For Library Use Only

Do Not Check Out

THE
NEW HANDBOOK
OF TEXAS

Ron Tyler, *Editor in Chief*

Douglas E. Barnett, *Managing Editor*

Roy R. Barkley, *Editor*

Penelope C. Anderson, *Associate Editor*

Mark F. Odintz, *Associate Editor*

The NEW HANDBOOK of TEXAS

IN SIX VOLUMES

Volume 2

AUSTIN
THE TEXAS STATE HISTORICAL ASSOCIATION
1996

Published by the Texas State Historical Association
in cooperation with the Center for Studies in Texas History
at the University of Texas at Austin.

Copyright © 1996 Texas State Historical Association, Austin, Texas. All rights reserved.
Printed in the United States of America.

ISBN 0-87611-151-7

10   9   8   7   6   5   4   3   2   1   96   97   98   00   01   02   03   04   05

Designed by David Timmons

The paper used in this book meets the minimum requirements of the
American National Standard for Permance of Paper for Printed Library Materials, Z39.48—1984.

This volume of the *New Handbook of Texas* is dedicated to
Lillie Cranz Cullen and Hugh Roy Cullen
in memory and recognition of their interest in the study of
Texas history and culture.

C

[CONTINUED]

CEDAR, TEXAS (Fayette County). Cedar was on Farm Road 609 five miles southwest of La Grange in Fayette County. It was originally settled before 1836 by Anglo-American colonists and incorporated into Fayette County by an act of the Republic of Texas[qv] on May 5, 1838. John Lewis was appointed justice of the peace. The community's name came from the many cedar trees in the area. During the late 1840s and 1850s a wave of German immigrants replaced most of the earlier settlers. A post office was established at the community in 1859, and a small cluster of businesses developed to meet the needs of the new settlers. Since there were many similar small communities in the vicinity, Cedar never grew much beyond a store, a saloon, a post office, a physician's office, and a large community hall. The cotton grown by local farmers was ginned at nearby Bluff, where residents also voted. Civic activities moved to nearby O'Quinn, and the local post office was discontinued in 1904. Cedar's store and saloon closed soon after, and in the 1980s only the cemetery remained to identify the site.

BIBLIOGRAPHY: Frank Lotto, *Fayette County: Her History and Her People* (Schulenburg, Texas: Sticker Steam Press, 1902; rpt., Austin: University of Texas Press, 1981). Leonie Rummel Weyand and Houston Wade, *An Early History of Fayette County* (La Grange, Texas: La Grange *Journal*, 1936).
Jeff Carroll

CEDAR, TEXAS (Limestone County). Cedar, in western Limestone County, was probably established in the 1870s. It grew up around a church and school built by freedmen from several nearby plantations (*see* RECONSTRUCTION). The community's school may have been the Cedar Creek school, which had thirty-six students and two teachers in 1896. The community was abandoned soon thereafter and was not shown on the 1948 county highway map.

BIBLIOGRAPHY: Walter F. Cotton, *History of Negroes of Limestone County from 1860 to 1939* (Mexia, Texas: Chatman and Merriwether, 1939).
Vivian Elizabeth Smyrl

CEDAR BAYOU. Cedar Bayou rises eleven miles northwest of Liberty in western Liberty County (at 30°07′ N, 94°59′ W) and runs south for forty-six miles to its mouth on Trinity Bay, southeast of Baytown (at 29°41′ N, 94°56′ W). The lower portion of the watercourse forms the boundary between Harris and Chambers counties. Cedar Bayou flows through flat terrain with local shallow depressions, surfaced by clays and sands that support loblolly pine and post oak forests. Navigation along Cedar Bayou had been established by 1854, and the bayou remained an important water route through the early 1900s, with fifteen to thirty miles navigable according to the season. Much of the upper two-thirds of Cedar Bayou had by 1982 been channeled to aid in flood control. In the 1980s a Chevron petroleum refinery and a U.S.X. Corporation steel plant were in operation on the creek's lower reaches.

BIBLIOGRAPHY: Jewel Horace Harry, *A History of Chambers County* (M.A. thesis, University of Texas, 1940; rpt., Dallas: Taylor, 1981).

CEDAR BAYOU, TEXAS. Cedar Bayou is at the intersection of Sjolander Road and the Southern Pacific Railroad, two miles north of State Highway 146 within what is now the city limits of Baytown in eastern Harris County. Though the founding date of Cedar Bayou is uncertain, the first recorded burial in the area was in 1810. In its early years and even as late as the 1930s, the community was used as a shipping port for bricks and other materials to Galveston Bay. A Methodist church was organized at Cedar Bayou in 1844, and the community's first school was founded in 1845. In 1870 a Masonic lodge was started in the area, and in 1871 John Peter Sjolander[qv] arrived at the community from his native Sweden. From 1870 until sometime after 1930 Cedar Bayou had a post office. In 1880 the community had thirty students under the instruction of William K. Gourley, and by 1900 there were sixty students with two teachers. By 1884 Baptist and Christian churches had been organized at the community. In 1890 the town had a population of 200, three general stores, several steam gristmills and cotton gins, and two brick manufacturers. In 1905 one Cedar Bayou school had six black students and one teacher, and a second school had ninety white students and three teachers. By 1914 Cedar Bayou had a population of 400, as well as five general stores, a boatbuilder, and an undertaker. In 1947 it reported a population of 500 and five businesses. The town was annexed in 1955 by the city of Baytown. In the early 1990s Cedar Bayou reported 1,287 inhabitants.

BIBLIOGRAPHY: Margaret Swett Henson, *History of Baytown* (Baytown, Texas: Bay Area Heritage Society, 1986). Houston *Chronicle*, June 13, 1937.
Timothy Nolan Smith

CEDAR BLUFF, TEXAS. Cedar Bluff was on Brown's Creek and Farm Road 2609, twelve miles northeast of Nacogdoches in northeastern Nacogdoches County. The community was first settled after the Civil War[qv] and was named for a small rise. A public school began operating there around 1900, and in 1908 it had an enrollment of forty-nine. The school later closed, though in the late 1980s the schoolhouse was still standing. By the early 1990s only a few scattered houses remained in the area.
Christopher Long

CEDAR BRANCH. Cedar Branch rises just south of Highland Park in Dallas in north central Dallas County (at 32°49′ N, 96°48′ W) and runs southwest for 1½ miles to its mouth on Turtle Creek, just south of Interstate Highway 35 East (at 32°48′ N, 96°49′ W). The area around the creek has been extensively developed.

CEDAR CREEK (Angelina County). Cedar Creek rises near Brandon School in Lufkin in central Angelina County (at 31°21′ N, 94°44′ W) and runs south for 20½ miles to its mouth on the Neches River (at 31°08′ N, 94°49′ W). The surroundings are typical of the East Texas piney woods: flat to moderately rolling terrain, surfaced by sandy and clay loams that support pine and hardwood forest.

――― (Bell County). Cedar Creek rises four miles northwest of Troy in north central Bell County (at 31°14′ N, 97°22′ W) and runs southwest for 8½ miles to its mouth on Belton Lake, near Morgan's Point Resort City (at 31°10′ N, 97°27′ W). The creek traverses nearly level to sloping and rolling terrain, surfaced by gravelly, loamy, and clayey soils. The area is used predominantly for agriculture.

――― (Bowie County). Cedar Creek rises just east of the Red River county line in extreme western Bowie County (at 33°26′ N, 94°45′ W) and runs southwest for six miles, through the southeastern corner of

Red River County, to its mouth on the Sulphur River, near the intersection of the Franklin, Morris, and Red River county lines (at 33°21′ N, 94°47′ W). The creek crosses flat to gently rolling terrain surfaced by sandy and clay loams that support grasses and mixed hardwoods and pines.

_____ (Brazos County). Cedar Creek rises a mile south of Peach Creek and three miles east of the Brazos River in southern Brazos County (at 30°30′ N, 96°18′ W) and flows south for four miles to its mouth on the Brazos River, 2½ miles from Clay Lake (at 30°27′ N, 96°18′ W). The stream traverses low to moderately rolling terrain surfaced by sandy and clay loams that support oak and pine forests with some mesquite and occasional grasses.

_____ (Brewster County). Cedar Creek rises on the northern slopes of Nine Point Mesa fifty-five miles southeast of Alpine in south central Brewster County (at 29°41′ N, 103°27′ W) and follows an arc to the north and east of Nine Point Mesa across a rolling tableland, then runs southeast through sharply eroded desert terrain for 13½ miles to its mouth on Nine Point Draw, on the broad, open flats northwest of the Rosillos Mountains (at 29°34′ N, 103°18′ W). Though the creek has flowing water through its entire length only after rainstorms, at least three permanent springs, including Cedar Springs to the west of Nine Point Mesa, feed portions of the creek before their waters again disappear underground. The banks of the creek, particularly in its upper reaches, support a variety of desert riparian vegetation, including juniper, hackberry, Mexican walnut, and numerous Texas persimmons. The area surrounding Cedar Creek was once predominantly semiarid grassland, but overgrazing by livestock virtually eliminated the grass. As a consequence, much of the area terrain was in the 1980s dominated by Chihuahuan Desert scrub. However, much of the land through which the creek passes belongs to the Terlingua Ranch Resort, and on this land some scattered grassland remnants near available water had begun by the mid-1980s to show signs of modest recovery.

_____ (Caldwell County). Cedar Creek rises east of Mendoza in northern Caldwell County (at 30°00′ N, 97°41′ W) and runs east for forty miles to its mouth on the Colorado River, six miles southeast of Bastrop in Bastrop County (at 30°02′ N, 97°17′ W). The surrounding flat to rolling terrain is surfaced by clay and sandy loams that support hardwoods and grasses.

_____ (Cherokee County). Cedar Creek rises a mile south of Alto in southern Cherokee County (at 31°39′ N, 95°05′ W) and runs southwest for six miles to its mouth on the Neches River, two miles southeast of the State Highway 21 bridge (at 31°34′ N, 95°09′ W). The stream is intermittent in its upper reaches. It traverses flat to gently rolling terrain surfaced by clay and sandy loams that support grasses and mixed hardwoods and pines.

_____ (Collin County). Cedar Creek rises three miles northeast of Farmersville in eastern Collin County (at 33°13′ N, 96°19′ W) and runs west for three miles to its mouth on Indian Creek, northeast of Farmersville (at 33°15′ N, 96°21′ W). The local terrain varies from flat with shallow depressions to rolling prairie with some steep slopes. The area soils are clay and sandy loams that support water-tolerant hardwoods, conifers, oaks, junipers, and grasses. The region has been used as crop and range land.

_____ (Dallas County). Cedar Creek rises in the Oak Cliff subdivision of Dallas in south central Dallas County (at 32°44′ N, 96°51′ W) and runs northeast for five miles to its mouth on the Trinity River, a quarter mile southeast of the Atchison, Topeka and Santa Fe line (at 32°45′ N, 96°47′ W). It runs through Wynnewood, Marsalis, and Moore parks on the back slope of the Austin chalk formation. Most of the area around the creek was subdivided for residential and commercial use by 1923. Where development permits, the stream's banks are wooded, with sugarberry and American elms, cedar elm, Osage orange, ash, red cedar, and various oaks.

_____ (Edwards County). Cedar Creek rises a half mile east of White Mountain Road in southeastern Edwards County (at 29°52′ N, 100°13′ W) and runs southeast for fifteen miles to its mouth on Pulliam Creek, three miles northwest of Barksdale (at 29°45′ N, 100°06′ W). The stream is intermittent in its upper reaches. It crosses flat terrain with local deep and dense dissection and steep slopes and benches, surfaced by shallow, stony clay loams that support oak, juniper, and mesquite.

_____ (Edwards County). Cedar Creek rises eight miles northwest of Carta Valley in west central Edwards County (at 29°54′ N, 100°33′ W) and runs east for nine miles to its mouth on the West Nueces River, at Farm Road 674 (at 29°54′ N, 100°25′ W). It crosses flat terrain with local deep and dense dissection, surfaced by shallow, stony soils that support oak, juniper, and mesquite.

_____ (Falls County). Cedar Creek rises two miles south of Perry and a quarter mile east of the Missouri Pacific tracks in northeastern Falls County (at 31°24′ N, 96°55′ W) and runs southwest for 5½ miles, around Buie Lake, to its mouth on the Brazos River, four miles northwest of Marlin (at 31°21′ N, 96°58′ W). The creek initially winds through level to sloping upland terrain surfaced by calcareous clayey soils that support mixed hardwoods and pines. Near the creek's mouth the terrain changes to a nearly level bottomland surfaced by clayey and loamy soils that support water-tolerant hardwoods and conifers.

_____ (Fayette County). Cedar Creek rises south of Farm Road 609 and a mile southwest of O'Quinn in west central Fayette County (at 29°48′ N, 97°00′ W) and runs northwest for five miles to its mouth on Buckner's Creek (at 29°51′ N, 97°01′ W). It cuts through rolling hills surfaced by fine sandy and clay loams that support oak and cedar with a dense understory of yaupon that provides good wildlife habitat. The eroded stream banks are quite steep and sometimes reach heights of thirty feet or more above the water. In open areas the stream provides water for cattle.

_____ (Fayette County). Cedar Creek rises a mile southeast of the Cedar Grove Church in north central Fayette County (at 29°58′ N, 96°50′ W) and runs south for 7½ miles to its mouth on the Colorado River, just east of La Grange (at 29°54′ N, 96°50′ W). The local rolling terrain is surfaced by loose and gravelly sands and sandy and clay loams. Most of the local land is suitable for unimproved pasture. In the 1980s much of the area was dotted with gas and oil wells.

_____ (Fayette County). Cedar Creek rises in a small stock tank eight miles north of La Grange in north central Fayette County (at 30°01′ N, 96°49′ W) and runs west for 6½ miles to its mouth on Rabbs Creek, a mile from the Colorado River (at 30°00′ N, 96°55′ W). The surrounding flat to rolling terrain is surfaced by clay and sandy loams that support dense thickets of cedar mixed with oak and yaupon.

_____ (Fayette County). Cedar Creek rises in western Fayette County (at 29°55′ N, 97°08′ W) and runs northeast for nine miles to its mouth on the Colorado River, just below Bartons Creek (at 29°58′ N, 97°04′ W). It traverses an area of rolling terrain surfaced by fine sandy loams and clays that support mixed oak and cedar with a yaupon understory that provides good wildlife habitat.

_____ (Fayette County). Cedar Creek rises between State Highway 159 and upper Lake Fayette in eastern Fayette County (at 29°57′ N, 96°45′ W) and runs through the lake and then continues southwest for 9½ miles to its mouth on the Colorado River, across from Mullins Prairie (at 29°52′ N, 96°46′ W). Below Lake Fayette the stream traverses flat to rolling terrain with local scarps surfaced by loose sandy gravel that is extracted for local use. Closer to the river the land has sandy loam topsoils and deep layers of clay mixed with gravel. These better soils support good crops of grain, pecans, and hay in the areas where they have not been removed by gravel producers.

_____ (Foard County). Cedar Creek rises five miles north of Vivian in northwestern Foard County (at 34°07′ N, 99°55′ W) and runs east for five miles to its mouth on Canal Creek, three miles north of Sugarloaf Mountain (at 34°05′ N, 99°48′ W). The area's steep to rolling slopes are surfaced by shallow and locally stony sandy and clay loams that support juniper, cacti, mesquite, oak, and sparse grasses.

_____ (Fort Bend County). Cedar Creek rises four miles southwest of

Needville in southern Fort Bend County (at 29°21′ N, 95°54′ W) and runs southeast for twelve miles, through southern Fort Bend and western Brazoria counties, to its mouth on the San Bernard River, two miles north of Danciger (at 29°14′ N, 95°48′ W). It crosses variable to flat terrain surfaced by clay that supports mixed hardwoods and pines along the creek's upper reaches and water-tolerant hardwoods, conifers, and a variety of prairie grasses toward its mouth.

_____ (Freestone County). Cedar Creek rises in south central Freestone County (at 31°36′ N, 96°09′ W) and runs northeast for 5½ miles to its mouth on Upper Keechi Creek, two miles south of Mount Zion (at 31°39′ N, 96°07′ W). It crosses terrain varying from rolling prairie to flat with local shallow depressions, surfaced by clay and sandy loams that support hardwoods, pines, conifers, and grasses. The area is used primarily as dry cropland and forest.

_____ (Freestone County). Cedar Creek rises three miles northwest of Dew in southern Freestone County (at 31°36′ N, 96°10′ W) and runs south for six miles to its mouth on Caroline Creek, four miles south of Dew (at 31°32′ N, 96°09′ W). The local terrain is rolling to flat prairie with local shallow depressions, surfaced by clay and sandy loams that support hardwoods, pines, conifers, and grasses. The area is used primarily as dry cropland and forest.

_____ (Grayson County). Cedar Creek rises four miles northeast of Howe in southeastern Grayson County (at 33°31′ N, 96°31′ W) and runs first northwest, then northeast, for four miles to its mouth on Choctaw Creek, three miles southeast of Sherman (at 33°35′ N, 96°33′ W). The local flat to rolling prairie with some steep slopes is surfaced by deep to shallow expansive clays and clay and sandy loams that support oak, juniper, water-tolerant hardwoods, conifers, and various grasses.

_____ (Grimes County). Cedar Creek rises two miles northeast of Navasota in southwestern Grimes County (at 30°24′ N, 96°03′ W) and runs southwest six miles to its mouth on the Navasota River (at 30°24′ N, 96°07′ W). The surrounding gently sloping terrain is surfaced by clays that support narrow stands of post oak–blackjack oak and elm–hackberry timber on the banks of the creek's lower channel. On March 18, 1687, the French explorer René Robert Cavelier, Sieur de La Salle,[qv] was murdered by members of his own party near the confluence of Cedar Creek and the Navasota River as he searched for the Mississippi. Settlement in the vicinity of the stream began in 1826 when Georgia planter Daniel Arnold took up a one-league tract of land on the middle creek extending west to the Navasota River and called the area Cross Roads. In 1848 James Nolan erected tents and other temporary structures and began to cultivate cotton on a small tract on the banks of the creek where it was paralleled by the La Bahía Road.[qv] During the 1850s four different stage lines established stops in the settlement, which became known as Navasota, in the 1990s the largest town in Grimes County.

BIBLIOGRAPHY: Grimes County Historical Commission, *History of Grimes County, Land of Heritage and Progress* (Dallas: Taylor, 1982).

_____ (Hill County). Cedar Creek rises seven miles northeast of Steiner Valley Park on Lake Whitney in northwestern Hill County (at 32°05′ N, 97°23′ W) and runs south for 6½ miles to its mouth on Lake Whitney, at Cedar Creek Park just west of Live Oak Resorts (at 31°59′ N, 97°23′ W). It crosses variable terrain surfaced by shallow, stony clays that support juniper, oak, and grasses. For most of the county's history, the Cedar Creek area has been used as range and crop land.

_____ (Hopkins County). Cedar Creek rises just south of Cumby in western Hopkins County (at 33°08′ N, 95°50′ W) and runs south for seven miles to its mouth on Turkey Creek, two miles west of Miller Grove (at 33°01′ N, 95°50′ W). It crosses generally flat terrain with locally shallow depressions, surfaced by clay and sandy loams that support water-tolerant hardwoods, conifers, and grasses.

_____ (Hunt County). Cedar Creek rises nine miles southeast of Greenville in south central Hunt County (at 33°06′ N, 96°06′ W) and runs southeast for two miles to its mouth on Lake Tawakoni, just south of Greenville Club Lake (at 33°00′ N, 96°01′ W). It crosses flat to rolling terrain surfaced by sandy and clay loams that support hardwoods and grasses. The area has been used mostly as range and crop land.

_____ (Johnson County). Cedar Creek rises 4½ miles northwest of Bono in western Johnson County (at 32°22′ N, 97°34′ W) and runs west for two miles to its mouth on the Brazos River, at the De Cordova Bend a half mile west of the Hood county line (at 32°21′ N, 97°36′ W). It runs through variable terrain surfaced by shallow, stony clay loams that support juniper, oak, cacti, and grasses. Throughout Johnson County's history, the Cedar Creek area has been used as range and crop land.

_____ (Kaufman County). Cedar Creek rises five miles north of Prairieville in east central Kaufman County (at 32°36′ N, 96°07′ W) and runs southeast into Van Zandt County ten miles east of Kaufman, then turns southwest to reenter Kaufman County. It runs for 35½ miles to its mouth on the Trinity River, a half mile south of Creslenn Ranch in central Henderson County (at 32°04′ N, 96°07′ W). In 1965 the stream was dammed a half mile south of Kemp to form Cedar Creek Reservoir in southeastern Kaufman and northern Henderson counties. The land surface drained by Cedar Creek is generally flat with locally shallow depressions and is surfaced by clay and sandy loams that support water-tolerant hardwoods, conifers, and grasses. The area has historically been used as range and crop land, though since the construction of Cedar Creek Reservoir, recreation has also become important.

_____ (Kimble County). Cedar Creek rises seven miles southwest of Segovia in southern Kimble County (at 30°19′ N, 99°42′ W) and runs northwest for 14½ miles to its mouth on Lake Junction, on the south Llano River opposite the Junction city limit (at 30°23′ N, 99°45′ W). The creek is generally free-flowing for six miles upstream from its mouth. Its only major tributary is intermittent Dry Cedar Creek, which joins Cedar Creek two miles south of Junction. The local flat terrain has deep and dense dissection and is surfaced by shallow soils that support oak, juniper, grasses, and some mesquite.

_____ (McCulloch County). Cedar Creek rises two miles west of Placid in northeastern McCulloch County (at 31°18′ N, 99°14′ W) and runs north for 14½ miles to its mouth on the Colorado River, seven miles northwest of Mercury (at 31°27′ N, 99°16′ W). The local terrain is generally flat with local depressions, surfaced by shallow, stony soils that support oak, juniper, and mesquite. For part of the creek's course the soils change to clay and sandy loams that support water-tolerant hardwoods, conifers, and grasses.

_____ (Milam County). Cedar Creek rises four miles south of Milano in southeastern Milam County (at 30°39′ N, 96°52′ W) and runs southeast for twenty-three miles to its mouth on the Brazos River, at the Burleson–Brazos county line fifteen miles northeast of Caldwell (at 30°38′ N, 96°36′ W). The area terrain is generally flat to rolling, with some local shallow depressions, and is surfaced by dark, calcareous clays and sandy loams that support mesquite, cacti, and grasses in the creek's upper reaches and water-tolerant hardwoods and conifers near its mouth.

_____ (Montague County). Cedar Creek rises near the Bowers oilfield in northeastern Montague County (at 33°48′ N, 97°30′ W) and runs four miles northeast to its mouth on the Red River, in northwestern Cooke County (at 33°51′ N, 97°28′ W). It crosses flat to rolling terrain with local escarpments, surfaced by sandy loam that supports hardwood forest, brush, and grasses.

_____ (Navarro County). Cedar Creek rises just west of the Corsicana city limits in central Navarro County (at 32°05′ N, 96°32′ W) and runs southeast for nine miles to its mouth on Richland Creek, six miles west of Richland (at 31°59′ N, 96°31′ W). The surrounding flat to rolling terrain is surfaced by clay and sandy loam that supports water-tolerant hardwoods and grasses.

_____ (Navarro County). Cedar Creek rises a mile east of Mildred in central Navarro County (at 32°03′ N, 96°23′ W) and runs east ten miles to its mouth on Richland Creek Reservoir, a mile east of the Eureka Church (at 32°02′ N, 96°16′ W). Before the reservoir was built in the 1980s the creek ran into Chambers Creek (at 32°03′ N, 96°14′ W). Cedar Creek traverses an area of low-rolling hills and prairies, surfaced by clay and sandy loams that support grasses and mesquite.

_____ (Robertson County). Cedar Creek, also known as Big Cedar Creek, rises 1½ miles southeast of Franklin in central Robertson County (at 31°33′ N, 96°28′ W) and runs southeast for twenty-seven miles, crossing both Robertson and Brazos counties, to its mouth on the Navasota River, a half mile northwest of the Brazos-Grimes-Madison county line (at 30°50′ N, 96°10′ W). The stream is intermittent in its upper reaches. Both Copperas and Bee creeks flow into Cedar Creek. The stream traverses nearly level to slightly sloping terrain that becomes level near its mouth. The local sandy loam soils support post oaks and grasses.

_____ (Stephens County). Cedar Creek (Big Cedar Creek) rises a mile north of Frankell in southeastern Stephens County (at 32°36′ N, 98°45′ W) and runs northeast thirty-six miles to its mouth on Possum Kingdom Lake, southeast of Farm Road 1148 (at 32°53′ N, 98°37′ W). The creek has been dammed to form Lake Necessity in its upper reaches. The surrounding generally flat terrain has local shallow depressions and is surfaced by clay and sandy loam that supports water-tolerant hardwoods and grasses.

_____ (Taylor County). Cedar Creek rises three miles north of Tuscola in east central Taylor County (at 32°14′ N, 99°44′ W) and runs north twenty miles to its mouth on Elm Creek, just across the county line in southeastern Jones County (at 32°32′ N, 99°43′ W). Cedar Creek is dammed to form Kirby Lake two miles south of Abilene. The land near the stream's source is rolling prairie surfaced by clay loams that support oak, juniper, mesquite, and grasses. Later in the stream's course the terrain becomes flat to gently sloping and is surfaced by silt loams that support mesquite and grasses.

_____ (Terrell County). Cedar Creek, also known as Cedar Arroyo, rises two miles south of U.S. Highway 90 in southeastern Terrell County (at 29°55′ N, 101°59′ W) and runs southeast for nine miles to its mouth on Palma Canyon, 1½ miles south of U.S. Highway 90 (at 29°53′ N, 101°51′ W). It traverses an area characterized by chalk deposits on rolling prairies. Soils in the area are generally dark, calcareous stony clays and clay loams that support oaks, junipers, and grasses.

_____ (Trinity County). Cedar Creek rises one mile northeast of Holly Cemetery in northwestern Trinity County (at 31°08′ N, 95°19′ W) and runs southwest for 6½ miles to its mouth on White Rock Creek, near White Rock Cemetery (at 31°04′ N, 95°23′ W). The surrounding flat to rolling terrain is surfaced by clay and sandy loam that supports conifers, water-tolerant hardwoods, and grasses.

_____ (Uvalde County). Cedar Creek rises six miles northwest of Montell in far northwestern Uvalde County (at 29°37′ N, 100°04′ W) and runs southeast for seven miles to its mouth on the Nueces River, a mile east of Montell (at 29°33′ N, 100°00′ W). Along the course gentle to steep slopes and bench terraces are surfaced by gravelly clay loam that supports scrub brush, sparse grasses, juniper, live oak, and mesquite.

_____ (Van Zandt County). Cedar Creek rises half a mile northeast of Elwood in northwest Van Zandt County (at 32°45′ N, 95°57′ W) and runs two miles north to its mouth on McBee Creek, just east of Farm Road 1395 (at 32°46′ N, 95°57′ W). The surrounding flat terrain with local shallow depressions is surfaced by clay and sandy loam that supports water-tolerant hardwoods, conifers, and grasses.

_____ (Waller County). Cedar Creek rises three miles west of Reids Prairie Church in northern Waller County (at 30°13′ N, 95°59′ W) and runs northwest for eight miles to its mouth on Beason Creek, a mile east of the Brazos River (at 30°14′ N, 96°05′ W). Local low and rolling hills and prairies are surfaced by sand and clay that support grasses and agricultural products.

_____ (Washington County). Cedar Creek rises midway between Burton and Carmine in western Washington County (at 30°10′ N, 96°38′ W) and runs north to form the western boundary between Lee and Washington counties, traveling about fifteen miles before reaching its mouth on Somerville Lake (at 30°18′ N, 96°38′ W). Its tributaries include Turkey, Black, and Tracy creeks. The stream traverses mostly level terrain surfaced with clay soils that support grasses and intermittent post oak woods.

CEDAR CREEK, TEXAS (Anderson County). Cedar Creek is at the intersection of Farm Road 322 and State Highway 294, by Cedar Creek nine miles southwest of Palestine in southwestern Anderson County. In 1932 Cedar Creek school district had a school serving forty-nine white pupils and a school serving seventy-three black pupils. In the 1930s the community had two churches, two schools, and a number of scattered dwellings. Cedar Creek school district was consolidated with Elkhart schools by 1955. In 1982 the community had a number of dwellings and, about ½ mile north of the crossroads, Cedar Creek church. The church was still on the site in 1985.

BIBLIOGRAPHY: Thomas Paul Jones, The Reorganization of the Public Schools of Anderson County, Texas (M.Ed. thesis, University of Texas, 1934).
Mark Odintz

CEDAR CREEK, TEXAS (Bastrop County). Cedar Creek is beside the creek for which it is named eleven miles west of Bastrop in west central Bastrop County. The area was settled as early as 1832, when Addison Litton was granted a league of blackland prairie on both sides of the creek. He and his wife, Mary Owen Litton, soon established their home there. They were joined by other pioneers, such as Jesse Billingsley and John Day Morgan,[qv] who built the first log cabin on the townsite. In January 1842 a Methodist minister preached to a full house at the Owens home on Cedar Creek, and the religious and social life of the community soon revolved around Methodist meetings. A local post office opened in 1852 with Elisha Billingsley as postmaster. A Presbyterian church was organized in 1855. Violence occurred in the small community during the Reconstruction[qv] era when a black justice of the peace and constable were elected. One man's refusal to allow Constable Ike Wilson to serve papers on him led to a shootout in which two black men and two white men were killed. By 1884 Cedar Creek had a population of 600 and served as a shipping point for cotton and country produce. The community's school, the Central Texas Normal Academy, closed its first annual session in June of that year, having enrolled 101 pupils. By 1896 the community's population had dropped to 250. In 1914 Cedar Creek had 225 residents, four general stores, a gin, a tailor, a doctor, and a cattle dealer. Oil drilling came to the area by 1913, and in 1928 a pool was discovered on the Yost farm four miles east of the community. Though not a major pool, the Yost oilfield was producing commercial quantities in the mid-1940s. The population reached 300 during these years but gradually declined afterward. In 1984 the community had six businesses and 145 people. At that time an annual homecoming picnic was being held the fourth Sunday of each May. In 1990 the population was still reported as 145.

BIBLIOGRAPHY: Bastrop Historical Society, *In the Shadow of the Lost Pines: A History of Bastrop County and Its People* (Bastrop, Texas: Bastrop *Advertiser*, 1955). William Henry Korges, Bastrop County, Texas: Historical and Educational Development (M.A. thesis, University of Texas, 1933). Bill Moore, *Bastrop County, 1691–1900* (Wichita Falls: Nortex, 1977).
Paula Mitchell Marks

CEDAR CREEK, TEXAS (Delta County). Cedar Creek was two miles southeast of Cooper, just south of the site of present City Lake, in southern Delta County. Settlement of the area began in the 1840s. The settlers soon organized Cedar Creek School under the direction of a Mrs. Strickland and by 1867 had established the Cedar Creek School District. In 1905 the school district enrolled forty-seven students and employed one teacher. Local residents organized the Cedar Creek Church in 1929; it met in the school, and T. M. McClain was the first pastor. The congregation sent a messenger to the Delta County Baptist Association meeting in 1931; however, the church was usually without a pastor. In 1949 Cooper Independent School District absorbed the local school, and the church closed soon after. The little community had disappeared from maps by 1964, and only Dawson Cemetery, near the old site, was identified on maps in 1984.

BIBLIOGRAPHY: Paul Garland Hervey, *A History of Education in Delta County, Texas* (M.A. thesis, University of Texas, 1951). Wilma Ross and Billie Phillips, *Photos and Tales of Delta County* (1976).

Vista K. McCroskey

CEDAR CREEK, TEXAS (Trinity County). Cedar Creek, on Cedar Creek four miles north of Apple Springs in northern Trinity County, was first settled around 1853 by William B. Womack and his family, who moved to the area from Simpson County, Mississippi. A school for black children was established before 1884. The school was later consolidated with Apple Springs school, but in the mid-1930s Cedar Creek still had a store and a number of houses. In the early 1990s only a few scattered houses remained.

BIBLIOGRAPHY: Patricia B. and Joseph W. Hensley, eds., *Trinity County Beginnings* (Groveton, Texas: Trinity County Book Committee, 1986).

Christopher Long

CEDAR CREEK, TEXAS (Waller County). Cedar Creek is near the intersection of State Highway 6 and Farm Road 2979, seven miles north of Hempstead in northern Waller County. Presumably named for the creek nearby, Cedar Creek existed by the middle of the 1880s when Henry Kloecker, a German immigrant, opened a cotton gin for local farmers. The gin remained in the Kloecker family until about 1902 or 1903, when a resident of Navasota in neighboring Grimes County purchased it. A school for local children had opened by 1892; in 1906 thirty-seven children attended classes, but the school had apparently closed by the 1930s. A cemetery which may have begun during the Civil War[qv] era lies at the northern edge of the community. A small number of citizens resided at Cedar Creek in 1990, and St. Luke Church was in the vicinity.

BIBLIOGRAPHY: Waller County Historical Commission, *Cotton Gins of Waller County* (Brenham, Texas, 1981). Waller County Historical Survey Committee, *A History of Waller County, Texas* (Waco: Texian, 1973).

Paul M. Lucko

CEDAR CREEK, TEXAS (Washington County). Cedar Creek, one of the earliest settlements in Washington County not on the Brazos River, was a mile north of the site of later Chapel Hill, on or near Cedar Creek. The community prospered with abundant lumber supplies from the vicinity's cedar trees. Under the Republic of Texas,[qv] a post office was established on March 23, 1837; James Hall was postmaster until 1840. Cedar Creek was the site of a large Methodist camp meeting on October 19, 1843, and the eighth Texas Conference of the Methodist Church was held there from December 29, 1847, until January 3, 1848. The community became a Methodist center during the 1840s. In November 1847 a Methodist church was built. A United States post office operated from 1846 until 1848, when Chapel Hill was founded nearby. Cedar Creek Academy transferred to the new settlement. With the growth of Chapel Hill, Cedar Creek declined and soon disappeared as a separate community.

BIBLIOGRAPHY: Homer S. Thrall, *History of Methodism in Texas* (Houston: Cushing, 1872; rpt., n.p.: Walsworth, 1976). Mr. and Mrs. Nate Winfield, *All Our Yesterdays: A Brief History of Chappell Hill* (Waco: Texian Press, 1969).

Carole E. Christian

CEDAR CREEK RESERVOIR. Cedar Creek Reservoir is three miles northeast of Trinidad on Cedar Creek in the Trinity River Basin in Henderson County (at 32°11′ N, 96°04′ W). The project is owned and operated by the Tarrant County Water Control and Improvement District No. 1 for municipal water supply. Construction started in April 1961 and was completed in 1965. The reservoir has a capacity of 679,200 acre-feet and a surface area of 34,000 acres at operating elevation of 332 feet above mean sea level. The drainage area above the dam is 1,007 square miles. The surrounding flat to rolling terrain is surfaced by sandy and clay loams that support water-tolerant hardwoods, conifers, and grasses.

BIBLIOGRAPHY: C. L. Dowell, *Dams and Reservoirs in Texas: History and Descriptive Information* (Texas Water Commission Bulletin 6408 [Austin, 1964]).

Seth D. Breeding

CEDAR GROVE, TEXAS (Brazoria County). Cedar Grove was twenty miles west of Angleton in extreme west central Brazoria County. A post office was established in 1886 and operated until 1887, when mail was transferred to Columbia. It was then reestablished by 1898 and functioned as late as 1911. The community was located in the area of Cedar Brake plantation, which belonged to the Dance family. Cedar Grove had a school with one teacher and fifty-two black pupils in 1896. State highway maps of 1936 showed scattered dwellings at the townsite, but by 1980 only the local cemetery remained.

Diana J. Kleiner

CEDAR GROVE, TEXAS (Harris County). Cedar Grove is on Farm Road 1942 four miles southwest of Crosby in east central Harris County. State highway maps in 1936 showed a church, a cemetery, and scattered dwellings at the townsite. In the 1980s the church and dwellings remained, and three cemeteries were located nearby.

Diana J. Kleiner

CEDAR GROVE, TEXAS (Kaufman and Van Zandt counties). Cedar Grove was ten miles northeast of Terrell and four miles north of U.S. Highway 80 in Van Zandt and Kaufman counties. In the mid-1840s families moved from the Red River valley to the waters of Duck Creek, a tributary of the Sabine River, and settled at the townsite. Included in the party were William H. McBee, an early Kaufman county commissioner; Adam P. Sullivan, the first county clerk; and William Gibbard, on whose farm a grove of cedars grew. The post office opened in 1850, and a town plat was filed with the county clerk in 1858. The Masonic lodge was chartered in 1868, and a local Grange[qv] existed by 1874.

The community was one of the oldest and most prosperous settlements in the county until 1872. That year the Texas and Pacific Railway bypassed it, and the settlement began to decline. The post office was closed in 1874, when merchants began moving to the railhead at Wills Point. The Masonic lodge survived until 1913. The Cedar Grove public school district was formed by the commissioners' court in 1885. Cedar Grove School became Cartwright School in Wills Point in 1930. A private academy, the Cedar Grove Male and Female Institute, opened in the 1880s, but its existence was brief. By 1990 the original cedars on William Gibbard's farm were no longer standing, and all that remained of the town was the cemetery.

Jack Stoltz

CEDAR HILL, TEXAS (Dallas County). Cedar Hill is on U.S. Highway 67 and the Atchison, Topeka and Santa Fe Railway, two miles north of the Ellis county line in the rolling hills of southwestern Dallas County. It was founded in the 1850s. A branch of the Chisholm Trail[qv] once passed through the area, connecting with the main trail near Fort Worth. A post office was opened at Cedar Hill in 1852. In 1897 the name was changed to Cedarhill, but by 1900 residents had reverted to the old spelling. In 1856 a tornado hit the tiny community, destroying most of its buildings and homes and claiming the lives of nine people. In 1890 the population had grown to 500. By 1915 Cedar Hill had three churches, two banks, and a number other businesses and professional services. In the 1980s the population grew dramatically, especially after 1989 when Joe Pool Lake opened nearby. Northwood Institute, founded in Michigan, moved to Cedar Hill in 1966.

In 1990 Cedar Hill had a population of 9,191 and 203 business establishments.

BIBLIOGRAPHY: *Memorial and Biographical History of Dallas County* (Chicago: Lewis, 1892; rpt., Dallas: Walsworth, 1976).

Carlton Stowers

CEDAR HILL, TEXAS (Floyd County). Cedar Hill is on Farm Road 97 fifteen miles east of Lockney and six miles west of the eastern edge of the Caprock escarpment in northwest Floyd County. Wheat farming is predominant in the area. The community may have been named for the cedars that grew locally or for a town in East Texas. Area settlement began during the late 1880s. A school was built in 1898 and designated a county school district by 1900. The nearby school named Union Bower doubled as a religious meeting hall. A Baptist church was built in 1900. In 1916 John Dillard had a store and post office at Alcino, two miles northwest of Cedar Hill. Dave Dillard built a store at Cedar Hill in the 1920s. During the 1930s and 1940s the town had a brick school, two churches, parsonages, a store, and an icehouse. Later a cafe and beauty shop were established. A grain elevator was built in the early 1960s. The school at Cedar Hill continued in operation until it was consolidated with the Floydada schools in 1950. Businesses in the 1980s included a co-op grain elevator, which processed twenty-five million pounds of wheat in 1985, and an upholstery shop. Assembly of God and Baptist churches are active in the settlement. The population of the community in the 1980s was about ten.

BIBLIOGRAPHY: Floyd County Historical Museum, *History of Floyd County, 1876–1979* (Dallas: Taylor, 1979).

Charles G. Davis

CEDAR HILL, TEXAS (Washington County). Cedar Hill was on Tommelson Creek in northwestern Washington County. Henry Eichholt, the first German settler of Washington County, farmed near Cedar Hill before the Civil War.qv During the war the Eichholt brothers' gristmill served Confederate soldiers and civilians. Cedar Hill's population, predominantly German immigrants and their descendants, was a center of Republican strength in Washington County during the 1880s. In 1883 the community was the site of tumultuous Republican meetings attended by blacks and Germans. Cedar Hill flourished from the 1880s through the early twentieth century. In 1896 it had its own German Baptist church, a public school, and baseball and horse clubs. The Eichholt gristmill still operated in 1896, and Cedar Hill was the site of an annual April Children's Fest. Cedar Hill's prosperity was based on agriculture. The settlement declined rapidly when nearby William Penn began to grow. Three cemeteries are all that marked Cedar Hill's location in 1988.

BIBLIOGRAPHY: W. O. Dietrich, *The Blazing Story of Washington County* (Brenham, Texas: Banner Press, 1950; rev. ed., Wichita Falls: Nortex, 1973). Mrs. R. E. Pennington, *History of Brenham and Washington County* (Houston, 1915). Charles F. Schmidt, *History of Washington County* (San Antonio: Naylor, 1949).

Carole E. Christian

CEDAR HILL STATE PARK. Cedar Hill State Park is on Farm Road 1382 and the northeastern shore of Joe Pool Lake, ten miles southwest of Dallas in southwestern Dallas County. The land is owned by the United States Army Corps of Engineers. It was first settled by the John Penn family, and during the 1990s the Penn farm structures were undergoing restoration. The 1,850-acre park is operated by the Texas Parks and Wildlife Department. It opened in May 1991 and has 335 camping sites in five camping areas: Shady Ridge, Eagle Ford, Lakeview, Hog Wallow, and Coyote Crossing. The park also has boat ramps, picnic areas, swimming areas, and fishing jetties. It is set in rolling hills with wooded areas of cedar, elm, Ashe juniper, and mesquite. Some tall-grass prairie is also present.

BIBLIOGRAPHY: Dallas *Morning News*, April 30, 1991. *Texas Parks and Wildlife*, August 1991.

Matthew Hayes Nall

CEDAR HOLLOW. Cedar Hollow begins east of Red Rock in southwestern Bastrop County (at 29°58′ N, 97°25′ W) and runs northwest to a point just west of Rockne (at 30°01′ N, 97°27′ W). Its lower reaches are known as Lower Cedar Valley. The local rolling prairie is surfaced by clay loams that support post oak woods.

CEDAR KNOB. Cedar Knob, also known as Cedar Mountain, is four miles northeast of Youngsport beside Stillhouse Hollow Lake in southwestern Bell County (at 30°59′ N, 97°39′ W). At an elevation of 850 feet above sea level, its summit rises 230 feet above the nearby lake.

CEDAR LAKE (Brazoria County). Cedar Lake, a teardrop-shaped lake under one mile in diameter, is near the Galveston county line nineteen miles east of Angleton in east central Brazoria County (at 29°12′ N, 95°05′ W). Before the construction of the Gulf Intracoastal Waterwayqv in 1948, the lake was fed by Cedar Lake Creek and the San Bernard River and drained into the Gulf of Mexico.

_____ (Gaines County). Cedar Lake is a large salt lake in the southern half of the Llano Estacado,qv twenty-five miles from Seminole in the north corner of Gaines County (at 32°49′ N, 102°16′ W). Its Spanish name was Laguna Sabinas. Its English name came from the gnarled scrub cedar that once dotted its edges. It is located in a semiarid region once considered part of the Great American Desert. The lake was a gathering place for wildlife as well as a stopping place for travelers as they moved from water source to water source across the region. In 1875 an official United States Army report described this strategic lake as being six miles long and four miles wide, as well as having "plenty of good water in numerous wells or rather dug springs in a ravine at the north end, and several large wells at the south end, of slightly brackish water but fit for use of men and animals." Wood and stone for building, the report continued, could be gathered in the bluffs. Both prehistoric and historic Indians often used the lake. It was a favorite camping place for the Comanches who traded there with the Comancheros.qv Some writers believed that Cedar Lake was the birthplace of the last Comanche war chief, Quanah Parker.qv After the Civil Warqv this vital water source was frequently used by white buffalo hunters as they systematically destroyed the last of the southern herd. The famous cowboy-detective Charles A. Siringoqv went there in the late 1870s and found the "camps black with genuine buffalo hides." It was there, too, that the famous hide hunter George Causeyqv killed 200 buffalo in 1882, believed to be the last sizable herd on the Staked Plains, if not in the larger southern High Plains (*see also* BUFFALO, BUFFALO HUNTING).

The United States Army used Cedar Lake in its forays against the Comanche Indians. Col. Ranald S. Mackenzieqv made an all-night forced march to the site in December 1874 but failed to catch the large group of Comanches he believed to be camped there. The following year Col. William R. Shafter,qv who later gained fame in the Spanish-American War, covered over 2,500 miles of the Llano Estacado during three scoutings for Comanches. He used Cedar Lake as his headquarters. During that campaign the able Indian fighter Lt. John L. Bullisqv led his Black Seminole scoutsqv in a dawn attack at the lake and scared off a large band of Indians. With the Indians on reservations, Cedar Lake continued its important role in the region as a ranching center. By the late 1870s cattleman C. C. Slaughterqv had established his huge Lazy S Ranch adjacent to Cedar Lake. By 1920 cotton farmers had surrounded the lake, and in 1935 the first productive oil well in the area was brought in. In 1936 the Texas Centennialqv Commission placed a historic marker at the north end of Cedar Lake identifying it as Quanah Parker's birthplace. In 1990 farms dominated the scene, and pump jacks dotted the edge and center of the lake.

BIBLIOGRAPHY: M. L. Crimmins, "Shafter's Explorations in Western Texas, 1875," West Texas Historical Association *Year Book* 9 (1933).

James I. Fenton, "Cedar Lake: Mirror of Staked Plains History," *Permian Historical Annual* 21 (1981).
James I. Fenton

CEDAR LAKE, TEXAS. Cedar Lake, on Farm Road 2611 just west of the Brazoria county line in southeastern Matagorda County, was named for a cedar brake surrounding a nearby lake. A post office operated there from 1848 until 1855. In September 1854 the name was changed to Dura, and in November, to Duroc. A post office known as Roweville operated from 1890 until 1893, when the community changed the name to Cedar Lake. At this time the community was in Matagorda County; formerly it had been part of Brazoria County. In 1896 Cedar Lake recorded ten residents, and Velasco served as the community's banking and railroad point. In 1906 the town had five schools and five teachers for 266 black pupils and one school and one teacher for six white pupils. A general store was established there by 1914, and in 1936 the township had one business and thirteen dwellings and was served by a metal-surfaced road. The community's post office closed sometime after 1930. In 1942 Cedar Lake had fifty residents and two businesses. Its reported population dropped to forty in 1967, then grew to 148 by 1969. By 1972 the Cedar Lakes School had been constructed two miles southwest of Cedar Lake. The community reported 148 inhabitants in 1990.

BIBLIOGRAPHY: James A. Creighton, *A Narrative History of Brazoria County* (Angleton, Texas: Brazoria County Historical Commission, 1975). Matagorda County Historical Commission, *Historic Matagorda County* (3 vols., Houston: Armstrong, 1986).
Diana J. Kleiner

CEDAR LAKE CREEK. Cedar Lake Creek, sometimes locally known as Cedar Bayou, rises in Old Ocean Swamp four miles southwest of Sweeny in southwestern Brazoria County (at 29°01′ N, 95°45′ W) and flows southeast for twenty-one miles, into the San Bernard National Wildlife Refuge,qv to its mouth on the Gulf Intracoastal Waterwayqv (at 28°50′ N, 95°32′ W). As late as the 1930s the stream passed through Cedar Lakes into the Gulf of Mexico. It serves as the Brazoria-Matagorda county line for 17½ miles. Cedar Lake Creek is banked by levees in its upper reaches. It traverses a flat, flood-prone area with local shallow depressions, surfaced by sandy and clay loam that supports water-tolerant hardwoods and grasses. As the creek nears the coast, the terrain shifts first to low levees, then to a brackish marshland in which thrive diverse plant and animal species, including waterfowl and numerous grasses. A number of the Confederate camps established along the coast in Matagorda and Brazoria counties were on Cedar Lake Creek and Cedar Lakes. Among these were Camp Cedar Bayou (also known as Camp Buchel after the area's commanding officer, Augustus Buchelqv), established in December 1863 on Cedar Lake Creek (then also called Cedar Bayou) and garrisoned with 1,273 troopers. In addition, Camp Cedar Lake, established by John Bankhead Magruderqv as one of a chain of Confederate forts extending along the Gulf of Mexico from just below Velasco to Wharton, was located on the western shore of Cedar Lake (probably what is now Cedar Lakes). Finally, a Camp Nellie, which from November 1862 to January 1863 hosted the Twenty-fifth Texas Cavalry Regiment, was located on a Cedar Bayou that very likely was the same stream as Cedar Lake Creek.

BIBLIOGRAPHY: Matagorda County Historical Commission, *Historic Matagorda County* (3 vols., Houston: Armstrong, 1986).

CEDAR LAKES. The Cedar Lakes, a group of shallow connected lakes, are located just south of the Gulf Intracoastal Waterway,qv beginning in Brazoria County two miles west of the Matagorda county line and continuing east for six miles to the mouth of the San Bernard River on the Gulf of Mexico (at 28°51′ N, 95°30′ W). The lakes measure just over a mile at their widest point. The area is brackish to saltwater marsh with a surface of mud and sand that supports grasses.
Diana J. Kleiner

CEDAR LAKE SLOUGH. Cedar Lake Slough is by the Horseshoe Bend of the Trinity River in southwestern Anderson County (at 31°46′ N, 95°52′ W). Much of it is in the Coffield State Department of Corrections facility. The 10½ mile long series of sloughs is an old channel of the Trinity River.

CEDAR LANE, TEXAS. Cedar Lane is on Caney Creek at the junction of Farm roads 457 and 521, twenty miles southeast of Bay City in east central Matagorda County. The original settlement clustered around a plantation store, with an approach through a lane of cedars. In 1912 the community secured its own post office and by that time was a stop on the Texas and New Orleans Railroad. By 1914 Cedar Lane had a population twenty-five and a telephone connection. In 1936 the community had a church, a school, two businesses, sixteen dwellings, and a paved thoroughfare. It also had its own school district. During the school year 1937–38 four teachers instructed eighty-five students. By 1949 Cedar Lane school had been consolidated with the Van Vleck Independent School District. In 1940 Cedar Lane had an estimated fifty inhabitants and two businesses and in 1967 fifty-seven residents and three business. In 1972 the settlement had a church, the Kennedy school, and several scattered dwellings. In 1990 Cedar Lane had a population of eighty-five and no businesses.

BIBLIOGRAPHY: Matagorda County Historical Commission, *Historic Matagorda County* (3 vols., Houston: Armstrong, 1986).
Stephen L. Hardin

CEDAR MILL, TEXAS. Cedar Mill was on the old road from Austin to Hamilton Valley (now Burnet) near the intersection of Farm Road 243 and Ranch Road 1174 in Burnet County. The first settler came in 1854. Alexander Barton, a miller, ran a sawmill, gristmill, and flour mill on the south fork of Oatmeal Creek. There were also merchants and a saddletree maker. The early settlers came from South Carolina, Missouri, and Illinois. During the 1860s an Austin-Burnet road was charted on more favorable terrain. This caused the citizens of Cedar Mill to move in the 1870s to a site north of the South San Gabriel River, where they called their new settlement South Gabriel.

BIBLIOGRAPHY: Darrell Debo, *Burnet County History* (2 vols., Burnet, Texas: Eakin, 1979).
Maxine B. Glimp

CEDAR MILLS, TEXAS. Cedar Mills was twenty-four miles northwest of Sherman in northwestern Grayson County. Settlement of the community began in the 1870s, when grist and saw mills were built in the cedar groves on the Red River. Cedar Mills quickly established itself as a community center for the mill operators and area farmers. Postal service began in 1872, and by the mid-1870s the town had a church, a school, and a number of businesses, including a hotel and racetrack. In 1884 the town had a population of 500. Cedar Mills was bypassed by the railroads. In 1890 the population dropped to eighty. Businesses left, and the post office closed in 1907. The community had fifty residents through the 1930s. During the early 1940s, however, the site was inundated by Lake Texoma.
David Minor

CEDAR MOUNTAIN (Burnet County). Cedar Mountain is just east of Lake Buchanan in western Burnet County (at 30°50′ N, 98°20′ W). It stands at an elevation of 1,415 feet above sea level, more than 300 feet above the surrounding countryside.

____ (Coke County). Cedar Mountain is near the Colorado River three miles southwest of Bronte in eastern Coke County (at 31°52′ N, 100°20′ W). With an elevation of 1,900 feet, its summit rises 120 feet above U.S. Highway 277, two miles east.

____ (Eastland County). Cedar Mountain is eight miles north of Cisco in northwestern Eastland County (at 32°29′ N, 98°59′ W) and has an elevation of 1,623 feet.

_____ (Llano County). Cedar Mountain is seven miles southeast of Oxford in southern Llano County (at 30°32′ N, 98°38′ W). At an elevation of 1,856 feet, the summit rises 800 feet above nearby Sandy Creek. The large, steep-sided plateau, five miles by two miles, stands in the Llano Basin, surrounded by rolling terrain with deep and dense dissection, surfaced by shallow, stony soils that support open stands of live oak and Ashe juniper.

CEDAR PARK, TEXAS. Cedar Park is on Cluck Creek and U.S. Highway 183 some sixteen miles northwest of Austin in southwestern Williamson County. In earlier days the community and the creek were named Running Brushy, after a heavy-flowing spring that formed the headwaters of the creek. In 1871 George Cluck made a cattle drive up the Chisholm Trail qv accompanied by his wife Harriet, who was the first woman to make the drive; in 1873 the Clucks bought the land which included Running Brushy Spring. The Cluck ranch and home became the nucleus for a community. A post office was authorized in February 1874 for the Running Brushy settlement. Joel Sutton served as postmaster until December 1874, when Harriet Cluck took the job, which she held for eight years. In 1882 the Austin and Northwestern Railroad was completed from Austin to Burnet, crossing the Cluck land in Running Brushy. The deed called for a sidetrack to be built. At this time the railroad company changed the name of the community to Brueggerhoff, the name of a partner of a company official. In 1887 Emmett Cluck, son of George and Harriet, renamed the town Cedar Park, after the parklike surroundings of his home. In 1892, when George Cluck sold the railroad company a lot adjoining the railroad, the deed called for a park and a building to house plants. For years the park was used as a community meeting place. Limestone for building became a major product of Cedar Park in the 1890s and remained important until about 1970. Cedar fence posts were also a major product during this period. Under the influence of the growth of nearby Austin, the local ranch land began to be used for housing in the 1960s, and between 1970 and 1980 the population of Cedar Park grew from 125 to over 3,000. On February 24, 1973, Cedar Park citizens voted to incorporate. In the 1980s Cedar Park comprised shopping centers, numerous other businesses, and rapidly multiplying dwellings. In the early 1990s it reported 206 rated businesses and more than 5,300 residents.

BIBLIOGRAPHY: Leonard T. Allen, *The Twentieth Century As It Unfolded for Me: An Autobiography* (1975). Clara Stearns Scarbrough, *Land of Good Water: A Williamson County History* (Georgetown, Texas: Williamson County Sun Publishers, 1973). T. U. Taylor, *The Chisholm Trail and Other Routes* (San Antonio: Naylor, 1936).
Frances W. Wynn

CEDAR POINT, TEXAS. Cedar Point, east of Beach City in extreme west central Chambers County, was the site of the Sam Houston's qv summer home on Trinity Bay known as Raven Moor. Houston purchased the home from John Iliam's wife, Tabitha Harris, in 1837 and used it until 1862. A centennial marker was placed near the site in 1936 and a county historical marker in 1986. A highly productive nearby oilfield developed in 1935 and was named for Cedar Point.

BIBLIOGRAPHY: Jewel Horace Harry, A History of Chambers County (M.A. thesis, University of Texas, 1940; rpt., Dallas: Taylor, 1981). Margaret S. Henson and Kevin Ladd, *Chambers County: A Pictorial History* (Norfolk, Virginia: Donning, 1988).
Diana J. Kleiner

CEDAR SPRINGS, TEXAS (Dallas County). Cedar Springs was on Cedar Springs Branch in the area of Oak Lawn in north central Dallas. It was on the original land grant of C. Grigsby. The site was first settled by troops working on the Military Road qv project under the command of Col. William G. Cooke, qv who ordered Capt. William Houghton to construct a temporary fort on Cedar Springs Branch in February 1841. Though the installation was abandoned a month later, the local spring formed an attractive watering spot that pioneer travelers believed had medicinal properties.

Two years later Dr. John Cole, a Peters colony qv settler, came to Texas to claim the 640-acre headright promised him by the Republic of Texas.qv The land Cole wanted was already owned by John Grigsby, a veteran of the Texas Revolution,qv but Grigsby eventually agreed to sell Cole 160 acres at one dollar an acre along Cedar Springs Branch. Cole immediately constructed a general store, stocked it with merchandise he had brought with him, and established his medical practice, reportedly the first in Dallas County. During the 1840s the area around Cole's store became a community and trade center that eventually included a gristmill, a blacksmith, and a Gold and Donaldson distillery. The community also had a school called Cedar Springs Institute.

In 1846 residents of the area elected John Neely Bryan qv to go to Austin and lobby the legislature to establish Dallas County. Later that year John Cole was elected the first probate judge of the county. Four years later Cedar Springs was involved in a county seat election in competition with Dallas and Hord's Ridge. Cedar Springs came in last. In 1929 the community was annexed by the city of Dallas.

BIBLIOGRAPHY: Dallas *Times Herald*, August 28, 1949, April 9, 1991.
Matthew Hayes Nall

CEDAR SPRINGS, TEXAS (Falls County). Cedar Springs, once known as Mill Tract, is on Farm Road 2027 nine miles south of Marlin in south central Falls County. It was named for several springs that flowed through a nearby cedar grove. In the early 1870s the community had a sawmill, a gin, and a store. In 1879 a post office was established, taking the name Viesca, in remembrance of the colonial settlement Sarahville de Viesca, which had been five miles north. The community had a population of thirty in the mid-1880s. In 1890 it had 100 residents, a general store, and a hotel. When the San Antonio and Aransas Pass Railway completed the section of track between Waco and Lexington in 1891, bypassing Viesca by six miles, many residents were drawn to the railroad and the newly established community of Lott. The population of Viesca fell to fifty by the mid-1890s. When the post office was discontinued in 1905, the community resumed the name Cedar Springs. In 1905 the community had a two-teacher school for sixty-six white students and a one-teacher school for eighty-one black students. Until the mid-1950s Cedar Springs served as the focus of a common-school district; this district was divided and consolidated with the Lott and the Rosebud school districts in 1955. Cotton and corn were the principal crops grown by farmers in the Cedar Springs area until the 1930s. At that time tomatoes were introduced as a specialty crop, and farmers also began to grow watermelons, cantaloupes, and sweet potatoes. Stock, in particular turkeys, increased in importance after 1960. The population of Cedar Springs fell to fifteen in the early 1930s but increased to fifty by 1939 and to seventy by 1945. A school, a church, and several residences marked the community on county highway maps in the late 1940s. Ninety residents were reported in 1970 and 1990.

BIBLIOGRAPHY: Roy Eddins, ed., and Old Settlers and Veterans Association of Falls County, comp., *History of Falls County, Texas* (Marlin, Texas?, 1947). Lillian S. St. Romain, *Western Falls County, Texas* (Austin: Texas State Historical Association, 1951). Vertical File, Texas Collection, Baylor University.
Vivian Elizabeth Smyrl

CEDAR SPRINGS, TEXAS (Upshur County). Cedar Springs, on U.S. Highway 259 sixteen miles northeast of Gilmer in extreme northeastern Upshur County, was first settled before the Civil War qv near a spring surrounded by large cedar trees. In the mid 1930s the community had a school and number of scattered houses. After World War II qv the school was consolidated with the Coffeeville school district and later became part of the Ore City Independent School District. In the mid 1960s Cedar Springs had a church and a few houses. Most of the approximately 100 residents worked the nearby Lone Star Steel Company. In 1990 Cedar Springs was a dispersed rural community.

BIBLIOGRAPHY: Doyal T. Loyd, *History of Upshur County* (Waco: Texian Press, 1987).

Christopher Long

CEDAR TOP PEAK. Cedar Top Peak, 5½ miles northwest of Lampasas in south central Lampasas County (at 31°07′ N, 98°15′ W), is said to have been named for the numerous cedar trees that grow on its slopes. At an elevation of 1,517 feet above sea level, its summit rises 150 feet above nearby U.S. Highway 183/190. It stands in an area of the Grand Prairie characterized by steep slopes and limestone benches, that give a stairstep appearance to the landscape. Shallow clay loams support grasses and open stands of live oak, mesquite, and Ashe juniper.

BIBLIOGRAPHY: *Lampasas, Texas* (Chicago: Poole Brothers, 1889?; rpt., Lampasas, 1972).

CEDARVALE, TEXAS. Cedarvale was on State Highway 243 twelve miles east of Kaufman in eastern Kaufman County. During the 1930s the community had an estimated population of twenty and three businesses. During the 1950s and early 1960s the population was estimated at forty, and no businesses were in operation.

David Minor

CEDAR VALLEY, TEXAS (Bell County). Cedar Valley is on Farm Road 2843 thirteen miles southeast of Killeen in southwestern Bell County. It had a school and several churches. In 1903 Cedar Valley School served forty-four students, and it was still in operation in 1948. In 1990 Cedar Valley had a listed population of only four but was the site of two churches, several scattered dwellings, and an air strip.

Mark Odintz

CEDAR VALLEY, TEXAS (Travis County). Cedar Valley is on U.S. Highway 290 twelve miles southwest of Austin in southwestern Travis County. Mark Thomas, an early settler, gave land for a school in 1867. A post office opened in 1872 with Peter Wuthrich as postmaster. By the mid-1880s Cedar Valley had two churches, a district school, and forty residents; area farmers shipped cotton, wool, and hides. The population of the community rose to 100 by the late 1930s but fell to fifty by 1949. The post office was discontinued in 1957, and mail for Cedar Valley was sent to Austin. The population increased to 150 in the late 1960s but stabilized at seventy from the 1970s through 1990.

BIBLIOGRAPHY: Mary Starr Barkley, *History of Travis County and Austin, 1839–1899* (Waco: Texian Press, 1963). John J. Germann and Myron Janzen, *Texas Post Offices by County* (1986).

Vivian Elizabeth Smyrl

CEDAR VALLEY LAND AND CATTLE COMPANY. The Cedar Valley Land and Cattle Company, Limited, was an English ranching syndicate with American headquarters in Kansas City. It was organized in 1884 by a Major Ewing, who had gone to London for that purpose. The stockholders elected Ewing as their general manager and authorized him to buy ranchland in Texas. In 1885 he purchased the T Anchor Ranch,[qv] consisting of 275,000 acres in Randall and Deaf Smith counties, from William B. Munson[qv] for $800,000. Included in the transaction were 25,000 cattle and 325 horses. Ewing hired Sam Dyer, brother-in-law of Charles Goodnight,[qv] as foreman. In 1885 Henry R. Hilton of Kansas City replaced Ewing as general manager, and Hilton hired Jim Moore of Wyoming as foreman. Charles J. E. Lowndes was employed as bookkeeper and remained in that position until 1900. After Moore resigned in 1887, Henry E. (Hank) Siders served six months as foreman and then was succeeded by Lee John Hutson,[qv] an English-born rancher and loan-company agent. Hutson hired the young Scottish aristocrat, Charles L. Gordon-Cumming,[qv] as a cowhand. Paul Phillips succeeded Hilton as general manager in 1889.

The ownership and utilization of land became an increasingly important issue, especially after the advent of the railroads drew nesters[qv] into the area. The fenced range of the Cedar Valley Company included school land and an additional 179,200 acres leased from the New York and Texas Land Company. Beset by small farmers and ranchers, the syndicate attempted to counter them by securing and enclosing the watering places. However, two smaller cattle operations from Iowa drove their herds onto unfenced company pastures and would not move them, claiming that they were actually grazing state land. To solve that problem, the syndicate entered into a contract in which they agreed to care for the intruders' stock for cash. Even so, certain terms of this agreement were violated, and this led to a bitter court battle that was settled in favor of the Iowa plaintiffs.

The Cedar Valley Company's insistence on leasing rather than buying let others crowd the ranch out of existence, particularly after the organization of Randall County in 1889. In 1895 the company forfeited its remaining leases. Hutson formed a partnership with Emmett Powers, leased the block pasture, and replaced the T Anchor brand with the Crescent G. In 1900 Hutson sold his interest to Vinson Roe but continued to control the ranch until 1902. Powers and Roe subsequently dissolved their partnership, and the remaining holdings were sold in small blocks to farmers and other ranchers. Although the Cedar Valley Land and Cattle Company thus passed into history, many of its former employees, including Lowndes, Hutson, and Gordon-Cumming, stayed to put down roots in the Canyon area.

BIBLIOGRAPHY: Laura V. Hamner, *Short Grass and Longhorns* (Norman: University of Oklahoma Press, 1943). C. Boone McClure, A History of Randall County and the T Anchor Ranch (M.A. thesis, University of Texas, 1930). C. Boone McClure, "A Review of the T Anchor Ranch," *Panhandle-Plains Historical Review* 3 (1930). Mrs. Clyde W. Warwick, comp., *The Randall County Story* (Hereford, Texas: Pioneer, 1969).

H. Allen Anderson

CEDRIC, TEXAS. Cedric, a mile west of Ralls in Crosby County, was laid out in 1911 by Julian Bassett[qv] in an effort to kill the infant town of Ralls. Bassett had opened the town of Crosbyton in 1908 and, in a successful attempt to secure the county seat for his town, built in 1911 the Crosbyton-South Plains Railroad from Lubbock to Crosbyton. The rail line crossed John R. Ralls's[qv] ranch, and Ralls decided in 1911 to open a town, named for him, on the railroad. Bassett, wishing to be rid of the competition posed by Ralls' townsite, refused Ralls a depot. He laid out Cedric, where he built four brick business buildings, which were never occupied, and a depot. Settlers in Ralls freighted supplies from the railroad stop in Cedric to their community. By 1915, when the Santa Fe Railroad bought the Crosbyton-South Plains Railroad and made Ralls a regular stop, Bassett had conceded that he could not destroy the rival settlement and sold Cedric to John Ralls, who moved Cedric's depot and sidewalks to Ralls.

BIBLIOGRAPHY: Lubbock *Avalanche-Journal*, June 10, 1951. Nellie Witt Spikes and Temple Ann Ellis, *Through the Years: A History of Crosby County* (San Antonio: Naylor, 1952).

David B. Gracy II

CEDRON CREEK. Cedron Creek rises three miles east of Meridian and one-half mile southeast of Pilot Knob in central Bosque County (at 31°56′ N, 97°35′ W) and runs east for 10½ miles to its mouth on Lake Whitney and the Brazos River, near Cedar Shores Estates (at 31°57′ N, 97°26′ W). Known as Cedral Creek when the Texan Santa Fe expedition[qv] crossed it in 1841, the stream was probably named for the cedar trees that grew along its banks.

BIBLIOGRAPHY: William C. Pool, The History of Bosque County (M.A. thesis, University of Texas, 1946).

CEE VEE, TEXAS. Cee Vee is on Farm Road 1440 twenty-three miles northwest of Paducah in northwest Cottle County. The settlement was founded on land which previously belonged to the CV Ranch. In 1927 Lafayette M. Hughes sold off property of the Mill Iron Ranch (*see* CONTINENTAL LAND AND CATTLE COMPANY), which included the CV land. A post office for the new settlement was granted in 1928 with William Newson as postmaster. Newson had requested the name of CV for the post office, and although postal officials forbade the use of initials, they accepted Cee Vee. A school, begun in 1928, functioned in the old Mill Iron Ranch headquarters until a new building was constructed in 1930. A gin was built around 1929, and Cee Vee grew to include a feed supply, a barbershop, and two general stores. Methodist, Baptist, and Church of Christ congregations had organized by 1929. Local businesses supplied a large isolated farming area. By 1940 Cee Vee had a population of fifty and two stores. The school continued to function through the late 1950s. The 1980 census reported a post office, one business, and a population of seventy-one in the community. In 1990 the population was still seventy-one.

BIBLIOGRAPHY: Carmen Taylor Bennett, *Our Roots Grow Deep: A History of Cottle County* (Floydada, Texas: Blanco Offset Printing, 1970).   *Charles G. Davis*

CEGO, TEXAS. Cego is on Farm Road 1950 seven miles southwest of Chilton in western Falls County. When it was founded in the early 1880s by a group of German-American farmers, the community was known as Pleasant Valley. A few years later, when residents applied to the postal department for a star route, the name of the town had to be changed because a Pleasant Valley, Texas, already existed. The name Cego was chosen in honor of a cotton picker who had worked on several of the local farms. The Cego post office was granted in 1895; it was discontinued ten years later, and mail for the community was sent to Eddy.

The Pleasant Valley school began serving the district in 1885 and continued to operated under that name until after 1900. In 1904 it had two teachers and 149 students. The population of Cego proper was thirty-five in 1910. Two churches, a school, and several businesses marked the community on county highway maps in 1948, and the number of residents was estimated at 200. The school at Cego was consolidated with the Chilton Independent School District in 1949. Although the population of Cego was listed as ninety-eight in the 1970s and 1980s, local residents maintained that the actual number was closer to fifty.

BIBLIOGRAPHY: Vertical File, Texas Collection, Baylor University.   *Vivian Elizabeth Smyrl*

CELE, TEXAS. Cele is two miles west of Farm Road 973 and seven miles north of Manor in northeastern Travis County. It was established in the 1890s and was supposedly named for Lucille Custer, daughter of a local store owner. A post office opened there in 1896 with John Pitts Johns as postmaster. When the office was discontinued briefly in 1899, the community's mail was sent to New Sweden. The Cele post office reopened that same year but was again discontinued in 1902, when mail was routed through Manor. From the 1930s to the 1960s the population of Cele was reported at twenty-five. Cele was still listed as a community in 1990.

BIBLIOGRAPHY: Mary Starr Barkley, *History of Travis County and Austin, 1839–1899* (Waco: Texian Press, 1963). John J. Germann and Myron Janzen, *Texas Post Offices by County* (1986).
Vivian Elizabeth Smyrl

CELERY CREEK. Celery Creek rises thirteen miles northwest of Menard in northern Menard County (at 31°03′ N, 99°56′ W) and runs southeast for seventeen miles to its mouth on the San Saba River, a mile west of Menard (at 30°55′ N, 99°47′ W). The creek traverses flat terrain with local deep dissections, surfaced by shallow and stony soils that support oak, juniper, mesquite, and grasses.

CELESTE, TEXAS. Celeste is on U.S. Highway 69 two miles southeast of the headwaters of the Sabine River and ten miles northwest of Greenville in northwest Hunt County. Like many towns in Hunt County, it was a product of railroad development. The townsite was platted in 1886 by the Gulf, Colorado and Santa Fe Railway three miles north of Kingston, on open prairie already crossed by the Missouri, Kansas and Texas line. This location was chosen in order to ensure that Kingston, whose elected officials had refused to offer incentives to attract the Gulf, Colorado and Santa Fe to build through their community, would be bypassed by the line as it put down tracks from Paris through Farmersville to Dallas. Celeste was named for the wife of a Santa Fe official. The two rail lines stimulated rapid growth. A Celeste post office opened in 1886, and a number of merchants moved their businesses from Kingston to Celeste. By 1888 three churches were holding services in the settlement. The population by the mid-1890s stood at 600, and the community maintained three gristmills and cotton gins, a bank, a weekly newspaper, and a graded public school. Celeste was incorporated in 1900, and its population increased from 671 that year to 850 on the eve of World War I.[qv] By 1914 the community had two banks, three cotton gins, a water works, an ice factory, and a weekly newspaper, as well as some thirty-five other businesses. It reported a population of 1,022 by 1926. Its high school and two elementary schools registered 500 students. Some fifty business establishments, including two banks and a newspaper, were in operation. After the 1920s, however, the population of Celeste fell from 803 in 1933 to 518 in the mid-1960s; businesses correspondingly declined, from thirty to sixteen. After the 1960s the town revived; in 1976 its population was 745. In 1982 the community, where World War II[qv] hero Audie Murphy[qv] once lived, had a bank, four churches, ten stores, and a school that enrolled 300 students. The population in 1990 was 733.

BIBLIOGRAPHY: W. Walworth Harrison, *History of Greenville and Hunt County, Texas* (Waco: Texian, 1976). Kathleen E. and Clifton R. St. Clair, eds., *Little Towns of Texas* (Jacksonville, Texas: Jayroe Graphic Arts, 1982).   *Brian Hart*

CELINA, TEXAS. Celina is on State Highway 289 and Farm Road 455, fifteen miles north of McKinney in north central Collin County. It was established in 1879 and named by John T. Mulkey for his native town, Celina, Tennessee. A post office opened in 1881. By 1884 the town had a population of 150, a school, a Methodist church, and a cotton gin and gristmill, as well as several general stores. However, the population declined to a low of fifty in 1892. In 1902, when the St. Louis, San Francisco and Texas Railway reached the area, the town moved to its present location, one mile south of the original site. Celina was incorporated in 1907. In 1915 it had the first road in the county built exclusively for automobiles, Celina Pike. By that time it also supported two banks, a newspaper, and a municipal water works. In 1921 Lone Star Gas organized the Farmers Gas Company to provide service to small rural towns, including Celina. Three years later Texas Power and Light began service to the town. Area residents receive electricity through the Grayson-Collin Electric Cooperative, organized in 1937. Like many rural towns, Celina shrank during the Great Depression,[qv] from 1,126 in 1920 to 994 in 1940. Following World War II,[qv] however, the town grew steadily. In 1950 there were 1,051 residents. By 1980 that number had increased to 1,520 and by 1990 to 1,737.

BIBLIOGRAPHY: Roy Franklin Hall and Helen Gibbard Hall, *Collin County: Pioneering in North Texas* (Quanah, Texas: Nortex, 1975).

J. Lee and Lillian J. Stambaugh, *A History of Collin County* (Austin: Texas State Historical Association, 1958).

David Minor

CELOTEX, TEXAS. Celotex is on Farm Road 668 and a branch line of the Atchison, Topeka and Santa Fe Railway seven miles southwest of Hamlin in northeast Fisher County. The industrial town was named Plasterco for a gypsum plant that was moved from Goodlett to Fisher County in 1907, after the Orient Railroad (*see* KANSAS CITY, MEXICO AND ORIENT RAILWAY) had built into the area. By the late 1920s the plant owned seventy-two company houses for workers. A commissary established at the site served all area settlers. The company built a community center with a seating capacity of 400 that functioned also as a church and movie theater. A school, several churches, a golf course, and other sports facilities were available. Although production declined during the late 1920s and 1930s as a result of the Great Depression,[qv] the industry survived. On March 15, 1945, Celotex Corporation bought the plant and changed the community's name to Celotex. The population was 100 in 1947, when the school was consolidated with the Hamlin schools. The Celotex community and industry still appeared on 1980 county maps, and the community was still listed in 1990. Plasterco Lake, on a branch of California Creek, is northwest of the factory.

BIBLIOGRAPHY: Lora Blount, *A Short History of Fisher County* (M.A. thesis, Hardin-Simmons University, 1947). E. L. Yeats and E. H. Shelton, *History of Fisher County*, (n.p.: Feather, 1971).

Charles G. Davis

CEMENT, TEXAS. Cement or Cement City was on the Missouri Pacific Railroad three miles west of downtown Dallas, south of the Trinity River and north of the old site of La Réunion[qv] in central Dallas County. The community was named for the two cement plants, its largest employers. Émile Remond arrived from France in 1856, acquired property in the La Réunion colony tract after it dissolved in 1857, and began a brick-making business. Because of an interest in geology he began experimenting with the white rocks on the west bank of the Trinity and discovered in the late 1880s that the area was ideal for lime and cement manufacturing. He later started the Iola Cement Plant, which existed for only a short time.

Around 1901 a group of Galveston investors heard of the cement-making potential of the area and organized the Trinity Portland Cement Company. The Texas and Pacific ran through the area. In 1907 the company opened, and families moved in to work. A local post office operated from 1907 until 1915. At that time Cement had a population of 500, telephone connections, a physician, and grocery, drug, and general stores. A short time later Cement City High School was built. On November 15, 1928, the Cement City school system merged with the Dallas Independent School District.

By 1931 Cement City was incorporated and had a population of 609 and eight businesses. By the mid-1930s the number of businesses had risen to fourteen. The area became so highly industrialized through its production of cement, one of Dallas County's most important products, that the residential area of the town declined; the population in the early 1940s was only 249. By 1951 the community was unincorporated. The population rose to 450 in 1960, the last time Cement is mentioned as an independent community.

BIBLIOGRAPHY: Dallas *Daily Times Herald*, May 28, 1949. Sidney A. Davidson, Jr., *General Portland, Inc.: The Dallas Plant Story* (Dallas: Taylor, 1987). Rose Mary Rumbley, *A Century of Class: Public Education in Dallas, 1884–1984* (Austin: Eakin Press, 1984).

Lisa C. Maxwell

CEMENT MOUNTAIN. Cement Mountain, eight miles east of Graham in southeastern Young County (at 33°07′ N, 98°27′ W), rises to a height of 1,350 feet, 200 feet above the surrounding prairies. It derives its name from boulders of conglomerate sandstone and gravel that surround it. The mountain was traversed by the Fort Worth–Fort Belknap road, built in 1851. Supply trains bound for Fort Belknap and, later, more distant frontier forts shared the road with stagecoaches and mail vehicles such as those of the Fort Worth–El Paso Mail until 1876 and other local lines carrying passengers and mail until the late 1880s, when advancing railroads hastened the end of coach-delivered mail. Alfred Lane, pioneer Palo Pinto County cattleman, Texas Ranger, and brother-in-law of Charles Goodnight,[qv] was attacked and killed by Indians on Cement Mountain in July 1864. After dreaming the previous night that his parents had been massacred by Indians, Lane, despite Goodnight's warnings of the hazardous trip back, attempted to return to his home in the Keechi valley after helping Goodnight herd cattle to nearby Elm Creek, near Fort Murray on the Young-Throckmorton county line. Lane was temporarily buried on the mountain, then later reinterred at a cemetery two miles west of Black Springs (now Oran) in Palo Pinto County. In 1877, when widespread cattle rustling prompted the formation of cattlemen's protective associations, Cement Mountain served as an original boundary landmark for District No. 1 of the Northwest Texas Cattle Raiser's Association (later part of the Texas and Southwestern Cattle Raisers Association[qv]). The mountain is dotted with the remains of the homesteads and graves of early-day settlers. Bennett School was established in 1893 at a place on the mountain called Toe Hole Gap. The Center Ridge community waxed, then waned, on the west end of the mountain, where only its cemetery remains.

BIBLIOGRAPHY: Graham *Leader*, April 20, 1972. J. Evetts Haley, *Charles Goodnight* (Norman: University of Oklahoma Press, 1949). J. W. Wilbarger, *Indian Depredations in Texas* (Austin: Hutchings, 1889; rpt., Austin: State House, 1985).

Steve M. King

CEMENT PRODUCTION. Cement production is the manufacture of hydraulic cement from rock usually quarried by the manufacturer. The principal cement product is Portland cement, patented in England in 1824 and originally used as a substitute for lime mortar, but small quantities of natural cement and pozzolana are also manufactured. Limestone and clay, or materials containing the same mineral constituents, are mixed in definite proportions to produce chemical reactions during a burning process. The finished product is an extremely fine dry powder, which when wet will become hard. Certain regions of Texas, particularly where the Edwards and other limestones outcrop, are ideal for cement production. Cretaceous limestones and shales or clays suitable as raw materials for Portland cement can be found in the Blackland Prairies, Grand Prairies, Edwards Plateau, and Trans-Pecos[qv] areas of Texas. Iron oxide, also required for cement production, is found in iron-ore deposits in East Texas. Gypsum, used as a retarder in cement, is available in north central Texas, Central Texas, and the Trans-Pecos region. Along the Gulf Coast, cement producers have used oyster shell for calcium carbonate, while a Texas High Plains cement plant near Amarillo has used impure caliche as its chief raw material.

In 1882 there were two cement factories in operation in San Antonio and one in Austin. As late as 1909 Texas had only three factories, but between 1909 and 1925 cement manufacturing in Texas showed an increase of 185 percent, and the production of cement was the state's twelfth-ranked industry. Cement production in 1929 reached a peak of 7,369,000 barrels, fell to 2,973,000 barrels in 1933, and rose to 8,036,515 barrels from ten plants in 1945, when Texas was the second-largest producer and consumer of cement in the United States. The principal use of cement is in concrete and reinforced concrete. After World War II[qv] one of the large-scale uses for cement in Texas was the manufacture of concrete blocks for construction; hundreds of small plants sprang up all over Texas to produce large, hollow building blocks from a semidry mixture of cement and fine aggregate, shaped in a steel or cast-iron mold by either tamping or vibration. For a time these plants produced for a market in which there was a great scarcity of other types of material—and for that reason showed immense profits. As the construction industry stabilized after the war, many of these small cement plants were shut down, while others adjusted to smaller profits and more regular production. But the concrete building block had become a prominent part of postwar Texas architecture.

By 1954 Portland cement production totaled 21,350,000 barrels valued at $53,500,000. Portland cement ranked next to petroleum minerals in 1964, when its production increased to 29,600,000 barrels valued at $94,128,000. In the same year masonry cement production totaled 950,000 barrels valued at $2,917,000. Figures for 1966 indicated that cement production for that year was 2 percent higher than the preceding year, with Portland cement production exceeding 31,000,000 barrels valued at $100,166,000, and masonry cement production decreasing to a total of 922,000 barrels valued at $3,013,000.

In 1970 Portland cement production was over 35,000,000 barrels valued at more than $107 million. Masonry cement production was 955,000 barrels valued at over $3 million. In that year Texas had nineteen cement producers located in Bexar, Dallas, Ector, Ellis, El Paso, Harris, Johnson, McLennan, Nolan, Orange, Potter, and Tarrant counties. By 1976 thirteen companies were operating eighteen cement plants in twelve counties. By 1978 construction materials were in short supply, deliveries were delayed, and plans were announced to build new plants in Comal and Williamson counties. With a value of $393 million, total production in that year made cement the state's top-value construction material. Production of both Portland and masonry cement continued to increase, reaching a high in the mid-1980s, when 10,242,000 short tons of Portland cement valued at over $532 million were produced, along with 310,000 short tons of masonry cement valued at over $22 million. By the late 1980s Texas was the nation's leading producer and consumer of Portland cement, which was then being prepared at thirteen plants in Bexar, Comal, Dallas, Ector, Ellis, Hays, McLennan, Nolan, and Potter counties. Revenues from the state cement tax grew from almost $3 million in 1970 to almost $6 million by 1987. Foreign exports of building cement in 1987 totaled 1,882 short tons, and domestic shipments totaled 332,534 short tons. In addition, Texas imported 745,349 short tons of foreign building cement and had domestic receipts of 202,323. Thereafter, production of both Portland and masonry cement slowly declined. In 1990 Texas producers manufactured 8,000,000 short tons of Portland cement valued at $320 million, and 145,000 short tons of masonry cement valued at almost $12 million.

CENIZO INDIANS. The Cenizo (Cenis, Ceniz, Seniso, Zenizo) Indians were well-known Coahuiltecan Indians of northeastern Mexico during the late seventeenth and early eighteenth centuries. Some entered Mission San Antonio Galindo Moctezuma (north of Monclova, Coahuila) in 1698, and shortly thereafter others entered San Francisco Solano Mission near the site of present Eagle Pass, Texas. In 1718, when San Francisco Solano was transferred to San Antonio and became known as San Antonio de Valero, some of these Cenizos moved with it. The baptismal records at Valero include such names as Censoc, Censoo, Senizco, Senixzo, Sinicu, and Siniczo, all of which seem to be variants of Cenizo. However, H. E. Bolton[qv] has identified two groups: Cenizo (with Siniczo as a synonym) and Sinicu (with Censoc, Censoo, Senizco, and Senixzo as synonyms). J. R. Swanton followed Bolton by listing Cenizo (Seniso) as separate Coahuiltecan bands. Reanalysis of the primary documents is needed in order to clarify this matter.

BIBLIOGRAPHY: Frederick Webb Hodge, ed., *Handbook of American Indians North of Mexico* (2 vols., Washington: GPO, 1907, 1910; rpt., New York: Pageant, 1959). Joseph Antonio Fernández de Jáuregui Urrutia, *Description of Nuevo León, Mexico (1735–1740)*, ed. Malcolm D. McLean and Eugenio del Hoyo (Monterrey: Instituto Tecnológico de Estudios Superiores, 1964). Esteban L. Portillo, *Apuntes para la historia antigua de Coahuila y Texas* (Saltillo: Tipografía "El Golfo de México" de Severo Fernández, 1886). J. R. Swanton, *Linguistic Material from the Tribes of Southern Texas and Northeastern Mexico* (Washington: Smithsonian Institution, 1940). *Thomas N. Campbell*

CENSUS AND CENSUS RECORDS. In 1744 the population of Texas, according to Henderson Yoakum's[qv] *History of Texas* (1855), was about 1,500, centered largely around San Antonio. There were a few small settlements on the Rio Grande and in East Texas near Nacogdoches. An official Spanish census of December 31, 1792, records 247 male mulattoes, 167 female mulattoes, 15 male Negroes, and 19 female Negroes in a total population for Texas of 1,617 males and 1,375 females. The estimated population of Texas was 7,000 in 1806, and it was not much greater fifteen years later when Stephen F. Austin[qv] founded his colony on the Brazos River. In 1826 a census of the Austin colony showed 1,800 persons, 443 of whom were slaves. The colonization period of 1821–35 brought many settlers; the population was estimated at 20,000 in 1831. In 1834 Juan N. Almonte,[qv] after a visit to Texas, placed the population at 24,700, including slaves. In 1836 there were probably 5,000 blacks, 30,000 Anglo-Americans, 3,470 Hispanics, and 14,200 Indians in Texas. A population of about 50,000 is indicated by the vote for the first president of the republic in 1836, and the vote of 1845, the last year of the republic, indicated a population of 125,000. In 1847 a partial enumeration was made showing a population of 135,000, of whom 39,000 were slaves. In a census of the state for 1848 the total population was given as 158,356, of whom 42,455 were slaves.

The first United States census was taken in 1850, when the Texas population comprised 154,034 whites, 397 free Negroes, and 58,161 slaves. The second United States census in 1860 gave Texas a population of 604,215. Growth in population was rapid until the Civil War;[qv] the decade of 1860–70 shows the smallest increase of population of any of the decennial periods for which enumeration of population has been made. Between 1870 and 1880 the population of Texas increased 94.5 percent to reach a total of 1,591,749. The census for 1900 ranked Texas sixth in the United States, with 3,048,710 residents. Each decade showed an increase in population; in 1930 Texas ranked fifth in population with 5,824,715. In 1940 Texas was ranked sixth again among states, but the population had grown to 6,414,824. A 19.7 percent increase between 1940 and 1950 brought the population to 7,677,832. In 1955 Texas had an estimated population of 8,657,000 and ranked sixth in the nation. The 1960 census recorded 9,579,677 persons living in Texas. By 1962 the population had reached the 10,000,000 mark, with 75 percent of all residents classified as urban. The official 1970 population was 11,196,730.

During the 1970s the majority (58.5 percent) of population growth in Texas was due to an influx of people from other states. In the 1980s the increase was attributed to immigration from other countries (76 percent of net migration was from foreign nations). In 1980 the Texas population stood at 14,229,191. By 1990 it had increased by 20 percent to 16,986,510. During the 1980s minority populations grew considerably in the state. Between 1980 and 1990 Hispanic population figures increased by 45 percent, African Americans[qv] by 17 percent, and whites by 10 percent. In 1990 the ethnic breakdown of the population was as follows: 10,291,680 non-Hispanic whites, 1,976,360 blacks, 4,339,905 Hispanics, and 378,565 other groups. During the 1980s the rural population continued to decline, reaching a low of 19.7 percent of the entire state population in 1990. The farm population constituted 1.1 percent of the state total. Overall, the growth in Texas population since 1970 had exceeded the growth of the nation as a whole.

The United States Bureau of the Census has reported the following population figures in Texas:
1850   212,592
1860   604,215

1870	818,579
1880	1,591,749
1890	2,235,527
1900	3,048,710
1910	3,896,542
1920	4,663,228
1930	5,824,715
1940	6,414,824
1950	7,677,832
1960	9,579,677
1970	11,196,730
1980	14,229,191
1990	16,986,510

BIBLIOGRAPHY: Barnes F. Lathrop, *Migration into East Texas, 1835–1860: A Study from the United States Census* (Austin: Texas State Historical Association, 1949). Rupert N. Richardson, *Texas: The Lone Star State* (New York: Prentice-Hall, 1943; 4th ed., with Ernest Wallace and Adrian N. Anderson, Englewood Cliffs, New Jersey: Prentice-Hall, 1981). Texas General Land Office, First Census of Austin's Colony, 1826 (MS, Barker Texas History Center, University of Texas at Austin).

CENTENARY, TEXAS. Centenary was six miles west of Mount Pleasant and three miles north of Monticello in southwestern Titus County. A post office was established there in 1885 with A. J. Hutchings as postmaster. Although the post office was closed in 1888, the community was still in existence the next year, when the Knights of Labor held a picnic there. The tannery located there was still in operation in 1889.

BIBLIOGRAPHY: Wright Patman, *History of Post Offices—First Congressional District of Texas* (Texarkana, Texas, 1946?). *Titus County Times*, July 5, December 31, 1889.

Cecil Harper, Jr.

CENTENARY COLLEGE. Centenary College, in Lampasas, Lampasas County, was founded by local Methodists in 1883, the centennial of the organization of the Methodist Church in the United States. It was the first coeducational college in Lampasas. The school was housed in two three-story buildings, and the college's enrollment in its first year was 174. The Reverend Marshall McIlhaney was the college's first president. The school sold its property in 1894 and moved classes to the vacant Park Hotel. The hotel was destroyed by fire in 1895, and Centenary College closed. The former Centenary College buildings were used by a Catholic boarding academy, St. Dominic's Villa, between 1900 and 1925. The site is marked with a Texas Historical Commission[qv] marker.

BIBLIOGRAPHY: Marker Files, Texas Historical Commission, Austin.

Mark Odintz

CENTENNIAL, TEXAS. Centennial, on Farm Road 123 sixteen miles northeast of Carthage in eastern Panola County, was established before 1850. The community's first school, founded around 1867, also served as a church. A post office operated in Centennial from 1875 until 1913. By the early 1890s the town had two general stores, a grist and saw mill, and a population of thirty. In 1906 it had a school with an enrollment of seventeen white students and another school with an enrollment of ninety-seven black students. By the mid-1930s Centennial had a store, a cemetery, and a number of houses. Its estimated population in 1936 was fifty. The Centennial schools were consolidated first with Midyett and later with Carthage schools, and by the mid-1960s only a cemetery and a few houses remained in the area. In the early 1990s Centennial was a dispersed community.

BIBLIOGRAPHY: Leila B. LaGrone, ed., *History of Panola County* (Carthage, Texas: Panola County Historical Commission, 1979). John Barnette Sanders, *Postoffices and Post Masters of Panola County, Texas, 1845–1930* (Center, Texas, 1964).

Christopher Long

CENTENNIAL INSTITUTE. Centennial Institute, at Cannon, was a private school that operated for twelve years. It was established by John A. and Joseph L. Cobb, L. H. Scruggs, and Julia Benson in the winter of 1876–77. Later the Mason and Eastern Star chapters used the building for meetings and renamed it Centennial Masonic Lodge No. 500. The building burned in 1888 and was never rebuilt.

BIBLIOGRAPHY: Dallas *Morning News*, November 10, 1936. Graham Landrum and Allen Smith, *Grayson County* (Fort Worth, 1960; 2d ed., Fort Worth: Historical Publishers, 1967). Mattie D. Lucas and Mita H. Hall, *A History of Grayson County* (Sherman, Texas, 1936).

John G. Johnson

CENTER, TEXAS (Fisher County). Center, also known as Center Point, is on a country road one mile south of U.S. Highway 180 and four miles west of Roby in western Fisher County. Center Point school was operating on a site 1½ miles east of the later site of the community by 1889. The school was moved to its current site sometime thereafter, and its name was changed to Center. In 1940 Center had the school, Fairview Church, and a number of scattered dwellings. The school was consolidated with that of Roby in 1947 but was briefly reopened several years later as the black school for the Roby district. In the 1980s all that remained in the community were a number of homes.

BIBLIOGRAPHY: Fisher County Historical Commission, *History of Fisher County, Texas* (Rotan, Texas: Shelton, 1983).

Todd Sloan

CENTER, TEXAS (Houston County). Center, a farming community on Farm Road 1733 four miles northwest of Kennard in eastern Houston County, was established before 1900. A school was in operation there by 1897, when it had an enrollment of fifty-four. In the mid-1930s the community had a church and a number of houses. After World War II[qv] many of its residents moved away, and by the mid-1960s only a church and a few widely scattered houses remained in the area. In the early 1990s Center was a dispersed rural community.

Christopher Long

CENTER, TEXAS (Limestone County). Center is at the intersection of State Highway 164 and Farm Road 1953, seven miles west of Groesbeck in eastern Limestone County. In the 1940s it had a church, two businesses, and twenty-five residents. By the late 1960s its population had increased to seventy-six. Construction of Lake Limestone in the mid-1970s may have provided a small boost to the local economy. By the late 1980s, however, only a store remained at Center, though in 1990 the community's population was still reported as seventy-six.

Vivian Elizabeth Smyrl

CENTER, TEXAS (Lubbock County). Center is a farming community on Farm Road 2902 eight miles northeast of New Deal and seven miles southeast of Abernathy (Hale County) in north central Lubbock County. The settlement formed near a school about 1½ miles south of where Center is now located. Around 1925 the school was moved to provide a more central location; it also served as a meeting place for church services. In 1935 Center and three neighboring districts consolidated to create the New Deal Rural School District. The old Center school continued to serve as a meeting place for religious services, but around 1950 it was torn down and replaced with a new church building. The Center church remained active in the 1980s.

Charles G. Davis

CENTER, TEXAS (Shelby County). Center is seventeen miles from the Louisiana border and 118 miles north of Beaumont at the center of Shelby County. In 1856 or 1857 J. C. and Margaret A. Wilson and Jesse Amason donated the land for the town. The community was involved in the Regulator–Moderator War.[qv] In an election called in January 1866 Center was voted the new county seat, but a number of people disputed the results, and no action was taken for some months. Finally, in August of that year some Center residents stole the county records and moved them to Center, thereby permanently establishing Center as the county seat. A post office opened there in 1866. Sam Weaver surveyed the community's site in 1869. In 1882 the town's frame courthouse burned, and it was replaced by J. J. E. Gibson's "Irish Castle," which still stood in the 1980s and was a popular tourist attraction. The town was incorporated in 1893. The Gulf, Beaumont and Great Northern Railway arrived at Center by 1904. Local telephone service was started in 1905 and became part of the Bell telephone system in 1915. Electrical power was available at Center by 1909. The town's growth has generally been slow and steady: its population grew from 1,684 in 1910 to 3,010 in 1940 and to 5,827 in 1980. The 1980 population tabulations showed 3,903 whites, 1,906 blacks, 5 Filipinos, and 13 Asian Indians. In the 1980s Center manufacturers processed timber and poultry products. Some tourist trade came from fishermen on Toledo Bend Reservoir. In 1985 local businesses included a newspaper, two banks, two movie theaters, two hospitals, and two nursing homes. Around that time the town also had four low-income housing projects. The Center Independent School District had an elementary, a junior high, and a high school, and there was also a private church school. Center's reported population in 1990 was 4,950.

BIBLIOGRAPHY: Patricia R. McCoy, *Shelby County Sampler* (Lufkin, Texas, 1982). Charles E. Tatum, *Shelby County: In the East Texas Hills* (Austin: Eakin, 1984).
Marleta Childs

CENTER, TEXAS (Smith County). Center is a small church community just west of Owentown and near the site of Camp Fannin[qv] in northern Smith County. The area was settled by the 1880s, when the local Methodist church was built. The church became the center of the community and was periodically rebuilt. In the church's early years, services were conducted by a circuit rider and held only on the second Sunday of each month. In 1903 Center had a one-teacher school for white students and a second one-teacher school for black students; each school reported an enrollment of thirty-seven. During the 1920s the community's white students attended classes in a crude, unpainted, one-story school with one teacher and an average of twenty-five pupils. By 1936 the white school had closed, but there were still seventy-two pupils and two teachers at the black school. During World War II[qv] Center grew because of its proximity to Camp Fannin. The Center church was on land used for the training camp, and the military used it as a chapel. After the war the church was returned to community use. By 1952 the Center school, along with others in the area, had been consolidated with the Winona Independent School District. In 1972 Center consisted of the church, a cemetery, and some scattered homes just outside Owentown. A 1985 map showed a church and cemetery at the site.

BIBLIOGRAPHY: Edward Clayton Curry, An Administrative Survey of the Schools of Smith County, Texas (M.Ed. thesis, University of Texas, 1938). "School Sights," *Chronicles of Smith County*, Fall 1969. Mrs. W. E. Zorn and Mrs. Betty Shamburger, "Center Methodist Church," *Chronicles of Smith County*, Spring 1967.
Vista K. McCroskey

CENTER FOR AMERICAN HISTORY. The Center for American History at the University of Texas at Austin is a special collections library, archive, and museum that facilitates research and sponsors programs on the historical development of the United States. The center was established in December 1991 as a unit in the university's General Libraries to consolidate and make more visible the university's extensive holdings documenting the historical development of the United States. In August 1994 the Center for American History was made an independent operating unit in the university. The center's divisions are the Eugene C. Barker Texas History Collections, the Littlefield Southern History Collections, the Congressional History Collections, the Sam Rayburn Library[qv] and Museum (located in Bonham, Texas), the Winedale Historical Center[qv] (located near Round Top, Texas), the Western Americana Collections, the Special Collections for American History, the University of Texas Archives, and the Oral History Program. Its research-collection strengths are the history of Texas, the South, the Southwest, the Rocky Mountain West, congressional history, and specific national topics. In 1995 the center director was Don E. Carleton. The center supports research and education by acquiring, preserving, and making accessible research collections and by sponsoring exhibitions, conferences, symposia, oral history projects, publications, fellowships, and grant-funded initiatives. The center, with the exception of its Winedale Historical Center and its Sam Rayburn Library and Museum, is located in Sid Richardson Hall on the University of Texas at Austin campus, adjacent to the Lyndon Baines Johnson Library.[qv] *See also* BARKER TEXAS HISTORY CENTER.
Katherine J. Adams

CENTER FOR ARCHAEOLOGICAL RESEARCH. The Center for Archaeological Research, at the University of Texas at San Antonio, was established as an organized research unit in September 1974; it is housed in the College of Social and Behavioral Sciences. The center has four major goals: to train students in archeology, to promote archeological research in southern and south central Texas, to carry out archeological surveys and other investigations required by state and federal legislation, and to aid local agencies and citizens needing the services of professional archeologists. The first director of the center, 1974–87, was Thomas R. Hester; its first associate director was Jack D. Eaton, who became acting director in 1987.

Public, or contract, archeology, surveys, assessments, and excavations for local, regional, state, and federal agencies have been integrated with the UTSA anthropology program. The Friends of Archaeology, a public-outreach program, was developed in 1985 and has more than 100 members in South Texas. In addition to its focus on the archeology of southern Texas, center projects have been carried out in other parts of the state, New Mexico, Mexico, Belize, and Guatemala. The Gateway Project, a two-year study funded in large part by the National Endowment for the Humanities, conducted excavations, historical research, and ethnohistoric studies of Indian groups concentrated in the missions of San Bernardo and San Juan Bautista,[qqv] south of the site of modern-day Piedras Negras, Coahuila. The Colha Project, administered by the center from 1979 to 1987 and focused on excavations at the Mayan site of Colha, an ancient community that specialized in stone-tool production in what is now northern Belize. The Río Azul project, a Mayan excavation site in Guatemala, was initially sponsored by the center in the mid-1980s.

The largest project carried out by the center in South Texas involved the study of the archeological resources of the Choke Canyon Reservoir, on the Frio River in Live Oak and McMullen counties. The reservoir basin encompassed 40,000 acres, in which archeologists discovered more than 300 prehistoric and historic sites and carried out major excavations at several. Numerous center projects have involved the archeology of downtown San Antonio, including excavations at the Alamo[qv] and in its environs. In the early 1990s the center studied nineteenth-century neighborhoods being razed for the construction of the Alamodome. In 1985 a long-forgotten earthworks of Santa Anna's army was found in the La Villita area of San Antonio and was fully excavated by center staff. Among other prehistoric site studies done by the center in southern Texas are the excavations at the Panther Spring Creek Site in Bexar County; a survey of the proposed Applewhite Reservoir, also in Bexar County; excavations at the Hinojosa Site in Jim Wells County; and fieldwork on the Leona River in Uvalde County.

The center's research programs, including those sponsored through governmental contracts and those funded through grants from foundations, are reported in nine publication series. The most active series are *Archaeological Survey Reports,* with more than 200 volumes issued through 1992, and *Special Reports,* with 18 volumes. The *Choke Canyon Series* was completed in 1986, with the publication of 12 volumes on the center's study of prehistoric and historic resources in that reservoir basin. The other series, with limited numbers published to date, include *Archaeology and History of the San Juan Bautista Mission Area, Coahuila and Texas; Colha Papers; Guidebooks in Archaeology; Regional Studies; Río Azul Interim Reports;* and *Working Papers.* The center's Archaeology Laboratory is a regional repository for prehistoric and historic archeological collections and records. Hundreds of collections from Texas, New Mexico, and Belize are curated in the laboratory, which has been directed by Anne A. Fox since 1975.

Thomas R. Hester

CENTER FOR BIG BEND STUDIES. The Center for Big Bend Studies is a program of Sul Ross State University in Alpine. It is dedicated, through public programming, instruction, research, and publication, to enhancing public understanding of the cultural and historical development of the Big Bend, the Trans-Pecos qv region of Texas, and adjacent areas in New Mexico and along the Texas-Mexican border. The center was conceived in the 1970s, and planning began in 1982. An endowment to finance operations was initiated in 1983, and the board of regents of the University of Texas System qv gave final approval to implement its activities in February 1987. The center is managed by a director; Earl Elam assumed that responsibility in August 1987. The center, located on the campus of Sul Ross State University, publishes a newsletter and the annual *Journal of Big Bend Studies.* The management encourages the use of collections in the Archives of the Big Bend, the Museum of the Big Bend, and the Bryan Wildenthal Memorial Library, as well as other resources that relate to the culture and history of the region.

BIBLIOGRAPHY: Alpine *Avalanche,* January 27, 1983, November 6, 1986, February 26, 1987. *Earl H. Elam*

CENTER CITY, TEXAS. Center City, on U.S. Highway 84 north of Bennett Creek in eastern Mills County, was settled about 1870. When the county was organized, the townsite was laid out with a large area in the center designated as the site for the new courthouse. Built around this square were various businesses, including several saloons, several dry goods stores, two blacksmith shops, a general store, and a drugstore. But Goldthwaite became the county seat. By 1874 Center City had a post office, a gristmill, and a school. After a survey in the early 1870s designated an ancient live oak standing in the town as the exact center of Texas, the name of the town, which had previously been Hughes Store, was changed to Center City. Controversy was to break out when the tree was later threatened with removal by construction of State Highway 7 (now U.S. 84). Citizens won out, and in 1984 the live oak was still standing fifty feet south of the highway in the middle of a dirt road between Goldthwaite and Evant. The tree is included in *Famous Trees of Texas* (1970, 1984). Although the tree's exact age is unknown, early settlers were said to have held justice court under its branches until a courtroom could be erected. Early school and church services were held there also. By 1880 Center City had a church, and in 1885 the community reported a population of 100. In 1910 it had three churches. By 1920 Center City's post office had been replaced by rural delivery from Goldthwaite. In the late 1940s Center City reported three stores and an estimated population of seventy-five. In 1970 and 1990 it reported a population of fifteen and no businesses.

BIBLIOGRAPHY: Hartal Langford Blackwell, *Mills County—The Way it Was* (Goldthwaite, Texas: Eagle Press, 1976). Flora Gatlin Bowles, *A No Man's Land Becomes a County* (Austin: Steck, 1958). John A. Haislet, ed., *Famous Trees of Texas* (College Station: Texas Forest Service, 1970; 3d ed. 1984). *Claudia Hazlewood*

CENTER CREEK. Center Creek rises just outside Decatur in central Wise County (at 33°14′ N, 97°35′ W) and runs south for 8½ miles to its mouth on the West Fork of the Trinity River, two miles east of Paradise (at 33°11′ N, 97°36′ W). The creek was probably named for its location in Wise County. It traverses nearly level to undulating terrain surfaced by light-colored soils with loamy or sandy surfaces over reddish or mottled clayey or loamy subsoils.

CENTER GROVE, TEXAS. Center Grove, a farming community on Farm Road 1309 four miles northeast of Lovelady in southern Houston County, was founded in 1925 as a combination of two earlier communities, Pine Grove and Center Hill. In the mid-1930s the settlement comprised a school and a number of houses. In 1966 the community had a school and an estimated population of 300. Many of its residents have since left. In the early 1990s a number of houses were still at the site.

BIBLIOGRAPHY: *Houston County Cemeteries* (Crockett, Texas: Houston County Historical Commission, 1977; 3d ed. 1987). Houston County Historical Commission, *History of Houston County, Texas, 1687–1979* (Tulsa, Oklahoma: Heritage, 1979). *Christopher Long*

CENTER HILL, TEXAS. Center Hill, also known as Corinth, is a farming community 1½ miles west of Kennard in east central Houston County. The settlement grew up around a school, known as Corinth or Old Corinth School, that was established in 1857. In the mid-1930s the community had a school, a church, a cemetery, and a number of houses. Its school was later consolidated with that of Kennard, and by the mid-1960s only a church and cemetery remained in the Center Hill area. In the early 1990s Center Hill was a dispersed rural community.

BIBLIOGRAPHY: Armistead Albert Aldrich, *The History of Houston County, Texas* (San Antonio: Naylor, 1943). *Houston County Cemeteries* (Crockett, Texas: Houston County Historical Commission, 1977; 3d ed. 1987). Houston County Historical Commission, *History of Houston County, Texas, 1687–1979* (Tulsa, Oklahoma: Heritage, 1979). *Christopher Long*

CENTER: A JOURNAL FOR ARCHITECTURE IN AMERICA. *Center* is published annually by the Center for American Architecture at the University of Texas at Austin and distributed through bookstores by Rizzoli International. The journal, which was founded in 1985, is based on annual symposia organized by the center. Each edition surveys a current topic in American architecture through essays, illustrations, and presentations of major architectural projects. Subjects have included studies of the Mediterranean influence in contemporary building, the New Regionalism, and Modernist visions of the city and their influence on American urban architecture. The publication is funded in part by endowments and grants from foundations and individuals. *Patricia Henderson*

CENTERLINE, TEXAS. Centerline, also known as Lystra, was a ranching and farming community in southeastern Jones County about twelve miles northeast of Abilene. Its name referred to its location near the center of the southern Jones county line. A school was begun there in 1885. At its peak as a community center, Centerline had a Methodist church, where the other denominations in the area also met to worship. In 1905 Centerline had three schools with a total enrollment of ninety-five students. In 1909 the local school had forty-one students and one teacher. After 1910 the school was called Lystra, a name it took from the local post office, which served the community from 1910 to 1912. The community had a blacksmith shop, cotton gin, and grocery store in 1917. It also had a Woodman hall and a baseball field. By 1927 enrollment at the Lystra school had grown to eighty, with two teachers. The school was consolidated with the Hawley district on July 6, 1949. The population of Centerline and the area it served declined after the 1920s, and by 1936 it reported only fifteen residents. Fort Phantom Hill Reservoir,^qv built beginning in 1937, covered part of the area where Centerline lay. Much of the area was annexed to Abilene during the 1950s. In 1988 Centerline existed only as the name of Voting Precinct No. 6 in Jones County.

Sandra Hollis

CENTER MILLS, TEXAS. Center Mills was a farming community near the headwaters of Long Creek in north central Johnson County. The settlement, named for its location equidistant from Fort Worth, Cleburne, and Weatherford, developed sometime before 1866. Its existence, however, was short; there is no evidence that the settlement survived into the 1870s.

David Minor

CENTER PLAINS, TEXAS. Center Plains is on Farm Road 145 nine miles west of Kress in southwestern Swisher County. Originally there were two separate communities, Auburn and Center Plains, in the area. The first local school was organized in 1893 and was located six miles west of Kress. The school occupied one other spot before in 1916 reaching its final location near what is now the site of the Center Plains Gin. The community of Auburn, to the north, was founded sometime before 1900 and had a school, a grocery store, and a blacksmith shop. In 1922 the two communities merged their schools and constructed a red brick schoolhouse. Many community affairs and church functions were held at this building. In 1947 the Center Plains school district was merged with the Kress district, but the old brick building continued to be used for various community functions. It, the gin, two stores, and surrounding farms made up the Center Plains community in the 1980s.

BIBLIOGRAPHY: Swisher County Historical Commission, *Windmilling: 101 Years of Swisher County History* (Dallas: Taylor, 1978).

H. Allen Anderson

CENTER POINT, TEXAS (Camp County). Center Point is just off Farm Road 2057 nine miles southeast of Pittsburg in southeastern Camp County. The site was originally settled by former slaves, beginning shortly after their emancipation in 1865. Because the major roads through the area crossed at the center of the community, the settlement came to be known as Center Point. Settlers in the area had established a church by 1873 and a school by 1889. These were the focus of the dispersed rural settlement. By 1897 the one-room, one-teacher school enrolled thirty-one black children. That year the school was listed in the county school superintendent's report as being in bad condition and worth only fifty dollars. The school term was 100 days.

In 1900 the residents of the community began a long and ultimately successful campaign to improve their school. By 1908 the school had two teachers, and bonds voted shortly thereafter financed a four-room school building in 1916. The General Education Board donated $1,700 for additional buildings, and Julius Rosenwald later made donations totaling $5,750, which were also used for buildings, including a library. By the 1935–36 school year the school had become in many respects one of the best schools in the county. Its physical plant included four buildings with ten classrooms and was valued at $14,000. Nine of the ten teachers who taught in the Center Point school had at least B.A. degrees, and, despite the fact that black teachers were typically paid less than white teachers with the same education and experience, the average teacher's salary at Center Point was higher than that at any other Camp County school, white or black. The school term was 176 days, only one day shorter than the longest school term in the county. The school enrolled 279 students, 129 in high school. Many of the high school students came from other districts that did not offer the upper grades.

During the late 1930s the population of the area began to decline, at first because of the Great Depression^qv and then in the 1940s and 1950s because of increased economic opportunities for blacks in urban areas. By 1938 the enrollment in Center Point High School had dropped to seventy-eight, and by 1955 the district had been consolidated with the Pittsburg Independent School District. The 1983 county highway map showed two churches, a cemetery, and a community center at the site.

BIBLIOGRAPHY: Hollie Max Cummings, An Administrative Survey of the Schools of Camp County, Texas (M.A. thesis, University of Texas, 1937). Artemesia L. B. Spencer, *The Camp County Story* (Fort Worth: Branch-Smith, 1974).

Cecil Harper, Jr.

CENTERPOINT, TEXAS (Hays County). Centerpoint (Center Point) was about five miles south of San Marcos in southern Hays County. It was a public school community in the late 1800s and early 1900s and continued to serve Mexican-American residents of the area after the initial consolidation of county schools. In the 1980s Centerpoint was the site of a historical marker recording the route of the Spanish colonial King's Highway, or Camino Real (*see* SPANISH TEXAS).

BIBLIOGRAPHY: Tula Townsend Wyatt, *Historical Markers in Hays County* (San Marcos, Texas: Hays County Historical Commission, 1977).

Daniel P. Greene

CENTER POINT, TEXAS (Hopkins County). Center Point, a farming community on Farm Road 2653 some twelve miles southwest of Sulphur Springs in southwestern Hopkins County, was settled before 1900. A public school was operating there by the early 1900s, and in 1905 it had an enrollment of fifty-one. By the mid-1930s Center Point had a school, a church, and a number of scattered houses. After World War II^qv most of the community's residents moved away. Its school was consolidated with the Miller Grove School District, and by the early 1960s all that remained of Center Point was the church and a few houses. In the late 1980s it was a dispersed rural community.

Christopher Long

CENTER POINT, TEXAS (Kerr County). Center Point is on the Guadalupe River eight miles southeast of Kerrville in southeastern Kerr County. The site became a focal point for business activity when early settler Dr. Charles de Ganahl opened a post office in his home on the north side of the river in November 1859. Ganahl called the post office Zanzenburg in honor of his ancestral home in the Austrian Tyrol. The new postmaster, Dr. G. W. Harwell, renamed the growing community Center Point in 1872, when the post office was moved to the south side of the river. It is reported that he chose the name because the settlement was halfway between Kerrville and Comfort, as well as halfway between Fredericksburg and Bandera. The area's potential as a farming and stock-raising center, its healthful climate, and its abundant game continued to attract settlers. Virginia Jordan (Wright) de Ganahl, Charles de Ganahl's widow, deeded 200 acres to the San Antonio and Aransas Pass Railway in 1888. She hoped to draw the center of population back to the north side of the river around a community to be called Ganahl. Although the community never developed, the Ganahl depot, located a mile north of central Center Point, ensured the town's position as a trade center for the surrounding region.

By 1900 Center Point had an estimated population of 500, permanent churches, a solid business community, public schools, and a growing reputation as a health and recreation resort. Early newspapers encouraged the growth of the region. The *Excelsior*, published by John A. Corbell and edited by D. C. Nowlin and J. M. Coleman, began as a bimonthly paper in 1878. Thomas A. Buckner^qv of Bandera County established the weekly Center Point *News* in 1905. It continued publication under various owners until it was absorbed by the Kerrville *Times* in 1924. The town was incorporated, for public school purposes only, in August 1889 and in April 1890 elected its first school trustees. In February 1913 it voted to complete incorporation and establish a commission government. A new vote in October of the same year, however, dissolved the municipality. Center Point held its position as area trade center until the 1920s, when the paved highway skirted the edge of town and surrounding towns developed their own transportation facilities. The town maintained a stable population and business community throughout succeeding years. In 1984 its population was estimated to be 800. Much like other towns in scenic Kerr County, Center Point has several small service and manufacturing businesses and attracts a steady stream of vacationers, retirees, and summer residents. The population in 1990 was 623.

BIBLIOGRAPHY: Bob Bennett, *Kerr County, Texas, 1856–1956* (San Antonio: Naylor, 1956; bicentennial ed., rev. by Clara Watkins: *Kerr County, Texas, 1856–1976*, Kerrville, Texas: Hill Country Preservation Society, 1975). Matilda Maria Real, A History of Kerr County (M.A. thesis, University of Texas, 1942).
Ganahl Walker, Jr.

CENTER POINT, TEXAS (Panola County). Center Point, a farming community on Farm Road 959 fourteen miles northwest of Carthage in northwestern Panola County, was first settled after the Civil War.qv In the mid-1930s the community had a store, a church, and a number of houses. After World War IIqv many of its residents moved away, but in the mid-1960s a church and a few scattered dwellings still remained in the area. In the early 1990s Center Point was a dispersed rural community.
Christopher Long

CENTER POINT, TEXAS (Trinity County). Center Point was a farming community in northern Trinity County. The town's name derived from its location halfway between Nogalus Prairie and Honest Ridge, both of which were common school districts. In 1923 the schools were consolidated, and a new school was built at Center Point. In the mid-1930s the community had a school, a church, and a number of houses. Its school later closed, and in the early 1990s only a few scattered houses remained in the area.

BIBLIOGRAPHY: Patricia B. and Joseph W. Hensley, eds., *Trinity County Beginnings* (Groveton, Texas: Trinity County Book Committee, 1986).
Christopher Long

CENTER POINT, TEXAS (Upshur County). Center Point, also known as Pleasant Grove, is a farming community just off Farm Road 1404, ten miles southwest of Gilmer in southwestern Upshur County. It was established before the Civil War.qv During the antebellum period (*see* ANTEBELLUM TEXAS) a school known as Pleasant Grove operated in the settlement. In the mid-1930s the community had a school, a cemetery, and a number of scattered houses. During the 1950s most of its residents moved away. Its school was consolidated with the Gladewater school district, and by the mid-1960s all that remained of Center Point was a cemetery and a few houses. In 1990 Center Point was a dispersed rural community.

BIBLIOGRAPHY: Doyal T. Loyd, *History of Upshur County* (Waco: Texian Press, 1987).
Christopher Long

CENTER UNION, TEXAS. Center Union is a rural community just off Farm Road 155 and six miles northeast of Smithville in eastern Bastrop County. In 1905 it had a one-teacher school for eighty black students. County highway maps showed two churches, a school, and several scattered houses in the area. The Center Union school was consolidated with the Smithville Independent School District in 1962. A community center and two churches marked the community on county maps in the 1980s.
Vivian Elizabeth Smyrl

CENTERVIEW, TEXAS. Centerview was on Farm Road 59 fourteen miles southwest of Athens in southwestern Henderson County. By 1906 a school was in operation at the site; that year it had an enrollment of sixty-three. In the 1930s the settlement had a church, a school, and a number of houses. After World War IIqv the community's school and church closed, and by the early 1990s only a cemetery and a few scattered houses remained in the area.
Christopher Long

CENTERVILLE, TEXAS (Dallas County). Centerville was on Duck Creek twelve miles northeast of Dallas in eastern Dallas County. The townsite is within what is now the city limits of Garland along Centerville Road between Miller Road to the north and Broadway Road to the southeast. The Eastern Hills Country Club and the western finger of Lake Ray Hubbard are to the east. The community was located on the original land grants of John Little to the east, J. Mills to the north, and J. W. Keen to the south. The site was reportedly settled in the 1850s. It had a school with fifty pupils and one teacher in 1896–97. In 1936 the community reported two businesses, a school district, and a population of ten. By 1940 Centerville had lost one of its businesses. The last available population figure for the community was ten, reported in the 1947–48 *Texas Almanac*.qv

BIBLIOGRAPHY: David S. Switzer, *It's Our Dallas County* (Dallas: Switzer, 1954).
Matthew Hayes Nall

CENTERVILLE, TEXAS (Henderson County). Centerville, a former county seat, was twelve miles northeast of Buffalo, six miles west of Eustace, and sixteen miles northwest of Athens in Henderson County. On March 14, 1848, the Texas legislature reduced the size of the county and ordered a survey to determine the new center, which was northeast of Buffalo and between North and South Twin creeks. James H. Starrqv donated 100 acres for the town of Centerville, and voters selected it as the county seat. On September 11, 1848, the first court session was held in the town, and Centerville was divided into lots and blocks. A post office was established there on January 18, 1849, but was discontinued on June 19. By May of the same year the county court had been moved back to Buffalo, where it remained until October 1850, when, after further reduction of the county to its present size, Athens was designated the county seat. As a result of these changes Centerville was abandoned. In 1991 the old townsite was on the shore of the huge Cedar Creek Lake, in an area that was booming with development.

BIBLIOGRAPHY: J. J. Faulk, *History of Henderson County* (Athens, Texas: Athens Review Printing, 1926). *Memorial and Biographical History of Navarro, Henderson, Anderson, Limestone, Freestone, and Leon Counties* (Chicago: Lewis, 1893).
Theo S. Daniel III

CENTERVILLE, TEXAS (Leon County). Centerville (Centreville), the county seat of Leon County, is at the intersection of State highways 7 and 75, Interstate Highway 45, and Farm Road 1119, between two branches of Keechi Creek in central Leon County. When it became clear that Leona was an inconvenient county seat and did not meet the legislative requirement for centrality within the county, Centreville, named for its location, was laid out as the new county seat in 1850. In October of that year the county records were moved to the new community. A courthouse was also erected that year, and a post office was opened in December. From 1852 to 1856 the *Leon Pioneer* was published in the community. It was succeeded by a series of newspapers, including the Centreville *Times*, the *Texas Times*, the *Experiment*, the *Leon Lone Star*, the *Democrat*, and the *Leon County News*. In 1990 the community was served by the Centerville *News*. School was first taught in the community in 1851 in the back of a store, and a church, shared by several denominations, was built about the same time. In 1853 Frederick Law Olmsteadqv stayed in the Centreville Hotel, a drafty log cabin. The original courthouse was replaced by a brick building in 1858.

During Reconstructionqv a Freedmen's Bureauqv agent and an infantry company were stationed in Centreville. The community was dealt a severe blow when it was bypassed by the International–Great Northern Railroad in 1872. In 1884 Centreville had an estimated population of 300 and a church, a school, a saloon, two hotels, two general stores, a steam gristmill, and a cotton gin. Its courthouse burned down and was replaced by a new structure in 1886. The community had a population of 318 in 1900. In 1907 Centreville's black school district had 163 pupils and three teachers, while its white schools had 92 pupils and two teachers. A bank was opened in the community in 1910, and by 1914 Centreville had changed the spelling of its name to Centerville and comprised an estimated 600 inhabitants. A black man accused of murdering a white was taken from the county jail and lynched in the community in November of 1915. The community incorporated in 1930, when it had declined to a population of 388 with some twenty businesses. The courthouse square was paved in the 1930s by a Work Projects Administration[qv] project. Centerville established an annual Black-Eyed Pea Festival in 1937. The community had grown to 961 residents and 42 businesses by 1950, but slowly declined to 836 residents by 1960 and to 805 by 1980. In 1990 its population was reported as 812, and the community had some thirty-five businesses.

BIBLIOGRAPHY: Leon County Historical Book Survey Committee, *History of Leon County* (Dallas: Curtis Media, 1986).

Mark Odintz

CENTERVILLE, TEXAS (Trinity County). Centerville, at the junction of State Highway 94 and Farm Road 358, nine miles northeast of Groveton in northeastern Trinity County, was founded in 1935 when a consolidated school was built in the area. Centerville's population reached 400 in the mid-1960s; most of the residents earned their livings from farming, ranching, or forestry. The community's population declined in the 1970s and 1980s; 1990 estimates put it at forty.

BIBLIOGRAPHY: Patricia B. and Joseph W. Hensley, eds., *Trinity County Beginnings* (Groveton, Texas: Trinity County Book Committee, 1986).

Christopher Long

CENTRAL, TEXAS (Angelina County). Central is on U.S. Highway 69 eight miles northwest of Lufkin in northwestern Angelina County. The community was settled before 1900 and was originally known as Central School, for a schoolhouse that served the surrounding farms. In the mid-1930s Central had a school, two churches, and several businesses. Many residents left the area after World War II,[qv] but in the early 1990s Central reported a population of 105 and had a school, a church, a cemetery, and three stores.

Christopher Long

CENTRAL, TEXAS (Bee County). Central is a predominantly Czech farming community on a road between Farm roads 1349 and 888 some four miles south of Beeville in southwestern Bee County. The settlement is named for its location midway between Beeville and Olmos. Central was first settled in 1874 by Henry T. Clare, a native of Missouri, and his sons, John, Bud, Gus, Hillery, and Thomas. James B. Madray and Tom and Henderson Allsup of Tennessee arrived around this same time. Later settlers included Charles Sugarek, Jim Doubrava, and Valentine, Stephen, and Frank Kubala, who arrived around 1889. In 1888 the San Antonio and Aransas Pass Railway was constructed between Skidmore and Alice; it ran five miles east of Central. The community's first schoolhouse was built sometime in the early 1890s, and in 1905 the school had one teacher and twenty-seven students. Around 1915 a larger school was built. In 1938 a second teacher was hired, and the school offered seven grades. In the 1970s grain, flax, broomcorn, and cotton were the principal local crops. After the Central school was consolidated with the Beeville Independent School District, its schoolhouse was converted into a community center, where parties and dances were still held in the late 1980s. At that time the community still gathered on the first Saturday of the month for a covered-dish dinner at the community center, and Central's largest annual event was the Fourth of July barbecue and dance. Also at that time the local gravel road was being transformed from a county road to a Farm Road at a cost of $400,000.

BIBLIOGRAPHY: Grace Bauer, *Bee County Centennial, 1858–1958* (Bee County Centennial, 1958). Grace Bauer (Lillian Grace Schoppe), The History of Bee County, Texas (M.A. thesis, University of Texas, 1939). Camp Ezell, *Historical Story of Bee County, Texas* (Beeville: Beeville Publishing, 1973). Mrs. I. C. Madray, *A History of Bee County* (Beeville, Texas: *Bee–Picayune*, 1939).

Robert D. Crangle, Jr.

CENTRAL, TEXAS (Cherokee County). Central, also known as Central High, was a dispersed community on Farm Road 851 eight miles southeast of Rusk in eastern Cherokee County. The area was first settled after the Civil War,[qv] but a distinct community did not form until the establishment of Central High School at the site in the early 1900s. In the mid-1930s Central, as the community that grew up around the school came to be called, comprised the school and a number of houses, with several stores nearby. Central High was consolidated with the Alto school district in 1955. In the early 1990s a church, a community center, and a few houses still remained in the area.

BIBLIOGRAPHY: Hattie Joplin Roach, *A History of Cherokee County* (Dallas: Southwest, 1934).

Christopher Long

CENTRAL, TEXAS (Van Zandt County). Central, a farming community several miles northeast of Grand Saline in northeastern Van Zandt County, was the site of a local school built in 1901 on land donated by Zack Waddill. The enrollment at the Central school reached forty-four in 1905. A three-room school was built at the community in 1916. Several area churches met in the school before relocating at Crossroads. In 1936 the county highway map showed a school and two churches at the townsite. The local school was consolidated with the Grand Saline Independent School District in 1947. By 1987 only a single church and cemetery remained at the site.

BIBLIOGRAPHY: Van Zandt County History Book Committee, *History of Van Zandt County* (Dallas, 1984).

Diana J. Kleiner

CENTRAL COLLEGE. Central College, in Sulphur Springs, began in 1877 as Sulphur Springs District Conference High School. In 1882, after being offered the presidency of the school by the board of directors, Rev. J. W. Adkisson drafted a charter to reorganize the school as Central College. The charter was granted in 1883, and control of the college was transferred to the Methodist Episcopal Church, South, with Adkisson as the first president. The college departments included arts and sciences, primary, preparatory, commercial, and music. The school had two literary societies, Kappa Tau and Belles Lettres. Central College enrollment ranged from 150 to 200. Its property was valued at $20,000. In 1894 a Central College professor, H. P. Eastman, from Indiana, purchased the college and continued operation under a new charter. At that time the name was changed to Eastman College and Conservatory of Music and Art. The institution operated under Eastman's leadership until it was destroyed by fire in 1900.

BIBLIOGRAPHY: Kenneth and Sidney Brice, *A Century of Memories* (n.d).

Bob and Michelle Gilbert

CENTRAL COLORADO RIVER AUTHORITY. The Central Colorado River Authority (*see also* LOWER COLORADO RIVER AUTHORITY *and* UPPER COLORADO RIVER AUTHORITY), a state authority related to control of the Colorado River, was established in 1935 by the Forty-fourth Texas Legislature. This state conservation and reclamation district is limited in area to Coleman County, and its headquarters are in Coleman, the county seat. In 1939 the Texas legislature remitted to the authority, for a period of ten years, 50 percent of the state ad valorem taxes collected for general revenue purposes from

Coleman County. The major activity of the authority has been the prevention of flood damage and the construction of soil-conservation and municipal water-supply projects on a section of the upper portion of the river system, including its tributaries. The authority has pioneered in the practice of constructing farm and ranch tanks that average some five acre-feet in capacity. By 1949 over 1,000 of these, some ranging in size up to 115 acre-feet in capacity, had been constructed. The river authority has also built terraces, spreader dams, and diversion channels for the farmers of the county. In these activities the farmers and the authority were assisted by the Soil Conservation Service and the Production and Marketing Administration of the United States Department of Agriculture. The authority also built a number of community lakes, including those at Gouldbusk, Novice, Talpa, and Santa Anna. It sponsored the construction of Hords Creek Lake, which was completed in 1948. During the 1960s the Central Colorado River Authority had constructed another major reservoir, Coleman Lake. The river authority is governed by a nine-member board of directors appointed by the governor to six-year overlapping terms. In the early 1990s its major function was water conservation and supply.

Comer Clay

CENTRAL FREIGHT LINES. Central Freight Lines, with headquarters in Waco and regional offices in Dallas, Fort Worth, Houston, and San Antonio, is one of the oldest continuously operating Texas motor carriers, the state's largest intrastate motor carrier, and a southwestern regional interstate motor carrier. The company was originally known as Central Forwarding and Warehouse Company, when William W. (Woody) Callan, Sr., founded it in 1925 with a single Model-T truck to transport goods from Dallas to Waco merchants. Callan, who was born in 1905 in Valley Mills, Texas, and attended Waco High School, Toby's Business School, and Baylor University, went to work for Sanger Brothers[qv] before joining the Weathered Transfer and Storage Company as an assistant to the warehouse foreman. There he learned the freight business by dealing with shippers, railroads, and trucklines at a time when horse-drawn floats and wagons carried goods between railroad stations and customers' places of business. At the time Callan founded Central, security in transportation could not be guaranteed, government regulation did not exist, and trucking lines were seldom considered dependable or reliable because the roads were not paved. During World War II[qv] Callan further broadened his experience by serving as a warehousing chief for army service and supply offices in Atlanta and at the Pentagon.

He was soon joined at Central by his brother, T. H. Callan, who for fifty-three years managed the company's Dallas facility, which grew into the world's largest freight facility owned and operated by a single motor carrier. The company incorporated in 1927, beginning with regular routes between Dallas, Fort Worth, and Austin, but promptly abandoned a route to Houston because of poor weather and road conditions. In 1929, as trucking regulations increased, the firm's household-goods business became Central Forwarding, and its general freight transporter was named Central Freight Lines. Central started regular service to Houston in 1933 and began to purchase intrastate operating authority from other companies, including a route between Austin and Houston from Austin Forwarding.

The Central Federal Credit Union opened in 1940, independently of Central Freight Lines but with membership limited to Central employees. Callan ran both Central Freight and Central Forwarding, and the companies shared facilities and equipment, but Central Freight expanded more rapidly and separated from Central Forwarding in 1951. In 1952 Central opened its first equipment-maintenance shop in Waco. The same year Callan initiated an employee stock-ownership plan and stepped down as president but remained chairman of the board. Under his leadership the Employees Profit Sharing and Retirement Plan was established in 1959. Before his death on March 17, 1987, Callan was active in local banking, helped organize KWTX Broadcasting Company in Waco, and promoted school career days and fairs. R. H. Linam served as president of Central from 1952 to 1979. Woody Callan, Jr., served as president from 1979 to 1992. Tom Clowe became president in 1992.

In the 1980s, as the company faced threats of unionization and deregulation of interstate trucking, Central acquired West Texas carriers Curry Freight Lines and Perry Motor Freight, purchased authority for additional points and short routes in West Texas from another company, and acquired seventy-six Texas intrastate points when Red Arrow Freight Lines ceased its Texas intrastate operations. In 1991 Central expanded into Oklahoma, with terminals in Oklahoma City and Tulsa, and implemented a hub-and-spoke system for its expanding operations. In 1992 it began serving more than 300 points in Arkansas, New Mexico, and Tennessee, and opened several new terminals.

In 1992 Woody Callan, Jr., and Diana Callan Braswell, the son and daughter of W. W. Callan, Sr., retired from Central and together sold their Central stock to the company and the profit-sharing and retirement plan, making Central a truly employee-owned company. Employee owners and other Central shareholders elected to sell Central to Roadway Services, Incorporated, in April 1993. Central became a wholly owned subsidiary in that company's regional carrier group, which includes Viking Freight System in the West, Spartan Express in the central and southern states, and Coles Express in New England. Central now serves more than 5,200 cities and towns in Texas, Louisiana, New Mexico, Oklahoma, Arkansas, and Tennessee and handles more than 3.5 million freight shipments annually, ranging from cotton to oilfield equipment. In addition, the firm provides import and export service through all major ports in its Southwest system and handles international shipments and hazardous materials. Central is non-union, employs nearly 4,000 people, and operates more than 7,000 trucks, tractors, and trailers through three hubs and seventy-three terminals. Revenue exceeded $230 million in 1992.

BIBLIOGRAPHY: N. A. Adamson, *Railroad and Motor Freight Movement in the Golden Triangle Area* (Beaumont: John Gray Institute, Lamar University, 1983). *Centrally Speaking*, October 2, 1992. Garland A. Smith, *Men of Achievement in Texas* (Austin: Garland A. Smith Associates, 1972).

Rajni Madan

CENTRALIA, TEXAS. Centralia is on Farm Road 357 fifteen miles northeast of Groveton in northeastern Trinity County. The area was settled around the time of the Civil War.[qv] In 1873 a public square was laid off at the townsite on the Ainsworth survey, and various businesses were begun. The community was named Centralia for its location between Nogalus Prairie and Apple Springs. A post office was established there in 1874, and by 1885 the community had a reported population of 150 and several steam sawmills and gristmills, two blacksmiths, two general stores, a district school, and a saloon. Centralia's population reached 300 by 1914, but the town began to decline after World War I.[qv] In the mid-1930s only a store, a chair factory, and seventy-five residents remained there. By the early 1970s the community's remaining businesses had closed. In 1990 Centralia was a dispersed community with twenty-six residents.

BIBLIOGRAPHY: Patricia B. and Joseph W. Hensley, eds., *Trinity County Beginnings* (Groveton, Texas: Trinity County Book Committee, 1986).

Flora G. Bowles

CENTRALIA DRAW. Centralia Draw rises thirteen miles northeast of Rankin in eastern Upton County (at 31°19′ N, 101°52′ W) and runs east for forty-five miles across Upton, Reagan, and Irion counties to its mouth on the Middle Concho River, just east of the Reagan–Irion county line in western Irion County (at 31°26′ N, 101°15′ W). The draw crosses Farm roads 1555, 1800, and 33 and runs through the Stiles community in north central Reagan County. Centralia Draw is on a natural floodplain and has a bed of sand, gravel, and mud substrate. Water-tolerant hardwoods, conifers, and grasses grow along its banks.

CENTRAL AND MONTGOMERY RAILWAY. The Central and Montgomery Railway Company was chartered on December 31, 1877. The track was planned to begin at some point on the Houston and Texas Central Railway between Navasota and Courtney in Grimes County and extend to Montgomery, Montgomery County, in the timber belt of East Texas—a distance of twenty-five miles. The initial capital was $150,000, and the principal place of business was Plantersville, Grimes County. The members of the first board of directors were G. Jordan, F. A. Hyatt, F. A. Rice, and William D. Cleveland, all of Houston; Thomas W. Blake and Jack Baker, both of Plantersville; James H. Price and J. E. McCombe, both of Montgomery; and David White, of White Hall in Grimes County. In 1878 the railroad built twenty-seven miles of track, from Navasota to Montgomery, and on September 2, 1882, George Sealy^{qv} bought the road and conveyed it to the Gulf, Colorado and Santa Fe Railway Company. However, due to an adverse court decision regarding the legality of the original sale, the Gulf, Colorado and Santa Fe reacquired the Central and Montgomery at a sheriff's sale in 1887.
S. G. Reed

CENTRAL NATIONAL ROAD. The Central National Road of the Republic of Texas^{qv} was planned by the Texas Congress, which, on February 5, 1844, established a five-man commission to select a right-of-way, see that it was cleared, and supervise the building of necessary bridges. The commissioners, William M. Williams, John Yeary,^{qv} Rowland W. Box, Jason Wilson, and James Bradshaw, were paid for their services in land, much of which they selected along the route chosen. George W. Stell of Paris was the surveyor. The road was to begin on the bank of the Trinity River not more than fifteen miles below the bank of the Elm Fork in Dallas County and run to the south bank of the Red River in the northwest corner of Red River County, opposite the mouth of the Kiamachi River. As surveyed, the route probably started at John Neely Bryan's^{qv} crossing on the Trinity River, a little north of the later site of the Dallas County Courthouse, ran east by north to the Dallas county line, crossed Rockwall County near Rockwall, and cut off the southeast corner of Collin County. It then crossed northwestern Hunt County north and west of Greenville, ran along the southeast line of Fannin County through the site of present Ladonia, proceeded northeast across Lamar County through Paris, and extended nine miles within the extreme northwest corner of Red River County along the Red River to Travis Wright's landing. This terminus, six miles above old Jonesborough, later became the site of Kiomatia; in 1844 it was the head of navigation on the Red River. To the north and east the Central National Road connected with the military road to Fort Gibson and old roads connecting the Jonesborough area with settlements in Arkansas. At its southern terminus it connected with the road opened in 1840 between Austin and Preston Bend on the Red River, in effect making an international highway between St. Louis and San Antonio. The international role that Congress may have visualized for the road was never fulfilled, however, because of population shifts that came with the westward movement of the frontier and the subsequent development of new towns and increased importance of other routes. *See also* NATIONAL ROAD.
BIBLIOGRAPHY: Clarksville *Northern Standard*, March 2, 1844. J. W. Williams, "The National Road of the Republic of Texas," *Southwestern Historical Quarterly* 47 (January 1944).

CENTRAL NAZARENE COLLEGE. Central Nazarene College, near Hamlin, was established for the Hamlin, San Antonio, and New Mexico districts of the Church of the Nazarene under the guidance of Rev. W. E. Fisher, superintendent of the Abilene and Hamlin districts. The college was chartered in 1909, when a board of directors and a building committee were elected. The charter provided for the teaching of the doctrine of salvation as set forth in the church manual, and the faculty had to meet church requirements for teaching of "sanctification." The school opened in 1911 with J. E. L. Moore as president and with grammar, academy, and junior college departments. Students were required to attend chapel, prayer meeting, Sunday school, and church services and to take Bible courses. The curriculum was primarily for ministerial students; their courses included Greek, Hebrew, church history, homiletics, and Bible. Courses in literature, commerce, speech, and music were also offered. Though it had no football or baseball program, the college encouraged physical education and later had a modified military-training program. Central became the only Nazarene college in Texas when it was merged with the Nazarene school at Pilot Point not long after 1911.

The physical plant, located just southwest of downtown Hamlin, included a gray stone administration building and two wooden dormitories on a campus of twenty-three acres. Library and laboratory facilities were inadequate for standard work, however. Throughout most of its eighteen years of existence, Central Nazarene College averaged between 100 and 150 students; in the 1922–23 session it had 122 students and graduated eight from the college department and fourteen from the academy department. In 1929, as the general economy faltered, President B. F. Neeley agreed to the consolidation of Central with Bethany Peniel College in Bethany, Oklahoma. The former administration building in Hamlin was used as a church by the local Nazarene congregation until it burned in 1934; a new church building replaced it in 1936.
BIBLIOGRAPHY: Hooper Shelton and Homer Hutto, *The First 100 Years of Jones County* (Stamford, Texas: Shelton, 1978).
H. Allen Anderson

CENTRAL PLAINS ACADEMY. Central Plains Academy, at Estacado in Crosby County, was founded in 1890 by Quakers who had opened a school there in the fall of 1882 for six pupils taught by Emma Hunt. The student body had increased to thirty-two by 1886, when the two teachers each received forty-five dollars a month as salary. In 1884 the school was made a high school and equipped with patented desks. In 1889 it was raised to junior college rank and named Central Plains Academy. It was the first institution of higher learning on the Llano Estacado.^{qv} Rev. Jesse H. Moore was made president of the college; he had an M.A. from Harvard University and a Ph.D. from Johns Hopkins University. Other teachers included E. C. Lewis and Elva Lewis, both master of arts graduates of Penn College. Mrs. Jesse H. Moore, bachelor of music from Johns Hopkins University, was teacher of music, voice, and violin. The two-year institution was originally housed in a new twenty-by-sixty-foot frame building next to the Quaker church, and the rest of the school was taught in the church. Enrollment grew to over 100 students; the first and only graduating class had eighteen students. In the spring of 1893 Central Plains Academy closed. The Quaker community was disintegrating as farmers left in discouragement due to drought and grasshoppers. *See also* RELIGIOUS SOCIETY OF FRIENDS.
BIBLIOGRAPHY: Roger A. Burgess, "Pioneer Quaker Farmers of the South Plains," *Panhandle-Plains Historical Review* 1 (1928). Crosby County Pioneer Memorial Museum, *A History of Crosby County, 1876–1977* (Dallas: Taylor, 1978). Crosby County Pioneer Memorial Museum, *Estacado: Cradle of Culture and Civilization on the Staked Plains of Texas* (Crosbyton, Texas, 1986; based on an M.A. thesis by John Cooper Jenkins).
Mary L. Cox

CENTRAL PLAINS COLLEGE AND CONSERVATORY OF MUSIC. Central Plains College, the first junior college in Plainview, was originally established in 1907 as Central Plains Holiness College on land given by Ferd Falkner. The school was intended to serve students from the Nazarene Church. L. L. Gladney of Mississippi accepted an invitation to become the institution's first president and soon persuaded the governing board to accept students of other denominations. After the college's name was changed to Central Plains College and Conservatory of Music, it opened, on September 18, 1907.

Within the first year some 159 students enrolled. The institution was coeducational but stressed military training. Students wore blue uniforms and kept strict schedules. Classes were taught from grade school through college; tuition ranged from thirty-five dollars a term for grades one through eight to $150 for nine months of college. Campus facilities included a three-story main building, two three-story dormitories, and a smaller music building. The college was set up to be self-sufficient and thus maintained a laundry and several barns and stables. By 1910 the campus had grown to about fifty acres. College classes included music, business, theology, liberal arts, and dressmaking. The enrollment was estimated at 152 in 1908 and 225 in 1909. After three years, however, the task of running the school became too great for the Nazarenes, who sold the college for $32,000 to the Methodist Church of Plainview on December 27, 1910. The institution was renamed Seth Ward College.qv

BIBLIOGRAPHY: Mary L. Cox, *History of Hale County, Texas* (Plainview, Texas, 1937). Vera D. Wofford, ed., *Hale County Facts and Folklore* (Lubbock, 1978).

Charles G. Davis

CENTRAL TEXAS COLLEGE. Central Texas College in Waco was founded in 1902 as Central Texas Academy by black Baptists to provide instruction from first grade to college. The academy became a college in 1907. Enrollment was small at the beginning but gradually peaked at almost 500 students. The first building was named Katy Ross Padgitt Hall, after a local white benefactor; an administration building was built in 1911. Students, recruited by visiting preachers in area churches, chose from a curriculum that included theological and teacher training, business, music, and a variety of trades, as well as academic courses in such fields as literature and drama. The all-black faculty numbered as many as eleven; they included local physicians and ministers who served on a part-time basis. The school had an unofficial but close relationship with New Hope Baptist Church of Waco. Central Texas College was governed by a board of trustees that included local black Baptist ministers. John W. Strong served as principal and then president from 1904 until 1928, when he moved to Chicago. After two other administrators served briefly, the school closed in 1931 due to financial difficulty. The campus site was obliterated by U.S. Highway 84 in the early 1950s.

BIBLIOGRAPHY: Dayton Kelley, ed., *The Handbook of Waco and McLennan County, Texas* (Waco: Texian, 1972).

M. Rebecca Sharpless

CENTRAL TEXAS COLLEGE–AMERICAN EDUCATIONAL COMPLEX. Central Texas College, Killeen, was approved in a Bell County bond election and opened on September 1, 1967. The first president of the college was Luis M. Morton, Jr. The campus is situated five miles west of Killeen on the south side of U.S. Highway 190 and was formerly part of Fort Hood. As the role of the college expanded to serve both the local community and military personnel around the world, three other educational institutions, the Research Institute for Advanced Technology, the American Technical Institute, and the Central Texas Vocational Skills Training Center were added to what became in 1984 the American Educational Complex College District. In addition to its Bell County facilities the complex runs a variety of programs at military installations around the world. In 1985 it served some 250,000 students, of whom about 15,000 attended the Killeen campus; 6,000 attended a campus at Fort Hood.

BIBLIOGRAPHY: Bell County Historical Commission, *Story of Bell County, Texas* (2 vols., Austin: Eakin Press, 1988). Judy Bicknell, "Education," *Killeen Magazine*, 1985.

L. M. Morton, Jr.

CENTRAL TEXAS AND NORTHWESTERN RAILWAY. The Central Texas and Northwestern Railway Company operated between Waxahachie and Garrett and was originally chartered as the Waxahachie Tap Railroad Company. When the Houston and Texas Central was planning to extend its route through Ellis County in 1870, the people of Waxahachie refused to offer a bonus for the new road for fear that undesirables might settle in a railroad town. The citizens soon realized their mistake, however, as the neighboring rival town of Ennis reaped the benefits of the railroad. The townspeople of Waxahachie, led by Justus W. Ferris, Henry W. Graber, John G. Williams, and C. D. Pickett, received a charter establishing the Waxahachie Tap on January 25, 1875. The city of Waxahachie contributed $13,600 in bonds. Construction on the 12.36-mile road between the county seat and Garrett, located three miles north of Ennis on the Houston and Texas Central, was completed by September 1879. On September 28, 1881, an amendment to the original charter of the Waxahachie Tap changed the name to Central Texas and Northwestern Railway Company. Members of the board of directors at that time included G. Jordan, Eber W. Cave,qv Robert M. Elgin, John O. Carr, and A. S. Richardson. In 1892 the company owned one locomotive, seventy-eight freight cars, and two passenger cars and earned $15,777 in passenger revenue, $67,744 in freight revenue, and $2,882 in other revenue. Earnings for 1895 had increased to $107,521. The road hauled lumber, grain, cotton, and flour. The Texas legislature authorized the purchase and consolidation of the CT&NW with the Houston and Texas Central, which occurred on August 22, 1901. In 1934 the Houston and Texas Central became part of the Texas and New Orleans Railroad Company, which was merged with the Southern Pacific in 1961.

BIBLIOGRAPHY: H. W. Graber, *The Life Record of H. W. Graber, A Terry Texas Ranger, 1861–1865* (1916; facsimile, *A Terry Texas Ranger*, Austin: State House, 1987).

Robert J. Haaser

CERDA, ALFREDO DE LA (1887–1902). Alfredo de la Cerda, rancher and suspected cattle thief, was born in 1887. He and his brother Ramón and their father owned the Francisco de Asís Ranch, which bordered the King Ranch.qv Alfredo's father was killed in 1900 by a Brownsville policeman. In 1901 the brothers were arrested and charged with rustling cattle from the King Ranch and changing the King brand from a "W" to "Bar-W". Ramón was in the process of branding cattle on King's El Saenz pasture when he was killed by ranger Anderson Yancey Bakerqv in an exchange of gunfire on May 16, 1902. Baker was supported financially and legally by Richard King, John B. Armstrong,qqv and the Lyman brothers. An inquest into the incident stated that Baker acted in self-defense. Six days after his death Ramón's body was secretly disinterred and appeared to have been dragged and mistreated. When word of the mistreatment was spread in the Brownsville Spanish-language newspaper, a local group known as the Red Club, which opposed the Texas Rangersqv and prominent ranchers, excoriated the rangers' actions. An ambush on Baker and two other rangers, Emmett Roebuck and Jesse Miller, occurred on September 9, 1902. Roebuck was killed, Baker was slightly wounded, and Miller was unhurt, although his horse was killed. Alfredo and five other men suspected in the ambush were arrested after an investigation by ranger captain John A. Brooks.qv Heroulano Berbier, who was to testify against Alfredo, was killed before he could do so.

An attempt to lynch Alfredo was prevented by the rangers, and he was freed on bond. He swore to kill Baker or pay $1,000 to anyone who killed him. Baker, however, acted first. At the time he was shot Alfredo had been trying on a pair of gloves at Tomás Fernández's store, on the corner of Elizabeth and Thirteenth in Brownsville. Baker shot Alfredo in the back with a rifle shortly before 5:00 P.M. on October 3, 1902. Baker and other rangers fled to Fort Brown, two blocks away, to avoid a gathering mob. Using money provided by the Kings and others, Baker was freed on bond. In September of 1903 Baker was acquitted of the killings of Ramón and Alfredo.

BIBLIOGRAPHY: Milo Kearney and Anthony Knopp, *Boom and Bust: The Historical Cycles of Matamoros and Brownsville* (Austin: Eakin

Press, 1991). Américo Paredes, *With His Pistol in His Hand: A Border Ballad and Its Hero* (Austin: University of Texas Press, 1958). J. Lee and Lillian J. Stambaugh, *The Lower Rio Grande Valley of Texas* (San Antonio: Naylor, 1954). William Warren Sterling, *Trails and Trials of a Texas Ranger* (Norman: University of Oklahoma Press, 1968). Walter Prescott Webb, *The Texas Rangers* (Boston: Houghton Mifflin, 1935; rpt., Austin: University of Texas Press, 1982).

Juan O. Sanchez

CERRACCHIO, ENRICO FILIBERTO (1880–1956). Enrico Filiberto Cerracchio, sculptor, was born in Castel Vetro Val Furtore, Italy, on March 14, 1880, the son of Memnato and Joseppa (Alterisio) Cerracchio. He studied both academic subjects and sculpture at the Institute Avellino in Italy. After graduating in 1898 he continued his studies in sculpture under Rafael Belliazzi. In 1900 Cerracchio immigrated to the United States and settled in Houston, where he sculpted commemorative monuments and busts for forty years. He became a naturalized citizen in 1905 and two years later married Marion Kowalski of Shamokin, Pennsylvania; they had a daughter and a son.

Cerracchio worked in a heroic, classicizing style, generally choosing bronze or marble as his medium. After World War I[qv] he won recognition with two sculptures commemorating the American doughboy: one was presented to Gen. Armando Diaz and accepted by the Italian government, and the other was presented to Gen. John J. Pershing[qv] by the city of Houston. Cerracchio's best-known Texas sculpture is probably the large bronze equestrian figure of Sam Houston[qv] (1924) located at the entrance to Hermann Park in Houston; the figure points toward the site of the battle of San Jacinto.[qv] Other well-known works by the sculptor include a marble portrait bust of the first Texas woman governor, Miriam A. Ferguson[qv] (1926), located in the Capitol,[qv] and a bronze memorial bust of Confederate major general John A. Wharton[qv] (n.d.), located in the State Cemetery.[qv] Cerracchio also executed portrait busts of such notables as Vice President John Nance Garner,[qv] Houston banker and public official Jesse H. Jones,[qv] physicist Albert Einstein, and Hollywood idol Rudolf Valentino. In later years he maintained a studio in Houston and one in New York City, where he was living at the time of his death, on March 20, 1956.

BIBLIOGRAPHY: *New York Times*, March 22, 1956. *Who Was Who in America*, Vol. 6.

Kendall Curlee

CERRITO CREEK. Cerrito Creek rises 5½ miles southwest of Mirando City in southern Webb County (at 27°23′ N, 99°03′ W) and runs southwest for sixteen miles to its mouth on San Juanita Creek, fifteen miles southeast of Laredo (at 27°20′ N, 99°15′ W). The creek rises in low-rolling terrain and descends to flat terrain with locally shallow depressions. Its soil bed is surfaced by clay and sandy loams. Grasses, mesquite, and chaparral grow along Cerrito Creek's upper reaches, and water-tolerant hardwoods and various grasses grow near its mouth.

CERRO ALTO MOUNTAIN. Cerro Alto Mountain is forty-five miles west of Dell City in northwestern Hudspeth County (at 31°57′ N, 105°58′ W). Its summit, with an elevation of 6,787 feet above sea level, is the highest point in the Hueco Mountains, which are composed of Permian limestone, some 250 million years old. The area is surfaced by shallow, stony soils that support scrub brush and grasses.

CERRO BOLUDO. Cerro Boludo is two miles north of San Jacinto Mountain in east central Presidio County (at 29°48′ N, 103°57′ W). Its summit, at an elevation of 4,740 feet above sea level, rises 740 feet over Little San Jacinto Creek, which runs along its southern edge. Its name is Spanish for "round (or bald) hill." Cerro Boludo is a Tertiary intrusion surrounded by sedimentary deposits of sandstones and conglomerates in the Alamito Creek valley. The surrounding terrain of desert mountains and rugged canyonland is surfaced by loose rubble. Local vegetation consists primarily of sparse grasses, cacti, and desert shrubs of conifers and oaks.

CERRO CASTELLAN. Cerro Castellan, less commonly known as Castolon Peak or Castellan Peak, is a prominent conical mountain rising from the desert floor about a mile northeast of the Castolon ranger station in Big Bend National Park,[qv] Brewster County (at 29°09′ N, 103°30′ W). The mountain is part of a series of summits once known as the Carazones Peaks. Cerro Castellan's peak reaches an elevation of 3,293 feet above sea level, and rises more than 1,000 feet above the terrain below. The geologic origin of the peak, like that of so many other topographic highs in this region of West Texas, is differential erosion—a resistant rock wearing away more slowly than rocks around it. Cerro Castellan is a high stack of volcanic rocks, including ash, lava, and tuffaceous rocks. It is capped by a dense lava flow underlain by various tuffs and basalts. A northwest-trending fault cuts the eastern flank of Cerro Castellan. Though little vegetation grows on the sheer cliffs and steep, pointed profile of its peak, the lower slopes of Cerro Castellan support a sparse growth of Chihuahuan Desert scrub, including most prominently such characteristic species as creosote bush and ocotillo. The name Cerro Castellan seems to mean "castle-warden's hill," though the reasons for this name's adoption are obscure.

BIBLIOGRAPHY: Virginia Madison and Hallie Stillwell, *How Come It's Called That? Place Names in the Big Bend Country* (Albuquerque: University of New Mexico Press, 1958).

CERRO DIABLO MOUNTAIN. Cerro Diablo Mountain is twelve miles southwest of Dell City in north central Hudspeth County (at 31°54′ N, 105°24′ W). It rises 5,717 feet above sea level and is surfaced with shallow, stony soils that support scrub brush and grasses.

CESTOHOWA, TEXAS. Cestohowa (originally Czestochowa) is on Farm Road 3191 and Cibolo Creek a mile west of State Highway 123 in northern Karnes County. It is a daughter settlement of Panna Maria, the oldest Polish settlement in America, and is named after the city in Poland where the famous painting of Our Lady of Czestochowa, the patroness of Polish Catholics everywhere, is enshrined. In 1873, as the population of Panna Maria grew, a group of about forty families decided to start a new community five miles north. They first built a small school that also served as a chapel. The priest came from Panna Maria once a month to say Mass and made special trips for other purposes. In 1877 land was donated for a church, which was completed on February 10, 1878, and placed under the patronage of the Nativity of the Blessed Virgin Mary; the church was remodeled in 1931 and repaired and painted again in 1973. By 1878 the town had 175 residents, a gristmill, a gin, and a school. By 1892 a bank was in operation in Cestohowa. During that decade the population reached 170 families. In 1898 some residents moved north and formed the new community and parish at Kosciusko in Wilson County. In 1902 others formed a new parish at Falls City. But Cestohowa continued to progress and at various times had two general stores, a cotton gin, and several blacksmith shops. The town had lost its bank and several other businesses by 1914. A Cestohowa post office was established in 1883 and discontinued in 1918, when local mail was routed through Falls City. In 1936 the community had only 100 residents. Its population was 200 in 1970. The first school in Cestohowa was St. Joseph's, a parochial school. In 1937 it was incorporated into the Karnes County public school system. A new eight-grade Cestohowa school was built in 1964, but declining enrollment led to its closure in 1974. As part of the Falls City schools, it reopened in 1975 as a three-grade school, operated a few years, and was closed again. In 1990 Cestohowa remained a lively community centered about its fine church building, a large parish hall, and a community center that occupied the former school building. That year its population was 110.

BIBLIOGRAPHY: Robert H. Thonhoff, History of Karnes County (M.A. thesis, Southwest Texas State College, 1963). Vertical Files, Barker Texas History Center, University of Texas at Austin (Karnes County, Texas).
Robert H. Thonhoff

CHABOT, FREDERICK CHARLES (1891–1943). Frederick Charles Chabot, diplomat and historian, was born in San Antonio on May 11, 1891, the son of Charles Jasper and Pauline Minter (Waelder) Chabot. After graduating from San Antonio High School in 1909 (with the "highest honors any graduate had received up to that time," according to his obituary), he embarked upon studies overseas at the Sorbonne and the University of Berlin, where he focused on music and languages. After returning to Texas, he had a brief career as a concert pianist and organist. He also apparently tried his hand in the insurance and real estate businesses, as well as doing historical research in 1915–16. Perhaps because his grandfather, George S. Chabot, had served in the British Foreign Service, Chabot decided to prepare for a career in the State Department by attending classes at George Washington University in Washington. In 1917 he found his first government employment working for the Library of Congress; by April of that year he was performing duties as a special agent of the Department of Justice. In June 1917 he embarked upon his career in the diplomatic service. During the next eight years he moved from posting to posting—Paris, Athens, Sofia, Rio de Janeiro, San Salvador, San José, and finally, in 1923, Caracas. His service in the diplomatic corps was not smooth: he had conflicts with superiors, was reprimanded several times for infractions of State Department rules, and, while serving in San Salvador, was arrested by local officials on what appeared to be trumped-up charges of being drunk and disorderly. His last chance for saving his career had been in Caracas, but his poor and sometimes incoherent reports from the field eventually moved the State Department to ask him to resign or face being fired. Despite protests that he was a victim of Republican politics, Chabot tendered his resignation in December 1924.

After returning to Texas he made a more positive contribution in the field of historical research. He published his first book, *The Alamo, Altar of Texas Liberty,* in 1931, and continued his writing and research on Texas and Mexican history for the remainder of his life. Through the auspices of the Yanaguana Society,qv founded by Chabot in 1933 and devoted to promoting the study of Texas history, he published and edited a number of brief books on a variety of topics. His most notable works are *With the Makers of San Antonio* (1937); *Excerpts from the Memorias for the History of Texas, by Father J. A. Morfi* (1932), a translation of those parts of Juan A. Morfi'sqv work that dealt with Indians in Texas; and *Texas in 1811,* a translation done in 1941. He also contributed articles dealing with the history of Texas to a local newspaper, the San Antonio *Light.* Other significant contributions made by Chabot include his locating thirteen original paintings by Theodore Gentilz,qv which were later placed in the Alamo,qv helping in the restoration of La Villitaqv and San José Mission in San Antonio, and compiling an album entitled *Pictorial Sketch of Mission San José* (1935). Chabot died of uremic poisoning while on a research trip to Mexico on January 18, 1943, and was buried in San Luis Potosí. At the time of his death, he had been preparing four more books for publication.

BIBLIOGRAPHY: Florence Elberta Barns, *Texas Writers of Today* (Dallas: Tardy, 1935). San Antonio *Light,* January 22, 1943. Vertical Files, Barker Texas History Center, University of Texas at Austin.
Michael L. Krenn

CHACON CREEK (Medina County). Chacon Creek rises four miles northwest of Castroville in east central Medina County (at 29°22′ N, 98°57′ W) and runs south for thirty-three miles to its mouth on Francisco Perez Creek, just south of the Frio county line and two miles east of the Missouri Pacific tracks (at 29°05′ N, 98°56′ W). Together the two creeks form the headwaters of San Miguel Creek. Chacon Reservoir, once known as Chacon Lake, is on Chacon Creek four miles north of Natalia. The creek passes initially through low-rolling hills and prairies surfaced by expansive clays that support grasses, mesquite, and chaparral. In its middle reaches the creek traverses low terrain surfaced by clays that support pecans, hardwoods, and grasses. Towards its mouth the creek moves through flat terrain with local shallow depressions, surfaced by clays that support water-tolerant hardwoods, conifers, and grasses.

_____ (Webb County). Chacon Creek rises six miles from Webb in central Webb County (at 27°43′ N, 99°22′ W) and runs southwest for twenty miles to its mouth on the Rio Grande, on the southern edge of Laredo (at 27°29′ N, 99°29′ W). In its lower reaches the creek is dammed to form Casa Blanca Lake. The surrounding flat terrain is surfaced by sandy clays that support mesquite, cacti, and grasses.

CHACON RESERVOIR. Chacon Reservoir (Chacon Lake) is on the southern end of the Medina Dam and Medina Diversion Dam irrigation system, four miles northwest of Natalia in southeastern Medina County. The lake's dam impounds water carried by Chacon Creek and surplus water from the Medina Canal, an irrigation channel supplied by water impounded upstream by the Medina Diversion Dam. The reservoir's capacity is estimated at 2,000 acre-feet. In 1989 local residents claimed that the reservoir was the place to catch Texas-size catfish.

BIBLIOGRAPHY: C. L. Dowell, *Dams and Reservoirs in Texas: History and Descriptive Information* (Texas Water Commission Bulletin 6408 [Austin, 1964]). Cyril Matthew Kuehne, S.M., *Ripples from Medina Lake* (San Antonio: Naylor, 1966).

CHADWICK, JOSEPH M. (1812–1836). Joseph M. Chadwick, military and topographical engineer and acting adjutant general under Fannin at Goliad, was born in Exeter, New Hampshire, in April 1812, the son of Peter Chadwick. He was admitted to the United States Military Academy at West Point on July 1, 1829, but resigned on April 30, 1831. He lived for several years in Illinois before his arrival about December 25, 1835, at Velasco, Texas, where he was appointed sergeant major of William Ward'sqv Georgia Battalion.qv The unit sailed to Copano and arrived at Refugio in January 1836, but fell back to Goliad, where it became part of James Walker Fannin, Jr.'sqv provisional regiment. Although he was defeated by Dr. Warren J. Mitchellqv in the election for regimental major by an 81–73 vote, Chadwick was appointed acting adjutant general when Fannin reorganized his staff about the middle of February 1836. As a military and topographical engineer Chadwick mapped Fort Defiance (La Bahíaqv) for his commander, and with John Sowers Brooksqv supervised the fortification of the Goliad presidio. Lewis M. H. Washington,qv who also served on Fannin's staff, described Chadwick as having "a native suavity of temper and urbanity of manner, which at once made him the Pride of the battalion."

Chadwick was sent to ensure Ward's prompt return from his mission to relieve Amon B. Kingqv at Refugio but got lost and returned to Goliad. With Fannin and Benjamin C. Wallace,qv he signed the articles of surrender to Gen. José de Urreaqv following the battle of Coletoqv and returned to Goliad a prisoner. On March 24 Chadwick and two or three others accompanied Fannin under Mexican escort commanded by Lt. Col. Juan Holzingerqv on a trip to Copano to determine the availability of a ship to transport prisoners to New Orleans. The records do not reveal the result, but the party returned to Goliad on March 26. Chadwick was murdered with the rest of Fannin's command in the Goliad Massacreqv by order of Antonio López de Santa Annaqv on March 27, 1836. For his service and sacrifice in the Texas cause, Chadwick's heirs received five land grants totaling 3,820 acres by 1846.

BIBLIOGRAPHY: Harbert Davenport, "Men of Goliad," *Southwestern Historical Quarterly* 43 (July 1939). Harbert Davenport Papers, Barker Texas History Center, University of Texas at Austin. Hobart Huson, *Refugio: A Comprehensive History of Refugio County from Aboriginal Times to 1953* (2 vols., Woodsboro, Texas: Rooke Foundation, 1953, 1955).

Craig H. Roell

CHADWICK, TEXAS. Chadwick was on Antelope Creek eight miles northwest of Lometa in western Lampasas County. In response to a growing need for a mill in the western part of the county, Henry A. Chadwick and his son, J. Milam, built a log dam on the Colorado River in 1879. They also built a sawmill, flour mill, and cotton gin at the site and later constructed a stone dam in front of the wooden one. The Chadwick Mills were soon in high demand, and wagons came from as far as San Angelo to use them. The settlement later became a freight station on the Gulf, Colorado and Santa Fe Railway, and the growing community took the name Chadwick. By 1900 the town had become a popular scenic resort, with a small hotel and an outdoor dance platform near the mills. Campers, fishermen, and other tourists were drawn to the area by the scenery and excellent hunting and fishing, and at one time Chadwick was one of the most famous inland fishing resorts in the state. Milam Chadwick was running a power plant at the mills by 1910. A post office, established in the community that same year, served about twenty-five people. At one time a school was located a quarter mile from the railway station. In the summer of 1915 the west bank of the Colorado River was washed out locally by heavy rains, and the river's course shifted so that it bypassed the dams at the Chadwick Mills. Attempts to restore operations failed, and eventually the mills were abandoned. The local post office was discontinued in 1918, and the railway station was closed in January 1941. All that is left of the once popular resort is a historical marker—placed at the former site of the mills in May 1971—and a cemetery.

BIBLIOGRAPHY: Ed Ellsworth Bartholomew, *800 Texas Ghost Towns* (Fort Davis, Texas: Frontier, 1971). Jonnie Ross Elzner, *Relighting Lamplights of Lampasas County, Texas* (Lampasas: Hill Country, 1974). William Leshner, "Lometa: A Coming Lampasas County Town," *Texas Magazine*, November 1910. Lewis B. Porter, Sr., *Take a Journey with Me from the Washboard* (Goldthwaite, Texas: Goldthwaite Eagle Press, 1976).

Alice J. Rhoades

CHAFFEE, ADNA ROMANZA (1842–1914). Adna Romanza Chaffee, army officer, son of Truman Bibbins and Grace (Hyde) Chaffee, was born on April 14, 1842, in Orwell, Ohio, and educated at a nearby country school. He joined the regular Sixth Cavalry on July 22, 1861, and saw action in the Peninsular campaign, the battle of Antietam, the battle of Fredericksburg, the Stoneman Raid, and the battle of Gettysburg, where he was wounded and narrowly escaped capture. Throughout 1864 he took part in Gen. Philip Sheridan's[qv] Virginia campaigns and was promoted to first lieutenant in February 1865.

After the Sixth Cavalry's reorganization in the summer of 1865, Chaffee was transferred to Austin, Texas, where he was appointed depot quartermaster on December 12, 1866. In March 1867 he resigned his commission with thoughts of going into business, but was persuaded to seek restoration to rank. After promotion to captain in October, he was assigned in February 1868 to Fort Griffin. On March 5 he successfully pursued a band of Quahadi Comanche warriors who had attacked a wagon train hauling lumber from the Mill Creek sawmill. Chaffee and his men found the Quahadis taking refuge near Paint Creek, encircled the camp, charged, and defeated them. Chaffee was brevetted a major for his actions. With his reputation as an Indian fighter established, he spent the next three years at various army camps in Texas chasing down outlaws and hostile Indians. The dogged persistence of Chaffee and his men on the Texas frontier soon gained them the name Chaffee's Guerillas.

Chaffee was transferred to Fort Riley, Kansas, in March 1871 and spent most of 1872 on detached duty at Oxford, Mississippi. After returning to Kansas, he was stationed briefly at Fort Harker and in April 1873 moved to Camp Supply, Indian Territory, in response to increased tension caused by hide hunters entering the southern plains. When the Red River War[qv] broke out in 1874, Chaffee was attached to Col. Nelson A. Miles's[qv] column, and on August 30 in Palo Duro Canyon[qv] his command was among the Sixth Cavalry forces in the front lines. With his famous exhortation, "Forward; if any man is killed I will make him a corporal!" Chaffee led his troops in a charge against a superior number of Cheyenne warriors, whom the cavalry then chased as far west as what is now Randall County. Chaffee was subsequently brevetted a lieutenant colonel. On October 14 he led a force against a hostile Indian camp located between Gageby and Sweetwater creeks. On March 31, 1875, he married Annie Frances Rockwell; they had three daughters and a son.

For a decade beginning in 1875 Chaffee and his command responded to troubles with the Apaches at Fort Verde, Arizona. He commanded the garrison in 1878, served as agent at the San Carlos Reservation in 1879–80, and participated in Gen. George Crook's expedition in 1883. He was transferred in 1884 to New Mexico and was at Fort Wingate when Geronimo and his Chiricahua Apache followers broke out of their reservation in 1885. Chaffee remained in southern Arizona and New Mexico until the chief surrendered in September 1886.

On July 7, 1888, with the Indian depredations at an end, he was promoted to major in the regular army and transferred to the Ninth Cavalry. For the next two years he supervised the construction of Fort Duchesne in southern Utah. He served as acting inspector general for the Department of Arizona from 1890 to 1893 and for the Department of Colorado until the fall of 1894. Chaffee then moved to Fort Robinson, Nebraska, and in 1895 conducted the restoration of the Bannock Indians to the Fort Hall reservation in Idaho. He served as an instructor at the Infantry and Cavalry School at Fort Leavenworth, Kansas, from November 1896 to June 1897, when he was appointed lieutenant colonel of the Third Cavalry.

With the outbreak of the Spanish-American War, Chaffee was made brigadier general (in May 1898) and commanded the Third Brigade of Gen. Henry W. Lawton's Second Division volunteers in Cuba. As a result of his performance in the capture of El Caney on July 1, he was promoted to major general. After a brief respite he returned to Cuba in December 1898, as chief of staff of the military government under Gen. Leonard Wood, a post he held until May 1900. Having lost his volunteer rank in reduction of the army, Chaffee was again appointed brigadier general of volunteers in April 1889 and then promoted to colonel in the regular United States Army in May 1899.

In July 1900 he was reappointed major general of volunteers and given command of the 2,500-man United States contingent in the joint relief expedition sent to put down the Boxer Rebellion in China. His troops took the gates of Peking on August 14, 1900, and relieved the city's besieged embassies. The success of that mission made Chaffee a celebrity among the troops and commanders as well as the Chinese. After his advancement to major general in February 1901, Chaffee was appointed military governor and commander of the United States forces in the Philippines, where he remained until October 1902. He commanded the Department of the East until October 1903; he helped organize the General Staff Corps and in January 1904 was named United States Army Chief of Staff, with the rank of lieutenant general. He served as grand marshal for President Theodore Roosevelt's inaugural parade on March 4, 1905, in which former Indian adversaries like Geronimo and Quanah Parker[qv] also participated. Afterward, he went on a good-will tour of Europe on behalf of the president. Chaffee stepped down from his position on January 15, 1906, and retired from the army two weeks later. He was subsequently named a member of the Board of Visitors of West Point. Later he and his wife moved to Los Angeles, California, where he served as chairman of that city's Board of Public Works and as first president of the Southwest Museum. Chaffee died of typhoid pneumonia on November 1, 1914, and was interred in Arlington National Cemetery.

BIBLIOGRAPHY: William Giles Harding Carter, *Life of Lieutenant General Chaffee* (Chicago: University of Chicago Press, 1917). *Dictionary of American Biography*. James L. Haley, *The Buffalo War: The History of the Red River Indian Uprising of 1874* (Garden City, New York: Doubleday, 1976). Sallie Reynolds Matthews, *Interwoven: A Pioneer Chronicle* (Houston: Anson Jones, 1936; 4th ed., College Station: Texas A&M University Press, 1982). Carl Coke Rister, *Fort Griffin on the Texas Frontier* (Norman: University of Oklahoma Press, 1956). *Webster's American Military Biographies* (Springfield, Massachusetts: Merriam, 1978). *Who Was Who in America*, Vol. 1.

H. Allen Anderson

CHAGUANE INDIANS. Near the end of the seventeenth century the Chaguane (Chaguame, Ohaguame) Indians were reported as living between the site of present Eagle Pass and the Nueces River. Later the Ohaguame (presumably a copying error for Chaguame) Indians were listed among the groups resident at the nearby mission of San Juan Bautista,qv and still later the name Chaguane was recorded at San Antonio de Valero Mission in San Antonio. It seems likely that these names refer to the same band of Coahuiltecan Indians. Chaguantapam, a similar name, also occurs in the records of San Antonio de Valero and may be a variant of Chaguane, but further study of the original documents is needed for demonstration of identity.

BIBLIOGRAPHY: Bexar Archives, Barker Texas History Center, University of Texas at Austin. Frederick Webb Hodge, ed., *Handbook of American Indians North of Mexico* (2 vols., Washington: GPO, 1907, 1910; rpt., New York: Pageant, 1959).

Thomas N. Campbell

CHAGUANTAPAM INDIANS. Some confusion surrounds the name Chaguantapam, which was recorded in 1690 by Damián Massanetqv for one of the Indian groups living north of Matagorda Bay on the upper courses of the Lavaca and Navidad rivers, apparently in what is now Lavaca County. Massanet noted that other Indian groups lived in this same area, but he gave a name for only one of them, the Muruam. He said that these Indian groups all lived by hunting bison and collecting wild plant foods. The name Chaguantapam, given by Massanet, was misread by a Spanish copyist as Chaguastapa, which in turn was misread as Chagustapa by J. R. Swanton, who listed Chaguantapam and Chagustapa as names for two separate Indian groups. The erroneous name Chagustapa should be stricken from the record. Swanton thought that the Chaguantapam spoke the Coahuilteco language, but they lived farther to the east than any Indian groups firmly identifiable as Coahuilteco speakers. It has been suggested that Chaguantapam may be a variant of the name Siaguan, but this does not appear likely, for in the same year, 1690, Massanet saw Chaguan (Siaguan) Indians on the Nueces River some 175 miles west of the area in which he encountered the Chaguantapams. H. E. Boltonqv stated that Chaguantapam Indians were present at San Antonio de Valero Mission in San Antonio, but there is no clear record of this. In the Valero registers the name Chaguantapam occurs only once, in a baptismal entry of 1737, and this was corrected by insertion of the name Mallei (Mayeye). If there were Chaguantapam individuals at Valero, they were never recorded as being baptized, married, or buried there.

BIBLIOGRAPHY: Lino Gómez Canedo, ed., *Primeras exploraciones y poblamiento de Texas, 1686–1694* (Monterrey: Publicaciones del Instituto Tecnológico y de Estudios Superiores de Monterrey, 1968). Frederick Webb Hodge, ed., *Handbook of American Indians North of Mexico* (2 vols., Washington: GPO, 1907, 1910; rpt., New York: Pageant, 1959). J. R. Swanton, *Linguistic Material from the Tribes of Southern Texas and Northeastern Mexico* (Washington: Smithsonian Institution, 1940).

Thomas N. Campbell

CHAIN SEVEN RANCH. The Chain Seven Ranch was a 5,500-acre ranch in Denton County owned by William C. Wrightqv from the mid-1850s to 1900. One source claims it was one of the largest horse ranches in the Southwest, with an estimated stock of over 1,000 horses. Another source places the number of cattle at the ranch as high as 2,000 for the period between 1875 to 1885. The brand was in the shape of two or possibly three number sevens linked or "chained" together (777). Wright thought the sevens would bring his ranch luck. The ranch also had holdings in Foard and Hardeman counties.

BIBLIOGRAPHY: Mary Jo Cowling, *Geography of Denton County* (Dallas: Banks, Upshaw, 1936). Gus L. Ford, ed., *Texas Cattle Brands* (Dallas: Cockrell, 1936).

Matthew Hayes Nall

CHALK BLUFF, TEXAS. Chalk Bluff is on Farm Road 933 some six miles north of Waco in northeast central McLennan County. It takes its name from the Austin chalk prevalent in the terrain overlooking the nearby Brazos River. A Moore family received land grants in the area in 1835, but actual settlement may not have occurred before the early 1850s. Both the Texas Central and the Missouri, Kansas and Texas railroads bypassed Chalk Bluff by about two miles in 1882. Thus, though area farmers had fairly easy access to markets, the community did not develop as a railroad town. Before 1900 Chalk Bluff had a school, a store, and a gin. In 1896 the Chalk Bluff school had forty-five students and one teacher. The White Rock Baptist Church moved to the community in 1908 and changed its name to Chalk Bluff Baptist Church. The Chalk Bluff school was consolidated with the Elm Mott school district in the 1930s. Several scattered houses marked Chalk Bluff on county highway maps in the 1930s and 1940s. Later the area was developed as a subdivision, and many local residents commuted to jobs in Waco.

BIBLIOGRAPHY: Dayton Kelley, ed., *The Handbook of Waco and McLennan County, Texas* (Waco: Texian, 1972). William Robert Poage, *McLennan County Before 1980* (Waco: Texian, 1981). Vertical File, Texas Collection, Baylor University.

Vivian Elizabeth Smyrl

CHALK CREEK (Kimble County). Chalk Creek rises seven miles east of Telegraph in south central Kimble County (at 30°18′ N, 99°47′ W). It runs northwest for thirteen miles to its mouth on the south Llano River, 6½ miles southwest of Junction (at 30°24′ N, 99°50′ W).

—— (Kinney County). Chalk Creek rises nine miles northwest of the intersection of Farm roads 3199 and 334 in northeastern Kinney County (at 29°31′ N, 100°10′ W) and runs south for 3½ miles to its mouth on the West Nueces River, five miles northwest of Farm Road 334 (at 29°29′ N, 100°12′ W). The surrounding flat terrain has local deep and dense dissection and is surfaced by dark, calcareous clays and clay and sandy loams that support oak, juniper, mesquite, and various grasses.

CHALK DRAW. Chalk Draw originates in Chalk Valley between Elephant Mountain and the Del Norte Mountains, about twenty-eight miles south-southeast of Alpine in north central Brewster County (at 30°02′ N, 103°29′ W) and runs south-southeast for thirty-eight miles. It skirts the west side of Santiago Peak, where it is joined by Calamity Creek, then parallels the western base of the Santiago Mountains to its mouth on Nine Point Draw, north of the Rosillos Mountains (at 29°36′ N, 103°14′ W). The course of the draw runs over Quaternary alluvial deposits derived from underlying Cretaceous limestones and from surrounding Tertiary igneous formations, such as those which form the Santiago Mountains. Chalk Draw drops from an elevation of 4,400 feet above sea level to about 2,670 feet. The area was once predominantly a semiarid grassland with abundant animal life, but overgrazing beginning at the close of the nineteenth century virtually destroyed this former biological community. In the 1980s the terrain was dominated by Chihuahuan Desert scrub, and the draw appeared to be an avenue for scrub encroaching into the remaining grasslands of the higher, more northern mountains. Large areas had been reduced to barren hardpan that would not support even creosote bush.

CHALK HILL, TEXAS. Chalk Hill is on a mail route from Longview in northeastern Rusk County. It was settled about 1875. During the 1940s it reported a population of twenty-five and one store. In 1978 the National Weather Service established a radar site at Chalk Hill that forecasts for the East Texas area.

BIBLIOGRAPHY: Dorman H. Winfrey, *A History of Rusk County* (Waco: Texian, 1961).

Megan Biesele

CHALK MOUNTAIN. Chalk Mountain is two miles northwest of Chalk near the Somervell county line in eastern Erath County (at 32°11′ N, 97°55′ W). It rises to an elevation of 1,200 feet above mean sea level.

CHALK MOUNTAIN, TEXAS. Chalk Mountain, on U.S. Highway 67 near the Somervell county line in southeastern Erath County, was named for a nearby elevation of white rock. Although the J. H. F. Skipper ranch, founded in the area in 1860, may have served as a prewar trading center, the community of Chalk Mountain was not itself established until later. The Chalk Mountain post office, established in 1876 with Elisha D. McCoy as postmaster, was originally in Somervell County. It was moved to Erath County by 1892. By 1890 Chalk Mountain had a gin, a school, and two churches, and by 1900 its population was eighty-one. A Masonic lodge was chartered there in 1904 and occupied the upper floor of a frame commercial building. Chalk Mountain did not prosper because local residents had good road access to Stephenville, and by 1910 its population had fallen to fifty. Its post office closed in 1927. In 1940 the population of Chalk Mountain was sixty-nine, and the town reported two businesses. Its population in 1980 was twenty-five, and meetings were still being held at the Masonic lodge. In 1990 Chalk Mountain's population was still listed as twenty-five.

BIBLIOGRAPHY: T. Lindsay Baker, *Ghost Towns of Texas* (Norman: University of Oklahoma Press, 1986). Vallie Eoff, A History of Erath County, Texas (M.A. thesis, University of Texas, 1937).

William R. Hunt

CHALK, WHITFIELD (1811–1902). Whitfield Chalk, millwright and soldier, was born on April 4, 1811, in Hertford County, North Carolina, the son of Rev. William Roscoe and Mary Elizabeth (Williams) Chalk. In 1823 the family moved to Maury County, Tennessee, from where Chalk immigrated to Texas in 1839. En route, all of his fellow steamboat passengers died of cholera; Chalk and the captain alone survived. Chalk first settled in Nashville, Milam County, but sometime later moved to the frontier community of Georgetown.

His military service to the Republic of Texas qv is said to have been nearly continuous after his arrival in the new country. He participated in the battle of Plum Creek qv on August 12, 1840, and the battle of Salado Creek qv on September 18, 1842. When the Somervell expedition qv was organized to retaliate against the raids of Mexican generals Rafael Vásquez and Adrián Woll qqv in 1842, Chalk was elected a lieutenant in Capt. John G. W. Pierson's qv company, the Milam Mounted Riflemen. When Col. Alexander Somervell qv ordered the disbanding of the expedition after the seizure of Laredo, Chalk chose instead to remain with the volunteers who elected William S. Fisher qv as their new commander and crossed the Rio Grande on the Mier expedition.qv Fisher's men exhausted their supplies of food, water, and ammunition at the battle of Mier on Christmas Day 1842, and were forced to surrender to the forces of Gen. Pedro Ampudia.qv Chalk and William St. Clair, however, hid under a pile of sugarcane and became the only two Texans to escape capture. They then made their way out of the town in the dark and joined the small force of men under George B. Erath qv that had been left north of the Rio Grande. Together they returned to Texas after Fisher and the rest of his men were marched off to captivity in Mexico City. For his role in the fighting in 1842 Chalk was ultimately awarded $402.50 and 320 acres of bounty land in Milam County. He returned to Georgetown, where, on August 5, 1844, he was elected major of the Second Regiment of the First Militia Brigade. After two years he resigned the commission. During the Mexican War qv Chalk served as a private in Capt. Shapley P. Ross's qv company of Texas Rangers,qv assigned to the defense of the frontier between the Little River and the San Gabriel River against Indian raids.

On August 9, 1847, Chalk married Mary Elizabeth Fleming. His brother, Rev. John Wesley Chalk, performed the ceremony. In 1848 Chalk was elected sheriff of Williamson County, and at the same time another brother, Ira Ellis Chalk, was elected district clerk. In 1850 Chalk was living in Milam County, where he was employed as a millwright. At the time he owned $3,000 in real estate. Ten years later he had moved to Belton, where he and Ira Chalk founded a lumber and grist mill on Salado Creek near Salado. By that time he owned $3,600 in real estate and some $400 in personal property.

In 1870 a special act of the state legislature awarded veterans' benefits to Chalk as a survivor of the Mier expedition, and in 1873 he joined the Texas Veterans Association.qv That same year he moved his family to Kempner in Lampasas County. In December 1881 Ira Chalk was charged with the murder of a deputy sheriff in Bonham. Whitfield Chalk died at his Lampasas County home on May 18, 1902. On Texas Independence Day, 1944, a marker was erected at his grave, with full military honors from the United States government. He had nine children.

BIBLIOGRAPHY: Dallas *Herald*, December 15, 1881. George B. Erath, "The Memoirs of George B. Erath, 1813–1891," *Southwestern Historical Quarterly* 26–27 (January–October 1923; rpts., Austin: Texas State Historical Association, 1923; Waco: Heritage Society of Waco, 1956). William S. Speer and John H. Brown, eds., *Encyclopedia of the New West* (Marshall, Texas: United States Biographical Publishing, 1881; rpt., Easley, South Carolina: Southern Historical Press, 1978). Charles D. Spurlin, comp., *Texas Veterans in the Mexican War: Muster Rolls of Texas Military Units* (Victoria, Texas, 1984). Houston Wade, comp., *The Dawson Men of Fayette County* (Houston, 1932). Olive Todd Walker, "Major Whitfield Chalk," *Southwestern Historical Quarterly* 60 (January 1957).

Thomas W. Cutrer

CHALK, TEXAS. Chalk, in southern Cottle County, was founded on land originally owned by W. Q. Richards as part of his 3D and Moon ranches. The rise in prices for farmland and severe drought in 1903 or 1904 led him to dig wells and plot a settlement. As the settlement was being developed between 1905 and 1907, it was known as Richards colony and as Dutch colony before assuming the name of Chalk in honor of James M. Chalk, who owned a gin and who became the first postmaster for the community in 1908. The town grew slowly, but some impetus was provided by the Oscar brothers, who started a store there in 1906. By 1915 the population of Chalk had reached forty-five. A school was not established in Chalk until 1914, probably because there were already three schools in the area. By 1940 the town had 100 residents and four stores. Its population later declined, and in 1945 its school was closed and local students were transferred to Paducah. By 1980 the population of Chalk numbered forty-five, although the community still retained its post office and had a cotton gin and a gas plant. The reported population in 1990 was still forty-five.

BIBLIOGRAPHY: Carmen Taylor Bennett, *Our Roots Grow Deep: A History of Cottle County* (Floydada, Texas: Blanco Offset Printing, 1970). Kathleen E. and Clifton R. St. Clair, eds., *Little Towns of Texas* (Jacksonville, Texas: Jayroe Graphic Arts, 1982).

William R. Hunt

CHALMERS, TEXAS. Chalmers was on State Highway 60 some five miles north of Bay City in northern Matagorda County. In the early 1900s the community was a stop on the Gulf, Colorado and Santa Fe Railway. A post office opened at the community in 1912, by which time Chalmers also reported a general store, a rice storehouse, and an estimated population of fifty. By 1914 the town had a telephone connection. Its post office closed in 1915, and local mail was dispatched to Bay City. In 1936 Chalmers comprised a school, a factory, one other business, and eight dwellings scattered around the junction of metal-surfaced and soil-surfaced roads. In 1940 Shell Oil was operating a refinery in the community, and the local school was still in operation. By 1949 the Chalmers school had been consolidated with the Bay City Independent School District, and by 1952 both the refinery and the school appear to have closed. In 1980 a few dwellings remained in the area along an unimproved dirt road. In 1989 the community was no longer shown on county road maps.

BIBLIOGRAPHY: Matagorda County Historical Commission, *Historic Matagorda County* (3 vols., Houston: Armstrong, 1986).

Stephen L. Hardin

CHALMERS, JOHN GORDON (1803–1847). John Gordon Chalmers, editor and political figure in the Republic of Texas,qv was born in Halifax County, Virginia, on August 25, 1803, the son of James Ronald and Sarah Lanier (Williams) Chalmers. After graduation from the University of North Carolina, Chapel Hill, he received his medical education at the University of Edinburgh, Scotland, where his uncle, Rev. Thomas Chalmers, was a leading theologian. On his return from Scotland, he served for several years in the Virginia legislature. In 1827 he married Mary Wade Henderson of Milton, North Carolina; they had seven children. Chalmers moved his family to Texas in 1840 and settled first in La Grange and then in Austin. He held office for a time as secretary of the treasury for the Republic of Texas under President Mirabeau B. Lamarqv and later chaired the committee that drafted the resolution approving the annexationqv of Texas to the United States. Chalmers helped establish the Democratic partyqv in Texas. In 1845 he became editor and proprietor of the Austin *New Era*.qv He also formed a partnership with Michael Cronicanqv to publish the Austin *Texas Democrat*.qv On January 1, 1847, he became involved in a heated argument with Joshua Holden; a fight resulted and Chalmers was mortally stabbed. He was buried in Oakwood Cemetery, Austin.

BIBLIOGRAPHY: Amelia W. Williams and Eugene C. Barker, eds., *The Writings of Sam Houston, 1813–1863* (8 vols., Austin: University of Texas Press, 1938–43; rpt., Austin and New York: Pemberton Press, 1970).

Virginia Roberts Gilman

CHALUPEC, BARBARA APOLLONIA (1894?–1987). Barbara Apollonia Chalupec [pseud. Pola Negri], screen actress, was born in Janowo, Poland, the daughter of a Hungarian tinsmith and his wife. She was evidently born on December 31, 1894, though she occasionally gave her birth year as 1897 or 1899. Pola was her childhood nickname, shortened from Apollonia; Negri she later took as her stage name after Italian poetess Adah Negri, her girlhood idol. As a youth she attended the boarding school of Countess Platen in Warsaw and

Barbara Apollonia Chalupec, better known as Pola Negri. From New York Journal-American, *July 1941. Courtesy HRHRC.*

studied at the Imperial Ballet School in St. Petersburg before entering the Philharmonia Drama School in Warsaw.

Negri made her stage debut in 1913 in Gerhardt Hauptmann's *Hannele* in Warsaw and appeared the following year in her first film, *Niewolnica Zmyslow*. Her stage work attracted the attention of Alexandr Hertz, a pioneer Polish film producer, who made several of her earliest films. She also starred in Max Reinhardt's pantomime play *Sumurun* in Warsaw, and in 1917, at Reinhardt's urging, she continued the role in Berlin. After World War Iqv she appeared in a series of German films, including *Carmen* and *Madame DuBarry* (*Passion*) both directed by Ernst Lubitsch. The two films subsequently became major hits in the United States. Offers began to pour in from Hollywood, and in 1922 Negri signed a contract with Famous Players–Lasky (later Paramount). Her arrival in New York was greated with great fanfare, and she quickly rose to stardom in such films as *Forbidden Paradise* (1924) and *Hotel Imperial* (1927). Known for her fiery temperament and her exotic looks, she became the prototypical "vamp" of 1920s Hollywood. She was romantically linked with Charlie Chaplin, and carried on a well-publicized affair with Rudolph Valentino, which lasted until his death in 1926.

With the advent of talkies in the late 1920s Negri's Hollywood career faltered, and in the early 1930s she returned to Europe. She made one film in France, *Fanatisme* (1934), before signing a contract with German film studio UFA in 1935. She made several well-regarded films in those years, including *Mazurka* (1935), *Moskou-Shanghai* (1937), and *Madame Bovary* (1937). She fled Germany after the outbreak of World War II,qv settled briefly in France, then sailed for the United States in 1940. Her arrival in New York was clouded by unfounded charges that she had had an affair with Hitler. She eventually cleared her name and attempted to make a comeback in Hollywood, but made only two films thereafter, *Hi Diddle Diddle* (1943) and *The Moonspinners* (1964).

In 1957 Negri moved to San Antonio with her longtime friend, Margaret West, who was from a prominent family of the city. They lived for a time in a suite in the Menger Hotel[qv] and later in a large home in Olmos Park. In her later years Negri lived in semiseclusion. She served on the board of directors for the San Antonio Symphony Orchestra[qv] and the San Antonio Little Theater. She was married twice, first to Polish count Eugene Domski in the late 1910s and in 1927 to Prince Serge Mdivani; both marriages ended in divorce. Pola Negri died of a brain tumor in San Antonio on August 2, 1987, and was buried in Los Angeles. She donated her personal library to Trinity University in San Antonio and gave a large collection of memorabilia, including several rare prints of her early films, to St. Mary's University there. She also left a large portion of her estate to St. Mary's, which established a scholarship in her name.

BIBLIOGRAPHY: *The International Dictionary of Films and Filmmakers*, Vol. 3. Pola Negri, *Memoirs of a Star* (New York: Doubleday, 1970). *Texas Parade*, October 1973. *Christopher Long*

CHAMBERLAIN, HIRAM (1797–1866). Hiram Chamberlain, Presbyterian minister, was born at Monkton, Vermont, on April 2, 1797. As a descendant of a New England family of Revolutionary War patriots, Protestant clergymen, physicians, and small farmers, he was raised in an intense religiosity unusual even for that era in the "Burned-Over District" of western Vermont and the New York frontier. In 1818 he made his profession of faith at Rev. Dr. Gardner Spring's Presbyterian church in New York City. Also that year he entered Middlebury College in Vermont, from which he graduated in 1822. Able to think of "but little except the duty of constant prayer and deep humiliation before God," he entered Andover Theological Seminary and dedicated himself to "missionary labors." After a year's study at Princeton, he graduated in 1825 from Andover, where he helped to establish the American Home Missionary Society. On October 16, 1825, he received ordination as a missionary from the New York Presbytery at Dr. Spring's church. For the next two decades (1825–45) he held numerous pastoral duties in Missouri, at churches in St. Louis, Dardonne, Boonville, New Franklin, Fayette, and St. Charles. He also served as an agent and promoter for Marion College, as well as editor and publisher of the St. Louis newspaper *Herald of Religious Liberty*.

The Presbyterian split in 1838 found Hiram decidedly in the old school. In addition, he severed his ties with the American Home Missionary Society the next year, apparently over the society's increasing support of the abolition movement. Though Chamberlain himself owned no slaves and seems to have disapproved of slavery,[qv] he, like many old-school ministers, believed that slaveholding was not forbidden in scripture and that the relation of master and slave was a civil and domestic institution in which the church had no power to legislate. He was also an ardent believer in the separation of church and state, dedicated "to wake up the attention of Protestants to the errors and evils of Roman Catholicism." Enlightenment, Chamberlain believed, came only through self-denial, noble resolution, and an unemotional adherence to Christian duty.

In 1845 he moved down the Mississippi River to Memphis, Tennessee, where he accepted new pastoral duties. Two years later he again moved sixty miles eastward to Somerville, where he agreed to oversee the building of a new church. Chamberlain moved to Brownsville, Texas, in 1850 to organize, build, and lead the first Protestant church on the lower Rio Grande. On February 23 he organized the First Presbyterian Church of Brownsville. With Melinda Rankin[qv] he opened an academy for young girls, Rio Grande Female Institute, in 1854. Chamberlain was an ardent secessionist and served as chaplain of the Third Texas Infantry throughout the Civil War.[qv] He accepted the surrender of the Confederacy as a sign of God's will that the Union remain intact.

On October 9, 1825, at Dorset, Vermont, he married Maria Morse, with whom he had three children, only one of whom, Henrietta King,[qv] lived to maturity. On April 19, 1836, at St. Charles, Missouri, Chamberlain married Sarah H. Wardlaw of Rockbridge County, Virginia; they had no children. At Pinckney, Missouri, on October 16, 1842, he married Anna Adelia Griswold of Wethersfield, Connecticut, who survived him and died at Brooklyn, New York, on November 24, 1882. They had seven children, five of whom lived to maturity. Chamberlain died on November 1, 1866, at the parsonage of his church in Brownsville.

BIBLIOGRAPHY: Florence Bell, *A History of the First Presbyterian Church of Brownsville, Texas* (1950?). Chamberlain and Morse Family Papers, King Ranch Archives, Kingsville, Texas. Tom Lea, *The King Ranch* (2 vols., Boston: Little, Brown, 1957). Melinda Rankin, *Twenty Years among the Mexicans: A Narrative of Missionary Labor* (Cincinnati: Central Book Concern, 1881). *Bruce S. Cheeseman*

CHAMBERLAIN, SAMUEL EMERY (1829–1908). Emery Chamberlain, soldier, adventurer, and artist, was born in Centre Harbour, New Hampshire, on November 27, 1829, and moved with his family to Boston at an early age. In 1844 he ran away to Illinois. On June 12, 1846, a month after the outbreak of the Mexican War,[qv] he joined the Alton Guards of the Second Illinois Volunteer Regiment, bound for Texas. When he reached San Antonio, he transferred to the First United States Dragoons of the regular army. After a number of misadventures in San Antonio, Chamberlain left that city with Gen. John E. Wool's[qv] corps bound for Mexico. He was fascinated with the Texas Rangers[qv]—so much so that he claimed to have been with them in the battle of Monterrey, which had already taken place before he left San Antonio. Chamberlain did, however, have many rollicking adventures with the rangers in Mexico—fighting guerillas, drinking in cantinas, and having countless love affairs with Mexican women. He also participated in and painted numerous pictures of the battle of Buena Vista. On March 22, 1849, he was listed as a deserter from the First Dragoons. He was back in Boston by 1854 and married Mary Keith on July 4, 1855; they had three children. Chamberlain touched Texas in several other ways. He rode with the notorious Texas scalphunter John Joel Glanton[qv] all over the northern Mexican frontier. In the Civil War[qv] he rose to brevet brigadier general and took the all-black Fifth Massachusetts Cavalry to Clarksville, near the mouth of the Rio Grande, after the war had ended. An extraordinary collection of 147 Mexican War watercolors by Chamberlain is owned by the San Jacinto Battlefield Museum. The pictures form a version of Chamberlain's unpublished masterpiece recounting his adventures in Texas, Mexico, Arizona, and California during and after the Mexican War. A brilliantly illuminated manuscript, part fact and part fiction, on which he worked all through the latter half of his life, *My Confession: the Recollections of a Rogue* (published in 1956), is perhaps the most vivid, revealing, earthy account of the life of an enlisted soldier in the war with Mexico. Chamberlain died on November 10, 1908.

BIBLIOGRAPHY: William H. Goetzmann, *Sam Chamberlain's Mexican War: The San Jacinto Museum of History Paintings* (Austin: Texas State Historical Association, 1993). *William H. Goetzmann*

CHAMBERLAIN, TEXAS. Chamberlain (Chamberlin) was on the Chicago, Rock Island and Pacific Railroad near the route of what is now U.S. Highway 54 ten miles northeast of Dalhart in southeastern Dallam County. In 1947 the community had a grocery store and a population of fifty and received its mail from Dalhart. After the Rock Island line ended its Panhandle operations in the early 1980s, the line was taken over by the St. Louis Southwestern Railway. By that time the Chamberlain site had been abandoned.

CHAMBERLIN, CHESTER HARVEY (1859–1922). Chester Harvey Chamberlin, engineer, was born at Natchez, Mississippi, on September 14, 1859. After receiving an A.B. degree from Stewart College in Clarksville, Tennessee, in 1879, he joined the Texas and Pacific Railway in 1881. He assisted in surveying routes for the line for two years before joining the Yazoo and Mississippi Valley Railroad as a construction engineer in 1883. Two years later he was hired by the Ferrocarril del Norte, a Guatemalan rail company, as a locating engineer. Chamberlin returned to the United States in 1886 and accepted a surveying position with the federal government. In 1889 he became a locating engineer and engineer of construction for the Nicaraguan Canal Railroad Company. After two years in this position, Chamberlin returned to the United States as assistant engineer for maintenance with the Texas and Pacific. He moved upward through the ranks of the company to chief engineer. He died in Dallas on July 14, 1922.

BIBLIOGRAPHY: *Who Was Who in America*, Vol. 1.   *Brian Hart*

CHAMBERS, BARZILLAI J. (1817–1895). Barzillai J. Chambers, pioneer and politician, was born in Montgomery County, Kentucky, on December 5, 1817, the son of Walker and Talitha Cumi (Mothershead) Chambers. He was commissioned a captain of the Kentucky volunteers by his uncle, Thomas Jefferson Chambers,qv and arrived in Texas in May 1837 as an aide-de-camp. After his discharge in 1838 he became a surveyor, first in South Texas, and in 1839 in Robertson County. In 1847 he was elected district surveyor of the Robertson Land District. He settled in Navarro County as a farmer and land dealer in 1855 and became an attorney in 1860. He was an ardent secessionist and served in the Texas State Troops in 1864. In 1867 with W. F. Henderson he donated the land for the establishment of Cleburne as the county seat of Johnson County. In 1871 he and J. W. Brown opened a private bank, from which Chambers retired in 1875. He was an alderman, and in the late 1870s he was an incorporator of a proposed narrow-gauge railroad from Dallas to Cleburne.

Politically, Chambers first gained notice with a newspaper article in 1868 opposing an interest-bearing national debt. He opposed ratification of the state Constitution of 1876 qv because of its homestead exemption and was defeated in his race for the legislature in 1876. He became a member of the Greenback partyqv after the Democratic national convention of 1876 refused to adopt as strong a greenback money plank as he wanted, and he began to publish a Greenback paper in Cleburne. In 1878 he was again defeated for the legislature as a Greenback party nominee in Johnson County. He was an active party organizer and writer and in March 1879 attended the Greenback national convention at Chicago, where he was elected the Texas member of the national executive committee. In 1880 he was nominated for vice president by the Union Greenback Labor party and later by the national Greenback party to promote harmony between the two factions. He was forced to end his campaign, however, after breaking two ribs in a fall from a train in July. He continued to be active in the Greenback party through 1884.

Chambers married Susan Wood in Limestone County in 1852, but she died the next year. In 1854 he married Emma Montgomery, who died after having one child. The child died in infancy. Chambers then married Harriet A. Killough in Johnson County in 1861, and they had one son and two daughters. Chambers was a Mason and a member of the Christian Church. He died on September 16, 1895.

BIBLIOGRAPHY: Alwyn Barr, "B. J. Chambers and the Greenback Party Split," *Mid-America* 49 (October 1967). H. L. Bentley and Thomas Pilgrim, *Texas Legal Directory for 1876–77* (Austin: Democratic Statesman Office, 1877). A. J. Byrd, *History and Description of Johnson County and Its Principal Towns* (Marshall, Texas: Jennings, 1879). *A Memorial and Biographical History of Johnson and Hill Counties* (Chicago: Lewis, 1892). Galveston *Weekly News*, March 18, July 15, 1880.   *Alwyn Barr*

CHAMBERS, CALEB WALLACE AND MARY EMMA. Caleb Wallace Chambers and his wife, Mary Emma Chambers, served as missionary and missionary-teacher, respectively, among the Alabama-Coushatta Indians in Polk County from 1899 until their retirement in 1936. The work of this husband-wife team among the Alabama-Coushattas went far beyond the usual responsibilities of a pastor and teacher and contributed substantially to the progress of these Indians during their thirty-seven years of service.

Caleb Wallace Chambers was born in Dover, Lafayette County, Missouri, on November 13, 1854. When he was thirteen, his family moved to Lexington in the same county, and Caleb grew up there. After attending private and public schools in Dover and Lexington, he entered Westminster College in Fulton, Missouri, in his twenty-second year. In the fall of 1878 he decided to devote his life as a minister in the Presbyterian Church.qv Under the auspices of the Lafayette Presbytery, he reentered college that fall to begin his ministerial studies. In 1884 he began his seminary course at McCormack Theological Seminary in Chicago, Illinois. Later, he spent a year in Clarksville, Tennessee, in the Divinity Department of Southwestern Presbyterian University. There he graduated in 1887 with the degree of B.D., after which he spent two years preaching as a licentiate under the care of the Lafayette Presbytery. Chambers came to Texas in September 1890 and, in Sherman, conferred with John L. Moore, then pastor of First Presbyterian Church of Sherman and president of home missions in the Dallas Presbytery. Chambers spent his first year in Texas at Henderson as stated supply of the Presbyterian church there, where he was ordained as a minister in November 1890. In the spring of 1892 he moved to Tyler and subsequently preached for a group of churches around Tyler, including the church at Troup, where he served until January 1899.

Mary Emma Daniel was born on June 9, 1868, at Rockwall, Texas. Her father, Rev. J. B. Daniel, was an organizer and first pastor of the First Baptist Church at Terrell. She was reared at Terrell and was a member of the first graduating class at Terrell High School (1886). She taught for three years in the public schools of Rockwall before entering Sam Houston Normal Institute (now Sam Houston State University) and graduating in a class of ten in 1890. After teaching one year in a private school in Willis, she became a member of the public school faculty in Troup. There she met Caleb Wallace Chambers, then pastor of the Presbyterian church. They were married in Terrell on December 28, 1892, and made their home in Troup for seven years.

Chambers began his missionary activities at the Alabama-Coushatta reservation in May 1899 and preached for more than a year before he and his family moved there in July 1900. At the reservation they found many obstacles. The church was a one-room frame building constructed a few years before they arrived. The school was a dilapidated structure with no desks, books, or blackboards. In warm weather classes were frequently held outside the building in a brush arbor. Many of the Indians could not speak English, and the Chambers did not know the Indians' language.

Devotedly the missionaries worked among their charges. Mrs. Chambers became the public school teacher, and Reverend Chambers served as pastor of the Presbyterian mission on the reservation. In addition to church and school work, the missionaries' duties included serving as advisors to the Indians in all sorts of situations and comforters in time of trouble, nursing the sick, holding deathbed vigils, and helping to provide food and clothing to destitute tribal members. Over the years the couple worked with others to interest government and social-welfare groups in improving conditions on the reservation. During their tenure a new school and a hospital were built, and federal and state funds were appropriated to purchase more land. Chambers took courses in nursing to fill the need for medical attention, as the Indians suffered from malaria and tuberculosis, as well as other diseases. He was very successful with this part of his work and became so efficient in his medical activities that it was seldom necessary to summon a physician to the reservation.

Many honors came to these missionaries in recognition of their service among the Alabama-Coushattas. In 1929, at the age of seventy-six, Reverend Chambers received a doctorate of divinity from Austin College in Sherman. Mrs. Chambers's outstanding work as teacher of the Alabama-Coushatta children was recognized by her invitation to charter membership in the East Texas chapter of the Delta Kappa Gamma Society,qv a women's national honor fraternity in education. This missionary couple retired in 1936 and moved to Livingston, seventeen miles west of the reservation. Chambers died on April 16, 1950, and was buried in Forest Hill Cemetery in Livingston. His wife died on August 29, 1956, and was also buried at Forest Hill.

BIBLIOGRAPHY: *Delta Kappa Gamma Bulletin,* Spring 1953. Files, Austin College Archives. Houston *Chronicle,* July 10, 1949. Nettie McClamrock, *History of the Alabama Indian Church: Indian Village, Polk County, Texas* (Beaumont, Texas?, 1944?). Vertical Files, Barker Texas History Center, University of Texas at Austin. Mary Donaldson Wade, *The Alabama Indians of East Texas* (Livingston, Texas: Polk County Enterprise, 1931; rev. ed. 1936).

Howard N. Martin

CHAMBERS, IOLA BOWDEN (1904–1978). Iola Bowden Chambers, music teacher, director of the Negro Fine Arts School, and a fifth-generation Texan, daughter of Andrew Mack and Amanda (Heflin) Bowden, was born at Holder, Texas, on October 18, 1904. Her father was a doctor. Iola developed an early interest in music and studied privately while attending the public schools at Holder and May. She attended the last two years of high school at Daniel Baker Academy in Brownwood and graduated in 1921. After receiving a diploma in piano from Daniel Baker College in 1923, she studied piano at the Washington Conservatory of Music, where she received a graduate diploma in piano in 1926. She returned to Texas and taught piano in May, Rotan, and Breckenridge, as well as at Baylor University, before moving to Georgetown in 1933 to teach at Southwestern University and complete her degrees, a B.F.A. (1935) and a B.A. (1936). She subsequently stayed at Southwestern University as instructor of music, teaching piano and harmony. She later taught piano pedagogy. She began a master's program at the Cincinnati Conservatory of Music in the summer of 1938 and completed it in the summer of 1941. She was an early white proponent of black education. In 1946 she and several of her piano students founded the Negro Fine Arts School, in which students from Southwestern University taught local African-American children to play the piano. The program was sponsored by the Student Christian Association at Southwestern University and was conducted at the First Methodist Church of Georgetown. The program, in operation from 1946 to 1966, added vocal music and art in later years.

The Negro Fine Arts School provided generations of black children an opportunity to learn music. It staged an annual recital, complete with a printed program, to showcase the students' accomplishments. It awarded scholarships to students going to college or pursuing other higher education. The school also helped to ease the transition from segregation to integration both in the Georgetown Independent School District and at Southwestern University. The first African-American student to enroll at Southwestern University was a student of Iola Bowden Chambers and an alumnus of the Negro Fine Arts School. Charles Miller, one of the first students in the Negro Fine Arts School and in 1993 an administrator for the Georgetown Independent School District, stated, "She was the one that came across the railroad tracks and helped us all. Miss Bowden was to Georgetown what Eleanor Roosevelt was to the United States, because she was one of the first." Bowden was promoted to assistant professor in 1948 and to associate professor in 1960. In addition to her work as a member of the music faculty and as director of the Negro Fine Arts School, she supervised the Junior Music Department at the university for years and was organist for the First Methodist Church in Georgetown for more than twenty years.

She was active in state and national professional organizations, including the American Guild of Organists, the National Federation of Music Clubs (in which she was a district officer), the Texas Music Teachers' Association, the National Guild of Piano Teachersqv (she served as a judge in the National Piano Playing Auditions), and the American College of Musicians. She was one of the founders of the Delta Nu chapter of Delta Omicron at Southwestern University and served as a national officer in that organization. She was a member of the Alpha Chi honor society. She published an article, "Musical Phrasing," in *Southwestern Musician* in June 1949. In 1955 Iola Bowden married Walter R. Chambers. She retired from Southwestern University in 1966, and the couple moved to Brownwood. After her retirement she continued to be active professionally and endowed a scholarship in music at Southwestern University. She died at her home in Brownwood on December 14, 1978, and was buried in May.

BIBLIOGRAPHY: Estill Franklin Allen, *Methodist History of May, Texas* (Brownwood, Texas: Howard Payne University, 1980). *Histories of Pride: Thirteen Pioneers Who Shaped Georgetown's African American Community* (Georgetown, Texas, 1993). Ralph W. Jones, *Southwestern University, 1840–1961* (Austin: Jenkins, 1973).

Martha Mitten Allen

CHAMBERS, THOMAS JEFFERSON (1802–1865). Thomas Jefferson Chambers, lawyer and land speculator, was born in Orange County, Virginia, on April 13, 1802, the youngest of twenty children of Thomas Chambers and the ninth of his second wife, Mary (Gore). His father died in 1815, leaving a small estate of less than $500. Soon after, the widow and her youngest children moved to Mount Sterling, Kentucky, where relatives lived. Chambers attended the academy of Joshua Worley in Georgetown, where he studied Latin, Greek, and the sciences. While teaching school to support himself he trained for the law by clerking for judges Jesse Bledsoe and James Clark in Lexington. Chambers was in debt, and when his mentor Clark declared the state's debtor relief laws unconstitutional in 1823, Chambers left Kentucky for Alabama. He was, however, always able to secure the patronage of influential men and was sponsored for the bar in Alabama by Supreme Court justice Abner S. Lipscomb. There is no evidence that Chambers encountered trouble in Alabama, but by 1826 he left for New Orleans and took passage for Veracruz. He traveled to Mexico City, where he lived with a Mexican family in order to learn the language and customs. For the next few years he supported himself by giving English lessons and translating for businessmen. He became acquainted with Vice Governor Victor Blancoqv of Coahuila and Texasqv and moved to Saltillo. With Blanco's influence Chambers became a certified surveyor and in 1829 was named surveyor general of Texas. He and land commissioner Juan Antonio Padillaqv were to survey claims and issue titles to Texans who had lived on their land before 1827 but remained without deeds.

The pair reached Nacogdoches by February 13, 1830, and Chambers sent out surveyors. In April Padilla's political enemies had him arrested on a bogus murder charge. This ended issuing titles and surveying until his replacement was named. Chambers became the paid agent at the legislature for residents of East Texas. On September 23, 1834, for his activities as surveyor he received eleven leagues of land that he located in Ellis, Navarro, Chambers, Liberty, and Hays counties. Besides their state commissions, Chambers and Padilla were engaged in large-scale land speculation. On February 12, 1830, the state granted them an empresarioqv contract to settle 800 families in northern Texas. Unfortunately the land assigned to them lay outside of Texas, and nothing was done with the contract. Chambers participated in a shady though not illegal purchase of land from Vincent Padilla, who had bought an unlocated eleven-league grant from the state in 1829 in accordance with the state law allowing native Mexicans to buy Texas tracts. On March 3, 1830, Vincent asked his kinsman, the land commissioner, to issue a title. A five-league tract was surveyed and title issued on March 28, 1830, to land stretching around Turtle Bay and down to Double Bayou in what is now Chambers County. Chambers bought the tract on June 23, 1830, and this purchase made him very unpopular in the area among settlers, some of whom had come as early as 1824.

Seeing the potential of Texas whetted his ambition. In Saltillo in the summer of 1830 he became a naturalized Mexican citizen with a special assurance from influential men that he would be given a bar examination and permission to practice law. But he did not receive a license until 1834 and was the only foreigner to hold one. During the Anahuac disturbances[qv] Chambers, with ties to the government, tried to stop the rebels and was accused of being a Tory. His enemies hanged him in effigy in Brazoria in July, and, his pride hurt, he published a pamphlet the following year defending his actions. One month after securing his license to practice law the legislature named him assessor general (state attorney) for Texas, a position he kept for only two months before resigning on May 7, 1834, without ever leaving Saltillo. In 1834 he and others worked to reform the judicial system to make it more responsive to Texas needs. One of the changes was the Chambers Jury Law, which provided for a jury of twelve in Texas and a verdict determined by a majority of eight. The legislature mandated a Texas supreme court on April 17, and two months later the governor named Chambers chief justice. He remained in office one year and five months but never presided over a court. By law he was to receive $3,000 a year, payable in land at the rate of $100 a league. He claimed a salary based on thirty leagues but located some claims on top of others. He located only thirteen of his leagues before the land offices were closed by the Texas Revolution.[qv]

In the fall of 1835 Chambers's toryish support of the authorities caused the General Council[qv] to denounce him. But after the Texas victory at Gonzales, he acquiesced in steps toward revolution. He did not join the attack against San Antonio. In January he asked the council for the rank of major general in return for raising and equipping 1,145 volunteers, the "Army of Reserve," in the United States to be marched to Texas by May 15. He intended to use his own credit in the amount of $10,000, which would be repaid by Texas. He left for Kentucky on February 23 via Nacogdoches. Though he did not return until June 1837, he sent some troops, not the 1,915 he claimed, to Texas after the battle of San Jacinto.[qv] His accounts totaling $23,621 were approved, but they were not paid because there was no money in the treasury. For service as major general he applied for a bounty of 1,280 acres, which he received in 1846.

Chambers became a founding member of the Texas Philosophical Society[qv] on December 5, 1837, and made an unsuccessful bid for the Texas Senate in 1838. He retired in 1839 to his house at Round Point, below Anahuac. He changed the name of that town to Chambersia and hired an agent to sell city lots, actions that antagonized old residents. He went to the United States to raise money by selling some of his land and left a nephew in charge of his local business. He then returned unsuccessful in May 1842 and discovered that his entire Padilla tract had been bought from the sheriff for back taxes by John O'Brian, who was living at Round Point. When the local court decided against Chambers, he ambushed and killed O'Brian. The Liberty court did not indict him, however, and he regained possession of the house. O'Brian's widow pursued the matter to the state Supreme Court, where she won in 1855. During this same time Chambers was in litigation with Charles Willcox,[qv] who claimed the town of Anahuac; the Texas high court decided in favor of Willcox in 1862. Chambers was also involved in numerous other suits over his various land claims.

After annexation[qv] Chambers tried to reenter politics but failed to beat incumbent William Fields[qv] in the election for the state legislature in 1849; in 1851 and 1853 he was defeated for the governorship. He received a charter for the Chambers Terraqueous Transportation Company in 1854. This company was to have constructed 4,000 miles of road and to have had a right-of-way 200 feet wide over land, rivers, lakes, and bays, for an amphibious vehicle. The unsuccessful machine was never put into operation.

Chambers County became a separate county in 1858 with the general's nephew, William Morton Chambers,[qv] as county judge. The pair represented the county in the Secession Convention[qv] in 1861. Chambers lost the gubernatorial race to Francis R. Lubbock[qv] in the fall of 1861. He allowed the Confederates to place a battery on his property in Anahuac to guard the mouth of the Trinity, including his own wharf. A company arrived in late 1862 to man the cannon at Fort Chambersia. Seeking a command, Chambers went to Richmond in 1862 but was unable to raise the required number of men. Instead, he became a volunteer aide to an officer in Hood's Texas Brigade[qv] and received a minor wound during the Seven Days' battles. He remained in Richmond with the futile suit that he be made a general to defend the Texas coast instead of John B. Magruder,[qv] then returned home in 1863 and again ran unsuccessfully for governor.

Chambers had married Annie Chubb on November 20, 1851; the couple had two daughters. He built a fine house on the bluff in Anahuac, one section of which still stood in 1990. On the night of March 15, 1865, the family was gathered in an upstairs parlor when an assassin fired a shotgun through the open window and killed Chambers. Though nobody was arrested, local people believed that Albert V. Willcox did it. The general was buried near his home. The next year his wife moved his body to the Galveston Episcopal Cemetery, and Charles Willcox bought Chambers's wharf, warehouse, and home from the widow. In 1925 the Texas legislature appropriated $20,000 to pay Chambers's descendants for his controversial claim to the site of the Capitol[qv] and other land in Austin.

BIBLIOGRAPHY: William Chambers, *Sketch of the Life of General T. J. Chambers of Texas* (Galveston: Galveston *News* Book and Job Office, 1853). Llerena B. Friend, The Life of Thomas Jefferson Chambers (M.A. thesis, University of Texas, 1928). Vertical Files, Barker Texas History Center, University of Texas at Austin.

Margaret Swett Henson

CHAMBERS, WILLIAM MORTON (1821–1892). William Morton Chambers, lawyer, county judge, and gubernatorial candidate, son of Landon Gore and Mary Green (Allen) Chambers, was born in Orange County, Virginia, on November 18, 1821. He was the oldest of nine children. He moved to Texas in 1844 and settled in Liberty County, where he read law and was admitted to the bar. In 1853 he published his *Sketch of the Life of General T. J. Chambers of Texas* as a campaign biography for his uncle, Thomas Jefferson Chambers,[qv] who was running for governor. William Chambers was elected chief justice of Liberty County in 1856 and became the first chief justice of the new Chambers County, which was named for his uncle in 1858. By 1860 he had accumulated an estate with twenty slaves, the whole valued at more than $20,000. Chambers was a delegate from Chambers County to the Secession Convention[qv] of 1861 and served in the Confederate Army during the Civil War.[qv]

By 1866 he had become county judge of Chambers County. He abandoned his former Democratic affiliations and joined the Republican party,[qv] which rewarded him with appointment as judge of the First Judicial District. Chambers was involved in the political turmoil of Reconstruction[qv] and charged with several misdemeanors on the bench. The Fourteenth Legislature, however, refused to convict him. In a reorganization of judicial districts he was given jurisdiction of Orange County, even though he was not a resident of that area. The Republican party nominated Chambers, who had served as a delegate to its national convention in 1872, as its gubernatorial candidate in 1876. As a Republican, with a somewhat tarnished reputation as a jurist, he stood little chance against the rejuvenated Democratic party,qv which had resumed its dominance in Texas in the 1873 election. The Democratic incumbent, Richard Coke,qv won by a better than three-to-one margin. In 1880 Chambers again served as a delegate to the Republican national convention. He also waged a pair of unsuccessful campaigns in the 1880s. In 1882 he lost his bid for a seat in the United States Congress, and in 1888 he failed in his attempt to become state attorney general on the Nonpartisan ticket. Chambers married Theodosia Gillard DeBlanc around 1848, and they had two children. He married Petronille Lacour in 1855 and Betty Keyes in 1879. He died late in 1892.

BIBLIOGRAPHY: Paul D. Casdorph, *A History of the Republican Party in Texas, 1865–1965* (Austin: Pemberton Press, 1965). William Chambers, *Sketch of the Life of General T. J. Chambers of Texas* (Galveston: Galveston News Book and Job Office, 1853). Jewel Horace Harry, A History of Chambers County (M.A. thesis, University of Texas, 1940; rpt., Dallas: Taylor, 1981). E. W. Winkler, *Platforms of Political Parties in Texas* (Austin: University of Texas, 1916).

Julianne Johnston and Robert Wooster

CHAMBERS OF COMMERCE. The first two chambers of commerce in Texas were chartered by the Republic of Texas.qv Houston founded its chamber on January 28, 1840, seventy-two years after the organization of the first chamber of commerce in the United States. The Galveston chamber was chartered on February 3, 1845. The United States census of 1850 listed thirty towns in Texas. Only ten towns had a population over 1,000, and Galveston, the largest, had only 4,177 residents. More than a decade after the Civil War,qv when Texas had seventy-five urban communities, several other cities organized commercial associations—Austin in 1877, Fort Worth in 1882, Gainesville in 1888, Hillsboro in 1890, Dallas in 1893, San Antonio in 1894, Marlin in 1898, Waco in 1899, and Port Arthur in 1899.

The commercial-organization movement gained full momentum during the first decade of the twentieth century. In 1900 Texas had 124 urban centers; forty-five additional towns appeared in the 1910 census. Growing urban populations awakened a competitive spirit among the businessmen of the various communities in quest of their full share of prosperity. Realizing the advantages of organized effort, businessmen in every city in Texas organized chambers of commerce before the decade ended.

While vigorously building their own communities, Texas business interests moved rapidly into a program of statewide cooperation. Chamber of commerce executives organized their statewide association in 1906. Two years later the Texas Business Men's Association was founded. It functioned successfully as the first statewide chamber of commerce until 1914, when its career was abruptly ended by a temporary court injunction secured by the state attorney general on grounds that the association engaged in politics. The charge was never proved, and the lawsuit was dismissed five years later. Local chambers of commerce had not been included in the injunction. Upon recommendation of the post–World War I Readjustment Conference, the Texas Chamber of Commerce was formed in April 1919 but was dissolved four years later because Texas businessmen preferred regional organizations. The powerful West Texas Chamber of Commerceqv was founded in February 1919. Although rudimentary commercial associations existed in other sections, additional regional chambers of commerce were not founded until 1926, when the present East Texas Chamber of Commerceqv was organized on March 24, and the South Texas Chamber of Commerceqv on November 16. The Lower Rio Grande Valley Chamber of Commerce began in 1944. Chambers of commerce have been the propelling force in promoting highways, transportation, industry, business, agriculture, tourism, new community facilities and services, and applying new techniques to keep abreast of constantly changing economic and political conditions. In 1988 the regional chambers of commerce merged to form the Texas Chamber of Commerce.

BIBLIOGRAPHY: Carl A. Blasdig, *Building Texas* (Brownsville, Texas: Springman-King, 1963). Vertical Files, Barker Texas History Center, University of Texas at Austin. *Carl A. Blasig*

CHAMBERS COUNTY. Chambers County (G-12), named for Thomas Jefferson Chambers,qv is a rural county less than twenty miles east of Houston in the Coastal Prairie region of Southeast Texas. The county is divided by the Trinity River. It comprises 616 square miles of level terrain that slopes toward Galveston Bay and the Gulf of Mexico, its southern and southwestern boundaries. The center point of the county is at 29°42′ north latitude and 94°41′ west longitude. The elevation rises from sea level to fifty feet. Chambers County has a subtropical, humid climate, with rainfall averaging forty-nine inches, a mean annual temperature of sixty-nine degrees, and a growing season averaging 261 days per year. The soils are chiefly coastal clay and sandy loam. The flora includes tall grasses, live oaks, cypress, pine, and cedar trees, as well as hardwoods along rivers and streams. The Southern Pacific and the Gulf, Colorado and Santa Fe provide railroad service, and Interstate Highway 10 was built through the county in 1955. The county's abundant coastal marshland has never supported a large population, but its watery lowlands support the rice cultureqv that yields the county's principal crop. Other farmers raise significant numbers of beef cattle, hogs, sheep, and poultry, as well as corn, feed grains, citrus fruits, vegetables, and some cotton. Natural resources include salt domes, industrial sand, and pine and hardwood timber; oil, gas, and sulfur are present in commercial quantities. The proximity to Houston enables many residents to commute to jobs in that city. Incorporated communities in Chambers County in 1994 were Anahuac, Baytown (in both Chambers and Harris counties), Beach City, Cove, Mont Belvieu (Chambers and Liberty counties), and Old River–Winfree. Hurricanesqv that have struck Chambers County include those of 1875, 1900, 1915, 1943, 1957, 1961, and 1983.

Archeological excavations in the county have produced artifacts dating to A.D. 1000. Karankawa, Coapite, and Copane Indians lived in the area when the first expeditions traveled the lower Trinity River. The land that became Chambers County formed part of the Atascosito (or lower Trinity River) District, a subdivision of Nacogdoches in Spanish Texas.qv By the late seventeenth century the French intruded on Spanish interests by trading with the Indians as far as the Sabine. French trader Joseph Blancpain'sqv expedition to the area along Galveston Bay and the lower Trinity in 1754 provoked Spanish efforts to protect the region with a system of missions guarded by adjoining presidios. In 1756 Spanish missionaries established Nuestra Señora de la Luz Missionqv near the site of present Wallisville, and, to gain strategic control of the lower Trinity, soldiers constructed San Agustín de Ahumada Presidioqv on its east bank near what is now the Chambers-Liberty county line. Missionaries worked with Orcoquiza Indians who inhabited the region. After the 1763 Treaty of Paris removed the French threat by awarding Louisiana to the Spanish, storms and constant Indian hostility resulted in removal of the missions to another location in 1766 and abandonment of the settlements by 1772. In 1805 Spanish troops landed at what is now Smith's Point to reinforce the Atascosito ("Marshy") community, but by 1812 few Spanish settlers had moved into the region. It was subsequently used by filibusters as a staging ground to mount attacks against Spanish Mexico.

By the early 1800s, Alabama and Coushatta Indians had arrived in the area from Alabama, assimilated the local Bidais and Orcoquizas, taken over their livestock trade with settlers along the Atascosito Road,qv and planted crops. A colony of French exiles from Napoleon's Grand Army under Charles François Antoine Lallemand,qv planning to free Napoleon and put his brother Joseph on the Mexican throne, attempted to establish themselves near the site of present Anahuac in 1818, but were driven out by the Spanish. Jean Laffiteqv left the area permanently around 1820.

Mexican influence in the area increased after the Mexican war of independence^qv from Spain in 1821, and Mexican place names replaced many earlier designations. In 1825 Perry's Point, the principal port of entry for the colonial grant, was renamed Anahuac, after the ancient capital of the Aztecs. American settlement began in 1821 at the invitation of the Mexican government. Some of Laffite's men stayed, and empresarios Haden Edwards, Joseph Vehlein, David G. Burnet, and Lorenzo de Zavala^qqv received grants in the area. The major part of what is now Chambers County became Vehlein's grant. T. J. Chambers received land for serving as chief justice of the Supreme Court of Coahuila and Texas^qv and, in 1829, as surveyor general. Chambers's home, built in 1835, today houses the county library. Other early settlers, largely from southern and western Louisiana, included Peter Ellis Bean, James Morgan, James Taylor White,^qqv and the Wallis family, which settled at the future site of Wallisville. White is believed to have introduced a herd of longhorn cattle^qv at Turtle Bayou in 1827; other farmers raised rice and cotton, and the lumber industry^qv became important by the 1850s. Antebellum education in Chambers County was private.

Struggles between Anglo settlers and Mexican authorities increased as officials sought to prevent further immigration from the United States and maintain control. The Mexican government established Fort Anahuac in 1830 and gave command of the port at Anahuac to John Davis Bradburn,^qv whose difficulties with the settlers culminated in the Turtle Bayou Resolutions^qv and the eventual withdrawal of the Mexican garrison. Bradburn also arrested Francisco I. Madero,^qv whose commission was to grant land titles to American immigrants. In a further foreshadowing of the Texas Revolution,^qv discontented settlers rose against Mexican rule in 1835 in a conflict set off by disagreements over Mexican tariff policy (*see* ANAHUAC DISTURBANCES). At the same time, others chose to get along with a lax Mexican government that levied no taxes and frequently failed to enforce the law. A substantial number of these moved eastward during the Texas Revolution.

In the 1840s, the western edge of the future county was developed. Among those who acquired land was Sam Houston,^qv who established a home at Cedar Point around 1837. The first post office was established at Anahuac, then known as Chambersea, in 1844. When the area became part of Liberty County after independence, land quarrels broke out, among them the notorious conflict between Charles Willcox^qv and Chambers, who, with property valued at more than half a million dollars by 1860, was the county's wealthiest resident.

Chambers County was formed in 1858 from Liberty and Jefferson counties, and organized the same year with Wallisville as its county seat. By 1860, census returns reported merino sheep, 26,632 cattle, and only 344 slaves countywide, a reflection of the importance of livestock in the local economy. Of sixty families that owned slaves in 1859, John White held thirty-three, and only twelve families among the remainder owned more than ten. Cotton growing increased in the antebellum period, but by 1860 only 100 cotton farmers operated in a county population of 1,508. Industry was confined to a steam sawmill and a shipyard.

Chambers County residents voted 109 to 26 for secession,^qv and many participated in the ensuing conflict. The Liberty Invincibles, formed in 1861, joined Company F of the Fifth Regiment of Texas Volunteers. Others joined the Twenty-sixth Regiment of Texas Cavalry, the Moss Bluff Rebels, which became Company F of the Twenty-first Regiment of Texas Cavalry, or Company B of the Texas State Troops. Fort Chambers was established by Confederate troops in 1862 to protect the Gulf Coast, and Union troops reached Liberty by July 1865, but no major fighting occurred in Chambers County.

During Reconstruction^qv the county began to recover from the hardships of war, but by 1870 its population had dropped to 1,503, below the prewar total. Roughly one-third of this number were black, and as many as fifteen African Americans^qv were property owners. The Freedmen's Bureau^qv opened a black school at Wallisville in 1869, and other black and white schools opened in 1871. By 1898 thirteen white schools were operating with an enrollment of 324, and ten black schools with 211. Local politics reflected a struggle for control between those seeking to institute reforms and others resistant to change. Among the most notable incidents was Gen. Joseph J. Reynolds's^qv attempt in 1869 to remove county and city officials who did not qualify under the Iron Clad Oath. Other conflicts arose from Ku Klux Klan^qv opposition to the Union League,^qv which sought to enroll black voters, and from other opposition to improvements in the lives of former slaves. In 1876 the election of local officials reflected passage of a new Texas constitution that overturned many Radical Republican reforms. Thereafter the white primary^qv and the poll tax remained as obstacles to civil rights.

The opening of a meat-packing plant in Wallisville in the 1870s reflected the continuing importance of ranching^qv in the Chambers County economy, though many cattlemen drove their herds north to Kansas City or shipped them after railroad service reached the area. The Whites and Jacksons maintained large ranches, and James Jackson introduced wire fencing on 26,000 acres in 1882. Price declines after the Civil War^qv kept cotton farming to a minimum. Brickmaking on Cedar Bayou supported a Galveston building boom in the 1870s, while other manufacturers turned to boatbuilding, particularly at the Turtle Bayou Shipyard. The lumber industry centered at Wallisville helped that city to grow in the 1880s and 1890s, while Anahuac remained unoccupied.

Because railroad routes reached no farther than the county's eastern and western borders by the 1890s, with the exception of a single branch line that provided freight service to the interior, Chambers County remained isolated and dependent on steamer traffic and other water transportation to Galveston. No important towns developed in the county until 1896, when settlers from the Midwest, who also developed the port at Bolivar, helped to complete the Gulf and Interstate Railway from Beaumont to Bolivar Peninsula. Later, important railroad towns developed at Winnie and Stowell, in the extreme northeastern part of the county. Railroads in the western part of the county were first built from Dayton to the Goose Creek oilfield^qv by Ross S. Sterling^qv and later taken over by the Southern Pacific.

A disastrous fire at the county's wooden courthouse destroyed early records in 1875, hurricanes in 1875 and 1900 damaged crops and livestock, and a smallpox epidemic in 1877 killed many residents. Though some farmers left Chambers County after the 1875 hurricane, total farms increased from 146 to 327 between 1870 and 1900. In the latter year the total acres in farms reached 366,436; farm value had increased tenfold in the previous ten years. General prosperity resulted in a near doubling of the population between 1880 and 1910 from 2,187 to 4,234. In 1900 county farmers owned a total of 49,000 cattle, the highest in the county's history.

Between 1910 and 1930, tenant farmers increased from roughly 27 percent to more than 35 percent of all farmers. Mules in use as draft animals reached a high of 1,022 in 1920. In the early 1900s, canal development by the Lone Star Canal Company^qv and other firms enabled some farmers to begin rice farming, while others in the eastern part of the county turned to truck farming. A total of 210,000 barrels of rice was harvested in 1903, and significant quantities of sweet potatoes, Indian corn, and sugar were produced by 1910. Lumber peaked at Wallisville in 1906, but declined during the panic of 1907. The largest local mill and the community's only important industry, Cummings Export Lumber Company, built by the Cummings brothers in 1898, closed in 1915 when another major hurricane blew through.

In 1906 Wallisville adopted a stock law to prevent pigs from running loose. Anahuac had become a boomtown. In 1908 Anahuac supporters filed suit and, in spite of Wallisville's genteel swine law, succeeded in making their town the county seat. Efforts to dissolve the county itself were made in 1915, 1923, and 1925 as conflicts developed over stock laws, prohibition,^qv and the county seat question; these were complicated by offers of lower taxes from Harris and Liberty counties, whose officials hoped to cash in on Chambers County oilfields.

Despite increased agricultural production, the Chambers County population declined from 4,234 to 4,162 between 1910 and 1920, then rose again to reach a high of 5,710 by 1930 as a growing oil boom brought new residents to the area. Barbers Hill oilfield,[qv] developed after 1918, reached its peak production of 8,082,000 barrels in 1933; the field was later serviced by five pipelines. Oilfields were subsequently discovered at Lost Lake, Anahuac, Monroe City, and Turtle Bay, and near Hankamer, and gas reserves were developed in the eastern part of the county. Oil production provided jobs and revenue that helped the county weather the Great Depression[qv] with relatively little discomfort, and brought in workers who increased the population to 7,511 by 1940. Transportation gains after 1926 included the extension of State Highway 146 from Anahuac to Stowell.

During World War II[qv] many Chambers County residents found employment in refineries and shipyards at Baytown, Houston, Beaumont, Port Arthur, and Orange. After September 1943 rice farmers employed German prisoners of war[qv] from camps in Liberty and Chambers counties. The establishment of the Fraternity of the White Heron, the Forward Trinity Valley Association, the Texas Water Conservation Association, and the Chambers-Liberty County Navigation District advanced area water interests, including the dredging of a channel from the Houston Ship Channel[qv] to Smith Point, Anahuac, and Liberty. The Trinity Bay Conservation District was started in 1949. Major highway improvements were made to Farm roads 563 and 565 and State Highway 73, later Interstate 10.

After the war the population grew to 7,871 by 1950 and 10,379 by 1960. By 1959 county farms totaled 483, of which roughly 62 percent were commercial and only 12.4 percent tenant-operated. Mining, contract construction, wholesale distribution, petroleum extraction, and natural-gas production were the chief county industries. Only four manufacturing firms were operating, among 112 mining and mineral establishments. By 1966, though the overall population continued to increase, no populated place in Chambers County had as many as 2,500 inhabitants; 22.5 percent of the population was described as living in poverty; and the population density was only nineteen persons per square mile. In this period, many black residents left for jobs in urban areas.

Growing national support for environmental preservation and passage of the 1967 National Environmental Policy Act had important effects on Chambers County. Relying upon an earlier study by the United States Army Corps of Engineers in preparation for the construction of a saltwater barrier across the Trinity River to aid rice farmers, improve river navigation, and provide increased water supplies for adjacent counties, in 1960 state legislators proposed a 23,200-acre reservoir and wildlife refuge that would inundate Wallisville. Despite protests, engineers purchased the townsite, the plan was approved in 1962, and work began. Excavations led to the unearthing of a primitive burial site and other historic discoveries. Ultimately, the project drew the interest of the Sierra Club, and other environmental groups as well as a representative of the commercial shrimping industry[qv] filed suit against several state and national agencies. In 1973 a United States district judge ordered construction stopped, when the project was 75 percent complete. The corps of engineers eventually wrote off the $23 million investment and in 1977 recommended a smaller project. Wallisville Heritage Park,[qv] established in 1979, henceforth preserved the townsite and some of the community's historic buildings.

Between 1970 and 1980 the rural population of Chambers County grew 52 percent, and in the early 1980s the total county population was 19,100. People of English[qv] origin comprised 27 percent, Irish[qv] 17 percent, French 6½ percent, African-American 14 percent, and Hispanic 3 percent. Forest products and cattle, along with rice and soybeans, potatoes, peaches, and pecans constituted the county's principal products. A total of 288 business establishments operated countywide, including sixteen manufacturing establishments with 400 employees. Oil and gas extraction, agribusiness, petroleum refining, and the manufacture of plastics and resins topped the list of industries. In the late 1980s, after a number of petroleum-industry-related accidents nearby, residents of Mont Belvieu were moved and the community was purchased by oil companies, which rebuilt it at another location. The county's three school districts included four elementary, three middle, and three high schools. Whereas in 1960 only 10 percent of the population had completed high school and fewer than 3 percent had completed college, 57.5 percent of the county population had completed high school and 10 percent had finished college in 1982.

Chambers County residents consistently supported Democratic presidential candidates up to 1920, but voted Republican in roughly half of subsequent elections, including those for Warren Harding in 1920, Herbert Hoover in 1928, Dwight Eisenhower[qv] in 1952 and 1956, Richard Nixon in 1972, Ronald Reagan in 1980 and 1984, and George H. W. Bush in 1988.

Several important wildlife areas are located in Chambers County, including Moody National Wildlife Refuge and Anahuac National Wildlife Refuge,[qv] at the juncture of Oyster Bay and East Bay. Lake Anahuac[qv] and Fort Anahuac Park were built in the 1940s, H. H. (Hub) McCollum Park in 1959, and Whites Park in 1965. The Texas Rice Festival, which began in 1969, is celebrated annually at Winnie-Stowell in September and October.

BIBLIOGRAPHY: Anahuac *Progress,* June 25, 1937. Jewel Horace Harry, A History of Chambers County (M.A. thesis, University of Texas, 1940; rpt., Dallas: Taylor, 1981). Margaret S. Henson and Kevin Ladd, *Chambers County: A Pictorial History* (Norfolk, Virginia: Donning, 1988). Ralph Semmes Jackson, *Home on the Double Bayou: Memories of an East Texas Ranch* (Austin: University of Texas Press, 1961).

Diana J. Kleiner

CHAMBERS CREEK. Chambers Creek, also known as Pecan Creek, rises at the junction of its north and south forks, 2½ miles southwest of Boz in west central Ellis County (at 32°17′ N, 96°58′ W) and runs first southeast, then northeast, and then south for sixty-seven miles to its mouth on Richland Creek, two miles north of the Freestone county line in southern Navarro County (at 31°58′ N, 96°12′ W). It is named for Thomas Jefferson Chambers,[qv] who in 1834 received the first land grant issued by the Mexican government (*see* MEXICAN TEXAS) in what is now Ellis County. The local terrain is flat with some shallow depressions and is surfaced by clay and sandy loams that support water-tolerant hardwood trees, conifers, and various grasses.

CHAMBERSVILLE, TEXAS. Chambersville is on a hill overlooking the rich farmland of the Blackland Prairies, near Farm Road 543 seven miles north of McKinney in northwestern Collin County. The town was named in honor of Elisha Chambers, a native of North Carolina who arrived in the county in 1847. Three years later he received a Peters colony[qv] land certificate for 320 acres near the East Fork of the Trinity River. In 1853 he provided land for the town's school, church, and cemetery. A post office was established there in 1894, with Jacob Bryan as postmaster. In 1903 the post office was discontinued, and local mail was routed through McKinney. Chambersville reported a population of forty from the 1950s through the early 1990s.

BIBLIOGRAPHY: Seymour V. Connor, *The Peters Colony of Texas: A History and Biographical Sketches of the Early Settlers* (Austin: Texas State Historical Association, 1959). Roy Franklin Hall and Helen Gibbard Hall, *Collin County: Pioneering in North Texas* (Quanah, Texas: Nortex, 1975). J. Lee and Lillian J. Stambaugh, *A History of Collin County* (Austin: Texas State Historical Association, 1958).

David Minor

CHAMBLISS, TEXAS. Chambliss, on Farm Road 545 seven miles northeast of McKinney in northeastern Collin County, was named in honor of Charles Chambliss, an early settler. In 1900 the community had a school, a church, a gin, and two stores. A post office was established there in 1898, but in 1903 it was closed, and local mail was rerouted through Anna, three miles northwest. From 1933 to the early 1990s the population of Chambliss was twenty-five.

BIBLIOGRAPHY: Roy Franklin Hall and Helen Gibbard Hall, *Collin County: Pioneering in North Texas* (Quanah, Texas: Nortex, 1975). J. Lee and Lillian J. Stambaugh, *A History of Collin County* (Austin: Texas State Historical Association, 1958).

David Minor

CHAMBODUT, LOUIS CLAUDE MARIE (1821–1880). Louis Claude Marie Chambodut, priest, was born on March 25, 1821, at Just-en-Chevalet, Loire, France. His parents, after giving him the best education their native town could afford, sent him to the Grand Séminaire of Lyons, where he completed with brilliant success a full course of philosophy and theology and was raised to the diaconate in December 1845. When Jean Marie Odin,qv vicar apostolic of Texas, called at the seminary for recruits, young Chambodut offered his services. On March 25, 1846, he was ordained a priest in the Cathedral of St. Louis, New Orleans, Louisiana, after which he proceeded to Galveston. He was then sent to Nacogdoches for five years, where he was responsible for practically all East Texas and part of Louisiana. About 1851 he was called to Galveston by Odin, who appointed him his vicar general. In 1853 Chambodut was one of a number of priests who ministered to the sick in the Galveston yellow fever epidemic. He was one of only a few clergymen to survive. The immense diocese covered the whole of Texas and part of Indian Territory, and the bishop spent his time visiting his widely scattered flock, so the administration of the affairs of the diocese rested heavily on the shoulders of the vicar general. To him the bishop now left the task of building the cathedral and episcopal residence. Along with serving as chaplain of the Ursuline Sistersqv of Galveston, Chambodut collected funds and personally supervised the construction of the initial building of St. Mary's Infirmary (*see* ST. MARY'S HOSPITAL), St. Mary's Orphanage,qv and St. Patrick's church in Galveston. In 1856 Chambodut embarked on a speaking tour across Texas to lecture on and answer questions about Catholicism.

In 1861 three Texas regiments went to the Army of Virginia and became famous as Hood's Texas Brigade.qv One company mustered in Galveston and adjacent counties was made up entirely of French settlers, descendants of the dispersed army of Napoleon. They were all Catholics, and Chambodut was a great favorite with them. After the Civil Warqv Gen. John B. Magruder showed his affection by giving the venerable Father Chambodut the gift of his sword. In 1880 while accompanying Bishop C. M. Dubuisqv on a trip to San Antonio, Chambodut fell ill; he died on December 7, and was buried at St. Mary's Cathedralqv in Galveston.

BIBLIOGRAPHY: Carlos E. Castañeda, *Our Catholic Heritage in Texas* (7 vols., Austin: Von Boeckmann–Jones, 1936–58; rpt., New York: Arno, 1976). Mary Angela Fitzmorris, Four Decades of Catholicism in Texas, 1820–1860 (Ph.D. dissertation, Catholic University of America, 1926). Galveston *Daily News*, December 8, 1880. *Interstate Index: A Journal of Progress*, June–July 1920.

Mary Ann Acosta

CHAMIZAL DISPUTE. The Chamizal dispute between Mexico and the United States was a boundary conflict over about 600 acres at El Paso, Texas, between the bed of the Rio Grandeqv as surveyed in 1852 and the present channel of the river. About 100 acres of the tract fell within the business district of the city. The dispute was based on the interpretation of the Treaty of Guadalupe Hidalgoqv of 1848 and the Treaty of 1884.qv These agreements specified that the boundary should be down the middle of the river along the deepest channel, regardless of any alterations in the banks or channels. The Treaty of 1884 also provided that the alterations had to result from such gradual natural causes as the erosion of alluvium and not from the cutting off of land by floods or sudden changes in the river's course. This provision followed the long-established doctrine of international law that when changes in the course of a boundary river are caused by a deposit of alluvium, the boundary changes with the river, but when changes are due to avulsion, the old channel remains the boundary.

The river continually shifted south between 1852 and 1868, with the most radical shift in the river occurring after a flood in 1864. By 1873 the river had moved approximately 600 acres, cutting off land that was in effect made United States territory. Eventually the land was settled and incorporated as part of El Paso. The controversy started in 1895, when Mexico made a claim for the putative owner of the land, Pedro I. García, whose title dated to 1827.

In 1910, in an effort to determine proper title to the land, Mexico and the United States agreed on rules of arbitration. A third member, a Canadian, was added to the International Boundary Commission (later the International Boundary and Water Commissionqv) to complete the task. The tribunal was to decide whether or not the change in the river's course had been gradual, whether or not the boundaries set by treaties in 1848 and 1853 were fixed, and whether or not the 1884 treaty applied. Mexico claimed that the boundary had never changed and therefore that the Chamizal was technically Mexican territory, while the United States claimed that the 1884 convention applied, that the boundary was the result of gradual erosion, and that the property therefore belonged to the United States.

The commission met on June 10, 1911, in El Paso. According to its proposed settlement, the part of the disputed tract lying between the riverbed, as surveyed in 1852, and the middle of the river in 1864 was declared United States territory; the remainder of the tract was declared part of Mexico. Since this decision divided the Chamizal (Spanish for "Chamiza Thicket") between the two countries, the United States considered that the proposal did not conform to the terms of the arbitration and refused to accept it. Mexicans regarded the American refusal to accept the verdict as evidence of unwillingness to negotiate in good faith on matters that did not meet United States interests.

Between 1911 and 1963 several more initiatives were undertaken by different presidential administrations to solve the Chamizal debate. One suggested compromise was that the United States would forgive Mexico's default on the Pious Fund of the Californias, which was intended for the perpetual support of missions and spread of Christianity in California, in exchange for El Chamizal. Other proposed compromises included exchange of other territory along the Rio Grande for the Chamizal, direct purchase of the tract, and inclusion of the Chamizal in the Rio Grande Rectification Project.qv

The entire tract was under the jurisdiction of the United States and the state of Texas. No suits for delinquent taxes were contested, on the grounds that the property was in disputed territory and therefore not subject to taxation. In fact, aside from the question of guaranteed titles to the land in the tract, no distinction was made between it and the rest of El Paso. The dispute continued to affect Mexico–United States relations adversely until President John F. Kennedy agreed to settle it on the basis of the 1911 arbitration award. It was hoped that settlement of the dispute would strengthen the "Alliance for Progress" and solidify the Organization of American States.

The dispute was formally settled on January 14, 1963, when the United States and Mexico ratified a treaty that generally followed the 1911 arbitration recommendations. The agreement awarded to Mexico 366 acres of the Chamizal area and seventy-one acres east of the adjacent Cordova Island.qv Although no payments were made between the two governments, the United States received compensation from a private Mexican bank for 382 structures included in the transfer. The United States also received 193 acres of Cordova Island from Mexico, and the two nations agreed to share equally in the cost of rechanneling the river. In 1964 President Adolfo López Mateos and President Lyndon B. Johnsonqv met on the border to end the dispute officially. On September 17, 1963, Senator John Sparkman of Alabama introduced in Congress the American-Mexican Chamizal Convention Act of 1964, which finally settled the matter. In October 1967, Johnson met with Mexican president Gustavo Díaz Ordaz on the border and formally proclaimed the settlement. *See also* BANCOS OF THE RIO GRANDE and BOUNDARIES.

BIBLIOGRAPHY: Thaddeus Amat, *Transcript of Record of Proceedings before the Mexican and American Mixed Claims Commission with Relation to "The Pious Fund of the Californias"* (Washington: GPO, 1902). Austin *American-Statesman*, October 29, 1967. Alan C. Lamborn, *Statecraft, Domestic Politics, and Foreign Policy Making: The El Chamizal Dispute* (Boulder: Westview Press, 1988). Sheldon B. Liss, *A Century of Disagreement: The Chamizal Conflict, 1864–1964* (University Press of Washington, D.C., 1965). César Sepúlveda, *La Frontera Norte de México, historia, conflictos, 1762–1982* (Mexico City: Editorial Porrúa, 1983). *Gladys Gregory and Sheldon B. Liss*

CHAMIZAL NATIONAL MEMORIAL. The Chamizal National Memorial is near the Cordova Bridge in south central El Paso, El Paso County. The 54.9-acre park, which commemorates the peaceful settlement of a ninety-nine-year-old boundary dispute between the United States and Mexico (*see* CHAMIZAL DISPUTE), is on part of the 193-acre site acquired from Mexico in the Chamizal settlement in 1963. Congress set aside the park site the same year, and it was opened to the public in 1973. The memorial hosts a variety of programs throughout the year, including the Border Folk Festival in October, the Siglo de Oro (Spanish Golden Age) Festival in February and March, the Border Jazz Festival in May, the Zarzuela Festival in July and August, and the Sixteenth of September "Grito" celebration. A state historical marker was placed at the site in 1968. In 1990 the park logged 205,073 visits. *Christopher Long*

CHAMP D'ASILE. Although Champ d'Asile, a colony of Bonapartist refugees founded on the Trinity River in 1818, endured barely six months, its impact on the future of Texas was strong. The concern aroused among United States and Spanish diplomats over this intrusion into disputed territory caused two immediate results. United States pressure forced pirate Jean Laffite[qv] and his men, who had assisted the French colonists, to leave Galveston. And French presence at Champ d'Asile precipitated the Adams-Onís Treaty[qv] of 1819, which eliminated the Neutral Ground[qv] agreement and established the Sabine River as the Louisiana-Texas boundary and the border between the United States and New Spain. The body of thought, art, and literature evoked in Paris around Champ d'Asile also had important long-term effects on Texas. Bourbon Spain still ruled Mexico in 1818, and the Mexican army marched against the colony. In Restoration France, therefore, artists and the liberal press could represent the failure of Champ d'Asile as a Bourbon attack against the remains of France's imperial glory. A mythic Champ d'Asile stirred French attachment to Texas, intermittently rekindled by journalists, which two decades later resulted in France's becoming the first European power to recognize the Republic of Texas.[qv] Champ d'Asile, the Bonapartist refugees, and Laffite the pirate persist as themes in French literature.

The idea of an armed expedition of Frenchmen into Texas apparently took form during Baron Henri Dominique Lallemand's stay in New Orleans early in 1817 but was soon appropriated by his elder brother, Baron Charles François Antoine Lallemand,[qv] on his arrival in the United States later in the year. In Philadelphia Charles Lallemand obtained the presidency of a company that had received from Congress a grant of four townships of land in Alabama for the purpose of colonizing French emigrants who would cultivate grapes and olives. Lallemand succeeded in imposing more than sixty refugee officers on the society for the purpose of selling colonial allotments for the benefit of the expedition. The sale of most of the allotments in the early days of December enabled the first contingent, led by Baron Antoine Rigaud,[qv] to sail from Philadelphia aboard the schooner Huntress on December 17. Shortly afterward the Lallemand brothers, with more officers and munitions, left New York for New Orleans aboard the brig Actress. Charles Lallemand and his group went on to Galveston on February 19, 1818, leaving Henri Lallemand behind to coordinate the dispatch of supplies and recruits. At Galveston the Frenchmen were the guests of Pierre and Jean Laffite, special agents of the Spanish government. The Laffites provisioned and transported the filibusters while reporting their activities to the Spanish consul in New Orleans. On March 10, with the aid of their hosts, the French left for the Texas mainland in small boats and ascended the Trinity River to a locale now unknown, near the site of the present town of Liberty. There they built their fortress, Champ d'Asile.

What Lallemand and his officers intended to do in Texas remains an open question. Lallemand had offered his services to Spain, but the viceroy had turned him down. At the same time an emissary of Lallemand's claimed to have made an arrangement with the insurgent congress to train a large number of recruits in a remote part of Texas, a project to have been financed by Mexican mine owners. One deserter from Champ d'Asile reported that the general spoke of the wealth and power the mines would give the filibusters, perhaps to be used to free the captive Napoleon; while other deserters not privy to their leader's private conversations called the expedition mysterious. Lallemand issued a manifesto claiming that the invaders, although organized into military units, were peaceable colonists dedicated to tilling the soil. However, there is no evidence of their having undertaken agriculture in a serious manner, and lack of food was one cause that led finally to the breakup of the encampment. In any case, the officers primarily dedicated themselves to building a fortress and manufacturing munitions. Their pretension to agriculture masked Lallemand's aggressive intent, though the objective of the aggression is not known.

There probably were never many more than 100 officers at the encampment at one time. The roster of all those whose names are known amounts to 149. In addition there were four women and four children, three enlisted orderlies, several servants and laborers, and a few others. The officers were organized into three companies, called cohorts, of infantry, foot cavalry, and artillery. Between two-thirds and three-quarters of them were French, and the rest were former Grande Armée officers of other nationalities. The latter formed the most discontented and unstable element of the expedition, and most of the desertions were from their ranks. The French themselves were divided, some partisans of Lallemand and others of Rigaud, the second in command, who was in charge during Lallemand's frequent absences. Learning while away that Spanish troops had been dispatched from San Antonio to expel the filibusters, Lallemand ordered the camp abandoned. By July 24 the retreating invaders were at Galveston Bay waiting to be returned to the island in the Laffites' boats. In August George Graham,[qv] a United States special agent, arrived at Galveston to inform Lallemand that the American government wanted the French to leave Texas. When Graham left, Lallemand and a few others went with him and Rigaud remained in command. In September a hurricane inundated the island, destroying the refugees' shelters and supplies. In October a Spanish officer arrived and commanded the French to leave. With aid of the Laffites, most of the filibusters were in New Orleans by the end of November.

The myth of Champ d'Asile took over after the collapse of the colony and the withdrawal of all the colonists. In Paris, artists and the liberal press opposed to Louis XVIII seized the image of Charles Lallemand and the unfortunate half-pay veterans depicted as soldiers of the plow. Led by Benjamin Constant,[qv] the newspaper *Minerva* raised funds to send veterans to Texas, then to bring them back to France after the colony dispersed. Jean-Pierre Béranger composed a touching song, and Louis Garneray, Charles Aubry, Charles Abraham Chasselat, and other artists prepared highly sentimental engravings and lithographs. Even wallpaper and labels on liqueur bottles represented an imaginary Champ d'Asile. Three books were published in

1819: Hartmann and Millard, *Le Texas, ou Notice historique sur le Champ d'Asile;* L. F. L'Heritier, *Le Champ d'Asile;* and *L'Héroine du Texas,* a fictionalized version of the love story of two real colonists. Although it was probably written in Paris, *L'Héroine* may be the first novel set in Texas. Philippe Brideau, the archvillain of Honoré de Balzac's novel *La Rabouilleuse* (1842; translated as *A Bachelor's Establishment*), was a colonist at Champ d'Asile. The most popular book featuring Champ d'Asile was first published in French in 1878: *Adventures of a French Captain, at Present a Planter in Texas, Formerly a Refugee of Camp Asylum,* whose author uses the pseudonym Girard Roy Just. In 1985, after extensive research in Texas, French novelist Jean Soublin published *Le Champ d'Asile* in which the Comanches play an expanded role. In this novel some of the survivors form a utopian colony, an imaginative conclusion that telescopes the Franco-Texan experience of the entire nineteenth century. *See also* FRENCH.

BIBLIOGRAPHY: *All the Banners Wave: Art and War in the Romantic Era, 1792–1851* (exhibition catalog, Brown University Department of Art, 1982). Nina Athanassaglou-Kallmyer, "Sad Cincinnatus: Le Soldat-Laboureur as an Image of the Napoleonic Veteran after the Empire," *Arts Magazine,* May 1986. Kent Gardien, "Take Pity on Our Glory: Men of Champ d'Asile," *Southwestern Historical Quarterly* 87 (January 1984). Betje B. Klier, "The Bayeux Tapestry and the Papier Peint of Dijon," in *The Consortium on Revolutionary Europe, 1750–1850: Proceedings,* 1992. Jesse Siddall Reeves, *The Napoleonic Exiles in America* (Baltimore: Johns Hopkins University, 1905). René Rémond, *Les Etats-Unis devant l'opinion française, 1815–1852* (2 vols., Paris: Armand Colin, 1962). Harris Gaylord Warren, *The Sword Was Their Passport: A History of American Filibustering in the Mexican Revolution* (Baton Rouge: Louisiana State University Press, 1943).

Kent Gardien and Betje Black Klier

CHAMPION, ALBERT (1816–1890). Albert Champion, South Texas settler, son of George and Marie (Bronzin) Champion, was born on May 9, 1816, in Revigno, Austria. In the early 1840s he settled in Mobile, Alabama, after several years at sea. He later moved to New Orleans, where he was joined by his younger brothers, Peter and Nicholas. When the village of Point Isabel, Texas (later Port Isabel), was founded, the Champions were among the first settlers. The brothers secured sail lighters and became engaged in transporting goods and passengers from shipside off the bar to the wharves at Point Isabel. Champion later established the United States Mail Stage Line, which he operated from about 1858 to 1873, when Point Isabel and Brownsville were connected by rail. During the 1850s he established two ranches, La Florida, the oldest in Cameron County, and La Gloria. In 1850 he married Estéfana Solís of Point Isabel. He held the appointive office of road commissioner for many years, and in 1873 Governor E. J. Davis[qv] appointed him pilot commissioner for the Brazos Santiago port. Champion suffered property damage from the occupation by federal troops during the Civil War.[qv] After the war he became a citizen of Brownsville, where he engaged in merchandizing and managed his ranches. He died there on September 20, 1890, and was buried in the Old City Cemetery.

BIBLIOGRAPHY: Brownsville *Herald,* January 17, 1937. Gilbert D. Kingsbury Papers, Barker Texas History Center, University of Texas at Austin. Joseph Kleiber, Letters, Archives, University of Texas at Brownsville.

A. A. Champion

CHAMPION, TEXAS. Champion, on Champion Creek and Farm roads 1230 and 2319, eight miles southwest of Roscoe in west central Nolan County, began in 1905. Alton Griffin ran the first store at the site, and later a gin and three churches opened there. A local post office operated from 1907 to 1909. Champion's population was fifty in 1940, when the town had a church, a store, and a blacksmith shop. By 1975 little remained at the site. Champion reported a population of sixteen in 1980 and 1990.

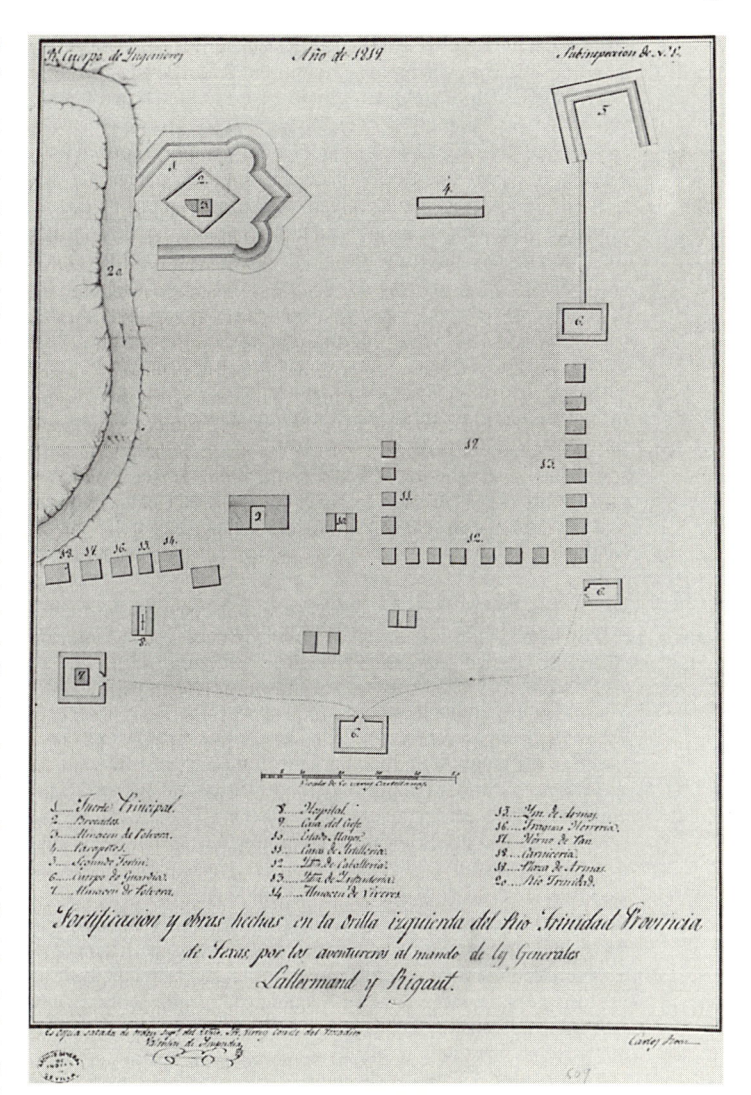

Fortificacion y obras hechas en la orilla izquierda del Rio Trinidad Provincia de Texas . . . , 1819. Original in Archivo General de Indias, Seville; Mapas y Planos, México 609. Photograph courtesy TSL. This plan of Champ d'Asile shows the main fort (1) at the top, left; the generals' headquarters (9) at left center; and the hospital (8), below headquarters and to the left, as well as other buildings and their relation to the Trinity River.

BIBLIOGRAPHY: E. L. Yeats and Hooper Shelton, *History of Nolan County* (Sweetwater, Texas: Shelton, 1975).

William R. Hunt

CHAMPION CREEK. Champion Creek rises at the confluence of its north and south forks in Champion Creek Reservoir in central Mitchell County (at 32°19′ N, 100°49′ W) and runs south for six miles to its mouth on the Colorado River, four miles west of State Highway 208 (at 32°17′ N, 100°52′ W). The North Fork of Champion Creek rises north of Farm Road 1982 two miles west of the Nolan county line (at 32°30′ N, 100°41′ W) and runs southwest for twenty-two miles before joining the South Fork of Champion Creek at the upper end of Champion Creek Reservoir, west of the intersection of Farm Road 2319 and State Highway 208 in east central Mitchell County (at 32°19′ N, 100°49′ W). The South Fork of Champion Creek rises three miles southeast of Bench Mountain in west central Nolan County (at 32°16′ N, 100°32′ W) and runs west for twenty-nine miles. The creeks traverse flat terrain with locally shallow depressions, surfaced by expansive clays that support water-tolerant hardwoods, conifers, and grasses.

CHAMPION CREEK RESERVOIR. Champion Creek Reservoir, an artificial lake on Champion Creek in the Colorado River basin, is seven miles south of Colorado City in east central Mitchell County (the lake's center point is 32°17′ N, 100°52′ W). The reservoir is owned and operated by Texas Electric Service Company, and its normal water capacity is 42,500 acre-feet. With an earthfill dam rising 2,109 feet above mean sea level, or 114 feet high locally, the reservoir is designed to hold a maximum of 90,200 acre-feet. Its water is used for industrial, recreational, and municipal purposes. The reservoir has a cut-channel emergency spillway at 2,091 feet above mean sea level and a service spillway at 2,083 feet above mean sea level. On May 28, 1957, before construction on the project began, the state authorized a permit to allow storage of 42,000 acre-feet and to annually divert 4,050 acre-feet of water for industrial use and 2,700 acre-feet for municipal use. General contractors Moorman, Dewitt, and Singleton began construction on May 5, 1958, and finished on April 30, 1959. They began impounding water in February of that year. A thirty-inch pipe through the dam has a valve control for downstream water requirements and connects to a pumping plant to supply water to Lake Colorado City.

CHANCE, JOSEPH BELL (1800–1839). J. B. Chance, pioneer surveyor and soldier in the war for Texas independence, son of William Alexander and Nancy Chance, was born near Nashville, Tennessee, on July 4, 1800. He married Nancy Braden on November 14, 1820, in Wilson County, Tennessee. They had four children. Chance came to Texas on January 7, 1830, and took the oath on February 27, 1830, swearing to "subject himself to the Constitution of the United Mexican States." He and his family settled on a league and a labor of land granted by the Mexican government in Stephen F. Austin's qv second colony in an area that is now part of Washington and Burleson counties. Chance served as a delegate from the Hidalgo District to the Convention of 1833.qv In early 1835 his name appeared on a petition to the Mexican government to establish Washington Municipality. His surveying office was located on Ferry Street in that town. Chance was a subscriber to the first effort to raise money for a Protestant minister in Texas. Mrs. Chance was also a frequent contributor to the Protestant ministry. She received a grant for twenty-four labores of land located adjacent to Belton on August 13, 1835.

Chance served in the Washington Company of volunteers under Capt. James G. Swisherqv from October 7 to December 3, 1835, and was a participant in the Grass Fight.qv On April 7, 1836, he raised a company of volunteers, the Washington Guards, and was elected their captain. He did not participate in the battle of San Jacintoqv but was detached to guard the baggage at the camp near Harrisburg on April 21, 1836. For his army service from March 20 to June 1, 1836, he received 640 acres of land now in Ellis County. Chance described his personal situation after San Jacinto: "Our greate distress in having to run from our homes, together with sickness and campaign after campaign ever since last fall has so exhausted my funds that I am well nigh ruined."

Chance was appointed deputy surveyor of District 2, Robertson County, and by July 1838 advertised plans "to run two or three compasses during the season . . . for gentlemen wishing to select lands in those parts." He surveyed 67,000 acres of land in the virgin wilderness that became parts of the present Bosque, Hill, McLennan, and Robertson counties. He died shortly after May 23, 1839, in Washington County.

BIBLIOGRAPHY: Eugene C. Barker, ed., *The Austin Papers* (3 vols., Washington: GPO, 1924–28). Joseph E. Chance, *Joseph Bell Chance and His Family* (1979). Malcolm D. McLean, comp. and ed., *Papers Concerning Robertson's Colony in Texas* (19 vols., Fort Worth: Texas Christian University Press, 1974–76; Arlington: University of Texas at Arlington Press, 1977–92). Worth Stickley Ray, *Austin Colony Pioneers* (Austin: Jenkins, 1949; 2d ed., Austin: Pemberton, 1970). *Telegraph and Texas Register*, July 23, 1838. Homer S. Thrall, *History of Methodism in Texas* (Houston: Cushing, 1872; rpt., n.p.: Walsworth, 1976).
Joseph E. Chance

CHANCE, SAMUEL (ca. 1790–?). Samuel Chance, one of Stephen F. Austin'sqv Old Three Hundredqv colonists, was born in Georgia about 1790. He and his partner, Joseph H. Polley,qv received title to a league of land in Brazoria County, Texas, on July 27, 1824. The census of the Colorado District in 1825 and the colony census of March 1826 classified Chance as a farmer, a stock raiser, and a single man. He married a daughter of Joseph San Pierreqv and applied for land adjoining San Pierre's on the Navidad River. In November 1830 the ayuntamientoqv at San Felipe appointed Chance commissioner to report on the best route for a road from Jennings's crossing on the Colorado River to Brazoria. He may have served as a private in William H. Patton'sqv Columbia Company during the Texas Revolutionqv in 1836. The Austin *Texas Sentinel*qv of October 7, 1841, listed a Sam Chance as owing direct taxes on property in Jackson County. The Fraimville area of Burleson County (*see* HIX, TEXAS) was originally settled by two brothers named James and Samuel Chance. A Samuel Chance lived in Milam County in 1850.

BIBLIOGRAPHY: Eugene C. Barker, ed., *The Austin Papers* (3 vols., Washington: GPO, 1924–28). Eugene C. Barker, ed., "Minutes of the Ayuntamiento of San Felipe de Austin, 1828–1832," 12 parts, *Southwestern Historical Quarterly* 21–24 (January 1918–October 1920). Lester G. Bugbee, "The Old Three Hundred: A List of Settlers in Austin's First Colony," *Quarterly of the Texas State Historical Association* 1 (October 1897). *Texas Gazette*, November 6, 1830. *Texas Sentinel*, October 7, 1841.

CHANCEVILLE, TEXAS. Chanceville, also known as Ward's Store, was five miles northwest of Maydelle in west central Cherokee County. It was established in 1886 by James and Emma Ward, who opened a general merchandise store known as Ward's Store. After James Ward's death in 1914, his son Francis Ward took over the business and expanded it, eventually adding a barbershop, shoe repair shop, clothes-pressing booth, and photo shop. Later, he opened several other businesses, including a gristmill, a woodworking shop, a blacksmith shop, a service station, a snack bar, and an icehouse. After World War Iqv and World War IIqv Ward also sold surplus military goods from his huge complex. The store became known as Chanceville, reportedly because locals would say if they could not find a particular item, there was a good chance Ward would have it. For many years the store complex served as the community center for area farms. Local residents often spent hours there pitching horseshoes or playing dominos or checkers. In later years Ward built a pool that served as the community swimming and baptizing pool. After Ward died in 1955, his store closed, and eventually the community lost its distinct identity. In the early 1990s only the empty store building and a few scattered houses remained in the area.

BIBLIOGRAPHY: *Cherokee County History* (Jacksonville, Texas: Cherokee County Historical Commission, 1986).
Christopher Long

CHANCEY, TEXAS. Chancey was ten miles west of Lufkin in western Angelina County. It was established around 1900 as a whistle stop on the St. Louis and Southwestern Railway. By 1915 a small sawmill center had grown up there. A post office operated at the community from 1915 to 1916, when the office closed and local mail was routed through Lufkin. By the mid-1930s Chancey was longer shown on maps of the area.

BIBLIOGRAPHY: Angelina County Historical Survey Committee, *Land of the Little Angel: A History of Angelina County, Texas*, ed. Bob Bowman (Lufkin, Texas: Lufkin Printing, 1976).
Christopher Long

CHANDLER, ASA CRAWFORD (1891–1958). Asa Crawford Chandler, biologist, was born in Newark, New Jersey, on February 19, 1891, the son of Frank Thomas and Augusta (Jappe) Chandler. He graduated from South Orange High School, New Jersey, in 1907, and later attended Cornell University (B.A., 1911) and the University of California (M.S., 1912; Ph.D., 1914). He taught at Oregon State Agricultural College from 1914 to 1918. Chandler was most well-known for his biology textbook, which was used by many universities and medical schools. This standard text on parasitology, first published in 1918 under the title *Animal Parasites and Human Disease*, went through nine editions, the last of which was entitled *Introduction to Parasitology with Special Reference to the Parasites of Man* (1955). Chandler was a second lieutenant in the Sanitary Corps, United States Army, in 1918–19. He was subsequently appointed instructor of biology at Rice Institute (now Rice University), where he remained until 1924. From 1924 to 1927 he was research director of the Hookworm Research Laboratory at the British School of Tropical Medicine and Hygiene in Calcutta, India. In 1927 he completed a highly influential helminthological survey of India. Upon his return to the United States he was appointed professor of biology at Rice Institute. From 1942 to 1947 he was special consultant to the United States Public Health Service on Malaria Control in War Areas. In 1952 he was appointed to the advisory panel on parasitic diseases at the World Health Organization. The same year, he held a Fulbright grant at the Fuad I Institute for Tropical Medicine in Egypt.

Chandler was a fellow of the American Association for the Advancement of Science, vice president of the American Society of Tropical Medicine and Hygiene (1938), and president of the American Society of Parasitologists (1950). He was a member in the American Academy of Tropical Medicine, the American Microscopical Society, the American Society of Naturalists, and Sigma Xi. In addition to his widely used textbook he wrote several other works, including *Anthelmintics and Their Uses* (with R. N. Chopra, 1928), *Hookworm Disease* (1929), and *The Eater's Digest*, a treatise on diet (1941).

Chandler married Belle Clarke on June 1, 1914, and they had three daughters. He was a Republican. He died suddenly of a heart attack on August 23, 1958, in a railway station in Rotterdam, Netherlands, shortly after he had arrived from New York by sea on his way to an international science meeting in Portugal, where he was to serve as honorary president of the Sixth International Congress on Tropical Medicine and Malaria.

BIBLIOGRAPHY: Dallas *News*, August 24, 1958. *Proceedings of the Philosophical Society of Texas*, 1958. *Who's Who in the South and Southwest*, Vol. 2.   Brian Jackson

CHANDLER, CLYDE GILTNER (1879–1961). Clyde Giltner Chandler, sculptor, was born in June 1879 in Evansville, Indiana, the daughter of William W. and Flora A. Giltner Chandler. The family moved to Dallas, Texas, in 1883. Clyde studied with Robert J. Onderdonk qv in Dallas and San Antonio and became the protégé of the Austin sculptor Elizabet Ney.qv From 1896 to 1898 she studied at the Massachusetts Normal Art School in Boston. Beginning in 1898 she taught "modeling and freehand drawing" at St. Mary's College in Dallas; from 1900 to 1902 she taught studio classes with Vivian Aunspaugh.qv

In September 1903, with a scholarship from the Dallas Art Association, Clyde Chandler moved to Chicago, where she studied for two years with Lorado Taft at the Art Institute. When he went to Florence, Italy, she accompanied him as his assistant. In 1906 she returned to Chicago, where she completed sculpture commissions for Bay City, Michigan, and South Bend, Indiana. In 1907 she received a second-place award at the Chicago Artists' Exposition, Art Institute of Chicago; she also exhibited at the Art Institute in 1908 and 1909. Between 1907 and 1912 she apparently maintained two residences, in Chicago and in Dallas, where she earned her living in a variety of temporary jobs—dressmaking, retail clothing sales, office clerk.

In 1912 the State Fair of Texas qv contracted with Chandler to do a sculpture as a memorial to Sydney Smith for his twenty-six years of service to the fair. In October 1916 *Gulf Clouds*, which she considered to be her best work, was installed at Fair Park. The bronze and grey granite sculpture, also called the Sydney Smith Memorial Fountain, is of a mother and three daughters representative of features in Texas geography. The seated mother represents Texas prairies; the left daughter represents the mountains; the Gulf, the third figure, adorned with draperies undulating like waves, lies at the feet of the other figures; a winged "Gulf Cloud" rises from the Gulf and symbolizes rain. The work, twelve feet high, thirty-five feet in diameter, and five tons in weight, was done in Chicago between 1912 and 1916. After *Gulf Clouds* was dedicated the sculptor lived in Chicago until 1936, when she moved to Santa Monica, California, and started a studio. She died on July 11, 1961, in Santa Monica.

BIBLIOGRAPHY: Jerry Bywaters, *Seventy-Five Years of Art in Dallas: The History of the Dallas Art Association and the Dallas Museum of Fine Arts* (Dallas: Dallas Museum of Fine Arts, 1978). Diana Church, *Guide to Dallas Artists, 1890–1917* (Plano, Texas, 1987). Frances Battaile Fisk, *A History of Texas Artists and Sculptors* (Abilene, Texas, 1928; facsimile rpt., Austin: Morrison, 1986). Esse Forrester-O'Brien, *Art and Artists of Texas* (Dallas: Tardy, 1935).   Diana Church

CHANDLER, ELI (ca. 1798–?). Eli Chandler, soldier and Indian fighter, was born in South Carolina about 1798. After sojourning in Madison County, Tennessee, where at least three of his children were born, he immigrated to Texas in 1835. During the Texas Revolution qv he served as a private in Capt. Sterling C. Robertson's qv ranger company, mustered into service on January 17, 1836. He reenlisted for a period of three months on June 30, but his unit cannot now be determined. The General Land Office qv reckoned his period of service from July 15 until November 15, 1836. On January 16, 1839, he played a conspicuous role in "Bryant's Defeat," a fight between settlers led by Capt. Benjamin Franklin Bryant and Ethan Allen Stroud qqv and a band of Anadarko Indians led by Chief José María.qv This fight took place near the falls of the Brazos River in what is now Falls County.

On March 29, 1841, Chandler was elected captain of a forty-five-man company of Robertson County Minute Men, which he led against the Indians in the battle of Pecan Creek in what is now Cooke County on April 21, 1841. On April 9, 1842, Alexander Somervell qv authorized Chandler to raise a company for the invasion of Mexico, and on May 13, 1842, Chandler's became the first company to report for the Somervell expedition.qv He apparently did not lead this unit to the Rio Grande, however, for on December 10, 1842, Sam Houston qv commissioned Chandler and Thomas I. Smith qv to raise a company of volunteers to remove the archives of the Republic of Texas qv from Austin to Houston. Although Houston admonished the two not to "be thwarted in the undertaking," the citizens of Austin prevented the removal of the nation's papers by force (*see* ARCHIVE WAR).

In 1843 Chandler was elected adjutant of the Snively expedition qv but disagreed violently with the battalion's commander, Jacob Snively.qv When the expedition broke up in frustration on June 28, 1843, Chandler was chosen leader of one faction, seventy-six men calling themselves the "Home Boys," which he led back to the Arkansas River in hopes of intercepting a Mexican convoy bound for Santa Fe. On July 9, after being disarmed by United States dragoons under Capt. Philip St. George Cooke, Chandler led his fragment back toward Austin.

During the Mexican War qv Chandler raised and commanded Company K of Col. John C. Hays's qv First Regiment, Texas Mounted Riflemen, and served in the Monterrey campaign. His son, Eli Chandler, Jr., served as a private in the company. In 1850 Chandler was farming in Robertson County with his thirty-five-year-old wife, Mary, a native of North Carolina, and their three young daughters. His estate was then valued at $2,220.

BIBLIOGRAPHY: Malcolm D. McLean, comp. and ed., *Papers Concerning Robertson's Colony in Texas* (19 vols., Fort Worth: Texas Christian University Press, 1974–76; Arlington: University of Texas at Arlington Press, 1977–92). Joseph Milton Nance, *After San Jacinto: The Texas-Mexican Frontier, 1836–1841* (Austin: University of Texas Press, 1963). Joseph Milton Nance, *Attack and Counterattack: The Texas-Mexican Frontier, 1842* (Austin: University of Texas Press, 1964). Charles D. Spurlin, comp., *Texas Veterans in the Mexican War: Muster Rolls of Texas Military Units* (Victoria, Texas, 1984). *Telegraph and Texas Register*, January 6, 1841. J. W. Wilbarger, *Indian Depredations in Texas* (Austin: Hutchings, 1889; rpt., Austin: State House, 1985). Amelia W. Williams and Eugene C. Barker, eds., *The Writings of Sam Houston, 1813–1863* (8 vols., Austin: University of Texas Press, 1938–43; rpt., Austin and New York: Pemberton Press, 1970).

Thomas W. Cutrer

CHANDLER, JESSE VAN BUREN (1892–1968). Jesse Van Buren Chandler, poet, was born on November 9, 1892, in Belton, Texas, the son of W. E. and Sarah (Dickey) Chandler. He married Helen Marie Airhart on July 24, 1915, and they had two sons. Chandler graduated from the University of Texas Dental School and practiced dentistry in Kingsville. He also was known as a writer of articles, short stories, and, under the name Van Chandler, poetry. He published two books of poetry, *Night Alone* (1947) and *Petals Fall* (1959), and his poems appeared in magazines and newspapers. He was editor of the fiftieth-anniversary issues of the El Campo *Citizen* and the Kingsville *Record*. He served as a member of the executive staff of the Southwest Writers Conference. He was appointed to the honorary position of Poet Laureate of Texas[qv] for the term 1959–61. He was also a district governor of Rotary International and an organizer of the Nueces Valley District Dental Society. Chandler died on January 9, 1968.

BIBLIOGRAPHY: Margaret Royalty Edwards, *Poets Laureate of Texas* (San Antonio: Naylor, 1956; rev. ed., 1966). Kleberg County Historical Commission, *Kleberg County, Texas* (Austin: Hart Graphics, 1979).

Margaret Royalty Edwards

CHANDLER, SAMUEL EZEKIEL (1861–1944). Samuel Ezekiel Chandler, minister and college president, son of Ezekiel and Sarah (Lemmen) Chandler, was born in Sumter County, South Carolina, on October 2, 1861. He received his B.A. degree at Davidson College, North Carolina, in 1884, his B.D. degree at Southwestern Presbyterian University in Clarksville, Tennessee, in 1888, and his D.D. degree at Davidson in 1905. From 1888 to 1890 Chandler was pastor at Brenham, Texas. He was professor of Bible at Austin College from 1897 to 1904, when he became pastor at Corpus Christi. He was president of Daniel Baker College at Brownwood in 1908 and professor of Greek at Austin Presbyterian Theological Seminary in 1909. He was pastor at Austin and Kingsville until 1902, when he again became president of Daniel Baker. He resigned the presidency in 1933 but continued as head of the Bible department until 1942. Chandler married Mary Olivia Becton of Sulphur Springs, and after her death he married Carrie Knox of Giddings, in 1897. He died at his home in Brownwood on September 20, 1944, and was buried in Greenleaf Cemetery.

BIBLIOGRAPHY: *Ministerial Directory of the Presbyterian Church, U.S.*, 1942. *Minutes of the Synod of Texas of the Presbyterian Church in the United States*, 1945.

Jeanette H. Flachmeier

CHANDLER, WELCOME WILLIAMS (1813–1870). Welcome Chandler, the first settler, farmer, county judge, postmaster, and store owner in Brown County, was born in North Carolina to William Hugh and Tebitha Elizabeth (Hodges) Chandler in January 1813. The family moved to Copiah County, Mississippi, where Chandler married Sarah Brown in 1834; they moved to Texas in 1854. That summer, Chandler, Samuel R. Coggin, and J. H. Fowler visited the Brown County area and resolved to settle there permanently. In July 1856 Chandler arrived with his wife, their eight children, J. H. Fowler (who became the first bridegroom in Brown County by marrying Chandler's daughter Mary Ann the following year, and who also brought the first herd of cattle to Brown County in December 1856), and seven slaves. On Pecan Bayou, just east of the site of Brownwood, they built the first dwelling in Brown County, a large log cabin. Chandler also operated the county's first store, a settlers' supply house, in his home. Although local mail service may have existed earlier, the first official post office in Brownwood was apparently established on February 20, 1860, and located in Chandler's house. Chandler was named postmaster, a position he held till January 23, 1867, when the post office was temporarily discontinued by the United States government.

On March 21, 1857, the first election in the county took place in the Chandler home, and Chandler was elected county commissioner; however, because of a mistake about county boundaries made by the state legislature, none of the officers elected in 1857 ever served. Instead they asked the legislature to correct its mistake, and it did so on February 8, 1858. The second election, on August 2, 1858, was also held in the Chandler home, and Chandler was elected chief justice (county judge). The first courthouse in the county, a log structure, was built on Chandler's farm in October 1858. Chandler was elected county treasurer on August 4, 1862. After the defeat of the Confederacy and the invalidation of county elections of the Civil War[qv] years, a new election of county officers was held on August 25, 1865, and Welcome Chandler rode with the results in less than a day to have them validated in Austin (140 miles from Brownwood), so that the county would not be without the rule of law. He was elected judge of the county board of appeals in 1869.

The Chandlers had five more children after arriving in Brown County. Their daughters Melissa and Laura Caldora were the first twins born in the county, and their daughter Ella was the second white child born there. The first Confederate flag in the county was made by Mrs. Chandler, her daughter Jane, and Mrs. Brooks W. Lee. It was first flown on February 23, 1861, when the residents of Brown County met in the Chandler home and voted to ratify the ordinance of secession.[qv] Chandler died in Williamson County, Texas, in May 1870 and was buried in Florence, Texas.

BIBLIOGRAPHY: Thomas Robert Havins, *Something about Brown: A History of Brown County, Texas* (Brownwood, Texas: Banner Printing, 1958). Tevis Clyde Smith, *Frontier's Generation* (Brownwood, Texas, 1931; 2d ed. 1980). James C. White, *The Promised Land: A History of Brown County* (Brownwood, Texas: Brownwood *Banner*, 1941).

Charlotte Laughlin

CHANDLER, TEXAS. Chandler is twenty-five miles northeast of Athens in northeastern Henderson County. The area, originally inhabited by Caddo Indians, was settled in 1859 by Alfonson H. Chandler as a one-store town called Stillwater, two miles north of what is now the site of Chandler. A post office was established in April 1873 and was named after Chandler in 1880. Around that time he donated land to the Texas and St. Louis Railway, and a settlement, named for him, developed by the tracks. By 1890 the town had a cotton gin, a mill, a school, and two churches. In 1910 the community incorporated. Chandler had two schools: one that in 1904 had two teachers and an enrollment of ninety-one white students, and another that in 1905 had one teacher and thirty-seven black students. By 1936 Chandler had 624 residents, three churches, two schools, and some twenty businesses, including the *Times* weekly newspaper, a canning factory, and a crate factory. By that time fruit farming had replaced cotton as the main source of income. The community's first mayor was elected in 1960, and in 1989 the town reported a population of 1,680 and forty businesses. In 1991 Chandler reported 1,678 residents and eighty-four businesses.

BIBLIOGRAPHY: *Chandler Area: Its History and People, 1880–1980* (Chandler, Texas: Chandler Historical Society, 1981). J. J. Faulk, *History of Henderson County* (Athens, Texas: Athens Review Printing, 1929).

Kent Willis

CHANDLER'S PEAK. Chandler's Peak, also called Chambers Peak, is four miles northwest of Novice in the northwestern corner of Coleman County. It has an elevation of 2,173 feet above sea level.

CHANDOR, DOUGLAS GRANVIL (1897–1953). Douglas Granvil Chandor, artist, the son of John Arthur and Lucy May (Newton) Chandor, was born on August 20, 1897, in Surrey, England. World War I[qv] began a few months after he completed his education at Radley, and at seventeen he joined the Life Guards, First Regiment of Household Cavalry. Later, he served as a member of the celebrated Scottish Lovat Scouts. In 1918 Chandor was discharged from the Scouts after contracting typhoid and severely damaging his knee. He recuperated in Surrey, then pursued his childhood interest, art. He enrolled at the Slade School in London, where he concentrated on developing his talent as a portraitist. In 1919 he received his first major commission, to paint Sir Edward Marshall-Hall, K.C. When it was displayed at the British Royal Academy Exhibition, the portrait attracted further offers for the young artist, including a commission to paint the Prince of Wales, a work he completed in 1921. The painting drew "half of London" to the Grieves Gallery. Two years later Chandor accepted an invitation to portray the prime ministers of the British empire at work during the Imperial Conference held in London at 10 Downing Street.

Although he was a critical success, Chandor's income did not stretch far enough to support a wife and child. In 1926 he and his wife, Pamela (Trelawny), whom he had married in 1920, traveled to the United States, where Chandor thought his prospects might be better. His first American exhibition, held at the Andrews Gallery in New York in March 1927, was well received and resulted in a number of commissions. Included among the invitations was a request to paint President Herbert Hoover, Vice President Charles Curtis, and the entire cabinet. Chandor's painting of Hoover, combined with his earlier portraits of British aristocrats, established his reputation as a painter of the world's political leaders. During his career he painted about 300 portraits. Significant subjects included President Gerardo Machado y Morales of Cuba, Prime Minister Winston Churchill, Queen Elizabeth II, Samuel T. (Sam) Rayburn,[qv] and President Franklin Roosevelt. His portrait of Eleanor Roosevelt is believed to be the only one for which she formally posed; he also painted Sara Delano Roosevelt and the wives of James and Elliott Roosevelt.

From 1926 until the mid-1930s Chandor's career demanded most of his time. He was divorced in 1932 and married Ina K. Hill of Weatherford, Texas, in 1934. He returned with his wife to her native city where they lived in the family mansion. For the rest of his career Chandor spent half of each year in New York and the remaining time in Weatherford, where he developed the grounds of his estate into a showplace that the Chandors named White Shadows Gardens. The house, which sat on a hill overlooking the city, was surrounded by an elaborate network of walls that enclosed an array of plants and trees, Chinese pagodas, a Japanese water garden, and a miniature replica of Mount Fujiyama. After World War II[qv] Chandor was commissioned to paint the "Big Three" (Churchill, Roosevelt, and Stalin) to celebrate the meeting at Yalta. He was never able to get to Moscow to paint Stalin. On January 13, 1953, two weeks after returning from London, where he completed his second portrait of Queen Elizabeth II, Chandor died of a cerebral hemorrhage. He had become an American citizen a few years before and requested that he be buried in his new home, Weatherford.

BIBLIOGRAPHY: Dallas *Morning News*, January 14, 15, 1953. London *Times*, January 15, 1953. Malcolm Vaughn, *Chandor's Portraits* (New York: Brentano's, 1942). Vertical Files, Barker Texas History Center, University of Texas at Austin.

David Minor

CHANEY, TEXAS. Chaney, on Farm Road 571 four miles east of Lake Leon in central Eastland County, was founded in the early 1880s when the Texas and Pacific Railway came through the area. A post office, possibly known as Chauncey, opened in 1902, with Amos G. Chaney as postmaster. The community did not develop beyond a one-store supply point for local ranches. Its rural school was consolidated with that of Alameda in 1939. Chaney's population was twenty-five in 1940 and thirty-five in 1980 and 1990.

BIBLIOGRAPHY: Homer Stephen, *The Frontier Postmasters* (Dublin, Texas: Dublin *Progress*, 1952).

William R. Hunt

CHANNEL, TEXAS. Channel, also known as Houston Terminals, was a residential community on the Houston Ship Channel[qv] in Harris County. A post office operated there from 1919 until 1920, when mail was delivered from Deepwater. Another post office operated from 1922 until 1923, when mail was delivered from Pasadena. The community's population was 100 in 1921, but the area was subsequently engulfed by industrial development, and the community was not shown on the 1936 county highway map.

Diana J. Kleiner

CHANNELVIEW, TEXAS. Channelview (Channel View), an oil refinery suburb of metropolitan Houston, is at the site where the San Jacinto River forms Old River, south of Interstate Highway 10 and the Missouri Pacific Railroad and eight miles southeast of Houston in eastern Harris County. It was named for its location on the northeastern curve of the Houston Ship Channel[qv] and was populated by blue-collar oil refinery workers and their families after oil discoveries in the area in 1916. After 1910, schools for both black and white students opened as ship channel industries grew. Beginning sometime before 1916 and continuing as late as 1942, the McGhee School served black students. The local white school had thirty-one pupils in 1925. A post office was established at the community in 1933, and the 1936 county highway map showed a sawmill, a school, several businesses, and multiple dwellings at the site. By 1938 the Channelview school district covered twenty square miles and employed one black teacher and seven white. Channelview reported a population of fifty and two businesses in 1940, and grew to 700 residents and twenty-three businesses by 1947. In 1967 a new Sinclair Petrochemical plant began production of isophthalic acid and metaxylene near the ship channel. At that time the town had a population of 7,860 and seventy-five businesses. Its population was 8,227 in the mid-1970s. In 1985 Channelview had 347 businesses. In the early 1990s it had a population of 26,115 and 385 businesses.

BIBLIOGRAPHY: Janet Roesler, "The Homecoming," *Third Coast*, April 1985. Barney Harold Scott, An Administrative Survey and Proposed Plan of Reorganization of Schools in Eastern Harris County, Texas (M.Ed. Thesis, University of Texas, 1940).

Claudia Hazlewood

CHANNING, TEXAS. Channing, the seat of Hartley County, is located on the Fort Worth and Denver City Railway in the southeastern part of the county. Of all the Panhandle[qv] towns associated with the XIT Ranch,[qv] only Channing can truly claim that it developed directly from that enterprise. It derived its original name, Rivers, from George Channing Rivers, paymaster of the railroad when it built through the county in the spring of 1888. Since the name Rivers duplicated that of another Texas town, the name was changed to Channing later that year. At the time that Willis D. Twichell[qv] platted its business district in 1891, Channing was general headquarters of the XIT. Albert G. Boyce,[qv] the ranch's general manager and a prominent early citizen, built the first house in the town. Boyce's "Poor Farm," the Rita Blanca Division headquarters, was less than two miles south of town. When

Tascosa was abandoned, several of its businesses were moved to Channing. By 1900 Channing had two lumberyards, two general stores, a school, and a grocery store, which also housed the post office. Although the town initially had several saloons, these were later voted out. Two elections, one in November 1896 and the other in May 1903, were required for Channing to replace Hartley as county seat. The original frame courthouse was moved to Channing on wheels by a group of XIT cowboys and was transformed into a hotel when the brick courthouse was built in 1906. Two years later, the local women's club established a public library, one of the earliest in the Panhandle.

The XIT, which conducted much of its business from Channing, was the town's chief customer until liquidation of the ranch in 1911. For a time thereafter, the real estate business thrived from the sale of XIT lands. Among the prominent citizens were the brothers James and William Powell[qv] of England, who were the first to breed Hereford cattle in the Panhandle. With A. G. Boyce, the Powells established the Channing Methodist Church. Walter Farwell, one of the family of XIT financiers, built his spacious summer home just outside Channing. His tree-lined driveway and his wife Mildred's southern hospitality became legendary. In addition, Farwell had on his estate a dam and artificial lake and a polo field on which he trained cow horses for the game.

On September 6, 1931, a fire destroyed seven buildings in the business district. Nevertheless, by 1940 Channing had a population of 475 with a high school, three churches, and five businesses, including a plant for grinding volcanic cinders and a cinder-block plant. Channing was incorporated in 1960 and grew as a shipping point and trade center for grains, feed, and livestock. By 1984, mainly because of the accessibility of Dalhart and Amarillo by U.S. highways 87 and 385, the population had decreased to 304. Six businesses were in operation. In 1990 the population was 277.

BIBLIOGRAPHY: Cordia Sloan Duke and Joe B. Frantz, *6,000 Miles of Fence: Life on the XIT Ranch of Texas* (Austin: University of Texas Press, 1961). J. Evetts Haley, *The XIT Ranch of Texas and the Early Days of the Llano Estacado* (Chicago: Lakeside, 1929; rpts., Norman: University of Oklahoma Press, 1953, 1967). James D. Hamlin, *The Flamboyant Judge: As Told to J. Evetts Haley and William Curry Holden* (Canyon, Texas: Palo Duro, 1972). Lillie Mae Hunter, *The Book of Years: A History of Dallam and Hartley Counties* (Hereford, Texas: Pioneer, 1969).

Jennie Rose Powell

CHAPA, FRANCISCO A. (1870–1924). Francisco A. Chapa, alderman and member of the board of education in San Antonio, was born in Matamoros, Tamaulipas, on October 4, 1870. When he was seventeen years old, he immigrated to New Orleans to continue his studies in pharmacy at Tulane University. He worked as a drugstore clerk in Matamoros and Brownsville in 1890 and later that year moved to San Antonio, where he worked as a pharmacist for four years before establishing his own drugstore, La Botica del León, on West Commerce and Santa Rosa, which he ran for thirty years. The store became well known to Mexican revolutionary leaders, including Emiliano Zapata, who was said to have passed through it on his way to his physician's office, which was on the second floor. Chapa served as a member of the local board of education from 1888 to 1906, some of the time as treasurer. In 1913 he was narrowly elected alderman for the third ward. He was apparently an alderman for at least two terms. He was also president of the San Antonio Retail Druggists' Association and a member of the Business Men's Club.

He was one of a handful of Texas-Mexican Republicans. He published *El Imparcial de Texas*, a conservative newspaper that resembled the *Imparcial* of Mexico City. Under his guidance the Texas *Imparcial* championed the dictator Porfirio Díaz and denounced the Mexican Revolution.[qv] Chapa is credited with delivering the Texas-Mexican vote to Oscar B. Colquitt[qv] in the Democratic gubernatorial primary in 1910. Colquitt went on to win the governor's seat and ultimately appointed Chapa a lieutenant colonel on his personal staff.

In this position Chapa was involved in political intrigue that was "legally and politically embarrassing" to him and Colquitt. The event concerned Gen. Bernardo Reyes, once one of the most powerful military associates of Mexican president Porfirio Díaz. After Díaz resigned during the Mexican Revolution in May 1911, Reyes attempted to assume political power in Mexico and used San Antonio as his base of operations. Chapa, a defender of the Díaz regime, aided Reyes's efforts by arranging meetings between Governor Colquitt and Reyes to discuss the deployment and use of the Texas Rangers[qv] along the border, with the intention of ensuring that the Rangers would not interfere with Reyes's revolutionary endeavors. Chapa probably assisted Reyes in other ways as well, for when the "Reyes Conspiracy" collapsed almost two dozen others, including Chapa, were accused of violating federal neutrality laws. Only Chapa, however, came to trial. In federal court in Brownsville he was found guilty by a jury allegedly reassured by presiding Judge Walter T. Burns that he would not be sentenced to prison. Burns fined Chapa $1,500 and stated that the "penitentiary is not the place for men of your kind." Chapa remained on the governor's staff, and Colquitt persuaded President William Howard Taft to issue a presidential pardon to Chapa.

Chapa's association with the governor and his apparent leadership among Texas Mexicans helped win Gregorio Cortez's[qv] struggle for justice in the murder case against him. Chapa spent ten years leading the legal fight for Cortez's pardon, which was granted in 1913. He was called to testify years later in a joint Texas House and Senate committee organized by Representative J. T. Canales[qv] to investigate alleged atrocities committed by the Texas Rangers against Texas Mexicans; Chapa refused to implicate the leader of the rangers.

He married Adelaide Rivas and had two daughters and a son. His son, Francisco, operated La Botica del León until it was demolished under urban renewal in 1970. Chapa died of pneumonia in San Antonio on February 18, 1924. At his funeral service at San Fernando de Bexar Cathedral,[qv] honorary pallbearers included his old friend and political ally, former governor Oscar B. Colquitt.

BIBLIOGRAPHY: Don M. Coerver and Linda B. Hall, "Neiman-Marcus: Innovators in Fashion and Merchandising," *American Jewish Historical Quarterly* 66 (September 1976). Américo Paredes, *With His Pistol in His Hand: A Border Ballad and Its Hero* (Austin: University of Texas Press, 1958). Vertical Files, University of Texas Institute of Texan Cultures, San Antonio.

Teresa Palomo Acosta

CHAPA, FRANK L. (1897–1985). Frank L. Chapa, Mexican-American politician, was born in San Antonio, Texas, on September 23, 1897, to Adelaida (Rivas) and Col. Francisco A. Chapa.[qv] He was a descendent of María Granados de Betancourt. He married Blanche Laborde, and they had one child. Chapa attended St. Peter and St. Paul School in New Braunfels, San Antonio public schools, and St. Mary's College (now St. Mary's University). On August 5, 1917, he entered military service at Camp Stanley and later was commissioned second lieutenant in the Texas National Guard.[qv] He was then assigned to the Central Cavalry Officers Training Camp at Leon Springs, where he was first lieutenant. In 1935 he served as adjutant of the Fifty-sixth Cavalry Brigade of the Texas National Guard and in the 124th Cavalry Brigade.

Chapa worked in his father's business, F. A. Chapa's Drug Store, from the late teens through the 1960s, when the store was destroyed for urban renewal. He was appointed assistant state service officer in 1926 and served until 1928. Under Governor Ross S. Sterling[qv] he was brevetted colonel and represented Texas at the first aeronautical and industrial exposition in Mexico City. He was also on Governor James Allred's[qv] staff from 1935 to 1939. During World War II[qv] Chapa was chief intelligence officer for the Southern Defense Command and received numerous commendations, including the Medal of Merit from the Mexican Ministry of Defense. He was a member of the Military Order of the World Wars and a founding member of the Texas Cavaliers.

He was one of six Tejanos to be included in *Texas Democracy*, a history of the Democratic party[qv] published for the Texas Centennial[qv] in 1936. He was a member of the American Legion, a director of the League of United Latin American Citizens[qv] Council 16 in the 1930s, and a member of the Granaderos de Galvez and Our Lady of Grace Catholic Church. He died on February 2, 1985, and is buried in the San Fernando Archdiocesan Cemetery.

BIBLIOGRAPHY: Frank Carter Adams, ed., *Texas Democracy: A Centennial History of Politics and Personalities of the Democratic Party, 1836–1936* (4 vols., Austin: Democratic Historical Association, 1937).

Cynthia E. Orozco

CHAPA, JUAN BAUTISTA (1627–1695). Juan Bautista Chapa was born Giovanni Bautista Schiapapria in 1627 in Albisola, Italy, and is now recognized as the "anonymous historian" of Nuevo León, Mexico, where he arrived in the mid-seventeenth century and served Governor Alonso De León[qv] and other governors as their secretary for over four decades. Chapa knew these officials well, traveled through the province extensively, and wrote his observations of developments in that far northern region in *Historia del Nuevo Reino de León de 1650 a 1690*. The chapters of this work that treat Texas analyze the motives, frustrations, and strategies of Spanish expansion to the rim of the empire and constitute one of the most important primary sources for history in early Spanish Texas.[qv] The expeditions Chapa participated in include De León's first expedition in search of René Robert Cavelier, Sieur de La Salle's[qv] Texas colony, from Cadereyta to the mouth of the Rio Grande, and his second, which is generally supposed to have reached Baffin Bay. Chapa also joined De León on his 1689 expeditions that found the ruins of La Salle's Fort St. Louis.

His observations are particularly important because of the political impartiality he maintained by writing the book secretly and anonymously. He was a well-educated man who knew Italian (including the Genoese dialect), Spanish, Latin, and Tuscan. He left behind a perceptive and well-crafted historical work. The authorship of the *Historia* remained a mystery until 1961, when the edition published by the Biblioteca de Nuevo León revealed his identity.

Chapa lived out his life in Nuevo León and married Beatriz Olivares de Treviño, daughter of one of Monterrey's elite families. They had four sons and two daughters. Chapa died in Nuevo León in 1695 and is recognized as the ancestor of the very numerous Chapa families of northeastern Mexico and South Texas. Norman P. Brown has researched the Chapa descendants in *Chapa: The First Four Generations*, which covers the period from 1651 to 1800. Juan Bautista Chapa's own ancestors have been documented by Amancio J. Chapa, Jr., of La Joya, Texas.

BIBLIOGRAPHY: Robert S. Weddle, *Wilderness Manhunt: The Spanish Search for La Salle* (Austin: University of Texas Press, 1973).

Eduardo J. Hinojosa

CHAPAMACO INDIANS. Attempts to establish an identity for the Chapamacos have resulted in much confusion, and even today the problem cannot be regarded as fully solved. In 1708, when first recorded under the name Chapamo, the Chapamacos were said to be one of twenty-nine remnant Indian groups then living in southern Texas, mainly south of present-day San Antonio. No document has been found that gives a more precise location for them. The registers of San Antonio de Valero Mission in San Antonio indicate that at least two Chapamaco individuals, both adult females, lived there between 1730 and 1748. That one of these women is identified in various entries by two names, Chapamaco and Secmoco, seems to indicate that both are variants of the same ethnic name. The second woman is identified by the ethnic name Sepunco, which on phonetic grounds appears to be a variant of the name Chapamaco. Some Chapamacos also entered Spanish missions near the Rio Grande in northeastern Coahuila. One male was recorded at San Bernardo in 1762 and two males at San Juan Bautista[qv] in 1772. Through error the name Chemoco has been equated with Secmoco. This resulted from confusing Mission San Francisco Solano of California with a mission of the same name in northeastern Coahuila. Other errors include the equation of Sencase with Sepunco, and Sinicu with Secmoco. No evidence supports either of these equations. J. R. Swanton listed Chapamaco, Chemoco, and Secmoco as three separate Texas Indian groups who probably spoke Coahuilteco. As Chapamaco and Secmoco seem to be variants of the same ethnic name, and Chemoco refers to an Indian group of California, the main residual problem is determining what language was spoken by the Chapamaco. They could have spoken Coahuilteco, but linguists today point out that languages other than Coahuilteco were also spoken in southern Texas. It therefore seems best to say that the language spoken by the Chapamaco remains undetermined.

BIBLIOGRAPHY: F. D. Almaráz, Jr., *Inventory of the Rio Grande Missions: 1772, San Juan Bautista and San Bernardo* (Archaeology and History of the San Juan Bautista Mission Area, Coahuila and Texas, Report No. 2, Center for Archaeological Research, University of Texas at San Antonio, 1980). Thomas N. Campbell, *Ethnohistoric Notes on Indian Groups Associated with Three Spanish Missions at Guerrero, Coahuila* (Center for Archaeological Research, University of Texas at San Antonio, 1979). Frederick Webb Hodge, ed., *Handbook of American Indians North of Mexico* (2 vols., Washington: GPO, 1907, 1910; rpt., New York: Pageant, 1959). P. Otto Maas, ed., *Viajes de Misioneros Franciscanos a la conquista del Nuevo México* (Seville: Imprenta de San Antonio, 1915). J. R. Swanton, *Linguistic Material from the Tribes of Southern Texas and Northeastern Mexico* (Washington: Smithsonian Institution, 1940).

Thomas N. Campbell

CHAPARROSA CREEK. Chaparrosa Creek rises in two branches near the Anacacho Mountains and the Kinney-Maverick county line in southeastern Kinney County (at 29°04′ N, 100°10′ W) and runs southeast for seventeen miles across the extreme northeastern corner of Maverick County to its mouth on Turkey Creek, near Johnson Lake in west central Zavala County (at 28°49′ N, 100°00′ W). The creek's West Prong rises in the southeastern corner of Kinney County (at 29°07′ N, 100°15′ W) and runs for eight miles to its confluence with the East Prong, which rises near the Anacacho Mountains (at 29°13′ N, 100°09′ W) and runs for fourteen miles. Members of the Bosque-Larios expedition,[qv] who were at the headwaters of the stream in 1675, reported that the Indians there called it Ona, which they said meant salty, but the Spaniards renamed the stream Rio de San Isidro Labrador. Father Damián Massanet,[qv] who encountered the stream nearer its mouth in 1691, wrote that the Indians called it Guanapacti. He also added another name, calling the stream Arroyo de San Lucas. The name Chaparrosa is derived from the Spanish word meaning scrub oak and refers to the thick growth which covers part of the area. The creek crosses flat terrain with local shallow depressions, surfaced by clay and sandy loams that support water-tolerant hardwoods, some conifers, and grasses.

CHAPEL HILL, TEXAS. Chapel Hill is off Farm Road 2088 fifteen miles northwest of Gilmer in northwestern Upshur County. It was probably established before 1900. In the mid-1930s the community had a church and a small number of scattered houses. Children attended school at Piney Grove or Mount Lebanon. In the mid-1960s Chapel Hill had a church and a few houses. In 1990 it had a store and a church.

BIBLIOGRAPHY: Doyal T. Loyd, *History of Upshur County* (Waco: Texian Press, 1987).

Christopher Long

CHAPEL HILL COLLEGE. Chapel Hill College was located at Daingerfield on land donated by Allen Urkhart to the Marshall Presbytery of the Cumberland Presbyterian Church. The school was chartered on February 7, 1850, and opened in February of 1852 in a two-story frame classroom building, with Rev. William E. Beeson^{qv} as president. A month later Chapel Hill College became the first college in Texas to provide for the free education of those entering the Presbyterian ministry, a response by the board of trustees to initial low enrollment. In addition to its preparatory program, the school offered college-level courses leading to a bachelor of arts degree. But the college was not well supported, perhaps because of its northern location, and in 1856 the property was transferred to the Texas Synod of the Cumberland Presbyterian church. The synod constructed a new brick building for the institution in 1858 and set an endowment-fund goal of $20,000, but before that goal could be met rumors of an impending invasion by Union forces in 1860 led Beeson to dismiss all of the college-level classes, leaving only the preparatory department in session. The college continued to operate through 1865 with only two full-time instructors and emerged from the war years free of debt and with plans for recovery. In 1869, however, Beeson resigned his post to become president of the newly formed Trinity University, and the Texas Synod transferred its support to that institution. Chapel Hill College lost its function as a college and continued as a secondary and preparatory school under the Marshall Presbytery until the early 1890s, when public schools opened and Chapel Hill closed.

BIBLIOGRAPHY: Robert Douglas Brackenridge, *Voice in the Wilderness: A History of the Cumberland Presbyterian Church in Texas* (San Antonio: Trinity University Press, 1968). Thomas H. Campbell, *History of Cumberland Presbyterian Church in Texas* (Nashville: Cumberland Presbyterian Publishing House, 1936).   *Carl L. McFarland*

CHAPLIN, CHICHESTER (1800–1874). Chichester Chaplin, jurist in Texas and Louisiana, was born in Ireland on November 17, 1800. He probably immigrated to southeastern Louisiana between 1810 and 1820. Marriage records of St. Tammany Parish reveal his marriage on October 10, 1824, to Tabitha Beall Edwards Aydelot, daughter of empresario^{qv} Haden Edwards.^{qv} Chaplin was then a fledgling lawyer. Tabitha died on November 24, 1827. Chaplin undoubtedly followed his father-in-law to the Nacogdoches area of East Texas, where he became a key figure in the Fredonian Rebellion^{qv} (1826), led by Haden and Benjamin W. Edwards,^{qv} along with Martin Parmer,^{qv} who later became Chaplin's second father-in-law. Edwards ordered an election held on January 1, 1826, to select an alcalde^{qv} for the Nacogdoches District. Chaplin actually received the most votes, but the losing candidate, Samuel Norris,^{qv} an American who had married a Spanish colonial woman and was the choice of the old settlers, appealed the election to the political chief of Texas, who declared Norris the legally elected candidate.

When the Fredonian Rebellion erupted in December 1826, Chaplin joined the Edwards forces in revolt, and when the rebellion collapsed he fled eastward across the Sabine River with the Edwards brothers and Parmer. The Chaplin family settled in Natchitoches, where, on June 4, 1827, Chaplin was named a justice of the peace for Natchitoches Parish, a post he held for less than a year. With his selection as a Louisiana justice in 1827, he began a judicial career in both western Louisiana and eastern Texas that spanned almost four decades (1827–64). In 1827–28 he served as probate judge and from 1829 to 1834 as parish judge of Claiborne Parish, Louisiana, newly formed from a portion of the original Natchitoches Parish.

Sometime late in 1833 or early in 1834 he returned to Jefferson County, Texas, where in 1836 he was chosen the first chief justice of the county. He served in that office for a short time and in 1838 was made a member of the Board of Land Commissioners of San Augustine County, Texas. Since he was in Texas before 1835, Judge Chaplin was awarded a Mexican land grant of a league in San Augustine County, on May 18, 1835. In December 1839 he received a headright grant of 640 acres in Jasper County from the Republic of Texas.^{qv}

By 1845, however, he was again in Louisiana serving as district attorney for Sabine Parish, a post he held until 1853, when he was installed as district judge of the parish. When a district court for the Sixteenth District was established in 1855, he began functioning as judge of both the old Ninth District Court and the new Sixteenth District Court, both headquartered in Sabine Parish; he held this dual post until December 1864. In 1865 Chaplin completed his public service as the attorney for the Natchitoches Parish police jury.

While he was a fugitive from the Fredonian Rebellion, Chaplin married his second wife, Emily Parmer. This marriage must have occurred in 1829 or 1830, probably in Natchitoches Parish. They had six children. In 1870 Chaplin was grand master of Phoenix Lodge No. 38 in Natchitoches. He died on October 14, 1874, and Emily died on August 9, 1878. Both are buried in the American Cemetery in Natchitoches.

BIBLIOGRAPHY: *Biographical and Historical Memoirs of Natchitoches Parish, Louisiana* (Tuscaloosa, Alabama: Mills Historical Press, 1985). George L. Crocket, *Two Centuries in East Texas* (Dallas: Southwest, 1932; facsimile reprod., 1962). Joe E. Ericson, *Judges of the Republic of Texas (1836–1846): A Biographical Directory* (Dallas: Taylor, 1980). Judge R. B. Williams, "The History of the Judiciary of Natchitoches Parish, Louisiana," *Natchitoches Genealogist*, April 1978.
Joe E. Ericson

CHAPMAN, AMOS (1837–1925). Amos Chapman, frontiersman, was born on March 15, 1837, of mixed white and Indian parentage in Michigan. Beginning in the late 1860s, he served as a civilian scout and interpreter for the United States Army and was often hired as a guide for settlers moving to Kansas and Colorado. In September 1868 he scouted for Maj. Joel H. Elliott's Seventh Cavalry detachment during Gen. Alfred Sully's campaign against the Southern Cheyennes from Fort Dodge, Kansas. That campaign led to the establishment of Camp Supply in Indian Territory, where Chapman subsequently served as an interpreter. There he married Mary Longneck, a daughter of the Cheyenne chief Stone Calf, and lived for a time among her tribe. They had six children. During the early 1870s he was involved in the army's attempts to keep whiskey peddlers and outlaws out of the reservations.

Chapman volunteered his services to Col. Nelson A. Miles's^{qv} regiment in July 1874 and scouted for Lt. Frank D. Baldwin.^{qv} While carrying dispatches for Miles on September 12, Chapman, William (Billy) Dixon,^{qv} and four troopers ran into a party of more than 100 Comanches and Kiowas near Gageby Creek, in what is now Hemphill County. In the resultant Buffalo Wallow Fight,^{qv} Chapman's left knee was shattered by a bullet while he was attempting to aid the fatally wounded George Smith. He managed to hold out until Dixon was able to reach him and carry him to the safety of the wallow. Subsequently, Chapman's injured leg was amputated by the post surgeon at Camp Supply. For their heroism he and his comrades were awarded the Medal of Honor, but the award was later revoked for Chapman and Dixon because they were civilians.

After the Red River War^{qv} Chapman, who thereafter wore an artificial leg, continued in his role as post interpreter. He worked vigorously on behalf of his wife's people and helped keep order during the excitement surrounding Dull Knife's flight in 1879. When James Monroe (Doc) Day^{qv} and other free-range cattlemen began running their herds on reservation lands, Chapman again wielded his influence to prevent bloodshed. He helped work out peaceful solutions, which included designating certain routes, such as the Deep Creek Trail, over which cattle could graze and be driven to the Kansas markets. After his retirement from government service, Chapman and his wife settled on a ranch four miles east of Seiling, Oklahoma. It was said that they "divided matters evenly." Sometimes they slept in a tepee, for instance. Chapman died on July 18, 1925, from injuries sustained in an accident with his spring wagon. At the time, he was preparing to lecture on his frontier days with a lyceum circuit. He was buried at Seiling.

BIBLIOGRAPHY: Wayne Montgomery, "Amos Chapman, Scout," *Frontier Times*, April–May 1972.
H. Allen Anderson

CHAPMAN, HELEN ELLSWORTH BLAIR (1817–1881). Helen Ellsworth Blair Chapman, letter writer from frontier Brownsville and Corpus Christi, the daughter of William and Emily (Welles) Blair, was born on April 4, 1817, in Westfield, Massachusetts, and educated at the Westfield Academy. She married 1st Lt. William Warren Chapman[qv] on August 29, 1838. As an army wife she lived in garrisons at various army posts including Fort Niagara, near Buffalo, New York (1838–41); Fort Columbus (Governors Island), New York (1841–47); Matamoros, Tamaulipas (January through mid-1848); and Fort Brown, Brazos Santiago, Point Isabel (mid-1848 through mid-1852), and Corpus Christi, Texas (mid-1852 until 1858). Her son was born in Fort Niagara, and her daughter was born at Fort Brown on October 23, 1851.

Helen Chapman was a literate and concerned citizen of the Texas frontier. Many of her letters to family, newspapers, and missionary organizations have been preserved, and they chronicle the early days of Brownsville and Corpus Christi, in many cases providing compelling portraits of the early citizens and events of the Rio Grande valley and the Corpus Christi area. Although the wife of the quartermaster at Fort Brown, Brazos Santiago, and Point Isabel, and consequently in a relatively secure situation, Mrs. Chapman witnessed and described the excitement and attractions of the frontier as well as its abuses. Notable were her observations on the lot of women and children in frontier society. Early during her Texas residence she initiated a letter campaign to friends in the East to bring charitable, religious, and educational influences to the Rio Grande valley and to Corpus Christi. By 1858, when the army transferred her husband to New York, she could point to many successes resulting from her letters. She had a high regard for the Mexican people and became an early advocate of equal civil rights for Mexican Americans[qv] when she realized that they were being denied the rights promised under the terms of annexation[qv] and the Treaty of Guadalupe Hidalgo,[qv] which ended the war with Mexico.

In 1851 Helen Chapman traveled to Mexico City and made many poignant observations concerning life in the Mexican capital. She resided in the North from 1858 until the end of the Civil War.[qv] William Chapman died in late 1859. He had engaged in many business ventures in both the Brownsville and Corpus Christi areas during his army tour there and had acquired substantial property in South Texas. Some of it was confiscated by the Confederate States of America during the Civil War and, in other instances, a few of her husband's former business associates denied their business relationship in an attempt to acquire her property. In her later years, she was involved in litigation to recover this property. After the Civil War she resided at various times in Corpus Christi and Columbia, South Carolina. Helen Chapman died on December 10, 1881, in Columbia, South Carolina.

BIBLIOGRAPHY: Helen Chapman, *The News From Brownsville: Helen Chapman's Letters from the Texas Military Frontier, 1848–1852*, ed. Caleb Coker (Austin: Texas State Historical Association, 1992). William W. Chapman Papers, Barker Texas History Center, University of Texas at Austin.
Caleb Coker

CHAPMAN, ROBERT MARTIN (1810–?). Robert Martin Chapman, Episcopalian missionary, was born in Petersburg, Virginia, on April 10, 1810. He became a deacon in 1838 at St. Stephen's Church in Pittsfield, Massachusetts. Early that year he corresponded with Mirabeau B. Lamar,[qv] then the vice president of Texas, and informed him of his desire to establish an academy in the republic. In October 1838 Chapman gained an appointment as foreign missionary of the Protestant Episcopal Church[qv] to Texas, where he arrived in late November. He boarded in Houston with the family of Col. William Fairfax Gray,[qv] a prominent settler and active layman of the church. In return for this assistance, he tutored the family children. Chapman spent most of his time in Houston, where he held church services in the Capitol, though he also ministered in Galveston and traveled to Velasco and Quintana. In March 1839 Gray circulated a petition to organize an Episcopal congregation in Houston, and Chapman presided over the first parish meeting on April 1, 1839. The vestry elected during this meeting formed the foundation of Christ Church in Houston, the second Episcopal church in Texas. During this time Rev. Leonidas Polk, missionary bishop of the Southwest, conducted the first visitation of a high Episcopal church official to the Republic of Texas.[qv] While in Texas, Chapman opened the Senate five times, held services for nine burials, solemnized five marriages, and baptized two children. He left Texas in June of 1839 apparently discouraged and unable to cope with the conditions of frontier life.

BIBLIOGRAPHY: Lawrence L. Brown, *The Episcopal Church in Texas, 1838–1874* (Austin: Church Historical Society, 1963). E. Clowes Chorley, "The Missionary March of the American Episcopal Church," *Historical Magazine of the Protestant Episcopal Church*, June 1933. Marguerite Johnston, *Houston, The Unknown City, 1836–1946* (College Station: Texas A&M University Press, 1991). Andrew Forest Muir, "William Fairfax Gray," *Historical Magazine of the Protestant Episcopal Church*, December 1959. DuBose Murphy, "Early Days of the Protestant Episcopal Church in Texas," *Southwestern Historical Quarterly* 34 (April 1931). DuBose Murphy, *Short History of the Protestant Episcopal Church in Texas* (Dallas: Turner, 1935). Rupert N. Richardson, *Texas: The Lone Star State* (New York: Prentice-Hall, 1943; 4th ed., with Ernest Wallace and Adrian N. Anderson, Englewood Cliffs, New Jersey: Prentice-Hall, 1981).
David L. Fisher

CHAPMAN, WILLIAM WARREN (1814–1859). William Warren Chapman, soldier and influential citizen of South Texas, the fourth child of James and Ethelinda (Preston) Chapman, Jr., was born in Springfield, Massachusetts, on January 31, 1814. He entered West Point on July 1, 1833, and graduated seventh in general order of merit, but second in military affairs, in the class of 1837. After West Point he served in the second Seminole war in Florida. He was stationed at Fort Foster on the Hillsborough River north of Tampa Bay from November 1837 until May 1838. He began as quartermaster of the fort but was commander at the time the fort was abandoned in the spring of 1838. After leaving Florida in May of 1838 he served briefly in Tennessee, where he assisted in the relocation of the Seminole and Cherokee Indians to the Western states.

On July 7, 1838, Chapman was promoted to first lieutenant in the Second Artillery. He married Helen Ellsworth Blair (*see* CHAPMAN, HELEN E. B.) in Westfield, Massachusetts, on August 29, 1838; they had a son and a daughter. Chapman was assigned to Fort Niagara near Buffalo, New York, from 1838 through 1841, during the Canadian border disturbances. From 1841 through mid-1846 Chapman served in the garrison at Fort Columbus, Governors Island, New York.

On May 11, 1846, he was promoted to captain. He joined the army of Gen. John E. Wool[qv] in San Antonio, Texas, as staff assistant quartermaster, traveled with Wool's column into Mexico, and fought in the battle of Buena Vista, February, 22–23, 1847 (*see* MEXICAN WAR). He was brevetted major for gallant and meritorious conduct in that battle. In November 1847 he left Wool's staff and became quartermaster of the army depot in Matamoros, Tamaulipas. Matamoros was then under martial law, and, in addition to his duties as quartermaster, Chapman was also appointed collector of revenue and given responsibility for the administration of civil government. With characteristic energy, he improved the city streets, the central plaza, and the schools of the Mexican city during his tenure.

Upon the termination of hostilities with Mexico in mid-1848, the army decided to build a new fort across the Rio Grande from Matamoros. Chapman selected the site and constructed the permanent military facility, known as Fort Brown. This fort replaced the original Fort Brown that had been bombarded by the Mexican army during May 3–9, 1846, while Zachary Taylor's qv army was otherwise occupied at the battles of Palo Alto and Resaca de la Palma qqv a few miles north. The city of Brownsville was laid out and developed simultaneously with the construction of the permanent Fort Brown. From mid-1848 until mid-1852 Chapman was the quartermaster at the fort. After the first year his duties were enlarged to include responsibility for the military depots at Brazos Santiago and Point Isabel, Texas. In 1850 he sent an expedition on the first official exploration of the Rio Grande to determine the navigability of the river and the economic potential of the region. Chapman and his wife were prominent and well-regarded citizens of early Brownsville.

In mid-1852 Chapman was appointed quartermaster of the new army headquarters in Corpus Christi under Gen. Persifor F. Smith.qv Chapman remained at the military facility until it was closed in 1857. During his military service in the fledgling community of Corpus Christi, Chapman was prominent in civic and business affairs, including a partnership with Richard King qv in the acquisition of the first tracts of land to be incorporated into the King Ranch.qv Thereafter during 1858 he was briefly assigned to the military depot at Fort Schuyler in New York. In 1859 he was transferred to Fort Monroe, Virginia. He died on September 28, 1859, at Old Point Comfort, Virginia. His son was a life-long resident of Corpus Christi.

BIBLIOGRAPHY: Helen Chapman, *The News From Brownsville: Helen Chapman's Letters from the Texas Military Frontier, 1848–1852*, ed. Caleb Coker (Austin: Texas State Historical Association, 1992). Chapman Papers, Barker Texas History Center, University of Texas at Austin.
Caleb Coker

CHAPMAN, TEXAS. Chapman, also known as Blossom Hill, is near Trammel's Trace qv eight miles east of Henderson in eastern Rusk County. The community was named for the family of a pioneer, John Chapman. A member of this family, Henry Chapman, fought at the battle of San Jacinto.qv The town's first postmaster was Francis M. Bridges, who was appointed in 1894. The post office at Chapman was discontinued in 1904, and local mail was sent to Henderson. Chapman's population grew from a reported figure of twelve in 1895 to 150 by 1940. From 1967 to 1990 its population was estimated at twenty. In the mid-1980s the community had three businesses and a community center.

BIBLIOGRAPHY: Garland Roscoe Farmer, *The Realm of Rusk County* (Henderson, Texas: Henderson *Times*, 1951). Dorman H. Winfrey, *A History of Rusk County* (Waco: Texian, 1961).
Megan Biesele

CHAPMAN CITY, TEXAS. Chapman City was west of Farm Road 112 and east of Lawrence Chapel in southeastern Williamson County. It grew up as the result of the discovery of oil in 1930 by a driller named Chapman on land owned by J. C. Abbott. Chapman City had one business and a population of ten in 1933 and twenty-five residents in 1940. Though there were still scattered dwellings marked on the 1946 county highway map in an area called Chapman Field, the community was dropped from the *Texas Almanac* qv population listings in 1949 and was not marked on the 1977 county highway map.

BIBLIOGRAPHY: Clara Stearns Scarbrough, *Land of Good Water: A Williamson County History* (Georgetown, Texas: Williamson County Sun Publishers, 1973).
Mark Odintz

CHAPMAN DRAW. Chapman Draw rises nine miles northeast of Menard in northeastern Menard County (at 31°01′ N, 99°41′ W) and runs southwest for nine miles to its mouth on the San Saba River, five miles east of Menard (at 30°55′ N, 99°43′ W). The surrounding flat to rolling terrain has local deep dissections and is surfaced by shallow and stony to moderately deep clay loams that support oak, juniper, mesquite, and grasses.

CHAPMAN RANCH, TEXAS. Chapman Ranch is on Farm Road 70 seven miles south of Corpus Christi in southeastern Nueces County. It is named for a family that purchased 34,000 acres of the King Ranch qv in 1919. A post office was established in 1926 with Charles C. Simpson as postmaster. A school in town was named Santa Cruz, the original name of the King Ranch water well at the site. High School students from Chapman Ranch now attend Corpus Christi schools. Chapman Ranch had a population of twenty-five in 1933 and 100 from 1945 to 1990.

BIBLIOGRAPHY: Nueces County Historical Society, *History of Nueces County* (Austin: Jenkins, 1972).
Karen S. Parrish

CHAPPEL, TEXAS. Chappel, previously known as Harrell's Chappel, is at the intersection of Farm roads 1031 and 501, near Cherokee Creek and five miles southwest of Bend in southeastern San Saba County. On November 7, 1854, David Matsler and his family settled near the site of future Chappel. Other early settlers in the area included the Rumsey and Poplin families, Ambrose Casey, E. M. Boyett, and three brothers, William A., David Donald, and James Milton Low. By the 1860s settlers were involved in stock raising, irrigation, and chairmaking. In the late 1880s Joab B. Harrell donated fifteen acres of land to the Methodist Episcopal Church, South. The new church building also served as a school until 1892, when a separate structure was erected for the school. The Keeney (Keeney's) post office was established beside Davis Creek near Chappel in 1879. The post office was operated by George Keeney in his home until a flood destroyed it on July 8, 1880. Mail was then sent to San Saba until 1891, when the Richards (Richard) post office was opened near Davis Creek in Mrs. Sabina A. Self's home. This office lasted less than a year because of a flood. Mail was routed to the Bend post office until the Chappel post office was opened in 1897. This post office was named after the church and served the community until 1917. In 1914 Chappel had two general stores and a population of twenty-five. The Chappel post office was reestablished in 1918 and operated until 1941. The estimated population of Chappel was sixty-nine from 1925 until 1939, when it fell to fifty. The number of local businesses also declined from ten in 1933 to two in 1939. Although the estimated population of Chappel remained at fifty from 1939 to 1964, the number of businesses fell to one in 1945. After 1964 there were no rated businesses reported in Chappel. The community's estimated population from 1966 to 1990 was twenty-five. In 1984 a church and a cemetery remained at the site.

BIBLIOGRAPHY: Alma Ward Hamrick, *The Call of the San Saba: A History of San Saba County* (San Antonio: Naylor, 1941; 2d ed., Austin: Jenkins, 1969). *San Saba County History* (San Saba, Texas: San Saba County Historical Commission, 1983).
Karen Yancy

CHAPPELL CREEK. Chappell Creek rises in southeastern Comanche County (at 31°46′ N, 98°22′ W) and runs seven miles northeast to its mouth on the Leon River, four miles southeast of Gustine (at 31°51′ N, 98°19′ W). It crosses flat terrain with local shallow depressions, surfaced by clay and sandy loams that support water-tolerant hardwoods, conifers, and grasses.

CHAPPELL HILL, TEXAS. Chappell (Chapel) Hill is located at the junction of Farm roads 1155 and 2447, fifty-seven miles northwest of Houston in southeastern Washington County. By 1847 the site was a trading locality, one mile from Cedar Creek settlement, an early Methodist center. Trader Jacob Haller's wife, Mary Hargrove Haller, bought 100 acres for the townsite; she named the town for her grandfather, Robert Wooding Chappell, an early settler. In 1849 she laid out and sold town lots. In the 1850s Chappell Hill grew rapidly as the center of large cotton plantations. Mary Haller established a post office in 1847, and missionary Robert Alexander qv organized the Chappell Hill Methodist Church the same year. In 1851 the Hubert Masonic Lodge (still functioning in 1988) was chartered. An academy was organized the previous year. The Methodist Texas Conference established Chappell Hill Male and Female Institute (1852) and Soule University (1856). Between 1854 and 1878 five Texas Methodist conferences were held at Chappell Hill. The town was incorporated on April 7, 1856. To obtain better transportation for their growing cotton harvests, Chappell Hill residents held a meeting in 1852 to encourage Houston businessmen to construct the Houston and Texas Central Railroad. In 1856 Chappell Hill planters William M. Sledge qv and Col. W. W. Browning organized the Washington County Rail Road, which held stockholders' meetings in Chappell Hill. With extension of the Washington County Railroad to Chappell Hill in 1859, the town became a distribution center. During the Civil War qv Chappell Hill had a Confederate quartermaster depot and a military hospital; Camp Felder qv was in the vicinity. The Twenty-first Texas Lancers were raised at Chappell Hill. The *Texas Ranger* newspaper was published there from 1851 to 1853.

From 1868 to 1870 the town had a Freedmen's Bureau qv school. Emancipation severely disrupted Chappell Hill's economy. The high mortality of the 1867 yellow fever epidemic resulted in the exodus of many surviving residents. The arrival of industrious Polish immigrants, principally farmers, beginning in the early 1870s and increasing after 1884, helped Chappell Hill remain a supply point. The population increased from 318 to 800 by 1878. Between 1853 and 1909 the town furnished seven state representatives, including two African Americans. qv In the 1870s the Grange, qv black and white Greenback clubs, and the temperance movement flourished. In 1889 Polish immigrants organized St. Stanislaus Catholic Church, one of the earliest Polish parishes in Texas. Town residents organized the Chappell Hill Circulating Library Association in 1893. The library was restored in 1964 and is in use today. As Brenham developed, however, Chappell Hill declined. Soule University closed in 1888, and Chappell Hill Female College closed in 1912.

Mayor-council government ended in 1884. Despite the establishment of the Farmer's State Bank in 1907, commerce declined in volume and variety between 1880 and World War I. qv By 1914 Chappell Hill had a population of 600. Residents increased to 1,000 by 1930, but the depression and postwar decline in the importance of cotton cultivation resulted in a commercial decline. The population was 300 in 1960. Beginning in the 1960s an influx of Houstonians revived commerce and renewed interest in the restoration of historic homes. The Chappell Hill Chamber of Commerce organized in 1970. Property values soared, and deposits at the Farmers State Bank—$500,000 in 1970—climbed to $5 million within a few years. The Chappell Hill Historical Society, founded in 1964, promotes historical preservation and maintains a museum. The town has more than twenty-five Texas historical markers and ten sites on the National Register, including the Main Street Historic District. The population, predominantly Anglo-American before the Civil War, had become predominantly Polish-American by the early twentieth century. Residents in the 1980s numbered 600. Chappell Hill voters rejected reincorporation in 1984. Annual events include the Bluebonnet Festival in April, the Scarecrow Festival in October, and the Independence Day Parade, in which the Chappell Hill children's kazoo marching band participates. The recently restored Masonic Cemetery contains the graves of Republic of Texas qv settlers and Confederate veterans. In 1990 the population was 310.

BIBLIOGRAPHY: W. O. Dietrich, *The Blazing Story of Washington County* (Brenham, Texas: Banner Press, 1950; rev. ed., Wichita Falls: Nortex, 1973). Ardita Berry Morgan, A Short History of Chappell Hill Female College (MS, Barker Texas History Center, University of Texas at Austin, 1953). Charles F. Schmidt, *History of Washington County* (San Antonio: Naylor, 1949). Vertical Files, Barker Texas History Center, University of Texas at Austin. Mr. and Mrs. Nate Winfield, *All Our Yesterdays: A Brief History of Chappell Hill* (Waco: Texian Press, 1969). Judy and Nath Winfield, Jr., Cemetery Records of Washington County, 1826–1960 (MS, Barker Texas History Center, University of Texas at Austin, 1974).

Carole E. Christian

CHAPPELL HILL FEMALE COLLEGE. Chappell Hill Female College, in Chapel (originally Chappell) Hill, Texas, began as Chappell Hill Institute, founded on land donated by Jacob and Mary Haller in 1850. It received a charter from the legislature on February 9, 1852, as a nondenominational school called Chappell Hill Male and Female Institute. Several Masons were members of the board of trustees. In 1852 a second building was constructed to keep the boys and girls apart. In 1853 Professor P. S. Ruter, former instructor at Transylvania University, Kentucky, became president. The school, now known as Chappelle Hill College, offered a variety of courses, including geology, chemistry, art, and music, and continued to board students. Elizabeth Knox from Pittsburg, Pennsylvania, supervised the female department, and Ruter's sister, Charlotte, was head of the music department.

Methodists who desired to replace the dying Rutersville College acquired Chappell Hill Male and Female Institute in 1854. Its enrollment had increased to 100. The Methodist Texas Conference decided to form Soule University from the institute's male department, and Chappell Hill Female College obtained a separate charter on August 29, 1856. The institution's objective was to educate girls in a Christian environment and to assure their acquisition of culture, discipline, and oratorical skills. Music and art received special emphasis. Despite the Civil War, qv two fires, and yellow fever epidemics in 1867 and 1869, Chappell Hill Female College continued, and even constructed a new building in 1872. The college was debt-free by 1873. It added a dormitory and music hall in the 1880s and served as a cultural center for the area, especially after Soule University closed in 1887. By 1885 students numbered 112, the school's real estate was worth $15,000, and the college was only $1,200 in debt.

By 1895, however, student enrollment had declined by half. In 1896 the college obtained additional income by enrolling seventy public school pupils, including fifty boys. During the 1890s the Texas Conference gave this institution more aid than it gave Southwestern University. In 1900 the trustees redesigned the curriculum in accord with the Methodist Church General Board of Education. Although the college received the property of Soule University to liquidate its debts, Chappell Hill Female College closed in 1912. Economic decline in the area, continuing fear of yellow fever, the rise of Texas public schools, and decreasing public support for girls' schools all probably contributed to the demise. The school's final enrollment was 112. The college building served as a public school until 1926, but only the school bell survived in the 1980s.

BIBLIOGRAPHY: W. O. Dietrich, *The Blazing Story of Washington County* (Brenham, Texas: Banner Press, 1950; rev. ed., Wichita Falls: Nortex, 1973). Arthur A. Grusendorf, The Social and Philosophical Determinants of Education in Washington County, Texas, from 1835 to 1937 (Ph.D. dissertation, University of Texas, 1938). Ardita Berry Morgan, A Short History of Chappell Hill Female College (MS, Barker Texas History Center, University of Texas at Austin, 1953). Vertical Files, Barker Texas History Center, University of Texas at Austin (Chapel Hill; Washington County). Washington County Scrapbook, Barker Texas History Center, University of Texas at Austin. Mr. and Mrs. Nate Winfield, *All Our Yesterdays: A Brief History of Chappell Hill* (Waco: Texian Press, 1969).

Carole E. Christian

CHAQUANTIE INDIANS. In 1700 the Chaquantie (Chacacante, Chaquanhe, Chicacanti) Indians lived on the Red River some sixty to seventy-five miles west of the Kadohadachos. This would place them in the area covered by present Lamar and Red River counties. Apparent variants of this name appear on several eighteenth-century maps, some showing the name north of the river, others south. The Chaquanties may have been the same people as the Canteys, who were listed as enemies of the Kadohadachos in records (1687) of the La Salle expedition.[qv] The Canteys have been identified as Lipan-Apache, but this identification is debatable. The geographic and historical facts lend more support to identification of the Canteys with the Chaquanties. Although it has been speculated that the Chaquanties were Caddoan, this has yet to be demonstrated.

BIBLIOGRAPHY: Frederick Webb Hodge, ed., *Handbook of American Indians North of Mexico* (2 vols., Washington: GPO, 1907, 1910; rpt., New York: Pageant, 1959). Pierre Margry, ed., *Découvertes et établissements des Français dans l'ouest et dans le sud de l'Amérique septentrionale, 1614–1754* (6 vols., Paris: Jouast, 1876–86).

Thomas N. Campbell

CHARAMUSCA CREEK. Charamusca (Cheremusca) Creek rises seven miles northwest of Freer in northwestern Duval County (at 27°55′ N, 98°44′ W) and runs northwest for eighteen miles to its mouth on the Nueces River, in southeastern La Salle County (at 28°06′ N, 98°50′ W). Its name is Spanish for a type of twisted candy. The surrounding flat terrain has local shallow depressions and is surfaced by clay and sandy loams that support water-tolerant hardwoods, conifers, and grasses.

CHARCO, TEXAS. Charco, on State Highway 239 some fourteen miles from Goliad in northwestern Goliad County, was settled by at least four members of Stephen F. Austin's[qv] Old Three Hundred.[qv] Spanish explorers in the eighteenth century recorded that an Indian village was located at this site. The Spanish charco means "pool" or "watering hole," a name suggested by the numerous bodies of water that once dotted the area. The name is also said to come from an Indian designation for the locality, referring to a petrified stump near a watering pool. A post office was established in the area in 1855 and was moved three times before it was discontinued in 1954. Settlers farmed corn, cane, hay, and especially cotton, and also raised cattle and mules; one local entrepreneur bred Shetland ponies, which for years were in demand throughout the United States and in some foreign countries. By 1904 Charco had a population of 113 and was a dry town, except for a short-lived saloon that was closed by the commissioner's court in 1906 and its owner "reimbursed for ingredients on hand." The first church for the community was built through the efforts of the widow of John Freeman Pettus,[qv] a veteran of the battle of San Jacinto.[qv] In time Charco had Methodist, Baptist, Church of Christ, Catholic, and Pentecostal churches. At one time the town had a druggist, a gristmill, two blacksmiths, two barbershops, two garages, two cotton gins, several piano teachers, three stores, and a variety of other shops. The last general store there had opened in 1903 and did not close until 1973. The community's population declined from 250 in 1925 to 150 by 1933 but stabilized at about 150 until the mid-1960s. In the 1930s the local one-room school became the short-lived Charco Independent School District. After the boll weevil[qv] killed the area's cotton crop, the gins closed, and cattle ranching again became the major industry. As sharecroppers moved on, the town dwindled. In the 1960s a television program described Charco as a ghost town, although population statistics from 1970 to 1986 reported sixty-one residents there. In 1990 the community's population was listed as sixty-eight.

BIBLIOGRAPHY: Goliad County Historical Commission, *The History and Heritage of Goliad County*, ed. Jakie L. Pruett and Everett B. Cole (Austin: Eakin Press, 1983).

Craig H. Roell

CHARCO CREEK (Goliad County). Charco Creek rises three miles northeast of Charco in northwestern Goliad County (at 28°46′ N, 97°35′ W) and runs southeast for seven miles to its mouth on the San Antonio River, two miles west of the Riverdale oilfield (at 28°41′ N, 97°34′ W). It traverses flat to rolling terrain with clay loam and sandy loam soils that support water-tolerant hardwoods and grasses.

CHARCO MARRANO CREEK. Charco Marrano Creek rises nine miles east of Cotulla in central La Salle County (at 28°24′ N, 99°05′ W) and runs south for twelve miles to its mouth on the Nueces River, sixteen miles southeast of Cotulla (at 28°14′ N, 99°04′ W). The name is Spanish for "filthy pond." In the creek's upper reaches the surrounding flat to rolling terrain has locally shallow depressions and is surfaced by dark clays that support grasses, mesquites, and cacti. In the creek's lowest reaches, clay and sandy loams support water-tolerant hardwoods and grasses.

CHARGOS CREEK. Chargos Creek, also known as Los Charco Creek, rises on the Webb county line just east of the El Ranchito oilfield in northern Zapata County (at 27°16′ N, 99°02′ W) and runs southwest for eleven miles to its mouth on Salomoneño Creek, four miles east of Farm Road 3169 (at 27°09′ N, 99°08′ W). It crosses flat to gently rolling terrain surfaced by sands and clay and sandy loams that support scrub brush, grasses, mesquite, chaparral, and scattered oak mottes. *Chargos* is probably a corruption of the Spanish word *charcos*, which means "puddles."

CHARITY GUILD OF CATHOLIC WOMEN. The Charity Guild of Catholic Women was founded in 1922 in Houston by a group of women headed by Mrs. Lucian Carroll. It was devoted to charitable works and had no bylaws (until 1947), dues, or time or place of meeting. Its early efforts included giving aid to the San José free clinic for Mexican-American women and children, supplying layettes, and supporting Christmas charities. The money came from an annual fundraising event and later also from membership dues. In 1953 the Charity Guild Shop opened in an abandoned filling station. The present building on Lovett Boulevard was purchased in 1960; a wing was added in 1965 and another in 1978. The shop serves as a resale shop and a meeting place for the parent organization and its various committees. In 1963 and 1972 the guild provided furnishings for Catholic maternity homes, and it continued thereafter to help maternity programs with an annual subsidy.

In 1940 a group from the guild joined the volunteer program as companion-escorts at Jefferson Davis Hospital. Later they assisted in follow-up work with premature baby, heart, tumor, and diabetic patients in Ben Taub General Hospital. In 1949 the guild offered volunteer aid to St. Joseph's Pediatric Department, an offer that led to the formation of the St. Joseph Auxiliary. In 1951 the guild went into Veterans Hospital (now Veterans Affairs Medical Center, Houston[qv]) as volunteers to form the local chapter of the National Catholic Community Service. A reorganization of the guild occurred in 1940. Regular meetings were scheduled in the homes of members, and everyone in attendance sewed layettes, an activity that continued in the late 1980s. Projects at that time included the shop, foster children and maternity programs of Catholic Charities, layettes, nursing scholarships, and the San José Clinic. The guild also continued to assist the St. Anthony Center for low-income elderly.

BIBLIOGRAPHY: Charity Guild of Catholic Women, Records, Houston.

Mrs. Hudson D. Carmouche

CHARLESTON, TEXAS. Charleston is on Farm Road 895 some nine miles east of Cooper in southeastern Delta County. It is bordered by Evans Branch on the east and McGuyer Branch on the west. The area, originally part of the D. A. Sey Survey, was within Hopkins County until Delta County was formed in 1870. Settlers in 1854 traveled from Charleston, South Carolina, and named the site for their former home. Local residents exploited the abundance of oak and elm trees, and the first local industry was hardwood lumbering. In 1857 a post office opened at the community, with Zachariah R. Terrell as postmaster. In 1861, during the Civil War,qv local citizens organized the first Texas militia brigade and chose to fight for the Confederacy. The Charleston school district was organized in 1867. When Delta County and its county seat, Cooper, were established in 1870, the new shipping center attracted much of Charleston's business. In 1884 Charleston had 250 residents, three cotton gins, several stores, two wagonmaking enterprises, a flour mill, a sawmill, a gristmill, a church, and a school. In 1890 mail was delivered triweekly from Paris. The population of Charleston had increased to 400 by 1892, when the community also had a weekly newspaper, the *News*, and a new municipal government. From 1892 to 1897 A. J. Street conducted a teacher-training school in the community. In 1904 the town had 183 inhabitants. Near Charleston, on May 19, 1910, a 500-pound meteorite fell to earth during the passage of Haley's Comet, bringing some publicity to the community. In the 1920s and 1930s Charleston reported a population of 225, a school, a church, a cemetery, and five or six businesses, including a factory. In 1930 the local school was merged with the Vasco, Cleveland, and Long Ridge districts. Ten years later the school was in East Delta Number 2 District. By 1950 Charleston's population was 150. A 1964 map showed two churches, a cemetery, and a cluster of dwellings at the site on Farm Road 895. By 1970 local children attended classes within the Cooper Independent School District. The Charleston post office closed in 1972. By 1976 area residents had built the Charleston Community Center. In 1990 the community's population was 120.

BIBLIOGRAPHY: Cooper *Review*, April 8, 1976. Paul Garland Hervey, *A History of Education in Delta County, Texas* (M.A. thesis, University of Texas, 1951). Wilma Ross and Billie Phillips, *Photos and Tales of Delta County* (1976). *Vista K. McCroskey*

CHARLIE, TEXAS. Charlie is on Farm Road 810 twenty-one miles northwest of Henrietta in northwestern Clay County. The community was called Big Wichita Valley in 1878, when Henry T. Dunn built a store just south of the Red River. Later Dunn sold the store to Charlie Taylor, and almost immediately the site became known as Charlie. For years the store was a popular trading post for county farmers and ranchers and some Indians from nearby Indian Territory (later Oklahoma). In 1882 a post office opened at the community. By the mid-1920s the population of Charlie surpassed 200. After the Great Depressionqv and World War II,qv however, the community's population count declined. The Charlie post office closed sometime after 1930. From the early 1970s through 1990 the community's population has been estimated at sixty-five.

BIBLIOGRAPHY: William Charles Taylor, *A History of Clay County* (Austin: Jenkins, 1972). *David Minor*

CHARLOTTE, TEXAS. Charlotte is at the junction of State Highway 97 and Farm roads 140, 1548, and 1333, in southwestern Atascosa County. Coahuiltecan Indian groups once roamed the site. Charlotte was carved from the Old Tobey Ranch, which at the time of its founding was owned by Jourdan Campbell and T. H. Zanderson. In 1910 the townsite was laid out by J. F. Edwards in the form of a wagon wheel, the streets forming spokes. In 1911 J. E. Franklin, from Missouri, offered to construct a railroad through the county. Landowners donated land to help finance the project; George F. Hindes and M. M. Davis are reported to have given thousands of acres. The name Charlotte was given by Dr. Charles Simmons, who aided in the development of Atascosa County. Towns in the county were named for all three of his daughters, Charlotte, Imogene, and Christine. In the early days cotton was the principle crop around Charlotte. At one time farmers waited in line for twenty-four hours, their wagons loaded, to have their cotton ginned. But ranching is still the basic industry, and some ranchers have developed fine herds of registered cattle. Some have also established dairy farms. Oil was discovered in 1946; there are now more than 700 producing oil wells in the school district.

The first store in Charlotte, built by J. M. Couser in 1910, was sold to W. M. Wilson. Other merchants were S. Fleischman, A. F. Hahn, A. K. McBride, John Neal, and Hugh Dixon, and the town had a drugstore, a hotel, a hardware store, and a blacksmith shop. Charlotte was incorporated on December 21, 1946. In 1963 the Charlotte Rotary Club sponsored the Charlotte Community Recreation Association, which organized a little league and a rodeo. The First Baptist Church was organized on January 21, 1914. Members set aside acreage of cotton to finance construction of their first building, which was replaced in 1951. The church supported a mission for the Spanish-speaking citizens of the community. The Methodist church was established in 1912, with twenty-three charter members. At first Charlotte was on a circuit with Fowlerton, Jourdanton, Poteet, and Christine. A parsonage was built in 1938, at which time the church became a station. The old building was replaced in 1950. St. Rose of Lima Catholic Church was established in 1909. It was served by Claretian Fathers from San Antonio. A new building was dedicated in honor of St. Mary on July 25, 1925. Improvements were made in 1944 and 1972. The first public school was conducted in 1913 by Mrs. Sauer, who held classes in a dance hall over a bakery. By 1914 a new building was constructed, and the school became an independent district by 1919. As enrollment increased the school started a four-year high school. In 1935 citizens voted bonds of $25,000 to construct a new school plant, and received a Public Works Administration grant of $23,000. The district added elementary and lunchroom buildings in 1948. A new gymnasium and an auditorium were built in 1950. In 1990 the population of Charlotte was 1,475.

BIBLIOGRAPHY: *Atascosa County Centennial, 1856–1956* (Jourdanton, Texas: Atascosa County Centennial Association, n.d.). *Atascosa County History* (Pleasanton, Texas: Atascosa History Committee, 1984). *Janie S. Tubbs*

CHARLTON, JOHN B. (1848–1922). John B. (Jack) Charlton, an Indian fighter known as the "Old Sergeant," was born on August 6, 1848, in Bowling Green, Virginia, into an old planter family. His father died when Charlton was nine, and the family lost its fortune during the Civil War.qv Charlton enlisted in 1865 and served for five years in Gen. William Graham's Light Battery K of the First United States Army Artillery. He reenlisted in April 1870 in Col. Ranald S. Mackenzie'sqv Fourth United States Cavalryqv and joined other recruits traveling west to forts Concho and Griffin from Texas Department headquarters in San Antonio. At Mountain Pass he encountered his first Indians, who attempted to steal the army mules. By encouraging soldiers without guns to find sticks that resembled weapons, he bluffed the Indians and averted the attack. He was subsequently assigned to Company F under Capt. Wirt Davis, promoted to corporal, and transferred to Fort Richardson.

Charlton escorted William T. Sherman and Randolph B. Marcyqqv on a frontier inspection tour that narrowly escaped the Kiowas in 1871. Charlton killed Kiowa chief Satankqv when the Indian escaped his chains en route to Jacksboro to stand trial for the Salt Valley Massacre. Before the year's end, Charlton also took part in Mackenzie's frustrating Blanco Canyon campaign, captured deserters between Weatherford and Hillsboro with Lt. Robert G. Carter,qv and achieved the rank of sergeant. In 1872 he accompanied the Mackenzie expedition to New Mexico across the Llano Estacadoqv and on September 29 was one of four men who remained uninjured in the initial charge on Mow-way'sqv camp at the North Fork of the Red River. A few days later he was twice wounded while saving Lt. Peter H. Boehm and another wounded man from the Comanches. Charlton participated in attacks on Kickapoo villages in Mexico with the Fourth Cavalry in early 1873. During the Red River Warqv he was a member of Lt. William A. Thompson's scouting party, which sighted tepees in

Palo Duro Canyon on September 27, 1874; Charlton won praise as a fighter in the ensuing battle of Palo Duro Canyon.qv In April 1875 he reenlisted at Fort Sill and accompanied the delegation under Dr. Jacob Sturm that induced Mow-way and Quanah Parkerqv to surrender to federal authorities. After that, Charlton trailed horse thieves and outlaws in Northwest Texas and the Indian Territory with Jack Stilwell, until, dissatisfied with army life and suffering from an abdominal rupture, he obtained his discharge in 1876.

He next began a freight service between Cheyenne and Deadwood, South Dakota, where he met Wild Bill Hickok, John Burwell (Texas Jack) Omohundro,qv and Buffalo Bill Cody. After the Meeker Massacre (1879), he was among civilian teamsters in Major Thornburg's cavalry column, which was ambushed by Utes at Milk Creek in western Wyoming and rescued after a six-day siege by Gen. Wesley Merritt. Charlton prospected in Alaska and South America, accompanied the Cole Circus as a horse trainer to Hawaii and Australia, and worked in Mexico as a grader for the Mexican Central Railroad. In 1884 he returned to Texas and settled in Brackettville as a stock raiser.

Officers of the Fourth Cavalry acknowledged Charlton's bravery, but he was never awarded the Medal of Honor. He wrote his memoirs in a series of letters to Lt. Robert G. Carter,qv who edited and in 1926 published them as *The Old Sergeant's Story*. Charlton married Letitia Walling in 1892 and later moved to Uvalde, where he spent his remaining years in failing health. He died of heart disease on March 5, 1922, and was buried in the old Post Cemetery at Fort Clark near Brackettville. His remains were later moved to Fort Sam Houston National Cemetery in San Antonio.

BIBLIOGRAPHY: Robert G. Carter, *On the Border with Mackenzie, or Winning West Texas from the Comanches* (Washington: Eynon Printing, 1935). Ernest Wallace, *Ranald S. Mackenzie on the Texas Frontier* (Lubbock: West Texas Museum Association, 1964).

H. Allen Anderson

CHARNWOOD INSTITUTE. Charnwood Institute was located at the corner of Fannin and Charnwood streets in Tyler. Professor John T. Hand, a Georgian, founded the boarding school in 1865 when he received a lease on Eastern Texas Female Collegeqv as partial payment for his services as president. He also acted as headmaster at Charnwood, which became coeducational after three years. The academic year was divided into two terms, one of four months and the other of six. This enabled the boys to harvest crops before the beginning of the fall term. Students from Smith and the adjoining counties attended, and enrollment was usually between sixty and seventy pupils. In 1868 the institute employed Professor Hand, Mary Spear, Mollie E. Moore (see DAVIS, MOLLIE E. M.), and Professor B. R. Lignoski. Other teachers included Madeline Oldham, Kate Walker, and Capt. Tom Smith. Hand served as president until 1874, when the school closed because of competition from other Tyler institutions. It reopened shortly thereafter as a girls' school, still named Charnwood Institute, and continued in operation until 1882.

BIBLIOGRAPHY: Vicki Betts, *Smith County, Texas, in the Civil War* (Tyler, Texas: Smith County Historical Society, 1978). Morris Burton, "Culture in the Cotton County," *Chronicles of Smith County*, Fall 1968. "The Miller House," *Chronicles of Smith County*, Spring 1964. Donald W. Whisenhunt, comp., *Chronological History of Smith County* (Tyler, Texas: Smith County Historical Society, 1983). Albert Woldert, *A History of Tyler and Smith County* (San Antonio: Naylor, 1948).

Carolyn Hyman

CHARQUITAS CREEK. Charquitas Creek rises five miles southwest of Lagarto in southeastern Live Oak County (at 28°04′ N, 97°59′ W) and runs east for four miles to its mouth on Lake Corpus Christi, four miles northwest of Sandia (at 28°04′ N, 97°55′ W). Its name is the diminutive of a Spanish word for pools of water. The surrounding terrain is flat with local shallow depressions and is surfaced by clay and sandy loams and occasional dark clays that support water-tolerant hardwoods, conifers, and grasses, with some mesquite, cacti, and brush along the creek's upper reaches.

CHARRERÍA. *Charrería*, the national sport of Mexico and a forerunner of the North American rodeo, originated among the Spanish conquistadors in the sixteenth century. *Charros*, or Mexican horsemen, adapted the equestrian contests of the Spaniards to produce a uniquely Mexican sport. By the nineteenth century these contests were essential elements of celebrations on large haciendas, especially those festivities celebrating the *herraderos* (brandings) and rodeos (round-ups). People came from miles around to take part in the celebrations and to watch *charros* exhibit their skills and compete against each other in daring competitions of horsemanship. *Charro* contests were also included at major fiestas and celebrations in Mexico, and single *charro* events, such as the *coleadero*, the forerunner of bulldogging or steer wrestling, were often used as holiday contests. It was at these fiestas and celebrations that Anglo-Texans first encountered and participated in the sport. *Charrería* was well known in Texas from the days of the republic, and by the 1860s such contests were included at Texas fairs. *Charrería* was also influenced by the *corridas*, or bullfights, in the *plazas de toros*, where the *coleaderos* and *jineteos de toros* (bull riding) were first popularized. *Charro* sports were included in the *corridas* through the nineteenth century, and this helps to explain the presence of bull riding, which is not a ranching chore, in both rodeo and *charrería*.

When the large haciendas in Mexico were divided as a result of the Mexican Revolution,qv *charros* feared the demise of the tradition, and so they called a *congreso* in Mexico City on July 4, 1921, and founded the Asociación Nacional de Charros. In 1933 the Federación Nacional de Charros was founded in Mexico City to govern the different *charro* associations that emerged, and in the late twentieth century this organization oversaw the *charro* associations in both Mexico and the United States. In order to compete in a *charreada*, or rodeo, all associations must be licensed by the federation, and competitors must be certified as *charros*. There are presently over 100 *charro* associations in the United States. Texas *charro* associations exist in Houston, San Antonio, Austin, and El Paso.

The differences between rodeo and *charrería* have developed since the 1920s; before then, athletes from Mexico, the United States, and Canada competed in all three countries with no problems regarding rules or eligibility. One outstanding difference between the contemporary rodeo and *charrería* is that rodeo is an individual sport, while *charrería* is a team sport. The *charreadas* are performed in a *lienzo*, or arena, which has two principal areas: one is sixty meters long and twelve meters wide, and the second is a circular area with a diameter of forty meters. Unlike the rodeo competitor, the *charro* does not compete for prize money but rather for the honor of the sport.

The *charreada* is highly ritualized, and the events follow a traditional sequence. The competition usually begins with a military march, or the "Marcha Zacatecas," played by a mariachi band. A procession follows, with representatives of the different *charro* associations riding horseback around the *lienzo* carrying flags and banners; they are followed by the president of the state *charro* association, the members of the competing teams, and perhaps a "*charro* queen." Once the opening ceremony is completed, the *cala de caballo*, the first of nine separate competitions, begins. During this event, the equivalent of dressage in traditional equestrian competition, judges evaluate the rider's control of the horse. The *charro* gallops from the end of the *lienzo* to the middle of the arena, where he must rein in his horse within a marked area twenty meters wide by six meters long. He must also lead the horse in right and left turns and in backward movements.

The second event is the *piale en lienzo*, during which three *charros* attempt to rope the hind legs of a horse, steer, or bull. The third event is the *coleadero*, sometimes called *colear* or *el coleo*. There are at least eight different methods of accomplishing this feat, but the classic move requires the *charro* to ride up, grab the bull by the tail, pass the tail under the *charro's* right leg, and make a sharp right angle turn, thereby flipping the bull on its back.

The fourth competition is the *jineteo de toros,* or bull-riding, during which the *charro* must ride the bull until it stops bucking. During *la terna,* which is the equivalent of team roping in a North American rodeo, riders must rope a calf as quickly as possible, one from the neck and the other from the hind legs. The *jineteo de yeguas* is bronco-riding. The seventh and eighth events are the *piales* and the *manganas,* where the *charro,* either on foot or on horseback, must rope the hind legs and the forelegs of a running mare and pull it off balance. The final event is considered the most difficult, the *paso de la muerte* or "death pass," where the *charro* rides his tame horse bareback and attempts to jump onto a wild horse and ride it until it stops bucking.

A *charro* may compete in only three events in the state or national competitions; only one individual from each association may compete in all events, and he is known as the *charro completo.* Competitors are judged for style as well as execution. *Charrería* is predominantly a male sport; women perform in only one event, the *escaramuza* (skirmish). *Escaramuza* teams consist of sixteen women who perform precision patterns while riding sidesaddle, often to musical accompaniment. This event is traditionally held at the conclusion of the *charreada. See also* RODEOS.

BIBLIOGRAPHY: *Charrería: The National Sport of Mexico* (photocopy, Benson Latin American Collection, University of Texas at Austin, 1970). Leovigildo Islas Escarcega, "Historical Synthesis of Charrería," *Artes de México,* 1967. Mary Lou LeCompte, "The Hispanic Influence on the History of Rodeo, 1823–1922," *Journal of Sport History* 12 (Spring 1985). Alfonso Rincón Gallardo, "Contemporary Charrería," *Artes de México,* 1967. Joe Torres, *La Charreada,* December 16, 1975 (videotape, Benson Latin American Collection, University of Texas at Austin). Maximo Vigil, "Mexican American Women Excel: La Charreada," *La Luz,* November 1978.

María-Cristina García

CHARRO DAYS. Charro Days is an annual four-day pre-Lenten celebration held in Brownsville in cooperation with Matamoros, Tamaulipas. The fiesta was organized in 1937 by the Brownsville Chamber of Commerce to recognize Mexican culture and was named Charro Days in honor of the *charros,* "dashing Mexican gentlemen cowboys." To encourage the wearing of regional costumes of Mexico, a booklet of patterns for Charro Days was issued in 1949. It features drawings of women's and men's traditional apparel from Michoacán, Oaxaca, Yucatán, and Chiapas, as well as other regions of the country. The *china poblana* dress and the *charro* suit are among the most popular costumes worn during Charro Days. The festival begins with the traditional Mexican *grito* (celebratory cry) at the Gateway International Bridge and with an exchange of words and gifts by the mayors of both cities. Since the earliest Charro Days fiesta, the celebrations have included parades complete with floats, as well as street dances, a rodeo, mariachi and marimba concerts, and ballet folklorico performances by school students. The festival has become very popular, and a Charro Days Fiesta organization has been established to oversee the extensive program, which includes several days of events.

BIBLIOGRAPHY: Robert B. Vezzetti and Ruby A. Wooldridge, *Brownsville: A Pictorial History* (Virginia Beach, Virginia: Donning, 1982). *With Furbelos and Buttons and Bows: Make Your Costume Now for Charro Days Fiesta* (Brownsville, Texas: Brownsville *Herald* and the Printcraft Shop, 1949). *Teresa Palomo Acosta*

CHARRO INDIANS. Charro is the Spanish name for an otherwise unidentified group of Indians represented at San Antonio de Valero Mission[qv] in San Antonio.

BIBLIOGRAPHY: Herbert Eugene Bolton, *Texas in the Middle Eighteenth Century: Studies in Spanish Colonial History and Administration* (Berkeley: University of California Press, 1915; rpt., Austin: University of Texas Press, 1970).

Thomas N. Campbell

CHASE, IRA CARLTON (1868–1933). Ira Carlton Chase, physician, was born in Oberlin, Ohio, on August 16, 1868, the son of Edwin R. and Malvina (Dayton) Chase. He was educated in the public schools of Flint, Michigan, and received a bachelor's degree from Oberlin College (1891), where he was associate editor of the Oberlin *Review* in 1890–91. In 1891 Chase was employed by the YMCA, which he served as physical director at Tyler, Texas, and then at Denison as general secretary. He taught physics and chemistry at Fort Worth University in 1893. The following year he became professor of chemistry and toxicology, assisted in the organization of the medical department of Fort Worth University, and was the first secretary of the faculty. In 1899 he received a medical degree from Bellevue Hospital Medical College in New York City. He then established a private practice in Fort Worth and continued teaching as professor of anatomy at Fort Worth Medical College. He was elected secretary of the Texas State Medical Association (*see* TEXAS MEDICAL ASSOCIATION) in 1904 and became the first editor in chief of the *Texas State Journal of Medicine* when it was established in 1905. Chase continued in these roles until 1910, when he went to Europe for two years for postgraduate training. Afterwards he served as dean of Fort Worth Medical College until that school merged with the medical department of Baylor University in Dallas in 1918. During World War I[qv] Chase served as chairman of the Council on National Defense, Medical Section, for Texas. He edited the *Texas Medical State Journal* through the war. Also during this time he served as contract surgeon for the Canadian government, in charge of the injured from three air fields near Fort Worth.

Chase exercised several official roles in professional societies. In 1920 he became the fifty-third president of the Texas State Medical Association. He served several terms as a Texas delegate to American Medical Association meetings (1910, 1918, and 1919), and he was a member of the Judicial Council of the AMA (1919–25). He became a fellow of the American College of Surgeons in 1915. He was active in establishing licensure and public policies for Texas, and he was acknowledged as an outstanding community leader in Fort Worth. The Exchange Club selected him as the city's Most Outstanding Citizen in 1932. This honor specifically referred to Chase's advocacy of the city council form of government for Fort Worth. Chase died of cancer at his home in Fort Worth on June 20, 1933. He was survived by two sons.

BIBLIOGRAPHY: Fort Worth *Star-Telegram,* June 21, 1933. *Texas State Journal of Medicine,* August 1933. *Chester R. Burns*

CHATAIGNON, MARIUS STEPHEN (1886-1957). Marius Stephen Chataignon, pastor of Sacred Heart Church in Galveston and United States Army chaplain, was born on September 17, 1886, in Cellieu, Loire, France, the son of Étienne and Benoîte (Cancade) Chataignon. He served in the French army and had an outstanding military career. He traveled to America in 1906 and studied for the priesthood at St. Joseph Seminary in Baltimore and then St. Mary's Seminary in La Porte, Texas. He was ordained on December 24, 1911, at St. Mary's Cathedral, Galveston,[qv] and was assigned as an assistant there the next day. He left the cathedral in 1917 and entered the army as a chaplain, then returned 1919 and became rector in 1924.

He again served as chaplain overseas from 1930 until 1945 and emerged at the end of the conflict as a full colonel, a rank infrequently bestowed on chaplains. Francis Joseph Cardinal Spellman of New York wrote of him in 1945, "I regard him as perhaps the best Chaplain in the whole Army." Chataignon was awarded the Legion of Merit by Gen. Dwight D. Eisenhower[qv] for services as corps chaplain in North Africa and Sicily. He also held the Cross of Merit from the

Italian government, the Distinguished Service cross, and the Bronze Star. He was affectionately called "Father Chat."

Father Chat was the first American to say Mass in St. Peter's Basilica after the occupation and led so many Americans to papal audiences that the pope began to recognize him and single him out in later visits. When the Bronze Star was awarded him in 1944, he was commended for performing "a highly important liaison mission with Vatican officials with a high degree of tact, integrity and wisdom." After the war Chataignon returned to Sacred Heart parish in Galveston, where he died on November 18, 1957. He is buried in Mount Olivet Cemetery in Dickson. He was survived by a sister, Mary Louise.

BIBLIOGRAPHY: Catholic Archives of Texas, Files, Austin.

Mary Ann Acosta

CHATFIELD, TEXAS. Chatfield is eleven miles northeast of Corsicana in northeastern Navarro County. It is named for Champion Chatfield, a pioneer who in 1838 established a trading post in an oak grove six miles west of Porter's Bluff; this was the future townsite of Chatfield. The trading post was on the San Antonio and Shreveport Trail and drew settlers to the area before the Civil War.qv Robert Hodge arrived in the area in 1849 and was reported to own more than 1,280 acres and 100 slaves. Chatfield was a center for the cause of secessionqv by the mid-1850s, when the community had a private school, a horse-powered gin, cotton and wool mills, a flour mill, a machine shop, a cemetery, and several churches—Disciples of Christ, Methodist, and Baptist. The community shipped cotton and grain. A Chatfield post office was established in 1867. The community's population reached 250 in 1885, and in 1887 its private school was replaced by a public school. The Elizabeth Institute, a preparatory and boarding school, was established there in 1896. By 1906 Chatfield had two public schools—one with two teachers and 105 white students and one with one teacher and 101 black students. Chatfield reached its peak in the 1890s, when it had a population of 500 and a daily stage to Rice, six miles away. In 1939 the community had a population of 300 and seven businesses, but its population subsequently declined. The local public school closed in 1951. Chatfield's population fell from 100 in 1954 to forty in 1990, when the community had a post office, a store, a volunteer fire department, a water supply company, the Methodist church, and two cemeteries.

BIBLIOGRAPHY: Wyvonne Putman, comp., *Navarro County History* (5 vols., Quanah, Texas: Nortex, 1975–84).

Todd Gantt

CHATMAN, JOSEPH ALVIN (1901–1967). Joseph Alvin Chatman, black physician and civic leader, was born on May 28, 1901, in Navasota, Texas, the youngest of five children of Sandy and Sally (Greer) Chatman. He attended public schools and was a seasonal cottonpicker at Mexia. At eighteen he was admitted to Prairie View Agricultural and Mechanical College (now Prairie View A&M University), where he played football and led an undefeated baseball team. Chatman then attended Fisk University in Nashville, Tennessee, where he took premed courses and remained on the honor roll despite heavy participation on both the varsity football and baseball teams. In 1926 he received an M.D. from Meharry Medical College in Nashville, Tennessee, third in his class. He began his medical career in Mexia, Texas, where he built the Chatman Hospital. He also published and coedited a weekly, *Open Forum*. He organized an insurance company, helped to establish a County Negro Fair, and was secretary of the Negro Chamber of Commerce. He received a bachelor of science degree in 1927 from Samuel Huston College (now Huston-Tillotson College) in Austin.

Chatman moved to Lubbock in 1939 and there founded the Chatman Medical and Surgical Clinic and Hospital, the first hospital for African Americans in Lubbock, completed in 1945. Nurses' quarters and quarters for ambulatory patients were added later. Chatman was active in state, local, and national medical organizations and was elected Lubbock "Man of the Year" for six consecutive years, until the award was discontinued. He was a member of the building committee for Lubbock City Hall, and his name is engraved on the building. He was an active volunteer for many years in the Community Chest, later the United Fund, and the March of Dimes. He fostered activities of the Negro Boys Club and was chairman of the board of directors. He also served as presiding judge of Precinct Eleven. He was a member of the Knights of Pythias and Masonic lodges and a devoted member and district trustee of the Methodist Episcopal Church, where he served on the Hospital and Homes Committee for the Northwestern Area. Governor Price Danielqv appointed Chatman in 1960 to the President's White House Conference on Youth and in 1964 to the Conference on the Aged. In 1955 Chatman was awarded an honorary doctor of humanities degree by Paul Quinn College and was the alumni speaker. In 1956 he received an achievement award from Prairie View A&M University and again served as an alumni speaker. On March 23, 1963, he was appointed by Governor John Connallyqv to serve on the board of directors of Texas Southern University, Houston, where he was chairman of the building committee.

Chatman was an ardent Democrat. He was the first black to be an official in the Democratic partyqv in Lubbock County and served as a delegate to the state Democratic convention. In 1963 at a testimonial dinner given by the Interdenominational Ministerial Alliance to honor Chatman as "a man of deeds," prominent Democrats sending congratulatory messages included Vice President Lyndon B. Johnson,qv Governor John Connally, Lieutenant Governor Preston Smith, and United States Representative George H. Mahon.qv Chatman was the author of various publications, including *History of Negroes in Limestone County* (1939) and *The Lone Star State Medical, Dental, and Pharmaceutical Association History* (1959). He married Ruth Morton on June 1, 1927; she died in December 1935. He married Emmalene Phea on May 2, 1955, and they had four sons. Chatman died on January 12, 1967, and was buried in the City of Lubbock Cemetery.

BIBLIOGRAPHY: Joseph Alvin Chatman Papers, Southwest Collection, Texas Tech University. Lubbock *Avalanche-Journal*, January 13, 1967.

Jeanne F. Lively

CHATT, TEXAS. Chatt is off Interstate Highway 35 some four miles south of Hillsboro in central Hill County. It apparently was established about 1884, when it was named Jessie for Jessie McClure, a pioneer settler who built and operated a general merchandise store there. A two-story school was built on land donated by W. A. Ficklin in 1896. By the 1905–06 academic year the school had sixty-eight students and two teachers. A post office operated in the community from 1896 to 1910. The town apparently adopted the new name Chatt sometime after the tracks of the Missouri, Kansas and Texas Railroad arrived, because the line already passed through another Texas town called Jessie. Chatt was identified on the 1984 county highway map, but only a cemetery was shown at the site.

BIBLIOGRAPHY: Hill County Historical Commission, *A History of Hill County, Texas, 1853–1980* (Waco: Texian, 1980).

Brian Hart

CHAUTAUQUA, TEXAS. Chautauqua was on the Texas and Pacific Railway, five miles east of Baird in northeast Callahan County. The town was established around 1900 and by 1915 had a population of 125. A post office was opened on July 23, 1907, with William T. White as postmaster. It was discontinued on April 30, 1914. By 1936 Chautauqua was not marked on maps.

BIBLIOGRAPHY: Brutus Clay Chrisman, *Early Days in Callahan County* (Abilene, Texas: Abilene Printing and Stationery, 1966).

John G. Johnson

CHAYOPIN INDIANS. The aboriginal homeland of the Chayopins has not been positively identified. They seem to have been first recorded under the name Cayupin by Juan Bautista Chapa,[qv] an early historian of Nuevo León who died in 1695. Although Chapa connected them with the northern part of Nuevo León, he failed to mention whether the Cayupins were native to Nuevo León or lived north of the Rio Grande and raided southward into Mexico. For the Texas area no documents refer to the Chayopins until San José y San Miguel de Aguayo Mission was established at San Antonio in 1720. The earliest reference to a Texas location for the Chayopins appears in a document of 1737. This and several later documents indicate that they were from an area southeast of San Antonio, lying mainly between the lower courses of the Nueces and San Antonio rivers, apparently in the general vicinity of modern Bee County. As no early French and Spanish travelers in Texas referred to encounters with Chayopins, and no Chayopins were ever recorded for northern Tamaulipas, it is possible that Chapa's Cayupins, along with other refugees from the northern frontier of Nuevo León, moved into the Bee County area in the early part of the eighteenth century.

Chayopin individuals and families are known to have entered at least three of the five Spanish missions of San Antonio. The documentary record, however, is limited, and it is difficult to extract much precise information. It is evident that initially the Chayopins were dissatisfied with the restrictions of mission life, for they sometimes deserted a mission to return to their home grounds. Reliable figures cannot be given for the number of Chayopins who went to each of the three missions, or for the number who remained in their homeland and never entered missions at San Antonio or elsewhere. Although the recorded evidence is none too clear, it appears that some Chayopin entered San José Mission not long after it was established at San Antonio in 1720, but they soon deserted this mission. Just when they deserted, or for what reasons, remains unknown. Apparently no Chayopins ever returned to this mission. A document of 1743 names the Chayopins as one of the nine Indian groups represented at Nuestra Señora de la Purísima Concepción de Acuña Mission when it was established in 1731. Just how many Chayopins came to this mission is unknown, but probably not many, since the Concepción marriage register, the only register that has survived, identifies only two Chayopin individuals (entries for 1745–46). Most of the Chayopin who entered missions seem to have been associated with San Juan Capistrano Mission. It is clear that Chayopins arrived at this mission sometime between 1731 and 1737. In 1738 all of them deserted the mission and returned to their former home in southern Texas. One document mentions that the Chayopin and Venado Indians, who both deserted at the same time, numbered over 150. In 1762 it was recorded that the principal Indian groups at San Juan Capistrano were Chayopin, Orejón, Pamaque, and Piguique, which all together consisted of fifty-one families with a total population of 203. Some Chayopins seem to have remained at San Juan Capistrano until the mission was secularized in 1794. One Chayopin individual, a young man of San Juan Capistrano known as Andrés, went to Nuestra Señora de la Candelaria Mission when it was founded in 1749 on the San Gabriel River in what is now Milam County, some forty-five miles northeast of Austin. At Mission Candelaria Andrés served as cook for the two missionaries. In 1752, one of the missionaries, Fray Juan José Ganzabal, was killed, and Andrés was charged with murder. The case was complex because the presidential commander, Capt. Felipe de Rábago y Terán, who had quarreled with the missionaries, was implicated. Neither the commander nor Andrés was ever convicted. During a lengthy investigation Andrés was taken to Coahuila, and it appears that he spent the remainder of his life at a Spanish mission near Monclova.

In 1769 two Indian men, one a Chayopin, the other an Apache, were imprisoned for theft in San Antonio. These men escaped from their cell and took refuge in a room where guns and ammunition were stored. Both were killed in a long gunfight with Spanish soldiers. The Chayopin was evidently from one of the San Antonio missions, probably San Juan Capistrano, for he was given Christian burial. The corpse of the Apache was hung in a tree outside of town. In the second half of the eighteenth century the name Chayopin was given to the San Antonio–La Bahía road crossing of the San Antonio River northwest of the site of present Floresville (Wilson County), and several nearby ranches had names that included the word Chayopin. These place names were frequently mentioned in travel documents of that period. In 1760 Fray Bartolomé García published a manual for use in administering church ritual in the Coahuilteco language. According to him, the Chayopins spoke this language. Though this has led most scholars to classify the Chayopin as Coahuilteco-speakers, linguists have recently asked whether the Chayopins spoke Coahuilteco before entering the San Antonio missions. This problem cannot be resolved unless a pre-mission sample of Chayopin speech is found in some heretofore unknown European document. Nothing was ever recorded about Chayopin culture.

Some confusion surrounds recognizable variants of the name Chayopin. A statement made by one missionary at San Antonio indicated that the names Chayopin and Tiopin refer to the same Indian group. Chayopin has sometimes been mistakenly equated with the names Tiopan and Sayupan, both variants of the name Siupam, which refers to an Indian group distinct from the Chayopins. Apparently because of the similarity in the names, the Chayopins have been confused with the Choyopans, a poorly recorded subdivision of the Tonkawa Indians. As yet no documentary evidence has been found that shows Chayopin and Choyopin to be names for the same people, and there is no basis for relating the Chayopins to the Tonkawas.

BIBLIOGRAPHY: Herbert E. Bolton, "The Founding of the Missions on the San Gabriel River, 1745–1749," *Southwestern Historical Quarterly* 17 (April 1914). Lyle Campbell and Marianne Mithune, eds., *The Languages of Native America: Historical and Comparative Assessment* (Austin: University of Texas Press, 1979). T. N. Campbell, "Coahuiltecans and Their Neighbors," in *Handbook of North American Indians,* Vol. 10 (Washington: Smithsonian Institution, 1983). Carlos E. Castañeda, *Our Catholic Heritage in Texas* (7 vols., Austin: Von Boeckmann–Jones, 1936–58; rpt., New York: Arno, 1976). Bartholomé García, comp., *Manual para admiministrar los santos sacramentos* (Mexico City, 1760). Marion A. Habig, *The Alamo Chain of Missions* (Chicago: Franciscan Herald Press, 1968; rev. ed. 1976). Frederick Webb Hodge, ed., *Handbook of American Indians North of Mexico* (2 vols., Washington: GPO, 1907, 1910; rpt., New York: Pageant, 1959). Alonso de León et al., *Historia de Nuevo León* (Monterrey: Centro de Estudios Humanísticos de la Universidad de Nuevo León, 1961). Proceedings for the Investigation of the Murder at San Xavier of Father Francisco Joseph Ganzábal and Juan Joseph Zains de Zeballos, February 21–September 30, 1752, Bexar Archives Translations, Vol. 24, Barker Texas History Center, University of Texas at Austin. M. K. Schuetz, "An Historical Outline of Mission San Juan de Capistrano," *La Tierra: Quarterly Journal of the Southern Texas Archaeological Association* 7 (1980). Robert S. Weddle and Robert H. Thonhoff, *Drama and Conflict: The Texas Saga of 1776* (Austin: Madrona, 1976).
Thomas N. Campbell

CHEAPSIDE, TEXAS. Cheapside is on Ranch Road 2067 twenty-one miles southeast of Gonzales in south central Gonzales County. The first settler to establish permanent residence there was Thomas Baker (1822–84), who moved to Gonzales County from the Natchez District of Mississippi and built a log cabin in the area in 1857. He was followed by several families whose forebears were immigrants from England. One of these settlers, Thomas Carter, laid out the town plat in lots ninety feet wide, except for the corner lots, which were ninety-five feet wide. The plat was destroyed by a fire without having been recorded. Dr. E. R. Henry, a local physician of English descent who was born in Cheapside, Virginia, named the settlement. The first post office for Cheapside was established on June 5, 1882, in DeWitt County, but it was moved a mile to the west, inside the Gonzales county line, in 1890 or 1891.

In its early years the economy of the Cheapside area was basically agricultural, with a heavy emphasis on cotton but including livestock, poultry, and grain. A combination cotton gin–gristmill was built by E. F. Elder in 1889 and sold in the same year to H. N. Smith. At one time the town had a broom factory, three grocery and general stores, a drugstore, a confectionery, a blacksmith shop, a hotel, a barbershop, and at least two saloons, complete with a resident deputy sheriff to keep order. The Masonic and Woodmen of the World lodges both maintained meeting halls. From about 1890 to 1913, A. T. Young ran a private school on Fulcher Creek. The Cheapside public school, during its heyday, offered grades one through nine and had from 120 to 135 students with three teachers. Local teams competed with those from nearby communities in baseball games and calf and goat roping. A Delco plant, installed in 1925, provided electricity for the two stores and four homes in the community until rural electrification arrived in 1939. The Cumberland Presbyterian Church was organized in 1874 at Bellevue and later moved to Cheapside. The Cheapside Baptist Church was organized in 1893. Bellevue Cemetery, two miles south, was established in 1876 and continues to serve the people of the rural community under the management of the Bellevue Cemetery Association. Its 325 marked graves hold the remains of veterans of every declared American war from the Civil War qv to the present.

With the coming of the Great Depression qv of the 1930s, cotton was no longer a profitable crop. In the 1940s the Cheapside gin was closed, and most of the farmland reverted to open pasture. By 1941 decreases in enrollment had reduced the school to a seven-grade, one-teacher school; and in 1949, with only eight students remaining, the school was consolidated with the Cuero Independent School District. By 1960 only one commercial business remained in Cheapside—a small grocery store operated by Joe Watson, who had purchased it from Earl L. Freeman in 1958. A fourth-class postal service occupied part of the store and helped it to survive. In February 1989 the Watson store closed and the post office with it. In 1990 the interdenominational Cheapside Community Church still held services every Sunday, the Cheapside Home Demonstration Club held regular meetings on the third Monday of every month, and the Cheapside Community Center, converted from an old schoolhouse, was still the site of frequent showers, suppers, and post-funeral gatherings. Former students of the Cheapside school held an annual reunion in June. The population of Cheapside stood at 150 in 1904, but it declined during the middle years of the century; from 1972 to 1989 a figure of thirty-one was regularly recorded.

BIBLIOGRAPHY: Margaret Briscoe, "Cheapside," *Junior Historian,* January 1950. Gonzales County Historical Commission, *History of Gonzales County* (Dallas: Curtis, 1986). Vertical Files, Barker Texas History Center, University of Texas at Austin. *W. Lamar Fly*

CHEEK, JAMES BRUCE (1895–1970). James Bruce Cheek, architect, was born on February 19, 1895, in Hillsboro, Texas, the only child of Bruce and Lenni Cheek. He moved to Dallas at the age of five and spent most of his life there. He enrolled in the University of Texas in 1913 but left to serve in the United States Navy during World War I.qv After the war he did not return to school, but began an apprenticeship with H. B. Thomson in 1918. Thomson designed robustly scaled, eclectic houses for Dallas gentry. Cheek had a hand in many of Thomson's best-known commissions from 1918 to 1920, particularly those along Swiss Avenue and in Highland Park. During the apprenticeship Cheek met Marion F. Fooshee,qv who become his partner about 1920, when they apparently opened an office in Wichita Falls. By 1925 they had returned to Dallas and established a small practice at 1901½ Harwood Street, now the site of the Dallas Museum of Art.qv They worked independently on small commissions but collaborated on larger work. Cheek designed numerous houses, mostly in Dallas, but also in Corsicana, Terrell, Tyler, and Wichita Falls. Always eclectic, much of his work was characterized by rich, well-crafted Spanish designs.

Fooshee and Cheek's nonresidential work included shopping centers, motels, gas stations, and participation in several buildings at Fair Park,qv including the Hall of State,qv the Aquarium, and the United States Federal Exhibits Building. While the exact nature of Cheek's participation in many of the firm's projects is unclear (with the exception of the Federal Exhibits Building, where he is individually credited as the associate architect), he was the primary creative force behind Highland Park Village qv (1929) in Highland Park, the first self-contained shopping center in the United States. Cheek and the developer, Hugh Prather, made trips to southern California, South Texas, and the 1929 World Exposition in Barcelona to study Spanish architecture. This, combined with the knowledge gained from studying and visiting Country Club Plaza in Kansas City, made both men unusually well prepared to invent a new building type, which received national attention when designed. Cheek was also a talented watercolorist and studied under the Dallas painter Charles Frank Reaugh.qv He was a childhood friend of muralist Reveau Bassett, whom he commissioned to work on several buildings, including the Highland Park Village Theater. During World War II,qv when private construction was halted, Cheek obtained appointment as architectural supervisor for the Federal Housing Administration. His area of responsibility encompassed Texas, New Mexico, Arkansas, Louisiana, and Oklahoma. He was a member and served as president of the Idlewild Club and was also a member of the Terpsichorean Club. In 1939 Cheek married Mary V. (Pat) Murphy. They had two daughters. He was a member of Highland Park Presbyterian Church and the American Institute of Architects. He practiced until the mid-1960s and died in Dallas on March 30, 1970. During the last twenty years of his life he designed many private vaults at Hillcrest Mausoleum. He is buried on its grounds in Hillcrest Memorial Park.

BIBLIOGRAPHY: *Architectural Record,* September 1931. Dallas *Morning News,* April 1, 1970. Duncan T. Fulton III, "Fooshee and Cheek," *Texas Architect,* November–December 1989. Anita Towes, "Spanish Colonial Revival Architecture in Dallas: The Work of Fooshee and Cheek," *Perspective* 13 (1984). *Duncan T. Fulton III*

CHEEK, TEXAS. Cheek is on State Highway 124 seven miles southwest of Beaumont in central Jefferson County. In 1906 it was laid out by and named for J. R. Cheek. The community was on the Gulf and Interstate Railway and was inhabited largely by rice farmers who used the Beaumont Irrigating Company's canal, which cut through Cheek and irrigated the surrounding farms. By 1925 Cheek's population was estimated to be forty. Although Cheek remained an identifiable community, its proximity to Beaumont probably reduced the number of services available at the site. Its post office was discontinued in 1928. The Cheek Common School District, organized in 1907 and bolstered by the construction in 1939 of a new school building by the Public Works Administration (*see* GREAT DEPRESSION), was consolidated with the South Park Independent School District of Beaumont in 1951. By the 1970s a large Goodyear chemical plant was nearby. The community reported a population of sixty-two in 1990.
Robert Wooster

CHEESELAND, TEXAS. Cheeseland was in northern Angelina County. Jacob Ferguson Humphrey, a native of Wales, moved to the site in 1844 and built a log cabin and stockade to protect his family and horses. The mail road from Alto to Homer and Rusk ran in front of Humphrey's house. On August 8, 1854, a post office opened with Humphrey as postmaster; the post office was closed on August 4, 1860. Before the Civil War,qv the Humphrey family grew lonely and offered Wenzel Hillenkamp and his family a free thirty-acre tract of land across the road. Hillenkamp, who had come from Prussia with his wife, Caroline, to escape a three-year period of compulsory military training, built a combination house, coach station, and post office and a whiskey and general store. At the store he sold Mrs. Hillenkamp's cheese, from which the settlement took its name, though it has been claimed that the original cheesemaker in the area was from the North. On November 10, 1860, the post office was reestablished with Hillenkamp as postmaster and named Cheeseland. Hillenkamp remained postmaster until he was removed by Reconstruction;[qv] he was reinstated in 1873. In the interim Martha Buckalew served as postmistress. After his reinstatement, Hillenkamp served until 1886, when the post office and store were moved to Wells in Cherokee County. The Humphreys continued to live at Cheeseland, and John Gill Humphrey, the only son of Jacob, took increasing responsibility for the blacksmith shop and farm. The Hillenkamps all died or moved away after the post office was moved to Wells.

BIBLIOGRAPHY: John N. Cravens, *Between Two Rivers: A History of Wells, Texas* (Wichita Falls: Humphrey Printing, 1974). John N. Cravens, *A History of Three Ghost Towns of East Texas* (Abilene, Texas: Abilene Printing and Stationery, 1970?).

John N. Cravens

CHEETHAM, TEXAS. Cheetham was on U.S. Highway 90A and the San Antonio and Aransas Pass Railway a mile east of Sheridan and twenty miles southwest of Columbus in west central Colorado County. The community was founded during the late 1880s as a station on the San Antonio and Aransas Pass line. In 1888 a post office, named Cheetham for the first postmaster, John A. Cheetham, was opened there. By 1890 the community comprised an estimated 150 inhabitants, and cordwood was the main product shipped from its railroad station. The next year a school was operating at Cheetham, and in 1896 the town was platted and recorded. The one-teacher Cheetham school served forty-seven pupils in 1904. Around 1906 speculators promoted the town to midwestern farmers, but Cheetham did not grow. In 1908 its post office was transferred to nearby Sheridan; it remained there until 1912, when the Cheetham office was reopened. Cheetham in 1914 had seventy-five inhabitants as well as a general store and Baptist and Methodist Episcopal churches. In 1920 the community once more lost its post office, and it appears to have gradually declined thereafter. It was no longer named on the county highway map by 1940. In 1981 all that remained of the community was a cemetery; the railroad line had long been abandoned.

BIBLIOGRAPHY: Colorado County Historical Commission, *Colorado County Chronicles from the Beginning to 1923* (2 vols., Austin: Nortex, 1986).

Mark Odintz

CHEISA, TEXAS. Cheisa was near the intersection of Cheisa Road and the Missouri, Kansas and Texas Railroad tracks, three miles southeast of Rowlett and ten miles northeast of downtown Dallas in northeastern Dallas County. It was named for John Cheisa, who settled in the area on Duck Creek before 1848. A store was moved from Rowlett to the Cheisa farm in the late 1880s, when the Missouri, Kansas and Texas line was built through the area. Cheisa was a railroad community by 1892; it had a switch on the railroad and eventually received a station. Its population was twenty-five in 1915, and it had twenty residents from the mid-1930s to the mid-1940s, after which no population statistics were available. In the 1980s the former townsite was within the city limits of Rowlett.

BIBLIOGRAPHY: Daniel Hardy, *Dallas County Historic Resource Survey* (Dallas: Dallas County Historical Commission, 1982).

Lisa C. Maxwell

CHEMICAL INDUSTRIES. Though "chemical industries," broadly defined, would include such industries as cement production, the sulfur industry, the cottonseed industry, the salt industry, and the oil and gas industry[qqv] the term is here considered as applying to those industries engaged in the production of chemical compounds most of which find industrial use directly or by further conversion. The production of chemicals in Texas makes up the largest manufacturing industry in the state. Chemical industries did not get a significant beginning in Texas until World War I.[qv] After a brief recession at the end of the war, the industry rose steadily until by 1925 state production figures showed that the value added by manufacture through chemical processes reached a total for the year of $1,126,000. Chemical production, exclusive of oil, salt, gas, and food industries, was the twenty-eighth ranking Texas industry. Legislative grants made in 1937 and 1938 to the Bureau of Industrial Chemistry at the University of Texas were repaid by the discovery of a number of new processes for the chemical utilization of Texas raw materials. Between 1939 and 1949 more than $750 million was invested in chemical plants in the state. During World War II[qv] with the development of petrochemical units to produce synthetic rubber and other strategic materials, the industry saw its biggest growth in the shortest period of time. After 1950 the enormous proliferation of the industry placed it first among all Texas manufactures in value added. Capital investment for new chemical-manufacturing plants and equipment totaled about $457 million in 1965—more than 40 percent of all new manufacturing investment in the state. In 1989 capital expenditures for the chemical and petrochemical industry accounted for 51 percent of manufacturing investment in the state.

In the United States Census Bureau's classification Chemicals and Allied Products, the number of production workers in Texas increased from 6,847 in 1939 to 17,475 in 1947. A total of 433 establishments was included in this classification, and the value added by manufacturing in 1947 was given as $234,496,000. In 1968 the Texas chemical industry employed more than 60,000 workers, mostly in the coastal area. The Houston vicinity, including Freeport, Bay City, and Texas City, had the heaviest concentration of plants. Second in size was the chemical industry of Beaumont–Port Arthur–Orange. Other major centers near the coast were Brownsville, Corpus Christi, Victoria, and Seadrift. Total chemical-plant investment in 1968 within a 150-mile radius of Houston was estimated at $7 billion. Inland centers of chemical production during the 1960s included Big Spring, Borger, Denver City, Longview, Odessa, and Pampa.

Historically, the principal growth of the chemical industry has been along the Gulf coast, but during the 1940s there were plants engaging in the production of soap and edible oils, sulfuric acid, and various synthetic catalysts in the Dallas area, while in the Laredo area antimony metal and antimony oxide were produced (*see* ANTIMONY SMELTER). In the 1990s, the industry continued to be concentrated on the coast and employed more than 116,000 people in 1992. Inland plants operated in Borger, Longview, and Midland. Chemical products accounted for 24 percent of the value of all manufacturing shipments in Texas, according to a 1989 survey. Producers of chemicals also led the state in paying the highest hourly wages. Workers in both petrochemical and chemical plants averaged between $16.92 and $18.69 an hour.

In the Brownsville area after World War II[qv] Carthage Hydrocol Company produced high-octane gasoline, alcohols, and other oxygenated materials. The Corpus Christi area also had a number of plants producing acetic acid, formic acid, and formaldehyde (Hoechst Celanese Corporation of America); soda ash, caustic soda, and chlorine from local salts and oyster shells (Southern Alkali Corporation); and corn starch, oils, and other corn products from milo maize. A $52 million plant for the production of electrolytic zinc and cadmium was also located in the Corpus Christi area, and near Port Lavaca ALCOA ran a large plant converting bauxite to aluminum by an electrolytic process. In the 1950s Wharton County sulfur production (Texasgulf[qv] and others) was the largest in the world (*see* SULFUR INDUSTRY). During the 1930s Dow Chemical Company invested more than $100 million in facilities at Freeport for a wide range of chemical production. The only tin smelter (*see* TIN SMELTING) in North America was located in Texas City, as was a carbon black manufacturing company. Monsanto Chemical Company, which operated out of Texas City originally, currently has plants in Alvin near Chocolate Bayou. Immediately after World War II a large variety of chemical industrial plants in the Houston area produced hydrocyanic acid, phosphate fertilizers, electrolytic chlorine, and caustic soda (Diamond Alkali–Diamond Shamrock qv), anhydrous hydrofluoric acid, sulphuric acid, and superphosphate fertilizers, hydrochloric acid and bone black, freon, phenathiazin, and DDT (DuPont-Grasselli Division), and ammonium sulphate (Phillips Chemical Company, a subsidiary of Phillips Petroleum). Shell Chemical Company also built and operated a $50 million plant for diversified chemical and petroleum products and research. At Baytown in conjunction with Humble Oil and Refining Company (now Exxon Company, U.S.A.qv), the largest petroleum refinery in the United States at the time, there was a toluene plant and a butyl rubber polymerization plant. In this area also General Tire and Rubber operated a large synthetic rubber plant (see SYNTHETIC RUBBER MANUFACTURE). In the Beaumont–Port Arthur–Orange industrial triangle, plants produced a variety of petrochemicals and organic chemicals, butane, synthetic rubber (B. F. Goodrich and Firestone Chemical Companies), and oxygen. McCarthy Chemical Company in Baytown operated the largest oxygen plant in the United States.

Major companies in operations in the 1990s included Dow Chemical, E. I. DuPont de Nemours and Company, Hoechst Celanese Chemical Group, Incorporated, Occidental Chemical Corporation, Quantum Chemical, ARCO, Huntsman Chemical Corporation, and Union Carbide Corporation. Many companies that manufacture chemicals in the state are also members of the Texas Chemical Council, the Austin-based state trade association of the industry.

Most of the new chemical plants after 1960 fell into one of three broad product categories: petrochemicals, based on oil and gas; industrial inorganics; and finished products, such as detergents, paints, and medicinal preparations. The greatest growth has come in the first of these three.

Petrochemicals. The largest-volume petrochemical product was ethylene, produced in more than a dozen Texas plants, most of them along the coast. Ethylene is an intermediate product, used in the making of dozens of chemicals. Some of these were polyethylene, made in larger amounts than any other plastic, vinyl plastics, styrene plastics and rubber, and cellulose acetate, as well as solvents, cleaning agents, antifreeze compounds, and many other products. The preparation of most of these petrochemicals was carried on in several phases, often in different plants, which were frequently connected by pipelines. The term "spaghetti bowl" has come into use to describe the elaborately interconnected production complexes that have grown up along the Houston Ship Channel and the Sabine-Neches Waterway and Sabine Pass Ship Channel.qqv Texas produced 70 percent of American ethylene production in 1989, making it the fifth largest producer in the world. Synthetic rubber, pioneer product of the state's petrochemical industry,qv was made in larger volume in 1968 and in a wider range of types than ever before. Ten Texas plants, along the coast from Houston to Beaumont–Port Arthur and also in Borger and Odessa, turned out various polymers and copolymers for use as rubber. In 1970 Texas produced 80 percent of the nation's synthetic rubber. Some of the basic building blocks of the petrochemical industry were compounds that could be separated or derived from either natural gas or petroleum: ethane and ethylene, butane and butylene, propane and propylene. Others, such as benzene, toluene, and xylene are produced only from oil. In spite of the occurrence of oil and gas in almost all parts of Texas, most petroleum refining was carried on along the coast, where low-cost water transportation could be used. The petrochemical industry, closely tied technologically and economically to refining, developed principally in already established refining centers.

Most major Texas petrochemical products were organic chemicals, but a few were not. Synthetic ammonia, made from the hydrogen contained in natural gas, was in rapidly increasing demand for use in agricultural fertilizers. It was made not only in the Houston area but also in East Texas and on the High Plains, where demand was strong for agricultural chemicals. Texas has been the leading state in production of fixed-nitrogen fertilizers, chiefly ammonia-based. Carbon black, used largely in tire rubber, was an important product of the Texas chemical industry. In the past most of the carbon black plants based their production on natural gas and were located in the gas fields of the Panhandle.qv However, the grades of black in demand for use in synthetic rubber in 1968 were more readily made from oil, and the industry has moved to the Gulf Coast, where petroleum-based feedstocks can be purchased from the large coastal refineries. Sulfur is a Texas petrochemical to the extent that large amounts have been recovered from hydrogen sulfide-bearing natural gas, mainly in the Permian Basinqv and Panhandle gas fields. Similarly, helium was extracted from natural gas at Amarillo, Dumas, Gruver, and Masterson, which were close to gas deposits that contained enough helium to justify its extraction.

Industrial inorganic chemicals. Aside from petrochemicals, the state's largest-volume chemical outputs were generally those derived from salt, sulfur, sea water, oyster shell, and other raw materials drawn mainly from reserves along the Gulf Coast. These inorganics include chlorine, soda ash, caustic soda, and sulfuric acid, all of which figure very importantly in a wide variety of chemical process operations. In 1963 Texas plants shipped more chlorine (valued at $23 million) and more caustic soda (valued at $36 million) than plants in any other state. Most of this came from production centers in or near Corpus Christi, Houston, and Port Neches.

Finished chemical products. The end products turned out by the chemical industry in Texas have fallen mostly into three categories: detergents and soaps, paints and varnishes, and pharmaceutical chemicals. Output of these products has been more heavily concentrated in Dallas than in any other Texas city. In fact, one Dallas plant accounted for most of the state's total employment in soap manufacture. In 1993 there were 167 producers of soap, cleaners, and toilet goods in the state, with $1.2 billion in gross sales. The making of paint and related products was a significant manufacture in Dallas and particularly in Houston. Seventy-eight paint plants in Texas shipped products valued at $118 million in 1963. In 1988 there were ninety plants that had gross sales exceeding $281 million. In 1993, the number of plants dropped to eighty-five but gross sales exceeded $416 million. After World War II the Texas drug industry was small and rather specialized. Substantial quantities of veterinary medicines were produced and also some synthetic organic chemicals for medical use. However, there were no major production centers in 1968. In 1987, seventy-one manufacturers in the state reported gross sales of $432,774,592. By 1993 there were eighty-seven producers of drugs in the state reporting revenues of more than $1 billion.

In response to the growing community concern about chemical pollution, several chemical companies joined Clean Industries 2000, a voluntary program of the Texas Natural Resource Conservation Commission, to reduce various types of pollution to 50 percent of 1987 levels by the year 2000. Members improve environmental management within their corporations and adhere to environmental regulations. Companies also organize and participate in various environmental outreach programs and projects. Texas members include Phillips 66, Howell Hydrocarbon and Chemicals, DuPont, and OxyChem. *See also* CARBON BLACK INDUSTRY *and* HELIUM PRODUCTION.

BIBLIOGRAPHY: M. A. M. Anari and Jared E. Hazelton, *The Chemical Industry of Texas* (College Station: Center for Business and Economic Analysis, Texas A&M University, 1992). Texas Chemical Council, *The Texas Chemical Industry* (n.p.: Union Carbide Corporation, n.d.). Texas Water Commission, *Clean Texas 2000 Environmental Partnership* (1992).
Robert H. Ryan

CHEMPANATAHU INDIANS. This name is recorded in the burial register of San Antonio de Valero Mission in San Antonio. It is linked with an adult female who died in 1737. Since no recognizable variant of the name Chempanatahu has been found in other documents, judgment must be withheld concerning its validity as an ethnic group name.

BIBLIOGRAPHY: San Antonio de Valero Mission, Baptismal and Burial Registers, San Antonio. *Thomas N. Campbell*

CHENANGO, TEXAS. Chenango, seven miles north of Angleton on State Highway 521 and the International–Great Northern Railroad in northeast Brazoria County, was named for a town in New York State. It grew up around nearby Chenango Plantation, where the original sugar house still stood in 1990. The 1,300-acre plantation, located roughly a mile west of the town, was originally part of the William Harris survey, to which acreage belonging to S. Richardson and Joshua Abbott was added for a total of more than 3,000 acres. Around 1835 Benjamin Fort Smith[qv] bought a portion of the property, and Monroe Edwards[qv] and his partner, Christopher Dart, purchased it for conversion from cotton to sugarcane production in 1836. Conflict over ownership between the partners resulted in resale of the plantation later. When James Love and Albert T. Burnley[qqv] were partners in the plantation from July 1841 to May 1848, it was known as Parker's (or Parking's) Point, the name also used by the local post office from June 1847 to July 1848. At a later date the plantation was owned by Captain Sharpe of the Eighth Texas Cavalry[qv] (Terry's Texas Rangers). In 1934 a black couple still lived in one of the slave cabins on Chenango plantation.

A post office was established at Chenango in 1869, discontinued in 1871, reopened in 1877, and closed sometime after 1930. The community had forty residents by 1884 and became a station on the International–Great Northern by 1890, when the town had two general stores and a population of thirty. In 1906 Chenango had a white school with two teachers and twenty-two pupils and a black school with 180 pupils and five teachers. A local cotton gin was operating by 1914. In 1929 the town had an estimated population of 100 and four businesses but by 1939 had declined to only fifty residents and two businesses. Voters in 1940 numbered twenty. By 1947 white children from Chenango attended school in Angleton and black children continued to attend a school in Chenango. That year the community had a single business, and Chenango Plantation raised cattle and feed. Though some oil production began by 1950, state highway maps of that year showed only an abandoned railroad station and Providence Church near the townsite; the community no longer appeared in the census.

BIBLIOGRAPHY: James A. Creighton, *A Narrative History of Brazoria County* (Angleton, Texas: Brazoria County Historical Commission, 1975). Abner J. Strobel, *The Old Plantations and Their Owners of Brazoria County* (Houston, 1926; rev. ed., Houston: Bowman and Ross, 1930; rpt., Austin: Shelby, 1980). *Merle Weir*

CHENEYBORO, TEXAS. Cheneyboro, on the banks of Richland Creek Reservoir four miles south of Navarro in south central Navarro County, was established in the early 1880s. It was named in honor of Francis Marion Cheney, an early settler who built his home from lumber that was cut from his land and milled at his sawmill on the banks of Richland Creek. This house survived into the 1980s, although it had been moved to a new site in central Navarro County. Cheney also built a brick commissary for his farmhands and a ticket depot for the Trinity and Brazos Valley Railway. The Rock Island and Pacific and the Burlington Northern and Chicago lines also once passed through this one-store supply point. In 1936 the community had a population of twenty, a church, a cemetery, and a few scattered dwellings. By 1940 its population had grown to fifty. In 1990 the site was marked only by a cemetery.

BIBLIOGRAPHY: Annie Carpenter Love, *History of Navarro County* (Dallas: Southwestern, 1933). Wyvonne Putman, comp., *Navarro County History* (4 vols., Quanah, Texas: Nortex, 1975–84). Alva Taylor, *History and Photographs of Corsicana and Navarro County* (Corsicana, Texas, 1959; rev. ed., *Navarro County History and Photographs*, Corsicana, 1962). *Carol M. Rushing*

CHENNAULT, CLAIRE LEE (1893–1958). Claire Lee Chennault, aviator and air force general, son of John Stonewall Jackson and Jessie (Lee) Chennault, was born on September 6, 1893, in Commerce, Texas. He was a descendant of eighteenth-century Huguenot immigrants, related to Sam Houston[qv] paternally and to Robert E. Lee[qv] maternally. At the age of one month he moved with his family to Gilbert, Louisiana. His mother died when he was five. He attended Louisiana State University and graduated from Louisiana State Normal College. On Christmas Day 1911 he married Nell Thompson; they had eight children. The marriage ended in divorce in 1946. Chennault married Anna Chan on December 2, 1947, and they had two children.

He taught in various southern towns, including Athens, Louisiana; Biloxi, Mississippi; and Louisville, Kentucky. With the American entry into World War I,[qv] he was commissioned a first lieutenant and became a flight instructor. From 1919 to 1923 he was with the border patrol; from 1923 to 1926 he served with the Hawaiian Pursuit Squadron; and from 1930 to 1936 he was a member of the United States Pursuit Development Board and leader of the Air Corps Exhibition Group ("Three Men on a Flying Trapeze"). Deafness and disagreements with his superiors over tactics forced his retirement in 1937. In the same year he became advisor to Chiang Kai-shek and the Chinese Air Force. In 1941 he organized the American Volunteer Group (Flying Tigers) in China. In March 1943 Chennault was promoted to major general and to command of the Fourteenth Air Force. His tour was marked by conflicts with the theater commander, Lt. Gen. Joseph Stilwell. Chennault was retired against his will in July 1945, as the defensive tactics he favored were regarded as obsolete by air corps strategists. He then organized and was chairman of the board of Civil Air Transport. He maintained homes in Taipei, Taiwan, and near Monroe, Louisiana.

He was the author of an autobiography and several works on fighter tactics. Among his many decorations were the Distinguished Flying Cross with cluster; Army and Navy Air Medal with cluster; Chinese Army, Navy, and Air Force Medal; Commander of the British Empire; Legion of Honor; Croix de Guerre with Palm; and Chevalier Polonia Restituta. He died of cancer on July 27, 1958, at the Ochsner Foundation Hospital in New Orleans and was buried in Arlington National Cemetery. Monuments were erected to him in Taipei, on the grounds of the Louisiana State Capitol at Baton Rouge, and at Chennault Air Force Base, Lake Charles, Louisiana.

BIBLIOGRAPHY: Keith Ayling, *Old Leatherface of the Flying Tigers: The Story of General Chennault* (Indianapolis and New York: Bobbs-Merrill, 1945). Martha Byrd, *Chennault: Giving Wings to the Tiger* (Tuscaloosa: University of Alabama Press, 1987). Anna Chennault, *Chennault and His Flying Tigers* (New York: Eriksson, 1963). Anna Chennault, *A Thousand Springs: The Biography of a Marriage* (New York: Eriksson, 1962). Claire Lee Chennault, *Way of a Fighter: The Memoirs of Claire Lee Chennault* (New York: Putnam, 1949). New York *Times*, July 28, 1958. Otha Spencer, *Flying the Hump: Memories of an Air War* (College Station: Texas A&M University Press, 1992). *Time*, August 4, 1958. Barbara W. Tuchman, *Stilwell and the American Experience in China, 1911–45* (New York: Macmillan, 1970). U.S. Air Force Historical Division, *The Army Air Forces in World War II*, ed. Wesley Frank Craven and James Lea Cate (7 vols., Chicago: University of Chicago Press, 1948–58). *James W. Pohl*

CHENOWETH, JAMES Q. (1841–1909). James Q. Chenoweth, lawyer, judge, and auditor of the United States Treasury, was born in Louisville, Kentucky, in 1841. He was raised in Harrison County, Kentucky, by his grandparents and attended the local public schools. He then studied law at the offices of Elmore, Keys, and Gunter in Montgomery, Alabama. The Civil War[qv] interrupted his studies, and he served in the Confederate Army for four years. After being discharged as a colonel he returned to his studies and in 1865 was admitted to the bar before being elected a senator in the Kentucky legislature. After his wife's death he resigned from the Kentucky Senate in 1872 and left for Texas. He moved to Bonham, where his legal and political skills led to his appointment by Governor Richard Coke[qv] as special district judge of the criminal courts of Fannin, Lamar, and Red River counties. Two years later Chenoweth served the first of two consecutive terms in the Texas legislature. In 1885 President Grover Cleveland appointed him auditor of the United States Treasury.

After Cleveland was defeated in 1888, Chenoweth returned to Texas. In 1892 he waged his first successful campaign for the position of Fannin county judge. After three terms, he worked as publisher of the Bonham *Daily Favorite* before accepting appointment as superintendent of the Confederate Home for Men (*see* TEXAS CONFEDERATE HOME) at Austin in 1903. Illness forced him to resign from this position. He spent the last year of his life in Virginia, where the Elks provided a home for him. He died there on June 20, 1909.

BIBLIOGRAPHY: W. A. Carter, *History of Fannin County, Texas* (Bonham, Texas: Bonham *News*, 1885; rpt., Honey Grove, Texas: Fannin County Historical Society, 1975). *Fannin County Folks and Facts* (Dallas: Taylor, 1977). Floy Crandall Hodge, *A History of Fannin County* (Hereford, Texas: Pioneer, 1966).
David Minor

CHENOWETH, JOHN M. (?–?). John Chenoweth, soldier and legislator of the Republic of Texas,[qv] arrived in Texas in 1835, apparently with Capt. John W. Peacock's company, the United States Invincibles. He is said to have paid his own way from Louisiana, where he left his wife and family. Chenoweth and his company joined the revolutionary army[qv] at Bexar on November 26, 1835. When Peacock was killed at the siege of Bexar,[qv] December 5–10, 1835, Chenoweth was elected to command of the company, which officially enlisted for the duration of the war on December 27. On December 25 Chenoweth requested that the General Council[qv] allow him to recruit a new company of volunteers to garrison Copano. His Invincibles were officially mustered into service in February 1836, and Chenoweth still commanded them as late as that month, when they were stationed at Refugio under Col. James W. Fannin, Jr.[qv] He was, however, detached from Fannin's command and given command of the garrison at Copano as he had requested. Soon thereafter Fannin's men, including most of the Invincibles, were captured and executed in the notorious Goliad Massacre.[qv] Chenoweth thereupon joined Sam Houston's[qv] army at Gonzales as a private and served in Capt. William H. Patton's[qv] Columbia Company of Col. Sidney Sherman's[qv] Second Regiment at the battle of San Jacinto.[qv] Houston commended him to James Collinsworth,[qv] chairman of the military committee, as "very active."

After San Jacinto, Chenoweth was elected captain of the Zavala Volunteers, on August 20, 1836. The company was assigned to the First Regiment of Gen. Thomas J. Green's[qv] brigade and stationed at Camp Johnston. From there Chenoweth ranged the coast gathering supplies and horses for the brigade. He paid for much of this material with his own money. Nevertheless, he reported to Gen. Mirabeau B. Lamar[qv] that his requisitioning of supplies resulted in many citizens' leaving the area and taking their livestock with them. Before July 6 he was promoted to major. The death of his wife in Louisiana necessitated his return there for several months in 1836. While still commanding his company, Chenoweth was furloughed to attend the First Congress of the Republic of Texas, to which he had been elected from Goliad County on October 3. During the spring term of the Harrisburg (now Harris) County district court, Chenoweth served on the grand jury.

On October 8, 1842, Houston denied Chenoweth's application for a commission to raise a company of rangers for the defense of the upper Colorado River frontier but instead appointed him to take charge of those Indians captured by Texans and return them to their homes in compliance with a recent treaty. On December 3, 1847, Chenoweth married E. H. Reed. He lived in Harrisburg County and then in Burleson County, where he was residing on September 12, 1850. He was awarded a 690-acre bounty certificate for his participation in the battle of San Jacinto, which he sold for sixty dollars. Later he received an additional 1,280-acre warrant, which he also sold.

BIBLIOGRAPHY: Daughters of the Republic of Texas, *Muster Rolls of the Texas Revolution* (Austin, 1986). John H. Jenkins, ed., *The Papers of the Texas Revolution, 1835–1836* (10 vols., Austin: Presidial Press, 1973). *Telegraph and Texas Register*, June 5, 1839. Texas House of Representatives, *Biographical Directory of the Texan Conventions and Congresses, 1832–1845* (Austin: Book Exchange, 1941). Amelia W. Williams and Eugene C. Barker, eds., *The Writings of Sam Houston, 1813–1863* (8 vols., Austin: University of Texas Press, 1938–43; rpt., Austin and New York: Pemberton Press, 1970).
Thomas W. Cutrer

CHENTI INDIANS. The Chenti (Chení) Indians are known only from the 1730s, when they were closely associated with the Lipan and other Apache groups in west central Texas, particularly along the San Saba River. They were probably one of several bands that later came to be spoken of collectively as the Lipan Apaches.

BIBLIOGRAPHY: Herbert E. Bolton, "The Jumano Indians in Texas, 1650–1771," *Quarterly of the Texas State Historical Association* 15 (July 1911). William Edward Dunn, "Apache Relations in Texas, 1718–1750," *Quarterly of the Texas State Historical Association* 14 (January 1911). Juan Agustín Morfi, *History of Texas, 1673–1779* (2 vols., Albuquerque: Quivira Society, 1935; rpt., New York: Arno, 1967).
Thomas N. Campbell

CHEOCAS. Hainai chief Cheocas was formally invested as governor of the Hainai Indians on August 8, 1721. At that time, when it was refounded by the Marqués de Aguayo,[qv] he assembled his people to be neophytes of Nuestra Señora de la Purísima Concepción de los Hainai Mission.

BIBLIOGRAPHY: Eleanor Claire Buckley, "The Aguayo Expedition in Texas and Louisiana, 1719–1722," *Quarterly of the Texas State Historical Association* 15 (July 1911).

CHEROKEE, TEXAS. Cherokee is on State Highway 16 some fifteen miles south of San Saba in southern San Saba County. The settlement of upper Cherokee Creek, from which the community took its name, dates to the early 1850s, when P. P. "Pop" Woodard established a ranch five miles west of the site of what is now Cherokee. The second oldest post office in the county was the Cherokee post office, which was moved several times before arriving at the site that it still occupied in the 1980s. It originally opened in 1858 in the home of J. R. Williams in Llano County, then moved in 1869 to the residence of Capt. John Williams in Hanna, a school community on Cherokee Creek in San Saba County. In June 1871 the office was moved to the Montgomery school community on the north bank of the creek, where it shared a building with William O. Handshey's store and the Landrum Hotel. The post office was moved again in September 1878 to the home of M. H. Wadsworth on the Jackson Branch of Cherokee Creek, then moved one last time in July of 1879 to James Samuel Hart's store in Cherokee. David Seth Hanna laid out the permanent townsite of Cherokee in 1878. By the mid-1880s the settlement had developed into the processing and marketing center of an active farming and ranching economy, and by the mid-1890s the town reported a population of 500. In the 1890s the agricultural economy of the Cherokee valley supported a hotel, several churches and schools, a number of processing and supply businesses, and various craft and professional services. Cherokee also became a county center of higher education when Francis Marion Behrns established the Cherokee Academy around 1894. Twice reorganized—first as the West Texas Normal and Business College (1896) and later as Cherokee Junior College (1911)—the school operated until its sale to the county school district in 1921. It then served the community as Cherokee High School until fire razed the main building in 1945. The school was rebuilt using its original façade. In the 1920s Cherokee supported a short-lived bank and two newspapers, and for the next several decades the number of residents remained stable at about 250. In 1990 Cherokee, with a population estimated at 175, served primarily as a supply and postal center for a stock raising and farming economy. Local agricultural production centered on sheep, poultry, and pecans.

BIBLIOGRAPHY: Alma Ward Hamrick, *The Call of the San Saba: A History of San Saba County* (San Antonio: Naylor, 1941; 2d ed., Austin: Jenkins, 1969). *San Saba County History* (San Saba, Texas: San Saba County Historical Commission, 1983). Alice Gray Upchurch, "A Sketch History of San Saba County," *Southwestern Historical Quarterly* 50 (July 1946).
Daniel P. Greene

CHEROKEE ACADEMY. Cherokee Academy, at Rusk in Cherokee County, was chartered on March 18, 1848. The charter provided that the academy was to be on a site designated for school purposes, that the school should be nondenominational, and that it should continue only so long as it devoted itself to the advancement of science and the promotion of useful knowledge. There is some question as to whether the academy was ever in operation, though meager sources in the form of deed records refer to it in 1851, and there is some evidence that in 1848 J. B. Mitchell was conducting a school that was transferred to Cherokee Academy. The school may have merged with the Stephens and Carter Academy established in 1851. The Commissioners Court of Cherokee County sold the site in 1869.

BIBLIOGRAPHY: *Cherokee County History* (Jacksonville, Texas: Cherokee County Historical Commission, 1986). Hattie Joplin Roach, *A History of Cherokee County* (Dallas: Southwest, 1934).

CHEROKEE BAYOU. Cherokee Bayou begins at the spillway and dam on Cherokee Lake in northern Rusk County (at 32°22′ N, 94°36′ W) and runs eight miles northeast to its mouth on the Black Slough in Gregg County (at 32°24′ N, 94°32′ W). The surrounding terrain varies from flat to rolling with local escarpments and is surfaced by deep, fine sandy loams that support pine and hardwood forests. The creek forms the Gregg–Rusk county line for part of its length.

CHEROKEE COUNTY. Cherokee County (F-21) is located in central East Texas, bordered on the north by Smith County, on the east by Rusk and Nacogdoches counties, on the south by Angelina County, and on the west by Anderson and Houston counties. It was named for the Cherokee Indians, who lived in the area before being expelled in 1839. Rusk, the county seat, is 130 miles southeast of Dallas and 160 miles north of Houston. The center of the 1,049-square-mile county is located near Rusk at 31°48′ north latitude and 95°10′ west longitude.

The soil surface in Cherokee County consists of sandy and clay loams interspersed with alluvial bottoms. Redlands cover a fourth of the county. A forest of shortleaf and loblolly pine with mixed hardwoods covers 57.6 percent of the land. Timber, rich soils, abundant water, oil, natural gas, clays, and iron ore lead the list of natural resources. The hilly terrain ranges from 250 to 570 feet above sea level. The Neches River forms the western boundary of the county and the Angelina River the southeastern boundary. Three major reservoirs lie wholly or partly within the county: Lake Palestine, Striker Creek Reservoir, and Lake Jacksonville.qqv The underlying Carrizo-Wilcox aquifer provides much of the water supply to municipalities. Average annual rainfall is 44.26 inches. The temperature ranges from an average low of 38° F in January to an average high of 94° F in July. The average growing season extends 258 days.

Early Indian habitation has been thoroughly investigated at the George C. Davis Site at Mound Prairie, six miles southwest of Alto. Evidence of all stages of southeastern Indian development has been found, beginning with the 12,000-year-old Clovis culture. Indian development reached its peak after the arrival of the Caddos about A.D. 780. The Early Caddoan Period, which lasted until about 1260, saw the development of Mound Prairie as a regional ceremonial center with three earthen mounds, the southwesternmost examples of the Mississippian mound-building culture. In the Late Caddoan Period, Mound Prairie was abandoned, but numerous sites show a continuing Caddo presence in the northern two-thirds of the county. At the time of European contact, two tribes of the Caddoan Hasinai Confederacy lived in the county: the Neches, in scattered hamlets between Mound Prairie and Alto, and the Nacachau, located north of the Neches.

The record of early European contact is somewhat vague. Luis de Moscoso Alvaradoqv may have passed through in 1542, and the French of the La Salle expeditionqv probably visited in 1686–87. A strong Spanish influence came into the area in 1690 with the establishment of San Francisco de los Tejas Mission in neighboring Houston County. The first documented entry of Europeans came on November 6, 1691, when the expedition of Domingo Terán de los Ríos and Father Damián Massenetqqv entered the county en route from San Francisco de los Tejas to the Red River. The mission was abandoned in 1693, and Europeans ignored the area until 1705, when French traders led by Louis Juchereau de St. Denisqv began to do business among the Hasinais. To counter the resultant growing French influence, Spanish authorities sent Capt. Domingo Ramónqv to establish a series of missions and a presidio in East Texas. On July 3, 1716, Ramón founded Nuestro Padre San Francisco de los Tejas Mission among the Neches Indians. In June 1719 French pressure led to the temporary abandonment of the mission, but the Marqués de Aguayoqv reoccupied the site on August 5, 1721, at which time it was renamed San Francisco de los Neches. The Spanish permanently abandoned the mission in 1730. Thereafter, a mission at Nacogdoches maintained the Spanish presence in the area.

The first land grant in the county went to Nacogdoches merchants William Barr and Peter Samuel Davenportqqv in 1798, but they did not settle there. The Indians for whom the county was named—the Cherokees—joined by Delawares, Shawnees, and Kickapoos, began settling north of the Camino Real (the Old San Antonio Roadqv) about 1820. Cherokee chiefs Bowl, Richard Fields, and John Dunn Hunterqqv tried unsuccessfully to obtain title to their land from the Mexican government. Anglo-American settlers began moving onto land claimed by Cherokees near Linwood in the late 1820s. Indian hopes suffered another blow when in 1826 David G. Burnetqv obtained an empresarioqv grant to lands north of the Camino Real, and the area south of the road fell to empresario Joseph Vehlein.qv

Rapid settlement began in 1834. The Houston-Forbes treaty (see FORBES, JOHN) of February 23, 1836, seemingly assured Cherokee neutrality, but the rejection of the treaty by the Texas Senate and the increased encroachment of settlers on Indian land led to violence. On October 5, 1838, Indians massacred members of the Isaac Killough family at their farm northwest of the site of present Jacksonville (*see* KILLOUGH MASSACRE). This led directly to the Cherokee Warqv of 1839 and the expulsion of all Indians from the county. White settlers quickly occupied the abandoned Indian farms, and the communities of Pine Town, Lockranzie, Linwood, and Cook's Fort developed. Cherokee County was marked off from Nacogdoches County on April 11, 1846, and was organized on July 13 of that year, with the town of Rusk as the county seat. Only one family lived at Rusk then.

The county's settlers were mostly from the South and brought with them the economic and social traditions of that region. The 1850 population of 6,673 was the third largest in the state. By 1860 the population had grown to 12,098, of whom 3,250 were slaves, two were free blacks, and fourteen were Spanish surnamed. Of the white families, 29 percent owned slaves, although only thirty-two plantations had twenty or more slaves; seven slaveholders in the county owned more than forty slaves. Cotton was important to the local economy, and in 1860 local farmers produced 6,251 bales of the fiber. The area's principal crops, however, were corn and wheat. County farmers produced more than 496,000 bushels of corn in 1860, and about 21,000 bushels of wheat (*see* COTTON CULTURE, CORN CULTURE, WHEAT CULTURE).

Cherokee County voters strongly supported secession,qv and twenty-four companies from the county entered Confederate service. The Confederate Army maintained two training camps, a prisoner of war camp, a large commissary depot, and conscription and field-transportation offices in the county. War demands allowed the development of two iron foundries and a gun factory.

After the war, despite a brief military occupation, Republicans had little impact and did not seriously challenge Democratic control. There was little evidence of Ku Klux Klan^{qv} or other terrorist activity in the county during Reconstruction.^{qv} Since then, the only serious challenge to Democratic control has come from the Populist party,^{qv} which carried the county with strong black support in 1894 and 1896, despite the leading role in the Democratic party of Governor James S. Hogg,^{qv} a native of Rusk. Democrats have carried the county in all presidential elections except those of 1956, 1968 (when George Wallace carried the county), and 1984. Republicans have never offered candidates for local offices and maintain only a minimal organization.

Baptists, who organized the first church in 1844, remain the largest religious denomination. Methodist and Presbyterian churches also appeared at Alto, Rusk, and Jacksonville in the 1840s. Blacks organized separate congregations shortly after obtaining freedom. Other Protestant groups appeared in the twentieth century. A Catholic parish has been active in Cherokee County since 1905, but it remained quite small until the recent influx of Hispanics.

Educational institutions began to develop in Cherokee soon after white settlement in the area. There was a secondary academy by 1848, and in 1850 Cherokee County had seventeen public schools and ranked first in the state in the number of school children attending (537 males, 446 females). In 1854 the county commissioners established forty-four school districts, which received some public assistance. Higher education was available as early as 1855 at Hale Institute in Rusk, but the most important institution of higher education was Larissa College, which opened in 1856. The Civil War^{qv} considerably disrupted education, but with Reconstruction came free public education for children of all races. Improved transportation in the twentieth century led to consolidation of the rural schools. There are now six independent school districts wholly in the county, while parts of three others extend into the northern part of the county. Desegregation came in the 1966–69 period. Higher education is now represented by two church-related junior colleges, Lon Morris College and Jacksonville College, and by North American Theological Seminary. By 1980, 49.6 percent of Cherokee County residents over age twenty-five had completed at least twelve years of school.

In addition to Rusk, several new towns appeared shortly after the organization of the county. Larissa, founded in 1846 in the northwest part of the county, became the largest town. Gum Creek, soon renamed Jacksonville, was founded in 1847. Alto was established on the Old San Antonio Road in 1851. Lone Star (originally Skin Tight), Knoxville, and Griffin were other pioneer communities.

Railroad construction and agricultural development, especially the expansion of cotton cultivation, helped the county to grow and mature between 1870 and 1900. In 1870 there were 1,216 farms and ranches in Cherokee County, and the county had a population of 11,079; by 1900, 3,683 farms and ranches had been established in the county, and the population had increased to 25,154. During this same period total acres in farms rose from 133,014 to almost 341,000; the number of improved acres more than tripled, from about 43,000 to almost 149,000.

The arrival of the railroads also drastically altered the settlement pattern. All the old towns except Jacksonville, Rusk, and Alto disappeared, unable to compete with the new railroad centers. The International–Great Northern (later the Missouri Pacific), built in 1872, gave rise to Troup and a relocated and revitalized Jacksonville. Between 1882 and 1885 the Kansas and Gulf Short Line built north-to-south through the county, producing new towns—Bullard, Mount Selman, Craft, Dialville, Forest, and Wells—and bringing rail service to Rusk and Alto. In 1905 the Texas and New Orleans produced Cuney, Reese, Turney, Gallatin, Ponta, and Reklaw. Maydelle appeared on the Texas State Railroad in 1910. The only new town not associated with a railroad was New Summerfield, which was founded as a market center in the late 1890s. The automobile and school consolidations led to the growth of the four central towns—Jacksonville, Rusk, Alto, and Wells—at the expense of the others, which today typically have only one or two stores.

The decline of farming, which began in the 1930s, and increased industrial job opportunities in the years during and after World War II^{qv} led to another major population shift. County population reached a peak of 43,970 in 1940, then declined to 38,694 in 1950, and to 33,120 in 1960 before dropping to its lowest point of 32,008 in 1970. Yet, during these same years, the population of the larger towns in the county increased. This indicated both emigration from the county to outside urban areas and migration within the county from the countryside to the towns.

Although no longer preeminent, agriculture remains important in the economy. Cotton replaced wheat as the major crop immediately after the Civil War, and continued to grow in importance into the twentieth century; in 1928 the county's cotton production reached its maximum (36,951 bales), and in 1929, 113,689 acres of Cherokee County farmland was devoted to its cultivation. But in the 1930s production fell sharply because of low prices and New Deal allotment programs; by 1940 cotton production utilized only about 45,000 acres in the county. Peaches became important after the introduction of refrigerator cars in 1893, and Cherokee County orchards produced a record of 1,204 carloads in 1912 before the San José scale and marketing troubles brought a decline. In the late 1930s, however, peach production revived somewhat (*see* FRUITS OTHER THAN CITRUS). From its beginnings at Craft in 1897, tomato culture grew until by 1917 Cherokee County produced 90 percent of the tomatoes shipped from Texas. Tomatoes remained a major product in the county until increased competition and marketing problems caused a sudden collapse in the 1950s. Since then, Cherokee County agriculture has centered on cattle and timber. The nursery industry dates from the 1880s and is of increasing importance in the New Summerfield–Reklaw area. Some truck farming still exists, and dairies remain significant. Some poultry production remains from the boom of the late 1950s. Sharecropping, which had been prevalent since Reconstruction, largely disappeared with farming. The typical Cherokee County farm of today is a beef-and-timber operation run as a sideline by a landowner with a job in town.

The twentieth century brought great improvements in transportation. The first automobile arrived in 1905; by the 1920s automobile ownership was commonplace. During the 1930s and 1940s the basic highway system was paved. Four federal and four state highways now cross the county, while hundreds of miles of paved farm-to-market roads network the rural areas. Rail transportation has been sharply curtailed. The last passenger train ran in the late 1960s, and in the early 1980s the Southern Pacific stopped all service, as did the Cotton Belt, south of Rusk. The first airport in the county was established at Jacksonville in 1934. The present county airport, built in 1961, has no scheduled airline service.

Sawmills provided the first industry, beginning with John Durst's^{qv} mill at the lower San Antonio Road crossing of the Angelina in 1832. Three times the rich iron ore deposits have produced important industries. Blast furnaces operated during the Civil War, in the 1884–1909 period, and during World War II. The industry led to the founding in 1888 of New Birmingham, which grew to be a city of some 2,000 inhabitants before collapsing completely as a result of the panic of 1893. Since World War II industry has led the private sector of the economy, employing around 30 percent of the private-sector work force. Jacksonville has become the industrial and commercial hub of the county. There, more than sixty firms make wood, metal, and plastic products. Altogether, some 114 manufacturing firms operated in the county in 1977. Oil was discovered in 1933, but technical and financial difficulties prevented development until 1934. Continuing discoveries produced an oil value of $51,379,910 by 1982. Currently, some 26 percent of the labor force works in professional and related services (a relatively high figure reflecting employment at the Rusk State Hospital[qv]), 22 percent in manufacturing, and 18 percent in wholesale and retail trade. Tourism is of growing importance, spurred by the establishment in 1971 of the Texas State Railroad State Historical Park.[qv]

The 1980 census counted 38,127 people in Cherokee County, representing a 19.1 percent increase over 1970. In 1990 the county population was 41,049. Ethnically, the county is 78 percent white, including around 6.6 percent Hispanics; 17 percent are black; and less than 1 percent are Asian and American Indian. Incorporated towns include Jacksonville, Rusk, Alto, Wells, New Summerfield, Cuney, and Gallatin. Reklaw is partly in Rusk County, while Troup and Bullard are mostly in Smith County.

BIBLIOGRAPHY: *Cherokee County History* (Jacksonville, Texas: Cherokee County Historical Commission, 1986). Fred Hugo Ford and J. L. Browne, *Larissa* (1930?; rev. ed., Jacksonville, Texas: McFarland, 1951). Jack Moore, *Angelina—Little Angel of the Tejas* (Jacksonville, Texas: Progress, 1967). Jack Moore, *The Great Jacksonville Circus Fight and Other Cherokee County Stories* (Jacksonville, Texas, 1971). Hattie Joplin Roach, *The Hills of Cherokee* (1952; rpt., Fort Worth, 1976). Hattie Joplin Roach, *A History of Cherokee County* (Dallas: Southwest, 1934).

John R. Ross

CHEROKEE CREEK (Briscoe County). Cherokee Creek rises in east central Briscoe County (at 34°31′ N, 101°03′ W) and runs north twelve miles to its mouth on the Prairie Dog Town Fork of the Red River (at 34°37′ N, 101°00′ W). It was on the JA Ranch[qv] properties and gave its name to Cherokee Camp, one of the ranch's twelve winter line camps. The creek crosses variable terrain surfaced by shallow to moderately deep silt loams that support mesquite and grasses.

_____ (Llano County). Cherokee Creek rises 5½ miles west of Magill Mountain in northwestern Llano County (at 30°54′ N, 98°52′ W) and runs northeast for forty-one miles to its mouth on the Colorado River in San Saba County (at 31°07′ N, 98°30′ W). The stream was identified as Marble Creek before 1841, but surveys in that year designate it as Mineral Creek. It was named Cherokee on November 4, 1854, by a deputy surveyor of the Fisher-Miller Land Grant.[qv] The name came either from a battle fought near the stream's mouth on December 25, 1839, between the Cherokee Indians and a group of frontiersmen under the command of Edward Burleson,[qv] or from the Cherokee wife (Polly Ann Rogers) of a settler in the area. At one point the creek is dammed to form a lake. The surrounding flat to gently sloping uplands are surfaced by clay and sandy loams that support live oak, mesquite, Ashe juniper, and grasses.

BIBLIOGRAPHY: Alma Ward Hamrick, *The Call of the San Saba: A History of San Saba County* (San Antonio: Naylor, 1941; 2d ed., Austin: Jenkins, 1969).

CHEROKEE INDIANS. The Cherokees call themselves Ani-Yunwiya, the "Principal People." They were indeed one of the principal Indian nations of the southeastern United States until pressure from advancing Europeans forced their westward migration. They were a settled agricultural people whose ancestral lands covered much of the southern Appalachian highlands, an area that included parts of Virginia, Tennessee, North and South Carolina, Georgia, and Alabama. The Cherokees' Iroquoian language and migration legends suggest that the tribe originated to the north of their traditional homeland. Cherokee society reflected an elaborate social, political, and ceremonial structure. Their basic political unit was the town, which consisted of all the people who used a single ceremonial center. Within each town, a council, dominated by older men, handled political affairs. Individual towns sent representatives to regional councils to discuss policy for the corporate group, especially issues of diplomacy or warfare. Towns typically included thirty to forty households clustered around a central townhouse that was used as a meeting place. Houses were square or rectangular huts constructed of locked poles, weatherproofed with wattle and daub plaster, and roofed with bark. Cherokee society was organized into clans, or kin groups. The clans were matrilineal, and marriage within the clan was prohibited. There were seven major Cherokee clans, each identified by a particular animal totem. A variety of clans was represented in each community and performed significant social, legal, and political functions.

The Cherokees' first contact with Europeans came in 1540, when members of a Spanish expedition led by Hernando De Soto (*see* MOSCOSO EXPEDITION) passed through Cherokee territory. After that brief encounter, more than a hundred years passed before the Cherokees had significant association with Europeans. The 1670s marked the beginning of sustained contact between the two cultures, and that contact influenced Cherokee lives in many ways. The Cherokees were quick to adapt many material elements of European culture to their own society, a characteristic that led to their designation as one of the "Five Civilized Tribes." They established a constitutional government with a senate, a house of representatives, and an elected chief. The Cherokees had a written language devised by the tribe's syllabary genius, Sequoyah. They valued education and often maintained schools for their children. The dress of the Cherokees also reflected their acculturative tendencies. Women wove cotton cloth and adopted a European style of dress. Men traditionally wore a turban, cloth tunic, or coat bound at the waist by a sash, skin leggings with garters below the knees, and moccasins. Although the Cherokees derived some advantages from interaction with European cultures, those were far outweighed by the negative effects of that contact. Throughout the eighteenth century the process of European empire building subjected the Cherokees to calamitous wars, epidemics, and food shortages, all of which resulted in declining population, shrinking territory, and weakening group identity. Between 1790 and 1820, many Cherokees, hoping to preserve what remained of their traditional culture, voluntarily migrated west of the Mississippi River and settled in the future Missouri, Arkansas, and Texas. Those who chose to remain on their ancestral land in the Southeast were ultimately forced to move west by the United States Indian removal policy, which was initiated in 1830. Between 1838 and 1839, 16,000 to 18,000 Cherokees were forcibly marched to their new home in northeastern Indian Territory. An estimated 4,000 died on the march, which has come to be known as the Trail of Tears.

Cherokees were first reported in Texas in 1807, when a small band, probably an offshoot of the Arkansas settlements, established a village on the Red River. In the summer of that year, a delegation of Cherokees, Pascagoulas, Chickasaws, and Shawnees sought permission from Spanish officials in Nacogdoches, the easternmost town in Texas, to settle members of their tribes in that province. The request was approved by Spanish authorities, who intended to use the immigrant Indians as a buffer against American expansion. For several years a small number of Cherokees drifted in and out of Texas. Subsequently, between 1812 and 1819, increasing population pressure in Arkansas compelled more Cherokees to migrate south. In the spring of 1819, Cherokees began settling in Lost Prairie, an area between the Sulphur Fork and the Red River in what is now Miller County, Arkansas,[qv] and within a year some 200 Cherokees had settled there. But they could not escape American competition for the land. By 1820 Anglo-Americans had established seven settlements in the valley of the Red River, and the Cherokees began to consider moving further south. In early 1820, Chief Bowl,[qv] also known as Duwali, led some sixty Cherokee families into Texas. They settled first on the Three Forks of the Trinity River (at the site of present Dallas), but pressure from prairie tribes forced them to move eastward into a virtually uninhabited region north of Nacogdoches now in Rusk County. They carved out farms on land that belonged to their friends, the Caddoes, a once powerful Indian confederacy that had been greatly reduced by warfare and epidemic diseases. By 1822 the Texas Cherokee population had grown to nearly three hundred.

While the Cherokees were establishing their homes in East Texas, the government of Texas passed from Spain to Mexico. Mexican officials, like their Spanish predecessors, welcomed the presence of Cherokees in Texas. Cherokee headmen, having learned the importance of holding legal title to real property, repeatedly petitioned Mexican authorities for a permanent land grant. Richard Fields,qv a Cherokee diplomat, conducted negotiations with the Mexican government in the early 1820s, and although Fields claimed that his tribe had been granted land north of the Old San Antonio Road qv between the Trinity and Sabine rivers, the Mexican government denied the claim. While the government delayed granting the Cherokees clear title to the land, the population of East Texas swelled. By the mid-1820s, Americans were drifting into the region south and east of the Cherokee settlement. Distrust developed between the two peoples as each felt its security threatened by the other. By the late 1820s the rapid influx of American settlers to Texas alarmed Mexican officials, who feared losing the province to the growing United States. The Law of April 6, 1830,qv prohibited further American immigration to Texas. At the same time, Mexican authorities resurrected their policy of using the Cherokees as a buffer against immigrant Americans. By 1830 the Cherokee population of Texas was approaching 400. The tribe was congregated in at least three but possibly as many as seven towns north of Nacogdoches along the Sabine River and its tributaries, including a stream now known as Cherokee Creek. In order to secure Cherokee aid, Mexican officials proposed giving the Cherokees the long-sought title to their land, but the Indians lacked the money and legal expertise to complete the complicated procedure. However, lingering hopes of securing legal rights to their land kept the Cherokees loyal to the Mexican government when Anglo-Texans began to protest Mexican rule in 1832. When the Texas Revolution qv erupted in 1835, the Cherokees still had not obtained title to their land, and their loyalty to Mexico placed them in a doubtful position with the revolutionary government in Texas. The Cherokees addressed the problem by declaring themselves neutral in the conflict between Texas and Mexico.

The Texas revolutionary government, anxious to ensure Cherokee neutrality, sent Sam Houston qv to counsel with the tribe in the fall of 1835. Houston, the newly elected commander of the Texan forces, was an adopted member of the Cherokee tribe and became an influential advocate of the Cherokee people. In November 1835 the Consultation,qv acting on Houston's recommendation, pledged to recognize Cherokee claims to the land north of the Old San Antonio Road and the Neches River and west of the Angelina and Sabine Rivers. The government also appointed John Forbes, John Cameron,qqv and General Houston as commissioners and empowered them to negotiate a treaty with the tribe. The resulting agreement established a reservation for the Cherokees in East Texas, and although it considerably reduced their landholdings, the Cherokees agreed to the accord because they believed it finally gave them a permanent home. The reservation included the future Smith and Cherokee counties as well as parts of Van Zandt, Rusk, and Gregg counties. Eight Cherokee leaders, including Duwali and Big Mush,qv signed the agreement in 1836. But the treaty was never ratified by the Texas government. Although a majority of the Cherokees had agreed to peace with the Texans, a militant faction of the tribe remained pro-Mexican, a fact that greatly complicated Texan-Cherokee relations.

After the battle of San Jacinto qv in 1836, Sam Houston was elected president of the new Republic of Texas.qv He advocated peace with all Texas Indians and worked diligently to enlist the Cherokees as allies in his attempts to negotiate with the warring western tribes. In the fall of 1836 the Cherokees agreed to provide a company of twenty-five rangers to patrol the frontier that lay west of their settlements. The following year the aging Cherokee leader Duwali consented to serve as the republic's emissary to the Comanches. Texas-Cherokee relations deteriorated again in 1838, however, when attacks on settlers in East Texas were blamed on a combined Cherokee-Mexican force. Before leaving office, Houston attempted to preserve peace between Texans and Cherokees by establishing a boundary line separating their territory, but the line only angered Anglo-Texans who were clamoring for land and saw the Cherokees as allies of their enemies, the Mexicans. Houston's successor as president, Mirabeau B. Lamar,qv wanted the Cherokees removed from Texas. He sent troops to occupy the Neches Saline (see NECHES SALINE, TEXAS) in Cherokee country, and when Duwali blocked the advance of the Texans, Lamar notified the old chief that his people would be moved beyond the Red River, "peaceably if they would; forcibly if they must." The president then appointed commissioners who were authorized to compensate the Cherokees for land and property they would leave behind. The Cherokees decided to fight for their land, and the resulting conflict came to be known as the Cherokee War.qv In the summer of 1839, a force of several hundred warriors led by Duwali met Texas forces in the battle of the Neches qv near the site of present Tyler. More than 100 Indians, including Duwali, were killed, and the remaining Cherokees were driven across the Red River into Indian Territory. Some Cherokees continued to live a fugitive existence in Texas, while others took up residence in Mexico. A few even continued the fight against the Texans but with little success. When Houston was elected to a second presidential term in 1841, he inaugurated an Indian policy calculated to forestall future hostilities with immigrant tribes. As a result of his peace policy, treaties were concluded with the remaining Texas Cherokees in 1843 and 1844.

The Cherokees forced north of the Red River were reunited with some 6,000 Cherokees already settled in the northeastern corner of Indian Territory. The arrival of the destitute newcomers naturally caused problems for longtime residents, but in 1846, the same year that Texas formally joined the Union, representatives of all the Cherokee factions met in Washington, D.C., and signed an agreement specifying that the lands belonging to the Cherokee nation were for common use.

The Civil War, however, divided the Cherokee Nation once again. John Ross, chief officer of the tribe, favored neutrality, but the Southern Rights party, led by Stand Watie, was determined to fight for the South. In late 1861, Ross, fearing Confederate invasion, allied the nation with the South. When Union troops took control of Cherokee territory in 1863, many "Southern" Cherokees fled to Texas, but after the war, most of them returned to their homes in Indian Territory. In the decades after the war, the Cherokees endured a succession of federal efforts to reduce their landholdings. According to terms of an 1866 treaty with the federal government, the tribe agreed to cede the Cherokee Outlet, an eight-million-acre tract extending westward from the edge of the Cherokee Nation into the Plains. The land had been set aside to guarantee that the Cherokees would have unobstructed access to buffalo.qv The terms of the cession were not concluded until 1893, when the land was purchased by the federal government for roughly $1.40 an acre and opened to white homesteaders, who became known as "Sooners." The Cherokees were exempted from the provisions of the Dawes Severalty Act of 1887, which required tribal land to be broken up into individual allotments, but the exemption was short-lived. The Curtis Act, passed in 1898, required the Cherokees to establish tribal rolls and allot land to individual members on the basis of those rolls. By 1907, when Oklahoma became a state, the Cherokee lands had been severely reduced.

From the 1840s until the 1960s, Cherokees sought compensation from Texas for lands lost in 1839. In the mid-1850s the tribe had sent William P. Adair to Washington, D.C., to petition Congress for permission to sue the state of Texas for the return of 1.5 million acres in East Texas. The state offered the Cherokees fourteen million acres in the Panhandle qv as compensation, but the tribe declined the offer. For the next hundred years, the Cherokees periodically renewed their claims against the state of Texas, but without success. The most recent case, filed in 1963 by Earl Boyd Pearce, chief counsel for the Cherokees, petitioned the state of Texas for redress of the 1839 grievances. In an ingenious plan, Pearce asked for compensation in the form of free education for a thousand Cherokees in state-supported Texas universities. In an opinion handed down in March 1964, Texas attorney general Waggoner Carr denied the validity of the Cherokee claim on the grounds that the state of Texas is not liable for claims against the Republic of Texas.

In the 1970s the Cherokee Nation once again became a federally recognized "sovereign" nation, just as it had been for much of the nineteenth century. The nation, with its capital at Tahlequah, Oklahoma, has a population of 165,000 spread over fourteen counties in the northeastern corner of the state. Another 10,500 Cherokees, known as the Eastern Band, occupy the 56,000-acre Qualla Boundary Reservation in North Carolina. The town of Cherokee, located fifty miles west of Asheville, is the hub of that reservation. In the 1980 federal census, a total of 1,366,676 people across the United States identified themselves as Cherokees. The Cherokee Nation preserves tribal culture and seeks economic opportunities to provide a better future for its members.

BIBLIOGRAPHY: Mary Whatley Clarke, *Chief Bowles and the Texas Cherokees* (Norman: University of Oklahoma Press, 1971). Dianna Everett, *The Texas Cherokees: A People between Two Fires, 1819–1840* (Norman: University of Oklahoma Press, 1990). Grant Foreman, *Sequoyah* (Norman: University of Oklahoma Press, 1938). Duane M. King, *The Cherokee Indian Nation: A Troubled History* (Knoxville: University of Tennessee Press, 1979). James G. Mooney, *Myths of the Cherokee* (Washington: Smithsonian Institution, Bureau of American Ethnology, 1900). Geoffrey Norman, "The Cherokee: Two Nations, One People," *National Geographic,* May 1995. E. W. Winkler, "The Cherokee Indians in Texas," *Quarterly of the Texas State Historical Association* 7 (October 1903). Dorman H. Winfrey and James M. Day, eds., *Texas Indian Papers* (4 vols., Austin: Texas State Library, 1959–61; rpt., 5 vols., Austin: Pemberton Press, 1966). Grace Steele Woodward, *The Cherokees* (Norman: University of Oklahoma Press, 1963).

Carol A. Lipscomb

CHEROKEE JUNIOR COLLEGE. Cherokee Junior College, in Cherokee, San Saba County, was operated by the Llano, and later by the Lampasas, District conference of the Methodist Episcopal Church, South. The college was housed in a building that had originally belonged to West Texas Normal and Business College. The Llano District conference bought the building from Francis Marion Behrns on April 4, 1911, for $20,000. C. A. Lehmberg was named president of Cherokee Junior College, which accepted students from 1911 until at least the fall of 1918, when a small enrollment was reported. On July 21, 1921, the property was sold to the school trustees of San Saba County for $20,000. The building was used as a public school until it burned on January 30, 1945. In 1978 Cherokee High School stood on the site, the entrance to the old college having been incorporated in the new structure.

BIBLIOGRAPHY: Alma Ward Hamrick, *The Call of the San Saba: A History of San Saba County* (San Antonio: Naylor, 1941; 2d ed., Austin: Jenkins, 1969). San Angelo *Standard Times,* December 24, 1978. Alice Gray Upchurch, "A Sketch History of San Saba County," *Southwestern Historical Quarterly* 50 (July 1946). Vertical Files, Barker Texas History Center, University of Texas at Austin (Cherokee, Texas).

Wesley N. Schulze

CHEROKEE VILLAGE. Cherokee Village, on Caney Creek halfway between Kilgore and Henderson in northern Rusk County, was a Cherokee Indian settlement at the time of the arrival in the area of the first white settlers. The site was identified on maps in the late 1830s and may have been the "Village of Chief Bowles" where the 1836 treaty with the Cherokees was signed. The settlement later disappeared, and no trace of it remains.

BIBLIOGRAPHY: Eugene W. McWhorter, *Traditions of the Land: The History of Gregg County* (Longview, Texas: Gregg County Historical Foundation, 1989). Albert Woldert, "The Last of the Cherokees in Texas and the Life and Death of Chief Bowles," *Chronicles of Oklahoma* 1 (June 1923).

Christopher Long

CHEROKEE WAR. The Cherokee War of 1839 was the culmination of friction between the Cherokee, Kickapoo, and Shawnee Indians and the white settlers in Northeast Texas. The Indians, who had obtained squatters' rights to the land from Spanish authorities, were promised title to the land by the Consultation;qv and on February 23, 1836, a treaty made by Sam Houston and John Forbes,qqv who represented the provisional government,qv gave title to the lands between the Angelina and Sabine rivers and northwest of the Old San Antonio Roadqv to the Cherokees and their associated bands. The treaty was tabled by the Texas Senate on December 29, 1836, and was declared null and void by that body on December 16, 1837, despite Houston's insistence that it be ratified. The Córdova Rebellionqv in August 1838 caused Thomas Jefferson Ruskqv to march on the Cherokees in an effort to intercept Vicente Córdova;qv but Córdova did not seek shelter among the Cherokees, and Rusk returned to the settlements. On October 16, 1838, Rusk, with 230 troops, pursued a band of Kickapoos, destroyed their village, and killed eleven warriors, including one renegade Cherokee. There were sporadic raids by the Indians during the fall of 1838 and spring of 1839.

After the discovery, in May 1839, of a letter in the possession of Manuel Floresqv exposing plans by the Mexican government to enlist the Indians against the Texas settlers, President Mirabeau B. Lamar,qv supported by popular opinion, determined to expel the East Texas Indians. In July 1839, Kelsey H. Douglassqv was put in command of approximately 500 troops under Edward Burleson, Willis H. Landrum,qqv and Rusk, and was ordered to remove the Indians to Arkansas Territory. The army camped on Council Creek, six miles south of the principal Cherokee village of Chief Bowlqv and dispatched a commission on July 12 to negotiate for the Indians' removal. The Indians agreed to sign a treaty of removal that guaranteed to them the profit from their crops and the cost of the removal. During the next two days they insisted they were willing to leave but refused to sign the treaty because of a clause that would give them an armed escort out of the republic. On July 15 the commissioners told the Indians that the Texans would march on their village immediately and that those willing to accept the treaty should display a white flag. Landrum was sent across the Neches to cut off possible reinforcements, and the remainder of the army marched on the village. The battle of the Nechesqv occurred a few miles west of Tyler, in what is now Henderson County. By sundown three Texans had been killed and five wounded; the Indians had lost eighteen. The Indians fled, and Douglass made camp. Pursuit was begun on the morning of July 16. A scouting party under James Carter engaged the Cherokees near the headwaters of the Neches River at a site now in Van Zandt County. The Indians sought shelter in a hut and the surrounding cornfields but were forced to abandon them after Carter was reinforced by the arrival of Rusk and Burleson. After thirty minutes of fighting the Indians were forced to the Neches bottom, where Chief Bowl was killed and a number of warriors were lost. After the last fighting near Grand Saline, it was estimated that more than 100 Indians had been killed or wounded in the engagements.

On July 21 the Texans marched toward the headwaters of the Sabine River along the route taken by the fleeing Indians. Numerous huts and fields were destroyed that afternoon, and several villages and more than 200 acres of corn were burned on the morning of July 22. The destruction continued during the pursuit of the Indians, which was not abandoned until July 24. Most of the Indians fled to Cherokee lands outside the republic. During the winter a small group under Chief Egg and John Bowles, son of Chief Bowl, attempted to reach Mexico by skirting the fringe of white settlements. Burleson, on a campaign against the Plains Indians, intercepted the Cherokees and attacked them near the mouth of the San Saba River on December 25, 1839. Egg and Bowles and several warriors were killed, and twenty-seven women and children were captured. This was the last important action against the Cherokees in Texas.

BIBLIOGRAPHY: Dianna Everett, *The Texas Cherokees: A People between Two Fires, 1819–1840* (Norman: University of Oklahoma Press, 1990).

CHERRY, EMMA RICHARDSON (1859–1954). Emma Richardson Cherry, artist and preservationist, was born in Aurora, Illinois, on February 28, 1859, the eldest of four children of James Perkins and Frances Ann (Mostow) Richardson. Her father was an architect and carpenter and built the Aurora City Hall. Since he was unable to finance her art education, she taught art at the university at Lincoln, Nebraska, for three years before going to New York for advanced study at the Art Students League. She married Dillon Brooke Cherry in Nebraska before she went to Paris for further lessons. Among the European artists with whom she studied at different times were Jules Joseph Lefebvre and Andre L'Hote in Paris and Vettore Zanetti-Zilla and Vicente Poveda y Juan in Italy.

The Cherrys moved from Denver to Houston about 1893 and later bought the home of William Marsh Rice,qv which had to be moved from its downtown location. At least one version of the story says that Mrs. Cherry bid twenty-five dollars for the ornate front door and perhaps some interior rails and, as the sole bidder, acquired the entire house; other versions say that her husband engineered the purchase through a sealed bid. In any event, preservation of the Rice house is due to Emma Cherry. The residence was eventually sold to the Harris County Heritage Society in 1954. Since 1959 it has been open to the public in the society's downtown Sam Houston Park.

Emma Cherry, one of the earliest professional women artists in Houston, worked in oils, watercolors, pastels, pencil, and charcoal; though at least one critic referred to her use of "modern" laws of color, she painted a number of traditional portraits while living in Houston and experimented with a number of styles. She was known for her paintings of flowers and in 1937 did a study of oleanders to be presented to President Franklin Roosevelt during his visit to Galveston. Her other subjects include landscapes and figures. The most readily accessible of her works are four murals done for the Houston Public Libraryqv under the auspices of the Public Works Administration. In addition to a depiction of the capitol of the Republic of Texasqv and the first home of Sam Houston,qv both in Houston, she did views of the homes of Robert E. Lee and Jefferson Davis.qqv Each of the four is mounted amid painted native flora and symbols appropriate to the subject.

She exhibited her work at the Metropolitan Art School and the National Academy of Design in New York City, the Art Institute of Chicago, the Witte Museumqv in San Antonio, and the Museum of Fine Arts, Houston.qv She was also represented at the Paris Salon, the French-Irish exhibition in London, and the Columbian Exposition in 1893. In 1926 she traveled in North Africa and Europe, studying in Rome, Venice, and Paris; she made periodic trips abroad throughout her life. She taught locally in her studio. In 1900 she organized the Houston Public School Art League, which later became the Houston Museum of Fine Arts; the league provided replicas of old masters and ancient statues for public schools.

Mrs. Cherry won the gold medal from the Western Art Association in Omaha, Nebraska, a landscape prize from the Southern States Art League, and a still-life prize at the Texas Artists Exhibit in Nashville, Tennessee. In Texas her portraits won awards in Austin, Dallas, and Houston. Her works are included in the permanent collections of the Society of Civil Engineers in New York, the Denver Art Association, the Elisabet Ney Museumqv in Austin, the San Antonio Art League,qv the Museum of Fine Arts in Houston, and in public libraries. Mrs. Cherry was a member of many of the leading art associations of the United States. After the death of her husband in 1937, she lived with her only child, Dorothy, the wife of Col. Walter H. Reid. With the help of a magnifying glass, Emma Cherry continued to paint until a few weeks before her death, on October 29, 1954.

BIBLIOGRAPHY: Frances Battaile Fisk, *A History of Texas Artists and Sculptors* (Abilene, Texas, 1928; facsimile rpt., Austin: Morrison, 1986). Esse Forrester-O'Brien, *Art and Artists of Texas* (Dallas: Tardy, 1935). Houston *Post*, October 30, 1954. *Margaret Swett Henson*

CHERRY, JOHNSON BLAIR (1901–1966). Johnson Blair Cherry, football coach and oilman, was born at Kerens, Navarro County, Texas, on August 7, 1901. He began his coaching career at Ranger after graduating from Texas Christian University in 1924. After three years at Ranger he moved to Northside High School in Fort Worth. In 1930 he was named head coach at Amarillo High School and thus embarked on a remarkable career that saw his fabled Sandies win eighty-six of ninety-one games and four state championships in seven years. In 1936 he married Florence Snodgrass of Amarillo; they had two children. Cherry was hired at the University of Texas in 1937 by Dana X. Bible,qv and served as first assistant on the Longhorn staff for ten years. When Bible retired after the 1946 season, Cherry was named head coach. He accepted the challenge of following Bible and gambled on a new formation, the "T." As executed by quarterback Robert Lawrence (Bobby) Layne,qv the formation was an immediate success. In Cherry's four years at Texas, he had one Southwest Conferenceqv championship, three postseason bowl games, and an overall record of 32-10-1. He resigned after the 1950 season, in which his Longhorns ranked number two nationally and became the school's first team to win all of its Southwest Conference games, to enter the oil business in Lubbock. Cherry was voted into the Texas Sports Hall of Fameqv shortly before his death in Lubbock on September 10, 1966. He was buried in Llano Cemetery, Amarillo.

BIBLIOGRAPHY: Joe B. Frantz, *The Forty-Acre Follies* (Austin: Texas Monthly Press, 1983). Denne H. Freeman, *Hook 'Em Horns: A Story of Texas Football* (Huntsville, Alabama: Strode, 1974). Vertical Files, Barker Texas History Center, University of Texas at Austin.

Jones Ramsey

CHERRY, WILBUR H. (1820–1873). Wilbur H. Cherry, soldier, printer, and publisher in the Republic of Texas,qv was born in Oswego, New York, on January 4, 1820, and at the age of fifteen ran away from home to join in the Texas Revolution.qv On November 21, 1835, he joined Capt. Andrew Briscoe'sqv company of Liberty Volunteers and subsequently participated in the siege of Bexar.qv After the Texas Revolution Cherry joined the Army of the Republic of Texas,qv on December 24, 1839; he received a bounty payment of thirty dollars for enlisting as a private in Second Lt. R. W. Lee's Company F of Col. Edward Burleson'sqv First Regiment, Infantry. He served briefly in Capt. Benjamin Y. Gillen's Company I and on May 19, 1840, transferred into Capt. Adam Clendenin's Company A at Galveston.

For a time thereafter Cherry worked as a printer in Austin and in Liberty. He moved to Galveston in 1843 and there, in 1844, with Michael Cronican,qv whom he had first met during the siege of Bexar, became a publisher of the Galveston *Weekly News*. Its first issue appeared on January 6, under the editorship of Richard D. Sebring, who soon bought out Cronican's interest in the paper. Although the *News* claimed to be politically independent, it was in fact staunchly anti-Houston in its editorial stand, largely in response to the Houston administration's antipathy toward the Texas Navy,qv whose home port was Galveston. When Sebring died in July 1844, Cherry brought Benjamin F. Nealqv into the partnership to form the firm of Cherry,

Neal, and Company. These two men then hired Willard Richardson[qv] as their new editor. Within a year, however, Cherry and Neal sold their shares of the paper to Richardson and printer Gideon K. Lewis.[qv] In February 1850, at age thirty-one, Cherry joined John M. Gibson in publishing the Galveston *Democratic Journal*, a Whig newspaper. Robert H. Howard was their editor. Cherry bought out Gibson in July 1851 and left the paper himself in June 1853.

Cherry was a member of the Texas Veterans Association.[qv] On August 8, 1847, he married Mrs. Catherine French, the Irish-born widow of George H. French.[qv] The couple had four children. Cherry died in Galveston on June 12, 1873. At the time of his death he was working as a printer at the Galveston *Weekly News*.

BIBLIOGRAPHY: Daughters of the Republic of Texas, *Defenders of the Republic of Texas* (Austin: Laurel House, 1989). Galveston *Daily News*, April 11, 1842, June 13, 1873. Marilyn M. Sibley, *Lone Stars and State Gazettes: Texas Newspapers before the Civil War* (College Station: Texas A&M University Press, 1983). *Telegraph and Texas Register*, August 16, 1844.

Thomas W. Cutrer

CHERRY BRANCH. Cherry Branch rises eighteen miles northwest of Burnet in northwestern Burnet County (at 30°59′ N, 98°24′ W) and runs south for two miles to its mouth on Deer Creek (at 30°58′ N, 98°24′ W). The local flat terrain has some deep dissections and is surfaced by shallow, stony soils that support oak, juniper, and mesquite.

CHERRY CREEK (Edwards County). Cherry Creek rises in south central Edwards County (at 29°43′ N, 100°20′ W) and runs south for seven miles to its mouth on the West Nueces River (at 29°39′ N, 100°23′ W). The surrounding flat terrain with local deep and dense dissection is surfaced by shallow, stony soils that support oak, Ashe juniper, mesquite, and grasses.

_____ (Jeff Davis County). Cherry Creek rises a mile northeast of Mount Livermore and seventeen miles northwest of Fort Davis in central Jeff Davis County (at 30°41′ N, 104°10′ W) and runs northeast for sixty-seven miles before running dry five miles southwest of Pecos in central Reeves County (at 31°14′ N, 103°34′ W). In its lowest reaches the stream is flanked by levees for two miles. It crosses gently sloping and rugged, variable terrain surfaced by soils that support Mexican buckeye, walnut, persimmon, desert willow, scrub brush, and sparse grasses.

_____ (Kerr County). Cherry Creek rises seven miles south of State Highway 27 in southeastern Kerr County (at 29°51′ N, 98°56′ W) and runs north for nine miles to its mouth on the Guadalupe River, four miles east of Center Point (at 29°56′ N, 98°58′ W). It traverses an area characterized by rocky outcrops in the steep terraces and benches of the Balcones Escarpment,[qv] surfaced by loams that support open stands of live oak, mesquite, and Ashe juniper.

_____ (Lamar County). Cherry Creek rises four miles southwest of Paris in southern Lamar County (at 33°35′ N, 95°37′ W) and runs southeast for eight miles to its mouth on the North Sulphur River, southwest of Gadston and a half mile south of the Delta county line (at 33°28′ N, 95°36′ W). The local flat to gently rolling terrain is surfaced by dark clays and deep loams that support grasses, oak, and juniper in the creek's upper reaches. At its mouth floodplains are surfaced by clay loams.

_____ (Real County). Cherry Creek, a spring-fed stream, rises five miles north of the Uvalde county line in southeastern Real County (at 29°41′ N, 99°40′ W) and runs southwest for twenty-nine miles to its mouth on the Frio River, near Garner State Park[qv] in Uvalde County (at 29°35′ N, 99°43′ W). It descends the eastern side of the Frio canyon in a winding course over a bed of limestone, gravel, and calcareous soil. The surroundings are typical of the heavily dissected canyonlands of the Balcones Escarpment on the southern edge of the Edwards Plateau, forested with open stands of live oak, mesquite, and Ashe juniper.

CHERRY GROVE, TEXAS. Cherry Grove was off State highways 19 and 154 some seven miles north of Sulphur Springs in north central Hopkins County. A public school was operating there by 1898, when it had an enrollment of fifty-two black students. In the mid-1930s Cherry Grove had a church, a school, a cemetery, and a number of scattered houses. After World War II[qv] most of its residents moved away. Its school was consolidated with the North Hopkins School District, and by the early 1960s a church and a cemetery remained at the site. In the late 1980s Cherry Grove was a dispersed rural community.

Christopher Long

CHERRY MOUND, TEXAS. Cherry Mound is on Farm Road 1753 some ten miles northeast of Sherman in northeastern Grayson County. Settlement at the site began in the mid-1850s, when the David Cherry family arrived and settled on a rise that provided a view of the countryside. In the 1940s the community there had a school, a church, two businesses, and a number of scattered dwellings. Cherry Mound served area farmers and cattle ranchers as a school and church community. In 1988 Cherry Mound was still named on the county highway map, though no structures were shown at the site.

BIBLIOGRAPHY: Graham Landrum and Allen Smith, *Grayson County* (Fort Worth, 1960; 2d ed., Fort Worth: Historical Publishers, 1967).

David Minor

CHERRY SPRING, TEXAS. Cherry Spring is on Cherry Spring Creek a half mile south of the Mason county line and 16½ miles northwest of Fredericksburg in northern Gillespie County. The site was originally settled by Dietrich Rode and William Kothe, who left Fredericksburg in search of land in 1852. According to some sources Rode had built a small Lutheran church at Cherry Spring in 1849 with lumber shipped from Austin. Later settlers included William Marschall, Conrad Ahrens, Ludwig Spaeth, and Adam Schneider. Cherry Spring was on the route from San Antonio to El Paso and thus enjoyed a moderate prosperity as a commercial center. A number of the early settlers were sheep ranchers. The Cherry Spring post office was established in 1858, and by 1860 the town had a population of 202, 142 of whom had German surnames. In 1897 John O. Meusebach[qv] was buried at Cherry Spring. The community's post office closed in 1912. Its population was estimated at forty in 1933 but by 1964 had fallen to nine. In the late 1960s, however, Cherry Spring grew, reaching a reported population of seventy-five by 1970. Its population was still seventy-five in 1990.

BIBLIOGRAPHY: Rudolph L. Biesele, *The History of the German Settlements in Texas, 1831–1861* (Austin: Von Boeckmann–Jones, 1930; rpt. 1964). Sara Kay Curtis, A History of Gillespie County, Texas, 1846–1900 (M.A. thesis, University of Texas, 1943). Joe Tatum, "History of the Gillespie County Livestock Industry," *Southwestern Sheep and Goat Raiser*, July 1946.

Martin Donell Kohout

CHERRY SPRING CREEK. Cherry Spring Creek, also known as Cherry Springs Creek, rises twelve miles northwest of Fredericksburg in Gillespie County (at 30°26′ N, 98°57′ W) and runs north for twelve miles to its mouth on Hickory Creek, three miles northwest of Prairie Mountain in Llano County (at 30°34′ N, 98°56′ W). The spring-fed stream traverses an area of the Llano basin characterized by flat to rolling terrain that in places is deeply dissected. Local soils range from shallow and rocky to deep sandy and clay loams and support open stands of live oak and juniper.

CHESTER, TEXAS. Chester is near the junction of U.S. Highway 287 and Farm Road 1745, thirteen miles northwest of Woodville in extreme northwestern Tyler County. The townsite is part of a five-league grant made to Gavino Aranjo on the old road from Nacogdoches to Liberty. In 1883 the Trinity and Sabine Railway routed its new line through the area one mile south of Peach Tree Village. Lots were sold near the line, and soon the Peach Tree Village post office and the Mount Hope Masonic lodge moved to the new town of Chester on the railroad. The town was named for Chester A. Arthur, who was at the time a senator from New York. The first postmaster at Chester was A. B. Green, who had been postmaster in Peach Tree Village. W. B. Carnes had a mercantile business in the town, and Dr. Whitehead of Mount Hope set up his son with a store there as well. Tom Seamans had a blacksmith shop, John Cobb a saloon, and Bill Lee a boardinghouse, where he also worked as justice of the peace. Jackson Riley had a large hotel, and John Lowe was constable. By 1890 the town had a sawmill, a school, two gins, and two churches. The population of Chester was reported as 176 in 1904, 300 in 1914, and as 250 from the mid-1920s to the mid-1940s, when it rose to 350. It continued to be reported at that level until the late 1960s, when it dropped to around 260. By 1980 the population had risen to 301, and by 1988, to 409. The community generally had from seven to ten rated businesses during this period. The local blackland soil is fine farmland; Chester in the 1980s was also surrounded by prime pine forests and for many years had seen sawmill activity. In 1986 the town comprised farmers and cattle raisers, three churches, several stores, substantial homes, a school, a post office, and good roads. Its population was reported as 285 in 1990.

BIBLIOGRAPHY: *It's Dogwood Time in Tyler County* (Woodville, Texas), 1963, 1967. Lou Ella Moseley, *Pioneer Days of Tyler County* (Fort Worth: Miran, 1975). Thomas Clarence Richardson, *East Texas: Its History and Its Makers* (4 vols., New York: Lewis Historical Publishing, 1940). WPA Writers' Program, *Texas: A Guide* (New York: Hastings House, 1940; rev. ed. 1969).
Megan Biesele

CHESTERVILLE, TEXAS. Chesterville is near the point where Farm Road 1093 crosses the Colorado-Wharton county line in southeastern Colorado County. The community is the product of a land-development program begun in 1894 when John Linderholm, a land promoter from Chicago, purchased 60,000 acres in the area in the name of the Southern Texas Colonization Company. The name of the community is taken from the surveyor who plotted the area, William P. Chester. Colonization efforts were successful. In cooperation with the railroad, settlers came to the area from many states in the Midwest, and a post office was established in 1895. At the height of its development Chesterville had a school, several churches, and some twenty businesses serving a population of between 150 and 200. Land in the area was, however, better suited to large rice-farming and stock-raising enterprises than it was to small farms; consequently the population of Chesterville fell to seventy-five by 1914 and to twenty-five by 1933. The community's post office closed in 1950, and after 1966, when the population was still reported as twenty-five, population statistics were no longer recorded. By the mid-1980s, only one business remained there to serve the needs of the large rice farms in the area.

BIBLIOGRAPHY: *Colorado County Sesquicentennial Commemorative Book* (La Grange, Texas: Hengst Printing, 1986).
Jeff Carroll

CHEVALLIE, MICHAEL H. (?–1852). Michael H. Chevallie (Chevaille, Chevalier), Texas Ranger and leader of Chevallie's Battalion in the Mexican War,[qv] was born in Richmond, Virginia. Although less known than John Coffee Hays, Benjamin McCulloch, and Samuel H. Walker,[qqv] Chevallie and Robert A. Gillespie[qv] contributed their share of action to produce the heroic images of the early Texas Rangers.[qv] Chevallie joined the rangers in the early days of their role as citizen soldiers. His skills fitted the ranger creed: ride, shoot, and fight, with weapons and fists. In a story that is often cited in ranger histories, an Englishman complained to a general that Chevallie had beaten him. The officer exclaimed, "Keep a sharp look out or he will beat you again." By 1841 Chevallie had entered Texas and was in the field with Hays's rangers. He scouted, escorted colonists, took part in the struggle against Mexican cavalry near Laredo in 1841, and engaged Comanches at Paint Rock.

In 1845 he joined Gillespie's company of Texas Mounted Rangers as first lieutenant. These troops entered federal service under Gen. Zachary Taylor[qv] for the protection of the frontier. Then came several years of service with Hays's rangers. As a major of the First Regiment, Texas Mounted Rifles, under Colonel Hays, Chevallie took part in the assault on Monterrey in 1846. In this battle rangers carried out a frontal charge and took Federation Hill, which commanded the Saltillo road. Chevallie's battalion, mustered into federal service on April 25, 1847, escorted supply wagons and fought Mexican guerrillas in northern Mexico for General Taylor. In addition, the battalion tried to protect Mexicans from Apache and Comanche raids. Chevallie's troops, composed of five companies, most with over 100 men each, never fought as a unit. Company commanders were Henry W. Baylor, Walter P. Lane,[qqv] Robert N. Taylor, James B. Reed (Reid), and George W. Adams. Disagreements between Gen. John E. Wool[qv] and Major Chevallie made the latter resign his commission on August 31, 1847. Lane was promoted to major and commanded the battalion to the end of the war. When Hays formed another regiment to keep communication and supply lines open between Veracruz and Mexico City for the armed forces under Gen. Winfield Scott, Chevallie rejoined him. Although not formally listed in the chain of command of Hays's new regiment, he was still called major and ably carried out his duties as contract buyer and commissary officer. As a "civilian-along-for-a-fight," Chevallie was praised for his quick-thinking actions in engagements with Mexican guerrillas at Teotihuacán and Zacualtipán. His admiration for Hays brought him to blows with another ranger who was impersonating Colonel Hays. After the Mexican War Chevallie and others stayed in Mexico and hunted for Indian scalps for bounties from the Mexican government. Chevallie died in Stockton, California, in 1852.

BIBLIOGRAPHY: John S. Ford, *Rip Ford's Texas*, ed. Stephen B. Oates (Austin: University of Texas Press, 1963). James K. Greer, *Colonel Jack Hayes: Texas Frontier Leader and California Builder* (New York: Dutton, 1952; rev. ed., Waco: Morrison, 1974). William J. Hughes, *Rebellious Ranger: Rip Ford and the Old Southwest* (Norman: University of Oklahoma Press, 1964). Frederick Wilkins, *The Highly Irregular Irregulars: Texas Rangers in the Mexican War* (Austin: Eakin Press, 1990).
Harold J. Weiss, Jr.

CHEYENNE, TEXAS. Cheyenne was on the W. F. Scarborough Ranch, nine miles north of Kermit in northern Winkler County. In 1926 oil was discovered in the county, and in 1927 the Scarborough field was found. Anticipating an oil boom in 1928, newcomers built a number of shacks at Cheyenne. A bond election was called by the Winkler County Commissioners Court in the amount of $75,000 to build a school. However, the bonds were cancelled, and the school was never built. Cheyenne lost in competition with another new town called Leck, located five miles to the west in the newly-discovered Leck oilfield.

Although a post office was established at Cheyenne in 1929, the townsite was returned to W. F. Scarborough the next year. He moved the post office to a site east of the newly constructed Texas–New Mexico Railway and near State Highway 82, which later became State Highway 18. A large building was constructed for the post office and a grocery store. Residences were built for the postmaster and the store keeper. A railroad section house and several smaller houses were erected also. Four businesses were reported at Cheyenne in 1933, but only one was still in operation in 1939, when a population of twenty-five was recorded. Shipping pens held the many cattle sent by railroad from Cheyenne during the 1930s and early 1940s. The railroad abandoned Cheyenne in the 1940s, and the post office closed in 1944.

BIBLIOGRAPHY: *A History of Winkler County* (Kermit, Texas: Winkler County Historical Commission, 1984).
Julia Cauble Smith

CHEYENNE DRAW. Cheyenne Draw rises a half mile south of the New Mexico border in the northeastern corner of Loving County (at 31°59′ N, 103°23′ W) and runs east for 4½ miles, then sinks in sand a mile east of the Winkler county line (at 31°59′ N, 103°18′ W). The flat to rolling desert terrain is surfaced by windblown sand, shale, siltstone, and locally active dunes that support small mesquites, yucca, and bear grass. The draw was named for Cheyenne, Texas, a post office and railroad station in Winkler County that is now a ghost town.

BIBLIOGRAPHY: Ed Ellsworth Bartholomew, *The Encyclopedia of Texas Ghost Towns* (Fort Davis, Texas, 1982).

CHEYENNE INDIANS. The Cheyenne Indians were one of the plains tribes of the Algonquian family. They were first encountered by white explorers in what is now South Dakota, but in 1868 the Cheyennes were moved to a reservation in Indian Territory. In 1874 they left the reservation and along with Comanches and Kiowas participated in the second battle of Adobe Walls.[qv]

BIBLIOGRAPHY: George Bird Grinnell, *The Cheyenne Indians, Their History and Ways of Life* (New Haven: Yale University Press, 1923). Evetts Haley, Jr., "Adobe Walls," *Junior Historian*, January 1948. Frederick Webb Hodge, ed., *Handbook of American Indians North of Mexico* (2 vols., Washington: GPO, 1907, 1910; rpt., New York: Pageant, 1959). E. Adamson Hoebel, *The Cheyennes, Indians of the Great Plains* (New York: Holt, 1960).

CHIAMON BAYOU. Chiamon Bayou rises just northwest of Bronson near the San Augustine county line in western Sabine County (at 31°22′ N, 94°01′ W). Before the development of the Sam Rayburn Reservoir, the stream ran southwest for 10½ miles to its mouth on Ayish Bayou, fifteen miles south of San Augustine (at 31°17′ N, 94°07′ W). Sam Rayburn Reservoir inundated the lower reaches of the creek. The surrounding nearly level terrain is surfaced by loam and clay that support patches of dense pine and hardwood forests. The area is used predominantly for agriculture and as forest land.

CHICAGO, ROCK ISLAND AND GULF RAILWAY. The Chicago, Rock Island and Gulf Railway Company was chartered on May 13, 1902, in the interest of the Chicago, Rock Island and Pacific Railway (Rock Island) to construct an extension of the Rock Island system from Fort Worth to Galveston. It had a capital stock of $15,000,000. The principal place of business was Fort Worth. The members of the first board of directors were M. A. Low of Topeka; N. H. Lassiter, S. B. Hovey, Henry C. Holloway, F. E. Dietrich, and W. G. Newby, all of Fort Worth; and J. B. Wilson of Dallas.

In 1903 the CRI&G built thirty-two miles of track between Fort Worth and Dallas. No track was built south of Dallas, as the Rock Island eventually acquired a 50 percent interest in the Trinity and Brazos Valley in order to reach Houston and Galveston. In December 1903 the CRI&G acquired and merged three other Texas subsidiaries of the Rock Island. The Chicago, Rock Island and Mexico Railway and the Choctaw, Oklahoma and Texas Railroad operated lines in the Texas Panhandle, while the Chicago, Rock Island and Texas Railway ran between Terral, Oklahoma, and Fort Worth. The merger created a 334-mile system. An extension from Amarillo to the Texas–New Mexico border near Glenrio, New Mexico, was completed in 1910. At Glenrio the CRI&G connected with another Rock Island line to Tucumcari, New Mexico. A connection at Tucumcari with what later became the Southern Pacific completed a through route between Memphis and the Pacific Coast. In 1916 the CRI&G owned fifty-five locomotives and 2,044 cars and reported passenger earnings of $848,000 and freight earnings of $2,476,000. In 1931 the line owned forty locomotives and 1,078 cars and reported passenger earnings of $778,000 and freight earnings of $5,500,000; that year it was listed as a Class I railroad.

No other major construction occurred until the late 1920s, when a series of new lines was projected for the Panhandle[qv] and adjoining states. The lines built included a route between Amarillo and Liberal, Kansas. The Texas portion opened as far as Stinnett in 1927 and was extended to Hitchland in 1929. Another Panhandle branch between Dalhart and Morse opened in 1930. In 1940 the CRI&G acquired the track of the Gulf, Texas and Western running seventy-five miles between Jacksboro and Seymour. However, the attempt to revive this line was unsuccessful, and it was abandoned in 1942.

The CRI&G was leased to its parent, the Chicago, Rock Island and Pacific Railway, on September 1, 1939. Both companies had entered receivership in 1933. The CRI&G was merged into the reorganized CRI&P on January 1, 1948, at which time the separate Texas organization ceased to exist. When merged, the CRI&G operated 732 miles of track that included the lease of ninety-six miles of the Burlington–Rock Island between Dallas and Teague.   *Nancy Beck Young*

CHICAGO, ROCK ISLAND AND MEXICO RAILWAY. The Chicago, Rock Island and Mexico Railway Company was chartered by the Chicago, Rock Island and Pacific Railway on December 17, 1900, to construct the Texas portion of the projected line between Liberal, Kansas, and Santa Rosa, New Mexico. The plan was to build from the northern boundary of Sherman County southwest 110 miles to the west line of Hartley County. The initial capital was $2 million, and the business office was in Twist, Hartley County. Members of the first board of directors included S. B. Hovey, J. C. McCabe, F. E. Deitrich, and M. V. Harris, all of Fort Worth; Robert Mather and J. M. Johnson of Chicago, Illinois; and M. A. Low of Topeka, Kansas. Construction took place in 1901 and 1902; ninety-two miles of track was laid from Texhoma, Oklahoma, through Dalhart, to Bravo, Texas. This line formed part of the Golden State Route of the Rock Island and Southern Pacific. In 1903 the CRI&M owned 459 railroad cars; earnings for that year included $96,637 in passenger revenue and $246,833 in freight revenue. On December 1, 1903, the line was merged into the Chicago, Rock Island and Gulf Railway.   *Chris Cravens*

CHICAGO, ROCK ISLAND AND PACIFIC RAILROAD. The Chicago, Rock Island and Pacific Railroad Company (Rock Island) was chartered in Delaware on December 16, 1947, as successor in reorganization to the Chicago, Rock Island and Pacific Railway. The new company, which also consolidated the Chicago, Rock Island and Gulf Railway, began operating on January 1, 1948, with 7,650 miles of track in fourteen states. Originally chartered in Illinois on February 27, 1848, as the Rock Island and LaSalle Rail Road Company, the road was renamed Chicago and Rock Island Rail Road Company on February 7, 1851, and Chicago, Rock Island and Pacific Railroad Company in 1866. In Texas the Rock Island operated 633 miles of main track plus joint ownership of the Burlington–Rock Island. Three main Rock Island routes crossed the state. The Midcontinent Route ran from Minneapolis–St. Paul to Fort Worth and Dallas and, with the Burlington–Rock Island, to Houston and Galveston. The other two main lines connected with the Southern Pacific at Tucumcari, New Mexico, to form through routes to the Pacific Coast. These were the Golden State Route, running from Chicago and Kansas City through Dalhart, and the Choctaw Route, which ran from Memphis and Oklahoma City through Amarillo. In addition to its Texas routes, the Rock Island also served the major railroad centers of St. Louis, Missouri, and Denver, Colorado. Two of the named passenger trains of the Rock Island operating across Texas were the Twin Star Rocket and the Golden State Limited.

The Rock Island acquired thirty-nine miles of the Wichita Falls and Southern Railroad between Graham and South Hanlon in 1955, but abandoned this line in 1969. The Rock Island had acquired a 50 percent interest in what later became the Burlington–Rock Island in 1906. The B–RI was operated separately until 1964, when it was merged into the parent companies. This allowed the Rock Island direct access to the Houston and Galveston markets. In addition, the

Rock Island owned 50 percent interest in the Galveston Terminal, 45 percent interest in the Great Southwest, and one-eighth interest in both the Houston Belt and Terminal and the Union Terminal Company at Dallas. Track abandonments by the Rock Island included the 12.5 miles between Dalhart and Wilco in 1960 and the forty-five miles between Amarillo and Stinnett in 1972. The fifty-four-mile branch between Bridgeport and Graham was sold to the Texas Export in 1973.

The Rock Island was one of the weaker major railroads, and reentered receivership in 1975. At that time the line had 609 locomotives and 27,736 freight cars. Attempts to sell the railroad to a stronger carrier were delayed by regulatory hearings while the financial and physical condition of the Rock Island continued to deteriorate. The line was unable to withstand the effects of a strike and ceased operations on March 31, 1980. However, major portions of the Rock Island in Texas were acquired by other railroads, including the Golden State Route by the St. Louis Southwestern and the Midcontinent Route from Kansas to Fort Worth by the Oklahoma, Kansas and Texas (now the Union Pacific). The jointly owned line between Dallas and Houston continued to be operated by the Burlington Northern. Most of the Choctaw Route, however, was abandoned.

George C. Werner

CHICAGO, ROCK ISLAND AND TEXAS RAILWAY. The Chicago, Rock Island and Texas Railway, a subsidiary of the Chicago, Rock Island and Pacific, was chartered on July 15, 1892, to build from a point on the north boundary of Montague County south to Weatherford in Parker County, a distance of seventy-five miles. The road was capitalized at $3 million, and the business office was located at Bowie. Members of the first board of directors included C. H. Thompson of Hennessey, Oklahoma; Joseph T. Harris of Belcher; M. A. Low and W. F. Evans of Topeka, Kansas; and John H. Matthews, Zachary T. Lowrie, and H. F. Weber, all of Bowie.

The Chicago, Rock Island and Texas Railway was organized to extend the Rock Island from Oklahoma into Texas. By 1893 fifty-five miles of track had been constructed from the Oklahoma-Texas state line to Paradise. In 1893 the charter was amended to authorized the line to open a branch to Fort Worth and Dallas. The track was extended thirty-six miles to Fort Worth by 1894, giving the road a total of ninety-one miles in Texas. Earnings for 1895 included $89,638 in passenger revenue, $325,378 in freight revenue, and $253 in other revenue.

Though the line to Weatherford was never built, another amendment authorized the construction of a branch to Graham. The track was completed from Bridgeport to Jacksboro, twenty-eight miles, in 1899, and opened to Graham, twenty-seven miles, in 1903. In 1903 the railroad operated a total of 147 miles of track in Texas, owned 1,150 freight cars, and earned $467,642 in passenger revenue, $930,200 in freight revenue, and $96,668 in other revenue. The Chicago, Rock Island and Texas was merged into the Chicago, Rock Island and Gulf Railway on December 1, 1903.

Chris Cravens

CHICAGO, TEXAS AND MEXICAN CENTRAL RAILWAY. The Chicago, Texas and Mexican Central Railway Company was chartered on September 16, 1880, to acquire the moribund Dallas, Cleburne and Rio Grande Railway. The DC&RG had completed fifty-three miles of narrow-gauge track between Dallas and Cleburne in 1879. In order to collect a promised bonus, the company ran one freight and one passenger train over the line, but service was then abandoned. At this time a number of prominent Dallas businessmen, including Alexander Sanger,qv J. B. Simpson, and A. T. Hardie, became involved in the project. These men secured investments from northern businessmen and a bonus of $50,000 to replace the narrow-gauge line with a standard-gauge road. The line would connect Dallas with the Gulf, Colorado and Santa Fe track at Cleburne. A new charter was taken out on September 16, 1880, under the name Chicago, Texas and Mexican Central Railway Company. The planned railroad was to connect Dallas with the Rio Grande in Kinney County and with the Red River in Lamar County.

The capital was $7,500,000, and the principal place of business was Dallas. The members of the first board of directors were Daniel H. Hale, Clinton B. Hale, and Thomas P. Robb, all of Chicago; Dwight K. Tripp of Washington, D. C.; and Simpson, Hardie, Thomas L. Marsalis,qv L. H. Fitzhugh, and T. A. Wilmans, all of Dallas. The line was acquired by the Gulf, Colorado and Santa Fe Railway Company in June 1882, and the GC&SF began the conversion to standard gauge the following month.

Cecil Harper, Jr.

CHICANA RESEARCH AND LEARNING CENTER. The Chicana Research and Learning Center, the first research and service project in the nation founded and run by and for Mexican-American women, opened in 1974 at the University Methodist Student Center in Austin, after an initial two-year period of fund-raising and program planning in Texas and other states. The CRLC was established by women in the Chicanoqv movement to focus attention on gender issues and roles. To denote its cultural ties and its concern with women's issues, CRLC adopted a logo consisting of an Aztec eagle and the universal symbol for female. Its board of directors was made up of women, and Evey Chapa became its executive director. She was already deeply involved in the movement and had previously worked as the associate director of Juárez Lincoln University.

The CRLC set out to accomplish two goals: to identify the social and educational barriers to Chicanas' progress and to develop Chicana-organized "bilingual-bicultural demonstration models" to overcome these barriers. During the center's two years of operation it identified issues for research and provided technical assistance and training programs to resolve the issues. Its small staff was assisted by many University of Texas at Austin volunteers. Together, the women organized projects in historical research, curriculum development, and human-resources training to address what they defined as the triple oppression faced by Mexican-American women—as women, as members of an ethnic minority, and as women within their culture.

The CRLC maintained communication with Chicanas in other states and inspired members to study their heritage and become involved in the Chicano movement. The CRLC sought scholarly and practical ways to address Chicanas' needs. For instance, its research efforts resulted in *La Mujer Chicana: An Annotated Bibliography* (1975), which listed 320 documents dealing with twelve areas, including feminism, history, labor, culture, machismo, politics, and health. *La Mujer Chicana: A Texas Anthology* (1976) was another of the organization's efforts to document Chicana history. Moreover, the CRLC was involved in organizing the first university course on Chicanas in Texas at the University of Texas at Austin in the spring of 1975, which Chapa, the CRLC executive director, taught. The bibliography, anthology, and course were considered a means to awaken intellectuals to the importance of Chicana studies.

The CRLC also encouraged members' political activities by maintaining files on Chicana conferences, leaders, and their other political and social-action efforts in the state. As a result of this work, the CRLC developed links to such public-service agencies as the Civil Rights Commission and the Texas Manpower Commission. The center also provided assistance for a handbook on women's rights with the Women's Law Caucus at the University of Texas Law School and for an anthology on Chicanas for Notre Dame University Press. The CRLC worked independently, however, on one of its most important ventures—the *"concientización y desarollo de la mujer"* ("consciousness raising for women") training sessions—in which some 500 individuals participated. The Chicana Research and Learning Center closed after two years due to lack of money.

BIBLIOGRAPHY: Evey Chapa, *Chicana Research and Learning Center: A Progress Report, April 1973 to August 1975* (Austin, 1975). Evey Chapa, *La Mujer Chicana: An Annotated Bibliography* (Austin: Chicana Research and Learning Center, 1976).

Teresa Palomo Acosta

CHICANA RIGHTS PROJECT. The Chicana Rights Project was established by the Mexican American Legal Defense and Education Fund[qv] in 1974 to address the legal rights of poor Mexican-American women. The project focused on discrimination in employment and health but also addressed education, housing, and credit. MALDEF was founded in 1968, and in 1974, shortly after Vilma Martínez of San Antonio became its first woman director, the Chicana Rights Project was initiated. The Ford Foundation provided funds for the project for San Francisco and San Antonio. In 1978 national director Patricia M. Vasquez coordinated the project out of the San Antonio office, and Carmen A. Estrada operated the San Francisco office. In 1980 the project was headed by Estrada in San Francisco, and Norma Solis, staff attorney, and Elsa Giron Nava, a full-time paralegal, operated in San Antonio.

The project consisted of three units—litigation, research, and community education. In 1975 it began monitoring the impact of the Comprehensive Employment and Training Act program on Mexican women in San Antonio. In 1976 the project filed the administrative complaint *Hernández, et. al v. Cockrell, et. al.* against the city of San Antonio. After the complaint was filed, the number of women and minority members in the San Antonio CETA programs rose from 20 to 50 percent. This case was unique at the time because it was one of a few in the nation filed under CETA on behalf of women that ended in an agreement. Consequently, CETA programs were restructured to designate women as a priority group.

The project also filed a class-action suit against the Texas Employment Commission[qv] seeking unemployment compensation benefits for pregnant women. It filed lawsuits in California and Texas to challenge sterilization abuses and cutbacks in health services. The project obtained compliance reviews and audits of the five largest banks in the San Antonio area under an executive order to assure equal employment opportunities for women.

The project initiated an informational pamphlet series in 1975. Some of the pamphlets were *Profile of the Chicana, A Statistical Fact Sheet* (1975, 1978), which included census data; *Chicanas: Women's Health Issues* (1978), which addressed abortion and sterilization abuse; *CETA: An Economic Tool for Women* (1979); and *Chicanas and Mental Health* (1979), which dealt with cultural sensitivity in mental health practices. *Hispanic Women: Immigration Issues* (1979) addressed the preference system, deportation hearings, voluntary departures, and immigrant rights; *Hispanic/Women's Employment Rights* (1980) focused on employment issues. *The 1980 Census: Impact on Hispanics and Women* and *Texas Women's Legal Rights Handbook,* a guide to federal and state laws, were both produced in English and Spanish in 1980.

Project members participated in panels, legal workshops, and community outreach at the local, regional, and national levels. The project served as a resource and liaison for Hispanic women's organizations in the United States. It also provided written and oral testimony to state and federal agencies.

The project depended on foundation grants. It received funds from the Ford, Rockefeller Family, Revlon, and Playboy foundations. Around 1982 the project staff noted that it was underfunded; by March 14, 1983, its director had resigned. When the project lost its funding, MALDEF discontinued it.

BIBLIOGRAPHY: Karen O'Connor and Lee Epstein, "A Legal Voice for the Chicano Community: The Activities of the Mexican American Legal Defense and Educational Fund, 1968–82," in *The Mexican American Experience,* ed. Rudolfo O. de la Garza et al. (Austin: University of Texas Press, 1985). Julian Samora Papers, Benson Latin American Collection, University of Texas at Austin.

Cynthia E. Orozco

CHICANO. Although the etymology of *Chicano* is uncertain, linguists and folklorists offer several theories for the origins of the word. According to one explanation, the pre-Columbian tribes in Mexico called themselves Meshicas, and the Spaniards, employing the letter *x* (which at that time represented a *sh* and *ch* sound), spelled it *Mexicas.* The Indians later referred to themselves as Meshicanos and even as Shicanos, thus giving birth to the term *Chicano.* Another theory about the word's derivation holds that Mexicans and Mexican Americans[qv] have historically transferred certain consonants into *ch* sounds when expressing kinship affection or community fellowship. In this manner, *Mexicanos* becomes *Chicanos.* The term has been part of the Mexican-American vocabulary since the early twentieth century, and has conveyed at least two connotations. Mexican Americans of some social standing applied it disparagingly to lower-class Mexicans, but as time passed, adolescents and young adults (usually males) used *Chicano* as an affirmative label expressing camaraderie and commonality of experience.

During the 1960s and 1970s, the designation gained mainstream prominence because of a civil-rights groundswell (*see* CIVIL-RIGHTS MOVEMENT) within Mexican-American communities. The catalyst in Texas was a dramatic farmworkers' march during the summer of 1966; the march from South Texas to Austin turned media attention to the plight of the state's army of agricultural field hands. Inspired by the courage of the farmworkers, by the California strikes led by Cesar Chavez, and by the Anglo-American youth revolt of the period, many Mexican-American university students came to participate in a crusade for social betterment that was known as the Chicano movement. They used *Chicano* to denote their rediscovered heritage, their youthful assertiveness, and their militant agenda. Though these students and their supporters used *Chicano* to refer to the entire Mexican-American population, they understood it to have a more direct application to the politically active parts of the Tejano[qv] community.

Almost from the initial mainstream appearance of *Chicano* during the 1960s, the Spanish-speaking population resented the word's broad usage, and this displeasure led to the cognomen's decline in general discourse by the late 1970s. The older generation remembered the word's earlier disparaging implications, and other Mexican Americans felt uncomfortable using *Chicano* in formal conversation. Most significantly, many Mexican Americans rejected the way self-styled Chicanos had taken the expression from its in-group folkloric context and appropriated it for common dialogue. It was this violation of folkloric norms that produced the word's repudiation from within by the early 1980s. *Mexican Americans, Hispanics,* or *Latinos* took its place. *Chicano,* however, remained a part of the overall in-group lexicon.

BIBLIOGRAPHY: José E. Limón, "Expressive Dimensions of Heterogeneity and Change: The Folk Performance of 'Chicano' and the Cultural Limits of Political Ideology," in *"And Other Neighborly Names": Social Process and Cultural Image in Texas Folklore,* ed. Richard Bauman and Roger D. Abrahams (Austin: University of Texas Press, 1981).

Arnoldo De León

CHICANO ART NETWORKS. The Chicano art networks established in Texas during the mid-1960s were part of a larger effort by Mexican-American literary, theatrical, and visual artists to foster Mexican-American aesthetics and venues. The networks were independent coalitions aligned philosophically with the Chicano[qv] movement, which emphasized cultural identity and political activism. In Texas the networks sprang from the artists' commitment to record their historical experiences in an Anglo environment. They composed in Spanish and *caló* (an argot; *see* PACHUCOS), worked indepen-

Flor i canto/Flor i canto dos, by Amado Peña, 1975. Poster. Mexican-American Art Collection, Benson Latin American Collection, University of Texas at Austin.

dently of the mainstream, and employed American Indian, Spanish, and Mexican perspectives in their work. Visual artists presented their art in posters and murals and believed such representational works were the most direct form of communication with their people.

Networks operated in distinct ways. Writers helped launch the Chicano Literary Renaissance[qv] in Texas by forming publishing collectives. These collaborations were limited by costs, but they produced important books. For instance, in 1976 poets Carmen Tafolla, Reyes Cárdenas, and Cecilio García-Camarillo, the first editor of *Caracol*, an important journal of the renaissance, jointly published *Get Your Tortillas Together*. Cárdenas and Tafolla later received awards in Texas and California, respectively, for their poetry. In 1977 *Caracol* published *NahuatliangDoing*, a book featuring twenty-three writers, more than half from Texas. The journal had called for poetry written in Spanish and English, as well as in Nahuatl, the language of the Aztecs. Chicano Artistas Sirviendo a Aztlán of Austin developed *'TA CINCHO* (1977), which spotlighted fifteen poets and an art piece called *Huelga* ("*Strike*") by Amado Peña, who later won national ac-

claim for his silkscreens. In 1978 CASA joined *Tejidos,* a literary journal, in producing *Encuentro Artístico Femenil*. This book emanated from an event at Juárez-Lincoln University on November 28, 1977. Both the event and book featured female writers associated with CASA and visual artists involved in Mujeres Artistas del Suroeste.[qv] Nineteen woman poets, musicians, painters, photographers, and other visual artists appeared in *Encuentro*. Literary networks also organized public readings, art exhibitions, and musical performances. During the 1970s the plays *Festival de Flor y Canto* and *Canto al Pueblo* were performed in Texas and elsewhere. Anthologies featuring the writers involved in the festivals often were the only means for new writers to appear in print. Collectively, the anthologies contained works by writers who formed the nucleus of Mexican-American literature in the 1980s and beyond. *Canto Al Pueblo*, for instance, featured novelist Rolando Hinojosa-Smith and poets Evangelina Vigil and Abelardo Delgado, all of whom later achieved prominence.

Less is known about the Chicano theater networks. Five groups thrived: Chicano Arts Theater and the Teatro de los Barrios, both of San Antonio; Teatro de los Pobres of El Paso; Teatro Chicano de Austin; and Teatro de los Malqueridos (Theater of the Abhorred) of Mercedes. These groups were affiliated with the Teatro Nacional de Aztlán, a national organization of Mexican-American theaters established in 1971 in California. Theatrical companies also tried to establish a "federation of Tejano theaters." In July 1978 they hosted the annual national Chicano theater festival in San Antonio. (*See also* MEXICAN-AMERICAN THEATER.)

When the Chicano art movement emerged, museums, galleries, art schools, and university art departments were Anglo institutions that preached the gospel of "art for art's sake." Artists were encouraged to produce a universal art with minimal references to time and place. Form was emphasized over content, which was trivialized (in the case of Pop art) or banished altogether (as in Minimalism). Some artists explored media emphasizing content, but most schools and museums pronounced the political themes of Chicano art provincial. Latino artists in the Southwest and elsewhere established art groups and cultural centers to publicize their work and ideas. One of the earliest groups was formed in San Antonio in late 1967. At different times it used the names Los Pintores de Aztlán, Tlacuilo, and Los Pintores de la Nueva Raza. It offered lectures on design and Chicano sensibility. Its exhibitions (1970, 1971) were among the earliest to feature Chicano art. In 1972 Los Pintores de la Nueva Raza reorganized as Con Safo, named after an expression on murals and other works that requested respect for Chicano art. Con Safo organized several exhibitions, including one that visited colleges and universities in Michigan in the spring of 1972. Con Safo broke up in 1975 following internal dissent over the definition of Chicano art. One group argued that Chicano art should not function solely as an "artistic arm of any political ideology," and formed Los Quemados ("the Burned Ones"). Con Safo was short-lived, but it enhanced the reputations of many of its members, who included Melesio Casas, Felipe Reyes, Santa Barraza, Carmen Lomas Garza, César Augusto Martínez, Carolina Flores, and Amado Peña. Other art networks active in Texas included the San Antonio art group Ladrones de la Luz (active ca. 1979) and the Austin groups El Grupo (active ca. 1967), Chicano Artistas Sirviendo a Aztlán (active ca. 1977), the League of United Chicano Artists (middle to late 1970s), and the Mujeres Artistas del Suroeste (1977 to the mid-1980s).

Some Chicano art groups used their programs and centers to affect their communities. San Antonio's Community Cultural Arts Organization, for instance, a city-funded agency established in 1979, produced more than 200 murals by 1992 at public-housing projects in the West Side barrio representing Mexican and Chicano history. Led by Anastacio "Tache" Torres and Rudy Treviño, who worked with students and former students from local high schools, the organization also operated a truancy program. The Performance Artists Nucleus, Incorporated, formed in San Antonio in 1979, spearheaded the reconstruction of the West Side's historic Teatro Guadalupe, which opened in 1984 as the Guadalupe Cultural Arts Center.qv In 1992 the Teatro Guadalupe was one of the largest Latino art organizations in the nation. The center sponsored programs in visual arts, music, literature, film, theater, and dance. It offered classes to the public and published *Tonantzín,* a periodical filled with artwork, literature, and listings of cultural activities. The center's eclectic, multidisciplinary approach was dedicated to community education and enrichment. Other organizations included Mexic-Arteqv (founded in 1984) and Galería sin Fronteras (1986) in Austin, the Instituto Chicano de Artes y Artesanías (1972–74) and El Centro Cultural de Aztlán (early 1970s) in San Antonio, the Southwest Chicano Art Center (middle to late 1970s) in Houston, and the Xochil Art and Culture Centerqv (late 1960s–1989) in Mission. La Peña,qv established in Austin in 1982, hosted literary, musical, and visual-arts events without the benefit of a center.

Chicano artists used exhibitions to share their work with people in the barrio and to legitimize their efforts nationally. Early exhibitions were modest affairs at community art galleries, colleges, or art centers. Pamphlets contained artists' statements and a checklist of works. In 1973 art historian Jacinto Quirarte published *Mexican American Artists,* an overview that prompted a traveling exhibition featuring their works. A Mexican-American art exhibition also took place at Trinity University in San Antonio in 1973. An accompanying symposium attracted artists and historians from around the nation. It received extensive media coverage and helped form a national network of Chicano artists. More ambitious exhibitions followed, such as the *Festival de Flor y Canto* and *Canto al Pueblo* celebrations. In the late 1970s Chicano art emerged as a national force. Corporations such as Illinois Bell Telephone and Exxon sponsored traveling exhibitions that opened museum doors to Mexican-American art. In 1977 the National Endowment for the Arts formed a National Task Force on Hispanic Arts to gather information on the movement and seek ways to support Mexican-American arts. Tejanos Luis Jiménez, Carmen Lomas Garza, Jacinto Quirarte, and Tomás Rivera served on the task force, with other artists, writers, and historians. *A Directory of Hispanic American Arts Organizations,* prepared by the Research Center for the Arts and Humanities in San Antonio, was published in 1982. As the artists won recognition, museums and galleries arranged special exhibitions. With foundation and corporation support, curators and exhibit organizers published illustrated catalogues with critical essays to accompany the exhibits. The success of these presentations varied. Several were organized by Anglo curators who knew little of the social and political contexts of Chicano art and imposed selection criteria based on formal qualities. Texas museums generally included Chicanos in exhibition planning. Artist Santos Martinez organized Dále Gas for the Contemporary Arts Museumqv of Houston (1977), and the San Antonio Museum of Artqv and the Guadalupe Cultural Arts Center co-organized Influence: An Exhibition of Works by Contemporary Hispanic Artists Living in San Antonio, Texas (1987).

In the mid-1970s the Chicano art movement lost its political base. Most Mexican Americansqv rejected the separatist ideology of the early years of the movement. Some Chicano artists joined the mainstream art world. Government funding diminished. Chicano artists who focused on social protest came under pressure. Many, however, had built on earlier alliances. In 1991 a traveling exhibit, Chicano Art: Resistance and Affirmation, 1965–1985, organized by the UCLA Wight Art Gallery, celebrated the legacy of the artists and art groups whose creativity had fueled the Chicano Renaissance. As Chicano writer collaborations diminished, literary festivals ended and state gatherings declined. Such regional publishing houses as Arte Público continued to produce Chicano literature. Chicano drama in Texas flourished only where performers, playwrights, and directors had a home base. In the 1990s the Guadalupe Cultural Arts Center in San Antonio was the most prominent in the field. Though Teatro Dallas presented Spanish-language productions, it ignored Chicano ideology. In Austin, Los Actores de Austin and the Colores Collective remained active but did not collaborate on productions.

BIBLIOGRAPHY: Leonardo Carillo et al., eds., *Canto al Pueblo: An Anthology of Experiences* (San Antonio: Penca, 1978). Richard Griswold del Castillo et al., eds., *Chicano Art: Resistance and Affirmation, 1965–1985,* Wight Art Gallery, University of California, Los Angeles, 1991. Jacinto Quirarte, ed., *Chicano Art History: A Book of Selected Readings* (Research Center for the Arts and Humanities, University of Texas at San Antonio, 1984).

Teresa Palomo Acosta and Kendall Curlee

CHICANO LITERARY RENAISSANCE. The Chicanoqv literary renaissance, a flowering of all forms of literature by Mexican Americansqv throughout the Southwest, started in 1965 with the Teatro Campesino (Farmworkers Theater) in California. In Texas, however, the renaissance started in 1969, with the publication of poet Abelardo Delgado's *25 Pieces of a Chicano Mind,* and lasted for about ten years of renewed literary activity among Mexican Americans in the state. The writers reaffirmed their ethnic identity and addressed their community through fiction, poetry, essays, and works of drama that responded to its political, economic, and social history. They also pioneered in Texas literature the use of "Spanglish," which combines English and Spanish into new words or mixes words of the two languages in the same passage. The literary movement in Texas achieved national stature with the 1971 publication of the novel *. . . Y no se lo tragó la tierra* (translated as *And the Earth did not Part*) by Tomás Riveraqv of Crystal City. The book was awarded the first Quinto Sol Award from Quinto Sol Publications, a Mexican-American publishing house in California. In 1973 Rolando Hinojosa-Smith of Mercedes won the prize for *Estampas del valle y otras obras (Sketches of the Valley and Other Works).* He received international recognition in 1976, when the Latin-American literary world honored him with the Casa de las Américas Award for *Klail City y sus alrededores.*

Other important works written by Tejanos during this period were *Hay Otra Voz Poems (There is Another Voice Poems)* by Tino Villanueva of San Marcos (1972) and *Viaje/Trip* by Raúl Salinas of Austin (1973). In 1975 Angela de Hoyos brought out *Arise Chicano! and Other Poems,* and in 1976, Carmen Tafolla, Reyes Cárdenas, and Cecilio García-Camarillo jointly issued *Get Your Tortillas Together,* a collection of their poetry. All these works depicted Mexican-American life in a style both lyrical and realistic. Other important writers to emerge in Texas were poets Evangelina Vigil Piñón, Rosemary Catacalos, and Ricardo Sánchez and playwrights Estela Portillo Trambley, Nephtali De León, and Carlos Morton.

Some of these writers were also published in Chicano literature anthologies produced in the Southwest and in the literary journals established in Texas. Two important periodicals were *Tejidos,* a quarterly published in Austin from 1973 to about 1978, and *Caracol,*qv a journal issued in San Antonio between 1974 and 1977. *Tejidos* and *Caracol* gave a voice to many working-class Tejanoqv writers, who brought to their pages penetrating themes and innovative writing styles. The influence of *Caracol* in particular was felt throughout the state because it published a large amount of poetry, as well as novel excerpts, criticism, and political articles. It also served as an important forum for announcing literary events. Its editor, Cecilio García-Camarillo, was an important poet of the movement. The establishment of *Caracol* also brought about the first network of Chicano writers in the state and helped them to find an audience. Poet Angela de Hoyos set up her own publishing house, M&A Editions, in San Antonio for this purpose as well.

Tejano writers participated in other Chicano renaissance events in the Southwest and organized some of the Flor y Canto festivals, which were named for the Aztec poetic vision of literature as a fusion of "flower and song." These events facilitated the emergence of additional writers. Tejanos attended the first Festival de Flor y Canto, which was held in Los Angeles, California, in 1973, and sponsored the second and third festivals, respectively, in Austin in March 1975 and in San Antonio in June 1976. Starting in 1976, anthologies based on these gatherings were published in California and Texas. The festivals later became known as Canto al Pueblo, and at least one such festival was held in Corpus Christi in 1978; that same year an anthology featuring works from the event was published. The Chicano literary renaissance also included dramatic performances organized by the Teatro Nacional de Aztlán, the Texas affiliate of which sponsored the sixth annual celebration in San Antonio in July 1975. The presentations allowed theater groups to continue the tradition of Mexican theaters and circuses, which had flourished in Mexico and later in Texas between the 1850s and 1950s.

The renaissance began to end when the annual literary gatherings moved from Texas to other states after the 1970s. *Tejidos* and *Caracol* ceased publication in the late 1970s. With the demise of these tools to nurture new and often self-taught writers (both hallmarks of the renaissance), this important period in Chicano literature in the state was complete. Nonetheless, its legacy was felt in subsequent decades. Mexican-American feminists continued to challenge traditional views. Their work provided the impetus for the 1981 *This bridge called my back: writings by radical women of color,* coedited by Cherríe Moraga and Texan Gloria Anzaldúa. In 1987 Anzaldúa followed this book with her own work in prose and poetry—*Borderlands = La Frontera: The New Mestiza.* Portillo Trambley, whose collection of short stories, *Rain of Scorpions and Other Writings,* was published in 1975, saw her plays produced throughout the Southwest and in New York, where her *Blacklight* won second place at the Latin American Theatre Festival in 1985.

Poet Rosemary Catacalos and poet-novelist Sandra Cisneros of Chicago both held Dobie Paisano writing fellowships (*see* PAISANO RANCH), as did novelist Genaro González. Rolando Hinojosa-Smith continued to write many well-received works in his Klail City Death Trip Series. He also was recognized as an outstanding prose stylist. Tino Villanueva established an international Mexican-American poetry journal, *Imagine,* on the East Coast in 1984. In Houston, Nicolás Kanellos continued to produce the *Americas Review* and established Arte Público Press, both of which introduced many Tejano writers. Some of the works produced during the Chicano literary renaissance in Texas were incorporated into university literature courses and found an audience outside the Mexican-American community; some also received scholarly attention. The Nettie Lee Benson Latin American Collection qv at the University of Texas at Austin has become a major repository of Chicano literature.

BIBLIOGRAPHY: Leonardo Carillo et al., eds., *Canto al Pueblo: An Anthology of Experiences* (San Antonio: Penca, 1978). Francisco Lomelí and Carl R. Shirley, eds., *Chicano Writers, First Series* (Detroit: Gale Research, 1989). Julio Martínez and Francisco A. Lomelí, eds., *Chicano Literature: A Reference Guide* (Westport, Connecticut: Greenwood, 1985). National Chicano Literature Festival, *Flor y Canto II: An Anthology of Chicano Literature from the Festival Held March 12–16, 1975 in Austin, Texas* (Albuquerque: Pajarito, 1975).

Teresa Palomo Acosta

CHICANO MURAL MOVEMENT. The Chicano mural movement began in the 1960s in Mexican-American barrios throughout the Southwest. Artists began using the walls of city buildings, housing projects, schools, and churches to depict Mexican-American culture. Chicano qv muralism has been linked to pre-Columbian peoples of the Americas, who recorded their rituals and history on the walls of their pyramids, and Mexican revolutionary-era painters José Clemente Orozco, Diego Rivera, and David Alfaros Siqueiros, collectively known as *los tres grandes,* who painted murals in the United States. Two other Latino predecessors were Antonio García and Xavier González,qv who painted murals in the 1930s under the auspices of the Work Projects Administration qv art projects. In 1933 at San Diego (Texas) High School, García produced *March on Washington,* which has since been moved to the Duval County Museum. It embodies the idea that President Herbert Hoover failed to rebuild the nation's finances after the stock-market crash of 1929 and that President Franklin Delano Roosevelt triumphed in putting Americans back to work. García also painted murals for Corpus Christi Cathedral qv and an academy in Corpus Christi. González, who went on to international acclaim as a sculptor, painted a mural for the San Antonio Municipal Auditorium in 1933. It was later removed because of public outcry over the "upraised fist and a palm with a bleeding wound" depicted in it.

During the Mexican-American artistic and literary renaissance that occurred throughout the Southwest in the 1960s and 1970s mural production became part of the effort of Hispanics to reinvigorate their cultural heritage, which was manifested in the rise of the Raza Unida party, the United Farm Workers Union, and the Mexican American Youth Organization,qqv all of which tried to affirm cultural identity and challenge racism. The mural movement depicted such cultural motifs and heroes as Quetzalcoatl from the pre-Columbian era, Francisco (Pancho) Villa qv from the revolutionary period, and Cleto L. Rodríguez qv from Tejano qv history. Nuestra Señora de Guadalupe qv (Our Lady of Guadalupe) is the only representation of a woman. Around the state, most of the artists, some formally trained and others self-taught, worked in collaboration with community volunteers, often teenagers who were recruited for specific projects, to fashion the murals.

In El Paso more than 100 murals have been painted since the mid-1960s. Manuel Acosta qv painted *Iwo Jima,* perhaps the earliest of the city's known Chicano murals, at the Veterans of Foreign Wars office in 1966. Carlos Rosas, Felipe Adame, and Gaspar Enríquez usually worked in conjunction with student painters. Mago Orona Gándara, one of the few known female muralists working in El Paso, has painted at least two as a solo artist, *Señor Sol* and *Time and Sand.* Two other women, Irene Martínez and Monika Acevedo, participated in the team that completed *Myths of Maturity* at the University of Texas at El Paso library in 1991. The murals, located throughout the city's various corridors, often depict themes common to Chicano muralism, such as mestizo heritage or social problems, but they also tell unique stories about the "merging of ideas, cultures, and dreams" along the United States–Mexico border. An attempt to preserve the murals, as well as to restore older ones or paint new ones, was sponsored in the early 1990s by the city's artists and the Junior League, which also published a brochure entitled *Los Murales, Guide and Maps to the Murals of El Paso.*

San Antonio also has a strong Chicano mural tradition, with the majority of murals concentrated on the city's predominantly Mexican-American West Side. The Cassiano public-housing project, for instance, has been the site of numerous murals, many of them painted under the direction of the Community Cultural Arts Organization, which was organized in 1979. CCAO chief artist Anastacio "Tacho" Torres has recruited teams of student artists to complete works that depict an array of subjects: labor leader César Chávez, lowriders,qv the San Antonio missions, Tejano military and political heroes, and others. More than 130 murals had been completed in the city by the early 1990s. Some have been privately commissioned for a variety of locales such as the convention center, Mario's Mexican Restaurant, and Our Lady of the Lake University. As in El Paso, efforts to record the existence of these works have occurred. In the early 1980s, for example, historian Ricardo Romo developed a slide show on them called "Painted Walls of the Barrio" for the University of Texas Institute of Texan Cultures.qv

In Houston, Leo Tanguma painted *Rebirth of our Nationality* on the wall of the Continental Can Company. Because of the politically charged content of Tanguma's mural art, several of his works have been erased. In Austin muralist Raúl Valdez has led volunteer teams in painting murals at several public sites on the city's predominantly

Mexican-American east side, including the Pan American Recreation Center. Some of his work, like Tanguma's, has been lost in recent years. *Los Elementos,* for instance, which was painted on the exterior of the Juárez-Lincoln University building in 1977, was destroyed in 1983; city officials could not save it when the building was sold to a new owner. Sylvia Orozco, codirector of Mexic-Arte,qv has also painted murals, among them one for the Chicano Culture Room in the student union building of the University of Texas at Austin. Murals have also been reported in Crystal City, Dallas, Lubbock, Levelland, Lockhart, and other cities. Whether in small or large towns, artists in the Chicano mural movement have offered an opportunity to the barrios' "untrained" painters. Art historians Shifra Goldman and Tomás Ybarra-Frausto call the murals a significant contribution to public art.

BIBLIOGRAPHY: *Arriba,* November 15–December 15, 1989. Shifra Goldman and Tomás Ybarra-Frausto, *Arte Chicano: A Comprehensive Annotated Bibliography of Chicano Art, 1965–1981* (Chicano Studies Library Publications Unit, University of California, Berkeley, 1985).

Teresa Palomo Acosta

CHICHITAME INDIANS. This is the name of one band of Chizo Indians, who are considered by some writers to be a branch of the Conchos. In the seventeenth and early eighteenth centuries the Chizos occupied the area now covered by northeastern Chihuahua, northwestern Coahuila, and the lower part of the Big Bend region of Trans-Pecos Texas.

BIBLIOGRAPHY: Charles W. Hackett, ed., *Historical Documents Relating to New Mexico, Nueva Vizcaya, and Approaches Thereto, to 1773* (3 vols., Washington: Carnegie Institution, 1923–37). Carl Sauer, *The Distribution of Aboriginal Tribes and Languages in Northwestern Mexico* (Berkeley: University of California Press, 1934).

Thomas N. Campbell

CHICKASAW INDIANS. The Chickasaws, a Muskogean-speaking tribe from the American Southeast, first encountered white men, probably members of De Soto's gold-seeking expedition, in the mid-sixteenth century. At that time the tribe occupied land now in Kentucky, Tennessee, Mississippi, and Alabama and lived from hunting and horticulture. They had semipermanent settlements and a moderately hierarchical society. In this they closely resembled other southeastern tribes, particularly the Choctaws, their closest linguistic relatives. In the early nineteenth century the tribe attempted to repel the white invaders but were defeated by the 1830s and, along with Choctaws, Creeks, Cherokees, and Seminoles, moved to lands west of the Mississippi River. In 1830, convinced that continued resistance to white settlement would be futile, Chief Levi Colbert led a delegation westward in search of a new Chickasaw homeland. The original plan called for the Chickasaws to settle on the southwestern edge of the new Choctaw domain, located in the southwestern corner of what is now Oklahoma, but Colbert and his group found this solution unacceptable. Fearing the warlike Plains Indians and unwilling to affiliate himself politically with the more numerous Choctaws, Colbert asked for permission to settle inside Mexican Texas,qv on lands along the Sabine River. Though this request was denied and the Chickasaws were instructed to settle in Indian Territory, as late as 1837 communities of Chickasaws and Choctaws lived inside Texas. Their small settlements, located near Nacogdoches along the Attoyac and Patroon rivers, pursued an independent course until the late 1830s, when, with the establishment of a Choctaw-Chickasaw confederation through the Treaty of Doakesville, the Texas Chickasaws joined their tribesmen in Indian Territory.

That did not end the Chickasaws' relationship with Texas, however. From the late 1830s into the 1840s, Plains Indians, notably the Comanches, used the open Texas frontier as a base for conducting raids into Chickasaw country. So frequent and destructive were these raids that for a time they affected relations between the United States and the Republic of Texas.qv In an effort to placate the Chickasaws, in 1843 the Texas government pledged to exert firmer control over the Red River borderlands. The treaty, known as the Treaty of Bird's Fort, accomplished little in the way of protecting Chickasaw property; nevertheless, it facilitated trade across the Red River. As a result, cross-border trade increased throughout the 1840s and 1850s, even though the benefits of the trade flowed unevenly southward. The high agricultural tariffs of the Republic of Texas served virtually to close its markets to Chickasaw goods, while lower tariffs in the United States allowed Texans to dominate markets within Indian Territory. In addition, Texas moonshiners found a ready market for their products in Chickasaw country, despite attempts by United States authorities to halt the liquor trade. Through the illicit liquor traffic, Texas merchants relieved the Indians of their annuity checks and contributed to the social disruption that followed removal.

By the late 1850s many Chickasaws, like numerous other Indians from the surrounding resettled tribes, were closely tied to the Southern plantation-slave system. This fact, combined with simple geography, kinship ties, and residual hostility toward the federal government, led them, along with the Cherokees, Choctaws, Creeks, and Seminoles, to ally with the Confederacy. It was a disastrous decision, for, ill-equipped to make war and divided internally, the South's Indian allies suffered greatly, physically as well as emotionally. After the war, as punishment, the Chickasaws and the other tribes allied with the South were forced to agree to another land cession. This, combined with the loss of slave labor and the general physical destruction brought on by war, contributed to renewed social disorganization within the group. The Indians were also forced to contend with numerous freedmen who fled to Chickasaw country to escape persecution in Texas. Because of its history as a slaveholding society, the Chickasaw nation was inhospitable toward the newly freed blacks. In the years following the Civil War,qv Chickasaw lands served as part of the great cattle "highway" between Texas and the marketplaces in Kansas. The Chisholm Trailqv was just one of these routes. Contact with cattle ranchers and other frontier whites had the effect of breaking down barriers between the Chickasaws and white men to the extent that, over time, tribal identity was lost, and the fortunes of the Indians fused with those of surrounding whites. Today, though Chickasaw communities continue to exist and a tribal government of a sort remains, Chickasaw independence has virtually disappeared.

BIBLIOGRAPHY: Arrell M. Gibson, *The Chickasaws* (Norman: University of Oklahoma Press, 1971). Monte Lewis, "The Chickasaw on the Texas Frontier," West Texas Historical Association *Year Book* 58 (1982). Francis Paul Prucha, *The Great Father: The United States Government and the American Indians* (2 vols., Lincoln: University of Nebraska Press, 1984). Robert F. Spencer et al., *The Native Americans* (New York: Harper and Row, 1965; 2d ed. 1977).

Monte Lewis

CHICKEN BAYOU. Chicken Bayou rises seven miles northwest of Center in western Shelby County (at 31°50′ N, 94°17′ W) and runs northeast for nine miles to its mouth on Flat Fork Creek (at 31°53′ N, 94°10′ W). The surrounding terrain varies from nearly level to moderately steep and is surfaced by sandy and clay loam that supports pine and hardwood forests.

CHICKEN RANCH. The "Chicken Ranch" in La Grange, Fayette County, made famous by the Broadway musical *The Best Little Whorehouse in Texas,* was perhaps the oldest continuously running brothel in the nation. Institutionalized prostitution in La Grange can be traced back to 1844, when a widow, "Mrs. Swine," brought three young women from New Orleans and settled in a small hotel near the saloon. Mrs. Swine became the first madam and began a tradition of interaction with the community and local lawmen that lasted almost 130 years. She and the girls and women who worked for her carried on a lucrative business, using the hotel lobby for entertaining and a room upstairs for services, until the Civil War,[qv] when she and a faithful prostitute named Tillie were run out of town as Yankees and traitors. After the war prostitution[qv] continued to operate in conjunction with the saloons in La Grange, but no official records were kept. By the end of the nineteenth century, prostitution had moved out of the hotels and into a red-light district on the banks of the Colorado River.

There Miss Jessie Williams (born Faye Stewart) bought a small house soon after her arrival from Waco in 1905. She continued the custom set by her predecessor of good relations with the law and ran the only respectable house on the banks of the Colorado River; she admitted politicians and lawmen but excluded drunkards. Through her connections she learned of an impending crusade against the red-light district, sold the house she owned in Waco, and bought two dwellings and eleven acres outside of the city limits of La Grange and two blocks from the Houston–Galveston highway. This became the location of the Chicken Ranch.

In 1917 two sisters arrived at the house and were taken in and promoted to "middle-management" positions by Miss Jessie. They were in charge of public relations and sent packages and letters to local boys fighting in World War I.[qv] One of the sisters eventually married an older, wealthy customer and moved to San Antonio, where she became, as one author says, "a beloved benefactor and patron of the arts." The other sister stayed in her middle-management position until her death. As the war ended and America entered the twenties, automobiles made the establishment accessible to many more customers. New prostitutes came and necessitated more rooms and new furniture. The rooms were simply built onto the main house in a haphazard fashion as needed, a style that continued until the closing of the place. Miss Jessie stayed on good terms with the sheriff, Will Lossein, who visited every evening to pick up gossip and get information on criminals who had visited the whorehouse and bragged of their exploits. Many crimes in La Grange were solved in this way. While the sheriff kept a tight grip on criminals, Miss Jessie ruled the house with a firm hand. Nothing exotic was allowed, and none of the bedroom doors had locks on them. Miss Jessie would walk the halls, and if she heard a customer giving one of her girls a hard time she would chase him out of the room and house with an iron rod and perhaps never admit him again.

As the Great Depression[qv] hit and the economy fell, Miss Jessie was forced to lower her prices. Though initially she still had plenty of clients, as times grew harder, customers were not so plentiful and the girls grew hungry. Miss Jessie therefore began the "poultry standard" of charging "one chicken for one screw." Soon chickens were everywhere, and the establishment became known as the Chicken Ranch. The girls were never hungry. Miss Jessie supplemented the income by selling surplus chickens and eggs. The economy began to turn around as the Civilian Conservation Corps[qv] began construction of Camp Swift near La Grange, and the shortage of men and money declined. The establishment used the same public-relations tactics in World War II[qv] as in the First World War, and the ranch began an economic recovery from the depression. As the war ended, Miss Jessie was confined to a wheelchair by arthritis but still ruled the house with her iron rod. She did so into the 1950s, when she was confined to her bed and cared for by her longtime nurse. She spent her last few years with her wealthy sister in San Antonio and died in 1961 at the age of eighty.

Edna Milton had arrived at the Chicken Ranch from Oklahoma in 1952 at the age of twenty-three. She soon took over for Miss Jessie and proved just as capable and entrepreneurial. When she bought the ranch from Miss Jessie's heirs for $30,000—much more than the property value—she already had established herself as a competent madam. She had a good relationship with the new sheriff, T. J. Flournoy, who had been elected in 1946 and had immediately put in a direct line to the Chicken Ranch, so he could replace the nightly visits of his predecessor with nightly calls. Edna also interacted with the community in the same ways Jessie had: social contact between the girls and the residents of La Grange was forbidden; girls saw the doctor weekly and shopped with local merchants; and commodities and supplies were bought from local stores on a rotating basis. Edna also continued Jessie's custom of giving money to local civic causes and became one of the town's largest philanthropists. The generosity of her donations points to the success of the ranch. During the 1950s the ranch reached its sixteen-girl maximum. On some weekends there was a line at the door, made of students and soldiers from the nearby military bases. One base even supplied transportation via helicopter to the ranch. A visit to the Chicken Ranch also became part of freshman initiation at Texas A&M.

A door attendant admitted only white, presentable, and sober men into the parlor, where chairs stood on both sides of the room. No cursing or drinking was allowed of the men, or the women for that matter. Edna charged a quarter for the jukebox, seventy-five cents for cigarettes, and a dollar for a Coke, steep prices for the sixties. The women asked for music and Cokes to promote business. The going rate for their services was fifteen dollars for fifteen minutes, though more expensive options were added in the sixties. A girl would have from five to twenty customers a day. After giving an estimated 75 percent to Edna, the prostitutes still made $300 a week and had no expenses. Edna took care of taxes, insurance, utilities, food (two meals a day), weekly doctor visits, two attendants, maids, a cook, and laundry bills. Even before profits from the Cokes, cigarettes, and jukebox, it has been estimated that the ranch had an income of more than $500,000 a year. All new employees were fingerprinted and photographed by Sheriff Flournoy before they could start work, and a criminal record of any kind prevented their employment. Flournoy caught a few women wanted on warrants this way. Once at the ranch, the women had to subscribe to strict rules written by Miss Edna.

The Chicken Ranch continued operating successfully until mid-1973. That year, consumer-affairs reporter Marvin Zindler from KTRK-TV in Houston ran a week-long exposé on the ranch. He claimed that his motive was inaction on the part of the Texas Department of Public Safety[qv] and local law officers to combat the organized crime and corruption allegedly evident at the ranch. All of the attention drawn to the ranch forced the governor, Dolph Briscoe, to meet with the head of the DPS, the state attorney general, and Zindler. At the meeting it was disclosed that the DPS had run a two-month surveillance on the Chicken Ranch and had failed to find evidence of connection with organized crime. However, the pressure on the governor was such that he could not ignore the problem. He scheduled a meeting with Sheriff Jim Flournoy and ordered the house closed. The sheriff, along with some of the citizens of La Grange, saw little reason to close the ranch, but thought he had to do it anyway. He informed Edna of the situation, and by Wednesday morning of the week following Zindler's exposé, August 1, 1973, the ranch was closed and the women had left. Flournoy left for his meeting with the governor with a petition signed by nearly 3,000 people, but upon arriving was informed that the governor had canceled the meeting when he heard the house was closed. Most of the ranch's employees had headed for Austin or Houston; only Edna and a few maids were left. Edna attempted to buy a house in La Grange, but her downpayment was returned. She subsequently got married and moved to an East Texas town where her husband owned several restaurants.

Although the Chicken Ranch was officially closed, the story was not over. Customers showed up for more than two years looking for the place. Zindler also came back for a follow-up story and in the midst of an argument with Sheriff Flournoy was pushed down. This resulted in a $3 million lawsuit against the sheriff. Many local people began contributing to Flournoy's cause by selling T-shirts and bumper stickers. Flournoy settled out of court for much less than $3 million.

The musical about the ranch was very successful. Edna had a silent role in the Broadway production, which was later turned into a movie. Two lawyers from Houston bought the building and land and in 1977 moved part of the building, in its original condition, to Dallas to open a restaurant named the Chicken Ranch. It opened in September 1977 with Miss Edna as the hostess, the building and furniture in their original condition, and a menu of mainly chicken dishes. The restaurant closed in January 1978. The building and furniture were auctioned off at the site of the restaurant in late June of that year in a foreclosure sale ordered by the Small Business Administration. Sheriff Flournoy resigned in 1980, saying that he and his wife were sick of hearing about the Chicken Ranch and did not want to hear that name again. When he died in October of 1982, his funeral was attended by Lieutenant Governor Bill Hobby and nearly 100 lawmen. He was credited with solving every murder and bank robbery in Fayette County during his thirty-four-year term. The Chicken Ranch had helped his criminal investigations.

BIBLIOGRAPHY: Austin *American-Statesman,* August 2, 1973, January 22, June 25, 1978. Jan Hutson, *The Chicken Ranch: The True Story of the Best Little Whorehouse in Texas* (New York: Barnes, 1980). Vertical Files, Barker Texas History Center, University of Texas at Austin (Jim Flournoy, La Grange, Texas). *Walter F. Pilcher*

CHICKEN SALAD CASE. The "Chicken Salad Case" was involved in the impeachment charges against James E. Ferguson qv in 1917. On February 11, 1915, the Thirty-fourth legislature passed a deficiency appropriations act providing $2,000 a year for two years for expenses incurred by former Governor Oscar Branch Colquitt qv for fuel, lights, water, and ice for the governor's mansion, and for food, including "chicken salad and punch," automobile repairs, feed, and stationery for his private use. Although Attorney General Benjamin F. Looney ruled the appropriation invalid, Ferguson signed the bill. Representative W. C. Middleton of Rains County brought suit and on June 12, 1915, was granted a temporary injunction by Judge George Calhoun of the Fifty-third District Court, Austin, restraining comptroller Henry Berryman Terrell qv from issuing warrants on the state treasury to cover these expenditures.

On appeal by Terrell to the state Supreme Court, transferred to the Court of Civil Appeals of Texas, Fourth District, San Antonio, Chief Justice William Seat Fly, qv on June 14, 1916, upheld the lower court, making the injunction perpetual in part. The court ruled that the legislature could appropriate for fuel, water, lights, and ice necessary for the Governor's Mansion, qv but not for groceries and other personal needs of the governor, which appropriation was held to be contrary to the provisions of the Constitution of 1876 qv on the governor's salary, casual deficiencies, and prohibition against appropriation for private purposes.

Meanwhile, Ferguson continued to purchase groceries with state money under this appropriation. When questioned before the House Investigation Committee of the Thirty-fifth Legislature on charges of misappropriated funds, he testified under oath that he would repay the state if the Supreme Court decided against him. But in spite of the adverse decision he failed to do so. In September 1917 the High Court of Impeachment held that Ferguson was guilty of a misapplication of appropriations made by the legislature for fuel, lights, ice, and incidentals, in that he used the same in the purchase of groceries, feed, automobile tires, and gasoline for his private use, and that his refusal to repay these funds constituted a continued misapplication of the public funds of Texas.

BIBLIOGRAPHY: *Proceedings . . . Charges against Governor James E. Ferguson* (Austin: Texas House of Representatives, 1917). *Record of Proceedings of the High Court of Impeachment on the Trial of Hon. James E. Ferguson, Governor, before the Senate of the State of Texas* (Austin: Texas Senate, 1917). Ralph W. Steen, The Political Career of James E. Ferguson, 1914–1917 (M.A. thesis, University of Texas, 1929). *Martha Sue Parr*

CHICKEN WAR. As the Texas manifestation of the War of the Quadruple Alliance in Europe, the Chicken War caused abandonment of the Spanish Franciscan missions in eastern Texas in 1719. With news that Spain and France were on opposing sides in the conflict, Lt. Philippe Blondel at the French post of Natchitoches, Louisiana, struck in June 1719 at the nearest Spanish target: San Miguel de Linares de los Adaes Mission, qv at a site near that of present Robeline, Louisiana. Finding only a lay brother and one soldier at the mission, Blondel and his detail of seven gathered up the sacred vestments and provisions, then raided the henhouse. As he mounted his horse after tying the chickens to the pommel of his saddle, the chickens flapped their wings, the horse reared, and the lieutenant was spilled in the dirt. His companions rushed to his aid. Taking advantage of the confusion, the lay brother dashed off into the woods.

After reaching Nuestra Señora de los Dolores Mission (at the site of present-day San Augustine, Texas) on June 22, 1719, the brother informed Fray Antonio Margil de Jesús qv of what he had been told by Blondel: Pensacola had been captured by the French, and a hundred soldiers were on their way from Mobile with the East Texas settlements as their objective. Lacking confidence in the Spaniards' relationship with the Indians, Father Margil viewed retreat as the only alternative. He packed his vestments and headed for Nuestra Señora de la Purísima Concepción Mission (in the area of present Nacogdoches County) to spread the alarm.

Capt. Domingo Ramón qv of Nuestra Señora de los Dolores de los Tejas Presidio, heeding the clamor of his soldiers and their wives, gathered citizens and livestock to withdraw toward San Antonio and await reinforcements. Margil, Isidro Félix de Espinosa, qv and two soldiers remained at Mission Concepción for twenty days "consoling" the Indians, who were reluctant to let them leave. They received word on July 14 that Ramón was withdrawing farther than agreed upon, and they set out to overtake the caravan at the border of Hasinai (Tejas) country. There they encamped until the end of September, when Espinosa resolved to go personally to San Antonio de Béxar and San Juan Bautista qqv to seek help. After traveling twenty leagues he encountered a volunteer relief expedition from San Juan Bautista and learned that no military support would be forthcoming. On October 3 the entire camp marched for San Antonio.

While Margil and the seven other friars took residence at San Antonio de Valero Mission, Espinosa went on to San Juan Bautista to make a personal appeal for military aid in recovering the missions. There he learned of the appointment of the Marqués de San Miguel de Aguayo qv as governor of Coahuila and Texas qv and of the military campaign Aguayo was mounting to reclaim eastern Texas for Spain. Despite Espinosa's urging, the Aguayo expedition qv was delayed a year and a half. In the meantime the war ended, and the operation, planned as one of reconquest, became merely one of reoccupation.

The Chicken War represented a costly overreaction by Spanish religious and military men to a feeble French gesture. The French made no aggressive move against Texas after Blondel's comical fiasco. Aside from causing a two-year hiatus in the Spanish missionary effort, the episode also disrupted the commercial aims of the French Company of the West. Directors of the company sent word to Jean Baptiste Benard de La Harpe, qv who had just established a trading post on the Red River in the area that is now Bowie County, that he was not to make war on the Spaniards but to pursue trade with them. The Spanish withdrawal following Blondel's raid left no one with whom he might trade.

BIBLIOGRAPHY: Isidro Félix de Espinosa, *Chrónica apostólica y seráphica de todos los colegios de propaganda fide de esta Nueva España,*

parte primera (Mexico, 1746; new ed., *Crónica de los colegios de propaganda fide de la Nueva España,* ed. Lino G. Caneda, Washington: Academy of American Franciscan History, 1964). Robert S. Weddle, *San Juan Bautista: Gateway to Spanish Texas* (Austin: University of Texas Press, 1968). Robert S. Weddle, *The French Thorn: Rival Explorers in the Spanish Sea, 1682–1762* (College Station: Texas A&M University Press, 1991).
Robert S. Weddle

CHICO, TEXAS. Chico is at the intersection of State Highway 101 and Farm Road 1810, five miles north of Bridgeport in northwestern Wise County. Settlement of the area began in the mid-1870s, when J. T. Brown, from Chico, California, moved to the area and opened a general store near Dry Creek. The settlement became a church and school community for area farmers. A post office was established in 1882. A decade later the tracks of the Rock Island Railroad reached the community. Soon thereafter Chico became a retail center for cotton farmers. The town remained economically dependent on agriculture until the early 1940s, when oil was discovered nearby. The population reached 1,000 in 1942. Although Chico billed itself as the oil capital of Wise County, it also was one of the leading producers of crushed stone for road construction. At one time the town had four large stone processing plants. Agriculture remained important; in the 1950s peanuts and cantaloupes replaced cotton as the primary crop. Chico was incorporated in 1950, but the population declined to 850 by the middle of the 1950s. In 1986 Chico had an estimated 890 residents, twenty-five businesses, and a weekly newspaper, the Chico *Times.* In 1990 the population was 800.

BIBLIOGRAPHY: John Clements, *Flying the Colors: Texas, a Comprehensive Look at Texas Today, County by County* (Dallas: Clements Research, 1984). Rosalie Gregg, ed., *Wise County History* (Vol. 1, n.p: Nortex, 1975; Vol. 2, Austin: Eakin, 1982).
David Minor

CHICO CREEK. Chico Creek rises two miles southwest of Guerra in Jim Hogg County (at 26°52′ N, 98°55′ W) and runs southwest for eight miles to its mouth on San Juan Creek, three miles southeast of Moss in eastern Zapata County (at 26°49′ N, 98°59′ W). The stream is dammed several times in its middle course. It traverses low-rolling to flat terrain surfaced by clay and sandy loams that support grasses, cacti, some mesquite, and chaparral.

CHICO SOUTH, TEXAS. Chico South, also known as Chicon, was on the International–Great Northern Railroad two miles northeast of Natalia in southeastern Medina County. It was named for its proximity to Chacon Creek. A post office was established at Chico South in 1871 with Robert S. Ragsdale as postmaster and was discontinued in 1880. School records indicate forty-three students attending a one-teacher school in Chico South in 1907. By the 1940s the settlement had been abandoned.

BIBLIOGRAPHY: John J. Germann and Myron Janzen, *Texas Post Offices by County* (1986).
Ruben E. Ochoa

CHICOLETE, TEXAS. Chicolete was thirteen miles east of Cuero in eastern DeWitt County. It was named for Chicolete Creek, though its school was originally called Hefner School for W. Hefner, who donated the land. The school began operation in 1880 and closed in 1942.

BIBLIOGRAPHY: Nellie Murphree, *A History of DeWitt County* (Victoria, Texas, 1962).
Nellie Murphree

CHICOLETE CREEK. Chicolete Creek rises near Stratton six miles southeast of Edgar in southeastern DeWitt County (at 29°09′ N, 97°10′ W) and runs eighteen miles southeast across the southwestern corner of Lavaca County to its mouth on the Lavaca River, south of Horseshoe Lake in northwestern Jackson County (at 29°05′ N, 96°49′ W). A major tributary, South Chicolete Creek, rises two miles south of the creek near Berry Pond in southeastern DeWitt County and flows ten miles to its confluence with Chicolete Creek (at 29°05′ N, 97°02′ W). The creeks cross flat terrain with local shallow depressions surfaced by clay and sandy loam that supports water-tolerant hardwoods, conifers, and grasses.

CHICONY (?–?). Chicony (She-co-ney) was the principal chief of the Comanche Indians in 1836, when Alexander Le Grand[qv] was sent by the Texas government to make a treaty with the Comanches. Chicony refused to make the treaty and swore eternal enmity to the white man.

BIBLIOGRAPHY: Henderson K. Yoakum, *History of Texas from Its First Settlement in 1685 to Its Annexation to the United States in 1846* (2 vols., New York: Redfield, 1855).
L. W. Kemp

CHICOTA, TEXAS. Chicota, near the Red River one mile north of Pat Mayse Lake and fifteen miles north of Paris in northern Lamar County, was established in 1879, when it received a post office. Capt. Robert Draper started a store at the site called Center Springs. From Indians trading at the store he heard of Checotah in Indian territory and chose the name for the post. In 1884 Chicota had a post office, four churches, and a district school with 100 white pupils and two teachers. The population was forty-five. The town grew to 225 residents in 1892. In 1914 Chicota had a population estimated at 100 and seven businesses. By 1936 it had a church, a cemetery, a couple of businesses, and a number of scattered dwellings. Throughout the 1940s and 1950s the population was estimated at 212. In 1980 Chicota had a cemetery, a school, four businesses, one church, three surrounding churches, and a number of scattered dwellings. In 1990 the population was estimated at 125.
Shannon Nunnelley

CHIGGER CREEK. Chigger Creek rises four miles northwest of Alvin in north central Brazoria County (at 29°29′ N, 95°20′ W) and runs northeast for twelve miles, passing south of Friendswood, to its mouth on Clear Creek, at the Galveston-Harris county line (at 29°30′ N, 95°10′ W). The creek is channeled as it passes through Hastings oilfield.[qv] The surrounding flat terrain has local shallow depressions and is surfaced by clay and sandy loam that supports water-tolerant hardwood, conifers, and grasses.

CHIHUAHUA, TEXAS. Chihuahua was six miles west of Mission in Hidalgo County. It was the name given to a 20,000-acre ranch by its owner, Ramon Vela, who moved his family to the site from Laguna Seca Ranch, twenty miles northeast. In 1910 Vela built a two-story colonial home, housing and store facilities for his employees, and a school which he supported. The Sam Fordyce branch of the St. Louis, Brownsville and Mexico Railway passed the settlement, and a stop at that location was named Chihuahua. Chihuahua reached its height during the first three decades of the 1900s. Upon the death of Vela in 1926 his heirs pursued other interests, and the old homestead and property were sold in the late 1940s. The house was razed, and no trace remains of the stately home or the village. As of 1990 a few cattle pens have been constructed on the village site. The railroad still passes by but has no stop or siding facilities.

BIBLIOGRAPHY: Frank Cushman Pierce, *Texas' Last Frontier: A Brief History of the Lower Rio Grande Valley* (Menasha, Wisconsin: Banta, 1917; rpt., Brownsville: Rio Grande Valley Historical Society, 1962). Mrs. James Watson, *The Lower Rio Grande Valley of Texas and Its Builders* (Mission, Texas, 1931).
Robert E. Norton

CHIHUAHUA EXPEDITION. The Chihuahua expedition of 1839–40 was undertaken by a caravan of Mexican traders from Chihuahua City, Chihuahua, that sought to open a direct trade with the United States by way of a shorter trail than the circuitous route through St. Louis, Santa Fe, and El Paso. In response to Mexican interest in trade after the opening of the Presidio del Norte entry to Texas in 1830, Henry Connelly,qv a Missouri physician and prominent Chihuahua merchant, organized a party of more than 100 men accompanied by fifty Mexican dragoons that left Chihuahua with 200,000 or 300,000 dollars in specie on April 2, 1839. They traveled northeast to the Rio Grande, crossed at the site of present Presidio, then went on to the headwaters of the Colorado and Brazos rivers, possibly between the Double Mountain and Clear Forks of the Brazos. Moving northeast, the party initially mistook the Canadian for the Red River, then proceeded to the Red, traveled downriver, and crossed at the mouth of the Wichita River into Indian Territory. There, a Delaware Indian band directed them to Fort Towson. Connelly proceeded east, reached the post in June, and presented the commandant, Maj. Henry Wilson, a passport issued at Chihuahua on April 1 by Governor Simón Elias Gonzales, authorizing him to pass with his party through the Republic of Mexico to the state of Arkansas. Connelly next took a steamboat to Louisiana to exchange his gold and silver for merchandise, then returned to Fort Towson in early September. He left Fulton, Arkansas, in April 1840 after delays for weather, with between sixty and eighty new wagons loaded with merchandise and a company of American equestrian circus performers carrying tents and equipment to entertain in Mexico. Connelly maintained cordial relations between the Mexicans and the inhabitants of the northern Texas settlements who might have inspected and taxed the party heavily on its return. Citizens were eager for the trade and dealt generously. The return route passed from Fort Towson into North Texas, through what became Red River, Lamar, Fannin, Grayson, Cooke, Montague, Clay, and Archer counties. The expedition passed the sites of Paris and Bonham, swung south of Sherman through Whitesboro, north of Gainesville and Muenster, and into the city limits of St. Jo in Montague County. Some six miles west, the travelers veered northward into the Cross Timbersqv between Montague and Nocona, where the caravan spent five weeks cutting through and traversing the muddy prairies. The remainder of the route passed northwest of the site of Montague, north of Brushy Mound, and northwest of Bowie. The next two or three hundred miles are uncertain, but the traders traveled several days near the Brazos, probably upstream. They hit their incoming route near Archer City and marched west past Seymour before turning south, likely passing near the sites of present Benjamin, Aspermont, and Colorado City. After fording the head branches of the Brazos, they found another part of their path near the site of modern Snyder at a branch of the Colorado, apparently south of some sandy and salty regions of the Brazos, and crossed the area of Big Spring. The route then ran southwest by Stiles, some seventy miles west of San Angelo, to the Pecos River. From near McCamey it passed near Comanche Springsqv at Fort Stockton, traveled a mile north of Alpine, then moved on through Paisano Passqv to the west and down the course of Alamito Creek to the site of Presidio on the Rio Grande.

On arrival, the traders spent forty-five days reaching a compromise on duty payments. Governor José Irigoyen,qv who had promised lower tariffs, had died, and full duties were now threatened. Eventually, the caravan crossed the Rio Grande, passed down its original trail along the Río Conchos, and arrived at the town of Chihuahua on August 27, 1840. Because of the tariff increases and unfavorable reports on the trail, the trip was not repeated, and use of the route was curtailed until the late 1840s. Connelly's route is sometimes called the Chihuahua Trail, though another Chihuahua Trail was developed to the west of Texas.

BIBLIOGRAPHY: Howard G. Applegate and C. Wayne Hanselka, *La Junta de los Ríos del Norte y Conchos* (*Southwestern Studies* 41 [El Paso: Texas Western Press, 1974]). Seymour V. Connor and Jimmy M. Skaggs, *Broadcloth and Britches: The Santa Fe Trade* (College Station: Texas A&M University Press, 1977). Carlysle Graham Raht, *The Romance of the Davis Mountains and Big Bend Country* (Odessa, Texas: Rahtbooks, 1963). Grant Foreman, *Advancing the Frontier* (Norman: University of Oklahoma Press, 1933; rpt. 1968). Josiah Gregg, *Commerce of the Prairies*, ed. Max L. Moorhead (Norman: University of Oklahoma Press, 1954). George Wilkins Kendall, *Narrative of the Texan Santa Fe Expedition* (2 vols., New York: Harper, 1844; rpts. Austin: Steck, 1935; n.p.: Readex, 1966). Thomas Maitland Marshall, "Commercial Aspects of the Texan Santa Fe Expedition," *Southwestern Historical Quarterly* 20 (January 1917). Ernest Lisle Reedstrom, *Bugles, Banners and War Bonnets* (Caldwell, Idaho, 1977). Rupert N. Richardson, *The Frontier of Northwest Texas, 1846 to 1876* (Glendale, California: Clark, 1963). Roy L. Swift and Leavitt Corning, Jr., *Three Roads to Chihuahua* (Austin: Eakin Press, 1988).

Roy L. Swift

CHIHUAHUAN DESERT RESEARCH INSTITUTE. The Chihuahuan Desert Research Institute was established in the spring of 1974 as a nonprofit scientific and educational organization. Its mission is to gather and publicize data on the Chihuahuan Desert of the United States and Mexico. Its activities include scientific investigation, instruction, and the operation and development of the Chihuahuan Desert Visitor Center. The institute's twenty-nine-member board of directors is assisted by a board of advocates. The organization was originally housed in an unused school building in Alpine, Texas. In 1984 the building was sold by the Alpine Independent School District, and the CDRI was moved to Honors Hall on the Sul Ross State University campus, also in Alpine. In 1989 the institute was moved to its present location in the Barton Warnock Science Building on the Sul Ross campus. There the CDRI staff conducts business, produces its publications and newsletters, and maintains the 2,000 volume W. Frank Blair Library.

The CDRI is supported through grants, donations, contributions, and membership. It had 500 members in 1991. It is endowed through a sister corporation, the Chihuahuan Desert Foundation, Incorporated, which was established in 1985. Research activities are generally funded through contracts and grants. The institute has studied fire ecology, restoration and revegetation of disturbed areas, organismal biology, systematics, range management, environmental impact, anthropology, and archeology, among other topics. The CDRI Board of Scientists meets annually, acts in an advisory capacity, and conducts a series of symposia at five-year intervals on the resources of the Chihuahuan Desert. The institute supports academic excellence through the annual presentation of an Innovative Research Award and the annual W. Frank Blair Award Competition for Excellence in Written Data Presentation. Educational activities include seminars, lectures, the publication of books and magazines, public school presentations, teacher training, and the production of films. The Institute's film series, *The Chihuahuan Desert Trilogy*, has won more than twenty international awards.

The Chihuahuan Desert Visitor Center, on State Highway 118 four miles south of Fort Davis, was established in 1978 with the purchase of 507 acres of wooded grasslands. The center, a desert museum, has been open to public since 1982. Development efforts have centered on the composition of a master plan, the design and construction of a forty-acre arboretum, the construction and maintenance of a 1,440-square-foot cactus and succulent greenhouse, the design and construction of the Modesta Canyon Nature Trail System, and the operation of a gift shop. Annual special events include a native plant sale held on the last weekend of April and a members-appreciation barbecue in late summer.

BIBLIOGRAPHY: Vertical Files, Barker Texas History Center, University of Texas at Austin.

Dennis J. Miller

CHILANO VILLAGE. The Chilano Indian village or group, probably Caddoan, was visited by the Moscoso expeditionqv in Northeast Texas in 1542.

BIBLIOGRAPHY: Frederick Webb Hodge, ed., *Handbook of American Indians North of Mexico* (2 vols., Washington: GPO, 1907, 1910; rpt., New York: Pageant, 1959).

CHILDER'S SLOUGH. Childer's Slough rises a mile south of Batesville Hill seven miles northwest of Batesville in north central Zavala County (at 29°02′ N, 99°43′ W) and runs southeast for eight miles to its mouth on Gallina Slough, a mile northwest of Batesville (at 28°58′ N, 99°39′ W). The surrounding terrain is flat with locally shallow depressions and is surfaced by expansive clays that support water-tolerant hardwoods, conifers, and grasses.

CHILD LABOR LEGISLATION. Child labor in Texas is regulated by (1) federal legislation contained in the Fair Labor Standards Act, forbidding oppressive child labor in interstate commerce, and (2) laws passed by the state legislature in 1993, included in the Texas Labor Code. The Texas Labor Code governs employment of children—defined as individuals under the age of eighteen—and empowers the Texas Employment Commission[qv] to adopt rules for ensuring the safety, health, and well-being of children in the workplace. The only limitation on the employment of children aged seventeen and eighteen is that the commission may prohibit employment of children of any age in hazardous occupations. Children under sixteen may not work more than eight hours a day or forty-eight hours a week, and they may not work during nighttime hours. These restrictions on hours do not apply to a given child if an application is made to the Texas Employment Commission and it determines that a hardship exists for that child. State law forbids employment of children under the age of fourteen except as specified by the Labor Code or by rules promulgated by the commission. Specific exceptions permit newspaper delivery, school-sponsored work-study, agricultural employment outside school hours, certain rehabilitation programs, and any nonhazardous work done under the supervision of a parent or other custodial adult in a business that is owned or operated by the parent or custodian. The Labor Code also authorizes the commission to allow employment of children under fourteen as television, radio, theater, or movie actors. In any place where the commission has good reason to believe young people subject to the Code may be working, the commission must be given full access to, and must be given all desired information regarding, such workers. Any violation of the Code concerning child labor is a Class C misdemeanor, punishable by a fine not to exceed $500.
Sally L. Ray

CHILDREN OF GOD. The Children of God movement was started in the late 1960s by David Brandt Berg, a former Christian and Missionary Alliance pastor. Berg, a native of Oakland, California, had followed in his father's footsteps as a minister in that denomination, gaining his first pastorate in Arizona in 1949. In 1950, however, he had a falling-out with certain of the church's leadership and resigned. That experience left him embittered and with a permanent distaste for organized religion. Berg's belief that God had a special destiny and mission for him developed shortly thereafter, and he began making personal claims as a "prophet for this generation." In 1968 with his wife Jane and four children, he moved to Huntington Beach, California, where he developed a small communal group of thirty-five charter members, basically from the youth counterculture. Early in 1969 he was convinced that a monstrous earthquake would soon destroy the California coastal cities; accordingly he and some fifty followers left for Arizona, where their disruption of church services and condemnation of organized churches soon resulted in their expulsion. Afterward, members of the rapidly increasing group wandered throughout much of the United States and Canada staging demonstrations and urging others to join. They adopted the name "Children of God," and their founder took the name Moses David, or "Mo." Many of his followers addressed Berg as "Father" Moses or "King" David and considered him their cult's main authority.

Toward the end of 1969, some 200 members of the COG established a 425-acre colony a few miles from the ghost town of Thurber, in Erath County, Texas. This acreage, known as the Texas South Clinic Ranch, was owned by the American Soul Clinic group, a nondenominational missionary organization headed by television evangelist Fred Jordan. Based on Berg's preachments, members used only biblical first names, gave to their commune their personal possessions, and divided themselves into twelve tribes (inspired by the twelve tribes of Israel), with each tribe responsible for certain work several hours a day, including camp maintenance, food preparation, procurement of food from neighboring towns, and care of livestock. Their main interest reportedly was in Bible study and discussions that often resembled those of nineteenth-century revivals. There was a Montessori school there for the colony's children. Rock music with religious lyrics was popular. Most members of the group had a history of drug use and claimed that they had conquered the drug habit through communion with God.

On Moratorium Day, October 31, 1970, COG members from the Thurber group parked their bus next to the campus of the University of Texas at Austin and made a dramatic appearance wearing sackcloth and carrying Bibles, to "witness Christ" among university students. By 1971 the Children of God claimed a membership of 4,000 in every state in the Union, mostly teen-agers and people in their early twenties. Although they saw themselves as a primitive or fundamentalist Christian organization run along the same lines as the Jesus People, the God Squad, Teen Challenge, and others, many outraged parents claimed that their children were brainwashed or hypnotized by leaders of the group and forcibly alienated from their families; indeed, Berg had often placed revolutionary emphasis on "forsaking all," including material possessions and allegiance to families. What was more, the COG allegedly became increasingly preoccupied with liberal, often permissive, sexual mores. According to several former COG members, Berg often led in discussions at the Thurber colony that always ended up on sexual subjects and often with mass lovemaking sessions. Even mate-swapping was sometimes allowed by the cult's leadership, who reportedly used the term "flirty fishing," or "f-fing," in reference to their practice of using sex to entice people to join or contribute to their organization.

Such charges may have been a major factor in the closing of the COG's Thurber colony. In November 1971 the colony was evicted from the property after a major disagreement with Fred Jordan and other American Soul Clinic associates. Subsequently, many members sought to join COG communes in other states and in foreign countries, particularly England, where in 1972 many such groups had been formed. David Berg set up his permanent headquarters in Europe, from which he published several books, a monthly periodical, and a series of "MO" letters that his followers considered equal in authority to the Bible. Most mainline evangelical groups and denominations have criticized Berg's writings as being often vague and contradictory, with no clear statement of belief.

BIBLIOGRAPHY: Deborah Davis, *The Children of God: The Inside Story* (Grand Rapids, Michigan: Zondervan, 1984). Deborah Cecil Edwards, An Analysis of Some Contemporary Alternatives to Denominational Christianity (M.A. thesis, University of Texas at Austin, 1976). San Antonio *Express*, February 22, August 19, 1972. David E. Van Zandt, *Living in the Children of God* (Princeton: Princeton University Press, 1991).

CHILDREN'S MEDICAL CENTER OF DALLAS. The Children's Medical Center of Dallas was established in 1948 as an umbrella organization to coordinate the activities of several previously existing children's health-care institutions located near each other on Maple Avenue, in the Oak Lawn section of Dallas. The oldest unit was a hospital serving infants up to age three, founded in 1913 in four tents on the grounds of Parkland Hospital as the Dallas Baby Camp by May

Forster Smith[qv] and the Dallas County Graduate Nurses Association. On May 16, 1914, the Baby Camp moved into a permanent frame structure on the hospital grounds, where it remained until 1930, when it moved into a new building designed by James B. Cheek at the corner of Maple Avenue and Turtle Creek Boulevard. Because the new facility had been made possible by a $100,000 gift from Tom L. Bradford, Sr., the Baby Camp was renamed Bradford Memorial Hospital for Babies. The second unit to become a part of the Children's Medical Center was the Presbyterian Clinic, an outpatient clinic organized in 1921 by Dr. Jack Perkins and Rev. William M. Anderson.[qv] It was originally housed in the basement of the First Presbyterian Church in downtown Dallas and subsequently acquired a new home in 1924 at the corner of Maple and Welborn streets. The facility was renamed Richmond Freeman Memorial Clinic after the son of the principal donors, Mr. and Mrs. Percy R. Freeman, Sr. The third organization, the Children's Hospital of Texas, opened in 1940 next door to the Freeman Clinic under the leadership of R. B. George.

These three facilities were joined in 1948 by the Ivor O'Connor Morgan Hospital for Tuberculous Children, which occupied a special wing of the Children's Hospital building. During the 1950s the four institutions slowly merged their administrative structures, and in 1967 they moved into a new complex adjacent to Parkland Memorial Hospital and the University of Texas Southwestern Medical Center.[qv] Several subsequent expansions allowed the Children's Medical Center, by the mid-1980s, to admit more than 9,000 inpatients annually and to attend over 115,500 outpatient visits. Children's has pioneered numerous medical procedures for children in Texas, including pediatric day surgery (1968), pediatric liver-transplant surgery (1984), sleep-disorder care (1987), preventive cardiology (1987), and pediatric heart-transplant surgery (1988). The medical center retains a close relationship with the University of Texas Southwestern Medical School; the chairman of the school's department of pediatrics serves as chief of staff at the center. In 1985 a holding company, Children's Health Services of Texas, was established to provide strategic planning, marketing, and management support. The same year Children's Medical Foundation of Texas was formed as the fund-raising and fund-management arm of the hospital.

BIBLIOGRAPHY: Children's Medical Center Files, Archives, Dallas Public Library. Dallas *Morning News,* March 16, April 1, 8, 10, 1913, January 1, 1930, October 16, 1940, February 1, November 24, 28, 1948, July 30, 1967. Dallas *Times Herald,* April 7, May 16, 17, 1914. Michael V. Hazel, "May Smith and the Dallas Baby Camp," *Heritage News* 10 (Summer 1985).

Michael V. Hazel

CHILDRESS, GEORGE CAMPBELL (1804–1841). George Campbell Childress, lawyer, statesman, and author of the Texas Declaration of Independence,[qv] son of John Campbell and Elizabeth (Robertson) Childress, was born on January 8, 1804, at Nashville, Tennessee. His sister Sarah later married James K. Polk, president of the United States. In 1826 he graduated from Davidson Academy (later the University of Nashville). He was admitted to the Tennessee bar in 1828 and married Margaret Vance on June 12 of that year. Their son was born in March 1835, and Margaret Childress died a few months later. Childress practiced law and for a brief period (September 1834–November 1835) edited the Nashville *Banner* and Nashville *Advertiser.* In December 1834 he made his first trip to Texas, where his uncle, Sterling C. Robertson,[qv] was organizing Robertson's colony.[qqv]

After spending some time raising money and volunteers in Tennessee for the Texas army, Childress left permanently for Texas. He arrived at the Red River on December 13, 1835, and reached Robertson's colony[qv] on January 9, 1836. The following February he and his uncle were elected to represent Milam Municipality at the Convention of 1836.[qv] Childress called the convention to order and subsequently introduced a resolution authorizing a committee of five members to draft a declaration of independence. Upon adoption of the resolution, he was named chairman of the committee and is almost universally acknowledged as the primary author of the document.

On March 19 President David G. Burnet[qv] sent Robert Hamilton[qv] and Childress, whose family was on friendly terms with President Andrew Jackson, to Washington as diplomatic agents for the Republic of Texas.[qv] They were instructed to negotiate for recognition of the republic. In late May 1836 their mission was terminated when they were replaced by James Collinsworth and Peter W. Grayson.[qqv]

On December 12, 1836, Childress married Rebecca Stuart Read Jennings; they had two daughters. Childress returned to Texas three times—in 1837, 1839, and 1841—to open law offices, first in Houston, then Galveston. Each time he was unsuccessful in establishing a practice that would support his family. On October 6, 1841, while living in Galveston, he slashed his abdomen with a Bowie knife and died soon thereafter. On August 21, 1876, Childress County was formed and named in his honor.

BIBLIOGRAPHY: Daughters of the Republic of Texas, *Founders and Patriots of the Republic of Texas* (Austin, 1963–). Cornelia Hood, The Life and Career of George Campbell Childress (M.A. thesis, University of Texas, 1938). Louis Wiltz Kemp, *The Signers of the Texas Declaration of Independence* (Salado, Texas: Anson Jones, 1944; rpt. 1959). Texas House of Representatives, *Biographical Directory of the Texan Conventions and Congresses, 1832–1845* (Austin: Book Exchange, 1941).

Joe E. Ericson

CHILDRESS, HUGH MARTIN, JR. (1835–1897). Hugh Martin (Mart) Childress, Jr., cattle dealer and traildriver, son of Rev. Hugh Martin and Susannah (Watters) Childress, Sr., was born in Bastrop County, Texas, on May 24, 1835. He was the third of four children of a Methodist minister; the eldest son, Lemuel, was killed accidentally at the Alamo before the siege. His parents, both Tennesseans, had migrated in 1832 from Alabama to Bastrop County; the elder Childress served as a militiaman and ranger there and later fought under Edward Burleson[qv] at the battle of Salado Creek.[qv] By 1856 the family had settled near Camp Colorado in Coleman County. Hugh, Jr., entered the stock business in Lampasas and Brown counties and in 1859–60 won contracts to supply beef to Camp Colorado. In 1861 he started a ranch at Post Oak Springs in western Coleman County and was taxed for 400 cattle valued at $2,000. During the Civil War[qv] Childress served with J. J. Callan's minutemen and in Company B under Henry Fossett at Camp Colorado. In January 1865 he fought in the battle of Dove Creek[qv] against Kickapoo Indians bound for Mexico. In April he collected cattle to drive to northern markets but lost his horse herd to Comanche raiders. A year later, with his holdings increased to over 8,000 head through purchase and consignment, Childress piloted a small herd from Coleman County to central Iowa. In June 1866 he started 2,500 cattle to Colorado over what became the Goodnight-Loving Trail,[qv] but lost both cattle and horses to Indians before reaching the Pecos.

He regularly sent herds to Kansas between 1867 and 1869 and in 1870 was a preeminent drover in West Texas. He trailed more cattle than John Hittson, John Chisum, or Charles Goodnight.[qqv] By this time he also had suffered $42,680 in stock losses. In 1872 Childress joined Hittson and others in sweeping the ranches along the Pecos near Las Vegas, New Mexico, and recovered 11,000 stolen cattle and 300 horses. The next year in several drives he took 10,000 head to Kansas, found no market, and turned his herds loose to graze with wandering buffalo[qv] herds; he later hired hunters to round them up. "There are few more widely known and persistent drovers tha[n] H. M. Childress," wrote cattle entrepreneur Joseph G. McCoy in his classic *Historic Sketches* (1874). But times were changing. When the Comanches burned his headquarters in 1874 in Coleman County, Childress left the trail and settled on a small ranch in Throckmorton County.

He pioneered in driving herds from west central Texas to Kansas markets as early as 1866 and was a major cattle dealer and drover for more than a decade after the Civil War. He dealt regularly with other stalwarts of the trade, and like many of them he abandoned the trail by the mid-1870s. He was never active in church work or politics. He married Hulda Ann Cox in Bell County in 1853, and the couple had four children. In 1888 Childress left Texas, settled on a small ranch in Grant County, New Mexico, and pursued his Indian-depredation claims, most of which were later paid. After he was accused of murdering ranchman Ed Moss, he fled into the Gila wilderness. He was killed by a sheriff's posse on the White House Ranch near Cliff on September 23, 1897.

BIBLIOGRAPHY: Tabitha L. Morgan and Frank D. Jenkins, comps., *Two Texas Pioneers Called Hugh Martin Childress* (Ballinger, Texas, 1978).
Harwood P. Hinton

CHILDRESS, TEXAS. Childress, the county seat of Childress County, is at the junction of U.S. highways 287, 62, and 83, in the central part of the county. The town is named for George C. Childress,qv author of the Texas Declaration of Independence.qv It developed out of two separate townsites, Childress City and Henry, which were platted about four miles apart on land previously occupied by the OX Ranch.qv When Childress County was organized upon the arrival of the Fort Worth and Denver City Railway in February 1887, the two towns contested for the position of county seat. In the first election, held on April 11, 1887, Childress City, which already had three businesses, won the honor. A wooden courthouse was built under the supervision of Amos J. Fires,qv the "Dean of the Panhandle Lawyers." However, the Donley County Court (to which Childress County was attached for judicial purposes at the time) canvassed the election and declared it illegal. R. E. Montgomery, the railroad's right-of-way and townsite agent, had always favored Henry as the county seat because of the rougher terrain at Childress City, which he claimed would prevent the railroad from building a depot there. Significantly, he had also purchased half the property in Henry. After the court's action, Montgomery proposed that the railroad give those owning lots in Childress City lots in Henry. Furthermore, when Henry was chosen county seat in another election, the company offered to change the name of Henry to Childress. Fires and his associates agreed to this compromise, and the businesses and residences were moved to the new Childress by September 1887.

The town then enjoyed a boom from the railroad, which constructed the Dwight Hotel, the section house, and the depot. The Childress Lumber Company opened for business soon afterward. Dr. J. H. Christler became the first physician and one of the town's first businessmen. Fires, who was elected county judge, started the first bank and helped organized the first school system. James S. Harrison began the town's first newspaper, the *Childress County Index* (later the Childress *Index*), in 1888. Four churches, Methodist, Baptist, Presbyterian, and Church of Christ, were established in Childress by 1889. The city was incorporated in 1890. It had a post office, a livery stable, a boarding house, a restaurant, three stores, a local YMCA, a theater, and a population of 621. There were also several saloons at first, but in 1904 a fatal shooting prompted the citizens to vote the town dry. In 1901, when the Fort Worth and Denver City began considering Childress as a division point, the citizens approved bonds and donated land to build shops, roundhouses, and terminal facilities. These businesses, in addition to the influx of farmers and homesteaders, provided more jobs and resulted in a population increase to 5,003 by 1910. Walter P. Chrysler served as general foreman of the Childress railroad shops in 1905 and 1906 before working as a master mechanic in Iowa and subsequently founding the Chrysler Motor Corporation. After a fire destroyed the first courthouse in 1891, an elaborate stone building was constructed and used until the present courthouse was built in 1939. For years a large windmill in the middle of Main Street served as the city's water source.

The railroad continued as the industrial mainstay of Childress into the 1940s. Construction of the Fort Worth and Denver Northern line from Childress to Pampa and increased activity in the railroad shops in Childress helped reduce the economic hardships of the Great Depressionqv in Childress. In 1941 a move on the part of the railroad to discontinue its shops was thwarted by the citizens, in cooperation with the Interstate Commerce Commission. Various social clubs and lodges helped to promote the community, as did Childress Army Air Fieldqv during its existence from 1942 to 1945. In the 1920s a brick high school building was completed. In 1929 the town had a second newspaper, the Childress *News,* which was published under various names until 1942, when it was leased by the Index. In 1947 the Childress *Reporter* was established. After the depression and Dust Bowlqv era, the advent of modern farm machinery and improved highways reduced the town's rate of growth; the population was 6,464 in 1940. Furthermore, the railroad experienced a decline, and by 1970 several shops in Childress had been torn down. Such companies as Lanchart Industries, Royal Park Fashions, and Fiberglass Corporation of America moved in to supplant the railroad as the town's economic mainstay. The population decreased from 6,399 in 1960 to 5,817 by 1980. Nevertheless, Childress has remained the "Gateway to the Panhandle" and an important agribusiness center, as attested by several cotton gins and grain elevators. The first commercially producing oil well in the area was drilled in 1961.

In 1984 Childress had 159 businesses rated by Dun and Bradstreet, several churches, three schools, a public library, a hospital, clinics, nursing homes, and an ambulance service. The town's attractive Fair Park contains a small zoo and numerous recreational facilities, and the country club has a nine-hole golf course. The Childress County Heritage Museum, housed in the former county jail, features industry exhibits, local Indian artifacts, and furnished period rooms. Annual events include the Old Settlers' Reunion in July. This celebration, initiated soon after the town's founding in 1887, features a nightly rodeo. In August is the annual Greenbelt Bowl football classic, a contest between selected high school all-stars from a three-state area. In 1990 Childress had a population of 5,055.

BIBLIOGRAPHY: Lana Payne Barnett and Elizabeth Brooks Buhrkuhl, eds., *Presenting the Texas Panhandle* (Canyon, Texas: Lan-Bea, 1979). Michael G. Ehrle, ed., *The Childress County Story* (Childress, Texas: Ox Bow Printing, 1971). Ray Miller, *Eyes of Texas Travel Guide: Panhandle/Plains Edition* (Houston: Cordovan, 1982). Paul Ord, ed., *They Followed the Rails: In Retrospect, A History of Childress County* (Childress, Texas: Childress Reporter, 1970). LeRoy Reeves, The History of Childress County (M.A. thesis, West Texas State College, 1951).
H. Allen Anderson

CHILDRESS ARMY AIR FIELD. Childress Army Air Field, a World War IIqv bombardier-training school under the Central Flying Training Command, occupied an area of 2,474 acres 2½ miles west of the Childress city limit. Construction of the field was announced on May 2, 1942, and began immediately thereafter. An activation ceremony was held in October, and Col. John W. White assumed command on November 24. The first class of cadets began training in February 1943 and graduated in May. Members of this class were dubbed the "Valentine of Steel" class, in reference to a dummy bomb that Mrs. White decorated as a Valentine to Hitler. Subsequent classes arrived at three-week intervals through the rest of the war and participated in an initial training program of eighteen weeks, later increased to twenty-four. Those who completed the work were designated flight officers or commissioned as second lieutenants. The base produced the first classes qualified in both precision bombing and dead-reckoning navigation. In 3½ years Childress graduated thirty-five classes of bombardier-navigators; its 4,791 graduates made a tenth of the total World War II air force bombardier production. The first "All-American Precision Bombing Olympics" was held at Childress in May 1943 with seven air fields participating. Such meets were held there and at other training bases at three-week intervals thereafter until April 1944. A special practice feature was skip-bombing on Lake Childress. A redeployment program for veteran bombardiers was instituted at the field to give retraining in line with development of bombing techniques. The War Department also established a prisoner of war camp at the base. Childress was renamed the 2,512th Army Air Forces Base Unit on July 1, 1944. After the field was closed on December 21, 1945, it was given to the city and transformed into a municipal airport.

BIBLIOGRAPHY: Lana Payne Barnett, and Elizabeth Brooks Buhrkuhl, eds., *Presenting the Texas Panhandle* (Canyon, Texas: Lan-Bea, 1979). Jeff S. Henderson, ed., *Childress, Texas: the Crossroads of Hospitality* (1961).

James L. Colwell

CHILDRESS COUNTY. Childress County (D-11), on the eastern edge of the Panhandle,qv is bounded on the east by Oklahoma, on the south by Cottle County, on the West by Hall County, and on the north by Collingsworth County. The county is named for George C. Childress,qv author of the Texas Declaration of Independence.qv The county seat, Childress, is located 116 miles southeast of Amarillo, on the Fort Worth and Denver Railway and U.S. Highway 287. The center of the county lies at approximately 34°35′ north latitude and 100°13′ west longitude. The county comprises 699 square miles of rolling prairies and rough riverbottoms. Its soils are a mix, usually a sandy loam mixed with alluvial sands from the county's many creeks and rivers. These soils support a variety of native grasses as well as cotton, wheat, and sorghum. Shin oak, mesquite, salt cedar, and hackberry grow in the bottoms. The county has a small yearly production of oil and gas, but minerals do not play a major role in the local economy. The elevation of the county ranges from 1,600 to 1,900 feet above sea level; the annual growing season averages 217 days, and annual precipitation averages 20.67 inches. The average minimum temperature is 26° F in January, and the average maximum is 99° in July. The major water feature of the county is the Prairie Dog Town Fork of the Red River, which bisects the county as it flows eastward towards the main channel of the Red River. This stream and its tributary creeks (Dry Salt Creek, East Salt Creek, and Spiller, or Buck, Creek) render much of the central and northern part of the county unfit for farming. Thus ranching retains a significant role in the local economy. Baylor Lake and Lake Childress, two small bodies of water, lie to the northwest of Childress and provide recreation.

Archeological discoveries along the banks of the Prairie Dog Town Fork of the Red River indicate that permanent Indian farming communities existed in the area now known as Childress County between A.D. 1000 and 1600. The Indians lived in half dugouts and used stone and bone tools; they made pottery and supplemented their diet with buffalo, deer, dogs, turtles, and mussels.

Apaches occupied the area from about 1600 to about 1700, when the more warlike Comanches entered the region to begin a rule of the Panhandle and South Plains of Texas until they were crushed by the United States Army in the Red River Warqv of 1874. As the Comanches retreated to reservations in Indian Territory during 1875 and 1876, buffalo hunters spread across the area. By the late 1870s the buffalo herds were exterminated and ranchers entered the local picture. The Texas legislature formed Childress County in 1876.

In 1879 the OX Ranch,qv owned by A. Forsythe and Doss D. Swearingen, was established in the southern part of the county. This large ranch occupied the entire southern half of Childress County and parts of Cottle and Motley counties. The Shoe Nail Ranch,qv owned by Chicago meat packer Gustavus Franklin Swift, was started in 1883 in the northern part of the county, while the Mill Iron Ranch spilled into the northwestern part of the county from Collingsworth County. These ranches dominated the local economy, and the unorganized county remained a sparsely populated ranching area until farmers began to appear in numbers during the early twentieth century. In 1890 the United States Agricultural Census enumerated 3,982 cattle in Childress County; in 1900 the number was almost 25,500.

Farms began to be established in the Childress County in the 1880s after the Fort Worth and Denver City extended its tracks into the area. This railroad began construction of its line from Fort Worth to the Texas–New Mexico border in 1881 and crossed into Childress County in April 1887. Organization of the county soon followed. A move to organize the county began even as the rails were being laid across it. A lively competition for the role of county seat developed between two townsites: Childress City, favored by most of the county residents, and Henry, the site favored by the railroad. In an election held in April 1887, county residents chose Childress City as their county seat, but soon changed their minds to accommodate demands and threats leveled by the railroad company. The Fort Worth and Denver City threatened not to stop in Childress City unless the election results were reversed, and sweetened its demand by offering lot owners in Childress City equal lots in Henry, the railroad's town. Using these tactics the FW&DC was able to force a new election in July 1887, and in the second election Henry became the county seat; its name was changed to Childress. The old Childress City disappeared as all its buildings were moved to the new town.

With both organization and a rail link to the East accomplished, farmers began to move into the county, settling on unclaimed or state lands and usually entering into stock farming to make a living. By 1890, 153 farms and ranches in the county encompassed almost 79,350 acres (including 39,671 acres classified as "improved" land), and the county's population had increased to 1,175. At this time county farmers planted only about 1,300 acres in cereal crops such as corn, oats, and wheat, and only fourteen acres in cotton. Population figures reflect a gradual shift in the county's economy during these years. The population swelled from twenty-five in 1880 to 1,175 in 1890 and 2,138 in 1900, as a small but steady stream of settlers moved into Childress County. By 1900 there were 262 farms and ranches in the county.

After the establishment of this base, farming expanded quickly in the county in the early twentieth century, as old ranches were divided and farmers opened more land to the cultivation of corn, wheat, and, especially, cotton. By 1910 961 farms and ranches were in operation in the county; cotton cultureqv occupied more than 45,000 acres of the county that year, and wheat was planted on more than 12,000 acres. Local farmers had also planted more than 6,300 fruit trees, mostly peach. By World War Iqv all readily tillable land in the county had been sold to the new farmers. The ranching industry survived, however, since the nonarable portions of the large ranches were sold to smaller ranchers during this same period; the county enumerated almost 12,900 cattle in 1910 and almost 12,000 in 1920.

The county's agricultural economy experienced a brief downturn after World War I, but quickly recovered and began to expand again in the 1920s. There were only 861 farms and ranches in the county in 1920, but by 1925 the number had jumped to 1,322, and by 1930 to 1,348. Cotton, already the county's most important crop by 1910, became even more important during this time. By 1930, almost 135,000 acres of county land was devoted to cotton cultivation. Wheat production also increased during this time, so that by 1930 over 40 percent of the land in the county was under cultivation. By this time poultry had also become a significant part of the local economy; in 1929 Childress county farmers owned almost 71,000 chickens and sold more than 289,000 dozen eggs. Smaller ranchers also increased their production, and in 1930 more than 18,719 cattle were counted in Childress County.

During the first half of the twentieth century, Childress County emerged as the center of a transportation network. The construction of the railroad through the county gave it an early advantage. Shortly after the turn of the century, the Fort Worth and Denver City moved its division point and shops from Clarendon to Childress, a process that began in 1901 and ended in late 1902. The addition of the railroad facilities boosted an already expanding economy and population. The construction of the Fort Worth and Denver South Plains Railway from Estelline to Plainview and Lubbock in 1927–28 further stimulated the Childress County economy because Childress served as the terminal for that branch line. Childress also served as the terminal for the Fort Worth and Denver Northern Railway, built from the main line at Childress to Pampa via Wellington and Shamrock during 1931 and 1932. Thus by the early 1930s Childress County's economy benefited from both the Fort Worth and Denver City's mainline and two of its major branch lines. Construction of the Fort Worth and Denver South Plains and the Fort Worth and Denver Northern lines in 1929 and 1932 led to a doubling of the yard force at the Childress shops of the Fort Worth and Denver City Railway.

Between 1900 and the early 1930s, this expansion of transportation facilities in Childress, combined with the expansion of agricultural activity in the county, resulted in a substantial increase in the local population. In 1900 only 2,138 people had been counted by the census in Childress County; by 1910 the population had jumped to 9,538, by 1920 to 10,933, and by 1930 to 16,044.

The hard years of the Great Depression,[qv] combined with effects of the Dust Bowl[qv] and farm mechanization, however, worked to reduce the number of small farmers and farm laborers in Childress County during the 1930s. Harvested cropland dropped from more than 183,000 acres in 1929 to only 114,467 in 1939; cotton production was reduced to about 57,000 acres, and the number of farms dropped from 1,348 to 904 during the same period. Railroad workers were also hurt during the depression, as the conversion from steam to diesel locomotives and the mechanization of some shop activities reduced the number of railroad employees during most of the decade. By 1940 the population of Childress County had declined to 12,149.

The presence of Childress Army Air Base[qv] probably kept the population from declining further during the 1940s; but after 1950 the population declined continuously, to a low of 6,505 in 1970. The loss is related to the great reduction in railroad operations and the unprofitability of small-scale farming. Though the county's population increased slightly to 6,950 in 1980, in 1992 only 5,953 people lived in Childress.

By the mid-1920s "improved" and paved roads linked Childress to Wichita Falls via Quanah, Vernon, and Electra, and to Amarillo via Memphis, Clarendon, and Claude. This major route, originally U.S. Highway 370, is now U.S. 287. "Improved roads" also linked Childress to Canadian by way of Wellington, Shamrock, Wheeler, and Mobeetie, while a more primitive dirt road ran from Childress to Paducah. During the 1930s and 1940s a network of crude farm-to-market roads developed. This system was paved during the 1950s and 1960s. By the 1980s U.S. Highway 287 ran through the county, U.S. 83 (from Laredo to Perryton) passed through Childress, and a complex system of paved farm-to-market roads was centered around that city and its larger road systems.

In the 1980s Childress County continued with an economy based on agriculture, both farming and ranching. Small oil discoveries made in 1961 contributed little to the local coffers; in 1982 production was only 8,472 barrels, and in 1990 it was about 13,600. Between 1961 and 1991 county production totaled 1,346,966 barrels, not a large output. On average, more than $22 million worth of agricultural products come out of the county every year. This production derives from cotton, wheat, and sorghum, as well as cattle and hogs. Farmers plant only about 158,000 acres of the county's 447,360 each year; ranching plays a larger local role. By the 1980s small industry in Childress included the manufacture of clothing, mobile homes, fences, and wood products. Because of this, by 1980 most of the county's population lived in that town. Other communities include Kirkland (1980 population 100), Carey (57), and Tell (51). Childress, the county seat and largest town, had an estimated population of 5,055 in 1992. The town is the home of the Greenbelt Bowl, a high school all-star football game.

BIBLIOGRAPHY: Michael G. Ehrle, ed., *The Childress County Story* (Childress, Texas: Ox Bow Printing, 1971). Paul Ord, ed., *They Followed the Rails: In Retrospect, A History of Childress County* (Childress, Texas: Childress *Reporter*, 1970). LeRoy Reeves, The History of Childress County (M.A. thesis, West Texas State College, 1951).

Donald R. Abbe

CHILDRESS CREEK. Childress Creek rises five miles northeast of Clifton in south central Bosque County (at 31°51′ N, 97°33′ W) and runs southeast for fifteen miles to its mouth on the Brazos River, in adjacent McLennan County (at 31°42′ N, 97°17′ W). It was originally known as Childers Creek for Capt. Goulsby Childers, an Indian fighter associated with George B. Erath's[qv] early expeditions through the region. The Childress Creek area was settled after the Civil War,[qv] when Cayote and Womack were developed.

BIBLIOGRAPHY: *Bosquerama, 1854–1954: Centennial Celebration of Bosque County, Texas* (Meridian, Texas: Bosque County Centennial Association, 1954). William C. Pool, *Bosque Territory* (Kyle, Texas: Chaparral, 1964).

CHILICOTAL MOUNTAIN. Chilicotal Mountain is in Big Bend National Park[qv] nine miles southeast of Panther Junction in southern Brewster County (at 29°12′ N, 103°09′ W). With an elevation of 4,108 feet above sea level, it rises 1,500 feet higher than Glenn Spring, two miles to the south. The mountain is a body of intrusive rock surrounded by shales and sandstones from the Cretaceous period, 66 million to 144 million years old. Its surface of shallow, stony soils supports scrub brush and grasses. *Chilicote* is the Spanish name for the coral bean bushes found on the mountain.

CHILILI INDIANS. The Chililis originally occupied a Tiguex pueblo of the same name in New Mexico, but, upon abandoning the village between 1669 and 1676 because of hostility of the Apaches, most of the inhabitants retired to the Tiguex villages on the Rio Grande.

BIBLIOGRAPHY: Frederick Webb Hodge, ed., *Handbook of American Indians North of Mexico* (2 vols., Washington: GPO, 1907, 1910; rpt., New York: Pageant, 1959).

W. E. S. Dickerson

CHILLICOTHE, TEXAS. Chillicothe is on U.S. Highway 287, State Highway 91, Farm Road 2006, and the Fort Worth and Denver and Santa Fe railroads in eastern Hardeman County. It was founded in the early 1880s and developed rapidly after the construction of the Fort Worth and Denver City Railway in 1887. The community, named by A. E. Jones for his hometown in Missouri, grew up on Wanderer's Creek near the headquarters of W. H. Worsham's R2 Ranch in the 1870s. The post office was established in 1883 with Charles E. Jones as postmaster. A fire destroyed the town in 1890, and citizens rebuilt south of the rail line rather than north. Pioneers include Sam L. Crossley, who became the first mayor in 1903, J. J. Britt, J. A. Shires, and W. L. Ledbetter. Wheat elevators were constructed in 1892–93, and the town was incorporated in 1907 with a population of 800. Additional rail service from the Kansas City, Mexico and Orient Railway began in 1908. Chillicothe is called the Iris Village because of the many iris gracing the town. The population was 1,411 in 1950, 1,161 in 1960, 1,116 in 1970, and 1,052 in 1980. Chillicothe has a hospital, a library, a newspaper, and other businesses. In 1990 the population was 816.

BIBLIOGRAPHY: Bill Neal, *The Last Frontier: The Story of Hardeman County* (Quanah, Texas: Quanah *Tribune-Chief*, 1966). Kathleen E.

and Clifton R. St. Clair, eds., *Little Towns of Texas* (Jacksonville, Texas: Jayroe Graphic Arts, 1982).

William R. Hunt

CHILTIPIN CREEK (Duval County). Chiltipin Creek rises sixteen miles northwest of San Diego in the Strake oilfield in northeastern Duval County (at 28°00′ N, 98°25′ W) and runs southeast for thirty miles to its mouth on San Fernando Creek, just northeast of Alice in central Jim Wells County (at 27°47′ N, 98°02′ W). It traverses flat terrain with local shallow depressions, rolling hills, and local escarpments, surfaced by clay and sandy loams that support water-tolerant hardwoods, conifers, grasses, and some scrub brush.

──── (San Patricio County). Chiltipin (Chilipin) Creek rises north of West Sinton in west central San Patricio County (at 28°04′ N, 97°40′ W) and runs east for forty-five miles to its mouth, on the Aransas River in western Aransas County (at 28°04′ N, 97°16′ W). In early days the creek flowed with fresh water and abounded in fish; however, by 1990 the freshwater seeps were gone, and saltwater discharges from oil wells had contributed to erosion and pollution problems. In 1870 Sidney G. Borden[qv] applied for a post office at Chiltipin Settlement, on the banks of the creek. The creek provided a natural boundary for the Coleman–Fulton Pasture Company[qv] after 1871. When the San Antonio and Aransas Pass Railway came through San Patricio County in 1886, Sinton was laid out on the south bank of the creek where the railroad crossed. In later times severe flooding from the creek necessitated extensive flood-control measures in the Sinton area. The name of the creek comes from *chilipitín* (early variant *chiltapin*, from Mexican Spanish *chiltipiquín*), which denotes the small, wild red peppers that grow abundantly in the area (called bird pepper elsewhere).

BIBLIOGRAPHY: *Dictionary of American Regional English*. Keith Guthrie, *History of San Patricio County* (Austin: Nortex, 1986).

Keith Guthrie

CHILTON, GEORGE WASHINGTON (1828–1883). George Washington Chilton, Confederate Army officer, was born on June 4, 1828, in Elizabethtown, Kentucky. He briefly attended Howard College at Marion, Alabama, but with the outbreak of the Mexican War[qv] he enlisted as a private in Capt. Christopher B. Acklin's Company B of Col. John C. Hays's[qv] First Regiment, Texas Mounted Rifles. After being discharged on September 13, 1846, he returned to Alabama, where he was admitted to the bar in 1848 and set up practice in Talladega. Chilton moved to Texas in 1851 and became an attorney in Tyler. The following year he married Ella Goodman of Tyler; the couple had two children. Chilton was a fiery orator, a member of the Knights of the Golden Circle,[qv] and outspoken in his proslavery beliefs. He favored reopening the African slave trade and believed that every white man should own a black to perform menial labor, thus saving the energies of the "master race" for "self-improvement." The owner of five slaves, Chilton believed that a life of physical labor was God's will for the black race and that slavery was an improvement over a life of barbarism in Africa. Chilton was elected as a delegate to the Secession Convention,[qv] served from January 28 until February 4, 1861, and then was elected major of Col. Elkanah Greer's[qv] Third Texas Cavalry[qv] regiment. Samuel Barron, a trooper in the regiment, said of Chilton that "whenever an opportunity offered, [he] showed himself to be brave and gallant." Chilton commanded a battalion of the regiment at the battle of Wilson's Creek, Missouri, on August 10, 1861, and received a slight gunshot wound to the head at the battle of Chustenahlah, Indian Territory, in December 1861. When the regiment's one-year enlistment period expired on May 8, 1862, new elections for officers were held, and J. J. A. Barker was elected to Chilton's place. For the last year of the war Colonel Chilton served as ordnance officer on the staff of Gen. Hamilton P. Bee.[qv] After the war he was elected to the United States House of Representatives but was refused his seat by the radical majority in Congress. In 1876 he was a presidential elector on the Democratic ticket. Chilton died in 1883 and was buried in Oakwood Cemetery, Tyler. He was the father of United States senator Horace Chilton.[qv]

BIBLIOGRAPHY: Samuel Barron, *The Lone Star Defenders: A Chronicle of the Third Texas Cavalry, Ross' Brigade* (New York: Neale, 1908; rpt., Waco: Morrison, 1964). Douglas Hale, "The Third Texas Cavalry: A Socioeconomic Profile of a Confederate Regiment," *Military History of the Southwest* 19 (Spring 1989). Sidney S. Johnson, *Texans Who Wore the Gray* (Tyler, Texas, 1907).

Thomas W. Cutrer

CHILTON, HORACE (1853–1932). Horace Chilton, lawyer and statesman, son of Ella (Goodman) and George W. Chilton,[qv] was born on December 29, 1853, near Tyler, Texas. His mother taught him at home until he began attending local schools, including Charnwood Institute,[qv] at the age of ten. He later spent one semester at Lynnland Institution in Glendale, Kentucky. He learned the printing business and at the age of eighteen published a tri-weekly newspaper at Tyler, the Tyler *Sun*. Later he studied law, was admitted to the bar in 1872, and began his practice in Tyler. Chilton was assistant attorney general of Texas from 1881 to 1883, delegate to the Democratic national conventions of 1888 and 1896, and the first native Texan to sit in the United States Congress. Governor James Stephen Hogg[qv] appointed him to succeed John H. Reagan[qv] in 1891. Although he sought election to the position, Roger Q. Mills[qv] defeated him to replace Reagan. In March 1895 Chilton was elected to follow Richard B. Coke[qv] in the Senate and served until March 3, 1901. He returned to his law practice in Tyler, but moved to Beaumont later in 1901 to become Governor Hogg's office manager for his oil operations at Spindletop oilfield.[qv] He returned to Tyler, and in 1906 he represented the city in his most famous case, a successful fight to keep the offices of the Cotton Belt (St. Louis Southwestern) Railroad in that town. Chilton married Mary W. Grinnan on February 20, 1877; they had five children. He moved to Dallas in 1906 and lived there until his death on January 12, 1932. He was buried in Oakwood Cemetery, Tyler. He was an Episcopalian.

BIBLIOGRAPHY: *Biographical Directory of the American Congress*. Robert W. Glover, ed., *Tyler and Smith County, Texas* (n.p.: Walsworth, 1976). C. W. Raines, *Year Book for Texas* (2 vols., Austin: Gammel-Statesman, 1902, 1903). Vertical Files, Barker Texas History Center, University of Texas at Austin. Albert Woldert, *A History of Tyler and Smith County* (San Antonio: Naylor, 1948).

Anne W. Hooker

CHILTON, ROBERT HENRY (1844–1901). Robert H. Chilton, pioneer oculist, was born in Cumberland County, Kentucky, in 1844 to J. Lewis and Martha (Freeman) Chilton. The family moved from Virginia to Kentucky in 1838. Robert attended common schools in Kentucky, where he showed an aptitude for science and medicine. He attended medical school in Louisville, Kentucky, and was on the staff of Louisville City Hospital by the time he was twenty-one years old. He began to study eye, ear, and throat diseases at this time. Chilton was a member of the Kentucky Medical Association. He graduated from Miami University, Oxford, Ohio, in 1870 and married S. A. Harrison in 1874. They had one child.

The Chiltons moved in 1880 to Dallas, where he was the first oculist in the Southwest. Chilton was a Mason and a member of the Christian Church, the American Medical Association, and the Texas State Medical Association (later the Texas Medical Association[qv]). He invested in real estate in Dallas and built the Chilton Building around 1890. During the later years of his practice he took Dr. John O. McReynolds[qv] as his medical partner. Chilton was one of the seventeen charter members of the first Dallas County Medical Society, organized in April 1884. He had a stroke and died on June 6, 1901, in his home in Dallas. He was buried in Dallas. Members of the Dallas Medical Association published a resolution honoring him.

BIBLIOGRAPHY: Dallas *Morning News,* June 8, 1901. Marie Louise Giles, The Early History of Medicine in Dallas, 1841–1900 (M.A. thesis, University of Texas, 1951). *Memorial and Biographical History of Dallas County* (Chicago: Lewis, 1892; rpt., Dallas: Walsworth, 1976). George Plunkett [Mrs. S. C.] Red, *The Medicine Man in Texas* (Houston, 1930).
Linda Sybert Hudson

CHILTON, TEXAS. Chilton is on State Highway 7 a mile east of U.S. Highway 77, twelve miles west of Marlin, and twenty-one miles south of Waco in northwestern Falls County. The first settlers in the Chilton area were five Missouri families who arrived in 1854. Newton B. Maxey, one of the early settlers, established a wagon line to Galveston to bring in supplies. In the first year of settlement John Wethers was mistakenly shot by another settler, who thought he was a bear. The man who shot him lost his mind and was sent back to Missouri. In 1873 the site was bought by James C. Gaither. The town was originally called Abney's Farm. In 1876 Lysias B. Chilton, in partnership with W. J. de Bardeleben, opened a store near the present site of Chilton. The post office opened in 1882 and was named after Chilton. When the San Antonio and Aransas Pass Railway built through the county in 1888, the town was moved closer to the tracks and officially designated Chilton by the Texas Townsite Company. Chilton then became one of several railroad stations in Falls County and served as a shipping center.

In 1884 it had a population of 100, a steam flour mill, a cotton gin, a Baptist church, a First Christian church, and a district school. By 1896 the Chilton school had three teachers. Population estimates for the early twentieth century vary widely, from 230 to 750 for the same period. They also fluctuate markedly afterward. By 1914 Chilton had a bank, three churches, a large lumberyard, two cotton gins, a new schoolhouse, a telephone system, and a weekly newspaper, the Chilton *Homeland.*

The first oil well in the county was brought in on Deer Creek southeast of Chilton in April 1922. During an attempt to find oil in 1924, hot artesian wells were discovered, and the water was piped throughout the town. In 1935 the Chilton school district had 585 students, 8 percent of the students in Falls County. By the mid-1950s, when the Chilton district was one of only four independent school districts in the county, the town's population reached 750. It stayed at that level until the mid-1970s, when the number of residents dropped to 310, which was still the reported population in 1990. In the 1930s the town had twenty-five businesses, but by 1966 the number had dropped to eleven. In 1988 Chilton had ten businesses, six churches, one school, a town hall, and a recreation center.

BIBLIOGRAPHY: William Leshner, "Rosebud, Lott, and Chilton, Texas," *Texas Magazine,* January 1911. Lillian S. St. Romain, *Western Falls County, Texas* (Austin: Texas State Historical Association, 1951).
Lisa C. Maxwell

CHILYMPIAD. The annual Chilympiad celebration, a custom that began in 1969 in Hays County, attracts thousands of onlookers and hundreds of contestants. The contest is a chili cookoff held the second week of September at the Hays County Civic Center in San Marcos. Winners automatically qualify for the world championship chili cookoff in Terlingua. The rules for entry require that all chili be made from scratch at the site of the contest and bar women from entering. In response to the latter rule, a separate cookoff was established in Luckenbach called Hell Hath No Fury Like A Woman Scorned. Its winners also qualify for the world championship contest. Some participants in the cookoff are serious, some come for the party, and not all aspects of the contest relate to the state championship. There are several smaller cookoffs for media representatives, college students, and local business people. There is an award for best showmanship, and many contestants use costumes, decorations, and themes to win. The Chilympiad also offers country and western dancing, arts and crafts, food booths, and a parade.

BIBLIOGRAPHY: Vertical Files, Barker Texas History Center, University of Texas at Austin.
Robin Dutton

CHIMNEY CREEK (Floyd County). Chimney Creek rises on the eastern edge of the Caprock in extreme eastern Floyd County (at 34°02′ N, 101°04′ W) and runs east six miles to its mouth on Mott Creek, eight miles west of Matador in western Motley County (at 34°03′ N, 100°59′ W). The surrounding moderately steep slopes with locally high relief are surfaced by shallow to moderately deep silt loams that support mesquite and grasses.

____ (Howard County). Chimney Creek rises five miles north of Forsan in southeast Howard County (at 32°11′ N, 101°21′ W) and runs northeast for seven miles, traversing the Signal Mountains, to its mouth on Beals Creek, six miles southeast of Coahoma (at 32°14′ N, 101°16′ W). Chimney Creek runs through flat to rolling terrain surfaced by shallow, stony sand that supports oak, juniper, grasses, and mesquite. Several ridges over 2,700 feet in elevation lie just east of the creek. The surrounding area is sparsely settled ranchland. The main source of the stream is Barnett Springs.

____ (Shackelford County). Chimney Creek rises just south of State Highway 180 six miles west of Albany in west central Shackelford County (at 32°43′ N, 99°25′ W) and runs seventeen miles northwest to its mouth on the Clear Fork of the Brazos River, in east central Jones County (at 32°45′ N, 99°37′ W). The surrounding flat to gently sloping terrain is surfaced by shallow to moderately deep silt loam that supports mesquite and grasses. The down-stream terrain becomes flat with local shallow depressions surfaced by clay and sandy loam that supports water-tolerant hardwoods, conifers, and grasses. Finally, at the creek's mouth resistant ledges and low cuestas are surfaced by shallow stony soils that support live oak, juniper, and grasses.

CHINA, TEXAS. China is on U.S. Highway 90 ten miles west of Beaumont in northwestern Jefferson County. The Texas and New Orleans Railroad was completed through the area in 1860, and a water stop was established amidst a grove of chinaberry trees near the community's present location; the stop was dubbed China Grove. A post office by that name was authorized in March 1887 but was discontinued within two months. Another office, using the shorter name China, was established in 1893.

Two miles east of China, Charlie Nash and Howell Land organized a separate community called Nashland, which had 174 residents in 1900. The new townsite plat was belatedly filed on October 30, 1902. When fire destroyed the older China depot to the west in 1906, the people of Nashland convinced railroad officials to move operations to the more populated community center. The railroad, however, stipulated that the new depot retain the name of China. The Nashland post office, established in 1900, was therefore renamed China.

Agriculture provided the community with its economic lifeblood, and rice warehouses made it a center for the area's rice farmers. The South China oilfield, discovered in 1939, provided further growth. Although the community's population fell from an estimated 350 during the mid-1920s to 200 by the early 1950s, new discoveries of oil and natural gas at nearby oilfields in 1960, 1975, and 1980 brought new growth. In 1971 residents voted 118 to 88 in favor of incorporation. By the mid-1980s China had a population of 1,351 and eighteen businesses. In 1990 the population was 1,144.

BIBLIOGRAPHY: L. I. Adams, Jr., *Time and Shadows* (Waco: Davis Brothers, 1971).
Robert Wooster

CHINA CANYON CREEK. China Canyon Creek rises near Summit two miles south of U.S. Highway 62/70 and six miles west of the Cottle county line in southeast Motley County (at 33°57′ N,

100°35′ W) and runs east for seven miles to its mouth on Salt Creek, a mile west of the Motley-Cottle boundary (at 33°58′ N, 100°31′ W). The area is sloping terrain, surfaced by shallow silt loams that support mesquite and grasses. The stream forms the main drainage for China Canyon.

CHINA CREEK (Fisher County). China Creek rises near Palava in southeastern Fisher County (at 32°36′ N, 100°19′ W) and runs northeast for ten miles to its mouth on the Clear Fork of the Brazos River, four miles southeast of Sylvester (at 32°41′ N, 100°12′ W). The surrounding flat to gently sloping terrain is surfaced by loose sand that supports scrub brush and grasses.

_____ (San Saba County). China Creek rises 8½ miles northwest of San Saba in central San Saba County (at 31°19′ N, 98°47′ W) and runs southeast for 9½ miles to its mouth on the San Saba River (at 31°13′ N, 98°45′ W). It crosses level to gently rolling uplands surfaced by clay and sandy loam that supports live oak, mesquite, Ashe juniper, and grasses.

_____ (Wilbarger County). China Creek rises at Harrold in northeastern Wilbarger County (at 34°04′ N, 99°03′ W) and runs northeast for fifteen miles to its mouth on the Red River, ten miles northeast of Electra in northwestern Wichita County (at 34°08′ N, 98°46′ W). It was first named Moore's Creek after a worker with the Memphis, El Paso and Pacific Railroad, but when the railroad company went bankrupt the land passed into other hands, and the stream was renamed China Creek for the dense growth of chinaberry trees on its banks. The surrounding flat to rolling terrain is surfaced by silt loams that support mesquite and bunch grasses. China Creek is dammed three miles north of Electra to form a municipally owned reservoir with a capacity of 695 acre-feet.

CHINA DRAW. China Draw rises two miles east of Boracho Peak in northwestern Jeff Davis County (at 30°56′ N, 104°21′ W) and runs northwest for seventeen miles before running dry five miles south of Plateau in south central Culberson County (at 30°59′ N, 104°33′ W). In the upper reaches China Draw crosses steeply to gently sloping terrain surfaced by shallow, stony soils that support scrub brush and grasses. Along its lower reaches the terrain is flat to rolling and surfaced by sandy soil that supports scattered oak mottes.

CHINA GROVE, TEXAS (Bexar County). China Grove is on U.S. Highway 87 nine miles east of downtown San Antonio in eastern Bexar County. It was settled around 1900. In the mid-1930s it had a school, a church, and a number of houses. With the expansion of the San Antonio metropolitan area after World War II[qv] the town grew gradually. It incorporated in the 1960s, and by 1970 the population was 254. In the 1970s the town name was used as the title of a Doobie Brothers song. In recent years China Grove has experienced steady growth, with the number of inhabitants increasing from 372 in 1980 to 872 in 1990.

Christopher Long

CHINA GROVE, TEXAS (Brazoria County). China Grove is twelve miles north of Angleton, two miles south of Rosharon, and west of State Highway 288 in northwest Brazoria County. It was named for the chinaberry trees planted for shade by Warren D. C. Hall,[qv] owner of the original land grant. Hall, who also raised figs and oranges, operated a plantation called China Grove for a time, then sold it in 1843 to Albert Sidney Johnston and Albert T. Burnley.[qqv] Johnston took over his partner's interest, operated the plantation until 1849, and sold it in 1852. The China Grove station on the Columbia Tap Railroad, across the tracks from the plantation, served the area from at least as early as 1877 to 1892, when the town of Custer was established. In 1896 a black school in China Grove had eighty-seven pupils, and in 1906 two local black schools had 108 pupils and two teachers; that year a local white school had seven pupils and one teacher. In 1947 China Grove was a common school district with both white and black schools, but by 1974 only a single building and scattered dwellings remained. Of the original plantation, only hedges of Cherokee roses, thought to have been planted by Johnston, remained in 1991.

BIBLIOGRAPHY: James A. Creighton, *A Narrative History of Brazoria County* (Angleton, Texas: Brazoria County Historical Commission, 1975).

Diana J. Kleiner

CHINA GROVE, TEXAS (Trinity County). China Grove was near the site of present Nogalus Prairie sixteen miles northeast of Trinity in northeastern Trinity County. It was settled in the 1850s. In 1858 a post office known as Beasly's Store opened in a store operated by Wyatt S. Beasly. In 1859 the name was changed to China Grove. The post office closed in 1860, and the mail was sent to nearby Nogalus Prairie. After the Civil War[qv] the community lost its separate identity.

BIBLIOGRAPHY: Patricia B. and Joseph W. Hensley, eds., *Trinity County Beginnings* (Groveton, Texas: Trinity County Book Committee, 1986).

Christopher Long

CHINA GROVE, TEXAS (Van Zandt County). China Grove, on Farm Road 1256 eight miles south of Canton in Van Zandt County, was probably named for the chinaberry trees near a spring on the John Henry Robertson farm. The community had a post office from 1891 to 1905, three mills and gins by 1892, and two stores at its zenith. In the early 1890s the China Grove school district was divided; China Grove School was moved east and Rock Hill School was moved northwest. China Grove School reached an enrollment of thirty-four in 1905, and Rock Hill had eighty-seven students in 1904. The China Grove Missionary Baptist Church, organized on June 12, 1914, met in China Grove School. Both schools were consolidated with the Bethel Independent School District by the 1950s. State highway maps of 1936 showed a church, a school, and scattered dwellings at China Grove, but by 1987 only the church remained. Morris Cemetery, on the nearby farm of Elijah Newton Morris west of Denman Crossroads on State Highway 19, dates to 1866.

Diana J. Kleiner

CHINA SPRING, TEXAS. China Spring (China Springs) is on Farm Road 1637 twelve miles northwest of Waco in northwestern McLennan County. Settlement of the area began as early as 1860, and the community was founded in 1867. It was named for a spring in a chinaberry grove. A post office was established at China Spring in May 1873 with Charles S. Eichelberger as postmaster. By the early 1880s the community had five steam cotton gins and gristmills, three general stores, a Methodist church, and 200 residents. Cotton, corn, and wool were the principal shipments from the area. Population estimates for the community fell to 100 in the early 1890s but rose to 250 by 1896.

China Spring became the focus of a rural high school district in the late 1920s; it joined with Bosqueville in 1963 to form the China Spring–Bosqueville Independent School District. Two years later China Spring became a separate independent school district. Two churches, a school, and a good number of houses marked the community on topographic maps in the mid-1970s. The population of China Spring was reported at 214 from the 1930s through the 1960s and at 181 in the 1970s through 1990.

BIBLIOGRAPHY: Dayton Kelley, ed., *The Handbook of Waco and McLennan County, Texas* (Waco: Texian, 1972). William Robert Poage, *McLennan County Before 1980* (Waco: Texian, 1981). Vertical File, Texas Collection, Baylor University.

Vivian Elizabeth Smyrl

CHINATI, TEXAS. Chinati is on Farm Road 170 and the Rio Grande in the foothills of the Chinati Mountains, six miles northwest of Adobes in southwestern Presidio County. The settlement began as a Mexican mining village. After irrigation was introduced along the Rio Grande, Chinati farmers began growing cotton. It received a post office in 1922. By 1930 the area farmed 600 acres of irrigated land. From 1931 until 1947 a store operated in Chinati; in January 1933 it was raided by Mexican bandits. By 1939 the post office had closed. The population of Chinati remained at ten until 1943, when a population of 250 was reported. The growth was a result of World War II[qv] and the activity around the Presidio County military bases. After the war the military bases closed, and Chinati declined. At the end of the 1980s the community remained unincorporated and received mail through Presidio.

BIBLIOGRAPHY: Virginia Madison and Hallie Stillwell, *How Come It's Called That? Place Names in the Big Bend Country* (Albuquerque: University of New Mexico Press, 1958). *Julia Cauble Smith*

CHINATI MOUNTAINS. The Chinati Mountains are between Pinto Canyon on the northwest and Cibolo Creek on the south and east in southwestern Presidio County (at 29°54′ N, 104°28′ W). Their elevations range from 4,605 to 7,728 feet above sea level. Chinati Peak is the highest point in the range, which is elliptical in shape and runs from northwest to southeast for fourteen miles. The Chinatis are a series of terraced and dissected mesas cut by rugged canyons in all directions, formed from several superimposed flows of igneous rock. Vegetation in the area consists primarily of sparse grasses, cacti, and desert conifer and oak shrubs. In the 1880s mining developed in the range when John Spencer found silver-bearing ore near the site of present Shafter. The Presidio Mine, which resulted from his strike, produced over $20 million worth of silver between 1883 and 1941.

BIBLIOGRAPHY: Paul H. Carlson, "The Discovery of Silver in West Texas," West Texas Historical Association *Year Book* 54 (1978).

CHINATI PEAK. Chinati Peak, the highest point in the Chinati Mountains, is located between Oso Creek on the east and Boulder Canyon on the west in southwestern Presidio County (at 29°57′ N, 104°29′ W). It rises 7,728 feet above sea level and is encircled by desert mountain peaks and rugged canyons with elevations of 4,500 to 7,000 feet. The Chinatis are a series of terraced and dissected mesas cut by canyons to form gently rolling to steep slopes. The peak is formed of metamorphic and intrusive igneous rocks. The surrounding vegetation consists primarily of sparse grasses, cacti, and desert scrub of conifers and oaks.

BIBLIOGRAPHY: J. A. Udden, *Geology of the Shafter Silver Mine District* (Austin: Von Boeckmann-Jones, 1904).

CHINESE. The Chinese were the first of the Asian immigrants to come to Texas, and until the influx of the Vietnamese[qv] in the 1970s they were also the most numerous. According to the 1980 census, the Chinese in Texas numbered 25,461, or less than two-tenths of one percent of the state's total population.

The Chinese first came to Texas, in two contingents, with the railroads. The first group, 250 contract laborers from California, arrived in January 1870 with the Houston and Texas Central, whose railhead was then at Calvert. Although their labor on the Houston–Dallas line was abruptly terminated after less than a year and most of them soon left the state, a few nevertheless remained in Robertson County. In 1880 these seventy-two were 53 percent of the 136 Chinese living in Texas. The second contingent, also from California, came in 1881 with the Southern Pacific, whose 3,000-person work force was, except for 400, all Chinese. When the line was completed in 1883, some of them, too, stayed in Texas. By 1890 the number of Chinese statewide had jumped to 710, of whom 225 (32 percent) were in El Paso County.

After reaching a peak of 836 in 1900, the Chinese population in Texas began to decline as a delayed reaction to the congressional enactment in 1882 of the Chinese exclusion law, which for the next six decades barred practically all further immigration from China. The decline would have been more precipitous than it was but for one of the rare occasions when the exclusion law was set aside. In 1917, when Gen. John J. Pershing[qv] returned to the United States from Mexico, after his fruitless pursuit of Francisco (Pancho) Villa,[qv] he was permitted to bring with him 527 Mexican Chinese who had assisted his troops during the invasion. Most of these "Pershing Chinese" settled in San Antonio and thereafter replaced those in El Paso as the largest Chinese community in Texas. Even with this infusion, the statewide Chinese population in 1930 was only 703, of whom 321 (46 percent) were in Bexar County.

The Chinese exclusion act was repealed in 1943, and American immigration laws were greatly liberalized in the following decades. As a result, the Chinese population in Texas boomed. From 1,031 in 1940 the statewide population soared to 25,461 in 1980, of whom 12,048 (47 percent) were in Harris County. In the 1950s Houston surpassed San Antonio as the center of Chinese life in the state.

These postwar immigrants from China were, in several respects, very different from their predecessors—so much so that the two groups and their descendants often have little to do with each other. Whereas the old immigrants had originated almost exclusively from the Canton region of south China and spoke only Cantonese, the new immigrants were generally from north and central China (though often by way of Taiwan or Hong Kong) and spoke Mandarin. Furthermore, the old immigrants were originally of peasant stock and had come to the United States initially as unskilled and illiterate contract laborers, such as railroad workers. Once in Texas, however, they had carved out for themselves niches in the service and commercial sectors of the urban economy—notably hand laundries, which required little capital and posed no economic threat to Caucasian males; chop houses and restaurants that served American food as well as ersatz Chinese food like chop suey; and retail groceries that often catered to Chicanos or blacks. The descendants of these older immigrants, though upwardly mobile, usually stayed in the business world. The new immigrants, on the other hand, have generally been products of China's elite culture and have tended toward professional careers in the sciences and engineering. Finally, the old immigrants had come to America not as permanent settlers. They were nearly all men—in 1910 only thirteen (2 percent) out of the 595 Chinese in Texas were women—and their primary purpose in coming to America was to earn money to support the families they had left behind in China and hoped eventually to rejoin. Because of this "sojourner" attitude on their own part as well as because of the exclusion law, which barred them from bringing their wives, a normal conjugal family society did not emerge among the Chinese Texans until the late 1920s or 1930s, long after they first arrived in the state. The new immigrants, on the other hand, usually came with their families as permanent residents.

Except in the 1870s, when most of the Chinese in Robertson County were sharecroppers and field hands on the cotton plantations near Calvert and Hearne, the Chinese Texans have always been overwhelmingly an urban population. As noted, they were successively drawn to the cities of El Paso, San Antonio, and Houston. Around the turn of the century in El Paso they were numerous enough to form a small but compact Chinatown.

Socially, the Chinese in Texas have always been a close-knit, inward-looking community, bound by their own awareness of the distinctiveness of their original Chinese culture as well as by a long history of discrimination in the United States. They have looked to themselves and their own institutions for support and protection. The foremost institution among all Chinese has been the patriarchal family, on whose behalf, for example, the old immigrants endured long periods of separation during the era of exclusion. Among both old and new immigrants it is not unusual for three generations to be under one roof, with the aged parents living with their adult children and their grandchildren. Aside from the family, other social groups have also played an important role, though probably more among the old immigrants and their descendants than among the new. These include the clan or family association (usually defined by a common surname), the district association (defined by a common county of origin in China), and the merchant association (descended from the secret society of an earlier era, e.g., the Hip Sing and On Leong associations). These organizations, either individually or collectively, looked after the general well-being of all Chinese; they claim, for example, to have kept the Chinese Texans off the welfare rolls during the Great Depression.qv

Politically, the Chinese have similarly kept to themselves. Until the end of exclusion, they were classified as aliens ineligible for citizenship and thus, except for the few who had been born in the United States, were denied the right to vote. In 1937 they successfully lobbied against an amendment to the Texas alien land law that would have driven the Chinese groceries out of business. They were not, however, otherwise active in Texas politics. They preferred to involve themselves instead in the politics of their native land. They contributed generously to China's struggle against Japanese aggression in the 1930s and early 1940s, when branches of the Chinese Nationalist party, or Kuomintang, were established in San Antonio and El Paso. Since the repeal of the exclusion act in 1943 and the triumph of the Communists in China in 1949, however, their ties to China have loosened considerably. In 1964 Tom J. Lee of San Antonio became the first Chinese Texan to be elected to the state House of Representatives. More recently, others have been elected to local office in Houston.

Culturally, Chinese Texans have retained, to varying degrees, some of the distinctive elements of the old world ways. Many prefer Chinese food to American, though the proliferation of Chinese restaurants since the 1970s has been due more to the changing tastes of the general public than to any Chinese demand. Most celebrate the Chinese (lunar) new year. And, under the influence of Confucianism, they tend to emphasize family solidarity and the value of education more than most other ethnic groups do. They have also attempted to pass on to the younger, American-born generation some knowledge of Chinese languages and culture. A Chinese school operated in San Antonio for more than twenty years beginning in 1928; another was founded in Houston in 1970. But such efforts have been of only limited success. By and large, the Chinese, despite an adherence to traditional values and practices, have assimilated into the mainstream of American life. In religion, many are Baptists.

BIBLIOGRAPHY: Francis Edward Abernethy and Dan Beaty, eds., *The Folklore of Texan Cultures* (Austin: Encino, 1974). Edward Eugene Briscoe, "Pershing's Chinese Refugees in Texas," *Southwestern Historical Quarterly* 62 (April 1959). Edward C. M. Chen and Fred R. von der Mehden, *Chinese in Houston* (Houston Center for the Humanities, 1982). Amy Elizabeth Nims, Chinese Life in San Antonio (M.A. thesis, Southwest Texas State Teachers College, 1941). Edward J. M. Rhoads, "The Chinese in Texas," *Southwestern Historical Quarterly* 81 (July 1977).
Edward J. M. Rhoads

CHINQUAPIN, TEXAS (Matagorda County). Chinquapin is on an unpaved road on Live Oak Bayou just north of the Gulf Intracoastal Waterwayqv and East Matagorda Bay, east of the Big Boggy National Wildlife Refuge,qv and eighteen miles southeast of Bay City in southeastern Matagorda County. It is surrounded by swampland. It and nearby Chinquapin Bayou were probably named for a type of tree in the area. The community, which has been in existence since at least the 1940s, was built on land that was once part of Bay Stock Farm, property owned by John J. LeTulle (a half brother of Victor Lawrence LeTulleqv). At one time Chinquapin had grown to around 100 cabins. In 1961 it was completely destroyed by Hurricane Carla; it gradually rebuilt, and by 1972 a landing strip and nineteen new dwellings had been added. The community appeared on 1989 highway maps. It is primarily a fishing village.

BIBLIOGRAPHY: Matagorda County Historical Commission, *Historic Matagorda County* (3 vols., Houston: Armstrong, 1986).
Rachel Jenkins

CHINQUAPIN, TEXAS (San Augustine County). Chinquapin is on Chinquapin Creek at the intersection of State Highway 103 and a country road, nine miles southeast of San Augustine in eastern San Augustine County. It was settled before 1900 and named for the nearby creek and the chinquapin trees that are common in the area. In 1904 Chinquapin had two schools serving 100 pupils and three teachers. In 1940 it had a business, an estimated population of twenty-five, two churches, and a number of dwellings. In the 1980s Chinquapin had a number of dwellings, a cemetery, and a church.
Mark Odintz

CHINQUAPIN, TEXAS (Van Zandt County). Chinquapin was twelve miles south of Canton in extreme south central Van Zandt County. In 1890 it had a school, that reached an enrollment of forty-six in 1904 and was consolidated with the Athens Independent School District by the 1950s. A cemetery and scattered dwellings marked the community on state highway maps in 1987. Chinquapin was still listed as a community in 1990.
Diana J. Kleiner

CHINQUAPIN CREEK. Chinquapin Creek, also known as Egg Nog Branch, rises just east of Venable in eastern San Augustine County (at 31°28′ N, 94°04′ W) and runs southwest for 10½ miles to its mouth on Ayish Bayou, at the east edge of Angelina National Forestqv twelve miles south of San Augustine (at 31°21′ N, 94°08′ W). The surrounding nearly level flood plain is surfaced by loam and clay that supports dense forests of pine and hardwoods. The area is used predominantly as forest land. The creek is named for the chinquapin trees that grow along its banks.

CHIPLEY, TEXAS. Chipley was four miles northwest of Whiteface in east central Cochran County. It was named for H. D. Chipley, an associate of Morton Smith, the land agent in charge of selling most of the holdings in Cochran County. Chipley was in charge of developing the site. The proposed town was surveyed and platted by Lee Secrest on April 2, 1926. R. F. Fox, who owned the land of the townsite, gave the streets and alleys for public use; plans were made to name the streets for locally prominent people. The fact that Chipley was between the rapidly growing railroad towns of Lehman and Whiteface probably accounted for the lack of interest in settlement. Chipley did have a small store, a service station, and a dance hall for a short time. Plans for the town were officially cancelled on August 18, 1945, and the site is now ranchland.

BIBLIOGRAPHY: Ed Ellsworth Bartholomew, *800 Texas Ghost Towns* (Fort Davis, Texas: Frontier, 1971). Elvis Eugene Fleming, *Texas' Last Frontier: A History of Cochran County* (Morton, Texas: Cochran County Historical Society, 1965).
H. Allen Anderson

CHIQUITA CREEK. Chiquita Creek rises in northwestern Ochiltree County (at 36°24′ N, 100°59′ W) and runs north for seven miles into Texas County, Oklahoma, to its mouth on Huckleberry Creek (at 36°38′ N, 101°00′ W), a short distance above the point where their waters drain into the North Canadian River. It rises in a barren area with shallow depressions surfaced by variable soils that support grasses and runs into flat to rolling terrain with local escarpments surfaced by deep, fine, sandy loam that supports brush, grasses, and limited hardwood forest. A trail, thought to be part of the Tascosa-Dodge or a cutoff in flood periods to the Jones and Plummer Trail,qv ran along the eastern edge of the creek and on northeastward.

BIBLIOGRAPHY: *Wheatheart of the Plains: An Early History of Ochiltree County* (Perryton, Texas: Ochiltree County Historical Survey Committee, 1969).

CHIRENO, TEXAS. Chireno is on State Highway 21 sixteen miles west of San Augustine and eighteen miles southeast of Nacogdoches in Nacogdoches County. Spanish pioneers first settled north of the site in 1790 on grants they received from the Spanish government. About 1837 John Newton Fall, of Georgia, was the first Anglo settler to secure land from José Antonio Chirino, for whom the town was named. Fall was reportedly responsible for much of the town's early development. In 1837 Samuel Martin Flournoy,qv of Mississippi, built a large two-story home that became Chireno's first post office. On May 22, 1846, the log and clapboard structure evolved into a stage stop known as the Halfway House. Other early Chireno families were those of Daniel Vail, brothers Randal and Sanford Wilson, G. W. Davis, William Stivers, and Joseph Stallings. By 1836 Chireno had several home schools with area ministers serving as teachers. The town organized the first public school by 1839. During the Civil War,qv amid rumors of an impending Union siege to capture Galveston, all the men in Chireno that were not too old left their homes to aid in defending the coast. Andrew Jackson Mast operated a tanyard with Joseph Stallings. They worked for the Confederate government six months out of each year providing boots for the troops. An associate, Craig Wilson, made saddles, harnesses, and other leather goods.

Reconstructionqv divided the community. The Freedmen's Bureauqv organized a branch in Nacogdoches, and by 1866 black soldiers had been sent to Chireno to ensure propriety in elections. In response, a chapter of the Ku Klux Klanqv was organized in Chireno to keep black voters from the polls. By 1870 Texas returned to the Union, and the period of unrest gradually came to a close.

In 1866 the appearance of oil near Chireno prompted the drilling of one of the first oil wells in Texas. Other wells were unprofitable and were eventually abandoned. Chireno's first cotton gin, a small hand-turned operation, preceded Jack Moss's successful water-driven mill and gin near the Cottingham Bridge in 1872. In 1912 the Angelina and Neches River Railroad came to Chireno from Lufkin, carrying both logs and passengers. Another railroad, later a part of the Santa Fe line, was constructed northwest of Chireno and was still used for hauling timber in the early 1990s, when Chireno's principal crops were cotton, corn, wheat, barley, and potatoes. Livestock also remained important in the local economy. The population of Chireno was 415 in 1990.

BIBLIOGRAPHY: Robert Bruce Blake Research Collection, Steen Library, Stephen F. Austin State University; Barker Texas History Center, University of Texas at Austin; Texas State Archives, Austin; Houston Public Library, Houston. Nacogdoches County Genealogical Society, *Nacogdoches County Families* (Dallas: Curtis, 1985).

Randell G. Tarín

CHIROPRACTIC. Chiropractors have worked in Texas since the early twentieth century, although chiropractic was not legally recognized in the state until 1949. Before then, chiropractors were frequently fined or jailed for practicing medicine without a license. One Waco chiropractor was arrested sixty-six times between 1915 and 1943. The Texas State Chiropractic Association opened a legal-defense department in 1938 and hired an attorney to defend the large number of indicted chiropractors. Chiropractic legislation was first proposed in 1917. This and subsequent attempts to gain recognition failed because of the strong opposition of the Texas Medical Associationqv and because Texas chiropractors were not united. The first state chiropractic association was formed in 1914, but the strength of organized chiropractic in Texas was compromised for decades by factionalism. Chiropractors divided into "straights," who insisted that treatment be limited to manual manipulation of the spine, and "mixers," who used other therapeutic elements such as water and heat. Representatives of both groups united in 1932 to form the Texas State Chiropractic Association, but this merger spawned the Texas Chiropractic Research Society, a new rival group of "straight" chiropractors. During the late 1930s and the 1940s both organizations competed for the right to specify licensure requirements.

Legislation establishing the Texas State Board of Chiropractic Examiners and establishing licensure procedures was finally adopted in 1949. In 1953 chiropractic became an approved treatment for Texas workmen's compensation claimants, and in 1973 some chiropractic services were approved for Medicare and Medicaid reimbursement. By 1987 more than 1,600 chiropractors were licensed to practice in Texas. The Texas State Chiropractic Association changed its name to Texas Chiropractic Association in 1973. It remains the largest chiropractic group in the state. All licensed chiropractors in Texas are eligible for membership. The TCA represents the interests of chiropractors to the state legislature and to state agencies such as the Texas Workers' Compensation Commission.qv The TCA also offers its members educational seminars for license renewal and professional development. *The Texas Journal of Chiropractic,* the official publication of the TCA, was preceded by the *Chiropractic Flash,* which was first published in 1934 and later named *The Texas Chiropractor.* In 1942 the TSCA printed and distributed *Chiropractic for Texans* as a public-relations effort.

Chiropractic education in Texas dates from 1908, when physician and chiropractor J. N. Stone established Texas Chiropractic College in San Antonio. The school was chartered by the state in 1913 and operated privately until the alumni association purchased it in 1948. It was moved from San Antonio to Pasadena in 1965. The Texas Chiropractic Association purchased the school in 1986 and operates it as a nonprofit institution. It is one of the twelve chiropractic colleges in the nation accredited by the Council on Chiropractic Education. About 300 students graduate from the four-year program each year. In 1982 Parker Chiropractic College in Irving opened; its first class graduated in 1986.

BIBLIOGRAPHY: Walter R. Rhodes, *The Official History of Chiropractic in Texas* (Austin: Texas Chiropractic Association, 1978). Jane G. P. Sherrill, Chiropractic in Texas, 1968 (M.Ed. thesis, University of Texas at Austin, 1970).

Megan Seaholm

CHISHOLM, JESSE (1805?–1868). Jesse Chisholm, Indian trader, guide, and interpreter, was born in the Hiwassee region of Tennessee, probably in 1805 or 1806. His father, Ignatius Chisholm, was of Scottish ancestry and had worked as a merchant and slave trader in the Knoxville area in the 1790s. Around 1800 he married a Cherokee woman in the Hiwassee area, with whom he had three sons; Jesse was the eldest. Sometime thereafter Ignatius Chisholm separated from Jesse's mother and moved to Arkansas Territory. Jesse Chisholm was evidently taken to Arkansas by his mother with Tahlonteskee's group in 1810. During the late 1820s he moved to the Cherokee Nation and settled near Fort Gibson in what is now eastern Oklahoma. Chisholm became a trader and in 1836 married Eliza Edwards, daughter of James Edwards, who ran a trading post in what is now Hughes County, Oklahoma. Chisholm took trade goods west and south into Plains Indian country, learned a dozen or so languages, established small trading posts, and was soon in demand as a guide and interpreter. Eventually he interpreted at treaty councils in Texas, Indian Territory, and Kansas.

He was active in Texas for nearly twenty years. While president of the Republic of Texas,qv Sam Houston,qv who probably met Chisholm at Fort Gibson between 1829 and 1833, called on him to contact the prairie Indian tribes of West Texas. Chisholm played a major role as guide and interpreter for several Indian groups at the Tehuacana Creek councilsqv beginning in Spring 1843, when he coaxed several tribes to the first council on Tehuacana Creek near the Torrey Brothers trading post eight miles south of the site of present Waco. Over the next year and a half he continued to offer his services to Houston, and on October 7, 1844, Chisholm got Comanches and others to attend a meeting at Tehuacana, where Houston spoke. In February

1846, while visiting the Torreys' post from a trip south of San Antonio, Chisholm was hired to bring Comanches to a council at Comanche Peak (Glen Rose today). The meeting was held on May 12. Finally, on December 10, 1850, Chisholm assembled representatives from seven tribes at a council on the San Saba River. At some of these meetings and on trading trips he was able to rescue captives held by the Indians.

By 1858 Chisholm ended his trips into Texas and confined his activities to western Oklahoma. During the Civil War[qv] he served the Confederacy as a trader with the Indians, but by 1864 he was an interpreter for Union officers. During the war Chisholm resided at the site of Wichita, Kansas; Chisholm Creek in the present city is named for him. In 1865, Chisholm and James R. Mead loaded a train of wagons at Fort Leavenworth and established a trading post at Council Grove on the North Canadian near the site of present Oklahoma City. Many of his Wichita friends followed, and their route later became the Chisholm Trail,[qv] which connected Texas ranches with markets on the railroad in Kansas. Chisholm attempted to arrange an Indian council at the Little Arkansas in 1865, but some tribes held out. In 1867, with the aid of Black Beaver, famous Delaware leader and guide, he induced the plains tribes to meet government representatives in a council that resulted in the Medicine Lodge Treaty. Chisholm died of food poisoning at Left Hand Spring, near the site of present Geary, Oklahoma, on April 4, 1868.

BIBLIOGRAPHY: Stan Hoig, *Jesse Chisholm: Ambassador of the Plains* (Niwot, Colorado: University of Colorado Press, 1991). Thomas Ulvan Taylor, *Jesse Chisholm* (Bandera, Texas: *Frontier Times*, 1939). Vertical Files, Barker Texas History Center, University of Texas at Austin.
T. C. Richardson

CHISHOLM CREEK. Chisholm Creek rises six miles southwest of Cuero in central DeWitt County (at 29°02′ N, 97°22′ W) and runs east for three miles to its mouth on the Guadalupe River, two miles southwest of Cuero (at 29°03′ N, 97°19′ W). The surrounding nearly level to gently sloping terrain is surfaced by clay and mud that supports water-tolerant hardwood, conifers, and grasses. The stream was named for Richard H. Chisholm, who with his family settled on the stream in 1829. His land grant is dated 1831.

CHISHOLM TRAIL. The Chisholm Trail was the major route out of Texas for livestock. Although it was used only from 1867 to 1884, the longhorn cattle[qv] driven north along it provided a steady source of income that helped the impoverished state recover from the Civil War.[qv] Youthful trail hands on mustangs[qv] gave a Texas flavor to the entire range cattle industry of the Great Plains and made the cowboy an enduring folk hero.

When the Civil War ended the state's only potential assets were its countless longhorns, for which no market was available—Missouri and Kansas had closed their borders to Texas cattle in the 1850s because of the deadly Texas fever[qv] they carried. In the East was a growing demand for beef, and many men, among them Joseph G. McCoy[qv] of Illinois, sought ways of supplying it with Texas cattle. In the spring of 1867 he persuaded Kansas Pacific officials to lay a siding at the hamlet of Abilene, Kansas, on the edge of the quarantine area. He began building pens and loading facilities and sent word to Texas cowmen that a cattle market was available. That year he shipped 35,000 head; the number doubled each year until 1871, when 600,000 head glutted the market.

The first herd to follow the future Chisholm Trail to Abilene belonged to O. W. Wheeler and his partners, who in 1867 bought 2,400 steers in San Antonio. They planned to winter them on the plains, then trail them on to California. At the North Canadian River in Indian Territory they saw wagon tracks and followed them. The tracks were made by Scot-Cherokee Jesse Chisholm,[qv] who in 1864 began hauling trade goods to Indian camps about 220 miles south of his post near modern Wichita. At first the route was merely referred to as the Trail, the Kansas Trail, the Abilene Trail, or McCoy's Trail. Though it was originally applied only to the trail north of the Red River, Texas cowmen soon gave Chisholm's name to the entire trail from the Rio Grande to central Kansas. The earliest known references to the Chisholm Trail in print were in the Kansas *Daily Commonwealth* of May 27 and October 11, 1870. On April 28, 1874, the Denison, Texas, *Daily News* mentioned cattle going up "the famous Chisholm Trail."

The herds followed the old Shawnee Trail[qv] by way of San Antonio, Austin, and Waco, where the trails split. The Chisholm Trail continued on to Fort Worth, then passed west of Decatur to the crossing at Red River Station. From Fort Worth to Newton, Kansas, U.S. Highway 81 follows the Chisholm Trail. It was, Wayne Gard observed, like a tree—the roots were the feeder trails from South Texas, the trunk was the main route from San Antonio across Indian Territory, and the branches were extensions to various railheads in Kansas. Between 1871, when Abilene ceased to be a cattle market, and 1884 the trail might end at Ellsworth, Junction City, Newton, Wichita, or Caldwell. The Western Trail[qv] by way of Fort Griffin and Doan's Store ended at Dodge City.

The cattle did not follow a clearly defined trail except at river crossings; when dozens of herds were moving north it was necessary to spread them out to find grass. The animals were allowed to graze along for ten or twelve miles a day and never pushed except to reach water; cattle that ate and drank their fill were unlikely to stampede. When conditions were favorable longhorns actually gained weight on the trail. After trailing techniques were perfected, a trail boss, ten cowboys, a cook, and a horse wrangler could trail 2,500 cattle three months for sixty to seventy-five cents a head. This was far cheaper than shipping by rail.

The Chisholm Trail led to the new profession of trailing contractor. A few large ranchers such as Capt. Richard King and Abel (Shanghai) Pierce[qqv] delivered their own stock, but trailing contractors handled the vast majority of herds. Among them were John T. Lytle[qv] and his partners, who trailed about 600,000 head. Others were George W. Slaughter[qv] and sons, Snyder Brothers, Blocker Brothers, and Pryor Brothers. In 1884 Pryor Brothers contracted to deliver 45,000 head, sending them in fifteen separate herds for a net profit of $20,000.

After the Plains tribes were subdued and the buffalo[qv] decimated, ranches sprang up all over the Plains; most were stocked with Texas longhorns and manned by Texas cowboys. Raising cattle on open range and free grass attracted investments from the East and abroad in partnerships such as that of Charles Goodnight and Irish financier John Adair[qqv] or in ranching syndicates such as the Scottish Prairie Land and Cattle Company and the Matador Land and Cattle Company.[qv] Texas tried to outlaw alien land ownership but failed. The XIT Ranch[qv] arose when the Texas legislature granted the Capitol Syndicate of Chicago three million acres for building a new Capitol.[qv]

The Chisholm Trail was finally closed by barbed wire[qv] and an 1885 Kansas quarantine law; by 1884, its last year, it was open only as far as Caldwell, in southern Kansas. In its brief existence it had been followed by more than five million cattle and a million mustangs, the greatest migration of livestock in world history.

BIBLIOGRAPHY: Wayne Gard, *The Chisholm Trail; with Drawings by Nick Eggenhofer* (Norman: University of Oklahoma Press, 1954). Wayne Gard, "Retracing the Chisholm Trail," *Southwestern Historical Quarterly* 60 (July 1956). Joseph G. McCoy, *Historic Sketches of the Cattle Trade of the West and Southwest* (Kansas City, Missouri: Ramsey, Millett, and Hudson, 1874; rpt., Philadelphia: Porcupine, 1974). Jimmy M. Skaggs, *The Cattle-Trailing Industry: Between Supply and Demand, 1866–1890* (Lawrence: University Press of Kansas, 1973). Donald E. Worcester, *The Chisholm Trail* (Lincoln: University of Nebraska Press, 1980).
Donald E. Worcester

CHISOS MINING COMPANY. The Chisos Mining Company, a major quicksilver producer, was established in 1903 at Terlingua, in southern Brewster County. Founded by Howard E. Perry,qv a Chicago industrialist, the Chisos reported the first recovery in 1903, and during the next three decades became one of the nation's leading producers of quicksilver. Initially the company processed the cinnabar ore in primitive retorts, where the silver liquid metal is recovered through a simple baking process. As production increased, Perry turned to more industrialized methods; in 1908 he installed a twenty-ton Scott Furnace to help boost production. Exploration continued, and in 1914 the company discovered one of the richest veins of cinnabar ore in the Terlingua district. This discovery coincided with the outbreak of World War I,qv and with the increased military demands for the product, the company entered its most successful period. In 1915 the Chisos installed a more modern thirty-ton rotary furnace; within one ten-day period in September 1916 the company shipped two carloads of quicksilver from Alpine, valued at more than $50,000. Although strict secrecy surrounded the operation, one long-time Chisos employee claimed that company profits averaged $2,000 a day during the early war years and yielded more than $1,250,000 in its best year. In 1934 two Texas geologists, E. H. Sellards and C. L. Baker,qqv cited the three-decade Chisos recovery at $12 million. Several factors contributed to the success. First, the property contained some of the richest ore in the quicksilver district; second, although he seldom went to the mine, Perry engaged men of outstanding caliber to supervise the onsite operations (metallurgist William Battle Phillipsqv and geologist Johan August Uddenqv); third, quicksilver prices peaked during World War I, the period of the mine's maximum recovery; and fourth, an abundance of cheap Mexican labor. The community of Terlingua grew up around the mine. Its some 1,000 inhabitants had access to facilities of modern civilization: a company-owned commissary and hotel, several excellent dwellings (for Anglo employees), a school, a company doctor, telephone service, a dependable water supply, and three-times-a-week mail delivery. Prior to the use of mechanized vehicles in the early 1930s, the mule-drawn wagontrains that delivered the quicksilver to the railroad at Alpine and Marathon supplied the settlement. Production declined during the late 1930s, and on October 1, 1942, the company filed for bankruptcy. The Esperado Mining Company purchased the Chisos assets and operated the mine unsuccessfully until the end of World War II.qv At that time most of the surface installations were demolished and sold for scrap. On December 6, 1944, Howard E. Perry died in his sleep in a Boston hotel en route to a Florida vacation.

BIBLIOGRAPHY: James M. Day, "The Chisos Quicksilver Bonanza in the Big Bend of Texas," *Southwestern Historical Quarterly* 64 (April 1961). Kenneth B. Ragsdale, *Quicksilver: Terlingua and the Chisos Mining Company* (College Station: Texas A&M University Press, 1976).
Kenneth B. Ragsdale

CHISOS MOUNTAINS. The Chisos Mountains are the heart of Big Bend National Parkqv in southern Brewster County (at 29°16′ N, 103°18′ W). They extend twenty miles from Punta de la Sierra in the southwest to Panther Junction in the northeast. Among the highest peaks in the range are Emory Peak (7,835 feet above sea level), Lost Mine Peak (7,535 feet), Toll Mountain (7,415 feet), and Casa Grande Peak (7,325 feet). Shallow, stony soils on the mountains support a flora that includes Douglas fir, aspen, Arizona cypress, maple, ponderosa pine, and madrone.

The Chisos Mountains and the surrounding lowlands sit in a sunken block bounded on the northeast by the Sierra del Carmen and Santiago Mountains and on the southwest by the Sierra de Santa Elena. The mountains were pushed up to elevations of more than 5,000 feet above sea level by a great deformation during the Cenozoic era. During this uplift, however, formations from the Cretaceous period, between 66 million and 144 million years old, were also pushed up, and are still found occasionally high in the mountains.

In the eighteenth century the Chisos Mountains became the base of the Mescalero Apaches, who raided the Spanish settlements in Coahuila and Neuva Vizcaya, south of the Rio Grande. In 1747 Governor Pedro de Rábago y Teránqv of Coahuila led the first full-scale European expedition into the Big Bend. In the 1770s and 1780s Lt. Col. Hugo Oconór and Col. Juan de Ugaldeqqv led several campaigns against the Mescaleros, who had moved down into northern Mexico, and succeeded in driving them as far north as the Guadalupe Mountains.qv In the nineteenth century the Comanche Trail,qv used by Comanche raiding parties striking into northern Mexico, passed through the Chisos Mountains. By this time, however, white settlers, traders, and soldiers were also using the pathways through the mountains, and eventually cattle ranchers replaced hostile Indians as the primary occupants of the range. Since 1944 the Chisos Mountains have been part of Big Bend National Park.

Several explanations of the origin of the name of the range have been offered over the years. One held that *chisos* means "ghost," and that the mountains were named for the ghost of the Apache chief Alsate, who hid in the mountains for a time. Another version was that *chisos* was the plural of *chis,* meaning "clash of arms" (*chischás* in Castilian), since some reported hearing battle sounds at night in the mountains as the ghosts of Spanish soldiers returned to fight again. A third story was that *chisos* was a corruption of the Spanish *hechizos,* "bewitchments" or "enchantments." The mountains were almost certainly named, however, for the Chizos Indians.

BIBLIOGRAPHY: Clifford B. Casey, *Mirages, Mysteries and Reality: Brewster County, Texas, the Big Bend of the Rio Grande* (Hereford, Texas: Pioneer, 1972). Walter Fulcher, *The Way I Heard It: Tales of the Big Bend* (Austin: University of Texas Press, 1959; rpt. 1973). Arthur R. Gomez, *A Most Singular Country: A History of Occupation in the Big Bend* (Santa Fe: National Park Service; Salt Lake City: Charles Redd Center for Western Studies, Brigham Young University, 1990). Elton Miles, "Terlingua and Los Chisos: The Place Names," *Journal of Big Bend Studies* 1 (January 1989). James B. and Margaret S. Stevens, "Stratigraphy and Major Structural-Tectonic Events along and near the Rio Grande, Trans-Pecos Texas and Adjacent Chihuahua and Coahuila, Mexico," in *Geology of the Big Bend and Trans-Pecos Region,* ed. Patricia Wood Dickerson et al. (San Antonio: South Texas Geological Society, 1990).
Martin Donell Kohout

CHISPA, TEXAS. Chispa was on the Southern Pacific Railroad and U.S. Highway 90, sixteen miles northwest of Valentine and six miles south of Chispa Mountain in northwestern Jeff Davis County. It was founded in 1882, when the railroad built through the area. A post office was established there in 1895 or 1896 but closed in 1900. For a time a branch railroad ran from Chispa to a coal mine near the Rio Grande, and in 1949 the siding, a section house, two dwellings, and the abandoned tunnel of the branch railroad remained at the site. By the early 1970s Chispa was only a stop on the railroad. The C. Means ranch was a half mile northeast. The town's name is Spanish for "spark."
Martin Donell Kohout

CHISPA MOUNTAIN. Chispa Mountain is two miles southeast of Lobo in southwestern Culberson County (at 30°48′ N, 104°43′ W). At an elevation of 5,200 feet above sea level, its summit rises 1,200 feet above U.S. Highway 90, two miles west.

CHISUM, ETHELYN MILDRED TAYLOR (1895–1983). Ethelyn Mildred Taylor Chisum, black teacher and administrator, was born in Dallas on June 9, 1895, the daughter of William Henry and Virgie M. (Collins) Taylor. After graduating from Prairie View State Normal and Industrial College in 1913, she taught in the public schools of Rock Creek (Smith County), Waxahachie, and Dallas (1916–23). On September 23, 1923, she married John O. Chisum, an optometry student. She did secretarial work from 1925 to 1928. In 1932 she became attendance teacher at Booker T. Washington High School in Dallas. In 1941 she became dean of the school, a position in which she served until her retirement in 1965. During her tenure as dean she earned a B.S. in 1936 and an M.S. in 1959 from Prairie View State College. Mrs. Chisum joined the staff of Southern Methodist University in 1967 to work with the Upward Bound program and remained with SMU until poor health forced her second retirement in November 1982.

She served as president of the Dallas Teachers Council, an affiliate of the National Education Association, from 1948 to 1958 and as an advisor to the council from 1959 to 1965. She was the NEA membership chairwoman for North Texas from 1955 to 1960. In 1956 she chaired the Dallas Negro Division to Improve the Texas Teachers Retirement Plan. She served on a special committee of the Texas Education Agency[qv] for the study of teacher-training programs (1955–57) and on the Constitution Committee of the Texas Association of Women Deans and Counselors (1962–64). She was a life member of the NEA and a member of the National Association of Women Deans and Counselors, the Texas Personnel and Guidance Association, and the Teachers State Association of Texas.[qv] She was a founder, president, and president emeritus of the Dallas Personnel and Guidance Club.

In addition to her involvement with professional organizations, Ethelyn Chisum was active in community and civic affairs. In the mid-1950s she served on the board of the Texas Commission on Race Relations. She was a member of the board of management of the Maria Morgan branch of the YWCA, a branch she helped establish in 1927 in order to make that program available to Dallas blacks. She also served as president of the North Park–Cedar Springs Civic League and as a member of the board of trustees for the Dallas Metropolitan Chapter of the March of Dimes. Before joining Knight's Chapel African Methodist Episcopal Church, she was an active member of the New Hope Baptist Church. She was also a member of Zeta Phi Beta Sorority; a member and president of the Priscilla Art Club, the oldest Dallas club for black women; and a member of the North Dallas Democratic Women's Club. She served as second vice president of the Prairie View Alumni Association from 1961 to 1963 and as a member of the executive committee from 1963 to 1965. She died on January 27, 1983. The John O. and Ethelyn M. Chisum Collection at the Dallas Public Library not only chronicles the careers of Ethelyn Chisum and her husband, but offers much information about the lives of African Americans[qv] in early twentieth-century Dallas.

BIBLIOGRAPHY: *Who's Who in American Education*, 23d. ed. *Who's Who of American Women*, 1966–67.
Mary M. Standifer

CHISUM, JOHN OSCAR (1895–1979). John Oscar Chisum, optometrist and civic leader, was born in Dallas on December 12, 1895, the son of Benjamin and Rosa Pauline (White) Chisum. After graduating as salutatorian from Dallas Colored High School in 1916, he worked briefly as a mortician. During World War I[qv] he served with the American Expeditionary Force in France. In 1925 he graduated from the Northern Illinois College of Otology and Optometry in Chicago and returned to Dallas, where he practiced optometry until his retirement in 1965. He was on numerous boards and committees of the Bethel African Methodist Episcopal Church. He was also an active member of Tommy Robinson American Legion Post No. 802 and was among the founders of the Moorland Branch of the Young Men's Christian Association, which served the Dallas black community. During the early 1950s Chisum gained fame as one of the leaders of a movement to halt the expansion of Love Field.[qv] He was first married to Goldie Belle Ramage in 1920; in September 1923 he married Ethelyn Mildred Taylor. Chisum died in Dallas on September 9, 1979, and was buried in Lincoln Memorial Park. After Ethelyn Chisum's[qv] death in 1983, the Chisums' foster niece, Ouida H. Parham, donated their extensive collection of papers, correspondence, photographs, and other objects to the Dallas Public Library. The collection, which covers the period from 1895 to 1983, is an outstanding source of information about life in black Dallas during the first half of the twentieth century.

BIBLIOGRAPHY: Biographical Files, Dallas Public Library.
Christopher Long

CHISUM, JOHN SIMPSON (1824–1884). John Simpson Chisum, pioneer cattleman, son of Claiborne C. and Lucinda (Chisum) Chisum, was born in Hardeman County, Tennessee, on August 16, 1824. His parents were cousins. He was reared on his grandfather's plantation, one of five children, and accompanied his parents and a group of relatives to Red River County, Texas, during the summer of 1837. Claiborne Chisum, probably the earliest settler in Paris, Texas, was public-spirited and wealthy. John Chisum worked as a store clerk in Paris, served briefly as a road overseer in Hopkins County, accumulated land, operated several small grocery stores, was a member of the I.O.O.F. Lodge, and held the office of Lamar county clerk from 1852 to 1854. With Stephen K. Fowler, a New Orleans investor, he filed on land in northwestern Denton County, purchased a partnership herd, and entered the cattle business with the Half Circle P brand. Chisum also managed herds for neighboring families and various partners and shared in the calves. He became an active cattle dealer in search of markets and drove a small herd to a packing house in Jefferson. By 1860 he was running 5,000 head of cattle, which he valued at $35,000, owned six slaves, and was considered a major cattleman in North Texas.

At the outbreak of the Civil War[qv] Chisum was exempted from service and placed in charge of several herds in his district. Early in 1862 he took a herd across Arkansas to the Confederate forces at Vicksburg but thereafter exhibited little interest in the Southern cause. In the fall of 1863, suffering from Indian raids and drought, he and other cowmen in the Denton area started moving herds to Coleman County, where they camped on the Concho River near its junction with the Colorado. He terminated ties with Fowler and received cattle for land. Chisum and his partners soon had 18,000 head grazing along the Colorado.

In the fall of 1866 he joined Charles Goodnight[qv] and others driving cattle to feed the 8,000 Navajos on the Bosque Redondo Reservation near Fort Sumner, New Mexico. Chisum wintered 600 steers near Bosque Grande, below Fort Sumner, and in the spring sold his herd and contracted to furnish additional cattle. The market vanished in 1868, when the army resettled the Navajos in Arizona. Chisum arranged to supply Goodnight, now ranching in Colorado, with Texas cattle for markets there and in Wyoming. For three years he delivered 10,000 head annually to Goodnight crews at Bosque Grande, for one dollar a head over Texas prices. During this period he adopted the Long Rail brand and the Jinglebob earmark for his herds.

In 1872 Chisum abandoned his base in Texas and established his headquarters at Bosque Grande; he claimed a range extending more than 100 miles down the Pecos. He loosed herds obtained from Robert K. Wiley, the Coggin brothers,[qv] and others in West Texas with his own for fattening and sought markets in New Mexico, Arizona, and Kansas. In the summer of 1874 Chisum won a contract to provide beef to several Apache reservations in New Mexico, only to have his operations crippled by marauding Indians. His total stock losses from 1868 to 1874 reached $150,000, the largest in the nation. In November of 1875 he transferred his livestock holdings, estimated at over 60,000 head of cattle, to Hunter, Evans, and Company, a St. Louis beef-commission house, which assumed his indebtedness, mostly for Texas cattle, of over $200,000. Chisum settled at South Springs, near Roswell, New Mexico.

As he helped Hunter and Evans gather cattle for markets, horse thieves and renegade Indians struck branding crews and horse herds. Lincoln County authorities and the army at Fort Stanton offered little help. Simultaneously, Chisum was drawn into the Lincoln County range war of 1878 by festering difficulties generated by his attorney,

Alexander A. McSween, and rancher John H. Tunstall, who defied Judge Lawrence G. Murphy's economic stranglehold on the county. In the summer of 1878, with both Tunstall and McSween dead and the county in chaos, Chisum and Hunter and Evans cleared their cattle from the Pecos. A small herd of Jinglebob heifers, wintering on the Canadian River in the Panhandle,[qv] was transferred to Pitser and James Chisum, John's brothers, as payment for their years of service. In 1879 the Chisums adopted the U brand and returned to South Springs, built a comfortable ranchhouse, improved their cattle, and became active in local and territorial livestock associations.

Chisum was a major figure in the southwestern cattle industry for nearly thirty years, eighteen of which (1854–72) were in Texas. He located immense herds on the open range near running water and controlled surrounding pastures by right of occupancy. He never claimed to be a traildriver, nor did he spend much time at the ranch or on the range. Personable and shrewd, he primarily was a cattle dealer who traveled in search of markets. His colorful and eccentric life epitomized the adventurous world of open-range cattle operations that set the tone for the industry after the Civil War. Chisum was reared in the Cumberland Presbyterian faith, never married, and took no interest in politics. He died of cancer at Eureka Springs, Arkansas, on December 22, 1884, and was buried in Paris, Texas.

BIBLIOGRAPHY: James Cox, *Historical and Biographical Record of the Cattle Industry* (2 vols., St. Louis: Woodward and Tiernan Printing, 1894, 1895; rpt., with an introduction by J. Frank Dobie, New York: Antiquarian, 1959). Harwood P. Hinton, Jr., "John Simpson Chisum, 1877–84," *New Mexico Historical Review* 31–32 (July 1956–January 1957).
Harwood P. Hinton

CHITA, TEXAS. Chita is on Farm Road 355 some nine miles southwest of Groveton in southwestern Trinity County. The area was first settled before the Civil War,[qv] but a community did not begin to develop there until the 1890s. A post office was established for the community in 1895, and a school was founded the next year. By 1914 Chita had a general store, a cotton gin and gristmill, a stone and sand company, and a reported population of sixty. Its post office closed in 1929, but in the mid-1930s Chita still had two businesses and a population of seventy-five. The community's population declined during the 1950s and 1960s but then began to grow because of the community's proximity to Lake Livingston. In 1990 Chita was a dispersed rural community with an estimated population of seventy-five.

BIBLIOGRAPHY: Patricia B. and Joseph W. Hensley, eds., *Trinity County Beginnings* (Groveton, Texas: Trinity County Book Committee, 1986).
Christopher Long

CHITTENDEN, WILLIAM LAWRENCE (1862–1934). William Lawrence (Larry) Chittenden, known as the poet-ranchman of Texas, son of Henry and Henrietta (Gano) Chittenden, was born on March 23, 1862, in Montclair, New Jersey, and educated in Montclair schools. As a young man he worked in his family's dry goods store and as a New York newspaper reporter. In 1883 Chittenden borrowed fifty dollars and made his way to Texas as a traveling dry goods salesman. To help pay his way he sent articles back to New York newspapers. In 1884 he visited Jones County to look over some land owned by his family and decided that ranching could be a profitable venture. Three years later he went into partnership with his uncle, former New York congressman Simeon B. Chittenden, and established a ranch at the foot of Skinout Mountain, seven miles northwest of Anson.

After his uncle's death in 1889, Chittenden bought the estate's ranch interest and further developed it. He began to write poetry and, according to legend, inspired by a comely San Angelo lass, wrote "The Odd Fellow's Ball" in 1885. His best-known poem, "The Cowboys' Christmas Ball," was first published in 1890 in the Anson *Texas Western*. It has been reprinted and anthologized many times since. Anson citizens staged a show called the Cowboys' Christmas Ball[qv] in 1934, and the poem has been reenacted annually since. G. P. Putnam's sons published a collection of Chittenden's Texas poems, *Ranch Verses*, in 1893. The book went through sixteen editions and earned the author the sobriquet "poet-ranchman." Chittenden moved from Texas to Bermuda in 1904 and, in 1909, Putnam's published *Bermuda Verses*. Some years later *Lafferty's Letters* was published. Chittenden's verse appeared in many periodicals throughout the country.

During his last years Chittenden had a home in Christmas Cove, Maine, where he began and served as sole financial supporter of a public library consisting of books autographed by their authors. He also founded the Children's League, a day nursery and fresh-air and convalescent home for underprivileged children. Chittenden never married. He died on September 24, 1934, in a New York hospital after undergoing surgery and was buried in Rosedale Cemetery, Montclair, New Jersey.

BIBLIOGRAPHY: Hybernia Grace, "Larry Chittenden and West Texas," West Texas Historical Association *Year Book* 13 (1937). *National Cyclopaedia of American Biography*, Vol. 16. *New York Times*, September 25, 1934. Jim Bob Tinsley, *He Was Singin' This Song* (Orlando: University Presses of Florida, 1981).
Shay Bennett

CHIZO INDIANS. The Chizo (Chiso) Indians were nomadic desert people who lived in the area now covered by northeastern Chihuahua, northwestern Coahuila, and the lower Big Bend region of Trans-Pecos Texas. They were also known under the alternate name of Taquitatome. The names of several Chisos bands are known: Chizo proper, Batayogligla, Chichitame, Guazapayogligla, Osatayogligla, Satapayogligla, and Sunigogligla. Some writers consider the Chizo as an eastern subdivision of the Concho Indians. The Chisos Mountains of the Big Bend National Park[qv] are believed to have been named for the Chizo Indians, whose range included the present park area.

BIBLIOGRAPHY: Jack D. Forbes, "Unknown Athapaskans: The Identification of the Jano, Jocome, Jumano, Manso, Suma, and Other Indian Tribes of the Southwest," *Ethnohistory* 6 (Spring 1959). Charles W. Hackett, ed., *Historical Documents Relating to New Mexico, Nueva Vizcaya, and Approaches Thereto, to 1773* (3 vols., Washington: Carnegie Institution, 1923–37). Carl Sauer, *The Distribution of Aboriginal Tribes and Languages in Northwestern Mexico* (Berkeley: University of California Press, 1934).
Thomas N. Campbell

CHOATE, TEXAS. Choate is seven miles southeast of Kenedy in southeastern Karnes County. It developed between Hondo and Cottonwood creeks on the road from Goliad to Kenedy and was named after James Monroe Choate, a prominent rancher of the area. Many of its settlers were from Oklahoma, and the area was known as the "Oklahoma" settlement. They were predominantly Baptists and Methodists. The post office of Choate was established in 1902 and was discontinued in 1909. A store, a school, a church, a blacksmith shop, and a cotton gin were built. The area's population was estimated at seventy-five from the 1930s until the 1950s, when a drought caused a decline. The school was closed in the 1960s; two churches and a cemetery still remained in the early 1980s. Choate was still listed as a community in 1990.

BIBLIOGRAPHY: Robert H. Thonhoff, History of Karnes County (M.A. thesis, Southwest Texas State College, 1963).
Robert H. Thonhoff

CHOATES, HARRY H. (1922–1951). Harry H. Choates, Cajun musician, was born in either Rayne or New Iberia, Louisiana, on December 26, 1922. He moved with his mother, Tave Manard, to Port Arthur, Texas, during the 1930s. Choates apparently received little formal education and spent much of his childhood in local bars, where he listened to jukebox music. By the time he reached the age of twelve he had learned to play a fiddle and performed for tips in Port Arthur barbershops. As early as 1940 he was playing in Cajun music bands for such entertainers as Leo Soileau and Leroy "Happy Fats" LeBlanc. Choates, who also played accordion, standard guitar, and steel guitar, preferred to play on borrowed instruments and may never have owned a musical instrument of his own.

Around 1946 he organized a band that he called the Melody Boys. Perhaps in honor of his daughter, Linda, he rewrote an old Cajun waltz, "Jolie Blone" (Pretty Blonde) and renamed it "Jole Blon." He recorded the song in 1946 for the Gold Star label, owned by Bill Quinn of Houston. "Jole Blon" became a favorite in the field of country and western music and a standard number in Texas and Louisiana clubs and dance halls. A year after Choates's recording, Aubrey "Moon" Mullican, a Texas-born singer and piano player, made an even bigger hit with the song. "Jole Blon," which Choates performed in the key of A instead of the traditional G, featured slurred fiddle notes and has been sung with both Cajun French and English romantic lyrics as well as nonsense lyrics with references to the "dirty rice" and "filé gumbo" of Cajun cuisine. Choates, who suffered from chronic alcoholism, sold "Jole Blon" for $100 and a bottle of whiskey.

He and his Melody Boys recorded over two dozen other songs for Gold Star in 1946 and 1947, including "Baisile Waltz," "Allans a Lafayette," "Lawtell Waltz," "Bayou Pon Pon," and "Poor Hobo," but none of those records earned Choates the success he achieved with "Jole Blon." He also recorded for the Mary, DeLuxe, D, O.T., Allied, Cajun Classics, and Humming Bird labels during his brief career. His recordings have been preserved on *Jole Blon*, an album by D Records of Houston that contains the Gold Star issues, and *The Fiddle King of Cajun Swing*, a compilation of Choates's works released by Arhoolie Records of El Cerrito, California, in 1982. Rufus Thibodeaux, a well-known Cajun fiddler, recorded an album entitled *A Tribute to Harry Choates* in the mid-1960s on the Tribute label. During the 1980s Cajun French radio stations in Jennings, Crowley, and Ville Platte, Louisiana, played Choates's music.

Choates, who could sing in French or English, became famous for his "Eh...ha, ha!" and "aaiee" vocal cries. A real crowd pleaser, he frequently played his amplified fiddle while dancing on the floor with his audience and stood on tiptoe while reaching for high notes. He merged traditional French Cajun music with the western swing music pioneered by such musicians as James Robert (Bob) Wills.[qv] He played jazz and blues as well as country music, including instrumental tunes like "Rubber Dolly," "Louisiana Boogie," "Draggin the Bow," and "Harry Choates Blues." As songwriter, instrumentalist, singer, and bandleader he raised Cajun music to national prominence.

Choates, whom one observer has characterized as "a Cajun Janis Joplin," also achieved a great deal of notoriety for his raucous lifestyle. Often performing while intoxicated and oblivious of his personal appearance, he wore a formerly white hat which, according to one of his band members, "looked like a hundred horses had stomped on it and then it had been stuck in a grease barrel." Choates was virtually illiterate and incurred the ire of musicians' union locals for ignoring contracts. Consequently, after the union in San Antonio blacklisted him and forced a cancellation of his bookings, his band broke up.

By 1951 Choates had moved to Austin, where he appeared with Jessie James and His Gang, a band at radio station KTBC. His estranged wife, Helen (Daenen), whom he had married in 1945, filed charges against Choates for failing to make support payments of twenty dollars a week for his son and daughter. Authorities in Austin jailed him pursuant to an order from a Jefferson County judge who found Choates in contempt of court. After three days in jail, Choates, unable to obtain liquor and completely delirious, beat his head against the cell bars, fell into a coma, and died, on July 17, 1951, at the age of twenty-eight. Although some of his fans believe his jailers may have killed him while attempting to calm him, Travis County health officer Dr. H. M. Williams determined that liver and kidney ailments caused his death. The James band played a benefit to raise money for Choates's casket, and Austin disk jockey Gordon Baxter secured funds to bury him in a Catholic cemetery in Port Arthur. Baxter and music historian Tim Knight of Groves raised money in 1979 and 1980 to purchase a granite grave marker with the inscription in Cajun French and English: "Parrain de la Musique Cajun"—"The Godfather of Cajun Music."

BIBLIOGRAPHY: John Broven, *South to Louisiana: The Music of the Cajun Bayous* (Gretna, Louisiana: Pelican, 1983). Houston *Chronicle*, July 23, 1989. Bill C. Malone and Judith McCulloh, eds., *Stars of Country Music* (Urbana: University of Illinois Press, 1975). John Morthland, *The Best of Country Music* (Garden City, New York: Doubleday, 1984). Irwin Stambler and Grelun Landon, *Encyclopedia of Folk, Country and Western Music* (New York: St. Martin's, 1969).

Paul M. Lucko

CHOCOLATE, TEXAS. Chocolate settlement was on Chocolate Bayou in northern Calhoun County. After Texas independence Sylvanus Hatch purchased a league of land near the stream, where he and his brother Joseph settled with their families in 1846. Hatch built a large home known as Agua Dulce near the bayou. Episcopalian services were held in the community, and Nelson E. Carrington served as a teacher. St. Paul's-on-the-Prairie Church was consecrated in 1870. The community school, which reported one teacher and thirty-one pupils in 1904, was consolidated with the Port Lavaca schools in 1918. The community subsequently declined, and by 1936 church services and school classes had ceased, and county highway maps no longer noted the townsite. Two tropical storms that struck in 1942 and 1945 virtually destroyed St. Paul's Church, erasing the last vestige of the community.

BIBLIOGRAPHY: Calhoun County Historical Commission, *Shifting Sands of Calhoun County, Texas* (Port Lavaca, Texas, ca. 1980).

Diana J. Kleiner

CHOCOLATE BAY. Chocolate Bay is at the mouth of Chocolate Bayou north of the west end of West Bay in Brazoria County (at 29°11′ N, 95°09′ W). It is crossed by the Gulf Intracoastal Waterway[qv] as it opens into West Bay. Francisco de Llanos and Gregorio de Salinas Varona[qqv] entered Chocolate Bay on November 4, 1690, and explored it by canoe, after searching for René Robert Cavelier, Sieur de La Salle's[qv] colony.

BIBLIOGRAPHY: A. C. Becker, Jr., "Chocolate Bay: Coastal Fishing as Sweet as Its Name," *Texas Fisherman*, April 1986. Herbert Eugene Bolton, "The Location of La Salle's Colony on the Gulf of Mexico," *Mississippi Valley Historical Review* 2 (September 1915); rpt., *Southwestern Historical Quarterly* 27 (January 1924).

CHOCOLATE BAYOU (Brazoria County). Chocolate Bayou rises a mile north of Manvel in northwest Brazoria County (at 30°00′ N, 95°23′ W) and runs southeast for thirty miles to its mouth on Chocolate Bay, thirteen miles west of Angleton (at 29°12′ N, 95°12′ W). Many members of the Old Three Hundred[qv] settled on Chocolate Bayou, and for a time the stream was considered the eastern boundary of Stephen F. Austin's[qv] first colony. The stream is intermittent in its upper reaches. It traverses flat terrain with local shallow depressions and rolling prairie, surfaced by clay and sandy loam and dark clays that support water-tolerant hardwoods, conifers, mesquite, grasses, cacti, and hardwoods mixed with pines.

———— (Victoria County). Chocolate Bayou rises a mile south of Guadalupe in south central Victoria County (at 28°44′ N, 96°56′ W) and runs southeast for twenty-five miles before emptying into Chocolate Bay, an inlet off Lavaca Bay, one mile south of Port Lavaca (at 28°35′ N, 96°39′ W). The creek crosses flat to rolling prairie surfaced by dark, commonly calcareous clay that supports mesquite, grasses, and cacti; through flat terrain surfaced by loam that supports water-tolerant hardwoods; and into brackish saltwater marsh surfaced by mud and sand in which grow rushes and grasses. Chocolate Bayou is intermittent in its upper and middle reaches.

CHOCOLATE BAYOU, TEXAS. Chocolate Bayou is on Farm Road 2917 between State Highway 35 and Farm Road 2403 in eastern Brazoria County. It is close to the bayou from which it takes its name on land originally in the Stephen F. Austin and James Franklin Perry qqv land grant. Emily Perry,qv who operated the Peach Point plantation qv on land near the site of present Chocolate Bayou, was Stephen F. Austin's sister. Although little remains of the ruins of the plantation, in its day it was a producer of cotton and sugar. In 1911 Chocolate Bayou received a post office. In 1914 it was on the St. Louis, Brownsville and Mexico Railway and had twenty-five residents, a general store, and two hay shippers. By 1925 Chocolate Bayou had a population of 150. Oil was discovered in 1946. In 1950 the population was fifty, and the post office had been discontinued. The community had lost its business by 1966, and in 1990 had sixty residents.

BIBLIOGRAPHY: Abner J. Strobel, *The Old Plantations and Their Owners of Brazoria County* (Houston, 1926; rev. ed., Houston: Bowman and Ross, 1930; rpt., Austin: Shelby, 1980).   *Chris Damon*

CHOCTAW, TEXAS. Choctaw was seven miles east of Sherman in eastern Grayson County. The first Anglo-Americans arrived in the area in the mid-1830s, led by Daniel Dugan. Initially the settlement that developed was called Dugan's Chapel. When the Texas and Pacific Railway built through the area, company officials apparently changed the name of the town to Choctaw. A post office operated for one year, 1874–75, then closed and reopened in 1884. In 1892 the town had a population of forty-two and three businesses. Choctaw served as a community center for area farmers. The post office closed again in 1918, and from 1918 to the 1930s the number of residents was estimated at twenty-five or below. Choctaw no longer appeared on county highway maps by the 1940s.   *David Minor*

CHOCTAW CREEK. Choctaw Crees rises 3½ miles southwest of Sherman in central Grayson County (at 33°37′ N, 96°42′ W) and runs northeast for thirty-eight miles to its mouth on the Red River, 2½ miles northwest of Anthony in western Fannin County (at 33°43′ N, 96°22′ W). It crosses into Cooke County just north of Ambrose. The surrounding flat terrain with local shallow depressions is surfaced by clay and sandy loams that support water-tolerant hardwoods, conifers, and grasses. Some tributaries to Choctaw Creek include South Branch, Cedar Creek, Mill Creek, and Cleveland Branch.

CHOCTAW INDIANS. The Choctaw Indians are the most numerous branch of the Muskogean language group, which also includes Chickasaw, Creek, Seminole, and Natchez. They are classed as one of the "Five Civilized Tribes." In historic times they inhabited the region of southeastern Mississippi and extreme southwestern Alabama, having migrated to that region from the west at an earlier, undetermined time. Choctaws are closely associated with the Chickasaws, and many of their early legends indicate that the two tribes descended from a common people. Apparently, after crossing the Mississippi, two brothers who had led the nation separated—the Chickasaws moving north and the Choctaws south.

The Choctaw tribe was divided into two moieties, which consisted of six to eight clans. Each clan was further divided into local groups that might consist of a group of towns or a single village, or, in rare occasions, a part of a village. These divisions dominated Choctaw social and ceremonial life. Marriage within a moiety was forbidden. Spouses were required to belong to opposite moieties, and children became members of their mother's group. Fathers had no authority over their children; rather, the children were watched over by their oldest maternal uncle. In addition to the moieties, the Choctaws were divided into three districts, each of which was led by a *mingo* or principal chief elected by the men of the district. Administrative ability, proven military status, and illustrious ancestors, were the three most prized qualities of a chief. The *mingo* was assisted by elected captains and subcaptains and was superior to the war chiefs. The three *mingos* would often convene at a national council meeting where issues of concern could be debated and discussed. Through this system, the Choctaws achieved an efficient and democratic political system.

Delivery of children was to be carried out by the mother with the least possible disruption to the family's lifestyle. Men played no role in the birthing process, and the mother received little assistance. When a child was born, a mare, a colt, a cow, a calf, a sow, and pigs were set aside for it with the provision that none of them could be sold or given away. In this way, when the child reached maturity and the stock formally became his, he had a good start in life. Adoption was common even among families with many children. The process was completed through the symbolic act of allowing the child to eat from the family bowl. At maturity, a Choctaw boy or girl had complete freedom to chose a mate, provided the spouse was from the other moiety. The young man would visit the family of his love and during the evening would toss small stones or sticks at the object of his affection. If the young woman was interested, she would play along; if not, she might leave the room in a rush. If accepted, the young man would leave and return a few days later with presents for his prospective in-laws. They would set a wedding date and prepare a feast and dance for the occasion. At the beginning of the party, the prospective bride and groom were led to separate cabins. The bride was then released to run toward a pole set up on a distant hill, and after she had been given a head start the groom was released to chase her. If he caught her, as he usually did unless the bride had for some reason changed her mind, the friends and family showered her with gifts and the marriage became official. Choctaw marriages lasted as long as both parties were satisfied. Separation or divorce was not disparaged, although all children were kept by the wife. Both monogamy and polygamy were accepted. In cases of polygamy, wives were usually sisters or at least close relatives. In rare cases where wives were unrelated, the husband was required to set up two or more residences.

Women generally performed the drudge work, laboring in the fields, making clothing, and preparing and storing food. Men were responsible for providing game, building houses, manufacturing tools, carrying out governmental duties, and protecting the tribe during wars. Apparently the Choctaws were less warlike than many of their neighbors but defended themselves bravely against any attacks. They rarely carried out offensive campaigns unless in retaliation for aggression against them. In such cases, the campaign was preceded by a war dance that might last eight days. Women sometimes accompanied the men to the battlefield to encourage them and supply them with arrows. Stealth and cunning were primary factors in Choctaw war making, like that of most other Indians. Aboriginal Choctaw homes were constructed of wooden posts, connected with lianas and covered with mud. The roofs were made from cypress or pine bark, and a hole was left in each gable end of the structure to allow smoke from the internal fire to escape. By the early nineteenth century, especially in Texas, these structures had been largely replaced by log cabins that were sparsely furnished. A cane bed, raised three or four feet off the floor and covered with deer or bear skins, served as table and chair as well. The Choctaws were primarily farmers. Corn was their most important crop, although they also raised beans, melons, pumpkins, peas, sunflowers, and tobacco. They cleared land by girdling trees and burning the undergrowth around their cabins and surrounding vicinity. Their agricultural proficiency often led to surpluses, which they sold or traded to neighboring tribes. Once cattle were introduced, they saved a portion of their surplus corn to feed their stock. Choctaws raised cattle with such success that they often sold excess to other Indians and white men living near by. Choctaw men and women in aboriginal times allowed their hair to grow long, and the men, like most other Indians, removed their scanty beards. They also customarily flattened the heads of infants with a piece of wood, which caused them at first to be known to white men as Flatheads. Their dress was similar to that of other southeastern Indians. Men wore deerskin breechclouts with a skin shirt and leggings in winter time. Women wore deerskin skirts and a shawl of skin, woven feathers, or the inner bark of a mulberry tree.

The first recorded European contact with the Choctaws was by members of Hernando De Soto's expedition in 1540. The Spaniards encountered Tuscaloosa, a *mingo,* from whom they demanded servants, canoes, and women. Tuscaloosa supplied carriers and rafts but delayed delivering women until De Soto and his army reached the town of Mabila. Upon reaching the town, Tuscaloosa, who had been a hostage, escaped and refused to grant any further concessions. A battle ensued in which Mabila was burned and hundreds or perhaps thousands of Choctaws and eighteen to twenty-two Spaniards were killed. The Spaniards, recovering from battle, remained in the area for another month and then moved on. Scattered incidental contacts with Europeans occurred in the following years, but not until 1700 did significant contact occur between Choctaws and Europeans.

American contact began in the late eighteenth century and became gradually more significant by the turn of the century. Between 1801 and 1830 the Choctaws signed a series of treaties with the United States, by which they ceded virtually all of their Mississippi lands in exchange for territory in Oklahoma. After the Treaty of Dancing Rabbit Creek (1830), the remaining Choctaw lands were ceded, and the Choctaws agreed to move to Oklahoma or apply for allotments under article 14 of the treaty. A census of the Choctaw population before removal indicated a total of 19,554. Approximately 12,500 migrated west, 2,500 died, and 5,000 to 6,000 remained east of the Mississippi. Of those migrating to Indian Territory, more than 700 split off to move to Texas, which was then part of Mexico. Apparently a few families had drifted into Texas earlier, for in 1830 ten to fifteen families lived on the Texas frontier.

Choctaws were participants in the Cherokee Treaty of February 23, 1836. Members of the tribe resided in Nacogdoches and Shelby counties in 1837 and were considered friendly. The Choctaws continually boasted that they had never made war on the white man and apparently remained at peace with the Texans during their residence in the republic. The Texas Senate refused to ratify the Cherokee Treaty, and further efforts to secure territory for the Cherokees and their allied tribes also failed. The Indians' situation deteriorated further when Mirabeau B. Lamar[qv] became president of the Republic of Texas.[qv] His aggressive policy toward the Indians resulted in a two-day battle at the headwaters of the Sabine with the Cherokees and their allies in July 1839. After their defeat, most of the Indians abandoned their homes and fled to Mexico or the United States. The Choctaws probably joined their kinsmen on their reservation in southeastern Oklahoma.

The United States census of 1910 showed 14,551 Choctaws in Oklahoma, 1,162 in Mississippi, 115 in Louisiana, 57 in Alabama, and 32 in other states, for a total of 15,911. The Department of Indian Affairs, however, showed more than 19,000 in Mississippi and more than 1,200 in Mississippi in 1916–19. The census count was apparently erroneous. In 1974 there were 3,779 Choctaws in Mississippi, and a 1975 census showed 9,018 in Oklahoma. Only 2,930 of these were half or more Choctaw.

BIBLIOGRAPHY: Jean Louis Berlandier, *Indians of Texas in 1830*, ed. John C. Ewers and trans. Patricia Reading Leclerq (Washington:: Smithsonian, 1969). Angie Debo, *The Rise and Fall of the Choctaw Republic* (Norman: University of Oklahoma Press, 1934; 2d ed., 1961). Arthur H. DeRosier, Jr., *The Removal of the Choctaw Indians* (Knoxville: University of Tennessee Press, 1970). Jesse O. McKee and Jon A. Schlenker, *The Choctaws: Cultural Evolution of a Native American Tribe* (Jackson: University Press of Mississippi, 1980). Carolyn Keller Reeves, ed., *The Choctaw before Removal* (Jackson: University Press of Mississippi, 1985). John R. Swanton, *The Indians of the Southeastern United States* (Washington: GPO, 1946). John R. Swanton, *Source Material for the Social and Ceremonial Life of the Choctaw Indians* (Washington: GPO, 1931). Dorman H. Winfrey and James M. Day, eds., *Texas Indian Papers* (4 vols., Austin: Texas State Library, 1959–61; rpt., 5 vols., Austin: Pemberton Press, 1966).

Jeffrey D. Carlisle

CHOCTAW, OKLAHOMA AND TEXAS RAILROAD. The Choctaw, Oklahoma and Texas Railroad Company was chartered on June 21, 1901, by the Choctaw, Oklahoma, and Gulf Railroad Company. The Choctaw ran from Memphis, Tennessee, through Oklahoma City to western Oklahoma. The CO&T was organized to extend the CO&G from the Oklahoma-Texas border near Texola to Amarillo. The capital was $1,680,000, and the business office was in Amarillo. Members of the first board of directors included J. W. McLoud of Little Rock, Arkansas, G. L. Blackford of Denison, Texas, Francis I. Gowan and Charles E. Ingersoll of Philadelphia, Pennsylvania, and Squire H. Madden,[qv] R. L. Stringfellow, and Wiley H. Fuqua,[qv] all from Amarillo. In 1902 the CO&T built ninety-eight miles to Yarnall, and, by utilizing trackage rights over other carriers, reached Amarillo. The CO&T completed its own line into Amarillo by late 1903. By this time the Choctaw and its Texas subsidiary had been acquired by the Chicago, Rock Island and Pacific Railway Company. The CO&T was merged into a Rock Island subsidiary, the Chicago, Rock Island and Gulf Railway Company, on December 1, 1903. The CRI&G completed an extension from Amarillo west to the Texas–New Mexico line at Glenrio in 1910. Another Rock Island line extended from Glenrio to Tucumcari, New Mexico, where a connection with what later became the Southern Pacific created a through route between Memphis and the Pacific Coast.

BIBLIOGRAPHY: William Edward Hayes, *Iron Road to Empire* (New York: Simmons-Boardman, 1953). Della Tyler Key, *In the Cattle Country: History of Potter County, 1887–1966* (Amarillo: Tyler-Berkley, 1961; 2d ed., Wichita Falls: Nortex, 1972). F. Stanley, *Story of the Texas Panhandle Railroads* (Borger, Texas: Hess, 1976).

H. Allen Anderson

CHOCTAW ROBINSON OAK. In the mid-1800s Hazel Dell was a tough settlement at a site on present Farm Road 1702 three miles north of its intersection with State Highway 36, midway between Comanche and Hamilton in Comanche County. A missionary Baptist preacher named William Robinson[qv] came to Central Texas in the late 1840s and was preaching in Erath County by 1855. In his later years he preached beneath an oak tree in Hazel Dell across the road from a store, post office, and saloon. He would lay his gun in the forks of the tree and preach sermons that sometimes lasted four hours. One group of Choctaws is said to have left during one of his sermons with the comment, "White man lie. Him talk too long." From this incident, Robinson acquired his nickname "Choctaw Bill," and the tree under which he preached became known as the "Choctaw Robinson Oak."

BIBLIOGRAPHY: Nancy V. Cooley, "Special Deputy to the Almighty," *Texas Parade,* November 1972. John A. Haislet, ed., *Famous Trees of Texas* (College Station: Texas Forest Service, 1970; 3d ed. 1984).

John A. Haislet

CHOICE, TEXAS. Choice is at the junction of Farm roads 417 and 2140, on the Atchison, Topeka and Santa Fe Railway seven miles

Louise (Mother Madeleine) Chollet. Courtesy Archives, Incarnate Word Generalate, San Antonio.

southeast of Center in southern Shelby County. It was founded about 1904 and given its name by the post office department. In 1914 Choice had a sawmill, two grocers, and a population estimated at 100. By 1925 the population had declined to an estimated twenty-five. The town grew again during the 1930s and by 1939 had an estimated population of 100. In 1946 Choice had a business, a cemetery, and numerous dwellings. In 1947 the population of the community was estimated as 150. It began to decline again in the 1960s and from 1972 through 1988 was reported as twenty. In 1990 Choice had a population of twenty-one.

Cecil Harper, Jr.

CHOKE CANYON STATE PARK. Choke Canyon State Park consists of two units beside the 26,000-acre Choke Canyon Reservoir. The 385-acre South Shore Unit is on State Highway 72 four miles west of Three Rivers in Live Oak County, and the 1,100-acre Callaghan Unit is on State Highway 72 eleven miles west of Three Rivers in McMullen County. The park was acquired in 1981 in a fifty-year cooperative agreement among the United States Bureau of Reclamation, the city of Corpus Christi, and the Nueces River Authority.[qv] Much of the area is former ranchland and is covered with the brushy scrub typical of South Texas. The abundant wildlife ranges from javelinas and white-tailed deer to Rio Grande turkeys and coyotes. Each unit provides picnic sites, restrooms, showers, a trailer dump station, campsites, a group shelter, a playground, and a boat ramp. The Callaghan Unit also has a swimming pool, boats to rent, a hiking trail, and a seasonal grocery store.

BIBLIOGRAPHY: Ray Miller, *Texas Parks* (Houston: Cordovan, 1984).

Christopher Long

CHOLLET, LOUISE (1846–1906). Louise (Mother Madeleine) Chollet, pioneer in health care, cofoundress and first superior general of the Sisters of Charity of the Incarnate Word[qv] of San Antonio, was born in Roanne, France, on February 7, 1846. She grew up in a devoted family and entered the Monastery of the Incarnate Word and Blessed Sacrament in Lyons, France, in 1867. She received the habit and with it was given the name of Sister Marie St. Madeleine of Jesus.

In December of the same year she arrived in Galveston; she made her profession of vows on May 31, 1868, in the Galveston Incarnate Word community. In March 1869, accompanied by two companions, she arrived in San Antonio at the request of Bishop Claude Dubuis,[qv] who appointed her superioress of the Sisters of Charity of the Incarnate Word of San Antonio, a position she held until 1872. She began a life dedicated to the sick, the orphans, and the poor when San Antonio was a mere frontier village. There were few doctors, and city and county hospitals were inadequately staffed and funded. The polluted riverwater and mud-soaked streets bred disease. In December 1869 Mother Madeleine opened the first private hospital in San Antonio. This hospital, which was probably also the first in San Antonio with a professional nursing staff, is known today as Santa Rosa Medical Center. In 1990 it was the largest Catholic hospital in the United States (*see* CATHOLIC HEALTH CARE).

Again serving as superioress from 1894 until 1906, Mother Madeleine oversaw the expansion of Santa Rosa, the founding of a number of schools in West Texas, the building of a permanent convent in 1899 on property purchased from George Washington Brackenridge,[qv] and the opening of Incarnate Word Academy, today known as Incarnate Word College. She died in San Antonio on July 20, 1906, after a long illness. Before her death the congregation had grown from three to 452 members and had established more than fifty religious institutions in five states, including thirty-four academies and schools, twelve hospitals, two orphanages, and two homes for the aged.

BIBLIOGRAPHY: Catholic Archives of Texas, Files, Austin. Sister Mary Helena Finck, C.C.V.I., *The Congregation of the Sisters of Charity of the Incarnate Word of San Antonio, Texas* (Washington: Catholic University of America, 1925). Incarnate Word Generalate Archives, San Antonio. Marilyn M. Sibley, *George W. Brackenridge* (Austin: University of Texas Press, 1973).

Sister Josephine Kennelly, C.C.V.I.

CHOME INDIANS. In the late seventeenth and early eighteenth centuries the Chome, apparently Coahuiltecans, ranged from northeastern Coahuila northward across the Rio Grande into the adjoining part of Texas south of the Edwards Plateau. The Chomes are not to be confused with the Alachome; both names appear in the same document.

BIBLIOGRAPHY: Mattie Alice Hatcher, trans., *The Expedition of Don Domingo Terán de los Ríos into Texas,* ed. Paul J. Foik (Preliminary Studies of the Texas Catholic Historical Society 2.1 [1932]). Frederick Webb Hodge, ed., *Handbook of American Indians North of Mexico* (2 vols., Washington: GPO, 1907, 1910; rpt., New York: Pageant, 1959).

Thomas N. Campbell

CHORRUCO INDIANS. The Chorruco (Charruco) Indians were an otherwise unidentified group, possibly Karankawan, that lived on the mainland of Matagorda Bay and kept Álvar Núñez Cabeza de Vaca[qv] with them for about six years. He stated that they took their name from the woods in which they lived.

BIBLIOGRAPHY: Frederick Webb Hodge, ed., *Handbook of American Indians North of Mexico* (2 vols., Washington: GPO, 1907, 1910; rpt., New York: Pageant, 1959).
Margery H. Krieger

CHRIESMAN, HORATIO (1797–1878). Horatio Chriesman, one of the Old Three Hundred,^{qv} colonial statesman, and military officer, was born in Virginia on August 13, 1797. He moved to Kentucky and then on to Missouri, where he worked as a surveyor and married Mary Kincheloe in 1818. In 1821 he chartered the schooner *Only Son* and prepared to move with William Kincheloe's^{qv} family to Texas. His wife died at New Madrid before the expedition started. Chriesman and other members of the party reached the Colorado River in Texas on June 19, 1822. He was surveyor of Stephen F. Austin's^{qv} colony from 1823 to 1836. As a captain of the colonial militia in 1824, he participated in several Indian fights and also fought the Fredonians (*see* FREDONIAN REBELLION). On July 8, 1824, he received title to one league and two labores of land in the area that became Fort Bend and Austin counties. In 1825 he married Augusta Hope. He was elected alcalde^{qv} at San Felipe in 1832 and signed the official call for the Convention of 1832.^{qv} He petitioned for the organization of Washington Municipality in 1835 and was defeated that year in the race for the office of regidor.^{qv} After attending the Convention of 1836,^{qv} Chriesman started east to move his family and others beyond the Trinity River; they had reached Jefferson County when they learned of the battle of San Jacinto.^{qv} In October 1837 Chriesman was one of a commission of five chosen to select a site for the capital of the republic. His offer of 700 acres near Washington-on-the-Brazos for the seat of government was rejected. He was still living in Washington County in 1842, when he was administrator of Thomas Gay's estate. Chriesman had eleven children. He later moved to Burleson County, where he died on November 1, 1878. The town of Chriesman in northern Burleson County, originally known as Yellow Prairie, was named for him.

BIBLIOGRAPHY: Eugene C. Barker, ed., *The Austin Papers* (3 vols., Washington: GPO, 1924–28). E. L. Blair, *Early History of Grimes County* (Austin, 1930). Lester G. Bugbee, "The Old Three Hundred: A List of Settlers in Austin's First Colony," *Quarterly of the Texas State Historical Association* 1 (October 1897). Louis Wiltz Kemp, *The Signers of the Texas Declaration of Independence* (Salado, Texas: Anson Jones, 1944; rpt. 1959). J. H. Kuykendall, "Captain Horatio Chriesman," in *One League to Each Wind: Accounts of Early Surveying in Texas,* ed. Sue Watkins (Austin: Von Boeckmann–Jones, 1964?). Andrew Jackson Sowell, *History of Fort Bend County* (Houston: Coyle, 1904; rpt. Richmond, Texas: Fort Bend County Historical Museum, 1974). Clarence Wharton, *Wharton's History of Fort Bend County* (San Antonio: Naylor, 1939).

CHRIESMAN, TEXAS. Chriesman is on the Atchison, Topeka and Santa Fe Railway just west of Farm Road 36 seven miles northwest of Caldwell in northwestern Burleson County. In the 1830s Alexander Thomson, Jr.,^{qv} brought a group of colonists to the site. They named the settlement Yellow Prairie for the high yellow grass that covered the surrounding prairie. The community became a station on the Gulf, Colorado and Santa Fe when it built through the area in 1880. Yellow Prairie had a post office from 1880 to 1884. In 1885 the post office and community were renamed Chriesman for Horatio Chriesman,^{qv} an pioneer in the region who spent the last years of his life in the area. The railroad station in the community continued to be known as Yellow Prairie through the early decades of the twentieth century. In 1890 Chriesman had an estimated population of 100, a school, a steam gristmill and cotton gin, and Methodist and Presbyterian churches. In 1904 a cucumber salting station was established in the community by the Price-Booker Manufacturing Company of San Antonio. In 1914 Chriesman had an estimated 175 inhabitants, telephone service, a bank, four general stores, and a cotton gin. The community's population declined from 200 in 1925 to 100 in 1930 and to fifty in 1950. The cucumber plant closed by 1930, when the community had eight businesses. The population was estimated at thirty inhabitants from 1972 to 1993. In 1988 the community had two churches, a number of scattered dwellings, and the Chriesman cemetery on a hill to the east of town.

BIBLIOGRAPHY: Burleson County Historical Society, *Astride the Old San Antonio Road: A History of Burleson County, Texas* (Dallas: Taylor, 1980).
Mark Odintz

CHRISMAN, JOHN H. (1821–1922). John H. Chrisman, pioneer settler in Coryell County, was born in Charleston, Indiana, on May 25, 1821. He married Samantha Minnis in Illinois and moved by 1846 to Arkansas, where his wife died. Leaving his two children temporarily, he returned to Illinois and married Sarah Mitchell. The couple reclaimed his children in Arkansas and moved to Texas, where they arrived at Fort Gates on April 4, 1854. With his second wife Chrisman had nine more children. He surveyed the original townsite of Gatesville in 1854 and made a plat map of Coryell County. He built the first Coryell County Jail in 1855 and served as justice of the peace from 1855 to 1861. At the same time, he sold dry goods and groceries for a period of three years, buying goods in Houston and hauling them to Gatesville in ox wagons. He carried mail between Gatesville and Comanche beginning in 1858. In 1859 Chrisman drove a herd of cattle to Shreveport, Louisiana. During the Civil War^{qv} he served with the Frontier Regiment^{qv} under James M. Norris and J. E. McCord.^{qqv} He was admitted to the bar on March 29, 1866, and practiced law in Gatesville, where he died at the age of 100 in February 1922.

BIBLIOGRAPHY: Clyde and Mabel Bailey, *Vignettes of Coryell County* (Gatesville, Texas: Gatesville Printing, 1976). H. L. Bentley and Thomas Pilgrim, *Texas Legal Directory for 1876–77* (Austin: Democratic Statesman Office, 1877). Coryell County Genealogical Society, *Coryell County, Texas, Families, 1854–1985* (Dallas: Taylor, 1986). Zelma Scott, *History of Coryell County* (Austin: Texas State Historical Association, 1965). Vertical Files, Barker Texas History Center, University of Texas at Austin.
Sylvia Edwards

CHRISTEN, TEXAS. Christen was at a site just north of what is now Laredo off Interstate Highway 35 in south central Webb County. The settlement was named for Joseph Christen, who patented land in the area in 1840. The area was gradually absorbed by Laredo, and in 1990 only the Christen Junior High School and a few older homes marked the site of the former settlement.
Christopher Long

CHRISTIAN, CHARLES (1919–1942). Charles (Charlie) Christian, musician, was born in Dallas, Texas, in 1919. He spent much of his youth in Oklahoma City, where he lived with his father and played bass and guitar in various small groups. He made his first experiments with an amplified guitar in 1937. When music critic John Hammond heard him in 1939, he persuaded Benny Goodman to employ Christian. Although barely twenty years old, Christian immediately became known among professional jazzmen for his new sounds and new ideas. Only one other electric guitar had been recorded on jazz records when the first Christian-Goodman records were issued. After that, his large creative contribution to modern jazz was widely recognized. Christian featured a down-stroke technique almost exclusively. His single-string solos, with altered chords, new melodic lines, rows of even beats, and contrasting dramatic aspects became the base from which musicians constructed an entirely new approach to jazz. Christian won Down Beat polls from 1939 through 1941 and in the Encyclopedia Year Book poll of 1956 was chosen "Greatest Ever." Always in delicate health, he died of tuberculosis in a Staten Island sanitarium on March 2, 1942, leaving behind a contribution that belies the brevity of his career.

BIBLIOGRAPHY: Arrigo Polillo, "Charlie Christian," in *I Grande del Jazz*, Vol. 48 (Milan: Fabbri, 1982; Audio Archives, Barker Texas History Center, University of Texas at Austin).

Joe B. Frantz

CHRISTIAN, EDWARD (1833–1888). Edward Christian, soldier and businessman, son of Samuel Patteson and Nancy (Patteson) Christian, was born in Buckingham County, Virginia, on January 10, 1833. When he was quite young the family moved to Marengo County, Alabama, where both his parents died around 1840. Christian may have been raised by his older brothers until, at about the age of twelve, he became a carpenter's apprentice. In 1851 he and another young carpenter, Simon Loomis, moved from Alabama to Texas, first to Bastrop and then to Austin, where they worked together as builders and lumber dealers. After the outbreak of the Civil War[qv] the partnership was dissolved, and Christian enlisted in the Confederate Army as a private in Company G, Sixteenth Texas Infantry. He served for the rest of the war and fought in the battles of Mansfield and Pleasant Hill (*see* RED RIVER CAMPAIGN). After the war he returned to Austin and again went into business with Loomis; in 1867 they established a planing mill and extensive lumberyards. Their firm, Loomis and Christian, prospered and became one of the largest lumber dealers in Texas. Christian also served as a vice president of City National Bank of Austin and on the board of trustees of the Deaf and Dumb Institute (later the Texas School for the Deaf[qv]). He was a member of the Independent Order of Odd Fellows and a Presbyterian. Christian married Matilda Horst on April 7, 1873; they had three children. He died in Austin on April 14, 1888, and was buried at Oakwood Cemetery.

BIBLIOGRAPHY: Frank Brown, Annals of Travis County and the City of Austin (MS, Frank Brown Papers, Barker Texas History Center, University of Texas at Austin). John Henry Brown, *Indian Wars and Pioneers of Texas* (Austin: Daniell, 1880; reprod., Easley, South Carolina: Southern Historical Press, 1978). Lewis E. Daniell, *Types of Successful Men in Texas* (Austin: Von Boeckmann, 1890).

Robert Christian

CHRISTIAN, JAMES TERRILL (1868–1950). James Terrill Christian, rancher, the second of the ten children of George Richard and Louisa (Terrill) Christian, was born near Moberly, Missouri, in 1868. In 1881 the family moved to a homestead on Lynn Creek, near Antelope, Jack County, Texas, where they engaged in ranching and the children received much of their elementary education. In 1889 Jim Christian and his older brother Paul rode west to the Panhandle[qv] and were employed as cowhands on the JA Ranch.[qv] Although Paul returned to the Jack County homestead after a year, Jim stayed on and was later joined by four younger brothers, Will, Ben, Robert, and Ernest. Robert and another cowhand were killed by lightning during a roundup in 1895.

During his fifteen years as a JA employee, Christian gradually worked his way up from horse wrangler to wagon boss. In 1900 he was made manager of the JA's Mulberry Creek Division, near Claude. On April 5 of that year he married Georgia Jones, whom he had known from his youth; the couple had four children. In 1902 Christian began homesteading two sections of choice land near the rim of Palo Duro Canyon in western Armstrong County and next to the tracts filed on by his brothers Ben and Ernest. He remained with the JA for another year and then began building up his own herd of cattle, which he branded with a Figure 3, similar to that of R. O. Watkins in Kaufman County. After their first two-room house burned in March 1904, the Christians were forced to build again. They also donated a plot of land for a schoolhouse.

Jim and Georgia Christian were both active in community affairs in Claude. He served for years on the school board, while she helped form Armstrong County's first Union Sunday school. They were members of the Disciples of Christ and charter members of the Panhandle-Plains Historical Society,[qv] which they helped to organize. Christian was a longtime Mason and Shriner and was active in the Texas and Southwestern Cattle Raisers Association.[qv] The Christians turned their ranching operations over to their sons in August 1929 and spent their retirement years in Claude. Christian died on March 28, 1950, from the effects of a stroke he had suffered in 1945; he was buried in Claude. Since the breakup and reduction of the JA properties, the Figure 3 remains one of the few ranch homesteads still owned by the family of the original founder. It is noted for its registered purebred Herefords and famous Cowboy Breakfasts held on the north rim of Palo Duro Canyon for tour groups and visiting notables.

BIBLIOGRAPHY: Armstrong County Historical Association, *A Collection of Memories: A History of Armstrong County, 1876–1965* (Hereford, Texas: Pioneer, 1965). Gus L. Ford, ed., *Texas Cattle Brands* (Dallas: Cockrell, 1936).

H. Allen Anderson

CHRISTIAN CHURCH (DISCIPLES OF CHRIST). The Disciples of Christ in Texas are a part of a movement started by Barton W. Stone in Kentucky in 1804, and by Thomas and Alexander Campbell and Walter Scott in Virginia, Pennsylvania, and Ohio between 1809 and 1823. The two groups united in 1832, and the church moved westward with the tide of migration. The earliest Disciples who came to Texas were led by Collin McKinney.[qv] They stopped on the border of Texas just east of Texarkana in 1824 and in 1831 moved on to the Hickman's Prairie and McKinney's Landing areas on the Red River in what is now Bowie County. A church was organized in 1841 with G. Gates as minister and Collin McKinney as elder. The families of the group gradually moved westward until they were all living in Collin and Grayson counties, where, in 1846, they organized Old Liberty or Mantua Church, which became the First Christian Church of Van Alstyne. From this early church sprang most of the Christian churches in North Texas. Their ministers included William McKinney, Collin M. Wilmeth,[qv] A. Cartright, J. H. O. Polly, R. C. Horn, and B. F. Hall. Education was provided by the Muse Academy, operated by J. C. Muse. In January 1836 an entire congregation of the Disciples moved by way of Texarkana into Texas under the leadership of Lynn D'Spain and Mansell W. Matthews[qv] and settled at Clarksville in Red River County. About 1841 Matthews moved to Rockwall and began preaching generally through North Texas. In 1836 the D'Spain family moved to Nacogdoches, where they established a church and where Hettie D'Spain married Joseph Addison Clark[qv] and became the mother of Addison and Randolph Clark,[qqv] founders of Add-Ran College (now Texas Christian University). In 1833 Dr. William Defee began preaching in Sabine, San Augustine, and Shelby counties. Antioch Church, four miles from San Augustine, was organized in the home of Rhoddy Anthony in 1836 and became the oldest continuous congregation in the area. A church at Rio Navidad had eight members in 1841 and heard a report of four other congregations of Disciples near by. In 1842 a church of 100 members was reported at San Patricio. In 1845 churches were reported at Live Oak Well in Fayette County with David B. Stout as minister, at Clear Creek with J. W. Cox as minister, in Washington County, and in Lamar County.

A fear of ecclesiastic control and a tendency toward biblical literalism and frontier individualism made these early Disciples wary of organization; nevertheless, a "co-operative" sprang up near Palestine as early as 1852 under the leadership of Carroll Kendrick, Samuel Henderson, and John B. Tyler. A statewide meeting of ministers was held at Thorp Spring as early as 1879 and was followed by annual meetings at Waxahachie, Bonham, Ennis, Bryan, Sherman, and Austin. At Austin in 1886 the Texas Christian Missionary Society was organized. This establishment of a society for home-mission work and a controversy over the use of instrumental music in worship services caused disagreement between conservative and liberal elements in the communion. The *Firm Foundation* at Austin became the journal for the conservatives; the *Christian Courier*qv spoke for the progressives after 1888. By 1906 the conservative elements broke off into the Church of Christ.qv

Executives of the Texas Christian Missionary Society from 1886 to 1959 were A. J. Bush, J. W. Holsapple, B. B. Sanders, J. C. Mason, A. B. Rogers, J. B. Holmes, Patrick Henry, Sr., and Chester Crow. In 1963 the name of the Texas Christian Missionary Society was changed to the Texas Association of Christian Churches. T. T. Swearingen was the executive until 1969. The Disciples of Christ (Christian Church) resolved at their annual assembly in 1956 to change their official name to Christian Church (Disciples of Christ). When the Christian Church (Disciples of Christ) in the United States and Canada made significant structural changes in the late 1960s, the Texas branch was designated one of thirty-six regions and named Christian Church (Disciples of Christ) in Texas. In 1975 the region was enlarged to include New Mexico, the panhandle of Oklahoma, and Liberal, Kansas, and the regional name was changed to Christian Church (Disciples of Christ) in the Southwest. The executive officer is called "regional minister." Serving in that position since 1969 have been Kenneth L. Teegarden, Harrell A. Rea, James C. Suggs, and M. Margaret Harrison. The purposes of the Disciples' Southwest Region are to engage in mission, witness and service among the people and social structures of the region, and to establish and nurture congregations, provide help, counsel and pastoral care to members, ministers and congregations, and relate them to the worldwide mission and witness of the whole church. In addition to their denominational work, Texas Disciples engage in ecumenical enterprises and belong to the Texas Conference of Churches.qv

In 1860 the Disciples of Christ had 2,500 members in Texas. In 1994 there were 103,130 members in 445 congregations. The denomination has had under its auspices, directly or indirectly, a number of Texas colleges: Carlton College, Carr-Burdette, Randolph College at Lancaster, Hereford College, Midland Christian College, Randolph College at Cisco, Bay View College, Patroon College, Mount Enterprise Male and Female College, Burnetta College, Add-Ran Jarvis College, Add-Ran College, Add-Ran Christian University, Jarvis Christian College, and Texas Christian University.qqv By 1949 all of the schools had been closed or absorbed into other institutions except Jarvis Christian College and Texas Christian University. The Disciples also operate the Juliette Fowler Homes,qv a benevolent institution in Dallas.

BIBLIOGRAPHY: Randolph Clark, *Reminiscences* (Wichita Falls: Lee Clark, 1919; rpt., Fort Worth: Texas Christian University Press, 1979). Winfred Ernest Garrison and Alfred T. De Groot, *The Disciples of Christ: A History* (St. Louis: Bethany, 1948; rev. ed. 1958). Colby D. Hall, *History of Texas Christian University* (Fort Worth: Texas Christian University Press, 1947). Chalmers McPherson, *Disciples of Christ in Texas* (Cincinnati: Standard, 1920).

Colby D. Hall and Kenneth L. Teegarden

CHRISTIAN CHURCH EDUCATION. During the first half of the twentieth century, the Christian Church (Disciples of Christ)qv had several schools directly or indirectly operating under its influence. They included Carlton College, Carr-Burdette College, Randolph College at Lancaster, Bay View College, Patroon College at Cisco, Mount Enterprise Male and Female College,qqv Add-Ran Jarvis College, Add-Ran College, Add-Ran Christian University, and Jarvis Christian College for Negroes. By 1949 most of these colleges had been closed or consolidated. There were four educational institutions affiliated with the Christian Church in 1967. They were Texas Christian University, Jarvis Christian College,qqv the Texas Bible Chair, and the Inman Christian Center.

The Texas Bible Chair, adjacent to the campus of the University of Texas at Austin, was founded to give students at the university the opportunity to study the Judeo-Christian tradition and the theology of the Disciples of Christ. The institution, founded in 1905 through the efforts of the Christian Women's Board of Missionaries and Mrs. M. M. Blanks of Lockhart, who contributed $30,000 to the building fund, offered students religion classes and Christian fellowship. The Christian Women's Board of Missionaries, renamed the United Christian Missionary Society, continued to sponsor the school except for a brief interruption during the Great Depression.qv The Christian Churches in Texas also offered support. The first director of the Bible Chair, Frank Jewett, oversaw the school until his retirement in 1946, when Paul Wassenich took over as director. In honor of Jewett's service to the school, the current library bears his name. In 1946 the Texas Bible Chair began its current close relationship with the University Christian Church. In response to several requests, Wassenich began to hold weekly church services in the TBC chapel. Eventually, the congregation outgrew the small chapel, and church members negotiated with the missionary society to expand the facilities. The society granted the church a ninety-nine-year lease in 1949 to build a new sanctuary next to the Bible Chair building. The growth of the church quickly outpaced the demands of the TBC, and in the early 1950s the missionary society transferred control of the TBC and its assets to the Texas Association of Christian Churches. In exchange for the land, the University Christian Church promised to contribute $25,000 to a permanent trust for the continued support of the Texas Bible Chair. Other financial support comes from the Texas Association of Christian Churches, Austin area churches, and individual donations. In the 1950s the original building of the TBC was demolished to make room for University Christian Church facilities. Housed in the church, the Texas Bible Chair continues to offer religious instruction to university students.

The Inman Christian Center, formerly the Mexican Christian Institute, was originally a settlement house founded in 1913 for Mexican Americansqv in the San Antonio area (*see* SETTLEMENT HOUSES). The founders were on the Christian Women's Board of Missions. Within the settlement house, Samuel G. Inman,qv director of Mexican missionary work for the Disciples of Christ, and Hugh McLellan, minister at Central Christian Church in San Antonio, established a school for the children of the neighborhood. In 1961 the institute changed its name to Inman Christian Center. Throughout the 1960s and 1970s the center offered kindergarten classes, health clinics, a library, boys' and girls' clubs, naturalization instruction, parents' forums, and cultural events to the mainly Hispanic community. In 1994 the center served low-income families, the elderly, and children through ministries of education, health, substance-abuse prevention and treatment, social services, and housing.

In 1994 the Christian Church continued to sponsor Texas Christian University in Fort Worth and Jarvis Christian College in Hawkins. Brite Divinity School,qv the theological seminary at TCU, prepares persons for Christian ministry. Although related and supported by the Christian Church, Brite maintains an ecumenical spirit as reflected in the denominational diversity of its student body and faculty. *See also* THORP SPRING CHRISTIAN COLLEGE.

Noel L. Keith and Kenneth L. Teegarden

CHRISTIAN COLLEGE OF THE SOUTHWEST. Christian College of the Southwest (formerly called Garland Christian College) was at the intersection of U.S. Highway 67 and Barnes Bridge Road, two miles north of downtown Mesquite in eastern Dallas County. The school was chartered in 1962 as Garland Christian College, a two-year liberal arts school, with plans to develop into a four-year institution. The college was affiliated with the Church of Christqv and was established to provide "a quality education in a Christian atmosphere under leadership of a Christian faculty." The institution opened in a temporary location on North Shiloh Road in Garland with an enrollment of 115 students.

In 1963, in order to illustrate the college's mission, the name was changed to Christian College of the Southwest. One year later, enrollment had increased to 160 students, and the college had acquired its new site, the location of a pioneer schoolhouse built by David Oates, an early Dallas County physician. In 1965 construction on the first building began at the new Mesquite site, and student enrollment at the temporary site in Garland had increased to 180. The board of trustees, headed by G. C. Whitefield, selected Willis E. Kirk as the college's first president. Later that year college officials announced a development program that included a fund-raising drive appealing to Dallas businesses and numerous Church of Christ congregations. In September 1966 the first permanent building was opened on the new 117-acre campus. By 1968 the Christian College of the Southwest had moved to its Mesquite campus and had an enrollment of 365. In March of that year the college established a Community Resources Program that brought numerous civic, industrial, and business leaders to the Mesquite campus as part of a lecture program. The college also initiated a program to give the institution senior status by 1970 with the addition of a third year of instruction in 1969 and a fourth year in 1970. As part of this program Christian College of the Southwest would also begin cooperative development with Abilene Christian College, Fort Worth Christian College, Lubbock Christian College, and Southwestern Christian College at Terrell. The student enrollment was 410. The school's academic divisions included languages and literature, social sciences, business administration, science and mathematics, education, Bible studies, and fine arts.

One year later the academic-administrative building, the gym, and the physical plant were completed. The college's basketball team, the Trojans, was ranked ninth in the nation, and the student body numbered over 400. The college was affiliated with the Texas Association of Colleges and Universities, the American Association of Higher Education, the American College Public Relations Association, Texas Junior College Association, and the Texas and American associations of Collegiate Registrars and Admissions Officers and was approved by the United States Department of Health, Education, and Welfare.

In 1971 financial problems forced Christian College of the Southwest to close. Later that year the college's campus was acquired by Abilene Christian College (now Abilene Christian University) as part of its ACC Metrocenter branch. The Mesquite campus was eventually closed when the branch became Abilene Christian University at Dallas and moved to a new campus in Dallas (*see* AMBER UNIVERSITY).

BIBLIOGRAPHY: Dallas *Morning News*, November 27, 1968, April 13, 1969. Vertical Files, Barker Texas History Center, University of Texas at Austin. Donald W. Whisenhunt, *The Encyclopedia of Texas Colleges and Universities* (Austin: Eakin, 1986). *Matthew Hayes Nall*

CHRISTIAN COURIER. The *Christian Courier*, the oldest regional newspaper of the Christian Church,qv was a continuation of the *Texas Courier*, published from 1878 to 1888 by Joseph Addison Clarkqv at Thorp Spring. The *Texas Christian* merged with the *Christian Courier* in 1888 and was published as a weekly in Dallas by William Kercheval Homan.qv It carried sermons, inspirational poems, and articles, as well as news from small towns, Indian Territory, and other states. Advertisements promoted such religious items as baptismal gowns and nonreligious items such as patent medicines. The newspaper continued as a weekly until the 1930s, when it was published monthly by a panel of three editors. By 1949 it was published in Fort Worth. In 1964, when it was published by the Texas Association of Christian Churches, a plan was implemented to publish different editions for each of five regions. In 1966 the *Courier*'s distribution to 32,000 families made it the most widely delivered Christian Church newspaper in the United States and Canada. Eventually nine area editions were published, but by the 1980s they were merged into a single newspaper. The Texas Association of Christian Churches was succeeded as publisher by the Christian Church (Disciples of Christ) in Texas. In 1972 that group merged with its counterpart in New Mexico to form the Christian Church (Disciples of Christ) in the Southwest. With offices in Fort Worth, that organization was still publishing the paper in 1993. At that time Carole Coffey was the editor and M. Margaret Harrison the executive editor. The paper had a distribution of 31,000 and was distributed primarily in Texas and New Mexico.

BIBLIOGRAPHY: Carter E. Boren, *Religion on the Texas Frontier* (San Antonio: Naylor, 1968). *Christian Courier*, April 1988. Chalmers McPherson, *Disciples of Christ in Texas* (Cincinnati: Standard, 1920).
Lisa C. Maxwell

CHRISTIAN MESSENGER. The *Christian Messenger*, a religious journal of the Disciples of Christ, was edited in the 1880s by Thomas R. Burnettqv at Bonham and later at Dallas. The May 16, 1894, issue announced that the *Christian Messenger* was being consolidated with the *Gospel Advocate*. Burnett became the editor for that paper.
Colby D. Hall

CHRISTIAN METHODIST EPISCOPAL CHURCH. In 1954 the General Conference of the Colored Methodist Episcopal Church met in Memphis and adopted a resolution changing the name of the church to the Christian Methodist Episcopal Church. The first Protestant church in Texas was a Methodist church established by William Stevensonqv from Arkansas in Pecan Point in 1815. Some African Americansqv belonged to this church. By 1837 several Methodist churches had a combined membership of thirty-six black and forty-five white members. African-American preachers were encouraged to hold services for other blacks, and their churches spread over Texas. In some areas blacks and whites held services together; in other areas white preachers held separate services for the two races. After 1844–45 when disagreement over slaveryqv caused the Methodists of the South to separate from those of the North, many slaves continued to worship with their masters, even after emancipation. Many former slaves later became members of the Colored Methodist Episcopal Church.

During the Civil War,qv Methodist Episcopal preachers followed the Union Army to the South and persuaded some black Methodists to join the Methodist Episcopal Church. A Texas District was established in 1865. The Methodist Episcopal Church, South, in its General Conference at New Orleans in 1866 declared that if black members so desired, the bishops were empowered to organize them into separate congregations, organize district and annual conferences, obtain suitable preachers, and appoint presiding elders to direct their affairs. By 1870, when the General Conference met in Memphis, Tennessee, African Americans, who had organized five annual conferences, asked for a separate organization. The General Conference agreed to ordain the men the new conference selected as bishops. In December 1870 the new Colored Methodist Episcopal Church was organized at Jackson, Tennessee.

The first CME church in Texas was established at Marshall in Harrison County. The East Texas Conference was one of the original conferences recognized at the Jackson organizational meeting. A West Texas Conference was organized in 1871. The first East Texas Annual Conference was held at Marshall on November 6, 1872. Later a Northwest Conference was organized, and in 1894 the Colored Methodist Episcopal Church established Texas College in Tyler, the center of the Colored Methodist Episcopal population in East Texas. Bishop M. F. Jamisonqv is given much of the credit for the establishment and success of the Colored Methodist Episcopal Church in Texas.

By the 1990s, the CME Church was divided into five Conferences and associated districts. These were the Northwest Texas Conference, the Dallas–Fort Worth Conference, the Central Texas Conference, the East Texas Conference, and the Southeast Texas Conference. A senior bishop presides over Texas. There were some 45,000 communicants in some 500 churches with 375 pastors in Texas as of 1990. That year the largest congregation was Cedar Crest Church in Dallas, with 1,500 members; the second-largest was BeBee Tabernacle–Coleman Cathedral in Houston, with 1,300 members.

BIBLIOGRAPHY: Cullen T. Carter, *History of the Tennessee Conference and a Brief Summary of the General Conferences of the Methodist Church* (Nashville: Parthenon Press, 1948). Hightower T. Kealing, *History of African Methodism in Texas* (Waco, 1885). Othal Hawthorne Lakey, *The History of the CME Church* (Memphis: CME Publishing House, 1985). Charles Henry Phillips, *The History of the Colored Methodist Episcopal Church in America* (Jackson, Tennessee: Publishing House of the CME Church, 1898). Walter N. Vernon et al., *The Methodist Excitement in Texas* (Dallas: Texas United Methodist Historical Society, 1984). Carter G. Woodson, *The History of the Negro Church* (Washington: Associated Publishers, 1921; 2d ed. 1945).

Charles E. Tatum

CHRISTIAN PREACHER. The *Christian Preacher*, the voice of the conservative wing of the Disciples of Christ in North Texas, was first published in 1875 under the name *Texas Christian Monthly* at McKinney, by Collin M. Wilmeth^qv and his brother James. Their father, Joseph Bryce Wilmeth, was one of the first settlers and public officials of Collin County and a cofounder of the first Christian Church^qv in the county. Following the Civil War^qv the Disciples of Christ established a society for home mission work, and a number of churches introduced the use of instrumental music in services. These actions produced a schism within the denomination and became a matter of public debate until the conservative elements separated in 1906 to form the Church of Christ. C. M. Wilmeth, assisted by his brother, entered the public debate with the publication of *Texas Christian Monthly*, originally produced at McKinney in 1875. Wilmeth moved the journal in 1877 to Dallas, where he established a publishing house in connection with the paper and renamed it the *Christian Preacher*. Although Wilmeth published church news and a calendar of coming events, most of the *Christian Preacher* was devoted to commentaries that attacked the "progressive" tenets of the other faction of the church. The editorials, demonstrative and flamboyant, often were a response to remarks published in the *Christian Messenger*,^qv a rival religious paper edited by Thomas R. Burnett.^qv These two publications acted as a public forum for members of the Disciples of Christ. The *Christian Preacher* ceased publication probably before the turn of the century.

BIBLIOGRAPHY: Colby D. Hall, *Texas Disciples* (Fort Worth: Texas Christian University Press, 1953). Chalmers McPherson, *Disciples of Christ in Texas* (Cincinnati: Standard, 1920). J. Lee and Lillian J. Stambaugh, *A History of Collin County* (Austin: Texas State Historical Association, 1958).

David Minor

CHRISTIAN SCIENCE. The earliest evidence of the appearance of Christian Science in Texas came in the 1889–90 *Christian Science Journal*, which, although it listed no churches in Texas, did mention two cities where Christian Science services were held, Austin and Galveston. The Texas Christian Science Institute in Galveston, managed by Ladd M. Waters, advertised for students that year. By 1899 there were ten Christian Science churches in Texas, including two each in Dallas and Houston. Christian Scientists in El Paso were holding regular Sunday services but were not incorporated as a church. There were also fifty-two practitioners (authorized healers) and three teachers in Texas. The Galveston school no longer existed, but Austin supported the Southern Christian Science Institute. Like its predecessor, this institute taught Christian Science, treated patients "both present and absent," and sold periodicals.

In 1908 seventeen different Texas cities, mostly east of what is now Interstate Highway 35, were the sites of Christian Science churches. Fifty-eight practitioners and eight teachers, the majority of whom were concentrated in the large cities, operated in the state. By 1955 there were sixty-five churches and thirty-eight societies in Texas. Since services were segregated in the 1950s, two "colored" societies, located in Dallas and Houston, existed to serve the religious needs of black Christian Scientists. A total of 228 practitioners, including four blacks, and seven teachers resided in Texas. In 1983 a total of sixty-six churches and thirty-two societies existed in eighty Texas cities and towns, Dallas and Houston having the greatest numbers. Christian Science college organizations held meetings on fourteen campuses including both public and private institutions. The Leaves, a Christian Science sanatorium in Richardson, provided practical but nonmedical health care for Christian Science patients. Christian Scientists were permitted to reside at the Leaves temporarily for the purpose of religious study. Although there was no official Texas committee on publication, Peter Vanderhof monitored the media and the legislature with regard to the interests of Christian Scientists and wrote *The Legal Rights of Christian Scientists in Texas* (1983).

BIBLIOGRAPHY: *Christian Science Journal* 7, 17, 26, 73, 101.

Mary Anne Norman

CHRISTINE, TEXAS. Christine is on Farm Road 140 ten miles south of Jourdanton in south central Atascosa County. It was founded in October 1909 as one of two towns promoted by developer C. F. Simmons and named after his daughters, Christine and Imogene. The community of Imogene never went beyond the planning stages, but by 1910 Christine had a post office, two hotels, a cafe, and a department store. Simmons also built the Artesian Belt Railroad to Christine from McDonna. A three-teacher school and Methodist and Baptist churches were added in 1911. By 1913 the school had 141 students.

Water problems plagued the town, but in 1916 a reservoir and water tower temporarily solved the problem. Lettuce, honey, and cattle became the main cash crops. Three cattle breeders and retail outlets for feed, lumber, and groceries served an estimated population of 600 in 1914. Christine became a stock-shipping point. The population of the town declined to 259 by 1925, however. In 1931 the number of residents had increased to 524, where it remained for a decade; during this time the number of recorded business varied from nine to fifteen. In 1936 the Christine school had seven teachers and 175 students.

Christine's population declined to slightly less than 300 during the 1940s and remained under 300 until 1982. The town had nine businesses in 1945 but only two in the late 1960s. The high school closed in 1948, and the school district was officially annexed to Jourdanton in 1954. During the 1950s a new water well was dug in Christine. In the early 1980s the Atascosa Mining Company and the San Miguel Power Plant were located there. In 1988 the population was 381, and one retail business was listed.

BIBLIOGRAPHY: *Atascosa County Centennial, 1856–1956* (Jourdanton, Texas: Atascosa County Centennial Association, n.d). *Atascosa County History* (Pleasanton, Texas: Atascosa History Committee, 1984). Margaret G. Clover, The Place Names of Atascosa County (M.A. thesis, University of Texas, 1952). C. L. Patterson, *Atascosa County* (Pleasanton, Texas: Pleasanton *Express*, 1938).

Linda Peterson

CHRISTMAS BAY. Christmas Bay is a protected bay on the coast of the Brazoria National Wildlife Refuge^qv west of Follets Island and south of Mud Island in Brazoria County (at 29°03′ N, 95°11′ W). It joins Bastrop Bay on the north. Access to the bay is through Cold Pass, south of Mud Island or through the Mud Cut which connects it to West Bay.

CHRISTMAS CREEK. Christmas Creek rises seven miles east of Axtell in northeastern Limestone County (at 31°41′ N, 96°52′ W) and runs southeast and then north for twenty-four miles to its mouth on the Navasota River, near Lake Mexia (at 31°39′ N, 96°37′ W). The surrounding flat to rolling prairie is surfaced by clay that supports mesquite, grasses, hardwood forest, and scrub brush. The stream was named by a group of surveyors who camped there on Christmas Day of 1855.

Ellen Maschino

CHRISTMAS MOUNTAINS. The Christmas Mountains are twelve miles northeast of Terlingua in southern Brewster County (at 29°26′ N, 103°27′ W). With an elevation of 5,728 feet above sea level, the highest peak in the mountains rises 2,050 feet above the Terlingua Ranch Lodge, a mile northeast. The area's shallow, stony soils support oak, juniper, mesquite, chaparral, cacti, scrub brush, and grasses.

CHRISTOPHER COLLEGE OF CORPUS CHRISTI. Christopher College of Corpus Christi was first organized in 1957 as Mary Immaculate Teacher Training Institute, an affiliate of the Catholic University of America. Christopher College was governed by the Sisters of the Incarnate Word and Blessed Sacrament,qv and its primary purpose was to furnish education for aspirants to the order. In January 1958 the institute was chartered by the state of Texas; classes began at Incarnate Word Academy. Shortly afterwards the institute began admitting nonmembers of the order to its classes, and in 1961 its name was shortened to Mary Immaculate College. A growing, more heterogeneous student body and a shortage of space led to a complete reassessment of the college in 1964. The following year the institution was reorganized as a junior college and in August 1965 was renamed Christopher College of Corpus Christi. In 1967 the coeducational college offered an associate of arts degree and was a member of the Southern Association of Junior Colleges, the American Association of Junior Colleges, and the Association of Texas Colleges and Universities.qv Because of inadequate financial support the college was closed on August 31, 1968.

BIBLIOGRAPHY: Donald W. Whisenhunt, *The Encyclopedia of Texas Colleges and Universities* (Austin: Eakin, 1986).

CHRISTOVAL, TEXAS. Christoval, also known as Delong and South Concho, is on Loop 110, U.S. Highway 277, Farm Road 2084, and the South Concho River, twenty miles south of San Angelo in southern Tom Green County. It is supposedly named, in Spanish, for Christopher Columbus Doty,qv an early settler. A Christoval post office was established in 1889, and by 1901 the local school had forty-six pupils and one teacher. In 1914 Christoval had a population of 200, two general stores, and a newspaper, the Christoval *Observer*. The Panhandle and Santa Fe Railway ran through town. From that decade through the 1930s 10,000 persons attended the Baptist encampment on the South Concho annually, and mineral waters in Christoval attracted visitors and settlers. In the 1930s the community had a population high of 544 and twenty businesses. State highway maps in 1936 showed two churches, multiple businesses, and scattered dwellings at the townsite. The population dropped to 400 by 1953 and to 216 by 1973. Businesses decreased from eighteen to four, despite the development of the local mohair industry. The population remained at 216 from 1973 to 1990, when the community had three churches, a school, and three business establishments; residents expected further decline resulting from a 1987 rerouting of U.S. Highway 277 to bypass the town. The forests of the town's Pugh Park, in which Mount Susan is located, reflect the original features of the area.

BIBLIOGRAPHY: Dallas *Morning News*, June 16, 1990.

Diana J. Kleiner

CHRISTY, WILLIAM H. (1791–1865) William H. Christy, soldier, lawyer, merchant, and friend of the Texas Revolution,qv was born on December 6, 1791, in Georgetown, Kentucky, the son of George and Mary (Cave) Christy. At the age of fourteen his parents died, leaving him in possession of a large estate. Christy was studying law at the time of the outbreak of the War of 1812. He left his books and joined the staff of Gen. William Henry Harrison and was later assigned as quartermaster and storekeeper at Fort Meigs, at the falls of the Maumee River in Ohio. On May 5, 1813, he distinguished himself in a fight with Tecumseh's Indians. Although twice wounded in an ambush, Christy escaped the melee to return with reinforcements and save the lives of many of his companions. Thereafter he was known as "the hero of Fort Meigs" and on March 9, 1814, was commissioned a second lieutenant in the First United States Infantry. He served under Andrew Jackson at the battle of New Orleans, and at the end of the war he resigned from the army, on October 1, 1816, to settle in Louisiana. He became a successful tobacco merchant in New Orleans but lost his savings to a dishonest partner in 1818 and once again took up the study of the law. On June 10 of that year he married Katherine P. Cenas of Philadelphia; the couple had two sons and a daughter.

Christy was most likely the "Colonel Christy of New Orleans" who became involved in the Long expeditionqv sometime in late 1819 or 1820. Together with John Austin and Benjamin Rush Milam,qqv he was helping José Félix Trespalaciosqv equip an expedition to assist the Mexican independence movement when these four men decided to join forces with James Long.qv The five sailed together with a group of men to Bolivar Point, near Galveston. Christy, Milam, and Trespalacios were then to sail on to Mexico, land somewhere near Tampico, and raise an army that would march north, while Long marched south from La Bahía.qv The history of Christy's group after their landing in Mexico is uncertain, but they were in Mexico City in October 1821 when Long and Austin arrived. After Long was killed there by a Mexican guard several months later, Christy, Milam, and Austin planned retaliation against Trespalacios, whom they held responsible for Long's death. Their plan was discovered, however, and they were imprisoned in Mexico City until about November 1821. Their release was obtained by Joel R. Poinsett,qv newly appointed United States envoy to Chile, who was passing through Mexico City. Christy, Milam, and Austin then sailed for the United States; they landed in Norfolk, Virginia, in December 1822.

Christy was admitted to the bar and from 1823 until 1833 served as a member of the New Orleans board of aldermen. In 1826 he completed a digest of the decisions of the Louisiana Supreme Court. By September 1835 he was chairman and treasurer of a New Orleans committee to aid Texas. He was reportedly sought out by numerous individuals interested in going there, many of whom he helped equip. On October 13, 1835, he chaired a meeting that raised money for the Texas cause. Adolphus Sterneqv made a plea at this meeting for volunteers, and the men who responded were organized as the New Orleans Greys.qv In January 1836 Christy was instrumental in helping Stephen F. Austin, Branch T. Archer, and William H. Wharton,qqv commissioners from Texas, to secure two loans totaling $250,000. Early in 1836 the United States government charged Christy with violating the neutrality law, alleging that he had aided José Antonio Mexía'sqv Tampico expeditionqv in November 1835. He was acquitted by the presiding judge.

Christy claimed to have pledged a great part of his personal fortune to the cause of Texas independence. After the battle of San Jacintoqv his friend Sam Houstonqv sent to Christy the saddle and bridle of Mexican general Martín Perfecto de Cosqv in appreciation of Christy's assistance to the revolution. Houston wrote that Christy's name would "never be uttered by the people of Texas unaccompanied by a prayer for his happiness and prosperity." Christy's continued interest in Texas was evidenced by his reported subscription in the mid-1830s to the Texas Railroad, Navigation, and Banking Company.qv

Christy was a staunch Whig who supported the presidential candidacy of his old commander William Henry Harrison. In 1850 he was appointed surveyor of customs at New Orleans, a position he held until 1854. He is remembered in New Orleans as one of the founders of the city's first home for orphans. He died on November 7, 1865.

BIBLIOGRAPHY: John Henry Brown, *History of Texas from 1685 to 1892* (2 vols., St. Louis: Daniell, 1893). Charles Adams Gulick, Jr., Harriet Smither, et al., eds., *The Papers of Mirabeau Buonaparte Lamar* (6 vols., Austin: Texas State Library, 1920–27; rpt., Austin: Pemberton Press, 1968). Francis B. Heitman, *Historical Register and Dictionary of the United States Army* (2 vols., Washington: GPO, 1903; rpt., Urbana: University of Illinois Press, 1965). John H. Jenkins, ed., *The Papers of the Texas Revolution, 1835–1836* (10 vols., Austin: Presidial Press, 1973). *National Cyclopaedia of American Biography*, Vol. 11. *Proceedings in the Case of the United States Versus William Christy* (New Orleans: Levy, 1836). *Telegraph and Texas Register*, October 31, November 14, 1835, February 28, 1837. Amelia W. Williams and Eugene C. Barker, eds., *The Writings of Sam Houston, 1813–1863* (8 vols., Austin: University of Texas Press, 1938–43; rpt., Austin and New York: Pemberton Press, 1970). James E. Winston, "New Orleans and the Texas Revolution," *Louisiana Historical Quarterly* 10 (July 1927). Dudley Goodall Wooten, ed., *A Comprehensive History of Texas* (2 vols., Dallas: Scarff, 1898; rpt., Austin: Texas State Historical Association, 1986).

Thomas W. Cutrer

CHROMČIK, JOSEF (1845–1910). Reverend Joseph Chromčik, Czech Catholic priest and missionary to Texas, was born in Řepčíne, near Olomouc, Moravia, to Martin and Marianna Pitschová Chromčik. After attending seminary school in Olomouc and graduating in 1866, he was ordained on July 5, 1869, and made assistant pastor at Lichnov, Moravia, on August 15, 1869. In 1872 he was administrator of a parish in Zenklebeu Stramberka, near Noveho Jičína. Answering a plea of Bishop Claude Dubuis,qv bishop of Galveston, Father Chromčik was assigned to America, using a prepaid ticket that was sent by the people of Fayetteville. He sailed to Cuba and New Orleans, and arrived in early December 1872 at Galveston, where no one greeted him. He made his way to Ellinger, where the townspeople took him in and, not knowing immediately who he was, gave him food, clothing, a feather bed, and a pillow. On December 25, 1872, he arrived at Fayetteville and celebrated his first Mass on that Christmas Day. He reestablished St. John's Parish and built the Chromčik School in 1875, after receiving a certificate to teach. He taught for fifteen years.

Father Chromčik was a linguist, and his knowledge of several languages enabled him to represent many nationalities as a community spokesman. Because of the difficulty many Czechs had in obtaining life insurance from eastern companies, Chromčik suggested establishing an insurance and fraternal group to serve Czech Catholics. On March 24 and 25, 1889, the Katolická Jednota Texaská (Czech Catholic Union of Texas) was established. Chromčik was chaplain of the group from 1890 to 1894, 1896 to 1898, and 1901 to 1910; he was also made director and counselor for life. In 1994 local Catholic lodges still carried his name. Father Chromčik was a an ecclesiastical judge (for the clergy in ecclesiastical cases). His mission trips by buggy or horseback to surrounding communities, including Ellinger, Bluff, Round Top, Granger, Dubina, and Warrenton, occasionally in treacherous weather, led him to request that passable roads and bridges between communities be built.

Letters to his homeland encouraged countrymen to come to the new land, which he described as a new free world. He sponsored many families in their journey to Texas, and on July 1878 he became a American citizen. In 1894 he returned to his homeland to celebrate the twenty-fifth anniversary of his ordination. A celebration was held with many young children carrying flowers honoring him. He returned with priests for new parishes. In 1894 he recorded 218 family names in the area surrounding Fayetteville. In 1994 a large number of those surnames still appeared.

On July 14, 1909, Chromčik celebrated forty years of priesthood. Father Peter Houst came to assist him. Chromčik died on April 7, 1910, and was buried in the Catholic Cemetery in Fayetteville. On October 19, 1932, a bronze statue of Father Chromčik was erected; it was moved southwest of St. John's Parish in 1969, where it stood in 1994. Children referred to him as their "Tatíček," meaning "dear loving father." A Texas historical marker was planned to be dedicated in September 1995, and plans were in progress for a reenactment of his arrival at the church in December 1997.

BIBLIOGRAPHY: *The Czech Texans* (San Antonio: University of Texas Institute of Texan Cultures, 1972). Estelle Hudson and Henry R. Maresh, *Czech Pioneers of the Southwest* (Dallas: South-West, 1934). Frank Lotto, *Fayette County: Her History and Her People* (Schulenburg, Texas: Sticker Steam Press, 1902; rpt., Austin: University of Texas Press, 1981). Marker Files, Texas Historical Commission, Austin. Leonie Rummel Weyand and Houston Wade, *An Early History of Fayette County* (La Grange, Texas: La Grange *Journal*, 1936).

Carol Jurajda Kitchen

CHRONICLE OF THE TIMES. The *Chronicle of the Times* was a weekly newspaper produced from 1855 to at least 1858 by Dugald MacFarlaneqv and his son-in-law Joseph Theall in Matagorda, which was at that time the Matagorda county seat. Its masthead included a star and snake.

BIBLIOGRAPHY: Marilyn M. Sibley, *Lone Stars and State Gazettes: Texas Newspapers before the Civil War* (College Station: Texas A&M University Press, 1983).

Rachel Jenkins

CHRONISTER, TEXAS. Chronister was a lumber community just north of Wildhurst in southern Cherokee County. It was named for C. J. Chronister, owner of the C. J. Chronister Lumber Companies, which built a large sawmill at the site in the late 1890s. In addition to the mill the company also erected managers' and workers' houses and later added a planing mill and a commissary. Just after 1900 the operation was bought by Joe Lipshitz (Lipshure), whose family continued to operate the mill until World War II.qv After 1900, however, Chronister lost its separate identity and by 1910 had been completely absorbed by Wildhurst. Both were gone by the early 1990s, when the surrounding area was covered with dense forests.

BIBLIOGRAPHY: *Cherokee County History* (Jacksonville, Texas: Cherokee County Historical Commission, 1986).

Christopher Long

CHUAPA INDIANS. It is not certain that Chuapa is an actual Indian group name. H. E. Boltonqv indicated that he had seen the name Chuapa in the registers of San Antonio de Valero of San Antonio Mission, but no one else has been able to find it in these registers. As Bolton did not cite a register entry number or a date, it is not possible to determine if he may have misread a personal or an ethnic name. No recognizable variant of the name Chuapa has been found in Spanish documents of the seventeenth and eighteenth centuries. J. R. Swanton listed Bolton's Chuapa among the Indian groups he thought might have spoken the Coahuilteco language, but this cannot be given serious consideration until the name Chuapa has been verified. F. H. Ruecking, Jr., mistakenly equated Chuapa with the name Chinipa, which refers to an Opata Indian village on the Río Sonora of northwestern Mexico, some 750 miles west of San Antonio.

BIBLIOGRAPHY: Frederick Webb Hodge, ed., *Handbook of American Indians North of Mexico* (2 vols., Washington: GPO, 1907, 1910; rpt., New York: Pageant, 1959). F. H. Ruecking, Jr., The Coahuiltecan Indians of Southern Texas and Northeastern Mexico (M.A. thesis, University of Texas, 1955). J. R. Swanton, *Linguistic Material from the Tribes of Southern Texas and Northeastern Mexico* (Washington: Smithsonian Institution, 1940).

Thomas N. Campbell

CHUBB, THOMAS B. (1811–1886). Thomas B. Chubb, Galveston shipmaster, the son of Thomas Chubb, was born in Charlestown, Massachusetts, on June 17, 1811. He left home in 1818 at the age of six or seven to serve on a United States frigate and was employed by the navy until 1823. After that he worked as a stevedore on the Boston docks, where he unloaded goods with horse and pulley, an innovation that almost precipitated a general strike on the waterfront. He engaged in the cod-fishing business and became involved in the coffee trade between South America and New York. After observing the use of slaves in the West Indies, he made a trip to the Congo and returned with 400 blacks to dispose of there. According to some sources, Chubb also acquired free blacks as crew members in the north and sold them into slavery[qv] in the south. He engaged in business in Boston, managed a circus, and built the Federal Street Theater. In 1827, in the United States Navy, he was a coxswain on the U.S.S. *Java*.

As conflict in the Southwest grew, Chubb sailed with a shipment of arms to Texas, where he offered his services, became friendly with Sam Houston,[qv] and in 1836 arrived in Galveston to accept an appointment as admiral of the Texas Navy.[qv] On January 24, 1857, he was accused in *State of Texas v. Thomas B. Chubb* of stealing slaves. He remained in Galveston until 1861, when he became commander of the steamer *Royal Yacht*, a Confederate Navy vessel. During the war he was a member of a militia group that watched for enemy vessels from a tower on the Galveston Strand. Chubb was captured at Galveston harbor, imprisoned at Fort Lafayette in the North, and condemned to death for engaging in the slave trade; he was exchanged when President Jefferson Davis[qv] threatened to avenge his death by executing ten men.

Chubb married Phoebe Briggs in 1828, and they had eight children. After her death in 1867, he married Mrs. Martha A. Sturgis the same year and sold his two-story "flat roof" house, which was built in 1859 and still stood in Galveston in the 1980s. Chubb served as harbormaster in Galveston from 1882 until his death at his summer home in Post Mills Village, Vermont, on August 26, 1886. He was buried in Galveston.

BIBLIOGRAPHY: Virginia Eisenhour, *Galveston, a Different Place* (Galveston, 1983). Earl Wesley Fornell, *The Galveston Era: The Texas Crescent on the Eve of Secession* (Austin: University of Texas Press, 1961). Arthur James Lyon Fremantle, *Three Months in the Southern States* (Edinburgh and London: Blackwood, 1863). Galveston *News*, August 28, 1890. Charles Waldo Hayes, *Galveston: History of the Island and the City* (2 vols., Austin: Jenkins Garrett, 1974). Marker Files, Texas Historical Commission, Austin.

Diana J. Kleiner

CHUCARETO CREEK. Chucareto Creek rises a mile northwest of Encinal in southwestern La Salle County (at 28°03′ N, 99°23′ W) and runs northeast fourteen miles to its mouth on Caiman Creek, twelve miles northeast of Encinal (at 28°09′ N, 99°10′ W). The surrounding low rolling terrain is surfaced by clay and sandy loam that supports grass, mesquite, and chaparral.

CHUMLEY, TEXAS. Chumley is on a country road off of Farm Road 353 three miles east of San Augustine in northeastern San Augustine County. In 1904 it had a school serving eighteen pupils and one teacher. In 1940 it had a cemetery and a number of dwellings. By the 1980s Chumley had a number of dwellings, a cemetery, and a church.

Mark Odintz

CHUPADERAS CREEK. Chupaderas Creek rises just east of Martinez in eastern Bexar County (at 29°25′ N, 98°20′ W). It formerly ran southeast for ten miles to its mouth on Calaveras Creek, three miles northeast of Elmendorf. After Calaveras Lake Dam was completed in 1969, the creek was inundated in its lower reaches, and it now enters the lake one mile west of Parita (at 29°20′ N, 98°17′ W). It traverses rolling terrain surfaced by clay loam that supports mesquite and grasses.

CHURCH OF THE ANNUNCIATION, HOUSTON. Annunciation Church, the oldest extant Catholic Church in Houston, is situated between U.S. Highway 59 on the east and the World Trade Center on the west. In 1866 the bishop of Galveston, Claude M. Dubuis,[qv] and Father Joseph Querat realized that a church larger than St. Vincent's, the first Catholic church in Houston, was needed for the increasing number of Catholics. For the new church the bishop purchased from Peter W. Gray[qv] the half block at Texas and Crawford streets for $2,000; the brick to be used in the construction was purchased from the old courthouse. Nicholas J. Clayton[qv] designed the structure, using the Gothic forms of European cathedrals suggested by Father Querat. In March 1869 Querat presented the plans to the parishioners, who chose the name Church of the Annunciation. The cornerstone was laid the following month, and two years later, on September 10, 1871, the church was dedicated. In 1878 St. Vincent's Church closed.

After the building of the new church, Father Querat purchased the other half of the block for a school, on January 3, 1873. At first only boys attended Annunciation School, but by September 1914 the school was coeducational. The school was closed in 1983, since most of its students came by that time from outside the parish.

The church was enhanced with a bell tower in 1871, and smaller twin towers were added in 1884. After the exterior of the church was refinished in 1916, other additions followed: a Pilcer pipe organ in 1924, air-conditioning in 1937, a marble shrine to Our Lady, Help of Christians, in 1945, and guards for stained-glass windows and a public address system in the 1950s. Five parishes were formed from Annunciation: St. Joseph (1879), St. Patrick (1880), St. Nicholas (1887), Sacred Heart (1897), and Blessed Sacrament (1910).

When the Galveston hurricane of 1900[qv] destroyed St. Joseph's Church, among the ruins of the belfry was found the original bell of old St. Vincent's Church. This bell was transported to Annunciation and later burnished for the diamond jubilee of the parish; it was put on display in the vestibule of the church. In 1953 the church provided the setting for the induction ceremonies of thirty-seven lay men and women into the Order of the Holy Sepulcher of Jerusalem, with James Cardinal McIntyre of Los Angeles as celebrant. Blanche Foley, a major donor to the church, was one of those honored. Among the pastors who have served Annunciation parish were George T. Walsh, Houston's first monsignor, and Anton J. Frank, the first native Houstonian ordained for the Diocese of Galveston; Frank was ordained in Annunciation Church and served his entire priestly ministry there. A state historical marker was placed at Annunciation in 1969, the centennial year of the parish. Annunciation Church is listed in the National Register of Historic Places.

BIBLIOGRAPHY: Houston *Press*, September 2, 1945, December 2, 1953. Mary Brendan O'Donnell, Annunciation Church—Catholic Mother Church of Houston (M.A. thesis, University of Houston, 1965).

Sister Mary Brendan O'Donnell

CHURCH ARCHITECTURE. In transplanting their native religions, immigrants brought to Texas particular requirements for houses of worship, as well as building traditions. Whether on a large or small scale, their chapels and churches were designed functionally to accommodate their practices in worship and aesthetically to satisfy certain values, within the economic means of the builders.

Spanish colonists erected chapels for their missions, presidios, and secular parishes. Regardless of size or location, a chapel invariably had a central hall either oblong or cruciform in shape, with a focus upon the altar. The naves were often flanked by sacristies or other rooms serving religious uses. The first chapels for the missions and presidial establishments were temporary palisaded shelters. However, at the missions that prospered, these were replaced by durable and handsome edifices reflecting the stylistic traditions of Spain and Mexico. While none of the ephemeral palisaded works remains, several durably built structures survive, including the chapel at San José y San Miguel de Aguayo Mission,[qv] a work in Churrigueresque style erected in 1768–82, and San Antonio de Valero Mission[qv] (the Alamo), a work in Baroque (Salamonica) style begun in 1744, both in San Antonio. The presidial chapels, mandated by official regulations, ordinarily were prominently located within a complex of shelters or an enclosure and were commonly of temporary wood or adobe construction. Some, however, were more permanent; Nuestra Señora de Loreto Presidio^{qv} near Goliad is a durable masonry work that has been restored. Secular parish churches were erected in San Antonio (Nuestra Señora de la Candelaria y Guadalupe Church) and Laredo (San Agustín Church) in 1728–49 and 1761–67, respectively. The former has been restored and is somewhat plain in appearance, but the latter is gone. (The present San Agustín Church was begun in 1871.)

Though the chapels surviving from Spanish Texas^{qv} served the needs of residents of Mexican Texas,^{qv} Anglo-American colonists brought Protestant religion—predominantly Baptist, Methodist, and Presbyterian—to Texas, along with customs for the construction of houses of worship. After meeting under trees, on porches, or in homes, they erected churches to serve basic needs. A church was often a simple box of logs, frame, or stone, with three or four openings per side and a gabled roof, above which rose a simple cross or belfry that identified the function of the building. Interiors were plain, often with only pews, benches, or chairs, a stove, a small piano or organ, and a pulpit. In time and with prosperity, numerous congregations and parishes began constructing churches with stylistic distinction. In imitation of early nineteenth-century fashions in the East, many edifices were in Greek Revival style. Although still on a simple rectangular plan similar to their predecessors, they were embellished with simple classical entablatures and porticoes. Among such churches built in antebellum Texas^{qv} is the First Methodist Episcopal Church, South, in Marshall (1860–61), a brick-walled building that has been much remodeled over the years. The Gothic Revival style, characterized by pointed arches, projection buttresses, and steeply pitched roofs, also appeared in many churches both before and after the Civil War.^{qv} Included among these were a number of Carpenter Gothic works, with board-and-batten walls, many of which are now gone; these were often built from plan prototypes developed in the eastern United States. However, numerous masonry-walled churches were also built, including St. Mary's Cathedral (1847–48) and Trinity Episcopal Church^{qqv} (1855–57), both in Galveston.

After the Civil War, African Americans,^{qv} who previously had worshipped in makeshift shelters, also erected buildings serving their religious needs. Located in segregated neighborhoods and central to their societies, numerous churches were, at first, executed in plain box-like forms with frame constructions. Baptist and Methodist churches were common, although Cumberland Presbyterian congregations also constructed buildings, sometimes with assistance from the national church. Eventually, numerous black houses of worship were built with substantial masonry walls, but designs remained staightforward, with simple stylistic details.

During the prosperous years of the late nineteenth century, large new Victorian Gothic churches, often designed by prominent architects, appeared, although small buildings continued to be constructed by small or rural congregations and parishes. Ornate buildings with polychromatic stone or brick walls, high towers, stained glass windows, and large naves or auditoriums were common. Catholic churches generally had traditional long, narrow naves; so did Lutheran and Episcopalian churches, though other Protestant churches commonly had wide auditoriums designed for good acoustics and sight lines. Christ Episcopal Church, Houston (1893), is a fine example of the traditional plan with beautiful interior woodwork, and the First Baptist Church of Dallas^{qv} (1890) is a noteworthy example of the new Protestant form. During the nineteenth and early twentieth centuries various ethnic groups also introduced their customs into church building. Particularly noteworthy are the edifices with painted interiors. Walls finished with wood were painted with patterns and forms representing architectural ornamentation and religious symbols meaningful to worshipers. Among the churches with painted interiors is the Praha Catholic Church (1891) in rural Fayette County.

Around 1900 the Richardsonian Romanesque style characterized many churches, particularly those of the Baptist, Methodist, and Presbyterian communions. Round-arched openings, polychromatic stonework, and lofty towers were typical features. Among the fine examples is the First Baptist Church, Beaumont (ca. 1900), now the home of the Tyrrell Historical Library. During the early decades of the twentieth century, although Gothic and Romanesque churches continued to appear, numerous Classical edifices were erected. Conforming to national trends in design, buildings were commonly crowned with domes and usually were entered through monumental porticoes supported by Classical columns. After World War II^{qv} modern concepts of space and form appeared. Rejecting traditional historical styles, architects used new forms, spaces, and decorative modes for numerous new churches. Nonetheless, traditional styles continued in popularity.

BIBLIOGRAPHY: Rex E. Gerald, *Spanish Presidios of the Late Eighteenth Century in Northern New Spain* (Santa Fe: Museum of New Mexico, 1968). Marion A. Habig, *The Alamo Chain of Missions* (Chicago: Franciscan Herald Press, 1968; rev. ed. 1976). Historic American Buildings Survey, *Texas Catalog*, comp. Paul Goeldner (San Antonio: Trinity University Press, 1974?). Terry G. Jordan, "The Traditional Southern Rural Chapel in Texas, " *Ecumene* 7 (March 1976). Max L. Moorhead, *The Presidio: Bastion of the Spanish Borderlands* (Norman: University of Oklahoma Press, 1975). Willard B. Robinson, "Houses of Worship in Nineteenth-Century Texas," *Southwestern Historical Quarterly* 85 (January 1982).

Willard B. Robinson

CHURCH OF CHRIST. The Church of Christ in Texas developed as a part of the westward advance of an American religious movement growing out of the Second Great Awakening that became known as the Restoration Movement or the Reformation of the Nineteenth Century. The movement sought to restore first-century Christianity and used the Bible as the sole religious authority. From this effort two movements evolved, the "Christians" of Barton W. Stone of Kentucky and the "Reformers" or "Reforming Baptists" led by Alexander Campbell of Pennsylvania; the two merged in 1832. Sharing this heritage today, in addition to the Church of Christ, are two other fellowships in the movement: the Christian Church (Disciples of Christ)^{qv} and the Churches of Christ. (Members of the Church of Christ, because of the church's strict congregational autonomy, often refer to the aggregate of congregations as Churches of Christ.) In 1824 Collin McKinney,^{qv} a signer of the Texas Declaration of Independence,^{qv} became the first known member of the Church of Christ to settle in Texas. William P. DeFee, who established the Antioch Church of Christ near San Augustine in 1836, was the first minister of the church to preach in Texas. The first Church of Christ in Texas was a church on wheels begun by Mansell W. Matthews,^{qv} a surgeon in the revolutionary army^{qv} and a member of the First and Seventh congresses of the Republic of Texas.^{qv} Many early immigrants to Texas were from Kentucky, Tennessee, and northern Alabama, where Stone's influence was strongest. José María Jesús Carbajal,^{qv} the first native Texan to become a member, lived in Alexander Campbell's home in Bethany, Virginia, from 1827 to 1830, when he brought back to Texas all of Campbell's writings. Early Texas Churches of Christ sprang from converted Baptist congregations; Thomas Washington Cox,^{qv} a Baptist minister, is credited with several of these conversions.

During the republic the Church of Christ grew in Deep East Texas and South Texas, and expanded west beyond the Colorado River. After statehood, immigration swelled the membership, especially after midcentury. Although many unheeded appeals for missionaries were made, the churches increased in membership chiefly through the efforts of men otherwise employed during the week who preached on weekends and during the summer months. The number of such ministers grew by 1860; more than 100 can be identified. Few churches had buildings of their own and often met in homes, schoolhouses, courthouses, union halls, or, during warm months, at campmeeting grounds. The first permanent church was built by John Henry Moore,qv an Indian fighter and founder of La Grange, Fayette County. By 1860 the church had 2,500 members in Texas, in fifty-three congregations scattered along the frontier in Montague, Parker, Erath, Burnet, and Gillespie counties and extending westward to Batesville in Zavala County. The Civil Warqv had little adverse affect on the churches, although many young men participated in the struggle. The churches continued to grow through vigorous evangelism.

By 1876 such itinerant preachers as W. H. Stewart, Silas Scarborough, and Thomas Nance began expansion on West Texas prairies and in the Panhandle.qv Several churches were started in West Texas by colonization, notably at Abilene, San Angelo, Lockney, and Lubbock. Similar ventures in Mexico began in 1896, when Collin McKinney Wilmethqv led an "Exodus to Mexico" that ended with his untimely death. In the next two decades ministers led more successful American colonies in Mexico, which ended in 1916 as a result of Pancho (Francisco) Villa'sqv activities.

Because the Churches of Christ had no organizational structure above the local church, evangelism depended heavily on individual efforts of frontier preachers and camp meetings. Later, cooperative ventures were undertaken by churches and individuals regionally, and in 1872 a state cooperative effort began through the efforts of Carroll Kendrick.qv In 1862 division in the Churches of Christ began on a national level when progressives and conservatives began differing over innovations in worship and clericalism. Texas churches were divided in San Marcos, Waco, Dallas, Waxahachie and other towns when organs, favored by the progressives, were introduced into the church service. A statewide division occurred at the state meeting in Austin in July 1886, when progressives established a Texas Christian Missionary Society to mimic the American Christian Missionary Society, founded in 1849. The conservatives believed that supracongregational organization and instrumental music had no scriptural basis. In 1906 the United States census officially divided the two groups into the Churches of Christ (conservatives) and the Disciples of Christ (progressives). While the Churches of Christ stressed the restoration principle, the Disciples were more ecumenical. In the 1960s another separation occurred between the Disciples and the Churches of Christ due to heightened ecumenical emphasis by the Disciples. In 1886 the undivided body had approximately 30,000 members, about evenly split between progressives and conservatives. However, by 1906, signs of more rapid growth among Churches of Christ were becoming evident. The increase over the Disciples of Christ was due largely to the labors of itinerant preachers and the agrarian nature of the Texas population. In the small-town and rural areas the militantly autonomous Churches of Christ grew most rapidly. Pulpit-centered churches were led by an aggressive, often combatant, ministry. In 1906 the Church of Christ had 627 congregations and 34,006 members. By the mid-twentieth century Texas accounted for 35 percent of the 450,000 members in the United States. The number of Texas congregations, stable since midcentury, reached 2,215 in the 1990s, when the membership numbered 292,585. Decline in Texas rural population brought a concomitant decline in rural churches. City churches increased after World War IIqv until recent decades, when growth leveled off. The greatest growth of the church occurred in the Dallas–Fort Worth area. Significant growth in recent decades has been only in suburban areas, and much of this is due to the mobility of church members.

The first Texas religious periodical published by a member of the Church of Christ was the short-lived *Christian Philanthropist,* edited by Carroll Kendrick, which merged with the *Gospel Advocate* of Nashville, Tennessee. By 1860 the *Gospel Advocate,* with a Texas department edited by Kendrick, and another conservative paper, the *American Christian Review* of Cincinnati, Ohio, had become the most influential among Texas members. The principal periodicals published in Texas have been the *Christian Messenger* (later *Burnett's Budget*), published in Bonham and Dallas from 1875 to 1916 and edited by Thomas R. Burnett;qv the *Christian Preacher,* which appeared in McKinney and Dallas from 1875 to 1895, edited by Collin M. Wilmeth; and the *Firm Foundation,* published in Austin from 1884 to 1983, edited by Austin McGary,qv G. H. P. Showalter (1908–54), and Reuel G. Lemmonsqv (1955–83). Still being published are the *Christian Chronicle* (founded in Abilene in 1942, now published in Oklahoma City, Oklahoma) and *Restoration Quarterly* (1957–), published in Abilene. Several regional religious newspapers are published by members of the Church of Christ.

The earliest Church of Christ (or Disciples of Christ) school was Mount Enterprise Male and Female College, established in 1851 in Rusk County; it closed in 1855. Joseph Addison Clarkqv conducted schools at Midway (Madison County) and Fort Worth before purchasing the school at Thorp Spring, Hood County, in 1873. With his sons he established Add-Ran College, which closed in 1890. At Tarrant, Hopkins County, Mary Fanning conducted a school for girls. Other ministers involved with schools were William C. McKinney and Peter Cartwright (Mantua Institute) and Carroll Kendrick (Salado). Schools established by the Churches of Christ include Burnetta College (Venus), 1896–1909; Carlton College (Bonham), 1865–1916; Carr-Burdette College (Sherman), 1893–1914; Clebarro College (Cleburne), 1909–17; Gunter Bible College (Gunter), 1903–28; Lampasas College (Lampasas), 1879–85; Lingleville Christian College (Lingleville), 1901–09; Lockney Christian College (Lockney), 1894–1918; Muse Academy (McKinney), 1857–87; Nazareth University (Dallas), 1886–90; Sabinal Christian College (Sabinal), 1907–17; Southland University (Denton), 1904–09; Terrell Bible College (Terrell), 1929–30; Thorp Spring Christian College (Thorp Spring), 1910–30; West Texas Normal and Business College (Cherokee), 1905–09; and Fort Worth Christian College. Current schools include Abilene Christian University (Abilene, founded in 1906); Lubbock Christian University (Lubbock, 1957); Southwestern Christian College (Terrell, 1948); and Amber University (Garland, 1971).

Belle Haven was the first home for orphans supported by the Churches of Christ in the West. Mrs. Jennie Clarke established this pioneer benevolent institution in her home at Luling in May 1898 and was the director until her death in 1929, after which the home was dissolved in July 1930, but not before fostering a home at Canadian (now Tipton Home, Tipton, Oklahoma) and Boles Homeqv at Quinlan. Current homes include Boles Home, Cherokee Children's Home (Cherokee), Gunter Home for the Aged (Gunter), the Christian Care Center (Mesquite), and Medina Children's Home (Medina).

BIBLIOGRAPHY: Carter E. Boren, *Religion on the Texas Frontier* (San Antonio: Naylor, 1968). Stephen Daniel Eckstein, *History of the Churches of Christ in Texas, 1824–1950* (Austin: Firm Foundation, 1963). Samuel S. Hill, ed., *Encyclopedia of Religion in the South* (Macon, Georgia: Mercer University Press, 1984). R. L. Roberts, "Expansion of Church of Christ in West Texas, 1870–1900," West Texas Historical Association *Year Book* 53 (1977).   R. L. Roberts

CHURCH HILL, TEXAS. Church Hill is nine miles northeast of Henderson in eastern Rusk County. The site was settled in the early 1850s by families from Georgia and was named for a tree-covered hill where they built a church. Plantations were established in the area. The first brick house in the county was reportedly built at Church Hill by a Dr. Prior, a planter from Virginia. The Church Hill Male and Female Academy operated in the 1850s under the auspices of the Presbyterian church. A post office was established in 1893 with George S. Strong as postmaster. In 1895 Church Hill had a population of thirty, a Methodist church, and a general store. The post office was discontinued in 1904, and mail was sent to Henderson. From 1932 to 1966 the reported population was thirty; it was fifteen from 1967 to 1990.

BIBLIOGRAPHY: Dorman H. Winfrey, *A History of Rusk County* (Waco: Texian, 1961). *Megan Biesele*

CHURCH HILL ACADEMY. Church Hill Academy, at Church Hill, nine miles northeast of Henderson in Rusk County, was a Presbyterian school established by an act of the Texas legislature on February 13, 1854. At that time it was called Church Hill Male and Female Academy. The institution was on land donated on September 2, 1853, by John C. Robertson,qv John Strong, and Samuel Watson, who were appointed to the board of trustees with Jackson Pryor, Anderson W. Smith, Newell Tullis, and William P. Wright. It was supervised by six Presbyterian ministers and run by John M. Becton.qv It is thought to have lasted until the Civil War.qv

BIBLIOGRAPHY: Garland Roscoe Farmer, *The Realm of Rusk County* (Henderson, Texas: Henderson *Times*, 1951). Dorman H. Winfrey, *A History of Rusk County* (Waco: Texian, 1961). *Megan Biesele*

CHURCHILL BRIDGE, TEXAS. Churchill Bridge is a community on the San Bernard River sixteen miles southwest of Angleton in southwestern Brazoria County. It was known as Bennett's Ferry when, on September 1, 1875, Lewis T. Bennett bought a ferry and 200 acres with improvements on the San Bernard River from Andrew S. Churchill, who had arrived in the county before March 1836. A local post office was established in February 1877, with Bennett as postmaster, but was discontinued by September. In 1886 Bennett's descendents sold some of the land, and the site came to be known as Churchill Place. According to some sources, it is likely that the post office was known as Bennett's Ferry, but the place was more often referred to as Churchill Ferry or Churchill Bridge. The ferry was replaced by a hand-operated drawbridge and then later by a modern bridge known as Sportsman Span, roughly a mile upriver from the original location. In the 1930s the community had scattered dwellings and several other buildings. Between 1943 and 1945 the town recorded a population of forty and two businesses. In 1988 the county highway map showed two businesses at the site and a development, Las Playas, nearby.

BIBLIOGRAPHY: James A. Creighton, *A Narrative History of Brazoria County* (Angleton, Texas: Brazoria County Historical Commission, 1975). *Diana J. Kleiner*

CHURCH MOUNTAIN. Church Mountain, also called Church Peak, is in the far southeastern corner of Nolan County, 2½ miles northeast of its boundary with Coke and Runnels counties (at 32°05′ N, 100°12′ W). At an elevation of 2,410 feet above sea level, Church Mountain rises 300 feet above nearby U.S. Highway 277.

CHURCH OF THE NAZARENE. The Church of the Nazarene is a Protestant, evangelical, perfectionist body that originated in the early twentieth century as a result of successive mergers of small perfectionist, or holiness, groups. Its official beginning as a national church occurred in Pilot Point, Texas, in 1908, when the Pentecostal Church of the Nazarene, formed the previous year from a union of the Church of the Nazarene on the West Coast and the Association of Pentecostal Churches in New York and New England, merged with the Holiness Church of Christ, a Tennessee-Arkansas-Texas group. Despite the name, the latter had no doctrinal connection with the religious body known as the Church of Christ.qv The Holiness Church of Christ was itself the result of the merging of two groups: the New Testament Church of Christ, organized in Milan, Tennessee, in 1894 and then expanded to rural areas of West Texas; and the Independent Holiness Church, with congregations in East Texas. These joined forces in 1904 at Rising Star, Texas, and contributed about 100 small churches to the Pilot Point merger of 1908. The number of Nazarene churches in Texas grew from 129 in 1916 to 134 in 1926 and 155 in 1936. Membership increased from 3,821 in 1916 to 8,646 in 1936. From 1908 to 1919, the organization was known as the Pentecostal Church of the Nazarene. Doctrinally, the Church of the Nazarene is of Methodist lineage. It subscribes to the view expounded by John Wesley that the moral depravity of the soul can be cleansed away by operation of the spirit of God in a religious experience subsequent to conversion. According to Nazarene belief, the experience, termed "entire sanctification" or "Christian perfection," is characterized by purifying of inner motives, although it does not perfect human judgment or preclude mistakes and temptations. Other doctrines of the Church of the Nazarene include those common to conservative Protestantism. Belief in the free agency of man and in universal atonement places this denomination among Protestant churches espousing Arminianism, a strongly antipredestinarian theology. In Texas the Church of the Nazarene is divided into four districts. Each district, led by a district superintendent, holds an annual assembly and is accountable to a General Assembly that convenes quadrennially and to a Board of General Superintendents. By 1966 Nazarene congregations in Texas numbered 280, with a membership of around 18,000. Total giving for all purposes exceeded $2.8 million, and church property in this state was valued at $13 million. In 1995, 32,745 members attended 337 churches in Texas. The total giving of the congregations was $25,897,083. The church's property values exceeded $134 million.

BIBLIOGRAPHY: Church of the Nazarene, *Manual of the Church of the Nazarene: History, Constitution, Government, Ritual* (Kansas City, Missouri: Nazarene Publishing House, 1932). Ernest W. Moore, Jr., History of the Church of the Nazarene in Texas (M.A. thesis, University of Texas, 1963). Timothy Smith and W. T. Purkiser, *Called unto Holiness: The Story of the Nazarenes* (2 vols., Kansas City, Missouri: Nazarene Publishing House, 1962, 1983). *Ernest W. Moore, Jr.*

CÍBOLA INDIANS. This name, which means "bison," was used by the Spanish to refer to various Indian groups that specialized in bison hunting. In the Texas area one group of Cíbola (Cíbolo, Cíbula, Síbolo, Síbula, Zívolo) lived in western Texas in close association with the nomadic branch of the Jumano Indians. In the late seventeenth century both groups were bison hunters and traders who traveled widely in Texas and northern Mexico. In the warm season they ranged the area between El Paso and the Hasinai country of eastern Texas but spent the winter in the Indian towns near the site of present Presidio. Such evidence as is available suggests that the Cíbola were originally occupants of the southern plains between the Pecos and Colorado rivers. They appear to have been displaced by the southward movement of Apache groups and to have moved into the Trans-Pecos region. Continued Apache pressure in the eighteenth century led to their disappearance as an ethnic group. Some Cíbolas were evidently absorbed by the Apaches and others by the Spanish-speaking population of northern Chihuahua. The linguistic affiliation of the Cíbola Indians remains unknown.

BIBLIOGRAPHY: Herbert E. Bolton, "The Jumano Indians in Texas, 1650–1771," *Quarterly of the Texas State Historical Association* 15 (July 1911). Jack D. Forbes, "Unknown Athapaskans: The Identification of the Jano, Jocome, Jumano, Manso, Suma, and Other Indian Tribes of the Southwest," *Ethnohistory* 6 (Spring 1959). Charles W. Hackett, ed., *Historical Documents Relating to New Mexico, Nueva Vizcaya, and Approaches Thereto, to 1773* (3 vols., Washington: Carnegie Institution, 1923–37). J. Charles Kelley, "Factors Involved in the Abandonment of Certain Peripheral Southwestern Settlements," *American Anthropologist* 54 (July–September 1952). J. Charles Kelley, "The Historic Indian Pueblos of La Junta de Los Rios," *New Mexico Historical Review* 27, 28 (October 1952, January 1953). J. Charles Kelley, "Juan Sabeata and Diffusion in Aboriginal Texas," *American Anthropologist* 57 (October 1955). Carl Sauer, *The Distribution of Aboriginal Tribes and Languages in Northwestern Mexico* (Berkeley: University of California Press, 1934). *Thomas N. Campbell*

CIBOLEROS. The ciboleros were Mexican buffalo hunters who operated on the Llano Estacado[qv] for nearly two centuries. Their name was derived from the Spanish *cíbolo*, the common term for buffalo.[qv] Although they were often associated with the Comancheros (*see* COMANCHERO) they were actually a distinct group whose primary objective was to hunt the shaggy bison for meat, hides, and sport. Like the Indians, the ciboleros considered the thrill of the chase as much a part of the hunt as the kill. Most of them operated out of Taos, Santa Fe, or the El Paso area, and they were an important factor in the eventual demise of the buffalo herds on the southern plains.

Since pre-Columbian times sedentary Pueblo Indians from the upper Rio Grande had ventured onto the plains to supplement their vegetable diet with buffalo meat whenever relations with plains tribes permitted. The acquisition of horses from the Spaniards made these annual journeys faster, easier, and more successful. Early Spanish expeditions into West Texas, beginning with that of Vicente de Zaldívar[qv] in 1598, hunted and even tried to capture and domesticate buffalo. Though the Pueblos and Spanish colonists of New Mexico obtained most of their meat and hides through barter with the plains nomads, they soon mastered many buffalo-hunting techniques. By the late seventeenth century ciboleros had begun to venture out in force onto the Llano Estacado.

They made their annual expeditions mainly to provide meat for their families during the winter. These hunts usually occurred during October, after they had harvested the crops at home and when the weather was still mild. Buffalo hides were in prime condition that time of the year, and the animals had migrated into the Canadian River breaks from their summer grazing ranges farther north and so were closer at hand. The ciboleros soon became legendary for their hunting prowess, their main weapons being bows and arrows or, more commonly, lances. They often dressed gaudily and sometimes rode their agile Spanish ponies bareback to prevent entanglement in gear. Racing to the side of a running buffalo, the cibolero drove the razor-sharp lance point into the animal's heart, quickly dismounted, often at great risk, to pull out the lance, and then remounted to continue the chase and kill as many animals as he could. A skilled lancer could bring down as many as twenty-five buffalo during a single chase, which often covered two or three miles.

The ciboleros traveled in groups numbering as many as 150 men, accompanied on occasion by their women and children. Even before the lancers finished their job, the other members of the party went to work skinning fallen animals, loading the meat onto horses or into wooden *carretas,* and hauling it back to their campsite, where they cut it Indian fashion into thin strips that they hung out to dry. The jerked slices were then beaten or kneaded with the feet, a process thought to help preserve them, and packed into the *carretas.* Most of the rest of the animal was used in various ways. The fat was cut into large chunks and made into tallow for cooking and manufacturing candles. After the tallow was drained off, the crunchy cracklings that remained were a favorite treat among the children. Hides were tanned into highly valued rugs and robes by scraping and kneading with repeated applications of buffalo brains. These robes came in handy during severe northers and blizzards. Horns were made into utensils and decorative objects, and the long hair from the neck and shoulders was made into coarse cloth or used as mattress stuffing.

To avoid conflict with plains Indians who were also after buffalo, the ciboleros brought along homemade bread, beads, and other trinkets to use as barter. Sometimes Indian hunting parties were given flour, sugar, coffee, and other provisions when they called on the cibolero camps.

On the return trip to the Rio Grande settlements with their carts laden with meat and other products, successful hunters rode proudly through villages in a triumphal procession, to the envy and admiration of the local populace. In their hometowns they received a hero's welcome and on the first night were treated to a fandango. Although most of their products were subsequently sold, they kept some of the meat for themselves to eat with frijoles.

By the beginning of the nineteenth century the ciboleros had become an important economic factor. They supplied food for the New Mexico settlements and hides for the rich Santa Fe–Chihuahua trade. Their buffalo jerky found ready markets throughout northern Mexico, while delicacies like dried buffalo tongues were hauled as far south as Mexico City, where they sold for as much as two dollars apiece. The expedition of Francisco Amangual[qv] in June 1808 encountered hunting parties in West Texas, and in the 1840s Josiah Gregg[qv] described their colorful manner of life in detail. The ciboleros also gained a thorough knowledge of the trackless prairies and inspired the Comancheros to begin their lucrative trading expeditions to the breaks and canyons of the Llano.

As early as 1832 ciboleros were reported to have killed between 10,000 and 12,000 bison each year. Such butchery resulted in increased antagonism on the part of the southern plains tribes by the 1850s. Attempting to protect their main source of livelihood, the Comanches warned the ciboleros to bring only a few pack animals with them and threatened on occasion to "take away all their animals and wagons." In southeastern Colorado skirmishes broke out between the ciboleros and Cheyennes, compelling the former to restrict their hunts largely to the Comanchería in the Texas Panhandle. Further serious Indian opposition was avoided until after the Civil War.[qv] By that time the ciboleros had begun replacing their flimsy carts with larger, more durable wagons capable of holding the jerked meat of forty-five buffalo. They were thus capable of depleting the herds even more. In addition, military officials in New Mexico and Indian Territory attempted to close the Llano Estacado to all native New Mexicans in an effort to curb the illicit activities of the Comanchero trade. Even so, many ciboleros managed to continue their activities until the decimation of the buffalo herds in the late 1870s by white hide hunters with their long-range rifles.

BIBLIOGRAPHY: Charles Leroy Kenner, *A History of New Mexican–Plains Indian Relations* (Norman: University of Oklahoma Press, 1969). Frederick W. Rathjen, *The Texas Panhandle Frontier* (Austin: University of Texas Press, 1973). *H. Allen Anderson*

CIBOLO, TEXAS (Frio County). Cibolo was near Dry Cibolo Creek at a site immediately north of present Farm Road 85 and seven miles west of Dilley in southwest Frio County. Around 1920 a schoolhouse was constructed in Cibolo; this school was one of the first in Frio County to offer an eleven-grade curriculum. By 1929 the community had two schools and several dwellings. Only one school operated in Cibolo by 1936. In 1974 three dwellings remained in the community, and by 1989 Cibolo appears to have been abandoned.

Ruben E. Ochoa

CIBOLO, TEXAS (Guadalupe County). Cibolo is on Farm Road 78 and Cibolo Creek, sixteen miles west of Seguin in western Guadalupe County. *Cíbolo* is Spanish for "buffalo." The banks of Cibolo Creek are quite steep, and along its entire course, which is the boundary between Guadalupe and Bexar counties, there are few places where pioneers could find a safe crossing before the development of bridges. It is said that Indians stampeded buffalo over the banks to disable them so they could be slaughtered. Jacob Schlather bought land in the area in 1867, and his son George built a store to supply neighboring settlers, who were mostly German. The store was sold to Charles Fromme in 1882, and the settlement became known as Fromme's Store. When the Galveston, Harrisburg and San Antonio Railway built through the area in 1877 the station was called Cibolo Valley. A post office called Cibolo opened in 1883. By 1890 the community had a church, a cotton gin, a general store, and 100 residents.

The Cibolo Valley school had one teacher and thirty-one students in 1904. O. Henry's (*see* PORTER, WILLIAM SYDNEY) story "The Smiling Valley of the Cibolo" was supposedly inspired by a visit to the area. In 1914 a second frame school building was constructed to accommodate the growing number of students. In 1916 the voters approved a bond for a new high school. The trustees, F. J. Werner, George Schlather, and Alfred Sahm, contracted for a two-story brick structure. The first graduates of Cibolo High School received their diplomas in 1920. The census of 1940 recorded a post office, a bank, nine businesses, and a population of 250. When the town was incorporated in 1968 the population was 398. The major economic influences on Cibolo have been Randolph Air Force Base^{qv} and the expansion of San Antonio. In the 1980s Cibolo grew dramatically along Interstate Highway 35, and many housing developments were planned. The town reported 657 residents in 1988 and 1,757 in 1990.

BIBLIOGRAPHY: Willie Mae Weinert, *An Authentic History of Guadalupe County* (Seguin, Texas: Seguin *Enterprise*, 1951; rpt. 1976).

Willie Mae Weinert

CIBOLO CREEK (Duval County). Cibolo Creek rises six miles south of Realitos in southern Duval County (at 27°24′ N, 98°32′ W) and runs southeast for thirty-five miles, crossing southwestern Jim Wells County, to its mouth on Palo Blanco Creek, one mile southeast of Falfurrias in northeastern Brooks County (at 27°12′ N, 98°08′ W). Its name means "bison" in Spanish. The surrounding flat to gently rolling terrain with local shallow depressions and escarpments is surfaced by shallow clay to deep sandy loams and loose sand that support scrub brush and grasses.

____ (Kendall County). Cibolo Creek rises ten miles northwest of Boerne in southwestern Kendall County (at 29°50′ N, 98°53′ W) and runs southeast for 100 miles, forming the Bexar-Comal and the Bexar-Guadalupe county lines and crossing Wilson County, to its mouth on the San Antonio River, five miles northwest of Karnes City in Karnes County (at 28°57′ N, 97°52′ W). The creek passes through steep slopes and benches in the upper reaches and flat terrain with local shallow depressions in the middle and lower reaches. Clay and sandy loams support oak, juniper, and mesquite in the drier regions and water-tolerant hardwoods, conifers, and grasses in the middle and lower reaches of the creek.

Cibolo Creek has been identified as the one called "Xoloton" by the Coahuiltecan Indians and "Bata Coniquiyoqui" by the Indians of the Tonkawan linguistic family. The second name was noted in 1691 by Father Damian Massanet,^{qv} but he called the stream "Santa Crecencia." Domingo Terán de los Ríos,^{qv} on the same expedition, named the creek "San Ygnacio de Loyola." Domingo Ramón^{qv} in 1716 called it "San Xavier," but the term "Cibolo" gradually came to be applied to the entire area. From the time of the expedition of the Marqués de San Miguel de Aguayo^{qv} in 1721 the stream was called "Arroyo del Cibolo" or "Río Cibolo." In 1768 the Marqués de Rubí^{qv} included Cibolo Creek in his list of sites for potential posts to solidify Spanish claims on Texas. Permanent settlement along Cibolo Creek was delayed until after the annexation of Texas to the United States. In the late 1840s and early 1850s the communities of Schertz, Tusculum (later Boerne), La Vernia, and the Pieper Settlement (later Bulverde) were established.

BIBLIOGRAPHY: Carlos E. Castañeda, *Our Catholic Heritage in Texas* (7 vols., Austin: Von Boeckmann-Jones, 1936–1958; rpt., New York: Arno, 1976).

____ (Presidio County). Cibolo Creek rises four miles southwest of Farm Road 2810 in central Presidio County (at 30°04′ N, 104°18′ W) and runs south for forty-one miles to its mouth on the Rio Grande, just west of Presidio (at 29°34′ N, 104°24′ W). It cuts through the eastern Chinati Mountains and is intersected by a major tributary, Osa Creek, which drains the northeast side of the mountains. Cibolo Creek crosses rocks of great variety, ranging in age from Permian to Quaternary, surfaced by sands and clay loams that support sparse desert shrubs. The first settlement on Cibolo Creek came in 1832 when Col. José Ynacio Ronquillo received a 2,500-square-mile grant from the Mexican government (*see* RONQUILLO LAND GRANT). He settled his family at El Cibolo, three miles north of Presidio del Norte. In 1857 Milton Faver^{qv} settled on the creek and ranched in the Chinati Mountains. John Spencer found valuable silver ore near Cibolo Creek in 1882, and the mining town of Shafter sprang up on the banks of the creek in the 1880s.

BIBLIOGRAPHY: John Ernest Gregg, History of Presidio County (M.A. thesis, University of Texas, 1933). Cecilia Thompson, *History of Marfa and Presidio County, 1535–1946* (2 vols., Austin: Nortex, 1985).

____ (Zavala County). Cibolo Creek rises eleven miles northwest of Crystal City in southeastern Zavala County (at 28°47′ N, 99°32′ W) and runs southeast for forty-seven miles through Frio County to its mouth on the Frio River, three miles southwest of Fowlerton in eastern La Salle County (at 28°27′ N, 98°53′ W). The surrounding low rolling to flat terrain with local dissections and locally shallow depressions is surfaced by deep to shallow clay and sandy loams that support scrub brush, cacti, and grasses in the creek's upper reaches and water-tolerant hardwoods and grasses in its lower. The section of Cibolo Creek in La Salle County extending twenty miles from its mouth has also been known as Jahuey Creek, where in 1856 William A. Waugh established his Jahuey Ranch; two years later, when La Salle County was established, Waugh was the county's only permanent white settler.

BIBLIOGRAPHY: Annette Martin Ludeman, *La Salle: La Salle County* (Quanah, Texas: Nortex, 1975).

CIBOLO SETTLEMENT, TEXAS. Cibolo Settlement, a ghost town on Cibolo Creek in Comal County, was established in 1846, when a road was blazed from New Braunfels to the Pedernales River. The route followed the Old San Antonio Road^{qv} southwest to the Cibolo and then followed an old Indian trail over the only convenient passage from the prairie over the Balcones Escarpment. Teamsters plying between New Braunfels and Fredericksburg settled in the fertile valley. Cibolo is reported to have been the site of a community school in the 1850s and 1860s, but its fate is unknown.

BIBLIOGRAPHY: Lillian Penshorn, A History of Comal County (M.A. thesis, Southwest Texas State Teachers College, 1950).

Oscar Haas

CIDWELL BRANCH. Cidwell Branch rises 2½ miles southwest of Nebo Mountain in southern Parker County (at 32°37′ N, 97°44′ W) and runs southwest for five miles to its mouth on Spring Creek (at 32°35′ N, 97°48′ W). It crosses nearly level to rolling terrain surfaced by shallow to deep clay and loam that support grasses. For most of the county's history the Cidwell Branch area has been used as rangeland.

CIENEGA CREEK (Jeff Davis County). Cienega Creek rises four miles northwest of Blue Mountain and twelve miles west of Fort Davis in central Jeff Davis County (at 30°35′ N, 104°06′ W) and runs northeast for twenty-one miles, although it disappears for about a mile just west of State Highway 17 and five miles southwest of Fort Davis. The Middle and Merrill forks of Cienega Creek join the stream just before this point, and the North and South forks join it just after it resumes flowing. Cienega Creek enters Limpia Creek a quarter mile south of State Highway 17 and five miles northeast of Fort Davis (at 30°38′ N, 103°49′ W). It traverses an area of steep to gentle slopes surfaced by shallow, stony soils that support scrub brush and sparse grasses. The name of the creek is apparently a corruption of Spanish *ciénaga*, "marsh."

____ (Presidio County). Cienega Creek rises four miles northwest of U.S. Highway 67 in central Presidio County (at 30°02′ N, 104°16′ W) and runs south thirty-two miles to its mouth on Alamito Creek, just northwest of Ocotillo (at 29°40′ N, 104°12′ W). Surrounding the creek, steep slopes of sedimentary deposits, desert mountain terrain, canyon land of volcanic rocks, and wash pediments of gravels and sand support sparse grasses, cacti, and desert shrubs. The creek was named for the Cienega Mountains. Milton Faver,^{qv} the first Anglo American to ranch on a grand scale in West Texas, established one of his three ranches on Cienega Creek in 1857.

BIBLIOGRAPHY: Leavitt Corning, Jr., *Baronial Forts of the Big Bend* (Austin: Trinity University Press, 1967).

CIENEGA MOUNTAIN. Cienega Mountain is sixteen miles south of Alpine in western Brewster County (at 30°07′ N, 103°39′ W). With an elevation of 6,562 feet above sea level, it rises 1,960 feet above State Highway 118, five miles to the east. The core of the mountain is a large intrusive body of the Tertiary period, between 2 million and 66 million years old. The region's shallow, stony soils support scrub brush and grasses.

CIENEGA MOUNTAINS. Cienega Mountains are three miles west of the Atchison, Topeka and Santa Fe Railway in south central Presidio County (at 29°47′ N, 104°10′ W). At an elevation of 5,315 feet above sea level, the summit rises 1,515 feet higher than Cienega Creek, on the western edge of the mountains. Cienega Mountains are formed by a Tertiary intrusion and are surrounded by alluvial deposits of pebbles and cobbles that support scrub brush, sparse grasses, and desert shrubs of conifers and oaks. In the 1880s Lawrence Haley ranched in the area of the Cienega Mountains. A legend claims that friendly Indians led him to the Valle de los Cienegas, or the Valley of the Marshes.

BIBLIOGRAPHY: Virginia Madison and Hallie Stillwell, *How Come It's Called That? Place Names in the Big Bend Country* (Albuquerque: University of New Mexico Press, 1958).

CIGAR MOUNTAIN. Cigar Mountain is 1½ miles northeast of Terlingua in southwestern Brewster County (at 29°20′ N, 103°36′ W). At an elevation of 3,301 feet above sea level, it rises 410 feet higher than the town. Its shallow, stony soils support scrub brush and grasses.

CIGAR SPRING. Cigar Spring is two miles northeast of Terlingua at the northern foot of Cigar Mountain in southwestern Brewster County (at 29°20′ N, 103°35′ W).

CIGARROA, LEONIDES GONZÁLEZ (1922–1973). Leonides González Cigarroa, physician and civic leader, son of Joaquín González Cigarroa, a physician, and Josefina González de la Vega, a pharmacist, was born in Tlalpam, Mexico, on December 19, 1922. His family moved to San Antonio when he was an infant, then to Laredo when he was fifteen. Cigarroa attended public schools in San Antonio and Laredo. He was trained as a concert pianist and eventually earned a degree from San Antonio College of Music, but at age ten he confided to his brother that he planned to become a surgeon. During his teenage years in Laredo he spent much of his free time at Mercy Hospital as an enthusiastic volunteer in the laboratories, emergency room, and X-ray department. He also observed surgery performed by his father and other physicians. Cigarroa received a B.S. degree from St. Edward's University in Austin in 1943 and graduated cum laude from Loyola University School of Medicine in Chicago in 1947. He completed an internship and a residency in general surgery at Cook County Hospital in Chicago. In 1946, when he was twenty-four years old, he became a United States citizen.

He returned to Laredo to begin an outstanding career in medicine and civic leadership. As a diplomate of the American Board of Surgery and a member of several professional organizations, he became chief of surgery at Mercy Hospital, civilian consultant in surgery at Laredo Air Force Base, and clinical professor of surgery at the University of Texas Health Sciences Center in San Antonio. He also served as surgical advisor to the vocational rehabilitation division of the Texas Education Agency[qv] and chairman of the Health Task Force of the Texas Urban Development Commission. He was especially concerned about education and child welfare. As a trustee of the joint Laredo Junior College and Laredo Independent School District Board, he and colleague Albert King headed a building committee for the college. The mathematics and science building that now bears Cigarroa's name, a library building, and four other buildings opened in 1968 and 1969. Cigarroa initiated a campaign for upper-level college instruction in Laredo that resulted in the establishment of a branch of Texas A&I University at Laredo Junior College. He also led a successful citizens' effort to have the University of Texas Medical Branch in Galveston organize an Area Health Educational Center in Laredo.

President Lyndon B. Johnson[qv] appointed Cigarroa to serve on the National Commission on Health Facilities, and President Richard M. Nixon named him to the Health Manpower Development Program Advisory Board, a program of the Office of Economic Opportunity. In 1970 Cigarroa was a delegate to the White House Conference on Children and that same year was made chairman of the state commission on drug use and abuse. He served on the State Board of Mental Health and Mental Retardation for several years (*see* TEXAS DEPARTMENT OF MENTAL HEALTH AND MENTAL RETARDATION). In 1967 he was chosen "Man of the Year" in Laredo. A high school that opened in Laredo in 1984 was named for him. The Human Resources and Leadership Conference for Migrants, sponsored by the Hogg Foundation for Mental Health,[qv] honored Cigarroa for his outstanding work to improve health in South Texas. Cigarroa married Margaret Giller, M.D., of Chicago, and the couple had six children, four of whom became physicians. Cigarroa died in 1973 and was buried in Laredo.

BIBLIOGRAPHY: Laredo *Times*, February 18, 1970. Vertical Files, Barker Texas History Center, University of Texas at Austin.

Megan Seaholm

CIMATAGUO INDIANS. H. E. Bolton[qv] reported Cimataguo as an Indian group name he had seen in the baptismal register of San Antonio de Valero Mission in San Antonio, and J. R. Swanton entered Cimataguo on his list of Indian groups who may have spoken the Coahuilteco language. Analysis of the Valero registers reveals that Cimataguo is given in a single entry (1748) as the personal nickname of a woman who, in five additional entries (1748–64), is clearly identified as a Pacuache Indian. Since no ethnic group name similar to Cimataguo has been found in other documents, it seems advisable to drop Cimataguo from the roster of Indian groups connected with Texas.

BIBLIOGRAPHY: Frederick Webb Hodge, ed., *Handbook of American Indians North of Mexico* (2 vols., Washington: GPO, 1907, 1910; rpt., New York: Pageant, 1959). J. R. Swanton, *Linguistic Material from the Tribes of Southern Texas and Northeastern Mexico* (Washington: Smithsonian Institution, 1940).

Thomas N. Campbell

CINCINNATI, TEXAS. Cincinnati, on the Trinity River in northern Walker County, was a riverport and an important ferry crossing during much of the nineteenth century. The settlement was founded in 1837 by James C. DeWitt and surveyed in 468 lots by Charles Brookfield. Water Street, on the west side, was a segment of the main road between Huntsville and Crockett and the site of the ferry crossing. The waterfront lots were all sold in 1836, but the town developed slowly during its first five years. Although there is no doubt that cotton was shipped from Cincinnati to Galveston on the Trinity, the volume handled is unclear. Records indicate numerous steamboats, as well as keelboats and flatboats, plying the Trinity between Galveston and points north. Although these boats stopped to load cotton or deliver goods at numerous points on the river, often at individual plantations or farms, towns such as Cincinnati frequently developed as central collection points. But navigation on the Trinity was difficult because of sandbars and fluctuations in water level, which often stranded boats for months; repeated attempts to improve the situation failed.

Cincinnati probably reached its peak in the early 1850s, when the town had a saloon, a grocery store, a cotton warehouse, a dry-goods store, a saddlery, a tannery, a cotton gin, a blacksmith shop, a wagonmaker, a stonemason, and two doctors. Estimates of the population during the early 1850s ranged from 200 to 600. A post office was established in 1866.

The major cause of the demise of Cincinnati occurred in 1853, when a traveler from Galveston brought yellow fever to the town. Perhaps as many as 250 people died, although the record is not clear. Rumors were wild and horrifying, but there are only a few specifically identified instances of yellow fever as the cause of death. No doubt a far greater number of people fled to escape the pestilence, and many never returned. The town began a steady decline. In 1872 the railroad connecting Houston and Dallas crossed the Trinity River fifteen miles downstream from Cincinnati, at Riverside. Ten years later the population of Cincinnati had decreased to thirty-five. In 1892 the post office closed.

BIBLIOGRAPHY: D'Anne McAdams Crews, ed., *Huntsville and Walker County, Texas: A Bicentennial History* (Huntsville, Texas: Sam Houston State University, 1976). Heather Hornbuckle, "Cincinnati: An Early Riverport in Walker County," *Texas Historian*, March 1978.

Gerald L. Holder

CINQUIN, JEANNE PIERRETTE (1845–1891). Jeanne Pierrette (Mother St. Pierre) Cinquin, foundress of the Sisters of the Incarnate Word of San Antonio[qv] and pioneer in health care and education, the daughter of Pierre and Claudine (Biellard) Cinquin, was born in Beaujeu, France, on May 22, 1845. On completing her education at the Ursuline Academy in Beaujeu, she entered the Monastery of the Incarnate Word in Lyons, where she was prepared for the mission in Texas. She received the habit and with it the name Sister Saint Pierre on August 6, 1868. Toward the close of the year she arrived in Galveston to join her missionary companions at St. Mary's Charity Hospital.

Bishop Claude Dubuis[qv] appointed sisters St. Pierre, Madeleine, and Agnes to begin a new foundation; they arrived in San Antonio in March 1869. At that time San Antonio was a mere frontier village recovering from the effects of two cholera epidemics that had broken out during the two previous decades. The worst epidemic recorded was that of 1849; it was followed by another in 1866, which, though not so severe, was sufficiently grave to arouse the anxiety of the people. But the community, with few doctors, no nurses, and no hospitals, experienced new hope when on December 3, 1869, Sister St. Pierre and her two companions opened the first hospital, known at that time as Santa Rosa Infirmary (now Santa Rosa Medical Center), to begin its long career of service to humanity.

In the spring of 1872 Sister St. Pierre was appointed superioress of her congregation, an office she held until her death. During her administration she recruited new members for the congregation; trained sisters for health care and education; and opened schools and hospitals throughout Texas and beyond its borders, a home for the aged, and an orphanage in San Antonio. Her letters reveal that she was a shrewd businesswoman and a wise and practical administrator, deeply spiritual and dedicated to serving the sick, the poor, and orphans. She died in her native France on December 19, 1891, at the age of forty-six. Her remains were transferred to San Antonio in 1895.

BIBLIOGRAPHY: *Sisters of Charity of the Incarnate Word of San Antonio, Texas* (Washington: Catholic University of America, 1925). Incarnate Word Generalate Archives, San Antonio. Martha Ann Kirk, "Ashes Could Not Stop Her: Mother St. Pierre and Community-Building in Texas," *Texas Journal* 11 (Fall–Winter 1988).

Sister Josephine Kennelly

CIPRES, TEXAS. Cipres is a mile west of Farm Road 1017 on the Rico gas and oilfield in northwestern Hidalgo County. The area was in Rancho Tale Perez until after 1890. In the early 1900s the land was subdivided for farming, and in 1909 J. H. Hinojosa planted cypress trees around a commissary and supply store. A post office, named for the trees, operated from 1913 until 1955 in a room in the ranch house. From 1925 through 1948 the community had one business and a population of twenty-five. In August 1990 a metal storage building, a small trailer, corrals, and a windmill remained at the site. Sidewalks and five salt cedars mark the former location of the house. Twenty people lived in the vicinity in 1990.

CIRCLE, TEXAS (Cherokee County). Circle is on Farm Road 2962 eight miles east of Rusk in eastern Cherokee County. The site was probably first settled after the Civil War.[qv] A local post office operated from 1898 to 1905. In the mid-1930s Circle had several stores, a church, and a number of houses. After World War II[qv] many residents left the area, but in the early 1990s a church, a school, a store, and a few scattered houses still remained.

Christopher Long

CIRCLE, TEXAS (Lamb County). Circle is at the intersection of U.S. Highway 70 and Farm Road 1842, five miles southeast of Springlake and six miles west of Olton in northeast Lamb County. It was on ranchland of Christopher C. Slaughter[qv] and was known as Punkin Center by 1928, when Abe Winkle established a store there. Later the town adopted the name of Circle for a curve in U.S. 70. D. G. Hobbs opened a cotton gin in 1936. The Hopewell Baptist Church was a mile west of the community. In the 1960s two businesses were active, although the church had been discontinued by 1968. The community still appeared on county maps of the 1980s and was still listed as a community in 1990.

BIBLIOGRAPHY: Evalyn Parrott Scott, *A History of Lamb County* (Sudan, Texas: Lamb County Historical Commission, 1968).

Charles G. Davis

CIRCLE BACK, TEXAS. Circle Back, at the junction of Farm roads 298 and 3397, in eastern Bailey County, was named for a ranch to the south whose brand was a circle on the backs of cattle. From 1918 to 1954 the settlement had a six-grade school and at one time about a dozen houses, a filling station, and a store–post office. Zue Smart ran the store, which burned in 1954. In 1949 the community, which served surrounding cattle and sheep ranches, had 100 people. By 1980 the population had dwindled to forty-nine, and by the mid-1980s only the Baptist minister and his wife and two children remained. In 1990 the population was reported as ten.

BIBLIOGRAPHY: LaVonne McKillip, ed., *Early Bailey County History* (Muleshoe, Texas, 1978).

William R. Hunt

CIRCLEVILLE, TEXAS. Circleville is on State Highway 95 one mile south of the San Gabriel River and seventy miles south of Waco in Williamson County. The town was settled in 1853 by three brothers, skilled craftsmen, James, Joseph, and William Eubank, and named for its semicircle of homes. In its early days it had a general store, a gristmill, a gin, a molasses press, tin and pewter shops, a blacksmith shop, a carding factory, a school, a church, and, from 1857 to 1911, a post office. The Kansas, Texas and Missouri Railroad ran through town in the 1880s; several train wrecks occurred there because of an ill-designed curve near the San Gabriel River. The school was consolidated with the Jonah school in 1949. In 1980 Circleville had a cattle auction barn, two stores, a tavern, and a population of fifty. In 1990 the population was forty-two.

BIBLIOGRAPHY: Clara Stearns Scarbrough, *Land of Good Water: A Williamson County History* (Georgetown, Texas: Williamson County Sun Publishers, 1973).

Clara Stearns Scarbrough

CÍRCULO CULTURAL ISABEL LA CATÓLICA. The Círculo Cultural Isabel la Católica (originally Círculo Social Femenino Mexicana) was a voluntary civic and social group organized in San Antonio in 1937 to improve conditions for Mexican women. Most of its activities focused on helping needy families. The first president was Carolina Malpica Munguía,qv and the first board member was María L. de Hernández.qv The board members scrutinized new members; organized fiestas on Halloween, Christmas, and for the group's anniversary in June; and attended to sickness and death of members and their families. Apparently the group used "Mixteca" as its theme song. Most members were married Mexican citizens. Membership ranged from twenty-one to forty-six. Members included Santos S. Herrera, who also belonged to Ladies LULAC.qv Lawyers Adolfo Garza and Gustavo C. Garcíaqv were honorary members. The circle met bimonthly on Sundays at the Biblioteca Mexicana, to which they donated curtains and plants. The Círculo Cultural was concerned with morality, order, and elevating the status of Mexican-American women. The group donated to the Mexican consul to help with the local *fiestas patrias*qv and in 1938 and 1939 sent delegates to the Cruz Azul Mexicanaqv convention. Members also distributed food and toys to their Mexican communities of origin at Christmas. The Círculo Cultural organized an exhibit of popular Mexican art at the Witte Museumqv in 1939. They no longer met after the early 1940s.

BIBLIOGRAPHY: Richard A. García, *Rise of the Mexican American Middle Class, San Antonio, 1919–1941* (College Station: Texas A&M University Press, 1991). Munguía Family Papers, Benson Latin American Collection, University of Texas at Austin. *Cynthia E. Orozco*

CISCO, TEXAS. Cisco, at the intersection of U.S. Highway 183 and Interstate Highway 20, in northwestern Eastland County, traces its history back to 1878 or 1879, when Rev. C. G. Stevens arrived in the area, established a post office and a church, and called the frontier settlement Red Gap. About six families were already living nearby, and W. T. Caldwell was running a store a half mile to the west. In 1881 the Houston and Texas Central Railway crossed the Texas and Pacific, which had come through the year before, at a point near Red Gap, and the settlement's inhabitants moved their town to the crossing. Three years later the town was officially recognized and a new post office granted; the town's name was changed to Cisco for John A. Cisco, a New York financier largely responsible for the building of the Houston and Texas Central.

Railroads continued to influence the development of Cisco as the Texas and Pacific acquired lots in the town and sold them to immigrants attracted by brochures touting the town as the "Gate City of the West" and promising half fares and generous baggage service for all settlers. Once settlers arrived, agricultural agents employed by the railroad advised them what and when to plant and on occasion provided the seed. During the 1880s a Mrs. Haws built and managed the first hotel, and Mrs. J. D. Alexander brought the first "millinery and fancy goods" to town. Following a practice common at the time, religious groups in Cisco met together for prayer meetings in the schoolhouse until they could build separate churches. By 1892 Cisco was a growing community with two newspapers, a bank, and an economy based on trade, ranching, fruit farming, and the limestone, coal, and iron ore available nearby. A broom factory and roller corn and flour mills were among the town's fifty-six businesses. But in 1893 a tornado hit Cisco, killing twenty-eight people and destroying or damaging most of its homes and businesses. Sources note that Mayor Conner of Dallas impressed fifty blacks to help clean up the wreckage in Cisco, and that among those whose businesses were affected was a Chinese laundryman.

Although Cisco played a relatively minor role in the Eastland County oil boom of 1919–21, its population grew rapidly at the time, with some estimates as high as 15,000; in the wake of the boom Cisco adopted a city charter and built a new railroad station that cost $25,000. Cisco was also in the background of a heated controversy between the Ku Klux Klanqv and its opponents that swept the county in the early 1920s (see RANGER, TEXAS). A Klan newsletter noted that Klan and anti-Klan forces had agreed to cease hostilities at Cisco, a fact that suggests a certain level of Klan activity in the town.

Probably the best-known event in Cisco history was the Santa Claus Bank Robbery.qv It occurred two days before Christmas of 1927, when four men robbed the First National Bank, taking $12,000 in cash and $150,000 in nonnegotiable securities. A chain of exciting events—including an attempt to steal a car foiled by a quick-thinking fourteen-year-old and a gun battle in which three people were killed, seven were injured, and two young girls were kidnapped—accounts for the many, often melodramatic, stories written about the robbery. One of the bandits eventually died of gunshot wounds, one served a prison sentence and was released, one died in the electric chair, and the last was lynched after shooting a jailer while trying to escape.

In the years following World War II,qv Cisco became increasingly dependent on oil and gas production, agriculture (primarily peanut cultureqv), and manufacturing. Cisco Junior College grew and was enrolling around 1,000 students in the early 1980s. In 1980 Cisco had a population of 4,517 and 154 businesses. That year residents applied to have the whole town named a historical district. They were inspired to seek recognition by a University of Houston professor who had come to Cisco to supervise the restoration of the Mobley Hotel, the first hotel owned by hotel magnate Conrad Hilton.qv In 1990 the population of Cisco was 3,813.

BIBLIOGRAPHY: Edwin T. Cox, *History of Eastland County, Texas* (San Antonio: Naylor, 1950). Fort Worth *Star-Telegram*, March 12, 21, 1967. Ruby Pearl Ghormley, *Eastland County, Texas: A Historical and Biographical Survey* (Austin: Rupegy, 1969). *Noel Wiggins*

CISCO JUNIOR COLLEGE. Cisco Junior College, in the north part of Cisco, is on the site of three previous colleges. Britton Training School, established by O. C. Britton in 1909, was its first forerunner. A leading North Texas newspaper proclaimed Britton's school to be "situated . . . on the highest peak in Eastland County, above the mosquito line, one of the best places in the West for a school of this kind." Britton closed during World War I,qv and Randolph College, a four-year baccalaureate school supported by the First Christian Church, replaced it in 1923. In 1932 Randolph officials reorganized the school as Randolph Junior College, but it closed in 1934.

Legislation signed by Governor W. Lee O'Danielqv on May 8, 1939, officially authorized the founding of Cisco Junior College. With a vacant campus available, the Cisco school board and superintendent Robert N. Cluck were able to organize the college in 1940 as a part of the Cisco Independent School District. Cluck served as the first president, while retaining his superintendency. Cisco High School principal O. L. Stamey acted as the new junior college's first dean and later (1947–54) as its first full-time president. The founders intended to benefit the people of Cisco and surrounding communities with both academic and vocational college-level courses.

The Cisco Chamber of Commerce raised funds to repair the Randolph Junior College property, acquired from Temple Trust Company in 1940 by Cisco Independent School District. Citizens contributed materially, and the junior college opened on September 10, 1940. Tuition, donations from the Cisco Chamber of Commerce, and funds from the National Youth Administrationqv and the War Department financed initial operations. The first-year enrollment totaled 124. During World War IIqv the college grew through its civilian pilot training and Cisco War Training School. The latter program trained female mechanics and was the first of its kind in the United States; it was supervised by the Texas State Board for Vocational Education. The G.I. Bill funded both academic and vocational training, thus causing enrollment to increase after the war, and the period from 1949 to 1956 put the college on a sound financial basis. In 1956 Cisco Junior College was separated administratively from Cisco Independent School District but retained the same tax district. A nine-member board of regents was to direct college operations thereafter.

From two buildings, one administrative classroom, and a dormitory on fifty acres of land in 1940, the Cisco Junior College plant expanded by 1984 to five dormitories, an administrative classroom building, a gymnasium, a science building, a student center, a library, two technical and vocational buildings, and a faculty office building. The campus had expanded to ninety-two acres. The college maintained branch campuses at Clyde and Abilene. In the late 1980s the college offered associate degrees in arts, science, applied arts, and applied science. Certificates were awarded for successful completion of study in specialized vocational fields. Numerous student employment, loan, grant, and scholarship programs were available. The Veterans Administration and the Texas Rehabilitation Commission[qv] also offered assistance to qualified students. The college received money from state appropriations for approved courses, tuition and fees, and college district taxes. Gifts, donations, oil and gas royalties, and auxiliary-enterprises income made up the remainder of the school's support.

Cisco Junior College is accredited by the Southern Association of Colleges and Schools and is a member of the Association of Texas Colleges and Universities,[qv] the American Association of Community and Junior Colleges, the National Junior College Athletic Association, and other associations. It maintains a dramatic theater, the Roof Garden, and publishes a semiannual humanities journal, the *Cross Timbers Review*.[qv] The school continues to pursue its goal of providing low-cost, quality education to residents of the Western Cross Timbers and Rolling Plains regions of North Central Texas. For the 1992–93 regular session the college had sixty-six faculty members and 1,835 students.

BIBLIOGRAPHY: Robert N. Cluck, The Organization and Operation of the Cisco Junior College (M.Ed. thesis, Hardin-Simmons University, 1943). Dallas *Morning News,* July 30, 1910. *Monte Lewis*

CISCO AND NORTHEASTERN RAILWAY. The Cisco and Northeastern Railway Company was chartered on December 4, 1918, to build seventy miles from Cisco in Eastland County to Graham in Young County. The capital was $500,000, and the business office was located at Cisco. Members of the first board of directors included Robert Q. Lee, William Reagan, E. B. Gude, D. K. Scott, G. D. Ward, A. J. Ward, C. H. Fee, J. J. Butts, J. R. Skinner, and J. W. Mancill, all from Eastland County. The road completed twenty-eight miles from Cisco to Breckenridge between August 1919 and October 1920, during the height of the Ranger oil boom. It paid 7.15 percent on capital stock, but all surplus was reinvested in the property. The Texas and Pacific bought a controlling interest in the road at the book value of $160 per share in January 1927. However, the Cisco and Northwestern continued to operate as a separate company and completed an additional thirty-seven miles from Breckenridge to Throckmorton in April 1928. The road ceased operations in 1942. *S. G. Reed*

CISNEROS V. CORPUS CHRISTI ISD. The Mexican-American struggle for access to the Texas public school system pursued a different strategy than that used by African Americans.[qv] As legal doctrine evolved after the Civil War,[qv] racial categories included only two groups, Caucasian and Negro. Segregation of blacks occurred by overt, legal definition—it was the law of the land—whereas segregation of persons of Mexican origin was done by covert shifts within the law, as they were classified as white. In Texas, school officials separated Mexican-origin children by "pedagogical analysis" or language deficiency. This practice was developed in 1930 to reinstate the system temporarily suspended by *Del Rio ISD v. Salvatierra,*[qv] a suit against separation by national origin. In the post–World War II era, Mexican-American organizations and strategists re-established the "other white" concept; they also stressed the absence-of-law tactic, whereby segregation was unconstitutional where no law existed permitting such action. Several successful suits between 1948 and 1957 established Mexican Americans[qv] as "a class apart"; in succeeding years only one court finding failed to support that designation, but others did not always find discrimination. State officials began using the "other white" and absence-of-law arguments to justify grouping black and Hispanic children to fulfill integration laws and to deny the existence of discrimination.

Cisneros v. Corpus Christi Independent School District (1970) was the first case to extend the U.S. Supreme Court's *Brown v. the Board of Education of Topeka, Kansas* decision (1954) to Mexican Americans. It recognized them as a minority group that could be and was frequently discriminated against. Such segregation and discrimination was ruled unconstitutional. The decision replaced the "other white" argument based on *Hernández v. State of Texas,*[qv] which had provided constitutional rights based on class discrimination where Mexican Americans had not been identified as a separate race. In 1968 José Cisneros and twenty-five other Mexican-American parents filed suit against the Corpus Christi Independent School District, charging operation of a dual school system at all levels on a *de facto* basis. The attorney for *Cisneros* was James de Anda, an experienced Mexican-American civil-rights lawyer who participated in the 1954 *Hernández* case before the Supreme Court and won the *Hernández v. Driscoll ISD*[qv] case in 1957. De Anda had begun that experience as an attorney for the American G.I. Forum.[qv] He argued that Mexican Americans were an identifiable minority group that had been illegally segregated by state action, whereas the school district maintained that since there was no history of state law requiring segregation, a dual school system could not exist. Judge Woodrow Seal found that the school board consciously fostered a system that perpetuated traditional segregation. This included a system that bused Anglo students to schools out of their neighborhoods, renovated old schools in black and Mexican-American neighborhoods rather than building new ones, assigned black and Hispanic teachers to segregated schools, and limited hiring of such teachers at other schools; the school board also lacked a majority-to-minority busing system. Judge Seal cited the "other white" argument as adjacent proof of segregation, but relied primarily on the application of unconstitutional segregation of Mexican Americans as an identifiable minority group based on physical, cultural, religious, and linguistic distinctions. The United States Department of Justice required further proof of historical evidence of segregation, and the school procrastinated on implementation of a plan to satisfy constitutional requirements. However, in 1975 the *Cisneros* case produced a new school system for Mexican-American and black children in Corpus Christi.

BIBLIOGRAPHY: Carlos M. Alcala and Jorge C. Rangel, "Project Report: De Jure Segregation of Chicanos in Texas Schools," *Harvard Civil Rights–Civil Liberties Law Review* 7 (March 1972). Carl Allsup, *The American G.I. Forum: Origins and Evolution* (University of Texas Center for Mexican American Studies Monograph 6, Austin, 1982). Carl Allsup, "Education Is Our Freedom: The American G.I. Forum and Mexican American School Segregation in Texas, 1948–1957," *Aztlán* 8 (Spring-Summer-Fall 1977). Guadalupe San Miguel, Jr., "Mexican American Organizations and the Changing Politics of School Desegregation in Texas, 1945–1980," *Social Science Quarterly* 63 (December 1982). Guadalupe San Miguel, Jr., "The Struggle Against Separate and Unequal Schools: Middle Class Mexican Americans and the Desegregation Campaign in Texas, 1929–1957," *History of Education Quarterly* 23 (Fall 1983). *V. Carl Allsup*

CISTERCIAN FATHERS. Our Lady of Dallas Abbey, the home of the Cistercians in Texas, is located in Irving off Highway 114, near Texas Stadium, Las Colinas, and the University of Dallas. It comprises thirty-six acres dotted with elevations and mesquite trees, and its brick buildings exhibit both modern and traditional architectural features. Its chapel, built in the early 1990s, is a massive limestone building with no veneers and few modern features; according to one critic, "the Cistercian church evokes 900 years of history, scholarship and prayer." The members of the community dedicate themselves exclusively to the love of God and the service of their fellow men. To be undivided in their loyalties they renounce marriage and individual ownership and subordinate their wills to the higher ideals of their institution. They belong to the world-wide Cistercian order, hence are called Cistercians. The name derives from Citeaux (in Latin, Cistercium), their parent abbey in Burgundy, founded as a reform branch of the Benedictine order in 1098. The Cistercians, who adopted the white habit and black scapular, quickly spread over all of Europe and influenced medieval life in numerous ways. Their constitutional document, the Charter of Charity, is said to have inspired parliamentary government. The Cistercians in Irving came from the abbey of Zirc in western Hungary, founded in 1182. Upon higher request, Zirc, cloistered at first, accepted full educational and teaching responsibilities in the latter part of the eighteenth century. Afterward the monk-priests also acquired academic degrees in the liberal arts and taught in one of the five modern college preparatory schools of the abbey. They trained generations of prominent public figures and intellectual leaders.

Hungarian monks living in the United States after the Communist takeover were invited by Bishop Thomas Gorman[qv] to the Diocese of Dallas–Fort Worth. They moved into their own monastery, built on the campus of the University of Dallas, in 1958. Five years later their priory was raised to the status of an abbey. Since then, buildings have multiplied on their grounds, and American vocations have increased their ranks. The Irving Cistercians follow a rigorous daily schedule. Their communal prayer life includes the recitation of the monastic office, made up largely of psalms, and on Sundays they also chant traditional Gregorian melodies. As teachers, they staff their own Cistercian Preparatory School for boys grades five through twelve, built on their premises in 1963, or serve as teachers or administrators at the University of Dallas. They carry out their priestly ministry in the abbey, as well as in parishes, convents, and military bases of the metropolitan area.

Individually, the monks are well-versed in languages and have earned advanced degrees in the classics, modern languages, science, history, music, philosophy, and theology. Some have published scholarly books and articles, given talks on a variety of subjects, or cultivated the fine arts on a highly professional level. Thus one can see attractive sculptures, paintings, ceramics, and prints all over the monastery. Collectively, the Cistercians contribute their spirituality, achievements, and cosmopolitan enthusiasm to the culture of North Texas.

BIBLIOGRAPHY: Dallas *Morning News,* May 29, 1992. Louis J. Lekai, *The Cistercians: Ideals and Reality* (Kent, Ohio: Kent State University Press, 1977). Louis J. Lekai, "Hungarian Cistercians in America," *Records of the American Catholic Historical Society of Philadelphia* 79 (December 1968).
Bede K. Lackner

CISTERN, TEXAS. Cistern is on State Highway 95 twelve miles northwest of Flatonia near the southwestern point of Fayette County. The community, first called Whiteside's Prairie and then Cockrill's Hill in honor of two early landowners, was settled during the 1850s on a hill overlooking fertile prairie land. Water wells in the area contained such high concentrations of minerals that residents were forced to build cisterns to trap rainwater for domestic use. By the time the post office was established in 1858, the community was known as Cistern.

The community life of this mixture of Anglo-American, German, and Czech residents centered around the Catholic and Lutheran churches, the school, the Harmony Club, and various fraternal organizations. In 1900 Cistern had a population of 150, a general merchandise store, a combination drugstore and saloon, a blacksmith shop and gin, and a physician. The post office closed in 1930. In 1950 the population was 150, and Cistern had two stores, two garages, and a consolidated high school employing five teachers. When the Muldoon oilfield was discovered between Cistern and Flatonia, wells began to dot the cotton fields. Cotton ceased to be a popular crop during the 1950s and 1960s, and landowners turned to ranching and the production of chickens. Many of the old fields were abandoned and reverted to pasture. Mail was delivered from Flatonia. During the 1980s the population dropped to seventy-five, and only three businesses remained in operation. The population was seventy-five in 1990.

BIBLIOGRAPHY: Frank Lotto, *Fayette County: Her History and Her People* (Schulenburg, Texas: Sticker Steam Press, 1902; rpt., Austin: University of Texas Press, 1981).
Jeff Carroll

CITIZEN'S PARTY OF HARRISON COUNTY. The Citizen's Party of Harrison County was the first of the so-called White Primary[qv] political parties formed after Reconstruction.[qv] In the years after the Civil War[qv] the black-dominated Republican party[qv] held a decided majority in the county. In an effort to end local Republican rule, a citizens' club, including most of the white voters, met and founded the party in the fall of 1878. The party was led by James F. Taylor, a former Whig and Constitutional Union party[qv] leader; Amory R. Starr,[qv] the son of James Harper Starr;[qv] Jonathon D. Rudd,[qv] Democratic Party[qv] county chairman; and other prominent citizens.

On October 12, 1878, the party held a nominating convention and selected William T. Scott,[qv] the county's wealthiest antebellum planter, to run for the lower house, as well as a slate of other candidates. The party presented itself as a nonpartisan citizens' group seeking to restore honest and efficient government to the county, though it was clearly an attempt by white traditional leaders to regain political power. In an attempt to sway the black vote, party leaders called for racial harmony and promised to protect political rights. The party also employed other tactics, including making its ballots similar to those used by the Republicans as a means of confusing illiterate black voters. The election was held on November 5, 1878, and at first it appeared that the Republicans had won most of the important contests. But Citizen's party leaders challenged the returns from one of the important districts, arguing that the box had been improperly located, and obtained an injunction from a Democratic district judge. When the Republican county judge refused to recognize the injunction, Citizen's party leaders seized the sheriff's and county clerk's offices, recounted the ballots, and issued themselves certificates of election. In a counter move, the Republican county judge issued certificates of election to Republican candidates. Outgoing Governor Richard Bennett Hubbard[qv] and incoming Governor Oran M. Roberts[qv] refused to intercede, and the Citizen's party candidates retained control of the offices. After 1878 the party became the vehicle for the white primary. Whites retained control of local offices until 1952, when the party was declared unconstitutional by a federal circuit court.

BIBLIOGRAPHY: Alwyn Barr, *Reconstruction to Reform: Texas Politics, 1876–1906* (Austin: University of Texas Press, 1971). Randolph B. Campbell, *A Southern Community in Crisis: Harrison County, Texas, 1850–1880* (Austin: Texas State Historical Association, 1983). Marshall *News Messenger,* April 6, 1952. Lawrence D. Rice, *The Negro in Texas, 1874–1900* (Baton Rouge: Louisiana State University Press, 1971).
Christopher Long

CITRUS FIESTA. The Citrus Fiesta is a two-week festival held annually in Mission to publicize the citrus industry of the region and to attract visitors. It occurs in December or January, depending on the harvest season. It was started by John H. Shary[qv] in the late 1920s. A royal court chosen from prominent valley families includes King Citrus, Queen Citrianna, the Princess of Orange Blossom, the Princess of Grapefruit Blossom, a lady-in-waiting, Princess Anna (who must be six years old), and her attendants, the Princess of Lime Blossom and the Princess of Lemon Blossom. The king's and queen's attendants include the royal crown bearer and four train bearers for the queen's train, which can be up to twenty feet long. Twenty-two duchesses are selected from valley communities. Crowns are designed for each new king, queen, and fiesta theme. The queen's gown was originally made of by-products from citrus plants.

The first annual fiesta was held in 1932 with the theme "Coronation and Pageant of Citrus." The one-day celebration included a coronation ceremony with Shary as King Citrus I and citrus exhibits, fruit-packing contests, a flying circus, a football game, and a parade. By 1934 the fiesta was expanded to two days with the addition of the Fiesta Style Show and the Fruit, Vegetable, and Flower Style Show, which features costumes made from local agricultural products. In 1936 the Texas Citrus Fiesta was officially incorporated as a nonprofit organization. By 1939 the celebration included an air show and a one-day school holiday so that Mission children could participate in the first day of the festival. In 1941 Lloyd M. Bentsen, Jr., was crowned king and the theme was "The Rio Grande Valley Serves America;" that year the tourist parade was introduced. From 1942 to 1946 the fiesta was cancelled due to World War II.qv In 1948 the Ex-Kings Association was formed and given the duty of selecting the new king. The following year the Texas Citrus Fiesta got its own building, and by 1950 it was underwritten by the Mission City Merchants and became self-supporting. The fiesta continued to become more elaborate through the 1950s, and in 1961 there was an unsuccessful attempt to move it to McAllen. C. B. Curtis carved a new queen's scepter out of an orange branch in 1963, and it became the first year that the Queen's gown was required to be all white and no longer had to be citrus products. By 1970 the Texas Citrus Fiesta had become a week-long celebration with a multitude of events, including skeet-shooting tournaments and the international motorcycle races.

By 1982 the Fruit, Vegetable, and Flower Style Show had been renamed the Product Costume Show to allow the use of other natural products as cover on costumes. The devastating freeze of 1983 that killed half the producing trees in the valley led to changes in the fiesta. The Parade of Oranges floats were allowed to be covered by natural products other than citrus, and the Products Style Show allowed the use of ashes and sawdust from destroyed trees. By 1989 the fiesta had been expanded to two weeks. Added to original activities and events were the Fiesta Fun Fair, which included the Little Fest for children, a petting zoo, and local food specialties.

BIBLIOGRAPHY: Marker Files, Texas Historical Commission, Austin.

Alicia A. Garza

CITRUS FRUIT CULTURE. Citrus fruit growing in Texas was probably begun by Spaniards who in the eighteenth century planted seven orange trees on the Laguna Seca Ranch north of Edinburg in what is now Hidalgo County. Oranges and satsumas, many from trees imported from Japan, were produced along the Texas coast in fairly large quantities as early as 1910, when 42,384 orange trees produced 10,694 boxes of oranges; shortly thereafter two citrus associations were formed—the Texas Citrus Growers' Association and the South Texas Citrus Fruit Growers' Association. The first commercial grove of grapefruit trees was planted in 1904; by 1925 approximately 80 percent of the Texas citrus crop consisted of grapefruit, the remainder of the crop being 15 percent oranges and 5 percent limes, lemons, tangerines, and kumquats. By that time the citrus fruit industry had centered in the Rio Grande valley,qv and more than 500 carloads of fruit were exported annually. Production along the coast to the east had practically disappeared. In 1932 there were 7,864,000 citrus trees in Texas, of which 5,966,369 were grapefruit, 1,671,758 were oranges, and the remainder were kumquats, limes, lemons, mandarins, satsumas, sour oranges, and tangelos. Hidalgo, Cameron, and Willacy counties were the largest producers. During the depression of the 1930s the growers, because of surplus production and a poor fresh-fruit market, started processing grapefruit juice, orange juice, frozen orange concentrate, and orange powder to solve their marketing problem.

Citrus fruits in the Valley, after the peak harvests of 1947 and 1948, suffered disastrous freezes in 1949 and 1951 which killed 7,000,000 of the 9,000,000 producing grapefruit and orange trees. In 1952 the citrus fruit industry began rehabilitation of its groves, while the canning industry in South Texas temporarily turned to vegetable canning. By 1959 the United States Department of Agriculture census reported that the industry had been rebuilt to the extent of 3,165,932 grapefruit trees on 2,299 farms and 2,428,543 orange trees on 2,129 farms. Approximately 39,201 lemon trees, which continued to have limited significance because of their lack of cold resistance, were reported on 298 farms; lesser production of limes, tangerines, kumquats, and other citrus fruits was also reported in that year. In 1964 the Texas citrus fruit industry produced 2,400,000 boxes of grapefruit valued at $8,016,000 and 1,000,000 boxes of oranges valued at $3,810,000. Tangerines, tangelos, and tangors, as well as limes, kumquats, and various ornamental hybrids such as calamondin and citrangequats, continued to have only small acreage in Texas. In 1966 Texas produced 5,600,000 boxes of grapefruit valued at $10,152,000 and 2,800,000 boxes of oranges valued at $5,808,000, placing it second and third, respectively, in the nation in production of these fruits. The 1967–68 crop harvested by December 1968, however, totaled only 2,800,000 boxes of grapefruit and 1,800,000 boxes of oranges. Production for the 1968–69 season was estimated to be 6,500,000 boxes of grapefruit and 4,100,000 boxes of oranges, a 126 percent increase over the 1966 crop and a 230 percent increase over the 1967 crop. Production for the 1970–71 season was estimated to be 10,000,000 boxes of grapefruit and 5,900,000 boxes of oranges of all varieties. In 1982–83 growers were able to sell grapefruit for only $2.16 a box and oranges at $4.65 a box. They sold a total of 16.9 million boxes with a value of $50,550,000. In 1985 Texas growers had 30,600 acres planted with citrus trees, with the majority of the acreage devoted to grapefruit and oranges. A freeze in 1983 had killed more than half of the state's 8,072,640 citrus trees. A freeze in 1989 wrecked citrus production in Cameron, Hidalgo, and Willacy counties. In 1991–92, grapefruit farmers harvested 65,000 boxes at $15.12 per box for a total gross of $982,800. That year, 30,000 boxes of oranges sold for $14.37 a box with a value of $431,100. Production of citrus fruits other than oranges and grapefruits continues to be limited.

BIBLIOGRAPHY: J. C. Bowen, The Citrus Fruit Industry of the Lower Rio Grande Valley of Texas (B.B.A. thesis, University of Texas, 1925). Mariita Cecilia Conley, The Role of the Labor Contractor in the Farm Labor Market of South Texas: The Case of the Citrus Industry (M.A. thesis, University of Texas at Austin, 1976). Federal-State Market News Service, *Marketing Texas Citrus* (1978). Camilo Martinez, The Mexican and Mexican-American Laborers in the Lower Rio Grande Valley of Texas, 1870–1930 (Ph.D. dissertation, Texas A&M University, 1987). Eldo Smith, *Progreso Haciendas: Citrus Fruit and Farm Lands in the Lower Rio Grande Valley of Texas* (Weslaco, Texas: Progreso Development Company, 1930?).

W. H. Friend

CITRUS GROVE, TEXAS. Citrus Grove is at the junction of two rural roads four miles northeast of Collegeport in southwestern Matagorda County. It was named for citrus orchards that were planted in the early 1900s. By 1910 the community was a stop on the St. Louis, Brownsville and Mexico Railway. That year the post office opened, and the population was twenty-five. In 1914 Citrus Grove had a gin, an express agent, a grocery and lumber business, a dry goods store, and a telephone connection. In 1925 the population had risen to fifty, but no businesses were registered. In 1936 Citrus Grove had eight scattered dwellings. In 1948, the last year that the settlement reported statistics, one business and fifty inhabitants were listed. As recently as 1989 the community still appeared on county maps, and in 1990 it was still listed as a community.

BIBLIOGRAPHY: Matagorda County Historical Commission, *Historic Matagorda County* (3 vols., Houston: Armstrong, 1986).

Stephen L. Hardin

CITY GOVERNMENT. Before 1836 there were in Texas no incorporated cities in the modern meaning of the term. The Spanish municipality included not only the settlement itself, but also large areas of surrounding territory that might cover thousands of square miles. Under Mexican rule, these settlements continued to serve as nuclei of the units of local government. With the advent of the Republic of Texas, the Texas Congress began enacting laws incorporating cities in the state. City charters could only be granted by the legislature until adoption of a constitutional home-rule amendment in 1912. With the passage of the enabling act the following year, numerous cities with more than 5,000 in population began writing and adopting charters. These charters set forth the type of government under which the city would operate, established the number of individuals to serve on the governing body, and authorized the city to perform many of the functions required when large numbers of individuals chose to live in close proximity to one another. The state constitution provided that the city charters could authorize the individual city to govern itself, subject only to the constitution and general laws of the state (*see* HOME RULE CHARTERS). For smaller cities, generally under 5,000 in population, the legislature, then and now, continues to set policy, and those "general law" cities are not authorized to perform any act or organize themselves in any fashion not expressly allowed by state law. Home rule cities in Texas now operate under one of two forms of city government: council-manager[qv] (251 of the 290 home-rule cities) and mayor-council[qv] (39 of the 290). The commission form of city government[qv] is now extinct in Texas; Portland, Oregon, is the only city of any size in the nation now operating under this form of local government.

BIBLIOGRAPHY: Terrell Blodgett, *Texas Home Rule Charters* (Austin: Texas Municipal League, 1994). Dick Smith, The Development of Local Government in Texas (Ph.D. dissertation, Harvard University, 1938).
Terrell Blodgett

CITY LAKE. City Lake was a natural lake on Little Mustang Creek a mile west of Ennis in eastern Ellis County (at 32°18′ N, 96°39′ W). Since the Bardwell Dam was completed in 1966 City Lake has become part of Bardwell Lake.

CIVIL AIR PATROL COMMISSION. The Civil Air Patrol Commission was established by the Sixty-second Texas Legislature in 1971 for the purpose of improving and promoting the Texas Civil Air Patrol, a voluntary civilian organization. The commission also promoted financing of the patrol and was active in aerospace education and training programs. Almost all of the state's air-oriented search-and-rescue operations were supplied by the Civil Air Patrol, and the commission helped in the deployment of the patrol's resources, manpower, and equipment for such emergencies. Working with the Texas Department of Public Safety,[qv] the commission was also involved in improving civil defense capabilities. The commission was composed of nine members appointed by the governor with concurrence of the Senate for six-year overlapping terms. Reports to the governor and the legislature were made by the commission. The commission was abolished after sunset review in 1981 (*see* TEXAS SUNSET ADVISORY COMMISSION).

CIVIL ENGINEERING. Civil engineers design and construct the elements of societal "infrastructure": facilities and systems related to water supply and treatment, sewage, and the protection of the environment; transportation systems; residential, commercial, manufacturing, and industrial structures; flood-control and other hydraulic projects; and projects made possible by geotechnical engineering. Since the turn of the century civil engineering has made remarkable contributions in Texas that have resulted in the enhanced protection of human health and wellbeing. In recent decades civil engineers have adopted advanced technologies in the area of information systems, automation, and telecommunications to improve the planning, design, construction, maintenance, and operation of infrastructure systems and in so doing to achieve cost savings and improved productivity. More such changes lie ahead.

Environmental Engineering. Every civilization in history has been located near an abundant fresh-water supply, for adequate potable water is essential for the development of any aggregation of human beings. A privately owned water-distribution system from wells was started in San Antonio in 1866, whereas large cities now operate public systems. Most of these depend on surface water impounded by dams, themselves designed and executed by civil engineers. People and industries have come to take water for granted and consider it an unlimited and free resource that should be delivered at minimal cost. But water supply may control the limits of industry in Texas. The estimated available surface and ground water supplies in Texas are estimated to be about 25 million acre-feet. Projected demands range from about 17 million to over 25 million acre-feet in the year 2000 and from 22 million to 30 million acre-feet in the year 2030. Estimated shortages range from 400,000 acre-feet (130 billion gallons) per year in 2000 up to about 5 million acre-feet (over 1.6 trillion gallons) in 2030. Of the total annual predicted water use in Texas in 2000 (25 million acre-feet, or 8.2 trillion gallons), drinking water represents more than 20 percent, irrigation[qv] and water for livestock account for about 63 percent, and industrial and manufacturing use constitute about 10 percent. Of the projected water use in 2030 (30 million acre-feet, or 9.8 trillion gallons) municipal use constitutes about 27 percent, industrial and manufacturing use about 18 percent, and irrigation about 50 percent. Development of such water supplies will require civil engineers to design and construct forty-one new dams and reservoirs to increase the safe yield of surface-water supplies. In addition, twenty-eight major pumping and conveyance facilities will be constructed to divert surface-water supplies from river basins in the state to the urban-industrial complexes by the year 2005. Civil engineers will also be called to dams, pipelines, distribution conduits, wastewater-collection systems, and other facilities to repair, replace, extend, and maintain the water in these areas.

Sanitary sewer construction was started in Dallas in 1881. Now, in almost every city in Texas, civil (environmental) engineers have designed and constructed municipal wastewater systems to transport wastewater to biological wastewater-treatment facilities. Approximately 60 to 70 percent of the water used for municipal purposes is returned as wastewater. New or upgraded facilities are required to be in compliance with the Water Pollution Control Amendments of 1972 and subsequent years. In the future, environmental engineers will be called on to design more efficient treatment facilities to enhance maximum recycling and reuse. Improved facilities have also resulted in the production of more sludges and biosolids. The amount of sludge generated by a city of 10,000 people is about a ton of dry solids or about 1,000 gallons of liquid sludge a day. Environmental engineers have designed facilities to convert sludge to beneficial biosolids through composting, and to energy through biodegradation in anaerobic digestion or incineration. The development of other innovative and cost-effective technologies offers opportunities for civil engineers to convert these wastes into usable resources. Liquid sludge has been mixed with clay to make bricks, for instance; organic solids burn in the kiln and reduce the requirement for auxiliary fuel.

Civil engineers have designed and constructed facilities for the treatment and disposal of municipal refuse, municipal and industrial sludges, industrial solid wastes and hazardous wastes. Protection of the health and safety of the public and maintenance of the quality of the environment are added challenges. The land has been the principal receptacle of these waste materials. Leachates from many waste disposal sites have flowed into usable groundwater supplies and polluted them. The volume and tonnage of municipal refuse and wastewater treatment plant sludges pose continued challenges to the civil engineer. Municipal refuse exceeds more than one ton per person annually. Available land for refuse disposal in sanitary landfills in the proximity of the urban-industrial centers is rapidly disappearing. Therefore, environmental engineers will have to develop further innovative, efficient technologies for the conversion of refuse to energy and for the reclamation of recyclable and reusable constituents of refuse. Environmental engineers have developed different technologies to treat contaminants in hazardous wastes by in situ bioremediation and restored the quality of water in contaminated aquifers. Hazardous wastes often pose potential health and environmental problems. Many exhibit possible carcinogenic, mutagenic, or other adverse properties. It falls within the purview of civil engineering to design and construct proper facilities to minimize contamination of surface and underground water and, in general, protect the environment. Environmental engineers will continue to address the protection of water resources, control of pollution, and disposal of hazardous wastes as well as the design and construction of facilities to provide safe drinking water and a clean environment. *See also* BOARD OF WATER ENGINEERS *and relevant articles beginning with* WATER *and* TEXAS WATER.

Transportation Engineering. Harbor, railroad, highway, and airport development depends upon civil engineering. Before 1851 transportation in Texas was confined to boat traffic along the coast and the lower reaches of a few rivers or to animal-drawn vehicles on the few and primitive roads to the interior (*see* RIVER NAVIGATION). As railroads*qv* developed, river transportation declined, but the Gulf ports were built up. All the thirteen deepwater ports in Texas today have artificial harbors dredged in relatively shallow areas. The port of Houston is fifty miles from deep water and was made possible in 1925 by dredging of the Houston Ship Channel.*qv* The second railroad west of the Mississippi River, the Buffalo Bayou, Brazos and Colorado Railway, was in Texas. The twenty miles running west from Harrisburg were begun in 1851 and put into service in 1853. By 1862 engineers had built some 492 miles of track, largely in the Gulf Coast area. Stimulated by grants of state land, a new era of railroad construction began about 1870, reaching a peak of 1,669 miles built in the year 1881 and 1,096 miles in 1882, at which time grants ceased. The 17,078 miles of track in Texas in 1932 declined to 15,586 miles by 1949, when several branch lines were abandoned because of highway competition.

Highways had a humble beginning. An early specification of the Republic of Texas*qv* called for a road thirty feet wide with tree stumps not to exceed twelve inches high. Under state law counties were responsible for all early highway work, but they naturally built more local roads than highways. In cities pavements were gradually introduced: creosoted wood blocks in 1875, asphalt in 1897, brick in 1899, concrete about 1910. But most pavements were limited to city streets or highways near large cities until the Highway Department was established in 1917 (*see* STATE DEPARTMENT OF HIGHWAYS AND PUBLIC TRANSPORTATION). By 1950 the department had developed 33,648 miles of paved highways. In 1945 the department began the construction of farm-to-market roads, and the building of expressways within all the larger cities began in 1949 (*see* HIGHWAY DEVELOPMENT). By 1970–80, Texas had the largest mileage of interstate highways in the United States and had a total highway system second to none in the nation. Approximately 70,000 miles of highway, the backbone of the state's transportation system, provided good access to markets and facilitated technical growth.

Aviation*qv* has also reaped the rewards of civil engineering. All major cities and many smaller towns in Texas have airports. In 1972, the Dallas–Fort Worth International Airport*qv* was the largest airport in the world. Though no longer the biggest, it has been expanded many times since then and serves as a major hub for air travel all over the world. Houston Intercontinental Airport*qv* is a major international hub and has fueled the industrial development of the state. Air traffic continues to grow in Austin, San Antonio, and other population centers. Texas is also the home of two major air carriers. American Airlines, one of the largest air carriers in the world is owned by AMR Corporation*qv* and headquartered in Fort Worth. Southwest Airlines*qv* has offices in Dallas. As a result of its innovative pricing structure, faster handling methods, and speedy turnaround of planes, Southwest has changed the face of the airline industry. Many low-cost carriers have developed nationwide, but none has been as successful as Southwest Airlines, which now serves both the east and west coasts.

Structural Engineering. Railroads and highways also need bridges, which are a product of structural engineering. The first bridge across the Brazos, the Waco Suspension Bridge,*qv* used Roebling wire rope, iron from New Jersey, and three million locally produced bricks. It was completed in 1870. Subsequently, John A. Roebling used similar cable for the Brooklyn Bridge in New York. The Houston Street viaduct (Dallas, 1911) and Paddock viaduct (Fort Worth, 1914) served as prototypes for similar concrete arch viaducts across the growing western United States. Other notable bridges are the Rainbow Bridge*qv* at Port Arthur and the Pecos High Bridge,*qv* a railroad bridge. Before 1940, Texas bridges for rail and for highways were reliable adaptations of forms and styles developed in the Midwest and Atlantic coastal states. After 1950 the Texas Highway Department achieved national recognition for applications with composite steel-concrete girders, prestressed concrete, expressway-interchange structures, and segmental construction of bridges. Research facilities at the University of Texas at Austin and Texas A&M University contributed to the success of these innovative bridge systems. Noteworthy steel bridges in Texas include bridges across the ship channels in Corpus Christi and Beaumont, the bridge over the Colorado River on the Capital of Texas Highway (Loop 360) in Austin, and a bridge across the Devils River canyon, which appeared to be much deeper before Amistad Reservoir*qv* was impounded. Ferguson Structural Engineering Laboratory of the University of Texas at Austin gained international recognition during the latter decades of the twentieth century. The company began activities in 1960 and took its current name in 1980. Research at the Ferguson Laboratory involves studies of the design, construction, and repair of bridges, buildings, and special-purpose structures. Laboratory facilities include a three-dimensional structural test facility, fatigue-testing capabilities that have been expanded with the procurement of new computer-based data systems and unique cable-test equipment, and advances in structural materials. At the lab, full-size components can be tested under random amplitude and frequency to simulate actual service conditions. Advanced stress-analyzing techniques such as stress analysis with computer-controlled thermal imaging and three-dimensional nonlinear finite element analysis are utilized to evaluate specimen behavior. Approximately two-thirds of the research conducted at Ferguson Laboratory is related to bridge structures. In 1995 the faculty of Ferguson Laboratory served code and specification authorities for steel, concrete, timber, masonry, and bridge structures, and its graduates held prominent industrial and faculty positions throughout the world.

The growth of Texas cities encouraged structural engineers to produce many tall buildings and brought about the growth of internationally prominent structural-design firms. Notable buildings of reinforced concrete include the Medical Arts Building (Dallas 1909), the Mills Building (El Paso, 1915), the Gulf Building*qv* (Houston 1929), and One Shell Plaza (Houston 1969). Each of these was one of the tallest buildings ever constructed at the time of its completion. Design firms from Houston (e.g., CBM, Incorporated, and Walter P. Moore, Incorporated) and Dallas (e.g., Ellisor and Tanner, Incorporated, and Datum, Incorporated) helped change urban skylines in Texas, other states, and other countries. Other unique tall structures include the San Jacinto Monument*qv* (1937) and the Hemisfair '68*qv* Tower in San Antonio (1966).

Texas structural engineers and petrochemical companies have also made major contributions to the offshore oil industry. Indeed, the earliest offshore platforms for radar installations in World War II*qv* were known as "Texas towers." Research and engineering design for ocean structures has been managed by large corporations with headquarters in Texas. Some of the largest such structures were built in the Gulf of Mexico.*qv*

Open spaces and the need for rapid transport have prompted Texas to become a leader in aircraft design and manufacture, another area in which structural engineering is practiced. The Lyndon B. Johnson Space Center^qv near Houston has been the source for development and application of structural plastics and very lightweight structural systems.

Hydraulic Engineering. Since Texas rivers have high flood flows, floods are a major problem (*see* WEATHER). More than 100 levee districts have been formed, and many miles of levees have been built. A levee system combined with river-channel improvement has reclaimed a large industrial area near the middle of Dallas. Many combined flood-control and power dams have been built. Olmos Reservoir^qv at San Antonio, built solely for flood protection, avoids all long-time storage. The first large reservoir constructed in Texas was a dam for power on the Colorado River at Austin in 1890. This dam failed in the flood of 1900 and was later rebuilt. The Medina River Dam for irrigation followed in 1912. By 1950 almost every major Texas river had at least one dam. In 1949 the total reservoir capacity was nearly three times that of ten years earlier; dams under construction subsequently increased the capacity another 80 percent. The Lower Colorado River Authority,^qv established in 1934, developed a unified power and flood-control program originally utilizing four, and later six, dams. When built, Mansfield Dam (at Lake Travis^qv), 270 feet high, was the fourth largest masonry structure in the world. The Brazos River Authority^qv has brought about similar control for the Brazos River. Denison Dam on the Red River impounds the huge Lake Texoma.^qv

A notable early hydraulic problem was the protection of Galveston after the catastrophic Galveston hurricane of 1900.^qv Structural engineers directed the building of a massive seawall and the raising of most of the city from three to ten feet by a giant earth-filling job that cost nearly twice as much as the wall.

Geotechnical Engineering. The development of theories, field equipment, and laboratory devices to characterize soils and rocks for the design and construction of foundations, embankments, pavements, and retaining structures began before 1925, when Austrian Karl Terzaghi's *Erdbaumechanik* was published. The book, along with technical articles in engineering journals, stimulated great interest and a burst of activity. The author traveled from Austria to the United States and lectured at various universities, including the University of Texas, in the summer of 1941. The development of geotechnical engineering, called soil mechanics and foundation engineering at first, began in Texas in earnest in the early 1930s, when Professor Raymond F. Dawson joined the University of Texas, and in 1942, when Professor Spencer J. Buchanan joined Texas A&M University. Soil-mechanics laboratories were established at the universities, and instruction began for both undergraduate and graduate students. Dawson established the Texas Conference on Soil Mechanics and Foundation Engineering. The first conference was in 1938. The eighth, in 1956, was the final one because the American Society of Civil Engineers had begun a division to serve geotechnical engineers in the United States. At the last Texas conference, which had the theme of geotechnical engineering for offshore structures, the proceedings included papers by Terzaghi and other notable authors, including Bramlette McClelland, who established the first major firm in Texas aimed exclusively at the practice of geotechnical engineering. McClelland's firm developed innovative techniques for the sampling of offshore soils and did research that led to improvements in the design of pile foundations. Many firms now are engaged in the practice of geotechnical engineering, several in each of the major cities in Texas. Undergraduate and graduate instruction is offered by several colleges of engineering in Texas, and research is conducted by faculty and students at these universities as well as at private and governmental agencies. The firms and agencies in the practice of geotechnical engineering are making use of steady advancements from research and are using modern methods in the development of facilities for transportation, water supply and treatment, industrial plants, the central city, and private dwellings. Geotechnical engineers have been active participants in the design and construction that has characterized the recent industrial growth in Texas and are contributing significantly to improvements in the environment.

CIVILIAN CONSERVATION CORPS. The Civilian Conservation Corps, proposed by President Franklin Roosevelt, operated nationwide between 1933 and 1942. it provided outdoor employment for 2.5 million young men working out of nearly 3,000 camps. The camps of 200 men each were supervised by the United States Army and the work projects by the departments of Agriculture and Interior, in cooperation with the state. At individual camps the CCC hired LEMs ("locally experienced men") to work as craftsmen and teachers, and professional architects and engineers to provide design assistance and construction supervision to enrollees. To be an enrollee, a young man was required to be seventeen to twenty-five years of age and from a family on relief. The pay was thirty dollars a month, of which twenty-five dollars was sent directly to the family. Veterans of World War I^qv were also eligible and were housed in separate camps.

At its peak in Texas the CCC operated camps with a capacity of 19,200 men. Assignment to states was random, so workers in Texas came from all over the country. Although most camps were devoted to soil-conservation and erosion-control projects, about twenty-five were responsible for the development of state parks. The average CCC enrollee in Texas was twenty years old and served two six-month terms. Participants performed heavy, semiskilled, outdoor labor; most worked on seeding, sodding, planting trees, banking slopes, or building roads and small dams. The enacting statute for the CCC forbade discrimination based on race, color, or creed. Still, the 200,000 black enrollees were often segregated, especially in the South. The CCC offered participants a variety of activities in addition to work. The young men could enroll for classes in camp or in local high schools or colleges and earn educational credits from the elementary to the college level. They could also participate in a sports program that often included baseball, football, and track.

The CCC declined as the economy recovered; the advent of World War II^qv brought prosperity and new priorities, and in the summer of 1942 the program ended. Nearly 50,000 Texans were enrolled in the CCC between 1933 and 1942. They left behind significant physical improvements to forest and farmland and passed on soil-conservation information to more than 5,000 farmers. In addition, CCC work in Texas was significantly responsible for development of the state's park system and its architectural legacy. Of the fifty-six state parks established through CCC efforts, thirty-one are still in existence, including Bastrop, Davis Mountains, Garner, Goliad, and Palo Duro Canyon state parks.^qqv Several CCC city and county parks also remain in Texas.

BIBLIOGRAPHY: John A. Salmond, *The Civilian Conservation Corps* (Durham, North Carolina: Duke University Press, 1967). James Wright Steely, *The Civilian Conservation Corps in Texas State Parks* (Austin: Texas Parks and Wildlife Department, 1986).

Kenneth E. Hendrickson, Jr.

CIVIL-RIGHTS MOVEMENT. Civil-rights campaigns in Texas are generally associated with the state's two most prominent ethnic minorities: African Americans and Mexican Americans.^qqv Mexican Americans have made efforts to bring about improved political circumstances since the Anglo-American domination of Texas began in 1836. African Texans have fought for civil rights since their emancipation from slavery^qv in 1865. Organized campaigns, however, were not launched until the early twentieth century.

Issues of immediate concern to Mexican Americans after the Texas Revolution^qv centered around racist actions. In the 1850s, Tejanos faced expulsion from their Central Texas homes on the accusation that they helped slaves escape to Mexico. Others became victims of Anglo wrath around the Goliad area during the Cart War^qv of 1857, as they did in South Texas in 1859 after Juan N. Cortina's^qv capture of Brownsville. Following the Civil War, both the newly freed slaves and

African-American college students protest segregation at the University of Texas, Austin, April 27, 1949. UT Texas Student Publications, Inc., Photographs, CAH; CN 02653. While UT admitted African Americans to some graduate and professional programs in 1950, it continued to exclude black undergraduates until 1956.

Tejanos faced further atrocities. In the 1880s, white men in East Texas used violence as a method of political control, and lynching[qv] became the common form of retaliation for alleged rapes of white women or for other insults or injuries perpetrated upon white society. Mexican Americans of South Texas experienced similar forms of brutality. The Ku Klux Klan,[qv] the White Caps, law officials, and the Texas Rangers,[qv] all acting as agents of white authority, regularly terrorized both Mexican Americans and black Texans.

De facto segregation followed emancipation. Freedmen found themselves barred from most public places and schools and, as the nineteenth century wore on, confined to certain residential areas of towns. By the early twentieth century, such practices had been sanctioned by law. Whites never formulated these statutes with Tejanos in mind, but they enforced them through social custom nonetheless. By the 1880s and 1890s, furthermore, minority groups faced legal drives to disfranchise them, though Anglos turned to a variety of informal means to weaken their political strength. African and Mexican Americans faced terrorist tactics, literacy tests, the stuffing of ballots, and accusations of incompetence when they won office. Political bosses in South Texas and the El Paso valley, meantime, attempted the Mexicans' domination through the controlled franchise.

In 1902 the legislature passed the poll-tax law (see election laws), and the next year Texas Democrats implemented the white primary.[qv] These mechanisms disfranchised blacks, and Mexican Americans for that matter, for white society did not regard Tejanos as belonging to the "white" race. Progressive reformers of the age viewed both minority groups as having a corrupting influence on politics. By the late 1920s, Texas politicians had effectively immobilized African-Texan voters through court cases that defined political parties as private organizations which could exclude members. Some scholars have estimated that no more than 40,000 of the estimated 160,000 eligible black voters retained their franchise in the 1920s.

Newer Jim Crow laws in the early twentieth century increased the segregation of the races, and in the cities, black migrants from the rural areas joined their urban compatriots in ghettoes. The laws ordinarily did not target Mexicans, but were enforced on the premise that Mexicans were an inferior and unhygienic people. Thus Tejanos were relegated to separate residential areas or designated public facilities. Hispanics, though mostly Catholic, worshiped in largely segregated churches. Blacks and Hispanics attended segregated and inferior "colored" and "Mexican" schools. As late as the mid-1950s, the state legislature passed segregationist laws directed at blacks (and by implication to Tejanos), some dealing with education, others with residential areas and public accommodations. Gov. R. Allan Shivers,[qv] who opposed the 1954 *Brown v. Board of Education* decision, went so far as to call out the Texas Rangers at Mansfield in 1956 to prevent black students from entering the public school (*see* MANSFIELD SCHOOL DESEGREGATION INCIDENT). Although Marion Price Daniel, Sr.,[qv] Shivers's successor, was more tolerant, the integration process in Texas was slow and painful. Supreme Court decisions in 1969 and 1971 ordered school districts to increase the number of black students in white schools through the extremely controversial practice of busing.

Violence in the era until the Great Depression[qv] years resembled that of the nineteenth century. In the ten-year period before 1910, white Texans lynched about 100 black men, at times after sadistic torture. Between 1900 and 1920, numerous race riots broke out, with black Texans generally witnessing their homes and neighborhoods destroyed in acts of vengeance. Similarly, Tejanos became victims of Anglo wrath for insult, injury, or death of a white man, and Anglos applied lynch law to Tejanos with the same vindictiveness as they did to blacks.

African and Mexican Americans criticized segregationist policies and white injustices via their newspapers, labor organizations, and self-help societies. Black state conventions issued periodic protests in the 1880s and 1890s. On particular occasions during the nineteenth century, communities joined in support of leaders rising up against perceived wrongs or in behalf of those unjustly condemned. Tejanos, for one, rallied behind Juan N. Cortina and Catarino Garza,qv and contributed to the Gregorio Cortez Defense Network, which campaigned for the defense of a tenant farmer named Gregorio Cortez,qv who killed a sheriff in Karnes County in self-defense in 1901.

The period between 1900 and 1930 saw continued efforts by minorities to break down racial barriers. In 1911 Mexican-American leaders met at the Congreso Mexicanistaqv in Laredo and addressed the common problems of land loss, lynchings, ethnic subordination, educational inequalities, and various other degradations. In 1919 the Brownsville legislator J. T. Canalesqv spearheaded a successful effort to reduce the size of the Texas Ranger force in the wake of various atrocities the rangers had committed in the preceding decade. La Agrupación Protectora Mexicana, founded in 1921, had as its intent the protection of farm renters and laborers facing expulsion by their landlords.

Much of the leadership on behalf of civil rights came from the ranks of the middle class. Black leaders established a chapter of the National Association for the Advancement of Colored Peopleqv in Houston in 1912, three years after the founding of the national organization; by 1930 some thirty chapters existed throughout the state. The association pursued the elimination of the white primary and other obstacles to voting, as well as the desegregation of schools, institutions of higher education, and public places. Tejanos established their own organizations to pursue similar objectives, among them the Orden Hijos de America (Order of Sons of Americaqv). The order was succeeded in 1929 by the League of United Latin American Citizens,qv which committed itself to the same goals of racial equality.

Mexican Americans and Black Texans continued their advocacy for equality during the depression era. In San Antonio, Tejanos founded La Liga Pro-Defensa Escolar (School Improvement Leagueqv), which succeeded in getting the city's school board to build three new elementary schools and make improvements in existing facilities. Mexican Americans in the Gulf Coast area near Houston and in El Paso organized the Confederación de Organizaciones Mexicanas y Latino Americanasqv in the late 1930s, also for the purpose of eradicating racist policies. The black movement, for its part, won increased white support in the 1930s from the ranks of the Association of Southern Women for the Prevention of Lynchingqv and from such prominent congressmen as Maury Maverick.qv

After World War II,qv Tejano war veterans founded the American G.I. Forum,qv and by the 1950s, LULAC and the Forum became the foremost Mexican-American groups using the legal system to remove segregation, educational inequities, and various other discriminatory practices. In 1961 the politically oriented Political Association of Spanish Speaking Organizationsqv joined LULAC and the G.I. Forum to pursuing the goal of mobilizing the Texas-Mexican electorate in an effort to prod mainstream politicians to heed the needs of Hispanics. African Americans, meantime, undertook poll-tax and voter-registration drives through the Democratic Progressive Voters League;qv the white primary had been declared illegal in 1944. During the 1960s the Progressive Voters League worked to inform black people about political issues and encouraged them to vote.

During the 1960s both African Americans and Mexican Americans took part in national movements intended to bring down racial barriers. Black Texans held demonstrations within the state to protest the endurance of segregated conditions. They also instituted boycotts of racist merchants. In conjunction with the National March on Washington in 1963, approximately 900 protesters marched on the state Capitol.qv The group, which included Hispanics, blacks, and whites, attacked the slow pace of desegregation in the state and Governor John Connally'sqv opposition to the pending civil-rights bill in Washington. By the latter half of the sixties, some segments of the black community flocked to the cause of "black power" and accepted violence as a means of social redress, though the destruction of property and life in Texas in no way compared to that in some other states. In a similar manner, Tejanos took part in the Chicanoqv movement of the era, and some, especially youths, supported the movement's militancy, its denunciation of "gringos," and its talk of separatism from American society. The Raza Unida partyqv spearheaded the movement during the 1970s; as a political party, Raza Unida offered solutions to inequalities previously addressed by reformist groups such as LULAC and the G.I. Forum. Members used demonstrations and boycotts and confrontational approaches, but violence of significant magnitude seldom materialized. The movement declined by the mid-1970s.

During the same period, the federal government pursued an agenda designed to achieve racial equality, and Texas Mexicans and Black Texans both profited from this initiative. The Twenty-fourth Amendment, ratified in 1964, barred the poll tax in federal elections, and that same year Congress passed the Civil Rights Act outlawing the Jim Crow tradition. Texas followed suit in 1969 by repealing its own separatist statutes. The federal Voting Rights Act of 1965 eliminated local restrictions to voting and required that federal marshals monitor election proceedings. Ten years later, another voting-rights act demanded modification or elimination of at-large elections.

After the 1960s several organizations joined LULAC and the G.I. Forum in the cause of equality for Mexican Americans. The Mexican American Legal Defense and Education Fund,qv founded in 1968, emerged as the most successful civil-rights organization of the late twentieth century. It focused on the state's inequitable system of financing schools, redistricting, and related problems. Working to see the increasing political participation of Tejanos and the removal of obstacles to Tejano empowerment was the Southwest Voter Registration Education Project.qv Groups at the city level that sought to help out barrio residents included COPS in San Antonio, and EPISO in the El Paso area. The struggle for civil rights also produced a number of favorable court decisions. Black Texans won a judicial victory in 1927 when the Supreme Court ruled in *Nixon v. Herndon* that the white primary violated constitutional guarantees. When the state circumvented the decision by declaring political parties to be private organizations that had the right to decide their own memberships, blacks again turned to the courts. Not until the case of *Smith v. Allwright* (1944) did the Supreme Court overturn the practice.

The post-World War II era came to be a time of increased successes for civil-rights litigants. The case of *Sweatt v. Painter*qv (1950) integrated the University of Texas law school, and in its wake several undergraduate colleges in the state desegregated. The famous case of *Brown v. Board of Education* (1954) produced the integration of schools, buses, restaurants, and other public accommodations. Mexican Americans won similar decisions that struck at discriminatory traditions. The decision in *Delgado v. Del Rio ISD* (1948) made it illegal for school boards to designate specific buildings for Mexican-American students on school grounds; *Hernandez v. Driscoll CISD*qv (1957) stated that retaining Mexican-American children for four years in the first two grades amounted to discrimination based on race; *Cisneros v. Corpus Christi ISD*qv (1970) recognized Mexican Americans as an "identifiable ethnic group" so as to prevent the subterfuge of combining Mexicans and blacks to meet integration; and *Edgewood ISD v. Kirby*qv (1989) held that the system of financing public education in the state discriminated against Mexican Americans. In another significant case, *Hernandez v. State of Texas*qv (1954), the United States Supreme Court recognized Mexican Americans as a class whose rights Anglos had violated through Jim Crow practices.

BIBLIOGRAPHY: Evan Anders, *Boss Rule in South Texas: The Progressive Era* (Austin: University of Texas Press, 1982). Alwyn Barr, *Black Texans: A History of Negroes in Texas, 1528–1971* (Austin: Jenkins, 1973). Arnoldo De León, *The Tejano Community, 1836–1900* (Albuquerque: University of New Mexico Press, 1982). Arnoldo De León, *They Called Them Greasers: Anglo Attitudes Toward Mexicans in Texas, 1821–1900* (Austin: University of Texas Press, 1983). Ignacio M. Garcia, *United We Win: The Rise and Fall of La Raza Unida Party* (Tucson: University of Arizona Mexican American Studies Research Center, 1989). Michael L. Gillette, "Blacks Challenge the White University," *Southwestern Historical Quarterly* 86 (October 1982). Michael L. Gillette, "The Rise of the NAACP in Texas," *Southwestern Historical Quarterly* 81 (April 1978). Darlene Clark Hine, *Black Victory: The Rise and Fall of the White Primary in Texas* (Millwood, New York: KTO Press, 1979). David Montejano, *Anglos and Mexicans in the Making of Texas, 1836–1986* (Austin: University of Texas Press, 1987). Merline Pitre, *Through Many Dangers, Toils and Snares: The Black Leadership of Texas, 1868–1900* (Austin: Eakin, 1985). Guadalupe San Miguel, Jr., *"Let All of Them Take Heed": Mexican Americans and the Campaign for Educational Equality in Texas* (Austin: University of Texas Press, 1987). James Smallwood, *Time of Hope, Time of Despair: Black Texans during Reconstruction* (London: Kennikat, 1981).

Arnoldo De León and Robert A. Calvert

CIVIL WAR. The sectional controversies that divided the North and South in the 1850s deeply troubled Texans (*see* ANTEBELLUM TEXAS). While most Texans had a strong attachment to the Union that they worked so hard to join in 1845, they expressed increasing concern over the attacks upon Southern institutions by Northern political leaders. Although only one Texas family in four owned slaves, most Texans opposed any interference with the institution of slavery,qv which they believed necessary for the continued growth of the state.

Many Texans considered the election of Abraham Lincoln to the presidency (November 1860) as a threat to slavery. They urged Governor Sam Houston qv to call a convention of the people to determine what course of action the state should take. Houston, devoted both to Texas and the Union, paid little heed to these requests, refusing to take any step that might aid secession.qv The demands for a convention increased, however, with the secession of South Carolina in December 1860 and the calling of state secession conventions in Mississippi, Florida, Alabama, Georgia, and Louisiana in early January. A group of secessionist leaders, including O. M. Roberts, John S. (Rip) Ford, George M. Flournoy, and William P. Rogers,qqv issued an address to the people calling for the election of delegates to a state Secession Convention qv in early January. Houston attempted to forestall the convention by calling a special session of the legislature and recommending that it refuse to recognize the convention. Instead, the legislature gave approval to the convention, on the condition that the people ratify its outcome by a final vote.

The convention, which assembled in Austin on January 28, 1861, was dominated by secessionists. On February 1 the delegates adopted an ordinance of secession by a vote of 166 to 8. This ordinance was approved by the voters of the state, 46,153 to 14,747, on February 23. The convention reassembled in early March, declared Texas out of the Union, and adopted a measure uniting the state with other Southern states in the newly formed Confederate States of America. Governor Houston, who refused to recognize the authority of the convention to take this action, refused to take an oath of allegiance to the new government, whereupon the convention declared the office of governor vacant and elevated Lieutenant Governor Edward Clark qv to the position. President Lincoln offered to send troops to assist Houston if he would resist the convention, but Houston rejected the offer rather than bring on civil conflict within the state. He retired to his home in Huntsville, where he died on July 26, 1863.

While the campaign for ratification of the secession ordinance was being waged in mid-February, the Committee of Public Safety

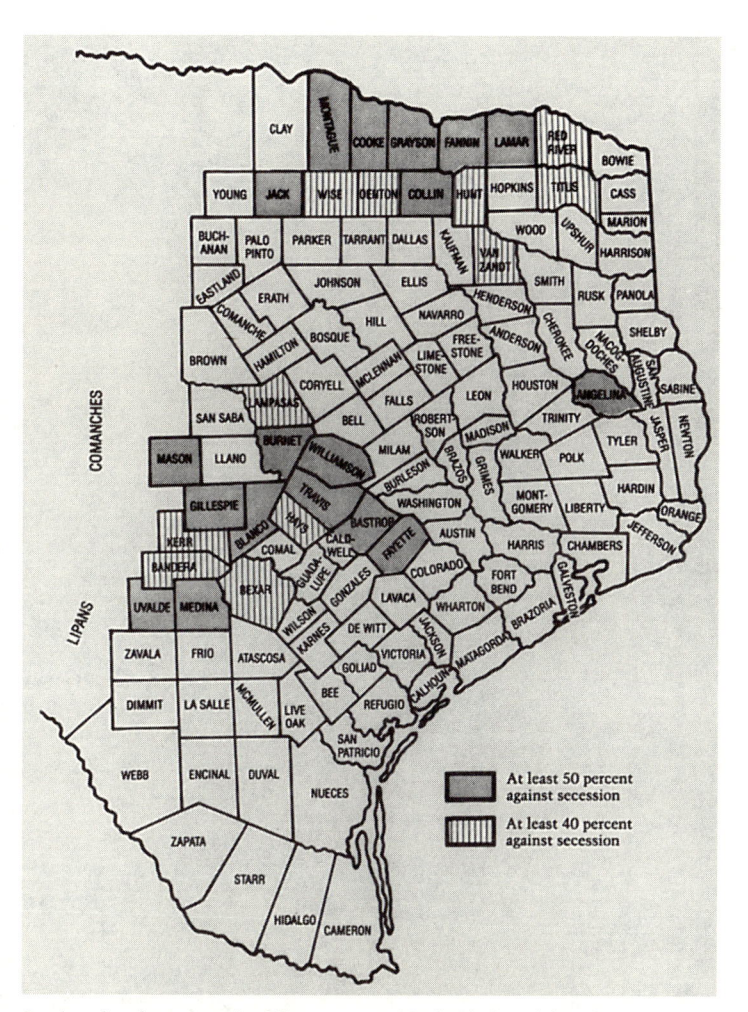

Popular referendum on secession, February 23, 1861. Map by Liz Conrad, from Secession and the Union in Texas *by Walter Buenger, Copyright © 1984. Courtesy University of Texas Press. Photograph courtesy CAH; CN 08486.*

assembled by the secession convention took steps to take over federal property in the state (*see* COMMITTEES OF PUBLIC SAFETY). The committee opened negotiations with Maj. Gen. David E. Twiggs,qv the commander of United States troops stationed in Texas. Twiggs, an aging Georgian in poor health, was awaiting orders from the War Department. On the morning of February 16, Benjamin McCulloch,qv a veteran Texas Ranger and Mexican War qv hero and now colonel of Texas cavalry, led at least 500 volunteers into San Antonio, where they surrounded Twiggs and his headquarters garrison. Twiggs agreed to surrender all federal property in Texas and evacuate the 2,700 Union troops scattered in frontier forts throughout the state.

The Committee of Public Safety authorized the recruiting of volunteer troops during late February and March 1861. In addition to troops recruited by Ben McCulloch, regiments of cavalry were enrolled by Henry E. McCulloch,qv Ben's younger brother, and John S. Ford, veteran ranger captain and explorer. The firing on Fort Sumter in April 1861 and the subsequent call for volunteers by Confederate president Jefferson Davis qv stimulated efforts by Texas authorities to raise additional troops. Governor Clark divided the state first into six and later into eleven military districts for recruiting and organizing the troops requested by Confederate authorities.

By the end of 1861, 25,000 Texans were in the Confederate army. Two-thirds of these were in the cavalry, the branch of service preferred by Texans. Lt. Col. Arthur Fremantle of the British Coldstream Guards, who visited Texas during the war, observed this fondness for

Surrender of General David E. Twiggs's federal forces and stores to Texas Confederate militia, San Antonio, February 16, 1861. Ambrotype. Courtesy TSL. This photograph was taken on Soledad Street in San Antonio, facing north, and is believed to be a scene associated with Twiggs's surrender. Terms of the surrender were negotiated in the Veramendi Palace, shown here in the center of the picture.

cavalry service: "it was found very difficult to raise infantry in Texas," he said, "as no Texan walks a yard if he can help it." Governor Clark observed that "the predilection of Texans for cavalry service, founded as it is upon their peerless horsemanship, is so powerful that they are unwilling in many instances to engage in service of any other description unless required by actual necessity."

Francis R. Lubbock,[qv] who defeated Clark by a narrow margin in the 1861 gubernatorial election, worked closely with Confederate authorities to meet manpower needs as the war expanded. Recruitment became more difficult as some of the early enthusiasm waned. The passage of a general conscription law by the Confederate Congress in April 1862 momentarily gave impetus to volunteering. Under this law all white males between the ages of eighteen and thirty-five were liable for military service. In September the upper age limit was raised to forty-five, and in February 1864 the age limits were extended to seventeen and fifty. The Confederate conscription laws did contain many exemptions, however, and for a time conscripted men could hire substitutes.

Approximately 90,000 Texans saw military service in the war. Governor Lubbock reported to the legislature in November 1863 that the army numbered 90,000 Texas residents, but this figure seems high for Texans in service at any one time. The 1860 federal census lists 92,145 white males between the ages of eighteen and forty-five years living in the state. Allowing for a slight increase in population during the four years of the war and considering that some Texans younger than eighteen and older than fifty served, one may say that between 100,000 and 110,000 Texans were potential soldiers.

Two-thirds of the Texans enrolled in the military spent the war in the Southwest, either defending the state from Indian attacks and Union invasion or participating in expansionist moves into New Mexico Territory. One regiment, recruited mainly in the Houston area, served under the colorful Rip Ford in South Texas. Ford commanded the military district of the Rio Grande, which extended from the mouth of the river for more than 1,000 miles to above El Paso. During the course of the war, Ford's men battled Union invaders, hostile Comanches, and Mexican raiders led by Juan N. Cortina.[qv]

Other Texas regiments patrolled North and West Texas. In May 1861 Col. William C. Young[qv] and the Eleventh Texas Cavalry, recruited in North Texas, crossed the Red River and captured federal forts Arbuckle, Cobb, and Washita. Another regiment, enrolled originally as state troops and known as the Frontier Regiment,[qv] patrolled Northwest Texas between the Red River and the Rio Grande. The regiment, commanded first by Col. James M. Norris and later Col. James E. McCord,[qqv] was transferred to Confederate service as the

Forty-sixth Texas Cavalry. Part of the regiment was later moved to the Houston area, and its place on the frontier was taken by state troops commanded by Brig. Gen. James W. Throckmorton,qv who was appointed commander of the northern military district by state authorities.

Texans played a major role in Confederate efforts to expand into New Mexico Territory. In June 1861 four companies of Ford's cavalry, under the command of Lt. Col. John R. Baylor,qv were ordered to occupy the extreme western part of Texas. Baylor reached Fort Bliss at El Paso in early July and later in the month moved into New Mexico. He occupied the small town of Mesilla, located on the left bank of the Rio Grande about forty miles north of El Paso. After a small skirmish, federal troops commanded by Maj. Isaac Lynde surrendered Fort Fillmore, on the opposite bank of the Rio Grande. On August 1, 1861, Baylor decreed the existence of the Confederate Territory of Arizona, with its capital at Mesilla and himself as the military governor.

Meanwhile, Henry H. Sibley,qv a West Point graduate and veteran soldier, convinced President Davis that the Confederates could capture New Mexico and Arizona. Sibley was commissioned brigadier general with orders to raise and equip a brigade of cavalry to drive federal forces from New Mexico. In August he established his headquarters in San Antonio, where he began recruiting men for the "Army of New Mexico." In early November the brigade, consisting of three regiments, began the long march to El Paso, nearly 700 miles distant. Sibley's brigade reached El Paso on December 14. On January 11, 1862, it marched to Mesilla, where Sibley assumed the command of Baylor's forces. Sibley moved northward along the west bank of the Rio Grande to Fort Craig, where he encountered Union forces commanded by Col. Edward R. S. Canby,qv perhaps Sibley's brother-in-law. The Confederates won a battle at nearby Valverde ford but were not strong enough to capture the fort (*see* VALVERDE, BATTLE OF). Sibley decided to bypass the fort and move northward to capture Albuquerque and Santa Fe. Morale in his army was low. Commissary supplies were virtually exhausted, the weather was bitterly cold, and many of the men were highly critical of Sibley himself. On March 26 his men fought a spirited battle with Colorado militia at Apache Canyon to the east of Santa Fe. Two days later a larger battle was fought in Glorieta Pass (*see* GLORIETA, BATTLE OF) between federals led by Col. Maj. John M. Chivington and Texans commanded by Col. William R. Scurry.qv In the fierce engagement the Texans drove the federals from the field. Late that afternoon, however, Scurry's supply train was captured by Union forces. The loss of the supply train was a major blow to Sibley's plans. With Union forces receiving reinforcements from Colorado and California, Sibley determined to retreat down the Rio Grande. By early May the Confederates were back at Fort Bliss, where Sibley issued an address praising his men for their sacrifices. Many of the Texans who served under Sibley blamed the commander for their failure and expressed the view that better leadership would have brought success to the campaign.

The defense of the Texas coastline was more successful than the New Mexico invasion. Brig. Gen. Earl Van Dorn,qv commander of the Texas district from April to September 1861, organized defense companies, authorized the use of slave labor for building fortifications, and worked to secure heavy cannons for coastal defense. His successor as district commander, Brig. Gen. Paul Octave Hébert,qv also made efforts to secure heavy ordnance, but with only limited success. Hébert concluded that he would be unable to prevent a landing on the coast and determined to fight the enemy in the interior.

In November 1861 Union naval forces began a series of harassing activities along the Texas coast. The Confederate patrol schooner *Royal Yacht* was partially burned, and Confederate positions near Aransas Pass, Port Lavaca, and Indianola were shelled. The naval blockade of the Texas coastline was intensified in 1862; the United States bark *Arthur,* commanded by Lt. John W. Kittredge, was especially active along the middle coast. In August Kittredge, commanding a small flotilla, attempted to capture Corpus Christi but was re-

Santos Benavides. Courtesy Laredo Public Library. Benavides attained the rank of brigadier general, becoming the highest-ranking Mexican American in the Confederate service. His troops pushed Juan Cortina and his force back into Mexico in 1861, and repelled a federal assault on Laredo in 1864.

pulsed by Confederates commanded by Maj. Alfred M. Hobby.qv Another, more successful, Union force commanded by Lt. Frederick Crocker destroyed a small fort at Sabine Pass and burned the railroad bridge at Taylor's Bayou.

The main Union attack against the Texas coast in 1862 was aimed at the state's largest seaport, Galveston (*see* GALVESTON, BATTLE OF). On October 4, 1862, a small Union fleet commanded by W. B. Renshaw sailed into Galveston harbor. Confederate artillery at Fort Point opened fire but was quickly silenced by superior Union gunpower. Renshaw demanded and received the surrender of the city. The loss of Galveston was followed by a change in Confederate command in Texas. General Hébert, who had never been popular with Texans, was replaced by Gen. John Bankhead Magruder,qv a Virginian with a reputation as an aggressive soldier. Magruder quickly made plans for the recapture of Galveston. He called for land forces to move across the railroad bridge from the mainland at night to surprise Union garrison troops, while two river steamers converted to gunboats, the *Bayou City*qv and the *Neptune,* sailed into the harbor to attack federal warships. The Confederate assault began shortly after midnight on New Year's Day, 1863. At 1:00 A.M., while federal troops slept, Magruder led his forces across the railroad bridge connecting the island and the mainland. Between 4:00 and 5:00 A.M., Confederate artillery opened fire on federal ships and positions along the waterfront. The two Confederate gunboats attacked the Union fleet soon thereafter. The *Neptune* was hit by a shell from the U.S.S. *Harriet Lane,*qv veered into shallow water, and sank. The *Bayou City* meanwhile moved alongside the *Harriet Lane.* The "Horse Marines"qv stormed aboard, captured the vessel, and hauled down her colors. Other Union ships in the harbor had troubles of their own. The Union flagship, the *Westfield*,^{qv} ran aground on Pelican Spit, and efforts by a sister ship, the *Clifton*,^{qv} to move her were unsuccessful. Three other small Union vessels, *Sachem*,^{qv} *Owasco,* and *Corypheus,* fired on Confederate troops near the waterfront without much success. In the midst of the excitement, the *Westfield* was rocked by an internal explosion caused by premature detonation as her commander, Renshaw, prepared to destroy the ship rather than risk capture. The explosion killed Renshaw and fourteen crewmen. Union naval forces now pulled out of the harbor, and the Union infantry soon surrendered to Magruder. Galveston was once again in Confederate possession.

Union naval forces continued to maintain a blockade of the Texas coastline throughout the war, but its effectiveness is difficult to measure. Ships loaded with cotton sailed out of Galveston and other Texas ports several times a week, while other vessels sailing from Havana and Caribbean ports returned with trade goods, munitions, and Enfield rifles. Unfortunately for the Confederacy, the Texas blockade runners, like those elsewhere in the South, were never adequately directed and organized for the highest degree of efficiency. Furthermore, the number of Union warships in the blockade increased with each passing month of the war. In an effort to tighten control of the Texas coastline, Maj. Gen. Nathaniel P. Banks,^{qv} the Union commander of the Department of the Gulf, with headquarters in New Orleans, planned a major operation in the fall of 1863. He intended to land a large military force near Sabine Pass, march overland to Houston, and capture Galveston. To this effort he assigned 4,000 troops of the Nineteenth Army Corps, commanded by Maj. Gen. William B. Franklin. Transport vessels carrying the troops were to be protected by four light-draft gunboats, the *Clifton, Sachem, Arizona,* and *Granite City.*

The Union fleet appeared off the upper Texas coast in early September. Franklin planned to move his gunboats up the narrow channel at Sabine Pass, knock out the guns of the small Confederate fort guarding the waterway, and bring his transport vessels into Sabine Lake,^{qv} where landings could be made. The only obstacle was the rough earthwork fortification known locally as Fort Griffin and defended by a battery of Confederate artillery of forty-seven men commanded by Lt. Richard W. Dowling,^{qv} an Irish barkeeper from Houston. On September 8, 1863, the four Union gunboats entered the channel and opened fire on Fort Griffin. The six cannon from the Confederate installation responded with high accuracy, firing 107 rounds in thirty-five minutes. The *Sachem* was hit on the third or fourth round and driven up against the Louisiana side of the channel, a helpless wreck. The Confederates then turned their fire on the *Clifton.* A cannonball cut her tiller rope, throwing her out of control, and she soon ran aground. Many of the crew jumped overboard and made it to shore, where they were captured by the Confederates. The two other Union gunboats, the *Arizona* and the *Granite City,* turned and withdrew from the pass. General Franklin, overestimating the size and nature of the Confederate defense, ordered a withdrawal back to New Orleans. Dowling and his men were awarded medals by the Confederate government for their victory.

Union troops were temporarily more successful in southern Texas. In November 1863, 7,000 soldiers commanded by General Banks landed at the mouth of the Rio Grande and captured Brownsville, cutting the important trade between Texas and Mexico. Banks then sent one wing of his army upriver to capture Rio Grande City and another column along the coast to capture Corpus Christi, Aransas Pass, and the Matagorda peninsula. General Magruder called upon state and Confederate authorities for additional forces to halt the advance. Fortunately for the Confederacy, many of Banks's troops were transferred to Louisiana, where a major Union offensive was planned for the spring of 1864. This allowed Confederate and state troops commanded by John S. Ford to retake most of the area occupied by Union forces. In the summer of 1864 Ford recaptured Brownsville and reopened the vital trade link with Mexico. By the end of the war the only Union holding on the lower Texas coast was Brazos Island.

Union campaigns in Arkansas and Louisiana in 1864 involved thousands of Texans. In March, General Banks moved an army of 27,000 men and a naval flotilla up the Red River toward Shreveport. He hoped to link up with federal troops under Gen. Frederick Steele, who was moving southward from Little Rock, and then extend federal control over Northeast Texas. In an effort to prevent this, Texas troops in Indian Territory commanded by Brig. Gen. Samuel Maxey^{qv}—Gano's Brigade,^{qv} Walker's Choctaw brigade, and Krumbhaar's battery, which was attached to Gano's brigade—were moved to Arkansas, where they joined Sterling Price in halting the Union advance at Camden.

Banks, meanwhile, continued his advance in northwest Louisiana. On April 8, 1864, part of his army was defeated at Sabine Crossroads, near Mansfield, by Confederates under the command of Richard Taylor.^{qv} Texans played a major role in the battle, which halted Banks's advance. Confederates resumed the attack the next day at Pleasant Hill, fourteen miles to the south, but superior Union numbers prevented a Southern victory (*see* RED RIVER CAMPAIGN). Once again Texas units—including Walker's Texas Division;^{qv} Thomas Green's^{qv} cavalry, which consisted of five brigades in three divisions led by Hamilton P. Bee, James Patrick Major, and William Steele;^{qqv} and Polignac's Brigade^{qv}—figured prominently in the fighting. Green, one of the most popular of all the Texans, was killed three days later while leading an attack on the retreating federals at Blair's Landing. Banks continued to retreat and in mid-May crossed the Atchafalaya River, thus ending attempts to invade Northeast Texas.

The large battles of the Civil War were fought beyond the Mississippi River, far from Texas. The state contributed thousands of men who participated in the great battles of the war. Texan Albert Sidney Johnston^{qv} was killed in the battle of Shiloh in April 1862 while commanding a major Confederate army. Another Texas officer, Gen. John Bell Hood,^{qv} lost the use of an arm at Gettysburg and a leg at Chickamauga. The Texas Brigade, originally commanded by Hood, had one of the finest reputations of any military unit. The brigade, including the First, Fourth, and Fifth Texas Infantry regiments, fought with honor at Gaines' Mill, Second Manassas, Sharpsburg, Gettysburg, and Chickamauga. A Texas regiment, the Eighth Texas Cavalry,^{qv} better known as Terry's Texas Rangers, distinguished itself on battlefields in Kentucky, Tennessee, Mississippi, Georgia, and South and North Carolina. Another brigade, commanded late in the war by Lawrence Sullivan Ross,^{qv} won praise for combat in Mississippi, Tennessee, and Georgia. Granbury's Texas Brigade,^{qv} commanded by Waco lawyer Col. Hiram B. Granbury,^{qv} also saw extensive action in Georgia and Tennessee. Granbury himself was killed in the futile Confederate assault at Franklin, Tennessee, in November 1864. Ector's Brigade,^{qv} consisting of the Tenth, Eleventh, Fourteenth, and Fifteenth Texas Dismounted Cavalry and commanded by Brig. Gen. Mathew Duncan Ector,^{qv} saw action in Tennessee, Mississippi, and Georgia and participated in Hood's invasion of Tennessee.

The task of recruiting and equipping the thousands of Texans in military service required diligent efforts by state authorities. Francis R. Lubbock, who served as governor during the first half of the war, was a most capable and energetic chief executive. At his request the legislature provided for reorganization of the state militia system, passed a revenue act raising taxes, and established the Military Board of Texas,^{qv} which had power to purchase military supplies and establish ordnance foundries and arms factories. Lubbock met frequently with Confederate political and military leaders in efforts to provide better cooperation in the war. Although Texas and the Southwest were cut off from the rest of the South with the fall of Vicksburg in the summer of 1863, Lubbock continued to emphasize the need for unity in support of the Confederacy.

The governor entered the military in December 1863 and did not seek reelection. In the contest to choose his successor, Pendleton

Murrah,qv a Harrison County lawyer and former state legislator, defeated Thomas Jefferson Chambers,qv four-time gubernatorial candidate and pioneer Gulf Coast rancher. The election centered upon support for the war effort. Although Murrah was less well known than Chambers, the Marshall lawyer benefited from Chambers's reputation as a political maverick and a critic of Jefferson Davis's administration. Most Texans regarded Murrah as the safer candidate. In office Murrah soon found himself involved in controversy with Gen. Edmund Kirby Smith,qv commander of the Trans-Mississippi Department. The disagreements related to a variety of relationships between the state and the central Confederate authority, including conscription laws, impressment of slave labor, transfer of Texas troops outside the war area, and supply matters. Particularly bitter was the controversy over government purchase of cotton, a disagreement that divided Smith, who had set up the national Cotton Bureau for purchasing and selling cotton, and Murrah, who developed a state plan for the same purpose. The matter was resolved in a meeting between Smith and Murrah at Hempstead in June 1864. Shortly thereafter, the governor requested that the people of Texas deliver their cotton to the army's agents for compensation and declared that the state would no longer compete with the military for the cotton.

The majority of Texans approved the efforts of governors Clark, Lubbock, and Murrah to support the Confederacy. Even so, Unionism remained strong in some sections of the state. This was especially true in some of the German counties in the Hill Countryqv and in a group of counties north of Dallas. Some of the early Texas Unionists such as James W. Throckmorton, who cast one of the eight votes against secession in the Secession Convention, and Ben H. Epperson,qv a leader of East Texans opposed to secession, accepted the Confederacy after Fort Sumter and vigorously supported the Southern cause. Others, such as David G. Burnet, Elisha M. Pease,qqv and Sam Houston, withdrew from public life and attempted to avoid controversy. Another group left the state or attempted to do so. Some of these, such as S. M. Swenson,qv the father of Swedish migration to Texas, and William Marsh Rice,qv a native of Massachusetts who made a fortune in the mercantile business in Texas, quietly left. Others joined the Union army in their efforts to defeat the Confederacy. Though most of the Mexican Americansqv from Texas who fought in the war joined the Confederate Army, some joined the Union Army, partly in memory of the events of the Texas Revolutionqv and its aftermath. The Second Texas Cavalry (U.S.), for example, was made up of mostly Texas Mexicans and Mexican nationals; the unit suffered a high desertion rate (*see* MEXICAN TEXANS IN THE CIVIL WAR). Some 2,132 whites and forty-seven blacks from Texas served in the Union Army. The best known of the Texans who supported the Union were Edmund J. Davis,qv a district judge who organized and commanded the First Texas Cavalry Regiment (Union), and Andrew J. Hamilton,qv Texas legislator and congressman, whom Lincoln appointed military governor of Texas after the war.

Texas Confederates dealt harshly with those attempting to assist the enemy. In August 1862 Fritz Tegener led sixty-five Unionists, mostly Germans from the Hill Country, in an unsuccessful attempt to cross the Rio Grande and flee from Texas. They were overtaken near the Nueces River by state troops commanded by Lt. C. D. McRae. Thirty-five of the Unionists were killed, and several others were wounded in the battle of the Nueces.qv Another fifty Union sympathizers were hanged in Gillespie County several weeks later. The greatest roundup of suspected Unionists occurred in Cooke and Grayson counties, north of Dallas. A citizens' court at Gainesville tried 150 individuals for Unionist activities. Some confessed, some were convicted, and thirty-nine were executed in what contemporaries called the Great Hanging at Gainesville.qv

The life of ordinary Texans was much affected by the war. Although the state suffered less economically than other Confederate states, many adjustments were necessary. The blockade resulted in shortages of many commodities, especially coffee, medicine, clothing, shoes, and farm implements. Homespun clothing was worn as in early days; Governor Lubbock was inaugurated in a homespun suit. The British visitor Colonel Fremantle reported that "the loss of coffee afflicts the Confederates even more than the loss of spirits; and they exercise their ingenuity in devising substitutes, which are not generally very successful." These substitutes included barley, corn, okra, peanuts, and sweet potatoes. Salt was so scarce that some Texans dug up the floors of their smokehouses and leached the dirt to recover the salt drippings. Thorns were used for pins, willow-bark extract and red pepper were mixed to substitute for quinine, and pieces of wallpaper served as writing paper. Several Texas newspapers suspended or discontinued operations for periods of time due to the lack of paper.

Hood's Texas Brigade, in camp. Courtesy Austin History Center, Austin Public Library; photo no. PICA 03674. Hood's Texas Brigade fought in most of the Virginia engagements. Its commander, John Bell Hood, went on to become commander of the Army of Tennessee.

On the other hand, trade with Mexico made more materials available to Texas than to other Confederate states. In return for cotton, Texans received military supplies, medicines, dry goods, food, iron goods, liquor, coffee, and tobacco. Matamoros, on the Rio Grande across from Brownsville, and Bagdad, Tamaulipas, a seaport village at the mouth of the Rio Grande, were the centers of this activity, in which hundreds of vessels from Europe and the United States engaged in a flourishing business. The trade was interrupted from time to time by Union military activities along the lower Texas coast, but even so it provided many items needed by Texans during the war.

The war brought other changes to Texas. Some adjustments were made in agriculture as farmers planted more corn to meet food needs and requests of the government to reduce cotton production. The absence of men away at the war front placed greater responsibilities and burdens upon women and children, who assumed increased duties. The shortage of free labor was partially offset by the increase in the number of slaves sent from other Southern states to Texas in an attempt to avoid the invading enemy armies. On occasion, military units were assigned harvesting duties.

Transportation was seriously affected by the war. The outbreak of fighting halted all railroad building for seven years, and difficulties in maintaining rolling stock caused existing service to be interrupted. General Magruder ordered segments of the Eastern Texas road and the Texas and New Orleans torn up for coastal fortifications. Several miles of track between Swanson's Landing and Jonesville in East Texas was taken up and relaid eastward from Marshall to Waskom for military purposes. Stagecoach lines continued to operate, but coaches were overcrowded and behind schedule. Roads and bridges suffered from lack of repair as labor and materials were diverted elsewhere.

The requirements of the military and the impact of the blockade caused rapid expansion of manufacturing in the state. The Texas State

Funeral of German patriots at Comfort, Texas, August 20, 1865. *Engraving published in* Harper's Weekly: A Journal of Civilization, *January 20, 1866. Photograph courtesy Special Collections Libraries, University of Texas at Austin. In August 1865, in the German community of Comfort, a funeral was held and a monument erected honoring Unionists who were killed in the battle of the Nueces.*

Military Board had the promotion of manufacturing as one of its responsibilities. Under its direction a percussion-cap factory and a cannon foundry were established in Austin. The board established a textile mill in the Texas State Penitentiary at Huntsville.qv During the war three million yards of cotton and wool cloth was produced at the Huntsville facility. The Confederate quartermaster department operated, or contracted for, facilities at Houston, Dallas, Austin, Tyler, Rusk, Paris, Jefferson, Marshall, Waco, and Hempstead for the manufacture of clothing, shoes, iron products, wagons, tents, harness, and saddles. A major ordnance works was established at Tyler, and smaller plants were located in or near Rusk, Jefferson, Houston, and Galveston (*see* GUN MANUFACTURE DURING THE CIVIL WAR). A beef-packing plant at Jefferson provided meat for the Confederate Army.

Although political and military leaders attempted to keep up the morale of Texans, military defeats in Georgia, Tennessee, and Virginia in late 1864 caused increased anxiety in the state. Newspaper editorials urged civilians to remain calm, and Governor Murrah and General Smith asked Texans to continue the struggle. News of Robert E. Lee'sqv surrender in April 1865, followed by that of Joseph E. Johnstonqv in North Carolina, made further resistance appear futile. Rip Ford defeated Union troops in the battle of Palmito Ranch,qv near Brownsville, on May 13, 1865, the last battle of the war. From captured prisoners Ford learned that Confederate forces were surrendering all over the South. Kirby Smith attempted to keep his command intact, but found his soldiers heading for their homes. Some Texans, including Murrah and former governor Clark, joined other Confederates fleeing to Mexico. On June 2, 1865, generals Smith and Magruder signed the formal terms of surrender for their commands, and on June 19 (Juneteenthqv) Gen. Gordon Grangerqv arrived in Galveston with Union forces of occupation. Reconstructionqv was in the offing. The Civil War had ended.

BIBLIOGRAPHY: Allen Coleman Ashcraft, Texas, 1860–1866: The Lone Star State in the Civil War (Ph.D. dissertation, Columbia University, 1960). Alwyn Barr, "Texas Coastal Defense, 1861–1865," *Southwestern Historical Quarterly* 65 (July 1961). Walter L. Buenger, *Secession and the Union in Texas* (Austin: University of Texas Press, 1984). Vera Lea Dugas, A Social and Economic History of Texas in the Civil War and Reconstruction Periods (Ph.D. dissertation, University of Texas, 1963). Robert Pattison Felgar, Texas in the War for Southern Independence, 1861–1865 (Ph.D. dissertation, University of Texas, 1935). Fredericka Meiners, The Texas Governorship, 1861–1865: Biography of an Office (Ph.D. dissertation, Rice University, 1974). Stephen B. Oates, "Texas under the Secessionists," *Southwestern Historical Quarterly* 67 (October 1963). *Official Records of the Union and Confederate Navies* (Washington: Department of the Navy, 1894–1927). David Paul Smith, *Frontier Defense in the Civil War: Texas' Rangers and Rebels* (College Station: Texas A&M University Press, 1992). *The War of the Rebellion: A Compilation of the Official Records of the Union and Confederate Armies*. Ralph A. and Robert Wooster, "'Rarin' For a Fight': Texans in the Confederate Army," *Southwestern Historical Quarterly* 84 (April 1981).

Ralph A. Wooster

CIVIL WAR INDUSTRY. Texas possessed few manufacturing establishments of significant size when she joined the Southern Confederacy in March 1861, but tremendous military requirements and the federal blockade soon forced the state to make every effort to encourage and expand manufacturing. Four agencies endeavored to supply the state and its troops with manufactured necessities: (1) the state, through both the Military Board of Texas[qv] and the penitentiary cloth factory, (2) the Confederate Army's quartermaster and ordnance shops (see GUN MANUFACTURING DURING THE CIVIL WAR), (3) extant private establishments and newly chartered wartime corporations, and (4) household industry.

The Military Board, established in 1862, built a percussion-cap factory and a cannon foundry at Austin, but only the cap factory contributed much, reportedly producing 100,000 caps during the last year of the war. The most important manufacturing plant, the Texas State Penitentiary at Huntsville,[qv] produced various cloth materials, including Osnaburgs, cotton jeans, and woolen plaids. The army reportedly received 1,419,364½ yards of cotton goods and 292,963½ yards of woolen goods from the factory between December 1, 1861, and December 18, 1863.

Texas troops received their initial clothing and equipage principally from local contributions. Ladies' aid societies spun, knitted, and sewed to outfit the volunteers from their communities. Throughout the war such household efforts were significant, but in 1862 the Confederate Quartermaster's Clothing Bureau began control of all clothing and equipage supply in the state. By January 1864 the army operated several major quartermaster depots and shops in Texas. Houston was the principal state depot, with shoe, tailor, tent, tin, and carpenter shops producing clothing, shoes, tinware, and wagon equipage. The Austin branch of the Houston depot produced shoes (principally), clothing, and miscellaneous items. The Tyler depot produced shoes and equipage. The San Antonio depot, tannery, and general shops produced shoes and general quartermaster supplies. Jefferson had a shoe factory and depot. The Marshall foundry (steam powered) produced skillets and camp kettles. And the Hempstead foundry (steam powered) produced skillets, camp kettles, and other metal products. Another branch of the Confederate quartermaster's department, the Field Transportation Bureau, established shops at Dallas, Tyler, Rusk, Mount Pleasant, Paris, Waco, and Hempstead. These shops employed civilian wheelwrights, blacksmiths, carpenters, saddlers, and harness-makers in the manufacture and repair of military transportation equipment. By February 1864 they were capable of producing 190 wagons, 6 ambulances, 900 sets of harness, and 360 saddles per month.

The legislature enacted several laws to encourage manufacturing. Two of these measures, passed on December 15, 1863, and November 7, 1864, respectively, granted 320 acres of land for each $1,000 worth of machinery set up by any concern before March 5, 1865. Few grants were made under these acts, however. In all, about forty manufacturing companies were chartered by special acts of the legislature during the war years, but little resulted from these paper incorporations. Typical of the companies chartered was the Fort Bend Manufacturing Company, authorized to manufacture cloth, fabrics, and wood, iron, or steel products. Companies designed to manufacture powder, iron, steel, bridges, cloth, and paper were chartered, but the results were disappointing.

BIBLIOGRAPHY: Robert Pattison Felgar, Texas in the War for Southern Independence, 1861–1865 (Ph.D. dissertation, University of Texas, 1935). Hans Peter Nielsen Gammel, comp., *Laws of Texas, 1822–1897* (10 vols., Austin: Gammel, 1898). Aldon Socrates Lang, *Financial History of the Public Lands in Texas* (Baylor Bulletin 35.3, Waco: Baylor University, 1932; rpt., New York: Arno Press, 1979). Frances Richard Lubbock, *Six Decades in Texas* (Austin: Ben C. Jones, 1900; rpt., Austin: Pemberton, 1968). James Lynn Nichols, *The Confederate Quartermaster in the Trans-Mississippi* (Austin: University of Texas Press, 1964). Charles W. Ramsdell, "The Texas State Military Board, 1862–1865," *Southwestern Historical Quarterly* 27 (April 1924).

James L. Nichols

CLAASSEN, ARTHUR (1859–1920). Arthur Claassen, choral and orchestral conductor, was born in Stargard, Prussia, on February 19, 1859. He studied at the Music School in Weimar, and as early as 1878 his youthful compositions aroused the attention of Franz Liszt, who gave him encouragement. From 1880 to 1884, Claassen was opera conductor in Göttingen and Magdeburg. Upon the recommendation of Leopold Damrosch, a disciple of Wagner, Claassen was chosen conductor of the New York Eichenkranz and, in 1890, of the Brooklyn Arion male singing societies. In nearly a quarter century under Claassen's baton, the Arion became one of the most celebrated choruses in the United States, earning him an audience with Kaiser Wilhelm II in 1900. Claassen conducted important American performances of Richard Wagner's *Liebesmahl der Apostel*, Felix Mendelssohn's *Midsummer Night's Dream* and Max Bruch's *Frithjof,* as well as a number of German operas. With the New York Liederkranz, he made recordings for Columbia Records after about 1910, and these were marketed in Texas.

In May 1913 Claassen was guest festival conductor for the Texas State Sängerfest, held in Houston. The Beethoven Männerchor of San Antonio was so impressed by his musicianship that in the spring of 1914 they invited him to become their permanent conductor. Thus Claassen became the first conductor of international reputation to assume full responsibility for a Texas musical organization. He took over the forty-three-voice male chorus and organized a sixty-voice women's chorus (the Mozart Society) to complement it. He also assumed charge of the sixty-member San Antonio Philharmonic (later the San Antonio Symphony Orchestra[qv]). In a newly refurbished Beethoven Hall he gave concerts of unprecedented sophistication in the Alamo City. An orchestral concert of March 15, 1917, is typical of Claassen's programming: Carl Maria von Weber's Euryanthe Overture, Robert Schumann's Piano Concerto, and Ludwig van Beethoven's Symphony No. 7, as well as light numbers by Liszt and himself. For the 1916 State Sängerfest, Claassen had combined all his forces for extensive excerpts from Wagner's *Die Meistersinger*. World War I[qv] signaled the decline of German ethnic prestige, however, and the influenza epidemic during the winter of 1918–19 brought concert life in San Antonio to a standstill.

Claassen's own compositions include the cantatas *The Battle and Festival Hymn,* the symphonic poem Hohenfriedberg, the Waltz-Idyll for string orchestra, and many songs and choruses. Claassen moved to San Francisco in July 1919 and died there on March 16, 1920.

BIBLIOGRAPHY: Theodore Albrecht, German Singing Societies in Texas (Ph.D. dissertation, North Texas State University, 1975). Theodore Albrecht, "101 Years of Symphonic Music in San Antonio," *Southwestern Musician/Texas Music Educator,* March, November 1975. *Baker's Biographical Dictionary of Musicians,* 7th ed. W. L. Hubbard, ed., *American History and Encyclopedia of Music* (12 vols., New York: Irving Squire, 1910), Vol. 5.

Theodore Albrecht

CLAIREMONT, TEXAS. Clairemont is at the intersection of U.S. Highway 380 and State Highway 208, fourteen miles southwest of Jayton and forty-three miles east of Post in central Kent County. The site was established as the county seat on land owned by R. L. Rhomberg when Kent County was organized in 1892. The town was named for Claire Becker, a relative of Rhomberg. A post office was established in December 1892 with Loulah Posey as postmistress. A courthouse and jail were constructed from local red sandstone and completed in 1895. By that time the town had several stores, a bank, a newspaper, and a hotel.

Although the Stamford and Northwestern Railway had bypassed Clairemont to the east by 1909, the town continued to prosper. Cotton and cattle ranching dominated the economy, and oil later became important. The population, a reported 150 during the 1930s and 1940s, grew to 300 in the 1950s, when the town's five businesses indicated a small-scale oil boom. Clairemont had several newspapers through the years, including the *Kent County Sentinel, Kent County News,* Clairemont *Enterprise,* and *Western Courier.* The lack of an adequate water source, declining cotton prices, and the removal of local oil camps, however, forecast an end to prosperity. After a two-year court battle Jayton became county seat in 1954. Loss of the county offices and consolidation with the Jayton schools in the 1950s caused a rapid decline. When the post office closed in 1970 Clairemont had two businesses and a population of thirty-five. The Clairemont courthouse burned shortly after the records were transferred to Jayton, and only the bottom story was preserved. Although several families lived in the area in the late 1980s, the sole resident of Clairemont was Margie (Ma) Hart. She operated the only remaining store—nicknamed the "Buzzer Den" for an earlier rash of rattlesnakes—which had become a popular local gathering place. In 1990 the population of Clairemont was recorded as fifteen.

BIBLIOGRAPHY: T. Lindsay Baker, *Ghost Towns of Texas* (Norman: University of Oklahoma Press, 1986). Jewell G. Pritchett and Erma B. Black, *Kent County and Its People* (Rotan, Texas: Rotan *Advance,* 1983). *Charles G. Davis*

CLAIRETTE, TEXAS. Clairette, on State Highway 6 some fifteen miles southeast of Stephenville in southeastern Erath County, was established when the Texas Central Railroad was constructed through the area in the early 1880s. The community was named for a popular brand of soap. In 1940 it had 275 residents, five businesses, several churches, and a post office. Changes in agriculture and transportation patterns subsequently reduced the town's prosperity. From 1968 until 1990 its population was estimated at fifty-five. The 1984 county highway map showed a church, a community hall, and three businesses at Clairette.

CLAM LAKE. Clam Lake is between the Gulf Intracoastal Waterway[qv] and State Highway 87, twenty-five miles south of Beaumont in southern Jefferson County (at 29°41′ N, 94°06′ W). It is fed by Salt Bayou and is roughly two miles long (east-west) and one mile wide (north-south) at its widest point. The Clam Lake oilfield, discovered in 1937, is just north of the lake. By 1984 it had produced over nineteen million barrels of oil.

BIBLIOGRAPHY: Railroad Commission of Texas, *Annual Report of the Oil and Gas Division,* 1984.

CLAMPITT, EZEKIEL (1805–1837). Ezekiel Clampitt, the oldest son of Nathan and Susanah Clampitt,[qv] was born in Wilson County, Tennessee, on June 14, 1805. He moved to Texas from Louisiana with his wife Catherine and son James in December 1825. He signed a petition denouncing the Fredonian Rebellion[qv] of 1827 and upholding the Mexican government. In March 1831 he received a Spanish land grant in Stephen F. Austin's[qv] second colony for one league near Gay Hill and homesteaded at Hidalgo Bluffs,[qv] overlooking the falls of the Brazos River. He farmed there until his death on March 27, 1837.

BIBLIOGRAPHY: Mrs. Harry Joseph Morris, comp. and ed., *Citizens of the Republic of Texas* (Dallas: Texas State Genealogical Society, 1977). Joyce Martin Murray, *Washington County, Texas, Deed Abstracts, 1834–1841* (Dallas, 1986). Worth Stickley Ray, *Austin Colony Pioneers* (Austin: Jenkins, 1949; 2d ed., Austin: Pemberton, 1970). Charles F. Schmidt, *History of Washington County* (San Antonio: Naylor, 1949). *Wayne Clampitt*

CLAMPITT, SUSANAH GRAVES (1781–1868). Susanah Clampitt, an early pioneer of Stephen F. Austin's[qv] second colony, was born on March 27, 1781, in Essex County, Virginia, and married Nathan Arnett Clampitt in Davidson County, Tennessee, on September 1, 1803. During their years farming in Wilson County, Tennessee, Susanah bore seven children. After Nathan's death in 1823, she moved to Texas in 1825 with her oldest son, Ezekiel Clampitt,[qv] and his family. She received a Spanish land grant in Washington County, one of the few women to hold a land title in her own name. She settled in Millican, Brazos County, where she married Moses Cummins.[qv] In 1841 Mrs. Clampitt gave two of her sons, Nathan and Francis G. Clampitt, 3,333 acres of her original land grant. She died on August 3, 1868.

BIBLIOGRAPHY: Mrs. Harry Joseph Morris, comp. and ed., *Citizens of the Republic of Texas* (Dallas: Texas State Genealogical Society, 1977). Joyce Martin Murray, *Washington County, Texas, Deed Abstracts, 1834–1841* (Dallas, 1986). Worth Stickley Ray, *Austin Colony Pioneers* (Austin: Jenkins, 1949; 2d ed., Austin: Pemberton, 1970). Charles F. Schmidt, *History of Washington County* (San Antonio: Naylor, 1949). *Wayne Clampitt*

CLANCLUIGUYGUEN INDIANS. In the eighteenth century this presumably Coahuiltecan band, also known as Clancluiguygu and Tlanchuguin, lived on the north bank of the lower Rio Grande between present Zapata and Rio Grande City.

BIBLIOGRAPHY: Gabriel Saldivar, *Los Indios de Tamaulipas* (Mexico City: Pan American Institute of Geography and History, 1943). *Thomas N. Campbell*

CLANTON, CLEORA (?–1968). Cleora Clanton, librarian, was born in Dallas to Susie E. Clanton. In 1915 she accepted a job with the Dallas Public Library and after a brief apprenticeship decided to make her career in library work. Over the next several years she served as a branch librarian, assistant librarian, and acting librarian before becoming head of the Dallas Public Library in 1927. She remained in this position for twenty-seven years. In it she worked for improved conditions and funding and oversaw the opening of the first branch library for the black community in Dallas. In the 1950s when librarians across the country were advised to remove all books on Communism from library shelves, she refused, noting that knowledge of Communism was not harmful. She led the campaign for construction of a new library building in downtown Dallas, which opened shortly after she retired. She began the use of bookmobiles in Dallas and implemented adult education in the library's film department. Cleora Clanton served as president of the Texas Library Association[qv] from 1931 to 1933. She was a member of the Oak Cliff Christian Church and, later, the First Community Church. She retired from the Dallas Public Library in 1955 and died in Dallas on September 16, 1968, survived by one brother and one sister. She was buried in Five Mile Cemetery.

BIBLIOGRAPHY: Dallas *Times Herald,* February 28, December 26, 1954, September 17, 1968. Larry Grove, *Dallas Public Library: The First 75 Years* (Dallas Public Library, 1977). *Debbie Mauldin Cottrell*

CLAPP, ELISHA (ca. 1803–1856?). Elisha Clapp, soldier and farmer, was born in Tennessee about 1803 and immigrated to Texas in 1822; he settled at Nacogdoches. He enlisted in Capt. Henry Wax Karnes's[qv] cavalry company on April 7, 1836, and participated in the battle of San Jacinto.[qv] Afterward he was detached to guard Mexican prisoners. He was discharged from the army on May 28, 1836. For his service Clapp received a labor of land in Houston County. On September 10, 1836, he was elected captain of a company of mounted rangers at his home at Mustang Prairie. Sam Houston,[qv] as commander in chief of the Texas army, ordered his company to "range from any point on the Brazos to Mr. Hall's Trading House on the Trinity" to intercept parties of raiding Indians. Clapp organized an expedition against the

Ionie Indians, who, according to one settler, "have been committing some depredations in the horse stealing way" on the frontier.

On May 31, 1837, President Houston nominated Clapp for a commission as captain and appointment to the command of the ranger company from Nacogdoches County. The Senate confirmed the nomination on June 13. Although Houston noted in his instructions to the auditor that Clapp was illiterate and that his muster roll must be monitored with special care, when Clapp moved to the Houston County community of Alabama he helped to organize and became one of the first eleven trustees of Trinity College, in April 1841. By March 1, 1849, he had moved to Leon County, where he and his wife, Rebecca Elizabeth (Robbins), and six of their eight children were living at the time of his death, which the *Texas Presbyterian*qv reported on December 6, 1851. Other sources state that he died in 1856. The value of his real property was estimated as $17,800.

BIBLIOGRAPHY: Daughters of the Republic of Texas, *Muster Rolls of the Texas Revolution* (Austin, 1986). Sam Houston Dixon and Louis Wiltz Kemp, *The Heroes of San Jacinto* (Houston: Anson Jones, 1932). *Houston County Cemeteries* (Crockett, Texas: Houston County Historical Commission, 1977; 3d ed. 1987). John H. Jenkins, ed., *The Papers of the Texas Revolution, 1835–1836* (10 vols., Austin: Presidial Press, 1973). Madison County Historical Commission, *A History of Madison County* (Dallas: Taylor, 1984). *Telegraph and Texas Register*, June 13, 1837, April 7, 1841. Gifford E. White, *1830 Citizens of Texas* (Austin: Eakin, 1983). Amelia W. Williams and Eugene C. Barker, eds., *The Writings of Sam Houston, 1813–1863* (8 vols., Austin: University of Texas Press, 1938–43; rpt., Austin and New York: Pemberton Press, 1970).
Thomas W. Cutrer

CLARA, TEXAS (Bee County). Clara was on the San Antonio and Aransas Pass Railway in southern Bee County. It was settled by E. O. Driscoll in 1857. When he donated the right-of-way to the railway in 1886, the settlement was named for his daughter. The community had a railroad switch and stock pens in 1946. Since that time most of the residents have moved away, and in the early 1990s only a few scattered houses remained.
Christopher Long

CLARA, TEXAS (Wichita County). Clara is on Farm Road 1813 and State Highway 240 twelve miles northwest of Wichita Falls in north central Wichita County. Development of the community began in April 1886, when Herman Specht filed the plat for a new town named in honor of his wife, Clara (Vogel). A Clara post office opened in 1886 but closed in 1892. The population reached thirty in 1890, a Lutheran church was built in 1900, and a one-room school served until 1929, when it joined Common School District No. 9. Clara grew to fifty residents by 1925, and the post office was open again from 1921 to 1925. In 1944 the school was consolidated with the Burkburnett school system. In 1936 Clara had a church, a cemetery, a school, and several businesses. From 1966 until 1990 the community reported 100 residents.

BIBLIOGRAPHY: Louise Kelly, *Wichita County Beginnings* (Burnet, Texas: Eakin Press, 1982).
David Minor

CLARDY, MARY M. (?–?). Mary M. Clardy, a late-nineteenth-century reformer, held positions in both the Prohibition party and the Texas state Farmers' Alliance.qv Her home was listed as Bexar when she attended the 1890 Prohibitionqv party state convention in Fort Worth as a member of the Committee on Platform and Resolutions. She was the only woman at that convention to serve in an official capacity. She advocated world trade markets for farmers in an 1890 article in the Farmers' Alliance newspaper, the *Southern Mercury*.qv She also contributed articles on the Populist party (*see* PEOPLE'S PARTY) and reform to the *National Economist*, the national Farmers' Alliance newspaper in Washington, D.C. In 1892 she was elected assistant state lecturer of the Farmers' Alliance of Texas, one of only three women elected to a state office in the Southern Farmers' Alliance. In 1892 the *Southern Mercury* gave her home as Sulphur Spring.

BIBLIOGRAPHY: Robert C. McMath, Jr., *Populist Vanguard: A History of the Southern Farmers' Alliance* (Chapel Hill: University of North Carolina Press, 1975). Melissa Gilbert Wiedenfeld, Women in the Texas Farmers' Alliance (M.A. thesis, Texas Tech University, 1983). E. W. Winkler, *Platforms of Political Parties in Texas* (Austin: University of Texas, 1916).
Melissa G. Wiedenfeld

CLARDY, TEXAS. Clardy is on Farm Road 905 fourteen miles southeast of Paris in southeast Lamar County. It grew up around the J. M. Dunlap store, in which the post office was established in 1899. James Dunlap, the storeowner and first postmaster, submitted a list of the surnames of six families living in the community from which the post office department chose the name. The post office was discontinued in 1907. In 1936 the community had a school, a church, and twenty-five residences within a one-mile radius. The population of Clardy peaked at fifty in the late 1940s, when one business, the local store, was in operation. In 1989 the community listed twenty-five telephone numbers, and the Bethel Baptist Church still held weekly church services and Sunday School classes.
Robert M. Towle

CLARE CREEK. Clare (Claire) Creek rises eight miles southeast of Jasper in northeastern Jasper County (at 30°52′ N, 93°53′ W) and runs southeast for nine miles to its mouth on White Oak Creek, in western Newton County (at 30°46′ N, 93°50′ W). It cuts through the gently undulating to hilly terrain surfaced by sandy and clay loam that supports loblolly, shortleaf, and longleaf pines. The area is used for timber production, woodland grazing, and pasturelands.

CLAREN, OSCAR VON (1812–1845). Oscar von Claren, naturalist, was born in Germany in 1812. As a colonist of the Adelsverein,qv he immigrated from Hannover to New Braunfels, Texas, probably early in 1845. His family correspondence indicated his interest in botany and wildlife of the New Braunfels area, and he collected turtles and snakes to sell to naturalists in Germany. He wrote *Indianer bei Neu Braunfels im Jahre 1845* (1845), a group of essays depicting Texas Indians. In October 1845, while on a collecting trip, Claren and his companion, Friedrich Wilhelm von Wrede,qv were killed by Indians near Manchaca Springs.

BIBLIOGRAPHY: Rudolph L. Biesele, *The History of the German Settlements in Texas, 1831–1861* (Austin: Von Boeckmann–Jones, 1930; rpt. 1964). S. W. Geiser, "A Century of Scientific Exploration in Texas," *Field and Laboratory* 7 (January 1939). Selma Metzenthin Raunick, "A Survey of German Literature in Texas," *Southwestern Historical Quarterly* 33 (October 1929). Solms-Braunfels Archives (transcripts, Sophienburg Museum, New Braunfels, Texas; Barker Texas History Center, University of Texas at Austin).
Clinton P. Hartmann

CLARENDON, TEXAS. Clarendon, on U. S. Highway 287 in central Donley County, is the county seat and chief commercial and shipping center of the county. Rev. Lewis Henry Carhart,qv a Methodist minister, promoted the colonization of the town through a partnership with his brother-in-law, Alfred Sully, of New York. The promoters bought railroad land scrip entitling them to 343 sections of land, most of which was in Donley County. In 1878 the Clarendon Land Investment and Agency Company, an English firm, began backing Carhart. The original site of Clarendon was on a flat at the junction of Carroll Creek and the Salt Fork of the Red River. There, on October 1, 1878, Carhart and his brother-in-law, W. A. Allen, established a "Christian Colony." Although tradition maintains that Clarendon was named in honor of Carhart's wife, Clara, it has also been argued that the name was borrowed from Clarendon, England, to compliment the British backers. The townsite was platted, and construction from such available materials as rock, adobe,qv and pickets began immediately. A post office was opened, and stagecoach communication with Mobeetie and Tascosa established. Supplies were freighted down the cattle trails from Dodge City. Soon Carhart and his associates attracted a substantial population. The church atmosphere in Clarendon (at one time the town had seven Methodist ministers) and the absence of bars caused the rowdier Panhandleqv inhabitants to call it "Saint's Roost." Indeed, the first edition of Edward E. Carhart'sqv Clarendon News (August 2, 1879) declared the town "a sobriety settlement." A public school was opened, and W. A. Allen made plans to establish a Methodist college, initially called Allenton Academy. In 1880, after L. H. Carhart left to resume his ministerial duties in East Texas, another of his brothers-in-law, attorney Benjamin Horton White, provided equally effective leadership for the colony. When Donley County was organized in 1882, Clarendon became the county seat and White was elected the first county clerk. A rock building originally used as a hotel was converted into a courthouse. White subsequently built a two-story frame hotel. Several stores, a meat market, a blacksmith shop, and a doctor's office were among the town's businesses by 1885.

In 1887, when the Fort Worth and Denver City Railway planned its line six miles south of the townsite, Clarendon's citizens voted overwhelmingly to move their homes and businesses to the tracks. Clarendon became a railroad division point and cultural center for the Panhandle, complete with an opera house. The first bank was organized in 1889, and a permanent brick-and-stone courthouse was completed in 1890. Homer Mulkey opened a photography studio in 1895. Although saloons and gambling dens flourished briefly in the Feather Hill section of town, these were shut down and cleared away in 1898 to make room for Clarendon College, which opened in the fall of that year. At about the same time, the Catholic populace built St. Mary's Academy. By then Clarendon had 200 residences, forty-six business establishments, six churches, and forty-five windmills. The town's reputation as a conservative bastion and the "Athens of the Panhandle" continued into the twentieth century.

In 1901 Clarendon was incorporated. The last legal hanging in the Panhandle occurred there on June 3, 1910. The city's independent school district purchased Clarendon College in 1927 and made it into a junior college. Since the town is located in a draw, its streets were frequently flooded until the 1930s, when the Work Projects Administrationqv built dams and terraces to turn the water away. The building of several gins and hatcheries attested to the town's increased importance as an agribusiness center. In 1950 Clarendon had eighteen businesses, ten churches, and a population of 2,577. By then the manufacture of cotton bags and covers had been added to the local light industry. In addition, Clarendon was a manufacturing center for farm and road equipment and leather goods. The population decreased from 2,172 in 1960 to 1,974 in 1970. In 1980 Clarendon had a population of 2,220 and seventy business establishments. Clarendon Lake is located to the northeast, and a small municipal airport is located southeast of town. The Clarendon Press, longtime publisher of western Americana, is in Clarendon. The two-story ranch home and studio of Clarendon's most famous citizen, western artist-illustrator Harold Dow Bugbee,qv which was built by his father in 1912, is northeast of town. Pete Borden's Boot and Saddle Shop contains an antique gun collection. The Donley County Museum features prehistoric specimens of local "Clarendonian Age" fossil beds, in addition to geological and historical artifacts. The original Saint's Roost townsite was inundated in 1968 by Greenbelt Reservoir. At that time the old cemetery was moved south on State Highway 70. In 1990 the population of Clarendon was 2,067.

BIBLIOGRAPHY: Virginia Browder, Donley County: Land O' Promise (Wichita Falls, Texas: Nortex, 1975). Willie Newbury Lewis, Between Sun and Sod (Clarendon, Texas: Clarendon Press, 1938; rev. ed., College Station: Texas A&M University Press, 1976).

H. Allen Anderson

CLARENDON COLLEGE. Two colleges, both known as Clarendon College, have operated at sites in Clarendon. The first, established in 1898 by the Methodist Episcopal Church, South, and administered as a junior college until 1926, was followed in 1927 by the present Clarendon College, a nonsectarian, state-supported, two-year college.

A Methodist minister, Rev. W. A. Allen, conceived the idea for Clarendon College in 1879, when he established Allenton Academy at old Clarendon. When the town moved to its present site on the Fort Worth and Denver City Railway in 1887, local citizens offered the Northwest Texas Methodist Conference four acres of land and promised to build a two-story building to relocate the college. Church leaders made it clear that they would build only if saloons were eliminated from the town. Rev. J. R. Henson, a local Methodist minister, led a campaign, which succeeded by 1902, to clear out the saloons in Clarendon's Feather Hill section and vote Donley County dry. In 1898, when the town's population was 2,756, construction began on the three-story building that housed president, administration, teachers, and students on Clarendon's ten-acre campus. The institution, known as Clarendon College and University Training School, was accepted by the conference and opened in the fall of that year with four teachers and twenty-one students. Classes were offered in all grades, and primary and intermediate departments existed until 1923. J. W. Adkisson, the first president, was followed by W. B. McKeown, J. Sam Barcus, G. S. Hardy, J. Richie Mood, G. S. Slover, R. E. L. Morgan, S. H. Condron, and, in 1984, Kenneth D. Vaughan.

Despite financial difficulty, by 1900 the school had a faculty of eight, property valued at $8,000, and 109 students. The first interscholastic football game in the Panhandleqv was played on December 5, 1903, when the Clarendon College Cowboys defeated neighboring Goodnight Academy 16 to 10. After a drop in enrollment in 1914, in 1916 Clarendon College had the largest enrollment of any junior college in the South. By 1919 the physical plant, with two additional frame dormitories and a new administration building, was valued at $175,000, and enrollment reached 350. The school added its third year of work in 1924 and its fourth in 1925 and was recognized as a four-year accredited institution. Baccalaureate degrees, awarded only in 1927, went to nineteen students.

After considering proposals to relocate the college at Amarillo, the Methodist Churchqv ceased supervision of the institution on August 15, 1927. School assets, valued at $654,749, were liquidated, and, on vote of the citizens, facilities were purchased by the Clarendon school board for the purpose of establishing a municipal junior college. In 1928 a vote to require a 20 percent ad valorem tax for support of the school was passed, and later the seven-member Clarendon College District voted a similar tax for the school's maintenance. In the 1960s the college moved to a new location, the former site of the home of pioneer rancher Thomas Sherman Bugbee,qv on a hill west of town. A new building complex was erected, and during the 1966–67 year, with a faculty of seventeen, enrollment reached 228. The college's Pampa Center, housed in Pampa's former Houston Elementary School, opened in December 1978 for night classes. In 1979 and 1980 vocational nursing programs were initiated with general hospitals in Shamrock and Childress. In 1980 the main campus maintained administration and classroom facilities, a physical education center, a fine arts building, a vocational-technological center, three dormitories, a cafeteria, and a library of over 19,000 volumes. During that year enrollment exceeded 400. Clarendon College is accredited by the Southern Association of Schools and Colleges and offers liberal arts and agriculture studies, as well as business and other vocational training. For the 1992–93 regular term, enrollment was 957 and the faculty numbered fifty-five.

BIBLIOGRAPHY: Virginia Browder, *Donley County: Land O' Promise* (Wichita Falls, Texas: Nortex, 1975). Macum Phelan, *History of Early Methodism in Texas, 1817–1866* (Nashville: Cokesbury, 1924); *A History of the Expansion of Methodism in Texas, 1867–1902* (Dallas: Mathis, Van Nort, 1937). Kate Talley, History of Clarendon College (M.A. thesis, West Texas State University, 1933).

H. Allen Anderson

CLARENDON LAKE. Clarendon Lake is a playa on the northeast edge of the Clarendon city limits in central Donley County (at 34°56′ N, 100°53′ W). It is used primarily for recreation. The surrounding terrain is flat to gently sloping surfaced by loose, sandy soil that supports mesquite, brush, and grasses.

CLAREVILLE, TEXAS. Clareville, located off Highway 59 and Farm Road 796 ten miles west of Beeville in southwestern Bee County, was established in 1874 and 1875 by Henry T. Clare and his sons. The community was first called Lomita, then received its present name in the late 1880s. Clare had come from Missouri to Texas in 1840 and later fought in the Mexican War.qv He married Ella Layton and in 1849 settled in Lavaca County, where he ranched. In 1856 he, his brother, and his five sons moved to the site of Central Community on Aransas Creek. In 1874 and 1875 they purchased and settled a large area of land that became Clareville. After enduring swarms of grasshoppers in 1879, they divided their land and sold to other settlers in the late 1880s. Businesses soon followed—J. H. Bell opened the first store in 1886. In 1898–99 a Clareville school had one teacher and forty-nine pupils. The arrival of the automobile and better roads focused the community's attention upon nearby Beeville, and businesses in Clareville closed. The estimated population of Clareville had fallen to fifty by 1940, and the schools were consolidated into the Skidmore-Tynan school system. In 1989 the community had a population of twenty-three.

BIBLIOGRAPHY: Grace Bauer, *Bee County Centennial, 1858–1958* (Bee County Centennial, 1958). Camp Ezell, *Historical Story of Bee County, Texas* (Beeville: Beeville Publishing, 1973). Mrs. I. C. Madray, *A History of Bee County* (Beeville, Texas: Bee-Picayune, 1939).

Adrian D. Ramirez

CLARK, ADDISON (1842–1911). Addison Clark, cofounder and first president of Texas Christian University, was born on December 11, 1842, in Titus (now Morris) County, Texas, the first of eleven children of Esther (DeSpain) and Joseph Addison Clark.qv He had some formal schooling but was educated primarily by his mother. He volunteered for the Confederate forces in 1862 and saw action as an officer. After the war he enrolled as an advanced student at Carlton College in Bonham. After graduation in January 1869, he married Sallie McQuigg; they had eight children. Clark and his brother Randolph Clarkqv moved to Fort Worth the same year and established a school there under the auspices of the local Disciples of Christ church.

In 1874 he moved to Thorp Spring where he, his brother, and their father opened a school they called Add-Ran College, after the first syllables of the brothers' first names. Addison was listed as president of the college from its opening in 1873, but he had remained in Fort Worth for a year to oversee the school there. Add-Ran Male and Female College, as it was officially called, also included a preparatory department. The school grew quickly, and in 1877 the Clarks built a larger facility across the road from the original building. Costs of construction and high operating expenses proved to be too much, and in 1889 the Clarks gave the institution to the Christian Church (Disciples of Christ)qv of Texas. Addison Clark continued as president, and the name was changed first to Add-Ran Christian Universityqv and later to Texas Christian University,qv although Clark was opposed to both name changes. In 1895, against his wishes, the university was moved to Waco. Clark remained president until 1899, when he stepped down. He continued to teach ancient languages until 1904, when he resigned from the faculty.

He also held pastorates in Waco and Amarillo until 1904, when he became president of Add-Ran Jarvis College in Thorp Spring, which occupied the same buildings as the original Add-Ran before its move to Waco. When Add-Ran Jarvis was forced to close in 1909, Clark moved to Mineral Wells to serve as pastor of the Disciples of Christ church. He died in Mineral Wells on May 12, 1911, and was buried in Thorp Spring.

BIBLIOGRAPHY: Joseph Lynn Clark, *Thank God We Made It* (Austin: University of Texas, 1969). Randolph Clark, *Reminiscences* (Wichita Falls: Lee Clark, 1919; rpt., Fort Worth: Texas Christian University Press, 1979). Jerome A. Moore, *Texas Christian University: A Hundred Years of History* (Fort Worth: Texas Christian University Press, 1974).

James M. Moudy

CLARK, BENJAMIN (1758–1838). Benjamin Clark, pioneer Red River County settler, was born in Dobbs County, North Carolina, in 1758. He fought in the American Revolution and by 1799 had settled in Tennessee. He moved to Arkansas Territory around 1814 and settled at Jonesborough on the Texas side of the Red River a few years later. In 1833 he founded Clarksville. Clark was a Methodist minister. He was married to Mary McLendon. He died in Clarksville in 1838 and was buried in Clarksville Cemetery.

BIBLIOGRAPHY: Pat B. Clark, *The History of Clarksville and Old Red River County* (Dallas: Mathis, Van Nort, 1937). Claude V. Hall, "Early Days in Red River County," *East Texas State Teachers College Bulletin* 14 (June 1931). *Red River Recollections* (Clarksville, Texas: Red River County Historical Society, 1986). Rex W. Strickland, Anglo-American Activities in Northeastern Texas, 1803–1845 (Ph.D. dissertation, University of Texas, 1937). George Travis Wright Family Papers, Barker Texas History Center, University of Texas at Austin.

Christopher Long

CLARK, CHARLES A. (?–?). Charles A. Clark was born in Louisiana and traveled to Texas in 1835 from New York. He entered service on January 28, 1836, as second corporal in Capt. Richard Roman'sqv Company B of Col. Edward Burleson'sqv First Regiment and took part in the battle of San Jacinto.qv He was discharged on June 17, 1836, and for his war service received a bounty warrant for 1,280 acres. On August 31, 1836, he enlisted in Capt. John Hart'sqv company, and on May 22, 1837, the Senate confirmed his appointment as a second lieutenant of permanent volunteers. For this term of enlistment he received an additional 1,280 acres.

Several other Charles Clarks were involved in Texas history of the same period. One, also a native of Louisiana, was a private in Capt. Thomas H. Breece'sqv company of Texas Volunteers that served in the siege of Bexar.qv This Clark was reportedly killed in the Goliad Massacre.qv Charles Henry Clarkqv died in the defense of the Alamo, and Charles Clarke, a lieutenant on the Sommervell expedition,qv was captured at the battle of Mier but soon released owing to his British citizenship.

BIBLIOGRAPHY: Daughters of the Republic of Texas, *Muster Rolls of the Texas Revolution* (Austin, 1986). James M. Day, *Black Beans and Goose Quills: Literature of the Texas Mier Expedition* (Waco: Texian Press, 1970). Sam Houston Dixon and Louis Wiltz Kemp, *The Heroes of San Jacinto* (Houston: Anson Jones, 1932). Thomas L. Miller, *Bounty and Donation Land Grants of Texas, 1835–1888* (Austin: University of Texas Press, 1967).

Thomas W. Cutrer

CLARK, CHARLES HENRY (?–1836). Charles Henry Clark, Alamo defender, was born in Missouri. He marched to Texas as a single man in November of 1835 in Capt. Thomas Breece's qv company of New Orleans Greys qv and took part in the siege of Bexar. qv Clark died in the battle of the Alamo qv on March 6, 1836.

BIBLIOGRAPHY: Daughters of the American Revolution, *The Alamo Heroes and Their Revolutionary Ancestors* (San Antonio, 1976). Daughters of the Republic of Texas, *Muster Rolls of the Texas Revolution* (Austin, 1986). Bill Groneman, *Alamo Defenders* (Austin: Eakin, 1990).

Bill Groneman

CLARK, EDWARD (1815–1880). Edward Clark, governor of Texas, was born in New Orleans, Louisiana, on April 1, 1815, the son of Elijah Clark, Jr., a brother of John Clark, governor of Georgia from 1819 to 1823. Edward Clark spent his early childhood in Georgia. After the death of his father in the early 1830s, he and his mother moved to Montgomery, Alabama, where he studied law and was admitted to the bar. In 1840 he was married to Lucy Long in Alabama, but his wife died within a few months. By December 1841 Clark had moved to Texas and opened a law practice in Marshall. In July 1849 he married Martha Melissa (Mellissa, Malissa) Evans of Marshall. The couple had four children.

Clark was a delegate to the Texas Constitutional Convention of 1845,qv a member of the first state House of Representatives, and a senator in the Second Legislature. He served on the staff of Gen. J. Pinckney Henderson in the Mexican War qqv and received a citation for bravery in the battle of Monterrey. From 1853 to 1857 he was secretary of state under Governor Elisha M. Pease.qv He was appointed state commissioner of claims in 1858 and was elected lieutenant governor of Texas on the independent Democratic ticket headed by Sam Houston qv in 1859.

When Governor Houston refused to take the oath of allegiance to the Confederacy in the spring of 1861, the Secession Convention qv declared the office of governor vacant and elevated Clark to the position. As governor, he moved quickly to address problems brought about by secession. Regiments commanded by John S. (Rip) Ford and Henry E. McCulloch qqv were mustered to protect the frontier, ad valorem and poll taxes were raised in an effort to stabilize the state's finances, and the state was divided into military districts for recruiting and organizing the troops required by the Confederate government. After the firing upon Fort Sumter and the outbreak of war, Clark worked closely with Confederate authorities to help obtain supplies for the army. The archaic state militia system was reorganized, and a system of training camps was built. Clark proceeded cautiously and within his constitutional powers. Even so, he exercised more authority and power than any previous Texas chief executive in recruiting, enrolling, and training troops, in purchasing weapons and supplies, and in communication with Confederate officials and governors of Mexican states.

He ran for election to a full term as governor in the autumn of 1861 but was defeated in an extremely close race by Francis R. Lubbock.qv Lubbock, who had the support of regular Democratic party qv leaders, received 21,854 votes, Clark, 21,730, and Thomas Jefferson Chambers,qv 13,733. Although there were widespread rumors of fraud, Clark accepted the outcome of the election without protest.

After he left the governor's office, he received a commission in the Confederate Army as colonel of the Fourteenth Texas Infantry regiment, which served as part of Walker's Texas Division qv in the repulse of the Union invasion in the Red River campaign qv of 1864. Clark was wounded in the leg while leading an attack at the battle of Pleasant Hill and subsequently discharged from the army. He was promoted to the rank of brigadier general before his discharge, but the promotion may not have been confirmed by the Richmond government.

When the Civil War qv ended, Clark fled to Mexico with other prominent civil and military leaders of the Southwest. He remained there only briefly and returned to his home in Marshall. After several business ventures, he resumed his law practice. He died on May 4, 1880, and was buried in Marshall.

BIBLIOGRAPHY: Edward C. Clark Papers, Barker Texas History Center, University of Texas at Austin. James T. DeShields, *They Sat in High Places: The Presidents and Governors of Texas* (San Antonio: Naylor, 1940). Tinsie Larison, "Edward Clark," in *Ten Texans in Gray*, ed. W. C. Nunn (Hillsboro, Texas: Hill Junior College Press, 1968). Ralph A. Wooster, "Texas," in *The Confederate Governors*, ed. W. Buck Yearns (Athens: University of Georgia Press, 1985).

Ralph A. Wooster

CLARK, EDWARD AUBREY (1906–1992). Edward A. Clark, lawyer, banker, and diplomat, was born on July 15, 1906, in San Augustine, Texas, to John and Lelia (Downs) Clark. He attended Southwestern University before finishing his undergraduate degree at Tulane University in New Orleans. He received a law degree in 1928 from the University of Texas. During the 1960s Southwestern University and Cleary College of Michigan awarded him honorary doctoral degrees for his philanthropic work done on behalf of the schools. Following law school, Clark served two terms as a county attorney in his hometown before moving to Austin to serve as assistant attorney general of Texas from 1932 to 1935 and assistant to Governor James Allred qv from 1935 to 1937. The governor appointed him secretary of state in 1937, when he was only thirty years old. After leaving the secretary of state's office, Clark remained in Austin and opened a private law practice with Everett Looney in December 1938. The firm eventually became Clark, Thomas and Winters, one of the most influential and successful firms in the state. Along with politics and law, Clark also had a reputation as an astute banker. He served on numerous boards and was the senior chairman of Texas Commerce Bank of Austin and the First National Bank of San Augustine. During World War II qv he was a captain in the United States Army.

For Clark, politics was always a primary interest, even after he officially left state government in 1938. He was a lobbyist and political strategist in both state and national politics. He was a mentor and advisor of vision and foresight to three generations of political leaders, including Lyndon Baines Johnson.qv Clark served as Johnson's legal counsel in 1948, when Coke Stevenson qv contested Johnson's seventy-one-vote victory in the United States Senate race. In 1965 Johnson appointed Clark United States ambassador to Australia. In 1969 Anne Clark, Edward's wife, published a book, *Australian Adventure: Letters From an Ambassador's Wife,* about their experiences. Clark was a devoted but conservative Democrat. In 1972, however, he supported John G. Tower's qv bid for the Senate. He stated that he believed "the best interests of Texas are served by having a senator from each major party. This assures us that on votes of vital interest to our state, Texans have a voice in both major parties." Despite protests from the faithful in both parties, Tower selected Clark to run his reelection campaign. Clark also supported Richard Nixon over George McGovern in the presidential election that year. Nixon appointed Clark in 1974 to the General Advisory Committee of the United States Arms Control and Disarmament Agency. In another departure from the Democratic fold in 1984, Clark served on a statewide nonpartisan steering committee to reelect Ronald Reagan.

His civic and community activities included serving on the board of regents of the University of Texas System qv from 1973 to 1979 and for many years as a trustee of both Southwestern University and the University of Texas Law Foundation. From 1983 to 1985, Clark served as president of the Texas State Historical Association.qv He was a fund-raiser extraordinaire for projects that benefited higher education and preservation of the Texas historical heritage. He was one of the first to recognize the need for a complete revision of the *Handbook of Texas* and served as chairman of the development committee for the revision project. In addition to his efforts for the *Handbook,* he was instrumental in raising funds for Southwestern University, the University of Texas Medical Branch, and the Lyndon Baines Johnson Library.qv He also organized the effort to finance construction of the State Bar of Texas qv headquarters and raised funds to purchase the telescope at the University of Texas McDonald Observatory.qv Clark's love of Texas history extended into his private life as well. He and his wife, Anne Metcalf Clark, whom he married on December 28, 1927, restored and maintained a home, Saddlefork Farm, in San Augustine. The couple's interest in the Southwest led them to acquire an extensive 7,000-volume Texana collection, which they subsequently donated to Southwestern University.

Among the many honors bestowed on Ambassador Clark was the Ima Hogg qv Historical Achievement Award. In 1967 the University of Texas Ex-Students' Association named him a distinguished alumnus. Twenty years later the University of Texas Law Alumni Association gave him the Outstanding Alumnus Award. The Edward Clark Centennial Professorship in Law was established at UT in his honor as well. Edward and Anne Clark were also awarded the Mirabeau B. Lamar qv Medal for Distinguished Contribution to Higher Education in recognition of their hard work and dedication to various schools in the state. Clark was a member of the Philosophical Society of Texas, the Knights of the Order of San Jacinto, the Sons of the Republic of Texas,qqv Kappa Sigma, and Phi Delta Phi Legal Fraternity. He was a member of St. David's Episcopal Church in Austin. He died on September 16, 1992, in Austin.

BIBLIOGRAPHY: Jon Newton, "A Tribute to Ambassador Edward A. Clark," *Southwestern Historical Quarterly* 96 (January 1993). Vertical Files, Barker Texas History Center, University of Texas at Austin.

Jon P. Newton

CLARK, GEORGE W. (1841–1918). George W. Clark, Confederate soldier, attorney, and state official, was born in Eutaw, Alabama, on July 18, 1841, the son of James Blair and Mary (Erwin) Clark. He was the youngest of seven boys in a family of nine children. He enrolled in October 1857 at the University of Alabama, Tuscaloosa, where he pursued undergraduate studies before the outbreak of the Civil War.qv In his final year there, 1860–61, the university was placed under military rule. In January 1861 a corps of cadets to which Clark belonged was taken by river steamer to Mobile, Alabama, and then to Montgomery, but its members were allowed to return shortly thereafter to Tuscaloosa and resume their studies. Clark remained at the university until the fall of Fort Sumter in April 1861. He graduated that June, enlisted in the Confederate Army as a private, and later became a third lieutenant in Lynchburg, Virginia, with the Eleventh Alabama Infantry. He and three of his brothers were in Gen. Robert E. Lee'sqv army. Two brothers were killed, and one lost his left arm. Clark participated in the Chancellorsville campaign, the battle of Gettysburg, and several other battles. He was wounded in July 1863 and August 1864. He eventually achieved the rank of lieutenant colonel. He was nearby in Danville, Virginia, when General Lee surrendered at Appomattox Courthouse.

At the end of the war Clark returned to Alabama and began studying law under his father's tutelage. He served as a justice of the peace from 1865 to 1867. In October 1866 he received his license to practice law. He sailed to Galveston, Texas, in January 1867 and traveled around the state for several months before he returned to Alabama to prepare for his permanent move. "The county in which I lived had about five Negroes to one white," he wrote in his memoirs, "and I knew that it would be impossible for me to remain there in case the Reconstructionqv measures passed, and these seemed certain, so I therefore began to look for a different location." The South was under Union military rule at the time (*see* FIFTH MILITARY DISTRICT), and a yellow fever epidemic along the Gulf Coast delayed Clark's return to Texas until December 1867. He settled for a short time in Waco, moved to Weatherford for a year, and returned to Waco in December 1868.

He became politically prominent as a member of the state Democratic committee in 1872 and helped to induce his friend Richard Cokeqv to run for governor. Clark lived with Coke's family in the spring of 1872 and acted as secretary of state under Governor Coke until the arrival of the regular appointee. He then took appointment

Edward A. Clark (left) with E. H. Perry, Sr., Herman Brown, Lyndon Baines Johnson, and Tom Miller at the Democrats' "Harmony Barbecue" following the 1940 state Democratic convention. Courtesy Lyndon Baines Johnson Library, Austin. In spite of efforts in 1940 to establish "harmony," Clark and other state Democratic leaders faced a growing ideological rift in the party.

in 1874 as Texas attorney general. From 1876 until 1878 he served as a Coke appointee on a commission to revise the laws of the state. He was appointed in November 1879 to fill a vacancy on the Texas Court of Criminal Appealsqv and served until October 1880, when he retired to resume his private law practice in Waco. He became a prominent railroad attorney.

In the spring and summer of 1887, Clark served as chairman of a successful campaign to defeat a bitterly controversial state constitutional amendment for prohibition.qv His name appeared often in daily newspaper accounts of the election held that August. "Indeed, the chairman of the prohibition State committee concedes the defeat of the amendment by 60,000," commented the Houston *Post*,qv "while the chairman of the anti prohibition committee [Clark] claims the victory by 100,000, and from the tenor of reports printed to-day it would appear that Judge Clark's figures are more nearly correct." The amendment lost by 91,000 votes. Clark was praised in the press for "the masterly manner in which he has managed the campaign." In 1892, as a candidate supported by railroad interests, Clark opposed James Stephen Hoggqv in his gubernatorial reelection bid. Hogg won the election and effectively ended Clark's political career.

Clark continued to practice law in Waco, but by 1908 he had begun to lose his sight. He was married in Austin on November 4, 1874, to Mary Pauline Johns, who died in Waco on May 6, 1903. They had two children. Clark died on March 28, 1918, after a six-week illness.

BIBLIOGRAPHY: Glynn Austin Brooks, A Political Survey of the Prohibition Movement in Texas (M.A. thesis, University of Texas, 1920). Dallas *Morning News,* March 29, 1918. Galveston *Daily News,* August 6, 1887. Houston *Daily Post,* August 6, 1887. *Doug Johnson*

CLARK, HORACE (1819–1909). Horace Clark, college president and minister, was born on July 7, 1819, in Charleston, Massachusetts, the only son of John and Catherine (Aldrich) Clark. He was raised by his mother after his father's death in 1821. Clark served four years under his uncle, who was a captain in the merchant marine. At fourteen he was pressed into the Portuguese navy in Rio de Janeiro, but the intervention of a Captain Brown and the United States consul brought about his release. In 1836 he and his mother moved to Alton, Illinois, and he entered Shurtleff College. He moved to Georgetown

College, Georgetown, Kentucky, in 1841 and completed his education. He and Martha Davis were married on March 30, 1844, in Macoupin County, Illinois.

Clark was the principal of Henry Academy, New Castle, Kentucky, from 1846 to 1850 and La Grange Collegiate Institute, La Grange, Texas, in 1851. On June 18, 1851, he accepted the position of principal at Baylor Female Department in Independence (see MARY HARDIN-BAYLOR UNIVERSITY). He served as secretary of the Baptist State Convention of Texas from 1856 to 1858 and in 1867, and he was corresponding secretary in 1861, 1864, 1868–70, and 1875. On September 18, 1858, he was ordained a minister by Independence Baptist Church. He resigned as principal in 1866, and during his year-long leave of absence, Baylor Female Department was organized into Baylor Female College, on September 28, 1866. Benjamin Simms Fitzgerald was named the first president of Baylor College. The following year Clark returned and was elected to replace him. He served until July 12, 1871. Later that fall, Clark opened Clark's Academy for young ladies in Houston. The school ceased to exist in seven or eight years.

About 1877 Horace Clark joined the Episcopal Church. His wife remained a Baptist. He was confirmed as a deacon in Christ Church, Houston, on November 22, 1878, where he served as assistant pastor. He was ordained to the priesthood at St. David's Church, Austin, on April 20, 1879, and accepted the rectorship of the Church of the Good Shepherd, Corpus Christi, in 1880; there he served for eighteen years. His wife died on January 9, 1896, in Corpus Christi. Clark was a Mason and served as grand chaplain of the Grand Lodge of Texas from 1876 through 1879, 1884–85, and 1901–02. He was grand chaplain of the Grand Royal Arch Chapter of Texas in 1869–70. He died on February 10, 1909, and was buried at Glennwood Cemetery, Houston. He was survived by three children.

BIBLIOGRAPHY: Robert A. Baker, *The Blossoming Desert—A Concise History of Texas Baptists* (Waco: Word, 1970). James Milton Carroll, *A History of Texas Baptists* (Dallas: Baptist Standard, 1923).

Samuel B. Hesler

CLARK, JAMES (1799–1838). James Clark, founder of Clarksville, Red River County, the son of Benjamin and Mary (McLendon) Clark, was born in 1799 in Sumner County, Tennessee. About 1814 he moved with his family from Tennessee to what is now southwestern Arkansas. He graduated from the University of Virginia at age sixteen and first entered Texas in 1819. He returned again by 1826 to trade with the Indians and to hunt. For most of the 1820s, however, he was living near Little River in what is now southwestern Arkansas, where he manufactured salt. In 1827 Clark was elected to the House of Representatives of the Arkansas Territory General Assembly as a representative of Miller County, Arkansas,qv which included parts of what is now northeastern Texas. He was reelected in August 1829 after his marriage, on July 15, 1829, to Isabella Hanks (see GORDON, ISABELLA H. H.), the widow of John Hanks. In late 1830 Clark moved to Jonesborough on the south side of the Red River in what is now Red River County, Texas. Though Mexico claimed Jonesborough as part of Texas, the settlement at that time was within the jurisdiction of Miller County, Arkansas Territory. The unsurveyed boundary line between the Sabine and Red rivers meant that Clark and his neighbors faced the uncertainty of not knowing whether they were living in Mexico or the United States. Clark was appointed postmaster for Miller County on December 10, 1830, but on December 31, 1830, he took an oath to Mexico to register his family for a Mexican land grant under the authority of Arthur Wavell'sqv colonization contract. Because of the Law of April 6, 1830,qv and the unsettled boundary with the United States, however, Mexico never issued titles to Wavell's colonists.

In 1831 Clark was appointed a justice of the peace for Miller County, and the next year he served as deputy clerk when Jonesborough became the county seat. In 1833 he was elected to represent Miller County in the Legislative Council, the upper body of the Arkansas Territory General Assembly. He moved his family in 1833 to Sulphur Fork Prairie, twenty-five miles south of Jonesborough, where he founded the settlement later named Clarksville, now the county seat of Red River County. On the outbreak of the Texas Revolutionqv the Red River settlements, known as Pecan Point to the South Texans, were invited to send a representative to the General Councilqv of the provisional governmentqv then meeting in San Felipe. Clark, appointed by a citizens' committee to represent the interests of Pecan Point, led a deputation of Red River settlers to Nacogdoches in December 1835; he arrived in San Felipe by January 11, 1836, with a letter of introduction from John Forbes.qv In April 1836 he was a member of a volunteer ranger expedition to gather information about Indian movements near the Red River settlements, and on July 14, 1836, he raised a company of mounted riflemen to join the fight for Texas independence. This company, known as the Red River Blues, was enlisted into service at Clark's home and was commanded by Capt. William Becknell.qv Clark served as first lieutenant. Though Clark was delayed along the way because of illness, the company traveled to the Lavaca River in South Texas and joined Gen. Thomas Jefferson Green'sqv brigade.

After the company was discharged in October 1836, Clark returned home. He and others supported the establishment of Red River County within the Republic of Texas,qv but Miller County, Arkansas, attempted similar jurisdiction at Jonesborough until 1838. On February 1, 1838, the Red River County Board of Land Commissioners awarded Clark 4,605 acres as his first-class headright grant. He later received another 320 acres from the Texas secretary of war as his bounty grant for serving three months in the army. Clark had a promising future as a leading figure in Clarksville and Northeast Texas, but he contracted a throat ailment while surveying land grants in early 1838 and never recovered. He died on May 2, 1838, and was buried in Clarksville Cemetery. He was survived by his wife and four children, and by his ward, Minerva Ann Hanks. In 1936 the state of Texas, as part of the Texas Centennial,qv placed a historical monument at his grave.

BIBLIOGRAPHY: James Clark Family Papers, Barker Texas History Center, University of Texas at Austin. Pat B. Clark, *The History of Clarksville and Old Red River County* (Dallas: Mathis, Van Nort, 1937). Claude V. Hall, "Early Days in Red River County," *East Texas State Teachers College Bulletin* 14 (June 1931). *Red River Recollections* (Clarksville, Texas: Red River County Historical Society, 1986). Rex W. Strickland, Anglo-American Activities in Northeastern Texas, 1803–1845 (Ph.D. dissertation, University of Texas, 1937).

Jeffrey D. Dunn

CLARK, JAMES ANTHONY (1908–1978). James A. Clark, author, columnist, and public-relations consultant and historian of the oil industry, was born in 1908 in Abita Springs, Louisiana, and grew up in Beaumont, Texas. He attended South Park Junior College (now Lamar University) and worked for Magnolia Petroleum Company cutting out oil-equipment parts. In 1927 he became sports editor for the Galveston *News*,qv and the same year found him in Beaumont, where he had a local beat as a reporter for the *Journal*. In 1931 Clark was assigned to interview Columbus M. Joiner,qv who had just brought in Daisy Bradford No. 3 and opened up the East Texas oilfield.qv In 1935, when James Allredqv became governor of Texas, Clark was appointed statehouse correspondent in Austin. From 1941 to 1946 he served the United States Army as an intelligence officer in Puerto Rico, the Pacific, and Japan. He left the army as a lieutenant colonel with a bronze star and after the war became public-relations manager for the Shamrock Hotel in Houston.

The publication of his first book, *Spindletop* (1952), with Michel T. Halbouty, gave Clark a position in the oil industry. He began a firm for public-relations consulting, the James A. Clark Company, and started a regular oil column, "Tales of the Oil Country," which he wrote for the next fourteen years. He also began research for other books on the oil industry. In 1954 he published *Three Stars for the*

Colonel: The Biography of Ernest O. Thompson, and in 1958 *The Tactful Texan: A Biography of Governor Will Hobby.* His other books include *The Chronological History of the Petroleum and Natural Gas Industries* (1963) and *The Last Boom* (1972). *Spindletop* is listed in John H. Jenkins III's^{qv} *Basic Texas Books.* Clark married Estelle Walton in 1934. In 1969 he established the Energy Research and Education Foundation in Houston. He died on April 5, 1978, in Houston.

BIBLIOGRAPHY: Houston *Post*, April 6, 1978. Vertical Files, Barker Texas History Center, University of Texas at Austin.

Jerrell Dean Palmer

CLARK, JAMES BENJAMIN (1831–1908). James Benjamin Clark, Civil War^{qv} soldier, lawyer, and university administrator, was born in Pitt County, North Carolina, in 1831 to William and Louisa Pearce (Lanier) Clark. He attended Franklin College, Tennessee, and in 1851 entered Harvard College, where he graduated in 1855 and enrolled in the law school. In 1857 he was admitted to the bar in Jackson, Mississippi. In the spring of 1861 Clark enlisted in the Eighteenth Mississippi Regiment, C.S.A.; he served for the rest of the war and became a captain. Afterward he moved to Harrodsburg, Kentucky, where he edited a newspaper and, on November 11, 1869, married Florence Anderson. On April 9, 1875, Clark moved to Bonham, Texas, where he practiced law for ten years. On the organization of the University of Texas in 1883, Clark became a member of the board of regents. On July 1, 1885, he was named proctor and custodian general of the university, a position he held until his sudden death in Austin on December 6, 1908. Clark Field, the baseball field at the university from 1928 to 1974, was named for him.

BIBLIOGRAPHY: Austin *Statesman*, December 7, 8, 1908. H. L. Bentley and Thomas Pilgrim, *Texas Legal Directory for 1876–77* (Austin: Democratic Statesman Office, 1877). Carl John Eckhardt, *One Hundred Faithful to the University of Texas at Austin* (197–?). Vertical Files, Barker Texas History Center, University of Texas at Austin.

Marie Giles

CLARK, JOHN C. (?–?). John C. Clark, officer of the Texas Navy,^{qv} was recommended to President Mirabeau B. Lamar^{qv} by Nathan Amory in Washington, D.C., on February 27, 1840, as "an old friend . . . with whom I passed several years in Venezuela." In that South American country Clark commanded several Colombian ships of war under Simón Bolívar during the revolution. Clark was commissioned into the Texas Navy by Secretary of the Navy Louis P. Cooke^{qv} on June 2, 1840, and commanded the Texas brig-of-war *Wharton*^{qv} from July until December 1841. In reaction to the raid of Rafael Vásquez^{qv} in March 1842, President Sam Houston^{qv} appointed Clark to the command of the Galveston coast guards. With the steamer *Laffite* and the sloop *Washington*, he was to intercept any Mexican troop or supply movements aimed at the upper Texas coast and was authorized to capture not only belligerent vessels but neutrals carrying contraband as well.

BIBLIOGRAPHY: Alex Dienst, "The Navy of the Republic of Texas," *Quarterly of the Texas State Historical Association* 12–13 (January–October 1909; rpt., Fort Collins, Colorado: Old Army Press, 1987). C. L. Douglas, *Thunder on the Gulf: The Story of the Texas Navy* (Dallas: Turner, 1936; rpt., Fort Collins, Colorado: Old Army Press, 1973). Charles Adams Gulick, Jr., Harriet Smither, et al., eds., *The Papers of Mirabeau Buonaparte Lamar* (6 vols., Austin: Texas State Library, 1920–27; rpt., Austin: Pemberton Press, 1968). Jim Dan Hill, *The Texas Navy* (New York: Barnes, 1962). Tom Henderson Wells, *Commodore Moore and the Texas Navy* (Austin: University of Texas Press, 1960). Amelia W. Williams and Eugene C. Barker, eds., *The Writings of Sam Houston, 1813–1863* (8 vols., Austin: University of Texas Press, 1938–43; rpt., Austin and New York: Pemberton Press, 1970).

Thomas W. Cutrer

CLARK, JOHN C. (1798?–1862). John C. Clark, Wharton County planter, member of the Old Three Hundred,^{qv} and Indian fighter, was born in South Carolina about 1798. He received little education and by 1822 had come to Texas, where he was injured in a fight with Karankawa Indians on the Colorado River in 1823. In June or July 1824 he was with Robert H. Kuykendall and Alexander Jackson, Sr.,^{qqv} in an Indian fight near Peach Creek. As one of Stephen F. Austin's^{qv} Old Three Hundred colonists, Clark received title to a sitio^{qv} of land now near Egypt in Wharton County in 1824. There he established one of the first plantations in the county, a spread of 4,428 acres. He was subpoenaed as a witness to testify against Aylett C. Buckner^{qv} in June 1825 and in April 1826 signed an affidavit concerning Tonkawa hostilities. In 1830 Clark sold the west half of his league to William J. E. Heard,^{qv} who paid fifty cents an acre for his 2,222 acres. In 1833 or 1834 Clark bought a mulatto named Sobrina, whom he may have married in 1837 and with whom he had three children. Sobrina had three other children. In 1850, when his real property was valued at $26,602, Clark had a total of fifty-one slaves; by 1860 he had real property valued at $132,145, personal property of $104,715, and forty-six slaves. He died in 1862, leaving a large estate of lands, slaves, and personal assets. His children, however, evidently did not learn of his death until after his property was sold in 1866 for $477,846.28 and the proceeds were turned over to the state. From 1863 to 1867 four sets of heirs claimed the estate, which by October 1867 was valued at about $380,000. On the basis of the Constitution of 1869,^{qv} which legitimized the children of couples who had lived together until the death of one party, the jury decided for the plaintiffs.

BIBLIOGRAPHY: Eugene C. Barker, ed., *The Austin Papers* (3 vols., Washington: GPO, 1924–28). Lester G. Bugbee, "The Old Three Hundred: A List of Settlers in Austin's First Colony," *Quarterly of the Texas State Historical Association* 1 (October 1897). Dallas *Herald*, October 12, 1867. J. H. Kuykendall, "Reminiscences of Early Texans," *Quarterly of the Texas State Historical Association* 6–7 (January, April, July 1903). Annie Lee Williams, *A History of Wharton County* (Austin: Von Boeckmann–Jones, 1964). Alice Mitchell Wright, An Abstract of Biographical Data in the Texas Supreme Court Reports, 1857–1874 (M.A. thesis, University of Texas, 1937).

CLARK, JOSEPH ADDISON (1815–1901). Joseph Addison Clark, preacher, journalist, and teacher, was born on November 6, 1815, in Shawneetown, Illinois, and named Zachariah by his parents, Thomas Dyson and Jane (Cunningham) Clark. He spent his childhood near Columbia and Clarksville, Tennessee. At twelve he assumed responsibility for his mother and two younger sisters when his father murdered a man in New Orleans and fled. His father was thought to have drowned in a shipwreck, but he survived and went to Texas, where he served in the Texas army after the Texas Revolution.^{qv} Clark and his father were reunited briefly in 1840. In 1826 the family moved to Alabama to be near Jane Clark's brother. During this time Clark managed to educate himself and took the name Joseph Addison because he admired the works of the British writer of the same name.

Clark moved to Texas with his sisters and mother in 1839. His mother died soon after the family landed at Matagorda. Clark and his sister Mary settled briefly in Austin, where he worked as a printer on the earlier Austin *Texas Sentinel.*^{qv} Delayed while attempting to return to Kentucky in 1841, Clark worked as a surveyor in East Texas. There he met Esther (Hetty) DeSpain, and they were married in 1842. They moved to Titus County because of the Regulator-Moderator War.^{qv} Through Esther's influence and after reading the debate between Alexander Campbell and Robert Owen, Clark became a Christian and spent most of his remaining life as a Christian educator, preacher, and journalist.

In Texas he was associated with the *Western Argus* in Bonham in 1847, the Rusk *Pioneer* in 1849, the Galveston *News*^{qv} in 1850, the Palestine *Advocate* in 1852, and the Bonham *Advertiser* in 1858. He conducted schools in Titus County in 1843, at Midway in 1855–56, and in Fort Worth from 1869 to 1873, before purchasing a school conducted by two church associates, H. D. Bantau and a man named Cook, at Thorp Spring. The Thorp Spring school opened in the fall of 1873 and was named Add-Ran College (now Texas Christian University) in memory of AddRan, Clark's first grandson. After moving to Thorp Spring Clark edited *The Texas Christian* and *The Add-Ran Student*. In 1879 he relinquished control of the school to his two sons, Addison and Randolph.

Clark published extensively in the *Gospel Advocate* of Nashville, Tennessee, and the *Firm Foundation* of Austin, Texas. He wrote a column in the former entitled "Briefs" beginning in 1890. He also published material directed to young people under the pen name "Uncle Joe" in the same paper. Clark died on January 11, 1901, in Thorp Spring.

BIBLIOGRAPHY: F. B. Baillio, *History of the Texas Press Association* (Dallas: Southwestern Printing, 1916). Joseph Lynn Clark, *Thank God We Made It* (Austin: University of Texas, 1969). Randolph Clark, *Reminiscences* (Wichita Falls: Lee Clark, 1919; rpt., Fort Worth: Texas Christian University Press, 1979). Houston *Post*, May 5, 1935.

R. L. Roberts

CLARK, JOSEPH LYNN (1881–1969). Joseph Lynn Clark, teacher, administrator, and author, was born in Thorp Spring, Texas, on July 27, 1881, the son of Ella Blanche (Lee) and Randolph Clark[qv] and nephew of Addison Clark.[qv] During his undergraduate days at Texas Christian University, he played baseball and assisted in the organization of the Texas Intercollegiate Athletic Association, the state's first intercollegiate sports organization. He graduated from TCU in 1906. From 1906 to 1909 he was an instructor in history and English at Add-Ran College and in 1909–10 an instructor at John Tarleton College (now Tarleton State University). He attended summer sessions at the University of Virginia in 1907 and at the University of California in 1915; he also did graduate work at Columbia University in 1917 and at the University of Texas in 1927–28 and 1932–33. He was married to Sallie Frances Chism on August 28, 1913.

In 1910 Clark was named secretary to Harry F. Estill,[qv] president of Sam Houston Normal Institute (now Sam Houston State University), and was soon given the additional duties of registrar, purchasing agent, bookkeeper, and librarian. He taught history at Sam Houston and was named head of the history department there in 1916. He wrote two school textbooks, *A New History of Texas* (1928) and *The Story of Texas* (1932); he also wrote, with Elton M. Scott, *The Texas Gulf Coast* (1955). His book *Thank God We Made It!* (1969) was an account of his family's role in higher education in Texas. Clark was one of the organizers and second president of the Texas College Classroom Teachers Association (later renamed the Texas Association of College Teachers[qv]). He was a longtime member, vice president, and fellow of the Texas State Historical Association.[qv] He was a cofounder and member of the Texas Commission on Interracial Cooperation, and it is possible that his was the first college course offered in Texas on race relations. Clark died in Houston on September 13, 1969, and was buried in Huntsville.

BIBLIOGRAPHY: Sam Hanna Acheson, Herbert P. Gambrell, Mary Carter Toomey, and Alex M. Acheson, Jr., *Texian Who's Who*, Vol. 1 (Dallas: Texian, 1937). Joseph L. Clark, *Texas Gulf Coast: Its History and Development* (4 vols., New York: Lewis Historical Publishing, 1955). Houston *Post*, September 14, 1969. *Sam Houston Alumnus*, August 1951. Vertical Files, Barker Texas History Center, University of Texas at Austin.

CLARK, M. B. (?–1836?). M. B. Clark, Alamo defender, was born in Mississippi. On January 27, 1836, he enlisted in the company of Capt. John M. Chenoweth[qv] in Texas. He may have been one of the volunteers who accompanied James Bowie[qv] to the Alamo. Louis Moses Rose,[qv] who left the Alamo before its fall, stated that he had seen Clark at the mission (*see* ALAMO, BATTLE OF).

BIBLIOGRAPHY: Robert Bruce Blake, "A Vindication of Rose and His Story," in *In the Shadow of History,* ed. J. Frank Dobie, Mody C. Boatright, and Harry H. Ransom (Publications of the Texas Folklore Society 15, Detroit: Folklore Association, 1939). Daughters of the American Revolution, *The Alamo Heroes and Their Revolutionary Ancestors* (San Antonio, 1976). Daughters of the Republic of Texas, *Muster Rolls of the Texas Revolution* (Austin, 1986). Bill Groneman, *Alamo Defenders* (Austin: Eakin, 1990). Phil Rosenthal and Bill Groneman, *Roll Call at the Alamo* (Fort Collins, Colorado: Old Army, 1985).

Bill Groneman

CLARK, RANDOLPH (1844–1935). Randolph Clark, teacher and minister, son of Esther Hettie (D'Spain) and Joseph Addison Clark,[qv] was born in Powelltown (now Waskom), Texas, on August 15, 1844, and educated at home. In the spring of 1864 he joined the Sixteenth Texas Cavalry, in which his brother, Addison Clark,[qv] had been serving the Confederacy since the spring of 1862. After the war he and Addison attended Carlton School in Kentucky Town and, later, Carlton College in Bonham. On July 5, 1870, he married Ellen Blanche Lee; they had seven children, including Randolph Lee Clark.[qv] Early in their education the two brothers decided to pursue teaching careers together. They took charge of the Male and Female Seminary of Fort Worth in 1869 and operated the school until 1874, when the town's railroad-boom atmosphere and the rowdy population it attracted made the downtown location unsuitable. When a land developer in Hood County offered them a large stone school building, Randolph opened Add-Ran Male and Female College at Thorp Springs in 1873. The following year, his responsibilities in Fort Worth fulfilled, Addison joined the school as president. In 1876 Randolph Clark took his family to West Virginia, where he completed a course of study in the physical sciences at Bethany College. Immediately upon his return to Thorp Spring, a dispute with the developer led the brothers to buy land nearby and construct their own building. Clark served Add-Ran College as vice president and full-time faculty member for twenty years, and under the Clark brothers' leadership the school gained a national reputation for educational excellence. He received an M.A. degree in literature from the college in 1896.

Clark was ordained a minister in the Disciples of Christ Church (now Christian Church[qv]) in 1873, and throughout his tenure with Add-Ran College he preached in communities throughout Central and North Texas. Addison was a minister in the same communion, but the word *Christian* was not included in the school's charter until 1890, when the Clarks officially deeded the property to the Disciples of Christ, the church from which the school's trustees had always been selected. When the institution moved to Waco in 1895, Clark stayed in Thorp Spring and taught at Jarvis college; when it closed in 1898, he opened Randolph College in Lancaster, at the request of citizens there. Two years later he founded Hereford College in Hereford, later called Randolph College and, still later, Panhandle Christian College. After 1910 Clark devoted his attention to various pastorates in the state, the Race Street Christian Church in Stephenville being his last. Texas Christian University awarded him an LL.D. degree in 1923, the year he served as chaplain of the Texas Senate. He died in Dallas on November 22, 1935, and was buried in Stephenville.

BIBLIOGRAPHY: Joseph Lynn Clark, *Thank God We Made It* (Austin: University of Texas, 1969). Jerome A. Moore, *Texas Christian University: A Hundred Years of History* (Fort Worth: Texas Christian University Press, 1974). Clarence R. Wharton, ed., *Texas under Many Flags* (5 vols., Chicago: American Historical Society, 1930).

Carey Goodwin

CLARK, RANDOLPH LEE (1871–1941). Randolph Lee Clark, teacher and school administrator, was born to Randolph and Ellen

(Lee) Clark in Fort Worth, Texas, on June 3, 1871. His father, a Confederate veteran and minister in the Disciples of Christ, cofounded Add-Ran College, a forerunner of Texas Christian University, at Thorp Spring in 1873. Clark, who in his youth sometimes worked as a cowboy on the XIT Ranch,qv received the B.A. degree between 1890 and 1895 from Add-Ran. In 1895 he began his teaching career. He entered the University of Chicago in 1897 but apparently earned no degree. Clark married Leoti Sypert in Holland, Texas, on December 18, 1898. The couple eventually had nine children.

In 1899 Clark was ordained to the ministry of the Disciples of Christ, but he never took a pastorate, and soon after his ordination he became involved in various educational activities. By 1902 he had accepted a teaching position at Add-Ran Christian University, where he became secretary of the faculty. In 1906 he left the college and assumed the duties of superintendent of schools at Iowa Park in Wichita County. He later held similar positions at Anson, Plainview, and Gainesville. From 1911 to 1913 he served as general agent for the Conference for Education in Texas. In 1915 he became superintendent of schools in Wichita Falls. He held the position for eight years and became known as an educational innovator. During his tenure a junior high school was constructed and night courses were first offered for black students. Recognizing that the children of Hispanic migrant workers in the area received little real education in Wichita Falls schools because they spoke little English and their teachers spoke little Spanish, Clark established a bilingual education program in 1922. He set up a two-grade school specifically for the children of non-English-speaking migrant workers and employed bilingual teachers to provide the students with both regular instruction and intensive English instruction.

He also established Wichita Falls Junior College, which eventually grew into Midwestern University,qv in 1922. He planned and won adoption of the junior college as a part of the local public school system. Clark believed that the new institution would provide inexpensive basic education, thereby reducing expenses for the parents of college-bound students and preparing those students for more advanced college work or for entrance into a profession. His leadership secured approval of an $850,000 bond issue to finance the construction of a junior-college building in 1922. The first classes met in this structure on May 5, 1924.

After receiving the M.A. degree from the University of Texas in 1924, Clark held a number of appointive and elective positions in the state educational system. He served as chairman of the board of examiners of the State Department of Education (*see* TEXAS EDUCATION AGENCY) and as a member of the State Textbook Committee. In addition, he was president of the Northwest Texas Teachers Association, the Texas Association of Junior Colleges, and the Texas State Teachers Association.qv He also served as vice president of the National Education Association. Clark died in Cisco on February 19, 1941.

BIBLIOGRAPHY: Louise Kelly, *Wichita County Beginnings* (Burnet, Texas: Eakin Press, 1982). *Brian Hart*

CLARK, ROBERT CARLTON (1877–1939). Robert Carlton Clark, teacher and historian, son of Sallie (McQuigg) and Addison Clark,qv was born at Thorp Spring, Texas, on March 4, 1877. In 1893 he graduated from Add-Ran College (later Texas Christian University). His early teaching was in the public schools of Mineral Wells and at Bay View College in Portland, Texas. While a graduate student at the University of Texas, he prepared transcripts of official documents in the national archives of Mexico. He was one of the early historians of Spanish-French relations on the Texas-Louisiana border. His earliest authoritative contribution, under the general title "The Beginnings of Texas," appeared in the January and July 1902 *Quarterly of the Texas State Historical Association* (now the *Southwestern Historical Quarterly*qv). In 1901–02 he held a graduate scholarship at the University of Wisconsin; in 1903 he was appointed fellow in American history at

the same university, where he was awarded a doctorate. He taught at Pennsylvania State College and later at the University of Oregon, where he became head of the history department. He was married first to Ann W. Wallace, with whom he had three children; he then married Marguerite Straugham, and they had two children. On December 4, 1939, he died in the classroom of a heart attack. He was buried in Eugene, Oregon. *J. L. Clark*

CLARK, THOMAS CAMPBELL (1899–1977). Tom Campbell Clark, attorney general of the United States and the first Texan to serve on the United States Supreme Court, was born in Dallas on September 23, 1899, to William H. and Jennie (Falls) Clark. He attended Virginia Military Institute in 1917–18 and received an A.B. degree from the University of Texas in 1921. After graduating in 1922 from the University of Texas School of Law, Clark practiced law in Dallas and was civil district attorney of Dallas County from 1927 until 1937. In 1924 he married Mary Ramsey, the daughter of Texas Supreme Court justice William F. Ramsey;qv they had three children.

In 1937 Clark joined the Roosevelt administration as an assistant to the United States attorney general. He worked first in the War Risk Litigation Section and then in the Antitrust Division. Clark became the department's chief of West Coast offices in 1940, and in 1942 he coordinated and directed the relocation and incarceration of American citizens of Japanese ancestry. He worked closely with the military to implement the program despite opposition to wholesale internment from his superior, Attorney General Francis Biddle. Clark later referred to his involvement in the Japanese-American relocation project as one of his biggest mistakes.

In 1942 Clark was appointed head of the War Frauds Unit of the Justice Department, where he prosecuted frauds uncovered by Senator Harry Truman. Clark became assistant attorney general in 1943 and headed the antitrust and criminal divisions until he became attorney general to President Truman in 1945. As attorney general, Clark supported the authority of the federal government. Thus he vigorously enforced the government's antitrust laws while successfully prosecuting the United Mine Workers Union and labor leader John L. Lewis for violating a federal no-strike injunction. Clark opposed states' rights when he successfully argued before the Supreme Court that the United States and not the individual states owned offshore oilfields in *United States v. California* (1947) (*see* TIDELANDS CONTROVERSY). In a similar vein, Clark helped develop Truman's national civil-rights policy in opposition to some of the states. Under Clark the Department of Justice initiated its first modern amicus brief on behalf of a civil-rights plaintiff in the restrictive-covenant case, *Shelley v. Kraemer* (1948), which resulted in a unanimous decision against race discrimination in housing contracts. Clark's support of a strong national government also extended to the defense of loyalty oaths and opposition to domestic dissent. He issued the first attorney general's list of subversive organizations and initiated prosecution of the leaders of the American Communist party under the Smith Act.

In 1949 he replaced Frank Murphy on the United States Supreme Court. He was generally considered a liberal member of the Vinson court and a more conservative justice during the years of the Warren court. Associate Justice Clark served for eighteen years. It is not surprising that the former attorney general who vigorously enforced the Smith Act usually voted to uphold McCarthy-era prosecutions. This put him in the minority in *Yates v. United States* (1957), which overturned the Smith Act convictions of fourteen Communist party officials, and in *Watkins v. United States* (1957), which curbed the investigations of the House Committee on Un-American Activities; and in the majority in *Barenblatt v. United States* (1959), which upheld a contempt conviction of a professor who refused to answer the committee's questions, and in *Rosenberg v. United States* (1959), which gave Congress control over the release of FBI files to defendants. As late as 1967 Clark dissented in *Keyishian v. Board of Regents,* when the court overturned the removal of a teacher for past political affiliations.

Clark joined the court at the beginning of the civil rights movement and consistently voted in favor of integration. In *Sweatt v. Painter*qv (1950) Clark's support of the majority opinion, which ordered the integration of the University of Texas law school, was particularly important. He also wrote the opinion in *Terry v. Adams* (1953), which struck down the white primaryqv in Texas. In 1954 he joined the unanimous decision in *Brown v. Board of Education of Topeka,* which declared racial segregation in public schools unconstitutional. A decade later he wrote an opinion for the unanimous upholding of the 1964 Civil Rights Act in *Heart of Atlanta Motel, Inc. v. United States.*

Clark's background of supporting federal authority was critical in extending federal constitutional protections in other areas. In *Mapp v. Ohio* (1961), Clark, the former federal prosecutor, extended the exclusionary rule to prevent the use of illegally seized evidence in criminal trials by state officials. Here he extended the protections of the Fourth Amendment to defendants in state trials and thus limited the powers of the states. In his opinion striking down prayer and Bible reading in public schools in *School District of Abingdon v. Schempp* (1963), Clark spoke as a justice from the "Bible Belt," reaffirming that "we are a religious people" but asserting that prayer should be kept out of public schools. In concurring in *Baker v. Carr* (1962), Clark ruled against state legislative apportionment practices that were discriminatory.

In 1967 his son William Ramsey Clark was appointed attorney general by President Lyndon B. Johnson.qv To avoid any conflicts of interest in cases his son might argue, Justice Clark retired from the bench. At the suggestion of Attorney General Ramsey Clark, Justice Tom Clark's seat was filled by Thurgood Marshall, the first black to serve on the Supreme Court. After retiring, Clark served on eleven of the United States circuit courts of appeals and in 1968 was appointed the first director of the Federal Judicial Center, where he studied the judicial system and worked for improvements in its administration. He also served as chairman both of the American Bar Association Section of Judicial Administration and of the National College of State Trial Judges. He died in New York City on June 13, 1977.

BIBLIOGRAPHY: Leon Friedman and Fred L. Israel, eds., *The Justices of the United States Supreme Court* (5 vols., New York: Chelsea House, 1969). Richard Kluger, *Simple Justice: The History of* Brown v. Board of Education *and Black America's Struggle for Equality* (New York: Knopf, 1976). *Supreme Court Reporter,* October 1977.

Paul Finkelman

CLARK, THOMAS MARSHALL (1856–1943). Thomas Marshall Clark, teacher and college officer, son of Esther (D'Spain) and Joseph Addison Clark,qv was born at Midway, Texas, on January 7, 1856. The family moved to Fort Worth in 1867. In 1873 Thomas's brothers, Addison and Randolph Clark,qqv settled at Thorp Spring in Hood County and established Add-Ran College, where Thomas was secretary-treasurer and teacher of music, dramatics, and languages. He married Alice Yantis in 1878, and they had one son. In 1894 the family moved to Portland, on Corpus Christi Bay, where Clark established Bay View College, a private school for girls. When the college was closed in 1917 he moved to Wichita Falls, where he taught until 1919, when he went to West Texas State Teachers College (now West Texas State University) at Canyon. He taught history and languages there until 1932. From 1934 to 1936 he taught at Cisco Junior College. After retiring in 1936 Clark lived at his home at Portland until his death, on April 21, 1943.

BIBLIOGRAPHY: Vertical Files, Barker Texas History Center, University of Texas at Austin.

Wallace R. Clark

CLARK, WILLIAM, JR. (1798–1871). William Clark, Jr., legislator, soldier, merchant, and signer of the Texas Declaration of Independence,qv was born in North Carolina on April 14, 1798. He married Martha B. Wall; they had four children. In 1835 the Clarks moved from Georgia, where they had become wealthy from merchandising and farming, to Sabine County, Texas. Clark and James Gainesqv represented Sabine Municipality at the Convention of 1836qv and signed the Declaration of Independence. After the convention Clark helped President David G. Burnetqv formulate a system of collecting and forwarding supplies to the army. He also served in 1836 as a member of the Board of Land Commissioners of Sabine County. He was elected to represent Sabine County in the House of the Second Congress in September 1837, but he resigned in April 1838 because of illness. Clark was still in Sabine County in April 1850 but probably moved to Nacogdoches County shortly thereafter. In 1859 he purchased the Planter Hotel in Nacogdoches, which he operated until his death, on January 3, 1871. Clark was a Methodist. In 1936 the Texas Centennialqv Commission placed a marker at the site of the Clarks' last home and a joint monument at the graves of Clark and his wife in Oak Grove Cemetery in Nacogdoches. Clark's son, who was also known as William Clark, Jr., was elected a representative to the state legislature in 1859 and to the Secession Conventionqv in 1861. This man's activities have sometimes been attributed to his father.

BIBLIOGRAPHY: *Southwestern Historical Quarterly,* Notes and Fragments, January 1920. Texas House of Representatives, *Biographical Directory of the Texan Conventions and Congresses, 1832–1845* (Austin: Book Exchange, 1941).

Cecil Harper, Jr.

CLARK, WILLIAM, JR. (1828–1884). William Clark, legislator and soldier, the son of Martha B. (Wall) and William Clark, Jr.,qv was born in Milledgeville, Georgia, on November 8, 1828. The family moved to Texas in 1835 and settled in Sabine County, where the junior Clark grew into adulthood. He served four months in Company K, Second Texas Mounted Volunteers, during the Mexican Warqv and participated in the battle of Monterrey. He was admitted to the bar in Shelby County in 1852 and practiced in San Augustine County. He settled permanently at Nacogdoches in September 1854. In the House of the Eighth Legislature (1859–61) Clark represented Nacogdoches County. When Governor Sam Houstonqv called the legislature into special session, Clark voted against calling the Secession Convention.qv However, he was elected to that convention and there voted for separation from the Union. He raised an infantry company at Nacogdoches. On January 13, 1862, his unit entered the Confederate Army as Company G, Twelfth Texas Infantry. He was elected the company captain and was eventually promoted to lieutenant colonel of the regiment. After returning home he resumed his law practice and served as attorney for Nacogdoches County and for the Houston, East and West Texas Railway Company. On July 11, 1867, Clark married Amelia Taylor, daughter of Charles S. Taylor,qv in Nacogdoches; they had ten children. Clark died on January 6, 1884, and was buried in the Oak Grove Cemetery in Nacogdoches.

BIBLIOGRAPHY: William DeRyee and R. E. Moore, *The Texas Album of the Eighth Legislature, 1860* (Austin: Miner, Lambert, and Perry, 1860). *Memorial and Genealogical Record of Texas (East)* (Chicago: Goodspeed, 1895; rpt., Easley, South Carolina: Southern Historical Press, 1982).

J. L. Bryan

CLARK, WILLIAM H. (1861–1931). William H. Clark, attorney, was born to William H. and Mary (McDowell) Clark near Brandon, Mississippi, on May 2, 1861. He attended Brandon Academy and graduated from the University of Mississippi in 1882. He returned to his hometown as principal of Brandon Academy immediately after receiving his college degree. He continued to study law in his spare time and resigned from the academy in 1883 to enter the law school at Cumberland University, Lebanon, Tennessee. He completed his legal education in 1885 and moved with his mother to Dallas, Texas. He worked in a series of positions—in the office of Seth Shepard,qv in the United States Court of Appeals in Washington, and subsequently in a number of other firms—before establishing a private practice in 1905. He married Virginia Maxey Falls of Brandon, Mississippi, on June 9, 1886. The couple raised seven children.

Clark was elected president of the Texas State Bar Association (*see* STATE BAR OF TEXAS) in 1897. At the time, he was the youngest attorney ever to hold this position. In a practice limited to civil law he successfully argued a number of cases before the United States Supreme Court, including *Brown Cracker and Candy Company v. City of Dallas*, in which he convinced the justices that a local ordinance reserving a portion of the city for bawdy houses violated the state constitution and state laws. Clark frequently advised committees of the state legislature in the framing of statutes. He was a Democrat and frequently served as a Dallas County delegate to the party's state conventions. He died in Dallas of a heart attack on September 17, 1931.

BIBLIOGRAPHY: Dallas *Morning News,* September 18, 1931. Frank W. Johnson, *A History of Texas and Texans* (5 vols., ed. E. C. Barker and E. W. Winkler [Chicago and New York: American Historical Society, 1914; rpt. 1916]).
Brian Hart

CLARK, WILLIAM THOMAS (1831–1905). William Thomas Clark, Union soldier and legislator, was born in Norwalk, Connecticut, on June 29, 1831, the son of Levi and Fanny Clark. At age thirteen he was forced to quit school and begin to support himself because of his family's extreme poverty. After a few years of doing odd jobs around Norwalk he took a job as a teacher and then began the study of law. Clark moved in 1854 to New York, where he was admitted to the bar. There in 1856 he married Laura Clark of Hartford. The couple immediately moved to Davenport, Iowa, where Clark began his practice. With the advent of the Civil War[qv] he raised the Thirteenth Iowa Infantry. On November 2, 1861, he was commissioned a first lieutenant in the regiment and appointed its adjutant. He saw action at the battles of Shiloh, Corinth, Vicksburg, and Atlanta. He was promoted to captain on March 6 and to major on November 24, 1862. On February 10, 1863, he was promoted to lieutenant colonel, and when Gen. James B. McPherson became the commanding officer of the Army of the Tennessee, Clark was named his adjutant general. Clark was brevetted to the rank of brigadier general "for gallant and distinguished service" at the battle of Atlanta on July 22, 1864, and to major general on November 24, 1865, for his distinguished service during the war.

At the end of the war he was transferred to Texas as a part of the United States force sent to check French expansionism in Mexico through the puppet emperor Maximilian. There he became involved in intrigue with Mexican general José Antonio Mexía,[qv] who promised to turn over Matamoros to the United States for $200,000. Generals Philip Sheridan[qv] and Ulysses S. Grant favored this scheme, but it was vetoed by President Andrew Johnson and Secretary of State William H. Seward.

Clark was discharged from the army on February 1, 1866, and moved to Galveston, where he helped to organize a bank, of which he became cashier. He also became active in the formation of chapters of the Union League[qv] and formed a close association with George T. Ruby,[qv] a leader of Galveston freedmen. In 1869 he was elected to the United States House of Representatives of the Forty-first Congress from the Third District of Texas. In Congress he labored to sell to the national government a vast region of West Texas for the sum of $40 million to be used to subsidize railroad building and Negro education in the state. Clark was defeated for reelection in 1871 by Dewitt Clinton Giddings[qv] despite Governor Edmund J. Davis's[qv] flagrant attempt to alter the election results and have him seated. Clark, in fact, returned to Washington and attempted to occupy his old seat but was expelled by the unanimous vote of his colleagues; Giddings was seated instead (*see* GIDDINGS-CLARK ELECTION CONTEST).

Clark was postmaster at Galveston from 1872 to 1874 and then secured a post in the Bureau of Internal Revenue, at which he served until his death in New York City on October 12, 1905. He is buried in Arlington National Cemetery. Historian Rossetter Gleason Cole referred to Clark as "the last of the carpetbaggers."

BIBLIOGRAPHY: Philip J. Avillo, Jr., "Phantom Radicals: Texas Republicans in Congress, 1870–1873," *Southwestern Historical Quarterly* 77 (April 1974). *Dictionary of American Biography.* Claude H. Hall, "The Fabulous Tom Ochiltree," *Southwestern Historical Quarterly* 71 (January 1968). Francis B. Heitman, *Historical Register and Dictionary of the United States Army* (2 vols., Washington: GPO, 1903; rpt., Urbana: University of Illinois Press, 1965). Carl H. Moneyhon, "Public Education and Texas Reconstruction Politics, 1871–1874," *Southwestern Historical Quarterly* 92 (January 1989).
Thomas W. Cutrer

CLARK, TEXAS (Liberty County). Clark is on State Highway 146 sixty miles northwest of Beaumont in northeastern Liberty County. During the 1840s the area was the site of Sam Houston's[qv] Grand Cane plantation on the Trinity River. The Grand Cane post office, established in 1846, was renamed Ironwood in 1869. The 1870 census listed seventy-six households in the Ironwood district, a largely agricultural area whose fertile soils supported dense forests. In 1900 the Ironwood post office was renamed Clark at the suggestion of postmaster Randolph Fields. As the lumber industry moved into northeastern Liberty County, the Cummings logging camp was established to the southwest, and the Milvid logging road was carved to the north and east. Clark became a voting precinct in 1924, and it was consolidated with Rye to form the Concord precinct in 1948. A few scattered buildings and a gravel pit still marked the site of Clark in 1990.

BIBLIOGRAPHY: Miriam Partlow, *Liberty, Liberty County, and the Atascosito District* (Austin: Pemberton, 1974).
Robert Wooster

CLARK, TEXAS (Van Zandt County). Clark was seven miles northeast of Canton in northeast Van Zandt County. It had a local school enrollment of fifty-three in 1904. In 1936 the town had the school, a business, and scattered dwellings. The school was consolidated with the Grand Saline Independent School District by the 1950s. In 1987 only a grain elevator remained to service area farmers.
Diana J. Kleiner

CLARKE, ANTHONY R. (?–?). Anthony R. Clarke, one of the Old Three Hundred[qv] and an alcalde[qv] at Nacogdoches, was the son of James and Catherine (Lynsen) Clarke. After corresponding with Stephen F. Austin[qv] between February and June 1824 about a move from East Texas to the Austin colony, Clarke received title to a labor of land in what is now Brazoria County on August 24, 1824. In January 1825 he still wanted his move to the colony kept secret lest he lose money on his improvements at Attoyac. He planned to move to San Felipe, get land with his sister, Mrs. Eliza Page, take two town lots and a labor to furnish timber and vegetables, and help his sister start a tavern. He was listed in the census of 1826 as a farmer and stock raiser, a single man aged over fifty, with two servants. In May 1827 he had a business in San Felipe. His character certificate, dated at San Felipe on December 23, 1829, stated that he was a native of New York and was fifty-five years old. Clarke reportedly died of cholera in Washington-on-the-Brazos.

BIBLIOGRAPHY: Austin Land Papers, Spanish Collection, Archives and Records Division, Texas General Land Office, Austin. Eugene C. Barker, ed., *The Austin Papers* (3 vols., Washington: GPO, 1924–28). Lester G. Bugbee, "The Old Three Hundred: A List of Settlers in Austin's First Colony," *Quarterly of the Texas State Historical Association* 1 (October 1897). Mrs. Harry Joseph Morris, comp. and ed., *Citizens of the Republic of Texas* (Dallas: Texas State Genealogical Society, 1977).

CLARKE, EDWARD A. (1808–1858). Edward A. Clarke (Clark), priest, son of Ignatius and Aloysia (Hill) Clarke and grandnephew of the first bishop of Cincinnati, was born in Marion County, Kentucky, in 1808. He and George W. Haydon^{qv} were the first American-born Catholic priests to settle and minister in Texas. Sometime before 1824 Clarke, along with his childhood friend Haydon, entered St. Thomas Seminary in Bardstown, Kentucky. Both transferred to St. Joseph College before graduation and ordination to the priesthood at St. Joseph's Cathedral in 1832. For the next few years Clarke served as missionary in a large district encompassing several counties. In 1836, after a brief assignment at St. Thomas Seminary, he was named co-assistant to the pastor of St. Louis Church in Louisville, a position also held by Haydon. In 1837 Clarke joined the faculty of St. Joseph College as professor of natural philosophy.

In 1839 Clarke and Haydon volunteered to go to Texas as missionaries, at the request of a number of Kentucky and Missouri Catholics planning to move to the young republic. After an initial delay due to conflicting reports about their pastoral qualifications, the two Kentucky priests set out for New Orleans, where they obtained canonical credentials from Bishop Blanc and a letter of introduction to President Mirabeau B. Lamar^{qv} from the Abbé Anduze, chaplain of the French fleet. Upon arrival in Texas, Clarke and Haydon visited a colony of Kentuckian settlers in Brazoria and then undertook a missionary tour of the republic. A few months later, using Richmond as a starting point, the priests made a second, longer, missionary tour of Texas, after which they separated for greater effectiveness. Haydon settled at Refugio, where he started to repair the old Spanish mission church, and Clarke moved to Brown's Settlement on the Lavaca River, where he helped the residents build a log church dedicated to St. Mary. The priests, however, continued to support each other; together they built a two-story log cabin amid the Lavaca farms, to serve as a school for children and adults. Eventually, the church entrusted all the English-speaking Catholics in the southwestern districts of the republic to Clarke's care.

Haydon died in October 1841. The loss of his lifelong friend was a deep blow for Clarke, but it made his pastoral commitment stronger. Using St. Mary's as a pivot, he traveled extensively during the next few years, ministering to Catholic settlers from the upper Navidad River to Victoria and Texana. In 1847 he was appointed resident pastor of St. Vincent de Paul, the oldest church in Houston, where he remained until 1856, when he became seriously ill. He returned to Kentucky to rest and died of consumption in Louisville on November 25, 1858.

BIBLIOGRAPHY: Ralph Francis Bayard, *Lone-Star Vanguard: The Catholic Re-Occupation of Texas, 1838–1848* (St. Louis: Vincentian Press, 1945). Catholic Archives of Texas, Files, Austin.

Aníbal A. González

CLARKE, MARY EMMA WHATLEY DUNBAR (1899–1990). Mary Whatley Clarke, western historian, country newspaper editor, and reporter, was born at Palo Pinto, Texas, on June 11, 1899, to Cephas Vachel and Narcissa Isabella (Abernathy) Whatley, Palo Pinto County pioneers. After her graduation from Mineral Wells High School, she taught in a private plantation school near Fort Gaines, Georgia. She later taught public school near Hobbs, New Mexico. She attended New Mexico State Normal in the summer of 1921. That year she married James Coleman Dunbar, publisher of the Norwood *Press* in Winnipeg, Canada. When Dunbar died in 1923, his widow became publisher of the paper. Although she had no previous newspaper experience, she learned the business well enough to publish the paper successfully for four years. In 1927 she sold the *Press* and purchased the *Palo Pinto County Star* in Palo Pinto, Texas.

The Palo Pinto weekly was a one-woman operation. Mary Dunbar wrote all the stories and editorials, sold advertising, managed the business operation, and supervised the press. During that time she was elected president of the West Texas Press Association, the first female so honored.

In 1943 she married Albany (Texas) banker Joe Clarke; they had one daughter. They moved to Fort Worth in 1946, when Clarke became executive vice president of the Fort Worth National Bank. Mary Clarke's first book was *Palo Pinto Story* (1956), a history of her native Palo Pinto County. It was followed by *Texas Sunbonnets,* a collection of her columns for the *Palo Pinto Star* published by the author in 1956. Her other books include *David G. Burnet* (1969); *Chief Bowles and the Texas Cherokees* (1971); *A Century of Cow Business,* a history of the Texas and Southwestern Cattle Raisers Association^{qv} published in 1977 to commemorate the organization's hundredth anniversary; *The Slaughter Ranches and Their Makers* (1979); and *John Chisum, Jingle Bob King of the Pecos* (1984), her final book. In addition, she edited *Life in the Saddle* by Frank Collinson (1963).

She also wrote 166 feature-length articles for the *Cattleman*^{qv} magazine, published by the Texas and Southwestern Cattle Raisers Association. The articles, published between 1943 and 1982, established her unique position as a woman writer on ranching and ranchers. For many years, she also wrote a monthly column for the magazine published by Fort Worth Children's Hospital, where she spent thousands of hours as a volunteer.

Mary and Joe Clarke were among the organizers of the Van Cliburn International Piano Competition in Fort Worth and the Jewel Charity Ball, which has raised more than $9 million for Cook–Fort Worth Children's Medical Center. The Clarkes traveled extensively, and Mary usually managed to include some type of cattle-raising operations in their itinerary. The Clarkes were on the maiden voyage of the *Andrea Doria,* the Italian luxury liner that later collided with a Swedish ship and sank in the Atlantic. Mary Clarke prized a commemorative cup and saucer marking the ship's maiden voyage. Regardless of their many trips, Mary and Joe Clarke always managed to be in Texas for the annual convention of the Cattle Raisers Association. Don C. King, secretary-general of the association for many years, recalled: "Mary Clarke was an institution at our convention with her pad and pencil, ready smile and quiet grace." She died on July 8, 1990, in Fort Worth. Joe Clarke died in 1971.

BIBLIOGRAPHY: Fort Worth *Star-Telegram,* July 9, 1990. *Southwestern Historical Quarterly,* Southwestern Collection, April 1991.

Cissy Stewart Lale

CLARKE AND COURTS PRINTING. Clarke and Courts Printing, with original headquarters in Galveston, was in business in Texas for over 100 years. Until the 1930s the company was the largest printing and lithography company in the region. It produced forms for state and local governments throughout Texas, for businesses, banks, and railroads, in addition to wedding invitations, stationery, and blank books. It also sold office furniture. Clarke and Courts developed from M. Strickland and Company, Printers, Lithographers and Blank Book Manufacturers, organized at Galveston by Miles Strickland in 1857. Strickland moved his printing press to Houston during the Civil War^{qv} but subsequently returned to Galveston. After the war Samuel Burke, an expert printer, became a partner in the business, and a bindery was added to the plant. After Robert Clarke purchased Burke's interest in the firm in 1870, the business came to be known as Strickland and Clarke. Known for its quality work, the company received a first prize at the Philadelphia Centennial Exposition for its blank-book business in 1876. George M. Courts, who had previously handled stationery for the Thompson Drug Company, purchased Strickland's interest, and in 1877 the two printers brought the first lithograph press in the state to Galveston, along with a crew to operate it. Clarke and Courts dates its origins to the partnership formed by the two men in 1879, in which Clarke managed the printing aspects of the business while Courts supervised the rest.

Traveling salesmen for Clarke and Courts marketed its products throughout Texas, western Louisiana, New Mexico, and Mexico. In the 1880s the firm's employees numbered between seventy-five and 100. In 1887, when the company won a blue ribbon at the State Fair of Texas,^{qv} it incorporated as Clarke and Courts. By 1890 the firm had completed its office on the Strand^{qv} in Galveston, designed by Nicholas J. Clayton,^{qv} as well as a plant and warehouse. The office came to be known as the "Texas House." In 1902 the firm subscribed $5,000 for seawall bonds to protect the city after the devastation of the Galveston hurricane of 1900,^qv which damaged the company's building and killed its head bookkeeper. Clarke and Courts printed the first newspapers after the disaster. In 1907 the firm installed the first offset press west of the Mississippi; thus began the company policy of acquiring every innovation in printing machinery as soon as it appeared and limiting the competition by refusing to sell old equipment. Eventually, Clarke and Courts offered customers an array of services ranging from printing, electrotyping, stereotyping, and bookbinding to box-manufacturing, lithographing, and zinc-engraving. Among its numerous printing projects was the printing of San Antonio city directories. In 1936, when the company renewed its charter and moved its headquarters to Houston, its service extended to customers in Texas, Louisiana, Oklahoma, New Mexico, Arkansas, Mexico, and Cuba. By 1976 Clarke and Courts operated plants in Galveston, Harlingen, and Houston, but faced growing computerization in the industry. The business closed in 1989. In 1994, as part of its rehabilitation and revitalization program, the city of Galveston planned to convert the Texas House into a residential building known as the Strand Lofts; its first floor was allocated to the Museum of Printing History. At the same time, space at the Houston building of the firm, renovated into a residential building known as Tribecca Lofts, was allocated to a display of printing machines and memorabilia curated by the Museum of Printing History.

BIBLIOGRAPHY: Andrew Morrison, *The Industries of Galveston* (Galveston?: Metropolitan, 1887). *Diana J. Kleiner*

CLARK LAKE. Clark Lake is a small, one-half mile long natural lake, half a mile south of the Brazos River, two miles north of the Rock Island, and one mile north of Donohoe Creek in Clark Bottom in northwest Waller County (at 30°12′ N, 96°08′ W). The surrounding flat to rolling terrain with local depressions is surfaced by clay and sandy loams that support water-tolerant hardwoods and conifers.

CLARK'S CHAPEL, TEXAS. Clark's Chapel was on Farm Road 713 six miles southeast of Lockhart in central Caldwell County. A camp meeting was held on land owned by William Alexander Clark in 1877, at which time the Clark's Chapel Methodist Church was organized. A post office was established there in 1899; it was called Ledford in honor of a local doctor and store owner, but residents of the community continued to use the name Clark's Chapel. Clark's Chapel became the focus of a common school district in 1886, but the school was consolidated with the Harmony Grove school in 1912. The church, which had about 150 members in 1890, continued to hold regular services until the mid-1940s. In the 1950s groups began to use the site for family reunions. In the 1970s and 1980s the grounds of the church and cemetery were kept by a cemetery committee.

BIBLIOGRAPHY: Mark Withers Trail Drive Museum, *Historical Caldwell County* (Dallas: Taylor, 1984). *Vivian Elizabeth Smyrl*

CLARKS CREEK (Harrison County). Clarks Creek rises two miles east of Longview in southwestern Harrison County (at 32°30′ N, 94°38′ W) and runs southeast for eleven miles, through Harrison County, to its mouth on the Sabine River, three miles east of Easton (at 32°24′ N, 94°32′ W). It was named for Isaac Clark, an antebellum settler in Harrison County. The surrounding nearly level to hilly terrain is surfaced by loam and clay that support dense patches of pine and hardwood trees. The land is used predominantly for agriculture.
_____ (Lavaca County). Clarks Creek rises a mile northeast of the intersection of Alternate U.S. Highway 77 and State Highway 95, at Yoakum in western Lavaca County (at 29°20′ N, 97°08′ W) and runs southeast for 33½ miles to its mouth on the Lavaca River, 6½ miles east of the intersection of Highway 77 and State Highway 111 (at 29°10′ N, 96°52′ W). Its course traverses rolling plains surfaced by variable soils. The area is used as range and improved pasture for cattle, with supplemental production of corn and grain sorghums and the flow from numerous oil and gas wells. The creek's name is probably derived from that of the families of Ben F. and John Clark, who lived in the area before 1840 and were active in the Clark-Hughes feud and the Petersburg-Hallettsville fight for the location of the county seat.

BIBLIOGRAPHY: Paul C. Boethel, *Colonel Amasa Turner, the Gentleman from Lavaca, and Other Captains at San Jacinto* (Austin: Von Boeckmann-Jones, 1963). Paul C. Boethel, *Sand in Your Craw* (Austin: Von Boeckmann-Jones, 1959).

CLARK SEMINARY. Clark Seminary, a private girls' school in Houston, was operated by Horace Clark^qv from 1872 to 1875. The classes were conducted on the second floor of the building occupied by the Houston Academy.^qv

BIBLIOGRAPHY: Carl Bassett Wilson, History of Baptist Educational Efforts in Texas, 1829–1900 (Ph.D. dissertation, University of Texas, 1934). *Carolyn Hyman*

CLARKSON, WILEY G. (1885–1952). Wiley G. Clarkson, architect, was born in Corsicana, Texas, on November 28, 1885. After attending the University of Texas for two years, he studied engineering at the Chicago Armour Institute of Technology and architecture at the Art Institute of Chicago. He returned to Corsicana in 1908 and operated a practice there until 1912, when he moved to Fort Worth. From 1919 to 1921 he collaborated with A. W. Gaines. After Gaines's death in 1921 he resumed his solo practice.

During the 1920s and early 1930s Clarkson designed a wide variety of works in Fort Worth, including the Texas Christian University Library (1925–27), Trinity Episcopal Church (1925–27), Sanger Brothers Department Store (1925–27), the YMCA Building (1925–27), the Woolworth Building (1925–27), and the Methodist Harris Hospital (1930), as well as numerous residences in the Ryan Place and River Crest sections of the city. Clarkson's early buildings were characterized by historical revival styles: Neoclassicism, Gothic, and Italianate. During the late 1920s, however, he began to experiment with the new Moderne or Art Deco idiom, and over the course of the next decade he produced many of the city's best examples of that style, among them the Sinclair Building (1929), the Masonic Temple (1930), the Collins Art Company (1932), the United States Courthouse (1933, with associate architect Paul Philippe Cret^qv), the Municipal Airport Administration Building (1936), North Side Senior High School (1937), W. C. Stripling Department Store (1937), Tarrant County Building and Loan Association (1938), and the City-County Hospital (1938–39). During World War II^qv Clarkson collaborated with the architectural firms of Joseph Roman Pelich, Preston M. Geren, Sr.,^qqv and Joe Rady on projects for the United States Housing Authority and the United States Army Corps of Engineers, including Liberator Village, Fort Worth; McCloskey Army Hospital, Temple; and Harmon Army Hospital, Longview. He also collaborated with Herbert Bayer, Gordon Chadwick, and A. George King on the design for the Fort Worth Art Center (1953), now the Modern Art Museum of Fort Worth.^qv

Clarkson was a charter member of the Texas Society of Architects and was president in 1942–43. He was also a founding member of the Fort Worth chapter of the American Institute of Architects and served as its president in 1948. He died in Fort Worth on May 5, 1952.

BIBLIOGRAPHY: Judith Singer Cohen, *Cowtown Moderne: Art Deco Architecture of Fort Worth, Texas* (Fort Worth: Texas Christian University Press, 1988). Judith Singer Cohen, "Wiley G. Clarkson," *Texas Architect*, November–December 1989. *Christopher Long*

CLARKSON, TEXAS. Clarkson is on Farm Road 1445 nine miles northeast of Cameron in northern Milam County. A post office operated there from 1889 to 1906. In 1903 the community had a one-teacher school for forty-three white students and a two-teacher school for 105 black students. Clarkson had a population of fifty in the 1940s, and the schools were consolidated with the Cameron Independent School District by the early 1950s. Clarkson had ten residents in 1990.

BIBLIOGRAPHY: Lelia M. Batte, *History of Milam County, Texas* (San Antonio: Naylor, 1956).

Vivian Elizabeth Smyrl

CLARKSVILLE, TEXAS (Cameron County). Clarksville was near the mouth of the Rio Grande, opposite the Mexican city of Bagdad. During the Mexican War[qv] a temporary army camp stood there, with William H. Clark,[qv] a civilian, in charge. Clark set up a country store and served as agent for the steamship lines using the port. The town quickly developed; houses were built up on stilts to be above high water. During the early part of the Civil War[qv] Clarksville thrived on the trade of the Confederate blockade-runners, but in 1863 it was captured by federals, who held it most of the time until the end of the war. The last battle of the war was fought four miles away at Palmito Ranch.[qv] In 1867 Clarksville was almost destroyed by a hurricane but survived during the days of the river steamer. In 1872 it received another blow when the railway was built from Brownsville to Point Isabel, and severe storms in 1874 and 1886 finished it. In 1953 the river had changed its course and flowed over the site of Clarksville.

BIBLIOGRAPHY: Houston *Chronicle*, April 19, 1926. Dick King, *Ghost Towns of Texas* (San Antonio: Naylor, 1953). Florence J. Scott, *Old Rough and Ready on the Rio Grande* (San Antonio: Naylor, 1935).

Cyrus Tilloson

CLARKSVILLE, TEXAS (Red River County). Clarksville, the county seat of Red River County, is at the junction of U.S. Highway 82, State Highway 37, and Farm roads 114, 412, 909, 910, and 1159, fifty-eight miles northwest of Texarkana near the center of the county. It was established by James Clark,[qv] who in 1833 moved to the area and laid out a townsite. Isaac Smathers is supposed to have built one of the first houses, a building that later became the home of Charles DeMorse.[qv] With the organization of Red River County in 1835, Clarksville defeated La Grange (later Madras) as the county seat. The town was incorporated by an act of the Texas Congress in 1837, and within a few years it became an educational and agricultural center. Clarksville Female Academy[qv] was founded in 1840 on Pine Creek and in 1844 moved to Clarksville; McKenzie College, four miles from Clarksville, opened in 1841; and the following year DeMorse began publication of the Clarksville *Northern Standard*.[qv] A post office opened in 1846, and in 1848 semiweekly mail service was instituted between Clarksville and Natchitoches, Louisiana.

In the town's early days, itinerant preachers, among them Mansell W. Matthews, John B. Denton,[qqv] Gilbert Clark, and Craig Shook, conducted religious services in a log schoolhouse. The First Presbyterian Church, believed to be among the oldest continually operating Protestant churches in the state, was organized at nearby Shiloh, four miles to the northeast, in 1833, and moved to the town in 1848. Baptist and Methodist churches were also organized before the Civil War.[qv]

From the late 1830s until the Civil War, Clarksville was the most important trading center in Northwest Texas. Steamboats brought goods from New Orleans by way of the Red River and delivered them to Rowland's Landing fifteen miles to the north. They were then hauled overland by wagon. During the 1850s new steam sawmills and cotton gins added to the town's importance. The first courthouse, a modest frame structure, was erected around 1840. In 1850 it was replaced by a larger brick structure at the center of a large public square; a brick jailhouse was built nearby in 1852. Within a few years of the town's founding, numerous mercantile establishments opened on and around the courthouse square, and by eve of the Civil War Clarksville's population had grown to 900.

The economy suffered a serious setback during the war and the early Reconstruction[qv] years, but by the beginning of 1870s business in Clarksville had begun to recover. The greatest impetus to the town's development came in 1872 with the completion of the Transcontinental Branch of the Texas and Pacific Railway. The coming of the railroad brought many new settlers and merchants to the area, and by 1885 Clarksville had a population of 1,200, five white and two black churches, a Catholic convent, three schools, two banks, two flour mills, and a weekly newspaper, the Clarksville *Times;* principal products included cotton, livestock, and grain. A new three-story limestone courthouse, designed in the Renaissance Revival style by W. H. Wison, was completed in 1884, a symbol of the town's continuing prosperity. In 1914 Clarksville had 3,000 inhabitants, a waterworks, two newspapers, an ice plant, and an electric power plant. But with the rise of Dallas, Paris, Bonham, and Texarkana during the 1870s and 1880s, the importance of Clarksville as a trading center had begun to decline.

In 1929 the estimated population reached 4,000. With the onset of the Great Depression[qv] in the early 1930s, many Clarksvillians found themselves out of work, and a large number left the area. By 1931 the population had dropped to 2,950. The number of rated businesses also declined from a high of 165 in 1931 to 104 in 1936. Particularly hard hit was the cotton wholesale and processing industry, which suffered from the combined effects of falling prices and the boll weevil.[qv]

In 1936 the economy began to turn around. Production of cotton increased 100 percent over the previous year, with the estimated value of the crop put at $1.9 million. During the mid-1930s oil was also discovered at Talco, sixteen miles south, and in 1936 more than 1,000 leases were filed with the county clerk's office. The oil boom brought a new wave of prosperity to the town, helping to mitigate the worst effects of the depression and fueling a wave of public and private construction. The population rebounded during the late 1940s, to an estimated 4,300 in 1952; the number of rated businesses that year also hit an all-time high of 210.

After World War II,[qv] however, Clarksville began to feel the effects of urban flight and the steady decline of agriculture. Between 1920 and 1980 the population of the county declined by one-half, and the number of farms dropped off sharply. The town subsequently weathered the decline of the oil industry. Heavily dependent on agriculture and oil for its livelihood, Clarksville saw a dramatic fall in its business and tax proceeds. During the 1980s one of the town's banks folded under the weight of bad farm and energy loans. The town was also rocked by scandal after a former Clarksville police chief was jailed for shooting a prisoner in the back, and a piece, aired nationally by CBS News, reported that the local housing authority was segregating white and black residents. In 1990 Clarksville had a population of 4,311, and ninety-five businesses. Leading industries in 1991 included livestock raising, light manufacturing, and oil and gas production.

BIBLIOGRAPHY: Pat B. Clark, *The History of Clarksville and Old Red River County* (Dallas: Mathis, Van Nort, 1937). Claude V. Hall, "Early Days in Red River County," *East Texas State Teachers College Bulletin* 14 (June 1931). *Red River Recollections* (Clarksville, Texas: Red River County Historical Society, 1986). Rex W. Strickland, Anglo-American Activities in Northeastern Texas, 1803–1845 (Ph.D. dissertation, University of Texas, 1937). Marker Files, Texas Historical Commission, Austin. Vertical Files, Barker Texas History Center, University of Texas at Austin.

Claudia Hazlewood

CLARKSVILLE, TEXAS (Travis County). Clarksville is just northeast of the intersection of the Missouri Pacific Railroad and West Tenth Street in west Austin, Travis County. The land, containing streams and steep hills, had previously been part of a plantation owned by Governor Elisha M. Pease.[qv] It is said that Pease gave the land to his emancipated slaves with the vain hope that they would remain near his mansion and be available for further service. Clarksville was founded in 1871 by Charles Clark, a freedman who changed his name from Charles Griffin after emancipation. Clark bought two acres of land from Confederate general and former Austin mayor Nathan G. Shelley[qv] and built a house on what is now West Tenth Street. He subdivided his land among other freedmen to start a community outside of Austin. Despite its isolation Clarksville came within the jurisdiction of Austin early in its history. Early Clarksville has been described by its older residents as a wilderness broken by an occasional dirt road and train tracks laid by the International–Great Northern Railroad in the 1870s. The Sweet Home Baptist Church served as the community meeting center. The church was organized in the home of Mary Smith on the Haskell homestead sometime before 1882, when the congregation purchased land on which to build a church. Rev. Jacob Fontaine[qv] served as the first minister. Elias Mayes,[qv] a black state legislator from Grimes and Brazos counties in the Sixteenth and Twenty-first legislatures, lived in Clarksville as early as 1875. He built a home on land purchased from Charles Clark in 1884. Many Clarksville residents worked in the cotton industry or farmed; others held jobs in surrounding communities. Leroy Robertson owned and operated a community store. In 1896 a school at Clarksville had an enrollment of forty-seven. In 1917 a new one-room schoolhouse was built and named Clarksville Colored School. It offered six grades.

Early in the twentieth century developers began to realize the land value of Clarksville, which lay near growing downtown Austin. Austin city policy aimed to concentrate the local black population in the east, and pressured black communities in west Austin, such as Clarksville and Wheatsville, to move. In 1918 the Austin school board closed the Clarksville school. Clarksville residents were later forced to use city services in east Austin or none at all. The 1928 master plan of the city of Austin recommended "that all the facilities and conveniences be provided the Negroes in this district, as an incentive to draw the Negro population to this area." Most Clarksville residents endured the lack of services, however, and refused to move. The community did experience two small emigrations to California, the first during World War I[qv] and the second in 1943. Clarksville maintained its school, which enrolled sixty-nine students in 1924, sixty-six in 1934, and seventy in 1940. Sometime in the 1960s the school building was moved to O. Henry Junior High School. The Sweet Home Baptist Church was rebuilt for a third time in 1935.

Until 1930 Clarksville residents used kerosene lamps, and the community remained surrounded by woods. In later years Clarksville began to feel the pressure of Austin's expanding white community, which filled the surrounding area with spacious, middle-class homes. In 1968 Clarksville residents unsuccessfully protested a state and local plan to build a highway along the Missouri Pacific Railroad, which extended along the western boundary of Clarksville. The completed MoPac Expressway cut through the community, causing twenty-six families to be relocated. Twenty-three families left of their own accord. The number of homes in Clarksville decreased from 162 in 1970 to less than 100 in 1976.

Residents of Clarksville began requesting Austin city funds for the improvement and preservation of their community in 1964, but dirt streets crossed the area until 1975, and a creek carrying sewage periodically flooded homes. In 1975 the Texas Historical Commission[qv] designated a two-block-wide strip of Clarksville as a historic district, and the city paved the streets with asphalt. In 1976 the Austin City Council approved the use of $100,000 from a federal housing and community-development grant to pave streets permanently, improve drainage, and expand the playground in Clarksville. Another $100,000 was designated for housing rehabilitation. The same year Clarksville residents and supporters defeated a plan to build a thoroughfare through the community connecting Interstate Highway 35 and the MoPac Expressway. The Clarksville Neighborhood Center, the third community center in Clarksville's history, opened in 1976 to provide information and referrals to community members. The center, remodeled from an old home with volunteer labor, also served as a base for community-improvement projects.

Land values in Clarksville rose with the municipal improvements, and in 1977 a development company began buying lots and building houses that attracted a young, predominantly middle-class white population to the community. Rent costs subsequently increased for the older residents. The Clarksville Community Development Corporation, formed in 1978, worked to establish community services and low-cost housing in the area to retain its black population and promote the return of former residents.

Historical markers stand outside the Sweet Home Baptist Church and the Clarksville Community Center. Some historic buildings, such as the Haskell homestead, have been restored. Clarksville was included in the National Register of Historic Places in 1976.

BIBLIOGRAPHY: Betty Fine et al., *Clarksville* (Corpus Christi: Mission Press, 1969). John Henneberger, *Clarksville: A Short History and Historic Tour* (Austin: Clarksville Community Development Corporation, 1978). Jennifer Sharpe, *Clarksville: Whose Community?* (Austin: Bread and Roses, 1982). Vertical Files, Barker Texas History Center, University of Texas at Austin. *Nolan Thompson*

CLARKSVILLE ACADEMY. Clarksville Academy opened in Clarksville, Red River County, in 1842 under the management of James Sampson. The coeducational school had separate classrooms for boys and girls and accepted students at elementary, high school, and college levels. The academic year was two sessions of five months each. In addition to such traditional subjects as grammar, history, math, Latin, and Greek, the school offered courses in French and Spanish. Enrollment reached only thirty-six by August 1846, and the school closed in 1847.

BIBLIOGRAPHY: Clarksville *Northern Standard,* December 10, 1842. Blewett Barnes Kerbow, The Early History of Red River County, 1817–1865 (M.A. thesis, University of Texas, 1936). B. E. Masters, A History of Early Education in Northeast Texas (M.A. thesis, University of Texas, 1929). *Marie Giles*

CLARKSVILLE CITY, TEXAS. Clarksville City is on U.S Highway 80 between Gladewater and White Oak in northeast Gregg County. The first settlers arrived in the area before 1845. There was a stagecoach stop at the home of William W. Walters, which was later owned and operated by Warren P. Victory. Though first known as Gilead, the post office was named Point Pleasant in 1852. It closed in 1867. The community withered when the railroad bypassed it in 1873 and Gladewater was established. With the advent of the East Texas oilfield[qv] in 1930, so many homes, businesses, and oil-company camps and offices sprang up along the highway that it was called the Main Street of Texas, and street numbers were designated from Longview to Gladewater. The area around George W. Clark's home on the site of the old stagecoach stop became known as Clarksville. After extensive paving projects and other civic improvements in the 1940s and the construction of Lake Gladewater in 1952, the nearby city of Gladewater had a high tax rate and was extending its boundaries. Industrialists in the area to the east became alarmed at the prospect of being taken into Gladewater and taxed more. A movement to incorporate, spearheaded by several oil companies and the L. W. Pelphrey Company, a general contractor specializing in oilfield construction, culminated in a vote to establish Clarksville City on September 14, 1956. Pelphrey was elected mayor and served until his death in August 1961. The bypassed portion of Old Highway 80 is named Pelphrey Drive in his honor. The population dwindled as drilling reached the state allowable and producing wells became automated. Cities Service Oil Company closed its office and camp in the early 1960s, and Sun Oil Company soon followed. After a population low of 359 in the 1960s, growth was steady. In 1990 Clarksville City had 720 residents and twenty businesses. The town has an elected mayor and council with a city manager form of government. The city hall was built in 1962 and doubled in size in 1991. The area is in the Gladewater Independent School District. A Texas historical marker for the old community of Point Pleasant is at the city hall.

BIBLIOGRAPHY: Norman W. Black and Ellie Caston, comps., *Guide to Gregg County's Historical Markers* (Longview, Texas: Gregg County Historical Museum and Gregg County Historical Commission, 1988). East Texas Council of Governments, *Regional Directory* (Kilgore, Texas, 1979). Eugene W. McWhorter, *Traditions of the Land: The History of Gregg County* (Longview, Texas: Gregg County Historical Foundation, 1989).

Nauty Byrd Pelphrey Mayer

CLARKSVILLE FEMALE ACADEMY. Clarksville Female Academy was first called Pine Creek Female Institute when it was established by Robert and Martha W. (Maum) Weatherred in 1840 on Pine Creek, fifteen miles north of Clarksville. The school was moved from Pine Creek to Clarksville in 1844, and the name was changed to Clarksville Female Academy, although the institution was often referred to as Mrs. Weatherred's School. Records indicate that fifty-eight pupils were enrolled in 1846. A Mrs. Gattis bought the school in 1852 and continued to operate it until the beginning of the Civil War,[qv] when a steady decrease in enrollment caused the school to close.

BIBLIOGRAPHY: Clarksville *Standard*, August 27, 1842, February 17, 1844. B. E. Masters, A History of Early Education in Northeast Texas (M.A. thesis, University of Texas, 1929).

CLARKSVILLE FEMALE INSTITUTE. Clarksville Female Institute was established in 1848 when the Ringwood Female Seminary,[qv] with Eliza A. Todd, wife of William S. Todd,[qv] as principal, moved from Boston in Bowie County to Clarksville in Red River County. The institute was bought by professor John Anderson in 1854 and became a part of the Clarksville Male and Female Academy.[qv]

BIBLIOGRAPHY: Marshall Vanderburg, The Presbyterians in Northeast Texas to 1920 (M.A. thesis, University of Texas, 1940).

Cecil Harper, Jr.

CLARKSVILLE MALE AND FEMALE ACADEMY. Clarksville Male and Female Academy originated in 1847 as Clarksville Male Academy, with A. J. Russell as superintendent. John Anderson, a Scottish Presbyterian minister, later became president and served for almost twenty years. Soon after the beginning of his presidency the name of the school was changed to Clarksville Classical, Mathematical, and Mercantile Academy. In 1854 Mrs. Eliza A. Todd's school, Clarksville Female Institute,[qv] was bought and consolidated with the Anderson school to form Clarksville Male and Female Academy. The school continued to function during the Civil War[qv] but closed in 1867.

BIBLIOGRAPHY: B. E. Masters, A History of Early Education in Northeast Texas (M.A. thesis, University of Texas, 1929).

CLARKSVILLE *STANDARD*. The Clarksville *Standard*, a weekly newspaper of Clarksville, Red River County, was the first and for many years the most important paper in Northeast Texas. It was founded as the *Northern Standard* by Charles DeMorse,[qv] who remained sole owner, publisher, and editor until his death in 1887. The first issue appeared on August 20, 1842, and bore the motto "Long May Our Banner Brave the Breeze—The Standard of the Free." The sparsely settled region, the lack of adequate roads and mail routes, and the numerous streams and rivers that could not be crossed during floods created serious problems, but by 1846 the paper had done so well that it was enlarged, the plant was moved into a new building, and an unsuccessful attempt was made to open a branch office at Bonham. In 1852 the name was changed from *Northern Standard* to *Standard*. In 1854 DeMorse erected a two-story brick building to house the paper and installed new equipment, including a cylinder press. The only other such press in Texas at the time was that of the Galveston *News*.[qv] In the following years the *Standard* was second in circulation among Texas newspapers and had agents as distant as Philadelphia, New York, and Boston.

While DeMorse, who was colonel of the Twenty-ninth Texas Cavalry, was away during the Civil War,[qv] the *Standard* was managed by John R. Woolridge. Although its size was reduced, publication continued throughout the war. In 1874 DeMorse closed the office and retired; but, persuaded by his friends, he purchased a Campbell press, installed it in the old building, and in 1879 resumed publication. After DeMorse's death in 1887 his daughter continued the publication of the paper for about a year.

The *Standard* was unusual because for forty-five years it was edited and published by a single individual whose personality, opinions, and hopes it reflected, and neither DeMorse nor his family desired that its control should pass even partially to any other. The files of the paper in the University of Texas at Austin library are almost complete. They constitute a valuable source for the study of the economic, social, and political life of Texas during the periods of the republic and early statehood.

BIBLIOGRAPHY: Ernest Wallace, *Charles DeMorse* (Lubbock: Texas Tech Press, 1943; new ed., Paris, Texas: Wright, 1985).

Ernest Wallace

CLARKWOOD, TEXAS. Clarkwood was on the Texas-Mexican Railway on a site that is now Woodland Park in Corpus Christi in eastern Nueces County. It was established in 1909 and was named for Z. H. Clark, a developer of the townsite. The post office was established in June of 1909 with John S. Byerley as postmaster. The town was part of the 1930s oil boom. The population of Clarkwood rose steadily from forty in 1925 to 350 in 1965. The number of businesses rose from five in 1936 to fourteen in 1965. Clarkwood was annexed to Corpus Christi by 1966. In 1972 the area was part of the Tuloso-Midway Independent School District.

BIBLIOGRAPHY: Nueces County Historical Society, *History of Nueces County* (Austin: Jenkins, 1972).

Robin Dush

CLAUDE, TEXAS. Claude, on U.S. Highway 287 in north central Armstrong County, is the county's largest town. It was originally named Armstrong City when the Fort Worth and Denver City Railway built through the county in 1887, but the name was soon afterwards changed to Claude, after Claude Ayers, the engineer who brought the first train through. Though E. H. Trice platted the town's business district in conformity with the railroad, which angles southeast to northwest, later additions, platted by various promoters including Samuel H. Graves, J. A. Parham, Lee Bivins,[qv] and R. A. Montgomery, were laid out by the compass. A post office was opened in June 1888 with Trice as postmaster.

When the county was organized in 1890, Claude won the contest with Washburn to be the county seat. Charles Goodnight,[qv] according to report, cast the tie-breaking vote. During the 1890s the town grew as a cattle-shipping point, with several stores, two saloons, two blacksmith shops, a livery stable, four churches, a bank, and a resident physician. J. M. White built the ornate, three-story Palace Hotel, which at that time was the largest in the Panhandle.[qv] W. S. Decker established a weekly newspaper, the Claude *Argus*, which later merged with the Goodnight *News* to become the Claude *News*.[qv] When the school district was organized in 1891, children attended classes in the Methodist church until a permanent schoolhouse was built. Before modern water and sewerage systems, Claude's residents went to the courthouse square for water at the public trough, which was shaded by a cottonwood tree. One early resident recalled that the old wooden courthouse "always smelled of tobacco and disinfectant."

After 1900 Claude was incorporated. A. P. McCubbins installed the first telephone system, and W. A. Wilson started the Armstrong County Abstract Company in 1907. The establishment of a flour mill and a grain company attested to Claude's increasing importance as an agribusiness center. By 1912 a permanent stone courthouse had replaced the wooden structure, and W. A. Warner had organized Troop 17, the first Boy Scout troop west of the Mississippi. Recreation and entertainment were provided by the community baseball league, the town band, and the annual chautauqua in August. During the 1930s several neighboring rural schools were consolidated with the Claude district. For years Claude had the only official-size gymnasium in the area, and the West Texas State College (now West Texas A&M University) basketball team used it on numerous occasions. In 1930 Claude had a population of 1,041. By 1940 its population had fallen to 761. In 1953 a new county jail was constructed out of the stones from the old one.

The proximity of Claude to Amarillo and the nearby Pantex Ordnance Plant (see PANTEX, TEXAS) has enabled it to maintain a stable population. Furthermore, Claude has gained a reputation in the movie industry; three motion pictures, *The Sundowners* (1960), *Hud* (1963), and *Sunshine Christmas* (1977), have been filmed there. Claude's population increased from 820 in 1960 to 992 in 1970 and 1,112 in 1980. In 1984 the town had twenty businesses. A city park, a rodeo arena, and a skeet range provide local recreation, and the public library remains the town's educational resource center. In 1990 the population was 1,199.

BIBLIOGRAPHY: Armstrong County Historical Association, *A Collection of Memories: A History of Armstrong County, 1876–1965* (Hereford, Texas: Pioneer, 1965). Arthur Hecht, comp., *Postal History in the Texas Panhandle* (Canyon, Texas: Panhandle-Plains Historical Society, 1960). Ray Miller, *Eyes of Texas Travel Guide: Panhandle/Plains Edition* (Houston: Cordovan, 1982). H. Allen Anderson

CLAUDE NEWS. The Claude *News*, a weekly newspaper published in Armstrong County, grew out of the Claude *Argus* first published by W. S. Decker in 1890. Around 1891 the *Argus* merged with the Goodnight *News* to form the Claude *News*, first published by J. H. Hamner and later by Thomas T. Waggoner. In the 1990s the publisher was Phil Miller, and Jason Cartwright was editor. The circulation was 831.

BIBLIOGRAPHY: *Texas Newspaper Directory* (Austin: Texas Press Service, 1991). Diana J. Kleiner

CLAUENE, TEXAS. Clauene, on U.S. Highway 385 ten miles south of Levelland in south central Hockley County, was one of the first settlements in the county. The area was opened for homesteading in the early 1920s. The site was once part of the Zavala Ranch and had more people and buildings than Levelland when that new community was designated the county seat. The name was derived from the catclaw bushes in the vicinity. Five families from Fort Stockton were the original settlers: the King family, G. E. Murray, L. E. Swafford, the Whites, and the Palmers. Mrs. Teague was the first teacher, and N. P. White had the first store. Brooksie Martin built a gin in 1923, one of the first in the county. Clauene did not develop much because of its proximity to Levelland. Its schools were consolidated with those of Levelland in 1946, and even church members, except for those of the Fellowship Baptist, gravitated from Clauene to Levelland churches. The population has remained stable with twenty-five in 1930, fifty in 1950, and twenty-four in 1970 and 1980. It was still reported as twenty-four in 1990.

BIBLIOGRAPHY: Lillian Brasher, *Hockley County* (2 vols., Canyon, Texas: Staked Plains, 1976). S. S. McKay

CLAWSON, TEXAS. Clawson is at the junction of U.S. Highway 69 and Farm Road 2021, six miles northwest of Lufkin in northwestern Angelina County. The St. Louis Southwestern Railway runs through the community, which was originally established as a sawmill town in the 1880s and became a rail shipping point around 1890. Clawson was named for the manager of the first mill built there, T. W. Clawson. The mill property was subsequently sold to Jack Caruthers, who built a larger sawmill on the site. Around 1890 Clawson had a large commissary for general merchandise, a post office, a church, a school, and tenant houses for the employees of the mill. Although Caruthers went bankrupt, a number of other lumber companies have operated mills in the vicinity of Clawson. The lumber manufacturer Grambling and Clark was listed there in 1902. Early in the twentieth century the Henderson Sand and Lumber Company operated a mill there. At the same time, two of Jack Caruthers's sons built a new mill near Clawson called the Pine Island Lumber Company. In 1907 the Caruthers brothers sold their mill to J. M. Burnett and Ashley Stroud. Shortly thereafter, Burnett and Stroud sold the property to J. H. Bivins and E. E. Blythe. Sawmilling at Clawson ended around 1911 when Bivins and Blythe went out of business.

Before 1904 Clawson had fewer than 100 people, but it did list a money order post office that year. By 1910, at the height of its prosperity as a mill center, it had grown to 250. In 1914 and 1915 the population was listed as 150, and the town had telephone service. In 1925 the population was still listed as 150, and from the end of the 1960s through 1990 it was reported as 195. Since 1926 Clawson has been receiving its mail from Lufkin.

BIBLIOGRAPHY: Archie Birdsong Mathews, The Economic Development of Angelina County (M.A. thesis, University of Texas, 1952). Megan Biesele

CLAY, NESTOR (1799–1835). Nestor Clay, pioneer, son of Thomas and Mary Jane "Polly" (Dawson) Clay, was born on January 6, 1799, in Daviess County, Kentucky. His father was a captain in the Revolutionary War, and Clay was a cousin of Henry Clay of Kentucky. Nestor Clay came to Texas in 1822 as a single man. In 1823 he returned to Kentucky to marry sixteen-year-old Nancy Wilson Johnson; the two returned to Texas in 1824 and settled near Independence, Washington County. Before leaving Kentucky, Clay had been a member of the Kentucky Senate, and he was a representative at the conventions of 1832 and 1833 qqv in Texas. He is not listed among the Old Three Hundred qv but received a Mexican land grant in Washington County on March 18, 1831. By 1834 he held title to 25,000 acres. The Clays had three children before Nancy died in 1834. Clay died in 1835 from wounds received during an Indian raid on Clay Creek in Milam County. Both he and his wife have been reinterred in Austin's Pioneer Cemetery. Clay's residence, known as Clay Castle, qv was completed by his brother, Tacitus, in 1836.

BIBLIOGRAPHY: Nestor and Tacitus Clay Papers, Barker Texas History Center, University of Texas at Austin. Betty Cantrell Plummer, *Historic Homes of Washington County* (San Marcos, Texas: Rio Fresco, 1971). Worth Stickley Ray, *Austin Colony Pioneers* (Austin: Jenkins, 1949; 2d ed., Austin: Pemberton, 1970). Gracey Booker Toland, *Austin Knew His Athens* (San Antonio: Naylor, 1958). Vertical Files, Barker Texas History Center, University of Texas at Austin. James L. Hailey

CLAY, TEXAS. Clay, originally known as Clay Station, on the Atchison, Topeka and Santa Fe Railway eight miles southeast of Snook in southeastern Burleson County, was founded as a stop on the Gulf, Colorado and Santa Fe Railway in the early 1880s. The town was named for local landowner A. M. Clay, who donated the tract on which the GC&SF depot was constructed. A post office was set up in 1884. In 1903 W. A. Lyon opened a general merchandise store, one of at least two in the early community. In 1911 a school was established. It was consolidated with the Snook Independent School District in 1949. Clay reported a population of 150 in 1925. In 1945 the community had a population estimated at 100 and four accredited businesses. The post office was discontinued during the 1960s, and by 1970 the town had declined to an estimated population of sixty-one and two businesses. In 1990 Clay still had an estimated population of sixty-one.

BIBLIOGRAPHY: Burleson County Historical Society, *Astride the Old San Antonio Road: A History of Burleson County, Texas* (Dallas: Taylor, 1980).

Charles Christopher Jackson

CLAYBANK, TEXAS. Claybank, 4½ miles east of Kilgore in south central Gregg County, was probably established after the Civil War.qv A post office operated from 1897 until 1902. Around 1900 the small settlement had a general store and a number of houses. By the early 1920s the community no longer appeared on maps.

Christopher Long

CLAY CASTLE. Tacitus C. Clay built a home in 1836 a mile west of Independence in Washington County and called it Ingleside. This four-story structure of native stone and cedar became known as Clay Castle because of the glassed-in ballroom on the third floor; the home survived seventy-five years until it sustained irreparable damage in the 1900 and 1915 Galveston storms. The land was granted to Tacitus's brother, Nestor Clay,qv by the Mexican government on March 18, 1831, and he began the construction. Nestor died in an Indian raid in Milam County in 1835, and Tacitus purchased half of his brother's league from his estate. Tacitus and Nestor were descendents of the Kentucky Clays and cousins to Henry Clay. Cotton produced on the Clay plantation was the first raised in Washington County. Tacitus's son, Capt. Thomas C. Clay, was a member of Hood's Texas Brigadeqv in the Civil War.qv He is reported to have used the "captain's walk," a large glass-enclosed walkway overhanging the hill upon which the home was built, to oversee his slaves at work in the fields below.

BIBLIOGRAPHY: Betty Cantrell Plummer, *Historic Homes of Washington County* (San Marcos, Texas: Rio Fresco, 1971).

James L. Hailey

CLAY COUNTY. Clay County (F-14) is on U.S. highways 287 and 82 on the Red River in north Texas, ninety miles northwest of the Dallas–Fort Worth area. The center of the county is at approximately 34°48′ north latitude, 98°15′ west longitude, near the county seat, Henrietta. The ninety-eighth meridian, which unofficially divides the United States into east and west, runs through the eastern part of the county. The county measures forty-six miles from north to south and twenty-five miles from east to west. The total land area is about 1,150 square miles. The terrain is nearly level to gently sloping. About a third of the county is prime farmland. The flora of most of the county is typical of the Cross Timbers and prairie, with grasses predominating. The northwest corner is in the Rolling Plains vegetation area, with taller grasses, mesquite, and cacti common. Trees, including mesquite, blackjack, post oak, and elm, are scattered throughout the county, but are more numerous along the streams. The elevation varies from 1,100 feet in the southwest to 900 feet in the east. The average rainfall is thirty inches a year. The average annual temperature is 64° F. Temperatures in January range from an average low of 28° F to an average high of 53° and in July from 73° to 98°. The growing season averages 229 days a year, with the last freeze in late March and the first freeze in mid-November. Snowfall averages six inches a year.

Clay County has many streams. The northern edge of the county is formed by the Red River; the Wichita River flows through the center of the county before dividing into two forks and emptying into the Red River. Other major streams include Turkey, Dry Fork, Hay, and East Post Oak creeks. Lake Arrowhead,qv in the western section of the county, is nine miles long and two miles wide and is used both as a source of water and for recreation. The fauna of Clay County is typical of North Texas, where deer, bobwhite quail, and migratory game birds provide excellent hunting. Mineral deposits in the county include building stone and clays for brick, tile, and ceramics. Oil was discovered near the site of present-day Petrolia in 1901 and has been an important asset to the county's economy. Oil production in 1990 was nearly 1.6 million barrels.

The Clay County area has long been the site of human habitation. Its earliest inhabitants were probably Archaic Age hunter-gatherers. Wichita and Taovaya Indians migrated into the area from what is now Kansas and Nebraska beginning in the middle of the eighteenth century. Despite their use of horses, which were introduced into the region by Spanish explorers, and their consequent facility as buffaloqv hunters, these peoples were heavily dependent on agriculture. The location of their lands placed them in conflict with the Lipan Apaches and Comanches, both of whom claimed the area and continued to visit it after they were removed to Oklahoma. The Indians often came into conflict with white settlers in the region after 1850, when federal troops forced them to move to reservations north of the Red River.

The earliest Europeans to visit the future county were Spanish explorers. Several early expeditions crossed Clay County, probably skirting the Cross Timbers. In 1759 Diego Ortiz Parrillaqv traveled through on his way to attack the Taovayas at the site of present Spanish Fort in Montague County, and in 1786 and 1787 Pedro Vial and José Mares qqv traversed the area while exploring possible routes from San Antonio to Santa Fe. In July 1841 the Texan Santa Fe expedition qv crossed the future county heading west. The Snively expeditionqv of 1843 cut across the northeast corner, and the California Trail cut across the southern section after 1849. In 1858, on an expedition to Oklahoma to punish the Comanches, Earl Van Dornqv followed an arc-shaped route through western Clay County as he traveled from Cottonwood Spring in Young County to what became known as the Van Dorn Crossing on the Little Wichita River; the expedition detoured eastward to join the California Trail at Brushy Mound.

The first settlers in the area were probably W. T. and Wess Waybourne, who came in the 1850s and built their homes on the south fork of the Wichita River two miles from the site of present-day Henrietta. Clay County was marked off from Cooke County on December 24, 1857, and named for Kentucky statesman Henry Clay; the population of the new county was only 109 in 1860. On the eve of the Civil War,qv Henrietta, the largest community, had ten homes and a general store. Indians, however, remained a constant threat at this time, and the army conducted regular patrols of the area. The county was organized in 1861, but it was largely abandoned the following year because of the removal of federal troops during the war. The 1870 census gave no population figures for Clay County, although a few ranchers and farmers remained near the Red River after most of the settlers had moved eastward to more populated regions.

With the establishment of Fort Sill in Indian Territory after the Civil War, settlers began to return to Clay County. Among the first permanent residents after the war was Henry A. Whaley,qv who raised grain and vegetables on his farm near the mouth of the Wichita River to sell to the army at Fort Sill. The county was reorganized on May 27, 1873, with Cambridge as the county seat, and during the 1870s a small but growing stream of new settlers moved in, attracted by good range and farm land. Most of the early settlers raised cattle, along with small crops of corn and cotton. In 1882 the Fort Worth and Denver Railway was built across the county through Henrietta. The town, which had been largely abandoned since the outbreak of the Civil War, bustled with new activity; after most of the residents of Cambridge moved there because of the railroad, Henrietta was incorporated and made the new county seat.

The railroad ushered in a boom. The population grew from a few hundred in 1870 to 5,045 by 1880. Buffalo hunters returning from the West shipped their hides from Henrietta, and the city became the principal trading center with nearby Fort Sill. In 1880 the county's 635 farms produced 1,155 bales of cotton and 92,766 bushels of corn; cattle numbered 58,763. Over the next twenty years cotton production grew to 3,774 bales, corn yields increased to 721,020 bushels, and the number of cattle rose to 91,212. Between 1890 and 1910 the population grew from 7,503 to 17,043. This surge was aided by the construction of two new railroads: the Gainesville, Henrietta and Western, a branch line of the Missouri, Kansas and Texas, which reached Henrietta in 1887; and the Wichita Valley Railway, which was constructed to Byers in 1904.

With the growth in population also came a marked increase in the county's farming economy. The number of farms grew from 766 in 1890 to 2,306 in 1910, and the number of acres under cultivation nearly tripled. At the turn of the century Clay County was primarily composed of ranches and farms, with the majority of its population living in rural areas. Before 1900 the leading crop was corn, but increasingly during the early years of the new century cotton took center stage. In 1890, 6,135 acres had been planted in cotton; by 1910 that figure had grown to 71,086; and by 1930 nearly one of every two improved acres—more than 80,000 in all—was given over to cotton production.

Cotton culture[qv] brought prosperity, but it had disastrous effects during the Great Depression.[qv] Many farmers borrowed heavily against future crops, encouraged by the unprecedented income earned by cotton in the 1920s. Moreover, about half of the farmers in Clay County in 1930 were tenant-sharecroppers who worked someone else's land for a share of the harvest. With the drop in cotton prices during the depression and the ensuing credit crunch, many farmers found it impossible to get by and were forced to give up farming permanently. Between 1930 and 1940 the number of farms in the county fell from 2,106 to 1,710, and over the next ten years the number dropped again by nearly a half. Hardest hit were the sharecroppers, who had little in the way of cash or assets to help them over tough times. Between 1930 and 1940 almost half of them were forced off the land, and within two decades virtually none of the tenants remained. The depression years permanently changed the face of the county's farming economy in other ways as well. After World War II[qv] cotton farming gradually gave way to cattle ranching, and by the late 1960s fully three-fifths of farm income came from livestock, principally beef cattle. That trend has continued. In the early 1990s cattle were grazed on three-fourths of Clay County land, and less than one-fourth was used for crops, chiefly wheat, cotton, pecans, and peaches.

Between the 1920s and the 1980s the county population declined slowly, from 16,864 in 1920 to 14,545 in 1930, 12,524 in 1940, 9,866 in 1950, 8,351 in 1960, and 8,079 in 1970. During the 1970s and 1980s the population grew slightly, increasing to 9,582 in 1980 and 10,024 in 1990, largely as the result of increasing emphasis on manufacturing. Henrietta was the largest community in 1990, followed by Petrolia, Byers, Bellevue, Dean, and Jolly.

Like most Texas counties, Clay County made significant improvements in education in the late twentieth century. In 1950 only 23.5 percent of adults twenty-five and older had a high school education, and only 4 percent had a college degree. In 1980, 50 percent of adults twenty-five and over had high school diplomas, and 7 percent had college degrees. In 1990 Clay County was divided into five school districts. White students constituted 97 percent of the student body, 2 percent were Hispanic, and .5 percent were black.

Politically, Clay County has been staunchly Democratic throughout most of its history. Although in 1861 its citizens did not vote like most Southerners, later generations did; with the exception of the 1928 and 1972 presidential elections, Clay County voters have consistently supported the Democratic party[qv] presidential candidates. In the election of 1920, 72.7 percent voted Democratic, and in 1956, 65 percent. Subsequently, Clay County voters increasingly turned to Republican candidates, particularly in statewide races, although most of the local offices remained firmly in Democratic hands.

The county economy depends on ranching, farming, oil, and manufacturing. Unemployment was only 1.1 percent in 1986, and although the jobless rate climbed afterward, it remained well below the statewide average. More than 82 percent of Clay County residents owned their homes. The average family weekly income of $335.45, however, remained lower than that of many other areas of the state. Many new jobs came from light manufacturing, introduced into the area in the 1970s and 1980s. As late as 1965, 181 people were employed in oil and gas operations and 241 worked in retail business, but in the early 1990s only a handful or oil workers remained. Mobile-home and wood-products plants, established during the 1970s and 1980s, added 189 jobs to the county's rolls and helped to offset losses in other areas. Local attractions include hunting and fishing, Lake Arrowhead State recreation Area,[qv] and the Pioneer Reunion Festival and Junior Stock Show, both held annually in Henrietta.

BIBLIOGRAPHY: Katherine Christian Douthitt, ed., *Romance and Dim Trails* (Dallas: Tardy, 1938). J. P. Earle, *History of Clay County* (Henrietta, Texas: Henrietta Independent Press, 1897). William Clayton Kimbrough, "The Frontier Background of Clay County," West Texas Historical Association *Year Book* 18 (1942). William Clayton Kimbrough, A History of Clay County (M.A. thesis, Hardin-Simmons University, 1942). William Charles Taylor, *A History of Clay County* (Austin: Jenkins, 1972).

Clark Wheeler

CLAY CREEK. Clay Creek rises in the Clay Creek oilfield four miles west of Independence in Washington County (at 30°17′ N, 96°23′ W) and runs north for five miles to its mouth on Yegua Creek, at the Burleson county line (at 30°21′ N, 96°25′ W). The surrounding moderately sloping terrain is surfaced mainly by clay that supports post oaks and grass. The creek was probably named for the Clay family, who settled in the area during the time of the republic.

BIBLIOGRAPHY: Joe B. Frantz and Mike Cox, *Lure of the Land: Texas County Maps and the History of Settlement,* ed. Roger A. Griffin (College Station: Texas A&M University Press, 1988).

CLAY HILL, TEXAS. Clay Hill, also known as Hick's Spring, is two miles north of U.S. Highway 84 and five miles northeast of Teague in west central Freestone County. It had a school and a gin owned by Johnny George. The school had an enrollment of nineteen in 1903, and church services were held in the school house. In the 1930s Clay Hill had the school and a few scattered dwellings. By 1989 only a church remained.

BIBLIOGRAPHY: Freestone County Historical Commission, *History of Freestone County, Texas* (Fairfield, Texas, 1978).

Chris Cravens

CLAY LAKE. Clay Lake is just east of the Brazos River in extreme southern Brazos County (at 30°26′ N, 96°16′ W). The half-mile lake is in a marshy area and drains into Franks Creek. It is surrounded by flat to rolling terrain with steep margins, surfaced by sandy loam that supports pecan, willow, and grasses.

Diana J. Kleiner

CLAY'S CORNER, TEXAS. Clay's Corner is west of Lazbuddie in southeastern Parmer County. A gin was operating nearby when in October 1953 Herbert and Vera Clay moved from Lamesa and established a grocery and general merchandise store for rural residents at the junction of Farm roads 145 and 214. As modern irrigation increased, several more farmers moved to the vicinity of the Clay store, among them James Robinson, noted for his champion greyhounds. In 1955 the Clays added a cafe and a hardware store to their growing business. A Farmers' Co-op elevator was erected nearby, probably in the early 1960s, and a fertilizer business was added to the community in 1961. During this time the Clays hosted annual Thanksgiving dinners and Easter egg hunts. The Clay establishment was a local gathering place and a refuge in time of foul or threatening weather.

BIBLIOGRAPHY: Parmer County Historical Commission, *Prairie Progress* (Dallas: Taylor, 1981).

H. Allen Anderson

CLAYS CREEK. Clays Creek rises near the Bell county line, a half mile south of Davilla in western Milam County (at 30°46′ N, 97°16′ W) and runs east for twelve miles to its mouth on the Little River, nine miles west of Cameron (at 30°48′ N, 97°08′ W). The surrounding rolling to flat terrain with local shallow depressions is surfaced by dark, calcareous clays and sandy loams that support mesquite, cacti, and grasses in the upper reaches of the creek and water-tolerant hardwoods and conifers in the middle and lower reaches. The creek is said to have been named for Nestor Clay,qv who was wounded in an Indian fight there in 1835.

CLAYTON, JOSEPH ALVEY (1817–1873). Joseph Alvey Clayton, soldier and community leader, was born in Marshall County, Tennessee, on December 30, 1817. He moved to Texas in the early part of 1835 and joined Capt. Amasa Turner'sqv company, but fought in the battle of San Jacintoqv as a private in the artillery under Lt. Col. James C. Neill.qv Clayton also saw action at the battle of Chapultepec during the Mexican War.qv He married Amanda Poole in Tennessee on June 1, 1847, and they had eight children. He lived near Washington-on-the-Brazos until 1852, when he settled near the site of present Kerens in Navarro County. Clayton represented Navarro County at the Secession Conventionqv early in 1861, and after hostilities began he served as the captain of a reserve company in the Nineteenth Infantry Brigade, Texas Militia. Clayton was a Baptist and Mason and took an active role in community affairs. He was twice involved in efforts to establish fairgrounds in the county. He died as a result of a farm accident on August 1, 1873, and was buried at Chatfield in Navarro County.

BIBLIOGRAPHY: Joe M. Daniel, "Navarro County Goes to War," *Navarro County Scroll*, July 12, 1965. Daughters of the Republic of Texas, *Muster Rolls of the Texas Revolution* (Austin, 1986). Sam Houston Dixon and Louis Wiltz Kemp, *The Heroes of San Jacinto* (Houston: Anson Jones, 1932). Louis Wiltz Kemp Papers, Barker Texas History Center, University of Texas at Austin. Wyvonne Putman, comp., *Navarro County History* (4 vols., Quanah, Texas: Nortex, 1975–84).

CLAYTON, JOSEPH ELWARD (1879–?). Joseph Elward Clayton, school principal and supervisor of programs to aid African Americansqv in Texas, was born on February 8, 1879, in Fulshear, Texas, the son of Joseph E. and Elizabeth Clayton. On December 27, 1899, he married Brittie White; they had two children. After completing his high school education in Houston, Clayton received his B.A. from Guadalupe College in Seguin in 1903. From 1908 to 1923 he was principal of the Clayton Vocational School in Manor. He was a lecturer at the Texas Department of Agriculture from 1907 to 1919. In 1924 he organized the National Self-Help Association and in 1930 was the supervisor and a lecturer for the Phoenix Aid and Development Association in Phoenix, Arkansas. In 1923 he began his long involvement in projects designed to move urban blacks to rural areas as part of self-help efforts. He purchased 2,000 acres of land in Texas, divided it into small farms, and invited blacks to move onto the land and support themselves away from urban areas. Clayton was a member of the Masons, the NAACP, and the Texas State Teachers Association.qv He was a Baptist. In 1933, although he maintained a Houston address, he was residing in Chicago, Illinois.

BIBLIOGRAPHY: *Who's Who in Colored America*, 1930–32.

Kharen Monsho

CLAYTON, NICHOLAS JOSEPH (1840–1916). Nicholas J. Clayton, architect, was born on November 1, 1840, in Cloyne, County Cork, Ireland, the son of Nicholas Joseph and Margaret (O'Mahoney) Clayton. In 1848, after the death of his father, he and his mother immigrated to Cincinnati, Ohio. Clayton's military records indicate that before the Civil Warqv he worked as a plasterer in Cincinnati, New Orleans, Louisville, Memphis, and St. Louis. Between 1862 and 1865 he served as a yeoman in the United States Navy. After his discharge in 1865, he returned to Cincinnati, where he was listed in city directories as a marble carver (1866), carver (1870), and architectural draftsman (1871). He traveled to Houston from Cincinnati in October 1871. In 1872 he moved to Galveston to take a position as supervising architect for the construction of the First Presbyterian Church, designed by the Memphis, Tennessee, architects Jones and Baldwin. He remained in Galveston and began the practice of architecture there.

Clayton was responsible for so many of the major public, commercial, and residential buildings constructed in Galveston during the 1870s, 1880s, and 1890s that Howard Barnstoneqv described this period in the city's history as the "Clayton Era." Clayton was a High Victorian architect. His buildings were exuberant in shape, color, texture, and detail. He excelled at decorative brick and iron work. His High Victorian predilections were evident not only in his buildings of the 1870s, but in those influenced by the Queen Anne movement of the 1880s, the Richardsonian Romanesque movement of the late 1880s and 1890s, and the revival of Renaissance classicism after 1890. What made Clayton's architecture so distinctive in late nineteenth-century Texas was the underlying compositional and proportional order with which he structured the display of picturesque shapes and rich ornament.

His first known independent work was St. Mary's Church (now St. Mary's Cathedralqv) in Austin (1873–84). He designed many parish churches and other institutional buildings in the Catholic dioceses of Galveston, Dallas, and Alexandria, Louisiana. He also produced major church and institutional buildings for Catholic religious orders, especially the Sisters of Charity of the Incarnate Word, the Ursuline Sisters, the Jesuits, and the Congregation of Holy Cross.qqv His religious architecture accounted for the broadest geographical distribution of his work outside Galveston. Clayton's major ecclesiastical works included St. Patrick's Church, Galveston (1874–77, reconstruction 1901–02); Eaton Memorial Chapel, Galveston (1878–79); Sacred Heart Church, Palestine (1890–03); Grace Episcopal Church, Galveston (1894–95); St. Patrick's Church, Denison (1896–98); Sacred Heart Cathedral, Dallas (1896–1902); and the dome of the second Sacred Heart Church, Galveston (1910). He also was the architect of St. Mary's Infirmary, Galveston (1874–76, demolished); Ursuline Academy, Dallasqv (1882, 1887–90, 1901–02, 1906–07, demolished); additions to Incarnate Word Academy, Houston (1888–89 and 1899, demolished; 1905, extant); St. Edward's University, Austin (1888–96, 1903, 1907); Ursuline Academy, Galvestonqv (1891–95, demolished); and St. Joseph's Infirmary, Houston (1892–94, 1895, demolished).

Among Clayton's foremost public buildings were the Galveston Electric Pavilion, the first building in Texas with electric lighting (1881, destroyed); Harmony Hall, Galveston (1881–83, demolished); the Masonic Temple, Galveston (1882–84, demolished); the Beach Hotel, Galveston (1881–83, destroyed); John Sealy Hospital,qv Galveston (1888–89, demolished); and the University of Texas Medical Department Building, Galveston (1888–91). Clayton served on an advisory board for the construction of the dome of the Capitolqv in Austin (1887) and was responsible for specifying furnishings for the building (1888).

His major commercial buildings included the International–Great Northern Railway General Offices Building, Palestine (1879, demolished); the Gulf, Colorado and Santa Fe Railway General Offices Building, Galveston (1881–82, 1892, destroyed); the Greenleve, Block, and Company Building, Galveston (1881–82, altered); the H. M. Trueheart and Company Building, Galveston (1881–82); the W. L. Moody Building, Galveston (1882–83, altered); the Galveston News Building (1883–84, defaced); the R. E. Stafford Bank and Opera House, Columbus (1886–87); the Clarke and Courts Building, Galveston (1890); the Adoue and Lobit Bank Building, Galveston (1890–91, defaced); the Hutchings-Sealy Building, Galveston (1895–96); the James Fadden Building, Galveston (1896–97); and the Star Drug Store Building, Galveston (1909).

Clayton was the architect of numerous houses, among which were

Bishop's Palace, Galveston, 1885–1892. Nicholas Clayton, architect. Photograph dated 1905. Courtesy Rosenberg Library, Galveston, Texas. Described as Nicholas Clayton's masterpiece, this mansion was built for the family of Walter Gresham. The Catholic Church purchased the building in 1923, and it served as the residence of the bishop of the Galveston diocese until 1959.

the Van Alstyne House, Houston (ca. 1878, demolished); the Adoue House, Galveston (1881–82, demolished); the Blum House, Galveston (1884–85, demolished); the Trueheart House, Galveston (1884–86, demolished); and the Gresham House, Galveston, also known as the Bishop's Palace (1885–92). Major concentrations of Clayton's buildings are in the Strand Historic District and the East End Historic District in Galveston.

During the course of his career, Clayton was twice involved in partnerships: with the engineer Michael L. Lynch in the firm of Clayton and Lynch (1877–81), and with Patrick R. Rabitt, Jr. in the firm of N. J. Clayton and Company (1890–99). Clayton was a founding member of the Texas State Association of Architects and a member of the Western Association of Architects. As a result of the Western Association's merger with the American Institute of Architects in 1889, Clayton became a member and fellow of the AIA. He served a term as vice president of the Southern Chapter of the AIA (1895–96).

His professional practice declined precipitously after 1900. Protracted litigation that he instigated after the controversial awarding of a commission to design a new Galveston County Courthouse in 1897 and the decline of new construction activity in Galveston in the aftermath of the Galveston hurricane of 1900[qv] were contributing factors. In March 1903 he declared bankruptcy. He never recovered financially. Although he continued in practice until his death, he never obtained subsequent major architectural commissions.

Clayton married Mary Lorena Ducie of Galveston on July 6, 1891. They had five children. Clayton was a parishioner of St. Patrick's Church. He was a member of the Galveston Garten-Verein and the Catholic Knights of America, the Knights of Columbus,[qv] and the Ancient Order of Hibernians. He died in Galveston on December 9, 1916, and is buried there at Calvary Cemetery. His architectural drawings and office records are deposited in the Galveston and Texas History Center of the Rosenberg Library[qv] and the Galveston County Historical Museum, both in Galveston, and the Barker Texas History Center[qv] and the Architectural Drawings Collection, both at the University of Texas at Austin.

BIBLIOGRAPHY: Howard Barnstone, *The Galveston That Was* (New York: Macmillan, 1966). Catholic Archives of Texas, Files, Austin. Galveston *Daily News*, February 20, 1972. Robert A. Nesbitt, *Bob's Reader: Galveston Island, Texas* (Galveston, 1985). Jim Steely, "The Fall and Rise of Nicholas Clayton," *Texas Architect*, March–April 1986. *Texas Highways*, January 1980.   Robert A. Nesbitt and Stephen Fox

CLAYTON, WILLIAM LOCKHART (1880–1966). William Lockhart Clayton, cotton merchant, was born on a farm near Tupelo, Mississippi, on February 7, 1880, to James Munroe and Martha Fletcher (Burdine) Clayton. He attended seven grades of public school in Tupelo and Jackson, Tennessee, where the family moved when he was six years old. Proficient in shorthand, he went to St. Louis in 1895 as personal secretary to an official of the American Cotton Company. From 1896 to 1904 he worked in the New York office of the American Cotton Company, where he rose to the position of assistant general

William L. Clayton. Copyright 1962, Houston Chronicle *Publishing Company. Reprinted with permission. All rights reserved.*

manager. In 1904 Clayton formed a partnership to buy and sell cotton with two members of a Jackson, Tennessee, family prominent in banking—Frank E. and Monroe D. Anderson,[qv] the former Clayton's brother-in-law. A younger brother, Benjamin Clayton,[qv] joined the firm in 1905. Anderson, Clayton and Company[qv] first opened its offices in Oklahoma City and experienced immediate success. In 1916 the firm moved its headquarters to Houston, where Clayton, as the partner most expert in foreign sales, led other cotton exporters in providing warehouse facilities, insurance, credit, and other services that European firms had formerly rendered. In 1920 the company reorganized as an unincorporated Texas joint-stock association. Later in the 1920s Clayton led the fight that forced the New York Stock Exchange to accept southern delivery on futures contracts, thus removing an impediment to the natural operation of the futures market.

When high tariffs and federal farm-price supports threatened to drive American cotton out of the world market in the late 1920s and early 1930s, Clayton's firm responded by establishing cotton-buying offices in Latin America and Africa in order to supply its foreign sales agencies with cotton at competitive rates. At the same time that Clayton was expanding his business abroad, he fought the farm policies of the New Deal. He opposed government supports of the agricultural market. Instead, he believed that if subsidies were necessary they should go straight to the farmer. Clayton joined the American Liberty League in 1934 but left the organization the following year, when it failed to accept his recommendations for public relations in Texas. In 1936 he renounced his earlier opposition to Roosevelt because of Secretary of State Cordell Hull's work for a reciprocal trade agreement, a cause Clayton had advocated for many years. Meanwhile, Anderson, Clayton and Company increased investments in cotton gins,

vegetable-oil mills, feed factories, experimental seed farms, and other enterprises related to processing cotton and similar commodities. From the beginning such investments had made the firm unique among cotton-merchandising organizations. Frank Anderson died in 1924, and Benjamin Clayton withdrew from the firm in 1929. The two remaining partners formed Anderson, Clayton and Company (Delaware) in 1930 and issued preferred stock. In 1940 Clayton retired from active management in the firm, but through several trusts he maintained control of the company until his death.

During World War I[qv] he served on the Committee of Cotton Distribution of the War Industries Board. In 1940 he was called to Washington to serve as deputy to the coordinator of inter-American affairs. For the next four years he held a variety of high-level positions with the Export-Import Bank, the Department of Commerce, and wartime agencies. From December 1944 until October 1947 he was assistant and then undersecretary of state for economic affairs, in which capacity he became a principal architect of the European Recovery Program, known commonly as the Marshall Plan. After his return to Houston in late 1947, he remained an occasional participant and frequent contributor to international conferences on world trade, the European Common Market, and related matters.

He contributed personally and through the Clayton Fund to a variety of religious, charitable, and educational institutions, most notably to Johns Hopkins University (of which he was a trustee from 1949 to 1966), Tufts University, the University of Texas, Susan V. Clayton Homes (a low-cost housing project in Houston), and the Methodist Church.[qv] Clayton married Susan Vaughan of Clinton, Kentucky, on August 14, 1902. They had a son who died in infancy and four daughters who survived them. Clayton died after a brief illness on February 8, 1966, and was buried in Glenwood Cemetery, Houston.

BIBLIOGRAPHY: Benjamin Clayton, *Notes on Some Phases of Cotton Operations: 1905–1929* (1965). Fredrick J. Dobney, *Selected Papers of Will Clayton* (Baltimore and London: Johns Hopkins Press, 1971). Lamar Fleming, Jr., *Growth of the Business of Anderson, Clayton and Company*, ed. James A. Tinsley (Houston: Texas Gulf Coast Historical Association, 1966). Ellen Clayton Garwood, *Will Clayton, A Short Biography* (Austin: University of Texas Press, 1958; rpt., Freeport, New York: Books for Libraries Press, 1971). Vertical Files, Barker Texas History Center, University of Texas at Austin. *James A. Tinsley*

CLAYTON, TEXAS. Clayton, at the junction of Farm Road 315 and State Highway 1970, sixteen miles southwest of Carthage in southwestern Panola County, was first settled around 1845 by Jacob Cariker, a native of Georgia. Cariker built a house two miles southwest of Reed's Settlement, one of the earliest communities in Panola County. During the early 1870s most of the white residents from Reed's Settlement moved to the Cariker site. A post office opened in 1874 under the name Clayton. Cariker, who suggested the name, had wanted to call the town Claybourne after one of his former slaves, but there was already another town with that name. Cariker instead chose Clayton, after Clayton, Alabama, said to have been the origin of several early settlers. The first store in Clayton was owned by Pleas Fite, who also opened the first saloon. By 1885 the town had a general store, a steam gristmill and cotton gin, two churches, a school, and a population of 130. The town's population reached 200 in 1914 but began to decline after World War I.[qv] In the mid-1930s Clayton had six stores, a factory, a school, and a number of houses; the estimated population in 1936 was 175. During the 1950s and 1960s the town's population continued to dwindle. In 1965 the school was consolidated with the Carthage school, and by the late 1960s the number of inhabitants had fallen to 125. In 1990 Clayton had one business and seventy-nine residents.

BIBLIOGRAPHY: *History of Panola County* (Carthage, Texas: Carthage Circulating Book Club, 1935?). Leila B. LaGrone, ed., *History of Panola County* (Carthage, Texas: Panola County Historical Commission, 1979). John Barnette Sanders, *Postoffices and Post Masters of Panola County, Texas, 1845–1930* (Center, Texas, 1964).

Christopher Long

CLAYTON DRAW. Clayton Draw is formed by the confluence of Bronco Mule Draw and Luckett Draw, five miles southwest of Dome Hill in south central Culberson County (at 31°20′ N, 104°30′ W). It runs southeast for twenty-one miles before running dry twelve miles north of Kent (at 31°14′ N, 104°12′ W). Water actually flows in only the first nine and last three miles of Clayton Draw, which traverses steep to gentle slopes surfaced by shallow to moderately deep clay and sandy loams that support scrub brush and sparse grasses.

CLAYTONVILLE, TEXAS (Fisher County). Claytonville is just west of Farm Road 419 ten miles southwest of Roby in southwestern Fisher County. It has had five different locations in the sparsely settled section of the county. The first school was conducted in a tent on the Walter Caves place in 1888, and the post office was established the same year. The office took its name from Rube Clayton, manager of an area ranch established in 1883. The community's meeting place was the attractive Eighteen Springs, the water source for the area. The post office closed before 1940, when the community had a school, three businesses, and sixty people. The population was twenty-one in 1980 and 1990.

BIBLIOGRAPHY: Lora Blount, *A Short History of Fisher County* (M.A. thesis, Hardin-Simmons University, 1947). E. L. Yeats and E. H. Shelton, *History of Fisher County,* (n.p.: Feather, 1971).

CLAYTONVILLE, TEXAS (Swisher County). Claytonville is on Farm Road 145 ten miles east of Kress in southeastern Swisher County. In the early 1950s M. C. Clayton, a cotton grower, moved his ginning business to the area from Bailey in Fannin County. He then built a grocery and cafe for his employees. Soon the Clayton Gin became a favorite gathering place for area farmers, and for several years the company hosted a community barbecue just before harvest. The gin was one of the first to compost gin waste and return it to the fields. In 1962 a Baptist church was established at Claytonville. In 1984 Claytonville reported a population of 116 and six businesses. The population was still 116 in 1990.

BIBLIOGRAPHY: Swisher County Historical Commission, *Windmilling: 101 Years of Swisher County History* (Dallas: Taylor, 1978).

H. Allen Anderson

A CLEAN, WELL-LIGHTED PLACE. A Clean, Well-Lighted Place, a short-lived but influential Austin art gallery opened by Dave Hickey in 1967, helped to launch the careers of a group of Texas artists who became prominent in the 1970s and 1980s. The gallery expanded on the legacy of Jermayne and Douglas MacAgy and James Johnson Sweeney, who introduced much contemporary art to the state through their directorships of Dallas and Houston museums in the early and mid-sixties. Hickey's gallery established a niche for unconventional contemporary art by young Texas artists that was further developed by Henry Hopkins, director of the Fort Worth Art Museum (now the Modern Art Museum of Fort Worth[qv]) from 1969 to 1974, gallery owners Janie C. Lee and Murray Smither of Dallas, and Fredericka Hunter of Houston.

A Clean, Well-Lighted Place was named after a short story by Ernest Hemingway. Hickey and his wife Mary Jane borrowed $10,000 and converted the downstairs portion of an old home at 2300 Rio Grande in Austin into an exhibition space. The gallery opened with a show of Jim Franklin's work. Franklin was a cartoonist who, with Glenn Whitehead, depicted the armadillo[qv] as antihero, in whose honor the Armadillo World Headquarters[qv] was named. Despite the gallery's links with the armadillo and other standard-bearers in what Hickey called "the great Texas tradition of weird enterprises," it remained distinct from Austin's counterculture by advocating a pop sensibility reminiscent of Andy Warhol's Factory studio in New York City.

Hickey perceived his role as that of a coach. He encouraged his artists to "do their own thing" while avoiding, if possible, the trap of using strictly Texas imagery. He promoted A Clean, Well-Lighted Place as a "pilot" gallery dedicated to showing the work of young artists, and it did, in fact, help to establish the careers of such artists as Barry Buxkamper, whose paintings, drawings, and sculptures used docile cows as their principal subject matter. Other artists closely associated with A Clean, Well-Lighted Place were George Green, whose green linoleum tile-coated wooden sculptures celebrate institutions such as the rodeo, Buicks, and Elvis Presley; Mel Casas, who combines images and words in paintings that address racism and other issues; and Luis Jiménez, who casts cars, motorcycles, vaqueros, and other cultural images in larger-than-life fiberglass sculptures. Hickey also exhibited the works of Jim Roche, a sculptor and painter who made potted ceramic "mama" plants with breasts, and works from Terry Allen's Juárez series, a collection of songs, drawings, and prints that chronicled the travels of two couples throughout the Southwest. Peter Plagens, Bobbie Moore, June Robinson, Earl Staley, Jack Boynton, Juergan Strunck, Vera Simons, and Willard Midgett also exhibited at A Clean, Well-Lighted Place.

In 1969 the Hickeys moved their gallery to a more spacious location at 600 West Twelfth, where they organized a series of successful exhibitions such as Six Sculptures by Six Artists (1970), which, in addition to the work of Roche and Green, displayed Harry Geffert's light sculptures, minimalist pieces by Scott Grieger, Jim Schinder's hanging tapestries of "found objects," and Haydn Larson's painted assemblages of scrap metal and farm tools. Old-Fashioned Painting (1970), which presented the work of abstract painters Stephen Mueller, Richard Mock, and Warren Davis, anticipated the 1980s revival of Expressionism by a decade.

Perhaps Hickey's most successful exhibition was South Texas Sweet Funk (1970), which featured many of the artists associated with A Clean, Well-Lighted Place and was held at St. Edward's University in Austin. The exhibition included the cadre of underground comic-book artists, among whom were Jim Franklin, Gilbert Shelton, and Steve Gosnell; sculptors George Green, Luis Jiménez, Jim Roche, and Robert Wade; Bobbie Moore, whose delicate drawings in colored pencil recast the suburban mothers of 1940s children's books in a sexual context, and many other artists. This exhibition crystallized the perception of these artists as a group, now defined by the name "Texas funk," that simultaneously attracted attention and confined the artists within a somewhat limiting regional categorization.

In September 1971 the Hickeys moved to New York City, where Dave ran a gallery and published critical articles on art and gallery reviews. A Clean, Well-Lighted Place closed several months after they left. As a critic and executive editor for *Art in America,* Hickey continued to write about Texas and to attract national attention to the artists working there. Jim Roche, George Green, Robert Wade, Jack Mims, and others established an artists' colony in the Oak Cliff area of Dallas that continued to feed the "Texas funk" mythos spawned by "South Texas Sweet Funk." Many of the artists whose work had been shown at Hickey's gallery and whose critical reputation continued to flourish, however, developed other forms.

BIBLIOGRAPHY: Jan Butterfield, "South Texas Funk," *Texas Observer,* January 8, 1971. Ron Gleason, "Interview: Dave Hickey," *Arts and Architecture,* Winter 1981. William H. Goetzmann and Becky Duval Reese, *Texas Images and Visions* (Archer M. Huntington Art Gallery, University of Texas at Austin, 1983). Dave Hickey, "The Texas to New York via Nashville Semi-Transcontinental Epiphany Tactic," *Art in America* 60 (September–October 1972). *Newsweek,* August 7, 1972. Roberta Smith, "Twelve Days of Texas," *Art in America* 64 (July–August 1976).

Kendall Curlee

CLEAR CREEK (Bell County). Clear Creek rises two miles southwest of Copperas Cove rises in western Bell County (at 31°06′ N, 97°53′ W) and runs ten miles northeast to its mouth on House Creek, in southwestern Coryell County (at 31°11′ N, 97°49′ W). The creek crosses rolling prairie into steep slopes and benches. Clays and clay loams support oak, juniper, grasses, and mesquite.

_____ (Brown County). Clear Creek rises four miles west of Brownwood in central Brown County (at 31°44′ N, 99°05′ W) and runs seventeen miles south to its mouth on the Colorado River, at the San Saba county line three miles southwest of Indian Creek (at 31°29′ N, 99°03′ W). The local rolling terrain is surfaced by clay loam that supports grasses and vine mesquite.

_____ (Burnet County). Clear Creek rises in two branches in eastern Burnet County. The West Branch of Clear Creek rises five miles northeast of Bertram (at 30°47′ N, 98°00′ W) and runs southeast for three miles. The East Branch of Clear Creek rises four miles northeast of Bertram (at 30°41′ N, 98°00′ W) and runs southeast for four miles. The two branches converge to form Cedar Creek (at 30°46′ N, 97°57′ W), which runs southeast for three miles to its mouth on the North Fork of San Gabriel River, five miles north of Liberty Hill in Williamson County (at 30°45′ N, 97°55′ W). Surrounding steep slopes and benches are surfaced by shallow clay loams that support juniper, live oak, mesquite, and grasses.

_____ (Burnet County). Clear Creek rises at the foot of Potato Hill six miles northwest of Burnet in western Burnet County (at 30°48′ N, 98°17′ W) and runs southwest for ten miles to its mouth on Inks Lake (at 30°45′ N, 98°23′ W). The surrounding rolling to flat terrain is surfaced by clay and sandy loams that support scrub brush, cacti, and grasses.

_____ (Colorado County). Clear Creek rises in two forks in Weimar in western Colorado County (at 29°42′ N, 96°47′ W) and runs southwest for 9½ miles to its mouth on the East Navidad River, a mile northwest of Oakland (at 29°37′ N, 96°51′ W). It crosses gently sloping terrain surfaced by dark clay, with some exposed alluvial sandstone, that supports oak, willow, sycamore, hackberry, and pecan, with an understory of wild grape and yaupon. Wildlife is abundant.

_____ (Coryell County). Clear Creek rises near Copperas Cove in southeastern Coryell County (at 31°07′ N, 97°56′ W) and runs southeast for 9½ miles, through southeastern Coryell and western Bell counties, to its mouth on the Lampasas River, near the Burnet county line (at 31°00′ N, 97°53′ W). It crosses gently sloping to sloping and undulating to rolling terrain surfaced by gravelly, loamy, and clayey soils and used predominantly as rangeland.

_____ (DeWitt County). Clear Creek rises a mile southeast of the Gonzales county line in southwest DeWitt County (at 29°06′ N, 97°35′ W) and runs northeast for fourteen miles to its mouth on Sandies Creek, five miles east of Westhoff (at 29°10′ N, 97°23′ W). Local variable terrain is surfaced by clay and sandy loam that supports grasses, mixed hardwoods, and pines.

_____ (Ellis County). Clear Creek rises three miles east of Rankin in southeastern Ellis County (at 32°11′ N, 96°42′ W) and runs east for five miles to its mouth on Chambers Creek, 4½ miles northwest of Emhouse in northern Navarro County (at 32°13′ N, 96°37′ W). It crosses flat to rolling terrain surfaced by shallow to deep sandy and clay loams that support scrub brush, cacti, and some hardwoods. For most of the county's history the Clear Creek area has been used as range and cropland.

_____ (Erath County). Clear Creek rises five miles northwest of Morgan Mill in northern Erath County (at 32°26′ N, 98°13′ W) and runs north for five miles to its mouth on Big Sunday Creek, one mile south of the Erath/Palo Pinto county line and five miles west of Patillo (at 32°30′ N, 98°15′ W). The surrounding steep slopes and rolling hills reach an elevation of 1,000 to 1,100 feet and are surfaced by sandy soils that support juniper, scrub brush, mesquite, cacti, grasses, and scattered oaks.

_____ (Fayette County). Clear Creek rises in a tank on the south slope of Hellers Hill in north central Fayette County (at 30°02′ N, 96°47′ W) and runs south and then east for fourteen miles to its mouth on Cummins Creek, 3½ miles north of Rek Hill (at 29°59′ N, 96°39′ W). It flows through Oldenburg and several unnamed flood control impoundments. Variable terrain is surfaced by clay, sand, and gravel that support oaks, cedar, occasional pines, and an understory of yaupon.

_____ (Fort Bend County). Clear Creek rises a mile west of the Blue Ridge oilfield in the northeast corner of Fort Bend County (at 29°35′ N, 95°29′ W) and runs east for forty-one miles, forming the southern boundary of Harris County and the northern boundary of Brazoria and Galveston counties, to its mouth on Galveston Bay (at 29°33′ N, 95°01′ W). The surrounding flat to rolling terrain is surfaced by sandy and clay loam that supports mixed hardwoods and pines.

_____ (Hemphill County). Clear Creek rises at the junction of its two branches in north central Hemphill County (at 36°04′ N, 100°19′ W) and runs south ten miles to its mouth on the Canadian River, at the southern boundary of the Gene Howe Wildlife Management Area (at 35°56′ N, 100°19′ W). The surrounding flat terrain with occasional rolling hills is surfaced by sand that supports sparse grasses and herbs.

_____ (Henderson County). Clear Creek rises two miles west of Meridith Cemetery in north central Henderson County (at 32°21′ N, 95°55′ W). It formerly ran southwest for fourteen miles to its mouth on Cedar Creek, just west of Caney City. With the construction of the Cedar Creek Reservoir in the early 1960s the lower four miles of the creek were inundated, and the creek now enters the lake near the Farm Road 2329 bridge (at 32°13′ N, 96°03′ W). The surrounding flat to rolling terrain is surfaced by sandy and clay loams that support water-tolerant hardwoods, conifers, and grasses.

_____ (Leon County). Clear Creek, also known as Forky Deer Creek, rises ten miles southwest of Centerville in southwestern Leon County (at 31°11′ N, 96°08′ W) and runs southwest for fourteen miles to its mouth on the Navasota River, on the Robertson county line (at 31°05′ N, 96°16′ W). It traverses nearly level terrain surfaced by sandy and loamy soils that support woods of pecan, elm, water oak, hackberry, post oak, and black hickory. Settlement in the vicinity began in the latter half of the nineteenth century. Flynn, a station on the Burlington–Rock Island Railway, is on the south bank of the upper creek; Vanetia is on the north bank of the lower creek.
BIBLIOGRAPHY: James Young Gates and H. B. Fox, *A History of Leon County* (Centerville, Texas: Leon County News, 1936; rpt. 1977).

_____ (Montague County). Clear Creek rises just north of State Highway 59 in east Montague County (at 33°42′ N, 97°36′ W) and runs southeast forty-seven miles, passing through Cooke County, to its mouth on Lewisville Lake, in northwest Denton County (at 33°16′ N, 97°03′ W). Clear Creek is one of the major streams of Denton County. It provided an important supply of clean water for early settlers of the Grand Prairie region. Fed by numerous tributaries, it drains the mostly deep, fine, sandy loam of the Blackland Prairie that supports grass and brush.

_____ (Montgomery County). Clear Creek rose in northern Montgomery County and originally ran south for seven miles to its mouth on the West San Jacinto River. By 1973, however, development of Lake Conroe resulted in the inundation of the creek.

_____ (Newton County). Clear Creek rises four miles west of Wiergate in northwestern Newton County (at 31°00′ N, 93°46′ W) and runs southeast for 7½ miles to its mouth on Yellow Bayou, three miles south of Burkeville (at 30°57′ N, 93°41′ W). It crosses the heavily forested country typical of much of Newton County.

_____ (Upshur County). Clear Creek rises two miles west of Piedmont in south central Upshur County (at 32°41′ N, 94°57′ W) and runs northeast for eleven miles to its mouth on Little Cypress Creek, a mile southeast of Graceton (at 32°41′ N, 94°48′ W). The surrounding flat to rolling terrain is surfaced by clay and sandy loam that supports water-tolerant hardwoods, conifers, and grasses.

_____ (Waller County). Clear Creek, also known as Fish Pond Creek, rises eight miles northeast of Hempstead in northern Waller County (at 30°11′ N, 95°59′ W) and runs twenty-two miles southwest to its mouth on the Brazos River, six miles south of Hempstead (at 30°00′ N, 96°05′ W). It forms the border between Waller and Austin counties and is fed by over forty tributaries, including Ponds Creek, Three Mile Creek, and the overflow from Becker Lake. Clear Creek crosses rolling East Texas timberlands to gently undulating coastal area surfaced by sandy and clay loams that support pines, oaks, grasses, and crops. During the Civil War[qv] both Camp Clear Creek and Camp Clever were located on Clear Creek. Other Confederate camps near the creek included Camp Carter, Camp Hempstead, Camp Herbert, and Camp Groce.[qv] Because of its location in Texas and its rail facilities provided by the Houston and Texas Central Railroad, Hempstead served as an intermediate organizing point for soldiers coming from Central and West Texas. The camps were built near Clear Creek because it provided water.

BIBLIOGRAPHY: Mildred W. Abshier, ed., *Waller County Whatnots* (Hempstead, Texas: Waller County Historical Commission and Waller County Historical Society, 1986).

CLEAR CREEK, TEXAS (DeWitt County). Clear Creek was near present Ranch Road 108 ten miles north of Yorktown in western DeWitt County, in an area predominantly settled by Germans. The community center was the Clear Creek school, organized in 1894 and sometimes called Sandgate. The school building also was used as a Methodist church. In 1926 the public school at nearby Nopal was merged with the Clear Creek school, which closed in 1951. By 1961 only Sandgate Cemetery marked the area. An earlier Clear Creek school may have been organized fourteen miles southeast in 1885 and operated until 1898; that building reportedly also doubled as a Methodist church.

BIBLIOGRAPHY: Nellie Murphree, *A History of DeWitt County* (Victoria, Texas, 1962).
Craig H. Roell

CLEAR CREEK, TEXAS (Hemphill County). Clear Creek, or Hogtown, was Hemphill County's first settlement and the forerunner of the county seat, Canadian. It rose on the north bank of the Canadian River, near its junction with Clear Creek, late in 1886 as a camp for the construction crews of the Southern Kansas (Panhandle and Santa Fe) Railroad. Soon the town won considerable notoriety as a "desperado city." Saloons, gambling dens, and stores were erected, and tents were pitched for temporary sleeping quarters. Sam Pollard, a local rancher, constructed a hotel and restaurant. The brothers John J. and George Gerlach,[qqv] who had operated a mercantile store for ranchers on Horse Creek since 1884, moved their one-room establishment to Hogtown.

The name Hogtown was supposedly derived from the town's generally shabby appearance and seamy atmosphere. One former resident, however, later stated that the town was so named because everyone was subject to the imperative "root, hog, or die." A dispute between Pollard and the railroad company over the price of town lots, along with the founding of Canadian on the south bank after completion of a bridge in 1887, led to Hogtown's rapid demise. Only a few settlers remained at the site, which was renamed Clear Creek. A schoolhouse, which doubled as a church, was in use until 1913. For years thereafter, a siding and flag station for the Santa Fe line retained the name.

BIBLIOGRAPHY: *Canadian Record*, September 9, 1937. Sallie B. Harris, *Cowmen and Ladies: A History of Hemphill County* (Canyon, Texas: Staked Plains, 1977). Glyndon M. Riley, The History of Hemphill County (M.A. thesis, West Texas State College, 1939). F. Stanley [Stanley F. L. Crocchiola], *Rodeo Town (Canadian, Texas)* (Denver: World, 1953).
H. Allen Anderson

CLEAR CREEK, TEXAS (Henderson County). Clear Creek was near the site of present Tool, twelve miles northwest of Athens in northwestern Henderson County. The site was settled before 1869, and at one time a church and a school were in the area. After World War II[qv] most of the residents left, and by the early 1990s only a few scattered houses remained.
Christopher Long

CLEAR FORK OF THE BRAZOS RIVER. The Clear Fork of the Brazos River rises east of Snyder in eastern Scurry County (at 32°40′ N, 100°45′ W) and runs east for thirty-seven miles, through Fisher, Jones, Shackelford, Throckmorton, Stephens, and Young counties, to its mouth on the Brazos River, near South Bend in southern Young County (at 33°01′ N, 98°40′ W). It passes near Fort Griffin[qv] in Shackelford County. It is dammed in Jones and Stephens counties and twice in Young County to form reservoirs for municipal water supply to nearby towns. A principal tributary, Hubbard Creek, joins the Clear Fork nine miles north of Breckenridge (at 32°54′ N, 98°53′ W). Other tributaries include Spring, Buffalo, Noodle, Bitter, and Fish creeks. The surrounding flat terrain with local shallow depressions is surfaced by clay and sandy loam that supports water-tolerant hardwoods, conifers, and grasses.

CLEAR FORK OF THE TRINITY RIVER. The Clear Fork, one of four forks that form the Trinity River, rises two miles south of Gibtown in extreme southeastern Jack County (at 32°59′ N, 97°55′ W) and flows east for five miles, then turns southeast and flows down a straight valley for fifty-six miles to its mouth on the West Fork of the Trinity River, just south of Lake Benbrook in southwestern Tarrant County (at 32°46′ N, 97°20′ W). In its upper reaches the stream traverses flat to rolling terrain surfaced by deep, fine sandy loams that support hardwood forest, brush, and grasses. The terrain southeast of Weatherford Lake is variable and surfaced by shallow, stony, clay loams. For most of the area's history the land that surrounds the Clear Fork has been used as range and crop land. In 1956 the fork was dammed seven miles east of Weatherford to form Weatherford Lake. In 1949 it was dammed in Tarrant County to form Lake Benbrook, ten miles southwest of Fort Worth. Like Lake Weatherford, Lake Benbrook was constructed in part to control the seasonal flooding of the Clear Fork.

CLEAR LAKE, TEXAS. Clear Lake is near the south shore of Lavon Lake, twelve miles southeast of McKinney in southeastern Collin County. The community was also on the Atchison, Topeka and Santa Fe Railway. In 1884 the United States government built and operated a distillery on the banks of nearby Clear Lake. The federal project attracted a small number of settlers to the area, and by 1890 the town of Clear Lake was established. A post office opened there in 1898, with Robert L. Palmer as postmaster; the office was discontinued sometime after 1930. For several years at the beginning of its existence the community was a principal provider of bois d'arc timber for Dallas, which experimented in using the wood to pave its streets. When Dallas abandoned the project, many residents left Clear Lake. Although located in the heart of the Blackland Prairie, the land surrounding Clear Lake was subject to seasonal flooding, which destroyed crops. The population of Clear Lake was estimated at seventy-five in 1910 and rose to 100 by 1914. From the 1930s to 1990 the estimated number of residents at the community remained at fifty, despite the construction of Lavon Lake in 1954.

BIBLIOGRAPHY: Roy Franklin Hall and Helen Gibbard Hall, *Collin County: Pioneering in North Texas* (Quanah, Texas: Nortex, 1975). Ellen Jeanene Walker, Agricultural Land Utilization in Collin County (M.A. thesis, Southern Methodist University, 1969).
David Minor

CLEAR LAKE CITY, TEXAS. Clear Lake City is on State Highway 3 a mile west of Clear Lake in southeast Harris County. In 1938 James Marion West[qv] sold 30,000 acres in southern Harris County, including the West family ranch, to Humble Oil and Refining Company (later Exxon Company, U.S.A.qv). In 1961 the National Aeronautics and Space Administration selected Houston as the site for its Manned Spacecraft Center (renamed the Lyndon B. Johnson Space Centerqv in 1973), built initially on a 1,000-acre tract of the former West ranch. Humble Oil announced plans in January 1962 to develop 15,000 acres of the West property near the Manned Spacecraft Center for residential and industrial use. Humble and Del E. Webb Corporation agreed to form a jointly owned company to develop the site. Their venture, Friendswood Development Company, became operational the following May. Governor John Connallyqv formally opened Clear Lake City on September 15, 1963. In 1968, the first year for which population statistics are available, 3,785 people lived in Clear Lake City. By 1970 the population had grown to 8,000, and in 1974 it was 16,000.

Clear Lake City was annexed to Houston in 1977. A utility shortage temporarily halted construction of new homes, but in 1988 the community led the Houston area in the sale of new, single-family homes. The diversified economy, which rests on the aerospace industry, retail business, and recreation and tourism, enabled Clear Lake City to weather the economic downturns that affected Houston during the 1980s. In fiscal year 1988 the Johnson Space Center, which employed 3,302 permanent civil-service employees, alone pumped almost $860 million into the Houston economy. Major aerospace contractors with local offices include Boeing, Ford Aerospace Corporation, McDonnell Douglas, and Martin Marietta. Tourists frequent numerous annual events in the area, including the Clear Lake Spring Fling and Boating Festival in April, the Lunar Rendezvous Festival in July, the Blessing of the Fleet in August, the Armand Bayou Nature Center Fall Festival in October, and the Christmas Boat Lane Parade.

Clear Lake City belongs to the Clear Creek Independent School District, which covers southern Harris County and northern Galveston County. This highly ranked school district had a 1988–89 enrollment of 20,725. The University of Houston–Clear Lake, authorized by the state legislature in 1971, began regularly scheduled classes in September 1974; this upper-level institution, located on 487 acres adjacent to the Johnson Space Center, had a fall 1988 enrollment of 7,196. The Clear Lake City Water Authority, a state agency established in 1963, is responsible for water and sanitary sewerage and drainage. It is the largest water authority in Texas and is funded through the sale of tax-exempt municipal bonds and water and sewer service. The estimated population of Clear Lake City in 1980 was 22,000.

BIBLIOGRAPHY: Houston *Chronicle*, December 29, 1938, August 25, 1941, September 19, 1961, January 18, 19, May 27, 1962, September 15, 1963, August 28, November 23, 1977, April 27, 1988. Houston *Post*, September 18, 1985, December 4, 1988. Vertical Files, Barker Texas History Center, University of Texas at Austin (Clear Lake City, Texas, Johnson Space Center). *Casey Edward Greene*

CLEAR SPRING, TEXAS. Clear Spring is at the intersection of Farm roads 25 and 578, nine miles northwest of Seguin in northwestern Guadalupe County. German immigrants came to the area in 1845. The community had a post office called Bernhardsville from 1874 to 1875, when the name was changed to Clear Spring. In the 1890s Clear Spring had a general store, a cotton gin, and a population of 100. The post office was discontinued in 1906, but the community remained. Clear Spring had two businesses and a school in 1946; the school was consolidated with the New Braunfels district by the 1950s. In 1990 a church and several businesses served a resident population of sixty.
Vivian Elizabeth Smyrl

CLEAR SPRINGS, TEXAS. Clear Springs is just south of Farm Road 1995 three miles west of Carroll in western Smith County. It was originally part of the Sheldon Graves Survey. In 1936 Clear Springs had two churches, a black elementary school, and a small collection of dwellings. Forty-two students attended the two-teacher school, which had been consolidated by 1952 with the Lindale Independent School District. Maps for 1973 and 1981 identify Clear Springs as a cemetery and a few scattered farms.

BIBLIOGRAPHY: Edward Clayton Curry, An Administrative Survey of the Schools of Smith County, Texas (M.Ed. thesis, University of Texas, 1938). *Vista K. McCroskey*

CLEARWATER, THERESA CLARK (1853–1938). Theresa Clark Clearwater, first teacher in Cameron County, daughter of William Henry Clark, was born on December 19, 1853, at Clarksville in Cameron County. In 1872 she received a state teaching certificate and, at a salary of fifty-five dollars a month, became the teacher of the first school in Cameron County and one of the first certified teachers in the area. In 1875 Theresa Clark married Joseph H. Clearwater; they had two children. After her husband died in 1879 in Tampico, Vera Cruz, she returned to Point Isabel, then moved to Brownsville, where she taught school from 1882 to 1936. She died on September 28, 1938; a Brownsville elementary school was named in her honor.

BIBLIOGRAPHY: W. H. Chatfield, *The Twin Cities of the Border and the Country of the Lower Rio Grande* (New Orleans: Brandao, 1893; rpt., Brownsville: Brownsville Historical Association, 1959). San Antonio *Express*, January 10, 1937. *Verna J. McKenna*

CLEARWATER, TEXAS. Clearwater is on Farm Road 1448 twelve miles south of Mount Vernon in southern Franklin County. It was originally between Cypress Creek and Dry Cypress Creek, but the streams were altered by the impoundment of Lake Cypress Springs and Lake Bob Sandlin. Clearwater was named for the water in Cypress Creek. Anglo settlement in the area began in the 1860s, and a community was in existence by the early 1870s. In the 1930s the community had a sawmill, a gin, a store, a church, and a school. The population was estimated at twenty-five in 1933 and at fifty in 1945. In 1985 Clearwater had a church and cemetery and widely scattered houses.

BIBLIOGRAPHY: Billy Hicks and Doris Meek, comps., *Historical Records of Franklin County, Texas* (Mount Vernon, Texas: Franklin County Historical Survey Committee, 1972). *Cecil Harper, Jr.*

CLEBARRO COLLEGE. Clebarro College originated in February 1909 when the Church of Christ in Cleburne invited Allen Booker Barret and Charles H. Roberson, formerly of Southland University, to establish a private school in that town. Several members of the Southland University faculty joined Clebarro College. Barret and Roberson became the owners of the school, which derived its name from Cleburne, Barret, and Roberson. The Cleburne Land Company donated twenty acres between Glen Rose and Granbury for a campus. Funds were sufficient to construct a three-story administration building and, three years later, a women's dormitory. Clebarro College offered elementary and secondary programs and two years of college, after which the students received bachelor's degrees. The new facilities were not ready for the first fall semester, and classes began on September 15 at the home of Judge J. A. Stanford. Sixty students enrolled. In addition to Bible classes, the college had teacher training, a commercial department, a vocal and instrumental music department, and departments of expression, oratory, and physical culture. By 1911–12 additional coursework in philosophy, sociology, political science, and education was offered, and the B.A., B.S., and B.Litt. degrees were conferred. Extracurricular activities at the college included literary societies, a debate club, and a choral club as well as sports for men and women. For a decade Clebarro College had an average enrollment of forty. By the end of World War I,qv however, the school found it was unable to sustain itself; it closed in the spring of 1919. In 1920 Dr. B. H. Turner purchased the physical plant from the trustees of the Christian Church and converted it into a hospital. The University of Texas never recognized Clebarro College as a standard junior college.

BIBLIOGRAPHY: Dudley M. Gordon, The History of Cleburne (M.A. thesis, University of Texas, 1929). M. Norvel Young, *A History of Colleges Established and Conducted by Members of the Churches of Christ* (Kansas City: Old Paths Book Club, 1949).

David Minor and Nancy Beck Young

CLEBURNE, TEXAS. Cleburne, the county seat of Johnson County, is on U.S. Highway 67 thirty miles south of Fort Worth. Its origin and growth can be attributed to its role as a crossroads and transportation center. The site was near the earliest Johnson County road, an old wagon trail that was used by soldiers traveling from Fort Belknap to Fort Graham. The location had an excellent water source on West Buffalo Creek that attracted travelers, including cattlemen from the nearby Chisholm Trail.qv During the Civil Warqv the site was used as a bivouac for Johnson County units marching off to war. This temporary facility, known as Camp Henderson, became a permanent settlement on March 23, 1867, when it became necessary to choose a new, centrally located county seat to replace Buchanan. The town was named in honor of Gen. Patrick R. Cleburne, under whom many of the men had fought during the Civil War.

Cleburne had a post office during its first year and a newspaper, the Cleburne *Chronicle*, in 1868. Cleburne Male and Female Institute, established by the Alvarado Baptist Association, operated between 1868 and 1872 as a church-related school. It was nonsectarian for a few more years before becoming the site of the first public school. The town was incorporated in May 1871 with a mayor-council form of government.

The importance of Cleburne as a transportation center was enhanced by the arrival of the railroad. In 1870 the population was 683; twenty years later the residents numbered 3,727. In 1881 the Gulf, Colorado and Santa Fe Railroad was completed from Fort Worth through Cleburne to Temple, and a secondary line connected Weatherford to Cleburne in 1887. The most important industrial contribution to the city was made by the Santa Fe Railroad, which in 1898 and 1899 constructed central machine shops in Cleburne, helping to double the city's population in the 1890s. In 1882 the Chicago, Texas and Mexican Central Railway connected Cleburne to Dallas. Two additional railroads maintained terminals in the city after 1900. The Dallas, Cleburne and Southwestern Railway completed a spur to Egan in 1902, and the Trinity and Brazos Valley, commonly called the "Boll Weevil," operated out of Cleburne from 1904 to 1924. The former line was sold to the Missouri, Kansas and Texas in 1910. The track out of Cleburne was abandoned after 1920. The Burlington and Rock Island used the Boll Weevil track from 1924 until 1932, when it too was abandoned. The Interurban out of Fort Worth served Cleburne for eighteen years after 1912. A local streetcar service operated from 1911 to 1917. Cleburne was still served by Santa Fe and Amtrak in 1990.

In 1909 the State Christian Junior College moved from Denton to Cleburne, where it operated as Clebarro Junior College until it closed in 1919. A Carnegie Library (*see* CARNEGIE LIBRARIES) was opened in 1904. Cleburne had a population of 12,820 in 1920. All four city banks failed in the 1920s, and a strike at the Santa Fe in 1922 further depressed the economy. The governor of Texas had to send Texas Rangersqv into the city to keep order during the strike. By 1940 Cleburne had a population of 10,558. During the 1930s a Civilian Conservation Corpsqv camp operated west of Cleburne with 200 workers. Among their projects was the construction of Cleburne State Recreation Park,qv which opened in 1941. German prisoners of war,qv kept in Cleburne during the latter part of World War II,qv were used as laborers on farms.

After 1945 proximity to the Dallas–Fort Worth region resulted in substantial growth in Cleburne. By 1990 the city had a population of 22,205, forty manufacturing facilities, a new regional hospital, and a community college extension center. A major area employer has been the Comanche Peak Nuclear Power Station in nearby Glen Rose. In 1990 Cleburne had a council-manager form of government, eight municipal parks, and Lake Pat Cleburne.qv Local cultural activities included a community theater group and Layland Museum, both housed in the old Carnegie Library building. A local preservationist society, Save Old Cleburne, sponsored an annual Candlewalk and Tour of Homes during the Christmas season.

BIBLIOGRAPHY: Frances Dickson Abernathy, The Building of Johnson County and the Settlement of the Communities of the Eastern Portion of the County (M.A. thesis, University of Texas, 1936). Dudley M. Gordon, The History of Cleburne (M.A. thesis, University of Texas, 1929). Ernest E. Guinn, A History of Cleburne, Texas (M.A. thesis, University of Texas, 1950). Johnson County History Book Committee, *History of Johnson County, Texas* (Dallas: Curtis Media, 1985). *A Memorial and Biographical History of Johnson and Hill Counties* (Chicago: Lewis, 1892). *Richard Elam and Mildred Padon*

CLEBURNE MALE AND FEMALE INSTITUTE. Cleburne Male and Female Institute, in Cleburne, was established in 1866 under the auspices of the Cleburne Baptist Church. In 1870 the Alvarado Baptist Association assumed control of the school. The first principal, J. R. Clark, was succeeded by W. B. Featherstone when the school was incorporated in 1872. The institute emphasized science, mathematics, and language. A maximum enrollment of 220 was recorded in 1874. With the opening of the Cleburne public school in 1875, enrollment declined, and in 1878 the institute was closed.

BIBLIOGRAPHY: Carl Bassett Wilson, History of Baptist Educational Efforts in Texas, 1829–1900 (Ph.D. dissertation, University of Texas, 1934). Joe P. Ross, "Requiem of a Cleburne School, 1868–1875," *Texana* 6 (1968). Donald W. Whisenhunt, *The Encyclopedia of Texas Colleges and Universities* (Austin: Eakin, 1986). *Herman L. Crow*

CLEBURNE STATE RECREATIONAL PARK. Cleburne State Recreational Park is located on Park Road 21 just south of U.S. Highway 67 and twelve miles southwest of Cleburne in southwestern Johnson County. The park originated in 1934 when a group of Cleburne businessmen purchased a few hundred acres of land at the present site and turned it over to the State Parks Board with the understanding that a park would be developed according to the arrangements that existed between the Civilian Conservation Corpsqv and the National Park Service. The land had been the home of Comanche raiding parties during the Civil War.qv In 1934 the CCC constructed a dam, a shelter, a residence for the park superintendent that still stands, and nature trails. In the park are deer, quail, and raccoons. The park covers 529 acres and has an artificial lake with a surface area of 116 acres. Because of its proximity to Six Flags Over Texasqv in Arlington, Cleburne State Recreational Park has become a popular camping spot.

BIBLIOGRAPHY: Ray Miller, *Texas Parks* (Houston: Cordovan, 1984). Vertical Files, Barker Texas History Center, University of Texas at Austin. *David Minor*

CLEGG, GEORGE AUSTIN (1872–1959). George Austin Clegg, quarter horseqv breeder and horse-show judge, son of Austin and Dower (Powers) Clegg, was born in Thomaston, Texas, on April 22, 1872. He attended the public schools of Thomaston, St. Joseph's College in Victoria, and Baylor University for a short while. He took a commercial course in San Antonio and at the age of eighteen began managing the large horse and cattle ranch owned by his uncle in DeWitt County. Clegg considered himself a riding, roping, and racing expert by 1895. He married Letetia Margaret Nichols of Cuero on July 12, 1897, and the couple had two children. They moved to Alice in 1904. There Clegg managed the 1,400-acre Taylor Brothers Farm and his own two 300-acre farms. In 1905 he laid the foundation for fine quarter-horse breeding when he bought a yearling colt, Little Joe, from Dow Shely (co-owner of Traveler) and four racing mares in Del Rio. In 1911 he began racing their offspring, with Pap Rebo as jockey. Clegg bought Hickory Bill, a racer, and two mares in 1911. His top quarter horses began with the breeding of Little Joe and the Hickory Bill mares. Old Sorrell, sired by Hickory Bill and sold in 1913, was the foundation stallion of the King Ranch[qv] remuda.

By 1916 Clegg owned ranches in Live Oak, Duval, and Jim Wells counties. By the early 1920s he owned about 300 pedigreed brood mares and large herds of beef and dairy cattle. With help from his son he ran a dairy near Alice. In 1929 Clegg was injured and his wife killed in an automobile accident. He gradually left his cattle management to others and focused exclusively on quarter-mile horse racing. Among famous Clegg horses were Jodie Click and Cotton Eye Joe (sires); Hickory Bill, Rondo, and Little Joe (racers); and Jiggs and Medina Sport (roping horses).

During the Great Depression[qv] Clegg lost his horses, cattle, and extensive ranch properties. He ran for sheriff in Jim Wells County in 1934 and lost. He then started working for the King Ranch, handled its race horses for several years, and in June 1952 delivered a boatload of King Ranch cattle to Cuba. He became a judge at horse shows and was nationally recognized for his knowledge of horses and his integrity. He died of cancer at the home of his daughter in Alice on January 10, 1959. In appreciation of his many accomplishments in horse breeding, the King Ranch donated the George Clegg Memorial Trophy to be presented annually to the grand champion of the Quarter Horse Show at the Jim Wells County Fair.

BIBLIOGRAPHY: Ellis A. Davis and Edwin H. Grobe, comps., *The New Encyclopedia of Texas* (2 vols., Dallas: Texas Development Bureau, 1925?; 4 vols. 1929?). Robert M. Denhardt, *The King Ranch Quarter Horses, and Something of the Ranch and the Men That Bred Them* (Norman: University of Oklahoma Press, 1976). Robert M. Denhardt, *Quarter Horses: A Story of Two Centuries* (Norman: University of Oklahoma Press, 1967). Agnes G. Grimm, *Llanos Mesteñas: Mustang Plains* (Waco: Texian Press, 1968).
Agnes G. Grimm

CLEGG, TEXAS. Clegg was on State Highway 59 sixteen miles southwest of George West in southwestern Live Oak County. It was named for George Clegg, a local rancher. A post office opened in 1913, about the same time as a Baptist congregation was organized. By the 1930s the town had a school, a store, three businesses, and a cotton gin. In 1940 the Baptists moved a church to the site. By 1950, however, the town had almost disappeared. Clegg's school was closed in 1948, and in 1949 only one business and twenty-five people were reported in the town. In 1958 the Clegg Baptist Church disbanded because of its shrinking congregation, and by the early 1980s only the town's old cemetery remained at the site.

BIBLIOGRAPHY: Ervin L. Sparkman, *The People's History of Live Oak County* (Mesquite, Texas, 1981).
John Leffler

CLEM, JOHN LINCOLN (1851–1937). John Lincoln Clem, army officer, was born in Newark, Ohio, on August 13, 1851. In May 1861 he attempted to enlist in the Third Ohio Volunteers but was rejected because of his youth. He attached himself unofficially to the Twenty-second Michigan Infantry and participated in the battle of Shiloh as a drummer. He enlisted shortly thereafter and participated in the battle of Chickamauga, in which, at the age of twelve, he shot a Confederate colonel who demanded his surrender. After the battle, the "Drummer Boy of Chickamauga" was promoted to sergeant and placed upon the roll of honor, the youngest soldier ever to be a noncommissioned officer in the United States Army. After participating with the Army of the Cumberland in many other battles, being twice wounded and a prisoner of war, he was discharged in 1864. He returned home and graduated from high school in 1870. After he attempted unsuccessfully to enter the United States Military Academy at West Point, President Ulysses S. Grant appointed him second lieutenant in the Twenty-fourth United States Infantry. Clem graduated from artillery school at Fort Monroe in 1875, transferred to the quartermaster department in 1882, and rose to the rank of major general by the time he retired in 1916. During his last years in the army he was the sole remaining Civil War[qv] veteran on active service. Clem spent a number of his army years in Texas. From 1906 to 1911 he was chief quartermaster at Fort Sam Houston; after retirement he remained in Washington for a few years, then returned to San Antonio. He married Anita Rosetta French in 1875. She died in 1899, and he married Bessie Sullivan of San Antonio in 1903. Clem was the father of two children. He died in San Antonio on May 13, 1937, and was buried in Arlington National Cemetery.

BIBLIOGRAPHY: John L. Clem, "From Nursery to Battlefield," *Outlook*, July 4, 1914. *National Cyclopaedia of American Biography*, Vol. C. *Texas Magazine*, November 1910. *Who Was Who in America*, Vol. 2.
Robert L. Talmadge

CLEMENS CREEK. Clemens Creek rises 1½ miles northeast of Belmont in northwestern Gonzales County (at 29°34′ N, 97°40′ W) and runs southeast to its mouth on the Guadalupe River (at 29°30′ N, 97°36′ W). It was probably named for Austin Clements, an early settler. The surrounding moderately rolling terrain is surfaced by sandy clay that supports mixed hardwoods and pines.

CLEMENTS, JOSEPH D. (?–?). Joseph D. Clements, early DeWitt colony[qv] settler and public official, was a prominent citizen of Gonzales. He arrived in Texas before April 1830, for it was then that he entered into a partnership with Green DeWitt[qv] to build a sawmill and gristmill on the Guadalupe River some twenty miles above Gonzales. The sawmill plans never came to fruition, but the DeWitt papers make repeated references to the gristmill.

In December 1834 Clements was elected to the Gonzales ayuntamiento[qv] as regidor[qv] and the next year served as a Gonzales delegate to the Consultation[qv] of 1835. In his capacity as regidor Clements became a leading figure in the events that led to the battle of Gonzales.[qv] When 100 Mexican dragoons arrived on the west bank of the Guadalupe River and demanded the town's tiny cannon, alcalde[qv] Andrew Ponton[qv] was out of town, and the responsibility of negotiating with Francisco de Castañeda,[qv] the commander of the Mexican detachment, fell upon Clements. When the Mexican detachment arrived on September 29, 1835, only eighteen local militiamen, including Clements—the "Old Eighteen"[qv]—stood ready to defend the river-crossing opposite Gonzales. On September 30 Clements informed Castañeda that Ponton had not returned but was expected shortly. If, however, the alcalde should fail to appear soon, Clements agreed to assume the responsibility of discussing the matter. Later that day Castañeda returned to find Clements waiting with a letter penned by him and approved by the Gonzales ayuntamiento. The letter stated emphatically that the men of Gonzales refused to surrender their ordnance. Clements ended his communication on a defiant note: "We are weak and few in number, nevertheless we are contending for what we believe to be just principles." Clements and the other members of the Old Eighteen were soon reinforced by volunteers from several surrounding settlements, and on October 2, 1835, during the battle of Gonzales the Texans attacked Castañeda's detachment and forced it to withdraw to San Antonio de Béxar (*see also* GONZALES "COME AND TAKE IT" CANNON).

Clements remained active in the revolution that his actions had helped instigate. In March 1836 he was appointed president of the commission to procure corn and meal for the Texas army. He is also reported to have sold provisions to the army at that time. The gristmill that he and DeWitt had established in 1830 was destroyed in 1836, most likely during the Runaway Scrape.[qv] In 1838 Clements served as president of the Board of Land Commissioners of Gonzales County.

BIBLIOGRAPHY: Edward Albert Lukes, *De Witt Colony of Texas* (Austin: Jenkins, 1976). Texas House of Representatives, *Biographical Directory of the Texan Conventions and Congresses, 1832–1845* (Austin: Book Exchange, 1941).

Stephen L. Hardin

CLEMENTS DRAW. Clements Draw is a valley, and sometimes a creek, that begins seventeen miles southeast of Eden near the southeastern corner of Concho County (at 31°06′ N, 99°36′ W) and runs northeast for five miles to South Brady Creek, 3½ miles south of Melvin in McCulloch County (at 31°09′ N, 99°34′ W). The valley begins at an elevation of 2,000 feet above mean sea level and ends at 1,810 feet.

CLEMONS, BASIL EDWIN (1887–1964). Basil Edwin Clemons, photographer, the firstborn of seventeen children of Lemuel Joseph and Sarah Alice (Clemmons) Clemmons was born in Lauderdale County, Alabama, on July 22, 1887. His parents were cousins. He attended grammar school in Alabama until his father, a farmer, moved the family to Ridgeway, Texas. At age sixteen, in 1903, Basil left Texas and journeyed to California. He was in San Francisco in 1906, when that city experienced its devastating earthquake. Clemons, who was well-read, became a self-taught photographer in Hollywood at the beginning of the movie era. Later, he trooped with the Tom Mix Wild West Show. In 1909 he returned to East Texas to visit his family before departing for Alaska, where he recorded the growth surrounding the gold discoveries in the Yukon River area. He introduced motion pictures to Alaskan residents by making and developing the first movies shown there. Clemons was responsible for bringing the first airplane into the snowy region and then preserved the sights of the frozen land with the first aerial photographs taken in Alaska. He was snow-blinded, however, and his eyesight was affected for the rest of his life. In Alaska Clemons became a Methodist. He later confided to his mother that he was a "sprinkled Methodist" because immersion in ice water would have frozen him to death. He joined the United States Army and trained at Fort Liscom, Alaska. In 1918 he was discharged as a private in the Ninth Company, 166th Depot Brigade. He eventually moved to Seattle, Washington, where he opened a photography studio.

In 1919, while traveling with a circus, he returned to Texas. There he received word that his studio had burned, but instead of returning to Seattle he headed west to Breckenridge. He chronicled on film every aspect of life in the small town as it boomed from oil production in 1920. When the oilfields declined, he remained and continued to photograph everyday happenings. His photographs included not only oil-derrick scenes, weddings, downtown display windows, rodeos, parades, and portraits of prominent citizens, but also funeral processions, Ku Klux Klan[qv] rallies, lakeside picnics, and the entire public school student body. His developing studio was his unusual home, an iron-wheeled gypsy wagon, ten feet long and six feet wide, which had been a cookshack used on a ranch. To develop photographs, he never measured the chemicals poured from jars. By tasting the finger he used to stir the mixture, he determined the correct proportions. He developed black-and-white and sepia-toned photographs. He also produced pictures on fabric and did hand-colored tinted prints. His skill was so perfected that he formulated a process for color developing before the Eastman Kodak Company. When he received a letter from Kodak in 1936, offering a fabulous amount, plus royalties, for his technique, Clemons had his teen-aged helper, Frank Pellizzari, Jr., type a refusal to the offer with the remark that the Kodak chemists should "figure it out for themselves." The trademark of his work was marking negatives with a fine pen and India ink so that the developed prints bore the subject label, date, and his signature in white lettering.

Clemons, a lifelong bachelor, believed in a simplified approach to living. As an eccentric, he did not follow conventional standards in his choice of habitat, dress, or diet. He wore jodhpurs and knee-high laced boots and traveled to photography sites in a stripped-down Model-T Ford. He declined social invitations, yet he always welcomed company and generously offered to serve visitors mulligan stew and bannock, a pancake-thin bread. From ground mesquite[qv] beans he made a weak tea-like beverage. At Thanksgiving he invited the entire community to share a harvest feast from his vast garden. His political affiliation is unknown. He belonged to both the American Legion[qv] and the Moose Lodge. In the Yukon he had served as secretary of the Alaska Kennel Club, similar to a chamber of commerce. Plagued by asthma and cataracts, Clemons gave up photography in 1949. He continued to live in his wagon, set on a lot where a car-wrecking yard had once been. Although his eyesight had failed, he still possessed a keen wit and sharp memory. With a chuckle he called his abode the "Atheneum of Breckenridge." He recognized visitors by the sound of their footsteps. His neighbors, the Pellizzaris, helped take care of him by cashing pension checks, buying groceries, and occasionally cooking his meals. Frail from suffering severe asthma attacks, Clemons died on June 22, 1964, in Breckenridge. He is buried beside his parents in Hopkins County, Texas. His Alaskan photographs are located at the University of Alaska Library-Fairbanks and in Juneau at the Alaska State Library. Pictures taken of Breckenridge and the surrounding area, dated from 1920 to 1949, were secured in 1985 by the Special Collections Division of the University of Texas at Arlington Libraries. In 1994 the Swenson Memorial Museum in Breckenridge acquired a similar group of his photos and organized the Basil Clemons Photograph Collection of Stephens County.

BIBLIOGRAPHY: Abilene *Reporter-News*, June 24, 1964. Dallas *Morning News*, January 14, 1940. Fort Worth *Press*, December 13, 1951. Betty Elliott Hanna, "Basil Clemons, Eccentric Photographer," *Frontier Times*, December–January 1975–76. Betty E. Hanna, *Doodle Bugs and Cactus Berries: A Historical Sketch of Stephens County* (Quanah, Texas: Nortex, 1975). Shirley Rodnitzky, "A Guide to the Basil Clemons Photograph Collection," Special Collections Division, University of Texas at Arlington Libraries, 1988. *Stephens County* (Breckenridge, Texas: Stephens County Sesquicentennial Committee, 1987).

Jean Ann (Pellizzari) Credicott

CLEMONS, LEWIS CHAPMAN (1816–1892). Lewis Chapman Clemons, soldier, was born in Christian County, Kentucky, on March 26, 1816, and moved to Texas in February 1833. On July 9, 1835, he enlisted as a volunteer in Capt. Philip H. Coe's[qv] ranger company, which served under Col. John H. Moore[qv] in a campaign against the Indians until August 31, 1835. During the Texas Revolution[qv] Clemons served in Capt. William W. Hill's[qv] Company H of Col. Edward Burleson's[qv] First Regiment, Volunteer Infantry, from March 1 though May 1, 1836, and fought in the battle of San Jacinto.[qv] In 1840 Clemons was a resident of Washington County, where he owned 378 acres of land and a stud horse. In June 1842 President Sam Houston[qv] appointed him captain of a ranger company, but in response to the raids of Raphael Vásquez and Adrián Woll[qqv] of that year Clemons, on September 25, enlisted as a private in Capt. Samuel A. Bogart's[qv] company of Col. James R. Cook's[qv] First Regiment of the South Western Army to participate in the Somervell expedition.[qv] Shortly thereafter, on October 17, he transferred to Philip Coe's company of the same regiment. Clemons was one of the men who returned from the Rio Grande with Gen. Alexander Somervell[qv] and so avoided the blunders of the Mier expedition.[qv] He died at Brenham in 1892. He was a member of the Texas Veterans Association.[qv]

BIBLIOGRAPHY: Daughters of the Republic of Texas, *Muster Rolls of the Texas Revolution* (Austin, 1986). Sam Houston Dixon and Louis Wiltz Kemp, *The Heroes of San Jacinto* (Houston: Anson Jones, 1932). Joseph Milton Nance, *Attack and Counterattack: The Texas-Mexican Frontier, 1842* (Austin: University of Texas Press, 1964). Amelia W. Williams and Eugene C. Barker, eds., *The Writings of Sam Houston,*

1813–1863 (8 vols., Austin: University of Texas Press, 1938–43; rpt., Austin and New York: Pemberton Press, 1970).

Thomas W. Cutrer

CLEMONS, TEXAS. Clemons (Clemens, Clemons Switch) is a rural community of scattered dwellings on the east side of Irons Creek near Farm Road 1458 seven miles northwest of Brookshire in southern Waller County. A switch on the Texas Western Narrow Gauge railroad was at the site. The community is named for an early settler, Martin Key Clemons, who operated a general store that also housed a post office from 1885 to 1888. A Clemons church existed as early as 1883 and a school by 1892. Clemons was a home of Edwin A. Waller,qv for whom Waller County is named.

Competition from neighboring Pattison, which had a railroad depot and a turntable, slowed Clemons's growth. The railroad ceased operations in 1899. A school for black children operated at Clemons in the 1930s. During the 1960s the community had two churches, Wades Chapel and Wesley Chapel, as well as five cemeteries. In 1990 a few homes remained in the community, and children attended classes in the Royal Independent School District in Brookshire.

BIBLIOGRAPHY: Mildred W. Abshier, et al., *Former Post Offices of Waller County* (Hempstead, Texas: Waller County Historical Society, 1977). Corrie Pattison Haskew, *Historical Records of Austin and Waller Counties* (Houston: Premier Printing and Letter Service, 1969). Waller County Historical Survey Committee, *A History of Waller County, Texas* (Waco: Texian, 1973).

Paul M. Lucko

CLEMVILLE, TEXAS. Clemville is on Farm Road 1468 just west of the Tres Palacios River, six miles northwest of Markham and twelve miles northwest of Bay City in northwestern Matagorda County. It was named for Charles T. Clem, who in the early 1900s was instrumental in developing several local oilfields. In 1911 Clemville secured its own post office. By 1914 the community had a general store, two hotels, two machinists, a dairy, a telephone connection, and an estimated population of 200. In 1933 the community still had 200 residents but only one business. In 1936 Clemville had three businesses, a church, and thirty dwellings. By 1949 the school had been consolidated with the Tidehaven Independent School District. In 1971 Clemville had a population of fifty-four and two businesses. In 1973 it had several dwellings and a church but no businesses. In 1990 the population was still estimated at fifty-four.

BIBLIOGRAPHY: Matagorda County Historical Commission, *Historic Matagorda County* (3 vols., Houston: Armstrong, 1986).

Stephen L. Hardin

CLEO, TEXAS. Cleo is on Farm Road 2291 ten miles northwest of Junction in northern Kimble County. Around 1860 Raleigh Gentry settled a mile south of the present location of Cleo. The first attempt to establish a community took place on March 11, 1880, when Thomas Riggs opened a post office initially called Viejo for Viejo Creek (now West Bear Creek), which flows west of the town. Postal and telegraph service was discontinued in May 1886 and transferred to Junction City (now Junction). The Viejo post office was reestablished on March 25, 1915, and John Simpson ran the postal business in his general store. In August 1920 Simpson sold the store and transferred the postmaster's duties to Sam L. Pearson. Pearson changed the name to Cleo, in honor of his niece Cleo Weston. Cleo was a supply point for campers, hunters, and fishermen in the 1920s and 1930s. During the Great Depressionqv years the unemployed also came to Cleo to find work cutting cedar. The Bear Creek School in Cleo closed in 1937, but the building continued to be used for social events. The population of Cleo was reported as between fifteen and thirty-six until 1966, when it was estimated at fifty-two. It was listed as eighty-one in 1974, when Cleo's last postmaster, Mrs. Josie Baylor Bishop, retired, and the post office was closed. The tourist trade had begun to decline earlier, when U.S. Highway 83 between Menard and Junction bypassed Cleo to the east. The community had a population reported as eighty-one in the mid-1980s. It was recorded as three in 1990.

BIBLIOGRAPHY: Frederica Burt Wyatt, "Kimble County," *Stalkin Kin*, May 1976.

Anthony B. Gaxiola

CLEON, TEXAS. Cleon was fifteen miles southeast of Center in southeastern Shelby County. A post office was established there in 1890 with Robert W. Field as postmaster. The community had a population of fifteen in 1896. The post office was closed in 1899.

Cecil Harper, Jr.

CLERK OF THE COUNTY COURT. The office of clerk of the county court, or county clerk's office, has been in existence since 1836, when it superseded the office of *escribano*qv of Spanish and Mexican Texas.qv Under the Constitution of 1876 qv the county clerk was to be elected biennially; in 1954, however, a constitutional amendment changed the term of office to four years. The main duties of the county clerk are to serve as clerk of the county court and the county commissioners' court,qv act as recorder of deeds and other instruments, issue marriage licenses, and take depositions. The clerk is also responsible for conducting countywide special and general elections and for handling absentee voting. In counties of less than 8,000 population the office of county clerk is combined with that of clerk of the district court.

BIBLIOGRAPHY: *Guide to Texas Laws for County Officials* (Austin: Texas Department of Community Affairs, 1988). Dick Smith, The Development of Local Government in Texas (Ph.D. dissertation, Harvard University, 1938).

Dick Smith

CLEVELAND, TEXAS (Delta County). Cleveland was near Farm Road 895 between Kensing and Vasco in eastern Delta County. The Edgar School, one of the county's first, opened there in 1883. The school was named for a local family, but the popularity of President Grover Cleveland led residents to change the name of the community in his honor in 1885. By 1889 citizens had also established the Cleveland Baptist Church, which sent a messenger to Delta County Baptist Association meeting that year. The school had thirty-six white students and one teacher in 1905. In 1939 it was consolidated into the East Delta School District. By 1964 Cleveland no longer appeared on maps.

BIBLIOGRAPHY: Paul Garland Hervey, A History of Education in Delta County, Texas (M.A. thesis, University of Texas, 1951). Wilma Ross and Billie Phillips, *Photos and Tales of Delta County* (1976).

Vista K. McCroskey

CLEVELAND, TEXAS (Liberty County). Cleveland is on U.S. Highway 59 forty miles northeast of Houston in northwestern Liberty County. The recorded history of the area began in 1836, when the General Land Officeqv offered land in the county in exchange for military service. In 1854 Father Peter La Cour, who was evidently the first priest resident in the county, built a church and convent near the present townsite. The community formed after 1878, when Charles Lander Cleveland deeded 63.6 acres of land to the Houston, East and West Texas Railway with a request that a station bear his name. Since 1900 Cleveland has served as the junction of this line (now the Southern Pacific) and the Gulf, Colorado and Santa Fe (now the Atchison, Topeka and Santa Fe). The town was not incorporated until 1935. The forests around Cleveland, including Sam Houston National Forest,qv which is located just to its north, are a resort for many inhabitants of the Houston area, who come to camp, hike, hunt, and fish. Cleveland has several historic sites and public recreational facilities, including two parks. The Austin Memorial Library Center offers a wide range of services to the community, and a Little Theater and annual rodeo provide entertainment. Commercially, Cleveland has been a shipping point for timber, lumber, and lumber byproducts since the 1870s. Oil, gas, cattle, farm products, and sand and gravel are important to the town's economy. The general trend toward urbanization of the entire area is reflected by the fact that in 1965 Liberty County was added to the Houston Standard Metropolitan Statistical Area. The population of Cleveland grew from 1,200 in 1930 to 5,977 in 1980. In the early 1980s an industrial park, new shopping centers, and new businesses were built to meet the growing demand. In 1990 the population was 7,124.

BIBLIOGRAPHY: *East Texas,* December 1940. Frank W. Johnson, *A History of Texas and Texans* (5 vols., ed. E. C. Barker and E. W. Winkler [Chicago and New York: American Historical Society, 1914; rpt. 1916]).
Barbara Smith

CLIBURN, RILDIA BEE O'BRYAN (1896–1994). Rildia Bee O'Bryan Cliburn, piano teacher and mother of pianist Van Cliburn, was born on October 14, 1896, in McGregor, Texas, to William Carey and Sirrildia (McClain) O'Bryan. Her father was a journalist and lawyer. She studied under Arthur Friedheim, a pupil of Franz Liszt's assistant, and passed the grand nineteenth-century virtuoso tradition on to her son, who revived and personified that tradition for audiences in the second half of the twentieth century. After early piano lessons from her mother and local teacher Prebble Drake, and after graduating from high school in Richmond, Texas, she studied at the Cincinnati Conservatory and later in New York, but was discouraged from pursuing a concert career by her father, a member of the Texas legislature and an associate of leading politicians of the day. She returned to Texas, where, in 1923, she married Harvey Lavan Cliburn, a native of Mississippi and a railroad employee who, shortly after their marriage, entered the oil business on the advice of his father-in-law.

An active, energetic person, Rildia Bee Cliburn came to motherhood at the relatively late age of thirty-seven; by that time, she had engaged in activities ranging from teaching piano lessons to running a riverfront mission in Shreveport, Louisiana. She began teaching her son while the family lived in Shreveport, where he was born, and continued teaching him as well as many other young pupils after the family moved to Kilgore, Texas, in 1940. After Van was catapulted to world fame as the winner of the first Tchaikovsky International Competition in Moscow in 1958, his mother frequently traveled with him and served as his manager until he withdrew from active concertizing in 1978. She resumed traveling with him when he renewed his concert career in the late 1980s. Cliburn always credited his mother as his most influential teacher and as a valued advisor up to the time of her death; he frequently said that she had better hands for playing the piano than his, and that, as his teacher, she could demonstrate anything she required him to do. After the death of her husband in 1974, Mrs. Cliburn shared Van's New York apartment until 1985, when they moved to the estate that had previously belonged to Kimbell Art Museum[qv] benefactor Kay Kimbell[qv] in the Westover Hills neighborhood of Fort Worth. There she lived her final years, lionized as the mother of an international concert star and musical celebrity. As long as her health permitted, well into her nineties, she circulated prominently in Fort Worth society at her son's side at cultural and church events (she was a lifelong, devoted Southern Baptist) and frequently entertained visiting musical artists. She died at the age of ninety-seven in Fort Worth on August 3, 1994, five days after suffering a stroke. At that time, construction had begun on the Rildia Bee O'Bryan Organ at Broadway Baptist Church in Fort Worth; it was projected that the instrument would be the largest organ in Texas at the time of its completion in October 1996.

BIBLIOGRAPHY: Abram Chasins and Villa Stiles, *The Van Cliburn Legend* (Garden City, New York: Doubleday, 1959). Fort Worth *Star-Telegram,* February 2, August 4, 1994. Howard Reich, *Van Cliburn* (Nashville: Thomas Nelson Publishers, 1993).
Wayne Lee Gay

CLICK, TEXAS. Click is on Barnett Branch near Sandy Creek in Sandy Valley, fifteen miles southeast of Llano in southeastern Llano County. It was granted a post office in 1880 with Benjamim F. Lowe as postmaster. The community was named for the large family descended from Malachi Click, an early settler. At one time it had a church, a school, and a store, but the post office was closed after 1940, and the population had declined to twenty by 1966.

BIBLIOGRAPHY: Wilburn Oatman, *Llano, Gem of the Hill Country: A History of Llano County* (Hereford, Texas: Pioneer, 1970).
James B. Heckert-Greene

CLICK CREEK. Click Creek rises in Paris just south of Loop 286 and east of Farm Road 1497 in central Lamar County (at 33°38′ N, 95°32′ W) and runs south for seven miles to its mouth on Hickory Creek, just northeast of Biardstown (at 33°33′ N, 95°31′ W). The surrounding flat to gently sloping terrain is surfaced by dark clay that supports grasses interspersed with some oak and hickory. The stream is named for Mathias Click, an early owner of the land.
Vista K. McCroskey

CLICK GAP. Click Gap is a pass in the southern Riley Mountains 2½ miles northwest of Click in Llano County (at 30°35′ N, 98°37′ W). The saddle between Hickory Bluff and Watson Mountain is crossed at an elevation of 1,386 feet by an unimproved dirt road linking local ranches. The pass rises 340 feet above Click and affords a commanding view of the more open terrain to the east. The local rolling to steep terrain is surfaced by shallow, stony soils that support open stands of live oak and mesquite.
James B. Heckert-Greene

CLIFF, TEXAS. Cliff, named for the rocky cliffs at nearby San Geronimo Creek, is on Farm Road 471 eighteen miles northeast of Castroville in northeast Medina County. The farming community was granted a post office in 1910 with Manuel Schuchart as postmaster. By 1914 Cliff had a post office, two general stores, and a school located on the north bank of San Geronimo Creek. Former students recalled that the sandy soil where the school was located would pack so hard that they could play tennis on it. The school had an enrollment of twenty in 1907. In 1926 a new school was built a mile south of the first and operated by the Maverick school district. In 1933 Cliff had a population of fifty and two businesses. In the mid-1940s the Maverick school district was consolidated with that of Medina Valley; by this time Cliff's general store had been abandoned. In the 1980s Cliff had a number of scattered dwellings along Farm Road 471, and a community hall occupied the former site of the Maverick school.

BIBLIOGRAPHY: John J. Germann and Myron Janzen, *Texas Post Offices by County* (1986).
Ruben E. Ochoa

CLIFF CREEK. Cliff Creek rises in a tank just west of Willow Springs in the northeast corner of Fayette County (at 29°58′ N, 96°36′ W) and runs south for 2½ miles to its mouth on Cummins Creek (at 29°57′ N, 96°37′ W). It is named for its steep banks; some are as deep as forty feet. The surrounding terrain is generally level to gently sloping and is used primarily as pasture for cattle.

CLIFFSIDE, TEXAS. Cliffside, five miles northwest of Amarillo in southern Potter County, became a station on the Fort Worth and Denver City Railway in 1888. No community developed until 1905, when a rural school was established. Mrs. Frances E. Boyles opened a post office in her husband's general store in 1908. William H. Bush dedicated the townsite on August 5, 1915. W. J. Williams, a surveyor, platted ten full blocks, consisting of three north-south and six east-west streets. Because of its proximity to Amarillo the Cliffside post office was discontinued in 1917, and mail was routed through Amarillo. By 1980 Cliffside only had a few small red buildings beside the railroad track. From the 1960s until 1990 the population estimates have been recorded at 206.

BIBLIOGRAPHY: Della Tyler Key, *In the Cattle Country: History of Potter County, 1887–1966* (Amarillo: Tyler-Berkley, 1961; 2d ed., (Wichita Falls: Nortex, 1972).
H. Allen Anderson

CLIFTON. The *USS Clifton,* a side-wheel steam ferryboat that saw action along the Texas coast during the Civil War,qv was built in Brooklyn, New York, in 1861. The United States Navy bought her in December of that year and placed acting lieutenant C. H. Baldwin in command. The *Clifton* left New York on February 22, 1862, and joined Commander David D. Porter's mortar flotilla at Ship Island, Mississippi, on March 18. She participated in the capture of forts Jackson and St. Philip below New Orleans in late April and had to be refloated by the *Sachem*qv when she ran aground below Fort Morgan in May. The *Clifton* also took part in the attack on the Confederate batteries at Vicksburg, Mississippi, in June. On June 28 she took a shot through her boiler that killed seven men, but she also assisted in the capture of Galveston (October 4–9). She captured the bark *H. McGuin* in Bay St. Louis near Gulfport, Mississippi, on July 18, 1863, and attacked Sibley's Brigadeqv on a reconnaissance up the Atchafalaya River and Bayou Teche in Louisiana on July 28. She was captured by the Confederates at Sabine Pass, Texas, on September 8. The *Clifton* ran aground at Sabine Pass on March 21, 1864, while trying to run the Union blockade and was burned by the Confederates to prevent her capture. *See also* SABINE PASS, BATTLE OF, *and* GALVESTON, BATTLE OF.

BIBLIOGRAPHY: *Dictionary of American Naval Fighting Ships* (8 vols., Washington: U.S. Navy, 1959-81). *Martin Donell Kohout*

CLIFTON, ELIZABETH ANN CARTER (1825–1882). Elizabeth Ann Clifton, rancher, merchant, and Indian captive, was born on March 29, 1825, in Alabama. In 1842, when she was sixteen, she married Alexander Joseph Carter, a free black. The couple had two children and lived with Carter's parents, Edmund J. and Susanna Carter, in Red River and Navarro counties before moving west to Fort Belknap in Young County, where they began raising stock and farming. Elizabeth Carter managed the ranch, soon as a full partner, while her husband and father-in-law ran a cargo transportation business. Though she was illiterate and epileptic, she also ran a boarding house, the Carter Trading House. In 1857 her husband and father-in-law were both mysteriously murdered. When Carter's estate was finally settled, his remaining assets were divided between his two grandchildren, Elizabeth Carter's married daughter and her young son. Mrs. Carter was not, however, made guardian of her son's property.

In 1858 Elizabeth Carter was briefly married to Lt. Owen A. Sprague, but Sprague disappeared eight months later. Elizabeth continued to be one of the most successful women on the frontier. The Trading House prospered after the Butterfield Overland Mailqv began stopping in Fort Belknap in 1858, and she still managed the ranch. When she was thirty-six years old, she married Thomas FitzPatrick, one of three Carter ranch cowhands, on August 26, 1862. FitzPatrick was murdered eighteen months later.

Elizabeth endured further calamity when her Young County ranch was attacked in the Elm Creek Raidqv of October 13, 1864, and she was taken captive by Plains Indians led by Comanche chief Little Buffalo. Elizabeth's daughter Mildred Susanna Durkin and Mrs. Durkin's infant son were murdered. The Indians took captive Elizabeth FitzPatrick, her thirteen-year-old son, and Elizabeth's two surviving granddaughters, Charlotte Durkin (Lottie), age 5 years, and Mildred Durkin (Milly), age 2 years. The son was killed shortly after his capture.

Mrs. FitzPatrick was held twelve months and twenty days in Kiowa chief Sun Boy's camp on the Arkansas River in northwestern Kansas. Her granddaughter Milly and several other children held in Comanche chief Iron Mountain's camp apparently froze to death early in 1854, though Elizabeth believed that Milly remained alive in captivity. The other grandchild, Lottie, spent nine months as captive of Comanches who tattooed her arms and forehead before releasing her.

Elizabeth was rescued on November 2, 1865, by Gen. J. H. Leavenworth and subsequently held at the Kaw Mission at Council Grove, Kansas. There she took care of another recently released woman, who was pregnant and in poor health, and the woman's two children. For the next ten months, Elizabeth was paid three dollars a week to nurse, cook, and sew clothes for a growing number of recently released captives. She complained on the released captives' behalf that they were not receiving adequate care, that arrangements for safe transportation to their homes were taking far too long, and that more should be done to free others still in captivity.

On August 27, 1866, almost two years after her capture, she and several others began the six-week trip home. Elizabeth FitzPatrick was reunited with her previously released granddaughter in Parker County. In 1869 Elizabeth married a Parker County farmer and widower, Isaiah Clifton. They moved to Fort Griffin with Lottie and Clifton's youngest four children in order to manage what remained of landholdings inherited by Lottie Durkin after her mother's death.

Elizabeth Clifton remained at Fort Griffin until her death on June 18, 1882. She was buried beside Isaiah Clifton, who predeceased her in 1880, in the oldest cemetery in Shackelford County. As late as 1877 she had wired the Office of Indian Affairs in Washington to report a rumor that her granddaughter, Milly Jane, might be living with a Kiowa woman named Ama. Elizabeth Clifton died penniless. *See also* INDIAN CAPTIVES.

BIBLIOGRAPHY: Barbara Neal Ledbetter, *Fort Belknap Frontier Saga: Indians, Negroes and Anglo-Americans on the Texas Frontier* (Burnet, Texas: Eakin Press, 1982). *Barbara A. Neal Ledbetter*

CLIFTON, JOHN M. (?–?). John M. Clifton, early settler and legislator, arrived in Texas in March 1836, bringing with him ninety-seven volunteers recruited from the area around Paducah, Kentucky. Clifton served as captain of the First Regiment from November 6, 1836, to December 5, 1837. His conditional certificate for land was issued in Shelby County in 1838, and his unconditional certificate was issued at Panola on July 5, 1841. The 1,280 acres of land were located in Harrison County and patented to him on December 13, 1848. He represented Harrison County in the House of Representatives of the Fourth Congress of the republic from November 11, 1839, until February 5, 1840.

BIBLIOGRAPHY: Texas House of Representatives, *Biographical Directory of the Texan Conventions and Congresses, 1832–1845* (Austin: Book Exchange, 1941). *Cecil Harper, Jr.*

CLIFTON, TEXAS (Bosque County). Clifton is at the junction of State Highway 6 and Farm Road 219, thirty-five miles northwest of Waco in southern Bosque County. It was founded in the winter of 1852–53, when the families of Samuel Locker, Monroe Locker, Frank Kell, and T. A. McSpadden settled in the vicinity. The town was named Cliff Town after the limestone cliffs that surround it. Over the years the name was altered to Clifton. The site was originally on the banks of Clear Branch. The Masonic hall and a log schoolhouse were the first public buildings. The post office was established in 1859. The First Presbyterian Church of Clifton was organized in 1861 and is the oldest church in continuous service in the county. The Baptists built the first church building in Clifton in 1884–85. After the Civil Warqv J. Stinnett built a flour mill that was powered by the Bosque River. It was replaced in 1868 by a limestone mill, which was eventually converted to the electric power plant that provided the first electricity for Clifton homes. A three-story school known as Rock School was built around 1870 and served the community for more than twenty years. In 1893 a new building was constructed on property donated to the Clifton school system.

In 1880 the Gulf, Colorado and Santa Fe Railway built a station a mile south of Clifton. Merchants moved their businesses closer to the railroad station, and the town thrived as a business and trade center. The Merchant Exchange and Flour Mill, the first steam flour mill in the Bosque valley, was established in 1887 or 1888. The Clifton *Record*, a newspaper that began publishing in 1895 under the ownership of W. C. O'Brian, continued to serve the community through the years. Clifton also served as the county seat between 1890 and 1892. Clifton

Lutheran College, later known as Clifton College, opened in 1896. The community was incorporated in 1901. An earlier attempt at incorporation in 1891 failed when the election results were declared invalid. A fire on December 23, 1906, destroyed a large portion of the business district, which was eventually rebuilt. The Clifton Volunteer Fire Department was organized in 1907. The town's need for a hospital was met by Dr. V. D. Goodall and Dr. S. L. Witcher in 1938. The Lutheran Sunset Home for the elderly was established in Clifton in 1954. The town had an estimated population of 204 in 1904 and 3,195 in 1990. It had 100 businesses in the 1980s. In the early 1990s an exotic-animal preserve open to tourists was located southwest of Clifton on Farm Road 3220.

BIBLIOGRAPHY: William C. Pool, *Bosque Territory* (Kyle, Texas: Chaparral, 1964).

Karen Yancy

CLIFTON, TEXAS (Van Zandt County). Clifton was at the juncture of Farm roads 47 and 2475, seventeen miles northwest of Canton in northwest Van Zandt County. It had a population of fifteen, a seasonal industry, and scattered dwellings by 1936 and a population of twenty-five in 1939, but by 1965 only a single business remained at the townsite. Both the *Enterprise* and *Bright Star* newspapers were produced there. No population figures were recorded after 1939.

Diana J. Kleiner

CLIFTON COLLEGE. Clifton College was organized on May 6, 1896, as the Lutheran College of Clifton, Texas. The school's charter was approved by the state government on May 26, 1896. The first building was dedicated on October 14, 1897, on land donated by N. Jacob Nelson and T. T. Hogevold; it was built by volunteer donations and labor. The school, which was financially supported by the Norwegian Lutheran Churches of America located in Texas, opened under the name Clifton High School on October 28, 1897. From 1907 to 1914 the Missouri Synod of German Lutherans helped support the college. The institution offered college courses for the first time in 1922. It was accredited in 1924 as a two-year college. In 1938 the high school was discontinued. The school's name changed from Lutheran College of Clifton, Texas, to Clifton Junior College on October 25, 1945, and to Clifton College on February 22, 1952. In 1954 the college merged with Texas Lutheran College in Seguin.

After the move the Clifton College administration building was sold to Carl Olsen, Sr., for his Gearwrench Manufacturing Company. In 1981 the building was dedicated as the Carl E. Olsen Fine Arts Building of the Bosque County Conservatory of Fine Arts. In 1982 a historical marker was placed on the building in commemoration of Clifton College. The remaining facilities of Clifton College were acquired by the Clifton Lutheran Sunset Home.qv This included an artifact collection of Jacob Olsen, an early Norwegian settler, which had been contributed to Clifton College in 1923. The collection became the core of the Bosque Memorial Museum. A log cabin like the Olsens' home has been reconstructed on the museum grounds.

BIBLIOGRAPHY: Bosque County History Book Committee, *Bosque County, Land and People* (Dallas: Curtis Media, 1985). Marker Files, Texas Historical Commission, Austin. William C. Pool, *Bosque Territory* (Kyle, Texas: Chaparral, 1964).

Karen Yancy

CLIFTON LUTHERAN SUNSET HOME. Clifton Lutheran Sunset Home, a nonprofit residence for the elderly and infirm, originated in 1954 when seventeen Evangelical Lutheran churches took over the facilities of Clifton Junior College in Clifton, after this college merged with Texas Lutheran College in Seguin. In 1960 the Lutheran Sunset Home Corporation expanded to include several American Lutheran churches. The home is administered by a board of nine chosen by the corporation. It has provided clinical facilities to the Texas Department of Mental Health and Mental Retardationqv and is certified by the Division of Service and Mission of the American Lutheran Church and by the Southern District of the Texas American Lutheran Church. The Clifton Lutheran Sunset Home maintained the Clifton Junior College Museum from 1954 until 1957, when the Bosque Memorial Museum Corporation was founded.

BIBLIOGRAPHY: Bosque County History Book Committee, *Bosque County, Land and People* (Dallas: Curtis Media, 1985). Vertical Files, Barker Texas History Center, University of Texas at Austin.

Karen Yancy

CLIFTY CREEK. Clifty Creek rises 1½ miles west of Millican in southern Brazos County (at 30°28′ N, 96°13′ W) and runs southeast for 4½ miles to its mouth on Big Creek, 1½ miles north of the Brazos River and the Brazos-Washington county line (at 30°25′ N, 96°11′ W). It crosses moderately rolling terrain surfaced by sandy and clay loam that supports oak and pine forests with some mesquite and grasses.

CLIMAX, TEXAS (Collin County). Climax is at the intersection of Farm roads 1377 and 2756, five miles east of McKinney in central Collin County. It was first settled by Williams Warden, a farmer who moved to Texas from Missouri in 1844. In 1850 Warden received a Peters' colonyqv land certificate for 640 acres near the East Fork of the Trinity River. He settled there with his family shortly thereafter. By the mid-1890s the community had two gins, a grain elevator, a school, a church, a hotel, and a general store. A post office was established in 1895. Six years later mail service was discontinued and rerouted to Farmersville. Climax has served as a retail point for area farmers for most of its history. Its population was estimated at forty from 1940 to 1990.

BIBLIOGRAPHY: Seymour V. Connor, *The Peters Colony of Texas: A History and Biographical Sketches of the Early Settlers* (Austin: Texas State Historical Association, 1959). Roy Franklin Hall and Helen Gibbard Hall, *Collin County: Pioneering in North Texas* (Quanah, Texas: Nortex, 1975). J. Lee and Lillian J. Stambaugh, *A History of Collin County* (Austin: Texas State Historical Association, 1958).

David Minor

CLIMAX, TEXAS (Nacogdoches County). Climax, on La Nana Bayou off U.S. Highway 59 eight miles south of Nacogdoches in southern Nacogdoches County, grew up around 1900 as a flag stop on the Texas and New Orleans Railroad. In 1910 the population was twenty-eight. At one time there were several stores in the area, but by the early 1990s only a few scattered houses remained.

BIBLIOGRAPHY: Nacogdoches County Genealogical Society, *Nacogdoches County Families* (Dallas: Curtis, 1985).

Christopher Long

CLINE, HENRY B. (1828–ca.1900). Henry B. Cline, Houston attorney and school official, the son of Daniel Cline and a woman whose maiden name was Yeats, was born in Adams County, Pennsylvania, on September 19, 1828. He was raised a Lutheran and graduated from the University of Pennsylvania with bachelor of laws and doctor of divinity degrees. He subsequently preached in various Protestant churches. He moved to New Orleans in the late 1840s and opened a boys' college that failed. He was admitted to the bar in New Orleans on November 9, 1853, and, according to one source, later edited the *Louisiana Statutes*. Cline moved to Texas in January 1861, married a teacher of the deaf and dumb at Woodville, and served for a time as justice of the peace in Tyler County. From 1867 until his death he lived in Houston, where he practiced law, mainly in abstracts and titles. Cline served as a member of the Constitutional Convention of 1875qv and in 1876 was on a committee to establish a public school system in Houston. Later he became supervisor and inspector of the Houston public schools. He was nominated for governor by the Lily-White Movementqv in 1896. After breaking his leg in a fall from a horse he died, at the age of seventy-two.

BIBLIOGRAPHY: H. L. Bentley and Thomas Pilgrim, *Texas Legal Directory for 1876–77* (Austin: Democratic Statesman Office, 1877). Vertical Files, Barker Texas History Center, University of Texas at Austin.

Carolyn Hyman

CLINE, RAOUL RENE DANIEL (1868–1924). Raoul Rene Daniel (R.R.) Cline, pioneer professor of pharmacy, was born in Woodville, Texas, on September 14, 1868. Shortly thereafter his family moved to Houston, where he attended public schools until, at the age of eleven, he was sent to live with an uncle in Gettysburg, Pennsylvania. He finished high school there and briefly attended Gettysburg College, then joined his sister, who had married a French chemist, in Montpellier, France. He studied pharmacy in Lille and received a B.S. degree from the University of Montpellier (1889). After returning to the United States, Cline graduated from the New York School of Pharmacy (1891). He then moved back to Houston, where he not only worked as a pharmacist, but also studied law under a local attorney and was licensed to practice. After practicing law for a short time, he resumed his education at Gettysburg College, where he obtained an M.S. in 1896.

His work experience was as varied as his education. While in France he taught English and science at a boys' school. In Houston he practiced both pharmacy and law. After James Kennedy, the first professor of pharmacy at the University of Texas Medical Branch (UTMB), resigned because of ill health, Cline was appointed professor of pharmacy and dean of the School of Pharmacy (1895). He held these positions until his death almost thirty years later, watching the graduating class grow from two to thirty-seven students, even though graduation from a school of pharmacy was not a requirement for licensure until five years after his death. In addition to his work in the School of Pharmacy, Cline was a regular lecturer on pharmaceuticals for the School of Medicine and on materia medica and therapeutics for the School of Nursing. In order to improve his teaching of pharmacy, he obtained an M.D. from UTMB in 1909.

Cline authored many articles in his field, as well as a textbook, *Pharmaceutical Technology*. He was a pioneer in encouraging women to achieve an education. In 1896 he was among a small group at UTMB who constructed and used the first X-ray machine in Texas. He was a member of the Texas State Pharmaceutical Association from 1892 and worked throughout his life to insure competent pharmacists and an adequate pharmacy board in Texas. He was appalled that his own state entered the twentieth century with "neither food, poison, nor pharmacy laws," and worked unceasingly to change this situation.

Cline married Anna Kaufman in 1898. She died suddenly in 1902, leaving a daughter, "Little Anna," whom Cline raised by himself. Cline died suddenly in the early morning of May 20, 1924, at the home of his daughter and her husband, C. P. Mann. Death was believed to be caused by a cerebral hemorrhage. His death occurred during the Texas Board of Pharmacy examination period in Houston. The examinations were halted for a day so that the members of the Pharmaceutical Board and the applicants, who included almost every member of the senior pharmacy class at UTMB, could go to Galveston for the funeral.

BIBLIOGRAPHY: Henry M. Burlage and Margot E. Beutler, *Pharmacy's Foundation in Texas: A History of the College of Pharmacy, 1893–1976* (Pharmaceutical Foundation of the College of Pharmacy, University of Texas at Austin, 1978). Galveston *Daily News*, May 21, 1924. *Texas State Journal of Medicine*, July 1924. *University Medical*, October 1895. *University of Texas Record*, July 1902, June 1903. *The University of Texas Medical Branch at Galveston: A Seventy-five Year History* (Austin: University of Texas Press, 1967).

Patricia L. Jakobi

CLINE, TEXAS. Cline is on U.S. Highway 90 and the Southern Pacific Railroad eighteen miles west of Uvalde in southwestern Uvalde County. The site was in Dawson County between 1858 and 1866. The community was first settled by Celeste Pingenot, from Castroville, who arrived with some cattle in 1870 and constructed a home on the south bank of Turkey Creek in 1871. During the 1870s he established a stagecoach depot complete with stables and corals, commonly referred to as the Turkey Creek Stage Stop. Pingenot also built a store and saloon near his home and established the Wallace Inn, named after his friend who brought mail to the site, William A. A. (Bigfoot) Wallace.[qv] Turkey Creek, as the settlement was called for most of the 1870s, was located near the Old Spanish Trail[qv] and was a rest stop for many travelers on their way west to Brackettville or to the silver mines near Chihuahua City, Mexico. Pingenot's small enterprise was the victim of cattle-thieving Indians and Mexican bandits during its first years of operation.

On July 14, 1878, a post office was established in Turkey Creek with Pingenot as postmaster. The name was officially changed to Wallace. August Cline, a German native, settled in Wallace in 1880 and took a job in Pingenot's general store. Cline became postmaster soon after the Texas and New Orleans Railroad reached the site in 1881. In 1883 the community was renamed Cline. By 1888 August Cline had moved the post office to his two-story rock house on the north side of Turkey Creek. Although the stage horses were cared for at Pingenot's stables and corrals, stage passengers dined at Cline's place. Celeste Pingenot's wife, Minnie, and her sister Sophie were gracious hostesses to railroad and mine workers, landladies to boarding teachers, and well-wishers to the numerous travelers who passed through the settlement in the 1880s. By 1892 Cline had an estimated population of seventy-five. In 1896 seventy-one students attended the one-teacher Cline school.

By 1914 many of Cline's seventy-five residents had telephone service. The Uvalde Asphalt Paving Company had established a business office, and four apiarists resided in the community. Cline had an estimated population of 150 by 1927 and was the terminus of a railroad spur from asphalt mines twenty miles southeast. Cline reached its highest estimated population of 250 in 1940. A resident of the community recalled that soldiers from Fort Clark maintained a contingent of cavalry near the Pingenot home during World War I.[qv] Although a school, a church, and two businesses remained in Cline in 1946, the population had dropped to an estimated fifty. The post office was discontinued in 1952. One year after the 1965 annexation of the Cline Independent School District to the Uvalde district, an estimated ten people lived in the community. Although there is evidence that ten residents remained in the community in 1974, Cline had by then lost its church, school, and businesses. The century-old Pingenot home was showcased in the 1982 publication *Uvalde Heritage Homes*. In 1990 an estimated ten people remained in Cline.

BIBLIOGRAPHY: Jane Knapik, *Uvalde Heritage Homes: From the Uvalde Leader-News Bicentennial Series, 1976* (Uvalde, Texas, 1982).

Ruben E. Ochoa

CLINE MOUNTAINS. The Cline Mountains are two miles south of Cline in southwestern Uvalde County (at 29°13′ N, 100°04′ W). At an elevation of 1,265 feet above sea level, the summit of Cline Mountain rises 250 feet above nearby U.S. Highway 90.

CLÍNICA DE LA BENEFICENCIA MEXICANA. Clínica de la Beneficencia Mexicana, a health clinic in San Antonio for the Mexican-descent community during the Great Depression[qv] and the 1940s, was a project of Beneficencia Mexicana, a Mexican-descent women's voluntary association. The clinic was supported by middle-class women for the poor on the West Side; they acted under the theme of "charity, order, and efficiency." In 1930 seven health clinics had been set up throughout the city in an effort to serve the poor during hard times. Nurses reported that the worst health conditions existed on the West Side, where most of the Mexican-descent community lived.

Ignacio E. Lozano,[qv] the editor of *La Prensa*[qv] in San Antonio, initiated the fund-raising project to build a health clinic. Contributions came from across the country and locally; voluntary associations like the Finck Cigar Factory Workers, Club Femenino Orquidia, and the Club de Jóvenes Católicos together donated $286. Caucasian businessmen such as the owners of the Finck Cigar Factory also contributed. In 1930, after *La Prensa* gathered $27,000 in seed money, Clínica Mexicana, a stone building in Spanish Colonial style, was constructed at 623 South San Saba. In 1931 Dr. Joaquin Gonzales served as superintendent. Efforts were also coordinated by the Junta de Beneficencia, a committee of middle-class individuals, most of whom seem to have been born in Mexico. Apparently, the committee eventually became an organization composed of women, with Alicia Lozano as president of the board of directors of Beneficencia Mexicana.

For a short time the clinic had financial problems and closed, but it was reopened. Clients paid twenty-five cents on the first visit, and the clinic made medical care available on request afterwards. Both Mexican-descent and Caucasian doctors served as volunteer staff. Matilde Elizondo, owner of La Gloria grocery and meat market, donated medical equipment to the clinic. The board of trustees was composed of men, probably doctors, and the board of directors was made up of women. Alicia Lozano was president until 1938, when María de los Angeles G. de Velasco replaced her. In 1938 a serious dispute over management resulted in a court settlement, and the women took over the clinic's management. Around 1949 the clinic served expectant mothers. At some time between 1942 and 1948 the clinic moved to 207 San Fernando Street.

BIBLIOGRAPHY: Richard A. García, *Rise of the Mexican American Middle Class, San Antonio, 1919–1941* (College Station: Texas A&M University Press, 1991). Frances Jerome Woods, Mexican Ethnic Leadership in San Antonio, Texas (Ph.D. dissertation, Catholic University of America, 1949; published as *Catholic University of America Studies in Sociology* 31 [1949]; rpt., New York: Arno Press, 1976).

Cynthia E. Orozco

CLINT, TEXAS. Clint, also known as Collinsburgh, is on the Southern Pacific Railroad at the intersection of State Highway 20 and Farm Road 1110, sixteen miles southeast of downtown El Paso in southern El Paso County. The story of the town, which was named for early settler Mary Clinton Collins, began when the San Elizario Corporation sold the townsite to J. A. Cole, who sold it to Thomas M. Collins in 1883. For several years after the establishment of the Clint post office in 1886, the settlement was identified as the San Elizario station on the Galveston, Harrisburg and San Antonio Railway. In 1890 the estimated population of Clint was 100, and the town had a general store, a fruit grower, and a hotel. Clint soon developed into an agricultural center. By 1896 the estimated population had increased to 150, including nine fruit growers and four alfalfa growers. The townsite was set up in 1909. By 1914 the estimated population of 400 supported three churches, two banks, a newspaper, and a tomato cannery. An estimated 600 residents lived at Clint in the late 1920s, but the number declined to 250 by the mid-1930s. By the late 1940s it had grown again to 550, then dropped to 417 in the early 1970s. In the late 1970s the estimated population was 1,120. It was 1,314 in the early 1980s and 1,883 in the late 1980s. In 1990 it was 1,035.

Martin Donell Kohout

CLINTON, TEXAS (DeWitt County). Clinton, former county seat of DeWitt County, was located on the west bank of the Guadalupe River five miles southwest of the site of present Cuero. The first settlers of the area were members of DeWitt's colony;qv the Richard Chisholm family settled in January 1829 and the Andrew Lockhart family later that March. The town gained notoriety during the Sutton-Taylor feud.qv Life in this area was rugged and perilous, despite DeWitt's settlements to the north and De León's colonyqv to the southeast. In the fall of 1829 Comanches kidnapped young Matilda Lockhartqv and three visiting companions as the children were gathering pecans in the Guadalupe riverbottom. The Lockhart girl was rescued, but she died from the effects of the ordeal; the other three children were never found. About 1839 Richard Chisholm began operating a ferry across the Guadalupe River about 3½ miles below the confluence of the river and Sandies Creek. He soon opened a store and a horse-driven gristmill that was used by settlers from as far away as Meyersville.

Clinton was not established until after the organization of DeWitt County on March 24, 1846. Chisholm, eager to have the new county seat located on his land, deeded 640 acres to friends with instructions to survey the land and try to induce the commissioners, among them Daniel Boone Friar,qv to accommodate his wishes. James Norman Smithqv surveyed the townsite, which was named Clinton in honor of the son of the empresarioqv Green DeWitt.qv Yet Chisholm's friends would not grant the commissioners the added land required for a county seat; instead Cameron, on the J. J. Tumlinsonqv survey east of the Guadalupe River, became county seat. As Clinton grew rapidly, its citizens contested the Cameron decision. Each town became county seat alternately several times, the last change being the result of an election in August 1850, which finally made Clinton the seat of government.

Clinton prospered. Court was held in a log house until a log courthouse was built at a cost of $400 in 1852. A frame building was erected in 1855 and followed by a two-story courthouse in 1858. The latter, insured for $8,000, was Clinton's last courthouse; it was moved to Cuero in 1876 when that town became county seat. William Cochran Blairqv organized Clinton's first church, Live Oak Presbyterian, in July 1849. Clinton Methodists organized in the 1850s. Both denominations held services in the log courthouse until 1856, when the Presbyterians built a church that they shared with the Methodists. Clinton had no school until about 1855, when Rev. and Mrs. James M. Connelly held classes as part of their Presbyterian ministry. During the Civil Warqv years Viola Case moved her Victoria Female Academyqv to Clinton when Victoria was threatened by Union invasion. Public school instruction began in the 1870s. The county's earliest Masonic lodge was established at Clinton; a two-story hall was built in 1852, to which the Cameron lodge then moved. Clinton's first hotel was a log house with outside dining facilities. A later two-story frame hotel had a reputation for its fresh oysters. Jesse O. Wheelerqv of Victoria operated a branch store at Clinton that achieved sales of $12,000 and $18,000 in 1850 and 1851 respectively. Among the town's lawyers were Henry Clay Pleasants and John W. Stayton.qqv The Clinton post office was established in October 1849.

William Read Scurryqv of Clinton, with Fielding Jones of Victoria, represented the Victoria district in the Secession Conventionqv (1861). During the Civil Warqv William J. Weisiger organized a company at Clinton, which later fought with George H. Giddings'sqv cavalry battalion in the Rio Grande area. During Reconstructionqv Clinton and other surrounding towns were occupied by troops based at Victoria. The traditional interpretation says that bad times following the war contributed to the notorious Sutton-Taylor feud, which originated in Clinton on Christmas Eve 1868, when Bill Sutton killed William "Buck" Taylor. The family feud that followed developed into the longest and most bloody in Texas history, and Clinton residents continued to be drawn into the fray. On June 20, 1874, R. P. "Scrap" Taylor and two others jailed at the town were lynched by Sutton sympathizers. The feud finally ended in Clinton with the killing of Jim Taylor and two companions by a Cuero posse on December 27, 1875.

Although the feud gave Clinton a bad reputation and caused many residents to move away, a more significant cause of the town's decline was the extension in 1873 of the Gulf, Western Texas and Pacific Railway to Cuero, across the river. The railroad induced many Clinton businesses and residents to move. In 1876 Cuero became county seat, and decline was then swift for Clinton. Clinton Methodists remained active until the 1870s. The Presbyterians moved in 1883 to Cuero. The

Masons moved their lodge to Yorktown in 1877, and the Clinton post office closed in 1886. The only available population estimate for Clinton dates from this period of decline and records 150 residents in 1885. Although the Clinton school served the surrounding rural community from 1881 until 1954, by 1900 there remained little evidence that the once prosperous town ever existed. The large cemetery is overgrown with brush.

BIBLIOGRAPHY: Roy Grimes, ed., *300 Years in Victoria County* (Victoria, Texas: Victoria *Advocate*, 1968; rpt., Austin: Nortex, 1985). Nellie Murphree, *A History of DeWitt County* (Victoria, Texas, 1962).

Craig H. Roell

CLINTON, TEXAS (Hunt County). Clinton is on Farm Road 3211 eight miles west-southwest of Greenville in west central Hunt County. It was established on land sold by J. M. Massey for five dollars to the St. Louis Southwestern Railway, which built through the area in 1887. Massey sold his land to the railroad on condition that a depot for a town be constructed on the property within five years of the sale date in 1887. The depot, named Clinton after an official of the line, was built the same year. A post office began operation in Clinton in 1888 and remained open until sometime after 1930, perhaps as late as the 1950s. In 1904 the community reported 138 residents. The population fell, however, from 100 in 1910 to eighty-eight in 1933, when the community had six businesses. By 1965, when the last population figures were reported, Clinton's population was thirty.

BIBLIOGRAPHY: W. Walworth Harrison, *History of Greenville and Hunt County, Texas* (Waco: Texian, 1976).

Brian Hart

CLINTON-OKLAHOMA-WESTERN RAILWAY. The Clinton-Oklahoma-Western Railroad Company of Texas was chartered on July 30, 1927, to build a line from the Oklahoma state line in Hemphill County, Texas, to Pampa, in Grayson County. The line was projected as the Texas extension of the Clinton and Oklahoma Western Railroad Company, which operated from Clinton, Oklahoma, to the Oklahoma-Texas line. The initial capital was $100,000, and the business office was originally located at Wichita Falls. Members of the first board of directors included Joe A. Fell of Vernon and Frank Kell,qv C. W. Cahoon, Jr., T. P. Duncan, L. N. Bassett, O. B. Womack, M. G. Scovell, Charles Crowell, Leslie Humphrey, and T. R. Boone, all of Wichita Falls. In June 1928 the Clinton and Oklahoma Western and the Clinton-Oklahoma-Western Railroad Company of Texas were acquired by the Atchison, Topeka and Santa Fe Railway Company. The fifty-six miles between Pampa and the state line was completed in 1929, and in 1931 an eleven mile branch was built from Heaton to Coltexo. Also, in 1931, the companies were leased to the Panhandle and Santa Fe Railway Company, which operated them until they were merged into the latter company on December 31, 1948.

Chris Cravens

CLIPPER, TEXAS. Clipper was three miles southwest of the site of present Jayton in east central Kent County. It had a gin, two stores, a drugstore, and a school in the 1890s. A post office was established in 1899 with John M. Kelly as postmaster. The first fraternal organization established in the county, a chapter of the Woodmen of the World, was founded in Clipper about 1896. The community flourished until Jayton was established on the Stamford and Northwestern Railway in 1907. The Clipper mail was rerouted through Jayton in February of that year, and Clipper was soon abandoned.

BIBLIOGRAPHY: Jewell G. Pritchett and Erma B. Black, *Kent County and Its People* (Rotan, Texas: Rotan *Advance*, 1983).

Charles G. Davis

CLODINE, TEXAS. Clodine is twelve miles northeast of Richmond and twenty-one miles southwest of Houston in Fort Bend County. The town was established around 1888 as a station on the San Antonio and Aransas Pass Railway and was possibly named by a railroad official for Clodine King of Houston. The settlement acquired a post office in 1893 and by 1896 had a general store, a Baptist church, and a population of fifty. In 1897 Clodine had a community school. By 1914 its population had dwindled to twenty-five, but by then residents had telegraph and telephone connections. In 1925 the population was reported as ten and in 1929 as seventy. The Texas and New Orleans Railroad bought the San Antonio and Aransas Pass line in 1934 and subsequently removed the depot and section houses at Clodine. In 1936 the town had a factory and several businesses. Clodine was the market and shipping point for surrounding farms and the Clodine oilfield in 1947. That year the community had a population of fifty. In 1990 its population was estimated at thirty-one.

BIBLIOGRAPHY: S. A. McMillan, comp., *The Book of Fort Bend County* (Richmond?, Texas, 1926). Vertical Files, Barker Texas History Center, University of Texas at Austin.

Stephen L. Hardin

CLOICE BRANCH. Cloice Branch (Cloice Creek) rises two miles west of Hewitt in south central McLennan County (at 31°28′ N, 97°14′ W) and runs northwest for 3½ miles to its mouth on the South Bosque River, near the city limits of Woodway (at 31°29′ N, 97°16′ W). The surrounding flat to rolling prairie is surfaced by dark, calcareous clays that support mesquite, cacti, and grasses. The stream was probably named for an early surveyor.

CLOPPER, NICHOLAS (1766–1841). Nicholas Clopper, early settler responsible for the acquisition of the Twin Sisters,qv was born in New Brunswick, New Jersey, on November 3, 1766. After unsuccessful business ventures in Pennsylvania and Maryland, he moved to Ohio about 1820. Two years later he moved to Texas to Stephen F. Austin'sqv colony, hoping to recoup his fortunes by trade and land speculation. For the rest of his life he divided his time between Ohio and Texas.

Clopper was one of the first to see the potential of Buffalo Bayou as a trade route between the Brazos area and the sea. He organized the Texas Trading Association in 1827 to conduct trade over the route. In 1826 he purchased the peninsula between Galveston and San Jacinto bays, now known as Morgan's Point. The sand bar blocking the entrance to San Jacinto Bay still bears his name. In 1835 Clopper presided over a meeting in Cincinnati, Ohio, which opened a subscription to purchase two cannons, the famous Twin Sisters, for the Texas revolutionaries.

Clopper married Rebecca Chambers in 1790, and they had eleven children. One of his sons, Andrew M., was a courier for President David G. Burnetqv during the Texas Revolution.qv Another was lost at sea in 1822 or possibly killed by Karankawa Indians on the Texas coast. Two other sons, Joseph C. and Edward N., came to Texas with Clopper at various times. Clopper died on December 2, 1841. The letters and journals of the family tell much about life and events in Texas at the time.

BIBLIOGRAPHY: Edward Nicholas Clopper, *An American Family* (Cincinnati, 1950). "Clopper Correspondence, 1834–1838," *Southwestern Historical Quarterly* 13 (October 1909).

Marilyn M. Sibley

CLOPTON, ALBERT GALLATIN (1828–1916). Albert Gallatin Clopton, doctor, soldier, and politician, was born near Eaton, Georgia, in 1828, the son of Alfred and Sallie (Kendricks) Clopton. He served in the Mexican War,qv studied law for a year, then abandoned law for medicine and graduated from the University of Louisiana in 1851. He moved to Camden, Arkansas, but shortly thereafter traveled to Texas and served for a time in the force of Texas Rangersqv under Shapley P. Ross.qv Clopton subsequently went back to Camden to practice medicine but returned to Texas in 1854 and settled at Douglassville, where he married Annie Matilda Henderson; they adopted two children. Clopton remained at Douglassville for six years working as a doctor and a farmer before moving to Jefferson just before the Civil War.qv In 1860 he owned a 245-acre farm and six slaves and raised twenty-two bales of cotton. He was a member of the Secession Conventionqv in 1861. He served as captain of Company D, First Texas Infantry, Hood's Texas Brigade,qv and acted as major of the regiment at the battle of Eltham's Landing in 1862. Soon afterward he transferred to the medical department. Clopton returned to Jefferson after the war. In April 1874 he was elected president of the Texas State Medical Association (see TEXAS MEDICAL ASSOCIATION). He was the first professor of physiology in the Medical Branch of the University of Texas at Galveston. He was a Methodist and was active in Confederate veterans' affairs. He died at Texarkana on June 21, 1916; his wife died the following day. Their double funeral was conducted at Jefferson, and Clopton is buried in Oakwood Cemetery, Jefferson.

BIBLIOGRAPHY: *Biographical Souvenir of the State of Texas* (Chicago: Battey, 1889; rpt., Easley, South Carolina: Southern Historical Press, 1978). Lucille Blackburn Bullard, *Marion County, Texas, 1860–1870* (Jefferson, Texas, 1965). Jefferson *Jimplecute*, June 22, 1916. George Plunkett [Mrs. S. C.] Red, *The Medicine Man in Texas* (Houston, 1930). William S. Speer and John H. Brown, eds., *Encyclopedia of the New West* (Marshall, Texas: United States Biographical Publishing, 1881; rpt., Easley, South Carolina: Southern Historical Press, 1978). Fred Tarpley, *Jefferson: Riverport to the Southwest* (Austin: Eakin Press, 1983). George T. Todd, *Sketch of the History of the First Texas Regiment, Hood's Brigade* (1909?; rpt., as *First Texas Regiment*, Waco: Texian Press, 1963). E. W. Winkler, ed., *Journal of the Secession Convention of Texas* (Austin, 1912). Ralph A. Wooster, "An Analysis of the Membership of the Texas Secession Convention," *Southwestern Historical Quarterly* 62 (January 1959).

CLOSE CITY, TEXAS. Close City, on Ranch Road 399 two miles north of U.S. Highway 380 and eleven miles west of Post in western Garza County, was on a site within the area purchased in 1906 by Charles William Postqv for his projected settlement. So many of the first inhabitants used tents for homes that the village was called Ragtown, but it was later renamed Close City. For a while Post encouraged construction there, until surveyors discovered that the site was eleven miles from the geographical center of the county and thus could not serve as the location of the county seat. Post ordered work to stop in Close City and proceeded to select the present site of Post. Close City consequently developed slowly. By 1920 it had a store, a school, two churches, and a population of fifty. Though the school consolidated with the Post Independent School District in the 1950s, the store and two churches were still present in the community in the 1980s. In 1990 Close City had a population of 107.

BIBLIOGRAPHY: Garza County Historical Survey Committee, *Wagon Wheels: A History of Garza County*, ed. Charles Didway (Seagraves, Texas: Pioneer, 1973).

Julius A. Amin

CLOSNER, JOHN (1853–1932). John Closner, Hidalgo County developer, the son of Swiss parents John and Elizabeth (Blumer) Closner, was born on March 24, 1853, in New Glaris, Wisconsin. The family moved to Minnesota and Iowa before moving to Texas in 1870 and settling in Bosque County. Closner began hauling freight to Fort Griffin in 1871, worked for railroad construction and streetcar companies in Oklahoma and Galveston, and spent 1876 to 1882 working on the extension of Jay Gould'sqv International–Great Northern Railroad in Mexico, where he contracted erysipelas, an infectious skin disease that continued to affect him for many years.

Left in financial distress when the railroad failed, Closner moved to Rio Grande City in 1883 with only fifteen dollars and became a stage driver to Peña Station.qv He later obtained the mail contract between Brownsville and Rio Grande City. In 1884 he moved to Hidalgo, then the Hidalgo county seat, bought a tract of land, and was appointed deputy sheriff by James L. Dougherty. Closner served as sheriff until 1889 and became tax collector; he became deputy United States marshall for a time and remained in these positions until his retirement as Hidalgo County Treasurer in 1919, when an audit of the county record office revealed that many records were missing. Some sources suggest that Closner may have been implicated. He and stock-raiser W. F. Sprague were involved in bankruptcy hearings from 1917 until July 4, 1919, facing creditors' claims of nearly $2 million.

At a time when banditry and cattle rustling were rife, Closner's tenure was marked by waves of border violence growing out of the Garza Warqv and the 1910 revolution by Francisco I. Maderoqv against the Mexican government of Porfirio Díaz. Closner survived several attempts on his life, including an 1899 assassination attempt by Pancho Garza, plotted by the Dougherty brothers, whom he had helped indict for stealing horses and, according to some accounts, for an effort to kill local officials and burn the town.

As one of the Rio Grande valley's largest landowners, Closner contributed most by promoting irrigationqv and diversified farming. He bought land at twenty-five cents to one dollar an acre and managed to acquire 45,000 acres by 1904. He constructed a canal system in 1895 to carry water from the Rio Grande to his alfalfa, banana, cotton, tobacco, and other crops and experimented successfully with growing a wide variety of fruits and vegetables. His sugarcane won a gold medal at the Louisiana Purchase Exposition in St. Louis in 1904.

Through his influence and a gift of 2,000 acres in 1904, Closner, with the help of Leonidas C. Hill, Sr.,qv Tom Hicks, and others, obtained the extension of the St. Louis, Brownsville and Mexico Railway from Harlingen to Samfordyce. In 1906, with William Sprague, he built a branch line of the railroad from San Juan Plantation,qv named for him by his wife, to the site of Chapin, which in 1908 he developed with Sprague and Judge Dennis Bangs Chapin. Closner and Sprague donated 1,400 acres to the development, which was renamed Edinburg in 1911, and arranged for an election on October 8, 1908, to make the town the county seat. To prevent resistance by those who objected, tents were set up to receive the county records, and men with wagons and mule teams made the move overnight. In 1907 Closner, William Briggs, and O. E. M. Jones were instrumental in founding East McAllen, today known as McAllen.

Closner gave Edinburg its first public school, served for years as president of the Edinburg State Bank and director of other Valley banks, and encouraged development of Edinburg's irrigation system. In 1902 he started a private telephone system, which later developed into the Hidalgo Telephone Company.

He married Ida Louise Cook at Galveston on August 19, 1876. In 1888 Closner was married for a second time, this time to Ann Sheridan Dougherty of Brownsville, with whom he had three children. After this wife died in 1903, he married Alice Dougherty, sister of his second wife, in 1904. In 1923 the family moved to Brownsville, where Closner lived in retirement until his death, on June 3, 1932.

BIBLIOGRAPHY: James Lewellyn Allhands, *Gringo Builders* (Joplin, Missouri, Dallas, Texas, 1931). Edinburg *Daily Review*, March 21, 1965. John Arthur Garraty, *Encyclopedia of American Biography* (New York: Harper and Row, 1974). Brian Robertson, *Wild Horse Desert: The Heritage of South Texas* (Edinburg, Texas: Hidalgo County Historical Museum, 1985). San Antonio *Express*, September 7, 1911. J. Lee and Lillian J. Stambaugh, *The Lower Rio Grande Valley of Texas* (San Antonio: Naylor, 1954). Valley By-Liners, *Roots by the River: A Story of Texas Tropical Borderland* (Mission, Texas: Border Kingdom Press, 1978).

Verna J. McKenna

CLOTHING MANUFACTURE. Clothing manufacture in Texas has increased slowly through a series of expansions and declines. At the beginning of the Civil Warqv five establishments in Texas were manufacturing wearing apparel, and during the war uniforms for Confederate troops were made at the Texas State Penitentiary at

Huntsville.qv By 1870 there were thirty-three establishments, but the census of 1889 reported only four plants. By 1899 the number had increased to eleven, but only 0.13 percent of the total value of the nation's ready-made clothes was produced in Texas, while 1 percent in 1939 was of Texas origin. At this time Texas ranked eleventh of all states in clothing manufacture. Until about 1910 the clothing manufacturers in Texas produced only men's clothing. Since that time there has been a shift to the production of women's apparel, but the manufacture of men's clothing, particularly pants and work clothes, engaged the major portion of the industry. The manufacture of apparel and related products by Texas producers in the twentieth century has been a "rags to riches" story in both the literal and figurative sense. Texas producers and designers have challenged successfully the hegemony of the New York and California industries. With 1,250 establishments employing 65,100 workers and an annual payroll of approximately $875 million in 1994, the industry was a statewide phenomenon with factories located in smaller communities as well as large cities. More than a fourth of the state's apparel-manufacturing enterprises were located in Dallas County; they had 12,305 employees and an annual payroll of $160,694,000. El Paso and Bexar counties were also centers of production.

By the late 1920s pioneer companies had emerged that manufactured clothing better suited to the regional tastes and seasonal demands of the Southwest. Such enterprises as Finesilver Manufacturing Company (1897, San Antonio), Lorch Manufacturing Company (1909, Dallas), Farah qv (1920, El Paso), Williamson-Dickie Manufacturing Company (1922, Fort Worth), Juvenile Manufacturing Company, now Santone Industries (1923, San Antonio), and the Haggar Company (1926, Dallas) produced men's work clothes and pants, ladies' cotton dresses, and children's play clothes. During the 1930s such Dallas companies as Nardis, Donovan, Marcy Lee and Justin McCarty capitalized on the marketability of the low-cost cotton house dress and produced new distinctive lines of sportswear, especially ladies' slacks, for national consumption. Texas had 73 clothing factories in 1917, 102 in 1929, and 103 in 1933. The receipt of federal contracts to manufacture large quantities of military uniforms during World War II qv enabled Texas firms to modernize plant machinery and expand national sales contacts. In 1942 manufacturers formed the Dallas Fashion and Sportswear Center, now the Southwest Apparel Manufacturers Association. This aggressive trade organization used advertisements in national fashion magazines, sponsored elaborate style shows, expanded the size and number of apparel markets held in Dallas, and published its own magazine, *Dallas Fashion and Sportswear* (later *Texas Fashions*) from 1942 to 1972.

Growth in the national importance of fashions designed and produced in Texas continued in the postwar period. In 1947 the state had 361 factories with 20,164 workers. The three Frankfurt sisters of Dallas, founders of the Page Boy Maternity Fashions Company, achieved national prominence. Seeking new labor markets, many of the pioneer firms decentralized manufacturing operations from large urban centers by placing factories in smaller communities throughout the state, especially along the border with Mexico. Producers introduced new lines of casual clothing made from wrinkle-resistant polyester fabric. Fashion-minded retailers, such as Neiman-Marcus qv in Dallas, produced a favorable fashion climate for the expansion of Texas apparel producers. Operating in a conservative economic environment, management successfully discouraged any meaningful unionization of workers by the International Ladies' Garment Workers' Union qv and the Amalgamated Clothing Workers of America, combined later as the Amalgamated Clothing and Textile Workers. In 1963 the manufacture of apparel and related items was, in number of employees and size of payroll, the fourth largest manufacturing industry in Texas. With 40,150 employees and a $124,809,000 payroll, the industry was outdistanced only by manufacturing of machinery, transportation equipment, and chemicals and allied products. A catalyst to the continued growth of the Texas industry was the opening of the $15 million Apparel Mart building in Dallas in 1964. By 1984 it was the nation's largest wholesale fashion market under one roof, having 2.3 million square feet of space in seven stories with 2,000 separate showrooms. The Apparel Mart attracted approximately 80,000 buyers annually. Such Dallas companies as Howard B. Wolf, Jerell, Prophesy, and Victor Costa established a special niche for themselves by upgrading the styling of garments targeted for a distinctive segment of the market. An emphasis on private corporate ownership and the passing on of traditional values from one generation to another brought about a continuity in ownership and longevity of existence among many Texas companies that were unprecedented in the national apparel industry. Competition from imports produced by low-cost labor began to alarm all Texas producers by the mid-1980s. By means of creativity in policy and audacity in action, however, such challenges were being met successfully.

BIBLIOGRAPHY: Shirley Barr, "The Texas Apparel Industry: Weaving a Pattern of Profits," *Texas Business,* August 1976. Carol T. F. Bennett, "An Economic Profile of the Texas Apparel Industry," *Texas Business Review* 52 (January 1978). Dorothy D. DeMoss, The History of Apparel Manufacturing in Texas, 1897–1981 (Ph.D. dissertation, Texas Christian University, 1981; New York: Garland Publishing, 1989). George Green, "ILGWU in Texas, 1930–1970," *Journal of Mexican American History* 1 (Spring 1971). Joe Carroll Rust, "The Texas Apparel Industry," *Texas Business Review* 34 (January 1960). Donald W. Whisenhunt, ed., *Texas: A Sesquicentennial Celebration* (Austin: Eakin Press, 1984).
Dorothy D. DeMoss

CLOUD, DANIEL WILLIAM (1814–1836). Daniel William Cloud, Alamo defender, son of Daniel and Nancy (Owens) Cloud, was born in Logan County, Kentucky, on February 20, 1814. He was a lawyer and, on his way to Texas, traveled through Illinois, Missouri, Arkansas, and Louisiana with Peter J. Bailey,qv also a lawyer from Logan County. Both men enlisted in the Volunteer Auxiliary Corps of Texas on January 14, 1836, at Nacogdoches, as did B. A. M. Thomas, William Fauntleroy, and Joseph G. Washington,qqv all of whom were also from Logan County, Kentucky. With these four men, Micajah Autry,qv and two others, Cloud traveled to San Antonio de Béxar and the Alamo. They arrived after February 11 and became members of the Tennessee Mounted Volunteers, commanded by William B. Harrison.qv Cloud died in the battle of the Alamoqv on March 6, 1836.

BIBLIOGRAPHY: Daughters of the American Revolution, *The Alamo Heroes and Their Revolutionary Ancestors* (San Antonio, 1976). Daughters of the Republic of Texas, *Muster Rolls of the Texas Revolution* (Austin, 1986). Phil Rosenthal and Bill Groneman, *Roll Call at the Alamo* (Fort Collins, Colorado: Old Army, 1985). San Antonio *Express,* November 24, 1901.
Bill Groneman

CLOUD, JOHN WORTH (1908–1990). John Worth Cloud, journalist, oil promoter, poet, and historian, was born on September 14, 1908, in Neosho, Missouri, the son of William Abner and Carrie June Cloud. He married Josie Herrington, teacher and poet, of Huntington, Texas, on December 31, 1936, and they had three children. Cloud attended Kemper Military Academy, Boonville, Missouri. From 1932 to 1939 he worked as fund-raiser and advertiser with various Texas oil companies (Sun Oil in Beaumont, Superior Oil in Houston, and Pioneer Exploration in Athens). He was editor, owner, and publisher of the Huntington *Weekly News,* the *Angelina County News,* and related newspapers from 1939 to 1950, when the Angelina plant burned with all the files. Cloud returned to involvement with oil exploration, which he combined with sixteen years as writer and Linotype operator for John McGaughey, owner and publisher of the Albany *News.* He retired in 1971, after which he worked another year at the Denton *Enterprise.* Mrs. Cloud taught school in Albany from 1953 to 1971; her autobiographical book, *The Way It Was,* was privately published in 1990.

Cloud's poetic history of the Albany–Fort Griffin area, *Legend of Old Stone Ranch,* handset at the Albany *News,* was proclaimed the "Official Epic Poem of Texas" by a joint Texas House and Senate resolution in 1968. Cloud was subsequently listed in the *International Who's Who Among Poets,* an English reference work. The Texas State Historical Survey Committee awarded the work "Best Historical Publication of the Year on Local or Regional History." In his eightieth year Cloud's dramatic presentation *The Shade of a Wandering Minstrel,* staged for friends at meetings of the American Association of Retired Persons and at a gathering at Christ the Servant Lutheran Church in Denton, drew kudos from critics. Cloud was a president and charter member of the Texas Historical Association of Albany, a member of the board of the Albany United Methodist Church and the local Boy Scouts of America, a director of the Lower Neches Valley Authority,qv state representative of the American Press Association, and a member of the Texas Press Association.qv He served as foster grandparent at Denton State School,qv was a recipient of the Chamber of Commerce Presidents Award, and was listed in *Who's Who in the South and Southwest.* He died on April 16, 1990, at Long Meadow Nursing Center in Denton.

BIBLIOGRAPHY: Albany *News,* June 26, 1969.

Charles E. Linck, Jr.

CLOUD, JOHN WURTS, SR. (1797–1850). John Wurts Cloud, Sr., early settler and planter in the Austin colony and the first known Episcopal priest in Texas, one of eight children of Adam and Mary (Grandin) Cloud, was born at Flanders, New Jersey, on February 27, 1797. He was a descendant of William Cloud, a Quaker from Wiltshire, England, who arrived in William Penn's colony in 1682, and of Robert Cloud of Delaware, who served in the American Revolution. John W. Cloud's father, Adam, was the first Episcopal clergyman in Mississippi. After studying at the Episcopal Academy in Cheshire, Connecticut, Cloud graduated from Yale College in 1823. He married Sarah Adeline Hull in Cheshire, Connecticut, in 1825; they had three children. Cloud served as a minister in Mississippi, then as a missionary in Connecticut, before being ordained in New York in 1829. However, he did not publicly practice his ministry after immigrating to Texas.

He arrived in the Austin colony before May 1831 and settled at Brazoria. In 1832 he was one of a committee of five Brazoria citizens that decided to attack the Mexican fort at Velasco. He then participated in the attack on June 26, 1832, one of the first engagements of the Texas Revolution (*see* VELASCO, BATTLE OF). Cloud became a division commander and served as a member of the convention of Brazoria Municipality, which framed an interim code of laws and performed other basic functions of government for a large area of Southeast Texas. In 1832 he opened a school, the first in Brazoria and one of the earliest in Texas, where such courses as Latin, Greek, geometry, trigonometry, surveying, philosophy, and chemistry were offered.

Cloud's first wife died of cholera in 1833, and he married Rebecca Johnston on November 1, 1837, in Harrisburg (now Harris) County. They had nine children. From about 1837 until 1845 Cloud was occupied primarily as a planter and stock raiser in Brazoria County. He served as a justice of the peace there from about 1838 to 1843 and was an associate county justice from 1839 to 1842. He moved to the Houston area in 1845 and lived briefly in Austin County before moving to Chappell Hill, Washington County, where he died on September 15, 1850.

BIBLIOGRAPHY: Andrew Forest Muir, "John Wurts Cloud, Priest and Planter," *Historical Magazine of the Protestant Episcopal Church,* September 1956. Raymond Houston Wilson, Sr., The Cloud family (MS, Genealogical Files, Barker Texas History Center, University of Texas at Austin).

Guy Maurice Cloud, Jr.

CLOUD BAYOU. Cloud (Clouds) Bayou rises a mile southwest of Alta Loma and State Highway 6 in western Galveston County (at 29°22′ N, 95°06′ W) and runs southwest for seven miles to its mouth on Halls Bayou, just northwest of Halls Bayou Camp in eastern Brazoria County (at 27°17′ N, 95°08′ W). The surrounding rolling to flat terrain is surfaced by sandy and clay loam that supports mixed hardwoods and pines.

CLOVER, TEXAS. Clover was near the Travis county line four miles east of Smithwick in southeastern Burnet County. A post office was established there in 1900. One early postal route map placed the Clover post office in western Travis County. Although the post office may have been in someone's home in Travis County when it was established around 1900, the focus of the community itself seems to have been in Burnet County. The post office was discontinued in 1914, and mail for the community was sent to Spicewood. Clover was not marked on county highway maps in the 1940s, but a few scattered houses were shown in the area; these were no longer marked in the 1980s.

BIBLIOGRAPHY: Darrell Debo, *Burnet County History* (2 vols., Burnet, Texas: Eakin, 1979).

Vivian Elizabeth Smyrl

CLOVERHILL, TEXAS. Cloverhill (Clover Hill, Clover Hill Church) is on Farm Road 69 five miles northeast of Quitman in north central Wood County. In 1856 the area was settled by families from Georgia and Alabama, who the next year built the Clover Hill Baptist Church on a hill covered with yellow clover. Before a school was established in the community, local children attended classes at Pleasant Grove, seven miles to the north. Another Clover Hill Baptist Church was reportedly organized in 1886, and by 1896 Clover Hill had a public school with thirty-one students. By 1911 the community also had two sawmills, a store, and a cotton gin. In 1917 the local school was destroyed by a storm, and in 1918 a new one was built. The cotton gin was closed around 1925, and by the mid-1930s Clover Hill comprised a church, a cemetery, two businesses, and a number of dwellings concentrated along the roads. In 1943 Bobby Manziel made the fourth major oilfield discovery in Wood County just a mile north of the community. The Manziel field, which led to a brief boom at Clover Hill, for a time produced a large percentage of Wood County's total oil output and was still in operation in 1988. Around the same time as the oilfield discovery Clover Hill received telephone and electric service. In 1944 the community's school was consolidated with the Quitman schools, and by 1960 all that remained at Cloverhill (now spelled as one word on maps) was the church and cemetery and a few widely scattered dwellings. The community did not grow significantly after Dry Creek was dammed in 1961–62 to form Lake Quitman, less than a mile to the northwest.

BIBLIOGRAPHY: *Wood County, 1850–1900* (Quitman, Texas: Wood County Historical Society, 1976).

Rachel Jenkins

CLOVERLEAF, TEXAS. Cloverleaf, north of Interstate Highway 10 between Channelview and Jacinto City in east central Harris County, began as a railroad station on the Beaumont, Sour Lake and Western Railway. The community was shown on the 1936 county highway map as an unnamed development. A local post office may have existed there briefly around 1950. By 1990 Cloverleaf, in the Houston metropolitan area, had two elementary schools, a junior high school, a high school, eighteen churches, and a population of 18,230.

Diana J. Kleiner

CLOWER, TEXAS. Clower was on Farm Road 773 ten miles southeast of Canton in southeastern Van Zandt County. In 1936 it had a school, a business, and scattered dwellings. By 1987 all that remained at the location was a tank farm and scattered structures along the roadway.

Diana J. Kleiner

CLUB CULTURAL RECREATIVO MÉXICO BELLO. The Club Cultural Recreativo México Bello, a social club for Mexican Americansqv in Houston, was founded in 1924. The founders included Alejandro and Isidro García;qv Alejandro was the first president. Among other goals, the club sought to "bring a closer understanding between the peoples of . . . Latin American countries and peoples of the United States." Because of its success, it became a model for subsequent Mexican-American clubs. The membership included both laborers and professionals, was limited to men who were "good, outstanding citizens," and never exceeded fifty. Most members were first-generation immigrants to the United States. They put on literary and musical programs and organized picnics and boat excursions on the Houston Ship Channel.[qv] They brought music and dance troupes from Mexico to the city auditorium. They also sponsored elaborate balls, to which they invited the leading citizens. Many of their dances and dinners were to raise money for the poor, especially new immigrants. The club also organized athletic activities for local youths, including baseball, basketball, and boxing.

The Club Cultural stressed adaptation into American society without loss of Mexican heritage. The bylaws of its constitution, drawn up in 1937, required that members speak Spanish at all the meetings, and the Mexican consul was a frequent guest at most of club activities. Many members also belonged to the Comité Patriótico Mexicano,[qv] and so the club helped to plan and coordinate the local celebration of Fiestas Patrias.[qv] Early meetings were held in the Rusk Settlement House, among other places, but in 1933 the club established headquarters at 1209 Shearn street. Among its many goals, it tried to promote positive relations between the governments of Mexico and the United States and organized banquets to honor dignitaries from both countries. In 1934, for example, these included Servando Barrera Guerra, the Mexican consul in Houston, who was feted at the Mexican Inn restaurant, owned by Félix Tijerina,[qv] and Mayor Oscar F. Holcombe,[qv] who was honored at another banquet and made an honorary member. A few years later the club also honored the governor of Nuevo León, Mexico, and Mayor Holcombe presented him the keys to the city. The club invited to its gatherings prominent scholars, journalists, and writers who addressed a variety of political, economic, and trade issues involving the United States and Latin America. The club also encountered discrimination from other ethnic groups. Most hotels and ballrooms in the city refused to rent to persons of Mexican origin, and so the club had difficulty finding rooms for such formal affairs as the annual Black and White Ball. Under the leadership of presidents Ramón Fernández and Fernando Salas Aldaz,[qqv] who worked closely with the Houston Chamber of Commerce, the club managed to get some of the better hotels to open their ballrooms to them.

Though membership was limited to men, the wives and daughters of members played a key role in coordinating the club's activities. The wife of the president, for example, always assumed responsibility for organizing dances and balls. In 1936 Olivia Rosales Ypiña organized a women's auxiliary México Bello club. The auxiliary disbanded after a few years, but reappeared in 1954 with the name Club Femenino México Bello, and Virginia de la Isla served as its first president. During this second tenure, the club opened its membership to women who were not related to México Bello members. In 1956 another women's México Bello club was founded in Port Arthur. Anita María García also organized a girls' México Bello club that organized sports teams, picnics, and parties.

After the 1960s the Club México Bello limited its activities, primarily because other clubs and organizations in the city duplicated its functions. It continued to sponsor the annual Black and White Ball, and, beginning in 1958, to put on an annual *quinceañera,* or debutante ball. In the early 1980s the club began to use both English and Spanish in its activities.

BIBLIOGRAPHY: Club Cultural Recreativo México Bello Collection, Houston Metropolitan Research Collection, Houston Public Library.
María-Cristina García

CLUB TERPSICORE. Club Terpsicore, a social club for Mexican-American women in Houston, was founded in 1937 by María Medrano, Edelia Cantú, Catalina and Virginia Gómez, and Hortensia and Lupe Quintanilla. It provided its members with social and recreational opportunities and also served the community. The club, named after Terpsichore, the mythological muse of dance, sponsored elaborate dances to raise money for various charities, among them the Salvation Army and the local tuberculosis ward. Members met once a week at the Cantú Photography Studios on Preston and Fannin streets to plan their activities. Membership in the club was limited to thirteen. Potential members were accepted on the basis of their "character." Members came from both working-class and middle-class families and from various areas of the city. They had to be single. Most of the young women were in their late teens and early twenties. Many of them had graduated from high school and worked as sales clerks or assisted their parents in the family business. A few worked as secretaries, a prestigious occupation for women in the community, since few employers hired secretaries of Mexican descent. The dances, with themes such as "A Night in Old Mexico," "Hawaiian Night," and the annual "White Ball," were held in some of the most elegant ballrooms in the city, among them the University Club, the Shiners' Hall, and the Empire Room of the Rice Hotel, which by the late 1930s had begun to rent to Mexican Americans. Their guests came from other clubs in the city: the Club Cultural Recreativo México Bello,[qv] the Club Internacional, the Club Tenochtitlán, the Club Chapultepec, and the Club Gardenia. The Mexican consul attended all their functions, as did the entire consular corps in Houston. The Club Terpsicore disbanded during World War II.[qv]

BIBLIOGRAPHY: Catalina Gómez Sandoval, Interview by Thomas D. Kreneck, February 3, 1989, Houston Metropolitan Research Collection, Houston Public Library.
María-Christina García

CLUETAU INDIANS. The name Cluetau is known from the registers of San Antonio de Valero Mission in San Antonio. Seven register entries for the period 1719–35 refer to one adult female. In three of these entries no ethnic identity is recorded; in two entries the woman is identified as a Sana; and in the two remaining entries she is identified as a Cluetau. This ambiguity makes it difficult to establish that Cluetau denotes a firm ethnic identity. Presumably there actually was an Indian group designated by this name, but the name, or some recognizable variant of it, has never been found in other documents. J. R. Swanton suggested that the Cluetaus may have spoken the Coahuilteco language. As there is no pre-mission information on Cluetau location and language, this suggestion is misleading.

BIBLIOGRAPHY: Frederick Webb Hodge, ed., *Handbook of American Indians North of Mexico* (2 vols., Washington: GPO, 1907, 1910; rpt., New York: Pageant, 1959). J. R. Swanton, *Linguistic Material from the Tribes of Southern Texas and Northeastern Mexico* (Washington: Smithsonian Institution, 1940).
Thomas N. Campbell

CLUTE CITY, TEXAS. Clute City, also known as Clute, is on Clute Lake and the Missouri Pacific Railroad between State highways 332 and 227, southeast of Lake Jackson and ten miles south of Angleton in south central Brazoria County. The site was one of the county's first plantations and is named for two Northerners who later acquired the property. Alexander Calvit,[qv] one of Stephen F. Austin's[qv] Old Three Hundred,[qv] and Jared E. Groce[qv] acquired about 4,800 acres of land there in 1824 for Evergreen Plantation.[qv] The plantation later became the Herndon sugar plantation, owned by John H. Herndon,[qv] who married Calvit's only daughter. Joseph Pegan, Soloman J. Clute, and several relatives including George and John Clute, founded a community near the plantation site after the Civil War.[qv] They acquired additional land from Herndon, who put it up for auction in the 1870s. A deed dated March 17, 1886, transferred ownership from Soloman Clute to George Clute for property known as Clute's Place. Soloman administered it until 1888 or 1889, when it was sold. The antebellum Eagle Island Plantation[qv] of William H. Wharton[qv] occupied the site of present Restwood Memorial Park.

In 1933 Clute had only two businesses and a population of ten. By

1937 the town had a school for white children with two teachers and two schools for black children with one teacher each. Growth increased in 1940, when Clute became part of the Brazosport industrial and port area. In 1950 Clute had a population of 700 and thirty-six businesses; in 1954 the residents numbered 3,200 and the businesses forty-five. A post office was established by 1943, and a new grade school was built in the 1950s. Clute was incorporated in May 1952 under the name Clute City, with a commission form of government; in 1955 the town changed its name back to Clute and adopted an aldermanic form of government. In 1974 Clute had six churches, including the True Honor Church; two schools, including Ogg School; and a railroad station. Clute changed its name to Clute City again in 1980. Its population rose to 7,000 in 1970, when it had ninety-five businesses; dropped to 6,023 in 1972; then rose again, reaching a high of 9,577 and 270 businesses in 1984. In 1990 the population was 8,910.

BIBLIOGRAPHY: Brazosport *Facts,* December 17, 1957. James A. Creighton, *A Narrative History of Brazoria County* (Angleton, Texas: Brazoria County Historical Commission, 1975).

Diana J. Kleiner

CLYDE, VANDER (1904–1973). Vander Clyde, who achieved international fame as Barbette, a female impersonator and trapeze and high-wire performer, was born on December 19, 1904, in Round Rock, Texas. His mother was a milliner, and he had a sister and at least one half-brother. Enamored of the circus after his mother took him to his first performance in Austin, Clyde began practicing on the clothesline in his mother's yard and working in the fields for money to go to as many circuses as possible. After graduating from high school at age fourteen, he traveled to San Antonio to answer a Billboard advertisement placed by one of the Alfaretta Sisters, "World Famous Aerial Queens." He joined the act on the condition that he dress as a girl, since his partner believed that women's clothes made a wire act more dramatic. He later performed in Erford's Whirling Sensation, in which he and two others hung by their teeth from a revolving apparatus.

During this period Clyde began developing a solo act in which he appeared and performed as a woman and removed his wig to reveal his masculinity at the end of the performance. After adopting the name Barbette, he traveled throughout the United States performing the act, which became quite popular. In the fall of 1923 the William Morris Agency sent him to England and then to Paris, where he opened at the Alhambra Music Hall. Barbette became the talk of Paris and was befriended by members of both American café society and French literary and social circles. In particular, his artistry was championed by French poet and dramatist Jean Cocteau. Inspired by Barbette's act, which he described as "an extraordinary lesson in theatrical professionalism," Cocteau wrote a review in the July 1926 issue of the *Nouvelle Revue Française,* "Le Numéro Barbette," which is considered a classic essay on the nature of art. As described by Cocteau, Barbette's acrobatics became a vehicle for theatrical illusion. From his entrance, when he appeared in an elaborate ball gown and an ostrich-feather hat, to an elaborate striptease down to tights and leotard in the middle of the act, Barbette enacted a feminine allure that was maintained despite the vigorous muscular activity required by his trapeze routine. Only at the end of the performance, when he removed his wig, did he dispel the illusion, at which time he mugged and flexed in a masculine manner to emphasize the success of his earlier deception. To Cocteau, Barbette's craftsmanship, practiced on the fine edge of danger, elevated a rather dubious stunt to the level of art, analogous to the struggle of a poet. Cocteau wrote about Barbette on several other occasions, and in 1930 he used the aerialist in his first film, *Le Sang d'un Poete* (*Blood of a Poet*), in which the bejeweled and Chanel-clad Barbette and other aristocrats applauded a card game that ended in suicide.

Although Clyde performed in such other European cities as Berlin, Hamburg, Copenhagen, Warsaw, Madrid, and Barcelona, his spiritual home remained in Paris, where he performed at venues such as the Casino de Paris, the Moulin Rouge, the Empire, and the Médrano Circus, in addition to the Alhambra Theater. His popularity peaked in the early 1930s, and his performing career ended in 1938, when he caught pneumonia after performing at Loew's State, a vaudeville theater in New York. His ailment left him crippled and required surgery and eighteen months of rehabilitation, during which time he had to learn to walk again.

Barbette. *Photograph by Man Ray. Paris? 1926. Gelatin silver print. 8½″ × 6¾″. Courtesy Collection of the J. Paul Getty Museum, Malibu, California, © 1928, Man Ray Trust/ADAGP-Paris/ARS-USA. Vander Clyde used the stage name "Barbette" when he performed as a circus aerialist, which he did in female dress. When he took his act to Europe in 1923, Clyde became the toast of Paris.*

Clyde continued to be involved with the circus by staging productions and training performers for Ringling Brothers–Barnum and Bailey, Cole Brothers, Clyde Beatty's, and other circuses. He spent his last years in Round Rock, where he lived with his sister Mary Cahill. He died at home on August 5, 1973. Late in life, and even posthumously, Barbette continued to inspire writers and poets: he was interviewed and subsequently profiled in a lengthy *New Yorker* article by Cocteau's biographer, Francis Steegmuller, and he was the subject of Albert Goldbarth's book-length poem, *Different Fleshes,* which won the Texas Institute of Letters [qv] award for poetry in 1980.

BIBLIOGRAPHY: Jean Cocteau, Francis Steegmuller, and Man Ray, *Le Numéro Barbette* (Paris: Jacques Damase, 1980). David Lewis Hammarstrom, *Behind the Big Top* (South Brunswick, New Jersey: Barnes, 1980). LeGrand-Chabrier, "Les Métamorphoses de Barbette," *Vu* 144 (December 17, 1930). New York *Times,* August 10, 1973. Francis Steegmuller, "An Angel, A Flower, A Bird," *New Yorker,* September 27, 1969. Francis Steegmuller, *Cocteau, A Biography* (Boston: Little, Brown, 1970). Vertical Files, Barker Texas History Center, University of Texas at Austin.

Kendall Curlee

CLYDE, TEXAS. Clyde is an incorporated community on Interstate Highway 20 and Farm Road 604, five miles west of Baird and eight miles east of Abilene in northwestern Callahan County. The site is on the Callahan Divide^{qv} between the Brazos and Colorado rivers; its elevation is 1,980 feet above sea level. The Texas and Pacific Railway was built through the area in 1880. Local sources have it that the railroad construction crew, which numbered 5,000, including many Chinese, gathered regularly at Robert Clyde's construction camp, just south of the tracks. Settlers moved in to the area, and the post office for the new community was commissioned in June 1881. In 1883 several Irish families moved to Clyde from Pennsylvania. Also around that time a group of Portuguese traveled to the area by the railroad and established a colony in the vicinity of Clyde; this colony was abandoned about 1900. A school and churches were formed at Clyde and met in local homes. A Methodist church organized at the community in 1884 and built a church building in 1904; a Baptist church began meeting in 1885 and built a church in 1907; a Catholic church was built in 1890, destroyed by Clyde's first tornado in 1895, and was later rebuilt. The local Church of Christ organized in the late 1880s and built its first building in 1904. Clyde had a population of 459 in 1910, some 610 in 1920, and 750 in 1925. At that time the town's forty-five businesses included five grocery stores, five dry goods stores, two banks, two drugstores, and two gins. In 1924 the transcontinental Bankhead Highway was routed through Clyde, facilitating faster transportation to nearby Abilene and consequently slowing Clyde's growth.

Clyde is built above an aquifer, and in 1926 its fruits and vegetables earned it the nickname "the California of Texas." Farmers often shipped their produce out by rail. Cattle and horses were raised on the area's abundant grasses. Oil production started about 1924 and through the 1980s continued to help diversify and stabilize the local economy. Clyde has had several bouts with severe weather. The bitterly cold winter of 1884–85 was followed by drought in 1886–87; later droughts occurred in 1930–36, 1949–57 (the longest), 1983–85, and in the summer of 1988 (possibly the worst). Clyde has also had several destructive tornadoes. The first one, in 1895, destroyed the Catholic church. On June 10, 1938, a tornado ripped through Clyde from the north, killing fourteen persons and destroying twenty-one homes and many other buildings, most notably the school. A freight train was also derailed. Temporary classes were held at the local churches. A third tornado, on April 28, 1950, killed five persons and destroyed four homes. The fourth twister, a less destructive one, struck east of Clyde on June 7, 1989.

The first newspaper for the town was named the Clyde *News*. The Clyde *Enterprise* was published from 1912 to 1950. A few other papers lasted briefly. The Clyde *Journal* began in 1972 and was still serving the area in 1989 as a weekly publication. By 1980 more rapid growth at Clyde had resumed. The census that year listed 2,562 residents, but according to the utility and telephone companies there were about 7,500 people in the Clyde area. It had become the largest town in the county. The post office doubled its capacity in 1987. For many years the public schools had been growing, and the town supported many churches. In the early 1990s Clyde had a population of 3,022 and some 130 businesses.

BIBLIOGRAPHY: Mrs. John Berry, "An Excessive Land," West Texas Historical Association *Year Book* 62 (1986). Brutus Clay Chrisman, *Early Days in Callahan County* (Abilene, Texas: Abilene Printing and Stationery, 1966). S. E. Settle, "Early Days in Callahan County," West Texas Historical Association *Year Book* 12 (1936).

Mrs. John F. Berry

COACOOCHEE (ca. 1810–1857). Coacoochee (Wild Cat), Seminole war chief, was born around 1810 to a sister of Micanopy, chief of the Seminole Nation, and King Philip (Emathla), chief of a Mikasuki band, in Mosquito County, Florida. He was captured with Osceola on October 21, 1837, under a white flag of truce and imprisoned in Fort Marion but escaped and became the war chief most respected by the United States Army after Osceola's death. From 1837 to 1840 he was effective in fighting and remaining free in the swamps of Florida. But Lt. Col. William S. Harney^{qv} captured Coacoochee's daughter and mother, whom Col. William Jenkins Worth^{qv} used to induce Coacoochee to come for negotiations. Coacoochee agreed to bring in the remainder of his band but took extensive advantage of his freedom and was captured by Maj. Thomas Childs and placed in irons. In October 1841 Colonel Worth finally sent Coacoochee to the Indian reservation in Arkansas Territory.

In December 1845 Indian agents took him to Texas on a peace mission to the Comanches, after which he devised a scheme for the confederation of tribes. Coacoochee spent four years traveling in Texas and Mexico promoting his scheme among various hostile Indian groups. In 1848 Maj. Robert S. Neighbors,^{qv} Texas superintendent of the Indian agency, accused Wild Cat of inciting the hostile Indians and thus hindering negotiations to move them to a Texas reservation. Coacoochee continued his promotional trips from the Arkansas reservation until December 1849. He had failed to obtain appointment as chief of the Seminole Nation, so with his following of Seminoles and blacks he went to the Brazos valley for the winter and for another attempt at recruiting. He managed to recruit some southern Kickapoo warriors, whom he led with the deserters from the reservation through Eagle Pass to Mexico. He and his followers were welcomed by the state of Coahuila, where they were placed on military reservations with supplies to defend the area against the forays of other hostile Indians. Coacoochee and his warriors were successful in this venture. They also fought against José M. J. Carbajal^{qv} in the so-called Carbajal's war and against Callahan's invasion of 1855 (see CALLAHAN EXPEDITION). The Black Seminole Indians and their sons became the Black Seminole scouts^{qv} at forts Duncan and Clark in the 1870s. In January 1857 Coacoochee contracted smallpox and died at Alto, Coahuila, Mexico.

BIBLIOGRAPHY: Arrell M. Gibson, *The Kickapoos, Lords of the Middle Border* (Norman: University of Oklahoma Press, 1963). John K. Mahon, *History of Second Seminole War, 1835–1842* (Gainesville: University of Florida Press, 1967). Edwin C. McReynolds, *The Seminoles* (Norman: University of Oklahoma Press, 1957). Kenneth Wiggins Porter, "Seminoles' Flight from Fort Marion," *Florida Historical Quarterly* 22 (January 1944).

Donald A. Swanson

COADY, TEXAS. Coady is two miles east of Lynchburg in east central Harris County. The 1936 county highway map showed a church and scattered dwellings at the townsite on the Beaumont, Sour Lake and Western Railway. A church, a water tank, an abandoned railroad station, and multiple dwellings were still at the site in the 1980s.

Diana J. Kleiner

COAHOMA, TEXAS. Coahoma, on Interstate Highway 20 ten miles northeast of Big Spring in east central Howard County, took its name from an Indian word meaning "signal." A nearby hill is called Signal Mountain. After the 1881 arrival of the Texas and Pacific Railway in the area, Coahoma grew into a retail trade center and shipping point. Its residents built their first school in 1891, and Gertrude McIntyre was the first teacher. By the time its second school was built in 1904, the town had a post office. Machinery and oilfield supplies became the most important goods distributed from Coahoma after the major oil strike of 1926. In 1928 the town had 600 residents, and its school district served 205 pupils. Between 1936 and 1956 the community's population rose from 620 to 802, and the number of commercially rated businesses went from eighteen to twenty-three. In 1960 the population was reported as 1,239, and in 1970 it was 2,000. In 1980 Coahoma had 1,069 residents, of whom 224 were Hispanic and none were black. At that time the community also had twenty-four businesses, a bank, and a post office. In the early 1990s it was an incorporated community with a population of 1,157 and forty-eight rated businesses.

BIBLIOGRAPHY: *Historic Howard County* (Big Spring, Texas: Howard County Survey Committee, n.d). Joe Pickle, *Gettin' Started: Howard County's First 25 Years* (Big Spring, Texas: Heritage Museum, 1980).

Noel Wiggins

COAHOMA DRAW. Coahoma Draw rises five miles northwest of Coahoma in north central Howard County (at 32°22′ N, 101°26′ W) and runs east for ten miles to its mouth on Guthrie Draw, just north of Interstate Highway 20 (at 32°19′ N, 101°17′ W). The local sand dunes are subject to wind erosion and dune migration and support scattered oak groves and bunch grasses.

COAHUILA AND TEXAS. In 1689–90 Alonso De León,qv governor of the Spanish province of Coahuila, extended his authority to include Texas. Early in 1691 he was succeeded by Domingo Terán de los Ríos,qv who was appointed governor of Coahuila and Texas. In 1693, however, Spain withdrew the Catholic missions from East Texas, and it was not until 1716 that Martín de Alarcón,qv who had been appointed governor of Coahuila in 1702, reextended his control over Texas. Alarcón was succeeded by the Marqués de Aguayo,qv whose activities resulted in the separation of the two provinces around 1726, during the time of his successor, Fernando Pérez de Almazán.qv The provinces were governed separately, with the capital of Texas at Los Adaesqv and that of Coahuila at Monclova.qv

By the Constitution of 1824qv the Mexican provinces of Nuevo León, Coahuila, and Texas were united as one state. Nuevo León was detached on May 7, 1824. A constituent congress was elected and assembled at Saltilloqv in August 1824, and a provisional governor was named for the state. A provisional chief was appointed for Texas in August 1824, and in December the Department of Texas was legally established as a subdivision of the state of Coahuila and Texas. The Constitution of Coahuila and Texasqv was adopted on March 11, 1827. The state was at first divided into three departments, but the number was eventually increased to seven: Saltillo, Parras, Monclova, Rosas, Bexar, Brazos, and Nacogdoches.

After some agitation Monclova replaced Saltillo as the capital of the state in March 1833. The legislature at Monclova passed several acts beneficial to Texas, creating new municipalities, dividing Texas into three departments, permitting the use of English in schools and public affairs, and allowing an additional representative from Texas. Also the Monclova government attempted to revise the judicial system, which had been particularly troublesome to Texans, by appointing Thomas J. Chambersqv superior judge of a three-district judicial circuit created for Texas, and by providing within this new system for trial by jury. Chambers was prevented from organizing the court system, however, by the ensuing difficulties in Coahuila.

When the Monclova legislature closed its session in April 1834, Coahuila lapsed into confusion. A rump meeting of the Monclova deputation in June declared against Antonio López de Santa Anna'sqv Plan of Cuernavaca. In July, Saltillo formed a state government in opposition to the Monclova faction, annulled the acts of the previous legislature, and appointed José María Goribar as military governor. The time for elections arrived amid growing party hostility, but before any serious collision occurred, the rival governments submitted their case to Santa Anna for arbitration. The Mexican president ordered that Monclova remain the seat of government and that a new election should be held for the entire state. Elections were held, but trouble arose almost immediately, and in protest against a decree providing for the wasteful sale of public land in Texas the Saltillo faction withdrew from the newly elected legislature. The national government was petitioned to nullify the elections which, it was alleged, had been conducted illegally. Martín Perfecto de Cos,qv military commandant for the eastern division of the Provincias Internas,qv supported the Saltillo faction in a stand against the Texas land sales and ordered a company of federal troops to disband the legislature at Monclova. After decreeing that the governor had the authority to change capitals, the legislature hastily adjourned on April 21, 1835. Agustín Viescaqv then called out the militia with the object of reducing Saltillo and, when threatened by General Cos, resolved to make Bexar (San Antonio) the capital of the department. In this he was supported by a number of Texans, and on May 25, accompanied by about 150 militiamen and twenty-odd Texans, he left Monclova with the archives. The military was ordered to prevent his crossing the Rio Grande, and he returned to Monclova to attempt a secret withdrawal to Texas aided by Benjamin R. Milam and John Cameron.qqv The party was captured and imprisoned, but most of the men escaped and eventually reached Texas. Viesca and the remaining members of the legislature were arrested in Coahuila. José Miguel Falcón, who was appointed governor, was replaced on August 8 by Rafael Ecay Músquiz, but neither man served. Ramón Músquiz,qv the vice governor under Viesca, took over the governorship on June 28, 1835. This overthrow of constitutional government, together with the arrest of the incendiary Viesca, precipitated long-smoldering resistance in Texas and led to the Texas declaration against Santa Anna. In November 1835 the Consultationqv declared Texas a separate state under the Constitution of 1824 and formed a provisional government. The severance of Texas and Coahuila was made final by the Texas Revolution and the Mexican War.qqv

BIBLIOGRAPHY: Vito Alessio Robles, *Coahuila y Texas en la época colonial* (Mexico City: Editorial Cultura, 1938; 2d ed., Mexico City: Editorial Porrúa, 1978). Hubert Howe Bancroft, *History of the North Mexican States and Texas* (2 vols., San Francisco: History Company, 1886, 1889).

COAHUILTECAN INDIANS. The lowlands of northeastern Mexico and adjacent southern Texas were originally occupied by hundreds of small, autonomous, distinctively named Indian groups that lived by hunting and gathering. During the Spanish colonial period a majority of these natives were displaced from their traditional territories by Spaniards advancing from the south and Apaches retreating from the north. The Spaniards had little interest in describing the natives or classifying them into ethnic units. There was no obvious basis for classification, and major cultural contrasts and tribal organizations went unnoticed, as did similarities and differences in the native languages and dialects. Spaniards referred to an Indian group as a *nación,* and described them according to their association with major terrain features or with Spanish jurisdictional units. Only in Nuevo León did observers link Indian populations by cultural peculiarities, such as hairstyle and body decoration. Thus, modern scholars have found it difficult to identify these hunting and gathering groups by language and culture.

The first attempt at classification was based on language, and came after most of the Indian groups were extinct. In the mid-nineteenth century, Mexican linguists designated some Indian groups as Coahuilteco, believing they may have spoken various dialects of a language in Coahuila and Texas (*Coahuilteco* is a Spanish adjective derived from *Coahuila*). Two friars documented the language in manuals for administering church ritual in one native language at certain missions of southern Texas and northeastern Coahuila. Neither these manuals nor other documents included the names of all the Indians who originally spoke Coahuilteco. In time, other linguistic groups also entered the same missions, and some of them learned Coahuilteco, the dominant language. Identifying the Indian groups who spoke Coahuilteco has been difficult. As additional language samples became known for the region, linguists have concluded that these were related to Coahuilteco and added them to a Coahuiltecan family. This encouraged ethnohistorians and anthropologists to believe that the region was occupied by numerous small Indian groups who spoke related languages and shared the same basic culture. Scholars constructed a "Coahuiltecan culture" by assembling bits of specific and generalized information recorded by Spaniards for widely scattered and limited parts of the region. This belief in a widespread linguistic and cultural uniformity has, however, been questioned. In Nuevo León, at least one language unrelatable to Coahuilteco has come to light, and linguists question that other language samples collected in the region demonstrate a relationship with Coahuilteco.

The early Coahuiltecans lived in the coastal plain in northeastern Mexico and southern Texas. The plain includes the northern Gulf Coastal Lowlands in Mexico and the southern Gulf Coastal Plain in the United States. It is bounded by the Gulf of Mexico[qv] on the east, a northwest-trending mountain chain on the west, and the southern margin of the Edwards Plateau[qv] of Texas on the north. The northeastern boundary is arbitrary. The course of the Guadalupe River to the Gulf of Mexico marks a boundary based on changes in plant and animal life, Indian languages and culture. The Coahuiltecan region thus includes southern Texas, northeastern Coahuila, and much of Nuevo León and Tamaulipas. The region has flat to gently rolling terrain, particularly in Texas. In Nuevo León and Tamaulipas mountain masses rise east of the Sierra Madre Oriental. The Rio Grande dominates the region. It flows across its middle portion and into a delta on the coast. Small drainages are found north and south of the Rio Grande. The coast line from the Guadalupe River of Texas southward to central Tamaulipas has a chain of elongated, offshore barrier islands, behind which are shallow bays and lagoons. The region's climate is megathermal and generally semiarid. Though rainfall declines with distance from the coast, the region is not a true desert. Álvar Núñez Cabeza de Vaca[qv] in 1534–1535 provided the earliest observations of the region. About 1590 colonists from southern Mexico entered the region by an inland route, using mountain passes west of Monterrey, Nuevo León. Tamaulipas and southern Texas were settled in the eighteenth century.

Hunting and gathering prevailed in the region, with some Indian horticulture in southern Tamaulipas. A wide range of soil types fostered wild plants yielding such foodstuffs as mesquite[qv] beans, maguey root crowns, prickly pear fruit, pecans, acorns, and various roots and tubers. The introduction of European livestock altered vegetation patterns, and grassland areas were invaded by thorny bushes. The deer was a widespread and available large game animal. Bison (buffalo[qv]) roamed southern Texas and northeastern Coahuila. Smaller game animals included the peccary and armadillo, rabbits, rats and mice, various birds, and numerous species of snakes, lizards, frogs, and snails. Fish were found in perennial streams, and both fish and shellfish in saline waters of the Gulf.

The Coahuiltecan area was one of the poorest regions of Indian North America. In it Indian groups became extinct at an early date. Documents written before the extinction provide basic information. European drawings and paintings, museum artifacts, and limited archeological excavations offer little information on specific Indian groups of the historic period. European and American archives contain unpublished documents pertinent to the region, but they have not been researched. Information has not been analyzed and evaluated for each Indian group and its territorial range, languages, and cultures. Group names and orthographic variations need study. Little is known about group displacement, population decline, and extinction or absorption. After displacement, the movements of Indian groups need to be traced through dated documents. As many groups became remnant populations at Spanish missions, mission registers and censuses should reveal much. Territorial ranges and population size, before and after displacement, are vague. Language and culture changes during the historic period lack definition. With such limitations, information on the Coahuiltecan Indians is largely tentative.

During the Spanish colonial period, hunting and gathering groups were displaced and the native population went into decline. Two invading populations—Spaniards from southern Mexico and Apaches from northwestern Texas plains—displaced the indigenous groups. As the Spaniards arrived, displaced Indians retreated northward, with some moving to the east and west. These groups, in turn, displaced Indians that had been earlier displaced. The Indians also suffered from such European diseases as smallpox and measles, which often moved ahead of the frontier. Spanish settlers generally occupied favored Indian encampments. Their livestock competed with wild grazing and browsing animals, and game animals were thinned or driven away. The Indians turned to livestock as a substitute for game animals, and raided ranches and Spanish supply trains for European goods. Poorly organized Indian rebellions prompted brutal Spanish retaliation. Most of the Indians left the immediate area.

In the north the Spanish frontier met the Apache southward expansion. In the first half of the seventeenth century, Apaches acquired horses from Spanish colonists of New Mexico and achieved dominance of the Southern Plains. In 1683–84 Juan Domínguez de Mendoza,[qv] traveling from El Paso eastward toward the Edwards Plateau, described the Apaches. The Apache expansion was intensified by the Pueblo Indian Revolt of 1680, when the Apaches lost their prime source of horses and shifted south to prey on Spanish Coahuila. Domínguez de Mendoza recorded the names of numerous Indian groups east of the lower Pecos River that were being displaced by Apaches. Variants of these names appear in documents that pertain to the northeastern Coahuila-Texas frontier. By the mid-eighteenth century the Apaches, driven south by the Comanches, reached the coastal plain of Texas and became known as the Lipan Apaches. The Lipans in turn displaced the last Indian groups native to southern Texas, most of whom went to the Spanish missions in the San Antonio area. By 1790 Spaniards turned their attention from the aboriginal groups and focused on containing the Apache invaders. In northeastern Coahuila and adjacent Texas, Spanish and Apache displacements created an unusual ethnic mix. Here the local Indians mixed with displaced groups from Coahuila and Chihuahua and Texas. Some groups, to escape the pressure, combined and migrated north into the Central Texas highlands.

The Spanish missions,[qv] numerous in the Coahuiltecan region, provided a refuge for displaced and declining Indian populations. Early missions were established at the forefront of the frontier, but as settlement inched forward, they were replaced. Because the missions had an agricultural base they declined when the Indian labor force dwindled. Missions were distributed unevenly. Some were in remote areas, while others were clustered, often two to five in number, in small areas. A large number of displaced Indians collected in the clustered missions, which generally had a military garrison (presidio) for protection. A few missions lasted less than a decade; others flourished for a century. Several moved one or more times. Eventually, all the Spanish missions were abandoned or transferred to diocesan jurisdictions.

The number of Indian groups at the missions varied from fewer than twenty groups to as many as 100. Many groups contained fewer than ten individuals. Missions in existence the longest had more groups, particularly in the north. Mission Indian villages usually consisted of about 100 Indians of mixed groups who generally came from a wide area surrounding a mission. Some came from distant areas. Although survivors of a group often entered a single mission, individuals and families of one ethnic group might scatter to five or six missions. Some Indians never entered a mission.

A majority of the Coahuiltecan Indians lost their identity during the seventeenth and eighteenth centuries. Their names disappeared from the written record as epidemics, warfare, migration, dispersion by Spaniards to work at distant plantations and mines, high infant mortality, and general demoralization took their toll. Small remnants merged with larger remnants. By 1800 the names of few ethnic units appear in documents, and by 1900 the names of groups native to the region had disappeared. Missions and refugee communities near Spanish or Mexican towns were the last bastions of ethnic identity.

The Indians caused little trouble and provided unskilled labor. Ethnic names vanished with intermarriages. By the end of the eighteenth century, missions closed and Indian families were given small parcels of mission land. Eventually, the survivors passed into the lower economic levels of Mexican society. In 1981 descendants of some aboriginal groups still lived in scattered communities in Mexico and Texas.

For this region and adjacent areas, documents covering nearly 350 years record more than 1,000 ethnic group names. Studies show that the number of recorded names exceeds the number of ethnic units by 25 percent. Names were recorded unevenly. Some come from a single document, which may or may not cite a geographic location; others appear in fewer than a dozen documents, or in hundreds of documents. Two or more names often refer to the same ethnic unit. A substantial number refer to Indians displaced from adjoining areas. Some groups became extinct very early, or later were known by different names. The best information on Coahuiltecan group names comes from Nuevo León documents. More than 60 percent of these names refer to local topographic and vegetational features. Others refer to plants and animals and to body decoration. Group names of Spanish origin are few. Fewer than 10 percent refer to physical characteristics, cultural traits, and environmental details. Some Spanish names duplicate group names previously recorded. A language known as Coahuilteco exists, but it is impossible to identify the groups who spoke dialects of this language. Also, it is impossible to identify groups as Coahuiltecans by using cultural criteria. The best information on Coahuiltecan-speaking groups comes from two missionaries, Damián Massanet[qv] and Bartolomé García. In 1690 and again in 1691 Massanet, on a trip from a mission near Candela in eastern Coahuila to the San Antonio area, recorded the names of thirty-nine Indian groups. On his 1691 journey he noted that a single language was spoken throughout the area he traversed. This language was apparently Coahuilteco, since several place names are Coahuilteco words. Coahuilteco was probably the dominant language, but some groups may have spoken Coahuilteco only as a second language. By 1690 two groups displaced by Apaches entered the Coahuiltecan area. Massanet named the groups Jumano and Hape. García (1760) compiled a manual for church ritual in the Coahuilteco language. He listed eighteen Indian groups at missions in southern Texas (San Antonio) and northeastern Coahuila (Guerrero) who spoke dialects of Coahuilteco. However, these groups may not originally have spoken these dialects. García included only three names on Massanet's 1690–91 lists. He also identified as Coahuilteco speakers a number of poorly known groups who lived near the Texas Gulf Coast. García indicates that all Indians reasonably designated as Coahuiltecans were confined to southern Texas and extreme northeastern Coahuila, with perhaps an extension into northern Nuevo León. Nineteenth century Mexican linguists who coined the term *Coahuilteco* noted the extension. The belief that all the Indians of the western Gulf province spoke languages related to Coahuilteco is the prime reason the Coahuiltecan orbit includes so many groups. Some scholars believe that the coastal lowlands Indians who did not speak a Karankawa or a Tonkawa language must have spoken Coahuilteco. Since the Tonkawans and Karankawans were located farther north and northeast, most of the Indians of southern Texas and northeastern Mexico have been loosely thought of as Coahuiltecan.

The ranges of the hunters and gatherers of this region are vague. Early Europeans rarely recorded the locations of two or more encampments, and when they did it was during the warm seasons when they traveled on horseback. Winter encampments went unnoted. Two or more groups often shared an encampment. The Indians probably had no exclusive foraging territory. Cabeza de Vaca recorded that some groups apparently returned to certain territories during the winter, but in the summer they shared distant areas rich in foodstuffs with others. The Mariames, for example, ranged over two areas at least eighty miles apart. The summer range of the Payaya Indians of southern Texas has been determined on the basis of ten encampments observed between 1690 and 1709 by summer-traveling Spaniards. The range was approximately thirty miles. Winter camps are unknown. The Pampopa and Pastia Indians may have ranged over eighty-five miles. The annual quest for food covered a sizable area.

The total Indian population and the sizes of basic population units are difficult to assess. The number of valid ethnic groups in the region is unknown, as are what groups existed at any selected date. Population figures are fairly abundant, but many refer to displaced group remnants sharing encampments or living in mission villages. Most population figures generally refer to the northern part of the region, which became a major refuge for displaced Indians. For group sizes prior to European colonization, one must consult the scanty information in Cabeza de Vaca's 1542 documents. The most valuable information on population lies in the figures for the largest groups at any time. The largest group numbered 512, reported by a missionary in 1674 for Gueiquesal in northeastern Coahuila. The Pacuaches of the middle Nueces River drainage of southern Texas were estimated by another missionary to number about 350 in 1727. Documents for 1747–72 suggest that the Comecrudos of northeastern Tamaulipas may have numbered 400. Limited figures for other groups suggest populations of 100 to 300. Cabeza de Vaca's data (1533–34) for the Mariames suggest a population of about 200. Estimates of the total Coahuiltecan population in 1690 vary widely. One scholar estimates the total nonagricultural Indian population of northeastern Mexico, which included desertlands west to the Río Conchos in Chihuahua, at 100,000; another, who compiled a list of 614 group names (Coahuiltecan) for northeastern Mexico and southern Texas, estimated the average population per group as 140 and therefore reckoned the total population at 86,000.

Descriptions of life among the hunting and gathering Indian groups lack coherence and detail. Only two accounts, dissimilar in scope and separated by a century of time, provide informative impressions. The first is Cabeza de Vaca's description of the Mariames of southern Texas, among whom he lived for about eighteen months in 1533–34. The second is Alonso De León's[qv] general description of Indian groups he knew as a soldier in Nuevo León before 1649. These groups ranged from Monterrey and Cadereyta northeast to Cerralvo. These two sources cover some of the same categories of material culture, and indicate differences in cultures 150 miles apart. De León records differences between the cultures within a restricted area. The two descriptions suggest that those who stress cultural uniformity in the Western Gulf province have overemphasized the generic similarities in the hunting and gathering cultures.

The Mariames (not to be confused with the later Aranamas) were one of eleven groups who occupied an inland area between the lower reaches of the Guadalupe and Nueces rivers of southern Texas. These groups shared a subsistence pattern that included a seasonal migration to harvest prickly pears west of Corpus Christi Bay. The Mariames are the best-described Indian group of northeastern Mexico and southern Texas. They spent nine months (fall, winter, spring) ranging along the Guadalupe River above its junction with the San Antonio River. In the summer they moved eighty miles to the southwest to gather prickly pear fruit. The Mariames numbered about 200 individuals who lived in a settlement of some forty houses. Each house was dome-shaped and round, built with a framework of four flexible poles bent and set in the ground. This was covered with mats. Poles and mats were carried when a village moved. During his sojourn with the Mariames, Cabeza de Vaca never mentioned bison hunting, but he did see bison hides. The principal game animal was the deer. In the Guadalupe River area, the Indians made two-day hunting trips two or three times a year, leaving the wooded valley and going into the grasslands. They carried their wood and water with them. They controlled the movement of game by setting grassfires. When traveling south, the Mariames followed the western shoreline of Copano Bay. When an offshore breeze was blowing, hunters spread out, drove deer into the bay, and kept them there until they drowned and were beached. The Indians also hunted rats and mice though rabbits are not mentioned. They killed and ate snakes and pulverized the bones for food. They collected land snails and ate them. They combed the prickly pear thickets for various insects, in egg and larva form, for food. Other faunal foods, especially in the Guadalupe River area, included frogs, lizards, salamanders, and spiders. The Mariames occasionally ate earth, wood, and deer droppings. During the April–May flood season, they caught fish in shallow pools after floods had subsided. They also pulverized fish bones for food. The Mariames depended on two plants as seasonal staples—pecans and cactus fruit. In the autumn they collected pecans along the Guadalupe, and when the crop was abundant they shared the harvest with other groups. They mashed nut meats and sometimes mixed in seeds. The prickly pear area was especially important because it provided ample fruit in the summer. When water ran short, the Mariames expressed fruit juice in a hole in the earth and drank it. In the winter the Indians depended on roots as a principal food source. Edible roots were thinly distributed, hard to find, and difficult to dig; women often searched for five to eight miles around an encampment. They baked the roots for two days in a sort of oven. Little is known about Mariame clothing, ornaments, and handicrafts. They may have used a net, described as 5.5 feet square, to carry bulky foodstuffs. Matting was important to cover house frames. The only container was either a woven bag or a flexible basket. The Indians used the bow and arrow as an offensive weapon and made small shields covered with bison hide. Several factors prevented overpopulation. The Indians practiced female infanticide, and occasionally they killed male children because of unfavorable dream omens. Men refrained from sexual intercourse with their wives from the first indication of pregnancy until the child was two years old. Mariame women breast-fed children up to the age of twelve years. Male contact with a menstruating women was taboo. Since female infanticide was the rule, Maraime males doubtless obtained wives from other Indian groups. The "bride price" was a good bow and arrow or a net. No Mariame male had two or more wives. Divorce was permitted, but no grounds were specified other than "dissatisfaction." Female infanticide and ethnic group exogamy indicate a patrilineal descent system. Cabeza de Vaca briefly described a fight between two adult males over a woman. Only fists and sticks were used, and after the fight each man dismantled his house and left the encampment. Little is said about Mariame warfare. Some behavior was motivated by dreams, which were a source of omens. The documents cite twelve cases in which male children were killed or buried alive because of unfavorable dream omens. Little is known about ceremonies, although there was some group feasting and dancing which occurred during the winter and reached a peak during the summer prickly pear hunt.

In his early history of Nuevo León, Alonso De León described the Indians of the area. In the same volume, Juan Bautista Chapa[qv] listed 231 Indian groups, many of whom were cited by De León. Some of the groups noted by De León were collectively known by names such as Borrados, Pintos, Rayados, and Pelones. A few spoke dialects designated as Quinigua. All were hunters and gatherers who consumed the food they acquired almost immediately. Some settlements were small and moved frequently. Some families occasionally left an encampment to seek food separately. One settlement comprised fifteen houses arranged in a semicircle with an offset house at each end. The women carried water, if needed, in twelve to fourteen pouches made of prickly pear pads, in a netted carrying frame that was placed on the back and controlled by a tumpline. In summer, prickly pear juice was drunk as a water substitute. The Indians of Nuevo León constructed circular houses, covered them with cane or grass, and made a low entrances. Each house had a small hearth in the center, its fire used mainly for illumination. A fire was started with a wooden hand drill.

The occupants slept on grass and deerskin bedding. The families abandoned their house materials when they moved. With eight or ten people associated with a house, a settlement of fifteen houses would have a population of about 150. The Indians of Nuevo León hunted all the animals in their environment, except toads and lizards. The animals included deer, rabbits, rats, birds, and snakes. The principal game animal was the deer. When a hunter killed a deer he marked a trail back to the encampment and sent women to bring the carcass home. The hunter received only the hide; the rest of the animal was butchered and distributed. The Indians used the bow and arrow and a curved wooden club. The club served as a walking aid, a weapon, and a tool for probing and prying. At night each man kept his club in easy reach. Both sexes shot fish with bow and arrow at night by torchlight, used nets, and captured fish underwater by hand along overhanging stream banks. The Nuevo León Indians depended on maguey root crowns and various roots and tubers for winter fare. In the summer they sought prickly pear fruits and mesquite bean pods. Maguey crowns were baked for two days in an oven, and the fibers were chewed and expectorated in small quids. When a food shortage arose, they salvaged, pulverized, and ate the quids. The Indians ate flowers of the prickly pear, roasted green fruit, and ate ripe fruit fresh or sun-dried on mats. Mesquite bean pods, abundant in the area, were eaten both green and in a dry state. The Indians pulverized the pods in a wooden mortar and stored the flour, sifted and containing seeds, in woven bags or in pear-pad pouches. Mesquite flour was eaten cooked or uncooked. The Indians added salt to their foods and used the ash of at least one plant as a salt substitute. In Nuevo León there were striking group differences in clothing, hair style, and face and body decoration. The men wore little clothing. No garment covered the pubic zone, and men wore sandals only when traversing thorny terrain. In some groups men wore rabbitskin robes. Women covered the pubic area with grass or cordage, and over this occasionally wore a slit skirt of two deerskins, one in front, the other behind. To the rear deerskin they attached a skin that reached to the ground, with a hem that contained sound-producing objects such as beads, shells, animal teeth, seeds, and hard fruits. On special occasions women also wore animal-skin robes. Males and females wore their hair down to the waist, with deerskin thongs sometimes holding the hair ends together at the waist. In some groups (Pelones), the Indians plucked bands of hair from the forehead to the top of the head, and inserted feathers, sticks, and bones in perforations in ears, noses, and breasts. Ethnic identity seems to have been indicated by painted or tattooed patterns on the face and the body. The face had combinations of undescribed lines; among those who had hair plucked from the front of the head, the lines extended upward from the root of the nose. Body patterns included broad lines, straight or wavy, that ran the full length of the torso (probably giving rise to the Spanish designations Borrados, Rayados, and Pintos.)

The descriptions by Cabeza de Vaca and De León are not strictly comparable, but they give clear impressions of the cultural diversity that existed among the hunters and gatherers of the Coahuiltecan region. The principal differences were in foodstuffs and subsistence techniques, houses, containers, transportation devices, weapons, clothing, and body decoration.

BIBLIOGRAPHY: T. N. Campbell, "Coahuiltecans and Their Neighbors," in *Handbook of North American Indians,* Vol. 10 (Washington: Smithsonian Institution, 1983). Thomas N. Campbell, *The Indians of Southern Texas and Northeastern Mexico: Selected Writings of Thomas Nolan Campbell* (Austin: Texas Archeological Research Laboratory, 1988).

COAL, TEXAS. Coal, nine miles east of Kosse in southern Limestone County, was named for the lignite coal mine in the area. The community had a post office for a brief time in 1898 and again from

1900 to 1901; when the office was discontinued, residents received their mail from Headsville in Robertson County. By the 1940s nothing remained in the area but the old mine.

BIBLIOGRAPHY: John J. Germann and Myron Janzen, *Texas Post Offices by County* (1986). Ray A. Walter, *A History of Limestone County* (Austin: Von Boeckmann–Jones, 1959).

Vivian Elizabeth Smyrl

COAL CREEK. Coal Creek rises a mile northeast of Willow City in northeastern Gillespie County (at 30°25′ N, 98°42′ W) and runs northeast for fourteen miles to its mouth on Sandy Creek, three miles southeast of Click in southern Llano County (at 30°32′ N, 98°35′ W). It crosses flat to rolling terrain surfaced by sandy loams that support open stands of live oak, mesquite, and grasses.

COAL KILN DRAW. Coal Kiln Draw rises just southeast of the Murr Ranch compound in northeastern Sutton County (at 30°39′ N, 100°09′ W) and runs northwest for 4½ miles to its mouth on Terrett Draw, just north of the Schleicher county line (at 30°43′ N, 100°10′ W). The surrounding gently rolling terrain is surfaced by shallow to deep loamy soils broken by occasional rock outcrops. Local vegetation includes grasses, with scattered stands of oak, juniper, and mesquite.

COAL AND LIGNITE MINING. Texas has an appreciable quantity of low to medium grade bituminous coal and a large quantity of average to high grade lignite. Bituminous coal is found in north central Texas in Pennsylvanian rocks in Coleman, Eastland, Erath, Jack, McCulloch, Montague, Palo Pinto, Parker, Wise, Young, and other counties. Cannel coal is found in considerable quantities in Maverick and Webb counties. Coal deposits in the Trans-Pecos[qv] area of West Texas occur in Brewster, Hudspeth, and Presidio counties. Earlier mines at Thurber[qv] in Erath County, Bridgeport in Wise County, Newcastle in Young County, and Strawn in Palo Pinto County produced large tonnages and in 1950 continued small-scale production for local use. Lignite, a low-grade coal, is found in a broad band of Tertiary Eocene strata that extends across the Coastal Plain[qv] from the Rio Grande near Laredo in South Texas to the Arkansas and Louisiana borders of East Texas, and in a group of intervening counties including Panola, Harrison, Marion, Gregg, Rusk, and Shelby. The largest source and best grades of lignite occur in the Wilcox Group of strata north of the Colorado River in East and Central Texas. In the period from 1895 to 1943, Texas mines produced more than twenty-five million tons of coal. Sixty thousand tons of lignite was mined in Texas in 1947. Deposits have been found in Angelina, Atascosa, Bastrop, Fayette, Freestone, Grimes, Harrison, Henderson, Hopkins, Houston, Limestone, McMullen, Milam, Panola, Robertson, Rusk, Titus, Van Zandt, and Walker counties. A thorough survey on which to base an accurate estimate of Texas coal and lignite resources has never been made, but it is estimated that there are 60,000 square miles of lignite territory with a supply of probably twenty billion tons of commercially valuable lignite. The coal belt is spottier and more difficult to estimate, but it is believed that the deposits exceed eight billion tons.

Coal was a significant energy source in Texas before the development of oil and gas. Early Texas settlers undoubtedly mined both coal and lignite from numerous outcroppings across the state for use in their homes, stores, and blacksmith shops. Commercial mining, however, did not begin until the 1880s. Coal production, first listed at 125,000 tons for Texas in 1884, declined for the next three years but climbed significantly from 1889 to 1901, when it reached 1,107,953 tons. In the mid-1880s, discoveries in northwestern Erath County led to operations that made it a leading coal-producing area in the state. The Texas and Pacific Coal Company established a company town at Thurber, which survived until the 1930s. After a slight recession in the industry in 1902–3, production surpassed the 1901 total in 1904, and began a steady climb to reach an all-time peak in 1913 at 2,429,920 tons. Totals declined slightly between 1914 and 1916, but soared to near the 1913 peak again in 1917 as the United States became involved in World War I.[qv] In the 1920s the industry underwent a sharp recession as competition from petroleum and electricity hurt the entire bituminous-lignite industry. The Texas decline was not unique. A brief rise took place in 1927, followed by a steady decline until 1935, when production fell to a thirty-year low of 757,529 tons. Mining practically ceased after World War II,[qv] and production totaled only 18,169 tons in 1950. The industry received a tremendous boost in the 1950s, however, when the Aluminum Company of America began using char produced from lignite at a plant near Rockdale. Production figures were not released after 1953, but the ALCOA operation was expected to consume approximately 300,000 tons of lignite a year.

Several methods have been used for extracting coal and lignite, including the pillar and stall, longwall, and strip mining. Mining was usually done formerly by hand with primitive tools, although gasoline locomotives were sometimes used. Most mines were small, yielding between 10,000 and 50,000 tons per year, and the bulk of coal produced was used within the state. Though railroads were early purchasers, they found the quality poor and used it only sparingly. Lignite was burned in homes, converted to briquettes used in boilers to produce steam for generating power, and reduced to activated carbon, a substance used as a clarifying agent in the sugar-refining industry. By-products of coal and lignite, including gas, coal tar, and char, were also obtained.

In the 1970s bituminous coal production resumed in the state after a long hiatus. Construction began on surface mines in southern Coleman County and the Thurber area of Erath County to produce coal for use as fuel in the cement industry. Construction continued on a Texas Utilities Company generating plant in Freestone County to be fueled with lignite from Freestone and Limestone County amounting to five million tons a year. Milam County lignite mining by the Industrial Generating Company produced fuel for electric power generation, while Harrison County lignite mined by Atlas Chemical Industries was processed into activated carbon. In 1975 the four strip mines in Texas produced a total of 11,002,000 short tons of lignite, representing an increase of 43 percent over the previous year and 172 percent over 1972. Subsequent production continued to increase for the next several years. The Texas Utilities Generating Company operated the state's largest producer, the Big Brown mine in Freestone County, and the Monticello mine in Titus County, which together produced more than 80 percent of the total, and planned a pilot *in situ* project to test the potential for gasifying Texas lignites in deep-basin beds. The remainder of the year's production came from the ALCOA Sandow strip mine in Milam County and the ICI United States Darco strip mine in Harrison County. The entire production was used within the state. Mining of cannel coals in the Santo Tomás district of Webb County, used mostly for boiler fuel, ceased from 1939 till 1978, when a surface mine was opened to produce coal for use in the cement industry. Coals of the Santo Tomás district were also demonstrated to have high gas, oil, and sulfur content, a fact that suggested their possible use as a source of petrochemical products. Leasing for lignite and coal continued strong, but was slower than in previous years, a decline indicating that easily attainable acreage had already been acquired. Several new mines, however, including the Martin Lake strip mine near Beckville in Panola County, were under development.

In the 1980s exploration for lignite resources continued, and bituminous coal was mined in the Eagle Pass section of Maverick County in South Texas. In 1986 lignite production totaled 48,346,000 tons, principally for the production of steam-generated electricity. By the 1990s, Texas was the nation's sixth leading coal producing state. As much as 99 percent of the product was lignite. A Milam County mine supplied electric power for alumina reduction, a Harrison County strip mine produced lignite used to make activated carbon, and other mines in Atascosa, Bastrop, Freestone, Grimes, Harrison, Limestone, Rusk, Panola, Titus, and Hopkins counties produced lignite for municipal, domestic, and industrial needs. Lignite reserves were estimated at approximately 23 billion short tons, and economically recoverable reserves of strippable lignite were estimated at nine to eleven billion tons. Other lignite resources of the Texas Gulf Coastal Plain, occurring as deep-basin deposits, were comparable in magnitude to near-surface resources.

BIBLIOGRAPHY: Thomas J. Evans, *Bituminous Coal in Texas* (Bureau of Economic Geology, University of Texas at Austin, 1974). Gary Warren Hamilton, Texas Lignite and the National Synthetic Fuel Effort (Master of Public Affairs Report, University of Texas at Austin, 1980). U.S. Bureau of Mines, *Minerals Yearbook*. University of Texas, *Texas Looks Ahead: The Resources of Texas* (Austin, 1944; rpt., Freeport, New York: Books for Libraries Press, 1968). David M. White and Olin B. Clemons, *Coal and Lignite* (Austin: Governor's Energy Advisory Council, 1977). *Dwight F. Henderson and Diana J. Kleiner*

COAL MINE, TEXAS. Coal Mine was on U.S. Highway 81 and the Missouri Pacific line in southeastern Medina County. Coal mines, worked by as many as 500 people at a time, precipitated the growth of mining camps southwest of Lytle in the 1880s. In 1881 the International–Great Northern Railroad built a rail line from Austin to Laredo that passed through Lytle. The community of Coal Mine developed on this line a mile southwest of Lytle and just north of the mining camps. The high-grade lignite produced at the mines was sold to the railroads until the advent of oil-burning locomotives. In 1888 Coal Mine consisted of a store, a bandstand, a main plaza, a dance hall, a Catholic church, and at least two schools. Thirty-eight students attended a one-teacher school there in 1907. By the 1940s Coal Mine consisted of a Catholic church and several dwellings, situated mostly north of the railroad tracks. Lytle annexed Coal Mine in 1969, and there were about 100 people living at the Coal Mine site in 1983.

BIBLIOGRAPHY: Castro Colonies Heritage Association, *The History of Medina County, Texas* (Dallas: National Share Graphics, 1983). *Ruben E. Ochoa*

COAPITE INDIANS. The Coapite (Coapiste, Guapica, Guapite) Indians were Karankawans who, when first reported by this name in the eighteenth century, lived on the Texas coast near Matagorda Bay, where they were closely associated with the Cujanes and Karankawas proper. In 1722 Espíritu Santo de Zuñiga Mission was established for these Indians near Matagorda Bay, but hostilities between Spaniards and Indians soon led to its removal. In 1754 the Spanish again attempted to missionize the Coapites and their Karankawan associates by establishing Nuestra Señora del Rosario Mission near the site of future Goliad. The Coapites were periodically in and out of this mission until as late as 1831. During this period a few Coapite Indians entered Nuestra Señora de la Purísima Concepción de Acuña Mission at San Antonio. Some of the Coapites also entered Nuestra Señora del Refugio Mission when it was founded in 1793 and were reported as being there until 1828. After this, remnants of the Coapite Indians seem to have merged with the group known to the Anglo American settlers as Karankawas, who disappeared in the middle of the nineteenth century.

BIBLIOGRAPHY: Herbert E. Bolton, "The Founding of Mission Rosario: A Chapter in the History of the Gulf Coast," *Quarterly of the Texas State Historical Association* 10 (October 1906). H. E. Bolton, "Records of the Mission of Nuestra Señora del Refugio," *Quarterly of the Texas State Historical Association* 14 (October 1910). Herbert Eugene Bolton, *Texas in the Middle Eighteenth Century* (Berkeley: University of California Press, 1915; rpt., Austin: University of Texas Press, 1970). William E. Dunn, "The Founding of Nuestra Señora del Refugio, the Last Spanish Mission in Texas," *Southwestern Historical Quarterly* 25 (January 1922). Frederick Webb Hodge, ed., *Handbook of American Indians North of Mexico* (2 vols., Washington: GPO, 1907, 1910; rpt., New York: Pageant, 1959). William H. Oberste, *History of Refugio Mission* (Refugio, Texas: Refugio Timely Remarks, 1942). *Thomas N. Campbell*

COAQUE INDIANS. The Coaque (Caoque, Cadoque, Cahoque, Capoque, Cayoque, Coaqui) Indians were encountered by Álvar Núñez Cabeza de Vaca[qv] in 1528 on the Texas coast. They occupied one end of an island that is usually identified as Galveston Island. The Coaques have been consistently identified with the Coco Indians, who were first known over 150 years later, at which time they lived on both sides of the Colorado River near the coast. It cannot be proved conclusively that these two names refer to the same people. A better case can be made for identification of the Coaque with the Akokisa Indians, who in the eighteenth century lived in the vicinity of Galveston Bay. Both occupied the same area, and there are phonetic similarities in the names.

BIBLIOGRAPHY: Adolph F. Bandelier, ed., *The Journey of Álvar Núñez Cabeza de Vaca and His Companions from Florida to the Pacific, 1528–1536* (New York: Barnes, 1905). Frederick Webb Hodge, ed., *Handbook of American Indians North of Mexico* (2 vols., Washington: GPO, 1907, 1910; rpt., New York: Pageant, 1959). *Thomas N. Campbell*

COASTAL CORPORATION. The Coastal Corporation, based in Houston, is a diversified energy company involved in refining and marketing, coal mining, natural-gas transmission, and exploration and production. The company has three United States refineries and one in Europe; owns coal mines in Utah and Kentucky; drills for oil and gas in the Rocky Mountains, Mid-Continent states, and overseas; maintains a pipeline in Kansas, Oklahoma, Texas, and other western states; conducts United States and international marketing of crude oil and petroleum products; and produces agricultural chemicals and liquid carbon dioxide. Its ANR Freight and Trucking subsidiary handles regional and long-haul freight through 228 terminals in forty states. Operations range from the United States to Canada, Europe, and Aruba.

The company began in 1951, when Oscar S. Wyatt, Jr., established a small natural-gas-gathering business in Corpus Christi. Wyatt, who had spent summers working in the oilfields as a young man, received a mechanical-engineering degree from Texas A&M, worked for Kerr-McGee and Reed Roller Bit, and was a partner in independent oil company Wymore Oil before founding Coastal. In 1955 the firm became the Coastal States Gas Producing Company, engaged in collecting and distributing natural gas from the South Texas oilfields. In the early 1960s Coastal purchased the Sinclair Oil Corpus Christi refinery and pipeline network and established a subsidiary called Lo-Vaca Gathering to supply natural gas to Texas cities and utilities. When Lo-Vaca curtailed its gas supplies and raised prices during the energy crisis of the early 1970s, customers sued Coastal. Regulators ordered the subsidiary to refund $1.6 billion in 1977, and Coastal spun off Lo-Vaca as Valero Energy to finance the settlement.

Wyatt expanded the company through a series of deals. With acquisition of Rio Grande Valley Gas he obtained a small South Texas pipeline. In 1973 he succeeded in a hostile takeover of Colorado Interstate Gas and changed its name to Coastal States Gas Corporation. Coastal also acquired the low-sulfur Utah coal operations of Southern Utah Fuel and New England pipelines through Union Petroleum in 1973, and California refining through Pacific Refining in 1976. With the acquisition of Belcher Oil in 1977, the company entered Florida petroleum marketing and transportation. Wyatt also made money on a number of other takeover bids.

In 1980 the company adopted the name Coastal Corporation, and Wyatt formed Coastal International Limited, a Bermuda corporation. Raymond M. Holliday, former chairman and chief executive officer of Hughes Tool, became president of the firm in 1981, and in 1984 Wyatt developed a plan to move company headquarters from Houston to his South Texas Ranch in Duval County. In 1985 Coastal purchased American Natural Resources of Detroit in a hostile takeover but failed in a 1989 attempt to acquire Texas Eastern. By 1987 company net sales totalled over $113 million; reserves included 26 million barrels of oil and 848 billion cubic feet of natural gas.

Before the Gulf War in 1991, Wyatt attempted to trade Coastal's refining and marketing assets for regular supplies of crude oil from Iraq. With Coastal director and former Texas governor John B. Connally,^qv Wyatt met with Saddam Hussein and flew twenty-one hostages out of Baghdad. Wyatt was later critical of Operation Desert Storm and was investigated for possible violation of the United States trade embargo.

By the 1990s Coastal's 20,000-mile pipeline network, including the Iroquois and Great Lakes pipeline, completed in 1991, and the Empire State Pipeline, completed in 1992, transported five billion cubic feet of natural gas daily. Coastal subsidiaries operated eight refineries, a fleet of tugs, tankers, and barges, and 962 convenience stores in thirty-three states. The company also sold Next Generation and Next Generation Plus diesel and unleaded auto fuels. Sales in 1991 totalled $9.549 billion.

BIBLIOGRAPHY: Vertical Files, Barker Texas History Center, University of Texas at Austin (Coastal Corporation, Oscar Wyatt). *Who's Who in the South and Southwest*, 1986–87.   Diana J. Kleiner

COASTAL PLAIN. The Texas Coastal Plain, a strip about a hundred miles wide extending from Nueces Bay to Galveston Bay,^qqv is underlain by sedimentary strata of Mesozoic (Lower and Upper Cretaceous) and Cenozoic age. These beds are mainly unconsolidated, and as a rule they dip gently toward the Gulf. The Upper Cretaceous strata outcrop along the interior portion of the Coastal Plain and extend to the Gulf in the subsurface; the remainder of the Coastal Plain is underlain by Tertiary and Pleistocene deposits, the latter lying immediately interiorward from and bordering the Gulf of Mexico.^qv Topographically, the Coastal Plain consists of three major physiographic divisions or belts that extend more or less parallel to the Gulf Coast. These divisions include: (a) the interior belt, consisting of an inner lowland plain that was sculptured out of the outcropping softer beds of the Upper Cretaceous; (b) the coastal belt, a low, flattish country, bordering on the Gulf of Mexico and underlain by the Beaumont clays and the Lissie formation, both of Pleistocene age; and (c) the intervening broad belt underlain mainly by sands and nonlimy clays, comprising the Central Dissected Belt. East of the Mississippi River, this intervening zone is often referred to as the Central Sandy Belt; in Texas, however, it has a few outcropping limy clay areas that are important agriculturally. Climatically, the Coastal Plain of Texas is divided into three major groups: the humid plains of forested East Texas, the moderately humid prairies, including the Black Prairies, and the subhumid plains of South Texas.

BIBLIOGRAPHY: William Bollaert, *Observations on the Geography of Texas* (London, 1850). Zachary Taylor Fulmore, *The Geography of Texas* (n.p.: Rand, McNally, 1908). Terry Jordan, *Texas: A Geography* (Boulder, Colorado: Westview Press, 1984). Frederic William Simonds, *Geographic Influences in the Development of Texas* (Austin: Journal of Geography, 1912).   E. H. Johnson

COASTAL ZONE. The Federal Coastal Zone Management Act of 1972 provided that coastal states develop resource-management programs to regulate coastal resources. The act defines the coastal zone as "coastal waters . . . and adjacent shorelands . . . extend[ing] inland only to the extent necessary to control shorelands, the uses of which have a direct and significant impact on the coastal waters." The act further clarifies "shoreline" as the "line of mean high tide, as determined by tide gauges." The Texas legislature responded with the Coastal Public Lands Management Act of 1973, which more broadly defined the state's coastal zone as "the geographic area comprising all the counties of Texas having any tidewater shoreline, including that portion of the bed and waters of the Gulf within the jurisdiction of the State of Texas." That jurisdiction extends to the Gulfward boundary of the state, 10.35 miles out into the Gulf of Mexico.^qv Governor Dolph Briscoe directed the General Land Office^qv to develop a coastal management program to be known as the Texas Coastal Management Program. A series of meetings subsequently held in coastal cities from Beaumont to Brownsville and as far upland as Dallas, Austin, and San Antonio, however, revealed concerns extending far inland. Cattlemen, manufacturers, oil and gas interests, and environmentalists all had an important interest in the Coastal Plain.^qv Moreover, the Texas Parks and Wildlife Department, the State Department of Highways and Public Transportation, the Texas Water Resources Board, the Railroad Commission,^qqv and other state agencies were involved in coastal management.

By 1975 the Texas Coastal Management Program had redefined the Texas coastal zone as "southwest along the coast from the Sabine to the Rio Grande, seaward into the Gulf of Mexico for a distance of 10.35 miles, and inland to include 36 counties." This zone is composed of eight geographic areas extending from the inner continental shelf to about forty miles inland. It includes all estuaries and tidally influenced streams and bounding wetlands. From north to south the areas are Beaumont–Port Arthur, Galveston–Houston, Bay City–Freeport, Port Lavaca, Corpus Christi, Kingsville, and Brownsville–Harlingen. The coastal zone as specified in 1975 includes 1,890 miles of waterfront. Of this, 74.6 percent is bays and estuaries and 373 miles faces the Gulf of Mexico. Eighty percent of the coast is behind a strip of barrier islands that include Matagorda, St. Joseph, Mustang, and Padre islands.^qv Except for three areas where the mainland is directly exposed to the Gulf, the islands and peninsulas form an almost continuous barrier shield, protecting the mainland from waves and storms. The total coastal zone comprises an area of more than 33,000 square miles. The coastal counties have one-third of the state's population, one-third of its economic activity, 40 percent of the national petrochemical industry, 25 percent of the national petroleum-refining capacity, and three of the ten largest seaports; yet they make up only about one-tenth of the total land area of the state. The zone is richly endowed with natural resources. Its mineral production, largely of oil and gas, has a value of nearly $1 billion a year. Another $156 million comes from commercial fisheries. The fertile soils along the coast produce agricultural products valued at $500 million a year. The beaches and waters attract about three million tourists who spend nearly $1.6 billion per year. In spite of the dangers from hurricanes^qv and beach erosion, development in the coastal zone has been continuous and rapid since the end of World War II.^qv Texas withdrew from the Federal Coastal Management Program in 1981 but continued to manage its coastal resources through the General Land Office.

BIBLIOGRAPHY: *Texas Coastal Legislation* (Austin: General Land Office and Texas Coastal and Marine Council, 1984). *Texas Coastal Management Plan, 1990–1991* (Austin: General Land Office, 1991).
          Art Leatherwood

COAT OF ARMS. The coat of arms of the Republic of Texas,^qv originally adopted by the Congress in December 1836, was finally established by an act of Congress on January 25, 1839. It was declared to be a white star of five points on an azure ground encircled by olive and live oak branches. The national seal bore the arms encircled by the words *Republic of Texas*. The Constitution of 1845^qv provided for the same seal with the words changed to *The State of Texas*. See also SEALS OF TEXAS.

BIBLIOGRAPHY: Hans Peter Nielsen Gammel, comp., *Laws of Texas, 1822–1897* (10 vols., Austin: Gammel, 1898).

COATS, MERIT M. (?–1827). Merit M. Coats (Coates), one of Stephen F. Austin's^qv Old Three Hundred^qv colonists, received title to a sitio^qv of land now in Waller County on July 19, 1824. No Merit M. Coats was listed in the colony census of 1826, but the census did list a Brown M. Coats, a farmer and stock raiser, a single man aged between twenty-five and forty and owner of two slaves. A Merrit M. Coates executed a will in Harris County on October 2, 1823. The will freed two slaves, Violet and her son, Carter. The claim was made that Coates kept Violet as his wife, and their daughter, Martha, was freed upon Coates's death in 1827. It is not clear if Carter was Coates's son.

BIBLIOGRAPHY: Lester G. Bugbee, "The Old Three Hundred: A List of Settlers in Austin's First Colony," *Quarterly of the Texas State Historical Association* 1 (October 1897). Andrew Forest Muir, "The Free Negro in Harris County, Texas," *Southwestern Historical Quarterly* 46 (January 1943).

COAYO INDIANS. The Coayos, an Indian group of southern Texas, was met by Álvar Núñez Cabeza de Vaca^qv together with Cutalchich, Maliacone, and Susola Indians at the "prickly pear grounds."

BIBLIOGRAPHY: Frederick Webb Hodge, ed., *Handbook of American Indians North of Mexico* (2 vols., Washington: GPO, 1907, 1910; rpt., New York: Pageant, 1959).
Margery H. Krieger

COBB, ARNETT CLEOPHUS (1918–1989). Arnett Cleophus Cobb, jazz tenor saxophonist, was born on August 10, 1918, in Houston. He was taught piano by his grandmother and went on to study violin before taking up tenor saxophone in the high school band. When he was fifteen he joined Louisiana band leader Frank Davis's band and performed in Houston and throughout Louisiana during the summer. He worked with trumpeter Chester Boone for two years and left to play with Milton Larkin in 1936. Cobb played with Larkin's band for six years as it successfully toured the country; its venues included the Apollo Theatre in Harlem and boxer Joe Louis's Rhumboogie Club in Chicago. Cobb turned down offers from both Count Basie and Lionel Hampton in 1939 but in 1942 accepted an offer from Hampton to take Illinois Jacquet's seat in his famous band. Although his fans doubted that anyone could successfully replace Jacquet, within a short time Cobb became as popular as Jacquet. Hampton rerecorded his theme song, "Flying Home No. 2," with Cobb as the featured soloist, and the excitement elicited by his uninhibited, blasting style earned him the label "Wild Man of the Tenor Sax." He was a major asset of the Hampton band for five years.

He left Hampton in 1947 and formed his own small group, which recorded a series of singles, including the hits "Dutch Kitchen Bounce," "Big Red's Dreams," and "When I Grow Too Old to Dream." After only seven months on the road Cobb was forced to disband the group and undergo spinal surgery and a long hospital stay because of Pott's disease, a tubercular condition of the vertebrae. He recovered and reorganized his group in 1950 and resumed touring in 1951. He quickly regained his popularity but in 1956 he became permanently disabled as a result of a car crash. Doctors advised against it, but a year later he was performing and touring coast to coast, although from this time on, he could not walk without crutches. Cobb was living in New Jersey at the time, but the long, cold, damp, northeastern winter made working too strenuous, so in 1959 he moved back to Houston permanently. From 1960 onwards he managed Club Ebony, performed locally with his own band and with other famous jazz performers, and toured to New York and Europe, all between stints in the hospital.

Cobb received a Grammy nomination in 1979 for best jazz instrumental performance. He shared a Grammy with B. B. King in 1984 for best traditional blues performance. In 1986 he founded the Jazz Heritage Society of Texas, which established the Jazz Archives at the Houston Public Library.^qv Cobb died in Houston on March 24, 1989, and was survived by his daughter.

BIBLIOGRAPHY: Larry Birnbaum, "Arnett Cobb: Soul-Wrenching Sax," *Down Beat*, April 1981. "A Feeling for Jazz: An Interview with Arnett Cobb," *Houston Review* 12 (1990). Barry Kernfeld, ed., *The New Grove Dictionary of Jazz* (London: Macmillan, 1988).
Kharen Monsho

COBB CAVERNS. Cobb Caverns is on the Cobb Ranch halfway between Florence and Georgetown in northwestern Williamson County. Although the cave had been known for several decades, it was not opened to the public until June 1962. A commercial trail follows a high-ceilinged, linear passage for 1,000 feet, past flowstone-coated walls, "totem poles," and boxwork. An additional 1,000 feet of passage is not open to tourists. Indian artifacts have been found in old campgrounds at nearby Cobbs Springs.

BIBLIOGRAPHY: James R. Reddell and Richard Finch, "The Caves of Williamson County," *Texas Speleological Survey* 2.1 (October 1963).
A. Richard Smith

COBB CREEK. Cobb Creek rises 1½ miles from Hillsboro in central Hill County (at 32°01′ N, 97°03′ W) and runs southwest for twenty-two miles to its mouth on Aquilla Lake near Vaughan (at 31°52′ N, 97°12′ W). The surrounding terrain varies from flat to rolling prairie and is surfaced by deep to shallow expansive clays, clay loams, and dark, commonly calcareous clays that support oak, juniper, mesquite, cacti, and water-tolerant hardwoods. For most of the county's history, the Cobb Creek area has been used as range and crop land.

COBB JONES CREEK. Cobb Jones Creek rises five miles east of Sulphur Bluff in northwestern Hopkins County (at 33°20′ N, 95°19′ W) and runs southeast for eleven miles to its mouth on White Oak Creek, ten miles northeast of Mount Vernon in Franklin County (at 33°19′ N, 95°09′ W). The surrounding nearly level to undulating terrain is surfaced by soil that is loamy with a clayey subsoil. The area is heavily wooded, with pines and hardwoods predominating.

COBLE, WILLIAM THOMAS (1875–1958). William Thomas Coble, rancher and oilman, was born on October 18, 1875, in Douglas County, Missouri. After his parents died, he was brought to Texas at age twelve by his grandfather, T. M. Johnson, who settled at Henrietta in Clay County. Coble earned fifteen dollars a month working as a farmhand for E. W. Grogan and over a period of five years saved $400. With this money he purchased twenty-five two-year-old steers in November 1896. He grazed them with the herd of John William Dunn on the Canadian River near Cheyenne, Oklahoma, and shipped them for $1.50 each to the Kansas City market. That venture, along with his earnings as a farmhand, netted him over $1,000.

Coble decided to stay in the cattle business and moved to the Panhandle^qv in the spring of 1899. There he bought forty-five cattle from Charles Goodnight^qv and ran them on a leased section ten miles north of Clarendon. After this herd doubled during the winter, Coble brought four sections of land on Moore Creek, just west of the Turkey Track Ranch^qv in Hutchinson County. Shortly afterward he made further land purchases. On November 16, 1905, he married Maud Roberts, daughter of James R. Roberts, former foreman of S. Burk Burnett's^qv Four Sixes Ranch.^qv The Cobles, the first couple to be married at Amarillo's new white frame Baptist church, established their home on North Julian Boulevard in Amarillo. They had a son who died young and a daughter, Catherine Elizabeth, who later married a son of James A. Whittenburg.qv In the meantime Coble continued supplementing his Hutchinson County holdings, and in 1916 he bought the original Turkey Track headquarters after the lease on it had expired. At that time he revived the famous Turkey Track brand. In all, he built up a vast ranching empire amounting to 105 sections of choice grazing land divided into thirty-two pastures and stocked with thousands of high-grade cattle. Later he acquired interest in several cotton farms in Hockley County.

He was also among the Panhandle ranchers who profited greatly from the oil boom of the 1920s. In 1918 the geologists Scott and Alba Heywoodqv explored the Turkey Track lands and found that they had oil potential. Subsequently, the Coble-Heywood Oil Company was organized with $75,000 capital. Coble served as president and Scott Heywood as general manager of the syndicate, which leased 10,000 acres of Turkey Track land and was among the first to pay a dividend. Phillips Petroleum drilled thirty consecutive producing wells on Coble's properties. Coble later formed the Coble-Whittenburg Oil Company with his in-laws and let out contracts for wells in the south Hutchinson County oil pool.

Coble was a member of the First Baptist Church in Amarillo and president of the Texas and Southwestern Cattle Raisers Associationqv from 1934 to 1936. He was also a benefactor of the Panhandle-Plains Historical Societyqv and supported that organization's museum in Canyon. In December 1938 Coble's wife died from injuries sustained in an automobile accident. He married Gladys Marion Martin on September 18, 1952, and moved into a house on Crockett Street in Amarillo. He died on June 13, 1958, and was buried in Llano Cemetery, Amarillo. His Turkey Track Ranch became part of the Whittenburg family's ranching empire.

BIBLIOGRAPHY: Hutchinson County Historical Commission, *History of Hutchinson County, Texas* (Dallas: Taylor, 1980). F. Stanley [Stanley F. L. Crocchiola], *The Early Days of the Oil Industry in the Texas Panhandle, 1919–1929* (Borger, Texas: Hess, 1973).

H. Allen Anderson

COBOLINI, LOUIS (1845–1928). Louis Cobolini, "father of the port at Brownsville," was born on December 13, 1845, in Trieste, Italy, then a part of the Austrian Empire. As a young man he fought under Giuseppe Garibaldi for Italian independence and unification, and as a result he could not return to his home, which remained under Austrian control. Cobolini immigrated to Galveston, Texas, in the mid-1860s. He began as a fish and fruit peddler but soon acquired a small fishing schooner and became a commercial fisherman. He joined the Screwmen's Benevolent Associationqv in December 1882, supported its strike in 1885, and at one time served as its vice president. He held both local and state offices in the Knights of Labor and in the Texas State Federation of Labor.qqv In 1894 Governor James Stephen Hoggqv appointed him state delegate to the National Farmers' Congress.

In the 1870s and 1880s Cobolini helped secure a federal project for a deepwater channel and port at Galveston. As he transferred his growing fishing business westward along the Texas coast, he helped to develop ports at Port Lavaca, Rockport, Aransas Pass, and Corpus Christi. In 1907 he moved his fishing operations to Port Isabel and settled in Brownsville. He served as Brownsville city alderman from 1910 to 1912 and as city commissioner in 1921–22. He was a strong advocate of municipally owned utilities and a nationally known lecturer on the cause of labor and the importance of seaport development.

By 1910, as secretary of the Brownsville Chamber of Commerce, Cobolini championed the more ambitious plan of a deepwater port for Brownsville itself. He insisted upon a major port and channel facility capable of handling ships drawing thirty feet of water. In 1911, with others, he helped organize the Brownsville Waterways Association, which employed him for both technical and political promotion of the Brownsville port project and sought federal funds through United States congressman John Nance Garner.qv In 1927 the Cameron County Commissioners Court also employed Cobolini to promote the project. Cobolini was married to Elizabeth Grupe; they had two sons. While conducting army engineers on a field trip over the proposed channel site in mid-February 1928, he became ill with pneumonia and died on February 27, 1928. A few months later Congress approved the Brownsville deepwater port project, and on May 14–16, 1936, Cobolini's granddaughter served as "Miss Port of Brownsville" for the port opening.

BIBLIOGRAPHY: Brownsville *Herald*, May 10, 1936. Ellis A. Davis and Edwin H. Grobe, comps., *The New Encyclopedia of Texas*, 4 vols., 1929?. Frank Cushman Pierce, *Texas' Last Frontier: A Brief History of the Lower Rio Grande Valley* (Menasha, Wisconsin: Banta, 1917; rpt., Brownsville: Rio Grande Valley Historical Society, 1962). James B. Wells Papers, Barker Texas History Center, University of Texas at Austin.

Edgar P. Sneed

COBURN, JAMES M. (?–?). James M. Coburn was the founder of the Hansford Land and Cattle Company, the Scottish syndicate that purchased the Turkey Track Ranchqv from C. S. Word and Jack Snider in 1882 and added to it the holdings of W. E. Anderson and T. S. Bugbeeqv in Hutchinson County. After emigrating from his native Scotland, he had established himself as a banker in Kansas City. He returned briefly to Scotland and organized the Hansford company to profit from the "Beef Bonanza." On acquiring the Turkey Track lands, company officials elected Coburn secretary and appointed A. H. Johnson general manager. In 1883, after Johnson was killed by lightning, Coburn appointed Thomas Logan Coffee range foreman and assumed the general managerial duties himself. Friction between the two men developed after Coffee apparently accumulated several head of cattle of his own, which he had allowed to run on the Turkey Track range. When Coburn tried to discharge Coffee, several cowhands stood by the foreman and sought to intimidate the Scotsman. Such lack of respect on the part of ranch employees led Coburn to hire Caleb B. (Cape) Willinghamqv as supervisor and maintain Kansas City as his home base. One Panhandle settler later recalled that Coburn was "a nervous, fractious man . . . scared of his own shadow." Apparently Willingham also served as Coburn's bodyguard and hired gun.

Coburn continued to make occasional visits to the Panhandle.qv He encouraged William (Billy) Dixonqv to take up a claim on three sections of Turkey Track land on Bent's Creek near the Adobe Walls site and operate the ranch store and post office. During the summers Coburn brought his wife and children, including several from a previous marriage, to the ranch. One summer one of the Coburn children was taken ill and died almost immediately. Since the Canadian River was up and the local minister could not get across, Coburn himself conducted the Episcopal burial service at the Turkey Track headquarters, with only the ranchhands and the Dixon family in attendance. When the river subsided, the body was shipped to Kansas City for interment in the family burial plot.

After Willingham moved to the Hansford company's ranch in New Mexico in 1893, Coburn began experiencing more troubles with the Panhandle spread. Company officials were concerned about increasing cattle thefts, and Coburn lacked the loyalty he needed from his employees to control them. His problems increased in 1897 after the Texas legislature passed the Four-Section Act,qv which he opposed. Coburn's quarrels with incoming nestersqv led to several lawsuits in Hutchinson County. He soon sold his Panhandle interests. After Willingham's resignation from the Hansford company in 1903, Coburn ran the New Mexico ranch himself for a few years, with J. M. Sanford and Cal Merchant assisting him. By 1915 the company had closed out its holdings altogether, and Coburn subsequently disappeared from the Texas ranching scene.

BIBLIOGRAPHY: Laura V. Hamner, *Short Grass and Longhorns* (Norman: University of Oklahoma Press, 1943). John L. McCarty, *Adobe Walls Bride* (San Antonio: Naylor, 1955).
H. Allen Anderson

COCHINO BAYOU. Cochino Bayou, also known as Coching Bayou and as Hog Creek, rises two miles southwest of Tadmor in southeastern Houston County (at 31°24′ N, 95°11′ W) and runs southeast for sixteen miles to its mouth on the Neches River, five miles north of Vair in northern Trinity County (at 31°22′ N, 95°10′ W). The surrounding flat terrain is surfaced by clay and sandy loams that support water-tolerant hardwoods, conifers, and grasses.

COCHRAN, ARCHELAUS M. (1839–1910). Archelaus (Arch) M. Cochran, physician and politician, was born to William M. and Nancy Jane (Hughes) Cochran at Columbia, Tennessee, on December 25, 1839. In the fall of 1843 the family moved to Dallas County, where his father was the first county clerk and his brother John represented the district in the state legislature. Arch was educated in the county's common schools and attended McKenzie College and the University of Louisiana in New Orleans, where he studied medicine. He completed his education about 1861 and returned to Texas to establish a medical practice in Dallas. His professional career was interrupted by the onset of the Civil War,qv and in June 1861 he enlisted in the Confederate Army as a third lieutenant in the Eighth Texas Cavalryqv (Terry's Texas Rangers). He was eventually promoted to captain and served in Texas, Louisiana, and Tennessee. He was captured at Arkansas Post and held at Camp Chase, Ohio, until the end of the war.

After release, Cochran returned to Dallas and reestablished his medical practice. In 1866 he married Laura Knight, who bore one child before her death in 1870. Cochran married Mary A. Collins the following year, and this couple had two children. Cochran was a Republican, a fact that contributed to his appointment to various federal positions in the years after 1870. He served in the state legislature in 1866 and in 1867 was elected to the Dallas City Council. He was elected again in 1872 but resigned his seat in April of the following year. President Rutherford B. Hayes appointed him postmaster of Dallas in 1879; Cochran held this position until 1883, when he was selected internal revenue collector for the Dallas district. He won the Republican gubernatorial nomination in 1886 and campaigned statewide against prohibitionqv in 1887. He also served as Texas commissioner to the 1890 Columbian Exposition. He died in Columbia, Tennessee, on August 4, 1910, while visiting his son there.

BIBLIOGRAPHY: Dallas *Morning News,* August 5, 1910.
Brian Hart

COCHRAN, JAMES (?–1847). James Cochran, pioneer merchant, farmer, and public official, was born in New Hampshire and taught school in various sections of the South before 1825, when he moved to Texas. He settled in San Felipe, where he became a successful merchant. At the approach of the Texas Revolutionqv he sold supplies to the Texas army. In October 1835, for example, the General Councilqv received $100 credit from Cochran with which to forward arms, ammunition, and other necessities to the army. Not long thereafter his store was burned in advance of the arrival of Antonio López de Santa Anna'sqv Mexican forces. In service with the Texas army, Cochran was detailed to assist in the evacuation of settlers during the battle of San Jacintoqv in April 1836. In 1837 he took up residence on a large tract of land at the mouth of Caney Creek on the west bank of the Brazos River, in what is now northeast Austin County. There he prospered in farming and stock raising and established the first mill and cotton gin in that part of the state. The county tax roll of 1838 listed Cochran as the owner of 15,468 acres of land, forty-four cattle, three horses, and ten slaves, an estate valued at more than $20,000. He represented Austin County in the House of the Fourth Congress of the republic, 1839–40, where he served on a committee to erect a monument to Benjamin R. Milam.qv Cochran died in 1847 and was survived by his wife and five children.

BIBLIOGRAPHY: Texas House of Representatives, *Biographical Directory of the Texan Conventions and Congresses, 1832–1845* (Austin: Book Exchange, 1941).
Charles Christopher Jackson

COCHRAN, JOHN HUGHES (1838–1928). John Hughes Cochran, state representative, was born to William M. and Nancy Jane (Hughes) Cochran on June 28, 1838, in Columbia, Tennessee. The family came to Texas in 1843 and settled in what became Dallas County, where William Cochran served as the first county clerk after the organization of the county in 1846. Cochran graduated from McKenzie College in Red River County in 1859. While a student he taught classes to earn money for tuition. Upon graduation he became commander of a company of Texas Rangersqv and in 1860 traveled with this unit to Young County. There he gathered census data and in June of that year married Martha Jane Johnson, a resident of the county; the couple raised six children. At the onset of the Civil Warqv Cochran enlisted as a private in Company C of the Sixth Texas Cavalry. He retired two years later, however, because of ill health and returned to Dallas County.

Almost immediately he was elected tax assessor and collector. He remained in office until 1866, when he declined to seek reelection. In 1873 he was elected as a Democrat to the Fourteenth Legislature. He was reelected to the Fifteenth and Sixteenth legislatures and in the latter was chosen speaker of the House. He returned as a representative in the Twenty-second and Twenty-third legislatures and again won election as speaker during the latter term. In 1887 President Grover Cleveland appointed Cochran postmaster of Dallas, and he remained in this position until Cleveland left office after the presidential election of 1888. Cochran apparently remained in Dallas County until 1894, when he moved to Nolan County and established himself as a farmer and stock raiser. He was elected county judge in 1896 and reelected twice. He refused to seek a fourth term and largely retired from political activity, although he served as an alternate delegate to the Democratic national convention at Baltimore in 1912.

In 1925 the Dallas Historical Societyqv asked Cochran to write a history of the county. *Dallas County* was completed in the spring of 1928 and distributed in November of that year. Cochran died on October 20, 1928, at Sweetwater.

BIBLIOGRAPHY: Dallas *Morning News,* October 21, 1928. *Biographical Encyclopedia of Texas* (New York: Southern, 1880).
Brian Hart

COCHRAN, ROBERT E. (1810–1836). Robert E. Cochran, Alamo defender, was born in New Jersey in 1810. He probably lived in Boston and then in New Orleans before immigrating to Texas in 1835. For a time he conducted business with Ammon Underwood.qv Cochran took part in the siege of Bexarqv and later served in the Alamo garrison as a member of Capt. William R. Carey'sqv artillery company. He died in the battle of the Alamoqv on March 6, 1836. Cochran County is named in his honor.

BIBLIOGRAPHY: Daughters of the American Revolution, *The Alamo Heroes and Their Revolutionary Ancestors* (San Antonio, 1976). Daughters of the Republic of Texas, *Muster Rolls of the Texas Revolution* (Austin, 1986). Bill Groneman, *Alamo Defenders* (Austin: Eakin, 1990).
Bill Groneman

COCHRAN, SAMUEL POYNTZ (1855–1936). Samuel Poyntz Cochran, businessman, was born to John Carr and Samuella Tannehill (Dewees) Cochran on September 11, 1855, at Lexington, Kentucky. He attended elementary school in Cincinnati, Ohio, and high school in Covington, Kentucky, where he graduated as valedictorian of his class in 1873. Although he passed examinations that qualified him to serve as a public school principal, he never took a full-time position as either a principal or a teacher. Instead, he was an occasional substitute teacher, but devoted the majority of his time to the fire-insurance business, which he entered at Cincinnati as an inspector in 1873. In 1874 he joined the J. W. Cochran and Son Insurance Company in Lexington. In 1876 he returned to Covington, where he operated a branch of the company until 1881. Cochran was also deputy United States marshal for the Eastern District of Kentucky from 1878 until 1880. He moved across the Ohio River to Cincinnati for a brief period in 1881 and worked as an agent for the Lancashire and the Phoenix insurance companies.

That year he moved to Dallas, Texas, where the Phoenix Company employed him as an itinerant agent. After three years of traveling the state by stagecoach, Cochran joined the insurance firm of Dargan and Trezevant in Dallas. On January 1, 1884, he became a partner in this company, which four years later became Trezevant and Cochran. When the senior partner retired in 1914, Cochran became the head of the firm, which had become one of the largest independent insurance agencies in the Southwest and served as the representative for ten national companies. He remained in this position until his retirement.

Outside of his business interests, Cochran devoted much of his time to work as a Mason. He became a Freemason in 1880 and joined Dallas Lodge No. 760 upon his arrival. He accumulated many of the group's honors and held many of its elective offices, including that of grand master of Texas Masons. He was instrumental in organizing the Dallas Scottish Rite Cathedral, a home for aged Masons in Dallas, and the Texas Scottish Rite Hospital for Crippled Children. He was also president of the Texas Scottish Rite Educational Association, which raised funds for a women's dormitory at the University of Texas. For these and other activities a $25,000 bronze statue was erected in Cochran's honor on the lawn of the Scottish Rite Cathedral in Dallas in 1920.

Cochran served on the board of directors of a number of Dallas institutions, including the Mutual Building Association (which he served as president from October 14, 1889, until his death), the American Exchange Bank, the United States Bond Mortgage Company, and the State Fair of Texas.qv He was a regent of the University of Texas from 1921 to 1924. He served as president of the Texas Society of the Sons of the American Revolution, 1924–28, and vice president of the national organization, 1927–29.

On July 3, 1883, he married Sue Webb Higgins of Lexington, Kentucky. After she died, Cochran married Regina Urbish of Dallas, in 1934. He was a Democrat and a Christian Scientist. He died at his home in Dallas on February 11, 1936.

BIBLIOGRAPHY: Dallas *Morning News*, February 12, 1936. Frank W. Johnson, *A History of Texas and Texans* (5 vols., ed. E. C. Barker and E. W. Winkler [Chicago and New York: American Historical Society, 1914; rpt. 1916]). *Who Was Who in America*, Vol. 1. *Brian Hart*

COCHRAN, TEXAS. Cochran is on State Highway 159 at the edge of the Raccoon Bend oilfield, nine miles northeast of Bellville in far northeastern Austin County. Settlement on the west bank of the Brazos River in this section of the county began in the early 1820s, but Cochran itself was not founded until about 1850. The town was named for James Cochran,qv original grantee of a large tract of land near what became the Cochran townsite. William Lange established a gin there, and L. T. Henton operated a general store during the community's early development. A post office operated at the community from 1884 until 1908, after which mail was delivered over a rural route from Bellville. A Junior Red Cross chapter was organized at the Cochran school in 1918. In 1933 the town had four businesses and a population estimated at twenty-five. By 1952 its population had increased to an estimated forty, but the number of local businesses had decreased to two. Oilfields had been developed nearby by the 1960s, and the local population had grown to 440 by 1966. By 1972, however, the population had declined to an estimated 116, at which level it remained through 1990. *Charles Christopher Jackson*

COCHRAN COUNTY. Cochran County (B-8), on the southern High Plains, is bordered on the west by New Mexico, on the north by Bailey County, on the east by Hockley County, and on the south by Yoakum County. It was named for Robert Cochran,qv who died at the Alamo. The center point of the county is 33°35′ north latitude and 102°50′ west longitude, some fifty miles west of Lubbock. Cochran County covers 783 square miles of level prairie with elevations varying from 3,500 to 3,800 feet above sea level; loamy or sandy soils predominate. Many small lakes dot the county, including Silver Lake, a small salt lake known to Spanish explorers as Laguna Quemado. Rainfall in the area averages 15.62 inches a year; the average minimum temperature in January is 23° F; the average high in July is 92° F. The growing season lasts 189 days. The county's agricultural income averages $50 million a year, derived from cotton, sorghums, wheat, and cattle; county farmers irrigate more than 110,000 acres. Mesquiteqv and grama grasses provide much of the ground cover.

According to archeological evidence, Indians hunted in the area that is now Cochran County 5,000 to 10,000 years ago. In the 1600s Kiowas and Apaches made war and hunted in the region after acquiring horses from the Spanish. In the 1700s, Comanches of the Quahadi or Antelope band took the area in battle; relying on buffalo huntingqv and raiding of other Indians and whites, they were dominant until the United States Army subdued them in the 1870s. In 1880, a detachment of Texas Rangersqv led by George W. Arringtonqv stopped at Silver Lake on the way from Yellow House Canyonqv to New Mexico in search for the legendary "Lost Lakes."

In 1876 Cochran County was formed by the Texas legislature from land previously assigned to Bexar and Young counties. It was a land of grass, sand hills, mesquite, jackrabbits, coyotes, bison, and pronghorn antelope. Until the 1920s, when farmers began to move into the area, the county's economy was dominated by ranches; the huge XIT Ranchqv controlled much of the land. In 1879 and 1880, the Capitol Reservation was surveyed, and in 1885 its land title passed to the XIT, which covered about 3,000,000 acres of land in the region. In 1887 XIT manager A. G. Boyceqv divided the XIT into seven divisions; Cochran County was within the southernmost division (known as Las Casas Amarillas, or Yellow Houses). The Yellow House division was used as the XIT's breeding range.

The 1890 census does not show any residents in the county, and in 1900 only twenty-five people lived there. In 1901 George Washington Littlefieldqv bought 238,858 acres, including some of Cochran county, for his great ranch; other parts of the county were ranched by C. C. Slaughter.qv The first headquarters of Slaughter's ranch was established in 1898 near the site of present-day Lehman, but was moved a year later to a site two miles southwest of Morton. For all his interest in cattle breeding to produce crossings of Herefords and shorthorns of record size, Slaughter foresaw other economic developments for West Texas. In 1907 he predicted that "the fertile Plains . . . will become the breadbasket of the great Southwest."

Nevertheless, as late as 1920 only fourteen ranches and farms had been established in the county, and only sixty-seven people lived there. During these first years of its existence, the judicial administration of the area was assigned to Hockley and Lubbock counties. A post office was located in the county at Mexline, now a ghost town, from 1903 to 1905. Another post office was established at Edwards in 1905, and named for the county's first storekeeper, Edward P. Kirkland, the postmaster. This post office closed in 1913. Until the 1920s, county residents got their mail from the Yoakum County post office of Bronco.

Cochran County began to grow rapidly after 1921, when Slaughter's heirs dissolved the Slaughter Cattle Company and began to sell its ranchlands to farmers. The area's limited rainfall had helped to deter settlement of the county for many years, but the new farmers tapped into underground water supplies a shallow depths. By 1925, there were fifty-six farms and ranches in Cochran County, which was now experiencing a minor farming boom. By 1930, 285 farms and ranches had been established in the county, and the population had increased to 1,963.

In 1924, after the influx of new farmers had begun, the county was formally organized, and a spirited political struggle ensued between Morton J. Smith, a rancher, and the Slaughter heirs. The Slaughter family, having failed on two earlier attempts to secure rail connections to their ranch, had founded Ligon four miles south of the site of Morton, in hopes that Ligon would become the county seat. Smith, meanwhile, was pushing to have the new town of Morton made county seat. In the 1924 election, Morton received seventy-nine votes to Ligon's twenty and thus became the county seat.

All of the towns presently in the county were established in the 1920s. When the Santa Fe Railroad built into Cochran County from Lubbock in 1925, the towns of Whiteface, Chipley, Lehman, and Bledsoe sprang up, and Ligon was moved four miles south to become Lehman. The railroad made Bledsoe Cochran County's largest town in the 1920s, but its population declined afterward as most of the county residents moved to Morton.

During the 1930s many residents were hurt by the Great Depression,[qv] and the Dust Bowl.[qv] The county had some of the worst sandstorms ever seen; new sand dunes as high as twenty-eight feet were reported. Nevertheless, the number of farms in the area increased to 431 by 1940, and cropland harvested in the county increased from 28,045 acres in 1929 to more than 90,500 acres in 1940. Many farmers in the county were turning to cotton during the 1930s, as land devoted to cotton production increased from about 5,300 acres in 1929 to almost 24,500 acres in 1940. By 1940 sorghum, which became the county's other important crop, was sown on more than 52,000 acres.

The discovery of oil in 1936 also helped to provide jobs and to stabilize the economy during this period. The first producing well in the county was drilled in 1936 at the Duggan ranch, south of Whiteface, and in 1938 Cochran County produced 95,458 barrels. Reflecting this growth during the 1930s, the county's population also increased significantly during this period, rising to 3,735 by 1940. The oil business boomed in Cochran County during World War II;[qv] production was 5,087,237 barrels in 1944. The area's agriculture also continued to grow; by 1947 county farmers worked on 108,000 producing acres, compared with 38,647 acres in 1935. Girlstown, U.S.A.,[qv] was established on Duggan ranchland near Whiteface in 1949, and a Lehman gasoline plant started operations in 1954. As the county economy continued to develop in the 1940s and 1950s, the population grew to 5,928 in 1950 and to 6,417 in 1960. After the 1960s, however, it declined. The population was 5,326 in 1970, 4,825 in 1980, and an estimated 4,377 in 1990.

The decline is largely traceable to the trend toward larger farms and does not necessarily indicate poor economic prospects for the future. Most Cochran County farm families live in Morton and commute to their jobs. Prosperity since the 1960s owes much to the tapping of underground water for irrigation, mostly for cotton raising. By 1986 the county included about 300,000 acres of cropland, 110,000 of which was irrigated. Cattle range comprises almost 191,500 acres of county land, and the county has a feed lot and a horse-meat packery. By the mid-1980s the Santa Fe Railroad had abandoned its tracks in the county.

Oil production has continued to be significant for the local economy since World War II. County wells produced almost 6,902,000 barrels in 1948, almost 7,348,000 barrels in 1956, more than 6,215,000 barrels in 1960, and more than 12,315,000 barrels in 1978. Production dropped in the 1980s before rising slightly again in the early 1990s. In 1990, it was almost 8,266,000 barrels. The cumulative total was more than 428,357,000 barrels by 1991.

State highways 214 (north–south), 114 (east–west), and 125 (east–west) serve the county. The county's communities include Whiteface (1980 population 463) and Bledsoe (125). Morton (1992 estimated population 2,597) is the county's largest town and its seat of government. Cultural events include a rodeo, county fair, and a museum.

BIBLIOGRAPHY: Elvis Eugene Fleming, *Texas' Last Frontier: A History of Cochran County* (Morton, Texas: Cochran County Historical Society, 1965).

John Leffler

COCKE, BARTLETT (1901–1992). Bartlett Cocke, architect, son of Emmett and Bessie Cocke, was born in Floresville, Texas, on October 30, 1901. He grew up in San Antonio, graduated from the University of Texas in 1922, and attended the School of Architecture at MIT. In 1924 he returned to San Antonio and began his apprenticeship as a draftsman with the Kelwood Company. Three years later he opened his own firm in partnership with Marvin Eickenroht, and was an architect for San Pedro Playhouse in 1929. In 1931 he began a sole proprietorship under his name.

During the Great Depression,[qv] as deputy district officer of West Texas of the Historic American Buildings Survey, Cocke produced dozens of detailed measured drawings of pre–Civil War Texas structures for HABS. He subsequently designed houses in San Antonio and surrounding towns, deriving inspiration from vernacular Texas ranchhouses and Greek Revival structures that he had encountered while working for HABS. These attracted widespread attention and were often featured in national architectural periodicals. In 1938, he won his first major public commission, to design a distinctive, efficient, downtown department store for Joske's of Texas on Alamo Plaza in San Antonio. His practice grew to include San Antonio public schools, industrial facilities and warehouses, office buildings, shopping centers, malls, and college and university campuses. He worked as architect for St. Mary's Hall, the Witte Museum,[qqv] the Frost Bank building, and Baptist Memorial Hospital, and he was an architect for North Star Mall. Over the years he worked with various architects, including Anton F. Heisler, Jr., and John Kell, Sr. Joint ventures with architect O'Neil Ford[qv] produced the master plan and all buildings for the campus of Trinity University (1950–81) and buildings for the University of Texas at San Antonio Health Science Center during the 1970s.

Cocke's firm developed a reputation as specialists in construction documents and project management. He was one of the first Texas architects to develop a plan for profit sharing for his employees. He became a member of the American Institute of Architects in 1935 and was elected to fellowship in the institute in 1961. He served as president of the San Antonio chapter of the AIA in 1940 and president of the Texas Society of Architects in 1944–45. He was appointed director of the Texas Board of Architectural Examiners in 1947 and reappointed in 1948 for a term of six years. Upon his retirement from practice in 1981, his firm was reorganized as Chumney, Jones and Kell. He received the Llewelyn W. Pitts Award, the society's highest honor, in 1981. In the 1980s Cocke became the first alumnus to be honored with a professorship in architecture in his name at the University of Texas at Austin.

Cocke married Mildred Hackett in 1925. They had two children. He died in San Antonio on March 17, 1992, and was buried there in Mission Burial Park South.

BIBLIOGRAPHY: *Alcalde* (magazine of the Ex-Students' Association of the University of Texas), February 1948. San Antonio *Express News*, March 19, 20, 1992. *Texas Architect*, November–December 1989.

Stephanie Hetos Cocke

COCKE, JAMES DECATUR (ca. 1815–1843). James Decatur Cocke, soldier and journalist, was born near Richmond, Virginia, about 1815. He was trained as an attorney but never practiced, taking up instead the printer's trade with the Mobile *Morning Chronicle*. He moved to Texas in 1837 with the ambition of starting a newspaper in Houston, and when Mirabeau B. Lamar^{qv} launched his campaign for the presidency in 1837 he sought to sell his press at Velasco to Cocke, an enthusiastic Lamar supporter. Cocke declined, however, stating that the expense of moving the press to Houston would equal its value. Theodore Léger and Algernon P. Thompson^{qqv} took up the project instead and began publication of *The People* in February 1838. Cocke then considered the purchase of a new press in New Orleans or partnership with George Washington Bonnell,^{qv} who also wished to found a paper in Houston and who had a new press on order. Cocke went so far as to issue a prospectus of his new paper, the *Banner of the Lone Star*, in January 1838, but he abandoned the project before the first issue was printed, fearing that it would be a "losing concern." Nevertheless, he remained a staunch supporter of Lamar's militant policy toward Mexico and won the sobriquet "Fighting Cock" for his attacks on Sam Houston's^{qv} administration. Samuel Alexander Roberts^{qv} referred to him as "the Bolingbroke, the kingmaker," of Texas politics.

In the summer of 1839 Cocke was rumored to be planning a newspaper for the new capital, Austin, but he denied the report in the August 15 issue of the Houston *Morning Star*.qv That fall he ran against D. W. Babcock for the post of colonel, First Regiment of the Second Brigade, Texas Militia. Cocke fought as a private at the battle of Plum Creek.^{qv} In August 1842 he was elected to a committee of correspondence to raise funds for the return of the Santa Fe prisoners (*see* TEXAN SANTA FE EXPEDITION). In reaction to the invasion of Texas by Adrián Woll^{qv} in 1842, Cocke raised a company of volunteers on Cypress Creek near Houston and led them, via Richmond and San Felipe, to San Antonio, where, on November 12, he enlisted as a private in Capt. Ewen Cameron's^{qv} company of Col. James R. Cooke's First Regiment, South Western Army, for the Somervell expedition.^{qv} A few days later Cocke transferred to the company of Capt. Gardiner Smith, perhaps because of the presence in that company of fellow editor Michael Cronican.^{qv} Cocke's letter of January 12, 1843, from Matamoros is one of the principal primary documents on the battle of Mier and Texan justification for undertaking the campaign. At Salado Cocke drew the first black bean and said to his friends, "Boys, I told you so; I never failed in my life to draw a prize." To a comrade he then commented, "They only rob me of forty years." Fearing that the Mexicans would strip his body after he was dead, he removed his pants and gave them to a companion whose own clothing was in worse shape. He was shot with the sixteen others who drew black beans on March 25, 1843. His last words were reported to have been "Tell my friends I die with grace." *See also* BLACK BEAN EPISODE.

BIBLIOGRAPHY: Donaly E. Brice, *The Great Comanche Raid* (Austin: Eakin Press, 1987). Thomas J. Green, *Journal of the Texian Expedition Against Mier* (New York: Harper, 1845; rpt., Austin: Steck, 1935). Charles Adams Gulick, Jr., Harriet Smither, et al., eds., *The Papers of Mirabeau Buonaparte Lamar* (6 vols., Austin: Texas State Library, 1920–27; rpt., Austin: Pemberton Press, 1968). Joseph Milton Nance, *Attack and Counterattack: The Texas-Mexican Frontier, 1842* (Austin: University of Texas Press, 1964). Marilyn M. Sibley, *Lone Stars and State Gazettes: Texas Newspapers before the Civil War* (College Station: Texas A&M University Press, 1983). Marilyn M. Sibley, ed., *Samuel H. Walker's Account of the Mier Expedition* (Austin: Texas State Historical Association, 1978).

Thomas W. Cutrer

COCKRELL, ALEXANDER (1820–1858). Alexander Cockrell, businessman and city builder, was born in Kentucky on June 8, 1820, to Joseph and Sally (Hunt) Cockrell. In 1824 the family moved to Johnson County, Missouri, where Cockrell's mother died while he was still a boy. When he was fourteen, he left his father and made his home with the Cherokees, learning their culture and language. He also learned the stock business. Cockrell first came to Texas in 1845 following runaway slaves. After service in the Mexican War^{qv} as a courier under Benjamin McCulloch,^{qv} Cockrell settled in Dallas, engaged in the stock business, and hauled freight with ox teams from Houston, Jefferson, and Shreveport. He married Sarah H. Horton (*see* COCKRELL, SARAH HORTON) on September 9, 1847, and established a claim on 640 acres in the Peters colony,^{qv} situated ten miles west of Dallas on Mountain Creek. On August 7, 1852, he purchased the part of John Neely Bryan's^{qv} homestead including the Dallas townsite and the Trinity River ferry concession.

The Cockrells moved from their White House Ranch to Dallas on March 21, 1853, the date the purchase became effective, and began operating a brick business, one of the variety of Cockrell enterprises that established the main lines of trade and development in Dallas. Assisted by his wife as bookkeeper (Cockrell was unable to read or write), Cockrell operated a sawmill, lumberyard, gristmill, and freighting business. He replaced the toll ferry with the first bridge across the Trinity River, which was authorized in 1854. The bridge and causeway gave the inhabitants of Hord's Ridge (now the Oak Cliff section of Dallas) better access to Dallas. To protect his toll bridge, Cockrell acquired hundreds of acres of land on the river. He built and rented several houses and store buildings and in 1857 began building a large and fine hotel, the St. Nicholas. On April 3, 1858, Cockrell was killed in a gunfight with a city marshal, Andrew M. Moore, leaving his widow with four children. Another child had earlier died in infancy. Cockrell was buried in his wife's private cemetery and later was moved to Greenwood Cemetery in Dallas.

BIBLIOGRAPHY: Frank M. Cockrell, *History of Early Dallas* (1944). Monroe F. Cockrell, *Destiny in Dallas* (1958). Monroe F. Cockrell, *The Early Cockrells in Missouri* (1966). Monroe F. Cockrell, *Sarah Horton Cockrell in Early Dallas* (1961). Dallas *Morning News*, November 24, 1991. *Memorial and Biographical History of Dallas County* (Chicago: Lewis, 1892; rpt., Dallas: Walsworth, 1976). John William Rogers, *The Lusty Texans of Dallas* (New York: Dutton, 1951; enlarged ed. 1960; expanded ed., Dallas: Cokesbury Book Store, 1965).

Joan Jenkins Perez

COCKRELL, JEREMIAH VARDAMAN (1832–1915). Jeremiah Vardaman Cockrell, congressman and judge, son of Joseph and Nancy Cockrell, was born near Warrensburg, Johnson County, Missouri, on May 7, 1832. In 1848 he made a trip to New Mexico, and in 1849 he went overland to California, where he settled at McKinney's Ranch on the Bear River and for two years engaged in mining and merchandising. He returned to Missouri in 1852, married Maranda J. Douglass, and began farming. During the Civil War^{qv} he served as a colonel in the Confederate Army and was wounded so seriously in 1864 that he was not able to engage in active service again. He took his family to Dallas, Texas, where they remained until the close of the war. He farmed in Grayson County until 1874, when he was admitted to the bar. Cockrell was a delegate to Democratic state conventions in 1878 and 1880. He moved to Jones County and in 1885 was appointed district judge of the Thirty-ninth District, a post he held until his election to Congress in 1893. He was elected as a Democrat to the Fifty-third and Fifty-fourth congresses. In 1896 he resumed farming and ranching in Jones County. He died at Abilene, Texas, on March 18, 1915, and was buried in the Masonic cemetery.

BIBLIOGRAPHY: *Biographical Directory of the American Congress*. William S. Speer and John H. Brown, eds., *Encyclopedia of the New West* (Marshall, Texas: United States Biographical Publishing, 1881; rpt., Easley, South Carolina: Southern Historical Press, 1978).

Anne W. Hooker

COCKRELL, SARAH HORTON (1819–1892). Sarah Cockrell, businesswoman and entrepreneur of Dallas, daughter of Enoch and Martha Horton, was born in Virginia on January 13, 1819, and in 1844 moved to Texas with her parents and six brothers and sisters. After her marriage on September 9, 1847, to Alexander Cockrell,^{qv} she lived in Dallas County until 1852, when Alexander purchased the remain-

Sarah Horton Cockrell, Dallas. From the collections of the Dallas Historical Society.

der of the original headright containing the settlement of Dallas. After the family moved into the town, Cockrell started a construction business, established a sawmill and gristmill, and erected a building for rental to business firms. His wife, in addition to her homemaking duties, kept the records, managed the money, and handled the correspondence for the businesses. After Alexander's death in 1858, Sarah took over the family enterprises. In 1859 she opened the St. Nicholas Hotel under her own management. When it burned in the fire that destroyed most of Dallas in 1860, she opened the Dallas Hotel, which later became the St. Charles.

In 1860 she received a charter from the Texas legislature to build an iron suspension bridge across the Trinity River. Construction was delayed by the dislocations of the Civil War,[qv] so that not until 1870 did she find investors for the Dallas Bridge Company, in which she retained the majority of the shares. In accord with social convention she never served on the bridge company's board but left formal membership to her son Frank and son-in-law, Mitchell Gray. In 1872 the bridge opened, linking Dallas with all major roads south and west; building this bridge has been called Sarah Cockrell's most significant contribution to the economic life of Dallas.

In 1872 she purchased a one-third interest in the city's second commercial flour mill, Todd Mills, and in 1875 bought the remaining mill stock. In partnership with her son and son-in-law, she formed S. H. Cockrell and Company at a time when flour milling was Dallas's major industry. During the 1880s she turned her attention to real estate and handled numerous deals each year; she not only purchased but sold, leased, and rented lands to railroads, business firms, churches, individuals, and the city of Dallas. In 1889 she handled fifty-three separate land deals and in both 1890 and 1891 more than twenty. In 1884 she opened the Sarah Cockrell Addition, a residential subdivision, and in 1885 she and her son Frank commissioned construction of the five-story Cockrell Office Building. In 1892 she owned approximately one-fourth of downtown Dallas, plus several thousand acres in Dallas County, as well as smaller properties in Houston, Mineral Wells, and Cleburne.

In 1868 she was a member of the Dallas County Agricultural and Mechanical Association, which then had only four other women among its 100-odd members. A stained glass window in the First Methodist Church at Ross Avenue and Harwood Street in Dallas commemorates her donations in 1870 and 1871 of land and money to the founding of that church. Sarah Cockrell was the mother of five children. She is remembered for her warm hospitality and her generosity to charitable causes and has been called Dallas's first capitalist. At the time of her death, on April 26, 1892, she was lauded for her leadership in Dallas's pioneer days as "a very mother in Israel . . . one of the founders of our city."

BIBLIOGRAPHY: Frank Cockrell, A History of Early Dallas (MS, Barker Texas History Center, University of Texas at Austin). Sarah Horton Cockrell Papers, Barker Texas History Center, University of Texas at Austin. Elizabeth York Enstam, "Opportunity Versus Propriety: The Life and Career of Frontier Matriarch Sarah Horton Cockrell," *Frontiers: A Journal of Women's Studies* 6 (Fall 1981). William L. McDonald, *Dallas Rediscovered: A Photographic Chronicle of Urban Expansion, 1870–1925* (Dallas: Dallas County Historical Society, 1978).

Elizabeth York Enstam

COCKRELL HILL, TEXAS. Cockrell Hill is a mile south of Interstate Highway 30 and downtown Dallas in southwest Dallas County. It was named for either Wesley Cockrell or his cousin Alexander Cockrell,[qv] an early Dallas county pioneer. The Cockrell place was known to travelers on the stage line that ran from Dallas to Fort Belknap and on to El Paso and the west. The settlement developed as an agricultural crossroads and by the late 1800s had a few scattered homes, a small store, and a school. Water became the overriding issue for the town's continued growth. Frank Jester, a local developer, laid out the plan for the modern community of Cockrell Hill in 1911. A first attempt at incorporation in 1925 proved unsuccessful, and the following year a vote to disincorporate was approved. The second incorporation passed on July 21, 1937, when the population was 459. The town grew to a population of 1,246 in 1941. Many of the new residents worked in war-related industries located in the surrounding areas. In 1952 the population was 2,194, and in 1990 it was 3,916.

BIBLIOGRAPHY: Dallas *Morning News*, May 23, 1945, October 10, 1948. Daniel Hardy, *Dallas County Historic Resource Survey* (Dallas: Dallas County Historical Commission, 1982). *Alan S. Mason*

COCO INDIANS. The Coco (Caaucozi, Caocasi, Cascossi, Coke, Quaqui, Quoaque) Indians were Karankawans who lived near the Gulf Coast between the Lavaca and Brazos rivers. They were most frequently linked with the lower Colorado River in the area now covered by Colorado, Wharton, and Matagorda counties. Most writers have identified the Coaque (Caoque) of Álvar Núñez Cabeza de Vaca[qv] with the Coco of the late seventeenth and eighteenth centuries, but this cannot be established beyond question. A. S. Gatschet equated the Biskatronge with the Coco without giving any apparent reason for doing so. The Coco Indians first became known through documents of the La Salle expedition,qv which recorded them under the name Quoaque. Coco was the most commonly used Spanish designation for these people; the Anglo Americans referred to the Coco as Coke. In the latter half of the eighteenth century the Coco were represented at various Spanish missions—San Antonio de Valero at San Antonio, San lldefonso and Nuestra Señora de la Candelaria on the San Gabriel River near the site of future Rockdale, Nuestra Señora del Rosario near the site of modern Goliad, and Nuestra Señora del Refugio qqv near the site that became Refugio. Some of the Coco remained in their ancestral area along the lower Colorado River, where they were encountered by Anglo American colonists in the early nineteenth century. Later these Coco merged with remnants of other Karankawan groups and became known as Karankawas. The Karankawa Indians became extinct by 1858.

BIBLIOGRAPHY: Herbert E. Bolton, "The Founding of the Missions on the San Gabriel River, 1745–1749," *Southwestern Historical Quarterly* 17 (April 1914). Herbert Eugene Bolton, *Texas in the Middle Eighteenth Century* (Berkeley: University of California Press, 1915; rpt., Austin: University of Texas Press, 1970). Herbert Eugene Bolton, ed., *Spanish Exploration in the Southwest, 1542–1706* (New York: Scribner, 1908; rpt., New York: Barnes and Noble, 1959). Albert S. Gatschet, *The Karankawa Indians, the Coast People of Texas* (Cambridge, Massachusetts: Peabody Museum of American Archaeology and Ethnology, 1891). Frederick Webb Hodge, ed., *Handbook of American Indians North of Mexico* (2 vols., Washington: GPO, 1907, 1910; rpt., New York: Pageant, 1959). John Gilmary Shea, *Discovery and Exploration of the Mississippi Valley* (New York: Redfield, 1852).

Thomas N. Campbell

COCOMA INDIANS. The Cocoma (Cocuma) Indians have been identified with the Macocoma, but the identity has yet to be fully demonstrated. When first encountered by the Spanish in 1675, the Cocomas lived in northeastern Coahuila and sometimes ranged northward across the Rio Grande into the southwestern part of the Edwards Plateauqv in Texas. However, in 1693 the Cocomas were also reported as a tribe that lived between Durango, Mexico, and the site of present Presidio, Texas. It is not certain that these two groups were the same people. The Cocomas of Coahuila and Texas were probably the same as the Macocomas of San Francisco Solano Mission (near the site of present Eagle Pass) and its successor, San Antonio de Valero, at San Antonio. J. R. Swanton evidently considered them to be the same, since he listed the Macocoma as a Coahuiltecan band but omitted the Cocomas from his list.

BIBLIOGRAPHY: Herbert Eugene Bolton, *Texas in the Middle Eighteenth Century* (Berkeley: University of California Press, 1915; rpt., Austin: University of Texas Press, 1970). Herbert Eugene Bolton, ed., *Spanish Exploration in the Southwest, 1542–1706* (New York: Scribner, 1908; rpt., New York: Barnes and Noble, 1959). Frederick Webb Hodge, ed., *Handbook of American Indians North of Mexico* (2 vols., Washington: GPO, 1907, 1910; rpt., New York: Pageant, 1959). J. R. Swanton, *Linguistic Material from the Tribes of Southern Texas and Northeastern Mexico* (Washington: Smithsonian Institution, 1940).

Thomas N. Campbell

COCOMEIOJE INDIANS. This name appears only in the records of San Antonio de Valero Mission in San Antonio, and its status remains in doubt. The Cocomeiojes may be the same as the Cocomeguas, a Coahuiltecan band that lived near Cadereyta in north central Nuevo León during the second half of the seventeenth century, but documentary proof of this has not been found.

BIBLIOGRAPHY: Herbert Eugene Bolton, *Texas in the Middle Eighteenth Century: Studies in Spanish Colonial History and Administration* (Berkeley: University of California Press, 1915; rpt., Austin: University of Texas Press, 1970). John R. Swanton, *The Indian Tribes of North America* (Gross Pointe, Michigan: Scholarly Press, 1968).

Thomas N. Campbell

CODMAN, TEXAS. Codman was on the Panhandle and Santa Fe Railway eight miles southwest of Miami in southern Roberts County. When the county was organized in 1889 the community was an election precinct with three legal voters, yet thirty-eight local votes were polled in the election of county officials. Local legend relates that during the legal battle between Miami and Parnell for the position of county seat, a patriotic Codman citizen named Buzzy sent his forty-two sons to vote. A post office was established at Codman in December 1892, discontinued in November 1893, reopened in July 1901, and closed a final time in May 1902. Codman reported a store, two grain elevators, and a population of twenty-five in 1947. Faster local transportation and U.S. Highway 60 later further diminished the community. A 1983 county highway map showed Codman as only a station on the Atchison, Topeka and Santa Fe Railway.

BIBLIOGRAPHY: Arthur Hecht, comp., *Postal History in the Texas Panhandle* (Canyon, Texas: Panhandle–Plains Historical Society, 1960).

H. Allen Anderson

CODY, CLAUDE CARR (1854–1923). Claude Carr Cody, teacher, mathematician, and university administrator, son of Madison Derrell and Fanny (Carr) Cody, was born in Covington, Georgia, on November 5, 1854. In 1875 he received an A.B. degree from Emory College with highest honors, and in 1878 Emory awarded him the A.M. degree. After three years he returned to Emory to receive an honorary doctorate. In 1898 he continued his studies at Cornell University. On January 20, 1879, Cody became professor of mathematics at Southwestern University in Georgetown, Texas. With great distinction he taught and served Southwestern for thirty-seven years. He also served as Southwestern's first dean and occasionally taught large numbers of students. In addition, at various times during his long tenure he was manager of the dormitories, secretary and chairman of the faculty, a member and secretary of the executive committee, treasurer of the university, and librarian. Known in his later years as the "Grand Old Man of Southwestern," he was "a leading candidate for the honor of being the most beloved teacher in the history of the institution" and was twice its acting president. One of Cody's greatest contributions to Southwestern and one of the toughest battles he had to fight was his role in the controversy that arose in 1910–11 over the proposal to move the university to Dallas. Cody's leadership against the proposal was important in keeping Southwestern in Georgetown, and Texas Wesleyan University (later Southern Methodist University) was founded in Dallas instead.

Cody published a biography of Southwestern's first president, *The Life and Labors of Francis Asbury Mood, D.D.* (1886), and, in collaboration with W. H. Bruce, several mathematics textbooks. He was an editor of the *Texas Methodist Historical Quarterly* and helped found the Texas Methodist Historical Association. He was a Democrat and participated in local and statewide religious and civic affairs and county politics.

On December 29, 1883, Cody married Martha R. Hughes, daughter of Judge Thomas Proctor Hughes.qv They had three sons, who, because of their close association with Southwestern, had a lifelong interest in the university. In the 1930s, as president of the board of trustees, Cody's eldest son, C. C. Cody, Jr.,qv played a major role in saving Southwestern from a crippling debt. Cody resigned his deanship in 1915. He died on June 26, 1923, and was buried in the I.O.O.F. Cemetery in Georgetown. The fund for a library at Southwestern was begun immediately after his death, and in 1939 the Cody Memorial Libraryqv was completed and dedicated to his memory.

BIBLIOGRAPHY: Claude Carr Cody Papers, Cody Memorial Library, Southwestern University. Ralph W. Jones, *Southwestern University, 1840–1961* (Austin: Jenkins, 1973). *Who's Who in America*, 1920–21.

Jon D. Swartz

CODY, CLAUDE CARR, JR. (1884–1959). Claude Carr Cody, Jr., otolaryngologist, was born in Georgetown, Texas, on September 9, 1884, the son of Martha R. (Hughes) and Claude Carr Cody.qv The elder Cody was professor of mathematics, dean of the faculty, and first official librarian at Southwestern University. Young Cody attended public schools in Georgetown, obtained both a B.A. (1904) and an M.A. (1905) from Southwestern, and in 1910 received an M.D. from Johns Hopkins University School of Medicine in Baltimore, Maryland. He then spent two years as intern and house surgeon of the First Surgical Division at Bellevue Hospital, New York City. He attended the University of Pennsylvania Graduate Medical School in 1920–21 and took further training in Vienna in 1931.

Cody moved in 1913 to Houston and practiced general medicine until 1917, when he joined the Army Medical Reserve Corps. He was soon called to active duty and served in France, Flanders, and New York before returning to Houston in 1919. After completing his training in Pennsylvania, he served as attending otolaryngologist at various Houston hospitals, including Southern Pacific (1913–17), Baptist (1922–26), Methodist (1924–26), and Jefferson Davis (1922–29). He was certified as a diplomate of the American Board of Otolaryngology in 1927, a year after he became consulting otolaryngologist at Methodist Hospital of Houston.qv In 1943 Cody was appointed professor and head of the Department of Otolaryngology at Baylor University College of Medicine. He served in these last two positions until his retirement in 1955.

He published numerous articles in his field as well as writings on medical education and medical economics. He helped establish the Harris County Medical Library in 1919. During his years as a trustee of the Houston Academy of Medicine (1919–38 and 1943–59) he worked to develop its library as well. Cody was also a trustee of Southwestern University from 1934 to 1959 and received an honorary D.Sc. from that school in 1940. In addition, he helped found the Houston Eye, Ear, and Throat Hospital, served as director of the Houston Chamber of Commerce in 1946, and was a steward of St. Paul's Methodist Church.

Among his many professional offices, Cody was president of the State Medical Association of Texas (later renamed the Texas Medical Associationqv) in 1946–47, the Texas Ophthalmological and Otolaryngological Society (1934), the Houston Academy of Medicine (1929), and the Harris County Medical Society (1923). He also chaired the Section on Laryngology, Otology, and Rhinology for the American Medical Association (1942–44) and served as a member of the Council on Medical Economics for the State Medical Association of Texas from 1936 to 1944, the last five years as its chairman. He was a life fellow of both the American Academy of Ophthalmology and Otolaryngology and the American College of Surgeons.

He married Florra Root in 1917 in Taylor. They had no children. Cody died in Houston on December 30, 1959.

BIBLIOGRAPHY: Reference Folder, Houston Academy of Medicine–Texas Medical Center Library, Harris County Medical Archive. *Texas State Journal of Medicine*, June 1946, February 1960.

Patricia L. Jakobi

CODY, SAMUEL FRANKLIN (1861–1913). Samuel Franklin Cody, frontier cowboy, Wild West showman and playwright, and pioneer of powered flight, was born at Birdville, Texas, on March 6, 1861. His father was a rancher, and at an early age Cody developed the skills necessary to be a cowboy. In 1874 he was separated from his family when their home was destroyed in an Indian attack. Believing his family had been killed, Cody became a wrangler at the Palo Pinto Ranch at the age of thirteen. He soon excelled at shooting, roping, knife throwing, riding, handling horses, buffalo hunting,qv and bronco busting. He worked the Chisholm, the Goodnight-Loving, and the Western trails.qqv Cody eventually became a trail boss on the route from Fort Worth to Dodge City. In 1881 he moved 3,247 cattle from the Panhandleqv to Montana. The same year he was offered the job of taking fifty ponies across the Atlantic to an English buyer named Blackburn-Davis. In England he met and married the buyer's daughter, Lela Davis. They had three sons. The Codys returned to Texas in 1882, but financial problems forced Cody to send his wife, who was expecting their second child, back to England. He worked as a wrangler for a while and eventually spent two years in the Yukon searching unsuccessfully for gold. He returned to Texas and, after working again as a trail boss, joined Adam D. Forpaugh's Wild West Show in 1887. He was billed as "Captain Cody, King of the Cowboys," and his act consisted of demonstrations of his skills as a marksman and cowboy. In 1889 his wife, inspired by the success of Buffalo Bill's Wild West Show, persuaded him to form his own show and bring it to London. The Great Codys, consisting of Cody, his wife, and their two oldest sons, was an immediate success. Along with the usual Wild West attractions, Cody wrote plays and melodramas for the show, including *The Klondyke Nugget, Calamity Jane,* and *Wild Alaska.* Although the Codys made their home in England, they took their show throughout Europe, where they enjoyed great popularity.

As a boy Cody had been taught the art of making kites by a Chinese cook on the trail. From that time on, he was fascinated with the mystery of the sky and the idea of conquering the air. Though kite building had always been a mere pastime, in 1899 Cody began to give serious thought to a purpose for his kites. After much experimenting he developed kites that could attain a height of 14,000 feet, a world record. Cody used these kites in his own meteorological research and was made a fellow of the Royal Meteorological Society for his contributions in this field. He developed a practical man-lifting kite that could ride in winds up to sixty miles per hour and take a man 1,000 feet up. In 1905 he built a set of kites for the British army and became an instructor in the use of the kites. He worked with Maj. Gen. Sir John Capper in developing the first English dirigible, the *Nulli Secundis*. Piloting the airship, Cody flew fifty miles, from Farnborough to the grounds of the Crystal Palace in London. This was not only a milestone in English aviation history but made England much more aviation-conscious.

In 1908 Cody turned his attention to building a heavier-than-air flying machine. After much work, testing, criticism, and skepticism, he designed and built a large aircraft of wood, metal, fabric, and a fifty-horsepower French engine. On the morning of October 16, 1908, near Farnborough, Cody flew it a quarter mile in what is recognized as the first powered sustained flight in Britain. Cody is to England what the Wright brothers are to the United States. Over the next five years, with much experimentation and numerous crashes, he developed additional planes including a biplane, a monoplane, and a seaplane. His biplane, *Cody's Flying Cathedral,* was then the largest plane in existence. He taught himself to pilot all of his planes, and he set a world record of forty miles for a cross-country flight, won the British Empire Michelin Cup contest in 1910, and won both the British and International divisions in the military airplane trials in 1913, in spite of the fact that he wrecked the plane he was planning to fly four weeks before the trials. Undaunted, he built a new plane from the parts of former planes.

Cody continued flying in spite of many accidents, always aware of the dangers and risks involved. In August 1913 his Cathedral VI broke up in the air and crashed. More than 50,000 people attended his funeral and burial in the Military Cemetery southeast of London. Known as the father of British aviation, Cody was awarded the silver medal by the Aeronautical Society for his services to aeronautics. His work stimulated public interest in aviation and led to the formation of the Royal Flying Corps and the Royal Naval Air Service.

BIBLIOGRAPHY: G. A. Broomfield, *Pioneer of the Air: The Life and Times of Colonel S. F. Cody* (Aldershot, Hampshire: Gale and Polden, 1953). Arthur S. G. Lee, *The Flying Cathedral* (London: Methuen, 1965).
Carol E. Williams

CODY, TEXAS. Cody (Cody Station) was near what is now Farm Road 1774, which parallels the Missouri Pacific Railroad, and three miles northwest of Magnolia, ten miles east of Plantersville, and thirteen miles northeast of Waller in far northeastern Waller County. The town was possibly named for Buffalo Bill Cody and had a post office from 1906, when 150 people lived in the area, until 1909. The Cody Sawmill Commissary housed the post office. A one-room school existed there in 1912. Cody was abandoned when the sawmill, after depleting the area's timber supply, closed. The town was probably gone by the time of World War I.qv

BIBLIOGRAPHY: Mildred W. Abshier, et al., *Former Post Offices Of Waller County* (Hempstead, Texas: Waller County Historical Society, 1977).
Paul M. Lucko

CODY MEMORIAL LIBRARY. The library at Southwestern University in Georgetown began with the founding of the school in 1873. Southwestern, a direct descendent of four of the earliest institutions of higher learning in the state, was founded by Francis Asbury Mood,qv who made building a library a high priority of the new school. Mood relied on the largess of fellow Methodists, and by 1876 the university catalogs showed regular donations of books and materials. Some 130 volumes were donated in 1876, including works of biography, history, theology, and English literature.

In 1880 Claude Carr Cody,qv a professor of mathematics, was named university librarian. He continued to build the collection by donations, making frequent and personal appeals to Texas Methodists. In 1885 he reported that Southwestern's library contained 785 volumes. During this time three student literary societies also maintained libraries for the use of their members. The Alamo, San Jacinto, and Alethean societies had together about 1,000 volumes in 1885. These books later were added to the main collection.

From 1892 to 1895 another faculty member, H. S. Hyer, served as librarian. His term is remembered chiefly for the acquisition of the books of Homer S. Thrall,qv a prominent Methodist author, whose books were the largest single gift that the library had received. Because library space was unduly small the old university chapel was refitted as a reading room in 1895. Special committees to deal with library operations were appointed in May 1897. Among their recommendations were a student-use fee for library operations and appropriations for the library.

After 1900 library development was accelerated. Library quarters were established in a new building completed in 1901. Margaret Mood McKennon, daughter of the founder, became the school's first full-time librarian in 1903. The same year also marked the first standing faculty committee for the library. By 1908 the collection contained 16,000 volumes, and the library's hours of operation had been extended to "every hour during school days."

In February 1910 students met to demand a separate library building. This demand led to plans for a three-story building supposedly modeled after the Library of Congress in Washington, but this building was never begun. The Southwestern library was a depository for United States government documents by 1915, when the staff had grown to three permanent employees and several student assistants. By 1935 library holdings had reached over 35,000 volumes and the library had been expanded to four rooms on the third story of the administration building.

In 1939 Cody Memorial Library was built on a lot east of the administration building. The new building, designed by a former student of Southwestern, Cameron Fairchild, consisted of three stories, was completed at a cost of approximately $81,000, and was partially financed by a Work Projects Administrationqv grant to the city. The fund for a library had been begun immediately after the death of Cody in 1923 and amounted to $46,000 at the time the library was built. The work started the last day of 1938, and the library formally opened on November 26, 1939. By the time the building was constructed, the total collection had grown to 54,890 volumes, and the staff included a librarian, an assistant librarian, and student assistants.

In 1966 a two-story, smooth limestone and glass building was constructed and connected to the original building. The older building was refurbished, and the two buildings were air-conditioned. The 1966 construction and renovation was made possible by a gift from the Brown Foundationqv of Houston and gifts from friends of Herman Brown,qv a member of the board of trustees for many years. Nearly 80,000 volumes were in the general collection by the end of 1966, and the staff numbered five, with four full-time librarians. The Edward A. Clark Collection, containing more than 2,400 volumes, was presented to Southwestern in July 1965 and placed in the new Special Collections Room. The Isabel Gaddis collection of the works of J. Frank Dobie,qv another Southwestern alumnus, was presented to the university in 1970 by the Charles N. Prothros of Wichita Falls. Nearly 1,000 Dobie items made up this collection. In 1982, a grant from the Pew Memorial Trust resulted in the computerization of library holdings through AMIGOS Bibliographic Council of Dallas.

By 1984 the size of the general collection had grown to 152,457, with an additional 6,718 titles in the Clark Texana Collection. Other special holdings at that time were the Bewick, Bible, Blake, and Meyer Hymnal collections. The full-time professional staff numbered fourteen, including five professional librarians. In 1988 the Cody Memorial Library became a part of the newly finished A. Frank Smith, Jr., Library Center and ceased to exist as an independent library.

BIBLIOGRAPHY: John Bigley, "Early Library Development at Southwestern University," *Texas Libraries* 45 (Fall 1984). Claude Carr Cody Papers, Cody Memorial Library, Southwestern University. Ralph W. Jones, *Southwestern University, 1840–1861* (Austin: Jenkins, 1973). Texas Library Association, *Handbook of Texas Libraries*, 1–4 (Austin, 1904–35).
John E. Bigley and Jon D. Swartz

COE, PHILIP HADDOX (1800–1852). Philip Haddox Coe, adventurer and soldier, was born in Georgia on January 10, 1800, and moved to Texas in December 1831 from Alabama. He settled in what is now Washington County. In 1834 he led a campaign against Indians from Fort Tenoxtitlán in Robertson's colony.qv In July 1835 he led one of four small companies that marched east to Fort Parker to relieve Capt. Robert M. Coleman.qv From there his company marched to Tehuacana Springs in what is now Limestone County in pursuit of a band of Tawakoni Indians that fled before his troops arrived. His company then spent several weeks in the field exhibiting a show of strength for the benefit of the Indians. Coe became a member of the General Councilqv in 1835, represented Washington County in the Consultation,qv and was appointed a recruiter of volunteers for the Texas army. He assumed command of a ranger force under the direction of Col. John Henry Mooreqv on July 9, 1835. He subsequently served as acting captain of the First Regiment of Volunteers from March 2 until April 10, 1836. He remained in the service of the Republic of Texasqv until June 2, 1836. During the battle of San Jacintoqv he was detailed to guard the baggage near Harrisburg. He received 640 acres of land as a result of his service. He also commanded a foray against an Indian raiding party at Tehuacana Springs in 1842, participated in an expedition against Rafael Vásquez,qv and served as a captain in the Somervell expeditionqv in October 1842. He and his wife, Elizabeth, had five children, born in Washington County. He died on December 14, 1852, at Coe Valley in Gonzales County.

BIBLIOGRAPHY: Worth Stickley Ray, *Austin Colony Pioneers* (Austin: Jenkins, 1949; 2d ed., Austin: Pemberton, 1970). Texas House of Representatives, *Biographical Directory of the Texan Conventions and*

Congresses, 1832–1845 (Austin: Book Exchange, 1941). Vertical Files, Barker Texas History Center, University of Texas at Austin.

James L. Hailey

COE, PHILIP HOUSTON (1839–1871). Philip Houston Coe, gambler, son of Elizabeth (Parker) and Philip Haddox Coe,[qv] was born in Gonzales, Texas, on July 17 or 18, 1839. On March 24, 1862, in Gonzales County he enrolled in William L. Foster's Company, which subsequently became Company D of Peter C. Woods's[qv] Thirty-sixth Texas Cavalry. He served without distinction in several companies and rose to the rank of lieutenant in Capt. William G. Tobin's[qv] Company F of Charles L. Pyron's[qv] Second Texas Cavalry. His service to the Confederacy ended on April 30, 1863. Coe may have later served with Ben Thompson[qv] under Emperor Maximilian in Mexico.

During the Civil War and Reconstruction[qqv] he learned to be a professional gambler, probably in Austin working with Thompson and Thomas Bowles. In late 1869 he was in Brenham, where his sister, Delilah, and her family lived. He met and gambled there with such notorious individuals as James Madison Brown, John Wesley Hardin, and William P. Longley.[qqv] Coe probably left Brenham for Kansas not long after; it was reported that he was in Saline, Kansas, during the summer of 1870. By May 1871 he was again with Ben Thompson, and the pair were partners in the operation of the Bull's Head Saloon in Abilene, Kansas, where James B. (Wild Bill) Hickok was city marshal. Although a number of incidents can be identified as probable causes of hard feelings between the gambler and the lawman, it is almost certain that the real base of their animosity involved a woman. On the night of October 5, 1871, Hickok shot Coe, who had been recklessly shooting in the street. Hickok's deputy was accidentally shot and killed—by the marshal himself—in the confusion. Immediately after the shooting Hickok drove the riotous Texas cowboys out of his town.

Coe lingered in agony for days and finally died on October 9. He was Hickok's last known victim. His body was transported back to Brenham and buried in Prairie Lea Cemetery. The following season the city fathers of Abilene, Kansas, chose peace and order over money and insisted that the Texas drovers take their cattle to other shipping points.

BIBLIOGRAPHY: Chuck Parsons, *Phil Coe, Texas Gambler* (Wolfe City, Texas: Henington, 1984). Joseph G. Rosa, *They Called Him Wild Bill* (Norman: University of Oklahoma Press, 1964; rev. ed. 1974). Floyd Benjamin Streeter, *Ben Thompson* (New York: Fell, 1957). W. M. Walton, *The Life and Adventures of Ben Thompson* (Austin, 1884; facsimile, Austin: Steck, 1956).

Chuck Parsons

COESFIELD, TEXAS. Coesfield is near Horseshoe Bend on the Red River, fifteen miles northeast of Gainesville in Cooke County. The town was given its name by Frank Liedke, a Civil War[qv] veteran, who moved to the area in 1867 and named the town after his hometown in Germany. After the Civil War Coesfield had a number of residents who were veterans that had moved to the area to farm. A post office opened there in 1883, and the town's population grew from twenty-five in 1884 to 150 in 1890. Its post office closed in 1906, and by 1933 the population of Coesfield had declined to eighty-one. By the mid-1980s only a few residents remained there.

BIBLIOGRAPHY: Gainesville *Daily Register*, Centennial Edition, August 30, 1948, A. Morton Smith, *The First 100 Years in Cooke County* (San Antonio: Naylor, 1955).

Robert Wayne McDaniel

COFFEE, AARON (1833–?). Aaron Coffee, Brazoria County planter, was born in Mississippi in 1833. He personally had twenty-five slaves, and the plantation he managed, Halcyon, had 132. In 1860 he owned real property valued at $100,000 and personal property valued at $167,350.

BIBLIOGRAPHY: Abigail Curlee Holbrook, "A Glimpse of Life on Antebellum Slave Plantations in Texas," *Southwestern Historical Quarterly* 76 (April 1973). Ralph A. Wooster, "Wealthy Texans, 1860," *Southwestern Historical Quarterly* 71 (October 1967).

Diana J. Kleiner

COFFEE, HOLLAND (1807–1846). Holland Coffee, Red River trader, the son of Ambrose and Mildred (Moore) Coffee, was born on August 15, 1807, probably in Kentucky. He was orphaned at age eleven and grew up in McMinnville, Tennessee, with an uncle, Jesse Coffee. In 1829 he arrived in Fort Smith, Arkansas, with Silas Cheek Colville,[qv] James Mayberry Randolph, and several others. There he established Coffee, Colville, and Company. He supplied local settlers, Indians, and trapping expeditions, and made contact with Sam Houston,[qv] who was living at the time among the removed Cherokees. In 1833 Coffee conducted a trapping expedition to the upper Red River. Afterward, he established a trading post at the old Pawnee village, probably the old north-bank village of the Taovayas near the site of present Petersburg, Oklahoma. He was a major link in completing the Camp Holmes treaty of August 24, 1835, the first treaty to authorize the relocation of eastern Indians to lands west of the Mississippi.

Coffee moved west to the mouth of Cache Creek, near Taylor, Oklahoma, in early 1836. He was respected by the Indians, became knowledgeable in Indian languages and customs, and ransomed many Indian captives.[qv] In April 1837 he was on Walnut Bayou, near Burneyville, Oklahoma, and by September he had moved across the river to Washita (Preston) Bend. Coffee was accused of aiding Indian depredations through trade—specifically by giving the Indians guns and whiskey in exchange for stolen cattle and horses—and was investigated by the Texas Congress. In the winter of 1837 he visited Houston, where he made satisfactory explanations to the government. On November 16, 1837, President Houston appointed him Indian agent, and on September 2, 1838, Coffee enacted a treaty between the Republic of Texas[qv] and the Kichai, Tawakoni, Waco, and Tawehash Indians at the Shawnee village, near the site of modern Denison. Coffee was elected to the Texas House of Representatives from Fannin County for the 1838–39 session. He married Sophia Suttenfield Aughinbaugh (*see* PORTER, SOPHIA) on January 19, 1839. Thereafter, he dissolved his partnership with Colville and turned to the development of Glen Eden Plantation[qv] in Grayson County. He furnished supplies for the Military Road[qv] expedition of William G. Cooke[qv] in the winter of 1840–41 and participated in framing the Texas Indian treaty of August 24, 1842. He developed the town of Preston near his trading post in 1845 and provided the supplies given to the Indians in the Comanche treaty of 1846.

On October 1, 1846, Coffee became offended over a remark about his wife and attacked Charles Ashton Galloway, a trader from Fort Washita, who stabbed him to death. Coffee had no children. He was entombed in a brick aboveground crypt at Glen Eden; his grave was removed to Preston Cemetery at the time of the impounding of Lake Texoma.

BIBLIOGRAPHY: Grant Foreman, *Pioneer Days in the Early Southwest* (Cleveland: Clark, 1926). Graham Landrum and Allen Smith, *Grayson County* (Fort Worth, 1960; 2d ed., Fort Worth: Historical Publishers, 1967). Audy J. and Glenna P. Middlebrooks, "Holland Coffee of Red River," *Southwestern Historical Quarterly* 69 (October 1965).

Morris L. Britton

COFFEE, TEXAS. Coffee, on Farm Road 69 and the banks of Coffee Creek, eleven miles southeast of Sulphur Springs in southeastern Hopkins County, was settled before 1900. In the mid-1930s it had a church, a school, and a cemetery. After World War II[qv] most of its residents moved away. Its school was consolidated with the Como school district, and by the early 1960s only a cemetery and a few houses remained in the area. In the late 1980s Coffee was a dispersed rural community.

Christopher Long

COFFEE CITY, TEXAS. Coffee City is off State Highway 155 twenty miles southeast of Athens in southeastern Henderson County. The largely residential community developed after the construction of nearby Lake Palestine in the early 1960s. The reported population of Coffee City in 1979 was 178; in 1990 it was 216.   *Christopher Long*

COFFEE CREEK (Hopkins County). Coffee Creek rises just southeast of Como in southeastern Hopkins County (at 33°03′ N, 95°27′ W) and runs southwest for six miles to its mouth on Carroll Creek, just east of the Como oilfield (at 32°59′ N, 95°29′ W). The surrounding flat to rolling terrain is surfaced by clay and sandy loams that support water-tolerant hardwoods, conifers, and grasses.

_____ (Palo Pinto County). Coffee Creek rises just east of State Highway 281 and three miles south of New Salem in southeastern Palo Pinto County (at 32°35′ N, 98°06′ W) and runs north for five miles to its mouth on the Brazos River, a mile north of New Salem (at 32°38′ N, 98°06′ W). It crosses an area of rolling hills surfaced by clay and sandy loams that support scrub brush, mesquite, cacti, and grasses.

COFFEE MILL CREEK. Coffee Mill Creek rises three miles north of Lake Bonham in north central Fannin County (at 33°45′ N, 96°08′ W) and runs east for twelve miles to its mouth on Coffee Mill Lake, in the southwestern corner of the Caddo National Grassland[qv] (at 33°44′ N, 96°00′ W). In the early days of Fannin County the road from the Red River to Bonham crossed the creek near a hole called Diamond Hole. A camper there nailed his coffee mill to a tree, then forgot it the next morning, whereupon Diamond Hole came to be known as Coffee Mill. Coffee Mill Creek crosses flat to rolling terrain surfaced by moderately deep to deep sandy and clay loams and dark, calcareous clays that support mesquite, hardwoods, native grasses, and cacti. For most of the county's history the Coffee Mill Creek area has been used as crop and range land.

BIBLIOGRAPHY: *Fannin County Folks and Facts* (Dallas: Taylor, 1977). Glenn A. Gray, *Gazetteer of Streams of Texas* (Washington: GPO, 1919). Floy Crandall Hodge, *A History of Fannin County* (Hereford, Texas: Pioneer, 1966).

COFFEE MILL CREEK LAKE. Coffee Mill Creek Lake is twelve miles northwest of Honey Grove in Fannin County (at 33°44′ N, 95°58′ W) It is on Coffee Mill Creek, a tributary of Bois d'Arc Creek, which is a tributary to the Red River. The lake was built in 1938 and is owned and operated by the United States Forest Service for recreational purposes. The reservoir has a capacity of 8,000 acre-feet and a surface area of 704 acres at the service spillway crest elevation of 496 feet above mean sea level. The drainage area above the dam is thirty-nine square miles.   *Seth D. Breeding*

COFFEE'S STATION. Coffee's Station, also known as Coffee's Trading Post, was operated by Holland Coffee[qv] and associates and occupied several locations on the Red River from 1834 to 1846. After leading a trapping expedition to the area of the forks of the Red River in early 1833, Coffee established the trading post near the "old Pawnee village." This was probably the abandoned north bank village of the Pani Piques (Taovayas or Wichitas) that Athanase de Mézières[qv] had named San Bernardo, across the river from the site of present Spanish Fort. The post housed thirty men and was surrounded by a picket fence. It was considered to be within the Choctaw Nation. Contacts were conducted out of the post that convened the plains Indians for the Camp Mason treaty negotiations of August 24, 1835, held near the site of present Lexington, Oklahoma.

Mexican agents tried to force evacuation of the post, and in early 1836 it was moved upriver to the mouth of Cache Creek, near the site of present Taylor, Oklahoma. Although later proved to be much in error, Coffee contended that this site was in Texas by virtue of being west of the 100th meridian. Various complaints were made that the post's trade encouraged Indian depredations, and members of the Texas House of Representatives recommended that it be placed under surveillance or even suppressed. By April it was moved downriver and located on Walnut Bayou, near the site of present Burneyville, Oklahoma. Abel Warren[qv] subsequently operated the post (called Warren's Post) at Walnut Bayou from 1836 to 1848 and later returned it to the Cache Creek site. In September of 1937 the post was moved across the river in Washita (Preston) Bend, a site north of modern Pottsboro, Texas. The early locations served the Comanches, Kiowas, Wichitas, Keechis, and Tawakonis primarily.

The last and lowest river location catered more to various eastern refugees and the removed tribes. Ransomed white captives were often brought to the post. In 1839 Coffee's Trading Post became a post office of the Republic of Texas,[qv] called Coffee's Station. After settling in Texas in 1837 Coffee turned his attention to landholdings and agriculture. In 1845 he developed the town of Preston near the site of his post. Thereafter the name Preston was used to designate the area, and the trading post was abandoned after Coffee's death in 1846. The site of Coffee's Post in what became Grayson County was inundated by Lake Texoma in the 1940s. A historical marker commemorating the post is located near the Preston Bend Cemetery, just north of Pottsboro.

BIBLIOGRAPHY: Herbert Eugene Bolton, ed. and trans., *Athanase de Mézières and the Louisiana-Texas Frontier, 1768–1780* (2 vols., Cleveland: Arthur H. Clark, 1914). Grant Foreman, *Pioneer Days in the Early Southwest* (Cleveland: Clark, 1926). Sherrie S. McLeRoy, "The Short Life and Hard Death of Holland Coffee," *True West*, December 1989. Audy J. and Glenna P. Middlebrooks, "Holland Coffee of Red River," *Southwestern Historical Quarterly* 69 (October 1965). Rex Wallace Strickland, "History of Fannin County, Texas, 1836–1843," *Southwestern Historical Quarterly* 33, 34 (April, July 1930). Vertical Files, Barker Texas History Center, University of Texas at Austin.
Morris L. Britton

COFFEEVILLE, TEXAS. Coffeeville is south of State Highway 155 and five miles west of Lake O' the Pines in the pine country of northeastern Upshur County. One account of the origin of the community's name claims that an early traveler spilled green coffee beans along the trail he was following, and the beans took root and grew. Another account explains that when Coffeeville was just a camping area, the smell of brewing coffee established its name. Actually, the community was named after the Coffee family, early settlers in the area. Coffeeville is one of the oldest settlements in East Texas. When Jefferson served as a riverport, Coffeeville was the goal of the first day's journey west from the port. Wagon trains moving west also stopped at Coffeeville for supplies, repairs, and recreation. Between 1845 and 1866 the Coffeeville area was settled by former plantation owners from Southern states. By 1852 a post office was established there. In the 1850s the community had Methodist and Presbyterian churches, three doctors, two dry-goods stores, two grocery stores, a drugstore, a Masonic lodge, an academy, and a large hotel. At its peak Coffeeville included several saloons, a bowling and pool hall, numerous blacksmith shops, and five churches. As late as 1867 the town had one of only four high schools in Upshur County; this school had an enrollment of seventy. During the Civil War[qv] and after, Coffeeville declined. Upon the request of Governor Edward Clark,[qv] the community voluntarily bore the burden of establishing and supporting a training camp for Confederate soldiers. After the war, however, the railroads bypassed Coffeeville, and the town's economy fizzled. Its population was 200 in 1887 and 153 by 1904. Its post office was closed in 1915. By 1936 the population of Coffeeville was down to fifty, and only two stores remained in 1940. Though a population of fifty was still reported in 1990, nothing of Coffeeville remained but a small church building.

BIBLIOGRAPHY: G. H. Baird, *A Brief History of Upshur County* (Gilmer, Texas: Gilmer *Mirror*, 1946). Claude W. Dooley, comp., *Why Stop?* (Odessa: Lone Star Legends, 1978; 2d ed., with Betty Dooley and the Texas Historical Commission, Houston: Lone Star, 1985). Doyal T. Loyd, *A History of Upshur County* (Gilmer, Texas: Gilmer *Mirror*, 1966).
Tommy J. Hicks

COFFEY, RICHARD (1823–1897). Richard (Uncle Rich) Coffey, pioneer rancher, Indian fighter, and teamster in the lower Concho River valley, was born in Georgia on February 14, 1823. He married Sarah Greathouse (Aunt Sallie) of Decatur County, Georgia, on October 5, 1849; the couple had six children. Coffey moved his family to Parker County, Texas, in 1855. While residing there he served in the Texas Rangers[qv] and assisted Capt. Lawrence Sullivan Ross in the rescue of Cynthia Ann Parker[qqv] on December 18, 1860. Coffey moved to Elm Creek, near the site of present Ballinger, Runnels County, in 1862. He and several of his cowboys constructed Picketville, a picket fort known as the first white settlement in Runnels County.

Sometime between 1865 and 1869 Coffey and his family moved to a location near the confluence of the Concho and Colorado rivers. He established the Flat Top Ranch, which extended into Runnels, Concho, and Coleman counties. His house was in Concho County. Reportedly, the Coffeys were the first white family to settle in that county. Coffey became a successful rancher but lost over 1,000 cattle and fifty-four horses to a band of Comanche Indians who attacked a group of Coffey's cattle drivers in 1871. When he filed a claim for his losses, the federal government refused to reimburse him. He rebuilt his herd but never achieved great wealth. He also acquired fame as a teamster and was often attacked by Indians. He and his employees transported salt in ox-drawn wagons from the Pecos River in Crane County for sale to his neighbors. Although he resided in Concho County, he also paid taxes in Coleman County and served on that county's first grand jury. A small settlement, Rich Coffey, Texas, existed briefly on the Coffey properties in Coleman County and had a post office from 1879 to 1882.

Distinguished by his bearskin clothes, buffalo robe and cape, as well as his long hair, the husky Coffey was the inspiration for a minor character in John H. Culp's novel *Born of the Sun* (1959). Coffey was a Baptist and a charter member of Masonic lodges in Brownwood, Coleman, and Paint Rock. He died on February 7, 1897, and was buried in Paint Rock.

BIBLIOGRAPHY: Hazie LeFevre, *Concho County History: 1858–1958* (2 vols., Eden, Texas, 1959). Bishop Powell, "Pioneering in the Concho Country: Rich Coffey," West Texas Historical Association *Year Book* 50 (1974). San Angelo *Standard Times,* May 27, 1973. D. D. Tidwell, "Rich Coffey of the Concho," *Texas Freemason*, November 1971. Vertical Files, Barker Texas History Center, University of Texas at Austin.

Paul M. Lucko

COGGIN BROTHERS. The Coggins were ranchers and developers of Brownwood. Moses J. (Mody) Coggin was born in Davidson County, North Carolina, on January 14, 1824. His brother Samuel Richardson Coggin was born there on February 23, 1831. They were two of nine children of Levi and Frankie (Lambeth) Coggin. The family moved to Tennessee in 1836 and to Mississippi in 1837. In 1851 Moses and Samuel moved to the vicinity of Rusk, Texas, where they established a business hauling freight to Bell County. In 1854 they purchased their first cattle herd and moved to Bell County. After losing about half the herd, they moved to Brown County in 1857. The brothers acquired large landholdings in Brown and Coleman counties and increased their herd. They moved cattle to Home Creek in Coleman County in 1860. In April 1862 Sam and Mody Coggin joined the Confederate Army. James and Frank Stiles, who ranched about four miles from the Coggins, tended the Coggin cattle during the early months of the Civil War.[qv] The Coggins' war tenure was brief, since they left the Confederacy and served in the state militia designed for frontier protection against the Comanches. They engaged in numerous Indian skirmishes. After the war the Coggins continued to be plagued by Indians and white cattle thieves.

When the trailing industry began on a large scale in 1866, the two cattlemen planned to market their own herds at Kansas railroads. By 1870 the firm had also contracted neighbors' cattle for delivery to the railheads. The Coggins sometimes developed and sold an entire herd to one buyer, thus avoiding the long drive. W. Clay Parks, a Coleman County rancher, formed a partnership with the Coggins in 1868. Their combined herds numbered over 25,000 head—a total ranking them among the largest operators in the state. In 1871 the three partners lost 7,000 cattle to Indian depredations, a loss of $175,000. Continued losses in Concho County compelled the Coggins to move back to Brown County to reestablish their herd. During the 1870s they engaged in money-making cattle arrangements with two of the state's most reputable cattlemen—John S. Chisum and Charles Goodnight.[qqv] In 1878 Coggin cattle also ranged near the Tongue River in southwestern Motley County and later in Dickens, Runnels, and Mitchell counties.

These cowmen, early advocates of herd improvement, sought constantly to upgrade their stock. The brothers constructed fences to allow the improvement of their herds more easily. They found themselves involved in the fence-cutting wars of the 1880s in Brown and Coleman counties (*see* FENCE CUTTING). Though cattlemen first, the Coggin brothers found farming profitable and raised wheat on their acreage along Clear Creek in west central Brown County. In 1888 they moved their Three Diamond Ranch to Terlingua Creek in Brewster County. There Frank Collinson served as ranch foreman. Although the venture was profitable, the Coggins left the Big Bend country in 1895 and leased land in Collingsworth, Wheeler, Donley, Gray, and King counties. In the early 1890s they pastured cattle in Indian Territory.

Sam and Mody Coggin never retired from the ranching business. They had ranched over much of Texas and what is now New Mexico and Oklahoma. Coggin cattle had grazed the Cross Timbers, the Concho country, the Panhandle,[qv] the Big Bend, and Indian Territory, as well as parts of Kansas, Colorado, and Montana. After 1903 the brothers largely confined their ranching to Brown County. They operated their home ranch in the southwestern part of that county and by 1899 had added the 4,400-acre Wright Ranch to their holdings. By 1902 their Grape Creek Ranch along the Colorado River in Runnels, Concho, and Coleman counties had expanded to nearly 20,000 acres. Fort Worth served as their principal market site during those years.

The first stone business house constructed in Brownwood was built by the Coggins in 1875 at a cost of $13,000. On March 31, 1881, the Coggin brothers established the banking firm of Coggin Brothers and Company. They became partners in a successful mercantile business in 1882. The Coggins were among the principal organizers of the Brownwood Roller Flouring Mills in 1885. On December 12, 1901, the Coggins and Henry Ford entered a partnership with James M. Ingle of Abilene, Texas, to form the Ingle Mining Company in Boise County, Idaho. The principal mineral produced was quartz.

Coggin Academy, established by the brothers on Coggin land in the 1870s, was one of the earliest schools in Brownwood. Later, this school became a part of the public school system and was known as Coggin Ward School. The brothers, generous supporters of the Cumberland Presbyterian Church, donated the site where Daniel Baker College was built in 1890. A tract of Coggin land for use as a city park was a gift to the city; the park still bears the name Coggin. Sam Coggin became the largest contributor to the fund established to secure the Carnegie Library for Brownwood (*see* CARNEGIE LIBRARIES). He also helped entice Santa Fe Railroad officials to build track toward Brownwood by donating subsidy funds to the railroad. Mody never married. He lived in Brownwood with a widowed sister and died about 1902. Samuel married the widow of E. L. Smith, the daughter of B. B. Lightfoot of Johnson County, on January 3, 1884. He died on October 1, 1910, and was buried in Brownwood. Folklorist Mody Coggin Boatright[qv] was a grandnephew of the Coggin brothers.

BIBLIOGRAPHY: Frank Collinson, *Life in the Saddle*, ed. Mary Whatley Clarke (Norman: University of Oklahoma Press, 1963). James Cox,

Historical and Biographical Record of the Cattle Industry (2 vols., St. Louis: Woodward and Tiernan Printing, 1894, 1895; rpt., with an introduction by J. Frank Dobie, New York: Antiquarian, 1959). Thomas Robert Havins, *Something about Brown: A History of Brown County, Texas* (Brownwood, Texas: Banner Printing, 1958). Buckley B. Paddock, *History of Central and Western Texas* (2 vols., Chicago: Lewis, 1911). Vertical File, Southwest Collection, Texas Tech University.

William Shive

COHEN, HENRY (1863–1952). Henry Cohen, rabbi, the son of David and Josephine C. Cohen, was born in London, England, on April 7, 1863. He attended a London Jewish boarding school and from 1878 to 1881 worked with the Board of Guardians, Britain's principal Jewish welfare agency. He studied at Jews' Hospital and Jews' College but did not graduate. In 1880 he traveled to Capetown Colony, South Africa, where he served as an interpreter for the British government. He returned home in 1883 and graduated from college in 1884, when he was ordained a rabbi. Cohen assumed his first assignment in Kingston, Jamaica, where Sephardic Jews composed a significant portion of the congregation. There he began to preach and develop a reform philosophy. In 1885 he became a rabbi at Woodville, Mississippi, where he taught romance languages at the female seminary, wrote poetry, and developed a strong community. In 1888 he moved to Galveston, Texas, as rabbi for Temple B'nai Israel, then comprising 175 families. In 1889 he married Mollie Levy; they had two children.

After the Galveston hurricane of 1900 qv Cohen served as a member of the Central Relief Committee, which kept law and order with the help of shotguns and ministered to people of all religions. He became nationally known for his work. He helped immigrants who arrived at the port of Galveston to find homes in less populated areas and families in the New York slums to move to various regions of the South and Midwest. He helped to establish Galveston's Jewish Immigrant Information Bureau in 1907 and later distributed relief for Mexican immigrants.

During World War I qv Cohen served as a lieutenant of the American Expeditionary Force in France and was responsible for getting Congress to provide Jewish naval chaplains. During the 1920s he battled the Ku Klux Klan, qv and in 1926 Governor Dan Moody qv appointed him to the Texas Prison Board (*see* PRISON SYSTEM). Cohen won statewide recognition as a prison reformer advocating segregation of hardened criminals from first offenders, better medical facilities, and vocational training, recommendations that were later adopted. Though he considered Jews to have only the citizenship of the country where they lived and joined the American Council for Judaism, he reacted to the restriction of immigration with efforts to build Jewish settlements in Palestine and support for the United Jewish Appeal.

In 1924 Cohen received an honorary doctor of Hebrew law degree from Hebrew Union College, in 1939 an honorary doctor of divinity from the Jewish Institute of Religion, and in 1948 an honorary doctorate from Texas Christian University. A recognized authority on the Talmud who was proficient in over ten languages, Cohen wrote *Talmudic Sayings* (1894) and did a study for the American Jewish Historical Society; published a number of monographs, including *Settlement of the Jews in Texas* (1894), *Henry Castro, Pioneer and Colonist* (1896), *The Galveston Immigration Movement, 1907–1910* (1910); and coauthored *One Hundred Years of Jewry in Texas* (1936?). In the 1890s he wrote articles for the *Texas Journal of Education,* along with translations and poems.

He was a member of the advisory board of Hebrew Union College and the Jewish Publication Society, president of the Texas Historical Society of Galveston, advisory chairman of the Lasker Home for Homeless Children, president of Seamen's Bethel, member of the Executive Council of the Central Conference of American Rabbis, founder and president of the Galveston Open Forum, deputy member of the Council of the Jewish Agency, twenty-year director of the Galveston Community Chest, and one of seven charter members of the Galveston Equal Suffrage Association. After an injury Cohen retired in September 1949 but continued to serve his congregation as rabbi emeritus. He died on June 12, 1952. His papers and library are housed at the Barker Texas History Center, qv University of Texas at Austin.

Henry Cohen, with his wife, Mollie Levy Cohen, and their children, Ruth and Henry. Galveston, after 1889. Courtesy Temple B'nai Israel Archives, Galveston. Photograph courtesy ITC.

BIBLIOGRAPHY: Henry Cohen Papers, Barker Texas History Center, University of Texas at Austin. A. Stanley Dreyfus, *Henry Cohen: Messenger of the Lord* (New York: Bloch, 1963). Houston *Post,* June 13, 1952. David G. McComb, *Galveston: A History* (Austin: University of Texas Press, 1986). Anne Nathan and Harry I. Cohen, *The Man Who Stayed in Texas* (New York: Whittlesey, 1941). New York *Times,* June 13, 1952. Ruthe Winegarten and Cathy Schechter, *Deep in the Heart: The Lives and Legends of Texas Jews* (Austin: Eakin Press, 1990).

James C. Martin

COHEN, ROBERT I. (1856–1934). Robert I. Cohen, merchant, was born in 1856 and reared in London, England. At age thirteen he left school and began working in his father's art and antique shop. Three years later, in 1872, he left London and immigrated to the United States through Boston. He joined a mercantile firm there and traveled throughout the United States and Canada for several mercantile firms over the next five years. In 1877 he arrived in Galveston, where he worked for merchants Levy and Weiss for four years before starting his own business. In his first business Cohen formed a partnership, Cohen and Schram. A year later the firm became Levy and Cohen, and subsequently Cohen and Michael. In 1889 Cohen founded Robert I. Cohen, a men's clothing store. He became the first Galveston merchant to branch into new techniques of selling, including advertising and window displays. He organized Galveston's first retail merchants' organization and added new merchandise in his own store, which eventually became a leading department store. In 1917 he purchased with his son, George S., the Foley Brothers Dry Goods store of Houston, which became one of the largest department stores in the South and Southwest, with branches in several major Texas cities. In 1919 Cohen became secretary and treasurer of the Houston Mill and Elevator Company; he eventually became president. He was treasurer of the Hebrew Benevolent Society and of the United Charities of Galveston. He was president of Congregation B'nai Israel for thirty years. Cohen married Agnes Lord in 1882; they had three children. He died on October 15, 1934, and was buried in the Hebrew Benevolent Association Cemetery.

BIBLIOGRAPHY: Galveston *Daily News,* April 26, 1932, October 16, 1934.
Natalie Ornish

COHEN, WILBUR JOSEPH (1913–1987). Wilbur Joseph Cohen, secretary of health, education, and welfare and university professor, was born in Milwaukee, Wisconsin, on June 10, 1913, the son of Aaron and Bessie (Rubenstein) Cohen. He married Eloise Bittel on April 8, 1938, and they became the parents of three children. He earned a bachelor's degree in economics from the University of Wisconsin in 1934. Cohen was on the Committee for Economic Security in 1934 and helped to draft the original Social Security Act. He began working for the Social Security Administration when it was established in 1935. By 1953 he had attained the position of director of the division of research and statistics. He left the agency in 1956 to become professor of public-welfare administration at the University of Michigan. From 1969 to 1980 he was professor of education at Michigan, where he also served also as dean of education from 1969 to 1978. He went to the University of Texas at Austin in 1980 as a professor for the Lyndon B. Johnson School of Public Affairs (*see* LYNDON BAINES JOHNSON LIBRARY).

In addition to his academic activities Cohen served as a consultant on aging to the United States Senate Committee on Labor and Public Welfare in 1956–57 and again in 1959. In 1960 President John F. Kennedy appointed him chairman of the President's Task Force on Health and Social Security, which made recommendations on Medicare, Social Security, and unemployment insurance. Cohen was a delegate to the General Assembly of the International Social Security Association in Turkey in 1961 and in the United States in 1964. He served as assistant secretary of the Department of Health, Education, and Welfare from 1961 to 1965, as undersecretary from 1965 to 1968, and as secretary from 1968 to 1969. He continued his work for Social Security outside of government by serving as cochairman of Save our Security from 1979 until his death. Cohen wrote *Retirement Policies in Social Security* (1957). He coauthored *Social Security: Programs, Problems and Policies* (with William Haber, 1960), *Social Security: Universal or Selective* (with Milton Friedman, 1972), and *Demographic Dynamics in America* (with Charles F. Westoff, 1977). He was also editor of *The New Deal: Fifty Years After* (1984) and *The Roosevelt New Deal* (1986).

Because of his many years of work with the Social Security agency and his later efforts to protect both Social Security and the Medicare program, Cohen has been called the "father of Social Security" and the "father of Medicare." He was the recipient of numerous awards, including a distinguished service award from HEW (1956), the Bronfman Public Health Prize (1967), the Rockefeller Public Service Award (1967), the Forand Award from the National Council of Senior Citizens (1969), and at least fifteen honorary degrees. He was a member of the American Public Welfare Association, the National Conference on Social Welfare, the Council on Social Work Education, the National Association of Social Workers, and the American Public Health Association.

He died on May 17, 1987, while in Seoul, South Korea, to attend an academic symposium on the cross-cultural aspects of aging. Memorial services were held in Ann Arbor, Michigan, Washington, D.C., and Austin, Texas. In August 1987 the federal government renamed the Health and Human Services North Annex in Cohen's honor, and in April 1988 the Wilbur J. Cohen Professorship in Health and Social Policy was established at the LBJ School of Public Affairs.

BIBLIOGRAPHY: Austin *American-Statesman,* May 18, 1987. Vertical Files, Barker Texas History Center, University of Texas at Austin. *Who Was Who in America,* Vol. 9 .
Vivian Elizabeth Smyrl

COHRON, LENORE (1900–?). Lenore Cohron (later known as Leonora Corona), operatic soprano, was born in Dallas on October 14, 1900, the daughter of Judge Cicero F. and Annie J. Cohron. She exhibited an interest in singing and acting as a child, but spent most of her youth studying piano with her mother, who remained her mentor and close companion throughout her career. Lenore was considered a child prodigy and gave solo recitals in Dallas. She attended Oak Cliff High School in Dallas before her family moved to Seattle. While living on the West Coast as a teenager, she became increasingly drawn to singing after hearing the Chicago Grand Opera and the Scotti Opera Company perform. These experiences inspired her to write a brief opera entitled "The Egyptian Tragedy," which was performed in Seattle. With some encouragement from prominent opera performers of the time, she determined to change her emphasis from piano to opera. She studied voice in New York and Italy and made her operatic debut around 1924 in Naples, where she changed her name to Leonora Corona.

Her career in Italy included singing five operas under Tullio Serafin, a future conductor at the Metropolitan Opera, and performing at La Scala in Milan. She sang in more than twenty-five European theaters before signing a contract with the Bracale Opera Company and touring in Havana and Puerto Rico. She signed a long-term contract with the Metropolitan Opera in 1927 and made her debut there in November of that year in the role of Leonora in Verdi's *Il Trovatore.*

Corona sang at the Met for eight seasons, performing in twelve operas during this time. Known particularly for her performances in Italian operas, she sang the leading roles in *Tosca, Aïda,* and *Don Giovanni.* During these years she also performed at Carnegie Hall and at the Opéra Comique in Paris. Critics praised both her vocal and dramatic powers and her picturesque beauty. Her tenure with the Met overlapped with that of two other Texans, Etheldreda Aves[qv] of Galveston and Rafaelo Diaz of San Antonio, and followed the career of Texan Lillian Eubank. Throughout this time Corona maintained ties to her hometown by returning to Dallas occasionally for concerts and other special events.

After her career with the Met concluded in 1935, she continued to perform professionally. She sang with such regional opera companies as the San Carlo Opera of Chicago, and presented recitals at both Town Hall and Carnegie Hall in New York. She appeared in a performance of *Cynthia Parker* at North Texas State Teachers College (now the University of North Texas) in Denton in 1939. Throughout her career she encouraged Americans to take a greater interest in opera. Despite her fame as a singer, virtually no information is available on Leonora Corona after the late 1930s. No obituary for her appeared in Dallas or New York papers, and it is not certain that she remained in this country in her later life.

BIBLIOGRAPHY: Dallas *Morning News,* April 29, May 2, 1928, June 25, 1932, April 7, 1933. Files, Library and Museum of the Performing Arts, Lincoln Center, New York Public Library. New York *Times,* November 16, 25, 1927, October 6, 1937. Vertical Files, Barker Texas History Center, University of Texas at Austin. *Debbie Mauldin Cottrell*

COIT, DANIEL PIERCE (?–1846?). Daniel Pierce Coit, judge and congressman, was born in Vermont. He had moved to Texas by 1835 and settled on a league at Tarquenton's Prairie in what would later become northern Liberty County. He was elected chief justice of Liberty County in 1836 and also served as president of the county board of land commissioners. He was appointed to guard Mexican officers imprisoned at Liberty from October 10, 1836, to January 6, 1837. He acted as vice president of a local organization that celebrated the first anniversary of the battle of San Jacinto.[qv] He was elected secretary of the Liberty township in 1837 and represented the county at the Fourth Congress of the republic from November 1839 to February 1840. Coit had married Elizabeth Hardin by 1835. He had three daughters, all born in Texas. Tax rolls indicate that he owned two town lots and twelve workhorses in 1840 and had title to over 8,000 acres of land. He had apparently died by 1846; his widow survived two subsequent husbands.

BIBLIOGRAPHY: Texas House of Representatives, *Biographical Directory of the Texan Conventions and Congresses, 1832–1845* (Austin: Book

Exchange, 1941). Gifford E. White, ed., *The 1840 Census of the Republic of Texas* (Austin: Pemberton, 1966; 2d ed., Vol. 2 of *1840 Citizens of Texas*, Austin, 1984).
Robert Wooster

COIT, TEXAS. Coit is on Farm Road 339 six miles northwest of Kosse in southwestern Limestone County. The site, at the center of a large farming area between Rocky Creek and the Little Brazos River, was settled by Ben Eaton, who set up a horse-powered gristmill there about 1848. A local post office was established in 1898 with William J. McAllister as postmaster, and W. J. Steele ran a gin. By 1871 the Houston and Texas Central Railway had been constructed through the area and had attracted more settlers. In 1900 B. B. Brooks opened a general store. The post office closed in 1905, however, and between 1910 and 1933 Coit's population rose from ten to only fifteen. In 1946 the community reported fifteen dwellings, one school, two churches, and two businesses, but its reported population had not changed. A single store existed at the townsite in 1955, and population estimates were unavailable after 1966, when Coit had eight buildings, Fairview Church, Clifton Cemetery, and three oil wells. After 1970 a church, the Clifton and Gunter cemeteries, and one business remained near the Coit oilfield.

BIBLIOGRAPHY: Ray A. Walter, *A History of Limestone County* (Austin: Von Boeckmann-Jones, 1959).
Holly Marshall

COKE, RICHARD (1829–1897). Richard Coke, Texas governor and United States senator, son of John and Eliza (Hankins) Coke, was born near Williamsburg, Virginia, on March 13, 1829. He entered William and Mary College in 1843 and in July 1848 was awarded a diploma in civil law. In 1850 he moved to Waco, then only a shantytown on the Texas frontier, where he soon earned a reputation as an able lawyer in both civil and criminal cases. In 1852 he married Mary Evans Horne of Waco, who was only fifteen years old. They had two daughters who died in infancy, and two sons, both of whom died before the age of thirty.

In 1859 Coke was appointed by Gov. Hardin R. Runnels[qv] to a commission that decided that Comanche Indians on the Brazos Indian Reservation[qv] should be removed from Texas. In 1861 Coke was a delegate to the Secession Convention[qv] in Austin and voted for secession.[qv] The next year he raised a company that became part of Joseph W. Speight's[qv] Fifteenth Texas Infantry and, as captain, served throughout the Civil War,[qv] except for a sixty-day leave in 1864. He was wounded at Bayou Bourbeau (Muddy Creek), near Opelousas, Louisiana, on November 3, 1863. In September 1865 he was appointed judge of the Nineteenth Judicial District by Gov. A. J. Hamilton,[qv] who valued Coke's integrity in spite of their political differences. Coke was elected associate justice of the state Supreme Court in 1866 but was removed a year later by Philip Henry Sheridan,[qv] the military commander. Coke won the Democratic nomination for governor in 1873 and, in a bitter and sometimes violent election, defeated Governor Edmund J. Davis,[qv] the Republican candidate, by a vote of 85,549 to 42,663. He took office in January 1874 in spite of Davis's resistance and an attempt of the Texas Supreme Court to nullify the election by its decision in the case *Ex parte Rodríguez*.[qv]

Governor Coke tried to restore financial order by cutting expenditures for public printing and the state asylums, but the cost of securing the safety of the Mexican border and combatting Comanche and Kiowa Indians on the western frontier offset such reductions. On one occasion he ignored threats of physical violence when he vetoed a popular bill for a subsidy to the International–Great Northern Railroad. The new governor was burdened with job applications, pleas for pardons, and requests for six-gun permits and for reward money to aid in the capture of criminals. Under the Constitution of 1876,[qv] adopted during his term, Coke served on a three-member board that supervised a new, decentralized system of public education. Vocational education benefited from the opening of the Agricultural and Mechanical College of Texas (now Texas A&M University), at which Coke made an eloquent speech. He was reelected governor by a ratio of three to one over William Morton Chambers,[qv] the Republican candidate. He was elected to the United States Senate in May 1876 and resigned the governorship in December. He began his first term as senator on March 4, 1877, replacing Morgan C. Hamilton.[qv]

Coke was generally regarded as an able and well-informed member of the Senate. "Old Brains," as his admirers called him, supported the Bland-Allison Act of 1878 and the Interstate Commerce Act of 1887. On grounds of unconstitutionality and extravagance, he opposed the Blair Bill for federal aid to the common schools. He also opposed the protective tariff, the suspension of silver coinage, and the Force Bill, which would have provided federal protection for voters and elections threatened by intimidation and violence. Meanwhile, Coke continued his involvement in Texas politics. He spoke as a strong opponent of prohibition[qv] throughout the state. In 1892 he traveled home to support the reelection of Gov. James S. Hogg[qv] over George Clark[qv] of Waco, Coke's former friend and campaign manager. Coke was reelected to the Senate in January 1883 and again in January 1889, both times by unanimous vote in the legislature. In 1894 he announced that he would not seek another term.

In the spring of 1897 he suffered from exposure while caring for his flooded Brazos valley farm and was ill for three weeks. He died at his home in Waco on May 14. After a state funeral, he was buried in Oakwood Cemetery, Waco. Information about Coke's religion is scanty; he was probably raised as an Episcopalian but in later years attended the Baptist Church. A white-bearded, hulking figure who towered six feet, three inches and weighed 240 pounds, Coke was a commanding presence. It is said that on the political platform he could bellow "like a prairie bull." His Senate speeches, while often ponderous, were factual, well-organized, and persuasive. He is considered one of the important leaders in Texas in the late nineteenth century.

BIBLIOGRAPHY: Merle Mears Duncan, "The Death of Senator Coke," *Southwestern Historical Quarterly* 63 (January 1960). *Governors' Messages: Coke to Ross (Inclusive), 1874–1891* (Austin: Archives and History Department, Texas State Library, 1916). Norman Kittrell, *Governors Who Have Been and Other Public Men of Texas* (Houston: Dealy-Adey-Elgin, 1921). Vertical Files, Barker Texas History Center, University of Texas at Austin.
John W. Payne, Jr.

COKE, TEXAS. Coke is on Farm roads 515 and 69, ten miles north of Quitman in northern Wood County. Though the area was settled as early as the 1850s, a community did not develop until the discovery of coal southwest of the area. By 1885 the community had received a post office called Coke, probably after that byproduct of coal production. By 1892 Coke had a population of 200, twelve businesses, a lawyer, a constable, a justice of the peace, and a teacher. By 1896 the population had fallen to twenty-five; ten years later the post office closed. By the 1930s Coke had a population of twenty-five, a number of dwellings, a business, a church, and a school. In 1942 the Amerada Petroleum Company made the second major oil discovery in the county, the Coke oilfield, just north of the community. It apparently had no lasting effect, as the population in Coke continued to be reported at twenty-five until the mid-1960s. Though the oilfield was still in operated in 1960, all that remained at Coke was a school and a number of dwellings. The population climbed to fifty-one in 1968 and to 130 in 1970. In 1972 it was 105, where it remained in 1990. In 1988 Coke had one business, a school, and two churches.

BIBLIOGRAPHY: *Wood County, 1850–1900* (Quitman, Texas: Wood County Historical Society, 1976).
Rachel Jenkins

COKE COUNTY. Coke County (F-12), in West Central Texas, is bounded on the east by Runnels County, on the south by Tom Green County, on the west by Sterling County, and on the north by Mitchell and Nolan counties. It was named for Richard Coke,[qv] a Texas governor. The county center is at 31°54′ north latitude and 100°33′ west longitude, about thirty miles north of San Angelo. The terrain includes prairie, hills, and the Colorado River valley; sandy loam and red soils predominate. The elevation varies from 1,800 feet in the south to 2,600 feet in the north, where Nipple Mountain, Meadow Mountain, Horse Mountain, and Hayrick Mountain are located. Its 911-square-mile area is drained by the north branch of the Colorado River and Yellow Wolf Creek. Native grasses include mesquite grass, needlegrass, sideoats, bunchgrass, and crabgrass. Ninety percent of Coke County's agricultural income of $10 million comes from cattle, sheep, goats, and horses. The rest is from cotton, sorghum, small grains, hay, fruits, and peanuts. Coke County is among the leading counties in sheep ranching.qv Extraction of sand and gravel is a minor industry, though the county has no manufacturing; county oil production of 2,249,804 barrels in 1982 earned almost $77 million. The annual rainfall is 20.48 inches. The average minimum temperature in January is 29° F; the maximum in July is 97°. The growing season lasts 226 days.

From about 1700 to the 1870s, Comanche Indians ranged the area that is now Coke County. They competed with the Tonkawa Indians to the east and the Lipans to the west for dominance of the Edwards Plateauqv and Colorado River valley. In 1851 Fort Chadbourne, in the northeast part of the future county, was established by the United States Army to protect the frontier; the fort was manned until the Civil War.qv The Butterfield Overland Mailqv ran through the area from 1858 to 1861.

Between 1860 and the early 1880s the only settlers in what became Coke County were ranchers attracted to open grazing land. J. J. Austin established his ranch headquarters near Sanco in 1875, and Pate Francher settled in the area in 1877, after he drove a cattle herd for John Austin and Joe McConnel to the Odom Ranch near Sanco. In 1882 the Texas and Pacific Railway began providing service to San Angelo, and settlers started coming into the region in somewhat larger numbers. Severe drought in the 1880s led to fence cuttingqv and its attendant quarreling, particularly on L. B. Harris's ranch: when landless cattlemen found that Harris had fenced in waterholes on the range, they destroyed $6,000 worth of his posts and wire. State authorities eventually settled the disputes.

The Texas legislature established Coke County in 1889, carving it out of territory previously assigned to Tom Green County; the county was organized that same year, with Hayrick as county seat. In 1889 the county's first newspaper, the Hayrick *Democrat,* began publication; shortly thereafter it was renamed the *Rustler.* By 1890 there were 163 farms and ranches in the county, and 2,059 people lived there. Only about 4,000 acres of the county was classified by the census as "improved" at this time. Ranchingqv dominated the local economy, and 13,806 cattle were counted in Coke County that year.

In 1891, after an election, the new town of Robert Lee became the county seat; Robert E. Leeqv had once served at Fort Chadbourne. That same year, the county's newspaper moved to the new county seat and was renamed the Robert Lee *Observer.* Early settlers named a new town Bronte, after English writer Charlotte Brontë; another was named Tennyson, in honor of the English laureate. By 1900, 480 farms and ranches had been established in the county, encompassing 605,842 acres. That year more than 46,000 cattle and about 17,500 sheep were counted in Coke County. Farming had also grown, for about 4,200 acres were planted in corn and almost 7,000 acres were devoted to cotton.

In 1907, when the Kansas City, Mexico and Orient Railway built tracks north out of San Angelo, the little towns of Tennyson, Bronte, and Fort Chadbourne lay near the line, and residents moved their business centers to enjoy the benefits of transportation. The county seat, Robert Lee, was not on the tracks, but managed to survive nonetheless.

In the first years of the twentieth century cotton cultureqv expanded significantly. By 1910 cotton was planted on more than 29,600 acres in Coke County; by 1920 cotton acreage had declined only slightly, to about 28,200 acres. Cotton production plunged sharply during the 1920s, however, apparently because of a boll weevilqv infestation, and by 1929 county farmers planted only 5,321 acres with cotton. These fluctuations in cotton production seem related to changes in the county's population that took place at about the same time. In 1910, near the height of the cotton boom in the county, 969 farms and ranches had been established in the county, and the population had grown since 1900 to 6,412. By 1920, after cotton production had begun to decline, there were only 721 farms and ranches in the area, and the county's population had dropped to 4,557. By 1925, as cotton production continued to drop, the number of farms had declined to 636.

But farmers were expanding their production of corn, wheat, and sorghum; in 1929 they harvested more than 55,300 acres of cropland in the county. Thousands of fruit trees were also planted during this time, and by 1920 about 18,000 fruit trees, including almost 14,000 peach trees, were growing in Coke County. Meanwhile, cattle ranching remained an important part of the economy. Though the number of cattle declined during the 1910s, by 1929 almost 31,000 cattle were grazing in the county. The number of farms and ranches in the county increased from 636 to 838 between 1925 and 1929. Meanwhile, the population of the county also began to recover; by 1930 there were 5,253 people living in the county.

The momentum of this recovery was lost during the Great Depressionqv of the 1930s. Cropland harvested in Coke County dropped more than 10 percent between 1930 and 1940, and the number of farms in the area fell again to 756. Hundreds of people left during the depression, and by 1940 only 4,593 remained.

Prospects for the local economy were greatly improved after 1942, however, when oil was discovered in the county. In November and December 1946, Sun Oil drilled the discovery well in the Jameson field in the northwest section of the county. In November 1948, Humble Oil Company (now Exxonqv) opened the Bronte field in the eastern part of the county. In 1949 numerous wells were drilled, and the Bronte and Fort Chadbourne fields were proved. The latter field was shut down for thirteen months from February 1952 by the Railroad Commissionqv to stop gas flaring. Production was resumed after the Lone Star Producing Company built a $3 million gas processing plant to utilize gas that was being wasted. Other oilfields drilled in the early 1950s included the North Bronte Multipay field; the McCutchen field, and the Wendkirk field. Production rose steadily into the 1950s but then began to drop. In 1948, Coke County produced almost 1,082,500 barrels of petroleum; in 1958, more than 12,795,000 barrels; in 1960, about 7,265,000; in 1978, almost 2,605,000; and in 1980, about 2,250,000. In 1990, production totaled 1,331,036 barrels. By 1991, since discovery in 1942, 209,281,131 barrels had been taken from Coke County lands. Tax money derived from oil profits helped the county to improve public services for its citizens. Modern schools were built in Bronte and Robert Lee; meanwhile, paving, road construction, and bridge improvements were made throughout the county. Oil money also helped to provide the county with a new courthouse, parks, and swimming pools.

The Robert Lee Dam, completed in 1969, impounded the E. V. Spence Reservoir which covers 14,950 acres and holds 488,750 acre-feet of water. Besides giving the Robert Lee area a reliable water supply, the lake is a valuable recreation site for fishermen, boaters, and swimmers. State highways 208 and 158 cross the county from north to south and east to west respectively, and U.S. Highway 277 crosses north–south through the eastern part of the county. Oil production accounts for the major share of income for the county. Income derived from its production is several times more than the county's income from agriculture. In the 1980s, Coke County maintained some 70,000 sheep and lambs and 30,000 cattle, along with smaller numbers of other livestock. About 500 acres were irrigated, and the county produced 47,000 bushels of wheat and more than 20,000 bushels of sorghum. Politically the county is stable in its voting habits; it was one of the sixty-two Texas counties that were still legally dry in 1986. By the late 1980s, Coke County had voted Democratic in every gubernatorial election since the 1950s, and had deviated to the Republican side only twice in presidential and senatorial elections (in 1972 and 1984.) The county's smaller communities include Bronte, Blackwell (partly in Nolan County), Sanco, Silver, and Tennyson. Robert Lee is the county seat and largest town. Recreation in the county centers around hunting and fishing at Lake Spence and Oak Creek Reservoir.qv

BIBLIOGRAPHY: Coke County Book Committee, *Coke County* (Lubbock: Specialty Publishing Company, 1984). Jewell G. Pritchett, *From the Top of Old Hayrick: A Narrative History of Coke County* (Abilene, Texas: Pritchett, 1980). Jessie Newton Yarbrough, *A History of Coke County, Home of the Rabbit Twisters: The Early Years to 1953* (1979).
William R. Hunt and John Leffler

COKE-DAVIS CONTROVERSY. In the election of December 1873 Richard Coke qv received 100,415 votes for governor against 52,141 for Edmund J. Davis.qv The election had been characterized by fraud and intimidation on both sides. Davis, the incumbent, proclaimed that he had a right to finish out his four-year term, and the "Semicolon Court,"qv in the case *Ex parte Rodriguez*,qv held that the election was illegal. Disregarding the court ruling, the Democrats secured the keys to the second floor of the Capitol and took possession. Davis was reported to have state troops stationed on the lower floor. The Travis Rifles (*see* TRAVIS GUARDS AND RIFLES), summoned to protect Davis, were converted into a sheriff's posse and protected Coke. On January 15, 1874, Coke was inaugurated as governor. On January 16 Davis arranged for a truce, but he made one final appeal for federal intervention. A telegram from President Ulysses S. Grant said that he did not feel warranted in sending federal troops to keep Davis in office. Davis resigned his office on January 19. Coke's inauguration restored Democratic control in Texas.

BIBLIOGRAPHY: Robert A. Calvert and Arnoldo De León, *The History of Texas* (Arlington Heights, Illinois: Harlan Davidson, 1990). Carl H. Moneyhon, *Republicanism in Reconstruction Texas* (Austin: University of Texas Press, 1980). Otis Singletary, "The Texas Militia during Reconstruction," *Southwestern Historical Quarterly* 60 (July 1956).
Curtis Bishop

COLABE CILLISTINE (ca. 1780–ca. 1865). Colabe Cillistine (Celestine, Sylestine), subchief or second chief of the Alabama Indian tribe, spoke four languages and served his tribe effectively in communications with other tribes and with government officials and white settlers from 1806 to 1865. He was the grandfather of Bronson Cooper Sylestine,qv tribal chieftain from 1936 to 1969. Colabe, as he was generally called by the Alabamas, was born around 1780 near Lafourche, Louisiana, and moved with his family to Texas by 1800. As a young man he became skillful in the use of other languages in addition to the Alabama tribal language: French, English, and the Mobilian trade language. In 1806 Antoneqv and Colabe were elected principal chief and second chief, respectively, of the Alabamas. Colabe served as an unofficial "prime minister" to Antone, attending numerous conferences relating to the Alabamas and translating for Antone when it became necessary. Colabe's name appears on several important documents involving the Alabamas. One of the most important was a petition for a permanent reservation that was presented to the Texas legislature on October 29, 1853. This petition was approved, and as a result the state of Texas purchased 1,110.7 acres of land for the Alabama Indian reservation. After the Alabamas moved onto their reservation during the winter of 1854–55, the tribal members expressed the need for an agent or reservation administrator to assist in tribal business matters, in contacts with government officials, and in relations with their white neighbors. On November 24, 1855, Colabe and other tribal leaders signed a request for the appointment of an agent, addressed to the Texas Senate and House of Representatives. Colabe continued to assist in tribal government activities but never rose above the rank of second chief. After an unusually long period of service to his people, he died around 1865. He was buried near the site of the present tribal cemetery, and the Alabama-Coushatta Tribal Council erected a monument in his honor at his gravesite. This monument was dedicated on June 23, 1990.

BIBLIOGRAPHY: Petitions of the Alabama Indian Tribe to the Texas Legislature (MSS, October 29, 1853, November 24, 1855, Texas Indian Papers, Texas State Archives, Austin).
Howard N. Martin

COLABROTE INDIANS. In 1683–84 Juan Domínguez de Mendozaqv led an exploratory expedition from El Paso as far eastward as the junction of the Concho and Colorado rivers east of the site of present San Angelo. In his itinerary he listed the names of thirty-seven Indian groups, including the Colabrotes, from which he expected to receive delegations. Nothing further is known about the Colabrotes, who seem to have been one of many Indian groups of north central Texas that were swept away by the southward thrust of the Lipan Apache and Comanche Indians in the eighteenth century.

BIBLIOGRAPHY: Herbert Eugene Bolton, ed., *Spanish Exploration in the Southwest, 1542–1706* (New York: Scribner, 1908; rpt., New York: Barnes and Noble, 1959). Charles W. Hackett, ed., *Pichardo's Treatise on the Limits of Louisiana and Texas* (4 vols., Austin: University of Texas Press, 1931–46).
Thomas N. Campbell

COLAS LARGAS INDIANS. The Colas Largas ("long tails") Indians are known only from a Spanish document of 1693 that lists them as one of fifty "nations" that lived north of the Rio Grande and "between Texas and New Mexico." This may be interpreted to mean the southern part of western Texas, since the document also mentions that the Apaches were at war with the groups named. Nothing further is known about the Colas Largas.

BIBLIOGRAPHY: Charles W. Hackett, ed., *Historical Documents Relating to New Mexico, Nueva Vizcaya, and Approaches Thereto, to 1773* (3 vols., Washington: Carnegie Institution, 1923–37).
Thomas N. Campbell

COLBERG, TEXAS. Colberg was near present Farm Road 3238 fifteen miles west of Austin in western Travis County. A post office opened there in 1883 with Ernst Hallmann as postmaster. In 1884 Colberg reported two churches, a district school, a steam gristmill and cotton gin, and forty residents. The post office was discontinued in 1885, and mail for the community was sent to Oak Hill.

BIBLIOGRAPHY: John J. Germann and Myron Janzen, *Texas Post Offices by County* (1986).
Vivian Elizabeth Smyrl

COLBERT'S FERRY. Colbert's Ferry became the main Red River crossing after Sherman and McKinney were established. It was located a half mile downriver from where the U.S. Highway 75/69 bridge now crosses, north of Denison in Grayson County. Joseph Mitchell, a Chickasaw, operated a ferry near the same location in 1842. He died in 1847, and around 1849 another Chickasaw, Benjamin Franklin Colbert, called on Joseph B. Earhartqv to establish a ferry. The early road from Mitchell's ferry had angled southwest to join the Preston road. After Sherman was founded, the Colbert Ferry road turned more directly south. Colbert's was the Red River crossing for the Butterfield Overland Mailqv from 1858 to 1861, and served stage lines thereafter. In 1860 M. A. McBride, utilizing the Texas side, challenged Colbert's exclusive service of the road. The controversy was eventually settled when Colbert obtained McBride's riverfront land. The Katy (Missouri, Kansas and Texas) Railroad crossing, built a half mile upriver from Colbert's in 1872, reduced traffic on the ferry. In July 1873 Colbert built a toll bridge. Within eleven months it was destroyed by floods, along with the Katy bridge. Ferry operations resumed, and the Katy began to rebuild. Colbert sold his bridge rights to the Red River

Bridge Company of Denison, which rebuilt the toll bridge in 1892. A flood in 1908 again destroyed both bridges. Ferry service was again resumed, this time with a powered boat that lasted until another toll bridge was built in 1915. In 1931 a free bridge was built adjacent to the railway bridge as a joint venture of Oklahoma and Texas. Opening of this bridge was delayed because of a lawsuit instigated by the toll bridge company. After considerable maneuvering between Governor W. H. D. (Alfalfa Bill) Murray qv of Oklahoma and Governor Ross Sterling qv of Texas, the free bridge was opened on July 25, 1931.

BIBLIOGRAPHY: Richard W. Fossey, "The Red River Bridge Conflict," *Red River Valley Historical Review* 1 (Autumn 1974). Ruth Ann Overbeck, "Colbert's Ferry," *Chronicles of Oklahoma* 57 (Summer 1979).
Morris L. Britton

COLD CREEK. Cold Creek rises eighteen miles southwest of San Saba in southwest San Saba County (at 30°58′ N, 98°56′ W) and runs south for eleven miles to its mouth on San Fernando Creek, at the southern foot of Smoothingiron Mountain in Llano County (at 30°50′ N, 98°55′ W). It traverses flat to rolling terrain, locally dissected, surfaced by sandy and clay loams that support open stands of live oak and mesquite.

COLD SPRING, TEXAS. Cold Spring was near the Gillespie county line a few miles from Loyal Valley, with which it has often been confused, in southeastern Mason County. It was settled in 1875 or 1876 and was named for a nearby spring.

BIBLIOGRAPHY: *Mason County Historical Book* (Mason, Texas: Mason County Historical Commission, 1976).
Alice J. Rhoades

COLDSPRING, TEXAS. Coldspring is at the junction of State Highway 150 and Farm roads 1514, 946, and 2025, sixty-five miles north of Houston in central San Jacinto County. According to local tradition, the settlement was named by Joseph Graves for the cold springwater found there. The first post office, named Coonskin, was opened in 1847. Within a year the office was renamed Fireman's Hill, and in 1850 the name was changed to Cold Spring, officially respelled Coldspring in 1894. The town, located on the Robert Rankin qv grant, became the county seat of newly established San Jacinto County in 1870. County government, agriculture, and lumbering provided the chief sources of income for Coldspring residents during the late nineteenth and early twentieth centuries. The courthouse burned in 1915, and the townsite was moved to its present, more elevated, site. The old town is now marked only by the old San Jacinto County Jail, which was placed on the National Register of Historic Places in 1980 and became a registered Texas landmark in 1982. The first bank in Coldspring opened in 1907, at which time the community had between 400 and 500 residents.

In 1926 the Delta Land and Timber Company built a commissary at Coldspring, which continued to rely heavily on the lumber industry.qv Five years later the company's sawmill plant was sold to the Kurth interests of Lufkin. A Civilian Conservation Corps qv camp for black youths operated at Coldspring from the early 1930s to 1937 and somewhat eased the devastating effects of the Great Depression qv for many local residents. Despite economic problems, the Gulf States Utility Company completed an electrical power line from Shepherd to Coldspring in 1936. In 1945 the Cold Springs oilfield was discovered southeast of town. The construction of Livingston Dam on the Trinity River in 1968 led to further development in the county. Coldspring residents voted to incorporate their city in 1969 by a 114-to-10 margin. Although additional exploratory drilling intensified during the late 1970s, the population of the county seat had declined from an estimated high of 750 in the early 1960s to 675 in 1970 and to 569 in 1980. Much of that decline was apparently due to shifts within the county itself, as seen in the growth of Shepherd, Camilla, and a variety of residential subdivisions. Despite the population trends, the number of rated businesses, which fell from twenty-five in 1960 to eighteen in 1971, had risen to twenty-nine by 1983. The weekly *San Jacinto Times* has served county residents since 1876. The population in 1990 was 538.

BIBLIOGRAPHY: Ruth Hansbro, History of San Jacinto County (M.A. thesis, Sam Houston State Teachers College, 1940). James Wright Steely, comp., *A Catalog of Texas Properties in the National Register of Historic Places* (Austin: Texas Historical Commission, 1984).
Robert Wooster

COLD SPRING CREEK. Cold Spring Creek, formerly known as Cold Creek, rises two miles west of U.S. Highway 87 in southeastern Mason County (at 30°34′ N, 99°02′ W) and runs east for 7½ miles to its mouth on Marschall Creek, just west of Loyal Valley in Llano County (at 30°35′ N, 98°57′ W). It got its name from the large springs which feed it. Rising in limestone hills on the eastern edge of the Edwards Plateau, the creek crosses flat to rolling terrain, with some steeper, rocky areas midcourse, surfaced by shallow and stony to deep sandy and clay loams that support grasses and open stands of live oak, Ashe juniper, and mesquite. Early settlers came to the creek's banks around 1858.

BIBLIOGRAPHY: *Mason County Historical Book* (Mason, Texas: Mason County Historical Commission, 1976). *Mason County News*, Centennial Edition, June 19, 1958.

COLD SPRINGS, TEXAS (Cherokee County). Cold Springs, fourteen miles south of Rusk on Farm Road 220 in southern Cherokee County, was first settled after the Civil War.qv In 1876 William Louis Byrd, a local farmer, deeded four acres for a church and school. A Methodist church was organized around the same time, and a school was in operation by 1884. During the 1930s the small community had a four-teacher school, a church, and a number of scattered houses. The school was consolidated with that of Alto in 1944. After World War IIqv many of the residents moved away, and in the early 1990s only the church and a few houses remained in the area.

BIBLIOGRAPHY: Marker Files, Texas Historical Commission, Austin.
Christopher Long

COLD SPRINGS, TEXAS (Coryell County). Cold Springs was fourteen miles southwest of Oglesby in southeastern Coryell County. It was named for a spring which flowed into Owl Creek. Tom and Elizabeth White gave land for a Baptist church in 1860. Residents received their mail from nearby Seattle, and children attended the Longview school. The establishment of the Fort Hoodqv military reservation in the 1940s and its expansion in 1953 forced residents of Cold Springs to relocate. In 1965 the Cold Springs name was given to a church two miles southeast of Flat at the intersection of State Highway 36 and Farm Road 184. A few scattered houses appeared on maps of the area.

BIBLIOGRAPHY: Coryell County Genealogical Society, *Coryell County, Texas, Families, 1854–1985* (Dallas: Taylor, 1986).
Vivian Elizabeth Smyrl

COLD SPRINGS FEMALE INSTITUTE. Cold Springs Female Institute, also known as Cold Springs Female Academy, was at Coldspring, at a site then part of Polk County but later in San Jacinto County. The school was incorporated on February 7, 1853, and opened under the guidance of Daniel Webster Steele in 1854. Four years later Steele moved to Pennington College in Trinity County, and B. T. Fore took over the school. Although the act of incorporation provided that the school be nonsectarian, the Tryon Baptist Association was providing support for the academy by 1858. The institute closed in 1861 due to a lack of patronage.

BIBLIOGRAPHY: Aline T. Rothe, History of Education in Polk County (M.A. thesis, University of Texas, 1934). Carl Bassett Wilson, History of Baptist Educational Efforts in Texas, 1829–1900 (Ph.D. dissertation, University of Texas, 1934).
Robert Wooster

COLDWATER, TEXAS (Dallam County). Coldwater was near Coldwater Creek in northern Dallam County. The school community had a store and a few scattered residences in 1947. Mail was delivered from Dalhart. Coldwater declined by 1950, after the consolidation of the county's school districts. The school was subsequently turned into a community hall for area farmers and ranchers.
H. Allen Anderson

COLDWATER, TEXAS (Sherman County). Coldwater, on Coldwater Creek in the central part of the county, became the county seat when Sherman County was organized in 1889. Some fifteen cowboys of the William B. Slaughter ranch (Coldwater Cattle Company) lived in the community, which in 1890 had the only post office in the county. By 1891 a hotel, a courthouse, a jail, and a mercantile store had been erected. Charles Randolph and George Loomis began the county's first newspaper, the *Sherman County Banner*, in July 1893. C. F. Williams based his windmill and well-drilling enterprise in Coldwater for a time. However, the railroads bypassed the community, and an election moved the county seat to Stratford in July 1901. By 1904 the only business left in Coldwater was George Loomis's store and post office. This post office closed in 1907. Though Coldwater continued as a ranch supply point, by 1940 only the old brick courthouse, often used as a rural church, remained. In the past several decades, the name of the community has been perpetuated by the Coldwater gas field.

BIBLIOGRAPHY: Sherman County Historical Survey Committee, *God, Grass, and Grit* (2 vols., Seagraves, Texas: Pioneer, 1971, 1975).
H. Allen Anderson

COLDWATER, TEXAS (Wood County). Coldwater was on a dirt road two miles south of Farm Road 852 and four miles southeast of Winnsboro in northeast Wood County. The settlement was inhabited by 1880. In 1884 a Cold Springs school district was established in the area, and in 1896 the one-teacher, one-room Cold Springs school enrolled thirty-one students. By 1905 the school, then known as Coldwater, had sixty-one students. By the 1930s the community had a number of farms scattered along country roads, a cemetery, and a school, known again as Cold Springs. In 1932 the school had fifty-five students in eight grades. By 1960 a few widely scattered dwellings and the Coldwater church and cemetery remained at the site. They were still there in 1988.
Rachel Jenkins

COLDWATER CREEK (Dallam County). Coldwater Creek rises in Cimarron County, Oklahoma (at 36°30′ N, 102°52′ W), and runs through northwest Dallam County, Texas, east across central Sherman County, and northeast across northwestern Hansford County, into Texas County, Oklahoma, where it proceeds northwest to its mouth on the North Canadian River (at 36°40′ N, 101°07′ W). It crosses flat to rolling hills surfaced by clay and sandy loam that supports hardwoods, brush, and grasses. The stream is sometimes known as Rabbit Ears Creek, after the two peaks called the Rabbit Ears near Clayton, New Mexico. These peaks were an important landmark and campsite on the Cimarron Cutoff section of the Santa Fe Trail.qv

_____ (Fayette County). Coldwater Creek rises in a tank just east of Farm Road 609 seven miles northeast of Flatonia in southern Fayette County (at 29°46′ N, 97°02′ W) and runs southeast for 5½ miles to its mouth on Rocky Creek, 1½ miles north of Engle in southern Fayette County (at 29°42′ N, 97°01′ W). The name is derived from several cold springs that join the creek near its head in an area generally known as the Black Jack Springs or Pin Oak community. The creek runs through variable terrain surfaced by sand and clay that support oak and cedar, with some hackberry, mesquite, and pecan. Until the 1960s cotton was produced there for ginning at Flatonia and Muldoon. Following the decline of cotton most of the land reverted to pasture for cattle, with some production of corn and hay.

COLE, CRISS (1918–1985). Criss Cole, Texas legislator and judge, was born on May 11, 1918, in Sawyer, Oklahoma, one of ten children of sharecroppers James M. and Drucy Cole. He spent his childhood on a farm near Avery, Texas. He worked in the Civilian Conservation Corpsqv near Golden, Colorado, before joining the United States Marines in 1940. He served in Iceland, New Zealand, and Guadalcanal. As a corporal, he was blinded in 1943 during a beach attack at Tarawa in the Gilbert Islands by a Japanese grenade, an injury for which he was later awarded a Purple Heart. He returned to civilian life, moved to Houston, completed high school work, worked for Reed Roller Bit and as a legal stenographer for the city's legal department, and took prelaw courses at the University of Saint Thomas. He received his law degree in June 1954 from the University of Houston law school. Cole was a member of the Texas House of Representatives from 1955 to 1962 and served in the Texas Senate from 1963 to 1970. In 1971 he was appointed to preside over what became in 1977 the 315th District Court, one of three courts handling juvenile cases in Harris County. He helped to pass bills establishing Padre Island National Seashoreqv and the University of Texas Institute of Texan Culturesqv at HemisFairqv in San Antonio, was instrumental in passing a measure banning racial discrimination by state and local governments, and was involved with measures for redistricting, loan-company regulation, multiple use and pollution of Texas waters, and vocational rehabilitation. In 1970, 1976, and 1977 he attended the National College for Juvenile Justice. Cole served as director of the Lighthouse for the Blind, vice president of the Texas Air and Water Resources Foundation, state general chairman for the Texas Society for the Prevention of Blindness, and state advocate for the Knights of Columbus.qv He was a member of the Houston and Texas Bar associations, a trustee of the University of Saint Thomas, and a founder and president of the Hope Center for Youth in Houston. In 1969 the legislature voted to name Austin's rehabilitation center for the blind in his honor. Cole married Joanne Spica on September 25, 1945; the couple had two sons. Cole died on June 21, 1985, in Houston and was buried in Houston National Cemetery.

BIBLIOGRAPHY: Houston Metropolitan Research Center Files, Houston Public Library. Mary Reincke, *American Bench: Judges of the Nation* (Minneapolis: Reginald Bishop Forster, 1977–). *Texas Bar Journal*, April 1986. *Texas Parade*, August 1974. Vertical Files, Barker Texas History Center, University of Texas at Austin.
Diana J. Kleiner

COLE, JAMES POPE (1814–1886). James Pope Cole, early settler of Galveston and chief justice of Galveston County, son of John and Susan Jane (Pope) Cole, was born on January 31, 1814, in Beaufort District, South Carolina. He graduated from South Carolina College (now the University of South Carolina) in 1832 with an A.B. degree. He taught school for three years near his home and pursued his legal studies under Robert W. Barnwell, then a member of Congress and afterward president of South Carolina College. Cole arrived in Galveston in 1839 and began a law practice. He served in 1842 in the Texas militia as a member of the Galveston Fusilier Company of the Fourth Militia Regiment. He rose to the rank of captain and served as judge advocate for the regiment. In 1854 he replaced his friend Gail Borden, Jr.,qv as secretary and agent of the Galveston City Company, which owned the site of Galveston. Cole was probate judge and served as city recorder for two years. He was sworn in as a county commissioner on August 16, 1856, and served as chief justice for the county commissioners' court from the August term of 1858 until July 18, 1864. As chief justice, he administered funds to the poor of Galveston County. He was an ardent secessionist and chaired a Committee of

Public Safety constituted to popularize secession.^{qv} Cole was a devout Baptist and a states'-rights Democrat. He was married on June 29, 1843, to Mary Jane Graham, daughter of a Scottish clergyman, James Graham, of Beaufort, South Carolina. Five of the couple's twelve children died as infants. Cole died on February 16, 1886, in Galveston.

BIBLIOGRAPHY: *Biographical Encyclopedia of Texas* (New York: Southern, 1880). Mary Edith Cole Papers, Texas Collection, Baylor University. Milton Harsteen Cole Papers, Texas Collection, Baylor University. Charles Waldo Hayes, *Galveston: History of the Island and the City* (2 vols., Austin: Jenkins Garrett, 1974). Mary Cole Farrow Long, *Stranger in a Strange Land: A Biography of Judge James Pope Cole, 1814–1886* (Belton, Texas: Bear Hollow, 1986).

Mary Cole Farrow Long

COLE, ROBERT G. (1915–1944). Robert G. Cole, Medal of Honor recipient, was born at Fort Sam Houston, Texas, on March 19, 1915. He entered service at San Antonio. Lieutenant Colonel Cole was a battalion commander of the 101st Airborne Division when they parachuted into France on D-Day (June 6, 1944). He was cited for "gallantry and intrepidity at the risk of his life" near Carentan, France, on June 11, 1944. He was personally leading his battalion in an attack on four bridges when the entire unit was pinned down by intense enemy rifle, machine-gun, mortar, and artillery fire. After an hour of the devastating fire from well-prepared and heavily fortified positions, which had inflicted numerous casualties, he issued orders to attack with fixed bayonets. With complete disregard for his own safety, he personally led the assault from in front of his troops. He charged on and led the remnants of his group across the bullet-swept ground and into the enemy position. His heroic action so inspired his men that a secure bridgehead across the Douve River was established. Cole was killed three months later, on September 18, 1944, by a sniper during "Operation Market Garden" while taking the bridge at Best, Holland. His mother, Mrs. Clara H. Cole, received his posthumous Medal of Honor while his wife and twenty-nine-month-old son looked on. He is buried in the American Battlefields Monuments Commission Cemetery in the Netherlands.

BIBLIOGRAPHY: Committee on Veterans' Affairs, United States Senate, *Medal of Honor Recipients, 1863–1973* (Washington: GPO, 1973). C. Ryan, *A Bridge Too Far* (New York: Simon and Schuster, 1974). Vertical Files, Barker Texas History Center, University of Texas at Austin.

Art Leatherwood

COLE CREEK. Cole Creek rises five miles northeast of Electra in northwestern Wichita County (at 34°04′ N, 98°51′ W) and runs northeast eleven miles to its mouth on Tenth Cavalry Creek, ten miles northeast of Electra and one mile south of the Oklahoma border (at 34°08′ N, 98°48′ W). The surrounding generally flat terrain is interspersed with local depressions and moderately steep slopes and is surfaced by moderately deep to shallow silt and clay loams that support mesquite, water-tolerant hardwood trees, and grasses. The area historically has served as crop and range land, although some urban development is present as well.

COLEGIO ALTAMIRANO. Colegio Altamirano, at Hebbronville, was founded by settlers of Spanish ancestry who wanted their children to learn Spanish culture. Dionicio Peña, Francisco Barrera Guerra, Tomás Barrera, José Ángel Garza, and Ascención Martínez founded the school in 1897. Students, many of whom went on to graduate from Hebbronville public schools, learned art, music, discipline, social graces, and the three Rs. Fiestas were held at the end of each term. The school operated until 1958.

BIBLIOGRAPHY: Jovita Gonzalez, "America Invades the Border Towns," *Southwest Review* 15 (Summer 1930). Hebbronville Chamber of Commerce, *Fiftieth Anniversary, Jim Hogg County* (Hebbronville, Texas, 1963).

Diana J. Kleiner

COLEGIO JACINTO TREVIÑO. In the 1960s the civil-rights movement among African Americans^{qv} and anti-Vietnam War protests gave impetus to Hispanic protest activities. Driven by anger and renewed cultural pride, Hispanics pressured public and private institutions to establish new organizations to correct social and political imbalances. In this spirit the Mexican American Youth Organization^{qv} voted unanimously at a statewide meeting during the Christmas holidays of 1969–70 to found Colegio Jacinto Treviño. The mission of the college was to "to develop a Chicano with conscience and skills, [to give] the barrios a global view, [and] to provide positive answers to racism, exploitation, and oppression." A core planning group of fifteen set the initial goal—a bilingual, bicultural program to train teachers of Hispanic children. Antioch College, in Yellow Springs, Ohio, agreed to lend its name to the development of a degree in education through its University Without Walls graduate program. In partial fulfillment of master's degrees in education from Antioch, fifteen students agreed to develop an undergraduate training program for teachers. The group was instructed by an adjunct volunteer faculty of university professors and others and supervised by a full-time Ed.D. Colegio Jacinto Treviño received small grants from the federal government, churches, and foundations. Income and expenses were shared among the graduate students. After a series of informal meetings in community centers, homes, and churches, the college settled into a two-story building in Mercedes, Texas. Enrollment ranged from fifteen to fifty students of high school and undergraduate age. The college had a constant flow of visitors who came to learn, advise, and even criticize.

Difficulties arose in the structure and governance of the college, criteria for selection of students and requirements for degrees. It was unclear how the school was to provide the broadest possible educational opportunities, compensate for past neglect, and also secure recognition of the school's degree. In addition to developing a teaching curriculum, the group proposed to provide a center of cultural dialogue encompassing a college press, a clearinghouse of information, and a distribution service for books in Spanish unavailable elsewhere in the country. To this end, members visited student groups and publishing houses in Mexico City. The first venture was to be a deluxe volume of art and poetry, "Semillas de liberación" ("Seeds of Liberation"). The college was managed by consensus, policy being set by a board of directors that met quarterly. The board's internal dynamics were political, intense, and eventually polarized in two identifiable camps. By the summer of 1971 irreducible tension resulted in the pulling away of one camp (some of whose members established another Hispanic center, Juarez-Lincoln University). Internal pressures were compounded by organized external efforts to close the college. Colegio Jacinto Treviño was closed in the mid-1970s.

BIBLIOGRAPHY: Victor Guerra-Garza, ed., *HOJAS: A Chicano Journal of Education* (Austin: Juárez-Lincoln University, 1976). Vertical Files, Barker Texas History Center, University of Texas at Austin.

Aurelio M. Montemayor

COLEMAN, ANN RANEY (1810–1897). Ann Raney Coleman, pioneer, was born on November 10, 1810, in Whitehaven, England, daughter of John Raney, a prosperous landowner and banker who went bankrupt and attempted to make a fresh start in Texas. In 1829 he sailed with his younger son for Austin's colony, where he became a teacher for James Briton Bailey's^{qv} family near Brazoria. Ann and her mother and sister joined him in 1832, after a harrowing sea voyage during which they hid in a closet while pirates ransacked the ship off the coast of Cuba. They arrived in Texas in time for Ann to help the Texans in the battle of Velasco^{qv} by making bullets and patches and carrying them fifteen miles on horseback to a hiding place in a hollow tree. After outrunning two Mexican spies on the return journey, she attended the reconciliation ball and was said to have so charmed Stephen F. Austin^{qv} as a dancing partner that he granted her father an additional league of land.

Both of Ann's parents died within a few months after the family was reunited in Texas, and in February of 1833 she married John Thomas, a cotton planter. They lived first on his plantation at Caney Creek, where their son Edmond was born, and later bought the old Bailey plantation on the Brazos. They fled to Louisiana during the Runaway Scrape^{qv} in 1836, losing most of their slaves and personal property in the process. Within a few months of their arrival in Louisiana, Thomas was hired to oversee the Bayou Grosse Tete plantations of Austin Woolfolk, the largest sugar planter in the state, and Ann was put in charge of allotting clothing and provisions to 100 slaves. In Louisiana she gave birth to a second son, who lived less than a year, and a daughter, Victoria; the older son died there.

After several years as tenants, the Thomases bought their own plantation at Pointe Coupee on the Mississippi. Against Ann's wishes Thomas mortgaged the land in order to raise operating capital. When he died in 1847 she was forced to accept a loan from John Coleman, a storekeeper who had been boarding with the family, to prevent the plantation from being sold. Coleman then used his advantage to pressure her into marrying him a few months later. He proved to be shiftless and abusive and allowed the estate to run into debt and be sold. They subsequently went to New Orleans, where Coleman abandoned her, and she took a job as a hotel housekeeper to support herself and her daughter.

Ann had some hope of alleviating her financial difficulties if she could make a trip to England, prove her father's bankruptcy a fraud, and claim his estate. After a journey to her homeland in the summer of 1854 failed to bring success, she yielded to Coleman's pleas to rejoin him. She lived with him in Powder Horn, Texas, for a year and supported the family by sewing. After divorcing Coleman in 1855 she moved to Matagorda, where she kept school and was soon joined by her daughter, whose husband had abandoned her. When she could get no more work in Matagorda, Ann moved in 1860 to Lavaca, where she supported her daughter and grandson by sewing and was shortly caught up in the Civil War.^{qv} She fled with her family to Indianola when federal soldiers shelled Lavaca in 1862 and returned to act as a caretaker for the house of a family that had retreated inland. When the federals burned Lavaca, she saved the house by passing buckets of water to her daughter, who poured them on the roof.

Plagued by poverty, she spent the remaining years of her life moving from town to town, wherever she could get a situation as a teacher or housekeeper. She scraped out an existence keeping schools at Bolivar Point, Hamshire, Hallettsville, Victoria, and Cuero. Citing her service in the battle of Velasco, she unsuccessfully petitioned the legislature for a pension. In the 1870s and 1880s she compiled a history of her long life for her niece in North Carolina; it was published in 1970 as *Victorian Lady on the Texas Frontier: The Journal of Ann Raney Coleman*. She died in Cuero in March 1897.   *C. Richard King*

COLEMAN, BESSIE (1892–1926). Bessie Coleman (Brave Bessie or Queen Bess), the world's first licensed black pilot, daughter of Susan Coleman, was born in Atlanta, Texas, on January 26, 1892, the twelfth of thirteen children. She grew up in Waxahachie. Her father left the family in 1900 to return to Indian Territory. Bessie, along with several siblings still living at home, helped ease the family's financial troubles by picking cotton or assisting with the washing and ironing that her mother took in. Upon graduation from high school she enrolled at the Colored Agricultural and Normal University (now Langston University) in Langston, Oklahoma. Financial difficulties, however, forced her to quit after one semester. She moved to Chicago, where a brother was then living, and attended beauty school for a time. She spent the early years of World War I^{qv} working as a manicurist at the White Sox Barbershop. She then operated a small but profitable chili parlor. Apparently in early 1917 Bessie Coleman married Claude Glenn, but she never publicly acknowledged the marriage, and the two soon separated.

In 1920 Coleman, acting on a lifelong dream of learning to fly,

Bessie Coleman, 1921–1926. Courtesy National Air and Space Museum, Smithsonian Institution; SI neg. no. 92-13721. Known as "Queen Bess," Coleman gained great fame as a stunt flier.

traveled abroad to attend aviation school in Le Crotoy, France, after she discovered that no American school would accept African Americans.^{qv} Robert S. Abbott, editor of the Chicago *Weekly Defender*, assisted her in contacting schools abroad. After studying for ten months in France she was issued a license on June 15, 1921, by the Fédération Aéronautique Internationale, giving her the distinction of being the first black person in the world to become a licensed pilot. She returned to the United States in 1921. Her goal, in addition to making flying her career, was to open a flying school for black students. In 1922 she made a second trip to Europe and during her studies took lessons from the chief pilot for the Fokker Aircraft Company in Germany.

Coleman's first American air show was at Curtiss Field, near Manhattan, on September 3, 1922. She followed the success of this show with exhibition flights all over the country, many of them in her native South. After several years of touring the East and West coasts, she traveled back to Texas and established her headquarters in Houston in 1925. Her first performance in Texas took place in that city on June 19, 1925. Her daredevil stunts and hair-raising maneuvers earned her the nickname "Brave Bessie." She primarily flew Curtiss JN-4D planes and army surplus aircraft left over from the war. During her trips she often gave lectures to schools and churches to encourage young black men and women to enter aviation. On one occasion in Waxahachie she refused to give an exhibition on white school grounds unless blacks were permitted to use the same entrance as whites. The request was granted, although blacks and whites remained segregated once inside. Early in her career she was presented a loving cup for her achievements from the cast of *Shuffle Along*, a black Broadway musical. By 1926, the year of her death, Coleman had become one of America's most popular stunt fliers.

She had her first major accident in 1924 while barnstorming in California, and she took a year off to recover. On April 30, 1926, she died during a test flight before a show sponsored by the Negro Welfare League in Jacksonville, Florida. About twelve minutes into the flight, the plane did not pull out of a nosedive as planned; instead, it did a somersault and dropped Bessie Coleman to her death. Her mechanic and publicity agent, William Wills, fell with the plane and died on impact. Although the charred condition of the wreckage prevented a full investigation, the crash was believed to have been caused by a loose wrench that jammed the plane's controls. After funeral services in Jacksonville, which were attended by hundreds of admirers, Coleman's body was returned to Chicago, where she had made her home. She is buried there in Lincoln Cemetery. Although her dream of establishing a flying school for black students never materialized, the Bessie Coleman Aero groups were organized after her death. On Labor Day, 1931, these flying clubs sponsored the first all-black air show in America, which attracted 15,000 spectators. Over the years, recognition of Coleman's accomplishments has grown. In 1977 a group of black female student pilots in Indiana organized the Bessie Coleman Aviators Club. In 1990 a street in Chicago was renamed Bessie Coleman Drive, and May 2, 1992, was declared Bessie Coleman Day in Chicago. In 1995 the United States Postal Service issued a thirty-two-cent commemorative stamp in her honor.

BIBLIOGRAPHY: Austin *American-Statesman,* September 6, 1993. Roger Bilstein and Jay Miller, *Aviation in Texas* (Austin: Texas Monthly Press, 1985). Dallas *Morning News,* September 8, 1993. Houston *Post-Dispatch,* May 1, 1926. Anita King, "Brave Bessie: First Black Pilot," Parts 1 and 2, *Essence,* May, June 1976. Doris L. Rich, *Queen Bess: Daredevil Aviator* (Washington: Smithsonian Institution Press, 1993). Vertical Files, Barker Texas History Center, University of Texas at Austin.

Roni Morales

COLEMAN, ROBERT M. (ca. 1799–1837). Robert M. Coleman, Indian fighter, soldier at the battle of San Jacinto[qv] and signer of the Texas Declaration of Independence,[qv] was born in Kentucky about 1799. He moved to Texas in 1831 and settled in what is now Bastrop County. In the summer of 1835 he commanded one of four volunteer companies organized to attack the Tawakoni Indians at Tehuacana Spring in what is now Limestone County. From September 28 to December 16, 1835, he commanded the Mina (Bastrop) Volunteers. His company was stationed near San Antonio in the siege of Bexar[qv] from December 5 to 10, 1835, but did not enter the town. Evidence suggests that he was elected as a delegate to the Consultation[qv] but may not have attended. Coleman was one of the four representatives from Mina to the Convention of 1836[qv] at Washington-on-the-Brazos, where he signed the Declaration of Independence. After the convention he joined the Texas army and was aide-de-camp to Gen. Sam Houston[qv] from April 1 to July 15, 1836, a period that included the battle of San Jacinto. After his discharge from the army, Coleman raised a regiment of rangers, of which he was colonel until at least November 30, 1836. For distributing a pamphlet in 1837 criticizing Houston's action at San Jacinto, Coleman was discharged from the army. He drowned about July 1, 1837, while bathing in the Brazos River at Velasco. He was survived by his wife and six children. The wife and oldest son were killed by Indians near Webberville in 1839. Coleman County, established in 1858, was named for him. A monument to him was set up in Freeport in 1931.

BIBLIOGRAPHY: Sam Houston Dixon, *Men Who Made Texas Free* (Houston: Texas Historical Publishing, 1924). Louis Wiltz Kemp, *The Signers of the Texas Declaration of Independence* (Salado, Texas: Anson Jones, 1944; rpt. 1959). William S. Speer and John H. Brown, eds., *Encyclopedia of the New West* (Marshall, Texas: United States Biographical Publishing, 1881; rpt., Easley, South Carolina: Southern Historical Press, 1978). Texas House of Representatives, *Biographical Directory of the Texan Conventions and Congresses, 1832–1845* (Austin: Book Exchange, 1941).

L. W. Kemp

COLEMAN, THOMAS ATLEE (1860–1923). Thomas Atlee (Little Tom) Coleman, rancher, son of Margaretta Susan (Atlee) and Thomas Matthew (Big Tom) Coleman,[qv] was born on June 5, 1860, in Goliad, Texas, and educated at the universities of Tennessee and Virginia. His father and paternal grandfather, Youngs Levi Coleman,[qv] helped found the Coleman-Fulton Pasture Company.[qv] His maternal grandfather, John N. Keeran,[qv] moved to Texas in 1867 and became a prominent rancher in Victoria County. Coleman ranched in Dimmit, La Salle, Webb, and other counties. From his office in San Antonio he supervised a spread that included the towns of Carrizo Springs, Catarina, Encinal, Cotulla, Artesia Wells, and Asherton. In addition he purchased the 1.5 million-acre Milmo Ranch in Mexico, for which he paid $3.5 million.

Not only did Coleman bring improved conditions and breeds to the range, but he improved Bermuda onions and citrus fruit and contributed greatly to the conversion of the lower reaches of Texas into an agricultural area. He sold a substantial amount of land to farmers interested in truck farming. At one time he entered into a partnership with John M. Green and Joseph F. Green[qv] (no kin to each other) to lease the 224,000-acre Catarina Ranch from David Sinton. After Sinton's death in 1900 Joseph Green took over the Coleman-Fulton Pasture Company as manager, and Coleman took Sinton's place on the board of directors, where he served until 1907. The company operated a ranch-supply store in Encinal named Green, Coleman, and Company. Coleman was also a large stockholder in Southwestern Casualty Insurance Company and general livestock agent for the International–Great Northern Railroad, as well as a member of Governor James E. Ferguson's[qv] personal staff.

Coleman married Birdie Keeran on June 16, 1886, and the couple had five children. Coleman was a member of Masonic organizations, the Elks, the Shriners, the San Antonio Country Club, the University Club, and the San Antonio Chamber of Commerce. He died on March 30, 1923, and was buried in San Antonio.

BIBLIOGRAPHY: Ellis A. Davis and Edwin H. Grobe, comps., *The New Encyclopedia of Texas,* 3d ed. Keith Guthrie, *History of San Patricio County* (Austin: Nortex, 1986). *History of the Cattlemen of Texas* (Dallas: Johnson, 1914; rpt., Austin: Texas State Historical Association, 1991). Coleman McCampbell, *Texas Seaport: The Story of the Growth of Corpus Christi and the Coastal Bend Area* (New York: Exposition, 1952). *Men of Affairs of San Antonio* (San Antonio Newspaper Artists' Association, 1912). A. Ray Stephens, *Taft Ranch* (Austin: University of Texas Press, 1964). Vertical Files, Barker Texas History Center, University of Texas at Austin. Clarence R. Wharton, ed., *Texas under Many Flags* (5 vols., Chicago: American Historical Society, 1930).

Keith Guthrie

COLEMAN, THOMAS MATTHEW (1833–1896). Thomas M. Coleman, pioneer Texas cattleman, the son of Lucy Catherine (White) and Youngs Levi Coleman,[qv] was born on August 15, 1833, at Liberty, Texas. The family moved to Gonzales and then Jackson County before moving to Goliad County. In the early 1850s Youngs Coleman bought San Patricio County land on Chiltipin Creek and at La Quinta on Corpus Christi Bay. The younger Coleman was associated with his father during this period as a rancher and cattleman in Goliad and San Patricio counties, and as foreman of operations headquartered at Rincon. In 1858 he and others formed the Star Cattle Company, which drove cattle to Chicago. He left the drive in 1859 to marry Margaret Susan Atlee of Athens, Tennessee, but the couple spent their honeymoon in New York trying to sell barrels of beef when poor market prices forced the company to slaughter more than 1,300 cattle and ship them east. The Colemans eventually had two children.

In 1871 Coleman was among the incorporators of the Rockport, Fulton, Laredo and Pacific Railroad, which became the Texas and Pacific in 1874. Also in 1871 at Rockport, Coleman and his father formed the Coleman, Mathis, Fulton Cattle Company with Thomas Henry Mathis, George Ware Fulton,[qq,qv] and J. M. Mathis. The firm shipped cattle and operated a Rockport packery that manufactured tallow and shipped rawhides to factories. The partners sold their own land to the cattle company, borrowing money to pay the bill, and bought land for the new partnership, thus consolidating a spread of some 265,000 acres in Aransas, Goliad, and San Patricio counties with ranges leased in Refugio and other counties. In 1879 the partnership dissolved because of personal conflicts. The Mathis partners dropped out, taking with them land and a promissory note. A new company with 165,000 acres was reorganized in 1879 as the Coleman-Fulton Pasture Company.[qv] Though Coleman was manager of the new company at its inception, Fulton replaced him as ranch-operations head with George W. Fulton, Jr.qv The elder Fulton borrowed money from David Sinton to help the company survive drought, and Coleman later sold most of his stock to Sinton and Charles P. Taft, both of Cincinnati, Ohio. Though he retained the Chiltipin Ranch, where he built a $150,000 mansion to rival that of Fulton at Rockport, Coleman never recovered from the financial burden of the project. At his death, the land was given to a relative in payment of a loan, and the mansion was torn down in 1930.

Coleman served under Capt. R. H. Belvin in a reserve company of the Twenty-ninth Brigade, Confederate States of America, and in San Patricio County as a deputy inspector of brands. He was appointed to the commissioners' court in 1889 and 1891 but resigned in 1892. He married Frances Humphreys in 1872, after the death of his first wife. He was elected county judge in 1894 and suffered a heart attack as he was about to open court at Sinton. According to commissioners' court records he died on February 11, 1896. Coleman's son Thomas Atlee Coleman,qv a prominent San Antonio businessman and rancher, purchased the Milmo Ranch in Mexico, a spread of over a million acres, for which he paid $3.5 million dollars.

BIBLIOGRAPHY: J. Frank Dobie, ed., *A Vaquero of the Brush Country* (Dallas: Southwest, 1929; new ed., Boston: Little, Brown, 1943). Keith Guthrie, *History of San Patricio County* (Austin: Nortex, 1986). J. Marvin Hunter, *Trail Drivers of Texas* (2 vols., San Antonio: Jackson Printing, 1920, 1923; 4th ed., Austin: University of Texas Press, 1985). Hobart Huson, *Refugio: A Comprehensive History of Refugio County from Aboriginal Times to 1953* (2 vols., Woodsboro, Texas: Rooke Foundation, 1953, 1955). Frank W. Johnson, *A History of Texas and Texans* (5 vols., ed. E. C. Barker and E. W. Winkler [Chicago and New York: American Historical Society, 1914; rpt. 1916]). Coleman McCampbell, *Saga of a Frontier Seaport* (Dallas: South-West, 1934).
Keith Guthrie

COLEMAN, WALTER MOORE (1863–1926). Walter Moore Coleman, author and teacher, son of William Ludlow and Maria Jane (Stewart) Coleman, was born in Chappell Hill, Texas, on December 21, 1863. After graduating from Sam Houston Normal Institute (later Sam Houston State University) in 1879, he served as principal of Belton High School, from 1884 to 1887. He subsequently earned a B.A. at Washington and Lee University, Virginia, in 1889, and studied at the University of Berlin in 1889 and at the Royal School of Science in 1890. He was professor of biology at Sam Houston Normal Institute from 1890 until 1908, when he began a year's research at the Physiological Institute of the University of Berlin. He was attached to London Hospital in 1909 and 1910. Coleman wrote *Hygienic Physiology* (1905) and was the coauthor of *First Course in Biology* (1908). He married Satis Narrona Barton on March 13, 1895, and lived in Corpus Christi until his death, in 1926.

BIBLIOGRAPHY: *Who Was Who in America*, Vol. 1.

COLEMAN, YOUNGS LEVI (1804–1881). Youngs Levi Coleman, pioneer rancher in San Patricio County, son of David Coleman and his first wife, née Hendrix, was born on July 6, 1804, in North Carolina. The family moved successively to South Carolina, Mississippi, Tennessee, and New York, where Coleman became an apprentice tailor. He moved to Texas in 1824 and on August 10, 1828, married Lucy Catherine White, daughter of Matthew G. White,qv at Liberty. The family ranched in Gonzales and Jackson counties and moved to Goliad County. In the early 1850s Coleman began buying land in San Patricio County and built a home on Chiltipin Creek. He and his son Thomas M. Colemanqv established ranch headquarters on the Rincon and ran cattle over thousands of acres of open rangeland. In 1871 Youngs and Tom joined Thomas H. Mathis, George W. Fulton,qqv and J. M. Mathis to form the Coleman, Mathis, Fulton Cattle Company. The partners sold the company their individually held ranch holdings to total 265,000 acres. The Rincon headquarters was turned into the operations headquarters for the new company, which was one of the first operations to introduce plank fencing and, in 1876, barbed wire.qv In 1879 the Mathis cousins withdrew from the partnership and took part of the land as their share of the business. The new company was called the Coleman-Fulton Pasture Companyqv and embraced 165,000 acres. Coleman gradually turned his interests over to his son Tom, since he refused to sign a loyalty pledge after the Civil War.qv He moved to Veracruz, where he purchased a sugar plantation. Family records state that he never returned to the United States; however, court records indicate that he served on juries and transacted other business regularly in San Patricio County. Amanda, Youngs's daughter, who married Ozias Newman, went to Mexico with her father, and eventually her husband and all her children except one moved to Mexico. Youngs died in 1881 and was buried in Mexico at his request. Amanda and one child are also buried on the Mexican plantation. Youngs's wife, Lucy, did not go to Mexico but stayed in the Colemans' Goliad home. She died in 1874 and is buried in Oak Hill Cemetery, Goliad.

BIBLIOGRAPHY: Keith Guthrie, *History of San Patricio County* (Austin: Nortex, 1986). A. Ray Stephens, *Taft Ranch* (Austin: University of Texas Press, 1964).
Keith Guthrie

COLEMAN, TEXAS. Coleman, the county seat of Coleman County, is at the junction of U.S. highways 84 and 283 and Farm Road 53 in the central part of the county. It had its origin in 1876 when R. J. Clow donated a 160-acre site on Hords Creek for a county seat. J. F. Gordon and R. S. Bowen surveyed the land, and town lots were sold. With its location on the Western Trail,qv Coleman boomed as a supply and recreation center for trail drivers bound for Dodge City, Kansas. The town was named after the county, which was named for Sam Houston'sqv aide Robert M. Coleman.qv Soon after the county was organized it had a courthouse in Coleman, built of lumber taken from elms found along Jim Ned Creek. The courthouse also housed bachelor quarters and a general store and was used for religious services and community gatherings. A second general store was moved to Coleman from Echo by a man named King. A cowboy shootout in front of this store led to a fatality and the first use of the town cemetery. In 1879 a private school was established with Anna Miles as teacher, and three years later a public school opened. A printer started the short-lived Coleman *Telegram* in 1877. In 1881 J. J. Callan published the Coleman *Voice*, which competed with the Coleman *Democrat*, published by Will Hubert, from 1897 until the papers merged as the *Democrat-Voice* in 1906. The population grew from 1,362 in 1904 to over 3,000 in 1912. The town prospered as school lands were sold to ranchers. The Santa Fe Railroad missed the town by five miles, but a spur line was built to it by 1886. After 1900 the economy shifted to cotton raising. The Great Depressionqv years hit county farmers hard, and many left their land to live in town. Coleman subsequently became been a meat-processing and wool center and a thriving manufacturing center producing brick and clay tile, clothing, leather goods, office supplies, and furniture. The population was 6,530 in 1954, 6,371 in 1960, and 5,608 in 1972, when the town had 138 businesses. Annual events include a stock show in January, a rattlesnake hunt and antique show in March, and a rodeo in July. In the city park is a replica of Camp Colorado.qv The population was 5,410 in 1990.

BIBLIOGRAPHY: Leona Bruce, *They Came in Peace to Coleman County* (Fort Worth: Branch-Smith, 1970). James T. Padgitt, "Early Day Coleman," West Texas Historical Association *Year Book* 28 (1952). Kathleen E. and Clifton R. St. Clair, eds., *Little Towns of Texas* (Jacksonville, Texas: Jayroe Graphic Arts, 1982).
William R. Hunt

COLEMAN COUNTY. Coleman County (J-12) is located in west central Texas. Coleman, the county seat and largest town, is sixty miles southeast of Abilene. The center point of the county is 31°45′

north latitude and 99°25′ west longitude. The county is bordered on the south by the Colorado River, on the north by Taylor and Callahan counties, on the west by Runnels County, and on the east by Brown County. Coleman County encompasses 1,280 square miles. It lies in the transitional area between the Edwards Plateau[qv] and the Rolling Plains and has some characteristics of each. Rolling hills dominated by mesquite brush and oaks predominate in the county. The county has an elevation range of 1,500 to 2,250 feet. The most significant topographic features include Jim Ned Peak (2,140′), Chandlers Peak (2,173′), and Robinsons Peak in the northern half of the county; and the Santa Anna Mountains (2,000′), Speck Mountain (1,520′) and Parks Mountain in the southern half. The flora and fauna of Coleman County are typical of west central Texas; species are mostly western, but some eastern plants and animals can be found. The flora consists of three natural types—mesquite-grassland savanna, upland scrub, and bottomland woodland along the creeks and the Colorado River. The fauna of the county includes such reptiles as yellow mud turtles, Texas map turtles, Western cottonmouth snakes, hognose snakes, Western diamond-backed rattlesnakes, coachwhips, horned toads, and the eastern tree lizard; birds such as turkeys, screech owls, wood ducks, turkey vultures, and red-tailed hawks; and such mammals as white-tailed deer, black-tailed jackrabbits, opossums, and ringtails. The natural resources of the county include oil, gas, rock, and clay. The northern half of the county is drained by Jim Ned and Hords creeks, which meet and flow into Pecan Bayou in neighboring Brown County. Both creeks have been dammed and have reservoirs on them, Coleman Lake[qv] on Jim Ned Creek and Hords Creek Lake[qv] on Hords creek. The southern half of the county is drained by the Colorado River. Grape and Bull creeks are the two major tributaries of the Colorado within the county. Coleman County has an average growing season of 235 days. It receives 26.82 inches of rainfall on the average annually. Temperatures range from a mean January low of 34° F to a mean July high of 96°.

Human occupation of the future Coleman County began 10,000 to 12,000 years ago, as archeological evidence along the Colorado indicates. Closer to modern times, the area was dominated by the Lipan Apaches and the Comanches. European exploration into the county was not frequent, but as many as four seventeenth-century Spanish explorations came through the area. In 1632 a Father Salas led an expedition to the upper Colorado; in 1650 captains Hernán Martín and Diego del Castillo[qqv] explored the western portion of the county. Four years later Diego de Guadalajara[qv] followed the same path as Martín and Castillo, and in 1683–84 Juan Domínguez de Mendoza[qv] established a short-lived mission somewhere near the confluence of the Concho and Colorado rivers. The exact location, however, is unknown and has been the subject of some debate. Some archeologists and historians put the mission site at the Concho-Colorado confluence, while others put it at the site of present-day Leaday in Coleman County.

Anglo exploration of the county came with the establishment of Camp Colorado.[qv] The camp was originally located in what later became Mills County, but in August of 1856 was moved to Mukewater Creek on the Jinglebob Trail of John Chisum[qv] in the eastern part of Coleman County. Because of disease the camp was moved in July 1857 twenty miles north to Jim Ned Creek. Camp Colorado was operated by the United States Army until the outbreak of the Civil War.[qv] In 1861–62 the camp housed state militiamen, and from 1862 to 1865 a company of Texas Rangers[qv] was stationed there. Some of the notables who served at Camp Colorado include Earl Van Dorn, John Bell Hood, Edmund Kirby Smith, Lawrence S. (Sul) Ross, and Fitzhugh Lee.[qqv] In 1870 the site was purchased by H. H. Sackett.

Coleman County was formed in 1858 from parts of Brown and Travis counties. Organization began in 1862 and was completed in 1864. The county was named for Robert M. Coleman,[qv] a signer of the Texas Declaration of Independence[qv] and an aide to General Houston at San Jacinto. After organization was completed settlers began moving into the county. Some of the more notable were Rich Coffey, William Day, Mabel Doss Day Lea,[qqv] and John Chisum. Chisum established a store at Trickham and maintained a ranch headquarters on Home Creek in the southern part of the county. Coffey established himself on a ranch between the site of present Leaday and Voss about 1866. He also served as a county commissioner, participated in the first county grand jury, and was part of a commission to select a new county seat. William Day ran a ranch in the southwestern corner of the county. His holdings sprawled from Grape Creek in the north, eastward to Elm Creek and then southward to the Colorado River. He died in June 1881 from injuries received in a cattle stampede. His wife, Mabel, whom he had married in 1879, continued to run the ranch for a time after his death. Because of debts she sold the ranch to homesteaders in 1904.

Camp Colorado served as the county seat from 1864 to 1876. But with an increasing population, a new county seat in a more central location was needed. In 1876 a commission was selected to find a suitable site. Early that year a tract on Jim Ned Creek was chosen as the site of the future city of Coleman. In July 1876 town lots were sold to settlers. The "second city" of Coleman County, Santa Anna, came into existence three years later. It had formerly been called Gap because of the cleft in the Santa Anna Mountains but changed names when the residents petitioned for a post office.

The years between 1880 and 1920 were prosperous for Coleman County. Agriculture dominated the local economy. In 1880 the county had a population of 3,603. There were 435 total farms with an average size of 389 acres. The estimated value of all farm products that year was $154,727. In 1890 the county's agriculture showed a modest growth, and the population had increased to 6,112. The number of farms had increased to 582, with an average size of 696 acres. The estimated value of farm products increased to $286,610 by 1890. Between 1880 and 1890 the number of sharecroppers increased significantly. In 1880 there were thirty-two sharecroppers in the county, or a little over 7 percent of the operating farmers. In 1890, however, there were seventy-six sharecroppers, or about 13 percent of the operating farmers. This trend continued into the twentieth century.

The local economy continued to grow overall, however. The county population increased through the first two decades of the twentieth century. In 1900 it stood at 10,077. By 1910 it had doubled. In 1910 farm products worth almost $6 million were produced and $821,102 worth were sold. Coleman also grew at a rapid pace, from 1,362 people in 1900 to 3,406 in 1910. In 1910 manufacturing concerns produced over $74,000 worth of goods in the town.

Between 1910 and 1920 the economy began to falter, particularly in agriculture. In 1917 only 12.74 inches of rain fell, and the cotton crop suffered. That year the cotton crop was 15,231 bales, but in 1918 it was only 916 bales. The drought became so bad that the city of Coleman had to import water. People moved away; the census of 1920 recorded only 18,805.

In the same decade the oil industry began in Coleman County. Natural gas had been discovered around Trickham, and in 1916 the wells were producing 2½ million cubic feet of gas a day. In 1917 oil was discovered north of Coleman on the J. P. Morris ranch. By the end of 1918 Coleman County had produced over 31,000 barrels of oil.

In the 1920s the agricultural economy of Coleman County was depressed. In 1919 the value of the crops grown was more than $10 million, but crops grown in 1924 were worth only a little over $6 million. Tenancy increased dramatically in the twenties. In 1920, 54.8 percent of Coleman County farmers were tenants. By 1925 tenants amounted to over 63 percent. The oil industry began to grow in this decade, however, and continued to grow for the next thirty years. In 1927 the county produced more than 400,000 barrels of oil.

Coleman County reached its highest population in 1930, with 23,669 people. This increase signaled no boom, however. Throughout the 1930s the farm economy was depressed, and the oilfields experienced only modest growth. The Great Depression[qv] hit county farmers hard, and tenancy continued to increase. In 1935 the number of tenants was almost twice that of farm owners. But oil continued to flow; in 1934 and 1935 the county produced almost 500,000 barrels of oil annually.

The years after the depression saw many changes in Coleman County. In the next four decades the county experienced a decrease in population, a stabilization of agriculture, and booming oilfields. The population of the county in 1940 was 20,571, a figure representing a net decline of 13 percent since 1930. For the first time in many years the farm segment of the economy began to improve. In 1945 only about one-third of the farm operators were tenants, and of these the largest group were cash tenants. The oilfields of the county were producing over a million barrels a year by 1948.

In 1950 the population of Coleman County had declined to 15,503, nearly 25 percent less than in 1940. Also by 1950 the urban population increased significantly. More than 42 percent of the county's population was urban by 1950, compared to a little less than 30 percent in 1940. The oil industry, centered in Coleman, accounted for this shift in population. Coleman had 6,530 people in 1950. Oil reached its peak in the county during the 1950s and early 1960s. In a period of about ten years Coleman County produced over three million barrels of oil a year. Agriculture continued its rise. With the loss of rural population, the number of holdings decreased, but the average size increased due to a greater reliance on machinery. In 1950 there were 1,596 farms with an average size of 485.7 acres. In 1954, however, the number of farms had decreased to 1,427, and the average size of each holding had increased to 526.7 acres. Tenancy continued to decrease. In 1950, 37.3 percent of the county's farmers were tenants. By 1954 tenancy had decreased to 34.5 percent. Again most of these were cash tenants.

In the 1960s and 1970s the economic trends of the previous two decades continued. The population of the county declined to 12,458 by 1960. For the first time in the county's history most of the population was urban. By 1960 the number of farms had decreased to 1,105 and earned an annual income of over $7 million. The petroleum industry began to slow down, however. In 1968 production was a little over a million barrels, less than half the yield of 1960.

The 1970s brought similar changes. In 1969 the county had 1,073 farms with a total area of 795,000 acres; the value of products of these farms was almost $9 million. By 1974 the number of farms had decreased to 847, and the total area under cultivation had also decreased, to 747,000 acres. However, the value of farm products sold annually had increased to $10 million. Oil production slowed further during the 1970s. In 1972 the county produced just over 700,000 barrels of oil; in 1976 the total was 643,000. Production increased during the 1980s, increasing to nearly one million barrels, but in the early 1990s it had fallen to about 700,000 barrels annually.

Politically Coleman County has been staunchly Democratic, though in the late twentieth century the Republican party qv made strong inroads, particularly in national and statewide races. Between 1952 and 1990 Republican presidential candidates have outpolled their Democratic counterparts in every election except those of 1964, 1976, and 1992. Republican candidates in gubernatorial and senatorial contests also fared well. In 1980 the county population had increased to 10,439 people, as compared to 10,288 in 1970. In 1990 the county population was 9,710.

BIBLIOGRAPHY: Coleman County Historical Commission, *History of Coleman County and Its People* (2 vols., San Angelo: Anchor, 1985).

Rusty Tate

COLEMAN FIELD. Coleman Field, at Coleman, was activated as a contract primary flying school in December 1940. It was operated by the Austin Flying Service. Flight training began in June 1941. The field was deactivated on November 15, 1944.

BIBLIOGRAPHY: Coleman County Historical Commission, *History of Coleman County and Its People* (2 vols., San Angelo: Anchor, 1985).

Robert E. Hays, Jr., Military Aviation Activities in Texas, World Wars I and II (M.A. thesis, University of Texas, 1963).

Art Leatherwood

COLEMAN-FULTON PASTURE COMPANY. Five South Texas entrepreneurs, cattlemen, and dreamers pooled their assets and wits in 1871 to form one of the largest cattle companies in Texas. Col. George Ware Fulton qv was the leader. He convinced Youngs Coleman, his son Thomas M. Coleman, Thomas Henry Mathis,qqv and his cousin, J. M. Mathis, to form the Coleman, Mathis, Fulton Cattle Company, with headquarters in the new town of Rockport.

Fulton came to Texas in 1837 from Philadelphia with a company of men to help in the Texas Revolution.qv He married Harriet G. Smith, eldest daughter of former governor Henry Smith.qv Youngs Coleman came to Texas shortly after the revolution and settled in Jackson County. By the early 1850s he was one of the largest landowners in San Patricio County. His son, Tom, was associated with his father and gradually took over the family ranching interests. The Mathis cousins were drawn to the South Texas in 1859. They were involved in trading with Mexico. T. H. joined the Confederate Army and after the war returned to South Texas as a trader and merchant. The cousins built a packery at the site of present Rockport and went into business with their own steamboat, the *Prince Albert*, shipping tallow, hides, and bones to the east.

The four men pooled their private landholdings to get the Coleman, Mathis, Fulton Cattle Company started and immediately began a campaign of acquiring additional land. At its peak the company controlled 265,000 acres of land that ran from Rockport westward through San Patricio County and spilled over into Live Oak, Bee, and Goliad counties. Some of the first fences in South Texas were put up by this company. Since this was before the advent of barbed wire,qv they used smooth wire and in one instance built a board fence that enclosed a sizable portion of the land near Rockport as a holding area for cattle awaiting their turn at the slaughterhouse. Later, after barbed wire was introduced, the partners continued fencing the entire ranch and put in cross fences to make individual pastures.

From the beginning they spent money like the storied cattle barons. This led to early financial trouble and heavy borrowing; however, early company records reveal that in 1878 the company declared a dividend of $214,624.19—partly with borrowed money. Personality conflicts and disagreements over finances, plus a prolonged drought, caused the partners to dissolve the company in 1879. Under the terms of the agreement the Mathis cousins received the Henry Bend Ranch near Mathis, as well as land in Live Oak and Goliad counties, a total of 47,000 acres.

The other three partners, Fulton and Youngs and Tom Coleman, formed the Coleman-Fulton Pasture Company to take the place of the dissolved organization. Youngs Coleman actually never took part in the management of the company, since he refused to pledge allegiance to the Union after the Civil Warqv and chose to buy a huge plantation in Mexico. He left Tom Coleman in charge of his interests. G. W. Fulton, Jr.,qv was brought into the company in 1884 and replaced Tom Coleman as ranch superintendent in 1885, thus causing a rift that had lasting effects on the company.

Financial problems beset the company, which now embraced 167,000 acres of land, primarily in San Patricio County. Fulton borrowed money from millionaire David Sinton, an acquaintance and college mate in Cincinnati. Continued borrowing finally gave Sinton the controlling interest in the company after he purchased the Coleman interests. At the death of Sinton his only daughter, Anna, the wife of Charles P. Taft, inherited control of the company. Taft was the half-brother of President William Howard Taft.

Despite financial problems the company became a leader in the ranching world in South Texas. Improved breeds of cattle were introduced in keeping with Colonel Fulton's desire to push forward. Originally the company offices were in Rockport, with the ranch headquarters at Rincon (eight miles north of Gregory). When the railroad came through San Patricio County in 1886 the office was moved to Rincon and later to Gregory, which was on the railroad. The last company office was in a two-story building constructed by the company in 1923 in Taft to house the company's two banks on the ground floor and company offices on the second floor.

By the late 1890s Sinton had full control of the company, had eliminated all debts, and had the cattle ranch on a paying basis. He had already bought the 224,000-acre Catarina Ranch in Dimmit County and installed a young attorney by the name of Joseph F. Green qv in 1896 as manager. In 1900 Green was made manager of the Coleman-Fulton Pasture Company. With the death of Sinton in 1900, and the assumption of management by Charles P. Taft, the ranch began to be known locally as the Taft Ranch. However, the official name, Coleman-Fulton Pasture Company, remained until the charter was officially dissolved in 1930.

From the time he took over the affairs of the ranch in 1900 until his death in 1926, Green was the driving force in the building of an agricultural and ranching giant; he subsequently presided over its sell-out. Green's instructions had been to develop the ranch in such a manner as to increase the value of the company's land. To bring this about he poured millions into the Taft Ranch, developing breeds of cattle and improving agriculture. The keystone in his plan was the formation of the town of Taft in 1904. When the first sweet water was discovered in Taft in 1909, the board of directors of Coleman-Fulton Pasture Company authorized Green to construct an agricultural-industrial complex in Taft. Eventually a meat-packing plant with a slaughterhouse and rendering plant, power plant, ice plant, creamery, hatchery, machine shop, cottonseed oil mill, cotton gins, and a feed mill were built. The plan was simple: to increase the value of the land by providing a market for the new farmers to sell their products.

The ranch became a leader in the opening of the area to agriculture by developing a system of company farms to pioneer different crops in the area. Shorthorn cattle were introduced, and an extensive dairy herd was formed that won national awards. La Quinta, a large mansion, was constructed in 1907 as the superintendent's home and also as a place to entertain the steady stream of national figures, including the president of the United States, William Howard Taft, who visited the ranch in 1909. Leaders in all fields were brought in to head the various ranch departments as the development continued and the sellout began in earnest.

Taft, which was a complete company town, was put on the market in 1921, after streets were built, sewers and water lines laid, power and telephone line strung, and a school built. Over 5,000 people attended the auction, which featured Taft town lots, farm tracts, and company businesses. By the time the charter expired in 1930 the vast ranch and all of its enterprises had been sold. Green purchased key businesses and land that were still owned by his heirs in 1990.

BIBLIOGRAPHY: Keith Guthrie, *History of San Patricio County* (Austin: Nortex, 1986). Dorothy Louise Nims, History of the Village of Rockport (M.A. thesis, Southwest Texas State Teachers College, 1939). May M. Watson and Alex Lillico, *Taft Ranch* (1935).

Keith Guthrie

COLEMAN LAKE. Coleman Lake, formerly Coleman Reservoir, is on Jim Ned Creek fourteen miles north of Coleman in Coleman County (at 32°02′ N, 99°28′ W). It is owned and operated by the city of Coleman for municipal water supply. Construction of the 3,200-foot-long earthfill dam, built by the R. N. Adams Construction Company, was started in August 1965 and completed on May 10, 1966; deliberate impoundment began in April 1966. The cost was well over $1 million. The reservoir has a capacity of 40,000 acre-feet with a surface area of 2,000 acres at the service spillway elevation of 1,717.5 feet above mean sea level and a capacity of 59,000 acre-feet with a surface area of 2,530 acres at the emergency spillway crest elevation of 1,726 feet above mean sea level. The drainage area above the dam, part of the Colorado River basin, is 292 square miles.

BIBLIOGRAPHY: C. L. Dowell and R. G. Petty, *Engineering Data on Dams and Reservoirs in Texas* (Texas Water Development Board Report 126 [3 pts., Austin, 1971–74]).

Seth D. Breeding

COLES, JOHN P. (1793–1847). John P. Coles (Cole), one of Stephen F. Austin's qv Old Three Hundred,qv was born in Rowan County, North Carolina, in 1793. He married Mary Eleanor Owen in Georgia in 1821. The couple moved to Texas as an Old Three Hundred family and reached the Brazos River in the spring of 1822. Coles received title to 8½ leagues of land in the area of present-day Burleson, Washington, and Brazoria counties on August 19, 1824. His cedar log cabin became the center of a community known as Coles' Settlement. Coles maintained a public house, where David Crockettqv was reported to have lost eighty dollars in a poker game on his way to the Alamo. According to inaccurate local tradition, when the signers of the Texas Declaration of Independenceqv rode from Washington-on-the-Brazos to spend the night at Coles' Settlement, the name of the village was changed to Independence. The census of March 1826 listed Coles's wife, a son, two daughters, five servants, and four slaves and noted that Coles was building a mill on Yegua Creek. Three other children were later born to the family.

Coles was alcaldeqv of Washington Municipality in 1828 and a delegate to the Convention of 1833qv at San Felipe de Austin. On July 2, 1835, he signed a petition for the organization of Washington Municipality. During the Texas Revolutionqv he moved his family east of the Neches and then joined William Warner Hill'sqv company, in which he served from July to October 1836. Coles was elected chief justice of Washington County in December 1836 and represented the county in the Senate of the Fifth Texas Congress, 1840–41. He died on January 19, 1847, and was buried at Independence. His original cabin was in good restored condition late in the twentieth century.

BIBLIOGRAPHY: E. L. Blair, *Early History of Grimes County* (Austin, 1930). Lester G. Bugbee, "The Old Three Hundred: A List of Settlers in Austin's First Colony," *Quarterly of the Texas State Historical Association* 1 (October 1897). Betty Cantrell Plummer, *Historic Homes of Washington County* (San Marcos, Texas: Rio Fresco, 1971).

Noel Grisham and L. W. Kemp

COLES CREEK. Coles Creek rises in northern Washington County (at 30°20′ N, 96°16′ W) and runs east for seven miles to its mouth on the Brazos River, two miles north of Washington-on-the-Brazos (at 30°21′ N, 96°10′ W). It was named for John P. Coles,qv who received a land grant on it from the Austin colony. The surrounding gently sloping to moderately steep terrain is surfaced by deep, fine sandy loam that supports hardwood forests and conifers. Toward the mouth of the creek the terrain levels, is marked by local shallow depression, and is surfaced by clay and sandy loam that supports water-tolerant hardwoods, post oak, and grasses.

COLE SPRINGS, TEXAS. Cole Springs was six miles north of Lexington in extreme northern Lee County. The area was settled before the Civil War.qv In 1856 residents organized the Cole Springs Baptist Church and constructed a log building to serve as the church and school. The structure burned down in 1901, and a new wooden frame church was constructed. The school enrolled thirty-four students during the 1905–06 school year. A new separate building was erected for the school in 1913 and continued to serve area children until the school was consolidated with the Lexington Independent School District. By the mid-1930s the community no longer appeared on state highway maps.

BIBLIOGRAPHY: Lee County Historical Survey Committee, *A History of Lee County* (Quanah, Texas: Nortex, 1974).

Christopher Long

COLETO, BATTLE OF. The battle of Coleto, the culmination of the Goliad Campaign of 1836,qv occurred near Coleto Creek in Goliad County on March 19 and 20, 1836. Originally called "the battle of the prairie" and "la batalla del encinal [oak grove] del Perdido [Creek]," it was one of the most significant engagements of the Texas Revolution.qv The battle, however, cannot properly be considered as isolated from the series of errors and misfortunes that preceded it, errors for which the Texas commander, James W. Fannin, Jr.,qv was ultimately responsible. The most exasperating decision confronting Fannin was whether to abandon Goliad after having fortified it, and if so, when. He had already been informed of Gen. José de Urrea'sqv advancing Mexican army by Plácido Benavides,qv after the defeat of Texas forces under Francis W. Johnson and James Grantqqv at the battles of San Patricio and Agua Dulce Creek.qqv The Mexican advance caused the Texans to abandon the port of Copano, thus making Goliad considerably less important strategically, as Fannin knew. He had received word that the Alamo had fallen as well. Still, he continued to fortify Fort Defiance, as he christened the La Bahíaqv presidio, and awaited orders from superiors to abandon the site, knowing also that a retreat would not be well received among his men, who were eager to confront the Mexicans.

More immediately consequential to the battle of Coleto was Fannin's dispatching Amon B. King'sqv men and then William Ward and the Georgia Battalionqqv to Refugio, a move primarily induced by the activities of Carlos de la Garzaqv and his rancheros, who were operating as advance cavalry for General Urrea. Not only did the decision to send Ward and King into Urrea's known path dangerously divide the Goliad garrison, thus reducing by about 150 the men Fannin would be able to bring against Urrea at Coleto Creek, but the move became the main reason Fannin waited so long to abandon Goliad. He refused to do so until he learned of King and Ward's fate, even after he received Sam Houston'sqv order to fall back to Victoria. Since King had taken the Goliad garrison's wagons and teams with him to Refugio, however, Fannin delayed his retreat further, awaiting the arrival of Albert C. Horton'sqv men from Guadalupe Victoria, who were bringing needed carts and twenty yokes of oxen garnered by army quartermaster John J. Linn.qv Accounts are not in agreement, but Horton apparently arrived by March 16. In addition, by capturing virtually all of Fannin's couriers sent to find King and Ward, Urrea learned the details of the Goliad commander's plans and schemed accordingly. Fannin, however, was unable to find out his opponent's true strength or position, though on March 17 Horton's cavalry did discover Col. Juan Moralesqv approaching with the Jiménez and San Luis battalions, 500 veterans of the battle of the Alamoqv whom Antonio López de Santa Annaqv had sent from Bexar to reinforce Urrea.

Fannin finally learned of King and Ward's defeat in the battle of Refugioqv from Hugh McDonald Frazerqv on March 17, but he still did not order the retreat to Victoria until the next day. March 18 was spent instead in a series of skirmishes between Horton's cavalry and Urrea's advance forces, which by then had reached Goliad. Fannin, thinking the fort was about to be besieged, kept the garrison on alert and attempted no retreat even that night, the result of a council decision based on Horton's observations. During this delay the oxen, which were to be hitched to the carts made ready for the removal to Victoria, were left unfed.

At last the Texans began their retreat, by 9:00 A.M. on March 19 under a heavy fog. Fannin insisted on taking nine cumbersome artillery pieces of various calibers and about 1,000 muskets, though he neglected to take enough water and food for more than a few meals. The carts were heavily loaded, the hungry oxen were tired and unruly, and progress was slow. Urrea, expecting to lay siege to the fort, was unaware of Fannin's departure until 11:00 A.M. But the Texans forfeited about an hour of their lead while crossing the San Antonio River; a cart broke down, and the largest cannon fell into the river and had to be fished out. Another valuable hour was lost when Fannin ordered the oxen detached for grazing after the column had proceeded about a mile past Manahuilla Creek. John Shackelford, Burr H. Duval, and Ira Westoverqqv protested this stop, arguing that the column should not rest until reaching the protection of the Coleto Creek timber. Shackelford particularly noted his commander's contempt for the Mexican army's prowess and his disbelief that Urrea would dare follow them—an assumption apparently common among Fannin's men.

Urrea had quickly left Goliad without his artillery and the full complement of his force in order to narrow Fannin's two-hour lead. Mexican sources indicate that he set out with eighty cavalrymen and 360 infantrymen. He discovered through his mounted scouts the location of Fannin's column and that the rebel force was considerably smaller than supposed, information that prompted him to return 100 infantrymen to Goliad to help secure Presidio La Bahía and escort the artillery ordered to join him as soon as possible. Horton's approximately thirty cavalrymen served as advance guards on all sides of Fannin's column. The unalert rear guard, however, which included Hermann Ehrenberg,qv failed to detect the Mexican cavalry. Meanwhile, the Texans had scarcely resumed march after resting the oxen before another cart broke down; its contents had to be transferred to another wagon. Fannin then sent Horton to scout the Coleto Creek timber, now in sight, when the Mexican cavalry emerged from behind them. Upon overtaking the lumbering Texan position at about 1:30 P.M., the Mexican commander ordered his cavalry to halt Fannin's advance toward the protective timber. Fannin set up a skirmish line with artillery while the column attempted to reach Coleto Creek, about two miles distant.

Perceiving the danger, he then formed his men into a moving square and continued toward the closer timber of Perdido Creek, which was less than a mile away when the Texans were overtaken by Mexican cavalry. Caught in a valley some six feet below its surroundings, the Texans were trying to get to the more defensible higher ground about 400 to 500 yards distant, when their ammunition cart broke down. While Fannin called a council to determine the feasibility of taking what ammunition they could and reaching the timber, Urrea, seeing his advantage, attacked.

With little water, and situated in an open prairie covered with high grass that occluded vision of their enemy, Fannin's men made ready their defense. Their hollow square was three ranks deep. Each man received three or four muskets. Bayonets, rifles, more than forty pairs of pistols, and abundant ammunition complemented this arsenal. The San Antonio Greys and Red Roversqqv formed the front line; Duval's Mustangs and others, including Frazer's Refugio militia, formed the rear. The left flank was defended by Westover's regulars, the right by the Mobile Greys.qv The artillery was placed in the corners (except when moved as needed), and Fannin assumed a command position in the rear of the right flank. In addition, an outpost of sharpshooters formed around Abel Morgan'sqv hospital wagon, which had become immobilized earlier when an ox was hit by Mexican fire.

Soon after Urrea's cavalry managed to stop Fannin's retreat, the Mexican general amassed his troops and attacked the square. The rifle companies under Morales assaulted the left, the grenadiers and part of the San Luis Battalion charged the right under Urrea's direct supervision, the Jiménez Battalion under Col. Mariano Salas attacked the front, and Col. Gabriel Núñez's cavalry charged the rear.

Sources differ widely about the numbers of men involved on March 19. Fannin defended his position with about 300 men. Urrea wrote that he had eighty cavalry and 260 infantry at the time the Texans were overtaken, a figure confirmed by Peña, who also stressed that most of the Mexican troops were Alamo veterans. Many Texas sources give unrealistically high numbers for Urrea's pursuit force. Clearly the Mexican general set out with only a small force of veteran troops to ensure catching Fannin, and left orders for a larger force, including artillery, to follow and aid in battling the Texans once they were caught. It seems likely that Urrea had between 300 and 500 men when he overtook Fannin, and after receiving reinforcements by morning, March 20, he had between 700 and 1,000.

The battle of Coleto lasted until after sunset on March 19. The Texans made effective use of their bayonets, multiple muskets, and nine cannons; their square remained unbroken. Dr. Joseph H. Barnard[qv] recorded that seven of his comrades had been killed and sixty wounded (forty severely), Fannin among them. The Mexican general was impressed with both the "withering fire of the enemy" and their ability to repulse his three charges. Ironically, Urrea retired because of ammunition depletion. His casualties were heavy as well, though accounts vary widely. He then positioned snipers in the tall grass around the square and inflicted additional casualties before Texan sharpshooters were able to quell these attacks by firing at the flashes illuminating the darkness. Ultimately, the Texans under Fannin suffered ten deaths on March 19.

Fannin's men hardly felt defeated and anxiously awaited Horton's return with reinforcements from Guadalupe Victoria. None came, however, for Horton was unable to cut through the Mexican lines. William Ward and the Georgia Battalion, defeated in the battle of Refugio, were close enough to hear the Coleto gunfire during their retreat to Victoria, but were exhausted and hungry. Urrea knew from captured couriers that Ward and Fannin would try to rendezvous at Victoria, so with the aid of Carlos de la Garza's men, he kept the Georgia Battalion isolated in the Guadalupe riverbottom until they surrendered. At the Coleto battlefield, Urrea posted detachments at three points around Fannin's square to prevent escape and kept the Texans on stiff watch throughout the night with false bugle calls.

Fannin's position became critical during the night because the lack of water and inability to light fires made treating the wounded impossible; the situation was made even more unbearable by a cold and rainy norther. The cries of the wounded demoralized everyone. The lack of water, which was required to cool and clean the cannons during fire, also guaranteed that the artillery would be ineffective the next day, especially considering that the artillerists had sustained a high number of casualties. Furthermore, ammunition was low. A council among Fannin and his officers weighing these facts concluded that they could not sustain another battle. The proposition to escape to the Perdido or Coleto creek timber under dark and before Urrea received reinforcements was rejected, since after much debate the men unanimously voted not to abandon the wounded, among whom the unwounded all had friends or relatives. They therefore began digging trenches and erecting barricades of carts and dead animals in preparation for the next day's battle. By the time this was completed, the Mexican position had been reinforced with munitions, fresh troops, and two or three artillery pieces from Goliad. Urrea placed his artillery on the slopes overlooking the Texan position and grouped for battle at 6:15 A.M., March 20.

After the Mexican artillery had fired one or possibly two rounds, Fannin was convinced that making another stand would be futile. Another consultation among his officers produced the decision to seek honorable terms for surrender for the sake of the wounded, and to hope the Mexicans would adhere to them. Fannin's men apparently drafted terms of surrender guaranteeing that they would be considered prisoners of war, that their wounded would be treated, and that they sooner or later would be paroled to the United States. But Urrea could not ratify such an agreement; he was bound by Santa Anna's orders and congressional decree to accept no terms other than unconditional surrender. He made it clear to Fannin in person that he could offer only to intercede on the Texans' behalf with Santa Anna. The extant document of capitulation, signed by Benjamin C. Wallace, Joseph M. Chadwick,[qqv] and Fannin, shows that the Texas commander surrendered his men "subject to the disposition of the supreme government"; but Fannin apparently did not make this fact clear to his men, since survivors' accounts indicate that the Texans were led to believe they were surrendering honorably as prisoners of war and would be returned to the United States. This discrepancy is significant only in light of the ultimate fate of Fannin's command. Nevertheless, traditional Texan renditions inaccurately imply some insidious conspiracy in the surrender episode.

Those Texans able to walk were escorted back to Goliad. Texas physicians were made to care for the Mexican wounded to the neglect of their own men. Many of the Texas wounded were not transported to Goliad for three days; Fannin himself was left on the field for two. Urrea, meanwhile, continued his advance to secure Guadalupe Victoria, from where he wrote Santa Anna recommending clemency for the Goliad prisoners. One week after Fannin's surrender, however, Santa Anna bypassed Urrea and ordered Col. José Nicolás de la Portilla,[qv] the commander at Goliad, to carry out the congressional decree of December 30, 1835, that captured armed rebels must be executed as pirates. Fannin's entire command, together with William Ward and the Georgia Battalion, were shot in the Goliad Massacre[qv] on Palm Sunday, March 27, 1836.

Although the battle of Coleto is usually considered meaningful only as a prologue to the massacre, it does have separate significance. The sequence of events underscores the tragedy of Fannin's inability to make timely decisions crucial for success. This disadvantage was worsened by his disrespect for the capabilities of his enemy and a reluctance, common in the Texas army, to coordinate campaigns. Urrea, by contrast, showed skill in staying alert to Fannin's plans, keeping the Texans inside the presidio an extra day, pursuing and catching them by taking advantage of every opportunity, and isolating Ward's men near Victoria while successfully battling Fannin's command at Coleto Creek. Still, the Texans, though most were relatively untrained volunteers, obeyed their commanders and withstood the onslaught of seasoned enemy troops. The intensity of this battle produced heroism on both sides.

The battle's greatest significance, however, remains bound up in its consequences. Urrea's victory gained him greater esteem in the army but also incurred the jealousy of other generals, especially Santa Anna, who had only recently suffered through his difficult victory at the Alamo. Ironically, the triumph caused overconfidence among Mexican leaders, who, like Santa Anna, now believed the campaign against the rebellion to be nearing a successful conclusion. Finally, it was the Goliad Massacre and not the defeat and surrender at Coleto Creek that soured United States opinion against Mexico and gave Houston and the Texas army the second half of the rallying cry that inspired victory at the battle of San Jacinto[qv]: "Remember the Alamo! Remember Goliad!" The assumed location of the Coleto battlefield is now maintained as Fannin Battleground State Historic Site[qv] by the Texas Parks and Wildlife Department[qv] and is near Fannin, Texas (once called Fanning's Defeat), on U.S. Highway 59 between Goliad and Victoria.

BIBLIOGRAPHY: Hubert Howe Bancroft, *History of the North Mexican States and Texas* (2 vols., San Francisco: History Company, 1886, 1889). Joseph H. Barnard, *Dr. J. H. Barnard's Journal: A Composite of Known Versions*, ed. Hobart Huson (Refugio?, Texas, 1949). Harbert Davenport, "Men of Goliad," *Southwestern Historical Quarterly* 43 (July 1939). John Crittenden Duval, *Early Times in Texas, or the Adventures of Jack Dobell* (Austin: Gammel, 1892; new ed., Lincoln: University of Nebraska Press, 1986). Hermann Ehrenberg, *Texas und Seine Revolution* (Leipzig: Wigand, 1843; abridged trans. by Charlotte Churchill, *With Milam and Fannin*, Austin: Pemberton Press, 1968). Joseph E. Field, *Three Years in Texas* (Greenfield and Boston, Massachusetts, 1836; rpt., Austin: Steck, 1935). Henry Stuart Foote, *Texas and the Texans* (2 vols., Philadelphia: Cowperthwait, 1841; rpt., Austin: Steck, 1935). Andrew Jackson Houston, *Texas Independence* (Houston: Anson Jones Press, 1938). Hobart Huson, *Refugio: A Comprehensive History of Refugio County from Aboriginal Times to 1953* (2 vols., Woodsboro, Texas: Rooke Foundation, 1953, 1955). John H. Jenkins, ed., *The Papers of the Texas Revolution, 1835–1836* (10 vols., Austin: Presidial Press, 1973). William Kennedy, *Texas: The Rise,*

Progress, and Prospects of the Republic of Texas (London: Hastings, 1841; rpt., Fort Worth: Molyneaux Craftsmen, 1925). John J. Linn, *Reminiscences of Fifty Years in Texas* (New York: Sadlier, 1883; 2d ed., Austin: Steck, 1935; rpt., Austin: State House, 1986). Abel Morgan, *An Account of the Battle of Goliad and Fanning's Massacre* (Paducah, Kentucky?, 1847?). Kathryn Stoner O'Connor, *The Presidio La Bahía del Espíritu Santo de Zúñiga, 1721 to 1846* (Austin: Von Boeckmann–Jones, 1966). José Enrique de la Peña, *With Santa Anna in Texas* (College Station: Texas A&M University Press, 1975). Jakie L. Pruett and Everett B. Cole, *Goliad Massacre: A Tragedy of the Texas Revolution* (Austin: Eakin Press, 1985). Antonio López de Santa Anna et al., *The Mexican Side of the Texan Revolution,* trans. Carlos E. Castañeda (Dallas: Turner, 1928; 2d ed., Austin: Graphic Ideas, 1970). Ruby C. Smith, "James W. Fannin, Jr., in the Texas Revolution," *Southwestern Historical Quarterly* 23 (October 1919, January, April 1920). David M. Vigness, *The Revolutionary Decades: The Saga of Texas, 1810–1836* (Austin: Steck-Vaughn, 1965). Dudley Goodall Wooten, ed., *A Comprehensive History of Texas* (2 vols., Dallas: Scarff, 1898; rpt., Austin: Texas State Historical Association, 1986). Henderson K. Yoakum, *History of Texas from Its First Settlement in 1685 to Its Annexation to the United States in 1846* (2 vols., New York: Redfield, 1855).

Craig H. Roell

COLETO CREEK. Coleto Creek is formed by the confluence of Fifteen-Mile Creek and Twelve-Mile Creek (at 28°52′ N, 97°14′ W) in Victoria County and flows southeast for twenty-five miles to its mouth on the Guadalupe River, six miles south of Victoria (at 28°42′ N, 97°01′ W). The stream forms part of the county line between Goliad and Victoria counties. In the area flat to rolling prairie is surfaced by permeable sand that supports mesquite and a variety of prairie grasses. The creek is impounded to form Coleto Creek Reservoir, which lies on the boundary of Victoria and Goliad counties. The stream was known as Coleto Creek as early as 1836. That year Texas revolutionary forces under James W. Fannin[qv] were defeated by a division of the Mexican army commanded by José de Urrea[qv] at the battle of Coleto,[qv] which was fought 2½ miles southwest of its banks. In 1850, when Clinton became the county seat of DeWitt County, the headstreams of Coleto Creek were named Three-Mile Coleto, Five-Mile Coleto, Twelve-Mile Coleto, Fifteen-Mile Coleto (the main stream), and Eighteen-Mile Coleto, the names signifying the distance from the stream to the courthouse door at Clinton. Although Cuero became county seat in 1876, the headstreams in 1949 were still known by their distances from Clinton. By the 1960s, however, the headstreams were considered separate creeks on county maps, with no reference to Coleto Creek in their names.

COLETOVILLE, TEXAS. Coletoville is near Coleto Creek Reservoir ten miles west of Victoria in Victoria County. The site was known in its early days as Steiner's Settlement, after Carl Steiner, who arrived from Germany in 1850. It took its present name from Coleto Creek, which, with Dry Creek, marked the community's boundaries. The Coleto Creek valley communities are part of the large area of German settlement in Victoria, DeWitt, and Goliad counties, which also includes Schroeder (Germantown), Arneckeville, Meyersville, and Yorktown. Steiner's Settlement produced 2,000 gallons of wine from the local wild Mustang grapes in 1860 alone. The Old Goliad Road, which carried Victoria-Goliad traffic through Coletoville, contributed to the town's early growth. The community had a store, a school, and the Coleto *Schuetzen Verein* (shooting club), as well as a *Gesangverein* (singing club) established in 1854, a Lutheran church founded in 1872, and a post office established in 1875. Trustees paid four dollars for the two-acre church site, upon which they also established a community cemetery without burial restrictions regarding creed. Most early Coletoville settlers are buried there.

Coletoville was one of the few German settlements that failed to prosper, however. The post office was closed in 1877, and the store was closed by 1884. The Gulf, Western Texas and Pacific Railway established a stop five miles away at Raisin in 1889, and the Goliad-Victoria road missed the community. Raisin emerged as the new business center. Local custom merges the two settlements into Raisin-Coletoville, the combined population of which remained about fifty from the early 1900s to 1986, when many residents were descendents of the pioneers. The rural school served the area into the 1940s, and the church was still active in 1986.

BIBLIOGRAPHY: Anne A. Fox and Katherine Livingston, *Historical Architectural and Archaeological Investigations at the Steiner-Schob Complex, Victoria County, Texas* (Archeological Survey Report 52 [Center for Archeological Research, University of Texas at San Antonio, 1979]). Terry G. Jordan, *German Seed in Texas Soil: Immigrant Farmers in Nineteenth-Century Texas* (Austin: University of Texas Press, 1966). Victoria *Advocate*, Progress Edition, March 10, 1963.

Craig H. Roell

COLEY CREEK, TEXAS. Coley Creek is east of Farm Road 223 sixty miles north of Houston in southeastern San Jacinto County. Early Anglo settlers of the area included the Emory Lovin and Rufus Hughes families. Residents of the agricultural community depended upon nearby Shepherd for stores and a post office. Numerous tram railroad lines in the area indicate former involvement in logging operations. Although the lines have been abandoned, the growth of Shepherd has in recent years sparked new development in the surrounding countryside.

BIBLIOGRAPHY: Ruth Hansbro, History of San Jacinto County (M.A. thesis, Sam Houston State Teachers College, 1940).

Robert Wooster

COLFAX, TEXAS. Colfax is eight miles southeast of Canton on Farm Road 16, at the headsprings of the Neches River in southeast Van Zandt County. The original community center was a log house used for religious services known as Cold Water. The name was changed to Tunnell's Chapel when Elisha Tunnell put up a church that also served as a school in the late 1870s. A local post office established after 1870 was maintained in private homes. The name Colfax, probably first used for the post office in the early 1880s, honored Schuyler Colfax, United States vice president from Indiana. Colfax was still a church community when the Methodist and Cumberland Presbyterian churches established a brush arbor on a nearby tract of land in 1885 and erected a tabernacle and bungalows for church services and camp meetings. Postal service was discontinued in 1905, and mail was delivered from Canton. A population recorded at thirty between 1885 and 1895 grew to 100 by 1933. At the community's zenith local residents raised fruits and vegetables, and Colfax had a brick schoolhouse, three churches, a cemetery, several businesses, and numerous residences. School enrollment reached 122 in 1906, and the Grange[qv] and Masonic lodge, revivals, and Sunday school met in the new school building. When the Van oilfield[qv] opened in 1929 and Van residents set up a school system, the new district absorbed Colfax, and the town's schoolhouse was torn down. The population of Colfax fell to twenty-eight by 1968 and was last recorded at thirty-five in 1974.

BIBLIOGRAPHY: William Samuel Mills, *History of Van Zandt County* (Canton, Texas, 1950). Van Zandt County History Book Committee, *History of Van Zandt County* (Dallas, 1984).

Diana J. Kleiner

COLINA, AGUSTÍN DE (16?–?). Agustín de Colina, a Franciscan priest, was stationed in 1687 at the struggling missions of La Junta de los Ríos[qv] (the juncture of the Rio Grande and the Río de Conchos), at the site of present Presidio, Texas, and Ojinaga, Chihuahua. There in the fall of that same year, widely traveled Cíbolo and Jumano Indians approached Colina and asked him for a letter that they could take to "the Spaniards who were coming and going among the Tejas" in East Texas. Not privy at this remote location to intelligence that Frenchmen had landed somewhere on the northern Gulf Coast, Colina made light of the request and countered with one of his own: the Indians should bring *him* a letter from "the other Spaniards."

In September 1688 five Cíbolos who had just returned from a journey to East Texas brought news that a "Moor" lived among a tribe situated near the Tejas. The foreigner was Jean Jarry,qv a Frenchman who had likely been a member of the Sieur de La Salle's qv colony at Fort St. Louis.qv Shortly thereafter, other Cíbolos arrived with details of strangers living among the Tejas Indians who had armor and long muskets. These foreigners were assuredly La Salle's men.

Colina reported this information to Juan Isidro de Pardiñas, the governor at El Parral. Pardiñas felt obliged to investigate the matter, and on November 3 issued an order that led to the formation of an expedition commanded by Gen. Juan Fernández de Retana qv of Presidio de Conchos. The Fernández expedition, however, was repeatedly delayed by Indian unrest in the La Junta area, and it did not depart for the land of the Tejas until sometime later.

Despite the joint efforts of Colina and a fellow priest (Joaquín de Hinojosa) to missionize the Indians at La Junta de los Ríos, conditions among the enemy nations of the locale forced them under orders from their superiors to abandon the fledgling missions and withdraw to Fernández de Retana's presidio. Both priests gave testimony before the departure of a military entrada that inflicted punishment on some of the offending Indian nations. Subsequently, news of the destruction of La Salle's colony reached Pardiñas at El Parral. He reacted by canceling the Fernández expedition, which had advanced as far as the Pecos River before returning with Chief Juan Sabeata qv and news of its own that the French settlement had been destroyed. After depositions at El Parral by Sabeata and other Indians, Pardiñas ordered General Fernández to return to his presidio. It is possible, but by no means certain, that Agustín de Colina continued to labor as a missionary in the La Junta region.

BIBLIOGRAPHY: Robert S. Weddle, *The French Thorn: Rival Explorers in the Spanish Sea, 1682–1762* (College Station: Texas A&M University Press, 1991). Robert S. Weddle, *Wilderness Manhunt: The Spanish Search for La Salle* (Austin: University of Texas Press, 1973).

Donald E. Chipman

COLITA (?–1852). Colita (Kalita, Coleto, Colluta), Coushatta Indian leader, was born during the mid-1700s, possibly in the village of Coosawda, on the Alabama River near the site of present Montgomery, Alabama. He served first as chief of the Lower Coushatta Village (also known as Colita's Village qv) on the Trinity River and succeeded Long King qv as principal chief of all the Texas Coushattas after Long King's death around 1838. Among Republic of Texas qv officials Colita was well known for tribal leadership and for his role in helping to maintain peaceful relations between Indians and white settlers in the lower Trinity River region. When white settlers fleeing eastward along the Coushatta Trace in the Runaway Scrape qv (1836) reached the Coushatta villages on the Trinity River, Colita directed the Coushattas' efforts to help the settlers cross the river and then to feed them.

In a letter to Gen. Sam Houston qv of August 17, 1838, S. C. Hirams, who lived near Colita's Village and acted as interpreter for him, reported that Colita talked with the Coushattas at Long King's Village to persuade them to remain peaceful. A German traveler, Friedrich W. von Wrede,qv wrote that while visiting Texas in October 1838, he contacted Colita, who informed him through Hirams that Houston had directed the Coushatta chief to go to a distant Indian village to warn its inhabitants against participating in the revolt at Nacogdoches.

Colita reported to President Mirabeau B. Lamar,qv in a letter written for him by Hirams on June 10, 1839, that difficulties had arisen between Coushattas and their white neighbors. In a letter to Colita on July 9, 1839, Lamar expressed regret that there had been disturbances between Indians and white settlers, and he announced the appointment of Joseph Lindley qv as agent for the Coushattas to serve as mediator in all future difficulties that might arise between these groups. On April 4, 1842, President Houston directed Gen. James Davis qv to visit the Alabamas and Coushattas and assure them of the protection of the Republic of Texas. He specifically asked Davis to send Colita to him for additional discussions of conflicts.

Colita continued to serve as leader of the Coushattas until his death on July 7, 1852, while on a hunting trip in the area of present Liberty County. He was thought to be 100 or older. A brief account of the life and death of this prominent Coushatta chief was included in the *Texas State Gazette* (*see* AUSTIN STATE GAZETTE) for July 17, 1852. A monument in honor of Colita was placed on Texas Highway 146 twelve miles north of Liberty by the Sophia Lee Harrison Chapter of the Daughters of the American Revolution.qv

BIBLIOGRAPHY: Miriam Partlow, *Liberty, Liberty County, and the Atascosito District* (Austin: Pemberton, 1974). Aline T. Rothe, *Kalita's People* (Waco: Texian Press, 1963). Amelia W. Williams and Eugene C. Barker, eds., *The Writings of Sam Houston, 1813–1863* (8 vols., Austin: University of Texas Press, 1938–43; rpt., Austin and New York: Pemberton Press, 1970). Dorman H. Winfrey and James M. Day, eds., *Texas Indian Papers* (4 vols., Austin: Texas State Library, 1959–61; rpt., 5 vols., Austin: Pemberton Press, 1966).

Howard N. Martin

COLITA, TEXAS. Colita, west of Farm Road 350 ninety miles north of Houston in west central Polk County, was one of a cluster of communities known collectively as the Louisiana Settlement. It was established around 1840 and named after Colita,qv a Coushatta Indian chief whose tribe had frequently camped at the site and had established friendly relations with the Texans during the Texas Revolution.qv The rural community had a post office from 1853 to 1909. Colita Academy, established in 1870, served local residents for twenty years. In 1900 Colita had a population of 100. In 1990 a church and two cemeteries remained near the site.

BIBLIOGRAPHY: *A Pictorial History of Polk County, Texas, 1846–1910* (Livingston, Texas: Polk County Bicentennial Commission, 1976; rev. ed. 1978). Aline T. Rothe, History of Education in Polk County (M.A. thesis, University of Texas, 1934). Carl Bassett Wilson, History of Baptist Educational Efforts in Texas, 1829–1900 (Ph.D. dissertation, University of Texas, 1934).

Robert Wooster

COLITA ACADEMY. Colita Academy was in Louisiana Settlement,qv at the site of present Colita in Polk County. The school was founded about 1870 and had a two-story pine building. It was officially nonsectarian, although Baptists were its chief supporters. Principals of the Colita institution included J. M. Pearson, Helen Lawson, a Professor Thomas, Rev. Kit Williams, Thornton Walker, and a Reverend Weymouth. Pupils ranged from seven to twenty-three years of age. Faced with competition from a growing public school system, Colita Academy was closed in 1894.

BIBLIOGRAPHY: Aline T. Rothe, History of Education in Polk County (M.A. thesis, University of Texas, 1934). Carl Bassett Wilson, History of Baptist Educational Efforts in Texas, 1829–1900 (Ph.D. dissertation, University of Texas, 1934).

Robert Wooster

COLITA'S VILLAGE. Colita's Village was the lower village of the three principal communities established by the Coushatta Indians on the Trinity River in the area of present Polk and San Jacinto counties. This major Coushatta village is mentioned in surveyors' field notes for thirteen original land surveys in this area. Coushatta chief Colita qv lived in this village, which was located on a great bend of the Trinity River at a site in present San Jacinto County. In 1840 the Republic of Texas qv Congress granted two leagues of land—one league included the Battise Village qv and the other included Colita's Village—to the Coushattas for permanent reservations. The land was surveyed and the field notes were filed, but the grants never became effective because white settlers had already claimed the land. Colita's Village was included in an earlier grant of land to William G. Logan,qv a merchant in Nacogdoches. Alexander Hamilton Washington qv purchased this land in 1840, and he permitted the Coushattas to continue living on his plantation. The men who operated steamboats on the Trinity River began calling the Logan league "Shirt-tail Bend" because they observed the Coushattas there wearing long, deerskin blouses that "looked like shirt-tails flapping in the breeze."

John R. Swanton quoted William Bollaert's qv estimate that in 1850 there were 500 warriors in the Battise Village and Colita's Village. The location of Colita's Village is shown on several maps produced by the General Land Office,qv including a map of the Polk County area dated 1856 and certified by the GLO on August 2, 1991.

During the early years of the Civil War,qv Colita's Village served temporarily as a Confederate naval station after the capture of Galveston by Union forces in October 1862. On December 18, 1862, Commander W. W. Hunter, Confederate States Navy, the superintendent of Texas coastal defenses, established his headquarters on the Logan league. His objective was to use the Indians in the vicinity to obstruct the Trinity River and prevent an invasion of East Texas. Five wagonloads of Confederate naval equipment and supplies were stored on A. H. Washington's plantation. Commander Hunter cooperated with Washington in preparing an active defense. Gen. John B. Magruder qv recaptured Galveston on New Year's Day, 1863 (see GALVESTON, BATTLE OF), and the naval station on the Logan league was abandoned in April 1863.

In 1855 the Texas legislature granted the Coushattas 640 acres of land for a permanent home. Because suitable land was no longer available in Polk County, however, the grant remained only a scrap of paper. The Alabama Indians had received a grant of Polk County land in 1854, and with the permission of the Alabamas, many of the Coushattas settled on this reservation in 1859. A few remained on the site of Colita's Village in San Jacinto County until 1906, when they joined the others on the Alabama-Coushatta Indian Reservation.

BIBLIOGRAPHY: Howard N. Martin, "Polk County Indians: Alabamas, Coushattas, Pakana Muskogees," *East Texas Historical Journal* 17 (1979). Howard N. Martin, "Texas Redskins in Confederate Gray," *Southwestern Historical Quarterly* 70 (April 1967). Texas General Land Office, *An Abstract of the Original Titles of Record in the General Land Office* (Houston: Niles, 1838; rpt., Austin: Pemberton Press, 1964). Gifford E. White, *1840 Citizens of Texas* (2 vols., Austin, 1983–84).

Howard N. Martin

COLITA TRACE. The Colita Trace connected two Coushatta Indian villages in the lower Trinity River region of Texas. The first of these villages, Colita's Village,qv was the lower Coushatta village on the Trinity in what is now San Jacinto County. The village at the other end of the trace was Long King's Village,qv the middle Coushatta village, located at the junction of Long King Creek and Tempe Creek, three miles north of the Trinity in Polk County. From a point on the east bank of the Trinity River opposite Colita's Village, the Colita Trace extended northwestward in Polk County, crossed Drew's Mill Creek and Copeland Creek, passed northeast of the site of present Goodrich, crossed Long King Creek, and proceeded to Long King's Village. The trail expedited travel and communications between Colita's Village and Long King's Village. It also merged with the Liberty-Nacogdoches Road qv near Colita's Village, and the Colita Trace thus served secondarily in the system of trails leading to hunting grounds in the Big Thicket qv and for trips to Atascosito or Liberty, near the mouth of the Trinity River. *Howard N. Martin*

COLLARD, ELIJAH SIMMONS (1778–1846). Elijah Simmons Collard, early settler and government official, was born November 9, 1778, in Augusta County, Virginia, the son of Joseph and Margaret Collard. As a child he moved with his family to Kentucky. On May 2, 1801, in Bullitt County, Kentucky, he married Mary Stark; the couple had eleven children, ten of whom lived to adulthood. Collard served in the War of 1812 as a private in the Upper Louisiana militia and later as a captain in the Missouri militia. A plaque commemorating this service has been placed at his gravesite. The family lived in Kentucky, Missouri, and Arkansas before moving to Texas. Preceded by at least three of his sons, Collard arrived in what would become Montgomery County in 1833 and was given a league south of the site of what is now Willis. There is some question whether he actually lived on this league. He later moved south to what became Walker County. As trouble developed with the Mexican authorities he became a member of the Consultation qv from Washington Municipality. On January 5, 1836, he became a member of the General Council.qv When Montgomery County was being organized in 1837, he was one of five commissioners chosen to select a county seat. In 1844 he served as a justice of the peace. When Walker County was established from Montgomery County in July 1846, he was selected county commissioner. He died March 13, 1846, and is buried in Gourd Creek Cemetery near New Waverly in Walker County. A Texas historical marker is at his gravesite.

BIBLIOGRAPHY: D'Anne McAdams Crews, ed., *Huntsville and Walker County, Texas: A Bicentennial History* (Huntsville, Texas: Sam Houston State University, 1976). William Harley Gandy, A History of Montgomery County, Texas (M.A. thesis, University of Houston, 1952). Texas House of Representatives, *Biographical Directory of the Texan Conventions and Congresses, 1832–1845* (Austin: Book Exchange, 1941).

Anne M. Rackley

COLLARD, WILLIAM E. (1839–1902). William E. Collard, attorney and judge, son of James H. and Julia (Robinson) Collard and grandson of Elijah S. Collard,qv was born in Conroe, Montgomery County, Texas, on October 3, 1839. He attended McKenzie College before the Civil War.qv During the war he enlisted with the Tenth Texas Infantry and transferred to the Fifteeneth Texas Infantry, where he served with Company B. He was admitted to the bar in 1865 and established his practice in Robertson County. He served as district judge from November 1880 until he was appointed to the Commission of Appeals on September 15, 1887. On April 15, 1891, he became judge of the Third District Court of Civil Appeals. In 1865 Collard married Mattie Glaize, who died in 1867. In 1868 he married M. E. Heth, and they had three children. He died on April 14, 1902.

BIBLIOGRAPHY: Lewis E. Daniell, *Personnel of the Texas State Government, with Sketches of Representative Men of Texas* (Austin: City Printing, 1887; 3d ed., San Antonio: Maverick, 1892). James M. Day, comp., *Texas Almanac, 1857–1873: A Compendium of Texas History* (Waco: Texian Press, 1967). Deborah D. Powers, *The Court of Appeals at Austin, 1892–1992* (Austin: State House Press, 1992).

Carolyn Hyman

COLLARDS CREEK. Collards Creek rises a mile east of Madisonville in central Madison County (at 30°57′ N, 95°53′ W) and runs southeast ten miles to its mouth on Bedias Creek, on the Walker county line (at 30°53′ N, 95°47′ W). The surrounding gently sloping to nearly level terrain is surfaced by sandy loam that supports pecan-elm, water oak-elm, willow oak-blackgum, and post oak-black hickory woods. Anglo-American settlement in the vicinity began during the 1830s. Pee Dee was on the west bank of the middle creek by the early 1830s. Madisonville was established west of the headwaters in 1854. The creek is named for Job Starks Collard, the original grantee of the land on which it rises.

BIBLIOGRAPHY: Madison County Historical Commission, *A History of Madison County* (Dallas: Taylor, 1984).

COLLECTORS' INSTITUTE. The Collectors' Institute was a private association of collectors of library materials, including books, manuscripts, documents, and maps, cosponsored by the Texas State Historical Association and the Harry Ransom Humanities Research

Center[qqv] of the University of Texas at Austin. It was organized on November 23, 1968, with more than 150 members. Between the fall of 1969 and 1980 twelve annual meetings were held, with programs of general interest in the area of publishing, authors, and collections. Speakers included Carl Hertzog, Hallie Stillwell, Lawrence Clark Powell, Archibald Hanna, J. Evetts Haley, and John Graves. In addition to annual meetings, workshops were held each spring. The workshop programs focused on questions of interest to collectors, such as identity, preservation, repair, and maintenance of printed and manuscript material.

Through 1973 transcripts of the meetings were published and distributed to the membership. Jenkins Garrett was president of the Collectors' Institute from 1968 through 1980. From its organization in 1968 through the fall of 1970 Kenneth Ragsdale, a fulltime staff member of the Texas State Historical Association, served as voluntary secretary and coordinator of the institute. In 1974 John Payne, a full-time employee of Humanities Research Center, volunteered to take over these responsibilities. He served through the fall meeting of 1980. The organization was discontinued after that meeting.

Jenkins Garrett

COLLEGE HILL, TEXAS. College Hill, seven miles south of DeKalb in southwestern Bowie County, was established in the early 1890s by W. H. Patty, who operated a gin and sawmill. A post office was granted in 1902 but discontinued in 1907. The population of College Hill reached 100 in 1915. In 1938 the school was consolidated with those in eight other communities to form the James Bowie Consolidated District. The building was located in Simms. College Hill had a store and a population of thirty in 1945. In 1984 it had a church, a cemetery, a business, and a few scattered houses. In 1990 the population was 116.

Claudia Hazlewood

COLLEGE HILL INSTITUTE. College Hill Institute, at Springtown in the northeast corner of Parker County, was chartered by the state of Texas in 1884. It operated for ten years under the guidance of president John W. McCracken and vice president D. P. Hurley. Springtown was also the home of the Springtown Male and Female Institute, and the community became known as the "educational center for northwest Texas." In 1894 the school closed.

BIBLIOGRAPHY: Dallas *Morning News*, May 21, 1939, June 1, 1941. Weatherford *Democrat*, August 11, 1939.

David Minor

COLLEGE OF THE MAINLAND. The College of the Mainland, located in Texas City, was launched in late 1966 when the voters of Dickinson, Hitchcock, La Marque, Santa Fe, and Texas City approved a building-bond issue of $2,850,000. The idea of a community college had begun in 1935. Herbert F. Stallworth, who previously had helped establish two colleges, was selected to head the new college in April 1967, and Fred A. Taylor was appointed dean of instruction. Classes were begun in temporary quarters in 1967. On March 21, 1970, the administration building, learning-resources center, math and science building, and technical-vocational building were completed, and the College of the Mainland moved to its new campus on Palmer Highway. On May 16, 1970, residents of the college district approved $4,750,000 for a second phase of construction. The campus was expanded to include a fine arts building, a physical education complex, and a student center. The math-science and technical-vocational buildings were improved. In 1984 a third addition to the technical-vocational building was constructed.

The college budget is supported by state appropriations (36 percent) and local property taxes (53 percent). Other sources of revenue are federal grants and funds raised by the College of the Mainland Foundation for scholarships. The college is governed by a seven-member board of trustees elected to six-year terms by the residents of the college district.

As an open-door, comprehensive community college, the College of the Mainland offers a university-parallel program offering associate in arts, associate in business administration, and associate in science degrees with a choice of forty majors (courses in this program transfer for credit to all Texas universities); a two-year associate in applied science degree in twenty-one career choices; a one-year diploma program in fifteen technical-vocational occupations; continuing education courses; and an active, service-oriented senior program for residents over fifty-five years of age. The college also offers adult basic-education courses; a developmental program in reading and writing skills; counseling in the areas of career planning, program development, and management of personal problems; a year-round schedule of plays, concerts, lectures, dance-ensemble performances, and art exhibits; community services, such as the use of campus recreational and meeting facilities; a wide range of student clubs and activities; an innovative cooperative-education program, which combines classroom instruction with on-the-job experience, with pay; and an extensive financial-aid program of grants, loans, scholarships, and part-time employment on campus.

The College of the Mainland received its accreditation from the Southern Association of College and Schools in 1969 and completed its second ten-year reaffirmation of accreditation in 1984. The college is also accredited by the Texas Education Agency, the Texas Higher Education Coordinating Board,[qqv] the American Institute of Banking, the Board of Nurse Examiners (*see* EXAMINING BOARDS), the National League for Nursing, the Texas Credit Union League, the Texas Real Estate Commission, and the Texas Commission on Law Enforcement Officer Standards and Education.

Student enrollment in the fall 1988 semester was 3,527; approximately 50 percent registered in the university-parallel program and 50 percent in the technical-vocational program. As of 1992 the college enrolled 3,890 students and employed 390 faculty members, many of whom were part-time.

BIBLIOGRAPHY: Vertical Files, Barker Texas History Center, University of Texas at Austin.

Mary Dahaczko

COLLEGE MOUND, TEXAS. College Mound is on Farm Road 429 five miles southeast of Terrell in eastern Kaufman County. A small group of settlers from Indiana and Tennessee moved into the area in the mid-1840s to establish one of the first communities in the county. The community is said to have been named in remembrance of an early plan to establish a college on the site, a plan never carried out. Soon the community had several stores, a cotton gin, a public school, and a church. The Methodist church was founded in 1845, and a cemetery was begun in 1846. W. T. Patton donated land in 1866 for a permanent site for the church. At one time five denominations shared the building—Methodist, Presbyterian, Christian, Missionary Baptist, and Primitive Baptist. The present building was built in 1897. According to some accounts, two saloonkeepers from nearby Elmo once attempted to disrupt church services in College Mound by heckling the minister. An unknown man, reportedly resembling Abraham Lincoln, took one of them outside and thrashed him, after which the two interlopers left and never again caused any trouble. The College Mound post office was opened in 1850, discontinued before the Civil War,[qv] reestablished after the war, and discontinued in 1874. John L. Beck, one of the original settlers, was the first postmaster. The school was consolidated with that of Terrell in 1949. In the late 1980s the Methodist church remained a vibrant force in the community, and many of its members were descended from the earliest settlers. At that time College Mound was a quiet community with a cluster of rural homes, a church, and a cemetery.

BIBLIOGRAPHY: T. Lindsay Baker, *Ghost Towns of Texas* (Norman: University of Oklahoma Press, 1986).

Jack Stoltz

COLLEGE OF NUESTRA SEÑORA DE GUADALUPE DE ZACATECAS. The College of Nuestra Señora de Guadalupe de Zacatecas, a Franciscan missionary college, was established under the auspices of the College of Santa Cruz de Querétaro^{qv} after several requests by the people of Zacatecas, some as early as 1686. The royal decree approving the college was issued on January 27, 1704, and arrived in Mexico in 1706. Antonio Margil de Jesús,^{qv} president of the newly established college, arrived in Zacatecas to take charge of his assignment in January 1707. Missionaries from the college entered Texas for the first time with Domingo Ramón's^{qv} expedition in 1716. In 1772 the college received the Texas missions previously administered by the College of Santa Cruz de Querétaro at the request of the latter. The final transfer papers of the mission field were in the hands of the viceroy on March 10, 1773. The Zacatecan missions founded in Texas were Nuestra Señora de los Dolores de los Ais, San Miguel de Linares de los Adaes, Nuestra Señora de Guadalupe de los Nacogdoches, Nuestra Señora del Espíritu Santo de Zúñiga, Nuestra Señora del Rosario, Nuestra Señora del Refugio, Nuestra Señora de la Luz, and San José y San Miguel de Aguayo.^{qqv} The college also did the initial missionary work along the lower Rio Grande between Laredo and the Gulf of Mexico between 1749 and 1766.

BIBLIOGRAPHY: Carlos E. Castañeda, *Our Catholic Heritage in Texas* (7 vols., Austin: Von Boeckmann–Jones, 1936–58; rpt., New York: Arno, 1976). Herbert Eugene Bolton, *Texas in the Middle Eighteenth Century* (Berkeley: University of California Press, 1915; rpt., Austin: University of Texas Press, 1970).

COLLEGEPORT, TEXAS. Collegeport is on Farm Road 1095 and the eastern shore of Tres Palacios Bay, half a mile north of Pelican Slough and two miles northeast of Palacios in southwestern Matagorda County. It was organized by the Hurd Land Company in 1908 as a promotion for selling acreage in Jonathan E. Pierce's^{qv} ranch. The company also established the Gulf Coast University of Industrial Arts. The combination of a port and the college gave the settlement its name. The community was organized in the early 1900s and secured a post office in 1909. It became a stop on the St. Louis, Brownsville and Mexico Railway in 1911. By 1914 it had a bank, the college, a weekly newspaper called the Collegeport *New Era,* and a population of 450. That year an agricultural crisis contributed to a decline in population. Ten years later in December an ice storm killed hundreds of cattle around Collegeport, and the packing house closed. In 1936 the town had a population of 200, six businesses, two schools, a college, two churches, and numerous dwellings. By 1938 the Collegeport Independent School District had been formed. In 1946 the population was still estimated at 200, but the number of businesses had dropped to three. By 1948 the Collegeport schools had been consolidated with the Palacios Independent School District. By 1952 the college, the church, and most local businesses had closed. From 1955 to 1965 the number of residents was estimated at 100. In 1988 Collegeport had one business, and in 1990 the estimated population was ninety-one.

BIBLIOGRAPHY: Frank J. Balusek, Survey and Proposed Reorganization of the Schools of Matagorda County, Texas (M.Ed. thesis, University of Texas, 1939). Matagorda County Historical Commission, *Historic Matagorda County* (3 vols., Houston: Armstrong, 1986).

Stephen L. Hardin

COLLEGE OF ST. THOMAS MORE. The College of St. Thomas More was founded as St. Thomas More Institute on December 26, 1981, by a group of parishioners of St. Patrick Cathedral^{qv} parish of Fort Worth. The purpose of establishing the institute was to erect "in Fort Worth a Roman Catholic liberal arts college devoted to teaching and learning within the tradition of Catholic arts and letters." In 1982 St. Thomas More Institute was incorporated under Texas law as the Fellows and Visitors of the Saint Thomas More Institute. James Patrick, institute provost, and Ronald Muller, dean of the new school, began to offer short courses in Fort Worth and Dallas in theology, philosophy, and literature. This informal curriculum existed under the auspices of the institute and was called the Common Tradition Curriculum. In 1983 St. Thomas More Institute moved into a donated building in Fort Worth. In that same year the first Cardinal Newman Lecture was hosted and the institute's first visiting professor addressed the school's community. By 1985, an annual budget had been established and the basic courses of a two-year curriculum leading to the associate of arts degree had been developed. In that same year a permanent home for the college was found in the university neighborhood of Fort Worth, when a building located on Merida Street was purchased by the school. The number of students in the Common Tradition Curriculum, in the meantime, had increased to approximately seventy-five, and another sixteen students were enrolled in the college curriculum. By this time, it was understood that the college had been established "to make accessible the great tradition of learning that celebrates language and literature, history, philosophy, and theology as the philosophic forms of the soul, seeking to give these an ordered existence and to make them accessible to every student."

Considerable expansion of the college occurred between 1986 and 1989. It acquired a second building on Lubbock Street, just around the block from the Merida Street edifice in Fort Worth. The college's library holdings were expanded through gifts and donations, and student enrollment grew to twenty-five. Meanwhile, in 1986, St. Thomas More's Oxford Studies Program, initiated at the Oxford suburb of Littlemore, England, was started. As the college continued to develop, in 1988 Judith Shank joined the institution as its fourth teaching fellow. In the fall of 1988 the school applied to the Texas Higher Education Coordinating Board^{qv} to become a degree-granting institution. In January 1989 the school became a college under Texas law and began its Rome term.

Between 1990 and 1994 the college's library volumes grew in number to about 6,000, housed in one of the two additional buildings that the college acquired. Student enrollment in the college curriculum increased to more than sixty, and the college began to offer some seminars "in ethics, history, and the liberal arts for area civic and business leaders." It also began sponsoring conferences and lectures throughout North Texas. In June 1994 the College of St. Thomas More was granted full accreditation as a two-year college by the Southern Association of Colleges and Schools.

BIBLIOGRAPHY: *North Texas Catholic,* August 5, 1994.

Patrick Foley

COLLEGE OF SAN FERNANDO DE MEXICO. The College of San Fernando de Mexico was established by Franciscans^{qv} in response to repeated requests that Mexico City be granted a college comparable with those at Querétaro and Zacatecas. A hospice for eight friars from the College of Santa Cruz de Querétaro^{qv} was opened on January 14, 1731, and the friars were instructed to remain in Mexico City until a seminary college was established. On January 27, 1731, the viceroy approved the project and appointed Father Alcántaro temporary president. Fray Isidro Félix de Espinosa^{qv} relieved Alcántaro in April 1731. The plans for the college were approved by the king of Spain on October 15, 1733. Two of the friars from the college who served in Texas were killed at San Sabá de la Santa Cruz Mission on March 16, 1758.

BIBLIOGRAPHY: Herbert Eugene Bolton, *Texas in the Middle Eighteenth Century: Studies in Spanish Colonial History and Administration* (Berkeley: University of California Press, 1915; rpt., Austin: University of Texas Press, 1970). Carlos E. Castañeda, *Our Catholic Heritage in Texas* (7 vols., Austin: Von Boeckmann–Jones, 1936–58; rpt., New York: Arno, 1976).

COLLEGE OF SANTA CRUZ DE QUERÉTARO. The College of Santa Cruz, the first institution for the propagation of the Catholic faith in America, was founded in 1683 in Querétaro, now capital of the state of Querétaro, Mexico, by Father Antonio Linaz de Jesús

María of Mallorca, Spain, a Franciscan friar and prefect of all missions in the Indies. Of the original nineteen priests who founded the College of Santa Cruz de Querétaro, nine served in Texas: Antonio Casañas de Jesús María, Damián Massanet, Francisco Hidalgo,qqv Miguel de Fontcuberta, Francisco Esteves, Antonio Borday, Antonio Perea, and José Diez. Many other Franciscansqv who served in Texas also came from this college. Under its direction two other colleges were founded to send missionaries to Texas, the College of San Fernando de México and the College of Nuestra Señora de Guadalupe de Zacatecas.qqv After the expulsion of the Jesuitsqv from New Spain, the College of Santa Cruz assumed the Jesuit missions in Sonora. In 1772, to offset that added burden, it withdrew its missionaries from Texas and turned the mission work in that province over to Zacatecas. The final transfer papers of the mission field were in the hands of the viceroy on March 10, 1773.

During its period of missionary endeavor in Texas the College of Santa Cruz de Querétaro founded the following missions: San Francisco de los Tejas,qv which became Nuestro Padre San Francisco de los Tejasqv in 1716, San Francisco de los Nechesqv in 1721, and San Francisco de la Espadaqv in 1731; Nuestra Señora de la Purísima Concepción de los Hainais, which became Nuestra Señora de la Purísima Concepción de Acuña;qv San José de los Nazonis,qv which became San Juan Capistrano;qv San Antonio de Valero;qv Santísimo Nombre de María;qv Santa Cruz de San Sabá;qv San Francisco Xavier de Náxara;qv Nuestra Señora de la Candelaria del Cañón;qv San Lorenzo de la Santa Cruz;qv San Francisco Xavier de Horcasitas,qv which became Nuestra Señora de Guadalupe;qv Nuestra Señora de la Candelaria;qv and San Ildefonso.qv

BIBLIOGRAPHY: Herbert Eugene Bolton, *Texas in the Middle Eighteenth Century: Studies in Spanish Colonial History and Administration* (Berkeley: University of California Press, 1915; rpt., Austin: University of Texas Press, 1970). Carlos E. Castañeda, *Our Catholic Heritage in Texas* (7 vols., Austin: Von Boeckmann–Jones, 1936–58; rpt., New York: Arno, 1976).

COLLEGE STATION, TEXAS. College Station, the home of Texas A&M University, is located just south of Bryan in southwest central Brazos County, and is crossed by State Highway 6, Farm roads 2154, 2347, 2818 and 60, and the Southern Pacific Railroad. Bryan and College Station adjoin to form the urban heart of Brazos County. The Houston and Texas Central Railway built through the area in 1860. In 1871 the site was chosen as the location of the proposed Texas A&M College, which opened in 1876. In 1877 a post office, College Station, was opened in a building near the railroad tracks, and the community took its name from the post office. A railroad depot was constructed in 1883; By 1884 the community had 350 inhabitants and two general stores. Faculty members generally lived on campus in housing provided by the university. College Station received electrical service in the 1890s; the population was 391 in 1900.

One of many electric interurban railwaysqv in Texas was established between Bryan and College Station in 1910, and over the next ten years the area just north of the campus developed as a business district. The interurban was replaced by a bus system in the 1920s. Children from the community attended school in neighboring school districts until 1920, when the A&M Consolidated School was established by the college to enhance its teacher-education programs. In the 1920s and 1930s, as the college grew, the community built in all directions. In the early 1930s the North Oakwood subdivision, at the northern end of College Station, voted to incorporate with Bryan.

In 1938 College Station incorporated, with John H. Binney as the first mayor. A zoning commission was established in 1939, and the city has maintained a tradition of managed growth. That same year the remaining faculty living on campus were told to move, and the need for housing in College Station grew more. In 1940 the town had 2,184 inhabitants (not including students) and sixty businesses, and a new school building was completed. In 1942 Ernest Langford, called by some the "Father of College Station," was elected mayor, an office he held for the next twenty-six years, during which he emphasized developing city services over commercial expansion. Lincoln High School for blacks was completed in 1942. College Station moved to council-manager city governmentqv in 1943. By 1950 it had 7,898 inhabitants, including students.

Texas A&M initiated a major expansion program in the 1960s, and College Station has grown with the school. The community grew from a population of 11,396 in 1960 to 17,676 in 1970, 30,449 in 1980, and 52,456 in 1990, thus increasing almost fivefold in thirty years. School desegregation was achieved rapidly after the black high school burned down in 1966, and a number of new schools have been built since the 1960s to accommodate population growth. Through its ties with the university, College Station has developed high-tech manufacturing industries and become a major research center.

BIBLIOGRAPHY: Glenna Fourman Brundidge, *Brazos County History: Rich Past—Bright Future* (Bryan, Texas: Family History Foundation, 1986).

Mark Odintz

COLLEY, RICHARD STEWART (1910–1983). Richard Stewart Colley, architect and city planner, son of Richard Bertram and Irene (Stewart) Colley, was born in Fort Worth, Texas, on June 18, 1910. Soon afterward his family moved to Yoakum, where he spent his school years. He entered the architecture program at the Agricultural and Mechanical College of Texas (now Texas A&M University) in 1926 but left in 1931 without a degree. From 1931 to 1933 he worked with a former classmate, architect Rodolfo Garza Madero, in Monterrey, Nuevo León. In 1934 he joined S. C. P. Vosper,qv his former professor at A&M, and Raiford Stripling to work on the restoration of the eighteenth-century Nuestra Señora del Espíritu Santo de Zúñiga Mission in Goliad for the National Park Service. In Goliad Colley met and married Margaret Hutcheson of Edna, Texas; the couple had two sons.

Colley moved to Corpus Christi in 1936 and worked for the architects Brock and Roberts until 1938, when he opened his own office. With the exception of an eighteen-month tenure as director of planning for the city of Corpus Christi (1944–45), he maintained an independent architectural practice until his death. His first two commissions were a Spanish Colonial Revival hacienda for Richard Hawn at the corner of Santa Fe and Hewitt (1939) and the Spanish Colonial Revival Sacred Heart Church on Comanche Street (1938–39). In these he demonstrated his interest in a regionally inflected modern architecture, although one still dependant on historic models.

During the 1940s he produced buildings, especially houses, that were simple and straightforward, stripped of historical detail but often bland. A more positive approach to modernism became evident in his work after 1949, as he began to respond to conditions of site and climate with the use of roof overhangs, sunscreens that doubled as wind baffles, building masses oriented to the prevailing breeze, integration of indoor and outdoor spaces, tropical plants, and provocative color combinations. The Trauerman (1949), Massad (1951), and Selby (1952) houses in Corpus Christi and the Stahl house (1951) in McAllen represent this tendency. During the 1950s the city of Corpus Christi commissioned Colley to design a series of buildings for a new municipal complex on Shoreline Boulevard. His designs, which included a city hall, a civic center and auditorium, and an exposition hall, were widely published in leading architectural journals. The works were hailed for their response to the climate of the Gulf Coast and for the architect's innovative structural solutions, such as his use of Lamella steel arches reinforced by concrete buttresses to span the 224-foot space in the civic center. Colley's major works in Corpus Christi include the D. N. Leathers Center II public-housing complex (1952), Memorial Coliseum (1953), the Hawn Building (1955), the Ada Wilson Hospital of Physical Medicine and Rehabilitation (1965), 4600 Ocean Drive (apartments, 1965–66), and houses for George S. Hawn

(1952), William E. Carl (1956), and I. Guy Braselton (1957). Colley was also responsible for multiple buildings in McAllen, Victoria, Houston, and Dallas.

In the early 1950s he became interested in the lift-slab method of construction developed by the Southwest Research Institute[qv] and used by architect O'Neil Ford[qv] for the new Trinity University campus in San Antonio. Colley built a number of buildings in South Texas using the new method and helped to refine the process. The most important projects on which he and Ford collaborated were the Crossroads Restaurant at the Great Southwest Industrial District in Arlington (1957), Texas Instruments[qv] Technical Laboratories in Houston (1957), and Texas Instruments Semiconductor Building in Richardson (1958). In these Colley was responsible for the innovative integration of supporting structure and mechanical servicing.

In the 1960s Colley received a series of commissions to design further buildings for Texas Instruments, and he planned and supervised the construction of buildings in Argentina, El Salvador, the Philippines, Hong Kong, Malaysia, and Japan. Among his other works were Richard King High School and the planetarium in Corpus Christi.

Colley was a member of the American Institute of Architects. In 1983 he was awarded an honorary doctorate by Texas Tech University in recognition of his contributions to the architecture of Texas. He died in Corpus Christi on October 21, 1983, and was buried at Seaside Memorial Park and Mausoleum. After his death his firm was reorganized by his employees as Colley Associates.

BIBLIOGRAPHY: Richard S. Colley, "Civic Buildings: Corpus Christi," *Progressive Architecture* 34 (February 1953). Corpus Christi *Caller*, May 9, 1950.
Mary Carolyn Hollers George

COLLEY CREEK. Colley Creek rises three miles north of Linden in central Cass County (at 33°03′ N, 94°22′ W) and runs southeast for 6½ miles to its mouth on Frazier Creek, five miles northeast of Linden (at 33°02′ N, 94°17′ W). The surrounding gently undulating to rolling terrain is surfaced by sandy loam that supports heavy woods of pines and hardwoods.

COLLEYVILLE, TEXAS. Colleyville, previously known as Coleysville, is a suburb of Fort Worth on State Highway 25 in northeastern Tarrant County. In the 1990s it was bounded on the north by Southlake, on the west by Richland Hills and Hurst, on the east by Grapevine and Euless, and on the south by Bedford. The area was first settled in the 1850s, and the communities of Spring Garden, Pleasant Run, Pleasant Glade, and Red Rock (later Bransford) eventually developed in an area that is now within the city limits of Colleyville. Hilburn (or Lilburn) Howard Colley, a physician and a native of Missouri, moved to Texas in 1880 and settled in Bransford soon after. He practiced in the area for forty years. His name became associated with a community that grew up around a store founded in 1914 south of Bransford. The surrounding area gradually came to be known as Coleysville and, later, Colleyville. Though the St. Louis Southwestern Railway ran through the community, the primary reason for Colleyville's growth has been its proximity to Fort Worth, where most of its residents have been employed. The earliest reported population for Colleyville was twenty-five in 1936, when the town had two businesses; by 1945 its population had increased to forty. Colleyville was incorporated on January 10, 1956, and by 1958 a population of 100 was recorded there. By 1964 the city had 1,491 residents and thereafter continued to grow, for a time by about 3,000 residents a decade. The town in the early 1980s became divided over the issue of development, with one group wanting to limit new construction to expensive, single-family homes on large lots and the other group wanting smaller lots and multifamily housing. In 1990 the population of Colleyville was 12,724.

BIBLIOGRAPHY: *Historic Resources Survey: Selected Tarrant County Communities* (Fort Worth: Historic Preservation Council for Tarrant County, 1990). Vertical Files, Barker Texas History Center, University of Texas at Austin.
John G. Johnson

COLLIER, JOHN C. (1834–1928). John C. (Marse) Collier, Cumberland Presbyterian minister and college president, was born on May 18, 1834, in the Kershaw District of South Carolina to Benjamin and Sarah Collier. Shortly after his birth the family moved to southern Pickins County, Alabama. As he grew older, to fulfill his decision to become a Cumberland Presbyterian minister, Collier enrolled in classes at Cumberland College in Tennessee. By 1855 he was ordained, and within a short time he moved to Texas to begin his ministry in McLennan and Bosque counties. He became a member of McLennan County Masonic Lodge. By the end of 1854 he had started his teaching career at Bosque Academy, and around 1856 he become associated with the Waco Female Seminary.[qv] When these schools consolidated to form Bosque College and Seminary,[qv] Collier became president of the school. On August 26, 1858, he married Mary Ellen (Mollie) Fowler. In 1860 Collier, given the nickname "Marse" by his students, sold Bosque Male College to the trustees on the condition that Sunday services would continue to be held at the college. By 1861 Bosque College had an enrollment of more than 400 students; Collier taught classes and was president. The Civil War,[qv] however, brought a gradual end to the college. A company of 100 was organized from among the male students in 1861, and in 1863 Collier resigned to become a scout in Ross's Brigade.[qv] Though not a chaplain, he preached to his fellow soldiers. During this period his wife taught a community school.

After the war, in September 1866, Collier opened Oakland College; in November of that year the school received its charter. Inadequate boarding facilities, however, forced him to move the college to Alvarado, where he opened Alvarado College by January 1868. During 1868 Collier served as pastor of the Cumberland Presbyterian churches in Alvarado and Mansfield. He was offered classroom and boarding facilities for his college, as well as a house for his family, on condition that the college move from Alvarado to Mansfield. The offer was accepted, and the move was begun in 1869. On July 9, 1870, Collier was one of thirteen Masons who organized Mansfield Lodge No. 331, and he was elected to serve as the first senior warden of the lodge. In 1871 Mansfield Male and Female College was chartered with Collier as president. During the first years of the college he also served as the first pastor of a Cumberland Presbyterian church in Fort Worth. In 1873 he began his first term (1873–75) as worshipful master of the Mansfield Masonic lodge, and in 1875 he dedicated the cornerstones of both the Mansfield lodge building and the new classroom facility for Mansfield Male and Female College. In 1879 he became the first superintendent of public schools and the first principal of a public secondary school in Fort Worth, but his college presidency and his performance of ministerial duties resulted in his dismissal by the end of his first year. In 1883–84 Collier again served as worshipful master of the Mansfield lodge. Around this time his oldest daughter, Allie Speer, a graduate of the New England Conservatory of Music, became a teacher in Mansfield Male and Female College. Collier closed the college in 1887 and bought Marvin College in Waxahachie.

In September 1887 he reopened Marvin College as Waxahachie College, with his daughter Allie Speer in charge of the female department. The school was not successful and in 1889 was sold at public auction. Collier then moved to Dallas, where he pastored a church and also attempted to open a school for girls in Oak Cliff, but this venture ended in failure. He and his family then moved to Walnut Springs, where Collier taught for the next few years. In 1896 he became the president of Buffalo Gap College, which, in 1897, achieved its peak enrollment of 318 students, with twenty-two applying for degrees. On August 18, 1898, he agreed to organize and become the president of Baird College in Baird. Though this college failed within a few years, Collier stayed in Baird, where he had purchased a home. With the merger of the United States (Northern) Presbyterian Church and the Cumberland Presbyterian Church in 1906, he became a member of the Abilene Presbytery of the United States Presbyterian Church. In 1909 his wife died. In 1914 a banquet was held in Waco to honor Collier, and he was presented with a purse containing eighty gold dollars to commemorate his eightieth birthday. In 1917 a banquet was held by former students in Dallas, and Collier received eighty-three gold dollars for his eighty-third birthday as a love offering from those who attended the banquet. On February 29, 1928, Collier died in Baird; he was buried in Dallas. *See also* PRESBYTERIAN CHURCH.

BIBLIOGRAPHY: Robert Douglas Brackenridge, *Voice in the Wilderness: A History of the Cumberland Presbyterian Church in Texas* (San Antonio: Trinity University Press, 1968). Tommie Clack, "Buffalo Gap College," West Texas Historical Association *Year Book* 35 (1959). Dallas *Morning News*, May 19, 1917, March 1, 1928. Mansfield *News-Mirror*, February 7, 1985. Carl L. McFarland

COLLIER CREEK. Collier Creek rises near Hopewell in north central Red River County (at 33°46′ N, 94°59′ W) and runs northeast for six miles to its mouth on the Red River, just east of Bachman Cemetery (at 33°47′ N, 94°55′ W). The stream is intermittent in its upper reaches. It crosses flat to gently rolling terrain with sandy and clay loam soils that support grasses and mixed hardwoods and pines.

COLLIN COUNTY. Collin County (C-18/19), is located in northeastern Texas thirty miles south of the Red River. McKinney, the county seat, is thirty-four miles northeast of Dallas. The county's center lies at approximately 33°11′ north latitude and 09°64′ west longitude. With the exception of a small portion of its western edge, Collin County's area of 851 square miles lies entirely within the Blackland Prairie region of Texas. The surface of the county is generally level to gently rolling, with an elevation ranging from 450 to 700 feet above sea level. Deep clayey soils over marl and chalk surface the central and western part of the county. Dark loamy alluvial soils, subject to flooding during the rainy season, lie in the eastern section. The western and central portions of the county are drained by the East fork of the Trinity River. The Elm fork of the Trinity drains the eastern section. Bois d' arc, oak, elm, ash, pecan, and post oak trees grow along the streams of the county but not in sufficient quantity for commercial use. Limestone and sand for making cement are the only mineral resources. Temperatures range from an average high of 96° F in July to an average low of 34° in January. Rainfall averages just under thirty-five inches a year, and the growing season extends for 237 days.

Branches of the Caddo Indians inhabited the area before the arrival of the first white settlers. Occasional outbreaks of violence occurred between the two groups, but there was no extended period of conflict since the Caddos withdrew from the county by the mid-1850s. The absence of organized Indian resistance, combined with the county's fertile soil and an offer of land grants by the Peters colony[qv] attracted settlers to the area in the early 1840s. Even with the offer of free land, the estimated population of the county was only 150 when it was demarked from Fannin County on April 3, 1846, and named for Collin McKinney,[qv] one of the first settlers of the county and a signer of the Texas Declaration of Independence.[qv] The original county seat was Buckner. Because this town Buckner was not within three miles of the center of the county, however, McKinney became the county seat in 1848. Like the county, McKinney was named for Collin McKinney.

The settlement of Collin County can be divided into two phases. The first occurred during the early period of the county's history, from 1840 to 1860. The second phase took place during and after the arrival of railroads. The settlements established before the construction of rail lines seldom survived if the railroads bypassed them. The majority of the first settlers of Collin County were farmers who lived near streams, where water and wood were easily obtained. They established small, family-operated farms that produced mostly wheat and corn. The slave and cotton economy that characterized most of the South, with its large plantations, failed to take hold in the county. In part this was a result of the lack of navigable rivers and railroads to transport cash crops to retail centers. The nearest market was Jefferson, more than 150 miles to the east. In addition, the farmers who settled the county were from the upper South and had little experience in slaveholding or raising cotton. In 1860 only 1,047 of the 9,264 residents were black, and the cotton harvest was of no significance.

These factors, plus the influence of James W. Throckmorton,[qv] a native of McKinney and Texas state senator, resulted in Collin County's vote against secession,[qv] 948 to 405, in 1861. Once Texas joined the Confederacy, however, more than 1,500 residents of the county enlisted in the defense of the South, led by Throckmorton, who rose to the rank of brigadier general. During the war isolated incidents of violence occurred between Union sympathizers and Confederates, including the participation of an undetermined number of county residents in the events that led to the Great Hanging at Gainesville[qv] in 1862. Outbreaks of violence continued after the war. Farmersville, twelve miles east of McKinney, was the site of one of the killings that took place during the Lee-Peacock feud. By 1869 gunplay between the two groups had ended. Except for the military appointments of a few public officials in 1867–68, the county remained under the control of the Democratic party[qv] during Reconstruction.[qv]

For the first thirty years of the county's history farmers had little incentive to take advantage of the fertile soil of the Blackland Prairie, considered the richest agricultural region of Texas. Between the 1840s and 1870s the lack of transportation facilities, limited markets, and absence of mechanized farm equipment restricted the agricultural production of the county. The arrival of the railroad removed these obstacles and initiated a fifty-year period of economic growth. In 1872 the Houston and Texas Central Railway, the first to reach the county, connected McKinney and Plano to tracks that reached as far south as Houston. The Missouri, Kansas and Texas followed four years later and was joined in a decade by the Gulf, Colorado and Santa Fe. By the mid-1890s six railroads crisscrossed the county, connecting farmers to retail markets throughout Texas. With an outlet for their products farmers began to cultivate the unplowed fertile land in the eastern and central sections of the county. Between 1870 and 1920 the number of farms and crop production increased dramatically. In 1870, 903 farms valued at just over three million dollars produced 674,565 bushels of corn, 4,371 bales of cotton, and 42,827 bushels of wheat. In 1920 the number of farms had increased to 6,001, with a value estimated at well over $84 million. Production of corn had increased to 2,574,689 bushels, cotton to 49,311 bales, and wheat to 956,412 bushels.

By the 1920s, twenty-three Collin County communities had voted road bonds totaling just under $4 million. New roads, combined with State Highway 289, provided county residents with easy access to Dallas, Fort Worth, and Waco. By the end of the decade thirteen communities had electricity, natural gas, and a telephone exchange. Three had a population of over 1,000. In 1920 the county seat had 6,677 residents, and the population of the county was 49,609.

During the next forty years, however, the population declined. The Great Depression,[qv] mechanization of farms, and employment opportunities outside the county contributed to the drop in population. Although Collin County did not suffer the extreme hardships that befell other areas of Texas, the number of county farms declined from 6,069 in 1930 to 4,771 by 1940. The value of all crops harvested dropped from just over $10 million to just over $6.5 million during the same period. As late as 1940 Collin County's unemployment rate stood at 19 percent.

By the mid-1950s the economy had recovered. The average value of farmland per acre increased from $58.91 in 1940 to $145.52 in 1954. In part this improvement was a result of the efforts of the Texas Research Foundation[qv] and the Collin County Soil Conservation District. The Texas Research Foundation, established at Renner in 1944, used the latest scientific discoveries to improve farming practices. In 1946 the Collin County Soil Conservation District was formed and planned the construction of 144 flood-retarding structures, including

Lake Lavon, to prevent the flooding of thousands of acres of rich bottomland in southeastern Collin County. Farmers also benefited from the electric cooperatives established by the Rural Electrification^{qv} Administration in the late 1930s. The Hunt-Collin Co-operative (1937), the Fannin County Electric Co-operative (1939), and the Grayson-Collin Electric Co-operative (1937) combined to bring electricity to the isolated communities of the county. New roads also assisted county farmers. In 1946 the county had 138 miles of paved roads. By the early 1970s the paved miles had increased to 2,333. The work of the Texas Research Foundation and improved soil-conservation practices increased the production of wheat, the county's primary cash crop, from 352,229 bushels in 1949 to 1,224,664 bushels in 1959.

The mechanization of farming, however, reduced the number of farms from 3,166 in 1950 to 2,001 in 1960. A corresponding decline in the county's population occurred. Historically the percentage of tenant farmers in Collin County was high; it reached a peak of 74 percent in 1925. By 1960 that figure had dropped to 38 percent. Because of the lack of business opportunities outside farming in the county, the majority of those forced to leave farming also left the county. The population decreased from 47,190 in 1940 to 41,247 in 1960.

Although agriculture, especially developing dairy farming, continued to be an important factor in the county's economy, by 1980 the introduction of light industry, combined with the growth of the Dallas metropolitan area, produced a successful diversified economy. In 1980 the number of business establishments totaled 2,388; 25 percent of the population was employed in manufacturing and 23 percent in wholesale and retail trade. Most of the population, 59 percent, worked outside the county. The economic growth between 1960 and 1980 accompanied a comparable population growth. Plano, eighteen miles northeast of Dallas, had the most dramatic increase of all Collin County towns: in 1960 Plano's population was 3,695, and twenty years later it was 72,331. Overall, Collin County's population increased from 41,692 in 1960 to 144,576 in 1980. Subsequently it continued to grow, largely as a result of the development of the suburbs in and around Plano. By 1990 the number of residents in Plano increased to 128,673, and the population of the county as a whole grew to 264,036, nearly double what it had been only a decade before. Many of the new arrivals in the county are from areas outside of Texas.

Though before 1970 the voters of the county were staunchly Democratic, from 1972 to 1992 they consistently chose Republican presidential candidates, and Republicans also made inroads in state and local races. Other changes have occurred. Due to the large number of young families that have moved to the area, the average age has dropped considerably, and education levels have been steadily rising. Hispanics, traditionally only a small minority in the county, now outnumber African-Americans,^{qv} and the number of Asians is increasing rapidly. In 1990 nearly 90 percent of the population was white, 6.9 percent black, 4.1 percent Hispanic, and 2.8 percent Asian. Collin County is well on its way to being one of the most densely populated counties in Texas. The largest city, Plano, overshadows the county seat as the business and educational center of the county. The diversified economy continues to diminish the number of farms. At its 150th anniversary the county little resembled what was settled in the 1840s.

BIBLIOGRAPHY: Roy Franklin Hall and Helen Gibbard Hall, *Collin County: Pioneering in North Texas* (Quanah, Texas: Nortex, 1975). J. Lee and Lillian J. Stambaugh, *A History of Collin County* (Austin: Texas State Historical Association, 1958). Ellen Jeanene Walker, Agricultural Land Utilization in Collin County (M.A. thesis, Southern Methodist University, 1969).
David Minor

COLLIN COUNTY COMMUNITY COLLEGE DISTRICT. The voters of Collin County approved the establishment of the Collin County Community College District, the election of a nine-member board, and a $70 million bond issue for the construction of two campuses on April 6, 1985. The first classes began in fall 1985, when 1,326 students met in high schools throughout the county. The central campus, on 155 acres near the intersection of U.S. highways 75 and 380 in McKinney, opened to over 2,000 students in January 1986.

In the fall of 1988 construction of a second campus was completed. The Spring Creek Campus, a 380,000-square-foot complex, is located on 110 acres at Spring Creek Parkway and Jupiter in east Plano. Besides classrooms, laboratories, and office space, this campus includes a physical education complex, a theater, a food-service area, a conference center, a learning-resource center, and a child-development center. The college has purchased 125 acres in southwest Collin County for the construction of a third campus. The college has encouraged county residents to use its facilities.

Collin County Community College District, the tenth largest college district in the state in 1989, was awarded full accreditation by the Southern Association of Colleges and Schools in the summer of that year. The district offers courses in thirty-five areas of study that satisfy general requirements for associate degrees in arts and sciences and are transferable to senior institutions. Students can earn an associate of applied science degree in twenty-five areas of study. Certificate programs help students reenter the job market by upgrading their skills in advertising art, management development, and several areas of office administration. A continuing-education program is offered. In addition, creative laboratories are offered in math, writing, science, arts and the humanities, social sciences, business, and industry. Programs emphasized at the Central Campus include fire science, engineering technology, nursing, and emergency medical technology. The Spring Creek Campus focuses on business, management, the sciences, art, and music. In the 1992–93 regular term the district enrolled 9,590 students. The 568-member faculty included many part-time teachers.
Larry Collins

COLLINGSWORTH COUNTY. Collingsworth County (D-11), on the eastern edge of the Texas Panhandle, is bordered on the east by Oklahoma, on the north by Wheeler County, on the west by Donley County, and on the south by Childress and Hall counties. The county is named for James Collinsworth,^{qv} the first chief justice of the Republic of Texas,^{qv} whose name was misspelled in the legislation that established the county. The center of Collingsworth County is located at approximately 100°15′ north longitude and 34°57′ west latitude, about five miles north-northwest of Wellington, the county seat. Wellington is ninety miles east-southeast of Amarillo. Collingsworth County occupies 894 square miles of rolling prairie and riverbreaks located to the east of the Texas High Plains. The county terrain is such that about half of its area is not suitable for farming. Therefore ranching remains strong in the county, balanced but not displaced by farms. The county's sandy and loam soils support a variety of native grasses as well as cotton, wheat, and grain sorghums. A small amount of oil and gas is produced in the northern part of the county. The land is broken by the Salt Fork of the Red River, which meanders eastward across the central portion of the county, as well as by its many tributaries, including Elm, Wolf, Spiller (or Buck), and Sand creeks. The elevation of the county ranges from 1,800 to 2,600 feet above sea level, the average annual maximum temperature is 99° F in July, the average annual minimum is 26° F in January, the average annual precipitation is 22.03 inches, and the growing season averages 212 days per year.

The area that is now Collingsworth County was occupied by Apaches from prehistoric times until about 1700, when Comanches and Kiowas moved in. These tribes dominated the Panhandle^{qv} until they were crushed by the United States Army in the Red River War^{qv} of 1874 and removed permanently to reservations in Indian Territory. The Panhandle was thus opened for settlement. In 1876 the Texas legislature formed Collingsworth County of land previously assigned to Bexar and Young counties.

Buffalo hunters who occupied the area during and just after the Indian wars slaughtered the great herds and opened the frontier for cattlemen. Ranchers first appeared within the borders of Collingsworth County during the late 1870s; the Rowe Brothers Ranch established its large holdings in southwestern Collingsworth county during 1878. In 1880 the United States census reported six people (three white and three black) living in Collingsworth County.

During the early 1880s a few huge ranches were formed and controlled most of the land in the county. In 1880 William and James Curtis claimed the southeastern part of the county for their Diamond Tail Ranch.qv During 1883 the Rocking Chair Ranch,qv an English venture like that of the Rowe brothers, bought alternate sections of most of the remaining land in the northeastern part of the county, as a means of controlling twice as much land as it actually owned.

During the late 1880s and early 1890s, however, great changes occurred in the ranching industry. The severe drought of 1885–87 and the even more destructive blizzard of 1886 wiped out many large ranches, while changes in Texas land laws made it more difficult for ranchers to control state lands desired by settlers. As a result the large ranches began to break up in the late 1880s and early 1890s and smaller spreads were established by newcomers, some of whom began farming on a limited scale. In 1890 there were eighty-nine farms and ranches in the county, eighty-seven of them 500 acres or smaller. About 19,800 cattle were counted in the area that year, while about 335 acres were devoted to the cultivation of wheat, corn, oats, and cotton. The census counted 357 people living in the county that year.

Immigration and economic development led to the county's political organization in 1890, when the growing population felt the need for local political control. In August of that year a petition of organization was circulated, and in September an election was held to choose county officers and a county seat. The site of a proposed town, Wellington, was elected over its competitors as the county seat. In 1891 the new city was platted, and the construction of a courthouse began.

Good wheat crops in 1889 and 1890 had indicated the land's agricultural potential, and newly arriving farmers and stock farmers eagerly purchased lands in Collingsworth County. By 1900 there were 218 farms in the area encompassing 584,692 acres (with 21,494 acres classified as "improved"), and the population had increased to 1,233. In the first years of the twentieth century agricultural development accelerated, and by 1910 the county had developed a mixed ranching and farming economy based on small and medium-sized ranches and cotton, corn, milo, and wheat farms. That year the census counted 806 farms in the county. Corn cultureqv occupied more than 26,000 acres, and cotton cultureqv took up almost 17,500; improved acres on the farms totalled almost 105,000 acres. The population of the county, 5,224, was quadruple that of 1900. By 1920 the county had 1,139 farms and ranches, with more than 49,500 acres planted in cotton and 80,200 acres devoted to various cereals, especially corn. By the late 1920s, all the land in the county suitable for farming was occupied, and in 1930 Collingsworth County maintained a mixed agricultural economy, with numerous cattle ranches and over 246,000 acres of farmland. Almost 26,400 cattle were counted in Collingsworth County that year, while local farmers planted corn, wheat, oats, alfalfa, milo, and, especially, cotton; about 162,000 acres was devoted to cotton production alone. In 1930 the census enumerated 2,112 farms and 14,461 residents in the county.

During the 1920s a dispute arose between Texas and Oklahoma over the actual location of the eastern boundary of the Texas Panhandle. After resurveying, and after a United States Supreme Court decision, the line was moved 3,800 feet to the east. Thus Lipscomb, Hemphill, Wheeler, Collingsworth, and Childress counties of Texas all grew slightly, at the expense of Harmon, Beckham, Ellis, and Roger Mills counties of Oklahoma (see BOUNDARIES).

Rail and highway systems that developed during the first half of the twentieth century helped to tie the area to national markets and to encourage economic development. In 1910 the Wichita Falls and Wellington Railway Company of Texas (which a year later became a Missouri, Kansas and Texas subsidiary) built a line from the Oklahoma-Texas border to Wellington. In 1932 the Fort Worth and Denver City Northern Railway Company built a line from Childress to Pampa via Wellington and Shamrock. Following the Federal Highway Aid Act of 1916 and the establishment of the State Highway Commission in 1917, many Texas counties began to build auto routes. Collingsworth County began its first road projects in 1917 by building unpaved roads. By the mid-1920s, good roads linked Wellington to Childress, Shamrock, Clarendon, and Memphis, while lesser routes tied the outlying towns and ranches to the major road system. During the 1930s and 1940s, paving and upgrading of the system began. Today a network of federal, state, and farm roads crisscrosses the county (see HIGHWAY DEVELOPMENT).

The Great Depression and Dust Bowlqqv interrupted Collingsworth County's expansion during the 1930s. The number of farms in the county fell from 2,112 to 1,358 between 1929 and 1940, and the population of the county dropped from 14,461 to 10,331 during the same period.

Since World War IIqv the population of the county has continued to decline steadily, partly due to the mechanization and consolidation of agriculture. Collingsworth County's population dropped to 9,139 in 1950, 6,276 in 1960, 4,755 in 1970, and 4,648 in 1980. It was estimated to be 3,573 in 1992.

Oil and gas reserves were discovered in the county in 1936, but only modest production resulted: in 1956 petroleum production totalled only 795 barrels, and in 1960, 779 barrels. Since the 1970s production has been more impressive but still quite limited. In 1978 about 19,120 barrels of oil were pumped from Collingsworth County lands, and 13,106 in 1982; in 1990 the county produced 8,595 barrels. By that year, almost 1,169,500 barrels of oil had been produced in Collingsworth County since 1936.

By 1982 the number of cultivated acres in Collingsworth County had declined to 156,000, as marginal lands were returned to ranching. During the 1980s agricultural production in Collingsworth County averaged around $28 million annually, with a healthy mix of cotton, grain, and beef production. Oil production, worth almost $650,000 a year, supplemented the economy. County communities include Dodson (1980 population 185), Dozier (30), Samnorwood (110), and Quail (92). The bulk of the county's population resides in Wellington, the county seat, which had an estimated population of 2,456 in 1992.

BIBLIOGRAPHY: Clyde Chestnut Brown, A Survey History of Collingsworth County, Texas (M.A. thesis, University of Colorado, 1934). *A History of Collingsworth County and Other Stories* (Wellington, Texas: *Leader* Printing, 1925). Estelle D. Tinkler, "Nobility's Ranche: A History of the Rocking Chair Ranche," *Panhandle-Plains Historical Review* 15 (1942).
Donald R. Abbe

COLLINS, ALBERT (1932–1993). Albert Collins, blues musician, was born on October 1, 1932, in Leona, Texas, the son of Andy Thomas. The family moved to Marquez when Albert was seven and to Houston when he was nine. He started his music career in Houston in 1952, recorded his first single, "The Freeze," in 1958 and the first of fifteen albums, *The Cool Sound Of Albert Collins*, in 1965. Called "the telecaster" for his guitar and the "iceman" for his particular music, he became famous for walking into the audience, and on one occasion into the parking lot, with a 300-foot extension cord, followed by the audience. Collins used his fingers, not a pick, to play the guitar; unorthodox minor tunings and a capo on the fingerboard produced his unusual sounds. In the early 1960s his album *Frosty* became his first gold album. In 1968 Collins moved from Texas to California with the group Canned Heat. Although he had numerous regional hits recorded on small labels in the 1960s and 1970s, in the late 1970s he signed with Alligator. His 1979 *Ice Pickin'* won the best blues album award from the Montreux Jazz Festival and was nominated for a Grammy. In 1983 he won the W. C. Handy award for best blues album of the year with *Don't Lose Your Cool,* and in 1986 he shared a

Grammy for *Showdown*. By the 1990s he had played in Carnegie Hall and appeared at the Live Aid Television benefit. His last album, *Molten Ice*, was released in 1992. A favorite in Austin, Collins yearly played three or four two-night stands at Antone's, a local club, and in 1991 taped a BBC special there. He also played at the annual Aqua-Fest and appeared on the PBS show, "Austin City Limits"[qv] in 1991. He died in Las Vegas on November 24, 1993.

BIBLIOGRAPHY: Austin *American-Statesman*, November 25, 29, 1993. Colin Larkin, ed., *The Guinness Encyclopedia of Popular Music* (Chester, Connecticut: New England Publishing Associates, 1992). *Newsweek*, December 6, 1993.

John G. Johnson

COLLINS, CARR P. (1892–1980). Carr P. Collins, insurance magnate and philanthropist, son of Elizabeth (Hopkins) and Vinson Allen Collins,[qv] was born at Chester, Texas, on May 12, 1892. His higher education was limited to one year at Southwest Texas State Teachers College (now Southwest Texas State University). In 1913 he was appointed first secretary of the Industrial Accident Board (*see* TEXAS WORKERS' COMPENSATION COMMISSION), which had been founded as a result of legislation sponsored by his father in the Texas Senate. Thus began a long career in insurance, highlighted by his founding of Fidelity Union Life Insurance Company in 1928. The company's rapid growth resulted from a novel stock-option plan partially devised by Collins. His most famous business endeavor, however, was the 1930s coast-to-coast radio selling of Crazy Crystals, dehydrated minerals from the springs at Mineral Wells, Texas. When reconstituted with water, they supposedly acted as a laxative. Sales reputedly reached $3 million a year before the Pure Food and Drug Administration declared the product fraudulent.

A fundamentalist Baptist and Democrat, Collins made a dramatic entry into politics in 1938 when he became advisor to evangelical gubernatorial candidate W. Lee O'Daniel.[qv] As governor, O'Daniel tried to appoint Collins to the state highway commission, thus breaking the tradition of giving each major section of the state a member; the Senate voted Collins down. After a bitterly disputed race for the United States Senate in 1941, in which O'Daniel narrowly defeated Lyndon B. Johnson,[qv] a Texas Senate investigating committee questioned Collins about a large undeclared gift of radio time to O'Daniel on Collins's Mexican station, XEAW. Collins claimed that the time was paid for by O'Daniel's friends but that he could not remember the donors and had kept no records of the contributions.

In the last three or four decades of his life Collins was deeply involved in a number of manufacturing and home-building ventures. He was also instrumental in the selection of premillennialist W. A. Criswell as pastor of the First Baptist Church of Dallas[qv] in 1944. He endowed the Texas Institute of Letters[qv] with a $1,000 annual award for the author of the best book about Texas, beginning in 1946. He helped bring Bishop College to Dallas in 1961 and also worked for better housing for blacks. His donation of Dallas property to Baylor University in 1961 was the largest gift ever made to the university at that time, and in 1979 Collins contributed $1 million to establish the Carr P. Collins Chair of Finance at Baylor. In 1914 he married Ruth Woodall, a schoolteacher from Hallsville; they had three children. Collins died on January 17, 1980.

BIBLIOGRAPHY: Dallas *Morning News*, January 19, 1980. George N. Green, *The Establishment in Texas Politics* (Westport, Connecticut: Greenwood, 1979). Dorothy Neville, *Carr P. Collins* (Dallas: Park, 1963).

George N. Green

COLLINS, HARRY WARREN (1896–1968). Harry Warren (Rip) Collins, athlete and law officer, the son of H. W. Collins, was born at Weatherford, Texas, on February 26, 1896. The Collinses moved to Austin, where their son attended Austin High School and quickly established a reputation as a versatile athlete. Collins was chiefly known for his ability to punt a football long distances with a peculiar spin that made the ball almost impossible to handle. His punting and running ability helped him lead his team to two consecutive state championships in 1913 and 1914.

Collins wanted to attend the University of Texas after graduation. The UT coach, however, questioned his desire and endurance after watching Collins leave a game because of an ankle injury. Consequently, Collins chose to attend Texas A&M University and was on the team when the heavily favored Longhorns took the field against the Aggies in 1915. Collins punted the ball twenty-three times that afternoon for an average of fifty-five yards per kick. The crazy spin he placed on the ball resulted in thirteen fumbles by Texas return men. One fumble set up the only touchdown scored that day, a run by Collins. The final score was 13-0.

Collins joined the United States Army and spent the fall season of 1916 playing on the Second Texas Infantry Team. After he returned to school in 1917 his punting ability became the team's main offensive weapon. Often the Aggies punted on second down. "I knew the quickest, farthest and safest way to get that ball down the field was to let him kick it down there," the coach explained years later. The strategy worked. In 1917 the Aggies went undefeated and unscored on. By the end of his college career Collins's punting ability was legendary; he is still regarded as the best punter in Southwest Conference[qv] history.

He was equally talented at throwing a baseball and as a high school pitcher had received a contract offer in 1915 from the Texas League.[qv] After the Aggies' undefeated football season Collins fulfilled his contractual obligations and became a starting pitcher for Dallas. He spent a year there and left in 1920 to join the New York Yankees. In his first season in the major leagues he was fourteen and eight and recorded two shutouts. He followed that with an eleven and five mark in 1921. At the end of that season he joined the Boston Red Sox. His longest stay with any one team was with the Detroit Tigers (1923–28). He finished his career in St. Louis (1929–31). During his eleven years as a starting pitcher Collins had an earned-run average of 3.99 and 108 wins against eighty-two losses. The victories included fifteen shutouts. Throughout his career he did spot duty as a relief pitcher, in which role he compiled a nine and seven record with five saves. He had only one home run, however, in 582 turns at bat. Collins returned to the Texas League in 1933 and played one season in Fort Worth before retiring from baseball.

He then joined the Texas Rangers.[qv] He was elected Travis county sheriff in 1940 and served for eight years. He became police chief of Bryan in 1950 and retired from law enforcement work in 1959. Collins died in Bryan on May 27, 1968, and was buried in College Station Cemetery.

BIBLIOGRAPHY: Austin *American*, May 29, June 27, 1968.

David Minor

COLLINS, JASPER (1870–1924). Jasper Collins, state legislator, was born on February 18, 1870, near Carthage, Texas, the son of John J. and Elizabeth (McDaniel) Collins. He attended private schools in Texas and Louisiana before receiving his bachelor of arts degree at the University of Texas in 1891. He then attended law classes and was licensed to practice law in 1892. Immediately afterward, he moved to Dallas, and in 1894 he returned to Carthage to practice law. In 1895 he became the editor and proprietor of the *Panola Watchman*, a job he held until 1905. Collins was elected state legislator in 1899 and served one term as the Democratic representative for Panola County. In 1904 as a presidential elector he cast a vote for William Jennings Bryan. He returned to Dallas in 1908 and worked there in real estate. He continued his political activity as a progressive by serving as chairman of the speakers' division of the statewide campaign for prohibition,[qv] a position in which he traveled around the state speaking on behalf of the cause. He was a member of the University Club, the Dallas Chamber of Commerce, the Knights Templar, and Hella Temple. He married Gertrude James of Memphis on February 16, 1907, and they had two sons. Collins was a Shriner, an Episcopalian, and a Democrat. He died in his Dallas home on January 2, 1924, of heart disease. He was buried in Grove Hill Cemetery with Masonic honors.

BIBLIOGRAPHY: Ellis A. Davis and Edwin H. Grobe, comps., *The Encyclopedia of Texas*, 2-vol. ed. Dallas *Morning News*, January 2, 1924. Vertical Files, Barker Texas History Center, University of Texas at Austin.
Carolyn Hyman

COLLINS, RICHARD M. (1815–?). Richard M. Collins, Brazoria County legislator, county official, and planter, moved to Texas from New York, probably around 1840. He received an unconditional certificate for land in Brazoria County on June 4, 1844. He represented that county in the Eighth Congress (1843–44) and was on a committee in 1845 to draft a resolution to the Senate expressing Brazoria County's aversion to certain diplomatic appointees. In August 1851 Collins was elected justice of the peace of precinct four in Brazoria. He was elected county commissioner in August 1856 and served until removed by military commander Gen. J. J. Reynolds[qv] on April 25, 1869. According to one source, Collins was a doctor who owned a plantation on Oyster Creek. In 1860 he was among the wealthiest citizens in the county, with real property valued at $44,070, personal property estimated at $85,324, and seventy-seven slaves. The 1870 census listed him as a stock raiser and farmer. Confederate veteran Ferrell Vincent, Collins, and others moved their families to Tuxpan, Vera Cruz, after the Civil War,[qv] formed the Tuxpan Land Company, and bought a half million acres in the area. Collins is believed to have died in Mexico, and his family did not return to Texas. The Tuxpan land was eventually confiscated by the Mexican government, and the colony came to an end.

BIBLIOGRAPHY: Abner J. Strobel, *The Old Plantations and Their Owners of Brazoria County* (Houston, 1926; rev. ed., Houston: Bowman and Ross, 1930; rpt., Austin: Shelby, 1980). *Telegraph and Texas Register*, January 8, 1845. Texas House of Representatives, *Biographical Directory of the Texan Conventions and Congresses, 1832–1845* (Austin: Book Exchange, 1941). Ralph A. Wooster, "Wealthy Texans, 1860," *Southwestern Historical Quarterly* 71 (October 1967).
Carolyn Hyman

COLLINS, VINSON A. (1867–1966). Vinson Collins, attorney and legislator, was born near Honey Island, Texas, on March 1, 1867, to Warren J. and Eboline (Valentine) Collins. After graduating from Sam Houston State Normal College (now Sam Houston State University) in 1893, Collins taught for six years in Grand Saline and studied law in his spare time. He passed the bar examination in 1901 and opened a law practice in Beaumont. During three terms in the Texas Senate (1910–14, 1916–17) he supported prohibition, woman suffrage,[qqv] and an eight-hour workday. In 1913 he wrote the state's first workmen's compensation laws. He was defeated by Martin Dies, Sr.,[qv] in a subsequent race for the United States House of Representatives. Although he was a member of the Ku Klux Klan,[qv] Collins entered the 1924 gubernatorial election without securing support from the Klan hierarchy. In the absence of official backing, he fought a bitter, unsuccessful campaign against the official Klan candidate, Felix D. Robertson.[qv] Collins was among the many Texas Democrats who bolted from the party rather than endorse Alfred E. Smith during the 1928 presidential race. He served on the board of regents for state teachers' colleges from 1935 to 1950. He maintained an active law practice in Dallas, Beaumont, and Livingston until his retirement in 1957. He first married Lizzie Hopkins, who died in 1900; he later married Nannie Kuykendall of Grand Saline. Collins died in Dallas on July 5, 1966, and was survived by six children. He was buried at Livingston.

BIBLIOGRAPHY: Norman D. Brown, *Hood, Bonnet, and Little Brown Jug: Texas Politics, 1921–1928* (College Station: Texas A&M University Press, 1984). Dallas *Morning News*, July 6, 1966.
Robert Wooster

COLLINS, TEXAS (Jasper County). Collins was on the Atchison, Topeka and Santa Fe Railway seventy-five miles north of Beaumont in north central Jasper County. The rail siding at Collins was established before 1918 on the Gulf, Beaumont and Great Northern Railway and was reportedly named after a black settler, Sebe Collins. In 1984 the railroad siding and a small gravel pit marked the locale.
Robert Wooster

COLLINS, TEXAS (Nueces County). Collins was forty miles west of Corpus Christi at a site that was in Nueces County and now is in Jim Wells County. The settlement was established in 1878 on the Los Preseños grant, a Mexican grant that was subdivided in 1878. N. G. Collins bought the northwest portion and platted the Collins townsite across San Fernando Creek from the town of Los Preseños. The Corpus Christi, San Diego, and Rio Grande Narrow Gauge Railroad laid track through the townsite en route to San Diego, Texas, in late 1878. That year the post office at Los Preseños was closed. Collins began to grow and soon replaced Los Preseños on maps. The post office occupied a room in Phil Hobbs's store, and Hobbs was postmaster. Residents of Los Preseños followed the post office to Collins. Early settlers included Oscar Staples, who taught school in Collins; Mrs. E. D. Sidbury, who had a lumberyard near the Becham House, which served as the meeting place for the Methodist Episcopal Church, South, until 1889; and Father Bard, who almost singlehandedly built the town's Catholic church. By 1880 Collins had a population of 500, a railroad station, a two-story hotel, several stores and eating places, and a few houses and small barns.

The town was a shipping and mail center for ranchers between Agua Dulce and San Diego. In 1885 the San Antonio and Aransas Pass Railway bypassed Lagarto, and many residents moved to Collins. But in 1888 the SAAP bypassed Collins and joined the Texas-Mexican Railway three miles west, on land belonging to the King Ranch.[qv] A new town, Kleberg, was established at the intersection, and Collins began to decline. The Becham House was moved to Kleberg to house railroad workers. In 1888 George Hobbs bought four lots in Kleberg and moved his two-story store in September. The post office remained in Collins, however, because postal authorities refused to grant Kleberg a post office.

In 1889 George Hobbs, George Newberry, and others built a twenty-by-forty-foot log schoolhouse in Kleberg. It was also used as a Protestant church. The Catholic church building that Father Bard built was moved to Kleberg, along with some stores. Kleberg changed its name to Alice in 1888 and continued to grow as Collins declined. In 1892 the post office was moved from Collins to Alice, and by 1900 Collins was a ghost town. The Old Collins Cemetery remains in southeast Alice.

BIBLIOGRAPHY: Corpus Christi *Caller-Times*, January 18, 1959. Neva Virginia Pollard, The History of Jim Wells County (M.A. thesis, Texas A&I University, 1945).
Agnes G. Grimm

COLLINS CITY, TEXAS. Collins City was a short-lived post office and flag stop on the International–Great Northern Railroad near Jacksonville in north central Cherokee County. It was named for Col. C. F. Collins, agent for the I&GN in Jacksonville in the 1870s. A local post office operated briefly from February through September 1877, but a town evidently failed to develop, and the mail service was discontinued.

BIBLIOGRAPHY: Hattie Joplin Roach, *A History of Cherokee County* (Dallas: Southwest, 1934).
Christopher Long

COLLINS CREEK. Collins Creek rises fourteen miles northwest of Albany in north central Shackelford County (at 32°57′ N, 99°22′ W) and runs eleven miles east to its mouth on the Clear Fork of the Brazos River, just north of Fort Griffin State Park (at 32°56′ N, 99°13′ W). According to sources, the creek was named for a man named Collins who was murdered nearby by the "Old Law Mob." The creek runs through steep slopes and benches surfaced by shallow clay loam that supports juniper, live oak, mesquite, and grasses to flat terrain with local shallow depressions surfaced by clay and sandy loam that supports water-tolerant hardwoods, conifers, and grasses.

BIBLIOGRAPHY: Don Hampton Biggers, *Shackelford County Sketches* (Albany, Texas: Albany News Office, 1908; rpt., ed. Joan Farmer, Albany and Fort Griffin, Texas: Clear Fork Press, 1974).

COLLINSON, WALTER JAMES (1855–1943). Walter James (Frank) Collinson, buffalo hunter, cattleman, and student of the frontier, was born on November 13, 1855, in Yorkshire, England. Shortly after his sixteenth birthday he left boarding school in Beverly and sailed for the United States aboard the *San Marcos*. He landed at Galveston, Texas, in the fall of 1872 and went to work on the Circle Dot, Judge George H. Noonan's qv horse ranch near San Antonio. In December 1873 Collinson went to work for rancher John T. Lytle qv in southeast Medina County, where he once helped round up and brand a herd of 3,500 cattle and drive them to the Red Cloud Indian Reservation in northwest Nebraska; there the stock was turned over to George Armstrong Custer. qv

In October 1874 Collinson became a partner in the two-wagon, six-mule buffalo-hunting outfit run by Jim White and Thomas L. (George) Causey. qv After buying supplies at Frank Conrad's store at Fort Griffin, Collinson moved westward onto the Llano Estacado qv and helped complete the destruction of the southern buffalo herd. In spring 1877 he returned to Fort Griffin with 6,000 tongues, 11,000 hides, and 45,000 pounds of dried meat (*see* BUFFALO, BUFFALO HUNTING).

He then headed westward toward New Mexico Territory, apparently to fight in the Lincoln County War of Billy the Kid fame (*see* MCCARTY, HENRY), but upon meeting cattlemen S. R. Coggin and Robert K. Wylie qv along the way, he changed his mind. He hired out to Coggin to go to Granada, Colorado, and return a herd of 8,000 Jinglebob cattle, recently purchased from John S. Chisum, qv to good grass in Texas. Collinson chose his old buffalo-hunting grounds on the Tongue River (now the South Pease), located at the eastern edge of the Staked Plains. There he ran the Jinglebob herd until 1881, when it was sold to the Matador Land and Cattle Company. qv For about the next fifteen years he ran stock, either as a partner or independently, on various West Texas ranches. In 1882 he joined S. R. and M. J. Coggin in running a ranch on the Colorado River. From there he made several trail drives northward to the Yellowstone River in Montana. Around 1900, in King County near his old Jinglebob Ranch, he became the partner of the pioneer Panhandle rancher Robert B. Masterson. qv

In 1887 Collinson married Jessamine Anne (Jesse) Bremmer, a Scot, at Lamar, Colorado, and honeymooned in England. The next year he returned to the Big Bend country in Southwest Texas, where he ran his own ranch through a series of drought years until 1895, with marginal success. Thereafter he lived in several places, among them Clarendon in the Panhandle, before moving in 1922 to El Paso, where he spent his last years. He died there in 1943 and was buried at Clarendon. He and his wife had ten children.

Frank Collinson's significance lies in the fact that not only did he literally follow the frontier for fifty years, but during his last ten years he recorded many of his experiences and impressions in interviews, letters, and a series of articles published in the popular magazine *Ranch Romances*. The bulk of these, now housed in the Panhandle-Plains Historical Museum qv library at Canyon, are rich in anecdote and offer valuable insights into the unfolding of the frontier, especially in West Texas. Collinson's observations on the clash between whites and Indians, on the cattle industry, on the buffalo slaughter, and on the little-publicized mustangers (*see* MUSTANGS) and ciboleros, qv as well as on the flora and fauna of the region, make a major contribution to our knowledge of the Southwest frontier, despite the fact that Collinson was given to occasional exaggeration. He also offered new information on notable personalities in the region, many of whom he knew personally, including John L. Bullis, Charles Goodnight, Quanah Parker, Francisco (Pancho) Villa, William A. A. (Big Foot) Wallace, qqv and John S. Chisum.

BIBLIOGRAPHY: Frank Collinson, *Life in the Saddle*, ed. Mary Whatley Clarke (Norman: University of Oklahoma Press, 1963).

James I. Fenton

COLLIN STREET BAKERY, CORSICANA. In 1896 August Weidmann, a young German immigrant, opened a bakery on Collin Street in Corsicana, with financial backing from Tom McElwee, local cotton buyer and opera-house proprietor. Weidmann's specialty was a fruitcake baked by a recipe he had brought with him from his native country. McElwee suggested the trade name DeLuxe Fruitcake for the product. In 1906 the business was moved to a location on Sixth Avenue, and there McElwee opened an exclusive hotel on the second floor of the bakery. Enrico Caruso, John J. McGraw, and Will Rogers were among the celebrities who stayed at the hotel at various times. In 1914 a Ringling Brothers circus troupe, in Corsicana for a performance, bought dozens of DeLuxe Fruitcakes to give as Christmas gifts to friends and relatives all over the United States and in Europe. As a result, the bakery received an overwhelming number of orders from the recipients for more cakes, and the company's mail-order business resulted.

McElwee died in 1946; Weidmann died the following year. Lee McNutt, R. F. Rutherford, Harry Montgomery, and H. T. Cook purchased the business from McElwee's widow. L. W. (Bill) McNutt, Jr., Lee McNutt's son, joined the firm in 1958, and in 1967 became company president. His two sons are also involved in the company's management. In 1967 the bakery moved to its current location at 401 West Seventh Avenue. Although there is a small retail outlet in the bakery that sells traditional bakery items, the emphasis of the business has continued to be its mail-order DeLuxe Fruitcakes. Company officials have rejected numerous offers from major food companies to distribute the fruitcakes. The cakes are available only through the bakery or by mail order and cannot be purchased in stores. From October through mid-December the company bakes 30,000 fruitcakes (75,000 pounds) a day and expands its force from fifty regular employees to more than 600. The cakes are shipped to all fifty states and more than 190 countries.

BIBLIOGRAPHY: Dallas *Morning News*, November 22, 1950, May 21, 1972. *Pecan Press*, December 1983.

Tommy W. Stringer

COLLINSVILLE, TEXAS. Collinsville is on U.S. Highway 377 eighteen miles southwest of Sherman in southwestern Grayson County. The first Anglo-Americans to settle in the area arrived in the late 1850s. Originally the community was called Springville, and land for the townsite donated by Joshua Miller. A post office operated there in 1857–58. In the late 1860s another town, Toadsuck, was established in the area. Following the Civil War qv L. M. Collins and her two sons arrived from Ann Arbor, Michigan, and established what many believe to be the first free school in the North Texas area. In 1872 a post office opened. Nine years later the Texas and Pacific Railway arrived. The railroad established the community as a shipping and retail point for area farmers. Sometime early in the 1890s residents voted to incorporate and rename their town in honor of Collins. By 1900 Collinsville had a population of over 600. That figure fluctuated little over the next five decades. The town had Methodist, Baptist, Christian, and Cumberland Presbyterian churches and fifty businesses. Beginning in the mid-1970s a ten-year growth in population occurred. In 1989 Collinsville had an estimated 911 residents and sixteen businesses. In 1990 the population was 1,033.

BIBLIOGRAPHY: Graham Landrum and Allen Smith, *Grayson County* (Fort Worth, 1960; 2d ed., Fort Worth: Historical Publishers, 1967).

David Minor

COLLINSWORTH, GEORGE MORSE (1810–1866). George Morse Collinsworth (Collingsworth), soldier, planter, and civil servant, was born in Mississippi in 1810. He was living in Brazoria, Texas, in 1832, when he participated in the battle of Velasco.qv In July of that year he was serving as secretary of the Brazoria Committee of Vigilance. In early October 1835 he raised a company of infantry from among the planters around the lower Colorado for service in the Texas army. With Benjamin Rush Milam,qv who had just returned to Texas after escaping from prison in Mexico, these men, numbering about fifty, captured the Mexican garrison at Goliad on October 9, 1835. Their victory cut off communication between San Antonio, then in possession of Mexican forces, and the Gulf of Mexico and secured valuable arms and supplies. At some time between October 10 and 17, 1835, Collinsworth left Goliad, either to recruit more men and gather supplies or to join the Texas army at San Antonio. Philip Dimmittqv was elected to take his place as commander at Goliad. Critical reports about Dimmitt persuaded Stephen F. Austinqv to write him on November 18, demanding that he turn his command over to Collinsworth. Volunteers then present in Goliad adopted resolutions protesting Austin's order, and the General Councilqv declined to intervene, so that Dimmitt continued in his position. In the meantime, on November 13, the provisional governmentqv voted a resolution of thanks to Collinsworth and his company for their victory at Goliad. On November 28, 1835, the General Council appointed Collinsworth captain of a company of infantry (*see also* GOLIAD CAMPAIGN OF 1835).

On December 11, 1835, the General Council elected Collinsworth collector of customs for the port of Matagorda. His resignation from the army was accepted on January 4, 1836. On January 12, 1838, he received a bounty warrant for 320 acres for his military service. He was nominated collector for the port of Matagorda on May 22, 1837. On January 16, 1839, he was elected collector of the revenue for the county of Matagorda, and on January 30, 1840, he was nominated commissioner to inspect the Matagorda County land office, a post for which he was confirmed on February 3. Collinsworth was elected collector of the revenue for the port of Calhoun on January 22, 1841, and justice of the peace for the fourth beat in Matagorda County on March 27, 1841. On February 9, 1845, he was confirmed as customs collector for Aransas District.

Collinsworth married Susan R. Kendrick on June 5, 1837, in Matagorda County, where they lived until about 1854. In 1857 he was a surveyor in Karnes County. He died in Matagorda County on April 18, 1866. A son, George M. Collinsworth, Jr., was born about 1840 and served as a private in Company B, Eighth Texas Cavalryqv (Terry's Texas Rangers).

BIBLIOGRAPHY: Eugene C. Barker, "Texan Revolutionary Army," *Quarterly of the Texas State Historical Association* 9 (April 1906). *Compiled Index to Elected and Appointed Officials of the Republic of Texas, 1835–1846* (Austin: State Archives, Texas State Library, 1981). Charles Adams Gulick, Jr., Harriet Smither, et al., eds., *The Papers of Mirabeau Buonaparte Lamar* (6 vols., Austin: Texas State Library, 1920–27; rpt., Austin: Pemberton Press, 1968). Louis Wiltz Kemp Papers, Texas State Archives, Austin. Amelia W. Williams and Eugene C. Barker, eds., *The Writings of Sam Houston, 1813–1863* (8 vols., Austin: University of Texas Press, 1938–43; rpt., Austin and New York: Pemberton Press, 1970).

Thomas W. Cutrer

COLLINSWORTH, JAMES (1806–1838). James Collinsworth, lawyer, jurist, and signer of the Texas Declaration of Independence,qv was born in Davidson County, Tennessee, in 1806, the son of Edmund and Alice (Thompson) Collinsworth. He attended school in Tennessee, studied law, and was admitted to the Tennessee bar in 1826. He was an ally of Andrew Jackson, Sam Houston,qv and other leading Tennessee politicians. From April 30, 1829, until early 1834, Collinsworth served as United States district attorney for the Western District of Tennessee. By 1835 he had moved to Matagorda, in the Brazos Municipality, Texas, and begun the practice of law. Along with Asa Brigham, John S. D. Byrom, and Edwin Wallerqqv he represented Brazoria in the Convention of 1836.qv

At the convention Collinsworth signed the Texas Declaration of Independence, introduced and guided to adoption a resolution making his fellow Tennessean Sam Houston commander in chief of the Texas army, became chairman of the military affairs committee, and served on the committee appointed to draft a constitution for the new Republic of Texas.qv After the convention adjourned, Houston, on April 8, 1836, appointed Collinsworth his aide-de-camp with the rank of major. After the battle of San Jacintoqv Gen. Thomas J. Ruskqv commended him for his bravery and chivalry.

From April 29 to May 23, 1836, Collinsworth served as acting secretary of state in President David G. Burnet'sqv cabinet. On May 26, 1836, because of his intimacy with President Andrew Jackson, he was designated a commissioner to the United States to seek assistance and possible annexation.qv The mission failed. Later in the year Collinsworth declined Houston's offer to make him attorney general of the Republic of Texas. Instead, on November 30, 1836, he was elected to a term in the Senate of the republic.

When the judiciary of the republic was organized, Collinsworth, on December 16, 1836, was appointed the first chief justice, a post he held until his death. Also in 1836 he helped organize the Texas Railroad, Navigation, and Banking Company,qv and the following year he helped found the city of Richmond. He was a charter member of the Philosophical Society of Texas,qv founded in 1837.

In 1838 Collinsworth was a candidate, along with Mirabeau B. Lamar and Peter W. Grayson,qqv for the presidency of the republic. The first published report of his candidacy was on June 30, 1838. On July 11, however, after a week of drunkenness, he fell or jumped off a boat in Galveston Bay and drowned. Most assumed he committed suicide. His body was recovered and taken by boat up Buffalo Bayou to Houston, where it lay in state in the capitol (*see* CAPITALS). Chief Justice Collinsworth was buried in the City Cemetery, Houston, under the direction of Temple Lodge No. 4; his was "the first Masonic funeral ever held in Texas." On August 21, 1876, Collingsworth County, its name misspelled in the act of the legislature establishing the county, was named in his honor. A state monument was placed at Collinsworth's grave in the old City Cemetery in Houston in 1931.

BIBLIOGRAPHY: Joe E. Ericson, *Judges of the Republic of Texas (1836–1846): A Biographical Directory* (Dallas: Taylor, 1980). Louis Wiltz Kemp, *The Signers of the Texas Declaration of Independence* (Salado, Texas: Anson Jones, 1944; rpt. 1959). Texas House of Representatives, *Biographical Directory of the Texan Conventions and Congresses, 1832–1845* (Austin: Book Exchange, 1941).

Joe E. Ericson

COLLWOOD, TEXAS. Collwood was on the Texas and New Orleans Railroad several miles north of Diboll in southern Angelina County. The settlement grew up during World War II,qv when J. V. Lankford and Sons of Redland moved a small sawmill to the site. The mill evidently closed just after the war, and within a short time most of the residents left the area. In the early 1990s only a few scattered houses remained.

BIBLIOGRAPHY: Angelina County Historical Survey Committee, *Land of the Little Angel: A History of Angelina County, Texas*, ed. Bob Bowman (Lufkin, Texas: Lufkin Printing, 1976).

Christopher Long

COLMENA CREEK. Colmena Creek rises five miles southwest of Freer in western Duval County (at 27°50′ N, 98°42′ W) and runs northwest for eighteen miles to its mouth on Black Creek, four miles north of Biel Lake in eastern Webb County (at 27°56′ N, 98°53′ W). Its name means "Beehive" in Spanish. The surrounding low rolling hills and prairies are surfaced by clay and sandy loams that support grasses and some mesquite. Near the creek's mouth the terrain becomes flat, and some water-tolerant hardwoods and conifers occur.

COLMESNEIL, TEXAS. Colmesneil is at the intersection of U.S. Highway 69 and Farm Road 256, nine miles north of Woodville in north central Tyler County. The town, sometimes referred to as Colmesneil Junction, was named for one of the first conductors on the Texas and New Orleans Railroad through the area. The T&NO line was crossed at Colmesneil by the Trinity and Sabine. In 1881 Jay Gould,qv of the Missouri, Kansas and Texas Railroad, secured a charter for the Trinity and Sabine and built sixty-six miles of track from Trinity to Colmesneil, which became a railroad center for Tyler County. It had the only turntable in the county at the end of the Waco, Beaumont, Trinity and Sabine line. The actual terminus of the railroad was not located in what today is thought of as downtown Colmesneil, but rather in what flourished for a time as a neighboring town called Ogden. The two towns had a long-standing feud, largely between the Manns and Sturrocks of Colmesneil and the Ogdens and Campbells of Ogden. The two towns were consolidated under the single name of Colmesneil in early 1888.

In 1889 Colmesneil shipped cotton and other products from Jasper, Newton, Sabine, San Augustine, and Angelina counties. Since the land around the town is too hilly for cultivation, local products were confined to timber and some cattle. The Yellow Pine Lumber Company operated a sawmill in Colmesneil in the 1880s. At one time Colmesneil was larger than Beaumont. The S. H. Meadows general store, owned and operated by the same family since 1892, is the oldest business establishment in Tyler County. The East Texas Hotel was built by Levi Fortenberry in 1888, bought by C. W. Matthews in 1916, and owned by Mrs. Easter Mann in 1986. The first post office in Colmesneil opened in 1882.

The population was at its height around 1890 at 1,016. By 1900 it was down to 632, and in 1931 it was 370, but by 1939 it was back to 1,000. In the late 1980s it was 600. Nearby Lake Tejas, fed by cool springs, provided water sports for a large East Texas area. At that time the town had a bank, a car dealership, several small grocery stores, and a good high school with an excellent sports record. In 1990 the population was 569.

BIBLIOGRAPHY: Fred I. Massengill, *Texas Towns: Origin of Name and Location of Each of the 2,148 Post Offices in Texas* (Terrell, Texas, 1936). Lou Ella Moseley, *Pioneer Days of Tyler County* (Fort Worth: Miran, 1975). S. G. Reed, *A History of the Texas Railroads* (Houston: St. Clair, 1941; rpt., New York: Arno, 1981). Thomas Clarence Richardson, *East Texas: Its History and Its Makers* (4 vols., New York: Lewis Historical Publishing, 1940).
Megan Biesele

COLOGNE, TEXAS. Cologne, on U.S. Highway 59 near the Victoria county line in eastern Goliad County, was established by two former slaves, Jim Smith and George Washington, as a place where freedmen could settle. Smith and Washington, who operated a freighting and passenger business from Indianola westward, bought 500 acres at the site on Perdido Creek. In 1870 the first families began moving into the settlement, initially called the Colony and later Perdido Community. The name Centerville was adopted after Jim Hall noted that the site was halfway between Goliad and Victoria. Until after the railroad was built the town excluded all white settlers.

In 1889 the Gulf, Western Texas and Pacific Railway established a depot at Centerville but named the stop Ira Station, the name by which the community was known for about ten years. Hall exchanged land for the depot for a lifetime job as station agent and the guarantee that the railroad would not abandon the station. The town became a cattle slaughtering and shipping center, reportedly with a hog rendering plant as well. In 1898 a post office was established under the name of Cologne through the efforts of William Young. The new name was adopted because the abattoirs made the community "such a sweet-smelling place." A Methodist church was established in 1880, then a Baptist, though both were destroyed in the 1930s. The Methodist church was rebuilt, but the Baptists began commuting to nearby Fannin. A one-room school served as the recreational center, and a permanent racetrack and a baseball team provided sport. In 1914 about thirty-five people were living in Cologne. The post office was discontinued in 1925, and the population declined to twenty-five by 1940. Thirty-five residents were recorded from 1970 through 1986. The railroad station and cattle pens no longer exist, though part of the original town is now the location of a large power plant. The town was mentioned in John F. Kennedy's June 1963 speech in Cologne, Germany, where the president said, "I bring you greetings from the cities of America, including the citizens of Cologne, Minnesota, Cologne, New Jersey, and even Cologne, Texas." In 1990 the population was eighty-five.

BIBLIOGRAPHY: Goliad County Historical Commission, *The History and Heritage of Goliad County*, ed. Jakie L. Pruett and Everett B. Cole (Austin: Eakin Press, 1983). Frank X. Tolbert, "Tolbert's Texas" Scrapbook, Barker Texas History Center, University of Texas at Austin.
Craig H. Roell

COLONIA. Colonias are unincorporated and unregulated settlements along the United States–Mexico border. They grew rapidly during the 1980s as thousands of legal and illegal immigrants, primarily Mexican but also Central American, settled in them because they could not pay for other housing. By 1989 an estimated 185,000 people lived in colonias in the border states of Texas, New Mexico, Arizona, and California. Many Texas colonias emerged during the 1960s. As the cotton market collapsed, farmers sold their lands to real estate developers who in turn sold small plots of land for as little as a thousand dollars down and a thousand dollars a year. Many low-income families, lured by the desire to own their own homes, built houses on these plots of land, even though they lay outside city limits, were unregulated, and had minimal public services and building requirements. Builders assured many of them, however, that public utilities would follow, and consequently thousands waited for water, some as long as ten to fifteen years. Cities were reluctant to shoulder the financial burden of providing services without remuneration to thousands of people. The El Paso public water utility, for instance, citing economic and planning considerations, imposed a morato-

Colonia Las Milpas, near Pharr. Photograph by Alan Pogue, 1979. Courtesy Alan Pogue, Austin. In 1995 Las Milpas still had no garbage pickup or sewage system.

rium in 1979 that halted the supply of water to new customers outside the city. The El Paso colonias continued to grow, however, as Mexican immigrants fled their deteriorating economy. Consequently, by 1989 an estimated 28,000 colonia residents lived near El Paso without water, and an additional 53,000 lived with minimal sewage treatment.

In the late 1980s high rates of dysentery, hepatitis, and tuberculosis among colonia residents drew nationwide attention. Residents transported and stored their own water, sometimes in large barrels that formerly held toxic chemicals; water wells were often polluted by cesspools and inadequate sewage plants. In 1987, the San Elizario school system, which accommodated the largest number of colonia children in El Paso County, reported that its high absentee rates were a result of the lack of water and that children suffered from numerous health problems, including skin rashes, diarrhea and vomiting, ringworms and lice.

Since the early 1980s community groups such as Valley Interfaith and the El Paso Interreligious Sponsoring Organization have called attention to the deplorable conditions in colonias and have urged colonia residents to seek public action. In 1987, EPISO, with help from the Southwest Voter Registration Education Project,qv registered more than 20,000 new voters in the city and county, and pressured the El Paso City Council to pass a resolution urging the water utility to reverse its moratorium; new county officials were also elected who threatened to sue the city to force it to provide water to the colonias. The colonias in El Paso won a major victory in 1988, when the city's public-service board, with the help of a low-interest loan from the Texas Water Development Board,qv agreed to build a water plant to treat twenty million gallons a day to serve up to 78,000 people by the year 2010.

In the lower Rio Grande valley, however, where colonias are more isolated and far from any major city, action has been slower. In 1988 Texas comptroller Bob Bullock proposed a widely supported $500 million plan to help build water and sewer plants for poor communities, but the state legislature failed to act on the plan. Opponents claimed that the colonias were the federal government's responsibility since the Immigration and Naturalization Service had been unable to curb illegal immigration. In 1988, Congressman Ronald D. Coleman, a Democrat from El Paso, introduced legislation to establish a United States–Mexico Border Commission to address a wide range of border problems, but no action was taken on the bill. In 1989 state senator Tati Santiesteban of El Paso introduced legislation to establish a state bond program to fund construction for running water and sewage systems. Such measures notwithstanding, in the 1990s the problems of the colonias were far from solved.

BIBLIOGRAPHY: Robert K. Holz and Christopher Shane Davies, *Third-World Colonias: Lower Rio Grande Valley, Texas* (Lyndon B. Johnson School of Public Affairs, University of Texas at Austin, 1993). *Life*, November 1987. New York *Times*, January 3, 1989. Exiquio Salinas, *The Colonias Factbook: A Survey of Living Conditions in Rural Areas of South Texas and West Texas Border Counties* (Austin: Texas Department of Human Services, 1988). *Texas Observer*, October 23, 1987. *Time*, October 17, 1988. — *María-Cristina García*

COLONY, TEXAS (Fayette County). Colony is on State Highway 95 nine miles northwest of Flatonia near the western boundary of Fayette County. It was established in 1880 by a group of migrants from Mississippi who intended to raise cotton in the fertile soil. The original name, Mississippi Colony, was shortened to Colony when the post office was established in 1884. By 1900 Colony had a store, a blacksmith shop, three Protestant churches, and a population of 141. In 1906 the post office closed, and mail was routed through Flatonia. The soil was easily eroded and soon lost its productivity, however, and during the first half of the twentieth century the land reverted to unimproved pasture. Although two churches remained in 1947, all other businesses had disappeared, and children attended school in nearby Cistern. Many area residents moved to other population centers, and the ranches were operated by absentee owners. The discovery of the Muldoon oilfield improved the financial situation of the landowners but came too late to rejuvenate the community itself. In the 1980s one church and a cemetery remained.

BIBLIOGRAPHY: Frank Lotto, *Fayette County: Her History and Her People* (Schulenburg, Texas: Sticker Steam Press, 1902; rpt., Austin: University of Texas Press, 1981). — *Jeff Carroll*

COLONY, TEXAS (Rains County). Colony is on Farm Road 779 eight miles southeast of Emory in southeastern Rains County. It was first settled in the late nineteenth century. By 1904 a three-teacher school had an enrollment of 140. In the mid-1930s the settlement had a school, a church, and a number of scattered dwellings. After World War IIqv the school closed, and in the early 1990s only a church and a cemetery remained. In 1991 the reported population was seventy. — *Christopher Long*

COLONY CREEK. Colony Creek rises twelve miles southeast of Breckenridge in southern Stephens County (at 32°32′ N, 98°47′ W) and runs southeast eighteen miles to its mouth on the Leon River, twelve miles southeast of Eastland in southeastern Eastland County (at 32°22′ N, 98°40′ W). It crosses flat to rolling terrain with local escarpments surfaced by deep, fine sandy loam that supports hardwood trees, conifers, brush, and grasses. In its lower reaches the stream flows through a flat, flood-prone area with local shallow depressions, surfaced by clay and sandy loams that support water-tolerant hardwoods, conifers, and grasses.

COLONY HILL, TEXAS. Colony Hill was on Farm Road 1750 near the site of the present Abilene Municipal Airport in northeastern Taylor County. Colony Hill school, named for a colony of Germans that had recently settled in the area, was started in 1878. In the early years of the settlement church services were held in the school building, until a Baptist Church was erected in 1898. In 1902 Colony Hill school served two teachers and eighty-one pupils. In 1921 the old plank school burned down and was replaced by a new brick building. The church and school were both gone by the 1940s, and by the 1980s the community site lay within the Abilene city limits.

BIBLIOGRAPHY: Juanita Daniel Zachry, *A History of Rural Taylor County* (Burnet, Texas: Nortex, 1980). — *Mark Odintz*

COLONY OF KENT. The Colony of Kent (City of Kent) was a short-lived mid-nineteenth-century British settlement on a horseshoe curve of the Brazos River, now known as Kimball's Bend, three miles north of Kopperl on Lake Whitney in what is now Bosque County. Its founders envisioned Kent as the commercial center of an elaborate colonization project of the Universal Emigration and Colonization Company of London. The colonists planned to sell cooperatively produced grain to nearby Fort Graham as well as in an expected export market. In addition, the colonists imagined Kent as a "Philadelphia on the Brazos," a manufacturing center with a navigable link to the Gulf of Mexico, and hence to world markets. In early September 1850 thirty families left Liverpool, England, and sailed for Texas, where they landed in Galveston. Apparently a second ship of colonists left England a short time later. The colonists included people of the middle class such as shopkeepers, bank clerks, bakers, and tailors. Sir Edward Belcherqv was to be in charge of overseeing the settlement, and Lt. Charles Finch MacKenzie was to be an on-site leader in charge of government. In November 1850 Jacob De Cordovaqv accepted a downpayment from Belcher, who represented the company and the roughly 100 emigrants already moving inland, as well as a similar number soon to disembark in Galveston, for 27,000 acres of Brazos riverbottom belonging to Richard B. Kimball, De Cordova's partner. Belcher had preceded the first of numerous proposed groups in order to inspect 60,000 acres now in Coryell County belonging to James Reily,^qv which company officials in London provisionally had purchased. De Cordova, Reily's agent as well, had guided Belcher to the Reily tract on Cow House Creek imagined by the vaguely communitarian colonists as "New Britain," but Belcher deemed it unsuitable. De Cordova then suggested the Kimball Bend lands, which Belcher and the emigrant leaders accepted after a survey by George B. Erath and Neil McLennan.^qqv As the first group of colonists moved inland from Galveston, cold, wet weather made travel difficult. Some became discouraged and turned back to go to Houston or New Orleans. The colonists, perhaps revealing diminished expectations after a very difficult month in Texas, selected an old name for the new site, "Kent." Kent was officially founded in January 1851 at the foot of a hill called Solomon's Nose. The townsite itself consisted of about forty acres. Belcher promptly returned to England, stopping briefly in New York City to finalize conditions of sale with Kimball. From London, Belcher foresaw Kent "at no very distant period" as the "*chief city* in Texas."

The colonization project reflected not only pervasive English emigration impulses of mid-century but specifically two years of constant promotion by George Catlin,^qv the preeminent American painter of Indians. Since 1840 Catlin had displayed his "Indian Gallery"—nine tons of artifacts and 600 oil paintings, enhanced periodically by Indians performances—throughout Britain and the continent, by which he had gained considerable attention, though not always respect, and no financial security. Despondent from the loss of his wife and son and decreasing interest in his gallery, Catlin turned to a new career as colonization expert, building on his reputation as one who knew the West. He mortgaged his gallery in order to promote and speculate on the proposed project in Texas. After two years of intensive, unremunerated promotion, Catlin abruptly resigned in August 1850 as Texas superintendent of the company, just weeks before departure of the first group of colonists. After the company refused Catlin his anticipated per capita recruitment fees, he continued to borrow in order to repay earlier creditors. When the Texas project failed and with it the company, Catlin faced creditors demanding several times the gallery's value, and the gallery passed in 1852 to an American industrialist, Joseph Harrison. Though not as tragic as the avoidable loss of dozens of settlers' lives, perhaps the most historically significant casualty was the Catlin Indian Gallery, which eventually reappeared in the Smithsonian.

Kent did not survive 1851; many of the settlers died before summer from exposure to bad weather. By the summer of 1852 only one immigrant remained in the Kent colony; the other survivors had departed for more developed areas. The land reverted to Kimball and De Cordova, in accordance with the verbal agreement between Kimball and Belcher. The expectant capitalists failed for several reasons. Because Belcher had made no arrangements for living quarters or provisions, his middle-class would-be farmers were stranded without the necessary means for production. Most settlers lived in mud and straw huts or dugouts. Only the on-site leader, MacKenzie, lived in a log house. Water was obtained from a large spring near Solomon's Nose. The settlers knew little about farming. Even so, De Cordova had proposed a demonstration farm to familiarize the colonists with local practices, but Belcher had blocked this offer, which could have saved the colony. MacKenzie regimented daily routine according to his military training, thereby provoking hostility and wasting time and energy. Essentially, the Kent settlers, described by one potential colonist as "persons of means, education and perhaps I may add delicate habits," were not accustomed to the deprivation and sacrifice necessary for the first years in a remote settlement, and had not been made aware beforehand. Catlin had painted an image of Texas frontier life that emphasized the glories of a presumed natural life, not the requisite hardships and hard work. Even if the colonists were not what De Cordova saw—"broken down English clerks, Superanuated Scotch officers or dissipated Irish boys"—the lamentable but predictable result was the death of ill-prepared and ill-selected British emigrants.

BIBLIOGRAPHY: Thomas W. Cutrer, *The English Texans* (San Antonio: University of Texas Institute of Texan Cultures, 1985). Brian W. Dippie, *Catlin and His Contemporaries: The Politics of Patronage* (Lincoln: University of Nebraska Press, 1990). Dorothy Waties Renick, "The City of Kent," *Southwestern Historical Quarterly* 29 (July 1925). Richard H. Ribb, George Catlin's Crash: "Texas Gamblings" and the Loss of His Indian Gallery (M.A. thesis, University of Texas at Austin, 1992).
Richard H. Ribb

COLONY SETTLEMENT, TEXAS. Colony Settlement, also known as Colony, is on Farm Road 3355 two miles east of U.S. Highway 181 and Normanna and eight miles northeast of Beeville in east central Bee County. In 1893 W. T. McCampbell sold 10,000 acres of his land to C. (or O.) M. Peterson, who journeyed to Chicago with hopes of returning with colonists to develop the area. The immigration of several Norwegian farmers from 1894 to 1898 led residents to call the community Norwegian Colony. Later, the area was called Mennonite Colony, then Colony Settlement. A Lutheran church was built there in 1912 but fell into disuse in the 1960s. A local school served one teacher and thirty-five pupils in 1898, and in 1926 the community constructed another school. The 1948 state highway maps indicate several scattered dwellings at the site. Although the school at Colony Settlement was no longer in operation in 1990, a number of families still lived at the site.

BIBLIOGRAPHY: Grace Bauer, *Bee County Centennial, 1858–1958* (Bee County Centennial, 1958). Camp Ezell, *Historical Story of Bee County, Texas* (Beeville: Beeville Publishing, 1973).
Adrian D. Ramirez

COLORADO, TEXAS. Colorado is two miles southeast of Smithville in southeastern Bastrop County. In 1905 it had a one-teacher school for fifty black students; the school was probably absorbed by the Smithville Independent School District in 1921. In the 1940s a church and several scattered houses marked the community on county highway maps, but by the 1980s only a cemetery and a church remained.
Vivian Elizabeth Smyrl

COLORADO CANYON. Colorado Canyon, through which the Rio Grande flows at the United States–Mexico border, begins south of Tapado Canyon (at 29°20′ N, 104°03′ W) and runs southeast of Farm Road 170 to a point west of Santana Mesa entirely within extreme southern Presidio County (at 29°18′ N, 103°58′ W). The canyon has rugged terrain with high relief surfaced by shallow, stony soils that support scrub brush, sotol, cacti, and sparse grasses.

COLORADO CITY, TEXAS (Fayette County). Colorado City, on the west bank of the Colorado River directly opposite La Grange in central Fayette County, never progressed beyond the plat stage. The town was designed in the late 1830s by John W. S. Dancy^qv and associate promoters to rival the promotion of La Grange by John H. Moore. Elaborate plans called for the development of 5,000 acres with 156 blocks of residential and commercial property. The proposed city was unanimously selected by the Congress as the capital of the Republic of Texas,^qv but President Sam Houston^qv vetoed the proposal because he wanted the capital to remain in Houston. When Mirabeau B. Lamar^qv succeeded Houston, he selected the site of what is now Austin as the capital, and the plan for Colorado City languished. One of the frequent floods along the Colorado River made the plan unfeasible, and most of the area was later included in the decentralized community of Bluff.

COLORADO CITY, TEXAS (Mitchell County). Colorado City, the county seat of Mitchell County, is on the Colorado River, Lone Wolf Creek, U.S. Highway 20/80, State highways 208 and 163, and the

Missouri Pacific Railroad, thirty-eight miles east of Big Spring and twenty-three miles south of Snyder in the north central part of the county. It has been called the "Mother City of West Texas" for its early origin as a ranger camp in 1877 and for its prominence as a cattlemen's center. In 1881 the town was chosen county seat and acquired a station on the new Texas and Pacific Railway. Local ranchers hauled in tons of buffalo bones (see BONE BUSINESS) for shipment to the East and loaded their empty wagons with provisions purchased from pioneer merchant William H. "Uncle Pete" Snyder^qv and others. When the town was granted a post office in 1881 Prince A. Hazzard became the first postmaster. Water was hauled to town from Seven Wells and elsewhere and sold at fifty cents a barrel. The first school, conducted in a dugout^qv in 1881, was moved to a building the next year, and soon a new building was built.

By that time the town had between 200 and 300 residents and was a cattle-shipping center. Ranchers drove their cattle to Colorado City from as far north as Amarillo, from as far south as San Angelo, and from eastern New Mexico. Great herds were held until rail cars were available. After shipment, cowboys were free to enjoy the town's amenities. Between 1881 and 1884 its five saloons multiplied to twenty-eight, and other businesses showed the same growth. The population was estimated as high as 6,000 in 1884–85. The boom slowed after the 1885–86 drought, however, and the 1890 population was 2,500.

In May 1881 W. P. Patterson, a prominent rancher, was shot down by Texas Rangers.^qv Citizens blamed the shooting on the rangers' feud with cattlemen, and the ranger camp was moved from town to Hackberry Springs, twenty miles southwest. When Amarillo developed with the arrival of the Fort Worth and Denver Railway in 1887 and when the Santa Fe Railroad reached San Angelo a year later, business in Colorado City declined sharply. During the 1890s salt mining was important to the local economy, but salt declined in importance after 1900.

A second boom between 1900 and 1906 followed the influx of farmers. The population of Colorado City was 3,000 in 1906. By 1910 the town had a new public school, a waterworks, and an electric plant. In 1914 the population was estimated at 1,500, and the town had two banks and a newspaper, the Colorado City *Record*. Though the drought of 1916–18 adversely affected local farmers, interest in oil increased. In 1916 the Consolidated Oil and Gas Company of Colorado was organized by local bankers, businessmen, and merchants to develop the area's oil and gas resources, and by 1920 oil production was a part of the local economy. The Col-Tex Refinery began operation in 1924. By 1926 a city hall had been built, the streets were paved, and a new sewage system was in operation.

In 1931 Colorado City had an estimated population of 4,761 and 200 businesses. By 1940 the population had increased to 5,213, but by 1945 the number of reported businesses had declined to 120. In the late 1940s increased oil activity in Mitchell, Scurry, Coke, and Borden counties caused some growth, and by 1949 the number of businesses in Colorado City had increased to 176. During the mid-1950s a drought, the longest on record, affected the area's agricultural production, particularly of cotton. In 1955 the population was 6,774. Lake Colorado City,^qv five miles southwest, and Champion Creek Reservoir,^qv six miles south, were built in 1959. The population was estimated at 6,400 in 1965. The Col-Tex Refinery closed in 1969, but in the early 1970s new industries were established, including a meat-packing operation and a mobile-home plant. Colorado City had 5,300 residents and 126 businesses in 1975. In 1988 it had a population of 5,549, a hospital, and 122 businesses. Local attractions include the Colorado City Museum and an annual rodeo. In 1990 the population was 4,749.

BIBLIOGRAPHY: Omer W. Cline, History of Mitchell County to 1900 (M.A. thesis, East Texas State Teachers College, 1948). *Lore and Legend: A Compilation of Documents Depicting the History of Colorado City and Mitchell County* (Colorado City *Record*, 1976).

William R. Hunt

COLORADO COLLEGE. Colorado College, in Columbus, was said to be the first Lutheran College in Texas. It was founded in 1857 by John Jacob and Gideon Scherer^qqv and their father, Jacob. J. J. Scherer was professor of ancient languages and president of the school. The board of trustees consisted of nine members, the majority of whom had to be members of the Evangelical Lutheran Church. Enrollment reached as high as 300. There were negotiations in 1868 to sell the three-story building to the First Evangelical Lutheran Synod of Texas. The IOOF Lodge purchased the school in 1871. The College was last reported functioning in 1886.

BIBLIOGRAPHY: Flachmeier Family Papers, Barker Texas History Center, University of Texas at Austin. William A. Flachmeier, *Colorado College and Its Founders* (1980?). William Franklin Ledlow, History of Protestant Education in Texas (Ph.D. dissertation, University of Texas, 1926). John Jacob Scherer Diary and Records, Microfilm, Barker Texas History Center, University of Texas at Austin.

William A. Flachmeier

COLORADO COUNTY. Colorado County (M-18), located about sixty miles above the Gulf of Mexico^qv in south central Texas, is bounded on the northeast by Austin County, on the southeast by Wharton County, on the south by Jackson County, on the southwest by Lavaca County, and on the northwest by Fayette County. It is roughly rectangular in shape except for a small strip extending to the southwest. The center point of the county is at 29°38′ north latitude and 96°32′ west longitude. The county was named for the Colorado River, which bisects it northwest to southeast. Columbus is the county seat. Colorado County is crossed by Interstate Highway 10, U.S. highways 90 and 90A, and State Highway 71, as well as by the Southern Pacific and Atchison, Topeka and Santa Fe railroads. The county includes 964 square miles of level to rolling land with elevations that range from 150 to 425 feet above sea level. The annual rainfall is forty-one inches. The average minimum temperature in January is 41° F, and the average maximum in July is 96°. The growing season lasts 280 days. From 11 to 20 percent of the land is considered prime farmland. Colorado County has several different soil sections: light-colored soils with clayey subsoils predominate in the southwest and northeast; poorly drained soils with cracking, clayey subsoils are found along the Colorado River; and loamy soils with cracking, clayey subsoils characterize the center. The northwest part of the county, in the Blackland Prairie area, supports elm, oak, pecan, and mesquite trees along streams. The remainder is a post oak savanna, where post oak, blackjack oak, and elm grow, with walnuts and pecans along streams.

Colorado County has been the site of human habitation for some 12,000 years. Archaic-age hunters and gatherers lived in the county on deer, bison, roots, and nuts. Within the historic period, the Coco branch of the Karankawa tribe hunted through the area, and Tonkawa Indians ranged up into the area from the south. When La Salle's^qv party camped on Skull Creek on January 20, 1687, the Frenchmen found an Indian village that they called the Hebemes. It is probable that the fourth expedition of Alonso De León^qv crossed the county in search of Fort St. Louis in 1689. Martín de Alarcón^qv traversed the area on his way to La Bahía^qv del Espíritu Santo in 1718, and in 1766 and 1767 the Marqués de Rubí^qv crossed the Colorado near the site of present Columbus on his tour of inspection of East Texas.

The territory that is now Colorado County was settled by Anglo colonists, many of whom belonged to Stephen F. Austin's^qv Old Three Hundred,^qv beginning in 1821. A number of families settled near Beeson's Ford,^qv several miles south of the site of present Columbus. In November 1822 the settlers along the Colorado River in the future Colorado and Wharton counties were authorized by the Mexican government to elect an alcalde.^qv Early in 1823 a skirmish was fought between a militia company from the settlement and a band of Cocos along Skull Creek. In August of that year the Baron de

Bastrop, Rawson Alley,qqv Austin, and a party of slaves surveyed 170 acres above the Atascosito Crossing qv on the Colorado. The site was to be the capital of Colorado Municipality and the headquarters of all the Austin colony, but the location was later abandoned in favor of San Felipe de Austin. The frequency of Indian raids in the area and the fact that more colonists were located on the Brazos than on the Colorado probably caused the change in plans. Between 1824 and 1834 sixty-one individuals received land grants from the Mexican government in the future Colorado County. Columbus grew up at the site of Dewees Crossing, five miles north of Beeson's Ford, in 1835 (*see* DEWEES, WILLIAM BLUFORD). When Sam Houston's qv army retreated from Gonzales after the battle of the Alamo,qv it camped on the east bank of the Colorado in Colorado County, and the Mexican army camped about two miles west of the river; the armies remained for seven or eight days. Other Mexican troops under Antonio López de Santa Anna qv arrived on March 25, 1836, and Houston ordered further retreat. During the Runaway Scrape qv hundreds of persons crossed the river at Benjamin Beeson's qv ford.

Colorado County, one of the original counties of the Republic of Texas,qv was formed in 1836 and organized in 1837, the first district court being held by Robert M. Williamson qv in April 1837 at Columbus, the county seat. By 1840 there were 249 heads of families and 319 slaves in the county. A German settlement grew up around the community of Frelsburg around 1839, and the first German university in the state, Hermann University, was chartered there in 1844. Men from Colorado County made up most of Company E, First Texas Mounted Riflemen, during the Mexican War.qv Cotton and corn were the main crops grown in the 1840s. Among the more notable plantations in the county was that of Robert Robson, who arrived from Dumfries, Scotland, about 1839 and built a concrete castle of homemade lime and gravel on his estate on the south bank of the Colorado River. The castle, surrounded by a moat crossed by a drawbridge, was probably the first building in Texas to have running water, and was a center of social life for the local planters. A steamboat, the *Flying Jenny*, ran from the castle up the Colorado to Austin. The county was heavily dependent on the river for transporting its crops in the 1840s and 1850s. Keelboats and flatboats operated in the early years of the county, and by the 1840s the *Moccasin Belle* and other steamboats carried cotton from the county to Matagorda. Water traffic was heavy until the Colorado became too blocked by a raft of floating and sunken timber. Railroads qv displaced river navigation qv after the Civil War.qv

By 1850 the county population was 2,257, including 644 black slaves. Corn, cotton, and tobacco were the primary crops. Farmers raised sheep, hogs, cattle, and dairy cows in significant numbers. Colorado County grew dramatically in the 1850s, reaching a population of 7,885, including 3,559 African Americans,qv in 1860. A significant plantation economy had emerged, based on cotton. Fourteen Colorado County men had fortunes of $100,000 each in 1860. That year the county had 397 farms, many of them small establishments that existed alongside of the great plantations. Slaveowning was widespread; of 306 slaveholders in the county, 160 held fewer than 5, while 12 had 50 or more and 4 had more than 100. In 1856 the county was the scene of what may have been one of the few attempted slave insurrections qv in Texas. According to local reports as many as 400 slaves plotted to arm themselves and fight their way to Mexico, but before they could act a slave gave the plot away, and several slaves were executed by hanging or by being whipped to death. In the 1850s new communities were founded at Osage and Oakland. Two other towns, Eagle Lake and Alleyton, grew up on the line of the Buffalo Bayou, Brazos and Colorado Railway, which began to build into the county in 1859. For a time Alleyton flourished as an important cotton-shipping point. The county's first newspaper, the *Colorado Citizen*, began publication in 1857 in Columbus. Colorado County had the fifth-largest cotton crop of all Texas counties in 1860, more than 14,000 bales. It also had four slaveholders who owned more than 100 slaves each. Alongside of the cotton and corn grown on the plantations and farms, sheep ranching qv reached its all-time peak in the county (6,034 head) in 1860. With almost 30,000 head, cattle ranching began to assume an important role in the county economy.

In 1860 the county voted in favor of secession qv 584 to 330. Most of the sizable number of German settlers were opposed to leaving the Union, and the predominantly German town of Frelsburg voted against the secession proposal 154 to 22. On the other hand, most of the Anglo settlers in the county favored secession. At least three "castles" of the Knights of the Golden Circle qv had been formed in Colorado County by December of 1860. During the Civil War, men from the county served in a number of military units; they formed companies in the Fifth Texas Cavalry and the Fifth, Thirteenth, and Seventeenth Texas Infantry regiments. Although there was no actual fighting in the county, the war devastated the county economy. The extent to which Colorado County had been dependent on slavery qv is shown by the drop in value of county farms from $3,066,070 in 1860 to $493,890 at the end of the war. While the value of livestock in the county fell by about half during the decade, the value of overall farm property fell by five-sixths. In spite of the decline of the county economy, the population continued to grow, reaching 8,326 in 1870.

Reconstruction qv was a difficult period of adjustment for county residents. Columbus was occupied by federal troops in June 1865, and was intermittently the site of small garrisons through 1870. Freedmen's Bureau qv agents stationed in Columbus opened schools for black children and attempted to mediate labor contracts between planters and freedmen. An organization similar to the Ku Klux Klan,qv composed of Colorado and Fayette County men and formed around a nucleus of Confederate veterans, was active in the county in the late 1860s. Several blacks from Colorado County held state and county office during and after Reconstruction, including county commissioner Isaac Yates, state representative B. F. Williams,qv and county commissioner Cicero Howard. A few lawless Colorado County whites attempted to intimidate black voters in 1873 by killing two freedmen, though the county nevertheless voted for Republican governor Edmund J. Davis qv that year and supported Republican presidential candidates from 1872 to 1884. In spite of the growth of one of the White Man's Union Associations qv in the county in the late 1870s, blacks continued to hold county office through the 1880s, elected a second black legislator, Robert Lloyd Smith,qv as late as 1894, and in 1896 helped produce the last Republican majority the county saw until the 1950s. The formation of the White Man's Reformation Association in 1894 and the White Man's party in 1902 restricted the black vote in primaries. The poll tax led to the official disfranchisement of black voters in the county by 1904 (*see* ELECTION LAWS *and* WHITE PRIMARY). From a peak of 3,990 voters in 1896, the number of voters declined some 62 percent to 1,518 eight years later. The county electorate did not again approach the voting levels of 1896 until the 1950s. With the exception of a strong third party showing in 1920, from the election of 1900 until the 1950s the county remained solidly Democratic. Subsequently, Colorado County supported Republican presidential candidates in 1952, 1956, 1968, and 1972, and from 1980 through 1992.

Feuding and violence occurred amid the postwar recovery. C. C. Herbert, a prominent planter and legislator, was murdered in 1867. Three local families, the Staffords, the Townsends, and the Reeses, were involved in a number of murderous incidents in the final decades of the nineteenth century and the early years of the twentieth century, including the Colorado County Feud.qv Meanwhile, further development of the railway network invigorated the economy. The Columbus Tap Railway, a branch line from Columbus to the Buffalo Bayou, Brazos and Colorado Railway, had been chartered before the Civil War but was not actually completed until 1867. This line was farther extended from Columbus to the west in 1873, linking the county with San Antonio and leading to the founding of Weimar. The San Antonio and Aransas Pass Railway built through the county in the late 1880s, and about 1900 the Gulf, Colorado and Santa Fe was built from Eagle Lake to Matagorda. The Missouri, Kansas and Texas later built across the northeastern tip of the county. The 1870s through the 1890s were decades of dramatic growth for the county. The number of farms grew between 1870 and 1880 from 456 to 1,666 and reached a peak of 2,992 in 1900. The county population more than doubled in the 1870s, reaching 16,673 in 1880, and then increased at a more moderate rate to a maximum of 22,203 in 1900. The value of farms increased fourfold between 1870 and 1880 and surpassed prewar levels by 1890. Colorado County's prosperity at this time was based on cotton, corn, and cattle. In 1880 cotton, the dominant agricultural product, was planted on 32,994 acres; corn acres totaled 28,711. The dependance of the county on cotton and corn reached its peak about 1900, when 69,093 acres was devoted to cotton and corn was grown on 39,861 acres. These two crops together accounted for 60 percent of improved acres in the county. Cattle raising reached a peak of 108,368 head in 1880 and declined thereafter to 34,879 head in 1900.

Substantial numbers of Europeans entered Colorado county after the Civil War. Germans,qv present in the area since the early 1830s, numbered 776 in 1870. This number increased to 1,328 by 1880, when 207 Austriansqv also lived in the county. The number of foreign-born whites in the county, mostly from Germany, Austria, and the future Czechoslovakia, reached its peak in 1890, when 2,376, or 22 percent of the whites in the county, were of foreign birth. The black population grew as well, reaching a peak of 46 percent of the county population in 1880; thereafter, while continuing to grow in absolute numbers, African Americans declined in relative terms to 43 percent of the whole by 1900.

After 1900 several new crops became important to county agriculture. Rice, which had been introduced in the county in 1898, became economically feasible with large-scale irrigation around the turn of the century and was grown on 15,000 acres in 1903. Sugarcane was also an important crop. A large sugar refinery was opened in the community of Lakeside in 1901. Dairy farming also grew in prominence during these years. The county had several creameries by 1913. However, cotton and corn remained the most important crops until the 1940s. In 1930, of the 87,200 acres of cropland harvested, 43,551, or 50 percent, was planted in cotton, and 28,052 acres, a further 32 percent, was planted in corn. In the 1930s and 1940s cotton declined in importance, amounting to only 7 percent of the cropland harvested in 1950, while farmers continued to grow substantial amounts of corn and began growing hay. Rice, grown on more than 40,000 acres in 1950, was the most important crop that year.

Farm tenancyqv rose and fell with the vagaries of the cotton market. Tenant farming had become a dominant feature of Colorado County agriculture by 1900, when 1,632, or 55 percent, of the county's 2,992 farms were occupied by tenants. Blacks were far more likely to become tenants than whites; in 1900, 59 percent of white farmers owned their land, while only 21 percent of black farmers were owners. Tenant farming declined somewhat in the early decades of the twentieth century to 47 percent in 1910 and 48 percent in 1920, only to shoot back up again during the Great Depressionqv to a record 60 percent of the 2,589 farms in 1930. During the 1930s and 1940s both the number of farms and the tenancy rate fell, and by 1950 only 29 percent of the county's 1,840 farms were worked by tenants.

After dropping 15 percent between 1900 and 1910 to 18,897, Colorado County's population remained relatively static during the twentieth century, numbering 19,129 in 1930, 17,638 in 1970, and 18,383 in 1990. The migration of blacks from the county started after 1900; they declined to 37 percent of the county population in 1910, 30 percent in 1940, 25 percent in 1950, and 17 percent in 1990. Mexican Americansqv formed 14 percent of the county population in 1980 and 15.4 percent in 1990. Since the early years of the century Columbus, the county seat and largest town, has been the home of 15 to 20 percent of the county's population. The town had 3,367 residents in 1990.

The county oil and gravel industries began to develop in the first decade of the twentieth century. Companies and individuals began to explore for oil in the county as early as 1901, though the first significant find did not occur until 1932. By 1990, 31,523,143 barrels of oil had been produced in the county. Digging gravel for commercial purposes began by 1906. The county had two gravel companies by 1910 and has been one of the leading producers of gravel in the state since the 1930s. In 1980 the economy was dominated by agribusiness, the extraction of sand and gravel, and oil and gas production. The county was third in the state in rice production. Other major crops were corn, hay, soybeans, oats, and sorghum. Hogs and cattle were the principal livestock, though dairying remained an important feature of the economy. In 1982, 94 percent of the land in the county was in farms and ranches and 20 percent of the farmland was in cultivation. In the 1980s, with cutbacks in the oil and gas industry and in gravel production, the county suffered a depressed economy. The same primary businesses had rebounded somewhat by 1990.

Colorado County has made slow but steady progress over the years in educating its citizens. The first schoolhouse in the county was built in Columbus in the early 1830s. By 1879 the county had sixty public schools, thirty-six for white students and twenty-four for black. In spite of the efforts of the public schools and several parochial establishments, as late as 1910, 14.5 percent of the county population was illiterate; the illiteracy level among black residents was more than twice as high at 30.5 percent. In 1950 only 1,170 county residents over age twenty-five, about 7 percent of the county population, had completed high school. Ten years later that number had more than doubled to 15 percent, and by 1980, 42 percent of county residents over age twenty-five were high school graduates. In 1980 Colorado County supported forty-six churches, with Catholic, Southern Baptist, and United Methodist as the largest communions. The county is well supplied with recreational facilities and tourist sites. With neighboring Washington, Fayette, and Austin counties, it forms part of the Texas Pioneer Trail. Columbus is rich in Victorian-era homes, a number of which are open to the public during the Magnolia Homes Tours the third weekend in May. The Attwater Prairie Chicken National Wildlife Refugeqv hosts a festival every October. In 1990 the incorporated communities in Colorado County included Columbus (pop. 3,367), Weimar (2,052), and Eagle Lake (3,551).

BIBLIOGRAPHY: Colorado County Historical Commission, *Colorado County Chronicles from the Beginning to 1923* (2 vols., Austin: Nortex, 1986).

Mark Odintz

COLORADO COUNTY CITIZEN. The *Colorado County Citizen*, a weekly newspaper, was established in Columbus in 1857 by James Davis Baker and named the *Colorado Citizen* by Rev. J. J. Scherer.qv Baker's younger brothers, Benjamin Marshall and A. Hicks Baker, owned minority interests in the newspaper. The paper supported Sam Houstonqv for president in 1860. The paper also opposed the abolitionqv of slavery and the dissolution of the union but became ardently secessionist when Abraham Lincoln was elected president. All three brothers joined the Confederate army; publication of the newspaper ceased during the Civil War.qv Hicks Baker was killed during the war, and James and Ben returned to Columbus to resume publication of the paper. When James became ill, the paper was sold to Fred Barnard, and its name was changed to the Columbus *Times*. In 1869 Barnard, who had subsequently sold the *Times*, started a second paper, resurrecting the name *Colorado Citizen*. The *Citizen* eventually ran the *Times* out of business. Barnard sold the paper to three Columbus law firm partners, Robert Levi Foard, Wells Thompson, and George McCormick,qqv in 1871; they sold it back to Barnard the following year. Ben Baker, who had been hired by Barnard to work on the new *Colorado Citizen*, bought the newspaper in 1873 and served as its editor and publisher until his death in 1907. The yellow fever epidemic in 1873 and a fire in 1880 caused brief suspensions of the publication of the paper. After Baker's death the *Citizen* survived repeated changes of ownership. Henry Hurr purchased the paper from W. L. Pendergraft in 1924 and changed the name to *Colorado*

County Citizen in 1927. Since February 17, 1993, it has been published by the Citizen Publishing Company, a group of local citizens. In the 1990s the paper had a circulation of 4,292.

BIBLIOGRAPHY: Colorado *Citizen,* August 15, 1857, May 6, 1869, April 28, 1911, December 30, 1926. Marilyn M. Sibley, *Lone Stars and State Gazettes: Texas Newspapers before the Civil War* (College Station: Texas A&M University Press, 1983). *Diana J. Kleiner*

COLORADO COUNTY FEUD. The Colorado County Feud, a series of gun battles between members of the Townsend family of Columbus, started during the 1898 Colorado County sheriff's race. The election pitted incumbent sheriff Sam Reese against his one time deputy, Larkin Hope. Former state senator Mark Townsend, who directed a political machine that had backed the winning candidate in each of the last nine sheriff's elections, dropped his backing of Reese and endorsed Hope. The move seemingly assured Hope of victory. But on August 3, 1898, Hope was killed by an unknown assailant in downtown Columbus. Immediately, suspicion centered on Jim Coleman, a close friend of Sam Reese's sons, Walter and Herbert. Townsend picked a new candidate, Will Burford, and, with feeling running high against the Reeses, Burford won the election. Less than a year later, on March 16, 1899, Sam Reese was killed in a gun battle on the street near where Hope died. Will Clements, Marion Hope, and Mark Townsend were among those shooting. Stray bullets killed Charles Boehme, a bystander, and wounded a boy named Johnny Williams. Even though the best evidence suggests that Reese had provoked the fight in which he was killed, his sons vowed to get revenge. In five more gunfights—on May 17, 1899, January 15, 1900, July 31, 1900, June 30, 1906, and May 17, 1907—five more men were killed and several others wounded. The dead included Reese's brother Dick, Burford's son Arthur, Will Clements's brother Hiram, and Jim Coleman. Also dead was another innocent bystander, Dick Gant. No one was ever convicted of any of the murders. Those accused included Mark Townsend, Jim Townsend, Step Yates, Will Clements, Walter Reese, Joe Lessing, Frank Burford, and Marion Hope. The Townsends, Reeses, Burfords, Clementses, Hopes, and Lessings were all related to each other, either directly or through marriage.

The feud had a direct effect on the economic wellbeing of Columbus. Boehme, a farmer, had been in town buying supplies when shooting erupted and he was killed. His death persuaded many area farmers to buy their supplies elsewhere. The peaceful citizens of Columbus, trying to end the feuding, asked the city council to reestablish the office of city marshal, which had been abolished some years earlier. For financial reasons, they refused. On August 7, 1906, the citizenry voted to abolish the corporation of the city of Columbus and turn the administration of the town over to the county. The town remained unincorporated for twenty years.

Many of the other participants in the feud died violent, early deaths. Marion Hope was killed in an accident in Gonzales County in 1911. That same year, Will Clements was shot from ambush in Matagorda County by a man with whom he had had an altercation a few days earlier. Jim Townsend was also killed in 1911, in a gun battle with a saloon keeper in Louise. Herbert Reese was killed in 1912, when a gun he was cleaning in his Columbus home accidentally discharged. Walter Reese died as the result of injuries received in an automobile accident in El Paso in 1919.

BIBLIOGRAPHY: Houston *Post,* March 17, 1899, January 17, August 1, 1900. John Walter and Lillian Estelle Reese, *Flaming Feuds of Colorado County* (Salado, Texas: Anson Jones Press, 1962). C. L. Sonnichsen, *I'll Die Before I'll Run—The Story of the Great Feuds of Texas* (New York: Harper, 1951; 2d. ed, New York: Devin-Adair, 1962). *Bill Stein*

COLORADO FEMALE ACADEMY. Colorado Female Academy, according to the Austin *Texas Democrat*[qv] of August 16 and 30, 1848, was to be opened in October 1848 at the French Legation,[qv] by C. W. Howell, president, and Mrs. Maria Howell, governess. The notice of the school specified a school year of two sessions of twenty-two weeks each and advertised the conveniences of Austin for visits of parents to students.

BIBLIOGRAPHY: Aloise Walker Hardy, A History of Travis County, 1832–1865 (M.A. thesis, University of Texas, 1938). Willie Madora Long, Education in Austin Before the Public Schools (M.Ed. thesis, University of Texas, 1952). *Carolyn Hyman*

COLORADO GAZETTE AND ADVERTISER. The *Colorado Gazette and Advertiser,* successor to the Matagorda *Bulletin,*[qv] was a four-column, four-page weekly newspaper published in Matagorda from May 1839 until sometime in 1843. The paper was published by James Attwell[qv] and originally edited by W. Donaldson, previously editor of the Matagorda *Bulletin.* In 1840 William Douglas Wallach[qv] became owner and editor and Attwell, who was later publisher of the Matagorda *Weekly Despatch,*[qv] continued as both printer and publisher. The paper had agents throughout Texas. Apparently there was little political rivalry between the *Gazette* and other contemporary Texas papers, though the paper seems to have leaned toward the policies of Sam Houston.[qv] A partial run of the paper is housed at the Texas State Library.[qv]

BIBLIOGRAPHY: Joe B. Frantz, Newspapers of the Republic of Texas (M.A. thesis, University of Texas, 1940).

COLORADO INDIANS. The Spanish name Colorado, meaning "red" or "painted," was given to many Indian groups in the New World, but only one of those can be related to the Texas area. The Colorados of northern Mexico were identified by the Spanish in the late seventeenth century. According to Spanish documentation, they were one of many tribes who inhabited the region between the city of Durango and La Junta de los Ríos,[qv] the junction of the Río Conchos and the Rio Grande near the site of present Presidio, Texas. The Colorados apparently ranged over the northern portions of the Mexican states of Coahuila and Chihuahua. In 1688 that tribe, along with the Tobosos and Cabezas, participated in an uprising against the Spanish settlements along the Texas-Coahuila border. The Jumanos and Terocodames, two groups from the Texas side of the Rio Grande, also joined in that revolt.

BIBLIOGRAPHY: Herbert E. Bolton, "The Jumano Indians in Texas, 1650–1771," *Quarterly of the Texas State Historical Association* 15 (July 1911). Charles W. Hackett, ed., *Historical Documents Relating to New Mexico, Nueva Vizcaya, and Approaches Thereto, to 1773* (3 vols., Washington: Carnegie Institution, 1923–37). Nancy Parrott Hickerson, *The Jumanos: Hunters and Traders of the South Plains* (Austin: University of Texas Press, 1994). *Carol A. Lipscomb*

COLORADO RANGER. The *Colorado Ranger* was a side-wheel steamer, commanded by Captain Powell, that operated on the Colorado River between Columbus in Colorado County and the head of "the raft on the Colorado" in Matagorda County during the early 1850s. Cargoes of cotton were off-loaded there and carried by wagons around the obstructing raft to the port of Matagorda. The steamer made a trip to Austin and arrived on April 7, 1851, amid public fanfare. On March 5, 1853, it hit an obstruction, tore its hull, and sank ten miles southeast of La Grange, Fayette County.

BIBLIOGRAPHY: Comer Clay, "The Colorado River Raft," *Southwestern Historical Quarterly* 52 (April 1949). *Democratic Telegraph and Texas Register,* March 28, 1851. *Jeff Carroll*

COLORADO RIVER. The Colorado River, measured in length and drainage area, is the largest river wholly in Texas. (The Brazos drainage basin extends into New Mexico.) It rises in intermittent draws in northeastern Dawson County (at 32°41′ N, 101°44′ W), flows generally southeastward for 600 miles across Borden, Scurry, Mitchell, Coke, and Runnels counties, and forms all or parts of the county lines between Coleman and Concho, Coleman and McCulloch, Brown and McCulloch, Brown and San Saba, Mills and San Saba, Lampasas and San Saba, Burnet and San Saba, and Burnet and Llano counties, before it bends to the east across southern Burnet County and continues its southeastern course across Travis, Bastrop, Fayette, Colorado, Wharton, and Matagorda counties to its mouth, on Matagorda Bay (at 28°36′ N, 95°59′ W). Its drainage area is 39,900 square miles, and its runoff reaches a volume of more than 2 million acre-feet near the Gulf. The major towns along the stream are Austin, Lamesa, Colorado City, Robert Lee, Ballinger, Paint Rock, Marble Falls, Bastrop, Smithville, La Grange, Columbus, Wharton, Bay City, and Matagorda. Important reservoirs on the Colorado include Lake Colorado City, Lake J. B. Thomas, Buchanan Lake, Inks Lake, Lake Lyndon B. Johnson, Lake Travis, and Town Lake[qqv] in Austin.

The Colorado River is probably the one called Kanahatino by Indians of the Caddoan linguistic family and Pashohono by some of the other Indian groups. It has also been identified as the stream that Juan Domínguez de Mendoza and Nicolás López[qqv] called San Clemente in 1684, and as the one René Robert Cavalier, Sieur de La Salle,[qv] named La Sablonnière ("Sand-Pit") in 1687. The name Colorado, Spanish for "red," is evidently a misnomer, for the water of the stream is clear and always has been, according to the earliest records of historians. Most authorities agree, however, that the name Colorado was first applied by Alonso De León[qv] in 1690, not to the present stream but to the Brazos, and there is considerable evidence to support the theory that the names of the two streams were interchanged during the period of Spanish exploration. The present names, however, were well established before the end of Spanish Texas.[qv] Other historic associations along the Colorado include the river's use as a route inland by early colonists, including several of the Old Three Hundred[qv] who settled on its banks; the establishment of Austin as the seat of government in 1839; and the fact that in 1844, when both England and France were working to prevent the annexation[qv] of Texas by the United States, the British minister in Mexico secured a written avowal from Antonio López de Santa Anna[qv] to recognize the independence of Texas with the Colorado River as its boundary.

The river flows across the rolling prairie near San Saba County, enters the more rugged Hill Country[qv] and the Llano basin, and passes through a series of canyons before it issues from the Balcones Escarpment[qv] at Austin. Above Austin the lands along the Colorado are generally rough, but below Austin the river traverses the flat, alluvial bottoms of the Coastal Plain, an important agricultural area. Principal tributaries of the river include the Pedernales, Llano, San Saba, and Concho rivers and Pecan Bayou, the most westerly "bayou" in the nation. With the exception of the bayou, the tributaries flow into the river from the Edwards Plateau[qv] and are spring-fed. Although the Colorado has a relatively small annual run-off with relation to its watershed, it has presented some of the most serious drainage problems in Texas. Early in the nineteenth century its slow current caused the formation of a raft, or log jam, which gradually grew upstream so that the river was navigable in 1839 for only ten miles above its mouth. By 1858 the situation in Matagorda and Wharton counties had become so bad that the state appropriated funds for the

Roy Inks Dam on the Colorado River, between Llano and Burnet counties, 1936–38. Courtesy Texas Department of Transportation/Randy Green. Inks Dam was one of several dams built on the Colorado in the 1930s for flood control and the generation of electricity.

construction of a new channel around the raft. The United States Army Corps of Engineers opened the channel in the mid-1800s, but since it was not maintained the raft filled it up. Teamsters unloaded vessels above the raft and carried the cargo to other teams that loaded it on other boats for shipment to Galveston and other Gulf ports. Shallow-draught vessels were at times able to ascend the Colorado to Austin.

After the Civil War qv the Colorado ceased to be a factor in transportation. The delta that developed after removal of the log jam, beginning in 1925, reached across Matagorda Bay as far as Matagorda Peninsula qqv by 1936; that year a channel was dredged through the new delta from the Gulf of Mexico to the town of Matagorda, thus forcing the river to deposit its flotsam and sediment directly into the Gulf. With removal of the raft, the community of Matagorda, formerly a major Texas seaport, gradually became landlocked. The present Caney Creek channel was the channel of the Colorado until about a thousand years ago, when the river cut into a wide estuary in the present Caney Creek area and redirected its flow to the west.

The need for a steady flow of water to irrigate rice farms in Wharton and Matagorda counties, combined with the necessity for flood-control measures, has presented more recent challenges. These have been met largely by the construction of Lake Travis and Lake Buchanan. Three smaller reservoirs in Burnet County—Inks, Johnson, and Marble Falls—produce power from water running over the Buchanan Dam spillway. The dam at Lake Austin, which is largely filled with silt, produces power from water flowing from the lakes above. Town Lake, a recreation site that divides north and south Austin, is the last impoundment in this section of the river; Town Lake and the lakes above Austin are known as the Highland Lakes. Conservation and use of the Colorado are overseen by three agencies established by the state legislature, the Lower, Central, and Upper Colorado River authorities,qqv and formerly the Colorado River Municipal Water District.qv

BIBLIOGRAPHY: Comer Clay, "The Colorado River Raft," *Southwestern Historical Quarterly* 52 (April 1949). James Cody, *Rivers of Texas: The Colorado River* (Los Cerrillos, New Mexico: San Marcos Press, 1974). Walter E. Long, *Flood to Faucet* (Austin: Steck, 1956). Matagorda County Historical Commission, *Historic Matagorda County* (3 vols., 1986–88). Byron D. Varner, *Lakeway: The First Twenty-five Years and Earlier Times on the Colorado* (Austin, 1988).

Comer Clay and Diana J. Kleiner

COLORADO RIVER MUNICIPAL WATER DISTRICT. The Colorado River Municipal Water District, established in 1949, was authorized to impound the storm and flood water and the unappropriated flow of the Colorado River and its tributaries, and also to distribute it to cities and other agencies for municipal, domestic, and industrial purposes. The enacting legislation was the first of its kind after World War IIqv and was used as the blueprint for subsequent municipal water districts. The district was originally brought into being and organized to furnish water to the member cities of Odessa, Big Spring, and Snyder. The board of directors governs the district and is composed of four representatives from each member city, appointed by the governing body of each city. The administration has a general manager, assisted by an administrative assistant and a staff of eighty-two employees. Although the cities own the district, it operates independently, subject to terms covered originally by a trust indenture. The district's charter was amended in 1961 and 1963 to permit use for mining (secondary recovery of oil), pollution prevention, and water-quality enhancement. In 1981 the service area was expanded to include the home counties of the original three member cities as well as thirty-one other cities in the vicinity. The principal office of the district is in Big Spring, Texas. By September 1952 the new district had developed a water-well field to provide water for Odessa and Big Spring. This well field was enlarged and for a short time artificially recharged during winter months with water from Lake J. B. Thomas.qv Surface water was injected into the de-watered aquifer and recovered in summer months to furnish water for peaking purposes. Upon completion of Lake J. B. Thomas the city of Snyder received its first water from this source on July 1, 1953. The district later contracted to furnish water-flood projects for oil companies; recovery of oil was doubled or tripled by this means. These contracts are subject to cancellation if water is needed for municipal use.

Initially the district installed 115 miles of pipeline, varying from twenty-one to thirty-three inches in diameter. A series of pump stations capable of delivering a total of 44 million gallons a day was developed. In 1994 the district operated twenty-one pump stations and pumped water through some 560 miles of pipeline. Pump capacity in 1994 was 150 million gallons a day. The district originally issued $11,750,000 in revenue bonds, then added $4,600,000 in 1958 for pipeline and terminal-storage construction and $2,750,000 in 1963 for additional pipeline. Bond funds, without assistance from the state or federal government, purchased land and financed the cost of a dam and channel for a lake, pipelines, and rights-of-way, a pair of eighty-million-gallon storage reservoirs, three fifteen-million-gallon reservoirs, twenty-one pump stations with microwave equipment for automatic operation of the system, basic equipment and supplies, and several houses for key employees at pump-station locations. The organization it has also invested several hundred thousand dollars in dam improvement, recreation facilities, and extensive studies for a new lake and other improvements. Since the district's inception in 1951, an aggregate of over 576 billion gallons of water has been supplied to cities and oilfield consumers; the district grossed over $263 million in revenue. As of January 1995 the face value of all original bond issues was $247,015,000, of which $198,355,000 was outstanding.

A permit was granted on September 1, 1965, by the Texas Water Rights Commissionqv authorizing the district to build a reservoir near Robert Lee in Coke County, which was scheduled to impound a maximum of 488,760 acre-feet of water on the Colorado River, and to divert 40,000 acre-feet per annum from this source. This permit, along with existing rights for Lake J. B. Thomas, authorizes the district to divert a total of 73,000 acre-feet annually from the Colorado River. Construction of the dam began in 1966 and was completed by 1970. The reservoir, E. V. Spence Reservoir, along with its related pipelines and other facilities, was financed through the sale of $30 million in revenue bonds. It supplied approximately 70 percent of Midland's water requirements in accordance with a sixty-year water-sales agreement.

Hardly had the system become operative in 1952 than the district made a presentation to the Board of Water Engineers to divert Deep Creek (Scurry County) into Lake Thomas to increase reserves. Though nothing came of this, the district continued seeking more supplies. A permit for a second reservoir on the Colorado River was granted June 11, 1959, but when the original site was changed from southern Mitchell County to Robert Lee in Coke County, the Lower Colorado River Authorityqv protested. Finally, the permit was granted on September 1, 1965, for 488,760 acre-feet (40,000 acre-feet annual diversion) at Lake E. V. Spence, costing $34,500,000. Completion was early in 1969 and dedication on June 15, 1969. Simultaneously, a 57.4-mile, forty-two-inch pipeline was laid to Moss Creek Lake and on to Big Spring, where the water was mixed with Lake Thomas water for that city and for Midland-Odessa. (Midland contracted for water from the district in 1966 and received first deliveries in 1970.)

By 1975 CRMWD began looking seriously at the USGS "Stacy" site on the Colorado River below Ballinger. It filed an application on October 11, 1977. After six months of hearings (the longest and costliest to that date) the Texas Water Commission overrode protests by LCRA and others and issued a permit on April 10, 1979. This was tied up in courts for five years until the Texas Supreme Court overruled lower courts in November 1984 and denied the permit. On rehearing, the case was remanded to TWC; in the meantime, Gov. Mark White insisted that the parties agree, and a permit for 554,340-acre-foot Lake O. H. Ivie (named for the CRMWD general manager) was issued on

May 14, 1985. Construction began in May 1987, and the reservoir was completed in March 1990. Unprecedented rains in December 1991 filled the lake to capacity in two years instead of the projected eight. This brought to 1,247,000 acre-feet the total impoundment permitted to CRMWD for its three supply reservoirs. Growing municipal demands, plus a brimming but unused lake, led CRMWD in 1991 to issue $115 million in bonds (supplemented with $9 million more in 1994) to finance a 157-mile pipeline from Lake Ivie via San Angelo to Odessa-Midland. At the time it was the longest and most expensive water-supply line in Texas under a single contract. All CRMWD water has to be pumped uphill, but this one required six pump stations to lift water 1,400 feet over the distance. Earlier, Midland, San Angelo, and the West Central Texas Municipal Water District (Abilene) had contracted for one-sixth of the water in place in Lake Ivie, and now San Angelo and Midland shared in pipeline costs for twenty-five million gallons a day to San Angelo and twenty million for Midland. The Big Spring junction was staked for ten million later to Big Spring. The first joint of pipe was laid on August 20, 1992, and the last on September 27, 1994. The system was activated in January 1995. A spin-off of the project was a half-million dollar communications control center at headquarters in Big Spring to enable a single operator to control twenty-one pump stations.

CRMWD pioneered in water-quality protection and enhancement, starting in 1951 by moving the Lake Thomas site upstream to avoid salty tributaries, then recovering lost watershed by plugging Bull Creek and diverting it through an 8,500-foot canal to Lake Thomas. District efforts also led to a Railroad Commission[qv] ban on salt-water disposal pits. Other efforts led to a diversion works on the Colorado River above Colorado City and Beals Creek below Big Spring. Poor-quality normal low-flow water was diverted to side reservoirs and sold to oil companies for repressuring. Later, a 9,000-acre-foot detention reservoir was installed above the notoriously salty (4,500 ppm chloride or better) Natural Dam Lake, ten miles west of Big Spring. Previously, salty playas west of Big Spring had been pumped behind Natural Dam, on Sulphur Draw, which becomes Beals Creek and empties into the Colorado River. Finally, a 28,000-acre-foot disposal lake for evaporation of surplus bad water was built in western Mitchell County. Altogether, the district had 93,860 acre-feet capacity in quality-control lakes. In all, CRMWD spent over $20 million in quality control, which by January 1, 1995, had prevented 645,000 tons of chlorides from entering Lake Spence.

Because Lake Spence ran into a critical drought before it could catch appreciable water, CRMWD planned, financed, and completed a forty-mile pipeline from Odessa to a well field it developed in Ward County, where it got water on May 26, 1971. In another rush job, the district laid a 51.89-mile pipeline from Lake Thomas to Sun Oil in Coke County in 1963, and later this line was used to pump water from Lake Spence to critically low Lake Colorado City and keep a Texas Utilities generating plant operative. The drought induced CRMWD in 1971 to institute a precipitation-enhancement program that, except for one year, operated continuously (as of 1995), making it the oldest in the nation. Drought also led on several occasions to "pump back" operations at Lake Thomas when levels dipped below the intake of the pump station. Pumps on barges at lower elevations boosted water by canals to a pumping pool formed by mounds around the intake. Thus CRMWD recovered 33.835 billion gallons of its best water for upgrading general quality. Because of the paucity of water in semiarid West Texas, the district provides aquatic recreational services, which by 1995 called for a $275,000 annual budget. The district was among the first to set up its own pension and health benefit plans.

BIBLIOGRAPHY: James H. Banks and John E. Babcock, *Corralling the Colorado: The First Fifty Years of the Lower Colorado River Authority* (Austin: Eakin Press, 1988).
Joe Pickle

COLORADO RIVER WESTERN RAILROAD. The Colorado River Western Railroad Company was chartered on February 11, 1955, to build from Altair in Colorado County northwest to a terminus two miles south of Alleyton, a distance of about nine miles. The initial capital was $41,000, and the business office was in Alleyton. The railroad was controlled by Texas Construction Materials Company. Members of the first board of directors included C. L. Griffin, C. B. Sheffield, Morris Hodges, Frank C. Brooks, Mrs. C. E. O'Meara, J. M. Carley, E. P. Gemmer, and Charles B. Whiter. In 1953, ten miles of main line and sidings was constructed and in operation from Altair to Helm. In 1958 the road became the property of the Texas and New Orleans Railroad Company.
Chris Cravens

COLORADO AND SOUTHERN RAILWAY. The Colorado and Southern Railway Company was chartered in Colorado on December 19, 1898, and operated in Wyoming, Colorado, and New Mexico. The company was formed on January 11, 1899, when the Colorado and Southern acquired the Union Pacific, Denver and Gulf Railway Company and the Denver, Leadville and Gunnison Railway Company, both formerly subsidiaries of the Union Pacific. In Texas, the Colorado and Southern controlled a rail system extending from Texline in Dallam County through Fort Worth and Dallas to Houston and Galveston, in addition to branches in the Panhandle,[qv] in the South Plains, and to Abilene. The Colorado and Southern system in Texas included ten railroads, of which eight were owned by the end of 1910. The oldest was the Fort Worth and Denver City Railway Company, which made direct connection with the Colorado and Southern at Texline. Other owned companies included the Wichita Valley Railroad Company, the Wichita Valley Railway Company, the Abilene and Northern Railway Company, the Stamford and Northwestern Railway Company, the Fort Worth and Denver Terminal Railway Company, the Wichita Falls and Oklahoma Railway Company, and a 50 percent interest in the Trinity and Brazos Valley Railway Company. The Trinity and Brazos Valley also owned a 25 percent interest in the Houston Belt and Terminal Railway Company, the Galveston Terminal Railway Company, and one-eighth interest in the Union Terminal Company at Dallas. The Trinity and Brazos Valley was reorganized as the Burlington–Rock Island in 1930. The Texas properties were expanded during the late 1920s with the construction of the Fort Worth and Denver South Plains Railway Company and the Fort Worth and Denver Northern Railway Company. The Colorado and Southern also owned the Wichita Falls and Oklahoma Railway Company of Oklahoma, which was built in 1924. On August 7, 1951, the Fort Worth and Denver City was renamed the Fort Worth and Denver Railway Company, and, on June 13, 1952, it merged all of the Colorado and Southern properties in Texas with the exception of the Burlington–Rock Island. The Burlington–Rock Island was dissolved in 1965, with the Colorado and Southern's one-half interest merged into the Fort Worth and Denver. In December 1908 the Chicago, Burlington and Quincy Railroad Company purchased the Colorado and Southern, which, however, continued to operate as a separate company. On March 2, 1970, the Burlington was one of the railroads merged to form the Burlington Northern Railroad, and the Colorado and Southern was subsequently merged on December 31, 1981. *See also* BURLINGTON SYSTEM, BURLINGTON–ROCK ISLAND RAILROAD.
George C. Werner

COLORADO STATION. Colorado Station, on the lower Colorado River, was also known as Station Colorado River and Post Colorado. It should not be confused with Colorado Camp or Fort Colorado, other garrisons in place during the republic. Colorado Station occupied two sites during its installation. The first was at Thomas Cayce's ferry near the site of present Bay City, Texas, in Matagorda County. This small army post was garrisoned from the latter part of November 1836 until June 1837 by a detachment of Permanent Volunteers, thirty to forty men, under the command of Capt. Andrew Neill[qv] and 1st Lt. James Campbell. Gen. Felix Huston[qv] ordered the establishment of the post to assist those traveling on official business, to prevent the use of the ferry and crossing of the Colorado there by army personnel traveling without proper orders, and to facilitate communications between army headquarters near Texana and the capital at Columbia. After Houston became the capital in May 1837, the republic army of both regulars and volunteers was reduced by two-thirds.

With the new capital in Houston it was necessary to establish a new army post higher up on the Colorado River to replace the one at Cayce's ferry. This second garrison was located at Mercer's Ferry, a major crossing on the Colorado at a site now in Wharton County near Egypt, Texas, on the west bank of the river. The new garrison was called Colorado Station, and less often it was referred to as Post Colorado. This area had also been the site of an encampment of the Texas army under Gen. Thomas J. Rusk,qv on May 20, 1836, but no post was established here until the location of the second Colorado Station.

Captain Neill and his men reached Mercer's about June 1, 1837, to set up camp and establish a post. Their duties were the same as those of the troops at the earlier Colorado Station, which had been abandoned within a week or two before the transfer to Mercer's. Most of the men at Colorado Station were ordered to nearby Post West Bernard Stationqv and Post Bernard in January 1838, leaving only a few men at Mercer's until about June 1838. In command of the men during this period were lieutenants Edward W. Sargent and Peter R. Garner, Second Regiment of Permanent Volunteers.

BIBLIOGRAPHY: Gerald S. Pierce, *Texas Under Arms: The Camps, Posts, Forts, and Military Towns of the Republic of Texas* (Austin: Encino, 1969).

Merle R. Hudgins

COLORADO TRIBUNE. The *Colorado Tribune*, earlier known as the *Colorado Herald*, was a weekly newspaper in Matagorda, which was at that time the Matagorda county seat. James Wilmer Dallamqv began the *Herald* in the summer of 1846, and it probably ran until at least early 1847. By August 1847 Dallam was planning to stop publishing the *Herald* and move his office to the new town of Indian Point, where he intended to publish a paper printed in English and German and called the *Emigrant*. However, after he died suddenly that month of yellow fever, Edward F. Gilbert bought the press and renamed the newspaper the *Colorado Tribune*. This paper, also a weekly, supported Zachary Taylorqv for president in 1848. It was put up for sale by Gilbert in late 1853. The *Colorado Tribune* continued to publish until at least 1854 and possibly later.

BIBLIOGRAPHY: Joe B. Frantz, Newspapers of the Republic of Texas (M.A. thesis, University of Texas, 1940). Marilyn M. Sibley, *Lone Stars and State Gazettes: Texas Newspapers before the Civil War* (College Station: Texas A&M University Press, 1983).

Rachel Jenkins

COLORADO VALLEY RAILWAY. The Colorado Valley Railway Company was chartered on April 26, 1897, to connect Colorado City, in Mitchell County, with San Angelo, seventy-five miles to the south in Tom Green County. The capital stock was $500,000. The members of the first board of directors were C. B. Holmes, Irving Wheatcroft, J. H. Burroughs, J. W. Reed, L. H. Brightman, W. C. Barron, F. Buchanan, J. B. Latham, and L. B. Murray, all of Robert Lee in Coke County, where the principal office was located. At a stockholders meeting held on July 21, 1897, the route was changed to run between Sweetwater and San Angelo via Robert Lee. In 1889 the railroad built seven miles of track from Sweetwater and was acquired by the Panhandle and Gulf Railway Company in that year.

Nancy Beck Young

COLORED FARMERS' ALLIANCE. In the 1880s black farmers in the South, like white farmers, faced economic problems resulting from falling commodity prices, rising farm costs, and high interest rates. Since the Southern Farmers' Alliance (*see* FARMERS' ALLIANCE) barred blacks from membership, a small group of black farmers organized the Colored Farmers' National Alliance and Cooperative Union in Houston County, Texas, on December 11, 1886. They elected J. J. Shuffer president and H. S. Spencer secretary. Richard Manning Humphrey, a white, accepted the position of general superintendent. After the alliance received a charter from the federal government in 1888, Humphrey began organizing chapters throughout the South. For a while he faced competition from a rival group, the National Colored Alliance, which appeared in Texas about the same time as the Colored Farmers' Alliance and was led by Andrew J. Carothers. In 1890 the two groups merged, and the next year the Colored Alliance claimed to have a membership of 1,200,000.

The Colored Alliance tried to help its members in a variety of ways. To educate them on how to become better farmers, it established a weekly newspaper, the *National Alliance*, published at Houston. It established exchanges in the ports of Charleston, Houston, Mobile, New Orleans, and Norfolk, through which the members bought goods at reduced prices and obtained loans to pay off mortgages. The alliance raised funds to provide for longer public school terms, and in some places it founded academies. Being a fraternal organization, the Colored Alliance solicited funds to help sick and disabled members. Its spokesmen advised black farmers that they could best alleviate racial prejudice by owning their own homes and avoiding debt. In pursuing these programs the Colored Alliance resembled other black organizations of that era that urged members to uplift themselves by hard work and sacrifice.

The Colored Alliance occasionally cooperated with the Southern Alliance. Both advocated the abolition of the Louisiana lottery, fearing it would lead farmers further into debt. To keep vegetable-oil prices low in comparison to the prices of animal fats, they opposed the Conger lard bill, a measure that attempted to impose taxes upon the production of vegetable oil. The two alliances sometimes joined forces in attempting to improve their business ventures. Despite their mutual support for some goals, however, the two organizations had sharp differences, as they revealed in a clash over the Lodge election bill, which promised federal protection to safeguard voting rights in the South. The Southern Alliance condemned that measure, while the Colored Alliance supported it.

The Colored Alliance was made up of landless people who picked cotton for white farmers. In September 1891 it called for cotton pickers throughout the South to strike unless they received wages of a dollar per hundred pounds, but the organization had neither the local leaders nor the means of communication necessary to unite its members in such a venture. Consequently, in most places the strike failed to materialize. When pickers in one Arkansas community actually tried to strike, whites forcefully crushed it and in the process killed fifteen strikers. In the months following the abortive strike, the Colored Alliance declined rapidly. The strike contributed to its demise.

BIBLIOGRAPHY: Jack Abramowitz, "The Negro in the Agrarian Revolt," *Agricultural History* 24 (April 1950). William F. Holmes, "The Arkansas Cotton Pickers' Strike of 1891 and the Demise of the Colored Farmers' Alliance," *Arkansas Historical Quarterly* 32 (Summer 1973). William F. Holmes, "The Demise of the Colored Farmers' Alliance," *Journal of Southern History* 41 (May 1975). Richard M. Humphrey, "History of the Colored Farmers' Alliance and Co-operative Union," in *The Farmers' Alliance History and Agricultural Digest*, ed. Nelson A. Dunning (Washington: National Farmers' Alliance, 1891). Floyd J. Miller, "Black Protest and White Leadership: A Note on the Colored Farmers' Alliance," *Phylon* 33 (Summer 1972). William W. Rogers, "The Negro Alliance in Alabama," *Journal of Negro History* 45 (January 1960).

William F. Holmes

COLQUHOUN, LUDOVIC (1804–ca. 1882). Ludovic Colquhoun, soldier and legislator, was born in Virginia in 1804 and moved to

Bexar County, Texas, in 1837. After the resignation of William H. Daingerfield,qv Colquhoun was appointed to the Senate of the Sixth Congress of the Republic of Texas and served from June through September 1842. He was characterized as staunchly anti-Houston in his political philosophy, in favor of immediate offensive war against Mexico. He objected, however, to the portion of the bill passed by the Senate authorizing an invasion that named Houston as commander "because of his inefficiency and inability to command an army with advantage to the country." When the United States government offered to mediate the hostilities between Texas and Mexico, Colquhoun changed his opinion and, according to the *Telegraph and Texas Register*,qv "went out to the West with the full determination to exert all his influence to prevent any expedition from starting for the Rio Grande."

Samuel Maverickqv filed suit against Colquhoun in a dispute over the ownership of a piece of land on Cibolo Creek, and while the case was being tried in San Antonio on September 11, 1842, Adrián Wollqv raided the town, taking captive all of the officers of the court, Colquhoun and Maverick among them. They were taken to Mexico and confined in Perote Prison.qv There Colquhoun made several copies of a map of the area between Veracruz and Mexico City that aided Thomas Jefferson Greenqv and several of his companions in their escape. Colquhoun was released on March 24, 1844, after intervention on behalf of the prisoners by United States ambassador Waddy Thompson.qv Colquhoun sailed from Veracruz for New Orleans on April 1 aboard the brig of war USS *Bainbridge* and returned to Galveston aboard the *Neptune*.

In 1850 Colquhoun was residing in San Antonio with his English-born wife, Frances, and working as a merchant. His real estate was valued at $15,000. With the outbreak of the Civil War,qv due to his reputation as a man of character and ability, he was appointed Confederate States depository. He died between April 1882 and April 1883.

BIBLIOGRAPHY: *Telegraph and Texas Register*, July 27, September 21, October 12, 1842. Texas House of Representatives, *Biographical Directory of the Texan Conventions and Congresses, 1832–1845* (Austin: Book Exchange, 1941).

Thomas W. Cutrer

COLQUITT, OSCAR BRANCH (1861–1940). Oscar Branch Colquitt, politician and governor, was born on December 16, 1861, at Camilla, Georgia, the son of Thomas Jefferson and Ann Elizabeth (Burkhalter) Colquitt, each of whom boasted some distinguished American ancestors. The family moved in 1878 to Daingerfield, Texas, where young Colquitt worked as a tenant farmer and attended the Daingerfield Academy one term. After a brief apprenticeship as a newspaperman, he founded the *Gazette* at Pittsburg, Texas, in 1884. He married Alice Fuller Murrell of Minden, Louisiana, on December 9, 1885, and the couple had four sons and one daughter. He sold the *Gazette* and published the *Times-Star* of Terrell, Texas, from 1890 to 1897. Colquitt served as state senator from 1895 to 1899 and was the author of delinquent-tax laws that earned him a statewide reputation. He was the state revenue agent during the last eight months of 1898 and, as the tax expert of a special tax commission, wrote the report that this commission submitted to the legislature in 1900. Colquitt acted as a paid lobbyist for several corporations during the sessions of 1899 and 1901 and also practiced law, having been admitted to the bar in 1900. He succeeded John H. Reaganqv as state railroad commissioner and served from 1903 to 1911.

He made an unsuccessful run for governor in 1906 and was elected governor in 1910 as an anti-prohibitionist. After being reelected in 1912, he held the office until 1915. His administration achieved a reform of the prison system,qv improvement in the physical plants and management of the eleemosynary institutions, great advancement in the educational system, and a number of measures designed to improve the lot of laborers. This program was adopted despite the open hostility of two legislatures, which resulted from the animosities engendered by the prohibitionqv question. Colquitt was pro-German from 1914 to 1916 and tried to secure the financial assistance of the German government in buying the New York *Sun*, which he planned to edit as a German propaganda organ. He failed in this venture, ran for the United States Senate in 1916, and received a large plurality over six opponents in the first primary. In the runoff, however, he was defeated by the incumbent, Charles A. Culberson.qv Although he remained interested in politics, Colquitt devoted the next decade to serving as president of a Dallas oil firm. In 1928 he bolted the Democratic partyqv and headed the "Hoover Democrats" of Texas. He then served as a member of the United States Board of Mediation from 1929 through 1933. He became a field representative of the Reconstruction Finance Corporation in 1935 and held this position until his death, on March 8, 1940. Colquitt was a self-made man, obstinate yet affable. Though not a polished orator, he was a convincing speaker and possessed of the "color that drew a crowd"; he was one of the most effective stump speakers in the history of Texas.

BIBLIOGRAPHY: Oscar Branch Colquitt Papers, Barker Texas History Center, University of Texas at Austin. James T. DeShields, *They Sat in High Places: The Presidents and Governors of Texas* (San Antonio: Naylor, 1940). Lewis L. Gould, *Progressives and Prohibitionists: Texas Democrats in the Wilson Era* (Austin: University of Texas Press, 1973; rpt., Austin: Texas State Historical Association, 1992). George P. Huckaby, Oscar Branch Colquitt: A Political Biography (Ph.D. dissertation, University of Texas, 1946). Norman Kittrell, *Governors Who Have Been and Other Public Men of Texas* (Houston: Dealy-Adey-Elgin, 1921). Ross Phares, *The Governors of Texas* (Gretna, Louisiana: Pelican, 1976).

George P. Huckaby

COLQUITT, TEXAS. Colquitt is on a spur off Farm Road 548 two miles south of the Rockwall county line in north central Kaufman County. The settlement was established sometime in the 1880s and throughout its history has served as a community center for area farmers. It was named for a family of pioneer settlers, a descendant of whom, Oscar B. Colquitt,qv became governor in 1911. At one time the town had a gin, a store, and several houses. Between 1910 and the early 1930s the population was just over 100. In the early 1940s it was estimated at twenty-five. Colquitt was still listed as a community in 1990.

BIBLIOGRAPHY: Ed Ellsworth Bartholomew, *The Encyclopedia of Texas Ghost Towns* (Fort Davis, Texas, 1982).

David Minor

COLSON, ESTHER NEVEILLE HIGGS (1902–1982). Neveille Colson, Texas legislator, was born on July 18, 1902, to Walter J. and Ollie (Jowers) Higgs in Bryan, Texas. She attended school in Bryan and entered Baylor University in Waco in 1923. After a year she took a teaching position in Iola, Grimes County. About 1925 she married Nall Colson, a local football coach. From 1930 to 1932 she continued her education at the Agricultural and Mechanical College of Texas (now Texas A&M University) and at Sam Houston State Teachers College (now Sam Houston State University). In 1932 Colson was elected to the Texas House of Representatives for District 27, and his wife accompanied him to the legislature to observe and assist. During the 1930s she also held jobs in the secretary of state's office and the Internal Revenue Service. She studied at the University of Texas but did not complete a degree. By early 1938 the Colsons were divorced, and Nall Colson had died.

Neveille Colson ran successfully for the Texas House of Representatives from the district her husband had served. In her tenure from 1939 to 1948 she promoted legislation to improve and fund juvenile corrections, education, and public roads, especially for rural areas. She was the first woman to get a constitutional amendment through the legislature and past a vote by Texas citizens; her bill (1946) ensured that road-use taxes would be directed specifically to the highway department for road construction.

She ran successfully for the Texas Senate in the Fifth District, comprising nine counties between Dallas and Houston, in 1948 and thus became the first female Texas representative elected to the Texas Senate. Her district encompassed more state facilities than any but the Austin area. She continued to champion the key interests of her east central Texas constituents—public roads and schools. In 1949 the legislature approved the Colson-Briscoe Act, allocating funds for statewide farm-to-market roads. With the help of federal funds this program enabled the Texas Highway Department nearly to double the number of paved rural roads in the state within two years (*see* HIGHWAY DEVELOPMENT). Colson was appointed to the Senate education committee and helped gain passage of the Gilmer-Aiken Laws[qv] in 1949.

The Texas Highway Department completed the state's longest girder bridge near Washington-on-the-Brazos in 1954. Colson's constituents succeeded in having it named for her, in appreciation for the farm-road legislation and funding she had sponsored to move rural school transportation and mail delivery "out of the mud," as she put it. Though soft-spoken, Colson held her own in the Senate for the remainder of her career. By 1955 she was on nineteen Senate committees and the legislative budget board. She chaired the Senate education committee from 1955 to 1957 and the public health committee from 1957 to 1964. For the 1955 ad interim session she served as president pro tem. Calling herself "the only full-time Senator," she could afford to devote most of her energy to legislation and visiting constituents because her parents supplemented her $3,000 biennial Senate salary.

Boundaries for Senate districts were redrawn in 1953 and again in 1966. The latter redistricting forced Colson into competition with incumbent Senator Bill Moore of Bryan to retain her seat. She lost the 1966 election, ending a twenty-eight-year career in the legislature. She subsequently assumed curatorship of the Sam Houston Memorial Museum[qv] at Huntsville. Upon retiring from the museum in 1977, she returned to Bryan, where she died on March 3, 1982, after spending her last years at a nursing home. Her remains were buried at the Bryan City Cemetery.

BIBLIOGRAPHY: Bryan–College Station *Eagle,* March 4, 1982. Dallas *News,* December 16, 1956. *Who's Who of American Women,* 1964–65.

Sherilyn Brandenstein

COLSTON DRAW. Colston Draw rises nine miles south of Fort McKavett in northwestern Kimble County (at 30°40′ N, 100°04′ W) and runs northwest for ten miles to its mouth on Terrett Draw, four miles southwest of Fort McKavett in Schleicher County (at 30°47′ N, 100°08′ W). The surrounding flat terrain with local shallow depressions is surfaced by clay and sandy loams that support water-tolerant hardwoods, conifers, and grasses.

COLT REVOLVERS. The first practical revolving-cylinder handgun was invented in 1831 by Samuel Colt of Hartford, Connecticut, and patented on February 25, 1836, the year of the Texas Revolution.[qv] Texas became a proving ground and nearly the only market for Colt's revolutionary product. Colt provided the struggling republic and frontier state with the increased firepower necessary to defend and advance itself. Colt revolvers were manufactured first in 1837 at Paterson, New Jersey, by the Patent Arms Manufacturing Company. Three principal variations of these five-shot Paterson Colt handguns were produced: the .28 caliber Pocket model, the .31 caliber Belt model, and the .36 caliber Holster model. The Republic of Texas[qv] ordered 180 of the .36 caliber Holster model revolvers for its navy in August 1839. Numbers of these rather delicate arms were issued to various Texas warships and served well in engagements against Mexico over the next four years. Colt was so pleased by the Texas purchase and with the performance of his product that he engraved the scene of the victorious naval battle fought off Campeche on May 16, 1843, by the Texas Navy[qv] on the cylinders of the 1851 Navy, 1860 Army, and 1861 Navy model Colts (in all, nearly 500,000 revolvers).

Many of the Paterson Colts purchased for the Texas Navy were ultimately used by the Texas army and in various quasimilitary expeditions. They are known to have been involved in the Council House Fight[qv] at San Antonio, as well as in the Texan–Santa Fe and Mier expeditions.[qqv] Most significant, however, were those revolvers reissued to units of the Texas Rangers.[qv] Among these border horsemen the Colt revolver first won its reputation as a weapon ideally suited to mounted combat. Using Paterson Colts purchased in 1843, Col. John Coffee Hays[qv] commanded a Ranger contingent in several uneven battles against depredating Comanches. Most notable was the contest in which Hays and fourteen rangers charged and routed nearly eighty Comanche warriors in a running battle along the Pedernales River in July 1844. Other victories against considerable odds at Nueces Canyon and Enchanted Rock reinforced the report of the Colt revolver's firepower. All of the forthcoming Walker and Dragoon model Colts (some 21,000 revolvers) carried a cylinder scene commemorating the so-called "Hays Big Fight" on the Pedernales. Colt himself came to call the Paterson Holster model revolver the Texas Arm, and present-day collectors generally refer to it as the Texas Model or Texas Paterson.

Although Colt's Paterson enterprise failed in 1842 because of inadequate sales, his early revolvers had won the devotion of frontier Texans, particularly those of the ranger force. Appropriately, it was a former Texas Ranger, Samuel H. Walker,[qv] who in conjunction with the demands of the Mexican War,[qv] put Colt back in business to stay. In November 1846 Captain Walker, then of the United States Mounted Riflemen, opened negotiations with Colt for the production of 1,000 improved revolvers. Familiar with the shortcomings of the Paterson arm, Walker specified a substantial new design incorporating a fixed trigger with guard and a loading lever beneath the nine-inch barrel. The massive revolver mounted a six-shot cylinder chambered for a .44 caliber conical bullet; the revolver weighed an unprecedented four pounds, nine ounces. Texas Ranger John S. (Rip) Ford[qv] claimed the new Walker Colt pistol was as powerful as the United States Model 1841 "Mississippi" rifle.

The Walker Colt inaugurated the era of perfected revolver design and manufacture. Colt established a new factory at Hartford, Connecticut, in 1848, and Colt's Patent Fire Arms Manufacturing Company (today the Firearms Division of Colt Industries) began regular production. By the time of Colt's death in 1862, a succession of ten improved revolver models had been introduced, and some 468,000 units manufactured. Before the Civil War[qv] the most popular of these in Texas was the .36 caliber 1851 Navy model, about which traveler Frederick Law Olmsted[qv] observed, "Of the Colt's [Navy] we cannot speak in too high terms.... There are probably in Texas about as many revolvers as male adults, and I doubt if there are one hundred in the state of any other make." During the war the few Texas arms manufacturers producing revolvers—Dance Brothers,[qv] for instance—patterned their limited output on the Colt Dragoon and Navy models.

The Colt revolver remained preeminent among such arms in Texas and throughout the West for the remainder of the nineteenth century. The 1873 Single Action Army model, known as the Peacemaker or simply six-shooter, became the standard sidearm of the postwar military, the Texas Rangers, and the majority of cowboys across the plains. Though restrictions against carrying handguns were applied in Texas during the 1880s, widespread possession declined only slowly.

Windmills, barbed wire[qqv] fences, and Colt revolvers have been credited with settlement of the Great Plains. The Colt revolver and Texas remain inextricably associated in history, symbolism, and romance. Colt collectors abound in the state.

BIBLIOGRAPHY: T. R. Fehrenbach, *Lone Star: A History of Texas and the Texans* (New York: Macmillan, 1968). John S. Ford, *Rip Ford's Texas,* ed. Stephen B. Oates (Austin: University of Texas Press, 1963). J. Evetts Haley, *The XIT Ranch of Texas and the Early Days of the Llano Estacado* (Chicago: Lakeside, 1929; rpts., Norman: University of Oklahoma Press, 1953, 1967). Charles Tower Haven and Frank A. Belden, *A History of the Colt Revolver* (New York: Morrow, 1940). Carroll C.

Holloway, *Texas Gun Love* (San Antonio: Naylor, 1951). Philip D. Jordan, "The Pistol Packin' Cowboy: From Bullet to Burial," *Red River Valley Historical Review* 11 (Spring 1975). Noel M. Loomis, *Texan–Santa Fe Pioneers* (Norman: University of Oklahoma Press, 1958). Watson Parker, "Armed and Ready: Guns on the Western Frontier," in *The American West: Essays in Honor of W. Eugene Hollon*, ed. Ronald Lora (University of Toledo, 1980). John E. Parsons, *The Peacemaker and Its Rivals: An Account of the Single Action Colt* (New York: Morrow, 1950). Ernest Lisle Reedstrom, *Bugles, Banners and War Bonnets* (Caldwell, Idaho, 1977). James E. Serven, *Colt Firearms* (Santa Ana, California: Serven, 1954). James E. Serven, *Conquering the Frontiers* (La Habra, California: Foundation, 1974). Walter Prescott Webb, *The Great Plains* (Boston: Ginn, 1931). Walter Prescott Webb, *The Texas Rangers* (Boston: Houghton Mifflin, 1935; rpt., Austin: University of Texas Press, 1982). R. L. Wilson, *Colt: An American Legend* (New York: Abbeville Press, 1985). R. L. Wilson, *Colt Heritage: The Official History of Colt Firearms* (New York: Simon and Schuster, 1950).

Richard C. Rattenbury

COLTEXO, TEXAS. Coltexo, an oil camp on Farm Road 1474 three miles northeast of Lefors in north central Gray County, was established in the late 1920s. The camp was named for the Col-Tex Refinery Company, which erected a carbon black plant (*see* CARBON BLACK INDUSTRY) on a spur of the Panhandle and Santa Fe Railway. Earl and Thelma Butterick operated a store there, and local mail came through Lefors. After the improvement of transportation in the area, many of the plant's employees moved to Lefors. The Coltexo community declined when carbon black lost its importance in the petroleum industry. In 1990 the population of Coltexo was recorded as five.

BIBLIOGRAPHY: Gray County History Book Committee, *Gray County Heritage* (Dallas: Taylor, 1985). Carl Coke Rister, *Oil! Titan of the Southwest* (Norman: University of Oklahoma Press, 1949).

H. Allen Anderson

COLTHARP, TEXAS. Coltharp was on Cochino Bayou twenty miles east of Crockett in eastern Houston County. The community, settled before 1860, derived its name from an early settler who owned a store and a mill. A post office operated there from 1857 until 1909. The town had Presbyterian, Methodist, and Baptist congregations by 1884. Between 1884 and 1891 it also had a school, a shingle mill, and several steam cotton gins, gristmills, and sawmills. The town served as a shipping point for cotton. In 1884 Coltharp had a population of 150 and thirteen businesses. On August 15, 1887, the construction of a local school was authorized. In 1890 the community had a population of fifty, six cotton gins, two general stores, two gristmills, a gunsmith, a blacksmith, a sawmill, a shingle and planing mill, a church, and a district school. In 1892 Coltharp's population was 100, and the town also had two constables, a justice, and a doctor. By 1896 it had a population of seventy-five and two businesses. The population was reported as 113 in 1900, the last year for which statistics were available. In 1925 the local school was closed, and its students transferred to the Kennard school. The community was not shown on the 1946 county highway map.

BIBLIOGRAPHY: Houston County Historical Commission, *History of Houston County, Texas, 1687–1979* (Tulsa, Oklahoma: Heritage, 1979).

Mike Smalley

COLTHARP-BEALL HOUSE. The Coltharp-Beall House, one of the earliest surviving structures in Van Zandt County, is on Farm Road 279 near the Henderson county line; it marks the original site of Edom on the north side of State Highway 64, five to six miles east of the present townsite. The house was built in 1849 by James Coltharp, who arrived from Georgia in 1846 with Capt. August Chandler Beall, who married Charlotte Elizabeth Coltharp on June 24, 1845. The Hamburg general store and post office was later built across the road. The site is located about halfway between Dallas and Shreveport, and the house served as an early stagecoach stop. Traveling preachers also stopped there in the 1850s and 1860s; the house was claimed to be the site of the area's first sermon. Coltharp family members established mills for processing lumber, flour, and cotton over the line in Henderson County before the Civil War.[qv] After the war, members of the Beall family purchased the one-story wooden house with a stone chimney as a residence. In 1990 the structure served as a reunion center for the Beall and Coltharp families.

BIBLIOGRAPHY: Van Zandt County History Book Committee, *History of Van Zandt County* (Dallas, 1984).

Diana J. Kleiner

COLTON, TEXAS. Colton, seven miles southeast of Austin in Travis County, was established by the McKenzie family about 1866. The community was first called Cotton, in reference to the area's staple crop, but its name was changed to Colton when the local post office opened in 1897. At that time Colton had a small store and ten to fifteen residents. Its post office was discontinued in 1902, and its mail was sent to Creedmoor. Colton had twenty-five residents in 1933 and fifty in 1939; its population was still reported as fifty in the 1980s and in 1990.

BIBLIOGRAPHY: Mary Starr Barkley, *History of Travis County and Austin, 1839–1899* (Waco: Texian Press, 1963). John J. Germann and Myron Janzen, *Texas Post Offices by County* (1986).

Claudia Hazlewood

COLUMBIA COLLEGE. Columbia College, at Van Alstyne in Grayson County, operated for just under a decade. As North Texas began to grow in the late nineteenth century a number of communities supported college-level institutions. Residents of Van Alstyne joined in 1889 to establish Columbia College. The school building had eight large rooms, among them a chapel with a stage. By 1894 the enrollment was 578. In the late 1890s a fire destroyed the school. Attempts to refinance failed, and the school never reopened.

BIBLIOGRAPHY: Mattie D. Lucas and Mita H. Hall, *A History of Grayson County* (Sherman, Texas, 1936).

David Minor

COLUMBIA *PLANTER*. The *Planter*, probably a successor to the Columbia *Planter's Gazette*[qv] and possibly the same paper, was published at Columbia between June 1843 and March 1845, when the paper was moved to Brazoria. It ceased publication sometime in 1846. Matthew Hopkins,[qv] one of the early editors, wrote and published in the paper a serial novel, *Marianna and Her Wrongs*. The five-column, four-page paper with a four-dollar subscription rate was published weekly on Saturdays. It included little political comment and much promotion of agriculture; it opened its office to meetings of agricultural associations.

BIBLIOGRAPHY: Joe B. Frantz, Newspapers of the Republic of Texas (M.A. thesis, University of Texas, 1940). Marilyn M. Sibley, *Lone Stars and State Gazettes: Texas Newspapers before the Civil War* (College Station: Texas A&M University Press, 1983). John Melton Wallace, *Gaceta to Gazette: A Checklist of Texas Newspapers, 1813–1846* (Austin: University of Texas Department of Journalism, 1966). WPA Historical Records Survey Program, *Texas Newspapers* (Houston: San Jacinto Museum of History Association, 1941).

COLUMBIA *PLANTER'S GAZETTE*. The *Planter's Gazette*, according to a checklist of Texas newspapers, was published by Samuel J. Durnett[qv] at Columbia from November 1842 until June 1843.

BIBLIOGRAPHY: Marilyn M. Sibley, *Lone Stars and State Gazettes: Texas Newspapers before the Civil War* (College Station: Texas A&M

University Press, 1983). John Melton Wallace, *Gaceta to Gazette: A Checklist of Texas Newspapers, 1813–1846* (Austin: University of Texas Department of Journalism, 1966). WPA Historical Records Survey Program, *Texas Newspapers* (Houston: San Jacinto Museum of History Association, 1941).

COLUMBUS, TEXAS. Columbus, the county seat and second largest city of Colorado County, is at the junction of Interstate Highway 10 and State Highway 71, sixty-five miles west of Houston, on a small rise south and west of a lazy horseshoe bend in the Colorado River. It is on the site of the legendary Indian village of Montezuma. Members of Stephen F. Austin's[qv] Old Three Hundred[qv] began arriving in the area in 1821; in late December Robert H. Kuykendall, his brother Joseph, and Daniel Gilleland[qqv] moved from a newly established settlement on the Brazos River, later known as Washington-on-the-Brazos, to a site on the Colorado River near that of present Columbus. By 1823 a small community had developed. It became known as Beeson's Ferry or Beeson's Ford,[qv] named for Benjamin Beeson,[qv] one of the original settlers, who operated a ferry across the Colorado River. In 1835 it was renamed Columbus, allegedly at the suggestion of a former resident of Columbus, Ohio. The town began as a river crossing and became the seat of local government in 1822, when Austin's colony was divided into two autonomous districts by Mexican governor José F. Trespalacios.[qv] Trespalacios had the Baron de Bastrop[qv] travel to the Colorado River District to supervise local elections. Gathering at Beason's Crossing, the residents elected John J. Tumlinson, Sr.,[qv] alcalde,[qv] Robert Kuykendall captain, and Moses Morrison[qv] lieutenant. Austin had intended to locate his headquarters here and even laid out a town the following year, but finally opted for a more promising location on the Brazos River. No doubt the frequent Indian attacks in the Colorado River District and poor drainage influenced his decision to relocate his headquarters.

By the time of the Texas Revolution,[qv] this settlement, now known as Columbus, was home to over twenty-five families, including that of William D. Lacey,[qv] one of the signers of the Texas Declaration of Independence.[qv] The community had a ferry, a cotton gin, a gristmill, a sawmill, and a small inn or boardinghouse for travelers. Sam Houston[qv] camped on the east bank of the Colorado River at Columbus from March 19 to 26, 1836, during the Runaway Scrape,[qv] as he retreated from Gonzales to San Jacinto. Although Houston had Columbus burned when he departed, a traveler noted in 1837 that the refurbished town had two public houses, two stores, half a dozen shanties, and quite a bit of gambling. Another traveler passing through Columbus around 1847 found the little town excited over a horse race; bets ranged up to $500. At that time Columbus had twenty houses, three stores, two taverns, and a blacksmith but showed no evidence of growth. Evidently, horse racing, betting, and drinking, along with chewing tobacco and spitting, were favorite pastimes in Columbus, as well as in most of Texas throughout the nineteenth century. The Beacon Hill Blood Stock Farm, owned by Dr. Robert H. Harrison,[qv] had a racetrack and was reportedly the best in the state. Eventually, the Columbus Quarter Horse Racetrack was established a few miles east of town. It was quite popular into the twentieth century.

Columbus was designated the county seat of Colorado County when the county was established in 1836. The following year the county was organized, and in April Judge Robert McAlpin (Three Legged Willie) Williamson[qv] reportedly convened the first district court in Colorado County in the shade of a large oak tree near the site of the present courthouse. The trunk of the tree, long since dead, still sports a historical plaque and for a time provided the background for yearly reenactments of the original court. Columbus was then the largest settlement in the county, with a population of 1,500. The following year, as a local story has it, lumber was cut from the pine forest near the site of present Bastrop for the construction of a courthouse. An obstruction was placed in the Colorado River near Columbus, and the logs were floated downriver, but the obstruction failed and the lumber was lost. The first of the county's three courthouses was finally constructed in 1847.

In 1839, a year after the lumber incident, Col. Robert Robson moved to Columbus from Dumfries, Scotland, and built a castle, complete with a drawbridge and moat, on the south bank on the Colorado River north of town. Robson's Castle was constructed of concrete made from locally produced lime and gravel. It was three stories high and had a large ballroom and roof garden. A cistern on the roof provided running water piped throughout the castle. Robson hosted many parties in the castle's ballroom, and Dr. Lawrence Washington, grand-nephew of President George Washington, held Episcopal services there. The foundations of the castle were undermined by a flood in 1869. In 1883 it was torn down, and a beef-packing plant was built on the site.

Columbus was incorporated on August 22, 1866, after the Civil War,[qv] under the legislative act of January 28, 1858. The latter half of the nineteenth century was marred by almost continual violence. A fresh wave of killings in 1906 prompted the citizens of Columbus to petition the mayor and city council to reestablish the office of city marshall, abolished in 1903. The council voted three to two against the measure. Incensed by the council's lack of responsiveness, the citizens then approached county judge J. J. Mansfield,[qv] who ordered an election to decide the fate of the city charter. By a vote of ninety-nine to thirty-five Columbus was disincorporated, and the county commissioners' court took over daily operation of city government. Columbus remained unincorporated until 1927, by which time the population had risen to 3,100. The population declined during the Great Depression[qv] and did not climb above 3,000 again until the mid-1950s.

The first major industry to arise in Columbus, apart from smithies, was a German cigar factory, established around 1840. As more Germans turned from tobacco to cotton production, the importance of the cigar factory declined, and it eventually ceased to operate; by 1880 tobacco production in the area was of little importance. The next major industry developed around cotton. Cottonseed oil was a very important commodity. In the early 1880s several oil mills were built in Colorado County. At least one of these was in Columbus, built by the Columbus Oil Company in 1881. But hard times came in 1884, and R. E. Stafford foreclosed on the mill. It was sold at public auction and dismantled. The 1870s showed a dramatic increase in cotton production in Colorado County. In 1880, 15,552 bales was produced; although this was only an 8 percent increase over the 14,438 bales produced in 1860, it was a full 456 percent increase over the 2,796 bales produced in 1870. This increase was accompanied by a similar growth in the number of farms, from 397 in 1860 to 456 in 1870 and 1,666 in 1880. Cattle production also peaked in the early 1880s, at 108,368 head. This increase prompted Stafford to establish the Columbus Meat and Ice Company in 1883 on the site of Robson's Castle near the north bridge. Stafford planned to take advantage of the large supply of local beef and ship it to markets in Europe and the North. The packing plant had a capacity of 250 cattle and forty tons of ice per day but normally processed only around 25 to 100 head per day.

Large deposits of sand and gravel in and around Columbus helped give birth to the next major industry to flourish in the area. Gravel pits were first dug by the Galveston, Harrisburg and San Antonio Railway just west of Glidden in 1906. By 1910 Columbus was virtually surrounded by gravel pits. Four additional companies were formed in that year alone. Gravel production has continued to be a major source of economic prosperity over the years, with only moderate declines during the Great Depression.[qv] In addition to its economic contribution, the prevalence of an inexpensive source of local gravel also made road construction affordable.

Columbus grew steadily after World War II,[qv] as the local economy became increasingly focused on recreational activities. For Columbus this focus centered on historic buildings and a down-home atmosphere. In 1961 a group of civic leaders organized the Magnolia Homes Tour, a nonprofit organization established to preserve the unique local culture, traditions, and heritage of Columbus as embodied in its historic buildings. Tours are conducted on the first and third Thursdays of each month and include the Stafford Opera House, the Senftenberg-Brandon House Museum, the Alley Log Cabin Museum, the Dilue Rose Harris^{qv} House Museum, and the Mary Elizabeth Youens Hopkins Santa Claus Museum. Other historic buildings in the area include the Confederate Memorial Museum, in the brick-based Water Tower (1883), the Brunson Building (1891), the Raumonda house (1887), the Gant house (ca. 1870), and the Colorado County Courthouse (1891). As of 1990 Columbus had four banks with assets totaling over $907,000, two elementary, one junior, and one high school with 1,569 students enrolled, a library, two weekly newspapers, and a radio station. The citizens were also served by three hospitals or clinics with a forty-bed capacity and four hotels with a total of 232 rooms.

BIBLIOGRAPHY: *Columbus, Texas: "The City of Live Oaks and Live Folks"* (Columbus: *Colorado County Citizen*, 1935). *Columbus, Texas Sesquicentennial, 1823–1973* (Columbus, Texas: Columbus Sesquicentennial, Inc., 1977). Fred I. Massengill, *Texas Towns: Origin of Name and Location of Each of the 2,148 Post Offices in Texas* (Terrell, Texas, 1936). Bill Stein, Paul Ussi, and Sarah Ussi, *Colorado County's Courthouses* (Columbus, Texas: Colorado County Historical Commission, 1991).

Don Allon Hinton

COLUMBUS FEMALE SEMINARY. Columbus Female Seminary, the first educational institution in Columbus, was founded through the effort of the Caledonia Masonic Lodge of Columbus. On February 3, 1851, shortly after the charter was granted, a committee was appointed to supervise construction of a two-story building to be used as a lodge hall and female seminary. The seminary was conducted by a board of trustees. If the school could not pay the teachers, the lodge agreed to pay the deficit. The board could discharge any teacher or expel or suspend any student at any time.

By 1859 more school rooms were needed. A corporation was formed, which included eight Masons and eighteen other citizens of Columbus, to build a school building and provide for the increased educational needs of the town. The school was named Colorado College. On December 27, 1859, the cornerstone was laid. In January 1860 P. Riley was principal and Misses Nannie Martin and Carrie E. Martin were assistants. The monthly charge ranged from two to five dollars. Pupils were charged from the time of entrance to the close of the session, and no refund was made except for protracted sickness. Evidently, the college building was completed by January 12, 1861, at which time the *Colorado Citizen* (see COLORADO COUNTY CITIZEN) states that Columbus Female Seminary had been placed under the control of Professor Riley and Rev. J. J. Loomis as principals. Miss Mary Haswell was music teacher. The seminary was no longer under Masonic sponsorship.

The school continued to operate for a number of years, sometimes under a board of trustees and at other times under individuals. It changed hands many times. The lower floor of the Masonic Institute building was rented to anyone who could provide the public with a good school. Riley ran it until around 1870, after which Mrs. Kate Oakes had a small private school in the Masonic building until after Christmas of 1871. On August 19, 1877, E. E. Riley advertised to teach a mixed school at the Masonic Academy, assisted by his sister. By October 4, 1877, the school had some forty students. On January 7, 1878, Professor F. M. Reager announced to parents and guardians that he would open a high school for males and females in the Masonic Academy. The next and last record of a school at the Masonic Academy was P. J. Oakes's announcement of a ten-month session to begin on the first Monday in September 1882. The school at the Masonic building must have ceased operation in 1883.

BIBLIOGRAPHY: James David Carter, *Education and Masonry in Texas, 1846 to 1861* (Waco: Grand Lodge of Texas, 1964). Colorado County Historical Commission, *Colorado County Chronicles from the Beginning to 1923* (2 vols., Austin: Nortex, 1986).

James G. Hopkins

COLUMBUS TAP RAILWAY. The Columbus Tap Railway Company was chartered on February 2, 1860. The Buffalo Bayou, Brazos and Colorado, the first railroad built in Texas, had mapped its route from Harrisburg through Alleyton to Austin up the east side of the Colorado River, bypassing Columbus. The citizens of Columbus, to protect their trade area, decided to build their own railroad to connect with the BBB&C at Alleyton. Six men were appointed commissioners to organize the company: Charles W. Tait, George W. Smith,^{qqv} A. M. Campbell, John G. Logue, W. E. Wallace, and Isam Tooke. The railroad had a capital stock of $300,000 divided into shares of $100 each. The charter authorized the company to establish a ferry across the Colorado River to be used until a bridge was constructed. From William Harbert^{qv} the commissioners bought a 2½-mile right-of-way 150 feet wide, extending from the east bank of the Colorado River to Alleyton. By orders of the commissioners, directors of the Columbus Tap Railway Company were elected on September 15, 1860. Of the six directors elected, Logue became president; he was soon succeeded by E. P. Whitfield. Tait was treasurer, and C. Windrow was clerk.

The Civil War^{qv} disrupted plans by slowing construction of the road, but two miles had been graded by January 15, 1861. The railway proved to be needed by the Confederate Army, and Gen. John Bankhead Magruder^{qv} ordered impressment of 100 men to work on its roadbed in 1863, though the project failed to reach completion in the war years. Some reports indicate that after the war in 1865 the line was built to the river, where the ferry gave Columbus rail service. Contemporary newspaper accounts, however, indicate that the track was not completed until 1867. The BBB&C contracted for the construction of a bridge in its own name, and after its completion in 1867 by Nathan Wheeler and John R. Brooks, the Austin was the first locomotive to cross the Colorado River into Columbus. The BBB&C was authorized to buy the Columbus Tap on September 21, 1866, but each railroad retained a separate legal existence until July 7, 1870, when the legislature authorized a merger. At that time the BBB&C amended its charter and changed its name to Galveston, Harrisburg and San Antonio.

James G. Hopkins

COLVILLE, SILAS CHEEK (1804–1844). Silas Cheek Colville, Red River trader, was born in eastern Tennessee on January 2, 1804, the son of Joseph and Martha (Cheek) Colville. He moved with his family to McMinnville, Tennessee, around 1810. In 1829 he went to Fort Smith, Arkansas, with Holland Coffee^{qv} and others and established Coffee, Colville, and Company. John S. Young, once secretary of state in Tennessee, was his brother-in-law, and Hugh Franklin Young^{qv} was his cousin. In 1834 Colville accompanied Coffee to establish a trading post at the old Pawnee village on Red River, but he soon returned to his home in Van Buren. In 1837 he joined Coffee at Walnut Bayou on the Red River. They soon moved to Preston Bend (now Preston, Grayson County). Colville and Coffee dissolved their partnership after Coffee's marriage in 1839. Colville then became associated with James A. Caldwell at Shawneetown, near the site of modern Denison. They had postal contracts for much of East Texas, some interest in a trading house in Austin, and an association with E. F. Edrington, an Indian trader. The partnership furnished supplies to the Republic of Texas.^{qv} Caldwell died in 1842.

Colville served on a committee to honor William Gordon Cooke,^{qv} who was commanding the Military Road^{qv} expedition. In a fight at Warren in the spring of 1841, he killed John Hart,^{qv} an old pioneer, once a merchant of Jonesboro. Hart had aggressively protested the land claims of Coffee in Preston Bend, without legal success. Colville was acquitted, yet he was killed by unknown assailants in 1844. The place of his death is unknown, although his will was probated in old Fannin County. He had never married. The site of his burial has yet to be discovered. Litigation over Colville's Red River land continued almost until 1900.

BIBLIOGRAPHY: Audy J. and Glenna P. Middlebrooks, "Holland Coffee of Red River," *Southwestern Historical Quarterly* 69 (October 1965).
Morris L. Britton

COMAL, TEXAS. Comal, eight miles southwest of New Braunfels in southern Comal County, is not to be confused with Comal Town or the Comal Creek Settlement. It was established as a community on the Old San Antonio Road in 1846 and became a railroad section station on the Missouri, Kansas and Texas Railroad about 1900. In the 1980s its forty inhabitants farmed, ranched, or worked at a nearby quarry. In 1990 the population of Comal was still reported as forty.

COMAL COUNTY. Comal County (L-15) is located in south central Texas on the divide between the Blackland Prairies and the Balcones Escarpment.qv Its largest city and county seat, New Braunfels, is twenty-nine miles northeast of San Antonio and forty-five miles southwest of Austin. The county's center lies at 29°48′ north latitude and 98°17′ west longitude. The county comprises 555 square miles of prairie and Hill Countryqv terrain. The eastern quarter, below the Balcones Escarpment, is gently rolling grass and crop land ranging in elevation from 600 to 750 feet above sea level. The Blackland Prairie soil of this section is loam with clay subsoils and is well suited for cultivation. The elevation of the northwestern three-quarters of the county ranges from 750 to roughly 1,500 feet above sea level. The loam in this section varies from shallow to deep and has proved better suited for grazing than for cultivation. The Hill Country terrain supports more timber—live oak, mesquite, and Ashe juniper—and fewer grasses than the prairies of eastern Comal County. Indigenous wildlife includes deer, doves, rabbits, turkeys, squirrels, ringtail cats, skunks, bobcats, and coyotes. Ranchers have also introduced several exoticsqv into the area, including axis deer,qv sika deer, and Barbados sheep. The annual precipitation averages 33.19 inches, and average temperatures range from a low of 40° F in January to a high of 96° in July; the growing season lasts 265 days. Mineral resources include limestone, sand, and gravel; these have become the basis of a construction-materials industry in the county.

The Guadalupe River and, since 1964, Canyon Lakeqv drain the central hills and valleys of the county. Cibolo Creek, which empties into the San Antonio River, forms the southwestern boundary of the county and is the primary drainage channel for that area. Numerous streams north and east of Canyon Lake flow north into the Blanco River in Hays County. The Balcones Fault zone of the Edwards Aquifer is the primary source of groundwater in Comal County.

Spanish explorers were familiar with the Comal Springsqv area but evinced little interest in settling the region. After the expedition of Domingo Terán de los Ríosqv of 1691, the Old San Antonio Roadqv crossed the Guadalupe River near the future site of New Braunfels. Subsequent French and Spanish expeditions, including those of the Marqués de Aguayo and Louis Juchereau de St. Denis,qqv commonly passed through what later became southeastern Comal County. In 1756 Comal Springs became the site of the short-lived Nuestra Senora de Guadalupe Mission, but, rather than fortify the mission against anticipated Comanche depredations, Spanish authorities closed it in 1758. Nearly a century passed before settlement became permanent, although a Mexican land grant of 1825 gave title of the area around the springs to Juan M. Veramendi.qv During the eighteenth century the springs and river (which had been called Las Fontanas and the Little Guadalupe respectively) took the name Comal, Spanish for "flat dish." It is thought that the name was suggested to the Spanish by the numerous small islands in the river or by the shallow basin through which the river runs.

The inhabitants of the region on the eve of settlement were primarily Tonkawa and Waco Indians, although Lipan Apaches and Karankawas also roamed the area. Early settlers' contacts with these peoples were generally uneventful. Nomadic Wacos who were camped at springs north of New Braunfels moved their camp west within a year of the founding of the settlement, and a village of some 500 Tonkawas on the Guadalupe River above New Braunfels initially welcomed German visitors. Notwithstanding the rapid influx of settlers in the 1840s and 1850s and isolated incidents of violence, county fathers and Indian leaders generally maintained peaceful relations.

Permanent settlement of the county began in 1845, when Prince Carl of Solms-Braunfelsqv secured title to 1,265 acres of the Veramendi grant, including the Comal springs and river, for the Adelsverein.qv In succeeding years thousands of Germansqv and Americans were attracted to the rich farm and ranch land around New Braunfels. Settlement progressed rapidly; in March 1846 the Texas legislature formed Comal County from the Eighth Precinct of Bexar County and made New Braunfels the county seat. The final boundary determination was made in 1858 with the separation of part of western Comal County to Blanco and Kendall counties. The first county elections were held on July 13, 1846. It is estimated that in 1850 New Braunfels was the fourth largest city in Texas. In 1854 the county commissioners divided the county into eight public school districts, and in 1858, long before they were required by law to do so, New Braunfels citizens voted to collect a tax for support of public schools. The population of the county grew 133 percent between 1850 and 1860, and numbered more than 4,000 on the eve of the Civil War.qv

Comal County was exceptional among the largely German counties of south and west central Texas in the strength of its 1861 vote in favor of secession.qv The county contributed three all-German volunteer companies—two cavalry and one infantry—to the Confederate cause. There is little to suggest that the county's support for the Confederacy reflected enthusiasm for slavery.qv Free labor predominated over slave in all counties with large German populations; a survey of 130 German farms in Comal and two other counties in 1850 revealed no slave laborers. By 1860, as Anglo-Americans settled alongside the German pioneers, blacks still made up less than 5 percent of county residents, and the family remained the primary source of labor. Comal County residents seem to have embraced the Southern cause because of their support of the larger cause of states' rights. But there is no record in the county of the violence between Unionists and Confederates that broke out in German counties to the northwest.

From the early years of its settlement Comal County supported diversified farming and ranching industries. Corn was almost universally cultivated by pioneers and quickly became a staple both of the German diet and of the local economy as a cash crop. It declined in importance relative to other crops and to livestock, however, during and after the Civil War as county ranchers and farmers began to produce commercially important amounts of cotton, wheat, oats, wool, dairy products,qv and beef.

As farming and ranching spread beyond the environs of New Braunfels into the Hill Country, the county seat developed as an important supply and processing center for products of the expanding agricultural frontier. Many immigrants brought manufacturing experience and commercial acumen to their new home and applied these skills to the products of local agriculture. Comal County never developed as a major cotton-producing area, but the crop played an important role in the local economy. Production rose from 1,220 bales in 1860 to a peak of more than 16,000 bales in 1900. Perhaps more significant, however, was early interest in cotton processing. The first cotton gin in the county was built in the mid-1850s, and by 1885 there were twenty. During the Civil War John F. Torreyqv imported machinery and looms to manufacture cotton textiles and laid the foundation of the Comal County cotton industry of the twentieth century. At almost the same time, another New Braunfels industrialist, George Weber, established the first cottonseed press in the state. Local businessmen also moved rapidly from sheep herding to woolen textiles. Production of raw wool expanded from 621 pounds in 1850 to 72,000 pounds in 1890, and in 1867 a company for the manufacture of woolen products was organized in New Braunfels.

County population growth slowed after the rapid expansion of the 1850s; from 4,030 in 1860 it reached 8,824 in 1920. In these years cotton and wheat peaked and were supplanted in importance by oats and dairy products. Oat cultivation surpassed 200,000 bushels annually; production of milk approached a million gallons and that of butter neared 200,000 pounds before 1920. Corn culture[qv] and livestock remained important sources of income. Production of corn reached as much as 439,000 bushels annually in the years after World War I,[qv] while the number of cattle, though fluctuating widely, grew to an annual average of about 20,000 head in the twentieth century. Near the end of the nineteenth century goat ranching[qv] also became a significant part of the county economy; in the 1930 agricultural census goats outnumbered sheep 22,176 to 15,457.

As county agricultural production expanded, so too did the scale of industry. The value of county manufactures grew inconsistently until the 1890s, when it increased nearly tenfold to more than $950,000; it grew again almost fivefold by 1920. Although the value of manufactured products approached $5 million in 1920, the number of manufacturers fell after 1900 from sixty to twenty-nine. Improvements in transportation and in power generation allowed a shift toward larger industrial concerns and the expansion of production. By the turn of the century the International–Great Northern and Missouri, Kansas and Texas railroads had replaced the stagecoach and oxcart in the passenger and freight-hauling business and linked the county with state and national markets. At the same time electricity began to replace water and steam power in New Braunfels industry. By the 1920s Comal County had established itself as a manufacturing and shipping center for textiles, garments, flour, and construction materials.

After World War I Comal County farming declined relative to ranching. Though the number of livestock, particularly cattle, sheep, goats, hogs, and poultry, remained relatively constant until 1960, production of the primary commercial crops of the nineteenth century, corn, cotton, and oats, fell in most decades after 1920. The agricultural censuses indicate that cotton cultivation ceased altogether in the 1950s. From a peak in 1920 of 439,182 bushels, corn production fell to slightly more than 60,000 bushels by 1970. The oat harvest in the same period dropped from 217,160 bushels to 40,814 bushels, while the number of cattle, goats and sheep, and poultry increased in most censuses through 1950. That year county ranchers raised 20,000 cattle, almost 60,000 sheep and goats, and 62,938 chickens, turkeys, and other barnyard fowl. By the end of the decade the number of goats alone surpassed 50,000.

By mid-century mixed stock raising and the production of hay and feed grains, particularly sorghum, supplanted the commercially important crops of the nineteenth century as the basis of Comal County's agricultural economy. After hybrid seeds became widely available in the 1950s, the yield from sorghum culture[qv] leapt from 3,958 bushels in 1940 to almost 250,000 bushels in 1969. Except during the decade of the Great Depression,[qv] the value of county farms and ranches rose steadily in the twentieth century, but the variety and number of agricultural enterprises in the area declined just as consistently. From a high of 899 in 1910, the number of Comal County farms dropped to 584 in the early 1980s; the bulk of agricultural income was increasingly concentrated in livestock and its products. In 1968 cash receipts from crops amounted to $385,000; that derived from livestock exceeded $2.6 million. That ratio held steady through the following decade; in 1985 cattle, goats, sheep, and poultry generated roughly 85 percent of the county's $8 million agricultural income.

As the diversified farms and ranches of the original Comal County agriculturalists gave way to the livestock economy of the twentieth century, local industrialists were increasing the scope and the scale of county manufactures. By 1982 fifty manufacturers, employing almost 30 percent of the county labor force, had a gross product of more than $188 million. The production of such construction materials as gravel, sand, limestone, crushed stone, and concrete, in addition to the manufacture of textiles and clothing and the milling of wheat and corn were still the mainstays of the industrial sector and accounted for much of its expansion. Metal and wood work and food processing also became important industries.

The county grew rapidly after World War II[qv] and boomed after 1970. From 16,357 residents in 1950, the population expanded by 21 percent in the subsequent decade and by the same amount in the 1960s, reaching 24,165 by 1970. In 1980 the figure was 36,446—a 50 percent increase from the previous census.

The emergence of tourism as a primary industry, as well as attendant increases in retail and service employment, explains much of the population growth. The county is located in the "corridor" along Interstate Highway 35 between San Antonio and Austin and in 1973 was included in the San Antonio Metropolitan Statistical Area. Between 1970 and 1984 the number of residents employed in trade nearly doubled, to 2,287; the number of jobs in service industries increased more than 600 percent, to 1,977; and employment in financial, insurance, and real estate businesses rose 400 percent.

Since its impoundment in 1964, Canyon Lake has transformed a rural stretch of the Guadalupe River valley in northern Comal County into one of the largest rural population centers in Central Texas. By 1984 more than eighty subdivisions had been built on the shores of the lake and in the hills surrounding it; the number of permanent residents is estimated at 12,000 to 15,000. The area is especially popular with retired people. Canyon Lake and the scenic river valley below the dam have also served as the focal point for revitalization of a tourist industry in the county that dates to the early years of the century, when the International–Great Northern Railroad promoted New Braunfels as a tourist destination for San Antonians. Capitalizing on the natural and historic attractions offered by the Guadalupe River, by Natural Bridge Caverns,[qv] and by the county's German heritage, tourism in the mid-1980s supported some thirty hotels and motels, as well as resort condominiums, around New Braunfels and Canyon Lake.

Comal County was founded and initially populated under the sponsorship of the Association for the Protection of German Immigrants in Texas. The county was perhaps one-half German-born in the 1850s. The influx of Americans from the old South and border states in subsequent years diluted the Germans' early predominance, and by 1890 only about one in five county residents was a native German. When the children of German immigrants are included in the 1890 figure, however, German stock still comprised roughly 75 percent of the county population. The flow of German immigrants dwindled after the Civil War, and by 1940 only 1.6 percent of county residents were native Germans; but their influence on the social and cultural life of the area endured. The first newspaper in the county, the *Neu Braunfelser Zeitung* (later the New Braunfels *Herald-Zeitung*[qv]), was published exclusively in German until after World War II. Social clubs and an annual celebration of the county's German heritage, the Wurstfest (begun in the 1960s), have also served to maintain the ethnic identity and cultural legacy of the original settlers. With the exception of Mexican immigrants, no other single foreign nationality settled in significant numbers in the area. Mexican immigration peaked during the period of the Mexican Revolution.[qv] The 1930 census recorded 3,662 ethnic Mexicans in the county, or 30.5 percent of the total population. Though there were nearly twice as many Hispanic-surnamed residents when they were next recorded in 1970, their number did not grow as quickly as the population of the county as a whole. By 1980, when 8,728 Mexican Americans[qv] were counted, they made up 24 percent of the county population. The 1860 census recorded only 193 African Americans^{qv} in Comal County, and in 1870, when blacks constituted 31 percent of the state population, they made up just 7.1 percent of the county total. By 1980 blacks constituted barely 1 percent of the area population.

Within the context of the state's historic loyalty to the Democratic party,^{qv} Comal County voters have been a remarkably independent lot. The county's antebellum voting record was unexceptional; in the four presidential elections in which it participated before secession, Comal County registered a nearly unanimous vote in line with the statewide majority. It voted Democratic in the first post–Civil War presidential vote in Texas, but produced solid Republican majorities in the next three elections. In 1888 and 1892 it supported the Democratic candidate. The county opted for the Republican Warren Harding in 1920, but by 1924 must have felt disowned by both major parties. Seventy-four percent of Comal County voters rejected both the Republican and Democratic nominees for Progressive leader Robert La Follette. Four years later, perhaps with prohibition^{qv} uppermost in voters' minds, the county returned to the Democratic fold (four years earlier than the state as a whole), where they remained through the worst years of the Great Depression. In 1940, when Texans voted by more than four to one to return Franklin D. Roosevelt to the White House, Comal County reverted to Republicanism. From 1940 through 1992 it has voted Democratic in only one presidential election, that of Lyndon B. Johnson^{qv} in 1964.

The influx of new residents as well as the expansion and transformation of the job market after 1970 dramatically improved the average educational level of citizens. In 1950 just 20 percent of the population over the age of twenty-five had completed high school. Steady improvement before 1970 raised that figure to 35 percent. In 1980, 60 percent of residents over twenty-five were high school graduates. The shift from an agricultural economy to one based on industry and tourism is reflected in the proportional growth of New Braunfels. In 1900 the city's 2,097 people made up less than 30 percent of the county's residents. In 1990 the 27,334 inhabitants were more than half the county population of 51,832.

BIBLIOGRAPHY: Rudolph Biesele, "Early Times in New Braunfels and Comal County," *Southwestern Historical Quarterly* 50 (July 1946). Edgar R. Dabney, The Settlement of New Braunfels and the History of Its Earlier Schools (M.A. thesis, University of Texas, 1927). Oscar Haas, *History of New Braunfels and Comal County, Texas, 1844–1946* (Austin: Steck, 1968). Terry G. Jordan, *German Seed in Texas Soil: Immigrant Farmers in Nineteenth-Century Texas* (Austin: University of Texas Press, 1966). Lillian Penshorn, A History of Comal County (M.A. thesis, Southwest Texas State Teachers College, 1950). Vertical Files, Barker Texas History Center, University of Texas at Austin (New Braunfels, Comal County). *Daniel P. Greene*

COMAL CREEK SETTLEMENT, TEXAS. Comal Creek Settlement, the second community established in Comal County, was begun in 1845 by settlers from New Braunfels. The pioneers raised grain and vegetables and grazed their cattle on the unfenced lands around the settlement. In 1856 the Comal Creek school had thirty-five tuition pupils and seven poor and orphan pupils. By 1948 the school was a part of the New Braunfels system, and the community had been incorporated into the city of New Braunfels. *Oscar Haas*

COMAL RIVER. The Comal River, said to be the shortest river in the United States, rises in a number of large springs in New Braunfels in southeastern Comal County (at 29°43′ N, 98°08′ W) and flows southeast for three miles to its mouth on the Guadalupe River, also in New Braunfels (at 29°42′ N, 98°07′ W). It has a number of small islands in its upper reaches, and its course crosses an area of the Balcones Escarpment characterized by low relief surfaces and moderately deep to deep sandy and clay loam soils that support live oak and Ashe juniper woods. Most of the land around the river has been developed by the city of New Braunfels or has been converted to cropland. The Comal was called the Guadalupe by some early Spanish explorers, two of whom, Domingo Ramón and the Marqués de San Miguel de Aguayo,^{qqv} knew the river in its lower regions. The name Guadalupe was still used as late as 1727, but after Pedro de Rivera y Villalón^{qv} identified the longer stream as the Guadalupe, the shorter was given the name Comal, Spanish for "flat dish," for the landscape along the riverbed. The abundant and reliable flow of the Comal provided power for the early industry of New Braunfels—gristmills and sawmills as well as flour and textile mills. With the development of alternative sources of power after 1900, much of the property along the banks of the river was converted to municipal parkland, including Landa Park^{qv} and Prince Solms Park.

Mary H. Ogilvie and Daniel P. Greene

COMAL SPRINGS. The Comal Springs, the largest group of natural springs in Texas, is on the northwestern edge of New Braunfels in southeastern Comal County (at 29°41′ N, 98°08′ W). After filtering through the Edwards and associated limestones, the springs' artesian flow issues from several fissures along the Comal Springs fault and feeds Landa Lake and the Comal River. In earlier centuries Tonkawas and other Indians camped near the springs. The Spanish explorer Damián Massanet^{qv} found a large group of Indians there when he visited the region in 1691. From 1756 to 1758 the springs were the site of a Spanish mission, Nuestra Señora de Guadalupe. In 1845 German settlers came to the area with Prince Carl of Solms-Braunfels^{qv} and called the springs Las Fontanas. The springs powered grist and saw mills in the 1860s, and a hydroelectric plant for New Braunfels from 1890 to 1950 and after 1978. Both Landa Lake and the Comal River continue to be popular recreation areas. The average flow from the springs between 1892 and 1978 has been estimated at 9,000 liters a second, but that flow and the variety of plant and animal life it supports are threatened by the falling level of the Edwards aquifer.

BIBLIOGRAPHY: Gunnar Brune, *Springs of Texas,* Vol. 1 (Fort Worth: Branch-Smith, 1981). Oscar Haas, *History of New Braunfels and Comal County, Texas, 1844–1946* (Austin: Steck, 1968). *Gunnar Brune*

COMAL TOWN, TEXAS. Comal Town, in eastern Comal County, retained its original name for more than 100 years, though since 1847 it has been part of New Braunfels, from which it is separated only by the Comal River. Settlement at the site began in 1846, when the husband of Maria A. Veramendi Garza began selling plots from the lands granted by Coahuila and Texas^{qv} to Juan Martín de Veramendi^{qv} in 1831. Comal Town maintained its own public school for some time after the settlement in 1847 became Ward Two of New Braunfels and in 1852 the second polling place for the town. The Comal Town school census of 1856 listed twenty-five tuition pupils and nineteen poor and orphan children. In 1947 the two Comal Town elementary schools were a part of the New Braunfels Independent School District.

Oscar Haas

COMAL UNION SCHOOL. On February 13, 1852, the Texas legislature granted the citizens of Comal Town, Comal County, a charter incorporating the German-American Union School, or Comal Union School. The school had six trustees, three German-speaking and three English-speaking. Both languages were taught. In 1864 the school was granted a portion of the taxes received by New Braunfels Academy.^{qv} The school continued for thirty years, progressing slowly because of competition from the academy, and finally became a New Braunfels ward school. In 1935, after being used as a school for black children for several years, the property was sold by the New Braunfels Independent School District to Mrs. Emma Schneider.

BIBLIOGRAPHY: Edgar R. Dabney, The Settlement of New Braunfels and the History of Its Earlier Schools (M.A. thesis, University of Texas,

1927). Hans Peter Nielsen Gammel, comp., *Laws of Texas, 1822–1897* (10 vols., Austin: Gammel, 1898).

COMANCHE, TEXAS. Comanche is located in the central part of Comanche County on U.S. highways 67 and 377. It was established in 1858, when John Duncan offered the county 240 acres on Indian Creek as a site for a county seat. The commissioners' court accepted the donation, and Ransom Tuggle was authorized to lay out the townsite. T. J. Nabors built the first house. The new town replaced Cora as county seat in May 1859. The first courthouse was a "picket house"—a structure of logs cut and split on the ground, set vertically in a ditch, and covered with boards also made on the ground. A post office was established in 1860. A newspaper, the Comanche *Chief*, began publication in 1873. The town, a supply base for Texas ranches during its early history, was incorporated in 1873. By 1892 Comanche had 2,500 residents, the Fort Worth and Rio Grande Railway, a daily stage, and numerous businesses. By 1915 the population was 4,500, and the town was a flourishing farm-market center and transportation center. By the close of World War II qv the population had grown to approximately 4,000. In 1945 a cheese plant, pecan and peanut shelling plants, granaries, and wool and mohair concerns were the chief businesses. The population was 3,832 in 1950. The city swimming pool was completed in 1953. The public library was established in 1960. That year, Comanche had a population of 3,415. In 1970 the town had a population of 3,933 and 108 businesses, mainly concerned with the marketing and processing of peanuts, fruits, and livestock. Industries produced camping trailers, air-conditioners, feeds, peanut products, and leather goods. The town has a county airport, two hospitals, several nursing homes, and a home for handicapped children. The construction of Procter Reservoir qv made possible a new water system. After 1970 a fairgrounds and high school were built. Also located in the city is the Comanche County Historic Museum, which attracts many visitors. A park is located three miles south of Comanche at Lake Eanes.qv In 1980–81 the town had 132 businesses and a population of 3,888. In 1990 the businesses numbered 105 and the residents 4,087.

BIBLIOGRAPHY: Comanche County Bicentennial Committee, *Patchwork of Memories: Historical Sketches of Comanche County, Texas* (Brownwood, Texas: Banner Printing, 1976). Vertical Files, Barker Texas History Center, University of Texas at Austin.

J. R. Eanes and Jeanne F. Lively

COMANCHE COUNTY. Comanche County (F-15), in central Texas, is bounded on the south by Mills County, on the west by Brown County, on the north by Eastland County and on the east by Hamilton and Eastland counties. The county is named for the Comanche Indians, whose territory once included the area. Comanche County covers 944 square miles of rolling land with elevations from 650 to 1,700 feet. The center of the county lies at 31°55′ north latitude and 98°40′ west longitude; the county seat, Comanche, is located about seventy miles southeast of Abilene. The area is drained by the North and South Leon rivers and their tributaries, which in turn flow into the Brazos River system. The northern part of the county is in the Western Cross Timbers region, which is characterized by light sand and loamy soils that support mixed timber of cedars, oaks, mesquites, and pecans. Southern Comanche County forms part of the southern edge of the Grand Prairie region and has dark waxy and dark loam soils. The county has a 238-day growing season and an average annual rainfall of 18.45 inches. In 1982 there were 1,350 farms in Comanche that produced a variety of agricultural products. Peanuts, pecans, grains, and hay account for about 40 percent of the county's $69 million annual agricultural income, while beef, dairy cattle, swine, sheep, and goats account for the remainder. The average minimum temperature in January is 32° F; the average maximum in July is 95°.

The area that is now Comanche County was dominated from the eighteenth to the mid-nineteenth centuries by the Comanche Indians. The Comanches' culture was well adapted to their life on the plains. Unlike some Indian tribes they organized raids and buffalo hunts without a tribal military society, but with a responsible hunt leader chosen as coordinator. Their prey included buffalo, elk, mustangs,qv longhorn cattle,qv and black bears of the Cross Timbers region; the last they used for their oil. They did not eat fish, wildfowl, dogs, or coyotes unless they were severely pressed for food. Comanches sheltered in the common plains type of tepee, made of tanned buffalo hides, standing twelve to fourteen feet high and resting on a framework of sixteen to eighteen poles. The entry was usually covered with a bearskin, and a flap at the peak vented smoke from winter fires.

White settlement in the area began with a colony organized by Jesse Mercer and others in 1854 on lands earlier granted by Mexico to Stephen F. Austin and Samuel May Williams.qqv F. M. Collier built the first log house in the county in 1855, and in 1856 the Texas legislature formed Comanche County from Coryell and Bosque counties; Cora was designated as the county seat. In 1859 the more centrally located town of Comanche became county seat. By 1860 the United States census counted 709 people living in the county; farming and ranching occupied 24,730 acres, about 1,880 acres of which was classified as "improved." Twenty-five residents owned slaves, but there were no large-scale plantations in the area. The population included only sixty-one slaves, and only two of the county residents owned as many as eight bondsmen; most of the slaveholders owned only one. Cattle ranching was by far the most important economic activity in Comanche County at that time, and over 14,700 head of cattle were counted in the area that year. Wheat and corn were the county's most important crops on the eve of the Civil War; only one bale of cotton was produced in the county in 1860.

The withdrawal of the United States Army during the Civil War qv left the settlers without protection and even without livestock after Indian raids. Home-guard companies were organized for defense, but many settlers fled and the white population shrank to about sixty by 1866.

With the war's end, military protection returned, and settlers were once more attracted to the county, many to participate in a range cattle boom. By 1870 the county had 126 farms and ranches, encompassing about 17,500 acres, and the population had increased to 1,001. By the 1870s the town of Comanche had become the political center for some fifty counties, both organized and unorganized, to the west and northwest. The Comanche *Chief*, which began to be published in 1873, was for some years the only newspaper in this part of Texas.

The people worked for economic and social stability and were impatient with outlaws. When the notorious John Wesley Hardin qv killed Brown County deputy sheriff Charlie Webb in Comanche in 1874 many local citizens resented Hardin's escape. In misguided retaliation, a mob of 300 residents of Brown and Comanche counties stormed the county jail where Joe Hardin (brother of the outlaw) and two of the outlaw's associates were being held. The three prisoners were lynched. Some months later John Hardin was arrested in Florida, tried for murder in Comanche, and sentenced to twenty-five years in prison.

By 1880 Comanche County had 1,985 farms and ranches that encompassed 190,482 acres. Ranching had expanded since the Civil War, and over 21,000 cattle, and 2,925 sheep were counted in Comanche that year. Farming had also markedly increased; the county's farms included 48,550 acres of improved land on which grains and cotton were produced. Over 14,200 acres were devoted to corn, the county's most important crop at that time, while cotton was grown on 9,301 acres that produced 2,098 bales.

As the economy of the area rapidly developed in the 1870s, its population increased almost eightfold, and by 1880, 8,608 people lived in Comanche county, including seventy-nine blacks. Agriculture was further encouraged in 1881 when the Texas Central Railroad began service in Comanche County and started carrying cattle and cotton to market. That many of the county's settlers came from

Southern states may have been a contributory factor to racial tensions that emerged in the 1880s. Amid economically desperate times and political unrest in 1886, the second occasion on which a black murdered whites resulted in all the black people being driven from the county by vigilantes. They have not returned in any number.

Between 1880 and 1900 the county's economy continued to grow rapidly despite periodic droughts, the savage winter of 1885–86, and the nationwide economic crisis that began in 1893. The number of farms and ranches in the area rose to 1,985 by 1890; by 1900 the 3,548 farms and ranches encompassed 522,273 acres. Almost 167,500 acres of farmland was classified as improved; on it farmers grew mostly cereals and cotton. Cotton had come to be the single most important crop in the county by 1890, when almost 35,000 acres of Comanche County land was devoted to the fiber. In 1900 the county planted more than 88,700 acres in cotton and produced 24,224 commercial bales.

Meanwhile, ranching continued to be crucial to the local economy, as more than 47,000 cattle were counted in 1890 and about 43,000 in 1900. More than 15,000 sheep were also found in the county in 1890, though the number of herds declined to only about 3,800 by 1900. Population growth during the last two decades of the nineteenth century reflected the economic development that took place during that period. The census enumerated 15,679 people in Comanche County in 1890 and 23,009 in 1900. The county's continued economic growth did not by any means inoculate local farmers against the many problems afflicting American farmers during the late nineteenth century, however, and in fact the People's (or Populist) party qv grew powerful in Comanche County politics during the 1890s; in the 1898 election, the Populist slate won a number of county offices.

Expansion of cotton farming had been responsible for much of the county's growth during the late nineteenth century. But the local economy was severely damaged between 1900 and 1930, after the boll weevil qv plague entered the area in the early twentieth century and killed the cotton boom. The infestation devastated cotton crops and helped to drive a third of Comanche County farmers out of business between 1910 and 1925. Land devoted to cotton production in the county dropped from almost 89,000 acres in 1900 to only 39,000 acres in 1910, and never again came near the peak production of earlier years. Meanwhile, the number of farms in the county dropped from 4,372 in 1910 to 3,015 in 1920 and to only 2,746 in 1925. The population of the county dropped accordingly from 27,186 in 1910 to 25,748 in 1920 and to 18,748 in 1930.

Some of the impact of the boll weevil was offset by the efforts of local farmers to diversify their production during the early twentieth century. An experimental crop of peanuts planted in 1907, for example, paved the way for the county's longtime leadership in peanut products. Local farmers also planted tens of thousands of fruit trees (mostly peaches) during this period; by 1920 more than 70,000 fruit trees were growing in the county. Poultry products also became a significant part of the local economy; by 1920, over 140,000 chickens were counted in the county, and in 1930 more than 672,000 dozens of eggs were sold by the county's farmers. Meanwhile, ranching and the dairy industry qqv remained strong. By 1930 the county had 28,000 cattle, not including almost 6,500 milk cows.

The discovery of oil at Desdemona in southeastern Eastland County in 1918 also helped to offset the worst effects of the boll weevil in Comanche County (see RANGER, DESDEMONA, AND BRECKENRIDGE OILFIELDS). Oil drillers moved into northern Comanche in the wake of the Eastland County discoveries and brought in wells at Sipe Springs, Sidney, Comyn, and Proctor; De Leon became an important supply center to the oilfields. The peak year for the Comanche County oil boom was 1920, when production was 328,098 barrels. The shallow wells at Sipe Springs were soon depleted, however, and the boom lasted only until 1924. Production continued at lower levels into the 1930s and beyond. In 1938, for example, the county produced about 22,000 barrels.

Local farmers suffered during the 1930s through the effects of the Great Depression and the Dust Bowl; qqv many recalled watching helplessly as the soil from their holdings blew away. Cropland harvested in the county dropped from 188,606 acres in 1929 to 153,604 in 1940. Nevertheless, perhaps because of the previous damage done to the local economy by the boll weevil infestation, Comanche County farmers were able to make their way through the thirties more successfully than farmers in many other counties in the state; in fact, the number of farms in the county actually grew slightly during this period, from 2,768 in 1920 to 2,911 in 1940. The county population grew during this time from 18,430 to 19,245.

From the 1940s to the 1960s, however, the mechanization of agriculture combined with other factors (such as the droughts of the 1950s) to depopulate the area. The population declined to 15,516 in 1950 and 11,865 in 1960. During the 1960s, though, it began to rise slowly. In 1970 11,898 people lived in Comanche County; in 1980, 12,900; and in 1992, an estimated 13,381.

After the droughts of the 1950s action was taken to assure the county of a reliable water supply. Lack of rain encouraged rainmaking experiments in 1951 and 1952 with funds raised in the county, but the experiments did not improve the situation. A more meaningful answer to drought came in 1960 when federal funding became available for a reservoir on the Leon River. At a cost of $15 million a dam and flood-control system began operation in 1967 to protect 40,200 acres of farmland in the Leon River floodplain and store water in Proctor Reservoir qv for use in Comanche, De Leon, and other towns.

Oil wells in the county are still producing. The 1982 production of 90,000 barrels was valued at just under $2.5 million; in 1990, production was 30,820 barrels. By 1991, 5,764,906 barrels had been pumped from Comanche County lands since oil was first found in the county in 1918.

In the 1980s, agricultural production in the county was fairly well balanced between farming and ranching. The United States agricultural census of 1982 reported 88,993 cattle in the county and an income of $20,675,000 from the sale of dairy products. There were also 9,388 goats, 10,387 hogs, and 6,660 sheep in the county. Comanche County produced 129,305 bushels of sorghum, 95,234 bushels of wheat, and 37,910 bushels of corn. More than 45,546,000 pounds of peanuts was produced in the county in 1982, placing Comanche second in the state in peanut production. Farmers in the county also harvested 2,469 acres of vegetables that year.

Meanwhile, the county also profited from related agribusinesses, nut shelling, and food processing, while other manufacturing contributed a value of $12.9 million in 1980. These industries, a modest oil production, and ever-growing agriculture gave the county an aggregate income of over $100 million that year. Of this, some $8,556,000 came from the fifty-five businesses registered in the county.

The county population centers include Comanche (1992 estimated population: 4,087); De Leon, the county's marketing center for peanuts (2,190); and Gustine (430). Principal highways are U.S. 67 (northeast to southwest), State Highway 36 (northwest to southwest), and State 16 (north to south). Tourist attractions include a January livestock show, a rodeo in July, a peach and melon festival in August, and Proctor Reservoir, with its five attendant county parks. Among distinguished Comanche County residents was the famed geologist Robert T. Hill qv (1858–1941), whose early investigations of fossils on Round Mountain near Sidney began an outstanding career.

BIBLIOGRAPHY: Comanche County Bicentennial Committee, *Patchwork of Memories: Historical Sketches of Comanche County, Texas* (Brownwood, Texas: Banner Printing, 1976). Eulalia Nabers Wells, *Blazing the Way: Tales of Comanche County Pioneers* (Blanket, Texas, 1942).
John Leffler

COMANCHE CREEK (Bexar County). Comanche Creek rises near the junction of Interstate Highway 410 and State Highway 16 in southern Bexar County (at 29°19′ N, 98°33′ W) and runs southeast for four miles to its mouth on Leon Creek, 1½ miles northwest of Cassin (at 29°16′ N, 98°31′ W). It traverses rolling terrain surfaced by clay loams that support mesquite and grasses.

_____ (Blanco County). Comanche Creek rises in rugged Hill Country[qv] terrain two miles south of Blowout in far northwestern Blanco County (at 30°25′ N, 98°34′ W) and runs north for 11½ miles to its mouth on Sandy Creek in southeastern Llano County (at 30°32′ N, 98°32′ W). It runs over the southeastern reaches of the Llano Uplift. The area is characterized by large outcroppings of exposed granite and numerous boulders interspersed with live oak, post oak, and short wild grasses. For long stretches the creekbed runs over bare rock and tumbled stones that form many small waterfalls. For thousands of years this area has been inhabited—in more recent centuries by Coahuiltecans, Tonkawas, Apaches, and Comanches. The earliest permanent settlement of the area was at Blowout.

_____ (Mason County). Comanche Creek rises a half mile southwest of Mason Mountain in north central Mason County (at 30°51′ N, 99°15′ W) and runs southeast for twenty miles, passing through Mason, to its mouth on the Llano River, southeast of Mason (at 30°39′ N, 99°08′ W). The creek rises in the limestone hills on the eastern edge of the Edwards Plateau and crosses rolling to steep terrain surfaced by shallow, stony and clayey soils, broken by an area of low-rolling to flat terrain surfaced by deeper loamy and clayey soils that support grasses and open stands of live oak, mesquite, and Ashe juniper. In the mid-1850s a stage line running from San Antonio to El Paso crossed the creek 120 miles from San Antonio. Comanche Indians reportedly often lay in ambush for the stagecoaches in the hills along the stream. Fort Mason was built in 1851 on one of the hills overlooking Comanche Creek, and a spring that runs down the hillside into the creek supplied the fort with water. In those days the creek had many deep pools and was a popular fishing spot. By 1928, however, it had become a generally dry watercourse with a sandy bottom.

BIBLIOGRAPHY: J. E. Grinstead, "Mason County, Texas," *Grinstead's Graphic,* August 1923. J. Marvin Hunter, "Brief History of Mason County," *Frontier Times,* November, December 1928; January, February, March 1929.

_____ (Maverick County). Comanche Creek rises a mile north of Farm Road 2644 and eight miles east of El Indio in southeastern Maverick County (at 28°30′ N, 100°11′ W) and runs northeast for thirty-three miles, passing through Rocky and Fishhook lakes, to its mouth on Comanche Lake, four miles west of Crystal City in southwest central Zavala County (at 28°41′ N, 99°54′ W). The creek is dammed to form Comanche Lake just west of Crystal City. The stream rises in flat terrain with locally shallow depressions, then in its lower reaches enters flat to rolling terrain with local scarps. Soils throughout the creek's course are expansive clays and support water-tolerant hardwoods, conifers, and grasses, interspersed in the creek's lower reaches with hardwood forest and some scrub brush.

_____ (Pecos County). Comanche Creek rises at Comanche Springs in Fort Stockton in central Pecos County (at 30°53′ N, 102°53′ W) and runs northeast for forty-three miles to its mouth on the Pecos River, three miles north of Girvin (at 31°06′ N, 102°24′ W). It crosses steep to rolling terrain surfaced by clay and sandy loams that support creosote bush, tarbush, mesquite, and juniper brush.

COMANCHE INDIAN RESERVATION. The Texas legislature passed a law on February 6, 1854, that established the Brazos Indian Reservation[qv] for the Caddos, Wacos, and other Indians, and also provided four square leagues of land, or 18,576 acres, for a Comanche reserve to be located at Camp Cooper on the Clear Fork of the Brazos in Throckmorton County. In compliance with the treaty of August 30, 1855, about 450 of the Penateka or southern Comanches settled on the reservation and were to be taught farming. The location had good hunting and water and had been selected by Maj. Robert S. Neighbors.[qv] The principal Indian village, established in a bend of the river, consisted of several hundred Indians and their chief, Ketumse, who lived there with his wives and many children.

Until the arrival of troops of the Second United States Cavalry,[qv] the Comanches were restive and difficult to control, but thereafter they acceded to the suggestion of Indian agent John R. Baylor[qv] to begin their farming effort. Baylor sent a farmer and laborer to assist them, and the first crops were planted—corn, melons, beans, peas, pumpkins, and other vegetables. The Comanches cultivated the crops remarkably well, but extreme drought kept them from producing all they needed.

A number of other factors prevented the Comanche reservation from being as successful as the one on the Brazos: the Kickapoos and northern Comanche bands raided the settlements, and the reservation Indians received the blame; the Penateka band itself was divided, Chief Sanaco leading away from the reservation a larger group than that which remained under Chief Ketumse; the reservation was too near the old Comanche trails to Mexico and to the west, and loiterers and troublemakers intruded from those trails; the reservation Indians left the reservation on hunting expeditions or to join marauding bands; unprincipled traders sold whiskey to the Comanches; the Indians were inadequately protected by federal troops, largely infantry untrained in Indian warfare; state troops were slow to intervene when federal aid was insufficient; and white settlers were hostile to the Indians.

On March 29, 1858, therefore, Major Neighbors recommended the abandonment of the Comanche reservation (as well as the Brazos reservation) and removal of the Indians to Indian Territory. Orders for their complete removal were issued on June 11, 1859. The two groups were consolidated at the Red River, and on September 1 Neighbors delivered them to agency officials in Indian Territory.

BIBLIOGRAPHY: George D. Harmon, "The United States Indian Policy in Texas, 1845–1860," *Mississippi Valley Historical Review* 17 (1930). Lena Clara Koch, "The Federal Indian Policy in Texas, 1845–1860," *Southwestern Historical Quarterly* 28 (January, April 1925). Kenneth F. Neighbours, *Indian Exodus: Texas Indian Affairs, 1835–1859* (San Antonio: Nortex, 1973). Virginia Pink No'l, The United States Indian Reservations in Texas, 1854–1859 (M.A. thesis, University of Texas, 1924).

W. E. S. Dickerson

COMANCHE INDIANS. The Comanches, exceptional horsemen who dominated the Southern Plains, played a prominent role in Texas frontier history throughout much of the eighteenth and nineteenth centuries. Anthropological evidence indicates that they were originally a mountain tribe, a branch of the Northern Shoshones, who roamed the Great Basin region of the western United States as crudely equipped hunters and gatherers. Both cultural and linguistic similarities confirm the Comanches' Shoshone origins. The Comanche language is derived from the Uto-Aztecan linguistic family and is virtually identical to the language of the Northern Shoshones. Sometime during the late seventeenth century, the Comanches acquired horses, and that acquisition drastically altered their culture. The life of the pedestrian tribe was revolutionized as they rapidly evolved into a mounted, well-equipped, and powerful people. Their new mobility allowed them to leave their mountain home and their Shoshone neighbors and move onto the plains of eastern Colorado and western Kansas, where game was plentiful. After their arrival on the Great Plains, the Comanches began a southern migration that was encouraged by a combination of factors. By moving south, they had greater access to the mustangs[qv] of the Southwest. The warm climate and abundant buffalo[qv] were additional incentives for the southern migration. The move also facilitated the acquisition of French trade goods, including firearms, through barter with the Wichita Indians on the Red River. Pressure from more powerful and better-armed tribes to their north and east, principally the Blackfoot and Crow Indians, also encouraged their migration. A vast area of the South Plains, including much of North, Central, and West Texas, soon became Comanche country, or Comanchería. Only after their arrival on the Southern Plains did the tribe come to be known as Comanches, a name derived from the Ute word Kumántcia, meaning "enemy," or, literally, "anyone who wants to fight me all the time." The Spaniards in New Mexico, who came into contact with the Comanches in the early eighteenth century, gave the tribe the name by which they were later known to Spaniards and Americans alike. Although the tribe came to be known historically as Comanches, they called themselves Nermernuh, or "the People."

The Comanches did not arrive on the South Plains as a unified body but rather in numerous family groups or bands. The band structure of Comanche society was not rigid, and bands coalesced and broke apart, depending on the needs and goals of their members. As many as thirteen different Comanche bands were identified during the historic period, and most probably there were others that were never identified. However, five major bands played important roles in recorded Comanche history. The southernmost band was called Penateka, or "Honey Eaters." Their range extended from the Edwards Plateau qv to the headwaters of the Central Texas rivers. Because of their location, the Penatekas played the most prominent role in Texas history. North of Penateka country was the habitat of the band called Nokoni, or "Those Who Turn Back." The Nokonis roamed from the Cross Timbers qv region of North Texas to the mountains of New Mexico. Two smaller bands, the Tanima ("Liver-Eaters") and the Tenawa ("Those Who Stay Downstream"), shared the range of the Nokonis. These three divisions are sometimes referred to collectively as Middle Comanches. Still farther north was the range of the Kotsotekas, or "Buffalo-Eaters." Their territory covered what is now western Oklahoma, where they often camped along the Canadian River. The northernmost band was known as the Yamparikas, or "Yap-Eaters," a name derived from that of an edible root. Their range extended north to the Arkansas River. The fifth major band, known as Quahadis ("Antelopes"), roamed the high plains of the Llano Estacado.qv

The Comanches remained a nomadic people throughout their free existence. Buffalo, their lifeblood, provided food, clothing, and shelter. Their predominantly meat diet was supplemented with wild roots, fruits, and nuts, or with produce obtained by trade with neighboring agricultural tribes, principally the Wichita and Caddo groups to the east and the Pueblo tribes to the west. Because of their skills as traders, the Comanches controlled much of the commerce of the Southern Plains. They bartered buffalo products, horses, and captives for manufactured items and foodstuffs. The familiar Plains-type tepee constructed of tanned buffalo hide stretched over sixteen to eighteen lodge poles provided portable shelter for the Comanches. Their clothing, made of bison hide or buckskin, consisted of breechclout, leggings, and moccasins for men, and fringed skirt, poncho-style blouse, leggings, and moccasins for women. Buffalo robes provided protection from cold weather.

But it was the horse that most clearly defined the Comanche way of life. It gave them mobility to follow the buffalo herds and the advantage of hunting and conducting warfare from horseback. Horses also became a measure of Comanche wealth and a valuable trade commodity. In horsemanship the Comanches had no equal. Children learned to ride at an early age, and both men and women developed exceptional equestrian skills.

Democratic principle was strongly implanted in Comanche political organization. Each tribal division had both civil or peace chiefs and war chiefs, but traditionally the head civil chief was most influential. Leaders gained their positions through special abilities or prowess, and retained their power only so long as they maintained the confidence of band members, who chose their leaders by common consent. Tribal decisions were made by a council of chiefs presided over by the head civil chief, but individuals were not bound to accept council decisions. Comanche society permitted great individual freedom, and that autonomy greatly complicated relations with European cultures.

By the early eighteenth century, Comanche bands had migrated into what is now North Texas. In 1706 Spanish officials in New Mexico documented the presence of numerous Comanches on the northeastern frontier of that province. As the Comanches moved south, they came into conflict with tribes already living on the South Plains, particularly the Apaches, who had dominated the region before the arrival of the Comanches. The Apaches were forced south by the Comanche onslaught and became their mortal enemies. The first documented evidence of Comanches in Texas occurred in 1743, when a small band, probably a scouting party, appeared at the Spanish settlement of San Antonio seeking their enemies, the Lipan Apaches. No hostilities occurred, but it was obvious that the Comanches believed that the Spanish and Apaches were allies. However, fifteen years passed before the Spanish learned the true strength of Comanche presence in Texas. In 1758 a force of some 2,000 Comanches and allied tribes attacked a Spanish mission built for the Apaches on the San Saba River near present Menard. Santa Cruz de San Sabá Mission was sacked and burned, and eight of its inhabitants, including two priests, were killed. A year later, a Spanish punitive expedition led by Col. Diego Ortiz Parrilla qv also met defeat at the hands of the Comanches and their allies in a daylong battle on the Red River near the site of present Spanish Fort.

By the mid-eighteenth century, the armed and mounted Comanches had become a formidable force in Texas. Spanish officials, lacking the resources to defeat them militarily, decided to pursue peace with the Comanches. A peace policy that utilized trade and gifts to promote friendship and authorized military force only to punish specific acts of aggression was inaugurated and remained in effect, with varying degrees of success, for the remainder of Spanish rule in Texas. The first success of the new Spanish policy came in 1762, when Fray José Calahorra y Saenz qv negotiated a treaty with the Comanches, who agreed not to make war on missionized Apaches. Continued Apache aggression made it impossible for the Comanches to keep their promise, and ultimately led Spanish officials to advocate a Spanish-Comanche alliance aimed at exterminating the Apaches. That policy was officially implemented in 1772, and with the help of Athanase de Mézières,qv a French trader serving as Spanish diplomat, a second treaty was signed with the Comanches. The Comanche chief Povea signed the treaty in 1772 at San Antonio, thereby committing his band to peace with the Spaniards. Other bands, however, continued to raid Spanish settlements. Comanche attacks escalated in the early 1780s, and Spanish officials feared the province of Texas would be lost. To avoid that possibility, the governor of Texas, Domingo Cabello y Robles,qv was instructed to negotiate peace with the warring Comanches. He dispatched Pedro Vial qv and Francisco Xavier de Chaves to Comanchería with gifts and proposals for peace. The mission was successful, and the emissaries returned to San Antonio with three principal Comanche chiefs who were authorized by their people to make peace with the Spanish. The result was the Spanish-Comanche Treaty of 1785, a document that Comanches honored, with only minor violations, until the end of the century. As Spanish power waned in the early years of the nineteenth century, officials were unable to supply promised gifts and trade goods, and Comanche aggression once again became commonplace. Comanches raided Spanish settlements for horses to trade to Anglo-American traders entering Texas from the United States. Those Americans furnished the Comanches with trade goods, including arms and ammunition, and provided a thriving market for Comanche horses.

In 1821 Mexico won independence from Spain, but the change of government had little impact in Comanchería. Though Mexican authorities in Texas continued the Spanish policy of pursuing peace with the Comanches, the unstable government in Mexico City failed to provide the resources necessary to accomplish the job with any permanence. Comanches continued to dominate much of Texas, both in trade and warfare. In the late 1820s several principal chiefs, including Paruaquibitse, Yncoroy, and Yzazona, established a tenuous peace with Mexican officials—possibly because of pressure from Osage Indians and other hostile tribes on their north. However, when two of the major peace chiefs died in the early 1830s, Comanche-

Mexican relations deteriorated once again, and Mexican officials began encouraging Shawnees, Cherokees, and other tribes to make war on the Comanches. The Mexican Colonization Law of 1824 encouraged foreign immigration to Texas, and settlers from the United States poured into the province. As the Anglo-American population grew, relations between Americans and Comanches began to deteriorate. The amity that had developed through mutually beneficial trade quickly disintegrated when the newly arrived Texans began surveying land that Comanches considered their traditional hunting ground, and the two soon became implacable enemies.

When Texans won their independence from Mexico in 1836 the Comanches and their allies were still in absolute control of the Texas plains. They frequently conducted raids on frontier settlements from San Antonio to northern Mexico. In May 1836 a particularly destructive raid occurred at Fort Parker, a settlement of some thirty-four persons near the Navasota River in the future Limestone County. Comanches and their Kiowa allies attacked the blockhouse, killed several settlers, and took five hostages, including nine-year-old Cynthia Ann Parker,qv who lived with the Comanches for twenty-four years. Parker became the wife of Chief Peta Nocona qv and the mother of Quanah Parker,qv the last great Comanche chief. In an effort to stop Comanche destruction on the Texas frontier, Sam Houston,qv first duly elected president of the Republic of Texas,qv instituted a policy aimed at establishing peace and friendship through commerce. Houston's peace efforts were hampered because the Texas Congress refused to agree to the one Comanche requirement for peace—a boundary line between Texas and Comanchería. Peace commissioners did succeed in negotiating a treaty with a band of Penateka Comanches led by Muguara, Muestyah, and Muhy, but the treaty was never ratified by the Texas Senate. When Houston left office in late 1838, Texan-Comanche relations were rapidly deteriorating and depredations were being committed by both sides.

Mirabeau B. Lamar,qv who succeeded Houston as president, abandoned the peace policy, which he considered a failure, in favor of waging war on the Comanche nation. Lamar's policy culminated in the Council House Fight,qv a tragic incident that occurred in San Antonio in the spring of 1840 when Texas officials attempted to arrest a Comanche peace delegation. Fighting broke out, and thirty-five Comanches, including twelve chiefs, were killed. The remaining thirty Comanches, primarily women and children, were imprisoned by the Texans. Seven Texans were also killed in the melee, and eight were wounded. But the violence was not over. In late summer Comanches launched a retaliatory raid. More than 500 warriors led by Buffalo Hump qv made a sweep through south Texas, devastating the towns of Victoria and Linnville and killing twenty-five Texans. After the Linnville raid of 1840,qv as the Comanches made their escape to the north, they were intercepted at Plum Creek near the site of present Lockhart and routed by Texan forces. Though some fifty Comanches were killed in the battle of Plum Creek,qv the Texans continued to seek retribution. In October an expedition under the command of Col. John H. Mooreqv traveled 300 miles up the Colorado River and destroyed a Comanche encampment near the site of present Colorado City. Having suffered a tremendous loss of leadership and manpower, the Penatekas moved beyond the Red River and out of the range of Texas forces. Lamar's policy had succeeded in removing the Comanches from the borders of Texas, but at a terrible cost to both sides.

In 1841 Sam Houston again became president of the republic and almost immediately reinstated his peace policy. Emissaries were sent to inform the various Indian groups that Texans wanted to end hostilities. As a result of their previous experience with the Texas government, the Comanches were suspicious of the peace overtures. They continued to raid in Mexico but generally avoided the Texas settlements. In 1844 Comanches finally agreed to attend a peace council at Tehuacana Creek. The treaty resulting from the Tehuacana Creek councils,qv signed by Buffalo Hump and other chiefs, called for peace and trade between Texans and Comanches, but once again no agreement was reached on a boundary to separate the two nations. Conflict was inevitable, and by 1845 relations between Texans and Comanches were again strained.

Texas was annexed to the Union in 1845, and the United States government took over the administration of Texas Indian affairs. Federal agents and Comanche leaders attempted to preserve peace despite frequent outbreaks of hostilities, as white settlement continued to encroach on Comanche hunting grounds. In 1849 the army established a line of forts to protect the frontier, but settlers rapidly pushed beyond the established cordon and became vulnerable to attacks by Comanches who were attempting to defend their traditional range. In an attempt to protect both settlers and Indians, two reservations were established in Texas in 1854. A 23,000-acre reservation on the Clear Fork of the Brazos, in what is now Throckmorton County, became home to some 350 Penateka Comanches whose band had been weakened by warfare with Texans, epidemic diseases, and depletion of the buffalo herds. Other Comanche bands, farther removed from white settlement, still freely roamed the plains. The establishment of reservations did not stop Indian raids, however. Frontier Texans, who coveted the Indians' land, blamed the reservation Indians for the continued depredations and demanded the removal of the reservations. In 1859, in response to complaints, the reservation Comanches were moved to Indian Territory, where they were given a tract of land near Anadarko and assigned to the Wichita Agency. However, since the reservation Indians had not been the perpetrators of the raids, removal of the reservations did little to solve the Texas Indian problem. Raids increased as the Civil Warqv left the frontier virtually unprotected, and the country west of a line from Gainesville to Fredericksburg was abandoned by settlers.

When the war ended, the federal government reestablished frontier defenses and resumed its treaty-making with the Plains tribes. The treaties were designed to open the region to white travelers and settlers by locating the nomadic tribesmen on reservations. The 1867 Treaty of Medicine Lodge Creek, the last treaty made with the Comanches, established a reservation for the Comanches, Kiowas, and Kiowa Apaches in southwestern Indian Territory between the Washita and Red rivers. The treaty did not greatly improve conditions in Texas, however, because the Comanches would not stay on the lands allotted them and continued to conduct destructive raids in Texas.

The Comanches, who saw their way of life rapidly vanishing, turned to a young Quahadi medicine man for leadership. Isa-tai qv (later known as White Eagle) called his people together for a Sun Dance in the spring of 1874 and promised victory over the whites. Inspired by the visionary leader, agitated warriors attacked buffalo hunters at Adobe Walls in Hutchinson County. The unsuccessful attack not only destroyed the Indians' faith in Isa-tai, but it also brought retribution from the United States government. In 1874 the army began a relentless campaign that became known as the Red River War.qv A concerted five-pronged attack was launched in the Panhandleqv for the purpose of driving all Indians to the reservation. Forces under the command of Col. Ranald S. Mackenzieqv surprised a Comanche camp in Palo Duro Canyon and destroyed their horse herd. Very few Indians were killed in the engagements, but their mounts and supplies were so depleted that they could not survive the winter on the plains and were forced to enter the reservation.

Once estimated to number in the thousands, the Comanche population, according to an 1875 reservation census, had been reduced to 1,597. Reservation life necessitated a complete restructuring of Comanche society as the government attempted to transform the hunters and warriors into farmers and stockmen. Their cultural values and beliefs were under constant attack as they were encouraged to take up the white man's ways. Unable to subsist themselves, and only begrudgingly supported by the government, Comanches suffered terribly. Many turned to peyoteqv religion to foster tribal unity during that difficult time.

The reservation period came to an end in 1901, when the Comanche reservation was broken up into allotments in severalty. According to provisions of the Jerome Agreement, each man, woman, and child would receive 160 acres of land, with additional acreage set aside for church, agency, and school use. Comanche leaders protested the allotment on multiple grounds, but the federal government upheld the agreement. Lands not allotted to the Indians were thrown open to the public, and whites soon outnumbered Indians on the former reservation. The post-allotment period was a difficult time for Comanches, who continued to lose their land as a result of financial reverses or fraudulent schemes. Many were forced to leave the vicinity of the old reservation to seek employment, and those who remained were divided by factionalism. World War II[qv] accelerated the breakup of Comanche society as members of the tribe left to find jobs in the defense industry or join the military service. In the postwar years, the Comanche population continued to disperse in search of economic opportunity.

In the 1960s the Comanches, encouraged by a resurgence of Indian nationalism, began to work together to rebuild their society. They underwent important political changes as a result of that initiative. They seceded from the Kiowa-Comanche-Apache Intertribal Business Committee, which had served as their government since passage of the Oklahoma Indian Welfare Act of 1936. Although they maintained ties with the Kiowas and Apaches, the Comanches established their own tribal government, which operates in a bustling complex near Lawton, Oklahoma. In 1995 the Comanches had an enrolled tribal population of 9,722 scattered across the United States. For them the pow-wow, or dance gathering, had become an important method of maintaining Comanche kinship. The People are also united by pride in their rich Comanche heritage, an element that has remained constant through years of tumultuous change.

BIBLIOGRAPHY: Morris W. Foster, *Being Comanche: A Social History of an American Indian Community* (Tucson: University of Arizona Press, 1991). William T. Hagan, *United States–Comanche Relations: The Reservation Years* (New Haven: Yale University Press, 1976; rpt., Norman: University of Oklahoma Press, 1990). Thomas W. Kavanagh, *Comanche Political History: An Ethnohistorical Perspective, 1706–1875* (Lincoln: University of Nebraska Press, 1995). Rupert N. Richardson, *The Comanche Barrier to South Plains Settlement* (Glendale, California: Clark, 1933; rpt., Millwood, New York: Kraus, 1973). Ernest Wallace and E. Adamson Hoebel, *The Comanches* (Norman: University of Oklahoma Press, 1952).

Carol A. Lipscomb

COMANCHE PEAK (El Paso County). Comanche Peak is a half mile northwest of Scenic Drive and a mile west of Newman Park in northwestern El Paso County (at 31°48′ N, 106°29′ W). The peak, at an elevation of 5,225 feet above sea level, rises 1,160 feet above Scenic Drive. Shallow, stony soils on the mountain support scrub brush and grasses.

_____ (Hood County). Comanche Peak is four miles south of Granbury in south central Hood County (at 32°23′ N, 97°48′ W). Its summit reaches a height of 1,230 feet above mean sea level. It was an early landmark in the area.

COMANCHE SPRINGS. Comanche Springs was in the southeastern part of the town of Fort Stockton in central Pecos County. The springs, the source of Comanche Creek, flowed from a fault in Comanchean limestone. In 1849 a reconnaissance party organized by United States Army captain William Henry Chase Whiting[qv] reached Comanche Springs. Whiting called the springs Awache, Comanche for "white [or wide] water," and described the water as being clear and abundant in fish and soft-shell turtles. José Policarpo Rodríguez,[qv] interpreter for the Whiting party, later said he gave the name Comanche to the springs. John C. Reid described Comanche Springs in 1856, saying the water came from the earth "like a sea monster." Reid said Comanche Springs received its name when a Comanche, covered in a wolf's hide, was killed while attempting to attack a party of travelers at the springs. United States Army lieutenant S. G. French noted in 1849 that Comanche Springs was an Indian campground on the Comanche Trail[qv] to Mexico. French said large wagontrains of immigrants traveling from Fredericksburg to Presidio passed by Comanche Springs. Camp Stockton, later Fort Stockton, a United States Army post, was established at Comanche Springs on March 23, 1859, to provide protection to travelers and mail service from raiding Indians. The springs supplied water for the camp. Comanche Springs was an important of irrigation water in Pecos County after 1875. In 1899 the spring flow was 1,900 liters a second. Heavy pumping from the Edwards-Trinity Aquifer caused the flow of Comanche Springs to decline after 1947. A county bathhouse, swimming pool, and pavilion were constructed at Comanche Springs in 1938. By March 1961 the springs had ceased flowing. The rare and endangered Comanche Springs pupfish lived there until the springs dried up.

BIBLIOGRAPHY: Gunnar Brune, *Springs of Texas*, Vol. 1 (Fort Worth: Branch-Smith, 1981). Pecos County Historical Commission, *Pecos County History* (2 vols., Canyon, Texas: Staked Plains, 1984). Clayton W. Williams, *Never Again, Texas* (3 vols., San Antonio: Naylor, 1969).

Glenn Justice

COMANCHE SPRINGS, TEXAS. Comanche Springs was two miles west of McGregor in western McLennan County. A post office was established there in May 1872, with John S. Elmore as postmaster; the office was discontinued in 1875. The community was bypassed in the early 1880s by the Texas and St. Louis and the Gulf, Colorado and Santa Fe railroads. Subsequently Comanche Springs was gradually abandoned as its residents moved their homes and businesses to the new town of McGregor.

BIBLIOGRAPHY: William Robert Poage, *McLennan County Before 1980* (Waco: Texian, 1981).

Vivian Elizabeth Smyrl

COMANCHE TRAIL. Though the Comanche Trail has long been named in the historical literature of the Southwest, only an occasional reference is made to it in contemporary records and documents. A map of West Texas made by J. H. Young in 1857 shows such a trail. The lower portion had two prongs, one crossing the Rio Grande about the vicinity of Boquillas and the other at Presidio. The two converged at Comanche Springs, near the site of Fort Stockton. From this point the trail extended north to cross the Pecos at or near Horsehead Crossing[qv] and continued northeasterly across the sand hills to the site of present Big Spring. From Big Spring it extended east of the Caprock[qv] past watering spots on Tobacco Creek, Mooar's Draw, and Gholson Spring. From this point there were two routes across the Staked Plains. One was up Yellow House Canyon by Buffalo Spring to the forks of the canyon in what is now Mackenzie State Recreation Area[qv] in Lubbock, thence up the north fork of the Double Mountain Fork of the Brazos, where there was running water just west of the site of present Abernathy. From there this branch extended to Sod House Spring, north of the site of present Littlefield. From this point it ascended Blackwater Draw to Portales Spring, to Tiban Spring, and thence to the Pecos near Fort Sumner. The alternative route from Gholson Spring extended southeast to Blanco Canyon and thence up that canyon and Running Water Draw, past the site of present Plainview about twenty miles, at which point the route left the draw and extended west to Spring Lake. From there it continued to Blackwater Draw, where it intercepted the Yellow House route fifteen miles east of the site of present Muleshoe. Young's map indicated that water could be had daily from Big Spring northward and northwest to the site of Fort Sumner, New Mexico. The upper portion of the trail from Plainview westward was possibly used by Francisco Vásquez de Coronado[qv] on his return to the Pecos.

BIBLIOGRAPHY: Joe Cunningham, "The Comanche Trail," *Texas Parade,* December 1952. Edward N. Todd, "The Comanche Trail," *Frontier Times,* July 1974.
William Curry Holden

COMANCHEROS. The Comancheros were natives of northern and central New Mexico who conducted trade for a living with the nomadic plains tribes, often at designated areas in the Llano Estacado.qv They cut trails followed by traders and later ranchers and settlers. They were so named because the Comanches, in whose territory they traded, were considered their best customers. The term, unknown in Spanish documents, was popularized during the 1840s by Josiah Greggqv and subsequently applied by United States Army officers who were familiar with Gregg's accounts. Initially, the Comancheros' lucrative practices were considered legitimate, and trade grew slowly. Increased demand for cattle in New Mexico, however, led to become "rustlers by proxy" who traded stolen cattle to the Indians. The resulting hostility between Indians and settlers led to army intervention in 1874 and the Comancheros' eventual demise.

Comancheros ranged east to the Wichita Mountains of Oklahoma, southeast as far as the Davis Mountains in Texas, and north to the Dakotas. The distinctive form of trade associated with them began with a treaty of 1786 between the Spanish governor of New Mexico, Juan Baptista de Anza, and the Comanche Indians of the plains, allowing trade between New Mexico and the Indians in return for Indian protection of Texas against intruders on Spanish territory.

At first many Comancheros cached their oxcarts or carretas and loaded their merchandise on burros before venturing into the trackless Comanchería. But by the 1840s Josiah Gregg, James W. Abert,qv and other American mapmakers found evidences of broad cart trails leading into the Canadian River valley. Randolph B. Marcyqv described the "old Mexican cartroad" in his 1849 survey. Lieutenant Abert, while at Bent's tradinghouse on the Canadian in September 1845, parleyed with a small group of Comancheros, and in 1853 some New Mexico traders helped guide Lt. Amiel W. Whippleqv across the Panhandle.qv During the first decades of the Comancheros' trade, their merchandise consisted largely of beads, knives, paints, tobacco, pots and pans, and calico and other cloth, as well as the metal spikes that Indians came to prefer over flint points for their arrows. Foodstuffs such as coffee, flour, and bread were also bartered. The majority of their excursions were to the Comanche and Kiowa villages on the Llano Estacado. Such expeditions, poorly organized and often risky, depended on the nature of relations with different tribes.

From about 1840 on, Comanches realized the commercial value of horses and raided the frontiers of both Texas and northern Mexico to secure animals not only for themselves but for trade to the Comancheros. The rising demand for cattle in New Mexico led to further raiding. Between 1850 and 1870 thousands of animals stolen by Indians were traded by Comancheros to merchants in New Mexico and Arizona who had contacts with government beef contractors. The addition of firearms, ammunition, and whiskey to the list of trade items from New Mexico likewise added to the trade's worsening reputation. Although the territorial governors of New Mexico attempted to regulate the trade by requiring licenses, Comancheros mainly neglected the law. Many American officials, particularly federal Indian agents, believed that trading was merely a cover-up for the New Mexicans' real purpose of inciting resentment and resistance against Anglo Texans. Certainly the traders and their Comanche customers shared a common dislike of Anglos, and as far as the victims of raids and thefts were concerned, the feeling was mutual.

As the sordid commerce in stolen property increased, the Comancheros began arranging specific meeting times and places with their Indian customers to conduct business away from any settlements. The remote Panhandle–South Plains area thus became an ideal trading ground for these transactions. Horses, mules, and cattle bearing Texas brands were exchanged for such items as tobacco, coffee, and whiskey at popular rendezvous sites like Mulberry Creek, on what became the JA Ranchqv range; Tecovas Springs, on the future Frying Pan Ranchqv northwest of the site of Amarillo; Sweetwater Creek, near the site of Mobeetie; Atascosa Creek, at the site of Old Tascosa (now Cal Farley's Boys Ranchqv); and Yellow House Canyon near the site of present-day Lubbock, known to the Comancheros as Cañón del Rescate (Canyon of Ransom). Another familiar trading site was at Las Lenguas (or Los Lingos) Creek near the future site of Quitaque. From a typical rendezvous, during which bargaining might last as long as three weeks, a shrewd Comanchero could take back with him a mule for five pounds of tobacco or a keg of whiskey, a good pack horse for ten pounds of coffee, or a buffalo robe for little or nothing.

Probably the most controversial aspect of the Comancheros' operations was the ransoming of captives, a practice dating back centuries. At first enterprising New Mexicans had bought only captive Indians for use as mine workers or servants, but as time went on they began accepting Mexican prisoners as well. Many traders reportedly made large profits from highborn captives they had ransomed from Comanches by holding them for a suitable "reward" from relatives in the settlements of Texas or northern Mexico or from American government officials.

The Civil Warqv momentarily left the Texas frontier practically defenseless and allowed the Indian raiders free access to livestock grazing in the Cross Timbers and Hill Countryqqv of central West Texas. Comancheros profited handsomely from this stock, much of it left unbranded as well as unattended, which they frequently traded to army posts, government Indian reservations, and ranchers for guns, ammunition, and whiskey to trade to the Indians. Noted traders like José P. Tafoyaqv maintained crude rock and adobe shelters at places like Las Lenguas or Tecovas Springs during the 1860s.

Comancheros often accompanied Comanches on cattle raids into Coleman County and environs in the 1870s. The days of the Comancheros were numbered, however, as Texas Rangersqv and United States Army patrols mounted increasing pressure on their Indian customers. Col. Ranald S. Mackenzieqv and other army commanders often enlisted, or perhaps conscripted, Comancheros to guide them to the camps of the Indians with whom they had traded. The final defeat of the Comanches and their allies in the Red River War,qv along with the extermination of the buffaloqv by hunters, ended the Comanchero trade. In the late 1870s Casimero Romero, José P. Tafoya,qqv Juan Trujillo, and others who had sometime engaged in the Comanchero trade settled for a time in the western Panhandle as peaceful *pastores.*

BIBLIOGRAPHY: J. Evetts Haley, "The Comanchero Trade," *Southwestern Historical Quarterly* 38 (January 1935). Charles Leroy Kenner, *A History of New Mexican–Plains Indian Relations* (Norman: University of Oklahoma Press, 1969). Frederick W. Rathjen, *The Texas Panhandle Frontier* (Austin: University of Texas Press, 1973).
H. Allen Anderson

COMBES, TEXAS. Combes is on Business U.S. Highway 77 and State Highway 107, bordering Harlingen in northwestern Cameron County. The site was originally the headquarters for the Combes Ranch, named for Charles B. Combes, a settler from Kentucky, who moved to the region during the early 1900s. The town developed after 1904, when the St. Louis, Brownsville and Mexico Railway built a line through the region. There is some debate as to whether the town was named for the ranch or for a Brownsville surgeon named Joe Combe. In January 1911 a post office was established there, and by 1915 the community had a population of 100. In 1920 the post office was closed, but it reopened in 1926. Combes had a population of 500 in 1929. In 1936 the town had a population of 100 and thirteen businesses, including a factory; at that time it also had five churches, a cemetery, a school, a tourist camp, and numerous dwellings and farm units. By 1949 Combes had twenty businesses and an estimated population of 400. The community was incorporated during the 1950s, and in 1956 it consisted of a central community surrounded by numerous scattered dwellings that fell within its corporate boundary. Throughout the 1960s its estimated population remained at 400, and in 1972 it reached an estimated 689. The population continued to steadily increase through the 1980s, reaching an estimated 2,042 in 1990.

Alicia A. Garza

COMBINE, TEXAS. Combine is at the intersection of Farm roads 3039 and 1389, twenty miles southeast of Dallas in Kaufman and Dallas counties. The settlement was probably established sometime in the late 1880s or early 1890s. From 1895 to 1903 a post office branch operated at the community. During the 1930s and 1940s the population of Combine was never reported as more than twenty-five. By the 1970s Combine was surrounded by the city of Seagoville, and Combine residents incorporated their community. The population of Combine increased from 297 in 1970 to 815 in 1988. In the early 1990s the population of Combine was reported as 1,398, and Combine occupied parts of both Kaufman and Dallas counties.

David Minor

COMBS, DAVID ST. CLAIR (1839–1926). David St. Clair Combs was born on May 26, 1839, in Johnson County, Missouri, the son of David and Rebecca (Burruss) Combs. In 1854 the family moved to Texas and settled near San Marcos, then a frontier town. In August 1861 at La Grange, Fayette County, Combs enlisted in Company D of the Eighth Texas Cavalry,qv better known as Terry's Texas Rangers. He fought in all major engagements in which the rangers participated through Chickamauga. While he was on furlough in Texas, he was transferred to the Trans-Mississippi Department, where he served to the end of the war. He fought in the battle of Palmito Ranchqv on May 13, 1865, the last engagement of the Civil War.qv After the war Combs was one of the first traildrivers; from 1866 to 1879 he drove cattle and horses to Louisiana, Kansas, Iowa, Nebraska, and the Dakotas. In 1880 he and his partners ranched near San Angelo, but in 1882 they moved ranching operations to Brewster County. In 1900 he established Combs Ranch, one of the largest ranches in Brewster County, near Marathon. As one of the last surviving members of the Eighth Texas Cavalry, Combs was instrumental in getting L. B. Giles to write his history of the regiment, *Terry's Texas Rangers* (1967); Combs's letter is the preface. Combs married Eleanora Browning on February 27, 1873, and they had two daughters and a son. Combs died on January 3, 1926, in San Antonio and was buried in San Marcos.

BIBLIOGRAPHY: J. Marvin Hunter, *Trail Drivers of Texas* (2 vols., San Antonio: Jackson Printing, 1920, 1923; 4th ed., Austin: University of Texas Press, 1985). Frank W. Johnson, *A History of Texas and Texans* (5 vols., ed. E. C. Barker and E. W. Winkler [Chicago and New York: American Historical Society, 1914; rpt. 1916]).

Nowlin Randolph

COMBS, JESSE MARTIN (1889–1953). Jesse Martin Combs, jurist and congressman, son of Frank and Mary (Beck) Combs, was born in Shelby County, Texas, on July 7, 1889. He was orphaned as a small child and raised by his maternal grandparents, Mr. and Mrs. Jesse Beck. After graduating from Center High School, Combs attended San Marcos State Teachers College (now Southwest Texas State University) and received his degree in 1912. He taught at several rural schools before becoming the Hardin county agent in 1914. Four years later he was admitted to the bar and elected county judge. He subsequently served as judge for the Seventy-fifth District Court, which served Tyler, Hardin, Liberty, Chambers, and Montgomery counties. He moved to Beaumont and sat on the Ninth Court of Civil Appeals from 1933 to 1943. He was also influential in developing Beaumont's South Park school district, and was president of the Board of Trustees of Lamar Junior College (now Lamar University) from 1940 to 1944.

In May 1944 Combs announced that he would challenge incumbent Martin Diesqv for the Second Congressional District seat. Faced with a difficult battle, the controversial Dies decided not to seek reelection. Combs served four terms in Congress as a key associate of fellow Democrat Samuel T. (Sam) Rayburn.qv As a member of the House Ways and Means Committee, Combs was influential in securing federal appropriations for housing, industrial, and water projects, such as those at Dam B and McGee Bend (see B. A. STEINHAGEN LAKE, SAM RAYBURN RESERVOIR). He opposed a large reduction in the capital-gains tax and supported President Harry Truman's 1947 loyalty order for government employees. Combs generally backed Truman in Congress, although he broke with the president over the Tidelands Controversy.qv Poor health led him not to seek reelection in 1952. He died of lung cancer on August 21, 1953, at Beaumont and was buried there in Magnolia Cemetery. He was a Baptist. Two sons and his wife of forty-two years, Katherine (Alford), survived the former congressman.

BIBLIOGRAPHY: Beaumont *Enterprise*, August 22, 1953. Dallas *Morning News*, August 23, 1953. New York *Times*, May 13, 1944, May 14, 1947, May 18, 1950, August 23, 1953.

Robert Wooster

COME CÍBOLAS INDIANS. These Indians are known only from a Spanish document of 1693 which lists the Come Cíbolas ("bison eaters") as one of fifty "nations" that lived north of the Rio Grande and "between Texas and New Mexico." This may be interpreted to mean the southern part of western Texas, since the document also mentions that the Apaches were at war with the groups named. Nothing further is known about the Come Cíbolas. They were evidently not the same as the Cíbolas, whose name occurs on the same list.

BIBLIOGRAPHY: Charles W. Hackett, ed., *Historical Documents Relating to New Mexico, Nueva Vizcaya, and Approaches Thereto, to 1773* (3 vols., Washington: Carnegie Institution, 1923–37).

Thomas N. Campbell

COMECRUDO INDIANS. The Comecrudo (Spanish for "raw meat eaters") Indians were a Coahuiltecan people who in the late seventeenth and eighteenth centuries lived in northern Tamaulipas. In the second half of the eighteenth century part of the Comecrudos lived along the south bank of the Rio Grande near Reynosa, and it may be inferred that they hunted and gathered wild plant foods on both sides of the river. At times the Comecrudo Indians were also referred to as Carrizo, a Spanish name applied to many Coahuiltecan groups along the Rio Grande below Laredo. In 1886 the ethnologist A. S. Gatschet found a few elderly Comecrudo near Reynosa who could still speak their native language. Gatschet's Comecrudo vocabulary and texts helped to establish the linguistic affiliations of many Indian groups of southern Texas and northeastern Mexico.

BIBLIOGRAPHY: Frederick Webb Hodge, ed., *Handbook of American Indians North of Mexico* (2 vols., Washington: GPO, 1907, 1910; rpt., New York: Pageant, 1959). Gabriel Saldivar, *Los Indios de Tamaulipas* (Mexico City: Pan American Institute of Geography and History, 1943). J. R. Swanton, *Linguistic Material from the Tribes of Southern Texas and Northeastern Mexico* (Washington: Smithsonian Institution, 1940).

Thomas N. Campbell

COME INDIANS. The Come Indians are known from a single Spanish document of 1683 in which they are identified only as "the people who eat." Since no native name is given, they cannot be related to other known groups. Their area seems to have been somewhere east of the Pecos in west central Texas.

BIBLIOGRAPHY: Charles W. Hackett, ed., *Pichardo's Treatise on the Limits of Louisiana and Texas* (4 vols., Austin: University of Texas Press, 1931–46).

Thomas N. Campbell

COMET, TEXAS. Comet was two miles from Jefferson in central Marion County. It had a post office from 1891 to 1905. In 1892 it had two general stores, and J. O. Jackson was postmaster. The population of the community was estimated at ten in 1896, and in 1899 thirty pupils attended the Comet school. By 1936 the community was not marked on the county highway map.
Mark Odintz

COMETA, TEXAS. Cometa is at the intersection of Farm roads 2691 and 393, ten miles west of Crystal City in far southwestern Zavala County. The Cometa area was the location of prehistoric Indian encampments and Spanish campsites; one such campsite was called the Loma de Cometas by Spanish transportation agents. With spring water, a large natural lake, free-roaming cattle, and fertile soil, land in the Cometa area was much sought after immediately after the Civil War.qv Part of the site was bought by people interested in establishing a commune. The first families to settle the area permanently were Grey (Doc) White and the Vivian family around 1867. They were joined by the Ramón Sánchez and Galván families in 1870 and by J. Fisher in 1871. Cattlemen ranched the Cometa area throughout the last quarter of the nineteenth century. Around 1885 T. A. Coleman established his ranch headquarters on Cometa hill and hired Charles Lindenborn as foreman. The ranch brand was in the shape of a comet, called *cometa* by the Mexican ranchhands. The county's first schoolhouse was constructed by teacher George Herman in 1885 near Cometa; twenty-five students attended that year. The schoolhouse also served the community as church and community center. Methodists, Baptists, and members of the Church of Christ used the facility. In the early 1890s Coleman constructed a building that served as the general store and later the post office. The Vivian Cemetery was established in the community sometime near the turn of the century.

By 1900 16 percent of Zavala County's population resided in the Cometa area. A post office was established in the community in 1905 with B. H. Erskine as postmaster. At that time Cometa farmers used artesian wells to irrigate small farms that produced watermelons, pumpkins, and tomatoes. Although harvests were bountiful, Cometa's farmers discovered that their produce spoiled in transit by oxcart and mulewagons to distant markets such as Eagle Pass.

In the early 1900s Thomas Edison and later the Edison Institute contracted with several Cometa farmers to grow experimental crops, including soybeans and guayule for use in the manufacture of various rubbers and plastics. The area was replete with registered and purebred stock, including Durham cattle, Duroc Jersey hogs, Hampshires, brown Leghorn chickens, thoroughbreds, and quarter horses. By 1920, however, Cometa was declining; the post office was discontinued in 1919, and the general store closed several years later. Nonetheless, local prosperity during the Great Depressionqv enabled farmers to donate fresh vegetables and corn to a growing number of migrants moving to the area from northern states. In 1942 the schoolhouse was closed. That same year Cometa had several irrigated and dry-land farms; although some vegetables were raised, most farmers produced oats for cattle grazing. By 1946 Cometa was a rambling community of farms and ranches with an estimated population of 100. In the 1980s Cometa's farmers contended with a rapidly falling water table. Vegetables and exotic crops were cultivated on only 500 acres in the area. The springs at Pendencia Creek had dried up in 1926. In 1988 the area was largely abandoned except for a scattering of small farms and the Vivian Cemetery.

BIBLIOGRAPHY: Florence Fenley, *Old Timers of Southwest Texas* (Uvalde, Texas: Hornby, 1957). R. C. Tate, History of Zavala County (M.A. thesis, Southwest Texas State Teachers College, 1942). Zavala County Historical Commission, *Now and Then in Zavala County* (Crystal City, Texas, 1985).
Ruben E. Ochoa

COMFORT, TEXAS. Comfort, the second largest town in Kendall County, is located at the junction of State Highway 27, U.S. Highway 87, and Interstate Highway 10, sixteen miles northwest of Boerne on the county's western edge. The town was laid out near the site of an Indian village in 1854 by Ernst Hermann Altgelt,qv though its history goes back to a group of Germans from New Braunfels that settled in 1852 along the banks of the Cypress Creek above its confluence with the Guadalupe River. Freemasons, freethinkers, and political activists, middle-class German families, and liberals from Bettina and Sisterdale settled the area. Townsmen organized the community along cooperative lines and steadfastly opposed formal local government. Comfort opened a school shortly after its founding, but not until 1892 was a church built. The town was a center of Union sentiment during the Civil Warqv and lost many young men at the battle of the Nuecesqv in 1862. A monument on a hillside across from the high school campus honors these dead. From 1856 until Kendall County was organized in 1862, Comfort competed with Kerrville to become the county seat of Kerr County; Kerrville won.

Early agriculture and commerce in the area depended on sheep and goats, grains, lime burning (see LIMEKILNS), masonry, building rock, lumber, and shingles. In the 1940s and 1950s, when the Hill Countryqv was an international wool and mohair center, Adolf Stieler of Comfort reigned as "Angora Goat King of the World." In the 1980s agribusiness continued to dominate the local economy, but hunting, fishing, sightseeing, and youth camps drew increasing numbers of tourists.

Much of the original townsite is listed in the National Register of Historic Places. Significant architectural sites include Bolshevik Hall, Turner Hall, a theater, and numerous half-timber and Victorian structures that survived a disastrous flood in 1978. A tradition of secular funerals was still widely observed in the twentieth century, and German turner (see TURNVEREIN MOVEMENT) activities and modern Volksmarsch celebrations continued. A local museum, volunteer and mutual aid organizations, and service and literary clubs provided informal governance. The population of the unincorporated town was over 1,400 in 1980, when the post office, established in 1856, still existed. In 1990 the population was 1,477.

BIBLIOGRAPHY: Guido E. Ransleben, *A Hundred Years of Comfort in Texas* (San Antonio: Naylor, 1954; rev. ed. 1974). Vertical Files, Barker Texas History Center, University of Texas at Austin.
Glen E. Lich

COMISARIO. A *comisario*, under Spanish and Mexican law, was an elected official who served in districts or precincts of around 500 inhabitants. The term of office was one year, and though a *comisario* might be reelected, he could not be compelled to serve more than one year in three. The *comisario* was subject to the ayuntamientoqv and might attend its sessions voluntarily or on summons; he had a voice but no vote in its deliberations. Duties of the *comisario* were to take the census of the precinct, keep a record of families moving into it and of the places from which they came, assist tax collectors, execute the orders of his superiors, arrest disturbers of the peace, and report undesirable persons to the alcalde.qv In addition, the *comisario* was invested with minor judicial authority similar to that of the alcalde.

BIBLIOGRAPHY: Eugene C. Barker, "The Government of Austin's Colony, 1821–1831," *Southwestern Historical Quarterly* 21 (January 1918). Hans Peter Nielsen Gammel, comp., *Laws of Texas, 1822–1897* (10 vols., Austin: Gammel, 1898). Henry Smith, "Reminiscences of Henry Smith," *Quarterly of the Texas State Historical Association* 14 (July 1910).

COMISIÓN HONORÍFICA MEXICANA. Chapters of the Comisión Honorífica Mexicana were organized by the Mexican Consulate throughout Texas and the United States in 1920–21 for the purpose of mutual aid, protection, and charity. Local chapters acted as the consul's official representative to Mexican-descent communities and to such United States authorities as school officials during at least the 1920s and 1930s. One source indicates that they may have continued to have a role in Mexican-American education for a while after World

War II.^qv They served as a liaison, helped maintain loyalty to Mexico, and resembled *sociedades mutualistas*.^qv The Mexican Consulate organized the *comisiones* in response to a call for assistance from Mexican immigrants when the 1920–21 recession hit. The Mexican government responded by forming three new consulates in the United States and organized *comisiones honoríficas* for men. They may have assisted with repatriation efforts in the early 1920s. The *comisiones* were often in rural towns, where they were especially important. They functioned under the jurisdiction of the regional consulate office closest to them. A large *comisión* in San Antonio and numerous other *comisiones* in area towns made up Division One, which included chapters in East, Central, and South Texas and Oklahoma, Kansas, and Nebraska; by 1927 Division One also had 163 chapters and 203 groups of Cruz Azul Mexicana,^qv a charitable women's organization. The *comisiones* admitted all men of Mexican-descent, regardless of citizenship, although United States citizens were unable to vote because of the group's affiliation with the Mexican consulate and, thus, the government of Mexico. The associations were composed of "respected members of the community," apparently including members of the working class, although workers were fewer than in the *sociedades mutualistas*. The Dallas chapter had twelve prominent men, and the Gonzales chapter in rural Texas was composed of five members. The Mexican consul was typically honorary president. The commissions held conventions annually, usually in San Antonio. In 1923 twenty-seven groups and twelve groups of Cruz Azul attended. At this meeting members discussed segregated schools, unity among *Mexicanos*, the need for a Mexican industrial school, and a fund for the "defense of those compatriots that have litigation in American tribunals."

The *comisiones* aided the consul in maintaining communication with colonia^qv residents. When a local issue was of importance to the consul, the commission kept him informed about it. The groups assisted in legal matters, immigration matters, labor complaints, social welfare, and issues of racial discrimination affecting the Mexican-descent community. They helped the consul register Mexican immigrants, fill out documents, and file complaints and claims against employers and administrators, especially as related to contracts and wages. In 1923 in San Antonio the groups promoted and distributed sample labor contracts because of complaints of labor exploitation. Since they sought to protect the Mexican-descent community, by custom they did not inform immigration officials of the status or whereabouts of undocumented workers. The *comisiones* provided services to Mexican-descent residents and immigrants in Texas. They offered help to persons of Mexican descent in almshouses, jails, hospitals, schools, factories, and fields, places where prejudice might be felt. In 1927 in Florence, members organized a fund drive to help bury Benito de la Cruz, a farmworker fatally injured during work. They also often sponsored educational conferences to celebrate Mexican holidays (*fiestas patrias*^qv). According to one scholar, *comisiones* were the most important organizations in facilitating the repatriation movement to Mexico during the Great Depression,^qv especially from rural Texas. They provided information about opportunities in the homeland, helped organize repatriation groups, and raised funds for transportation. In 1931 the Maxwell *comisión honorífica* arranged for the resettlement of thirty-six families to the Don Martín colony. The Austin chapter helped destitute families with transportation to the border in 1931 and 1932. The Houston chapter and the Cruz Azul raised money for fifty families being repatriated in 1931. The Kenedy and Kyle chapters appointed committees to visit the Eighteenth of March colony and Matamoros settlements in Mexico in 1939 to study land, housing, and employment conditions. Little is known of the *comisiones* after 1940.

BIBLIOGRAPHY: Francisco E. Balderrama, *In Defense of La Raza: The Los Angeles Mexican Consulate and the Mexican Community, 1929 to 1936* (Tucson: University of Arizona Press, 1982). *Dictionary of Mexican American History* (Westport, Connecticut: Greenwood Press, 1981). Manuel Gamio, *Mexican Immigration to the United States* (Chicago: University of Chicago Press, 1930; rpt., New York: Arno Press, 1969). R. Reynolds McKay, Texas Mexican Repatriation during the Great Depression (Ph.D. dissertation, University of Oklahoma, 1982). Julie Leininger Pycior, La Raza Organizes: Mexican American Life in San Antonio, 1915–1930, as Reflected in Mutualista Activities (Ph.D. dissertation, University of Notre Dame, 1979). Mark Reisler, *By the Sweat of Their Brow: Mexican Immigrant Labor in the United States, 1900–1940* (Westport, Connecticut: Greenwood Press, 1976). Emilio Zamora, Mexican Labor Activity in South Texas, 1900–1920 (Ph.D. dissertation, University of Texas at Austin, 1983).

Cynthia E. Orozco

COMITÉ PATRIÓTICO MEXICANO. The Comité Patriótico Mexicano (Mexican Patriotic Committee) is a community-based organization that sponsors social, cultural, and educational activities to celebrate the Mexican cultural heritage. The first *comités patrióticos* (also known as *juntas patrióticas*), emerged during the late nineteenth century in cities with large Mexican-origin populations in Texas and throughout the Southwest. In cities such as Houston and El Paso, the *comités* worked closely with the Mexican consulate to promote activities that fostered better relations between Mexico and the United States and a mutual appreciation of the cultures on opposite sides of the border. The *comités* sponsored the annual local celebrations of *fiestas patrias*,^qv which were among the most widely attended civic celebrations in communities around the state. The *comités* also sponsored parades, banquets, and dances that attracted persons of all nationalities and cultures.

The *comité patriótico* played an important social and psychic role, especially in communities where Mexican Americans^qv were a minority of the population. People of Mexican descent, many of them immigrants, keenly felt the pressure to abandon their heritage and assimilate to the dominant culture. Though most struggled to adapt to the social and economic mainstream, they did not want to do so at the expense of their cultural identity. The *comité*'s activities helped Mexican Americans to maintain their cultural ties to the homeland and encouraged them to take pride in their heritage.

A Junta Patriótica Mexicana existed in El Paso as early as 1897. Together with the Mexican consulate and the local *sociedades mutualistas*,^qv the Junta Patriótica organized the annual sixteenth of September festivities, which were celebrated by Tejanos and Anglos alike. In Houston the Comité Patriótico Mexicano, organized during the 1930s, was composed of representatives from the most important social, civic, and political organizations in the Mexican-American community, such as the Sociedad Mutualista Obrera Mexicana, the Sociedad Mutualista Benito Juárez, Council No. 60 of the League of United Latin American Citizens,^qv the Club Cultural Recreativo México Bello,^qv and the Port Houston Lion's Club. As in other cities, the Houston Comité Patriótico Mexicano played an important role in the community-wide celebration of *fiestas patrias*, which oftentimes included a parade through the downtown area and a variety show at City Coliseum with popular entertainers from all over the Americas.

BIBLIOGRAPHY: Arnoldo De León, *Ethnicity in the Sunbelt: A History of Mexican-Americans in Houston* (University of Houston Mexican American Studies Program, 1989). Mario T. García, *Desert Immigrants: The Mexicans of El Paso, 1880–1920* (New Haven: Yale University Press, 1981). María T. Reyna Collection, Houston Metropolitan Research Collection, Houston Public Library. Mariano Rosales Ypiña Collection, Houston Metropolitan Research Center, Houston Public Library.

María-Cristina García

COMMERCE, TEXAS. Commerce is at the juncture of State highways 50, 11, 24, and 224, fifteen miles from Greenville in northeastern Hunt County. It owes its origins to William Jernigin, a pioneer merchant in partnership with Josiah Hart Jackson in nearby Cow Hill, who in 1872 opened a mercantile store on the site of the northwest corner of the present town square to take advantage of a new trade route that developed with the building of a new bridge on the South Sulphur River. The community grew up around Jernigin's store and apparently received its name on one of Jernigin's business trips to Jefferson. Jernigin had his merchandise sent to "commerce," since his small community did not have a name. In 1885, the year of incorporation, Commerce had twelve businesses in addition to a hotel and livery stable, a wood shop and wagon factory, and a steam mill and gin, as well as a church and school. In 1887 the St. Louis Southwestern Railway (the Cotton Belt) connected Commerce with Texarkana, Sherman, and Fort Worth. During the 1890s Commerce gained additional rail outlets to Ennis and Paris with the arrival of the Texas Midland Railroad. Commerce has been a college town since 1894, when William L. Mayo[qv] moved his East Texas Normal College from Cooper to Commerce to benefit from the rail connections and to collect a $1,000 bonus offered by the community.

By 1910 the population of Commerce had risen to 2,818, and the town had a flour mill and cottonseed oil mill, four cotton gins, a roundhouse, rail yards and machine shops, and four banks; East Texas Normal College enrolled 900 students. The population continued to grow until the 1950s, even though growth was limited during and after 1930. In the early 1950s the roundhouse was abandoned, and the machine shops were moved to Tyler. In 1956 passenger service to Commerce was discontinued. Also during this period the many cotton gins of Commerce began to close; the last one shut down in 1978. The population fell from 5,889 in 1950 to 5,789 in 1960. The college became part of the state college system in 1917 and began to grow rapidly, as the "baby boom" generation entered college. East Texas State College, which became a university in 1965, began to replace cotton and the railroads as the basis of the economy. In addition, the Commerce Industrial Development Association, formed in 1956, began to attract manufacturers. The population of Commerce was 9,534 in 1970, 8,136 in 1980, and 6,825 in 1990. The decline in enrollment at East Texas State University, from nearly 10,000 students in 1975 to 7,135 in 1984, ended in the late 1980s. Manufacturers in Commerce include United States Brass and Montgomery Controls, Sherwood Medical, Manatee Homes, and American Wood. Commerce is the second largest town in Hunt County.

BIBLIOGRAPHY: W. Walworth Harrison, *History of Greenville and Hunt County, Texas* (Waco: Texian, 1976). Mack W. Mullins, The History of Commerce, Texas (M.A. thesis, East Texas State Teachers College, 1949). Billie and Otha Spencer, eds., *The Handbook of Commerce, Texas* (Commerce: Friends of the Commerce Public Library, 1985).
Harry E. Wade

COMMISSIONER OF EDUCATION. The office of commissioner of education, established as an appointive position by the Gilmer-Aiken Laws[qv] in 1949, replaced the elective office of State Superintendent of Public Instruction (1884–1949).[qv] The commissioner was to be elected by the State Board of Education,[qv] with the consent of the Texas Senate, and was to serve as director of the Texas Education Agency.[qv] Other duties included supervising the Texas Council of Public Junior Colleges and appointing, with approval of the board of directors of the Texas Education Agency, the superintendents of the Texas School for the Deaf and Texas School for the Blind.[qq,qv] By 1970 supervision of junior colleges was no longer part of the commissioner's duties. In 1991 selection of the commissioner of education was changed to nomination by the board with appointment to a four-year term by the governor and confirmation by the Senate. If the governor does not approve of the candidate, he can ask the board for other nominations.
John G. Johnson

COMMISSIONERS CREEK. Commissioners Creek rises four miles east of Tarpley in south central Bandera County (at 29°41′ N, 99°13′ W) and runs southwest for 5½ miles to its mouth on Hondo Creek, 1½ miles south of Tarpley (at 29°38′ N, 99°16′ W). It runs through an area of the Edwards Plateau characterized by steep slopes and limestone benches and surfaced by shallow clay loams that support open stands of Ashe juniper and live oak interspersed with grassy clearings.

COMMISSIONERS OF DEEDS. The appointment by the governor of one or more commissioners of deeds in each state, territory, and foreign country was authorized by the legislature in 1846 to replace the consuls of the Republic of Texas.[qv] These commissioners served two-year terms and were to have the same authority as notaries public in Texas. The last commissioner of deeds served under Preston Smith in 1971.

BIBLIOGRAPHY: Seymour V. Connor, "A Preliminary Guide to the Archives of Texas," *Southwestern Historical Quarterly* 59 (January 1956).
Dick Smith

COMMISSION FORM OF CITY GOVERNMENT. The commission form of city government, also known as the Galveston Plan, was devised in Galveston in 1901 and became one of the three basic forms of municipal government in the United States. (The others are mayor-council and council-manager.) Under the commission plan voters elect a small governing commission, typically five or seven members, on an at-large basis. As a group the commissioners constitute the legislative body of the city responsible for taxation, appropriations, ordinances, and other general functions. Individually, each commissioner is in charge of a specific aspect of municipal affairs, e.g., public works, finance, or public safety. One of the commissioners is designated chairman or mayor, but his function is principally one of presiding at meetings and serving in ceremonial capacities. Thus the commission plan blends legislative and executive functions in the same body.

The invention of the commission plan was a direct result of the Galveston hurricane of 1900.[qv] An estimated 6,000 lives were lost, and millions of dollars worth of property was swept away. Fearful that the island city might never recover its prosperity under the leadership of the incumbent city council, a group of wealthy businessmen known as the Deep Water Committee devised a plan to have the governor appoint a commission to govern the city during the rebuilding period. To appease opponents who contended that appointed government was undemocratic, the plan was altered to provide for popular election of two of the five commissioners. This plan went into operation one year after the great storm. Court challenges to the constitutionality of the partially appointive government led the legislature to make the office of all five commissioners elective, and in this form the commission plan became popular across Texas and the nation.

Galveston's apparent success with the new type of government inspired Houston to adopt the plan in 1905 and Dallas, Fort Worth, El Paso, Denison, and Greenville to follow in 1907. By then sometimes referred to as the Texas Idea, the commission plan began to be noticed nationally and to be regarded as a progressive reform. Des Moines, Iowa, was the first city outside Texas to adopt the commission plan. The Des Moines version included nonpartisan balloting, merit selection of employees, and the direct-democracy devices of initiative, referendum, and recall. Although Dallas, Fort Worth, and some other Texas cities also used direct democracy, Des Moines was able to take credit for making commission government a package of reforms often billed as the Des Moines Plan.

Usually supported by chambers of commerce and other businessmen's groups, the commission plan spread rapidly from 1907 to 1920. In this period about 500 cities, including seventy-five in Texas, adopted commission charters. (Exact figures are not available because of poor reporting and imprecise definitions.) Leading figures of the Progressive Era,[qv] including Theodore Roosevelt and Woodrow Wilson, endorsed the plan. Reformist periodicals such as *Outlook* and *McClure's* praised the idea. Historians have generally regarded the

Galveston–Des Moines plan as an important aspect of the progressivist thrust toward expertise and efficiency. Some progressive reformers, however, questioned the plan because they viewed it as an effort by business interests to take influence away from the working class.

To a significant extent the commission plan served as a precursor to the popular council-manager form of city government. Richard S. Childs, often called the father of the city manager plan, worked through the Short Ballot Organization and the National Municipal League to make the manager plan rather than the commission plan the progressive idea of choice for business-minded reformers. Childs and others pointed out that the specific departmental interests of commissioners often caused internal squabbling and that the absence of a chief executive could result in a lack of leadership. Manager charters, many argued, could retain the beneficial aspects of the Galveston–Des Moines system, such as the short ballot, at-large voting, nonpartisanship, the merit system, and direct democracy, but could replace leaderless bickering with businesslike management in the corporate model.

Indeed, after World War I[qv] very few cities adopted the commission plan, and many existing commission cities shifted to the manager system; a few reverted to mayor-council charters. From a peak in 1918 of about 500, commission plan cities had dwindled to only 177 by 1984. In contrast, there were 3,776 mayor-council and 2,523 council-manager cities in that year. Even Galveston abandoned its own child when the island city adopted manager government in 1960. Because at-large balloting is intrinsic to the commission concept and since at-large elections may dilute minority voting strength, some southern cities, including Shreveport, Jackson, and Mobile, have dropped the commission plan because of suits brought under the Voting Rights Act of 1965 and subsequent amendments. In Texas as of May 1993 there were no true commission forms of government. Twenty-seven cities had manager-commission governments, but they were more like mayor-council government than the original commission form.

BIBLIOGRAPHY: Chandler Davidson, ed., *Minority Vote Dilution* (Washington: Howard University Press, 1984). Dewey W. Grantham, *Southern Progressivism: The Reconciliation and Progress and Tradition* (Knoxville: University of Tennessee Press, 1983). *Municipal Year Book, 1984* (Washington: International City Management Association, 1984). Bradley Robert Rice, *Progressive Cities: The Commission Government Movement in America, 1901–1920* (Austin: University of Texas Press, 1977). Martin J. Schiesl, *The Politics of Efficiency: Municipal Administration and Reform in America, 1880–1920* (Berkeley: University of California Press, 1977).   Bradley R. Rice

COMMISSION ON LAW ENFORCEMENT OFFICER STANDARDS AND EDUCATION. The Commission on Law Enforcement Officer Standards and Education, established in 1965, was composed in 1993 of fourteen members: five ex-officio members, including the commissioner of higher education (*see* TEXAS HIGHER EDUCATION COORDINATING BOARD), the commissioner of the Texas Education Agency,[qv] the director of the Texas Department of Public Safety,[qv] the attorney general, the director of the governor's Office of Criminal Justice Division, and nine citizens appointed by the governor with concurrence of the Senate for six-year overlapping terms. An executive director appointed by the commission is the chief administrative officer.

The commission tries to improve training of law enforcement officers and to direct research in this field. It establishes mandatory standards for qualifications for training peace officers and county jailers and is authorized to certify training programs as having attained minimum standards, to certify instructors, and to certify law enforcement officers as having achieved certain standards of education, training, and experience. The program was voluntary under the original law, but 1969 amendments made such training and education mandatory for all peace officers. A 1971 amendment established minimum requirements and training standards for all reserve officers. In 1981 the legislature mandated the agency to license officers and in 1987 extended the mandate to licensing armed public-security officers and certifying hypnotic investigators, telecommunicators, and inspectors of home-owners' insurance. The commission program includes a system of regional training centers, junior college programs in police science, and introductory courses for high school seniors. In 1993 the agency issued licenses to new peace officers, jailers or guards of county jails, and reserve law-enforcement officers. In 1987 it had sixty-three employees and a budget of $1,929,306. In 1992 the appropriations had increased to $3,758,825, and the number of employees had dropped to fifty-three.

COMMISSIONS OF APPEALS. At different times in the history of Texas, commissions of appeals have been established to assist various courts. The first one was established by the legislature on July 9, 1879, to determine, with the consent of the parties involved, cases pending in the Supreme Court and the Court of Appeals. The commission was composed of three lawyers appointed by the governor. On July 9, 1881, the legislature passed an act which provided for the continuance of the commission, and the courts were authorized to refer civil cases without the consent of those involved. In 1891 Texas had two commissions, each with three members; these were abolished when the system of appellate courts was organized to consist of the Supreme Court, Courts of Civil Appeals, and the Court of Criminal Appeals. In 1918, because the Supreme Court was several years behind with its docket, another Commission of Appeals was established in two sections with three commissioners each. Decisions had to be submitted and accepted by the Court of Civil Appeals of the Supreme Court. Later in 1945, when the Supreme Court was expanded to nine members, that commission was abolished. A commission consisting of two members was set up to assist the Court of Criminal Appeals in 1925. The commissioners were appointed by the court for two-year terms and had to meet the requirement of at least ten years' service as lawyers or judges. In the latter half of the twentieth century the commission went into virtual inactive status. The last commissioner of appeal was appointed in August 1981. In the 1990s the office still existed, but no commissioners were serving.

BIBLIOGRAPHY: Keith Carter, "The Texas Court of Criminal Appeals," *Texas Law Review* 11 (December 1932, February, April, June 1933). Robert W. Stayton and M. P. Kennedy, "A Study of Pendency in Texas Civil Litigation," *Texas Law Review* 21, 23 (April 1943, June 1945). John C. Townes, "Development of the Texas Judicial System," *Southwestern Historical Quarterly* 2 (July, October 1898).

Margaret Waters

COMMISSION ON SERVICES TO CHILDREN AND YOUTH. The Commission on Services to Children and Youth was established by the Sixty-second Texas Legislature in 1971 to be composed of twenty-eight members, eighteen of whom were appointed by the governor with the concurrence of the Senate for overlapping terms of six years; the remaining were permanent ex officio members who were heads of various Texas state commissions and departments. The eighteen appointed members were to be widely representative of the racial, ethnic, and economic makeup of the state's population, and six of them were required to be younger than twenty-one years of age at the time of appointment. The commission was to assist in the coordination of services to state agencies and programs as they related to children and youth. It periodically reported its findings to the legislature in matters relevant to the protection, growth, and development of children, and recommended modification in state programs or proposed new ones. It encouraged public and private organizations in the state to participate in youth development programs, and it performed duties assigned to it by the governor or legislature that pertained to the White House conferences on children and youth. The commission was abolished on recommendation of the Texas Sunset Advisory Commission qv on September 1, 1985.

COMMITTEES OF PUBLIC SAFETY (Civil War). A Committee of Public Safety was appointed by the first session of the Secession Convention qv in February 1861 to carry out the secession program in case of opposition by Unionists. Of top priority was the seizure of all military equipment in Texas held by the United States Army. John C. Robertson qv served as chairman. The committee was given extensive powers that were gradually strengthened. All of the fifteen members had military experience. Benjamin McCulloch, Henry McCulloch, and John S. Ford qqv were named colonels and ordered to raise an army with which to fight the Unionists and ensure the safety of citizens until the Confederate Army should become effective. A subcommittee was appointed to call on Governor Sam Houston qv in order to assure that he would not exercise his powers in conflict with the convention. They found Houston agreeable to this and also found that he had received a letter from Gen. David E. Twiggs, qv Union commander at San Antonio, giving the conditions under which he would surrender the Union forces. A subcommittee was appointed to confer with Twiggs.

Twiggs, a Southerner, had written the federal commander on January 15 asking to be relieved by March 4, but had received no reply. Twiggs appointed a committee of his officers to consider surrender, but the committee could not agree and Twiggs hesitated as he had received no orders. Ben McCulloch had raised a cavalry company of 400 men. When he reached San Antonio he was joined by volunteer companies that enlarged his force to 1,000. When Twiggs saw the show of force he surrendered his post and all other posts in Texas. Between February 18 and April 13 all federal posts were surrendered or abandoned. A large number of Texas counties also appointed Committees of Public Safety to give general protection.

BIBLIOGRAPHY: Jack W. Gunn, "Ben McCulloch: A Big Captain," *Southwestern Historical Quarterly* 58 (July 1954). Stephen B. Oates, "Texas Under the Secessionists," *Southwestern Historical Quarterly* 67 (October 1963). Anna Irene Sandbo, "The First Session of the Secession Convention of Texas," *Southwestern Historical Quarterly* 18 (October 1914). Dudley Goodall Wooten, ed., *A Comprehensive History of Texas* (2 vols., Dallas: Scarff, 1898; rpt., Austin: Texas State Historical Association, 1986).

John G. Johnson

COMMITTEES OF SAFETY AND CORRESPONDENCE. Committees of Safety and Correspondence similar to those in the American Revolution were organized in Texas as early as 1832. At first these bodies were not hostile to the Mexican government. Their purpose was to secure the organization of the militia for defense against Indians. Later, they kept people in touch with developments and made possible organized, effective resistance in the Texas Revolution.qv On May 8, 1835, Mina (Bastrop) appointed its committee of safety and correspondence for the general diffusion of information. A few days later organizations at Gonzales and Viesca were formed. A committee for the jurisdiction of Columbia met on August 15, 1835. Other communities established similar committees, and before the end of that summer apparently all precincts had such organizations.

BIBLIOGRAPHY: Hans Peter Nielsen Gammel, comp., *Laws of Texas, 1822–1897* (10 vols., Austin: Gammel, 1898). Rupert N. Richardson, *Texas: The Lone Star State* (New York: Prentice-Hall, 1943; 4th ed., with Ernest Wallace and Adrian N. Anderson, Englewood Cliffs, New Jersey: Prentice-Hall, 1981). Forrest T. Ward, "Pre-Revolutionary Activity in Brazoria County," *Southwestern Historical Quarterly* 64 (October 1960).

Ora Lee Capp

COMMUNITY PROPERTY LAW. In the Texas matrimonial property system there are two kinds of property: separate property (solely owned by a spouse) and community property (owned in common in equal shares by both spouses). All property acquired during marriage by either spouse is presumed to be community property, and a spouse who asserts that particular property is separate property must prove its sole ownership. The principle of community property is derived from the law of Castile and ultimately from Visigothic custom. The other states that use this system are California, Louisiana, New Mexico, Arizona, Idaho, Nevada, Washington, and Wisconsin. During marriage all the earnings of both spouses and the revenues from the separate property acquired during marriage are community property. Between spouses, community property may become separate property by a gift or sale for a separate property consideration, or since 1980 by a partition or exchange entered into either before or during marriage. Separate property may be converted into community property by sale for a community property consideration. Otherwise, as long as its identity can be traced, separate property retains its character, but if separate property is commingled with community property so that it cannot be traced, the whole commingled mass is deemed common. Since 1987 spouses have been able to agree in writing that all or any part of their community property will belong to the survivor of them. Prior to 1913, and in large measure from 1929 to 1968, management of community property was vested in the husband. Since 1967 management of community property is clearly divided between the spouses according to its source. Each spouse has control of his or her earnings, the profits of separate property, and recoveries from personal injury for loss of earning power, but if that common property over which one spouse has sole management power is mixed or combined with that which is subject to the sole control of the other spouse, the resulting mixture is subject to joint control of the spouses. Spouses may, however, agree to manage their community property as they may choose. *See also* SEPARATE PROPERTY LAW.

BIBLIOGRAPHY: William Q. DeFuniak and Michael J. Vaughn, *Principles of Community Property*, 2d ed. (Tucson: University of Arizona Press, 1971). William Orr Huie, *The Community Property Law of Texas* (Kansas City, Missouri: Vernon Law Book Company, 1960). Joseph W. McKnight and William A. Reppy, Jr., *Texas Matrimonial Property Law* (Charlottesville, Virginia: Michie, 1983).

Joseph W. McKnight

COMO, TEXAS. Como is an incorporated community on East Caney Creek at the junction of State Highway 11 and Farm Road 69, on the Louisiana and Arkansas Railway eight miles southeast of Sulphur Springs in southeastern Hopkins County. The area was first settled around 1846 when Ferdinand Carroll established a teamsters camp on the Jefferson Road on East Caney Creek. In 1858 Red Collins and Lonnie Ticer opened a store in the vicinity, and a second store opened in 1866. A post office, named Bacchus, was established for the community in 1870, but the office was renamed Carroll's Prairie in 1876. In the late 1870s the East Line and Red River Railroad was built through the town, and in 1879 the name of the community was changed to Carrollton. In 1894, to avoid confusion with the town of Carrollton near Dallas, the name was changed to Como, at the suggestion of local settlers who were from Como, Mississippi. By 1885 the town had a population of 200 and six general stores, two steam gristmills and cotton gins, a wagonmaker, a blacksmith, and a saloon. Lignite coal was discovered on the property of J. F. Smith, and by 1900 it had become one of the town's leading industries. A settlement of miners of Mexican descent developed east of Como near the mines. In 1910, after much of the town, which had been located south of the railroad tracks, burned down, the townspeople laid out a new town north of the tracks. It was built around a square with a bandstand in the middle. In 1914 Como had a population of 900, Baptist, Methodist, and Christian churches, two banks, an electric light plant, and a weekly newspaper, the Como *Headlight*. The community was incorporated in 1932. In the early 1930s most of the local mines closed down. Many Como residents moved away, and by 1933 the town's population was only 392. In 1948 Como had five churches, a ten-teacher school, sixteen businesses, and an estimated population of 450. After that the town grew slowly, and in 1989 it reported a population of 625 and thirteen businesses. In the early 1990s it had 585 residents and twenty-nine businesses.

BIBLIOGRAPHY: Sylvia M. Kibart and Rita M. Adams, eds., *Pioneers of Hopkins County, Texas,* Vol. 1 (Wolfe City, Texas: Henington, 1986).

J. E. Jennings

COMOCARA INDIANS. The Comocaras are known from a single Spanish document of 1683 that does not clearly identify their area. They seem to have lived somewhere in west central Texas. Their affiliations remain unknown.

BIBLIOGRAPHY: Charles W. Hackett, ed., *Pichardo's Treatise on the Limits of Louisiana and Texas* (4 vols., Austin: University of Texas Press, 1931–46).

Thomas N. Campbell

COMO INDIANS. The Como Indians, a group living inland from the Quitoles, was met by Álvar Núñez Cabeza de Vaca[qv] in South Texas between 1528 and 1534.

BIBLIOGRAPHY: Frederick Webb Hodge, ed., *Handbook of American Indians North of Mexico* (2 vols., Washington: GPO, 1907, 1910; rpt., New York: Pageant, 1959).

Margery H. Krieger

COMPROMISE OF 1850. The results of the Mexican War[qv] (1846–48) brought Texas into serious conflict with the national government over the state's claim to a large portion of New Mexico. The claim was based on efforts by the Republic of Texas,[qv] beginning in 1836, to expand far beyond the traditional boundaries of Spanish and Mexican Texas to encompass all of the land extending the entire length of the Rio Grande. Efforts to occupy the New Mexican portion of this territory during the years of the republic came to naught (see TEXAN SANTA FE EXPEDITION).

In the early months of the Mexican War, however, federal troops, commanded by Gen. Stephen W. Kearny, easily occupied New Mexico. Kearny quickly established a temporary civil government. When Texas governor J. Pinckney Henderson[qv] complained to United States secretary of state James Buchanan, the latter replied that, though the matter would have to be settled by Congress, Kearny's action should not prejudice the Texas claim. By the provisions of the Treaty of Guadalupe Hidalgo,[qv] Mexico relinquished all claim to territory north and east of the Rio Grande. The treaty did not, however, speak to the issue of the Texas claim to that portion of New Mexico lying east of the river.

By this time New Mexico and all other lands ceded to the United States by Mexico had become embroiled in the slavery[qv] controversy. Southern leaders insisted that all of the new territory be opened to slaveholders and their human property. Northern freesoilers and abolitionists were determined to prevent such an opening and so resisted the claims of Texas to part of the area in question. Texas attempted to further its claim by organizing Santa Fe County in 1848, with boundaries including most of New Mexico east of the Rio Grande. In New Mexico military and civilian leaders then petitioned the federal government to organize their area into a federal territory. Texas governor George T. Wood[qv] responded by asking the legislature to give him the power and means to assert the claim of Texas to New Mexico "with the whole power and resources of the State." Soon afterward his successor, Peter H. Bell,[qv] made a more moderate request, asking only for authority to send a military force sufficient to maintain the state's authority in that area. Bell then sent Robert S. Neighbors[qv] west to organize four counties in the disputed area. Although he was successful in the El Paso area, Neighbors was not welcomed in New Mexico.

Publication of the report of Neighbors's mission in June of 1850 led to a public outcry in Texas. Some persons advocated the use of military force; others urged secession. Bell reacted by calling a special session of the legislature to deal with the issue. Before the session began, the crisis deepened. New Mexicans ratified a constitution for a proposed state specifying boundaries that included the territory claimed by Texas. Also, President Millard Fillmore reinforced the army contingent stationed in New Mexico and asserted publicly that should Texas militiamen enter the disputed area he would order federal troops to resist them. Southern political leaders responded by sending Governor Bell offers of moral and even military support.

Meanwhile, the United States Congress was grappling with the issue. On January 16, 1850, Senator Thomas Hart Benton of Missouri introduced a bill that would have had Texas cede all land west of 102° longitude and north of the Red River to the United States for $15 million. The bill would also divide Texas into two states. Soon afterward, Senator John Bell of Tennessee offered a resolution that would have divided Texas into three states. Then a Senate committee, chaired by Henry Clay of Kentucky, reported a bill that would have given Texas an unspecified sum in exchange for ceding all lands northwest of a straight line from the El Paso area to that point on the 100th meridian that intersects the Red River. None of these efforts proved successful.

Finally, Senator James A. Pierce of Maryland introduced a bill that offered Texas $10 million in exchange for ceding to the national government all land north and west of a boundary beginning at the 100th meridian where it intersects the parallel of 36°30′, then running west along that parallel to the 103d meridian, south to the 32d parallel, and from that point west to the Rio Grande. The bill had the support of the Texas delegation and of moderate leaders in both the North and South. Holders of bonds representing the debt of the Republic of Texas[qv] lobbied hard for the bill, for it specified that part of the financial settlement be used to pay those obligations. The measure passed both houses of Congress in the late summer of 1850 and was signed by President Fillmore.

Though there was some opposition in Texas to accepting the proffered settlement, voters at a special election approved it by a margin of three to one. The legislature then approved an act of acceptance, which Governor Bell signed on November 25, 1850. The boundary act and four additional bills passed at about the same time, all dealing with controversial sectional issues, came to be known collectively as the Compromise of 1850.

BIBLIOGRAPHY: William Campbell Binkley, *The Expansionist Movement in Texas, 1836–1850* (Berkeley: University of California Press, 1925). Holman Hamilton, *Prologue to Conflict: The Crisis and Compromise of 1850* (Lexington: University of Kentucky Press, 1964). Kenneth F. Neighbours, "The Taylor-Neighbors Struggle over the Upper Rio Grande in 1850," *Southwestern Historical Quarterly* 61 (April 1958).

Roger A. Griffin

COMPTROLLER OF PUBLIC ACCOUNTS. The office of comptroller of public accounts was established by Article IV, Sections 1 and 23 of the Constitution of 1876.[qv] As a state office it was first established by the Constitution of 1845[qv] and superseded a similar office originally established in 1835 and made part of the Treasury Department during the Republic of Texas[qv] in 1836.

The comptroller is elected and serves for four years. The major duties of the office are keeping accounts of state funds, acting as tax administrator and collector for the state, and furnishing research and statistics for estimating revenue. The comptroller submits financial reports to the governor and the legislature with statements on the previous fiscal year, outstanding appropriations, and estimates of anticipated revenue.

The comptroller's office is composed of a number of divisions designed to carry out various tasks. The Administration Area includes budget, support services, training, and personnel divisions to monitor agency expenditures and funds, maintain agency inventories, and train and keep records on personnel. The Audit Area conducts audits on twenty-eight state taxes, including the sales tax, which is the state's largest single revenue source. An Internal Audit Area provides an independent review of the office's accounting activities. The Communications Area provides taxpayer information to the public, while the Enforcement Area has several operations that collect delinquent taxes, file criminal complaints, issue licenses, and execute various other tax-related procedures. A Data Processing division disseminates information through the agency's computer network. Other areas of operation in the comptroller's office include Fiscal Management, Revenue Management, Legal/Policy, Local Government, and State Accounting Operations. These divisions prepare economic forecasts, process tax returns and license applications, assist counties and cities in collecting revenue, handle claims against the state, and issue annual expenditure reports. The comptroller's office had a budget totaling over $115 million in 1991, when about 2,800 employees worked in the agency.

Laurie E. Jasinski

COMSTOCK. The hydraulic hopper dredge *General C. B. Comstock* was built for the United States Army Corps of Engineers in 1895; the hull was built at Perth Amboy, New Jersey, and the internal mechanisms were supplied by the Bucyrus Steam Shovel and Dredge Company of South Milwaukee, Wisconsin. The ship was named for Cyrus B. Comstock, a prominent nineteenth-century corps of engineers officer. The *Comstock* was ordered for service in Galveston and designed for southern climates, with a metal-sheathed wooden hull and an airy, well-ventilated superstructure. She had the modern conveniences of her era: comfortable, well-furnished accommodations, hot and cold running water, and electric lighting.

The *Comstock* was 177 feet long and 35½ feet wide, and drew twelve feet. The two hoppers together held 600 to 650 cubic yards. The dredging system was based on two centrifugal dredging pumps, separately powered, each operating a fifty-foot, jointed suction pipe with interchangeable drags, one set for use in mud or clay and one for use in sand. The pipes were raised and lowered with steam cranes and derrick booms; they were designed to lift automatically over obstructions on the sea floor, and the *Comstock* could turn without raising the pipes.

The *Comstock* traveled to Galveston on her own keel in the summer of 1895 and spent most of her career there. The dredge was a very efficient machine that moved material at a cost of approximately 7.4 cents a cubic yard during her first year in Galveston. Wages for forty-two people operating her twenty-four hours a day ran to $2,030 a month in 1896. She could move four or five full loads in a ten-hour day; the hoppers could be discharged in 7½ minutes.

The *Comstock* suffered wear and tear from the demanding work schedule and accident and storm damage over the years. After being driven ashore by the Galveston hurricane of 1900,[qv] she could not be freed until a channel fifty feet wide and eight feet deep was dug to release her. She was converted from coal to oil in 1902 and overhauled several times. After 1910 she was lent to the Wilmington Corps District and sent to work first at Aransas Pass and afterward at Freeport. On February 17, 1913, she caught fire off the mouth of the Brazos River and burned to the water line. The crew was quickly rescued by fishermen from Quintana and the life-saving crew from Surfside, but the *Comstock* was a total loss. She was relocated during jetty construction in June 1987 and investigated and identified in 1988. The artifacts are in a collection at Corpus Christi Museum.

BIBLIOGRAPHY: Lynn M. Alperin, *Custodians of the Coast: History of the United States Army Engineers at Galveston* (Galveston: U.S. Army Corps of Engineers, 1977). C. B. Comstock Collection (Corpus Christi Museum of Science and History). *Engineering News*, November 7, 1895. Galveston *Daily News*, September 1, 1895, February 18, 1913.

Kay G. Hudson

COMSTOCK, TEXAS. Comstock is on U.S. Highway 90, State Highway 163, and the Southern Pacific Railroad, twenty-nine miles northwest of Del Rio in south central Val Verde County. About 6,000 years ago prehistoric people lived in the nearby caves and rockshelters. They left behind caches of seeds, bits of clothing, tools, burial sites, and cave art. Modern settlement of the area began in the 1800s and was aided by the advent of the railroad. The Galveston, Harrisburg and San Antonio Railway built tracks through the county in 1882 and 1883. Comstock was established as a station on the railroad and was named for John B. Comstock, a railroad dispatcher. Although the original townsite, called Sotol City, was built east of the current Comstock, it was moved to Comstock's present site to make use of water from a nearby natural lake. In 1888 a post office was granted to the small town. The same year George Washington Ames opened the Ames General Store, which sold groceries, lumber, salt, livestock feed, and ranch supplies. From 1888 until 1910 the Deaton Stage Line operated a six-horse stagecoach that changed teams four times between Comstock and Ozona. The company delivered mail and hauled freight. In 1889 the Phillips Hotel began to serve travelers stopping overnight in Comstock. In 1890 the D. C. Denny Lumber Yard was established; it was later converted into Uncle Denny's Saloon and Billiard Hall. By 1901 a public school at the community had one teacher and reported an enrollment of eighty-nine students. In 1925 the population of Comstock was 200. Ten businesses operated there by 1931, but the number dropped to eight during the late years of the Great Depression.[qv] During World War II[qv] the town had fifteen businesses and a population of 400; in the 1950s it had five businesses and a population of 300; by the early 1990s Comstock had twelve businesses and a population of 375.

BIBLIOGRAPHY: Kathleen E. and Clifton R. St. Clair, eds., *Little Towns of Texas* (Jacksonville, Texas: Jayroe Graphic Arts, 1982).

Julia Cauble Smith

COMYN, TEXAS. Comyn, on Farm Road 1496 in eastern Comanche County, was settled about 1875. The community was first called Theney for W. F. Matheney, who operated a trading post. In 1881, when the Texas Central Railroad built through the town and opened a depot there, the community's name was changed to Comyn, for M. T. Comyn, the construction foreman of the railroad; the local school, however, was still called Theney. In 1909 a post office was established in Comyn. The town also had a lumberyard, a blacksmith shop, a cotton gin, a number of stores, and a Woodmen of the World lodge. In 1918 the Humble Pipe Line Company built a pipeline connecting Comyn with the Humble company's terminal at Webster. The company also began building a tank farm, and a large tent city sprang up at the site, but construction ceased in 1919 and the people moved on. Between 1924 and 1926 the Humble Pipe Line Company extended the Comyn pipeline west to Kempner and extended the trunk line between Comyn and Webster. A large school complex was built in Comyn in 1924. Decreasing oil production in West Texas led to Comyn's decline. Low attendance forced its school to close in 1952, and its post office closed in the late 1950s. Comyn's estimated population in 1939 was thirty and in 1974 and 1990 was twenty-seven. In 1976 the town had a Baptist church, a Humble Oil Company (later Exxon Company, U.S.A.) office, and the Shell Peanut Company. By 1980 most businesses had moved out of the community, although the oil company still had an office and pipeline pumping station there.

BIBLIOGRAPHY: T. Lindsay Baker, *Ghost Towns of Texas* (Norman: University of Oklahoma Press, 1986).

Tracey L. Compton

CONA INDIANS. The Conas, a semisedentary group called Teya by the Spaniards, was identified with the Hainais. Their settlement was visited by Francisco Vásquez de Coronado[qv] and his army in 1541.

CONCAN, TEXAS. Concan (Con Can) is on the Frio River and State Highway 127 in north central Uvalde County. According to local lore, the town was named after "coon can," a Mexican card game. Though the site may have been settled as early as 1840, the first log cabin with a chimney was built there in the 1860s by Theophilus Watkins.qv The settlement was awarded a post office in 1880, and J. A. Robinson became the first postmaster. By 1884 Concan had grown to an estimated 150 residents, and a blacksmith shop had been established there; wool and beef were transported from the town to the nearest railroad station at Uvalde. In 1890 about 100 people lived in Concan, and the community had a cotton gin, a blacksmith, and a wagonmaker. The town declined in the early 1890s, however. Its post office was discontinued in 1894 and was not reopened until 1900, when John S. Caddel and his brother began operating a store there. In 1914 Concan had a post office and general store. During the late 1920s the population of Concan was about twenty, and the town had begun to attract tourists; by 1929 the Shut In, on the west bank of the Frio, had become the center of the town. A sawmill was opened at the community in the late 1930s to harvest the cedar, wild cherry, cypress, and walnut trees in the Frio Canyon, and by 1939 Concan had grown to about seventy-five residents. A 1946 map showed a church and a small collection of buildings at the site. The population level remained fairly stable from the early 1940s to the early 1970s, when the town included a post office, a church, two stores, and a community center. By that time the town and the surrounding area had become a popular tourist spot. During the fall and winter, hunters, in search of deer, doves, and wild turkeys, stayed in Concan; during the spring and summer, visitors came to enjoy the clear waters of the Frio River. Concan had seventy-one residents in 1990.

BIBLIOGRAPHY: *A Proud Heritage: A History of Uvalde County* (Uvalde, Texas: El Progreso Club, 1975). *John Leffler*

CONCEPCIÓN, BATTLE OF. The battle of Concepción occurred on October 28, 1835, the opening engagement in the siege of Bexar.qv After the skirmish at Gonzales on October 2 (the battle of Gonzalesqv), the Texas army under Stephen F. Austinqv grew to 400 men as it advanced on San Antonio. Gen. Martín Perfecto de Cos,qv with a Mexican army that peaked in size at 750 men in late October, fortified the plazas in San Antonio and the Alamo mission (San Antonio de Valero) across the river.

On October 27 Austin ordered James Bowie and James W. Fannin, Jr.,qqv to lead ninety men from San Francisco de la Espada Mission to locate a protected position closer to the town. The four companies of Andrew Briscoe, Robert M. Coleman, Valentine Bennet,qqv and Michael Goheen explored the other missions and briefly engaged Mexican scouts before reaching Concepción. There the officers decided to camp for the evening rather than return to the main army as Austin had directed. The Texans occupied a wooded bend in the San Antonio River protected by an embankment, and sent out pickets to warn of a Mexican attack. A few cannon shots from the town failed to inflict losses.

Cos seized the opportunity to attack the separate force the next day, sending out Col. Domingo de Ugartecheaqv with 275 men and two cannons before dawn. The 200 Mexican cavalry drove in the Texan guards in early morning fog and formed on the west side of the river. Lt. Col. José María Mendoza led the smaller infantry and artillery forces across the stream to attack from the east. Mexican volleys crashed through the trees overhead, but inflicted no casualties among the Texans until Bowie moved Coleman's company to meet the advance. Then one man fell mortally wounded. The Texans responded with accurate rifle fire that drove back three Mexican charges and killed or wounded most of the infantry and artillerymen in about thirty minutes. Then the Texans counterattacked and captured one of the cannons. Mexican cavalry covered the retreat of the infantry and cannoneers who survived.

Austin and his other troops rushed to the field when they heard firing, but arrived too late to do more than hurry the Mexican withdrawal. Austin urged an assault on the town, but most of his officers believed San Antonio too well fortified. Mexican losses included fourteen killed and thirty-nine wounded, some of whom died later. Texas losses included one killed and one wounded.

BIBLIOGRAPHY: Alwyn Barr, *Texans in Revolt: The Battle for San Antonio, 1835* (Austin: University of Texas Press, 1990).
Alwyn Barr

CONCEPCION, TEXAS. Concepcion is on Farm Road 716 and Macho Creek, fourteen miles southeast of Benavides and twenty-eight miles southwest of San Diego in southeastern Duval County. It was named after Santa Cruz de Concepción, a land grant from the Spanish government to Francisco Cordente. Concepcion is one of the oldest towns in Duval County. Its post office was established in 1873, with Rafael F. Salinas as postmaster. By 1884 Concepcion had 600 residents and three general stores. Around this time Don Julian Palacios established himself as the leading local rancher, owning almost 3,000 sheep. He also served as a justice of the peace. In 1892 the town had a population estimated at 100, four general stores, two blacksmiths, and a shoemaker. In the 1906–07 school year sixty-four pupils attended the Concepcion school. In 1913 Concepcion fell victim to the political maneuvers of Duval County political boss Archer Parr,qv who sought to split the county to organize Pat Dunn County.qv Concepcion had had a voting box of its own for more than thirty years, but Parr's supporters, seeking to ensure the selection of Benavides as the seat of the new county, drew a precinct boundary through Concepcion and forced its voters to travel either to Mazatlan, about ten miles away, or to Benavides to cast their ballots. Pat Dunn County never became a reality because the legislation authorizing it violated the state constitution. In 1914 the population of Concepcion was estimated at 150, and over the next fifteen years estimates varied from a low of seventy-five in 1925 to a high of 500 in 1927. From the mid-1930s until the mid-1960s the population was usually reported as seventy-five. In the late 1940s the town had six businesses and was a trade center for the Concepcion oilfield. The Concepcion school was consolidated with the Benavides Independent School District sometime between 1955 and 1968, when the town had a few scattered dwellings, a church, and one business. In the early 1970s Concepcion's population was estimated at twenty-five, where it remained through 1990. *Martin Donell Kohout*

CONCEPCION CREEK. Concepcion Creek rises nine miles west of Benavides in central Duval County (at 27°34′ N, 98°38′ W) and runs southeast for seventeen miles to its junction with Agua Poquita Creek to form Los Olmos Creek, eight miles south of Benavides (at 27°30′ N, 98°27′ W). Concepcion Creek was formerly known as Rosalia Creek, after the Spanish Santa Rosalia land grant made to Rafael Ramirez. The surrounding flat terrain with local shallow depressions is surfaced by clay and sandy loams that support water-tolerant hardwoods, conifers, and grasses.

CONCEPCIÓN DE AGREDA PUEBLO. Concepción de Agreda, the Indian pueblo attached to Nuestra Señora de Guadalupe de la Purísima Concepción de los Hainais Mission, was reorganized and named by Martín de Alarcónqv on his inspection tour of Texas in 1718.

BIBLIOGRAPHY: Carlos E. Castañeda, *Our Catholic Heritage in Texas* (7 vols., Austin: Von Boeckmann–Jones, 1936–58; rpt., New York: Arno, 1976). Fray Francisco Céliz, *Diary of the Alarcón Expedition into*

Texas, 1718–1719, trans. F. L. Hoffman (Los Angeles: Quivira Society, 1935; rpt., New York: Arno Press, 1967).   *Winifred W. Vigness*

CONCHAMUCHA INDIANS. In 1683–84 Juan Domínguez de Mendoza^{qv} led an exploratory expedition from El Paso as far eastward as the junction of the Concho and Colorado rivers east of the site of present San Angelo. In his itinerary he listed the names of thirty-seven Indian groups, including the Conchamuchas, from whom he expected to receive delegations. Nothing further is known about the Conchamuchas, whose name is Spanish for "much shell" and suggests that they lived near the Concho River, so named because of its abundant freshwater mussel shells. The Conchamuchas seem to have been one of many Indian groups of north central Texas that were swept into oblivion by the southward thrust of the Lipan Apache and Comanche Indians in the eighteenth century.

BIBLIOGRAPHY: Herbert Eugene Bolton, ed., *Spanish Exploration in the Southwest, 1542–1706* (New York: Scribner, 1908; rpt., New York: Barnes and Noble, 1959). Charles W. Hackett, ed., *Pichardo's Treatise on the Limits of Louisiana and Texas* (4 vols., Austin: University of Texas Press, 1931–46).   *Thomas N. Campbell*

CONCHATÉ INDIANS. Juan Antonio Padilla's^{qv} report on Texas Indians in 1820 listed the Conchatés as being a branch of the Nadacos or Anadarko "nation," which lived between the Trinity and Sabine rivers. They had aided José Bernardo Gutiérrez de Lara^{qv} at the time of the Gutiérrez-Magee expedition.^{qv}

CONCHO, TEXAS. Concho is on Ranch Road 1929 and the Concho River, seven miles northeast of Paint Rock in northeastern Concho County. It had a post office from 1905 until sometime after 1936. Its first school opened in 1906–07 with one teacher. The community had a cotton gin and a Woodmen of the World lodge in 1908 and a general store and a blacksmith in 1914. In 1936, in addition to the school and the post office, Concho had two businesses and a scattering of other buildings. In 1940 its seven-grade school had two teachers and an average daily attendance of thirty-one students. By 1955 the Concho school district had been consolidated with that of Paint Rock. Concho's reported population stood at twenty in 1914, declined to fifteen by 1925, rose to fifty by 1939, and dropped to thirty by 1968. A 1987 topographical map showed a cemetery and one occupied building at the community.

BIBLIOGRAPHY: Gus Clemens, Jr., *The Concho Country* (San Antonio: Mulberry Avenue, 1980). Hazie LeFevre, *Concho County History: 1858–1958* (2 vols., Eden, Texas, 1959). W. C. Montgomery, *Have You Ever Heard of the Great Concho Country?* (Ballinger, Texas, 1908). Vernon Lee Rucker, A Proposed Reorganization of the Concho County, Texas, Public Schools (M.Ed. thesis, University of Texas, 1940).   *Mary M. Standifer*

CONCHO COUNTY. Concho County (H-13), in Central Texas, straddles the northern edge of the Edwards Plateau.^{qv} The county derives its name from the Concho (or "Shell") River, which in turn was named for the large number of mussels found there. The center of the county lies at approximately 31°20′ north latitude and 99°52′ west longitude. Paint Rock, the county seat, is situated in the north central part of the county on U.S. Highway 83, approximately thirty miles east of San Angelo and 150 miles northwest of Austin. Concho County comprises 992 square miles with an elevation of 1,600 to 2,100 feet above mean sea level. The terrain in the north is rolling, with steep slopes and benches, while that to the south, on the Edwards Plateau, is flat but broken by numerous deep creekbeds. The thin and stony soil of the Edwards Plateau supports oak, juniper, and mesquite, while the clay loams to the north sustain grasses, mixed with oak, juniper, and mesquite in the northwest and with mesquite in the north central region. The county is drained by the Concho River, which flows east to west across the northern part, and by the Colorado River, which forms the northeastern county line. Major creeks, or creek systems, include Dry Hollow, Kickapoo, Duck, Mustang, Brady, and South Brady. The creekbeds were originally thick with elm, live oak, and post oak trees. Of the total county area, 11 to 20 percent is considered to be prime farmland. Temperatures range from an average low of 33° F in January to an average high of 97° in July. Rainfall averages twenty-three inches; snowfall, three inches; and the growing season, 228 days per year. The climate, on the whole, is mild and dry. Natural resources include oil and gas, limestone, caliche, dolomite, and bituminous coal. In 1982, 218,748 barrels of oil and 1,982,444 thousand cubic feet of gas-well gas were produced in the county.

The two sites of Indian activity in Concho County that have drawn the most attention lie along the bluffs of the Concho and Colorado rivers. About a mile west of Paint Rock, above the Concho, are found some of the most noted Indian pictographs in Texas (*see* PAINT ROCK). To the east of Paint Rock on the Colorado, the area of O. H. Ivie Reservoir^{qv} has been the scene of the most intensive archeological investigation in the county. Evidence here indicates occupation as early as 10,000 to 8,000 B.C. The area was attractive for its plentiful food, water, and lithic resources, and for the protective high cliffs along the river. The diet of the groups who camped here may have consisted of such plant foods as yucca, prickly pear, mesquite beans, pecans, and grass seeds, as well as fish, mussels, prairie chickens, and wild turkeys. Deer would not have been abundant, and buffalo^{qv} may not have been generally available until the late Archaic Period (ca. A.D. 1100). In 1981 this area marked the farthest point north that ring middens and burned-rock middens had been discovered.

Around 1500 Athabascan-speaking Indians associated with the prehorse Plains culture lived in this part of Texas. In the 1600s the Jumanos established themselves along the Concho and traded with the Spaniards. Seeking protection against the Lipan Apaches, in 1683 the Jumanos requested that the Spaniards establish a mission in their territory. In response to this request Juan Domínguez de Mendoza^{qv} led an expedition in 1684 that built a temporary mission, San Clemente, at a location that has been fixed variously west of Ballinger, near the confluence of the Concho and Colorado, on the South Llano, and on the San Saba a little west of Menard. After several months, however, attacks by the Apaches forced the Spaniards to withdraw. By 1771 the Jumanos had apparently been absorbed by the Lipans. A map of Texas in 1776 places the area of Concho County within the domain of the Lipans, which extended southward from the Colorado River. The territory above the Colorado belonged to the Comanches, and that east of the Colorado to the Tonkawas. By about 1840 the Comanches had overrun the area of Concho County and pushed as far south as the vicinity of modern Austin. By the late 1850s the Lipan Apaches had reestablished control over the Concho valley, though Comanches continued to raid along the river in the 1860s and 1870s. The last significant conflict in the area between Indians and whites ended with the 1874 campaign of Ranald S. Mackenzie,^{qv} which drove the remaining Indians out of the region and forced them onto reservations.

The area of present-day Concho County was included in the Fisher-Miller Land Grant^{qv} of 1842. By 1845 the Adelsverein^{qv} (the Society for the Protection of German Immigrants in Texas) had secured complete rights to the Fisher-Miller contract. In 1847 John O. Meusebach,^{qv} after concluding a peace treaty with the Comanches, sent surveyors into the tract on behalf of the society. The area surveyed included much of the land along the banks of the Concho River now in Concho County. Although the colonization contract stipulated that the lots surveyed should be as nearly square as possible, the survey marked off long lots along the Concho. This may have been done to increase access to a water supply, since rain in the region is sparse. The Concho country did not yet attract immigration, however, as it lay beyond the farming frontier where Indian attacks were frequent.

The next notable settlement in the area took place in 1849, when Robert S. Neighbors^{qv} led a small expedition in search of a wagon route to El Paso. American interest in establishing routes to the West had been intensified in 1848 by the acquisition of the Mexican Cession and by the discovery of gold in California. Neighbors's group, which included John S. Ford,qv crossed the southern part of the future Concho County, following the course of Brady Creek. The route that Neighbors subsequently recommended, known as the Upper Route, passed just south of the county; it was used extensively by emigrants and the military.

The legislature formed Concho County out of Bexar County in 1858, but it was not organized until 1879. In the meantime, in the early to middle 1860s, cattlemen began to move into the open range in Concho and adjacent counties. John S. Chisum,qv the first large-scale cattleman in the county, established a string of cow camps on the Concho River in the northeastern part of the county in 1862 or 1863. He moved his headquarters to New Mexico in 1873, though he still had a camp on the Concho near the site of present-day Paint Rock in the fall of that year. There is no record of his activity in the area after 1875. Other large early operations included the U-Bar and OH Ranch, or Concho Cattle Company, which first ran cattle about 1878, and the Davies and Holland Ranch. Both of these operated in the 1880s and 1890s. For the most part, however, ranching in Concho County was relatively small-scale.

As the Texas farming frontier advanced, cattle drives shifted from the more easterly Chisholm and Shawnee trailsqqv to the Western Trail.qv The Western Trail began in South Texas and pushed northward through the center of Concho County, crossing the Colorado River at the Concho-Coleman county line. Near the site of present-day Eden the Goodnight-Loving Trailqv branched off from the Western Trail and led toward New Mexico. By the mid-1880s, however, most of the grazing land in Concho County had been enclosed. In 1888 the Gulf, Colorado and Santa Fe Railway completed a line from Ballinger, in Runnels County, to San Angelo, in Tom Green County, giving Concho County ranchers their closest rail access to markets. It was another two decades, however, before railroads built into Concho County itself.

Concho County was organized in 1879, after the required petition was signed by at least seventy-five voters. There being no established community in the county, the vote to select officers and a site for the county seat was held near Mullins Crossing on the Concho. The location chosen for the county seat was at a ford on the Concho about a mile below the mouth of Kickapoo Creek, twelve miles west of the confluence of the Concho and Colorado rivers, and five miles south of the Concho-Runnels county line. The county seat was named Paint Rock, after the nearby pictographs. The town developed steadily. By 1884 it had an estimated population of 100 and had become a shipping center for pecans, wool, hides, and mutton (the cattle were routed elsewhere). In 1886 a permanent courthouse was constructed.

Eden, on Hardin Branch in the south central region of the county, was established in 1882. By 1931, when Paint Rock had reached its peak population of 1,000, Eden had surpassed it with 1,194. Thereafter the population of Paint Rock declined and that of Eden remained relatively constant. The southwestern part of the county saw the development of several early communities, but none of them attained any size, and the names of all but one have disappeared from the map. These included Kickapoo Springs, Erskine, and Vigo, which succeeded one another on virtually the same location on Kickapoo Creek. Ruth and Live Oak (the latter still marked on the 1963 county map) were situated approximately ten miles and eight miles southwest of Eden, respectively. In the west central part of the county grew up the small communities of Vick and Henderson Chapel and, around the turn of the century, the more substantial community of Eola. In 1988 Eola was the third largest town in the county. Lowake, on the Concho, San Saba and Llano Valley Railroad in the far northwestern corner of Concho County, was established in 1909. Concho, a small community on the Concho River about seven miles northeast of Paint Rock, maintained itself through the 1960s. Millersview, in the east central region, acquired a post office in 1903 and in 1988 was the fourth largest community in the county. In the southeast, the communities of Pasche, Welview, and Lightner grew up along the railroads that entered the county around 1910, but none of these has survived.

At the time of the first census, most settlers had come from Arkansas, Tennessee, Mississippi, Alabama, and Kentucky, in that order. A map of nineteenth-century cultural distributions in the county shows the eastern half dominated by the "Appalachian hill folk" culture, a way of life imported chiefly from the Appalachians and Ozarks and oriented to a subsistence economy. The western half of the county had a blend of the Appalachian culture and that of the middle-class upper South, which embraced grain and cotton farming and was oriented to a market economy.

Between 1910 and 1912 three railroad lines were completed into or through Concho County. The Concho, San Saba and Llano Valley was completed from Miles, in southwestern Runnels County, to Paint Rock in 1910. In 1911 the Fort Worth and Rio Grande Railway completed a line across the southeastern corner of the county, and in 1912 the Gulf, Colorado and Santa Fe finished a line from Lometa, in Lampasas County, to Eden. All of these lines have been abandoned, that to Paint Rock in the mid-1930s and those to Eden and through the southeastern corner in 1972.

The population grew steadily from 800 in 1880, the date of the county's first census, to 1,427 in 1900. Over the next ten years the figure jumped to 6,654, the greatest increase in the county's history. Part of this growth may have been stimulated by the work of the Pecan, Colorado, Concho Immigration Association, which operated during the 1890s on behalf of Concho and ten other counties. The influx was also doubtless encouraged by a number of wet years between 1895 and 1910, which, together with the introduction of improved dry-land-farming techniques, made agriculture appear more viable. In addition, an act of the state legislature in 1895 made the purchase of public land easier by reducing the price and allowing forty years for payment at 3 percent interest. After peaking at 7,645 in 1930, the population of Concho County began a steady decline that was intensified by the drought of 1950–56. In 1980 the population stood at 2,915.

The population of Concho County has remained overwhelmingly white. Fewer than twenty black residents have been enumerated in every census year except 1920, when 198 were reported, and 1930, when 82 were counted. It is difficult to trace the presence of Hispanics in the county because they were apparently not recorded separately from Anglos until recently. In 1980, the first year in which they were specifically enumerated, Hispanics in Concho County numbered 806, or 28 percent of the total population.

In the mid-twentieth century, concentrations of ethnic groups in the county included pockets of Germansqv in the northwest corner and a cluster of Swedesqv on the Concho-McCulloch county line. In 1970 over 100 Czechsqv resided in the vicinity of Eola, in the far west central part of the county. A 1971 map of religious affiliation showed, in the extreme northwest corner, a Catholic simple majority with substantial Lutheran and Reformed representation. In the extreme southeast, Baptists were a simple majority and Methodists had a significant presence. Elsewhere in the county Baptists were an absolute majority and Methodists a minority.

The local economy, based originally on cattle, soon embraced sheep ranchingqv and farming. In 1988, when Concho County was the leading sheep-producing county in Texas, 60 percent of its $15 million in farm income came from sheep, cattle, and goats, and the leading crops were grains and cotton. In 1982 farms and ranches occupied 95 percent of the county. Sheep were first introduced into the county in the 1870s and by 1890, the year of the first enumeration, numbered 41,724. After a coyote-eradication campaign between 1917 and 1922 the number of sheep soared, increasing from 41,802 in 1920 to 220,533 in 1930. Most shepherds employed in the care of these flocks were

Mexican-American *pastores*.qv Angora goats also became an important resource. Their numbers increased from 197 in 1900 to 4,248 in 1920 and 18,483 in 1930. The largest increase in cattle came between 1880 and 1900, when the number reached 56,182. This figure was reduced by almost half over the next decade, when farming became widespread, and fell to a low of 11,903 in 1940. After that date the number of cattle rose again, reaching a total of 26,364 in 1969.

The number of farms in Concho County increased dramatically between 1900 and 1910, the decade of swiftest population growth. The total of 865 farms in 1910, compared to 119 in 1900, marks the second highest recorded level, next to the top figure of 1,137 reached in 1930. Subsequently the number of farms declined to 376 by 1982. Though farm acreage fell slightly during the period of rapid growth between 1900 and 1910, the number of improved acres increased more than tenfold. Of the land under cultivation, by far the most was devoted to cotton, a crop that dominated Concho County agriculture until the 1930s, partly because it is relatively drought resistant. The number of acres devoted to cotton culture qv rose from 591 in 1900 to 38,734 in 1910. By 1930 the figure had soared to 72,381 acres (65 percent of the acres harvested).

With cotton cultivation came tenant farming. In 1900 only four of the county's 119 farms had been operated by tenants. By 1910, more than half the farms in the county were tenant-operated. A drought in 1917–18 reduced both the total number of farms and the number operated by tenants, so that by 1920 owner-operated farms were slightly more numerous. As the number of acres planted in cotton doubled between 1920 and 1930, however, the number of tenant farmers soared. During this decade, also, sharecropping became a prominent feature of Concho County agriculture. In 1930, 449 farms were operated by owners and 682 by tenants, of whom 619 were sharecroppers—a greater than tenfold increase in sharecroppers since 1920.

The dramatic increase in cotton production in Concho County reflected the fiber's growing importance both at home and abroad. But by 1928 prices began to signal a glut in the market. With the onset of the international depression, revenues from cotton plummeted. Between 1928–29 and 1932–33, the average gross income per cotton-farm family fell nationwide from $735 to $216. Beginning in 1933 the federal government undertook a series of measures designed to limit the amount of cotton grown. Other factors discouraging production included an increased import allowance on foreign-grown cotton, the introduction of synthetics, and a shortage of labor during World War II.qv In 1940 cotton still claimed the most acres in Concho County, but the number had fallen to 29,301, while sorghum culture,qv which now occupied 21,556 acres, had made heavy inroads on former cotton lands. By 1969 cotton cultivation accounted for 10,837 acres, or 11 percent of acres harvested. The drop in cotton acreage resulted in the displacement of large numbers of tenant farmers throughout the South. Between 1930 and 1950, the number of rented farms in Concho County rose from 63 to 164, but the number of farms worked by sharecroppers fell from 619 to 25. In 1910 sorghum grains were second in importance to cotton in Concho County, with 10,241 acres in cultivation. By 1950 sorghum had surpassed cotton, and wheat culture qv had risen to rough parity; that year sorghum was grown on 33,346 acres, cotton on 30,502, and wheat on 25,803 acres. In 1969 wheat claimed 27,397 acres (27 percent of acres harvested) and sorghum, 22,698 acres (23 percent of acres harvested). Like cotton, sorghum and wheat are relatively drought resistant. In 1982, 7 percent of Concho County farmland was irrigated.

Manufacturing has never become established in Concho County on a significant scale. One manufacturing establishment was reported in 1982, and the county has seldom recorded more than that figure.

Between 1930 and 1940 the Great Depressionqv reduced the number of farms in Concho County by more than half (1,137 to 483), while the population declined from 7,645 to 6,192. Federal programs provided some relief: between 1933 and 1940 the Concho County Agricultural Adjustment Office disbursed $1,649,465 to county farmers and ranchers. Federal programs also made possible soil and range conservation measures, which were then implemented for the first time on a wide scale. Terracing and contour farming were introduced, and funds became available for the construction of dams, tanks, and wells, and for the eradication of prickly pear cactus. In 1940 Concho County became part of a soil-conservation district. The use of tractors also seems to have become prevalent during the 1930s, as the number of mules, which had averaged 1,717 in the three census years since 1910, dropped to 257 in 1940.

In the early decades, education in Concho County was largely a matter of one-teacher country schools. By 1940 the county had four independent school districts, in the incorporated communities of Paint Rock, Eden, Eola, and Millersview, and ten common-school districts. A study conducted that year found significant differences in the education offered by these districts. The common schools had a more limited curriculum and also placed greater instructional demands on their teachers, having too few instructors for the number of grades taught. In addition, fewer than half of the teachers in the common schools had completed bachelor's degrees (8 of 23), while virtually all of the teachers in the independent school districts had done so (46 of 47). By 1955 the total number of districts had been reduced to four and by 1989 to two, Paint Rock and Eden. Between 1950 and 1960, the percentage of Concho County residents over the age of twenty-five who had completed high school doubled, rising from 10 to 21 percent.

In national elections, Concho County has most often voted Democratic, although the Republican party qv won some of them in the twentieth century. The Republicans' first presidential victory in the county was a twenty-vote win for Herbert Hoover over Alfred E. Smith in 1928. Subsequent victories were registered by Dwight D. Eisenhower qv in 1952 and 1956, Richard M. Nixon in 1972, and Ronald Reagan in 1984. On the Democratic side, the most massive victories were recorded by Franklin D. Roosevelt and Harry S. Truman, who polled more than 1,000 votes in each election between 1932 and 1948, while opponents received fewer than 200. The county voted for Democrats in 1988 and 1992. Third parties have never carried a national election in Concho County, although the Socialists beat the Republicans in 1912 and 1916 and made a strong third-place showing in 1920.

In 1990 the population of Concho County was 3,044. The largest towns were Eden and Paint Rock. Attractions included boating, hunting, fishing, the Paint Rock pictographs, and the Concho County Fair, which is held annually in August and September.

BIBLIOGRAPHY: Gus Clemens, Jr., *The Concho Country* (San Antonio: Mulberry Avenue, 1980). *Concho Herald*, October 11, 1940. Irene Henderson, The History of the U-Bar and O H Ranch (M.A. thesis, Southwest Texas State Teachers College, 1939). Hazie LeFevre, *Concho County History: 1858–1958* (2 vols., Eden, Texas, 1959). John A. Loomis, *Texas Ranchman: The Memoirs of John A. Loomis,* ed. Herman J. Viola and Sarah Loomis Wilson (Chadron, Nebraska: Fur Press, 1982). Orlando L. Sims, *Cowpokes, Nesters, and So Forth* (Austin: Encino, 1970).
Mary M. Standifer

CONCHO RIVER. The Concho River rises in three branches known as the North Concho, the Middle Concho, and the South Concho. The North Concho, the main branch and a perennial stream, originates two miles north of the Glasscock county line in southern Howard County (at 31°07′ N, 101°24′ W) and flows southeast for eighty-eight miles across Glasscock, Sterling, Coke, and Tom Green counties to its confluence with the South and Middle Concho rivers, a mile north of Goodfellow Air Force Base in central Tom Green County (at 32°27′ N, 100°27′ W). The three forks become known as the Concho River at this juncture. San Angelo Dam, which became known as O. C. Fisher Dam (*see* O. C. FISHER LAKE) was completed on the North Concho in 1951. The Middle Concho rises in southern

Sterling County (at 31°38′ N, 101°13′ W) and runs south and then east for sixty-four miles through Irion County to Twin Buttes Reservoir[qv] in western Tom Green County and then to its mouth on Lake Nasworthy[qv] (at 31°23′ N, 100°31′ W). The South Concho rises half a mile east of U.S. Highway 277 in central Schleicher County (at 30°51′ N, 100°35′ W) and flows north for thirty-six miles through Twin Buttes Reservoir, which was built on the branch in 1963, and Lake Nasworthy, which was completed in 1930, to its confluence with the North Concho River (at 31°27′ N, 100°25′ W). The consolidated Concho River flows east for fifty-eight miles across Tom Green and Concho counties to its mouth on the Colorado River, one-half mile west of the Coleman county line and one mile south of the Runnels county line in eastern Concho County (at 31°34′ N, 99°43′ W). Along its route it is joined by fifteen tributaries. Construction of the Simon W. Freeze Dam on the Colorado River, sixteen miles below the confluence of the Colorado and Concho, and the O. H. Ivie Reservoir[qv] (formerly Stacy Dam and Reservoir) has flooded the lower reaches of the Concho; water in the reservoir was impounded in 1990. The Concho River and its branches traverse a 246-mile path, crossing caliche beds and wash deposits on flat and rolling terrain, dissecting massive limestone, and ending on steep slopes and benches of limestone and marl. The surrounding soils are generally dark and calcareous stony clays and loams, dark brown to red-brown calcareous sandy clays and loams, and red-brown to gray-brown sandy and clay loams. Vegetation along the river consists primarily of water-tolerant hardwoods and conifers, grasses, scrub brush, creosote bush, cacti, oak, juniper, and mesquite.

The river is named for Spanish *concha,* "shell." When Hernán Martín and Diego del Castillo[qqv] explored the area in 1650, they found large quantities of mussel shells that yielded freshwater pearls. Their report was so enthusiastic that Diego de Guadalajara[qv] returned to the area four years later; unfortunately, the yield proved to be only about one decent pearl per 100 mussels, and any notion of systematic harvesting was abandoned. Although the river was first called Río de las Nueces because of the many pecans found in the area, the name Concho became the most widely used by the mid-nineteenth century. Some of the best-known Indian pictographs in Texas are found on bluffs along the Concho a mile west of Paint Rock. The river attracted many early Indian tribes, but the Comanches controlled it by the mid-1800s. In 1862 or 1863 John S. Chisum[qv] established a ranch on the Concho near its confluence with the Colorado. Fort Concho, a military installation designed to protect travelers and settlers from Indian attack, was established in 1867 at the confluence of the North Concho and the combined Middle and South branches, which offered a steady supply of water.

BIBLIOGRAPHY: Candace Beaver, "Stone Age Art Gallery," *Texas Highways,* July 1988. Carlos E. Castañeda, *Our Catholic Heritage in Texas* (7 vols., Austin: Von Boeckmann–Jones, 1936–58; rpt., New York: Arno, 1976). Roger N. Conger et al., *Frontier Forts of Texas* (Waco: Texian Press, 1966). Duford W. Skelton and Martha Doty Freeman, *A Cultural Resource Inventory and Assessment at Camp Swift, Texas* (Texas Archeological Resource Report No. 72, Austin: Texas Archeological Survey, University of Texas at Austin, 1979). Del Weniger, *The Explorers' Texas* (Austin: Eakin Press, 1984).

Julia Cauble Smith

CONCHO, SAN SABA AND LLANO VALLEY RAILROAD. The Concho, San Saba and Llano Valley Railroad Company was chartered on April 2, 1909, with authority to build a railroad from northeast Tom Green County southeast to a connection with the San Antonio and Aransas Pass in either Kerr or Kendall counties. The initial capital was $250,000, and the business office was located at Miles in Runnels County. Members of the first board of directors included D. E. Sims, W. A. Norman, S. Roach, W. C. Scarritt, and T. K. Wilson, all from Paint Rock in Concho County; T. C. Wynn of San Angelo; and R. A. Love of Kansas City, Missouri. The CSS&LV built two disconnected segments from connections with the Gulf, Colorado and Santa Fe Railway Company. Initial construction began in April 1909, and the 16.5-mile line between Miles and Paint Rock opened in December of that year. Construction of the longer route between San Angelo and Sterling City, forty-three miles, began in August 1909 and opened a year later. Work on the CSS&LV was financed by the Atchison, Topeka and Santa Fe, which acquired the railroad in August 1910. Citizens along the line made donations amounting to $140,973, of which $40,000 was contributed in San Angelo and Tom Green County. A prior agreement between the Santa Fe and the city of San Angelo stated that no additional cash donations would be requested for any Santa Fe extension built from San Angelo. The $40,000 was returned and used to finance Santa Fe Park as well as other parks in San Angelo. The CSS&LV was leased to the Gulf, Colorado and Santa Fe in 1914. By the mid-1930s improved roads had siphoned off much of the traffic and the line between Miles and Paint Rock was abandoned in April 1937. The balance of the CSS&LV was merged into the GC&SF in December 1948. However, operations between San Angelo and Sterling City were discontinued in July 1958, and the line was abandoned the following year.

BIBLIOGRAPHY: James M. Day, "Railroading along the Concho: A History of the Concho, San Saba, and Llano Valley Railroad Company," West Texas Historical Association *Year Book* 38 (1962).

George C. Werner

CONCORD, TEXAS (Angelina County). Concord was seven miles east of Zavalla in eastern Angelina County. The area was first settled by Col. T. L. Mott and his family, who moved to Texas from Alabama in the late 1850s. Around 1860 the Motts and several other families established a church, which they named Concord after a reference in the Bible's second book of Corinthians. The church and a school established at the community by 1900 continued to operate until the 1960s, when the area was inundated by newly built Sam Rayburn Reservoir. The church and the Mott family cemetery were moved to Zavalla, and the school was merged with the Zavalla school district. The original log cabin and corn crib of the Mott family were purchased by Mrs. Bennie Polk Morgan of Jasper, who moved them to a site in Jasper County.

BIBLIOGRAPHY: Angelina County Historical Survey Committee, *Land of the Little Angel: A History of Angelina County, Texas,* ed. Bob Bowman (Lufkin, Texas: Lufkin Printing, 1976).

Christopher Long

CONCORD, TEXAS (Cherokee County). Concord is six miles north of New Summerfield in extreme northeastern Cherokee County. The town is thought to have been named by early settlers from Concord, Massachusetts. According to local historians, Concord was settled by the Martin family from Tennessee around 1850. In the 1930s and 1940s Concord was on a mail route from Jacksonville. It recorded a business and twenty residents in 1930 and two businesses, three churches, and fifty residents in 1940. The Concord school was established in 1884 and was consolidated with the Carlisle Independent School District in 1948. In 1987 Concord was reported to have two churches, two businesses, and ninety-seven families. It was on a mail route from Troup.

BIBLIOGRAPHY: *Cherokee County History* (Jacksonville, Texas: Cherokee County Historical Commission, 1986). Fred Tarpley, *1001 Texas Place Names* (Austin: University of Texas Press, 1980).

Tracy Don Sears

CONCORD, TEXAS (Houston County). Concord was off State Highway 7 eight miles east of Crockett in east central Houston County. It was established after the Civil War.[qv] A Presbyterian church was founded there in 1875, and around the same time a school began operating in the church; later a separate school building was constructed. In 1897 the school had an enrollment of forty-six. During the mid-1930s the small community had a church, a cemetery, and a number of houses. After World War II[qv] many local residents moved away, and by 1990 only a church and a few widely scattered houses remained in the area.

BIBLIOGRAPHY: Houston County Historical Commission, *History of Houston County, Texas, 1687–1979* (Tulsa, Oklahoma: Heritage, 1979).

Christopher Long

CONCORD, TEXAS (Hunt County). Concord is at the intersection of State Highway 66 and Farm Road 3211, just southwest of Greenville in central Hunt County. The first available population statistics indicate that ten persons lived there in 1936, when two local businesses were in operation. Concord's population was reported as 100 from the 1940s through the mid-1960s, and three businesses operated at the community for the first part of this period. From the 1970s to 1990 Concord reported a population of thirty.

Brian Hart

CONCORD, TEXAS (Leon County). Concord is on the Burlington Northern Railroad, State Highway 7, and Farm Road 39, some ten miles northwest of Centerville and eight miles south of Jewett in western Leon County. A community was established at the site between 1856 and 1893, though a Concord Baptist Church and a Concord Cemetery were at the site before a community developed there. The name was probably for the hometown of the community's first settlers, who were from Concord, Massachusetts. The local post office operated from 1884 until 1904 and was located at the crossroads between Concord and Robbin. After 1904 mail was routed to Jewett. After the construction of the Trinity and Brazos Valley Railway through the area in 1908, the post office was reestablished in 1909. In 1956 the post office building was destroyed by fire, and the office was moved to the Concord school building where it was still housed in 1990. After the arrival of the railroad, Concord's population grew to 175, served by a variety of businesses. The community's Methodist church was built in 1915 and was still active in 1990. Concord had schools for white and black students, and the combined enrollment in 1939 was 581. In 1940 Concord had a population of 280, a church, a school, and a central business district with at least seven businesses, including a factory. In 1948 the community had a store, a garage, a post office, and a barbershop; that year its schools were consolidated with the Centerville schools. In the early 1950s Concord's major companies, the Texas Pipe Line Company and the Magnolia Pipe Line Company, closed and transferred their employees. In 1990 Concord had the post office and a senior citizens center (both located in the school building), as well as two churches and a cemetery. That year the community had twenty-eight residents.

BIBLIOGRAPHY: Leon County Historical Book Survey Committee, *History of Leon County* (Dallas: Curtis Media, 1986). Fred Tarpley, *1001 Texas Place Names* (Austin: University of Texas Press, 1980).

Maria Elena Kruger

CONCORD, TEXAS (McLennan County). Concord was on the old Corsicana Road five miles northeast of Waco in McLennan County. It was settled by brothers Martin, Wilson, Mark, and George Bird, who moved to the area in the early 1850s from Concord, North Carolina, and who gave the community its name. In 1866 the Tehuacana Baptist Church of Christ was organized, and in 1872 the church was moved to the site of what is now the Concord cemetery. By the 1880s the town had a school, a general store, and a cotton gin, and the church was eventually moved to a site near them. By 1900 Concord was a switch on the International–Great Northern Railroad. The Concord school merged with several others to form the La Vega school district in 1924. In 1950 the church was moved to a site near Bellmead, where it was still located in the 1980s. By 1970 the cemetery was all that remained of Concord.

BIBLIOGRAPHY: Dayton Kelley, ed., *The Handbook of Waco and McLennan County, Texas* (Waco: Texian, 1972).

Harold T. Purvis

CONCORD, TEXAS (Rusk County). Concord, one of the oldest settlements in Rusk County, is 5½ miles east of Mount Enterprise in the southeastern part of the county. The town reportedly got its name from the general harmony among its early settlers. In the 1930s the community had twenty-five residents and six businesses. During the 1940s Concord had 125 inhabitants, four businesses, and a school. Its population began to decrease during the 1950s, and by the 1980s it had fallen to twenty-three, where it remained in 1990.

BIBLIOGRAPHY: Fred Tarpley, *1001 Texas Place Names* (Austin: University of Texas Press, 1980). Dorman H. Winfrey, *A History of Rusk County* (Waco: Texian, 1961).

Megan Biesele

CONCORD, TEXAS (Upshur County). Concord, on Farm Road 2263 seven miles northeast of Gilmer in north central Upshur County, was probably established before 1900. Around the turn of the century two schools were operating there; during the 1906–07 school year they had a combined enrollment of eighty-nine. In the mid-1930s the community had a school, a church, a store, a sawmill, and a number of scattered houses. After World War II[qv] many of its residents moved away, and the school was consolidated with the Gilmer school district. By the mid-1960s all that remained of the community was a church, a cemetery, and a few houses. The church and cemetery were still shown on county highway maps in the 1980s.

BIBLIOGRAPHY: Doyal T. Loyd, *History of Upshur County* (Waco: Texian Press, 1987).

Christopher Long

CONCORD, TEXAS (Wood County). Concord is on Farm Road 778 two miles northwest of Hainesville and 5½ miles southeast of Quitman in south central Wood County. It was probably settled in the 1870s and by the early 1880s had a one-teacher school known as the Concord Academy. By 1891 the area had a church, called Hubbard's Chapel Baptist Church, after settler Hubbard Moseley (or Mosley), who donated land to the church. In 1896 seventy-six white and thirty-eight black students were taught by two teachers in one-room schools. In 1932 seventy-seven white students attended classes in nine grades taught by three teachers, and forty-five black students attended classes in seven grades taught by one teacher. A few years later Concord's schools closed, and the community had only a church and a number of scattered dwellings. In 1960 a single dwelling and the church remained at the site, but by the late 1970s several more dwellings were in the vicinity.

BIBLIOGRAPHY: Adele W. Vickery and Ida Marie Turner, comps., *Cemeteries of Wood County* (3 vols., Mineola, Texas, 1970–71). *Wood County, 1850–1900* (Quitman, Texas: Wood County Historical Society, 1976).

Rachel Jenkins

CONCORD CHURCH, TEXAS. Concord Church is three miles west of Elmwood and eleven miles north of Palestine in northern Anderson County. In the 1930s the community had a church, a district school, and a number of scattered dwellings. In 1932 the Concord school served thirty-seven white pupils. By 1955 the community school had been consolidated with that of Elmwood, and in 1985 Concord Church was a small crossroads community with a church, a cemetery, and several homes.

BIBLIOGRAPHY: Thomas Paul Jones, The Reorganization of the Public Schools of Anderson County, Texas (M.Ed. thesis, University of Texas, 1934).

Mark Odintz

CONCORDIA, TEXAS. Concordia is on Farm Road 3354 twenty-two miles southwest of Corpus Christi in southwestern Nueces County. It was established around 1911 by Herman Moerbe and by

Germans from Fayette and Lee counties. During the mid-1930s a school and a church were at the site, but by the early 1990s only a few scattered houses remained.

BIBLIOGRAPHY: Nueces County Historical Society, *History of Nueces County* (Austin: Jenkins, 1972).
Christopher Long

CONCORDIA UNIVERSITY AT AUSTIN. In the late nineteenth century Texas Lutherans of the Missouri Synod determined to build a local school to prepare their own young men for the ministry. After three short-lived attempts to establish such a college, in New Orleans in 1883, in Giddings in 1894, and at Clifton in the early twentieth century, they succeeded after World War I[qv] with the founding in Austin of Lutheran Concordia College of Texas, the name by which the school was known until 1965, when it became Concordia Lutheran College. In 1921 the Texas district requested the Missouri Synod to establish and maintain the institution. The school opened as a boys' secondary school—modeled after the German *Gymnasium*—preparatory for the ministry. The first president, Dr. Henry Studtmann, remembered that the district chose Austin because it was beautiful, it was the capital city, and especially because the University of Texas was located there. In 1925 the synod's board of directors and the district's board of control purchased twenty acres at the northern city limits, two miles from the Capitol[qv] and one mile from the university. The next year they laid the cornerstone for the first building, Kilian Hall.

This structure was named after Rev. John Kilian,[qv] who led 500 Lutheran Wends[qv] to America from Prussia and Saxony in 1854. Its architecture, designed by the firm of Harvey P. Smith[qv] and Arthur Fehr, won an award from the Architects' Guild of Texas. The building features a pink Spanish tile roof and hand-carved front doors made by Austin artist Peter H. Mansbendel.[qv] Classes began in Kilian Hall on October 26, 1926. Twenty-six students slept on the second floor on rented army cots until permanent beds arrived, read from a library furnished with donated books, cleared the campus of underbrush, and cut out their own baseball field.

From the beginning the laity supplemented synod and district financing with donations, even farm produce and goats that the college picked up in a truck it purchased for that purpose. Extensive lay involvement required two lay organizations: the College Association to coordinate giving and an advisory board. By 1929 increased enrollment demanded a new classroom building, but the depression brought financial hardship for the school and successive decreases in enrollment from a high of fifty-eight in 1929 to a low in 1934 of twenty-five students. At one time the board questioned keeping the school open. After World War II[qv] expansion began again with the addition of six significant new buildings in the next fifteen years. Studtmann retired in 1948, and George J. Beto,[qv] who had been a member of the faculty since 1939 and who later directed the state prison system[qv] in Huntsville, followed him in the presidency. A junior college curriculum was added in 1951, women began matriculating in 1955, and general education received more emphasis by the end of the fifties. High school classes were discontinued in 1967, Concordia was accredited by the Southern Association of Colleges and Schools in 1968, and in 1979 the synod authorized Concordia to become a four-year baccalaureate college. The first bachelor's degrees were awarded in 1982. In 1990 the school had fourteen buildings on the original twenty acres, including a 70,000-volume library, and a student population of more than 600. In 1993 the school joined nine other Missouri Synod colleges and universities to form the Concordia University System, and in 1995 the school was renamed Concordia University at Austin.

BIBLIOGRAPHY: William Henry Bewie, *Missouri in Texas: A History of the Lutheran Church–Missouri Synod in Texas, 1855–1941* (Austin: Steck, 1952).
Louann Atkins Temple

CONCRETE, TEXAS. Concrete is on U.S. Highway 183 eight miles north of Cuero in northern DeWitt County. James Norman Smith[qv] laid out the town in 1846; it was thus the county's earliest townsite, and its nucleus was the old Upper Cuero Creek settlement, which dates from 1827. The town was named for the early adobe concrete used in local buildings and homes. A Cumberland Presbyterian church was established in 1846, the first church in DeWitt County; a two-story structure later replaced the original log building and served both Methodists and Masons. Methodists were active in Concrete until the 1890s. Concrete College, chartered in 1856, was one of the best-attended boarding colleges in Texas and established Concrete as an education center. It operated until 1881. The Baptists were active in Concrete from 1865 to 1881, when Rev. John Van Epps Covey,[qv] a professor at Concrete College, was there. Primary school sessions were held in the Presbyterian church, but there was no regular school in Concrete until 1855, when a two-room schoolhouse was built. Reverend Covey and his wife taught at this school, which became known as Covey Academy. The Concrete public school was established in 1880. A post office opened in 1853. In 1870 Concrete received mail twice daily, had seven stores, a two-story hotel, a blacksmith, a mule-driven gin, Baptist and Presbyterian churches, a Masonic lodge, and the college. An 1885 directory shows a population of 200, a steam cotton gin, a gristmill, Baptist and Methodist churches, and daily stages to Gonzales and Cuero. The local economy thrived on cotton, pecans, livestock, and hides. The town suffered after the Gulf, Western Texas and Pacific Railroad built through to the south and Cuero was established as a railhead. The population of Concrete declined to 100 by the mid-1890s, and the post office was discontinued in 1907. By 1933 only twenty-five residents and four businesses were recorded. The Baptists held regular services until 1948. In the 1940s seventy-five people supported four businesses and several schools. Forty-six residents were listed in 1985 and 1990, and the 1983 county highway map indicated one business.

BIBLIOGRAPHY: Nellie Murphree, *A History of DeWitt County* (Victoria, Texas, 1962).
Craig H. Roell

CONCRETE COLLEGE. The first school in Concrete, DeWitt County, was conducted by James Norman Smith,[qv] who had taught President James K. Polk in his native state of Tennessee. What developed after legislative charters in 1856 and 1873 was a typical nineteenth-century rural college. Dr. Robert Peebles[qv] and other pioneer Concrete settlers sponsored and lobbied for the school, the administration of which was entrusted under the charter of 1856 to J. M. Baker, F. M. Taylor, Josh Stevens, J. R. North, and Francis J. Lynch.[qv] Rev. John Van Epps Covey[qv] began teaching in the community about 1864, and by the mid-1870s a ten-acre campus had taken shape along Coon Hollow. The main building measured 150 by fifty feet, with a kitchen and dining room attached. Coeds shared the stone house of the Covey family, and the male students were assigned to more primitive, two-room frame buildings.

Covey's curriculum favored the classics and business. Music and penmanship were offered, and farming techniques were taught in a cultivated area adjacent to the college. More than a dozen instructors taught an annual average of perhaps 100 students during the twenty-year existence of the college. Rev. Woodlief Thomas, vice president of the institution, and Professor J. D. Bradfors saw to it that Hebrew, Greek, and Latin fundamentals were covered; Professor Grothus taught German; professors Hueber, Woolsey, and Bonney conducted classes in business and commerce; Misses Anna Stell and Adlia Debery taught the students of the primary school (some pupils were admitted before the age of twelve), and Mrs. Eisenmeyer and Miss Tunn molded the social amenities in the "ladies department." Mrs. Covey taught sewing, and musical talents were developed by professors Young and Fuchs.

Covey was a New Yorker who earned the doctor of divinity degree from Madison College and later taught in Tennessee. After 1854 he served as teacher and Baptist preacher in Palestine, Marshall, Trinity, and Hallettsville, before he took up duties at Concrete. Although he required no particular religious confession of prospective students, Concrete College was Baptist-oriented; the school's financial status was a concern of the Texas Baptist Convention.

The census officer who visited the campus in 1870 recorded the names of students who resided on the campus. Most of the boarders that year were males ranging in age from twelve to twenty, and most were Texans. But Indiana, Germany, and England also contributed to the student body. During the peak enrollment year of 1873–74, 250 students attended classes, and the 100 boarders came from twenty Texas counties scattered from the Brazos to the Rio Grande. A fee of $100 covered tuition, room, and board for a five-month semester. For a time the institution was the largest boarding school in the state.

The student's day at Concrete was well regulated, and his attire was carefully scrutinized. Firearms, profane language, alcohol, gambling, and smoking were all strictly forbidden. Public oral examinations were held on Fridays, and graduation was a social event lasting three days, with concerts each evening. Notable graduates of Concrete included Rudolph Kleberg, William Henry Crain, and George W. Saunders.qqv Measles and influenza ravaged the student population in 1871 and 1872, and in 1873 the Gulf, Western Texas and Pacific Railway arrived in Cuero, thus shifting emphasis away from Concrete. The development of public schools within the county also probably contributed to the school's decline. The year 1881 marked the last class at Concrete College. Covey went on to McMullen College at Tilden and later returned to the ministry. He died in Cotulla in 1898.

BIBLIOGRAPHY: Robert W. Shook, "Covey's College at Concrete," *East Texas Historical Journal* 6 (March 1968). Dorothy House Young, The History of Education in DeWitt County (M.A. thesis, University of Texas, 1943).

Robert W. Shook

CONCUGUYAPEM INDIANS. The Concuguyapem (Couguyapem) Indians, apparently Coahuiltecan in speech, lived on the north bank of the Rio Grande between present Zapata and Rio Grande City. They are known only from the middle eighteenth century.

BIBLIOGRAPHY: Gabriel Saldivar, *Los Indios de Tamaulipas* (Mexico City: Pan American Institute of Geography and History, 1943).

Thomas N. Campbell

CONE, HORACE (1820–1885). Horace Cone, lawyer, editor, legislator, and railroad pioneer, was born in Virginia in 1820, the son of a Baptist minister and nephew of Spencer Cone, a famous New York clergyman. He received his early education in Baltimore before moving to Pennsylvania. He left college in 1837 and set out for Montgomery, Alabama, ran out of cash by the time he reached Augusta, Georgia, and walked the remaining distance to Montgomery, carrying only a knapsack made from his cloak. He walked twenty-eight miles a day through the dangerous Creek Indian Nation, where the Creek Indian War had just ended and tensions remained high. After less than a year in Montgomery, Cone pressed on to Tuscaloosa, Alabama, and studied law under prominent lawyer Harvey W. Ellis. Three years later, having relocated to Marion, Alabama, he opened his own law practice. He later entered a law partnership with Col. George W. Gale in Cahaba, Alabama. In this venture Cone received much recognition before the bar. While in Cahaba during the early 1840s, he met and married Amarantha E. Roberts. They moved to Brazoria, Texas, in 1850. In 1853 he was elected to the Texas House of Representatives.

In 1857 Cone resettled in Houston. Three years later, as attorney of the Texas and New Orleans Railroad, he was called to New York, where he remained until January 1861. There he observed Northern sentiments and wrote a series of letters home to Texas discussing his observations. By the time the Civil Warqv began, Cone had returned to Houston and reopened his law practice with partner George Goldthwaite.qv He was reelected to the Texas House in 1861 and spoke publicly of his experiences in the North. He shared the House leadership with M. M. Potter of Galveston. When Speaker of the House Constantine W. Buckleyqv resigned, Cone was offered the speakership, but refused. He was appointed chairman of the finance committee, and the House of Representatives needed his experience to endure the bickering and hostile financial battles that erupted during the Ninth Legislature. In a time of hardship for the entire state, Cone had to preside over an unpopular tax bill and a furor over legislators' compensation that fractured the government. During the session he lobbied unsuccessfully for a Houston–New Orleans railroad as a "military necessity." He also took a bold stand and presented a petition to the House for a special act to allow Peter Allen, a free black barber who had fought for the Confederate Army at Shiloh, to reside in the state. Cone was defeated, and Allen was not allowed to remain free. During the war Cone served as a colonel on the staff of Gen. John Bankhead Magruder.qv He was also judge advocate–general of the military district of Texas, with duties "arduous and fraught with great responsibility."

After the war Cone took his family to New York for several years. He returned to Texas in October 1874 to become editor of the *Daily Telegraph*. He assumed the editorship in May 1875 but resigned the next year due to ill health. The Dallas *Weekly Herald* bemoaned that the "vigorous, terse, incisive style of putting fact, fancies or argument which was so characteristic of Mr. Cone's writing is now wanting." By the summer of 1876 Cone was employed as the right-of-way agent for the Houston and Texas Central Railway line to Shreveport. During the early 1880s he was also associated with the Houston East and West Texas Railway. At this time he became involved with an ambitious plan to build a track from Columbia, Texas, to the Pacific via San Antonio. He and others traveled to France and secured a multimillion-dollar loan for the project before returning. But upon his return in October 1885, Cone died suddenly and the plan collapsed. He was survived by at least one daughter.

BIBLIOGRAPHY: *Biographical Encyclopedia of Texas* (New York: Southern, 1880). James A. Creighton, *A Narrative History of Brazoria County* (Angleton, Texas: Brazoria County Historical Commission, 1975). Dallas *Weekly Herald*, May 29, 1875, June 17, 1876, September 12, 1888. *House Journal of the Ninth Legislature, First Called Session, February 2, 1863–March 7, 1863* (Austin: Texas State Library, 1963).

Mark Dallas Loeffler

CONE, STEPHEN ELSEMERE (1893–1970). Stephen Elsemere Cone, West Texas grain dealer and real estate and oil man, was born on November 9, 1893, at Yarrellton, Texas, one of nine children of Mr. and Mrs. Jesse M. Cone. At age ten he began his business career with a hive of bees. Later he sold his beekeeping enterprise to finance his education at East Texas Normal School (now East Texas State University) in Commerce. After a year there he attended St. Louis University. In October 1915 Cone was called home by his father's death. He never returned to college.

While living with his mother and younger siblings on the family farm, he began working for C. E. Parks in the grain business. He later purchased the entire interests of the company and in 1927 bought W. K. Dickenson's grain elevator. Over the next two years Cone established elevators in Muleshoe, Bovina, Hereford, Amherst, and Anton. By the early 1930s he was one of the largest dealers in sorghum and sudan grass seed in the Southwest. He later entered the real estate business. In partnership with Col. "Sheb" Williams of Paris, Texas, he bought about 20,000 acres in eastern Lubbock County and sold off parcels of land to newcomers. In addition Cone managed a number of farms, some of which he owned and some of which were owned by others. He also leased land on which he grew cotton and row crops. In 1928 he began buying and selling oil rights on West Texas lands. His most active period in this business came in 1940–41, and a considerable share of his fortune resulted from it. In 1953, however, he suffered a series of strokes that left him an invalid and compelled his retirement.

Cone first married Fern Parks on May 18, 1921, and they had a daughter; they were divorced in 1932. He married Adeline Zeigenhalz on February 6, 1938; they had another daughter and a son. This marriage ended in divorce in 1952. On December 7, 1952, Cone married Lola Meek Ross. He died at his home on May 1, 1970, and was buried in Resthaven Memorial Park in Lubbock. He was survived by his wife, three children, and six grandchildren.

BIBLIOGRAPHY: Seymour V. Connor, ed., *Builders of the Southwest* (Lubbock: Southwest Collection, Texas Technological College, 1959). Lubbock *Avalanche-Journal*, May 1, 2, 1970.   *H. Allen Anderson*

CONE, TEXAS (Crosby County). Cone is on U.S. Highway 62 thirty-four miles northeast of Lubbock in Crosby County. The community was established in 1901 and named for early settler James Stanton Cone. A post office opened there around 1903. "Uncle" Charlie Travis donated land for a school, and on February 14, 1905, the Cone school district was founded. After 1939, when Cone had an estimated 150 residents, the town decreased in population; in 1965 the Cone school district was consolidated with the schools of Ralls. In 1988 the community had the post office, three businesses, and fewer than fifty residents.

BIBLIOGRAPHY: Crosby County Pioneer Memorial Museum, *A History of Crosby County, 1876–1977* (Dallas: Taylor, 1978).
Edloe A. Jenkins

CONE, TEXAS (Milam County). Cone was on the Gulf, Colorado and Santa Fe Railway ten miles southeast of Cameron in central Milam County. It was named for Robert Newton Cone, who moved to the area from Alabama after the Civil War.qv The community had a post office from 1884 to 1886 and a one-teacher school for twenty-two students as late as 1903. The Cone school was consolidated with the Hoyte school district in 1918. By the 1940s no evidence of Cone was shown on the county highway map.

BIBLIOGRAPHY: Milam County Heritage Preservation Society, *Matchless Milam: History of Milam County* (Dallas: Taylor, 1984).
Vivian Elizabeth Smyrl

CONEJERO INDIANS. The Conejero (Conexero) Indians were a Plains Apache band who roamed along the Canadian River valley in northeastern New Mexico and the western Texas Panhandle, as well as in western Kansas and southeastern Colorado, during the seventeenth century. The name is Spanish for "rabbit people" and may have been derived from the types of dwellings they built. In the light of contemporary Spanish documents, the Conejeros appear to have been an early band of Lipan Apaches. Apparently they had some contacts with the French in the Mississippi valley. These contacts were not always friendly, however; in 1695 some Chipayne Apaches visiting Picurís Pueblo reported that white men from the east had attacked a band of Conejeros in western Kansas. In 1706 Juan de Ulibarri conferred with Conejeros in the vicinity of present Cimmaron, New Mexico. After the Comanches invaded the Southern Plains during the early eighteenth century, nothing more was mentioned of the Conejeros; it is possible that they were among the Plains Apache bands that were wiped out or scattered by Shoshonean invaders, although they may have subsequently merged with the Jicarilla Apaches in New Mexico.

BIBLIOGRAPHY: José M. Espinosa, *Crusaders of the Rio Grande: The Story of Don Diego de Vargas and the Reconquest and Refounding of New Mexico* (Chicago: Institute of Jesuit History, 1942). John Upton Terrell, *The Plains Apache* (New York: Crowell, 1975). Alfred B. Thomas, *After Coronado: Spanish Exploration Northeast of New Mexico, 1696–1717* (Norman: University of Oklahoma Press, 1935). Albert H. Schroeder, *A Study of the Apache Indians: The Mescalero Apaches*, Part III, Vol. 1 (New York: Garland, 1974).
H. Allen Anderson

CONEJO INDIANS. The Conejo (Spanish for "rabbit") Indians are considered to be a subdivision of the Conchos, a Uto Aztecan group of northern Chihuahua. In a Spanish document of 1693 the Conejos were identified as living north of the Rio Grande, presumably in what is now Trans-Pecos Texas, but in the first half of the eighteenth century the Conejos were known only from the lower Conchos River in Chihuahua.

BIBLIOGRAPHY: Charles W. Hackett, ed., *Historical Documents Relating to New Mexico, Nueva Vizcaya, and Approaches Thereto, to 1773* (3 vols., Washington: Carnegie Institution, 1923–37). Carl Sauer, *The Distribution of Aboriginal Tribes and Languages in Northwestern Mexico* (Berkeley: University of California Press, 1934).
Thomas N. Campbell

CONEJOS CREEK. Conejos Creek rises a mile south of the Uvalde county line and nineteen miles northwest of La Pryor in far northwestern Zavala County (at 29°04′ N, 100°05′ W) and runs south four miles to its mouth on Muela Creek, sixteen miles northwest of La Pryor (at 29°02′ N, 100°05′ W). *Conejos* is the Spanish word for rabbits. The surrounding low relief terrain is surfaced by sands and gravels. Local vegetation includes grasses, pecan trees, and other hardwoods.

CONEY, DONALD (1901–1973). Donald Coney, university librarian, was born on February 21, 1901, in Jackson, Michigan, the son of Glenn E. and Eunice Frances (Diffenbaugh) Coney. He received a B.A. degree in 1925 and an A.M. degree in library science in 1927 from the University of Michigan. He married Dorothy Bell Petit on July 2, 1925; they had two children. Coney worked as librarian of the University of Delaware in 1927–28. He moved to the University of North Carolina in 1928 as assistant librarian and in 1931 became professor of library science and assistant director of the School of Library Science. From 1932 to 1934 he worked at the Newberry Library in Chicago as supervisor of technical processes. In 1934 he accepted a position as director of the University of Texas library, a post he held until 1945. During his years at UT the library grew from 474,000 to 770,000 volumes; some of the university's most important acquisitions were in the archives, the Latin American Collection, the Texas Collection, and the rare book collection. Also during Coney's tenure, the university library began publishing the *Library Chronicle of the University of Texas*.

Coney became university librarian and professor of librarianship at the University of California at Berkeley in 1945 and remained there until his retirement in 1968. At Berkeley he saw the library grow from 1,300,000 to 3,000,000 volumes; the staff increased from 175 to more than 400. In addition to his library duties he was a member of the Buildings and Campus Development Committee and influenced the design of several buildings on campus, including the Student Union, Hertz Hall, Zellerbach Auditorium, the Art Museum, and Wurster Hall. Coney was vice chancellor for administration at Berkeley in 1955–56. He was also chairman of the Committee for Arts and Lectures from 1955 to 1970, though he retired in 1968. He served on the executive board of the Council of the American Library Association and was a member of several other professional organizations. He died on February 10, 1973. *See also* UNIVERSITY OF TEXAS LIBRARIES.

BIBLIOGRAPHY: *Dictionary of American Library Biography* (Littleton, Colorado: Libraries Unlimited, 1978). Vertical Files, Barker Texas History Center, University of Texas at Austin.
Vivian Elizabeth Smyrl

CONFEDERACIÓN DE ORGANIZACIONES MEXICANAS Y LATINO AMERICANAS. The Confederación de Organizaciones Mexicanas y Latino Americanas del Estado de Texas was founded at a state convocation of Texas-Mexican self-help organizations in Port Arthur on November 27, 1938. Its attempt to coordinate efforts of various groups in the state to improve the "moral, economic, and cultural betterment" of Mexicans place it as a historical bridge between the earlier mutual-aid societies (*sociedades mutualistas*qv) and the later civil-rights groups. Its original name was Confederación de Organizaciones Mexicanas, but it soon assumed a broader title to include state residents of Mexican descent born in either the United States or Mexico. The Mexican consuls in Houston and Galveston issued a call in July 1938 to Texas-Mexican organizations to a meeting called the Convención Regional de Organizaciones Mexicanas de las Jurisdicciones Consulares de Galveston, Beaumont, y Houston. Efforts were made to establish El Congreso del Pueblo de Habla Española (Spanish-speaking Congress) to ensure basic rights for all Spanish-speaking people in the United States.

The Galveston convention participants set up a coordinating committee, which spent the remainder of the summer forming regional alliances that led to COMLA the following November. The committee contacted social, recreational, and other civic groups in all the consular districts around the state, including the Cruz Azul Mexicana,qv a women's charitable organization, hoping to bring all these groups under COMLA's banner. COMLA worked to improve the cultural life of Mexican children by organizing libraries and cultural enrichment programs. In Houston the organization took a slightly different name, La Federación de Sociedades Mexicanas y Latino Americanas. Under consul Luis L. Duplán it worked to improve its constituents' health, educational, and social conditions, in some cases cooperating with the Rusk Center (*see* SETTLEMENT HOUSES), a settlement school that provided social services to the Mexican immigrant community in the city. At one time FSMLA joined COMLA in temporarily removing signs posted in public places in Wharton that declared, "Mexicans not Allowed." COMLA held at least four annual conventions, beginning in 1938 and was considered somewhat successful for a time in addressing the Mexican community's major concerns. At what may have been its last annual convention in Galveston in 1941 it focused on the specific issue of segregation. FSMLA apparently lasted through World War II.qv

BIBLIOGRAPHY: Arnoldo De León, *Ethnicity in the Sunbelt: A History of Mexican-Americans in Houston* (University of Houston Mexican American Studies Program, 1989).

Teresa Palomo Acosta

CONFEDERATE AIR FORCE. The Confederate Air Force, Incorporated, also known as the Ghost Squadron, is an nonprofit educational organization dedicated to preserving, in flyable condition, a complete collection of aircraft flown by all the military in World War II.qv In addition it provides museum buildings for the permanent protection and display of the aircraft as well as nonflying artifacts from the same period. The idea for the organization began in 1951, when a group of former military pilots around Mercedes began to acquire surplus fighter aircraft. In visiting various disposal facilities they realized that the 300,000 aircraft produced by the United States during World War II, were about to be melted down for scrap metal; in the process an irreplaceable part of the world's heritage was about to be lost.

The first aircraft, a P-40 Warhawk, was acquired in 1951 by Lloyd Nolen, a flight instructor during World War II. In 1952 he sold the P-40 to purchase a P-51 Mustang, but because of the Korean War, the air force recalled all P-51s in civilian hands. Interest in the old warbird grew; the small group of former military pilots pooled resources and purchased a surplus P-51 Mustang in 1957. The group grew, and when someone painted Confederate Air Force on the Mustang they had a name. That day marks the unofficial birthday of the organization. The airfield at Mercedes became Rebel Field, and the mystique was born. Their high-spirited camaraderie also provided the rank of "colonel" to each member. In 1959 the group acquired two navy F8F Bearcats. The collection has grown to include military aircraft from all the nations engaged in World War II.

By 1963 the CAF had acquired one of each of the ten American fighter planes from World War II. By 1967 the force had signed two movie contracts for films depicting air battles of World War II. In a British film entitled *The Battle of Britain,* the CAF was commissioned to do the flying in return for two British "Spitfires" and three German ME-109s to go into the flying museum. Another film commitment was *Tora, Tora, Tora,* a story depicting the Japanese preparations for and the bombing of Pearl Harbor. By 1972 all of the available bombers, helicopters, trainers, and gliders had been added. By 1974 a fine collection of fighters, bombers, transports, and trainers of the Royal Air Force, German Luftwaffe, and Imperial Japanese Navy, as well as a fleet of replica Japanese aircraft, had been added.

By 1968 the group had outgrown the small airfield at Mercedes, and they moved to the old Harlingen Aerial Gunnery School facility at Harlingen. They renamed their new facility Rebel Field and remained there until 1991, when they moved to the dryer climate and more central location of Midland. In 1983 the American Airpower Heritage Foundation, Incorporated, was formed to develop financial support for the CAF. In 1990 two additional corporations were established: the American Airpower Heritage Flying Museum, to obtain and maintain legal title to CAF aircraft, and the American Airpower Heritage Museum, responsible for the acceptance, preservation, and display of all nonflying artifacts, relics, and documents, as well as onsite display of aircraft. The Confederate Air Force remains the flying organization. In 1993 the CAF was composed of some 10,000 members, organized into ninety units called Wings, Squadrons, and Detachments, located throughout the United States and in France, England, New Zealand, and Australia. The corporation holds title to 140 aircraft. Most are in flying condition and are regularly flown in air shows throughout the country.

BIBLIOGRAPHY: John Covington, "The Confederate Air Force," *Junior Historian,* January 1968. *The Ghost Squadron of the Confederate Air Force: A Pictorial History of the Preservation of the World's Greatest Combat Aircraft of World War II* (N.p.: Taylor Publishing Company, 1975). Philip Makanna, *Ghosts: A Time Remembered* (New York: Holt, Rinehart and Winston, 1979). *Texas Star,* March 4, 1973. Vertical Files, Barker Texas History Center, University of Texas at Austin.

Art Leatherwood

CONFEDERATE RESEARCH CENTER. The Confederate Research Center at Hillsboro was established in 1964 as part of the Hill Junior College History Complex, which includes the center, the Audie L. Murphyqv Gun Museum, and the Hill Junior College Press. The center is dedicated to scholarly research in such fields as the Civil War,qv the Confederate States of America, and the role of Texas in the war and the Confederacy. It houses a 3,500-volume library, as well as numerous periodicals and booklets. It possesses an extensive microfilm collection of newspapers published in Texas during the Civil War. Of particular interest is the center's collection of documents relative to the war in Texas, including post returns from federal garrisons in the state, 1846–61; service records of all of the members of Hood's Texas Brigade,qv as well as information, records, and memorabilia dealing with that unit; many unpublished manuscripts; and letters and diaries written by Texas Confederate soldiers. The Confederate Research Center sponsors, among other events, the Civil War Round Table of Texas and an annual Confederate history symposium.

BIBLIOGRAPHY: Hill County Historical Commission, *A History of Hill County, Texas, 1853-1980* (Waco: Texian, 1980).

Brian Hart

CONFEDERATE REUNION GROUNDS STATE HISTORICAL PARK. The Confederate Reunion Grounds State Historical Park is at the junction of Farm roads 2705 and 1633, in central Limestone County. The park encompasses seventy-four acres. By 1990 it was a day-use-only park, and the cost for visitors was two dollars a day for each motor vehicle. The park services included restrooms, hiking trails, a playground, and picnicking areas. Fishing and swimming were allowed in the lake. The park was the site of the Joseph E. Johnston^{qv} Camp No. 94, Confederate States of America, established in 1889. In 1897 the camp purchased seventy acres of land in which to hold reunions. Each year in August, Civil War^{qv} veterans and their families and friends would gather. A pavilion was built in 1893 and was used by various musical bands at the encampment. The Texas Parks and Wildlife Department^{qv} assumed management of the grounds in 1983. By the early 1990s the park had several historical and architectural attractions, such as the 1872 Heritage House, the 1893 dance pavilion, and Mordecai "Give-em-Hell" Yell's two-story log cabin. One popular feature is the Miss Mamie Kennedy 1914 Confederate Flirtation Walk along the Navasota River. Other special features include the picnic pavilion, two scenic footbridges, a low-water dam, a Val Verde cannon, and a natural spring known as Colonel's Spring.

BIBLIOGRAPHY: *A Family History of Limestone County* (Dallas: Taylor, 1984).
Chris Cravens

CONFEDERATE WOMAN'S HOME. The Confederate Woman's Home was opened in 1908 to care for widows and wives of honorably discharged Confederate soldiers and other women who aided the Confederacy. Residents were required to be at least sixty years of age and without means of financial support. The home was initially acquired and operated by the United Daughters of the Confederacy.^{qv} In 1903 the organization established a Wives and Widows Home Committee, which raised funds for the home and oversaw its construction. In 1905 the organization purchased a half block of property north of Austin, and in 1906 A. O. Watson, a prominent Texas architect, was hired to design a rusticated concrete-block building on the site. The two-story facility, constructed in 1906–07, had fifteen bedrooms. At its opening on June 3, 1908, three women were admitted to the home; by 1909 it housed sixteen. The United Daughters of the Confederacy operated the home until 1911, relying solely on donations to cover expenses. A bill to confer the home to the state was vetoed by Governor Samuel Willis Tucker Lanham^{qv} in 1905. In 1907 a constitutional amendment providing for state ownership of the home was rejected by Texas voters. The amendment was resubmitted to the voters in 1911 and passed by a wide margin. The property was deeded to the state. At the time of the transfer, the institution had eighteen residents.

The state placed the eleemosynary institution under a six-member board of managers. In 1913 the state constructed a large two-story brick addition, designed by Page Brothers, architects, which included twenty-four new bedrooms. To accommodate the growing number of ailing patients, a brick hospital building was built in 1916, with a hospital annex added eight years later. The institution was placed under the Board of Control^{qv} in 1920, and housed between eighty and 110 residents from 1920 through 1935. By the late 1930s new admissions to the home were decreasing and most of the surviving women were in poor health. From 1938 to 1945, the population of the home fell from eighty-seven to fifty-five. In 1949 the home fell under the jurisdiction of the Board of Texas State Hospitals and Special Schools. During the late 1950s, the nine remaining residents were consolidated into one hospital wing. In 1963 the last three residents were moved to private nursing homes at state expense, and the facility was closed. The state sold the property in 1986. The home cared for more than 3,400 indigent women over a period of fifty-five years. It was popular with the Austin community, and was the site of many community events over the years.

BIBLIOGRAPHY: Barbara Ann Stocklin, *The Texas Confederate Woman's Home: A Case Study in Historic Preservation and Neighborhood Conservation Planning* (M.A. thesis, University of Texas at Austin, 1991).
Barbara Stocklin-Steely

CONFERENCE OF SOUTHWEST FOUNDATIONS. The Conference of Southwest Foundations traces its origin to 1949, when Dr. Robert L. Sutherland,^{qv} then director of the Hogg Foundation,^{qv} Mrs. Lemuel Scarbrough of the Scarbrough Foundation, and Mary E. H. Butt^{qv} of the Butt Foundation learned that each had made a grant in support of the same program at the University of Texas. This caused them to wonder about other foundations in the state and the possible value of bringing them together to share information about their programs. The first meeting, hosted by the Hogg Foundation, Miss Ima Hogg,^{qv} Mrs. Scarbrough, and Mrs. Butt, was held in Austin on April 8, 1949. Donors and trustees of ten Texas foundations attended. Representatives of the Carnegie Foundation, Rockefeller Foundation, General Education Board, and Southern Education Foundation presented the program and led the discussions. The meeting was such a success that the group voted to meet the following year; several Houston foundations present offered to host the gathering. The group continued to meet in this informal way for the next eight years. During this period the conference planning, staffing, and operation was essentially a project of the Hogg Foundation, assisted by other foundations with a variety of support. The meetings were called the Conference of Texas Foundations and Trust Funds. Attendance was by invitation, limited to grant-making foundations.

At the time the conference was formed, Texas foundation philanthropy was in its first generation. The foundations were still very closely related to living donors, most of whom were running the foundations themselves with the help of their business or personal office staffs. The funds were, for the most part, modest and often dependent on donations from good business years and favorable investment returns. The donors avoided publicity about their foundations, lest they be swamped with requests for funds far beyond the size of their foundations. The annual conferences were attended by foundation donors and their families, trustees, persons who were considering establishing foundations, bank trust officers, and executives of the few staffed foundations. Because this was the only meeting of its kind, foundation representatives from other parts of the country often attended.

After the group had met for eight years, a plan for formal organization was proposed and adopted at the Eighth Annual Conference, held in Corpus Christi in April 1956. The organization was chartered in the state of Texas as a not-for-profit organization. The name was changed to Conference of Southwest Foundations in order to extend membership to foundations in other states in the region. The conference was incorporated in the state of Texas in October 1975, and a 501(c)(3) exemption was granted by the Internal Revenue Service in January 1976. Although the Conference of Southwest Foundations was the first, and for many years the only, organization of its kind, gradually groups of foundations and grantmakers began to be formed throughout the country in other regions, states, and metropolitan areas. The Council on Foundations has given encouragement and definition to these groups and provided a network structure and annual staff-development opportunities. Formal relationship to the council is maintained through the council's Committee on Regional Associations of Grantmakers, on which the Conference of Southwest Foundations serves.

The conference sponsors two major meetings a year: the annual conference in the fall and the mid-year board and committee meetings in the spring. The annual conference is a two-day educational meeting held in various locations around the region. It offers a full schedule of sessions, workshops, site visits, and other activities. The mid-year board and committee meeting is a two-day working meeting for board and committee members. A seminar or educational session is often included. The conference publishes a quarterly newsletter for members and outstanding papers presented to the annual conferences. At the beginning of 1992 active membership in the Conference stood at 154 member foundations from Texas, Oklahoma, Arkansas, New Mexico, Arizona, and Colorado. By 1994 the annual meetings were attended by 300 to 400 persons. With the maturation and professionalization of foundations in the Southwest, the composition of the group has changed over the years. Although donors or their families (some in the third generation now) still represent a high percentage of the active participants, about 50 percent of the conference participants are foundation staff. Despite the many changes the years have brought to the field of philanthropy, the basic purpose of the conference remains the same as in the early years "to promote wise foundation administration and to enhance the ability of each member to fulfill its charitable mission."

BIBLIOGRAPHY: Ima Hogg Papers, Barker Texas History Center, University of Texas at Austin.   *Maud W. Keeling*

CONFERENCIA DE MUJERES POR LA RAZA. The Conferencia de Mujeres por la Raza, also known as the National Chicana Conference, was the first interstate assembly of Mexican-American feminists organized in the United States. It was held at the Magnolia Park YWCA in Houston on May 28–30, 1971. An estimated 600 women from twenty-three states attended it. Elma Barrera organized the event. Many of the participants were students, social workers, and other progressives, who differed greatly from the women who had declared two years before, at the 1969 Denver, Colorado, Youth Conference, that Chicanas did not want to be liberated. The women at the Houston conference represented the radical elements of Mexican-American women's political movements. Nonetheless, they were linked to earlier, more moderate women's groups, such as Cruz Azul Mexicana[qv] and Ladies LULAC.[qv] In the new era of Chicano[qv] politics, a few women had emerged as leaders of the Mexican American Youth Organization[qv] and the newly formed Raza Unida Party.[qv] They gathered to organize stronger positions regarding women's roles. Gender discrimination, abortion, and birth control were given as much importance at the conference as inadequate educational opportunities, racism, welfare support, and employment discrimination, issues always at the heart of the Mexican-American civil-rights agenda. In addition, conference speakers urged the participants to work to change society.

The meeting consisted of four major workshops on education and employment, sex and birth control, marriage and child care, and religion. Each seminar produced resolutions, calling, for example, for free abortions, free birth control, free sex education, and twenty-four-hour child-care centers in Mexican-American communities. One resolution also noted that men bore responsibility for the upbringing of children. The conference participants were not, however, united. A sizable portion of them feared that the Anglos at Magnolia Park YWCA, who had helped plan the event, sought to split the Chicano movement along male and female lines. An estimated half of the delegates walked out of the meeting, urging that the conference focus on racism, not sexism. Betita Martínez, a feminist, and one of the protestors, criticized the meeting's failure to focus on poor or working-class women.

BIBLIOGRAPHY: Rosaura Sánchez and Rosa Martínez, eds., *Essays on la Mujer* (Los Angeles: Chicano Studies Center Publications, University of California, 1978). Marta Vidal, *Chicanas Speak Out: Women, New Voice of La Raza* (New York: Pathfinder Press, 1971).
Teresa Palomo Acosta

CONFERENCIA PLÁSTICA CHICANA. The international Plástica Chicana Conference was held September 13–16, 1979, in Austin to focus on the historical and cultural significance of Chicano[qv] art. The four-day event was sponsored by Mujeres Artistas del Sudoeste[qv] and the League of United Chicano Artists and obtained support from the Texas Commission on the Arts,[qv] the City of Austin, the University of Texas, and the Pan American Recreation Center. Artists and art critics from the United States and Mexico discussed the roots of Latino-generated art and evaluated the first decade of Chicano-movement art. Conference participants included muralist Ray Patlán, Amado Peña, and Emmy-winning filmmaker Susana Racha. They were joined by Raquel Tibol, Mexican scholar of muralist David Alfaro Siqueiros and biographer of painter Frida Kahlo, and Shifra Goldman, authority on Chicano art. In addition, members of the Mexican fine arts community contributed to twenty-four workshops on such topics as folk art, photography, and lithography. The conference was held at several sites around the city, including the University of Texas, St. Edward's University, and several East Austin locations, such as the Pan American Recreation Center, Galería Tonantzín, and Zaragoza Park. It opened in East Austin with an exhibition called Espejo Del Pueblo/1979. A highlight of the conference was an exhibit of thirty works by Manuel Alvarez Bravo unveiled at the Texas Memorial Museum.[qv]

BIBLIOGRAPHY: Orozco Family Papers, Benson Latin American Collection, University of Texas at Austin.   *Teresa Palomo Acosta*

CONGREGATION BETH ISRAEL, HOUSTON. Congregation Beth Israel in Houston is the oldest Jewish house of worship in Texas. Its beginnings can be traced to the founding of a Jewish cemetery on West Dallas Street in 1844. The congregation was organized as an orthodox synagogue in 1854, and its twenty-two members, many of western European origin, obtained a charter for the Hebrew Congregation of the City of Houston on December 28, 1859. The institution started a religious school in 1864 and incorporated as the Hebrew Congregation Beth Israel in 1873, adopting the Polish minhag. Efforts to introduce the Reform style of worship, which began as early as 1868 with the adoption of the *minhag America* custom of prayers, were completed with the adoption of the Union Prayer Book in 1898 and the Basic Principles in 1943, which transformed the congregation from an Orthodox to an American Reform Jewish congregation. A new state charter was obtained in 1895. The Franklin Avenue Temple Beth Israel was completed in 1874, and a new temple at Austin Street and Holman Avenue in 1925 included the Abe M. Levy[qv] Memorial Hall. In 1945 the mausoleum at the cemetery on West Dallas was expanded, and new classrooms were added in 1950. In 1873 the congregation joined the Union of American Hebrew Congregations. The Hebrew Congregation Beth Israel was renamed Congregation Beth Israel in 1945. Its important early members included the president of the Houston National Exchange Bank, Henry S. Fox, and Morris Levy, one of the founders of the Houston Ship Channel[qv] Company. Chief rabbis of the congregation have included Henry Barnstein (later Barnston), who arrived in 1900, and Hyman Judah Schachtel,[qv] who came in 1943. The congregation publishes the *Beth Israel News*.

BIBLIOGRAPHY: Anne Nathan Cohen, *The Centenary History of Congregation Beth Israel of Houston* (Houston, 1954).
Diana J. Kleiner

CONGREGATION EMANU EL, HOUSTON. Congregation Emanu El of Houston was organized as a Reform Jewish congregation. Its first formal meeting was held on June 8, 1944. The preamble to its constitution expresses the reform views of the founders: "believing that Judaism is a religion of perpetual growth and development, we hold that, while loyal to the fundamental teachings thereof, we are and by virtue of the genius of Israel, ought to be, free to interpret and restate the teachings of Israel of the past in light of the present, and that each succeeding generation in Israel is free to reformulate the truths entrusted in the Providence of the God of our fathers." The second meeting was held at Central Presbyterian Church on July 11, 1944. Temporary officers were elected: president, Nathan Klein; vice presidents, A. I. Lack and Mose M. Feld; secretary, William Nathan; and treasurer, Herman Cohen. Temporary board members were also elected. The name chosen means "God Be With Us," and Rabbi Robert I. Kahn, chaplain, United States Army, who was in the Pacific, was invited to the pulpit as soon as he would be discharged. Until then Rabbi Alan S. Green of Troy, New York, was chosen to lead Emanu El.

Negotiations were begun toward purchasing twenty-seven acres on Old Richmond Road (now called Bissonnet) for a cemetery. Emanu El Memorial Park was dedicated on September 29, 1946, and the oval in the center was preserved for a future chapel. The Kagan-Rudy Cemetery Chapel was dedicated in September 1983. The congregation held its first high holy day services at St. Paul's Methodist Church, religious school was held at MacGregor Elementary School, and Shabbat services were held at Central Presbyterian Church. On January 10, 1945, the congregation authorized Herman Cohen to purchase seven acres opposite Rice Institute (now Rice University) on Sunset Boulevard. By the time of the second annual meeting in 1946, the congregation had grown to 603 members. In 1947 the congregation voted to accept plans and proceed with building a permanent home. The cost of the land, furnishings, and building was estimated at $750,000, of which pledges had been secured in excess of $400,000. Mackie and Kamrath and Lenard Gabert were selected as architects. The Fretz Construction Company was awarded the building contract. The dedication of the building was held on September 9, 1949, when the congregation had 722 members. The original building comprised 65,000 square feet with a sanctuary seating 855 persons and Feld Hall seating an additional 1,800 persons for religious services. At that time these areas formed one of the largest spaces in the world under a cantilever roof, two-thirds of an acre without pillars. In 1975 the Freda and Jackie Proler Chapel and the Robert I. Kahn Gallery were added. In 1978 Rabbi Roy A. Walter became the senior rabbi, succeeding Rabbi Kahn, who was named rabbi emeritus. The membership in 1975 was 1,500 families; in 1988 it was 2,100 families. Two mottoes flank the pulpit: "to do justly, love mercy, walk humbly with God" and "ye shall be a light unto the nations".

BIBLIOGRAPHY: Natalie Ornish, *Pioneer Jewish Texans* (Dallas: Texas Heritage, 1989).

Myra Lipper

CONGRESO MEXICANISTA. The Congreso Mexicanista, sometimes referred to as El Primer Congreso Mexicanista, met in Laredo from September 14 to 22, 1911. Clemente Idar,qv whose family owned and published *La Crónica,*qv proposed the meeting to organize the Gran Liga Mexicanista de Beneficencia y Protección (Great Mexican League for Benefit and Protection) to advance education, culture, and civil rights for Mexican Americans.qv The Idars invited the OCH (Orden Caballeros de Honor), members of lodges and *sociedades mutualistas,*qv all Mexican consuls in the state, and Texas-Mexican journalists. They also issued a special invitation to women from the region, including Nuevo Laredo, Tamaulipas. *La Crónica* furnished free advertising for the conference and, in a series of articles, called on all Texas Mexicans to send representatives. The Congreso was scheduled to coincide with the celebration of el Diez y Seis de Septiembre, Mexican independence day, and an OCH convention. Workshops focused on social oppression and the Texas-Mexican economic situation. Soledad de la Peña spoke on the need to educate women. The *congreso* established the Gran Liga Mexicanista de Beneficencia y Protección and the Liga Femenil Mexicanista to promote cultural and moral values among Texas Mexicans, provide protection from abuse by public authorities, and combat segregation of Texas Mexican students. Nicasio Idarqv was chosen the leader of the Gran Liga, and Jovita Idar,qv his daughter, was elected president of the Liga Femenil, which emphasized free education for poor Texas Mexican children. Both organizations took the motto "Por la Raza y Para la Raza."

BIBLIOGRAPHY: José E. Limón, "El Primer Congreso Mexicanista de 1911," *Aztlán* 5 (Spring, Fall 1974).

Teresa Palomo Acosta

CONGRESS OF THE REPUBLIC OF TEXAS. The Constitution of the Republic of Texasqv provided for a two-house Congress. The House of Representatives was to be made up of "not less than twenty-four nor more than forty members," until such time as the population of the republic should exceed 100,000. When the population exceeded this number the house was to be made up of "not less than forty nor more than one hundred members provided that each county was entitled to at least one representative." Members of the House served one-year terms. A member had to be twenty-five or older, a citizen of the republic, and a resident of his district for six months. The House chose its speaker and had sole power of impeachment. The Senate was to have a membership numbering "not less than one-third nor more than one-half that of the House." The Senate was also chosen by districts that were as nearly equal as possible to the population of free men. Each district was entitled to no more than one member. A senator had to be thirty or older, a citizen of the republic, and a resident of his district for one year. Senators served three-year overlapping terms, with one-third of the members being elected each year. The Senate chose its own officers and president pro tem and had sole responsibility to try impeachments. Each house was to judge election and qualification of its own members. A quorum in either house was two-thirds of its membership. Members were to receive pay as fixed by law, but no change could be made in salary in the session in which the change was made.

The first Congress, which convened at Columbia on October 3, 1836, was made up of thirty representatives and fourteen senators. Lorenzo de Zavala,qv as vice president, was president of the Senate until October 22, when Mirabeau B. Lamarqv was inaugurated. Ira Ingramqv was elected speaker of the House, and Richard Ellisqv was elected president pro tem of the Senate. Since members of the House were elected for one-year terms, each Congress lasted only one year. In its short history, the Republic of Texas had nine congresses.

BIBLIOGRAPHY: Hans Peter Nielsen Gammel, comp., *Laws of Texas, 1822–1897* (10 vols., Austin: Gammel, 1898). Texas House of Representatives, *Biographical Directory of the Texan Conventions and Congresses, 1832–1845* (Austin: Book Exchange, 1941).

Ralph W. Steen

CONKLINE CREEK. Conkline Creek rises three miles north of Childress in south central Childress County (at 34°27′ N, 100°15′ W) and runs north, almost parallel to U.S. Highway 83, for nine miles to its mouth on the Prairie Dog Town Fork of the Red River (at 34°33′ N, 100°10′ W). The land through which it runs was once part of the OX Ranch.qv It crosses flat to rolling terrain surfaced by loams that support grasses, mesquite, and cacti.

CONLEN, TEXAS. Conlen, on U.S. Highway 54 and the Chicago, Rock Island and Gulf Railway in eastern Dallam County, was founded in 1903. It was named for Capt. J. H. Conlen, a Spanish–American War veteran who supervised the building of the Rock Island tracks from Liberal, Kansas, to Santa Rosa, New Mexico, through Sherman, Dallam, and Hartley counties in Texas. During the 1930s Conlen was noted for its high school girls' basketball team, which was sponsored by the Conlen Mercantile Company and which won the state championship in 1934. The community is allied by geography and trade with Stratford in Sherman County. Conlen survived the disastrous dust bowlqv years and later revived its grain-based economy with the introduction of irrigation wells. Conlen reported four businesses and a population of 150 in 1940; by 1948 its population had decreased to sixty-two, with three businesses. In 1990 Conlen's population was reported as sixty-one.

BIBLIOGRAPHY: Lillie Mae Hunter, *The Book of Years: A History of Dallam and Hartley Counties* (Hereford, Texas: Pioneer, 1969). Sherman County Historical Survey Committee, *God, Grass, and Grit* (2 vols., Seagraves, Texas: Pioneer, 1971, 1975).

H. Allen Anderson

CONLEY, JAMES MICHAEL PATRICK (1892–1978). James M. P. (Snipe) Conley, baseball pitcher, was born on April 25, 1892, to Michael and Rose Daily Conley in Schuylkill Haven, Pennsylvania. He left school at age twelve to help his family by working for the Pennsylvania and Reading Railroad. Two years later he moved to another town to work in a shoe factory. For entertainment he started playing baseball, developed as a pitcher, and eventually joined the company team. Soon he was playing semi-pro ball at night and working during the day. Conley signed with the original Bloomer Girl's baseball team and while on tour was hired by the Baltimore Orioles. John "Jack Quinn" Picus, an Oriole pitcher, taught Conley to throw the spitball. "Snipe hunting" was a popular prank at the time, and Baltimore veterans used it to initiate rookies. Conley was taken on a hunt, dutifully held the bag, and thereafter was known as "Snipe." In 1914–15 he played for the Baltimore Federals. While in Johnsonburg, Pennsylvania, for an off-season game, he agreed to pitch for the Dallas Submarines. With the variously named Texas League[qv] Dallas team he became a famed spitball thrower. Between 1916 and 1927 he led the club to three championships, the first in 1917, when he won twenty-seven games, including nineteen consecutively. In 1955 his games-won record of 211 was tied, but his consecutive victories remained intact for the first century of Texas League baseball (1888–1987). In 1918 Conley played briefly with the National League's Cincinnati team, but returned to Dallas in time to help Dallas earn its second pennant. In 1926 he managed the team to its third. In 1927 he was hired as manager of the Jackson, Mississippi, team in the Cotton States League. In 1928 he managed the Midland semi-pro club and later the same year went to work for the Big Lake Oil Company[qv] and became playing manager of its team, the Texon Oilers.[qv] During the World War II[qv] inactivity in semi-professional baseball, Conley continued his interest in the game by coaching amateur and youth teams. He retired from the Big Lake Oil Company in 1957 to Robert Lee, moved to Arizona, and eventually returned to Robert Lee. He was an excellent all-around player known for his down-to-earth attitude, loyalty, and good sportsmanship. Always a popular player with Dallas fans, he returned in 1941 to pitch two games with the Dallas Rebels. Under Texas League rules he could still use his spitball pitch; 3,000 fans saw him win on Snipe Conley Day, July 27. In 1973 Conley was inducted into the Texas Sports Hall of Fame.[qv] He was Catholic. He married Rosebud Stuart of Dallas in 1917. To this union two sons were born. In 1943 Conley married Mary Lee Reese. He died on January 5, 1978, in Robert Lee and is buried in Wheatland Cemetery, Dallas.

BIBLIOGRAPHY: Dallas *Morning News*, September 2, 1923. Bill O'Neal, *The Texas League, 1888–1987: A Century of Baseball* (Austin: Eakin Press, 1987). Joseph L. Reichler, ed., *The Baseball Encyclopedia*, 6th ed. (New York: Macmillan, 1985). San Angelo *Standard Times*, July 28, 1941, May 11, 1969.

Jane Spraggins Wilson
FCOSF

CONNALLY, JOHN BOWDEN, JR. (1917–1993). John Bowden Connally, Jr., thirty-eighth governor of the state of Texas, was born on a farm near Floresville, Texas, on February 27, 1917, one of eight children of John Bowden and Lela (Wright) Connally, Sr. He attended Harlandale High School in San Antonio, graduated from Floresville High School, and entered the University of Texas in 1933. He was elected president of the UT Student Association for 1938–39 and received his law degree from the UT law school in 1941. Connally passed the state bar examination in 1938 and began his career in government and politics in 1939 as secretary (legislative assistant) to Representative Lyndon B. Johnson,[qv] Connally's "mentor, friend and benefactor." It was the beginning of a close personal relationship that was storied but often stormy, and lasted until Johnson's death in 1973. Connally met Idanell (Nellie) Brill of Austin at UT and they were married on December 21, 1940. They had four children. Their eldest, Kathleen, eloped in 1958 at age sixteen and the same year died of an apparently self-inflicted gunshot wound.

Connally was commissioned in the United States Naval Reserve in 1941. As a fighter director aboard aircraft carriers, he went through nine major air-sea battles in the Pacific Theater. Aboard the USS *Essex* he endured fifty-two consecutive hours of Japanese kamikaze attacks in April 1945. He attained the rank of lieutenant commander and came home a hero. After returning to civilian life, Connally headed an investors' group of war veterans that owned and operated Austin radio station KVET (1946–49). He also joined an influential Austin law firm and during this period served as campaign manager in LBJ's 1946 reelection to Congress and successful 1948 Senate race. He then served as LBJ's aide until 1951, when he became Sid W. Richardson's[qv] legal counsel, a position he held until Richardson's death in 1959. Connally earned a reputation both as "Lyndon's boy" and as a "political mastermind" and expert strategist. His political credo was "Fight hard and rough, but when the battle is over, forget and dismiss." Connally managed five of LBJ's major political campaigns, including reelection to the United States House of Representatives in 1946, the 1941 and 1948 races for the United States Senate, the unsuccessful bid for the Democratic presidential nomination in 1960, and the election to the presidency in 1964. In LBJ's pivotal 1948 Senate race against former governor Coke R. Stevenson,[qv] Connally, as LBJ's campaign manager, was publicly linked to the suspicious late report of 200 votes in Box 13 from Jim Wells County, which had provided LBJ's eighty-seven-vote margin of victory. Connally denied any tie to vote fraud, but acknowledged that he had learned a lesson in managing LBJ's unsuccessful 1941 race for the Senate, when Johnson's seemingly decisive 5,000-vote lead had been whittled away by late election returns from East Texas. LBJ lost the 1941 race by 1,311 votes. In 1948 Connally instructed South Texas campaign operatives to *under*state their early returns in the vote canvassing because, he claimed, "we had been bitten once. It would not happen again."

Connally also ably assisted in various political turf skirmishes, including fights to control the state Democratic party.[qv] In these he was a field operative or grass-roots political ally of both LBJ and Speaker of the House Sam Rayburn,[qv] who considered themselves leaders of the state party's "moderate conservative wing." One major struggle for party control was fought in 1952–56 against the "right-wing Shivercrats," led by Governor Allan Shivers,[qv] who bolted in 1952 and led a "Democrats for Eisenhower" move that helped the Republican presidential candidate carry Texas. A second, and longer-running, feud that extended through Connally's tenure as governor was with liberal senator Ralph Yarborough. Divisions between liberal and conservative-moderate Democrats became a personal feud between Lyndon Johnson and Yarborough, and Connally found himself embroiled in the feud because of his close ties to Johnson.

Connally served as secretary of the navy in 1961 in the cabinet of Democrat President John F. Kennedy. He won his first political race as a candidate for governor the next year. He was tall, handsome, personable, and articulate; his speech reflected his debate, drama, and declamation training in high school and college. He was also well-schooled in politics and government and had profited from his experience as Sid Richardson's legal counsel. Connally entered the race against a large field of candidates, including Governor Price Daniel, Sr.,[qv] who was seeking a fourth term. A poll showed that Connally had only 4 percent of the votes at the outset. But in addition to wealthy backers such as the oilman Richardson, he had a strong grass-roots network of politically astute supporters. Connally won a 1962 runoff by 26,000 votes. The next year he survived serious gunshot wounds inflicted in the Kennedy assassination.[qv] He speculated that both he and JFK might have been the assassin's targets. He was reelected by a 3-to-1 vote margin in 1964 and won a third term in 1966 with 72 percent of the vote.

Connally had grown up on his family's South Texas cotton farm in the hard-scrabble status of "a barefoot boy of mule-plowed furrows." His accomplishments as governor "epitomized the big man of Texas" and "personified the Texas establishment as the Texas establishment wanted to see itself." He considered himself "a conservative who believed in active government." He had a vision of moving Texas into a dynamic era and entered the governorship saying that his administration should emphasize one of three crucial issues of the day: education, race relations, or poverty. He chose to be "an education governor" both because he believed that the most enduring way to address social problems was through education and because he "had a farm boy's dream to become the governor of the intellectuals and of the cultivated." Connally effectively used his political skills to increase taxes substantially in order to finance higher teachers' salaries, better libraries, research, and new doctoral programs. He considered this the crowning achievement of his administration. He promoted programs to reshape and reform state government, to develop the state's tourism[qv] industry (including his endorsement of liquor by the drink and pari-mutuel betting), to establish a state fine arts commission and a state historical commission (see TEXAS COMMISSION ON THE ARTS *and* TEXAS HISTORICAL COMMISSION), and to establish the University of Texas Institute of Texan Cultures,[qv] which was initiated as part of HemisFair '68,[qv] a state-supported world's fair at San Antonio.

After leaving the governor's office in 1969 Connally joined Vinson and Elkins, a large law firm in Houston named for William Ashton Vinson and James A. Elkins,[qv] both early principals in the firm. The same year, he was named a member of President Richard M. Nixon's foreign-intelligence advisory board and assumed a favored position among Nixon's advisors (it was said that "If Connally is not for a matter, the President won't do it"). In 1971 he became Nixon's secretary of the treasury and earned a reputation as "a tough American statesman." He sought to address the nation's growing trade deficit and inflation by such mechanisms as currency devaluation and a price freeze. In 1972 he spearheaded a Democrats for Nixon organization that helped the Republican president carry Texas. Connally switched parties from Democrat to Republican in 1973, three months after LBJ's death. In the wake of the bribery-related resignation of Vice President Spiro Agnew in October 1973, Nixon passed word that he would name Connally to fill the vacancy. This would have put Connally in a strong position to run for president in 1976. Nixon and Connally had privately mused about starting a new Whig-type party in the tradition of Henry Clay and Daniel Webster. But Democrats and Republicans alike in the Senate erupted in a "firestorm of protest." Warnings went up that if Nixon pursued the appointment, some powerful Senate Democrats "would be determined to destroy Connally." This was during the height of the Watergate scandal, which ultimately forced Nixon to resign. Nixon named House minority leader Gerald Ford vice president but said that he intended to support Connally for the 1976 GOP nomination. In the aftermath, Connally rejoined Vinson and Elkins but soon confronted a criminal prosecution for alleged bribery and conspiracy in a "milk-price" scandal. He was acquitted after a trial in federal court.

Connally's aborted effort to win the GOP's presidential nomination in 1980 was short-lived. He was hurt in part by a "wheeler-dealer" identification reminiscent of LBJ, and a press criticism that he was a political "chameleon." He was also damaged by a 1977 bank partnership he entered into with two Arab sheiks and an ill-advised or misunderstood speech he delivered to the National Press Club in Washington, D.C., that was interpreted as having anti-Semitic overtones. Connally raised and spent $11 million on the fourteen-month campaign but dropped out of the primaries, having gained the binding commitment of only one GOP convention delegate. He felt himself to be a victim of the Watergate scandal. After he lost his bid for the presidential nomination in 1980, he left politics and government.

In February 1982 Connally, a man of some wealth, took mandatory retirement from Vinson and Elkins. In 1981 he went into the business of real estate development with his former political protégé, Ben Barnes. In the partnership Connally was the "intimidating Olympian eminence," and Barnes was the "sometimes overpowering salesman and legman." Both had superb business and political contacts in the state and nation "and saw no reason why the values of their political life could not work equally well in their business life." The partners "conducted business," however, "as if they were campaigning for higher office." They signed personal notes on loans bearing short-

Governor John Connally and President Lyndon Baines Johnson aboard Air Force One. Photograph by Yoichi R. Okamoto, September 28, 1967. Courtesy Lyndon Baines Johnson Library, Austin. Connally and Johnson are shown here during a trip to inspect flood damage in South Texas and the Rio Grande valley in the wake of Hurricane Beulah.

term interest at 18 percent and by June 1983 had sixteen major projects under way totaling $231 million. It was a boom time in the Texas petroleum industry, with world oil prices ranging up to thirty-seven dollars a barrel. When the oil price collapsed, the state's economy collapsed. Connally and Barnes were out on a limb that broke and took them with it, along with many other wealthy Texans and most of the state's major financial institutions (see BANKS AND BANKING). The fiasco led Connally to acknowledge that "we were moving too far too fast and paying dearly for it." He declared bankruptcy, and he and Nellie held a globally publicized auction of their holdings and expensive personal belongings to apply the proceeds to their debt. The positions Connally held in law and business had taken him to the high echelons of corporate America. He was a director of the Coastal Corporation, Kaiser Tech, Kaiser Aluminum, Methodist Hospital of Houston,[qv] and Maxxam, Incorporated. He had earlier served on the boards of the New York Central Railroad, U.S. Trust, Pan American Airways, the Andrew Mellon Foundation, Greyhound Corporation, Ford Motor Company, Signal Companies, First City Bank Corporation, Superior Oil Company, Falkenbridge Nickel, and American General Insurance. He was a member of the State Bar of Texas,[qv] and the American, Houston, and District of Columbia Bar associations. Connally died on June 15, 1993, at the Methodist Hospital of Houston, where he was being treated for pulmonary fibrosis. He was buried in the State Cemetery[qv] in Austin. He was survived by his wife, a daughter, Sharon C. Ammann, and two sons, John Bowden III and Mark.

BIBLIOGRAPHY: Robert A. Caro, *The Years of Lyndon Johnson* (New York: Knopf, 1982–). John Connally, with Mickey Herskowitz, *In History's Shadow: An American Odyssey* (New York: Hyperion, 1993). D. B. Hardeman and Donald C. Bacon, *Rayburn: A Biography* (Austin: Texas Monthly Press, 1987). Lyndon Baines Johnson, *The Vantage Point: Perspectives of the Presidency, 1963–1969* (New York: Holt, Rinehart and Winston, 1971). Doris Kearns, *Lyndon Johnson and the American Dream* (New York: Harper and Row, 1976). William Manchester, *The Death of a President* (New York: Harper and Row, 1967). Merle Miller, *Lyndon: An Oral Biography* (New York: Putnam, 1980). Richard M. Nixon, *RN: The Memoirs of Richard Nixon* (New York: Grosset and Dunlap, 1978). James Reston, Jr., *The Lone Star: The Life of John Connally* (New York: Harper and Row, 1989).

Walter H. Gray

CONNALLY, THOMAS TERRY (1877–1963). Tom Connally, United States senator, was born on a farm in McLennan County, Texas, on August 19, 1877, to Jones and Mary Ellen (Terry) Connally. Jones Connally was a Confederate veteran. Tom, the only surviving son of the couple, took a law degree from the University of Texas in 1898 and was elected to the state House of Representatives unopposed in 1900 and 1902. He was a progressive in his opposition to monopolies and to the powerful Senator Joseph Weldon Bailey.qv Connally declined to run for a third term. He practiced law for several years in Marlin and married a local belle, Louise Clarkson, in 1904. He was Falls County prosecuting attorney from 1906 to 1910 and was in and out of local politics for the next decade, while building up a prosperous law practice and establishing himself in the Methodist Churchqv and several fraternal orders.

In 1916 Connally ran for the vacant Eleventh District seat in the United States Congress, a jurisdiction centered in Waco. After defeating two opponents without a runoff, he was elected and placed on the House Foreign Affairs Committee. He became something of a foreign-policy spokesman for the Democrats in the 1920s, urging the Republican administrators to settle their differences with Mexico and to cease invading Caribbean republics. In 1928 Connally ran against United States Senator Earle B. Mayfield,qv a Klansman who had been elected during the heyday of the Ku Klux Klan.qv Connally successfully urged voters to "turn out the bedsheet-and-mask candidate" and in his first term fought President Herbert Hoover's efforts to raise the tariff, levy a national sales tax, and aid business and mortgage holders at the expense of consumers and homeowners.

During Franklin D. Roosevelt's first term as president, Connally was a stalwart New Dealer, seldom differing with the administration. Like any senator he looked after the largest interest groups in his state, writing relief bills for cattle ranchers, cotton farmers, and oilmen. The most far-reaching solutions were devised for the oil industry, which was facing a glut. Prostrate in the early 1930s, the major oil companies and leading independent operators were demanding state and federal aid. The Connally Hot Oil Act of 1935 effectively outlawed the interstate shipment of oil produced in violation of the new state quotas and was fiercely resisted by many independent drillers and processors. Connally first parted significantly from Roosevelt when the senator opposed the president's attempt to change the United States Supreme Court, the court-packing plan of 1937.qv The measure failed in the Senate. Also in 1937 Connally led the filibuster against the antilynching bill and fought diligently for the southern differential in the wage and hour law.

Connally was a traditional southern internationalist who resisted the isolationist tide and the neutrality acts of the middle and late 1930s. He led the Senate battle for the arms-embargo repeal in 1939 (the Cash and Carry Act) and for the Lend Lease Act of 1941. As chairman of the Senate Foreign Relations Committee from 1941 to 1947, he was one of the handful of Americans who devised the United Nations and its charter. Together with Arthur Vandenburg, he helped to determine bipartisan foreign policy during Harry Truman's administration, including the establishment of the North Atlantic Treaty Organization. He served another stretch as chairman of the Senate Foreign Relations Committee from 1949 to 1953.

During the war years Connally and his fellow Texas senator, W. Lee O'Daniel,qv supported the Republican–Southern Democratic coalition more often than any other southern duo. In 1942 Connally led the ten-day filibuster against the repeal of the poll tax. The Smith-Connally Act of 1943 extended the power of the president to seize strike-bound war plants, a measure that Connally believed helped the war effort.

In his years of prominence in the 1930s and 1940s Connally was the best showman in the Senate. A contemporary politician, describing the 200-pound, white-haired Connally, decreed him to be "the only man in the United States Senate who could wear a Roman Toga and not look like a fat man in a nightgown." By the early 1950s, however, Connally had lost some of his effectiveness. Moreover, his notions of party loyalty were distasteful to the powerful tidelands oil lobby. The lobby wanted a strong leader who would support whichever 1952 presidential nominee embraced state ownership of offshore oil lands (see TIDELANDS CONTROVERSY). After they found their candidate in state attorney general M. Price Daniel, Sr.,qv whose speeches effectively linked Connally with the unpopular Truman administration, Connally retired.

Connally and his first wife had one son, Ben C. Connally. Mrs. Connally died in 1935. In 1942 the senator married Lucile (Sanderson) Sheppard, the widow of Senator Morris Sheppard.qv Connally died on October 28, 1963.

BIBLIOGRAPHY: Tom Connally and Alfred Steinberg, *My Name Is Tom Connally* (New York: Crowell, 1954). *Dictionary of American Biography.* George N. Green, *The Establishment in Texas Politics* (Westport, Connecticut: Greenwood, 1979).

George N. Green

Tom Connally (left) speaks to fellow Texas senator Morris Sheppard (second from right). Prints and Photographs Collection, Morris Sheppard file, CAH; CN 08126. First voted into public office in 1900, Connally never lost an election.

CONNALLY HOT OIL ACT OF 1935. The Connally Hot Oil Act of 1935 came about as a result of the federal government's attempts to deal with the problem of hot oilqv—petroleum produced in violation of state and federal quotas and regulations. In the early 1930s the overproduction of oil, largely a result of the East Texas oil boom, was adversely affecting the oil market. As part of the National Industrial Recovery Act in 1933 the federal government enacted regulation prohibiting the transport of petroleum that exceeded state quotas of production. The United States Supreme Court struck down the NIRA, including the petroleum-related provision, thereby prompting the federal government to seek new legislation in the attempt to stop hot oil.

Senator Thomas Connally of Texas sponsored a bill known as the Connally Hot Oil Act. It became law on February 22, 1935. In general, the law was intended to protect foreign and interstate commerce against "contraband oil" and encourage the conservation of United States crude-oil deposits. It prohibited the shipment of hot oil. Under the law the president had the power to prescribe regulations and require certificates of clearance for petroleum and petroleum products to be moved interstate. It called for the establishment of boards to issue certificates. Boards could conduct hearings and investigations regarding the enforcement of the act, and the United States District Courts had exclusive jurisdiction regarding judicial matters and disputes over denied permits. Violators of the law paid a fine of up to $2,000 and were sentenced to as much as six months' imprisonment. The federal government could seize the contraband oil, though it had the option to return it to the original owner in cases of extreme hardship.

Though the legislation was intended to expire on June 16, 1937, it was maintained afterwards as a permanent law. There was some debate as to the law's effects on the transport of other fuels such as coal and timber, and many independent oil producers vehemently opposed the government regulations. However, in 1937 four federal courts upheld the Connally Act, which was later administered by the Federal Petroleum Board, a part of the Department of the Interior.

BIBLIOGRAPHY: Gerald Forbes, *Flush Production: The Epic of Oil in the Gulf-Southwest* (Norman: University of Oklahoma Press, 1942). Wayne Gard, "Hot Oil in Texas," *New Republic,* January 30, 1935. Samuel Barrett Pettengill, *Hot Oil* (New York: Economic Forum, 1936). Erich W. Zimmermann, *Conservation in the Production of Petroleum,* Petroleum Monograph Series, Vol. 2 (New Haven, Connecticut: Yale University Press, 1957).
Laurie E. Jasinski

CONNELL, JOHN (?–?). John Connell, pioneer settler and merchant, son of an immigrant Irish blacksmith, was born in Pennsylvania and moved to Texas as a young man with Sterling C. Robertson[qv] in 1826. He established a mercantile business near Austin and soon acquired considerable property. In 1830 he married Matilda T. Roberts, daughter of Texas pioneer Elisha Roberts;[qv] they had two children. Connell was chosen as a delegate from Mill Creek, now in Austin County, to the Convention of 1832.[qv] He died at Viesca, Milam County, in 1834. In 1850 his wife donated a portion of the family estate, 120 acres of a one-league tract east of the Lampasas River on Noland Creek, once the site of the Connell home, to Bell County as a site for the new county seat, which soon became known as Belton. Matilda Connell was remarried in 1835 to Samuel T. Allen[qv] of New York. Connell's son, John H., Jr., became a prominent farmer and stock raiser in Bell and Williamson counties and served with the Confederate forces during the Civil War.[qv]

BIBLIOGRAPHY: *A Memorial and Biographical History of McLennan, Falls, Bell, and Coryell Counties* (Chicago: Lewis, 1893; rpt., St. Louis: Ingmire, 1984). Texas House of Representatives, *Biographical Directory of the Texan Conventions and Congresses, 1832–1845* (Austin: Book Exchange, 1941).
Charles Christopher Jackson

CONNELL, JOHN HENRY (1867–1943). John Henry Connell, whose first name may have been James, director of the Texas Agricultural Experiment Station and developer of the concept of regional agricultural research, the son of John Tinsley and Orpha (Salmon) Connell, was born in Walnut Hill, Arkansas, on July 9, 1867. He entered Mississippi A&M College (now Mississippi State University) in 1884 and graduated in 1888 with a bachelor of science degree. Thereafter he worked as an agriculturalist and continued his education. In 1893, after directing research on tick fever[qv] and cottonseed rations for steers, Connell earned a master of science degree, also from Mississippi A&M.

That same year he accepted the directorship of the Texas Agricultural Experiment Station (*see* AGRICULTURAL EXPERIMENT STATION SYSTEM). He shared the belief of the Texas A&M Board of Directors that experimental substations, later known as agricultural research and extension centers, should be established in each area of Texas that had distinct soil and climate characteristics. As director, he traveled the state, solicited sites for substations, and listened to farmers. He crusaded for farmers' institutes and wrote popular articles that related to fundamental, as well as practical, problems faced by farmers. Connell insisted that government funds be spent according to congressional intent and for the benefit of the largest number of farmers. Through farmers' congresses at Texas A&M, he expanded the reputation of the experiment station and the college, obtained greater cooperation among farmers, and educated them about the latest scientific discoveries. These included the adaptability of corn varieties to different Texas soils; information about the life cycle of the Texas tick, knowledge resulting in an inoculation program by George Curtis and Mark Francis;[qv] and the influence of cottonseed oil products upon the butter industry (*see* COTTONSEED INDUSTRY).

When Connell resigned from the experiment station in 1902 to become associate editor and assistant general manager of *Texas Farm and Ranch,* he had developed a statewide system of substations. The locations and number of stations changed to meet the changing needs of Texas agriculture. Although others, such as Seaman Knapp,[qv] made important contributions to agricultural extension in the state, Connell seems to have done the most to foster the Texas Agricultural Extension Service.[qv] He continued to emphasize agricultural education with *Texas Farm and Ranch.* He became president of Oklahoma A&M College (now Oklahoma State University) in 1908. There he enjoyed the support of his friend William (Alfalfa Bill) Murray[qv] and served until 1914. He subsequently moved to Dallas and served for twenty-five years as executive secretary and vice president of the Dallas Automobile Association.

Connell was married to Maud Brock. He was a member of the First Methodist Church, the Masons, and the Sons of the American Revolution. He died in Dallas on May 26, 1943, and was buried in Grove Hill Cemetery, Dallas.

BIBLIOGRAPHY: Dallas *Morning News,* May 27, 1943. Irvin M. May, Jr., "J. H. Connell, Aggie Administrator: The Texas Years," *Red River Valley Historical Review* 3 (Winter 1978). Philip R. Rulon, *Oklahoma State University since 1890* (Stillwater, Oklahoma, 1975). *Texas Farm and Ranch,* June 14, 1902.
Irvin M. May, Jr.

CONNELL, WILSON EDWARD (1858–1936). Wilson Edward Connell, banker, was born on April 12, 1858, in Bell County, Texas, to William A. and Louisa (Wills) Connell. The family moved to Brown County when he was two years old. He entered the ranching business at the age of fourteen and, working with his father's cattle during most of the year, attended school only in the winter. By the time he was sixteen, he was self-supporting and took charge of a herd belonging to a partnership that included his father and his brother G. H. He worked with the cattle for four years and received 25 percent of the calves. Within a couple of years Connell sold his share of the stock for $11,000 and promptly invested the proceeds in a merchandising and cattle operation in Sweetwater.

On January 30, 1881, he married Hattie Millican of Comanche County. They had six children. Connell moved to Midland in 1886 to open a branch of his Sweetwater store. Soon he entered the banking business. He first operated a partnership under the name Connell Brothers and Scharbauer, which he later renamed W. E. Connell and Company. Around 1888 he changed the name again and chartered the First National Bank of Midland. After serving as a principal stockholder, cashier, and general manager for ten years in Midland, Connell transferred to the First National Bank of Fort Worth in Tarrant County. He served as cashier for several years before being named vice president. During his tenure the bank moved to a new ten-story "skyscraper" at the corner of Seventh and Houston in downtown Fort Worth. In 1912 Capt. Martin B. Loyd, the first president of the bank, died; his last words were, "Damn my soul, you'll never fill this building." With his passing, Connell was named president. Under his leadership, the bank building not only filled but doubled in size. In 1931 he was elected chairman of the board. He stayed with the bank the remainder of his life. In addition, he had an interest in twenty West Texas banks.

Connell owned several cattle ranches that totalled 100,000 acres. He usually held 3,000 to 5,000 cattle. He was vice president and a stockholder of the Dublin Oil Mills. From 1920 until his death he served as treasurer of the Texas and Southwestern Cattle Raisers Association.qv He was also a director of the Texas and Pacific Railway and vice president and stockholder of the Cicero Smith Lumber Company. Connell was appointed to the War Finance Corporation during World War Iqv and was named a district officer of the Reconstruction Finance Corporation in 1932. He was a member of many clubs and a Baptist. He died at his home on May 5, 1936, and was buried at Greenwood Cemetery, Fort Worth. He was survived by his widow and five children.

BIBLIOGRAPHY: James Cox, *Historical and Biographical Record of the Cattle Industry* (2 vols., St. Louis: Woodward and Tiernan Printing, 1894, 1895; rpt., with an introduction by J. Frank Dobie, New York: Antiquarian, 1959). Fort Worth *Star-Telegram*, May 5, 1936. Buckley B. Paddock, *History of Texas: Fort Worth and the Texas Northwest Edition* (4 vols., Chicago: Lewis, 1922). *Who Was Who in America* (Chicago: Marquis, Vol. 2.
Kristi Strickland

CONNELL, TEXAS. Connell is on the Southern Pacific Railroad east of State Highway 105 and eight miles east of Beaumont in west central Orange County. The western end of a siding on the Texas and New Orleans Railroad was called Diana as early as 1905. At that time the Anderson brothers owned a mill 1½ miles to the east, at the approximate site of what would later be called Connell. By 1913 the eastern end of the siding was known as Connell, after the president of the Reese-Corriher Lumber Company, G. H. Connell. The company's new mill at Connell had a daily capacity of 75,000 board feet. Also in 1913 a post office was established for the community. In 1920 the West Lumber Company of Harris County acquired the Connell mill. At that time the local population was estimated to be 400. As available timber was cut out, however, sawmill operations slowed throughout the area. The West Lumber Company began selling its lands and moving its machinery at Connell by 1924, when the local post office was discontinued. During the 1960s and 1970s the old sawmill site became an increasingly popular residential area, as the population from Vidor, Rose City, and Beaumont pushed farther east.

BIBLIOGRAPHY: *Gulf Coast Lumberman*, September 1, 1913.
Robert Wooster

CONNELLEE, CHARLES ULRICH (1851–1930). Charles Ulrich Connellee, surveyor and state legislator, son of Sadosa T. and Lucy A. (Woods) Connellee, was born on August 21, 1851, in Scott County, Kentucky. After studying in the agricultural and mechanical department of the University of Lexington, he taught school in Scott County. In 1874 he was elected county surveyor, but in October of the same year he moved to Texas, where he established a real estate business in Dallas. In January 1875 he bought and staked out a public square on 320 acres centrally located in Eastland County. The tract had originally been surveyed by C. S. Betts. In May, Connellee and two partners, Jack S. Dougherty and J. B. Ammerman, surveyed the town of Eastland and were influential in getting the new community made county seat. During the early 1880s Connellee was a leader in efforts to eradicate Texas feverqv and improve cattle breeds for the area ranches. In 1887 he was elected as representative from the Forty-second District in the Twenty-first and Twenty-second legislatures. In 1911 he was a member of the board that located and established the state tuberculosis colony. He served as a regent of the College of Industrial Arts (now Texas Woman's University) from 1925 until his death. Connellee married Mattie E. Payne on April 22, 1875. They had four children. After her death he married Lulu Ostrom, on September 1, 1888. On June 14, 1894, he married Tully Hardeman. On March 15, 1924, he married Mrs. Bula B. Whittington. Connellee died in Fort Worth on December 2, 1930, and was buried in Eastland.

BIBLIOGRAPHY: Edwin T. Cox, *History of Eastland County, Texas* (San Antonio: Naylor, 1950). Lewis E. Daniell, *Personnel of the Texas State Government, with Sketches of Representative Men of Texas* (Austin: City Printing, 1887; 3d ed., San Antonio: Maverick, 1892). Fort Worth *Star-Telegram*, December 3, 1930. Ruby Pearl Ghormley, *Eastland County, Texas: A Historical and Biographical Survey* (Austin: Rupegy, 1969). Carolyne Lavinia Langston, *History of Eastland County* (Dallas: Aldridge 1904).

CONNELL AND EUBANK RANCHES. The first ranch in Ochiltree County was established by Thomas Connell and J. D. (Dee) Eubank, both of whom came from Burnet County. In 1876 Connell and Eubank drove cattle from Winters, in Runnels County, to seek a suitable ranch site. They initially attempted the valley of the Purgatoire River in Colorado, but two successive hard winters there decimated their herds. With about thirty cattle left, the two young cowmen headed south from Kansas. They camped at a small playa near the site of present-day Perryton on December 20, 1878. They decided Wolf Creek was the most promising location for their ranch, herded their longhorn cattleqv into the creek draw, and occupied the dugoutqv recently vacated by their friends Alfred H. and D. Wilborn Barton,qqv who had moved into the abandoned Jones and Plummer stockade farther downstream (*see* JONES AND PLUMMER TRAIL). Another neighbor was Charles A. Dietrich, who helped them round up wild mustangs and often cooked for them. Within two years Connell and Eubank had increased their individual herds and established their own ranches, Eubank in eastern Ochiltree County and Connell two miles to the east in Lipscomb County.

Just before this separation, Dee's letters had prompted his brother, Henry T. Eubank, to move his family to Wolf Creek from McCulloch County, where he had served as county sheriff. In 1887 Henry Eubank registered a Triangle F brand. Two years later, when Ochiltree County was organized, he was elected a county commissioner. From 1894 to 1900 he served as county judge. Dee Eubank helped establish Ochiltree County's first school, known locally as "Raw Hide College," across Wolf Creek from his homestead. In later years the Eubank heirs leased the ranch property and eventually sold it to Carl Freeman.

Tom Connell, who recorded a D brand in 1881, built a comfortable ranchhouse with a stone fireplace on Wolf Creek in western Lipscomb County. The county line was his property's western boundary. In 1886 he erected a fence along a strip two miles wide and eight miles long and connected it with the old drift fence (*see* PANHANDLE DRIFT FENCES) to the south. In 1885 Connell married Jannie Watson at Mobeetie; they had two sons and two daughters. When Lipscomb County was organized in 1887, Connell was elected its first county judge. He also established a mercantile and butcher shop in Lipscomb. Business was conducted there in a way most unusual, even for the frontier. Connell would hang a fresh beef carcass in his shop, place a pencil and tablet near the meat block, go away, and leave the door unlocked. Each customer would cut off the portion of meat he wanted, weigh it on Connell's scales and write his name and the amount of purchase on the pad. At his convenience the customer looked up the judge and paid him. Connell ran this meat business successfully for several years before selling it and moving in 1905 to Canadian, where he and his wife spent their remaining years.

The Eubank and Connell ranches were never large like that of their neighbor, Henry W. Cresswell.qv They have remained basically intact, although under different brands and owners. The site of Connell and Eubank's original dugout on Wolf Creek is now on the Walter Daniel ranch.

BIBLIOGRAPHY: Millie Jones Porter, *Memory Cups of Panhandle Pioneers* (Clarendon, Texas: Clarendon Press, 1945). Pauline D. and R. L. Robertson, *Cowman's Country: Fifty Frontier Ranches in the Texas Panhandle, 1876–1887* (Amarillo: Paramount, 1981).
H. Allen Anderson

CONNELLY, HENRY C. (1800–1866). Henry C. Connelly, merchant, the son of John Donaldson and Frances (Brent) Connelly, was born in what is now Spencer County, Kentucky, in 1800. After obtaining a degree in medicine he practiced in Liberty, Missouri, in

1828. In less than a year he closed his office and joined a trade caravan for Chihuahua. There he began to clerk for Ludwell Powell and soon bought Powell's store. In 1839 he organized and conducted a caravan across western and northern Texas in an attempt to establish a route shorter than the Missouri-Chihuahua trail. He and his party were delayed on the way by bad weather and by getting lost (*see* CHIHUAHUA EXPEDITION). When the Connelly party finally reached Fort Towson the commander of the fort, Maj. Henry Wilson, was unsure if he should allow a party of more than 100 men with eighty wagons to cross into United States territory to trade. Correspondence on the question reached the secretary of war before the decision was made to let the expedition pass. On the return trip in 1840 Connelly again found his progress impeded by bad weather. In addition, due to a change in the Mexican government, there was a question as to the amount of impost duty the expedition had to pay. The venture proved to be so unprofitable that the trail was not used again.

In 1843 Connelly formed a partnership with Edward J. Glasgow of St. Louis in order to take advantage of the Santa Fe trade with Missouri and Chihuahua. He continued to live in Chihuahua until after the Mexican War.[qv] When Stephen W. Kearny approached Santa Fe, Connelly acted as an emissary for Gen. Manuel Armijo. Thereafter he moved to Santa Fe and established a large mercantile business. In 1860 and 1864, President Abraham Lincoln appointed Connelly territorial governor of New Mexico. Connelly was married twice, to women of Mexico. He died of accidental poisoning in July 1866.

BIBLIOGRAPHY: Stella M. Drumm, ed., *Down the Santa Fe Trail and into Mexico: The Diary of Susan Shelby Magoffin, 1846–1847* (New Haven, Connecticut: Yale University Press, 1926). Grant Foreman, *Advancing the Frontier* (Norman: University of Oklahoma Press, 1933; rpt. 1968). Josiah Gregg, *Commerce of the Prairies*, ed. Max L. Moorhead (Norman: University of Oklahoma Press, 1954). George Wilkins Kendall, *Narrative of the Texan Santa Fe Expedition* (2 vols., New York: Harper, 1844; rpts. Austin: Steck, 1935; n.p.: Readex, 1966).

Morris L. Britton

CONNER, ARTHUR BENJAMIN (1881–1971). Arthur Benjamin Conner, agronomist and developer of sorghum for use in Texas, son of Richard Benjamin and Jane Conner, was born in Rosebud, Texas, on October 20, 1881. He graduated from Texas A&M in 1904 with a B.S. in agriculture and worked as a scientific assistant for the United States Department of Agriculture at Chillicothe until 1911. During this time he tested hundreds of sorghum varieties and became responsible for distributing dwarf yellow milo, the principal sorghum grown in Texas for the next twenty-five years (*see* SORGHUM AND SORGHUM CULTURE). In 1911 Conner became vice director of the Texas Agricultural Experiment Station (*see* AGRICULTURAL EXPERIMENT STATION SYSTEM). He completed an M.S. at Texas A&M in 1923 and three years later became acting director of the station. In 1928 he became director, a post he held until 1944. In 1948 he received the first honorary doctor of agriculture degree awarded by Texas A&M University.

As station director, Conner wanted experiment stations to be like model farms. His scientific goals included prevention and cure of plant diseases[qv] and diseases of animals, adaptation or breeding of fruits and vegetables for Texas soils and climate, soil fertility and agricultural chemistry, and research on livestock feeds, forestry, cotton, and agricultural economic problems. He recognized and supported Harris P. Smith's development of the mechanical cotton stripper, Paul Mangelsdorf's studies of corn, and Ray E. Dickson's[qv] soil conservation research. The Soil Conservation Act of 1935 was written by Conner, Representative James Paul Buchanan,[qv] and Dickson, and supported in the United States House of Representatives by Marvin Jones,[qv] chairman of the House Agricultural Committee. Under Conner's direction the Texas Agricultural Experiment Station expanded research to areas of diverse soil, climate, and agricultural conditions. He cooperated with the United States Department of Agriculture to establish the Southwestern Great Plains Research Center near Amarillo and entered into joint relations with John Tarleton College (now Tarleton State University) at Stephenville. In addition to research on sorghum, soil fertility, and conservation, he supported and helped make possible the introduction of the Chinese elm to Texas, the development of the sore-mouth vaccine, and the development of new varieties of cotton, corn, oats, and wheat, as well as work on controls for the cotton flea hopper.

Conner was a member of the American Association for the Advancement of Science, the American Genetic Association, the American Society of Agronomy, and the Philosophical Society of Texas.[qv] He lived near Rosebud with his wife, Nettie. He was a Methodist. He died on August 4, 1971, and was survived by his wife and two sons. *See also* AGRICULTURE, CORN AND CORN CULTURE, COTTON AND COTTON CULTURE, WHEAT PRODUCTION.

BIBLIOGRAPHY: Arthur B. Conner Papers, Texas A&M University Archives. Vertical Files, Barker Texas History Center, University of Texas at Austin.

Irvin M. May, Jr.

CONNER, JEFFIE OBREA ALLEN (1895–1972). Jeffie O. A. Conner, home economist and teacher, was born near Waco on August 17, 1895, the daughter of Jeff D. and Meddie Lillian Estelle Allen. After graduating from Mary Allen Seminary in 1912, she earned a teacher's diploma from Prairie View State Normal and Industrial College (now

Jeffie O. A. Conner. George Sherman and Jeffie O. A. Conner Papers, Texas Collection, Baylor University, Waco, Texas.

Prairie View A&M University) in 1914. She taught in county schools from 1914 to 1923. She married George Sherman Conner, a physician, on September 19, 1923; they had no children.

Beginning in 1923, Mrs. Conner served as cooperative extension agent for the rural black population of McLennan County. Her home-demonstration program instructed farm families in scientific gardening practices, nutritious methods of food preparation and preservation, and home sanitation. In the schools she concentrated on improving nutrition and on preventing the spread of disease by showing children how to make individual drinking cups from used tin cans instead of drinking from a common dipper. At the same time, she continued her own formal education by earning a B.S. in home economics from Prairie View in 1934. In 1935 she became supervisor of home-demonstration work for seventeen East Texas counties. She traveled from one to another and stayed in private homes because hotels refused to accommodate blacks. She incorporated her professional experience into graduate work at Prairie View and received her M.S. in 1944 after completing a thesis entitled "A Study of 460 Negro Farm Families in Three Texas Counties." In 1946 she did additional coursework at Cornell University.

She resigned in 1948 to become supervisor of McLennan County schools, a position she held until 1957. She presided over the Texas Association of Colored Women's Clubs from 1955 to 1959 and was active in Waco civic affairs and in the New Hope Baptist Church. Governor John Connally[qv] appointed her to the Governor's Committee on Public School Education in 1967, and she served on the Waco Human Relations Commission from 1969 to 1972. Jeffie Conner's awards included an honorary doctor of humanities degree from Paul Quinn College, a citation from Prairie View A&M University for outstanding service in the humanities, and a woman-of-the-year award from Zeta Beta Phi sorority. She died in Waco on June 10, 1972, and was buried in Greenwood Cemetery.

BIBLIOGRAPHY: George S. and Jeffie O. A. Conner Papers, Texas Collection, Baylor University. Waco *News-Tribune*, January 13, 1967. Patricia Ward Wallace, *A Spirit So Rare: A History of the Women of Waco* (Austin: Nortex, 1984).

Judith N. McArthur

CONNER, JOHN COGGSWELL (1842–1873). John Coggswell Conner, congressman, was born in Noblesville, Indiana, on October 14, 1842. In 1861 he received an appointment to the United States Naval Academy in Annapolis, Maryland. He withdrew soon afterwards, enlisted in the United States Army, and obtained a commission. He served during the Civil War[qv] as a first lieutenant in the Sixty-third Indiana Infantry. After the war he unsuccessfully sought a seat in the Indiana House of Representatives. He rejoined the army in 1866 and this time received a captain's commission in the Forty-first Regiment, United States Infantry. He served in Texas with that unit until November 29, 1869. Between 1866 and 1869 he settled in Sherman. In 1869 he campaigned successfully in Texas as a Democrat for a congressional seat. Described by the New York *Times* as a "Democratic carpetbagger from Indiana," Conner was the lone Democrat representing Texas in the state's first congressional delegation since the Civil War. He was reelected in 1871 to the Forty-second Congress, defeating his Republican opponent with over 75 percent of the vote.

When Conner arrived in Washington his right to be seated in Congress received a strong challenge from a number of House Republicans. John P. Shank of Indiana moved that Conner be denied his seat until the House Committee on Elections reviewed the legitimacy of his campaign. Benjamin Butler, Republican from Massachusetts, supported Shank's motion and introduced evidence that claimed Conner had conducted himself less than honorably as an army officer in Texas. Shank's motion was defeated, and Conner took his seat. Predictably, once in Congress Conner opposed Republican-initiated Reconstruction[qv] legislation designed to assist freedmen, such as enforcement acts for the Fifteenth Amendment. On the other hand he supported economic measures that benefited his region and frequently found himself aligned with the Texas Republicans on such matters as currency, railroads, and tariffs. Relations with the Indians occupied much of Conner's congressional attention. He sought greater protection from the Indians on the Texas frontier, charging that while the government honored its treaties with Indians, the Indians failed to abide by the agreements. In his opinion Indians were an obstacle to progress, and as a result he opposed any government policies designed to aid them.

Because of a lingering illness Conner did not seek renomination for the Forty-third Congress in 1872. He died in Washington on December 10, 1873, and is buried in the Old Cemetery, Noblesville, Indiana.

BIBLIOGRAPHY: *Biographical Directory of the American Congress*, 1971.

Philip J. Avillo, Jr.

CONNER, JOHN EDWIN (1883–1989). John Edwin Conner, teacher, college dean, and author, the son of Harriet (Williamson) and William Trustan Conner, was born on November 21, 1883, at Field Creek, Llano County, Texas. Shortly after he was born, the family moved to Pontotoc, Mason County, where they lived until 1904 (except for the years 1888 to 1890, spent in Santo, Palo Pinto County). His father ran a general store, farmed, and occasionally built houses; his mother was postmistress at Pontotoc. In 1891 or 1892 a school district was formed at Pontotoc with William Conner as the first school board president. From 1890 onward, John Conner worked on the family farm and also did a variety of other work, learning at one point about setting type. During his youth his recreation included attending Mollie Bailey[qv] shows and playing baseball. With the shortened and sometimes missing school years at that time it was not until May 1904 that he graduated from high school, first in a class of two. In 1904 it was required that Pontotoc High School graduates pass the state examination for the first-grade teacher's certificate. During Conner's last two or three years at Pontotoc, the superintendent was E. C. Broyles, great-grandfather of the William Broyles who later edited *Texas Monthly*.[qv] Broyles had a profound influence on Conner, exciting his interest in history and teaching him how to write clearly and persuasively. Above all, he taught him how to edit his own work. Broyles, in addition to his other work, published more than one small-town newspaper, and in the early summer of 1904 he hired Conner to run for him the newspaper Broyles owned in Eden.

Before the next year, Conner took a job in a one-room school at Katemcy at sixty-five dollars a month for five months. During the next two school years, he taught at two other one-room schools. In 1907 he went to Eden as principal and teacher of a three-room school, and in 1908 he became high school principal and teacher in Eldorado. There were eleven grades in Eldorado, and for the first time he found it feasible to teach only some, rather than all of the subjects the students were supposed to master. There were normal schools at several places by 1904, and Conner attended two of them (at Denton and at San Marcos). In 1911 he graduated from Southwest Texas Normal. On August 27, 1911, he married Fannie Johnson; they had three children. During the 1911–12 school year he was principal of the high school at Ozona, and in the fall of 1913 he became superintendent of schools at Sanderson, where he remained until 1918. The years at Sanderson were the years of Francisco (Pancho) Villa,[qv] and an unofficial militia was formed to defend the town, of which Conner was a leader.

In the fall of 1919 Conner left Sanderson to become superintendent at Marfa, a somewhat larger and more prosperous place than Sanderson. Beginning in 1917 he taught in several summer sessions and teacher's institutes at Sul Ross Normal in Alpine. He became acquainted with Robert Bartow Cousins,[qv] who had been appointed president of the new college to be built in Kingsville, and in 1923 Cousins offered Conner a job there. To qualify for the position Conner entered the University of Texas in June 1923. In May 1924 he was inducted into Phi Beta Kappa, and in August of that year was granted an A.B. degree in American history; his M.A. was granted in 1927. During the 1924–25 school year he was superintendent at Odessa. Conner and his family arrived in Kingsville on June 1, 1925, and South Texas State Teachers College (later Texas A&M University at Kingsville) opened on June 7 of that year. This school had been planned by the legislature in 1911 as a source of teachers for the local Mexican-American population. Cousins and his staff faced a formidable task in starting the new college. There were few potential students. More than half the population of the area spoke little English, and few of the English speakers had finished high school. What students there were had trouble getting to Kingsville, as there were almost no paved roads and the only public transportation was by rail, which had inconvenient schedules for local routes. The new college also at first had few facilities and a library with fewer than 1,000 volumes. Conner became engaged at once in recruiting students and was soon acting as publicity man and lobbyist—producing press releases, contacting school superintendents, and approaching legislators. He made himself available as a speaker all over the area and talked to graduating classes, to Rotary, Kiwanis, and Lions clubs, to Boy Scout groups, and to parent-teacher associations. Robert J. Kleberg[qv] and J. K. Northway of the King Ranch[qv] had pushed strongly for the college to be located in Kingsville and were disappointed that graduates of the college were not going to be useful to the ranch's plans. Northway in particular began to push for a change in the purpose of the college so he could get more technical help from its graduates. In 1929 the school became the Texas College of Arts and Industries, and Conner became dean of the college. In the next ten years he taught classes and promoted the college, helped develop a museum, and struggled to get approval for the college from the Southern Association of Colleges and Secondary Schools. As early as the summer of 1925 people were bringing to Conner's office collectible materials, primarily, at first, World War I[qv] weapons. Very soon the materials became more diversified, and from 1928 onward Conner sought out materials, specimens, and contributions for the museum. After World War II[qv] he no longer had administrative responsibilities, and could spend more of his time on the collection. During the 1940s his vision gradually began to fail. While he was on leave from the campus during 1942–45, he became the historian at the quartermaster depot at Fort Sam Houston. He completed his first published book, *The Centennial Record of the San Antonio Service Forces Depot (1845–1945)* in 1945. He retired from the university in May 1954, whereupon he served as the director of the school's museum until 1964. He also began to write a history of Texas, intended for public school children. *Your Texas and Mine* appeared in 1961 and was followed by *The Flags of Texas* in 1964. Though he was engaged in writing, his museum collecting continued until 1967, when he left the area for a time. In 1976 the collection was moved to its current location and dedicated as the John E. Conner Museum.[qv] Conner continued to write until the end of his life, though his eyesight prevented him from rewriting or editing his writings. His daughter-in-law pulled some of his reminiscences together into a book, *A Great While Ago*, published in 1983. On his 100th birthday Conner was honored with a encomium from the governor, which was printed in the *Congressional Record*. In September 1988 he was the oldest living graduate of the University of Texas and the oldest living holder of a Phi Beta Kappa key. He died on September 1, 1989, in Corpus Christi at the age of 105 and was buried at Bellevue Cemetery.

BIBLIOGRAPHY: Vertical Files, Barker Texas History Center, University of Texas at Austin. Victoria *Advocate*, September 3, 1989.

William J. Conner

CONNER, LINCOLN GUY (1860–1920). Lincoln Guy Conner, rancher and founder of Canyon, was born on March 4, 1860, near Boonville, Missouri. Earlier, his father had established a flour mill, and the community that grew up around it was known as Conner's Mill. After suffering severe economic losses during the Civil War[qv] the family moved to Grayson County, Texas. There Conner met Queenie Victoria Younger, whom he married on January 19, 1884. They made their home on a 600-acre tract in Clay County near Bellevue, east of Henrietta, where Conner had previously built a small herd of cattle.

In the summer of 1887 the Conners moved their 350 cattle into the Panhandle,[qv] stopping first at Quitaque, near the future site of Plainview. On Christmas Day 1887 Conner surveyed and located section 34, block B5 in Randall County, near the T Anchor Ranch[qv] headquarters. He bought this land from the state for three dollars an acre on April 2, 1888, and constructed a half-dugout (*see* DUGOUT) from logs hauled from nearby Palo Duro Canyon.[qv] Here he established a general store and post office, and in the spring of 1889 he laid out the townsite of Canyon City. When Randall County was organized on July 27, the Conner dugout served as a voting place. Conner's daughter Mamie, the oldest of three children, was the first white child born in the county.

To attract settlers to Canyon City, the Conners began donating town lots to anyone willing to built a home or business building. Conner opened the town's first real estate office and gave thirty acres to the Santa Fe Railroad for a depot and cattle pens. He also donated lots for a county courthouse, schools, and churches. In 1891 he built the two-story Victoria Hotel, which he named for his wife. Conner expanded his ranching and real estate ventures steadily over the next two decades and became one of Canyon City's most prosperous citizens.

As a charter member of Canyon's First Baptist Church and Masonic lodge, Conner contributed generously to the improvement of his community's civic and educational institutions and sought to have Palo Duro Canyon made a national park (*see* PALO DURO CANYON STATE SCENIC PARK). His crowning achievement was the donation of forty acres near his residence and $2,000 for the establishment of West Texas State Normal College (now West Texas A&M University) in 1910. He died on December 30, 1920, and was buried in Dreamland Cemetery, Canyon. Victoria Conner continued her husband's philanthropic works and was the undisputed leader of the local Pioneer Club until her death on March 27, 1946. Conner Park, Canyon's first city park, is named for the Conners. In 1967 a historical marker was placed on the site of the original Conner dugout in Canyon.

BIBLIOGRAPHY: Harley True Burton, "A History of the JA Ranch," *Southwestern Historical Quarterly* 31 (January 1928). Canyon *News* November 15, 1928, July 20, 1939, April 4, 1946. Swisher County Historical Commission, *Windmilling: 101 Years of Swisher County History* (Dallas: Taylor, 1978). Mrs. Clyde W. Warwick, comp., *The Randall County Story* (Hereford, Texas: Pioneer, 1969).

H. Allen Anderson

CONNER, WALTER THOMAS (1877–1952). Walter Thomas (W. T.) Conner, Southern Baptist theologian and professor, son of Philip Orlander and Frances Jane (Monk) Conner, was born at Center (now Rowell), Arkansas, on January 19, 1877. The family moved to the West Texas community of Tebo (now Tye), eight miles west of Abilene, when Walter was fifteen. Because of straitened finances Conner's attendance at the academy of Simmons College (now Hardin-Simmons University) and Baylor University was intermittent. He received an A.B. degree from Baylor in 1906; in 1908 he received both a Th.B. from Baylor Theological Seminary (which chartered in March 1908 as Southwestern Baptist Theological Seminary) and an A.M. degree from Baylor University. In order to prepare for a teaching post at Southwestern, Conner matriculated at Rochester Theological Seminary in 1908; he received a B.D. degree there in 1910. He studied at the University of Chicago and Southern Baptist Theological Seminary, in Louisville, Kentucky, where he received his Th.D. degree in 1916. His thesis was on "Pragmatism and Theology." Baylor University awarded Conner an honorary D.D. degree in 1920. When Southern Baptist Theological Seminary began to award the Ph.D. degree instead of the Th.D., Conner availed himself of the opportunity of upgrading his Th.D. to Ph.D. status with an additional thesis on the topic "The Idea of Incarnation in the Gospel of John" in 1931.

Conner was pastor of several churches. He was ordained by Harmony Baptist Church, Caps, Texas, in 1899, where he was serving as pastor. He served as pastor at Baptist churches at Eagle Lake, Rock Island, East Bernard, Blum, Rio Vista, Godley, and Handley. While a student at Rochester, he served as pastor of the Baptist church in Wheatville, New York. He was the first pastor of Seminary Hill Baptist Church (now Gambrell Street Baptist Church) in Fort Worth. In the Southern Baptist Convention, Conner often lectured at conferences and assemblies and spoke at state and national conventions. The Southern Baptist Foreign Mission Board utilized him as a counselor and advisor in selecting missionary candidates.

Conner's enduring legacy to Southern Baptist life lies in his thirty-nine-year teaching career at Southwestern Baptist Theological Seminary. He joined Southwestern in 1910, when the school moved from Waco to Seminary Hill (now in Fort Worth). In the classroom he endeavored to make theology practical rather than speculative; in the faculty his recommendations for prospective teachers were tantamount to administrative approval; and in the administration his long tenure provided continuity from the first president to the third. Systematic theology was Conner's main responsibility, and he soon distinguished himself as the preeminent Southern Baptist theologian during the 1930s and 1940s. As a theologian he was at home among both laymen and scholars. His lectures and books were written with the layman in mind, but they display an underlying academic depth and extensive knowledge of his field. His theology reflects the influence of three former professors: Benajah H. Carroll qv of Baylor, A. H. Strong of Rochester, and E. Y. Mullins of Louisville. But Conner's theology still displays his own acumen; his theological works reflect a biblical rather than systematic approach. Conner's complete theological system is best expressed in his works *Revelation and God* (1936) and *The Gospel of Redemption* (1945). He wrote fifteen books and numerous articles for professional journals and other periodicals. He was a member of the Southwestern Society of Biblical Study and Research, and in 1946 he delivered the Wilkinson Lectures at Northern Baptist Theological Seminary, Chicago.

Conner married Blanche E. Horne, a Baylor University classmate, on June 4, 1907; they had six children. Conner died on May 26, 1952, and was buried in Mount Olivet Cemetery, Fort Worth.

BIBLIOGRAPHY: *Encyclopedia of Southern Baptists* (4 vols., Nashville: Broadman, 1958–82). James Leo Garrett, Jr., "The Bible at Southwestern Seminary during Its Formative Years: A Study of H. E. Dana and W. T. Conner," *Baptist History and Heritage* 21 (October 1986). James Leo Garrett, Jr., The Theology of Walter Thomas Conner (Th.D. dissertation, Southwestern Baptist Theological Seminary, 1954). Samuel S. Hill, ed., *Encyclopedia of Religion in the South* (Macon, Georgia: Mercer University Press, 1984). Stewart Albert Newman, *W. T. Conner: Theologian of the Southwest* (Nashville: Broadman Press, 1964). Jesse J. Northcutt, "Walter Thomas Conner, Theologian of Southwestern," *Southwestern Journal of Theology* 9 (Fall 1966). *Who's Who in America*, 1950–51. Stephen M. Stookey

CONNER CREEK. Conner Creek rises one mile south of Mount Vernon in eastern Houston County (at 31°24′ N, 95°05′ W) and runs northeast for six miles to its mouth on the Neches River, on the Angelina county line (at 31°25′ N, 95°01′ W). It was probably named for W. M. Conner, the original grantee of land near its head. The surrounding flat terrain is surfaced by clay and sandy loam that supports water-tolerant hardwoods, conifers, and grasses.

CONNERLY, DORIS HAYNE (1897–1987). Doris Hayne Connerly, lawyer and librarian, daughter of Robert Henry and Louise (Hale) Connerly, was born in Austin, Texas, on November 7, 1897. As the director of the Legislative Reference Division of the Texas State Library qv she served the public and members of legislative, executive, and judicial bodies for thirty-four years (1928–62). The Texas Senate, House of Representatives, and State Library and Historical Commission (*see* TEXAS STATE LIBRARY AND ARCHIVES COMMISSION) all passed resolutions honoring her upon her retirement. She graduated from the University of Texas School of Law in 1919 and was among the first women lawyers in Texas. After practicing with a prominent Houston law firm for four years, she returned to Austin to become the librarian of the University of Texas law school and to help take care of her invalid mother. In 1928 she was appointed state legislative librarian, a post she held until retirement. She was also acting state librarian from September 1950 through August 1951.

In 1948 Miss Connerly was the first person to be named "Public Employee of the Year," chosen as outstanding among 35,000 state employees (exclusive of college staffs) by the Austin chapter of the American Society for Public Administration. In 1978 she was among fourteen attorneys commended by the Travis County Women Lawyers' Association for their role in establishing the legal profession as a career option for women. She was a member of the State Bar of Texas, qv the Governor's Committee on Interstate Cooperation, the American Judicature Society, the Colonial Dames of America, qv and Kappa Alpha Theta sorority.

Her legal and public service interests followed family tradition. Her father, grandfather, and an uncle were attorneys. Her great-grandmother, Sarah Josepha Hale, was editor of the popular women's magazine *Godey's Lady's Book* from 1837 through 1877 and was an influential advocate for the advancement of women's rights. Doris Connerly's great-grandfather, James Wright Simmons, qv was secretary of the treasury of the Republic of Texas qv in the administration of President Mirabeau B. Lamar. qv She died on November 17, 1987, at College Station, Texas.

BIBLIOGRAPHY: Vertical Files, Barker Texas History Center, University of Texas at Austin. David M. Greathouse

CONNOR, CONNIE YERWOOD (ca. 1908–1991). Connie Yerwood Connor, pioneer in public health in Texas and the first black physician named to the Texas Public Health Service (now the Texas Department of Health qv), the oldest daughter of Dr. Charles R. and Melissa (Brown) Yerwood, was born in Victoria, Texas, around 1908. She decided to become a doctor when she was a young girl. She and her sister Joyce, who also became a doctor, accompanied their father on house calls in his largely rural practice in Gonzales County. At first they traveled by horse-drawn buggies, later by automobile. Connor attended public school in Austin and graduated from the Samuel Huston College Academy in 1925. She received the bachelor of arts degree *cum laude* from Samuel Huston College (now Huston-Tillotson College). In 1933 she graduated *cum laude* from Meharry Medical School. She began her residency in pediatrics but became interested in public health. She earned a scholarship to study public health at the University of Michigan and returned to Texas in 1937, when she joined the Texas Public Health Service. During the early years of her work with the state health agency, Connor was responsible for training midwives in East Texas. She also served as a consultant in setting up health clinics that offered services such as well baby clinics and prenatal care to the rural poor of Texas. In the beginning her duties were limited to work among the black population in East Texas, but as the need and demand grew she eventually worked with all cultures throughout the state. She led the state's efforts in early periodic screening diagnosis, treatment, and chronic diseases for pregnancy and pediatrics. When she retired on August 31, 1977, she was director of health services.

Connor was president of the Lone Star Medical, Dental, and Pharmaceutical Association, qv secretary of the Charles H. Christian Medical Society, and a member of the Texas Medical Association. qv When she retired she received outstanding service awards from the Texas Department of Health, the commissioner of health, and the staff of the maternal and child health division. She was the first black to be appointed to serve on the Human Relations Committee, the predecessor of the Human Rights Commission (a local group of the Texas Commission on Human Rights). She was appointed to the first board of trustees of the Mental Health–Mental Retardation Center of Austin and Travis County. She also served on the boards of the Austin Child Guidance Center, Austin Evaluation Center, Citizens Advisory Committee to the Juvenile Board of Travis County, Girl Scouts, YWCA, and Travis County Grand Jury Association. She was a trustee of Samuel Huston College for fifteen years and was one of the board members who signed the merger agreement of Huston-Tillotson College in 1952; she continued on the board after the merger. Her retirement on March 22, 1991, was the culmination of over fifty-four years of service to the college. At her retirement from the board of trustees of the college she received its highest award, the Crystal Ram with Golden Horns. She was the second person to receive this prestigious award. She also received several awards as outstanding alumna from both Huston-Tillotson College and Meharry Medical College and an honorary degree of doctor of sciences from Samuel Huston College.

Connor was active in the Wesley United Methodist Church, where she served as chairman of the board of trustees. Even when she was traveling throughout the state as a young woman, she returned to Austin every weekend to teach a Sunday school class. She was a lay leader and received a distinguished service award from Church Women United for services in religious leadership. For fifteen years she served as grand treasurer in the Order of the Eastern Star. She was a member of Alpha Kappa Alpha sorority, the Links, Incorporated,qv the American Association of University Women,qv the Community Welfare Association, and many other organizations. Connor died on June 11, 1991, in Austin, and was buried in Evergreen Cemetery.

BIBLIOGRAPHY: Austin *American-Statesman*, March 2, 1986, June 15, 16, 17, 1991. Vertical Files, Barker Texas History Center, University of Texas at Austin.
Kharen Monsho

CONNOR, WILLIAM OTT (1852–1934). William Ott Connor, financier, son of William J. and Julia C. (Hines) Connor, was born in Hamburg, Tennessee, on October 8, 1852, and moved to Texas with his mother and other children from Corinth, Mississippi, in 1859, after his father died. They settled in Jefferson. After moving to Dallas Connor became a salesman for Sanger Brothers (*see* SANGER, ALEXANDER) in 1878 and in 1881 became manager, a position he held until April 1, 1920, at which time he became president of the Republic National Bank. He served as first president of the trade league that helped to build Dallas into a wholesale center by inducing jobbers to pay for transportation of merchants to the city. Connor was the first mayor of Highland Park, a member of the first park board in Dallas, chairman of the board of directors of Republic National Bank and Trust Company, and a director of many Dallas corporations. He married Lula J. Mays on June 8, 1882, and they had two children. He later married Hattie Crowdus, and they had one child. Connor died on February 5, 1934.

BIBLIOGRAPHY: Dallas *Morning News*, February 6, 1934. *Memorial and Biographical History of Dallas County* (Chicago: Lewis, 1892; rpt., Dallas: Walsworth, 1976). *Who Was Who in America*, Vol. 2.
Carolyn Hyman

CONNOR, TEXAS. Connor, on Farm Road 1428 eight miles east of Madisonville in Madison County, was established in the mid-1800s. Rufus M. Connor and James S. Connor were postmasters at the local post office, which operated from 1890 until 1905. The general store was also run by Jim Connor. The population of Connor was 101 in 1900. The area raised livestock and fruits, vegetables, and cotton. Several general stores, a blacksmith shop, a cotton gin, and a gristmill operated at the time. A two-room Black Oak School was established in 1880; one room was for the boys, and the other was for the girls. A single teacher sat between the rooms and taught arithmetic, English, history, and spelling. David Green donated land for South Bethel School and a Methodist church. Several other churches including a Baptist church and a Church of Christ were built in the community. The population was fifty in the 1930s, when Connor had a school and scattered dwellings. In 1989 a general store was in operation at the site.

BIBLIOGRAPHY: Madison County Historical Commission, *A History of Madison County* (Dallas: Taylor, 1984).
Ellen C. Short

CONNOR CREEK. Connor (Conner) Creek rises a mile south of Sewell oilfield in southeast Young County (at 33°05′ N, 98°27′ W) and runs southeast four miles to its mouth on Possum Kingdom Lake (at 33°00′ N, 98°29′ W). It was named for Delaware chief John Connor, who was granted a league of land by the Republic of Texasqv on which the creek was located. The surrounding rolling hills are surfaced by clay and sandy loams that support scrub brush, mesquite, grasses, live oak, and juniper.
Barbara A. Neal Ledbetter

CONNOR CREEK, TEXAS. The Connor Creek community, named after Delaware Indian chief John Connor, was near the junction of Connor Creek on Possum Kingdom Lake in southeast Young County. It was on part of a league given to Chief Connor on October 13, 1857, by the Texas legislature for his services to Texas. An estimated fifty families lived in the area in the 1880s. The Connor Creek school had twenty-four pupils in 1881 and 1897 and twenty-one in 1904. The community used the Finnis Cemetery four miles east in Jack County. In 1930 scattered residences were in the area, but Connor Creek was no longer identified on maps.
Barbara A. Neal Ledbetter

CONOLEY, TEXAS. Conoley was on Farm Road 486 four miles southeast of Thorndale in southwestern Milam County. It was named for Malcolm Campbell Conoley, a Presbyterian minister who came to the area in 1859. The community became a voting precinct in 1875. A church, a school, and a few scattered houses marked its location on county highway maps in 1941. The school was consolidated with the Thorndale Independent School District in 1946. Only the church and a cemetery appeared in 1988.

BIBLIOGRAPHY: Lelia M. Batte, *History of Milam County, Texas* (San Antonio: Naylor, 1956). Milam County Heritage Preservation Society, *Matchless Milam: History of Milam County* (Dallas: Taylor, 1984).
Vivian Elizabeth Smyrl

CONQUISTA CREEK. Conquista Creek rises just east of Fashing oilfield in western Karnes County (at 28°53′ N, 98°07′ W) and flows northeast for ten miles to its mouth on the San Antonio River, three miles southwest of Falls City (at 28°57′ N, 98°03′ W). It traverses flat to rolling terrain surfaced by clay and sandy loam that supports water-tolerant hardwoods and grasses.

CONRAD, EDWARD (1811–1836). Edward Conrad, early soldier and politician, the son of John and Elizabeth (Kittera) Conrad, was born in Philadelphia in April 1811. He traveled to Texas through Natchitoches, Louisiana, in December 1835. On December 10, 1835, at Nacogdoches, he was made second lieutenant of the United States Independent Volunteer Cavalry under Benjamin L. Lawrence. At Bexar the company was consolidated with the Kentucky company of James Tarleton on December 25, 1835. On February 8, 1836, Conrad applied for land in Stephen F. Austin'sqv colony, stating that he was single, a printer by trade, and had emigrated from Pennsylvania. Conrad was one of four representatives from Refugio Municipality at the Convention of 1836qv at Washington-on-the-Brazos and there signed the Texas Declaration of Independence.qv He also served as a member of the committee to draft the Texas constitution. He left the convention early, however, to join the Texas army as a lieutenant in the regular infantry. Sam Houston[qv] later sent Conrad to New Orleans to recruit troops. On March 29, 1836, the day after he arrived in New Orleans, Conrad appears to have enrolled as a lieutenant under Francis W. Thornton.[qv] While serving with the company, he died at Victoria, Texas, on July 13 or 14, 1836.

BIBLIOGRAPHY: Hobart Huson, *Refugio: A Comprehensive History of Refugio County from Aboriginal Times to 1953* (2 vols., Woodsboro, Texas: Rooke Foundation, 1953, 1955). Louis Wiltz Kemp, *The Signers of the Texas Declaration of Independence* (Salado, Texas: Anson Jones, 1944; rpt. 1959).

L. W. Kemp

CONRAD, FRANK EBEN (1842–1892). Frank Eben Conrad, frontier merchant, was born on May 4, 1842, at Rockford, Illinois. After his parents' death in Tampa, Florida, he was taken to San Antonio, Texas, and reared by an uncle and aunt. He was clerking in his uncle's store at the outbreak of the Civil War.[qv] He enlisted in Hood's Texas Brigade[qv] and served with the organization until the end of the war. Upon the Union reoccupation of Fort McKavett in 1868, Conrad was appointed post trader. In 1871 he became post trader at Fort Griffin, where he established an enviable reputation as a frontier merchant. During the Indian campaigns from 1872 to 1875, Fort Griffin was Ranald S. Mackenzie's[qv] supply base, and Conrad's post store did a thriving business with the soldiers. Upon the conclusion of the Indian campaigns, the buffalo[qv] kill in Texas got under way, and Conrad's store supplied buffalo hunters with guns, large quantities of ammunition, and provisions of all kinds. Conrad grubstaked the hunters, advanced them cash, accepted orders for cash to their skinners, and bought their hides as they were freighted in from the range. Conrad provided an iron safe from which his cash payments were made and in which the hunters and employees deposited their money. For these services he became known as a banker.

By 1875 the drovers of South Texas had blazed the Western Trail[qv] to Kansas. Conrad's post store was for the first few years the only provisioning point on the trail, and later his store in the town of Fort Griffin and a new store at Albany continued to get a major share of the drovers' trade. At various times he had partners in his general merchandise business, the best known of whom was Charles Rath.[qv] Conrad and Rath moved their $40,000 stock from the post store to the town of Fort Griffin in December 1879. When they became associated as partners, the buffalo kill was about over, but they bought large quantities of buffalo bones (*see* BONE BUSINESS) and specialized in drovers' supplies and supplies for ranchmen moving into the area. In 1880 Rath withdrew from the partnership; Conrad continued under the name of Conrad and Company and in 1881 opened a branch business at Albany. In 1882, when that town became the terminus of the Texas Central Railroad, he moved to Albany, advertising, as he had in Fort Griffin, that he carried the largest stock of merchandise west of Fort Worth. In the middle 1880s Conrad became one of the largest wool buyers on the frontier, did a thriving business in buffalo robes, continued to buy bones, and did a wholesale business in pecans.

In 1889 his advertisement in an Albany paper stated that his business had been established since 1870 and summarized his career: "We were here in Early Times. We were here in Indian Times. We sold goods in Soldier Times. We did a little business here in Buffalo Times. We went slow here in Hard Times. We handled wool here in Sheepmen's Times. We boomed things here in Booming Times." Having acquired a ranch in Shackelford County, Conrad retired in 1891 to devote his time to ranching. He was married twice. All that is known of his first wife is that she was from Tennessee and that he divorced her sometime prior to 1880; they had one son. On April 22, 1881, Conrad married Rose Ellen Matthews; they had five children. He committed suicide in Albany on May 4, 1892.

BIBLIOGRAPHY: Don Hampton Biggers, *Shackelford County Sketches* (Albany, Texas: Albany News Office, 1908; rpt., ed. Joan Farmer, Albany and Fort Griffin, Texas: Clear Fork Press, 1974). Carl Coke Rister, *Fort Griffin on the Texas Frontier* (Norman: University of Oklahoma Press, 1956).

J. R. Webb

CONROE, TEXAS. Conroe, the county seat of Montgomery County, is on Interstate Highway 45 at the junction of the Missouri Pacific and the Atchison, Topeka and Santa Fe railroads, seven miles southeast of Lake Conroe in central Montgomery County. In 1881 Houston lumberman Isaac Conroe established a sawmill on Stewarts Creek two miles east of the International–Great Northern Railroad's Houston–Crockett line on a tract of land in the J. G. Smith survey, first settled in the late 1830s. A small tram line connected the mill to the I–GN track, but Conroe soon transferred his operations down the tracks to the rail junction, where his new mill became a station on the I–GN. In January 1884 a post office was established at the mill commissary, and, at the suggestion of railroad official H. M. Hoxey, the community took the name Conroe's Switch, in honor of the Northern-born, former Union cavalry officer who founded it and served as its first postmaster; within a decade the name was shortened to Conroe.

In the mid 1880s the Gulf, Colorado and Santa Fe Railway extended its Navasota–Montgomery spur eastward through the town, which thus became the only junction of major rail lines in the county. Conroe Mill School was established in 1886, and not long afterward the community's first black school was founded at Madeley Quarters, south of town. A lumber boom beginning in the late nineteenth century in the Piney Woods of eastern and central Montgomery County attracted scores of settlers to Conroe. By 1889 the population had climbed to an estimated 300. In that year Conroe replaced Montgomery as county seat. A residence donated by Isaac Conroe served as a temporary courthouse until a permanent brick structure could be erected in 1891. By the early 1890s Methodist, Presbyterian, and Baptist congregations were organized in the town; they initially shared a single house of worship. Simultaneously, black residents founded Baptist and African Methodist Episcopal congregations.

By 1892 the community had become a shipping center for lumber, cotton, livestock, and bricks, and had five steam-powered saw and planing mills, several brickyards, a cotton gin, a gristmill, several hotels and general stores, and a population of 500. The Conroe Independent School District was established in 1892, combining twelve nearby common school districts, and within a year a second white school was established in the town. By 1896 the community's first weekly newspaper, the *Courier*, had been founded.

During the late nineteenth and early twentieth centuries Conroe briefly shipped local tobacco. In 1900 a four-room schoolhouse for white pupils of all grades was constructed, and the local black school was transferred to the building abandoned by the whites. Since 1900 most black residences have been in a district on the southeastern edge of town. In 1902 the town's first white high school class graduated. Three years later a public school library was established. In April 1903 a private coeducational vocational school for blacks was founded by Dr. Jimmie Johnson on a seven-acre tract in northeast Conroe and quickly began to attract students from around the state. Funds for support of the institution were solicited from black churches, conventions, and organizations throughout the nation; local white residents also made financial contributions to the school and provided its students with employment in their homes and businesses. By the end of World War I[qv] the college's enrollment had climbed above 400.

By 1900 Conroe was Montgomery County's largest community. It was incorporated in 1904 with a population of 1,009, and its first mayor and city council were elected the following year. In 1906 the first electric lighting appeared in the town when an electrical generating plant was constructed on nearby Stewarts Creek. About 1910 the community's first Catholic church was constructed, and the first black public school was established. Over the next two decades the Conroe Independent School District was expanded to encompass twenty-five square miles. Some 617 pupils were enrolled in the district by 1913. Six years later the first black high school in Conroe was established.

The prosperity of the local agriculture and timber industries in the early twentieth century enabled Conroe to continue its rapid early growth despite severe fires in 1901 and 1911, which destroyed much of the business district near the courthouse square. Southwest of town in 1913 the Delta Land and Timber Company established one of the most extensive milling operations in the South; the company eventually employed 700 people. In addition to its many churches and schools, by 1914 Conroe had two banks, five grocery and hardware stores, two dry-goods stores, two drugstores, a cotton gin, a waterworks, a planing mill, numerous sawmills, box factories, cross-tie mills, two weekly newspapers, the *Courier* and the *Montgomery County Times*, and an estimated population of 1,374. The population continued to climb for the next several years, reaching an estimated 1,858 in the mid-twenties and an estimated 2,457 by 1931.

A sanitarium was established in Conroe in 1920. The community acquired its first fire truck in 1921, and two years built its first fire station. In 1922 the courthouse grounds became the scene of communal violence when a black mill worker accused of rape was lynched. In the mid-1920s the Dr Pepper Company^qv opened a soft-drink plant in the community. In 1925 the Conroe Independent School District was enlarged to its present size, 330 square miles, with the inclusion of fifteen rural common schools and 600 additional pupils scattered through central and southern Montgomery County. Children from discontinued schools were transported in private buses to schools in Conroe.

After years of sustained growth, the town's prosperity was threatened in the late 1920s by the dwindling of the improperly managed local timber supply. Then in 1930 the spreading effects of the Great Depression^qv struck Montgomery County, drastically curtailing lumber production and forcing many mills to close. In November 1930 Conroe's only bank abruptly failed and pushed many residents and institutions into financial doldrums for many years. Faced with precipitous declines in revenue, Conroe's schools struggled to complete full terms. But the community's fortunes began to improve on December 13, 1931, when George W. Strake^qv discovered oil seven miles southeast of town, thus marking the opening of the Conroe oilfield^qv and triggering an oil boom in the county. Within weeks the local economy had revived, as many petroleum wholesalers, retailers, and service companies and thousands of workers entered the town. By 1933 the population was an estimated 5,000, and eighty-four business were reported in the community. The Conroe school district, rescued from financial distress by the discovery of oil within its boundaries, became one of the wealthiest in the state, and its enrollment began to grow rapidly. A new black high school was built in 1933, and a new white elementary school and a junior high were soon constructed. A community center and a swimming pool were completed by the district in the early 1940s.

The oil revenues and population influx of the 1930s lent Conroe a boomtown atmosphere. It briefly claimed more millionaires per capita than any other town in the United States. During the early 1930s streets were paved for the first time, and U.S. Highway 75 was extended through the town. The thirty-seven-room State Hotel was completed in 1933. The ornate Crighton Theater was erected on the courthouse square in 1935. In 1936 a new courthouse was constructed, and two years later a county hospital was completed not far from the courthouse square. That year the population surged to an estimated 10,000, but it soon began to subside as production in the Conroe oilfield crested and began a gradual decline. By 1941 the population stood at an estimated 4,624.

During World War II^qv the town's lumber industry revived, but it never regained its earlier preeminence and lapsed into a steady decline after 1950. Its former position was increasingly assumed by chemical firms, including a carbon black factory (*see* CARBON BLACK INDUSTRY) and a recycling plant, established after the oil discovery. The Montgomery County Airport, three miles northeast of town on Farm Road 1484, was constructed during the war as a military facility but since 1945 has served as a local airfield. In 1946 the Montgomery County Library was established in Conroe. A new black high school constructed in the early 1950s remained the pride of the black community until Conroe's schools were desegregated in 1968. By 1952 Conroe had a population estimated at 7,313 and 340 businesses. The population climbed to an estimated 9,192 in 1961 and 11,969 in 1972.

With the construction of Interstate Highway 45, increasing numbers of Houstonians took up residence on the margins of Conroe. Lake Conroe was impounded in the late 1960s and early 1970s, seven miles northwest on the West Fork of the San Jacinto River, further stimulating local growth. In addition to the familiar lumber and petrochemical concerns, a number of new manufacturing and engineering firms have been established in Conroe. The population reached an estimated 18,034 by 1982. Conroe Independent School District had an enrollment of 8,873 in 1971 and 15,112 by 1976. In 1980 the district employed 1,200 teachers in twenty-eight schools. Conroe Normal and Industrial College has struggled for survival since the depression; by 1980 enrollment had been reduced to 176. In the 1980s Conroe had two hospitals, a nursing home, ten medical clinics, nineteen churches, three radio stations, a television station, a cab company, a new sewage treatment plant, and a newspaper named the *Daily Courier*. The population grew to 27,610 by 1990.

BIBLIOGRAPHY: Robin Navarro Montgomery, *The History of Montgomery County* (Austin: Jenkins, 1975). Montgomery County Genealogical Society, *Montgomery County History* (Winston-Salem, North Carolina: Hunter, 1981). *The Choir Invisible: An Early History of Montgomery County* (Montgomery, Texas: Montgomery Historical Society, 195?).

Charles Christopher Jackson

CONROE OILFIELD. Conroe field is an elliptical-shaped oil-producing area in south central Montgomery County. It was discovered by a young wildcatter, George W. Strake,^qv but its development was the quick work of Humble Oil and Refining Company (now Exxon^qv), the Texas Company (Texaco^qv), and a number of independents. The original field drew production from an average depth of 5,050 feet in the Upper Cockfield and Main Conroe sands, which overlie a deep-seated, faulted salt dome of Eocene age. The source of primary recovery was a strong water drive and gas-cap expansion. Reservoir pressure has been closely observed since April 1933 and has been maintained by gas and water injections, obviating the need for secondary recovery. Between its discovery on December 13, 1931, and January 1, 1993, the field produced more than 717 million barrels of oil. Although the field held large volumes of gas, many early operators regarded gas as a nuisance and a danger and wasted it through venting or flaring until 1935, when the practice became illegal. The field is significant because its flush production reestablished the Texas Gulf Coast as a major oil-producing province after thirty years of intensive prospecting. Conroe field was named for the county seat, situated five miles to the southeast.

Several early exploration attempts in the area of Conroe field proved unsuccessful before and during the 1920s. Gas seeps on the Rhodes farm in Montgomery County captured the interest of a number of local amateur oilmen as early as 1919. They formed Crystal Creek Oil Company and consolidated a block of 5,000 acres in and around the Ransom house survey. Although the acreage later proved to be a part of Conroe field, the company could not finance the drilling of a test and dropped the leases. In 1924 El Saline Petroleum Company No. 1 Outlaw was staked in the G. W. Wagers survey and drilled to 1,961 feet. Finding only gas, the operators abandoned it. The Kelly-Barker No. 1 Juergens was staked in the D. James survey two miles west of Conroe in 1929. Drilling to a depth of 3,662 feet encountered no oil. In January 1930 the No. 1 Juergens was junked.

Although amateurs and independents had found no production in the area, several major oil companies took leases and began geophysical studies there. After refraction seismography and torsion balance were used, no oil-bearing structure was found and most of the leases were allowed to expire. Although seismography was important to Gulf Coast exploration by the late 1920s, it offered no evidence of the deep-seated domal structure. That evidence came from a wildcat well drilled by George W. Strake, who became interested in the area. He put together a block of 9,300 acres and spudded a poor-boy well, the Strake No. 1 South Texas Development Company, in the Theo Slade survey on August 30, 1931. He drilled the well to a depth of 5,033 feet, where it began to spray fifteen million cubic feet of gas and 200 barrels of condensate a day. The discovery was given little attention because it produced only gas and condensate and because oilmen regarded the Cockfield sands as unproductive. At the end of 1931, Conroe field reported annual production of 1,000 barrels of oil from one well. Although Strake had found oil, he still had no money to develop the field. In March 1932 his company, Strake Oil Corporation, contracted with Humble Oil and Refining Company. Strake Oil assigned six leases to the major company for $100,000 and agreed to drill four wells for Humble to a depth of 5,500 feet at a maximum cost of $50,000 each. Strake Oil brought in the No. 2 South Texas Development Company, staked 2,400 feet south of the No. 1, at a depth of 5,026 feet on June 5, 1932. It flowed 900 barrels of oil a day and was considered the discovery well in the Conroe field because it sank into the Main Conroe sand and produced large quantities of oil. Although there were other operators in the field, Strake and Humble delayed the drilling of additional wells for several months.

One reason for delayed development by Strake and Humble may have been the emergency proration rules set up in the field by the Railroad Commission[qv] of Texas when only five wells had found production. The regulations covered drilling practices, casing procedure, and well spacing, all designed to preserve the highly unstable reservoir. The gas-charged shallow sands and the deeper soft, unconsolidated domal formation made drilling and development risky. Several wells in the field cratered. The rig in one instance and the Christmas tree in another sank out of sight into their holes. Several wells caught fire. There were blowouts in a number of wells. Water, mud, and cement were pumped into difficult wells to stabilize them. Relief holes were drilled to minimize the force of reservoir gas. But it was the Harrison and Abercrombie Oil Company No. 1 M. H. Alexander, located in the John McHorse survey, that caused a major problem for all field operators.

The No. 1 Alexander was completed to a total depth of 5,094 feet and flowed 120 barrels of oil in its first hour on December 12, 1932. At the end of 1932 the field had sixty drilling rigs at work and reported an annual production of 2,630,000 barrels of oil. But early in January 1933 as the field was poised for the greatest year of its development, the No. 1 Alexander cratered when the casing, well-head connections, and tubing began to sink. The casing split and the well began to flow out of control. A short time later, the hole bridged over and production decreased to an estimated ten barrels a day. By March the No. 1 Alexander was quiet, and flush field production began as 258 wells flowed oil and sixty-two rigs drilled for new oil. As development in the field continued, the Railroad Commission temporarily separated the Upper Cockfield sand production from the main field and set the Cockfield allowable at 10,000 barrels of oil a day. Daily allowable for the main field was fixed on June 1, 1933, at 60,000 barrels of oil, based 50 percent on acreage and 50 percent on potential, on twenty-acre units. Although operators agreed to the regulations, they were unprepared for the events of June 20, 1933. On that day the No. 1 Alexander roared to life again when the bridge that checked its wild production gave way, allowing unrestricted flow. On August 10, 1933, with the field only 57½ percent developed and with the renegade well gushing, production reached a peak daily flow of 92,000 barrels of oil, exceeding its allowable by 32,000 barrels. As late as September 13 the runaway well continued to shower the countryside with nearly 11,000 barrels of oil daily as pumps were installed to skim the oil from the surface for storage. Since the No. 1 Alexander was using its own allowable in addition to that of other wells, operators petitioned the Railroad Commission to increase field allowable to assure them their proportion of production. The request was denied because the depression economy could not absorb the great volume of oil. The commission actually reduced the field allowable by the end of 1933. With their petition rejected, field operators realized that any solution to the problem of the No. 1 Alexander had to come from their own initiative. In October 1933 Humble, aided by several other operators, made a deal with Harrison and Abercrombie by which Humble agreed to pay the owners of the fugitive well $300,000 cash for the privilege of killing it in the producing horizon. Harrison and Abercrombie would continue to own all oil produced from the No. 1 Alexander above the well allowable. If the well were not killed, it would remain the property of Harrison and Abercrombie. If the plan were successful, Harrison and Abercrombie would assign to Humble the fifteen acres surrounding the No. 1 Alexander. It was estimated that Humble spent $365,000 to drill a relief well, kill the outlaw well, and preserve the reservoir by January 16, 1934. The crater of the No. 1 Alexander was estimated to be 600 feet deep and 200 feet wide at the top. The well had produced more than 1,250,000 barrels of oil.

In 1933, the year of its greatest development, the field produced 21,483,279 barrels of oil from 679 wells—ten times more than in 1932. A large part of production left the field by pipeline. Eight gathering systems took crude to two trunk lines owned by Tide Water Pipe Line Company and Channel Transport and Pipe Line Company, which linked Conroe field with the Houston Ship Channel.[qv] Three other pipelines, operated by Humble Pipe Line Company, Texas Pipe Line Company, and Sun Pipe Line Company, carried crude to refineries owned by the parent companies. In the field, Strake had constructed Conroe Refining Company to handle a daily capacity of 250 barrels of oil, and several other small refineries were under construction at year's end. Two gas plants operated in the field—Humble, with a daily capacity of 6.72 million cubic feet, and Midland, with a daily capacity of 12.5 million cubic feet.

By early 1934 the field was in the last stage of development and covered 17,000 proved acres. During the year six gas wells were completed and daily gas production for the field reached thirty million cubic feet. Oil-well drilling declined during the year as operators observed the twenty-acre spacing rule. In 1934 crude production declined to 17,761,000 barrels. Throughout the remainder of the decade, it generally slipped downward as gas production climbed. By the end of 1941, after ten years of production, Conroe field reported an increased annual gas yield to 1,598,942,000 cubic feet from thirteen wells, while crude figures slid to 11,614,880 barrels. By 1942, with the increased wartime demand for crude, production rose, and by 1944 crude yields soared to an all-time annual high of 23,207,917 barrels of oil as gas production surged to 2,930,385,000 cubic feet. At the end of the war, crude production began a general downward trend as gas production maintained or escalated yields. By the end of 1951, after twenty years of production, the field reported yearly yields of 13,989,299 barrels of oil and 5,226,669,000 cubic feet of gas. On August 1, 1956, the commission permanently separated the Upper Cockfield formation into a new field by that name, leaving production from the Main Conroe sands in the original field. Throughout the 1960s the mature field continued reduced crude and enlarged gas production. At the end of 1971 new short-lived production improved annual yields of both oil and gas. In 1978 Conroe field was unitized, retaining the twenty-acre spacing. By the 1990s the field no longer produced dry gas or condensate, but its cumulative gas yield since 1970 was 16,403,142,000 cubic feet. By January 1, 1993, the field that reestablished the Gulf Coast region as an oil province reported cumulative crude production of 717,258,952 barrels.

BIBLIOGRAPHY: William E. Galloway et al., *Atlas of Major Texas Oil Reservoirs* (Austin: University of Texas Bureau of Economic Geology,

1983). Frank J. Gardner, *Texas Gulf Coast Oil* (Dallas: Rinehart Oil New Company, 1948). Railroad Commission of Texas, *Annual Report of the Oil and Gas Division* (Austin, 1952). Edgar Wesley Owen, *Trek of the Oil Finders: A History of Exploration for Petroleum* (Tulsa: American Association for Petroleum Geologists, 1975). David F. Prindle, *Petroleum Politics and the Texas Railroad Commission* (Austin: University of Texas Press, 1981). *Julia Cauble Smith*

CONSAVVY LAKE. Consavvy Lake is near Farm Road 1213 and Monahans Draw eight miles southeast of Midland in central Midland County (at 31°54′ N, 101°58′ W). The lakebed is composed of sand, gravel, and mudstone substrata with shallow, sandy loam. Scrub brush and grasses grow around the lake.

CONSIDERANT, VICTOR PROSPER (1808–1893). Victor Considerant, founder of La Réunion,qv a colony near Dallas, was born in Salins, France, on October 12, 1808. After a short service in the French army he resigned to devote his energies to popularizing and applying the utopian ideas of Charles Fourier. Considerant was one of the leading democratic socialist figures in France during the volatile revolutionary period of 1830 to 1850 and functioned as the international leader of the Fourierist movement. Because of his participation in the abortive insurrection of June 13, 1849, against Louis Napoleon Bonaparte, Considerant was forced to flee to Brussels. There he was contacted by Albert Brisbane,qv an American Fourierist, who interested him in colonization efforts in Texas. Considerant visited the United States in 1852–53 and accompanied Brisbane on a trek that eventually took him through North and Central Texas. His enthusiasm for the land, climate, and people of Texas induced him to establish the European Society for the Colonization of Texas upon his return to Belgium. He set forth elaborate plans for a Texas colony in *Au Texas*, published in Paris in 1854, and in *The Great West*, published the same year in New York. In these two books he called for a joint European-American venture at La Réunion and proposed the ultimate establishment of a network of colonies throughout the Southwest connected by commercial, cultural, and educational ties to the original commune. Early in 1855 agents sent by Considerant bought about 2,500 acres of land on the banks of the Trinity River near Dallas. Before adequate provision had been made for them, however, nearly 200 colonists made their way to La Réunion; when Considerant and his wife, Julie, and mother-in-law, Clarisse Vigoureux, arrived with more colonists in June 1855, the settlement was completely disorganized. It never fully recovered from that state.

Fourier had advocated societal reform through communal societies that he called phalansteries. During his politically active period, from 1843 to 1849, however, Considerant deviated from pure Fourierism and came to advocate republican political activism, direct democracy, and the voluntary association of capital and labor in various types of cooperatives, rather than rigid communalism. He thus planned for La Réunion to be a loosely structured experimental commune administered by a system of direct democracy. The participants would share in the profits according to a formula based on the amount of capital investment and the quantity and quality of labor performed. When La Réunion collapsed in 1859 due to financial insolvency, Considerant, discouraged but not disillusioned, moved to San Antonio, where he unsuccessfully attempted to raise funds for another commune. Unable to fulfill his dreams in Texas and still under a ban of deportation from France, he became an American citizen and farmed in Bexar County until 1869, when he and his wife returned to Paris. There he lived as a teacher and socialist sage of the Latin Quarter and died on December 27, 1893.

BIBLIOGRAPHY: Jonathan Beecher, *Charles Fourier: The Visionary and His World* (Berkeley: University of California Press, 1986). Clarisse Coignet, *Victor Considérant: sa vie, son oeuvre* (Paris: Félix Alcan, 1895). Victor Prosper Considerant, *Au Texas* (Paris: Librairie

Victor Prosper Considerant. Courtesy Lycée Victor Considerant, Salins, France.

Phalanstérienne, 1854; ed., with additions, by Rondel V. Davidson, Philadelphia: Porcupine, 1975). Victor Prosper Considerant, *Du Texas: Premier Rapport à mes amis* (Paris: Librarie Sociétaire, 1857). Rondel V. Davidson, *Did We Think Victory Great? The Life and Ideas of Victor Considerant* (New York: University Press of America, 1988). Rondel V. Davidson, "Victor Considerant and the Failure of La Réunion," *Southwestern Historical Quarterly* 76 (January 1973). Betje Black Klier, "Des Fouriéristes au Texas: la famille Considerant à San Antonio," *French Review* 68 (May 1995). *Rondel V. Davidson*

CONSOLIDATED VULTEE AIRCRAFT CORPORATION. Consolidated Vultee Aircraft Corporation was formed by a merger of Consolidated Aircraft Corporation, founded by Reuben H. Fleet in 1923 in Buffalo, New York, and Vultee Aircraft, a California airplane builder. In Texas it operated a mile-long facility, known locally as the Bomber Plant, built in 1942 on 563 acres on the west side of what is now Carswell Air Force Base qv at Fort Worth. The company used the site to fulfill contracts for planes it had no room to build at its San Diego factory and produced more than 3,000 B-24s, as well as C-87 cargo planes there. The Fort Worth plant, one of five factories including ones at Tulsa, Willow Run (Michigan), Dallas, and San Diego, was later used for production of F-16 fighter planes. At one time the Fort Worth plant employed up to 38,000 workers, including women, many of whom came from small towns like Cleburne, Decatur, and Denton. The company became part of General Dynamics Corporation's Convair division in 1954. During the war the firm, which began making trainers and seaplanes and commercial passenger and cargo planes, produced more B-24 Liberator bombers and PBY Catalina patrol bombers than any other United States corporation.

BIBLIOGRAPHY: Jacob Goodwin, *Brotherhood of Arms: General Dynamics and the Business of Defending America* (New York: Times

Books, 1985). Roger W. Lotchin, *Fortress California, 1910–1961: From Warfare to Welfare* (New York: Oxford University Press, 1992).

Diana J. Kleiner

CONSTABLE. Under the constitutions of 1836, 1845, and 1861,qqv a constable was elected biennially from each militia captain's precinct. Under the Constitution of 1866qv the term was extended to four years, and under the Constitution of 1869qv five constables were appointed for four-year terms by the county board. The Constitution of 1876qv provided for the biennial election of a constable from each justice of the peace precinct. A constitutional amendment in 1954 lengthened the term of office to four years. Duties of the constable include serving processes, attending the sessions of the justice court, and, in general, performing the usual duties of precinct peace officers.

BIBLIOGRAPHY: *Guide to Texas Laws for County Officials* (Austin: Texas Department of Community Affairs, 1988). Dick Smith, The Development of Local Government in Texas (Ph.D. dissertation, Harvard University, 1938).

Dick Smith

CONSTANT, BENJAMIN (1767–1830). Benjamin Constant was born Henri Benjamin Constant de Rebècque in November 1767 to Louis Arnold Juste de Constant and Henriette Pauline Chandieu in Lausanne, Switzerland, where his Protestant family had been exiled from France upon the revocation of the Edict of Nantes. His mother died in childbirth, and Constant's health was never good. After living and studying in Holland, Belgium, England (Oxford), Scotland (Edinburgh), and Germany (Protestant University, Erlangen), he allied himself with Mme. de Staël, whom Napoleon later exiled from Paris. They lived in Germany and Switzerland. Aside from his longstanding relationship with Germaine de Staël, Constant was married twice. In 1789 he married Wilhelmenie Luise Johanne von Cramm; they were divorced in 1795. Constant married Charlotte von Hardenberg in 1808. He had no children from either marriage, but it is believed that he did have a daughter, Albertine, with Mme. de Staël. In 1814 he returned to Paris, where he championed freedom of the press and condemned as "turncoats" those who rallied to Napoleon on his return from Elba. Constant went into hiding but emerged to have an interview with the former emperor, who persuaded him to prepare a liberal revision of the constitution: *L'Acte additionnel aux constitution de l'Empire*. After Waterloo, Constant fled to England, where he published *Adolphe* (1817), the first psychological novel. In 1818 and 1819 he supported the Bonapartist colony of Champ d'Asile,qv Texas, first through his newspaper, the *Minerva*. In this publication he built an exotic image of Texas, which he manipulated as a political tool in opposition to the restored monarchy of Louis XVIII. The *Minerva* sponsored a fund-raising campaign for half-pay imperial veterans going to Texas. Although the "subscription" was initially successful, Constant's role as a political voice was damaged when the colony failed and a scandal erupted over the donations. His newspaper collapsed, but the image of Texas propagated by the liberal Constant and his Bonapartist allies endured in France for several generations. After losing the *Minerva* in 1818, Constant was elected to the Chamber of Deputies for the next twelve years—the forum from which he continued to fight for freedom of the press—and his enemies questioned his citizenship. Tall, thin, hunchbacked, and having to wear glasses, he was a frequent target of caricaturists. After the July Revolution in 1830, Louis Philippe became "king of the French" (a constitutional monarch), and Constant was elected president of the Council of State months before his death. He died on December 8, 1830, almost destitute, but his reputation was strengthened by the posthumous publication of his letters and manuscripts.

BIBLIOGRAPHY: *Benjamin Constant: Political Writings*, trans. and ed. Biancamaria Fontana (Cambridge University Press, 1988). Cecil Patrick Courtney, *A Guide to the Published Works of Benjamin Constant* (Oxford: Voltaire Foundation at the Taylor Institution, 1985). *La Grande Encyclopédie: Inventaire raisonné des sciences, des lettres et des arts* (Paris: Lamirault, n.d.). René Rémond, *Les Etats-Unis devant l'opinion française, 1815–1852* (2 vols., Paris: Armand Colin, 1962).

Betje Black Klier

CONSTANTINEAU, HENRY A. (1861–1940). Rev. Henry A. Constantineau, first provincial of the second American province of the Oblates of Mary Immaculateqv and first president of Our Lady of the Lake University, was born in 1861 in Lowell, Massachusetts, and educated in the public schools there. After his graduation in 1879, he began a business career. After three years in banking, however, he went to the University of Ottawa, Canada, under the jurisdiction of the Oblate congregation, to study theology and philosophy. He was admitted to the Oblates on September 30, 1883, and ordained a priest on May 26, 1888. After his ordination, Father Constantineau taught at the University of Ottawa in the Commercial Department. By 1892 he was named secretary of the university and six years later was appointed its rector. At this time Laval University conferred on him the degree of doctor of divinity.

Ill health compelled him to resign in 1901, and the Oblate provincial sent him to San Antonio, Texas, with the hope that a warm climate would restore him to health. Because of his business acumen Constantineau was commissioned in 1902 by the Oblate provincial of the United States to purchase property on McCullough Avenue, San Antonio, to build a seminary. The San Antonio Philosophical and Theological Seminary (see OBLATE SCHOOL OF THEOLOGY) was opened in 1903. A year later the second American province of the Oblate congregation was established, with San Antonio as headquarters and Constantineau as provincial.

As early as the summer of 1903 he began his lifelong work for the Sisters of Divine Providenceqv of San Antonio. At that time he gave a series of lectures at the summer normal school of Our Lady of the Lake. The superiors of the Congregation of Divine Providence realized their need for such a priest to aid them in financial matters and especially to assist them to be recognized as a congregation by the Sacred Congregation of Religious in Rome. By 1904 Constantineau and Father Albert Antoine, O.M.I., were working with the sisters on a new constitution to be sent to Rome for approval. The approval was obtained provisionally in 1907 and finally in 1912. During this period, Father Constantineau was named delegate superior of the sisters by the bishop of San Antonio. When the congregation came under the jurisdiction of the Sacred Congregation of Religious in 1912, Constantineau was appointed business advisor for the sisters.

The Congregation of Divine Providence opened Our Lady of the Lake College in San Antonio in 1911, and Constantineau was named president. He held the position until his death. During his tenure the college built four new buildings, between 1920 and 1937, and gained recognition from such accrediting agencies as the Southern Association of Schools and Colleges and the Association of American Universities. As an expert in finance Constantineau helped the college and the congregation to become financially sound.

As provincial and later as provincial procurator, Father Constantineau also served the congregation of Oblate missionaries. One work is especially noteworthy. Oblate priests had served the Catholic Churchqv in the southern part of Texas and northern Mexico since the time of Bishop Jean M. Odin.qv As early as the middle of the 1870s they had planted bananas and grapes in the Texas Valley, but without sufficient water to produce much. Father Constantineau saw that the Rio Grande could supply a system of irrigation for this section of Texas so as to raise citrus and other fruits. With the help of John J. Conway, a wealthy citizen from the Midwest, he worked out a system of irrigation on the 17,000 acres of La Lomita Ranch (*see* LA LOMITA MISSION).

In 1913, when a violent persecution of the church began in Mexico, Constantineau, in an attempt to keep the Mexican clergy from being completely wiped out, obtained permission from the Congregation of Divine Providence for the use of the Oblates' Castroville properties as a seminary for Mexicans. Father Constantineau died on July 9, 1940, at Our Lady of the Lake College, where he had lived almost as an invalid during the last months of his life. He was buried in the Oblate Cemetery, San Antonio.

BIBLIOGRAPHY: University Archives, Our Lady of the Lake University, San Antonio. *Sister Mary Generosa Callahan, C.D.P.*

CONSTITUTIONAL ADVOCATE AND BRAZORIA ADVERTISER. The *Constitutional Advocate and Brazoria Advertiser* was published as a weekly at Brazoria from about August 1832 to the last of July 1833 by Daniel W. Anthony.qv The paper's motto was from Horace's *Odes,* "Incedimus per ignes, suppositos cineri doloso" ("We walk through fires hidden beneath deceptive ashes"). When Stephen F. Austinqv protested that the paper was anti-Mexican, Anthony wrote him explaining why the paper had carried an account of the acts of the central committee established in October 1832 and emphasizing the need of a consistent policy. The paper gave notice of the Convention of 1833qv and of the outbreak of a cholera epidemic. It probably ended when Anthony died of cholera in the summer of 1833. The paper may also have been called the *Constitutional Advocate and Texas Public Advertiser.* Its name reflected the sentiment of the period in favor of a Texas government and constitution separate from that of Coahuila (*see* COAHUILA AND TEXAS).

BIBLIOGRAPHY: Eugene C. Barker, ed., *The Austin Papers* (3 vols., Washington: GPO, 1924–28). Eugene C. Barker, "Notes on Early Texas Newspapers," *Southwestern Historical Quarterly* 21 (October 1917). James A. Creighton, *A Narrative History of Brazoria County* (Angleton, Texas: Brazoria County Historical Commission, 1975). Marker Files, Texas Historical Commission, Austin. WPA Historical Records Survey Program, *Texas Newspapers* (Houston: San Jacinto Museum of History Association, 1941).

CONSTITUTIONAL AMENDMENTS. Article XVII, Section 1, of the Constitution of 1876 qv provides that two-thirds of all members of each house of the Texas legislature may propose amendments at any regular biennial session and specify the date on which proposed amendments will be submitted to the voters. Members of the legislature may also propose amendments at special sessions as long as the subject of them have been included among the session's purposes for convening. Since the days of the Constitution of the Republic of Texasqv publicizing an amendment has been required. The proposed amendment must be published twice in all newspapers that print official notices. The first printing can appear no sooner than sixty and no later than fifty days before an election, and the second is published on the same day of the following week. The secretary of state's office is responsible for preparing explanatory statements and arranging for newspaper publication. Explanatory statements require approval by the attorney general. A copy of the complete text of each amendment is also posted in every county courthouse at least thirty days before the election. An amendment is adopted if it receives a favorable majority of the votes cast on it. Most amendments are voted on in the November general election or in a special election called by the legislature. The legislature prepares the ballot language for each amendment.

In various Texas constitutions there has never been any limitation on the number of amendments proposed. By the end of 1950 the legislature had proposed 193 amendments, and 107 had been adopted by the voters. By the time of the Constitutional Convention of 1974,qv the legislature had submitted 343 amendments to the voters since 1876. Of this number, 219 had been approved. By the end of 1994, 521 amendments had been proposed, and 353 had been approved by Texas voters. The record number of amendments proposed in any one election year was twenty-five in 1987.

In 1972 an amendment was passed that allowed proposed constitutional amendments to be considered and adopted during special sessions, the only time Section 1 has been amended. The new language in Section 1 allowed for the proposal of amendments for revising the constitution. This opened the door to the possibility of comprehensive revision. On November 7, 1972, voters approved the adoption of an amendment that called for the establishment of a constitutional revision commission and for the convening of the Sixty-third Texas Legislature as a constitutional convention at noon on the second Tuesday in January 1974, for the purpose of writing a new constitution to be submitted to the voters of Texas. Proposals to voters in the November 4, 1975, election included eight amendments that, except for the Bill of Rights, composed a new constitution for Texas. All were rejected by the voters.

BIBLIOGRAPHY: Howard A. Calkins, "The Need for Constitutional Revision in Texas," *Texas Law Review* 21 (May 1943). James Dickson, "Erratic Continuity: Some Patterns of Constitutional Change in Texas since 1975," *Texas Journal of Political Studies* 14 (Fall–Winter 1991). Janice C. May, *Amending the Texas Constitution, 1951–1972* (Austin: Texas Advisory Commission on Intergovernmental Relations, 1972). Seth Shepard McKay, *Seven Decades of the Texas Constitution* (Lubbock, 1942). *Practicing Texas Politics* (Boston: Houghton Mifflin Company, 1971). L. C. Reithmayer, "Amendments to the Texas Constitution," *Southwestern Social Science Quarterly* 22 (September 1941). Irvin Stewart, "Constitutional Amendments in Texas," *Southwestern Political Science Quarterly* 3 (September 1922).

Howard A. Calkins

CONSTITUTIONAL CONVENTION OF 1866. On November 15, 1865, Andrew Jackson Hamilton,qv provisional governor of Texas, issued a proclamation fixing January 8, 1866, as the date for an election of delegates to a constitutional convention to meet at Austin on February 7. The number of delegates was to be equal to the number of members in the Texas House of Representatives, and no person excluded from President Andrew Johnson's general amnesty proclamation was eligible as a delegate unless pardoned by the president. Few former secessionists were barred from voting for constitutional delegates. When the delegates assembled, it became apparent that there were two strong factions in the convention—radical Unionists and radical secessionists—with the extremes of each group holding most power. Among the extreme Unionists I. A. Paschal, A. H. Latimer, Robert H. Taylor, and E. J. Davis qqv were the most prominent, while J. W. Throckmorton and John Hancock qqv represented the moderate Union view. O. M. Roberts, James W. Henderson, T. N. Waul, and former governor Hardin R. Runnels qqv were of the uncompromising wing of the secessionist party. Throckmorton, who opposed secessionqv but had fought as a Confederate soldier, was elected president of the convention by a coalition of moderate Unionists with the extreme and moderate wings of the secession party.

Matters of organization and arguments over requiring the delegates to take the constitutional oath consumed the time of the convention for the first three days. On the fourth day Hamilton's message outlining what would be expected of the convention was received and read. The governor made it clear that half measures would not satisfy the United States government and warned the delegates that hasty action might postpone indefinitely the day Texas would be represented in Congress. As minimum requirements for restoration of normal relations with the Union he recapitulated the points formerly set out: that the right of secession must be specifically denied; that acquiescence must be given to the abolition of slavery;qv that a fair and impartial determination of the social and political status of freedmen must be arrived at; and that the debt incurred by the state in the prosecution of the war must be repudiated.

The question of secession appeared on February 13 in an ordinance presented by Latimer that declared the Secession Ordinance null and void *ab initio.* This ordinance represented the view that the right of secession had never existed, as against the view that the right existed until the end of the war. This resolution was referred to a committee on the condition of the state. Division in the committee over the *ab initio* question qv resulted in majority and minority reports. After a long and bitter debate the delegates decided that the ordinance was merely null and void and made no reference to dates.

On the question of the abolition of slavery the members agreed that the Thirteenth Amendment, by then a part of the Constitution, had abolished slavery and that since they had taken the oath to support that Constitution, they had indirectly abolished slavery. They reasoned, therefore, that a direct and formal ratification of the amendment was not necessary and voted to allow the taking of the constitutional oath to suffice.

With greater unanimity than on most questions, the members agreed that neither slavery nor involuntary servitude, except as a punishment for a crime, should exist in Texas and that freedmen should be protected in their rights of person and property. The right to sue and be sued, to contract and to be contracted with, should likewise be theirs. Freedmen should be prosecuted in the courts under the same rules as obtained for whites, and they should be allowed to testify in court in cases that involved one of their own number. They also agreed that they should testify in such other cases as the legislature might deem proper. The idea of black suffrage found little support even among the radicals, and blacks were banned from holding public office.

The fourth question that the convention had been specifically enjoined to consider, that of repudiating the war debt, was disposed of with relatively little friction. The war debt, together with the entire civil debt incurred from January 28, 1861, to August 5, 1865, was repudiated.

The convention had at first delegated to itself legislative and constituent powers supreme and final; but on March 27, after it had declared secession null and void, cancelled the war debt and fixed the status of freedmen, it voted to submit to the electors the proposed changes in basic government known as the Constitution of 1866. The convention adjourned on April 2, 1866.

BIBLIOGRAPHY: Claude Elliott, *Leathercoat: The Life History of a Texas Patriot* (San Antonio, 1938). Carl H. Moneyhon, *Republicanism in Reconstruction Texas* (Austin: University of Texas Press, 1980). Rupert N. Richardson, *Texas: The Lone Star State* (New York: Prentice-Hall, 1943; 4th ed., with Ernest Wallace and Adrian N. Anderson, Englewood Cliffs, New Jersey: Prentice-Hall, 1981).

Claude Elliott

CONSTITUTIONAL CONVENTION OF 1868–69. Gen. Winfield Scott Hancock,qv commander of the Fifth Military Districtqv (Texas and Louisiana) under Congressional Reconstruction,qv called an election to be held in each Texas county seat between February 10 and 14, 1868, to determine whether a constitutional convention should be held and to elect delegates to such a convention. Democrats were opposed to the convention, but the Radical Republicans won easily by a vote of 44,689 to 11,440. Of those who voted for a convention, 36,932 were black. In all of Texas only 818 blacks voted against the calling of a convention, while 52,964 (41,234 whites and 11,730 blacks) of the registered voters failed to vote. The convention assembled at Austin on June 1, 1868. The ninety delegates consisted of eighty whites and ten blacks. Six of the ninety had been members of the Constitutional Convention of 1866.qv Most of the delegates had been antebellum opponents of the Democrats and represented Republicans of varied interests. The Democrats, being in the minority, generally served as a balance between the different Republican factions, casting votes with one particular group to counteract the proposals of another. The Republicans were basically divided into four blocs, with no one faction really dominating. The largest bloc was led by A. J. Hamilton and supported Governor Elisha M. Pease.qv It represented Unionist strongholds in Northeast Texas and supported agricultural and commercial interests, law and order, and black civil rights. James Winwright Flanaganqv headed the second bloc, which represented East Texas interests. It favored economic development, state division, and railroad interests, but did not favor benefits for freed slaves. The third bloc represented Unionist supporters from western counties and included Morgan C. Hamilton, Edmund J. Davis, James P. Newcomb, and Edward Degener.qv This group also supported state division, but had broad views on extending black civil rights. George T. Ruby,qv a black agent for the Freedmen's Bureauqv schools, led the fourth block and supported black civil rights and free education.

The purpose of the convention was simply to write a constitution, but it was apparent from the beginning that the delegates wished to address broader issues. The convention soon became a contest between different factions pursuing their own agendas. The first trial of strength came in the organization when the radicals elected E. J. Davis over Judge Colbert Caldwellqv to be president of the convention. Progress on the constitution was exceedingly slow because the delegates gave so much time to such controversial matters as the division of Texas, railroad charters, and lawlessness in the state. Another key issue considered was the ab initio question qv regarding the legality of state laws passed under Confederate rule. Funds for the expenses of the convention were exhausted on August 31, while the factions were still debating and before they had begun the consideration of a constitution. The convention, therefore, adjourned and did not get back into session until the first Monday in December, the money to complete its sessions having been raised by a special tax. About ten days before adjournment the delegates got down to the business of writing a constitution and, in addition, by their acts bound the first legislature to assemble after the adoption of the constitution to ratify the Thirteenth and Fourteenth amendments. On February 8, 1869, the convention broke up in confusion, having devoted less than a month's time to the task for which it had convened. Forty-five of the ninety delegates signed the partially assembled constitution. The Constitutional Convention of 1866 remained in session only fifty-five days, completed a constitution, and spent $70,000. By contrast, the 1868–69 convention was in session 150 days, did not complete a constitution, and spent over $200,000.

By order of the convention an election was held in July, when the proposals of the convention were approved by the electorate as the Constitution of 1869.qv

BIBLIOGRAPHY: Hans Peter Nielsen Gammel, comp., *Laws of Texas, 1822–1897* (10 vols., Austin: Gammel, 1898). Carl H. Moneyhon, *Republicanism in Reconstruction Texas* (Austin: University of Texas Press, 1980). Charles W. Ramsdell, *Reconstruction in Texas* (New York: Columbia University Press, 1910; rpt., Austin: Texas State Historical Association, 1970). John Sayles, *The Constitutions of the State of Texas* (1872; 4th ed., St. Paul, Minnesota: West, 1893).

Claude Elliott

CONSTITUTIONAL CONVENTION OF 1875. The Constitutional Convention of 1875 was the result of the determination of the Democrats of Texas to eliminate the radical Constitution of 1869.qv A strong movement to have the changes in that document made by a legislative joint committee and then submitted to the voters failed in the House of Representatives because of a belief that the electorate would resent such a centralized method of providing a new organic law. The legislature then called an election in August 1875, in which voters approved a convention to prepare a new constitution and elected three delegates from each of the state's thirty senatorial districts. The time before the constitutional convention was marked by a number of Democratic measures designed to undo many Republican acts previously passed. The centralized school system was weakened. State salaries and expenditures were cut, and the governor was stripped of his powers to appoint some state officers and declare martial law.

The convention, presided over by Edward B. Pickett,qv met in Austin on September 6, 1875, and adjourned on November 24. The new Constitution of 1876,qv which was adopted by a vote of fifty-three to eleven, was submitted to the people in an election on February 15, 1876. Seventy-five of the members of the convention were Democrats, fifteen, including six black men, were Republicans. Before the convention had gone far with its work one of the black members resigned, and his place was taken by a white Democrat. One of the members had helped write the Constitution of 1845;qv eight had been members of the Secession Conventionqv of 1861; one had served in the Constitutional Convention of 1866;qv not a member had taken part in the Constitutional Convention of 1868–69.qv About forty of the delegates were members of the Grange;qv a number had been commissioned officers in the Confederate Army; three had served in the United States Army. Leigh Chalmers was chosen as secretary of the convention. Standing committees, each consisting of five to fifteen delegates, were appointed and covered issues including federal relations, suffrage, education, crime, railroads, and public lands. Agricultural and law-oriented interests controlled much of the agenda. In an effort to reverse the perceived Republican excesses of the previous years, restrictions were placed on salaries, expenditures, taxes, and the state debt. State banks were abolished, some activities of corporations and railroads were limited, and term limits were placed on many public offices.

The majority of the convention believed so firmly in economy that they refused to employ a stenographer and would not allow the proceedings of the convention to be published. The document that they prepared provided for short terms of office, low salaries, and limited powers for officials and indicated generally a lack of faith in government. These features were the results of the reaction of the members of the convention to the events of the Civil War and Reconstruction,qqv through which they had just passed.

BIBLIOGRAPHY: Alwyn Barr, *Reconstruction to Reform: Texas Politics, 1876–1906* (Austin: University of Texas Press, 1971). J. E. Ericson, "The Delegates to the Convention of 1875," *Southwestern Historical Quarterly* 67 (July 1963). Seth Shepard McKay, *Making the Texas Constitution of 1876* (Philadelphia: University of Pennsylvania, 1924). Caleb Perry Patterson et al., *State and Local Government in Texas* (New York: Macmillan, 1940).
Ralph W. Steen

CONSTITUTIONAL CONVENTION OF 1974. Recognizing the need for a new state constitution, the Sixty-second Texas Legislature passed a resolution in May 1971 that called for the establishment of a constitutional revision commission and for the convening of the Sixty-third Legislature as a constitutional convention at noon on the second Tuesday in January 1974. The proceeding was to be a limited convention, meaning that the Bill of Rights could not be changed. After a two-thirds vote the resolution was presented to the voters of Texas as Constitutional Amendment Number 4 on November 7, 1972, and, by a vote of 1,549,982 to 985,282, the voters approved the adoption of the amendment, which became Article XVII, Section 2 of the Constitution of 1876.qv In February 1973, following the mandate of the amendment, the Sixty-third Legislature established a constitutional revision commission to "study the need for constitutional change and ... report its recommendations to the members of the legislature not later than November 1, 1973." The legislature appropriated $900,000 for the work of the commission. The thirty-seven members of the commission were appointed by a committee composed of Governor Dolph Briscoe, Lieutenant Governor William P. Hobby, Attorney General John Hill, Speaker of the House of Representatives Marion Price Daniel, Jr.,qv Chief Justice of the Supreme Court Joe R. Greenhill, and Presiding Judge of the Court of Criminal Appeals John F. Onion, Jr.; the appointments were ratified and confirmed by the legislature. Only thirty-nine legislators signed a motion of nonconcurrence. Had a legislative majority rejected the slate, a new thirty-seven-member commission would have had to be nominated by the committee. Robert W. Calvert, former speaker of the Texas House of Representatives and former chief justice of the Texas Supreme Court, was named chairman of the commission, and Mrs. Malcolm Milburn, former president of the Texas Federation of Republican Women, was named vice chairman. The other members of the commission were Loys D. Barbour, Roy R. Barrera, Bill Bass, George Beto,qv Tony Bonilla, Mrs. Mary Beth Brient, Mrs. David F. (Ann) Chappell, Barbara Culver, William Donnell, Beeman Fisher, Peter T. Flawn, M. F. "Mike" Frost, Clotilde Garcia, Mrs. C. F. (Sibyl) Hamilton, Bill Hartman, Zan Holmes, Mrs. Faye Holub, Leon Jaworski,qv Leroy Jeffers, Andrew Jefferson, Jr., Page Keeton, W. James Kronzer, Jr., Earl Lewis, Honore Ligarde, Wales Madden, Jr., Mark Martin, Janice May, Mark McLaughlin, L. G. Moore, Raymond Nasher, E. L. Oakes, Jr., Don Rives, Preston Shirley, Jim W. Weatherby, and Ralph W. Yarborough.

The commission held its first meeting in March 1973. After holding nineteen public hearings across the state, it presented its recommendations for a new constitution to the legislature on November 1, 1973. The proposed document represented the first thorough attempt to draft a new constitution for Texas since the Constitutional Convention of 1875.qv On January 8, 1974, the Sixty-third Legislature convened as a constitutional convention, meeting as a unicameral body in the chamber of the House of Representatives, with Lieutenant Governor Hobby presiding as temporary chairman. Speaker of the House of Representatives Price Daniel, Jr., of Liberty County, was elected president of the convention, and State Senator A. M. Aikin, Jr.,qv of Lamar County, was elected vice president. Also during the first week of proceedings, the permanent rules of the convention were adopted, and the delegates were appointed to the eight substantive and five procedural committees. Daniel, with approval of the convention, named the following delegates to head the convention committees: Neil Caldwell, of Brazoria County, chairman of the committee on finance, and H. Tati Santiesteban, of El Paso County, vice chairman; Craig A. Washington, of Harris County, chairman of the committee on local government, and Charles Evans, of Tarrant County, vice chairman; Dan Kubiak, of Milam County, chairman of the committee on education, and Bill Braecklein, of Dallas County, vice chairman; Robert Maloney, of Dallas County, chairman of the committee on the legislature, and Ron Clower, of Dallas County, vice chairman, L. DeWitt Hale, of Nueces County, chairman of the committee on the judiciary, and Oscar H. Mauzy, of Dallas County, vice chairman; Bob Gammage, of Harris County, chairman of the committee on general provisions, and Hilary B. Doran, Jr., of Val Verde County, vice chairman; Bill Meier, of Tarrant County, chairman of the committee on the executive, and Jim Vecchio, of Dallas County, vice chairman; A. R. Schwartz, of Galveston County, chairman of the committee on rights and suffrage, and James R. Nowlin, of Bexar County, vice chairman; Matias (Matt) Garcia,qv of Bexar County, chairman of the committee on rules, and Richard S. Geiger, of Dallas County, vice chairman; Jack Hightower, of Wilbarger County, chairman of the committee on administration, and Joe Allen of Harris County, vice chairman; Nelson W. Wolff of Bexar County, chairman of the committee on submission and transition, and Gene Jones, of Harris County, vice chairman; Max Sherman, of Potter County, chairman of the committee on style and drafting, and Tim Von Dohlen, of Goliad County, vice chairman; Pike Powers, of Jefferson County, chairman of the committee on public information, and Eddie Bernice Johnson, of Dallas County, vice chairman.

James F. Ray, who served as executive director of the commission, was appointed executive director of the convention. Upon the completion of its work the convention was to submit a proposed new constitution to the voters of Texas for their approval or rejection. The convention was originally planned to last ninety days and adjourn on May 31, 1974, but members soon voted by a two-thirds majority to extend that time for sixty days, the maximum allowed, to July 30. With the legislators as delegates, divisive politics became a major obstacle to completing the task at hand. Some argued that the hands-off policy of the state executive branch prevented positive leadership. The most controversial issue was a right-to-work provision in the constitution. Labor groups strongly opposed the measure, while antilabor factions pressured the delegates for support. An election primary in May 1974 also served as a political distraction for many legislators campaigning for reelection.

More than $3 million in appropriations was spent on the convention. After seven months the constitutional convention closed, on July 30, 1974, having failed by three votes (118 for, 62 against, and 1 not voting) to produce a document to submit to the voters. In 1975 the legislature did approve a new constitution in the form of eight amendments approved by the normal amendment process. The Bill of Rights remained unchanged, but the eight amendments went before the voters on November 4, 1975, in a special election. They were all defeated. One legacy of the 1974 constitutional convention was a large body of written material on the Texas constitution.

BIBLIOGRAPHY: John E. Bebout and Janice C. May, *The Texas Constitution: Problems and Prospects for Revision* (Texas Urban Development Commission, Institute of Urban Studies, University of Texas at Arlington, 1971). George D. Braden, *Citizens' Guide to the Proposed New Texas Constitution* (Houston: Institute for Urban Studies, 1975). Janice C. May, *The Texas Constitutional Revision Experience in the '70s* (Austin: Sterling Swift, 1975). Janice C. May, "Texas Constitutional Revision: Lessons and Laments," *National Civic Review* 66 (February 1977). *Practicing Texas Politics*, 8th ed. (Boston: Houghton Mifflin Company, 1992). *The Texas Constitutional Revision Commission of 1973* (Austin: Texas Advisory Commission on Intergovernmental Relations, 1972). Nelson Wolff, *Challenge of Change* (San Antonio: Naylor, 1975).   *Mary Lucia Barras and Houston Daniel*

CONSTITUTIONAL UNION PARTY. After the demise of their party in the mid-1850s Whig partisans searched for another organization that could win elections and bring them to power. For a time some drifted into the American (Know-Nothing) party,qv but its nativism cost it votes and alienated some of the more prominent former Whigs. By 1859 a new party, generally called the Opposition party, had emerged. It attracted disaffected Democrats worried about the growing radicalism of their former party. It also attracted a sizable percentage of the new voters of the state and most ex-Whigs and unconditional Unionists. The Opposition party, led by its gubernatorial candidate, the former Democrat Sam Houston,qv swept the majority of the statewide elections that year. Another member of the party and another former Democrat, Andrew Jackson Hamilton,qv was elected to the United States House of Representatives from the Second District. In 1860 the Opposition party, minus much of its Democratic support, became the Constitutional Union party, and a state organizational meeting was held at Marshall, Texas.

Starting in the spring of 1860 members of the Opposition began to call for the nomination of either Millard Fillmore or Sam Houston for president. Houston had much more appeal to the Democratic strain of the party than the former Whig president, but neither candidate had much support outside of the lower South. On April 27 a small group of Governor Houston's East Texas friends, who were supporters of the new party, assembled in Tyler for the primary purpose of electing four delegates to the national convention, which was to be held at Baltimore in May. These delegates were Anthony B. Norton, Abram M. Gentry, Benjamin H. Epperson, and Lemuel D. Evans.qqv At the Baltimore convention the Texas delegation worked for the nomination of Houston, but John Bell, an ex-Whig from Tennessee, received the nomination, defeating Houston on the second ballot by a vote of 125 to 68.

In 1860 four viable candidates ran for the presidency: Abraham Lincoln, the Republican; John C. Breckinridge, the southern Democrat; Stephen A. Douglas, the northern Democrat; and Bell. In Texas, Republicans were so disliked that Lincoln was not even on the ballot. Douglas had a few supporters, but the Texas campaign was really between Bell and Breckinridge.

Two weeks after being rejected at Baltimore, Houston accepted a presidential nomination offered him at a San Jacinto celebration in April. Eventually, however, as former Whigs who were not already allied with the other parties began to rally to Bell, Houston lost his out-of-state newspaper support, and in August he withdrew his candidacy and became an active backer of the Constitutional Union party. Even before Houston's withdrawal, Whig Unionists in East Texas were organizing for Bell. They had strong support from the Marshall *Harrison Flag*. A number of other Texas newspapers supported the Bell-Everett ticket, including the Austin *Southern Intelligencer*,qv the Belton *Independent*, the Columbus *Colorado Citizen*, the Fort Worth *Chief*, the McKinney *Messenger*, the Quitman *Express*, and the Weatherford *News*. Some of these were well-established Whig publications, others were independent Democratic journals that had long supported Houston, and a few were recently founded Constitutional Union newspapers.

Elsewhere in the state, Union clubs sprang up. The Galveston Constitutional Union party, one of the first to organize, almost appeared to be a gentleman's club; its members included a number of respected longtime Island City citizens and ex-Whigs. In Jackson County, Constitutional Unionists met at Texana on August 11 and elected as chairman Clark L. Owen,qv a veteran of the Texas Revolutionqv and one of the wealthiest men in the state. The Travis County Union Club organized in Austin on September 3, and members appointed an executive committee of correspondence. San Antonio Union party rallies began in September and were well attended. Union meetings were held in a number of counties between the San Antonio-Austin area and Galveston, including Colorado and Fayette. In Central Texas the party organized in Corsicana, Waco, Georgetown, and elsewhere.

Until August 1860 the race much resembled earlier contests between the Democrats and the Whigs. Partisan accusations, not concern for the Union, held center stage. Fear that the election of Lincoln might precipitate a crisis changed the tone of the Constitutional Unionists, however. The party lost heavily to the regular Democrats in a statewide election on August 6, and party leaders began to call for fusion with the Douglas Democrats. Constitutional Unionists repeatedly described themselves as the party most capable of saving the Union. The hybrid nature of the party was reflected in the election in early September of two Unionist Democrats, George W. Paschalqv of Travis County and John H. Robson of Colorado County, and two old-line Whigs, William Stedmanqv of Rusk County and Benjamin H. Epperson of Red River County, as presidential electors. Unionist campaigners, however, faced a militant opposition motivated by suspected abolitionist plots within Texas, as well as by a growing belief in the need for southern solidarity. Attempts at fusion that might have restored the effective coalition of 1859 failed. Democrats voted for the Democratic candidate, and Breckinridge carried the state 47,561 to 15,402, with only three counties—Bandera, Gillespie, and Starr—voting for Bell.

In the 1860 election, calls to save the Union could not overcome party loyalty and party history. Germans and Mexican Texans well remembered that many of the leaders of the Constitutional Union party had been Know-Nothings. Democrats saw the nomination of Bell and the failure to focus clearly on Unionism early in the campaign as definite signs that the Constitutional Unionists were simply Whigs in new garb. Even the last-minute attempt to combine with the Douglas Democrats and the claim that only they could keep Abraham Lincoln out of the White House failed to broaden their appeal significantly.

Abraham Lincoln won the 1860 election, although he received no votes in Texas. His victory caused a popular movement for secession^{qv} in Texas and the rest of the South. But the Constitutional Union party had already split along former partisan lines before the election, and with the growth of secession sentiment the fragile coalition collapsed entirely.

BIBLIOGRAPHY: James Alex Baggett, "The Constitutional Union Party in Texas," *Southwestern Historical Quarterly* 82 (January 1979). Walter L. Buenger, *Secession and the Union in Texas* (Austin: University of Texas Press, 1984). John V. Mering, "The Slave-State Constitutional Unionists and the Politics of Consensus," *Journal of Southern History* 43 (August 1977). David M. Potter, *The Impending Crisis* (New York: Harper, 1976). Frank H. Smyrl, "Unionism in Texas, 1856-1861," *Southwestern Historical Quarterly* 68 (October 1964). John B. Stabler, A History of the Constitutional Union Party (Ph.D. dissertation, Columbia University, 1954).

Walter L. Buenger and James Alex Baggett

CONSTITUTION OF COAHUILA AND TEXAS. The Constitution of 1824^{qv} of the Republic of Mexico provided that each state in the republic should frame its own constitution. The state of Coahuila and the former Spanish province of Texas were combined as the state of Coahuila and Texas.^{qv} The legislature for the new state was organized at Saltillo in August 1824, with the Baron de Bastrop^{qv} representing Texas. More than two years was spent on the framing of a constitution, which was finally published on March 11, 1827.

The constitution divided the state into three departments, of which Texas, as the District of Bexar, was one. The Catholic religion was made the state religion; citizens were guaranteed liberty, security, property, and equality; slavery^{qv} was forbidden after promulgation of the constitution, and there could be no import of slaves after six months. Citizenship was defined and its forfeiture outlined. Legislative power was delegated to a unicameral legislature composed of twelve deputies elected by popular vote; Texas was allowed two of the twelve. The body, which met annually from January through April and could be called in special session, was given wide and diverse powers. In addition to legislative functions, it could elect state officials if no majority was shown in the regular voting, could serve as a grand jury in political and electoral matters, and could regulate the army and militia. It was instructed to promote education and protect the liberty of the press.

Executive power was vested in a governor and vice governor, elected for four-year terms by popular vote. The governor could recommend legislation, grant pardons, lead the state militia, and see that the laws were obeyed. The vice governor presided over the council and served as police chief at the capital. The governor appointed for each department a chief of police, and an elaborate plan of local government was set up. Judicial authority was vested in state courts having charge of minor crimes and civil cases. The courts could try cases but could not interpret the law; misdemeanors were tried by the judge without a jury. Military men and ecclesiastics were subject to rules made by their own orders. Trial by jury, promised by the constitution, was never established, nor was the school system ever set up. The laws were published only in Spanish, which few Anglo-Texans could read. Because of widespread objections to government under this document, the Convention of 1833^{qv} proposed a new constitution to give Texas statehood separate from Coahuila (*see* CONSTITUTION PROPOSED IN 1833).

BIBLIOGRAPHY: Vito Alessio Robles, *Coahuila y Texas en la época colonial* (Mexico City: Editorial Cultura, 1938; 2d ed., Mexico City: Editorial Porrúa, 1978). Nettie Lee Benson, "Texas as Viewed from Mexico, 1820–1834," *Southwestern Historical Quarterly* 90 (January 1987). *The Constitution of Mexico, and of the State of Coahuila and Texas* (New York: Ludwig and Tolefree, 1832). Hans Peter Nielsen Gammel, comp., *Laws of Texas, 1822–1897* (10 vols., Austin: Gammel, 1898). Henderson K. Yoakum, *History of Texas from Its First Settlement in 1685 to Its Annexation to the United States in 1846* (2 vols., New York: Redfield, 1855).

S. S. McKay

CONSTITUTION OF 1824. Constitutional government in Texas began with the Mexican federal Constitution of 1824, which, to some degree, was patterned after the United States Constitution but resembled more the Spanish Constitution of 1812. Congress was made the final interpreter of the document; the Catholic religion was made the state faith; and the church was supported by the public treasury. The president and vice president were elected for four-year terms by the legislative bodies of the states, the lower house of Congress to elect in case of a tie or lack of a majority. There were numerous limitations on the powers of the president. The Congress was composed of two houses meeting annually from January 1 to April 15. The president could prolong the regular session for an additional thirty days and could call extra sessions. Deputies in the lower house served two years, while senators were selected by their state legislatures for four-year terms. The judicial power was vested in a Supreme Court and superior courts of departments and districts. The Supreme Court was composed of eleven judges and the attorney general. There was no particular effort to define the rights of the states in the confederacy. They were required to separate executive, legislative, and judicial functions in their individual constitutions, which were to be in harmony with the national constitution, but local affairs were independent of the general government.

Stephen F. Austin^{qv} conferred with the Mexican leaders who framed the Constitution of 1824, and Juan José María Erasmo Seguín^{qv} represented Texas in the constituent assembly; the farmers of Austin's colony contributed several hundred bushels of corn to help pay Seguín's expenses. The Anglo-Americans in Texas were not represented, and the instrument was never submitted to a vote of the people for ratification.

BIBLIOGRAPHY: *Constitución federal de los Estatos Unidos Mexicanos sancionada por el Congreso General Constituyente el 4 de Octubre de 1824* (Guadalajara: Poderes de Jalisco, 1973). *Crónicas: constitución federal de 1824* (Mexico City: Comisión Nacional para la Conmemoración del Sesquicentenario de la República Federal y del Centenario de la Restauración del Senado, 1974). *Manifesto del congreso general a los mejicanos* (Mexico City: Imprenta del supremo gobierno de los Estados-Unidos Mexicanos, 1824).

S. S. McKay

CONSTITUTION OF 1845. The Constitution of 1845, which provided for the government of Texas as a state in the United States, was almost twice as long as the Constitution of the Republic of Texas.^{qv} The framers, members of the Convention of 1845,^{qv} drew heavily on the newly adopted Constitution of Louisiana and on the constitution drawn by the Convention of 1833^{qv} (*see* CONSTITUTION PROPOSED IN 1833), but apparently used as a working model the Constitution of the republic for a general plan of government and bill of rights.

The legislative department was composed of a Senate of from nineteen to thirty-three members and a House of Representatives of from forty-five to ninety. Representatives, elected for two years, were required to have attained the age of twenty-one. Senators were elected for four years, one-half chosen biennially, all at least thirty years old. Legislators' compensation was set at three dollars a day for each day of attendance and three dollars for each twenty-five miles of travel to and from the capital. All bills for raising revenue had to originate in the House of Representatives. Austin was made the capital until 1850, after which the people were to choose a permanent seat of government. A census was ordered for each eighth year, following which adjustment of the legislative membership was to be made. Regular sessions were biennial. Ministers of the Gospel were ineligible to be legislators.

The governor's term was two years, and he was made ineligible for more than four years in any period of six years. He was required to be a citizen and a resident of Texas for at least three years before his election and to be at least thirty years of age. He could appoint the attorney general, secretary of state, and supreme and district court judges, subject to confirmation by the Senate; but the comptroller and treasurer were elected biennially by a joint session of the legislature. The governor could convene the legislature and adjourn it in case of disagreement between the two houses and was commander-in-chief of the militia. He could grant pardons and reprieves. His veto could be overruled by two-thirds of both houses.

The judiciary consisted of a Supreme Court, district courts, and such inferior courts as the legislature might establish, the judges of the higher courts being appointed by the governor for six-year terms. The Supreme Court was made up of three judges, any two of whom constituted a quorum. Supreme and district judges could be removed by the governor on address of two-thirds of both houses of the legislature for any cause that was not sufficient ground for impeachment. A district attorney for each district was elected by joint vote of both houses, to serve for two years. County officers were elected for two years by popular vote. The sheriff was not eligible to serve more than four years of any six. Trial by jury was extended to cases in equity as well as in civil and criminal law.

The longest article of the constitution was Article VII, on General Provisions. Most of its thirty-seven sections were limitations on the legislature. One section forbade the holding of office by any citizen who had ever participated in a duel. Bank corporations were prohibited, and the legislature was forbidden to authorize individuals to issue bills, checks, promissory notes, or other paper to circulate as money. The state debt was limited to $100,000, except in case of war, insurrection, or invasion. Equal and uniform taxation was required; income and occupation taxes might be levied; each family was to be allowed an exemption of $250 on household goods. A noteworthy section made exempt from forced sale any family homestead, not to exceed 200 acres of land or city property not exceeding $2,000 in value; the owner, if a married man, could not sell or trade the homestead except with the consent of his wife. Section XIX recognized the separate ownership by married women of all real and personal property owned before marriage or acquired afterwards by gift or inheritance. Texas was a pioneer state in providing for homestead protection and for recognition of community property.

In the article on education the legislature was directed to make suitable provision for support and maintenance of public schools, and 10 percent of the revenue from taxation was set aside as a Permanent School Fund.qv School lands were not to be sold for twenty years but could be leased, the income from the leases becoming a part of the Available School Fund.qv Land provisions of the Constitution of 1836 were reaffirmed, and the General Land Officeqv was continued in operation.

By a two-thirds vote of each house an amendment to the constitution could be proposed. If a majority of the voters approved the amendment and two-thirds of both houses of the next legislature ratified it, the measure became a part of the constitution. Only one amendment was ever made to the Constitution of 1845. It was approved on January 16, 1850, and provided for the election of state officials formerly appointed by the governor or by the legislature.

The Constitution of 1845 has been the most popular of all Texas constitutions. Its straightforward, simple form prompted many national politicians, including Daniel Webster, to remark that the Texas constitution was the best of all of the state constitutions. Though some men, including Webster, argued against the annexationqv of Texas, the constitution was accepted by the United States on December 29, 1845.

BIBLIOGRAPHY: Hans Peter Nielsen Gammel, comp., *Laws of Texas, 1822–1897* (10 vols., Austin: Gammel, 1898). Annie Middleton, "The Texas Convention of 1845," *Southwestern Historical Quarterly* 25 (July 1921). John Sayles, *The Constitutions of the State of Texas* (1872; 4th ed., St. Paul, Minnesota: West, 1893). *Vernon's Annotated Constitution of the State of Texas* (Kansas City: Vernon Law Book Company, 1955).

S. S. McKay

CONSTITUTION OF 1861. After the Texas voters ratified secessionqv from the Union on February 23, 1861, the Secession Conventionqv reconvened. Convention delegates believed it their duty to direct the transition of Texas from a state in the United States to one of the Confederate States of America. As part of that duty they amended the Constitution of 1845.qv In most instances the wording of the older constitution was kept intact, but some changes were required to meet new circumstances. The words United States of America were replaced with Confederate States of America. Slaveryqv and states' rights were more directly defended. A clause providing for emancipation of slaves was eliminated, and the freeing of slaves was declared illegal. All current state officials were required to take an oath of loyalty to the Confederacy, and all existing laws not in conflict with the constitutions of Texas or the Confederate States were declared valid. Amending the constitution was also made easier. This constitution was as remarkable for what it did not do as for what it did. It did not legalize the resumption of the African slave trade, a move advocated by some leaders of the secession movement. It did not take an extreme position on the issue of states' rights. It did not substantially change any important law. It was a conservative document partly designed to allay fears of the radical nature of the secessionists and to ease the transition of Texas into the Confederacy.

BIBLIOGRAPHY: Walter L. Buenger, *Secession and the Union in Texas* (Austin: University of Texas Press, 1984).

Walter L. Buenger

CONSTITUTION OF 1866. The Constitutional Convention of 1866,qv in addition to other actions in compliance with presidential Reconstruction,qv proposed a series of amendments to the fundamental law, which came to be known as the Constitution of 1866. The governor's term was increased to four years and his salary from $3,000 to $4,000 a year. He was prohibited from serving more than eight years in any twelve-year period. For the first time the governor was given the item veto on appropriations. He was empowered to convene the legislature at some place other than the state capital should the capital become dangerous "by reason of disease or the public enemy." The comptroller and treasurer were elected by the voters to hold office for four years.

The Senate was set to number from nineteen to thirty-three members and the House from forty-five to ninety; legislators were required to be white men with a prior residence of five years in Texas. Terms of office were to remain the same as before, but salaries of legislators were raised from three dollars a day to eight dollars, and mileage was increased to eight dollars for each twenty-five miles. A census and reapportionment, based on the number of white citizens, was to be held every ten years.

The Supreme Court was increased from three judges to five, with a term of office of ten years and a salary of $4,500 a year. The chief justice was to be selected by the five justices on the court from their own number. District judges were elected for eight years at salaries of $3,500 a year. The attorney general was elected for four years with a salary of $3,000. Jurisdiction of all courts was specified in detail. A change was made in the method of constitutional revision in that a three-fourths majority of each house of the legislature was required to call a convention to propose changes in the constitution, and the approval of the governor was required.

Elaborate plans were made for a system of internal improvements and for a system of public education to be directed by a superintendent of public instruction. Separate schools were ordered organized for black children. Lands were set aside for the support of public schools, for the establishment and endowment of a university, and for the support of eleemosynary institutions. The legislature was empowered to levy a school tax. An election in June ratified the proposed amendments by a vote of 28,119 to 23,400; the small majority was attributed to dissatisfaction of many citizens with the increase in officials' salaries.

BIBLIOGRAPHY: Hans Peter Nielsen Gammel, comp., *Laws of Texas, 1822–1897* (10 vols., Austin: Gammel, 1898). Charles W. Ramsdell, *Reconstruction in Texas* (New York: Columbia University Press, 1910; rpt., Austin: Texas State Historical Association, 1970). John Sayles, *The Constitutions of the State of Texas* (1872; 4th ed., St. Paul, Minnesota: West, 1893). *Vernon's Annotated Constitution of the State of Texas* (Kansas City: Vernon Law Book Company, 1955).

S. S. McKay

CONSTITUTION OF 1869. The Constitutional Convention of 1868–69,qv called in compliance with the Congressional Reconstruction Acts of 1867, broke up without completing a constitution. Its work was gathered up under orders of the military officers, published as the Constitution of 1869, and accepted by the electorate. The preface of the bill of rights of the new document reflected the sentiments of its makers in its condemnation of nullification and secession.qv The Constitution of the United States was declared to be the supreme law. Slaveryqv was forbidden, and the equality of all persons before the law was recognized. The House of Representatives was set at ninety members and the Senate at thirty. One-third of the senators were chosen biennially, and their term of office was increased from four to six years. Sessions were held annually.

The salary of the governor was increased to five thousand dollars a year. The attorney general and secretary of state were appointed by the governor; other officials were elected by the voters. The Supreme Court was reduced from five to three judges and the term reduced to nine years, one new judge to take office every third year. All judicial offices were appointive. All elections were held at the county seat and had to continue through four consecutive days. A poll tax was authorized; its receipts, along with the income from the school lands and one-fourth of the annual taxes, went to the school fund. The office of state superintendent of public instructionqv was continued, and school attendance was made compulsory. An immigration bureau was authorized; county and local government was outlined in detail; blacks were included as voters; homesteads were to be given gratis to actual settlers; mineral rights were released to landowners; the legislature was forbidden to grant divorces or authorize lotteries; all qualified voters were to be qualified jurors; and the legislature was permitted to prohibit the sale of liquor near colleges, except at county seats. Permission for the legislature to call a new constitutional convention was withheld, but the amendment procedure was unchanged.

This constitution, formulated under pressure from Washington, was disputed by a large constituency of Texans. Many felt that it was one of the longest and most unsatisfactory of Texas constitutions. Over the years, however, alternate interpretations have pointed out some positive goals that delegates tried to achieve such as the establishment of a common school system, centralized law enforcement, and broader civil rights. The programs, implemented by greater taxation, drew heavy criticism from many citizens, and though it may have laid some of the foundations for a strong educational system, as well as strengthening the branches of state government, the Constitution of 1869 sparked much controversy among political and social factions in Texas.

BIBLIOGRAPHY: Hans Peter Nielsen Gammel, comp., *Laws of Texas, 1822–1897* (10 vols., Austin: Gammel, 1898). Charles W. Ramsdell, *Reconstruction in Texas* (New York: Columbia University Press, 1910; rpt., Austin: Texas State Historical Association, 1970). Betty Jeffus Sandlin, The Texas Constitutional Convention of 1868–1869 (Ph.D. dissertation, Texas Tech University, 1970). John Sayles, *The Constitutions of the State of Texas* (2d ed., St. Louis: Gilbert, 1884; 4th ed., St. Paul, Minnesota: West, 1893).

S. S. McKay

CONSTITUTION OF 1876. The Constitution of 1876 is the sixth constitution by which Texas has been governed since independence from Mexico was achieved in 1836. It was framed by the Constitutional Convention of 1875qv and adopted on February 15, 1876, by a vote of 136,606 to 56,652, and it remains the basic organic law of Texas. The constitution contains some provisions that are uniquely Texan, many of which are products of the state's unusual history. Some, for example, may be traced to Spanish and Mexican influence. Among them are sections dealing with land titles and land law in general, debtor relief, judicial procedures, marital relations and adoption, and water and other mineral rights. Other atypical provisions may be attributed to the twin influences of Jacksonian agrarianism and frontier radicalism—both prevalent when Texas first became a state and both widely supported by the bulk of immigrants to Texas before the Civil War.qv Those influences produced sections prohibiting banks and requiring a stricter separation of church and state than that required in older states. Reconstruction, under the highly centralized and relatively autocratic administration of Governor Edmund J. Davisqv and his fellow Radical Republicans, prompted provisions to decentralize the state government. Upon regaining control of both the legislative and executive branches of the government, the Democrats determined in 1874 to replace the unpopular Constitution of 1869.qv They wanted all officials elected for shorter terms and lower salaries, abolition of voter registration, local control of schools, severely limited powers for both the legislature and the governor, low taxation and state expenditures, strict control over corporations, and land subsidies for railroads.

Early in 1874 a joint legislative committee reported an entire new constitution as an amendment to the Constitution of 1869. Because the document had not been prepared by a convention and because of the possibility that its adoption might antagonize the federal government, the legislature rejected the proposal. On the advice of Governor Richard Coke,qv the next legislature submitted the question of a constitutional convention to the voters, who, on August 2, 1875, approved the convention and elected three delegates from each of the thirty senatorial districts. In the convention, which convened on September 6, seventy-five members were Democrats and fifteen, including six blacks, were Republicans. Not one had been a member of the Convention of 1868–69,qv forty-one were farmers, and no fewer than forty were members of the Patrons of Husbandry (the Grangeqv), the militant farmers' organization established in response to the Panic of 1873. In the convention the Grange members acted as a bloc in support of conservative constitutional measures. To assure that the government would be responsive to public will, the convention precisely defined the rights, powers, and prerogatives of the various governmental departments and agencies, including many details generally left to the legislature.

The Constitution of 1876 began with a lengthy bill of rights. It declared that Texas was a free and independent state, subject only to the Constitution of the United States, that all free men have equal rights, and that the writ of habeas corpus could not be suspended or unduly delayed. The article also forbade religious tests for office, unreasonable searches, and imprisonment for debt, and it guaranteed liberty of speech and press, the right of the accused to obtain bail and to be tried by a jury, and the right of citizens to keep and bear arms. The legislative article defined the powers and limitations of the legislature in great detail. The legislature was to be composed of two houses, a Senate to consist of thirty-one members and a House of Representatives never to exceed 150 members. Senators and representatives were to serve terms of four and two years, respectively. Legislators were to receive mileage allowance and not more than five dollars a day for the first sixty days of each session and two dollars a day thereafter. The legislature, which was to meet biennially, could incur no indebtedness greater than $200,000 and could establish no office for longer than two years. It was required to levy taxes on all property in proportion to its value and to hold its sessions in Austin. The executive article provided for seven officers—governor, lieutenant governor, secretary of state, comptroller of public accounts, treasurer, commissioner of the land office, and attorney general. All except the secretary of state were to be elected by the voters for a term of two years but with no limitations on eligibility for new terms. All salaries were reduced, that of the governor from $5,000 to $4,000. The governor was empowered to convene the legislature in special sessions, to call out the militia to execute the laws, to suppress insurrections, to protect the frontier against hostile Indians, and to veto laws and items in appropriations bills; his veto, however, could be overridden by a two-thirds vote of both houses. The governor was also empowered to make certain appointments, fill vacancies, and cause the laws to be faithfully executed but was given no control over local or other elected state officials. The judicial article provided for a supreme court, a court of appeals, district courts, county courts, commissioners' courts, and justices of the peace. All judges were to be elected by popular vote, with terms of six years for the supreme and criminal appeals courts, four years for the district courts, and two years for all other courts. The number of district courts was placed at twenty-six, but the legislature was authorized to establish others as needed. The Texas Supreme Court,[qv] composed of three judges, was vested with appellate jurisdiction in civil cases only, and the court of appeals, composed of three judges, was vested with appellate jurisdiction over all criminal cases and certain classes of civil cases. The district courts received original jurisdiction (in criminal cases) over felonies and over misdemeanors involving official misconduct and (in civil cases) over a long list of classes of suits. The district courts were given appellate jurisdiction over the county courts in probate matters. The article also mandated a court in each organized county with original jurisdiction over misdemeanors not granted to the courts of justices of the peace and certain civil cases and appellate jurisdiction in cases originating in the justice of the peace courts. The courts of the justices of the peace, not fewer than four or more than eight in each county, were granted jurisdiction in civil and criminal matters involving not more than $200 in controversy or in penalties. The commissioners' court was to consist of the county judge and four elected commissioners, one from each commissioner's precinct.

The article on education drastically changed the system established by the Republicans in 1869. In the first section the framers ordered the legislature to establish and make provision for the support and maintenance of an efficient system of public free schools but then added provisions that made that directive impossible. To support the system the article authorized the legislature to levy a poll tax of one dollar on all male inhabitants between the ages of twenty-one and sixty and to appropriate not more than one-fourth of the general revenue. In addition, it set aside as a perpetual fund all proceeds from lands previously granted to the schools, including all the alternate sections of land already reserved for the state or afterwards reserved out of grants to railroads or other corporations (as specified in the Constitution of 1866[qv]), and the proceeds from the sale of one-half of all other public lands (as prescribed by an act of the legislature in 1873). The document abolished the office of state superintendent, founded a board of education composed of the governor, comptroller, and secretary of state, eliminated compulsory attendance, provided for segregated schools, and made no provision for local school taxes. The Constitution of 1876 provided for the establishment of the University of Texas and made Texas A&M, which had been founded by the legislature in 1871, a branch of it. The constitution further required the legislature to establish an institution of higher education for the instruction of the black youth of the state. To support the university and its branches the constitution set aside one million acres of the public domain, with all sales and proceeds therefrom to be placed in a Permanent University Fund.[qv] It also provided that proceeds from the lands previously granted for the establishment and maintenance of the university (including the fifty-league grant by the legislature in 1858 but not the one-tenth of the alternate sections of land granted to railroads) and all future grants would permanently belong to the university.

The constitution also provided for precinct voting and mandated a poll tax, but not as a prerequisite for voting. It provided for homestead grants of 160 acres to heads of families and eighty acres to single men eighteen or more years of age, and for protection against the forced sale of a homestead for debt. It declared railroads to be common carriers, forbade their consolidation and further aid in grant of money or bonds, and authorized the legislature to enact regulatory laws, including maximum freight and passenger rates. To promote the construction of new track, the document authorized the legislature to grant the railroads sixteen sections of public land for each mile of road constructed. It prohibited the state from chartering banks but mandated the legislature to enact general laws for the establishment of private corporations other than banks, that would provide fully for the adequate protection of the public and individual stockholders.

Overall, the Constitution of 1876 complied with public opinion. It provided for biennial sessions of the legislature, low salaries for public officials, precinct voting, abolition of the road tax, and a return to the road-working system; for a homestead exemption clause, guarantees of a low tax rate, a less expensive, locally controlled, segregated school system, and a less expensive court system; for county and justice of the peace courts; and for popular election of officers. It also prohibited the registration of voters and grants of money or bonds to railroads. The document was adequate for a rural people engaged principally in subsistence farming, but not for an urban-industrial-commercial society. Very few changes were made during the first half century of the constitution's existence, but since then it has been changed at a steadily increasing rate. Changes are made through amendments submitted to the voters by consent of two-thirds of the members of each house of the legislature and approved by a majority of those voting. Of ninety-nine amendments submitted by September 1928, only forty-three were adopted, but by 1980 the voters had approved 235 proposals. No provision was made in the constitution for calling another constitutional convention. On several occasions there has been considerable agitation for a new document, but the voters defeated a proposal for a constitutional convention in 1919, and in 1975 they rejected an extensive revision prepared by the legislature. The constitution's more than 63,000 words make it one of the most verbose of state constitutions. Its wealth of detail causes it to resemble a code of laws rather than a constitution. Its many requirements and limitations on both state and local governments make it one of the most restrictive among state constitutions. Some of its passages are so poorly drafted as to need clarification for understanding, and others have been declared by the Texas Supreme Court to be beyond interpreting. Finally, since many of its provisions relating to the same subject are scattered widely throughout the text, a detailed index is necessary.

Most of the numerous amendments have dealt with the legislature, the judiciary, public education, and state finances. Those relating to the legislature have generally removed existing limitations on legislative action. Changes in the article on the judiciary have been so sweeping that the article has been almost completely rewritten. Alterations in provisions relating to public education have also removed original limitations and permitted expansion of the public school system. Provisions relating to the state's financial system have been altered to permit adoption of new expenditure programs and exploitation of new sources of revenue. Other constitutional changes have relieved some of the burden of detail imposed on the governor's office in 1876, revamped the basic suffrage requirements, altered the method of chartering municipal corporations, lengthened the term of office for many state and local officials, and established an ever-growing number of specifically allocated funds in the state treasury. In spite of its cumbersomeness, of its need for frequent amendment, and its occasional obscurity, however, Texans have continued to hold on to the Constitution of 1876.

BIBLIOGRAPHY: Wilbourn E. Benton, *Texas: Its Government and Politics* (Englewood Cliffs, New Jersey: Prentice-Hall, 1961; 4th ed. 1977). Joe E. Ericson, An Inquiry into the Sources of the Texas Constitution (Ph.D. dissertation, Texas Tech University, 1957). Hans Peter Nielsen Gammel, comp., *Laws of Texas, 1822–1897* (10 vols., Austin: Gammel, 1898). Seth Shepard McKay, *Making the Texas Constitution of 1876* (Philadelphia: University of Pennsylvania, 1924). Rupert N. Richardson, *Texas: The Lone Star State* (New York: Prentice-Hall, 1943; 4th ed., with Ernest Wallace and Adrian N. Anderson, Englewood Cliffs, New Jersey: Prentice-Hall, 1981).

Joe E. Ericson and Ernest Wallace

CONSTITUTION PROPOSED IN 1833. Misgovernment in Texas and revolution in Mexico led the central committee of San Felipe to call the Convention of 1833,[qv] which, as one of its actions, framed and approved a state constitution that was submitted to the Mexican Congress for approval. The proposed constitution was typically Anglo-American, being modeled on the Massachusetts Constitution of 1780, which happened to be available. It provided for a legislature to be composed of a Senate and a House of Representatives, elected biennially. The state was to be divided into ten electoral districts, with one representative for each hundred voters. The governor was to be at least twenty-seven years old and a resident of the state for three years preceding election. His term of office was to be two years, and he should not serve more than four out of any period of six years. He was to have the usual executive powers, but legislation was to be passed over his veto by simple majority vote in both houses of the legislature.

The judiciary was to include a Supreme Court, three district courts, and such inferior courts as the legislature should determine. The jurisdiction of the offices of alcalde, *comisario,* and *sindico procurador*[qqv] was to be fixed by law. Judges were to be elected by the legislature for terms of six years, removable by impeachment by vote of two-thirds of both houses of the legislature. The Supreme Court was to be composed of a superior judge acting with the district judges, a majority forming a quorum.

The franchise was proposed for all male citizens twenty-one years old, and officials were to be elected directly. The projected bill of rights of twenty-seven articles included a guarantee of trial by jury, prohibited illegal search and seizure, and guaranteed other due-process rights. It also affirmed liberties of free speech but did not address religious liberty. The legislature was to establish free schools. It was declared that no banking institution would exist under the constitution, and only gold, silver, and copper coins would be considered legal tender.

Stephen F. Austin's[qv] mission to Mexico City to bear the petitions of the convention and the proposed constitution resulted in his imprisonment and was a significant development in the chain of events that led to the Texas Revolution.

BIBLIOGRAPHY: Hubert Howe Bancroft, *History of the North Mexican States and Texas* (2 vols., San Francisco: History Company, 1886, 1889). Eugene C. Barker, *The Life of Stephen F. Austin* (Nashville: Cokesbury Press, 1925; rpt., Austin: Texas State Historical Association, 1949; New York: AMS Press, 1970). David B. Edward, *The History of Texas* (Cincinnati: James, 1836; rpt., Austin: Texas State Historical Association, 1990). Henderson K. Yoakum, *History of Texas from Its First Settlement in 1685 to Its Annexation to the United States in 1846* (2 vols., New York: Redfield, 1855).

S. S. McKay

CONSTITUTION PROPOSED IN 1874. Like the document proposed by the Constitutional Convention of 1974,[qv] the Constitution of 1874 was written and then rejected by a sitting legislature instead of the traditional constitutional convention. In 1874 it was the Democratic reaction against Reconstruction[qv] that brought about the constitution. A common desire for a new organic law, however, did not mean agreement on what such a document should contain. The legislature's rejection of the 1874 document was just one step in a constitutional struggle that ultimately produced a very different, and successful, organic law—the Constitution of 1876.[qv] The process of writing the 1874 constitution was unusual. As Democrats regained control of their state government in 1873 and 1874, they made writing a new constitution one of their main goals. Initially, however, the legislature's efforts for constitutional reform focused almost exclusively on the method of revision rather than the substance of it. Governor Richard Coke[qv] and the legislature's Democratic leadership sought to block a constitutional convention, the traditional means of reform, and have a legislative committee write the new document instead; an appointive commission was also proposed. A majority of the house of representatives, however, considered anything but a convention "anti-Democratic." Superior parliamentary maneuvering produced a temporary victory for the proposal to have a legislative committee draft the new constitution. The Senate approved that document, but the House rejected it. This defeat produced such a public outcry for a constitutional convention that Coke convened a special session of the legislature to call the 1875 convention. Ultimately the public overwhelmingly approved the Constitution of 1876, an organic law whose style and substance was without precedent in Texas and had only recently emerged in the nation as a whole.

The 1874 document can best be understood in comparison with the state's other post–Civil War constitutions. In terms of substance the 1874 organic law had much in common with constitutions Democrats wrote in 1866 and Republicans drafted in 1869, as all three of these documents provided for a stronger and more expensive state government (although the 1869 constitution was longer and contained more technical detail). Among the more important similarities were stipulations of annual sessions of the legislature, a state superintendent for education, higher salaries for state officials, and the traditional lack of controls on state and local taxing powers. A distinctive feature that the 1874 document shared only with that of 1869 was the absence of the usual constitutional prohibition on banks (*see* BANKS AND BANKING). The 1874 constitution also contained measures designed to exclude African Americans[qv] from the political process by introducing a poll tax and by giving the hated Republican measure of voter registration constitutional standing. Further reinforcing the antiblack character of the 1874 document was its absence of provisions found in the 1869 constitution that affirmed the equality and rights of blacks.

While the resemblances between the 1874 constitution and the earlier documents are notable, the differences between that organic law and the Democratic-prepared Constitution of 1876 are even more striking. The disparity between the 1874 and 1876 documents reflects the scope of the division that emerged in the state Democratic party[qv] after Reconstruction. Grangers dominated the 1875 constitutional convention, and their work stood in stark contrast to the legislative-written 1874 document. Though the 1874 organic law increased government power, the 1876 constitution imposed unprecedented controls on it. Using the technique quickly gaining popularity in other states, north and south, the 1875 convention employed the device of constitutional maximums. For example, not only were tax rates and the salaries of state officials lowered, but the legislature lost the authority to increase these measures in the future. The 1875 convention also refused to act against black voting as the 1874 legislature had because such measures threatened poor whites as well as blacks. Points of similarity did exist, such as continuing to allow a maximum one-fourth of all the state's tax revenue to go to education (this was legislatively mandated until 1879). The continuity of the 1874 document with the 1866 and 1869 constitutions and its discontinuity with the 1876 organic law fitted a pattern: active-government state constitutions written in the 1860s and early 1870s were followed by restrictive ones starting later in the 1870s, especially in the North.

BIBLIOGRAPHY: John Walker Mauer, Southern State Constitutions in the 1870s: A Case Study of Texas (Ph.D. dissertation, Rice University, 1983). John Walker Mauer, "State Constitutions in a Time of Crisis: The Case of the Texas Constitution of 1876," *Texas Law Review* 68 (June 1990).

John Walker Mauer

CONSTITUTION OF THE REPUBLIC OF TEXAS. The Constitution of the Republic of Texas (1836), the first Anglo-American constitution to govern Texas, was drafted by a convention of fifty-nine delegates who assembled at Washington-on-the-Brazos on March 1, 1836 (see CONVENTION OF 1836). A constitution was adopted by the convention fifteen days later and ratified by a vote of the people of the republic on the first Monday in September 1836.

The ever-present threat of attack by Mexican cavalry tended to stifle originality in the document. Almost of necessity the haste to complete their task led delegates to lift portions from the Constitution of the United States and from several contemporary state constitutions. The use of such models produced a document embodying some familiar features. Like the United States Constitution it was admirably brief (less than 6,500 words) and contained generous grants of power to state officials, especially the chief executive. Furthermore, great numbers of specific limitations and restrictions upon government often found in state constitutions of the time were avoided. Finally, the well-known words and phrases of older American constitutions were preserved, making understanding easier.

Typical American features included a short preamble; separation of the powers of government into three branches—legislative, executive, and judicial; checks and balances; slavery;[qv] citizenship, with "Africans, the descendents of Africans, and Indians excepted"; a Bill of Rights; male suffrage; and method of amendment. The legislature was bicameral, the two houses being the Senate and the House of Representatives (see CONGRESS OF THE REPUBLIC OF TEXAS). The executive resembled the American presidency, and the four-tiered judiciary system comprised justice, county, district, and supreme courts, of which the district courts were the most important.

Some of the constitution's atypical provisions undoubtedly reflected Jacksonian ideas current in the states from which many delegates had come; fourteen, for example, came from Tennessee. Ministers and priests were declared ineligible to hold public office. Imprisonment for debt was abolished, and monopolies, primogeniture, and entailment were prohibited. Terms of office were short, ranging from one year for representatives to four years for some judges. Annual elections were required.

Among the most important provisions adapted from Spanish-Mexican law were community property, homestead exemptions and protections, and debtor relief. Contrary to common-law practice in the American states, Texas courts were not separated into distinct courts of law and equity.

The amending process was so complex that, although in the ten-year life span of the constitution several amendments were suggested, none was ever adopted. Amendments could be proposed in one session of Congress, referred to the next session for a second approval, and then submitted to a popular vote.

Of nearly paramount importance at the time of adoption were provisions relating to land. The document sought in many ways to protect the rights of people in the unoccupied lands of the republic, lands that were the main attraction to the immigrants who had come to Texas. In its "Schedule," for example, the constitution affirmed "that all laws now in force in Texas . . . shall remain in full force." Later, in the "General Provisions," a citizen who had not received his land grant was guaranteed "one league and one labor of land" if the head of a family; single men over seventeen years were assured of "the third part of one league of land"; and orphan children "whose parents were entitled to land" were declared eligible for all property rights of their deceased parents. The constitution also sought to void all "unjust and fraudulent claims."

Preference of the predominantly Anglo-American settlers for the legal system they had known "back in the states" is apparent in a provision that called for the introduction of the common law of England as early as practicable and declared it the rule to be used in deciding all criminal cases. Although the constitution of 1836 was a revolutionary document written and adopted in haste, it was a product of the social and economic conditions of the time as well as of the constitutional and legal heritage of Texas, the southern and western states, and the United States. Therefore, Anglo-Americans immigrating to the Republic of Texas[qv] found institutions of law and government in accord with their experience. *See also* LAW.

BIBLIOGRAPHY: George D. Braden, ed., *The Constitution of the State of Texas: An Annotated and Comparative Analysis* (2 vols., Austin: Advisory Commission on Intergovernmental Relations, 1977). Hans Peter Nielsen Gammel, comp., *Laws of Texas, 1822–1897* (10 vols., Austin: Gammel, 1898). John Sayles, *The Constitutions of the State of Texas* (2d ed., St. Louis: Gilbert, 1884; 4th ed., St. Paul, Minnesota: West, 1893). Rupert N. Richardson, "Framing the Constitution of the Republic of Texas," *Southwestern Historical Quarterly* 31 (January 1928).

Joe E. Ericson

CONSULAR SERVICE OF THE REPUBLIC OF TEXAS. The consular service of the Texas nation evolved from a single general agency established in New Orleans in 1835 by the commissioners, Stephen F. Austin, William H. Wharton, and Branch T. Archer,[qqv] and sent to the United States by the provisional government.[qv] Its purpose was to secure outside aid in the form of trade and financial assistance for Texas. William Bryan,[qv] the first New Orleans agent, was succeeded by Thomas Toby (see TOBY AND BROTHER COMPANY) in June 1836. It was during Toby's appointment that the term *consul* first came into use in the republic. On December 10, 1836, David White was appointed Texas agent in Mobile. A few days later President Sam Houston named John Woodward[qqv] consul general and instructed him to open an office in the port of New York and to establish branches at Boston, Baltimore, and Philadelphia. In April 1837 Houston appointed Nathaniel Townsend[qv] consul for New Orleans. Up to this time the consular service was an embryonic, unorganized branch of the government, under the supervision of the president. An attempt to establish a definite system was made by the passage of a joint resolution on December 15, 1837, containing general instructions for the formation of the service. The organization was placed under the supervision of the secretary of state. Some degree of order was achieved, but poor communications and a lack of interest in Texas plagued the Texas consuls in both Europe and the United States and prevented an efficient organization. Growing chiefly through the initiative of individual consuls, the consular service expanded on both sides of the Atlantic. European service was first established as early as 1838 with a consular appointment to France, but confusion about the appointment and the ongoing negotiations for a commerce treaty forestalled the service's definite role in Europe for several years. The service ended in 1845 with the annexation[qv] of Texas to the United States.

Because of its nebulous organization a definitive analysis of the service is not possible, but the following consulates are known to have been established: *New Orleans,* 1835, Nathaniel Townsend, Thomas Toby, William Bryan, P. Edmunds; *New York,* 1836, John Woodward, Charles H. Forbes, August W. Radcliff, John Brower;qv *Mobile,* 1836, David White, George Dobson, Walter Smith, Thomas J. Fettyplace; *Baltimore,* 1838, Henry H. Williams;qv *Natchitoches,* 1838, John F. Cortes, Thomas H. Airey; *Philadelphia,* 1838, John L. Hodge, Cyrus Joy, Francis G. Smith; *Charleston,* 1838, James Hamilton,qv Thomas L. Hamilton; *Vicksburg,* 1839?, S. W. Rudder; *Key West,* 1839, Joseph P. Brown; *Boston,* 1839, Thomas A. Dexter, Nathaniel Amory;qv *Natchez,* 1840, Lyman Potter; *Cincinnati,* 1841, Benjamin Drake, Alexander H. McGuffey; *Detroit,* 1841, Calvin C. Jackson; *Bangor,* 1841, Moses Patton; *Norfolk,* 1841, Samuel G. Taylor; *St. Louis,* 1842, Edward Hutawa; *Richmond,* 1842, William B. Hamilton; *Marseille* (France), 1841, John Willis, Louis Grousset; *Paris* (France), 1840, Theodore Barbey, Henri Castro,qv Pierre Brunet; *Bordeaux* (France), 1842, Paul E. Dumon; *Cette* (France), 1843, Maly E. Dumon; *Rouen* (France), 1842, M. Ladeur, M. Largillier; *Bayonne* (France), 1845, August Furtado; *London* (England), 1841, Arthur Ikin,qv John Barnes, William Kennedy,qv Lockland M. Rate; *Liverpool* (England), 1841, Francis B. Ogden; *Glasgow* (Scotland), 1843, John Graham Stewart; *Greenock* (Scotland), 1843, John Roxburgh; *Falmouth* (England), 1842, Alfred Fox; *Plymouth* (England), 1842, Thomas Were Fox; *Kingston-upon-Hull* (England), 1843, John Atkinson; *Newcastle-upon-Tyne* (England), 1843, William Henry Brockett; *Dublin* (Ireland), 1843, Thomas Snow; *Amsterdam* (Netherlands), 1842, Louis J. Herckenrath; *Rotterdam* (Netherlands), 1843, Joshua J. Crooswyck; *Antwerp* (Belgium), 1843, Maximilian Van Den Bergh; *Bremen* (Germany), 1844, Henry F. Fisher.qv

BIBLIOGRAPHY: Alma Howell Brown, "The Consular Service of the Republic of Texas," *Southwestern Historical Quarterly* 33 (January, April 1930).

CONSULTATION. The Consultation grew out of a proposed meeting of Texas representatives to confer on the prerevoltionary quarrel with Mexico. This idea was first advocated by opponents of revolution in the early summer of 1835 in Mina Municipality. Moderate and radical elements endorsed the concept to present a unified front. A meeting in Columbia on August 15 first used the term *consultation,* perhaps to avoid the revolutionary connotations that the word *convention* implied in Mexican politics. There was not complete agreement on the power of this body. Some treated it as sovereign, but others insisted that the gathering was to investigate, counsel, and recommend to the people and denied that it could assume legislative or constitutional functions. Though originally set for October 15, the Consultation was delayed until November 1 by the eruption of military hostilities earlier in the month, at the insistence of delegates-elect and army officers. On October 16 thirty-one members assembled at San Felipe and recognized the legitimacy of a Permanent Councilqv for a two-week period. Enough of the delegates gathered on November 1 to begin deliberations, but no actual quorum existed until the fourth. They chose Branch T. Archerqv to preside.

The Consultation was not completely representative of all of Texas—no delegates served from the war zone districts of Bexar, Goliad, Refugio, Victoria, or San Patricio, and less than half of those elected attended from Bevil, Mina, and Matagorda. A total of fifty-eight of the ninety-eight credentialed delegates attended the Consultation. These factors weakened the influence of Stephen F. Austin,qv who remained with the Texas army, because several of the absent delegates had strong affiliations with him. John A. Wharton and Henry Smithqqv directed the faction opposed to the Austin group, headed by Don Carlos Barrett.qv Each group had the support of about a third of the delegates; the resulting balance of power led the Consultation toward compromise. The participants were experienced in Texas affairs—more than one-third had been local leaders during the earlier phases of the dispute with Mexico. The average delegate had resided in Texas longer than seven years and was thirty-eight years old, but many of those who had been identified with the land-speculating scandals in the Coahuila and Texasqv state legislature or those who had strongly favored conciliation with Mexico failed to win election. Most of the representatives were from the moderate movement that had sought a course between submission and revolution.

Three issues dominated Consultation deliberations—the purpose of the war, the power and structure of government, and the virtues of different leaders. Barrett, as leader of the Austin forces, favored endorsement of the Constitution of 1824.qv Pragmatic arguments supported this position, since there was hope that Mexican liberals might still rally to support Texas. The Wharton-Smith line of thought grew out of more overtly anti-Mexican attitudes and sought an immediate declaration of independence. On November 7 the Consultation, by a vote of 33 to 14, endorsed establishment of "a provisional government upon the principles of the Constitution of 1824." Yet, at the same time the delegates declared that Antonio López de Santa Annaqv had already dissolved the social compact and that Texas had the right to declare its independence.

Smith chaired the committee on the provisional government. The Consultation approved an interim structure called the Organic Law on November 13. The delegates abolished Mexican political titles and positions such as political chief. Otherwise, the Organic Law reflected a spirit of balance and hesitation. It established an executive along with a general council, made up of a representative from each municipality chosen by his delegation, to assist the governor. Its members had no legislative authority unless "in their opinion the emergency of the country requires" it, and could levy import duties but no other taxes. The governor was to have "full and ample" executive authority, including being head of the military forces, and could be given additional powers that the council thought necessary. The Organic Law also provided for judiciary and treasury departments. Structurally the Organic Law suffered from an unsound political concept in that the governor and council shared many of the same powers on the assumption that they would work together. The delegates chose the disputatious Smith as governor over Austin by 30 to 22. The Consultation displayed a deferential attitude toward the army in the field. It designed a land policy to reassure the soldiers who feared that while they sacrificed, the speculators would carry off the spoils. In three separate articles the Organic Law nullified the "fraudulent" grants made by the last state legislature, reaffirmed the benefits of earlier emigration policies to citizens who had not yet received their land, and ended all transactions for the duration of the war. The Consultation also provided for land grants of unspecified amounts for each volunteer.

The Wharton-Smith faction pushed for a regular army, disciplined by conventional military rules and subject to oversight by the civil government. The Consultation on November 13 passed both the Organic Law and a measure concerning the military. It provided for militia organization but also established a regular army with two-year enlistments and United States Army regulations; Sam Houstonqv won unanimous election as commander, with the rank of major general. However, the Consultation made no attempt to assert its will over existing bodies of volunteer troops who elected their own officers, had little discipline, and served for unspecified enlistments. As a result, the regular army was not recruited. The Consultation refused to reconsider this arrangement on November 14, the day of its adjournment.

The focus on moderation and compromise held the Consultation together but left Texas without a clear course to its future in terms of leadership, purpose, structure of government, or military authority. The body left a legacy of uncertainty leaning toward anarchy.

BIBLIOGRAPHY: Paul D. Lack, *The Texas Revolutionary Experience:*

A Political and Social History (College Station: Texas A&M University Press, 1992).

Paul D. Lack

CONSUMER CREDIT COMMISSIONER. The Office of Consumer Credit Commissioner was established in 1967 to enforce the provisions of the Texas Credit Code. This office replaced the Office of Regulatory Loan Commissioner, established in 1963 as part of the Texas Regulatory Loan Act. The regulatory loan commissioner, appointed by the finance commission, was responsible for the regulation of licensed agencies engaged in making loans of up to $1,500, and he could promulgate regulations to implement the act. By 1970 the maximum loan amount had been increased to $2,500. At that time the agency had thirty-seven employees. In addition to regulating loan companies, the new office was to license and examine lenders who made installment loans to purchase motor vehicles. In 1978 pawn shops came under supervision of the commission. The Sixty-second Legislature placed loans made by vending-machine operators to tavern keepers under the commission, and the Sixty-third Legislature extended regulation to lenders whose sole purpose was to finance insurance premiums. In 1975 the act was amended to conform with the federal Truth in Lending Act, with the commission responsible for enforcement of the changes. The commission also began to register sellers of consumer goods and mobile homes on credit. From 1967 to 1973 the commission had joint responsibility with the attorney general's qv office over deceptive trade practices. In 1980 responsibility to regulate financing of insurance premiums was transferred to the State Insurance Board. Complaints about credit-card sales are also handled by the commission. The policy-making body of the commission is the nine member Finance Commission, which hires the commissioner. Since 1990 appropriations have been around $1.2 million, and the number of employees has been around thirty.

John G. Johnson

CONTEMPORARY ARTS MUSEUM. The Contemporary Arts Museum, in Houston, is one of the oldest institutions of its kind. Since 1948, when its founders, Walter I. Farmer, Robert Preusser, Alvin Romansky, Karl F. Kamrath, Edward M. Schiwetz,qqv and Robert D. Straus, first chartered the Contemporary Arts Association, it has presented the Houston public with aesthetic ideas and works of art. The association began as an alliance among artists, art patrons, architects, and business people who wanted to sponsor the exhibition of contemporary arts as a supplement to the traditional programming of the Museum of Fine Arts qv in Houston. The original charter established the association as a nonprofit organization to be supported by membership dues and run by volunteers. In October 1948 the first exhibition, This Is Contemporary Art, opened in two galleries lent by the Museum of Fine Arts. One of the most important exhibits of the museum's earlier years was a presentation of paintings and drawings by Van Gogh in 1951. At that time, comprehensive showings of his works had been limited to New York and Chicago. In addition, the Houston exhibit included four pieces that had never before been exhibited in the United States.

As a result of the enthusiastic response, the association became a museum with its own building in 1949 and, in 1955, hired its first professional director, Jermayne MacAgy.qv Under her the museum began to organize series of thematic exhibitions in which contemporary arts were presented in a historical context. During her tenure was presented one of the most memorable exhibitions ever shown in Houston, Totems Not Taboo: An Exhibition of Primitive Art (1959), which included over 200 rare examples of primitive art from all over the world. Despite the fact that under MacAgy's leadership the museum enjoyed an improved reputation, inner association conflicts and budgetary problems led to her dismissal in 1959. In the early 1960s a series of directors, Robert C. Morriss, Donald Barthelme,qv and Wilson Burdett, ran the museum, which increasingly emphasized the performing arts and film. Southwestern art was emphasized in the early 1970s, including such exhibits as 12/Texas, a 1974 exhibition of twelve Texas artists, many of whom gained national recognition as a result.

The museum quickly outgrew its first home. The building itself had already been moved in 1954, when the original property it stood on was sold. In 1970 a drive was begun to build a new facility by Sebastian J. Adler, who had been appointed director in 1966. The present building, a distinctive parallelogram structure of stainless steel designed by Gunnar Birkerts and Associates, opened in 1972. The inaugural exhibition of ten commissioned artists included a forty-eight-foot-long pipe sculpture by Robert Grosvenor, Newton Harrison's *Portable Farm (Survival Piece No. 6)*, which consisted of planted herbs, fruits, and vegetables, and Ellen Van Fleet's tiered collection of urban animals entitled *New York City Animal Levels*. Adler expanded the staff of the growing museum and hired its first curator, Jay Belloli. In June 1976 a storm flooded the lower level of the museum, damaging many irreplaceable records and several pieces from the exhibitions then on display. Houston citizens responded immediately with donations and a special fund-raising drive that enabled the museum to reopen in March 1977.

The Contemporary Arts Museum is a noncollecting museum, unique among institutions of its size in the number of major, documented exhibitions mounted each year. The exhibition policy is to examine recent trends in contemporary arts and their precedents through both thematic shows and retrospectives of work by seminal figures. The 11,107-square-foot upper gallery is devoted to these exhibitions, and the lower-level, 2,000-square-foot Perspectives gallery focuses on medium-sized shows of new developments in the arts. Exhibitions have included a series first begun in 1981 entitled "The Americas," which examined traditional topics in contemporary art, and has featured such artists as Frank Stella, Andy Warhol, Frank Freed,qv and Melissa Miller. Catalogues with essays, bibliography, biography, and reproductions accompany each exhibition.

The museum has several education programs with emphasis on promoting art appreciation through classes for children and adults as well as an extension program that teaches children art after school. In addition the Visiting Artists Lecture Series supplements exhibitions by bringing exhibiting artists to the museum to discuss their work. The museum also offers lectures by visiting curators, critics, and scholars, as well as films and symposia. The museum shop offers books and catalogues.

Since 1979 the museum has expanded its programs. By 1982 a circulating exhibitions program was increasing the museum's audiences as museum-originated shows traveled to other cities in the United States and abroad. Additionally, a publication distribution project through national and international library exchange and retail outlets had strengthened awareness of the museum. In the early 1990s the museum had a professional staff of twelve and approximately 55,000 visitors annually.

BIBLIOGRAPHY: Cheryl A. Brutvan, Marti Mayo, and Linda L. Cathcart, *In Our Time: Houston's Contemporary Arts Museum* (Houston: Contemporary Arts Museum, 1982). Contemporary Arts Museum (Houston), *Annual Report*. Vertical Files, Barker Texas History Center, University of Texas at Austin.

Sally Johnson

CONTENT, TEXAS (Colorado County). Content is four miles south of Weimar near the junction of Farm roads 155 and 2144 in the northwestern corner of Colorado County. The site was probably settled during the Civil War,qv and in 1865 a post office named Content was opened there. A school, organized in the community by the 1870s, served thirty-two students in 1879. The Content post office closed in 1880, and residents received their mail from nearby Weimar. In 1904 the one-teacher Content school served fifty-six pupils. In 1940 the community comprised the school and scattered dwellings. At various times Content also had stores and a cotton gin. By the 1950s the Content school had consolidated with that of Weimar. A

German community named New Bielau was contiguous with Content; the two settlements shared churches and a school board. In the 1980s both communities were served by the New Bielau community center and the Trinity Evangelical Church.

BIBLIOGRAPHY: Colorado County Historical Commission, *Colorado County Chronicles from the Beginning to 1923* (2 vols., Austin: Nortex, 1986).

Mark Odintz

CONTENT, TEXAS (Runnels County). Content, near Ranch Road 382 fourteen miles northeast of Winters in northeastern Runnels County, was founded by storekeeper Daniel W. Hale in 1881 and named by him "for the contentment of this valley." Hale became the first postmaster in 1882. Content had a school in 1882 and a hotel in 1888. At some time it had several stores, two gins, a lime kiln, and a blacksmith shop. In 1890 Content was the county's second largest town, with 200 people. The post office name was changed to Tokeen in 1905. The Santa Fe Railroad extension missed Content in 1909, and most residents moved to Goldsboro. The post office was closed in 1916, and after that the name was changed back to Content. The settlement had a population of twenty-five in 1940 and 1960. In 1970 there were only three houses left.

BIBLIOGRAPHY: Charlsie Poe, *Runnels Is My County* (San Antonio: Naylor, 1970).

CONTINENTAL AIRLINES. Continental Airlines, the fifth-largest air carrier in the United States in 1993, traces its roots back to Varney Speed Lanes. Varney began service in El Paso in 1934 with six employees, including two pilots. Its headquarters moved back and forth between El Paso and Albuquerque for the next few years. In 1937 the company moved its main offices to Denver. Robert F. Six became president in 1938 and held the position for more than twenty years. The airline changed its name to Continental and slowly increased its service to a growing number of cities in the 1940s and 1950s. By 1957 the airline served thirty-six cities in Texas, New Mexico, Colorado, Oklahoma, Kansas, and Missouri. Continental dramatically expanded its position in the Southwest by purchasing Pioneer Airlines in 1957. Pioneer started operations in 1945 with its headquarters in Dallas, and by 1957 it flew to twenty-two cities in Texas and New Mexico. Continental purchased its first jets in 1958.

Continental Airlines remained prosperous through the 1960s and 1970s, then went into a major slump in the late 1970s. Between 1978 and 1983 the company had a series of bad years, with losses of over $500 million. In 1981 Francisco D. (Frank) Lorenzo and his Texas Air[qv] Corporation began to take over the debt-ridden Continental. With their labor agreements about to expire, Continental's employees opposed the takeover bid. When the takeover was completed the following year, Lorenzo merged Texas International, another Texas Air affiliate, with Continental. Labor problems threatened the new airline, and Continental shortly filed for reorganization under Chapter 11 of the bankruptcy code. Lorenzo resumed operations with the workers still on strike and succeeded in defeating the unions. Continental moved its corporate headquarters to Houston in 1983 and, pursuing a strategy of low fares and hiring nonunion employees, worked its way out of bankruptcy by 1986.

Texas Air purchased three further airlines in 1986—Eastern, Frontier, and People's Express. Continental Airlines absorbed People's Express along with New York Air, another Texas Air affiliate, in the same year. In 1987 Continental made 1,500 flights daily, and served 141 cities as the nation's third-largest carrier. In spite of their dramatic expansion, Texas Air and Continental once again faced hard times in the late 1980s. Rising fuel prices and declining passenger traffic led to heavy losses in 1988 and 1989. Part of Eastern Airlines was sold to Donald Trump in 1988, and the remainder of Eastern went into bankruptcy in 1990 and liquidation in 1991. Frank Lorenzo left Texas Air in 1990. When Eastern airlines went into bankruptcy and was removed from the control of Texas Air, Texas Air was renamed Continental Airlines Holdings in 1990, to reflect its primary remaining air operation. Continental once again declared bankruptcy in 1990, a year in which it lost a further $340 million. Continental was purchased by Air Canada in 1992 and emerged from bankruptcy the following year. In 1993 Continental's 319 airplanes served 136 United States cities and fifty-seven foreign cities.

BIBLIOGRAPHY: *The Texas 500: Hoover's Guide to the Top Texas Companies* (Austin: Reference Press, 1994). Vertical Files, Barker Texas History Center, University of Texas at Austin.

Mark Odintz

CONTINENTAL LAND AND CATTLE COMPANY. The Continental Cattle Company, as it was originally called, was formed in 1881 by William Edgar Hughes, John N. Simpson,[qq v] and John W. Buster. Having recently purchased J. R. Couts's interest in the Hashknife Ranch[qv] and the Millett brothers' operation in Baylor County, Hughes and Simpson became president and vice president, respectively, of the company, which had offices in Dallas and St. Louis. Buster served as general manager, and several smaller stockholders formed the firm's core. Seeking to acquire more land and cattle, the company established the Mill Iron Ranch in the lower Texas Panhandle.

According to tradition, the Mill Iron brand had its origin when a cowboy working for Simpson found an unbranded calf. Since he had no branding irons with him, he appropriated an iron from a nearby mill to burn his claim on the maverick. Simpson, who held the water rights on Bitter Lake, near the Pease River, first used the brand on his small herd of cattle. The Continental Company then bought these cattle and adopted the Mill Iron as its official brand.

After establishing a dugout[qv] headquarters in Hall County, Hughes and his associates began buying a number of small herds, of 200 to 300 each, between the Red and Pease rivers and started leasing sections near water for three cents an acre. Before long the Mill Iron grew to a total of 162,736 acres and encompassed portions of Hall, Childress, Motley, and Cottle counties. Ranches bordering the Mill Iron included the OX, Shoe Nail, Shoe Bar, Quitaque (Lazy F), Diamond Tail, and Matador.[qq v] The Mill Iron also maintained a feeding ranch on the Powder River in Montana, where herds were driven in the spring for summer fattening. The Montana property also supplied most of the cow ponies for the Mill Iron. Since these horses were above average in size, the Mill Iron soon became noted for big horses and big men. Once when an epidemic of glanders broke out among the horse herds in Texas, the local veterinarian drove thirty-five Mill Iron horses into Brewster Canyon, where they were shot. Many of them were favorites of individual cowboys, and they could not bear to watch, much less do the job themselves; from then on they avoided the canyon. Periodic visits by Hughes from his Denver residence were always dramatic occasions, especially when he arrived with his hunting dogs in his colorful, trim coach.

On February 5, 1884, Hughes and his associates reorganized and incorporated their ranching enterprise as the Continental Land and Cattle Company, with their main office in St. Louis. Two years later the company absorbed the holdings of Hughes and Simpson in the Hashknife Ranch and moved its cattle to the Mill Iron range. During its heyday the Mill Iron branded between 10,000 and 12,000 calves annually; in 1890, 25,000 calves were reported. In 1896 the Mill Iron bought the adjoining 152,320-acre Rocking Chair Ranch,[qv] thus extending its holdings into Collingsworth and Wheeler counties.

In 1885 the coming of windmills[qv] ended the ranch's dependence on surface tanks and springs, which usually dried up during prolonged droughts. Wells were drilled as watering places in isolated pasture recesses. Two Mill Iron pastures were fenced with the coming of barbed wire[qv] and used to hold the bulls rounded up in the fall to be placed in the pasture or shipped to market. Not until 1887 was a permanent headquarters built on the ranch at Windmill 62, four miles south of Estelline. Prior to that the only ranch structures on the Mill

Iron were dugouts and chuck wagons. Foreman R. D. Green lived in the ranch headquarters house, which burned in 1897 and was replaced by a new headquarters located in Estelline. "Colonel" Hughes stayed in both houses during his occasional visits.

In an attempt to save money Continental continued to drive Mill Iron cattle to Montana until 1894, when it finally joined its neighbors in utilizing the railroad shipping points at Estelline, Giles, Childress, and Clarendon. Not until 1898 did the Mill Iron begin improving its herds of longhorn cattle[qv] by adding 2,000 grade cattle from the JA[qv] and 1,000 full bloods from the JJ. That year the cowhands undertook the hazardous job of dehorning the Texas stock, and over the next few years the ranch built up higher-quality, blooded herds.

By the 1890s, when settlers began homesteading on the range's school sections, Hughes and his associates were able for a time to buy and trade lands with them and keep them outside the Mill Iron's best pastures. But by 1913 they were compelled to reduce both their range and its herds. William J. Lewis[qv] leased 10,000 acres of Mill Iron range on which to run his Spurs, and also bought 12,000 head of Mill Iron cattle. The Crews brothers of Childress bought the Mill Iron's Rocking Chair range and herd; by 1916 these transactions had left the firm with only 5,000 cattle. In the meantime the company's large shareholders continued to absorb the interests of the smaller ones until the organization became W. E. Hughes and Company. On March 7, 1916, Hughes was named president of the firm and by October was its sole owner. Just before his death two years later, he sold the remaining Mill Iron cattle and gave the headquarters house in Estelline to Bob Green and his wife for their years of faithful service. Although the Hughes heirs continued ranching in the Panhandle on a limited basis, the Continental Land and Cattle Company had ceased to exist. Highways and farming establishments now cross the range where Mill Iron cattle once grazed.

BIBLIOGRAPHY: Inez Baker, *Yesterday in Hall County* (Memphis, Texas, 1940). Laura V. Hamner, *Short Grass and Longhorns* (Norman: University of Oklahoma Press, 1943). Pauline D. and R. L. Robertson, *Cowman's Country: Fifty Frontier Ranches in the Texas Panhandle, 1876–1887* (Amarillo: Paramount, 1981).
H. Allen Anderson

CONTRABANDO MOUNTAIN. Contrabando Mountain is located three miles northwest of Lajitas on the Brewster-Presidio county line (at 29°19′ N, 103°48′ W); its summit is in southeastern Presidio County. With an elevation of 3,214 feet above sea level, it rises some 560 feet above Contrabando Creek, one half mile northwest. The area's variable soils support scrub brush and grasses. Contrabando means "contraband" or "smuggling" in Spanish, perhaps a reference to extralegal trade in various commodities that has long flourished along the United States–Mexico border. Among the most notorious local smugglers were the Domínguez brothers, Patricio (Picho), Marcelino, and Juan, who were active in southwestern Brewster County in the 1920s and 1930s. Juan was executed by Mexican lawmen just across from Lajitas around 1930, and Marcelino died in a shootout with American officers a few years later.

CONTRABANDO WATER HOLE. Contrabando Water Hole, a natural lake, is on the western edge of Contrabando Mountain in southeastern Presidio County (at 29°19′ N, 103°48′ W). It is set in desert mountain terrain. Its volcanic rock is surfaced by light reddish-brown to brown sand, clay loam, and rough stone. Sparse grasses, cacti, and desert shrubs grow in the area.

CONVENT OF THE INCARNATE WORD AND BLESSED SACRAMENT. The Convent of the Incarnate Word and Blessed Sacrament, in Brownsville, was established on March 20, 1853, when the Sisters of the Incarnate Word and Blessed Sacrament[qv] laid the cornerstone of the first convent of that order in America. The four sisters first assigned to do missionary work in the United States were Sister Mary St. Clare (Frances Valentine[qv]), Sister Mary St. Ange (Euphemie Barre), Sister St. Ephrem (Peroline Satin), and Sister St. Dominic (Benoit Ravier), who left Lyons, France, on March 18, 1852. Their assignment was to do missionary work and teach in South Texas. They arrived in New Orleans on May 11, 1852, then traveled to Galveston, where they were instructed in English and Spanish by Ursuline Sisters[qv] and Louis Claude Marie Chambodut,[qv] vicar general of Bishop J. M. Odin.[qv] While in Galveston a Miss Martignat entered the order as Sister St. Joseph.

Upon their arrival in Brownsville in 1853 the sisters moved into an unfurnished former warehouse to begin their school while their first convent was being built. For their bilingual pupils they translated from French and printed textbooks on a small hand press. In 1854 they were joined by sisters Stanislaus Deideu, Mary Louise Murray, and Mary of the Cross Murray. The sisters taught without interruption through Indian raids, yellow fever epidemics, and the Civil War[qv] until 1867, when the convent was destroyed by a hurricane.

Donations of land and money for a new building persuaded the bishop to reopen the convent and school, and by December 25, 1868, a New Orleans French-style convent, built at a cost of $20,000, was ready for occupancy. The convent, which served as a day and boarding school for girls, received its charter from the state of Texas in 1885. The sisters opened a school for boys near the female academy in 1890. The academy had two departments, one in Spanish and one in English, until 1902, when the Spanish department was closed. The Oblates of Mary Immaculate[qv] asked the sisters to teach at their parochial school in 1905. When St. Francis School was established in 1916 the sisters were asked to teach there as well. Because the two parochial schools caused a reduction in attendance at the Boy's School of Incarnate Word Academy, that building was used for Our Lady of Guadalupe School, an institution for poor girls. In 1967 the sisters moved to Villa Maria. An official Texas historical marker has been placed at the former site of the convent on East St. Charles Street in Brownsville.

BIBLIOGRAPHY: Sister Mary Xavier Holworthy, I.W.B.S, *Diamonds for the King* (Corpus Christi, 1945).
Alicia A. Garza

CONVENTION OF 1832. The Convention of 1832, held at San Felipe de Austin, followed the Anahuac Disturbances,[qv] the battle of Velasco,[qv] and the Turtle Bayou Resolutions,[qv] in which many Texans pledged their support to then-liberal Antonio López de Santa Anna.[qv] Fifty-five delegates, none of whom were Tejano,[qv] represented sixteen districts and met from October 1 through October 6, 1832. The largely Tejano-populated San Fernando de Béxar (San Antonio) and Victoria did not send a delegation. Delegates from La Bahía (Goliad), who arrived after the meeting had adjourned, approved what had been done.

Stephen F. Austin[qv] was elected president of the convention and Francis W. Johnson[qv] secretary. The convention adopted a series of resolutions requesting the extension of tariff exemption to Texas for three years; modification of the Law of April 6, 1830,[qv] to permit more general immigration from the United States; the appointment of a commissioner to issue land titles in East Texas; donation of government lands for the maintenance of primary schools to be conducted in Spanish and English; and a request of the ayuntamiento[qv] of Nacogdoches to prevent white encroachment on lands guaranteed to Indians in East Texas. The convention also established a plan for organizing a militia and committees of vigilance, safety, and correspondence, which could disseminate news quickly in case of an emergency. In its most controversial decision the convention adopted a motion to request separate statehood from Coahuila. After some debate, it carried. William H. Wharton[qv] was selected to present the resolutions to the Mexican Congress and state legislature of Coahuila and Texas.[qv] Rafael Manchola[qv] of the Goliad delegation was to accompany him.

For several reasons the resolutions were never presented. Refusal of San Antonio to cooperate with the convention made it appear that only the colonists who had come from the United States were dissatisfied. The political chief of the province, Ramón Músquiz,[qv] ruled that the meeting was unauthorized and therefore illegal; Austin apparently thought that the petition for statehood was premature; and Santa Anna had not yet taken over the national government from Anastasio Bustamante.[qv]

BIBLIOGRAPHY: Eugene C. Barker, *The Life of Stephen F. Austin* (Nashville: Cokesbury Press, 1925; rpt., Austin: Texas State Historical Association, 1949; New York: AMS Press, 1970). Hans Peter Nielsen Gammel, comp., *Laws of Texas, 1822–1897* (10 vols., Austin: Gammel, 1898).
Ralph W. Steen

CONVENTION OF 1833. The Convention of 1833 met at San Felipe on April 1 as a successor to the Convention of 1832,[qv] to which San Fernando de Béxar (San Antonio) had refused to send delegates. While Stephen F. Austin[qv] was visiting the Mexican settlements in an effort to secure their cooperation, less patient settlers called the new convention, which met on the day that Antonio López de Santa Anna[qv] took power. The political chief in San Antonio, Ramón Músquiz,[qv] again disapproved of the meeting. Approximately fifty-six delegates attended, including Sam Houston,[qv] a delegate from Nacogdoches. William H. Wharton[qv] presided, and Thomas Hastings[qv] was secretary. The convention petitioned anew for repeal of the anti-immigration section of the Law of April 6, 1830,[qv] asked for more adequate Indian defense, judicial reform, and improvement in mail service, sought tariff exemption, and passed resolutions prohibiting African slave traffic into Texas. Delegates also proposed to split Coahuila and Texas.[qv] Assuming that the petition for statehood would be granted, a committee of which Houston was chairman prepared a constitution for submission to the Mexican Congress. This document was a model of republicanism fashioned, surprisingly, after the Massachusetts constitution of 1780, which happened to be on hand. It provided for trial by jury, habeas corpus, freedom of the press, and universal suffrage (*see* CONSTITUTION PROPOSED IN 1833). David G. Burnet[qv] was chosen to head a committee on preparing a memorial to the Mexican government extoling the merits of the constitution and organization of the state government. Juan Erasmo Seguín, Dr. James B. Miller,[qqv] and Austin were chosen to present the petitions to the government, but since Seguín and Miller were unable to go, Austin went to Mexico alone. The convention adjourned on April 13.

BIBLIOGRAPHY: Stephen F. Austin, "Explanation to the Public Concerning the Affairs of Texas, by Citizen Stephen F. Austin," *Quarterly of the Texas State Historical Association* 8 (January 1905). Eugene C. Barker, *The Life of Stephen F. Austin* (Nashville: Cokesbury Press, 1925; rpt., Austin: Texas State Historical Association, 1949; New York: AMS Press, 1970). Eugene C. Barker, ed., *The Austin Papers* (3 vols., Washington: GPO, 1924–28). Holland Edwards Bell, The Texas Convention of 1832 (M.A. thesis, University of Texas, 1907). John Henry Brown, *History of Texas from 1685 to 1892* (2 vols., St. Louis: Daniell, 1893). E. W. Winkler, "Membership of the 1833 Convention of Texas," *Southwestern Historical Quarterly* 45 (January 1942). Henderson K. Yoakum, *History of Texas from Its First Settlement in 1685 to Its Annexation to the United States in 1846* (2 vols., New York: Redfield, 1855).
Ralph W. Steen

CONVENTION OF 1836. The Convention of 1836 wrote the Texas Declaration of Independence[qv] and the Constitution of the Republic of Texas,[qv] organized the ad interim government,[qv] and named Sam Houston[qv] commander in chief of the military forces of the republic. The call for the convention to meet at Washington-on-the-Brazos was issued by the General Council[qv] of the provisional government[qv] over the veto of Governor Henry Smith[qv] in December 1835, and the delegates were elected on February 1, 1836. The convention met on March 1, 1836, in near-freezing weather in an unfinished building belonging to Noah T. Byars and Peter M. Mercer,[qqv] his business partner. The building was rented for use of the convention by a group of Washington business men who, incidentally, never got around to paying the rent. Forty-four delegates were assembled on the first day of the convention. Fifty-nine delegates finally attended its sessions. Andrew Briscoe[qv] did not arrive until March 11. Twelve of the members were natives of Virginia, ten of North Carolina, nine of Tennessee, six of Kentucky, four of Georgia, three of South Carolina, three of Pennsylvania, three of Mexico (including two born in Texas), two of New York, and one each of Massachusetts, Mississippi, New Jersey, England, Ireland, Scotland, and Canada. Only ten of the delegates were in Texas as early as January 1830; two of them arrived in 1836. Sam Houston, Robert Potter, Richard Ellis, Samuel P. Carson, Martin Parmer, and Lorenzo de Zavala[qv] had all had political experience in Mexico or the United States in state or national government, several in both. James Collinsworth[qv] presided as temporary chairman, and Willis A. Faris[qv] was secretary pro tem. After the examination of credentials of the members, the permanent officers were elected; Richard Ellis was president and Herbert Simms Kimble[qv] was secretary. The Declaration of Independence was adopted on March 2, and members began signing it on March 3. The convention then proceeded to the writing of the constitution and election of ad interim government officials. With the report of the approach of the Mexican army, the convention adjourned in haste in the early morning hours of March 17.

BIBLIOGRAPHY: Louis Wiltz Kemp, *The Signers of the Texas Declaration of Independence* (Salado, Texas: Anson Jones, 1944; rpt. 1959). Paul D. Lack, *The Texas Revolutionary Experience: A Political and Social History* (College Station: Texas A&M University Press, 1992).
Ralph W. Steen

CONVENTION OF 1845. The Convention of 1845 was called by Anson Jones[qv] to meet in Austin to consider the joint resolution of the United States Congress proposing the annexation[qv] of the Republic of Texas[qv] to the United States. The convention assembled on July 4, 1845. Thomas Jefferson Rusk[qv] was elected president of the convention, and James H. Raymond[qv] was secretary. By a vote of fifty-five to one, the delegates approved the offer of annexation. Richard Bache[qv] of Galveston was the lone dissenter. Subsequently, the convention prepared the Constitution of 1845[qv] for the new state. Rusk appointed several committees to examine legislative, executive, judicial, and general provisions of the constitution, as well as a committee of five to prepare convention rules. Of the fifty-seven delegates elected to the convention, eighteen were originally from Tennessee, eight from Virginia, seven from Georgia, six from Kentucky, and five from North Carolina. Considered the most able body of its kind ever to meet in Texas, the convention included men of broad political experience such as Thomas J. Rusk, James Pinckney Henderson, Isaac Van Zandt, Hardin R. Runnels, Abner S. Lipscomb, Nicholas H. Darnell, R. E. B. Baylor, and José Antonio Navarro.[qqv] The convention adjourned on August 28, 1845.

BIBLIOGRAPHY: *Journals of the Convention* (Austin: Miner and Cruger, 1845; rpt., Austin: Shoal Creek, 1974). Annie Middleton, "The Texas Convention of 1845," *Southwestern Historical Quarterly* 25 (July 1921).
Ralph W. Steen

CONVERSE, TEXAS. Converse is on Farm Road 1976 thirteen miles northeast of downtown San Antonio in northeastern Bexar County. It was named for the chief engineer of the Southern Pacific Railroad, a Major Converse, who in 1877 bought a tract of land including the townsite. A post office was established in 1878, and by 1885 a population of thirty was reported. In 1896 the town had a saloon, two cotton gins, and a grocery. In 1990 the community, originally settled by German farmers, reportedly had the oldest 4-H Club in Texas.

A singing society, the Salatrillo Liederkranz, had been active for many years. The population in 1946 was 175; by 1965 the town had twenty-two businesses and 900 residents. Converse has become a suburb of San Antonio. In 1990 the community had a population of 8,887, and in 1991 it had seventy-three businesses.

Minnie B. Cameron

CONVICT LEASE SYSTEM. The convict lease system in Texas functioned in much the same manner and for many of the same reasons as it did in the other states of the former Confederacy. In the years immediately after the Civil War[qv] a variety of factors associated with the Confederate defeat brought about substantially higher levels of lawlessness. At the same time, persistent shortages of funds in the state treasury effectively tied the hands of prison officials, who found they could not house and care for the larger number of individuals sentenced to the penitentiary. Leasing the prison and the inmates to private individuals appeared to offer the best and, in the view of many, the only solution to the problems.

The first leases in Texas came about in 1867, when two railroad companies headquartered in the state hired prison inmates to help construct their roadbeds. The parties to these early agreements, despite the enthusiasm that greeted them, did not anticipate all of the problems inherent in such a contractual arrangement. The most difficult problem resulted from the conflict between the profit motive of the contractors, who wanted to get the most labor possible from the prisoners at the least cost, and the interests of the state, which wanted at least a minimal effort to provide adequate food, clothing, and shelter for the prisoners. Owing to the many difficulties encountered in the course of administering the early leases, state officials abrogated the contracts after only a few months, and the prison inmates were returned to the penitentiary.

Prison problems intensified through the next few years, as chronic overcrowding and lack of adequate funding fostered a general breakdown of morale among prison employees and a concurrent decline in discipline and growth of resentment among the inmates. The findings and conclusions of several legislative investigations all pointed to the seemingly unresolvable nature of the problems, given the limited resources available to the state. By late March 1871 the governor and most legislators agreed that another lease of the penitentiary had to be undertaken. Accordingly, on April 29, 1871, state officials entered an agreement with Ward, Dewey, and Company of Galveston. The men leasing the prison, A. J. Ward, E. C. Dewey, and Nathan Patton, all had reputations as successful businessmen, and Patton, the preeminent politician among the three, had particularly close ties to the administration of the Republican governor, Edmund J. Davis.[qv] The terms of the lease agreement gave the lessees full use of all prison facilities and property, including inmates, for a period of fifteen years. The prisoners could be placed at whatever labor the lessees directed, subject to minimal state regulation and control.

For their part, Ward, Dewey and Company agreed to assume financial responsibility for all costs necessary for the support and maintenance of the institution. These would include food, clothing, and medical care for the prisoners, as well as salaries for guards and prison officials. In addition, the lessees obligated themselves to make annual payments to the state for the labor of the prisoners. For the first five years of the lease, the labor payment totalled $5,000 annually. It increased to $10,000 for each of the next five years and reached $20,000 annually for each of the remaining five years.

For the first few months of the lease all parties to the agreement seemed pleased. Ward-Dewey made a number of improvements and additions to the prison, restored discipline and order among the inmates, and evinced a genuine concern, according to inspection reports, for the care and treatment of the prisoners. This mood of satisfaction was short-lived, however, and by the spring of 1873 reports of abuse and neglect of prisoners began to be heard regularly in the state capital. Repeated attempts by the governor and other state officials to force a strict compliance with the regulations for inmate care proved futile, and for the remaining years of the Ward-Dewey lease reports of mistreatment of prisoners persisted.

The year 1873 also witnessed the beginnings of financial difficulties for the prison lessees. In May, Ward-Dewey appealed to state officials for a delay in making the company's already-overdue annual payment to the state. After much debate and disagreement, state officials agreed to the delay, fearing that to do otherwise might cause the lessees to abandon their lease and return the prison to state control. The financial difficulties did not improve, however, and they, along with continuing reports of prisoner abuse and mistreatment, plus growing political differences between Ward-Dewey and the administration of the Democratic governor, Richard B. Hubbard,[qv] led eventually to the resumption of state control of the penitentiary in early 1877.

Shortly after terminating the Ward-Dewey lease, the state entered into a short-term agreement with a firm headed by John H. Burnett,[qv] a Galveston cotton merchant and long-time acquaintance of Governor Hubbard. This temporary arrangement, concluded to spare the state the financial burden of operating the prison, gave state officials time to advertise and prepare for a new long-term lease. By December 1877 all preparations had been completed and all requirements met, so the state entered into an agreement with the firm of Cunningham and Ellis.

Ed H. Cunningham and L. A. Ellis both owned substantial agricultural property in the counties to the south and west of Houston, where they raised sugarcane, along with some feed grains and cotton. During their lease, which lasted until 1883, Cunningham and Ellis sublet the prison inmates to private farmers, small industries, and railroad companies. Over the tenure of their lease Cunningham and Ellis earned handsome profits, paid several hundred thousand dollars into the state treasury, and made substantial improvements to prison facilities, including constructing the branch penitentiary at Rusk. But to a significant degree, the financial success of the Cunningham and Ellis lease served as its undoing. Influential members of the legislature, with substantial support from the public, began to question the financial desirability of continuing the lease. Editorials in *Texas Siftings*[qv] fed the controversy. The principal question was whether the state should resume control of her penitentiaries, hire out the prisoners directly to private individuals, and reserve for the state treasury the profits that had gone previously to Cunningham and Ellis. The sentiment for resumption grew until, in the spring of 1883, the legislature refused to renew the lease and the state prison system reverted to state control.

For the next thirty years the income from the labor of state prison inmates formed a significant portion of total state revenues. The prisoners worked at many of the same jobs as under the lessees and, increasingly, through the latter decades of the nineteenth and early twentieth centuries on large state-owned farms located through the eastern and southeastern parts of the state. The decision to purchase farmland on which to place the prisoners arose primarily from the belief that farm work was the ideal type of labor for the generally unskilled inmates. In addition, state-owned and operated farms represented a wise investment of the state's money and would better enable state prison employees to care properly for the inmates. In spite of the handsome and dependable earnings that came from prison labor, however, by the first decade of the twentieth century a spirit of reform had emerged in the state against convict leasing.

The beginning of the end for convict lease in Texas came in the fall of 1908, when a young reporter for the San Antonio *Express* began a series of investigative articles on the inner workings of the Texas prison system. Revelations of long-term abuse and neglect of inmates, along with allegations of mismanagement, corruption, and indifference on the part of elected leaders to the hellish prison living conditions, led to a public demand for change. Newspapers in all parts of the state, expressing the sentiments of Progressive era[qv] civic and religious groups in the towns and cities, featured editorials calling for legislative action to bring all prisoners back under the exclusive control of the state and implement new prison policies to provide better care for the inmates.

The public pressure for change reached the point that Governor Thomas M. Campbell,qv nearing the end of his second term of office, called a special session of the legislature to meet in the summer of 1910. Out of this session came laws providing for a major revamping of the prison system. A modified administrative structure, enabling closer accountability, was established, new work programs and policies were implemented, and the private employers of prison inmates were told that no labor contracts would be extended beyond the expiration dates already in force. By January 1, 1914, all prisoners were to be back under the exclusive control of the state, working within the walls of the prison, on state-owned farms, or on private property that the state had acquired under long-term rental agreements. The state actually succeeded in terminating all of its leases by the end of 1912. See also PRISON SYSTEM.

BIBLIOGRAPHY: Herman L. Crow, Political History of the Texas Penal System, 1829–1951 (Ph.D. dissertation, University of Texas, 1964). James Robertson Nowlin, A Political History of the Texas Prison System, 1849–1957 (M.A. thesis, Trinity University, 1962). Penitentiary Papers, Texas State Archives, Austin. Donald R. Walker, Penology for Profit: A History of the Texas Prison System, 1867–1912 (College Station: Texas A&M University Press, 1988).

Donald R. Walker

CONWAY, GORDON (1894–1956). Gordon Conway, artist, only child of John Catlett and Tommie (Johnson) Conway, was born at Cleburne, Texas, on December 18, 1894. Her father descended from colonial and revolutionary era patriots in Tidewater Virginia that included a collateral ancestral line from the mother of President James Madison. After the Civil Warqv he moved to Texas, where he succeeded in business, became an active Episcopal layman, and served as mayor of Cleburne. Around 1900 the family moved to Dallas, where he expanded his chain of lumberyards, established lumber firms in Dallas and Fort Worth, and became a well-known civic and social leader before his death in 1906. His daughter, Gordon, the last of the family line, had no children from a seven-year marriage to businessman Blake Ozias that ended in divorce in France in 1927. Gordon Conway's mother also descended from early American leaders, including the Samuel Adams family of Massachusetts and Joseph Johnson, the first Virginia governor elected by a vote of the people. One Johnson line later moved to Texas and settled in Whitesboro, Paris, and Cleburne. Tommie Johnson Conway established the pattern of a glamorous, nomadic lifestyle that included sporadic educational efforts for Gordon at the National Cathedral School in Washington, D.C., a Lausanne girls' school, and brief art lessons in Rome. She was a champion of her daughter's career and her lifelong companion.

During a brief but prolific twenty-two-year career (1915–37), Gordon Conway won international acclaim in the fields of commercial graphic art and costume design for stage and film in New York, London, and Paris. She made around 5,000 finished drawings, including illustrations for at least 26 publications and 33 advertising clients. With assignments ranging from one to 80 costumes per show, she designed graphics and costumes for at least 119 stage productions for both theater and cabaret. She costumed 47 films. Conway helped democratize Parisian haute couture and popularize the severe elements of modern design. Starting out during the golden age of American illustration, she was a self-taught, free-lance artist who worked without apprentices and models. A significant but often overlooked aspect of her career—and rare for women of the era—was Conway's ability to create a popular public persona, which expanded her network of clients. She was in the vanguard of the new business enterprises of advertising and public relations at the beginning of the twentieth century.

She excelled in several genres best reviewed in two stages: her New York period (1915–20) and her European period (1921–36). Highlights of her New York period included silhouette art for mass print media and color billboards, posters, and promotional graphics touting Broadway theater and cabaret productions. She was a spirited and determined twenty-year-old in 1915 when she launched her career at *Vogue* and *Vanity Fair*. Recognizing her native talent, Heyworth Campbell—publisher Condé Nast's first art director—insisted that Conway forget academic art school. He urged her to take classes at the Art Students League and to study magazine and advertising illustration with tutors. Campbell joined another Conway mentor, *Vanity Fair* editor Frank Crowninshield, in helping her establish a popular public image. These editors also marshaled her innate flair for whimsy and parody by commissioning covers and narrative vignette pages spoofing New York society girls involved in World War Iqv charity work. Also publishing Conway's drawings of bright young sophisticates was Condé Nast rival *Harper's Bazaar*, whose editor, Henry B. Sell, encouraged Conway's talent and introduced her to the art work of their new cover artist, Erté. These successes led to other publications and diverse advertising clients such as the Delage and the Franklin motor car companies, Huylers chocolates, Neiman-Marcus,qv and Hallmark watches. The National City Company (New York) commissioned a series of her posters for a nationwide advertising campaign to attract women as securities investors.

Conway's stage collaboration represents some of the best talent in theater and cabaret production in New York, including Broadway clients Cohan and Harris, Comstock and Gest, Hitchcock and Goetz, the Selwyns, the Shuberts, Robert Milton, and Ned Wayburn. In 1916 her first stage assignment for the new cabaret field glamorized exhibition dancers in silhouette illustrations for newspaper advertisements, window cards, menus, and wine lists. This led to jobs including costumes and graphics for cabaret shows at such venues as the Palais Royal (1920), starring Conway's friend and most frequent client, Dorothy Dickson, and dance partner-husband Carl Hyson. Conway's first musical in 1917, for which she designed costumes and graphics for Raymond Hitchcock and E. Ray Goetz, led to silhouette illustrations for theater reportage in the New York *Times*, the Selwyn Theatre's program cover and page designs, and graphics for such acclaimed plays as *Tea for Three* (1918) and *Listen Lester* (1919). Conway's lively, colorful billboards and posters attracted a spectator following. These posters promoted such seminal musical comedy productions as *Oh, Lady! Lady!!* (1918), which was ordered by F. Ray Comstock and the Princess Theatre team of Jerome Kern, Guy Bolton, and P. G. Wodehouse, who are credited with defining the American musical comedy. Conway's professional aspirations materialized in 1920 when she was hired to create a total design concept for the stage. She coordinated the visual images through costuming and graphics for Alice Duer Miller's *The Charm School*, directed by Robert Milton with music by Jerome Kern. Recognizing the artist's multifaceted talent, and capturing the essence of her public image, *Vanity Fair* labeled Conway "the soul of versatility."

Conway married in 1920 and moved to Europe because of her husband's business ventures. Her European period was distinguished by magazine cover and color illustration and consumer advertising art as well as costume design and poster art for theater, cabaret, and film. She advanced her career in London and Paris, in spite of six years of inconvenient moves back and forth across the English Channel due to Ozias's jobs. These frequent relocations added stress to her professional life. From 1923 to 1931, when film work eclipsed print and stage orders, Conway illustrated for the "Great Eight" magazine consortium in London. Championed by editor Peter Edward Huskinson, she produced scores of illustrations and original fashion-design pages, especially for *The Tatler* and *Eve: The Lady's Pictorial*, which featured more than thirty of her color covers. British advertising clients included the department stores of Harrods, Debenham and Freebody, and Selfridges. In her Paris studio, Conway received the prestigious

Gordon Conway's painting for cover of Eve *magazine, August 8, 1928. Watercolor and ink on paper. Gordon Conway Collection, Theatre Arts Collection, HRHRC, University of Texas at Austin. Conway, a costume designer and fashion illustrator, is remembered best for her depiction of independent "new women."*

job of interpreting various Parisian couture collections and offering her original designs for *La Donna*, an Italian women's magazine in Milan.

Between 1922 and 1928 she produced such cabaret art as her coordinated concept for costumes, sets, and graphics for the Club Daunou *Midnight Follies* in Paris, and occasional designs for the Casino de Paris. On the forefront of the London cabaret craze, she created costumes and graphics for most editions of Carl Hyson's *Midnight Follies* at London's Hotel Metropole and other venues. As the major designer for British cabaret legend Percy Athos, Conway made some of her most exotic and erotic costumes and sparkling graphic designs as part of her unified design scheme for his *New Princes' Frivolities*.

London theater commissions expanded between 1921 and 1931 with stage producers Charles B. Cochran, Dion Titheradge, Bertie A. Meyer, Albert de Courville, and such transatlantic talent as Guy Bolton and P. G. Wodehouse, and for megastars the Dolly Sisters. She costumed mid-1920s Broadway musical productions in London such as George and Ira Gershwin's *Tip-Toes* and Rodgers and Hart's *Peggy-Ann*, as well as the 1924 all-British musical *Patricia* and *Wonder Bar* in 1930. These four popular shows, among others, starred Dorothy Dickson, who was at the time the toast of West End musical comedy. After the ambitious 1930 *Charlot's Masquerade*, featuring scene sets and elegant costumes, Conway's last noteworthy stage production was the 1934 *Why Not To-night?*, choreographed by the young Agnes de Mille. These shows drew rave reviews for her promotional graphics and striking costume ensembles.

In 1927, during major print-media and stage offerings in London, where she and her mother now lived, Conway began free-lance silent-film work for *Confetti*, directed by Graham Cutts. Cutts joined with directors Victor Saville, Walter Forde, and Maurice Elvey, writer Douglas Furber, cameraman Roy Overbaugh, publicist W. J. "Bill" O'Bryen, and production-manager Chandos Balcon, in encouraging Conway's ambitions beyond costuming, in such areas as art direction, lighting, casting, and marketing. Her futuristic costuming for *High Treason* won acclaim in 1929, the same year that Cutts hired her for another hit, *The Return of the Rat*. He told the press that "dresses worn by British film actresses have often been criticized by cinemagoers . . . [so he] determined that this reproach shall not be levelled against his cast." A longtime advocate of "better-dressed British films," Conway added: "I hope to see every studio with its own designer and dressmaking staff, as they have in Hollywood."

Until 1934, when illness limited her commissions to print and stage art, other Conway movie collaborators included Tom Walls, Tim Whelan, Basil Dean, and the young Michael Powell. In addition to Dorothy Dickson, Dickson's daughter Dorothy Hyson, and Jessie Matthews, other noted film and stage stars she dressed included Cicely Courtneidge, Edna Best, Heather Thatcher, Annette Benson, and Evelyn Laye, as well as stars who later moved to Hollywood—Benita Hume, Madeleine Carroll, Wendy Barrie, and Anne Grey. Conway also was heralded for costuming such early-1930s British film classics as *Sunshine Susie, The Faithful Heart, Jack's the Boy, Love on Wheels, Rome Express, The Good Companions, Waltz Time, It's a Boy, The Ghoul, I Was A Spy, The Fire Raisers, A Cuckoo in the Nest, Friday the 13th, Aunt Sally, The Constant Nymph*, and *Red Ensign*.

Conway's early successes were for Gainsborough studios, a part of the newly reorganized Gaumont-British Picture Corporation, which contracted and elevated her to executive "Dress Designer." Determined to compete with Hollywood's global domination, the company pushed hard to increase production that included Conway's remarkable record of twelve feature films released in 1932, followed by nineteen in 1933. She was the only woman member of the hardworking executive team, headed by British-film pioneer and producer Michael Balcon. She worked ten-hour days, seven days a week, on a hectic schedule with debilitating deadlines and delays, on a meager budget, and in inadequate facilities that caused her to move her design studio and fitting area into her Bryanston Court flat. In this grinding atmosphere, she took full responsibility for her mother and their active social life. The bright spots in her professional life were close relationships with friends and colleagues, especially her tiny but talented and dedicated staff—including the young Margaret Furse—along with artisans at the London stores executing her designs. Because of Conway's vision and flair for marketing, the already demanding design and management job mushroomed to include media relations and promotional schemes to increase female audiences that yearned to emulate the new roles of professional women on the screen. Press coverage likewise singled out Conway herself as an example for aspiring professional women. Typical headlines proclaimed that she was "A Woman Prophet Of Film Fashion [in the] New Post In British Films," and one of the "Film Stars who Never Act."

Gordon Conway had the distinction of serving as the head of the first autonomous wardrobe department in the history of British film, and one of the rare female film-production executives in the world at that time. Her professional rewards, however, came at a high price, for she was like contemporaneous Hollywood image-makers who had brilliant but limited film careers due to stress and ill health. Even with big Hollywood salaries and lavish studio ateliers, famed designers like Texas-born Travis Banton[qv] suffered from deeply felt clashes of taste with actresses and management, and from the pressure to compromise aesthetic judgment and produce showy, extravagant, and commercial images at a maddening pace. Conway agreed with most film-design pioneers that costuming was a device to delineate a character's role on the screen, as well as a screen-viewer's guide to women's dress. Such designers' efforts should be viewed in historical perspective: an Academy Award for costume art was not established until 1948.

Throughout her career Gordon Conway worked long, arduous hours to become a respected and highly paid illustrator and costume designer. This was a rare accomplishment for a woman in these competitive fields not known for exceptional pay. After financial reversals due to the Great Depression,qv she doubled her efforts as a shrewd financial manager and increased commissions to maintain the sophisticated lifestyle she shared with her mother. However, her high-profile, demanding career led to ill health that forced her into early retirement in 1937, at forty-three years of age. Her return to New York also was occasioned by events leading to World War II.qv Conway lived the last two decades of her life at Mount Sion in Caroline County, Virginia, an eighteenth-century property inherited from her father's family. She earned a modest living by managing the place and became a pioneer in historic preservation by restoring the house and protecting the land and neighboring landmarks from a military-base expansion. She died on June 9, 1956, after years of painful malignancies. She is buried alongside her parents and maternal grandmother in the Oakland Cemetery in Dallas.

Credited early in her career as a major image-maker, Conway captured the essence of a popular type of woman that emerged during World War I in urban areas and consumer centers on both sides of the Atlantic. Her images portrayed tall, sleek, svelte, agile, sophisticated, independent, and self-assured women like Conway herself, who was the quintessential New Woman extoled in upscale publications, consumer advertisements, and female roles showcased in musical-comedy, cabaret, and motion-picture productions. Conway's New Women are young, red-headed females of two kinds: the whimsical, playful, supple imp, and the alluring, sensual, graceful cosmopolite. Her images both reflected and shaped the aspirations of millions of women yearning for economic, political, physical, sexual, social, and cultural freedom before and after legislation awarding suffrage and property rights to women in the United States and Great Britain. Gordon Conway's drawings feature striking, streamlined, and sleek lines that highlight uncluttered forms in an asymmetrical balance enlivened by bold, vivid, and flat color combinations. Even her early Art Nouveau-inspired drawings from the mid-teens feature controlled curvilinear and organic lines, before graduating into her signature geometric, rectilinear, and austere style. In addition to vibrant colors, another strength of Conway's art is the presentation of motion by her figures. The interplay of shapes displays a disciplined and stylized expression of compressed power and energy. In 1928 she explained the central focus of her style: "My experience...has served to strengthen my conviction that the most telling and striking effects are usually secured by carefully studied simplicity." Articles by Gordon Conway include "Fashions from the Films," *Picture Show*, April 28, 1928; "Dressing the Talkies," *The Film Weekly*, September 2, 1929; and "Frocks for Films," *The Bioscope British Film Number*, 1929. Gordon Conway's art recalls the spirit of an age. Her New-Woman images capture the essence of the Jazz Age, as well as a popular feminine look defined by a sensual but naive charm. Both her life and work reflect the era between the world wars, which honored vitality, experimentation, light-hearted rebellion, exuberance, optimism, hope, and most of all, possibilities.

BIBLIOGRAPHY: Martha Banta, *Imaging American Women: Idea and Ideals in Cultural History* (New York: Columbia University Press, 1987). Elizabeth Leese, *Costume Design in the Movies* (Bembridge, Isle of Wight: BCW, 1976). Bobbi Owen, *Costume Design on Broadway: Designers and Their Credits, 1915–1985* (New York: Greenwood Press, 1987). Susan Perez Prichard, *Film Costume: An Annotated Bibliography* (Metuchen, New Jersey: Scarecrow Press, 1981). David Schaff, "Gordon Conway," *Horizon*, May 1980. David Schaff, "That Red Head Gal": Fashions and Designs of Gordon Conway, 1916–1936 (Washington: American Institute of Architects Foundation, 1980).

Raye Virginia Allen

CONWAY, TEXAS. Conway, on Interstate Highway 40 in southern Carson County, traces its beginnings to 1892, when the Lone Star School, said to be the first rural school that endured in the Panhandle, was established for the children of area ranchers and homesteaders. A post office opened in the area in 1903. Perhaps inspired by the previous arrival of the Chicago, Rock Island and Gulf Railway, J. D. Delzell and P. H. Fisher platted a town, which they named in honor of former county commissioner H. B. Conway in 1905. The one-room schoolhouse was subsequently moved there. Edward S. Carr opened a mercantile store in 1907 and assumed the duties of postmaster. A railroad depot, a grocery store, and a blacksmith shop were soon added, and a steam-operated threshing machine served area wheat farmers. An interdenominational community church was erected in 1912. During the 1920s the town formed a community club and began an annual community fair. In 1943 the Conway school district was merged with that of Panhandle. The old brick school building was subsequently used as a community center. From a low of twenty-five persons in 1925, the town reached an estimated population of 125 in 1939. In 1969 it had 175 residents, but by 1970 it reported a population of fifty, two grain elevators, four service stations, three cafes, and a general store. The post office was discontinued by 1976, and some of these businesses have since closed. The population was still listed as fifty in 1990.

BIBLIOGRAPHY: Jo Stewart Randel, ed., *A Time to Purpose: A Chronicle of Carson County* (4 vols., Hereford, Texas: Pioneer, 1966–72).

H. Allen Anderson

COOK, ABNER HUGH (1814–1884). Abner Cook, carpenter, architect, and contractor, was born near Salisbury, North Carolina, on March 15, 1814, the son of William and Susanna (Hill) Cook. He seems to have served an apprenticeship at Salisbury under the tutelage of Samuel Lemly, a master builder and gentleman farmer. Lemly built a bridge over the South Yadkin River (1824–25) to the designs of Ithiel Town and built the First Presbyterian Church, Salisbury (1826), a brick temple-form structure with freestanding portico in the Roman Ionic manner. In 1835, at age twenty-one, Cook moved to Macon, Georgia, where he may have found work on the construction crew for two imposing Greek Revival buildings, the Georgia Female College and the Monroe Railroad and Banking Company, both built to the designs of Elam Alexander. When the panic of 1837 brought building to a halt, Cook moved to Nashville, Tennessee. He seems to have taken careful note of the Hermitage, Andrew Jackson's country place, and of other recent Greek Revival work, but there was little work to be had in Nashville, and he moved to Texas in 1839.

Cook arrived in Texas just as the fledgling republic was beginning the construction of a new capital city on the western frontier, to be called Austin. By the summer of 1839 Cook was there and in partnership with a New York carpenter, Heman Ward. They did little work on the public buildings, but instead occupied themselves with private commissions for houses and furniture. Ward soon drifted back to the Gulf Coast, but Cook put down roots in the community. In October 1839 he and five others founded the first Presbyterian church in Austin, indeed, the first church in Austin. Cook later built the congregation's first log church with his own hands. On September 15, 1842, he married a widow, Mrs. Eliza T. Logan, with whom he had four sons. During the trying days when the capital was removed from Austin, little building was done, and for two years Cook was a partner of Jacob Higgins in the ownership of a lumbermill in Bastrop.

In 1847, a year after Texas entered the Union, Cook built a large residence for Thomas William Ward,qv veteran of the Texas Revolution,qv commissioner of the General Land Office,qv and one of the wealthiest men in Austin. Ward's was a two-story frame house with a single-story portico, late Federal in style and not unlike the Lewis Utzman House in Salisbury, built between 1814 and 1819, possibly by Cook's mentor Samuel Lemly. Several years later Cook built a single-story brick house in the Federal style for his friend Dr. William Copeland Philips[qv] (1854), and a two-story frame house in the same style for another friend, Dr. Samuel G. Haynie.[qv] Cook soon bought the latter house and lived in it for the rest of his life. From summer 1848 until early 1850 he was at Huntsville, supervising the construction of the Texas State Penitentiary.[qv] Back in Austin Cook was contractor for woodwork on the 1852 state Capitol, built to the designs of his partner and fellow carpenter John Brandon, who seems to have had no experience in the planning of large public buildings.

Early in the 1850s Cook built his own brick kiln on the banks of Shoal Creek and became part owner of another lumber mill near Bastrop, thus assuring his building projects of a dependable and economical supply of building materials. About the same time he seems to have purchased Minard Lafever's *The Beauties of Modern Architecture* (1835), a volume that deeply influenced Cook's subsequent projects. The earliest work to show the change was a farmhouse for William S. Hotchkiss, later owned by Beriah Graham,[qv] which, though a single story, is prefaced by a box-columned portico with a weighty entablature. The Hotchkiss-Graham House also seems to have been the first of Cook's houses to feature an X-and-stick balustrade, a Federal motif that became one of Cook's trademarks. Next was a house for John Milton Swisher,[qv] which was two stories, brick, with two sets of paired columns, Greek Ionic in detail and proportion. In 1854 Cook began three great brick houses with Greek Ionic porticoes stretching across their front. These were houses for State Treasurer James H. Raymond[qv] and State Comptroller James B. Shaw,[qv] and the Governor's Mansion.[qv] The building committee for the mansion consisted of Raymond, Shaw, and Governor Elisha M. Pease,[qv] who was the first occupant of the mansion and who later bought Shaw's place and named it Woodlawn Mansion.[qv] In 1856–57 Cook switched to the Greek Doric for houses for Washington L. Hill and Mary and Reuben Runner, now known as the Neill-Cochran House and Westhill, respectively. For the door frames, window frames, and mantels of these houses Cook designed simplified, abstracted versions of the shouldered architraves illustrated in Lafever's book.

In the era of Reconstruction,[qv] professionally trained architects began to move to Austin, and Cook began to leave design to the architects and to concentrate on construction. He was contractor for the North Building at the State Lunatic Asylum (1874–75), for the First National Bank Building (also known as Cook's Corner) at Sixth and Congress (1875–76), and three stores in a business block, 912, 914, and 916 Congress (1875–76), all built to the Victorian designs of architect Jacob Larmour.[qv] Cook's largest residential project of the postwar era was a two-story Italianate house for cattle baron Seth Mabry at Twelfth and Lavaca (1876). Cook's last great work was the construction of the west wing of the main building of the newly founded University of Texas. This High Victorian Gothic building, designed by Frederik E. Ruffini,[qv] was dedicated in September 1883, just a few months before Cook's death. Like many of Cook's works, Old Main has been demolished, but most of his Greek Revival houses of the 1850s remain, a testament to his skill as a master builder.

Cook was the most significant designer of Greek Revival buildings in antebellum Texas.[qv] Such works as the Pease-Shivers House (Woodlawn), the Governor's Mansion, and the Neill-Cochran House combined a monumentality of form and a sophistication of detail rarely seen in Texas since the days of the Franciscans.[qv] He died on February 22, 1884, in Austin and was buried in Oakwood Cemetery.

BIBLIOGRAPHY: Kenneth Hafertepe, *Abner Cook: Master Builder on the Texas Frontier* (Austin: Texas State Historical Association, 1992). Hank Todd Smith, ed., *Austin, Its Architects and Architecture* (Austin Chapter, American Institute of Architects, 1986). Vertical Files, Barker Texas History Center, University of Texas at Austin. Roxanne Williamson, *Austin, Texas: An American Architectural History* (San Antonio: Trinity University Press, 1973).
Kenneth Hafertepe

COOK, FREDERICK ALBERT (1865–1940). Frederick Albert Cook, son of Dr. Theodore A. and Magdalena Koch, was born at Callicoon Depot, New York, on June 10, 1865. He successively became a physician, polar explorer, and Texas oil promoter. He attended Columbia and New York universities and received his M.D. in 1890 from the latter. In 1899 he married Libby Forbes, who died in childbirth in 1890. On June 10, 1902, he married Marie Fidele Hunt; they had one daughter and were divorced in 1923. Cook served as a surgeon with the Arctic expedition of Robert E. Peary in 1891–92 and the Belgian Antarctic expedition in 1897–99. He led expeditions to Mount McKinley between 1903 and 1906 and achieved a modest reputation as an explorer, despite charges, subsequently well documented, that his claim to the first ascent of Mount McKinley in 1906 was fraudulent.

Cook started one of the most publicized controversies in the early part of the century after his 1907–09 "race" to the North Pole against Peary. After returning to claim he had reached the pole on April 21, 1908, besting Peary's achievement by a year, Cook was at first acclaimed, then questioned when Peary and others charged him with fakery. Most observers eventually concurred with the University of Copenhagen's finding that Cook's evidence did not substantiate his claims. Cook disappeared from public view for a year, then emerged to write and lecture in defense of his record. As World War I[qv] neared, however, the number of speaking engagements offered to him dwindled. In 1917 Frank G. Curtis, president of New York Oil Company, organized the Cook Oil Company and made Cook its president. Cook resigned this position in 1918 to work as a geologist in the Texas oilfields. In 1922 he organized the Petroleum Producers Association at Fort Worth; it consolidated several financially weak companies and sold stock to subsidize field operations. Cook attracted investors through intense promotional campaigns utilizing the writing and salesmanship of S. E. J. Cox and H. O. Stephens. In 1923 his extravagant assurances of future oil production caught the attention of journalist Don H. Biggers[qv] and federal district attorneys investigating widespread reports of fraud committed by the Petroleum Producers Association and other oil-lease promoters. A federal grand jury at Fort Worth indicted 400 individuals after hearing evidence for seven months.

The trial, at Fort Worth, of Cook and other PPA officers began on October 16, 1923. Defense attorneys included former United States senator Joseph W. Bailey[qv] and William (Wild Bill) McLean, Jr. A carefully presented case by the prosecution, including 283 witnesses, convinced jurors that Cook, Cox, and others had committed fraud by dispersing stock-sales revenues as dividends, claiming income from nonproducing wells, and otherwise misrepresenting the company's position. Cook's stiff sentence—fourteen years, nine months, and a $12,000 fine—expressed the court's disdain for him and, perhaps, for the insulting, unscrupulous tactics of Bailey and the drunkenness of several other defense attorneys. Cook was paroled from Leavenworth in 1930 and pardoned by President Franklin Roosevelt in 1940 as an act of mercy for a dying man. Cook died in New Rochelle, New York, on August 5, 1940, and was buried there.

BIBLIOGRAPHY: Hugh Eames, *Winner Lose All: Dr. Cook and the Theft of the North Pole* (Boston: Little, Brown, 1973). Andrew A. Freeman, *The Case for Doctor Cook* (New York: Coward-McCann, 1961).
William R. Hunt

COOK, GUSTAVE (1835–1897). Gustave Cook (Cooke), lawyer and judge, son of Nathaniel and Harriet Anthony (Herbert) Cook, was born in Lowndes County, Alabama, on July 3, 1835. After traveling to

Texas alone in 1850, he found work as a clerk in a drugstore. During this time he educated himself and began to study law. Judge John B. Jones^{qv} later directed his studies, and in 1855 Cook was admitted to the bar. On July 13, 1853, he married Eliza Jones; they had four children. Cook was clerk of the district court of Fort Bend County and from 1856 to 1858 served as county judge. He favored secession.^{qv} In 1861 he enlisted as a private in the Eighth Confederate Cavalry,^{qv} Terry's Texas Rangers. He served for the duration of the war and saw action in numerous engagements, including Shiloh, Murfreesboro, and Chickamauga. He received six or seven wounds during the war and reached the rank of colonel.

Cook moved to Houston in 1870 to practice law and was elected to the Thirteenth Legislature in 1872. He was appointed judge of the criminal court for the district comprising Galveston and Harris counties in 1874 and held the position until he resigned on October 1, 1888. He was a delegate from Texas to the Philadelphia Peace Convention in 1866 and a delegate in 1876 to the Democratic state convention at Galveston, where he opposed endorsing the constitution submitted to the legislature. In 1887, as an antiprohibitionist, he canvassed a great portion of the state, and in 1888 he helped to campaign for the reelection of Roger Q. Mills^{qv} to Congress. In 1890 Cook ran in the convention for the Democratic nomination for governor but was defeated by James S. Hogg.^{qv} In 1892 he moved to San Marcos for his health. He died there in 1897.

BIBLIOGRAPHY: Lewis E. Daniell, *Types of Successful Men in Texas* (Austin: Von Boeckmann, 1890). Norman Kittrell, *Governors Who Have Been and Other Public Men of Texas* (Houston: Dealy-Adey-Elgin, 1921). *Memorial and Genealogical Record of Southwest Texas* (Chicago: Goodspeed, 1894; rpt., Easley, South Carolina: Southern Historical Press, 1978). Rupert N. Richardson, *Texas: The Lone Star State* (New York: Prentice-Hall, 1943; 4th ed., with Ernest Wallace and Adrian N. Anderson, Englewood Cliffs, New Jersey: Prentice-Hall, 1981). William S. Speer and John H. Brown, eds., *Encyclopedia of the New West* (Marshall, Texas: United States Biographical Publishing, 1881; rpt., Easley, South Carolina: Southern Historical Press, 1978).

COOK, JAMES (1797–?). James Cook, a partner with William B. DeWees^{qv} as one of Stephen F. Austin's^{qv} Old Three Hundred^{qv} families, was born in Bowling Green, Kentucky, in 1797 and was probably in Texas by 1820. On August 3, 1824, he and DeWees received title to a sitio^{qv} of land now in Colorado County. Cook was possibly the J. Cook who was elected third sergeant of the San Felipe militia on July 10, 1824, and also possibly the James Cook who voted in the alcalde^{qv} election held at Rawson Alley's^{qv} house in January 1825. In the census of 1826 he was listed as a single farmer and stock raiser aged between twenty-five and forty, the partner of James McNair.^{qv}

By 1829 a James Cook was among the soldiers stationed at a small stockade built in 1828 to protect incoming colonists and located at the site of future Matagorda; in 1831 this Cook was awarded a Matagorda town lot for his work against the Indians. It was probably the Austin colonist James Cook, brother of Hamilton L. Cook, who married the widow Maria (sometimes given as Mariah) Cummins Ross. Mrs. Ross owned property known as Cedar Island on Bay Prairie, northeast of the site of present Bay City in Matagorda County. The couple had two children. By April 1836 Cook was serving as postmaster at Cedar Island, later known as Cook's Island, on the mail route between San Felipe and Matagorda. Though records of the Daughters of the Republic of Texas^{qv} indicate that Austin colonist James Cook served in the army during the Texas Revolution,^{qv} this may actually have been James R. Cooke,^{qv} who did not arrive in Texas until 1834. A local history, citing probate records, indicates that both James and Maria Cook had died by the end of 1836, but Republic of Texas postal records suggest that Cook served as postmaster as late as 1839.

BIBLIOGRAPHY: Eugene C. Barker, ed., *The Austin Papers* (3 vols., Washington: GPO, 1924–28). Lester G. Bugbee, "The Old Three Hundred: A List of Settlers in Austin's First Colony," *Quarterly of the Texas State Historical Association* 1 (October 1897). Daughters of the Republic of Texas, *Founders and Patriots of the Republic of Texas* (Austin, 1963–). James M. Day, comp., *Post Office Papers of the Republic of Texas* (2 vols., Austin: Texas State Library, 1966–67). Matagorda County Historical Commission, *Historic Matagorda County* (3 vols., Houston: Armstrong, 1986).

Rachel Jenkins

COOK, JIM (1861–1940). Jim Cook, cattleman and raconteur, son of Mart Cook, was born on February 25, 1861, in Washington County, Arkansas. When the Civil War^{qv} broke out, Mart enlisted in the Confederate Army and served as a captain under Gen. Sterling Price. Afterward he moved to Texas, rounded up cattle, and sought out a market in Kansas. Jim and his brother Al grew up in the saddle. In 1866 the Cooks were perhaps among the first to drive cattle north to Honeywell, Kansas. The boys' mother died later that year, and their father was reportedly killed by Indians in 1867. Jim and Al went to live with an uncle and cousin who were also ranchers. Until 1876 Jim remained at his uncle's ranch; he was then put in charge of a herd of 1,000 steers to be trailed north to Kansas and fattened on the grasslands there. While on the trail, according to his earliest account, some of Cook's fellow cowboys started calling him Jim Lane and Kid Boss. The nicknames stuck with him for several years. In the fall of 1876 Cook and a partner started their own ranch on the South Fork of the Llano River in Kimball County. Cook remained there until 1880, when he sold his interest.

Both Jim and Al, who sometimes went by the alias of Taylor Williams, worked for O. J. Wiren, foreman of the Quitaque Ranch.^{qv} In 1881, when the Quitaque was sold to Charles Goodnight^{qv} and Wiren purchased the Two Circle Bar on the upper Brazos from Jesse Hitson, the Cooks stayed with Wiren. Indeed, Jim "Lane," who was made wagon boss, was said to have owned an interest in the Two Circle Bar, although the records show no such evidence. He reportedly ran his own herd at the ranch and won notoriety among the cowboys as a "hard man to work for and inconsiderate of his men." However, he remained with Wiren five years before leaving "for reasons of my own," as he later stated. At that time Cook reportedly "put a notice in the *Fisher County Call* refusing to answer to Lane any more to anyone."

In 1888 he was hired by the Capitol Freehold Company as foreman for the XIT Ranch's^{qv} Escarbada Division. Aggressive and overbearing and often carrying a pair of six-shooters, Cook was nearly always at odds with cow thieves from "across the line" and occasionally with his own men. When he met a visiting young lady from Kansas City at La Plata, he fell in love with her, and according to several old cowboys, was instrumental in getting the Escarbada headquarters declared a post office so that letters from his lady would be delivered directly to him. Eventually they were married.

When Deaf Smith County was organized on October 3, 1890, Cook was elected its first sheriff, but he was ousted a year later because of his needless killing of a cowboy. In later years he boasted that since La Plata had no cemetery he had to "kill a man to start one." Whether or not this was true, he was finally acquitted after judicial wrangling and a change of venue to Amarillo. Possibly to escape the effects of the scandal, Cook and his wife turned up in South Dakota for a short time and then homesteaded near Monument, New Mexico. They became the parents of a daughter, whom Cook managed to raise after his wife died. His brother, Al, eventually made his home in Las Cruces.

Beginning in the early 1900s, Jim Cook traveled throughout the western United States and Canada, prospecting and working as a wilderness-park guide in his attempt to find or re-create the way of life he had known during the early years of the Cattle Kingdom. In 1912 he published a booklet entitled *The Canadian Northwest as It Is Today*, in which he described his experiences on a pack trip into the Canadian wilds in 1910–11. Cook's eccentricities increased in the

1920s when he proposed to open a central detective agency in Austin to recover stolen cattle, an information bureau to locate choice homesteads, and a home for aged cowboys. As he recounted his early adventures to enthralled listeners, facts became submerged in plausible fantasy. He made his later travels in a battered Model T with his daughter and two granddaughters.

While Cook was living in Albuquerque during the 1930s, T. M. Pearce of the University of New Mexico conducted a series of interviews with him for the New Mexico Folklore Society. These formed the basis for the book *Lane of the Llano* (1936). In this work Cook related his alleged birth in Llano County in 1858, his capture by Comanches as a boy, his wanderings with the tribe and marriage to the chief's daughter White Swan, his role as a scout in Ranald S. Mackenzie's qv Palo Duro campaign, his alleged involvement with John S. Chisum qv and Billy the Kid (*see* MCCARTY, HENRY), and the death of White Swan from a rattlesnake bite, all mixed with convincing descriptions of the arid land, with its flora and fauna and harsh realities. One contemporary called the book "a bunch of the worst lies that would make Bill Burns, Zane Grey, and John Cook green with envy," and J. Evetts Haley admitted that an accurate biography of Cook could never be written as long as the man failed to distinguish between truth and fiction. However, for the remainder of his life, Jim Cook was lionized by college students, faculty, and others who saw him as a living symbol of the vanished frontier. He died in January 1940 and was buried in the Oddfellows Cemetery in Goldthwaite.

BIBLIOGRAPHY: J. Evetts Haley, *The XIT Ranch of Texas and the Early Days of the Llano Estacado* (Chicago: Lakeside, 1929; rpts., Norman: University of Oklahoma Press, 1953, 1967). *Deaf Smith County: The Land and Its People* (Hereford, Texas: Deaf Smith County Historical Society, 1982).   H. Allen Anderson

COOK, JOHN R. (1844–1917). John R. Cook, soldier, hunter, and author, noted for his narrative of buffalo hunting qv in the Panhandle, qv was born at Mount Gilead, Ohio, on December 19, 1844. In 1857 he moved with his parents to Lawrence, Kansas, thence to Peru, Indiana, where the family remained until 1861. Cook joined Company E, Twelfth Kansas Infantry, at Lawrence, Kansas, on September 2, 1862, and, after defending the Kansas border against guerrillas and operating in the Arkansas region, he was mustered out of the service at Little Rock, Arkansas, on June 30, 1865. He located 160 acres in Labette County, Kansas, in 1867 and became the township constable. In 1873 he traveled to Denison, Texas; later the same year he returned to Kansas. In the spring and summer of 1874 he prospected around Santa Fe, New Mexico; in the fall he went to the Texas Panhandle, where he arrived for the first big year of buffalo hunting. He remained in Texas until 1879 and was one of the organizers of Wheeler County. He returned to Kansas, became a temperance orator, met and married Alice Victoria Maddux in 1883, and moved to the Dakota Territory. In 1892 he moved to Eugene, Oregon, in the Cascade Mountains; there he wrote *The Border and the Buffalo* (1907). In 1906 he returned to Kansas, where he died on March 25, 1917. He was buried in the Kansas Soldier's Home at Fort Dodge, Kansas.

BIBLIOGRAPHY: John R. Cook, *The Border And The Buffalo: An Untold Story Of The Southwest Plains* (Topeka, Kansas: Crane, 1907; Rpt., New York: Citadel Press, 1967).

COOK BRANCH. Cook Branch, also known as Cook Creek, rises just north of Grounds in east central Houston County (at 31°25′ N, 95°23′ W) and runs northeast for five miles to its mouth on San Pedro Creek, two miles east of Refuge (at 31°30′ N, 95°22′ W). The surrounding flat terrain is surfaced by clay and sandy loam that supports water-tolerant hardwoods, conifers, and grasses.

COOKE, EDWARD F. (1875–1931). Edward F. Cooke, clinical pathologist, was born on August 24, 1875, in Oldham, Lancashire, England, the eldest of the five children of H. C. and Elizabeth Ann (Fenton) Cooke. The family moved to Council Bluffs, Iowa, in 1890 and to Galveston, Texas, the following year. After attending Ball High School, Cooke went to work as an office boy for a shipping firm. In 1894 he entered the University of Texas Medical Branch, where he obtained his M.D. in 1897. In 1898, after completing most of a year's internship at St. Mary's Infirmary (*see* ST. MARY'S HOSPITAL) in Galveston, Cooke left to begin contract practice at a Montgomery County sawmill. In 1900 he moved to Ellis County and set up practice, first in Waxahachie and subsequently in Forreston. He moved to Houston in 1907 and limited his practice to clinical pathology two years later. He was chairman of pathology, histology, and bacteriology at the Texas Dental College and pathologist at Methodist and Jefferson Davis hospitals and at St. Joseph's Infirmary. He served as a captain in the medical corps during World War I; qv after the war he maintained his association with the military through the Medical Reserve Corps, in which he attained the rank of lieutenant colonel.

While still in Ellis County, Cooke was appointed chairman of the Committee on Public Health and Legislation for the county medical society and in that capacity worked to secure enforcement of laws regulating medical practice. After transferring his membership to the Harris County Medical Society in 1907, he served as secretary (1908–10), president (1910), delegate to the state association (1912–14), and member of the Council on Medical Defense (1914–16). During this same period he served as secretary (1907–13) and president (1913–14) of the Southern Texas District Medical Society. He was also president of the Texas Pathology Society and was a charter member of the American Society of Clinical Pathologists (1922). Cooke married Pearl Florence McClusky of Galveston on June 10, 1899. They had four children. He died on January 8, 1931, in Houston after a brief illness. He was a Mason.

BIBLIOGRAPHY: Houston *Post*, January 9, 1931. *Texas State Journal of Medicine*, May 1931.   Patricia L. Jakobi

COOKE, FRANCIS JARVIS (1816–1903). Francis Jarvis Cooke, Texas revolutionary fighter and merchant, was born on July 13, 1816, in Beaufort, Carteret County, North Carolina, the son of Henry M. and Frances Barry (Buxton) Cooke. Mrs. Cooke died in February 1833. Henry Cooke, a successful merchant, shipper, and collector of customs, remarried the following January and soon departed for Texas with his new wife, Naomi, and with Francis and his six brothers and four sisters. On the journey Henry grew ill and died, on March 4, 1835, in Randolph, Tennessee. Naomi returned to North Carolina, but all eleven children continued to Texas, where they arrived on April 3, 1835. They originally settled in Matagorda County and planted crops, but were forced by a flood to flee. In Montgomery County they settled in a log cabin by a creek, but were again flooded out; this time they lost all they owned. They moved to higher land, were helped by neighbors, and started over again.

Francis and his brother Tom heard William B. Travis's qv plea for help from a courier and, with ten or twelve others from the area, joined Col. Albert C. Horton's qv company on its way to join James W. Fannin, Jr. qv The two brothers traveled to Victoria and there volunteered with seventeen others to transport a wagonload of lead and powder from Dimitt's Landing qv to the main army at Beeson's Ford. qv They were successful in this mission and fortunate to have volunteered for it, as most of the men who stayed at Victoria were killed. In the meantime, the rest of the Cooke family was fleeing in the Runaway Scrape; qv they eventually returned to their home after the war.

At Beeson's, Tom and Francis joined Capt. Robert J. Calder's qv company, in which Francis and his brother fought at the battle of San Jacinto. qv The night before the battle a friend in his company, Benjamin Brigham, asked someone to stand guard duty in his place, since he had been on duty the last two nights. Francis gave Brigham his bed for the night. Brigham was one of the first to be killed the next day in battle, and it is said that Mirabeau B. Lamar qv wrote his poem on the battle after viewing the body of Brigham and others. Francis Cooke continued to serve for a short time after the battle and served as one of Santa Anna's guards.

After the war he received 320 acres of land for his service from March 17 to June 20, 1836, and later 640 acres of land for his part at San Jacinto. In 1842 he enlisted again in the army for three months in Col. Joseph L. Bennett's qv regiment to take part in the campaign against Adrián Woll, qv though he did not join the Mier expedition. qv He served in the Texas Rangers qv for six weeks in 1843.

Cooke tried his skills as a merchant in both Houston and Brenham. While in Brenham, he fell ill and was nursed back to health by Mr. and Mrs. Hugh McIntyre, Sr. On December 28, 1845, he married their niece, Emily Stockton. He was involved as a partner in businesses in Brenham, Houston, Chappell Hill, and Hempstead before retiring to his farm near Hempstead. He and Emily had eleven children, one of whom grew up to be "Senator" Annie Cooke, an influential figure in Texas politics in the first half of the twentieth century. Cooke died on November 11, 1903, and was buried in Salem Cemetery, near Howth. He was a member of Holland Masonic Lodge No. 1 of Houston and of the Texas Veterans Association.qv Emily died on September 4, 1908. In 1936 the state had a Texas Centennial qv monument placed at their graves, probably under the influence of Annie Cooke.

BIBLIOGRAPHY: F. J. Cooke, "Brigham and I," *Educational Free Press*, March 1902. J. Marvin Hunter, Sr., "Frank J. Cooke Was at the Battle of San Jacinto," *Frontier Times*, February 1951. Louis Wiltz Kemp Papers, Barker Texas History Center, University of Texas at Austin. Vertical Files, Barker Texas History Center, University of Texas at Austin.
Walter F. Pilcher

COOKE, JAMES RUSSELL (1812–1843). James Russell Cooke (Cook), soldier, was born on May 8, 1812, in Clinton, Georgia, the son of John and Mary Ellen (Hampton) Cooke. The family moved to Alabama Territory in 1817. By 1835 Cooke had moved to Washington County, Texas. On December 25, 1835, he joined Capt. Peyton S. Wyatt's qv company of Huntsville (Alabama) Volunteers, but was on furlough on February 29, 1836, a fact that no doubt saved him from sharing the fate of his comrades at the Goliad Massacre.qv He was elected first lieutenant of Capt. Henry Wax Karnes's qv cavalry company and participated in the battle of San Jacinto.qv From June 5 through November 5, 1836, he served as acting captain of the company.

On December 19, 1837, Cooke married Sarah Ann Lott. They raised two sons on Doe Run Creek near Washington, Washington County, Texas. Upon receiving a commission from Sam Houston qv on August 10, 1842, Cooke "cheerfully commenced recruiting volunteers" in Washington County for the Somervell expedition.qv With the organization of the volunteers at San Antonio, Cooke was first appointed inspector general and mustering officer of Alexander Somervell's qv Army of the South West and then, on November 10, was elected colonel of the First Regiment of the Second Brigade. He played a conspicuous role in the capture of Laredo and Guerrero, but when Somervell suggested that the expedition be broken up and return to San Antonio, Cooke is said to have replied, "we cannot break *up* this expedition, the men will mutinize, they are determined to cross the Rio Grande and fight the enemy, but my advice is to fling every impediment in its way and let it break itself up." As Somervell's authority over his men deteriorated, Cooke resigned his command. Nevertheless, he remained in a position of some authority and was largely responsible for returning the rump of Somervell's army to San Antonio intact, while the second half of the command remained on the Rio Grande under William S. Fisher qv preparing for the disastrous Mier expedition.qv

According to the Clarksville *Northern Standard,*qv Cooke was killed in the streets of Washington by a man named Adkins, "with whom he had some difficulty." The *Telegraph and Texas Register*qv elaborated, stating that "in a drunken row" on March 31, 1843, Cooke "cut his friend Adkins, who in turn shot and killed Cook." Cooke's tombstone says he died on March 30. He was the uncle of Judge Gustave Cook,qv a colonel of the Eighth Texas Cavalry.qv

BIBLIOGRAPHY: Daughters of the Republic of Texas, *Muster Rolls of the Texas Revolution* (Austin, 1986). Sam Houston Dixon and Louis Wiltz Kemp, *The Heroes of San Jacinto* (Houston: Anson Jones, 1932). *Memorial and Genealogical Record of Southwest Texas* (Chicago: Goodspeed, 1894; rpt., Easley, South Carolina: Southern Historical Press, 1978). Joseph Milton Nance, *Attack and Counterattack: The Texas-Mexican Frontier, 1842* (Austin: University of Texas Press, 1964). *Telegraph and Texas Register*, August 10, 1842. Gifford E. White, *1830 Citizens of Texas* (Austin: Eakin Press, 1983).
Thomas W. Cutrer

COOKE, JOHN (?–?). John Cooke was a partner of Isaac Hughes qv as one of Stephen F. Austin's qv Old Three Hundred qv families. The two received title to a league and a labor of land now in Harris County on August 10, 1824. The census of March 1826 classified Cooke as a farmer and stock raiser, a single man aged between twenty-five and forty. At one time he served as a surveyor for the Coahuila and Texas qv government. The ayuntamiento qv of San Felipe de Austin, meeting on December 15, 1830, to examine titles granted to settlers in Austin's first colony, ruled that Cooke and Hughes had abandoned the country in 1826 without improving their land and that the titles were null and void.

BIBLIOGRAPHY: Eugene C. Barker, ed., "Minutes of the Ayuntamiento of San Felipe de Austin, 1828–1832," 12 parts, *Southwestern Historical Quarterly* 21–24 (January 1918–October 1920). Lester G. Bugbee, "The Old Three Hundred: A List of Settlers in Austin's First Colony," *Quarterly of the Texas State Historical Association* 1 (October 1897). Virginia H. Taylor Houston, "Surveying in Texas," *Southwestern Historical Quarterly* 65 (October 1961). *Texas Gazette*, May 8, 1830.

COOKE, LOUIS P. (1811–1849). Louis P. Cooke, early Texas legislator, son of George W. and Jemina W. Cooke of Sharpsburgh, Bath County, Kentucky, was born in Tennessee in 1811. The was the oldest of three sons. He attended the United States Military Academy at West Point but did not graduate. In 1835 he joined a New York volunteer battalion under command of Edwin Morehouse.qv The battalion did not arrive in time for the battle of San Jacinto,qv but Cooke was elected lieutenant colonel in the Texas army in 1836. As a member of the Third Congress from Brazoria, he was an adherent of Mirabeau B. Lamar.qv He served as secretary of the navy under Lamar from May 1839 until December 1941 and was elected to the Sixth Congress from Travis County. Cooke introduced the Homestead Exemption Law and was a member of the committee that chose Austin for the capital. In company with John Nolan and George Barrett, Cooke was involved in a shooting scrape in downtown Austin with Capt. Mark B. Lewis.qv Nolan was killed, and a friend of Nolan accidentally shot and killed Alex Peyton, who tried to stop the affray. Lewis fled, but was killed later by Cooke and Barrett. Judge R. E. B. Baylor qv issued a warrant for Cooke and Barrett, charging them with Lewis's murder. Cooke retained James S. Mayfield qv to defend him, and the trial moved to Bastrop. The jury was deadlocked with all but one of twelve finding Cooke guilty. Cooke escaped in December 1843 before a second trial could be held and went to Corpus Christi, where he obtained employment as a brickmaker with John A. F. Gravis, a friend and fellow Lamar partisan. During the Comanche raid on Corpus

Christi 1844, Cooke was wounded with an arrow in the side of his head and lost an eye. When the Mexican War[qv] broke out he accompanied the United States Army under Gen. Zachary Taylor[qv] to the Rio Grande. He later built a house in Brownsville. He and his wife, Mary, died of cholera during the 1849 epidemic there, leaving four children.

BIBLIOGRAPHY: William S. Speer and John H. Brown, eds., *Encyclopedia of the New West* (Marshall, Texas: United States Biographical Publishing, 1881; rpt., Easley, South Carolina: Southern Historical Press, 1978). Texas House of Representatives, *Biographical Directory of the Texan Conventions and Congresses, 1832–1845* (Austin: Book Exchange, 1941). Homer S. Thrall, *A Pictorial History of Texas* (St. Louis: Thompson, 1879). A. E. Wilkinson, "Author of the Texas Homestead Exemption Law," *Southwestern Historical Quarterly* 20 (July 1916).

Frank Wagner

COOKE, REGINA TATUM (1902–1988). Regina Tatum Cooke, painter and journalist, was born on August 22, 1902, in Corsicana, Texas, the daughter of Reese and Frances Hunter Tatum. She grew up in Dalhart, where her father was a district judge; her mother, a painter and homemaker, died when Regina was a child. At age fifteen Regina accompanied her father on a visit to Taos, New Mexico. She graduated from Dalhart High School as salutatorian of her class, and subsequently attended Ward-Bellmont Junior College, a girls' school in her father's home state, Tennessee. After graduating with honors she studied under the Swedish artist Birger Sandzen at Bethany College in Lindsborg, Kansas. She also studied at Broadmoor Art Academy before receiving a bachelor's degree in art from Colorado College in Colorado Springs. She married and spent the next five years in Denver, where she bore a son and exhibited her work at the Denver Art Museum. After her divorce in 1930 she returned to Dalhart.

Regina Cooke won prizes for works exhibited at the Tri-State expositions held in Amarillo in 1931–32. In 1933 the Dust Bowl[qv] prompted her to move to Taos, which became her permanent home. There she studied with Walter Ufer for two years and was heavily influenced by his realistic depiction of colorful southwestern subjects. She worked in the Regionalist style popular at the time, painting landscapes featuring the Rockies of Colorado and the mountains of New Mexico and Texas. She also painted still lifes of arrangements that typically might include garden flowers, pottery, or Indian and Mexican art objects. Cooke received several commissions from the WPA. She painted a series of reconstructions of Southwestern missions, later published in *Mission Monuments of New Mexico* (1943); she also painted the landscape backgrounds for a series of dioramas now in the collection of the Museum of Fine Art in Santa Fe. During the war years she taught art in several schools in southern California.

Upon her return to Taos in 1948, Cooke began her career as chronicler of the arts at the Taos *Star*, where she was the society and arts editor. She subsequently worked at *El Crepúsculo de la Libertad* before she became arts editor at the Taos *News* in 1959. For years Cooke reported on art events in Taos, building up a vast reserve of knowledge on its art community. She was not just an observer, however, but a participant who helped to found the Taos Art Association in 1952 and served as its first secretary. She also started the Taos municipal schools' art collection in 1948 and helped to found the Taos Little Theater.

Cooke won more than 100 state and national newspaper awards for her articles. In 1969 she received the New Mexico Press Women's Woman of Achievement Award, and in 1987 the Taos Press Women established an award in her name to recognize women who have contributed most to the arts in New Mexico. Cooke continued to write a weekly column for the Taos *News* and submit occasional articles to *Southwest Art* after her retirement in 1971. She died on September 3, 1988. Her work is included in the collections of the Museum of New Mexico and the Museum of Fine Art, both in Santa Fe.

BIBLIOGRAPHY: Peter Haskins Falk, ed., *Who Was Who in American Art* (Madison, Connecticut: Sound View, 1985). Reginald Fisher and Edgar Hewitt, *Mission Monuments of New Mexico* (Albuquerque: University of New Mexico Press, 1943). Mary Carroll Nelson, *The Legendary Artists of Taos* (New York: Watson-Guptill, 1980). Taos *News*, September 8, 1988.

Kendall Curlee

COOKE, WILDS K. (1820–?). Wilds K. Cooke, physician and state legislator, was born in 1820, probably in Kentucky. He moved to Texas in 1840 and settled in Robertson County. He served as a representative in the Ninth Congress of the republic and in the First Texas Legislature and as a senator in the Third Legislature. Cooke practiced medicine near Springfield, Texas, in Limestone County. He is listed in the 1850 Census as a physician and in the agricultural census of that year as a farm owner.

BIBLIOGRAPHY: Texas House of Representatives, *Biographical Directory of the Texan Conventions and Congresses, 1832–1845* (Austin: Book Exchange, 1941). Ray A. Walter, *A History of Limestone County* (Austin: Von Boeckmann–Jones, 1959).

Carolyn Hyman

COOKE, WILLARD RICHARDSON (1888–1966). Willard Richardson Cooke, gynecology professor, was born in Galveston on September 6, 1888, to Dr. Henry P. and Caroline (Richardson) Cooke. He represented the seventh generation of physicians in his family; his father had also practiced in Galveston and served as one of the first deans at the University of Texas Medical Branch (1898–1901). His mother was the daughter of Willard Richardson,[qv] an early editor of the Galveston *Daily News* (see GALVESTON NEWS). Cooke was educated at Miss Jackie Andrews' Private School in Galveston and attended Ball High School and the Episcopal High School of Virginia. He received an undergraduate degree from the University of Texas in 1910 and an M.D. from UTMB in 1912, graduating first in his class. Cooke served an internship at John Sealy Hospital[qv] in 1912 and in 1913 began a forty-seven-year affiliation with the Department of Obstetrics and Gynecology at UTMB. In 1922 he advanced to associate professor. In 1924 he was appointed chairman and professor of the department; he maintained the chairmanship until 1954 and his professorship until he retired in 1959. He once estimated that he had delivered more than 5,000 babies and taught some 3,000 physicians during his professional career. He published more than seventy articles and was the author of a widely used textbook, *Fundamentals of Gynecology* (1935).

Cooke served as president (1942–44) of the American Association of Obstetrics and Gynecology, founding member and president of the Texas Association of Obstetricians and Gynecologists, founding member and president (1935) of the Central Association of Obstetrics and Gynecology, governor of the American College of Surgeons, vice president of the American Gynecological Society (1955–56), and secretary of the Galveston County Medical Society (1918). He was a director of the American Board of Obstetrics and Gynecology from 1935 to 1955. Cooke also served as an associate editor of both the *American Journal of Obstetrics and Gynecology* and *Medical Times*. In 1947 physicians who had served as residents under Cooke formed the Willard R. Cooke Club. That club, which meets annually, is now open to all former residents of the Department of Obstetrics and Gynecology at UTMB.

In 1914 Cooke married Aline Ruth Austin, the daughter of Galveston's first mayor under commission government. She died in 1956. They had three children, one of whom was killed in Germany during World War II.[qv] Throughout his life Cooke maintained a strong interest in boat building, boating, and photographing marsh birds and their rookeries. He died in an Austin Hospital on March 16, 1966.

BIBLIOGRAPHY: Galveston *News*, March 17, 1966. *Obstetrics and Gynecology*, October 1957. *Texas State Journal of Medicine*, May 1966. *The*

University of Texas Medical Branch at Galveston: A Seventy-five Year History (Austin: University of Texas Press, 1967).

Patricia L. Jakobi

COOKE, WILLIAM GASTON (1820–1890). William Gaston Cooke, early settler, the son of Henry Marchant and Frances (Buxton) Cooke, was born at New Bern, North Carolina, on December 20, 1820. He came to Texas in 1835 with ten brothers and sisters to claim land granted to their father, who died en route. Two of his older brothers, Thomas and Francis J., joined the troops at San Jacinto and left him in charge of the family. Cooke and his family were forced to flee from the Mexicans during the Runaway Scrape,qv and near Richmond on the Brazos River they participated in a minor skirmish with the Mexicans. Cooke resided in Montgomery County until 1840, when he moved to Houston to work as a carpenter. He subsequently moved to Navarro County and bought a farm. In 1853 he bought a farm of 125 acres in Ellis County, where he remained until his death. During the Civil Warqv he was in the state militia but saw no action. He was a member of the Christian Church, a school trustee, a Mason, and a member of the Farmers' Alliance.qv He was married to Angeline Salmon in Harris County. After her death he married Catherine Kendall, in 1850; they had ten children. Cooke died in 1890.

BIBLIOGRAPHY: *Memorial and Biographical History of Ellis County* (Chicago: Lewis, 1892; rpt. as *Ellis County History*, Fort Worth: Historical Publishers, 1972). Agnes R. G. Smith, *Back When and Now: History of the Family of Agnes Rust Gordon Smith* (San Angelo, 1976).

Steven A. Brownrigg

COOKE, WILLIAM GORDON (1808–1847). William Gordon Cooke, soldier and statesman, son of Adam and Martha (Riddell) Cooke, was born at Fredericksburg, Virginia, on March 26, 1808. He was trained in the family drug business. He moved to New Orleans to continue his career and on October 13, 1835, volunteered for the New Orleans Greys.qv He arrived with the second company at Velasco, Texas, on October 25, 1835, and was elected first lieutenant the next day at Quintana. After arrival at Bexar on November 8, 1835, Cooke was elected captain of his company and raised volunteers to storm the town. Cooke led the party that captured the priest's house on the main plaza, thus forcing the Mexican capitulation, and received the flag of surrender, which he sent to Col. Francis W. Johnson,qv commanding officer (*see* BEXAR, SIEGE OF).

Cooke then volunteered for the Matamoros expedition of 1835–36.qv As captain he led the reformed San Antonio Greys to Goliad. Shortly after Sam Houston'sqv arrival and impassioned speech there, Cooke offered his services to the Texas army and was sent with his company to Refugio, where they were joined by Col. James Walker Fannin, Jr.,qv and the Georgia Battalion.qv Fannin ordered Cooke to San Patricio to reinforce Maj. Robert C. Morris.qv Cooke was subsequently left in command there when Morris, Johnson, and Col. William Grant proceeded to the Rio Grande.

Cooke received Grant's letter stating his intentions to join the Mexican Federalists and, after relaying this news to Fannin, was ordered to fall back to Goliad, where he arrived on February 12, 1836. He was then sent with two Mexican prisoners to Washington-on-the-Brazos, where he joined Houston's staff as assistant inspector general. Cooke went with Houston to Gonzales and there assisted in organizing the troops. At the battle of San Jacintoqv he served on Houston's staff with the rank of major. Cooke was in charge of the guard on the prisoners when Antonio López de Santa Annaqv was captured. He prevented the angry Texans from executing Santa Anna so that he could be brought before General Houston.

When Houston went to New Orleans to recover from wounds received in the battle, Cooke accompanied him, but soon returned to Texas to serve as chief clerk of the War Department. In October 1836 he was appointed stock commissioner in Houston's first administration and was responsible for issuing stock certificates and certificates to fund the public debt. He served in this office until the spring of 1839. In November 1836 Houston appointed Cooke acting secretary of war and on January 31, 1837, inspector general, an office he held until July 31, 1837. Cooke then retired from the army because of ill health and opened two drugstores in Houston. On June 9, 1837, he was made official signer of the president's name to promissory notes of the Republic of Texas,qv a job necessitated by injuries to Houston's arm that were aggravated by illness. The position lasted until November 11, 1839.

Cooke reenlisted in the army around October 1838 and received a commission as quartermaster general of the republic. In March 1840 Mirabeau B. Lamarqv named him commissioner to sign treaties with the Comanches, and in this role he took part in the Council House Fightqv in San Antonio on March 19, 1840.

On August 18, 1840, Cooke was appointed colonel of the First Regiment of Infantry, the unit that laid out the Military Roadqv from the Little River to the Red River. Fighting Indians and starvation along the way, Cooke explored and mapped much of north central Texas. He established Fort Johnson and Fort Preston on the Red River and Cedar Springs Post on the Trinity River; at this post were the first structures built by white men at the future site of Dallas. Cooke's success in this venture prompted a grand military ball in his honor, held in the Senate chamber at Austin on February 27, 1841, and a nomination for vice president of the republic. He declined the latter and accepted instead an appointment from Lamar in April 1841 as senior commissioner on the Texan Santa Fe expedition.qv

Cooke assisted Lamar in promoting and organizing the expedition and was to have been the chief civil authority in Santa Fe. On September 17, 1841, he was deceived by the traitor Capt. William G. Lewis and surrendered the Texans' arms. Cooke and his men were marched to Mexico City and imprisoned in Santiago Prison on December 26, 1841. They were released on June 14, 1842, and stayed at Waddy Thompson'sqv house in Mexico City and then in Jalapa, Vera Cruz, until passage could be arranged. Cooke arrived at Galveston aboard the United States brig *Boxer* on August 10, 1842.

Ignoring his pledge not to take arms against Mexico under pain of death, he immediately joined with Gen. Edward Burlesonqv to expel the Mexican general Adrián Wollqv from San Antonio. On September 22, 1842, Cooke was wounded in Capt. John C. Hays'sqv charge on the cannon at Arroyo Hondo. On October 25, 1842, Houston appointed him quartermaster general and chief of the subsistence department, in which capacity Cooke helped organize the infamous Snively expedition and the Somervell expedition,qqv of which he was a member until February 1, 1843.

Seeking further revenge, Cooke went to New Orleans to join Edwin Ward Mooreqv on his expedition to the Yucatán. They sailed on April 15, 1843, in the sloop-of-war *Austin*.qv Cooke participated in engagements with the Mexican steamships *Montezuma* and *Guadaloupe* (*see* MONTEZUMA AFFAIR), and after the *Independencia* joined the Texan fleet, he twice accompanied her on raiding expeditions, hoping to capture prisoners to exchange for those held in Mexican prisons. The first expedition resulted in the capture of the Mexican ship *Glide,* and the second brought back news to Moore that Houston had declared him a pirate, charges against which Cooke later defended him. They returned to Galveston on July 14, 1843, and Cooke received an appointment from Gen. Sidney Shermanqv as adjutant general of the Texas militia.

Cooke was elected representative from Bexar County to the House of the Ninth Congress on September 2, 1844, and served his term as chairman of the Committee on Military Affairs. Partly as a result of his efforts on Commodore Moore's behalf, Cooke was appointed by President Anson Jonesqv in December 1844 to replace Morgan Calvin Hamiltonqv as secretary of war. Cooke, who had become the last commander of the regular Texas army when the troops were disbanded in 1841, was now responsible for raising troops and supplies for the United States army of occupation under Gen. Zachary Taylor.^qv He served in this office until the spring of 1846, when he ran unsuccessfully for the Congress of the United States. He lost to Timothy Pillsbury^qv by a narrow margin. On April 27, 1846, Cooke was appointed the first adjutant general of the state of Texas by Governor James Pinckney Henderson.^qv He served in this office until his death.

Cooke was a Protestant and a grand royal arch captain of Holland Masonic Lodge No. 36 in Houston. On August 16, 1844, he married Ángela María de Jesús Blasa Navarro, daughter of Luciano Navarro and niece of José Antonio Navarro.^qv They had one son. Cooke died of tuberculosis on December 24, 1847, at his father-in-law's ranch in Seguin. He was buried in nearby Geronimo and, on March 2, 1937, reinterred in the State Cemetery,^qv Austin. Cooke's Camp, near San Antonio, Cooke County, and Cooke Avenue in San Antonio were named for him.

BIBLIOGRAPHY: Allen F. Adams, *The Leader of the Volunteer Grays: The Life of William G. Cooke, 1808–1847* (M.A. thesis, Southwest Texas State University, 1940). Joseph Milton Nance, *After San Jacinto: The Texas-Mexican Frontier, 1836–1841* (Austin: University of Texas Press, 1963). Texas House of Representatives, *Biographical Directory of the Texan Conventions and Congresses, 1832–1845* (Austin: Book Exchange, 1941). Harry Warren, "Col. William G. Cooke," *Quarterly of the Texas State Historical Association* 9 (October 1905). Tom Henderson Wells, *Commodore Moore and the Texas Navy* (Austin: University of Texas Press, 1960).

Steven A. Brownrigg

COOKE COUNTY. Cooke County (B-17) is located in north central Texas, on the Oklahoma border. The approximate center of the county is at 33°40′ north latitude and 97°15′ west longitude. Gainesville, the county seat and largest population center, is located seven miles south of the Red River and seventy-one miles north of Dallas. The county comprises 905 square miles. The central section of the county is part of the Grand Prairie; it is flanked by a small section of the Eastern Cross Timbers on the east and the Western Cross Timbers on the West. The rolling terrain is surfaced by mixed soils ranging from sandy to loam and from red to black. Grassy prairie predominates in the west. The county is forested mainly with blackjack oak, post oak, and hackberry, and with elm, pecan, walnut, and cottonwood along the creeks and rivers. The altitude increases from 700 feet on the eastern border to nearly 1,000 feet in the west. The northern quarter of Cooke County drains into the Red River, and the remaining three-quarters is part of the watershed of the Elm Fork of the Trinity River. Three lakes are found within the county's boundaries: Lake Kiowa, Hubert H. Moss Lake, and Lake Texoma. A fourth lake, Lake Ray Roberts, dammed in Denton County, covers much of southwestern Cooke County. Temperatures range from an average high of 96° F in July to an average low of 32° in January. The average rainfall is about thirty-four inches a year. The growing season extends for 226 days.

Before the coming of Anglo-American settlement Cooke County stood on the borderlands between the Caddo Indians to the east and the Comanches in the west. The first Europeans to visit the county may have been Spaniards on expeditions during the sixteenth, seventeenth, and eighteenth centuries, but no permanent settlements were made. The county was included in the Cameron land grant, a Mexican grant of 1828, but no settlers came.

Cooke County was established by an act of the Texas legislature on March 20, 1848, and named for William G. Cooke,^qv a hero of the Texas Revolution.^qv The boundaries of the original county encompassed its present area, along with territory that became Montague, Clay, Wise, and Jack counties. Cooke County assumed its present boundaries in 1857. It was crossed by several early trails, including the Mormon Trail, a branch of the Chisholm Trail,^qv and the Butterfield Overland Mail^qv route. Settlements in the northern extension of the Peters colony^qv reached the southeastern edge of the county by the late 1840s. Fort Fitzhugh was established in 1847 to protect area settlements against Indian raids, the last of which occurred in the western part of the county in January 1868. Early settlers employed Daniel Montague^qv to locate a site for a county seat fifteen miles west of the Grayson county line. They planned to name the town Liberty, but the state rejected that name because another settlement near Houston had claimed it. Col. William F. Fitzhugh,^qv commander at the fort, proposed that the town be named for his former commander, Gen. Edmund Pendleton Gaines.^qv Gainesville, founded in 1850, has been the county seat since the organization of the county. The southern and eastern parts of the county were settled by people primarily from Tennessee, Arkansas, and Missouri. The western part had only scattered settlements prior to the late nineteenth century, when German land speculators founded the towns of Muenster in 1889 and Lindsay in 1891.

The Denison and Pacific Railway reached Gainesville on November 7, 1879, from the east; it later became the Missouri, Kansas and Texas (Katy) Railroad. The Gulf, Colorado and Santa Fe connected Gainesville and Denton on January 2, 1887, on its way to meet the Atchison, Topeka and Santa Fe at Purcell, Indian Territory. These links provided for the first time a north–south rail line from Chicago to Galveston. The Katy was later extended west toward Wichita Falls.

The earliest settlers brought slaves with them, but not in the numbers that accompanied migrants from the Deep South to East Texas. The slave population of Cooke County in 1860 was 369, 10.9 percent of the total. Although in 1861 the county's citizens voted more than 61 percent against secession,^qv sentiment for the Confederate cause was so potent during the Civil War^qv that in October 1862 an estimated forty-two men were executed because they were believed to have participated in a pro-Union conspiracy (see GREAT HANGING AT GAINESVILLE).

During most of its history Cooke County has voted for Democrats. From 1884 to 1916 the county gave more than 75 percent of its votes to Democratic presidential candidates; William Jennings Bryan received 83.2 percent over William McKinley in 1896. Democratic congressman and senator Joseph Weldon Bailey^qv came from Cooke County. The Democratic hegemony continued through the Great Depression^qv and the New Deal era. Harry Truman received 53.1 percent of the votes in the 1948 presidential election. From 1948 to 1992, however, Cooke County voted for Republican nominees for president, except in 1964, when Lyndon B. Johnson^qv received 65.7 percent.

Education in Cooke County is conducted predominantly by nine independent school districts. Both Catholic and Protestant private education is available in the county, too. The county is also the home of Cooke County College, founded in 1924, and Gainesville State School for Girls,^qv a reformatory.

Points of interest in the county include the Frank Buck Zoo, located in Leonard Park in Gainesville; Morton Museum in downtown Gainesville; and a center for diabetic children at Camp Sweeney east of Gainesville. Camp Howze,^qv a military training base during World War II,^qv had a troop capacity of 39,963. The installation was abandoned in 1946. Structural remains of support beams, storage towers, and various foundations in the camp can still be seen from Farm Road 1201 northwest of Gainesville. Cultural events in the county that attract the greatest number of visitors include the annual Germanfest in Muenster the last weekend in April. Festivities include traditional German foods, beer, booths, a bicycle rally, and the German Fun Run. Other events in the county are the Octoberfest in Lindsay and Sam Bass^qv Days in Rosston. A popular attraction in Gainesville is the driving tour of the Victorian homes on Church, Denton, and Lindsay streets.

Throughout its history Cooke County has been heavily agricultural. In 1900 it had 3,307 farms, averaging 142.4 acres. The farms were almost equally divided between those owned by the people who worked them (44.1 percent) and those worked by sharecroppers (42.2 percent), with a handful of cash-rent farmers. Farm income in 1900 was more than $2.2 million. Cattle in 1900 numbered 48,765.

Corn production was 1.68 million bushels—1.5 percent of the state's corn crop. The oats yield stood at 840,790 bushels, 218,330 more than wheat production. At the turn of the century, Cooke County ginned 11,332 bales of cotton. The years between World War I^{qv} and the depression saw cotton production peak at around 20,000 bales a year. The emigration of the Dust Bowl^{qv} and depression years reduced cotton production to 8,906 bales in 1936. Cotton production was only 1,540 bales in 1956, but rose to 6,200 in 1965. No cotton gins were operating in the county in 1984.

The 1920s was a bad decade for agriculture across the South, for the bottom dropped out of the cotton market. Cooke County was hit hard. The number of farmers owning the land they worked decreased from 1,299 in 1920 to 720 in 1930, a 44.6 percent decrease in one decade. Conversely, the number of sharecroppers increased from 1,390 in 1920 to 1,848 in 1925, but dropped to 1,673 in 1930 as tenant farmers went broke and moved away. The New Deal years saw the trend reverse somewhat. By 1940, 51.9 percent of the farms in the county were operated by tenants, either cash-renters or sharecroppers. The same year, the number of farms in Cooke County had dropped to 2,530, only 76.5 percent of the number at the turn of the century, partly because smaller farms were being consolidated. Only large farms—those of more than 180 acres—increased in number in the late 1930s; between 1935 and 1940 farms greater than 700 acres increased from sixty-five to eighty-two.

Dairying continued to grow as the chief agribusiness. The number of cows and heifers kept mainly for milking increased from 7,929 in 1930 to 11,565 in 1940. As cotton production decreased and the cattle industry increased, corn production rose. In 1934, 78,840 bushels of corn was harvested for grain; in 1939 the total was 465,671 bushels. Wheat production increased in the 1934–39 period by 62.75 percent. By World War II, then, Cooke County had changed from being part of the Cotton Belt to being a part of the West, that is, a cattle-producing area.

Agriculture still dominates the economy of Cooke County, for 77.9 percent of the county's total area is occupied by farms. Fifty-seven percent of the acreage is pasture or rangeland. In the 1978 agricultural census the value of all agricultural products sold was about $26,095,000, and 81.8 percent of it derived from the livestock industry. Of the income from livestock, 36.7 percent came from dairy products and 58.7 percent from the sale of cattle and calves. Cooke County is still cattle country.

The crops grown in the county also reflect the predominance of livestock. Corn culture^{qv} is decreasing, though sorghum culture^{qv} increased slightly during the 1970s. Wheat and oats are the primary crops: 756,571 bushels of wheat were grown in 1978, and 862,543 bushels of oats. Peanuts and hay are also important, though by 1978 cotton production had fallen to 5 percent of the peak yield of the early 1920s. By 1978, 58 percent of the farms in Cooke County were owned by the farmers, and only 11 percent were worked by tenants. Individuals or single families owned 87.4 percent of the farms. Of the 93,304 acres of harvested cropland in 1978, 73,608 were fertilized. The average market value of all machinery and equipment for each farm in 1978 was $19,037.

The county's major mineral resources are oil and gas. The first oil well started operation on November 9, 1924, two miles east of Callisburg. From 1924 to 1982 oil production was 4,288,009 barrels. The total value of oil production in 1983 was $131,899,471.

Manufacturing in the county, according to the 1977 manufacturing census, was valued at $79,500,000. The oil value in 1982 stood at $131,899,471. The wages paid in 1982 amounted to about $171 million. Property in the county in 1981 was assessed at $548,210,089. Taxable sales for 1982 amounted to $103,877,358.

Cooke County's population has remained relatively stable in the last hundred years. The 1880 census counted 20,391 inhabitants. By 1900 the figure had reached 27,494. Postwar urban migration brought the number of residents to 22,146, its lowest twentieth-century level, in 1950. The 1980 census counted 27,656. The population of the county was 93.46 percent white and 4.36 percent black in 1980. The largest town in the county is Gainesville, with a 1980 population of 14,081. It had almost doubled in size since 1900, when it registered 7,874 residents. Other incorporated areas were Muenster (1,408), Lindsay (581), Valley View (514), Callisburg (281), and Oak Ridge (200).

Cooke County is served by two federal highways, U.S. Highway 82, running east and west, and U.S. Highway 77, running north and south. In the early 1960s Interstate Highway 35 was built across the county from north to south. There is no longer any railroad service in the county. Carload lots can be delivered from one of the eighteen or so freight trains that transit the county daily on the AT&SF. Automobile registration in 1981 stood at 28,612. The county has one daily newspaper, the Gainesville *Daily Register,* which has been published continuously since 1890, and two weeklies. Radio station KGAF-AM broadcasts from Gainesville. The population of Cooke County was 30,777 in 1990.

BIBLIOGRAPHY: Wanda Joan Cabaniss, Santa Fe Depot, Gainesville, Texas: An Adaptive Use Proposal (M.A. thesis, University of Texas at Austin, 1981). Michael Collins, *Cooke County, Texas: Where the South and West Meet* (Gainesville, Texas: Cooke County Heritage Society, 1981). A. Morton Smith, *The First 100 Years in Cooke County* (San Antonio: Naylor, 1955).
Robert Wayne McDaniel

COOKE CREEK. Cooke Creek rises a mile east of Rusk in east central Cherokee County (at 31°48′ N, 95°07′ W) and runs northeast for eight miles to its mouth on Mud Creek, a mile south of Reklaw (at 31°50′ N, 94°59′ W). The surrounding flat to gently rolling terrain is surfaced by clay and sandy loam that supports mixed hardwoods and pines. The creek was probably named for James Cooke, the original grantee of the area.

COOK'S FORT. Cook's Fort, three miles southeast of Rusk in Cherokee County, was built in late 1839 or early 1840 by a military company under the command of Capt. G. K. Black for protection of the settlers against hostile Indians. The fort, named in honor of Joseph Thomas Cook, who owned the land and had the primitive fort and stockade built, became a gathering place for new settlers in the area and gave them a sense of security while they scouted for a location of their own. There were no Indian attacks, and no soldiers were stationed nearby. The Cherokee Indians had been removed in 1839 to Indian Territory.

Cook and his wife, Mary (Moore), had come from South Carolina through Alabama and Mississippi before they arrived in the San Augustine area in the early 1830s. By 1834 they were in Nacogdoches. Most of their eleven children, if not all, came with them and lived at the fort. Cook had received Mexican grants of a league and a labor of land. After Texas independence, he spent three months with Capt. Michael Costley's^{qv} company of rangers (September 11–December 11, 1836), for which service he received 320 acres of land. Several of his children and his sons-in-law received warrants for land.

His son James Cook owned the league of land adjoining that of his father. On it he built a store and blacksmith shop. This was the beginning of a settlement that had an estimated population of 250, including slaves, by 1846, when Cherokee County was formed from Nacogdoches County. At that time the locating commission looked favorably on Cook's Fort as the county seat. It was centrally located, on the well-traveled Nacogdoches–Neches Saline Road,^{qv} and near the road to Fort Houston. It is said that James Cook was opposed to making Cook's Fort the county seat because that function would interfere with his large-scale farming interests. Thus a new town was formed and called Rusk. Those not engaged in farming moved to the new town, and the little settlement at Cook's Fort declined.

Several hundred acres of land including the fort site are still owned by Cook's descendants, who received a Texas Land Heritage

Award in 1967 for having a farm in continuous operation for over 100 years. Many of the Bibles, furniture, and silver the Cooks brought to Texas were destroyed in a fire. In the nearby Salem Cemetery Joseph and Mary Cook are buried on land they donated for the cemetery. A Texas Centennial qv marker was placed by the state of Texas at the site of Cook's Fort in 1936.

BIBLIOGRAPHY: Helen Wooddell Crawford, *Cemeteries of Mid Cherokee County, Texas* (1973). Ogreta W. Huttash, *Historical Markers of Cherokee County, Texas* (Jacksonville, Texas, 1982). Thomas L. Miller, *Bounty and Donation Land Grants of Texas, 1835–1888* (Austin: University of Texas Press, 1967). Mrs. Harry Joseph Morris, comp. and ed., *Citizens of the Republic of Texas* (Dallas: Texas State Genealogical Society, 1977). Gerald S. Pierce, *Texas Under Arms: The Camps, Posts, Forts, and Military Towns of the Republic of Texas* (Austin: Encino, 1969). Hattie Joplin Roach, *The Hills of Cherokee* (1952; rpt., Fort Worth, 1976). Hattie Joplin Roach, *A History of Cherokee County* (Dallas: Southwest, 1934). Gifford E. White, *Character Certificates in the General Land Office of Texas* (1985).

Ogreta W. Huttash and Chris Martin

COOKS POINT, TEXAS. Cooks (Cookes) Point, on State Highway 21 eight miles east of Caldwell in Burleson County, is one of the oldest communities in the county. It was named for Silas L. Cooke, a surveyor who lived in the area during the days of the Republic of Texas.qv The community began as a crossroads settlement at the point where the old Colonial Road from Washington-on-the-Brazos and Independence to Tenoxtitlan and Nashville crossed the Old San Antonio Road.qv The first recorded trading post in the area was that of Gabriel Jackson, who built a two-story log house nearby and operated a store on the first floor. He dealt with settlers, the first of whom in the area were of Anglo-American descent, and also with local Indians. In 1854 Judge A. S. Broaddus led a wagon train, stretching over a mile long, of eighty whites and 120 blacks from Virginia to Cookes Point. After the Civil Warqv German and Czech settlers began moving into the area, and by 1884 the developing community had a population of about 100. The first church organized in the area was Methodist. Judge Broaddus and his party established a Baptist church in 1881; the Germans established a German Methodist church; and the Czechs later established a Brethren church. In 1990 the community had two churches, the Cooks Point United Methodist Church and the Unity of the Brethren. The first public school was built about 1880 and was operated by the Cooks Point Independent School District until 1973, when it merged with the Caldwell district. The original community was built on either side of the Old San Antonio Road. There was a general store, a gin, and a post office that was established in 1874 and discontinued in 1913. The Houston and Texas Central Railway arrived in the community in 1913. When State Highway 21 was built, the general store was moved south to face the new highway; the store still operated in 1990, when the community reported a population of about sixty and continued as a hub for cattle ranches and dairy, cotton, grain, and hay farms. Cooks Point lies along the Austin Chalk Formation, and many oil wells have been drilled around the community.

BIBLIOGRAPHY: Malcolm H. Addison, *Reminiscences of Burleson County, Texas* (Caldwell, Texas, 1886; rpt., Caldwell: Caldwell Printing, 1971). Burleson County Historical Society, *Astride the Old San Antonio Road: A History of Burleson County, Texas* (Dallas: Taylor, 1980).

Catherine G. Alford

COOKS SLOUGH. Cooks Slough rises near Farm Road 55 four miles northeast of Sevenmile Hill and seven miles northwest of Uvalde in central Uvalde County (at 29°20′ N, 99°50′ W) and runs southeast seventeen miles to its mouth on the Leona River, two miles southeast of Uvalde near the Fort Inge Historical Site (at 29°10′ N, 99°46′ W). In the creek's upper reaches steep to gently sloping terrain is surfaced by very shallow to shallow and stony clay and loam that supports sparse scrub brush and grass; along the lower section the terrain changes to flat with locally shallow depressions, surfaced by deep loam and clay that support water-tolerant hardwoods, conifers, and grass.

COOKVILLE, TEXAS. Cookville is at the intersection of U.S. Highway 67 and the St. Louis Southwestern Railway, seven miles northeast of Mount Pleasant in eastern Titus County. In 1867 Andrew B. Cook opened a general store on the major road leading from Omaha to Mount Pleasant. The community was originally called Clay Hill when the post office was established in 1870, but in 1880 the name was changed to Cookville in honor of Cook. Cookville began to grow in the late 1870s, when it became a station on the narrow-gauge East Line and Red River Railroad. By 1884 the town had an estimated population of 500 and was a major shipping and supply center for farmers in eastern Titus and western Morris counties. During the 1890s the population of the town dropped from 600 to 250. During the early years of the twentieth century it began to grow again. By 1914 Cookville had a bank, a telephone company, several stores, and 800 residents. The economy was linked directly with the prosperity of the cotton farmers in the area. When the price of cotton plummeted in 1920, the bank and a number of other businesses were forced to close. By 1925 the population had fallen to 420. In 1990 Cookville had one business and a population of 105.

BIBLIOGRAPHY: John Marion Ellis II, *The Way It Was: A Personal Memoir of Family Life in East Texas* (Waco: Texian Press, 1983). Traylor Russell, *History of Titus County* (2 vols., Waco: Morrison, 1965, 1966; rpt., n.p.: Walsworth, 1975).

Cecil Harper, Jr.

COOL, TEXAS. Cool is a small incorporated town on U.S. Highway 180 eleven miles west of Weatherford in western Parker County. Cool was incorporated after 1960 and was first shown on county maps in the mid-1960s. By 1969 it had an estimated population of 506. In 1970 the census reported only 21 people living in Cool, but by 1978 its population was estimated at 253. The census reported 202 people in Cool in 1980 and 214 in 1990.

John Leffler

COOLEY, DANIEL DENTON (1850–1933). Daniel Denton Cooley, real estate developer and prominent Houston businessman, known as the "Father of Houston Heights" in Harris County, the son of Robert William and Eliza Maria (Stone) Cooley, was born on April 15, 1850, probably in Pennsylvania. He was raised in Binghamton, New York, where he attended public school and business college. As a young man he settled in Ashland, Nebraska, where he worked in a mercantile business and served as cashier for the First National Bank under president Oscar Martin Carter. In 1887 Cooley became a director, treasurer, and general manager of Carter's newly formed Omaha and South Texas Land Company, for which he worked until the company was dissolved in 1895. The Omaha and South Texas Land Company was a subsidiary of the American Loan and Trust Company, which was responsible for the purchase on May 5, 1891, of 1,765 acres of land west of downtown Houston. The property, twenty feet higher in elevation than the downtown area, came to be known as Houston Heights. At the time it was one of the country's largest real estate projects. Cooley's home was one of the first houses in the division. He installed the electric lights by hooking wires from the house to the electric trolley. Marmion Park, at the site of the former Cooley residence, contains a pavilion modeled after Cooley's home, which was razed in 1965. Cooley School was named in his honor and built on land donated by the company. Cooley played a key role in establishing the school, and he was one of only two living persons in the city for whom a school had been named. It served the community until the 1970s. After the Heights incorporated in 1896, Cooley was elected alderman in April 1897. Later he served as chairman of the joint city and county committee that built Jefferson Davis County Hospital. Cooley helped to organize St. Stephen's Mission in 1895 and served as warden until it disbanded in 1904. He also served on the vestry and assisted in the formation of another Episcopalian mission that became St. Andrew's Church.

Cooley was a Shriner and a member of the Fraternal Hall Association. His wife was especially active in the Houston Heights Women's Club, and he and his wife donated property for a clubhouse for the organization. He was associated with the South Texas National Bank, the Houston Electric Company, and the Electric Street Railway Company. He served as president of the State Land Oil Company, which later merged with Gulf Oil Corporation,qv and the Houston Railway Company, which became part of the Houston and Texas Central line. In 1903 Cooley became a partner in the insurance firm of Childress and Taylor, which later became Cooley, Schweikart, and Seaman. He married Helen Grace Winfield on February 5, 1883. Among his three sons was Ralph Cooley, a pioneer in restorative dentistry. A grandson, Denton Arthur Cooley, became a world-famous cardiovascular surgeon. Cooley died in Houston Heights on November 22, 1933, and was buried in Glenwood Cemetery.

BIBLIOGRAPHY: Sister M. Agatha, *The History of Houston Heights, 1891–1918* (Houston: Premier Printing, 1956). Houston *Chronicle*, October 22, 1912, November 22, 1933, October 17, 1965. Houston *Post*, November 23, 1933. Houston Metropolitan Research Center Files, Houston Public Library. Marie Phelps McAshan, *A Houston Legacy: On the Corner of Main and Texas* (Houston: Gulf, 1985).

Gayle Davies

COOLIDGE, DANE (1873–1940). Dane Coolidge, naturalist and writer of western novels, the son of Francis and Sophia (Whittemore) Coolidge, was born in Natick, Massachusetts, on March 24, 1873. The family moved to Los Angeles in 1877, and Coolidge subsequently grew up on his father's orange farm at Riverside, California. He received his B.A. from Stanford University in 1898 and studied at Harvard University in 1898–99. During the summers Coolidge collected animals for Stanford University, the British Museum, the United States Biological Survey, the United States National Zoological Park, and the New York Zoological Park. In 1900 he worked as a field collector for the United States Natural History Museum.

After returning to the United States Coolidge became a western wildlife photographer specializing in desert animals. He also spent a good deal of time in mining towns, on Indian reservations, on roundups, and with Texas Rangersqv on the Rio Grande, collecting material for stories. He wrote some forty novels of Western life and was considered an expert on Indian and cowboy lore. His novels with a Southwest or Texas setting include *The Texican* (1911), *The Law West of the Pecos* (1924), *Lorenzo the Magnificent: The Riders from Texas* (1925), *Jess Roundtree, Texas Ranger* (1933), and *Ranger Two-Rifles* (1937). Coolidge also contributed about a hundred short stories to such magazines as *Harper's Weekly, Leslie's Weekly, Red Book,* and *Sunset.* His nonfiction works, many illustrated with his own photographs, included *Fighting Men of the West* (1932), *Texas Cowboys* (1937), *Death Valley Prospectors* (1937), *Arizona Cowboys* (1938), *Old California Cowboys* (1939), *The Navajo Indian* (1930), *Navajo Rugs* (1933), and *The Last of the Seris* (1939), the last three written with his wife.

Coolidge married Mary Elizabeth Burroughs (Roberts) Smith, a sociologist, on July 30, 1906, in Berkeley, California. He served for thirty-five years as director of the San Francisco Boys' Club. He was a Unitarian and belonged to the American Society of Mammalogists, the Authors League of America, and the California Writers Club. Coolidge died in Berkeley on August 8, 1940. His wife survived him.

BIBLIOGRAPHY: *American West,* November–December 1977. Dane Coolidge Collection, Bancroft Library, University of California, Berkeley. Dane Coolidge Pictorial Collection, Bancroft Library, University of California, Berkeley. *National Cyclopaedia of American Biography,* Vol. 35. Jon Tuska and Vicki Piekarski, eds., *Encyclopedia of Frontier and Western Fiction* (New York: McGraw-Hill, 1983). *Twentieth-Century Western Writers* (Detroit: Gale Research, 1982; 2d ed., Chicago: St. James Press, 1991). *Who Was Who among North American Authors, 1921–1939* (2 vols., Detroit: Gale Research, 1976). *Who's Who in America,* 1933–34.

Carolyn Hyman

COOLIDGE, TEXAS. Coolidge is at the intersection of State Highway 171 and Farm Road 73, eleven miles northwest of Mexia in northern Limestone County. It was established in 1903 while the Trinity and Brazos Valley Railway was laying track between Hillsboro and Mexia and was named in honor of a stockholder in the company. When the post office opened in 1903, the name was misspelled as "Cooledge"; the error was not corrected until 1930. The townsite was a mile northeast of Armour, from which residents moved their homes and businesses to be nearer the railroad. Coolidge was incorporated in 1905, and by 1910 had a population of 500. By 1914 Coolidge had two banks, a weekly newspaper, and a variety of businesses. By the early 1930s the population had risen to 1,169. The community experienced a serious setback in 1942, when the railroad decided to abandon its track through the town; however, the decline in population that resulted proved to be moderate. In the early 1950s the number of residents was estimated at 1,062. The population fell to 786 in the early 1970s but rose to 864 in the late 1980s; 748 residents were reported in 1990. Coolidge was the focus of a large independent school district that covered much of northern Limestone County.

BIBLIOGRAPHY: John J. Germann and Myron Janzen, *Texas Post Offices by County* (1986). Ray A. Walter, *A History of Limestone County* (Austin: Von Boeckmann-Jones, 1959).

Vivian Elizabeth Smyrl

COOL SPRINGS, TEXAS. Cool Springs, on Farm Road 1651 just off State Highway 19 four miles south of Canton in south central Van Zandt County, appeared on state highway maps in 1987 as the site of a church and cemetery near Tundra.

Diana J. Kleiner

COOMBES, ZACHARIAH ELLIS (1833–1895). Zachariah Ellis Coombes, lawyer, state legislator, and Confederate soldier, son of William and Ivy (Green) Coombes, was born in Nelson County, Kentucky, on March 30, 1833. The family moved to Dallas in 1843 as early members of the Peters colonyqv and originally settled just west of the Trinity River. As a young man Coombes returned to Kentucky for his education. On December 10, 1856, he married Rebecca Finch Bedford in Dallas. The couple had seven children.

In June of 1858 Coombes was employed by the Brazos Agency to conduct a school on the Brazos Indian Reservationqv in Young County. He remained as head of the school until the federal government abandoned the reservation system in Texas the next year. Official records and written accounts of those who visited the school indicate that he was a competent teacher. On the Indian reservation he began the study of law and kept a diary that was subsequently published.

In the spring of 1862 he entered the Confederate Army as a member of Trezevant C. Hawpe'sqv Thirty-first Regiment of Texas Calvary. He was promoted to lieutenant in April 1863 and to captain of Company G in June of that year. He was elected county judge of Dallas County in the June 1866 election, during presidential Reconstruction.qv Coombes and the other Dallas County elected officials were removed in November 1867 as "impediments to Reconstruction" after repeated assertions by the local Freedmen's Bureauqv agent that they refused to protect black lives and property.

Shortly thereafter Coombes resumed the study of law and in 1870 began an active and successful law practice. In addition, he maintained an active interest in politics. He was an alderman of Dallas in 1871, a delegate to the state Democratic convention in May 1884, and a member of the state House of Representatives in 1885. He was a Mason, for a time grand master of the state body. He was a member of the Pioneer Association of Dallas County and of the Christian Church. He died on November 25, 1895, and was buried in Dallas.

BIBLIOGRAPHY: Barbara Neal Ledbetter, comp., *The Fort Belknap of Yesterday and Today* (1963). Murl L. Webb, "Religious and Educational Efforts among Texas Indians in the 1850's," *Southwestern Historical Quarterly* 69 (July 1965).   *Cecil Harper, Jr.*

COON CREEK (Bosque County). Coon Creek rises three miles southeast of Womack in eastern Bosque County (at 31°49′ N, 97°27′ W) and runs northeast for ten miles to its mouth on the Brazos River (at 31°51′ N, 97°20′ W). The South Prong of Coon Creek rises three miles northeast of Cayote (at 31°48′ N, 97°26′ W) and runs northeast for five miles to its mouth on Coon Creek, three miles above the main stream's mouth. The area has flat to rolling terrain surfaced by shallow, stony clay loams that support juniper, mesquite, and grass.

_____ (Fayette County). Coon Creek rises in open pastureland a half mile north of Warrenton in north central Fayette County (at 30°01′ N, 96°44′ W) and runs east for five miles to its mouth on Cummins Creek (at 30°00′ N, 96°40′ W). It crosses gently rolling terrain surfaced by shallow sandy loam that in the past has produced good crops of cotton and corn. Since the 1950s the land has been used primarily as pasture for cattle and horses. Halfway in its course the creek passes through a small flood-control pool, and near its mouth there is evidence of sand and gravel extraction.

_____ (Fort Bend County). Coon Creek rises just southeast of Rosenberg in central Fort Bend County (at 29°32′ N, 95°52′ W) and runs southeast for twelve miles to its mouth on Big Creek (at 29°29′ N, 95°50′ W). The local terrain is variable surfaced by calcareous clay that supports mixed hardwoods and prairie grasses.

_____ (Henderson County). Coon Creek, once known as Otter Creek, rises just west of Athens in central Henderson County (at 32°13′ N, 95°50′ W) and runs southwest for seventeen miles to its mouth on Catfish Creek, four miles west of Springfield in northwestern Anderson County (at 31°59′ N, 95°51′ W). The surrounding flat to rolling terrain is surfaced by sandy and clay loams that support water-tolerant hardwoods, conifers, and grasses.

COON CREEK, TEXAS. Coon Creek is on Farm Road 56 two miles south of Lake Whitney in southeastern Bosque County. It is named for Coon Creek which runs through it. John Jackson Smith[qv] and his wife, Margaret, were wealthy plantation owners in Mississippi who bought several thousand acres that became known as Smith Bend in 1854. Their son, Burton Smith, came with horses, cattle, and slaves ahead of his parents. He died before his parents arrived, and his grave was the first in the Smith Bend–Coon Creek Cemetery. In 1936 Coon Creek had a church, a business, a school, and a number of scattered dwellings. In the 1940s the little schools of Coon Creek, Meridian, Clifton, and Valley Mills were consolidated. By 1970 the town had a church, one business, and a community hall. In 1990 four or five large cattle ranches operated in the area, and about twenty families lived in Coon Creek, five of which are direct descendants of the founders of the area. On October 29, 1978, a Texas historical marker was placed at the cemetery's entrance, and a dedication ceremony was held.

BIBLIOGRAPHY: Bosque County History Book Committee, *Bosque County, Land and People* (Dallas: Curtis Media, 1985). Whitney *Messenger,* November 9, 1978.   *Mr. and Mrs. Marshall V. Bonds*

COON MOUNTAIN. Coon Mountain is just east of State Highway 279 and two miles south of Pecan Bayou in northwest Brown County (at 31°57′ N, 99°07′ W). With an elevation of 1,550 feet, its summit rises 100 feet above the bayou. It is surrounded by rugged terrain and rolling prairie surfaced by clay loams that support mesquite, various grasses, and mixed hardwoods. Coon Mountain was last labeled on a 1936 county highway map.

COONS, BENJAMIN FRANKLIN (1826–1892). Benjamin Franklin Coons, merchant, was born in St. Louis, Missouri, in 1826, the son of David and Mary Coons. He led wagon trains to Santa Fe in 1846, 1847, and 1848, and by September 1848 had established himself as a merchant in El Paso del Norte and elsewhere in Chihuahua. Coons bought ranch property near El Paso del Norte from Juan María Ponce de León[qv] in 1849 and leased the main buildings and six acres to the United States government for $250 dollars a month as the site for the first military post in the area. He then proceeded to build a tavern, warehouse, stables, and store just west of the army post. Hoping to capitalize on the potential market, he established a partnership with Lewis and Groesbeck of San Antonio in 1850. Financial difficulties began almost immediately, however. The first wagon train, plagued by unscrupulous drivers and a scarcity of water, took nearly five months to travel from San Antonio, and most of the shipment was ruined as a result. Also, that summer Coons absorbed a loss totalling nearly $18,000, having accepted several bills of credit that later proved to be forgeries.

He went to California in late 1850, regained a measure of financial security, and returned to El Paso early in 1851. Unfortunately for him, when the United States troops left Coons' Rancho[qv] in September, 1851, Coons lost his most reliable source of income and was soon forced to default on his property payments. His ranch repossessed, he returned to California to seek yet another fortune. He apparently achieved some measure of success herding sheep, moved back to St. Louis in 1856, and married Sophie Delor in 1859. Later censuses listed him as a farmer and teamster. Coons died in St. Louis on December 14, 1892. The Franklin community (later renamed El Paso) and the Franklin Mountains are said to have been named for him.

BIBLIOGRAPHY: Myra McLarey, "Letters to Jenny: A Self-Portrait of Benjamin Franklin Coons," *Password* 34 (Summer 1989). Leon C. Metz, "Franklin," *El Paso Magazine,* August 1985.

Myra McLarey

COONS' RANCHO. Coons' Rancho was at a site now in downtown El Paso. In 1827 Juan María Ponce de León,[qv] a wealthy merchant in El Paso del Norte, Mexico, bought some 211 acres bounded to the south and west by the Rio Grande. He dug an irrigation ditch and began growing grapes and wheat on the site, which became known as Ponce's Rancho. A flood in 1830 washed away an adobe[qv] hut used to house Ponce's workers, thus forcing him to rebuild on higher ground, but the same flood nearly doubled his holdings by eroding into El Paso del Norte. After the Mexican War,[qv] when the rancho became part of the United States, Ponce sold it to a St. Louis trader named Benjamin Franklin Coons,[qv] whereupon it became known as Coons' Rancho or Franklin. When Maj. Jefferson Van Horne[qv] reached the El Paso area in September 1849 he stationed four companies of the Third Infantry on the rancho, six acres of which Coons rented to the United States Army for $4,200 a year. Troops remained at the "Post Opposite El Paso [del Norte]" until late 1851, when they were transferred to Fort Fillmore in New Mexico. The loss of income from the army, combined with other business reverses, ruined Coons financially, and Ponce repossessed the rancho. A post office was established there under the name of El Paso in 1852. After Ponce died that same year, his wife and daughter sold the property for $10,000 to a trader from Kentucky named William T. (Uncle Billy) Smith. Smith divided the rancho and began selling tracts, but sold out to the El Paso Company, which included Josiah F. Crosby[qv] and other prominent local citizens. They hired Anson Mills[qv] to survey the property. Mills completed the job in February 1859, by which time the property had gained another thirty-five acres, thanks to the changing course of the Rio Grande. The property eventually became the site of El Paso.

BIBLIOGRAPHY: Leon C. Metz, *Turning Points in El Paso* (El Paso: Mangan, 1985). W. H. Timmons, *El Paso: A Borderlands History* (El Paso: Texas Western Press, 1990). *Martin Donell Kohout*

COONVILLE, TEXAS. Coonville is on Farm Road 2694 two miles east of Shelbyville in southeastern Shelby County. The area was originally occupied by plantations. The Carroll Colored Methodist Episcopal Church was organized in the late 1870s on land owned by Thomas and John Carroll. During the early years of the twentieth century the community also had a school, which in 1903 enrolled twenty-eight children. In 1983 Coonville had the church and scattered houses.

BIBLIOGRAPHY: Charles E. Tatum, *Shelby County: In the East Texas Hills* (Austin: Eakin, 1984). *Cecil Harper, Jr.*

COOPER, ARTHUR BYRON (1850–1916). A. B. Cooper, early settler and leader in Motley County, son of Dr. James and Elizabeth (Juryens) Cooper, was born in York, Pennsylvania, on July 25, 1850, and educated in Ohio. While serving as an army scout under George A. Custer,qv he camped on Tee Pee Creek in Motley County. Later, on his way back to Texas, he met and married a Swedish immigrant waitress, Anna Benson Nelson, on December 3, 1878, at Denver, Colorado. Cooper and his bride headed for Dallas, where they bought a team, a wagon, and household goods. By following the Rath-Reynolds Trail, a trail made by buffalo hunters hauling hides to market, they arrived at Tee Pee City, a thriving buffalo hunters' camp, in February 1879.

With Anna's savings, Cooper filed on land in 1879 and bought three sections of railroad land, the first survey in this area. He set up a general store in their dugoutqv and in 1880 was appointed postmaster of Tee Pee City. When Cooper was away freighting, Mrs. Cooper served the cowboys and settlers; the buffalo-hide trade had gone with the buffalo.qv In 1882 the second of four Cooper children, Nora, became the first white girl born in the area. When Motley County was organized in 1891 Cooper was one of the first four commissioners. He served as a trustee when the Tee Pee City school was built in 1895 of rock quarried from the Cooper claim. Cooper went on bond for Sheriff Joe Beckham in 1891, but Beckham turned outlaw, and the Coopers lost their land in 1893. Anna Cooper fought the court, claiming that her money had purchased the land, and eight years later she was awarded the homestead. In 1898 Cooper, then forty-eight, left for the Klondike to prospect for gold, leaving the family to ranch, farm, and raise grapes for a living. He died at Cordova, Alaska, on November 25, 1916, and was buried at Sitka. Although Tee Pee City was deserted around the turn of the century, Mrs. Cooper remained at her old claim, where she died in 1932.

BIBLIOGRAPHY: Harry H. Campbell, *The Early History of Motley County* (San Antonio: Naylor, 1958; 2d ed., Wichita Falls: Nortex, 1971). Eleanor Traweek, *Of Such as These: A History of Motley County and Its Families* (Quanah, Texas: Nortex, 1973). *Marisue Potts*

COOPER, DILLARD (ca. 1816–ca. 1878). Dillard Cooper, pioneer settler, was born in South Carolina about 1816. He and his wife, Lucinda, lived in Alabama and Tennessee before moving to Texas. Cooper traveled to Texas with Capt. John Shackelford'sqv Red Rovers.qv The company landed at Copano Bay in January 1836 and shortly thereafter was sent to join James W. Fannin'sqv command. Cooper was slightly wounded at the battle of Coletoqv but escaped the Goliad Massacre.qv After Texas independence, he lived in Hays County and subsequently settled on a tract of land on the east bank of Cummins Creek in Colorado County, granted to him by the Republic of Texas.qv The 1860 census described him as a farmer with a personal estate of $3,500. He and Lucinda were the parents of five children. After Lucinda's death Cooper married a widow, Mrs. E. E. Gholson, in October 1878. His account of the Goliad Massacre was published in the Columbus *Citizen* on July 30, 1870. He died at Columbus after 1878.

BIBLIOGRAPHY: Colorado County Historical Commission, *Colorado County Chronicles from the Beginning to 1923* (2 vols., Austin: Nortex, 1986). Harbert Davenport, Notes from an Unfinished Study of Fannin and His Men (MS, Harbert Davenport Collection, Texas State Library, Austin; Barker Texas History Center, University of Texas at Austin). Carolyn R. Ericson and Frances T. Ingmire, comps., *First Settlers of the Republic of Texas* (2 vols., Nacogdoches, Texas: Ericson; St. Louis, Missouri: Ingmire, 1982; Printed first by Cruger and Wing, Austin, 1841.). Ira T. Taylor, *The Cavalcade of Jackson County* (San Antonio: Naylor, 1938).

COOPER, MADISON ALEXANDER, JR. (1894–1956). Madison Alexander Cooper, Jr., novelist and philanthropist, was born in Waco, Texas, on June 3, 1894, the son of Madison Alexander and Martha Dillon (Roane) Cooper. He entered the University of Texas in September 1911; after graduating with a B.A. degree in English in 1915, he returned to Waco to work in the family grocery business, the M. A. Cooper Company. He entered the first officers' training camp at Leon Springs, Texas, in May 1917, was commissioned a second lieutenant, and served in France during World War I.qv He was promoted to captain before his discharge and return to Waco in May 1919. He worked for the Cooper Company for ten years and then tried other business ventures on his own. Beginning in 1924, often anonymously, he sponsored many civic programs in Waco. In 1943, as a memorial to his parents, he set up the Madison Alexander Cooper and Martha Roane Cooper Foundation. In 1954, after a legal battle with J. R. Milam, Jr., Cooper sold his interests in the Cooper Grocery Company to Milam, and the business was renamed the J. R. Milam Company.

During the 1920s Cooper began writing short stories and sold a few. In the early 1930s, he took three correspondence courses in creative writing from Columbia University. He was known locally as a wealthy, eccentric, bachelor businessman and did not reveal his ambition as a writer, so that when his novel *Sironia, Texas* (which he worked on for eleven years), was published by Houghton Mifflin in 1952, it came as a surprise to most people. The two-volume novel was 1,731 pages long and made publishing history as the longest novel in English originally published in book form. It presents the life of a small Texas town from 1900 to 1921 and combines an impressive array of naturalistic social detail with the conventions of Victorian novels. The book involves eighty-three characters in twenty-one separate plot lines and traces the conflict between the town's decaying Southern aristocracy and its rising merchant class. Though Cooper denied any intended resemblance, some characters and events of the novel are composites of real people and events. For example, Cooper based his character Calvin Thaxton on Pat Morris Neffqv and the Southern Patriots on the Ku Klux Klanqv of the 1920s. The full extent to which *Sironia* is an exposé of real citizens of Waco is obscure, for, perhaps significantly, Cooper directed in his will that his literary files be burned unread. He received the Houghton Mifflin Literary Fellowship Award for the novel, and in 1953 the Texas Institute of Lettersqv awarded him the McMurray Bookshop Award for the work. The novel was a New York *Times* best-seller for eleven weeks. The publicity subsided, however, and his second novel, *The Haunted Hacienda* (1955), the first volume of a planned trilogy, went largely unnoticed. In his later years Cooper also wrote book reviews for the Dallas *Morning News*.qv

He died on September 28, 1956, and was buried with Presbyterian rites in Oakwood Cemetery, Waco. He left his entire estate of almost

$3 million to the Cooper Foundation, the income of which was to be used for the betterment of Waco. By 1984 the foundation held total assets of $6.2 million and had awarded 321 grants amounting to more than $4.9 million to various Waco projects.

BIBLIOGRAPHY: Vertical Files, Barker Texas History Center, University of Texas at Austin. Madison Cooper Papers, Texas Collection, Baylor University, Waco. Marion Travis, *Madison Cooper* (Waco: Word Books, 1971).

John Dennis Anderson

COOPER, OSCAR HENRY (1852–1932). Oscar Henry Cooper, university president and state education officer, the son of Dr. William Henry and Katherine Hunter (Rosser) Cooper, was born in Panola County, Texas, on November 22, 1852. He attended Marshall University (1865–66) and went on to Yale University, where he received the B.A. degree in 1872, graduating first in his class. His first teaching position was at Woods Post Office near Panola, Texas. He served as president of Henderson Male and Female College from 1873 to 1879 and for two years as an instructor at Sam Houston Normal Institute (now Sam Houston State University). He returned to Yale in 1881 to serve as a tutor and studied at the University of Berlin in 1884–85. Upon his return, he was principal of Houston High School (1885–86). He served as state superintendent of public instruction from 1886 to 1890. Among the reforms during his tenure were the foundations for county supervision, uniform textbooks, and standards for high schools. Cooper served as superintendent of Galveston schools from 1890 to 1896. At the time it was the highest-paying educational position in Texas. The Galveston school system received international acclaim under Cooper's leadership, when it received one of eight gold medals for the best schoolwork in America at the Paris Exposition—it was the only city in the South included on the list. In 1892 Cooper was placed at the helm of the state-established School of Methods, for preparing teachers. In 1896 he resigned his Galveston position and moved his family to Carthage, his boyhood home.

Cooper, a Texas Baptist layman, served as president of Baylor University from 1899 to 1902 and president of Simmons College (now Hardin-Simmons University) from 1902 to 1909. Both colleges saw a marked increase in scholarships, gifts, and enrollment under his direction. During his tenure as president at Baylor the school's degrees were recognized for the first time by eastern schools, the Department of Pedagogy was established, and the Department of Theology was expanded. The Waco school also received gifts of $75,000 each from F. L. Carroll of Waco and George W. Carroll[qv] of Beaumont for two new buildings. At the time these were the largest donations ever given in Texas to higher education. At Simmons College Copper greatly increased curriculum standards, entered into an aggressive building program, secured the entire estate of James Simmons for the school, and named Jefferson D. Sandefer[qv] as his successor. Cooper's efforts resulted in a doubling of enrollment.

After resigning from Simmons in 1909, Cooper established Cooper's Boys School in Abilene, which he headed until February 1915. He left the school to return to Simmons as chairman of the faculty and to head the department of education and philosophy. From 1928 to 1930 he served as a part-time professor of history and the philosophy of education at the University of Texas. He wrote numerous articles calling for a state university and chaired a subcommittee of the Texas State Teachers Association[qv] that issued a proposal for the establishment of a state institution of higher learning, thus playing a leading role in the establishment of the University of Texas (1882). He was one of the founders of the Texas State Teachers Association, served on the executive board of the Conference for Education in Texas (1907), chaired the State Educational Survey (1921), and served one term as president of the Association of Texas Colleges (1923). He contributed a multitude of writings and official reports on education, lectured extensively on the public education system, wrote a prospectus, "The Conditions and Prospects of the Public School System of Texas," and authored an American history text entitled *The History of Our Country* (1898). Cooper was a member of Phi Beta Kappa and was awarded honorary doctorates by Peabody College in Nashville, Tennessee, in 1891, by Baylor University in 1914, and by Simmons College in 1925. In 1902 he was made a fellow of the Texas State Historical Association.[qv] Cooper's contributions to education in Abilene led the city to name its second high school in his honor.

Cooper married the former Mary Bryan Stewart, granddaughter of James H. Starr,[qv] on November 24, 1886. The couple had four children. Cooper died in Abilene on August 22, 1932.

BIBLIOGRAPHY: Mary Baggett, The Life and Works of Dr. Oscar Henry Cooper: Texas Educator (M.A. thesis, Hardin-Simmons University, 1945). James Milton Carroll, *A History of Texas Baptists* (Dallas: Baptist Standard, 1923). L. R. Elliott, ed., *Centennial Story of Texas Baptists* (Dallas: Baptist General Convention of Texas, 1936). Ina Alice Hollis, Life and Work of O. H. Cooper (M.A. thesis, University of Texas, 1925). Thomas E. Turner, *The Presidents of Baylor* (Waco: Baylor University, 1981). Vertical Files, Barker Texas History Center, University of Texas at Austin.

Stephen M. Stookey

COOPER, SAMUEL BRONSON (1850–1918). Samuel Bronson Cooper, politician, son of Rev. A. H. and Elizabeth Cooper, was born in Caldwell County, Kentucky, on May 30, 1850. The family moved to Texas in 1850, and the elder Bronson, a Methodist minister, died in 1853. Samuel was raised by an uncle and worked on a farm as a boy. He was admitted to the bar in 1872. He married Phoebe Young on October 15, 1873. He was elected county attorney of Tyler County in 1876 and again in 1878. He also helped in the early educational efforts of John Henry Kirby.[qv]

Cooper served two terms in the state Senate, from 1880 to 1884, and was president pro tem during his second term. He wrote a bill granting each Confederate veteran 1,280 acres of state land. In 1885 President Grover Cleveland named him collector of internal revenue at Galveston, a position he held until 1888. Cooper ran unsuccessfully for district judge in 1889 but was elected in the Second Texas District to the first of six consecutive terms in the United States House of Representatives in 1892. He was defeated by Moses L. Broocks[qv] in 1904 but came back to beat Broocks in 1906 for a position in the Sixtieth Congress, only to lose to Martin Dies[qv] in the 1908 race. While a member of the Congress, Cooper served on the House Ways and Means Committee. He helped secure $600,000 in federal appropriations to link Beaumont with the Port Arthur ship channel. With Cooper's support, a nine-foot-deep channel was dug in 1908; later improvements tied Beaumont to the Sabine-Neches Waterway[qv] and made the city a deepwater port.

Cooper was chairman of the Texas delegation to the Democratic convention in Kansas City (1904). In 1910 President William Howard Taft appointed him to the Board of General Appraisers, a customs court that sat at New York. Cooper was affiliated with the Masonic lodge, the Independent Order of Odd Fellows, the Knights of Pythias, and the Benevolent and Protective Order of Elks. He died in New York on August 21, 1918, after a short illness. His funeral and burial were in Beaumont. He was survived by four of his five children, his wife having died in 1911. One of his daughters, William (Willie) Chapman Cooper, married William P. Hobby,[qv] and another married S. W. Sholars, congressman from Tyler County.

BIBLIOGRAPHY: Lewis E. Daniell, *Personnel of the Texas State Government, with Sketches of Representative Men of Texas* (Austin: City Printing, 1887; 3d ed., San Antonio: Maverick, 1892).

Robert Wooster

COOPER, WILLIAM (?–?). Evidently multiple William Coopers lived in colonial Texas. Two of them were members of Stephen F. Austin's[qv] Old Three Hundred.[qv] Though it is impossible to sort the biographical facts about these two men with any final confidence, one of them was associated with Matagorda County and the other with Waller and Austin counties. On August 10, 1824, the latter received title to 1½ sitios^qv of land in what is now Waller County and two labors^qv of land now part of Austin County. He was probably the man classified in the 1826 census as a farmer and stock raiser, aged between forty and fifty, with a household including his wife, aged between twenty-five and forty, three sons (the oldest between sixteen and twenty-five), two daughters, two servants, and three slaves. Though the evidence is far from conclusive, he was probably the "Cow" Cooper who with his wife, Sarah (James) of South Carolina, immigrated to Texas from Tennessee in 1822. They eventually settled near San Felipe, where he reportedly ran a small store and owned a large number of cattle. A small collection of the papers of this William Cooper is housed at the Barker Texas History Center.^qv He was probably the "Cow" Cooper whose stock ranch was located on the east side of the Brazos River below San Felipe, though "Cow" was also the nickname of a Cooper who came to Texas from Miller County, Arkansas, possibly with Henry Jones and William Rabb,^qqv sometime before November 1822.

Also, by 1828 or 1829 a "Sawmill" Cooper, evidently another man, was running a store in San Felipe with a partner called Cheves, probably Henry Cheves or Chevis. This may have been the William Cooper above. Evidently "Sawmill" Cooper received his nickname from having worked in the lumber business; one account claims he was mangled while working at a sawmill. The William Cooper who, with partner Moses Morrison^qv on July 24, 1824, received a sitio of land in what is now Matagorda County was probably the man listed in the 1825 census of the Colorado district and classified in the 1826 census as a farmer and stock raiser, a single man aged between twenty-five and forty.

The young William Cooper who was killed about five miles from his parents' residence in a fight with Indians on Caney Creek in November 1830 was probably the son of the Austin colonist "Cow" Cooper. Another son, James Cooper, went with Barzillai Kuykendall^qv to Fort Tenoxtitlán, where he shot off the thumb of one of the Waco Indians who had reportedly killed his brother and then had to hide to avoid capture by Mexican authorities. One of the William Coopers was *síndico procurador*^qv at San Felipe de Austin in 1829. "Sawmill" Cooper, partner of Henry Cheves, died before January 10, 1832, when the *Texas Gazette*^qv at San Felipe de Austin carried a notice by J. B. Miller and Henry Cheves, administrators of Cooper's estate. In January 1834 William B. Travis^qv examined the papers of the estate of one William Cooper, possibly the same deceased Cooper whose lands included a half league on the San Bernard River and one at the mouth of Buffalo Bayou. In April 1836 William and Amos Cooper sold several horses to the Texas army on credit and by 1838 still had not received payment; it is possible that this was the remaining Austin colonist.

BIBLIOGRAPHY: Eugene C. Barker, ed., *The Austin Papers* (3 vols., Washington: GPO, 1924–28). Eugene C. Barker, ed., "Minutes of the Ayuntamiento of San Felipe de Austin, 1828–1832," *Southwestern Historical Quarterly* 21–24 (January 1918–October 1920). Lester G. Bugbee, "The Old Three Hundred: A List of Settlers in Austin's First Colony," *Quarterly of the Texas State Historical Association* 1 (October 1897). William Cooper, Papers, Barker Texas History Center, University of Texas at Austin. Robert E. Davis, ed., *The Diary of William Barret Travis* (Waco: Texian Press, 1966). J. H. Kuykendall, "Reminiscences of Early Texans," *Quarterly of the Texas State Historical Association* 6–7 (January, April, July 1903). Noah Smithwick, *The Evolution of a State, or Recollections of Old Texas Days* (Austin: Gammel, 1900; rpt., Austin: University of Texas Press, 1983). Rex W. Strickland, Anglo-American Activities in Northeastern Texas, 1803–1845 (Ph.D. dissertation, University of Texas, 1937). Vertical Files, Barker Texas History Center, University of Texas at Austin. J. W. Wilbarger, *Indian Depredations in Texas* (Austin: Hutchings, 1889; rpt., Austin: State House, 1985).
Rachel Jenkins

COOPER, TEXAS (Delta County). Cooper, the county seat of Delta County, is at the junction of State highways 24 and 154, some twenty-four miles southwest of Paris in the south central portion of the county. It was founded in 1870 and named for L. W. Cooper of Houston, one of the sponsors of the bill to organize the county in 1870. A post office was established there in 1871, and the town was incorporated with aldermanic government in 1881. Cooper quickly emerged as the market center for the new county and by 1885 reported 300 residents. The construction of the Texas Midland Railroad further spurred the town's growth. In 1896 Cooper comprised 1,000 residents, two churches, and a school, as well as a bank, a shoemaker, a hotel, a grocery store, a wagonmaker, two blacksmith shops, two feed mills, two steam cotton gins and corn mills, two weekly newspapers (the Delta *Courier* and the *People's Cause*), three drugstores, and seven general stores. Cooper continued to grow rapidly during the early 1900s. Its population reached a reported high of 2,563 by 1925, thereafter remaining fairly stable. It declined slightly during the 1930s, grew during the 1950s, and declined again in the 1980s. In 1970 Cooper reported sixty businesses, including seed-cleaning plants and some thirty-eight dairies. The city's population was 2,349 in the early 1950s and 2,258 in 1970. Cooper in the early 1990s was a commercial and shipping center for the surrounding agricultural region. In 1991 the incorporated town reported seventy businesses and a population of 2,197.
Christopher Long

COOPER, TEXAS (Houston County). Cooper was on State Highway 21 nine miles southwest of Crockett in southwestern Houston County. It was probably established around 1900. In the mid-1930s the small community had a church, a cemetery, and a number of houses. After World War II^qv many of the residents moved away, and by the early 1990s only a church and a few widely scattered houses remained in the area.
Christopher Long

COOPERATIVES. Cooperatives are business organizations owned and controlled by the patrons of the business, their primary aim being service to patrons and not profit to stockholders. Each common stockholder is limited to one vote regardless of the number of shares he owns, any money left over after meeting business costs must be returned to the patrons in proportion to the amount of business each has done with the cooperative. The amount of interest paid on shares is limited by law to 8 percent and is usually held at 4 percent or less. Cooperatives with 85 percent farmer membership are exempt from federal income taxation, but all nonmember business is subject to taxation. In Texas cooperation has been a preponderantly rural activity, with the early farm cooperatives closely allied with general farm organizations. After the Grange^qv was established in 1873, affiliated grocery and supply stores were organized, and by 1887 there were 150 stores doing an annual business of almost $2 million. Such cooperatives, however, had largely died out by 1890. For several years beginning in 1878, cotton was handled by the Grange on a commission basis through the Texas Co-operative Association.

From 1905 to 1914 the Farmers' Educational and Co-operative Union was active in sponsoring more than 100 cooperative cotton gins and warehouses and in organizing the cooperative buying of farm supplies. The Texas Farm Bureau^qv Federation did the same sort of work in the early 1920s and in addition sponsored associations to market tomatoes and ribbon cane syrup in East Texas and watermelons in South Texas. Early cooperatives were incorporated under ordinary corporation law, however, most of those organized between 1920 and 1931 were incorporated under a law called the Society Act of 1917. This act, revised in 1925 and 1949 and called the Co-operative Marketing Act, regulated cooperatives as late as 1968. By around 1949 there were more than 1,000 cooperative associations in Texas, about half of which were cotton gins. The remainder included grain elevators and warehouses, cottonseed oil mills: marketing associations for citrus fruits, watermelons, tomatoes, pecans, mohair, cotton, and livestock, rural electrification[qv] cooperatives, grocery stores, bookstores, student housing, insurance companies, credit unions, and grain and feed supply stores. In addition there was one large wholesale concern, the Consumers' Co-operative Association of Amarillo and Dallas, which was owned cooperatively by about sixty local associations.

In 1966 there were more than 700 cooperative associations in Texas, about half of which were cotton gins. By 1994, the number of agricultural cooperatives had dropped to 400. Texas cooperatives in 1994 included cotton gins, grain elevators, marketing associations for fruits and vegetables, poultry, peanuts, and dairy and livestock products, rural electrification cooperatives, rural telephone cooperatives, production credit associations, credit unions, farm supply stores, college housing, bookstores, and grocery stores. Also included were cottonseed oil mills, cottonseed breeding associations, cotton compresses, cotton and grain marketing associations, and wholesale farm supply associations. Trade associations for cooperatives in the state included the Texas Federation of Cooperatives, the Texas Cotton Ginners Association, and the Texas Electric Cooperatives, Incorporated. These organizations were assisted in research, service, and educational activities by the Agricultural Cooperative Service of the United States Department of Agriculture, by the Texas Agricultural Experiment Station[qv] and the Texas Agricultural Extension Service[qv] of Texas A&M University, and by the Texas Credit Union League.

BIBLIOGRAPHY: Stanley Hack, *Legal Aspects of Small Business' Use of Cooperative Arrangements* (Madison: University of Wisconsin, 1964). Texas Department of Agriculture, *1948 Cooperative Marketing Act: Chapter 8 Revised Statutes* (Austin, 1968).

COOPER CREEK (Garza County). Cooper (Coopers) Creek rises four miles south of Post in southwestern Garza County (at 33°08′ N, 101°24′ W) and runs southeast for fourteen miles to its mouth on the Double Mountain Fork of the Brazos River, near U.S. Highway 84 (at 33°03′ N, 101°15′ W). The surrounding steeply to gently sloping terrain is surfaced by shallow stony clay and sandy loams that support oak, mesquite, grasses, and scrub brush.

——— (Scurry County). Cooper Creek rises in extreme northern Scurry County (at 32°58′ N, 100°54′ W) and runs northeast for ten miles to its mouth on the Double Mountain Fork of the Brazos River, eight miles southeast of Clairemont in southeastern Kent County (at 33°06′ N, 100°51′ W). The surrounding moderately steep slopes, with locally high relief, are surfaced by shallow to moderately deep silt loam that supports mesquite and grasses.

COOPER CREEK, TEXAS. Cooper Creek, two miles east of Denton on a creek in Denton County, attracted settlers because of the water and the available timber. It was established about 1900 and has served as a church and school community. By 1990 Cooper Creek was in the city limits of Denton, and only the Cooper Creek Baptist Church and Cooper Creek Cemetery were left as a reminder of its past.

BIBLIOGRAPHY: Edward Franklin Bates, *History and Reminiscences of Denton County* (Denton, Texas: McNitzky Printing, 1918; rpt., Denton: Terrill Wheeler Printing, 1976). Denton *Record-Chronicle,* September 25, 1960.
David Minor

COOPER MOUNTAIN. Cooper Mountain, in southeastern Kent County (at 33°01′ N, 100°51′ W), has an elevation of 2,706 feet above mean sea level. The surrounding terrain of moderately steep slopes, with some locally high relief and highly eroded in some areas, is surfaced by shallow to moderately deep silt loam soils that support mesquite and grasses.

COOPWOOD, BETHEL (1827–1907). Bethel Coopwood, soldier, lawyer, judge, and historian, was born on May 1, 1827, in Lawrence County, Alabama. He moved to Texas in 1846 and fought in a cavalry regiment in the Mexican War.[qv] In 1854 he moved to California, where he was admitted to the bar. He returned to Texas and became recognized as an able lawyer and Spanish scholar in the lower Rio Grande valley. In 1859 he married Josephine Woodward; they eventually had fourteen children. Coopwood entered the Confederate Army as a captain in the cavalry and served until 1863. After the Civil War[qv] he spent a year in Coahuila. He contributed articles to and wrote book reviews for early issues of the Texas State Historical Association[qv] *Quarterly,* in which he published "Notes on the History of La Bahía del Espíritu Santo" in 1898–99 and "The Route of Cabeza de Vaca" in 1899–1900. Judge Coopwood died in Austin on December 26, 1907.

BIBLIOGRAPHY: Wayne R. Austerman, "'Old Nighthawk' and the Pass of the North," *Password,* Fall 1982. Austin *Statesman,* December 29, 1907.
Margery H. Krieger

COOTAJANAM INDIANS. The Cootajanam (Cootajan) Indians, apparently Coahuiltecan in speech, lived along the lower Rio Grande. In the middle eighteenth century they were reported to have had settlements on the north bank of the river in the area of present Cameron and Hidalgo counties.

BIBLIOGRAPHY: Gabriel Saldivar, *Los Indios de Tamaulipas* (Mexico City: Pan American Institute of Geography and History, 1943).
Thomas N. Campbell

COPANE INDIANS. The Copane (Cobane, Coopane, Kopano) Indians were Karankawans who, in the eighteenth century, lived in the middle section of the Texas coast, mainly on and between Copano and San Antonio bays. Little is known about the Copanes other than that they were represented at the coastal missions of Nuestra Señora del Rosario and Nuestra Señora del Refugio between 1751 and 1828. It seems likely that the Copane Indians who survived the mission period joined remnants of other Karankawan groups that became known as the Karankawa Indians. All Karankawan groups became extinct by 1858.

BIBLIOGRAPHY: Herbert E. Bolton, "The Founding of Mission Rosario: A Chapter in the History of the Gulf Coast," *Quarterly of the Texas State Historical Association* 10 (October 1906). H. E. Bolton, "Records of the Mission of Nuestra Señora del Refugio," *Quarterly of the Texas State Historical Association* 14 (October 1910). Herbert Eugene Bolton, *Texas in the Middle Eighteenth Century* (Berkeley: University of California Press, 1915; rpt., Austin: University of Texas Press, 1970). William E. Dunn, "The Founding of Nuestra Señora del Refugio, the Last Spanish Mission in Texas," *Southwestern Historical Quarterly* 25 (January 1922). Frederick Webb Hodge, ed., *Handbook of American Indians North of Mexico* (2 vols., Washington: GPO, 1907, 1910; rpt., New York: Pageant, 1959). William H. Oberste, *History of Refugio Mission* (Refugio, Texas: Refugio Timely Remarks, 1942).
Thomas N. Campbell

COPANO, TEXAS. The long-abandoned port, and later town, of Copano was at what is now called Copano Point on the northwestern shore of Copano Bay, thirty miles north of Corpus Christi in southeastern Refugio County. The townsite is practically inaccessible by land, but can be reached by boat from Bayside, the nearest town, five miles to the south. Copano was named for the Copane Indians who frequented the area and during the Spanish and Mexican eras was known as El Cópano. The town is believed to have served as a port and rendezvous for pirates and smugglers and may have been in use as a port as early as 1722. Copano was used as a port of entry by Spanish governor Bernardo de Gálvez[qv] during the 1780s, but from the time of Spanish and Mexican Texas^qqv through revolutionary times, there was little more at Copano than a customhouse or warehouse and a fresh-water tank. Nevertheless, the port played an important role during the colonial and revolutionary periods. In 1834 Gen. Juan N. Almonte,^qv on an inspection tour for Mexican president Antonio López de Santa Anna,^qv reported Copano to have the deepest port in Texas.

Between 1828 and 1835 groups of colonists passed through the port on their journeys from Europe to settlement in Texas. Groups of Irish^qv arrived during 1833 and 1834. One large group of Irish colonists was struck by cholera during the voyage from New York, and many arrived in Texas only to be buried on the Copano beach. The port of Copano became strategically important to both the Mexican and Texas armies during the Texas Revolution.^qv On September 20, 1835, Mexican general Martín Perfecto de Cos^qv and his army landed at Copano on their way to Goliad and Bexar. The next month Gen. Sam Houston^qv issued orders that Copano be fortified. The Texans held the site and used it as a port of entry for supplies and provisions until March 1836, when the port fell to the Mexicans under Gen. José de Urrea.^qv When Maj. William P. Miller^qv and his Nashville Company of volunteers anchored at Copano in late March 1836, they were captured by the Mexicans. The port was used by the Mexicans to receive reinforcements and to evacuate their wounded and prisoners. After they withdrew from the area in May 1836, the Texans once again gained control of the port. The famous "Horse Marines"^qv incident occurred on the beach at Copano on June 3 and June 17, 1836, when Maj. Isaac W. Burton's^qv Mounted Rangers captured Mexican vessels, men, and supplies.

Settlement of Copano began around 1840 under the direction of James Power.^qv Associated with Power in the townsite project were Robert J. Walker, Duncan S. Walker, and Robert H. Hughes. The first home built at Copano was constructed by Joseph E. Plummer, Jr., around 1840. The Plummer cemetery is a mile north of the Copano townsite. By 1852 a dozen homes had been built in Copano, all of shell concrete made from materials found on the beach. A small school and two stores were constructed in the town. One store housed the post office, which operated between 1851 and 1867. Three wharves stretched into the town's harbor, described by a visitor as being "by far the safest harbor on the entire [Texas] coast." Cotton, hides, and tallow were principal products shipped through the port. Copano thrived during the Civil War.^qv Most Southern ports were blockaded, but because Copano was located on an inlet, ships could be loaded there unobserved by Union forces and then slip out to sea. However, in response to blockade running, a Union gunboat fleet anchored at Copano in 1864, and the town's inhabitants fled and remained away until the Yankees left a few days later. Various efforts to connect the town by railway to Goliad and San Antonio failed, and the inhabitants traveled to Refugio and the interior on an old military road that went north fourteen miles to the Refugio Mission, and later over a longer, more traveled highway that paralleled the bluff above Mission Bay, crossed Melon Creek, and then turned westward to Refugio. Throughout Copano's existence, an adequate fresh-water supply was difficult to maintain. The water problem, combined with the absence of a railroad and efficient interior transportation route, led to the demise of the town. Most residents moved to nearby Refugio, and by the 1880s Copano was abandoned.

BIBLIOGRAPHY: Hobart Huson, *El Copano: Ancient Port of Bexar and La Bahia* (Refugio, Texas: Refugio *Timely Remarks*, 1935). Hobart Huson, *Refugio: A Comprehensive History of Refugio County from Aboriginal Times to 1953* (2 vols., Woodsboro, Texas: Rooke Foundation, 1953, 1955).
June Melby Benowitz

COPANO BAY. Copano Bay, just west of Rockport off Refugio and Aransas counties, is a twelve-by-six-mile extension of Aransas Bay (at 28°07′ N, 97°07′ W). The bay was first explored in 1766 by Diego Ortiz Parrilla,^qv who named it Santo Domingo, but after the port of Copano was established in 1785 and named for the Copane Indians in the area, the bay became known as Copano Bay. The surrounding flat, marshy terrain is surfaced by sand and dark clays that support mesquite and grasses.

COPANO BAY STATE FISHING PIER. Copano Bay State Fishing Pier, sometimes called Copano Bay Causeway State Recreation Park, is on State Highway 35 at Copano Bay, six miles north of Fulton and forty-one miles northeast of Corpus Christi in Aransas County. It is a six-acre park with a fishing pier, available for day use only. The park has group facilities, restrooms, picnicking, fishing, boat ramps, swimming, a museum exhibit, and a historic structure. The pier was established in 1967 when the Texas State Highway Department (later the State Department of Highways and Public Transportation^qv) built a new causeway and turned the old causeway over to the Parks and Wildlife Commission, which made it into a lighted fishing pier. The park is operated as a concession rather than by the Texas Parks and Wildlife Department.^qv It is open twenty-four hours daily from Memorial Day through Labor Day and from dawn to early afternoon the rest of the year. There is a small user fee charged. The pier is three miles south of Goose Island State Park^qv on Park Road 13, where full camping facilities are available.

BIBLIOGRAPHY: Ray Miller, *Texas Parks* (Austin: Cordovan, 1984). Robert Rafferty, *Texas Coast* (Houston: Texas Monthly Press, 1986).
John G. Johnson

COPANO CREEK. Copano Creek rises in northeastern Refugio County (at 28°26′ N, 97°11′ W) and runs for twenty-four miles southeast to its mouth on Copano Bay (at 28°12′ N, 97°01′ W). The surrounding flat to rolling prairie is surfaced by expansive clay that supports hardwoods, pines, and prairie grasses. The area includes the rich Greta oilfield.

COPE, EDWARD DRINKER (1840–1897). Edward Drinker Cope, naturalist, the son of Alfred and Hannah Cope, was born on July 28, 1840, in Philadelphia, Pennsylvania. He studied at Westtown Academy, 1849–53, the University of Pennsylvania, 1860–63, and the Smithsonian Institution. On August 14, 1865, while teaching at Haverford College (1864–67), he married Annie Pym; they had a daughter. Cope made field studies of fossil vertebrates in the East and became an authority on paleontology and zoology. He was for a time employed by the Hayden and Wheeler surveys (the former was later known as the United States Geological and Geographical Survey of the Territories).

When Cope made his first trip to Texas in the summer of 1877, he was in competition with fellow paleontologists to be the first to identify the fossils of the West; therefore, when he employed Jacob Boll^qv to collect for him, it was in secret. On this journey Cope first recognized the existence of Permian amphibians, which represented a late geologic age before unknown in America. His published papers on his findings included "Descriptions of Extinct Batrachia and Reptilia from the Permian Formation of Texas" in *Proceedings of the American Philosophical Society* (1877–78) and "On the Zoological Position of Texas" in the *Bulletin* of the United States National Museum (1880).

In recognition of his work on Texas geology and fossil vertebrates, Cope was employed by the Geological Survey of Texas during the summer of 1892 (*see* GEOLOGICAL SURVEYS OF TEXAS). With William F. Cummins,^qv state geologist, Cope went to the Panhandle,^qv where he discovered the fossil fields that came to be known as the Clarendon Beds of the Upper Miocene and Lower Pliocene age and the Blanco Beds of the late Pliocene; these contained fossils of mammalian quadrupeds that had come from South America and giant mastodons from Southern Africa. Cope also worked in Palo Duro Canyon.^qv The mammal fossils collected on the trip were sent to the Museum of the Texas Geological Survey.

The findings of Cope's two journeys to Texas were published in at least thirty separate articles, including a series of five entitled "Contribution to the History of the Vertebrata of the Permian Formation of Texas" in *Proceedings of the American Philosophical Society* (1881–85). Published in the *Proceedings of the Academy of Natural Science, Philadelphia* (1892), was "A Contribution to a Knowledge of the Blanco Beds of Texas," and in the *American Naturalist* (1885–92) were "Pliocene Horses of Southwestern Texas," "Glyptodon from Texas," "On a Skull of the Equus excelsus Leidy from the Equus Beds of Texas," and "The Age of the Staked Plains." Cope's work made possible the identification of mammalian life that marked the close of the Pliocene age in America.

Cope was an assiduous collector and prolific writer. He named about one-third of the fossil vertebrates then known, published more than 600 articles and editorials, and owned and edited the *American Naturalist* for nineteen years. He was a member of national and foreign geological, philosophical, and scientific societies, and collected extensively in Europe, Canada, Mexico, and the United States. From 1889 until his death on April 12, 1897, he was professor at the University of Pennsylvania.

BIBLIOGRAPHY: *Dictionary of American Biography.* S. W. Geiser, *Naturalists of the Frontier* (Dallas: Southern Methodist University, 1937; 2d ed. 1948). Henry Fairfield Osborn, *Cope, Master Naturalist: The Life and Letters of Edward Drinker Cope* (Princeton: Princeton University Press, 1931). *Clinton P. Hartmann*

COPE, MILLARD LEWIS (1905–1964). Millard Cope, newspaper publisher, was born on December 31, 1905, to James A. and Hattie B. (Parkerson) Cope in Sonora, Texas, where at the age of twelve he began working for the local newspaper setting type by hand for a nickel a stick (about two column inches). As a student at Sonora High School he was elected the first chairman of the executive board of the Texas High School Press Association when it was organized at Baylor University in 1922. In 1925, during his third year at Howard Payne College (now Howard Payne University), he was elected president of the Texas Intercollegiate Press Association. He received his bachelor's degree in journalism in 1927 after a senior year at the University of Missouri, where he covered the state capitol for the student newspaper. In 1958 he was Howard Payne "Man of the Year," and in 1959 he received the University of Missouri's Honor Award for Distinguished Service to Journalism.

After graduating he joined the staff of the San Angelo *Morning Times,* newly begun in 1927 by Houston Harte,[qv] as a morning edition of the San Angelo *Standard.* His next assignment, from 1930 to 1936, was as publisher of the Sweetwater *Reporter* when it was purchased by Harte and Bernard Hanks of Abilene (*see* HARTE-HANKS COMMUNICATIONS). After its sale he was assigned to the Dallas office of the Texas Daily Press League, from where in 1940 he went to Denison as publisher of the Denison *Herald.* In January 1945 he was made publisher of the *News Messenger* in Marshall, where he remained for seventeen years and where his service to journalism brought him to national attention. He was director of the Associated Press (1959–64) and president of the Southern Newspaper Publishers Association (1957). By appointment of Governor Allan Shivers[qv] in 1953 and reappointment by Governor Price Daniel[qv] in 1959 he was a founding director of what is now the Texas Historical Commission[qv] and of the Texas Historical Foundation. In 1956 he served as a member of the Texas Commission on Higher Education, with supervisory responsibility over eighteen Texas institutions of higher learning. Governor Daniel also appointed him a member of the Texas Civil War Centennial Commission, for which service he received an award from the national commission. In 1963 President John F. Kennedy appointed him to the national advisory council for the Peace Corps. Cope became publisher of the San Angelo *Standard-Times* in August 1962.

During his many years as publisher of small Texas dailies Cope discovered and trained a number of young men and women who went on to establish national reputations of their own. Most notable of these were brothers James and Bill Moyers of Marshall, Lloyd May (Cissy) Stewart of Cleburne, and Jack Maguire of Denison. Although Cope did not openly profess a party affiliation, he was a conservative. Bill Moyers, who named his older son Cope, later wrote of his mentor, "In a way he was to small-town publishing in the 40s and 50s what William Allen White was to small-town editing, although White's reputation spread through his writing, and Millard's through personal character." Cope married Margaret Kilgore of San Angelo on December 12, 1931. They had a son and a daughter. He was a Presbyterian. He died on January 4, 1964, and was buried in San Angelo.

BIBLIOGRAPHY: Vertical Files, Barker Texas History Center, University of Texas at Austin. Mrs. Will E. Wilson and Deolece Parmelee, *The First Quarter Century* (Austin: Texas Historical Foundation, 1979). *Max S. Lale*

COPELAND, MURRAY MARCUS (1902–1982). Murray Marcus Copeland, cancer specialist, was born in McDonough, Georgia, in 1902. He received a B.S. from Oglethorpe University in 1923 and an M.D. from Johns Hopkins University School of Medicine in 1927. He was also trained in surgery and oncology at the Mayo Clinic Memorial Hospital for Cancer in New York City and Union Memorial Hospital in Baltimore. In 1955 he received an honorary D.Sc. from Oglethorpe. His position as clinical instructor at Johns Hopkins and the University of Maryland Medical School (1937–42) was interrupted by World War II,[qv] when he took command of the 142nd General Hospital in the South Pacific. He was discharged as a colonel in 1945 and received the Legion of Merit. After the war Copeland was professor of oncology and chairman of the Department of Oncology at Georgetown University School of Medicine (1947–60). While in Washington, D.C., he also served as consultant in surgery for Gallinger Municipal Hospital and Special Consultant to the Public Health Service, Cancer Control Branch.

In 1960 he joined the M. D. Anderson Hospital for Cancer Research (*see* UNIVERSITY OF TEXAS SYSTEM CANCER CENTER) as professor of surgery, associate director of education, and vice president for international affairs of the University Cancer Foundation. At the age of 69 he was asked to assume the directorship of the National Large Bowel Cancer Project, a position he held for ten years (1971–81).

Copeland was the author of over more than scientific articles. With Charles F. Geschickter he wrote *Tumors of the Bone* (three editions—1931, 1936, and 1949). He was the recipient of twelve national and international awards, including the President's Medal (1965) and the Distinguished Service Award (1972) from the American Cancer Society. In 1964–65 he was national president of the American Cancer Society, and in 1970 he served as secretary general of the Congress of the International Union Against Cancer. He was the first chairman of the American Joint Committee for Cancer Staging and End Result Reporting. The second edition of the *Manual for Staging in Cancer* (1983) is dedicated to Copeland's memory. In 1931 Copeland married Jean Brown. They had no children. He died on April 2, 1982, after a long illness, at Hermann Hospital in Houston.

BIBLIOGRAPHY: Houston *Post,* April 3, 1982. Reference Folder, Houston Academy of Medicine–Texas Medical Center Library, Harris County Medical Archive. *Texas Medicine,* August 1982. *Patricia L. Jakobi*

COPELAND, TEXAS. Copeland is just south of Tyler in Smith County. The area was settled as early as 1899, when the community was granted a post office named Coplen with Robert E. Burns as postmaster. In May 1904 the post office moved to Flint. By 1973 the name was spelled Copeland, and the community had several dwellings, a cemetery, and the Copeland Macedonia Church. Copeland was still on maps in 1985 and was still listed as a community in 1990. *Vista K. McCroskey*

COPELAND CREEK. Copeland Creek rises 1½ miles east of St. Jo in extreme east central Montague County (at 33°42′ N, 97°29′ W) and runs south for 4½ miles to its mouth on the Elm Fork of the Trinity River, 1½ miles southeast of St. Jo (at 33°39′ N, 97°29′ W). The surrounding flat to rolling terrain is surfaced by deep to shallow sandy and clay loam that supports hardwood, oak, and juniper trees, and grasses.

COPENHAGEN, TEXAS. Copenhagen was in the area of the present Center Plains cemetery on Farm Road 179, nine miles west of Hale Center in west central Hale County. It was formed around 1900. When its post office was opened in 1902 the post office department substituted the name Copenhagen for the settlement's original name, Center Plains. Although Copenhagen never developed into a town, its post office served the surrounding area until 1907, when the promise of a railroad led residents to move to the newly founded town of Norfleet nearby.

BIBLIOGRAPHY: Mary L. Cox, *History of Hale County, Texas* (Plainview, Texas, 1937).
Charles G. Davis

COPEVILLE, TEXAS. Copeville is on State Highway 78 eight miles southwest of Farmersville in southeastern Collin County. It was originally a mile west of the present townsite and was named for one of the earliest settlers to arrive in the area, Miles Cope. With his father and brother, Cope organized the community in the 1850s. In 1877 Thomas King surveyed and mapped a townsite for Copeville. The following year a post office was established. By 1885 the community had a church, a school, a cotton gin, a sawmill, a flour mill, and a general store. In 1886 the Gulf, Colorado and Santa Fe laid tracks one mile east of Copeville. Shortly thereafter, residents moved their houses and businesses to the line to take advantage of the railroad. Copeville served as a shipping point for area farmers until the 1930s. Between 1885 and 1890 the town was a principal supplier of bois d'arc timber for Dallas, where it was used experimentally as paving material. In 1915 the population of Copeville may have reached 300. However, the Great Depression,qv mechanization of farming, and job opportunities offered in the Dallas metropolitan area combined to retard the growth of the community. In 1926 the population estimate had fallen to 240, where it remained throughout the 1920s and 1930s. A further decline to 150 was reported in 1943; this estimate remained constant until the early 1970s. In 1947 the town had two churches, five businesses, and a school. In 1986 and 1990 Copeville had 106 residents and seven businesses.

BIBLIOGRAPHY: Roy Franklin Hall and Helen Gibbard Hall, *Collin County: Pioneering in North Texas* (Quanah, Texas: Nortex, 1975). J. Lee and Lillian J. Stambaugh, *A History of Collin County* (Austin: Texas State Historical Association, 1958).
David Minor

COPITA, TEXAS. Copita was eight miles southeast of Concepcion and twenty miles southeast of Benavides in southeastern Duval County. It had a general store by 1910, when it was described as a development of "farm and garden tracts." The population was estimated optimistically at "sixty total now" with "others coming in rapidly." A post office was established in 1911 with Edwin M. Flickinger as postmaster. By 1914, when the population was somewhat more realistically estimated at forty-five, Copita had a general store, a cotton gin, a well driller, and a hotel. The post office was closed in 1922, and by the late 1940s the town was down to only one business. By the late 1960s the Copita school had been consolidated with the Ramirez Independent School District, and the town had scattered dwellings, the Iglesia Adventista del Septima Dia (Seventh Day Adventist church), and a cemetery. By 1990 only the Copita cemetery was shown on maps of the area.
Martin Donell Kohout

COPPELL, TEXAS. Coppell is on Interstate Highway 635, U.S. Highway 121, Interstate Highway 35, the Elm Fork of the Trinity River, and the St. Louis Southwestern Railway, seven miles from Farmers Branch in the extreme northwest corner of Dallas County. The community is bordered by Irving, Grapevine, and Carrollton and is northeast of Dallas–Fort Worth International Airport.qv Grapevine Creek, Denton Creek, and Cottonwood Branch flow through the city. The area was on the original land grant of J. A. Simmonds. President Sam Houston qv and Republic of Texas qv troops camped on Grapevine Creek during negotiations with area Indian tribes in an effort to enlist their aid in defending the republic against attacks by Mexican troops in 1843.

The site was first settled in the mid-1800s by James Parish, from Goliad. In 1887 the community secured a post office. It was originally named Gibbs Station, after Texas lieutenant governor Barnett Gibbs,qv a large landowner in the area. In 1888 construction of the St. Louis, Arkansas and Texas Railway through the town was completed. In 1892 the post office was renamed Coppell, in honor of a railroad employee and pioneer settler of the region, George A. Coppell. In 1914 the settlement had two churches, two general stores, two blacksmiths, a bank, a hardware store, telephone service, a population of 450, and dealers in poultry, livestock, and lumber. However, by 1926 the population had decreased to 200, where it remained for three decades.

In 1936 the Work Projects Administration qv built a park on Grapevine Creek that included a half mile of walkways, three bridges, and a dam. The park was located in groves of oak, pecan, and cottonwood trees. Four years later the community had ten businesses, including a cotton gin. It also had a school and two churches. During this time Coppell produced a variety of agricultural products, including cotton, wheat, oats, sweet potatoes, peanuts, and melons. The community grew slowly but steadily in the 1950s and in 1956 formed a city government, which established a city zoning plan. By 1960 Coppell had six businesses and a population of 666. In 1962 the community was incorporated, and seven years later Coppell had set up a tax structure and constructed a new jail.

In the 1970s the town expanded northward into southern Denton County, built a new courthouse, and completed the General Telephone Company building (1972). Two years later Dallas–Fort Worth Regional Airport opened and a municipal utilities district was established. By this time Coppell had adopted the council-manager form of government and had a population of 2,500, ambulance service, police and fire departments, six churches, and schools. The population grew from 1,751 in 1981 to 3,826 in 1984. The number of businesses more than doubled also, growing from fourteen in 1981 to thirty-one in 1984. In 1984 a $16.3 million bond was approved to improve the street system, construct a new civic center and three new fire stations, increase the size of the park system, and install an emergency-warning system. Three years later Coppell secured the Coppell Mail Center, a bulk mail-sorting plant for the federal postal service.

In 1990 Coppell had a population of 16,881. The population was composed of primarily upper-middle-class homeowners with an average age of thirty-five, an average income of $66,000, and a house valued at $117,000. In 1991 Coppell's budget tripled from its 1985 level, and the community was developing a 116-acre park system that included two lakes, hike and bike trails, paddle boats, playgrounds, picnic areas, a Frisbee golf course, a community pool, and baseball, soccer, and football fields. The community also had established a curbside recycling program and had increased the size of its library system.

BIBLIOGRAPHY: *Dallas Guide and History* (Washington: WPA Writers' Program, 1940). Dallas *Times Herald*, March 12, 1984.
Matthew Hayes Nall

COPPERAS COVE, TEXAS. Copperas Cove, once spelled Coperas Cove, is at the intersection of U.S. Highway 190 and Farm Road 116, twenty-four miles southwest of Gatesville in southern Coryell County. In the 1870s the community centered around a small store about two miles southwest of the present townsite. Late that decade residents of the community applied for a post office under the name

Cove, but postal authorities rejected the name because a Texas post office by that name already existed. The name Coperas Cove was then submitted, inspired by the mineral taste of the water in a nearby spring. The Coperas Cove post office was established in March 1879 with Marsden Ogletree as postmaster.

A feeder route of the Chisholm Trail[qv] passed through Coperas Cove, making the cattle industry of primary importance to the local economy. When the Gulf, Colorado, and Santa Fe Railway built its track across the southern corner of Coryell County in 1882, residents of Coperas Cove moved their community two miles to the northeast in order to take better advantage of the rail service. By 1884 the town had a steam gristmill–cotton gin, five general stores, a hotel, and 150 residents. By the mid-1890s the population had risen to 300, and residents had voted to form their own school district. Although cattle production continued to be important to the local economy, area farmers began to devote more of their resources to the production of cotton, small grains, and feed crops, and by 1900 farming was the dominant occupation.

The spelling of the community's name was officially changed in 1901; at that time Copperas Cove had an opera house, three hotels, and a variety of businesses. A local private bank opened in 1906. By the time residents elected their first mayor in 1913, the population had grown to 600. The number of residents continued to increase through the 1920s, to a high of 650 in 1929. Copperas Cove began to decline with the onset of the Great Depression[qv] in the early 1930s. The local bank failed, several businesses closed, and many people left to look for work in other areas. By the 1940s only 356 residents remained.

Copperas Cove received a much-needed boost in the early 1940s, when the United States government chose southeastern Coryell and northwestern Bell counties as the site for Camp Hood, a new military training center. By the 1950 census the community had grown to 1,052 residents. When the military established Fort Hood[qv] as a permanent base in 1950, Copperas Cove began to grow at an even faster rate, and the city limit eventually extended southwest into Lampasas County. The population was estimated at 4,567 in 1960, at 10,818 in 1970, and at 19,469 in 1980. Most of the new residents were either attracted by the job opportunities associated with Fort Hood or chose to remain in the area after retirement from the military. By 1990 Copperas Cove had several manufacturing establishments, a wide variety of businesses, a hospital, and a population of 24,079.

BIBLIOGRAPHY: Clyde and Mabel Bailey, *Vignettes of Coryell County* (Gatesville, Texas: Gatesville Printing, 1976). Coryell County Genealogical Society, *Coryell County, Texas, Families, 1854–1985* (Dallas: Taylor, 1986). Jerry K. Smith and Patrick D. McLaughlin, *Copperas Cove, City of Five Hills: A Centennial History* (Burnet, Texas: Eakin Press, 1980). Vivian Elizabeth Smyrl

COPPERAS CREEK (Bastrop County). Copperas Creek rises on the northern outskirts of Bastrop State Park[qv] in central Bastrop County (at 30°08′ N, 97°16′ W) and runs south five miles to its mouth at the Colorado River (at 30°04′ N, 97°17′ W). It begins in sandy uplands, passes through pine forest, and ends on the loamy Colorado River floodplain. A sawmill on the creek bank in the 1840s produced lumber for many buildings in Bastrop and San Antonio.
BIBLIOGRAPHY: Bastrop Historical Society, *In the Shadow of the Lost Pines: A History of Bastrop County and Its People* (Bastrop, Texas: Bastrop *Advertiser*, 1955).

_____ (Caldwell County). Copperas Creek rises just east of Delhi in eastern Caldwell County (at 29°50′ N, 97°23′ W) and runs southeast for 16½ miles to its mouth on Peach Creek, four miles east of Waelder in Gonzales County (at 29°42′ N, 97°14′ W). The surrounding flat to rolling prairie, with local escarpments, is surfaced by fine, sandy loams and dark, calcareous clays that support hardwood forest, mesquite, and grasses.

_____ (Caldwell County). Copperas Creek rises four miles southeast of Tilmon in southeastern Caldwell County (at 29°43′ N, 97°31′ W) and runs northwest for six miles to its mouth on Plum Creek, three miles southeast of Brownsboro (at 29°45′ N, 97°35′ W). The surrounding rolling prairie is surfaced by shallow clay loams that support mesquite, mixed hardwoods, and grasses.

_____ (Eastland County). Copperas Creek rises near Rising Star in southwestern Eastland County (at 32°06′ N, 98°58′ W) and runs southeast for twenty-four miles to its mouth on Proctor Lake in Comanche County (at 32°01′ N, 98°35′ W). It traverses flat to rolling terrain surfaced by sandy soil that supports scrub brush and grass.

_____ (Kimble County). Copperas Creek rises 3½ miles northeast of Roosevelt in western Kimble County (at 30°31′ N, 100°00′ W) and runs southeast for 3½ miles to its mouth on the North Llano River, four miles east of Roosevelt (at 30°29′ N, 99°59′ W). Three three main tributaries to the creek are: East Copperas Creek, which rises in northwest Kimble County and is twenty-four miles long; Middle Copperas Creek, ten miles long; and West Copperas Creek, fifteen miles long. Nick B. and Jennie (Blackwell) Coalson, natives of Illinois, settled at the junction of East and West Copperas creeks in 1866. They raised corn and hunted native deer and turkey.
BIBLIOGRAPHY: Ovie Clark Fisher, *It Occurred in Kimble* (Houston: Anson Jones Press, 1937).

_____ (Robertson County). Copperas Creek rises five miles west of Wheelock in south central Robertson County (at 30°53′ N, 96°26′ W) and runs east seven miles to its mouth on Cedar Creek, one mile northeast of Wheelock (at 30°55′ N, 96°23′ W). The surrounding nearly level terrain is surfaced by sandy loams that support post oaks and grasses.

COPPER BREAKS STATE PARK. Copper Breaks State Park, on the Pease River and State Highway 6 twelve miles south of Quanah in Hardeman County, was established in 1970. From its original 1,889 acres, this scenic area has been expanded to nearly 1,933 acres featuring rugged canyons and a seventy-acre lake made by an earthen dam. "Breaks" refers to the fractures and faults that define the limited waterways of the park. Small amounts of copper, insufficient for commercial purposes, can be found in the area clay. Facilities for picnicking, camping, swimming, boating, fishing, hiking, and horseback riding are provided. A small historical museum exhibit is available, and a portion of the official Texas longhorn herd (*see* LONGHORN CATTLE) is maintained in the park, which is located near the historic Medicine Mounds[qv] and the site of Cynthia Ann Parker's[qv] recapture in December 1860.

BIBLIOGRAPHY: Ross A. Maxwell, *Geologic and Historic Guide to the Texas State Parks* (Bureau of Economic Geology, University of Texas at Austin, 1970). George Oxford Miller, *Texas Parks and Campgrounds: Central, South, and West Texas* (Austin: Texas Monthly Press, 1984). H. Allen Anderson

COPPER PRODUCTION. Copper was first reported in Texas by Capt. Randolph B. Marcy[qv] in his exploration of the Red River in 1852. In 1864 a small amount of high-grade copper ore was smelted in Archer County; a part of this ore is said to have been used for percussion caps for the Confederate Army during the Civil War.[qv] After the war, Gen. George B. McClellan[qv] became interested in the copper deposits in North Central Texas and organized a company that started a mine near the Pease River in Foard County. The remains of the resulting shaft were still called the Old McClellan Mine in 1950. Subsequent trial shipments of copper ore made from Baylor, Clay, Hardeman, King, Knox, and Stonewall counties did not encourage commercial development. About 1885 copper production in connection with silver began at the Hazel Mine near Van Horn in Culberson County; this production continued, with intermittent periods of inactivity, until 1942 and produced about a million pounds of copper. Between 1926 and 1928 about 12,500 tons of low-grade ore, averaging nine ounces of silver to the ton and 0.42 percent copper, were shipped from the Van Horn–Allamoore district of the Trans-Pecos[qv] area; in 1929 new underground developments produced ore of 1.53 percent copper. The total amount of copper produced in the state between 1885 and 1944 was 1,251 short tons, of which 60,000 pounds were produced in 1940, 128,000 pounds in 1942, and 230,000 pounds in 1944. Other mines in the Trans-Pecos area that have produced copper in small amounts are the Sancho Panza, Black Shaft, and Pecos. There are known deposits of copper in Burnet and Llano counties. The last reported copper production using ore from within the state was eighteen tons in 1952, valued at $8,712; it mostly used ore from the old Hazel Mine in Culberson County. During the mid-1950s most of the Texas copper mines were inoperative. Large deposits of ore were known to exist in the North Texas region but were not developed because of their low copper content.

Despite the state's relative lack of ore, copper refineries have been established in Texas to supply regional demand for metal goods and to make use of readily available fuel for metal plants. A copper refinery was established at El Paso by Dr. W. H. Nichols of Nichols Copper and was later acquired by Phelps Dodge Corporation; the refinery employed 750 persons by the 1950s. Eventually up to 30 percent of all the copper processed in the United States was produced at this refinery. Much of the refined material was subsequently manufactured by Phelps Dodge Copper Products Corporation into wire, tubes, and pipe for use in the building industry. In 1966 this refinery and a copper smelter were operating in El Paso County, using ore from Mexico, New Mexico, and Arizona to produce refined copper, copper anode, and copper sulfate. A copper refinery was also established by the American Smelting and Refining Company at Amarillo. In the 1970s Phelps Dodge Refining Corporation began an expansion of its copper refinery at El Paso and reached full operation at its copper-rod mill (copper rod is used for cable and electrical wire). The ASARCO qv El Paso metallurgical smelter produced blister and anode copper from ores and concentrates mined outside of Texas. In a joint venture with Phelps Dodge, the firm planned to test a new process to reduce its emission of pollutants. ASARCO established a department of environmental services and curtailed smelter operations during the year to control sulfur-dioxide pollution of the atmosphere. In 1975 ASARCO completed its refinery at Amarillo and began production of refined copper.

Plans were made in 1980 to modernize the ASARCO smelter and to increase its capacity to 135,000 tons per year by 1991. Copper continued to be refined at the ASARCO plant in Amarillo and by Phelps Dodge at its El Paso refinery. Phelps Dodge Copper Products Company, the manufacturing division of the corporation, planned to add a continuous casting copper-rod mill to its facilities in El Paso by 1982. In 1986 the United States Environmental Protection Agency issued final rules on arsenic emissions from copper smelters, requiring the El Paso smelter and two other plants to install additional air-pollution control equipment to comply with standards. By 1990 the Texas Copper Company, a subsidiary of Mitsubishi Metals Corporation and four other Japanese firms, was at work on a new 250,000-ton-per-year copper smelter at Texas City, and Tatsumi Texas planned to construct a marine service terminal for raw materials destined for the smelter.

BIBLIOGRAPHY: Floyd E. Ewing, "Copper Mining in West Texas," West Texas Historical Association *Year Book* 30 (1954). Elias H. Sellards, W. S. Adkins, and F. B. Plummer, *The Geology of Texas: Bibliography and Subject Index of Texas Geology* (Austin: Bureau of Economic Geology, University of Texas, 1933). *Texas Parade*, October 1954. University of Texas, *Texas Looks Ahead: The Resources of Texas* (Austin, 1944; rpt., Freeport, New York: Books for Libraries Press, 1968). U.S. Bureau of Mines, *Minerals Yearbook*.

John Q. Anderson and Diana J. Kleiner

COPPINI, POMPEO LUIGI (1870–1957). Pompeo Coppini, sculptor, was born in Moglia, Mantua, Italy, on May 19, 1870, the son of Giovanni and Leandra (Raffa) Coppini. He grew up in Florence, where he was a student at the Accademia di Belle Arte and there studied under Augusto Rivalta. He graduated with highest honors in 1889. On March 5, 1896, Coppini immigrated to the United States with very little money and no knowledge of English. On February 27, 1898, he married Elizabeth di Barbieri of New Haven, Connecticut; he became an American citizen in 1902.

Coppini, hearing of Frank Teich's qv search for a sculptor, moved to Texas in November 1901. He was commissioned to model the statue of Jefferson Davis qv and other figures for the Confederate monument (1901–03) subsequently erected on the Capitol qv grounds in Austin. Other Texas commissions followed, one of the best known being the Littlefield Fountain Memorial (1920–28) at the University of Texas at Austin. He also did the seven bronze statues along the south mall of the university grounds, all of which were associated with the Littlefield commission except the sculpture of George Washington (completed 1955). Coppini's Texas works include a statue of Rufus C. Burleson qv at Baylor University in Waco (1903), the monument to Sam Houston qv at Huntsville (1910), a monument at Gonzales in commemoration of the first shot fired for Texas independence (1910), a statue of a Confederate soldier at Victoria (1911), busts of Albert Sidney Johnston, Robert E. Lee, qqv Jefferson Davis, and Stonewall Jackson for the Confederate monument at Paris, Texas (1903), and a group statue called *The Victims of the Galveston Flood* (1903–4), which was given to the University of Texas, Austin. Coppini also modeled the equestrian monument to Terry's Texas Rangers (the Eighth Texas Cavalry qv) on the Capitol grounds (1905–07), the Charles H. Noyes Memorial in Ballinger (1918–19), the John H. Reagan qv Memorial in Palestine, with its personification of the "Lost

Pompeo Coppini working on the central figure for the Alamo cenotaph, San Antonio, 1938. San Antonio Light Collection, ITC.

Cause" (1911), and the bronze doors of the Scottish Rite Cathedral in San Antonio (dedicated 1926). One of his best-known works is a statue of George Washington in Mexico City (1911).

Coppini lived and worked in San Antonio until 1916, when he moved to Chicago for financial reasons. Three years later he moved to New York City to facilitate the production of the Littlefield Fountain Memorial. He was assisted on this and other major projects by sculptor Waldine Tauch,qv who began studying with Coppini in 1910 and continued to work with him as his colleague and foster daughter until his death. In 1937 Coppini established a studio at 115 Melrose Place in San Antonio in order to work on a major commission for the Texas Centennial,qv the cenotaph to the heroes of the Alamo (1937–39) on Alamo Plaza in San Antonio. Other Centennial commissions awarded to Coppini were the commemorative half-dollar (1934) and the Hall of Stateqv bronze statues of Stephen F. Austin, Thomas J. Rusk, William B. Travis, James W. Fannin, Mirabeau B. Lamar,qqv and Sam Houston (1935–36). Coppini's contributions to the state were recognized in 1941, when he was awarded an honorary doctor of fine arts degree by Baylor University. Recognition and appreciation of his work extended to Italy, for in 1931 he was decorated "Commendatore" of the Crown of Italy for his contribution to art in America.

Coppini is represented in the United States by thirty-six public monuments, sixteen portrait statues, and about seventy-five portrait busts. When expressing his own attitudes toward art and sculpture, he often criticized modernism, which he attributed to a general lack of screening of pupils in art schools. He thought that art training should be a regular branch of learning in a university, with strict standards that would assure adherence to classic and academic artistic traditions. He emphasized the importance of individual instruction from experienced artists. From 1943 to 1945 he was head of the art department of Trinity University in San Antonio. In 1945 he and Tauch cofounded the Classic Arts Fraternity in San Antonio (renamed Coppini Academy of Fine Arts in 1950). Coppini died in San Antonio on September 26, 1957, and was buried in Sunset Memorial Park in a crypt of his own design. He was survived by his wife and his foster daughter. The San Antonio studio now serves as a museum of Coppini and Tauch's work.

BIBLIOGRAPHY: Pompeo Coppini, *From Dawn to Sunset* (San Antonio: Naylor, 1949). Coppini-Tauch Papers, Barker Texas History Center, University of Texas at Austin. Patricia D. Hendricks and Becky D. Reese, *A Century of Sculpture in Texas, 1889–1989* (Huntington Art Gallery, University of Texas at Austin, 1989). Vertical Files, Barker Texas History Center, University of Texas at Austin.

COPYRIGHTS IN THE REPUBLIC OF TEXAS. On March 15, 1836, the delegates to the Convention of 1836 qv voted to add to the Constitution Article II, Section 3, authorization for patents and copyrights, but provided that three years elapse before beginning these. In 1838 Congress made an attempt to pass a special law authorizing copyright of a map for five years, but this failed to pass. On November 20, 1837, Secretary of State Robert A. Irionqv recommended in his annual report to Congress that the republic grant copyrights. On January 28, 1839, President Mirabeau B. Lamarqv approved an act which provided "patent" rights, running for fourteen years, on "composition of matter, liberal arts, sciences or literature, books, maps or charts," to citizens and those who had filed intentions of becoming citizens, upon payment of a thirty-dollar fee. Only three copyrights were issued, and of the copyrighted works but one was published, George William Bonnell'sqv *Topographical Description of Texas, To Which is Added an Account of the Indian Tribes* (Austin: Clark, Wing, and Brown, 1840). The imprint of this small volume is unique in that it states the copyright was secured in the Republic of Texas.qv Inasmuch as two of the three works registered in the republic were never published and the third was registered in the United States as well as in Texas, when Texas was admitted into the Union, there was no necessity for Texas copyrights to be incorporated into the United States copyright system, and no action was taken.

BIBLIOGRAPHY: Andrew Forest Muir, "Patents and Copyrights," *Journal of Southern History* 12 (May 1946). *Andrew Forest Muir*

CORA, TEXAS. Cora, the first seat of Comanche County, was about sixteen miles southeast of Comanche on the South Leon River in southeastern Comanche County. The county was formed and organized in 1856, and the next year F. A. Thomson and J. E. Bouldin donated eighty acres of the W. H. Murray survey, overlooking the river, for a county seat. The site was beside the Fort Gates and Fort Phantom Hill Road that had already brought people into the area. The community applied for a post office to be called Troy, but the application was denied since there was already a Troy in Bell County. Thomas C. Frost, county land agent, suggested the name Cora, for Miss Cora Beeman, daughter of Maj. Alonzo Beeman of Moffat, Bell County. This name was accepted, and James M. Cross, who had opened the first store in Cora in 1857, was appointed postmaster. Within a year, the community had two stores and a steam saw and grist mill. The town of Cora flourished until 1858, when some Comanche County land was made part of Hamilton County. This left Cora too far from the center of Comanche County to qualify as the county seat. The town of Comanche was created, and the county government moved there in July 1859. Though Indian problems slowed the local settlement rate after 1858, the 1860 census showed Cora to be a community of twenty-five houses, of which twenty-three were occupied. The 136 individuals reported as residents at that time made up nearly 20 percent of the county population and included twelve farmers or stock raisers, four mechanics, three merchants, two wagonmakers, two blacksmiths, two wagoners, two millers, a house carpenter, a schoolteacher, and a trader. Cora declined, and its post office closed in 1867. Old building foundations were visible at the site as late as 1880. By 1900, however, nothing remained of the community but the cemetery, which is today situated well back on private property. The few grave markers left by the 1990s in the unfenced cemetery dated from between 1859 and 1893; the cemetery also included many unmarked graves. Part of the log structure that had served as the first courthouse had been moved to a site on the bluff overlooking the river, where it was used as a residence.

BIBLIOGRAPHY: Marker Files, Texas Historical Commission, Austin. Margaret and Samuel J. C. Waring, *Comanche County Gravestone Inscriptions* (Vol. 3, Comanche, Texas, 1981). Eulalia Nabers Wells, *Blazing the Way: Tales of Comanche County Pioneers* (Blanket, Texas, 1942). *Margaret Tate Waring*

CORAL SNAKE. The coral snake found in Texas (*Micrurus fulvius tenere*) is the only black, red, and yellow crossbanded serpent whose red and yellow bands touch: "Red against yellow kills a fellow." Its uncommon look-alikes, the milk and scarlet snakes, have red and yellow bands separated by narrow black rings: "Red against black, poison lack." The coral's black bands, in contrast, are as broad as its red ones and are separated by bright sulfur rings; the head and tail are marked only with black and yellow, and, unlike those of nonvenomous snakes, the coral's body bands continued uninterrupted across its belly. The bright colors of the coral snake may serve both as a warning signal and as camouflage, for at night, when red appears as gray, on the dappled forest floor its alternating light and dark make the snake's shape less discernible to owls and other predators. The bold contrast between the bands of *M. fulvius* seems to deter small mammalian carnivores. In defense against them the coral may tuck its foreparts under its trunk while waving its elevated yellow and black banded tail tip back and forth in imitation of its head threatening to strike.

Coral snake venom is largely composed of neurotoxically destructive peptides and is, therefore, more deadly than the venom of any other North American reptile. A lethal dose for an adult human being is as small as five to ten milligrams, dry weight—several times more virulent than the venom of the western diamondback rattler (*see* RATTLESNAKES). Since its toxic peptides spread rapidly through the blood stream, the application of a tourniquet and immediate hospital administration of antivenin are probably appropriate in cases of severe poisoning. Although intense pain usually accompanies a bite, heavy envenomation is often difficult to determine because the central nervous system may not manifest symptoms for several hours. Still, few people are harmed by coral snakes: only 1 percent of all snake bites are by coral snakes, and fewer than 10 percent of these are fatal. Though locally common in suburban neighborhoods throughout all of the state but far West Texas, *M. fulvius* is so secretive and nonaggressive toward human beings that only those who handle the snake are often bitten. The rigid fangs, which are longitudinally grooved pegs rather than hollow hypodermic tubes, are less than one-eighth inch in length and are unlikely to penetrate shoes or even most clothing, although corals can pierce a pinch of skin anywhere on the body. If molested, the coral snake is a quite determined biter that flips its head from side to side and snaps sharply.

Texas coral snakes average about two feet in length. The record is nearly twice the average. They are most often seen in spring and fall, when they forage abroad on cool, sunny mornings; during hot weather their activity is mostly crepuscular or nocturnal. Their prey is chiefly other snakes, some as big as the coral itself, which are overcome by means of the potent venom. *M. fulvius* has an extended reproductive season, perhaps because of its small home range; because of the low sensory perception in males, which sometimes makes it difficult for them to find a mate; and because the larger of a pair of introduced corals, usually the female, sometimes tries to eat its prospective mate. The coral snake breeds from late summer to late spring and lays its clutches in midsummer. The three to five eggs, one and three-eighths inches in length by three-eighths inch in diameter, are deposited beneath loose ground cover or a layer of soil to prevent their drying; they hatch after some two months into young 6½ to 7½ inches long, which resemble adults. *See also* REPTILES.

BIBLIOGRAPHY: Robert E. Kuntz and Thomas G. Vermersch, *Snakes of South Central Texas* (Austin: Eakin Press, 1986). Alan Tennant, *The Snakes of Texas* (Austin: Texas Monthly Press, 1984). Alan Tennant, *The Snakes of Texas: A Texas Monthly Field Guide* (Austin: Texas Monthly Press, 1985).
Alan Tennant

CORAZONES PEAKS. Corazones Peaks is a pair of extremely steep and jagged mountains on the northeast edge of the Christmas Mountains seventy miles south of Alpine in south central Brewster County (at 29°30′ N, 103°26′ W). The peaks are part of a series of residual topographic highs developed on a single large Tertiary Age igneous intrusion into the Upper Cretaceous Boquillas formation. Their summits are about 1½ miles apart on an east-west line and rise in forbidding, near-vertical rock faces and broken inclines some 1,500 feet above the surrounding desert floor. At its summit the western peak reaches an elevation of 5,319 feet above sea level and the eastern peak 5,045 feet above sea level.

The peaks owe their high topography to the fact that they consist of rather dense, resistant igneous rocks, while the surrounding terrain is composed of the less resistant, flaggy Boquillas limestone, which is removed during weathering and erosion. Although the peaks themselves, especially at their upper elevations, are almost entirely bare rock, the lower slopes and the surrounding desert lowland support a sparse growth of Chihuahuan Desert scrub, including such characteristic species as lechuguilla, creosote bush, ocotillo, and sotol. The origin of the name Corazones ("hearts") is obscure. A popular explanation is that a cleft in one of the mountains makes it resemble a heart.

BIBLIOGRAPHY: Virginia Madison and Hallie Stillwell, *How Come It's Called That? Place Names in the Big Bend Country* (Albuquerque: University of New Mexico Press, 1958).

CORBET, TEXAS. Corbet is on Farm Road 2452 six miles southwest of Corsicana between Briar and Cedar creeks in Navarro County. It is bisected by the St. Louis Southwestern Railway. The area was first settled by a Colonel Cook in 1866 as a community named Cook's Schoolhouse. After the railroad arrived, the station was first named Waters and later renamed Corbet. The post office operated from 1893 through 1929. Corbet had one school in 1906, when it had an enrollment of fifty-seven students and one teacher. By 1914 Corbet had a population of 300. In 1945 it had two stores and a population of 100. In 1970 the population had decreased to eighty, where it remained in 1990.

BIBLIOGRAPHY: Annie Carpenter Love, *History of Navarro County* (Dallas: Southwestern, 1933). Wyvonne Putman, comp., *Navarro County History* (5 vols., Quanah, Texas: Nortex, 1975–84). Alva Taylor, *History and Photographs of Corsicana and Navarro County* (Corsicana, Texas, 1959; rev. ed., *Navarro County History and Photographs*, Corsicana, 1962).
David Allen

CORDELE, TEXAS. Cordele is on Farm Road 530 in northeastern Jackson County. In 1897 the New York and Texas Land Company[qv] sold acreage along Sandy Creek, which was later renamed Brushy Creek, to settlers. Soon after, a Dr. Stapleton—who was the settlement's first postmaster—named the town after his hometown, Cordele, Georgia. By 1914 Cordele had become a shipping center with a post office, but by 1925 the community had only eight residents. The local population gradually increased and reached 176 in 1968. From 1972 through 1990 the number of residents at Cordele was reported as seventy-four.
Stephen L. Hardin

CORDERO Y BUSTAMANTE, MANUEL ANTONIO (1753–1823). Manuel Antonio Cordero y Bustamante, governor of Coahuila and acting governor of Texas, was born in Cádiz, Spain, in 1753. He became a cadet in the Spanish army on December 1, 1767, and he held the same rank in America on September 6, 1771. He served in the Zamora Infantry, the Dragoons of Spain and Mexico, and the presidial companies of Janos and San Buenaventura. Between 1777 and 1790 he fought in twenty-five campaigns in the Provincias Internas,[qv] four of them as subordinate and the rest as commander. He captured or killed 472 enemies and rescued six prisoners. He signed a peace treaty with the Mimbreños and Gileños in 1787. For ten months during 1790 and 1791 he had military command of Nueva Vizcaya, where he chased marauders and punished rebelling Indians who threatened the ranches. In a four-month campaign during 1794 he again subjugated the Gileña and Mimbreña Apaches who rose against the Presidio of Janos. In 1795 he directed an expedition against the Mescaleros at Presidio del Norte. On December 27, 1796, he became commander of troops operating on the Coahuila frontier. During the years 1795 to 1800 he built up the defenses of Coahuila and founded numerous towns and settlements. From March 27, 1797, until December 1798 he was interim governor of Coahuila. He then served as governor until 1817.

Cordero became assistant governor of Texas in 1805 and held the office of acting governor of Coahuila and Texas[qv] until November 7, 1808. Tensions were high during his tenure in Texas because of the Louisiana Purchase. In September 1805 he arrived at San Antonio with orders to reinforce the posts of Orcoquisas, Nacogdoches, and Adaes. Until 1810 he remained in Texas, with the intention of establishing settlements on the Trinity, Brazos, Colorado, San Marcos, and Guadalupe rivers. Only San Marcos de Reve on the San Marcos and Santísima Trinidad de Salcedo on the Trinity were established. Cordero also established Palafox Villa[qv] in 1810. He encouraged immigration from the interior provinces of Mexico and attempted to bar North American colonists. He ordered all slaves entering Texas from Louisiana to be freed. Zebulon Pike[qv] described him as "five feet ten inches in height . . . fair complexion, and blue eyes . . . wears his hair turned back, and in every part of his deportment was legibly written

'The Soldier.'... Well-read and introspective, with a bachelor's fearlessness for his personal safety, he was one of the ablest Spanish military commanders on the frontier." In 1814 Cordero married Juan Ignacio Pérez's^{qv} twenty-four-year-old daughter Gertrudis. Cordero became commandant general of the Western Interior Provinces in 1822 and was promoted to field marshal general, a position he held until his death in Durango in the spring of 1823.

BIBLIOGRAPHY: Vito Alessio Robles, *Coahuila y Texas en la época colonial* (Mexico City: Editorial Cultura, 1938; 2d ed., Mexico City: Editorial Porrúa, 1978). Nettie Lee Benson, "Texas Failure to Send a Deputy to the Spanish Cortes, 1810–1812," *Southwestern Historical Quarterly* 64 (July 1960). Carlos E. Castañeda, *Our Catholic Heritage in Texas* (7 vols., Austin: Von Boeckmann–Jones, 1936–58; rpt., New York: Arno, 1976). Jack D. L. Holmes, "Showdown on the Sabine: General James Wilkinson vs. Lieutenant-Colonel Simón de Herrera," *Louisiana Studies* 3 (Spring 1964). Zebulon Montgomery Pike, *An Account of Expeditions to the Sources of the Mississippi and through the Western Parts of Louisiana* (Philadelphia: Conrad, 1810).

Jack D. L. Holmes

CÓRDOVA, VICENTE (1798–1842). Vicente Córdova, Nacogdoches official during the Mexican period and leader of the Córdova Rebellion,^{qv} was born in 1798. He was evidently well educated and was among the largest landholders in Nacogdoches in the late Mexican period. He served at various times as alcalde,^{qv} primary judge, and regidor.^{qv} He was for several years captain of a militia company and during the battle of Nacogdoches^{qv} in 1832 fought on the side of the local citizens. He supported the Texas Revolution^{qv} as long as it espoused a return to the Constitution of 1824^{qv} but opposed the call for Texas independence. Córdova married María Antonia Córdova on July 29, 1824; the couple evidently had several children.

In the fall of 1835 Córdova secretly began to organize local resistance to the Texan revolutionaries, though as late as 1836 he was elected primary judge for the department. During this period he kept the Mexican government informed of his attempts to "foster the favorable feelings which the faithful Mexicans here have always entertained" toward Mexico. He negotiated with Chief Bowl^{qv} of the Cherokee Indians and their allies, promising the Indians possession of hunting grounds and other rewards. In August 1838 he assembled a large group of Mexican loyalists and Indians on an island in the Angelina River, but the Córdova Rebellion, as it was called, was quickly suppressed.

Afterward, Córdova, accompanied by a small group of Mexicans, Indians, and blacks, attempted to flee to Matamoros, Tamaulipas. The group was discovered encamped near Waterloo (now Austin) and several days later fought a battle with the Colorado volunteers led by Edward Burleson^{qv} on Mill Creek near the Guadalupe River. Córdova was apparently severely wounded but managed eventually to make his way to Mexico. He returned to Texas with Gen. Adrián Woll^{qv} and assisted in the occupation of San Antonio in September 1842. He was killed shortly thereafter in the battle of Salado Creek,^{qv} September 18, 1842.

BIBLIOGRAPHY: Robert Bruce Blake Research Collection, Steen Library, Stephen F. Austin State University; Barker Texas History Center, University of Texas at Austin; Texas State Archives, Austin; Houston Public Library, Houston. Nacogdoches Archives, Steen Library, Stephen F. Austin State University; Barker Texas History Center, University of Texas at Austin; Texas State Archives, Austin. Joseph Milton Nance, *After San Jacinto: The Texas-Mexican Frontier, 1836–1841* (Austin: University of Texas Press, 1963). Joseph Milton Nance, *Attack and Counterattack: The Texas-Mexican Frontier, 1842* (Austin: University of Texas Press, 1964).

Robert Bruce Blake

CORDOVA ISLAND. Cordova Island, also known as Isla de Córdoba, is not a true island, but is located on both sides of the current channel of the Rio Grande in El Paso and Ciudad Juárez, Chihuahua, Mexico. In 1899 the United States and Mexico dug a channel across the heel of the horseshoe-shaped peninsula to control the flood-prone Rio Grande, but left the original riverbed, which wound to the north around the island, as the international boundary. Thus the 385-acre tract was part of Mexico, though it lay north of the Rio Grande, for most of the twentieth century. During prohibition^{qv} Cordova Island was a notorious haven for smugglers; it was almost completely surrounded by American soil, but lay outside the city limits of Juárez. The famous Hole in the Wall, a saloon and gambling parlor, flourished just a few yards from the border in defiance of United States and Mexican authorities, before it was finally torn down in January 1931. In 1963 the treaty that settled the Chamizal Dispute^{qv} transferred 193 acres on Cordova Island to the United States in exchange for an equal area further downstream. In the 1990s the channel of the Rio Grande bisected the old island from east to west, and Interstate Highway 110 crossed it from north to south.

CÓRDOVA REBELLION. Late in the summer of 1838 a group of Nacogdoches citizens accidentally uncovered a plot of rebellion against the new Republic of Texas.^{qv} This incident, known as the Córdova Rebellion, at first appeared to be nothing more than an isolated insurrection by local malcontents. Later evidence, however, indicated the existence of a far-reaching web of conspiracy.

A volatile mixture of political and social forces existed in the Nacogdoches area during the 1830s. For the most part, former citizens of the United States controlled the newly formed government of the republic. They lived in constant fear of repression by the Mexican government, from which they recently had declared independence. Before 1836 Texans of Hispanic descent made up the largest segment of the population of Nacogdoches. The end of the Texas Revolution,^{qv} however, brought an influx of American settlers into the area. Many older inhabitants, resenting this intrusion, understandably remained loyal to Mexico. Indians, represented principally by the Cherokees, made up the third major ethnic group. These Indians, a settled people who engaged in agriculture, desired clear title to the land they occupied. Attempts to secure this title from Mexico before 1832 were unsuccessful. During the Texas Revolution, Texas officials promised the Cherokees title to their lands in return for neutrality. The agreement, never ratified, was declared null and void in 1837.

In late 1836 several sources reported to President Sam Houston^{qv} that the Cherokees had concluded a treaty with Mexico for a combined attack on Texas. It would be a war of extermination, and the Indians would receive title to their land in return for their allegiance. Vicente Córdova,^{qv} a financially comfortable Nacogdochian who had served his community as alcalde,^{qv} judge, and regidor,^{qv} maintained contact with agents of the Mexican government during this period. On August 4, 1838, a group of Nacogdochians searching for stolen horses was fired upon by a party of Hispanics. Finding evidence that suggested the presence of a large assembly of people, they returned to Nacogdoches and reported their discovery. After being informed on August 7 that at least 100 Mexicans led by Córdova were encamped on the Angelina River, Thomas J. Rusk^{qv} called up the Nacogdoches squadron and sent a call to nearby settlements for reinforcements. On August 8 Houston issued a proclamation prohibiting unlawful assemblies and carrying of arms and ordered all assembled without authorization to return to their homes in peace. Two days later the leaders of the rebellion replied with their own proclamation, signed by Córdova and eighteen others. It stated that they could no longer bear injuries and usurpations of their rights. They had, therefore, taken up arms, were ready to die in defense of those rights, and only begged that their families not be harmed. On the same day Rusk learned that the insurrectionists had been joined by local Indians, who brought their number to approximately 400. After ascertaining that the rebellious band was moving toward the Cherokee nation, Rusk sent Maj. Henry W. Augustine^{qv} with 150 men to follow them.

Rusk, ignoring Houston's orders not to cross the Angelina River, took his remaining troops and marched directly toward the Cherokee village of Chief Bowl.qv En route Rusk learned that the rebellious army had been overtaken near Seguin and defeated. After communicating with local Indians, who disavowed any knowledge of the uprising, Rusk and his volunteer army returned to Nacogdoches.

Houston remained in Nacogdoches throughout the insurrection, writing letters of reassurance to his friend Bowl, and issuing orders to Rusk. Houston trusted the Cherokees' loyalty and hoped to keep peace with Bowl. Rusk, on the other hand, distrusted the Cherokee leadership and thought that a show of force was necessary. Rusk disobeyed Houston's orders and often bypassed him completely by sending reports to Vice President Mirabeau B. Lamar,qv who was in closer agreement with Rusk's views.

The leaders of the insurrection escaped arrest and went into hiding. Córdova eventually made his way to Mexico. Thirty-three alleged members of the rebellion, all with Spanish surnames, were arrested and indicted for treason in the Nacogdoches District Court. Because of the "distracted state of public feeling" a change of venue to neighboring San Augustine County was granted to all but one of the defendants. José Antonio Menchaca,qv one of those tried in San Augustine County, was found guilty of treason and sentenced to hang, while the remaining defendants were found not guilty or had their cases dismissed. After several former jurors claimed to have been pressured in their decisions, President Lamar pardoned Menchaca, only four days before his scheduled execution.

The capture of two Mexican agents after the rebellion produced new evidence pointing to an extensive Indian and Mexican conspiracy against Texas. On about August 20, 1838, Julián Pedro Miracle qv was killed near the Red River. On his body were found a diary and papers that indicated the existence of an official project of the Mexican government to incite East Texas Indians against the Republic of Texas. The diary recorded that Miracle had visited Chief Bowl and that they had agreed to make war against the Texans. On May 18, 1839, a group of Texas Rangers qv defeated a party of Mexicans and Indians, including some Cherokees from Bowl's village. On the body of Manuel Flores,qv the group's leader, were found documents encouraging Indians to follow a campaign of harassment against Texans. Included were letters from Mexican officials addressed to Córdova and Bowl. Although Bowl denied all charges against his people and Houston maintained his belief in their innocence, President Lamar became convinced that the Cherokees could not be allowed to stay in Texas. The Cherokee Warqv and subsequent removal of the Cherokees from Texas began shortly thereafter.

BIBLIOGRAPHY: Mary Whatley Clarke, *Chief Bowles and the Texas Cherokees* (Norman: University of Oklahoma Press, 1971). James T. DeShields, *Border Wars of Texas,* ed. Matt Bradley (Tioga, Texas, 1912; rpt., Waco: Texian Press, 1976). Joseph Milton Nance, *After San Jacinto: The Texas-Mexican Frontier, 1836-1841* (Austin: University of Texas Press, 1963). Walter Prescott Webb, *The Texas Rangers* (Boston: Houghton Mifflin, 1935; rpt., Austin: University of Texas Press, 1982). Dorman H. Winfrey and James M. Day, eds., *Texas Indian Papers* (4 vols., Austin: Texas State Library, 1959-61; rpt., 5 vols., Austin: Pemberton Press, 1966).
Rebecca J. Herring

CORDWOOD CREEK. Cordwood Creek rises just north of Farm Road 576 and four miles west of Moran in southeastern Shackelford County (at 32°33′ N, 99°15′ W) and runs for five miles northeast to its mouth on Deep Creek, just west of Moran (at 32°33′ N, 99°11′ W). The surrounding rolling hills are surfaced by clay and sandy loams that support scrub brush, mesquite, cacti, and grasses.

CORINE, TEXAS. Corine was a farming community twenty-two miles northwest of Rusk and eight miles west of Jacksonville in northwestern Cherokee County. The site was evidently first settled after the Civil War.qv A post office opened there in 1888, and a school by 1892. In 1896 Corine had a reported population of ten. Its post office closed in 1906, and by the mid-1930s the community was no longer shown on the county highway map. In the early 1990s only a few scattered houses remained in the area.
Christopher Long

CORINTH, TEXAS (Denton County). Corinth is six miles southeast of Denton in Denton County. It celebrated its 100th anniversary in 1980. The community was named by the Dallas and Wichita Railway, which built tracks through the townsite in 1880. Corinth had a population of 461 in 1970, 1,264 in 1980, and 3,944 in 1990. The town's growth was a result of the economic development that occurred in the 1970s along Interstate Highway 35 between Dallas and Denton. Although Corinth in the 1980s continued to be the home of a few independent farmers, most of its residents commuted to Lewisville, Denton, or Dallas for employment.
David Minor

CORINTH, TEXAS (Henderson County). Corinth was on Farm Road 753 six miles southwest of Athens in southern Henderson County. In the mid-1930s the settlement had a school, a church, and a number of houses. The school later closed, and by 1990 Corinth was a dispersed rural community with a church and a few scattered houses.
Christopher Long

CORINTH, TEXAS (Jones County). Corinth is on U.S. Highway 277 eight miles southwest of Stamford in north central Jones County. It relies upon Stamford and Anson for postal and other services. Its population was reported as twenty-five from 1940 until 1990.
William R. Hunt

CORINTH, TEXAS (Lee County). Corinth is 3½ miles north of Giddings in south central Lee County. A school known as Corinthian was in operation there by 1900 and in 1905-06 had twenty black students. For a time the school building was also used as a church. In the mid-1930s the community had the combined school and church building, a cemetery, and a few scattered dwellings. By the early 1950s the local school had been annexed to the Giddings Independent School District. In 1982 only the church and cemetery marked the site of the community.
Christopher Long

CORINTH, TEXAS (Marion County). Corinth was at the intersection of Farm roads 1324 and 248 and State Highway 49, on the Missouri Pacific Railroad three miles northeast of Jefferson in central Marion County. In 1936 the community had a school, a church, a factory, three roadside businesses, and a number of scattered dwellings. The Corinth school in 1938 was a one-room schoolhouse which accommodated forty black elementary school students and one teacher. The local school was consolidated with those of Jefferson by 1955, and by 1962 only the church and cemetery remained at Corinth. By 1983 the church was gone, and the cemetery was no longer marked on the county highway map.

BIBLIOGRAPHY: Jack Reed Harvey, Survey and Proposed Reorganization of the Marion County Schools (M.A. thesis, University of Texas, 1940).
Mark Odintz

CORINTH, TEXAS (Milam County). Corinth is on Farm Road 1915 some ten miles west of Cameron in western Milam County. It was settled by Czechs and Germans in 1847 and was named for the biblical city of Corinth, Greece. Corinth served as the judicial seat of Precinct Six until 1892, when the office of the justice of the peace was moved to Buckholts. The school at Corinth had two teachers and ninety-seven students in 1903. The 1941 county highway map showed a cemetery, a school, and several scattered houses at the site. The local school was consolidated with the Buckholts district in 1950. Only a cemetery marked the community's location on the 1988 county highway map.

BIBLIOGRAPHY: Lelia M. Batte, *History of Milam County, Texas* (San Antonio: Naylor, 1956). Milam County Heritage Preservation Society, *Matchless Milam: History of Milam County* (Dallas: Taylor, 1984).

Vivian Elizabeth Smyrl

CORINTH, TEXAS (Panola County). Corinth is just off Farm Road 315 sixteen miles southwest of Carthage in southwestern Panola County. It was settled around the time of the Civil War[qv] and developed around a church called Corinth. A school was in operation there by the mid-1890s; in 1897 it had an enrollment of forty-one black students. In the mid-1930s the community had a church, a school, a cemetery, and a number of houses. Its school was later closed, and its students were transferred to the Carthage or Gary schools. By the mid-1960s only a church, a cemetery, and a few scattered dwellings remained in the area. In 1990 Corinth was still a dispersed rural community.

Christopher Long

CORINTH, TEXAS (Van Zandt County). Corinth, originally known as Hatton, was on Farm Road 1255 some eight miles northeast of Canton in central Van Zandt County. Though whites had settled in the area earlier, the townsite was part of the Cherokee Nation from 1836 to 1840. The site was a stage stop between Marshall and Dallas from 1848 to 1873, when the Texas and Pacific Railway began operations in the area. In 1886 James Richardson, whose headright included the future townsite, donated the land for a church, a school, and a cemetery. When a post office was established there in 1888, the town was called Hatton, for James Thomas Hatton, the first postmaster and the father-in-law of James Kuykendall, who taught the first area school in 1849. The Corinth Missionary Baptist Church cemetery dates to 1874. The town was renamed Corinth by a member of the James J. Kuykendall family when the local post office was discontinued in 1906. A school building built at the community by 1890 also served the Baptist congregation. The building was replaced in 1899. The school had an enrollment of forty-two in 1906, and was replaced in 1916 by a third schoolhouse that was later sold to the church. By the 1890s the town had a population of fifty, three stores, three school buildings, a gristmill and gin, a blacksmith shop, a sawmill, and a broom manufacturer. In 1936 the church, cemetery, school, a single business, and scattered dwellings remained, but no population figures were available for the community. In 1940 its school was consolidated with the Grand Saline Independent School District. By 1981 only the church, the cemetery, and scattered dwellings along the road survived. Corinth is chiefly known as the birth and burial place of aviator Wiley Post.[qv]

BIBLIOGRAPHY: Van Zandt County History Book Committee, *History of Van Zandt County* (Dallas, 1984).

Diana J. Kleiner

CORINTH SCHOOL COMMUNITY, TEXAS. The Corinth School Community was in southeastern Ellis County. It began when the one-room Corinth School was built in 1870. The Corinth Baptist Church and churches of other denominations met in the school. In 1894 the school had fifty-two students. Eventually the schoolhouse was moved to Ensign, and the Corinth School Community ceased to exist.

BIBLIOGRAPHY: Edna Davis Hawkins, et al., *History of Ellis County, Texas* (Waco: Texian, 1972).

Lisa C. Maxwell

CORLEY, TEXAS. Corley is on the St. Louis Southwestern Railway three miles west of Maud in southern Bowie County. The community was named for John C. Corley, an early settler. A post office was established there in 1882 with J. Carr Turner as postmaster, and by 1884 the town had a sawmill, a gristmill, a gin, a store, a hotel, and a population of seventy-five. By 1890 the community's population had reached 100, but in 1896 it was reported as only fifty. The Corley post office was discontinued in the 1950s. In 1982 the town had a reported population of thirty-five and no rated businesses. In 1990 the population of Corley was still reported as thirty-five.

BIBLIOGRAPHY: J. J. Scheffelin, *Bowie County Basic Background Book* (n.d.).

Cecil Harper, Jr.

CORN CREEK. Corn Creek rises four miles southwest of Placid in northeastern McCulloch County (at 31°16′ N, 99°14′ W) and runs north for eighteen miles to its mouth on the Colorado River, three miles northwest of Mercury (at 31°27′ N, 99°11′ W). The surrounding flat to rolling prairie is surfaced by clay and sandy loams that support vegetation ranging from water-tolerant hardwoods, conifers, and grasses to scrub brush and mesquite.

CORN CREEK HILLS. The Corn Creek Hills are three miles north of Rochelle in northeastern McCulloch County (at 31°16′ N, 99°14′ W). The highest peak in the range rises 1,957 feet above mean sea level and 200 to 250 feet above the surrounding countryside.

CORN CULTURE. Corn, sometimes called maize, covers Texas chronology from prehistoric to present times. Tripsacoid (Tripsacum and teosinte) cobs, close relatives of corn, have been found in caves in the Hueco Mountains; the chapalote corn race existed in pre-Spanish Texas. Spanish explorers of the early 1500s found Indians growing corn in East Texas, and the Spanish carried on corn culture at the Rio Grande valley settlements and the Texas missions. They ate the grain as a basic ingredient in tortillas, tamales, posole, and atole.

Texas aborigines were major transmitters of prehistoric corn culture from Mexico to the lands that make up the eastern half of the United States. Centuries later the corn-hog-cotton (and wheat) agriculture from the South was fully reborn in Texas. Small farmers, planters, and slaves seeded their corn in rows, cultivated it with hoes, plows, horses, mules, and oxen, and cut and shocked the maturing crop. They held countless shucking frolics, or bees, and ground the kernels by water and horse-powered mills or hand-operated grinders. Much as they had done in the old South, these newcomers to the Mexican province, the Lone Star republic, and eventually the state of Texas ate the bountiful grain as roasting ears, cornbread, mush, hominy and hominy grits, parched corn, dodgers, pone, hoecake, pudding, porridge, popcorn, and fritters, and in other forms. They consumed it with pork, beef, wild game, and molasses, and washed it down with corn whiskey. They also fed it to their livestock as grain, fodder, and ensilage. For well over a century, corn was a major source of human food and the number-one feed crop.

Corn is an extremely versatile plant. Texans used cobs for jug and bottle stoppers, smoking pipes, tool handles, corn shellers, back scratchers, torches, fishing floats, and, most importantly, firewood and meat-smoking fuel. Corn and corn liquor served as a medium of exchange. For example, settlers each paid Stephen F. Austin[qv] ten to twenty bushels of the grain annually to cover the expenses of their deputy to the Mexican Congress, Erasmo Seguín.[qv] Shucks or husks served as writing paper, wrapping for foods such as tamales, sausages, ash cakes, and fruits, and mattress and pillow stuffing. Even the stalks and leaves had multiple uses. Settlers used them as sub-roofing, roof thatching, scarecrows, light fencing, erosion stoppage, and emergency material for the construction of shelter.

The corn plant was more than an economic necessity to Texans; it was an integral part of their way of life. Shucking bees were a major component of social life during the nineteenth century. Corn dolls, uses of the grain in games, the prevalence of whiskey-drinking sprees and corncob fights, and the references to corn in language, humor, literature, music, and poetry attest to the importance of the versatile plant as a cultural ingredient.

Until recent years the principal area of corn growing in Texas was the eastern half, where rainfall and soil conditions were most favorable. During the middle of the nineteenth century corn was the dominant grain crop. Texas produced over six million bushels, twenty-five times as much as all other grain crops combined, in 1849. In 1859 the figure was over sixteen million bushels of corn, more than six times the total of all other grains.

Corn made substantial gains on cotton acreage during the Civil War.qv The Confederate government encouraged production of more corn and less cotton, since the former was critically needed as food for the war effort and the cotton crop could not be readily marketed through the Union naval blockade. After the war, and for the century and more since, the relative importance of corn declined in Texas because of the resurgence of cotton, vast increases in wheat production, and more recently a shift to other feed grains such as sorghum (see SORGHUM AND SORGHUM CULTURE) and soybeans. As opposed to cotton and wheat, most of the state's corn crop goes to local consumption, primarily as livestock feed on the farms where it is produced.

In 1913 Texas planted some seven million acres in corn and harvested an average of twenty-one bushels per acre. The acres had dropped to a low of 500,000 in the mid-1970s. However, the development of new hybrids increased plantings in the late 1970s and early 1980s. In 1980 feed-corn acres reached one million. Commercial sweet corn added 1,800 acres in that year, although it should be noted that thousands of additional acres of sweet corn are grown annually in home gardens. Improved strains, more scientific cultivation and fertilization, and expansion of irrigation increased yields of corn in Texas from 10 to 25 bushels an acre during the nineteenth and early twentieth centuries to 90 to 120 bushels in 1975–80.

In the late 1930s and early 1940s Collin, Williamson, Fannin, and Guadalupe counties led the state in corn production. Thirty years later the record producers were Williamson, Lavaca, Bell, Collin, Falls, and Hill counties. By the early 1980s the pattern had shifted dramatically to irrigated lands in the High Plains of the western Panhandle,qv where Parmer, Castro, Hale, Lamb, and Deaf Smith counties were in the forefront. In the late 1970s corn ranked third in cash receipts among the crops of Texas. By the early 1980s it placed fourth, behind cotton, wheat, and sorghum grain.

Over the last 100 years technology has completely altered the corn culture of Texas. Gasoline-powered tractors, gang plows and harrows, multiple-row planters, pesticides, herbicides, and mechanical corn pickers have banished the old equipment to antique stores and museums, while farms have declined sharply in number and grown in size. Change has been the rule in varieties and uses of corn, in geographical areas of production, and in mechanization. The one constant element has been the great and continued importance of the golden grain to the economy of Texas.

BIBLIOGRAPHY: Paul Wallace Gates, *Agriculture and the Civil War* (New York: Knopf, 1965). Lewis C. Gray, *History of Agriculture in the Southern United States to 1860* (Washington: Carnegie Institution, 1933; rpt., Gloucester, Massachusetts: Peter Smith, 1958). Nicholas P. Hardeman, *Shucks, Shocks, and Hominy Blocks: Corn as a Way of Life in Pioneer America* (Baton Rouge: Louisiana State University Press, 1981). Paul Mangelsdorf, *Corn: Its Origin, Evolution, and Development* (Cambridge: Belknap Press of Harvard University, 1964).

Nicholas P. Hardeman

CORNELIA, TEXAS. Cornelia was eighteen miles southeast of George West in Live Oak County. It was founded in 1913, when the San Antonio, Uvalde and Gulf Railroad built tracks into the area, and was named for Cornelia (Cox) Staples, the wife of Henry Staples, who owned the townsite land. The community was granted a post office in 1915, and around that time a store opened there. Staples donated two acres for a cemetery that was used by the local Mexican-American population. Cornelia lost its post office in 1918, and by the next year its store had closed. A 1936 county highway map shows only a railroad depot at the site. After the Nueces River was dammed in 1958 to form Lake Corpus Christi, the railroad tracks were moved, the graves from Cornelia's cemetery were removed, and the site was inundated by the new lake.

BIBLIOGRAPHY: Live Oak County Historical Commission, *The History of the People of Live Oak County* (George West, Texas, 1982).

John Leffler

CORNELIASON CREEK. Corneliason Creek rises a mile south of Bells in extreme east central Grayson County (at 30°34′ N, 96°24′ W) and runs northwest for eight miles to its mouth on Mill Creek, three miles southwest of Ambrose (at 33°39′ N, 96°26′ W). The surrounding flat to rolling prairie is surfaced by dark, commonly calcareous clays and sandy and clay loams that support mesquite, pine, mixed hardwood trees, cacti, and various grasses.

CORNELL, TEXAS. Cornell was near the Angelina River in northern Angelina County. The settlement was established after the Civil War.qv Some lumbering was done there before 1900; later most residents earned their living from farming. By 1990 only a few scattered houses remained in the area.

Claudia Hazlewood

CORNERSVILLE, TEXAS. Cornersville is on State Highway 11 and the Louisiana and Arkansas Railway some eighteen miles southeast of Sulphur Springs in southeastern Hopkins County. It was named for its location near the corners of Hopkins and Franklin counties. Dr. J. P. Anderson operated a store and practiced medicine in the community in 1869. The population was composed chiefly of workers in a pottery. A post office called Grotton opened in 1901, with Eugenia A. Payne as postmaster, and operated until 1905. A school named Cornersville was operating by 1905, when it had an enrollment of 105. In the mid-1930s Cornersville had two churches, a cemetery, a business, and a number of scattered dwellings. By 1948 the business had closed, but an oil refinery had been erected a quarter mile east of the center of town on the Louisiana and Arkansas Railway. In the late 1980s the community had two churches, two cemeteries, and a business. It was still listed as a community in 1990.

J. E. Jennings

CORNETT, TEXAS. Cornett is on Farm Road 2888 ten miles northeast of Hughes Springs in northwestern Cass County. It was settled before the Civil Warqv and was first named Hamil's Chapel and then Troup, for Troup County, Georgia, the original home of many of its early settlers. The name was changed to Cornett in honor of the G. T. Cornett family, who owned land in the area. A post office was established at the community in 1901 and operated until 1906. In 1933 Cornett had two rated businesses and a population of fifty-three. By 1964 it reported forty residents and no rated businesses. In 1986 Cornett had an estimated population of thirty, a church, and a community center. In 1990 its population was still listed as thirty.

BIBLIOGRAPHY: *History of Cass County People* (Atlanta, Texas: Cass County Genealogical Society, 1982).

Cecil Harper, Jr.

CORNETTE, JAMES PERCIVAL (1908–1986). James Percival Cornette, university president and writer, was born in Charleston, Mississippi, on November 17, 1908. He spent most of his early years in Kentucky and graduated from Russellville High School. After completing his baccalaureate degree at Kentucky Wesleyan in 1929, he earned his master's degree from the University of Virginia in 1930, and his Ph.D. from George Peabody College for Teachers in 1938. He began his academic career as a teacher and coach in Clark County, Kentucky, and later taught at the high school in Mattoon, Crittenden County. From there he went on to teach at Western Kentucky State College (now Western Kentucky University) in Bowling Green as an associate professor of English for fourteen years before moving to Baylor University in Waco, Texas, where he served as an academic dean. He married Mary Elizabeth Lawson on February 26, 1930, and they had three sons.

In January 1948 Cornette moved to Canyon to assume the duties of executive vice president and intern at West Texas State College (now West Texas A&M University), and on October 2 he succeeded Joseph A. Hill[qv] as president of that institution. At a time when the concept of regional private support was unknown, Cornette immediately set out to expand the college into a "state-funded, regionally-endowed" university dependent on area contributions for its "niceties." During his twenty-five years as president the Kilgore Research Center was established on campus, and the Nance Ranch, site of various agricultural programs, was begun east of Canyon. Every building on campus was either constructed or renovated, and many programs were launched and expanded. Cornette expanded the athletic program and also helped start a financial-aid program for students.

He was a member of the National Education Association, the Texas State Teachers' Association,[qv] Rotary International, and Phi Kappa Delta. He served as president of the American Association of State Colleges and Universities, chaired that organization's National Committee on Legislation, and was on the board of directors of the American Association of Colleges for Teacher Education. He was also a president of the Council of Presidents of Texas Senior Colleges. In 1962 Cornette was named "Man of the Year" by the Amarillo *Globe-News* for his contributions to the Panhandle area.

He was the author of *A Biography of John Henry Clagett* (1938) and *A History of the Western Kentucky State College* (1941); with A. L. Cross he coauthored the Modern Language Handbooks, a series of English textbooks for grades five through eight. He published numerous articles and wrote more than forty television programs on literary subjects, especially his favorite poet, Robert Frost. His dream of university status for West Texas State College came true in the fall of 1963. By the time he stepped down in 1973 the university's enrollment had increased from 1,300 to nearly 8,000. After his retirement Cornette served a year as chancellor and then retired as president emeritus. The new university library, completed in 1973, was named in his honor.

Cornette was a member of the Panhandle-Plains Historical Society[qv] and served as its president from 1963 to 1965. In 1965 he and his wife, who had studied art, opened the Canyon Art Gallery near the university campus. Cornette was a director of the Amarillo Area Foundation and a trustee of High Plains Baptist Hospital. He was a Baptist, a Mason, and a president of the Llano Estacado Council of the Boy Scouts of America. He died at High Plains Baptist Hospital in Amarillo on November 16, 1986, and was buried in Dreamland Cemetery in Canyon.

BIBLIOGRAPHY: Joseph A. Hill, *More Than Brick and Mortar* (Amarillo: Russell Stationery, 1959). Ruth Lowes and W. Mitchell Jones, *We'll Remember Thee: An Informal History of West Texas State University* (Canyon: WTSU Alumni Association, 1984). Vertical Files, Barker Texas History Center, University of Texas at Austin.

H. Allen Anderson

CORN GAP. Corn Gap is a break in a line of hills 1½ miles south of Walnut Springs in northern Bosque County (at 32°02′ N, 97°44′ W). It is in a part of the Grand Prairie characterized by level to hilly terrain with locally deep dissection and some steep limestone slopes. Area soils range from shallow and stony to deep clay loams that support oak, juniper, mesquite, and grasses.

CORN HILL, TEXAS. Corn Hill was on Willis Creek and Interstate Highway 35 two miles south of Jarrell in north central Williamson County. The site was settled in 1855 by Judge John E. King as a stage stop on the road between Georgetown and Fort Gates and was named for the hill on which the judge's house sat. A post office was established there that same year. Growth seems to have been slow in Corn Hill until the 1870s and 1880s. A store was built in the town in 1869 and a gin about 1871; by 1884 Corn Hill was a thriving community with 250 inhabitants, four churches, three gins, two mills, a Masonic lodge, a weekly newspaper (the *Express*), and a school (Corn Hill Academy). Cotton was ginned in a large steam gin and shipped from the town. Corn Hill had a hotel and a population of 350 in 1896 and may have had as many as 500 residents in 1910, but thereafter the community rapidly declined. In 1909 it became clear that the Bartlett and Western Railway would bypass Corn Hill, and a new town, Jarrell, was laid out nearby on the proposed line. Between 1910 and 1920 the post office, the Masonic lodge, and many other of Corn Hill's buildings were moved to Jarrell, and by the end of this period Corn Hill was virtually abandoned. In 1973 the hotel was the only building still standing in Corn Hill.

BIBLIOGRAPHY: Clara Stearns Scarbrough, *Land of Good Water: A Williamson County History* (Georgetown, Texas: Williamson County Sun Publishers, 1973).

Mark Odintz

CORNUDAS, TEXAS. Cornudas is at the intersection of Farm Road 2317 and U.S. Highway 62/180, forty-two miles northwest of Sierra Blanca in north central Hudspeth County. It was named for the Cornudas Mountains, fourteen miles to the north. The settlement was founded by 1938, when Mrs. Willie Tinnin was appointed postmistress of a local post office that closed within a year. At that time the community served several cattle ranches, and there was a Standard Oil pumping station about six miles south. Cornudas continued to be shown on maps of the area through the mid-1980s, at which time it had several businesses and scattered dwellings. A church and a school were near the pumping station.

Martin Donell Kohout

CORNUDAS MOUNTAINS. The Cornudas Mountains lie eighteen miles northwest of Dell City in north central Hudspeth County and southern Otero County, New Mexico (with a center point of 32°02′ N, 105°32′ W). At 7,023 feet above sea level, the summit of San Antonio Mountain, just south of the Texas–New Mexico line, is the highest point in the Cornudas; the other two prominent peaks in Hudspeth County are Chattfield Mountain at 6,247 feet and Washburn Mountain at 5,697 feet. The Washburn and Persimmon springs on Washburn Mountain were known to nineteenth-century travelers and were shown on maps of the area from the 1860s and 1870s. The springs flowed from the Tertiary intrusive rocks, over two million years old, that constitute the core of the Cornudas Mountains; in the 1980s both springs were dry. The soils in the Cornudas are shallow and stony and support scrub brush and grasses. The name *Cornudas*, Spanish for "horned," presumably refers to the way the mountains protrude from the surrounding terrain.

CORONADO EXPEDITION. In 1536 Álvar Núñez Cabeza de Vaca[qv] took to Mexico City a report of people who lived in large houses in the Seven Cities of Cíbola,[qv] in the northern part of New Spain. To verify Cabeza de Vaca's statements, Viceroy Antonio de Mendoza sent Marcos de Niza[qv] to the north in the spring of 1539. After Niza's confirmation of the report, Mendoza, on January 6, 1540, appointed Francisco Vázquez de Coronado[qv] to lead an expedition to conquer the area. That expedition, gathered at Compostela for Mendoza's review in February 1540, included 1,000 men, 1,500 horses and mules, and cattle and sheep for the expedition commissary. Two vessels under command of Hernado de Alarcón were sent up the coast to support the land forces.

Coronado made his final preparations at Culiacán and, on April 22, 1540, set out with an advance guard of 100 men ahead of the main force under Tristán de Luna y Arellano.[qv] The route, roughly paralleling the west coast of Mexico, led through Sinaloa and Sonora to the Zuñi village of Háwikuh. This settlement, one of the group of villages called Cíbola by Niza and Granada by the Spaniards, was at the site of present Agua Caliento or Ojo Caliente in southeastern Arizona. Háwikuh was stormed and taken on July 7, 1540.

From there an exploring party under Pedro de Tovar made its way to Tusayán, the Hopi villages. García López de Cárdenas led a force to the Grand Canyon of the Colorado River. Intrigued by the tales of an Indian named Bigotes, Coronado sent Hernando de Alvarado[qv] east through Tiguex (the area along the Rio Grande in the vicinity of Bernalillo, New Mexico) to Cicúique (the Pecos pueblo that became present Rowe, New Mexico). There an Indian called El Turco[qv] acted as guide to the plains and told of the wonderful Quivira[qv] province. An unsuccessful attempt to get in touch with Alarcón's naval expedition, which had sailed through the Gulf of California and into the Colorado River, was made by Melchior Díaz, who went out from Corazones.

Coronado spent the winter of 1540–41 at Tiguex, on the Rio Grande, and on April 23, 1541, moved east from the Rio Grande to Cicúique, down the Río Cicúique or Pecos to a bridge that had been thrown across the river, probably between present Anton Chico and Santa Rosa, and into vast level plains that are identifiable as the Llano Estacado[qv] of eastern New Mexico and the Texas Panhandle. At "*barrancas* like those of Colima," present Palo Duro and Tule canyons, Coronado held a council of his captains in which it was determined that the army should return to Tiguex while Coronado took a small force to the north in search of Quivira. The army under Luna y Arellano took the most direct route from the canyons to the Pecos River, passed salt lakes, and arrived at the river thirty leagues below the bridge, apparently at the site of later Fort Sumner, New Mexico. From there Arellano's company went up the river, crossed the bridge, found Cicúique hostile, and went to the camp at Tiguex to await the return of Coronado.

From the ravines or canyons, Coronado, with thirty men on horses and six men on foot, proceeded to the north "by the needle." On St. Peter and Paul's Day, July 29, 1541, he arrived at the "river below Quivira" (probably the Arkansas), which flowed to the northeast. Down this river, at or near the edge of the plains, was Quivira. The unrewarding quest having ended, the expedition spent the winter of 1541–42 at Tiguex on the Rio Grande, where Coronado received a head injury in falling from a horse. In the spring of 1542 the expedition returned to Mexico on the route by which it had come.

BIBLIOGRAPHY: Herbert Eugene Bolton, *Coronado: Knight of Pueblos and Plains* (New York: Whittlesey; Albuquerque: University of New Mexico Press, 1949). Arthur Grove Day, *Coronado's Quest: The Discovery of the Southwestern States* (Berkeley: University of California Press, 1940; rpt., Westport, Connecticut: Greenwood Press, 1981).
David Donoghue

CORONAL INSTITUTE. Coronal Institute, in San Marcos, was founded by Orlando Newton Hollingsworth[qv] in 1868. It was a private, coeducational school and offered military training to boys. In 1869–70 the faculty was six men and two women, and enrollment was 130. Hollingsworth sold the school to R. H. Belvin on January 2, 1871. In 1875 the school was valued at $20,000. On June 26, 1875, the San Marcos district of the Methodist Episcopal Church, South, purchased the school, and J. H. Bishop became president. Succeeding presidents were Rev. E. S. Smith, R. O. Roundsavall, J. E. Pritchett, W. J. Spillman, A. A. Thomas, Sterling Fisher, and V. A. Godbey. The school, chartered in 1879, reached its peak of development in 1900 with twelve faculty members, property valued at $35,000, and a library of 900 volumes. However, enrollment never grew large enough for the increased investments in the school. In 1903 129 students enrolled.

Coronal offered coursework in English, history, mathematics, Latin, German, Spanish, physiology, physiography, physics, biology, chemistry, bookkeeping, agriculture, botany, domestic science, drawing, and music. During the presidency of Sterling Fisher in the first decade of the twentieth century, the school constructed a dormitory for boys and a new main building with a girls' dormitory. The total value of the plant was estimated at $115,000. Coronal Institute was affiliated with the University of Texas and with Southwestern University. Nearly 500 students received diplomas of high school level from the time the school first granted them in 1880 until it was discontinued in 1917.

When the United States entered World War I[qv] the government rented the facilities from the Methodist Episcopal Church for use as a barracks and training ground. After the war S. M. Melton leased the property and operated it under the name Coronal Military Academy. Enrollments were low, and the project was abandoned in 1919. The main building was converted into an apartment house, and the boys' dormitory became a hospital.

BIBLIOGRAPHY: Lewis N. Hale, "Texas Schools and Colleges," *Texas Magazine*, August 1912. William Franklin Ledlow, History of Protestant Education in Texas (Ph.D. dissertation, University of Texas, 1926). R. S. Morgan, Development of San Marcos as an Educational Center (M.A. thesis, University of Texas, 1936). Herschel C. Walling, comp., *History of Coronal Institute* (San Marcos, Texas: Hays County Historical and Genealogical Society, 1991).
Nancy Beck Young

CORPRON, CARLOTTA (1901–1988). Carlotta Corpron, a photographer whose work has been called "light-poetry," was born in Blue Earth, Minnesota, on December 9, 1901, the daughter of Dr. Alexander Corpron. In 1905 the family moved to India, where Dr. Corpron served as a medical missionary. While growing up, Carlotta attended a strict English boarding school in the Himalayan mountains. Although no art courses were taught at the school, the loneliness that she experienced there encouraged an independent spirit that later surfaced in the originality of her photographs. In 1920 she returned to the United States to study art at Michigan State Normal College (now Eastern Michigan University) in Ypsilanti. She graduated in 1925 with a B.S. in art education, then attended the Teachers' College of Columbia University. There she studied art education and fabric design and was awarded her M.A. in 1926. From 1926 to 1928 she taught at the Women's College of Alabama (now Huntington College) in Montgomery. After a summer sojourn in Europe she accepted a teaching post at the University of Cincinnati School of Applied Arts, where she taught from 1928 to 1935. In 1933 she bought her first camera for use as a teaching aid in a textile design course.

In 1935 she moved to Denton, Texas, to teach advertising design and art history at Texas State College for Women (now Texas Woman's University), a post she held until her retirement in 1968. She spent the summer of 1936 refining her photographic technique at the Art Center in Los Angeles in order to prepare to teach a course in photography. She continued the experimentation begun in Cincinnati to produce her earliest group of photographs, her "Nature Studies" series. In such works as *Coral and Starfish* (1944) she focused on the abstract patterns of natural forms. She occasionally manipulated an image to accentuate geometric forms, as in *Design with Oil Tank* (1942), a print composed of two overlapping negatives. Encouraged by the progressive art department at TWU and by her own conviction that her experimental work prompted creativity in her students, Corpron began to produce even more inventive studies. In a series she called "Light Drawings" she captured linear patterns of light by swinging her camera in front of the moving lights of carnival rides. In *A Walk in Fair Park, Dallas* (1943), the original subject matter was dematerialized to a pattern of light and motion that anticipated her abstract work.

In 1942 Corpron led a light workshop at Texas Woman's University for photographer Laszlo Moholy-Nagy. Although he praised her rap-

Light Follows Form. *Photograph by Carlotta Corpron, 1946. Gelatin silver print. 10 7/16" × 13 3/16". © Amon Carter Museum, Fort Worth, Texas. Carlotta Corpron Collection. Photographer Carlotta Corpron filtered light through Venetian blinds or glass onto a plaster cast, experimenting with the play of light on the three-dimensional form.*

port with her students, Moholy-Nagy did not encourage Corpron's independent photography. More influential on her work was the arrival of Gyorgy Kepes, who came to Denton to write a book in 1944. His interest in Corpron's work prompted her to produce several series of photographs that were the most original of her career. At his suggestion Corpron experimented by placing white paper cut in simple shapes within a perforated box that was open at one end. When flashlights were shined through the holes onto the paper shapes, interesting patterns of light and shadow were reflected. The resulting abstract photographs comprised Corpron's "Light Patterns" series. In her "Light Follows Form" series she extended her exploration of the modeling properties of light to three-dimensional form. In this series, she used light filtered through Venetian blinds or glass to dramatize a plaster cast of a Greek head.

She also experimented with solarization, a process in which already exposed negatives are exposed. Works such as *Solarized Calla Lilies* (1948) convey a surreal elegance, but Corpron favored more original methods of expression. She regarded her "Space Compositions" and "Fluid Light Designs" series as her best work. In the former she used still lifes composed of eggs, nautilus shells, or glass paperweights, usually combined with a curving reflective surface, to produce an illusion of receding three-dimensional space. She emphasized distortions of form that occurred in her egg photographs by experimentation during the development process. In *Fun With Eggs* (1948), for example, she combined vertical and horizontal negatives to achieve an ambiguous pictorial space. In her series "Fluid Light Designs," she produced her most fully abstract works by photographing the play of light on rippled plastic.

In 1945 Corpron met Alfred Stieglitz, a leader of avant-garde photography in the United States. He admired the beauty and strength of her work but died before he could mount an exhibition of her photographs. Corpron participated in more than five group exhibitions, including the 1952 Abstraction in Photography exhibition at the Museum of Modern Art in New York, and was the subject of solo exhibitions at the Dallas Museum of Art qv (1948), the Louisiana Art Commission in Baton Rouge (1952), the Art Institute of Chicago (1953), the University of Georgia in Athens (1953), the Woman's University of North Carolina, Chapel Hill (1954), and Ohio University in Athens (1955). In the late 1950s poor health and limited financial resources forced her to limit her hours in the darkroom in order to concentrate on teaching.

The inclusion of Corpron's photographs in the San Francisco Museum of Art's exhibition Women of Photography: An Historical Survey in 1975, followed by her first solo exhibition in a New York gallery in 1977, sparked a revival of interest in her work. Thereafter she was represented in important group exhibitions at the Dallas Museum of Art (1978), the International Center of Photography in New York (1979), the University of Missouri in St. Louis (1980), and the San Francisco Museum of Modern Art (1980). Solo exhibitions of her work were held at the Galleria del Milione in Milan, Italy (1978), Texas Woman's University (1980), and the Amon Carter Museum qv in Fort Worth (1980). Carlotta Corpron died on April 17, 1988. Her work is included in the collections of the Museum of Modern Art in New York City, the Art Institute of Chicago, the New Orleans Museum of Art, the Dallas Museum of Art, and the Amon Carter Museum in Fort Worth.

BIBLIOGRAPHY: Paula E. Bennett, "Carlotta Corpron," *Photographic Portfolio* 2 (June 1979). Mabel E. Maxcy, "A Creative Approach to Photography," *Texas Trends in Art Education,* Autumn 1960. Margaretta Mitchell, *Recollections: Ten Women of Photography* (New York: Viking, 1979). Martha A. Sandweiss, *Carlotta Corpron: Designer with Light* (Austin: University of Texas Press, 1980). Kendall Curlee

CORPUS CHRISTI, BATTLE OF. The battle of Corpus Christi occurred during the summer of 1862, while the coast of Texas from Cavallo Pass to Corpus Christi was under blockade by the USS *Arthur.*qv The *Arthur's* commander, acting lieutenant John W. Kittredge, was bold and aggressive, and his activities over a period of seven months caused grave concern to Texas military officials and near panic among coastal residents. However, Cavallo Pass was protected by Fort Esperanza at Saluria, and the intracoastal waterway remained open to commerce. The *Arthur,* with a draft of fourteen feet, was unable to cross the shallow inlets to pursue small vessels trafficking in cotton and other goods. The situation changed, however, when Kittredge received from New Orleans two light-draft vessels, the steamer *Sachem*qv and the yacht *Corypheus.* With the yacht he captured two Confederate sloops, the *Reindeer* and the *Belle Italia,* and converted them into armed gunboats. Then, on August 12, Kittredge brought his "mosquito fleet" into Corpus Christi Bay, where the USS *Corypheus* overtook and captured the Confederate schooner *Breaker.*

On August 13 Kittredge, under a flag of truce, landed at Corpus Christi and insisted on his right to inspect all United States government buildings there, but was rebuffed by Confederate major Alfred M. Hobbyqv and threatened to take the city by force. Kittredge agreed to a forty-eight-hour truce to allow civilians to evacuate but forbade military preparations during that time. Although he had no more than 100 men aboard his five vessels, Kittredge—with one Parrott gun, eight thirty-two-pounders, and a twelve-pound howitzer—was better armed than the Texans ashore.

The 700 defenders of Corpus Christi were local volunteers and the four companies of the Eighth Texas Infantry battalion under Hobby's command. Hobby had defied Kittredge and let him know that the Texans intended to resist. The defenders depended largely upon their only artillery pieces, three old smoothbore cannons, one eighteen-pounder and two twelve-pounders. Hobby and his men had neither training in the use of artillery nor combat experience. Two of the local volunteers, however, had both. Felix A. von Blücherqv was a veteran of the Mexican War,qv and Pvt. Billy Mann, home from the army on sick leave, was a combat veteran. Both men provided an invaluable service in the defense of their city.

When the forty-eight-hour truce ended and no attack came, Hobby took advantage of darkness to move his men and guns to earthworks erected by Gen. Zachary Taylor's^qv army of occupation in 1845. The move was accomplished without detection and brought the Texans within 400 yards of the *Sachem.* Early on the morning of August 16 the Confederates began firing, striking both the *Sachem* and the *Corypheus.* Both sides exchanged fire for several hours before Kittredge withdrew. No further action occurred until August 18, when thirty-two sailors were landed with a howitzer about a mile south of the battery. The federals advanced firing, backed by supporting fire from the ships. About 600 yards before reaching the battery, they were repulsed by a cavalry charge led by Capt. James A. Ware and hastily withdrew to their ships. Only one Confederate soldier was killed in the battle, despite the large number of shells fired at the battery and about the city. Hobby and one Union sailor were wounded, although not seriously. It was clearly a victory for the Texans, despite Kittredge's official report that his landing party had faced an overwhelming enemy force and had inflicted many casualties. Blücher and Mann both received field promotions from Gen. Hamilton P. Bee.^qv

Although the battle of Corpus Christi was acclaimed throughout the state as the "Vicksburg of Texas," the victory brought no permanent security to the city's citizens. The defending soldiers were soon withdrawn, leaving the city vulnerable to forays by a United States military force that occupied nearby Mustang Island during 1863–64. Many citizens, faced with starvation, offered allegiance to these forces in exchange for food and protection, and Corpus Christi remained a divided and stricken city for the duration of the war.

BIBLIOGRAPHY: Corpus Christi *Caller,* December 25, 1903. Corpus Christi *Ranchero,* August 19, 1862. *The War of the Rebellion: A Compilation of the Official Records of the Union and Confederate Armies.*

Norman C. Delaney

CORPUS CHRISTI, CATHOLIC DIOCESE OF. The Diocese of Corpus Christi, called by Pope Pius XII "the diocese with the most beautiful name," was until 1912 part of the Vicariate of Brownsville. The area's Catholic origins date to sixteenth-century missionary work of Franciscans,^qv of which little remains except for the La Bahía presidio and chapel at Goliad State Historical Park^qv and the foundation of Nuestra Señora del Refugio Mission at Refugio, the last mission to be established in Texas (1795). After his appointment as first bishop of Texas, Jean Marie Odin^qv visited Corpus Christi in 1850 to explore his territory. He found about thirty Catholic families, mostly of Hispanic descent, in the town. By 1888 that population was about 1,500. In 1883 the Catholic population in the Vicariate of Brownsville (the area between the Nueces River and the Rio Grande) was more than 40,000—of whom at least 37,500 were Hispanic. There were twelve churches, twelve chapels, twenty-one priests, a school for boys under twelve, three academies for girls, and five convents.

Catholic congregations of women^qv were critical in the progress of the diocese. The Sisters of the Incarnate Word and Blessed Sacrament,^qv in Brownsville since 1852, sent one of their members to Europe to recruit volunteers for expansion into Victoria. After a crisis-ridden journey marked by several deaths, the small group of missionaries returned in 1866 and founded Nazareth Academy^qv in Victoria the next year. In 1871 Sisters of the Incarnate Word and Blessed Sacrament in San Antonio came to Corpus Christi and opened a school that operated first in a home given up by the parish priest. The school moved several times before reaching its current location at the Incarnate Word Convent and Academy on South Alameda. The school was accredited by the state in 1885. With a rule based on that of the Sisters of the Incarnate Word and Blessed Sacrament with adaptations favoring nursing, the Sisters of Charity of the Incarnate Word^qv was founded by Bishop Claude Marie Dubuis,^qv who saw the dire need for nurses. At the invitation of Bishop Peter Verdaguer,^qv the sisters came to Corpus Christi in 1905 to administer Spohn Hospital.^qv The Religious Sisters of Mercy, a branch of the Sisters of Mercy,^qv began work in Refugio in 1875. In 1894 they moved to Laredo and initiated work that led to the establishment of Mercy Hospital.

In 1911, after Verdaguer's twenty-year administration of the vicariate, there were in the area thirty-two priests, fifteen churches with resident pastors, and sixty chapels and stations requiring visitations. Historian Carlos E. Castañeda^qv suggested that the "poor mission life in most of my Vicariate" referred to by Verdaguer may be partly a result of the delay of diocesan status. After the Diocese of Corpus Christi was established in 1912, Paul J. Nussbaum^qv served as its first bishop from 1913 until his resignation in 1920. During those years the diocese endured the destructive storms of 1916 and 1919, an influenza epidemic, and the burden of priests and nuns fleeing persecution in Mexico who looked to the church in Texas for assistance. During the tenure of Emmanuel B. Ledvina,^qv bishop from 1921 to 1949, there was much building (and rebuilding after storms) of missions, as well as of churches and schools in urban areas. Major funding came from the Catholic Church Extension Society, in which Ledvina had held office from 1907 to 1921, and the American Board of Missions. Mariano S. Garriga^qv was named in 1936 as coadjutor with right of succession; he assumed full administration of the diocese upon Ledvina's resignation in 1949. Garriga was born in Port Isabel, and was the first native Texan to become a Catholic bishop. A favored project of his was the education of boys for the priesthood, and the minor seminary operated by the Jesuits^qv opened in Corpus Christi in 1960. Garriga attended only the first session of the Second Vatican Council, but he carried the spirit of ecumenism back to the diocese, where he organized multifaith activities. His last project was the initiation of a drive to raise funds for a chapel of Perpetual Adoration in Corpus Christi Cathedral.^qv

Several months after Garriga's death in 1965, the see's four southernmost counties were separated to form the Catholic Diocese of Brownsville.^qv The counties remaining in the Corpus Christi diocese were Aransas, Bee, Brooks, Duval, Jim Hogg, Jim Wells, Kleberg, Kenedy, Live Oak, Nueces, Refugio, San Patricio, Webb, Zapata, and parts of LaSalle and McMullen—an area of 17,294 square miles. The fourth bishop of Corpus Christi, and the first after the division, was the Irish-born Thomas J. Drury, whose tenure, from 1965 to 1983, was marked by the turmoil following the Second Vatican Council and by legal conflicts over the estate of Sara Kenedy East.^qv Drury's expansion of diocesan activities from two to thirty-two departments included the establishment of Catholic Charities, the Office of Catholic Schools, the Catholic Youth Organization, the mission to Arteaga, Coahuila, the Family Life Bureau, the Department of Hispanic Affairs, the Catholic Telecommunications Center, the Pastoral Center, the Senate of Priests, and the Council of Religious. In 1966 he established the weekly *Texas Gulf Coast Register* (later called *Texas Gulf Coast Catholic*) as the official newspaper of the diocese. The name was changed to *South Texas Catholic* in 1980. Diocesan resources sustained damage from Hurricane Celia in 1970, when hundreds of people fled to temporary Red Cross headquarters set up in the basement of the cathedral.

René H. Gracida, installed as bishop in 1983, has been an outspoken opponent of restrictive immigration, abortion, and the death penalty. In 1994 the Catholic population of the diocese was 349,500 (of a total population of 740,250), served by eighty-four parishes and forty-seven missions. Sixty-nine of the parishes had resident pastors. The diocese had two homes for the aged, three retreat houses, three hospitals, and nine special centers for social services. Catholic congregations of men^qv in the diocese numbered seventeen; of women, thirty-two. The diocese had six monastery-residences for priests and brothers and twenty-eight convents for sisters. Twenty-nine Catholic elementary and secondary schools enrolled 6,364 students. *See also* CATHOLIC CHURCH, CATHOLIC HEALTH CARE, CATHOLIC JOURNALISM.

BIBLIOGRAPHY: Corpus Christi *Caller,* February 22, 1965. Carlos E. Castañeda, *Our Catholic Heritage in Texas* (7 vols., Austin: Von

Boeckmann–Jones, 1936–58; rpt., New York: Arno, 1976). Houston *Chronicle*, January 19, 1964. James Talmadge Moore, *Through Fire and Flood: The Catholic Church in Frontier Texas, 1836–1900* (College Station: Texas A&M University Press, 1992). *New Catholic Encyclopedia* (16 vols., New York: McGraw-Hill, 1967–74). Sister Genevieve Palmer, "Bishop Ledvina, Second Bishop of Corpus Christi," *Texas Gulf Coast Catholic*, April 14, 1978.   Jana E. Pellusch

CORPUS CHRISTI, TEXAS. Corpus Christi, a seaport at the mouth of the Nueces River on the west end of Corpus Christi Bay,qv is the county seat of Nueces County and the largest city on the South Texas coast. It lies at the junction of Interstate 37 and U. S. highways 77 and 181, 210 miles southwest of Houston. The city's transportation needs are also served by the Texas Mexican, Southern Pacific, and Missouri Pacific railways and Corpus Christi International Airport. In prehistoric times the area was inhabited by various tribes of the Karankawa Indian group, which migrated up and down the Coastal Bend region. It not known who the first Europeans were to visit the area, but it seems most likely that Álvar Núñez Cabeza de Vaca qv and his band were the first Europeans who actually set foot on the site. The Spanish, however, largely ignored the region until the 1680s, when Frenchmen under René Robert Cavelier, Sieur de La Salle,qv established a colony in Texas. Spanish authorities dispatched an expedition to the area in 1689 under Alonso De León,qv but the Corpus Christi Bay area remained unknown and unexplored until 1747, when Joaquín Prudencio de Orobio y Basterra qv led an expedition down the Nueces River, reaching the bay on February 26. After Orobio's return, José de Escandón,qv governor and captain general of Nuevo Santander,qv proposed founding a settlement at the mouth of the Nueces called Villa de Vedoya. In the summer of 1749, fifty families accompanied by a squadron of soldiers and two priests set out to colonize the area, but because of prolonged drought and a lack of adequate provisions they gave up before reaching their goal.

In 1787 Manuel de Escandón, son of José de Escandón, proposed another settlement at the mouth of the Nueces, but the project never advanced beyond the planning stages. In the late 1780s and early 1790s Spanish authorities considered moving Nuestra Señora del Refugio Mission to the mouth of the Nueces, but abandoned the idea because of continuing friction with the Lipan Apaches. During the 1830s two further failed attempts were made to establish colonies at the mouth of the Nueces. German nobleman Baron Johann von Rachnitz qv tried to found a German settlement there, but the ship carrying the colonists was prevented from landing by the French during the Pastry War. Around the same time, abolitionist Benjamin Lundy qv proposed the establishment of a colony of former slaves at the site; however, he dropped the plans after the outbreak of the Texas Revolution. The area thus remained uninhabited until September 1839, when Henry Lawrence Kinney qv and his partner William P. Aubrey established a trading post on the west shore of Corpus Christi Bay, reportedly near what is now the 400 block of North Broadway. Kinney and Aubrey quickly developed a brisk illegal trade with Mexico. In 1841 Capt. Enrique Villarreal,qv a rancher from Matamoros who had been granted the land by the Mexican government, led a force of 300 men to reclaim his property and seize the arms stored at Kinney's stockade. Kinney, who at the time reportedly had only eight men under his command, however, managed to negotiate an agreement to purchase the land. Kinney and Aubrey's post soon became the focus of trade in the area. Attacks by Mexican bands forced the abandonment of the post in 1842, but Kinney returned a short time later and reestablished his business. A post office opened the same year with Aubrey as postmaster. By the mid-1840s the settlement—now known as Corpus Christi ("the Body of Christ")—was a small village. An English visitor described it as consisting of "Colonel Kinney's fortified house, about a half dozen stores, and a grog shop or two"; another visitor around the same time reported that the village had some fifty families. In 1846 the town became county seat the of newly formed Nueces County. It was incorporated on April 25, 1846, but because no public officials were elected, the corporation was repealed, and the town was not reincorporated until February 16, 1852.

In September 1845 Gen. Zachary Taylor's qv army encamped nearby, and in the late 1840s numerous fortune-seekers passed through to join wagon trains headed for California, but few settlers put down permanent roots. In 1852 Kinney organized a state fair—reportedly the first in Texas—in an attempt to put Corpus Christi on the map, but it proved to be a failure and did little to spur the town's growth. A yellow fever epidemic struck the town in 1854, decimating the population, and difficulty in obtaining fresh water plagued the city throughout the 1850s. The chief impediment to growth, however, was the lack of a deepwater port, a problem that occupied the town's leaders for the next seventy years. Large ships, unable to enter Corpus Christi Bay, were forced to anchor offshore where supplies were offloaded onto lighters, shallow-draft vessels capable of navigating the narrow, twisting channels of the bay. Kinney, undismayed by the problems, continued to promote the town, placing glowing advertisements in northern newspapers and in Europe, which breathlessly described the natural beauty and business opportunities of the area. Some immigrants came and the population grew slowly, but the town continued to reflect something of a frontier character through the early 1850s. Public drunkenness and lawlessness were common. For many years there was no effective city government. By the middle of the decade, however, the situation began to change. The first schools opened around 1854, and by the eve of the Civil War qv the town had several established churches and several fraternal lodges. During the 1850s steamships of the Morgan Lines qv began making regular stops, and the volume of trade through the city gradually increased. By 1859 it was reported that some forty-five vessels carried on trade between Corpus Christi and Indianola alone. In 1860 the population reached 1,200 and the town reported four teachers, one music instructor, three ministers, a priest, three doctors, and eight lawyers. Men, however, outnumbered women, with seventy-three more men than women, a reflection of the town's continuing frontier character. Nearly one-third of all of all residents were foreign born.

During the early years of the Civil War, Corpus Christi served as an important crossroads for Confederate commerce. In defiance of the Union blockade, small boats sailed inside the barrier islands transporting goods from the Brazos River to the Rio Grande or delivering them for overland transport to Mexico. In an effort to halt the trade, Union forces seized Mustang Island qv in September 1863 and bombarded Corpus Christi on two occasions. They did not occupy the town until the end of the year. Military occupation continued until the early 1870s, but the town's economy quickly recovered, in large measure due to the growth in sheep and cattle ranching in the surrounding region. Between 1870 and 1880 Corpus Christi was the center of a wool market. But the growth of the cattle industry had the greatest impact on the town's economy in the postbellum period. During the great cattle boom of the 1870s Corpus Christi emerged as an important shipping point for cattle from the South Texas plains, and in the 1880s packing houses, stockyards, and markets for hides, tallow, and other cattle by-products flourished.

As the city grew in importance as a shipping center, efforts were made to improve access to the ocean. In 1874 the main sea channel was dredged to a depth of eight feet to allow large steamers to navigate. The railroad also reached the town in the mid-1870s. The Corpus Christi, San Diego and Rio Grande Narrow Gauge Railroad was organized in 1875, and by 1881 it was extended to Laredo as the Texas Mexican Railway. In 1885 Corpus Christi was a city of some 4,200 residents, with three banks, a customhouse, railroad machine shops, an ice factory, carriage factories, several hotels, Episcopal, Presbyterian, Methodist, Catholic, and Baptist churches, and two newspapers, the *Caller* and the *Critic*. The decades of the 1800s and 1890s brought other signs that Corpus was developing into a modern city. Many of city's streets were paved for the first time, a street railway system was built in 1889, and a public water system opened in 1893. In 1890 New York promoter Elihu H. Ropes[qv] announced plans to build a deepwater seaport that would make Corpus Christi a combined "Chicago of the Southwest" and "Long Branch of the South." His scheme collapsed in the national depression of the early 1890s, but the town continued to develop rapidly nonetheless. Growth was most impressive in the eight years from 1906 to 1914, when bank deposits increased ten-fold, from $300,000 to $3 million and property values rose from $1,290,000 to $7,455,000.

By 1914 Corpus Christi was served by four railroads, the Texas Mexican, the San Antonio and Aransas Pass, the St. Louis, Brownsville and Mexico, and the San Antonio, Uvalde and Gulf. The expanding network of links with the outside world contributed to the town's rapid development. The railroads aggressively promoted the city and the surrounding countryside, offering inexpensive fares in the hope that new residents and farmers would increase the rail business. Rail agents similarly promoted the city as a tourist center, billing it as a all-year resort "where the weary can come to rest, the invalid can come for health, and the gay devotee come for pleasure." During the teens, the Texas State Epworth League of the Methodist Church held its annual encampment in the city, and some 5,000 to 8,000 visitors each year took advantage of excursion rates to spent several weeks on the shore. Many others also came to the city, fueling a construction boom for hotels, cottages, and boardinghouses. A city administration elected in 1913 headed by mayor Roy Miller adopted an aggressive program of modernization. In three years it paved twelve miles of streets, laid twenty-six miles of storm and sanitary sewers, installed a modern water system, organized a paid fire department with two "triple-motor" pumpers, and constructed a new city hall and municipal wharf.

The efforts, however, all seemed to come to naught on September 14, 1919, when the city was hit by a powerful hurricane that destroyed much of the North Beach area and the central business district and killed some 350 to 400 people. The tremendous economic loss convinced civic and business leaders that for the city to recover and prosper it would be necessary finally to build a deepwater port. Various city and local organizations lobbied the federal authorities to build a thirty-foot-deep channel from the gulf to a protected harbor in the city. In 1922 President Warren G. Harding approved a rivers and harbors act that authorized construction of the ship channel. Dredging and construction began the following year. Finally, on September 14, 1926, seven years to the day after the hurricane hit, the jubilant city celebrated the opening of its deepwater port. The impact on Corpus Christi was immediate. In just ten years, from 1920 to 1930, the city's population more than doubled, growing from 10,522 to 27,741. The town's new-found prosperity was also apparent in other ways: in 1927 the first "skyscraper," the Nixon Building, was finished, and by 1930 two other modern office buildings and a large hotel, the Plaza, dotted the central business district.

Growth slowed during the years of the Great Depression.[qv] The number of businesses fell from 920 in 1931 to 710 in 1933, but the discovery of oil in the county in 1930 and the continued development of the port of Corpus Christi helped to offset the depression's worst effects. Between 1931 and 1941 the town's population more than doubled again, climbing from 27,741 to 57,301. In the years after World War II[qv] Corpus Christi continued to grow rapidly. By 1952 the city had 108,053 residents and 2,845 businesses. Already in 1948 the port was twelfth in volume of business in the United States, and it ranked ninth in the United States and second in Texas in 1969, when it handled more than twenty-nine million tons of cargo. A new system of channels forty feet deep and 400 feet wide was completed in 1965, assuring entry of the latest supertankers into the port.

Corpus Christi exports cotton, grain sorghums, and wheat. Its coastal shipments include fuel oils, gasoline, crude petroleum, and natural gas. Other major contributors to the income of the Corpus Christi area are petroleum and natural gas, manufacturing, agriculture, fishing, Truax Field,[qv] and tourism. The region has become the center of a large petroleum and petrochemical industry. Its six oil refineries are located in close proximity to 1,500 oil wells. Short-distance pipelines connect Corpus Christi to one of the nation's largest supplies of natural gas. Oil and gas production in the county was valued at 277 million dollars in 1987. Twenty-two docks in the Corpus Christi port handle only petrochemicals and petroleum products. Other manufactured goods of importance are metals, stone products, glass, chemicals, and gypsum products. Corpus Christi, in addition to its port facilities for agricultural products, also has some food processing, meat packing, and cottonseed oil manufacturing. Corpus Christi and nearby Aransas Pass are the commercial fishing headquarters of the area, and the city is a seafood-processing center. Truax Field, formerly the Corpus Christi Naval Air Station, adds more than $40 million annually to the economy.

The Corpus Christi metropolitan area offers numerous recreational facilities. Opportunities for boating, swimming, fishing, camping, and birdwatching are provided by Padre Island National Seashore, Aransas National Wildlife Refuge, the Rob and Bessie Welder Foundation and Refuge, Goose Island State Park, and Lake Corpus Christi State Recreation Area.[qv] The area includes historic Fort Lipantitlán, Fort Marcy, the San Patricio cemetery, and a number of historic homes. Annual events include Buccaneer Days, the All-Texas Jazz Festival, the Navy Relief Festival, the New Year's Day Swim, and the Cinco de Mayo celebration. Major cultural attractions include the Corpus Christi Museum, the Art Museum of South Texas,[qv] a symphony orchestra, and a little theater. Del Mar College and Texas A&M University at Corpus Christi provide higher education in the area. Del Mar Technical Institute, a branch of Del Mar College, and the University of Texas at Austin Marine Science Institute[qv] in nearby Port Aransas offer specialized training.

In recent years the city has continued to grow steadily. In 1968 the number of residents topped the 200,000 mark for the first time, and in 1990 the population reached 250,000. Over the same period the number of businesses grew from 3,900 to 4,500. In 1992 Corpus Christi was an ethnically diverse city with a population of 257,453; approximately 50 percent of the population was Hispanic, 43 percent white, 4 percent African American, and 3 percent Asian and other.

BIBLIOGRAPHY: Eugenia Reynolds Briscoe, *City by the Sea: A History of Corpus Christi, Texas, 1519–1875* (New York: Vantage, 1985). *Corpus Christi: 100 Years* (Corpus Christi *Caller-Times*, 1952). Dan E. Kilgore, "Corpus Christi: A Quarter Century of Development, 1900–1925," *Southwestern Historical Quarterly* 75 (April 1972). Dan Kilgore, *Nueces County, Texas, 1750–1800: A Bicentennial Memoir* (Corpus Christi: Friends of the Corpus Christi Museum, 1975). Coleman McCampbell, *Saga of a Frontier Seaport* (Dallas: South-West, 1934). Coleman McCampbell, *Texas Seaport: The Story of the Growth of Corpus Christi and the Coastal Bend Area* (New York: Exposition, 1952). Mary A. Sutherland, *The Story of Corpus Christi* (Corpus Christi Chapter, Daughters of the Confederacy, 1916). Bill Walraven, *Corpus Christi: The History of a Texas Seaport* (Woodland Hills, California, 1982). WPA Writers' Program, *Corpus Christi* (Corpus Christi *Caller-Times*, 1942).
Christopher Long

CORPUS CHRISTI ACADEMY. Corpus Christi Academy was chartered by the Texas legislature for a twenty-year period beginning on February 16, 1858, with thirteen leading citizens of the town as incorporators. Charles A. Russell, A. F. von Blücher, Charles Løvenskiold,[qv] Walter Merriman, H. A. Gilpin, and George W. Kinney were members of the first board of trustees. The academy was funded by shares that sold for thirty dollars each. The money was used to pay for a building, equipment, and the salaries of principal Charles Løvenskiold and the school's first teachers, Prof. M. P. Crafts, Mary H. Gordon, and Mrs. Julia L. Marsh. Mrs. Marsh had a controversial career at the school. After being indicted in 1862 for aggravated assault on her own two children, she was implicated in the attempted suicide of one of the school's students after she had allegedly whipped him with a "latigo colorado" (red lash). In 1862 she was again indicted for assault, this time on the principal, M. P. Crafts. Corpus Christi Academy charged monthly tuition and was open to both boys and girls. It was not church-related. During the Civil War,qv when Mrs. Rosalie Priour was its only teacher, the institution languished. When the victorious Union Army marched into Corpus Christi, Julia Marsh was appointed postmistress, a position she held from 1865 to 1867. She then resumed her work at Corpus Christi Academy. Her notorious severity with pupils and disputes with the board of trustees regarding her salary may have contributed to the academy's decline. In addition, the board insisted on paying teachers only with funds received from the state. When a law was passed in May 22, 1873, providing for free public schools in Texas, state aid to the Corpus Christi Academy was suspended, and it closed permanently.

BIBLIOGRAPHY: Gladys Gibbon, Education in Corpus Christi, Texas, 1846–1900 (M.S. thesis, Texas A&I University, 1941). Sister Jeanne Francis Minner, Early Development of Education in Corpus Christi, 1848 to 1909 (M.A. thesis, Catholic University of America, 1950).

Frank Wagner

CORPUS CHRISTI ARMY DEPOT. The temporary post established by Zachary Taylorqv in 1845 at Corpus Christi was designated Fort Marcy, for Secretary of War William Marcy. The name was seldom used, and it fell into complete disuse when another Fort Marcy was founded in New Mexico Territory; the Texas site was usually called Corpus Christi instead. In September 1852 Gen. Persifor F. Smithqv announced his intention to move United States Army headquarters in Texas from San Antonio to Corpus Christi on December 1 of that year. The post at Corpus Christi had a garrison of 150 to 200 men between the end of the Mexican Warqv and Smith's decision. The place was chosen largely because Smith had been ill from the day he arrived in San Antonio, and he found the climate and food in Corpus Christi more healthful; he was said to have particularly liked the local oysters. There were complaints about the location from some of his subordinates, especially the quartermaster, who found San Antonio more central to the forts the depot was to supply. Smith also sought to establish an army general hospital at Corpus Christi on land offered by Col. Henry L. Kinney,qv but his design was frustrated by a conflict between Senator Sam Houstonqv and Secretary of War Jefferson Davis.qv Smith was transferred to Leavenworth, Kansas, and died in the spring of 1858. In 1856 Col. J. K. F. Mansfield, inspector general of the United States Army, pointed out the disadvantages of Corpus Christi as a supply depot for such distant forts as Fort Bliss, Fort Mason, and Fort Worth. The depot was closed in January of 1852 but regarrisoned in 1869–70 and again in 1880–81. The present Corpus Christi Army Depot was activated in 1961 on the site of the Corpus Christi Naval Air Station and is the army's main helicopter overhaul and repair facility. By the late 1980s it was the largest single employer in South Texas.

BIBLIOGRAPHY: M. L. Crimmins, ed., "Colonel J. K. F. Mansfield's Report of the Inspection of the Department of Texas in 1856," *Southwestern Historical Quarterly* 42 (October 1938, January, April 1939). Francis Paul Prucha, *A Guide to the Military Posts of the United States, 1789–1895* (Madison: State Historical Association of Wisconsin, 1964).

Frank Wagner

CORPUS CHRISTI BAY. Corpus Christi Bay is a large saltwater estuary at the mouth of the Nueces River (at 27°46′ N, 97°15′ W). It is protected from the waves and storms of the Gulf of Mexico by Mustang Island. The bay is entirely in the jurisdiction of Nueces County, though its northern shoreline is the boundary of San Patricio County. Corpus Christi Bay is one of the few natural harbors on the Texas coast. The growth of the city of Corpus Christi is largely due to its maritime location. The port complex, which developed since the opening of the ship channel in 1926, has led the Corpus Christi area to economic prominence on the Texas coast. The port, connected by the ship channel to the Gulf of Mexico, has provided for increasing manufacturing and the processing of seafoods and agricultural food items. The bay has also contributed an array of mineral resources.

Corpus Christi Bay may have been first sighted by Alonso Álvarez de Pinedaqv on Corpus Christi Day 1519, the day he claimed the territory for his king. Alonso De León,qv who first crossed and named the Nueces River at the head of the bay on April 4, 1689, may also have seen the bay. Capt. Joaquín de Orobio y Basterra was instructed by Governor José de Escandónqv in 1746 to explore and settle the Gulf Coast from Tampico to the San Antonio River. Orobio describes the great bay at the mouth of the Río de las Nueces and states that he named it for St. Michael the Archangel. The first reference to Corpus Christi Bay by its present name appears in reports by Col. Diego Ortiz Parrillaqv in 1766. Perhaps the first landowner on the bayshore was Blas María de la Garza Falcón,qv who had holdings fifteen miles south of the Nueces River in 1746. Henry Lawrence Kinneyqv opened a store on Live Oak Point in 1838. Gen. Zachary Taylorqv landed troops at the site of present Corpus Christi on July 31, 1845, and the community developed as a result.

Through the efforts of Congressman John Nance Garner,qv a local harbor was authorized by President Warren G. Harding on September 22, 1922, and a channel twenty-one miles long and a minimum of twenty-five feet deep was dredged connecting Corpus Christi Bay with the Gulf of Mexico. The channel enters through the jetties at Aransas Pass. The bay is also crossed by the Gulf Intracoastal Waterway.qv Since the original opening of the port facilities in 1926 the channel has been gradually deepened and widened. Plans to improve the port further to accommodate supertankers of up to 500,000 dead-weight tons—including offshore mooring facilities—have been considered.

Corpus Christi Bay has developed into a major recreational area. The mild climate, the waters protected by the barrier islands, and the abundant sunshine draw thousands of both summer and winter tourists to the area.

BIBLIOGRAPHY: Robert H. Ryan and Charles W. Adams, *Corpus Christi: Economic Impact of the Port* (Bureau of Business Research, University of Texas at Austin, 1973). Bill Walraven, *Corpus Christi: The History of a Texas Seaport* (Woodland Hills, California, 1982). WPA Writers' Program, *Corpus Christi* (Corpus Christi *Caller-Times*, 1942).

Art Leatherwood

CORPUS CHRISTI *CALLER-TIMES*. The Corpus Christi *Caller-Times* began with the consolidation in 1929 of two newspapers, the *Caller and Daily Herald,* started as the *Caller* in 1883, and the *Times,* founded in 1917. Newspapermen Eli Merriman, Ed Williams, and W. P. Caruthers had established the *Caller,* which was named after the San Francisco *Call.* In 1910 the *Caller* merged with another local paper, the *Herald,* and became the Corpus Christi *Caller and Daily Herald.* One of the *Caller*'s original stockholders was King Ranch founder Richard King,qqv and the King Ranch maintained its interest in the paper until the 1920s.

W. E. Pope, a state legislator, purchased the Corpus Christi *Daily Democrat* in 1917, renamed it the *Times,* and sold it in 1928 to Houston Harteqv of San Angelo and Bernard Hanks of Abilene, founders of Harte-Hanks Communications.qv The next year Harte-Hanks bought the *Caller* from the King Ranch, and the two papers were combined as the Corpus Christi *Caller-Times.* The paper has outlasted more than two dozen newspapers published in the city since the first two, the Corpus Christi *Gazette*qv and the *Star,* were published in the 1840s.

When the newspaper observed its 100th birthday on January 23, 1983, it gave the city a bayfront monument, *Wind in the Sails,* by sculptor Kent Ullberg. In the mid-1980s the *Caller-Times* had a combined daily circulation of 82,800, with 69,050 on Saturdays and 91,400 on Sundays. The *Caller* appeared in the morning, the *Times* in the afternoon, and the *Caller-Times* on Saturdays and Sundays. In May 1987 the *Caller-Times* switched to producing morning editions only and in 1994 had a weekly circulation of 72,604 and a Sunday circulation of 104,245.

BIBLIOGRAPHY: Marker Files, Texas Historical Commission, Austin.
Margaret Ramage

CORPUS CHRISTI CATHEDRAL. There was no Catholic church in Corpus Christi until 1855, though the name of the bay and subsequently the city was derived from the Catholic Spanish. Mass and other services were at times conducted at the home of Richard Powers at the corner of Broadway at Lipan, the future site of Corpus Christi Cathedral. Father Bernard O'Reilly was the first resident pastor assigned to Corpus Christi in 1853. By the end of that year, work on a church had begun at a location on Tancahua Street, about two blocks northwest of the present cathedral. By 1855 services were being held in the incomplete building, which was finished in 1857. O'Reilly wrote in 1856 that his congregation consisted of nineteen families and that he paid $5,000, and still owed $1,400, for the church. Because of the Irish origins of some of these families, as well as of Father O'Reilly himself, the church was called St. Patrick's. According to an observer of the time, the church was a rectangular adobe qv structure forty feet long and almost forty feet wide. A small belfry rose from the middle of the façade; the roof was slightly vaulted for the entire length. Solid board shutters covered rectangular, plain glass windows. Above the front entrance were a small portico and a wooden cross. In the gloomy interior were the sacramental and worship accoutrements: confessional, baptismal font, two rows of pews, communion rail, altar, north wing for the sacristy. A south wing for the sisters' chapel was built after the Sisters of the Incarnate Word and Blessed Sacrament qv came to Corpus Christi in 1871.

Dominic Manucy, qv first vicar apostolic of Brownsville, moved to Corpus Christi from Brownsville in 1875. He described St. Patrick's as "a small church that is tumbling down" and solicited funds from residents and from the Society for the Propagation of the Faith. Work on a new church, a frame building on Carancahua Street, began in 1880; services were held in late 1882. Completion of the church was aided by donations of time and labor by the architect-builder, Charles Carroll. The old church was reportedly torn down in 1882. The Vicariate Apostolic of Brownsville was elevated to the rank of a diocese, taking the name of the see city, Corpus Christi, with St. Patrick's as the cathedral. Paul Nussbaum qv served as the first bishop from 1913 until his resignation in 1920. Pope Benedict XV appointed Emmanuel B. Ledvina qv to succeed Nussbaum in 1921. Due to Ledvina's illness, in 1936 Pius XII named Mariano S. Garriga qv diocesan coadjutor. The bishops began a fund drive for the building of a new cathedral. A site at Upper Broadway and Lipan streets known as City Bluff, overlooking Corpus Christi Bay, was donated by the John G. Kenedy, Jr., family. An old Kenedy family home on the property was moved to allow for construction. Ground was broken on March 1, 1939. The cornerstone was laid on March 1, 1940; on July 17, Corpus Christi Cathedral was dedicated.

The building is 176 feet long and 90 feet wide; it rests on 18 feet of reinforced concrete footings. The construction is of reinforced concrete, structural steel, and solid masonry brick walls eighteen inches thick. C. L. Monnot of Oklahoma was architect of the Spanish Mission-style structure. The roof of red Spanish clay tile is surmounted by two asymmetrical tower domes, 125 feet and 97 feet in height, of glazed terra-cotta. The three bells of the old cathedral were transferred to the shorter tower; the taller holds a thirty-two-bell carillon and has a clock in each of its four walls. Three copper doors lead from the Upper Broadway street frontage into the narthex, or vestibule, which has a Saltillo tile floor. On the right as one faces the interior of the church is a shrine to St. Anthony of Padua; on the left, to the Sorrowful Mother. Both statues are of Italian Carrara marble. Walls of gray Carthage veinless marble reach to the ornamental plaster cornice surrounding the ceiling. The nave has a distinctive ceiling studded with heavy oak beams. Around the nave is a four-foot-high wainscot of cream-colored Tavernelle Clair marble, capped and based with verde antique marble from Maryland. The floor is cream-colored terrazzo, bordered with ecclesiastical-design Spanish tile. An open choir at the rear overlooks the nave. Left of the main aisle are a shrine to Our Lady of Guadalupe and the Blessed Sacrament Chapel. Twelve Corinthian columns represent the twelve apostles. A communion rail of hand-wrought iron and white Alabama marble separates the nave from the sanctuary. At the north end of the rail is the pulpit, with body of cream Tavernelle and base and cap of verde antique. At the opposite end is the baptismal font of green marble, ringed with clover leaves—a tribute to the church's Irish history. The sanctuary is flanked by the priests' sacristy on the south and the servers' sacristy on the north. The right-side altar is dedicated to St. Joseph, the left to the Virgin Mary. Statues of St. Patrick and St. Thérèse of Lisieux stand in the upper rear of the sanctuary. Artist Emil Frei executed the stained-glass windows (the upper row portraying Eucharistic motifs, the lower depicting devotional acts) and the glass Stations of the Cross along the nave walls. A crypt, Emmanuel Chapel, was built in the basement below the main altar for the burial of the bishops and remodeled in 1985. Bishops Nussbaum, Ledvina, and Garriga are buried there. Total cost of the building and appointments at the time of construction was about $425,000. Capacity of the cathedral when built was said to be 1,100 persons; it is now reported to be 2,000.

The last Mass was said in the old cathedral—for Charles Carroll, its architect—on February 8, 1951, by diocesan chancellor Adolph Marx, the last priest to be ordained there. Dismantling of the building began in 1951. The name of the church was passed on to a new St. Patrick's parish established shortly after the new cathedral.

In 1978 a man with a history of mental problems attacked the sanctuary of Corpus Christi Cathedral, damaging the tabernacle, the candelabra, and the ten-foot marble statues of Mary and Joseph. In 1988 renovations to the cathedral included alterations in the apse, conversion of a room above the main sacristy into a pontifical sacristy, and construction of the Blessed Sacrament Chapel. The chapel was designed by historical architect James G. Rome, and seats twenty-four. There are now three chapels in the building. The cathedral was recorded as a state historic landmark in 1991. Although its distinctive façade can still be seen from Corpus Christi Bay, the cathedral is now surrounded by the city's business district. In 1953 the cathedral parish claimed 536 families as parishioners. In mid-1994, that figure was 950 families.

BIBLIOGRAPHY: *Corpus Christi Times,* July 16, 1940. James Talmadge Moore, *Through Fire and Flood: The Catholic Church in Frontier Texas, 1836–1900* (College Station: Texas A&M University Press, 1992). Sister Mary Xavier, *A Century of Sacrifice: The History of the Cathedral Parish, Corpus Christi, Texas, 1853–1953* (Corpus Christi, 1953).
Jana E. Pellusch

CORPUS CHRISTI COLLEGE-ACADEMY. Corpus Christi College-Academy, a boarding and day school for boys in junior and senior high school, was conducted by the Order of St. Benedict. Its five buildings, three miles west of Corpus Christi, were located on a forty-acre campus donated to Bishop Emmanuel Boleslaus Ledvina qv by John Dunn, Jr. His cousin, John B. Dunn, donated part of his museum collection to the school, which included Indian relics, fossil remains, antiques, and souvenirs of pioneer days. The school was approved by the state Department of Education. Annual enrollment was approximately 200. In 1972 a hurricane destroyed some of the buildings and the school was closed.

BIBLIOGRAPHY: Albert M. Schreiber, *When the Bishop Blesses* (San Antonio: Standard, 1943).

Eva Beth Wood

CORPUS CHRISTI *GAZETTE*. There were two newspapers known as the Corpus Christi *Gazette* during the nineteenth century. The first was announced in a prospectus published in the Austin *Texas Democrat*qv in November 1845. The first issue appeared on January 1, 1846, with Samuel Bangs qv and George Fletcher as publishers and the chief justice of Nueces County, José de Alba, as editor. The paper ceased publication on April 2, 1846. Though no more than half the run exists in archives, the *Gazette* is significant as a source of information about the Corpus Christi of its day. The sixth issue, for example, contains a detailed list of the officers at Corpus Christi, San Antonio, and St. Joseph Island in February 1846.

BIBLIOGRAPHY: Lota M. Spell, "Samuel Bangs: The First Printer in Texas," *Southwestern Historical Quarterly* 35 (April 1932).

Frank Wagner

CORPUS CHRISTI *GAZETTE*. The second Corpus Christi *Gazette* was started in January 1873 by James B. and Francis E. Barnard as a successor to the Corpus Christi *Advertiser*. It was originally issued as a weekly on Saturdays but was transformed into a daily (except Mondays) on January 1, 1876, with a weekly issue summarizing the news in a thirty-two-column folio. The *Gazette* prospered as Benjamin F. Neal's qv *Nueces Valley* declined. Neal died in July 1873, and his successors were less able and competitive than he. Other newspapers such as William Maltby's *Ledger* and Edward Williams's *Free Press* caused losses in circulation of the *Gazette* so that it suspended publication in 1878. Barnard's *Gazette* is one of the chief news resources for Corpus Christi history throughout the post-Reconstruction period.

BIBLIOGRAPHY: WPA Writers' Program, *Corpus Christi* (Corpus Christi *Caller-Times*, 1942). WPA Historical Records Survey Program, *Texas Newspapers* (Houston: San Jacinto Museum of History Association, 1941).

Frank Wagner

CORPUS CHRISTI DE LA ISLETA MISSION. Corpus Christi de la Isleta, the first mission and pueblo in Texas, was established by Antonio de Otermín and Fray Francisco de Ayeta qqv in 1682 and was maintained by Franciscans qv for Christianizing the Tigua Indians, who accompanied Otermín on his retreat to the El Paso area after his unsuccessful attempt to recover New Mexico in the winter of 1681–82. To the Tiguas, the mission church is known as San Antonio, after their patron saint, and they call the pueblo Ysleta del Sur. The site was also known by the Spaniards as Corpus Christi de la Isleta. The present church was constructed in 1851. Its distinctive silver-domed bell tower was added in 1897. In 1881 the Jesuits qv took over the church and renamed it Nuestra Señora del Monte Carmelo. Fire severely damaged the structure in 1907, but it was soon repaired.

The mission pueblo is estimated to have been 3½ leagues southeast of the site of modern Ciudad Juárez. Shortly after its founding as an Indian pueblo, twenty-one families of Spaniards were living at Ysleta. At that time Ysleta was on the south side of the Rio Grande. There, on May 19, 1692, Gov. Diego de Vargas granted possession of the church and convento to the Catholic Church qv in the person of Fray Joaquín de Hinojosa. For the next 160 years Franciscan missionaries were constant in their ministry to the spiritual needs of the people of Ysleta, but frequent shifting of the main channel of the river resulted in changes in location of the settlement. In 1726 and again in 1766 the inspectors Pedro de Rivera y Villalón and the Marqués de Rubí,qqv respectively, reported Ysleta on the east and then north side of the river. In 1758, however, Ysleta was located by Bernardo de Miera y Pacheco on the south bank of the Rio Grande. The most significant move, however, occurred in the period from 1829 to 1831. As a result of flooding, the river altered its course to the south and west, leaving Ysleta on the north bank of the main channel. Because the old channel was also active, Ysleta, Socorro, and San Elizario were situated on a twenty-mile-long island that ranged in width from two to four miles. According to the 1841 census Ysleta had 731 inhabitants: 456 Spanish and 275 Indians. By the terms of the 1848 Treaty of Guadalupe Hidalgo,qv the main current of the Rio Grande was the international boundary between the United States and Mexico; hence Ysleta became United States territory.

In 1878, in the aftermath of the Salt War of San Elizario,qv Ysleta replaced San Elizario as county seat of El Paso County; in 1884 El Paso became county seat. In the interest of preserving tribal culture, the Tiguas drew up a constitution and set of bylaws to it in 1895. The most dramatic change in life in Ysleta in modern times, however, followed the completion of Elephant Butte dam in 1916 and the subsequent development of an extensive irrigation system. A rising water table, increased soil salinization, and the onset of San Jose scale in fruit trees led to the substitution of a salt-tolerant variety of cotton for the traditional vineyards and orchards of the area by the late 1920s. Gradually, the community lost its agricultural land as the urban environment grew. In 1955 Ysleta, with a population of some 40,000, was annexed by El Paso over the protests of the residents. The Texas legislature recognized the Tiguas as an Indian tribe and requested transfer of federal responsibility for them to the state in 1967. The following year President Lyndon B. Johnson qv recognized the tribe and transferred responsibility to the State of Texas.

BIBLIOGRAPHY: J. J. Bowden, *Spanish and Mexican Land Grants in the Chihuahuan Acquisition* (El Paso: Texas Western Press, 1971). W. H. Timmons, "The Church of Ysleta—Recent Document Discoveries," *Password* 28 (Fall 1983). W. H. Timmons, *El Paso: A Borderlands History* (El Paso: Texas Western Press, 1990).

Rick Hendricks

CORPUS CHRISTI MUSEUM. The Corpus Christi Museum, accredited by the American Association of Museums, is a general museum with collections and exhibits in natural history, art, and history. Mixed with traditional permanent exhibits are touch tables, live animal displays, and changing exhibits of local artworks. Museum programs such as treasure hunts and fact hunts, Saturday matinee movies, and public performances on the Front Porch Stage encourage community involvement. The museum was founded as a junior museum in 1956 by schoolteachers from the Corpus Christi Independent School District as a private institution. It became a department of the city of Corpus Christi in 1967. That same year, the museum moved into a 25,000-square-foot facility at the current site in the Bayfront Arts and Sciences Park, and in 1972, 28,000 square feet of space was added. Although the museum is principally funded by the city of Corpus Christi with an annual contribution from the Corpus Christi Independent School District, private support is provided by the Friends of the Corpus Christi Museum and the Corpus Christi Museum Auxiliary. Volunteers from the auxiliary contribute their time to support various functions of the museum. The Junior League offers a puppet program at the museum, and Coastal Bend Archeological Society volunteers work with the museum staff on field projects. The educational programs of the museum include a fourth-grade science program developed cooperatively with the Corpus Christi Independent School District and a variety of exhibit-based programs offered to school groups. The museum offers annual summer classes for elementary schoolchildren and archeology field projects for high school students and adults.

Significant science collections include the Jones Herbarium (flora of the Texas Coastal Bend), the Andrews Collection (shells and shores of Texas), the Kirn and Quillen Bird Egg and Nest collections, the R. D. Camp Collection of Non-marine Shells, and the Carl Young Collection of Marine Shells. Also included in the science collections is a great variety of natural history specimens. The history and anthropology collections include prehistoric Indian artifacts, the artifacts from the Padre Island Spanish shipwrecks of 1554,qv and a wide variety of historical artifacts donated by the residents of South Texas. The art collection includes the Kenedy Collection of largely nineteenth-century oil paintings by European School painters and the works of contemporary Coastal Bend artists. The museum has a 10,000-volume library for research on its collections and an archive that includes the "Doc" McGregor Photograph Collection. The museum maintains exhibit areas devoted to geology, marine life, mammals, birds, prehistoric and historic archeology, anthropology, decorative and fine arts, and historical topics, including Naval Aviation in South Texas. The Friends of the Museum publishes a monthly periodical, *Museum Notes,* and a series of Occasional Papers on topics of interest to the museum. They also support research projects undertaken as part of the function of the museum.

BIBLIOGRAPHY: Paula and Ron Tyler, *Texas Museums: A Guidebook* (Austin: University of Texas Press, 1983).   *Richard R. Stryker, Jr.*

CORPUS CHRISTI PASS. Corpus Christi Pass, between Padre Island and Mustang Island in southeastern Nueces County (at 27°39′ N, 97°12′ W), was the principal entrance to Corpus Christi Bay before it silted up. The main channel later ran through Aransas Pass.

BIBLIOGRAPHY: Glenn A. Mitchell, The Geography of Nueces County, Texas (M.A. thesis, University of Texas, 1959). Nueces County Historical Society, *History of Nueces County* (Austin: Jenkins, 1972).   *Diana J. Kleiner*

CORPUS CHRISTI, SAN DIEGO AND RIO GRANDE NARROW GAUGE RAILROAD. The Corpus Christi, San Diego and Rio Grande Narrow Gauge Railroad Company was chartered on March 18, 1875, to connect Eagle Pass and Laredo with Corpus Christi by way of San Diego, Texas. As in many cases, the state land grant did not help the financing of the railroad because the land was worth little. The people responsible for the development of the railroad were Uriah Lott, Perry Doddridge,qqv David Hirsch, J. B. Mitchell, George F. Evans, N. Gossett, William I. Rogers, and Herman Chamberlain, all of Corpus Christi; M. M. Levy and Henry Goldsmidt, both of Laredo; Leon Blumqv of Galveston; and C. W. Hurley, F. W. Schaffer, and Frank David, all of San Diego. On January 1, 1878, the railroad opened twenty-five miles of track between Corpus Christi and Banquete. In 1879 the line was extended twenty-seven miles from Banquete to San Diego. Richard King and Mifflin Kenedyqqv ensured the continuation of the project, which was renamed Texas Mexican Railway Company on June 25, 1881.   *Nancy Beck Young*

CORPUS CHRISTI STATE SCHOOL. Corpus Christi State School was opened in June 1970 as a residential facility for the Texas Department of Mental Health and Mental Retardation.qv It was damaged by Hurricane Celia on August 3, 1970, and resumed partial operations by 1971. The 211-acre campus is on land formerly belonging to the Cliff Moss Airport. Thirty-five buildings provide 214,000 square feet of space that includes rooms for 410 mentally retarded individuals. The budget for 1993 was $22 million. Residents receive medical, recreational, speech and hearing, occupational, physical therapy, dental, and outreach services. Community services include Bay to Bay Infant Stimulation, for babies to three years old; Maverick County Association, with a program in Eagle Pass; the Beeville Living Complex; Kenedy Apartment Living Program; Windrush Apartment Living in Corpus Christi; Alice Workshop: Beeville Adult Habilitation Service; Crystal City Adult Habilitation Service; Dilly Adult Habilitation Center; Ingleside Adult Habilitation Center; and Karnes City Adult Habilitation Center. The school opened with 250 students in 1970. It increased to 566 students in 1980, with changes in the classification of the mentally retarded to include both resident and nonresident students. In 1990 the school had 394 clients.

Ray Valdez

CORRAL CREEK (Bowie County). Corral Creek rises two miles south of Wake Village in southeastern Bowie County (at 33°24′ N, 94°07′ W) and runs southeast for three miles to its mouth on Howard Creek, at the northeast corner of the federal correctional institution at Texarkana (at 33°23′ N, 94°04′ W). The local soils are clayey.

_____ (Potter County). Corral Creek rises in northwestern Potter County (at 35°37′ N, 102°00′ W) and runs southwest for eight miles to its mouth on the Canadian River (at 35°28′ N, 102°05′ W). It traverses an area of densely dissected gullies and low hills where shallow soils support sparse vegetation. Near the mouth of the creek, the terrain becomes flat to rolling with local escarpments and is surfaced by deep, fine sandy loam. Though some hardwoods border the creek at its mouth, the primary vegetation continues to be brush and grasses. The stream was formerly on the property of the LIT and LX ranchesqqv and was on the land taken over by the Robert Benjamin Mastersonqv interests in 1906.

BIBLIOGRAPHY: Pauline D. and R. L. Robertson, *Cowman's Country: Fifty Frontier Ranches in the Texas Panhandle, 1876–1887* (Amarillo: Paramount, 1981).

_____ (Reagan County). Corral Creek rises between Farm Road 2600 and the Reagan-Glasscock county line in northeastern Reagan County (at 31°38′ N, 101°22′ W) and runs southeast for six miles to its mouth on Indian Creek (at 31°35′ N, 101°19′ W). It crosses an area of limestone and dolomite substrate surfaced by shallow and stony soils that support oak, juniper, and some mesquite.

CORRIDOS. The *corrido* in its usual form is a ballad of eight-syllable, four-line stanzas sung to a simple tune in fast waltz time, now often in polka rhythm. *Corridos* have traditionally been men's songs. They have been sung at home, on horseback, in town plazas by traveling troubadours, in cantinas by blind *guitarreros* (guitarists), on campaigns during the Mexican Revolutionqv (1910–30), and on migrant workers' journeys north to the fields. Now they are heard frequently on records and over the radio. These ballads are generally in major keys and have tunes with a short—less than an octave—range. Américo Paredes, the preeminent scholar of the *corrido* of the lower Rio Grande border area, remarks: "The short range allows the *corrido* to be sung at the top of the singer's voice, an essential part of the *corrido* style." In Texas this singing has traditionally been accompanied by a guitar or *bajo sexto,* a type of twelve-string guitar popular in Texas and northern Mexico.

In its literary form the *corrido* seems to be a direct descendent of the *romance,* the Spanish ballad form which developed in the Middle Ages, became a traditional form, and was brought to the New World by Spanish conquistadors. Like the *romance,* the *corrido* employs a four-line stanza form with an *abcd* rhyme pattern. Paredes surmises that *corrido* is ultimately derived from the Andalusian phrase *romance corrido,* which denoted a refrainless, rapidly sung romance. With the noun dropped, the participle *corrido,* from a verb meaning "to run," itself became a noun.

The *corrido,* like the romance, relates a story or event of local or national interest—a hero's deeds, a bandit's exploits, a barroom shootout, or a natural disaster, for instance. It has long been observed, however, that songs with little or no narration are still called *corridos* if they adhere to the *corrido*'s usual literary and musical form.

Besides its music, versification, and subject matter, the *corrido* also employs certain formal ballad conventions. In *La lírica narrativa de México,* Vicente Mendoza gives six primary formal characteristics or conventions of the *corrido.* They are: (1) the initial call of the *corridista,* or balladeer, to the public, sometimes called the formal opening; (2) the stating of the place, time, and name of the protagonist of the ballad; (3) the arguments of the protagonist; (4) the message; (5) the farewell of the protagonist; and (6) the farewell of the *corridista*. These elements, however, vary in importance from region to region in Mexico and the Southwest, and it is sometimes difficult to find a ballad that employs all of them. In Texas and the border region, the formal opening of the *corrido* is not as vital as the balladeer's *despedida* (farewell) or formal close. Often the singer will start the *corrido* with the action of the story to get the interest of the audience, thus skipping the introduction, but the *despedida* in one form or another is almost never dropped. The phrase *Ya con esta me despido* ("With this I take my leave") or *Vuela, vuela, palomita* ("Fly, fly, little dove") often signals the *despedida* on the first line of the penultimate or final stanza of the song.

In the middle to late 1800s several ballad forms—the *romance, décima,* and *copla*—existed side by side in Mexico and in the Southwest, and at this time the *corrido* seems to have had its genesis. By 1848, however, the remote outposts of northern Mexico already belonged to the United States as a result of the Texas Revolution, the Mexican War, and the Treaty of Guadalupe Hidalgo.[qqv] The *romance* tradition in California dwindled with the Anglo-American migration and takeover, and a native balladry did not develop there until the *corrido* form was imported by Mexican immigrants in this century. New Mexico, on the other hand, remained somewhat isolated from modern Mexican and Anglo-American currents and retained much of its archaic Spanish tradition.

The border area of the lower Rio Grande and South Texas, however, was different. There the *corrido* seems to have had a separate and perhaps earlier development than elsewhere. Events in Texas between 1836 and 1848 resulted in the colonization of the lower Rio Grande area by white empresarios (*see* EMPRESARIO). The gradual displacement or subjugation of the Mexican people there provided the basis for more than a century of border conflict between the Anglos and the Mexicans. During the struggle against the Anglos, the *corrido* form developed in the area and became extremely popular. In Paredes's words, the borderers' "slow, dogged struggle against economic enslavement and the loss of their own identity was the most important factor in the development of a distinct local balladry."

The border *corrido* developed after 1848 and reached its peak at the height of cultural conflict between 1890 and 1910, at least ten years before the zenith of the Mexican *corrido* during the Mexican Revolution. The border *corridos,* in short, dramatic form, picture a heroic struggle against oppression and rival the Mexican *corridos* in quality, if not in quantity. Border heroes such as Ignacio and Jacinto Treviño and Aniceto Pizaña[qv] are depicted in *corridos* of this time defending their rights against the Americans. But the epitome of the border *corrido* hero was Gregorio Cortez.[qv] In *With His Pistol in His Hand,* Paredes discusses the legend, life, and *corridos* of Cortez. Despite Cortez's notoriety among South Texas Anglos, the ballads portray him as a peaceful *Mexicano* living in South Texas at the turn of the century. When Cortez's brother is shot, allegedly for no good reason, Cortez is pursued over South Texas by as many as 300 *rinches,* or Texas Rangers.[qv] Following the pattern, the *corridos* picture Cortez goaded into action, fighting against outsiders for his own and the people's independence.

The border ceased to be a distinct cultural area in the early 1900s. Improved communications and means of travel linked the south bank of the Rio Grande more with the interior of Mexico and the north bank more with Texas and the United States. The idea of a boundary caused the borderer to begin to see himself as a Mexican or American. *Corridos* in Mexico embodied epic characteristics during the revolutionary period. Although these *corridos* were known in Texas, few if any new *corridos* of border conflict were composed after about 1930. With the borderer's loss of identity went the *corrido* of border strife. The *corrido* tradition itself did not die in Texas, however; it merely changed during and after the 1930s.

At the same time that border strife was waning, labor demands of developing agribusiness in Texas were pulling more and more Texas-Mexican borderers into migrant farmwork. The decades of the 1920s through the 1950s were particularly frustrating for Texas Mexicans, who held the lowest status in the economy of South Texas. In these years were composed and sung hundreds of *corridos* about bad working conditions, poverty, and the hopelessness of the Texas-Mexican migrant agricultural worker.

In the late 1940s and in the 1950s, as Texas-Mexican music in general became commercialized, so did the *corrido.* With local *guitarreros* and *conjuntos* (musical groups), the new Texas-Mexican recording companies produced many *corridos.* These recorded songs, however, were usually about such sensational subjects as barroom shootings or drug smuggling. *Corridos* about migrant work were never recorded, for they were considered too politically inflammatory for fledgling recording companies and new radio stations. Not until the Kennedy assassination[qv] did Texas-Mexican *corridos* have a subject that would reinvigorate the genre. During the months following Kennedy's death, dozens of Kennedy *corridos* were composed, recorded, and broadcast on Spanish-language radio stations in Texas and across the Southwest. In contrast to the usual commercial *corridos* of the time, those about John Kennedy often resembled the older, heroic *corridos.* The new ballads spoke for Mexican Americans[qv] who identified with Kennedy's struggles and ideas. After the mid-1960s and the beginnings of the Chicano[qv] movement, *corridos* continued to thrive. Their subjects were Chicano leaders and ideals of economic justice and cultural pride. *See also* MÚSICA NORTEÑA, TEXAS-MEXICAN FICTION, TEXAS-MEXICAN CONJUNTO.

BIBLIOGRAPHY: Dan W. Dickey, "Tejano Troubadours," *Texas Observer,* July 16, 1976. Dan W. Dickey, *The Kennedy Corridos: A Study of the Ballads of a Mexican American Hero* (Center for Mexican-American Studies, University of Texas at Austin, 1978). Vicente T. Mendoza, *El corrido mexicano* (Mexico City: Fondo de Cultura Económica, 1954). Vicente T. Mendoza, *Lírica narrativa de México: El Corrido* (Mexico City: Universidad Nacional Autónoma de México, Instituto de Investigaciones Estéticas, 1964). Américo Paredes, Ballads of the Lower Border (M.A. thesis, University of Texas, 1953). Américo Paredes, El Corrido de Gregorio Cortez: A Ballad of Border Conflict (Ph.D. dissertation, University of Texas, 1956). Américo Paredes, *A Texas-Mexican Cancionero: Folksongs of the Lower Border* (Urbana: University of Illinois Press, 1976). Américo Paredes, *With His Pistol in His Hand: A Border Ballad and Its Hero* (Austin: University of Texas Press, 1958). Merle Simmons, *The Mexican Corrido as a Source of an Interpretive Study of Modern Mexico, 1870–1950* (Bloomington: University of Indiana Press, 1957). Dan W. Dickey

CORRIGAN, TEXAS (Bee County). Corrigan (Corrigan Settlement), six miles east of Skidmore on Aransas Creek in southern Bee County, was established in 1835 by Irish immigrants and received its name some thirteen years later. The community's earliest settlers included James O'Reilly and Jeremiah O'Toole; O'Toole had moved from Ireland to New York in 1825. In 1826, with hopes of obtaining land from the Mexican government (*see* MEXICAN TEXAS), O'Toole and O'Reilly visited the area on Aransas Creek. After returning to New York, O'Toole took his family aboard the *New Packet,* which arrived in Texas in 1829. Five years later he acquired 12,000 acres on Aransas Creek. In 1835 the family built a home at a site on the San Patricio–La Bahía road. The area's early settlers attempted ranching but were hindered in their efforts and sometimes forced to flee in the face of Indian attacks and raiding Mexicans. When O'Toole's daughter, Ellen, married Irish immigrant John Corrigan in 1848, the couple built their home on O'Toole's land, and the hamlet that developed was subsequently named Corrigan Settlement. In 1871 Ellen (O'Toole) Corrigan and her brother Martin O'Toole transferred to the bishop of Galveston several acres for a Catholic church and cemetery; the Sacred Heart of Jesus Church and the Campo Santo cemetery were constructed at the site. In 1898 the settlement had a school with one teacher and ten students. By 1936 the community had four or five scattered dwellings. The cemetery, marked by a state historical marker, remained in 1990, when several families resided on nearby lands. At that time the area was still referred to as Corrigan.

BIBLIOGRAPHY: Grace Bauer, *Bee County Centennial, 1858–1958* (Bee County Centennial, 1958). Camp Ezell, *Historical Story of Bee County, Texas* (Beeville: Beeville Publishing, 1973). Rachel Bluntzer Hébert, *The Forgotten Colony: San Patricio de Hibernia* (Burnet, Texas: Eakin Press, 1981). *St. Joseph's Catholic Church: 50th Anniversary, 1927–1977* (Beeville, Texas, 1978?).

Adrian D. Ramirez

CORRIGAN, TEXAS (Polk County). Corrigan is at the junction of U.S. highways 59 and 287 and Farm roads 352 and 942, about 100 miles north of Houston in north central Polk County. Although for several years a few sawmills and farms had been established in the area, the real impetus for community settlement came in 1881, when the Houston, East and West Texas Railway was completed through northern Polk County. The town was named for Pat Corrigan, conductor of the first train through the newly developed site. In 1882 the Trinity and Sabine Railway was also built through the town. Lumber companies, drawn by the good rail connections and huge pine forests, greatly expanded their operations in the Corrigan vicinity; in 1881–82, for example, seventeen sawmills, including the Allen and Williams mill, operated nearby. As the mills continued production, churches and a variety of businesses, including hotels, stores, and gins, opened at Corrigan. A post office opened at the community in 1883; nine years later the Corrigan Index, the first of several newspapers to be published there, printed its first issue. The local economy was diversified by a bottle works, stone quarries, sand pits, and continued agricultural production (especially of cotton, tomatoes, poultry, stock, and dairy products). This diversity allowed Corrigan to withstand periodic depressions in the lumber industry, like the one that closed area sawmills between 1904 and 1907. Timber nonetheless remained the mainstay of the town's economic and social structure. Particleboard plants and the Edens and Burch sawmill, leased by the Corrigan Lumber Company in 1946, proved particularly important. The weekly Corrigan *Times*, begun in 1953, continued to publish in the 1980s. The town's population, which numbered 461 in 1900, grew to 1,420 in the early 1950s before declining to 986 by 1960. Subsequent growth, however, nearly doubled the population by 1985, when some 1,770 persons lived in the incorporated town. In 1991 the population of Corrigan was reported as 1,816, with sixty-one businesses.

BIBLIOGRAPHY: Hamilton Pratt Easton, History of the Texas Lumbering Industry (Ph.D. dissertation, University of Texas, 1947). *A Pictorial History of Polk County, Texas, 1846–1910* (Livingston, Texas: Polk County Bicentennial Commission, 1976; rev. ed. 1978).

Robert Wooster

CORSICANA, TEXAS. Corsicana, county seat and largest city of Navarro County, is in the central portion of the county fifty-eight miles southeast of Dallas at the junction of Interstate 45, U.S. highways 75 and 287, and State highways 22 and 31. It was established in 1848 to serve as the county seat of newly-established Navarro County. José Antonio Navarro,[qv] a hero of the Texas Revolution[qv] after whom the county was named, was given the honor of naming the new town; he suggested Corsicana after the island of Corsica, the birthplace of his parents. David R. Mitchell, an early area settler, donated 100 acres for a townsite, and with the assistance of Thomas I. Smith, platted the land and began selling lots. The new town was centered near a log tavern built in 1847 and owned and operated by Rev. Hampton McKinney. The first courthouse, a two-room log structure, was constructed in 1849, and served as a church, meeting hall and civic center until a new frame building was constructed in 1853. The first school, taught by Mack Elliot and a man named Lafoon, opened in the old courthouse in 1847, and a short time later the Corsicana Female Literary Institute[qv] began operating. Within a few years of the town's founding, a large number of mercantile establishments opened on and around the courthouse square, and new brick courthouse—a symbol of the town's growing prosperity—was erected in 1858. The first newspaper, the *Prairie Blade,* was founded in 1855; it was replaced by the *Express* in 1857, which in turn was replaced by the *Observer* on the eve of the Civil War.[qv]

By 1850 Corsicana's population had already grown to some 1,200, 300 of whom were reportedly black slaves. Not surprisingly given the town's large number of slaveholders, Corsicanans supported Breckinridge over the Fusionist slate of candidates in the presidential election of 1860; and in February 1861, when had the election was held on the secession issue, the vote was almost unanimous, 213 in favor and only three opposed. At outbreak of the war in April 1861 townspeople held a mass demonstration on the courthouse square in favor of the Confederacy, and appeals were made for volunteers to serve in the Confederate Army in Virginia. The first company, the "Navarro Rifles" commanded by Capt. Clinton M. Winkler,[qv] was organized in August 1861; four additional companies were organized in the town by 1863. After the war Union soldiers, commanded by Capt. R. A. Chaffee, occupied the town. Corsicana, however, witnessed little of the bitter strife experienced by many Texas towns during Reconstruction:[qv] Chaffee enlisted a number of former slaves as policeman, but avoided provoking the townspeople, and at one juncture even came out in support of former Confederate officer C. M. Winkler who had caned a Union soldier after the man had insulted him. The town's economy suffered a serious setback during the war and the early Reconstruction years, but by the beginning of 1870s business had begun to recover. In 1871 the town's first bank opened, operated by two men named Adams and Leonard, and in 1874 Union troops finally were withdrawn.

The greatest spur to the town's development, however, came in November 1871 with the completion of the Houston and Texas Central Railroad. The coming of the railroad brought numerous settlers and new merchants, among them the Sanger Brothers,[qv] the Padgitts and others, who established stores near the new depot on East Collin Street. The construction of the Texas and St. Louis Railway (later the Cotton Belt) in 1880 prompted further commercial development, and by the mid-eighties Corsicana had become the leading trading and shipping center for a large area of the northern blacklands. In 1872 the town was incorporated with a mayoral form of government, and in 1880 a public school system was organized. The decade of the eighties also saw the establishment of a city fire department, a municipal water works, the installation of the first telephone system, and the construction of the State Orphans Home and the Odd Fellows Orphans Home. By 1885 Corsicana had a population of approximately 5,000, three Presbyterian, a Catholic, a Baptist, and three Methodist churches, as well as three blacks churches, an oil factory, a gristmill, two banks, and four weekly newspapers—the *Courier,* the *Observer,* the *Messenger,* and the *Journal*; principal products included cotton, grain, wool, and hides.

By the early 1890s the rapidly expanding city had outgrown its water supply, and the following year civic leaders formed the Corsicana Water Development Company with the aim of tapping a shallow artesian well in the area. Drilling began in the spring of 1894; but instead of water, the company hit a large pocket of oil and gas. The find—the first significant discovery of oil west of the Mississippi River—led to Texas's first oil boom: within a short time nearly every lot in the town and in the surrounding area was under lease, and wells were being drilled within the city limits: five in 1896, and fifty-seven the following year. The first oil refinery in the state was built in 1897, and by 1898 there were 287 producing wells in the Corsicana field.[qv] The oil find attracted numerous oil men from the East, among them Edwy R. Brown,[qv] H. C. Folger, W. C. Proctor, C. N. Payne, and J. S. Cullinan,[qv] founder of the Cullinan Oil Company, which later evolved into the Magnolia Oil Company. The discovery of oil transformed Corsicana from a regional agricultural shipping town to an important oil and industrial center, spawning a number of allied businesses, including the Johnston-Akins-Rittersbacher shops (later known as American Well Prospecting Company), producer of the newly-invented rotary drilling bits. In 1900 Corsicana had grown to 9,313 inhabitants, with three banks, twelve newspapers, eight hotels, forty-nine retail stores, a cotton mill, thirty-two doctors, and thirty-five saloons. The presence of the latter was a cause of great concern to many Corsicanans and led to a growing temperance movement in the city that culminated in the passage of prohibition law in November 1904. The closing of the saloons had some short-term benefits, but bootleggers rapidly filled the gap, serving the needs of the legions of oilfield workers.

The oil boom brought a new wave of prosperity to the town. A new courthouse—the one still in use in 1990—was completed in 1905, and in 1917 the Corsicana Chamber of Commerce was founded. The decades after 1900 also saw significant improvements in transportation. The Corsicana Transit Company converted from mule-drawn cars to electric trolleys in 1902; in 1912 the Trinity and Brazos completed a line between Corsicana and Houston; and in 1913 the Texas Electric Railroad instituted hourly service to and from Dallas. In 1923 a second, even larger oil deposit, the Powell oilfield, was discovered, unleashing a new oil boom. Within a few months Corsicana's population swelled to unprecedented heights; some estimates placed the number of residents as high as 28,000 during the peak months of the oil frenzy. New construction transformed the face of the city, and street lights were installed for the first time to control the increased traffic. During the height of the Powell field boom 550 wells in and around the city produced an estimated 354,000 barrels per day. As the boom subsided, the population dropped—to 11,300 in 1925—but it rebounded at the end of the decade, reaching 15,202 in 1930. With the onset of the Great Depression in the early 1930s many Corsicanans found themselves out of work. The number of rated businesses declined from a high of 780 in 1931 to 500 in 1936. Particularly hard hit was the cotton wholesale and processing industry, which suffered from the combined effects of falling prices and the boll weevil.qv The oil industry helped to mitigate the worst effects of the depression, however, and by the end of the decade the Corsicana economy was already beginning to show signs of a rebound. On the eve of World War II qv Corsicana had five banks, a daily newspaper (the *Daily Sun*), three movie theaters, three hospitals, three hotels, a cotton mill, a refinery, and two oil pumping stations. The reported population in 1940 was 17,500, of whom 77% were white and 23% black. Corsicana grew again during the war. In 1942 Air Activities of Texas opened a large flight training center where thousands of pilots received basic training, and in 1942 Bethlehem Steel took over the American Well Prospecting Plant, expanding the production of rotary drills.

Corsicana's leading industries during the 1950s included the Texas-Miller Products Company, a leading producer of hats; the Oil City Iron Works; the Wolfe Brand Company, producer of chili and tamales; several textile plants; the Bethlehem Supply Company; and the Collin Street Bakery,qv a leading producer of fruitcakes. The latter, founded at the end of the nineteenth century by German immigrant August Weidmann and William Thomas McElwee, developed into one of Corsicana's best known industries, shipping their DeLuxe fruitcakes to all fifty states and 195 countries around the world. The oil business, however, continued to form the mainstay of the town's economy. Huge oil profits fostered great wealth in Corsicana, and during the early 1950s there were said to be at least twenty-one millionaires in the town; the per capita income—$1,222 in 1953—was claimed to be the highest of any Texas city. In 1956 a new oilfield was discovered in East Corsicana, and within months 500 wells—nearly one in every backyard—had been drilled.

Since that time Corsicana has experienced steady, if not spectacular, growth. The population reached 20,750 in 1965 and 25,189 in 1991.

The number of businesses saw a sharp drop, from 550 in 1965 to 394 in the mid-1970s, but the number rebounded, and in 1991 the town reported 485 businesses. The leading industries in 1991 included oil and gas extraction, meat packing, fruit and vegetable canning, the printing of business forms, and manufacture of prepared foods, furniture, chemical and rubber products, and oil field machinery.

BIBLIOGRAPHY: Corsicana Chamber of Commerce, *Facts about Corsicana, Texas* (Corsicana: Stokes Printing, 1935). C. L. Jester, *Short History of Navarro County and Corsicana* (Austin: University of Texas Library, 1943). Annie Carpenter Love, *History of Navarro County* (Dallas: Southwestern, 1933). Marker Files, Texas Historical Commission, Austin. Carl Mirus, "A Short History of the Corsicana Shallow Oil Field," *Navarro County Scroll*, 1956. William Polk Murchison, *Corsicana in Civil War and Reconstruction Days* (University of Texas Bulletin 2546, December 8, 1925). William Polk Murchison, *The Early History of Corsicana* (University of Texas Bulletin 2746, December 8, 1927). Wyvonne Putman, comp., *Navarro County History* (5 vols., Quanah, Texas: Nortex, 1975–84). Alva Taylor, *History and Photographs of Corsicana and Navarro County* (Corsicana, Texas, 1959; rev. ed., *Navarro County History and Photographs*, Corsicana, 1962). Vertical Files, Barker Texas History Center, University of Texas at Austin.
Christopher Long

CORSICANA FEMALE LITERARY INSTITUTE. Corsicana Female Literary Institute, in Corsicana, was established in 1857 and first housed in the Navarro County Courthouse. The school moved from the courthouse when a new two-story, cedar-log building called "the academy" was constructed. The lower part of the building was used for education during the week and for church on Sundays. The upper floor was used by the Masonic lodge. Tuition in 1860 was $10 per session for junior classes, $12.50 for middle classes, and $15 for senior classes. Latin or French cost five dollars more, and music with instruments was twenty-five dollars extra. The charge for room and board was between eight and ten dollars per session. Around 1870 the school's stockholders sold the property to the Masons.

BIBLIOGRAPHY: Annie Carpenter Love, *History of Navarro County* (Dallas: Southwestern, 1933). *Memorial and Biographical History of Navarro, Henderson, Anderson, Limestone, Freestone, and Leon Counties* (Chicago: Lewis, 1893). Alva Taylor, *History and Photographs of Corsicana and Navarro County* (Corsicana, Texas, 1959; rev. ed., *Navarro County History and Photographs*, Corsicana, 1962).
Julie G. Miller

CORSICANA FIELD. Corsicana Field, at Corsicana, was a contract primary flying school operated by Air Activities of Houston, Texas. The base opened in March 1941 and closed in October 1944.

BIBLIOGRAPHY: Robert E. Hays, Jr., Military Aviation Activities in Texas, World Wars I and II (M.A. thesis, University of Texas, 1963). *History of AAF Training Command* (Fort Worth: Headquarters Air Training Command, 1941).
Art Leatherwood

CORSICANA OILFIELD. Corsicana field is an elliptical-shaped oil and gas producing area located in and around Corsicana in central Navarro County. It is significant because it was the first Texas field to produce oil and gas in important quantities. American Well and Prospecting Company, a water-well contractor, discovered it accidentally on June 9, 1894, while seeking a new water source for the city of Corsicana. The field produces from a pinch-out trap in an Upper Cretaceous sandstone reservoir at an average depth of 1,050 feet. The source of its primary recovery was a combined gas-cap and water drive. Its secondary recovery is the result of a number of saltwater flood projects initiated in the 1950s. Between 1896 and January 1, 1993, the field produced nearly 44 million barrels of oil. From 1900 through

1909 gas from the early field supplied fuel for domestic and industrial uses in Corsicana and other Texas cities.

In 1893 civic leaders of Corsicana needed a dependable water supply to promote commercial development. They contracted with American Well and Prospecting Company, operated by H. G. Johnston, Elmer Akins, and Charles Rittersbacher, to drill three water wells for the city. On June 9, 1894, the drillers took the first well to a depth of 1,027 feet, where they encountered oil. Although the producing formation was cased off, oil continued to rise to the surface outside the casing. When residents learned of the oil in the water well, interest in prospecting for oil in the area grew. On September 6, Ralph Beaton and H. G. Damon, local citizens, joined with an experienced Pennsylvania oilman, John Davidson, to organize the Corsicana Oil Development Company. The company took a twelve-year mineral lease from A. and Bertha Bunert and entered an agreement with John H. Galey of Pittsburg, Pennsylvania, on September 14, 1894. Galey agreed to drill five wells for the company at his own expense in exchange for an undivided one-half interest in all oil and gas leases owned by Corsicana Oil Development. The first well was staked 200 feet south of the water well drilled by American Well and Prospecting and was completed on October 15, 1895. It had an initial flow of 2½ barrels of oil a day. The second well was a dry hole. The third well was staked at Fourth and Collins streets in town and was completed in May 1896 with an initial yield of twenty-two barrels of oil a day. Three additional wells were producing by the end of 1896, when annual production of 1,450 barrels of oil was reported.

By 1897 it was evident that commercial quantities of oil could be produced in the area, and development of the field moved to the east, northeast, and southeast of the original site. Although the early wells were small producers, prospectors sank so many wells that Corsicana oil flooded an already-limited Texas market, where the demand was only for use in local field development and for shipment to Austin and Dallas for making gas. With the only refinery in Texas located at Sour Lake, Corsicana operators at times found no market for their crude. At those times, they poured surplus oil on the ground. Waste in the field resulted in the passage on March 29, 1899, of the first Texas statutory regulation of the drilling, casing, plugging, and abandoning of oil and gas wells to end irresponsible producing and dumping. By the time dumping of crude was outlawed in Texas, Corsicana had found a dependable outlet for its oil. In 1897 Mayor James E. Whitesell and town leaders invited Joseph S. Cullinan,[qv] a successful Pennsylvania oilman, to come to Corsicana to advise in the development of the field. Cullinan was so interested in the oil potential of the area that he became a participant in its development. He contracted with several operators to buy 150,000 barrels of oil for fifty cents a barrel. He agreed to lay gathering lines, construct storage tanks, build a refinery, and find a market for Corsicana oil. He began the process of fulfilling his agreement, but those who had offered financial backing in his project lost confidence in the oil-producing ability of the area and withdrew from the contract. The resourceful Cullinan then turned to out-of-state capital to fund the $150,000 project. By the end of 1897 the field had increased annual yields to 65,975 barrels of oil from forty-seven wells.

Early in 1898, with a refinery under construction and storage tanks in place to handle production, operators continued to add producing wells to the field. Early operators in the field besides the J. S. Cullinan Company and Corsicana Oil Development Company included Consumers Petroleum Oil Company, Lone Star Petroleum Company, Corsicana Cotton Oil Company, Co-operative Oil Company, Navarro Oil Company, Southern Oil Company, Southern Development Company, and Verna Petroleum Oil Company. By midsummer of 1898, rotary drilling replaced cable tools in the field. Rotary rigs worked well in the soft formations of the field and were quick and economical. At the end of 1898, when 342 additional wells were completed and yearly yields had sharply increased to 544,620 barrels of oil, the stills at the new Cullinan refinery were fired. After the first shipment left the refinery on February 24, 1899, the price of Corsicana crude rose from $.50 a barrel to $.98 and to $1.10 by May 1900. In response to the higher price for crude in 1899, producers increased their annual production to 668,483 barrels.

By July 1900, when the field covered an area of twelve to fifteen square miles around Corsicana, the Cullinan refinery was processing 1,500 barrels of crude a day. Half of the crude was made into gasoline and kerosene and half into illuminating oil. The field reached its peak primary annual production of oil in 1900, when 839,554 barrels were brought to the surface, along with natural gas valued at $20,000. Most of the gas sold in Texas for domestic and industrial purposes was produced in Corsicana until 1909, when other areas developed gas reserves. Oil drilling and yields for 1901 and 1902 declined under the pressure of newly discovered gusher production in coastal salt-dome reservoirs at the Spindletop and Sour Lake oilfields.[qqv] In 1903 a second crude-processing plant, Central Oil Refinery, was built at Corsicana. Production continued a general decline from 1903 through 1918, though some years showed increases and a modest number of new well completions. In 1919 shallow production at Powell was added to Corsicana annual yields, boosting them to 305,335 barrels of oil in 1921. By 1923, when Powell shallow outputs were separated from those of Corsicana, production totals from the old field slid to 292,000 barrels of oil annually, and by 1929 the annual yield was 225,000 barrels. After 1930 and throughout the 1940s production in the mature field settled into yearly yields of less than 170,000 barrels of oil.

Beginning in December 1949, field production was revitalized by mergers with two old fields and by the beginning of secondary recovery projects. In 1950 Rice field, a nearby pool that was discovered in 1909, was consolidated with Corsicana, and in 1953 Angus field, a pool found before 1915, was combined with it. In 1950, when all the original wells had been abandoned for fifteen years, a water-flood project began in the field. Other floods that injected salt water into oil-bearing horizons were initiated in 1952, 1954, and 1956. These secondary recoveries brought annual production in the seventy-year-old field to a remarkable 1,611,055 barrels of oil and 17,859,000 cubic feet of gas in 1965. By 1975, when the field had been giving up oil for eighty years, production dropped to 328,901 barrels of oil, a figure that exceeded the 1905 production. In 1985 continued secondary recoveries forced up 378,474 barrels of oil and 4,981,000 cubic feet of casinghead gas. On January 1, 1993, the first commercial Texas field reported annual production of 196,645 barrels of oil and 3,091,000 cubic feet of casinghead gas. Cumulative production for the field reached 43,965,138 barrels of oil by that time, after ninety-nine years of operation.

BIBLIOGRAPHY: William E. Galloway et al., *Atlas of Major Texas Oil Reservoirs* (Austin: University of Texas Bureau of Economic Geology, 1983). Frank A. Herald, ed., *Occurrence of Oil and Gas in Northeast Texas* (University of Texas Bureau of Economic Geology Publication 5116, Austin, August 15, 1951). Henry A. Ley, ed., *Geology of Natural Gas* (Tulsa: American Association of Petroleum Geologists, 1935). George C. Matson and Oliver B. Hopkins, The Corsicana Oil and Gas Field, Texas, in *Contributions to Economic Geology, 1917* (Washington: GPO, 1917; U.S. Geological Survey Bulletin 661-F). Edgar Wesley Owen, *Trek of the Oil Finders: A History of Exploration for Petroleum* (Tulsa: American Association for Petroleum Geologists, 1975). John S. Spratt, *The Road to Spindletop* (Dallas: Southern Methodist University Press, 1955; rpt., Austin: University of Texas Press, 1970). Charles Albert Warner, *Texas Oil and Gas Since 1543* (Houston: Gulf, 1939). Daniel Yergin, *The Prize: The Epic Quest for Oil, Money and Power* (New York: Simon and Schuster, 1991).   Julia Cauble Smith

CORSICANA STATE HOME. Corsicana State Home, formerly the State Orphans' Home, was established in 1887 by an act of the Twelfth Legislature to support, educate, and care for orphan or dependent children. It opened on July 15, 1889, and housed fifty-four children the first year. In 1932 the home reached a peak enrollment of 890. During the 1940s the enrollment began to decline, and by 1945 the facility housed only 443 children. By 1948 the orphanage, located three miles west of the Corsicana business district, had twenty-one brick structures and a number of small frame cottages, barns, and outbuildings on 417 acres. In its early years the home operated its own independent school district with a grade school, junior high, and high school. In addition to academic subjects the school offered courses in various vocational fields, including cosmetology, mechanics, printing, agriculture, home economics, and business. Until the 1960s the institution also operated its own farms, dairy, creamery, laundry, cannery, store, power plant, bakery, kitchen, and hospital. Older children worked part-time in these operations and thus received practical training. In 1957 the institution was renamed Corsicana State Home. The home was integrated in the mid-1960s and is now operated under the administration of the Texas Youth Commission.qv After World War II qv the school was closed down, and children from the home began to attend the Corsicana public schools. In 1989 the institution served sixty-six children.

BIBLIOGRAPHY: Files, Texas Youth Commission, Austin. Texas State Board of Control, *Report*.

James W. Markham and William T. Field

CORTES, TEXAS. Cortes was on the New York, Texas and Mexican Railway between Markham and the Colorado River at a site a mile north of what is now State Highway 35 in north central Matagorda County. It was named for H. W. Cortes, president of the Moore–Cortes Canal Company headquartered there, and served as a depot stop and a post office from 1901 to 1903, the year newly founded Markham opened a post office further west on the railroad. At its height the community had a hotel run by A. A. Moore, who was also postmaster. Until it moved to Markham, the Cortes post office was also used by residents of the nearby community of Northern Headquarters. Cortes is not shown on the 1936 county highway map.

BIBLIOGRAPHY: Matagorda County Historical Commission, *Historic Matagorda County* (3 vols., Houston: Armstrong, 1986).

Rachel Jenkins

CORTEZ LIRA, GREGORIO (1875–1916). Gregorio Cortez, who became a folk hero among Mexican Americans qv in the early 1900s for evading the Texas Rangers qv during their search for him on murder charges, was a tenant farmer and vaquero qv who was born on June 22, 1875, near Matamoros, Tamaulipas, to Román Cortez Garza and Rosalía Lira Cortina, transient laborers. In 1887 his family moved to Manor, near Austin. From 1889 to 1899, he worked as a farm hand and vaquero in Karnes, Gonzales, and nearby counties on a seasonal basis, and this transiency provided him with a valuable knowledge of the region and terrain. Around that time he owned two horses and a mule. He had a limited education and spoke English. On February 20, 1890, he married Leonor Díaz, with whom he had four children. Leonor began divorce proceedings against Gregorio in early 1903, alleging as part of her petition that Gregorio had physically and verbally abused her during the early years of their marriage and that she had remained with him only out of fear. Her divorce was granted on March 12, 1903. On December 23, 1904, Cortez married Estéfana Garza of Manor while in jail. He was married again in 1916, perhaps to Ester Martínez. According to folklorist Américo Paredes, before his encounter with Sheriff Morris on June 12, 1901, Cortez was considered "a likeable young man," who had not been in much legal trouble. Historian Richard Mertz, however, interviewed acquaintances of the Cortezes who claimed that in the 1880s Gregorio, his father, and brothers Tomás and Romaldo were involved in horse theft, an act Chicano qv historians have typically interpreted as resistance to racial oppression. A charge of horse theft against Romaldo around 1887 was dropped due to lack of evidence, and a similar charge against Tomás about the same time ended with an executive pardon from Governor Lawrence S. Ross.qv Paredes has noted, however, that in the early 1900s Tomás was sentenced to five years in the penitentiary for horse theft.

The event that propelled Cortez to legendary status occurred on June 12, 1901, when he was approached by Karnes county sheriff W. T. "Brack" Morris because Atascosa county sheriff Avant had asked Morris to help locate a horse thief described as a "medium-sized Mexican." Deputies John Trimmell and Boone Choate accompanied Morris in their search, and Choate acted as the interpreter. Choate questioned various Kenedy residents, including Andrés Villarreal, who informed them that he had recently acquired a mare by trading a horse to a man named Gregorio Cortez. Morris and the deputies then approached the Cortezes, who lived on the W. A. Thulmeyer ranch, ten miles west of Kenedy, where Gregorio and Romaldo rented land and raised corn. According to official testimony, Choate's poor job of interpreting led to major misunderstanding between Cortez and Choate. For instance, Gregorio's brother Romaldo told Gregorio, "*Te quieren*" ("Somebody wants you"). Choate interpreted this to mean "You are wanted," suggesting that Gregorio was indeed the wanted man the authorities were seeking. Choate apparently asked Cortez if he had traded a "*caballo*" ("horse") to which he answered "no" because he had traded a "*yegua*" ("mare"). A third misinterpretation involved another response from Cortez, who told the sheriff and deputies, "*No me puede arrestar por nada*" ("You can't arrest me for nothing"), which Morris understood as "*A mi no me arresta nadie*" and translated as "No white man can arrest me." Partly as a result of these misunderstandings Morris shot and wounded Romaldo and narrowly missed Gregorio. Gregorio responded to the sheriff's action by shooting and killing him. Cortez fled the scene, initially walking toward the Gonzales-Austin vicinity, some eighty miles away. His name was soon on the front page of every major Texas newspaper. Shortly after the incident, the San Antonio *Express* lamented the fact that Cortez had not been lynched. Meanwhile, Leonor and the children, Cortez's mother, and his sister-in-law María were illegally held in custody while posses mobilized to catch Cortez.

On his escape, Cortez stopped at the ranch of Martín and Refugia Robledo on Schnabel property near Belmont. At the Robledo home Gonzales county sheriff Glover and his posse found Cortez. Shots were exchanged, and Glover and Schnabel were killed. Cortez escaped again and walked nearly 100 miles to the home of Ceferino Flores, a friend, who provided him a horse and saddle. He now headed

Gregorio Cortez (seated, center) and his guard, ca. 1901. Photography Collection, HRHRC, University of Texas at Austin. Gregorio Cortez became a folk hero when, in self-defense, he killed the Karnes County sheriff. Newspapers considered his subsequent flight—which involved posses of hundreds of men—front-page material.

toward Laredo. The hunt for "sheriff killer" Cortez intensified. Newspaper accounts portrayed him as a "bandit" with a "gang" at his assistance. The *Express* noted that Cortez "is at the head of a well organized band of thieves and cutthroats." The Seguin *Enterprise* referred to him as an "arch fiend." Governor Joseph D. Sayers[qv] and Karnes citizens offered a $1,000 reward for his capture. Cortez found it more difficult to evade capture around Laredo since Tejanos typically served as lawmen in the region. Sheriff Ortiz of Webb County and assistant city marshall Gómez of Laredo, for instance, participated in the hunt. While anti-Cortez sentiment grew, so did the numbers of people who sympathized with the fugitive. Tejanos, who saw him as a hero evading the evil *rinches,* also experienced retaliatory violence in Gonzales, Refugio, and Hays counties and in and around the communities of Ottine, Belmont, Yoakum, Runge, Beeville, San Diego, Benavides, Cotulla, and Galveston. By the time the chase had ended at least nine persons of Mexican descent had been killed, three wounded, and seven arrested. Meanwhile, admiration of Cortez by Anglo-Texans also increased, and the San Antonio *Express* touted his "remarkable powers of endurance and skill in eluding pursuit." The posses searching for Cortez involved hundreds of men, including the Texas Rangers. A train on the International–Great Northern Railroad route to Laredo was used to bring in new posses and fresh horses. Cortez was finally captured when Jesús González, one of his acquaintances, located him and led a posse to him on June 22, 1901, ten days after the encounter between Cortez and Sheriff Morris. Some Tejanos later labeled González a traitor to his people and ostracized him.

Once he was captured, a legal-defense campaign began and a network of supporters developed. The Sociedad Trabajador Miguel Hidalgo in San Antonio wrote a letter of support that appeared in newspapers as far away as Mexico City. Pablo Cruz,[qv] the editor of *El Regidor* of San Antonio, played a key role in the defense network, which was located in Houston, Austin, and Laredo. Funds were collected through donations, *sociedades mutualistas,*[qv] and benefit performances to provide for Cortez's legal representation. B. R. Abernathy, one of his lawyers, proved to be the most committed to attaining justice for him. Cortez went through numerous trials, the first of which began in Gonzales on July 24, 1901. Eleven jurors, with the exception of juror A. L. Sanders, found him guilty of the murder of Schnabel. Through a compromise among the jurors, a fifty-year sentence for second-degree murder was assessed. The defense's attempt to appeal the case was denied. In the meantime a mob of 300 men tried to lynch Cortez. Shortly after the verdict, Romaldo Cortez, whom Sheriff Morris had wounded, died in the Karnes City jail. On January 15, 1902, the Texas Court of Criminal Appeals[qv] reversed the Gonzales verdict. The same court also reversed the verdicts in the trials held in Karnes and Pleasanton. In April 1904 the last trial was held in Corpus Christi. By the time Cortez began serving life in prison for the murder of Sheriff Glover, he had been in eleven jails in eleven counties. While in prison he worked as a barber, an occupation that he probably pursued throughout his years of incarceration. Cortez also enjoyed the empathy of some of his jailers, who provided him the entire upper story of the jail as a "honeymoon suite" when he married Estéfana Garza.

Attempts to pardon him began as soon as he entered prison. After Cruz died, Col. Francisco A. Chapa,[qv] the politically influential publisher of *El Imparcial* in San Antonio, took up the Cortez case; he has been considered the person most responsible for his release. Ester Martínez also petitioned Governor Oscar B. Colquitt[qv] for his release. The Board of Pardons Advisers eventually recommended a full pardon. Even Secretary of State F. C. Weinert[qv] of Seguin worked for Cortez's pardon. Colquitt, who issued many pardons, gave Cortez a conditional pardon in July 1913. Once released, Cortez thanked those who helped him recover his freedom. Soon after, he went to Nuevo Laredo and fought with Victoriano Huerta[qv] in the Mexican Revolution.[qv] He married for the last time in 1916 and died shortly afterwards of pneumonia, on February 28, 1916. His story inspired many variants of a *corrido* (see CORRIDOS) called "El Corrido de Gregorio Cortez," which appeared as early as 1901. The ballad was similar to those that depicted Juan Nepomuceno Cortina and Catarino Garza.[qq,qv] Américo Paredes popularized the story of Gregorio Cortez in *With His Pistol in His Hand: A Border Ballad and Its Hero,* which was published by the University of Texas Press in 1958. Between 1958 and 1965 the book sold fewer than 1,000 copies, and a Texas Ranger angered by it threatened to shoot Paredes. In subsequent decades, however, the book has been recognized as a classic of Texas Mexican prose and has sold quite well. Cortez's story gained further interest when the movie *The Ballad of Gregorio Cortez* was produced in 1982.

BIBLIOGRAPHY: Richard J. Mertz, "No One Can Arrest Me: The Story of Gregorio Cortez," *Journal of South Texas* 1 (1974).

Cynthia E. Orozco

CORTINA, JUAN NEPOMUCENO (1824–1894). Juan Nepomuceno (Cheno) Cortina (Cortinas), Mexican folk hero, was born on May 16, 1824, in Camargo, Tamaulipas, the son of Estéfana and Trinidad Cortina. His aristocratic mother was one of the heirs of a large land grant in the lower Rio Grande valley, including the area that surrounded Brownsville. The family moved to that land when Cortina was still young. In the Mexican War[qv] Cortina served as a part of an irregular cavalry during the battles of Resaca de la Palma and Palo Alto[qq,qv] under Gen. Mariano Arista[qv] of the Tamaulipas Brigade. After the war he returned to the north bank of the river, where he was indicted at least twice by a Cameron County grand jury for stealing cattle. Although Cortina frequently appeared in public, his political influence among Mexicans prevented him from being arrested.

In the decade following the Treaty of Guadalupe Hidalgo,[qv] Cortina came to hate a clique of judges and Brownsville attorneys whom he accused of expropriating land from Mexican Texans unfamiliar with the American judicial system. He became a leader to many of the poorer Mexicans who lived along the banks of the river. The incident that ignited the first so-called Cortina War occurred on July 13, 1859, when Cortina saw the Brownsville city marshall, Robert Shears, brutally arrest a Mexican American who had once been employed by Cortina. Cortina shot the marshall in the impending confrontation and rode out of town with the prisoner. Early on the morning of September 28, 1859, he rode into Brownsville again, this time at the head of some forty to eighty men, and seized control of the town. Five men, including the city jailer, were shot during the raid, as Cortina and his men raced through the streets shouting "Death to the Americans" and "Viva Mexico." Many of the men whom Cortina had sworn to kill, however, escaped or went into hiding.

When several of the town's leading citizens appealed to Mexican authorities in Matamoros, the influential José María Carbajal[qv] crossed the river to negotiate with Cortina. Cortina agreed to evacuate the town and retreated to the family ranch at Santa Rita in Cameron County, where, on September 30, 1859, he issued a proclamation asserting the rights of Mexican Texans and demanding the punishment of anyone violating these rights.

In the ensuing days, tensions remained high in Brownsville. A town posse captured Tomás Cabrera, one of Cortina's men. About twenty citizens of the town formed a group called the Brownsville Tigers, and, assisted by a militia company from Matamoros, moved against Cortina, who was reported to be at his mother's ranch some six miles upriver. With two cannons the Brownsville-Matamoros force launched a half-hearted attack, which Cortina easily repulsed; the "Tigers" lost their cannons and retreated in complete disarray. Cortina was idolized by many of the poorer Mexicans on both sides of the river, and his small army grew as recruits joined his ranks. He demanded that Cabrera be released and threatened to burn the town. In the first part of November an undisciplined company of Texas Rangers[qv] commanded by Capt. William G. Tobin[qq,qv] arrived.

Cabrera was hanged the next day, and an unsuccessful attack was launched against Cortina. Cortina issued a second proclamation on November 23 asking Governor Sam Houston^qv to defend the legal interests of Mexican residents in Texas.

By early December a second company of rangers, commanded by John Salmon (Rip) Ford,^qv arrived, as did Maj. Samuel P. Heintzelman^qv with 165 regulars. Cortina, who was reported to have over 400 men by this time, retreated upriver, laying waste to much of the lower Valley. On December 27 Heintzelman engaged Cortina in the battle of Rio Grande City; Cortina was decisively defeated, losing sixty men and his equipment. He retreated into Mexico and next appeared at La Bolsa, a large bend on the Rio Grande below Rio Grande City, where he attempted to capture the steamboat *Ranchero*, owned and operated by two of his antagonists, Richard King and Mifflin Kenedy.^qqv With the approach of the steamboat, Major Ford and his rangers crossed into Mexico, secured the south bank, and forced Cortina to retreat. Col. Robert E. Lee,^qv now in command of the Eighth Military District, arrived in the lower Valley determined to restore peace and threatening to invade Mexico if necessary. Cortina, however, had retreated into the Burgos Mountains, where he remained for more than a year.

With the secession^qv of Texas from the Union, Cortina appeared on the border again and started the second Cortina War. In May 1861 he invaded Zapata County and attacked the county seat, Carrizo. He was defeated by Confederate captain Santos Benavides^qv and retreated into Mexico; Cortina lost seven men in the fray, while eleven others were captured by Benavides and hanged or shot.

On May 5, 1862, during the period of French intervention in Mexico, Cortina helped to defend San Lorenzo at Puebla. He saw action at Matamoros and, envisioning himself as an independent and powerful caudillo, briefly cooperated with the imperialists. Later he fought in central Mexico and was at Querétaro at the execution of Maximilian. In 1863 Cortina proclaimed himself governor of Tamaulipas and was promoted to general of the Mexican Army of the North by President Benito Juárez. Cortina appointed himself governor again in 1866 but immediately relinquished the office to General Tapia. Cortina returned to the border in 1870, and forty-one residents of the Valley, including a former mayor of Brownsville, signed a petition asking that he be pardoned for his crimes because of his service to the Union during the Civil War.^qv The petition failed in the Texas legislature on its second reading, in 1871. In subsequent years, stockmen in the Nueces Strip accused Cortina of leading a large ring of cattle rustlers. Subsequent American diplomatic pressure was largely responsible for his arrest in July 1875 and his removal to Mexico City. He died in Atzcapozalco on October 30, 1894.

BIBLIOGRAPHY: Rodolfo Acuña, *Occupied America: A History of Chicanos* (2d ed., New York: Harper and Row, 1981). Arnoldo De León, *They Called Them Greasers: Anglo Attitudes Toward Mexicans in Texas, 1821–1900* (Austin: University of Texas Press, 1983). Charles W. Goldfinch and José T. Canales, *Juan N. Cortina: Two Interpretations* (New York: Arno Press, 1974). J. Fred Rippy, "Border Troubles along the Rio Grande, 1848–1860," *Southwestern Historical Quarterly* 23 (October 1919). Paul Schuster Taylor, *An American-Mexican Frontier, Nueces County, Texas* (Chapel Hill: University of North Carolina Press, 1934). Jerry Don Thompson, *Sabers on the Rio Grande* (Austin: Presidial, 1974).

Jerry Thompson

CORWIN, TEXAS. Corwin, near the Colorado River twenty-two miles southeast of Burnet in southeastern Burnet County, was settled in the mid-1850s. A post office was established there in 1870, with Thomas T. Word as postmaster. It was discontinued in 1882 but reestablished in 1884. That year Corwin had a district school, a steam gristmill and cotton gin, three churches, and seventy-five residents; cotton and wool were the principal shipments from the area. By 1896, however, the community's population had dropped to twenty. The post office was discontinued in 1899, and mail for the community was sent to Double Horn. Area children attended the Lewis School, which opened in 1888; it operated until 1913, after which time students attended the school at Spicewood. The community was not shown on the 1948 county highway map.

BIBLIOGRAPHY: Darrell Debo, *Burnet County History* (2 vols., Burnet, Texas: Eakin, 1979).

Vivian Elizabeth Smyrl

CORYELL, JAMES (1803–1837). James Coryell, for whom Coryell County was named, was born near West Union, Ohio, in 1803, the son of Lewis and Sarah (Voshall) Coryell. He left home at the age of eighteen and made his way to Texas. He was in San Antonio in 1831, when he joined James and Rezin P. Bowie^qqv on an exploring expedition to the San Saba region in search of silver mines. After his return to San Antonio, Coryell went with Arnold Cavitt to a site near that of Marlin and made his home with the Cavitt family. In 1835 he explored the Leon River country and located his headright near the mouth of Coryell Creek in what is now Coryell County. During the spring and summer of 1836 he was a member of Sterling C. Robertson's^qv ranging company, and in the fall of 1836 he joined Capt. Thomas H. Barron's^qv company. On May 27, 1837, while encamped near the falls of the Brazos River, Coryell and two companions were raiding a bee tree a short distance from the camp when they were attacked by Indians. His two companions escaped, but Coryell was shot and killed. His burial place is not known.

BIBLIOGRAPHY: Zelma Scott, *History of Coryell County* (Austin: Texas State Historical Association, 1965).

Carolyn Hyman

Juan Cortina, 1864. Courtesy Carlos Larralde Collection, Long Beach, California.

CORYELL CHURCH, TEXAS. Coryell Church is on Farm Road 185 five miles northwest of Oglesby in eastern Coryell County. The settlement grew up around the county's first Baptist church, which was established in 1854, and became known as Coryell Church; because no effort was made to establish a post office there, a more formal name for the community was unnecessary. In 1888 a new church building was completed on land donated by Green Franks and Henry Hall. Coryell Church thrived as long as the family farms in the area continued to operate. The school at the community had sixty-one students and one teacher in 1904. No population estimates were available for Coryell Church, but as late as the 1940s, a church, a business, and a number of residences were shown at the site on county highway maps. Gradually, however, small farms in the area were absorbed by larger operations, and the population of the community dwindled. Services at the church were held with reduced frequency. In 1970 the church building was designated as a Texas historical landmark, but in 1982 the church was declared unsafe and torn down. Only the cemetery remained to mark the Coryell Church community on county highway maps.

BIBLIOGRAPHY: Coryell County Genealogical Society, *Coryell County, Texas, Families, 1854–1985* (Dallas: Taylor, 1986).

Vivian Elizabeth Smyrl

CORYELL CITY, TEXAS. Coryell City is on Farm Road 929 ten miles northeast of Gatesville in northeastern Coryell County. It was known as Rainey's Creek when the county was organized in 1854; a post office by that name began operating by the creek in 1857. By 1860 nearly seventy families lived in the Rainey's Creek vicinity. The community became known as Coryell in the early 1870s. By the 1880s Coryell had a church, a district school, two steam cotton gins, and 200 residents; area farmers shipped cotton, wool, and grain. Coryell grew slowly through the first third of the 1900s, but after the late 1930s it began to decline. The number of residents fell from a peak of 406 in 1939 to 150 in 1943. The population was reported to be 175 from the mid-1940s through the mid-1960s and 125 from 1968 through 1990. The post office at Coryell City was discontinued in 1958, and mail for the community was sent to Gatesville and Valley Mills.

BIBLIOGRAPHY: Coryell County Genealogical Society, *Coryell County, Texas, Families, 1854–1985* (Dallas: Taylor, 1986). John J. Germann and Myron Janzen, *Texas Post Offices by County* (1986). Zelma Scott, *History of Coryell County* (Austin: Texas State Historical Association, 1965).

Vivian Elizabeth Smyrl

CORYELL COUNTY. Coryell County (H-16), in central Texas about 210 miles inland from the Gulf of Mexico, is bordered by Hamilton, Bosque, McLennan, Bell, and Lampasas counties. Gatesville, the county seat, is on U.S. Highway 84 and State Highway 36, about eighty miles north of Austin and 114 miles southwest of Dallas. The county's center lies about four miles southwest of Gatesville at approximately 31°23′ north latitude and 97°48′ west longitude. The present county comprises 1,031 square miles of plateaus and grasslands in the Grand Prairie region, with elevations ranging from 600 to 1,493 feet above sea level. Its two principal streams are the Leon River, which drains the northern and eastern parts of the county, and Cowhouse Creek, which drains the western and southern areas. Soils vary widely in the county, but most are alkaline with limestone underneath. Indigenous trees include red cedar, live oak, Spanish oak, burr oak, shin oak, cedar elm, hackberry, pecan, redbud, Mexican plum, buckeye, ash, and Eve's necklace; native grasses include bluestems, gramas, and buffalo grass. Approximately 25 percent of the county is considered prime farmland. The fauna includes deer, armadillos, skunks, coyotes, bobcats, opossums, ring-tailed cats, badgers, foxes, raccoons, and squirrels, as well as assorted birds, fish, and reptiles. The climate is temperate; the average minimum temperature is 33° F in January, and the average maximum is 97° in July. The growing season averages 244 days annually, and the rainfall averages about thirty-two inches.

Archeological evidence suggests that Central Texas, including Coryell County, has supported human habitation for at least 12,000 years. The hunting and gathering peoples who had established themselves along the Leon River by 4500 B.C. were probably ancestors of the Tonkawa Indians, who resided in the area in the eighteenth and nineteenth centuries. Another Central Texas tribe, the Lipan Apaches, became neighbors of the Tonkawas sometime after 1300. In later years Kiowas sometimes resided in the area, and the Comanches occasionally passed through.

The area that became Coryell County was part of the Milam Land District, assigned by the Mexican government for settlement first to Robert Leftwich,qv in 1825, and later to Sterling C. Robertson.qv Some of the land was surveyed as early as 1835, but few settlements existed before the late 1840s, when the United States established Fort Gates and other military posts along the frontier to protect incoming residents from Indians. The line of frontier forts was moved farther west in the early 1850s, and Fort Gates was abandoned in 1852. Settlers in the Fort Gates area numbered about 250 at that time, and they began to campaign for a county seat. In 1854 the legislature established Coryell County and named it in honor of frontiersman James Coryell,qv an early landholder. Residents chose the site for Gatesville, the county seat, in an election held in May 1854.

Besides Fort Gates, settlements established in Coryell County in the 1850s included Mound, Coryell Church, Rainey's Creek (Coryell City), Langford Cove (Evant), Boyd's Cove (Bee House), the Grove, Henson's Creek, Spring Hill, Station Creek, Turnover, and Lincolnville. The 1860 census showed the county's free population to be 2,360; 81 of this number were slaveholders, who owned a total of 306 slaves. The majority of residents were from the Old South. Of the heads of households in 1860, the largest number (115) were from Tennessee, forty were from Alabama, and thirty-seven each from Kentucky and North Carolina.

Unlike neighboring McLennan County, Coryell County had few large plantations. Most of its resources were devoted to stock raising and subsistence farming. The 1860 production included 25,000 cattle, 8,500 hogs, 3,800 sheep, 61,000 bushels of corn, 18,000 bushels of wheat, and forty-nine bales of cotton.

Although Coryell County residents owned relatively few slaves, the prevailing sentiment was decidedly in favor of secession.qv In the fall of 1860 residents held several mass meetings advocating secession and the formation of militia companies. James M. Norrisqv represented the county at the Secession Conventionqv in January 1861 and voted to leave the Union; Coryell County voters approved the ordinance later that year by a margin of 293 to 55. Several companies from Coryell County volunteered for duty in the Confederate Army or to help protect frontier settlers from Indians. Gatesville became headquarters of the Second Frontier District, under the command of Maj. George B. Erath.qv Local sources give little record of Coryell County during Reconstruction.qv Election returns for 1869 showed the county choosing Andrew J. Hamilton over Edmund J. Davisqqv for governor by a unanimous vote, 259 to 0; the vote indicated that the Radical Republicans had been banished by that time and the Democrats restored to power.

In national politics, Coryell County was staunchly Democratic from the end of Reconstruction through the late 1960s. However, voters chose Richard Nixon in 1972, Ronald Reagan in 1980 and 1984, and George Bush in 1988 and 1992. Occasional third parties, such as the Greenbackers, Populists, and Progressives, drew a sizable portion of the vote, but never enough to swing the county's overall election results. Residents generally voted Democratic in state elections.

Before the Civil War,qv schools in Coryell County were operated as private or subscription institutions, with state funds supplementing the budgets. The legislature enacted a system of public schools in 1870, and by 1872 Coryell County had twenty teachers and nineteen schools for nearly 600 schoolchildren. Nearly every community either had its own school or was near a community that did. As in many Texas counties, however, extensive schooling was for many children a luxury that took second place to helping on the family farm. As late as 1940 fewer than 9 percent of the population over the age of twenty-five had completed high school. Large-scale consolidation of common schools into independent school districts took place in the 1930s and 1940s, making it possible to use available resources more efficiently. After World War II qv the percentage of residents who finished school gradually rose. By 1960 nearly 18 percent were high school graduates, and by 1980 the number represented 72 percent of the population over twenty-five.

In the early years of Coryell County few communities had their own preacher; itinerant ministers went from place to place, sometimes staying two or three months in a town. Among the earliest churches established in the county were a Baptist church at Coryell Church in 1854 and a Methodist church at Gatesville in 1854. The first Presbyterian church was organized at Rainey's Creek in 1858. A Christian church was in operation by the mid-1860s, and Germans and Wends qqv brought the Lutheran church to the area, establishing St. John's in Coryell City in 1889. Coryell County had no Catholic church until 1940, when an influx of military families diversified the area's religion; before that, Catholics had to travel to Lampasas or Waco in order to attend services. In the early 1990s, the county had approximately 100 churches, representing fifteen different faiths; Southern Baptist, United Methodist, and Church of Christ were the largest communions.

Like most areas in the South, Coryell County suffered a severe economic decline after the Civil War and throughout Reconstruction. Between 1864 and 1866 the county lost 63 percent of its tax base. About a third of the lost property was in slaves; the rest came from declines in farm acreage, farm value, and livestock value, each of which had fallen 30 to 50 percent by the time of the 1870 census. Recovery was slow because transportation was poor and the economy was so dependent on stock raising and farming.

The county economy began to recover in the late 1860s. The overall population more than doubled between 1870 and 1880, rising from 4,124 to 10,924, and the market for agricultural products increased. The 1880 census reported 1,546 farms in the county, up from 279 ten years earlier, and the amount of improved land rose from 11,831 acres in 1870 to 83,258 acres in 1880. Field crops such as corn, wheat, oats, and cotton took up about 65 percent of the improved land, while livestock dominated the rest. By 1880 the county had nearly 23,000 cattle, 10,300 hogs, and 4,300 sheep. A branch of the Chisholm Trail qv passed through the county, and the area around Copperas Cove served as a camping ground for traildrivers. When the arrival of the railroad made long trail drives unnecessary, Copperas Cove continued to prosper as a shipping point for cattle. Coryell County ranchers reported more than 46,000 cattle and 19,800 hogs in 1890, but by 1900, due to the influx of new residents from the Old South, farming had become the dominant occupation; cotton, corn, and oats were raised on more than 65 percent of the county's 200,000 improved acres.

Two railroads were completed through Coryell County in 1882: the Texas and St. Louis Railway laid a narrow-gauge track from Waco to Gatesville, and the Gulf, Colorado and Santa Fe crossed the southern tip of the county near Copperas Cove, making its way from Belton to Lampasas. The arrival of the railroads prompted the establishment of Oglesby, Lime City, and Leon Junction, and provided new economic opportunities for Mound, Gatesville, and Copperas Cove. A third railroad company, the Stephenville North and South Texas, laid track from Hamilton to Gatesville in 1911, providing the northwestern part of the county with easier access to rail service and making the communities of Ireland and Levita more important commercial centers.

Between 1880 and 1900 the population of Coryell County nearly doubled again, rising to 21,308 by the turn of the century. Most of the incoming residents were from other parts of Texas or from other southern states; some, however, came from other countries. New immigrants arrived from Germany in the 1880s and 1890s via Galveston, Lee, and Fayette counties, and from Mexico soon after the turn of the century. In 1930, 145 residents of Coryell County were native Germans, and 352 were native Mexicans. As for African Americans,qv some former slaves left the county after the Civil War, but most stayed either to continue working for their former owners or to start new lives on their own. One group settled in Lincolnville, about four miles west of Gatesville. Between 1880 and 1950, the number of black residents in the county increased at roughly the same rate as the white population; blacks represented from 2 to 3 percent of the county's total population during those years. The permanent establishment of Fort Hood in 1950 changed the ethnic makeup of the county. By the early 1980s, 22 percent of the county's 56,767 residents were of British descent, 21 percent were German, 19 percent were black, 8 percent were Hispanic, 2 percent were Asian, and 0.6 percent were Indian; the remaining percentage was unspecified.

For the first third of the twentieth century, roughly 30 to 50 percent of the county's improved acreage was devoted to cotton culture,qv with production generally ranging from 18,000 to 30,000 bales annually; the county's record crop of nearly 58,000 bales occurred in 1906. Production totals fell in the 1930s, as low yields and the onset of the Great Depressionqv persuaded farmers to devote more of their resources to feed crops and livestock. In 1940 farmers planted 50,500 acres in cotton, compared to the 109,000 acres they had planted ten years earlier; in the late 1950s, cotton was grown on fewer than 17,000 acres. No cotton production was reported in the early 1980s.

Farmers and ranchers kept more of their land as pasture for livestock. Sheep and goat ranching,qqv which had been first introduced to the area in the 1850s and 1860s, gradually increased in importance in the 1930s. Production of wool rose from 32,800 pounds in 1920 to 665,700 in 1940, while mohair production increased from about 16,000 to 121,300 pounds; these two industries declined somewhat in the 1960s and 1970s as cattle production increased. The cattle industry remained fairly stable between 1900 and 1940, with the amount of stock on hand averaging about 35,000 head. The number of cattle rose to nearly 48,000 in the late 1960s and to 93,000 in the early 1980s.

Tenant farming and sharecropping, which had accounted for the operation of a third of the county's farms in 1880, increased steadily in the early twentieth century, peaking at 58 percent in 1930. The depression forced some people, many of them tenants, to give up farming and look for work elsewhere. The establishment of Camp Hood in the early 1940s took approximately 225 square miles of land in southern Coryell County, eliminating two dozen communities and nearly 1,200 farms. Although some small farmers in other areas of the county managed to keep their land, the trend was toward larger farming and ranching operations; the number of farms in the county fell from 3,101 in 1930 to 1,841 in 1950 and 991 in 1982, while the average size of a farm rose from 188 acres in 1930 to 268 acres in 1950, and to 627 acres in the early 1980s. In 1950, 28 percent of the farms were run by tenants, and by 1982 that figure had fallen to 12 percent.

By virtue of its rural environment and relatively small population Coryell County escaped many of the hardships suffered by more urban areas during the depression of the 1930s; nevertheless, relief programs were necessary to see local residents through the difficulties that they did experience. Among these programs were two camps established by the Civilian Conservation Corpsqv—one at Mother Neff State Parkqv to construct park buildings and tourist facilities, and one at Gatesville as a soil-conservation and brush-control detail.

The United States involvement in World War II brought an end to the depression; on a local level, new war industries paved the way for a dramatic increase in the population of Coryell County. Among the military facilities built in and near the county in the 1940s were Camp Hood, the Bluebonnet Ordnance plant, and a camp for German prisoners of war.qv Because of the large number of soldiers, construction workers, and other government employees who came to the area during the war years, there was a severe housing shortage, and many local families offered rooms for rent in their homes. When the military decided in 1950 to make Fort Hood a permanent base, the population of Copperas Cove mushroomed, from 1,052 in 1950 to 4,567 in 1960 and to 10,818 in 1970. During the same period Gatesville's population grew by only 800, from 3,838 to 4,683.

The St. Louis Southwestern of Texas abandoned its track to Gatesville in 1972, leaving the town without rail service; the branch to the northwest had been discontinued in the 1940s. However, in the 1970s and 1980s, Gatesville was chosen as the site for several new units of the Texas Department of Corrections (see PRISON SYSTEM). The Gatesville State School for Boys,qv established in 1887, closed in the early 1970s, and the facility became the Gatesville Unit of TDC. Mountain View School for Boys,qv established in 1962, was also transferred to TDC in 1975 to provide relief for overcrowded conditions at the Goree Unit Women's Prison in Huntsville. The Hilltop Unit, a minimum-security prison for men, opened in 1981. In all, more than 1,000 people worked for the prison system at Gatesville, making TDC one of the county's largest employers.

In the early 1980s, 88 percent of the land in Coryell County (exclusive of Fort Hood) was devoted to farms and ranches. About 20 percent of the farmland was under cultivation, with oats, wheat, and sorghum accounting for 94 percent of the 101,000 acres harvested; other crops were hay, potatoes, sweet potatoes, peaches, and pecans. Eighty percent of the county's agricultural receipts came from livestock and livestock products, the most important ones being cattle, sheep, wool, Angora goats, mohair, hogs, and turkeys. Although agriculture continued to be an important part of the local economy, farm receipts represented less than 8 percent of the county's total income. Professional and related services, manufacturing, wholesale and retail trade, and public administration employed 68 percent of the workforce in the 1980s; 10 percent of the workforce was self-employed, and 8 percent was employed outside the county. Coryell County had 56,767 residents in 1980, a 60 percent increase over the 1970 population of 35, 311. The county's population in 1990 was 64,213, according to census records.

BIBLIOGRAPHY: Coryell County Genealogical Society, *Coryell County, Texas, Families, 1854–1985* (Dallas: Taylor, 1986). Jerry K. Smith and Patrick D. McLaughlin, *Copperas Cove, City of Five Hills: A Centennial History* (Burnet, Texas: Eakin Press, 1980). Zelma Scott, *History of Coryell County* (Austin: Texas State Historical Association, 1965).
Vivian Elizabeth Smyrl

CORYELL CREEK. Coryell Creek, named for James Coryell,qv rises four miles northeast of Jonesboro in northern Coryell County (at 31°38′ N, 97°49′ W) and runs southeast for twenty-eight miles to its mouth on the Leon River, six miles southeast of Gatesville (at 31°23′ N, 97°35′ W). The surrounding flat to rolling terrain has local shallow depressions and is surfaced by shallow, stony clay loams that support juniper, oak, mesquite, and grasses in the upper and middle reaches of the creek. Along the creek's lower reaches grow water-tolerant hardwoods and conifers.

CORYELL VALLEY, TEXAS. Coryell Valley is on Farm Road 929 six miles northeast of Gatesville in northeastern Coryell County. It has also been known as Coffey, in honor of Smith Coffey, an early settler. The community had a church and a schoolhouse by the early 1870s. The Coryell Valley school had twenty students and one teacher in 1904. Only the church marked the community on county highway maps in the 1980s.

BIBLIOGRAPHY: Coryell County Genealogical Society, *Coryell County, Texas, Families, 1854–1985* (Dallas: Taylor, 1986).
Vivian Elizabeth Smyrl

CORZINE, SHELBY (?–1839). Shelby Corzine, early senator and jurist, came to Texas from Alabama in February 1835 and settled near San Augustine. He was wounded at the battle of Horseshoe Bend in Alabama in 1814. In October 1836 he was elected senator to the First Congress of the Republic of Texas but resigned on December 16, 1836, to accept appointment as judge of the First Judicial District. This position automatically made him also an associate justice of the first Supreme Court of the Republic. In 1838 he was made a member of the commission to lay out the boundary line between Texas and the United States. Early in 1839 Corzine presided over the only treason trial in San Augustine County, in which thirty Mexicans were tried for participating in the Córdova Rebellion.qv Corzine died on February 8, 1839, in San Augustine and was buried there. He and his wife, Sarah, had three children.

BIBLIOGRAPHY: Adele B. Looscan, "Harris County, 1822–1845," *Southwestern Historical Quarterly* 18–19 (October 1914–July 1915). *Telegraph and Texas Register,* February 20, 1839. Texas House of Representatives, *Biographical Directory of the Texan Conventions and Congresses, 1832–1845* (Austin: Book Exchange, 1941). Vertical Files, Barker Texas History Center, University of Texas at Austin.
Edd Miller

COS, MARTÍN PERFECTO DE (1800–1854). Martín Perfecto de Cos, Mexican general, the son of attorney Martín Perfecto de Cos, was born in Veracruz in 1800. He became a cadet in the Mexican army in 1820, a lieutenant in 1821, and a brigadier general in 1833. In September 1835 Cos was sent by Antonio López de Santa Annaqv to investigate the refusal of Texans at Anahuac to pay duties imposed after Santa Anna had established himself as president of Mexico with centralized powers (see ANAHUAC DISTURBANCES). General Cos dispersed the legislature of Coahuila and Texas,qv then in session at

General Cos, *possibly after William H. Croome, ca. 1848. Engraving. 2¼″ × 2″. From John Frost,* Pictorial History of Mexico and the Mexican War . . . *(Philadelphia: Charles Desilver, 1869), p. 169. Courtesy Benson Latin American Collection, University of Texas at Austin.*

Monclova, landed 300 men at Matagorda Bay, established headquarters in San Antonio, and declared his purpose of ending resistance in Texas. He intended to arrest several Texas critics of Santa Anna. His demands were resisted; a force of Texans under Stephen F. Austin and Edward Burleson qqv held the Mexican troops in the siege of Bexar qv until Cos surrendered after an attack led by Benjamin R. Milam qv in December 1835. Cos and his men were released on their pledge not to oppose further the Constitution of 1824.qv Texans believed the pledge was broken when Cos returned in the spring of 1836 to command a column in the attack on the Alamo. On April 21, 1836, he reached San Jacinto with reinforcements, crossing Vince's Bridge just before the Texans destroyed it. He was taken prisoner by Sam Houston qv in the general surrender and later released, after which he returned to Mexico and in the Mexican War qv commanded a post at Tuxpan. Cos died in Minatitlán, Vera Cruz, on October 1, 1854, while serving as commandant general and political chief of the Tehuantepec territory.

BIBLIOGRAPHY: Hubert Howe Bancroft, *History of the North Mexican States and Texas* (2 vols., San Francisco: History Company, 1886, 1889). Alwyn Barr, *Texans in Revolt: The Battle for San Antonio, 1835* (Austin: University of Texas Press, 1990). Claudia Hazlewood

COST, TEXAS. Cost is on State Highway 97 six miles west of Gonzales in central Gonzales County. It formed as a community when German settlers began arriving in the area during the 1890s. The community was first known as Oso, but its name was changed to Cost when its post office was established in 1897 in Samuel C. Hindman's store. The first shot in the war for Texas independence (*see* TEXAS REVOLUTION) was fired a mile east of the site of Cost on October 2, 1835. In downtown Cost, on March 14, 1937, Governor James Allred qv dedicated a monument commemorating this event. The first business in the original settlement was a general store opened by pioneer rancher J. B. Wells for employees on his 10,000-acre ranch to the west. A saloon followed, but both it and the store were closed by 1890. An influx of German cotton farmers led to the need for a cotton gin, and in 1892 William Muenzler moved his gin from Cummins Creek in Fayette County to Oso. This gin continued as a Muenzler family operation until 1923, when it was purchased by W. F. Gandre. The Gandre family closed it in 1950, when cotton was no longer significant to the area as a cash crop.

From 1895 until the 1920s the community always had a physician living there. In 1896 Adolph Tolle opened a blacksmith shop, which was sold to R. C. Schauer in 1902; it was eventually converted into a garage that operated until the 1960s. Another garage was operated at the community by Paul Muenzler from 1928 until the onset of World War II.qv After the war he operated on that site the Cost Lumber Company until it closed in the late 1950s. A public school served the community from 1897 until 1959, when the local population declined, and Cost students were transferred to the Gonzales schools. A telephone line connected Gonzales and Cost in 1909. Methodist, Lutheran, Roman Catholic, and Assembly of God church members attended services in nearby Monthalia. A Baptist church met in Cost from 1916 until 1952. An important part of the community's social life centered on the Cost Hot Well, a strong-flowing, artesian sulfur spring that was developed into a spa in 1925. It was popular until sometime after World War II. The most significant event in the community's history was the 1939 organization there of the highly successful Guadalupe Valley Electric Cooperative by 100 charter members. The cooperative's headquarters was later moved to Gonzales. By the 1990s cotton farming in the area had been superseded by poultry and livestock farming and by the production of feed grains. The 1990 population of Cost was reported as sixty-two, and its businesses included a grocery store, a feed and fertilizer store, a welding shop, an oilfield chemical supply house, and a field office of the Guadalupe Valley Telephone Cooperative.

BIBLIOGRAPHY: Allen H. Chessher, *Let There Be Light: A History of the Guadalupe Valley Electric Cooperative* (San Antonio: Naylor Company, 1964). Gonzales County Historical Commission, *History of Gonzales County* (Dallas: Curtis, 1986).
Esther and Raymond Juengermann

COSTLEY, MICHAEL (1809–1837). Michael Costley, soldier and Texas Ranger, was born in 1809. Though he may have moved to Texas as early as 1827, his arrival was more likely in the spring of 1832. He settled first in the San Augustine area and then in Nacogdoches. He served in the Texas army from June 22 to September 22, 1836, and, under Hugh McLeod,qv patrolled the Bexar Road between the Angelina and Neches rivers in the summer of 1836. Costley recruited a company of mounted rangers called the First Company of Texas Rangers qv and served as its captain from September 11 to December 11, 1836, when Sam Houston qv discharged him and his company for refusing to obey orders. In 1836 or 1837 he founded the town of Douglass in Nacogdoches County. Costley had married Mahalah Mussett, daughter of William Mussett, by bond (i.e., by written agreement in the absence of a priest) on January 18, 1827, probably in Missouri, and they had a son. Without obtaining a divorce, Costley married Elizabeth Reed, daughter of Jacob Reed, in September 1837 in Nacogdoches County, and they had two sons. Costley's bigamy set the stage for years of litigation among his heirs. He died of a pistol wound inflicted by W. R. D. Speight, the first district clerk of Nacogdoches County, on November 16, 1837. At the time of Costley's death, he and Joseph S. Able were operating a store, Costley and Able, in Douglass.

BIBLIOGRAPHY: Robert Bruce Blake Research Collection, Steen Library, Stephen F. Austin State University; Barker Texas History Center, University of Texas at Austin; Texas State Archives, Austin; Houston Public Library, Houston. Carolyn Reeves Ericson, *Nacogdoches, Gateway to Texas: A Biographical Directory* (2 vols., Fort Worth: Arrow-Curtis Printing, 1974, 1987). Thomas L. Miller, *Bounty and Donation Land Grants of Texas, 1835–1888* (Austin: University of Texas Press, 1967). Amelia W. Williams and Eugene C. Barker, eds., *The Writings of Sam Houston, 1813–1863* (8 vols., Austin: University of Texas Press, 1938–43; rpt., Austin and New York: Pemberton Press, 1970).
L. W. Kemp

COTLAND, TEXAS. Cotland was a post office in west central Newton County. It was started in 1850, presumably near the plantation of Thomas Stuart McFarland,qv who sold his San Augustine County home (also called Cotland) to Jacob Garrett in 1838 and moved to what was to become Newton County. After first settling at Belgrade, he relocated near the site of Bleakwood. The Cotland post office served Newton County residents until 1860. Bleakwood was granted a post office seven years later.

BIBLIOGRAPHY: Newton County Historical Commission, *Crosscuts: An Anthology of Memoirs of Newton County Folk* (Austin: Eakin, 1984).
Robert Wooster

COTNER, ROBERT CRAWFORD (1906–1980). Robert Crawford Cotner, history professor, son of Thomas Ewing and Nina Dot (Crawford) Cotner, was born at Cleveland, Ohio, on November 1, 1906. He earned his B.A. from Baylor University (1928), his M.A. from Brown University (1929), and his Ph.D. from Harvard University (1959). Before beginning his career at the University of Texas in 1940, he was associated with Midland High School (1929–31), Henderson State College in Arkansas (1931–35), and Stetson University in Florida (1935–40). He taught social and urban history at the University of Texas from 1940 until his retirement in 1977, moving from instructor (1940), to assistant professor (1949), associate professor (1960), professor (1969), and professor emeritus. He was a visiting professor at the University of Virginia in the summer of 1957 and at the University of Kentucky in the summer of 1965.

Cotner's scholarly contributions were many. Of most enduring value were his publications on Texas governor James Stephen Hogg.qv In 1951 he edited Hogg's papers to produce *Addresses and State Papers of James S. Hogg,* and in 1959 his *James Stephen Hogg: A Biography,* considered the standard work on Hogg, was published. The book won the Summerfield G. Roberts Award of the Sons of the Republic of Texasqv and an award from the American Association for State and Local History. Governor Price Daniel, Sr.,qv gave a reception at the Governor's Mansionqv on June 8, 1959, to launch the biography of Hogg, and Cotner displayed in his office a photograph of Vice President Lyndon B. Johnsonqv presenting a copy of the biography to President John F. Kennedy. Cotner also edited some ten books and wrote numerous chapters in books, articles, and book reviews in scholarly journals. In 1960 he was named a fellow of the Texas State Historical Association.qv He was a member of the Texas Institute of Lettersqv and at different times president of the East Texas Historical Association and the West Texas Historical Association.qqv

In addition, he served on the membership committees of the Western Historical Association, Southern Historical Association, and Southwestern Social Science Association; on the program committees of the Organization of American Historians and the East Texas Historical Association; on the executive committee of the Southern Historical Association; on the board of directors of the East Texas Historical Association; and as book review editor for the *Southwestern Historical Quarterly*qv and the *West Texas Historical Association Year Book.* In 1979 the East Texas Historical Association honored him with the Ralph W. Steenqv Service Award, and in 1957 the Texas Heritage Foundation awarded him its National Medal for his contributions to scholarship. As a teacher he developed innovative history courses and had an important influence on several generations of students. Cotner died at his home in Austin on September 23, 1980. He was a Baptist. He was survived by his wife Elizabeth (Breihan), a son, a daughter, and a grandchild.

Norman D. Brown

COTONAME INDIANS. In the second half of the eighteenth century the Cotoname (Catanamepaque, Cotomane, Cotonan) Indians lived on both sides of the Rio Grande below the sites of Camargo and future Rio Grande City, where they were sometimes called Carrizo, a Spanish name applied to many Coahuiltecan groups along the Rio Grande below Laredo. In 1886 a few Cotoname Indians were still living at La Noria Ranch in southern Hidalgo County and at Las Prietas in northern Tamaulipas. At that time the ethnologist A. S. Gatschet was able to obtain a short Cotoname vocabulary which demonstrated that this group spoke a Coahuiltecan language.

BIBLIOGRAPHY: Frederick Webb Hodge, ed., *Handbook of American Indians North of Mexico* (2 vols., Washington: GPO, 1907, 1910; rpt., New York: Pageant, 1959). Gabriel Saldivar, *Los Indios de Tamaulipas* (Mexico City: Pan American Institute of Geography and History, 1943). J. R. Swanton, *Linguistic Material from the Tribes of Southern Texas and Northeastern Mexico* (Washington: Smithsonian Institution, 1940). Cyrus Thomas and John R. Swanton, *Indian Languages of Mexico and Central America and Their Geographical Distribution* (Washington: GPO, 1911).

Thomas N. Campbell

COTTAM, CLARENCE (1899–1974). Clarence Cottam, biologist and conservationist, son of Thomas P. and Emmaline (Jarvis) Cottam, was born in St. George, Utah, on January 1, 1899. He was raised in this rural community and worked as a farm and ranch hand. His concern for wildlife led him to dedicate himself to wildlife research and conservation. He attended Dixie College in 1919–20 and the University of Utah in the summer of 1923; he graduated A.B. from Brigham Young University in 1926 and received a master's degree there in 1927. While there he was principal of the Alamo, Nevada, schools. From 1927 to 1929 he was instructor of biology at Brigham Young. In 1929 Cottam became a junior biologist on the research staff of the United States Biological Survey in Washington, and by 1934 he was senior biologist in charge of food-habits research. He earned his Ph.D. at George Washington University in 1936. In 1939 the United States Biological Survey became the United States Fish and Wildlife Service, and Cottam eventually served as chief of wildlife research in the agency. He became assistant director in 1945 and remained in that position for eight years. In 1954, after twenty-five years of government work, he returned to Brigham Young University as professor of biology and the dean of the College of Biological and Agricultural Sciences. A year later he agreed to help organize and to become the head of the Rob and Bessie Welder Wildlife Foundation and Refugeqv in Sinton, Texas, where he served as director until his death.

Cottam was involved in conservational causes and affiliated with several conservational and humanitarian organizations. In 1969 he fought against the use of a highly toxic pesticide in Texas, arguing that it would harm the Gulf Coast bays. He also helped research the long-range effects of DDT and campaigned for the control of its use. He was involved in the establishment of the Island National Seashore on the Gulf of Mexico and the expansion of the Arkansas Wildlife Refuge. He was an advocate of the cause to save the whooping crane,qv bald eagle, brown pelican, and other endangered species. Among his many memberships, Cottam belonged to the Wildlife Society of America (president, 1949–50), the National Parks Association (president or chairman of the board, 1960–74), the Outdoor Writers Association of America, the Ecological Society of America, the Soil Conservation Society of America, the American Forestry Association, the Society for Range Management, the National Academy of Sciences, the Texas Academy of Science,qv and the Texas Ornithological Societyqv (president, 1957). His published works include *Food Habits of North American Diving Ducks* (1939), *Insects: A Guide to Familiar American Insects* (1951), *Whitewings: The Life History, Status, and Management of the White-winged Dove* (1968), and numerous magazine articles for such periodicals as *Audubon Magazine, National Parks Magazine,* and *Living Wilderness.* Cottam's honors include the National Audubon Society's Distinguished Service Award (1961) and a citation from the National Wildlife Federation in 1964 for his work in conservation. He also received similar recognition from the Audubon Naturalist Society, Brigham Young University, and the Department of the Interior.

On May 20, 1920, Cottam married Margery Brown; they had four daughters. Cottam was a Mormon. He died on March 30, 1974, and was buried at Orem, Utah.

BIBLIOGRAPHY: *New York Times,* April 3, 1974. *Something about the Author* (Detroit: Gale Research, 1981). *Who's Who in the South and Southwest,* Vol. 11.

Lauren Williams

COTTEN, FRED RIDER (1894–1974). Fred Rider Cotten, businessman and local historian, the son of J. T. and Sarah Ida (Rider) Cotten, was born on June 21, 1894, in Weatherford, Texas. After graduating from Weatherford High School he attended the University of Texas, where he was managing editor of the *Daily Texan.*qv He graduated from UT and remained in Austin to study law, then took a job as a legal aid in the Department of Justice in Washington. Among his first assignments was an investigation of the German torpedoing of the British luxury liner Lusitania in 1915.

When his father died, Cotten abandoned his legal career and returned to Weatherford to assume the responsibilities of managing his father's undertaking business and furniture store. He rarely sent out bills, never imposed a carrying charge on his customers, and often accept one-dollar payments from families who drove into town to update their accounts. He refused to sell furniture that he believed was cheaply made and would not last. For years he was the Democratic chairman of Precinct Four in Weatherford. He was city commissioner during the Great Depressionqv and worked diligently to establish a local public works authority. His efforts enabled many persons to find employment during the 1930s and provided the city with newly paved streets. As a city official Cotten borrowed money to help provide facilities the town needed and secured the loans by his personal note. It reportedly took him twenty years to retire the debt he incurred during the depression years.

Cotten's interest in his native town extended to its history as well. Gradually his library grew to include a vast amount of literature on the history of Texas and on the growth of Weatherford and Parker County. In 1962 he was elected president of the Texas State Historical Association.qv At various other times he held the presidencies of the West Texas Historical Association,qv the Texas Funeral Directors' Association, the Texas Retail Furniture Dealers' Association, and the Texas Swine Breeders' Association. Cotten died on September 7, 1974, at Harris Hospital in Fort Worth and was buried in Weatherford. He was survived by his wife, Mary (Akard), a son, and a daughter.

BIBLIOGRAPHY: Joe B. Frantz, "In Memoriam: Fred R. Cotten," *Southwestern Historical Quarterly* 78 (April 1975). *Southwestern Historical Quarterly*, Clippings, July 1973.   *David Minor*

COTTEN, GODWIN BROWN MICHAEL (ca. 1791–?). Godwin B. M. Cotten was born about 1791. He may have been the G. B. Cotten who was an aide of José Álvarez de Toledo y Duboisqv in the battle of the Medina Riverqv on August 18, 1813. At any rate, he published the Louisiana *Gazette* in New Orleans in 1815 and the Mobile *Gazette* at Mobile, Alabama, from 1816 to 1819. He arrived in Stephen F. Austin'sqv Texas colony on August 10, 1829, and on September 25 at San Felipe de Austin began publication of the Texas *Gazette*.qv In 1830 he agreed to publish in his paper all orders, decrees, and advertisements of the ayuntamientoqv of San Felipe in return for two town lots. During the paper's first year Cotten suspended publication for nearly three months in order to release his equipment for printing the *Translation of the Laws, Orders and Contracts of Colonization, from January, 1821, up to This Time, in Virtue of Which Col. Stephen Austin Has Introduced and Settled Immigrants in Texas, with an Explanatory Introduction*—one of the earliest pamphlets, if not the earliest one, printed in Texas. He sold his paper in January 1831 and in March of that year had a log house at the mouth of the Brazos for the entertainment of travelers. He also acquired title to a league of land on the west bank of the Colorado River about five miles southwest of the site of present Bay City in what is now Matagorda County on December 15, 1830. He resumed publication of the *Gazette* in December 1831 and in early 1832 moved the paper to Brazoria, where it was issued as the *Texas Gazette and Brazoria Commercial Advertiser*.qv In July 1832 Cotten sold the paper to Daniel W. Anthony,qv but he continued his work in Anthony's employ through January 1833. On March 27, 1834, he announced his intention to practice law in Austin's colony.

BIBLIOGRAPHY: Eugene C. Barker, "Notes on Early Texas Newspapers," *Southwestern Historical Quarterly* 21 (October 1917). Douglas C. McMurtrie, "Pioneer Printing in Texas," *Southwestern Historical Quarterly* 35 (January 1932). Ike H. Moore, "The Earliest Printing and First Newspaper in Texas," *Southwestern Historical Quarterly* 39 (October 1935).

COTTINGHAM, IRVIN ALEXANDER (1866–1934). Irvin Alexander Cottingham, civil engineer, the son of James and Margaret Cottingham, was born at St. Mary's, Texas, on October 14, 1866. After his graduation from the Agricultural and Mechanical College of Texas (now Texas A&M University) in 1886, he settled in Houston, where he began work as a civil engineer. He was an assistant engineer for the Southern Pacific Railroad in 1889, division engineer for the Galveston, Harrisburg and San Antonio Railway until 1904, and engineer and assistant general manager of the Houston and Texas Central Railway from 1904 to 1916; from 1916 to 1918 he was in charge of valuation work for the Sunset-Central Lines. He was subsequently engaged in private practice and consulting for the Southern Pacific lines in Texas and Louisiana. He retired in 1932. Cottingham married Hester Kyle in 1892, and the couple had six children. He died on November 8, 1934.

BIBLIOGRAPHY: Houston Press Club, *Men of Affairs of Houston and Environs* (Houston: Coyle, 1913). *Who Was Who in America*, Vol. 1.   *Diana J. Kleiner*

COTTLE, GEORGE WASHINGTON (1811–1836). George Washington Cottle, early Texas colonist and Alamo defender, son of Jonathan and Margaret Cottle, may have been born in Tennessee or in Hurricane Township, Missouri, in 1811. His parents came to Texas on July 6, 1829, to settle in Green DeWitt's colonyqv on the Lavaca River. He married his first cousin, Eliza Cottle, on November 7, 1830, but the marriage was annulled on October 7, 1831. They had one daughter. Cottle received a league of land at the headwaters of the Lavaca River near Gonzales on September 12, 1832. Records indicate that on January 4, 1835, he married Nancy Curtis Oliver. They had twin sons, born after Cottle's death. When Mexican troops arrived south of Gonzales in September 1835, Cottle was one of the messengers sent to gather reinforcements. He returned to fight in the battle of Gonzalesqv on October 2. In February 1836 he lent a yoke of oxen to Capt. Mathew Caldwell'sqv company. He enlisted in the Gonzales Company under Lt. George C. Kimbellqv on February 24 and rode with thirty-two others to the Alamo on March 1. Cottle was killed on March 6, 1836, at the battle of the Alamo,qv alongside his brother-in-law, Thomas Jackson.qv Cottle County was named for him.

BIBLIOGRAPHY: Carmen Taylor Bennett, *Cottle County, My Dear: Where the 'Pan' Joins the 'Handle'* (Floydada, Texas: Blanco Offset Printing, 1979). Daughters of the American Revolution, *The Alamo Heroes and Their Revolutionary Ancestors* (San Antonio, 1976). Gonzales County Historical Commission, *History of Gonzales County* (Dallas: Curtis, 1986). Mildred Watkins Mears, *Cottle County Scrapbook* (Waco: Texian Press, 1963). Ethel Zivley Rather, "DeWitt's Colony," *Quarterly of the Texas State Historical Association* 8 (October 1904). William S. Speer and John H. Brown, eds., *Encyclopedia of the New West* (Marshall, Texas: United States Biographical Publishing, 1881; rpt., Easley, South Carolina: Southern Historical Press, 1978). Amelia W. Williams, A Critical Study of the Siege of the Alamo and of the Personnel of Its Defenders (Ph.D. dissertation, University of Texas, 1931; rpt., *Southwestern Historical Quarterly* 36-37 [April 1933–April 1934]).   *Paul N. Spellman*

COTTLE COUNTY. Cottle County (A-12), in the rolling prairieland of Northwest Texas below the High Plains, is bordered on the north by Childress County, on the west by Motley County, on the south by King County, and on the east by Foard and Hardeman counties. U.S. highways 62/70 (east to west) and 62/83 (north to south) are its main roads. The county was named for George Cottle,qv who died at the Alamo. Cottle County has an area of 900 square miles; its center point is at 34°05′ north latitude and 100°15′ west longitude, midway between Lubbock and Wichita Falls. The terrain is rough in the west and level in the east. Gray, black, sandy, and loam soils predominate. The county drains through the Pease, Tongue, and Little Wichita rivers. Elevations vary between 1,600 and 2,100 feet above sea level. The average annual rainfall in the county is 22.12 inches. The average minimum temperature in January is 27° F, and the average maximum in July is 97°. The growing season lasts 219 days. The county produces an annual average income of $33 million from cotton, grains, guar, beef cattle, and alfalfa. Irrigated acres total 10,000. The county produces modest amounts of oil—135,489 barrels, for instance, in 1990.

The area that is now Cottle County was occupied by Apache Indians until about 1700, when Comanches moved into the region. Comanches of the Wanderers-Who-Make-Bad-Camps band controlled the area until the 1870s, when they were driven away by the United States Army. The buffalo^{qv} herds that once roamed the area were exterminated by intensive hunting during the mid-1870s. The Texas legislature established Cottle County in 1876 and attached it for administrative purposes to Fannin County until 1887, when it became attached to Childress County.

In the fifteen years between the county's inception and its formal organization, it remained largely a grazing area. Some cattle were apparently brought in from New Mexico, and ranches such as the OX, SMS, and Matador^{qqv} established their headquarters in the area. The census of 1880 showed only twenty-four persons living in Cottle County. Between that year and 1890 the pace of growth quickened with the arrival of such settlers as J. J. McAdams, who had his headquarters at the site of present Paducah, and J. H. Cansler, who had a dugout^{qv} on Buck Creek. In 1886 a post office was established at Ottie Springs, near the present site of Paducah. The census counted fifty farms and ranches in Cottle County in 1890, when the population was 240 and growing.

A killing on the county line in 1889 induced residents to petition for county organization so that the suspect's trial could be held in the county. Cottle County was organized in 1892, with Paducah as county seat; four public school districts were established that year. Cottle County voters supported the Democratic candidate for president in 1892 and continued to support Democrats in national races through 1992, with the single exception of 1928. In 1893 the county's first newspaper, the Paducah *Post*, began to print, and the state legislature authorized a $12,000 bond to build a county jail.

Droughts^{qv} held back early settlers; pioneer H. P. Cook remembered that "it didn't rain enough in 1892, '93, and '94 to wet my shirt." Public-works projects such as the building of a new courthouse and the construction of roads to Crowell, Childress, and Kirkland helped sustain the community. By 1900, 122 farms and ranches were operating in the county and the population had increased to 1,002. The area continued to be dominated by the cattle industry; only 7,758 acres of the county's farmland was classified by the census as "improved" in 1900, while more than 43,000 cattle were counted in Cottle County that year. Between 1900 and 1930 the farming sector of the county developed rapidly, however, as an expansion of cotton culture^{qv} brought hundreds of new farmers. In 1890 only fifty acres of Cottle County land had been planted in cotton, but the building of a gin in the county in 1898–99 indicated local interest in the crop; farmers no longer had to travel to the gin at Quanah, some forty-five or fifty miles away in Hardeman County. In 1900 cotton was planted on 749 acres of Cottle County; in 1910, more than 17,000. Cotton farming in the county particularly accelerated between 1910 and 1930; in 1920, almost 45,500 acres was planted in cotton, and by 1930 cotton cultivation had expanded to 133,467 acres.

County farmers also moved into other areas of agricultural production during this time. Wheat culture^{qv} expanded from only 100 acres in 1900 to almost 11,500 acres in 1929; sorghum culture^{qv} also became important for local farmers. By 1929, almost 131,300 acres of cropland was harvested in the county. Poultry production^{qv} also began to become significant for the county's economy; by 1929, almost 44,000 chickens were counted on local farms, and that year Cottle County farmers sold almost 132,000 dozen eggs. Thousands of fruit trees were also planted in the area during this period. More than 7,500 fruit trees were growing in the county by 1920, producing mainly peaches but also pears, plums, and apples.

This economic development of the county during the early twentieth century was aided and encouraged by a growing transportation network. Auto roads between Paducah, Childress, and Matador were completed by 1910, making the movement of people and products easier. Prospects for the county were enhanced in 1909, when the Quanah, Acme and Pacific Railroad reached the county. The county's first hard-surfaced road was built in 1913 from Paducah to Dunlap.

Cottle County grew considerably between 1900 and 1930, as the number of farms steadily increased. The census counted 506 farms in the county in 1910, 686 in 1920, 832 in 1925, and 1,047 in 1930. The population rose from 1,002 in 1900 to 4,396 in 1910, 6,901 in 1920, and 9,395 in 1930. This trend was reversed during the 1930s by the Great Depression and the Dust Bowl.^{qqv} Cotton production in the county plunged; by 1940, only about 59,000 acres was devoted to the crop. About one-third of the county's farmers were forced out of business during this period, and by 1940 only 700 farms remained in Cottle County. Unfortunates sometimes sought shelter in the county jail, and everyone deplored the dust storms. Lyrical tributes to "The Beautiful Dust" appeared in the Paducah *Post*: "The dust, the dust, the beautiful dust; on the evil and on the just, From the North and from the South; in the eyes, the nose, the mouth . . . Bear it calmly since you must . . . Wear it bravely as a crown. Ope' your mouth and gulp it down." Farmers and other residents received some help from New Deal recovery measures; some women were paid for sewing done at WPA Sewing Rooms, for example. Nevertheless the local economy was battered, and more than 20 percent of the county's residents left. By 1940, only 7,072 people remained.

After the 1940s the mechanization of agriculture combined with other factors, such as the severe droughts of the 1950s, to continue depopulating the area. The cotton crop produced only 3,227 bales of cotton in 1953, and by 1960 only 387 farms were operating in the county. The county's population dropped to 6,099 by 1950, to 4,207 by 1960, to 3,204 by 1970, and 2,947 by 1980; in 1990 residents numbered 2,247. Despite this decline, however, the county was moderately prosperous in the late 1980s. Paducah, the county's only sizable town, is still the county seat. In cooperation with King County, Cottle County holds a rodeo and livestock show every April; in January a Cottle County calf and pig show is held.

BIBLIOGRAPHY: Carmen Taylor Bennett, *Our Roots Grow Deep: A History of Cottle County* (Floydada, Texas: Blanco Offset Printing, 1970).
John Leffler

COTTON, GILES (ca. 1814–?). Giles (Jiles) Cotton, former slave and member of the Texas legislature, was born around 1814 in South Carolina. He may have been the son of a white plantation overseer and a slave mother. He arrived in Texas around 1852 and became a favored slave of Logan Stroud of Limestone County. He worked as a teamster transporting goods from the port of Galveston to the Limestone area. Sometime after emancipation he moved to the area of Calvert in Robertson County, where he worked as a farmer. Voters from Robertson, Leon, and Freestone counties elected him to the Texas House of Representatives in 1870. Although he reportedly missed many sessions of the Twelfth Legislature, he served on the Agriculture and Stock Raising Committee and supported legislation that made Calvert the Robertson County seat. The United States census for 1870 reported that Cotton and his wife, Rachel, could neither read nor write and lived with their seven children. Cotton apparently died before 1880.

BIBLIOGRAPHY: J. Mason Brewer, *Negro Legislators of Texas and Their Descendants* (Dallas: Mathis, 1935; 2d ed., Austin: Jenkins, 1970). Walter F. Cotton, *History of Negroes of Limestone County from 1860 to 1939* (Mexia, Texas: Chatman and Merriwether, 1939). Doris Hollis Pemberton, *Juneteenth at Comanche Crossing* (Austin: Eakin Press, 1983). Merline Pitre, *Through Many Dangers, Toils and Snares: The Black Leadership of Texas, 1868–1900* (Austin: Eakin, 1985).
Paul M. Lucko

COTTON, TEXAS. Cotton, on the headwaters of Bedias Creek three miles northeast of Bedias in northeastern Grimes County, was named for the principal crop of the region. Settlement in the vicinity of the townsite began in the mid-1830s. In the late 1840s a small frame schoolhouse, which doubled for many years as the meetinghouse of the First Baptist Church of Bedias, was constructed on nearby Simes

Creek. In 1890 the community's first cotton gin was established by R. S. Callender, who also operated a general store. Mail was delivered to the community over a rural route from Bedias. In 1900 Cotton reported a population of fifteen. By 1936 it reported one business and a population of twenty-five. The number of residents continued to be reported at that level through the late 1940s, after which no population statistics were available.

BIBLIOGRAPHY: Grimes County Historical Commission, *History of Grimes County, Land of Heritage and Progress* (Dallas: Taylor, 1982).

Charles Christopher Jackson

COTTON BOWL. The Cotton Bowl is the stadium in which the annual Cotton Bowl Classic football game is played. The stadium, located in Fair Park qv in Dallas, is the second stadium at the site. In the 1890s unsuccessful attempts were made to build a wooden stadium there to host a world-championship prizefight. In 1921 the first stadium, with a seating capacity of 15,000, was constructed on the site of the future Cotton Bowl and named Fair Park Football Stadium. It was used for community events and football games, and was never filled until it sold out for the 1923 football game between Baylor and Southern Methodist University. In 1930 ground was broken for the construction of the Fair Park Bowl on the site of the Fair Park Football Stadium. The 46,000-seat stadium was completed in time for a football game on October 26, 1930. The cut-and-fill construction lowered the playing surface twenty-four feet below the original ground level. The dirt that was removed was placed around the field, so that the back seats were fifteen feet above the street. In addition to football games the stadium was used for such events as the Cavalcade of History during the Texas Centennial qv Exposition (1936), an outdoor play with 250 actors. That same year President Franklin D. Roosevelt spoke to 40,000 in the stadium. A milestone in the history of the stadium occurred on January 1, 1937, when the first Cotton Bowl Classic was played before a crowd of 17,000 between the Texas Christian University Horned Frogs and Marquette University; TCU won 16 to 6. The Cotton Bowl Classic, which reflected the new name the stadium had acquired, was the idea of J. Curtis Sanford, a Dallas oilman who lost $6,000 on the first game. Within three years the game was being called "Sanford's Folly," and in 1940 the 12,000 paid customers were not enough to prevent Sanford's losing $20,000. In 1941 Sanford arranged a partnership with the Southwest Conference,qv and the game between Texas A&M and Fordham University sold 45,507 tickets. After this first sellout, every subsequent game was sold out. World War II qv did not suspend the Cotton Bowl, as it did some other Dallas events. In 1944 a team composed of soldiers from Randolph Field in San Antonio played the University of Texas Longhorns. The score was the first tie at the Cotton Bowl Classic.

With the growing popularity of the Cotton Bowl games, the stadium was in need of expansion and renovation. Its design made maintenance difficult. Heavy rain during a tropical storm in 1947 washed dirt onto the playing field. The previous year Mayor Woodall Rogers had called for the sale of bonds to support renovation. These $100 bonds matured in thirty years and allowed the purchaser to buy reserved tickets for any event at the Cotton Bowl during that time. The proceeds virtually rebuilt the old stadium in 1948 and added 21,431 seats, bringing the seating capacity to 67,431. The next year more improvements increased the seating capacity to 75,504 and added new team dressing rooms, a three-story press box, and an automatic lawn-sprinkler system.

The opening baseball game of the Texas League qv season, attendance 53,748, was played at the Cotton Bowl on April 11, 1950, and pitted the Dallas Eagles against Tulsa. In 1952 the Dallas Texans played in the Cotton Bowl after Dallas was awarded a National Football League franchise, but poor fan support led to the team's moving to Baltimore the following year. Two other professional football teams, the Dallas Cowboys qv and an American Football League team named the Dallas Texans,qv had the Cotton Bowl as their home stadium at one time. The AFL Dallas Texans played there from 1960 through 1962 before moving to Kansas City. The Dallas Cowboys were at the bowl from their formation in 1960 until Texas Stadium was completed in Irving in 1971. On January 1, 1967, in the National Football League championship game, the Cowboys lost to the Green Bay Packers at the Cotton Bowl, 34 to 27.

The Cotton Bowl, however, is best known for the Cotton Bowl Classic, which until the demise of the Southwest Conference matched the winner of that conference with a highly rated team from some other conference or an independent team such as Notre Dame. Beginning in 1937, the game was been a showcase for future NFL stars and for winners of prestigious college football awards. The 1937 game featured Texas Christian University quarterbacks Sammy Baugh, later Washington Redskins quarterback and a member of the NFL Hall of Fame, and Davey (Robert David) O'Brien,qv who won the Heisman trophy in 1938 and later played for the Philadelphia Eagles. In 1946 Bobby (Robert Lawrence) Layne,qv future quarterback of the Detroit Lions, led Texas over Missouri. The 1948 game was the first to match undefeated and nationally ranked teams—Southern Methodist University (9–0–1), ranked number 3, and Penn State (9–0–0), ranked number 4. A black member of the Penn State team was the first African American to play in the Cotton Bowl. The 1954 game is best remembered for the off-the-bench tackle of Rice's Dickie Maegle by Alabama's Tommy Lewis. Syracuse University (10–0) and the University of Texas (9–1) played in 1960, the first time a national championship was decided by the Cotton Bowl Classic. The 1970 game was the outstanding bowl game of the season. Notre Dame (8–1–1), which had had a policy since 1925 of playing no postseason games, agreed to play the number-one-ranked University of Texas (10–0). Texas scored with a minute and eight seconds left to win both the game and the Longhorns' second national championship. The 1971 game was a rematch between Texas (10–0) and Notre Dame (9–1). Joe Theismann led the Irish to a 24-to-11 win and ended UT's thirty-game winning streak.

Heisman Trophy winners who have played in the Cotton Bowl Classic are Doak Walker (1949), Ernie Davis (1961), Roger Staubach (1964), John Cappilletti (Penn State, 1973), Bob Golic (Notre Dame, 1978), Bo Jackson (Auburn, 1986), Tim Brown (Notre Dame, 1988), and Troy Aikman (UCLA, 1989). Outland Trophy winners have been Bud Brooks (Arkansas, 1954), Tommy Nobis (UT, 1965), Lloyd Phillips (Arkansas, 1966), Bill Stanfill (Georgia, 1968), and Dave Rimington (Nebraska, 1981–82). Lombardi Award winners in the Cotton Bowl have been Walt Patulski (Notre Dame, 1971), Wilson Whitley (Houston, 1976), Kenneth Sims (UT, 1981), Dave Rimington (Nebraska, 1982), and Tony DeGrate (UT, 1984). Winners of the Walter Camp Award have been Ken MacAfee (Notre Dame, 1977) and Doug Flutie (Boston College, 1984). Davey O'Brien Award winners who have played in the Cotton Bowl Classic have been Earl Campbell (UT, 1978), Mike Singletary (Baylor, 1981), and Doug Flutie (Boston College, 1985). The Maxwell Award has gone to Davey O'Brien (TCU, 1938), Doak Walker (SMU, 1947), Roger Staubach (Navy, 1963), Tommy Nobis (Texas, 1965), and Doug Flutie (Boston College, 1984). Some others who have played in the Classic and become professional football stars are Kenny Stabler (Alabama, 1968), Tobin Rote (Rice, 1950), Vito "Babe" Parilli (Kentucky, 1952), Jim Brown (Syracuse, 1957), King Hill and Frank Ryan (Rice, 1958), and Joe Montana (Notre Dame, 1977).

The Classic was first televised nationwide in 1953, and in 1958 a long-term contract with CBS sports was signed, the same year the Cotton Bowl Parade was first held. The parade was televised by CBS for the first time in 1964. By 1992 it had become an important Dallas event, with an attendance downtown of 150,000 and a television audience of twenty million. That year the parade had forty-seven floats, six helium balloons, and ten marching bands, with a total participation of 5,000. The next year, however, the parade was canceled because lost television coverage had caused a loss of financial support from businesses.

In addition to the Cotton Bowl Classic the annual football game between the University of Texas and the University of Oklahoma is played in the stadium. Southern Methodist University played its home games there until Texas Stadium was built. By the 1990s the Cotton Bowl was supported by Mobil Oil and was called the Mobil Cotton Bowl Classic. In 1993–94 the Cotton Bowl was renovated, after a great deal of controversy. The $2.8 million expense was authorized by the city of Dallas to prepare for hosting part of the 1994 World Cup Soccer Tournament. It required the removal of some seats to expand the field and the replacement of the artificial turf with natural grass.

Sporting events have not been the only entertainment at the Cotton Bowl. Every Independence Day a display of fireworks has been held. General Douglas MacArthur spoke before a crowd in the bowl. Such religious leaders as Norman Vincent Peale and Billy Graham have spoken there. In addition, in the early days USO shows were performed at the Cotton Bowl. Frank Sinatra and Elvis Presley appeared there, and rock concerts occurred at the bowl into the 1990s.

BIBLIOGRAPHY: Dallas *Morning News*, June 11, 1992. Dallas *Times Herald*, October 12, 1985. Carlton Stowers, *Cotton Bowl Classic: The First Fifty Years* (Dallas: Host Communications, 1986).

Lisa C. Maxwell

COTTON CENTER, TEXAS (Fannin County). Cotton Center is on Farm Road 271 five miles southeast of Bonham in central Fannin County. The community was established in 1912 by George Williams when he built a cotton gin there. Throughout its history the settlement has served as a community center for area farmers. In 1966 it had a store and a cotton gin. In 1990 the population of Cotton Center was estimated at five.

BIBLIOGRAPHY: *Fannin County Folks and Facts* (Dallas: Taylor, 1977). Floy Crandall Hodge, *A History of Fannin County* (Hereford, Texas: Pioneer, 1966).

David Minor

COTTON CENTER, TEXAS (Hale County). Cotton Center is in a cotton-growing area twelve miles southwest of Hale Center in western Hale County. The area was developed in the late 1800s, primarily by ranchers. In 1907 the Plainview line, built through Hale County by the Santa Fe Railroad company, introduced both cash crops and a new wave of settlers arriving primarily from Oklahoma and East Texas. The community came into existence in 1925 with the consolidation of the local Bartonsite, Anchor, and Norfleet schools. In that year J. C. Brown, who is credited with naming the community, laid out a townsite and opened a cotton gin. In 1935 a local post office opened, and the first irrigation well was established. After World War II[qv] irrigation wells proliferated, pumping water from the Ogallala aquifer. On June 2, 1965, a tornado struck Cotton Center, killing one person, injuring three, and destroying several houses. During the 1980s the community was centered around the Cotton Center school system, which at that time served a district of about 130 square miles. In 1984 the community reported seven businesses and a population of 260, though the school district's population was estimated as around 800. In 1990 Cotton Center's population was reported as 205.

BIBLIOGRAPHY: Wilfred C. Bailey, "Cotton Center, Texas, and the Late Agricultural Settlement of the Texas Panhandle and New Mexico," *Texas Journal of Science* 4 (December 30, 1952). Mary L. Cox, *History of Hale County, Texas* (Plainview, Texas, 1937). Robert E. Simmons et al., eds., "Cotton Center: Reflections on the Cultural and Social Development of a West Texas Community," *Hale County History* 10 (1980).

Julia M. Payne

COTTON-COMPRESS INDUSTRY. The cotton-compress industry developed in antebellum Texas[qv] because of the need to lower the cost of transporting cotton on sailing vessels. Before the introduction of power cotton compressors, or hydraulic compressors, workers known as screwmen used screwjacks to pack and stow bulky bales of cotton for shipment by sea. Compressors, which reduced bales received from cotton gins to roughly half their former size, were first acquired in port. By 1860 more than $500,000 had been invested in the industry at Galveston. Despite the innovation, however, workers by 1866 had established at Galveston a Screwmen's Benevolent Association,[qv] which in the 1870s became the largest and strongest labor organization in the city. As cotton culture[qv] spread into the Texas hinterland after the Civil War,[qv] compresses were built in many Texas towns in addition to the port cities. The development of communications and the extension of railroads into the state's cotton-producing regions revolutionized the Texas cotton trade. The compress industry was a major factor in this change because it made the long-distance transportation of cotton by rail economically feasible. Interior cotton markets developed and disrupted the old factorage system. Cotton compression became a major industry in Texas in terms of capital invested and labor employed. Hydraulic compressors replaced screwmen with teams who opened bales received at the warehouse, "spider" men who climbed into the compress to position each bale under its heavy jaws, and others who retied and packed the compressed bales. By World War I[qv] screwmen had largely disappeared.

When the Railroad Commission[qv] came into existence in 1891, it soon provided rules and regulations governing the movement of cotton by rail; thus the cotton-compress industry was one of the first to feel the effects of this regulatory agency. Measures adopted by the commission encouraged overdevelopment of the industry in the interior and intensified a struggle for control of cotton between port and hinterland interests. After the 1920s the geographical growth of the cotton-compress industry in Texas was westward and southward, as cotton culture shifted to the High Plains and the Rio Grande valley, and policies of the Commodity Credit Corporation became a factor in the movement. The most important influence on the industry, however, was the development in the 1890s of processes to compress cotton to a high density at gins and thus eliminate the need for cotton compresses. Cotton was initially compressed in two densities, standard bales for domestic mills at roughly twenty-two pounds per cubic foot and high-density bales for overseas export at roughly thirty-two pounds per cubic foot. Owners of the compressing processes at gins attempted to get the Texas Railroad Commission and the Interstate Commerce Commission to set carload rates for cotton so compressed. The commissions refused to do so because of a belief that such a rate system would revolutionize the cotton trade and result in great losses to small operators in the cotton industry. In the early 1970s, however, the National Cotton Council devised a universal density for a new twenty-four-inch-wide bale at twenty-eight pounds per cubic foot; this density could be used for all purposes. With the adoption of this new standard, gin-manufacturing companies created universal-density presses for packaging, and compressors at warehouses were almost entirely phased out or replaced by gin service. By that time, prospects indicated a continued deterioration of a once-flourishing industry, though as late as 1979 cotton contributed $1 billion to the state economy and made up 10 percent of all agricultural production in Texas.

BIBLIOGRAPHY: Karen G. Britton, *Bale o' Cotton* (College Station: Texas A&M University Press, 1992). Louis Tuffly Ellis, The Texas Cotton Compress Industry: A History (Ph.D. dissertation, University of Texas, 1964). *Fortune*, November, December, 1945. James V. Reese, "Evolution of an Early Texas Union: The Screwmen's Benevolent Association of Galveston, 1866–1891," *Southwestern Historical Quarterly* 75 (October 1971). A. C. Taylor, History of the Screwmen's Benevolent Association (M.A. thesis, University of Texas at Austin, 1968).

L. Tuffly Ellis

COTTON CULTURE. Cotton was first grown in Texas by Spanish missionaries. A report of the missions at San Antonio in 1745 indicates that several thousand pounds of cotton were produced annually, then spun and woven by mission craftsmen. Cotton cultivation was begun by Anglo-American colonists in 1821. In 1849 a census of the cotton production of the state reported 58,073 bales (500 pounds each). In 1852 Texas was in eighth place among the top ten cotton-producing states of the nation. The 1859 census credited Texas with a yield of 431,645 bales. This sharp rise in production in the late 1850s and early 1860s was due at least in part to the removal of Indians, which opened up new areas for cotton production. The Civil War[qv] caused a decrease in production, but by 1869 the cotton crop was reported as 350,628 bales. The introduction of barbed wire[qv] in the 1870s and the building of railroads[qv] further stimulated the industry. In 1879 some 2,178,435 acres produced 805,284 bales. The 1889 census reported 3,934,525 acres producing 1.5 million bales. The cotton crop in 1900 was more than 3.5 million bales from 7,178,915 acres.

Additional factors contributed to the increase in cotton production during the last years of the nineteenth century. A specially designed plow made it possible to break up the thick black sod, and the fertile prairie soil produced as much as one bale per acre in some areas. Beginning in 1872, thousands of immigrants from the Deep South and from Europe poured into the Blackland Prairie of Central Texas and began growing cotton. Some of the newcomers bought small farmsteads, but most worked as tenant farmers or sharecroppers for landowners who controlled spreads as large as 6,000 acres. Cotton planting began in the spring, cultivation occurred during the summer, and harvesting by hand-picking began in late August. Tenants lived in houses on the landowners' property and supplied their own draft animals, tools, and seed; for their year of work, after the cotton was ginned, they received two-thirds of the value of the cotton. The landowner received one-third. Sharecroppers furnished only their labor, while the landowner supplied animals, houses, seed, and tools, and at the end of the cotton season the sharecroppers received half the value of the crop. In both cases tenants and sharecroppers, whether white or black, bought such goods as shoes, medicines, and staple food items from the landowners' commissaries, and the landowners kept the accounts. After the cotton was sold and the accounts settled, the tenant or sharecropper often had little or no hard cash left over. This socially enforced debt peonage, known as the crop-lien system, began after the Civil War and continued in practice until the 1930s.

Increased cotton production led to technological improvements in cotton ginning[qv]—the process of separating cotton fibers from their seeds, cleaning the fibers, and baling the lint for shipment to market. In 1884 Robert S. Munger[qv] of Mexia revolutionized the slow, animal-powered method of "plantation ginning" by devising the faster, automated "system ginning," the process in use today. Cotton compresses, huge machines that reduced 500-pound bales to about half their ginned, or flat-bale, size for convenience in shipping, were constructed along railroad rights-of-way in many towns. The relocation of compresses from port cities such as Galveston to interior cotton-growing areas allowed farmers to sell their crops directly to buyers, who represented textile mills on the East Coast, and the buyers to send the cotton directly to the mills by rail rather than by ship. As telegraph lines spread westward, cotton could be bought and sold on the world market faster than ever before. Not only were the fibers sold, but also the cottonseed was crushed for cooking oil, hulls were converted to cattle feed, and portions of the plant were used to make an early type of plastic.

Technology and a world demand for cotton products, however, could not offset the devastation of the boll weevil.[qv] Farmers first saw the ravaging effect of the weevil, which had spread northward from Mexico, near Corpus Christi during the 1890s. Within a few years, boll weevil damage affected crops throughout Texas and the Cotton Belt, the cotton-growing states of the Deep South. Farmers used calcium arsenate dust and other pesticides to reduce the damage from boll weevils and such pests as the pink bollworm.[qv] Agents of the United States Department of Agriculture and the county extension service, which was begun at Texas A&M College, set up demonstration farms and experiment stations and visited individual farms to show farmers how to improve their crops through better methods of cultivation. A high demand for cotton during World War I[qv] stimulated production, but a drop in prices after the war led many tenants and sharecroppers to abandon farming altogether and move to the cities for better job opportunities.

Factors that caused the decline of cotton production in the state after the 1920s were the federal government's control program, which cut acreage in half, the increase in foreign production (the state had been exporting approximately 85 percent of the total crop), the introduction of synthetic fibers, the tariff, the lack of a lint-processing industry in Texas, and World War II,[qv] which brought a shortage of labor and disrupted commerce. During the Great Depression[qv] of the 1930s, many former tenants and sharecroppers returned to farmwork, but after the United States entered World War II in 1941, farmworkers moved again to the cities for work in war-related industries. After the war, when steel and rubber became available to manufacturers again, farmers began to mechanize their methods of planting, cultivating, and harvesting, thus eliminating the need for tenants and sharecroppers, many of whom did not return to farmwork, and leading to new practices in cotton production that remain in use today. Cotton culture is now characterized by fewer but larger farms, fewer farmworkers and increased use of machines, widespread irrigation,[qv] better pest and weed control methods, alterations to the cotton plant that make it easier to harvest mechanically, and greater cooperation among farmers for marketing.

The most notable change in the production of cotton in the twentieth century was the geographical shift from East and Central Texas to the High Plains[qv] and the Rio Grande valley.[qv] Large production in the latter areas was obtained by extensive use of fertilizers and irrigation. Cotton requires fertile soil for profitable yields. It should be grown only on naturally fertile soils or on soils enriched by inoculated and properly fertilized legumes, barnyard manure, or commercial fertilizer. If the land has any appreciable slope, it should be terraced or contoured to prevent soil erosion and conserve water. Legumes, both summer and winter, play an important part in building up soil fertility and in making cotton production more profitable. The time for planting cotton varies greatly in the different sections of Texas. It is best not to plant until the soil has warmed up enough to ensure quick and uniform germination. Planting too early often results in stunted plants, poor stands, and lower yields. One-half to one bushel of fuzzy seed or from ten to fifteen pounds of delinted seed per acre is usually planted, the amount depending upon the section of the state. West Texas farmers usually plant a smaller quantity of seed per acre than East Texas growers. In the eastern part of the state, cotton is planted mostly on medium-high beds to allow better drainage and to enable the soil to warm up quicker in the spring, while in West Texas and other sections with low rainfall, cotton is planted below the level of the land. The seed are planted from one to two inches deep, the depth depending upon the condition of the soil and the amount of moisture present at planting time. If the plants are too close together they are thinned when they have four to six leaves. Larger yields are obtained in Texas from early thinning than from late thinning. A good spacing is about twelve inches between plants, with one or two plants per hill. This spacing helps to make the plants fruit earlier than would a wider spacing and usually results in higher yields. Cotton should be harvested as early as possible because profits are often greatly reduced by allowing the open cotton to be exposed to the wind and rain. Bad weather causes considerable shedding of the seed cotton from the bolls and lowers the grade and value of the fiber.

Because of a shortage of laborers and the destructiveness of sudden storms, cotton growers in the Lubbock area developed a means of rough-harvesting cotton during the 1920s. The first mechanical harvester consisted of fence posts attached to a draft animal and dragged between rows to dislodge the cotton. The method also broke off bolls, leaves, and sticks and mixed them in the fiber. A wagon or sled with an open groove down the center of the bed proved to be a better device. Horses or mules pulled the sled through the fields to harvest the cotton. Though these methods were faster, however, they both resulted in cotton with a high trash content that brought a much lower price than hand-picked or hand-snapped cotton. Mechanical strippers, which followed, pulled the boll off the plant by means of revolving rollers or brushes. Strippers are used to harvest cotton in the Plains region, where plants are small and grow close to the ground. Another type of harvester is the spindle picker. This machine does not strip cotton from the stalk but pulls locks of cotton from the bolls by means of revolving grooved or barbed spindles. The spindles add moisture to the locks to make them cling to the barbs, and rubber doffers loosen the cotton, which is then blown into a steel basket. Spindle pickers are used in areas of high rainfall where plants grow tall before they are defoliated.

In 1971 Lambert Wilkes of College Station, working with the Texas Agricultural Extension Service[qv] and Cotton Incorporated (a research division of the National Cotton Council), devised the concept of harvesting cotton by module. The steel module builder consists of a box large enough to hold 15,000 pounds (ten to twelve bales) of seed cotton, a cab, and a hydraulic tramper. Cotton from strippers or spindle pickers is emptied directly into the box, and an operator in the cab compresses the cotton with the tramper. When the box is full, a tractor pulls it forward, leaving on the turnrow a "loaf" of cotton that is eight feet high by eight feet wide by thirty-two feet long. The module is covered with a polyethelene tarpaulin and marked for field identification with a harmless spray. A specially designed module mover, a modified flatbed trailer, picks up the module and carries it to the gin, where it is unloaded into the cotton storage yard or directly under the suction telescope for ginning. In 1990, 74 percent of the Texas cotton crop was gathered by strippers and 26 percent by spindle pickers. Seventy percent of that crop was ginned from modules, and 30 percent from trailers.

Machines at the gin clean the trash from the fibers. The lint is baled in a universal-density press that eliminates the need for the old-fashioned compress, and the bale is packaged in synthetic bagging. During the baling process a sample is automatically removed. It may be sent to United States Department of Agriculture classing offices in various parts of the state. Increasingly often, however, high-volume instrument classing occurs at offices near the gins. Once the cotton grower or producer knows the class and value of his cotton, he sells it to buyers around the world by means of computers. A great deal of Texas cotton is exported, especially to Japan and South Korea.

Cotton has many uses besides clothing, linens, draperies, upholstery, and carpet. As early as 1813, nitrocellulose, or gun cotton, for explosives was made from raw cotton. In 1868 the combination of nitrocellulose and camphor made celluloid, an artificial plastic. Contemporary uses include fertilizer, paper, tires, cake and meal for cattle feed, and cottonseed oil for cooking, paint, and lubricants.

See also AGRICULTURE, COTTONSEED INDUSTRY, COTTON COMPRESS INDUSTRY, TEXTILE INDUSTRY, FARM TENANCY, SLAVERY, ANTEBELLUM TEXAS, RECONSTRUCTION, LATE NINETEENTH-CENTURY TEXAS, PROGRESSIVE ERA, *and* TEXAS IN THE 1920S.

BIBLIOGRAPHY: Karen G. Britton, *Bale o' Cotton* (College Station: Texas A&M University Press, 1992). Robert L. Haney, *Milestones: Marking Ten Decades of Research* (College Station: Texas Agricultural Experiment Station, 1989). M. Rebecca Sharpless and Joe C. Yelderman, Jr., eds., *The Texas Blackland Prairie: Land, History, and Culture* (Waco: Baylor University, 1993).

Karen Gerhardt Britton, Fred C. Elliott, and E. A. Miller

COTTONDALE, TEXAS. Cottondale is on Farm Road 2123 ten miles southwest of Decatur in south central Wise County. Its settlement began in the early 1850s, and it is one of the oldest communities in the county. B. F. Banks, a local landowner, offered to provide land to anyone who would build a house or business on it. When one of the early settlers, John Bridges, the town's blacksmith, planted cotton near the banks of Salt Creek and had a plentiful crop, residents began referring to the area as Cotton Valley. The rapid growth of the community prompted a request for postal service, and because the name Cotton Valley was already in use by another town, postal authorities substituted the designation Cottondale. The Cottondale post office was established in 1875. The town's growth was limited both because it was bypassed by the railroads and because area cotton production declined. The Cottondale post office closed in 1912, and the town's only school closed in 1933. Cottondale's population was reported as eighty-seven from the early 1930s through the late 1940s, when it dropped to twenty. In the mid-1960s it rose to seventy-five and was reported at that level in 1967, after which no further statistics were available. The 1984 county highway map showed three churches in the vicinity of Cottondale.

BIBLIOGRAPHY: Rosalie Gregg, ed., *Wise County History* (Vol. 1, n.p: Nortex, 1975; Vol. 2, Austin: Eakin, 1982).

David Minor

COTTON FLAT, TEXAS. Cotton Flat is 3½ miles south of Midland on State Highway 349 in central Midland County. It developed as a farming community when Henry Mayer Halff[qv] broke up the local Quien Sabe Ranch[qv] around 1910 by dividing it into family farms. By 1911 a school district had formed in the area, and Lula Countiss served as teacher. Since the community was unnamed, Countiss and her sister selected Cotton Flat by drawing from possible names they had placed in a hat. The Cotton Flat school building was also used for Sunday school and church services. Later a church was constructed in the community. In the 1940s the Cotton Flat school district was consolidated with the Midland Independent School District. In the 1990s Cotton Flat had a number of residences and a Baptist church and parsonage, a grocery store, a mobile home park, and a service station.

BIBLIOGRAPHY: Midland County Historical Society, *The Pioneer History of Midland County, Texas, 1880–1926* (Dallas: Taylor, 1984).

Julia Cauble Smith

COTTON GIN, TEXAS. Cotton Gin, on Farm Road 1366 twelve miles west of Fairfield in western Freestone County, was established in 1848 near the site of a mule-powered cotton gin built by Dr. James S. Wills. Wills constructed the first store in the community and served as postmaster when the post office was established in 1851. The 1860 census reported that the town had 508 residents. By the 1870s it had a dozen stores, four churches, and a weekly newspaper, the *Herald*. Many residents moved to nearby Mexia when the Houston and Texas Central Railway bypassed Cotton Gin in 1872. The community's population continued to decline as cotton production and ginning decreased in the county. The town had a population of 206 in 1904, and its post office was discontinued four years later. Cotton Gin reported a population of seventy-five from 1945 to about 1960 and sixty by 1964. Its population had dropped to twenty-eight by 1968 and continued to be reported at that level in 1990.

BIBLIOGRAPHY: Freestone County Historical Commission, *History of Freestone County, Texas* (Fairfield, Texas, 1978).

Timothy Palmer

COTTON GINNING. To attract settlers to his colony in Spanish Texas,[qv] empresario[qv] Stephen F. Austin[qv] advertised the richness of the lands along the Brazos and Colorado rivers as suitable for growing cotton as a cash crop. Jared Ellison Groce,[qv] one of the first colonists, moved to Texas from Alabama in January 1822 and bought land on the banks of the Brazos River near the site of present-day Hempstead. Groce's cotton crops far surpassed his expectations. When his son Leonard completed his education in Georgia in 1825, the young man brought home to Texas what is believed to be the first cotton gin used in Austin's colony. By 1828 there were four to five cotton gins in Austin's colony, and by 1860 there were approximately 2,000 in Texas.

Before cotton can be spun into yarn or thread and woven into cloth, the fibers must be separated from their seeds. In 1793 Eli Whitney had invented the cotton gin, a shortened term for "cotton engine." Whitney's patented machine featured a wooden cylinder with iron teeth or spikes, a grooved breastwork of brass or iron through which the spikes could pass but the seeds could not, and a brush cylinder behind the breastwork to clear cotton fibers from the spikes. Ginned seed cotton, or lint, was carried in baskets or allowed to fall into a lint room for storage. The lint was then packed by foot or wooden pestle into a sack and taken to market. H. Ogden Holmes, a South Carolina mechanic, received a patent in 1796 for improvements to the cotton gin that included saw disks passing between flat metal ribs and continuous emptying of the roll box, ginning principles in use today. The cotton gin enabled a worker who had formerly cleaned five pounds of cotton a day by hand to "gin" fifty pounds of cotton a day. The success of the cotton gin led to increased production of short-staple cotton throughout the South.

In Texas, Austin offered land bounties to colonists willing to grow cotton and to blacksmiths and carpenters willing to build cotton gins. As early as 1825 primitive gin manufacturing took place near San Augustine. Gin manufacturing occurred in East Texas for two reasons: cotton production in the area made a local market, and the forests provided ample lumber for the construction of individual cotton gins, or "gin stands." Gin stands were placed on the raised floor of a two-story, frame gin house. In the open space beneath the ginning floor, horses or mules harnessed to levers walked in circles, turning a large horizontal drive wheel. A bevel gear connected the drive wheel to a vertical pulley wheel. A leather belt on the pulley passed through the floor and attached to a smaller pulleys on the gin stand that turned the saw and brush shafts, thus ginning the cotton.

Even with this technology, the ginning process remained labor intensive. Workers brought hand-picked seed cotton from the field to the gin house in baskets, where it was stored in bins or stalls on the ginning floor until time to be ginned. Workers then placed the seed cotton on a flat tray and raked it from the tray into the gin stand. The lint fell through a hole in the floor into the "lint room" at one end of the gin house, where it was stored until ready for baling. Cotton was not baled inside the gin house. Workers carried basketloads of cotton from the lint room to a yard press, which consisted of a wooden screw with a plunger to compress cotton inside the bale box. Mules or horses harnessed to long sweeps walked in a circle around the press to raise and lower the screw. Workers wrapped the bale with flour sacks or old clothes and tied the bale with ropes or iron straps, removed it from the press box, and placed it on the ground. The bales, which weighed between 400 and 500 pounds, were taken by oxcart, by raft, or by steamboat to such ports as Galveston or Velasco, where they were compressed into smaller bales for shipment to textile mills in New England and Great Britain. This process, with modifications to the gin stand, remained commonplace for almost a century.

During the 1870s the Blackland Prairie became the primary cotton-growing region of the state due to the development of a plow that would break up prairie soil, construction of rail lines, and heavy immigration from the Deep South and from Europe. Cotton flourished so well in the Blackland Prairie that customary ginning methods no longer worked. During the 1870s a condenser connected by a flue to the rear of the gin stand added a cleaning function and formed batts of lint for faster baling, but the overall process remained slow.

Robert S. Munger[qv] of Mexia, Limestone County, brought an end to "plantation ginning." Munger's continuous "system ginning," developed between 1883 and 1885, moved, ginned, and baled cotton faster than ever before. His fan-driven pneumatic system suctioned seed cotton by means of a pipe, or "telescope," from the wagon into an air stream. Cotton moved first to a separator, from which it dropped to a distributor, usually a conveyor belt, that carried it to feeders mounted above each of a "battery," or series, of three to five gin stands. Seed was dropped through a conduit or blown through piping to a seed house a few yards from the gin building. After it was cleaned, the lint was carried by air stream through a single flue to a master condenser, as opposed to individual condensers behind each gin stand, where the lint was formed into a batt. The batt then slid down a chute into the charging box of the bale press. Munger brought the bale press indoors, placing a double box on a turntable at one end of the ginning floor. As one box filled with cotton from the condenser, the other box, already full of cotton, was compressed into a bale. Compression in the first indoor presses was achieved by means of a screw, but hydraulic rams soon replaced the screws. The bale was wrapped with jute or burlap bagging, tied with iron straps, and secured with metal buckles. Workers then rolled each bale out of the box, weighed and tagged it for identification, and moved it to the bale dock.

Munger's revolutionary system used steam engines to power the gin plant. After about 1910, diesel engines replaced steam power. As rural electrification[qv] spread, electric motors took the place of diesel engines, and remain the power source used today. Munger kept the gin plant open at Mexia for research purposes but moved to Dallas, where he began manufacturing components for system ginning as early as 1887. In 1899 he united his company with others to form Continental Gin Company in Birmingham, Alabama. Texas remained a manufacturing center for ginning systems and auxiliary equipment until the 1960s, when most companies were absorbed by Continental Gin Company (now Continental Eagle Corporation) of Prattville, Alabama or Lummus Cotton Gin Company (now Lummus Corporation) of Columbus, Georgia.

Individuals could not afford to buy and install Munger's expensive system ginning outfits. Groups of farmers formed cooperative associations to sell stock, build custom gin plants, and offer a variety of services. During ginning season, which lasted from late August through late December, the gin operated eighteen to twenty-four hours a day. Farmers, tenants, and sharecroppers brought their hand-picked cotton to the gin in wagons, often lining the roads for miles. After the cotton was ginned, farmers sold their seed to the ginner to cover ginning costs and their crop to buyers. Cotton buyers cut samples from bales and classed the cotton according to grade, staple length, color, and character (smoothness and cleanliness). Classing determined the quality and thus the value of the cotton. Once the value and price were established, farmers settled their accounts with merchants and bankers. Tenants and sharecroppers settled their accounts with the landowner. During World War II,[qv] many farm workers moved to the cities. Those landowners who continued to grow cotton used tractors and various attachments to mechanize their planting and cultivating methods, transported their cotton to the gin in trailers, and adopted methods of mechanical harvesting. Rough harvesting by means of sleds made of fence slats began during the 1920s on the High Plains, where a shortage of laborers plus rapid changes in weather that could destroy an entire crop within minutes made faster harvesting essential. Based upon the such variables as rainfall, plant height, and degree of defoliation, two types of harvesters became commonly used. Cotton growers in the High Plains relied on "strippers," while those in the Rio Grande valley and Coastal Bend used "spindle pickers."

In 1971 Lambert Wilkes, working for the Texas A&M Agricultural Extension Service and Cotton Incorporated, authored the module concept of harvesting cotton. The module is a steel box on wheels that is placed at the turnrow. Harvesters strip or pick basket loads of cotton and empty them into the boxes, which can hold up to twelve bales. A tramper compresses the seed cotton tightly into the box. When the box is full, a tractor pulls the box away, leaving the module of cotton behind. A tarpaulin is placed over the top of the module. A specially designed truck carries the module to the gin, where it is offloaded intact. Because this cotton is very dirty, a great deal of auxiliary cleaning machinery is added to the ginning process. The press turns out bales of uniform density and size, thus replacing the compress, and automatic bagging machines prepare the bales for shipment. High volume instrument classing now grades cotton with more consistency, and marketing of cotton takes place by computer. However, the purpose of the cotton gin remains unchanged: to ensure the best-quality fiber possible. *See also* COTTON CULTURE, COTTON COMPRESS INDUSTRY, COTTONSEED INDUSTRY.

BIBLIOGRAPHY: Karen G. Britton, *Bale o' Cotton* (College Station: Texas A&M University Press, 1992). M. Rebecca Sharpless and Joe C. Yelderman, Jr., eds., *The Texas Blackland Prairie: Land, History, and Culture* (Waco: Baylor University, 1993). Elizabeth Silverthorne, *Plantation Life in Texas* (College Station: Texas A&M University Press, 1986). Algernon L. Smith, *Continental Gin Company and Its Fifty-two Years of Service* (Birmingham: Continental Gin Company, 1952). Raymond E. White, "Cotton Ginning in Texas to 1861," *Southwestern Historical Quarterly* 61 (October 1957). Karen Gerhardt Britton

COTTON LAKE. Cotton Lake, fed by Cotton Bayou, is 1½ miles south of Cove in northwestern Chambers County (at 29°48′ N, 94°48′ W). It is roughly one mile long and one mile wide at its widest dimensions. The surrounding area of tidal marshland provides an excellent habitat for waterfowl.

COTTON PALACE. After the end of the Civil War,[qv] with the development of the fertile agricultural lands of the Brazos and Bosque valleys, cotton culture[qv] became the mainstay of Waco's economy. It continued as such until World War II.[qv] For many years Waco was recognized as one of the major inland cotton markets in the nation. Consequently, in 1894 plans were laid for a fair and exposition center in Waco to be named the Texas Cotton Palace. A large main building was erected in Padgitt Park, and the first event held there, in November 1894, was highly successful. In January 1895 the building was destroyed by a spectacular fire, and the Cotton Palace was not reactivated until 1910. That year, with an elaborately expanded facility, the project was launched again, and it continued uninterrupted for the following twenty-one years as one of the most successful such expositions in the nation. More than eight million people passed through its turnstiles. On November 3, 1923, attendance hit a one-day record of 117,208. In addition to its spectacular opening-day parades, the exposition featured agricultural and livestock exhibits, competitions and contests of many sorts, art shows, horse racing, athletic events, and operatic and concert attractions. The Queen's Ball was the city's major social occasion each year. In 1931, however, the palace became a casualty of the Great Depression.[qv] In the fall of 1940 the cornerstone from the Cotton Palace's main building, bearing the names of the directors, was mounted upon a monument of gray granite at Lovers Leap in William Cameron Park.

BIBLIOGRAPHY: Lavonia Jenkins Barnes, *Texas Cotton Palace* (Heritage Society of Waco, 1964). *Farm and Ranch*, October 28, 1911. *Gulf Messenger*, October 1894. Dayton Kelley, ed., *The Handbook of Waco and McLennan County, Texas* (Waco: Texian, 1972).
Roger N. Conger

COTTON PATCH BAYOU. Cotton Patch Bayou rises in Pasadena in southeast Harris County (at 29°43′ N, 95°11′ W) and runs northwest for 2½ miles through an urban industrial area to its mouth on Buffalo Bayou, one mile northeast of the Houston Ship Channel[qv] turning basin (at 29°44′ N, 95°12′ W).

COTTONSEED INDUSTRY. Cottonseed, which is separated from cotton lint in the ginning process, is considered a separate crop because of its distinctive uses and economic importance. The processing of cottonseed was one of the earliest large-scale industries to be established in Texas. By 1900 it was the second most important industry in the state in value of product, superseded only by lumber. By the end of the nineteenth century Texas had become the leading processor of cottonseed in the nation. Although the cottonseed industry declined in importance during the twentieth century relative to other industries within the state, it continued to maintain a significant presence. The many uses of cottonseed oil also helped to make Texas an early leader in the manufacture of such food products as cooking oil, vegetable shortening, margarine, and salad oil. In the early 1990s the cottonseed industry of Texas continued to lead that of all other states.

After cotton has been ginned, mills reduce the seed to four products—linters, hulls, cottonseed oil, and meal. Out of every ton of cottonseed received at the mill, hulls represent over 25 percent of the weight; oil, about 16 percent; and meal, 45 percent. In terms of value, oil is the most significant product, followed by meal, which itself is worth more than the combined value of hulls and linters.

Linters, the short fibers left clinging to the hulls after ginning, are almost pure cellulose. They are used in batting for mattresses and upholstery, industrial textiles, surgical dressings, and high-quality paper products. They also play a chemical role in the production of plastics, film, rayon, acetate, explosives, and other products. During World War II[qv] and the Korean War, almost all of the American production of linters was used in the manufacture of smokeless powder for artillery shells.

Hulls have been used to provide roughage in feed since the latter decades of the nineteenth century. In the early decades of the cottonseed-oil industry they were also used as fuel for the mills. The ashes of the hulls were useful as fertilizer and could be bleached to produce lye for making soap. Today, in addition to their use in feed, hulls are used as mulch, packing material, and raw material for various chemical industries. They are also useful in restoring potash and minerals in depleted soils.

Cottonseed oil, produced from the meat of the seed, is further refined for use in shortening, mayonnaise, salad oil, cooking oil, and margarine, as well as cosmetics, nitroglycerine, composition roofing, and other products.

Meal, the remains of the seed after the oil has been extracted, can be rendered as flakes, cakes, or pellets, depending on its intended use. Cottonseed meal has a high protein content and plays an important role as a supplement to livestock feed and natural forage.

Long before the Civil War,[qv] upland farmers east of the Mississippi River had used whole cottonseed as a fertilizer for wheat, oats, corn, and other crops. In Texas during the 1800s the seed was used almost exclusively as a supplemental cattle feed. One report exists of its use in 1875 to fuel a Texas flour mill, before the arrival of rail transport had made coal accessible and economical. For the most part, however, through most of the nineteenth century the seed was considered a waste product and a nuisance. It piled up in great quantities (two pounds of seed are separated out for every pound of cotton lint ginned), and it gave off a foul odor as it decomposed. It could not be burned, for heaps of it would continue to smoulder even after a rain storm. Various uses for the oil were known, but inadequate technology hindered production of the oil into the 1880s. The most challenging problems centered around removal of the linters and the hard hull.

Notwithstanding these difficulties, efforts to exploit cottonseed persisted in the United States from the late eighteenth century onward. The first commercially successful cottonseed-oil mill in the United States was built in Natchez, Mississippi, in 1834. The first mill in Texas was built by Leonard Waller Groce[qv] in 1836 near Brenham. Groce used the oil to make soap and paint, lubricate machinery, and fuel lamps. The first commercial oil mill established in Texas was reportedly at High Hill, three miles northwest of Schulenburg in Fayette County, in 1848. One or two mills are said to have operated in the state during the 1850s, and 1860 saw the incorporation of the

Texas Cotton Seed Oil and Manufacturing Company. In 1867 a New York concern built a mill in Galveston, oriented to the export trade. An oil mill in Hempstead reported doing business worth $3,000 in 1869. In 1870 twenty-six mills were reported throughout the country; each of the two in Texas was said to be grossing $20,000 annually. In April 1871 the East Texas Cotton, Woolen, and Cotton Seed Oil Manufacturing Company received a charter to build a mill within three miles of Marshall. Other mills established in the state during the 1870s included one in Columbus (1876) and one in Dallas (1878). The number of mills in the United States had risen to forty-five in 1880, when Texas mills were located in Brazos, Dallas, Galveston, Grayson, Grimes, Robertson, and Waller counties. The Grayson County mill was grossing $100,000 annually, and the one in Waller County, $90,000. By 1882 fourteen mills were in the state, located in Brenham, Bryan, Columbus, Dallas, Galveston, Houston, Navasota, San Antonio, Waco, and Weimar and in Falls, Fayette, Jefferson, and Waller counties. The combined production of these mills amounted to some five million barrels or more, and the mill in Galveston ranked as one of the largest in the country. By 1885 the number of Texas mills had risen to twenty-three.

Between 1870 and 1880 cottonseed overtook flaxseed as the chief source of vegetable oil in the United States. The development of the cottonseed industry was propelled by improved technology in processing, which was notable from 1869 onward, and by the development of markets for cottonseed products. Demonstrated uses for cottonseed oil made the seed commercially valuable during the 1850s, and New Orleans and Mobile became centers of production. Hopes for using the oil as a lubricant for machinery and source of illumination were dashed, however, by the rise of the petroleum industry after 1859.

The first major market for the oil developed in the 1870s in Europe, where manufacturers had learned to mix cottonseed oil with olive oil to mask its flavor and then market the hybrid as olive oil. When Italian olive growers learned of the ruse, however, they succeeded in imposing a high tariff on cottonseed oil about 1881. United States exports, which had accounted for three-fourths of the country's oil production in the late 1870s, plunged. Luckily a new market was formed in the meantime with the invention of oleomargarine by a Frenchman in 1870; oleo was being produced in the United States by 1873. Soon cottonseed oil was being substituted for animal fat in oleo production. In 1886 the United States dairy industry was able to get a stiff excise tax imposed on oleo, but European markets continued to import large quantities of oil for their oleo industry. Another important market developed in the 1880s for a product known as compound lard, which contained a large percentage of cottonseed oil in place of hog lard. By 1890 the manufacture of compound lard consumed perhaps one-third of the cottonseed oil produced in the United States.

Because cottonseed is bulky and perishable, it has been more economical to locate cottonseed mills near the source of supply. That circumstance helps to explain the front rank that Texas took within the national cottonseed industry toward the end of the nineteenth century, for Texas had become the leading cotton-producing state by 1880 (see COTTON CULTURE). It remained the largest cotton grower throughout the following century, into the early 1990s. The development of the seed industry in the state was also encouraged by the rapid expansion of the Texas rail system between 1870 and 1900. In 1880 the cottonseed industry ranked twelfth in the state in value added by manufacture and fourteenth in value of product. By 1890 it ranked fifth in the state in value of product, and by 1900 it ranked second in that category. In the 1899 census Texas stood in first place with 102 mills, South Carolina ranked second with 48, and the nation as a whole reported 357. In 1902 Texas led with 142 mills, Georgia placed second with 70, and the nation as a whole registered 530.

The amount of seed crushed had risen dramatically, from a national total of 80,000 tons in 1870 to 1,000,000 tons in 1891, 2,000,000 in 1898, and 3,524,780 in 1902, when Texas mills alone crushed 872,985 tons. The proportion of seed being crushed had also risen significantly. Nationally, mills in 1880 had crushed about one-seventh of the total cottonseed production. In 1901 mills in Texas, Oklahoma Territory, and Indian Territory crushed an estimated 60 percent or more of the seed from that region.

Securing an adequate supply of seed in good condition was a perennial concern for mill operators. Poor roads and the expense of transportation contributed to the problem and tended to confine the buying area of the mill to the surrounding environs. Water transport, which was cheaper than rail, could extend the buying reach of the mill. Although railroads were used to some extent in transporting raw seed, they were especially important in shipping the oil and linters. Because the hulls and meal were the heaviest components of the seed and had less value than the oil and linters, it was more economical to sell them nearby than to ship them far away.

In the early 1880s mill owners in Texas and Arkansas formed syndicates to regulate the price paid for seed and so moderate competition. About 1884 these syndicates combined to form the American Cotton Oil Trust. By the fall of 1886 this group controlled 88 percent of the crushing capacity of the country. In 1888 Louisiana sued to have the trust dissolved, and in 1889 it was reorganized as a corporation, the American Cotton Oil Company. Its chief competitor was the Southern Cotton Oil Company, organized in New Jersey in 1887. The properties of the latter company were purchased in 1901 by the Virginia-Carolina Chemical Company. Smaller corporations and independent mills also existed. In 1949 it was estimated that half the mills in the country were owned by groups and half were independent.

With the establishment of the industry on a firm footing, trade organizations began to be formed. The Cotton Seed Crushers Association, whose proceedings were published in New Orleans, was established and holding meetings by 1879. The Texas Cotton Seed Crushers' Association was organized in Waco in 1894, and the Inter-State Cotton Crushers' Association was formed in Memphis, Tennessee, in 1897. In addition to addressing other matters of business concern, the Texas and interstate associations established publicity bureaus in the early 1900s to educate the public in the use of cottonseed products. Many of the uses enumerated, such as the lubrication of harness and making of laundry soap, quilts, and mattresses, suggest that individuals were buying products directly from the mill for household use. The Texas publicity bureau was aided in its work by the Dallas-based *Farm and Ranch*,[qv] whose editor-in-chief, John H. Connell,[qv] was a wholehearted booster of cottonseed.

One of the publicists' chief goals was to persuade local farmers to use meal, rather than the whole seed, as a feed supplement. For some years oil was the only cottonseed product that found a market in the United States, but meal was valued highly by European farmers, who fed it to their beef and dairy cattle. In 1906 it was said that Hamburg made the market for Texas meal just as Liverpool made the market for Texas cotton. By 1909, however, most of the hulls, cake, and meal were being used within the state, while much of the production of linters was going out of state and most of the oil was being shipped to Europe (some was going to China and Japan). The growing use of cake and meal by Texas ranchers contributed significantly to the state's cattle industry in the twentieth century, for the feed supplement helped cattle to survive drought and harsh winters and helped to make ranching in semiarid regions possible. As research advanced, the usefulness of cottonseed meal in horse and swine feed was also demonstrated, while later in the twentieth century progress was made toward adapting it for poultry feed.

Along with exhortations to "locate and foster markets," early association members in Texas were urged to advertise in their local papers and to make a special point of addressing women, who made most of the decisions about household consumption. In spite of these appeals, most oil-mill managers generally may have been like the one in

Austin, who was reported in 1919 not to advertise at all. With the exception of the oil, most of the products of that mill were consumed locally, and inventory was seldom carried over from one year to the next.

If the mills themselves did not advertise, companies that used cottonseed products in their own manufactures did. Procter and Gamble, for instance, which already bought large quantities of cottonseed oil to produce Ivory soap, developed a vegetable shortening based on cottonseed oil in the early 1900s. When the new product, Crisco, was introduced in 1912, the company conducted a major advertising campaign. Producers of vegetable food products also sought to exploit public concern over conditions in the slaughterhouses and meat-packing industry by touting the purity and healthfulness of their products.

Research continued to develop new uses for cottonseed derivatives. Cellulose from linters became an important material in the manufacture of acetate fiber, one of the early synthetic fibers, by 1920 and a component of early plastics in the late 1920s. By 1929 a substantial amount of cottonseed oil was being used in prepared salad dressing. Research was also being conducted on the cotton plant itself. By 1939 A&M College had developed a strain of cotton that produced much seed and little lint.

The start of the season for cottonseed-oil mills varied by region according to the time of cotton harvesting. The season for the adless Austin mill usually began in August and lasted seven or eight months, with another two to three months spent on repairs. Although the repairs might have been finished in less time, the work was drawn out to provide continued employment for some workers and to serve as an inducement for them to remain in the area.

In 1909 most of the 194 Texas mills employed between five and fifty workers, 99 percent of whom were male. Laborers in cottonseed mills worked a longer week than in any other industry in the state, most of them clocking seventy-two hours a week or more. Ten years later conditions at the Austin mill seem to have been similar. Most workers there were unskilled Mexican and African Americans who worked twelve-hour shifts. Before World War I[qv] unskilled workers at the Austin mill had earned a dollar a day and skilled ones, two dollars. By 1919 those wages had risen to $2.25 and $4.50, respectively. Oil refineries required a more skilled work force than mills.

Between 1900 and 1915 the cottonseed industry in Texas continued its strong expansion, boosted by improved technology and the invention of new products. In 1915, its peak year, Texas had 233 of the 882 oil mills in the country. Soon, however, the number began a steady decline. By 1919 state mills were down to 200, reduced in part, perhaps, by the effect of federal regulations of the price of cottonseed during World War I. Also, a major cause of the decline was the fact that the industry had overexpanded, developing a crushing capacity that exceeded the supply of cottonseed. Some mills sought to offset the shortage of seed by crushing peanuts after the cottonseed season ended, while the Austin mill experimented in 1918 and 1919 with pressing dried coconut meat imported from California.

Despite hope that the expansion of cotton growing in Texas would alleviate the problem, overcapacity continued to plague the industry. The situation became even more severe after the Texas cotton acreage control law of 1931–32[qv] reduced the number of acres that could be planted with cotton. While the number of mills dropped, however, the capacity of the remaining mills increased, and the industry remained a significant one in the state. In 1909 it ranked third among state industries in value of product. In 1930 it ranked second in that category, and in 1939, third, while placing eighth in the number of employees and ninth in the value added by manufacture. Cottonseed also ranked high as a cash crop for Texas farmers, trailing only cotton lint and sometimes wheat in the period 1937 to 1940. During the 1940s the added income from cottonseed helped Texas cotton growers withstand the competition from synthetic fibers.

Demand for vegetable-oil products soared during World War II.[qv]

In the early 1940s Texas cottonseed mills, still faced with overcapacity, imported and crushed a large tonnage of northern soybeans. The demand for oilseed encouraged an expansion of peanut production in Texas and the development of flaxseed cultivation along the Gulf Coast. The Texas cottonseed industry sponsored oilseed research in cooperation with the Texas Agricultural Experiment Station, the Texas Research Foundation,[qqv] and other organizations, and the Texas Cottonseed Crushers Association provided A&M College with an experimental mill. Research in the uses of other oilseeds and their expanded cultivation in turn presented cottonseed with oilseed competitors. By the late 1950s soybeans had become the largest oilseed crop in the country, although cottonseed continued to dominate the oilseed category in Texas.

From 1929 to 1955 the number of mills in Texas counted by the federal census dropped from 176 to eighty-nine. The number of persons employed by the mills also declined, as did the value of product and the value added by manufacture. During the mid-1950s hopes for renewed vitality in the industry rested on the development of new products, such as a recently developed meal processed especially for poultry and an ice cream substitute called mellorine, which replaced butterfat with vegetable oil and sold for about half the price of the dairy product.

A further decline in the number of mills was presaged by the advent of solvent extraction of oil. By 1949 five mills that used solvent extraction had been built nationally, including one in Abilene. Mills using this technology had a larger capacity than others and needed to operate year-round to achieve efficiency. In the mid-1950s, however, the ranks of Texas mills still included small, "cotton-patch" mills, which performed only the first stages of processing, in addition to the larger, "terminal" mills, which performed such further operations as refining the oil, mixing formula feed, and manufacturing other products. Although Texas mills were fewer in number in the 1950s, they had a larger total capacity than in the 1940s and were crushing, on average, close to 90 percent or more of the seed produced each season. Cottonseed remained an important cash crop in Texas, placing second after cotton lint in 1957 and 1958, with sorghum grain a distant third.

In the postwar years the center of the cottonseed industry in Texas shifted to the west, as cotton growing itself shifted from East Texas to the southern High Plains. By 1955 Lubbock had become the largest cottonseed-processing center in the world, a distinction it continued to hold in the early 1990s. Lubbock was also the site of the world's first commercial cottonseed-flour mill. The venture was unprofitable, however, and lasted only from 1973 to 1975; flour production remained an unrealized facet of the industry in the early 1990s. By the mid-1950s cottonseed oil refineries had also moved west and were in operation in Lubbock, Abilene, and El Paso, as well as other cities. By the late 1940s the manufacture of food products incorporating cottonseed oil had also become an important industry in the state. At that time the chief centers in Texas for the production of mayonnaise, margarine, shortening, and salad dressing included Dallas, Fort Worth, Houston, San Antonio, and Sherman.

During the 1960s the shift in cotton growing to the western part of the state and from small farms to large irrigated farms continued. At the same time, there was a trend away from cotton growing and toward the cultivation of grain and other crops. In the early 1960s cottonseed ranked third as a source of cash farm income, behind cotton lint and sorghum grain. By 1965 it had slipped to fifth place, behind lint, sorghum grain, rice, and wheat. It ranked sixth in 1987–89.

In the latter decades of the twentieth century researchers continued to explore new uses for cottonseed derivatives. Cottonseed oil remained the most important component of the seed, being used extensively as a cooking oil and in a wide range of food products. Though soybean oil still dominated the vegetable-oil market nationally, cottonseed remained supreme among oilseed crops grown in Texas. Although the number of mills in the state had dropped to nineteen by 1983, Texas continued to be the leading producer of cottonseed products. In 1990 Texas mills crushed 2,049,000 tons of seed worth $239,686,000, and produced 48 percent of the cottonseed oil exported by the United States. For Texas farmers who were able to grow cotton profitably, it was often the added income from the seed that made the difference.

BIBLIOGRAPHY: *Cottonseed and Cottonseed Based Industries: Their Place in the Economy of Texas* (Austin: Cotton Economic Research, University of Texas, in cooperation with the Cotton Research Committee of Texas, 1959). Alonzo Bettis Cox, *The Cottonseed Crushing Industry of Texas in Its National Setting* (Austin: Cotton Research Committee of Texas, 1949). Vera Lea Dugas, "Texas Industry, 1860–1880," *Southwestern Historical Quarterly* 59 (October 1955). *The History of Cotton in Texas* (Natural Fibers Information Center, Bureau of Business Research, University of Texas at Austin, 1989). Lynette Boney Wrenn, *Cinderella of the New South: A History of the Cottonseed Industry, 1855–1955* (Knoxville: University of Tennessee Press, 1995). W. D. Wright, "Cotton Seed Products in Texas," in *Studies in the Industrial Resources of Texas: Studies by Texas Applied Economics Club* (University of Texas Bulletin 3, Austin, 1915). *Mary M. Standifer*

COTTONWOOD, TEXAS (Callahan County). Cottonwood, on Farm Road 880 eight miles northwest of Cross Plains in southeastern Callahan County, was originally settled by J. W. Love in 1875 or 1876 and named for cottonwood trees growing in the area. Dr. H. O. Broadnax built the first store, and the region's agricultural prospects appealed to farmers who migrated from East Texas. A post office was established in 1882, and for some years Cottonwood was the area's trading center. The population was 350 in 1890, when a weekly newspaper, the *Prodigal*, edited by C. J. Wilson, was published. The town was remarkable in its early days for violence, including a couple of main-street shootouts with fatal results. Pioneers included Jim Champion, Dan Robinson, John Breeding, and Green and Henry Robinson. Early merchants included Bill Orr, Fred Griffin, Elias Norton, and J. F. Coffey. A fruit and vegetable cannery opened in 1903. Cottonwood faded with the advent of the automobile era and a shift of agricultural emphasis from fruit and vegetable farming to ranching. The population was reduced to 300 by 1915 and 120 in 1940. In 1980 and 1990 the population was sixty-five.

BIBLIOGRAPHY: Brutus Clay Chrisman, *Early Days in Callahan County* (Abilene, Texas: Abilene Printing and Stationery, 1966). *William R. Hunt*

COTTONWOOD, TEXAS (Lamar County). Cottonwood is a church community at the intersection of Farm Road 38 and a dirt road just east of Cottonwood Creek and twelve miles west of Paris in western Lamar County. By 1896 Cottonwood School reported one teacher and twenty-two pupils. Maps for 1936 showed the community with a school, a church, and a cluster of dwellings. Students from Cottonwood attended Central Independent School District by 1957 and by 1970 the North Lamar Independent School District. The church and cemetery, along with a few scattered homes, still appeared on maps of the area in 1984.

BIBLIOGRAPHY: Thomas S. Justiss, An Administrative Survey of the Schools of Lamar County with a Plan for Their Reorganization (M.A. thesis, University of Texas, 1937). *Vista K. McCroskey*

COTTONWOOD, TEXAS (McLennan County). Cottonwood is on Farm Road 2114 four miles northeast of West in the northern corner of McLennan County. The area was settled by German immigrants who moved there from Washington County in the early 1880s. Cottonwood became the focus of a common school district in 1884 and continued to function as such until 1948, when the school was consolidated with the West Independent School District. A school, a church, and several scattered residences marked the community on county highway maps in the late 1940s. Cottonwood had only a few houses in the 1950s, and by the 1980s one business was all that appeared on county highway maps of the area. Cottonwood was still listed as a community in 1990.

BIBLIOGRAPHY: Martin Luther Bannister, The Historical Development of the Public School System of McLennan County (M.A. thesis, Baylor University, 1945). Vertical File, Texas Collection, Baylor University. *Vivian Elizabeth Smyrl*

COTTONWOOD, TEXAS (Madison County). Cottonwood is on State Highway 21 five miles southwest of Madisonville in southern Madison County. Settlement in the vicinity began as early as the mid-1800s, but no community formed at the site until about 1880. In 1885 J. R. Day donated two acres on the south bank of Iron Creek for a school. A small schoolhouse was erected there, and the community was named for the stand of cottonwood trees growing at the site. Eleven years later the school had one instructor and an enrollment of forty-eight. In 1894 the settlement acquired a post office and became known as Neal, after the family of postmaster John A. Heath's mother. In 1907 the post office was discontinued, and the community reverted to its former name. Around 1900 a syrup mill, a cotton gin, and a general store were in operation at the community. A two-room school building was constructed there in 1913, and shortly thereafter an interdenominational church. State Highway 21 was extended through the vicinity in the early 1930s. Enrollment at Cottonwood's seven-grade elementary school was twenty in 1936. By the late 1930s the community had two businesses and a population of fifty. In 1944 the Cottonwood school was consolidated with the Madisonville Independent School District. In 1945 Cottonwood's population was an estimated seventy, but by 1949 it had fallen to an estimated thirty-five. Thereafter its population remained virtually unchanged for more than four decades; it stood at an estimated forty in 1992, when the community had a church and a business.

BIBLIOGRAPHY: Madison County Historical Commission, *A History of Madison County* (Dallas: Taylor, 1984).

Charles Christopher Jackson

COTTONWOOD, TEXAS (Martin County). Cottonwood, on State Highway 137 ten miles north of Stanton in central Martin County, was named for the cottonwood trees set out by Jim Shriver, the town blacksmith. Its inhabitants considered themselves part of the Lenorah community, a few miles west. Cottonwood centered around Shriver's blacksmith shop, which was later bought by M. L. Koonce and converted into a community store. The community was principally known as the site of dances and boxing matches held on a concrete slab near the store. After reaching its peak in the 1930s, Cottonwood declined and ceased to exist by the 1950s.

BIBLIOGRAPHY: Martin County Historical Commission, *Martin County, Texas* (Dallas: Taylor, 1979). *Noel Wiggins*

COTTONWOOD, TEXAS (Wood County). Cottonwood, on Farm Road 779 three miles northwest of Golden in southwestern Wood County, was probably named for nearby Cottonwood Creek. It was originally located a mile southeast of its present site, and in the 1970s the Cottonwood cemetery still marked the community's original site. In 1884 a Cottonwood school district was established, and by 1896 it served twenty-seven students. By 1905 it served fifty-nine students. In the 1930s the community consisted of a number of farms concentrated along country roads, two businesses, and a school that in 1932 had seventy students in eight grades. Though the school and businesses no longer appeared on maps for 1959, the Cottonwood church and widely scattered dwellings were still in the area. Maps for the late 1980s showed a business about half a mile from the church.

BIBLIOGRAPHY: Adele W. Vickery and Ida Marie Turner, comps., *Cemeteries of Wood County* (3 vols., Mineola, Texas, 1970-71).

Rachel Jenkins

COTTONWOOD ARROYO. Cottonwood Arroyo rises near U.S. Highway 385 in eastern Oldham County (at 35°24′ N, 102°16′ W) and runs northeast five miles to its mouth on the Canadian River, near the Potter county line downstream from Cal Farley's Boys Ranch[qv] (at 35°30′ N, 102°11′ W). It traverses moderately steep slopes, with locally high relief, surfaced by shallow to moderately deep silt loams, severely eroded in some places, that support mesquites and grasses. The Tascosa stock pens are on Farm Road 1061 south of the mouth of the arroyo.

COTTONWOOD BRANCH. Cottonwood Branch, a spring-fed intermittent stream, rises five miles northwest of Lometa in western Lampasas County (at 31°15′ N, 98°27′ W) and runs southwest for nine miles to its mouth on the Colorado River, about 1½ miles south of U.S. Highway 190 (at 31°12′ N, 98°32′ W). It crosses an area of the Grand Prairies characterized by flat to rolling hills with steep margins. The creek then passes into a region on the eastern edge of the Edwards Plateau characterized by steeply to moderately sloping hills. The area soils are shallow and stony sandy and clay loams that support vegetation including scrub brush, cacti, grasses, and open stands of live oaks, Ashe junipers, and mesquites. Elms can be found in some areas upstream.

COTTONWOOD CANYON. Cottonwood Canyon is a half-mile-long canyon in the Brady Mountains five miles south of Lohn in northwest McCulloch County (at 31°15′ N, 99°26′ W). The top of the canyon is 1,900 to 1,950 feet above mean sea level and the base is 1,800 feet. The headwaters of the East Fork of Big Elm Creek run through the canyon.

COTTONWOOD CREEK (Armstrong County). Cottonwood Creek rises in east central Armstrong County (at 35°02′ N, 101°15′ W) and runs east for nine miles, passing north of Goodnight, to its mouth on the Salt Fork of the Red River near the Donley county line (at 35°04′ N, 101°07′ W). The creek traverses sloping mesquite plains with loamy soils. It was on the JA Ranch[qv] and later the Goodnight Ranch.[qv]

____ (Armstrong County). Cottonwood Creek rises in north and south forks in southeastern Armstrong County. The forks run east for seven miles and join near the county line (at 34°54′ N, 100°56′ W) to form Cottonwood Creek, which runs for two miles to its mouth on Mulberry Creek in Donley County (at 34°48′ N, 100°56′ W). The creek traverses flat to gently sloping plains surfaced by loam that supports mesquite. It is on the JA Ranch[qv] holdings.

____ (Baylor County). Cottonwood Creek rises six miles northeast of Mabelle near U.S. Highway 82/277 in northeast Baylor County (at 33°41′ N, 99°04′ W) and runs north through remote ranchland for seven miles to its mouth on the Wichita River, near the upper end of a diversion reservoir (at 33°46′ N, 99°02′ W). The creek crosses rolling hills with clay and sandy soils that support scrub brush, cacti, and grasses.

____ (Baylor County). Cottonwood Creek rises four miles west of Red Springs in extreme western Baylor County (at 33°37′ N, 99°28′ W) and runs south through farmland for three miles to its mouth on the Brazos River (at 33°35′ N, 99°28′ W). It runs through an area of gullies and low hills with shallow soils and sparse vegetation.

____ (Bell County). Cottonwood Creek rises one mile southwest of Troy in northeastern Bell County (at 31°11′ N, 97°20′ W) and runs southeast for twelve miles through Bell County to its mouth on Big Elm Creek, one mile southwest of Seaton (at 31°04′ N, 97°15′ W). It runs through nearly level to sloping terrain surfaced by clayey soils and used predominantly for agriculture.

____ (Callahan County). Cottonwood Creek rises three miles southeast of Spring Mesa in southeast Callahan County (at 32°15′ N, 99°13′ W) and runs south for ten miles to its mouth on Turkey Creek, two miles northwest of Cross Plains (at 32°09′ N, 99°11′ W). The creek runs through flat land to rolling hills surfaced with deep sandy loam that supports brush and grasses. The town of Cottonwood, located near the creek's midway point, was named after nearby Cottonwood Springs. Settlement in the area began in the mid-1870s.

____ (Colorado County). Cottonwood Creek, formerly known as Waterhole Creek, rises near Farm Road 155 between the New Bielau community center and Trinity Church, three miles south of Weimar in western Colorado County (at 29°38′ N, 96°46′ W), and runs southwest 7½ miles, past Oakland, to its mouth on the Navidad River (at 29°35′ N, 96°50′ W), where the river forms the boundary between Colorado and Lavaca counties. Although before 1960 ample crops of cotton were produced in the area, the fields have mostly reverted to rangeland. The creek crosses rolling terrain surfaced by clay soils that support stands of cottonwood mixed with sycamore, oak, pecan, and hackberry along the banks of the creek.

____ (Coryell County). Cottonwood Creek rises five miles northeast of Copperas Cove in southern Coryell County (at 31°12′ N, 97°52′ W) and runs northeast for five miles to its mouth on Cowhouse Creek, sixteen miles southwest of Gatesville (at 31°14′ N, 97°49′ W). It traverses steep slopes and benches surfaced by shallow clay loam that supports juniper, live oak, mesquite, and grasses.

____ (Coryell County). Cottonwood Creek rises sixteen miles north of Copperas Cove in west central Coryell County (at 31°22′ N, 97°51′ W) and runs northeast for eight miles to its mouth on the Leon River, two miles west of Gatesville (at 31°24′ N, 97°45′ W). It traverses flat to rolling terrain, with local deep dissections, surfaced by shallow, stony clay loams that support juniper, oak, mesquite, and grasses.

____ (Cottle County). Cottonwood Creek rises eight miles northeast of Paducah in central Cottle County (at 34°06′ N, 100°06′ W) and runs south for twelve miles to its mouth on the North Wichita River (at 33°58′ N, 100°07′ W). It traverses rolling terrain and steep slopes surfaced by shallow clay and sandy loams that support juniper, cacti, and sparse grasses.

____ (Culberson County). Cottonwood Creek, also known as Cottonwood Draw, rises nine miles northeast of Dome Hill in central Culberson County (at 31°30′ N, 104°22′ W) and runs southeast for forty-five miles before running dry five miles northeast of Toyah in central Reeves County (at 31°23′ N, 103°45′ W). It cuts across flat terrain with local steep slopes upstream. Downstream the terrain is gently sloping to steep and surfaced by shallow, stony sand that supports creosote bush, cacti, scrub brush, and sparse grasses.

____ (Dallas County). Cottonwood Creek rises west of Interstate Highway 45 a mile south of Hutchins in southern Dallas County (at 32°38′ N, 96°42′ W) and runs southeast 9½ miles to its mouth on Tenmile Creek, a mile from the confluence of Tenmile Creek and the Trinity River (at 32°34′ N, 96°36′ W). It crosses flat to rolling prairie, with occasional steep slopes, surfaced by dark clay soils that support juniper, oak, and mesquite.

____ (DeWitt County). Cottonwood Creek rises six miles northwest of Yorktown in central DeWitt County (at 29°03′ N, 97°29′ W), runs south for five miles, and joins Woods Creek to form Twelvemile Creek (at 29°00′ N, 97°26′ W). Cottonwood Creek traverses flat terrain with local shallow depressions, surfaced by clayey and sandy loams that support water-tolerant hardwoods, conifers, and grasses.

____ (Dickens County). Cottonwood Creek rises just west of the Dickens-King county line and four miles south of Dumont in northeastern Dickens County (at 33°44′ N, 100°32′ W) and runs northeast for ten miles to its mouth on the North Wichita River, one mile north of Farm Road 193 and five miles east of Dumont (at 33°48′ N, 100°27′ W). The creek received its name from stands of cottonwood trees that grew near a series of springs in northwest King County. The trees remain, although the springs are now mostly dry. Before the springs went dry, the creek had been filled with sand from erosion. The surrounding terrain of moderately steep slopes is surfaced by shallow to moderately deep silt loams in which grow mesquites and grasses. The creek was once a nesting place for wild turkeys.

____ (Dickens County). Cottonwood Creek rises near U.S. Highway 82 four miles south of McAdoo in western Dickens County (at 33°39' N, 101°00' W) and runs southeast for ten miles to its mouth on Duck Creek, two miles northwest of Soldier Mound (at 33°34' N, 100°53' W). The surrounding flat to rolling terrain is surfaced by sandy, clay, and silt loams that support oak, scrub brush, mesquite, and grasses. Much of the area was owned by the Spur Headquarters Ranch in the early 1970s.

____ (Ellis County). Cottonwood Creek rises 2½ miles southwest of Palmer in central Ellis County (at 32°22' N, 96°43' W) and runs east for 5½ miles to its mouth on Grove Creek, just east of U.S. Highway 75 a mile east of Palmer (at 32°24' N, 96°39' W). The creek traverses flat to rolling prairie surfaced by dark, calcareous soil that supports mesquite trees, various grasses, and cacti. Throughout the county's history the area has been used as range and crop land.

____ (Ellis County). Cottonwood Creek rises one mile east of Red Oak in northern Ellis County (at 32°31' N, 96°46' W) and runs southeast for three miles to its mouth on Brushy Creek, 2½ miles northwest of Palmer (at 32°30' N, 96°43' W). The creek traverses flat to rolling prairie surfaced by dark, calcareous soils that support mesquite trees, cacti, and various grasses. The land in this area has been used as range and crop land.

____ (Erath County). Cottonwood Creek rises near Dublin in southwestern Erath County (at 32°05' N, 98°20' W) and runs east eight miles to its mouth on Green Creek, one mile northwest of Alexander (at 32°04' N, 98°13' W). The creek is dammed in its upper reaches. It flows first through flat to rolling terrain with local escarpments, surfaced by deep, fine sandy loam soils that support brush and grasses. Toward the creek's mouth the terrain changes to steep slopes and benches surfaced by shallow clay loams that support juniper, live oak, mesquite, and grasses.

____ (Falls County). Cottonwood Creek rises within the southern city limits of Lott in western Falls County (at 31°12' N, 97°02' W) and runs southeast for thirteen miles to its mouth on Pond Creek, one mile southwest of Rosebud (at 31°04' N, 97°00' W). It is intermittent in its upper reaches. The creek traverses flat to rolling prairie surfaced by dark, calcareous clays that support mesquite trees, cacti, and grasses.

____ (Fort Bend County). Cottonwood Creek rises in the Orchard Dome oil and gas field, 1½ miles southeast of Orchard in western Fort Bend County (at 29°34' N, 95°56' W), and runs southeast for nine miles to its mouth, where it merges with Coon Creek to form Big Creek (at 29°29' N, 95°50' W). The creek traverses variable terrain surfaced by impermeable soil that changes to calcareous clay and supports mixed hardwoods and prairie grasses.

____ (Freestone County). Cottonwood Creek rises less than a mile west of Fairfield in central Freestone County (at 31°43' N, 96°11' W) and runs northeast and then southeast for twenty miles to its mouth on Tehuacana Creek, four miles northeast of Young (at 31°54' N, 96°05' W). The creek traverses flat to rolling prairies with local shallow depressions, surfaced by clay and sandy loams that support hardwoods, pines, conifers, and grasses. The area is primarily forest and dry cropland.

____ (Gillespie County). Cottonwood Creek rises in north central Gillespie County (at 30°29' N, 98°55' W) and runs north for four miles to its mouth on Hickory Creek, at the foot of Putnam Mountain three miles southwest of the town of Prairie Mountain in Llano County (at 30°33' N, 98°55' W). The creek traverses an area of the Llano basin with flat to rolling terrain, locally dissected and covered by sandy and clay loams. Local vegetation consists primarily of open stands of live oak and mesquite.

____ (Guadalupe County). Cottonwood Creek rises five miles east of New Berlin in southern Guadalupe County (at 29°27' N, 98°01' W) and runs northeast for nine miles to its mouth on the Guadalupe River, four miles southeast of Seguin (at 29°32' N, 97°56' W). The creek traverses rolling prairie surfaced by clay loams that support mesquite and grasses.

____ (Hays County). Cottonwood Creek, intermittent in its upper reaches, rises a mile northeast of Hunter in the southern tip of Hays County (at 29°51' N, 98°01' W) and runs southeast for seventeen miles to its mouth on York Creek, four miles north of Kingsbury in Guadalupe County (at 29°44' N, 97°52' W). It runs through clay and shale based soils that support the cultivation of food and fiber crops.

____ (Hill County). Cottonwood Creek rises four miles northwest of Itasca in north central Hill County (at 32°11' N, 97°14' W) and runs southwest for eleven miles to its mouth on Aquilla Creek, 4½ miles southeast of Blanton (at 32°03' N, 97°16' W). The creek traverses rolling to flat terrain surfaced by shallow stony clay and sandy loams that support juniper, cacti, scrub brush, and grasses. The area has been used as range and crop land.

____ (Hill County). Cottonwood Creek, one of at least two creeks by that name in the county, rises two miles north of Itasca in northeastern Hill County (at 32°10' N, 97°10' W) and runs northeast for 5½ miles to its mouth on Island Creek, in extreme northern Hill County three miles southeast of Grandview in Johnson County (at 32°15' N, 97°08' W). The creek traverses flat to rolling terrain surfaced by dark, commonly calcareous clays that support mesquite trees and cacti. The area has served as range and crop land.

____ (Hood County). Cottonwood Creek rises 15½ miles northwest of Granbury and one mile south of the Parker county line in northwest Hood County (at 32°32' N, 97°56' W) and runs north for five miles to its mouth on Kickapoo Creek, just southwest of Buckner in southwestern Parker County (at 32°35' N, 97°54' W). The creek traverses steeply sloping terrain surfaced by shallow sandy soils and clay loams that support junipers, live oaks, mesquites, and various grasses. The area drained by the creek historically has served as rangeland.

____ (Hutchinson County). Cottonwood Creek, sometimes known as Coldwater Creek, rises four miles north of Stinnett in central Hutchinson County (at 35°53' N, 101°27' W) and runs south for twelve miles to its mouth on the Canadian River, four miles north of Borger (at 35°44' N, 101°24' W). It crosses flat to rolling plains with sandy and clayey soils that support mesquites and various grasses. The stream was part of the Hansford Land and Cattle Company's Turkey Track Ranch.[qv] Much of it remains in the Whittenburg family holdings (*see* WHITTENBURG, JAMES ANDREW), and the old Dial townsite is located on the creek.

BIBLIOGRAPHY: Pauline D. and R. L. Robertson, *Cowman's Country: Fifty Frontier Ranches in the Texas Panhandle, 1876-1887* (Amarillo: Paramount, 1981).

____ (Johnson County). Cottonwood Creek rises four miles northeast of Alvarado in eastern Johnson County (at 32°26' N, 97°08' W) and runs southeast for fifteen miles to its mouth on the North Fork of Chamber Creek, a half mile south of Maypearl in western Ellis County (at 32°18' N, 97°04' W). The stream, intermittent in its upper and middle reaches, traverses flat to rolling prairie surfaced by dark, commonly calcareous clays that support mesquite, cacti, and grasses. The area has been used as range and crop land.

____ (Jones County). Cottonwood Creek rises one mile southeast of Funston and five miles east of Anson in east central Jones County (at 32°44' N, 99°47' W) and runs northeast eleven miles to its mouth on the Clear Fork of the Brazos River, south of Lueders (at 32°48' N, 99°37' W). The creek traverses flat to gently sloping terrain surfaced by moderately deep to shallow silt loam soils that support mesquite and grasses.

____ (Karnes County). Cottonwood Creek rises three miles southwest of Choate in southeastern Karnes County (at 28°44' N, 97°46' W) and flows northeast for six miles to its mouth on Hondo Creek, two miles east of Couch (at 28°47′ N, 97°43′ W). The stream traverses flat to rolling terrain with clay and sandy loam that supports water-tolerant hardwoods and grasses.

_____ (Kent County). Cottonwood Creek rises at Jayton in northeastern Kent County (at 33°16′ N, 100°35′ W) and runs northeast for four miles to its mouth on Short Croton Creek, in Kent County near the Stonewall county line (at 33°18′ N, 100°33′ W). The creek traverses moderately steep-sloped terrain surfaced by shallow to moderately deep silt loam soils that support mesquite and grasses.

_____ (Leon County). Cottonwood Creek rises three miles west of Normangee in southwestern Leon County (at 31°01′ N, 96°11′ W) and runs south five miles to its mouth on West Caney Creek, in far northwestern Madison County (at 30°58′ N, 96°11′ W). The creek traverses gently sloping to nearly level terrain surfaced by sandy and loamy soils that support intermittent pecan, elm, water oak, hackberry, post oak, black hickory, and mesquite trees along the creek. Settlement near the stream began in the mid-nineteenth century. Normangee, east of the creek, was established around 1900.

_____ (Limestone County). Cottonwood Creek rises three miles west of Prairie Hill in northwestern Limestone County (at 31°38′ N, 96°50′ W) and runs southeast for eighteen miles to its mouth on Big Creek, three miles southeast of Otto in Falls County (at 31°25′ N, 96°46′ W). The terrain through which the creek passes is generally low rolling to flat prairie surfaced by dark, calcareous clays and sandy loams that support mesquite, scrub brush, cacti, and grasses.

_____ (Lipscomb County). Cottonwood Creek rises eleven miles southeast of Higgins in southern Lipscomb County (at 36°05′ N, 100°16′ W) and runs northeast for ten miles to its mouth on Wolf Creek, four miles east of Lipscomb (at 36°15′ N, 100°12′ W). It traverses flat to rolling terrain with local escarpments, surfaced by deep, fine sandy loams that support native vegetation including mesquite shrubs and grasses.

_____ (Matagorda County). Cottonwood Creek rises five miles north of Bay City in northeastern Matagorda County (at 29°04′ N, 95°58′ W) and runs southeast for seventeen miles, passing through downtown Bay City, to its mouth on Peyton Creek, five miles northeast of Wadsworth (at 28°54′ N, 95°54′ W). The creek is banked by levees in its upper reaches. It traverses low-rolling to flat terrain with some local dissection, surfaced by deep to shallow sandy and clay loams with some dark, commonly calcareous clays that support grasses and hardwoods.

_____ (Montague County). Cottonwood Creek rises twelve miles northeast of Bonita in northeastern Montague County (at 33°46′ N, 97°33′ W) and runs northwest for eight miles to its mouth on the Red River, eighteen miles north of Bonita (at 33°54′ N, 97°35′ W). It traverses generally flat to rolling terrain with local escarpments and shallow depressions, surfaced by clay and sandy loams that support hardwood trees, conifers, brush, and grasses. The area has served as crop and range land.

_____ (Motley County). Cottonwood Creek rises ten miles northeast of Matador in north central Motley County (at 34°08′ N, 100°44′ W) and runs north for six miles to its mouth on Hornica Creek, two miles south of the North Pease River (at 34°11′ N, 100°44′ W). An early Matador Ranch^qv map shows Cottonwood Creek located on average grazing land. The area is sloping terrain surfaced by shallow silt loams that support mesquite and grasses.

_____ (Nolan County). Cottonwood Creek rises 1½ miles north of Interstate Highway 20 and four miles west of Roscoe in northwestern Nolan County (at 32°26′ N, 100°37′ W) and runs northeast for forty-four miles to its mouth on the Clear Fork of the Brazos River, 2½ miles north of U.S. Highway 180 and 2½ miles southwest of Royston in central Fisher County (at 32°47′ N, 100°21′ W). Hardwoods, scrub brush, and grasses grow upstream; mesquite and grasses grow along the middle reaches of the creek; and scattered oak mottes and occasional freshwater marshes appear along the lower reaches. The creek rises in flat to rolling terrain with local scarps, runs through an area of moderately steep slopes with local reliefs, and ends in flat to rolling terrain.

_____ (San Saba County). Cottonwood Creek rises 3½ miles northeast of Richland Springs in northern San Saba County (at 31°19′ N, 98°56′ W) and runs northeast to its mouth on the Colorado River, at a point where the Colorado serves as the San Saba and Mills county line (at 31°24′ N, 98°49′ W). The creek runs through moderately to steeply sloping hills surfaced by clay and sandy loam that supports live oak, mesquite, Ashe juniper, and grasses.

_____ (Scurry County). Cottonwood Creek rises seven miles east of Snyder in east central Scurry County (at 32°45′ N, 100°47′ W) and runs northeast for nine miles to its mouth on Rough Creek, twelve miles northeast of Snyder (at 32°50′ N, 100°44′ W). The creek, intermittent in its upper reaches, traverses moderately steep slopes with locally high relief, surfaced by shallow to moderately deep silt loams that support mesquite and grasses.

_____ (Stephens County). Cottonwood Creek rises near Farm Road 717 in southeastern Stephens County (at 32°33′ N, 98°42′ W) and runs east for four miles to its mouth on the North Fork of Palo Pinto Creek, two miles north of the Eastland county line (at 32°33′ N, 98°37′ W). The creek traverses rolling hills to flat terrain with local deep dissections, surfaced by shallow and stony to clay and sandy loams that support live oak, juniper, grasses, cacti, scrub brush, and mesquite.

_____ (Tarrant County). Cottonwood Creek rises near Helen Winsler Park within the city limits of Arlington in southeastern Tarrant County (at 32°45′ N, 97°13′ W) and runs east for 3½ miles to its mouth on Robinson Creek, three miles southeast of Grand Prairie (at 32°46′ N, 97°09′ W). The stream is intermittent in its upper reaches. It traverses flat to rolling terrain surfaced by dark, commonly calcareous clays that support mesquite, grasses, and cacti. For most of Tarrant County's history, the Cottonwood Creek area has been used as crop and range land.

_____ (Travis County). Cottonwood Creek rises five miles north of New Sweden in northeastern Travis County (at 30°28′ N, 97°29′ W) and runs southeast for thirteen miles to its mouth on Wilbarger Creek, six miles east of Manor (at 30°19′ N, 97°28′ W). It traverses generally flat to rolling terrain with steep margins, surfaced by sandy loams that support willow and pecan trees in the upper reaches of the creek and water-tolerant hardwoods, conifers, and grasses in the lower reaches.

COTTONWOOD DRAW. Cottonwood Draw rises on Hannold Hill, five miles north of Panther Junction within Big Bend National Park^qv in south central Brewster County (at 29°23′ N, 103°11′ W), and runs east for five miles to its mouth on Tornillo Creek, five miles southeast of the Grapevine Hills (at 29°24′ N, 103°06′ W). The draw traverses steep to gentle slopes surfaced by variable soils that support scrub brush and grasses.

COTTONWOOD MOTT CREEK. Cottonwood Mott Creek, also called Mott Creek, rises north of U.S. Highway 62/70 on the eastern edge of the Caprock^qv escarpment in extreme western Motley County (at 33°58′ N, 101°01′ W) and runs northeast for eight miles to its mouth on the Middle Pease River, eight miles northwest of Matador (at 34°04′ N, 100°57′ W). A Matador Ranch^qv line camp (*see also* COTTONWOOD MOTT LINE CAMP) was established on the creek near several springs known as Mott Camp Springs. These springs continued to flow until the mid-1970s. Much of the creek's drainage area was considered average to superior grazing land. The creek traverses gently rolling hills with some moderately steep slopes, surfaced by shallow to moderately deep silt loams that support mesquite and grasses.

COTTONWOOD MOTT LINE CAMP. Cottonwood Mott, named for the motte or cluster of trees that grew near some weeping springs on the headwaters of the Middle Pease River, is the site of what was probably the first house in Motley County. The log house was built by Frank Collinson twelve miles west of Matador in the winter of 1878 and was originally part of a line camp shared by the Jinglebob and Hall Ranch cowboys, whose job was to ride the line between ranges, pushing their respective herds back toward their headquarters. Perhaps because of its distance from the civilizing forces even of the ranch center, Cottonwood Mott was the site of at least two gunfights. A shoot-out occurred on January 1, 1880, when line riders Jim Barbee of the Jingle Bob Cattle Company and Jim Harkey of J. M. Hall's Spur Cattle Company disagreed over the singing of "Yankee Doodle." Taking offense at Harkey's song, Barbee drew his gun and mortally wounded him; Harkey drew and killed Barbee. Two freighters from San Saba witnessed the shooting, notified authorities, and helped bury the two side by side in a grave only eighteen inches deep and dug with an ax.

After Henry H. Campbell[qv] bought the Jinglebob herd and its free-range claim from the Coggin brothers[qv] and R. K. Wylie of Brownwood in 1881, the line camp was controlled by the Matador Ranch[qv] and was later purchased by the Matador Land and Cattle Company.[qv] From March 23, 1883, to September 21, 1885, Frank M. Drace served as postmaster of Old Lyman from the family home at Cottonwood Mott, offering mail service to the sparsely settled region. In 1888 Drace became enraged at Mose Harkey, a boarding Matador hand, and drew on him. The two exchanged shots and Harkey died the next day, thus becoming the second member of the family to die in a shoot-out at Cottonwood Mott.

The log cabin was replaced by a box strip house, and Cottonwood Mott, one of at least twenty line camps of the Matador Ranch, served as a batch camp or home to cowboys and their families until the ranch was split up in 1951. A Texas historical marker for the camp was granted in 1986.

BIBLIOGRAPHY: Dee Harkey, *Mean As Hell* (Albuquerque: University of New Mexico Press, 1948). Matador *Tribune,* August 22, 1940. W. M. Pearce, *The Matador Land and Cattle Company* (Norman: University of Oklahoma Press, 1964). Eleanor Traweek, *Of Such as These: A History of Motley County and Its Families* (Quanah, Texas: Nortex, 1973).
Marisue Potts

COTULLA, TEXAS. Cotulla, the county seat of La Salle County, is twenty-seven miles north of Encinal on U.S. Interstate Highway 35 in the northwestern part of the county. The town was named for Joseph Cotulla, a Polish immigrant. After learning that the International–Great Northern Railroad intended to extend its tracks into La Salle County in the early 1880s, Joseph Cotulla worked to build a town on the present site of Cotulla. In 1881 he provided 120 acres of land to induce the railroad to build into the county, and by 1882 a railroad depot had been built and lots in the new town had begun to be sold. By 1883 the town had been granted a post office, and several new buildings had been constructed, including a general store, a hotel, and a jail. In a special county election held that year Cotulla was designated the county seat, and the town began a period of rapid growth. By 1890 it had a population of 1,000, three general stores, two weekly newspapers, two churches, a saloon, a bank, a corn mill, and a cotton gin.

Cotulla developed a reputation as a rough place during its early years. According to one story, railroad conductors announced the town by calling out,"Cotulla! Everybody get your guns ready." Three sheriffs and nineteen residents are said to have lost their lives in gunfights in the town. Nevertheless, civilized institutions were also evolving; by 1885 Cotulla had a school enrolling 135 students, and by 1886 the town had a debating society that discussed such topics as "Should the education of a woman be co-equal of that of a man?" By 1892 Cotulla had a hotel, four general stores, three saloons, a meat market, two grocery stores, and daily stage service to supplement its railroad connection. School records for 1896 and 1906 show a separate school for fifteen black children.

Cotulla's economy has been largely based on sheep and cattle ranching. By 1914 the community had 1,800 residents, three hotels, two banks, two restaurants, an ice plant, an electric power plant, and a movie theater. In the mid-1920s new elementary and high schools were built. By 1931 Cotulla had a population estimated at 3,175 and seventy-five businesses. The population remained relatively stable and perhaps actually grew during the 1930s. A free public library was built in 1937, and by 1941 Cotulla had 3,633 residents and eighty businesses. In 1947 fifty-four businesses were reported. In 1949 the town built its first airport, and during the early 1950s the discovery of oil in the area helped to bolster the economy. In 1954 Cotulla had 4,425 residents, who supported ninety-two businesses. In 1961 the town had a population of 3,960 and seventy-two businesses. By 1971 it had an estimated 3,814 people and forty-seven businesses.

In 1974 the mayor of Cotulla was of Mexican descent, as were several members of the town council and two-thirds of the population. Since Cotulla had no industry, however, many residents lived in the town only part-time and seasonally migrated north to look for work. In 1982 Cotulla had a population of 3,912 and seventy-four businesses. In the early 1980s Ida and Ben Alexander donated the Alexander Memorial Library. The La Salle County Historical Commission sponsors the Brush Country Museum in the center of town. In 1990 the population of Cotulla was 3,694.

BIBLIOGRAPHY: Annette Martin Ludeman, *La Salle: La Salle County* (Quanah, Texas: Nortex, 1975). San Antonio *Express,* October 11, 1954. WPA Writers' Program, *Texas: A Guide* (New York: Hastings House, 1940; rev. ed. 1969).
John Leffler

COUCH, TEXAS. Couch, on the north bank of Hondo Creek off State Highway 239 seven miles southeast of Kenedy in southeastern Karnes County, was named for D. F. Couch, who was instrumental in bringing settlers from Oklahoma Territory in the early 1890s. The general vicinity of Couch, a rich farming area, was popularly known as the Oklahoma settlement for many years. In the early 1890s Andrew J. Harryman bought sixty acres of land from J. M. and T. Y. Pettus. Eighteen acres of this tract were surveyed and platted as the townsite of Couch. The town had a general store, a post office, a hotel, a Methodist church, and a public school. The post office was established in 1896 and closed in 1909. After the main road from Kenedy to Goliad was moved two miles south of Couch, its post office was moved in 1909 to Runge, and the community declined. State highway maps for the 1960s name the community but show no buildings at the site.

BIBLIOGRAPHY: Robert H. Thonhoff, History of Karnes County (M.A. thesis, Southwest Texas State College, 1963).
Robert H. Thonhoff

COUGHRAN, TEXAS. Coughran was four miles southeast of Pleasanton near the termination of Farm Road 1334 and the Missouri Pacific line in east central Atascosa County. The settlement was named for W. A. "Abe" Coughran, who in 1912 began to develop the town and in 1913 built a store, a bank, a gin, a school, and a post office and located artesian wells to make the place attractive to prospective settlers. Coughran also donated the right-of-way for the San Antonio, Uvalde and Gulf Railroad the same year. In 1914 the community had a population of 100, a weekly newspaper called the Coughran *Observer,* a hotel, and several retail and manufacturing establishments. The school had sixty-six students in 1913. During the 1920s Coughran marketed cotton and watermelons. Although the population dropped to fifty, a new school building was constructed in 1924 and enlarged in 1933 to accommodate 134 students. The reported population dropped to twenty-five in the mid-1930s but rose again to fifty in the 1940s and remained at that figure until 1964. In 1956 the school was consolidated with the Pleasanton schools. In 1986 the area was owned by the Eichelberger family, who operated the Big Oak Antiques complex.

BIBLIOGRAPHY: *Atascosa County Centennial, 1856–1956* (Jourdanton, Texas: Atascosa County Centennial Association, n.d.). *Atascosa County History* (Pleasanton, Texas: Atascosa History Committee, 1984). Margaret G. Clover, The Place Names of Atascosa County (M.A. thesis, University of Texas, 1952).   *Linda Peterson*

COULTERVILLE, TEXAS. Coulterville, also known as Culver, was in Buckner's Prairie, fifteen miles east of Bay City in eastern Matagorda County. In 1888 William D. Culver became the first postmaster, and by 1891 a community with two general stores, one owned by Culver, had developed. The following year the population was 125; the settlement supported nine businesses, including six general stores, and had a justice, a constable, and a physician. In 1894 Lemuel P. Coulter became postmaster, and the following year the post office name was changed to Coulterville. By 1896 Coulterville had 200 residents, a justice, a constable, a physician, and five general stores. In 1899 the voting precinct was still named Culver. When the Cane Belt Railroad came through the county in 1901 a Culver railroad stop was founded four miles south of Bay City. In 1904, the last year population estimates are available for the community, Coulterville reported 161 residents. In 1911 its post office was discontinued, and the mail was rerouted through Bay City. In 1936 Coulterville was not labeled on the county highway map, but a number of dwellings remained in the area. By 1952 maps showed nothing at the site. A Culver school was located near Citrus Grove in the western part of the county from at least 1917 until its consolidation with the Palacios schools in the late 1930s.

BIBLIOGRAPHY: Matagorda County Historical Commission, *Historic Matagorda County* (3 vols., Houston: Armstrong, 1986).
Rachel Jenkins

COUNCIL BRANCH. Council Branch rises four miles north of Lingleville in western Erath County (at 32°18′ N, 98°23′ W) and runs southeast four miles to its mouth on the North Bosque River, eight miles northwest of Stephenville (at 32°16′ N, 98°21′ W). It runs through flat to rolling terrain with local escarpments, surfaced by deep, fine sandy loam that supports hardwood trees, conifers, brush, and grasses. Downstream, steep slopes and benches are surfaced by shallow clay loams that support juniper, live oak, mesquite, and grasses.

COUNCIL CREEK. Council Creek rises at the foot of Potato Hill, six miles northwest of Burnet in western Burnet County (at 30°49′ N, 98°17′ W), and runs west for six miles to its mouth on Lake Buchanan (at 30°49′ N, 98°20′ W). The creek traverses low-rolling to flat terrain surfaced by clay and sandy loams that support scrub brush, cacti, and grasses.

COUNCIL CREEK, TEXAS. Council Creek was an early settlement on Council Creek and what is now Farm Road 2341, ten miles northwest of Burnet in western Burnet County. Local tradition has it that the creek and the community were named for a meeting of local residents trying to settle a difficulty. The meeting was called a "council of war," but the dispute was settled peacefully. The Council Creek area was settled about 1856 by several families from Illinois. By the early 1860s the community had a grist and saw mill, a turning lathe, and a leather shop; cedar shingles, hardwood lumber, and furniture were among the earliest commodities produced by area residents. The first schoolhouse in the vicinity, often referred to as Cedar College for the material from which it was made, also doubled as a church building. In 1896 the Council Creek school had one teacher and forty students. The school burned before 1912, and a new building had to be built. After being moved to several different locations, the school was finally consolidated with the Burnet Independent School District in 1951. The school and a few houses marked the community on county highway maps in the 1940s, but by the 1980s the only evidence of the old settlement was Fry Cemetery. A subdivision called Council Creek Village was established to the west of the old Council Creek community site in the early 1960s. Most residents of Council Creek Village were newcomers to the area, attracted by the resort facilities offered by Lake Buchanan.

BIBLIOGRAPHY: Darrell Debo, *Burnet County History* (2 vols., Burnet, Texas: Eakin, 1979).   *Vivian Elizabeth Smyrl*

COUNCIL HOUSE FIGHT. In the Council House Fight thirty Penateka Comanche leaders and warriors, as well as some five women and children of the tribe, were killed by Texas troops at San Antonio on March 19, 1840. The event is said to have hardened Comanche hostility to whites in Texas. From the time of the first white settlements in Texas Comanche warriors and American frontiersmen had skirmished. In 1840 the Penatekas, driven by the fear of Cheyenne and Arapaho attacks along the northern frontier of Comanche territory, the losses suffered in several smallpox epidemics, and the successes of Texas Rangers[qv] against them, sought to make peace with Texas. When Comanche peace representatives arrived at San Antonio in January 1840, commissioners of the Texas government demanded the return of all captives held by the Penatekas. In addition, Texas officials insisted that the Comanches abandon Central Texas, cease interfering with Texan incursions, and avoid all white settlements.

In response to the Texans, thirty-three Penateka chiefs and warriors, accompanied by thirty-two other Comanches, arrived in San Antonio on March 19, 1840. The prominent peace chief Muk-wah-ruh headed the delegation, which brought only a few prisoners, namely several Mexican children and Matilda Lockhart,[qv] a sixteen-year-old white girl. Matilda, who had been captured with her sister in 1838, claimed that her captors had physically and sexually abused her. Burn scars, coupled with the mutilation of her nose, supported her stories. She also said that fifteen other captives remained in Comanche hands and that the tribe's leaders intended to ransom these hostages one at a time (*see* INDIAN CAPTIVES).

When Texan commissioners demanded the release of the other captives Matilda had mentioned, Muk-wah-ruh replied that these prisoners were held by Comanche bands beyond his authority. Failing to comprehend the diffuse nature of Comanche political authority, the commissioners rejected the chief's explanation. Texas soldiers entered the Council House, where the peace talks were being held, and the commissioners informed the assembled chiefs that they were to be held as hostages until the remaining captives were released. In response to these threats, the Comanche chiefs attempted to escape and called to their fellow tribesmen outside the house for help. In the ensuing melee, Texans attacked several Indians while soldiers killed most of the Comanches who remained in the Council House courtyard. A single Comanche woman was freed by Texas authorities and ordered to secure the release of the white captives in exchange for twenty-seven Comanches captured in the fight. The Penateka leaders refused to respond to Texas demands, and most of the Texans' captives escaped.

The Council House Fight outraged Comanche sensibilities, for they considered ambassadors immune from acts of war. Led by Buffalo Hump,[qv] the Penatekas retaliated by raiding deep into Texas. Comanche hatred of Texans, who were regarded as treacherous, continued throughout the warfare era and contributed much to the violence of the frontier.

BIBLIOGRAPHY: John Holland Jenkins, *Recollections of Early Texas*, ed. John H. Jenkins III (Austin: University of Texas Press, 1958; rpt. 1973). Noah Smithwick, *The Evolution of a State, or Recollections of Old Texas Days* (Austin: Gammel, 1900; rpt., Austin: University of

COUNCIL-MANAGER FORM OF CITY GOVERNMENT. The newest of the three major forms of city government, the council-manager form quickly gained acceptance among cities of all sizes and continued in 1994 to be the most popular form in American cities of more than 10,000 population. In Texas this form is even more dominant: 251 of the 290 home-rule cities in Texas operate with a city council as a policy body and a city manager as the chief executive-administrative officer of city government. The plan's original features included a mayor elected from among the city council members after all of them assumed office. The council was nearly always elected at large, received no pay, and spent little time at city hall. Today, in most council-manager cities, mayors are elected at large. Other council members may be elected at large, at large by place, or by district. In larger cities they spend a considerable amount of time on their city duties. The plan continues to be adopted yearly by a number of cities and dropped by few. Amarillo, the first city in Texas to adopt the council-manager form of government, abandoned its commission government for the new plan in 1913. In 1914 Taylor and Denton adopted the council-manager plan. By 1947 there were fifty-eight council-manager cities in Texas. Austin is the largest city in Texas that elects its city council at large by place. Austin also pays its mayor and council members a great deal more than, for instance, Dallas. The norm for Texas cities is token pay, consistent with the original concept of the council-manager plan, which placed policy responsibility in a part-time elected body, and management of the city's business in a professional city manager. Today, most city managers have graduate degrees in public or business administration and may be paid as much as $150,000 a year. The salary is partially in recognition of the stress under which managers operate, particularly in large cities. Managers serve at the pleasure of their city councils and sometimes must bear the brunt of attacks that sometimes should be levied against the governing body. Because of this, contracts and severance agreements are becoming more prevalent. Under these, if a manager is involuntarily dismissed, he receives a specified amount of termination pay.

BIBLIOGRAPHY: Terrell Blodgett, *Texas Home Rule Charters* (Austin: Texas Municipal League, 1994). *The Municipal Year Book, 1993* (Washington: International City-County Management Association, 1993). Matthew Murguia, Councilmember Remuneration in Texas Council-Manager Cities (M.A. thesis, University of Texas at Austin, 1984). James H. Svara, *Official Leadership in the City: Patterns of Conflict and Cooperation* (New York: Oxford University Press, 1990).

Terrell Blodgett

COUNT DRAW. Count Draw, through which an intermittent stream runs, begins six miles northeast of the Black Hills and five miles east of Farm Road 1111 in east central Hudspeth County (at 31°29′ N, 105°16′ W) and runs northeast for four miles to its mouth in Bond Tank, two miles southwest of the Black Mountains (at 31°32′ N, 105°14′ W). Intermittent runoff from Bond Tank enters Miller Draw, a half mile to the north. The draw crosses steeply to gently sloping terrain surfaced by variable soil that supports scrub brush and grasses.

COUNTRY CAMPUS, TEXAS. Country Campus, on State Highway 19 some twelve miles northeast of Huntsville in northeastern Walker County, was established during World War II.qv The community was begun in 1942 as a German prisoners of warqv camp with a capacity to house 4,800 men. The camp's construction began on May 12, 1942, and its formal opening was observed on September 18 of that year. The camp commander was Lt. Col. H. E. Fischer. The camp had housing and medical facilities, a clothing shop, a barbershop, a laundry, a bakery, a cafeteria, a commissary, a gymnasium, a guardhouse, a fire station, and a motor pool. In addition, clubs for both officers and enlisted personnel were provided. Prisoners held at the camp were leased as laborers to local farmers. The camp was deactivated on January 25, 1946, and the property was donated by the government to Sam Houston State Teachers College (later Sam Houston State University) and renamed the Sam Houston Country Campus. The buildings were adapted to serve as dormitories, administrative offices, classrooms, and recreational facilities. Buses shuttled students between the country and main campuses. A post office was established at the site in 1948, with Mrs. R. H. Maxwell as postmistress. In 1949 the community reported a population of 1,000, and by 1952 it reported 500 residents and three businesses. Its post office closed in 1964, when the town reported 425 residents and one business. By 1968 the population had decreased to 121, and by 1972 the community reported only sixty inhabitants and no businesses. In the 1980s some of the old buildings, a golf course, and pastureland remained at the site. Country Campus in 1990 comprised sixty residents.

BIBLIOGRAPHY: Walker County Genealogical Society and Walker County Historical Commission, *Walker County* (Dallas, 1986).

James L. Hailey

COUNTS CREEK. Counts Creek rises five miles northwest of Morgan Mill in northern Erath County (at 32°25′ N, 98°15′ W) and runs east for eight miles to its mouth on the North Paluxy River, 1½ miles east of Morgan Mill (at 32°24′ N, 98°09′ W). The creek passes through steep-sloped terrain surfaced by shallow, sandy soil that supports juniper, scattered oak, and grasses.

COUNTY ATTORNEY. Though the *síndico procurador*qv of the Spanish and Mexican municipality seems to have performed the functions of a county attorney, no constitutional provision was made for a similar official after Texas independence until 1866. Under the constitutions of 1866 and 1869,qqv a county attorney was appointed by the county board for a four-year term. With the adoption of the Constitution of 1876 qv the office became elective, and the term was changed to two years. A constitutional amendment changed the term back to four years in 1954. The main duties of the county attorney are to represent the state in the justice of the peace and county courts, defend suits in which the county is interested, and serve as legal advisor to county and precinct officials. If the county has no district attorney, the county attorney also represents the state in district courts.

BIBLIOGRAPHY: *Guide to Texas Laws for County Officials* (Austin: Texas Department of Community Affairs, 1988). Dick Smith, The Development of Local Government in Texas (Ph.D. dissertation, Harvard University, 1938).

Dick Smith

COUNTY AUDITOR. The office of county auditor was established in specified counties by the state legislature in 1905. The provisions of the law have been changed several times, but in the late 1980s counties with a population of more than 10,000 were required to have an auditor and other counties might have one if the county board so wished. The auditor is appointed by the district judge and serves for two years. His main duties are to countersign all warrants on the county treasury, examine the treasurer's reports and all claims against the county, advertise for bids on county supplies, and exercise general oversight over the financial books and records of the county.

BIBLIOGRAPHY: *Guide to Texas Laws for County Officials* (Austin: Texas Department of Community Affairs, 1988). Dick Smith, The Development of Local Government in Texas (Ph.D. dissertation, Harvard University, 1938).

Dick Smith

COUNTY COMMISSIONERS' COURT. During the Republic of Texas qv the county board was composed of the chief justice (county judge qv) and the justices of the peace of the county; under the constitutions of 1845, 1861, and 1866,^qqv it was composed of the chief justice and four elective commissioners; and under the Constitution of 1869,^qv of any three of the five justices of the peace of the county. The county commissioners' court or county board, as established by the Constitution of 1876,^qv was composed of the county judge, as presiding officer, and four commissioners elected from precincts for two-year terms. A constitutional amendment adopted in 1954 changed the term of office to four years. The commissioners' court has none of the functions of a court but is the general governing body of the county. It establishes a courthouse and jail, appoints numerous minor officials such as the county health officer, fills vacancies in the county offices, lets contracts in the name of the county, builds and maintains roads and bridges, administers the county's public welfare services, performs numerous duties in regard to elections, sets the county tax rate, issues bonds, adopts the county budget, and serves as a board of equalization for tax assessments.

BIBLIOGRAPHY: *Guide to Texas Laws for County Officials* (Austin: Texas Department of Community Affairs, 1988). Dick Smith, The Development of Local Government in Texas (Ph.D. dissertation, Harvard University, 1938).
Dick Smith

COUNTY COURTHOUSES. County courthouses, symbols of self-government, are among the most substantial and attractive public buildings erected in Texas. In county seats, county courthouses occupy prominent positions on public squares, land often donated by town founders as sites for governmental structures. According to law each county is obligated to construct a "convenient building for holding courts." Spaces for courtrooms, offices, storage vaults, and other functions are essential. To accommodate changing needs and artistic tastes, many counties have erected three or more courthouses since their organization.

The county courthouse provides space for the state judicial system and for public business. The Texas Constitution provides for district courts with jurisdiction over felony criminal offenses and over civil suits and other matters. County courts have jurisdiction over misdemeanors and minor civil matters. The county commissioners' court,^qv consisting of county commissioners and a presiding county judge,^qv all elected by popular vote, conducts county business. Among other officials using county courthouses are the county tax assessor, county attorney, district attorney, justice of the peace, sheriff,^qqv county clerk, and district clerk. Because being a county seat gives a community prestige, competition among towns seeking the honor has often been spirited; "county seat wars" were common during the settlement of Texas.

As they brought other traditions, immigrants also brought architectural customs into Texas. Although the first governmental activities of any county were ordinarily conducted in a residence or a temporary log structure, soon work was underway on a hall of justice that reflected the origins of settlers in its style. During the Republic of Texas^qv era, courthouses, small in size and enhanced by simple decorative features, were patterned after court buildings in the south and southeast United States, with a courtroom on the ground floor and offices, usually four, on the second. No examples of this type of courthouse remain.

In antebellum Texas,^qv courthouses became larger and more substantial in construction. Brick or stone often rivaled wood as the building material of choice. Cubical in form and generally with a hipped roof and a cupola, the courthouses displayed simple Greek Revival details, similar to those of public buildings in Virginia and other southeastern states. Offices were on the first floor, and courtrooms were typically located on the second floor. Ordinarily the first floor was divided into quadrants by corridors extending through the building and meeting in the center. These allowed entrances on four sides, providing equal prominence to all sides of the public square on which the building was located.

After the Civil War,^qv during which virtually no construction occurred, these antebellum architectural traditions of interior spatial arrangement were continued, but as the economy recovered, decorative features progressively reflected a transition from Classical simplicity to Victorian ornateness. During the last quarter of the nineteenth century, courthouses were crowned with the mansard roofs of the Second Empire style or were enhanced with bracketed cornices and other features of the Italianate mode. The Parker County Courthouse, Weatherford (1885), by the firm of Dodson and Dudley, represents the former style, and the Wilson County Courthouse, Floresville (1884), by Alfred Giles,^qv the latter. Floor plans with second-story courtrooms, often two stories in ceiling height, continued in use, but buildings were larger and more complex.

At the end of the nineteenth century, numerous prospering counties replaced earlier halls of justice with large, picturesque edifices. Buildings appear in Romanesque Revival styles, with polychromy and Roman-arched openings; in Renaissance Revival style, with Classical details based upon Renaissance buildings in Europe; and in composite styles, with forms and features from manifold modes combined in a single building. The Fayette County Courthouse, La Grange (1890–91), by J. Riely Gordon,^qv exemplifies the Romanesque; the Tarrant County Courthouse, Fort Worth (1893–95), by Gunn and Curtis, the Renaissance; and the Coryell County Courthouse, Gatesville (1897–98), the composite.

Early in the twentieth century, following national trends of design that were heavily influenced by the World's Columbian Exposition of 1893 in Chicago and the teachings of the École des Beaux Arts in Paris, Texas courthouses conformed to the Neoclassical Revival style or Beaux-Arts Classicism. In planning they still largely followed earlier practices with symmetrical compositions of forms and spaces, although they often had rotundas providing impressive interior centers of circulation. On the exteriors, columns, pediments, and domes are characteristic features. Excellent examples include the Hays County Courthouse, San Marcos (1908), by the younger Charles Henry Page^qv and Brothers, and the McLennan County Courthouse, Waco (1901–02), by J. Riely Gordon.

Beginning in the 1930s some courthouses were designed in Moderne style, with a decorative vocabulary based upon clean forms, repetitive lines, and new materials. Buildings continued to be symmetrical in composition, but Classical details were stripped away and new arrangements of forms appeared. Representative is the Travis County Courthouse, Austin (1930–36), by Page Brothers. After World War II^qv former eclectic principles of design for courthouses were rejected by modernizing architects. Functionalism and economy produced entirely new types of courthouses. An example is the addition to the Brazoria County Courthouse, Angleton (1975–77), by Wyatt C. Hedrick.

Nineteenth-century courthouses are now protected, to a limited extent, by a law intended to encourage their preservation. This law was passed after concerned legislators and citizens became alarmed over the destruction of old courthouses to make room for the new.

BIBLIOGRAPHY: Willard B. Robinson, *Gone from Texas: Our Lost Architectural Heritage* (College Station: Texas A&M University Press, 1981). Willard B. Robinson, *The People's Architecture: Texas Courthouses, Jails, and Municipal Buildings* (Austin: Texas State Historical Association, 1983). Willard B. Robinson, "The Public Square as a Determinant of Courthouse Form in Texas," *Southwestern Historical Quarterly* 75 (January 1972). Willard B. Robinson and Todd Webb, *Texas Public Buildings of the Nineteenth Century* (Austin: University of Texas Press, 1974).
Willard B. Robinson

COUNTY HEALTH AUTHORITY. In 1891 the county judge was empowered by the legislature to appoint a part-time county physician to make and enforce local quarantine regulations, but in 1909 the office was abolished and the position of county health officer was established. The county health officer had to be a licensed physician of good standing. He was appointed biennially by the county commissioners' court^{qv} and was charged with giving medical care to people in jails and poorhouses and to those on the pauper rolls of the county. In addition, he cooperated with the State Department of Public Health (*see* TEXAS DEPARTMENT OF HUMAN SERVICES) in matters relating to quarantine, inspection, disease prevention, and vital statistics. Legislation passed in the 1980s replaced the designation "county health officer" with "county health authority." The health authority's duties could be delegated among the staff of the local county health department.

BIBLIOGRAPHY: Texas Advisory Commission on Intergovernmental Relations, *Handbook of Governments in Texas* (Austin, 1973–).

Dick Smith

COUNTY JUDGE. The county judge, called "chief justice" by early constitutions, was appointed by the Congress of the Republic of Texas^{qv} for four-year terms until the office was made elective in 1841. The term of office was shortened to two years in the constitutions of 1845 and 1861.^{qqv} Under the Constitution of 1866^{qv} the name was changed to county judge, and the term was again four years. The office was abolished by the Constitution of 1869^{qv} but was reestablished with an elective two-year term by the Constitution of 1876.^{qv} A constitutional amendment passed in 1954 increased the term of office to four years. The main duties of the county judge are to serve as presiding officer of the county commissioners' court,^{qv} judge of the county court, and budgeting officer of the county; he also has numerous duties pertaining to elections. In counties having fewer than 3,000 students the county judge serves as ex officio county school superintendent.

BIBLIOGRAPHY: *Guide to Texas Laws for County Officials* (Austin: Texas Department of Community Affairs, 1988). Dick Smith, The Development of Local Government in Texas (Ph.D. dissertation, Harvard University, 1938).

Dick Smith

COUNTY LINE, TEXAS (Anderson County). County Line was a rural post office community just east of a country road extension of Farm Road 1615 by the Henderson county line in northwestern Anderson County. The County Line post office operated from 1903 to 1906. In the 1930s the site had several scattered dwellings, but by 1982 all that remained of County Line was a cemetery.

Mark Odintz

COUNTY LINE, TEXAS (Camp County). County Line is on Farm Road 557 some thirteen miles from Pittsburg in far southeastern Camp County. It was named for its proximity to the Upshur and Morris county lines. The settlement was in existence by 1884. Originally the area was heavily wooded, and the settlers made their livelihood by converting the forests into shingles that were marketed in Greenville. As the timber was used up, the land was converted to farms, until County Line was almost entirely an agricultural community. It had a church, a cemetery, and a gristmill by 1888. Later a larger building was constructed there to serve as a church, school, and Woodman hall. In 1935 the school offered only the first seven grades of classes and had an enrollment of twenty-four. During the 1930s the population of the area began to decline, and by 1955 the local school had been consolidated with the Pittsburg Independent School District. Lake O' the Pines was constructed in the late 1950s, and its waters reach to within a mile of County Line. In 1960, though the church and cemetery were still in use, many of the houses in the area had been abandoned. In 1983 the community had two stores, a church, the cemetery, and several houses.

BIBLIOGRAPHY: Hollie Max Cummings, An Administrative Survey of the Schools of Camp County, Texas (M.A. thesis, University of Texas, 1937). Artemesia L. B. Spencer, *The Camp County Story* (Fort Worth: Branch–Smith, 1974).

Cecil Harper, Jr.

COUNTY LINE, TEXAS (Cochran County). County Line, a settlement in the northeast corner of Cochran County, was named for its location near the Cochran-Hockley county line. The community developed around the Union Sunday School that was established there in 1935. The County Line Baptist Church was organized in 1945, and a church building was constructed soon thereafter. In 1965 the community consisted of a gin, a store, and a few residences.

BIBLIOGRAPHY: Elvis Eugene Fleming, *Texas' Last Frontier: A History of Cochran County* (Morton, Texas: Cochran County Historical Society, 1965).

Melissa G. Wiedenfeld

COUNTY LINE, TEXAS (Hale and Lubbock counties). County Line is at the intersection of Farm roads 179 and 597, twelve miles west of Abernathy and twenty-four miles northwest of Lubbock on the Lubbock and Hale county line. It grew up around a school begun in the early 1900s, though settlers were living in the area before then. The school was first known as Murray, then as Harold County Line, and eventually just as County Line. It was consolidated with the Abernathy school in April 1935. An early settler in the area was J. C. Turner, who operated the first store in the early 1920s. Other longtime residents included the Pettis, Harrell, Murray, Rice, Claxton, Vaughn, and Noble families. During the 1930s and 1940s County Line grew to include three grocery stores, two blacksmith shops, two garages, and a gin. In the mid-1980s active businesses at the community were the County Line Co-Op Gin and the Teakell Independent Gin. Ike Bennett, ginner of the County Line Gin, was 1985 Ginner of the Year for the state of Texas. Also in the 1980s the County Line Baptist Church, founded about 1910, remained active with an average weekly attendance of around thirty-five. A store operated at the community until March 1986. Although the *Texas Almanac*^{qv} reported a population of thirty at County Line in the mid-1980s, local estimates noted only between ten and fifteen permanent residents there. At that time increased migrant employment sometimes raised the total to near fifty during ginning seasons. In the 1980s the community of County Line was bordered by the Anton-Irish Clear Fork oilfield, and most of the area's oil rights were under the jurisdiction of Amoco Oil, which maintained an office near the community. The *Texas Almanac* continued to report a population of thirty for County Line in the early 1990s.

BIBLIOGRAPHY: Mary Louise McDonald, The History of Lubbock County (M.A. thesis, University of Texas, 1942).

Charles G. Davis

COUNTY LINE, TEXAS (Rains County). County Line is on Farm Road 275 some seven miles north of Emory in northern Rains County. The site was first settled about 1840 by William Garrett. Supplies for early settlers were freighted from Jefferson. The first cotton gin there was built by Sam Matthis and Bill Stamps. After the Civil War^{qv} the school that served the community was called Union Valley. During the 1930s the settlement had a church, school, and post office. Its school and post office closed after World War II,^{qv} and in the early 1990s only the church and a few scattered houses remained. In 1991 County Line reported a population of forty.

Anna May Schrimsher

COUNTY LINE, TEXAS (Wood County). County Line is a church and school community on Farm Road 2966 two miles east of Yantis in northwestern Wood County, near the Hopkins county line. A County Line school existed by 1905, when it had one teacher and twenty-eight students. In 1932 the County Line school district had thirty-nine students in eight grades. The 1947 discovery of the Yantis oilfield just to the east of County Line appeared to have no lasting effect on the community, and by the late 1950s it consisted of only a church and widely scattered dwellings along country roads. The 1988 county highway map showed a church at the site. *Rachel Jenkins*

COUNTY ORGANIZATION. The origin of the Texas county is found in the municipality, the unit of local government under Spanish and Mexican rule. Municipalities were rather large districts embracing one or more settlements and the surrounding rural territory. There were twenty-three of them by 1836, when Texas won her independence from Mexico. The government of the municipality was vested in an *ayuntamiento*qv (council), composed of at least one alcalde qv (judge), a varying number of regidors (aldermen; *see* REGIDOR), a *síndico procurador*qv (attorney), an *alguacil*qv (sheriff), and an *escribano*qv (secretary).

Under the Republic of Texas qv the municipalities became counties, but the Spanish-Mexican influence on their government was negligible. The new local governments were based on the county as found in the southern United States. The chief governing body of the county during the republic was a county board, composed of the chief justice of the county court (appointed by Congress) and elective justices of the peace, although in 1845 four elective commissioners were substituted for the justices of the peace. The other officers were the sheriff, coroner, and clerk (all elected), a tax assessor (appointed by the county board), and a surveyor (appointed by Congress). New counties could be established if 100 free male inhabitants living in an area containing at least 900 square miles petitioned the government. By 1845 Texas had thirty-six regular counties.

County government under the Constitution of 1845 qv varied only slightly from that under the republic, the major changes being the election of all officials and the establishment of a few new offices. By the end of 1860 the number of organized counties had increased to 122. When Texas entered the Confederacy in 1861 and adopted a new state constitution, no changes were made in county government, nor were any really significant ones made by the Constitution of 1866.qv The government set up by that constitution lasted only a short while because of the passage of the Reconstruction qv Acts in 1867. Under the military rule that followed, many local elected officials were removed indiscriminately and either were not replaced or were replaced by appointees. This constitution lasted until 1870, when the government was reorganized under the Constitution of 1869.qv By the end of 1870 the state had 129 organized counties. Under the Constitution of 1869 the government of the county was again in the hands of an elected county board and several other elected officers, but actual administration, up to 1873, when the radical element was overthrown, was virtually a continuation of the Reconstruction government. No real changes were made until the adoption of the Constitution of 1876.qv

This constitution contains much detail about the organization of county government. The chief governing agency continued to be a county board, the county commissioners' court,qv but provision was also made for a county judge, county attorney, county tax assessor, county surveyor, and county treasurer,qqv as well as for the offices of constable, sheriff, justice of the peace, and clerk of the county court.qqv In addition, there were several statutory officers, the most important of which were the county superintendent of schools and the county auditor.qqv The constitution was also specific about the establishment of new counties: no new county from unorganized territory could be smaller than 900 square miles and should be square if possible; new counties demarked from established counties should contain not less than 700 square miles.

Early responsibilities of county governments included road construction and maintenance, law enforcement, and tax collection. As populations increased, however, county operations expanded to include such additional programs as health and social welfare, solid-waste management, and housing and community development. Environmental protection and floodplain development controls have also become concerns of county government. Texas has had 254 counties since the organization of Loving County in 1931. Voters adopted a home-rule provision in 1933, but the measure proved to be unworkable and was repealed in 1969. (*See also* DEFUNCT COUNTIES.)

BIBLIOGRAPHY: Dick Smith, The Development of Local Government in Texas (Ph.D. dissertation, Harvard University, 1938). *Units of Local Government in Texas* (Municipal Studies No. 15, Austin: Bureau of Municipal Research, University of Texas, 1941). *Dick Smith*

COUNTY SCHOOL TRUSTEES. The office of county school trustee was established in 1911. A board was made up of one trustee from each of the four commissioners' precincts and a chairman from the county at large. All were elected for two years. The main duties of the trustees were to divide the county into school districts, consolidate districts, establish new districts, hear appeals from the county superintendent, and apportion the common school fund among the districts according to scholastic population. In 1978 the legislature abolished state funding for county school trustees, and most counties chose not to continue the offices with local funds. *Dick Smith*

COUNTY SUPERINTENDENT OF SCHOOLS. In 1887 the Texas legislature gave the county commissioners' court qv in each county the optional privilege of establishing a separate office of county superintendent of schools, and in 1905 authorization was given for the office, after a favorable election initiated by the voters. In 1907 the office became mandatory in all counties with a scholastic population of more than 3,000. The county superintendent was usually elected but, under certain conditions, could be appointed by the county school trustees. The term was originally two years but was changed to four years in 1930. In counties where no superintendent was elected or appointed, or where the office had been abolished, the county judge served as ex officio county superintendent. There were 167 Texas counties with county superintendents in May 1945. The main duties of the superintendent were to serve as secretary and executive officer of the county school trustees, hold teachers' institutes, supervise the common school districts, approve vouchers drawn against the school fund, and distribute textbooks. In 1978 the legislature terminated state financial support for the office of county superintendent, leaving individual counties the option of continuing the office with local funds. Only a few counties chose to continue the office. In most cases the duties of county superintendent of schools was transferred to the local commissioners' court or divided among the school districts.

BIBLIOGRAPHY: Texas Advisory Commission on Intergovernmental Relations, *Handbook of Governments in Texas* (Austin, 1973–). *Dick Smith*

COUNTY SURVEYOR. The county surveyor was appointed by Congress under the Republic of Texas,qv but the Constitution of 1845 qv made the office elective for a two-year term, and each succeeding constitution has had a similar provision; in 1954 the term of office was increased to four years by constitutional amendment. Duties included surveying land for the county and recording and examining field notes of surveys made in the county. With the disappearance of open land the importance of the office decreased, and in many counties the office has remained vacant. An independent surveyor is often contracted to fulfill the functions of the office.

BIBLIOGRAPHY: *Guide to Texas Laws for County Officials* (Austin: Texas Department of Community Affairs, 1988). Dick Smith, The Development of Local Government in Texas (Ph.D. dissertation, Harvard University, 1938). *Dick Smith*

COUNTY TAX ASSESSOR-COLLECTOR. The office of county tax assessor-collector is constitutionally required for counties with a population exceeding 10,000. In smaller counties the duties of the office may be carried out by the sheriff. The Constitution of 1876 qv specifies that the county tax assessor-collector be elected biennially; however, in 1954 a constitutional amendment changed the term of office to four years. The duties of the office have included both the determination of property values and the collection of taxes, but in 1982 the appraisal duties were reassigned to the chief appraiser of the district. The county tax assessor-collector is also responsible for motor-vehicle registration and voter registration.

BIBLIOGRAPHY: *Guide to Texas Laws for County Officials* (Austin: Texas Department of Community Affairs, 1988).

Vivian Elizabeth Smyrl

COUNTY TREASURER. The Constitution of 1876 qv provides for the biennial election of a county treasurer in each county. During the Republic of Texas qv the duties of the office were performed by the county clerk. The Constitution of 1845 qv provided for a separate officer appointed by the county board, but in 1850 the office was made elective with a term of two years. This provision has been maintained under each of the succeeding constitutions. A constitutional amendment in 1954 increased the term of office to four years. The chief functions of the county treasurer are to receive county funds and disburse them as directed by the county commissioners' court.qv He also examines the books of all county officers who receive any money.

BIBLIOGRAPHY: *Guide to Texas Laws for County Officials* (Austin: Texas Department of Community Affairs, 1988). Dick Smith, The Development of Local Government in Texas (Ph.D. dissertation, Harvard University, 1938).

Dick Smith

COUPLAND, THEODORE VAN BUREN (1836–1890). T. V. Coupland, military officer, lawman, and government official, was born on October 16, 1836, in Jefferson County, Alabama, the son of Hugh and Harriet (Macmillan) Coupland and a grand nephew of Texas governor Andrew Jackson Hamilton and Texas senator Morgan C. Hamilton.qqv He settled in Austin, Texas, before the Civil War qv and served as deputy sheriff in Travis County until secession,qv when, along with other Unionists and Masons in Central Texas, he moved to Mexico and later New Orleans. In that federally occupied city, Coupland joined a socially and politically prominent group, accepted a commission as a major in the First Texas Cavalry, U.S.A.qv He was mustered out in 1865. On December 21 of that year he married Frances Flanders, daughter of a New Orleans ship owner and niece of a Louisiana governor. Until 1883 Coupland held appointments as collector of customs for the port of New Orleans and as deputy clerk of the United States circuit court. In 1883, Coupland, his wife, and their son Frank Hamilton Coupland returned to Texas to land the elder Coupland inherited from his uncle, Senator Hamilton, on Brushy Creek in Williamson County. There Coupland farmed and ranched until his death, on January 3, 1890. Ostensibly because of his and his wife's family's extensive connections with developing rail lines in Louisiana, Texas, and Mexico, the community of Coupland, in southern Williamson County on the Missouri, Kansas and Texas Railroad, was named for him in 1887.

BIBLIOGRAPHY: *History of Texas, Together with a Biographical History of Milam, Williamson, Bastrop, Travis, Lee and Burleson Counties* (Chicago: Lewis, 1893). Vertical Files, Barker Texas History Center, University of Texas at Austin. John L. Waller, *Colossal Hamilton of Texas* (El Paso: Texas Western Press, 1968). *Glen E. Lich*

COUPLAND, TEXAS. Coupland is on State Highway 95 twenty-five miles northeast of Austin in Williamson County. The town was established and lots were sold in 1887, when the Bastrop and Taylor Railway was under construction. Coupland was named for Maj. Theodore van Buren Coupland, who settled in the area at that time.

The post office was begun in 1889, with John Goetz as postmaster. By 1900 the town was a prosperous meeting place for the German and Swiss farmers who had settled in the surrounding area. In the early 1980s Coupland had a population of 135, a church, a post office, a bank, an eight-grade school, a gin, a grain elevator, a community center, a restored depot and museum, a construction company, a grocery store, and the Old Coupland Inn, a popular eating establishment. In the early 1990s Coupland continued to report a population of 135.

BIBLIOGRAPHY: Clara Stearns Scarbrough, *Land of Good Water: A Williamson County History* (Georgetown, Texas: Williamson County Sun Publishers, 1973). *Clara Stearns Scarbrough*

COUPS DE FLÈCHES INDIANS. The Coups de Flèches Indians were reported in 1807 on the Texas-Louisiana border in association with Hasinais, Tawakonis, and Anadarkos.

BIBLIOGRAPHY: Frederick Webb Hodge, ed., *Handbook of American Indians North of Mexico* (2 vols., Washington: GPO, 1907, 1910; rpt., New York: Pageant, 1959). *Margery H. Krieger*

COURTHOUSE CEDAR. An eastern red cedar tree growing near the southwest corner of the courthouse square beside the Brazos County Courthouse in Bryan has grown at the site of five Brazos County courthouses. The tree was a sapling in January 1841, when the Congress of the Republic of Texas qv established Navasota (now Brazos) County. That spring, county officers were elected and the first term of district court convened in Joseph Ferguson's home, near the Ferguson Springs crossing of the Navasota River. At that time the sapling grew beside Ferguson's cabin, which served as the county's first courthouse. Later that year Boonville was chosen as the county seat, and a new courthouse was built there. The cedar sapling did not grace courthouse grounds again until 1854, when a two-story frame building was erected on the previous Boonville site. At this time Harvey Mitchell, called by some "the father of Brazos County," decided to plant native shrubs and trees around the new courthouse. He moved the little red cedar that had grown near the Ferguson log cabin to the new courthouse grounds. In 1866 Bryan, three miles to the west, became the Brazos county seat. In 1879 a new brick courthouse was built on the present courthouse square, and Mitchell moved the historic cedar to the new site, its third courthouse home. The brick courthouse was adjudged unsafe after about twenty years and was replaced in 1891 by a stone building. The present courthouse, built in 1957, towers protectively above the red cedar tree, whose existence is interwoven with the history of Brazos County.

BIBLIOGRAPHY: John A. Haislet, ed., *Famous Trees of Texas* (College Station: Texas Forest Service, 1970; 3d ed. 1984).

John A. Haislet

COURTHOUSE MOUNTAIN. Courthouse Mountain, with an elevation of 2,986 feet above sea level, rises 380 feet above the Salt Fork of the Brazos River and is sixteen miles south of Ralls in southwestern Crosby County (at 33°26′ N, 101°24′ W). Shallow loams on the mountain support short grasses, sand sagebrush, and mesquite.

COURTLANDT PLACE HISTORIC DISTRICT. The Courtlandt Place Historic District is one of Houston's earliest elite residential subdivisions. Modeled on suburban planning developed in St. Louis and known as the "private place," the district is an example of neighborhoods built as small private enclaves in response to the urban chaos of Houston in the early 1900s. Courtlandt Place centers around a one-block-long, tree-lined, divided boulevard, where eighteen examples of early twentieth-century architectural styles flank the street. The residential enclave began in 1906, when the Courtlandt Improvement Company purchased the land and laid out the subdivision on the southern edge of the city; the first houses were built in 1909. Gateways at the end of the central boulevard limited access to residents only, while deed restrictions stipulated land use, minimum cost, and house size. The Courtlandt Association, founded in 1912 by property owners, enforced these restrictions until the 1930s. Residences were built for entertaining at home; among them were houses designed by Sanguinet and Staats, Birdsall P. Briscoe, John F. Staub, and Warren and Wetmore.qqv Courtlandt Place served as a model for Montrose in 1910, but subsequently was replaced by new designs for suburban living. Early residents were the old elite of Houston, known for their "congeniality in philosophy and politics," and frequently related. The district was admitted to the National Register of Historic Places in 1979 and received a Texas historical marker in 1989.

BIBLIOGRAPHY: Howard Barnstone, *The Architecture of John F. Staub: Houston and the South* (Austin: University of Texas Press, 1979). Stephen Fox, *Houston Architectural Guide* (Houston: American Institute of Architects, Houston Chapter, 1990). Houston Metropolitan Research Center Files, Houston Public Library.

Diana J. Kleiner

COURTMAN, HENRY (1808–1836). Henry Courtman, Alamo defender, was born in Germany in 1808. He traveled to Texas from New Orleans as a member of Capt. Thomas Breece'sqv company of New Orleans Greysqv and took part in the siege of Bexar.qv Courtman remained in Bexar and died in the battle of the Alamoqv on March 6, 1836. His brother, George F. Courtman, was killed in the Goliad Massacre.qv

BIBLIOGRAPHY: Daughters of the American Revolution, *The Alamo Heroes and Their Revolutionary Ancestors* (San Antonio, 1976). Daughters of the Republic of Texas, *Muster Rolls of the Texas Revolution* (Austin, 1986). Bill Groneman, *Alamo Defenders* (Austin: Eakin, 1990). Walter Lord, *A Time to Stand* (New York: Harper, 1961; 2d ed., Lincoln: University of Nebraska Press, 1978).

Bill Groneman

COURTNEY, TEXAS (Grimes County). Courtney is on the Southern Pacific Railroad at the western end of Farm Road 2 in extreme southwestern Grimes County. It was established about 1860 when the Houston and Texas Central Railway extended a line south of Navasota through the vicinity of Red Gully Creek. The site was first settled by slaveholding Anglo-American immigrants in the early 1820s. Local tradition has it that Stephen F. Austinqv colonist Jared E. Groceqv acquired the tract on which the town was later founded for the price of a riding pony and a bolt of cloth. On his plantation, known as Groce's Retreat,qv Groce built a cotton gin and a sawmill, but a community did not develop among the local cotton farmers until the railroad built into the area. In 1860 a post office was opened there; W. J. Calloway, the operator of a general merchandise store, was the postmaster. The settlement was named in honor of Courtney Ann Fulton Groce, wife of J. E. Groce's son, Leonard Waller Groce.qv The Houston and Texas Central Railway constructed a large freight platform, a depot, and a telegraph office in the town, which quickly became a shipping center for cotton and other agricultural produce. The Courtney Male and Female School was in operation from 1869 to 1870. In 1871 the Mount Zion Missionary Baptist Church was organized by the Reverend Prince Kiel. A two-story Grange hall stood nearby during the 1870s. In 1885 the community's population was an estimated 200. Around 1900 Courtney had a blacksmith shop, a gristmill, a cottonseed oil mill (*see* COTTONSEED INDUSTRY), two cotton gins, three general stores, and a number of churches and schools. A new two-story brick schoolhouse was erected in 1913. By 1936 the community's population had increased to an estimated 250. Courtney's population declined after World War II,qv and by 1949 the town had an estimated fifty residents and two businesses. In 1990 the population of Courtney was estimated at fifty-five.

BIBLIOGRAPHY: Lester G. Bugbee, "The Old Three Hundred: A List of Settlers in Austin's First Colony," *Quarterly of the Texas State Historical Association* 1 (October 1897). Grimes County Historical Commission, *History of Grimes County, Land of Heritage and Progress* (Dallas: Taylor, 1982).

Charles Christopher Jackson

COURTNEY, TEXAS (Martin County). Courtney is in south central Martin County on land that had previously served as headquarters of the Christopher C. Slaughterqv ranch. The community was named for John H. Courtney, who in 1889 began farming there and who donated land for a school, which opened in 1907. A rural school district was organized in 1916, and Courtney became an independent school district in 1927. In 1949 the Badgett school was consolidated with that of Courtney, and in the 1950s the Courtney and Stanton schools were consolidated. Baptists and Methodists joined to build a union church, known as the Courtney Tabernacle, in 1924. The Baptists built a new building in 1941, and the Methodists disbanded in 1954. Church of Christ and Primitive Baptist congregations also met in Courtney. The 1984 county highway map showed a church at Courtney.

BIBLIOGRAPHY: Vernen Liles, Pioneering on the Plains: The History of Martin County, Texas (M.A. thesis, University of Texas, 1953). Martin County Historical Commission, *Martin County, Texas* (Dallas: Taylor, 1979).

Noel Wiggins

COURTNEY CREEK. Courtney Creek rises north of Interstate Highway 10 near Farm Road 1776 in western Pecos County (at 30°56′ N, 103°05′ W) and runs northeast for thirty-one miles, crossing U.S. Highway 285 twelve miles northwest of Fort Stockton, to its mouth near Imperial Reservoir, eight miles west of Imperial (at 31°15′ N, 102°50′ W). The creek is on the eastern edge of the Trans-Pecosqv region. It traverses an area of steep to gentle slopes with mostly shallow, loamy soils that support mesquites, sparse grasses, and cultivated row and cover crops.

COURT-PACKING PLAN OF 1937. In 1937 President Franklin D. Roosevelt proposed a reorganization of the judiciary that included his controversial "court-packing" plan. This plan would allow the president to appoint a new Supreme Court justice whenever an incumbent judge reached seventy and failed to retire; a maximum of six judges could be named in this manner. Roosevelt's proposal to reorganize the federal courts began a year of crisis. Even though he was at the peak of his power after the election of 1936, much of his opposition was still entrenched in the judiciary, as evidenced in the decisions invalidating such New Deal measures as the National Recovery Act, the Agricultural Adjustment Act, and the Guffey Coal Act of 1935.

In Texas the court-packing proposal served to crystallize sentiment that was already going against the New Deal. For much of the Texas delegation in Washington, largely composed of rural conservatives, the president's request symbolized a desire for unlimited power. The three Texans who led the fight against the court plan were Vice President John Nance Garner, Representative Hatton W. Sumners, and Senator Thomas T. Connally.qqv

On February 5, 1937, Roosevelt, without any advance warning, presented the proposed bill to a group of congressional leaders, including Garner and Sumners. From the start, Garner loathed the plan and thought that it would be a threat to party harmony. He began covertly to rally the opposition. Sumners, as chairman of the House Judiciary Committee, determined immediately that he would oppose the plan. He decided that the reorganization bill would not come up in his committee, because he knew that if it was reported out, it would pass in the House. He also wanted time to promote opposition among his colleagues and the people. Because of Sumners's opposition as well as his own misgivings about the bill, majority leader

Samuel T. (Sam) Rayburn[qv] helped convince the president that it would be unwise to bring the bill up in the House. Roosevelt therefore had it introduced in the Senate. Meanwhile, Sumners began to travel about the country making speeches about constitutional government. The bill never left his committee.

While Sumners was engaged in the House, Connally was active in the Senate, where he was a member of the Judiciary Committee. Up to this point he had supported the president, but he thought the court plan was unconstitutional. With the measure sidetracked from consideration in the House, the Senate Judiciary Committee occupied center stage, where Connally proved a formidable opponent. First, he addressed the Texas legislature and made it clear that he opposed the plan. Second, he organized a series of prominent Texas lawyers to testify before the Senate Judiciary Committee. Their condemnation of the bill attracted nationwide attention.

In the midst of this struggle, Garner left for home. Immediately, rumors circulated that he had walked out on Roosevelt. In spite of pleas from the president, Garner did not return to Washington. But when Senator Joseph T. Robinson died, Roosevelt chose Garner to represent him at the funeral. On the train back to Washington, Garner conferred with Senate leaders and concluded that the president's plan was finished. Upon his return to Washington, Garner saw the president and told him the bill was dead. Eventually, Garner was given credit for smoothing over the crisis, but he had also rendered himself persona non grata with the administration.

Not all Texans joined Garner, Sumners, and Connally in opposing the court plan. Most notable in support of the bill were Maury Maverick,[qv] who introduced it in the House, and Morris Sheppard.[qv] But with Garner, Sumners, and Connally providing legislative skill on the other side, the bill was defeated.

BIBLIOGRAPHY: Tom Connally and Alfred Steinberg, *My Name Is Tom Connally* (New York: Crowell, 1954). Lionel V. Patenaude, "Garner, Sumners, and Connally: The Defeat of the Roosevelt Court Bill in 1937," *Southwestern Historical Quarterly* 74 (July 1970). Lionel V. Patenaude, *Texans, Politics and the New Deal* (New York: Garland, 1983). Bascom N. Timmons, *Garner of Texas* (New York: Harper, 1948).

Lionel V. Patenaude

COURTRIGHT, TIMOTHY ISAIAH (1845–1887). Timothy Isaiah (Longhair Jim) Courtright, two-gun marshal of Fort Worth, was born in Sangamon County, Illinois, in the spring of 1845, the son of Daniel Courtright. He married Sarah Elizabeth Weeks in 1870 and had at least three children. At seventeen he served in the Civil War[qv] as a member of the Seventh Iowa Infantry under Gen. John Logan, who later took him to New Mexico to work as a hired gun on the Logan ranch. During his Civil War service Cartwright won high praise for bravery at Fort Donelson and Vicksburg and acquired the nickname Jim, a mistake for Tim. After the war he served as an army scout and acquired the name Longhair, after the style in which scouts often wore their hair. Courtright always wore two six-shooters, butts forward, and drew from the right hip with the right hand. According to most students of the matter, he and Robert Clay Allison[qv] were faster on the draw than Wild Bill Hickok, Wyatt Earp, and Bartholomew (Bat) Masterson.[qv] Mrs. Courtright was also an excellent shot, and the couple traveled with a Wild West show as companions of Hickok.

In 1873, near Fort Worth, the Courtrights tried farming. After the farm failed, they moved to town, where Courtright worked as city jailer and in 1876 was elected city marshal by three votes. Since its incorporation as a city in 1873, Fort Worth had attracted the negative elements of a frontier town. Gambling, drinking, prostitution, and crime became rampant, but much of this vice brought income to the city, and Courtright soon learned that his job was not to clean up but simply to keep peace. While he was marshal, any attempts he made to enforce laws or make reforms met with the disapproval of the merchants. They told him to stop the flow of blood, but not that of liquor. In 1879 Courtright ran for a fourth term and was defeated by S. M. Farmer, after which the ex-marshal hung out around town, opened a detective agency that failed, spent time gambling and drinking, and then was invited to New Mexico.

His stay there was brief. After being accused of involvement in two murders, he escaped territorial authorities and returned to Fort Worth, where he opened the T. I. Courtright Commercial Detective Agency. When Texas Rangers[qv] and a New Mexico official arrived in the city to arrest him, an estimated 2,000 armed citizens challenged them. Although initially taken into custody, Courtright later escaped with the aid of friends. Eventually he returned to New Mexico, where he was acquitted due to insufficient evidence. In Fort Worth he was hired temporarily as deputy marshall during the Great Southwest Strike[qv] of 1886. Against the wishes of striking railroaders, he attempted to move the trains and, when two killings occurred, was blamed for siding with the railroads.

Courtright's career was brought to an end on February 8, 1887. Luke Short, a former friend of his, shot and killed him in one of the most famous gunfights in western history—and, contrary to the movie legends, one of the few face-to-face shootouts. The reason for the killing was never determined, though Short and Courtright were rivals for control of gambling interests in Fort Worth.

The question of Courtright's popularity in Fort Worth is moot. Though citizens protested his arrest by New Mexico legal authorities and turned out in droves for his funeral, they soundly defeated him in his attempt at reelection for a fourth term as marshal. Court records show that he was a bully and a brawler, and he was never endorsed by the Fort Worth *Democrat,* the city's leading newspaper. Nevertheless, his funeral procession was six blocks long, the largest the city had seen. Courtright is buried at Oakwood Cemetery in Fort Worth.

BIBLIOGRAPHY: Oliver Knight, *Fort Worth, Outpost on the Trinity* (Norman: University of Oklahoma Press, 1953). F. Stanley [Stanley F. L. Crocchiola], *Jim Courtright* (Denver: World, 1957). Mack H. Williams, comp., *The News-Tribune in Old Fort Worth* (Fort Worth: News-Tribune, 1975).

Carol E. Williams

COUSHATTA CREEK. Coushatta (originally Caschatta or Cachate) Creek rises three miles northeast of Alleyton in northeastern Colorado County (at 29°45′ N, 96°27′ W) and runs southeast for 15½ miles to its mouth on the San Bernard River, just north of the Atchison, Topeka and Santa Fe crossing (at 29°40′ N, 96°16′ W). The stream runs through broad, rolling to level coastal prairies with deep soils. The land is used for pasture or, where the terrain is level, for the production of rice. The lower part of the creek's course bisects the Attwater Prairie Chicken National Wildlife Refuge.[qv] The creek is named for the Coushatta Indians.

COUSHATTA INDIANS. The Coushattas (Koasatis), an important Muskogean-speaking Indian tribe, had moved to village sites near what is now Montgomery, Alabama, when discovered by the French at the beginning of the eighteenth century. This tribe was a member of the Upper Creek (or Muskogee) Confederacy and has always been closely associated with the Alabama (Alibamu) Indian tribe. When the English defeated the French, and the latter began leaving the territory east of the Mississippi River after 1763, many Alabamas and Coushattas left their homes on the Alabama River and migrated to Louisiana. Of several villages the Coushattas established in various sections of Louisiana, the largest was near the mouth of Quicksand Creek on the east bank of the Sabine River about eighty miles south of Natchitoches, Louisiana. In the 1780s the Coushattas began drifting across the border into Spanish Texas.[qv] There they were welcomed by the Spanish officials in Nacogdoches, Texas, who expected them to strengthen the bulwark of friendly tribes on the eastern border of Texas. During the early nineteenth century the Coushattas blazed an important trail from their Sabine River village westward to La Bahía.qv This trail, known as the Coushatta Trace,qv was a wilderness thoroughfare used by Indians, adventurers, and smugglers journeying between Louisiana and Mexico.

To control this traffic through the heart of Texas, the Spanish posted Coushattas at strategic points along the Trinity River to serve as sentinels and scouts. They were to inform the Spanish in Nacogdoches of any activity on the Coushatta Trace or the Trinity River. In 1830 about 600 Coushattas were living in or near three Coushatta communities, and the population living in independent villages reached its zenith. They hunted, gathered, fished, and farmed, and they traded with white settlers. In what is now San Jacinto County, where the Coushatta Trace crossed the Trinity River, was the Upper Coushatta Village (Battise Villageqv). This village site was on the opposite side of the Trinity River from the site of Onalaska in Polk County and is now under the waters of Lake Livingston. John R. Swanton quoted William Bollaert'sqv estimate that in 1850 there were 500 Coushatta warriors in the Battise Village and Colita's Village.qv Long King's Village,qv the Middle Coushatta village, was at the confluence of Tempe Creek and Long King Creek, in Polk County about two miles north of the present site of Lake Livingston Dam on the Trinity River. This village could be called the headquarters of the Coushatta Tribe: here lived Long King,qv the principal chief above all other Coushatta chiefs. The village's importance in the Big Thicketqv during the 1830s was further evidenced by the trails that radiated from it like spokes from the hub of a wheel. The location of Long King's Village is shown on various maps prepared by the General Land Officeqv in Austin. The last in this series of GLO maps indicating the continued existence of this village is dated 1856.

Colita,qv one of the best-known Indian chiefs in East Texas, lived in the Lower Coushatta Village. He succeeded Long King as principal chief in the latter part of the 1830s. His village was on the Logan league in what is now San Jacinto County, in a great bend of the Trinity River called the Shirt-tail Bend by the steamboat sailors. As indicated in the estimate for the Battise Village, the population of Colita's Village remained at a substantial level until at least 1850. The Coushatta chiefs Long King, Tempe,qv and Long Tomqv all had creeks named after them in Polk County. In addition to these chiefs and Colita, other Texas Coushatta chiefs were Ben-Ash,qv Canasa Gimingu, Chickasaw Abbey, Mingo, Payacho, Pia Mingo, and Usacho. The Coushattas remained neutral during the Texas Revolutionqv at the request of Gen. Sam Houston.qv But during the Runaway Scrape,qv when Texas families fled before Antonio López de Santa Anna'sqv advancing Mexican army, the Coushattas fed and cared for white settlers who surged through their villages. During the early years of the Republic of Texas,qv Mexican agents tried to incite counterrevolution in several areas and apparently were able to influence Kickapoos and members of other Indian tribes in East Texas. Coushatta chief Colita, however, managed to maintain peaceful relations with the white settlers. Nonetheless, the Coushattas could not entirely avoid the turmoil of the period 1836–39. A Comanche raiding party approached Long King's Village from the north in 1839; in the valley of Long King Creek the Coushattas defeated and turned back the invaders.

For nearly a century after 1763 the Coushattas were compelled to move from one place to another in search of permanent homes. Whenever white men wanted the land on which Coushattas happened to be living, the Indians moved. Their prospects seemed to brighten when the Congress of the Republic of Texasqv in 1840 granted two leagues of land (including Battise Village and Colita's Village) to the Coushattas for permanent reservations. Though the land was surveyed and the field notes filed, the grants were never made effective because white settlers had already claimed the land. In the 1850s two events further darkened the Coushatta prospects. First, in 1852, Chief Colita died. He had been such an effective leader that the Galveston Newsqv editorially lamented his passing. His death left the tribe leaderless at a critical time. Second, the Coushattas failed to obtain land for a reservation. Though the Texas legislature in 1855 granted them 640 acres for a permanent home, suitable land was no longer available in Polk County, and the grant remained only a scrap of paper. Fortunately for the Coushattas, however, their kinsmen, the Alabamas, had received a grant of Polk County land in 1854. With the permission of the Alabamas, most of the Coushattas settled on this reservation in 1859. A few remained on the site of Colita's Village in San Jacinto County until 1906, when they joined the others on the Polk County reservation. See also ALABAMA-COUSHATTA INDIANS.

BIBLIOGRAPHY: David B. Edward, *The History of Texas* (Cincinnati: James, 1936; rpt., Austin: Texas State Historical Association, 1990). Mattie Austin Hatcher, *The Opening of Texas to Foreign Settlement, 1801–1821* (University of Texas Bulletin 2714, 1927). *A Pictorial History of Polk County, Texas, 1846–1910* (Livingston, Texas: Polk County Bicentennial Commission, 1976; rev. ed. 1978). John R. Swanton, *Early History of the Creek Indians and Their Neighbors*, Smithsonian Institution, Bureau of American Ethnology Bulletin 73 (Washington: GPO, 1922). Dorman H. Winfrey and James M. Day, eds., *Texas Indian Papers* (4 vols., Austin: Texas State Library, 1959–61; rpt., 5 vols., Austin: Pemberton Press, 1966). Howard N. Martin

COUSHATTA-NACOGDOCHES TRACE. The Coushatta-Nacogdoches Trace was a trail used primarily by Coushatta Indians on trips from their village on the Sabine River to Nacogdoches, Texas. The large village was on the east bank of the Sabine River, opposite the mouth of Quicksand Creek. Dr. John Sibley,qv the American Indian agent in Natchitoches, Louisiana, wrote that this Coushatta village was approximately eighty miles south of Natchitoches. From the village the combined Coushatta-Nacogdoches Trace and the Coushatta Traceqv ran northwestward across Newton County and northern Jasper County to the Kisatchie Wold,qv a continuous ridge from the Mississippi River floodplain to the lower Rio Grande valley in Texas. At this point the Coushatta Trace turned westward along the Kisatchie Wold, and the Coushatta-Nacogdoches Trace continued in a northwest direction, traversing southern San Augustine County, crossing Attoyac Bayou north of its confluence with the Angelina River, and continuing to Nacogdoches.

An 1820 map of Louisiana and Mississippi, published by H. S. Tanner of Philadelphia, shows the route of the trail from the Coushatta village on the Sabine River to Nacogdoches. The Spanish post of Nacogdoches was an important factor in the pattern of living developed by the Coushatta and Alabama Indian tribes in the Big Thicket.qv Nacogdoches served as governmental administration center, military post, source of supplies and presents, and a market for deer hides, bear oil, and other items sold by the Indians near Nacogdoches. The increasing significance of Coushatta contacts with this trading and distribution center led to the development of a nearly straight trail from the Coushattas' village on the Sabine to Nacogdoches. The Spanish commandant at Nacogdoches maintained a record, the Nacogdoches Diary of Daily Events, which includes references to visits of Coushattas for various purposes.

BIBLIOGRAPHY: Isaac Joslin Cox, "The Louisiana-Texas Frontier," *Quarterly of the Texas State Historical Association* 10, 17 (July 1906, July, October 1913). John Sibley, *A Report From Natchitoches in 1807* (New York: Museum of the American Indian, Heye Foundation, 1922). Howard N. Martin

COUSHATTA TRACE. The Coushatta Trace was a road from Louisiana into Texas that was used by the Coushatta Indians in their hunting and trading activities. It was an important middle road between the better-known and Spanish-patrolled Atascosito Roadqv along the Texas coast and the Old San Antonio Roadqv farther inland. The first group of Coushattas migrated to Louisiana in approximately 1766, following a group of Alabamas who had established a village on the Opelousas River and soon thereafter established a large village on the Sabine River near the mouth of Quicksand Creek. They opened a path from their village southwestward to La Bahía,qv and perhaps farther, known to early American settlers as the Coushatta Trace. This trail was not much more than a narrow path barely suitable for riders on horseback. In the field notes for a survey of a tract of land now in Polk County a Mexican surveyor called a section of this trail a *sendal* or footpath. It led to the best crossings of streams or rivers and proceeded straight across the country. Gen. Sam Houstonqv chose the route at its crossing of the Brazos in his retreat in 1836. Trains of packmules loaded with merchandise in transit from Louisiana to Mexico used the route, and field notes for some of the surveys along the Coushatta Trace refer to it as the "contraband trace." There is no indication that the Coushatta Trace was ever patrolled by Spanish or Mexican military units, and it probably was a favorite route for contraband traders. Also, the trail was used by several early settlers coming into Stephen F. Austin'sqv colony. Jared E. Groce,qv one of the Old Three Hundredqv colonists, moved to Texas in 1821 and established a settlement in the area that is now Waller County at the crossing of the Coushatta Trace and the Brazos River. Francis Hollandqv also traveled the Coushatta Trace from Louisiana to Austin's colony in 1822 with a large party of relatives.

In organizing the Austin colony for governmental purposes, the ayuntamientoqv of San Felipe used portions of the Coushatta Trace to establish boundaries of the Bastrop and Viesca precincts. Titles or grants to land, beginning in 1821, frequently refer to the Coushatta Trace to establish location. For example, Merrit M. Coates, on July 19, 1824, received title to a square league of land on the east side of the Brazos, 2½ linear leagues above the Coushatta crossing. The deed records of Austin County for July 13, 1824, show that land about a quarter league above the Coushatta crossing of the Brazos was granted to William Smeathers (*see* SMOTHERS, WILLIAM).

Although the Coushatta Trace and the Atascosito Road were the most important roads through Austin's colony, the actual route of the Coushatta Trace has been discovered only generally and recently. After tracing indications of the route on surveyor's field notes for 3,000 land grants in the Texas counties along the probable route, Howard N. Martin identified a map of the trace. The trail extended from the Coushatta village on the Sabine River through the area of ten present Texas counties and merged with the Atascosito Road in Colorado County. From the Coushatta village on the Sabine River, one major trail led eastward to Opelousas, Louisiana, and another, the Coushatta-Nacogdoches Trace,qv extended northwestward to the post of Nacogdoches, where the Coushattas traded and received presents from the Spanish. The Coushatta Trace began at the village on the Sabine and proceeded through the area of present Newton and Jasper counties, using the same path as the Coushatta-Nacogdoches Trace, to the Kisatchie Wold.qv It then turned westward along this ridge, crossed the Neches River near the mouth of Shawnee Creek, and passed through the Alabama Indian villages of Cane Island and Peachtreeqqv in what is now northwestern Tyler County. Continuing to follow the Kisatchie Wold westward, the Coushatta Trace moved through the site of present Moscow in Polk County, crossed the Trinity River near the Battise Villageqv of the Coushattas, and passed through the area of present San Jacinto County and the southeastern corner of Walker County.

In the area of present Montgomery County the Coushatta Trace passed along the eastern side of the San Jacinto River, crossed this river near the Iron Mound league, and turned west. It ran south of the site of present Montgomery and then passed through what is now Waller County to the Coushatta crossing of the Brazos River. A General Land Officeqv map of Austin County shows the Coushatta Trace extending from the William C. Whiteqv survey at the Coushatta crossing to the James Cumminsqv five-league mill tract south of Bellville, through the Miles N. Allenqv survey, and from there across the San Bernard River to merge with the Atascosito Road at the Rawson Alleyqv survey, on the east bank of the Colorado River in Colorado County. The merged Atascosito Road–Coushatta Trace traversed the area of several Texas counties en route to La Bahía or Goliad.

This trail became so traveled that the Mexican government erected Fort Teran in 1831 at the Coushatta Trace crossing of the Neches River as a means of controlling the movement of settlers into Texas. Later, stagecoach and horse mail routes were established along sections of this trace. When new counties were organized in Texas after 1845, one of the principal responsibilities of the commissioners' court in each county was to "view" and establish new roads, and these new roads gradually replaced the Coushatta Trace. Only a few sections of this trail remained in use in the 1990s: an example is the paved ten-mile section of Farm Road 350 west of Moscow in central Polk County.

BIBLIOGRAPHY: Eugene C. Barker, ed., "Minutes of the Ayuntamiento of San Felipe de Austin, 1828–1832," 12 parts, *Southwestern Historical Quarterly* 21–24 (January 1918–October 1920). Leland C. Bement, *Buried in the Bottoms: The Archeology of Lake Creek Reservoir, Montgomery County, Texas* (Texas Archeological Survey, University of Texas at Austin, 1987). E. L. Blair, *Early History of Grimes County* (Austin, 1930). Julia Kathryn Garrett, "Dr. John Sibley and the Louisiana-Texas Frontier, 1803–1914," *Southwestern Historical Quarterly* 45–49 (January 1942–April 1946). Thomas Clarence Richardson, *East Texas: Its History and Its Makers* (4 vols., New York: Lewis Historical Publishing, 1940). Dudley Goodall Wooten, ed., *A Comprehensive History of Texas* (2 vols., Dallas: Scarff, 1898; rpt., Austin: Texas State Historical Association, 1986). Howard N. Martin

COUSINS, ROBERT BARTOW (1861–1932). Robert Bartow Cousins, educator, son of Isaac William and Mary Elizabeth (Bennet) Cousins, was born in Fayetteville, Georgia, on July 21, 1861. On the day of his birth his father, a surgeon in the Confederate Army, was serving under Gen. Francis Bartow in the first battle of Bull Run; Bartow was killed in that battle, and Isaac Cousins reportedly named his son in the general's honor. Since the family farm was in the path of William T. Sherman'sqv devastating March to the Sea, young Robert spent his early boyhood in a world of near-poverty and limited schooling. At one time his mother had her own backyard school for area children, but after the county schools were finally reestablished, Cousins eagerly absorbed books and decided early in life on a teaching profession.

He studied at the University of Georgia and received his B.A. degree in 1882. Although he read law in the office of a prominent Florida attorney and passed the bar exam in Atlanta, he continued to pursue a teaching career. He moved to Texas and taught Latin and Greek at the high school in Longview. There he married Dora M. Kelly on September 5, 1885. Their first child, a daughter, died in infancy, but five more children were born to the couple. Cousins served for two years as school superintendent at Mineola, then for sixteen years at Mexia, where he gained a statewide reputation as a school administrator. In 1897–98 he served as president of the Texas State Teachers Associationqv and in 1902 became an assistant to John L. Wortham in the business office of the Texas State Penitentiary at Huntsville.qv

In 1904 Cousins was elected state superintendent of public instruction; under his leadership between 1905 and 1910, several important educational reforms were introduced, including state accreditation, public school taxes, and the upgrading of standards for teachers. Cousins helped organize the Texas Conference for Education in 1907, and in 1909 he became a member of the Texas State Library and Historical Commission.qv In 1910 he resigned his superintendency to become president of West Texas State Normal College (now West Texas State University) at Canyon, which he had helped establish. He carefully selected the faculty of the college and formulated the high standards for which it became noted. He and Joseph A. Hillqv coauthored a textbook, *American History for Schools* (1913), which was adopted by public schools in several southern states. Cousins's youngest son died of meningitis at the age of thirteen, and in his memory Cousins instituted the Gregg Cousins Loan Fund at West Texas State. In the summer of 1918 he resigned his presidency to go into business at Longview. At the ceremony in which he relinquished the position to Hill, Cousins placed on Hill's finger a gold ring symbolic of "the purity and permanency of the invisible values which this, our college, seeks to develop." This presidential ring has since been passed on to each succeeding WTSU president. The first women's dormitory at the college was built in 1920 and named in Cousins's honor.

Cousins remained at Longview until 1921, when he became superintendent of the Houston public schools. There he engaged in constructive reform until 1924, when he accepted the presidency of the new South Texas State Teachers College (now Texas A&M University at Kingsville). Although he tackled this new position with characteristic zeal, Cousins always regarded West Texas State as his "favorite child" and kept up with its progress. He took leave in 1926 to do graduate work at the University of Chicago and was given an LL.D. degree by Southwestern University at Georgetown in 1930. In 1929 he reorganized the curriculum of South Texas State College and changed its name to Texas College of Arts and Industries, seeking to provide a broader program worthy of greater financial support. However, the Great Depression[qv] reduced state funds, so that Cousins and the regents had to seek alternative sources of financing. In the long run his tireless efforts proved successful for the university. Cousins was a longtime member of the Texas State Teachers Association. On March 3, 1932, he died of influenza. He was buried in Kingsville Cemetery.

BIBLIOGRAPHY: Joseph A. Hill, *More Than Brick and Mortar* (Amarillo: Russell Stationery, 1959). Ruth Lowes and W. Mitchell Jones, *We'll Remember Thee: An Informal History of West Texas State University* (Canyon: WTSU Alumni Association, 1984).

H. Allen Anderson

COUSINS, WALTER HENRY (1878–1942). Walter Henry Cousins, pharmacist, poet, and historian, the son of Henry Clay and Frances Cousins, was born on August 18, 1878, near Whitson, Texas. He attended Whitson, Walker, and Haunted Hill schools. In 1898 his family moved west to Haskell County, where Walter worked as a bronco buster on the MN Ranch in Haskell, Throckmorton, and Knox counties. He was also camp cook for trail drives across Oklahoma during this period. In 1902, after an apprenticeship, he became a licensed druggist. That year he also married Sue Reeves McClendon. They eventually had two children. Cousins was appointed a member of the State Board of Pharmacy[qv] in 1913 and became secretary in 1920. He held this office until December 1, 1941, when ill health forced him to retire. He bought and became editor of the *Southern Pharmaceutical Journal* in Dallas in 1915. That year he was elected secretary-treasurer of the Texas Pharmaceutical Association,[qv] and in 1918 he became president of the National Association of Retail Druggists. He owned drugstores in Munday and Wichita Falls.

He helped to establish the Texas Cowboy Reunion[qv] at Stamford in 1930 and served as historian, vice president, and president of the Reunion Association. He was author of *Cuz* (1922) and "Range Poems" in Lona Shawver's *Chuck Wagon Windies* (1934). He also wrote numerous poems, ballads, and articles that appeared in pharmaceutical journals and Texas Cowboy Reunion publications. He died in Dallas on February 6, 1942.

BIBLIOGRAPHY: *Cattleman*, March 1942. Vertical Files, Barker Texas History Center, University of Texas at Austin.

Laura Simmons

COUTCHMAN, TEXAS. Coutchman was on Farm Road 489 five miles west of Streetman in northern Freestone County. The site was settled around 1850 and was named for William Coutchman and his family, who owned much land in the area. At one time the town had about 300 residents, two Masonic organizations, a grocery store, a gin, and a school. It also had four churches—one Methodist, two Baptist, and an Assembly of God. A post office was established in 1894 in W. T. Stubbs's grocery store. By 1905 the post office had closed. At one time the community's school had an attendance of more than fifty, but it was eventually consolidated with the Wortham school district. In the 1930s the community had only a few scattered dwellings, and by the late 1980s it was no longer shown on county highway maps. Blues singer and guitarist Blind Lemon Jefferson[qv] was born in the area and spent some of his youth there.

BIBLIOGRAPHY: Freestone County Historical Commission, *History of Freestone County, Texas* (Fairfield, Texas, 1978).

Chris Cravens

COVE, TEXAS. Cove is at the junction of Farm Road 565 and Interstate Highway 10, thirty-five miles east of Houston in western Chambers County. The settlement was named for its protected location on Trinity Bay and was once called Winfree's Cove, after pioneer settler A. B. J. Winfree. An Indian graveyard is nearby. In 1871 William Icet operated what was reputedly the first cotton gin in the county at Cove. Although the gin was sold and moved in 1880, Icet and his sons, W. S. and H. C. Icet, ran a shipyard there until 1915. The family also operated a sawmill at the Cove settlement. Fishing has been of considerable importance to area residents. The first school opened at the community in 1885, and the Cove post office was established in 1894. The community's school district was consolidated with the Barbers Hill schools in 1937. The Cove population, estimated to be 150 in 1920, had declined to about forty by the late 1940s. The construction of large plants for United States Steel, Houston Lighting and Power, and MoBay Chemical along nearby Cedar Bayou led to new growth in the community. In 1970 Cove reported a population of 106. The town was incorporated in 1973 and had 645 residents by 1980. In 1990 its population was 402.

BIBLIOGRAPHY: Kendon L. Clark, *Diamond in the Rough: A History of Cove, Texas, 1824–1900* (Ozark, Missouri: Yates Publishing Company, 1982). Jewel Horace Harry, *A History of Chambers County* (M.A. thesis, University of Texas, 1940; rpt., Dallas: Taylor, 1981).

Robert Wooster

COVE CITY, TEXAS. Cove City was on Farm Road 1006 just south of Orange and about twenty-five miles east of Beaumont in eastern Orange County. A Cove school, named for the contour of land formed by the confluence of Adams Bayou and the Sabine River, was operating at the community by 1883. The establishment of the Cove school district encouraged further community development, as did the influx of new workers to Orange shipbuilding plants during World War I.[qv] In 1954 residents voted, 120 to 109, to incorporate Cove City. The census of 1960 set its population at 1,749; by 1970 that figure had fallen to 1,578. By 1974 Cove City had been annexed by its larger northern neighbor, Orange. In the 1980s the area remained largely urban.

BIBLIOGRAPHY: Allie Bland, "History of the Cove School," *Las Sabinas: The Official Quarterly Publication of the Orange County Historical Society* 5 (Spring 1979).

Robert Wooster

COVE SPRING, TEXAS. Cove Spring (Cove Springs), a farming community four miles east of Melrose in eastern Nacogdoches County, was settled before the Civil War[qv] and was the site of one of the earliest churches in the county. In 1858 Daniel H. Vail donated thirty acres there for a church and school. The community has for many years been the site of an annual reunion and singing convention the second Sunday in October. In the early 1990s a church, a cemetery, and a few scattered houses still remained in the area.

BIBLIOGRAPHY: Nacogdoches County Genealogical Society, *Nacogdoches County Families* (Dallas: Curtis, 1985).
Christopher Long

COVE SPRINGS, TEXAS. Cove Springs, off U.S. Highway 175 some eighteen miles northwest of Rusk in northwestern Cherokee County, was first settled in the 1850s. It was named for a spring on the old Neches Saline Road, a frequent stopping point for travelers. A local school was in operation by 1896, when it had an enrollment of twenty-three. A Methodist church was organized at the community before 1900, and the Cove Springs Baptist Church was established in 1932. At its height on the eve of World War II qv Cove Springs had two churches, several businesses, and a number of houses. After the war many residents left the area, but in the early 1990s two churches and a few businesses still remained.

BIBLIOGRAPHY: *Cherokee County History* (Jacksonville, Texas: Cherokee County Historical Commission, 1986).
Christopher Long

COVEY, JOHN VAN EPPS (1821–1898). John Van Epps Covey, Baptist minister and educator, was born in Fenner County, New York, on February 11, 1821. He graduated from Madison College (later Colgate) in 1845 and married Mrs. Louisa Renshaw Fastwood. He was ordained a Baptist minister in 1847. In 1856 the Coveys moved to Palestine, Texas, where Covey became the head of Franklin College,qv a Masonic school. Within a year they moved to Hallettsville, where he became the president of Alma Institute.qv From Hallettsville the next move was to DeWitt County, where, at Concrete, Covey established what was later known as Concrete College.qv He was its head from 1865 to 1881. For a time he taught in McMullen Collegeqv and was active in raising funds. After the death of his wife in 1882 Covey returned to the ministry and preached in and around Cotulla, where he died on January 13, 1898.

BIBLIOGRAPHY: Robert W. Shook, "Covey's College at Concrete," *East Texas Historical Journal* 6 (March 1968). Ed Wildman, Concrete College and Its Founder (M.A. thesis, Southwest Texas State Teachers College, 1944).
Ed Wildman

COVEY CHAPEL, TEXAS. Covey Chapel, also known as Ratama and as St. Mary's, is on Farm Road 85 some nine miles west of Dilley in far southwestern Frio County. The community was the site of brush arbor meetings held by a Reverend Roberts who arrived on horseback. The cemetery and St. Mary's Church were started at the site in 1909 and 1916, respectively, on land donated by local resident Bernard Brown. In 1929 the community had a church and scattered dwellings. By 1936 the name of the community was Ratama; it had a church, two cemeteries, one business, and about ten dwellings. In 1947 St. Mary's Church was destroyed by a storm, and Masses were then held in the homes of Wesley Carroll and Hubert Dunn. By 1949 the community was known as Covey Chapel and as St. Mary's. In 1950 the newly rebuilt St. Mary's Church was again the religious center of the community. In 1974 very few dwellings remained around the church and cemetery. The Covey Chapel Cemetery and the St. Mary's Church and Cemetery were at the site in 1989.

BIBLIOGRAPHY: *Frio County, Texas: A History* (Pearsall, Texas: Frio Pioneer Jail Museum Association, 1979). Vertical Files, Pearsall Public Library, Pearsall, Texas.
Ruben E. Ochoa

COVINGTON, BENJAMIN JESSE (1869–1961). Benjamin Covington, a black physician in Houston, was born in 1869 near Marlin, Texas, the son of Ben and Georgiana Covington, former slaves. As a young man he worked on a farm and attended school near Marlin. Around 1885 he entered Hearne Baptist Academy, where he supported himself as janitor and bell ringer. After graduating in 1892 he taught school but encountered hostility from some members of the white community who thought his salary was too high for a Negro.

Following a stint as a bookkeeper he entered Meharry Medical College in 1895. While still a student at Meharry he spent several months practicing medicine in Wharton, Texas, on a temporary permit. Covington graduated from Meharry in 1900. After another brief stay in Wharton he moved to Yoakum, where other doctors received him more favorably.

In 1903 Covington moved to Houston with his wife, Jennie Belle Murphy Covington,qv whom he had married in 1902. Covington practiced general medicine in Houston for fifty-eight years. He is best known as one of the five physicians who helped establish Houston Negro Hospital (now Riverside General Hospitalqv in 1925. His formula for the treatment of influenza, which he considered a form of yellow fever, was very successful and was used by United States medical officers. He was active in the push for improved public facilities and public health conditions. He helped reorganize the Lone Star Medical, Dental, and Pharmaceutical Association,qv a professional association of black physicians, and served as secretary-treasurer for ten years and as president in 1920. Over the course of his career Covington took fifty-one post-graduate "refresher and modernization" courses at Prairie View, Tuskegee, Flint-Goodridge (New Orleans), and the Mayo Clinic.

Covington belonged to the Omega fraternity, Young Men's Christian Association, Masonic lodge, and Business and Professional Men's Club. He was also a member of Antioch Baptist Church, where he accompanied the choir on his violin. He also taught himself to play the piano, mandolin, and cornet.

During World War IIqv Covington received citations from presidents Franklin D. Roosevelt and Harry Truman commending him for his services to the Selective Service System. The Masonic lodge established a medical college scholarship in his honor. Covington died on July 21, 1961, and was buried in Paradise Cemetery (North). He was survived by his wife and daughter, Ernestine Jessie Covington Dent. In 1994 a Texas historical marker was placed at the site of the Covington home at 2219 Dowling Street.

BIBLIOGRAPHY: Howard H. Bell, "Benjamin Jesse Covington, M.D., 1869–1961," *Journal of the National Medical Association* 55 (September 1963). Benjamin Covington Collection, Houston Metropolitan Research Center, Houston Public Library. Albert Walter and Jessie Covington Dent Papers, Amistad Research Center, Tulane University. Martin Kaufman et al., eds., *Dictionary of American Medical Biography* (2 vols., Westport, Connecticut: Greenwood, 1984). Fred Nahas, ed., *Houston: City of Destiny* (New York: Macmillan, 1980).
John S. Gray III

COVINGTON, JENNIE BELLE MURPHY (1881–1966). Jennie Belle (Ladybelle) Murphy Covington, African-American civic leader, was born on September 21, 1881, in Clinton, DeWitt County, Texas, the daughter of Rachel Thomas. She was raised in Dement by her aunt and uncle, Jane and Will Jones. As a girl she developed a great love of gardening and frequently ordered seeds from New Orleans. She attended Guadalupe College in Seguin, where she worked as a seamstress for the wife of the college president, David Abner, Jr.qv She married Dr. Benjamin Jesse Covingtonqv on September 30, 1902, at the Second Baptist Church in Seguin. After living for a short period in Yoakum the Covingtons moved to Houston in 1903.

Jennie Covington was a founder of the Blue Triangle Branch of the Young Women's Christian Association and served as the first chairwoman of its committee on administration. She was also a cofounder and first head of the Houston Commission on Interracial Cooperation and served for more than a decade as chairman of the Texas Commission on Interracial Cooperation. She was a member of the executive board of the Texas Commission on Race Relations in the mid-1950s, a member of the first board of the Negro Child Center, and a member and first chairman of the Houston Settlement Association. Mrs. Covington also served with the Women in Yellow and with the Ladies in Gray, groups that assisted Jefferson Davis Hospital and the Houston Negro Hospital (later Riverside General Hospital), respectively.

She was a charter member of the YWCA Garden Club and won numerous blue ribbons at garden shows. She also belonged to the Married Ladies Social, Art, and Charity Club; the Ada Miller Band; and the Court of Calanthe. She was an ardent member of the Antioch Baptist Church on Robin Street.

Because Houston hotels were segregated, the Covingtons hosted many prominent black Americans who visited the city, including Marian Anderson, Booker T. Washington, Roland Hayes, William Pickens, and Anne Brown. Jennie Covington was among the first group of women honored by the YWCA with an Award of Distinction "for outstanding community leadership and service." She received recognition as an Ideal Mother from Antioch Baptist Church and as Woman of the Year from the Gamma Omega chapter of Zeta Phi Beta sorority. In her honor the Women's Auxiliary of the Houston Medical Forum established the Jennie B. Covington Award, an award for nursing students. The Covingtons had one daughter. Jennie Covington died on October 8, 1966, survived by her daughter, one brother, and two sisters. She was buried in Paradise Cemetery (North) in Houston. In 1990 her daughter and grandchildren dedicated electronic chimes at Antioch Baptist Church in honor of her and her husband. In 1994 a Texas historical marker was placed at the site of the Covington home at 2219 Dowling Street.

BIBLIOGRAPHY: Howard H. Bell, "Benjamin Jesse Covington, M.D., 1869–1961," *Journal of the National Medical Association* 55 (September 1963). Benjamin Covington Collection, Houston Metropolitan Research Center, Houston Public Library. Albert Walter and Jessie Covington Dent Papers, Amistad Research Center, Tulane University. Houston *Post*, October 10, 1966. Fred Nahas, ed., *Houston: City of Destiny* (New York: Macmillan, 1980). Ruthe Winegarten, *Finder's Guide to the 'Texas Women: A Celebration of History' Exhibit Archives* (Denton: Texas Woman's University Library, 1984).

Mary M. Standifer

COVINGTON, TEXAS. Covington is on State Highway 171 twelve miles north of Hillsboro in north central Hill County. The community originated through the efforts of James J. Gathings,qv who moved to Texas from Mississippi in 1852 and purchased thousands of acres of land near what is now the Covington townsite. He established a large and successful farming and ranching concern, initially based on slave labor, and set aside 100 acres of his ranch for a town, which he named for his wife, Martha Wall (Covington). Lots were offered free to families who would establish homes, build a school, and prohibit the manufacture and sale of alcoholic beverages. Gathings's generosity was due in part to his desire to open a retail center for his other business, a factory that produced saddles, boots, wagons, flour, clothes, and almost any other item needed by settlers. A steam mill and gin provided farmers with a further incentive to make Covington their place of business, and the community became their retail point. Gathings himself became postmaster of the community when its first post office opened in 1855. To attract more families to Covington, he and his brother Philip established Gathings College in the early 1860s. The school operated till 1885, at one time enrolling 200 students. By 1870 Covington had a population of nearly 500. The town suffered its first setback when the Missouri, Kansas and Texas Railroad bypassed it. In 1904, however, the tracks of the Trinity and Brazos Valley Railway reached the community. For the next three decades Covington served area farmers and ranchers as a shipping and retail center. The Great Depression,qv however, ended its period of sustained growth. During the 1930s the Trinity and Brazos no longer stopped in Covington. In addition, World War II,qv the growth of Waco and the Dallas–Fort Worth area, and the construction of state and federal highways combined to end Covington's growth. Beginning in 1945 its population began a steady decline, from 450 to 270 by the late 1980s. The community reported only one business in 1988. In 1990 the population was 238.

BIBLIOGRAPHY: Hill County Historical Commission, *A History of Hill County, Texas, 1853–1980* (Waco: Texian, 1980).

David Minor

COWAN CREEK. Cowan Creek rises about two miles southwest of Tow in extreme northeastern Llano County (at 30°52′ N, 98°29′ W) and runs east for two miles to its mouth on Lake Buchanan, a half mile from the intersection of Ranch roads 2241 and 3041 (at 30°52′ N, 98°27′ W). It traverses an area of the Llano basin with flat to rolling terrain, covered with soils ranging from sandy to clay loams that support open stands of live oak and mesquite. David and Gideon Cowan and their mother, Ruth, were the earliest settlers in the Tow area on the west bank of the Colorado River; they arrived in 1852 from Tennessee.

COW BAYOU (Jasper County). Cow Bayou, formed by the junction of Gum Slough and Dognash Gully, rises eleven miles south of Buna in southeastern Jasper County (at 30°16′ N, 93°56′ W) and runs south-southeast for thirty miles to its mouth on the Sabine River, at Bridge City in Orange County (at 30°01′ N, 93°45′ W). With the development of rice farms in Orange County during the early twentieth century, Cow Bayou was used as a source of water for irrigation canals. The bayou, which is intermittent in its upper reaches, was long an important avenue of transportation and saw extensive barge traffic by 1911. In 1963 Congress approved a measure to improve the bayou by constructing a channel 100 feet wide and thirteen feet deep for 7.7 miles from its mouth to Orangefield, where a large (300′ x 500′ x 13′) turning basin was projected. However, a number of oil wells at Orangefield blocked the right-of-way, and only the first seven miles of channel was dredged. In 1967 planners deemed the channel adequate for navigation and flood control, even without the turning basin. At that time four industrial concerns operated terminal and transfer facilities on Cow Bayou. Two fishing camps and a number of boat ramps and wharves were also present.

BIBLIOGRAPHY: James E. Johnson, An Economic History of Orange County, Texas, Prior to 1940 (M.A. thesis, Lamar State College of Technology, 1966).

____ (McLennan County). Cow Bayou rises in two forks in southern McLennan County. North Cow Bayou rises about six miles southeast of McGregor (at 31°22′ N, 97°21′ W) and runs southeast for eighteen miles to join South Cow Bayou, which begins four miles north of Moody (at 31°21′ N, 97°22′ W) and runs southeast for eighteen miles. Cow Bayou proper begins at the confluence of these two branches, two miles northwest of Mooreville in northwestern Falls County (at 31°19′ N, 97°08′ W) and runs east for ten miles to its mouth on the Brazos River, four miles northeast of Chilton in Falls County (at 31°19′ N, 97°00′ W). Cow Bayou traverses flat to rolling prairie with locally steep slopes, surfaced by dark, expansive clays and clay loams. Local vegetation consists primarily of oak, juniper, mesquite, cacti, and grasses. The creek was supposedly named for wild cattle that used to graze on its banks.

COWBOY, TEXAS. Cowboy was on Deep Creek twenty miles northeast of Brady in the northeastern corner of McCulloch County. Settlers came to the area in the late 1870s. A post office opened there in 1879; by the mid-1880s, Cowboy had a church, a district school, and a population of eighty. At that time area residents shipped cattle, hides, wool, and pecans. By 1896 Cowboy's population had fallen to fifty, and its post office had been discontinued. Its school was consolidated with the Rochelle district in the 1940s. A church and a cemetery marked the location of the community on the 1987 county highway map.

BIBLIOGRAPHY: Wayne Spiller, comp., *Handbook of McCulloch County History* (Vol. 1, Seagraves, Texas: Pioneer, 1976; vol. 2, Canyon, Texas: Staked Plains Press, 1986).

Vivian Elizabeth Smyrl

COWBOY ARTISTS OF AMERICA MUSEUM. The Cowboy Artists of America Museum is the national headquarters of the Cowboy Artists of America, which was organized in June 1965 by a group of western artists in a tavern in Sedona, Arizona. The group was formed for the purpose of perpetuating the history and culture of the American West through fine art in all mediums and carrying on the realistic, representational tradition of such western artists as Frederick Remington and Charles Russell. As of the early 1990s the group had thirty-six artist members; twelve former ones were deceased.

The idea for the museum was proposed by five Texans—Lloyd D. Brinkman, William F. Roden, Walter Hailey, Jr., John H. Duncan, and Robert R. Shelton—and three-fourths of the twenty-six founders were from Texas. There had been some dissent among the members over the choice of location, but Kerrville was finally selected when the city presented both a plan and the necessary financing. In 1979 Shelton got a $1 million commitment for the museum, and the Cowboy Artists of America Museum Foundation was chartered by the state of Texas in September 1980. Duncan was elected president and Shelton secretary-treasurer. Architect O'Neil Ford qv of San Antonio was engaged to design the building. Groundbreaking was held in Kerrville on April 21, 1981. A fund-raising drive was begun on this date to obtain thirty founding sponsors who would pledge a minimum of $100,000 each. This, with other contributions, would provide the building funds and begin an endowment fund to provide operating expenses. On October 15, 1981, a contract was signed with Leo Blanchard and Associates of Fredericksburg to construct the facility. The founding director, Griffiths C. Carnes, began work on October 31, 1981, to supervise construction of the facility, continue to raise endowment funds, plan the grand opening, and direct operations of the facility thereafter. With over 400 contributors, the museum opened to the general public on April 24, 1983; the completed cost was $2.5 million. As part of the opening ceremonies, each of the Cowboy Artists of America members left his handprint, boot print, and signature on the cement patio in back of the museum.

The museum is located on ten acres of land donated by William F. Roden of Midland. The site overlooks the Guadalupe River. The 14,366-square-foot building was designed to blend with the southwestern environment and was built entirely of materials from the region. It contains a number of galleries, a library that includes an extensive video collection, a lecture gallery, and a guest house and studio for the use of member artists.

The museum was to be a place where the Cowboy Artists of America could exhibit its members' works and show its influence as a valid art movement. There is a continuous rotating exhibition of fine art of the American West by living and deceased members of the Cowboy Artists, with a minimum display of three pieces for each member at all times. In addition, at least four special exhibits of works that have significance to the ongoing history of western America are produced annually. The museum presents numerous workshops, seminars, and lectures for art students and the general public. It has also worked with Schreiner College to provide lectures and private instruction. The museum houses a library of Western American history and art that also serves as a repository for information about each cowboy artist's work.

BIBLIOGRAPHY: Don Dedera, *Visions West: The Story of the Cowboy Artists of America Museum* (Kerrville, Texas: Cowboy Artists of America Museum, 1983). Susan Hallsten McGarry, "The Cowboy Artists of America Museum, Kerrville, Texas," *Southwest Art* 12 (May 1983). Tommie Pinkard, "Cowboy Artists Find a Home," *Texas Highways,* September 1983.

Griffiths C. Carnes

COWBOYS' CHRISTMAS BALL. A frontier dance at Anson impressed William Lawrence Chittenden qv so much that he later wrote a poem about the event. He was staying overnight at the Star Hotel, where a Christmas dance was held annually in appreciation of the patronage of ranchers and cowboys. He watched the cowboys and their ladies dance the square, the schottische, the heel and toe polka, the waltz, and the Virginia reel. From his observations there, and perhaps at later dances, he wrote his poem "The Cowboys' Christmas Ball."

Some uncertainty exists as to which dance was the model for the poem; the years 1885 and 1887 are the most common dates given by writers. The poem was first published in the Anson *Texas Western* on June 19, 1890, after the Star Hotel had been destroyed by fire earlier in the year and information about the old hotel was being sought. In 1893 the poem appeared in the first volume of *Ranch Verses,* a collection of Chittenden's poems. John A. Lomax qv and his brother Alan published it in their book *Cowboy Songs and Other Frontier Ballads* in 1910. Gordon Graham, a cowboy folklorist from Colorado, set the poem to music and sang it at the Anson ball in 1946, and it became a common practice to have a soloist sing the ballad before the ball.

Dances were held at Christmas in Anson at irregular intervals with little regard for the poem for several decades following its publication. In 1934 the event was revived under the title Cowboys' Christmas Ball by Leonora Barrett, Anson teacher and folklorist. This first reenactment was held in the high school gymnasium and continued on an annual basis thereafter. The Anson dancers attempted to retain the old dance customs, steps, and songs. The men bowed and the women curtsied. The music was slow enough to allow the dances to be done in an unhurried manner and with much grace.

Because the Anson group performed dances not done by any other group in the National Folk Festival, they were invited to the festival in Chicago in 1937. Gertrude Knox, Washington folklorist, invited them to the festival in Washington in 1938; there they danced on the White House lawn. At later dates they performed their folk dances in St. Louis, St. Petersburg, Denver, and various cities in Texas.

The Anson group incorporated in 1937. A board of directors was named, and the event was copyrighted. In 1940, because of increased interest and attendance, Pioneer Hall was built as a permanent home for the ball, which had become a three-day event before Christmas each year. The dance has brought dignitaries, writers, and visitors from all over the nation to Anson. The dances are still presented in a frontier atmosphere, and the pioneer steps have been preserved.

BIBLIOGRAPHY: Hybernia Grace, "Larry Chittenden and West Texas," West Texas Historical Association *Year Book* 13 (1937).

Juanita Daniel Zachry

COWBOY STRIKE OF 1883. In the two decades after the Civil War qv the open-range cattle industry dominated the Great Plains, then died and was replaced by closed-range ranching and stock farming. In West Texas during the 1880s new owners, representing eastern and European investment companies, gained control of the ranching industry and brought with them innovations threatening to many ranchhands. Previously, cowboys could take part of their pay in calves, brand mavericks, and even run small herds on their employers' land. New ranch owners, interested in expanding their holdings and increasing their profits, insisted that the hands work only for wages and claimed mavericks as company property. The work was seasonal. It required long hours and many skills, was dangerous, and paid only an average of forty dollars a month. The ranch owners' innovations, along with the nature of the work, gave rise to discontent.

In 1883 a group of cowboys began a 2½-month strike against five ranches, the LIT, the LX, the LS, the LE, and the T Anchor, qqv which they believed were controlled by corporations or individuals interested in ranching only as a speculative venture for quick profit. In late February or early March of 1883 crews from the LIT, the LS, and the LX drew up an ultimatum demanding higher wages and submitted it to the ranch owners. Twenty-four men signed it and set March 31 as their strike date. The original organizers of the strike, led by Tom Harris of the LS, established a small strike fund and attempted, with limited success, to persuade all the cowboys in the area of the five ranches to honor the strike. Reports on the number of people involved in the strike ranged from thirty to 325. Actually the number changed as men joined and deserted the walkout.

Newspapers from as far away as Colorado covered the dispute and reported that the strikers planned fence burnings, attacks on ranchers, and indiscriminate killing of cattle. Strike leaders offered assurance that they planned only a peaceful and legal protest. In fact, no violence occurred. Press opinion favored the owners. News reports spoke of threatened violence and referred to Harris as "bold and bad." The *Texas Livestock Journal* argued that some cowboys were worth "almost any money as faithful servants" and that these cowboys were entitled to all that ranchmen could "afford to pay." But the *Journal* indicated that the owners were the best and fairest judges of what they could afford.

Ranchers found effective means of dealing with the strikers that required no force. Officials at the T-Anchor and the LE fired striking employees on the spot. The LS and the LIT offered a slight increase in wages and fired workers if they refused that offer. Owners and managers continued with roundup plans by hiring replacement workers at temporarily increased wages. Many of the replacement workers were in fact strikers who asked to return to work. After 2½ months the strike was so weakened that the May roundup occurred without incident. The last press mention of the strike was in the Dodge City *Times* on May 10. After the walkout the Panhandle[qv] was plagued with an outbreak of rustling that many contemporaries blamed on frustrated strikers. It is likely that some strikers, without work and short of money, resorted to rustling, then drifted on to other ranges or other jobs.

Whatever the causes of their failure to organize effectively, the strikers were finally unable to overcome the obstacles they found in the cattle industry. While some historians claim that the strike reflected the international labor movement, others consider it an interesting but isolated incident that had no lasting repercussions for either cowboys or the cattle industry.

BIBLIOGRAPHY: Ruth Alice Allen, *Chapters in the History of Organized Labor in Texas* (University of Texas Publication 4143, Austin, 1941). B. Byron Price, "Community of Individualists: The Panhandle Stock Association, 1881–1891," in *At Home on the Range*, ed. John R. Wunder (Westport, Connecticut: Greenwood, 1985). Donald F. Schofield, *Indians, Cattle, Ships, and Oil: The Story of W. M. D. Lee* (Austin: University of Texas Press, 1985). Robert E. Zeigler

COW CREEK (Brewster County). Cow Creek rises fifteen miles northwest of Bullis Gap (*see* BULLIS GAP RANGE) and 7½ miles southeast of the Southern Pacific Railroad in eastern Brewster County (at 30°00′ N, 102°37′ W) and runs southeast for nineteen miles to its mouth on San Francisco Creek, ten miles northeast of Bullis Gap (at 29°54′ N, 102°27′ W). The creek traverses flat terrain with local shallow depressions, surfaced by clay loams and sandy loams that support water-tolerant hardwoods, conifers, and grasses.

____ (Burnet County). Cow Creek rises eight miles southeast of Burnet in southeast central Burnet County (at 30°40′ N, 98°09′ W) and runs southeast for twenty-one miles to its mouth on Lake Travis, a mile above Lago Vista in Travis County (at 30°29′ N, 98°01′ W). The creek, which is intermittent in its upper reaches, traverses generally flat to rolling terrain with local escarpments and steep slopes and benches. Local soils of shallow clay and sandy loams support juniper, live oak, mesquite, and grasses.

____ (Coke County). Cow Creek rises a mile northeast of Hayrick Mountain and eight miles northeast of Robert Lee in northeastern Coke County (at 31°59′ N, 100°24′ W) and runs south for seven miles to its mouth on the Colorado River, six miles southwest of Bronte (at 31°51′ N, 100°23′ W). The creek crosses the McCutchen oilfield near State Highway 158. The local terrain is flat to rolling with steep margins and is surfaced by shallow to deep sandy clay loam soils that support oak, juniper, elm, and grasses.

____ (Coke County). Cow Creek rises near Ross Cemetery two miles north of Jones Peak in northeastern Coke County (at 32°01′ N, 100°20′ W) and runs north for two miles to its mouth on Bouzier Creek, three miles south of Blackwell (at 32°03′ N, 100°20′ W). The creek traverses terrain with moderately steep slopes and locally high relief, surfaced by shallow to moderately deep silt loam soils that support mesquite and grasses.

____ (Coleman County). Cow Creek rises near Robinson Peak eight miles northwest of Coleman in northern Coleman County (at 31°57′ N, 99°30′ W) and runs east-northeast for eight miles to its mouth on Jim Ned Creek (at 31°58′ N, 99°22′ W). The stream runs through terrain that is 1,600 to 1,900 feet above sea level. It traverses an area of flat land and rolling hills surfaced by clay and sandy loams that support scrub brush, mesquite, cacti, and grasses.

____ (Duval County). Cow Creek rises four miles northeast of Seven Sisters in northern Duval County (at 28°02′ N, 98°29′ W) and runs north for twenty-five miles to its mouth on the Nueces River, ten miles south of Tilden in north central McMullen County (at 28°19′ N, 98°31′ W). The creek passes through an area of low-rolling hills and prairies with local shallow depressions, surfaced by clay and sandy loams that support scrub brush, cacti, grasses, and some mesquite.

____ (Erath County). Cow Creek rises just north of Bunyan in western Erath County (at 32°10′ N, 98°22′ W) and runs eight miles southwest to its mouth on Armstrong Creek in northeastern Comanche County (at 32°06′ N, 98°29′ W). The creek, which is dammed in its middle reaches, traverses flat to rolling terrain with local escarpments, surfaced by shallow gravels and loams that support buffalo grass and a few short grasses.

____ (Fort Bend County). Cow Creek rises a mile north of Damon and eighteen miles west of Angleton (Brazoria County) in southern Fort Bend County (at 29°19′ N, 95°44′ W) and runs east twelve miles, largely along the Fort Bend-Brazoria county line, to its mouth on the Brazos River, at the northwest corner of the Ramsey state prison farm in Brazoria County (at 29°20′ N, 95°36′ W). Cow Creek is channeled in its upper reaches, and its tributaries include Bee and Turkey creeks. It traverses flat to rolling terrain surfaced by sandy and clay loams that support mixed hardwoods, conifers, grasses, and palmetto.

____ (Kinney County). Cow Creek rises just north of the Southern Pacific tracks and ten miles southwest of Brackettville in southwestern Kinney County (at 29°16′ N, 100°34′ W) and runs southwest for seventeen miles to its mouth on the Rio Grande, two miles northwest of the western end of the Maverick-Kinney county line in far southwestern Kinney County (at 29°07′ N, 100°41′ W). Grasses grow along the length of the creek. Sparse scrub brush grows around the creek's upper reaches, oak and juniper in its middle stretch, and water-tolerant hardwoods and conifers along its lower reaches. The creek rises in steep to gently sloping terrain and runs through rolling prairie before ending in flat terrain with locally shallow depressions.

____ (McCulloch County). Cow Creek is formed by the confluence of the East and West forks of Cow Creek. The East Fork rises eight miles north of Brady in north central McCulloch County (at 31°15′ N, 99°20′ W) and runs north for 8½ miles to the point where it joins the West Fork, three miles east of Lohn (at 31°20′ N, 99°21′ W). The West Fork rises six miles northwest of Brady in north central McCulloch County (at 31°12′ N, 99°24′ W) and runs north for ten miles to join the East Fork. Cow Creek runs north from this confluence for 7½ miles to its mouth on the Colorado River, three miles northeast of Fife (at 31°25′ N, 99°19′ W). It traverses generally flat terrain with local shallow depressions and clay and sandy loam soils that support water-tolerant hardwoods, conifers, and grasses.

____ (Milam County). Cow Creek rises two miles north of Yarrellton in northwestern Milam County (at 30°59′ N, 97°05′ W) and runs southeast for eight miles to its mouth on McFall Branch, five miles northwest of Cameron (at 30°55′ N, 97°01′ W). The surrounding flat to rolling prairie is surfaced by dark, calcareous clay that supports mesquite, cacti, and grasses.

____ (Val Verde County). Cow Creek rises two miles northeast of Sevenmile Gap and Farm Road 1024 in south central Val Verde County (at 29°46′ N, 101°10′ W) and runs south twenty-one miles to its mouth on Amistad Reservoir, five miles northwest of Box Canyon on the Mexican border (at 29°31′ N, 101°13′ W). Its course traverses a flat, densely dissected terrain of clay and massive limestone, forming a deep and winding canyon. Area soils of dark, stony, calcareous clays and clay loams support oaks, junipers, grasses, and mesquites. The creek was named for the cows that shelter in the natural caves formed in the bluffs along its course.

COWDEN, WILLIAM HENRY (1853–1933). William Henry Cowden, cattleman, was born on October 6, 1853, in Shelby County, Texas, the oldest son and second of twelve children born to William Hanby and Carrie (Liddon) Cowden. He grew up in Palo Pinto County, where his parents moved in 1855 to establish a ranch. He helped look after the domestic stock from the time he was a small boy and later assisted his father as a cowboy on the range and trail. His formal education was limited to attending a rural school during the winter months of his early youth. By 1875 he had started his own operation on Walnut Creek in Palo Pinto County with a herd of between seventy-five and 100 head. In 1879 he took 700 cattle belonging to him and his father to Paint Creek in Haskell County for a year.

In 1880 he married Mary Salvage, daughter of Benjamin Salvage, a newspaper printer from Rome, Georgia. After Salvage's death his widow married Alonzo Edwards, the rancher from whom the Cowdens purchased their JAL-branded herd in 1882. Will and Mary Cowden had eleven children, two of whom died in infancy. Cowden and his brothers, George Edgar and John Motherwell Cowden, ranged their cattle on the Double Mountain Fork of the Brazos in Kent County for a year and then trailed them through Midland to the White Sand Hills range in what is now Lea County, New Mexico. By 1885 they had established their JAL ranch, which they operated jointly for the next twenty-five years, with headquarters in New Mexico and business offices in Midland (*see* COWDEN RANCH).

In 1890 Will Cowden helped found the First National Bank of Midland and was installed as its president, a position he retained for thirty-six years. He remained involved in the JAL venture until 1892, when he sold his interest to his brothers and W. C. Cochran, a brother-in-law. The following year, in partnership with J. W. Gibson, he stocked a ranch with 2,000 steers in the Creek Nation of the Indian Territory. He also bought forty sections in Andrews County, which he fenced and stocked with 400 steers, and 60,000 acres of property in Crane County, which he operated with his sons. In 1904 he bought another ranch in Frio County.

Throughout his active years as a banker and independent rancher, Cowden maintained his family home in Midland, where he resided until his retirement from the bank in 1926. At that time he and his wife moved to San Antonio, where he resided until his death, on July 20, 1933.

BIBLIOGRAPHY: James Cox, *Historical and Biographical Record of the Cattle Industry* (2 vols., St. Louis: Woodward and Tiernan Printing, 1894, 1895; rpt., with an introduction by J. Frank Dobie, New York: Antiquarian, 1959). Gus L. Ford, ed., *Texas Cattle Brands* (Dallas: Cockrell, 1936). Gil Hinshaw, *Lea, New Mexico's Last Frontier* (Hobbs, New Mexico: Hobbs *Daily News-Sun*, 1976).

H. Allen Anderson

COWDEN RANCH. The Cowden, or JAL, ranch originated in 1882, when the brothers George, John M., and William Henry Cowden^{qv} bought 100 cattle and the JAL brand from Alonzo Edwards in Palo Pinto County. The brand's origin remains a mystery; theories claim that it came from the initials of John A. Lynch, James A. Lawrence or John Allen Lee, all of whom were early West Texas ranchers. The Cowdens ran their herd along the Double Mountain Fork of the Brazos River north of Colorado City for about a year. In 1883, however, they began trailing their cattle west to the rail town of Midland and thence to the Monahans Sandhills area, where sufficient water holes could be found. By December of that year they had moved about 1,000 head of stock to a site on Monument Draw in the sandy area of southeastern New Mexico, three miles west of the Texas line.

During the next two years the Cowdens' JAL cattle reportedly were scattered all the way from Midland to the Carlsbad area of New Mexico and as far south as Horsehead Crossing^{qv} on the Pecos River. In 1885 they selected a more suitable site on Monument Draw, where grass was more abundant, and dug wells, over which they placed windmills. By then they had between 6,000 and 7,000 cattle. They built a three-room adobe^{qv} ranchhouse on the draw by the end of 1886 and set up business headquarters in Midland, then the nearest shipping point on the Texas and Pacific line.

For twenty-five years the Cowden Cattle Company operated the JAL ranch, which at its peak covered one-fourth of Lea County, New Mexico, and portions of adjacent Texas counties. At first, only the three elder Cowden brothers and two brothers-in-law made up the firm, but in time it came to include the younger brothers, Liddon, Rorie, and Eugene Cowden. Not until 1895 did the Cowdens utilize barbed wire;^{qv} then they fenced over 300 sections. They kept no line camps at first, paid no lease on their grass, and owned none of their JAL range, although they later bought forty acres around their wells. Over the years the JAL herd multiplied to some 40,000 head and eventually necessitated line camps at various watering places.

After the turn of the century the influx of homesteaders into Lea County resulted in the rapid reduction of the JAL range. In 1912, after New Mexico became a state, John M. Cowden bought the interests of his brothers and continued to operate the ranch from the headquarters in Midland until all of the land was sold. The town of Jal, New Mexico, was founded at the ranch's Muleshoe Camp and named for the Cowdens' brand. The other Cowden brothers became independent ranchers and businessmen in West Texas or New Mexico; William H. Cowden, in particular, owned ranchland in Crane County and later in Frio County.

BIBLIOGRAPHY: Gus L. Ford, ed., *Texas Cattle Brands* (Dallas: Cockrell, 1936). Gil Hinshaw, *Lea, New Mexico's Last Frontier* (Hobbs, New Mexico: Hobbs *Daily News-Sun*, 1976).

H. Allen Anderson

COW GAP. Cow Gap, a pass in the Brady Mountains, is about eight miles north of Brady in north central McCulloch County (at 31°15′ N, 99°23′ W). The elevation of the pass is 1,770 feet above mean sea level. Several early cattle trails used this pass through the mountains. The West Fork of Cow Creek runs through Cow Gap.

COWHEAD MESA. Cowhead Mesa is an isolated remnant of the Llano Estacado^{qv} located east of the Caprock^{qv} escarpment near Post in Garza County. The mesa rises more than 100 feet above the surrounding terrain near the head of the Double Mountain Fork of the Brazos River. This natural landmark was a focus of settlement and aesthetic expression for prehistoric and historic Indians and early white travelers. It is on private property.

Images carved into the steep sides of the sandstone mesa depict human beings, animals, and buildings and are attributed to the Comanche or Kiowa-Apache Indians of the late eighteenth or nineteenth century. The rock art panel depicts mounted figures with long lances and small round shields and figures with long coats and hats, thought to represent Indians and Spaniards. Other figures include a turtle and a four-legged, horned animal. Buildings topped with crosses may be missions; one building appears to be burning. The South Plains Archeological Society has photographed and documented the rock art panel.

A prehistoric Indian occupation site on top of the mesa was recorded in 1957 by Emmett Shedd of Post. He and others directed the South Plains Archeological Society's excavations of an area twenty-three by forty meters on the north end of the mesa between 1960 and 1965. Late Archaic (Ellis and Williams dart points) and Late Prehistoric (Harrell arrow points, ceramics) components have been identified, dating from around 2000 B.C. to A.D. 1700. Other artifacts recovered include scrapers, bifaces, lithic debitage, ceramics, mano and metate fragments, burned rocks, boiling stones, bison bone, charcoal, mussel shell, and snail shell. Six sandstone hearths were found, varying from thirty-five to eighty centimeters in diameter and constructed of layers of slabs or groups of large, rounded cobbles on flat surfaces or in shallow basins. Collections and records of the South Plains Archeological Society excavations are held by Frank Runkles of Post, Texas. Late nineteenth and early twentieth century inscriptions on the mesa are names, dates, and brands from the ranching era, and include the Square and Compass brand (see SQUARE AND COMPASS RANCH). The mesa may have been a landmark during the early ranching period. The name Cowhead Mesa probably was assigned during this period, but its origin is unknown.

BIBLIOGRAPHY: Garza County Historical Survey Committee, *Wagon Wheels: A History of Garza County,* ed. Charles Didway (Seagraves, Texas: Pioneer, 1973). Aaron D. Riggs, Jr., "Petroglyphs of Garza County, Texas," *Transactions of the Regional Archeological Symposium for Southeastern New Mexico and Western Texas* 1 (1965). Frank A. Runkles, "The Garza Site," *Bulletin of the Texas Archeological Society* 35 (1964).
Margaret Ann Howard

COW HOLLOW CREEK. Cow Hollow Creek rises four miles north of U.S. Highway 62/70 and one mile west of the Motley-Cottle county line in extreme eastern Motley County (at 34°03′ N, 100°32′ W) and runs north-northeast through remote ranchland for ten miles to its mouth on the Middle Pease River, in west central Cottle County (at 34°08′ N, 100°26′ W). This confluence occurs within the Matador Wildlife Management Area, twelve miles northwest of Paducah. The area around the creek, both in Motley and Cottle counties, was included in the Matador Ranch qv holdings. The creek traverses sloping terrain surfaced with shallow silty soils that support mesquite and grasses.

COWHOUSE CREEK. Cowhouse Creek rises three miles west of Priddy in northeastern Mills County (at 31°36′ N, 98°32′ W) and runs southeast for ninety miles through Hamilton and Coryell counties into Bell County, where it reaches its mouth on Belton Lake, north of the Fort Hood military reservation (at 31°10′ N, 97°35′ W). The creek, which is intermittent in its upper reaches, is named for the natural shelters formed by limestone bluffs along its banks. It traverses variable terrain surfaced by stony clay loams and fine sandy loams that support vegetation ranging from juniper, oak, mesquite, chaparral, cacti, and grasses, to hardwood trees, conifers, and brush.

COWHOUSE MOUNTAIN. Cowhouse Mountain is three miles north of State Highway 218 in the extreme southern corner of Comanche County (at 31°44′ N, 98°27′ W). Its summit, at an elevation of 1,672 feet above sea level, rises 172 feet above the highway.

COWLEECH FORK OF THE SABINE RIVER. The Cowleech Fork of the Sabine River rises two miles northwest of Celeste in northwestern Hunt County (at 33°19′ N, 96°13′ W) and runs southeast for about forty miles, passing Celeste and crossing U.S. Highway 69, then running between the two municipal reservoirs just east of Greenville before reaching its mouth on the Pawnee Inlet of Lake Tawakoni, about three miles west of Lone Oak (at 33°00′ N, 96°01′ W). Its tributaries include Hickory and Wolf creeks. The Cowleech Fork, which is intermittent in its upper reaches, traverses generally flat land surfaced with clay loams and clayey sand loams that support grasses and water-tolerant hardwoods. For most of the county's history, the Cowleech Fork area has been used as crop and range land.

BIBLIOGRAPHY: W. Walworth Harrison, *History of Greenville and Hunt County, Texas* (Waco: Texian, 1976). Vertical Files, Barker Texas History Center, University of Texas at Austin (Lake Tawakoni).

COWL SPUR, TEXAS. Cowl Spur was on Farm Road 2854 and the Atchison, Topeka and Santa Fe, six miles west of Conroe in west central Montgomery County. The town was named after a spur and siding on the Gulf, Colorado and Santa Fe. During the early 1930s the Day Lumber and Timber Company had a timber mill there. In 1938 Day Lumber sold out to Daniel's Lumber Company and Retail Lumber and Building Materials. They changed the name to the People's Lumber and Building Materials Company soon after. In the 1940s the town had thirty dwellings and three businesses, including a sawmill and a railroad station. From 1940 to 1965 the population of Cowl Spur was reported at fifty. By 1965 the area had become part of the Conroe Independent School District.

BIBLIOGRAPHY: Montgomery County Genealogical Society, *Montgomery County History* (Winston-Salem, North Carolina: Hunter, 1981).
Rebecca L. Borjas

COWTRAP LAKES. The Cowtrap Lakes, a group of three shallow, connected lakes linked to the Gulf Intracoastal Waterway,qv are near the Matagorda county line in south central Brazoria County (at 28°51′ N, 95°31′ W). Each of the three nearly circular lakes is less than a mile in diameter. The surrounding area of brackish to saltwater marsh is made up of muds and sands that support rushes and grasses.

COX, ALONZO BETTIS (1884–1968). Alonzo Bettis Cox, teacher and authority on cotton marketing, son of Van Buren and Manerva (Compton) Cox, was born in Hamilton County, Illinois, on April 2, 1884. Ten months later his family moved to a farm in Erath County, Texas. After receiving his A.B. (1911) and M.A. (1914) degrees from the University of Texas, Cox went to the University of Wisconsin, where he earned his doctorate in 1920. In 1938 he received an honorary LL.D. from Abilene Christian College (now Abilene Christian University); he had served as president of ACC in 1911–12.

In 1922, after two years at the Agricultural and Mechanical College of Texas (now Texas A&M University) as chief of the Division of Farm and Ranch Economics in the Texas Agricultural Experiment Station (see AGRICULTURAL EXPERIMENT STATION SYSTEM), Cox was asked to take charge of cotton-marketing research for the United States Department of Agriculture in Washington, D.C. In 1924–25 he served as an agricultural economist representing the department in Europe.

In 1926 he accepted a position as professor of cotton marketing at the University of Texas. He established the University of Texas Bureau of Business Research in 1927 and served as its director from 1927 to 1942. From 1945 until his retirement in 1957 Cox devoted his time to teaching and research in cotton marketing. In 1947 he organized and became the permanent supervisor of the Cotton Merchandising Research Committee (now the Natural Fibers Information Center at the University of Texas), a unit of the Texas Cotton Research Committee (see TEXAS FOOD AND FIBERS COMMISSION). Under Cox's supervision the committee achieved international prestige as the headquarters of a worldwide program to standardize scientific cotton testing. He also initiated the annual Cotton Merchandizing Clinics, held between 1948 and 1958, that brought together cotton merchants, manufacturers, and researchers to discuss all aspects of cotton production and marketing in Texas. Cox was the organizer and chairman of the Texas Cotton Committee, a policy-making body, in 1927. In 1939 he was a member of the planning committee for the Texas Cotton Research Congress, which held its first meeting in Waco in 1940. In 1942, as chairman of the Foreign Markets Committee of the Texas Statewide Cotton Committee, Cox helped prepare the "Charter for Cotton," which set forth the fundamental economic principles governing the cotton industry and the postwar demands of cotton farmers.

Throughout his professional career Cox served on many state, national, and international committees. In 1939 he was a member of the State Intercollegiate Schools of Business Administration Committee, and in 1941 he was appointed a member of the Social Science Research Council, organized to plan postwar agricultural adjustments in the South. In 1943 he was a member of the Texas Postwar Planning Commission. That year he was a special consultant on cotton-price fixing for the United States government. In 1945 he was appointed a member of a federal committee to study merchandising of cotton and cotton products.

Cox served as an advisor to the National Cotton Council of America and the American Cotton Shippers Association. He was a member of many associations, including the American Farm Economics Association, the Southwestern Political and Social Science Association, and the American Economic Association. He wrote several books and numerous papers and articles. In 1922 he published, with Bonney Youngblood, *An Economic Study of a Typical Ranching Area on the Edwards Plateau of Texas*. In 1949 he published *The Cottonseed Crushing Industry of Texas in its National Setting*. He was published frequently in the leading cotton and economic publications in the United States. In 1952 he was selected to write the section on cotton for the *Encyclopaedia Britannica*. He was invited to address the International Cotton Congress in Prague in 1933 and in Cairo in 1937 and 1951.

Cox married Sue Merle Sheppard in 1911, and they had three children. After his first wife's death he married Irene Shannon Brezeale of Llano, in 1933. Cox was a Democrat and a member of the University Avenue Church of Christ in Austin. He died on December 25, 1968, and was buried in Austin Memorial Park. The A. B. Cox Memorial Library houses Cox's private collection at the Bureau of Business Research, University of Texas at Austin. *See also* COTTON CULTURE.

BIBLIOGRAPHY: Vertical Files, Barker Texas History Center, University of Texas at Austin. *Who's Who in America*, 1952–53.

Margaret T. Herring

COX, CHARLES HUDSON (1829–1901). Charles Hudson Cox, businessman and artist, was born at Liverpool, England, in 1829. In 1889 he immigrated to Waco, Texas, as a cotton buyer and continued to develop his considerable talent as an artist. He was soon persuaded to teach a class in watercolor painting, which was eagerly accepted by the young ladies of the city, and which he continued for a decade. Finding charm and inspiration from the hillsides and wildflowers of the Bosque Valley, Cox made these the subjects of most of his Texas paintings, which were usually small and signed C. H. Cox. In 1901 he was instrumental in organizing the Waco Art League, which is still in existence today. That same year he became seriously ill. At his doctor's recommendation he undertook a trip to the mountains of Colorado; but instead of improving, he died there, at Boulder, on August 7, 1901. His body was returned to Waco and buried in Oakwood Cemetery. The newspaper obituary records that the funeral was attended by a son, Edward L. Cox, of Galveston. In 1983 the Historic Waco Foundation officially dedicated a room in the restored C. C. McCulloch Mansion as the C. H. Cox Gallery, where about twenty of Cox's nostalgic paintings are on permanent exhibit.

BIBLIOGRAPHY: Waco *Times-Herald*, August 26, 1901. Waco Art League, Minutes.

Roger N. Conger

COX, GEORGE WASHINGTON (1879–1963). George Cox, director of the Texas Department of Public Health (now the Texas Department of Health[qv]), was born in Gonzales County, Texas, in 1879. After working on his parents' farm and his brother's ranch, he decided that he wanted to be a doctor, like his father and grandfather before him. He obtained a medical degree from Tulane University in 1906, after studying at Polytechnic College in Fort Worth, the University of Texas, Vanderbilt University, and Northwestern University. In 1907 Cox began his public-service career as a quarantine officer appointed by Governor Thomas M. Campbell[qv] to stations in Galveston, Brownsville, and Corpus Christi. After working as assistant surgeon for the Gulf Coast Railroad and practicing privately in Corpus Christi, Ozona, and Del Rio, Cox was appointed to the State Board of Health by Governor James Allred[qv] in 1935. The next year he became director of the board.

He was as controversial as he was successful. He was constantly criticized for being so outspoken on health issues, but what he accomplished was significant. During his tenure, he concentrated on pollution, garbage and sewage disposal, and particularly disease control. In this period deaths due to contagious diseases dropped sharply: syphilis by 74 percent; malaria, 99 percent; typhoid fever, 98 percent. In addition, maternal death rates decreased by 84 percent, and infant mortality decreased by 54 percent. Cox also lobbied heavily for the construction of a new State Board of Health headquarters building and twenty-two county health units. When he retired in 1954, due to the lingering problems of insufficient funds and resources, he commented, "I feel I had better take a rest and go fishing." He died on October 29, 1963, leaving one son. Cox was married to Maud French. He was buried at Rosehill Memorial Park in Corpus Christi.

BIBLIOGRAPHY: Vertical Files, Barker Texas History Center, University of Texas at Austin.

Justin Lien

COX, PARIS (1846–1888). Paris Cox, founder of Estacado, a Quaker colony in Crosby County, was born near Asheboro, North Carolina, on October 17, 1846, to Gideon and Asenath Cox, who raised their six children with a strong Quaker persuasion. As a young man Cox was drafted by the Confederate States of America to serve in the Civil War.[qv] Because of his pacifism, he purchased a legal exemption and moved to Westfield, Indiana, where he met and married Mary C. Ferguson, a young schoolteacher. Cox first went into business with his father-in-law in a sawmill. When the supply of lumber began to dwindle the business suffered, and he sought another opportunity in the West. He joined a group of buffalo hunters and traveled to the Llano Estacado[qv] of West Texas. One evening while they were camped above the Caprock[qv] west of pioneer Henry C. Smith's[qv] house on a hill overlooking a particularly beautiful site, Cox reportedly said, "Here, by the will of God, will be my home." In 1876 he returned to Texas and secured authority to sell land to settlers at twenty-five cents an acre. His colonists became the first settlers on the High Plains of Texas.

In late 1878 Cox revisited the site he had loved. He hired Hank Smith to dig a community well and to break and plant thirty acres of land with various crops in the summer of 1879. In the fall of 1879 Smith wrote that water was found at sixty-five feet and sent samples of good crops he had grown on the thirty-acre Crosby County farm. Encouraged by the news, Cox and his family, then including wife Mary and two sons, and three other families left for the plains. Cox built a sod house at the site. The others decided to live in tents. The winter of 1879 was a severe one, and the early spring brought high winds that blew away the tents and belongings of the other three families, who returned to Indiana. Cox and his family stayed on, planted, cultivated, and harvested excellent crops of corn, oats, millet, sorghum, melons, potatoes, and garden vegetables. A son and daughter were added to their family. Before long several friends and relatives began to arrive in covered wagons. In 1881 Cox persuaded his father and mother to come to the new colony. By the summer of 1882 the settlement comprised ten families.

In 1879 a town was established and named Marietta, in honor of Cox's wife. When the county was organized in 1886, the name was changed to Estacado because the state already had a post office named Marietta. Estacado became the county seat of Crosby County, and ten surrounding counties were attached to the county for judicial purposes. In a general election held on November 2, 1886, Cox was elected district clerk. From 1880 to 1890 the colony flourished. Paris Cox died of throat cancer on November 2, 1888, and was buried in the Estacado Cemetery. *See also* RELIGIOUS SOCIETY OF FRIENDS.

BIBLIOGRAPHY: Roger Andrew Burgess, The History of Crosby County, Texas (M.A. thesis, University of Texas, 1927). Crosby County Pioneer Memorial Museum, *Estacado: Cradle of Culture and Civilization on the Staked Plains of Texas* (Crosbyton, Texas, 1986; based on an M.A. thesis by John Cooper Jenkins). Crosby County Pioneer Memorial Museum, *A History of Crosby County, 1876–1977* (Dallas: Taylor, 1978). W. Hubert Curry, *Sun Rising on the West: The Saga of Henry Clay and Elizabeth Smith* (Crosbyton, Texas: Crosby County Pioneer Memorial Museum, 1979). Lawrence L. Graves, ed., *A History of Lubbock* (Lubbock: West Texas Museum Association, 1962). Nellie Witt Spikes and Temple Ann Ellis, *Through the Years: A History of Crosby County* (San Antonio: Naylor, 1952).

Jeanne F. Lively

COX, THOMAS B. (1785–?). Thomas B. Cox was born in Alabama in 1785 and moved to Texas in March 1822 with his wife, Cynthia, as a member of Stephen F. Austin's[qv] third colony. His grant was located in what is now Walker County. He served at the siege of Bexar[qv] and was mustered into the Texas army on January 24, 1836, as a private in Capt. John Chenoweth's[qv] company. He was one of only four members of the company to escape death at the Goliad Massacre.[qv] He later served as a private in Capt. Thomas H. McIntire's company of Col. Sidney Sherman's[qv] Second Regiment, Texas Volunteers, at the battle of San Jacinto.[qv] In February 1845 a bill for the relief of Thomas B. Cox was passed by the Texas legislature.

BIBLIOGRAPHY: Daughters of the Republic of Texas, *Muster Rolls of the Texas Revolution* (Austin, 1986). Sam Houston Dixon and Louis Wiltz Kemp, *The Heroes of San Jacinto* (Houston: Anson Jones, 1932). *Telegraph and Texas Register,* February 22, 1845. Gifford E. White, *1830 Citizens of Texas* (Austin: Eakin, 1983).

Thomas W. Cutrer

COX, THOMAS WASHINGTON (1815–1852). Thomas Washington Cox, Baptist preacher and soldier, was born in Alabama in 1815 and immigrated to Texas in 1838 or 1839. In 1840 he was living in Fayette County, where he owned 300 acres of land, a gold pocketwatch, and one metal clock. He soon organized and was elected pastor of churches at La Grange, Travis, and Independence and was named the first moderator of the Baptist Union Association in the state. As moderator, he called for the first convention of Texas Baptists in June 1840. He became a follower of the teachings of Alexander Campbell, however, and, according to nineteenth century Baptist historian John B. Link,[qv] "serious reports of bad conduct followed him from Alabama." In 1841, therefore, after confrontations with Z. N. Morrell,[qv] he was excluded from the church in La Grange and retained the pulpit of the other two only by narrow margins. "He afterwards became more interested in horse-racing and gambling than in preaching," wrote Link.

Cox was elected justice of the peace for Fayette County on January 20, 1842, but soon thereafter was elected second lieutenant in Capt. William M. Eastland's[qv] Company B of Brig. Gen. Alexander Somervell's[qv] Army of the South West. Cox participated in the Somervell and Mier expeditions,[qqv] was captured at the battle of Mier, and took part in the escape attempt led by Ewen Cameron[qv] at Salado on February 11, 1843. He was one of only four of Cameron's men to make his way back to Texas, the others being recaptured and subjected to decimation by firing squad after the notorious Black Bean Episode.[qv]

On September 16, 1849, the anniversary of the release of the Mier prisoners, Cox introduced a motion to a meeting at La Grange to form a monument committee to raise funds for a memorial to the dead of the Mier expedition and the Dawson Massacre.[qv] He also proposed that the remains of Nicholas M. Dawson's and William S. Fishers's[qqv] men be reinterred on Monument Hill (*see* MONUMENT HILL–KREISCHE BREWERY STATE HISTORICAL PARK). He was the only Mier man named to the Texas Monument Committee. On September 16, 1850, Cox, called "a man of great eloquence," met with the Mier and Dawson survivors at a reunion at Monument Hill and delivered the main address of the observation.

When Robert S. Neighbors[qv] returned from his reconnaissance into what is now New Mexico in 1850 and reported that area's intention of setting up an independent territorial government, the citizens of Fayette County appointed Cox to a committee to report on the "insurrectionary movements in the county of Santa Fe." Cox's committee considered New Mexico's actions "an outrage upon the State of Texas" and resolved to call upon the government of the United States to maintain Texas sovereignty there. Failing assistance from the national government, however, the members of the committee proposed to equip a "military force to put down the insurrection" and threatened secession from the Union if the state's boundaries of December 19, 1836, giving Texas all of New Mexico east of the Rio Grande, were not respected. Cox died in Bastrop County on February 6, 1852, of what the Austin *Texas State Gazette* called "congestion of the brain."

BIBLIOGRAPHY: James Milton Carroll, *A History of Texas Baptists* (Dallas: Baptist Standard, 1923). *Compiled Index to Elected and Appointed Officials of the Republic of Texas, 1835–1846* (Austin: State Archives, Texas State Library, 1981). *Telegraph and Texas Register,* June 24, 1840, December 21, 1842, February 15, 1843. *Texas State Gazette,* October 13, 1849, July 13, September 28, 1850, February 14, 1852. Houston Wade, *Notes and Fragments of the Mier Expedition* (La Grange, Texas: La Grange *Journal,* 1936).

Thomas W. Cutrer

COX, TEXAS. Cox, a farming community on Farm Road 2796 eleven miles northeast of Gilmer in northeastern Upshur County, was established around 1890 and named for a family of local settlers. A school was in operation there around 1900, and during the 1906–07 school year it had an enrollment of sixty-seven. In the mid-1930s the community had a sawmill, a school, and a number of scattered houses. After World War II[qv] many of its residents moved away, and its school was consolidated with the La Fayette school district. By the mid-1960s all that remained of Cox was a church, a cemetery, and a number of houses. Its population was estimated at 300. Many of the community's residents worked at the nearby Lone Star Steel Plant. In 1990 Cox had a church and one store.

BIBLIOGRAPHY: Doyal T. Loyd, *History of Upshur County* (Waco: Texian Press, 1987).

Christopher Long

COX BAY. Cox Bay is an inlet bound by Lavaca Bay in northeastern Calhoun County (at 28°38′ N, 96°31′ W). The bay was named for Thomas Cox, who settled on the shoreline. During the 1820s and 1830s Cox Point, a peninsula that extends into the bay, served as a point of entry for American immigrants (*see* MEXICAN TEXAS, REPUBLIC OF TEXAS). About 1832, while in the employ of George Sutherland,[qv] early settler Samuel C. A. Rogers[qv] operated a trading post on Cox Point. Huisache Creek and Huisache Cove empty into Cox Bay northeast of Cox Point. The community of Point Comfort is on the extreme northwestern edge of the bay.

BIBLIOGRAPHY: Samuel C. A. Rogers, Reminiscences, Barker Texas History Center, University of Texas at Austin.

COX BRANCH. Cox Branch rises four miles east-northeast of Walnut Springs in northern Bosque County (at 32°06′ N, 97°42′ W) and runs south for almost five miles to its mouth on Steele Creek (at 32°02′ N, 97°40′ W). The creek traverses flat to rolling prairie surfaced by dark clay loam soils over limestone. Local vegetation includes oak, juniper, mesquite, and grasses.

COX CREEK (Limestone County). Cox Creek rises just over two miles west of Oletha in the southern corner of Limestone County (at 31°24′ N, 96°28′ W) and runs south 6½ miles to its mouth on Steele Creek (at 31°19′ N, 96°26′ W). The area's light brown and dark grey sandy loams formerly supported a hardwood forest that was used for lumber production. Because the region is located along the Mexia–Talco fault zone, it is rich in natural gas production. It is possible the creek was named for George W. Cox, one of the first twelve pioneer settlers of Limestone County, who received a land grant of one-quarter league on January 21, 1835.

BIBLIOGRAPHY: Ray A. Walter, *A History of Limestone County* (Austin: Von Boeckmann–Jones, 1959).
Kenneth E. Austin

COX DRAW. Cox Draw, also known as Riggs Draw, is a valley with an intermittent stream. It rises 1½ miles northeast of Beard Mountain in northwestern Pecos County (at 30°50′ N, 103°30′ W) and runs northwest thirteen miles to its mouth on Sandia Creek, a half mile north of Interstate Highway 10 in southeastern Reeves County (at 30°58′ N, 103°35′ W). Its course crosses an area of canyonlands and steep to gentle slopes over volcanic rocks, then ends on flat terrain with mountain wash deposits. The land surface consists of rough stony areas, generally light reddish-brown to brown sands, and clay loams that support scrub brush, grasses, creosote bush, and cacti.

COXEY'S ARMY. In the wake of the 1893 panic Jacob Sechler Coxey of Massillon, Ohio, a businessman and reformer interested in fiat money, prepared to lead an army of jobless men to Washington to induce Congress to issue legal-tender currency to be spent on roads and other improvements. His appeal drew response from as far as the Pacific Coast, where contingents of his army were formed. In charge in Los Angeles was Lewis C. Fry. Fry and his men set out on foot from Los Angeles on March 16, 1894, and later boarded a freight train. Several towns gave them food and sped them onward. On March 21 the mayor of El Paso wired Governor James Stephen Hogg,qv asking him to request the War Department to place the garrison at Fort Blissqv at the service of the state to repel the expected invasion. Hogg refused, assuring him that Texas was able to enforce its laws and asking him to report any violations.

On the evening of March 22 Fry and 700 men arrived in El Paso and marched to the city hall, where they were fed and allowed to camp for the night. The next evening they marched to the railroad yards to await an eastbound train. As the railroads held back trains suited to their purpose, the men camped near the tracks for two days. They boarded a Southern Pacific freight on Easter, March 25, 1894, the day Coxey led his men out of Massillon. Seventy miles east of El Paso, trainmen uncoupled the cars on which the men were riding and left them stranded on the Finlay switch, in a barren region. The only inhabitants within miles were a few Mexican families, and no supplies of food or water were within reach. Indignant at this action, Governor Hogg insisted that the railroad company that brought the men into the state should carry them on through. Some of the hungry men walked to Sierra Blanca, twenty miles farther east, and a few were able to hop trains.

Except for several beeves donated by ranchmen and food sent by El Paso people, Fry's men still had nothing to eat three days later. Their plight aroused increasing sympathy. Six El Paso citizens telegraphed the governor that "the infamy of the Southern Pacific in hauling these men from California into the desert, refusing to haul them farther, is without parallel for barbarity." Dallas residents met and endorsed the governor's order that the Southern Pacific transport Fry's men to a place of refuge. The railroad's general manager refused until El Paso people raised money for a special train. At Finlay and Sierra Blanca the men crowded into this train of five coaches and two baggage cars and arrived in San Antonio on the afternoon of March 29. They were then transferred to a freight train of the International–Great Northern and stopped briefly in Austin early the next morning, but the police denied their wish to see the governor. After stops at Taylor, Hearne, and Palestine, the weary travelers—packed so densely that many could not lie down—arrived in Longview on March 31. They transferred to a Texas and Pacific train for Texarkana and there on April 1, 1894, to the Iron Mountain line. Some reached Washington weeks after Coxey was arrested on May 1, 1894, for carrying a banner and walking on the grass.

BIBLIOGRAPHY: Dallas *Morning News,* April 1, 1894. Donald LeCrone McMurry, *Coxey's Army: A Study of the Industrial Army Movement of 1894* (1929; rpt., New York: AMS Press, 1970).
Wayne Gard

COX HOLLOW. Cox Hollow rises ten miles west of Hud in extreme north central Scurry County (at 32°57′ N, 100°52′ W) and dips to the southeast, then travels northeast for a total of twelve miles to its mouth on the Double Mountain Fork of the Brazos River, just north of the Scurry-Kent county line and fifteen miles southeast of Clairemont (at 32°58′ N, 100°41′ W). The creek crosses an area of dissected gullies and low hills with shallow soils that support brush and grasses.

COX LAKE. Cox Lake, a shallow lake a half mile wide and more than a mile long, is northwest of Christmas Bay, twelve miles east of Angleton and three miles north of the Gulf of Mexico in east central Brazoria County (at 29°04′ N, 95°14′ W). The lake is fed by Bastrop Bayou.

COXVILLE, TEXAS. Coxville was fifteen miles southwest of Bastrop in western Bastrop County. A post office was established there in 1888, with John A. J. Cox as postmaster. In the 1890s the community also had a general store, a corn mill and gin, a Baptist church, and a district school. Its post office was discontinued in 1906, and by the late 1940s no evidence of Coxville was shown on county highway maps.

BIBLIOGRAPHY: Bill Moore, *Bastrop County, 1691–1900* (Wichita Falls: Nortex, 1977).
Vivian Elizabeth Smyrl

COYABEGUX INDIANS. The Coyabegux (Cagabegux and Coiaheguxee) Indians, an otherwise unidentified group mentioned to Henri Joutelqv in 1687 by the Ebahamos, were said to be northwest of the Colorado River in what was mainly Tonkawan territory.

BIBLIOGRAPHY: Frederick Webb Hodge, ed., *Handbook of American Indians North of Mexico* (2 vols., Washington: GPO, 1907, 1910; rpt., New York: Pageant, 1959).
Margery H. Krieger

COYANOSA DRAW. Coyanosa Draw, formed by the junction of Antelope Draw and Musquiz Creek in southwestern Pecos County (at 30°39′ N, 103°20′ W), runs north for sixty-two miles to its juncture with Hackberry Draw, five miles south of the Pecos River (at 31°17′ N, 103°07′ W). The draw runs through steep to gently sloping terrain surfaced by variable soils that support creosote bush, tarbush, and sparse grasses. It crosses Interstate Highway 10 sixteen miles west of Fort Stockton.

COYANOSA, TEXAS. Coyanosa is at the intersection of Farm roads 1776 and 1450, twenty-six miles northwest of Fort Stockton in northwestern Pecos County. It was originally settled as a ranching community. A post office was established there in 1908 and discontinued in 1918. Numerous water wells were drilled in the area during the 1950s to irrigate nearby cotton farms. No population statistics were available for the community until 1958, when it reported 200 residents. Around this time the post office was reopened. By 1961 Coyanosa reported eight businesses and an estimated population of 600. Greatly increased fuel prices in the mid-1970s made irrigation unprofitable and forced most nearby cotton farms out of business. By the mid-1970s the population of Coyanosa had declined to 270. Its population was still recorded as 270 in the early 1990s, when the community also reported seven rated businesses.

BIBLIOGRAPHY: Pecos County Historical Commission, Pecos County History (2 vols., Canyon, Texas: Staked Plains, 1984).

Glenn Justice

COY CITY, TEXAS. Coy City, also known as Appleville, is on Farm Road 99 some ten miles west of Karnes City in western Karnes County. It was named after the family of Trinidad Coy, whose forebears were among the first Spanish settlers of Texas. When the Butler, Nichols, and Adams ranches were subdivided into farms, John W. Roberts and his family were the first to settle at the site in 1916. In 1918 "Dad" Ratliff built a store for the farming community, and the place was briefly called Appleville because about all one could buy there was "red sodey pop and apples." Shortly after World War I[qv] Jenny Van Winkle built another store on the Appleville site, and Bud Wattle built a cotton gin nearby. R. J. Polasek built a new gin about a mile west, soon to be joined by another store and a café. R. H. Coats, who operated the store, called the place Coats City, but the name was changed to Coy City after the Coy family. A post office was established there in 1930 and served some thirty residents and two businesses. By 1939 the community reported a population of 100 and four businesses. It peaked in the late 1940s with 150 inhabitants and five businesses. The Pullin School, later renamed Coy City School, and the Pullin Church, replaced in 1945 by the Coy City Baptist Church, were built in the community. After the great drought of the 1950s the population of Coy City dwindled, and by the late 1960s it had only eighty-five residents and one business. By the 1980s its population had fallen to around thirty, and eventually its stores, cotton gin, school, and post office were closed. In 1990 the community reported a population of thirty, and only the Baptist church and a small cluster of residences remained.

BIBLIOGRAPHY: Robert H. Thonhoff, History of Karnes County (M.A. thesis, Southwest Texas State College, 1963).

Robert H. Thonhoff

COYOTE CREEK (Armstrong County). Coyote Creek rises at the breaks of the Llano Estacado[qv] in Palo Duro Canyon[qv] in south central Armstrong County (at 34°54' N, 101°19' W) and runs southwest for six miles to its mouth on the Prairie Dog Town Fork of the Red River (at 34°50' N, 101°24' W). It traverses terrain with moderately steep slopes and locally high relief, surfaced by shallow to moderately deep silt loams that support rangeland grasses and mesquite. Coyote Creek is in the western part of the JA Ranch.[qv]

——— (Runnels County). Coyote Creek begins at the confluence of Big and Little Coyote creeks, five miles southeast of Winters in central Runnels County (at 31°53' N, 100°00' W), and runs southeast for ten miles to its mouth on Elm Creek, 3½ miles northeast of Ballinger (at 31°48' N, 99°56' W). Mesquite and grasses predominate near its upper reaches and water-tolerant hardwoods, conifers, and grasses downstream. The creek rises in flat to gently rolling terrain, then runs onto land with local shallow depressions and an expansive clay surface.

COYOTE LAKE. Coyote Lake, one of the largest natural salt lakes in the Panhandle[qv] of Texas, is ten miles southwest of Muleshoe in Bailey County (at 34°06' N, 102°53' W). It was a favorite campsite for Comanche Indian tribes and early buffalo hunters. During the 1880s Coyote Lake became a watering spot for the vast XIT Ranch.[qv] The area is surfaced by mostly barren loose sands that support scrub brush and some tall grasses and vine mesquite.

BIBLIOGRAPHY: Bailey County History Book Commission, *Tales and Trails of Bailey County, 1918–1988* (Dallas: Taylor, 1988).

COYOTE PEAK. Coyote Peak is three miles east of Farm Road 569 and five miles south of the Sabana River in southwestern Eastland County (at 32°08' N, 99°02' W). Its summit, at an elevation of 1,882 feet above sea level, rises 152 feet above the nearby road.

COYOTE SPRINGS. Coyote Springs, also called Indian Springs, was seven miles south of the New Mexico state line in northeastern Loving County (at 31°54' N, 103°29' W). The springs flowed from red sandstone overlain by Quaternary sands and gravels. The surrounding desert terrain is flat to rolling, covered by sheets and dunes of silt and sand and by Triassic deposits of shale, siltstone, sandstone, and gravel. Soil of the area is brownish-red loamy fine sand in depths of eight to twelve inches. Local vegetation includes small mesquite, yucca, bear grass, and sparse range grasses. The springs were at one time called Indian Springs for the Lipan village located there in the mid-eighteenth century. Two Christianized Indians, Francisco Romero and Joseph Antonio Miraval, stopped at the springs in 1763 and reported that Lipans were living there. In 1893 the Johnson brothers established a ranch on land around the springs. During the twentieth century farmers and ranchers sank wells and sapped the water table, and the springs ran dry.

BIBLIOGRAPHY: Gunnar Brune, *Springs of Texas,* Vol. 1 (Fort Worth: Branch-Smith, 1981).

COZART, TEXAS. Cozart, a farming and post office community fourteen miles southwest of Carthage in southwestern Panola County, was probably established in the 1890s. A post office had opened there by 1901. At its height around the turn of the century, the community had a store, a mill, and a number of houses. When the Timpson and Henderson Railway bypassed Cozart in 1903, the local post office was closed, and within a short time the community was abandoned. Most of its residents moved to nearby Ragley, a stop on the railroad.

Christopher Long

CRABAPPLE, TEXAS. Crabapple is on Crabapple Creek about 10½ miles north of Fredericksburg in northern Gillespie County. The area was originally settled sometime in the mid-1800s by Friedrich Wellgehausen, Jacob Land, Adam Pehl, Mathias Schmidt, Nicolas Rusche, James Riley, Heinrich Keese, and Jacob and Adam Fries. Almost without exception, these early settlers were of German origin. A school had been established in Crabapple by 1867, and during the 1880s a Lutheran congregation was founded. In 1897 St. John's Lutheran Church was built there. The Crabapple post office operated from 1894 to 1910. Maps dating from the 1960s showed a school, a church, and several cemeteries at Crabapple.

BIBLIOGRAPHY: Don Hampton Biggers, *German Pioneers in Texas* (Fredericksburg, Texas: Fredericksburg Publishing, 1925). Ella Amanda Gold, The History of Education in Gillespie County (M.A. thesis, University of Texas, 1945).

Martin Donell Kohout

CRABAPPLE CREEK. Crabapple Creek rises a mile northwest of Hilltop in northern Gillespie County (at 30°25' N, 98°59' W) and runs northeast for twenty-eight miles to its mouth on Sandy Creek, about a mile west of State Highway 16 in southern Llano County (at 30°33' N, 98°43' W). The stream, which is intermittent in its upper reaches, rises in the hills of the eastern Edwards Plateau and crosses into an area of the Central (or Llano) basin. It runs through flat to rolling terrain surfaced by loamy and clayey soils that support grasses and open stands of live oak, mesquite, and Ashe juniper.

CRABB, TEXAS. Crabb (Crabb Switch) is on Farm Road 762 below the bend of the Brazos River five miles southeast of Richmond in Fort Bend County. The area was originally owned by Old Three Hundred[qv] colonists Joseph and Abner Kuykendall.[qqv] After the death of Joseph Kuykendall in the 1870s, his widow Eliza Jane married John C. Crabb. In 1879 the Gulf, Colorado and Santa Fe Railway built through the site, and the town got its name because Eliza Jane Kuykendall Crabb owned the property the railroad used as right-of-way. In 1896 the town had a gin, a district school, a Methodist church, two fruit growers, two doctors, and a population of 400. The next year the community had a school for black students. The settlement acquired a post office in 1894 but lost it in 1900. Despite the fact that Crabb was served by the railroad, its population dwindled, and by 1933 it was reported as 100. In 1936 Crabb comprised two churches, one business, and several dwellings along a paved road. Its population was listed as fifty by 1953, and as about forty from the mid-1960s until the mid-1980s. In 1988 and 1990 Crabb's population was reported as 125.

BIBLIOGRAPHY: Clarence Wharton, *Wharton's History of Fort Bend County* (San Antonio: Naylor, 1939). Stephen L. Hardin

CRABB'S PRAIRIE, TEXAS. Crabb's Prairie, near the junction of State Highway 75 and Farm Road 1696 and some seven miles northwest of Huntsville in central Walker County, was named for Hillary M. Crabb, who served as a county judge and Texas legislator. Crabb settled during the early 1830s on land now in Walker County; he received title to 4,000 acres on February 11, 1835. After Texas won its independence, newly arriving settlers congregated around Crabb's homestead. Crabb's Prairie was connected to Huntsville by a road built in 1846 and was on the stage route that linked Huntsville and Navasota. In 1901 the Cook Springs Baptist Church was built in the area and a school was established near the Alexander homestead. The Crabb's Prairie school offered seven grades in 1911. In 1936 the community had three businesses, two schools, and a church, surrounded by numerous farm dwellings. In the 1980s Crabb's Prairie was served by one business and the nearby Baptist church; local students attended school in Huntsville.

BIBLIOGRAPHY: D'Anne McAdams Crews, ed., *Huntsville and Walker County, Texas: A Bicentennial History* (Huntsville, Texas: Sam Houston State University, 1976). Walker County Genealogical Society and Walker County Historical Commission, *Walker County* (Dallas, 1986). James L. Hailey

CRACKER'S BEND, TEXAS. Cracker's Bend was between Nogalus Prairie and Druso near the Houston county line in northern Trinity County. The community was first settled before 1900 and at one time had a mill and a number of houses. After World War II[qv] most of its residents moved away, and in the early 1990s only a few scattered houses remained.

BIBLIOGRAPHY: Patricia B. and Joseph W. Hensley, eds., *Trinity County Beginnings* (Groveton, Texas: Trinity County Book Committee, 1986). Christopher Long

CRAFT, JUANITA JEWEL SHANKS (1902–1985). Juanita Craft, civil rights activist, was born on February 9, 1902, the only child of David and Eliza (Balfour) Shanks, in Round Rock, Texas. Her grandparents had been slaves; her father was a high school principal, and her mother was a teacher and seamstress. After completing high school in Austin, Juanita attended Prairie View State Normal and Industrial College (now Prairie View A&M University) and received a certificate in dressmaking and millinery in 1921. Later she received a teaching certificate from Samuel Huston College (now Huston-Tillotson College) in Austin. After briefly teaching kindergarten in Columbus, she moved to Galveston in 1922. She married and worked as a drugstore clerk in Galveston for three years. When her marriage ended, she moved to Dallas, where she was employed as a maid at the Adolphus Hotel from 1925 to 1934. She subsequently worked as a dressmaker until her marriage to Johnny Edward Craft on October 2, 1937. He died in 1950.

Joining the Dallas branch of the National Association for the Advancement of Colored People[qv] in 1935 marked the beginning of Mrs. Craft's long service as a civil rights activist. A dynamic force in the organization and throughout the state during the 1940s, she was appointed Dallas NAACP membership chairman in 1942 and in 1946 was promoted to Texas NAACP field organizer. She and Lulu Belle White[qv] of Houston organized 182 branches of the NAACP in Texas over a period of eleven years. In 1944 she became the first black woman in Dallas County to vote. In 1946 she was the first black woman deputized in the state to collect the poll tax.

She emerged as a leader in the civil rights movement in Dallas after her appointment as Youth Council advisor of the Dallas NAACP in 1946. Her work with the youth unit became a prototype for other NAACP youth groups throughout the country. In 1955 she attempted to enroll the first black student at North Texas State College (now North Texas State University), thus precipitating a battle that was eventually won through litigation. That same year her youth group spearheaded the picketing of the State Fair of Texas[qv] to protest the policy of admitting blacks only on Negro Achievement Day. From 1961 through 1964 she led the Youth Council in picketing lunch counters, restaurants, theaters, and public transportation to protest segregation. In 1967 she initiated an investigation of fraudulent trade-school practices in black communities in Dallas; it resulted in the passage of legislation establishing rules for such schools.

Juanita Craft was a Democratic precinct chairman from 1952 to 1975 and served two terms on the Dallas City Council between 1975 and 1979. She was a member of the Munger Avenue Baptist Church, the Democratic Women's Club, the YWCA, the League of Women Voters,[qv] and the National Council of Negro Women. She participated on numerous local, state, and national boards, including those of the Urban League of Greater Dallas, Goals for Dallas, Dallas United Nations, the Governor's Human Relations Committee, and the NAACP. During her fifty years of public service she received the Linz Award, Dallas's highest civic award (1969), the NAACP Golden Heritage Life Membership Award (1978), and the Eleanor Roosevelt Humanitarian Award for public service (1984). In 1985 the NAACP recognized her fifty years of service to the organization. She visited the White House on invitations from presidents Kennedy, Johnson, and Carter, the last of whom later called her "a living treasure." In 1985 she was one of seventy-two black women featured in Women of Courage, a traveling photographic exhibit sponsored by the Arthur and Elizabeth Schlesinger Library at Radcliffe College. The Dallas Parks and Recreation Department dedicated the Juanita Jewel Craft Recreation Center to celebrate Mrs. Craft's seventy-second birthday in 1974. The Juanita Craft Foundation was established in 1985 to further her ideals. She died on August 6, 1985, and was buried in Austin. The Craft Foundation donated her home to the Dallas Park and Recreation Department. She had no children but claimed to have "adopted the world."

BIBLIOGRAPHY: Juanita Craft, Oral History Interviews by David Stricklin and Gail Tomlinson, 1984 (Transcripts, Dallas Public Library). "Texas Women: A Celebration of History" Archives, Texas Woman's University, Denton. Chandler Vaughan, ed., *A Child, the Earth, and a Tree of Many Seasons: The Voice of Juanita Craft* (Dallas: Halifax, 1982). Mamie L. Abernathy-McKnight

CRAFT, TEXAS. Craft, formerly known as Independence, is on U.S. Highway 69 two miles south of Jacksonville in northern Cherokee County. The community was called Craft after a local post office was established in 1891 and named Craft for Thomas J. Craft, its first postmaster. The first railroad built through the area was Rusk Transportation, which in 1875 connected Rusk, southeast of Craft, with Jacksonville to the north. This line became the Kansas and Gulf Short Line in 1881 and was acquired by the St. Louis, Arkansas and Texas in 1887 and subsequently by the St. Louis Southwestern of Texas in 1891. The first carload of tomatoes ever shipped from Texas rolled out of

Craft on June 14, 1897. Tomatoes and the railroad brought prosperity to the community for several decades. The local population, estimated at ten in 1896, was fifty by 1925. In its prime Craft had the post office, a depot, a church, a three-teacher school, two general stores, and two tomato-packing sheds. In 1929, however, its post office was discontinued. Increasing urbanization and the decline of agriculture in the area reduced Craft's population, which was estimated at twenty-one from 1972 through the early 1990s. In the mid-1980s the community consisted of a church, a store, and a scattering of houses. A Texas Historical Commission^{qv} marker was erected at the old townsite on U.S. 69 in 1985.

BIBLIOGRAPHY: *Cherokee County History* (Jacksonville, Texas: Cherokee County Historical Commission, 1986). Hattie Joplin Roach, *The Hills of Cherokee* (1952; rpt., Fort Worth, 1976).

Bernard Mayfield and Phyllis Aswell

CRAFTON, TEXAS. Crafton is on Farm Road 2127 some two miles east of the Jack county line in northwestern Wise County. Settlement of the community began in the late 1870s after the removal of Comanche Indians from the area. A post office was established there in 1878. Among the first settlers was George R. Craft, who filed a claim for 160 acres near the headwaters of Indian Creek. In 1883 a town was laid out on part of Craft's land, and subsequently the community took the name Crafton. Crafton was within a mile of the Butterfield Overland Mail^{qv} route and by 1890 had three churches, a district school, a cotton gin, a hotel, steam flouring mills, a half dozen other businesses, and an estimated population of 200. In 1909 a tornado swept through Crafton, destroying all its churches, the school, a cotton gin, two stores, and seven residences. Although the town rebuilt after the tornado, it did not as successfully weather economic change. Crafton was originally a retail point for area farmers, but it suffered both from being bypassed by the railroads in the later 1800s and from declining cotton production in the early 1900s. In 1917 its post office was discontinued, and by the mid-1920s its population had declined to 168. In 1950 the community had an estimated fifty residents and one business. In 1986 and 1990 its population stood at twenty.

BIBLIOGRAPHY: Rosalie Gregg, ed., *Wise County History* (Vol. 1, n.p: Nortex, 1975; Vol. 2, Austin: Eakin, 1982).

David Minor

CRAIG, TEXAS (Lamar County). Craig (Craigs) was a farming community on U.S. Highway 271 and several dirt roads 1½ miles northwest of Pattonville and 8½ miles southeast of Paris in eastern Lamar County. The area was settled by 1883, when the Craigs post office opened. The post office closed after only two years, but a school was established in the community by 1936. By 1957 the school had been absorbed into the East Lamar common school district. Craig was not shown on a 1964 topographic map of the area.

BIBLIOGRAPHY: Thomas S. Justiss, An Administrative Survey of the Schools of Lamar County with a Plan for Their Reorganization (M.A. thesis, University of Texas, 1937).

Vista K. McCroskey

CRAIG, TEXAS (Rusk County). Craig is on State Highway 322 eight miles north of Henderson in north central Rusk County. The site, adjacent to the J. W. Crim plantation, was settled in 1834. Crim donated the land for an early church. A post office operated under the name Crim from 1887 to 1893 and from 1902 until sometime after 1904. In 1945 the community had a church, a school, and a cemetery. After World War II^{qv} the name Craig or Craig Community gradually supplanted the name Crims Chapel. In 1980 the settlement had two churches and a cemetery.

BIBLIOGRAPHY: Dorman H. Winfrey, *A History of Rusk County* (Waco: Texian, 1961).

Megan Biesele

CRAIG-TRANQUIL, TEXAS. Craig-Tranquil was a church community 3½ miles northeast of Cooper in central Delta County. The area was settled by 1854, when local residents deeded property to the Craig-Tranquil Methodist Episcopal Church, South. The Tranquil school had opened by 1905, when it enrolled twenty-six pupils and employed one teacher. In 1928 this school merged with the nearby Craig Prairie school to form the Craig-Tranquil district. In 1949 this system was divided between the Enloe and Cooper school districts. By 1964 the community was no longer shown on maps.

BIBLIOGRAPHY: Paul Garland Hervey, A History of Education in Delta County, Texas (M.A. thesis, University of Texas, 1951). Wilma Ross and Billie Phillips, *Photos and Tales of Delta County* (1976).

Vista K. McCroskey

CRAIN, JOEL BURDITT (1813–1887). Joel Burditt Crain, soldier, was born September 8, 1813, in Tennessee, the son of Ambrose and Mary (Burditt or Burdett) Crain. He settled in San Augustine County, Texas (at a site now in Nacogdoches County), in October 1834. He joined Capt. William Kimbro's San Augustine Company on March 15, 1836. He was in the skirmish at San Felipe when Santa Anna's army first arrived there, and his cousin, Robert Taylor Crain, was slightly wounded in the head by an *escopeta* ball there. His company joined Sam Houston^{qv} at Groce's Retreat^{qv} and was ordered down to San Felipe to guard that crossing. They burned the town, crossed to the other side, and entrenched. During the battle of San Jacinto,^{qv} Sam Houston, in an attempt to disguise himself, wore the cap and rode the horse of Sergeant Major Crain. As sergeant major, Crain received the sword from Juan Nepomuceno Almonte^{qv} at the surrender and carried the dispatches concerning the surrender to the authorities in Nacogdoches County. Crain married Sarah Elvina Smith on October 3, 1837; they had ten children, eight of whom lived to adulthood. Joel and Sarah lived in Nacogdoches County, then moved to Henderson in Rusk County, then to McLennan County. Crain received 640 acres for having participated in the battle of San Jacinto. In 1853, on the Brazos, seven miles south of Waco, he built one of the first sawmills in the county. He was also the first to plant cotton in the prairie portion of McLennan County. Crain died on January 18, 1887, and was buried in the Harris Creek Cemetery. In 1972 an official Texas historical marker was placed at his grave.

BIBLIOGRAPHY: Sam Houston Dixon and Louis Wiltz Kemp, *The Heroes of San Jacinto* (Houston: Anson Jones, 1932). Dayton Kelley, ed., *The Handbook of Waco and McLennan County, Texas* (Waco: Texian, 1972). *A Memorial and Biographical History of McLennan, Falls, Bell, and Coryell Counties* (Chicago: Lewis, 1893; rpt., St. Louis: Ingmire, 1984).

Eleanor Hanover Nance

CRAIN, WILLIAM HENRY (1848–1896). William Henry Crain, Texas senator and United States congressman, was born in Galveston, Texas, on November 25, 1848, the son of William Davis and Emily Matilda (Blake) Crain. His parents, while still youths, emigrated separately from New York City to Texas before 1836. Young Emily Blake narrowly escaped death in the Linnville Raid of 1840,^{qv} when Comanche Indians sacked and burned Linnville. She and William Davis Crain were married in Matagorda in 1844; after he died in 1854 their son was sent to New York City under the care of Peter F. Harrington, who educated him. Young Crain attended the Christian Brothers' School and received both the A.B. and the M.A. degrees from St. Francis Xavier College. He began the study of law at Indianola, Texas, in the firm of Stockdale and Proctor in 1869 and was admitted to the bar in 1871.

Crain was elected district attorney for the Twenty-third Judicial District in 1872 and served until 1876, when he was elected to the Texas Senate as a Democrat; he resigned in 1878, when he moved to Cuero. He canvassed the state for the Democratic party^{qv} during several presidential elections. He served as a member of the national Democratic convention in 1880 and that same year was an elector for the unsuccessful Winfield Scott Hancock. In 1884, with the support of James B. Wells,^{qv} Crain was elected as a Democrat from the Seventh

District to the Forty-ninth United States Congress. He served in the five succeeding congresses, where he opposed prohibition qv and, unlike most Texas Democratic congressmen, opposed the free coinage of silver in the 1890s and supported President Grover Cleveland's fiscal policies.

He was known as a "beautiful and fluent speaker." He was married to Angeline G. Mitchell, the granddaughter of James Kerr,qv in the Catholic church at Indianola in July 1873. The couple's six children married into prominent Texas ranching families, including those of Gustav Schleicher, James A. McFaddin, John Dunn,qqv and W. R. Rathbone. Crain died in Washington, D.C., on February 10, 1896, and was buried in Cuero.

BIBLIOGRAPHY: *Biographical Directory of the American Congress.* Lewis E. Daniell, *Personnel of the Texas State Government, with Sketches of Representative Men of Texas* (Austin: City Printing, 1887; 3d ed., San Antonio: Maverick, 1892). William S. Speer and John H. Brown, eds., *Encyclopedia of the New West* (Marshall, Texas: United States Biographical Publishing, 1881; rpt., Easley, South Carolina: Southern Historical Press, 1978). Clarence R. Wharton, ed., *Texas under Many Flags* (5 vols., Chicago: American Historical Society, 1930).

Craig H. Roell

CRAMAYEL, JULES EDOUARD DE (1798–1871). Jules Edouard Fontaine, Viscount de Cramayel, was the fourth of seven children born to Jean François Fontaine, Marquis de Cramayel, and Marie Josephine de Folard. He was born in 1798 in France and entered on a diplomatic career in 1818. He held successively the post of secretary of the legations at Stockholm, Madrid, Vienna, Hanover, Lisbon, and Naples. As chargé d'affaires ad interim to Texas from January 1843 to January 1844 he reported frequently on what he believed to be the fraudulent practices of Henri Castro qv in bringing French emigrants to Texas, and he urged the French foreign minister to take steps to prevent further recruitment of colonists in France. Plagued by ill health, appalled at frontier conditions, and concerned over the revival of the question of annexation,qv he nonetheless fulfilled his duties and compiled massive and detailed memoranda on the civil administration and military and naval organization of the Republic of Texas.qv Although commended by the foreign minister when he left Texas, he remained without further assignment until 1848, when he traveled as minister plenipotentiary to Copenhagen. In 1849 he became an officer in the Legion of Honor. He died a bachelor in Paris in 1871.

BIBLIOGRAPHY: Nancy Nichols Barker, "The Republic of Texas: A French View," *Southwestern Historical Quarterly* 71 (October 1967).

Nancy N. Barker

CRANDALL, TEXAS. Crandall is at the intersection of U.S. Highway 175 and Farm roads 148 and 3039, nine miles west of Kaufman in west central Kaufman County. The catalyst for its development was the decision of the Texas Trunk Line Railway to lay tracks through the area in 1880. Rev. C. F. Crandall gave the railroad a right-of-way through his land, and the community that quickly developed there was named in his honor; it became a shipping point for area farmers. In 1881 a post office branch was opened at the community. By 1884 the town had a gristmill, a cotton gin, a church, a school, and a population of fifty. Its population grew to an estimated 150 by 1890 and to 251 by 1904. By the mid-1920s Crandall had an estimated 750 residents and fifty businesses, including two banks. Its population dropped slightly during the Great Depression qv years, and some Crandall residents moved to work in the cities during World War II.qv In 1943 Crandall had 500 residents. In 1988 it had 1,207 residents and fifteen businesses, and in 1990 it had 1,652 residents.

BIBLIOGRAPHY: Robert Richard Butler, History of Kaufman County, Texas (M.A. thesis, University of Texas, 1940).

David Minor

CRANE, CARL JOSEPH (1900–1982). Carl Joseph Crane, aviation pioneer and inventor, was born in San Antonio on October 20, 1900, the son of John Paul and Ida (Witmer) Crane. At age ten he witnessed the birth of aviation qv in Texas when, at Fort Sam Houston, Capt. Benjamin Foulois first flew experimentally the only airplane owned by the United States government, a pusher-type, twenty-five-horsepower Wright Brothers biplane. Crane studied at St. Mary's University, San Antonio, and the University of Dayton (Ohio), where he received the bachelor (1924) and the master of mechanical engineering (1934) degrees. After graduating from the United States Army Advanced Flying School at Kelly Field (see KELLY AIR FORCE BASE) in 1925, he spent two years with the First Pursuit Group at Selfridge Field in Michigan, and then for five years was a flight instructor at Kelly, Brooks, and Randolph fields in Texas. In 1929 he teamed with William C. Ockerqv to devise revolutionary flying systems and to write the world's first manual for instrumental flight, *Blind Flight in Theory and Practice* (1932).

On August 23, 1937, at Wright-Patterson Air Force Base, with assistance from G. V. Holloman and Raymond Stout, Crane made the world's first fully automated landing, for which he had designed the key instruments. He served in military aviation until 1949. During World War IIqv he performed training and logistics duties in the United States, then served overseas with the Ninth Air Force and attained the rank of colonel. He was senior air officer with the Army Advisory Group in China, 1948–49. In more than sixty years as a pilot, Crane flew almost every experimental and production craft, from the earliest biplane to jet aircraft.

Among his more than 100 patented inventions were radio signaling equipment for use in aircraft trainers, which was licensed for use in the Link Trainer; the Navitrainer, designed with Colonel Ocker; the B-3 Drift Meter; the Gyro Panoramic Sextant; and numerous other navigational devices. He had inventions on the drawing board and patents pending when he died.

Crane was a member of the Daedalians and of the Institute of Navigation, a fellow of the American Institute of Aeronautics and Astronautics, and the holder of the Mackay Trophy, the Distinguished Flying Cross, and distinguished alumnus awards from both St. Mary's and the University of Dayton. In 1979 he (and Ocker, posthumously) received the Flight Safety Foundation's Pioneer Award. Crane married twice and had five children. He was a devout Catholic. He died on April 26, 1982, in San Antonio.

BIBLIOGRAPHY: Carl J. Crane, Interviews by Maj. Gen. William Allen Harris, 1980, Oral History Program, University of Texas Institute of Texan Cultures, San Antonio. San Antonio *Express News*, September 15, 1979, April 28, 1982. San Antonio *Light*, April 28, 1982.

Deolece M. Parmelee

CRANE, EDWARD E. (1883–1959). Edward E. Crane, attorney, law professor, and university regent, was born in Cleburne, Texas, on December 11, 1883, the son of Eula Olatia (Taylor) and Martin McNulty Crane.qv He graduated from the University of Texas with B.Litt. and L.L.B. degrees in 1906 and entered practice with his father's law firm in Dallas. Crane received a commission as first lieutenant in the field artillery in 1917 and served in France until 1919. He returned to Dallas after the war and continued to practice law. Governor Dan Moodyqv appointed him to the board of regents of the University of Texas in June 1927; Crane served on the board until January 1933 and made perhaps his most significant contribution as chairman of the Board for Lease of University Lands. He joined the University of Texas law faculty at the end of his term as regent in 1933 and taught until 1941. At the university he was instrumental in establishing the legal aid clinic. Crane was appointed regional attorney for the Office of Price Administration in 1942 but retired later that year to resume private practice. On June 12, 1937, he married Mrs. Donna (Roberts) Fitzgerald, widow of Hugh Nugent Fitzgerald.qv She died in 1938. Crane was a Baptist, a Mason, and a Democrat, and held membership in the

American, Texas, and Dallas bar associations. He died in Dallas on October 9, 1959, and was buried at Grove Hill Cemetery.

BIBLIOGRAPHY: Edward Crane Papers, Barker Texas History Center, University of Texas at Austin. Ellis A. Davis and Edwin H. Grobe, comps., *The Encyclopedia of Texas*, 2-vol. ed. Dallas *Morning News*, October 11, 1959. *National Cyclopaedia of American Biography*, Vol. 44. Vertical Files, Barker Texas History Center, University of Texas at Austin. *Vivian Elizabeth Smyrl*

CRANE, HUBERT HAMMOND (1893–1959). Hubert Hammond Crane, architect, was born in Louisville, Kentucky, on April 25, 1893, the son of William Franklin and Lilborne (Hammond) Crane. In 1912–13 he attended the University of Louisville. During World War I qv he served as lieutenant of field artillery and was awarded the Silver Star and Purple Heart. In 1919 he received a major's commission in the Red Cross as chief of motor operations for Europe. Crane remained in Europe until 1920, when he returned to the United States to become a draftsman for Dallas architect David R. Williams.qv In 1922 he started his own architectural practice in Dallas but moved to Fort Worth just before the stock-market crash of 1929. Beginning in the 1930s Crane's background in European architecture enabled him to remodel historic residences and design traditional ones in the Ridglea, Monticello, Crestwood, River Crest, and Westover Hills areas. His designs were based on Georgian, Colonial, French Provincial, and early New England styles. His functional Cubistic design in white concrete for the Dr Pepper Bottling Plant (1938) was a notable stylistic departure. This forward-looking composition showed the influence of European Functionalist architects, whose simply massed, rhythmic designs featured white stucco or concrete surfaces, flat roofs, and large expanses of glass. At the time, the Dr Pepper Companyqv building was the largest monolithic concrete structure in Fort Worth. This striking design proved to be Fort Worth's most outstanding and enduring example of the new, European style known as the International Style. Crane had three assignments in the Federal Public School Building Program: the South Hi-Mount Elementary School (1936), an addition to the Washington Heights Elementary School (1936), and an addition to the Circle Park Elementary School (1935). He was associated with five other Fort Worth architects on the city's two United States Housing Authority public-housing complexes (1938–40). During World War II qv he designed housing projects for military and civilian installations in Texas and Oklahoma for the federal Public Housing Authority. After the war he continued in private practice through the 1950s.

Crane was a charter member of both the Texas Society of Architects and the Fort Worth Chapter of the American Institute of Architects, which he served as president in 1953. He was a director of the Texas Society of Architects from 1949 to 1951 and from 1957 to 1959. He traveled throughout Texas in the 1940s and 1950s as guest lecturer to high school and college students and worked to improve education in architectural programs and techniques. He inaugurated the national Architect in Training Program (1957) and the local Craftsmanship Award. Crane regularly contributed poetry and prose to architectural and trade journals under the pen names Hubertus Junius, Herodotus Jones, Pete Pausanius, and Jonny Vitruvius. In June 1959 he was elected a fellow of the American Institute of Architects for his achievements in literature, education, and service to the institute. He married Julia Meade Starkey on June 6, 1919, and the couple had three sons. Crane died of cancer in Fort Worth on August 26, 1959.

BIBLIOGRAPHY: Judith Singer Cohen, *Cowtown Moderne: Art Deco Architecture of Fort Worth, Texas* (Fort Worth: Texas Christian University Press, 1988). Fort Worth *Star-Telegram*, August 27, 1959. *Texas Architect*, May 1959. *Judith S. Cohen*

CRANE, JOHN (?–1839). John Crane, early settler and soldier in the Texas revolutionary army, probably a native of Virginia, married Mary (called Polly) De Lozier and with her moved from Virginia to Tennessee, where he was a private in the Tennessee cavalry and served as a sergeant in the Tennessee militia in the War of 1812. In 1834 he moved to Texas and settled in what is now Walker County as a member of Joseph Vehlein'sqv colony. Crane raised a company of volunteers for the siege of Bexarqv in 1835 and the next year participated in the Runaway Scrape,qv during which he cared for his own family and that of his son-in-law, who was with the army at the battle of San Jacinto.qv From June 30 to September 30, 1836, Crane served in the Texas army in John M. Wade'sqv cavalry company. He was killed in the battle of the Nechesqv during the Cherokee Warqv in July 1839.

BIBLIOGRAPHY: D'Anne McAdams Crews, ed., *Huntsville and Walker County, Texas: A Bicentennial History* (Huntsville, Texas: Sam Houston State University, 1976). *John Crane McVea*

CRANE, MARTIN MCNULTY (1855–1943). Martin McNulty Crane, lawyer and politician, the son of Martin and Mary (McNulty) Crane, was born on November 17, 1855, at Grafton, Taylor County, West Virginia. After his mother died, his father took the four-year-old boy to Kentucky and subsequently to Stewart County, Tennessee, where the elder Crane died suddenly in 1860. For the next ten years friends of the family raised Crane. At the age of seventeen he left Stewart County and moved to Johnson County, Texas.

For a number of years he worked on a farm and attended school. Later he supplemented his income by teaching. During this time he also prepared himself for a legal career. In 1877 he was admitted to the bar. Although quite young and new to the area, Crane established such a favorable reputation that in 1878 voters elected him prosecuting attorney. He was reelected in 1880 but declined to stand for renomination in 1882. In part this decision was a result of family obligations. On January 22, 1879, Crane had married Eulla Olatia Taylor, and by 1882 the couple had three children and little financial security. To remedy the situation, Crane concentrated on his private legal practice. Ultimately, the Cranes had five daughters and three sons. In 1884, however, Crane's supporters persuaded him to return to politics. That year he was elected representative of the Thirty-sixth District to the Nineteenth State Legislature. After the term, family responsibilities again prevented him from running for reelection. In 1886 he returned to private practice. He devoted the next four years to his growing legal career.

For years he sympathized with the economic disadvantages North Texas farmers suffered. He approved of many of the programs suggested by the Farmers' Allianceqv and was alarmed at the unregulated power held by railroads, oil companies, and metropolitan banks. As a result of these sympathies Crane, a Democrat, aligned himself with the faction of the party that supported the reform efforts of future governors James S. Hogg and Charles Allen Culberson.qqv This commitment to progressive politics, combined with his legal skills, attracted a group of influential Democrats who in 1890 persuaded Crane to run for office. In 1890 voters elected him state senator from the Twenty-first District (Johnson, Ellis, and Hill counties). In the Twenty-second Legislature he served on a special committee established by Governor Hogg that successfully lobbied for the bill establishing the Railroad Commission.qv Two years later Crane was elected lieutenant governor. In 1894 he resigned from that office to campaign for attorney general. The voters elected him, and for the next four years he distinguished himself in a series of precedent-setting cases, including the case enforcing the new Texas antitrust laws against the Waters-Pierce Oil Company (*see* WATERS-PIERCE CASE). Crane represented Texas against the United States in the Greer Countyqv case, in which Greer County was declared to be north and east of the true Texas state line and became part of Oklahoma.

When some tried to nominate Crane for governor, he withdrew, perhaps prematurely, after failing to secure as many delegates as he expected. He returned to private practice in 1899 and for the next forty-four years managed a successful law firm in Dallas. In 1906, in a well-publicized debate with Senator Joseph Weldon Bailey[qv] of Houston, Crane argued against politicians' practice of accepting fees from businesses. In 1917 he was chief counsel in the impeachment proceedings against Governor James Ferguson.[qv] During the early 1920s he served as head of the Dallas County Citizens League, organized in 1922 to oppose the political influence of the Ku Klux Klan.[qv] On August 3, 1943, after a brief illness, Crane died, at the age of eighty-eight. He was buried in Oak Hill Cemetery, Dallas.

BIBLIOGRAPHY: Frank Carter Adams, ed., *Texas Democracy: A Centennial History of Politics and Personalities of the Democratic Party, 1836–1936* (4 vols., Austin: Democratic Historical Association, 1937). Martin McNulty Crane Papers, Barker Texas History Center, University of Texas at Austin. M. M. Crane, "Recollections of the Establishment of the Texas Railroad Commission," *Southwestern Historical Quarterly* 50 (April 1947). Dallas *Morning News*, August 4, 1943. Lewis E. Daniell, *Personnel of the Texas State Government, with Sketches of Representative Men of Texas* (Austin: City Printing, 1887; 3d ed., San Antonio: Maverick, 1892). *Texas Bar Journal*, November 1943. *Who's Who in America*, 1946–47.

David Minor

CRANE, ROYSTON CAMPBELL, SR. (1864–1956). Royston Campbell Crane, Sr., son of Catherine Jane (Shepherd) and William Carey Crane,[qv] was born on February 16, 1864, in Independence, Washington County, Texas. After graduating in 1884 from Baylor University, where his father was president, he acquired a law degree at the University of Texas and moved at age twenty-two to Roby, the county seat of recently organized Fisher County. There he was elected county attorney and subsequently held various other county offices. In 1899 Crane moved to Abilene and shortly thereafter to Sweetwater, where he became a partner in the Ragland law office.

He was an energetic promoter of West Texas. He started a newspaper, the *Call*, at Roby; in Sweetwater he served two terms as mayor and worked to keep the Kansas City, Mexico and Orient Railway shops. He also led efforts to obtain a proposed West Texas A&M College. In the 1930s he acquired $200,000 from the Texas Centennial[qv] Historical Advisory Committee to mark historic spots in West Texas. He was an avid document collector and knowledgeable historian. In 1923, with Rupert N. Richardson of Simmons College (now Hardin-Simmons University), he developed the idea of a West Texas Historical Association[qv] and recruited for leadership J. M. Radford, Jewel Davis Scarborough,[qv] and B. E. McGlammery of Abilene, W. C. Holden[qv] of McMurry College, and L. G. Kennamer of Abilene Christian College. On April 19, 1924, an organizational meeting convened in the Taylor County Courthouse, the association was given form, and Crane was elected president, a position he held until 1950. His frequent contributions to the West Texas Historical Association *Year Book* and his collection of West Texas historical materials became an important source for the study of regional history.

Crane was married to Mamie Douthit; they had three children, two of whom died in infancy. Royston Crane, Jr.,[qv] originated the comic strips "Wash Tubbs and Easy" and "Buzz Sawyer." On January 20, 1956, at the age of ninety-one, Crane died in Sweetwater.

BIBLIOGRAPHY: Marvin E. Burgess, "Royston Campbell Crane," West Texas Historical Association *Year Book* 32 (1956).

Joe R. Baulch

CRANE, ROYSTON CAMPBELL, JR. (1901–1977). Royston (Roy) Campbell Crane, Jr., award-winning cartoonist, son of Mamie (Douthit) and Judge Royston Campbell Crane, Sr.,[qv] was born in Abilene, Texas, on November 22, 1901. He grew up in Sweetwater and began taking correspondence courses in drawing. His father, an eminent historian and jurist, encouraged Roy's interest in writing and drawing by paying him fifteen cents a week to keep an illustrated diary. In high school he did all of the art work for the annual. His first newspaper cartoon was printed in the Dallas *Evening Journal* on the day of America's entry into World War I.[qv] In 1918 he started college at Simmons College (now Hardin-Simmons University) but transferred to the University of Texas within a year. Not entirely satisfied with the art department at UT, he attended the Chicago Academy of Fine Arts for a year. After a year in Chicago he returned to Austin. At the University of Texas Crane drew and wrote for the *Daily Texan*,[qv] the university newspaper, and was the art editor for the *Cactus*, the university annual. He was elected to Sigma Delta Chi, an honorary journalism fraternity, and Phi Kappa Psi, a social fraternity. In 1921, while he was still in school, he began work with the Austin *American-Statesman*[qv] as an artist and reporter.

Crane traveled throughout the Southwest and Europe before beginning his first full-time job as a cartoonist with the New York *World* in 1922. He worked there until 1924, when he received an offer from NEA, a Scripps-Howard news-feature organization in Cleveland. In Cleveland he developed one of the first adventure comic strips, "Wash Tubbs," and followed it with the color strip "Captain Easy" in 1933. In 1943 he received an offer from King Features to write a new comic strip, "Buz Sawyer," which dealt with the adventures of the title character, a Navy pilot, and air crewman Roscoe Sweeney. To ensure the accuracy of his cartoon characters' adventures, Crane went several times to sea on naval destroyers and aircraft carriers. "Buz Sawyer" was eventually carried by over 500 newspapers in the United States, twenty South American newspapers, several papers in Canada, and papers in three Scandinavian countries. In 1944 Crane was honored by Rear Adm. A. W. Radford, acting deputy chief of naval operations, for the comic strip. In 1951 the National Cartoonists' Society named him Cartoonist of the Year and awarded him the Billy De Beck Memorial Award. Crane also received the Best Story–Strip Award (1966) and the Reuben Award for Outstanding Cartoon Work (1950). He was an avid supporter of the arts; in 1965 he established the Roy Crane Award in the Arts at the University of Texas for outstanding student creativity in all branches of the arts.

Crane was a member of the National Cartoonists' Society, the Aviation-Space Writers Association, and the United States Navy League (honorary). He was also listed in Who's Who in America. He married Evelyn Cecile Hatcher, also a former student of the University of Texas, on February 8, 1927, and they had two daughters, one of whom was Miss Florida in 1953. Crane died on July 8, 1977, in Orlando, Florida.

BIBLIOGRAPHY: *Texas Ranger*, January 1947. *Daily Texan*, March 28, 1958. Maurice Horn, ed., *The World Encyclopedia of Comics* (New York: Chelsea House, 1976). Vertical Files, Barker Texas History Center, University of Texas at Austin.

Rebecca H. Green

CRANE, WILLIAM CAREY (1816–1885). William Carey Crane, Baptist pastor, editor, and college president, was born in Richmond, Virginia, on March 17, 1816, the son of William and Lydia (Dorset) Crane. After receiving lessons from private teachers he attended Mount Pleasant Classical Institute in Amherst, Massachusetts, and Virginia Baptist Seminary (now Richmond College). In 1833 he moved to New York and attended Hamilton Literary and Theological Institute and Madison (now Colgate) University. In 1834 he entered Columbian College (now George Washington University), from which he received an A.B. degree in 1836 and an A.M. in 1839. Crane taught in Georgia from 1837 to 1839 and was ordained to the Baptist ministry in Baltimore, Maryland, in 1838 at the age of twenty-two. During this period he married Alcesta Flora Galusha of Rochester, who died in 1840. In March 1839 he accepted a pastorate at Montgomery, Alabama, where he became acquainted with the family of Margaret Lea Houston.[qv] In Alabama Crane also met William Milton Tryon and James Huckins,[qqv] who, together with Robert Emmett Bledsoe Baylor,[qv] later became the major organizers of Baylor University. Crane married Jane Louisa Wright, also of New York, in 1841. Three years after her death in 1842, he married Catharine Jane Shepherd of Mobile, Alabama. The couple had nine children, eight of whom lived to maturity. During the 1840s Crane held pastorates in various communities in Mississippi, including Columbus, Vicksburg, and Yazoo City. He served as president of Mississippi Female College (1851–57), Semple Broaddus College in Mississippi (1859–60), and Mount Lebanon College in Louisiana (1860–63). At Mount Lebanon he was also coeditor of the *Mississippi Baptist*. He was the cofounder and vice president of the Mississippi State Historical Society and for two years was the general agent of the American Tract Society. He also served as secretary of the Southern Baptist Convention from 1851 to 1863 and as its vice president four times in the 1870s and 1880s.

In 1863 Crane moved to Texas to accept the pastorate of the First Baptist Church in Houston, but at the urging of supporters of Baylor University he visited Baylor at Independence and was offered the presidency of the university, effective January 1, 1864. He subsequently refused the pastorate of the Houston church and served as Baylor president for twenty-two years until his death in 1885. Crane's leadership and the expenditure of his own funds enabled Baylor to survive hard times during the Civil War and Reconstruction.qqv During the last years of his presidency, Texas Baptists debated whether to merge Baylor and Waco universities. Crane and the Baylor "Old Guard" fought to keep the school at Independence, although it became obvious that a move was inevitable.

Crane served as pastor of the Independence Baptist Church for eighteen years (1864–67 and 1869–84) and was active in the Texas Baptist State Convention. He was a prolific author and wrote a classic biography of Sam Houston.qv Crane was the first president of the Texas State Teachers Associationqv and was chairman of the committee that recommended the founding of Sam Houston Normal Institute (now Sam Houston State University). He was a leader in the reorganization of the Texas public school system after Reconstruction. In 1866 he was invited to address the Texas legislature and urged it to establish a graduate and professional school at Austin, where graduates of existing universities could pursue higher learning. He also served on the committee of teachers that drafted the resolution in favor of establishing a state university, but was absent at the vote and opposed the resolution. He favored state support of both public and private higher education, an idea strongly opposed by many of his fellow Baptists, but he believed state funds should be allocated to existing schools rather than spent on a state university that would undermine them.

Crane died on February 27, 1885; he was the first Baylor president to die in office. He was originally buried in Independence, but in 1937 the Texas Centennialqv Commission had his body reinterred in the State Cemeteryqv at Austin. Crane County is named in his honor.

BIBLIOGRAPHY: *Biographical Encyclopedia of Texas* (New York: Southern, 1880). James Milton Carroll, *A History of Texas Baptists* (Dallas: Baptist Standard, 1923). Lois Smith Murray, *Baylor at Independence* (Waco: Baylor University Press, 1972). *Texas Historical and Biographical Magazine,* 1891. E. Bruce Thompson, "William Carey Crane and Texas Education," *Southwestern Historical Quarterly* 58 (January 1955).

Travis L. Summerlin

CRANE, TEXAS. Crane, on U.S. Highway 385 and State Highway 329 in eastern Crane County, was named for Baylor University president William C. Crane.qv It is the seat and only town of the county and has the county's only post office, which was founded in 1908. The discovery of oil in the county in 1926 led to the county's organization the next year and to Crane's development as an oil boomtown. Its early residents had to put up with board sidewalks, unpaved roads, and limited services—including hauling their own water—until permanent housing and city utilities were built. Schools and other amenities were established at Crane as the local oil resources were exploited. Crane's population was reported as 1,420 in 1940, as 2,156 in 1950, as 3,796 in 1960, as 3,427 in 1970, and as 3,622 in 1980, when the town had a library, a swimming pool, and some 104 businesses. These included a steel foundry, a concrete plant, a nursing home, and a hospital (that was enlarged in 1962). A special edition of the *Crane News* in 1972 celebrated the county's production of one billion barrels of oil. In the 1980s the town was the service center for the region's flourishing oil industry. In 1990 the population of Crane was reported as 3,533.

BIBLIOGRAPHY: Fort Worth *Star-Telegram,* August 31, 1952. Midland *Reporter-Telegram,* February 27, 1949.

William R. Hunt

CRANE COUNTY. Crane County (G-8), at the western edge of the Edwards Plateauqv in Southwest Texas, is bounded on the north by Ector County, on the east by Upton County, on the south by Pecos County, and on the west by Ward County. It was named for William Cary Crane,qv a president of Baylor University. Crane County comprises 795 square miles of rolling prairie, bounded on the south and west by the Pecos River, which, with Juan Cardona Lake,qv drains the land. The center of the county lies at 31°25′ north latitude and 102°30′ west longitude, about forty miles south of Odessa. Rainfall averages 12.97 inches annually. The elevation varies from 2,400 to 3,000 feet above sea level. The average minimum temperature in January is 29° F; the average maximum in July is 96°. The growing season lasts 225 days, but there is very little farming. Cattle raising brings in about $1.5 million annually. Manufacturing income averages $1.4 million annually, derived largely from steel and concrete products. The county is among state leaders in oil and gas production. In 1982 oil production of almost 27,000,000 barrels earned $810,652,695.

The area that is now Crane County was within the territory of the Lipan Apaches, who were among the originators of the plains culture common to Apaches, Comanches, Kiowas, and other Indians. This part of the Pecos country may have been crossed by Spanish explorer Felipe de Rábago y Teránqv in 1761, and some of the early California-bound American travelers passed through Castle Gap and Horsehead Crossing.qqv

Crane County was formed in 1887 from land previously assigned to Tom Green County the same year, but for many years the area's scant rainfall deterred settlement. In 1890 only fifteen people lived in Crane County; as late as 1900 the United States census enumerated only fifty-one people and twelve ranches in the county. Almost 17,650 cattle and 3,750 sheep were counted that year.

The county seems to have experienced a brief burst of settlement during the first years of the twentieth century; census figures show that in 1910 there were seventy-one farms or ranches in the county, and that the population by that year had risen to 331. Almost no crop production was reported for the county that year, however, and in any case most of the new settlers had moved away by 1920, when only eight ranches, thirty-seven people, and about 4,700 cattle were reported. As late as 1918 the county had no roads, although the Texas and Pacific Railway crossed the northwest corner and the Panhandle and Santa Fe crossed the southern tip.

The area only began to develop after oil was discovered in the county in 1926, when an oil boom attracted thousands to the county. O. C. Kimmison opened a realty office and platted a townsite, where he named the streets of what became the town of Crane for his daughters and sons. He also invited a preacher to hold services in the area; according to county tradition, local gamblers resented the gesture and gave Kimmison a beating for it.

Crane County was attached to Ector County for administrative purposes until 1927, but with (according to one estimate) 6,000 oil boomers in the area by that time, the county was ready for organization. The town of Crane, bustling with as many as 4,500 fortune-seekers, was designated as the county seat, and citizens organized to build a courthouse. Water was a scarce commodity. People paid a dollar a barrel for water brought from a well seven miles east of town, or, if prosperous, paid $2.25 a barrel for better water from Alpine. Water was too precious then for any use but cooking or home-made whiskey; women sent their laundry to El Paso. According to the census 2,221 people were living in Crane County in 1930.

The county became one of the most productive oil counties in the state. In 1938 more than 5,494,600 barrels of oil was produced in the area; in 1944 more than 9,557,500 barrels was pumped, and in 1948 production was 16,851,698 barrels. Almost 27,377,800 barrels was produced in 1956, almost 30,731,500 in 1960, almost 34,092,000 in 1978, and about 26,866,000 in 1982. In 1990 the county produced almost 19,026,000 barrels of oil. By the beginning of 1991 almost 1,552,324,000 barrels of oil had been produced in the county since discovery in 1926.

Thanks almost exclusively to the oil industry Crane County's population rose to 2,841 in 1940, 3,956 in 1950, 4,699 in 1960, and 4,172 in 1970. In 1980, 4,600 people lived in the county, and in 1992 the area had an estimated population of 4,652. Highways in the county include U.S. Highway 385 and Farm Road 1053 (north to south); U.S. Highway 67/385, which crosses the southeast corner; and State Highway 329, Farm Road 11, and Farm Road 1223 (west to east). The town of Crane (1992 estimated population 3,553) is the county's only community and its seat of government. In 1992 business establishments in the town included a foundry and a surfboard manufacturer. Tourist attractions included historic pioneer trails and Horsehead Crossing on the Pecos River.

BIBLIOGRAPHY: *Crane News,* 40th Anniversary Edition, June 15, 1967.
John Leffler

CRANES MILL, TEXAS. Cranes Mill, a stock-raising community seventeen miles northwest of New Braunfels in central Comal County, was named for J. B. Crain, who built a mill at the Gum Spring crossing on the Guadalupe River in the early 1850s. The spelling became Crane when a post office was established there before the Civil War.qv Postal service to Cranes Mill may have been interrupted just after the war, but by 1872 August Engel, a minister, teacher, and storeowner, ran the community's post office in his store. His son succeeded him and was postmaster there until the rural mail route from Fischer's Store was established. The Cranes Mill community recorded a population of twenty-five until the 1940s. The Cranes Mill school was eventually consolidated with a nearby school district. The remains of the town disappeared under Canyon Lake when it began filling in the 1960s, but in the 1980s a lakeside park still carried the name Cranes Mill.

BIBLIOGRAPHY: Oscar Haas, *History of New Braunfels and Comal County, Texas, 1844–1946* (Austin: Steck, 1968).
Oscar Haas

CRANFILL, JAMES BRITTON BUCHANAN BOONE (1858–1942). J. B. Cranfill, Baptist leader, was born in Parker County, Texas, on September 12, 1858, the son of Eaton and Martha Jane (Galloway) Cranfill. As a young man he was converted to the Baptist religion in a brush-arbor meeting in Coryell County. Although he received no college or seminary education, from 1877 to 1878 he taught at a country school at Crawford, McLennan County. He married one of his pupils, Olivia (Ollie) Allen, on September 1, 1878. He learned about medicine from his father, passed the state medical examination, and early in 1879 was licensed as a doctor. He practiced general medicine at Turnersville, in Coryell County, from 1879 to 1882. In 1880 he also opened J. B. Cranfill's Cash Store in Turnersville. In 1881 he established the Turnersville *Effort,* a monthly paper devoted to combating mob rule and saloons. He moved to Gatesville in 1882 and began publishing the weekly Gatesville *Advance.* These journalistic ventures led to his move in 1886 to Waco, where he established and edited the Waco *Advance.* This daily paper represented Texans who wanted to add a prohibitionqv amendment to the state constitution. Cranfill served as financial secretary of Baylor University in 1888–89 and as superintendent of Baptist mission work in Texas from 1890 to 1892.

While superintendent of state missions, he initiated publication of the *State Mission Journal.* He was ordained a Baptist minister in 1890 and toured the South in 1892 as the national Prohibition party candidate for vice president of the United States.

In 1892 Cranfill and M. V. Smith, a Belton pastor, acquired the *Western Baptist,* which they brought from Dallas to Waco and renamed the *Texas Baptist Standard* (*see* BAPTIST STANDARD). During his tenure as editor of the *Standard,* Cranfill engaged in a heated controversy, called the Paper War, with Samuel A. Hayden,qv editor of the Texas *Baptist and Herald.*qv The controversy centered around the state convention's administration of organized, cooperative mission work among Texas Baptists, which Hayden distrusted. After fire destroyed the *Standard's* Waco plant in 1894, Cranfill moved the paper to Dallas and continued as editor until 1904. In that year a confrontation with Hayden on a train en route to the Southern Baptist Convention at Nashville, Tennessee, induced Cranfill to sell the *Standard* to George W. Carroll.qv

Cranfill remained an active Baptist leader in his later years. He edited the *Baptist Tribune* from 1905 to 1907 and was vice president of the Baptist General Convention of Texas in 1928. He also served as a trustee of Southwestern Baptist Theological Seminary from 1909 to 1942, and of the Relief and Annuity Board from 1920 to 1942. In a more secular vein, he pushed for Trinity River canalization, believing the project crucial to the future prosperity of Dallas. Cranfill wrote several books, including *Courage and Comfort* (1895), *Cranfill's Heart Talks* (1906), *Cranfill's Chronicles* (1916), *From Nature to Grace* (1924), and *From Memory* (1937). He was also the joint author of R. C. Buckner's *Life of Faith and Works* (1915). Cranfill compiled and edited humorous treatises and sermons by Benajah Harvey Carroll and James Milton Carroll.qqv He edited B. H. Carroll's *Interpretation of the English Bible* (1914) and J. M. Carroll's *A History of Texas Baptists* (1923), as well as three books of sermons by George Washington Truettqv: *We Would See Jesus* (1915), *A Quest for Souls* (n.d.), and *God's Call to America* (1923). Cranfill died in Dallas on December 28, 1942.

BIBLIOGRAPHY: Robert A. Baker, *The Blossoming Desert—A Concise History of Texas Baptists* (Waco: Word, 1970). *Baptist Standard,* April 1, 1959. James Milton Carroll, *A History of Texas Baptists* (Dallas: Baptist Standard, 1923). L. R. Elliott, ed., *Centennial Story of Texas Baptists* (Dallas: Baptist General Convention of Texas, 1936). *Encyclopedia of Southern Baptists* (4 vols., Nashville: Broadman, 1958–82).
Travis L. Summerlin

CRANFILLS GAP, TEXAS. Cranfills Gap is at the intersection of State Highway 22 and Farm Road 219, forty-two miles northwest of Waco and fourteen miles southwest of Meridian in western Bosque County. The town is near a gap in a mountain on the border between Bosque and Hamilton counties. It is named for George Eaton Cranfill, who had settled near the site by 1851. Although the immediate area was a focus of settlement by 1858, the first sign of organized community development occurred in May 1879, when Sam Cranfill succeeded in moving a nearby Hamilton County post office, opened one month earlier by Samuel B. Crawford, across the county line into Cranfills Gap. The area may have had a horse-powered cotton gin at this time; Riley and Bud Ford opened the first store in 1882. By 1890 the town had two more stores, a blacksmith shop, a saloon, and two physicians. St. Olaf Kirche, a Lutheran church constructed of rock, was built in a rural Norwegian community in 1886 a few miles from Cranfills Gap. As the membership grew and more people lived in the gap, the parishioners grew tired of driving to the country for services and built a new brick church in Cranfills Gap in 1917. The old rock church, marked by a state historical marker, was still standing in 1989 and was used on special occasions.

The First Security State Bank, backed by Colorado capital, opened in 1910. Hoping to attract a railroad, the town moved from its first location in the gap to its present site just east of the ridge in 1913. However, the citizens' hopes for rail transportation never materialized. Local ranchers operated a wool and mohair association during the mid-1920s. A newspaper, the *News,* appeared weekly in 1918; the *Enterprise* was published weekly between 1933 and 1935. Cranfills Gap was the first town in the nation to sell more than its quota in the Fourth War Loan Drive of World War II.[qv] In the 1980s the community school, a consolidation of eleven former districts, served a large part of the surrounding countryside. Estimates indicate that town size fluctuated greatly through the years. The population reached a peak of 600 around 1940. The town was incorporated in 1980, when its population was 341. Residents may have supported as many as twenty-five businesses in the 1940s, but by 1980 only nine rated businesses remained. Cranfills Gap sponsors two annual festivals—the Septemberfest and in December the Lutefisk Feast. In 1990 the population was 269.

BIBLIOGRAPHY: *Bosquerama, 1854–1954: Centennial Celebration of Bosque County, Texas* (Meridian, Texas: Bosque County Centennial Association, 1954). *Farm and Ranch,* April 1945. William C. Pool, *Bosque Territory* (Kyle, Texas: Chaparral, 1964). Thomas Clarence Richardson, "Bosky Dells Where the Bosque Swells," *Farm and Ranch,* November 1926.

Patricia L. Duncan

CRANFORD, JOHN WALTER (1859–1899). John Walter Cranford, lawyer, Texas senator, and United States congressman, son of James Heflin and Caroline Nancy (Bettis) Cranford, was born near Grove Hill, Alabama, on July 28, 1859. In 1865 the family moved to Hopkins County, Texas, where both of Cranford's parents died, his mother in 1865 and his father in 1872. Thus orphaned at the age of thirteen, Cranford worked to support himself and to attend school but left without graduating when he had an opportunity to study law. After reading with Sam J. Hunter of Fort Worth and judges J. K. Milam and J. A. B. Putman of Sulphur Springs, he was admitted to the bar in 1880 and became a junior partner in the firm of Hunter, Putman, and Cranford in Sulphur Springs. He was later a partner in the firm of Cranford and Garrison and subsequently with the firm of Cranford, Garrison, and Keasler.

In November 1888 Cranford ran successfully as the Democratic nominee for the Texas Senate from the Fifth Senatorial District. He was reelected in 1892. He served in the Twenty-first, Twenty-second, and Twenty-third legislatures and was elected president pro tem of the Twenty-second Legislature. In 1896 he was elected from the Fourth Congressional District to the Fifty-fifth Congress of the United States. He easily defeated J. H. (Cyclone) Davis,[qv] the populist candidate, and M. W. Johnson, a Gold-Standard Democrat.

Cranford married Medora Ennis at Sulphur Springs in 1880. They had four children. The oldest, Walter Ennis Cranford, established the law firm of Armstrong, Cranford, Barker, and Bedford in Galveston, notable for maritime, insurance, and corporate law. During his term with the Fifty-fifth Congress, Cranford suffered from poor health, caused in part by the illness of his wife, who died in 1898. He was given an indefinite leave of absence for illness on January 17, 1899, and died on March 3 of that year in Providence Hospital, Washington, D.C. His body was accompanied by a committee of nine United States senators and eleven members of the United States House of Representatives to Sulphur Springs, where it was interred in the city cemetery.

BIBLIOGRAPHY: *Biographical Souvenir of the State of Texas* (Chicago: Battey, 1889; rpt., Easley, South Carolina: Southern Historical Press, 1978). John Henry Brown, *Indian Wars and Pioneers of Texas* (Austin: Daniell, 1880; reprod., Easley, South Carolina: Southern Historical Press, 1978). Dallas *Morning News,* March 3, 1899.

Bob and Michelle Gilbert

CRANZ, TEXAS. Cranz, apparently named after a local family, was just east of the Caldwell county line in northwestern Gonzales County. A post office operated there from 1905 to 1913. By 1914 Cranz had a telephone connection, a cotton gin, a blacksmith shop, and a population of fifty. In 1922 the town had three businesses and continued to report fifty inhabitants. By 1948 its population was still listed at fifty, but the number of businesses had dropped to one. Cranz was no longer shown on the county highway map by 1965.

Stephen L. Hardin

CRASCO CREEK. Crasco Creek rises four miles northwest of the town of Rock Island in semiopen prairie in southern Colorado County (at 29°35′ N, 96°36′ W) and runs southeast for 10½ miles to its mouth on Skull Creek, two miles southwest of Altair (at 29°33′ N, 96°29′ W). The stream crosses the Rock Island North and the Tait gas fields and runs through nearly level prairie with deep, fine sandy loam surface soil over a mottled clay subsoil. This land is used primarily as cattle pasture and for natural gas production. Near Skull Creek it is also used for gravel production and for rice-growing.

CRASH AT CRUSH. A plaque fifteen miles north of Waco in McLennan County marks the site of the "Crash at Crush." On September 15, 1896, more than 40,000 people flocked to this spot to witness one of the most spectacular publicity stunts of the nineteenth century—a planned train wreck. The man behind this unusual event was William George Crush, passenger agent for the Missouri, Kansas and Texas Railroad. In 1895 Crush proposed to Katy officials that the company stage a train wreck as an attraction; he planned to advertise the event months in advance, sell tickets to transport spectators to and from the site on Katy trains, and then run two old locomotives head-on into each other. The officials agreed.

Throughout the summer of 1896 bulletins and circulars advertising the "Monster Crash" were distributed throughout Texas. Many newspapers in Texas ran daily reports on the preparations, and some papers outside the state carried the story. As Crush had predicted, the Katy offices were flooded with ticket requests. The engines, Old No. 999, painted a bright green, and No. 1001, painted a brilliant red, were displayed in towns throughout the state. Thousands turned out to look at them.

As the arena for his spectacle, Crush selected a shallow valley just north of Waco, conveniently located close to Katy's Waco-Dallas track. In early September 500 workmen laid four miles of track for the collision run and constructed a grandstand for "honored guests," three speaker's stands, two telegraph offices, a stand for reporters, and a bandstand. A restaurant was set up in a borrowed Ringling Brothers circus tent, and a huge carnival midway with dozens of medicine shows, game booths, and lemonade and soft-drink stands was built. Finally, workmen erected a special depot with a platform 2,100 feet long, and a sign was painted to inform passengers that they had arrived at Crush, Texas.

George Crush told a reporter that he expected a crowd of around 20,000. The first of thirty-three fully loaded excursion trains arrived at daybreak on September 15, and by 3:00 P.M. more than 40,000 people were on the grounds picnicking, listening to political speeches, and waiting for the great crash. Two dollars bought a round-trip ticket from anywhere in the state, and some passengers were obliged to ride on top of the cars because there was no room left inside.

At 5:00 P.M. engines No. 999 and 1001 squared off at opposite ends of the four-mile track. Crush appeared riding a white horse and trotted to the center of the track. He raised his white hat and after a pause whipped it sharply down. A great cheer went up from the crowd as they pressed forward for a better view. The locomotives jumped forward, and with whistles shrieking roared toward each other. Then, in a thunderous, grinding crash, the trains collided. The two locomotives rose up at their meeting and erupted in steam and smoke. Almost simultaneously, both boilers exploded, filling the air with pieces of flying metal. Spectators turned and ran in blind panic. Two young men and a woman were killed. At least six other people were injured seriously by the flying debris.

The Katy wrecker-trains moved in to remove the larger wreckage, and souvenir hunters carried off the rest. People began to leave for home, the tents, stands, and midway booths came down, and by nightfall Crush, Texas, ceased to exist. The Katy quickly settled all damage claims brought against it with cash and lifetime rail passes. As for George Crush, the railroad fired him that evening but relented and rehired him the next day. He continued to work for the Katy until his retirement. In the early twentieth century Scott Joplin[qv] commemorated the event in his march "Great Crush Collision." It has been surmised that the spectacle drew its huge audience in part because it occurred at a time of economic distress when railroads symbolized to many the evils of the big business "octopus" and were a target of attack for populist politicians.

BIBLIOGRAPHY: E. L. Connally, *Crash at Crush: Famous Duel of the Iron Monsters* (Waco: Texian Press, 1960). Allen Lee Hamilton, "Train Crash at Crush," *American West,* July–August 1983. Houston *Chronicle,* August 19, 1956. George B. Ward, The Crash at Crush (M.A. thesis, University of Texas at Austin, 1975).   *Allen Lee Hamilton*

CRAVENS, KATHRYN COCHRAN (1898–1991). Kathryn Cochran Cravens, radio personality and actress, was born in Burkett, Texas, on October 27, 1898, the daughter of John Calvin and Rose Ann (Hudson) Cochran. Her father was a rural physician in Coleman County, and her mother worked at the local post office. Kathryn studied at the Horner Institute of Fine Arts in Kansas City, Missouri; Henry Kendall College (now the University of Tulsa) in Tulsa; Morse School of Expression in St. Louis; and New York University. In 1919 she began her career as an actress with Fox Films in Hollywood. Throughout the 1920s she worked in silent films, stock theater companies, and radio theater. In 1922 she married Rutherford Rector Cravens; the couple was divorced in 1937.

In 1928 a St. Louis station hired Kathryn Cravens as a radio performer. She moved into radio news in the early 1930s, when another local station gave her her own program, entitled "News Through a Woman's Eyes." In 1936 she moved to New York City and went to work for CBS. When the network began broadcasting her news program nationwide, she became one of the first women news commentators to broadcast coast-to-coast. In 1937, in an effort to disprove criticism that the airline industry was unsafe, she traveled throughout the country for broadcasts and articles and was subsequently dubbed "the Flying Reporter." After this year of travel she began her own syndicated column of articles, feature stories, and poems. In 1941 she returned to radio broadcasts from New York.

Towards the end of World War II[qv] Cravens became the first woman accredited as a wartime radio correspondent when she was assigned to cover Europe, Asia, and the Middle East. She was one of the first broadcasters from Berlin following the Allied victory in 1945. In Potsdam she was arrested by Soviet authorities after entering the postwar conference site before the arrival of Allied political leaders. She was held briefly with a correspondent from the London *Sunday Times* and suspended from broadcasting for seventy-two hours. Undaunted, Cravens continued her coverage in Europe. She located and broadcast live interviews with numerous displaced persons in Europe who had relatives in the United States. In the postwar period she traveled to twenty-two countries, filing reports for the Cowles Broadcasting Company and the Mutual Broadcasting System. For her services overseas she received a special citation from the United States Army. She later covered elections in the Balkans and early Palestinian riots, as well as presidential news conferences and major social events. During her radio career Cravens interviewed numerous well-known individuals, including United States presidents Herbert Hoover, Franklin D. Roosevelt, Harry S. Truman, and Dwight Eisenhower; Italian dictator Benito Mussolini; entertainers James Cagney and Shirley Temple; author George Bernard Shaw; and Pope Pius XII.

In 1951 Coward-McCann published Cravens's only novel, *Pursuit of Gentlemen.* The manuscript for the novel won first prize from the National League of American Penwomen in 1948. Shorter works by Cravens were published in *Cosmopolitan,* the New York *Times,* and the *Christian Science Monitor.* Kathryn Cravens was active in the Texas Club of New York City, the National League of American Penwomen, the League of Women Voters, several press clubs, and the Christian Church. Noted for her stylish appearance, she was frequently voted best-dressed woman in radio and one of the ten best-dressed women in the United States. She returned to Texas from New York City in 1962 and lived in retirement in her family home in Burkett, where she died on August 29, 1991. She was survived by several nieces and nephews.

BIBLIOGRAPHY: Dallas *Times Herald,* October 2, 1962. New York *Times,* August 31, 1991. San Angelo *Standard Times,* January 18, 1970. *Texas Parade,* November 1951. Vertical Files, Barker Texas History Center, University of Texas at Austin. *Who's Who of American Women,* 1970–71.   *Debbie Mauldin Cottrell*

CRAVENS, ROBERT M. (?–?). Robert M. Cravens, early Lamar County settler and participant in the battle of San Jacinto,[qv] immigrated to Texas before May 30, 1831, when he received a league in Stephen F. Austin's[qv] second colony. In 1833 he opened a trading post at the mouth of Sanders Creek, in what is now Lamar County. The area at that time was under the jurisdiction of Arkansas, and in 1835 Cravens signed a petition submitted to Miller County, Arkansas, asking that a new township be established. At the beginning of the Texas Revolution,[qv] however, he joined the revolutionary army;[qv] he served as a private in Company C, First Regiment of Texas Volunteers, at the battle of San Jacinto. He returned to Lamar County, where he died before February 14, 1838, when Samuel M. Fulton,[qv] administrator of Cravens's estate, applied for his headright certificate.

BIBLIOGRAPHY: Sam Houston Dixon and Louis Wiltz Kemp, *The Heroes of San Jacinto* (Houston: Anson Jones, 1932). A. W. Neville, *The History of Lamar County, Texas* (Paris, Texas: North Texas, 1937; rpt. 1986).

CRAWFISH CREEK. Crawfish Creek rises fourteen miles southwest of Floydada and four miles west of Farm Road 378 in southwestern Floyd County (at 33°53′ N, 101°32′ W) and runs twenty-two miles southeast to its mouth on the White River, a mile south of the intersection of Farm roads 651 and 193 in northern Crosby County (at 33°47′ N, 101°14′ W). It crosses flat to rolling terrain with local escarpments, surfaced by deep, fine sandy loam that supports hardwood trees, conifers, brush, and grasses.

CRAWFISH DRAW. Crawfish Draw rises on the Caprock at an elevation of about 3,300 feet above sea level, ten miles west of Hale Center in western Hale County (at 34°02′ N, 102°00′ W), and runs southeast for about thirty-six miles, passing near Cotton Center and Petersburg in the farmlands of southern Hale County, then running into southwestern Floyd County, where it ends about half a mile west of Allmon and fourteen miles southwest of Floydada (at 33°53′ N, 101°32′ W). The draw is usually a dry creekbed with numerous playas[qv] along its course, but excessive rains can flood portions and make county roads impassable. Crawfish Draw traverses mostly flat to gently sloping terrain, surfaced by sandy loams that support brush, grasses, and, farther away from the draw, post oak. Crawfish Creek rises near the mouth of the draw.

CRAWFORD, EMMARETTA CARA KIMBALL (1829–1906). Emmaretta (Emaretta) Crawford [pseud. Cara Cardelle], compiler and possible author of *Letters from an Early Settler of Texas,* was born on April 13, 1829, in Wallingford, Connecticut, one of three children of Isaac and Abigail (Stevens) Kimball. Her parents died when she was a child, and Emmaretta was educated by an aunt in Massachusetts. In 1851 she traveled to Columbus, Texas, to join her brother, J. A. Kimball, a Baptist minister who operated a school. There she taught music and met William B. DeWees,qv an early settler. Together they collaborated on a book, first published in 1852, entitled *Letters from an Early Settler of Texas;* it was purportedly correspondence by DeWees that had been discovered, compiled, and published by his niece, Cara Cardelle. Doubt exists that DeWees himself wrote the letters, although his presence in Texas during the time the letters were said to have been written, 1819 to 1852, has been confirmed. Emma Crawford's son claimed she wrote the entire manuscript from DeWees's reminiscences. A written agreement between Emmaretta Kimball and DeWees, dated October 7, 1852, states that the two "have by mutual assistance written and produced" the manuscript and that Emmaretta "compiled" it. The introduction to a reprint (1968) of the book left the controversy unresolved. An earlier manuscript by the pair, "Life on a Frontier or Adventures of Will Dewey by Cara Cardelle," was apparently destroyed in a house fire in Killeen. Emmaretta Kimball married Marquis Lafayette Crawford on June 11, 1855. The couple had six children. They moved from Columbus to Salado, where Crawford died in 1903. Emmaretta died on her birthday in 1906 and was buried at Brady, Texas.

BIBLIOGRAPHY: Vertical Files, Barker Texas History Center, University of Texas at Austin.

Nancy Baker Jones

CRAWFORD, KATHERINE LESTER (1864–1947). Katherine Crawford, artist and art patron, was born in May 1864 in Oxford, Mississippi, the daughter of Dr. J. D. and L. Josephine (Oliver) Lester. On December 11, 1879, she married Lucius Quintus Cincinnatus Lamar, Jr., in Lafayette County, Mississippi; they had a son. In 1885 her husband became a personal secretary for his father, Secretary of the Interior L. Q. C. Lamar, Sr., and Katherine served as her father-in-law's hostess for his household in Washington, D.C. About 1887 Katherine Lamar moved to Paris, France, enrolled in the Académie Julien, and studied under Adolphe Bouguereau, Jules Clement Chaplain, Albert Durand, and Edmond Louis Dupain. After traveling, sketching, and painting throughout Europe, she returned to the United States in 1892 and moved to Dallas as an art instructor for Professor Jones' Female College. By 1894 she was head of the art department at North Texas Female College (later Kidd-Key College) in Sherman. In 1895 she established a school of art at 189 San Jacinto Street in Dallas.

On October 9, 1896, she married William Lyne Crawford,qv an attorney. They had one son and lived, along with her son from her first marriage, in an elegant Eastlake mansion at 3709 Ross Avenue. Mrs. Crawford presented several salons and opened an art gallery in her home, the first private gallery in Dallas. The Crawford Gallery displayed the family collection of statuary and 300 paintings and held annual exhibitions of work by European, American, and regional artists. It was at the time one of the finest privately owned collections in the Southwest and was open to the public by appointment. The Crawford home was also decorated with Mrs. Crawford's own work. In the dining room she painted a large mural depicting a feast scene of the Roman god Bacchus, and she decorated the breakfast rooms with Western rural landscapes and scenes from Texas history. She was particularly skilled as a portrait artist, and several of her portraits of noted Dallasites were displayed in her home.

Around 1920 she worked with the Dallas *Morning News*qv to establish and lead the Texas Art League, an organization devoted to bringing students and European instructors together to study all branches of art. She planned to develop the league into an academy of design and include in it a permanent gallery. Although a famous German court painter, Kunz-Meyer, participated in the league, there is no evidence that the academy evolved as planned. Katherine Crawford died in Dallas on March 4, 1947, and was buried in Oakland Cemetery there. After her death, the extensive Crawford collection was dispersed. Some items were sold; others were given to museums.

BIBLIOGRAPHY: Diana Church, *Guide to Dallas Artists, 1890–1917* (Plano, Texas, 1987). Frances Battaile Fisk, *A History of Texas Artists and Sculptors* (Abilene, Texas, 1928; facsimile rpt., Austin: Morrison, 1986). William L. McDonald, *Dallas Rediscovered: A Photographic Chronicle of Urban Expansion, 1870–1925* (Dallas: Dallas County Historical Society, 1978). *Who's Who of the Womanhood of Texas*, Vol. 1 (Fort Worth: Texas Federation of Women's Clubs, 1923–24).

Diana Church

CRAWFORD, LEMUEL (1814–1836). Lemuel Crawford, Alamo defender, was born in South Carolina in 1814. He enlisted in the service of Texas in early October 1835 and served until December 26 of that year as an artilleryman under Col. James C. Neill.qv He probably took part in the siege of Bexar.qv Crawford reenlisted on February 11, 1836, and served in the Alamo garrison, probably as a member of Capt. William R. Carey'sqv artillery company. He died in the battle of the Alamoqv on March 6, 1836.

BIBLIOGRAPHY: Comptroller's Records, Texas State Archives, Austin. Daughters of the American Revolution, *The Alamo Heroes and Their Revolutionary Ancestors* (San Antonio, 1976). Bill Groneman, *Alamo Defenders* (Austin: Eakin, 1990).

Bill Groneman

CRAWFORD, ROBERT (1815–1888). Robert Crawford, Methodist minister and soldier, was born in the Abbeville District of South Carolina on May 15, 1815, and moved with his family to Tennessee as a boy. He became a Methodist on September 22, 1834, and moved to Texas in 1835. At Nacogdoches on January 14, 1836, he enlisted for six months in the Volunteer Auxiliary Corps. At the battle of San Jacintoqv he served as a private in Capt. Robert James Calder'sqv Company K of Col. Edward Burleson'sqv First Regiment, Texas Volunteers.

Crawford is said to have assisted in the construction of the first Methodist church west of the Mississippi River, that at Washington-on-the-Brazos, during the winter of 1837–38, and was licensed to "exhort" on March 18, 1838. He was a pallbearer for Martin Ruter.qv He was licensed to preach on September 14, 1839. In 1840 he was living in Fayette County and owned four town lots in Rutersville, one slave, and a metal clock. On November 5 he became a charter trustee of Rutersville College. On December 25 of that year he was present at the organizational meeting of the Texas Conference of the Methodist Episcopal Church, where he was assigned to the pulpit at Nashville-on-the-Brazos.

Lewis W. Kemp and Sam Houston Dixon,qqv in *Heroes of San Jacinto*, wrongly identify Crawford as the Robert M. Crawford who served as a private in Capt. William S. Fisher'sqv company on the Mier expedition.qv This Crawford escaped from captivity in Mexico City while doing forced labor on the Tacubaya road. But at the time of the battle of Mier, Rev. Robert Crawford was attending the Methodist convention of December 22–27, 1842, which transferred him to the Methodist mission at Victoria.

In 1850 Crawford was living in Fannin County. He is said to have graduated "late in life" from medical school in Galveston. In 1874 he retired from the pulpit of the Northwest Texas Conference of the Methodist Church.qv He died on December 5, 1888, in the Robertson County community of Franklin and was survived by his wife and four children. He was a member of the Texas Veterans Association.qv

BIBLIOGRAPHY: Dallas *Morning News*, December 6, 1888. Daughters of the Republic of Texas, *Muster Rolls of the Texas Revolution* (Austin, 1986). Sam Houston Dixon and Louis Wiltz Kemp, *The Heroes of San Jacinto* (Houston: Anson Jones, 1932). Thomas J. Green, *Journal of the Texian Expedition Against Mier* (New York: Harper, 1845; rpt., Austin: Steck, 1935). *Texas Christian Advocate*, December 13, 1888.

Thomas W. Cutrer

CRAWFORD, ROBERTA DODD (1897–1954). Roberta Dodd Crawford, black contralto, also known as Princess Kojo Tovalou-Houenou, was born in 1897 in the black Tank Town section of Bonham, Texas, the oldest daughter among eight children born to Joe and Emma (Dunlap) Dodd. As a child she attended Washington School and later worked as a waitress at Curtis Boarding House. Her singing talent brought her to the attention of several Bonham women who arranged for her to perform at the Alexander Hotel and at several Bonham churches. With help from benefactors, she attended Wiley College at Marshall for two years, then entered Fisk University, where she studied with Roland Hayes. About 1920 she entered the University of Chicago, where for the next six years she studied voice with Madame Herman Devries. In 1926 she debuted at Kimball Hall and received favorable reviews from the Chicago *Tribune* and the Chicago *Defender*. While in Chicago she married Capt. William B. Crawford of the Eighth Illinois Regiment.

Two years later she performed at the First United Methodist Church in Bonham, where her program combined Italian, French, German, Spanish, and English art songs and operatic arias with Negro spirituals and at least one "primitive African melody." She then left for France to become a student of Blanche Marchessi in Paris. In 1931 she made her French debut by singing selections in five languages at the Salle Gaveau. Now widowed, she met Kojo Marc Tovalou-Houenou (or Marc Tovalou Quenum), a doctor and lawyer and Pan-African activist from Porto Novo, the capital of Dahomey in French West Africa. Some sources also refer to him as a prince. They married in 1932; he died about 1938. After his death, his widow returned to Paris. Unable to secure funds from her African property, she worked in the National Library of Paris and during World War II[qv] joined the Red Cross and sang in churches and canteens for American soldiers. Suffering from anemia, she relied on friends for financial help and credited a Fort Worth physician with saving her life by getting surplus food coupons for her. She reportedly spent time in a concentration camp during the German occupation of France, but was released. In 1948 she returned to Bonham, but her poor physical and emotional health left her unwilling to perform again. She later moved to Dallas.

Roberta Crawford sang in several cities in the United States and at Spellman and Tuskegee universities as well as in Europe. She had no children. She died on June 14, 1954, in Dallas and was buried in Gates Hill Cemetery in Bonham.

BIBLIOGRAPHY: Bonham *Daily Favorite*, June 15, 1954, November 25, 1973. *Fannin County Folks and Facts* (Dallas: Taylor, 1977). Juanita C. Spencer, *Bonham—Town of Bailey Inglish* (Wolfe City, Texas: Henington, 1977). Pat Stephens, ed., *Forgotten Dignity: The Black Community of Bonham...1880–1930* (Bonham, Texas: Progressive Citizens, 1984).
Nancy Baker Jones

CRAWFORD, WALTER JOSHUA (1873–1924). Walter J. Crawford, lawyer, son of J. S. and Lou (Eddins) Crawford, was born in Mount Vernon, Texas, on February 25, 1873. He moved to Austin as a child and graduated from the University of Texas in 1894. He received his law degree three years later, then moved to Beaumont and established a successful law practice. Among his partners was Stuart R. Smith.[qv] Crawford married Cora Shults in 1901, and they had two children. Although never a candidate for public office, Crawford became an active booster of both Beaumont and the Democratic party. As a civic leader he served as director of the local chamber of commerce and of the Gulf National Bank of Beaumont. He was also a Mason and a Methodist. As a major stockholder of the Beaumont *Enterprise*,[qv] Crawford convinced his friend William P. Hobby[qv] to leave a position with the Houston *Post*[qv] to become editor, manager, and half-owner of the paper in 1907. Crawford also served as Hobby's campaign manager during his successful race for lieutenant governor in 1914 and gave the nominating speech before Hobby's second term two years later. He died in Jefferson County of a stroke on February 19, 1924.

BIBLIOGRAPHY: Frank W. Johnson, *A History of Texas and Texans* (5 vols., ed. E. C. Barker and E. W. Winkler [Chicago and New York: American Historical Society, 1914; rpt. 1916]).
Robert Wooster

CRAWFORD, WILLIAM CARROL (1804–1895). William Carrol Crawford, the last surviving signer of the Texas Declaration of Independence,[qv] son of Archibald and Nancy (Carroll) Crawford, was born in Fayetteville, North Carolina, on September 13, 1804. He was related to Charles Carroll, the last surviving signer of the United States Declaration of Independence. The family moved to Georgia, where both parents died about 1821. Crawford was a tailor's apprentice from 1821 or 1822 until 1830, when he became a Methodist minister and was assigned to a circuit in Alabama. In 1834 he married Rhoda Jackson Watkins. Later, because of ill health, he moved to Texas with his wife's family. The caravan arrived in January 1835 and settled near the site of Shelbyville. The Crawfords became the parents of nine children. Crawford and Sydney O. Penington[qv] represented Shelby County at the Convention of 1836[qv] at Washington-on-the-Brazos and there signed the Declaration of Independence. In 1859 Crawford moved to Pittsburg, Camp County, where he was postmaster from 1874 to 1881. His wife died on January 18, 1881, and Crawford moved to Hill County, where he lived until 1884, when he moved to Alvarado, Johnson County, to live with a daughter. He died on September 3, 1895, while he was visiting his son in Erath County. He was buried in Cow Creek Cemetery, about five miles north of Dublin. In 1936 his remains were reinterred in the State Cemetery.[qv]

BIBLIOGRAPHY: Louis Wiltz Kemp, *The Signers of the Texas Declaration of Independence* (Salado, Texas: Anson Jones, 1944; rpt. 1959). Texas House of Representatives, *Biographical Directory of the Texan Conventions and Congresses, 1832–1845* (Austin: Book Exchange, 1941).
L. W. Kemp

CRAWFORD, WILLIAM LYNE (1839–1920). William Lyne Crawford, lawyer and legislator, was born on January 23, 1839, in Clay County, Kentucky, the son of Jeptha D. and Catherine Crawford. He moved to Texas with his parents in 1843, first to Harrison County and later to Marion County. He attended McKenzie College and studied law with David B. Culberson.[qv] Crawford joined the Confederate Army in 1861 and served as lieutenant colonel of the Nineteenth Texas Infantry. After the Civil War[qv] he returned to Jefferson and was admitted to the bar in 1866. He was a member of the Constitutional Convention of 1875.[qv] In 1880 he and his brother, M. L. Crawford, moved their law partnership, Crawford and Crawford, from Jefferson to Dallas, where William became a noted criminal and civil lawyer who tried cases of nationwide importance. He was a member of the House of Representatives of the Twenty-second Legislature, 1891–92. Crawford was married to Love Alley. On October 1, 1896, he married Katherine Lester Lamar, a widow with a son. Katherine studied in the Julien School in Paris, France; taught at Professor Jones Female College; and as an art collector built a private gallery on the side of the Crawford house on Ross Avenue. Crawford had one daughter and three sons. He died on February 17, 1920, and was buried in Oakland Cemetery, Dallas. *See* CRAWFORD, KATHERINE LESTER.

BIBLIOGRAPHY: Dallas *Morning News*, February 18, 1920. William L. McDonald, *Dallas Rediscovered: A Photographic Chronicle of Urban Expansion, 1870–1925* (Dallas: Dallas County Historical Society, 1978). *Men of Texas* (Houston: Houston *Post*, 1903). John William Rogers, *The Lusty Texans of Dallas* (New York: Dutton, 1951; enlarged ed. 1960; expanded ed., Dallas: Cokesbury Book Store, 1965). *Who Was Who in America*, Vol. 1.

CRAWFORD, TEXAS. Crawford is at the intersection of State Highway 317 and Farm Road 185, eighteen miles west of Waco in western McLennan County. Settlement of the area began in the 1850s and centered around Tonk Crossing (also called Crawford Crossing), a ford of the Middle Bosque River two miles east of the present town. The community was probably named for Nelson Crawford, who graded the river crossing. As early as 1867 the inn at Crawford was used as a changing station by the Brownwood stage line. A Crawford post office was established in 1871 with John Hamlin as postmaster. In 1881 the Gulf, Colorado and Santa Fe Railway laid track from Temple to Fort Worth, passing two miles west of Crawford. The focus of the community shifted to the railroad, and by 1890 Crawford had steam flour and corn mills, two general stores, three groceries, a cotton gin, four churches, and 400 residents; cotton, wheat, hides, and corn were the principal shipments from the area.

In the 1880s and 1890s Crawford had a series of short-lived weekly newspapers, among them the *Yeoman*, the *Democrat*, the *Banner*, and the *Advance*. The Crawford *Sun* was established in 1928, and except for the years 1943 to 1947 continued to be published weekly until 1969, when it merged with the McGregor *Mirror*. When Crawford was first established, community affairs were managed by a group of five or six elected trustees. Residents voted to incorporate on August 12, 1897, by a vote of fifty-one to forty-two; it may have been at that time that the city adopted a mayor-council form of government. A private bank opened in Crawford in 1901 and was reorganized eight years later as the First National Bank of Crawford. The town reached one of the high points in its development in 1910, when it had 600 residents and thirty-five businesses. The depression hit the community hard, forcing the bank and several other businesses to close. The population fell to 491 in the early 1930s and to 471 in the early 1940s. Still, Crawford was the only town of any size in northwestern McLennan County, and as such it was the natural focal point when small area schools began to consolidate with those in larger towns in the 1930s and 1940s. By the mid-1940s the Crawford Independent School District encompassed nearly seventy-eight square miles. The population of Crawford fell to 425 in the 1950s but rose again to 480 in the 1960s; it remained fairly stable through the 1970s but rose sharply in the 1980s, as more residents decided to live in Crawford and commute to work in Waco or nearby McGregor. The population was reported at 667 in the late 1980s. In 1990 it was 631.

BIBLIOGRAPHY: Martin Luther Bannister, The Historical Development of the Public School System of McLennan County (M.A. thesis, Baylor University, 1945). Dayton Kelley, ed., *The Handbook of Waco and McLennan County, Texas* (Waco: Texian, 1972). William Robert Poage, *McLennan County Before 1980* (Waco: Texian, 1981). Vertical File, Texas Collection, Baylor University.

Vivian Elizabeth Smyrl

CRAWFORD CREEK. Crawford Creek rises just west of Central in northwestern Angelina County (at 31°26′ N, 94°49′ W) and runs southwest for ten miles to its mouth on the Neches River, six miles west of Hudson (at 31°19′ N, 94°54′ W). It traverses flat to rolling terrain surfaced by sandy and clay loams that support water-tolerant hardwoods, conifers, and grasses.

CRAWFORD MOUNTAIN. Crawford Mountain, with an elevation of 1,470 feet above sea level, is six miles west of Palo Pinto in Palo Pinto County (at 32°47′ N, 98°22′ W). It was named for A. G. (Al) Crawford, who settled just north of the mountain on the Brazos River. The surrounding slopes are surfaced by clay and sandy loams that support scrub brush, cacti, grasses, and mesquite.

CRAZYCAT MOUNTAIN. Crazycat Mountain is three quarters of a mile south of the southwestern corner of the Franklin Mountains State Park[qv] in northwestern El Paso County (at 31°48′ N, 106°30′ W). Its peak, at an elevation of 4,564 feet above sea level, rises 465 feet above Arroyo Park, an El Paso city park about three quarters of a mile south. Local soils are shallow and stony and support scrub brush and grasses.

CREAGER, RENTFRO BANTON (1877–1950). Rentfro Banton (Rene B.) Creager, Republican party[qv] leader, was born at Waco, Texas, on March 11, 1877, son of Francis Asbury Warwick and Katherine (Rentfro) Creager. In 1898 he received a B.S. degree from Southwestern University, where he was awarded an LL.D. in 1930. After graduation from the law school of the University of Texas in Austin in 1900, he began practice in Brownsville. Before 1916, when he became the gubernatorial candidate of the Republican party in Texas, Creager served as a collector of customs at Brownsville under presidents Theodore Roosevelt and William H. Taft. Upon the death of Henry F. MacGregor[qv] of Houston in 1923, Creager was elected the Texas member of the Republican National Committee, a position he held until his death. He retained a firm leadership in the state Republican party and played a prominent role in national Republican politics for many years. At the Republican national convention of 1920 he delivered the only speech seconding the nomination of Warren G. Harding. After Harding's election, the president-elect and Mrs. Harding visited Creager at his home in Brownsville. The presidential party also fished at nearby Port Isabel. Creager was offered the post of ambassador to Mexico by both President Harding and President Calvin Coolidge, but declined. He was the first national committeeman to come out in support of Herbert Hoover for the 1928 presidential nomination. Likewise, he was in the forefront of the movement to secure the 1936 nomination for Kansas governor Alfred Landon. Creager was a close friend of and floor leader for Senator Robert A. Taft at the Republican national convention of 1948. In addition to his political activities, he was president of an oil company. He died on October 28, 1950, in Brownsville. He was survived by four children and his widow, the former Alice Terrell, whom he had married on February 3, 1904.

BIBLIOGRAPHY: Austin *American*, October 29, 1950. Paul D. Casdorph, *A History of the Republican Party in Texas, 1865–1965* (Austin: Pemberton Press, 1965). Donald J. Lisio, *Hoover, Blacks, and Lily Whites* (Chapel Hill: University of North Carolina Press, 1985). Roger M. Olien, *From Token to Triumph: The Texas Republicans since 1920* (Dallas: Southern Methodist University Press, 1982). *Who's Who in America*, 1950–51.

Paul D. Casdorph

CREAGLEVILLE, TEXAS. Creagleville, on Farm Road 17 just south of U.S. Highway 80 and the Missouri Pacific line ten miles northeast of Canton in northeastern Van Zandt County, may have been named for Henry Creagle, a resident of the county when it was organized in 1848. Creagleville had a church and cemetery in 1890 and a school that reached an enrollment of sixty-one in 1904. In 1936 Creagleville had a school, a church, two cemeteries, and multiple dwellings. By the 1950s the local school had been consolidated with the Grand Saline Independent School District, and by 1987 the county highway map showed only a church and the cemeteries at the site.

BIBLIOGRAPHY: Mary E. Valandingham, *Early Scholastic Records for Van Zandt County* (Center, Texas, 1968).

Diana J. Kleiner

CREAMER, TEXAS. Creamer, about six miles east of Comanche in Comanche County, was founded around 1910 and named for Jasper Creamer, who built its first store. The community's pioneer settlers included the Fowlers, Sligers, Burks, and Thomases. After 1910 the community developed quickly, and by 1933 it reported a population of 100 and one business. But the settlement declined rapidly after 1945, when its population was reported as forty. By the late 1950s Creamer was gone.

BIBLIOGRAPHY: Comanche County Bicentennial Committee, *Patchwork of Memories: Historical Sketches of Comanche County, Texas* (Brownwood, Texas: Banner Printing, 1976).

Julius A. Amin

CREAM LEVEL, TEXAS. Cream Level, a farming community eight miles southeast of Canton in southeastern Van Zandt County, was probably named for nearby Cream Level Creek. The town school was built by 1890 and reached an enrollment of thirty-eight in 1905; it was consolidated with the Martins Mills Independent School District by the 1950s. A post office operated at Cream Level from 1888 until 1891, after which mail was delivered from Martins Mills. In 1890 Cream Level had a general store, a corn mill and gin, and a population of thirty-five, but it subsequently declined. Cream Level was not shown on the 1936 county highway map.

BIBLIOGRAPHY: Mary E. Valandingham, *Early Scholastic Records for Van Zandt County* (Center, Texas, 1968).

Diana J. Kleiner

CREAM LEVEL CREEK. Cream Level Creek rises four miles northwest of Martins Mills in southeastern Van Zandt County (at 32°29′ N, 95°46′ W) and runs south for almost 11½ miles to its mouth on Kickapoo Creek, a half mile south of the Henderson county line (at 32°21′ N, 95°46′ W). It traverses flat to rolling prairie surfaced by clay and sandy loam that supports mesquite, grasses, cacti, and mixed hardwood and pine forests.

CREASY, TEXAS. Creasy was a farming community five miles south of Kennard in southeastern Houston County. It was established around the time of the Civil War qv and named for early settlers William Harrison Creasy and Mary Elizabeth Johnson Creasy, grandparents of Governor Allan Shivers.qv In the mid-1930s the community had a church, a cemetery, and a number of houses. After World War II qv most of its residents moved away, and in the early 1990s only a cemetery and a few widely scattered houses remained there.

BIBLIOGRAPHY: *Houston County Cemeteries* (Crockett, Texas: Houston County Historical Commission, 1977; 3d ed. 1987).

Eliza H. Bishop

CREATH, JOSEPH WARNER DOSSEY (1809–1881). Joseph Creath, Baptist missionary, son of William Creath, was born in Mecklenburg County, Virginia, on February 3, 1809. He and four of his brothers became preachers. After graduation from Virginia Baptist Seminary (now Richmond College) in 1837, he began a ministry that lasted forty-four years. He and his wife were commissioned as missionaries to Texas in 1846, the first two Home Missions appointees by the newly formed Southern Baptist Convention. From the time Creath began his work at Huntsville in 1846 until his death, he worked to strengthen virtually every facet of Baptist work in Texas. He served churches in Huntsville, Anderson, Cold Springs, and San Antonio, acted as president of the Southern Baptist Convention in 1876, and presided over the Texas Baptist Convention. From 1863 to 1865 he ministered to Confederate soldiers at the behest of the Texas Baptist Convention. He played a leading role in raising funds to support Baylor University and for over two decades was connected with the school as a trustee; at one time he was president of the board of trustees. Creath was the father of two children. When his first wife, Frances (Drake), died, he married C. A. Lea, a relative of Sam Houston.qv He died near Cameron, Milam County, Texas, on July 28, 1881.

BIBLIOGRAPHY: James Milton Carroll, *A History of Texas Baptists* (Dallas: Baptist Standard, 1923). Frank W. Johnson, *A History of Texas and Texans* (5 vols., ed. E. C. Barker and E. W. Winkler [Chicago and New York: American Historical Society, 1914; rpt. 1916]). Benjamin F. Riley, *A History of the Baptists of Texas* (Dallas, 1907). *Texas Historical and Biographical Magazine*, 1891. Robert George Torbit, *History of the Baptists* (Philadelphia: Judson, 1950).

Jerry F. Dawson

CREATH, TEXAS. Creath, on Farm Road 1733 near Wilcox Branch, some fifteen miles northeast of Crockett in eastern Houston County, was established around 1900 by M. B. Creath, who operated the community's general store and cotton gin. A post office opened there in 1904, with Creath as postmaster. In the mid-1930s the community had a store, a number of houses, and an estimated population of 100. After World War II qv many of its residents moved away, and by the early 1990s only a few widely scattered houses remained.

Christopher Long

CRECY, TEXAS. Crecy, on Farm Road 233 eleven miles northeast of Groveton in northeastern Trinity County, was settled after the Civil War qv by the Terry family. A post office was established there in 1899, and in 1900 Crecy had two general stores and a population of twenty-five. The community began to decline during the 1930s. Its post office closed in 1936, and after World War II qv many of its residents moved away. In 1990 only a store and a few scattered houses remained in the area.

BIBLIOGRAPHY: Patricia B. and Joseph W. Hensley, eds., *Trinity County Beginnings* (Groveton, Texas: Trinity County Book Committee, 1986).

Christopher Long

CREDIT UNION DEPARTMENT. The Credit Union Department was established in 1969 to enforce the Texas Credit Union Act, passed that year by the Sixty-first Legislature. It superseded the Credit Union Advisory Commission established in 1949. That commission was composed of five members, appointed by the governor from a list submitted by credit unions in Texas. Its purpose was to confer with and advise the Banking Commission on policies and problems relating to credit unions. The 1969 act enlarged the Credit Union Commission to six members, who are appointed by the governor, with the concurrence of the Senate, to six-year, overlapping terms. The new commission served as an advisory board to the Credit Union Commissioner, who determined whether applications for charters met the requirements of the Texas Credit Union Act. The legislature added three members in 1981, and the commission's role was changed from advisory to supervisory. Six of the members must be credit union directors, officers, or committee members or have five years' experience in a credit union in Texas. Three members are representatives of the general public and may have no connection, other than as customers, with any credit union. The Credit Union Commissioner is appointed by the commission. He oversees the examination, supervision, and regulation of all credit unions doing business in Texas, except federal credit unions organized under federal law. At the end of 1991 the department had twenty-seven employees, who supervised 357 credit unions, twelve of which were in the process of liquidation. The 345 active credit unions had assets of $5.7 billion. Appropriations for 1992 were $1,257,756 and for 1993, $1,253,997.

John G. Johnson

CREE, THOMAS BOGER (1847–1927). Thomas Boger Cree, Panhandle qv pioneer, was born on May 19, 1847, in Green Park, Pennsylvania, son of John Dunbar Cree, who worked as a horse and mule inspector for the federal government. When the Civil War qv broke out, fourteen-year-old Thomas joined his father in Washington, D.C.; he served as a teamster in the Union Army for two years. In 1866 or 1867 he went to Chicago to work for the Union Pacific Railroad. He was assigned to the construction company that built the first transcontinental railroad line and served as corral boss. He was present at the ceremonial driving of the golden spike at Promontory Point, Utah, on May 10, 1869. Cree afterward helped build the Missouri, Kansas and Texas (Katy) line to Fort Worth in the early 1870s. About that time he met and married Melissa Ballard, a niece of Jesse Chisholm,qv for whom the Chisholm Trail qv was named. The Crees had eight children.

Throughout the 1880s Cree did construction work with various railroads. In 1886 he started working for the Fort Worth and Denver City, which was building its line from Vernon into the Texas Panhandle. His family accompanied him as the railroad pushed northwest. Near the future townsite of Panhandle City, in Carson County, Cree built a dugout qv home and at his wife's request planted a bois d'arc sapling to help break the monotony of the prairie grass. Thomas

Cree's bois d'arc tree, located just off U.S. Highway 60 near Panhandle, was for years a familiar landmark on the treeless plain; on October 23, 1963, Governor John Connally^qv dedicated it as a historical landmark. Unfortunately, the tree, which had survived droughts, blizzards, summer heat, and sandstorms, was killed by herbicides sprayed on nearby crops in 1970.

In 1888 Cree filed a claim and erected a sod house near the head of McClellan Creek in Gray County. He assisted in the establishment of Panhandle City and helped organize its first church in 1889. In 1892 the Crees sold their land near Panhandle and settled on choice ranchland near Cheyenne, Oklahoma. In 1902, after a blizzard wiped out half of their herd, the Crees bought four sections in northeastern Wheeler County, Texas, and leased another four. There Thomas and Melissa Cree spent their remaining years. Mrs. Cree died in 1916 and her husband on July 23, 1927. They were buried in the Rankin (now the White Rose Reydon) Cemetery in Wheeler County.

BIBLIOGRAPHY: Jo Stewart Randel, ed., *A Time to Purpose: A Chronicle of Carson County* (4 vols., Hereford, Texas: Pioneer, 1966–72).
H. Allen Anderson

CREECHVILLE, TEXAS. Creechville is four miles east of Ennis in east central Ellis County. It was established in the late 1890s and served as a community center for the cotton farmers in the area, who built a cooperative gin. A post office operated in Creechville from 1899 until 1903. The community had a school, known as Village Creek. By the 1930s this school had been consolidated with the Ennis public schools. Creechville had an estimated population of twenty from the early 1930s, when population statistics were first reported, through the mid-1960s, after which no further statistics were available. In the 1980s the site was surrounded by cattle ranches and wheat farms.

BIBLIOGRAPHY: Edna Davis Hawkins, et al., *History of Ellis County, Texas* (Waco: Texian, 1972).
David Minor

CREEDMOOR, TEXAS. Creedmoor is at the intersection of Farm roads 1327 and 1625, fifteen miles southeast of Austin in southern Travis County. Though in the 1850s the site had general stores, a grocery, a meat market, a drugstore, a barbershop, a blacksmith shop, and an ice cream parlor, the name Creedmoor did not appear until the establishment of the community's post office in 1880. Some sources say the town was originally called Willow Springs; others say it was first called Creekmoor but was renamed Creedmoor by settlers who wanted the name to express their faith. Dr. Jacob T. Wilhite,^qv once the country's foremost authority on rabies and the founder and director of the Pasteur Institute at the Austin State Hospital, was born in Creedmoor. The town's population grew from twenty in 1896 to 150 by 1915. In 1921 a cyclone destroyed its four-room school and one of the local gins. The town suffered a drought in 1925. A 1946 map showed Creedmoor with a school, two churches, seven businesses, and more than thirty dwellings. In the 1950s it had two gins, and cotton was still a major local industry. Under threat of annexation by Austin in 1982, Creedmoor became the ninth community in Travis County to incorporate. In 1990 Creedmoor reported a population of 194, a store, a post office, and the San Francisco Catholic Church.

BIBLIOGRAPHY: *Alcalde* (magazine of the Ex-Students' Association of the University of Texas), April 1927. Austin *American-Statesman*, January 17, 1982. Mary Starr Barkley, *History of Travis County and Austin, 1839–1899* (Waco: Texian Press, 1963).
Donna P. Parker

CREEK, THOMAS E. (1950–1969). Thomas E. Creek, Medal of Honor recipient, was born in Joplin, Missouri, on April 7, 1950, the son of Ross F. Creek, Sr., of Amarillo, Texas. He attended Palo Duro High School in Amarillo and enlisted in the United States Marine Corps at San Diego, California. Lance Corporal Creek was a member of Company I, Third Battalion, Ninth Marines, Third Marine Division. Near Cam Lo, Vietnam, on February 13, 1969, he was a rifleman in action against the enemy. His squad was providing security for a resupply convoy when a mine detonated, destroying one of the vehicles and halting the convoy. The marines immediately came under heavy fire from a concealed enemy force. Creek moved into open terrain to fire on the enemy and was seriously wounded by enemy fire. A grenade landed between Creek and several companions. He fell on it and took the full force of the explosion, thus saving the lives of his fellow marines. He is buried in the Llano Cemetery, Amarillo.

BIBLIOGRAPHY: Dallas *Morning News*, April 21, 1970. Committee on Veterans' Affairs, United States Senate, *Medal of Honor Recipients, 1863–1973* (Washington: GPO, 1973).
Art Leatherwood

CREEK, TEXAS. Creek, on Farm Road 1280 fifteen miles southwest of Crockett in southwestern Houston County, was established after the Civil War^qv and named for its location on Big Creek. A school began operating there around 1885, and a post office opened in 1888. By the early 1890s the settlement had an estimated population of 150 and several gristmills and gins, as well as a blacksmith, sawmill, chair factory, and general store. The town began to decline in the 1920s, and by the mid-1930s only a church, a cemetery, and a few houses remained. In the early 1990s Creek was a dispersed rural community with a church and cemetery.

BIBLIOGRAPHY: Armistead Albert Aldrich, *The History of Houston County, Texas* (San Antonio: Naylor, 1943). Houston County Historical Commission, *History of Houston County, Texas, 1687–1979* (Tulsa, Oklahoma: Heritage, 1979).
Christopher Long

CREEK INDIANS. The Creek Indians were a confederation of tribes that belonged primarily to the Muskhogean linguistic group, which also included the Choctaws and Chickasaws. The Muskogees were the dominant tribe of the confederacy, but all members eventually came to be known collectively as Creek Indians. Most of the Creeks descended from groups living in six towns: Cusseta, Coweta, Areka, Coosa, Hoithle Waule, and Tuckabatchee, all within the confines of the future Alabama and Georgia. These groups most probably formed the confederacy. Later, the Creeks established the practice of adopting conquered tribes and accepting bands fleeing from English, French, and Spanish attacks. By these methods the Alabama, Coushatta, Hitchitee, Tuskegee, and Natchez Indians eventually became Creeks. The Creek confederacy inhabited a large portion of what later became Alabama and Georgia. They, like other Muskhogean tribes, apparently migrated to that region from the west in prehistoric times. The confederacy was divided into two districts, the Upper Creeks, centered on the Coosa and Tallapoosa Rivers, and the Lower Creeks, residing near the Flint and Chattahoochee. In early historic times, the Creek population was variously estimated at 11,000 to 24,000, distributed among fifty to eighty towns and outlying villages.

The Creeks divided their towns into White (Peace) or Red (War) classifications. White towns hosted councils for concluding peace, adopted conquered tribes, and enacted most laws and regulations for internal affairs. Red towns declared war, planned military expeditions, and held diplomatic councils. Although members of white clans were associated with peace, they were expected to fight during wars; indeed, advancement in civil rank was largely dependent upon military achievement. The entire Creek population was divided into clans that cut across towns and families alike. Members of a particular clan were considered close relatives even though they might have never seen each other before. Clan members had unlimited claims on each other's services. Because of the perceived kinship of clan members, marriage within a clan was strictly forbidden. Clans varied in size and stature. The Wind Clan, for example, had members in all of the towns of the confederacy and enjoyed special privileges as an aristocratic caste.

Clan membership was determined by a child's mother. Although the father's clan was respected, he had little role in his children's upbringing. Instead, the men of the mother's clan saw to a child's development. At times the clan would arrange marriages without consulting the principals, but more often the male would initiate the courtship on his own. He would send a female relative to consult with the women of his prospective bride's family, who would in turn consult her brothers and maternal uncles. The girl's father might also be consulted out of courtesy, but he had no authority in the final decision. If the men approved, the prospective husband was informed of the decision and sent gifts to the females of the girl's family. If the gifts were accepted, the marriage was considered consummated. There was usually little or no ceremony involved, for the man simply moved into his new wife's dwelling and lived with her family. The marriage was not considered permanent, however, until the new husband harvested his first crop, supplied his wife with game, and built her a house. Polygamy was common among the Creeks, although each wife usually lived in a separate home. If plural wives were sisters they might share a home, and sometimes unrelated wives lived in the same house without apparent jealousy. In all cases, the first wife had to approve of all subsequent wives, and if a husband attempted to ignore his wife's advice he might be punished as an adulterer by his wife's clan. Divorce could be sought by either spouse but was rare when children were involved. When it did occur, children and property remained with the wife.

Creek families lived in dwellings that consisted of one to four buildings, depending on the size and wealth of the family. Structures were rectangular and framed with sturdy poles. The walls were plastered with mud and straw. The roofs were of cypress-bark shingles. Generally, one structure was the cooking area and winter quarters, one was the summer lodge, another acted as a granary, and others served other functions. Near each dwelling the Creeks planted a small private garden where the women of the family grew corn, beans, tobacco, and other crops. Outside the town a larger plot of land was used for the communal field in which the main food supply was grown. Each family possessed its own plot in the common field, but the entire tribe worked the land together, starting at one end and finishing at the other. When the time arrived, each family harvested its own plot and stored the produce in a private granary. Surplus crops could be donated to the public store, which was used to feed visitors, supply war parties, or help feed families whose supplies failed. Corn, beans, squash, pumpkins, and melons were grown in abundance. The Lower Creeks also grew rice. Hickory nuts and acorns were a source of sustenance. Hunting deer and bear and fishing also supplemented the food supplies. Each town had its own hunting range, and the Creeks were careful not to trespass on other towns' preserves. Each town council carefully regulated hunting to prevent the depletion of game animals.

The Creeks, like other southeastern Indians, wore garments of animal skins, although feathers and natural vegetable products were sometimes used. Breechclouts were the standard dress for Creek men, who often wore skin shirts and were more likely than surrounding tribes to wear leggings. Women wore skirts that extended almost to their knees and often, during the summer months, nothing else. Children often went naked until they reached puberty. With the advent of European contact, Creek dress became a blend of Indian and European styles. Leggings and breechclouts were often made of red or blue woolen goods, and if the Indian wore a shirt it was usually obtained through trade.

European contact had other profound effects upon the Creeks. Although Hernando De Soto's expedition in 1540 made the first European contact with the Creeks, it had little impact. A century and a half later, however, the Creeks became caught in the European struggle for control of the New World. Spaniards in Florida, Frenchmen in Louisiana, and Englishmen in Georgia and South Carolina all attempted to win the allegiance of the Creek confederacy. Sporadic warfare with Choctaws, Chickasaws, and Cherokees added to the Creeks' problems. By the 1770s the English regarded the Creek confederacy as their most powerful opponent. The American Revolution brought a new expansionistic nation to the Creeks' doorstep. In the first decade of the nineteenth century, the Creeks ceded some of their territory to the land-hungry Americans, but in 1811 the Creek council passed a law forbidding further land sales. Unfortunately for the Creeks, during the War of 1812 a group known as the Red Sticks attacked and killed several American families. The American government responded by sending an army under Andrew Jackson to put down the perceived uprising. Jackson and his men decisively defeated the Red Sticks at the battle of Horseshoe Bend and forced the Creeks to cede a vast amount of their territory to the United States in the Treaty of Fort Jackson, signed in 1814. Over the next two decades, numbers of Creek Indians moved to Indian Territory, after signing treaties exchanging their former homelands for land in Oklahoma. By 1836 the last of the Creeks surrendered their lands and were taken to Indian Territory to join their progressive kinsmen who had moved a decade earlier. In 1836, 14,609 Creeks journeyed to Oklahoma. Some of them split off to live with the Alabama-Coushatta Indians in Texas, but most eventually moved to join their countrymen in the Indian Territory. The Standing Committee on Indian Affairs reported "Coushatta, Alabama, Biloxi, and Muskogee" living in Nacogdoches and Liberty counties in 1837. The first three tribes had resided there for fifty years, but the Muskogees had lived there only for three years. These four groups were estimated to include 150 warriors and were considered to be pacific toward the Texas government. By 1849 an estimated fifty Creek Indians still resided in Texas.

The Creeks in Indian Territory assumed the balance of power in their region. They suffered raids from the wild Plains Indians but soon assumed leadership, defended their borders, and encouraged the Plains tribes to make peace with each other and the Texans. Both Mexicans and Sam Houston[qv] attempted to enlist the Creeks' aid against their respective enemies, but the Creeks remained neutral. The Creeks held several meetings with the Plains tribes and counseled them to renounce their nomadic life and take up farming. In 1855 several thousand Comanches, apparently impressed with the Creeks' prosperity, approached the United States to apply for a tract of farmland, but the government never acted on the request. Apparently not all of the Creeks were so peaceful, however. Citizens of Gainesville reported in 1866 that they were daily suffering raids on their cattle and horse herds. A Chickasaw Indian informed them that he had seen a group of Creek Indians driving 750 cattle, identified as belonging to two Texans, across the Red River. The same region occasionally suffered a murder or a scalping, although the responsible Indians were not identified and might not have been Creeks.

Currently, most of the Creek Indians, Muskogees in particular, live southwest of the Cherokees and northwest of the Choctaws in central eastern Oklahoma. At the time of removal in 1832–33, the Creek population was 21,733. Of that population, 17,939 were Muskogees.

BIBLIOGRAPHY: Angie Debo, *The Road to Disappearance: A History of the Creek Indians* (Norman: University of Oklahoma Press, 1941). Grant Foreman, *The Five Civilized Tribes* (Norman: University of Oklahoma Press, 1934). Michael Green, *The Creeks: A Critical Bibliography* (Bloomington: Indiana University Press, 1979). John R. Swanton, *The Indians of the Southeastern United States* (Washington: GPO, 1946). Dorman H. Winfrey and James M. Day, eds., *Texas Indian Papers* (4 vols., Austin: Texas State Library, 1959–61; rpt., 5 vols., Austin: Pemberton Press, 1966).

Jeffrey D. Carlisle

CRENSHAW, TEXAS. Crenshaw was four miles southeast of Barclay in southern Falls County. In the 1880s it was established as ranch headquarters for William Anderson Barclay[qv] and named for a friend of Barclay's called Crenshaw, who managed the local store and gin. A

Crenshaw post office operated from 1903 until 1911. No evidence of the community was shown on county highway maps in the 1940s.

BIBLIOGRAPHY: Lillian S. St. Romain, *Western Falls County, Texas* (Austin: Texas State Historical Association, 1951).

Vivian Elizabeth Smyrl

CRESPO, MANUEL (1903–1989). Manuel Crespo, a builder of the Hispanic community in Houston, was born on November 12, 1903, in Orense, Spain. His father died two years later, and his mother supported the family by raising cattle on a small farm. The children attended a local school in the town, where Manuel earned the equivalent of a high school education and received the highest grades in his class. On March 2, 1920, he purchased third-class accommodations on the *Vigo*, bound for the United States. After spending a day in New York, he traveled by train to Houston, Texas, visited friends for a few days, and then moved on to Fort Worth, where he got a job as a dishwasher.

In May 1923 Crespo returned to Houston and settled in Magnolia Park. He lived by sharpening knives in a peddler's cart. In 1925 he bought and remodeled a Model-T truck to carry his wares around the city. His new business enabled him to meet many different people, and he spent his evenings studying English. In 1927 Crespo injured his left eye while he was sharpening a knife. He required several operations, and his doctor recommended that he go into another line of work. In 1928 he moved to Baytown to work at the Humble Oil (now Exxon[qv]) Refinery.

In 1931 Crespo returned to Houston to manage the Mexican Funeral Home, on Navigation, for fifteen dollars a week. He studied for his mortuary license and eventually bought out the three owners. He renamed the business Crespo Funeral Home and in 1934 moved it to a two-story house on Canal. On October 21, 1934, he married Emily (Emalie) Meyer, and they moved into the rooms above the mortuary. They had two sons. Emily was secretary-treasurer of the Crespo Funeral Home. In 1937 the family moved the business to 2516 Navigation, where they remained for the next fifty years.

In 1940 Crespo took a leave of absence to recover from a skin infection on his hands and joined the Houston Police Department as a detective; he was the city's first Hispanic police officer. The Mexican-American neighborhoods faced a difficult juvenile-delinquency problem, and the police department needed Spanish-speaking officers. Spanish-speaking Anglo-American officers worked under Crespo, and some apparently resented him; in 1946, upon returning from a brief vacation, he found his desk had been broken into and his records stolen. He resigned the next day and returned to the funeral home.

In 1926 he organized the city's first Hispanic soccer club for youngsters; a year later he organized the city's first soccer league. Crespo provided his players with uniforms, purchased their equipment, and transported them to their games, which were often as far away as Galveston and San Antonio. He also organized and sponsored various softball and volleyball teams. In 1932 he joined the Woodmen of the World, Lodge No. 2333, also known as El Campo Laurel, one of the first predominantly Hispanic organizations in the city. It had over 250 members. He served as financial secretary and chairman of the organization. In 1932 he joined the Club Cultural Recreativo México Bello,[qv] which sponsored numerous social, cultural, and recreational activities in the community. When his membership was revoked two years later, he and six other men organized the Club Internacional, which operated for ten years.

Crespo, on the advice of Manuel C. Gonzales[qv] from San Antonio and with the help of Juvencio Rodríguez, Mariano Hernández, and John Henry Duhig, founded the League of United Latin American Citizens[qv] Council No. 60 in Magnolia Park in 1934; it was chartered in 1935. Other founding members included John J. Herrera, Felix H. Morales, Felix Tijerina,[qqv] Isidro García, Dr. Angel González, and Manuel M. Ortiz. The first meetings were held at the Crespo Funeral Home. In October 1935 a small group of LULAC members, including Crespo, Herrera, Morales, and Tijerina, defected from Council No. 60 and organized themselves into the Latin American Club of Harris County, which addressed the same issues, including health, education, language, citizenship, employment, and equal opportunity. LAC initiated a drive to increase the number of poll-tax payments among Hispanics, to ensure their representation in elections. It also formed a Boy Scout troop for Mexican-American boys and organized such youth groups as the Club Recreativo Tenochtitlán. In 1939 the members of LAC overcame their differences with LULAC.

In 1938 Crespo helped to found the Federación de Sociedades Mexicanas y Latino Americanas, an umbrella organization that worked with the Mexican consul in Houston to defend the rights of Mexican Americans.[qv] In 1941 the federation was successful in getting Wharton County to remove signs that read "No Mexicans Allowed" from commercial establishments. They also provided the Harris County Grand Jury with recommendations on how to curb juvenile delinquency. Crespo served on the board of directors until the group dissolved at the end of the war. He was a member of the Eagles, the Elks, and Familias Unidas. In 1940 he helped to found the Mexican Chamber of Commerce, which promoted the interests of Mexican-American businesses. In 1956 he organized a local chapter of the Lion's Club for the Hispanic community. The Port Houston Lion's Club had 175 members, which made it the second-largest Lion's Club in the Houston area. Crespo served as the first president and was later elected to various other posts.

During the late 1950s he became a member of the local Viva Kennedy Club and later of the Political Association of Spanish-Speaking Organizations[qv] of Harris County. He met President Kennedy at the Rice Hotel in Houston the day before the Kennedy assassination.[qv] In 1963 a group of community leaders, which included Félix Tijerina, E. P. Leal, and a Reverend Calderón, approached Crespo and asked him to run in the citywide election for District D of the City Council. Crespo hesitated, but after twenty-five local businessmen pledged donations of at least $500 to his campaign, he accepted. The money did not come through, however, and Crespo ended up spending over $15,000 of his own savings for the political campaign. PASSO provided volunteers. Crespo came in second, with 42,500 votes, 6,000 fewer than Homer Ford. Crespo was later asked to run for mayor but refused. He voted for John F. Kennedy and Lyndon B. Johnson,[qv] but he also campaigned for Richard M. Nixon, Gerald Ford, and Ronald Reagan.

Crespo served as an usher for ten years at Our Lady of Guadalupe Church. When he and his wife purchased a home on Live Oak they joined Blessed Sacrament Church. In the early 1980s Vice President George H. W. Bush presented Crespo with an award for being a "Pioneer of Houston." His picture hangs in the Houston Police Academy Museum. Crespo died in Houston on July 14, 1989, and was buried in the Catacombs Mausoleum, Garden of Gethsemane Cemetery.

BIBLIOGRAPHY: Arnoldo De León, *Ethnicity in the Sunbelt: A History of Mexican-Americans in Houston* (University of Houston Mexican American Studies Program, 1989). Thomas H. Kreneck, *Del Pueblo: A Pictorial History of Houston's Hispanic Community* (Houston: Houston International University, 1989). *María-Cristina García*

CRESSON, TEXAS. Cresson is at the intersection of U.S. Highway 377 and State Highway 171, seventeen miles south of Fort Worth on the Hood-Johnson county line. The town was named for John Cresson, captain of a wagon train that camped in the area before the Civil War.[qv] Cresson later built several houses and a general store on the site of the future town. Stagecoaches operated as early as 1856 from Jacksboro and Weatherford to Cresson and from Cresson to Cleburne, Waco, Granbury, and Stephenville. Around the town longhorn cattle[qv] grazed on land leased from the state. Early settlers included the Stewarts, who came from Kentucky in 1860, the Slocums, who operated the Stage Coach House, the Fidlers, who built the first hotel, and W. W. Wolf, who owned and operated the first cotton gin. In 1887 the Fort Worth and Rio Grande Railway was built through Cresson and extended to Granbury, the county seat. The railroad bolstered the economy in Cresson by opening the Fort Worth and Granbury markets to the town's agricultural products and livestock. When the Santa Fe Railroad was extended through the county in the same year, it crossed the Fort Worth and Rio Grande at Cresson. A post office was also established in 1887.

By 1890 Cresson had a population of thirty-five, a lumberyard, and three stores. The First Methodist Church was established in 1894; a tornado later destroyed the building, and a new one was built in the 1960s. The First Baptist Church was established in 1896. The population of Cresson reached 100 that year. By 1905 the town had two banks, eight general stores, a drugstore, a lumberyard, two doctors, a justice of the peace, and a constable who employed two deputies. In 1904 Cresson had a reported population of 279. The population remained fairly constant until the early 1970s, when it was reported at 208. In 1988 the town continued to have a population of about 200 and eight businesses and was primarily a ranching and retirement community. Two manufacturing companies were operating: Tex-Star Industries, which manufactures stucco, and a fertilizer company, Hyponex. Children in grade school are bused to Acton, and middle and high school students are bused to Granbury. Two museums—the Hal S. Smith Machinery Museum and Sturdy's Prairie Box Museum—have functioned in Cresson, but both are now closed. In 1990 the population was 208.

BIBLIOGRAPHY: Thomas T. Ewell, *History of Hood County* (Granbury, Texas: Gaston, 1895; rpt., Granbury Junior Woman's Club, 1956). Vertical Files, Barker Texas History Center, University of Texas at Austin (Hood County). *Rhonda L. Callaway*

CRESSWELL, HENRY WHITESIDE (1830–1904). Henry Whiteside (Hank) Cresswell, range cattleman in the Texas Panhandle, the son of John Cresswell, was born at Fairfield House, Lancashire, England, in 1830. At sixteen he immigrated with his father and brothers to Huron County, Ontario. In Canada, by his own account, he was engaged twice before he was twenty-one. That seemed to have ended his romantic history, as he remained a lifelong bachelor. In 1856 he left Canada, stayed for a time in Missouri, and then spent about twelve years prospecting in Colorado, New Mexico, and Arizona. During that time he became increasingly interested in cattle. About 1870 he purchased 100 cows and started a dairy farm near Pueblo, Colorado. This enterprise was occasionally beset with attacks from hostile Indians until Cresswell returned from a visit to his brother in Canada with a breech-loading gun he had bought in New York City for $300. This new weapon proved effective against the Indians, who did not bother him again. In 1874 Cresswell first registered his Bar CC brand in Colorado. His success under adverse conditions won him many friends, including Charles Goodnight,[qv] and attracted the attention of several wealthy, influential businessmen. In 1877 he formed the Cresswell Land and Cattle Company with the brothers J. A. and M. D. Thatcher and O. H. P. Baxter.

That same year Cresswell established his Bar CC headquarters in Ochiltree County, Texas, with a foundation herd he drove south from Colorado. As his acreage and cattle expanded, he became a favorite among ranchers and their families throughout the upper Panhandle.[qv] He had a benign attitude toward homesteaders who came into his range, and his employees likewise benefited from his generosity, as he encouraged them to start their own herds. His word was said to be as good as some men's oaths. The town of Cresswell, founded by the Klapp brothers, was named for him.

After British investors reorganized the Bar CC as the Cresswell Ranch and Cattle Company in 1885, Cresswell stayed on as head of the ranch until 1889. In the meantime he entered into a partnership with A. J. (Tony) Day and ran cattle in the Indian Territory, using a Turkey Track brand different from that of the Turkey Track Ranch.[qv] For fifteen years Cresswell and Day operated there and near Grand Rivers, South Dakota, and Billings, Montana. When nesters began crowding into these northwestern states the partners moved their operations to the Canadian province of Saskatchewan, where they leased a large tract for two cents an acre. They stocked it by buying herds from various ranches in New Mexico and West Texas and shipping on four consecutive railroads. In 1896 they moved a herd of 10,000 cows to Canada from the F Ranch, on the head of the Pease River, which Cresswell purchased from L. R. Moore of Kansas City.

While engaged in this expensive but successful Canadian cattle operation Cresswell suffered an infection in his foot that became gangrenous. Despite three operations at the hospital in Medicine Hat, Alberta, he died, on January 29, 1904. Tony Day carried on the business until 1908, when he sold the Canadian ranch to Gordon, Ironsides, and Fares of Winnipeg. Hank Cresswell is remembered in the Panhandle as a "range cattleman with few equals and no superiors."

BIBLIOGRAPHY: Laura V. Hamner, *Short Grass and Longhorns* (Norman: University of Oklahoma Press, 1943). Pauline D. and R. L. Robertson, *Cowman's Country: Fifty Frontier Ranches in the Texas Panhandle, 1876–1887* (Amarillo: Paramount, 1981). *Wheatheart of the Plains: An Early History of Ochiltree County* (Perryton, Texas: Ochiltree County Historical Survey Committee, 1969). *H. Allen Anderson*

CRESSWELL, TEXAS. Cresswell was on Wolf Creek about two miles west of the Ochiltree County Cemetery in central Ochiltree County. The town was founded in 1887 by brothers Gus, John, and Edward P. Klapp, and named for Henry Whiteside Cresswell,[qv] on whose Bar CC range (see CRESSWELL RANCH) the site was located. Richard S. Cutter and his sons brought in lumber from Dodge City and elsewhere to construct several frame buildings and to open a lumberyard there. Cutter also began the first Sunday school in the area. John Klapp served as the town doctor, and his brother Ed opened a general store. In addition, Ed and his wife, Hannah, planted a cherry orchard and built a greenhouse for vegetables. A post office was established at the Klapp store in November 1888. Cresswell was in the running against Ochiltree to become county seat in 1889, but began to decline after railroads came to the area. By January 1897 its post office had been discontinued. Some of the buildings constructed by the Cutters were moved to Ochiltree or sold for ranchhouses, and Cresswell was abandoned.

BIBLIOGRAPHY: Pauline D. and R. L. Robertson, *Cowman's Country: Fifty Frontier Ranches in the Texas Panhandle, 1876–1887* (Amarillo: Paramount, 1981). *Wheatheart of the Plains: An Early History of Ochiltree County* (Perryton, Texas: Ochiltree County Historical Survey Committee, 1969). *H. Allen Anderson*

CRESSWELL RANCH. The Cresswell (or Bar CC) Ranch was established in 1877 by the Cresswell Land and Cattle Company of Colorado. This syndicate was formed when O. H. P. Baxter and the brothers J. A. and M. D. Thatcher, owners of bank stocks, mines, and farms, decided to back Henry W. Cresswell,[qv] who was enthusiastic about building up a ranch in the Panhandle.[qv] Accordingly, Cresswell drove a herd southward and selected as headquarters a site in Ochiltree County on a small tributary of the Canadian known as Home Ranch Creek. He marked his cattle with the Bar CC brand he had first registered in Colorado and cropped their left ears. Another Colorado herd trailed to the area in 1878 increased the Bar CC cattle to 27,000 head. Soon Cresswell expanded his range and became a favorite personality among his neighbors, including Robert Moody, Joseph Morgan,[qv] Dee Eubank, Tom Connell (see CONNELL AND EUBANK RANCHES), and the Cator brothers (see CATOR, JAMES HAMILTON). When Morgan died of smallpox in 1883, Cresswell aided the family and bought the Morgan Triangle cattle from the widow. Eventually the Bar CC range covered 1,250,000 acres that extended from the Canadian north to the state line. The great Panhandle drift fence^qv was erected across this range.

In order to move his headquarters to a more central location, Cresswell bought from Alfred H. Barton^qv the old picket stockade and storehouse built by Charles Edward Jones and Joseph H. Plummer^qqv on Wolf Creek in eastern Ochiltree County. In 1882 the Prairie Cattle Company^qv offered to buy out Cresswell, whose herd by then was estimated to be over 31,000 head. Although that deal fell through, some of the Prairie stockholders succeeded in joining the Bar CC operation in 1885. A new syndicate, composed of these English investors along with the old cattle company, was formed and called the Cresswell Ranch and Cattle Company. It bought the ranch for $1.5 million, and Cresswell retained $20,000 interest.

This transfer took some time, and it proved a time of troubles. The Cresswell Ranch was plagued in 1885–86 by a slump in the market, the "Big Die-up"^qv that winter, a prairie fire, and wolves. Nevertheless, Cresswell doggedly overcame his financial losses by purchasing 11,000 cattle from Charles Goodnight^qv and fattening them in Indian Territory. The new company retained Cresswell as head of the ranch, and he remained with the Bar CC until 1889. James McKenzie, a Scot from Kansas City, was named general manager, and W. J. Todd, who had counted cattle in the transfer, became superintendent. Laura V. Todd recalled how she and her infant son traveled by train to Dodge City from Trinidad, and then for two days by horse-drawn buggy from Dodge to the ranch headquarters, where she lived in a tent until a new frame house was completed. Mrs. Todd brought potted plants and had furniture shipped in by mule freight. She tells of an infestation of bedbugs and the death of her baby in 1886. By Christmas she had a second son, Jep, and joined in efforts to give the cowboys a real celebration, complete with a dance, wild turkeys for the feast, and a multitiered cake decorated with store-bought candles. Jack Meade, Dave Pope, Archie King, Dave Lard, O. R. McMordie, and Edward H. Brainard,^qv who was later made range foreman, were among the Bar CC cowhands who helped host that memorable Christmas gathering.

In January 1894 the Barcee post office was established at the ranch headquarters with Laura Todd as postmistress. Until then mail had been left there for distribution to area settlers. The office lasted only until May 1895, when mail was routed to Ochiltree. By then the Cresswell company had more than 25,000 cattle, including purebred shorthorn and Hereford bulls, and 300 saddle horses. However, fluctuating cattle prices and pressures of settlers caused the company to decline. Around 1900 it closed its operations and divided the ranch. Snyder and Sears of Kansas City bought the last of the original Bar CC herd. The brand, made with two irons, was used until 1937 by the ranch of Mrs. John Jones and her son-in-law, F. C. McMordie, located on Home Ranch Creek, the site of Cresswell's first headquarters.

BIBLIOGRAPHY: Laura V. Hamner, *Short Grass and Longhorns* (Norman: University of Oklahoma Press, 1943). Arthur Hecht, comp., *Postal History in the Texas Panhandle* (Canyon, Texas: Panhandle-Plains Historical Society, 1960). *A History of Lipscomb County, Texas, 1876–1976* (Lipscomb, Texas: Lipscomb County Historical Survey Committee, 1976). Pauline D. and R. L. Robertson, *Cowman's Country: Fifty Frontier Ranches in the Texas Panhandle, 1876–1887* (Amarillo: Paramount, 1981). *Wheatheart of the Plains: An Early History of Ochiltree County* (Perryton, Texas: Ochiltree County Historical Survey Committee, 1969).

H. Allen Anderson

CRESTONIO, TEXAS. Crestonio, on the Texas-Mexican Railway twenty miles southwest of Benavides in southern Duval County, was founded in 1902 and named after Creston King, the son of local landowner W. R. King. A post office was established there in 1913, with Charlie D. Adams as postmaster, and by the next year a cotton gin was operating in Crestonio. From the 1920s to the 1940s the population of the town was estimated at twenty-five. Its post office closed in 1944. In 1947 Crestonio had a school and church, but by 1955 the school had been consolidated with the Realitos school district. By 1975 the community consisted of a few scattered dwellings. Crestonio was no longer shown on a 1990 map of the area.

Martin Donell Kohout

CRESWELL, TEXAS. Creswell, a post office community near the site of what later became Ash, ten miles southwest of Crockett in southwestern Houston County, was probably established after the Civil War.^qv A post office opened there in 1870, and by the mid-1870s the community had a store and a number of houses. Its post office was discontinued in 1877, and by the mid-1930s Creswell was no longer shown on the county highway map. No trace of the settlement remained in 1990.

Christopher Long

CRET, PAUL PHILIPPE (1876–1945). Paul Philippe Cret, architect, was born in Lyons, France, on October 23, 1876, the son of Paul Adolphe and Anna Caroline (Durand) Cret. He attended a *lycée* in Bourg and studied architecture at the École des Beaux Arts in Lyons and the École des Beaux Arts, Paris, where he graduated in 1903. At the Paris school he was awarded the Rougevin Prize and the Grand Medal of Emulation, both in recognition of his remarkable skill as a draftsman. In 1903 he was invited to teach architecture at the University of Pennsylvania, where he remained until his retirement in 1937.

During his long tenure at Penn, Cret was recognized as one of the foremost practitioners of the "Beaux-Arts" style, and his work left a lasting impact on the built environment of the United States, forming a bridge between the end of Beaux-Arts historicism and the rise of modernism. Cret's early buildings—among them the Pan American Union Building in Washington (1907–10), the Indianapolis Public Library (1917), and the Detroit Institute of Arts (1927)—evinced a refined classicism that represented the best traditions of the Beaux-Arts style. By the late 1920s, however, he began to experiment with a new, radically stripped-down classicism, exemplified by his Folger Shakespeare Library (1930–37) in Washington, that was more attuned to the growing modern movement.

In 1930 the regents of the University of Texas hired Cret as the university's supervising architect and commissioned him to draw up a general development plan for the campus. Cret's scheme, which he formally submitted in 1933, was based on general Beaux-Arts principles of balance, axial arrangements, and symmetry. It called for four "principal aspects" or malls extending in the four cardinal directions from the main building, which would serve as an ordering concept for the buildings and monuments of the campus. In front of the main building and tower was a great courtyard framed on the west by Cass Gilbert's^qv library, and on the east by Herbert M. Greene's^qv Garrison Hall. A main north-south axis was formed by Littlefield Fountain, the tower, and the Home Economics Building; and a primary east-west axis featured the Union and Architecture buildings, the pavilions of the main building, and a proposed open-air theater. The remainder of the campus was subdivided into "secondary" areas, with the buildings generally arranged around large courtyards.

Cret argued that the malls and the other main features of the plan should not be altered. But he recognized the importance of introducing a plan that was flexible enough to meet the changing demands of the university, and he proposed what art historian Carol McMichael has called an "elastic formal plan" that allowed for variety in placement and design of individual buildings, as well as a certain amount of freedom for future development. The combination of formal, axial planning and informal, casual arrangements was in many respects unique in the design of American college campuses and has been widely admired. Since the 1930s the university campus has grown well beyond the confines of the area in Cret's development plan, and subsequent architects have ignored the spirit of his scheme, but the central part of the campus still bears the unmistakable imprint of Cret's work.

In 1931 the board of regents also commissioned Cret to design a new library on the site of Frederick E. Ruffini's^qv Old Main Building. Cret proposed several different designs, but the regents eventually opted for a large axially planned building in a Mediterranean-influenced Beaux-Arts style topped by a thirty-one-story tower. The great tower, the only structure at the time that competed with the dome of the state Capitol^qv on the Austin skyline, became the centerpiece of the university's campus, and formed, in Cret's words, "the image carried in our memory when we think of the place."

Between 1930 and the early 1940s Cret, working in association with the firm of Greene, LaRoche, and Dahl and Robert Leon White,^qv designed eighteen additional buildings for the campus. These included the Home Economics Building (now Mary Gearing Hall), the Texas Union Building, the Architecture Building (now Goldsmith Hall), and an auditorium (now Hogg Auditorium). Most of the buildings, like the tower, were characterized by a Mediterranean revival style. Only the Texas Memorial Museum,^qv designed in association with John F. Staub,^qv embraced the stripped-down classicism Cret had first employed in the Folger Shakespeare Library along with curving forms of the Moderne.

In addition to his work for the University of Texas, Cret designed the United States Courthouse (1933) in Fort Worth, built in association with Wiley G. Clarkson.^qv In 1937 ill health forced Cret to resign from the University of Pennsylvania. His last important work was the Federal Reserve Bank (1935–37) in Philadelphia. He died of a heart ailment in Philadelphia on September 8, 1945.

BIBLIOGRAPHY: Architectural Archives, Fine Arts Library, University of Pennsylvania, Philadelphia. Elizabeth Greenwell Grossman, Paul Philippe Cret: Rationalism and Imagery in American Architecture (Ph.D. dissertation, Brown University, 1980). Carol McMichael, Paul Cret at Texas: Architectural Drawing and the Image of the University in the 1930s (Austin: Archer M. Huntington Art Gallery, University of Texas, 1983). Carol McMichael, Paul Philippe Cret at the University of Texas: A Study of Style and the Communication of the University's Image in the 1930s (M.A. thesis, University of Texas at Austin, 1979). Theo B. White, Paul Philippe Cret, Architect and Teacher (Philadelphia: Art Alliance Press, 1973). *Christopher Long*

CRETE, TEXAS. Crete, also known as East Prairie and as Possum Walk, is off Farm Road 358 some eleven miles north of Groveton in north central Trinity County. It was established in the 1870s by settlers from De Ridder, Louisiana, and was originally known as East Prairie. The East Prairie school was in operation by 1884. In 1902 a post office was established there, and the name of the community was changed to Crete for the Biblical reference to the Mediterranean island. This name was still in use in the 1980s, though some residents also referred to the area as Possum Walk. By 1914 Crete had a general store, Baptist and Christian churches, two cotton gin and gristmill combinations, and a reported population of 250. Its post office closed in 1928, but in the mid-1930s the community still had one business and a population of seventy-five. After World War II^qv many residents moved away from the area. In the early 1990s Crete was a dispersed rural community.

BIBLIOGRAPHY: Patricia B. and Joseph W. Hensley, eds., Trinity County Beginnings (Groveton, Texas: Trinity County Book Committee, 1986). *Christopher Long*

CREUZBAUR, ROBERT (?–?). Robert Creuzbaur, surveyor and draftsman, was associated with the General Land Office^qv of Texas as a mapmaker during the mid-1800s. He probably came to Texas in the mid-1840s. Two of his maps are of particular importance. In 1848 he was commissioned to compile topographic information for a map of Texas for Jacob de Cordova,^qv a land promoter. Creuzbaur also made a map from notes compiled by John S. (Rip) Ford^qv on his exploring expedition in 1849 showing the route from Austin to Paso del Norte. This map was published for emigrants, and it gave the distances from one water hole to another, as well as pertinent landmarks and detailed descriptions of the nature of the soil and terrain. This map is included in Creuzbaur's Guide to California and the Pacific Ocean (1849). Creuzbaur also drew up a map of Austin in 1853. Sometime during the 1850s he married the daughter of Eli Kirk of Austin. In 1861 he invented the Sea King, a type of gunboat designed to fight Yankee blockaders. A joint committee from both houses of the Texas legislature appropriated $500 to enable Creuzbaur to present his plans to Confederate authorities in Richmond. After the Civil War^qv he moved north and settled in Brooklyn, New York, where he was still living in 1899. Copies of his maps are in the Barker Texas History Center,^qv University of Texas at Austin, and at the General Land Office in Austin.

BIBLIOGRAPHY: Austin History Center Files. Frank Brown, Annals of Travis County and the City of Austin (MS, Frank Brown Papers, Barker Texas History Center, University of Texas at Austin). Larry Jay Gage, "The Texas Road to Secession and War: John Marshall and the Texas State Gazette, 1860–1861," Southwestern Historical Quarterly 62 (October 1958). Kenneth F. Neighbours, "The Expedition of Major Robert S. Neighbors to El Paso in 1849," Southwestern Historical Quarterly 58 (July 1954).

CREVEL DE MORANGET (?–1687). Usually referred to as Moranget, Crevel de Moranget was the son of Nicolas Crevel. His Christian name is not known. His mother was the sister of René Robert Cavelier, Sieur de La Salle,^qv and Abbé Jean Cavelier.^qv His grandfather was Jean Cavelier, a wealthy merchant of Rouen, France, where Crevel de Moranget probably was born. As a young man, Crevel de Moranget enlisted in La Salle's company and with the rank of lieutenant sailed with his uncle from La Rochelle, France, in July 1684 to seek the mouth of the Mississippi via the Gulf of Mexico. He is portrayed in accounts of the La Salle expedition^qv as young, brash, and hotheaded, given to creating unpleasant situations—traits that led eventually to La Salle's murder and his own, as well as that of two companions. He probably contributed also to the destruction of Fort St. Louis.^qv

After La Salle's ships arrived on the Texas coast in January 1685, Moranget and Henri Joutel^qv went ashore near Cedar Bayou with a detail of soldiers and marched up Matagorda Island looking for a place to unload the ships. The vessels followed in the offing until they reached Cavallo Pass, then the only entrance to Matagorda Bay.

The storeship Aimable^qv wrecked while trying to enter the bay, and the cargo piled up on the beach was pillaged by Karankawa Indians. Sent to recover the stolen goods from the native village, Moranget proceeded "with great display of arms and a threatening attitude" and frightened the Indians away. His men helped themselves to Indian as well as French goods and hauled away the loot in two of the Indians' canoes. Overtaken by nightfall while returning to the French camp, the lieutenant permitted his men to go ashore and build a fire. The Karankawas attacked during the night with a shower of arrows that killed two men and severely wounded a third, while Moranget received an arrow through the arm. Thus began the bad relations between the Frenchmen and the natives that culminated in the Fort St. Louis massacre.

Despite his imprudence, Moranget was often trusted with important tasks. In June 1685, after his wound had healed, he was ordered by La Salle to conduct the colonists to a new site above the head of Lavaca Bay. In the spring and summer of 1686, he accompanied La Salle on his first journey to the "Cenis" (Hasinai Indians) in eastern Texas, on which twenty men went and eight returned. It may have been on this journey that Moranget aroused the hatred of Pierre Duhaut, for Duhaut's brother, Dominique, was one of those lost. Duhaut, it has been suggested, "detested Moranget for having abandoned him [his brother?] during the expedition of 1686." In any event, Duhaut conspired in Moranget's murder, which took place in a hunting camp as La Salle and seventeen men neared the Cenis a second time, on March 17, 1687. The trouble began with an argument over marrow bones, with Moranget acting in his customary officious manner. But that was only the spark that brought to the surface a long-simmering hatred. In the middle of the night, Duhaut's coconspirator, the brooding surgeon Liotot—who had attended Moranget's arrow wound and been repaid with constant abuse—laid open the skulls of Moranget, La Salle's servant Saget, and the Shawnee hunter Nika with an axe. Two days later, when La Salle came to investigate his nephew's extended absence, he was lured into an ambush by Duhaut's lackey, Jean L'Archêveque.qv Duhaut fired the fatal shot, an act—though not without other motivation—that was made necessary by the previous slayings.

BIBLIOGRAPHY: Paul Chesnel, *History of Cavelier de La Salle, 1643–1687*, trans. Andrée Chesnel Meany (New York: Putnam, 1932). Francis Parkman, *The Discovery of the Great West* (London: Murray, 1869; *La Salle and the Discovery of the Great West*, new ed., New York: New American Library, 1963). Marc de Villiers, *L'expédition de Cavelier de La Salle dans le Golfe du Mexique* (Paris: Adrien-Maisonneuve, 1931).

Robert S. Weddle

CREWS, TEXAS (Gregg County). Crews was also known as Swamp City, probably because of its location near the swamps of the Sabine River in Gregg County. It was named for Dr. C. C. Crews, a dentist in Longview and the donor of the land on which the Crews Baptist Church was built. The town was founded by 1931, when its population was reported as 300; its population had decreased to fifty by 1966. Oil provided the main industry and occupation of the inhabitants. The community was no longer shown on the 1984 county highway map.

CREWS, TEXAS (Runnels County). Crews, at the junction of Farm roads 53 and 382 in northeastern Runnels County, was named for C. R. Crews, a Ballinger businessman. A school opened there in 1888, and in 1892 J. D. Wise and a Mr. Broughton established a post office and store in Crews, with Wise as postmaster. In 1922 the community's post office closed. Crews had one business and 150 residents in 1940. Its school closed in 1948, and the local Baptist church disbanded in 1968. In 1970 the Methodist church was all that remained of Crews.

BIBLIOGRAPHY: Charlsie Poe, *Runnels Is My County* (San Antonio: Naylor, 1970).

William R. Hunt

CRIB CREEK, TEXAS. Crib Creek, off Farm Road 357 near Helmic in northern Trinity County, was first settled before the Civil Warqv and is said to have been named for a small corn crib built by Caddo Indians and found by early settlers in the area. By 1896 the community had a school, which that year had one teacher and thirty-two students. The local school was consolidated with the Hackberry school in 1915. In the 1930s there were still a number of houses in the area, but after World War IIqv many of the residents moved away. In the early 1990s only a few scattered houses remained there.

BIBLIOGRAPHY: Patricia B. and Joseph W. Hensley, eds., *Trinity County Beginnings* (Groveton, Texas: Trinity County Book Committee, 1986).

Christopher Long

CRIER, JOHN (1801–1840s). John Crier (Cryer), one of Stephen F. Austin'sqv Old Three Hundred,qv moved to Texas from Arkansas under the colonization law of March 1825. His character certificate stated that he was a twenty-four-year-old widower with five slaves, a daughter, and a son, Andrew, who eventually served in Sam Houston'sqv army during the Texas Revolution.qv As an Old Three Hundred colonist, Crier received title to a sitioqv of land in what is now Matagorda County on June 6, 1827, though sometime before 1836 he may have settled in the territory of Fayette County. The Austin *Texas Sentinel*qv of August 5, 1841, listed Crier as delinquent on direct taxes due in Colorado County in 1840. He was killed by Indians near Fayetteville, Fayette County, probably in the 1840s, and was buried on the edge of Ross Prairie (*see* ROSS PRAIRIE, TEXAS).

BIBLIOGRAPHY: Lester G. Bugbee, "The Old Three Hundred: A List of Settlers in Austin's First Colony," *Quarterly of the Texas State Historical Association* 1 (October 1897). Leonie Rummel Weyand and Houston Wade, *An Early History of Fayette County* (La Grange, Texas: La Grange *Journal*, 1936).

CRIER CREEK. Crier Creek rises 2½ miles northeast of Ellinger near the Fayette county line in northwestern Colorado County (at 29°51′ N, 96°40′ W) and runs south for 8½ miles to its mouth on the Colorado River, near the Shaws Bend community (at 29°46′ N, 96°40′ W). It traverses level to gently sloping terrain surfaced by dark gray, silty loam topsoils lying over mottled clay subsoils. These cover beds of gravel that are mined near the Colorado River for use in construction. Vegetation along the creek is often dense mixed oak and cedar, but in open areas the land is good for pasture and hay crops. The stream is probably named for John Crier,qv one of Stephen F. Austin'sqv Old Three Hundredqv colonists. Crier explored the area before settling near Matagorda in 1827.

CRIMMINS, MARTIN LALOR (1876–1955). Martin Lalor Crimmins, army officer, herpetologist, and military historian, was born on April 4, 1876, in New York City, the son of John D. and Lily (Lalor) Crimmins. From September 1891 to October 1895 he attended Georgetown College, Washington, D.C., after which he studied at the University of Virginia Medical School from November 1895 to May 1898. Shortly before graduation he joined the Rough Riders (*see* FIRST UNITED STATES VOLUNTEER CAVALRY) in San Antonio with the help of Theodore Roosevelt, a family friend. Crimmins was commissioned second lieutenant, Sixty-ninth Volunteer Infantry, on August 29, 1898. The following month he was commissioned second lieutenant, United States Army, and assigned to the Eighteenth Infantry regiment at Cavite, Luzon, Philippines. Thereafter, promotions continued until he reached his final rank of colonel on April 23, 1921. In 1926 he was retired for physical disability in the line of duty and moved to San Antonio, Texas. During his military service he traveled extensively in Europe, Asia, and Alaska.

As a herpetologist Crimmins did pioneer work in the field of snake-bite treatment, a subject on which he assisted medical experts in many experiments and lectured throughout the United States. He inoculated himself with serum until he became immune and then gave blood transfusions to snake-bite victims. In April 1953 he received the Walter Reed Award "in recognition of courageous service to mankind." He devoted his later years to writing, mostly on historical subjects. More than 200 of his articles appeared, in publications that included the West Texas Historical Association *Year Book*, *Southwestern Historical Quarterly*, *Frontier Times*,qqv New Mexico *Historical Review*, *Journal of the American Military Institute*, *U.S. Infantry Journal*, *Military Surgeon*, *Army & Navy Courier*, *Military Engineer*, *Southern Medical Journal*, and *Texas State Journal of Medicine*. He was active in various scientific and historical associations in Texas. On January 16, 1901, Crimmins married Margaret Custis Cole. On May 19, 1918, he married Josephine Yost. He died in San Antonio on February 5, 1955.

BIBLIOGRAPHY: Chris Emmett, *In the Path of Events with Colonel Martin Lalor Crimmins, Soldier, Naturalist, Historian* (Waco: Jones and Morrison, 1959). Vertical Files, Barker Texas History Center, University of Texas at Austin.

Paul Adams

CRIOLLO. In New Spain a criollo was a person born in the New World to Spanish-born parents. A criollo, although legally equal to a peninsular,qv was treated differently with regard to royal appointments to high colonial offices in administration, the military, and the church. The stigma of being born in America emerged from the difficulty of distinguishing between pure criollos and mestizos. In Spain it was also widely believed that exposure to the tropical sun in the New World retarded the development of children born there. Criollos therefore ranked one step below peninsulars on New Spain's social ladder. On the frontier of the Spanish empire, criollos held more important positions in the colonial administration because of the scarcity of peninsulars and their reluctance to serve in remote regions. The highest offices were usually reserved for the Spanish-born, and criollos and mestizos shared the other military and civil appointments. Criollos and mestizos also fared well in church positions because of their connections with local parishes. Social fluidity promoted miscegenation on the frontier, and the lines between criollos and mixed bloods quickly eroded.

BIBLIOGRAPHY: Oakah L. Jones, *Los Paisanos: Spanish Settlers on the Northern Frontier of New Spain* (Norman: University of Oklahoma Press, 1979). Lyle N. McAlister, "Social Structure and Social Change in New Spain," *Hispanic American Historical Review* 43 (August 1963). Magnus Mörner, *Race Mixture in the History of Latin America* (Boston: Little, Brown, 1967). David J. Weber, *New Spain's Far Northern Frontier* (Albuquerque: University of New Mexico Press, 1979).

Joan E. Supplee

CRISP, DOWNING H. (?–1844). Downing H. Crisp, naval officer, was born in England, the son of a commander in the Royal Navy. He was said to have once been a midshipman in the Royal Navy himself. He joined the Texas Navy qv in 1836 and was assigned as second lieutenant of the *Austin*.qv On October 4 Crisp saved the twenty-six-man crew of the Mexican brig *Segunda Fama*, which had been run aground by a norther on Blanquilla Reef near Lobos Island. In November he took part in the joint Texas-Yucatán raid on Tabasco. Funds acquired when the city paid a ransom demand of $25,000 allowed Crisp to purchase much-needed supplies and remain at sea until the end of February 1841, but he became seriously ill with the yellow fever that ravaged the fleet.

On March 24 he was assigned by Commodore Edwin W. Moore qv to command of the Texas war schooner *San Bernard*.qv After a season of patrolling off the Texas coast to intercept smugglers and to make surveys and maps, Crisp and the *San Bernard* conveyed Texas agent James Webb qv to Veracruz. They reached port on May 31 but were denied landing rights by Mexican officials. Crisp wished to exchange calls with the officers of the American and British vessels anchored there, but felt such acute embarrassment over his ragged uniform—Texas naval officers were not paid for years on end—that he exchanged courtesies by letter and signal only. After lingering off the coast until the end of June, he steered for the Yucatán. While crossing the Bay of Campeche his rotten topmast was carried away, however, and he was compelled to return to Galveston, where he arrived on June 20.

President Mirabeau B. Lamar qv was unable to negotiate a permanent peace with Mexico and once again ordered his fleet to the Yucatán. Crisp and the *San Bernard* sailed from Galveston on December 11, 1841, and arrived at Sisal on December 29; they once again patrolled between the Yucatán port and Veracruz and occasionally as far north as Tuxpan. Crisp and his men participated in the capture of the Mexican merchant vessel *Progreso* on February 6 and the *Doric*, the *Doloritas*, and the *Dos Amigos* in April. Off Tampico Crisp was ordered back to Galveston with dispatches and reports but returned to Moore and the rest of the Texas fleet on April 24. On July 19 Crisp was confirmed in grade as lieutenant.

At the end of this cruise he returned to Galveston, where in early September he reported his ship badly worm-eaten. He had been authorized to have her repaired at New Orleans, but no funds were provided to pay for the work. On September 18 the *San Bernard* was driven ashore by a hurricane, and for want of the $500 required to refloat her and have her repaired, she became a deserted, rotting hulk in Galveston harbor. On December 21, 1842, Crisp wrote to Sam Houston qv that the condition of his ship was "destitute and deplorable" and that for want of funds he and his officers were subsisting on the charity of the citizens of Galveston. They received neither pay nor rations from the government, and Crisp discharged his enlisted men, ate his pet pig, and at last in January 1843, having raised $27.08 by selling a broken bell and several pieces of old copper, departed for England in hopes of securing a berth in a European ship.

Crisp returned from England to take command of the *Austin* in January 1844. With a treaty of annexation qv pending, Sam Houston urged the United States to take Crisp into its naval service at his present rank, stating that he was "worthy of [his] rank" and was a gentleman "*who will obey orders.*" Before a treaty could be arranged, however, Lieutenant Crisp died, on June 3, 1844, of yellow fever in Galveston. His brief history of the navy of the Republic of Texas is preserved in the William Bollaert qv papers at the Barker Texas History Center,qv University of Texas at Austin.

BIBLIOGRAPHY: Jim Dan Hill, *The Texas Navy* (New York: Barnes, 1962). Tom Henderson Wells, *Commodore Moore and the Texas Navy* (Austin: University of Texas Press, 1960). Amelia W. Williams and Eugene C. Barker, eds., *The Writings of Sam Houston, 1813–1863* (8 vols., Austin: University of Texas Press, 1938–43; rpt., Austin and New York: Pemberton Press, 1970).

Thomas W. Cutrer

CRISP, JOHN H. (ca. 1797–1888). John H. Crisp, planter and physician, was born in North Carolina about 1797. He practiced medicine in western Tennessee and northern Mississippi before moving to Texas shortly before 1855, when he purchased 1,476 acres of land on the east bank of the Colorado River northwest of Columbus in Colorado County. By 1860 he reportedly owned 800 acres of improved land worth $32,000, which produced 6,000 bushels of corn and 260 bales of cotton annually. He owned 146 slaves—the second largest number in the county. The value of his personal property at that time was recorded as $98,200. In 1867 Crisp sold his holdings in Texas and joined the Confederate exodus to South America. He died on July 8, 1888, near the colony of American expatriates at Americana, Brazil.

BIBLIOGRAPHY: Colorado County Historical Commission, *Colorado County Chronicles from the Beginning to 1923* (2 vols., Austin: Nortex, 1986). Ralph A. Wooster, "Wealthy Texans, 1860," *Southwestern Historical Quarterly* 71 (October 1967).

Charles Christopher Jackson

CRISP, WILLIAM M. (?–?). William M. Crisp, early settler and legislator, arrived in Texas on November 5, 1837, and on March 21, 1839, received his conditional certificate for land in Red River County. He was tax assessor of Red River County in 1840 and received an unconditional certificate in Lamar County on August 2, 1841. He served as associate justice of Lamar County in 1841–42 and as representative from Lamar County to the Seventh Congress. Crisp was elected chief justice of Lamar County on February 3, 1845, but resigned in September. In 1850 he was a farmer and stock raiser in Hopkins County.

BIBLIOGRAPHY: Texas House of Representatives, *Biographical Directory of the Texan Conventions and Congresses, 1832–1845* (Austin: Book Exchange, 1941).

CRISP, TEXAS. Crisp is on Farm Road 660 ten miles east of Waxahachie in east central Ellis County. It was named for Charles F. Crisp, a speaker of the United States House of Representatives. The community was settled in the late 1880s or early 1890s, and a post office opened there in 1892. Crisp's population was not reported as more than 100 until the mid-1920s, when it was estimated at 120; it was reported at that level through the mid-1960s. In the late 1960s, however, the number of residents began to decline, and had fallen to ninety by 1968. Crisp's population was still reported as ninety in 1990.

David Minor

CRISWELL CREEK. Criswell Creek rises about a mile west of the Southern Pacific tracks and 2½ miles southwest of West Point in northwestern Fayette County (at 29°54′ N, 97°03′ W) and runs northeast for about five miles, crossing the Southern Pacific tracks, State Highway 71, and the Missouri, Kansas and Texas tracks, before reaching its mouth on the Colorado River (at 29°58′ N, 97°01′ W). South of West Point the creek traverses an area with a fine sandy loam surface soil over a very firm clay subsoil. This land is of marginal value for agriculture and is used primarily as cattle pasture. Between West Point and the Colorado River the stream runs through gently rolling terrain surfaced by firm calcareous clay layers overlying gravel deposits. This land produces good corn and hay crops, but much of the soil has been stripped to allow access to the gravel. The creek is probably named for John Yancy Criswell, an original settler in the area who in July 1835 accompanied John Henry Moore qv in an expedition against the Tawakoni (or Tehuacana) Indians.
BIBLIOGRAPHY: Leonie Rummel Weyand and Houston Wade, *An Early History of Fayette County* (La Grange, Texas: La Grange *Journal*, 1936).

A second Criswell Creek rises a mile east of U.S. Highway 77 and two miles northeast of the community of Swiss Alp in central Fayette County (at 29°48′ N, 96°54′ W) and runs east through steeply rolling pastureland for 6½ miles to its mouth on Williams Creek, on the floodplain of the Colorado River a mile southwest of the community of Mullins Prairie (at 29°50′ N, 96°49′ W). The creek traverses an area of hills and prairies with some local shallow depressions, surfaced by clay and sandy loam soils that support hardwoods, conifers, mesquite, and grasses. Despite its steep slopes, much of this land produced cotton until the 1960s, and was consequently eroded. By the 1980s most of the area hillsides had stabilized and had been converted to pastureland, while the level terrain near the mouth of the creek still produced good crops of maize and hay.

CRITTENDEN, GEORGE BIBB (1812–1880). George Bibb Crittenden, United States, Texas, and Confederate States army officer, was born on March 20, 1812, in Russellville, Kentucky, the eldest son of John Jordan and Sally (Lee) Crittenden. The elder Crittenden was United States attorney general and a senator. George Crittenden graduated from West Point with the class of 1832 and was brevetted a second lieutenant in the Fourth United States Infantry. He fought in the Black Hawk War before he resigned on April 30, 1833, to study law at Transylvania University. He later moved to Texas and accepted a commission in the Army of the Republic of Texas.qv In 1842 he served as second lieutenant of Capt. William Ryon's company in the unfortunate Mier expedition qv and was captured by Mexican forces after the battle of Mier. On January 14, 1843, he was declared unfit to travel by a Mexican army surgeon and placed in a hospital at Matamoros. By the end of February former president Andrew Jackson had interceded on Crittenden's behalf to secure his release from Antonio López de Santa Anna.qv In 1846, at the start of the Mexican War,qv Crittenden rejoined the United States Army as a captain in the Mounted Rifles and was brevetted major for "gallant and meritorious conduct" at the battles of Contreras and Churubusco. Although he was cashiered in August 1848, he was reinstated to his former rank the following March and in 1856 had risen to the rank of lieutenant colonel.

Soon after the outbreak of the Civil War qv Crittenden entered the Confederate Army as an infantry colonel; he was commissioned a brigadier general on August 15, 1861, and a major general on November 9, 1861 and given command of the Southern effort to liberate Kentucky. In January 1862 he took command of Brig. Gen. Felix Kirk Zollicoffer's small army, unfavorably located at Mill Springs, Kentucky, and there was ingloriously defeated by Union forces under Brig. Gen. George H. Thomas at the battles of Mill Springs and Logan's Crossroads. Crittenden was said to have been drunk on the field, and an outraged public demanded his removal from command. He was subsequently placed in charge of Gen. Albert Sidney Johnston's qv reserve corps at Iuka, Mississippi. His career was shattered beyond repair, however, when he was discovered drunk at his post with his troops "in a wretched state of discipline." He was arrested and subjected to a court-martial by Maj. Gen. William J. Hardee.

Crittenden resigned from the army on October 23, 1862, but continued to serve in various subordinate roles in western Virginia under the command of Gen. John S. Williams. After the war he lived in Frankfort, Kentucky, where he was appointed state librarian. He died on November 27, 1880. He was a member of the Whig party qv and the brother of Thomas Leonidas Crittenden, a major general in the Union army; their father, the author of the Crittenden Compromise, remained an ardent Unionist until his death in 1863.

BIBLIOGRAPHY: Patricia L. Faust, ed., *Historical Times Illustrated Encyclopedia of the Civil War* (New York: Harper and Row, 1986). Francis B. Heitman, *Historical Register and Dictionary of the United States Army* (2 vols., Washington: GPO, 1903; rpt., Urbana: University of Illinois Press, 1965). Joseph Milton Nance, ed., *Mier Expedition Diary: A Texas Prisoner's Account by Joseph D. McCutchan* (Austin: University of Texas Press, 1978). Jon L. Wakelyn, *Biographical Dictionary of the Confederacy* (Westport, Connecticut: Greenwood, 1977). Ezra J. Warner, *Generals in Gray* (Baton Rouge: Louisiana State University Press, 1959).
Thomas W. Cutrer

CRITZ, RICHARD (1877–1959). Richard Critz, lawyer and judge, was born in Starkville, Mississippi, on October 16, 1877, the son of George Edward and Ella (Richards) Critz. When he was fourteen the family moved to Williamson County, Texas, where Critz went to school. He attended Southwestern University for a short time, then studied law in a Georgetown law office while teaching in the local public schools. He was admitted to the bar in 1902 and practiced until 1910 at Granger, where he also served for some years as city attorney. He returned in 1910 to Georgetown to become county judge, a post he held until 1918, after which he continued to practice there until 1927. Around 1920 Critz assisted the young Georgetown district attorney, Daniel James Moody, Jr.,qv in his prosecution of sundry local members of the Ku Klux Klan.qv When Moody became governor in 1927 he appointed Critz to the Commission of Appeals to the state Supreme Court, on which Critz remained until elevated in 1935 to associate justice of the Supreme Court by appointment of Governor James Allred.qv Critz's judicial opinions are noteworthy for unusual conciseness and clarity, as well as for their logic and numerical abundance. He helped establish a judicial pattern for regulating the oil industry and was influential in the development of the substantial-evidence rule. He was defeated for renomination in the Democratic primary of 1944 and left the bench at the end of the year to practice law as a member of an Austin firm. On January 18, 1906, Critz married Nora Lamb of Granger; they had two sons and two daughters. Justice Critz was a Democrat and a Methodist. He died on April 1, 1959, and was buried in Capital Memorial Gardens, Austin.
BIBLIOGRAPHY: Sam Hanna Acheson, Herbert P. Gambrell, Mary Carter Toomey, and Alex M. Acheson, Jr., *Texian Who's Who*, Vol. 1 (Dallas: Texian, 1937).
W. St. John Garwood

CROCKERY CREEK. Crockery Creek rises just east of the Hood-Erath county line in northwestern Hood County (at 32°27′ N, 98°02′ W) and runs north for six miles, past the eastern edge of Lipan, to its mouth on Kickapoo Creek, a mile northeast of Lipan (at 32°32′ N, 98°02′ W). The creek traverses an area of steeply sloping terrain surfaced with shallow sandy soils that support juniper and scattered oak trees, as well as various grasses. The vicinity has generally been used as rangeland.

CROCKET, GEORGE LOUIS (1861–1936). George Louis Crocket, minister and historian, was born on June 3, 1861, at San Augustine,

Texas, the son of George L. and Louisa Alexander (Sharp) Crocket. He received degrees of B.Litt. and B.D. from the University of the South and the Theological Seminary, Sewanee, Tennessee, in 1886. He was ordained a deacon of the Protestant Episcopal Church[qv] in 1886 and served as rector of Christ Church, San Augustine, Texas, from 1887 to 1929. Crocket founded Christ Church, Nacogdoches, and St. Cyprian's Church, Lufkin. After retiring from the active ministry in 1929, he was professor of history emeritus and dean of students at Stephen F. Austin State Teachers College, Nacogdoches (now Stephen F. Austin State University). Crocket's pursuit of historical studies was a lifelong avocation. In 1932 he published *Two Centuries in East Texas*, the chief product of his labors in Texas history. His ink sketches of early Texas educational institutions are preserved in the Barker Texas History Center,[qv] University of Texas at Austin. His original maps and charts, along with his collection of other historical materials, were bequeathed to the college at Nacogdoches. At the time of his death on January 3, 1936, Crocket was president of the East Texas Historical Society.[qv]

BIBLIOGRAPHY: Robert Bruce Blake, *Historic Nacogdoches* (Nacogdoches, Texas: Nacogdoches Historical Society, 1939). Geo. L. Crocket, *Memories and Visions: An Address Delivered at the Commencement of the San Augustine Public School, June 5th, 1906* (Houston: Coyle, 1906). Vertical Files, Barker Texas History Center, University of Texas at Austin (G. L. Crockett).

Rose Sharp Brewer

CROCKETT, DAVID (1786–1836). David (Davy) Crockett, frontiersman, congressman, and defender of the Alamo,[qv] son of John and Rebecca (Hawkins) Crockett, was born in Greene County, East Tennessee, on August 17, 1786. In 1798, two years after the Crocketts opened a tavern on the road from Knoxville to Abingdon, Virginia, John Crockett hired his son out to Jacob Siler to help drive a herd of cattle to Rockbridge County, Virginia. Siler tried to detain David by force after the job was completed, but the boy escaped at night by walking seven miles in two hours through knee-deep snow. He eventually made his way home in late 1798 or early 1799. Soon afterward he started school, but preferred playing hooky and ran away to escape his father's punishment. This "strategic withdrawal," as Crockett called it, lasted 2½ years while he worked as a wagoner and day-laborer and at odd jobs to support himself. When he returned home in 1802 he had grown so much that his family did not recognize him at first. When they did, he found that all was forgiven. Crockett reciprocated their generosity by working for about a year to discharge his father's debts, which totaled seventy-six dollars, and subsequently returned to school for six months.

On October 21, 1805, Crockett took out a license to marry Margaret Elder of Dandridge, Tennessee, but was jilted by her, perhaps justly, since local legend intimated that he was a less than constant suitor. He recovered quickly from the experience, courted Mary (Polly) Finley, and married her on August 14, 1806, in Jefferson County; they remained in the mountains of East Tennessee for just over five years. Sometime after September 11, 1811, David, Polly, and their two sons, John Wesley and William, settled on the Mulberry Fork of Elk River in Lincoln County, Tennessee; they moved again in 1813, to the Rattlesnake Spring branch of Bean's Creek in Franklin County, Tennessee, near what is now the Alabama border. Crockett named his homestead Kentuck.

He began his military career in September of that year, when he enlisted in the militia as a scout under Major Gibson in Winchester, Tennessee, to avenge an Indian attack on Fort Mimms, Alabama. On November 3, under Andrew Jackson, Crockett participated in the retributive massacre of the Indian town of Tallussahatchee. He returned home when his ninety-day enlistment for the Creek Indian War expired on the day before Christmas, and reenlisted on September 28, 1814, as a third sergeant in Capt. John Cowan's company. He arrived on November 7, the day after Jackson took Pensacola, and spent his time trying to ferret out the British-trained Indians from the Florida swamps. After his discharge in 1815 as a fourth sergeant Crockett arrived home and found himself again a father. Polly died the summer after Margaret's birth, although she had been in good health when David returned.

On May 21, 1815, Crockett was elected a lieutenant in the Thirty-second Militia regiment of Franklin County. Before summer's end he married Elizabeth Patton, a widow with two children (George and Margaret Ann), and he explored Alabama in the fall with an eye towards settlement. He nearly died from malaria—was reported dead—and astonished his family with his "resurrection." By about September of the next year the Crocketts had moved to the territory soon to become Lawrence County, Tennessee, rather than Alabama. They settled at the head of Shoal Creek, and David continued his political and military career. He became a justice of the peace on November 17, 1817, a post he resigned in 1819. He became the town commissioner of Lawrenceburg before April 1, 1818, and was elected colonel of the Fifty-seventh Militia regiment in the county that same year.

New Year's Day 1821 marked a turning point in Crockett's career. He resigned as commissioner to run for a seat in the Tennessee legislature as the representative of Lawrence and Hickman counties. He won the August election and, from the beginning, took an active interest in public land policy regarding the West. After the session concluded he moved his family to what is now Gibson County in West Tennessee. He was reelected in 1823, defeating Dr. William E. Butler, but was in turn defeated in August 1825 in his first bid for a seat in Congress. In 1826, after returning to private business, Crockett nearly died when his boats carrying barrel staves were wrecked in the Mississippi River. When he was brought to Memphis he was encouraged to run again for Congress by Maj. M. B. Winchester and won election over Gen. William Arnold and Col. Adam Alexander to the United States House of Representatives in 1827. He was reelected to a second term in 1829 and split with President Andrew Jackson and the Tennessee delegation on several issues, including land reform and the Indian removal bill. In his 1831 campaign for a third term, Crockett openly and vehemently attacked Jackson's policies and was defeated in a close election by William Fitzgerald.

By this time Crockett's reputation as a sharpshooter, hunter, and yarn-spinner had brought him into national prominence. He was the model for Nimrod Wildfire, the hero of James Kirke Paulding's play *The Lion of the West*, which opened in New York City on April 25, 1831. *Life and Adventures of Colonel David Crockett of West Tennessee* was published in 1833 and reprinted the same year under the more accurate title of *Sketches and Eccentricities of Colonel David Crockett of West Tennessee*. Much of the same material spilled over into the first few issues of a series of comic almanacs published under Crockett's name from 1835 to 1856 that, as a whole, constituted a body of outrageous tall tales about the adventures of the legendary Davy rather than the historical David Crockett.

Building in part upon his growing notoriety, Crockett defeated the incumbent Fitzgerald in 1833 to return to Congress. The following year he published his autobiography, written with the help of Thomas Chilton, *A Narrative of the Life of David Crockett of the State of Tennessee*, the only work that he actually authored. It was intended to correct the portrayal given by Mathew St. Clair Clarke in *Sketches and Eccentricities* and to deny Crockett's authorship of that account, which did not bear Clarke's name. The *Narrative* was also a campaign biography of sorts, for Whig politicians were touting Crockett as an anti-Jackson candidate for the presidency in 1836. On April 25, 1834, he began a three-week triumphal tour of the eastern states, and his "campaign swing" was recorded in the first of two Whig books published the next year under his name, *An Account of Colonel Crockett's Tour to the North and Down East*. The second, a negative *Life of Martin Van Buren*, was issued less than three months later.

Crockett apparently thought himself a serious candidate, but he was likely only a convenient political tool to the Whigs, an independent frontiersman with a national reputation perhaps the equal of Jackson's who opposed Jackson on key political issues. The point became academic, however, when Crockett lost his 1835 congressional campaign to Adam Huntsman, a peg-legged lawyer supported by Jackson and by Governor Carroll of Tennessee, by 252 votes.

Disenchanted with the political process and his former constituents, Crockett decided to do what he had threatened to do—to explore Texas and to move his family there if the prospects were pleasing. On November 1, 1835, with William Patton, Abner Burgin, and Lindsey K. Tinkle, he set out to the West, as he wrote on the eve of his departure, "to explore the Texes well before I return." At this point he had no intention of joining the fight for Texas independence.

The foursome reached Memphis the first evening and, in company with some friends congregated in the bar of the Union Hotel for a farewell drinking party, Crockett offered his now famous remark: "Since you have chosen to elect a man with a timber toe to succeed me, you may all go to hell and I will go to Texas." They set off the next day. Their route was down the Mississippi River to the Arkansas and then up that river to Little Rock; overland to Fulton, Arkansas, and up the Red River along the northern boundary of Texas; across the Red River, through Clarksville, to Nacogdoches and San Augustine; and on to San Antonio.

At San Augustine the party evidently divided. Burgin and Tinkle went home; Crockett and Patton signed the oath of allegiance, but only after Crockett insisted upon the insertion of the word "republican" in the document. They thus swore their allegiance to the "Provisional Government[qv] of Texas or any future republican Government that may be hereafter declared." Crockett had balked at the possibility that he would be obliged to support some future government that might prove despotic.

That Texas had changed his plans was indisputable. His last extant letter, written on January 9, 1836, was quite clear:

"I must say as to what I have seen of Texas it is the garden spot of the world. The best land and the best prospects for health I ever saw, and I do believe it is a fortune to any man to come here. There is a world of country here to settle.... I have taken the oath of government and have enrolled my name as a volunteer and will set out for the Rio Grand in a few days with the volunteers from the United States. But all volunteers is entitled to vote for a member of the convention or to be voted for, and I have but little doubt of being elected a member to form a constitution for this province. I am rejoiced at my fate. I had rather be in my present situation than to be elected to a seat in Congress for life. I am in hopes of making a fortune yet for myself and family, bad as my prospect has been."

Government service in Texas would rejuvenate his political career and, as he stated elsewhere, provide the source of the affluence he had unsuccessfully sought all his life. He intended to become land agent for the new territory.

In early February Crockett arrived at San Antonio de Béxar; Antonio López de Santa Anna[qv] arrived on February 20. On the one hand Crockett was still fighting Jackson. The Americans in Texas were split into two political factions that divided roughly into those supporting a conservative Whig philosophy and those supporting the administration. Crockett chose to join Col. William B. Travis,[qv] who had deliberately disregarded Sam Houston's[qv] orders to withdraw from the Alamo, rather than support Houston, a Jackson sympathizer. What was more, he saw the future of an independent Texas as his future, and he loved a good fight.

Crockett died in battle of the Alamo[qv] on March 6, 1836. The manner of his death was uncertain, however, until the publication in 1975 of the diary of Lt. José Enrique de la Peña. Susanna Dickinson,[qv] wife of Almaron Dickinson,[qv] an officer at the Alamo, said Crockett died on the outside, one of the earliest to fall. Joe,[qv] Travis's slave and the only male Texan to survive the battle, reported seeing Crockett lying dead with slain Mexicans around him and stated that only one man, named Warner, surrendered to the Mexicans (Warner was

David Crockett, by John Gadsby Chapman. Oil on canvas. 24½″ × 16½″. Courtesy HRHRC, University of Texas at Austin. This painting is a copy of a life-sized portrait executed by Chapman in 1834 and since lost in a fire at the Texas Capitol. It features Crockett as his legend portrays him, with his rifle and coonskin cap.

taken to Santa Anna and promptly shot). When Peña's eyewitness account was placed together with other corroborating documents, Crockett's central part in the defense became clear. Travis had previously written that during the first bombardment Crockett was everywhere in the Alamo "animating the men to do their duty." Other reports told of the deadly fire of his rifle that killed five Mexican gunners in succession, as they each attempted to fire a cannon bearing on the fort, and that he may have just missed Santa Anna, who thought himself out of range of all the defenders' rifles. Crockett and five or six others were captured when the Mexican troops took the Alamo at about six o'clock that morning, even though Santa Anna had ordered that no prisoners be taken. The general, infuriated when some of his officers brought the Americans before him to try to intercede for their lives, ordered them executed immediately. They were bayoneted and then shot. Crockett's reputation and that of the other survivors was not, as some have suggested, sullied by their capture. Their dignity and bravery was, in fact, further underscored by Peña's recounting that "these unfortunates died without complaining and without humiliating themselves before their torturers."

Coincidentally, a work mostly of fiction masquerading as fact had put the truth of Crockett's death before the American public in the summer of 1836. Despite its many falsifications and plagiarisms, Richard Penn Smith's *Col. Crockett's Exploits and Adventures in Texas . . . Written by Himself* had a reasonably accurate account of Crockett's capture and execution. Many thought the legendary Davy deserved better, and they provided it, from thrilling tales of his clubbing Mexicans with his empty rifle and holding his section of the wall of the Alamo until cut down by bullets and bayonets, to his survival as a slave in a Mexican salt mine.

In the final analysis, however, no matter how fascinating or outrageous the fabrications were that gathered around him, the historical David Crockett proved a formidable hero in his own right and succeeded Daniel Boone as the rough-hewn representative of frontier independence and virtue. In this regard, the motto he adopted and made famous epitomized his spirit: "Be always sure you're right—then go a-head!"

BIBLIOGRAPHY: James Wakefield Burke, *David Crockett* (Austin: Eakin Press, 1984). Richard Boyd Hauck, *Crockett: A Bio-Bibliography* (Westport, Connecticut: Greenwood, 1982). Dan Kilgore, *How Did Davy Die?* (College Station: Texas A&M University Press, 1978). Michael A. Lofaro, ed., *Davy Crockett* (Knoxville: University of Tennessee Press, 1985). James A. Shackford, *David Crockett: The Man and the Legend* (Chapel Hill: University of North Carolina Press, 1956).

Michael A. Lofaro

CROCKETT, JOHN McCLANNAHAN (1816–1887). John McClannahan Crockett, second mayor of Dallas, state representative, and lieutenant governor of Texas, son of Robert McClannahan and Elizabeth (White) Crockett, was born in Lancaster, South Carolina, on December 26, 1816. His father was a South Carolina state representative, and his grandfather, Robert Crockett, was a Revolutionary War soldier. He attended Franklin Academy in Lancaster, entered the mercantile business in Camden, South Carolina, moved to Obion County, Tennessee, in 1836 as a partner in a general store, and there married Catherine W. Polk on March 17, 1837. He began reading law in 1841 and received a license to practice in 1844.

In 1847 he traveled with his wife to Paris, Texas, where they stayed for several months while Crockett worked as a bookkeeper and played his violin at village and country parties. They moved the next year to Dallas, where John's brother-in-law, William H. Hord,[qv] was county judge. Crockett opened a law practice and served as deputy county clerk his first year in Dallas. In 1850 he was appointed commissioner of the Mercer colony.[qv] He was elected state representative from the Dallas area in 1851. In 1852 he joined John H. Reagan[qv] and another man in investigating Peters colony[qv] troubles. He participated in many court trials and was a law partner of John Jay Good[qv] in Dallas in the early 1850s. He was first master of Tannehill Masonic Lodge in Dallas, chartered on June 24, 1850. He was elected mayor of Dallas in 1857 and served three terms. He was meteorological observer in Dallas for the Smithsonian Institution in 1859. In 1861 he was elected lieutenant governor of Texas. In 1863 he decided not to stand for reelection and declined to enter the race for governor, although he had a supportive constituency. Instead, he returned to the Dallas area to become superintendent of the Confederate arms factory at Lancaster (see LANCASTER, TEXAS). Crockett was an incorporator of Dallas Grain, Elevator, and Flouring Company in 1872 and a charter member of the executive committee of the Dallas Pioneers Association in 1875. He and his wife had no children. He died at their farm near Dallas on August 4, 1887, and he and Catherine are buried in the Old Masonic Cemetery in Dallas.

BIBLIOGRAPHY: Dallas *Morning News*, January 25, 1928. George Jackson, *Sixty Years in Texas* (Dallas: Wilkinson Printing, 1908; rpt., Quanah, Texas: Nortex, 1975). *Memorial and Biographical History of Dallas County* (Chicago: Lewis, 1892; rpt., Dallas: Walsworth, 1976). William S. Speer and John H. Brown, eds., *Encyclopedia of the New West* (Marshall, Texas: United States Biographical Publishing, 1881; rpt., Easley, South Carolina: Southern Historical Press, 1978).

John Alan Hord

CROCKETT, TEXAS. Crockett, the county seat and largest community in Houston County, is at the junction of U.S. Highway 287 and State highways 7, 19, and 21 in the central part of the county. When Houston County was established in 1837, Andrew Edwards Gossett,[qv] an early settler from Tennessee, donated land for the county seat. Gossett and his father, Elijah Gossett,[qv] named the settlement for David Crockett,[qv] a former neighbor in Tennessee. Crockett is said to have camped near the townsite in January 1836 on his way to San Antonio. County officials chose the site because of its proximity to the Old San Antonio Road.[qv] The town was incorporated on December 29, 1837, and a post office opened there on March 31, 1838. During the early years mail was delivered twice a month, and a stagecoach ran at intervals from Nacogdoches. In 1839 raids by the Alabama-Coushatta and Cherokee Indians forced the town's residents to take shelter in the fortified log courthouse. Several early schools operated in the vicinity of Crockett, among them Crockett Academy, built a half mile east of the courthouse about 1855. Several early newspapers were published in the town, including the Crockett *Printer*, begun in 1853 by Oscar Dalton, and the Crockett *Argus*, first published in 1857.

During the Civil War[qv] Crockett served as a mustering point and training center for Confederate forces. In 1865 the courthouse and most of the town burned, so that most of the county's early records were lost. In 1872 the Houston and Great Northern Railroad was built through Crockett, thus assuring its place as a regional trading center and spurring the growth of the lumber industry[qv] in the region. By 1885 the town had a bank, a hotel, an opera house, and several schools; Baptist, Methodist, and Presbyterian churches; a weekly newspaper, the Texas *Patron*; and an estimated population of 1,200. A school for black girls, later known as Mary Allen Junior College, opened in Crockett in 1886. In 1904 a lignite mine was opened just south of the town and at its height around 1910 produced twenty-five carloads a day. Wildcatting for oil began around the same time, but local oil was not produced commercially until 1934. Although the decline of the timber industry after World War I[qv] affected the economy of county, Crockett continued to prosper during the 1920s and 1930s, reaching a population of 3,063 in 1925 and 4,441 in 1936, when it had twenty-one businesses.

After World War II[qv] Crockett grew steadily; it topped the 5,000 mark in the early 1960s and reached 7,000 during the 1980s. In 1990 the town had a population of 7,024 and 180 rated businesses. The local economy was based on agriculture and the production of furniture, plastics, chemicals, and clothing. Attractions in Crockett include its many old homes, a Fiddlers Festival in June, and a rodeo in July.

BIBLIOGRAPHY: Armistead Albert Aldrich, *The History of Houston County, Texas* (San Antonio: Naylor, 1943). Houston County Historical Commission, *History of Houston County, Texas, 1687–1979* (Tulsa, Oklahoma: Heritage, 1979). *Houston County Cemeteries* (Crockett, Texas: Houston County Historical Commission, 1977; 3d ed. 1987).

Eliza H. Bishop and Christopher Long

CROCKETT COUNTY. Crockett County (J-10) is located in southwestern Texas on the western edge of the Edwards Plateau.[qv] It is bounded on the west by the Pecos River, which separates it from Terrell and Pecos counties. Its northern border is formed by Crane, Upton, Reagan, and Irion counties, while Schleicher and Sutton counties border it on the east and Val Verde County on the south. Ozona, the county seat and only town, is located eighty-two miles southwest of San Angelo. The center point of the county is at 30°41′ north latitude and 101°21′ west longitude. Crockett County comprises 2,806 square miles. The terrain consists of deep, narrow, steep-walled canyons and flat mesas in the southern and western areas. Broad valleys and flat divides characterize the northern part. The northeastern part is a large flat divide separating the Colorado River and Rio Grande basins. The surface geology is Cretaceous. The soils are dark, calcareous, stony clays and clay loams. The western half of the county is desert shrub savanna, and the eastern half is juniper, oak, and mesquite savanna. Altitudes vary from 1,500 feet above sea level in the southwest to 2,800 feet above sea level in the northwest. Temperatures vary from an average low of 32° F in January to an average high of 96° in July. The average rainfall is eighteen inches per year. The growing season extends across 233 days. Numerous draws, dry most of the year, drain the county during floods and empty into the Devils and Pecos rivers. Johnsons Run and Howard Draw bisect the central area before reaching the Devils and the Pecos, respectively, in Val Verde County. Live Oak Creek runs to the south from the northwest and enters the Pecos at Lancaster Hill. The dry bed of Spring Creek originates in the northeastern corner of the county and extends northeast to the Middle Concho River.

Early important sources of water for prehistoric people and early travelers were Live Oak Spring and Cedar Springs, which once provided strong flows in western Crockett County. Among the first people to take water from the springs were the early inhabitants of Gobbler Shelter, located on a small tributary canyon of Live Oak Creek. Prehistoric people lived over long periods of time in the shelter, where they left artifacts. Spaniards first passed through the area of Crockett County in 1590, when Gaspar Castaño de Sosa^{qv} brought the first Europeans through the isolated canyonland. Castaño led a mining expedition from Monclova, Chihuahua, to the northern New Mexico pueblo of Santo Domingo. His party of 170 men, women, and children is thought to have traveled up Johnsons Run and crossed the western section of the future Crockett County to reach the Pecos River. On May 22, 1684, Juan Domínguez de Mendoza^{qv} and his expedition crossed the Pecos River and camped at a site Domínguez called San Pantaleón now in Crockett County. At that time several Indian tribes lived in the area, among them Lipan Apaches and Tonkawas. Comanches drifted into the area during the eighteenth century, displacing earlier inhabitants.

John Coffee Hays^{qv} led an expedition through the county in 1849, charting waterholes for a freighting and stagecoach route from San Antonio to El Paso. In 1852 Col. Joseph Mansfield of the United States Army inspected the road from El Paso to San Antonio. After determining that travelers along the route needed more military protection against Indian attacks, he recommended establishing a new post on Live Oak Creek just above its juncture with the Pecos River. In response to Mansfield's recommendation, Fort Lancaster was founded on the east bank of Live Oak Creek August 20, 1855. When Texas seceded from the Union less than six years later, the fort was abandoned. A small Confederate unit held it for a short time, but soon left it. After the war the former fort was used only as a subpost. After 1874 it fell into complete decay. Following the Civil War,^{qv} Anglo-Americans moved into the frontier region and took up the unoccupied lands, but Indian depredations discouraged settlement until the United States sent troops to the frontier posts. The Texas legislature provided three battalions of rangers for protection of the area in September 1866. Another subpost, Camp Melvin, was established in 1868 at the river crossing where Domínguez de Mendoza had camped. A post office opened on November 2, 1868, under the name Pecos Station, but the designation was changed to Camp Melvin in December 1868. Although the post office closed in 1870, the subpost operated until 1871. Camp Melvin was important as a stage crossing and mail station, rather than a military installation.

On January 12, 1875, Crockett County, named for David Crockett^{qv} of Alamo^{qv} fame, was formed from Bexar County and attached to Kinney County for judicial purposes. It included the future Sutton and Schleicher counties and parts of the future Val Verde, Kinney, and Edwards counties. From the earliest settlement the economy was dependent on sheep and cattle ranching. In 1880 Crockett County reported fifteen farms, valued together at more than $44,500. Livestock consisted mostly of beef cattle, sheep, and hogs, which were in the aggregate worth $14,500. The county that year had 127 white residents, of whom eight were foreign-born. With the threat of Indian attack past in the 1880s, sheep and cattle ranchers were enticed to the new county by cheap grassland available for lease from both the railroad and the state. Among the first settlers was W. P. Hoover. The Hoovers located on the Pecos River near Cedar Springs and above the mouth of Howard Canyon in 1881. There they leased railroad land at five cents an acre. In 1885 Val Verde County was organized and Crockett County became a subsidiary of it. Two years later, on March 15, 1887, Crockett County was reduced to its present size when Sutton and Schleicher counties were cut away. Even with less territory in 1890, the county noted an increase in the number of farms to twenty-three. The mostly owner-operated ranches reported livestock valued at more than $222,000. Sheep numbered more than 35,000 and cattle more than 22,000. By 1890 the population increased to 194, still all white. Thirty-two were foreign-born.

Several short-lived communities formed in Crockett County in the 1880s and 1890s. Mobile ran a post office during 1880 and 1881, while Wight managed one from 1880 through 1883. Bullisford was a post office from February through September 1882. A post office was established in Ellis in 1885, but it was later moved to Edwards County. Emerald was located eight miles east of Ozona, where a post office opened in 1890 and the first school in the county was built in 1891. Hembrie, in northwestern Crockett County, maintained a post office from 1890 to 1911 and a school some of those years. Hinde, also in the northwestern part of the county, had a post office from 1891 to 1906 and ran a school until 1902. Mozart had a post office for the first ten months of 1899.

Crockett County was organized on July 7, 1891, when an election was held at Couch Well, or Eureka, to choose the county seat from three contending communities. The election was inconclusive, but Ozona, where E. M. Powell had already drilled a prolific water well and donated land for public buildings, became the county seat by the end of the year as the other communities failed to develop. The new county seat grew slowly for the first decade. In 1891 it received a post office and Mrs. J. W. Odom organized a union Sunday school. The same year the first school opened. A frame courthouse was built by the end of the year. A Baptist church was organized in 1892 and a Church of Christ in 1895. In 1899 a hotel opened. In 1900 stagecoach service began.

In the presidential election of 1892 the newly organized county gave 178 votes to the Democrat, Grover Cleveland, and 16 votes to the third party, but none to the incumbent Republican president, Benjamin Harrison. In the 1896 and 1900 elections voters turned to the Republican candidate, William McKinley. No results are available for 1904, but from 1908 through 1920 the county returned to the Democratic column. In 1924 and 1928 the Republican candidates again won the county. Voters returned to the Democratic fold in 1932 and supported Franklin D. Roosevelt and Harry Truman through the 1948 election. In 1952 and 1956, when the war hero and Republican candidate Dwight D. Eisenhower^{qv} won the presidency by large margins, Crockett County voters also gave him decided victories. They narrowly supported Republican candidate Richard Nixon in 1960. Lyndon B. Johnson^{qv} won the county in 1964, as did Hubert Humphrey in 1968, when George Wallace, the American Independent candidate, received 279 votes. When the Democratic party^{qv} swayed too far to the left for Crockett County residents in 1972, they gave their votes to Republican candidate Nixon. In 1976, after the Watergate scandal, Democrat James E. Carter won the county by two votes. From 1980 through 1988 the county voted Republican. In the 1992 election Democratic candidate William J. Clinton barely won the county with 653 votes to George Bush's 623 and H. Ross Perot's 368.

In 1900 Crockett County reported seven manufacturing establishments, which employed seven people and paid more than $3,700 in wages for the manufacture of $15,300 worth of products. By 1920 nine manufacturers employed twenty-one workers at a total wage of $42,500 and produced more than $93,600 in goods. Throughout the 1940s only one manufacturer was in business. In 1950 two producers were reported, but throughout the 1960s and 1970s that number was again reduced to one. In 1982 three manufacturers reported production valued at $100,000. In 1987, 1 percent of the population was employed in manufacturing, 26 percent in wholesale and retail trade, and 13 percent in professional services.

In 1900 the population had grown to 1,591, of whom eight were black and 90 were foreign-born. The eighty-five farms comprised 1.7 million acres and declared a worth of almost $4.4 million. Most ranches were operated by owners, who worked almost 121,000 cattle and 91,000 sheep. By the 1910 census the number of sheep climbed to almost 110,000 and the number of goats increased to nearly 9,000, while the number of cattle slipped to just under 45,000. These figures marked the deterioration of the range through overgrazing and the effects of droughts.[qv] In 1910 the number of farms had declined to seventy-nine and the acreage to 1.3 million acres, but the value of ranches had increased to $6.6 million. Foreign-born residents, mostly from Mexico, numbered 284 of the total population of 1,296. African Americans[qv] numbered 4, and the 550 females constituted less than one-half the total. In 1920 the population was 1,500. Agriculture prospered again by that year, when ninety-nine farms, worth more than $16.8 million, were in operation. Sheep, at almost 156,000, far outnumbered all other livestock and illustrated a continued shift in livestock production from cattle to sheep ranching.[qv]

On May 30, 1925, oil was discovered on L. P. Powell's ranch in north central Crockett County. Though many ranchers sold mineral leases to oil companies for large sums of cash, oil companies exerted no other overt influence on the economy or politics of the county in the 1920s; no oil boom occurred, and no oil companies opened offices in the county, mainly because of the lack of railroads and highways. Exploration in the 1930s and 1940s, however, brought good oil and gas production in several fields, including the prolific Todd Ellenburger field, opened in 1945. Over the decades oil companies paid large royalties to Crockett County mineral owners, and that wealth contributed to the independence and maverick spirit maintained in the county into the 1990s. Oil brought a rise in county population to 2,590 by 1930. Included in that number were 713 Hispanics and 40 blacks. Only 5 residents claimed to be foreign-born. Although oil money eased the lives of ranchers, the raising of livestock continued to dominate the economy. Ranches numbered 134, and most ranchers now hired managers to supervise operations. The number of cattle dropped by 1930 to fewer than 33,500, but sheep increased by more than 300,000 to almost 460,000 head and continued to outnumber all other livestock by far. In 1940 more than 18,000 cattle were reported and sheep declined to slightly more than 390,000. The value of ranches moved upward to $13.5 million, but most were again managed by their owners. The population of the county in 1940 was 2,809, of whom 191 were foreign-born and 115 were black. In 1950 county residents numbered 3,981. Approximately 10 percent (380) were high school graduates and 3 percent (110) were college graduates. During the 1950s sheep and goats exceeded 515,000, more than three times the number of cattle. By 1954 livestock in the county was valued at almost $3.2 million and the number of ranches had grown to 147, mostly owner-operated. In 1959 the number of farms had declined to 123 as livestock values had risen to almost $3.6 million. A decade later the value of livestock reached more than $6.2 million, and the number of farms reached an all-time high of 169. Slightly more than 43 percent of the owners lived on their farms. The 1960 population of 4,209 included 126 nonwhite residents and 2,045 women. By 1970 the population of Crockett County had decreased slightly to 3,885, including 60 blacks. High school graduates made up 47.8 percent and college graduates 7.3 percent of the population.

The 1980 population of 4,608 was 44.5 percent Hispanic and less than 1.2 percent black. In 1982 the value of livestock was almost $13 million, and the number of farms was 154. In 1985 nearly 93 percent of the land was taken up by ranches and farms; less than 1 percent was cropland. Livestock, mostly sheep, Angora goats, and beef cattle, made up 93 percent of the county's farm and ranch economy. Also in the 1980s, the county reported 725 miles of public roads, more than 4,000 registered vehicles, a branch line for rail freight, 38 registered aircraft, and a municipal airport. The nine churches of the county served a membership of about 4,300 people. The largest communions were Catholic, Southern Baptist, and United Methodist. In the 1980s the county had one school district with four schools and 1,000 students. By 1990 the population of Crockett County had declined slightly to 4,078, of whom 2,021 were Hispanic and 39 were black. Ozona had 3,181 residents. In the early 1990s the ranching economy continued, strongly supplemented by oil and gas. Hunting leases and tourism also contributed to the economy. The county faced environmental problems of overgrazing, undesirable brush and weeds, water shortages, and water erosion on its range.

BIBLIOGRAPHY: Crockett County Historical Society, *History of Crockett County* (San Angelo: Anchor, 1976). *Julia Cauble Smith*

CROCKETT CREEK. Crockett Creek rises three miles east of Stephenville in central Erath County (at 32°12′ N, 98°07′ W) and runs northeast for six miles to its mouth on Indian Camp Creek (at 32°17′ N, 98°05′ W). The surrounding land is flat to rolling, with local escarpments and a surface of deep, fine sandy loam that supports post oak and various short grasses.

CROCKETT STATE SCHOOL. In 1927 the Texas legislature authorized the state Board of Control[qv] to establish a correctional facility for delinquent black girls. Not until 1945, however, did the legislature appropriate funds for such a facility. In August 1946 the Board of Control entered into a lease agreement with the federal government for use of the former prisoner of war camp near Brady, McCulloch County. Brady State School for Negro Girls opened to students in February 1947. By the end of August 1947 forty-eight girls had been admitted. Before the establishment of the Brady school, there was no facility in the state that would admit delinquent black girls.

When the school came under the direction of the State Youth Development Council in 1949, some improvements to the Brady site had been made, but the expense of operating a small school in a facility designed for several thousand prisoners prompted the council to seek a more suitable location. In 1950, in an effort to cut expenses and to be near a larger black population, the school was moved to a 125-acre farm near Crockett in Houston County. Crockett State School for Girls, which was called the Colored Girls Training School at Crockett until the institution was integrated in 1966, was placed under the administration of the Texas Youth Council in 1957. In addition to academic courses, the educational program included sewing, housekeeping, child care, and cooking, as well as vocational courses in cosmetology and janitorial work. The school had an enrollment of 209 in 1972 but closed in 1973. Its name was changed to Crockett State Home on December 13, 1973, and the facility was used as a home and educational center for dependent and neglected children until 1975.

In 1975 Crockett State School reopened as a correctional institution for boys and had a capacity of about a hundred students. Its accredited education program included academic courses and work in horticulture, auto mechanics, and shop. In the late 1980s the legislature appropriated funds to expand the facility in order to provide relief for overcrowded conditions at other schools. Crockett State School had an enrollment of 148 in June 1991.

BIBLIOGRAPHY: Emma L. M. Jackson, *Petticoat Politics: Political Activism among Texas Women in the 1920's* (Ph.D. dissertation, University of Texas at Austin, 1980). Texas Youth Council, *Report to the Governor*, Austin, 1949–. *Vivian Elizabeth Smyrl*

CROIX, TEODORO DE (1730–1792). Teodoro de Croix, soldier and government official in New Spain, was born in Prévoté castle near Lille, France, on June 20, 1730. He entered the Spanish army at age seventeen and was sent to Italy as an ensign of grenadiers of the Royal Guard. In 1750 he transferred to the Walloon Guards, bodyguards of the Bourbon kings of Spain. He was promoted to the rank of lieutenant in 1756 and was decorated in Flanders with the Cross of the Teutonic Order, which gave him the title of caballero. In 1760 Caballero de Croix was made a colonel in the Walloon Guards. In 1766, when his uncle Francisco, Marqués de Croix, went to New Spain as viceroy, Teodoro accompanied him as captain of the viceregal guard. The viceroy shortly appointed him governor of Acapulco. He became inspector of troops for New Spain with the rank of brigadier in December of that year and served in that capacity until 1770. The next year the Marqués de Croix ended his term as viceroy, and Teodoro sailed with him for Spain in company with José Bernardo de Gálvez Gallardo,[qv] who was retiring as inspector general. Poor sailing weather held up the voyage for five months in Havana. Thus Gálvez's young nephew, Bernardo de Gálvez,[qv] fresh from his first frontier command in Chihuahua, was able to overtake him and join the group for the rest of the voyage.

Croix's career undoubtedly benefited not only from his uncle's status but also from the close alliance of the Gálvez and Croix families. The subsequent careers of both the two older men and their nephews—which followed a well-planned course—testify, if not to a Croix-Gálvez power scheme, at least to their tremendous influence at court. While the elder Croix became commandant-general of the Spanish Army, José de Gálvez advanced to the important post of minister of the Indies. Don José thus was able to implement his recommendation for separating New Spain's northern provinces form the viceroyalty to deal more effectively with the Indian problem. Teodoro de Croix was named commandant general of the new Provincias Internas[qv] jurisdiction and assumed his duties on January 1, 1777, the same date that Bernardo de Gálvez became acting governor of Louisiana.

As commandant general Croix found himself facing the animus of the reigning viceroy, Antonio María de Bucareli y Ursúa,[qv] who had been deprived of a portion of his jurisdiction. Croix saw little improvement in frontier conditions from the work of Hugo Oconór,[qv] a Bucareli appointee, who had undertaken a reshuffling of presidios to establish a new defense line to conform with the Royal Regulations of 1772 (see NEW REGULATIONS FOR PRESIDIOS). The staggering toll of Indian depredations all across the frontier convinced him of Oconór's incompetence. Croix faced the necessity of reorganizing the presidial line again. He ultimately returned some of the forts to their original position and buttressed them with a secondary line of fortified towns. In August 1777 Caballero de Croix left Mexico to inspect his jurisdiction. The entourage crossed the Rio Grande near San Juan Bautista[qv] on December 24 and remained in what is now Texas until January 22, 1778. At Monclova, San Antonio, and Chihuahua, Croix convened war councils to discuss with frontier officers the means of confronting the Apache menace that was common to all the Interior Provinces. Out of the juntas came a request for the new governor of Louisiana, Bernardo de Gálvez, to join Croix in the Apache campaign, uniting a Louisiana force to 2,000 troops the commandant general hoped to obtain from the crown. Such plans, which might have enhanced the stature of both men, were doomed by the prospect of Spain's entry into the war that the North American colonists were waging against England.

Croix built up a more extensive military establishment over the entire northern frontier than any that had existed previously, with 4,686 militiamen and presidials under arms from Texas to Sonora. With his departure, however, the bulk of his policy was abandoned. On February 13, 1783, he was promoted to lieutenant general and relieved of his duties to become viceroy of Peru. Two years later his friend Bernardo de Gálvez, having achieved notable successes in the war with England, was appointed viceroy of New Spain to succeed his late father, Matías de Gálvez. If the Croix and Gálvez families had achieved a colonial dynasty, it was short-lived. Bernardo died in office in November 1786. Caballero de Croix served as viceroy of Peru from April 6, 1784, to March 25, 1790. In 1791 he was made a colonel in the king's bodyguard and a commander in the Teutonic Order. He died in Madrid in 1792.

BIBLIOGRAPHY: Herbert Eugene Bolton, ed. and trans., *Athanase de Mézières and the Louisiana-Texas Frontier, 1768–1780* (2 vols., Cleveland: Clark, 1914). H. I. Priestley, *José de Gálvez, Visitor-General of New Spain, 1765–1771* (Berkeley: University of California Press, 1916). Alfred Barnaby Thomas, trans., *Teodoro de Croix and the Northern Frontier of New Spain, 1776–1783* (Norman: University of Oklahoma Press, 1941).

Robert S. Weddle

CROMWELL, CARL G. (1889–1931). Carl G. Cromwell (the Big Swede), oilman, was born to Swedish immigrants John Nels and Hannah (Anderson) Cromwell on January 26, 1889, in Seabrook, Pennsylvania. As the oldest of six children he took an oilfield job at age sixteen to help his family. He worked in major fields in Pennsylvania, Illinois, and Oklahoma and became one of the industry's most knowledgeable drillers. After service with the 358th Infantry at Camp Travis in San Antonio, Texas, during World War I,[qv] he returned to Oklahoma and married Luella Lundsford in 1919. They soon moved to Texas, where Cromwell drilled around Burkburnett, Cisco, and other booming areas.

In mid-1921 Frank T. Pickrell, vice president of Texon Oil and Land Company, contracted with Cromwell to drill on university lands in Reagan County. For almost two years the Cromwells, including a baby daughter, Carlene, lived in a shack on an isolated well site. Cromwell persevered, with only intermittent help from a constantly changing, inexperienced crew. Finally, on May 28, 1923, the famed Santa Rita No. 1 (see SANTA RITA OIL WELL) blew in, and the event heralded great wealth for the University of Texas. Subsequently, Cromwell became drilling superintendent of the Texon Company's rapidly expanding field around the camp of Santa Rita. He also acquired his own leases and became known as an honest, generous, free-spirited wildcatter.

Cromwell, Pickrell, and Clayton W. Williams,[qv] company engineer, experimented in drilling deeper than the average 3,000 feet. On January 20, 1926, Williams located a site and Cromwell's crews began work. In late November 1928, because of mounting expenses and problems, Cromwell was directed to shut down. Instead, he disregarded orders and went into hiding. On December 4, at 8,525 feet, University 1-B, the world's deepest well (until 1931) came in.

Cromwell was also an entrepreneur and aviation[qv] pioneer. He looked to the airplane to replace time-consuming automobile travel and named his first plane the *Miss Carlene*. He established an airport in San Angelo and, on November 1, 1929, inaugurated airline service between that city and Dallas, Fort Worth, and San Antonio. He was director of a San Angelo insurance company. He was also a Lutheran, a Democrat, a Mason, and an American Legionnaire. While on a business trip he was killed in an automobile accident near Sheffield, Pennsylvania, on September 27, 1931.

BIBLIOGRAPHY: Samuel D. Myres, *The Permian Basin: Petroleum Empire of the Southwest* (2 vols., El Paso: Permian, 1973, 1977). Martin W. Schwettmann, *Santa Rita: The University of Texas Oil Discovery* (Austin: Texas State Historical Association, 1943; rpt. 1958).

Jane Spraggins Wilson

CRONEIS, CAREY GARDINER (1901–1972). Carey Gardiner Croneis, geologist, teacher, and university administrator, was born on March 14, 1901, in Bucyrus, Ohio, the son of Frederick William and Nell (Garner) Croneis. He received a B.S. degree from Denison University, Granville, Ohio, in 1922, an M.S. degree from the University of Kansas in 1923, and a Ph.D. from Harvard in 1928. He was an instructor in geology at the University of Kansas (1922–23), the University of Arkansas (1923–25), and Harvard, Radcliffe, and Wellesley (1925–28). He worked on geological surveys in Arkansas, Kansas, and Illinois. In 1928 Croneis went to the University of Chicago, where he was assistant professor of geology, associate professor (1931–41), and professor (1941–44). He organized the geology section of the Chicago Museum of Science and Industry and was curator of paleontology at the Walker Museum, University of Chicago (1928–44). At the Century of Progress World's Fair he was in charge of the geology section (1933) and chief of basic sciences (1934). He produced films on geology for the University of Chicago and the National Park Service.

During World War II[qv] he was a consultant for the National Defense Research Committee and in this capacity helped plan coastal defenses for the Brownsville, Texas, area. He also helped select the proving grounds for the United States Chemical Warfare Service in the Republic of Panama. In 1944 he was named president of Beloit College in Wisconsin. He designed the geology department at Rice University in 1953, and in January 1954 he became the provost there and the first Harry C. Wiess professor of geology. Croneis was named acting president of Rice in 1960; in 1961 he became the university's first chancellor. He maintained a teaching load along with administrative responsibilities and was also involved in Houston civic affairs. He was chairman of the Houston City Charter Committee and is credited with influence in the decision to establish the Manned Spacecraft Center (now the Lyndon B. Johnson Space Center[qv]) near Houston. Croneis was the founding president of the Houston Council on World Affairs, a charter member of the Texas Academy of Science,[qv] and a member of the Centennial Committee of the American Museum of Natural History in New York City. He was editor of Harper and Row's Geoscience Series (from 1941), associate editor of the *Journal of Geology* (1930–45), and author of *Geology of the Arkansas Paleozoic Area* (1930) and numerous scientific articles. He coauthored *Down to Earth* with W. C. Krumbein (1936).

Croneis, a Phi Beta Kappa, was awarded nine honorary doctorates during his career; in 1967 he received the highest honor in professional geology, the Sidney Powers Memorial Medal, from the American Association of Petroleum Geologists, and the same year he was presented a gold medal by the Association of Rice Alumni for distinguished service to the university. He was elected a fellow of the World Academy of Art and Science. In 1970 the American Federation of Mineralogical Societies established in his honor five two-year scholarships for graduate study in earth sciences. Croneis was president of the Philosophical Society of Texas[qv] in 1971. He retired as chancellor emeritus of Rice University on August 31, 1971.

He was married to Grace Williams on September 15, 1923, and they had two daughters. Croneis died in Houston on January 22, 1972, and was cremated. Memorial services were held at Rice Memorial Chapel.

BIBLIOGRAPHY: Houston *Chronicle*, January 23, 1972. Houston *Post*, January 23, 1972. *Proceedings of the Philosophical Society of Texas*, 1972. *Who's Who in the South and Southwest*, Vol. 11.

CRONICAN, MICHAEL (ca. 1809–1849). Michael Cronican, soldier and newspaperman, was originally from Boston, Massachusetts, where he learned his trade as a printer. He traveled to Texas as a volunteer in Capt. William G. Cooke's[qv] company of New Orleans Greys[qv] in 1835 and fought in the siege of Bexar,[qv] after which he received a furlough as a result of illness and left for New Orleans. His original company was murdered at Goliad during his absence (*see* GOLIAD MASSACRE). Though sources have called him a veteran of San Jacinto, Cronican did not return to Texas until several days after the battle. He later served as an express rider for the Texas army and received bounty and donation certificates for his military service.

In 1839 Cronican operated the Fayetteville Hotel, located between San Felipe and Houston. He had joined the Masons by 1840, and the records of Temple Lodge No. 4 show him again working as a printer. After Gen. Adrián Woll's[qv] attack on San Antonio in September 1842, Cronican joined Capt. Charles K. Reese's[qv] company, which took part in the Mier expedition.[qv] He escaped the fate of the other soldiers by feigning death to avoid capture and returned to Texas. In June of the next year he helped found the Galveston *News*,[qv] then sold his share to pursue other interests. He and John S. Ford[qv] purchased the *Texas National Register*[qv] of Austin in 1845, and the two founded the Austin *Texas Democrat*[qv] a year later. Also in 1846 he and Ford were named public printers by the state legislature, of which body Cronican's brother, James, was a member. Two years later Cronican moved to San Antonio and with James A. Glasscock[qv] founded the *Western Texian*. Cronican died there during the cholera epidemic of 1849, and James was appointed administrator of his estate. In addition to his brother, Cronican was survived by a son. The *Northern Standard* (*see* CLARKSVILLE STANDARD), noting his death, characterized Cronican as a warm-hearted man, a printer, and, in his late years, a sprightly editor.

BIBLIOGRAPHY: Sam Houston Dixon and Louis Wiltz Kemp, *The Heroes of San Jacinto* (Houston: Anson Jones, 1932). Joe B. Frantz, Newspapers of the Republic of Texas (M.A. thesis, University of Texas, 1940). Louis Wiltz Kemp Papers, Barker Texas History Center, University of Texas at Austin. *Frontier Times*, July 1939, September 1941. Galveston *Daily News*, October 8, 1895. Clarksville *Northern Standard*, June 2, 1849.   *Helen B. Frantz*

CROOKED BRANCH. Crooked Branch rises five miles southeast of Martindale in western Caldwell County (at 29°49′ N, 97°46′ W) and runs south for four miles to its mouth on Callihan Creek, two miles northeast of Fentress (at 29°46′ N, 97°46′ W). The stream traverses flat to rolling prairie surfaced by dark, calcareous clay that supports mesquite, cacti, and grasses.

CROOKED CREEK (Anderson County). Crooked Creek rises five miles southwest of Palestine in southwestern Anderson County (at 31°41′ N, 95°40′ W) and runs southwest for 5½ miles to its mouth on the Trinity River, two miles west of Sulphur Springs (at 31°38′ N, 95°43′ W). The stream is intermittent in its upper reaches, and its banks are heavily wooded in places with mixed pine and hardwood trees. The surrounding nearly level to moderately steep terrain is surfaced by sandy, clayey, and loamy upland soils. The area is used mainly as woodland and for agriculture.

──── (Jack County). Crooked Creek rises four miles southwest of Newport in northeastern Jack County (at 33°24′ N, 98°06′ W) and runs south for just under eight miles to its mouth on the West Fork of the Trinity River, ten miles north of Jacksboro (at 33°20′ N, 98°08′ W). It traverses gently to steeply sloping terrain surfaced with clay and sandy loam soils that support scrub brush, cacti, mesquite, and live oak trees. The area has generally been used as range and crop land and for mineral production.

──── (Lavaca County). Crooked Creek rises near Farm Road 155 four miles northeast of Sublime in eastern Lavaca County (at 29°30′ N, 96°44′ W) and runs southwest for 9½ miles to its mouth on the Navidad River, 3½ miles south of Sublime (at 29°25′ N, 96°47′ W). The intermittent stream is dammed several times to provide water for cattle; these small impoundments also provide recreational fishing and some waterfowl habitat. The local soils have a deep sandy clay surface layer that is somewhat poorly drained. The rolling land along the stream, which is in an area locally called "the post oaks," is used primarily as unimproved range for cattle and is an excellent wildlife habitat.

──── (Van Zandt County). Crooked Creek rises northeast of Myrtle Springs and just over a mile north of Interstate Highway 20 in northwestern Van Zandt County (at 32°37′ N, 95°55′ W) and runs northeast for almost nine miles to its mouth on Mill Creek, east of State Highway 19 and almost two miles northwest of Fruitvale (at 32°42′ N, 95°50′ W). Artifacts of the Caddo Indians have been found along the creek. It traverses flat terrain with local shallow depressions, surfaced by clayey and sandy loams that support water-tolerant hardwoods, conifers, and grasses.

CROOKED CREEK, TEXAS. Crooked Creek, a farming community eight miles north of Canton in north central Van Zandt County, was originally settled on Crooked Creek and had a school by 1890. In 1936 the settlement had a school, two churches, and scattered dwellings, but by the 1980s it was no longer shown on the county highway map.
Diana J. Kleiner

CROOKED DRAW. Crooked Draw, through which runs an intermittent stream, rises a mile south of U.S. Highway 377 in west central Edwards County (at 29°55′ N, 100°31′ W) and runs eight miles southeast to its mouth on the West Nueces River (at 29°54′ N, 100°26′ W). It crosses flat terrain with local deep and dense dissection, surfaced by shallow, stony soils that support oak, juniper, and mesquite.

CROOKED HOLLOW. Crooked Hollow, a valley in southwestern McCulloch County, begins about eight miles north of the Calf Creek community (at 31°06′ N, 99°29′ W) and runs northeast for seven miles to a point five miles west of Brady (at 31°08′ N, 99°25′ W). An intermittent stream runs through the hollow, carrying water from an elevation of 1,950 feet above mean sea level to Brady Reservoir, which stands at 1,750 feet.

CROOKED LAKE. Crooked Lake, a small inland body of water, is five miles northeast of Richmond in north central Fort Bend County (at 29°39′ N, 95°43′ W). The lake drains to the east into Oyster Creek and is adjoined to the east by the Jester correctional facility. The surrounding flat to rolling prairie supports trees and prairie grasses. Crooked Lake was shown on the Fort Bend county land grant map of 1898, but was not named on the 1987 county highway map.

CROOKER, JOHN HENRY (1884–1975). John Henry Crooker, attorney, was born on July 15, 1884, in Mobile, Alabama, the son of Norman W. and Margaret (Kelton) Crooker. His father died while Crooker was quite young, and his mother moved the family to the north side of Houston. Crooker left school after the seventh grade and held a number of jobs before turning to local politics and law. He became a deputy constable and subsequently the clerk of a justice of the peace court, where he observed lawyers and read law independently; he obtained a law license in 1911. He became justice of the peace shortly thereafter and was elected district attorney of Harris County in 1914.

As a vigorous "law-and-order" district attorney, Crooker cleared the criminal docket during his first term and closed down Houston's vice district in 1917. After the Camp Logan race riot later that year, he arrested the persons thought to have been guilty but was thwarted in his effort to try military personnel in the state courts. However, he was invited to assist in the military courts-martial held in San Antonio. In the summer of 1918 Crooker resigned from office to accept a commission in the army with the rank of major. He served briefly in California and on the judge advocate general's staff in Washington before returning to Houston and private law practice in 1919. There he joined with Rufus Clarence Fulbright[qv] to form the firm of Fulbright and Crooker (now Fulbright and Jaworski). Crooker directed litigation for the firm and managed it after Fulbright became resident partner in a new office of the firm in Washington in 1927. When Crooker retired in 1960, the firm had thirty partners.

Crooker crusaded against the Ku Klux Klan[qv] in the twenties and played a key role in the legal maneuvers that preserved Lyndon B. Johnson's[qv] election to the United States Senate in 1948. He was active in the business and real estate development of Houston. From 1920 to 1922 he was the principal owner of Houston's minor-league baseball club, the Houston Buffs; he sold his interest to the St. Louis Cardinals. Later he built the Ben Milam Hotel. He was elected to the board of directors of the First National Bank of Houston in 1943 and continued to serve on the board of its successor, First City National Bank.

Crooker was reared a Catholic, but he joined the Episcopal Church in his late teens. He married Marguerite Malsch, the daughter of Hortense S. Ward,[qv] in 1913, and the couple had two sons. Crooker joined the Grey Lodge of the Masonic order in 1908 and was elected grand master of the Grand Lodge of Texas in 1933. He died in Houston on August 14, 1975.

BIBLIOGRAPHY: Robert V. Haynes, *A Night of Violence: The Houston Riot of 1917* (Baton Rouge: Louisiana State University Press, 1976). *Texas Bar Journal*, January 1976.

Newton Gresham and James A. Tinsley

CROSBY, JOSIAH FRAZIER (1829–1904). Josiah Frazier Crosby, judge, legislator, and secessionist leader, was born on January 3, 1829, in Charleston, South Carolina, the son of William and Mary Ann (Frazier) Crosby. His father was a merchant. The family moved to Alabama a few years after Josiah's birth, and after the death of his father in 1837 the boy was adopted by his uncle Josiah J. Crosby, a lawyer, who brought him to Texas. Crosby was educated by private tutors, including Joel Ankrim, and in 1844 began reading law with another uncle, William Crosby, and James Willie,[qv] the former attorney general of Texas, in Brenham. On January 10, 1848, an act of the legislature admitted Crosby to the state bar despite his minority, and he was appointed district attorney of the Third Judicial District. In 1850 he married the daughter of Judge Thomas Johnson, but two years later she died, and Crosby was forced by illness to resign his position.

His former tutor, Ankrim, who had become district judge in El Paso County, convinced Crosby to move west to recover his health. In the spring of 1852 Crosby, Ankrim, and several others bought an ambulance and mule team in San Antonio and attached themselves to one of William T. Smith's wagon trains for the two-month journey to San Elizario.

Crosby threw himself into the civic affairs of his new home. In July 1852 he was appointed, along with James Wiley Magoffin and Hugh Stephenson,[qqv] to a committee investigating Indian attacks. In 1853 Crosby was appointed to the Texas House of Representatives, where he advocated the passage of laws designed to curb Indian depredations. He also sponsored railroad legislation and campaigned for a rail link between Central Texas and the El Paso area. In 1854 he was elected district attorney of the Eleventh Judicial District, but shortly thereafter was elected to the legislature and resigned the office of district attorney. In Austin he met Josephine Bremond of Philadelphia; they were married on August 30, 1856, and eventually had eight children. Crosby was reelected to the legislature in 1856, but that same year his friend and mentor Ankrim resigned and left El Paso County. A year later Crosby was elected district judge to replace him.

Crosby also became the attorney for the freighter Smith, nicknamed Uncle Billy, who had purchased Coons' Rancho[qv] and tried with little success to promote it as a townsite. Smith wanted to sell the property and concentrate on his freighting business, but Crosby advised him to keep the property, as it would doubtless become valuable someday. Smith, however, insisted on selling, and Crosby was a member of the syndicate that bought the ranch and hired Anson Mills[qv] to survey it and lay out the townsite that became the city of El Paso. In the 1850s Crosby helped establish a local Masonic lodge and built up an extensive private library. He was also linked to the temperance movement and served as a delegate to the state Democratic convention.

In the late 1850s he became a forceful advocate of secession. He was a delegate from Texas to the Charleston convention that met on April

23, 1860, to select the Democratic presidential candidate, and on July 28, 1860, he denounced the Northern Democrats at a mass meeting in San Antonio.

At the time Crosby was suffering from lung disease, so he returned to El Paso to recover and resumed the district judgeship. He ruled that a Fort Bliss deserter had been within his rights in leaving the army, since the United States was no longer recognized as a legitimate government. Shortly thereafter, when the Civil War[qv] broke out, Crosby left to join the Confederate Army. He was acting quartermaster general on Henry H. Sibley's[qv] feckless invasion of New Mexico and later adjutant general on the staff of Gen. Edmund Kirby Smith.[qv] On Smith's orders he spent nine months in Europe buying arms and munitions. He returned to Texas in early 1865 and spent the remaining months of the war serving under Governor Pendleton Murrah.[qv]

In December 1865 a Union judge in New Mexico began ordering the seizure of property belonging to Confederate sympathizers, including Crosby, Magoffin, and Stephenson, in El Paso. They argued successfully before the New Mexico Supreme Court that the jurisdiction of the New Mexico courts did not extend to El Paso, and on March 28, 1868, in *United States vs. Hart*, the United States Supreme Court upheld the New Mexico Supreme Court ruling. A companion case, *United States vs. Josiah F. Crosby, Henry S. Gillett, and James S. Gillett,* confirmed the decision.

In October 1865, the war over, Crosby settled in Houston, where he practiced law and became vice president and general manager of the Texas and New Orleans Railroad and president of the Street Railroad Company of Houston. He maintained ties to El Paso, however, and in 1883 he and Anson Mills built the Grand Central Hotel there. The hotel, the largest in the state, opened on February 13, 1884, but was destroyed by fire on February 11, 1892. In 1886 Crosby returned to El Paso, from where he promoted mining and railroad activities in Chihuahua. He went to New York to open a law office in 1893 but soon returned to El Paso. He died there on January 3, 1904, and was buried in Concordia Cemetery. Crosby, a devout Episcopalian, would doubtless have been appalled when vandals desecrated his tomb, apparently for purposes of Satanic ritual, in March 1989.

BIBLIOGRAPHY: *Biographical Encyclopedia of Texas* (New York: Southern, 1880). J. Morgan Broaddus, *The Legal Heritage of El Paso* (El Paso: Texas Western College Press, 1963).

Martin Donell Kohout

CROSBY, STEPHEN (1808–1869). Stephen Crosby, General Land Office[qv] commissioner, was born in South Carolina in 1808. He moved to Alabama about 1830 and worked as a steamboat captain on the Alabama River. In Alabama he married Eliza Green; they had one child. Crosby settled in Texas in 1845 and in 1848 became chief clerk in the General Land Office. He was elected commissioner in 1851 as a Democrat. He served in that office until 1858, and it is to his credit that clear titles can be proved for most landholdings in Texas. Crosby then joined the Know-Nothing party (*see* AMERICAN PARTY) and was defeated in the next election. He returned to the Democratic camp in 1862 and served in his former post until he was removed from office in 1867 by the Reconstruction[qv] military government. He died in Austin on August 5, 1869. Crosby County is named for him. In 1930 the state placed a monument at his grave.

BIBLIOGRAPHY: Crosby County Pioneer Memorial Museum, *A History of Crosby County, 1876–1977* (Dallas: Taylor, 1978). Zachary T. Fulmore, *History and Geography of Texas As Told in County Names* (Austin: Steck, 1915; facsimile, 1935). Nellie Witt Spikes and Temple Ann Ellis, *Through the Years: A History of Crosby County* (San Antonio: Naylor, 1952)

Charles G. Davis

CROSBY, TEXAS. Crosby is on Farm Road 2100 near the Southern Pacific tracks two miles north of State Highway 90 and just outside the Houston city limits in eastern Harris County. The town was named for G. J. Crosby, a railroad construction engineer. Charlie Karcher opened the first store there in 1865, and the town quickly became a retail and shipping center for lumber and agricultural products from between the San Jacinto River and Cedar Bayou. A post office opened at the community in 1877, and in 1884 Crosby reported a population of fifty, a school, a Baptist church, and a general store. By 1891 it still had fifty inhabitants, as well as a Methodist church, two livestock stables, and a general store. Local legend reports that the community had received the nickname Lick Skillet by 1898. In 1905 it had one school with four teachers and 122 students. There were 300 people in Crosby in 1925 and 600 in 1929, when it became a banking center. Its population fell to 300 during the Great Depression[qv] but grew to 750 during World War II[qv] and then rose to 900, where it remained for most of the next twenty-five years. Crosby reported fifty businesses and a population of 2,500 in 1976. In the early 1990s Crosby reported 238 businesses and a population estimated at 1,888, though considerably more people lived in the area at that time.

Timothy N. Smith

CROSBY COUNTY. Crosby County (C-10) is on the eastern edge of the southern High Plains, bounded on the west by Lubbock County, on the north by Floyd County, on the east by Dickens County, and on the south by Garza County. It was named for Stephen Crosby,[qv] a Texas land commissioner during the mid-nineteenth century. U.S. Highway 82 runs west to east across the county, and State highways 207 and 651 are major north-to-south roads. The center of the county lies at 33°37′ north latitude and 101°18′ west longitude, about thirty miles east of Lubbock. Most of the western half of Crosby County, flat land covered by rich loam, lies above the Caprock,[qv] and the eastern part of the county and its southwestern corner are broken country below the Caprock. Drainage is to the forks of the Brazos River, White River, and numerous playas.[qv] Blanco Canyon crosses the county from northwest to southeast; at Mount Blanco the canyon is about 250 feet deep and 1½ miles wide, and is traversed by the White River. The county covers 911 square miles; its altitude ranges from 2,100 to 3,200 feet, and the average annual rainfall is 21.01 inches. Vegetation includes mesquite, hackberry, cottonwood, cedar, catclaw, cacti, and grasses, particularly curly mesquite, grama, salt, and sage. The average minimum temperature in January is 26° F; the average maximum in July is 94°. A growing season of 206 days yields $45 million average annual income from cotton, sorghums, wheat, corn, soybeans, sunflowers, cattle, hogs, and poultry. Irrigated land totals 125,000 acres.

Artifacts dating back 13,000 years to the early Paleolithic era have been discovered in Crosby County. Flint-pointed darts used with the atlatl (a type of spear-thrower) have been found and identified as Clovis, Eden, Agate Basin, Angostura, Folsom, Plainview, Meserve, Scottsbluff, and Sandia points. The darts were used to hunt the mammoth, mastodon, saber-toothed tiger, and giant ground sloth, all of which disappeared some 8,000 years ago. The early people of the area were rovers who hunted and gathered plants and differed from neighboring peoples in weapons and tools. In more modern times the area of Crosby County was inhabited by the Comanches, mounted hunters and warriors who dominated much of the South Plains in the eighteenth and nineteenth centuries until their buffalo-based culture gave way to settlers and superior technology.

United States Army forces commanded by Col. Ranald S. Mackenzie[qv] fought the Comanches at the battle of Blanco Canyon[qv] in the future county in 1871. The campaign established what became known as the Mackenzie Trail, used by the first settlers in Crosby County in the late 1870s. From 1874 to 1877 buffalo hunters entered the area, where they took part in the slaughter that exterminated the great buffalo[qv] herds. The hunts marked the end of an era. In 1876 the Texas legislature formed Crosby County from lands previously attached to the Young and Bexar districts.

The first permanent settler in the area was Henry Clay Smith,[qv] who arrived in 1878 and hauled lumber by ox team from Fort Worth to build his "Rock House" in Blanco Canyon; Smith set up a small cattle ranch. In 1879 Paris Cox^{qv} established a Quaker colony at Marietta on thirty-two sections purchased from the state for twenty-five cents an acre. Ample underground water supported the efforts of the Religious Society of Friends,^{qv} and Cox helped early settlers by planting corn, oats, sorghum, melons, and vegetables. In 1880 the census counted eighty-two people living in the county, including one black. Only two farms had been established in the county by that time.

The Quaker colony flourished for a while as a cultural and economic center and attracted merchants and settlers; in 1882 the colony established one of the first schools on the high plains. Crosby County was formally organized after elections held in 1886, with Estacado (the new name of the town formerly called Marietta) designated as the county seat. Open-range grazing continued until the mid-1880s, when barbed wire^{qv} was introduced and small ranchers and farmers began competing for the land. By 1890 the population of the county was 345. As more settlers moved in to establish farms and ranches, the influence of the Quakers declined and the religious orientation of the community was lost. In 1891 Emma became the seat of government. Until the early twentieth century, the county remained dominated by such large ranches as the St. Louis Cattle Company, the Two-Buckle Ranch,^{qv} the C. B. Livestock Company (founded in 1901) and smaller spreads. Thanks to plentiful grass and sufficient water holes, and despite the lack of rail transportation in early days, the beef-cattle industry thrived. In 1900, 30,618 cattle were counted in Crosby County, and in 1910 holdings were about the same.

The transition from the era of the giant cattle ranch to one of mixed farming and ranching accelerated during the early twentieth century, when many farmers moved into the area to grow cotton. Only 103 acres was devoted to cotton culture^{qv} in 1900 and only 324 in 1910. Gins were built at Emma in 1908 and at Lorenzo in 1914, and by 1920 more than 45,400 acres in the county was planted in cotton. The arrival of railroads helped to stimulate economic development between 1905 and 1930, and railroad expansion into the county was closely connected to efforts to subdivide and sell old ranchlands to new farmers. In 1908 the Bar-N-Bar Ranch began selling acreage to farmers. Between 1909 and 1911 the Stamford and Northwestern and the Santa Fe railroads laid tracks into the region, but bypassed Crosby County. In 1911 local investors, including the C. B. Livestock Company, which owned 80,000 acres in the county, raised $75,000 to induce the Crosbyton–South Plains and the Santa Fe to build forty miles of track between Lubbock and Crosbyton. Owners of the C. B. Company hoped to use the new railroad connection to help them sell plots of land in the new settlements they planned to establish at eight-mile intervals between Crosbyton and Lubbock. The towns of Cedric, Lorenzo, and Idalou (the last in Lubbock County) were founded as a result. Emma, the county seat, faded away after the railroad was routed four miles to the north of the town. In 1912 Crosbyton became the new county seat. As development proceeded, the population of the county grew. As late as 1910 only 1,765 people lived in Crosby County, but in 1920 the census counted 6,084 residents.

Farming continued to develop rapidly in the county throughout the 1920s, as the number of farms increased to 1,114 in 1924 and to 1,739 in 1929. In 1924 cotton was planted on more than 81,200 acres in the county, and by 1929 more than 133,467 acres was devoted to the fiber. As more farmers acquired land from the breakup of large ranches, sorghum and wheat culture^{qqv} also expanded, and some farmers began fruit production as well. By 1920 more than 15,000 fruit trees were growing in the county, producing mostly apples and peaches (see FRUITS OTHER THAN CITRUS). Poultry production^{qv} also became a significant part of the local economy during this time; by 1929 farmers in the county owned almost 83,000 chickens, and that year sold more than 395,000 dozen eggs. Meanwhile, livestock continued to be important. Almost 15,000 cattle were counted in Crosby County in 1920, and more than 15,556 in 1929. The county's population figures reflected this farming expansion. By 1930, 11,023 people lived in Crosby County.

The county was hit hard during the 1930s by the Great Depression and Dust Bowl.^{qqv} Cotton production plunged, especially during the drought of 1933–34, and the county lost 451 farms between 1930 and 1940. On the eve of World War II,^{qv} only 1,288 farms remained in Crosby County, and the population of the county had dropped to 10,046. Federal control programs and the market needs of the war resulted in a general diversification of crop and livestock production, though cotton continued to be an important crop. Soil-conservation projects were another result of lessons learned during the Dust Bowl. The first soil-conservation district in the county was formed in 1941 to assist in crop rotation, soil building, irrigation, mesquite^{qv} eradication, and terrace building. The mechanization of farms, which had begun in the 1930s, also helped to stimulate new crop production. Machinery was too expensive for most small farmers, however, and its utilization was one significant reason for the demise of family farms that became obvious in Crosby County by the late 1950s and continued afterwards.

For most of the period since World War II the population of Crosby County has slowly declined. It grew from 9,582 in 1950 to 10,347 in 1960. It dropped, however, to 9,085 in 1970, 8,859 in 1980, and 7,304 in 1990. The discovery of oil in the county in 1955 helped to stabilize and diversify the economy. Oil production was about 41,000 barrels in 1956, 113,300 in 1960, 267,700 in 1978, and 734,300 in 1990. By 1991 more than 14,122,000 barrels of oil had been produced in the county since 1955. Crosby County voters have supported Democratic presidential candidates for most of the county's history. Between 1888 and 1992 they voted for Republicans in national elections only three times, in 1928, 1972, and 1984. In 1990 the economic base of the county appeared stable, with truck farming and oil production contributing significantly. Communities included Ralls, Lorenzo, Farmer, Kalgary, Owens, Robertson, and Wake. In 1992 Crosbyton, the county seat and largest town, had a population of 2,026. For residents and tourists the county offers such attractions as White River Reservoir, Silver Falls,^{qqv} and Blanco Canyon.

BIBLIOGRAPHY: Crosby County Pioneer Memorial Museum, *A History of Crosby County, 1876–1977* (Dallas: Taylor, 1978). Nellie Witt Spikes and Temple Ann Ellis, *Through the Years: A History of Crosby County* (San Antonio: Naylor, 1952).
John Leffler

CROSBYTON, TEXAS. Crosbyton, county seat of Crosby County, is on U.S. Highway 82 on the Llano Estacado^{qv} a few miles west of Blanco Canyon and thirty-six miles east of Lubbock near the county's center. It was named for General Land Office^{qv} commissioner Stephen Crosby,^{qv} and lies in the center of a productive dairying and farming area. This territory was still cattle country when, in 1902, the C. B. Livestock Company purchased 90,000 acres from the Kentucky Cattle Company. By 1912 a 10,000-acre demonstration farm was under the C. B.'s supervision, with Judge L. Gough serving as farm manager. From about 1907 to 1915 the company engaged in land sales, promoting the area as a great cotton-growing region, and thereby aiding the growth of Crosbyton. In January 1908 the C. B. Livestock Company surveyed a townsite, and in February Crosbyton was opened and town lots were sold. Another opening sale took place in June of that year, and the next month the Crosbyton post office was established, with Julian M. Bassett as postmaster. The Crosbyton Inn, a three-story hotel that became noted for its hospitality, was also constructed in 1908. On September 17, 1910, Crosbyton won, by a vote of 198 to 120, a county-seat election over Emma, and after a court fight Crosbyton became the county seat. A few months later, on April 10, 1911, the first train left on the Crosbyton–South Plains Railroad. From the period of World War I^{qv} through the 1920s the population of Crosbyton and Crosby County grew steadily. The effects of the Great Depression,^{qv} however, were heavily felt in the county and contributed to the 8.9

percent decrease in county population between 1930 and 1940. In spite of this, during the decade the town of Crosbyton increased in population from 1,250 to 1,615 and gained roughly twenty more businesses. Crosbyton's first hospital opened in August 1947, and the Crosbyton Municipal Airport was dedicated in 1975. On May 1, 1976, the Federal Energy Research and Development Administration awarded a $2.4 million research grant to Texas Tech University for a solar power project at Crosbyton. In addition, the United States Department of Energy signed a $2.5 million contract with Texas Tech for construction of a sixty-five-foot mirrored dish 2½ miles south of Crosbyton. At the time it was the largest single solar collector in the world and was designed to reduce energy costs by converting solar power to electricity for use by the city-owned power plant. Recognizing the town's need for both a community center and a museum, Zina Lamar set up a foundation in 1958 to finance the construction, operation, and maintenance of the Crosby County Pioneer Memorial Museum. The building includes an auditorium and a kitchen as well as exhibit space for numerous artifacts of area pioneers. The museum's façade is a replica of the front of Henry Clay (Hank) Smith's[qv] rock house, the first home on the West Texas Plains. Crosbyton, a marketing center for hogs, wheat, and grain sorghum, was also at one time the home of the world's largest cotton gin. In 1980 the town had fifty-five businesses and a population of 2,289. In 1990 the population of Crosbyton was 2,026.

BIBLIOGRAPHY: Crosby County Pioneer Memorial Museum, *A History of Crosby County, 1876–1977* (Dallas: Taylor, 1978). Crosbyton Golden Jubilee, *Blanco Canyon Cavalcade: Official Souvenir Program* (Crosbyton, Texas, 1958). Kathleen E. and Clifton R. St. Clair, eds., *Little Towns of Texas* (Jacksonville, Texas: Jayroe Graphic Arts, 1982). Nellie Witt Spikes and Temple Ann Ellis, *Through the Years: A History of Crosby County* (San Antonio: Naylor, 1952). *Edloe A. Jenkins*

CROSBYTON-SOUTHPLAINS RAILROAD. The Crosbyton-Southplains Railroad was chartered on April 6, 1910, to build from a point in Dickens County to Lubbock, with a branch from Crosbyton to Plainview, for a total distance of 120 miles. The capital was $150,000, and the principal place of business was Crosbyton. The members of the first board of directors were Julian M. Bassett,[qv] Roger M. Bassett, William D. Petzel, and Joseph C. Johnson, all of Crosbyton; Avery Coonley of Riverside, Illinois; and John Stuart Coonley and Prentiss L. Coonley, both of Chicago, Illinois. In 1910 J. S. Coonley and J. M. Bassett began construction of nearly thirty-nine miles of track from Lubbock to Crosbyton, where the Coonley and Bassett Live Stock Company wished to promote the colonization of a large tract of land. Cash bonuses of more than $43,000 were given by citizens of Lubbock and of Crosby County along with right-of-way to aid in the construction of the line. The Crosbyton-Southplains opened on April 10, 1911. The Atchison, Topeka and Santa Fe purchased the railroad on August 1, 1915, and changed its name to South Plains and Santa Fe on August 17, 1916. The former Crosbyton-Southplains line was sold to the Crosbyton Railroad, which began operation in January 1990. However, the line was abandoned before the end of that year due to lack of business.

BIBLIOGRAPHY: Crosby County Pioneer Memorial Museum, *A History of Crosby County, 1876–1977* (Dallas: Taylor, 1978). *Jeanne F. Lively*

CROSS, JOHN S. (1816–?). John S. Cross, a Brownsville merchant and rancher, was born on August 16, 1816, the third of seven children of John and Margaret Joiner Cross of South Carolina. Some sources suggest that he was a black man or had some black ancestry, while others make no mention of race. He arrived in Brownsville in 1850 and began raising cattle. He settled in Matamoros, Tamaulipas, in 1857 and opened a dry-goods and general store there during in 1862, having been forced to abandon his cattle business in 1859 due to raids and thefts. His Matamoros establishment eventually came to occupy a half block in the heart of the town and included a warehouse for arms and ammunition, lumber, and furniture from which heavy shipments were made in carts to towns in the interior of Mexico. By 1892 Cross was the owner of a Matamoros bakery that supplied the needs of a large portion of the population. He eventually accumulated an estate valued at over $100,000.

Following a pattern already well established by border merchants of conducting operations on both sides of Rio Grande, Cross established a Brownsville operation. In 1880 he formed a partnership with his son Meliton (or Middleton), J. S. and M. H. Cross. They opened a lumberyard and wholesale stores in Matamoros and operated a branch store in Brownsville. The Brownsville wholesale house made riverboat shipments as far as Roma. Cross also renewed his stock-raising operation, which, by 1892, amounted to 3,000 cattle as well as horses and mules, on 9,000 acres. As late as 1906 Cross had a home and a commercial building constructed for him in Brownsville; both buildings still exist, as does the mansion built in American style for Meliton in Matamoros in 1885. Cross probably died after 1906 but before 1921, when the home was sold.

BIBLIOGRAPHY: Betty Bay, *Historic Brownsville: Original Townsite Guide* (Brownsville, Texas: Brownsville Historical Association, 1980). John Henry Brown, *Indian Wars and Pioneers of Texas* (Austin: Daniell, 1880; reprod., Easley, South Carolina: Southern Historical Press, 1978). W. H. Chatfield, *The Twin Cities of the Border and the Country of the Lower Rio Grande* (New Orleans: Brandao, 1893; rpt., Brownsville: Brownsville Historical Association, 1959). Loren Schweninger, *Black Property Owners in the South, 1790–1915* (Urbana: University of Illinois Press, 1990). *Anthony Knopp*

CROSS, MATTIE RUTH (1887–1981). Ruth Cross, novelist, the oldest of four children of Dr. Walter D. and Willie Alta (Cole) Cross, was born in Sylvan, Texas, on December 25, 1887. After moving around the South while her father, a former high school principal, finished his medical education, Ruth returned with her family to Sylvan, in rural Lamar County, where she attended local schools. Strongly influenced by her mother, a music teacher versed in Greek and Latin, Ruth excelled in her studies and graduated Phi Beta Kappa from the University of Texas. She had enrolled in college in 1904 and worked her way through by teaching in small Texas and Oklahoma towns. When an eye malady impaired Ruth's vision, her mother traveled to Austin to assist with her coursework. After her mother died, Ruth depended upon friends to read and take notes for her. She was awarded a B.A. in creative writing in 1911 and then taught in Longview, emphasizing oral work in her Latin and German classes in order to spare her eyes.

Writing fiction, however, remained her first ambition. After studying for a summer at the University of Chicago, she subsidized her creative efforts with stints as a housekeeper, travel companion, interior decorator, and real-estate broker in New York, Nevada, and California. Undeterred by almost a decade of rejection, she began selling her "cotton field" tales to *Holland's* magazine. Her literary career then bloomed quickly. In 1922 Louis B. Mayer based a movie on her short story "A Question of Honor." Two years later Harper published her first novel, *The Golden Cocoon*, which was greeted by favorable reviews and printed in five editions. After paying Cross $25,000 for the movie rights, Warner Brothers in 1925 filmed this saga of a farm girl from the Black Hills who survives heartbreak as the governor's mistress and then leaves her glamorous life in Austin to struggle as a writer in New York City.

Flushed with the additional success of a one-act play on the Keith vaudeville circuit, Ruth Cross in 1924 married George W. Palmer, a horticulturist and financier. Together they bought and renovated Edendale, a forty-acre farm estate outside Winsted, Connecticut, home to fellow Texas writers Dorothy Scarborough,[qv] Annie Laurie

Williams, and Maurice Crain. Over the next two decades, Cross published five novels: *The Unknown Goddess* (1926), *Enchantment* (1930), *The Big Road* (1931), *Soldier of Good Fortune* (1936), and *Back Door to Happiness* (1937). She also wrote two works of nonfiction, *Eden on a Country Hill* (1938) and *Wake Up and Garden* (1942), and numerous stories and articles for magazines. Always enthusiastic about her fruits and flowers, she contributed to Heinz's "Magazine of the Air" on WABC radio and broadcast an original program called "Your Garden and Home."

Just before her husband's death in 1947, Cross sold Edendale. She lived for a few years in New York City and then moved to Winnfield, Louisiana, her mother's hometown, to be near the families of her sister and brother. In 1975 she donated her papers to Northwestern State University at Natchitoches, which a year later published her final book, *The Beautiful and the Doomed*. Although her first novel established Cross as a writer of note, her subsequent books did not live up to its promise. Drawing on memories of her childhood, she set many of her tales in "Law's Chapel," a fictional counterpart of Sylvan, and critics commended her realism and local color in both *The Golden Cocoon* and *The Big Road*. When her characters left Texas for Broadway and the big cities, however, her "riotous imagination" tinged the plot with melodrama in such books as *Enchantment*. But even when Cross was out of the critical eye, she continued to write; at the age of eighty-eight she was planning a novel about her psychic experiences. She died in Winnfield on September 30, 1981.

BIBLIOGRAPHY: Florence Elberta Barns, *Texas Writers of Today* (Dallas: Tardy, 1935). Vertical Files, Barker Texas History Center, University of Texas at Austin.

Sylvia Whitman

CROSS, TEXAS (Grimes County). Cross, on U.S. Highway 39 and the Burlington–Rock Island Railroad in northwestern Grimes County, was established about 1900, when farm families in the vicinity of Morgan Creek began moving to the proposed route of a new Trinity and Brazos Valley Railway line where it crossed D. D. Sheffield's ranch. Settlement began in the area during the 1830s, but no community appeared until the coming of the railroad in 1900. By 1900 a post office had been established with T. H. Ware, operator of a general merchandise store, as postmaster. In 1907 the Trinity and Brazos Valley was extended through the townsite. The Spring Hill Free Will Baptist Church was soon organized. In its early development the town served as a ranching-supply center and supported a blacksmith shop, a drugstore, a cotton gin, a fraternal hall, and several general stores. By 1920 a school was in operation near the townsite at the intersection of the Case and Democrat roads, the junction that seems to have inspired the community's name. In the early 1920s the post office was discontinued, and rural mail delivery from Iola began. In 1949 the local school was incorporated into the Iola school system. Cross reported a population of ten in 1900 and fifty in 1936, when the community supported two businesses. Thereafter, the number of residents remained virtually unchanged for decades; in 1990 it stood at an estimated forty-nine, and no rated businesses were reported.

BIBLIOGRAPHY: Grimes County Historical Commission, *History of Grimes County, Land of Heritage and Progress* (Dallas: Taylor, 1982). Fred I. Massengill, *Texas Towns: Origin of Name and Location of Each of the 2,148 Post Offices in Texas* (Terrell, Texas, 1936).

Charles Christopher Jackson

CROSS, TEXAS (McMullen County). Cross is on State Highway 16 eight miles north of Tilden in north central McMullen County. It was named for Samuel G. Cross, who opened a grocery store on the site in 1924. The community was originally known as Nopal when it was founded around the mid-1870s; by 1883 it included a small store, two houses, and a one-room schoolhouse. It had a post office from 1889 to 1891, and for a time was designated by the McMullen County commissioners' court as a legal voting place. In 1925 the name was changed to Cross, and the community was granted a new post office under that name. In 1930 a one-room schoolhouse still stood on the site; a larger, stone schoolhouse was built in 1938. During the 1930s and part of the 1940s the town had a small grocery store. In 1933 an estimated fifteen people lived in the settlement. The post office was closed in 1934, and the school closed in 1945. In the late 1940s Cross had twenty-five residents, a few houses, and one business. By 1952 the business had closed, and the old schoolhouse was used as a community center for elections and religious revivals. A 1988 highway map showed one business on the site. In the mid-1980s the community was also known as Franklin Settlement.

BIBLIOGRAPHY: Joe Pate Smyer, A History of McMullen County (M.A. thesis, University of Texas, 1952).

John Leffler

CROSS BAYOU. Cross Bayou rises six miles southwest of Waskom in southeastern Harrison County (at 32°26′ N, 94°09′ W) and runs northeast for 15½ miles, through southeastern Harrison County and Caddo Parish in Louisiana, to its mouth on Cross Lake, three miles northwest of Shreveport, Louisiana (at 32°31′ N, 93°45′ W). The banks of the stream are heavily wooded in places with pine and hardwood trees. It traverses nearly level to rolling terrain surfaced by loamy and clayey soils used predominantly for agriculture.

CROSS BRANCH. Cross Branch rises just south of the Bosque-Somervell county line and one-half mile southeast of Seven Knobs in northwestern Bosque County (at 32°08′ N, 97°46′ W) and runs northeast for seven miles to its mouth on the Paluxy River, one-half mile southwest of Glen Rose in Somervell County (at 32°14′ N, 97°46′ W). The stream, intermittent in its lower reaches, traverses terrain with some steep slopes, surfaced by shallow clay and sandy loams that support juniper, live oak, and mesquite trees. The area is subject to seasonal flooding and is used as range and crop land.

CROSS CREEK. Cross Creek rises just northwest of the convergence of the Lee, Milam, and Williamson county lines in southeast Williamson County (at 30°27′ N, 97°11′ W) and runs southeast through Williamson, Milam, and Lee counties for seven miles to its mouth on Middle Yegua Creek, six miles northwest of Lexington in Lee County (at 30°25′ N, 97°07′ W). The banks of the stream are wooded in places with mesquite trees. It runs through gently sloping terrain surfaced by loamy and clayey soils used predominantly for agricultural purposes.

CROSS CUT, TEXAS. Cross Cut, at the junction of Farm roads 279 and 2940 in northwestern Brown County, was originally called Cross Out because it was across the county and out of the usual way of travel. Its founder was John M. Bloodworth, who opened a store in 1878 and served as the first postmaster. When the post office opened in 1879, the name of the town was changed to Cross Cut. The town remained small during the nineteenth century but grew somewhat in the early 1920s with oil production in the region. The population declined during the Great Depression,[qv] and the school was consolidated with the Williams school in 1930. In 1940 Cross Cut had one store and seventy-nine people. By 1980 the population had fallen to forty-five.

BIBLIOGRAPHY: Kathleen E. and Clifton R. St. Clair, eds., *Little Towns of Texas* (Jacksonville, Texas: Jayroe Graphic Arts, 1982).

Dorothy C. Ashton

CROSSENVILLE, TEXAS. Crossenville, eight miles from Edgar in eastern DeWitt County, was settled by the J. M. Alexander family in 1850. By 1858 six other families had arrived, including that of George W. Crossen, for whom the settlement was named and who established a store there that operated until after the Civil War.[qv] The

Crossenville school was established in 1859 and taught by Bill Edgar, Sr., who commuted from Edgar. In 1880 a frame building replaced the community's original log schoolhouse. The school operated until 1925, when it was consolidated with the Stratton school, three miles to the southeast. Baptist "elm tree meetings" were held in the Crossenville area from 1926 to 1935.

BIBLIOGRAPHY: Nellie Murphree, *A History of DeWitt County* (Victoria, Texas, 1962).
Nellie Murphree

CROSSETT, TEXAS. Crossett, seven miles northwest of McCamey in southwest Upton County, was established on October 10, 1925, by Mrs. Minnie Crossett, barely two weeks before major oil discoveries brought on a regional oil boom. For a brief time in the late 1920s the community had a post office (granted in 1926), three hotels, a barbershop, several cafes and beer halls, a nightclub, and a number of homes. Although the Crossett post office was discontinued in 1928, in 1929 the settlement's population was reported as 200. By the 1930s, however, competition from nearby McCamey caused the community to decline. It reported only two businesses and fifty people during the 1930s and 1940s. County maps in the 1980s gave no indication of the town other than the location of the Crossett oilfield south of U.S. Highway 385.

BIBLIOGRAPHY: Nancy Ethie Eagleton, *On the Last Frontier: A History of Upton County, Texas* (El Paso: Texas Western Press, 1971). John Leeds Kerr and Frank Donovan, *Destination Topolobampo: The Kansas City, Mexico & Orient Railway* (San Marino, California: Golden West, 1968).
Charles G. Davis

CROSSMAN, ROBERT (1810–1836). Robert Crossman, Alamo defender, son of Samuel V. Crossman, was born in Pennsylvania in 1810. He traveled to Texas by way of New Orleans as a member of Capt. Thomas H. Breece's qv company of New Orleans Greys.qv Crossman took part in and was wounded in the siege of Bexar.qv He later served in the Alamo garrison as a member of Capt. William Blazeby's qv infantry company. Crossman died in the battle of the Alamo qv on March 6, 1836.

BIBLIOGRAPHY: Daughters of the American Revolution, *The Alamo Heroes and Their Revolutionary Ancestors* (San Antonio, 1976). Daughters of the Republic of Texas, *Muster Rolls of the Texas Revolution* (Austin, 1986). Bill Groneman, *Alamo Defenders* (Austin: Eakin, 1990).
Bill Groneman

CROSS MOUNTAIN. Cross Mountain, or Kreuzberg, is just north of Fredericksburg, a quarter mile west of Farm Road 965 (at 30°18′ N, 98°52′ W).

CROSS PLAINS, TEXAS. Cross Plains, at the junction of State highways 36 and 206 in southeastern Callahan County, was established as a post office in 1877. The settlement had previously been known as Turkey Creek and Schleicher. In 1880 Cross Plains had twenty-five residents, a cotton gin, a gristmill, a wagonmaker, and a store; by 1885 it had a population of 175. In 1902 the short-lived Cross Plains *Herald* was published and edited by J. D. Grains. The Cross Plains *Review*, first published and edited by Belmont L. Shields, began publication in 1909 and continued into the 1980s. By 1910, the year the town incorporated, the population had grown to 600. The Texas Central Railroad reached Cross Plains in 1912, and the town became a trading center for cotton and other crops. The discovery of oil in 1925 at Pioneer and adjacent fields set off a boom. The population in Cross Plains reached 1,229 in 1940 and remained relatively stable into the 1980s. Robert E. Howard qv lived in Cross Plains during his most productive writing period. In 1980 the town had a new high school and post office, two motels, four restaurants, and eight churches. The Missouri, Kansas and Texas Railroad, which absorbed the Texas Central, had abandoned its track in Cross Plains by this time. In 1990 the population was 1,063.

BIBLIOGRAPHY: Brutus Clay Chrisman, *Early Days in Callahan County* (Abilene, Texas: Abilene Printing and Stationery, 1966). Kathleen E. and Clifton R. St. Clair, eds., *Little Towns of Texas* (Jacksonville, Texas: Jayroe Graphic Arts, 1982).

CROSSROADS, TEXAS (Camp County). Crossroads is on U.S. Highway 271 four miles southeast of Pittsburg in southern Camp County. It grew up around the Union Baptist Church, often called Crossroads Baptist Church, which was organized between 1885 and 1887. The church building was enlarged between 1888 and 1890 and used for both a church and a school. By 1897 the one-teacher, ungraded school served a scholastic population of fifty-two. In 1901 the trustees for the church and school purchased a little over three acres of land to the south of the church and built a separate school building. A new church was constructed in 1924. By 1935 the school had three teachers and offered eight grades. The scholastic census that year indicated that the district had ninety-seven white children of school age. There were also thirty-nine black children of school age living within the district, but they attended school in other districts. By 1955 all of the common school districts in the area had been consolidated with the Pittsburg Independent School District. In 1983 Crossroads had the church, a cemetery, and widely scattered houses.

BIBLIOGRAPHY: Artemesia L. B. Spencer, *The Camp County Story* (Fort Worth: Branch-Smith, 1974).
Cecil Harper, Jr.

CROSS ROADS, TEXAS (Delta County). Cross Roads, known at various times as Union, Clem, and Hog Wallow, is a small black community at the intersection of Farm roads 2949 and 128, four miles northwest of Enloe in northwestern Delta County. It is bordered to the southwest by the East Fork of Big Creek. The Cross Roads school opened as Hog Wallow School in 1895. In 1903 Emmett C. Norwood opened a post office and called the settlement Clem, in honor of a prominent county family. The postal service ended after four years, and residents soon began to call the community Cross Roads for its location. Cross Roads appeared on maps as an unidentified community in 1936. It had a large school, one business, and a cluster of dwellings at the intersection of Farm Road 128 and a dirt road. By 1960 the school had been absorbed by the Cooper Independent School District. In 1964 the community's population was twenty-five. Cross Roads still appeared on maps in 1984 and had ten inhabitants in 1990.

BIBLIOGRAPHY: Paul Garland Hervey, A History of Education in Delta County, Texas (M.A. thesis, University of Texas, 1951). Wilma Ross and Billie Phillips, *Photos and Tales of Delta County* (1976).
Vista K. McCroskey

CROSS ROADS, TEXAS (Denton County). Cross Roads, at the intersection of U.S. highways 377 and 380, four miles east of Denton in east central Denton County, came into existence as a result of the construction of Lake Dallas, which was completed in November 1927. In 1945 Cross Roads reported a population of fifty. By 1978 the number of residents had increased to 215, and in 1988 the population was estimated at 390. In 1990 it was 361.

BIBLIOGRAPHY: C. A. Bridges, *History of Denton, Texas, from Its Beginning to 1960* (Waco: Texian Press, 1978).
David Minor

CROSSROADS, TEXAS (Harrison County). Crossroads is named for its location at the intersection of Farm roads 31, 2625, and 2199, nine miles southeast of Marshall in southeastern Harrison County. The settlement was founded before 1897, when the Crossroads school served twenty-three pupils. In 1904 the community had four schools serving 416 black pupils and sixty-three white pupils. In 1965 Crossroads had two general stores facing each other across Farm Road 31, and in 1990 the site had two churches, a cemetery, and several scattered dwellings. *Mark Odintz*

CROSS ROADS, TEXAS (Henderson County). Cross Roads is at the junction of Farm roads 59 and 3441 in southwestern Henderson County. The area was originally settled in 1846. The earliest settlement was called Science Hill. In 1885 the Wildcat post office was opened at the site with George B. Thompson as postmaster. By 1892 the community had three cotton gins, a general store, and several other establishments, but the Wildcat post office closed in 1905. The community was also referred to as Thompson's Mill because of a water-powered mill built in 1871 by D. M. Thompson on Wildcat Creek. Cross Roads, as a named community, traces its origins to the early 1890s. A brush-arbor camp meeting of Baptists was held at the point where the road from Athens to Wildcat Ferry and the road from Malakoff to Palestine crossed, and gave the location the name "Cross Roads." The first permanent building in the area was a church, which was erected after the Union-Center school moved from Thompson's Mill to the Cross Roads location. In 1908 a one-room school was erected; it was taught by Sam Holland, who later became district judge of Henderson County. In the early part of the twentieth century numerous gins, gristmills, and other businesses supportive of an agricultural community thrived at Cross Roads. There was a post office there until World War I,[qv] and a courthouse was built to house the justice of the peace court.

In the mid-1920s, as a result of the merger of various smaller schools in the area, the Cross Roads Consolidated School was established. From the 1920s through the end of World War II[qv] the school was expanded and upgraded. The Work Projects Administration[qv] made several improvements to the school facility, and in the late 1940s the Cross Roads Independent School District was formed as the consolidation of eight common school districts in the general vicinity. After a disastrous fire in 1953 much of the school plant was rebuilt. In 1990 the Cross Roads Independent School District comprised 75,000 acres and had 500 students. Cotton and ranching were the most important agricultural activities in the district, particularly in the Trinity River bottom, but other areas produced various truck crops and fruit. Discoveries of oil and gas in the 1940s and 1950s contributed to a brief resurgence. A population of 135 was reported in 1988 and 1990.

BIBLIOGRAPHY: Henderson County Historical Commission, *Family Histories of Henderson County, Texas, 1846–1981* (Dallas: Taylor, 1981). Donna Paxton Holmes, *Cross Roads School and Community* (Austin: Nortex, 1986). Michael J. Vaughn, *The History of Cayuga and Cross Roads* (Waco: Texian Press, 1967). *Michael J. Vaughn*

CROSSROADS, TEXAS (Hopkins County). Crossroads (Cross Roads), at the junction of State Highway 154 and Farm Road 1567, ten miles south of Sulphur Springs in south central Hopkins County, was settled before 1900. By 1905 a public school there had an enrollment of fifty-two students. In the mid-1930s Crossroads had the school, a store, and a number of scattered houses. After World War II[qv] most of the residents moved away. The school was consolidated with the Sulphur Springs school district, and the store later closed; by the early 1960s only a few houses remained at the site. In the early 1990s Crossroads was a dispersed rural community. *Christopher Long*

CROSS ROADS, TEXAS (Milam County). Cross Roads (Crossroads) is near the intersection of Farm Roads 979 and 2027, twelve miles northeast of Cameron in northeastern Milam County. In 1941 it had a school, a business, and twenty-five residents. The population was thirty-five in 1990.

BIBLIOGRAPHY: Lelia M. Batte, *History of Milam County, Texas* (San Antonio: Naylor, 1956). *Vivian Elizabeth Smyrl*

CROSS ROADS, TEXAS (Navarro County). Cross Roads (Crossroads), two miles southeast of Frost in northwestern Navarro County, was established in 1868 by J. A. Tullos and other area plantation owners at the intersection of two roads. A post office opened there in 1877, and by the mid-1880s the community had several cotton gins, four or five stores, Methodist and Baptist churches, a broom factory, and an estimated population of fifty. The town began to decline in the late 1880s, after the St. Louis, Arkansas and Texas Railway bypassed it, and most of the residents and all of the businesses moved to the newly established town of Frost on the railroad. The post office closed in 1888, and by 1900 Cross Roads was completely deserted.

BIBLIOGRAPHY: Alva Taylor, *History and Photographs of Corsicana and Navarro County* (Corsicana, Texas, 1959; rev. ed., *Navarro County History and Photographs*, Corsicana, 1962). *Christopher Long*

CROSSROADS, TEXAS (Panola County). Crossroads, near the site that became Horton, twelve miles northeast of Carthage in northeastern Panola County, was established after the Civil War.[qv] A school was operating there by 1897, when it had an enrollment of forty-six. In the mid-1930s the settlement had a church, a school, and a number of houses. Its school was later consolidated with the DeBerry school, and by the mid-1960s only a cemetery and a few scattered houses remained in the area. *Christopher Long*

CROSS ROADS, TEXAS (Upshur County). Cross Roads (Crossroads), eight miles southwest of Gilmer on the old Gilmer–Big Sandy highway in southwestern Upshur County, was probably established around 1900. In the mid-1930s it had a church, a school, and a number of houses. After World War II[qv] many of its residents moved away, and the school was consolidated with the Big Sandy school district. By the mid-1960s all that remained of the community was a few scattered houses, among them the Gage House, one of the oldest houses in the county. Nearby was the Lone Pilgrim Primitive Baptist Church.

BIBLIOGRAPHY: Doyal T. Loyd, *History of Upshur County* (Waco: Texian Press, 1987). *Christopher Long*

CROSSTIMBER CREEK. Crosstimber Creek rises near Oak Dale in northeastern Hopkins County (at 33°17′ N, 95°32′ W) and runs southeast ten miles to its mouth on White Oak Creek, four miles north of Saltillo in eastern Hopkins County (at 33°15′ N, 95°21′ W). The stream, intermittent in its upper reaches, traverses generally flat terrain with local shallow depressions and clay loam and sandy loam soils that support water-tolerant hardwoods, conifers, and grasses.

CROSS TIMBERS. The Cross Timbers of Texas is two long and narrow strips of forest region that extend parallel to each other from Oklahoma southward to Central Texas between the ninety-sixth and ninety-ninth meridians and form a marked contrast to the prairies of the state. The Eastern (or Lower) Cross Timbers, a narrow band of blackjack and post oak, separates the region of Black Prairies on the east from the Grand Prairies on the west. The Eastern and Western Cross Timbers are formed by a narrow band of woodland extending along Red River. Toward the south the Eastern Cross Timbers belt spans the ninety-seventh meridian from the Red River to the Brazos River. Beginning in the eastern half of Cooke County, it extends southward through the eastern parts of Denton, Tarrant, and Johnson counties and the western parts of Grayson, Dallas, Ellis, and Hill counties. The average width of the Eastern Cross Timbers does not exceed fifteen miles, and its features disappear near the Brazos at Waco. The altitude of the belt is slightly higher than that of the surrounding prairies. The soil of the Eastern Cross Timbers differs from that of the Western in that the Eastern is more fertile and therefore produces larger trees and a wider variety of trees and shrubs. In pioneer times the band of timber was a famous landmark. It was also a formidable obstacle to travelers because of the density of growth. It served as a dividing line between the hunting grounds of the Plains Indians and East Texas Indians. Comanches raided east of the Cross Timbers in the early years, and the Wichitas and others used the wood in the Cross Timbers. Indians used the Cross Timbers as a north-south avenue that afforded secrecy from enemies. Cross Timbers oaks are used for firewood, railroad ties, and poles, but the most important function of the timber belt is preserving water. The timber prevents rain water from immediately running off the surface and causes much of it to soak into sand that supplies artesian water for hundreds of wells to the east and south of the Cross Timbers. The region is well adapted for truck farming. Cotton and corn are also grown.

The Western (or Upper) Cross Timbers comprises an irregularly bounded wooded region in north central Texas, extending in a generally southward direction through Montague, Wise, Jack, Parker, Hood, Erath, and Comanche counties. Topographically, much of the Western Cross Timbers is characterized by rough features, in contrast to the smooth outlines of the lands both to the east and to the west. The region at large, underlain by nonlimy geologic materials, is not easily eroded; constructional areas are few, and where they do occur, at the foot of longer slopes, they are of small extent. Since the region has a subhumid climate, its natural vegetation would ordinarily be grass; its scrubby tree growth results from edaphic features. The Western Cross Timbers is underlain by three larger groups of geologic formations: the Trinity sands of the Comanchean or Lower Cretaceous, the hard rocks of the various Pennsylvanian formations, and the Continental Red Beds materials of the Wichita formation in the Lower Permian. Owing to the fact that the parent materials are prevailingly noncalcareous, both the soils and the natural vegetation of the Western Cross Timbers areas differ sharply from soils of adjacent areas underlain by either "hard" or "soft" formations that are also highly calcareous. In fact, outcrops of the Paluxy sands are interspersed among calcareous materials to the east of the Trinity sands; without exception, the narrow belts of Paluxy sand outcrops support a growth of hardwoods, forming ribbons of woodland in an area where grasses would normally predominate. Topographic types in the region vary with the major geologic formations that outcrop in the area. The Trinity sands area at the east is a plain much of the surface of which is now so eroded as to forbid its use agriculturally. The Pennsylvanian outcrops form a plateau dissected by the channels of major streams that have been cut considerably below the surface level. The portion of the Western Cross Timbers underlain by the Wichita formation is a hilly and maturely dissected; in it the woodland vegetation is more scattered and more dwarfed than is the case in eastward-lying areas of the region. Soil and variations parallel both the topography and the geologic materials. The natural vegetation is a woodland predominantly made up of dwarfed post oaks. Short grasses occur over much of the area in localities where the woodland growth is sparse. Some of the areas underlain by deep sands support a growth of tall grasses. Among the Pennsylvanian outcrops occur scattered exposures of hard limestones; without exception, such exposures are characterized by a typical savanna landscape, comprising scattered mesquite shrubs underlain by a floor of sod-forming short grasses. The Western Cross Timbers country presents a landscape unexpected in West Texas. The region has been important chiefly for its mineral resources. Portions of the Trinity sands area are now important in peanut culture qv as well as for the growing of small fruits. In pioneer days the woodland growth on the Trinity sands supplied fuel for settlers on the western frontier of Texas as well as timber for log houses. The Trinity sands outcrop is an important intake area for meteoric water that forms important aquifers to the east where the formation continues in the subsurface. This was an important influence on early settlement as underground water was available from shallow wells dug into the Trinity sands. (*See also* LOWER PLAINS.)

BIBLIOGRAPHY: William Bollaert, *Observations on the Geography of Texas* (London, 1850). Edward Everett Dale, *The Cross-Timbers: Memories of a North Texas Boyhood* (Austin: University of Texas Press, 1966). Zachary Taylor Fulmore, *The Geography of Texas* (n.p.: Rand, McNally, 1908). Terry Jordan, *Texas: A Geography* (Boulder, Colorado: Westview Press, 1984). Frederic William Simonds, *Geographic Influences in the Development of Texas* (Austin: Journal of Geography, 1912).

CROSS TIMBERS, TEXAS. Cross Timbers, in northern Johnson County, was named for its location on the edge of the western Cross Timbers.qv The site was settled about 1853, and a post office opened there in 1870. By 1885 the community reported a population of 100, a school and church, and several businesses, including a cotton gin and gristmill. In 1890 Cross Timbers reported a population of 200. Though in 1896 the community school had one teacher with twenty-five students, by 1900 the school apparently no longer existed. Both the Missouri, Kansas and Texas and the Gulf, Colorado and Santa Fe lines bypassed the settlement in the 1880s. The Cross Timbers post office closed in 1904, and by 1910 the original community had apparently ceased to exist. In 1990 an incorporated Cross Timbers in Johnson County, in the Fort Worth metropolitan area, reported a population of 245.
Brian Hart

CROSS TIMBERS REVIEW. The *Cross Timbers Review*, a journal of poetry, fiction, history, criticism, biography, pen-and-ink drawings, reviews, and interviews, began in 1983 when Cisco Junior College president Norman Wallace approved the journal's concept as developed by editor Monte Lewis, poetry editor Cleatus Rattan, and fiction editor Ken Hammes. Lawrence Clayton of Hardin-Simmons University was literary-criticism editor, and Kenneth Neighbours of Midwestern State University was history and biography editor. Cisco Junior College publishes the review semiannually, using the college's press at Cisco. The first issue appeared in spring 1984. With the exception of poetry, the journal features material relative to the Southwest, especially the Cross Timbersqv region of Texas and Oklahoma. *Cross Timbers Review* was nominated for the Understanding Poetry Award for the decade of the 1980s.
Monte Lewis

CROSSVILLE, TEXAS. Crossville, four or five miles east of Copperas Cove on the Coryell-Bell county line, was named for early Bell County settler James M. Cross. Families began moving into the area before the Civil War.qv A post office opened there in 1872 with Martin W. Warren as postmaster, but closed in 1881. In 1880 the community had a population of forty. The townsite and area farms and ranches were absorbed by Camp Hood (*see* FORT HOOD) in the early 1940s, and most Crossville residents relocated in Copperas Cove.

BIBLIOGRAPHY: Jerry K. Smith and Patrick D. McLaughlin, *Copperas Cove, City of Five Hills: A Centennial History* (Burnet, Texas: Eakin Press, 1980).
Vivian Elizabeth Smyrl

CROSSVILLE MOUNTAIN. Crossville Mountain (Crossville Peak) is just northeast of Gray Army Airfield in Fort Hood military reservation in southwestern Bell County near the Coryell county line (at 31°06′ N, 97°50′ W). Its summit, at an elevation of 1,100 feet above sea level, rises 100 feet above Gray field.

CROTON, TEXAS. Croton is on Farm Road 2470 and a branch of Little Croton Creek, eight miles northeast of Dickens in north central Dickens County. The settlement, originally named Frankfort, was established around 1888 and served as a community center for the surrounding area. Many of the settlers were employed by the nearby Matador and Pitchfork ranches.qqv In the first county seat election in March 1891 Frankfort was one of three sites on the ballot. Although no town received enough votes to be declared the winner, Frankfort withdrew from the race. A school was built there in 1892 and named Noview for a grove of cottonwood trees. Later the community name was changed to Croton Flat, presumably for nearby Croton Creek. By 1922 residents had built a new two-story school that served as a community center, church, and voting station. In 1933 the school was consolidated with the Patton Springs school, several miles northwest of Croton. Croton was reported to have two stores and 100 residents in 1948. One store and a Baptist church were still in operation by the early 1970s. In the 1980s Croton appeared on county maps, but no businesses were indicated.

BIBLIOGRAPHY: Fred Arrington, *A History of Dickens County: Ranches and Rolling Plains* (Quanah, Texas: Nortex, 1971).

Charles G. Davis

CROTON BREAKS. The Croton Breaks is a 250-square-mile area of rough land below the escarpment of the Llano Estacado^{qv} (at 33°35′ N, 100°44′ W). The breaks encompass the southwest quarter of Dickens County between Dickens on the north and John Bell Canyon on the south. The region is severely eroded, marked with densely dissected gullies and low hills, a typical badlands topography with shallow topsoil or none. Plants are few. In 1879 the Matador Land and Cattle Company,^{qv} which owned nearly half a million acres in Motley, Floyd, Dickens, and Cottle counties, owned most of the land in the Croton Breaks. Cattle often were lost in the breaks and could not be rounded up in the spring. Stories of a lost lead mine in the Croton Breaks near Dickens are typified by the version in J. Frank Dobie's^{qv} *Legends of Texas* (1924). Some locals claim the rangeland received its name from the bitter water found in the Little and Big Croton creeks, which run through the breaks. Others claim that a tribe of "Croton Indians" were in the vicinity in the 1860s.

Richard Allen Burns

CROTON CREEK. Croton Creek rises in several small springs north of Dickens in central Dickens County (at 33°39′ N, 100°50′ W). Throughout much of its southeastward course it traverses the Croton Breaks, a rugged region of canyons and broken terrain surfaced by shallow silt loams that support mesquite and grasses. The stream is intermittent in its upper stages. It becomes a flowing stream after its junction with Little Croton Creek near the mouth of Fortyone Canyon, seven miles south of U.S. Highway 82 in southeastern Dickens County (at 33°31′ N, 100°38′ W). Little Croton Creek rises four miles north of Dickens (at 33°41′ N, 100°49′ W) and flows thirty miles. Croton Creek flows across the northeast corner of Kent County to its mouth on the Brazos River, in northwest Stonewall County fifteen miles northwest of Aspermont (at 33°17′ N, 100°25′ W). From an initial elevation of 2,700 feet Croton Creek descends 1,000 feet during its course of sixty-five miles.

BIBLIOGRAPHY: Fred Arrington, *A History of Dickens County: Ranches and Rolling Plains* (Quanah, Texas: Nortex, 1971). Dickens County Historical Commission, *Dickens County: Its Land and Its People* (Lubbock: Craftsman Printers, 1986).

CROTON PEAK. Croton Peak is in Big Bend National Park^{qv} nine miles northwest of Panther Junction in southern Brewster County (at 29°22′ N, 103°21′ W). With an elevation of 4,601 feet above sea level, it rises 1,240 feet above Croton Spring, two miles south. The peak is formed by the southwestern end of a sheet-like intrusion of alkalic quartz syenite, the northeastern end of which forms the Paint Gap Hills. The peak's shallow, stony soils support scrub brush and grasses.

CROUCH, CARRIE JOHNSON (1887–1967). Carrie Johnson Crouch, county historian, was born in Graham, Texas, on September 10, 1887, the second of six children born to Clark Wesley and Martha Blanche (Eichelberger) Johnson. Her father was the Republican nominee for governor in 1912. In 1909 she married Eugene A. Crouch of McKinney. She wrote *Young County: History and Biography*, first published in 1937 and republished with revisions by the Texas State Historical Association^{qv} in 1956 as *A History of Young County, Texas*. She also wrote a brief history of Fort Belknap, published by the Graham *Leader*. Mrs. Crouch was a Republican and served as county chairman from 1942 until 1952. She was active in the Methodist Church, the Poetry Society of Texas,^{qv} and the Fort Belknap Genealogical Association. She and her husband had one child, a daughter. Carrie Crouch died on May 23, 1967, in Graham.

BIBLIOGRAPHY: Young County Historical Commission, *Roots in Young County* (Dallas: Taylor, 1978).

Barbara A. Neal Ledbetter

CROUCH, JOHN RUSSELL (1916–1976). John Russell (Hondo) Crouch, humorist, writer, and owner and self-proclaimed mayor of Luckenbach, Texas, was born on December 4, 1916, in Hondo, Texas, to Ione and Harry Crouch, a telegraph operator for the Southern Pacific Railroad. Hondo Crouch was an All-American swimmer at the University of Texas, where he was awarded a degree in physical education in 1941. After training as a navigator in the Air Corps at Garner Field in 1942, he settled down to raise sheep, goats, and cattle near Fredericksburg. He was swimming coach at various Texas children's camps from the 1930s until the 1970s. In 1964 he was president of the Hall of Fame for UT athletes and in 1975 was influential in persuading the university to build the Texas Swim Center. From 1963 to 1975, under the pen name Peter Cedarstacker, Crouch wrote about 600 "Cedar Creek Clippings" for the Comfort *News*. Through his characters from the mythical town of Cedar Creek he satirized politics, government, ecology, deer hunters, social life, and everyday country problems and celebrations. In 1971 he bought Luckenbach, a small community established as an Indian trading post by German immigrant Albert Luckenbach in 1849. There Crouch presided as mayor over a population of three plus a single parking meter. As "clown prince" he brought to life the town's motto, "Everybody's Somebody in Luckenbach." He held zany celebrations, such as the Luckenbach World's Fair, the first Texas "women only" chili cookoff, Return of the Mud Daubers, and no-talent contests. Crouch participated in a Folklife Festival for Texas at the Smithsonian Institution in 1964. On July 4, 1976, Luckenbach received national attention for celebrating the Non-Buy Centennial, protesting the commercialization of the bicentennial of the Declaration of Independence. Crouch was a Republican. He was married for thirty years to Helen Ruth (Shatzie) Stieler, daughter of the 1945 "Goat King of the World," Adolf Stieler of Comfort, and they had four children. Crouch died of a heart attack on September 27, 1976, in Blanco.

BIBLIOGRAPHY: John Davidson, "The Man Who Dreamed Up Luckenbach," *Texas Monthly*, July 1984. Becky Crouch Patterson, *Hondo, My Father* (Austin: Shoal Creek, 1979). Carlton Stowers, "Hondo Crouch and His Backwoods Camelot," *Dallas Morning News Scene Magazine*, December 15, 1974.

Becky Crouch Patterson

CROW, TEXAS. Crow is at the intersection of Farm Road 778, U.S. Highway 80, and the Missouri Pacific Railroad, fourteen miles southeast of Quitman in southeastern Wood County. The site was called Graham when a railroad station was built there in 1876. When the town received a post office in 1906, it was renamed Crow in honor of Wilson Crow, who worked at a local sawmill. Sometime before 1900 Burrell Cannon, an employee of the nearby Rucker sawmill, is said to have built an airplane that flew. Crow at one time had a number of stores and a saloon, reported to be the last saloon in Wood County. By 1910 the community had two churches and a district school. A few years later it had a population of seventy-five, a telephone connection, and four businesses, including a blacksmith shop and a cotton gin. Though lots were platted at Crow, the town never grew. After the local timber supply was exhausted, the sawmills closed down, and much of the population left. In the 1930s Crow had a population of 100, a number of dwellings, a church, three businesses, and a school, which in 1932 had an enrollment of eighty-eight students in nine grades. At that time Crow was still a station on the Texas and Pacific Railway. By 1956 post office had closed. The church and school closed by 1960. Over the next decade the population gradually declined and in 1970 was reported at twenty-five. By the early 1980s U.S. Highway 80, which borders the community, had been expanded to four lanes, and Crow had gained a few new dwellings. The 1988 highway map shows several businesses, and the community reported a population of twenty-five in 1990.

BIBLIOGRAPHY: *Wood County, 1850–1900* (Quitman, Texas: Wood County Historical Society, 1976). *Rachel Jenkins*

CROW CREEK (Cass County). Crow Creek rises four miles north of Marietta in northwestern Cass County (at 33°14′ N, 94°32′ W) and runs northwest for three miles to its mouth on the Sulphur River (at 33°16′ N, 94°33′ W). It crosses gently undulating to rolling terrain surfaced by loam soils that support pine and hardwood forests.

――― (Wheeler County). Crow Creek rises a few miles east of Shamrock in southeastern Wheeler County (at 35°14′ N, 100°11′ W) and runs southeast for six miles into Collingsworth County, where it reaches its mouth on Elm Creek (at 35°07′ N, 100°06′ W). The stream crosses rolling to steep-sloped terrain surfaced by shallow clay and sandy loams that support primarily juniper and sparse grasses. During the 1880s and early 1890s Crow Creek was included in the vast rangeland owned or leased by the Rocking Chair Ranch.qv

CROWELL, CAROLINE (1893–1972). Caroline Crowell, physician for the University of Texas in Austin, the daughter of William James and Frances (Eakins) Crowell, was born on May 17, 1893, in Avondale, Pennsylvania. She received a B.A. degree in 1916 from Bryn Mawr and a B.S. degree in industrial chemistry in 1918 from Pennsylvania State College. During World War Iqv she worked as a chemist in a munitions factory; after the war she worked as an industrial chemist with the Corning Glass Works in New York before attending the University of Pennsylvania Medical School, where she received her M.D. in 1925. After serving her internship at Woman's Hospital, Philadelphia, she moved to Austin, Texas, where she was a staff physician at the University of Texas Student Health Center from 1926 until her retirement in 1965. At the time of her move to Texas she was one of only two doctors on the university campus and the only woman physician in Austin. From 1929 to 1932 she volunteered her services as night resident physician at Brackenridge Hospital.qv Dr. Crowell was the niece of the noted nineteenth-century artist Thomas Eakins; she donated to the university's art museum two of her uncle's works, *At the Piano* and *A Portrait of a Lady*. She died on August 28, 1972, in Austin and was buried in Austin Memorial Park. She was survived by brothers, nieces, and nephews.

BIBLIOGRAPHY: Vertical Files, Barker Texas History Center, University of Texas at Austin.

CROWELL, CHESTER THEODORE (1888–1941). Chester T. Crowell, newspaperman and writer, was born on October 14, 1888, in Cleveland, Ohio, to William Theodore and Adelaide (Chichester) Crowell. The family moved to Texas while he was a young boy. He attended public schools in Beaumont, Houston, and San Antonio, won a writing contest, and was recognized by the San Antonio *Express*. The paper offered him a job as soon as he graduated from high school. In 1907 Crowell moved to Mexico City to become the managing editor for the *Mexican Herald*. At the time, he had difficulty understanding and communicating in Spanish, yet by the time he left Mexico in 1909 he was translating and writing fluently in both English and Spanish. Upon returning to San Antonio, Crowell once again worked for the *Express*, this time as an editorial writer. In 1911 he became managing editor for the Austin *American-Statesman*,qv where he remained until 1916, when he became a staff correspondent for the Dallas *News* for a year. In 1923 he became an editorial writer for the New York *Evening Post*. From this time until his death in 1941, he did free-lance writing. In 1924 Crowell was awarded the O. Henry Short Story Award for his short story "Margaret Blake." Another story, "Ruth," was included in a book of the world's 100 best. Yet another of his short stories was published in the O'Brien collection of 1924, entitled *The Twenty Best Stories of the Year*. Crowell was a member of the Authors League of America. He was also a Democrat and paid careful attention to politics. When he moved to Washington, he was appointed special assistant to the secretary of the treasury. After resigning from this position, he wrote *Recovery Unlimited: The Monetary Policy of the Roosevelt Administration* (1936), one of his best-known books. Crowell first married in 1911. He and his wife, Mary Frances (Beaulac), had five children. On October 24, 1937, Crowell married Evelyn Miller Pierce, a Dallas-born writer and the daughter of Lieutenant Governor Barry Miller.qv Their marriage was a short one, for Crowell died on December 27, 1941. He was buried in Washington.

BIBLIOGRAPHY: Sam Hanna Acheson, Herbert P. Gambrell, Mary Carter Toomey, and Alex M. Acheson, Jr., *Texian Who's Who*, Vol. 1 (Dallas: Texian, 1937). Dallas *Morning News*, December 27, 1941. Vertical Files, Barker Texas History Center, University of Texas at Austin. *Who's Who in America*, 1934–35. *Aly Clyburn*

CROWELL, GRACE NOLL (1877–1969). Grace Noll Crowell, poet, daughter of Adam and Sarah (Southern) Noll, was born in Inland, Iowa, on October 31, 1877. In 1901, after receiving her B.A. from the German-English College in Wilton, Iowa, she married Norman H. Crowell, with whom she had three sons. She moved in 1917 to Wichita Falls, Texas, and two years later to Dallas, where she spent the rest of her life. Norman Crowell died in 1953.

Grace Crowell's poems appeared in major magazines throughout the United States and abroad. Her first book of poetry, *White Fire* (1925), was awarded first prize by the Texas Poetry Society. In 1935 she was designated Poet Laureateqv of Texas. Three years later she was awarded the Golden Scroll Medal of Honor as National Honor Poet. Also in 1938 the Golden Rule Foundation designated her American Mother of the Year, and *American Women*, a biographical publication, selected her as one of ten Outstanding American Women. Baylor University awarded her an honorary doctorate in 1940. Among many subsequent honors, she was also selected as honorary chancellor of the National Federation of State Poetry Societies in 1965.

In the early 1940s Grace Crowell was called "the most popular writer of verse in America." Dale Carnegie called her "one of the most beloved poets in America." Magazine and newspaper articles often commented on her widespread popularity, on the visitors from other parts of the United States and abroad who stopped by her Dallas home, and on her massive correspondence with grateful readers. Her husband quit his job to manage her career. She published over thirty-five books of poetry, stories for children, and poem and prose devotions. *Her Songs for Courage* went into twenty-five printings. In 1977 a reprint of her 1965 collection of poems appeared as *The Eternal Things: The Best of Grace Noll Crowell*. She died on March 31, 1969, and was buried at Hillcrest Mausoleum in Dallas.

BIBLIOGRAPHY: Dallas *Morning News*, April 1, 1969. *Notable Women of the Southwest* (Dallas: Tardy, 1938). Beatrice Plumb, *Grace Noll Crowell* (New York: Harper, 1938). Texas Mothers Committee, *Worthy Mothers of Texas* (Belton, Texas: Stillhouse Hollow, 1976). *Betty S. Flowers*

CROWELL, TEXAS. Crowell, on U.S. Highway 70, State Highway 6, and Farm Road 98 in central Foard County, was organized in 1891

and named for George T. Crowell, owner of the townsite. M. F. Thacker sold lots and became the first postmaster in 1891. In 1860 Texas Ranger captain Lawrence Sullivan (Sul) Ross[qv] had defeated a band of Comanche Indians on the Pease River near the site of Crowell and rescued Cynthia Ann Parker.[qv] Foard County was organized the year after the town was founded, and Crowell was voted county seat. It quickly became a trade center and the largest town in the county. Before the railroad was built, mail was carried to Crowell from Vernon. By 1900 Crowell had 500 residents and a number of businesses, including a hotel, a cotton gin, and a gristmill. The first train of the Kansas City, Mexico and Orient Railway reached the town in 1908. Crowell was incorporated that year, and a boom followed. The population was 1,500 by 1925. The *Foard County News* was published by J. L. Harper beginning in 1891. Crowell thrived after oil was discovered in the county in 1927 and weathered the Great Depression[qv] reasonably well. The community suffered heavy tornado damage in April 1942. Ten people were killed, 125 hurt, and 1,500 left homeless; 90 percent of the business buildings and homes were destroyed. The Red Cross, WPA, and Civilian Conservation Corps[qv] helped during the emergency, and eventually the town was rebuilt. The population climbed to 1,922 in 1950 and stood at 1,509 in 1980, when the town had twenty-seven businesses. Agribusiness and the manufacture of sporting goods are the leading industries. Tourist and recreation attractions include the Crowell Firehall Museum and Copper Breaks State Park, eight miles to the north in Hardeman County. In 1990 the population of Crowell was 1,230.

BIBLIOGRAPHY: Bailey Phelps, *They Loved the Land: Foard County History* (Quanah, Texas: Quanah *Tribune-Chief*, 1969). Kathleen E. and Clifton R. St. Clair, eds., *Little Towns of Texas* (Jacksonville, Texas: Jayroe Graphic Arts, 1982).
William R. Hunt

CROWLEY, MILES (1859–1921). Miles Crowley, congressman and judge, was born on February 22, 1859, in Boston, Massachusetts. He was educated in the public schools and worked for a time as a longshoreman. In the 1870s he moved to Galveston, Texas, where he was assistant chief of the Galveston Fire Department and studied law. He was admitted to the bar in 1892. That year he was elected a member of the Texas House of Representatives, and in 1893–94 he served in the Texas Senate. He was elected as a Democrat to the Fifty-fourth Congress and served from March 4, 1896, to March 3, 1897. He afterward resumed his private practice in Galveston rather than running for reelection. From 1904 to 1912 he served as county attorney and in 1920 became judge of the county court, an office he held until his death, on September 22, 1921. He was buried in Calvary Cemetery, Galveston.

BIBLIOGRAPHY: *Biographical Directory of the American Congress*. Galveston *News*, September 23, 1921.
Anne W. Hooker

CROWLEY, TEXAS. Crowley is at the crossroads of Farm roads 1187 and 731, two miles west of Interstate Highway 35 and fifteen miles south of downtown Fort Worth in Tarrant County. About 1848 pioneers began to farm near Deer Creek in the area. The first recorded burial was in 1857. The settlement was moved to its present site when the Gulf, Colorado and Santa Fe Railway built pens and laid tracks there. The first station depot was constructed in 1885. The community was named for S. H. Crowley, master of transportation for the railroad. A post office was established in 1882. Crowley is shown as a town on the 1885 *Railroad and County Map of Texas*. Dairy farming, the railroad, ranching, and related businesses were the principal economic activities in this area. A Presbyterian church was established in 1895. The Crowley post office was moved to the Hayes brothers' general store in 1896. Door-to-door delivery of mail did not begin until April 1972. A two-story concrete building served as the first school (1905). In 1907–08 the school had 120 students. The Continental Bank and Trust Company opened in 1907. Crowley set a per capita record during World War II[qv] for purchasing United States Defense Bonds. The Crowley volunteer fire department was formed in 1950. An election for the incorporation of Crowley was held on February 3, 1951. The first elected mayor was "Chick" Race, who held office from 1953 to 1957. Incorporation helped the town to obtain a water system, natural gas, and a sewage system in the 1960s. On September 3, 1972, the town council moved to change the designation of Crowley from town to city. A park board was established in 1971 to take care of ten acres of land donated to the city. Crowley had a population of 275 in the late 1920s and 1930s, 500 by the end of World War II, and 2,583 in 1970. In 1980 the population had doubled to 5,852. In 1990 Crowley had a population of 8,301, a student enrollment of 4,971, and 134 businesses.

BIBLIOGRAPHY: James Burke, Jr., *Burke's Texas Almanac and Immigrant's Handbook for 1879* (Houston, 1879; facsimile, Austin: Steck-Warlick, 1969). Fort Worth *Star-Telegram*, February 11, 1951, July 3, 1957. Fred I. Massengill, *Texas Towns: Origin of Name and Location of Each of the 2,148 Post Offices in Texas* (Terrell, Texas, 1936).
Kathryn M. Yockstick and Alta Lee Futch

CROWN, TEXAS. Crown is east of Farm Road 1334 ten miles west of Jourdanton in west central Atascosa County. It was a settlement of freed slaves and was first known as Lagunillas but was renamed Crown in 1900, when a post office was established. The name is said to have come from the crown trademark on a sewing machine. John W. Crouch was the first postmaster. In 1904 Lagunillas School in Crown had fifty-four students. By 1914 Crown had a population of twenty-five, a gin, a general store, and the Crown School (formerly Lagunillas School) with 244 students. The Crown post office closed in 1923. The population had grown to fifty in 1925 but declined to fifteen by 1933, the year that the school was consolidated with the schools in Charlotte. A boll weevil[qv] infestation wiped out the area's cotton farmers in 1937. In 1990 a few widely scattered dwellings, one business, and some oil wells on the edge of the Big Foot oilfield were at the site.

BIBLIOGRAPHY: *Atascosa County Centennial, 1856–1956* (Jourdanton, Texas: Atascosa County Centennial Association, n.d.). *Atascosa County History* (Pleasanton, Texas: Atascosa History Committee, 1984). Margaret G. Clover, The Place Names of Atascosa County (M.A. thesis, University of Texas, 1952).
Linda Peterson

CROWNEST CREEK. Crownest (Crows Nest) Creek rises near State Highway 208 in southern Coke County (at 31°42′ N, 100°26′ W) and runs southeast for eighteen miles to its mouth on the Concho River, four miles east of Harriet and seven miles southwest of Miles in northeastern Tom Green County (at 31°32′ N, 100°15′ W). It runs through isolated ranchland with flat terrain surfaced by clay and sandy loams that support conifers and grasses.

CROWN MOUNTAIN. Crown Mountain is in Big Bend National Park[qv] five miles southwest of Panther Junction in south central Brewster County (at 29°16′ N, 103°16′ W). With an elevation of 7,010 feet above sea level, it rises 1,760 feet above the Basin Ranger Station, two miles northwest. The shallow, stony topsoil of the mountain supports Douglas fir, aspen, Arizona cypress, maple, ponderosa pine, and madrone.

CROWNOVER, JOHN (1774–1842). John Crownover, an early settler, was born on October 7, 1774, to Benjamin and Rachel (Jasper) Crownover, who lived in Union District, South Carolina. Benjamin Crownover served in the Revolutionary War in South Carolina and received 200 acres of land for his service. In 1830 John Crownover moved to Texas from Arkansas with his wife, Elizabeth, and one daughter. He applied for land in May 1835 under Stephen F. Austin's[qv] fifth contract. His grant was located in Madison County. John Crownover married Elizabeth Chesney in South Carolina about 1793. Their first three children were born there. They moved to Buncombe County, North Carolina, then to Hardin County, Kentucky, to Illinois, and later to Arkansas and Texas. They had eleven children. Their grown children preceded them to Texas. John C. Crownover, who settled in Fayette County, arrived in 1824 as one of the Old Three Hundred.qv His sister, Mary Crownover Rabb,qv who published *Travels and Adventures in Texas in the 1820's*, came with her husband, John Rabb.qv John Crownover's will was dated August 18, 1842, and recorded in the Fayette County Courthouse at La Grange in 1843. Elizabeth died in 1844. The name Crownover derives from the name Wolfert Gerretse van Kouwenhove, the first of this family from the Netherlands, who sailed to New York in 1625.

BIBLIOGRAPHY: Eugene C. Barker, ed., *The Austin Papers* (3 vols., Washington: GPO, 1924–28). Worth Stickley Ray, *Austin Colony Pioneers* (Austin: Jenkins, 1949; 2d ed., Austin: Pemberton, 1970). Villamae Williams, *Stephen F. Austin's Register of Families* (Nacogdoches, Texas: Ericson, 1984). *Zoe Phillips Boozer Harris*

CROWNOVER BRANCH. Crownover Branch rises in the generally flat floodplain of the Colorado River a mile northwest of Plum in west central Fayette County (at 29°57′ N, 96°57′ W) and runs east for two miles to its mouth on the Colorado River, directly across from Rabbs Prairie (at 29°56′ N, 96°55′ W). The area soils have firm, thick calcareous clay layers and are well suited to agriculture, producing good crops of grain and hay and providing improved pasture for cattle. In large areas, particularly near Plum and near the mouth of the creek, the topsoil has been removed to gain access to beds of gravel. The creek name is derived from that of the family of John Crownover,qv who arrived with the Rabb family in time to become one of Stephen F. Austin'sqv Old Three Hundred.qv

BIBLIOGRAPHY: Leonie Rummel Weyand and Houston Wade, *An Early History of Fayette County* (La Grange, Texas: La Grange *Journal*, 1936).

CROWTHER, TEXAS. Crowther was on a county road off Farm Road 99 fourteen miles northeast of Tilden in northeastern McMullen County. It was named for Samuel Crowther, a transplanted Englishman who owned the townsite and who was the community's first postmaster. The town began between 1900 and 1902 as an ambitious real estate project conducted by the Boston and Texas Corporation. The developers, hoping to develop an agricultural center on their 1,600-acre townsite, cleared land and built a large reservoir and other irrigation projects. They offered farmland for $10 to $12 per acre and town lots for $10 to $100 and advertised in such northeastern states as Massachusetts, New York, and Pennsylvania. Crowther was granted a post office in 1902 and grew moderately over the next ten years, partly thanks to land buyers from New England. By 1905 the community had a three-story hotel and before 1910 also had three stores, an ice plant, and a butcher shop. At its height the town had 300 residents and about fifty homes. After 1910, however, it declined rapidly, in spite of vigorous promotion by the developers. By 1920 all of the businesses in the town had closed, and it was soon afterwards deserted. In 1965 only one family lived on the site, but Crowther appeared on state highway maps as late as 1988.

BIBLIOGRAPHY: Joe Pate Smyer, A History of McMullen County (M.A. thesis, University of Texas, 1952). Marker Files, Texas Historical Commission, Austin. *John Leffler*

CROZIER, HARRY BENGE (1891–1970). Harry Benge Crozier, journalist, was born on July 27, 1891, in Paint Rock, Texas, the son of Henry John and Sallie (Benge) Crozier and grandson of William Cocke Young.qv He attended Southwestern University but left school in 1912 to work for the San Antonio *Express* (see SAN ANTONIO EXPRESS-NEWS), thus beginning a writing career that spanned almost sixty years. He covered Capitolqv news events and legislative sessions from 1913 to 1931, first with the *Express* and later with the Galveston *News*,qv the Fort Worth *Record* (see FORT WORTH STAR-TELEGRAM), and the Dallas Morning *News*.qv

Although never far from newspaper work, Crozier continued his writing career in allied fields; he was editor of the Texas and Southwestern Cattle Raisers Associationqv publication the *Cattleman*,qv which he and Tad Moses took over and modernized with a new format that lasted thirty years. He was also public-relations director for the American Petroleum Institute in New York, public-relations director for the Texas Centennialqv in 1936, and director of information for the Texas Department of Health.qv Crozier worked in the political campaigns of Senator Thomas Terry Connallyqv and presidential candidates Al Smith and Wendell Willkie. Governor Coke Stevensonqv appointed him to the Texas Unemployment Compensation Commission (now the Texas Employment Commissionqv) in the early 1940s and in 1945 appointed him chairman of that agency. In January 1945, in a show of opposition to Stevenson, a solo session of the Texas Senate (the House was not convened) refused to approve Crozier's nomination to the chairmanship. The state Supreme Court, ruling on the legality of the session, rendered a split decision, which had the effect of leaving Crozier in the position. He served as chairman until 1953; he also served as executive director of the TEC from 1945 until 1953. He pursued public-relations work in the 1950s and returned to journalism about 1960 by joining Stuart Long's news service at the state Capitol.

Crozier was a member of Sigma Delta Chi, a professional journalism fraternity; Kappa Alpha, a social fraternity; and the American Legion.qv In 1918 he married Grace Younger; they had one son. After their divorce he married Ruth Hey. Crozier died on July 14, 1970, in Austin, and was buried in the State Cemetery.qv

BIBLIOGRAPHY: Austin *American-Statesman*, November 9, 1946, December 26, 1948, May 18, 1952. Vertical Files, Barker Texas History Center, University of Texas at Austin.

CROZIER, ROBERT HOSKINS (1836–1913). Robert Hoskins Crozier, Presbyterian minister and author, son of Hugh and Nannie (Oliver) Crozier, was born in Coffeeville, Mississippi, on January 28, 1836. He received an A.B. degree at the University of Mississippi in 1857 and an A.M. in 1859. From 1857 to 1861 he was principal of Eureka Male Academy at Eureka, Mississippi. He was captain of Company I, Thirty-third Mississippi Infantry, C.S.A., from 1861 to 1865. From 1867 to 1871 he was principal of Hickory Plains Institute and from 1871 to 1872 was president of Lonoke College, Prairie County, Arkansas. He was licensed to preach in 1872 and ordained a Presbyterian minister by the Arkansas Presbytery in 1873. He was pastor at Sardis and Monroe, Mississippi, from 1872 to 1888, when he moved to Texas and served at Palestine, first as pastor and subsequently as pastor emeritus, from 1888 to 1913. Arkansas College at Batesville, Arkansas, awarded him an honorary doctorate in 1889. Crozier did much writing in addition to his teaching and preaching. His books include *Confederate Spy* (1866), *The Bloody Junto, or the Escape of John Wilkes Booth* (1869), *Fiery Trials* (1882), *Hal Gilman* (1883), *Araphel* (1884), *Care of Hegobar* (1885), *Deep Water* (1887), and *Golden Rule, a Tale of Texas* (1900). Crozier died in Palestine on July 16, 1913.

BIBLIOGRAPHY: *Southwestern Historical Quarterly*, News Items, October 1913.

CRUDGINGTON, JONATHAN WILFORD (1859–1934). Jonathan Wilford Crudgington, jurist, son of Eli Crudgington, was born in Roane County near Knoxville, Tennessee, in 1859. His father fought with distinction in the Union Army during the Civil Warqv and returned afterward to the farm to raise his four children. In 1870 the family moved to Rockwall County, Texas, east of Dallas. Seven years later they moved to another farm near Breckenridge in Stephens County. Crudgington received a common school education and developed a regard for his health; from an early age he put emphasis on daily exercise and cold baths each morning.

About 1880 he formed a partnership with his brother James and began railroad contracting. Among other projects they pushed to get the Fort Worth and Denver City line through the Panhandle^{qv} and graded the Tascosa Cut in northwestern Potter County. Crudgington was in the new rail town of Amarillo for the festivities when the county was officially organized in 1887. In 1889, after studying law under Judge William Veale in Breckenridge, he was admitted to the bar. A year later he married the judge's daughter, Alliene. Four sons and three daughters were born to them.

During the height of the Populist movement in the 1890s (*see* PEOPLE'S PARTY), Crudgington was elected Stephens county judge. He moved to Palo Pinto in 1902 and two years later to Amarillo, where he joined the law firm of his brother-in-law, John Veale. He immediately became involved in the city's prohibition^{qv} battle, which the drys eventually won in 1908. From that time on Crudgington participated in or initiated several civic improvements in Amarillo. With Veale, James C. Paul,^{qv} and the brothers Henry A. and Millard C. Nobles,^{qv} he built the city's streetcar system in 1907. He helped initiate the building of Amarillo's first municipal auditorium in 1921 and was the first vice president of the Tri-State Fair commission in 1923; largely through his efforts alcoholic beverages were forbidden on the fairgrounds. His greatest civic triumph was the successful legal battle over ownership of the Potter County Courthouse square property, a case he carried to the state Supreme Court. Crudgington was known as a brilliant orator. He served two terms in the Texas legislature (1914–18) and was a leader in the statewide prohibition effort. He also supported the founding of West Texas State Normal College (now West Texas A&M University) in Canyon and encouraged the fledgling institution to rebuild after the disastrous fire of 1914. Crudgington was also a prime mover in the Santa Fe Railroad's successful fight to build into Amarillo from Washburn and connect with its Pecos Valley line in 1908. Later, in 1925, he helped Albert S. Stinnett^{qv} to secure the Rock Island line from Liberal, Kansas, to Amarillo.

Crudgington was an elder in the First Presbyterian Church of Amarillo, where he taught a Sunday school class for twenty-seven years. He was moderator of the synod of the Presbyterian Church^{qv} in Texas in 1928 and also served as a member of the church's permanent judicial commission. He died of a heart attack at his home on Tyler Street on June 17, 1934, and was interred in Memorial Park Cemetery, Amarillo.

BIBLIOGRAPHY: Amarillo *Daily News*, June 18, 1934. Della Tyler Key, *In the Cattle Country: History of Potter County, 1887–1966* (Amarillo: Tyler-Berkley, 1961; 2d ed., Wichita Falls: Nortex, 1972).

H. Allen Anderson

CRUGER, JACOB W. (1819–1864). Jacob W. Cruger, early Texas printer, was born in Dansville, New York, in 1819. He moved to Texas in June 1836 with his younger brother, James F. Cruger,^{qv} and an older friend, Dr. Francis Moore, Jr.^{qv} After serving in the Army of the Republic of Texas^{qv} from June 6 to September 22, 1836, Cruger served as a clerk in the War Department, engaged in the mercantile business with his brother, was for a time in 1837 postmaster of Houston, and served as assistant secretary to the Texas Senate. In June 1837 he became a partner with Moore in the ownership and management of the *Telegraph and Texas Register*,^{qv} an alliance that lasted fourteen years. Cruger acted as business manager and Moore as editor.

In April 1839 Cruger founded the first daily newspaper in Texas, the Houston *Morning Star*,^{qv} which was published from the *Telegraph* office but was independent of it. Cruger and Moore inherited the current public printing contract when they purchased the *Telegraph*. When Austin became the capital in 1839 Cruger turned the *Morning Star* over to his brother James, then founded the Austin *Texas Sentinel*^{qv} in 1840, in association with George W. Bonnell.^{qv} Bonnell and Cruger were also able to secure the new public printing contract. When the Austin paper failed in 1842 because of the removal of the government offices, Cruger returned to Houston and continued his activities there. He and Moore again received the public printing contract in 1844. Joel Miner^{qv} and Cruger teamed up in the summer of 1845 to publish the Austin *New Era*,^{qv} a paper that carried the proceedings of the annexation^{qv} convention. In April 1851 Cruger sold his interest in the *Telegraph* to Moore and merged his own *Morning Star* with it.

Cruger was opposed to Sam Houston's^{qv} policies, and his papers reflected this opposition. At the beginning of the Civil War^{qv} he joined the Confederate Army and served as aide-de-camp to Richard Montgomery Gano,^{qv} whose cavalry detachment ranged through the Trans-Mississippi Division and Indian Territory. Cruger died on November 30, 1864, in Bell County, of a disease contracted during his military service.

BIBLIOGRAPHY: C. Richard King, "Public Printing in the Republic of Texas," *Texana* 6 (Winter 1968). Addie Roy, History of the *Telegraph and Texas Register*, 1835–1846 (M.A. thesis, University of Texas, 1931). Madeleine B. Stern, *Imprints on History: Book Publishers and American Frontiers* (Bloomington: Indiana University Press, 1956).

A. E. Skinner

CRUGER, JAMES F. (?–1874). James F. Cruger, merchant and publisher, the brother of Jacob W. Cruger,^{qv} accompanied his brother and Francis Moore, Jr.,^{qv} to Texas in 1836 from Danville, New York. After settling in Houston, they first engaged in the mercantile business, but James Cruger was soon alone when his brother and Moore entered newspaper work and purchased an interest in the *Telegraph and Texas Register*.^{qv} Though Cruger remained in the store, he later spent much of his time assisting his brother in his newspaper enterprises. In 1841 his name was substituted for that of his brother as publisher of the Houston *Morning Star*,^{qv} and at this time the *Star* changed from a daily to a triweekly edition. Cruger died in Houston in 1874.

BIBLIOGRAPHY: Joe B. Frantz, Newspapers of the Republic of Texas (M.A. thesis, University of Texas, 1940). Mary Glasscock Frazier, Texas Newspapers during the Republic (March 2, 1836–February 19, 1846) (M. Journ. thesis, University of Texas, 1931). Douglas C. McMurtrie, "Pioneer Printing in Texas," *Southwestern Historical Quarterly* 35 (January 1932). *Southwestern Historical Quarterly*, Texas Collection, April 1944.

CRUGER, WILLIAM R. (1840–1882). William R. Cruger, frontier sheriff, the son of Nicholas and Elizabeth (Robert) Cruger, was born on May 30, 1840, at Albany, Georgia. He moved to Shackelford County, Texas, in 1874, assisted in the county's organization, and named the county seat Albany for his birthplace. Fort Griffin was then a thriving town and had become a rendezvous for outlaws, thieves, and other desperate characters. In 1876 John M. Larn^{qv} was elected sheriff and appointed Cruger deputy sheriff. Early in 1877, in an attempt to restore order in a Fort Griffin saloon, Cruger participated in a gunfight in which three men were killed and he and the county attorney were wounded. Larn resigned, and Cruger was appointed his successor on April 20, 1877. His jurisdiction over thirteen unorganized Texas counties extended to the New Mexico line. Acting on a warrant from the Albany court, Cruger arrested Larn, who on the night of his arrest, June 23, 1878, was shot and killed in an Albany jail, presumably by members of the Fort Griffin Vigilance Committee. This was the last vigilante killing in the county. Cruger was reelected sheriff and served until his resignation on July 20, 1880, when the commissioners' court passed a resolution attesting to his courage and fearlessness as a law officer and declaring that the thanks of the citizens of the western frontier were due him for ridding the frontier of lawless characters. Cruger was married to Mary R. Boynton; they had one child. On May 29, 1882, while serving as city marshal of Princeton, Tennessee, Cruger was shot and killed by a drunken prisoner whom he had failed to search. He was buried in Albany, Georgia.

BIBLIOGRAPHY: Dallas *Herald*, January 27, 1977. J. R. Webb, "Henry Herron, Pioneer and Peace Officer during Fort Griffin Days," West Texas Historical Association *Year Book* 20 (1944). *J. R. Webb*

CRUIAMO INDIANS. These Indians are known only from a Spanish document of 1693 which lists them as one of fifty "nations" that lived north of the Rio Grande and "between Texas and New Mexico." This may be interpreted to mean the southern part of western Texas, since the document also mentions that the Apaches were at war with the groups named. Nothing further is known about the Cruiamos.

BIBLIOGRAPHY: Charles W. Hackett, ed., *Historical Documents Relating to New Mexico, Nueva Vizcaya, and Approaches Thereto, to 1773* (3 vols., Washington: Carnegie Institution, 1923–37).
Thomas N. Campbell

CRUILLAS, JOAQUÍN DE MONTSERRAT, MARQUÉS DE (1700–1771). Joaquín de Montserrat, Marqués de Cruillas, was born in Valencia, Spain, in 1700. After a distinguished military career that included campaigns in France, North Africa, Gibraltar, and Italy, he gained administrative experience as governor of Badajoz and as commandant general of Aragon. In late life he served from October 6, 1760, to August 25, 1766, as the forty-fourth viceroy of New Spain.

The Marqués de Cruillas replaced an interim viceroy who had served briefly as successor to the Marqués de las Amarillas.[qv] And it was his bad luck to govern during really difficult times. Cruillas reached Mexico City shortly after the San Sabá massacre (1758) and the failed punitive campaign (1759) of Diego Ortiz Parrilla.[qv] His tenure also witnessed Spain's shifting role from neutral observer to active combatant in the Seven Years' War, the transfer of Louisiana from France to Spain near the end of that war, the costly and dramatically increased militarization of Mexico, the outbreak of horrible smallpox epidemics that claimed nearly 100,000 lives in just Mexico City and Puebla, and the sweeping inspection of frontier outposts conducted by the Marqués de Rubí.[qv] It is little wonder that the policies of this overburdened administrator, especially as they affected Texas, have drawn criticism.

Cruillas no doubt erred in choosing Felipe de Rábago y Terán,[qv] only recently exonerated of crimes committed at the San Xavier missions,[qv] to replace Ortiz Parrilla as the commander of San Luis de las Amarillas Presidio. Cruillas charged Rábago with the task of missionizing the Lipan Apaches at or near the ruins of San Lorenzo de San Sabá Mission, and he stressed the importance of establishing new forts and missions to the northwest of San Sabá—thereby linking Texas more closely with New Mexico. Rábago allowed the Lipans to influence his decisions and approved two new missions on the upper Nueces River between San Sabá and San Juan Bautista.[qv] The new missions, San Lorenzo de la Santa Cruz and Nuestra Señora de la Candelaria del Cañón, were not approved by the viceroy, and they seriously weakened the defenses of the presidio at San Sabá, as a permanent detachment of soldiers had to be assigned to the missions, and the presidio itself had to share provisions with those beleaguered outposts.

Near the end of his tenure as viceroy, the Marqués de Cruillas was obliged to receive two unwelcome royal appointees. The Marqués de Rubí, commissioned separately in Spain by King Charles III, was to carry out an all-encompassing inspection of presidios on the northern frontier of New Spain; and José Bernardo de Gálvez Gallardo[qv] was to serve as visitor general of public finance. The Rubí report was a devastating commentary on the condition of Spain's frontier garrisons, while Gálvez's overarching powers exceeded those of the viceroy himself. When the Marqués de Cruillas objected to the latter, he was replaced with the more compliant Marqués de Croix. The former viceroy returned to Spain and died at Valencia in 1771.

BIBLIOGRAPHY: Donald E. Chipman, *Spanish Texas, 1519–1821* (Austin: University of Texas Press, 1992). *Diccionario Porrúa de historia, biografía y geografía de México* (3d ed., 2 vols., Mexico City: Editorial Porrúa, 1970, 1971). Robert S. Weddle, *The San Sabá Mission* (Austin: University of Texas Press, 1964). *Donald E. Chipman*

CRUMP, WILLIAM DORSEY (1844–1940). William Dorsey Crump, town founder, son of Robert Henry and Sara (Dorsey) Crump, was born in Louisville, Kentucky, on August 21, 1844. Before his service in the Confederate Army, he attended the University of Kentucky. In 1874 he moved to Texas, settled near the site of present Oak Cliff, and three years later married Mary King of Dallas. In June 1890 Crump moved his family to the South Plains region, where he helped organize and build the town of Lubbock. Crump was a Mason and a member of the Disciples of Christ Church. He was elected county judge in 1898 and served two terms. With others, he set up the Ripley Townsite Company, which established the town of Shallowater. Crump died on January 18, 1940.

BIBLIOGRAPHY: Seymour V. Connor, ed., *Builders of the Southwest* (Lubbock: Southwest Collection, Texas Technological College, 1959).
Roy Sylvan Dunn

CRUNK'S LAKE, TEXAS. Crunk's (Krunk's) Lake, on the boundary between Lee and Burleson counties two miles east of Dime Box, was named for Nicholas S. Crunk, a participant in the battle of San Jacinto,[qv] who is buried nearby. In the 1940s it was a resort for picnics and fishing parties.

BIBLIOGRAPHY: Lee County Historical Survey Committee, *A History of Lee County* (Quanah, Texas: Nortex, 1974). *Julia Jones*

CRUSEVILLE, TEXAS. Cruseville was just off U.S. Highway 259 six miles north of Nacogdoches in northern Nacogdoches County. The area was probably settled before the Civil War[qv] and during its early years was known variously as Cruse's Store and as Cruseville; the latter name was used in 1880 when a post office opened. Its post office closed in 1882, reopened in 1893 under the name Thrash, after store owner Lee H. Thrash, and closed the following year. The community apparently declined after 1900, and by the 1930s it no longer appeared on highway maps. In the early 1990s only a few scattered houses remained in the area.

BIBLIOGRAPHY: Richard W. Haltom, *The History of Nacogdoches County, Texas* (Nacogdoches, 1880; rpt., Austin: Jenkins, 197-).
Christopher Long

CRUTCHERS CREEK. Crutchers Creek rises six miles south of Texarkana in the southeastern corner of Bowie County (at 33°21' N, 94°05' W) and runs south for three miles to its mouth on the Sulphur River, in Cass County (at 33°18' N, 94°04' W). The creek, which is intermittent in its upper reaches, has been dammed to form Kennedy Lake. The soils along the banks are loamy, and the land is heavily wooded, with various pines and hardwoods predominating. The stream was probably named for William Crutcher, the original grantee of the surrounding land.

CRUZ, PABLO (1866–ca. 1910). Pablo Cruz, publisher, was born in Monclova, Coahuila, in 1866 to Cruz Valdez and Viviana Cárdenas de Cruz. In 1877 he moved with his family to Floresville, Texas, where they lived for five years. He married Zulema Palanco, and they had seven children. His son Paul helped initiate the Order of Sons of America,[qv] a Mexican-American civil-rights organization, in San Antonio. In 1888 Cruz began publishing and editing *El Regidor*, a weekly Spanish-language newspaper. It was one of a few Spanish-language newspapers^{qv} in San Antonio in the late nineteenth century. During the Spanish-American War *El Regidor* sided with the United States over Cuba. Cruz was also involved in printing and publishing books. He was recognized as a supporter and promoter of education, public welfare, and civic causes.

In 1901 Cruz used *El Regidor* to inform readers about the Gregorio Cortez^{qv} case and collect defense funds. His efforts reached Mexico, and a ballad sung there referred to Cruz as a "prominent brother" and an "upright Mexican" for aiding Cortez. Cruz coordinated fund-raising efforts and hired lawyers, Judge B. R. Abernethy of Gonzales and Samuel Belden of San Antonio, for defense. The first trial resulted in a death penalty, but the lawyers appealed, and the Texas Court of Criminal Appeals^{qv} reversed the decision. According to one source, the appeal addressed the issues of illegal arrest and arrest without a warrant, and the court ordered a change of venue because of local knowledge of the case. Cruz also employed attorneys for trials of Cortez in Wharton, Karnes, and Nueces counties. When Cruz died around 1910, Col. Francisco A. Chapa,^{qv} publisher of *El Imparcial*, continued the movement to defend Cortez. The family continued *El Regidor* until 1916.

BIBLIOGRAPHY: Américo Paredes, *With His Pistol in His Hand: A Border Ballad and Its Hero* (Austin: University of Texas Press, 1958). *A Twentieth Century History of Southwest Texas* (2 vols., Chicago: Lewis, 1907).   *Cynthia E. Orozco*

CRUZ Y AROCHA, ANTONIO (?–?). Antonio Cruz y Arocha, Alamo defender and courier, was one of a number of native Texans who joined Capt. Juan N. Seguín's^{qv} company for six months' service during the Texas Revolution.^{qv} He took part in the siege of Bexar^{qv} and later served in the Alamo garrison as a member of Seguín's cavalry company. Cruz left the Alamo on February 25, 1836, along with Seguín, to rally reinforcements for the Alamo. He later served with Seguín in the battle of San Jacinto.^{qv}

BIBLIOGRAPHY: Daughters of the American Revolution, *The Alamo Heroes and Their Revolutionary Ancestors* (San Antonio, 1976). Daughters of the Republic of Texas, *Muster Rolls of the Texas Revolution* (Austin, 1986). Bill Groneman, *Alamo Defenders* (Austin: Eakin, 1990).   *Bill Groneman*

CRUZ AZUL MEXICANA. Cruz Azul Mexicana, a charitable organization, was established in 1920 by Mexican-American women in San Antonio to help poor Mexican families. The organization was likely affiliated with other Cruz Azul groups in the country. It was similar to the Cruz Azul (Blue Cross) in Mexico and took on the motto "Charity, Abnegation, and Patriotism." Its influence was eventually felt beyond the city in the rural towns of south central Texas, such as Asherton, Castroville, Charlotte, Mackay, Luling, and Phelan. It set up an affiliate in Malakoff in East Texas.

Cruz Azul Mexicana grew out of the mutual-aid societies (*see* SOCIEDADES MUTUALISTAS) that Texas Mexicans organized beginning in the last quarter of the nineteenth century as a means to unite themselves to combat ethnic discrimination and economic uncertainty. The *mutualistas* themselves originated in Mexico, where several had been organized by 1869 to provide medical and funeral insurance and recreational and educational benefits to the poor and working classes. Moreover the ideal of mutualism was also evident in the founding of the first workingman's central—the Gran Círculo de Obreros—in Mexico in 1870. The formation of the Cruz Azul may have also been an effort to expand the active but limited role women played in the Texas-Mexican mutualist societies. Of the nineteen traditional mutualist associations in San Antonio between 1915 and 1930, only seven permitted both men and women to join and hold office; two others organized women's auxiliaries, and two more were composed almost exclusively of women.

The women who established Cruz Azul Mexicana were probably of the upper class, like the members most charitable organizations. These women set out to serve poor people who earned a few cents an hour as unskilled laborers, laundresses, or pecan shellers. Women were generally the officeholders of the Cruz Azul Mexicana; early leaders were María Luisa Garza, a journalist who served as president, and Delfina Tafolla, who served as vice president. Santiago Tafolla, Delfina's father and an officer of Orden Amigos del Pueblo and Orden Hijos de América (*see* ORDER OF SONS OF AMERICA^{qv}), was its first vice president. The Comisión Honorífica, a service organization that had been established by men, and the Cruz Azul Mexicana both operated under the supervision of the Mexican Consulate in San Antonio.

One of the major projects of Cruz Azul was a public clinic funded by $4,000 from a fund-raising drive. The clinic was set up in 1925 and operated with the assistance of doctors of Mexican descent, who saw over 200 colonia^{qv} residents each month. These patients received both medical attention and food. The clinic also distributed health-information brochures, such as one directed at mothers called *Circular for Mothers*. In addition, the Cruz Azul Mexicana collaborated with other service organizations to assist with disaster relief.

The Cruz Azul established such educational projects as a library in San Antonio in 1925. Books to supply it came from donors in Chihuahua and Coahuila. The library also subscribed to periodicals and newspapers from Mexico and South Texas. Another of its academic efforts was to set up Spanish-language classes.

In conjunction with the Comisión Honorífica, Cruz Azul offered legal assistance in the form of sample contracts available in both English and Spanish, prepared by the Mexican Consulate. These were intended to protect workers whose rights could be compromised in contracts. The organization also provided legal assistance to Mexican immigrants facing litigation.

Cruz Azul held annual meetings in San Antonio with other Comisiones Honoríficas to determine group action on social and economic causes. Projects included a legal-defense fund and proposals to build monuments to such heros as Gen. Ignacio S. Zaragoza^{qv} and to organize a Mexican industrial school. Working with the local Mexican Consulate, Cruz Azul and the Comisión Honorífica also planned a census of Texas Mexicans in San Antonio to ascertain their living conditions. Later, when the group expanded its base of operations to other cities in the state, it published a monthly magazine first named *Revista Azul* and later renamed *Revista Nacional*. To fund all these activities, Cruz Azul apparently relied on such fund-raising activities as theatrical performances, public dances, and bazaars. The organization's reserve fund grew from little over $1,000 in 1924 to $4,500 in 1928.

Although the Cruz Azul was not a political organization, it influenced politicians to protect Texas Mexicans. The organization made Governor Pat Neff^{qv} an honorary member despite both his alleged affiliation with the Ku Klux Klan^{qv} and his endorsement of the death penalty. A month after Neff was inducted as an honorary Cruz Azul member, the group joined with other mutualistas and the Mexican Consulate and urged the governor to commute the death sentence of a Mexicano named Pedro Sánchez. Sánchez, who had been in the Marlin jail for a "minor offense" at the time that the jailer was murdered by two other inmates, had been sentenced to be hanged for "complicity in the murder." Jordan Israel, one of the two inmates hanged for the murder, had testified during his trial that Sánchez had no knowledge of the plan to kill the jailer. Governor Neff apparently relied on the opinion of the Court of Criminal Appeals as well as the efforts of the Mexican Consulate and Mayor O. B. Black of San Antonio in making his decision to grant executive clemency and change Sánchez's sentence to life imprisonment.

The coming of the Great Depression^{qv} and forced repatriation of numerous Texas Mexicans put an end to many civic groups in the Mexican community in San Antonio, especially the mutualistas. These events also likely meant the demise of the Cruz Azul, which relied on individual benevolence for maintaining its projects. Such groups as the Order of Knights of America and the League of United Latin American Citizens,[qqv] which replaced the Cruz Azul Mexicana and its peer organizations as the agents for social change in the Texas Mexican community, emphasized individual legal rights over "economic co-operativism."

BIBLIOGRAPHY: Armanda List Arzubide, *Apuntes sobre la prehistoria de la revolución* (Mexico City, 1958). Victor B. Nelson Cisneros, "La clase trabajadora en Tejas, 1920–1940," *Aztlán* 6 (1975). John M. Hart, Anarchist Thought in Nineteenth-Century Mexico (Ph.D. dissertation, University of California at Los Angeles, 1971). Julie Leininger Pycior, La Raza Organizes: Mexican American Life in San Antonio, 1915–1930, as Reflected in Mutualista Activities (Ph.D. dissertation, University of Notre Dame, 1979).   *Teresa Palomo Acosta*

CRUZ CALLE, TEXAS. Cruz Calle, also known as Vera Cruz, is on Farm roads 716 and 1329, sixteen miles southeast of Benavides and twenty-five miles south of San Diego in southeastern Duval County. The earliest record of the community is from the Vera Cruz school, which had eighty pupils during the 1906–07 school year. By the late 1940s the community had the school and a few scattered dwellings. By the late 1960s, when the community was first identified as Cruz Calle on maps of the area, the Vera Cruz school had been consolidated into the Premont Independent School District. Cruz Calle was still listed as a community in 1990.   *Martin Donell Kohout*

CRYER CREEK, TEXAS. Cryer Creek, at the intersection of Farm roads 2930 and 1126, four miles north of Barry in northwest Navarro County, took its name from that of a nearby creek. Settlers thought a fall in the stream sounded like a woman crying. The site was first settled in 1845 by William Melton, who before 1855 was joined by a number of other settlers. Dock Garlington and Wilt Stokes opened a general store there in 1878; this store still existed in 1962, when it was run by Minnie Garlington Walker. In 1879 Bud Conger opened the Cryer Creek post office, which was moved to Barry in 1907. By 1884 Cryer Creek had a district school, two stores, three churches, three steam cotton gin–gristmills, and a population of 100. The population rose to 150 in 1890 and peaked at 200 in 1892, but the town began to decline after the Texas and St. Louis Railway bypassed it. The Cryer Creek school had eighty-five students in 1906. In the 1930s the community consisted of a church, a school, a cemetery, and a number of scattered dwellings, and from 1936 to the end of the 1960s it reported seventy-five residents. From 1970 to 1990 the population was reported as fifteen.

BIBLIOGRAPHY: Fred Tarpley, *1001 Texas Place Names* (Austin: University of Texas Press, 1980). Alva Taylor, *History and Photographs of Corsicana and Navarro County* (Corsicana, Texas, 1959; rev. ed., *Navarro County History and Photographs*, Corsicana, 1962).
Molly McKee

CRYERS BRANCH. Cryers Branch rises just north of Goldthwaite in central Mills County (at 31°29′ N, 98°33′ W) and runs southwest six miles to join South Browns Creek (at 31°28′ N, 98°37′ W). The stream crosses steep slopes and benches surfaced by shallow clay loam soils that support juniper, live oak, mesquite, and grasses. It was probably named after the Cryer brothers, who established ranches in the area during the 1880s.

CRYSTAL BEACH, TEXAS. Crystal Beach, also known as Patton, stretches seven miles along State Highway 87 in the middle of Bolivar Peninsula in Galveston County. Although the site was settled in the early twentieth century, the only recorded activity was that in the community of Patton, one of several names adopted by residents of the area in its early years. A Patton Beach post office operated from 1898 to 1900. Patton was a railroad stop until the railroad ceased operation in the early 1940s. Around then the name of the community was changed to Crystal Beach.

The town was incorporated in 1971. At least four efforts to disincorporate were made in the mid-1980s, and a vote to disincorporate was successful in 1987. Afterward, supporters of incorporation and those of disincorporation alternated with successful campaigns for votes and battles in court. The community was not incorporated in 1990.

Although its 1990 population of full-time residents was recorded as 787, other estimates placed the figure as high as 1,600. Crystal Beach was thus the largest community on the peninsula in population as well as land area. Officials estimated that 80 percent of Crystal Beach property owners were "weekenders," so the summer, weekend, and holiday population was greatly expanded. In 1990 Crystal Beach had a bank, a hotel, and a supermarket, and most of the real-estate agencies on the peninsula had their headquarters there.

BIBLIOGRAPHY: A. Pat Daniels, *Bolivar! Gulf Coast Peninsula* (Crystal Beach, Texas: Peninsula, 1985). Houston *Chronicle*, May 10, 1982. Vertical Files, Barker Texas History Center, University of Texas at Austin (Bolivar Peninsula).   *A. Pat Daniels*

CRYSTAL CITY, TEXAS. Crystal City, the county seat of Zavala County, is at the intersection of U.S. Highway 83, Farm roads 393, 16, 1433, 65, and 582, and the Missouri Pacific Railroad, one mile north of the Dimmit county line in south central Zavala County. Two land developers, Carl F. Groos and E. J. Buckingham, developed the town in the early 1900s. In 1905 they purchased the 10,000-acre Cross S Ranch, sold off most of the land as farms, and platted the townsite of Crystal City, named for the clear artesian water of the area. The town received a post office in 1908, the same year the Crystal City and Uvalde Railway provided the first rail service to the community and the first school building was erected. Crystal City was incorporated in 1910, when it had an estimated 530 inhabitants, and by 1914 the community had a bank, three general stores, and the weekly *Chronicle*. In 1928 the county voted to make Crystal City the county seat, and that same year the community added a city manager to its mayor-council government. As soon as the railroad reached Crystal City, the community became a major shipping point for winter vegetables. At first onions were the major crop, but by the 1930s the city developed a reputation as the "Spinach Capital of the World." In 1936 the first annual spinach festival was held, and the following year a statue of the cartoon character Popeye,[qv] that mighty consumer of spinach, was erected across from the city hall. Carrots, tomatoes, peppers, and other vegetables were also marketed, and a vegetable cannery was opened in 1932.

Under the stimulus of agricultural growth the population rose from an estimated 800 in 1920 to 6,609 in 1930, then fell slightly to 6,529 in 1940. The majority of residents in the 1930s were Mexican or Mexican-American migrant laborers who followed a seasonal cycle of spinach in the winter, onions in the spring, and beet or cotton work in the summer and fall. A government report of 1941 estimated that 97 percent of the 5,500 Mexican Americans[qv] living in Crystal City at that time were migrant laborers. Making Crystal City their home base, most of these workers lived in slum conditions with poor services and limited educational opportunities. During World War II[qv] an alien internment camp was built on the site of a prewar labor camp on the edge of town. Japanese[qv] were relocated to the camp from all over the country, and a sizable group of Japanese nationals caught by the war in the United States or in a number of South American countries were also interned at the camp. After the camp closed in 1947, the area was converted to low-rent housing, and the schools built there became part of the Crystal City ISD. In 1945 the California Packing Corporation, later the Del Monte Corporation, built an extensive canning plant just northwest of Crystal City. Since that time it has been the largest single employer in the area. The company added a can-manufacturing plant in 1958 and expanded its Crystal City facilities several times in the 1970s and 1980s.

The employment opportunities offered by Del Monte helped increase the population of the community to 7,195 in 1950 and 9,101, a probable all-time high for Crystal City, in 1960. The 1960s were a period of dramatic political change for the town. In spite of the fact that Mexican Americans had formed 80 percent or more of the city's population since the 1930s, the Anglo minority had kept a tight hold on city government and school administration. Frustration over several controversial attempts at urban renewal in the late 1950s and over continuing educational discrimination led to the increasing politicization of Crystal City's Hispanics. In 1963 and much more successfully in 1969, Crystal City Mexican Americans sought to gain control of key city and school-board positions in the "Crystal City Revolts".[qv] Among the important outgrowths of this political movement was the formation of the Raza Unida party[qv] in 1970, which soon assumed statewide importance and dominated Crystal City politics until it splintered into factions in 1977. These political changes had a deep impact on the ethnic composition of Crystal City's government. Before 1971, with only a single exception, only Anglos had been selected as city managers, while from 1971 through the 1980s only Mexican Americans held that position. Similarly, the school superintendents had all been Anglo from 1908 to 1971, and from 1971 to 1990 they were all Mexican American. After Mexican Americans secured control of the city public schools in 1970, most Anglo students withdrew to private schools, and the public schools were 98 percent Mexican American through the 1980s.

The population declined somewhat during the 1960s, to 8,104 in 1970, and remained relatively static through the 1980s. In 1990 Crystal City's 8,263 residents represented almost 70 percent of the county population. The annual November spinach festival, which was halted by World War II, was resumed in 1982.

BIBLIOGRAPHY: David Montejano, *Anglos and Mexicans in the Making of Texas, 1836–1986* (Austin: University of Texas Press, 1987). John Staples Shockley, *Chicano Revolt in a Texas Town* (Notre Dame, Indiana: University of Notre Dame Press, 1974). Zavala County Historical Commission, *Now and Then in Zavala County* (Crystal City, Texas, 1985).
Mark Odintz

CRYSTAL CITY REVOLTS. In 1963 and again in 1969, Mexican Americans[qv] in Crystal City organized against Caucasian domination of city hall and the public school system. The result was an electoral victory for Hispanic Texans for the first time since the city's incorporation in 1910.

The 1963 movement was led by Juan Cornejo, a local representative of the Teamsters Union at the Del Monte cannery in Crystal City, and the Political Association of Spanish-speaking Organizations.[qv] PASSO succeeded in getting more Mexican Americans to pay the poll tax and vote. In addition, the Mexican Texans organized the large migrant farm-labor pool affiliated with the Teamsters at Del Monte. The Hispanics selected a slate of five candidates, who became known as *los cinco*, from among the poor and undereducated Mexican Texans, to run for the city council. The group faced intimidation by the political establishment. Several workers at the Del Monte plant were fired for wearing campaign buttons, for instance; but Teamsters officials intervened, and their jobs were reinstated. Texas Rangers[qv] were called in, reportedly to provide protection for the Mexican Americans. Agricultural leaders doubled hourly pay for their workers, and Del Monte went into overtime production to keep workers from voting. *Los cinco*, however, gained widespread support, and all five candidates defeated the five incumbents in a close election.

The newly elected all-Mexican-American city council and the succeeding administration had trouble governing the city because of political factions among the new officials. Cornejo was selected mayor from among the five new council members, but eventually his apparent quest for total control of city government led to his loss of support. A new group made up of both Caucasians and middle-class Mexican Americans, the Citizens Association Serving All Americans, announced its plans to run candidates for countywide offices in 1964, with the goal of ousting politicians that it considered dominated by "outside interests," an allusion to the roles of PASSO and the Teamsters in the elections of 1963. CASAA won the constable and commissioner seats and ran three Mexican-American and two Caucasian candidates in the city council election in 1965. The Hispanic activists did not repeat their poll-tax drive to bolster their voting bloc, and CASAA won.

In 1967 the Mexican American Youth Organization[qv] was founded by three Chicanos, including José Ángel Gutiérrez at Crystal City High School. In 1969, after a conflict about the ethnicity of cheerleaders, the school compromised to establish a cheerleading squad of three Caucasian and three Mexican-American girls. But in June the school board invalidated the compromise. The following November 100 Mexican-American students and their parents took a long list of grievances to the school board. In December 1969, when the board denied the charges of discrimination and refused to act on them, 200 Mexican-American students went out on strike, with their parents' support. The boycott soon extended to both the middle and elementary schools. The United States Department of Justice sent a team to intervene in the crisis, probably in response to the visit by three striking students to its Washington headquarters. The federal officials negotiated a settlement that obliged the board to meet most of the students' demands, including bilingual, bicultural education, better testing programs, and more cultural celebrations. The following January the Raza Unida Party,[qv] which was founded almost immediately after the successful student boycott, received enough votes to win seats on the school board and the city council.

BIBLIOGRAPHY: John Staples Shockley, *Chicano Revolt in a Texas Town* (Notre Dame, Indiana: University of Notre Dame Press, 1974).
Teresa Palomo Acosta

CRYSTAL CITY AND UVALDE RAILROAD. The Crystal City and Uvalde Railroad Company was chartered on April 19, 1909, to connect the Galveston, Harrisburg and San Antonio Railway near Uvalde with Crystal City, a distance of forty-one miles. The capital stock was $50,000. The principal place of business was Crystal City. The members of the first board of directors were A. R. Ponder of Missouri; A. R. Byrd, Sr., and E. J. Buckingham, both of San Antonio; E. R. Byrd and William J. Byrd, Jr., both of Dimmit County; and J. A. Weir and Carl F. Groos, both of Uvalde. Buckingham planned the railroad to reach his land in Zavala County to ship his produce. Area landowners gave a bonus of $345,000. By December 1909 the railroad had completed forty-one miles from Uvalde Junction to Crystal City. The following year two lines were built from Crystal City, one of twelve miles to Carrizo Springs and a forty-two-mile line to Gardendale. In 1911 twenty-six miles was opened from Gardendale to Fowlerton. On April 4, 1912, the railroad was renamed San Antonio, Uvalde and Gulf Railroad Company.
Nancy Beck Young

CRYSTAL CREEK (Montgomery County). Crystal (Chrystal) Creek rises in two branches in east central Montgomery County (at 30°16′ N, 95°22′ W). The East Fork rises at Willis in north central Montgomery County (at 30°26′ N, 95°29′ W) and runs for sixteen miles southwest to meet the West Fork, which rises on the northeastern edge of Conroe (at 30°20′ N, 95°26′ W) and runs for seven miles east to their confluence. Crystal Creek then flows south for six miles into the West Fork of the San Jacinto River, six miles south of Conroe (at 30°12′ N, 95°24′ W). The creek crosses flat to rolling terrain surfaced by deep, fine sandy loam that supports conifers into flat terrain with local shallow depressions, surfaced by clay and sandy loam that supports water-tolerant hardwoods, conifers, and grasses.

_____ (Presidio County). Crystal Creek rises near the southeast side of the base of Antelope Mesa in east central Presidio County (at

29°54′ N, 103°51′ W) and runs southeast for twenty miles to its mouth on Terlingua Creek, in southwest Brewster County (at 29°41′ N, 103°42′ W). Its course crosses desert mountain terrain, canyonland of volcanic deposits, and moderate to steep slopes of clay and limestone, surfaced in some areas by generally light reddish-brown to brown sand and clay loams that support sparse grasses, cacti, and desert shrubs.

CRYSTAL FALLS, TEXAS. Crystal Falls is at the intersection of Farm roads 1481 and 578, on the Clear Fork of the Brazos River in northwest Stephens County. It evolved during the 1870s, when settlers began to come into the region, and was named for a small waterfall nearby. Caravans of hide wagons stopped there during the brief buffalo boom of the 1870s. A post office was granted to Joseph C. Reavis in 1877, and by 1892 the town had grown to include a general store, a gristmill, livery stables, a steam gin, a flour mill, a Union church, a doctor, a blacksmith, and a population of 175. In 1900 Crystal Falls was the largest town in the county. The short-lived oil boom of 1918–21 pushed the population to 1,200 residents, who supported numerous businesses, including a bank, a hotel, and two restaurants. Rapid decline came in 1921, when oil prices plummeted, and every bank in Stephens County went bankrupt, save one in Breckenridge. Although it acquired a station on the new Cisco and Northeastern Railway during the 1930s and 1940s Crystal Falls had a population of only 150 and one surviving business. The post office closed in the early 1940s. After the 1950s the population declined further; from 1974 until 1990 it was estimated at ten. In 1980 a church and cemetery were indicated on county maps.

BIBLIOGRAPHY: Betty E. Hanna, *Doodle Bugs and Cactus Berries: A Historical Sketch of Stephens County* (Quanah, Texas: Nortex, 1975). Loy W. Hartsfield, A History of Stephens County (M.A. thesis, University of Texas, 1929).
Charles G. Davis

CRYSTAL LAKE. Crystal Lake, a natural lake seven miles east of Palestine in eastern Anderson County (at 31°45′ N, 95°30′ W), drains into Stills Creek. In the mid-1980s it was used for recreation by the Crystal Lake Country Club, which has been in operation there since 1875.

CRYSTAL LAKE, TEXAS. Crystal Lake is a rural church and recreation community by Crystal Lake on U.S. Highway 84 and the Texas State Railroad, eight miles east of Palestine in eastern Anderson County. In the 1930s the community had a number of dwellings, a golf course, and a school belonging to the Swanson Spring school district. The school served forty-nine pupils in 1932, but by 1955 had been consolidated with the Palestine school. In 1982 Crystal Lake had Antioch Church and several scattered dwellings; by 1985 one business was located there. The nearby Crystal Lake has fishing and camping facilities and is used by the Crystal Lake Country Club.

BIBLIOGRAPHY: Thomas Paul Jones, The Reorganization of the Public Schools of Anderson County, Texas (M.Ed. thesis, University of Texas, 1934).
Mark Odintz

CUCHENDADO INDIANS. The Cuchendados, an otherwise unidentified group met by Álvar Núñez Cabeza de Vaca^{qv} in southern Texas between 1528 and 1534, seem to have been the most westerly coastal Indians he met before going inland.

BIBLIOGRAPHY: Frederick Webb Hodge, ed., *Handbook of American Indians North of Mexico* (2 vols., Washington: GPO, 1907, 1910; rpt. New York: Pageant, 1959).
Margery H. Krieger

CUELLAR, ADELAIDA (1871–1969). Adelaida Cuellar, founder of the tamale stand that grew into the El Chico restaurant chain, was born on May 30, 1871, near Matehuala, Nuevo León, Mexico. In 1892 she and Macario Cuellar crossed into Texas and were married in Laredo. At the time they spoke no English. They worked on ranches in small Texas towns before settling as sharecroppers in Kaufman. In 1926, with twelve children to support, Mrs. Cuellar decided to supplement the family income by selling homemade tamales at the Kaufman County Fair. The tamale stand was a success, and the venture was repeated the following year. Soon after, sons Frank and Amos opened a Mexican cafe in Kaufman with Mama Cuellar, as she was called, doing the cooking. The cafe closed after two years, as the Great Depression^{qv} tightened its grip on the community. Eventually, using her recipes, several of the sons opened Mexican restaurants in the East Texas towns of Terrell, Wills Point, Malakoff, and Tyler, as well as in Oklahoma City, Oklahoma, and Shreveport, Louisiana. All of these ventures closed by the end of the 1930s.

In 1940 Mrs. Cuellar's sons Macario and Gilbert moved to Dallas and opened a restaurant, El Charro, in the Oak Lawn neighborhood. The menu featured Mama's tastiest recipes, and eventually most of the family moved to Dallas to help with the popular business. Within three years the restaurant was profitable, and the family began to expand its interests into other parts of Dallas and Fort Worth, Waco, and Houston. By this time, the restaurants had become known as El Chico and the Cuellar sons as "Mama's boys." The family expanded and diversified the business rapidly, entering the frozen food business in 1955 and opening restaurants throughout the Southwest. By the time Mama Cuellar died, the El Chico Corporation was involved in twenty separate business enterprises, from restaurant franchising to canning. Adelaida Cuellar was a member of Holy Trinity Catholic Church in Dallas. She died on April 13, 1969, in Dallas and was buried at Calvary Hill Cemetery.

BIBLIOGRAPHY: Dallas *Morning News*, April 14, 1969, June 17, 1984. Dallas *Times Herald*, February 15, 1970. Bill Porterfield, "Dallas Founders," *D Magazine*, July 1976.
Gerald D. Saxon

CUELLAR, JESÚS (?–1841). Jesús (Comanche) Cuellar, member of the Texas cavalry during the revolution, bore the name Comanche from having been a Comanche captive. In 1833 he was an alferez in the Mexican army in Tamaulipas. He was a guide for Domingo de Ugartechea^{qv} in November 1835 and was ranked as a lieutenant under Martín Perfecto de Cos^{qv} at the siege of Bexar^{qv} in December 1835, when he deserted the Mexican forces, reported to Edward Burleson^{qv} the weakness of Bexar's defenses, and offered himself as a guide for the Texans into San Antonio. Opposed to Antonio López de Santa Anna^{qv} because of an injury Santa Anna had inflicted on his brother, Cuellar joined Dr. James Grant^{qv} for the proposed Matamoros expedition of 1835–36,^{qv} but got only as far as Goliad, where he joined the troops of James Walker Fannin, Jr.^{qv} Cuellar devised a scheme for the defeat and capture of José de Urrea's^{qv} army and led Urrea's men into a pass where he expected Fannin to trap them, but Urrea retreated to San Patricio before Fannin could attack. Cuellar was later sent to Refugio to give warning to William Ward^{qv} and from Refugio went to join the Texas army. The General Council^{qv} designated Cuellar a captain. He died at Goliad in 1841.

BIBLIOGRAPHY: Harbert Davenport, "Captain Jesús Cuellar, Texas Cavalry, Otherwise 'Comanche,'" *Southwestern Historical Quarterly* 30 (July 1926). Hobart Huson, *Captain Philip Dimmitt's Commandancy of Goliad, 1835–1836* (Austin: Von Boeckmann–Jones, 1974). Vertical Files, Barker Texas History Center, University of Texas at Austin.

CUERO, TEXAS. Cuero is at the convergence of U.S. highways 183, 77A, and 87, in central DeWitt County. It is the largest city in the county and the county seat. The first post office in DeWitt County was established in May 1846 in Daniel Boone Friar's^{qv} store, four miles north of the present site; it was also called Cuero (later Old Cuero). Cuero is named after Cuero Creek, which the Spanish had called Arroyo del Cuero, or Creek of the Rawhide, in reference to the Indians' practice of killing wild cattle that got stuck in the mud of the creekbed. When the Gulf, Western Texas and Pacific Railway was extended from Indianola to San Antonio, the Cuero site was chosen as a midway stopping point in the construction of the line. Although the tracks were not completed to Cuero until January 1873, construction of business establishments and homes was begun as early as November 1872. Among the first residents were Benjamin McCulloch and Gustav Schleicher.qqv Schleicher, who surveyed the railroad, platted the new town for his Cuero Land and Immigration Company, and Robert J. Klebergqv surveyed the site in January 1873.

The city government was organized in the summer of 1873; the town was incorporated on April 23, 1875, and it replaced Clinton as county seat in 1876. Cuero grew as Clinton declined, and after the great hurricanesqv of 1875 and 1886 people came from Indianola. Among the significant early businesses were Otto Buchel's bank, J. R. Nagel's hardware, and H. Runge and Company, a branch of Henry Runge'sqv Indianola-based store and bank, which was operated in Cuero by Edward Mugge, Sr. Mugge was joined by William Frobese, Sr., and Emil Reiffert, Sr., when the firm moved its operating base to Cuero after the hurricane that destroyed Indianola in 1886. These men are credited with much of Cuero's early expansion. Rudolph Klebergqv began publishing the weekly Cuero *Star* in June 1873. Other Cuero newspapers were the *Deutsche Rundschau*, a German-language paper established by William T. Eichholz in 1880; Lee Chaddock's Cuero *Sun*, in operation by the early 1890s; the Cuero *Bulletin*, established in the 1880s by Samuel L. Kyle and later absorbed by the *Star*; the *Constitution*, a populist paper published in the 1890s by Fay Carothers; the *Daily Hustler*, issued by James C. Howerton from July to November 1894; and the Cuero *Daily Record*, founded in November 1894 by Howerton, H. G. Woods, and B. S. Wright. Howerton became sole owner of the *Record*, which absorbed the *Star* and *Deutsche Rundschau*, and is Cuero's longest running newspaper.

Professor David W. Nash opened Guadalupe Academy (also known as Nash's School or Cuero Institute), a coeducational private school, in September 1873; it operated until about 1910. The Cuero Independent School District was formed in 1892; white, black, and Mexican-American students attended separate schools. Among the German social associations were the Order of Sons of Hermannqv and a turnverein (see TURNVEREIN MOVEMENT). Episcopalians organized the first Cuero congregation in 1874, and Catholics founded a church and school in 1876. Methodists built a church in 1884; Baptists organized in 1877 under Rev. John Van Epps Coveyqv and Presbyterians in 1878. German Lutherans had organized by 1880, and their congregation grew substantially from the Indianola migrations of 1886.

Cuero prospered despite a period of lawlessness and a disastrous fire in April 1879. Citizens organized the Home Protection Club, which drilled regularly as a military unit and aided law officers when necessary (see SUTTON-TAYLOR FEUD). Shipping opportunity increased in 1886 when the San Antonio and Aransas Pass Railway connected Cuero to Houston; good dirt roads and two free iron bridges across the Guadalupe River also served the community. The town's proximity to the river provoked much discussion of Cuero's commercial future through an inland waterway that was proposed but never completed. By 1887 Cuero recorded a population of 2,500, mostly Anglos and Germans.qv Rudolph Kleberg recorded in his *Description of the Resources of DeWitt County, Texas: The Immigrant's Handbook* (1887) that Cuero had an opera house, two large schools, a fire department, and a hotel. Truck farming became an important industry, as did cotton, poultry, and livestock. The Cuero *Record* reported in late 1886 that the town had a railroad machine shop and a $50,000 steam-powered cotton textile factory with sixteen looms, but also noted that there was much cattle rustling in the area. By the mid-1890s Cuero also had one of the state's largest cottonseed oil mills, capable of producing eighty tons a day; there were also three large cotton gins, an ice factory, two bottling plants, a cigar factory, a tannery, a private electric company, and the first of three hospitals. The Cuero turkey industry was already shipping processed birds nationwide by 1906, though the renowned Turkey Trotqv parade did not begin until 1912.

Cuero had an estimated population of 3,422 in 1904 and 3,671 by the mid-1920s, at which time the town had an assessed value of $3.7 million. The power dam on the Guadalupe River, which formed part of the community's privately owned hydroelectric plant, was the largest in the state. Cuero pioneered the turkey-raising industry in south central Texas and became one of the largest poultry markets in the Southwest. The city also supported large cattle, dairy, and meatpacking industries and produced pecans, cottonseed oil and products, and feeds. Its Crescent Valley Creamery was one of the largest independent creameries in the South in 1935. Oil speculation began in 1919, although a successful well was not hit until after 1929.

The city's population rose to 5,474 by the mid-1940s and reached 7,498 in the next decade. By 1949 the broiler-chicken industry had passed turkeys as the second most important source of livestock income. The Cuero Livestock Commission records show Cuero as the largest shipper of cattle in the state in 1942 and 1943, with more than 800 carloads exported per year. The commission, established in 1940, sold $251,750 worth of stock that same year; sales jumped to $1.3 million in 1941, $3.5 million in 1942, and $4.7 million in 1943.

Cuero's population peaked about 1969 at 7,800 and had declined to 6,920 by the mid-1970s. Agribusiness still dominated the local economy, though the turkey and cotton industries had declined in significance. In the mid-1980s the population reached 7,124, and the city supported 142 businesses. The county courthouse, built in 1895–96, was restored in 1955–57. The DeWitt County Historical Museum was established in Cuero about 1974. The population in 1990 was 6,700.

BIBLIOGRAPHY: Roy Grimes, ed., *300 Years in Victoria County* (Victoria, Texas: Victoria *Advocate*, 1968; rpt., Austin: Nortex, 1985). Nellie Murphree, *A History of DeWitt County* (Victoria, Texas, 1962). Vertical Files, Barker Texas History Center, University of Texas at Austin.

Craig H. Roell

CUERO CREEK. Cuero Creek rises eight miles northeast of Cuero in north central DeWitt County (at 29°15′ N, 97°13′ W) and runs southwest for eight miles to its mouth on the Guadalupe River, three miles northwest of Cuero (at 29°09′ N, 97°19′ W). It traverses flat to rolling terrain surfaced by moderately permeable soil that supports mixed hardwoods and pines.

CUERO FIELD. During World War IIqv Cuero Field, located at Cuero Municipal Airport, two miles west of Cuero in DeWitt County, was a United States Army Air Forces training field. It was approved by the government as a primary training facility in January 1941 and established on February 6, 1941. Brayton Flying Service, headed by Clyde E. Brayton, was located at the airport and was awarded the government contract to manage the training operations. All instructors and mechanics were civilian, though the army rigidly supervised the training. The nine-week course included classes in meteorology, navigation, aircraft identification, and aircraft engines. Training included five hours on the Link simulation trainer and sixty-five hours' actual flying time. The capacity was 290 cadets. Thousands of pilots who graduated from Cuero Field went on to serve in World War II. The Brayton Flying Service School payroll brought about $145,000 a month into Cuero's economy. The commanding officers of Cuero Field, until the date of its deactivation on August 31, 1944, were Capt. James H. Price and majors Shepler W. Fitzgerald and Timothy F. O'Keefe. After the school closed, the government retained one hangar to repair and service army planes, and Brayton, an aviation pioneer, moved to Houston to become president of Red Arrow Freight Lines.

BIBLIOGRAPHY: Cuero *Record*, November 15, 1944.

Craig H. Roell

CUERO QUEMADO INDIANS. This name, which is Spanish for "burnt skin," was applied to a Coahuiltecan-speaking band that ranged both sides of the lower Rio Grande during the second half of the eighteenth century. Cuero Quemado may have been a local Spanish name for a downstream group of Tepemaca Indians, who occupied the Rio Grande valley in the area between Laredo and Rio Grande City. The Cuero Quemados were sometimes known as Quemado Indians.

BIBLIOGRAPHY: Frederick Webb Hodge, ed., *Handbook of American Indians North of Mexico* (2 vols., Washington: GPO, 1907, 1910; rpt., New York: Pageant, 1959). Gabriel Saldivar, *Los Indios de Tamaulipas* (Mexico City: Pan American Institute of Geography and History, 1943). Rudolph C. Troike, "Notes on Coahuiltecan Ethnography," *Bulletin of the Texas Archeological Society* 32 (1962).

Thomas N. Campbell

CUESTA. A cuesta is a hill or ridge with one face steep and the opposite face gently sloping. The term, from Spanish, is used by geologists to describe a feature of Texas topography. When strata are tilted, the more resistant layers form cuestas, or hogbacks, with the dip slopes of the upper surfaces forming one flank and the escarpment where the resistant rock breaks off forming the other. On the lower slopes, where the rocks are less resistant, are more gentle gradients. Place names in Texas that incorporate the term include Cuesta del Burro qv in Presidio County and Cuesta Blanca qv in Brewster County.

Henry T. Fletcher

CUESTA BLANCA. Cuesta Blanca is 3½ miles southeast of Terlingua in southwestern Brewster County (at 29°18' N, 103°34' W). The summit, at an elevation of 2,860 feet above sea level, rises some 375 feet above the Terlingua post office, three-quarters of a mile to the north. Soils on Cuesta Blanca are shallow and stony and support sparse vegetation. The name is Spanish for "white hill."

CUESTA DEL BURRO. Cuesta del Burro ("Donkey Hill"), a range of hills, is located between Cleveland Flats on the northwest and Perdiz Creek on the east in central Presidio County (at 30°07' N, 104°23' W). The range has elevations from 4,913 to 6,100 feet above sea level. Needle Peak (at 30°02' N, 104°29' W), with an elevation of 5,662 feet above sea level, and the Black Hills (at 30°00' N, 104°15' W), with an elevation of 5,569 feet above sea level, are located in Cuesta del Burro. The range, composed of rhyolite and later-aged conglomerate, stands in desert mountain terrain cut by rugged canyons. The area is surfaced by loose rubble that supports sparse grasses, cacti, and scrubby desert conifers and oaks.

CUEVAS CREEK. Cuevas Creek rises six miles northeast of El Indio in south central Maverick County (at 28°33' N, 100°13' W) and runs southwest for twelve miles before emptying into Saus Creek a mile north of the Rio Grande in southwest Maverick County (at 28°31' N, 100°20' W). Chaparral, mesquite, and various grasses grow in the area's clayey soil, which surfaces low-rolling hills and prairie. *Cuevas* is Spanish for "caves."

CUEVITAS, TEXAS (Hidalgo County). Cuevitas is a colonia (*see* COLONIAS) off Farm Road 886 one mile north of the Rio Grande in extreme southwestern Hidalgo County. A settlement called Las Cuevas (Spanish for "the Caves"), dating to the Mexican Republic, was north of the site of present Cuevitas. It was the site of an encounter between Mexican armed rebels and Confederate soldiers that resulted in the death of three teamsters and the theft of the entire wagon train they were driving. The community of Las Cuevas continued to exist into the 1940s. But by 1976 it had been replaced by the colonia, which had forty-eight dwellings and a population of 242. By 1986 it had forty-two dwellings and a population estimated at 189. It received its water from the La Joya Water District.

BIBLIOGRAPHY: *Colonias in the Lower Rio Grande Valley of South Texas: A Summary Report* (Policy Research Project Report No. 18, Lyndon B. Johnson School of Public Affairs, University of Texas at Austin, 1977). J. Lee and Lillian J. Stambaugh, *The Lower Rio Grande Valley of Texas* (San Antonio: Naylor, 1954).

Alicia A. Garza

CUEVITAS, TEXAS (Jim Hogg County). Cuevitas is on Farm Road 649 eight miles south of Guerra in Jim Hogg County. The site was a part of José de Escandón's qv land grant. Indian hostility and revolutions in Mexico prevented settlement in the area until the late 1800s. Brothers J. and F. Guerra founded the town when they established a ranch and general store. A post office was established there in 1894, and the town had a church, a cemetery, and a school. Most of the community's residents have been in some way related to one another. Cuevitas achieved brief stardom when in an episode of "Gunsmoke," Matt Dillon and Chester referred to the town as the worst place to live. The town at one time served as a retail point for cattle ranching in southern Jim Hogg County. The population of Cuevitas was reported as eighty in 1915, twenty-five from 1939 until the 1960s, and twelve in 1990.

BIBLIOGRAPHY: Hebbronville Chamber of Commerce, *Fiftieth Anniversary, Jim Hogg County* (Hebbronville, Texas, 1963). Vertical Files, Barker Texas History Center, University of Texas at Austin.

Justin Lee Elmore

CUITAO INDIANS. The Cuitao (Cuitoa, Cuitoat) Indians were known only in the seventeenth century. Their location hinges upon identification of a river referred to by the Spanish as Río Nueces. This was not the present Nueces River of southern Texas but a river much farther north. Two schools of thought have emerged concerning the identity of this river. One school identifies it as the Colorado River in west central Texas, and the other identifies it as either the Red River or Canadian River of Texas and Oklahoma. Since each identification leaves certain important details unexplained, the status of the Río Nueces remains undetermined. However, it is important to note that, regardless of river identification, the Cuitao area was either in north central Texas or that portion of Oklahoma north of it. A. H. Schroeder's suggestion that the Cuitaos were probably a Wichita group therefore appears reasonable. The phonetic resemblance of Cuitao to Quitaca may be significant, especially since the Quitaca Indians seem also to have been a Wichita group.

BIBLIOGRAPHY: Hubert Howe Bancroft, *History of the North Mexican States and Texas* (2 vols., San Francisco: History Company, 1886, 1889). Herbert E. Bolton, "The Jumano Indians in Texas, 1650–1771," *Quarterly of the Texas State Historical Association* 15 (July 1911). Herbert Eugene Bolton, ed., *Spanish Exploration in the Southwest, 1542–1706* (New York: Scribner, 1908; rpt., New York: Barnes and Noble, 1959). George E. Hyde, *Indians of the High Plains: From the Prehistoric Period to the Coming of Europeans* (Norman: University of Oklahoma Press, 1959). Albert H. Schroeder, "A Re-Analysis of the Routes of Coronado and Oñate into the Plains in 1541 and 1601," *Plains Anthropologist* 7 (February 1962). S. L. Tyler and H. D. Taylor, "The Report of Fray Alonso de Posadas in Relation to Quivira and Teguayo," *New Mexico Historical Review* 33 (October 1958).

Thomas N. Campbell

CUJACO AND CUJALO INDIANS. The Cujacos and Cujalos, apparently two separate groups, are listed among twenty Indian groups that joined Juan Domínguez de Mendoza qv on his journey from El Paso to the vicinity of present San Angelo in 1683–84. Since Mendoza did not indicate at what point the two groups joined his party, it is not possible to determine their range or affiliations. However, the Indians between the Pecos River and the San Angelo area were being hard pressed by Apaches at this time, and it seems likely that the two groups ranged between these two localities.

BIBLIOGRAPHY: Herbert Eugene Bolton, ed., *Spanish Exploration in the Southwest, 1542–1706* (New York: Scribner, 1908; rpt., New York: Barnes and Noble, 1959).
Thomas N. Campbell

CUJANE INDIANS. The Cujane (Cohanni, Coxane, Cujano, Guyane, Kohani, Qujane, Quxane) Indians were Karankawans who, when first mentioned by this name in the early eighteenth century, lived on the Texas coast near Matagorda Bay, where they were closely associated with the Coapites and the Karankawas proper. At this time they seem to have ranged between the Colorado and Guadalupe rivers, but later this range was extended westward along the coast at least as far as Aransas Bay. In 1722 Espíritu Santo de Zúñiga Mission was established near Matagorda Bay for the Cujanes and their Karankawan associates, but it was soon abandoned because of frequent hostilities between Spaniards and Indians. In the 1730s a few Cujane Indians were persuaded to enter Nuestra Señora de la Purísima Concepción de Acuña Mission at San Antonio. In 1745, when Espíritu Santo de Zuñiga Mission was moved to the vicinity of present Goliad, some of the Cujanes came but soon deserted the mission. Then in 1754 Nuestra Señora del Rosario Mission was established in the Goliad area for the Cujanes, whose name at this time became a general name for all Karankawan groups except Copanes. The Cujane Indians were in and out of this mission until it was secularized in 1831. When Nuestra Señora del Refugio Mission was founded in 1793, some of the Cujanes took up residence there, remaining until it was abandoned in 1828. The Cujane Indians who did not enter missions continued to live along the nearby coast. Soon after Anglo American colonization of the coastal region the Cujanes began to lose their ethnic identity among the coastal Indians generally referred to as Karankawas, who disappeared about 1858. Attempts have been made to identify the Cujane Indians with several groups named in records of the La Salle expedition,qv particularly Ebahamo, Kouan, Kouyam, and Quinet. Since all of these groups evidently lived in or not far from the original Cujane area, sound correspondences in names provide the only basis for identification. Quinet and Kouan seem to be phonetically most similar to Cujane, but this needs the support of reliable documentary evidence. Identification of the Quevene of Álvar Núñez Cabeza de Vacaqv with the Cujane is dubious because 175 years or more separate the initial records of these groups.

BIBLIOGRAPHY: Herbert E. Bolton, "The Founding of Mission Rosario: A Chapter in the History of the Gulf Coast," *Quarterly of the Texas State Historical Association* 10 (October 1906). H. E. Bolton, "Records of the Mission of Nuestra Señora del Refugio," *Quarterly of the Texas State Historical Association* 14 (October 1910). Herbert Eugene Bolton, *Texas in the Middle Eighteenth Century* (Berkeley: University of California Press, 1915; rpt., Austin: University of Texas Press, 1970). William E. Dunn, "The Founding of Nuestra Señora del Refugio, the Last Spanish Mission in Texas," *Southwestern Historical Quarterly* 25 (January 1922). Frederick Webb Hodge, ed., *Handbook of American Indians North of Mexico* (2 vols., Washington: GPO, 1907, 1910; rpt., New York: Pageant, 1959). William H. Oberste, *History of Refugio Mission* (Refugio, Texas: Refugio Timely Remarks, 1942).
Thomas N. Campbell

CULBERSON, CHARLES ALLEN (1855–1925). Charles Allen Culberson, state attorney general, governor, and United States senator, son of Eugenia (Kimball) and David Browning Culberson,qv was born in Dadeville, Alabama, on June 19, 1855. His father was active in Texas and national politics. Eugenia Culberson belonged to the Crawford family of Georgia, a member of which, William Harris Crawford, had been a United States senator, minister to France, secretary of war, and secretary of the treasury in the early nineteenth century. The Culbersons moved to East Texas in 1856. Charles attended school at Gilmer and Jefferson, entered Virginia Military Institute in 1870, graduated in 1874, and later graduated from the University of Virginia law school. He was admitted to the bar at Daingerfield, Texas, in 1877

The Texas Hercules Tackles the Trust Monster, by Elmer Burruss. Original published in Texas Sandwich, *January 27, 1895. Texas Newspaper Collection, CAH; CN 08522. Reproduced from Maury Forman and Robert A. Calvert,* Cartooning Texas: One Hundred Years of Cartoon Art in the Lone Star State *(College Station, Texas: Texas A&M University Press, 1993), p. 14. Governor Culberson received approbation when he enforced antitrust legislation. This political cartoon portrays him as Hercules, taking on insurance, cottonseed, coal, and oil trusts.*

and was elected county attorney of Marion County shortly thereafter. He married Sally Harrison, daughter of William M. and Elizabeth Ann (Epperson) Harrison of Jefferson, in 1882. The couple moved in 1887 to Dallas, where Culberson practiced law in the firm Bookout and Culberson.

After being elected attorney general in 1890 by an overwhelming margin, Culberson was involved in several landmark federal cases, including the successful defense of the newly established Railroad Commission.qv He was reelected in 1892. Two years later, with the help of Edward Mandell House,qv he became governor. The People's partyqv was at the height of its popularity in the 1890s, but Culberson, conservative and penny-pinching in a period of mostly national depression, and his efficient political allies easily beat back the Populist gubernatorial challenge in both 1894 and 1896. The most talked-about event of his administration was the proposed prizefight featuring James J. Corbett, heavyweight champion of the world, and Bob Fitzsimmons, challenger (1895). An old political foe from East Texas, Dan Stuart, and others had already expended a fortune promoting the fight in Dallas when Culberson called the legislature into special session and passed a law making prizefighting a felony. Corbett later described the action as nothing but a grandstand play for the voters, but the fight was cancelled. The next year Roy Beanqv staged an outdoor "championship" fight just across the border in Mexico.

During the hectic days of the Spanish-American War, E. M. House was quietly working to get Culberson into national office. On January 25, 1899, the Texas House and Senate sitting jointly elected Culberson to succeed Roger Q. Millsqv as senator. Thus was launched a senatorial career that lasted twenty-four years. Culberson served as Senate Democratic minority leader from 1907 to 1910 and served on numerous legislative committees, the most important of which was the Committee on the Judiciary, of which he was chairman from 1913 to 1919. He was forced to resign as minority leader in 1910 due to physical problems exacerbated by alcoholism. One Democrat stated in 1910 that Culberson had been "in a comatose state for five years." Periodic trips to health resorts and spas earned him the derisive title "sick man of the Senate." Culberson announced early for reelection in 1910 and drove potential contenders from the field, but persistence of frailties including Bright's disease made rivalry certain in the campaign of 1916. Because another "breakdown" in April 1913 had left him unable to campaign, he depended on seniority, friends, and inertia to carry him through and never set foot in Texas during the campaign. Voters were not told of his illness or dependence on alcohol. Culberson's duties increased sharply in 1917. He introduced measure after measure regarding espionage, foreign relations, sabotage, and other wartime matters during Woodrow Wilson's presidency. At last the senator's health, never robust, broke under the strain. He was unable to take to the stump for the campaign of 1922. His illness and the opposition of the Ku Klux Klan[qv] brought about the first political defeat he had ever suffered.

Any evaluation of Culberson is difficult because of his caution and a reserve bordering on aloofness. These qualities with his intellect and good looks made him a tempting target for opponents. Many contemporaries speculated on how far he could have risen had he been a brash, forceful politico with more "color." In his favor were the respect in which the king-maker House and other prominent men held him, his undoubted abilities as a lawyer, his reputation for adhering to party discipline, his honesty, and his ideas regarding strict accountability for the public purse. While residing in Washington, Culberson died of pneumonia on March 19, 1925. He was returned to Fort Worth for burial in the Harrison family plot. He was survived by his wife, their only child, Mary, and his only sibling, Robert Upton Culberson.

BIBLIOGRAPHY: Lewis L. Gould, *Progressives and Prohibitionists: Texas Democrats in the Wilson Era* (Austin: University of Texas Press, 1973; rpt., Austin: Texas State Historical Association, 1992). James William Madden, *Charles Allen Culberson* (Austin: Gammel's Bookstore, 1929). Charles Seymour and Edward M. House, *The Intimate Papers of Colonel House* (4 vols., Boston: Houghton Mifflin, 1926). Robert Lancaster Wagner, The Gubernatorial Career of Charles Allen Culberson (M.A. thesis, University of Texas, 1954).

Robert L. Wagner

CULBERSON, DAVID BROWNING (1830–1900). David Browning Culberson, lawyer, soldier, and politician, was born in Troupe County, Georgia, on September 29, 1830, the son of David B. and Lucy (Wilkerson) Culberson. After leaving Brownwood Institute, La Grange, Georgia, he read law at Tuskegee, Alabama, in the school of William B. Chilton, chief justice of Alabama. He was admitted to the bar in 1850 and began practice in Dadeville. In 1856 he moved to Texas and settled in Upshur County, where he practiced law in partnership with Gen. Hinche P. Mabry[qv] until 1861, when he moved to Jefferson. Culberson was a member of the Texas legislature from Upshur County during the session 1859–60; he resigned his seat because he opposed secession[qv] and his district favored it. When the Civil War[qv] began he aided in raising the Eighteenth Texas Infantry, of which he became lieutenant colonel. After service in the Vicksburg area in 1862 and 1863 his health broke, and he was assigned to Austin as adjutant general of Texas. In the winter of 1864 he was elected to the legislature from Cass, Titus, and Bowie counties and resigned his military position to accept.

Culberson attended the Democratic state convention in 1868 and served as a presidential elector. As a prominent Jefferson lawyer he was one of the defense attorneys in the Stockade Case[qv] of 1869, and he helped defend accused murderer Abe Rothschild in a much-publicized trial in 1878. Culberson was elected in 1873 to the state Senate; he resigned when he was elected to the Forty-fourth Congress of the United States. He was reelected for ten successive terms and served from March 4, 1875, to March 3, 1897. In office he supported prohibition[qv] and opposed federal interference in state government. In 1876 he favored the repeal of the Specie Act, and in 1888 he introduced antitrust legislation in Congress. Though he was in sympathy with many of their political goals, Culberson campaigned against the Populists in the 1890s, attacking them as a divisive force in state politics. On June 21, 1897, he was appointed by President William McKinley to the committee to codify the laws of the United States. He served in this capacity until his death.

On December 8, 1852, he married Eugenia Kimball; they had two sons, one of whom, Charles A. Culberson,[qv] became governor of Texas. Culberson was a Mason and an Odd Fellow. He died in Jefferson on May 7, 1900, and was buried in Girard Cemetery.

BIBLIOGRAPHY: Alwyn Barr, *Reconstruction to Reform: Texas Politics, 1876–1906* (Austin: University of Texas Press, 1971). *Biographical Directory of the American Congress* (Washington, D.C.: GPO, 1859–). *Biographical Encyclopedia of Texas* (New York: Southern, 1880). Robert C. Cotner, *James Stephen Hogg: A Biography* (Austin: University of Texas Press, 1959). Lewis E. Daniell, *Personnel of the Texas State Government, with Sketches of Representative Men of Texas* (Austin: City Printing, 1887; 3d ed., San Antonio: Maverick, 1892). Sidney S. Johnson, *Texans Who Wore the Gray* (Tyler, Texas, 1907). William S. Speer and John H. Brown, eds., *Encyclopedia of the New West* (Marshall, Texas: United States Biographical Publishing, 1881; rpt., Easley, South Carolina: Southern Historical Press, 1978). Marcus J. Wright, comp., and Harold B. Simpson, ed., *Texas in the War, 1861–1865* (Hillsboro, Texas: Hill Junior College Press, 1965).

Anne W. Hooker

CULBERSON, OLIN WELLBORN NICHOLS (1886–1961). Olin Culberson, son of William Albert and Martha Artemesia (Richardson) Culberson, was born at Turnersville, Coryell County, Texas, on October 26, 1886. He was taught by his parents at Culberson Select School, a family enterprise, and afterward labored as a railroad worker in Hillsboro until 1911. That year he was appointed deputy clerk of Hill County. The following year he married Mary Lou Rochelle of Hubbard; the couple had one daughter.

In 1918 Culberson resigned his office to serve in World War I.[qv] Upon returning to Hillsboro, he was twice elected county clerk of Hill County. In that office he discovered and exposed a $263,000 road-bond fraud. In 1925 he became county judge. During his two terms on the bench he used the recovered bond-fraud money to construct needed roads and bridges. He refused to run for a third term, moved to Edna, and purchased an interest in a dry-goods store. He moved in 1932 to Austin, where he was asked to accept a position with the Railroad Commission[qv] in order to conduct a rate investigation of the Lone Star Gas Company. First as chief examiner and later as chief of the gas utilities division, he conducted sixteen major rate investigations for the commission. These antagonized certain gas interests, pressure groups sought his removal, and in 1939 he was discharged.

The following year, as a reform candidate, Culberson bested eighteen opponents and was elected railroad commissioner. He was reelected three consecutive times. In addition to proposing a weekly meeting of the railroad commissioners and insisting on ten days' notice for all public hearings, he was responsible for other important rulings. Political appointees were replaced by graduate petroleum engineers. The flaring of casinghead gas was stopped, and its return to the well became mandatory. A malodorant was added to natural gas (*see* NEW LONDON SCHOOL EXPLOSION). Annual inspections of liquefied petroleum gas installations in schools and public buildings were established. Culberson implemented a new system of oil accounting and fought freight-rate discrimination against Southwest Texas. While on the Railroad Commission, he earned a reputation as an uncompromising champion of independent oil producers.

Culberson served the Texas Firemen's and Fire Marshals' Association as secretary for over forty years, and he was active in many charitable organizations. He died on June 22, 1961, and was buried in the

State Cemetery^{qv} in Austin. In 1963 the Olin Culberson Memorial Research Center, a center for the study of cardiovascular diseases, was dedicated at Scott and White Memorial Hospital^{qv} in Temple.

BIBLIOGRAPHY: Olin Culberson Scrapbook, Barker Texas History Center, University of Texas at Austin. Houston *Press*, June 24, 1961. Vertical Files, Barker Texas History Center, University of Texas at Austin.

Robert Stephen Peel

CULBERSON, TEXAS. Culberson was on Black Cypress Bayou ten miles southwest of Linden in southwestern Cass County. A post office was established there in 1883 with I. S. Lacy as the first postmaster. In 1884 the community had a school, two churches, a gristmill, a gin, a general store, and a population of fifty. In 1890 the population of Culberson was reported as 100, but by 1896 it had declined to thirty. The post office was closed in May 1904 and the mail sent to Lassater in Marion County. On the 1936 highway map, a factory, and several houses are shown near the site where Culberson was probably located but was not named. By 1983 the area was entirely rural.

BIBLIOGRAPHY: Wright Patman, *History of Post Offices—First Congressional District of Texas* (Texarkana, Texas, 1946?).

Cecil Harper, Jr.

CULBERSON COUNTY. Culberson County (H-5) is located in the Trans-Pecos region of West Texas. It is bordered by New Mexico to the north and by Hudspeth, Reeves, and Jeff Davis counties in Texas. Van Horn, the county seat, is approximately 120 miles east of El Paso in the southwestern part of the county. The county's center lies about thirty-six miles northeast of Van Horn at approximately 32°27′ north latitude and 104°29′ west longitude. Interstate Highway 10 and U.S. Highway 80 cross southern Culberson County from east to west; U.S. Highway 90 enters the county from the south and terminates at Van Horn; and U.S. highways 62 and 180 cross the county's northwestern corner. The Missouri Pacific Railroad crosses southern Culberson County, paralleling Interstate 10; the Southern Pacific crosses the county's southwestern corner; and a spur of the Atchison, Topeka and Santa Fe enters northeastern Culberson County from New Mexico and ends at Rustler Springs.

Culberson County comprises 3,815 square miles of terrain that varies from mountainous to nearly level, with elevations ranging from 8,751 feet on Guadalupe Peak, the highest spot in the state, to 3,000 feet. The county is in the Rio Grande basin. Soils in Culberson County are primarily shallow and stony, with some clay and sandy loams and sand. Vegetation consists of scrub brush, grasses, cacti, creosote bush, post oak, chaparral, oak, juniper, mesquite, yucca, and agave, with Douglas fir, aspen, Arizona cypress, maple, and madrone trees in the Guadalupe Mountains. The Guadalupes are also the home of several endangered or locally rare plant species, including bigtooth maple, ponderosa pine, chinquapin oak, Rocky Mountain juniper, Texas madrone, and Mexican buckeye, and of the only elk in Texas. Dolomite, gypsum, limestone, salt, silver, copper, lead, zinc, barite, and molybdenum are among the minerals found in Culberson County. The climate is mild and dry, with an average minimum temperature of 30° F in January and an average maximum of 94° in July. The growing season averages 224 days a year, and the average annual precipitation is ten inches. Less than 1 percent of the land in Culberson County is considered prime farmland.

Today Culberson County is best known as the site of Guadalupe Mountains National Park,^{qv} which includes Guadalupe Peak and is a major tourist attraction. The Guadalupes and the county's other mountains, such as the Delaware, Beach, Wylie, Sierra Diablo, Van Horn, Apache, and Baylor^{qv} ranges, made the area ideal for Indians seeking protection from their enemies and a remote home base from which to launch attacks. The earliest sign of human occupation in the area, found in the Guadalupes, is a 12,000-year-old Folsom point. Later, hunter-gatherers probably inhabited the mountains only during the summer; they also left artifacts, as well as pictographs. The most famous indigenous inhabitants of the mountains, the Apaches, arrived about 600 years ago. They harvested agave, yucca, and sotol when meat was unavailable, and their agave-roasting pits are still visible in the Guadalupes.

The area that was to become Culberson County was largely untouched by Spanish exploration, due to its forbidding topography. In 1583, however, Antonio de Espejo^{qv} became the first European to see the Mescalero Apaches, on the prairie just east of the Guadalupe Mountains. Beginning about 1630 the Mescaleros were raiding the more populous Plains Navajos and Pueblos from the Guadalupes; fifty years later they had added El Paso del Norte^{qv} to their list of targets. By the beginning of the eighteenth century Comanches from the Llano Estacado^{qv} had ended the Apache domination of western Texas, and the Mescaleros, based in the Guadalupes, restricted their raids to a smaller geographical area. Their ferocity, however, was unaffected, and the Mescaleros became one of the most feared of all Indian groups in Texas. Their presence, combined with the area's isolation, ensured that the area would not become popular with white settlers.

By the middle of the nineteenth century, however, emigrants were seeking new routes to connect central and eastern Texas with El Paso and California. The 1849 gold rush increased the demand for such roads, and exploration by the whites occurred with breathtaking speed. In May 1849 John S. (Rip) Ford and Maj. Robert S. Neighbors,^{qqv} returning to Waco from El Paso, skirted the Guadalupe Mountains and described Guadalupe Canyon. In July 1849 an expedition led by Lt. Francis Theodore Bryan^{qv} camped at Guadalupe Pass while retracing the Ford-Neighbors route to confirm its suitability for a wagon road to the west. In September 1849 Capt. Randolph Barnes Marcy^{qv} came in sight of the Guadalupes while returning from Santa Fe to Fort Smith, Arkansas.

Also in 1849, the Van Horn Wells were supposedly discovered by Maj. Jefferson Van Horne,^{qv} en route to El Paso. The wells became known as one of the few dependable water sources in the vast emptiness of West Texas; ten years later the army considered them sufficiently important to establish a cavalry outpost there under Lt. James Judson Van Horn^{qv} (no relation to Jefferson). Lieutenant Van Horn commanded the station until 1861, when he was taken prisoner by Confederate troops who seized the wells. The town of Van Horn, founded some twenty years later, was named for him.

The signing of the Treaty of Guadalupe Hidalgo^{qv} also increased knowledge of the area. John Russell Bartlett,^{qv} appointed a boundary commissioner by President Zachary Taylor,^{qv} traveled through the area on his way to El Paso to negotiate the United States–Mexico border. Bartlett reached what would become Culberson County in early November 1850. He found the Guadalupes "a dark, gloomy-looking range, with bold and forbidding sides." Bartlett suggested that the proposed transcontinental railroad be built along a route south of the Guadalupes, where "the country is quite open and apparently level."

Thanks in part to Bartlett's favorable report, a surveying party under Capt. John Pope^{qv} passed through the area in 1853, seeking a potential railroad route; Pope returned the following year to search in vain for an artesian water supply. A prospector named Thomas Owen or Owens reportedly discovered the Hazel Mine in 1856, but the Mescaleros and the Civil War^{qv} forced him to abandon the area for twenty-five years.

Despite the efforts of Bartlett and Pope, the next phase of exploration involved stagecoaches rather than steel rails. In March 1857 John Butterfield received a contract to carry mail twice a week from St. Louis and Memphis to San Francisco; three months later John Birch received a contract to carry mail semimonthly from San Antonio to San Diego, California. The Butterfield Overland Mail^{qv} route entered what would become Culberson County from the east, crossed the Rustler Hills, more or less followed the Delaware River west, and then went up and over Guadalupe Pass. The first westbound Butterfield coach arrived at the Pinery, a station in the Guadalupes, in late September 1858. Within a year, however, the Butterfield route was shifted to the south to take advantage of the protection afforded by forts Davis and Stockton. Birch's San Antonio–San Diego Mail Route,qv nicknamed the Jackass Mail, began operation in July 1857. By 1860 it had been shortened to connect San Antonio and El Paso, and was discontinued in 1861 because of the outbreak of the Civil War.

After the war the demand for a transcontinental railroad mounted. Before such a project could become a reality, however, the government decided it needed to wipe out the Apaches, who, led by their great chief Victorio,qv a Warm Springs Apache, and augmented by Mescaleros from the Fort Stanton Reservation, carried out a brilliant raiding campaign in the late 1860s and throughout the 1870s. Various military expeditions were sent in pursuit of the Apaches, but most stopped short of actually following them into the mountains. In December 1869, however, Troop F of the Third Cavalry under Lt. Howard B. Cushing left Fort Stanton, New Mexico, and entered the Guadalupes in pursuit of the Indians. Cushing's men found two Apache camps and destroyed the Indians' winter stores of food and clothing.

In May 1870 another detachment of troops left Fort Quitman under Maj. Albert Morrow. At Pine Springs in the Guadalupes, Morrow's men rendezvoused with reinforcements from Fort Davis, pressed up McKittrick Canyon in search of the Indians, and got lost. They did manage to discover and destroy one ranchería of seventy-five lodges, which the Apaches had abandoned.

By this time a ranching boom had begun in the Trans-Pecos, and the demand for rangeland for longhorn cattle qv sealed the fate of the Apaches. Thanks to Victorio's tactical brilliance, they managed to elude the military for another ten years, but the federal cavalry and the Texas Rangersqv had the advantage. Victorio himself was finally killed in Mexico in 1880, and in January 1881 a company of rangers under George W. Baylorqv ambushed the last surviving band of Apache raiders in Bass Canyon in the Sierra Diablo Mountains; it was the last big Indian fight in Texas.

In 1881 the long-awaited railroad link to the West finally became a reality, although not without its share of controversy. Under Jay Gould,qv who had bought the line a year before, the Texas and Pacific Railway was building westward from Fort Worth to El Paso. Meanwhile Collis P. Huntington's rival Galveston, Harrisburg and San Antonio Railway was building eastward from El Paso in order to complete its own link to central and eastern Texas. For a time no one was sure which road would prevail, but in November 1881 Gould and Huntington reached an agreement by which the Texas and Pacific would stop at Sierra Blanca, in Hudspeth County, and the two lines would share the track from Sierra Blanca to El Paso.

With the completion of the Texas and Pacific, white settlement of the area began in earnest. Among the pioneer settlers in what would become Culberson County were Ed Hamm, George Bristow, railroad agent Jack Veats, and the families of R. P. (Perry) Bean, A. A. (Gus) Cox, Sebastian (Ben) De Anda, J. H. Beach, and Robert K. Wylie.qv Local mountain ranges were eventually named after the last two. The towns of Van Horn, Plateau, and Kent grew up along the railroad, and ranchers pushed up into the Guadalupes themselves. The influx of ranchers continued for the next three decades, and Van Horn grew into a prosperous cattle-shipping center. In 1911 a new county, named after David B. Culberson,qv was separated from El Paso County. When Culberson County was organized in 1912, Van Horn was chosen as county seat. In 1920 the population of the county was only 912, of whom 910 were white. Perhaps reflecting the prevalence of ranching and the lack of urban centers, males outnumbered females 539 to 373. Ten years later the population had climbed to 1,228, 638 of whom were classified as white and 583 as Mexican. In subsequent years the population continued to increase: to 1,653 in 1940, 1,825 in 1950, 2,794 in 1960, and 3,429 in 1970. Between 1970 and 1980 the population declined slightly, to 3,315, but in 1982 had risen to 3,616. The 1982 population was mostly of Hispanic (63 percent), English (16 percent), or Irish (12 percent) descent.

Extraction of minerals has long been important in Culberson County, although rumors of fabulously wealthy gold mines in the Guadalupes seem to be mere wishful thinking. Around 1875 an old prospector named Ben Sublett strode into a saloon and casually tossed a buckskin pouch full of gold nuggets onto the bar, hinting broadly that he had discovered them in the Guadalupes. All efforts to get him to reveal the exact location of his find were unsuccessful; he took his secret to the grave in 1892, leaving his son to search in vain for the mine. Gen. Lew Wallace, the author of *Ben-Hur* and governor of New Mexico from 1878 to 1881, said he found references in the Spanish archives in Santa Fe to rich gold deposits in the Guadalupes, but the exact location had been lost. The Apache chief Geronimo also claimed that the Spanish had mined the area, and that the Guadalupes contained the richest mines in North America. More recent opinion holds such claims unlikely.

Other minerals have been less elusive. Between the late nineteenth century and the mid-twentieth century the Hazel Mine yielded about a million pounds of copper and more than two million ounces of silver. In the 1940s acidic sulfur earth was produced at Rustler Springs for use as a fertilizer and soil conditioner, and the Apache Mountains were the site of the largest barite deposit in Texas, which was mined from open pits during the 1960s. A mica quarry operated in the early 1980s in the Van Horn Mountains to mine mica schist for oilfield use, but the sustained production of sheet mica had not been achieved. Culberson County was also producing copper, bedded gypsum from surface mines, brucitic marble, molybdenum, crushed rhyolite, silver, Frasch sulfur, and talc in the 1980s.

Oil was discovered in the county in 1953, but annual production was only 320 barrels in 1956. In the late 1950s and early 1960s, however, production soared, reaching 184,208 barrels in 1958, 725,953 barrels in 1960, and 1,289,000 barrels in 1963. Production declined in subsequent years, to 873,868 barrels in 1968, 653,830 barrels in 1976, and 284,525 barrels in 1980, before rebounding to 1,102,644 in 1982. Two years later it had fallen again, to 642,932 barrels, and in 1990 Culberson County produced 409,238 barrels.

Ranching has traditionally been more important than farming in the local economy, although the cattle population in Culberson County decreased between 1920 and the early 1980s. The number of cattle dropped from 48,974 in 1920 to 40,563 in 1930, 27,144 in 1940, 18,883 in 1950, and 8,805 in 1960, then rose to 22,745 in 1969 and roughly 29,000 in 1982. The number of farms increased from forty-seven in 1920 to fifty-two in 1930 and peaked at eighty-one in 1940; in subsequent decades the number of farms remained relatively stable, with seventy in 1950, seventy-six in 1959, eighty in 1969, and seventy in 1982.

Shortage of water has always been a principal obstacle to agriculture in Culberson County. In the late 1930s, when local stockmen began using spreader dams and other techniques to conserve more of the precious rainwater, the county agricultural agent described Culberson County as "a strictly ranching area." In September 1948, however, a well was brought in at Lobo, one mile from the headquarters of William Cameron's ranch, and the Cameron Company began selling plots of land to farmers. Other wells were put down and fitted with more efficient pumps, but they proved prohibitively expensive to operate; by the late 1960s virtually all had been abandoned.

The story of the local cotton industry follows the pattern of farming in general in the county. Culberson County had been the only county in Texas never to produce a bale of cotton, but in 1949 Darwin Brewster grew the first on a 500-acre farm near Lobo. The bale was ginned at Tornillo, in El Paso County, and proudly displayed at the main intersection in downtown Van Horn; Brewster himself was honored by the chamber of commerce. In 1950, 1,295 acres planted with cotton in the county produced 1,114 bales. The county's first cotton gin was built the next year and ginned about 6,000 bales that fall;

two more gins were built in subsequent years. In 1959 cotton farmers planted 6,215 acres and produced 11,130 bales. But Culberson County's cotton boom was short-lived, thanks largely to the water shortage. Ten years later cotton was planted on only 3,585 acres that produced 3,415 bales, and by 1982 cotton land had fallen to 1,656 acres that produced only 1,324 bales.

Culberson County has generally voted Democratic, although Republicans won some presidential and statewide races in the late twentieth century. Republican presidential candidates won in the 1972 and 1984 elections, but Democrats Michael Dukakis and Bill Clinton managed to garner a majority of the votes in the 1988 and 1992 elections respectively. Democratic officials have also continued to maintain control of most county offices. In the 1982 primary 94 percent voted Democratic and 6 percent Republican, with a total of 630 votes cast.

As early as 1899, when the first Old Settler's Reunion was celebrated in Van Horn, the residents of Culberson County realized the potential benefits of attracting outside visitors; as one writer put it, Culberson County "is the kind of raw-mountain, raw-grasslands country that breeds mystics and imaginative, lyrical chambers of commerce." The Old Settler's Reunion became an annual event and remained so until 1958, when Frontier Day took its place. By the early 1980s Frontier Day had in turn been replaced by the Big Country Celebration, held in Van Horn in June. With the completion of U.S. Highway 62 in 1926, the increasing viability of automobile travel, and the relative proximity of Carlsbad Caverns in New Mexico, the Big Bend in Presidio County, and the Guadalupe Mountains in northern Culberson County, tourism became increasingly important in the local economy.

County employment statistics bear out the increasing importance of tourism and the declining importance of agriculture. In the 1930, 1940, 1950, and 1960 censuses more people were employed in agriculture than in any other field. In 1970 agriculture had slid all the way to third, behind the mining and service industries. Ten years later, 23 percent of the labor force was employed in agriculture and mining, 23 percent in wholesale and retail trade, and 12 percent in other counties. In 1982, 828 Culberson County residents were employed in the service and related industries, while only seventy-three were employed in agriculture. By 1982, when Culberson County ranked 237th among Texas counties in agricultural cash receipts, tourists spent $17,432,000 there. In 1990 the county population was 3,407; Van Horn was the largest community.

BIBLIOGRAPHY: Don Kurtz and William D. Goran, *Trails of the Guadalupes: A Hiker's Guide to the Trails of Guadalupe Mountains National Park* (Champaign, Illinois: Environmental Associates, 1978). Alan Tennant, *The Guadalupe Mountains of Texas* (Austin: University of Texas Press, 1980). Rosa Lee Wylie, *History of Van Horn and Culberson County* (Hereford, Texas: Pioneer, 1973).

Martin Donell Kohout

CULEBRA CREEK. Culebra Creek rises three miles west of Helotes in western Bexar County (at 29°35′ N, 98°45′ W) and runs southeast for twelve miles to its mouth on Leon Creek, one mile west of Interstate Loop 410 (at 29°28′ N, 98°38′ W). It traverses rolling terrain surfaced by clay loam and expansive clay soils that support mesquite and grasses. The name is Spanish for snake.

CULLEN, EZEKIEL WIMBERLY (1814–1882). Ezekiel Wimberly Cullen, early legislator, jurist, and lawyer, was born in 1814. He moved from Georgia to Texas in 1835 and settled at San Augustine, where he established a law practice. In 1835 he joined the Texas revolutionary forces and participated in the siege of Bexar.qv While representing San Augustine County in the House of Representatives of the Third Congress of the republic (1838–39), where he was chairman of the education committee, he sponsored the Cullen Act, which started land endowments for public schools and universities, thus laying the basis for an eventual Texas public-education system. In 1839 President Mirabeau B. Lamarqv appointed Cullen to judgeship of the First District, vacant after the death of Shelby Corzine.qv Cullen practiced law in San Augustine until 1850, when he was appointed purser in the United States Navy. He lived for a time in Pensacola, Florida, and later in Washington, D.C. He returned to Texas in 1871 and opened a law office in Dallas, where he lived until his death in 1882. Noted oilman and philanthropist Hugh Roy Cullenqv was his grandson. The Ezekiel Cullen Building on the University of Houston campus, constructed in 1950, was named in his honor.

BIBLIOGRAPHY: *Hall of Remembrance: The Heroes and Heroines of Texas Education* (Dallas: Texas Heritage Foundation, 1954). Texas House of Representatives, *Biographical Directory of the Texan Conventions and Congresses, 1832–1845* (Austin: Book Exchange, 1941). Vertical Files, Barker Texas History Center, University of Texas at Austin.

Christopher Long

CULLEN, HUGH ROY (1881–1957). Hugh Roy Cullen, oilman and philanthropist, son of Cicero and Louise (Beck) Cullen and grandson of Ezekiel W. Cullen,qv was born on July 3, 1881, in Denton County. His formal education was limited to a few years in the public schools in San Antonio. He married Lillie Cranz on December 29, 1903; they had four daughters and one son, Roy Gustave Cullen, who died in 1936. At the age of sixteen Cullen worked for a cotton broker; he later went into that business for himself and also dealt in real estate. He moved to Houston in 1911 and entered the oil business in 1918. His policy of drilling deep wells was so successful that he became known as the "king of the wildcatters." He made major discoveries in the Houston area, notably at Pierce Junction, Blue Ridge, Rabb's Ridge, Humble, and the O'Connor field. He owned half of the South Texas Petroleum Company and later formed the Quintana Petroleum Company. Cullen took an active interest in politics throughout his life. Since he was firmly dedicated to states' rights, much of his energy was spent in opposition to the New Deal. He promoted W. Lee O'Danielqv for governor in 1938 and 1940 and for senator in 1941. Although Cullen aided the Dixiecrat movement in 1948, he normally supported Republican candidates, particularly Dwight D. Eisenhowerqv in 1952. He gave more than $11 million each to his favorite projects, the University of Houston and Houston hospitals. In 1947 he established the $160 million Cullen Foundationqv to provide for continual aid to education and medicine. By 1955 he had given away an estimated 90 percent of his fortune. Cullen served in many capacities during his career, including chairman of the board of regents of the University of Houston, vice president of the Texas World Fair Commission in 1939, and director of the Boy Scouts of America. He received honorary degrees from the University of Pittsburgh in 1936, Baylor University in 1945, and the University of Houston in 1947. He was an honorary member of the American Hospital Association and a member of the Sons of the Republic of Texas.qv Cullen died in Houston on July 4, 1957.

BIBLIOGRAPHY: Edward Kilman and Theon Wright, *Hugh Roy Cullen* (New York: Prentice-Hall, 1954). Houston *Post*, July 5, 1957. *Who's Who in America* (1956–57).

Rita Crabbe

CULLEN FOUNDATION. The Cullen Foundation, of Houston, was established on March 31, 1947, by Hugh Roy Cullenqv and his wife, Lillie C. Cullen, to be devoted wholly to public charitable purposes in Texas. Before the establishment of the foundation, the Cullens had made large gifts to the University of Houston, Texas Medical Center,qv Baylor University College of Medicine, and Texas Southern University, as well as significant contributions to the Houston Symphony Society, the Houston Museum of Fine Arts,qv the Boy Scouts, the YMCA, and other organizations. The donors designated three trustees at the time the foundation was established. The trust indenture provided for succession of trustees and for an increase in the number of trustees to five upon the death of the last to die of the donors. The foundation, when established, held $10,000 in cash, together with South Texas oil properties. The assets of the foundation as of December 31, 1983, were $110,423,136.

By 1983 the foundation had made grants totaling $136,137,000 to charity, education, medicine, and other causes in sums ranging from $1,000 to $7 million. The University of Houston, to which Mr. and Mrs. Cullen personally gave significant contributions, has been the largest single beneficiary of the foundation. In 1989 the foundation had assets of $159,358,629 and income of $19,750,928. Grants for 1989 were $6,399,438, ranging from $5000 to $1 million. The $1 million was to Briarwood-Brookwood, Incorporated.

BIBLIOGRAPHY: *The Hooper Directory of Texas Foundations*, 1990. Houston *Chronicle*, April 1, October 28, 1947, August 15, 1957, April 10, 1962, May 1, 1968. Edward Kilman and Theon Wright, *Hugh Roy Cullen* (New York: Prentice-Hall, 1954). Patrick J. Nicholson, *In Time: An Anecdotal History of the First Fifty Years of the University of Houston* (Houston: Pacesetter, 1977).

Joseph C. Graf

CULLEOKA, TEXAS. Culleoka, on a spur off Farm Road 982 near the banks of Lavon Lake ten miles east of McKinney in east central Collin County, is named after the Tennessee hometown of its early settlers. It was formed in the late 1880s following the construction of a general store in 1887. In 1892 its population was twenty, and by 1900 a mill and cotton gin were operating there. From 1893 to 1906 Culleoka had a post office serving an estimated population of fifty. After 1906 mail for the community was sent to McKinney. Over the next several decades the population of Culleoka grew to 150, where it remained until the late 1940s. In the 1930s the town had a high school, three or four businesses, and four churches. It began to decline in the late 1940s, in part due to the growth of nearby Plano and also because of the disruption of the area caused by the completion of Lavon Dam in 1954 and the resulting large reservoir. The community still existed in 1990.

BIBLIOGRAPHY: Roy Franklin Hall and Helen Gibbard Hall, *Collin County: Pioneering in North Texas* (Quanah, Texas: Nortex, 1975).

David Minor

CULLINAN, JOSEPH STEPHEN (1860–1937). Joseph Stephen Cullinan, oilman, was born on December 31, 1860, near Sharon, Pennsylvania, the oldest son and second of eight children of John Francis and Mary (Considine) Cullinan. At the age of fourteen he began working in the Pennsylvania oilfields and learned to perform virtually every task associated with oil production. In 1882 he joined Standard Oil, and he eventually held several managerial positions in that company. He left Standard in 1895 to organize his own company, Petroleum Iron Works, an operation that manufactured steel storage tanks.

When oil was discovered in Corsicana, Texas, in 1894, local developers invited Cullinan to Texas to advise them on production and marketing techniques. In Corsicana he organized the J. S. Cullinan Company, which later became Magnolia Petroleum Company.qv Among the contributions that Cullinan made to the Corsicana oil industry were the introduction of oil as a fuel for locomotives, the use of natural gas for lighting and heating, and the utilization of oil to settle dust on the city's streets. South of Corsicana, Cullinan constructed a refinery that began operation in 1899 and was the first such facility west of the Mississippi. In addition, in 1899 he was instrumental in persuading the Texas legislature to enact the state's first petroleum-conservation statute.

Cullinan moved his operations to Beaumont shortly after the Spindletop discovery in 1901 (*see* SPINDLETOP OILFIELD). There he founded the Texas Company (later Texacoqv) in 1902; he served as company president until he lost control of the stock in a proxy fight with eastern investors in 1913. When he moved his operations and the Texaco headquarters to Houston in 1905, Cullinan established that city as the focal point of the oil industry in the Southwest. He remained active in the industry after his resignation as president of Texaco. Eventually he founded ten companies involved in the exploration, production, refining, and marketing of Texas petroleum, and he was instrumental in developing oil deposits in the Sour Lake, Humble, and East Texas oilfields.qqv

Cullinan served as president of the Houston Chamber of Commerce from 1913 until 1919 and supported development of the Houston Ship Channel.qv He also constructed the North Side Belt Railway around the city in 1922. During World War Iqv he was special advisor to the Food Administration under Herbert Hoover. He was a patron of the Museum of Fine Arts, the Houston Symphony Orchestra,qqv and Houston Negro Hospital. From 1928 to 1933 he was chairman of the Mount Rushmore National Memorial Committee. He married Lucy Halm on April 14, 1891; they had five children. Cullinan died of pneumonia while visiting his friend Herbert Hoover in Palo Alto, California, on March 11, 1937.

BIBLIOGRAPHY: John O. King, *Joseph Stephen Cullinan* (Nashville: Vanderbilt University Press, 1970). Tommy W. Stringer, "Joseph Stephen Cullinan, Pioneer in Texas Oil," *East Texas Historical Journal* 19 (Fall 1981).

Tommy W. Stringer

CULLINAN, NINA J. (1899–1983). Nina J. Cullinan, patron of Houston arts and parks, daughter of Lucie (Halm) and Joseph S. Cullinan,qv was born in Washington, Pennsylvania, in 1899. She was one of five children. Joseph Cullinan was a founder of the Magnolia Petroleum Companyqv and helped organize the Texas Company in Beaumont shortly after the oil strike at Spindletop oilfieldqv in 1902. The Cullinans moved to Beaumont when Nina was three. She grew up in Houston, attended Houston public schools, a prep school, and Ogontz College in Pennsylvania.

After college she followed her family's tradition of actively participating in civic life. She was a founding member of the Contemporary Arts Museum,qv the Society For Performing Arts, and the Houston Balletqv Foundation. She also served on boards of the Museum of Fine Arts,qv the Municipal Arts Commission, the Fine Arts Advisory Council of the University of Texas, and the American Federation of Art. She was a leading benefactor of the Houston Symphony Orchestra.qv In the 1950s she funded the building of the Cullinan Hall of the Museum of Fine Arts, designed by Ludwig Mies van der Rohe.

Nina Cullinan's philanthropy extended to other sectors of city life; she was a member of the boards of the Child Guidance Center, the Houston Mental Health Society, and the National Parks Commission. At her death she willed $4 million, more than half of her estate, to the Houston Parks Board for the development of new park space. In 1978 she was honored by the Society of Texas Architects for her donation to the Museum of Fine Arts for Cullinan Hall. She was among four Houstonians honored in 1982 by Mayor Kathryn J. Whitmire for contributions to the arts, and the same year a dinner was held in her honor by the Texas Project for the Archives of American Art. Nina Cullinan frequently made anonymous donations and placed few restrictions on charitable gifts. She died in Houston on February 22, 1983.

BIBLIOGRAPHY: Houston *Post*, July 1, 1956, October 31, 1982, February 23, 24, 25, 1983. Victoria *Advocate*, June 17, 1985.

Carol Brown

CULLUM, LANDON HAYNES (1889–1961). Landon H. (Shino) Cullum, oilman, the son of Jacob Davis and Eudona (Haynes) Cullum, was born in Dallas, Texas, on February 25, 1889. He studied engineering and participated in athletics at the University of Texas. In 1911–12 he worked on the construction of an interurban rail line between Waco and Dallas for Stone and Webster; the following year he worked for the Pacific Railroad Maintenance of Way Department. From 1913 to 1915 he was an engineer for the Gulf Oil Corporation, first at Beaumont and later in the Wichita Falls area. He was a zone agent in the land department from 1915 to 1918.

In 1918 he joined J. J. Perkins, Frank Kell,qqv and R. O. Harvey to form the Harvey Lease Account, one of the strongest and most profitable independent oil firms in the state. They opened the South Electra field and operated in the North Texas, Ranger, Desdemona, and other fields. In 1922 the firm was sold to Magnolia Petroleum Companyqv for a seven-figure sum. Cullum and Perkins formed the Perkins-Cullum Production Company, which successfully operated in many fields in Texas and Oklahoma. Cullum was one of the organizers of the Texas Division of the Mid-Continent Oil and Gas Association, president of the North Texas Oil and Gas Association in 1935–36, and active in other independent oil groups. His other business interests included buildings in Wichita Falls, farms, and ranches.

He was a member of the first board of trustees of Hardin Junior College at Wichita Falls. He served from 1941 to 1957, during which time Hardin became a four-year college, expanded its campus, added a graduate department, and changed its name to Midwestern University. He was active in University of Texas projects, including the Athletic Council, the Committee of Seventy-five Development Board, and the Ex-Students' Association, of which he was president. He was instrumental in securing passage of the first oil conservation and proration laws in Texas. He was a member of the Independent Petroleum Association of America, a director of City National Bank from 1927 until his death, and a director of the local chamber of commerce and Community Chest. He was a member of the First Presbyterian Church and a thirty-second-degree Mason. On May 28, 1921, he was married to Leila Beall Anderson of Wichita Falls; they had three children. Cullum died on August 15, 1961, and was interred in the mausoleum at Crestview Memorial Park, Wichita Falls.

BIBLIOGRAPHY: *Alcalde* (magazine of the Ex-Students' Association of the University of Texas), May 1940, December 1949. Ellis A. Davis and Edwin H. Grobe, comps., *The New Encyclopedia of Texas*, 2-vol. ed. John D. Palmer, "Glimpses of the Desdemona Oil Boom," West Texas Historical Association *Year Book* 15 (1939). Vertical Files, Barker Texas History Center, University of Texas at Austin. *Who's Who in the South and Southwest*, Vol. 2.   *Louise Kelly*

CULLUM, ROBERT BROOKS (1912–1981). Robert Brooks Cullum, cofounder of Tom Thumb–Page Food Stores and civic leader, son of Ashley Wilson and Eloise (Brooks) Cullum, was born on May 10, 1912, in Dallas. While attending North Dallas High School he was quarterback on the football team despite his short height of 5′6″. He continued as quarterback during his single term at Kemper Military School in Missouri before transferring to Southern Methodist University, where he received his bachelor of science in journalism in 1933. Cullum planned on a career in advertising, but the Great Depressionqv left him unable to find a job. Therefore, he went into his father's wholesale food business after graduation. On July 6, 1934, he married Dorothy Rogers; they had four children.

Cullum and his brother Charles both worked in the small family business his father had started. In the 1940s their biggest client was Toro Food Stores, a failing food chain. The owner fled to South America owing the Cullums $200,000. In 1948 the Cullum brothers took over the Toro Food Chain in order to avoid bankruptcy, took out a loan, and renamed the chain Tom Thumb. The first advertising, designed by Bob Cullum, was placed in the Dallas *Morning News*qv in 1948. In 1966 the brothers bought out Page Drug Stores. Eventually the two chains merged as Tom Thumb–Page. In 1981 the chain included 132 grocery stores, meat-packing plants, and a wholesale business that supplied restaurants and hotels.

In 1962 Cullum received the Linz Award for civic service to Dallas and the Brotherhood Citation of the National Conference of Christians and Jews. In 1964 he was named the Dallas Press Club's Headliner of the Year. He was president of the Dallas Chamber of Commerce and in 1964–65 was one of three negotiators responsible for the Dallas–Fort Worth Regional Airport (now Dallas–Fort Worth International Airportqv). From the 1950s he was active on the board of the State Fair of Texas;qv he served as president of the board from 1967 to 1979. In 1972 he was president of the Dallas Citizens Council. In October of 1979 the Dallas City Council named a street near Fair Park Robert B. Cullum Boulevard.

Cullum served on the boards of many businesses, including Dallas Power and Light Company, the Dr Pepper Company,qv and Republic National Bank of Dallas. He was director emeritus of Dallas Federal Savings and Loan Association and the director of the Dallas Council of World Affairs, the American Red Cross, the Dallas Zoological Society, and the Texas Research Foundation.qv He was a trustee of the Callier Center for Communication Disorders and of the Southwestern Medical Foundation (*see* UNIVERSITY OF TEXAS SOUTHWESTERN MEDICAL CENTER, DALLAS). He was a member of the board of governors of Southern Methodist University and the Dallas–Fort Worth airport. He belonged the National Association of Food Chains and the Super Market Institute, of which he was president in 1966–67. He was a member of the Cotton Bowlqv Athletic Association and the Southern United Methodist Alumni Association. He was a Methodist and belonged to a variety of clubs, including the Chaparral, City, Koon Kreek, and Dallas country clubs. He died on December 11, 1981, in Dallas and is buried in Hillcrest Mausoleum.

BIBLIOGRAPHY: Dallas *Morning News*, December 12, 1981. *Who Was Who in America*, Vol. 8.   *Lisa C. Maxwell*

CULP, TEXAS. Culp was ten miles west of Hillsboro in west central Hill County, the Cross Timbers section of the county. The site was likely settled during the late nineteenth century by William Myers,

Nina Cullinan in Cullinan Hall. Photograph by Dan Hardy. Houston, 1958. Courtesy Houston Metropolitan Research Center, Houston Public Library. Arts patron Nina Cullinan funded the building of Cullinan Hall of the Museum of Fine Arts, Houston, in the 1950s.

Mose Reed, and Cicero Beck. Local mineral-water springs, near which a hotel and bathhouse stood, won for the community a reputation as a health resort. A community school enrolled sixty students and employed one teacher during the 1905–06 school year. Though a post office operated locally from 1892 until sometime after 1930, Culp reported no population or business statistics during the twentieth century. The site was inundated by Aquilla Lake in the 1970s, though a church belonging to the community was still standing in 1990.

BIBLIOGRAPHY: Hill County Historical Commission, *A History of Hill County, Texas, 1853–1980* (Waco: Texian, 1980). Brian Hart

CULP BRANCH. Culp Branch rises eight miles northeast of Denton in north central Denton County (at 33°21′ N, 97°06′ W) and runs southeast for seven miles to its mouth on the Elm Fork of the Trinity River, five miles northeast of Denton (at 33°17′ N, 97°02′ W). It traverses low-rolling to flat terrain surfaced by sandy and clay loams that support hardwood trees, scrub brush, cacti, and various grasses. The area has served as crop and range land.

CUMBERLAND COLLEGE. Cumberland College, in Leonard, was founded by the Texas Synod of the Cumberland Presbyterian Church in 1911 as a coeducational institution. Its board of trustees consisted of Rev. J. W. Pearson, Joe F. Hall, John W. Groves, W. W. Witcher, and B. B. Braly. At the founding meetings Pearson was elected temporary president of the college. The campus included a three-story, twelve-room brick classroom building and a two-story, thirteen-room dormitory for women. In addition to the college campus, valued at $28,000, the college owned eleven lots in Leonard.

On September 12, 1911, Cumberland opened with thirty-four students. The first teachers were Pearson, professor of Greek and philosophy; Rev. DeCosta Howard Dodson, president and professor of mathematics; John F. Baker, instructor of telegraphy; Diana C. Miles, art teacher; and Gladys Marie Everett, music director. During the spring term of the first year Rev. W. J. Lackey was the dean of theology and business manager. Enrollment for the 1912–13 school year was twenty-two; George Medders was appointed professor of science and English. That year a primary department, under Maud Lackey, opened as an experiment. During the 1914–15 school year W. J. Jackey became the president, and the following year Rev. W. A. Boone, employed by the board of trustees of Cumberland Presbyterian Theology Seminary to teach theology in Cumberland College, took over. In 1914 the Cumberland Presbyterian General Assembly provided ministerial aid funds for Cumberland College.

Financial problems plagued the institution from the beginning. In 1911 the Texas Synod formulated plans to obtain funding through donations, and the trustees of the synod were granted a loan of $6,000. The loan and outside donations did enable the synod to purchase the college, but at the end of the first year, income did not cover expenses. In 1916 Rev. I. V. Stine collected over $8,000 in cash and promissory notes, but the hope of making the school financially viable ended with Stine's death in May 1917. On December 28, 1917, at a meeting of the Texas Synod, the board of trustees of Cumberland College recommended that the school be closed on January 8, 1918, and the property be sold. The campus was sold to the city of Leonard, and the classroom building became Leonard High School. This building and the women's dormitory were subsequently demolished. The site is now the location of the Leonard public schools.

BIBLIOGRAPHY: Ben Burrus et al., *A People Called Cumberland Presbyterians* (Memphis: Frontier, 1972). Thomas H. Campbell, *History of Cumberland Presbyterian Church in Texas* (Nashville: Cumberland Presbyterian Publishing House, 1936). *Fannin County Folks and Facts* (Dallas: Taylor, 1977). Carl L. McFarland

CUMBY, ROBERT H. (1825–?). Robert H. Cumby, Texas legislator and Confederate Army officer, was born on August 24, 1825, in Charlotte County, Virginia. In 1836 he moved with his family to Lafayette County, Mississippi. There he married and resided until 1849, when he moved to Rusk County, Texas. He became a prominent planter and one of the wealthiest men in the county; in 1860 he owned $22,600 in land and $38,000 in personal property, including thirty slaves. He was elected to the Eighth Texas Legislature in 1859 and served as a representative until 1961. At the outbreak of the Civil War[qv] he raised Company B of Col. Elkanah Greer's[qv] Third Texas Cavalry, also known as the South Kansas–Texas Regiment. The regiment was organized at Dallas on July 13, 1861, and after serving under Gen. Benjamin McCulloch[qv] in Arkansas and Missouri was transferred east of the Mississippi River and became part of Ross's Texas Brigade.[qv] When the regiment's one-year enlistment period expired on May 8, 1862, new elections for officers were held, and Cumby was elected colonel. Other outstanding officers in this regiment included M. D. Ector, Walter P. Lane, Hinche P. Mabry, and George W. Chilton.[qqv] Because he was in poor health, however, Cumby could not assume command and deferred to Lane. He resigned from command of the regiment and in 1864 was appointed brigadier general, Fourth Division, Texas State Troops. After the war he moved to Dallas, where he served as a constable. Cumby, Texas, was named for him.

BIBLIOGRAPHY: Samuel Barron, *The Lone Star Defenders: A Chronicle of the Third Texas Cavalry, Ross' Brigade* (New York: Neale, 1908; rpt., Waco: Morrison, 1964). Douglas Hale, "The Third Texas Cavalry: A Socioeconomic Profile of a Confederate Regiment," *Military History of the Southwest* 19 (Spring 1989). Marcus J. Wright, comp., and Harold B. Simpson, ed., *Texas in the War, 1861–1865* (Hillsboro, Texas: Hill Junior College Press, 1965). Thomas W. Cutrer

CUMBY, TEXAS. Cumby, on the Louisiana, Arkansas and Texas track a half mile north of Interstate Highway 30 in western Hopkins County, was settled in 1842 by D. W. (Wash) Cole. It was named Black Jack Grove because of its location near a grove of Black Jack oak trees. The oak grove, just west of the present-day business district, was used as a camp by Texas Rangers[qv] during the days of the Republic of Texas.[qv] Freight wagoners traveling on the Jefferson road to the interior also used the grove as a campground. The Black Jack Grove post office opened in 1848 in the home of the first postmaster, John D. Matthews. Three years later D. W. Cole bought the grove from Elizabeth M. Wren as part of a tract of 307 acres. Cole ran a store, sold town lots, and donated land for a Masonic lodge that was chartered in 1852. In February 1857 the Black Jack post office was renamed Theodocias, and James M. Brown was postmaster. In May 1858 the post office again became Black Jack Grove.

By 1860 Black Jack Grove was a thriving settlement with physicians, tradesmen, and blacksmiths. The town had also earned a reputation as a tough frontier town, where the worst people in the county congregated and violent fights were common. On Christmas Day 1866 a gun battle over a horse race resulted in the death of five men. During the Civil War[qv] men from Black Jack Grove formed Company K of Col. William B. Sims's Ninth Texas Cavalry. Jim P. Williams was elected captain and Mose Brown first lieutenant. At the battle of Elkhorn, Company K was the first to plant its flag in the Union battery.

The East Line and Red River Railroad reached Black Jack Grove in 1880, and the town gradually began to lose its roughness. In 1886 the railroad and post office, in an attempt to change the town's reputation, suggested that the community be renamed. Congressman David B. Culberson[qv] suggested naming the town after his friend Robert H. Cumby,[qv] a Confederate veteran. The Independent Normal College opened in Cumby in 1895 and operated until 1905. In 1911 the town had two banks, two lumberyards, three gins, a cottonseed oil mill, and a tin shop. By 1948 Cumby had twelve stores, six churches, a broom factory, and several other small businesses. The town reached a peak population of 925 in 1929. The number of residents gradually declined to a low of 405 in 1970 before increasing to 647 by 1980. In

1985 Cumby had six small businesses and an estimated population of 690. In 1990 the population was 571.

BIBLIOGRAPHY: Florene Chapman Adams, *Hopkins County and Our Heritage* (Sulphur Springs, Texas: 197–?). Wright Patman, *History of Post Offices—First Congressional District of Texas* (Texarkana, Texas, 1946?). C. G. Orren, The History of Hopkins County (M.A. thesis, East Texas State Teachers College, 1938). *Texas Magazine*, February 1911.

Bob and Michelle Gilbert

CUMINGS, JAMES (?–1825). James Cumings, one of Stephen F. Austin's qv Old Three Hundred qv settlers and one of seven sons of Anthony and Rebekah Cumings, qv received a Mexican land grant of five leagues and one labor in what is now Austin County and a league now in Brazoria County, on August 16, 1824. The tract, bisected by Palmetto (later Mill) Creek, lay seven miles north of San Felipe. The five-league grant, called a hacienda, was given in exchange for the building and operation of a grist and saw mill to serve Austin's first colony. James entered into a contract with his brothers, John and William, to fulfill those obligations. On August 26, 1825, shortly before his death, James willed to William and John the hacienda and its improvements, to be divided equally between them. He left another league of land, near Brazoria, to be divided between his sisters, Rebecca and Sarah. Cumings never married.

BIBLIOGRAPHY: Virginia H. Taylor, *The Spanish Archives of the General Land Office of Texas* (Austin: Lone Star, 1955). Vertical Files, Barker Texas History Center, University of Texas at Austin.

Tim Cumings

CUMINGS, JOHN (?–1839). John Cumings, one of Stephen F. Austin's qv Old Three Hundred qv colonists and one of seven sons of Anthony and Rebekah R. Cumings, qv was a successful businessman in Austin's colony who also served as an emissary from Austin to the Cherokee Indians. He had been a captain of militia in Lewis County, Kentucky, in 1811. He received title to a league of land now in Brazoria County on July 2, 1824. However, he made his residence with other family members on Palmetto (later Mill) Creek seven miles north of San Felipe. John and his brothers James and William Cumings qqv entered into a contract to construct a gristmill and a sawmill on the creek in 1825. The 1826 census lists John as between twenty-five and forty-five years old, unmarried, with three slaves. On at least two occasions Stephen F. Austin dispatched him as an emissary to the Cherokees; one of these was Austin's attempt to dissuade the Indians from taking part in the Fredonian Rebellion qv in Nacogdoches in the winter of 1826–27. James died in 1824 and left the mills and a five-league grant to be divided between William and John. William died in 1828. By 1832 John and his sister, Rebecca, were managing the mills as well as an inn at the San Felipe–Washington crossing on Mill Creek. John continued in these endeavors until his death on April 22, 1839. He never married.

BIBLIOGRAPHY: Vertical Files, Barker Texas History Center, University of Texas at Austin (James Cumings, John Cumings).

Tim Cumings

CUMINGS, REBEKAH RUSSEL (ca. 1757–1832). Rebekah Russel Cumings, one of Stephen F. Austin's qv Old Three Hundred qv colonists, was born in Loudoun County, Virginia, to Samuel and Sarah Moore Russel around 1757. Before 1777 she married Anthony Cumings, a Loudoun County property owner. The couple soon moved to what is today Lewis County, Kentucky, on the Ohio River. They had seven sons and two daughters. Rebekah was widowed by 1797. In 1822, with her three unmarried sons, James, William, and John Cumings, qqv and daughters Rebecca and Sarah, she traveled to Texas and became part of Austin's original colony. She received title to a league and two labores of land now in Brazoria and Waller counties on July 21, 1824. However, she made her home north of San Felipe in the vicinity of the sawmill and gristmill built by her sons on Palmetto (later Mill) Creek, now in Austin County. The 1826 census of Austin's colony lists her as a head of household with two daughters and three slaves. Rebekah Cumings died in 1832. Her daughter Rebecca was engaged to William B. Travis, qv who died in the Alamo; in 1843 she married David Y. Portis. qv

BIBLIOGRAPHY: James A. Creighton, *A Narrative History of Brazoria County* (Angleton, Texas: Brazoria County Historical Commission, 1975). Archie P. McDonald, *Travis* (Austin: Jenkins, 1976). Vertical Files, Barker Texas History Center, University of Texas at Austin (James Cumings, Rebekah Cumings).

Tim Cumings

CUMINGS, WILLIAM (?–1828). William Cumings, one of Stephen F. Austin's qv Old Three Hundred qv colonists and a son of Anthony and Rebekah Cumings, qv received title to a league of land in what is now Brazoria County on July 21, 1824. However, he lived with other family members on Palmetto (later Mill) Creek, north of San Felipe in Austin County. He served in the War of 1812 and was with a force of Kentuckians at the battle of the Thames. In 1822 he accompanied his mother, two sisters, and brothers James and John Cumings qqv to Texas. The three brothers entered into an agreement to construct and operate a gristmill and a sawmill on Palmetto Creek. William journeyed back to Lewis County, Kentucky, where, on December 20, 1825, he married Lucinda Ruggles. The 1826 census lists him as aged twenty-five to forty, with a wife aged eighteen to twenty-five, two slaves, and two servants. The couple settled on Palmetto Creek near the family mills and had one son. Cumings died at his residence on September 2, 1828, and the following year his widow returned with young Samuel to Kentucky.

BIBLIOGRAPHY: Lester G. Bugbee, "The Old Three Hundred: A List of Settlers in Austin's First Colony," *Quarterly of the Texas State Historical Association* 1 (October 1897). Worth Stickley Ray, *Austin Colony Pioneers* (Austin: Jenkins, 1949; 2d ed., Austin: Pemberton, 1970). Texas General Land Office, First Census of Austin's Colony, 1826 (MS, Barker Texas History Center, University of Texas at Austin).

Tim Cumings

CUMMINGS, DAVID P. (1809–1836). David P. Cummings, surveyor and Alamo defender, son of David and Elizabeth (Cathers) Cummings, was born at Lewistown, Pennsylvania, in 1809. He traveled to Texas by sea from New Orleans and arrived in mid-December of 1835. He walked to San Felipe with the intention of joining a ranger unit for action against Indians. Once there he sold his best rifle for thirty dollars, met Sam Houston, qv and presented him with a letter of introduction from his father. Houston advised him to obtain a horse and proceed to Goliad, where he would later meet him. Cummings traveled to Gonzales and then San Antonio, where he joined the garrison in late January or early February 1836. He left San Antonio sometime after February 14 to survey lands titled to him on Cibolo Creek and returned to San Antonio and the Alamo with the relief force from Gonzales. He entered the Alamo with this group on March 1. Cummings died in the battle of the Alamo qv on March 6, 1836.

BIBLIOGRAPHY: Daughters of the American Revolution, *The Alamo Heroes and Their Revolutionary Ancestors* (San Antonio, 1976). Bill Groneman, *Alamo Defenders* (Austin: Eakin, 1990). John H. Jenkins, ed., *The Papers of the Texas Revolution, 1835–1836* (10 vols., Austin: Presidial Press, 1973). Walter Lord, *A Time to Stand* (New York: Harper, 1961; 2d ed., Lincoln: University of Nebraska Press, 1978). Phil Rosenthal and Bill Groneman, *Roll Call at the Alamo* (Fort Collins, Colorado: Old Army, 1985).

Bill Groneman

CUMMINGS, FRANKLIN (1823–1874). Franklin Cummings, attorney, developer, and mayor of Brownsville, was born in Portland,

Maine, on September 18, 1823, the son of Cyrus Cummings, a Methodist minister. He married Ann Mildred Jones in April 1850 and moved with his bride to Brownsville. He was attracted to the area because of its great potential as a deep-sea port. He was a graduate of Wesleyan University, with an LL.B. degree, and an early partner of Stephen Powers,qv who established the first law office in Brownsville. In 1851 he was appointed to succeed Powers as postmaster; he held this office for seven years. He was also a judge and one of the early mayors of the city. He was one of the group of men who financed the building of the First Episcopal Church in Brownsville in 1851. Cummings served as county commissioner of Cameron County, as an officer in the Texas State Troops at Fort Brown during the Civil War,qv and as a member of the Committee of Public Safety after the Cortina raid (*see* CORTINA, JUAN N.). He was one of the men to whom a charter was issued to build the Rio Grande Railroad, a link between Brownsville and Point Isabel (now Port Isabel). He died in Brownsville in 1874 and was survived by six children, including Joseph Franklin Cummings.qv

BIBLIOGRAPHY: Betty Bay, *Historic Brownsville: Original Townsite Guide* (Brownsville, Texas: Brownsville Historical Association, 1980). W. H. Chatfield, *The Twin Cities of the Border and the Country of the Lower Rio Grande* (New Orleans: Brandao, 1893; rpt., Brownsville: Brownsville Historical Association, 1959). James Heaven Thompson, A Nineteenth Century History of Cameron County (M.A. thesis, University of Texas, 1965). *Eleanor Russell Rentfro*

CUMMINGS, JAMES DELL (1895–1981). James Dell (Mr. Jim, Mr. Pipeliner) Cummings, inventor, son of James H. and Lula (Shaw) Cummings, was born on December 28, 1895, in Washington County, Kansas. He and his twin sister, Belle, and other sister, Clara, and brothers John and Willie attended a one-room log school built on land donated by his parents. Jim worked on the family farm north of Morrowville, Kansas, and was a farmer after he finished school. He was adaptable and was always able to envision ways of doing things easier and then to make the equipment necessary for the work. In 1923, while observing men putting a pipeline across his farm, he thought there must be a better way to fill the ditch than using teams of men with shovels and mules. Consequently, he built the first bulldozer and was able single-handedly to backfill one and one-sixth miles of ditch the first day, as compared to a team's average of 500 to 700 feet a day. He soon had a contract to fill the ditch, as well as orders for more bulldozers.

He continued to see the problems of the pipeline and oilfield industry and to invent equipment to solve the problems. By 1976 he held sixty-eight patents for machines to streamline the work and is sometimes given the credit for making it possible for the United States to win World War II.qv Other equipment he designed included a sidewinch to reach over steep embankments to move dirt, a sideboom that would lift 1,000 pounds of pipe, a three-roller pipe cradle to permit a heavy machine to move readily and easily along a line, a coating and wrapping machine to apply hot tar evenly around a pipe and wrap it with insulating material, an automatic pipe-protection processor, a machine for cold-bending pipe, a thermostatically controlled tar kettle to heat and agitate dope en route, a machine to clean and coat insides of pipes, and a mechanism to quickly apply weight material to line pipe in water jobs.

Mr. Jim was made lifetime counselor of the Agricultural and Mechanical College of Texas (later Texas A&M University). In December 1964 he was recognized by national and international pipeline contractors with an honorary lifetime membership in the Pipeline Contractors Association, marking the first time anyone other than a contractor had received the honor. He was married on March 6, 1918, to Ora Belle Frager. They had two sons. In partnership with two others he founded Crutcher-Rolfs-Cummings, Incorporated, in Houston, a firm that manufactured and sold his equipment and later expanded to include engineering. The company also worked on oil pipelines of its own in World War II and put in pipelines all over the world. Cummings received the Presidential E (Excellence) Award from the United States Department of Defense on October 12, 1964.

After leaving Houston the family moved to Victoria, Wimberley, and then to San Marcos in 1943, where Cummings used his creative mind to improve farming and ranching techniques. His Green Valley Farm, a showplace for demonstrating better ways to farm, proved that proper automatic equipment can feed many thousands of cattle as cheaply as one farmer can feed 100. His Green Valley Livestock Commission Company sold the stock in its own auction ring, where buyers sat in comfortable theater seats in an air-conditioned arena that seated 400. Cummings supported the 4-H, the Hays County Youth Association, and the Hays County Civic Center. He and his wife gave generously to Hays Memorial Hospital, where their donations provided modern equipment for the facility and a trust for continuing support of the hospital (the facility has since been closed). Cummings died in San Marcos on May 27, 1981.

BIBLIOGRAPHY: Vertical File, Tula Townsend Wyatt Collection, San Marcos Public Library, San Marcos, Texas. *Mary Compton*

CUMMINGS, JOSEPH FRANKLIN (1851–1912). Joseph Franklin Cummings, teacher, son of Ann Mildred (Jones) and Franklin Cummings,qv was born in Brownsville, Texas, on July 16, 1851. He attended Wesleyan University in Middletown, Connecticut; his uncle, Joseph Cummings, was president of the university. On leaving Wesleyan, he entered West Point, from which he graduated in 1876; he was subsequently assigned to the Third United States Cavalry. He served in the Indian wars of 1876 and 1877 and was promoted to the rank of first lieutenant. After he retired from the army, he was employed in 1888 as a teacher in Galveston. He returned to Brownsville in July 1888 to organize the local public school system. Within two years a new school building was finished, on a site that was part of Washington Park. Because the school was well organized and thoroughly disciplined, Cummings became known as the founder of the Brownsville school system. Later, Cummings Junior High School was named for him. He also organized the first company of the Brownsville Rifles and was made its captain. In 1896 he married Katherine Garriga of Point Isabel (now Port Isabel); she was the sister of Mariano Simon Garriga,qv Bishop of the Catholic Diocese of Corpus Christi.qv The couple had one son. Cummings died in Washington, D.C., in 1912 and was buried in his mother's family burial plot in Maryland.

BIBLIOGRAPHY: W. H. Chatfield, *The Twin Cities of the Border and the Country of the Lower Rio Grande* (New Orleans: Brandao, 1893; rpt., Brownsville: Brownsville Historical Association, 1959).
Pierre Joseph Vivier, Jr.

CUMMINS, JAMES (?–1849). James (Jack) Cummins, farmer and public official, born about 1773, became interested in Texas as early as July 15, 1819, while operating a salt business on the south side of the Caddo River in Arkansas. He was in Texas before June 1822 and settled on the east bank of the Colorado River, opposite the community at Beason's Ferry, site of the present town of Columbus. While he was returning east for his family, an Indian raid on his vacant settlement destroyed his corn crop and left his family without provisions when they arrived on the Colorado. He became alcaldeqv at San Felipe de Austin on August 16, 1823, and served for four years. On July 7, 1824, as one of Stephen F. Austin'sqv Old Three Hundred,qv he was granted six leagues and a labor of land now in Colorado and Austin counties; his land bonus was granted because he was building a saw and grist mill. The census of March 1826 listed him as a farmer and stock raiser aged over fifty. Cummins and his wife, Rebecca, were the parents of six children. His home was a community center on the Colorado River, and he took an active part in all colonial affairs, serving on committees, drafting petitions, and carrying on an extensive correspondence with Stephen F. Austin. He was with the group of settlers who went to Nacogdoches to put down the Fredonian Rebellionqv but was too old to take part in the Texas Revolution.qv He lived on Cummins Creek, now in Colorado County, until his death in 1849.

BIBLIOGRAPHY: Eugene C. Barker, ed., *The Austin Papers* (3 vols., Washington: GPO, 1924–28). Eugene C. Barker, ed., "Minutes of the Ayuntamiento of San Felipe de Austin, 1828–1832," 12 parts, *Southwestern Historical Quarterly* 21–24 (January 1918–October 1920). Lester G. Bugbee, "The Old Three Hundred: A List of Settlers in Austin's First Colony," *Quarterly of the Texas State Historical Association* 1 (October 1897). Colorado County Historical Commission, *Colorado County Chronicles from the Beginning to 1923* (2 vols., Austin: Nortex, 1986).

CUMMINS, MOSES (1785–1841). Moses Cummins, early settler, was born in 1785 in the County of Kentucky, Virginia, now Jefferson County, Kentucky. He married Ruth Ann Griffith on October 23, 1805; she died in 1825. He arrived in Texas from Kentucky in February 1829, and was listed in the 1830 census in Washington County as forty-four years old, a widower with one son, three daughters, and three "dependents," presumably slaves. That census gives his profession as schoolteacher, but it is known that he also worked as a surveyor. He got married again, sometime between 1830 and 1838, to Susanah G. Clampitt,qv who had immigrated to Texas in 1825 or 1826. Cummins probably served in the Texas volunteer army from October 8 to December 22, 1835. He is not listed on the muster rolls of the Army of the Republic of Texas,qv however, and apparently did not receive any of the bounty or donation lands (*see* LAND GRANTS) given to everyone whose military service could be confirmed. In 1838 he was awarded a first-class land certificate confirming his grant as a settler of Stephen F. Austin'sqv colony. On April 17, 1841, Cummins signed his last will. It was probated on May 31, 1841, so he died sometime within that six-week period.

BIBLIOGRAPHY: Daughters of the Republic of Texas, *Founders and Patriots of the Republic of Texas* (Austin, 1963–). Gifford E. White, *1830 Citizens of Texas* (Austin: Eakin, 1983). *Tory Crook*

CUMMINS, ROBERT JAMES (1881–1960). Robert James Cummins, engineer, son of James and Mary (Douglas) Cummins, was born in Mountmellick, Ireland, on March 1, 1881. He attended public schools in County Antrim and preparatory school in Dublin. He received a bachelor of engineering degree in 1899 and a bachelor of arts in 1900 from Queen's College of the Royal University of Ireland, Galway. He immigrated to the United States shortly afterward and worked for ten years as a civil engineer in Detroit, Michigan, both for the city and as a private consultant with Grasset Concrete Steel Company.

In 1910 Cummins formed the consulting firm of Adams and Cummins and moved to Houston, where development of port facilities occupied much of his time for the next fifty years. For twenty-five years he was a member of the Houston Port Commission and for fifteen of those years served as vice chairman. He laid out the harbors and designed the original facilities for the ports of Brownsville and Corpus Christi. He designed other major port facilities in Freeport, Port Arthur, Beaumont, and Orange. At the time of his death, wharves he had designed were under construction at a cost of $200,000 to $500,000 along the Houston Ship Channel.qv In addition to his consulting practice, from 1918 to 1921 Cummins taught a senior class in engineering at Rice Institute (now Rice University). During the 1930s he served as engineering adviser to the Reconstruction Finance Corporation. He acted as adviser for the construction of the San Francisco–Oakland Bay Bridge and on several construction programs of the Metropolitan Water District of Southern California. He received the United States Navy Certificate of Achievement in 1945 for his part in the design of the navy hospital in Houston.

As a pioneer in welded, multistoried construction, Cummins was largely responsible for its popularity along the Gulf Coast. He was structural engineer on numerous major construction projects, notably the San Jacinto Monument (*see* SAN JACINTO MONUMENT AND MUSEUM) and the First City National Bank Building in Houston. He was a member of the American Society of Civil Engineers and president of the Texas section in 1940. Also, he was technical adviser to the International Boundary Commission (*see* INTERNATIONAL BOUNDARY AND WATER COMMISSION), chairman of the board of directors of the Travelers Aid Society, and director of the Houston Chamber of Commerce. On April 4, 1926, Cummins married Sascha Morrison in Houston. He was a member of the Rotary Club and Central Presbyterian Church. He died in Houston on June 11, 1960, survived by his widow, a son, and two daughters.

BIBLIOGRAPHY: Joseph L. Clark, *Texas Gulf Coast: Its History and Development* (4 vols., New York: Lewis Historical Publishing, 1955). Texas Legislature, *Senate Journal*, 1848. Vertical Files, Barker Texas History Center, University of Texas at Austin. *Uel Stephens*

CUMMINS, WILLIAM FLETCHER (1840–1931). William Fletcher Cummins, Methodist minister and geologist, the son of John and Rebecca (Roper) Cummins, was born at Springfield, Missouri, on June 13, 1840. He attended St. Charles College. Though his father, a Methodist minister, objected to his study of geology, Cummins accompanied a geological expedition to Texas in November 1859. In 1860 he was licensed to preach by the East Texas Conference of the Methodist Church and subsequently served as pastor of various churches in Chambers, Liberty, Van Zandt, Lampasas, Llano, Bell, and Ellis counties. He served in Arkansas with the Confederate Army during the Civil War.qv Cummins wrote about being a member of the Ku Klux Klanqv in 1866–67. His job with the Klan was to play on the superstitions of the newly freed blacks. He bought a half interest in the Waxahachie *Argus* in 1868 and served as editor for a short while. He also worked as a right-of-way agent and tried the real estate business. Cummins also worked with the United States Geological Survey in Parker and Archer counties. Copper deposits located in that area were used for making percussion caps for the Confederate Army during the Civil War. As assistant state geologist for North Texas in 1888, he discovered and named the Strawn, Canyon, and Cisco formations. For a number of years he did field work for Edward D. Cope,qv a paleontologist from Philadelphia. Cummins's list of collections was included in the Texas Geological Survey's *Second Annual Report* (1891–94), and an account of his work was published in the *Journal of Geology* (November–December 1908). Efforts to locate artesian water took Cummins to Mexico in 1909. Various oil and railroad companies employed him as geologist. Cummins married Mrs. Minnie C. Bullion Darnell in Weatherford, Texas, on March 17, 1871. They had three children. He spent his last years at his home in El Paso, where he died on January 8, 1931. He was buried at Evergreen Cemetery in El Paso.

BIBLIOGRAPHY: William Fletcher Cummins Papers, Barker Texas History Center, University of Texas at Austin. El Paso *Herald*, January 9, 1931. El Paso *Post*, January 9, 1931. *Memorial and Biographical History of Dallas County* (Chicago: Lewis, 1892; rpt., Dallas: Walsworth, 1976). Henry Fairfield Osborn, *Cope, Master Naturalist: The Life and Letters of Edward Drinker Cope* (Princeton: Princeton University Press, 1931). Macum Phelan, *History of Early Methodism in Texas, 1817–1866* (Nashville: Cokesbury, 1924); *A History of the Expansion of Methodism in Texas, 1867–1902* (Dallas: Mathis, Van Nort, 1937).

CUMMINS CREEK (Ellis County). Cummins Creek rises near the city limit of Ennis in southeastern Ellis County (at 32°19′ N, 96°38′ W) and runs southeast for 18½ miles to its mouth on Chambers Creek, three miles north of Corsicana in northeastern Navarro County (at 32°10′ N, 96°28′ W). The creek traverses flat to rolling terrain surfaced by shallow to deep sandy and clayey loams that support scrub brush, cacti, and some hardwoods. For most of the history of the county, the Cummins Creek area has been used as range and crop land.

____ (Lee County). Cummins Creek rises near Giddings in Lee

County (at 30°11′ N, 96°55′ W) and runs southeast through Lee, Fayette, and Colorado counties for sixty-five miles to its mouth on a horseshoe bend of the Colorado River, opposite Columbus (at 29°43′ N, 96°31′ W). The stream is named for James Cummins,qv one of Stephen F. Austin's qv Old Three Hundred,qv who was granted the land at its mouth in 1824. Cummins built a sawmill and gristmill there in 1826. The stream, known to the Spanish as San Benave, was also called Mill Creek before acquiring the name of the pioneer. Cummins Creek is a major tributary of the Colorado River and was for many years subject to extensive flooding. Throughout its course and along its tributaries a large number of flood-control impoundments built through programs of the United States Department of Agriculture provide both flood protection and opportunities for recreation. Soils along the stream vary in composition but are generally erosible. Before 1960 the Cummins Creek watershed produced large quantities of cotton and corn. Most of this land has reverted to pasture for cattle and horses. The densely wooded banks, especially along the lower reaches of the creek, provide good stands of native pecans and excellent wildlife habitat.

CUNDIFF, TEXAS. Cundiff is on Farm Road 1810 ten miles northeast of Jacksboro in northeastern Jack County. Settlement of the area began in the mid-1850s. Harrell Cundiff was one of the first settlers. The threat of Indian raids forced many settlers to abandon their homesteads in the 1860s. Following the removal of Indians from Jack County in the mid-1870s, settlers began returning to the Cundiff area. Not until the early 1890s, however, was a permanent community established. In 1891 Walker Moore subdivided a tract of land into small farms and laid out a townsite, which he named Cundiff. The town had a post office from 1891 to 1918. By the early 1900s it also had a cotton gin, a blacksmith shop, four stores, and a school. From 1940 to 1988 the town's population remained at approximately fifty residents. In 1990 it was forty-five.

BIBLIOGRAPHY: Thomas F. Horton, *History of Jack County* (Jacksboro, Texas: Gazette Print, 193-?). Ida Lasater Huckabay, *Ninety-Four Years in Jack County* (Austin: Steck, 1949; centennial ed., Waco: Texian Press, 1974).

David Minor

CUNEY, NORRIS WRIGHT (1846–1898). Norris Wright Cuney, politician, the fourth of eight children born to a white planter, Philip Minor Cuney, and a slave mother, Adeline Stuart, was born on May 12, 1846, near Hempstead, Texas. He attended George B. Vashon's Wylie Street School for blacks in Pittsburgh, Pennsylvania, from 1859 to the beginning of the Civil War.qv Afterward he wandered on riverboats and worked at odd jobs before he returned to Texas and settled in Galveston. There he met George T. Ruby,qv president of the Union League.qv Cuney studied law and by July 18, 1871, was appointed president of the Galveston Union League. He married Adelina Dowdie on July 5, 1871, and to their union were born a son and a daughter, Maud Cuney-Hare.qv

Cuney was a supporter of Edmund J. Davis,qv and his career in the 1870s and 1880s was a mixture of success and failure. In 1873 he was appointed secretary of the Republican State Executive Committee. He was defeated in the race for mayor of Galveston in 1875 and for the state House and Senate in 1876 and 1882 respectively. But in appointed offices and as a dispenser of patronage, Cuney was powerful. From his appointment as the first assistant to the sergeant-at-arms of the Twelfth Legislature in 1870, he went on to serve as a delegate to every national Republican convention from 1872 to 1892. In 1873 he presided at the state convention of black leaders at Brenham (see BLACK STATE CONVENTIONS). He became inspector of customs of the port of Galveston and revenue inspector at Sabine Pass in 1872, special inspector of customs at Galveston in 1882, and finally collector of customs of the port of Galveston in 1889.

In 1883 Cuney was elected alderman on the Galveston City Council from the Twelfth District, a post that left him time to work simultaneously as a leader of the Republican partyqv and a contracting stevedore. In 1886 he became Texas national committeeman of the Republican party, the most important political position given to a black man of the South in the nineteenth century. One historian of the Republican party in Texas characterizes the period between 1884 and 1896 as the "Cuney Era."

In order to lead Texas blacks to increased prosperity, in 1883 Cuney bought $2,500 worth of tools and called together a group of black dockworkers, which he eventually organized into the Screwmen's Benevolent Association.qv He carried this fledgling organization into open competition. He was also strongly committed to education. He was appointed a school director of Galveston County in 1871 and supported the black state college at Prairie View (now Prairie View A&M University).

Cuney was first grand master of the Prince Hall Masons in Texas from 1875 to 1877. He also belonged to the Knights of Pythias and the Odd Fellows. He died on March 3, 1898, in San Antonio and was buried in Lake View Cemetery, Galveston.

BIBLIOGRAPHY: Maud Cuney Hare, *Norris Wright Cuney: A Tribune of the Black People* (New York: Crisis, 1913). Virginia Neal Hinze, Norris Wright Cuney (M.A. thesis, Rice University, 1965).

Merline Pitre

CUNEY, PHILIP MINOR (1808–1866). Philip Minor Cuney, soldier, plantation owner, and legislator, the son of Richard Edmond and Tabitha (Wells) Cuney, was born of Swiss descent in Rapides Parish, Louisiana, in 1808. After the death of his first wife in 1834, he moved to Texas around 1840 and settled in Austin County, where he took up farming. In 1842 he married Eliza Ware; they had three children. Cuney, a Whig, was elected to the House of Representatives of the Republic of Texasqv in 1843. He became a prosperous cotton planter and, with Oliver Jones,qv was Austin County delegate to the Convention of 1845,qv which voted for annexationqv to the United States. On July 13, 1846, Cuney was elected brigadier general of the First Brigade of the Fourth Division of the Texas Militia. Also in 1846 he was elected to the state Senate and represented Austin and Fort Bend counties in the First and Second legislatures until 1848. On February 22, 1848, he was elected a state delegate to the national Democratic convention in Baltimore. In 1851 he was a candidate for the state Senate. On his plantation, Sunnyside, twelve miles southeast of Hempstead on Iron Creek, Cuney had 2,000 acres and 105 slaves by 1850. Among them was Adeline Stuart, who bore him eight children and whom he eventually set free. Among their sons was Norris Wright Cuney,qv who became a prominent politician in Galveston. On September 26, 1851, Cuney married Adeline Spurlock, daughter of James L. and Eliza Spurlock, also of Austin County. Cuney died at his Austin County home on January 8, 1866. He was a member of the Texas Veterans Association.qv

BIBLIOGRAPHY: Austin *Southern Intelligencer*, January 25, 1866. Clarksville *Northern Standard*, December 16, 1843, March 18, 1848. Maud Cuney Hare, *Norris Wright Cuney: A Tribune of the Black People* (New York: Crisis, 1913). Virginia Neal Hinze, Norris Wright Cuney (M.A. thesis, Rice University, 1965). *Members of the Legislature of the State of Texas from 1846 to 1939* (Austin: Texas Legislature, 1939). *Telegraph and Texas Register*, June 11, 1845. Texas House of Representatives, *Biographical Directory of the Texan Conventions and Congresses, 1832–1845* (Austin: Book Exchange, 1941). *Texas State Gazette*, June 21, 1851.

Thomas W. Cutrer

CUNEY, TEXAS. Cuney is at the junction of U.S. Highway 175 and Farm Road 855, twenty-two miles northwest of Rusk in northwestern Cherokee County. The site was first settled by freed slaves just after the Civil Warqv and was known for a time as Andy, after Andrew Bragg, a former slave and the first black landowner in the area. A community, however, did not grow up until around 1902, when the settlement became a flag stop on the newly built Texas and New Orleans Railroad. Around 1914 H. L. Price, the cashier at the Farmers and Citizens Savings Bank in Palestine, and several other local investors formed a development company and platted a townsite. They named the town Cuney in honor of Price's son, Cuney Price, who in turn had been named for Norris Wright Cuney,[qv] a prominent black politician and head of the Republican party[qv] in Texas. A Cuney post office was authorized in 1917, and by the early 1920s the town had two general stores, a blacksmith shop, several cotton gins, an eleven-grade school, a drugstore, and a hotel. In 1929, when U.S. Highway 175 was paved, most of the town's businesses moved to the highway, a mile north of the railroad. The town's population reached 100 in 1929 but declined during the early 1930s; in 1936 only twenty-five residents and six businesses were reported. Afterward the population grew steadily, from seventy-five in 1952 to 170 in 1990. When Cuney was incorporated in November 1983 it became the first incorporated black community in Cherokee County. A number of businesses closed after World War II,[qv] but in the late 1980s the town still sustained a post office, two grocery stores, an arts and crafts shop, a beauty shop, a garage, and a sawmill.

BIBLIOGRAPHY: *Cherokee County History* (Jacksonville, Texas: Cherokee County Historical Commission, 1986). Hattie Joplin Roach, *A History of Cherokee County* (Dallas: Southwest, 1934). Marker Files, Texas Historical Commission, Austin.   *Christopher Long*

CUNEY-HARE, MAUD (1874–1936). Maud Cuney-Hare, black musician and writer, was born in Galveston on February 16, 1874, to Adelina (Dowdy) and Norris Wright Cuney.[qv] After graduating from Central High School in Galveston in 1890, she studied piano at the New England Conservatory of Music, where she successfully resisted the pressure that white students exerted on the school's administrators to have her barred from living in the dormitory. She also studied privately with biographer Emil Ludwig and Edwin Klare. She taught music at the Texas Deaf, Dumb, and Blind Institute for Colored Youths in 1897 and 1898; at the settlement program of the Institutional Church of Chicago during 1900 and 1901; and at Prairie View State College (now Prairie View A&M University), Texas, in 1903 and 1904.

As a folklorist and music historian she was especially interested in African and early American music. She collected songs in Mexico, the Virgin Islands, Puerto Rico, and Cuba, and was the first music scholar to direct public attention to Creole music. She contributed to *Musical Quarterly, Musical Observer, Musical America,* and *Christian Science Monitor* and for years edited a column on music and the arts for *The Crisis,* the journal of the National Association for the Advancement of Colored People.[qv]

After marrying William P. Hare in 1906, she made her home in Boston and traveled in the East to give recitals and lectures. She participated in the artistic life of Boston and founded the Musical Art Studio to promote concerts and a little theater movement in the black community. *Antar,* her play about an Arabian Negro poet, was staged in Boston under her direction in 1926. She was the author of *Creole Songs* (1921); *The Message of the Trees* (1918), a collection of poetry; and *Norris Wright Cuney: A Tribune of the Black People* (1913), a biography of her father. She is best remembered for the highly regarded *Negro Musicians and Their Music* (1936). She died in Boston on February 13, 1936, and was buried beside her parents in Lake View Cemetery, Galveston.

BIBLIOGRAPHY: Rayford W. Logan and Michael R. Winston, eds., *Dictionary of American Negro Biography* (New York: Norton, 1982).   *Judith N. McArthur*

CUNNINGHAM, ABEL SEYMOUR (1810–1860). Abel Seymour Cunningham, a Republic of Texas[qv] congressman and participant in the Texas Revolution and the Mexican War,[qv][qv] was born on December 8, 1810, in Hardy County, Virginia. He moved to Texas in 1835 and settled in Victoria County. During the Texas Revolution he volunteered as a private in the army and served from April 1 to July 12, 1836,

Norris Wright Cuney. From Maud Cuney-Hare, Norris Wright Cuney, A Tribune of the Black People *(New York: Crisis Pub. Co., 1913), frontispiece. Prints and Photographs Collection, Norris Wright Cuney file, CAH; CN 01074.*

in a Captain Smith's company of cavalry. In the spring of 1842 he served in Capt. John T. Price's[qv] company under Col. Clark L. Owen[qv] in the expedition to crush the invasion of Texas by Rafael Vásquez.[qv] Cunningham represented Victoria County in the House of the Ninth Congress of the republic from December 2, 1844, to June 28, 1845, and was a member of the annexation[qv] convention that summer. He joined Col. Benjamin McCulloch's[qv] rangers in 1846, after the outbreak of the Mexican War. In the 1840s he was a Victoria alderman and joined the Victoria bar. He was kept on retainer by the board to represent the city in land cases before the Texas Supreme Court. Cunningham was married to Martha McGrew. He died on March 28, 1860, in Victoria.

BIBLIOGRAPHY: Roy Grimes, ed., *300 Years in Victoria County* (Victoria, Texas: Victoria *Advocate,* 1968; rpt., Austin: Nortex, 1985). Victor Marion Rose, *History of Victoria* (Laredo, 1883; rpt., Victoria, Texas: Book Mart, 1961). Texas House of Representatives, *Biographical Directory of the Texan Conventions and Congresses, 1832–1845* (Austin: Book Exchange, 1941).   *Craig H. Roell*

CUNNINGHAM, ALBERT BENJAMIN (1888–1962). Albert Benjamin Cunningham, teacher and mystery novelist, son of Nathan Decatur and Sarah Ann (Shafer) Cunningham, was born at Linden, West Virginia, on June 22, 1888. His father was an itinerant Baptist minister, and the family moved frequently. During his boyhood, Cunningham roamed the West Virginia hillsides and became an interested observer of flowers, trees, herbs, and other plant life of the region. His observations were later reflected in such works as *Old Black Bass* (1922).

In June 1905 Cunningham enlisted in the regular army. After serving only two months and three days he was discharged because of a strained heart resulting from dragging a cannon. He enrolled at

Muskingum College in New Concord, Ohio, and in 1913 received a bachelor of arts degree. He married Jean Gregory on June 18, 1912. Cunningham received a B.D. degree from Drew University at Madison, New Jersey, in June 1915. He served in pastorates and worked at various other jobs to support himself but decided on a teaching career. He attended New York University and received his M.A. degree in 1916, followed by a Litt.D. from Lebanon (Ohio) University in 1917. In New York he wrote *The Manse at Barren Rocks* (1917). His academic career was interrupted during World War I,qv when he volunteered to serve as a chaplain, but he was discharged because he contracted influenza and pneumonia during the epidemic that swept the country. After the war ended, he returned to New York University, where in 1929 he received a Ph.D. in sociology and psychology. He taught English for the rest of his career. He was dean of Lebanon University in 1916–17 and dean of the College of Puget Sound from 1919 to 1922. He taught in the English department at Washington State College from 1922 to 1925, was professor of English at State Teachers College, Shippensburg, Pennsylvania, from 1926 to 1929. In 1929 he accepted a position at Texas Tech University in Lubbock, Texas, where he taught English for twenty years. He retired in 1945 as professor emeritus and subsequently devoted full time to his freelance work.

Cunningham wrote forty-two books on a variety of themes. His twenty volumes of detective fiction, comprising the ABC Mystery series published by E. P. Dutton and Company, were his best known. Only one of his mysteries, *Death of a Bullionaire* (1947), is set in West Texas, where he spent the last years of his life; the others are set in his native West Virginia. One of his favorite protagonists was a homespun and shrewd Kentucky sheriff, Jess Roden. Cunningham's most popular mystery, *Death Rides a Sorrel Horse* (1946), was translated into German, Italian, Spanish, and French for printings in Mexico, South America, Canada, and Europe. Several of his mysteries were serialized, and many were included in detective-fiction digests. Because his publisher thought his more serious novels dealing with social problems appealed to a different audience from that of the detective fiction, Cunningham assumed the pseudonym Garth Hale for those works. *The Victory of Paul Kent* (1948) was perhaps his best-known in this category. He used the pen name Estil Dale to test the appeal of one novel, *The Last Survivor* (1952).

Cunningham was a member of Tau Kappa Alpha and Pi Kappa Delta. He was a Mason, Odd Fellow, and Knight of Pythias, as well as a Methodist and Republican. He died on September 24, 1962, and was survived by his wife, Jean. They had no children. Cunningham was buried at Resthaven Cemetery in Lubbock.

BIBLIOGRAPHY: Dallas *Times Herald*, November 9, 1947. Lubbock *Avalanche-Journal*, September 25, 1962.
Jeanne F. Lively

CUNNINGHAM, EUGENE (1896–1957). Eugene Cunningham [Leigh Carder], novelist, was born in Helena, Arkansas, on November 29, 1896, the son of Ira Eugene and Istalena Adkins (Stradley) Cunningham. The family apparently moved from Arkansas to St. Augustine, Florida, and then to Texas in 1898. Cunningham attended public schools in Dallas and Fort Worth from 1903 to 1911. From 1914 to 1919 he served in the navy in the Asiatic, Pacific, and Atlantic fleets; in the Mexican campaign; and in the Cruiser Escort Squadron in the war zone (1917). After World War Iqv he was a soldier of fortune in Central America. He served in the naval reserve until 1923, and during World War IIqv he reenlisted and worked in naval intelligence. Cunningham began writing for military publications in 1914 and after his discharge in 1919 spent two years as the Central American correspondent for the London *Wide World Magazine*.

After several years in San Francisco in the early 1920s, he moved to El Paso, where he held several jobs while establishing himself as a writer. He served as book-review editor for the El Paso *Times* from the mid-1920s to 1936 and for the *New Mexico Magazine* from 1936 to 1942. In 1922 Cunningham published *Gypsying through Central America* and in 1924 *The Trail to Apacaz*, his first western novel. During the 1930s he hit his stride as an author. He came to rank among the best Western writers who aimed at a middle ground between sophisticated stories and pulp novels. His tales involved an "intricately plotted contest between good and evil" and displayed a sure understanding of the psychology of gunmen. Among the best known of his violent books were *Riders of the Night* (1932), which involved the deaths of some seventy men, and *Buckaroo* (1933), in which three Texas Rangers qv kill about 300 villains. His other works of fiction included *Diamond River Man* (1934), *Texas Sheriff* (1934), *Trail of the Macaw: Soldiers of Fortune in Banana Land* (1935), *Redshirts of Destiny* (1935), *Quick Triggers* (1935), *Pistol Passport* (1936), *Whistling Lead* (1936), *The Ranger Way* (1937), *Texas Triggers* (1938), *Gun Bulldoggers* (1939), *The Red Ranger* (1939), *The Spiderweb Trail* (1940), *The Buscadero Trail* (1951), *Gunsight Chance* (1951), and *Riding Gun* (1956). Under the pen name Leigh Carder he wrote *Outlaw Justice* (1935), *Border Guns* (1935), and *The Bravo Trail* (1938).

His most successful book was probably *Triggernometry* (1934), a nonfiction study of famous gunfighters, which went through several editions and was reissued in 1941 as *Gunfighters All*. In 1986 *Triggernometry* was named one of the thirty-six best nonfiction Western books of all time by the Western Writers of America. Cunningham's other writings included screenplays for television and numerous short stories. The television program "Wagon Train" adopted a number of his plots. He edited the nonfiction *Buckboard Days*, by Sophie A. Poe (1936), and with W. H. Hutchinson prepared the works of Eugene Manlove Rhodes for publication after Rhodes's death. He also edited Thomas Cruse's *Apache Days and After* (1941). From time to time Cunningham also worked as a political speechwriter.

He married Mary Caroline Emilstein in 1921. The family moved from El Paso to the San Francisco area in 1942. Cunningham served as vice president of the American Fiction Guild and was an avid collector of cowboy songs, both in English and in Spanish. He died in San Francisco on October 18, 1957. He was survived by his wife, one son, and two daughters.

BIBLIOGRAPHY: Florence Elberta Barns, *Texas Writers of Today* (Dallas: Tardy, 1935). Eugene Cunningham Collection, Huntington Library, San Marino, California. Carol Ann Price, "Eugene Cunningham and the El Paso Southwest," *Password*, Summer 1983. Jon Tuska and Vicki Piekarski, eds., *Encyclopedia of Frontier and Western Fiction* (New York: McGraw-Hill, 1983). *Twentieth-Century Western Writers* (Detroit: Gale Research, 1982; 2d ed., Chicago: St. James Press, 1991).
Martin Donell Kohout

CUNNINGHAM, JAMES (1816–1894). James Cunningham, soldier, was born in Warren County, Tennessee, in 1816. In 1835 he married Susannah Tate. He served in the Alabama Mounted Militia in the Florida Indian Wars from October 23, 1837, until his discharge in 1838 at Fort Payne, Alabama. In 1839–40 he immigrated to the Republic of Texasqv with his wife and two small children and obtained a land grant in what is now Morris County. During the 1840s he moved to Bastrop, Travis, and Williamson counties. The Cunninghams moved in 1855 to a wilderness then known as the Upper Leon River Country and settled on Mountain Creek in what is now Comanche County. They were among the first families in that part of Texas, the entering wedge of Anglo-American occupation of the Plains. After coming to Texas, James and Susannah had ten more children. Five of their sons and a son-in-law served as Texas sheriffs.

Cunningham organized a volunteer company in June 1858 to protect the Comanche County area and reported to Governor Hardin Runnelsqv that the company was in service and that he was elected to its command. Until the cessation of Comanche depredations, he and his sons were involved in virtually every Indian battle in or from Comanche County. In 1861 Cunningham was elected captain of a Comanche County company of minutemen. In February he and his men appeared at Camp Coloradoqv in response to Confederate general Henry McCulloch'squv appeal for state troops to wrest that post from the United States Cavalry. Despite the general evacuation of the Northwest Texas frontier during the Civil War,^{qv} the Cunninghams remained, and James served as captain of the Comanche County Company of the Second Frontier District, commanded by Maj. George B. Erath.^{qv} Five of his sons also served as both officers and enlisted men. The Cunninghams participated in Indian fights at Rush Creek, Buffalo Gap, Tater Hill, Blanket Creek, Salt Mountain, Brown Creek, Cow House Creek, and Hog Creek. Captain Cunningham commanded the Comanche County Company in the ill-advised and botched fight with the Kickapoo Indians at the battle of Dove Creek^{qv} in Tom Green County on January 8, 1865.

Cunningham operated a ranch of 9,000 acres in Comanche County until his death at his home in 1894, when he was survived by his wife and all of his twelve children. He is buried at Newburg Cemetery, Comanche County; his grave is designated with a Texas historical marker. His home, a Texas historic landmark, is the oldest residence in Comanche County. The reunion of his and Susannah's descendants, the oldest continuous family reunion in Texas, celebrated its centennial in 1989, in recognition of which the Texas Historical Commission^{qv} placed a marker on the Cunningham family reunion grounds in Newburg.

BIBLIOGRAPHY: Comanche County Bicentennial Committee, *Patchwork of Memories: Historical Sketches of Comanche County, Texas* (Brownwood, Texas: Banner Printing, 1976). Jean Connor, *A Short History of Morris County* (Daingerfield, Texas: Daingerfield Bicentennial Commission, 1975). Fort Worth *Record*, August 25, 1907. F. Lee Lawrence, "The Cunningham Legacy: To Grandma and Grandpa with Love," in *Cunningham Family Centennial Reunion* (Tyler, Texas, 1989). Billy Bob Lightfoot, The History of Comanche County, Texas, to 1920 (M.A. thesis, University of Texas, 1949). William Wilson Straley, comp., *Pioneer Sketches: Nebraska and Texas* (Hico, Texas: Hico Printing Company, 1915). Eulalia Nabers Wells, *Blazing the Way: Tales of Comanche County Pioneers* (Blanket, Texas, 1942).

F. Lee Lawrence

CUNNINGHAM, LEANDER CALVIN (1810–1896). Leander Calvin Cunningham, soldier, attorney, and prohibitionist, was born in East Tennessee on July 10, 1810, the son of James and Margaret (Cunningham) Cunningham. At the age of five he moved with his family to Alabama; he studied law and was admitted to the bar at Hanceville, Alabama, in 1832. He moved to Texas with two of his older brothers, Andrew and David, in April 1833, and became the first lawyer in the frontier community of Mina, now Bastrop. In May 1835 Cunningham was delegated by the ayuntamiento^{qv} of Mina to deliver to the ayuntamiento of Nacogdoches information regarding Indian raids on the western frontier and to attempt to formulate a mutual-defense agreement. On September 7, 1835, he served as secretary to a meeting held at Mina to discuss the crisis precipitated by the arrival of Gen. Martín Perfecto de Cos^{qv} in Texas with an army of occupation. On December 10, 1835, Cunningham was appointed by the General Council,^{qv} as representative of the Mina District, to assist James W. Fannin, Jr.,^{qv} in recruiting volunteers and collecting supplies for the Texan army then besieging Bexar (*see* BEXAR, SIEGE OF).

Cunningham and a few of his neighbors from Mina are said to have marched to San Antonio in an attempt to relieve Col. William B. Travis's^{qv} besieged forces at the Alamo, where they found that they could not penetrate the Mexican lines. Thereupon he enlisted as a private in Capt. Jesse Billingsley's^{qv} Company C of Col. Edward Burleson's^{qv} First Regiment, Texas Volunteers, and fought at the battle of San Jacinto.^{qv} It is said that he attended Sam Houston^{qv} when the general was wounded on the field. On July 1, 1836, a J. Cunningham volunteered for three months' service in Capt. L. P. Cook's company of Col. Edwin Morehouse's^{qv} First Regiment of the First Brigade of the Texas Volunteer Army.

In 1838 Cunningham married a widow, Ann Sloan Slaughter, of Frankfort, Kentucky. The couple had six children. Cunningham served in the House of Representatives of the Second Congress of the Republic of Texas and as chief justice of Bastrop County for three consecutive two-year terms; he resigned in 1840. On December 31, 1844, he was elected notary public of Bastrop. He was also instrumental in the establishment in 1840 of Bastrop Academy,^{qv} a forerunner of Texas A&M University. About 1845 Cunningham ceased the practice of law and entered the mercantile business. By 1850 his property, including a number of slaves, was assessed at $40,000.

On October 9, 1852, he was named to the board of commissioners of the Colorado Navigation Company, of which Thomas J. Hardeman,^{qv} also of Bastrop, was president, and on May 28, 1853, Cunningham chaired a meeting in Bastrop in support of internal improvements; those present at the meeting urged the state to give direct financial support to the construction of railroads. Cunningham also chaired the 1853 meeting of the Bastrop County Democrats that endorsed the candidacy of Elisha M. Pease^{qv} for governor and William R. Scurry^{qv} for Congress.

In September 1853 Cunningham was selected to represent Bastrop County at the Texas Temperance Convention at Austin. Bastrop, the first community in the state to "banish the liquor traffic," had voted itself dry on September 10. Cunningham was appointed one of the ten "permanent officers" of the convention and was also appointed to a committee of nine to draft the convention's resolutions. On December 27 he was one of seven signers of a proclamation, published in the *Texas State Gazette* (*see* AUSTIN STATE GAZETTE) attacking "those stupendous curses of the land—Dram Shops."

In 1859, after twenty-six years in Bastrop, Cunningham moved to Alleyton when the railroad pushed west to that community. There he erected a large warehouse and operated a commission business until 1872, then moved to Columbus upon the completion of the Columbus Tap Railway. In 1869 he moved to Austin, where he spent three years in the lumber trade. In January 1874, once again following the railhead, he moved to Waelder to become the railroad's agent. After a few months he resigned his agency to open a lumberyard, which he operated until 1892. Later he opened a furniture business, and a contemporary account noted that he kept "an excellent assortment of furniture of all kinds, besides paints and oils, and also deal[t] in coffins." After the death of his wife in June 1895 Cunningham moved to Seguin to live with a daughter. He died there on December 24, 1896, and was buried at Waelder. Cunningham was a member of the Texas Veterans Association,^{qv} a devout Methodist, and "a pronounced Prohibitionist."

BIBLIOGRAPHY: *Compiled Index to Elected and Appointed Officials of the Republic of Texas, 1835–1846* (Austin: State Archives, Texas State Library, 1981). Daughters of the Republic of Texas, *Muster Rolls of the Texas Revolution* (Austin, 1986). Sam Houston Dixon and Louis Wiltz Kemp, *The Heroes of San Jacinto* (Houston: Anson Jones, 1932). John H. Jenkins, ed., *The Papers of the Texas Revolution, 1835–1836* (10 vols., Austin: Presidial Press, 1973). Frank W. Johnson, *A History of Texas and Texans* (5 vols., ed. E. C. Barker and E. W. Winkler [Chicago and New York: American Historical Society, 1914; rpt. 1916]). *Telegraph and Texas Register*, December 12, 1835. *Texas State Gazette*, October 9, 1852, June 11, July 30, September 24, November 29, December 27, 1853.

Thomas W. Cutrer

CUNNINGHAM, MICHAEL ANGELO (1889–1959). Michael Angelo Cunningham, superintendent of the Jefferson County Tuberculosis Hospital in Beaumont for twenty years, was born in Malvern, Iowa, on August 24, 1889, the son of Michael and Margaret (Aistrope) Cunningham. He attended schools in Malvern and received a medical degree from Creighton Medical College in Omaha, Nebraska, in 1913. After an internship at St. Mary–Corwin Hospital in Pueblo, Colorado, he became assistant superintendent of the Iowa State Sanatorium at Oakdale. Afterwards he became medical director of Holy Cross Sanatorium in Deming, New Mexico. In 1939 he became medical director and superintendent of the Jefferson County Tuberculosis

Hospital in Beaumont, Texas. In 1935 Cunningham joined thirty-eight other physicians to establish the American College of Chest Physicians. Like Cunningham, most of these physicians were busily involved in the treatment of patients with tuberculosis. Cunningham served for fifteen years as a director of the Texas Tuberculosis Association. He was also a member of the National Tuberculosis Association, the American Trudeau Society, the Jefferson County Medical Society, the Texas Medical Association,[qv] the American Medical Association, and the Southwestern Medical Association. He married Harriett M. Miller of Waterloo, Iowa, and they had a son. Cunningham was a Mason. He died in Beaumont on September 20, 1959.

BIBLIOGRAPHY: Beaumont *Enterprise*, September 21, 1959. Beaumont *Journal*, September 21, 1959, *Texas State Journal of Medicine*, December 1959.
Chester R. Burns

CUNNINGHAM, MINNIE FISHER (1882–1964). Minnie Fisher Cunningham, woman suffrage[qv] leader and leading liberal Democrat, the daughter of Horatio White and Sallie Comer (Abercrombie) Fisher, was born on March 19, 1882, on Fisher Farms, near New Waverly, Texas. Her father was a prominent planter who served in the House of Representatives of the Seventh Texas Legislature in 1857–58. He introduced her to politics by taking her to political meetings at Huntsville. After having been educated by her mother, Minnie passed a state examination to earn a teaching certificate when she was sixteen. She taught for a year before enrolling in the University of Texas Medical Branch at Galveston. In 1901 she became one of the first women to receive a degree in pharmacy in Texas; she worked as a pharmacist in Huntsville for a year, but she later said that inequity in pay "made a suffragette out of me." In 1902 she married Beverly Jean (Bill) Cunningham, a lawyer and insurance executive. His successful race for county attorney as a reform candidate was her first taste of the campaign trail, but the marriage was unhappy, in part because of her increasing political activity and his alcoholism.

The Cunninghams moved to Galveston in 1907. By 1910 she was elected president of the Galveston Equal Suffrage Association and toured Texas to speak for the cause. In 1915 she was elected to the first of four annual terms as president of the Texas Woman Suffrage Association (subsequently the Texas Equal Suffrage Association[qv]). The number of local auxiliaries quadrupled during her first year in office, largely because of her leadership. In 1917 she moved to Austin, opened state suffrage headquarters near the Capitol,[qv] and began a campaign

Minnie Fisher Cunningham (right) campaigning for the United States Senate, 1928. Courtesy Austin History Center, Austin Public Library; photo no. PICA 16817.

In 1928 Minnie Cunningham became the first woman in Texas to run for the United States Senate.

that culminated in legislative approval for woman suffrage in state primary elections in 1918.

In 1919 Carrie Chapman Catt, president of the National American Woman Suffrage Association, persuaded Minnie Cunningham to lobby Congress for the Nineteenth Amendment. When the amendment finally was passed and submitted to the states for ratification, Cunningham said she "pursued governors all over the west" and urged them to ratify it. That same year, she helped organize the National League of Women Voters and became its executive secretary. Twenty years later Eleanor Roosevelt recalled that Cunningham's address at the league's second annual convention made her feel "that you had no right to be a slacker as a citizen, you had no right not to take an active part in what was happening to your country as a whole."

Minnie Cunningham was widowed in 1927 and traveled to Texas to settle her husband's estate. The following year she became the first Texas woman to run for the United States Senate. She challenged Earle B. Mayfield,qv the incumbent, with a platform that advocated prohibition,qv tariff reduction, tax reform, farm relief, flood control, cooperation with the League of Nations, and opposition to the Ku Klux Klan.qv She finished fifth of six in the primary, carrying only her home county, Walker. She then campaigned for Thomas T. Connally,qv the runner-up, who edged out Mayfield in the runoff.

From 1930 to 1939 Cunningham worked in College Station as an editor for the Texas A&M Extension Service. She returned to Washington in 1939 to work as an information specialist for the Women's Division of the Agricultural Adjustment Administration.qv President Franklin Delano Roosevelt is credited with having given her the nickname by which she later became widely known, "Minnie Fish." She resigned in 1943 to protest a rule impeding the flow of information to farmers.

In 1944, at the Democratic state convention, anti-Roosevelt forces elected "uninstructed" delegates to the national convention, effectively disenfranchising the voters of Texas. Outraged, Roosevelt supporters elected their own slate of delegates at a rump convention. When a coalition of liberal Democrats failed to draft J. Frank Dobieqv as a candidate for governor, Cunningham ran herself. Angry that the incumbent governor, Coke Stevenson,qv did not take a public stand on the split, she ran an outspoken campaign, calling on Stevenson to declare his views, and prevented his leading the anti-Roosevelt delegation to the national convention. Stevenson won the primary by a landslide. Nevertheless, in a field of nine candidates, Cunningham finished second.

In 1946 she retired to Fisher Farms in New Waverly to raise cattle and pecans, but she continued to campaign for the Democratic partyqv and organized ad hoc committees to support liberal causes. When the board of regents fired the president of the University of Texas, Homer P. Rainey,qv she opposed the regents' decision and supported Rainey's unsuccessful bid for the governorship. In the wake of the Supreme Court ruling in *Brown vs. Board of Education* she supported civil rights on her local school board. In 1952 she stumped for Adlai Stevenson for president and Ralph Yarborough for governor. Prepared to mortgage her farm to ensure the continuation of a liberal voice in Texas journalism, she played a pivotal role in founding the *Texas Observer*qv in 1954. Also in the 1950s she helped start Democrats of Texas, an organization of liberals. In 1960, at the age of seventy-eight, she managed the campaign headquarters for John F. Kennedy in New Waverly. Minnie Cunningham died on December 9, 1964, and was buried in New Waverly.

BIBLIOGRAPHY: Minnie Fisher Cunningham Papers, Houston Metropolitan Research Center, Houston Public Library. John Carroll Eudy, "The Vote and Lone Star Women: Minnie Fisher Cunningham and the Texas Equal Suffrage Association," *East Texas Historical Journal* 14 (Fall 1976). Patricia B. Nieuwenhuizen, Minnie Fisher Cunningham and Jane Y. McCallum: Leaders of Texas Women (Senior thesis, University of Texas at Austin, 1982). *Notable American Women: A Biographical Dictionary* (4 vols., Cambridge, Massachusetts: Harvard University Press, 1971–80). *Texas Observer*, November 21, 1958. Vertical Files, Barker Texas History Center, University of Texas at Austin.   *Patricia Ellen Cunningham*

CUNNINGHAM, ROBERT W. (1804?–1836). Robert W. Cunningham, Alamo defender, the oldest of seven children of David and Anna (Jennison) Cunningham, was born in Ontario County, New York, on October 18, 1804 or 1806. He lived with his family in Indiana, Kentucky, and Arkansas before he came to Texas. In 1832 he worked as a cargo flatboatman on the Mississippi River to New Orleans. From New Orleans he wrote to his family informing them that he would be staying there. By March 4, 1833, however, he had moved to Texas, where he received title to a league of land on Skull Creek in Austin's colony. In 1836 Cunningham wrote to his family to inform them that he had joined the Texas army. He took part in the siege of Bexarqv as a sergeant and second gunner in Capt. T. L. F. Parrott'sqv artillery company. He remained in Bexar after the battle as a private in Capt. W. R. Carey'sqv artillery company. Cunningham was a single man. He died in the battle of the Alamoqv on March 6, 1836.

BIBLIOGRAPHY: Daughters of the American Revolution, *The Alamo Heroes and Their Revolutionary Ancestors* (San Antonio, 1976). Daughters of the Republic of Texas, *Muster Rolls of the Texas Revolution* (Austin, 1986). Bill Groneman, *Alamo Defenders* (Austin: Eakin, 1990). Phil Rosenthal and Bill Groneman, *Roll Call at the Alamo* (Fort Collins, Colorado: Old Army, 1985).   *Bill Groneman*

CUNNINGHAM, TEXAS. Cunningham is on Farm Road 196 near the North Sulphur River, twenty miles southeast of Paris in southeastern Lamar County. The town was named for Sam Cunningham, a landowner who encouraged settlement in the community. Its post office was established in 1912. By 1915 the population had risen to 350, and the town included two churches, a newspaper called the *Inland Journal*, three general stores, a printer, a sawmill, and a physician. The number of residents had decreased to 200 by the 1940s and continued to decline slowly. In the 1980s Cunningham had three churches, a school, a few businesses, and a population of 110, which remained at that level in 1990.   *John M. Santry*

CUNQUEBACO INDIANS. The Cunquebaco Indians were one of twenty Indian groups that joined Juan Domínguez de Mendozaqv on his journey from El Paso to the vicinity of present San Angelo in 1683–84. Since Mendoza did not indicate at what point the Cunquebacos joined his party, it is not possible to determine their range or affiliations. However, the Indians between the Pecos River and the San Angelo area were being hard pressed by Apaches at this time, and it seems likely that the Cunquebacos ranged somewhere between these two localities.

BIBLIOGRAPHY: Herbert Eugene Bolton, ed., *Spanish Exploration in the Southwest, 1542–1706* (New York: Scribner, 1908; rpt., New York: Barnes and Noble, 1959).   *Thomas N. Campbell*

CUPOLA MOUNTAIN. Cupola Mountain is eight miles west of the Rio Grande and a mile north of the Black Gap Wildlife Management Area in eastern Brewster County (at 29°40′ N, 102°51′ W). With an elevation of 3,935 feet above sea level, it rises 1,100 above Big Canyon, two miles to the east. Its shallow, stony soils support oak, juniper, and some mesquite.

CUPPLES, GEORGE (1816–1895). George Cupples, pioneer surgeon and civic leader, son of Robert and Camilla (Campbell) Cupples, was born in Berwick County, Scotland, on October 13, 1816. After two years as assistant surgeon with the British Auxiliary Legion in the Spanish service, he returned to Scotland and graduated in medicine at the University of Edinburgh in August 1838. From 1839 to 1843 he studied at the University of Paris. On the advice of Dr. Ashbel Smith,qv Cupples moved to Texas in 1844 in search of health for his wife, Alexia (Bourland), whom he had married in 1843. He settled in San Antonio as a member of Castro's colony.qv He was surgeon for the Second Regiment under John C. (Jack) Haysqv during the Mexican War.qv As first surgeon of the Seventh Regiment of Texas Mounted Volunteers, he served in the Confederate Army in 1861 and 1862, became medical director of the Eastern Military District of Texas in December 1862 and in June 1864 became medical director and inspector of the cavalry corps in the Trans-Mississippi Department.

Cupples was a notary public in Bexar County in 1847. In 1851 he was elected county commissioner and alderman at San Antonio. He was president of the Bexar County Medical Society in 1853, became city health physician in 1854, and was president of the San Antonio board of health in 1866 and again in 1873. He served as the second president of the Texas Medical Associationqv in 1853 and served as president again in 1878. In 1876 he helped found the West Texas Medical Association. As chairman of the association's section on state medicine and public hygiene in 1886, he headed the committee on legislation and advocated regulation and licensing of physicians. He was a member of the American Medical Association and Texas delegate to its national meetings in 1853, 1881, and 1884. He was also delegate to the International Medical congresses in 1876 and 1887 and in 1893 represented Texas at the Pan-American Medical Congress at Washington. Cupples was noted as an innovative surgeon and is thought to have been the first doctor in Texas to use anesthetics. After the death of his first wife in 1860, he married Mrs. Laura L. Sheaban in 1871. He was an Odd Fellow, a Democrat, and a Presbyterian. He died at his home in San Antonio on April 19, 1895.

BIBLIOGRAPHY: *Biographical Encyclopedia of Texas* (New York: Southern, 1880). Frederick Charles Chabot, *With the Makers of San Antonio* (Yanaguana Society Publications 4, San Antonio, 1937). Pat Ireland Nixon, *The Medical Story of Early Texas, 1528–1853* (Lancaster, Pennsylvania: Lupe Memorial Fund, 1946). William S. Speer and John H. Brown, eds., *Encyclopedia of the New West* (Marshall, Texas: United States Biographical Publishing, 1881; rpt., Easley, South Carolina: Southern Historical Press, 1978).   Robert Read Nixon

CURANDERISMO. *Curanderismo* is the art of folk healing by a *curandero*, the healer par excellence in the folk medicineqv practiced by Texas Hispanics. Healers can be either male or female and may even specialize in their practice. The three most common types of *curanderos* are the *yerbero* (herbalist), the *partera* (midwife), and the *sabador* (masseur). Though the *curandero* has the skill to treat a wide variety of illnesses, he is the only healer in the culture who can treat *mal puesto*, illnesses caused by witchcraft. He is thought to have been given a *don de Dios* (a gift from God) to heal the sick, and he learns his healing art through apprenticeship under another *curandero* or a spiritual manifestation. His chief adversary in the struggle between good and evil is Satan and those who have made secret pacts with him—the *brujos* or *brujas* (witches). Along with the treatment of *mal puesto*, *curanderos* also treat *mal de ojo* (the evil eye) and *susto* (loss of spirit). Typically, the *curandero* works on three levels, the material, the spiritual, and the mental. He may prescribe a herbal remedy or conduct a religious ritual. Quite often, a practitioner is called upon to treat the physical symptoms that patients believe come from supernatural causes.

Brujos—who frequently take the form of *lechuzas* (barn owls), cats, turkeys, or coyotes—may use their evil powers to cause many different problems, from prolonged serious illnesses (physical and mental) or death to bad luck in business and love. They can cause one person to fall uncontrollably in love with another. Any long-lasting, serious illness that does not respond to a medical doctor's treatments may be attributed to *brujería*. *Brujos* use rituals, incantations, and potions and powders, which, when near the victim, bring on the desired illness. The agent is sometimes put into the victim's drink or food, or it may be a powder spread across his path or placed in his house or yard. *Brujos* may also use a victim's photograph, hair, fingernail clippings, or other item to cast a spell. *Brujería* is particularly feared because it can penetrate even the sanctity of one's home. Though certain amulets and rituals are helpful in protecting one from *brujería*, the only sure protection is to live a sinless life—a claim few will make. Once a victim of the *brujo*'s spell, a person has only one source of help—the *curandero*. (Although the local Catholic priest should theoretically be able to help, the *curandero* is in practice the one usually consulted). When one suspects he is the victim of *brujería*, he will seek out a *curandero* even if he has to travel hundreds of miles. The ratio of *curanderos* to population is very small, and residents of rural Texas often have to travel to population centers. In the diagnosis phase of treatment, the healer uses divination (by, for instance, looking into a glass of clear water), pulsing (holding the patient's wrist to feel the pulse, which reveals more to the *curandero* than just the rate of heartbeat), or clairvoyance (including seances). If the healer diagnoses the problem as *brujería*, he must then identify the kind of witchcraft used and often the one who wanted the hex put on the victim, as well as the *brujo* who perpetrated the evil. If one delays treatment, however, the *curandero* may not be able to counter the hex.

The *curandero*'s treatment may consist of rituals, herbal remedies, potions, or countermagic, depending on what the illness is. Pedrito Jaramillo,qv the most famous *curandero* in Texas, used *recetas* (prescriptions) that involved drinking water at certain intervals or some equally simple treatment. He claimed that he could not cure anyone, but that patients could be cured by their faith in God. His patients included many Anglos. Sometimes the treatment may consist of contacting the *brujo* through supernatural means or directly and demanding that the hex be removed. If the *brujo* refuses, the *curandero* may hex the hexer. Part of the cure may consist of identifying and locating the hexing agent (e.g., a small bag of cursed items hidden in the victim's home or yard) and removing it. If dolls were used, they must be found and destroyed. The treatment may also involve the removal of objects magically injected into the victim's body (e.g., a lizard or worm). Love hexes using the victim's photograph may be counteracted with rituals involving countermagic, including rolling the victim's picture face-to-face with a picture of Christ, placing it on a small altar, and using prayers and religious rituals. The *curandero*'s rituals consistently use such Catholic symbols as crucifixes, rosaries, and holy pictures.

BIBLIOGRAPHY: Joe S. Graham, "The Role of the *Curandero* in the Folk Medicine System of West Texas," in *American Folk Medicine*, ed. Wayland D. Hand (Berkeley: University of California Press, 1976). Wilson M. Hudson, ed., *The Healer of Los Olmos and Other Mexican Lore* (Dallas: Southern Methodist University Press, 1951). Ari Kiev, *Curanderismo: Mexican-American Folk Psychiatry* (New York: Free Press, 1968). Eliseo Torres, *The Folk Healer: The Mexican-American Tradition of Curanderismo* (Kingsville, Texas: Nieves Press, 1983).
                                                                                                    Joe S. Graham

CURETON, CALVIN MAPLES (1874–1940). Calvin Maples Cureton, chief justice of the Texas Supreme Court, the son of William E. and Mary Jane (Odle) Cureton and grandson of Capt. J. J. (Jack) Cureton,qv was born on September 1, 1874, near Walnut Springs, Bosque County, Texas. In 1889, after four years at Central College in Walnut Springs, Cureton began moving his father's cattle from Bosque County to the Trans-Pecos region. In 1892–93 he attended the University of Virginia, where he absorbed much Jeffersonian political and social philosophy. The depression that followed the panic of 1893 interrupted his education, but he soon found new interests in the Texas political campaigns of the middle 1890s and served as state secretary on the executive committee of the People's partyqv during the campaign of 1896. During this time he and his brother, H. J. Cureton, published and edited the *Southern Arena*, a monthly magazine. Cureton studied law privately and was admitted to the bar in 1897. During the Spanish-American War he served with Company I, Third Texas Infantry.

In 1898 he became a junior law partner to Judge O. L. Lockett of Meridian, and three years later, on April 28, 1901, he married Nora Morris. After Lockett was elected district judge in 1905, Cureton and his brother practiced law together until 1913. Cureton served two terms, 1909–13, in the Texas legislature and in 1913 became first assistant in the office of state attorney general Ben Looney. He was elected attorney general in 1918 and held this position until Governor Pat M. Neff[qv] appointed him chief justice of the Texas Supreme Court in 1921. Cureton was elected to the court in 1922 and served until his death in 1940. His time on the bench was a period of industrial and oil activity in Texas, and his interpretation of the law promoted development of Texas resources. He also wrote many opinions concerning water and irrigation rights. Chief Justice Cureton died in Austin on April 8, 1940, of chronic heart disease and was buried in the State Cemetery.[qv]

BIBLIOGRAPHY: William C. Pool, *Bosque Territory* (Kyle, Texas: Chaparral, 1964). Vertical Files, Barker Texas History Center, University of Texas at Austin.
William C. Pool

CURETON, J. J. (ca. 1826–1881). J. J. (Jack) Cureton, one of the first settlers of Palo Pinto County, was born about 1826 and came to Texas during the Mexican War[qv] with Company H of Col. Archibald Yell's[qv] regiment of Arkansas volunteers. After being discharged at San Antonio in 1846, he returned to Arkansas and married Elizabeth Price. In 1852 he joined the gold rush and took some cattle to California; in the winter of 1854 he returned to Texas, where he settled on Keechi Creek. He was in command of his neighbors at a battle at Salt Creek in 1858, and in December 1860 he was a member of a group of citizen soldiers that met and killed Chief Peta Nocona.[qv] On March 15, 1861, he enlisted in the Confederate Army and raised a company of which he was elected captain. After serving until 1863 he returned home to become captain of a company of militia in the Frontier Regiment.[qv] In 1870 Cureton guided an immigrant train of seventy persons overland to California, and from 1876 to 1880 he served as sheriff of Bosque County. He died on May 12, 1881, and was buried in the family cemetery near Walnut Springs. A grandson, Calvin Maples Cureton,[qv] served as attorney general of Texas from 1918 to 1921 and chief justice of the Texas Supreme Court from 1921 to 1940.

BIBLIOGRAPHY: J. Marvin Hunter, *Trail Drivers of Texas* (2 vols., San Antonio: Jackson Printing, 1920, 1923; 4th ed., Austin: University of Texas Press, 1985). Buckley B. Paddock, *History of Texas: Fort Worth and the Texas Northwest Edition* (4 vols., Chicago: Lewis, 1922).
Carolyn Hyman

CURRIE, THOMAS WHITE (1879–1943). Thomas White Currie, Presbyterian minister, professor, and seminary president, son of David Mitchell and Ira Ione (White) Currie, was born on a farm near the Carolina Cemetery, not far from Durango, Texas, on January 23, 1879. After working as a clerk in grocery and clothing stores, he received an A.B. degree from Austin College in 1907. He taught chemistry for a year at Austin College and then went to Austin, where in 1911 he received an M.A. in history from the University of Texas and a B.D. from Austin Presbyterian Theological Seminary. At about this time he also became secretary of the Young Men's Christian Association at the University of Texas, a position he held until 1920. Upon graduation he was made assistant in English Bible at the seminary and, in 1922, president of the institution. He served as professor of church history and president there until his death. His chief interest at the seminary was to produce good ministers for the Southwest and for missionary areas.

Currie was granted honorary doctorates by Austin College in 1915 and Daniel Baker College in 1937. He was made an honorary member of Phi Beta Kappa in 1942 at the University of Texas. The chapel at the seminary was completed under his direction in 1942. In 1921 he was elected moderator of the Synod of Texas of the Presbyterian Church in the United States and in 1930 of the General Assembly. In 1925 he represented the church at the Universal Christian Conference on the Life and Work of the Churches at Stockholm, Sweden, and at the Pan-Presbyterian Conference at Cardiff, Wales. He was a representative in 1937 at the World Conference on Faith and Order in Edinburgh, Scotland.

In addition to his other duties, from December 1932 till the summer of 1937 he served as preacher at Highland Park Presbyterian Church in Dallas. He was interested in improving race relations and served for a time on the board of Tillotson College, a black college in Austin (now Huston-Tillotson College). He served as chairman of the Committee on Cooperation and Union of the General Assembly of the Presbyterian Church, U.S., and helped devise the first written plan of union with the Presbyterian Church, U.S.A. He was a member of the committee that compiled Presbyterian Expansion in the Synod of Texas of the Presbyterian Church, U.S. (1927) and the author of *Studies in the Psalms* (1941).

On August 26, 1913, Currie married Jeannette Ella Roe at the First Presbyterian Church of Colorado City, Texas. Their three sons entered the Presbyterian ministry, and their daughter became a director of Christian education. After a week's illness following a stroke, Currie died in Temple on April 22, 1943. He was buried in Oakwood Cemetery, Austin.

BIBLIOGRAPHY: Thomas White Currie, Jr., *Austin Presbyterian Theological Seminary: A Seventy-fifth Anniversary History* (San Antonio: Trinity University Press, 1978). *Ministerial Directory of the Presbyterian Church, U.S.* (Presbyterian Church in the United States, 1898, 1942–). *Who's Who in America*, 1940–41.
Thomas W. Currie, Jr.

CURRIE, TEXAS (Navarro County). Currie is on State Highway 14 near its junction with Farm Road 641, twenty-five miles south of Corsicana in south central Navarro County. It is made up of two earlier communities, Center Point and Rabbit Hill. The Houston and Texas Central Railway passed through the community in 1871. In 1883 the town was little more than two or three farms. Currie had a post office from 1901 to 1907. The town had become almost nonexistent until a revival in the 1920s. Oil was discovered in the immediate area, and the post office was reestablished in 1921. This boom was short, but Currie managed to retain a population of 125 in 1958. The post office had been closed again by that date. The population had dropped to twenty-five by 1970 and remained at the level through 1990, when a few homes and oil pumps still stood.

BIBLIOGRAPHY: Annie Carpenter Love, *History of Navarro County* (Dallas: Southwestern, 1933). Alva Taylor, *History and Photographs of Corsicana and Navarro County* (Corsicana, Texas, 1959; rev. ed., *Navarro County History and Photographs*, Corsicana, 1962). Charles P. Zlatkovich, *Texas Railroads* (Austin: University of Texas Bureau of Business Research, 1981).
Brian Bruckner

CURRIE, TEXAS (Travis County). Currie was on the Houston and Texas Central Railway five miles east of Austin in east central Travis County. A post office called Tate opened nearby in May 1887 with Isaac M. Tate as postmaster. This office was passed on to Ben N. Shropshire in February 1888, and the name was changed to Currie. It was discontinued by 1890, and mail for the community was sent to Austin.

BIBLIOGRAPHY: John J. Germann and Myron Janzen, *Texas Post Offices by County* (1986).
Vivian Elizabeth Smyrl

CURRY, ARTHUR RAY (1889–1966). Arthur Ray Curry, librarian and state supervisor of the WPA Statewide Library Project, son of

James Silas and Ella Annie (Ray) Curry, was born on March 21, 1889, in Cleburne, Texas. He attended public schools in Cleburne and graduated from Southwestern Christian College (later Southland University) in 1909. He attended the University of Texas in 1910–11 and taught in public schools in 1911–12 and at Abilene Christian College in 1912–13. In 1916 he received his B.A. degree from the University of Texas. After graduation he taught at Abilene Christian College, Greenville High School, and Allen Academy[qv] in Bryan. He entered the University of Illinois in 1919 and graduated in 1921 with a bachelor of library science degree.

From 1923 to 1925, after working in the library of the University of Oklahoma for two years, Curry served as secretary of the Public Library Commission of Indiana. He then returned to Texas, where he was hired by E. M. Waits, president of Texas Christian University, as librarian of the new Mary Couts Burnett Library.[qv] He served as librarian from 1925 until 1933, when he, along with a number of other professors, was dismissed due to financial problems at the university. In 1934 Curry was hired as librarian of the Rosenberg Library[qv] in Galveston, a position he held until 1936.

He was appointed state supervisor of the WPA Statewide Library Project in 1937. In that position he was responsible for founding hundreds of school and public libraries, providing assistance in operating bookmobile services, granting some of the first library services to blacks, and purchasing many books (7,000 volumes between 1938 and 1940 alone, and double that number before the project's completion). In addition he gave public speeches promoting support for his work and contributed articles to *News Notes* (later the *Texas Library Journal*). He resigned his post in 1941, when the project was declining as the country turned its attention to war.

From 1942 to 1947 Curry worked at the Tyler district office as a field-worker for the State Department of Public Welfare (now the Texas Department of Human Services[qv]). In 1947 he took the position of reference librarian at Sam Houston State Teachers College in Huntsville, where he also taught. He worked at the college until his retirement in 1959, then moved to Corpus Christi.

Curry was a life member of the American Library Association. He served as treasurer and later vice president of the Texas Library Association[qv] and as treasurer of the Southwest Library Association. He belonged to the Oklahoma and Indiana state library associations, and while working in Galveston he belonged to the Rotary Club and the Open Forum. His interest in poetry was lifelong, and he was a member of a poetry or literary society wherever he lived. In his youth he joined the Christian Church (Disciples of Christ)[qv] at the urging of his mother, and his religious views were not wholly accepted at Abilene Christian College. In later years his religion was not oriented to a church. He and Marguerite Lewis were married on May 28, 1924, in Indianapolis, Indiana. They had two children. Curry died on October 30, 1966, in Corpus Christi.

BIBLIOGRAPHY: Sheila Winship, Arthur Ray Curry (M.A. thesis, University of Texas, 1966). *Sheila Gail Winship Davis*

CURRY, TEXAS (Milam County). Curry was three miles northeast of Cameron in northern Milam County. In 1903 it had a one-teacher school with forty-two white students and a one-teacher school with eighteen black students. The community did not appear on county highway maps in 1941. *Vivian Elizabeth Smyrl*

CURRY, TEXAS (Stephens County). The exact location of Curry is unknown; the townsite may be submerged beneath Hubbard Creek Reservoir in Stephens County. The community was named for J. C. Curry, who settled in the county in 1881. In the 1920s an oil discovery in the Curry area brought about a boom, during which the settlement had a school, a carbon plant, several other businesses, and a population of 300. By 1930, however, the oil was exhausted, and the town quickly declined. *Julius A. Amin*

CURRY COMB BRANCH. Curry Comb Branch rises six miles west of Gorman just north of State Highway 6 in southern Eastland County (at 32°15′ N, 98°46′ W) and runs southeast six miles to its mouth on the Sabana River, four miles southwest of Gorman near the Comanche county line (at 32°11′ N, 98°44′ W). It traverses rolling hills surfaced by clay and sandy loams that support scrub brush, mesquite, cacti, live oak and juniper trees, and grasses.

CURRY COMB RANCH. The Curry Comb Ranch began in 1875 when W. C. Young of Fort Worth purchased 300 stock cattle and employed Ben Galbraith, a young Irishman from Illinois, to care for them. The cattle were kept in Tarrant County for a year and then moved to Shackelford County in 1876, when Galbraith was made an equal partner and the YG brand was adopted. Three years later the herd was moved to Garza County, and headquarters were set up in a dugout[qv] on Yellowhouse Creek about ten miles north of the future site of Post. In 1880 the Llano Cattle Company, with capital stock of $400,000, was organized with W. C. Young as president and Ben Galbraith as manager. Sam S. Gholson, a neighboring cowman, turned in 2,500 cattle and received $50,000 in stock. E. T. Ambler of Fort Worth and J. C. Lycon of Dallas became influential stockholders, and some of the employees on the ranch acquired a few shares each. The YG brand was soon superseded by the Curry Comb, a peculiar brand similar to one registered in June 1875 by J. H. Cage in Erath County.

The company purchased a tract of land measuring about ten by twelve miles in the northwest quarter of Garza County. Yellowhouse Creek ran through the northeast part of the tract, and several small creeks, with sources in springs at the base of the Caprock[qv] of the Llano Estacado,[qv] crossed the Curry Comb range, which was surveyed by Jasper Hays. The pasture was fenced in 1883, and headquarters was moved to a new, two-story frame house about three miles from the site of Post. After failing health forced Galbraith to resign his managerial position and return to Illinois that summer, he was succeeded by Rollie C. Burns.[qv] Trouble with nesters, mostly small free-rangers, on the north boundary resulted in instances of fence cutting[qv] during 1883 and 1884. At one time hired gunmen were called in to try to remedy the situation, but the problem was eventually brought under control as more settlers fenced their property. Even so, the unpleasantness that resulted caused Burns to resign after a difficult year as manager.

The capacity of the Curry Comb Ranch, which covered 200 sections, was found to be 8,000 to 10,000 cattle of all ages. The Llano Cattle Company carried on until 1907, when the cattle were disposed of and the land was sold to C. W. Post,[qv] who colonized the arable lands and founded the town named for him. The Curry Comb brand was discontinued at that time but later was revived by W. V. (Cap) Roy, a Garza county commissioner, whose ranch and homestead were located east of Justiceburg.

Between 1880 and 1908 J. H. Gage ran about 10,000 to 12,000 cattle on Texas ranges and on land leased in Oklahoma and Colorado. His Curry Comb brand was subsequently passed down through his son, Day Cage, of Stephenville.

BIBLIOGRAPHY: Gus L. Ford, ed., *Texas Cattle Brands* (Dallas: Cockrell, 1936). Garza County Historical Survey Committee, *Wagon Wheels: A History of Garza County*, ed. Charles Didway (Seagraves, Texas: Pioneer, 1973). William Curry Holden, *Rollie Burns* (Dallas: Southwest, 1932; rpt., College Station: Texas A&M University Press, 1986). Jesse Wallace Williams, *The Big Ranch Country* (Wichita Falls: Terry, 1954; 2d ed., Wichita Falls: Nortex, 1971).

William Curry Holden

CURRY CREEK. Curry (Curry's, Currie's) Creek rises (at 30°02′ N, 98°36′ W) in three branches in east central Kendall County and runs southeast fifteen miles through mostly sloping limestone terrain of the Hill Country^{qv} to its mouth on the Guadalupe River, in western Comal County (at 29°53′ N, 98°28′ W). It was named for an early settler on its banks. Area soils of generally stony clay and clay loam support oak, juniper, some mesquite, and grasses. The surrounding countryside is used primarily for ranchland. Settlers established homesteads on the creek beginning in the 1840s, and Judge William E. Jones established a sawmill there in 1850. Several years later John S. Hodges built a grist and saw mill on the creek. During this time a community called Curry's Creek Settlement developed. Edge Falls, named after settler George Edge, who established a homestead near the falls, is located on Curry Creek near Kendalia in Kendall County (at 29°55′ N, 98°30′ W). During rainy seasons water falls twenty-five feet off a rock ledge into a pool ninety feet long and 125 feet wide. Springs flow from cracks in the surrounding rock walls near the pool, and ferns and watercress grow along the banks. Edge Falls was a popular private park and appeared on area tourist maps from the 1930s through the 1960s. It was closed to the public in the 1970s.

BIBLIOGRAPHY: Austin *American*, July 21, 1954. Kendall County Historical Commission, *A History of Kendall County, Texas* (Dallas: Taylor, 1984). Vertical Files, Barker Texas History Center, University of Texas at Austin (Kendalia, Texas).

CURRY'S CREEK SETTLEMENT. Curry's (Currie's) Creek Settlement, three miles west of the site of present Kendalia in east Kendall County, was named for an early settler. It consisted of a number of homesteads along a five-mile stretch of Curry Creek. The settlement was founded about 1847 when Samuel B. Patton established a homestead at the site. Patton later became the first county judge of Blanco County. Early settlers included Judge William Jones, who established a sawmill on Curry Creek in 1850. John S. Hodges built a saw and grist mill. Parson Daniel Rawls,^{qv} one of the Old Three Hundred,^{qv} built the first cotton gin in the county in 1853. Another early settler by the name of Robison built a gristmill that also served as the location for a Masonic lodge chartered in 1858. The charter was moved to Blanco a year later. By the late 1850s Curry's Creek Settlement comprised more than 100 residents, supported by a farming and ranching economy. George Wilkins Kendall introduced sheep ranching in the area in the 1850s. A local post office opened in 1863 but closed in 1900; postal records had been transferred to nearby Kendalia in 1895. The population of Curry's Creek Settlement began to decline in 1880. Kendalia held a centennial celebration for the founding of the settlement in 1947. By the 1980s a few graves and remnants of homesteads were the only remaining signs of Curry's Creek Settlement.

BIBLIOGRAPHY: Kendall County Historical Committee, Kendall County Scrapbook (Kendalia, Texas, Public Library). Kathleen E. and Clifton R. St. Clair, eds., *Little Towns of Texas* (Jacksonville, Texas: Jayroe Graphic Arts, 1982).
Laurie E. Jasinski

CURTIS, DORIS S. MALKIN (1914–1991). Doris S. Malkin Curtis, geologist, was born in Brooklyn, New York, on January 12, 1914, the daughter of Meyer and Mary (Berkowitz) Malkin. She earned a bachelor's degree from Brooklyn College in 1933 and then a master's (1934) and doctorate (1949) in geology from Columbia. In the 1940s and from 1959 to 1979 she worked as a paleontologist, stratigrapher, and geologist for the Shell Oil Company; she was based in New Orleans until 1975, when she was transferred to Houston. She also taught geology at the University of Houston (1949–51), the University of Oklahoma (1954–59), and Rice University (1979–91). From 1951 to 1954 Doris Curtis served as a research geologist for Scripps Institute of Oceanography at the University of California. Her professional memberships included the United States National Committee on Geology of the National Academy of Sciences, the American Association of Petroleum Geologists, and the Houston Geological Society. She was president of the American Geological Institute in 1980–81 and president of the Society of Economic Paleontologists and Mineralogists in 1978–79; at the time of her death she was president of the Geological Society of America. She was also a member of the League of Women Voters. In 1979, with Dorothy Jung Echols, she formed Curtis and Echols, a geological consulting firm that operated out of suburban Houston. Dr. Curtis wrote more than thirty articles; her special research interests included the United States Gulf Coast and Gulf Coast petroleum geology. She married a Shell Oil Company engineer in 1950, and the marriage ended in divorce. She died in Houston on May 26, 1991. Survivors included one sister and two nieces.

BIBLIOGRAPHY: *American Men and Women of Science*, 17th ed.
Debbie Mauldin Cottrell

CURTIS, HINTON (?–1846). Hinton Curtis, soldier, farmer, and member of Stephen F. Austin's^{qv} Old Three Hundred,^{qv} received title to a league of land now in Matagorda County on August 10, 1824. In 1826 he was listed as a farmer and stock raiser between the ages of twenty-five and forty and married to Sarah A. Curtis; he owned one slave. In October 1829 he was named administrator of the estate of James F. Tong.^{qv} He served in Capt. John Austin's^{qv} company at the battle of Velasco^{qv} in 1832 and at the battle of San Jacinto^{qv} as a private in Capt. William H. Patton's^{qv} Fourth Company—the so-called "Columbia Company"—of Col. Sidney Sherman's^{qv} Second Regiment, Texas Volunteers. Curtis died at Matagorda on December 28, 1846. He had no children. James B. Hawkins was named administrator of his estate.

BIBLIOGRAPHY: Lester G. Bugbee, "The Old Three Hundred: A List of Settlers in Austin's First Colony," *Quarterly of the Texas State Historical Association* 1 (October 1897). Daughters of the Republic of Texas, *Muster Rolls of the Texas Revolution* (Austin, 1986). Sam Houston Dixon and Louis Wiltz Kemp, *The Heroes of San Jacinto* (Houston: Anson Jones, 1932). *Texas State Gazette*, October 24, 1829. Gifford E. White, *1830 Citizens of Texas* (Austin: Eakin, 1983).
Thomas W. Cutrer

CURTIS, JAMES, SR. (ca. 1779–1836). James Curtis, Sr., one of the Old Three Hundred,^{qv} was born around 1779 in Spotsylvania County, Virginia, to Frances (Carter) and Rice Curtis III. The family moved to Davidson County, Tennessee, sometime before 1789. Curtis married Sarah Hercules on May 13, 1802. They had nine children. He served in the Tennessee Militia in 1809 and may have served in the United States Army during the War of 1812. Curtis moved to Alabama sometime after 1820. The family was in Texas by late 1823. On August 3, 1824, as one of the Old Three Hundred, Curtis was given a sitio^{qv} of land on the west side of the Brazos River, now in Burleson County. He was a stock raiser. In 1831 he moved his family to Bastrop County and lived either with or near his orphaned grandsons, James and John Stewart. Curtis served in the revolutionary army^{qv} and may have participated in the siege of Bexar.^{qv} He fought at the battle of San Jacinto^{qv} in Jesse Billingsley's^{qv} company, but battle officers' reports that estimated Curtis to be in his mid-sixties were incorrect. He died in the late summer of 1836 in Bastrop County. His gravesite has not been found, but it is presumed that he was buried in a lost family burial ground somewhere in Bastrop County.

BIBLIOGRAPHY: Lester G. Bugbee, "The Old Three Hundred: A List of Settlers in Austin's First Colony," *Quarterly of the Texas State Historical Association* 1 (October 1897). Daughters of the Republic of Texas, *Muster Rolls of the Texas Revolution* (Austin, 1986). Sam Houston Dixon and Louis Wiltz Kemp, *The Heroes of San Jacinto* (Houston: Anson Jones, 1932). Kenneth Kesselus, *History of Bastrop County, Texas, Before Statehood* (Austin: Jenkins, 1986). Marion Day Mullins, *First Census of Texas, 1829–1836, and Other Early Records of the Republic of Texas* (Washington: National Genealogical Society, 1959).

Villamae Williams, *Stephen F. Austin's Register of Families* (Nacogdoches, Texas: Ericson, 1984).

Corine Thomas and Charles L. and Linda A. Reid

CURTIS, JAMES, JR. (ca. 1806–1849). James Curtis, Jr., Old Three Hundred^qv settler, was born around 1806 near Whites Creek in Davidson County, Tennessee, to Sarah (Hercules) and James Curtis, Sr.^qv Between 1820 and 1823 the family left Tennessee for Alabama. Curtis married Polly Ann Hide in Jefferson County, Alabama, on June 11, 1823. They accompanied James's parents to Texas. On August 19, 1824, he received title to a sitio^qv on the east side of the Brazos River in what is now Brazos County. He later moved to Bastrop County to be near other Curtis family members. Curtis and his wife were recorded on the 1829 census of Stephen F. Austin.^qv He may have been the James Curtis who served under Henry S. Brown^qv on an Indian campaign in 1829. Curtis served in the army under Edward Burleson^qv from July 27, 1837, to November 9, 1837. He was a private in Jesse Billingsley's^qv company on the expedition against Adrián Woll^qv in 1842 and was also mentioned by John H. Jenkins^qv as one of four men attacked by Comanches during a mustang hunt near Plum Creek in July 1842. Apparently Polly died sometime after 1829, and Curtis married Tamer C. Gray before 1843. They had one daughter. They were divorced in 1848, and he subsequently married a woman named Rebecca. Curtis died of consumption, probably in the summer of 1849 in Bastrop County. A notice appeared in the *Texas State Gazette* listing his brother Elijah Curtis, appointed in July 1849, as the administrator of his estate.

Many Texas historians have confused James Curtis, Jr., with his father, James Curtis, Sr. The younger Curtis does not appear on the list of Old Three Hundred members compiled by Stephen F. Austin, which is on file at the General Land Office.^qv This list only shows a "James Curtis." The presumption is that it meant James Curtis, Sr. However, Lester G. Bugbee^qv listed both Curtises as members of the Old Three Hundred.

BIBLIOGRAPHY: Lester G. Bugbee, "The Old Three Hundred: A List of Settlers in Austin's First Colony," *Quarterly of the Texas State Historical Association* 1 (October 1897). John Holland Jenkins, *Recollections of Early Texas*, ed. John H. Jenkins III (Austin: University of Texas Press, 1958; rpt. 1973). Kenneth Kesselus, *History of Bastrop County, Texas, Before Statehood* (Austin: Jenkins, 1986). Marion Day Mullins, *First Census of Texas, 1829–1836, and Other Early Records of the Republic of Texas* (Washington: National Genealogical Society, 1959). *Texas State Gazette*, August 25, 1849.

Corine Thomas and Charles L. and Linda A. Reid

CURTIS, NANNIE AUSTIN (1861–1920). Nannie Curtis, lecturer and temperance reformer, was born on June 22, 1861, in Hardin County, Tennessee (one source claims Texas), the daughter of Rev. D. J. and Julia Ann (Couch) Austin. She was a distant relative of Moses and Stephen F. Austin.^qqv Her early education was acquired in Tennessee according to one source, and Mississippi according to another. She reportedly moved to Texas with her family as a young girl.

When Frances Willard organized the first Woman's Christian Temperance Union^qv in Texas in Paris in May 1881, Nannie Austin was among the women participating in the founding. On June 12, 1881, she married W. J. Webb in Mississippi. The couple had four sons, one of whom died in infancy. Nannie Webb was elected secretary of the Texas WCTU at the first state convention in 1882, but she later resigned the office, as she said, "on account of numerous and persistent babies." Her husband died in 1891 in California, where the family had moved for his health. Nannie Webb returned to Texas in 1892 and spent a year in Bivins (Cass County) and the next two years teaching in Queen City (Cass County). She married I. S. Curtis of Texarkana in June of 1893 or 1894. In 1895 she taught at Central College in Sulphur Springs (Hopkins County) and then entered North Texas Female College (later Kidd-Key College) in Sherman for a two-year course in oratory.

Nannie Curtis began a long and successful career on the lecture platform after completing her training in public speaking. She became a renowned Chautauqua lecturer, known as the "Queen of the Southern Platform." Her crusade for prohibition^qv in local elections attracted the attention of the national WCTU, and in 1900 she became WCTU state organizer for Texas. In 1906 or 1907 she was elected to the board of national lecturers and became a national organizer. She was also a member of the national executive committee and the official board, the lawmaking arm of the organization. She took over the presidency of the state branch of the Texas Woman's Christian Temperance Union in 1909 and served until her death in 1920. She also served at one time as editor of the *Texas White Ribbon*, the state WCTU paper. In addition, she contributed articles to numerous periodicals around the country and collaborated on a Texas medical journal known as the "Red Back."

Like most WCTU members, Nannie Curtis believed that putting the ballot in women's hands would bring national prohibition closer to actuality, and she campaigned across the South for both causes, earning the nicknames "Henry Clay of her sex" and "silver-tongued orator of Dixie." Firmly committed to the progressive coalition in Texas politics, she celebrated passage of legislation permitting women to vote in the state primary by founding the Texas Woman's Democratic League in 1918. As chairwoman, she urged women to do their part toward cleaning up state politics by paying their poll taxes and voting and supporting lobbying efforts for woman suffrage^qv and constitutional statewide prohibition. As president of the Texas WCTU, she joined the leaders of other women's organizations in 1918 in organizing the female vote behind Governor William Hobby's^qv successful primary campaign against James Ferguson.^qv Ferguson, the antireform candidate and an old enemy of the prohibitionists, had been denounced by Curtis's WCTU earlier, during his fight with the University of Texas.

Curtis undertook speaking tours for liberty bonds during World War I,^qv led the Armenian Relief Commission in Texas, and was an annual delegate to the Southern Sociological Congress. As a member of the Child Welfare Conference, she was one of 250 women called to discuss national welfare in Washington, D.C., in 1920. After many years as a Baptist, she joined the Methodist Church after her marriage to I. S. Curtis. She was a member of both the Lincoln and the International Lyceum lecture bureaus. She died in Dallas on March 29, 1920, and was buried in Oakland Cemetery. She was survived by three sons. On June 15, 1920, the Texas Senate recognized her contribution to social reform in a resolution of appreciation.

BIBLIOGRAPHY: Austin *American*, March 30, 1920. May Baines, *A Story of Texas White Ribboners* (1935?). Minnie Fisher Cunningham Papers, Houston Metropolitan Research Center, Houston Public Library. Dallas *Morning News*, March 30, 1920. Alexander Caswell Ellis Papers, Barker Texas History Center, University of Texas at Austin. Lewis L. Gould, *Progressives and Prohibitionists: Texas Democrats in the Wilson Era* (Austin: University of Texas Press, 1973; rpt., Austin: Texas State Historical Association, 1992). *Home and State*, April 15, 1920. Sinclair Moreland, *The Texas Women's Hall of Fame* (Austin: Biographical Press, 1917). Texas Woman's Christian Temperance Union Scrapbook, Barker Texas History Center, University of Texas at Austin. *Woman's Who's Who of America* (New York: American Commonwealth, 1914).

Judith N. McArthur

CURTIS, STEPHEN (ca. 1806–?). Stephen Curtis, a black politician in the Reconstruction^qv era, was born into slavery^qv around 1806 in Virginia. He was skilled in carpentry. He was living in Brazos County in 1867, when he served as a delegate to the Republican state convention in Houston, where he was a member of the Platform and Resolutions Committee. He reportedly armed himself after a threat on his life. Curtis was elected to the Constitutional Convention of 1868–69^{qv} and served on the Committee on Immigration. He voted for the division of Texas into more than one state and unsuccessfully introduced a resolution to investigate Ku Klux Klan^{qv} activities. Curtis was one of five black delegates who signed the document produced by the convention. He also helped establish a special committee to investigate racial violence that occurred in 1868 at Millican in Brazos County. The 1870 national census reported that Curtis, who could neither read nor write, lived in a household in Brazos County with five other adults and four children, all named Curtis.

BIBLIOGRAPHY: J. Mason Brewer, *Negro Legislators of Texas and Their Descendants* (Dallas: Mathis, 1935; 2d ed., Austin: Jenkins, 1970). Merline Pitre, *Through Many Dangers, Toils and Snares: The Black Leadership of Texas, 1868–1900* (Austin: Eakin, 1985). Vertical Files, Barker Texas History Center, University of Texas at Austin.

Paul M. Lucko

CURTIS, WILLIAM RILEY (ca. 1845–1901). William Riley Curtis was born about 1845 in Jacksboro, Texas, where he grew up a ragged orphan and learned self-sufficiency at an early age but was denied the education he coveted. He worked for several years learning the cattle business from William S. Ikard.^{qv} He earned some of his first money riding for Oliver Loving,^{qv} driving herds to Shreveport, Louisiana, and up the Chisholm Trail^{qv} to Kansas. For a time he served as a Texas Ranger. He married Alice V. Ghormley of Weatherford on May 18, 1869; they made their home in Jacksboro. To their union were born three sons and a daughter.

In 1870 Bill Curtis and his younger brother, Jim C., purchased Mose Dameron's small herd of Diamond Tail Ranch^{qv} cattle. They grazed this herd along Cache Creek near Fort Sill after securing a government contract to sell beef to Fort Reno and Fort Sill in the Indian Territory. Soon they accumulated enough wealth to build up ranches on both Cache Creek and the Wichita River. After the expiration of the contract compelled them to seek other pastures, the Curtises established their ranch headquarters near Cambridge in Clay County. There Bill was dealt a severe blow with the accidental death of his brother in 1878. At the same time, he realized that his land was too crowded for good grazing and therefore moved his cattle north to Grosebeck Creek, near the site of present Quanah.

Curtis formed a new partnership with Thomas J. Atkinson, one of a family of Jack County pioneers. With the help of a cowboy, Sam Bean, the partners early in 1879 selected for their headquarters a site on Gypsum Creek, in southeastern Childress County. Later they moved this new headquarters to the junction of Doe and Buck creeks in Collingsworth County. Since their families resided in Henrietta, where the children had better educational opportunities, the partners never constructed a permanent ranchhouse. However, the Curtis and Atkinson families enjoyed summers on the ranch; the Atkinsons brought their own hired nurse and trail cook, along with appropriate camping equipment. Over the next few years Curtis secured more government contracts for reservation beef sales and delivered herds to the Kansas markets.

In the early 1880s George Loving, son of Oliver Loving, made a proposition whereby Curtis could sell out to British capital for a handsome sum and Loving himself could make a $100,000 commission. Curtis accepted, the contract was drawn up, and Loving went to Scotland to form a company and bring back prospective investors to see the Diamond Tail. Despite the ranch's crude living conditions, the Scotsmen were impressed and offered Curtis $1.25 million for the place, which he accepted. Before the deal could be completed, however, Curtis was indicted for shooting a lawyer from Henrietta who tried to kill him. Although he was acquitted, this turn of events caused the Scotsmen to call off negotiations. Due to their initial lack of trust, Curtis later turned down a second offer from Scotland, proposing that he retain one-quarter interest and manage the ranch himself. George Loving lost his commission, and the Diamond Tail remained in the possession of Curtis and Atkinson.

Curtis was widely known for generosity. After Giles emerged as the Diamond Tail's main shipping point with the arrival of the Fort Worth and Denver City Railway in 1887, Curtis began hosting an annual barbecue. A highlight of that event was his presentation of a baby carriage to every baby named for him during that year. When the lean years of the late 1880s caught up with Curtis, he brought in Sam Lazarus,^{qv} a man with remarkable financial skills, as a receiver to put the ranch in the black again. On February 11, 1893, when a blizzard swept across the Panhandle,^{qv} Curtis saved the Diamond Tail cattle by riding ahead of them in a heavy Arctic suit. With a pair of wire clippers he cut every fence in his path, allowing the herd to pass through and find safety. Beginning in 1895, Curtis moved most of his cattle to Chavez County, New Mexico. His oldest son, Jim, managed the cattle there and bought out several smaller ranches. Curtis, in the meantime, bought and sold whole herds at Amarillo, holding them on open range near the numerous playas until sold and then shipping them out to the buyers by rail.

On December 1, 1901, Curtis and W. H. Harrell, an Amarillo cattleman and longtime friend, caught the Fort Worth and Denver City train from Amarillo to Memphis, Texas, on business. While making their way to the diner as the train neared Giles, Curtis jostled a passenger whose gun dropped to the floor and discharged accidentally, giving Curtis a fatal wound. A special train from Clarendon rushed him to Fort Worth, but he lived only a few days. The president of the FW&DC road, who was a friend of Curtis, ran a special train to Henrietta to bear the body home for burial. Curtis's last request to his family was complete forgiveness for the careless man whose gun had killed him. For many years the Curtis children and their families continued ranching activities in New Mexico, and some of them made their homes in Amarillo, where their heirs still reside. Several years after Curtis's death, George L. Rickard,^{qv} a one-time Diamond Tail cowboy since grown rich, used the brand on his herd of 50,000 head in South America as a tribute to his former boss.

BIBLIOGRAPHY: Inez Baker, *Yesterday in Hall County* (Memphis, Texas, 1940). Virginia Browder, *Donley County: Land O' Promise* (Wichita Falls, Texas: Nortex, 1975). Laura V. Hamner, *Short Grass and Longhorns* (Norman: University of Oklahoma Press, 1943). Pauline D. and R. L. Robertson, *Cowman's Country: Fifty Frontier Ranches in the Texas Panhandle, 1876–1887* (Amarillo: Paramount, 1981).

H. Allen Anderson

CURTIS, TEXAS. Curtis is at the junction of State Highway 63 and Farm Road 777, eighty miles north of Beaumont in central Jasper County. It was known as Byerly's Gin until the mid-1940s, when the Beech Grove post office was moved to the site and renamed after the son of postmaster Adam Byerly. The Jasper-Newton Electric Cooperative maintained a suboffice at Curtis by 1948, when the community's population was estimated to be 150. In 1986 Curtis had several residences, a church, a store, and a small helicopter plant.

Robert Wooster

CURTIS FIELD. Curtis Field, a United States Army flying field on U.S. Highway 283 3½ miles north of Brady in central McCulloch County, was named for Mayor Harry L. Curtis of Brady, who proposed the site as an auxiliary field for the army. At the time it was built it was the only army air field named for a living person. Construction of the airport began in November 1940, and a primary flying school from Love Field^{qv} in Dallas moved to Curtis Field. Classes began on March 23, 1941, with eighty students; as many as 500 were enrolled at one time. Facilities at the 354-acre field included a headquarters building and annex, a ground school, an infirmary, three barracks, and four hangars. Three auxiliary fields within a ten-mile radius were used for training purposes. The school, originally for primary flight training, was used for basic training twice in its history but had reverted to primary training when it was closed on August 4, 1945, and became the Brady municipal airport. Some 10,000 student flyers were graduated. About 85 percent of the instructors and students were native Texans.   *Robert W. Stewart*

CURTRIGHT, TEXAS. Curtright was on the Sulphur River fifteen miles northwest of Linden in northern Cass County. The site was settled in the late 1860s and was first called White Sulphur Springs when the post office was established there in 1875. In 1884 it had a population of seventy-five and three churches, as well as a district school, a gristmill, a gin, and a store. In 1887 the name of the town was changed to Curtright, probably in honor of the Curtright family who lived there. Its post office was closed in 1890, and by 1936 Curtright no longer existed as a named community.   *Cecil Harper, Jr.*

CUSENBARY DRAW. Cusenbary Draw, a drainage ditch infrequently filled with water, begins a fourth of a mile north of the Edwards county line and east of Cusenbary Road in south central Sutton County (at 30°17′ N, 100°32′ W) and runs northwest for sixteen miles until it meets Cauthorn Draw west of U.S. Highway 277 (at 30°25′ N, 100°42′ W). The draw traverses the gently rolling limestone terrain of the western Edwards Plateau, and the area is surfaced by shallow to deep loamy soils occasionally broken by rock outcrops. Local vegetation is mainly range grasses with scattered small stands of oak, juniper, and mesquite.

CUSHING, EDWARD BENJAMIN (1863–1924). Edward Benjamin Cushing, president of the board of regents of Texas A&M, son of Matilda (Burke) and Edward Hopkins Cushing,qv was born in Houston on November 22, 1863. On February 18, 1888, he married Florence Abbey Powars. He entered A&M as a member of its second class in 1877. After his graduation in 1880, he worked for the Southern Pacific Railroad at Houston, first as an axman and rodman, then as assistant general manager, and then as maintenance-of-way engineer (1912). Early in 1917 he was commissioned a major and sent overseas as an officer of the Seventeenth Engineers, American Expeditionary Force. He served on the staff of Gen. John J. Pershing.qv For his services he was awarded the French Croix de Guerre. In 1919 Cushing became a federal bank examiner and at the time of his death was receiver for the First National Bank at Granger, Texas. He was appointed to the A&M board of directors (now regents) in 1912 and became president of the board in 1913. He also served as president of the Texas A&M Association of Former Students. Cushing was an Elk and a Mason. He died at Houston on February 17, 1924. On November 23, 1927, the Texas A&M library was named the Cushing Memorial Library.

BIBLIOGRAPHY: *National Cyclopaedia of American Biography*, Vol. 21. Vertical Files, Barker Texas History Center, University of Texas at Austin.   *Hugo Ellis*

CUSHING, EDWARD HOPKINS (1829–1879). Edward Hopkins Cushing, newspaperman and horticulturist, was born in Royalton, Vermont, on June 11, 1829, to Daniel and Nancy (Anthony) Cushing. His father was a farmer and trader, and his mother was the daughter of a prominent Puritan family in Providence, Rhode Island. Hopkins grew up on a farm and showed an early interest in books and learning. He entered Dartmouth at the age of sixteen and graduated in 1850. Hoping to establish himself in a fresh, new land, he traveled to Texas, where he intended to devote himself to teaching. During his first few years in Texas, he taught first at Galveston and later at Brazoria and Columbia. In Columbia he wrote for the local newspaper, the *Democrat and Planter*. Soon he acquired part ownership in the paper, and by the mid-1850s he had exchanged a career in education for one in journalism.

In 1856 he acquired control of the Houston *Telegraph* (*see* TELEGRAPH AND TEXAS REGISTER) from Dr. Frances Moore,qv whom he replaced as editor. In his role as editor and publisher of the *Telegraph* for the next thirteen years, Cushing was a tireless booster for the city. His interests were wide-ranging, and he used the columns of his paper to promote southern manufacture, railroads, education, Texas authors, and horticulture and scientific agriculture. The flowers at his estate, Bohemia, were among the most complete collections in the United States. Cushing published books by Texas writers, among them Mollie Evelyn Moore Davis'sqv *Poems* (1867), Maud Jeannie Young's *Familiar Lessons in Botany* (1873), and John Sayles'sqv *A Treatise on the Practice of the District and Supreme Courts of the State of Texas* (1875). When hostilities severed ties with northern publishers, Cushing printed some of the only textbooks available during the Civil War.qv Among his reprints and adaptations of prewar editions of popular northern books were three volumes of the New Texas Series published in May 1863. He was also a tough but compassionate competitor. In the late 1850s he battled Willard Richardson'sqv Galveston *News*qv for dominance in the area, but when his adversary was wiped out by a fire in 1863, Cushing sent newsprint so that Richardson could continue publishing.

Cushing became a staunch Southern-rights Democrat and in 1860 supported John C. Breckinridge for president. He played a key role in publicizing an alleged plot of abolitionists and blacks to overthrow slaveryqv in Texas, thus contributing to the growth of secessionism in the Lone Star State. Cushing established a pony-express route between Houston and army headquarters in Louisiana, with correspondents at important points to convey news from the front. Jefferson Davisqv noted his actions, and John B. Magruderqv offered him a commission on his personal staff. The *Telegraph* never suspended publication during the Civil War, although Cushing was forced on occasion to use butcher's paper and wallpaper to keep his press running. During Reconstruction,qv because the *Telegraph* took a position unfavorable to carpetbaggers, Governor Edmund J. Davisqv advised Andrew Johnson against political pardon for Cushing and suggested hanging him.

Cushing married Matilda Burke. A few years after the war he sold the *Telegraph* and used the proceeds to purchase a wholesale and retail book and stationery business, which he ran until his death, on January 15, 1879.

BIBLIOGRAPHY: Sam Hanna Acheson, *35,000 Days in Texas: A History of the Dallas "News" and Its Forbears* (New York: Macmillan, 1938). E. B. Cushing, "Edward Hopkins Cushing: An Appreciation by His Son," *Southwestern Historical Quarterly* 25 (April 1922). S. W. Geiser, *Horticulture and Horticulturists in Early Texas* (Dallas: University Press, 1945). S. W. Geiser, "Men of Science in Texas, 1820–1880," *Field and Laboratory* 26–27 (July–October 1958–October 1959). Donald E. Reynolds, *Editors Make War: Southern Newspapers in the Secession Crisis* (Nashville: Vanderbilt University Press, 1970). Emory M. Thomas, "Rebel Nationalism: E. H. Cushing and the Confederate Experience," *Southwestern Historical Quarterly* 73 (January 1970). Vertical Files, Barker Texas History Center, University of Texas at Austin.   *Donald E. Reynolds*

CUSHING, THOMAS HUMPHREY (?–1822). Thomas Humphrey Cushing, army officer, was born in Massachusetts, where he enlisted as a sergeant in the Sixth Continental Infantry in January 1776. He succeeded Isaac Guion in 1799 as commander of United States troops on the Mississippi and Tombigbee rivers, with headquarters near Natchez. He supervised the construction of American frontier forts in Mississippi Territory, particularly Fort Stoddart. Cushing was commissioned a colonel on September 7, 1805, was named commander of the posts west of the Mississippi the following May, and was ordered by Gen. James Wilkinsonqv to leave for Natchitoches with several cannons and howitzers. He was to prevent Spanish violations of American territory east of the Sabine River during the Neutral Ground^{qv} dispute. He negotiated with Simón de Herrera^{qv} in August 1806 but failed to reach any agreement. Hostilities were avoided when Wilkinson arrived and signed the Neutral Ground agreement on November 6, 1806. Cushing was commissioned a brigadier general on July 2, 1812. He was honorably discharged on June 15, 1815, and died on October 19, 1822.

BIBLIOGRAPHY: Francis B. Heitman, *Historical Register and Dictionary of the United States Army* (2 vols., Washington: GPO, 1903; rpt., Urbana: University of Illinois Press, 1965). Jack D. L. Holmes, ed., "Fort Stoddart in 1799: Seven Letters of Captain Bartholomew Schaumburgh," *Alabama Historical Quarterly* 26 (Fall, Winter 1964). Jack D. L. Holmes, "Showdown on the Sabine: General James Wilkinson vs. Lieutenant-Colonel Simón de Herrera," *Louisiana Studies* 3 (Spring 1964).

Jack D. L. Holmes

CUSHING, TEXAS. Cushing, on State Highway 204 and Farm Road 225, eighteen miles northwest of Nacogdoches in extreme northwestern Nacogdoches County, was founded in 1902, when the Texas and New Orleans Railroad announced that it would lay track. The community was named for Edward Benjamin Cushing,^{qv} an official with the railroad. A local post office opened in 1902, and the town was laid out the following year. In 1904 regular passenger service began on the railroad. The railroad spurred the development of the lumbering industry in the northwestern corner of the county, and Cushing quickly developed as a shipping center for the numerous sawmills in the region. The town incorporated in 1905 and by 1914 had a bank, a hotel, a weekly newspaper named the *Enterprise*, twenty-eight businesses, and an estimated population of 600. By 1925 the population reached a high of 1,500. During the 1930s the town began to decline, as a result of the Great Depression^{qv} and the deforestation of the surrounding area. By 1950 the population fell to 473. Afterward the number of residents remained steady, but many of the town's businesses have closed. In 1965 Cushing still had thirty-seven rated businesses; by the early 1990s it had seven. The reported population in 1990 was 465.

BIBLIOGRAPHY: Nacogdoches County Genealogical Society, *Nacogdoches County Families* (Dallas: Curtis, 1985). *Christopher Long*

CUSHNEY, WILLIAM H. (1819–1852). William H. Cushney, early newspaperman, was born in Fonda, New York, on September 15, 1819. He went to Augusta, Georgia, in 1835 as foreman in the office of the *Constitutionalist* before moving to Texas in 1840 and serving for a time in the Texas army. Cushney settled in Austin in 1845. He published the Austin *Texas Democrat*^{qv} for a time before founding the Austin *State Gazette*^{qv} in August 1849. Cushney married Lydia Jane Brown, sister of Frank Brown,^{qv} in 1846, and they became the parents of two children. Cushney died, probably of tuberculosis, on November 24, 1852, while visiting a friend's home in Independence, Washington County; he was buried with Masonic honors at Oakwood Cemetery in Austin.

BIBLIOGRAPHY: Frank Brown, Annals of Travis County and the City of Austin (MS, Frank Brown Papers, Barker Texas History Center, University of Texas at Austin). Clarksville *Northern Standard*, February 24, 1849, December 18, 1852. Marshall and the Texas State Gazette, 1860–1861," *Southwestern Historical Quarterly* 62 (October 1958). Marilyn M. Sibley, *Lone Stars and State Gazettes: Texas Newspapers before the Civil War* (College Station: Texas A&M University Press, 1983). *Texas State Gazette*, October 6, 1849, December 4, 1852.

Vivian Elizabeth Smyrl

CUSSETA, TEXAS. Cusseta is on the fringes of the Cusseta Mountains 11½ miles northwest of Linden in northwestern Cass County. The community was first settled in the early 1850s and was named for Cusseta, Alabama, the hometown of John Robin Heard, an early settler. A post office was established there in 1856, and the town was probably a supply point for plantation owners who lived in the area. By 1884 Cusseta reported two gins, a gristmill, a school, and a population of 100. By 1896 its population had fallen to fifty. In 1914 the population of the community was 100, but by 1933 it had fallen to sixty, with two rated businesses. In 1990 Cusseta reported thirty residents and no rated businesses.

BIBLIOGRAPHY: *Cass County Cemeteries: Texas Records* (Atlanta, Texas: Cass County Genealogical Society, 1976).

Cecil Harper, Jr.

CUSSETA MOUNTAINS. The Cusseta Mountains, three peaks with altitudes of 632, 620, and 596 feet above mean sea level, are located less than a mile northwest of Cusseta in northwestern Cass County (at 33°10′ N, 94°28′ W), in a gently rolling to hilly area with an altitude varying from 350 to 400 feet above mean sea level. The local soils are loamy and sandy, and the land is heavily wooded, with pines and various hardwoods predominating. When the Cusseta community was settled in the early 1850s, it was named for Cusseta, Alabama, hometown of John R. Heard, an early settler. Presumably the Cusseta Mountains took their name from the community.

CUSTER, ELIZABETH BACON (1842–1933). Elizabeth Bacon Custer, the only surviving child of Judge Daniel and Eleanor Sophia (Page) Bacon, was born at Monroe, Michigan, on April 8, 1842. At twenty Libbie, as she was called, graduated as valedictorian from the Young Ladies' Seminary and Collegiate Institute in Monroe. Shortly after, she met Capt. George Armstrong Custer.^{qv} His meteoric rise to brigadier general before Gettysburg, where he emerged as a national hero, overcame her father's objections to their courtship. They were married on February 9, 1864.

From the beginning, Libbie's charm and attractiveness helped advance her husband's military career. She socialized with powerful Republican congressmen and senators, thereby countering their suspicions that Custer had ties to the Democrats. Moreover, her husband's superior, Gen. Philip H. Sheridan,^{qv} admired Libbie so greatly that he gave her the table on which Gen. Ulysses S. Grant had written the terms of surrender accepted by Gen. Robert E. Lee^{qv} at Appomattox.

After the Civil War^{qv} Sheridan, anticipating military action against Mexico, ordered Custer, now major general of volunteers, to march a cavalry division from Alexandria, Louisiana, to Hempstead, Texas. Elizabeth accompanied the troops in August 1865 and later wrote of her hardships in her second book, *Tenting on the Plains*, published in 1887. Her early response to Texas was mixed. She found homes, even of the well-to-do, often poorly constructed. Moreover, many Texans struck her as violent and trigger-happy men who threatened both the federal troops and their local supporters. She was appalled that, despite a Union victory, some Texans were still trading slaves late in 1865.

Many planter aristocrats, however, welcomed the Custers warmly. Leonard Groce^{qv} and his family, of Liendo Plantation^{qv} on Clear Creek, nursed Libbie when she fell ill with malaria. After Custer became chief of cavalry in Texas, the couple moved to Austin, where they resided at the Asylum for the Blind. They continued associating with wealthy planters, who introduced them to the pleasures of breeding hunting dogs. Overall, whatever her criticism of the state, Libbie saw great economic potential in Texas and tried unsuccessfully to interest her father in investing in Texas land. After Custer became lieutenant colonel of the Seventh Cavalry in 1866, Elizabeth's prized Texas serapes decorated their quarters at forts Riley, Leavenworth, and Lincoln.

Following her husband's death at the Little Bighorn, on June 25, 1876, Elizabeth learned that Grant, now president, had charged Custer with disobeying orders and held him responsible for the destruction of his battalion of 221 men by Sioux and Cheyenne warriors. Throughout her fifty-seven years of widowhood, Mrs. Custer worked untiringly to defend her husband's reputation and transform him into a hero for boys. She influenced a number of writers, including Frederick Whittaker, Gen. Edward S. Godfrey, Gen. Nelson Miles,qv and Frederick Dellenbaugh. In addition, Elizabeth published two other books, *Boots and Saddles* (1885) and *Following the Guidon* (1890). In all her works, her husband emerged as an exemplary son, brother, husband, and conscientious commanding officer.

Since army men and the public alike saw Elizabeth as a model wife and devoted widow, many Custer critics withheld their comments during her lifetime. Elizabeth survived, however, until April 4, 1933. A year later, Frederic Van de Water published *The Glory-Hunter*, and the reappraisal of Custer's character and career began. By then much of the historical record had been irretrievably lost.

BIBLIOGRAPHY: John M. Carroll, ed., *Custer in Texas: An Interrupted Narrative* (New York: Sol Lewis–Liveright, 1975). Elizabeth B. Custer Collection, Little Bighorn Battlefield National Monument, Crow Agency, Montana. Elizabeth B. Custer Manuscript Collection, Western Americana Collection, Beinecke Rare Book and Manuscript Library, Yale University, New Haven, Connecticut. Lawrence A. Frost, *General Custer's Libbie* (Seattle: Superior, 1976). Shirley A. Leckie, *Elizabeth Bacon Custer and the Making of a Myth* (Norman: University of Oklahoma Press, 1993).
Shirley A. Leckie

CUSTER, GEORGE ARMSTRONG (1839–1876). George Armstrong Custer, Union Civil War general and western Indian fighter, was born in New Rumley, Ohio, on December 5, 1839, the son of Emanuel and Maria (Ward-Kirkpatrick) Custer. He grew up in New Rumley and Monroe, Michigan, and realized his ambition in 1857 when he was appointed to the United States Military Academy at West Point. He graduated in 1861 at the bottom of his class but won distinction in the Civil Warqv as a cavalry officer. At twenty-three he was made brigadier general of volunteers, and at twenty-five he earned the rank of brevet major general. With his long blond hair set off by a red tie, a sailor's blouse, and a blue jacket agleam with gold, the "boy general" cut a dashing figure. Admired by some, envied and disliked by others, he captured the public's imagination and became a popular hero in the North.

At the end of the war Custer was assigned to duty in Texas as part of Gen. Philip H. Sheridan'sqv effort to prevent Confederate retrenchment in Mexico under the emperor Maximilian. During an uneventful five-month stay in Hempstead and Austin, which ended when he was mustered out of the volunteers on February 1, 1866, Custer alienated many in his command by strict enforcement of regulations prohibiting foraging, lawlessness, and destruction of private property; by the same enforcement he won the gratitude of many Texans, who found him a generous and courtly soldier.

Effective September 1866, Custer, whose regular army rank was captain, was appointed lieutenant colonel of the newly formed Seventh United States Cavalry regiment, the position he held when he died ten years later. He served on the southern plains against the Cheyennes, Comanches, Kiowas, and Arapahos. Controversy followed him—he was court-martialed in 1867—but he gained a reputation as an Indian fighter in November 1868, when the Seventh Cavalry destroyed a Cheyenne village on the Washita River in what is now Oklahoma. After Reconstructionqv duty in the South, Custer returned to the plains, this time to Dakota Territory, and led the Seventh Cavalry on the Yellowstone expedition in 1873, the Black Hills expedition in 1874, and the fateful Sioux expedition in 1876.

Three military columns took the field in the spring of 1876—from forts in Wyoming, Montana, and Dakota—with the intention of trapping the Sioux and forcing them onto the reservation. Custer accompanied the Dakota column in command of the Seventh Cavalry. He was given independent command on June 22 with orders to cut off the Indians' escape to the south of their expected location on the Little Bighorn River. When his scouts found the Indian village on the morning of June 25, Custer decided to attack at once. He assigned 135 men to guard his packtrain and divided the remaining 515 men into three battalions; he took command of five companies. The Seventh was expecting at least 1,000 warriors but encountered double that number. Two of the battalions were besieged on the bluffs above the Little Bighorn, where they were relieved two days later; Custer's men, meanwhile, had proceeded north about four miles to strike the village downstream and, on the afternoon of June 25, were utterly annihilated.

There is controversy about where the blame for the massacre lies—on Custer or on his battalion commanders Reno and Benteen. There was also contemporary controversy, which began as soon as the news of disaster reached the East. The Centennial year, 1876, was a year of vigorous discussion and appraisal of America. It was also a presidential election year. Custer was championed in the Democratic press as a martyr to Republican mismanagement, and Democratic Texans chose to remember him as a friend, "the Stuart of the North . . . once our foe, but a generous and manly one." Papers throughout the state clamored for the right to raise a volunteer force: "Texas deserves the honor of attempting to wipe out the Sioux," the Austin *State Gazette*qv insisted. Resolutions passed at a public meeting in Dallas, and a reunion of Hood's Texas Brigadeqv in Bryan praised Custer as "a rare and magnanimous officer." The state legislature passed a resolution of condolence, subsequently published as a congressional document, noting that Custer had "endeared" himself to Texans by his frontier service.

Custer's wife, Elizabeth (Bacon), whom he married in 1864, lived to the age of ninety-one. The couple had no children. She was devoted to his memory, wrote three books about him, and when she died in 1933 was buried beside him at West Point. Her *Tenting on the Plains* (1887) presents a charming picture of their stay in Texas. Custer's headquarters building in Austin, the Blind Asylum, located on the "Little Campus" of the University of Texas, has been restored.

BIBLIOGRAPHY: John M. Carroll, ed., *Custer in Texas: An Interrupted Narrative* (New York: Sol Lewis/Liveright, 1975). George W. Cullum, *Biographical Register of the Officers and Graduates of the U.S. Military Academy at West Point, New York* (8 vols., New York [etc.]: D. Van Nostrand [etc.], 1868–1940). George Armstrong Custer, *My Life on the Plains, or Personal Experiences with Indians* (New York: Sheldon, 1874). Charles K. Hofling, *Custer and the Little Big Horn* (Detroit: Wayne State University Press, 1981). Jay Monaghan, *Custer* (Boston: Little, Brown, 1959). William L. Richter, "'A Better Time is in Store for Us': An Analysis of the Reconstruction Attitudes of George Armstrong Custer," *Military History of Texas and the Southwest* 9 (1971).
Brian W. Dippie

CUSTER CITY, TEXAS. Custer City, on Ranch Road 2896 some ten miles northeast of Gainesville in northeastern Cooke County, was established in 1876 by Jim Jones, who built a cotton gin and a flour mill there. The settlement was originally called Centennial City because it was founded during the nation's centennial; it was later renamed to honor Gen. George Armstrong Custer.qv Its post office operated under the name Custer City from 1877 until 1902. The community grew relatively rapidly and by 1882 had a population of 300 and a cotton gin and flour mill, as well as a school, sawmill, blacksmith shop, store, and church. It declined almost as quickly as it had developed, and in 1892 had only twenty-five residents, two mills, a blacksmith, and a general store. In 1978 the community still had a church and scattered dwellings. The church was still shown on the 1986 county highway map.

BIBLIOGRAPHY: A. Morton Smith, *The First 100 Years in Cooke County* (San Antonio: Naylor, 1955).
Brian Hart

CUSTIS, PETER (1781–1842). Peter Custis, born in 1781 in Accomack County, Virginia, was the first trained naturalist appointed to a United States government exploring party. For four months in 1806, before the expedition was turned back by Spanish opposition, he performed a wide-ranging scientific survey of the Red River in what is now Louisiana, Arkansas, and Northeast Texas. Though many have viewed the Red River expedition[qv] as both a scientific and diplomatic failure, Custis deserves recognition as the first trained naturalist to work in Texas and the near Southwest.

He entered the University of Pennsylvania in 1804 as a medical student and became a protégé of Benjamin Smith Barton, America's leading academic naturalist. President Thomas Jefferson's selection of Custis for his Red River exploring party came after a consideration of several famous naturalists, including William Bartram, Constantine Samuel Rafinesque, and Alexander Wilson, none of whom was available at the time the position was filled. Custis was appointed by Secretary of War Henry Dearborn in February 1806. He was to receive three dollars a day plus expenses. Although Thomas Freeman was the sole field leader and Capt. Richard Sparks the ranking officer of the party, Custis was one of its two diarists, and the expedition is sometimes referred to as the Freeman and Custis expedition.

Custis's Red River work suffered in three respects. Most important was his inexperience as a naturalist, which made him cautious in declaring new species, though he did declare twenty-one new ones and propose seven new scientific names. Today only a pair of vertebrates can be credited to him. Second was the loss or misplacement of his botanical collections; only two specimens, both of them plants first collected in 1806, survive. Finally, Custis's work was not well published, for it appeared in garbled form in an almost unnoticed government report. A brief article concerning the first leg of the exploration was published in the *Philadelphia Medical and Physical Journal* in 1806, but most of Custis's discoveries and his manuscript reports were forgotten. His notes, on 267 species of plants and animals inhabiting the Red River valley, are today an invaluable reference for environmental history.

Custis received little acclaim for his work and was not invited to join Jefferson's planned but never accomplished 1807 Arkansas River expedition, perhaps because he was finishing his M.D. degree that year. Later in 1807 he collected plants for Barton. By 1808 he had settled in a position as a doctor in New Bern, North Carolina. He died there on May 1, 1842, leaving a plantation and slaves to his wife and six children, several of whom were named after prominent naturalists.

BIBLIOGRAPHY: Dan L. Flores, "The Ecology of the Red River in 1806: Peter Custis and Early Southwestern Natural History," *Southwestern Historical Quarterly* 88 (July 1984). Dan L. Flores, ed., *Jefferson and Southwestern Exploration: The Freeman and Custis Accounts of the Red River Expedition of 1806* (Norman: University of Oklahoma Press, 1984).

Dan L. Flores

CUSTOMS SERVICE OF THE REPUBLIC OF TEXAS. The need for the government revenue and taxation program that would be considered least onerous by Texans prompted the General Council[qv] to enact a revenue tariff law in December 1835. This and subsequent enactments established what came to be known as the Customs Service of the Republic of Texas. Revenue districts designated were Galveston, Sabine, Brazos, Matagorda, Jackson, Aransas, La Bacca (Lavaca), Copano, and Maximilian.

At the Convention of 1836[qv] any earlier customs systems were declared void, and the republic enacted the formation of the customs service in December 1836. In June 1837 administration of customs was placed under the Treasury Department, and collectors of customs were appointed by the president, subject to confirmation by the Senate. Sometime later a comptroller of customs was made responsible for administering revenue laws. Lower-ranking officers were to be selected at each district port of entry by the respective collectors, the districts being designated as Aransas, Matagorda, Brazos, Galveston, Sabine, and San Augustine. In 1839 the district of La Vaca was carved from Matagorda district, and in 1841 the Matagorda and La Vaca districts were consolidated into the district of Calhoun. In 1842 a northeastern district, Red River, was established, and in 1845 Red River, Bowie, Harrison, Rusk, and part of Nacogdoches counties were organized as the Soda Lake district.

For collection of revenue and enforcement of the tariff, customhouses were maintained at Galveston, Aransas Pass, Linnville, Port La Vaca, Copano, Point Bolivar, Sabine Pass, Matagorda, Velasco, Sabine City, San Augustine, Port Calhoun or Cavallo, San Luis, and various river landings. The buildings were usually frame structures of from one to three rooms, poorly furnished and equipped. Employees of these offices were, for the most part, few in number and inadequate for preventing evasion of the tariff laws. At Galveston the officials included a collector and deputy collector, each of whom was paid $2,000 a year; a cashier, $1,600; a bookkeeper, $2,000; an entry clerk, $1,600; a permit clerk, $1,600; a storekeeper, $1,400; an impost clerk, $1,600; a boarding officer, $1 500; two boatmen at $90 a month each; and nine inspectors and an appraiser, paid for the days they were actually employed. In number and salary Galveston employees were the exception rather than the rule, for Galveston was the chief port of entry to Texas and the most important revenue district as well. Gail Borden, Jr.,[qv] served as Galveston collector from 1837 to December 1838, when Dr. Willis Roberts assumed charge. Roberts was succeeded by Alden A. M. Jackson in December 1839. Borden returned to the customhouse in January 1842 and continued as collector until relieved by James H. Cocke in January 1844.

Galveston trade from June 1, 1837, to March 1839 was largely confined to the import of manufactured goods, assorted groceries, and liquors from New Orleans and New York. The economic condition of Texas forced her into an unfavorable balance of trade until 1842. During the year of greatest importation, 1839, Texas commerce expanded to the ports of Europe, and by 1844 the trade included Trieste, Antwerp, Cork, Dunkirk, London, Liverpool, and Le Havre. Statistics compiled from reports of collectors of customs, the comptroller of customs, and the secretary of the treasury indicate that the Texas treasury received a total of $1,984,423.62 from customs between June 1837 and October 1846.

BIBLIOGRAPHY: R. E. L. Crane, *The Administration of the Customs Service of the Republic of Texas* (M.A. thesis, University of Texas, 1939).

R. E. L. Crane, Jr.

CUT, TEXAS. Cut, a farming community on State Highway 19 six miles south of Crockett in south central Houston County, was established in 1872 as a watering stop on the Houston and Great Northern Railroad. The settlement was originally known as Paso or Paso Switch, but its name was changed to Cut around 1900. A Cut post office operated from 1903 to 1918. At its height around 1914 the settlement had a sawmill, two general stores, and an estimated population of fifty. The community began to decline during the 1920s, and by the mid-1930s only a store and a few houses remained. After World War II[qv] most of its residents moved away. By the early 1990s Cut was abandoned.

BIBLIOGRAPHY: Houston County Historical Commission, *History of Houston County, Texas, 1687–1979* (Tulsa, Oklahoma: Heritage, 1979).

Christopher Long

CUTALCHICH INDIANS. The Cutalchich (Cultalchulches) Indians, an otherwise unidentified group met by Álvar Núñez Cabeza de Vaca[qv] during his journey through South Texas in 1528–34, lived inland near the Maliacones and Susolas and were a nomadic, gathering group.

BIBLIOGRAPHY: Frederick Webb Hodge, ed., *Handbook of American Indians North of Mexico* (2 vols., Washington: GPO, 1907, 1910; rpt., New York: Pageant, 1959).

Margery H. Krieger

CUTHAND, TEXAS. Cuthand, ten miles south of Clarksville in southern Red River County, was called Enterprise when planters began settlement there about 1850. In the late 1860s E. A. Mauldin established a gristmill and cotton gin at the site, and Samuel T. Arnold opened a general store. A post office was granted to the community in 1867, and its postmaster, Cornelius Crenshaw, named it for Cuthand Creek. The community had a population of 130, two gins, a church, and a school by 1880. Cuthand's population reached 150 in 1890 but declined to sixty by 1896. It was reported as ninety-one in 1914 and as ninety-six from 1920 through 1956. The Cuthand post office was closed in the 1950s, and in 1986 Cuthand reported a population of thirty-two and no businesses. In 1990 its population was 116.

Claudia Hazlewood

CUTHAND CREEK. Cuthand Creek rises near Byrdtown in eastern Lamar County (at 33°41′ N, 95°23′ W) and runs southeast into Red River County, traveling a total of thirty-three miles to its mouth on the Sulphur River, three miles southeast of the Harts Bluff community in southeastern Red River County (at 33°23′ N, 94°54′ W). The stream, which is intermittent in its upper reaches, was named for the Delaware Indian Cuthand, who is said to have lived on its banks. Cuthand Creek traverses flat to gently rolling terrain surfaced by clay and sandy loam that supports grasses and mixed hardwoods and pines.

CUTHBERT, TEXAS. Cuthbert was on Farm Road 1229 some fourteen miles northwest of Colorado City in northwestern Mitchell County. The community began in 1890 when D. T. Bozeman, a teacher in a nearby country school, settled in the area and built a wagonyard and a store. A post office was granted to the community in 1891, with Bozeman's wife, Ellen, as postmistress; the office was named for a family friend, Thomas Cuthbertson. A school was started at the community in 1893 but lasted only four years. Bozeman installed a telephone switchboard in his home in 1904, and his wife served as the operator for local subscribers. In 1907 a new county school district was established in Cuthbert. During the teens and early 1920s Cuthbert grew to include two stores, a church, a blacksmith shop, a gin, a school, and a telephone office. In 1920 the T. and P. Abrams No. 1 oil well, one of the first commercial oil ventures in the Permian Basin,qv was drilled just over a mile north of the town. A post office, two businesses, and a population of twenty-five were reported at the community in 1936, the year that its school was consolidated with that of Colorado City. After World War IIqv the improvement of rural roads in the area led to Cuthbert's decline as it lost its trade to Colorado City. The Cuthbert post office was discontinued about 1960, when the town reported one business and a population of twenty-five. By 1974 only a cemetery and scattered farms remained in the area.

BIBLIOGRAPHY: T. Lindsay Baker, *Ghost Towns of Texas* (Norman: University of Oklahoma Press, 1986). Ed Ellsworth Bartholomew, *The Encyclopedia of Texas Ghost Towns* (Fort Davis, Texas, 1982). *Lore and Legend: A Compilation of Documents Depicting the History of Colorado City and Mitchell County* (Colorado City *Record*, 1976).

Charles G. Davis

CUTOFF MOUNTAIN. Cutoff (Cut Off) Mountain, ten miles east of Hamilton in eastern Hamilton County (at 31°44′ N, 97°57′ W), has an elevation of 1,280 feet above sea level. It is separated by a narrow valley from a range of low peaks to the east; this separation is probably the origin of its name. Soils in the area are clay and clay loams and support oak, juniper, and grasses.

CUTRER, LEWIS WESLEY (1904–1981). Lewis Wesley Cutrer, attorney, civic leader, and mayor of Houston, was born in Osyka, Mississippi, on November 5, 1904, one of four children of Judge Richard Wiltz and Elizabeth (Lewis) Cutrer. He was reared in Magnolia, Mississippi, and received his law degree from the University of Mississippi in 1926. Cutrer moved to Houston in 1928, having been encouraged by his father-in-law, who had been impressed with the vitality of the city while he was on a business trip to Texas. Cutrer made Houston his adopted city for the next fifty-three years.

After about two years of practicing law in two firms, he became an assistant city attorney when Walter Monteith was mayor of Houston (1929–33). Later, when Oscar F. Holcombeqv defeated Monteith in 1934, Cutrer joined with the ousted Monteith to organize a new law firm. They practiced together until 1939. Cutrer served as city attorney from 1941 until 1947 under mayors C. A. (Neal) Pickett and Otis Massey. He supported Mayor Roy Hofheinzqv in his election campaigns in 1952 and 1954. In 1955–56 he served as general counsel for the Houston Independent School District.

Cutrer made his first race for mayor in 1957, when he defeated longtime mayor Oscar Holcombe. He was unopposed in the 1959 election. In 1961 he defeated councilman Louie Welch in a run-off election. In 1963 Cutrer once again ran for mayor against Welch. This time, however, voters failed to return him to office, primarily because of increased residential-water rates brought about by the Lake Livingstonqv project, which he had promoted. During his six-year administration Cutrer secured needed revenue by pushing through a bond issue, solved the controversy over the new charity hospital, and improved Houston's inadequate bus system. He considered his chief accomplishments, however, to be the development of the Lake Livingston project and the construction of Houston Intercontinental Airport.qv Lake Livingston, a man-made lake that was part of the Trinity River Project, solved Houston's industrial water shortage. The city and the Trinity River Authorityqv agreed on terms to permit expansion of water supply to the year 2010. The change encouraged large industries to move to Houston and to expand existing plants in Harris and Chambers counties. Although voters rejected the project during Cutrer's administration, his successor, Louie Welch, won voter approval for the program a year after he replaced Cutrer. In successfully launching the project of acquiring a jet-age airport for Houston, Cutrer laid the groundwork for aviation changes and improvements that were realized later. His own administration bought the site, won new and improved air routes for Houston from the Civil Aeronautics Board, and hired professional planners to start mapping out the new facility. Cutrer also ordered an end to racial segregation in Houston city buildings, lunch counters, and swimming pools during the early 1960s. At the end of his mayoralty he returned to the private practice of law.

He served on the board of trustees of the United States Conference of Mayors and was president of the Texas Municipal League.qv He was a former president of the Texas City Attorneys' Association and president and director of the American Municipal Association. Cutrer was a Mason and a member of the board of stewards of St. Luke's United Methodist Church. He married Catherine Hopson on October 11, 1927, and they had three children. He died in a Houston hospital after a brief illness on May 7, 1981, and was buried in Memorial Oaks Cemetery.

BIBLIOGRAPHY: Houston *Post*, June 15, July 15, 1956, September 10, 1959, May 9, 1981. David G. McComb, *Houston: The Bayou City* (Austin: University of Texas Press, 1969; rev. ed., *Houston: A History*, 1981).

Brooke Tucker

CUT AND SHOOT, TEXAS. Cut and Shoot (Cut 'n Shoot, Cut N Shoot) is six miles east of Conroe and forty miles north of Houston in eastern Montgomery County. It was apparently named after a 1912 community confrontation that almost led to violence. According to the different versions of the story, the dispute was either over the design of a new steeple for the town's only church, the issue of who should be allowed to preach there, or conflicting land claims among church members. A small boy at the scene reportedly declared, "I'm going to cut around the corner and shoot through the bushes in a minute!" The boy's phrase apparently remained in residents' minds and was eventually adopted as the town's name. Population statistics were not reported for the community until the mid-1970s, when the number of residents was fifty. By 1980 the incorporated community reported a population of 809 and had built a new city hall and supported a school and several businesses. Cut and Shoot had a post office by the mid-1980s. The community's population was reported as 903 in 1990.

BIBLIOGRAPHY: William Harley Gandy, A History of Montgomery County, Texas (M.A. thesis, University of Houston, 1952). Robin Navarro Montgomery, *Cut 'n Shoot: The Roy Harris Story* (Austin: Eakin Press, 1984).

Robin N. Montgomery

CUYLER, ROBERT HAMILTON (1908–1944). Robert Hamilton Cuyler, teacher and geologist, was born in Austin, Texas, on May 28, 1908, the son of Henry and Sarah (McBryde) Cuyler. The family moved to North Carolina in 1911 and returned to Austin six years later. Cuyler graduated from high school in Austin at the age of fifteen. He then enrolled at the University of Texas and received his B.A. in 1926, M.A. in 1927, and Ph.d. in 1931. In 1927 he married Esther Arsinoe Solcher and began his teaching career with an instructorship in the UT geology department. By 1935 he had risen to assistant professor, and in 1939 he was promoted to associate professor. As a teacher he was popular for his high standards and the camaraderie he shared with his students. His professional interests were mainly focused on the study of micropaleontology and subsurface geology. In addition to his teaching, Cuyler worked in the oil industry, in association with John F. Camp of San Antonio. In 1940 Cuyler proposed the "Well Logging Project" to the WPA, which for the next two years made "copies of all logs and other subsurface data on wells drilled in Texas." Cuyler was active in several professional associations, including the American Association of Petroleum Geologists and the Geological Society of America; he was a member of the University Presbyterian Church.

Cuyler entered the United States Army Air Force as a first lieutenant in July 1942 and was promoted to captain in 1943. While in the armed forces he served as assistant director of the Ground Training Technical Advisory Unit, Central Instructors School, in Randolph, Texas, where pilots used his handbook, *Maps, Charts, and Aerial Photographs*, in training. Cuyler was killed on a training mission near Blanco on March 13, 1944. He was posthumously granted a Legion of Merit Medal in 1945.

BIBLIOGRAPHY: Austin *American*, March 15, 1944. Fred M. Bullard, "Robert Hamilton Cuyler (1908–1944)," *Bulletin of the American Association of Petroleum Geologists* 28 (August 1944). *Daily Texan*, March 16, 1944, December 21, 1945.

Kris Ercums

CUYLER, TEXAS. Cuyler was a rural school community on the Panhandle and Santa Fe Railway between Panhandle and White Deer in eastern Carson County. The school district was organized sometime between 1907 and 1910 and was named for Cornelius C. Cuyler, one of the New York owners of the White Deer lands. According to former students, classes were held in a one-room frame house until 1913, when a two-room schoolhouse, complete with a horse shed and other outbuildings, was opened there. The school also served for other community purposes, including as a church and Sunday school. After a long succession of teachers, the Cuyler school was consolidated in 1934 with those of Panhandle and White Deer. The building remained on its original site until the early 1960s, when its new owners had it moved to Pampa. Although the community is gone, in the early 1980s the Cuyler Siding grain elevator remained near the railroad track, just off U.S. Highway 60.

BIBLIOGRAPHY: Jo Stewart Randel, ed., *A Time to Purpose: A Chronicle of Carson County* (4 vols., Hereford, Texas: Pioneer, 1966–72).

H. Allen Anderson

CYCLONE, TEXAS. Cyclone, on the Cyclone Branch of Camp Creek and on Farm Road 964, is eleven miles east of Temple in eastern Bell County. The community was founded about 1883 by several Czech families. A post office was opened there in 1886, and, according to popular tradition, the settlers opted to name it Cyclone because when they gathered to decide on its name, one of them quipped that "it would take a cyclone to get this bunch together." In 1890 Cyclone had a general store and seventy-five inhabitants. A gin and mill was operating in the town by 1892, the Cyclone school had forty-two pupils and one teacher in 1903, and the population of the town had grown to a peak of 102 in 1904. The Cyclone post office closed in 1906. The community had four businesses as late as 1948, but by 1964 there were no businesses reported there, and Cyclone had seventy-five inhabitants in scattered dwellings. Its population dropped to fifty-five in 1968 and to forty-five in 1988. The population of Cyclone was still reported as forty-five in 1990.

BIBLIOGRAPHY: Temple *Daily Telegram*, April 17, 1936.

Mark Odintz

CYCLONE BRANCH. Cyclone Branch rises just east of Zabcikville in eastern Bell County (at 31°04′ N, 97°09′ W) and runs south for four miles to its mouth on Camp Creek, about a mile southeast of Ratibor (at 31°00′ N, 97°09′ W). The stream runs through nearly level to sloping terrain surfaced by clayey soils used predominantly for agriculture.

CYPRESS, TEXAS (Franklin County). Cypress is on State Highway 37 some ten miles southwest of Mount Vernon in southwestern Franklin County. It was settled in the 1850s and named for Cypress Creek, which ran through the area before the impoundment of Lake Cypress Springs. In 1896 the community had a one-room, one-teacher school with an enrollment of fifty. During the 1930s Cypress had two businesses, a church, a school, and a cemetery. In 1990 the community had an estimated population of twenty and no rated businesses.

BIBLIOGRAPHY: Billy Hicks and Doris Meek, comps., *Historical Records of Franklin County, Texas* (Mount Vernon, Texas: Franklin County Historical Survey Committee, 1972).

Cecil Harper, Jr.

CYPRESS, TEXAS (Harris County). Cypress is on U.S. Highway 290 twenty miles northwest of Houston in northwestern Harris County. Various Atakapan Indian tribes once inhabited the area, but they quickly died out when white settlers moved into the area. German immigrants began settling along Cypress Creek in the 1840s near where some Anglo-Americans were already ranching. In the 1980s many of the original settler families were remembered through streets and schools that bore their names, like Huffmeister Road and Matzke Elementary. In 1878 a dance hall was built on Huffmeister Road, but it burned a few years later. Settlers soon rebuilt it with the financial support of the Cypress Gun and Rifle Club, this time using corrugated tin. Tin Hall was still a popular dance hall more than a century after its construction. The first Cypress school was built in 1884. The original one-room school later developed into the Cypress–Fairbanks Independent School District, which in the 1980s served the second largest area of the state's school districts, surpassed only by the Houston ISD. With the discovery of oil along the Gulf Coast in 1904, the Cypress area began to develop rapidly. A hot artesian well was discovered by surprised drillers only a mile from Cypress. This find resulted in the Houston Hotwell Sanitarium and Hotel; the well was frequently sought for the healing powers its mineral waters supposedly provided. In the 1980s the site was occupied by the Hot Wells Shooting Range. Rice and dairy farming were the main occupations of Cypress residents until the suburbanization of the area began in the 1950s. Because of the local interest in farming, the Cy-Fair Rodeo has been a favorite community event since its establishment in 1944 by Forrest Arnold. In the mid-1980s the community proper was unincorporated and had fewer than 100 residents, but the greater Cypress area was a suburb of Houston composed of many subdivisions and thousands of inhabitants. In 1990 Cypress reported a population of 260.

BIBLIOGRAPHY: *The Heritage of North Harris County* (n.p: North Harris County Branch, American Association of University Women, 1977). WPA Writers Program, *Houston* (Houston: Anson Jones, 1942).

Mauri Lynn Smith

CYPRESS CREEK (Angelina County). Cypress Creek rises about two miles southeast of Zavalla in southeastern Angelina County (at 31°09 N, 94°23' W) and runs south for 9½ miles to its mouth on the Neches River in Jasper County (at 31°03' N, 94°23' W). The surroundings are typical of the East Texas Piney Woods, with low to moderately rolling terrain surfaced by shallow to deep red sandy clay and sandy loam soils that support mixed pine and hardwood forests.

_____ (Blanco County). Cypress Creek rises in rugged Hill Country[qv] terrain about 3½ miles northwest of Buffalo Peak in northern Blanco County (at 30°25' N, 98°27' W) and runs east for 25½ miles to its mouth on the Pedernales River, slightly less than a mile north of Hammetts Crossing, where Ranch Road 962 crosses the Pedernales in far western Travis County (at 30°21' N, 98°08' W). In addition to cypress, the surrounding loamy clay soils also support Ashe juniper, live oak, mesquite, and grasses. In 1849 a group of Mormon homesteaders settled by the Cypress Mill Springs, a short distance upstream from the site of what became the Cypress Mill community. They used the springs, which rise in the bed of the creek, as a water supply, and built a mill just below the springs to cut cypress lumber. In 1854 William Evans filed the first official land claim on Cypress Creek, and three years later he established a mill on the creek just below the site abandoned by the Mormons. Despite this and subsequent exploitation of the cypress trees along this stretch of the creek, many of the trees still stood in the 1980s, when they were among the oldest and largest trees in Blanco County. One cypress growing at Cypress Mill has been measured as eighty feet high, with a thirty-foot circumference and a nine-foot diameter. It is reckoned to be some 2,500 years old.

BIBLIOGRAPHY: Gunnar Brune, *Springs of Texas*, Vol. 1 (Fort Worth: Branch–Smith, 1981).

_____ (Cass County). Cypress Creek rises along the northern city limits of Queen City in northeastern Cass County (at 33°09' N, 94°09' W) and runs northeast for ten miles to the point where it joins Little Cypress Creek to form Cypress Slough, three miles north of Cass (at 33°14' N, 94°03' W). The stream, which is intermittent in its upper reaches, traverses nearly level to gently rolling terrain surfaced by mostly loamy soils. Originally the area was heavily wooded, with pines and various hardwoods predominating.

_____ (Hays County). Cypress Creek rises about a mile west of Mount Sharp in western Hays County (at 30°06' N, 98°14' W) and runs southeast for 14½ miles to its mouth on the Blanco River in Wimberley (at 29°59' N, 98°06' W). The stream is intermittent in its upper reaches. Live oak and Ashe juniper trees grow in the primarily limestone and chalk soils found along its banks.

_____ (Jasper County). Cypress (Big Cypress) Creek rises just over six miles west of Kirbyville in western Jasper County (at 30°38' N, 94°00' W) and runs southeast for thirty-one miles, crossing into Newton County before reaching its mouth on the Sabine River, 2½ miles north of Deweyville (at 30°20' N, 93°46' W). The stream, which is intermittent in its upper reaches, cuts through the heavily forested areas of southern Jasper and Newton counties. The creek initially traverses an area of gently undulating terrain; closer to its mouth the land is flatter.

_____ (Kerr County). Cypress Creek rises 1½ miles east of State Highway 16 in northeastern Kerr County (at 30°06' N, 99°03' W) and runs southeast for nineteen miles to its mouth on the Guadalupe River, at Comfort in Kendall County (at 29°58' N, 98°54' W). The stream, which is intermittent in its upper reaches, runs through an area characterized by the steep slopes and benches of the Balcones Escarpment, with shallow clay loam soils that support cypress, Ashe juniper, live oak, and mesquite.

_____ (Polk County). Cypress Creek rises in southeastern Polk County about 4½ miles west of the intersection of the Polk, Tyler, and Hardin county lines (at 30°31' N, 94°37' W) and runs southeast through Hardin County for thirty-nine miles to its mouth on Village Creek, three miles east of Kountze (at 30°22' N, 94°15' W). The only major tributary of the stream is Flat Cypress Creek, which rises just over 1½ miles south of the Polk county line (at 30°28' N, 94°34' W) and passes through swampy terrain in its upper reaches before joining Cypress Creek just over 1½ miles south of Honey Island (at 30°22' N, 94°25' W). Cypress Creek traverses heavily wooded areas typical of Hardin County and was used to raft logs to Beaumont lumbermills before the expansion of the railroads in the late 1800s.

_____ (Travis County). Cypress Creek rises four miles east of Jonestown in northern Travis County (at 30°29' N, 97°52' W) and runs south for four miles to its mouth on Lake Travis, eight miles northwest of Austin (at 30°27' N, 97°52' W). It traverses an area of steep slopes and benches, surfaced by shallow clay loams that support juniper, live oak, mesquite, and grasses.

_____ (Waller County). Cypress Creek rises at the point where Snake Creek and Mound Creek join (at 29°57' N, 95°54' W), nine miles southeast of Waller in eastern Waller County, and runs northeast through Waller and Harris counties for forty-nine miles to its mouth on Spring Creek, 3½ miles northwest of Humble (at 30°02' N, 95°19' W). The creek traverses terrain in which stretches of coastal prairie are interspersed with forested areas of pine and oak, with a number of other native Big Thicket[qv] trees growing near the streams. Stephen F. Austin[qv] made the first land grant on Cypress Creek, to John Callihan in 1835. The grant was part of Austin's fifth colony. In 1838 the Republic of Texas[qv] granted much of the land along Cypress Creek in headright certificates to individuals living in Texas at the time that independence was declared. Many of the grantees, however, never settled on their land. Most of the first settlers along the creek were German immigrants who began arriving in the 1840s and 1850s and eventually dominated the northwest part of the county.

BIBLIOGRAPHY: *The Heritage of North Harris County* (n.p: North Harris County Branch, American Association of University Women, 1977).

CYPRESS CREEK, TEXAS. The Cypress Creek community, also known as Cypressville, is ten miles southeast of Kerrville in eastern Kerr County. It was named after a tributary of the Guadalupe River and comprises some fifty farms and ranches along about thirty miles of secondary and tertiary roads between Comfort and Kerrville. One of the first settlements in what is today Kerr County, the picturesque, originally German-speaking community has been the subject of numerous paintings and many historical, literary, and linguistic studies, as well as an archeological study that suggests that the well-watered valley has been inhabited for nearly 10,000 years. The first two German families, Wiedenfeld and Schladoer, arrived in 1852. The pattern in which other families and individuals—Saur, Boerner, Steves, Lich, Hoerner, Zink, Lindner, Voigt, Nagel, Nuernberger, Allerkamp, Schellhase, Holekamp, Karger, Mohrhoff, Reeh, and others—followed typifies an extended process of cluster migration, dispersal, and settlement. Linked by kinship, friendship, and politics and bolstered by Reconstruction-era prosperity, a high birth rate, and unusually low infant mortality, the population grew to over 150 within thirty years. Many came from New Braunfels, Sisterdale, Bettina, and Kerrville, but some came directly from Europe. There were also English, Anglo-American, and Hispanic settlers. Plans to organize a township never materialized; however, a cemetery, shooting club, militia, and school—but no churches—were established early in the history of this liberal, freethinking community. A sawmill-gristmill named Perseverence Mill, constructed by Ernst Altgelt[qv] in 1855, served both the Cypress Creek community and the adjacent town of Comfort. A women's literary club maintained an active membership for over a hundred years. Droughts[qv] of the 1950s and declining agricultural productivity in the 1960s lowered the population to about a hundred. The community grew again in the late 1960s with the completion of Interstate Highway 10, which put San Antonio within commuting distance. The population of the community was estimated at 200 in 1988. Historical markers located on the Sturdy Oak Farm commemorate the cemetery and a nexus of prehistoric sites. German place names abound in the community, including the colorful Hasenwinkel Creek, a small tributary. Among many historic homesteads, the most prominent is the Karger-Keidel ranchhouse (1860s and 1897), which German-Texan architect Albert Keidel inherited and extended between 1945 and 1950, thereby creating the prototype of Hill Country[qv] German vernacular architecture[qv] later popularized in Fredericksburg, Austin, and San Antonio.

BIBLIOGRAPHY: Francis Edward Abernethy, *Built in Texas,* Publications of the Texas Folklore Society 42 (Waco: E-Heart Press, 1979). Francis Edward Abernethy, ed., *T for Texas: A State Full of Folklore,* Publications of the Texas Folklore Society 44 (Dallas: E-Heart, 1982). Glen E. Lich, *The German Texans* (San Antonio: University of Texas Institute of Texan Cultures, 1981). Guido E. Ransleben, *A Hundred Years of Comfort in Texas* (San Antonio: Naylor, 1954; rev. ed. 1974). Vertical Files, Barker Texas History Center, University of Texas at Austin.
Glen E. Lich

CYPRESS MILL, TEXAS. Cypress Mill is on Farm Road 962 thirteen miles northeast of Johnson City in northeastern Blanco County. The area was settled in the late 1860s, when Wilhelm Fuchs and his family built a mill on Cypress Creek. The community that developed there was at first called Fuch's Mill; the name Cypress Mill came into use after a post office opened in 1874. By the mid-1880s the community had grist and saw mills, a cotton gin, and 130 residents. The principal shipments made by area farmers were cotton, cattle, and wool. Cypress Mill reached a peak population of 200 around 1900 but began to decline soon thereafter, and by the early 1940s its population had fallen to thirty. Its population rose to sixty by the late 1940s, and several houses and a business marked the community on county highway maps, but in 1958 the Cypress Mill post office was discontinued. The community's population was reported at seventy-six in 1970 and at fifty-six in 1980 and 1990.

BIBLIOGRAPHY: Blanco County News, *Heritage of Blanco County* (Dallas: Curtis Media Corporation, 1987).
Vivian Elizabeth Smyrl

CZECHS. Czechs are a Slavic people from Bohemia, Moravia, and parts of Silesia. Among the first Czechs to arrive in Texas were the writer Carl Postl[qv] (Charles Sealsfield), who may have visited the Texas-Louisiana borderland as early as 1823; Frederick Lemský,[qv] who arrived in 1836 and played the fife in the Texas band at the battle of San Jacinto; Bohumir Menzl, a Catholic priest who moved to New Braunfels in 1840; and Anthony M. Dignowity.[qv] Rev. Josef Arnošt Bergman,[qv] however, can best be described as the "father" of Czech immigration to Texas. Soon after arriving at the Austin County community of Cat Spring, Bergman began writing to his friends in Europe about the opportunities that awaited future immigrants. His letters stimulated Bohemian and Moravian immigration.

The first immigrants were chiefly poor laborers from the area around Nepomuky and Čermna in northeastern Bohemia. On August 19, 1851, headed by Josef Šilar, they began the long, circuitous journey that took them to Hamburg, Liverpool, New Orleans, and eventually Galveston. Dangerous and unhealthful traveling conditions reduced the group's numbers by half. Two years later, a second group of immigrants from the same geographical area came to Texas. Their leader, Josef L. Lešikar,[qv] who had been influenced by Bergman's letters, had helped organize the first group. In the following years many groups of immigrants came from Moravia, particularly the eastern part of that province. The transatlantic voyage grew less dangerous, and Galveston became established as the preferred port of entry. Cat Spring continued to be the point of dispersal for the immigrants. The Central Texas counties of Austin, Fayette, Lavaca, and Washington had early Czech settlements, and Fayette County in particular became established as the center of Czech population in Texas.

About 700 Czechs had established themselves in Texas by the time of the Civil War.[qv] By 1900 the number of foreign-born Czechs in the state had climbed to 9,204, and by 1910 to 15,074. After this time, however, Czech immigration decreased; foreign-born Czechs numbered 14,781 in 1920, 14,093 in 1930, and 7,700 in 1940, although the number of Czech "foreign white stock" (defined by the United States Bureau of the Census as those who spoke Czech at home during childhood) had climbed to 62,680 by that year.

During the years of greatest immigration before World War I,[qv] the abundance of good, relatively inexpensive farmland in Texas undoubtedly provided the chief motivation for the immigrants, most of whom had been small landowners who saw little chance for economic achievement at home. Political and religious oppression and military conscription in the Austrian Empire also encouraged emigration.

By the twentieth century approximately 250 Czech communities had been settled in Texas, especially in Blackland Prairie areas where farming looked promising. The greatest concentration was found in Lavaca and Fayette counties, though Czech settlement extended into Washington, Burleson, and Brazos counties. North of this strip was a larger belt of Blackland Prairie, where more scattered Czech communities were located in an area running northeast from Williamson County through Bell County and into McLennan County, with smaller offshoots to the north in Hill, Ellis, and Kaufman counties. Most of the other Czech communities were in the Coastal Prairie, with concentrations in Wharton, Fort Bend, Victoria, and a few South Texas counties.

Two basic characteristics of the Czechs in Texas lie at the heart of their social structure: the extremely close-knit family unit and the attitude toward land. The typical Czech farm family was a largely self-contained economic and social unit whose main purpose was to cultivate the land. Farming was a way of life not clearly separated from other life goals and not seen merely as a way of making money. The rural Czech settlements were characterized by such cooperative institutions as the beef club, designed to provide each member family with a supply of fresh beef weekly during the spring and summer. Settlements also often had an egalitarian social structure, a characteristic that helps to explain the Czechs' pronounced enthusiasm for American democratic ideals. Communities became established, and social clubs and organizations began to proliferate, first on a local, then on a state, level. The result was the establishment of fraternal organizations such as the SPJST (Slovanská podporující jednota statu Texas, known in English as the Slavic Benevolent Order of the State of Texas) in 1897; and the KJT (Katolická jednota texaská) in 1888 and the KJZT (Česko-řimská katolická podporující jednota žen texaských) in 1897, Czech Catholic organizations for men and women, respectively. Each of these organizations grew out of a national Czech fraternal order but split away to become a Texas institution.

Perhaps as many as 90 percent of the Czech immigrants were Catholics in their homeland, and the majority of these maintained an allegiance to the Catholic Church[qv] in Texas. Their first church, a small log structure, was built at Ross Prairie in 1859. The most important pioneer Czech priest in Texas was Rev. Josef Chromčík, who arrived in Fayetteville in 1872. A significant minority of the immigrants were Protestants, however. Several independent congregations (the first had been established at Wesley in 1864) were organized into the denomination known as the Unity of the Brethren in 1903, chiefly through the efforts of Rev. Adolf Chlumský. Members of this group considered it to be a continuation of the traditional Czech religious movement of the same name, which had been suppressed by the Austrians in the seventeenth century. The Czechs in Texas also included freethinkers, who openly challenged all religious authority, but in general the freethinking movement among the Czechs was much less significant in Texas than it was in other parts of the United States, especially in the Midwest, where it often dominated Czech-American culture.

Organized education in the Czech language began early in Texas. Bergman was conducting lessons in both Czech and German at Cat Spring as early as 1855. In 1859 Josef Mašík became perhaps the first formal Czech teacher in the United States when he opened his school at Wesley. The Catholic school he built in 1868 in Bluff (later Hostyn), with Terezie Kubálová as the first teacher, may have been the first of its kind in the United States. Czechs were also especially active in establishing schools in Lavaca County late in the nineteenth century. The first school to offer instruction in both Czech and English was established at Praha in 1870. Although instruction in Czech in the public schools declined rapidly in the late nineteenth century, Czech-American clubs and organizations continued to advocate study of the language, particularly at the college and university level. The continued promotion of such study in the late twentieth century is significant, for language is the most important indicator of Czech ethnic identity.

Because the majority of Texas immigrants came from Moravia, the Czech spoken in Texas is largely characterized by Moravian dialects, which vary to some extent from the Bohemian dialects spoken by most Czech-Americans. Czech-language journalism has been very active in the state over the years. Thirty-three newspapers and periodicals have been published. As of 1993 one weekly newspaper, *Našinec*, published at Granger, and one monthly, *Hospodář*, published at West, were still being published entirely in Czech. Other periodicals such as *Vestnik* and the *Brethren Journal* contained sections printed in Czech.

A wealth of oral literature has also been preserved in Texas, including stories, proverbs, and especially folk songs. Singing and dancing were the most popular forms of folk art maintained in Texas, but other forms, such as certain games and elaborate wedding rituals, have been preserved. In addition, certain ethnic foods, such as the pastry *koláč*, have become well known to virtually all Texans.

In spite of the development of such ethnic institutions as the fraternal organizations and the ethnocentric Brethren Church and efforts to preserve the Czech language and folklore, Czech-American leaders have generally argued for full participation in the political and economic life of the state and nation. Community leader Augustin Haidušek,[qv] in the late nineteenth and early twentieth centuries, articulated assimilationist ideals most prominently and influentially.

Friction between Czechs and Anglo-Americans was most pronounced during the Civil War. Many recent immigrants did not fully understand the conflict between North and South, and at the same time they were suspect as foreigners. Most significantly, virtually none of them had any allegiance to the institution of slavery,[qv] not only for moral reasons, but also because the concept of slavery was alien to their system of intensive family farming.

Ethnic pride among Czechs in Texas perhaps reached its height during World War I and immediately afterwards, for it was spurred by popular enthusiasm for the newly founded free state of Czechoslovakia. Such groups as the Czech National Alliance, which identified with the Czech cause in Europe, found support among the Czechs in Texas. As measured by the widespread use of Czech in churches, fraternal organizations, journalism, and books, as well as the preservation of ethnic music and other folk arts, Czech ethnicity remained strong in the state until World War II.[qv] Beginning in the 1960s, as part of a national interest in ethnic awareness, Czech ethnic festivals and celebrations became increasingly popular, although the use of the language continued to decline.

In the mid-1980s a Czech society, Texana Českeho Puvodu (Texans of Czech Ancestry), was formed to organize a celebration of the Texas Sesquicentennial and the role of Czechs in Texas history. Related projects included compiling community histories, pioneer registries, family histories and information on Czech cemeteries, schools, and churches. In the early 1990s the SPJSP had more than 140 lodges statewide and maintained the Czech Heritage Museum in Temple. The Fayetteville Museum also contained many items on Czech history and culture. The Czech Heritage Society had at least twelve chapters in Texas. A number of Czech festivals were held in the state annually, including Czech Fest in Rosenberg, Czhilispiel in Flatonia, Westfest in West, and the National Polka Festival in Ennis. Several radio stations in Central Texas regularly played Czech music. As of the 1990 census, 168,023 people in Texas were of at least partial Czech descent.

BIBLIOGRAPHY: Christian Sisters Union Study Committee, *Unity of the Brethren in Texas, 1855–1966* (Taylor, Texas: Unity of the Brethren, 1970). William Philip Hewitt, The Czechs in Texas: A Study of the Immigration and Development of Czech Ethnicity, 1850–1920 (Ph.D. dissertation, University of Texas at Austin, 1978). Estelle Hudson and Henry R. Maresh, *Czech Pioneers of the Southwest* (Dallas: South-West, 1934). Clinton Machann, ed., *The Czechs in Texas* (College Station: Texas A&M University Department of English, 1979). Clinton Machann and James W. Mendl, *Krásná Amerika: A Study of the Texas Czechs, 1851–1939* (Austin: Eakin Press, 1983).

Clinton Machann

D

DABBS, ELLEN LAWSON (1853–?). Ellen Lawson Dabbs, physician, early women's-rights activist, and reform writer, the daughter of Col. and Mrs. Henry M. Lawson, was born in Rusk County on April 25, 1853. She attended school in Rusk and Upshur counties. After a brief teaching stint she enrolled in Furlow Masonic College in Americus, Georgia, from which she graduated first in her class. She returned to Texas and taught school for five years before meeting J. W. Dabbs, a merchant from Sulphur Springs. Dabbs, a widower, had four children from his first marriage; the marriage of J. W. Dabbs and Ellen Lawson produced five more children. After the birth of her children Mrs. Dabbs attended the College of Physicians and Surgeons in Keokuk, Iowa, and a school of midwifery in St. Louis, Missouri.

In 1890 she returned to Sulphur Springs, where she practiced medicine and acquired an interest in a newspaper. In 1891 she moved to Fort Worth, where she wrote in support of various reforms. She eventually became a writer for the *National Economist,* a National Farmers' Alliance newspaper based in Washington, D.C., and in 1892 she served as a delegate from Texas to the National Farmers' Alliance and Industrial Union convention at St. Louis. That same year she was also a delegate to the state Woman's Christian Temperance Union[qv] convention and presided as the state chairman of the Woman's Southern Council.

Ellen Dabbs helped organize the state's first suffrage society, the Texas Equal Rights Association,[qv] and served in 1893 as corresponding secretary and a member of the publication committee. The following year she helped found a local auxiliary in Fort Worth and was elected corresponding secretary. She addressed the Dallas chapter on the need for the moral influence of women in politics and legislation and defended women's rights in the Dallas *Morning News.*[qv] In 1893 she organized the Texas Woman's Council (later the State Council of Women of Texas) at the State Fair of Texas[qv] in Dallas, for the purpose of bringing women's organizations concerned with philanthropy, social reform, education, literature, and the fine arts to an increased awareness of one another's activities. During her second term as president the council became a state affiliate of the National Council of Women, and Mrs. Dabbs was the presiding officer in 1895 when the Texas Woman's Council laid the cornerstone for a permanent women's building on the state fairgrounds in Dallas.

BIBLIOGRAPHY: Texas Equal Suffrage Association Scrapbook, Austin History Center. Melissa Gilbert Wiedenfeld, Women in the Texas Farmers' Alliance (M.A. thesis, Texas Tech University, 1983). Frances E. Willard and Mary A. Livermore, eds., *American Women* (2 vols., New York: Mast, Crowell, and Kirkpatrick, 1897; rpt., Detroit: Gale Research, 1973–). *Melissa G. Wiedenfeld*

DABNEY, ROBERT LEWIS (1820–1898). Robert Lewis Dabney, Presbyterian theologian, teacher, and author, was born on March 5, 1820, in Louisa County, Virginia, the son of Charles and Elizabeth R. (Price) Dabney, Jr. After private study of Greek, Latin, and mathematics, he attended Hampden-Sydney College and the University of Virginia, where he received an M.A. degree in June 1842. He spent two years managing his mother's farm and teaching his younger brother and sisters before he went to Union Theological Seminary at Hampden-Sydney in November 1844. He graduated in theology in May 1846 and in 1846–47 did missionary work in his home county. He was pastor at Tinkling Spring, Augusta County, from July 1847 until August 1853. Dabney married Margaret Lavinia Morrison on March 28, 1848, and they became the parents of three sons, two of whom died of diphtheria in 1853. In 1853 Dabney was awarded an honorary D.D. degree and elected to the chair of ecclesiastical history and polity at the seminary. He also preached regularly at the local Presbyterian church and was professor of mental and moral philosophy at Hampden-Sydney College. In 1859 he was transferred to the chair of systematic and polemic theology, a position he held until 1883.

Although he initially opposed secession,[qv] Dabney came to believe that the North was wicked and that the South had Christian motives in the war. He served the Confederate Army as chaplain in 1861 and then as chief of staff for Thomas J. (Stonewall) Jackson in 1862. After an illness forced him out of the service he continued his labors for the seminary and preached and wrote voluminously. He spent considerable time after the war exploring the possibilities of transplanting the Old South to Australia or Brazil. He never abandoned his belief that the South's cause had been right and that slavery[qv] was sanctioned by scripture. He remained bitter about the race issue and opposed both black education and black suffrage. Ever eager to migrate to the West, he acted on the advice of his physician and took the appointment to the chair of mental and moral philosophy at the University of Texas in 1883.

In 1884 Dabney and R. K. Smoot, Presbyterian pastor at Austin, opened the Austin School of Theology, to which they gave their services without compensation. Although Dabney became totally blind in 1890 and retired from the university faculty in 1894, he continued to live an active life. He delivered courses of lectures at Louisville Theological Seminary, Davidson College, and Columbia Theological Seminary and wrote prolifically both privately and for publication. Many of his articles were printed in the *Presbyterian Quarterly.* Among his books were *Life and Campaigns of Lieut-Gen. Thomas J. Jackson* (1866), *Defense of Virginia* (1867), and *Sensualistic Philosophy of the Nineteenth Century* (1887). Dabney and his wife moved to Victoria in 1895 to live with their son. Dabney died there on January 3, 1898, and was buried at the Union Theological Seminary cemetery in Richmond, Virginia.

BIBLIOGRAPHY: *Dictionary of American Biography.* Thomas Carey Johnson, *The Life and Letters of Robert Lewis Dabney* (Richmond, Virginia: Presbyterian Committee of Publication, 1903). David Henry Overy, Robert Lewis Dabney: Apostle of the Old South (Ph.D. dissertation, University of Wisconsin, 1967). *Daniel A. Penick*

DABNEY, TEXAS. Dabney, also known as Whitesmine, was a mining community at the southern end of Farm Road 1022, six miles south of Cline in far southwestern Uvalde County. An asphalt-mining operation was opened by the Lathe Carbon Company at the site in 1888.

In 1891 J. G. Smyth purchased 20,000 acres in southwestern Uvalde County that encompassed a portion of the Nueces River and the Lathe Company mining site. In 1906 thirty-one students attended the one-teacher Dabney school. The mine was closed in 1900 and reopened sometime after 1913, most probably in 1923, by a former employee of the Uvalde Rock Asphalt Company, R. L. White, who, after having left his former employers in 1918, returned for a source of raw limestone asphalt to supply his San Antonio–based Alamo Paving Company. White was married to Smyth's daughter Ethel and controlled a small interest in the property. He concluded an agreement with the remainder of the Smyth Ranch owners on September 14, 1923, that permitted his White's Uvalde Mines Company to mine and remove rock asphalt. Beginning in 1923 the Asphalt Belt Railroad transported the raw material to a siding, called Whites, on the San Antonio, Uvalde and Gulf Railroad. By 1928 the Whites Mine Corporation had developed a new process to manufacture on site a cold-mix paving material; the company began to market the new product during the Great Depression.qv

In 1935 White brought the mine to full production. In 1941 he took advantage of a proviso in the contract permitting him to pay a lump sum in order to cancel the lease portion of the agreement and permit the removal of 56,000 additional tons of asphalt without further compensation. A legal dispute over the removal of the additional asphalt reached the Texas Supreme Court in 1947, and the court exacted a sizable judgment against White and White's Uvalde Mines. By 1946 Dabney had been abandoned except for one dwelling, although a mining operation three miles southeast appears to have been in full operation.

The population of Dabney in 1966 was estimated at twenty-five. In the early 1970s a shortage of available railroad cars forced White's mine operators to turn to trucks for their transportation needs. In 1988 Dabney had an estimated population of thirty, two mines, and one business near the railroad depot. In 1990 the Vulcan Materials Company, based in San Antonio, operated the mines at Dabney. According to the plant manager in Dabney there were no longer any people living at the site; the seventy employees were transported by a company bus each day from their homes in Uvalde and Sabinal.

BIBLIOGRAPHY: *A Proud Heritage: A History of Uvalde County* (Uvalde, Texas: El Progreso Club, 1975). Texas Supreme Court, *Texas Reports: Cases Adjudged in the Supreme Court* (Austin: Gammel-Statesman, 1903–63).
Ruben E. Ochoa

DACOSTA, TEXAS. DaCosta, on U.S. Highway 87 ten miles from Victoria in southeastern Victoria County, was established in 1860 when the San Antonio and Mexican Gulf Railway completed its route from Victoria to Port Lavaca. The railroad station was named for Alfred DaCosta, a Morgan Linesqv agent and ship captain at Indianola. The railroad was destroyed during the Civil Warqv but was rebuilt, and DaCosta became a center of rural activity. A post office was established there in 1903, and a local social center and dance hall, which also housed the Guadalupe Sons of Herman Lodge, was built. Around 1900 the town was the site of a rice-farming enterprise in which 3,000 acres were put under cultivation. The venture, undertaken by a group of New Yorkers, was unsuccessful. The next year a Japanese group assumed sponsorship but was similarly unfortunate. Both projects failed because the rice fields did not have sufficient drainage in wet years. The community did, however, develop into an important center for cotton ginning, a business dating locally to the early 1900s. In 1963 DaCosta was the only community in Victoria County with two gins, which averaged about one-fifth of the county's annual ginning enterprise. Both gins were still operating in the mid-1980s. Though the community's post office was discontinued in the early 1950s, in 1986 the DaCosta Hall remained one of the most popular social and dance halls in the county. The DaCosta common school joined the Bloomington Independent School District in 1961. DaCosta's population, which was reported as about 100 from the 1920s to 1960, fell to 85 over the next decade and in 1990 was 89.

BIBLIOGRAPHY: Victoria *Advocate*, Progress Edition, March 10, 1963.
Craig H. Roell

DACUS, TEXAS. Dacus is at the junction of Farm Road 1486 and the Burlington Northern Railroad, a half mile from Lake Creek and twenty-two miles northwest of Conroe in the northwestern corner of Montgomery County. The town was named for J. B. Dacus, an early settler. French explorer René Robert Cavelier, Sieur de La Salleqv camped in the area on February 15 and 16, 1687. He found an Indian village of about forty huts in the vicinity. One of the first permanent white settlers in the area was Francis A. B. Wheeler, who established a homestead on the site around 1823. In order to encourage settlement, Wheeler offered small tracts of free land to families who met with his approval. A post office was established at the community in 1889 and remained in operation until around 1955. In its early days it was known as a farmers' post office and received mail semiweekly. Edwin E. A. Goodin was the postmaster. Around 1907 the Trinity and Brazos Valley Railway reached Dacus. By 1915 the community had two general stores, two stock breeders, a stock dealer, a hotel, a blacksmith, and a population of 100. By 1946 the railroad had been taken over by the Burlington Northern and Rock Island; that year Dacus had a few dwellings, a church, a business, and the railroad station. By 1962 the Chicago, Rock Island and Pacific had taken over the railroad line, and Dacus had a church and scattered dwellings. Its population was 161 in 1973, the last year for which statistics were available. In 1990 the community comprised a general store, a Baptist church, and a few houses.

BIBLIOGRAPHY: Robin Navarro Montgomery, *The History of Montgomery County* (Austin: Jenkins, 1975).
Will Branch

DADS CORNER, TEXAS. Dads (Dad's) Corner, twelve miles northwest of Archer City in north central Archer County, was established during the oil boom of the early 1920s and was named for oilman C. M. "Dad" Joiner.qv The community was never large and declined with the slowing of the boom. By the mid-1930s it reported one rated business and a population of fifty; residents numbered fifty for several decades, although by the mid-1950s no businesses were reported at the community. The population of Dads Corner had declined to twenty by the mid-1960s, when population statistics were last available. The 1984 county highway map showed one business at Dads Corner.

BIBLIOGRAPHY: Leta Byrne Gage, Archer County through Ninety-Eight Years (M.A. thesis, East Texas State College, 1957). Winnie D. Nance, A History of Archer County (M.A. thesis, University of Texas, 1927).
Brian Hart

DAFFAN, KATIE LITTY (1874–1951). Katie Litty (Miss Katie) Daffan, author, teacher, journalist, and clubwoman, was born on July 29, 1874, in Brenham, Texas, daughter of Laurence A. and Mollie (Day) Daffan. She attended public schools in Denison and Corsicana, graduated from Hollins Institute in Virginia, and was a special history student at the universities of Texas and Chicago. She taught elementary school in Ennis and San Augustine and high school history in Houston, served as principal of a girls' school in Dallas, and taught summer sessions in the normal schools of East Texas. She was elected first vice president of the Texas State Teachers Associationqv and was named to the State Text-Book Board by Governor T. M. Campbell.qv When she was named superintendent of the Confederate Woman's Homeqv in Austin in 1911, she became the first woman in Texas appointed to head a state institution; she remained superintendent until her resignation in 1918.

Miss Katie was literary editor for the Houston *Chronicle*qv from

1921 to 1928 and feature columnist for the Ennis *Daily News* from 1936 to 1950. She also wrote or edited *New Orleans* (1906), *Woman in History* (1908), *My Father as I Remember Him* (1908), *The Woman on Pine Springs Road* (1910), *As Thinketh a Woman* (poems, 1911), *Texas Hero Stories* (1912), *History of the United States* (1924), and *Texas Heros* (1924), which was adopted as a textbook for third, fourth, and fifth grade students in Texas.

She served five terms as president of the Texas Division of the United Daughters of the Confederacy,qv was third vice president general of the UDC, and was a life member of its executive board. In addition, she served as president of the Texas Woman's Press Association (1908–09), state historian of the Daughters of the American Revolutionqv (1909–10), state secretary to the General Federation of Women's Clubs (1909), and first vice president of the Texas State Historical Associationqv (1912, 1913, 1914); she was a member of the Daughters of the Republic of Texas,qv a charter member of Houston Pen Women, a board member of the Houston Public Libraryqv (1904–29) and of the Houston Board of Recreation (1922–29), and first president of the Houston Storyteller's Club (1922–29).

Miss Katie was twice appointed sponsor for Texas to the General Confederate reunions and in May 1913 was appointed sponsor for the South to the General Confederate Reunion held in Chattanooga, Tennessee—the highest social honor conferred upon a woman of the South. The Katie Daffan Chapter of the United Daughters of the Confederacy at Denton was named in her honor. She was also secretary for life of Hood's Texas Brigade,qv in which her father had served.

Although reared a Baptist, she was converted to Catholicism in 1938. Throughout her life she was an ardent Democrat and in her last writing still spoke strongly in favor of states' rights and the "Brave Cause of the South." She was married briefly in 1897 to Mann Trice, then assistant attorney general for the state of Texas. They had no children. Katie Daffan died in Ennis on May 22, 1951, after being hit by a car near her home.

BIBLIOGRAPHY: Virginia Duff, "In Memory of Miss Katie Daffan," Texas House of Representatives *Journal* (52d leg., reg. sess., 1951). *Who's Who in America*, 1946. Andrea Ivie Webb

DAFFAN, LAWRENCE AYLETT (1845–1907). Lawrence Daffan, Texas railroad official and Confederate soldier, was born on April 30, 1845, in Conecuh County, Alabama, to John Warren and Mary Julia (Jones) Daffan. The family moved to Montgomery, Texas, in 1849. Daffan first worked carrying the United States mail between Montgomery and Washington-on-the-Brazos in 1859 and 1860. In 1861 he enlisted in the Confederate Army as a private and was sent to Virginia, where he served under Capt. William H. Hutcheson as a member of Company G, Fourth Texas Regiment, Hood's Texas Brigade.qv He fought for the Confederacy in numerous engagements, including the battles of Second Bull Run and Antietam. He was captured at Lenore Station, Tennessee, on November 19, 1863, and was confined at Rock Island Prison, Rock Island, Illinois, until June 19, 1865. He reached his home in Navasota on July 6, 1865.

In October 1865 Daffan entered the service of the Houston and Texas Central Railway. He served first as brakeman, then advanced to passenger conductor, trainmaster, superintendent of the Second Division, and finally general agent of transportation, the position he held at the time of his death. Daffan was a lifelong Democrat and Baptist. He was also a member of the Ku Klux Klan,qv a Knight Templar, a Shriner, and a charter member of the Houston Elks Lodge. He married Mollie A. Day of Brenham on January 23, 1872, and they had six children, including Katie L. Daffan.qv Daffan died at his home in Ennis on January 28, 1907, and is buried there in Myrtle Cemetery.

BIBLIOGRAPHY: Katie Daffan, *My Father As I Remember Him* (Houston: Gray and Dillaye, 1907?). Andrea Ivie Webb

DAFFAN, TEXAS. Daffan, seven miles northeast of Austin and just south of U.S. Highway 290 in eastern Travis County, served in the 1930s and 1940s as a station on the Texas and New Orleans Railroad. The community's population was reported as twenty from the 1930s through the 1960s. The 1985 county highway map identified Daffan, but showed no buildings at its site. Vivian Elizabeth Smyrl

DAGGER POINT. Dagger Point is a landing on the western shore of San Antonio Bay in the northern tip of the Aransas National Wildlife Refugeqv in southwestern Calhoun County just east of the Aransas-Calhoun county line. In 1952 a triangulation station and a single dwelling were the only structures on the sand mounds. By 1985 the station was gone.

DAGGETT, EPHRAIM M. (1810–1883). Ephraim M. Daggett, merchant, legislator, and early promoter of Fort Worth, was born in Upper Canada on June 3, 1810. The family moved to Indiana in 1820 and in 1830 settled in Chicago, where in 1833 Daggett became an Indian trader. In April 1840 the Daggetts moved to Shelby County, Texas, where they participated as Regulators in the Regulator-Moderator War.qv At the beginning of the Mexican Warqv Daggett joined Col. George T. Wood'sqv regiment as a second lieutenant, but he was soon promoted to captain and attached to Col. John C. (Jack) Hays'sqv rangers.

At the close of the war Daggett returned to Shelby County, which he represented in the state legislatures of 1851 and 1853. He became interested in West Texas, however, after a trip there in 1849, and in 1854 he settled in Tarrant County. He opened a store in Fort Worth and worked for Fort Worth to replace Birdville as county seat. When the Texas and Pacific Railway planned its line through Fort Worth, Daggett donated ninety-six acres for a depot and tracks. After the arrival of the railroad Daggett devoted most of his time to the promotion of Fort Worth. In 1878 he ran unsuccessfully for Congress on the Greenback ticket. He was twice married. He and his first wife, the former Pheniba Strauss, had one son. His second wife was the former Caroline Norris Adams. Daggett died in Fort Worth on April 19, 1883.

BIBLIOGRAPHY: Stanley Farrington, "A Texas Giant," *Junior Historian*, March 1945. William S. Speer and John H. Brown, eds., *Encyclopedia of the New West* (Marshall, Texas: United States Biographical Publishing, 1881; rpt., Easley, South Carolina: Southern Historical Press, 1978). John Henry Brown, *Indian Wars and Pioneers of Texas* (Austin: Daniell, 1880; reprod., Easley, South Carolina: Southern Historical Press, 1978). Carolyn Hyman

DAHL, GEORGE LEIGHTON (1894–1987). George L. Dahl, architect, was born in Minneapolis, Minnesota, on May 11, 1894, the son of Norwegian immigrants Olaf G. and Laura (Olsen) Dahl. He studied architecture at the University of Minnesota and received his bachelor's degree in 1920. After earning a master's degree from Harvard in 1923, he spent two years in Rome as a fellow at the American Academy. He returned to the United States in 1925 and worked briefly for architecture firms in New York and Los Angeles before moving to Dallas in 1926 to work for Herbert M. Greene'sqv company, a large firm that at the time was constructing a number of buildings for the University of Texas. Dahl eventually became a partner in the firm and designed two dozen buildings for the university over the next two decades. During the 1920s he also designed a number of large commercial buildings for clients in Dallas, including the Volk Brothers Building, the Titche-Goettinger Company Building, and the Neiman-Marcusqv store. In contrast to contemporaries O'Neil Ford and Howard R. Meyer,qqv who developed their own unique styles, Dahl, as critic David Dillon noted, remained a stylistic chameleon who produced works to suit the needs and tastes of his clients. His early works ranged from Renaissance Revival to Second Empire and Spanish Colonial. Dahl is best known for his work on the 1936 Texas Centennialqv Exposition at

The Hall of State lit up for the Texas Centennial Exposition, Dallas, 1936. From the collections of the Dallas Historical Society. Dallas architect George Dahl oversaw planning and construction of twenty-six Art Deco buildings for the Texas Centennial Exposition, which were finished in just nine months.

Fair Park in Dallas, a complex of twenty-six Art Deco–style buildings designed by ten firms. He oversaw the planning and construction of the entire fair, which was completed in the astonishingly brief period of only nine months. The complex is now recognized as one of the best preserved assemblages of depression-era architecture and in 1986 was designated a national historic landmark.

Dahl was among the first Texas architects to have a nationwide practice and was among the pioneers in fast-track design, which allowed for actual construction to begin even before the design was finished. He is also credited with designing the nation's first drive-through bank, the Hillcrest State Bank in University Park (1938). By the time he retired in 1973, Dahl's firm had produced about 3,000 projects—over 100 of them in Texas—with an estimated value of over $2 billion. Among his best-known later works in Texas are the Dallas Methodist Hospital, Owen Art Center at Southern Methodist University, the Dallas *Morning News*[qv] building, and the LTV Aerospace Center. His work also included thirty-two stores for Sears, Roebuck and Company and fifteen prisons for the Texas Department of Corrections (*see* PRISON SYSTEM). Dahl was married twice—in 1921 to Lillie E. Olsen, with whom he had one daughter, and in 1978 to Joan Renfro. He was a Presbyterian, president of the Dallas Rotary Club (1936–37), director and a leading patron of the Dallas Opera for many years, a member of the Dallas City Advisory Committee from 1943 to 1945, and a member of the Greater Dallas Planning Council from 1948 to 1956. He contributed articles to *Architectural Forum*, *American Architect*, and other professional journals and was the author of *Portals, Doorways and Windows of France* (1925). Dahl died of cancer on July 18, 1987, at the age of ninety-three at his home in Dallas.

BIBLIOGRAPHY: Sam Hanna Acheson, Herbert P. Gambrell, Mary Carter Toomey, and Alex M. Acheson, Jr., *Texian Who's Who*, Vol. 1 (Dallas: Texian Press, 1937). *American Architects Directory*. Architectural Drawings Collection, Architecture and Planning Library, University of Texas at Austin. David Dillon, *Dallas Architecture, 1936–1986* (Austin: Texas Monthly Press, 1985). Kenneth B. Ragsdale, *The Year America Discovered Texas—Centennial '36* (College Station: Texas A&M University Press, 1987). *Texas Architect*, November–December 1989.

Christopher Long

DAILEYVILLE, TEXAS. Daileyville, on Escondido Creek eight miles south of Helena in central Karnes County, was founded by the brothers C. P. and David Dailey in 1869. There the road from Wofford's Crossing on the San Antonio River forked, one branch going to Beeville and the other following the west side of the San Antonio River to Goliad. A post office was established at the fork on July 5, 1870. The same year Professor Shives of Goliad built a store and named it Shives Store. For a short while it was operated by J. A. Addington, who called the place Addingtonville. But the name Daileyville prevailed, and by 1884 the community had a population of fifty served by a gristmill and cotton gin. That same year, however, the local post office was discontinued, and its records were moved to Helena. On September 6, 1886, the Butler-Elder feud erupted at the Daileyville store; it eventually resulted in the death of a Karnes County sheriff and several others. The Dailey brothers operated their store there for another year, then moved to Kenedy Junction in 1887.

BIBLIOGRAPHY: Robert H. Thonhoff, History of Karnes County (M.A. thesis, Southwest Texas State College, 1963).

Robert H. Thonhoff

DAILY, RAY KARCHMER (1891–1975). Ray Karchmer Daily, eye surgeon and author, was born in Vilnius, Lithuania, in 1891 and arrived in the United States at age fourteen with her parents, Anna and Kalman Karchmer, who took the family to Denison, Texas. From high school in Denison she went directly to the University of Texas Medical Branch in Galveston, where she became one of the first women to graduate from a Texas medical school. She interned at Women's Hospital in Philadelphia because that was the only hospital in the country with a dormitory for women. In 1914 she returned to Houston to marry Louis Daily, M.D., whom she had met in medical school.

The doctors formed a joint practice, and each took turns maintaining the practice while the other studied in Europe. In 1923–24 Ray remained in Vienna, Austria, to specialize in ophthalmology. She returned to Houston to work as a clinician and became an eminent surgeon specializing in cataract removal. She served on the Houston school board for many years, was elected president of it twice, and helped in founding the University of Houston. She worked as an ophthalmologist at Memorial and Jefferson Davis hospitals and as a clinical professor of ophthalmology at Baylor University College of Medicine. She became the first woman president of the medical staff at Memorial Hospital in Houston and in the 1950s served as president of the medical staff of Jefferson Davis Hospital. She produced films on surgical procedures that Harvard and other medical schools used, and wrote nine books, some in collaboration with her husband and their son, Dr. Louis Daily, Jr.

She served as vice president of the American Academy of Ophthalmology and Otolaryngology. On June 10, 1970, she received from the University of Texas Medical Branch the Ashbel Smith[qv] Distinguished Alumni Award. Dr. Ray Daily practiced until age eighty-three. She died on November 28, 1975, in Houston.

BIBLIOGRAPHY: Houston *Chronicle*, May 31, 1970. Natalie Ornish, *Pioneer Jewish Texans* (Dallas: Texas Heritage, 1989).

Natalie Ornish

DAILY TEXAN. The *Daily Texan*, student newspaper of the University of Texas at Austin, began as a weekly in 1900, when two privately owned campus newspapers, the *Calendar* and the *Ranger*, were joined to form the *Texan*, with Frederick Garland (Fritz) Lanham[qv] as the first editor. In 1904 the student assembly took charge of operating the paper, and by 1907 the *Texan* was published twice a week. A student referendum in 1913 made the *Texan* a daily newspaper, and its first issue as such appeared on September 24, 1913; on that date the *Daily Texan* became, according to its editors, the first college daily in the South. The student body elected an editor and a managing editor annually, and the paper supported itself by selling advertisements and by collecting part of an optional fee charged by the Students' Association in support of student government and publications. A student-faculty conference in 1921 led to the formation of Texas Student Publications, Incorporated, a nonprofit organization that was to issue, publish, and distribute the *Daily Texan*, the *Longhorn Magazine*, the *Cactus* (yearbook), and such other publications that might in the future be authorized. The *Daily Texan* fostered both the university song "The Eyes of Texas"[qv] and the name "Longhorns" for the university football team. Over the years the newspaper, with the aid of national news-gathering sources, provided the university community with coverage of local, state, national, and international news. By 1925 the newspaper was eight pages long and had a circulation of 5,500. The *Texan* occasionally took editorial stands that were unpopular in many areas of the state, as well as with some legislators, university administrators, and regents. The resulting controversies have led to a colorful history.

The original TSP charter provided for student domination of its board of directors and guaranteed that the student editors of the various publications would play an important role in policy-making. The charter contained two clauses, however, that would later lead to controversy: the first, included by law, limited the corporation to a fifty-year charter, leaving it vulnerable to renewal difficulties; the other clause provided that in the event of the corporation's dissolution, its assets would revert to the University of Texas Board of Regents (see UNIVERSITY OF TEXAS SYSTEM). During the 1930s the charter for TSP was revised several times, in effect giving the board of regents the authority to approve changes in the charter and subjecting all actions taken by the TSP board of directors to the approval of the regents. The *Texan* saw relatively little controversy in the 1940s, primarily because everyone was so much in favor of the war effort. In the mid-1950s, however, the paper's editor, Willie Morris, took outspoken stands against segregation and a Congressional bill to lower taxes on the oil and gas industries. His response to censorship was to print blank space where a controversial editorial was to have run or to substitute a conspicuously innocuous piece with a title like "Let's Water the Pansies." In the summer of 1956, after Morris's departure on a Rhodes Scholarship, the regents changed the student editor seats on the TSP board to nonvoting positions. Then in 1963 the regents changed the editorship of the *Texan* from an elected to an appointed position; in the face of strong opposition from the students, however, the decision was reversed the next year. In the late 1960s and early 1970s the *Texan* sometimes published controversial editorials, including ones critical of the country's involvement in Vietnam and also of university regent Frank C. Erwin.[qv] The battle that developed between Erwin and the *Texan* received state and national coverage, including an account in the New York *Times*. When the TSP charter came up for renewal in 1971, negotiations between the board of regents and the board of TSP eventually led to a compromise in which the assets of TSP (which were estimated by some to be as high as $600,000) became the property of the university. Student publications would continue to be published as an auxiliary enterprise of the university. In the 1980s and 1990s the editorship of the *Texan* remained a position elected by the student body; however, the editor's control of the paper was limited to the editorial page, while the rest of the paper was the responsibility of the managing editor, an appointed position.

The *Daily Texan* has been a consistent standout among college newspapers in the United States and has won several prestigious awards, including the Pacemaker Award from the Associated Collegiate Press in 1965, 1969, 1971, and 1985 and the Gold Crown Award from Columbia Scholastic Press in 1984, 1989, and 1990. Many of its editors and other staff members have gone on to become widely respected writers and news professionals, among them author Willie Morris; journalists Bill Moyers, Walter Cronkite, Larry Price, and Dan Malone; producer Mary Walsh; news executives Karen Elliott House, Lisa Beyer, and Deborah Howell; editors Mark Morrison and John Reitz; and cartoonists Sam Hurt and Berke Breathed. In the early 1990s the *Texan* had a circulation of 32,000 in the fall and spring and 21,000 during the summer sessions. It employed 250 to 300 persons during the fall and spring semesters, and 125 to 150 persons in the summer.

BIBLIOGRAPHY: Mike Godwin, "The *Daily Texan* Does Not Belong to You (but it used to)," *Utmost,* October 1987. Vertical Files, Barker Texas History Center, University of Texas at Austin.

DAINGERFIELD, WILLIAM HENRY (1808–1878). William Henry Daingerfield, legislator, diplomat, and early San Antonio mayor, was born in 1808 at Alexandria, Virginia. He attended the University of Virginia in 1828–29, farmed in Maryland, and later practiced law. In October 1837, he moved to San Antonio, Texas, where he was elected mayor in 1838. He became chief justice of Bexar County the same year and in 1839 was appointed commissary of purchases of the Army of the Republic of Texas.qv He was senator from Bexar County in the Fifth and Sixth congresses of Texas, 1840–42, but resigned on February 5, 1842, to become secretary of the treasury. In February 1844, he became Texas chargé d'affaires in the Netherlands, where he remained until annexation.qv His letter book kept on missions to the Netherlands, Belgium, and the Hanse towns is in the Texas State Archives.qv In 1860 Daingerfield moved to the District of Columbia and opened a law office near Washington. He died in September 1878 at his residence in Prince George County, Maryland.

BIBLIOGRAPHY: Biographies of Leading Texans (MS, Texas State Archives, Austin). Galveston *Daily News,* October 2, 1878. Galveston *News,* September 10, 1878. Galveston *National Intelligencer,* August 7, 1857. New Orleans *Daily Picayune,* November 7, 1843. Texas House of Representatives, *Biographical Directory of the Texan Conventions and Congresses, 1832–1845* (Austin: Book Exchange, 1941).

Redding S. Sugg, Jr.

DAINGERFIELD, TEXAS. Daingerfield, the county seat of Morris County, is on the Louisiana and Arkansas Railroad at the intersection of State highways 11 and 49 and U.S. Highway 259, in the south central part of the county. It is claimed that the first Europeans to visit the area camped by a spring near what is now the center of town around 1740. In 1830 Capt. London Daingerfield and a band of about 100 men fought a bloody battle with Indians near the spring. Daingerfield was killed, and the town that began to grow up in the area in the early 1840s was named in his honor. S. R. Shaddick started the first school in 1840. The town was named county seat of Paschal County, a judicial county in the Republic of Texas, and courts for the southern division of Red River County were held there in 1844. A post office was opened in 1846. William A. McClintock, who was traveling through the area in 1846, noted in his diary that the town consisted of "three or four cabins scarce fit for pigsties." By the early 1850s the town began to grow. Sylvia Academy, a private school for girls, opened around 1850, and in 1852 the Marshall Presbytery of the Cumberland Presbyterian Church founded Chapel Hill College, which continued to operate until 1870.

More rapid development began after the Civil War.qv In 1877 Titus County, which had originally included Daingerfield and the surrounding area, was divided, and Daingerfield became the county seat of the new Morris County. The same year the Louisiana, Arkansas and Texas track was laid a half mile southeast of the town. After a large fire destroyed most of the town in 1879, the majority of the businesses moved to the railhead, which is the present site of the town.

By 1904 the population in Daingerfield had grown to 699, and the town's industries included a chair factory, a tannery, a hat factory, a cotton gin, and a flour mill. In 1931 the town reported a population of 818 and thirty-eight businesses. The greatest growth, however, came during and after World War IIqv with the opening of the Lone Star Steel Company and the United States Navy Bureau of Ordnance Aerophysics Laboratory. Between 1945 and 1961 the population tripled, from 1,032 to 3,133. Between the early 1960s and the late 1980s it remained fairly constant at approximately 3,000. The town's principal employers in 1980 included the Lone Star Steel Company, a garment factory, a chemical factory, and a roofing-products factory. In 1985 the Daingerfield Independent School District comprised three elementary schools, a junior high school, and a high school, with a total enrollment of 2,250. Boating, swimming, camping, and hunting facilities are available at Daingerfield State Recreation Area, Ellison Creek Reservoir, and Lake O' the Pines; qqv Monticello, Welsh, Texarkana, and Caddo lakes are all located within twenty-five miles of Daingerfield. In 1990 the population was 2,572.

BIBLIOGRAPHY: Morris County Scrapbook, Barker Texas History Center, University of Texas at Austin. Thomas C. Minter, A History of Morris County (M.A. thesis, East Texas State Teachers' College, 1952).

Terrell W. Connor, Jr.

DAINGERFIELD STATE RECREATION AREA. Daingerfield State Recreation Area is off State Highway 49 two miles east of Daingerfield in south central Morris County. The 551-acre park includes an eighty-acre lake and was established in 1935 as a Civilian Conservation Corpsqv project. It was opened to the public in 1938. During the Civil Warqv the area was a center of iron manufacture where factories made guns and other metal products. The flora is mixed pine and hardwood forest. Park facilities include camp and picnic sites, a 2½-mile hiking trial, a boat ramp, a playground, and a fishing pier.

BIBLIOGRAPHY: Vertical Files, Barker Texas History Center, University of Texas at Austin.

Christopher Long

DAIRY ADVISORY BOARD. The Dairy Advisory Board, established by the Forty-second Texas Legislature in 1931, was a three-member board appointed for two-year terms by the governor with the concurrence of the senate. One member represented the dairy processing industries, one the dairy production industries, and one the consumers. The board acted as an advisory body to the commissioner of agriculture to determine proper apparatus for testing butterfat content and component parts of milk. In 1972 the Babcock test was the official dairy test used in Texas. The legislature provided for the approval of other testing equipment as it became available, contingent upon certain standards. The Texas legislature abolished the board in 1993.

DAIRY CATTLE. Very few cattle used exclusively for dairy purposes were found in Texas before the 1880s. Before that, of course, most farmers, planters, and townspeople kept cows, drank milk, and made butter and possibly cheese, but the cattle that produced for them were almost all general purpose and were also used for beef and as draft animals. Since the cattle industry in Texas mostly stemmed from Spanish or Mexican roots, and longhorn cattleqv were known as "exceedingly poor milkers," early Texas milk cows produced small quantities of milk compared to late-twentieth-century Holstein cattle. Very likely, a few Durhams, Devons, and Ayrshires were brought into Texas by Anglo-Americans before the Civil War,qv since those breeds were present in other southern states. Before the 1880s, however, there was only a small amount of commercial production from dairy cows near the larger towns and among German-Americans in Texas. The only place such commercial milk production existed was in the rougher, non-planting land around such towns, and thus the few cattle used primarily for dairy purposes could be found in those regions. There were probably already grade or mixed versions of both Jerseys and Holsteins in Texas, but in 1880 the first purebred Jerseys were imported, and in 1884 the first purebred Holstein calves were born in the state. These became the two main breeds in Texas dairy history. In the late 1800s and early 1900s Jerseys coming from other southern states were far more popular than any other dairy breed. One reason was that they were more resistant to tick fever (*see* TEXAS FEVER) than Holsteins or Ayrshires imported from the north. A second, more significant, reason for their popularity was that until the mid-1900s most milk was marketed as cream, butter, or cheese rather than as whole milk, and Jerseys produced milk with a high butterfat content. In

1949, 75 percent of the estimated 1,283,000 milk cows in Texas were Jerseys.

About 1950 the dairy business entered an era of revolutionary change. A combination of forces—including widespread artificial insemination, which greatly improved the milk-production potential of each animal—allowed a phenomenal decline in the number of dairy cows without much corresponding decline in total dairy production. As early as 1948 Texas had thirty artificial-breeding associations. Milk producers began to specialize in dairying and as a result made changes in feeding and general management that aided cows with a greater genetic capacity for producing milk. Consequently there were phenomenally rapid increases in production per animal in Texas and in the United States. Dairy cattle numbers in Texas declined from 1,283,000 in 1949 to 297,921 in 1974, with little decline in the total amount of milk produced. Not only did the number of dairy animals decline strikingly, so did the number of farmers engaged in producing milk. In 1945 there were 321,223 farms that reported sales of dairy products; in 1974 only 13,687 farms reported having dairy cattle. Though the number of dairy cattle in Texas reached a low point in 1974, the number of dairy farms dropped still lower, and by 1987 there were 5,899 farms that sold dairy products—but they reported having 356,538 dairy cows, an increase of more than 58,000 over the 1974 figure. Total milk production had increased as well, but increases in production per animal leveled off after the early 1970s. In 1987 the relatively small number of dairy farmers in Texas sold more than a half billion dollars in dairy products.

There was also a rapid and striking change in the pattern of milk marketing that began about the mid-1900s; the change had a dramatic effect on dairy breed preference in Texas. Before the mid-1900s the largest percentage of milk had been marketed as cream, butter, or cheese instead of as whole milk. Consequently butterfat production was a primary objective. From the 1950s onward, however, dairymen sent most Texas milk to market as whole milk. Since they were paid only a small premium for butterfat production, and most of their money was earned on pounds of milk sold, farmers rapidly switched to Holsteins, which produced much milk, but little fat. By the 1980s only a few herds of purebred registered Jerseys and Guernseys were left in Texas. Furthermore, mixtures of those breeds were not to be found in commercial dairy herds in the state. Neither did most commercial dairies milk any purebred Jerseys or Guernseys along with their Holsteins to keep butterfat production from dropping too low; this was because it was not generally feasible to run 1,400-pound Holsteins in the same pastures, lots, and barns with 700-pound Jerseys and Guernseys, because of injuries inflicted by the larger and heavier breed. Though in 1989 Texas ranked first in the nation in the number of all cattle, beef cattle, sheep, lambs, and goats, it ranked tenth in the number of dairy cows. Receipts for wholesale milk from 380,000 Texas dairy cows made up about 7 percent of all Texas farm receipts in 1989, though only 6,000 Texas farms reported milk sales in that year. In the early 1990s, 95 percent of the dairy industry in Texas was located east of a line running from Wichita Falls to Brownwood to San Antonio to Corpus Christi. Leading milk-producing counties at that time were Erath, Hopkins, Comanche, and Johnson, which together produced nearly 44 percent of the milk in Texas. At that time most Texas dairies were members of one of four marketing cooperatives, of which Associated Milk Producers, Incorporated, was the largest. Average annual milk production per cow in 1990 was 14,645 pounds; in 1991, 14,258 pounds; and in 1992, 14,867 pounds. In the early 1990s the major dairy products manufactured in Texas included ice cream; condensed, evaporated, and dry milk; creamery butter; and cheese.

BIBLIOGRAPHY: Lewis C. Gray, *History of Agriculture in the Southern United States to 1860* (Washington: Carnegie Institution, 1933; rpt., Gloucester, Massachusetts: Peter Smith, 1958). *E. Dale Odom*

DAIRY INDUSTRY. Throughout the nineteenth century Texas milk production was for the most part a haphazard, subsistence-type enterprise. Town dwellers as well as farm families kept milk cows, drank fresh milk, and made butter and cheese. Cheese manufacturing was the first dairying enterprise to become specialized and removed from the farm. After the Civil War,[qv] cheese makers of the old dairy belt stretching from New York to Wisconsin produced most of the cheese consumed in Texas. Even as late as the 1930s cheese manufacturing in Texas was small-scale. Gail Borden[qv] established a condensed-milk plant at Bordenville in 1872, but most of the canned milk sold in Texas during the nineteenth century was produced and processed in the northern states. Texas farmers, however, continued to produce most of the fresh milk and butter consumed in the state. As cities became larger, nearby enterprising farmers established milk routes to deliver milk and butter to residents. Very slowly, specialization in butter manufacturing developed. Several small creameries established in the 1880s failed, but by 1900 twelve creameries were in operation in Texas.

Thereafter, the market for cream separators expanded rapidly as farmers saw the advantage of marketing their surplus. They sold cream to local creameries, or shipped it on the railroad to distant ones, and fed the skim milk to the hogs. A Texas Dairymen's Association was founded at Waco in 1918, and although it did not survive World War I,[qv] it did help to promote commercial dairying. By 1914 about 100 creameries in Texas were producing over five million pounds of butter annually. Nevertheless, a dozen times that much was still produced at home, and most of it was consumed on farms where it was produced.

Most of the milk produced in Texas continued to be consumed as fluid milk. Specialization in processing, packaging, and marketing developed slowly in the early twentieth century, as urban growth and technological progress took place. Effective machines for pasteurizing milk first came on the market in 1895, and in the same year a steam-powered bottle washer was patented. Fear of tuberculosis and undulant fever brought demands for pasteurization from urban residents, who were drinking milk from cows they never saw. Most of the cities in Texas had adopted compulsory pasteurization by 1927, when 874 cities in the United States had such ordinances. In the rural areas of the state, the earlier patterns of production and marketing had changed little by the end of the 1920s. The number of creameries had grown little since 1914, but pounds of butter sold had increased to 14,634,612 by 1929.

In the 1930s the dairy industry in Texas began changing rapidly as national companies like Borden established processing plants and distributing centers in the state. Several organizations like the Southwestern Dairy Association were already in existence, and in 1939 Texas had 228 dairy-products plants in operation. Separating milk and selling cream continued, but non.specialist dairy farmers who lived far from cities were no longer restricted to selling cream. Better roads and rubber-tired vehicles brought dependable and regular milk routes, enabling farmers to sell a few cans a day as grade B milk to cheese plants, of which the first in the state was established in 1928. All along, however, most of the Texas milk production continued to take place in the eastern third of the state.

Growth accelerated as World War II[qv] brought an unusual increase in demand for dairy products, and Texas farmers responded by increasing production. The number of dairy cows in Texas had been increasing slowly since 1900, growing from 1,034,000 in 1914 to 1,146,768 in 1939, but during the war the number increased to 1,594,000. Milk production increased accordingly. After the war, however, expansion brought new problems as milk prices declined. Almost all grade A milk producers were by then wholesaling their product to processors, and dairy farmers complained that they were at the mercy of the handlers who purchased their milk. Such conditions led to the establishment and growth of producer bargaining associations. The South Texas Producers Association had already emerged in the Houston area during the 1930s. After World War II it was joined by the North Texas Producers Association and other regional producers' organizations. Dairy farmers were also aided by the advent of federal marketing orders in Texas in 1949. By the 1980s all milk sold in the state was marketed under federal marketing orders. One North Texas dairy farmer said, "I've milked by candle light, lantern light, and electric light, but never got fair tests or fair prices until we got a federal marketing order and the North Texas Producers Association."

Lower prices and hard times in the late 1940s were only a prelude of things to come. During the later 1950s milk-price wars broke out in Texas. Gallon jugs were sold by gasoline stations, and small retailers engaged in cutthroat competition. Cheap transportation brought fluid milk from Wisconsin and Minnesota to drive Texas prices down. General instability led to mergers of small regional producer organizations into huge multimarket associations. By 1969 Associated Milk Producers, Incorporated, had emerged. With over 40,000 producer-members from Texas to the Canadian border, it dominated milk marketing in mid-America. Although its power was diminished in the 1970s, in the 1980s most Texas producers were still marketing milk as members of that organization. General price stability at profitable levels for efficient producers was the rule through the 1970s, but a growing national dairy surplus posed a threat to Texas milk producers.

In the years from World War II to the 1980s the structure of Texas dairying underwent revolutionary changes in addition to the changes in marketing already described. Most striking was the decline in the number of milk cows, from 1,594,000 in 1945 to 355,000 in 1971, after which the decline continued at a much slower pace; in 1983 there were 335,000 on Texas farms. The number of producers declined sharply as well, and in 1981 there were only 2,600 commercial dairy farms in Texas. But total milk production slipped only from 3,750,000 pounds in 1948 to 3,680,000 pounds in 1982. The release of millions of acres of land normally devoted to cotton between 1930 and 1940 stimulated dairy production. With the growth of large, specialized dairy farms new practices were instituted, including improved herd management and expansion of artificial-insemination programs. Jersey, Holstein, and Guernsey cattle became the dominant breeds. The shift toward grade A production and participation in pasture-improvement programs also played a part. As a result of these factors annual production per cow grew from 2,820 to 11,459 pounds between 1925 and 1982.

In the 1980s milk production still centered in the eastern part of the state, with more than 90 percent produced east of a line from Wichita Falls to Brownwood to San Antonio to Corpus Christi. No longer, however, did urban counties lead in milk production. Until the 1950s Harris, Dallas, Tarrant, and Bexar counties usually led as milk producers. In the 1980s Hopkins, Erath, and Wise counties were leading; these three counties accounted for about 30 percent of the state's product, and Hopkins County alone produced 16 percent of the Texas total. Texas generally ranked in the top ten states of the nation in milk production during the 1970s and 1980s, and Texas farmers received a gross income of $504,583,000 from milk in 1980.

Although Texas has never been important in cheese and butter manufacture, it is a major ice cream manufacturing state and since the 1950s has led the nation in mellorine production, usually producing about half the annual national product. Noticeable changes in the processing and marketing of dairy products took place between World War II and the 1980s. There was a big decline in the number of dairy plants as many small firms disappeared. Home delivery of milk virtually ceased. Finally, supermarkets like H-E-B[qv] collectively became more important as processors and retailers of milk and dairy products than national dairy firms like Borden. *See also* DAIRY PRODUCTS *and* BLUE BELL ICE CREAM.

BIBLIOGRAPHY: William Bennett Bizzell, *Rural Texas* (New York: Macmillan, 1924). Earle Cabell, Interviews, Oral History Collection, University of North Texas Archives, Denton. Samuel Lee Evans, Texas Agriculture, 1880–1930 (Ph.D. dissertation, University of Texas, 1960). U.S. Department of Agriculture, *Trends in the Production and Disposition of Milk* (Southern Co-operative Bulletin 19, Washington: GPO, 1951).
E. Dale Odom

DAIRY PRODUCTS. Throughout the nineteenth century not much commercial processing of dairy products took place in Texas, and the state imported almost all of its condensed milk and cheese from the northern dairy states. Creameries, primarily to produce butter, were established in several North Texas towns such as Greenville, Alvarado, Terrell, and Weatherford in the late 1880s. They were premature, and most of them failed. Supply and markets continued to grow, however, so that by 1900 twelve and by 1913 eighty-nine creameries were in operation in the state. Even though the amount of butter produced in Texas grew from 4,982,000 pounds in 1918 to 25,083,000 in 1930, Texas was importing at least fifteen carloads of butter monthly during most of the 1920s.

Until World War II[qv] and even afterward, many small-town, and most rural, residents continued to produce their own milk and make their own butter. Around the growing cities, however, specialized dairies were producing fluid milk in large quantities by the late 1920s, and although many continued to sell directly to the consumer, demands for pasteurization increased the need for processing and interposed a handler between producers and consumers. Between 1889 and 1929 sales of fresh milk increased from 6,527,000 to 75,148,000 gallons annually; in the latter year the state's dairy farmers produced 412,708,000 gallons. During the 1930s more processing plants were established, and by 1939 Texas had 228 dairy-product factories, including twenty-two cheese plants, nine condensed and evaporated milk plants, sixty-six creamery butter plants, and 131 plants making ice cream. Of course, most of these were also engaged in pasteurizing and bottling whole milk. Expansion of production generally continued through World War II and up to the 1950s.

The structure of dairy-product manufacturing changed rapidly in the thirty years following 1950. The number of dairy establishments declined as large commercial manufacturers took control of the industry. At the same time, the number of milk cows declined as production per cow increased. By 1967 the state had 139 dairy-product firms operating, and a decade later, except for cottage cheese and ice cream producers, so few manufacturers that *Texas Dairy Statistics* no longer reported total production or number of businesses. This meant that fewer than three firms were engaged in production. While Texas ranked consistently in the top fifteen states of the nation in milk production, butter production had fallen by the 1970s to less than one-fifth that of 1930, and less than 1 percent of the amount produced in the United States. Cheese production was also insignificant. But Texas remained a major producer of ice cream and up to the early 1980s led the nation in mellorine manufacture, usually turning out about half of the national product. Consequently, Texas, while it was not important in most manufactured dairy products, remained an important dairy state; in 1982 dairy products made up 5.4 percent of the value of Texas agricultural production. In 1992, 5.6 percent of farm income was from dairy products. Dairy products reported included 123,670,000 gallons of frozen dessert (56,031,000 gallons of ice cream), 20,603,000 gallons of ice milk, and 2,268 gallons of milk sherbet. Total production of milk in 1992 was 5,590,000,000 pounds. Of this 5,549,000,000 was sold to plants and dealers. The average price was $13.70 a hundred pounds. Cash receipts for milk in 1992 totaled $760,213,000.

BIBLIOGRAPHY: Denton *Record-Chronicle*, June 28, 1984. Samuel Lee Evans, Texas Agriculture, 1880–1930 (Ph.D. dissertation, University of Texas, 1960).
E. Dale Odom

DAISETTA, TEXAS. Daisetta is at the southern junction of Farm roads 770 and 834, on a salt dome forty-one miles northwest of Beaumont in eastern Liberty County. Local storeowner Newt Farris named the town by combining the names of Daisy Barrett and Etta White. Daisetta was founded in the wake of the discovery of the nearby Hull oilfield in 1918, although planters and lumbermen had occupied the area as early as 1850. The Daisetta post office was established in 1921. The town was rebuilt after a devastating fire in 1924. Daisetta's economy, like that of its sister community of Hull, two miles north, depended largely upon oil. Several newspapers served Hull and Daisetta during the 1930s and 1940s. Among these were the *Progressive Outlook,* the *Liberty County News,* the *Liberty County Press,* and the *Hull-Daisetta News.* Despite the proximity of Hull, Daisetta residents maintained a strong independent identity, voting to incorporate their town in 1946, 1955, and 1961. Daisetta's population level, however, dropped as oilfield production declined. Although once Daisetta had an estimated 3,000 residents, the population was 1,764 in 1950 and 1,177 in 1980, when Daisetta had twenty-three businesses. In 1990 its population was 969.

BIBLIOGRAPHY: Miriam Partlow, *Liberty, Liberty County, and the Atascosito District* (Austin: Pemberton, 1974). Robert Wooster

DAISY, TEXAS. Daisy was six miles north of Emory in northern Rains County. The area was first settled around the time of the Civil War.qv A post office operated at the site from 1886 to 1904. Around 1900 the area had a mill and a store, but by the mid-1930s the community was no longer shown on maps. Christopher Long

DAKIN, TEXAS. Dakin, a dispersed farming community in eastern Young County, was a station on the Chicago, Rock Island and Gulf Railway. The 1936 county highway map indicated Dakin had three houses on State Highway 24 (later U.S. Highway 380) and a cemetery, three additional houses, and a school three miles south on an unimproved road. By the early 1980s only a cemetery named Center Ridge remained at the site. John G. Johnson

DALBY CREEK. Dalby Creek rises just east of the Red River county line in extreme western Bowie County (at 33°25′ N, 94°44′ W) and runs southwest for four miles through the southeastern corner of Red River County to its mouth on Wright Patman Lake (at 33°21′ N, 94°44′ W). Before the construction of the lake in the mid-1950s Dalby Creek entered the Sulphur River near the intersection of the Franklin, Morris, and Red River county lines (at 33°20′ N, 94°44′ W). The stream crosses flat to gently rolling terrain surfaced by sandy and clay loam that supports grasses and mixed hardwoods and pines. The stream is probably named for Philip A. Dalby, the original grantee of the land near its head.

DALBY SPRINGS. Dalby Springs is the collective name for what was originally four springs about 11½ miles south of DeKalb in southwestern Bowie County (at 33°22′ N, 94°41′ W). Archeological evidence indicates that the springs were used by prehistoric peoples for thousands of years. In 1687 the French explorer Henri Joutelqv found the Upper Natchitoches tribe of Caddo Indians living at the springs. Anglo settlement there began in 1839, when Warren Dalby and his family moved to the area. In the 1850s the springs began to be known for their medicinal value, and by the time of the Civil Warqv a community, known as Dalby Springs, had grown up around them. During the 1870s an observer reported that there were frequently as many as fifty to seventy-five people there to drink the springwater. The same observer claimed that this water was "good for dyspepsia, diseases of the skin and kidneys and also for diseases of females. It is a sovereign remedy for barrenness. If Abraham and Sarah had visited this spring Isaac would have figured fifty years earlier in Biblical history." Although the springs still flowed weakly in the 1980s, by that time several pitcher-pump wells were in use to obtain the water. A state historical marker is located at the church that stands south of the springs.

BIBLIOGRAPHY: Gunnar Brune, *Springs of Texas,* Vol. 1 (Fort Worth: Branch–Smith, 1981). Gunnar Brune

DALBY SPRINGS, TEXAS. Dalby Springs is a community eleven miles from DeKalb in southwestern Bowie County. It was named for the nearby Dalby Springs. Settlement in the area began in 1839 with the arrival of Warren Dalby and his family. In the 1850s the springs were discovered to have medicinal properties, and as word spread, people began to visit the area to drink from the springs. Buildings were erected to accommodate travelers, and in 1860 a post office was established there, with Joseph G. Dalby as postmaster. By 1884 the town had a church, a school, five mills, five gins, and a population estimated at 250. During the 1890s a newspaper called the *Guest* was published there. By 1900 the community's population had fallen to 186. It continued to be reported at about that level until the 1950s, when it fell to fifty. In 1984 Dalby Springs reported an estimated population of sixty and no rated businesses. In 1990 its population was estimated at 141.

BIBLIOGRAPHY: Bowie County Scrapbook, Barker Texas History Center, University of Texas at Austin. J. J. Scheffelin, *Bowie County Basic Background Book* (n.d.). Cecil Harper, Jr.

DALE, TEXAS. Dale is on Farm Road 1854 some seven miles northeast of Lockhart in Caldwell County. It was named for the valley in which it is located. A post office was established there in 1880 when the Missouri, Kansas and Texas line built through the town, and in 1885 Dale had seventy-five residents, three general stores, and a steam gristmill and cotton gin. The community shipped cotton. By 1905 the local school had 112 pupils and two teachers. Dale grew to 250 residents and fifteen businesses by 1914. Its population declined to 200 between 1925 and 1943. In 1936 the county highway map showed numerous residences at the townsite, as well as two schools, two churches, and several businesses, including a seasonal industry. In 1947 the community's population reached 275, but was recorded at 126 from 1970 until the early 1990s, when fourteen businesses were reported there. Scott E. Wagner

DALE CREST, TEXAS. Dale Crest is between Farm Roads 857 and 1255 southeast of Grand Saline in extreme eastern Van Zandt County. It had likely developed by 1900 and may have taken its name from local resident Lemuel Dale or the Reverend George Dale, a Baptist minister. By the 1980s most residents had moved away, and state highway maps showed only a single church remaining at the townsite.

BIBLIOGRAPHY: Van Zandt County History Book Committee, *History of Van Zandt County* (Dallas, 1984). Diana J. Kleiner

DALHART, TEXAS. Dalhart, the county seat of Dallam County, straddles the border of Dallam and Hartley counties in the northwest corner of the Texas Panhandle. The original settlement was platted early in 1901 by W. J. Blair and Charles W. Thornton when the Chicago, Rock Island and Pacific Railway built west from Liberal, Kansas, and crossed the Fort Worth and Denver City line. The site of the crossing was known for a time as Twist Junction. J. H. Conlen supervised the laying of the Rock Island tracks and made an old boxcar into a section house on the site. Later the settlement was named Denrock, a combination of the names of the two railroads; in 1901 Robert B. Edgell named his new newspaper the Denrock *Sun.* But when postal authorities objected, the town adopted the name Dalhart, combining the first syllables of the names of the two counties in which it is located. On June 11, 1901, Ora D. Atkinson and other promoters incorporated the Dalhart Town Company, and the first and only sale of lots was held on July 20. Dalhart was incorporated as a town on May 6, 1902, and as a city on April 6, 1904. It replaced Texline as Dallam county seat, as a result of an election on February 21, 1903. From that time on, Dalhart quickly grew as a shipping center for the XIT Ranchqv and other area ranches. The activities of the W. P. Soashqv Land Company also contributed significantly to Dalhart's progress.

C. E. Williams, a noted well driller, built the town's first water tower in 1906. Previously, it had been necessary to buy water at twenty cents a barrel from barrels lining the railroad tracks.

By 1912 Dalhart had a population of 3,500. The two railroad lines, which erected machine shops, roundhouses, and a lever control tower, contributed to the town's prosperity, and Dalhart played a major role in establishing the Enid, Ochiltree and Western and other small railways. In addition, it had three banks, a flour mill, a large grain elevator, a planing mill, a modern utilities system, a hospital, an ice plant, several hotels and churches, and a high school athletic program serving an ever-expanding agricultural area. When oil companies began drilling in the Panhandle,[qv] Dalhart was among the first towns to sell oil leases. The Dallam County Public Library, the first county library in Texas, opened for circulation in January 1921. Dalhart's population was further increased with the development of its East Heights addition in 1928.

During the drought years of the 1930s Dalhart was notorious for its "black dusters" (see DUST BOWL). R. S. (Uncle Dick) Coon, a wealthy businessman who owned the DeSoto Hotel, became legendary for his generosity to depression-stricken farmers and cowboys. In August 1934 Dalhart became the site of one of the first three erosion-control demonstration projects in Texas, sponsored by the federal land bank, and the first to be devoted specifically to wind erosion. The Work Projects Administration and National Youth Administration[qqv] also had chapters in Dalhart. Dalhart Army Air Field[qv] was established about two miles southwest of town.

In 1990 Dalhart remained an agribusiness center for a wide area of Texas, Oklahoma, and New Mexico. In addition to cattle feedlots, a bottling plant, and feed and meat processing plants, Dalhart is noted for its schools, hospital, and nursing home. The Dalhart *Texan* has served as the area newspaper since December 11, 1902. The Rock Island shops continue to help furnish the city's payrolls. Three U.S. highways, 87, 385, and 54, converge at Dalhart. Since 1936 Dalhart has been the home of the XIT Ranch Reunion and Rodeo, held in August. It was the XIT Reunion Association that built the landmark *Empty Saddles* monument and later established the XIT Museum. Another community event is the annual Railroad Week. Two miles south of Dalhart is Rita Blanca Canyon, site of Rita Blanca Lake. The city's population increased from 5,899 in the 1950s to 6,854 in the 1980s. In 1990 it was 6,246.

BIBLIOGRAPHY: Cordia Sloan Duke and Joe B. Frantz, *6,000 Miles of Fence: Life on the XIT Ranch of Texas* (Austin: University of Texas Press, 1961). David B. Gracy II, "Selling the Future: A Biography of William Pulver Soash," *Panhandle-Plains Historical Review* 50 (1977). Lillie Mae Hunter, *The Book of Years: A History of Dallam and Hartley Counties* (Hereford, Texas: Pioneer, 1969). F. Stanley [Stanley F. L. Crocchiola], *The Dalhart, Texas, Story* (Nazareth, Texas, 1975).
H. Allen Anderson

DALHART ARMY AIR FIELD. Dalhart Army Air Field, two miles southwest of Dalhart, was activated in September 1942 and consisted of a 3,000-acre field; two auxiliary fields were added later. Though originally intended for glider training, the field came to be used for B-17 and B-29 training and for fighter planes to be used in conjunction with bombers. It was closed early in 1946, and the property went to the city of Dalhart. Since that time, several of the remaining buildings have been used as the Dalhart municipal airport.

BIBLIOGRAPHY: F. Stanley [Stanley F. L. Crocchiola], *The Dalhart, Texas, Story* (Nazareth, Texas, 1975). *H. Allen Anderson*

DALLAM, JAMES WILMER (1818–1847). James Wilmer Dallam, legal scholar, newspaper publisher, and author, the son of Francis Johnson and Sarah (Wilmer) Dallam, was born in Baltimore, Maryland, on September 24, 1818. Following his graduation in 1837 from Brown University, where he was elected to Phi Beta Kappa, he studied law in Baltimore in the office of Reverdy Johnson. In 1839 Dallam moved to Matagorda, Texas, where he quickly made a place for himself in the frontier community. In 1844 he went to Washington, D.C., to compile *A Digest of the Laws of Texas: Containing a Full and Complete Compilation of the Land Laws; Together with the Opinions of the Supreme Court*. Published in Baltimore by John D. Troy in 1845, Dallam's *Digest*, as the work is familiarly known, has been called the "lawyer's Bible" and has gone through several printings: 1881, 1883, and 1904. His *Opinions of the Supreme Court of Texas from 1840 to 1844, Inclusive*, was published as a separate book in 1883, a reprint of the second part of the 1845 edition. Because modern Texas jurisprudence is based on the laws in effect in the republic, the *Digest* has retained its importance. In 1845 Dallam returned to Matagorda, where he married Annie Fisher, daughter of Samuel Rhoads Fisher.[qv] Their one child, Annie, was born in March 1847. Dallam founded and edited for a brief time a weekly paper in Matagorda, the *Colorado Herald*, the first issue in July 1846, carrying the motto: "Give me liberty to know, to utter, and to argue freely, above all liberties." In 1847 he was invited to establish a newspaper in Indianola. While making arrangements in New Orleans, he died of yellow fever on August 20, 1847. He was buried in Matagorda. The youthful lawyer–codifier–editor was a prodigious worker; besides his serious works in the law and in the newspaper field he wrote two short romances founded on incidents of Texas history. *The Lone Star, a Tale of Texas* was published in 1845, and *The Deaf Spy*, in 1848, after his death. Dallam County was named in his honor.

BIBLIOGRAPHY: James D. Lynch, *The Bench and Bar of Texas* (St. Louis, 1885). John C. Townes, "Development of the Texas Judicial System," *Southwestern Historical Quarterly* 2 (July, October 1898). Clarence Wharton, "Early Judicial History of Texas," *Texas Law Review* 12 (April 1934).
Kate Dallam Gregory

DALLAM COUNTY. Dallam County (A-2) is located in the far northwestern corner of the Texas Panhandle; its western border abuts New Mexico, and its northern boundary borders Oklahoma. The county seat, Dalhart, is located on the Dallam-Hartley county line in the south central part of the county. Texline, the county's only other incorporated town, is at the intersection of U.S. Highway 87 and the New Mexico border. The county's center lies at approximately 36°15′ north latitude and 102°35′ west longitude. Dallam County comprises approximately 1,505 square miles of the rolling grasslands of the Panhandle.[qv] The terrain is marked by numerous dry arroyos and by the intermittent Rita Blanca, Carrizo, and Coldwater creeks, all of which drain into the Canadian River. The county's sandy, sandy loam, loam, and salty clay loam soils support a variety of natural grasses and trees, as well as numerous crops, including wheat, corn, milo, sorghum, and other grain products. Ranching, the county's dominant industry, utilizes the abundant grasses to produce large numbers of beef cattle, along with some hogs and horses. The annual rainfall averages 17.38 inches, and the temperatures range from an average low of 19° F in January to an average high of 92° in July. The growing season averages 178 days annually.

Until white settlement reached it in the 1870s the Dallam County region existed as just a small portion of the huge, vacant High Plains that stretch from Texas to Canada. The earliest Plains Apache inhabitants were followed by the nomadic Comanches and Kiowas in their quest for buffalo and booty. Due to its proximity to both the Canadian River and New Mexico, this region undoubtedly witnessed the comings and going of Comancheros, ciboleros, and pastores[qqv] as they ventured eastward from New Mexico into Comanchería.

With the removal of the Comanches and Kiowas to Indian Territory as a result of the Red River War[qv] in 1874–75, the Anglo-American frontier moved into the region. Dallam County, named for James W. Dallam,[qv] Republic of Texas lawyer and newspaper editor, originated from the Bexar District in 1876. However, no exploitation of the area actually occurred until about six years later. On January 10, 1882, the Capitol Freehold Land and Investment Company^qv received approximately two-thirds of the county as part of its famous XIT Ranch^qv holdings. Buffalo Springs, in the northern part of the county, served as the first headquarters of the XIT. Between 1882 and 1887 only XIT cowboys and a few other settlers occupied the county. In 1887 and 1888 the Fort Worth and Denver City Railway was built through the county as it extended its line from Amarillo into New Mexico and Colorado. On May 14, 1888, the road reached Texline, the railroad's choice of a new division point. Perico, twelve miles southeast, began as a shipping point for the XIT. By 1890 the population of the county had reached 112. In 1891 the county was organized with Texline as its seat. Organization led to the county's first election, in which John V. Farwell^qv was chosen county judge and H. Willis, T. H. Hardin, J. L. Baughn, and J. B. Stevens county commissioners.

In 1900 and 1901 the Chicago, Rock Island and Pacific Railroad, building from Enid, Oklahoma, and Tucumcari, New Mexico, crossed Dallam County. A settlement soon developed at the point where the Rock Island crossed the Fort Worth and Denver. The town, named Dalhart because it is in both Dallam and Hartley counties, developed around the Rock Island shops and roundhouse built in 1901. Dalhart prospered, and as a result of an election held early in 1903 it became the county seat. Conlen, in the eastern part of the county, was founded on the Rock Island line that year. Later, in 1931, the town of Kerrick was laid out on the North Plains and Santa Fe line, which ran through the county's northeast corner from Stratford to Boise City, Oklahoma.

Ranching dominated the Dallam County economy in its early years. The few jobs not dependent on ranching were tied to the local railroads. However, in the first two decades of the twentieth century farmers began making their way into the county. Whereas only four farms, comprising 1,280 acres total, existed in the county in 1900, 210 farms covering more than 48,000 acres were producing by 1910. The large ranches had been broken up by then, and extensive land sales continued into the 1920s. By the mid-1930s over one-third of the county was classified as cropland. The primary crop, wheat, was supplemented by such grains as corn, milo, and millet. The Great Depression and Dust Bowl^qqv dealt harshly with Dallam County's economy, yet the ranchers and farmers pulled through. From the 1940s on, the farm and ranch economy grew and prospered. By 1980, when farm crops worth $40,700,000 and livestock worth $34,877,000 were marketed, the county agricultural economy had reached a balance that continued to the 1990s.

The transportation system of the county is centered around Dalhart. The two railroads in the town contribute to the local economy as employers of local citizens and as haulers of local goods. The highway system, however, plays a much larger role. As early as 1920 Dalhart had a strategic location on two major U.S. Highways. U.S. 54, running from Liberal, Kansas, to Tucumcari, New Mexico, passes through Dalhart and eastern Dallam County, and U.S. 87 runs from Amarillo to Colorado Springs via Dalhart and Dallam County. U.S. 287 cuts across the northeast corner of the county. Dalhart and Texline have both benefited from these roads and from the network of farm and ranch roads extending throughout the county. Dalhart is become the largest town in the northwest Panhandle because it is a crossroads for commerce and travel. Perico has become a mere ghost town, and Conlen and Kerrick, both declining rural communities, are allied by location with the Sherman County trade area.

Dallam County has continued to prosper on a diversified economic base of ranching, farming, and transportation, with Dalhart as the nucleus. From its meager 112 people in 1890 the county population grew to 4,001 by 1910 as farmers settled the area. Between 1920 and 1930 the population rose from 4,528 to 7,830. Afterward, until the 1990s, the population remained relatively stable, with changes coming as realignments in the local economy and not through continued expansion. The population, 6,494 in 1940, grew to 7,640 by 1950, then decreased to 6,302 in 1960 and 6,012 in 1970. In 1980 the county numbered 6,531 occupants; in 1990 the population was 5,461 with 425 living in Texline and 4,001 of Dalhart's 6,246 residents living in Dallam County. Politically, like many of the counties in the Panhandle, Dallam County generally voted Republican in the late twentieth century. From the early 1950s through 1992 Democratic presidential candidates outpolled their Republican opponents only twice, in 1964 and 1976. Republicans also made inroads in local and statewide elections as well, although as late as 1982, 89 percent of the county's electorate voted in the Democratic primary. The Dalhart *Texan* is the county's sole newspaper, and the chief cultural event is the annual XIT Reunion and Rodeo, held at Dalhart in August. Lake Rita Blanca, just across the line in Hartley County, provides recreation. Rita Blanca National Grasslands^qv covers several hundred acres in the north central part of the county.

BIBLIOGRAPHY: T. Lindsay Baker, *Ghost Towns of Texas* (Norman: University of Oklahoma Press, 1986). Lillie Mae Hunter, *The Book of Years: A History of Dallam and Hartley Counties* (Hereford, Texas: Pioneer, 1969). William D. Mauldin, "The Coming of Agriculture to Dallam County," West Texas Historical Association *Year Book* 13 (1937). Sherman County Historical Survey Committee, *God, Grass, and Grit* (2 vols., Seagraves, Texas: Pioneer, 1971, 1975).

Donald R. Abbe and H. Allen Anderson

DALLARDSVILLE, TEXAS. Dallardsville (Dollardsville), on Farm Road 1276 sixty miles northwest of Beaumont in east central Polk County, was named for John J. Dollard, a young schoolteacher and doctor, who also served as postmaster after the community secured a post office in 1877. In 1888 the Dallardsville school was organized. Trustees included S. D. McNeiley, E. G. Sims, and Hardy Vickers. By 1890 the town had seventy-five residents, three churches, and a public school; cotton and wool were the primary shipments from area farmers. The community's population fell to twenty by 1925, and its post office was discontinued in 1929. Subsequent discoveries of oil and natural gas at the Segno fields to the south, however, led to new growth. The local post office was reinstated by the late 1940s, and by the mid-1960s the community's population was reported as 350. In 1983 and 1984 additional oil and gas fields were found to the north and west of town at the Dallardsville fields. In 1990 the town's population was still recorded as 350.

BIBLIOGRAPHY: *A Pictorial History of Polk County, Texas, 1846–1910* (Livingston, Texas: Polk County Bicentennial Commission, 1976; rev. ed. 1978).

Robert Wooster

DALLAS, CATHOLIC DIOCESE OF. The Catholic Diocese of Dallas, previously part of the Diocese of Galveston, was established on July 15, 1890, by Pope Leo XIII. It covered all the northern part of the state; its southernmost counties, from west to east, were Yoakum, Terry, Dawson, Borden, Mitchell, Coke, Runnels, Coleman, Brown, Mills, Hamilton, Bosque, Hill, Navarro, Henderson, Smith, Rusk, and Panola. Thomas Francis Brennan,^qv the first bishop, was consecrated on April 5, 1891. Before he was transferred in February 1893 to St. John's, Newfoundland, he established a diocesan Catholic newspaper, the *Texas Catholic* (*see* CATHOLIC JOURNALISM). This was the first diocesan newspaper published in Texas. In 1892 El Paso, Hudspeth, and Culberson counties were added to the diocese. At the conclusion of Bishop Brennan's tenure the Diocese of Dallas comprised twenty-five churches with resident pastors, nineteen mission churches, four hospitals, and nine academies with a combined enrollment of about 1,500 students. The diocese served a Catholic population of about 20,000, about 9,000 of whom had been born in America.

Succeeding Bishop Brennan was Bishop Edward Joseph Dunne,^qv from the Diocese of Chicago, who was installed on January 17, 1894. During his administration (1894–1910) the Catholic population of the diocese rose to an estimated 62,000, the number of churches increased to fifty-nine, and the number of hospitals to six. Educational facilities included thirty-one parochial schools, with a combined enrollment of about 5,700, and Holy Trinity College and Academy, founded by the Vincentian Fathers^qv in 1907. Bishop Dunne's tenure also saw the construction of the present Dallas cathedral, the Catedral Santuario de Guadalupe, which was completed in 1902.

Bishop Dunne died in Green Bay, Wisconsin, on August 5, 1910, and Rev. Joseph Patrick Lynch^qv was appointed to succeed him. Lynch was consecrated on July 12, 1911, in Sacred Heart Cathedral. During his term of office (1911–54) the Catholic population increased to about 96,000 and the number of parishes to ninety-five. Parochial schools included nineteen high schools, with about 2,000 students, and fifty-two elementary schools, with about 14,000 students. In 1911 Holy Trinity College and Academy became the original University of Dallas,^qv which closed in the late 1920s because of financial difficulties. The boundaries of the diocese were also redrawn as three new dioceses were formed: El Paso in 1914, Amarillo in 1926, and Austin in 1947. In 1953 the Church of Saint Patrick, in Fort Worth, was raised to the status of co-cathedral, and the diocese was renamed the Diocese of Dallas–Fort Worth. The diocese received an auxiliary bishop in 1942 and a coadjutor bishop in 1952, The latter office, with right of succession, was filled by Bishop Thomas Kiely Gorman.^qv

Gorman became the fourth bishop of the diocese after the death of Bishop Lynch on August 19, 1954. His tenure (1954–69) saw the revival of the *Texas Catholic* and the reopening of the University of Dallas, which received its first students in the fall of 1956. In 1961 the diocese was divided again in order to form the Diocese of San Angelo.^qv Holy Trinity Diocesan Seminary was established in 1965, and St. Jude Chapel was opened to serve downtown Dallas. Ninety-six parishes served a Catholic population of about 188,000, while eleven high schools and fifty-two elementary schools had enrollments of approximately 4,000 and 18,250, respectively. The number of Catholic hospitals in the diocese remained at six (*see* CATHOLIC HEALTH CARE).

Gorman resigned in 1969 and was succeeded by Thomas A. Tschoepe, who was installed on October 29, 1969. When Bishop Gorman's resignation was announced, the diocese was divided to form the Diocese of Dallas and the Diocese of Fort Worth.^qv During Bishop Tschoepe's tenure six new missions and fourteen parishes were established. Tschoepe also oversaw the establishment of many new programs, including, among others, the Catholic Community Fund, an annual fund drive; the Diocesan Youth Ministry; the Deaf Apostolate; the Hispanic Ministry Office; the Black Catholic Ministry Office; the office of the Justice and Peace Commission; the Office for Pastoral Training; the permanent diaconate; and the Dallas Catholic Television Network. In 1976 Bishop Tschoepe renamed Sacred Heart Cathedral the Cathedral Santuario de Guadalupe. The boundaries of the parish were changed again in 1986 with the establishment of the Diocese of Tyler.^qv After that division the Diocese of Dallas comprised nine counties—Grayson, Collin, Dallas, Ellis, Navarro, Fannin, Hunt, Rockwell, and Kaufman.

Bishop Tschoepe retired in December 1990 and was succeeded by Charles Victor Grahmann, who had become coadjutor bishop of the diocese in February 1990. On January 1, 1993, the diocese comprised fifty-six parishes, seven missions, and a Catholic population of 262,605 out of a total population of 2,546,402. The diocese supported one Catholic hospital, a health-care center, a home for the aged, one specialized home, three day-care centers, and three special centers for social services, as well as the University of Dallas and the seminary. It also supported three diocesan and parochial high schools, with an enrollment of 1,259; twenty-nine diocesan and parochial elementary schools, with an enrollment of 9,038; and one nonresidential school for handicapped children.

BIBLIOGRAPHY: Thomas P. Cloherty, History of the Diocese of Dallas (MS, Catholic Diocese of Dallas Archives, 1970). James Tucek, *A Century of Faith: The Story of the Diocese of Dallas* (Dallas: Diocese of Dallas, 1993).

Sister Lois Bannon, O.S.U.

DALLAS, TEXAS. Dallas is on the Trinity River^qv in the center of Dallas County in North Central Texas. It is crossed by Interstate highways 20, 30, 35, and 45. The city was founded by John Neely Bryan,^qv who settled on the east bank of the Trinity near a natural ford in November 1841. Bryan had picked the best spot for a trading post to serve the population migrating into the region. The ford, at the intersection of two major Indian traces, provided the only good crossing point for miles. Two highways proposed by the Republic of Texas^qv soon converged nearby. Unknown to Bryan, however, he had settled on land granted by the republic to the Texan Land and Emigration Company of St. Louis, headed by William S. Peters.^qv Bryan eventually legalized his claim, and the extensive promotional efforts of the Peters colony^qv attracted settlers to the region. In 1844 J. P. Dumas surveyed and laid out a townsite comprising a half mile square of blocks and streets. The origin of the name Dallas is unknown. Candidates include George Mifflin Dallas, vice president of the United States, 1845–49; his brother, Commodore Alexander J. Dallas, United States Navy; and Joseph Dallas, who settled near the new town in 1843. When Dallas County was formed in 1846, Dallas was designated as the temporary county seat; in 1850 voters selected it as the permanent county seat over Hord's Ridge (Oak Cliff) and Cedar Springs, both of which eventually came within its corporate limits. The Texas legislature granted Dallas a town charter on February 2, 1856. Dr. Samuel Pryor, elected the first mayor, headed a town government consisting of six aldermen, a treasurer-recorder, and a constable.

Dallas quickly became a service center for the rural area surrounding it. By the 1850s it had dry-goods stores, groceries, a drugstore, an insurance agency, a boot and shoe shop, brickyards, and saddle shops, as well as a weekly newspaper, the Dallas *Herald*,^qv founded in 1849. In 1852 French immigrant Maxime Guillot^qv established the first factory, manufacturing carriages and wagons. Alexander and Sarah Horton Cockrell,^qqv who purchased Bryan's remaining interest in the townsite for $7,000 in 1852, built a three-story brick hotel, a steam sawmill, and a flour mill. With the breakup of the nearby La Réunion^qv colony in the late 1850s, skilled European craftsmen and artists moved into Dallas, including brickmakers, cabinetmakers, tailors, milliners, brewers, and musicians. By 1860 the population was 678, including ninety-seven African Americans^qv as well as French, Belgians, Swiss, and Germans.^qqv On July 8, 1860, a fire originating in the W. W. Peak Brothers Drugstore spread to the other buildings on the square and destroyed most of the businesses. Suspicion fell on slaves and Northern abolitionists; three slaves were hanged, and two Iowa preachers were whipped and run out of town. In 1861 Dallas voters voted 741 to 237 to secede from the Union. Dallas was selected as one of eleven quartermaster and commissary posts in Texas for the Trans-Mississippi Army of the Confederacy. After the war, freed slaves flocked to Dallas in search of jobs and settled in freedmen's towns on the periphery of the city. By 1870, the population was about 3,000.

The key to economic expansion had always been better transportation in and out of the region. Early attempts to navigate the Trinity River had proved impractical. Dallas businessmen turned their attention to securing rail service and succeeded in attracting the Houston and Texas Central in 1872 and the Texas and Pacific in 1873, making Dallas one of the first rail crossroads in Texas. Like Atlanta, Dallas found itself in a strategic geographical location for the transport of abundant regional products to northern and eastern manufacturing plants. Cotton became the region's principal cash crop, and Elm Street in Dallas was its market. Dallas became the world center for the leather and buffalo-hide trade. Merchants who opened general stores along the railroad route as rail construction crept north settled in Dallas and founded their flagship stores there. By 1880 the population had more than tripled, to 10,385.

During the last quarter of the nineteenth century, banking and insurance emerged as major industries under the leadership of such men as William Henry Gaston, William L. Cabell,^qqv and J. T. Trezevant. With their close involvement in civic affairs, Dallas businessmen launched the State Fair of Texas,^qv organized a board of trade, and founded a merchants exchange to promote the city's favorable business climate. Dallas acquired telephones (1881), electricity (1882), and several daily newspapers, principally the Dallas *Morning News*^qv (1885) and the Dallas *Times Herald*^qv (1888). Having annexed the neighboring town of East Dallas on January 1, 1890, Dallas ranked as the most populous city in Texas in 1890, with 38,067 residents. Three years later, in the wake of a national financial panic, five Dallas banks and several industries failed. Cotton prices dropped to less than five cents a pound. Only sixty-two new manufacturing firms were established in Dallas during the 1890s. The panic also affected unionized labor, which had just begun to organize: the American Federation of Labor granted a charter to the Trades Assembly of Dallas in 1899. Among its early causes was championship of the eight-hour workday and legislation outlawing the firing of union members.

By the turn of the century the economy had recovered, and Dallas was the leading book, drug, jewelry, and wholesale liquor market in the Southwest. It was the world's leading inland cotton market, and it still led the world in manufacture of saddlery and cotton-gin machinery. Its population stood at 42,638. In 1905 businessmen formed the 150,000 Club, aimed at increasing the city's population to 150,000 by 1910. Although the numerical goal was not met until 1920, the population did increase to 92,104 by 1910, and the city doubled in area to 18.31 square miles, partly through annexation of Oak Cliff in 1904. Dallas built its first steel skyscraper, the fifteen-story Praetorian Building, in 1907.

In the second decade of the twentieth century Dallas began to implement the city plan commissioned from George E. Kessler^qv after a disastrous flood in 1908. Oak Cliff and Dallas were connected by the Houston Street Viaduct, at the time the longest concrete structure in the world; the Union Terminal Company^qv consolidated six downtown railroad depots; and the railroad tracks were removed from Pacific Avenue. Dallas was selected as the site for a Federal Reserve Bank^qv in 1914, and Ford opened an auto assembly plant in the city. A wave of immigrants from Mexico helped swell the population to 158,976 by 1920, when Dallas ranked as the forty-second-largest city in the nation. The post–World War I era was marked by the reemergence of the Ku Klux Klan.^qv With 13,000 members, the Dallas chapter was the largest in Texas, and the national "imperial wizard" was a Dallas cut-rate dentist named Hiram Wesley Evans.^qv Some 75,000 citizens greeted Evans on "Klan Day" at the 1923 State Fair. The Dallas *Morning News* led the attack on the Klan, helping Ma (Miriam A.) Ferguson^qv defeat Dallas judge Felix Robertson,^qv the Klan candidate, in a Democratic runoff for governor in 1925. Dallas women had been in the forefront of movements in Texas for reform in child-welfare practices, pure food and drink legislation, sanitation, and other causes. By 1920 they were also entering the workforce in increasing numbers. In 1927 the local chapter of the National Association of Business and Professional Women estimated that there were 15,000 women working in 125 occupations, trades, and professions in Dallas. Dallas was also a major center for the textile industry,^qv which employed many women as dressmakers (*see* DALLAS GARMENT WORKERS' STRIKE). Minority businessmen also began to organize. The Dallas Negro Chamber of Commerce (later re-named the Dallas Black Chamber of Commerce^qv) was organized in 1925, and the Mexican Chamber of Commerce (now the Hispanic Chamber of Commerce) was formed in 1940.

The Great Depression^qv put 15,000 Dallasites on the relief roles by 1933, and retail sales and bank deposits plummeted. The population, which had soared to 260,475 by 1930, climbed only to 294,734 in 1940. The pain of the depression was eased somewhat for Dallas by the discovery of oil in East Texas in 1930. Dallas bankers such as Nathan Adams^qv of the First National Bank were the first in the nation to conceive of the idea of lending money to oil companies using oil reserves in the ground for collateral. Dallas soon became a center for petroleum financing. In a massive engineering effort begun in 1930, the channel of the Trinity River was moved, straightened, and confined between levees to prevent future flooding. Dallas businessmen also succeeded in making Fair Park^qv the site of the Texas Centennial^qv celebration, thus providing work for local builders, contractors, advertisers, concessionaires, and construction workers. The city played host to ten million visitors, including President Franklin D. Roosevelt. One of the premier suburbs in Texas, Highland Park,^qv developed within Dallas during the early part of the twentieth century. In it was built the first large-scale shopping center in the nation, Highland Park Village,^qv in 1931. Highland Park incorporated, and its battles with Dallas over annexation lasted into the 1940s.

Until World War II,^qv Dallas ranked as a minor manufacturing center in the nation. Its three leading industries were food processing,^qv apparel manufacturing, and printing and publishing. Then war-related industries, such as North American Aviation, pushed industrial employment in Dallas to more than 75,000 in 1944. Dallas businesses experienced a boom after World War II comparable to that following the coming of the railroads. In 1949, five new businesses opened each day and thirteen new manufacturing plants opened every month. In 1950 the population stood at 434,462. During the 1950s and 1960s, Dallas became the nation's third-largest technology center, with the growth of such companies as Ling-Tempco-Vought (LTV Corporation^qv) and Texas Instruments.^qv In 1957 two developers, Trammell Crow and John M. Stemmons, opened a Home Furnishings Mart that grew into the Dallas Market Center, the largest wholesale trade complex in the world (*see* TRAMMELL CROW COMPANY). The opening of Dallas–Fort Worth International Airport^qv in 1974 attracted numerous corporate headquarters to Dallas and consolidating the city's reputation as a national financial and business center. The population grew from 679,684 in 1960 to 844,401 in 1970, and from 904,078 in 1980 to 1,006,877 in 1990. The 1990 census reported the ethnic groups in the city as white, 47.67 percent; black, 28.88 percent; Hispanic, 20.88 percent; Asian, 2.18 percent; and American Indian, .48 percent. Racial integration of public facilities began on August 15, 1961, when a carefully orchestrated plan sent African Americans to lunch counters and businesses throughout the city for equal service. This plan, which proceeded without incident, was the work of a biracial committee appointed by the Dallas and Negro chambers of commerce, which devised a publicity campaign and notified business owners in advance. Integration of the public schools proceeded more slowly, and the school district remained under court supervision in 1994.

Dallas suffered its most traumatic experience on November 22, 1963, when President John F. Kennedy was assassinated while riding in a motorcade through Dealey Plaza, only yards from the site where John Neely Bryan had settled in 1841 (*see* KENNEDY ASSASSINATION). Two days later, his alleged assassin, Lee Harvey Oswald,^qv was killed before television cameras by a Dallas nightclub owner, Jack Ruby.^qv In 1989, after twenty-five years of debate about how the city should commemorate the event, the Sixth Floor, a museum, opened in the former Texas School Book Depository.^qv In 1993 Dealey Plaza was declared a National Historic Landmark District, the city's second after Fair Park.

The religious composition of the city has changed considerably over the years. Early Protestant settlers looked to traveling missionaries for religious services. The first Episcopal parish was organized in 1856. Catholics celebrated the first Mass in Dallas in 1859. Permanent places of worship were built as the city began to grow: Lamar Street Methodist (later First Methodist), City Temple Presbyterian, and First Baptist,^qv all in 1868. Early black churches included Bethel African Methodist Episcopal (1869–72), New Hope Baptist (1872), and St. Paul Methodist (1873). The first Jewish synagogue, Temple Emanu-El,^qv was built in 1873, and the first Catholic parish was established in 1872, when Dallas was still in the Diocese of Galveston. Congregationalists organized in 1875, Seventh Day Adventists in 1876, Lutherans in 1878, Unitarians in 1889, Christian Scientists in 1894, and Mormons in 1897. The variety of communions helped to make Dallas a religious stronghold by the turn of the century, and the continued growth of churches marked Dallas as a city of churchgoers. In the early 1980s, Dallas had six churches among the nation's 100 largest: First Baptist, Lovers Lane United Methodist, Cliff Temple Baptist, Beverly Hills Baptist, First United Methodist, and East Grand Baptist. Three more on the list were in suburbs: Highland Park United Methodist, Highland Park Presbyterian, and Park Cities Baptist. Subsequently, as the population has diversified, so have the religious faiths. Buddhists, Eastern Orthodox, Hindus, Muslims, and Sikhs are now found in Dallas. Southern Baptists have the largest representation in the Dallas area, followed by Catholics, black Baptists, and United Methodists.

The Art Saloon of Adolph Gouhenant (actually a photograph gallery), located on the south side of the courthouse square in the 1850s, was an early expression of artistic interest in Dallas. An 1857 diary reference to a visit "to the court house to look at the paintings of the Hudson scholars" may mark the earliest art exhibit in Dallas. Art shows at the annual state fairs after 1886 exposed the public to art, while plans for the Carnegie Library, which opened in 1901, included an upstairs art gallery. The success of early shows there, which featured such regional artists as Frank (Charles F.) Reaugh and Edward G. Eisenlohr,[qqv] led to the organization of the Dallas Art Association, which began assembling a permanent collection. After several moves and name changes, the Dallas Museum of Art[qv] now occupies a building designed by Edward Larrabee Barnes in the Dallas Arts District. By 1873 Dallas had a theater, Field's Opera House, where the first performance of an opera in the city took place in February 1875. The influx of German immigrants with the railroads led to the formation of the Dallas Frohsinn, a male singing society and member of the Texas State Sängerbund,[qv] which hosted statewide singing meets in 1883, 1892, 1904, and 1914. The Dallas Symphony Orchestra[qv] traces its roots to performances in 1900, and the Dallas Opera was launched in 1957. By the early 1920s Dallas was home to one of the earliest radio[qv] stations in Texas, WFAA.

During the 1920s and 1930s popular music was centered in the Deep Ellum[qv] district on the eastern edge of downtown, close to one of Dallas's original freedmen's towns. Major black jazz[qv] and blues[qv] musicians such as Huddie "Leadbelly" Ledbetter and Blind Lemon Jefferson[qqv] performed at Ella B. Moore's Park Theater, Hattie Burleson's dance hall, and other local clubs. Today Dallas has a wide variety of popular music and entertainment venues including the Summer Musicals, Starplex, and productions by the Dallas Jazz Orchestra, the Classical Guitar Society, the Dallas Chamber Orchestra, the Dallas Black Dance Theater, and the U.S.A. Film Festival. Dramatic productions in the nineteenth century were available as early as 1872 in Thompson's Variety Theater. The Little Theater of Dallas was established in 1921 and won the national Belasco Cup several times; it was followed by such other companies as the Civic Theater, the New Theater League of Dallas, and the critically acclaimed Margo (Margaret Virginia) Jones[qv] company. The Dallas Theater Center was founded in 1955 and is housed in a building on Turtle Creek designed by Frank Lloyd Wright. Other groups include Theatre Three, Teatro Dallas, the Dallas Children's Theater, and the Dallas Shakespeare Festival.

Educational institutions have been present in Dallas since its earliest years. Private schools and academies preceded the founding of the public school system in 1884. The present Dallas Independent School District, with more than 130,000 students, is the eighth largest school district in the nation. Institutions of higher learning include Southern Methodist University, founded in 1911; Paul Quinn College, a formerly black private institution that moved from Waco in 1990; Bishop College, another historically black institution founded in Marshall in 1881; and the University of Texas Southwestern Medical School, founded in 1943. Several campuses of Dallas County Community College, established in 1965, are located within the city.

Sporting events and teams in Dallas have their roots in the nineteenth century, when horse racing was popular enough to support a Dallas Jockey Club, founded in 1869. Horse racing was a major attraction at the State Fair of Texas from 1886 until 1909. The national bicycling craze inspired the formation of the Dallas Wheel Club in 1886, and races were held at Cycle Park from its construction in 1896 until its conversion to an open-air theater. Baseball was played in Dallas as early as 1877, when a touring team played a local team. By 1882 Dallas had its first semiprofessional team, the Brown Stockings, which won the league championship in 1883 and 1884. The Dallas Hams, a professional team, won the Texas League[qv] pennant in 1888; Dallas continued to field minor league teams until 1970. Football made its first appearance in Dallas with the organization of a Dallas Football Club in 1891. A team formed at Dallas High School in 1900 is thought to have been the first high school team in Texas. SMU sent a team to the 1935 Rose Bowl, and Doak Walker drew crowds to the Cotton Bowl[qv] in the late 1940s. Two professional teams, the Dallas Cowboys and the Dallas Texans,[qqv] competed for fans in the early 1960s, until owner Lamar Hunt moved the Texans to Kansas City in 1963. The Dallas Cowboys (who now play in Irving) won Superbowl titles in 1972, 1978, 1993, and 1994. Dallas's first professional basketball team, the Chaparrals, was moved to San Antonio, but the new franchise, the Dallas Mavericks,[qv] was organized in 1980. Dallas also hosts a professional soccer team, the Sidekicks, and an NHL hockey team, the Dallas Stars.

In 1907 Dallas voters adopted the commission form of city government[qv] to replace the aldermanic system. In 1930 the Citizens Charter Association won voter approval for the council-manager form of city government;[qv] an amendment in 1949 provided for direct election of the mayor. The CCA and the Dallas Citizens Council, a small group composed of business leaders, dominated local government until a 1971 lawsuit forced election by districts rather than at large. A 1992 amendment expanded the council to fourteen single-member districts, with the mayor elected at large.

Dallas purchased Fair Park from its owners in 1904 and continues to maintain this National Historic Landmark through a contract with the State Fair of Texas. Other municipal facilities include the City Hall, designed by I. M. Pei; the Dallas Convention Center, the Dallas Public Library, the Dallas Zoo, Union Terminal, and Love Field.[qv] The city also owns the Dallas Museum of Art, the Morton Meyerson Symphony Hall, the Dallas Zoo, and the Dallas Arboretum. Most of the cultural institutions are operated by private, nonprofit entities under contracts with the city.

Bryan's original survey for Dallas used the Trinity River as the western boundary, with streets laid out at right angles to the river. A competing survey drawn by Warren A. Ferris,[qv] done for John Grisby, was laid out at 45 degrees off cardinal directions. A third survey made for the Peters colony laid out sections using cardinal directions. The results are an odd series of doglegged streets downtown. Annexation of adjacent communities added another layer of surveying patterns to the Dallas street map. Although the first residential subdivision, the Cedars, was built south of downtown in the 1880s, most residential development has been toward the north and east. Segregated housing confined African Americans to a few overcrowded areas. Violence occurred as blacks began to integrate neighborhoods in South Dallas during the 1950s. Freedman's Town, the oldest of the freedmen's towns, in the State-Thomas area northeast of downtown, virtually disappeared with commercial development in the 1980s except for a historic cemetery that was literally unearthed during the widening of Central Expressway. The principal Hispanic barrio, immediately north of downtown, has also been displaced by commercial development.

The building boom of the 1970s and 1980s produced a distinctive contemporary profile for the downtown area, influenced by nationally prominent architects. At the same time, the establishment of the West End Historic District in the 1980s preserved a group of late-nineteenth-century brick warehouses that have been adapted for use as restaurants and shops. Similar efforts have been made in Deep Ellum, where the 1920s-era storefronts now house clubs and restaurants. The Dallas Park Department oversees some 406 parks that cover

50,000 acres. White Rock Lake,qv Bachman Lake, and Lake Cliff are surrounded by parks, and city-owned greenbelts follow the waterways in the city including White Rock Creek, Turtle Creek,qv and the Trinity River.

Modern historic preservation efforts began in the 1970s with the formation of the Historic Preservation League. The city's Landmark Commission has designated numerous buildings and several neighborhoods as landmarks, including Swiss Avenue, Munger Place, South Boulevard–Park Row, and State-Thomas. Fair Park is the largest Art Deco art and architecture district in the world. Old City Park,qv a museum of architectural and cultural history on the site of Dallas's oldest public park, is located just south of downtown.

BIBLIOGRAPHY: Sam Hanna Acheson, *Dallas Yesterday*, ed. Lee Milazzo (Dallas: Southern Methodist University Press, 1977). William L. McDonald, *Dallas Rediscovered: A Photographic Chronicle of Urban Expansion, 1870–1925* (Dallas: Dallas County Historical Society, 1978). Darwin Payne, *Dallas: An Illustrated History* (Woodland Hills, California: Windsor, 1982). John William Rogers, *The Lusty Texans of Dallas* (New York: Dutton, 1951; enlarged ed. 1960; expanded ed., Dallas: Cokesbury Book Store, 1965). WPA Writers' Program, *The WPA Dallas Guide and History*, ed. Maxine Holmes and Gerald D. Saxon (Denton: University of North Texas Press, 1992).

Jackie McElhaney and Michael V. Hazel

DALLAS ARCHEOLOGICAL SOCIETY. The Dallas Archeological Society was started in 1936 as a study group interested in the geology, paleontology, and archeology of the Dallas area. It had no formal organization until 1940, when the group decided to concentrate on archeology. A constitution and bylaws were adopted, officers elected, and the present name selected. The purpose of the organization is to bring together persons interested in the prehistory of the area for the purpose of systematic study, scientific investigation, and publication of relevant material. Membership is open to anyone interested in archeology. The society had a charter membership of thirteen. Activities of the society include archeological investigation of historic and prehistoric sites, regular meetings, and publication of a newsletter. In addition to sponsoring excavations and reconnaissance, the society cooperates with educational institutions, museums, and government agencies in surveying and recording sites affected by construction, flooding, or agricultural operations. The society newsletter, the *Record*, began publication in 1939; it announces the activities of the members and publishes scientific papers of interest to them.

BIBLIOGRAPHY: Vertical Files, Barker Texas History Center, University of Texas at Austin (Archeology).

Paul Lorrain

DALLAS ART INSTITUTE. The Dallas Art Institute, established in 1926 by artists Kathryn Hail and Olin Herman Travis,qv was initially located at 1215½ Main Street. It was the first art school in Dallas to offer instruction in several fields. Painting and drawing were emphasized, with classes offered in portraiture, landscape and still-life painting, composition, and life drawing. Classes in sculpture, commercial art, and fashion drawing were also available. In 1927 Kathryn Hail Travis organized the Ozark Summer School, an adjunct of the institute, in Cass, Arkansas, an abandoned sawmill town in the Ozark Mountains. The summer classes enabled students to sketch and paint outdoors in a naturally beautiful environment. The institute operated with a faculty of eight and had some 200 students until the early 1930s, when the Great Depressionqv placed a damper on attendance.

The Dallas Art Institute was subsequently reorganized with a civic board, and in 1931 moved to the grounds of the Civic Federation at 2419 Maple Avenue. Another series of changes was instituted in the summer of 1932 in an attempt to establish the institute as the preeminent art school in the Southwest. Architect Thomas D. Broad was named executive director, a new position, to act as liaison between the board of trustees and the school. Associate instructors were hired to conduct special classes in such areas as outdoor sketching, watercolor, ceramics, and stage design, thus extending the range of learning opportunities available to the students. Finally, a series of lectures and exhibitions was inaugurated to serve the Dallas community. By 1934 two degrees were offered by the school: a certificate of attainment earned after a three-year course, and a diploma awarded after four years of study.

The Dallas Art Institute exerted its greatest influence from 1931 to 1935. Its location at the corner of Maple Avenue and Alice Street placed the school in a thriving art colony that included the Southwest School of Fine Arts, the Klepper Sketch Club, and the Alice Street Art carnivals sponsored by the Dallas Art League,qv which met nearby. Director Olin Travis championed the work of the new generation of regionalist artists and hired Allie V. Tennant, Alexandre Hogue, Thomas M. Stell, Jr., Harry P. Carnohan, Jerry Bywaters,qqv and other leaders of the regionalist group to teach at the institute. Stell's emphasis on draftsmanship and his interest in early Italian and Flemish artists were particularly influential in shaping the styles of his students.

In 1935 the need for larger quarters prompted the institute to move to a remodeled residence at 2503 McKinney Avenue. The institute moved to the school wing of the Dallas Museum of Fine Arts (now the Dallas Museum of Artqv) in 1938, where it remained until 1941. At that time the trustees of the Dallas Art Association decided to establish their own museum school, and the Dallas Art Institute moved to a new location at 1912½ Main. By 1945 the school had closed, but its impact on Texas art continued through its graduates who became professional artists and teachers, among whom Merritt T. Mauzey, William Lester,qv Everett Spruce, Florence McClung, Bertha Landers, Lloyd Goff, and Michael G. Owen, Jr., were some of the most distinguished.

BIBLIOGRAPHY: Jerry Bywaters, *Seventy-Five Years of Art in Dallas: The History of the Dallas Art Association and the Dallas Museum of Fine Arts* (Dallas: Dallas Museum of Fine Arts, 1978). Dallas *Morning News*, August 28, 1982. Esse Forrester-O'Brien, *Art and Artists of Texas* (Dallas: Tardy, 1935). Rick Stewart, *Lone Star Regionalism* (Austin: Texas Monthly Press, 1985).

Kendall Curlee

DALLAS ARTISTS LEAGUE. The Dallas Artists League, a group of artists, scholars, and patrons formed during the Great Depression,qv became a forum for promoting the regionalist aesthetic in the Southwest. The group was founded in May 1932 by arts patron May Selley Wyche, who envisioned a contemporary version of English coffeehouse meetings. In the beginning the group met on a weekly basis at the Wyche home on Alice Street near the Dallas Art Institute.qv The league was led by artists Nina Peeples and Vivian Stanley.

Every Tuesday night Cyril and May Wyche offered dinner at cost to some twenty to forty artists, after which a lecture was presented by a local or visiting person involved in the arts. A wide range of topics was discussed. In some of the outstanding lectures presented in the first year, for example, C. L. Lundell spoke on Mayan excavations, Stanley Marcus lectured on contemporary bookmaking, Talbot Pearson spoke on the Little Theater movement, and David R. Williams and O'Neil Fordqqv lectured on early Texas and contemporary architecture. The league meetings also served as an arena for debate on the nature of art; regionalist art was promoted by such members as Henry Nash Smith and John H. McGinnis,qqv both of whom were associated with the *Southwest Review*,qv and artists Jerry Bywaters and Alexandre Hogue.qqv The league published a magazine edited by Bywaters, *Southwestern Arts* (1932–33), which focused on regionalist interests.

The Dallas Artists League provided an opportunity for local painters, sculptors, and craftsmen to exchange information and discuss problems on a regular basis. Harry P. Carnohan,qv for example, shared his knowledge of contemporary European art and his interest in early Italian Renaissance painters in a number of lectures after his return from Paris in 1932; Bywaters described his meetings with Diego Rivera and other Mexican muralists after a trip to Mexico City; artists Edward G. Eisenlohr, Frank E. Klepper,qqv Dorothy Austin, Ruby Stone, Lloyd Goff, Perry Nichols, and Velma Davis reported on their experiences. Speakers were frequently grilled with questions and opposing points of view in an atmosphere that Bywaters described as "stimulating" and "often rowdy."

From 1932 to 1935 the league also sponsored the Alice Street art carnivals, which were influential in building a local following for regionalist artists. Inspired by the Washington Square art festivals in Greenwich Village, the Dallas Artists League staged the first art carnival on June 29–30, 1932. Both ends of Alice Street were closed off by the city, and seventy-six artists displayed their wares. Although sales were modest, the artists were encouraged by the attendance of 7,000 people and the positive publicity generated by the event. The league sponsored fairs at Alice Street for the following three years, each year attracting more participating artists and visitors. No carnival was organized in 1936, since many of the league members were involved in preparations for the Texas Centennial qv Exposition.

After the new museum building was erected at Fair Park in 1936, the locus of Dallas's art activity shifted to the Dallas Museum of Fine Arts (now the Dallas Museum of Art qv), and interest in the Dallas Artists League waned. The art carnival was moved to the grounds of the Dallas Museum of Fine Arts in 1939, where it was sponsored by the Museum League. The Lone Star Printmakers and the Printmakers Guild of Dallas, established in 1938 and 1940, respectively, provided new arenas for the exchange of ideas and mutual support among artists.

BIBLIOGRAPHY: Jerry Bywaters, *Seventy-Five Years of Art in Dallas: The History of the Dallas Art Association and the Dallas Museum of Fine Arts* (Dallas: Dallas Museum of Fine Arts, 1978). Dallas *Morning News*, October 1, 1933. Jerry Bywaters Collection on the Art of the Southwest, Southern Methodist University. Rick Stewart, *Lone Star Regionalism* (Austin: Texas Monthly Press, 1985).

Kendall Curlee

DALLAS BAPTIST UNIVERSITY. Dallas Baptist University, in the southwest Oak Cliff section of Dallas, is the modern successor to Decatur Baptist College, originally named Northwest Texas Baptist College, which was founded in 1891 by the Northwest Texas Baptist Association. Decatur was chosen as the site for the school because of its central location, because of its "healthful and invigorating" climate, and because local Wise County citizens donated the land and pledged a $15,000 endowment. The classes of 1892–93 met in rented rooms in the old Opera House on East Main Street in Decatur. After the dedication on September 6, 1893, the college officially moved to the newly constructed administration building, three-fourths of a mile south of the Decatur courthouse. Three years later several of the churches that had pledged financial support failed to meet their obligations, and the college was sold at auction for $13,000 to pay off the creditors. In 1897 the Baptist General Convention of Texas purchased the property for $7,000 and changed the name of the institution to Decatur Baptist College. From 1898 to 1965 Decatur Baptist College operated as a church-affiliated coeducational junior college to prepare students for Baylor University. It was controlled by a board of trustees elected by the Baptist General Convention of Texas. Financial support was based on a $20,000 endowment and a $10,000 annual contribution from the Baptist Executive Board, supplemented by private donations and by the fees collected for tuition and board. Decatur Baptist College was accredited by the Southern Association of Colleges and by the Texas Education Agency qv and was a member of such organizations as the Texas Junior College Association and the American Association of Junior Colleges. The policy of Decatur Baptist College was "distinctly Christian and unswervingly Baptistic," and students were expected to attend church services and chapel regularly. Two Bible courses were required for graduation. By 1959 the college offered courses in fine arts, business, languages, and vocational training as well as religion. Decatur Baptist College typically employed twelve faculty members and enrolled an average of 150 students, most of whom came from within a fifty-mile radius of Decatur. Of Decatur Baptist College's six presidents J. L. Ward, who held the office from 1900 to 1907 and 1914 to 1950, was most influential in the development and expansion of the institution. During his forty-three years as president, Reverend Ward worked to increase enrollment and to establish a firm financial foundation for the school. By 1958 Decatur Baptist College claimed the distinction of being the oldest junior college in the world and possessed property valued at $250,000. In 1965 the college was moved to its present location in Dallas, its name was changed to Dallas Baptist College, and in 1968 it became a four-year institution. It gave its first baccalaureate degrees in 1970. The college was renamed Dallas Baptist University on January 1, 1985, and began offering graduate degrees in education, religion, and business administration. The Decatur property was purchased at auction by a local resident, Coke L. Gage, who donated the administration building and one acre of land to the Wise County Historical Association. The building houses the Wise County Heritage Museum and provides auditorium facilities for the local Little Theater group. For 1992–93 the school had 114 faculty and 2,712 students for the regular term and 2,124 students for the summer session. There were also 887 extension or continuing education students.

BIBLIOGRAPHY: Decatur Baptist College *Catalogue*, 60th Anniversary ed., 1948–59. Rosalie Gregg, ed., *Wise County History* (Vol. 1, n.p: Nortex, 1975; Vol. 2, Austin: Eakin, 1982). Mary Cates Moore, *Centennial History of Wise County* (Dallas: Story Book, 1953).

B. Jane England

DALLAS BLACK CHAMBER OF COMMERCE. The Dallas Black Chamber of Commerce is the oldest African-American Chamber of Commerce in Texas. In 1926, impatient with the limited direction from Booker T. Washington's National Negro Business League, businessmen in Dallas established the Dallas Negro Chamber of Commerce to promote economic progress among members of their race. Although the chamber maintained an affiliation with the National Negro Business League, leaders believed that "integrating the Negro community into the life of Greater Dallas" should remain the members' principal goal. The chamber initially consisted of 100 members directed by W. E. Clark. A period of intensive organizational activity occurred between 1933 and 1939, during Antonio Maceo Smith's qv tenure as executive secretary. Under Smith's leadership the chamber and its full-time staff counseled black owners of small retail establishments such as barber and beauty shops, grocery stores, restaurants, service stations, and funeral homes and encouraged African Americans qv to patronize businesses owned by members of their race. The chamber established an employment service in the early 1940s. It lobbied on behalf of the Negro Plumbers Association, the Negro Movie Operators Union, the Negro Golf Association, and other interest groups and called for improved schools, housing, and law enforcement in the black community. The staff also published an African-American directory for Dallas. Frequently the chamber organized civic leagues, prepared petitions, and arranged conferences with local governmental officials. While endorsing some white political candidates, the chamber campaigned for the employment of black law officers, for public housing, and for street improvements in black neighborhoods. Partly because of the chamber's efforts, the federal government provided financial support for the Hall of Negro Life qv at the Texas Centennial qv Exposition in 1936. The chamber also engaged in campaigns designed to encourage blacks to pay their poll taxes. Working with the National Association For the Advancement of Colored People qv and other political groups such as the Democratic Progressive Voters League and the Council of Negro Organizations, the chamber supported racial equality and opposed the Democratic party's white primary qqv in Texas. After a disturbance between black soldiers and Dallas police in 1943, the chamber helped organize a biracial committee that sought to improve interracial relations in the city. The chamber also played important roles in desegregating Texas State Fair qv facilities and in developing the Hamilton Park subdivision for black residents.

During the 1950s and 1960s the chamber sponsored urban renewal projects for black neighborhoods. In the 1960s it helped move Bishop College qv from Marshall. Under the leadership of J. H. Glenn in 1964, the chamber sponsored a study of black consumers in Dallas County which showed that the county's 169,000 African Americans contributed as much as $150 million annually to the local economy. By the 1970s the chamber was increasing cooperation with the Dallas Chamber of Commerce and other branches of the United States Chamber of Commerce. The chamber offered market surveys, public relations services, advertising assistance, and financial advice to local businesses. Under H. Ron White's presidency in 1975, the chamber changed its name to Dallas Black Chamber of Commerce. Chamber leaders attended symposia on "institutional racism," promoted tourism in Dallas, and attempted to place more African Americans on city boards and commissions. Although a self-study committee in 1971 criticized apathy among the nearly 500 chamber members and expressed concerns about the organization's future, by the early 1990s the Dallas Black Chamber of Commerce had from 900 to 1,100 members and still provided seminars and workshops for small businesses, promoted Dallas to blacks from other geographic locations, worked closely with the Dallas Convention and Visitors Bureau, and published a newsletter. Presidents of the chamber have included Antonio Maceo Smith (1933–39), Maynard H. Jackson, Sr. (1939–40), and John W. Rice (1942–62).qqv In 1981 Helen Giddings became the chamber's first woman president, although the organization had admitted women members as early as 1942. Other Texas cities established Negro chambers of commerce following the Dallas lead. The Texas Negro Chamber of Commerce, a federation of the local chambers, began in 1936 and patterned itself after the Dallas Negro Chamber of Commerce. A statewide organization of black chambers of commerce still operated in the early 1990s.

BIBLIOGRAPHY: Dallas Negro Chamber of Commerce Collection, Texas-Dallas History and Archives Division, Dallas Public Library. Tempie Virginia Strange, The Dallas Negro Chamber of Commerce: A Study of a Negro Institution (M.A. thesis, Southern Methodist University, 1945).
Paul M. Lucko

DALLAS CHRISTIAN COLLEGE. Dallas Christian College, a private, four-year coeducational college of the Christian church, is located in Farmers Branch, on a twenty-two-acre campus. In May 1949 forty men met in Dallas at the invitation of Vernon M. Newland to plan the founding of a Bible college that would recruit and train a "Bible-believing, evangelistic ministry." As a result of this meeting, Dallas Christian College opened for classes in 1950, with thirty-four students in facilities shared by Cole Park Christian Church in Dallas. Vernon Newland served as the school's first president. As the student body grew, the college was twice moved to larger locations. The second move, in 1967, was to the present location in Farmers Branch. Between 1974 and 1985, in an attempt to provide both Christian education for younger students and a preparatory program for its entering students, the college operated a twelve-grade school, Heritage Christian Academy, on the campus. The academy closed in 1985. In 1986 the college had an enrollment of 120, a full-time faculty of six, and a part-time faculty of twenty-one. Its library contained approximately 35,000 volumes. The school is approved by the Veterans Administration, the United States Department of Health, Education, and Welfare, and the United States Immigration Service for the enrollment of students eligible for benefits or supervised by these agencies. Dallas Christian College is accredited by the American Association of Bible Colleges. Degrees offered include bachelor of arts, bachelor of science in religion, bachelor of science in education, bachelor of science in music, and associate degrees in secretarial science, general education, and pastoral ministries.
Cecil Harper, Jr.

DALLAS, CLEBURNE AND RIO GRANDE RAILWAY. The Dallas, Cleburne and Rio Grande Railway Company was chartered on November 23, 1876, as the Dallas and Cleburne Railroad. The D&C was unable to secure financing and reorganized on July 31, 1879, as the Dallas, Cleburne and Rio Grande. The company planned to build from Dallas to Brownwood, about 150 miles. The initial capital was $250,000, and the business office was located at Dallas. Members of the first board of directors included Alfred Davis, W. J. Keller, S. J. Adams, A. F. Hardie, W. R. Wheelock, Alexander Sanger,qv F. M. Cockrell, W. C. Howard, and J. T. Eliot, all from Dallas. The Dallas and Cleburne Railroad had been chartered on November 23, 1876, to build a narrow-gauge line between Dallas and Cleburne, but the capital could not be raised and the road was reorganized as the Dallas, Cleburne, and Rio Grande. In 1879 the company built fifty-three miles of narrow-gauge track from Dallas to Cleburne. The company ran a freight and passenger train over the tracks to collect a promised bonus, but service was then abandoned. The right-of-way passed to the Chicago, Texas and Mexican Central Railway Company in 1880.
Chris Cravens

DALLAS, CLEBURNE AND SOUTHWESTERN RAILWAY. The Dallas, Cleburne and Southwestern Railway Company was chartered on June 3, 1902, by W. D. Myers and W. A. McDonald of Cleburne to build fifty miles from Cleburne in Johnson County to Dallas. The capital was $200,000, and the business office was in Cleburne. Members of the first board of directors included A. C. Irvine of Cooke County; J. E. Fesler of Grayson County; Myers and McDonald, both of Johnson County; and C. C. Nelson, B. P. McDonald, and C. H. Osbun, all from Bourbon County, Kentucky. In 1903 investors from Fort Scott, Kansas, had built the only track, a 9.32-mile line from Egan on the Missouri, Kansas and Texas Railway Company of Texas (Katy) in eastern Johnson County to Cleburne, the county seat. The Dallas, Cleburne and Southwestern was operated under contract by the Katy and subsequently leased to that company. However, the lease was terminated during the Katy's receivership, and the Dallas, Cleburne and Southwestern was not included in the reorganized Katy system. A separate receiver was appointed for the Dallas, Cleburne and Southwestern who operated the line from April 1, 1923, through June 30, 1923, at which time service was discontinued. The company was abandoned in 1925. During the railroad's short duration, a depot and terminal facility were located on East Chambers Street in Cleburne. The railroad was sometimes called the "DC" or "Old Betsy."
Richard Elam

DALLAS COLLEGE. Dallas College, probably an outgrowth of Dallas Male and Female College, was the result of a long period of agitation for a good Baptist college in the Dallas area. By September 1878 the Elm Fork Baptist Association and the Baptist Educational Association of Northern Texas had raised sufficient funds to open the school near the site of the fairgrounds in Dallas. The appointed faculty included instructors in chemistry, music, languages, fine arts, and theology. The school was divided into primary, preparatory, and collegiate departments. Tuition ran from two to five dollars, depending on the level of instruction. G. W. Rogers, the first president, was followed by C. H. Hobbs. The school closed in 1881 for lack of students.

BIBLIOGRAPHY: Carl Bassett Wilson, History of Baptist Educational Efforts in Texas, 1829–1900 (Ph.D. dissertation, University of Texas, 1934).

DALLAS COUNTY. Dallas County (E-18), in north central Texas, is bordered by Kaufman and Rockwall counties to the east, Tarrant County to the west, Denton and Collin counties to the north, and Ellis County to the south. Dallas is the county seat and largest city. The county's center point is at 32°30′ north latitude and 94°30′ west longitude. Dallas County comprises 902 square miles of the primarily flat, heavy Blackland Prairie. Elevations in the county range from 382 to 584 feet above sea level. The Elm Fork and West Fork of the Trinity River meet near downtown Dallas. The county is drained by the Trinity River and its tributaries, including White Rock, Mountain, Fivemile, Tenmile, Muddy, Duck, Turtle, and Mesquite creeks. These streams feed reservoirs for municipal water and recreational use, including Lake Ray Hubbard, Lake North, Joe Pool, Mountain Creek and White Rock Lakes. The terrain is generally undulating. The eastern two-thirds of the county and the land along the western border is surfaced by slightly acidic clayey soils with loamy topsoil. The rest of the county's soil is alkaline and loamy. The county has tall grasses with pecan and oak trees along streams and mesquite on the prairies. Though the rich soil is the main mineral resource of Dallas County, gravel and sand have been mined from the Trinity floodplain, cement has been made from the local soft limestone, and bricks have been manufactured from the county's clay. Temperatures range from an average high of 95° F in July to an average low of 36° in January. The average rainfall is thirty-six inches a year. The growing season lasts 235 days.

The primary Indians in the region were the Anadarkos, a Caddoan group, who settled in villages along the Trinity River. Probably the first European contact with the area occurred when the Moscoso expedition[qv] entered the northeastern corner of the future Dallas County in 1542. In the eighteenth century French explorers and traders were in the vicinity. In 1760 a missionary from Nacogdoches, José Francisco Calahorra y Saenz,[qv] made treaties with the Indians throughout the area. In 1819 or 1820 sixty Cherokee warriors and their families arrived from Arkansas under the leadership of Chief Bowl,[qv] a Scots–Indian. After a three-year battle between them and the local Caddos, during which the Cherokees lost a third of their warriors, the Cherokees withdrew. In 1837 rangers from an expedition under the command of Lt. A. B. Benthuysons, the first Anglo-Americans to see the future county, camped on Turtle Creek after an engagement with Indians fifty miles to the north. By 1840 American explorers had begun to enter the area. The first to remain was John Neely Bryan,[qv] who arrived in the autumn with his dog and a Cherokee friend, Ned.

The future Dallas County east of the Trinity was then part of Nacogdoches County, and the part west of the Trinity belonged to Robertson County. The area was an ideal place to settle because of its rich soil and ample water. The Republic of Texas[qv] was planning to build the Military Road[qv] from Austin through the site of future Dallas to the Red River. Other roads leading to Jefferson, Houston, and the Gulf Coast soon crossed at Dallas. The underlying Austin chalk made a firm foundation for roadways. The location on the Trinity was even more valuable because at the time it was thought that the river was navigable from the Gulf of Mexico[qv] (*see also* RIVER NAVIGATION). Settlers found useful trees, including post oak, bois d'arc, pecan, and mesquite;[qv] both Indians and settlers ate mesquite beans. The available game included deer, buffalo, bear, and jackrabbits. Settlers in the area had difficulties with Indians, however, and many had settled for protection at Fort Bird, one of eight forts built on the Military Road, located near the site of present-day Euless. In 1841 the Republic of Texas had authorized the Texas Emigration and Land Company, also known as W. S. Peters and Associates or the Peters colony[qv] to recruit settlers for a 1,300-square-mile area. The people at Fort Bird were unable to claim their land legitimately because of Bryan's claim on the banks of the Trinity. In January 1841 Bryan convinced some settlers to move near his cabin at the site he had christened Dallas. Indians continued to attack outlying settlements in the vicinity, and in 1843 Sam Houston,[qv] president of the Republic of Texas, went to Grapevine Springs, later called Coppell, to meet with Indian leaders. When the chiefs failed to show up, the meeting was rescheduled at Fort Bird, and in 1843 a treaty was signed that kept the Indians west of the site of present-day Fort Worth. By the mid-1840s there were several other communities in the area in addition to Dallas. Farmers Branch, in northwestern Dallas County, the location of the Peters colony field office, had more residents than Dallas at the time. Cedar Springs, 3½ miles northwest of Dallas, and Hord's Ridge, the predecessor of Oak Cliff, were competing with Dallas for settlers.

In 1845 voters in the future Dallas County approved the annexation[qv] of Texas to the United States by a vote of 29 to 3. On March 30, 1846, Dallas County was officially formed by order of the state legislature from portions of Nacogdoches and Robertson counties, and named probably for George Mifflin Dallas, vice president of the United States under James K. Polk (*see* DALLAS, TEXAS). At Dallas, the temporary county seat, a log cabin was built to serve as a courthouse. In 1850 an election was held to find a permanent county seat. A runoff election was held after the first vote yielded 191 votes for Dallas, 178 for Hord's Ridge, and 101 for Cedar Springs. Dallas beat Hord's Ridge 244 to 216 in the runoff. By 1850 Dallas County had a population of 2,743, and by 1860 the number of residents had almost tripled to 8,665. Though the slave population rose faster than the white population, Dallas County had fewer slaves that some other Texas counties. In 1850 the 207 slaves were 8 percent of the population, but by 1860 slaves constituted 12 percent of the population. These 1,074 slaves were owned by 228 slaveholders. In 1850 the county had two churches and ten one-teacher public schools with a total of 170 pupils. The population resided on 278 farms with a value of $175,502. The largest crop was corn, with 94,870 bushels, and cotton was a minor crop with only 44 bales. Cotton was originally grown primarily for home use, but by 1849 Farmers Branch had the first cotton gin in the county. By 1860 wheat was a major Dallas County crop, and many gristmills had been constructed to grind the grain. In 1850 stockmen raised more hogs (6,089) than cattle, but by 1860 cattle numbered 35,431 and sheep 20,974, while hogs numbered only 16,113.

In 1861, Dallas County's citizens voted overwhelmingly for secession.[qv] The area was not invaded during the Civil War,[qv] but ten companies were mustered in the county and 1,300 Dallas County men fought for the Confederacy. The county population rose during the war, however, in spite of the exodus of soldiers. In 1861, since Dallas County was the food-producing center for North Texas, the Confederate government established a general quartermaster's and commissary headquarters for the army of the Trans–Mississippi Department there. Officers and their families moved to the county. Slaveholders from other areas of the South moved into Dallas County with their slaves in order to avoid attack by Union troops. Lancaster, in southern Dallas County, was the site of a pistol factory. After the war came a prosperous era. The population rose from 8,665 in 1860 to 13,414 in 1870, with the black population growing more rapidly than the white. Dallas residents were urged by newspapers to comply with their conquerors as the best way to recover from the loss of the war. People from other areas of the South, primarily Tennessee, Missouri, Arkansas, Georgia, Alabama, South Carolina, and Mississippi, moved to Dallas, for they saw North Texas as a new land with plenty of opportunity to grow wheat, which did not require slave labor as cotton did.

After Reconstruction[qv] Dallas County voted Democratic until 1928, when it voted overwhelmingly for Herbert Hoover, the Republican candidate, who faced the "wet" Catholic Alfred E. Smith in the election. Subsequently, Dallas County voters maintained their Democratic voting habits until 1952, when they voted for Dwight D. Eisenhower.[qv] Afterwards, until the 1990s the county voted overwhelmingly for the Republican candidate, including Richard Nixon in 1960. The exception was the 1964 election, when Texan Lyndon B. Johnson[qv] won the county.

Between 1880 and 1920, Dallas County remained primarily rural and agricultural, although manufacturing was growing. Cotton peaked in 1900, when the county produced 41,012 bales. After 1900 the cotton crop declined every year. Hogs, horses, and cattle other than dairy cattle were also at their peak in 1900. Wheat and oats had their largest crops in 1920—584,399 and 1,448,541 bushels, respectively. In 1920 the county had its largest number of farms, 5,379. After that year, farms became less numerous every decade as farming became less important in Dallas County and manufacturing became increasingly significant. In 1860 the county had fifteen manufacturers that produced $341,239 worth of products; in 1920 the 492 manufacturers produced more than $116 million worth of products and employed 8,708 people. The population kept pace with the rapid expansion of manufacturing. It rose sixfold, from 33,477 in 1880 to 210,551 in 1920. By 1900, 70 percent of the population resided in Dallas, Oak Cliff, Carrollton, Lancaster, Garland, Grand Prairie, Mesquite, and Richardson. The proportion of black to white residents remained stable at around 15 percent black and 85 percent white.

The lack of transportation in Dallas County during the antebellum period slowed the county's growth. From 1843 to 1850 Houston, Texas, and Shreveport, Louisiana, were the nearest markets, and goods had to be shipped by oxen. By the 1860s Jefferson, Texas, was the nearest market and port. In spite of its great distance from markets, Dallas County had the advantage of being at the crossroads of two Republic of Texas roads, the Military Road from Austin to the Red River, completed in 1846, which crossed the Trinity at Dallas, and Preston Road. In 1846 Dallas County Commissioners approved the building of roads to contiguous counties. The easy fordability of the Trinity River in Dallas County increased the trade traffic. Optimistic attempts to make the river navigable failed, however. The Trinity had seven or eight crossings in the antebellum period, including Dawdy's Ferry, Record Crossing, California Crossing (used by Forty-niners on their way to California), and Eagle Ford, where a community was founded. But later, even the fords could not prevent the river from becoming a barrier to growth of the Dallas County economy. The first bridge across the river in Dallas County was built by Alexander Cockrell in 1855, but it survived only a few years before it was washed away in one of the Trinity's frequent floods. In 1872 a toll bridge was built. When purchased by the county in 1878 it became a free bridge. Dallas County also needed a railroad to ship its agricultural goods to market and continue its growth. In 1872 the Houston and Texas Central Railroad built through Dallas County from south to north, and such communities as Hutchins, Oasis, Wilmer, and Richardson were founded on the line. In 1873 the Texas and Pacific Railroad ran through Dallas from east to west and gave rise to many other communities, including Grand Prairie and Mesquite. By 1885 Dallas County had five railroads. Two of them, the Dallas and Wichita, which had become part of the Missouri, Kansas and Texas line in 1881, and the Dallas, Cleburne and Rio Grande, originated in Dallas. Dallas had tracks running in every direction, and they changed hands and names frequently. Other communities—Rowlett, Carrollton, Irving, Rylie, Simonds, Seagoville, Sachse—were founded on the railroad lines. Farmers Branch and Kleberg grew as a result of their contact with the railroads, and other communities disappeared as the tracks bypassed them. By 1910, Dallas County had ample transportation, with 1,200 miles of public roads and 295.36 miles of railroads. Four years later fourteen railroads served the county, including ten steam and four electric. Two of the steam lines, the Missouri, Kansas and Texas and the Texas and Pacific, had their general offices at Dallas. Four electric interurban railways[qv] provided transportation between Dallas County communities and other nearby towns, such as Fort Worth and Sherman, beginning in 1902. Only one interurban remained by 1935, as cars increased in number.

Throughout its history Dallas County had a vigorous Hispanic population, but it was difficult to detect in official records because until the 1960s Mexican Americans[qv] were listed as white in the census and were not enumerated as a separate group. In 1839 Mexican traders were in the Dallas area, and in 1850 Dallas County had its first Hispanic resident listed in the census. Downtown Dallas had Hispanic businesses by 1875. The arrival of the railroad attracted Mexican settlers both as railroad workers and as passengers on their way to agricultural jobs. The Mexican-American population increased from 2,838 in 1920 to 5,901 in 1930.

The years of the Great Depression and World War II[qv] accelerated changes in Dallas County that had actually begun in the 1920s. After 1920 the county became less rural and more urban, as manufacturing became the primary source of employment. The number of Dallas County farms sharply declined, from 5,379 to 4,830, between its peak in 1920 and 1930. The depression hastened the decline; by 1940 the number of farms had declined 35 percent from its 1920 high, and their value had dropped 61 percent. Agricultural production had declined drastically as well, though cotton declined less than other crops. Between 1940 and 1950 agriculture remained primarily stable. Livestock became much less significant. Between 1920 and 1950, however, cattle raised for nondairy uses more than tripled in number. While agriculture was declining, manufacturing was seeing rapid development. People were leaving farms in rural Dallas County and surrounding counties to move to Dallas and other Dallas County communities. During the Great Depression unemployment became a problem in the county, and the city and county government applied to the Reconstruction Finance Corporation for relief. In 1933 the County Board of Welfare and Employment reported fewer cases than before. Manufacturing became increasingly important from 1920 to 1947. The number of manufacturers more than doubled to 1,068 by 1947, with 38,936 employees—more than four times the number of 1920—and products valued at almost $2.5 million. World War II brought defense factories to Dallas County that supplied jobs for young people from rural areas. Communities such as Grand Prairie, grew up around these plants. The county had two airports in 1931 and twenty-one by the late 1940s. The population almost tripled between 1920 and 1950, when it reached 614,799. The percentage of African Americans[qv] dropped only slightly, from 15 percent to 13 percent. Dallas remained the largest community, with a population of 432,927, but other communities were expanding rapidly. In 1950, Dallas County was 89.8 percent urban.

As Dallas County became more urban and industrialized the education of its residents improved. In 1940, 34 percent had received at least a high school education, but by 1990, 77 percent had completed high school. The number of high school graduates continued to rise until the 1980s, when it began to level off. Although the number of schools and students increased, the number of school districts dropped from thirty-five in 1948 to fifteen in the 1980s. These comprised 284 elementary, 69 middle, and 62 high schools, as well as special-education and vocational schools. In the 1990s the Dallas County Community College District operated seven campuses. By 1949 public and private colleges in the county included Southern Methodist University, Dallas Theological Seminary, and Baylor College of Dentistry. Others, such as the University of Texas at Dallas in Richardson and Amber University in Garland were founded later. Besides the colleges there were a variety of technical and vocational schools teaching almost every conceivable skill.

Farming became insignificant in Dallas County compared to manufacturing. The number of farms declined from 3,519 in 1950 to 927 in 1987, though the average value of each farm rose more than twentyfold. Wheat production increased through the mid-1980s and began to fall again, but still remained above the 1950s level. Other crops dropped dramatically, especially cotton, which declined to its lowest level since 1850. The number of horses remained stable, at around 3,000 from 1950 to the 1980s, but all other livestock decreased dramatically. Manufacturing, in contrast, grew rapidly. The number of manufacturers in Dallas County more than tripled between 1947 and 1987, from 1,068 to 3,616. The number of employees in manufacturing grew even more rapidly, from 38,996 to 182,500. In addition to manufacturing, other businesses were burgeoning as well. Every major industry at least tripled its number of employees between 1953 and 1989. The three largest employers in 1953 were manufacturing, retail trade, and wholesale trade. By 1989 jobs in the service industry, primarily hotels, were employing the most people—314,777. Retail trade followed with 189,678, and manufacturing employed 184,698. This boom time lasted into the early 1980s for all types of employers. Subsequently, between 1980 and 1989, construction fell off by 33 percent and manufacturing declined.

The population increased rapidly from 1950 to the 1990s, as it had throughout the county's history. By 1950, 89.8 percent of Dallas County was considered urban. In 1950 the whole county was officially classified as the Dallas Metropolitan Statistical Area by the census bureau. The population tripled between 1950 and 1990, from 614,799 to 1,852,810. While both the black and white populations increased, the percentage of blacks in the population grew from 13 percent in 1950 to 20 percent in 1990. In 1980 the Hispanic population made up 9 percent of the population, but by 1990 it was 17 percent. In the 1980s the county had thirty-one district courts, twenty-one county courts, and twelve justices of the peace, as well as twenty-five fire departments, twenty-four police departments, and four jails. Thirty-five hospitals were in operation. A number of lakes provided recreation or supplied water within the county, including Bachman, Ray Hubbard, Mountain Creek, Texaco, Vilbig, and White Rock. The county had more than 28,000 acres in parks—one county park and 572 municipal parks. A number of museums were located in Dallas County, including the Dallas Museum of Art, the Science Place,[qqv] and the Mexican American Cultural Heritage Center. The county had a plethora of special events, including the State Fair of Texas,[qv] the Dallas Grand Prix, the Cotton Bowl[qv] Classic football game, and the Byron Nelson Golf Classic. Interstate highways 20, 30, 35E, and 635 and U.S. highways 67, 75, 81, and 175 crossed the county, in addition to other prominent roads.

BIBLIOGRAPHY: Darwin Payne, *Dallas: An Illustrated History* (Woodland Hills, California: Windsor, 1982). Anne Stark, A History of Dallas County (M.A. thesis, University of Texas, 1935). WPA Texas Writers' Project, *Dallas: Guide and History* (1940). Lisa C. Maxwell

DALLAS COUNTY COMMUNITY COLLEGE DISTRICT. The Dallas County Junior College District was established in May 1965 and changed its name in 1972 to Dallas County Community College District. The district was established to operate a system of public junior colleges in Dallas County. In the fall of 1966 El Centro College, the first of seven, opened in a remodeled eight-story department store building in downtown Dallas. The school enrolled 4,000 freshman students in 1966 and had an total enrollment of 6,099 in the fall of 1974. The district opened Eastfield College and Mountain View College in 1970; their enrollments were 6,895 and 5,340, respectively, in 1974. Richland College opened in 1972 and had an enrollment of 8,257 in 1974. Three more colleges were opened. Cedar Valley and North Lake began in 1977, and Brookhaven opened in 1978. The colleges were planned for expansion to a capacity of 10,000 each. They offer courses equivalent to the first two years of standard university work, leading to associate degrees in arts and sciences. In addition, courses are offered leading to associate degrees in applied arts and applied sciences in technical and occupational fields, including nursing, data processing, programming, drafting, electronics, culinary arts, mid-management, pattern drafting and draping, chemical technology, dental assisting, secretarial work, and library assisting. By 1981–82 the district had a combined enrollment of 42,374. By 1990–91 it had increased to 51,588, of which 37,273 students were in continuing education as compared to 20,182 in 1981–82. In 1981–82 the faculty numbered 2,021 and in 1990–91 2,939; the majority were part-time. In 1993 J. William Wenrich served as chancellor.

DALLAS COWBOYS. The Dallas Cowboys, a professional football team, began on January 28, 1960, when the National Football League awarded the league's thirteenth franchise to Clinton W. Murchison, Jr.,[qv] and Bedford Wynne for the sum of $600,000. In 1952 another NFL franchise played in Dallas, but it later moved to Baltimore. Because the franchise was sold after the college draft, Murchison, Wynne and the general manager, Tex Schram, were forced to select their roster of players from a pool composed of players from the existing twelve NFL teams. The owners selected native Texan Tom Landry to be the team's first coach. Landry had played for the University of Texas and for the New York Giants. He had also been the defensive coach for the Giants between 1955 and 1959. Despite Landry's experience and expertise, the Cowboys had difficulty overcoming the disadvantages of missing the college draft that first year. The team, an unusual mixture of veterans and free agents, did not win a single game in an 0-11-1 first season. The Cowboys were beset by poor attendance and little success. None of the first six seasons produced a winning record until 1966, when Dallas won their initial championship, taking the Eastern Conference title with a 10-3-1 mark and barely losing to the Green Bay Packers 34-27 in the NFL championship game. That game repeated itself the following season when the Cowboys again fell to the Packers, dropping a 21-17 decision in the title game that became known as the Ice Bowl because of the 13 degree-below weather.

The Cowboys captured the National Football Conference championship in 1970 and repeated in 1971. Whereas they lost to Baltimore 16-13 in the Super Bowl after the 1970 season, they won their first Super Bowl the next year with a decisive, 24-3 victory over the Miami Dolphins behind most valuable player quarterback Roger Staubach. Dallas also changed homes in 1971, moving from the Cotton Bowl near downtown to plush Texas Stadium in nearby Irving. Under the direction of the innovative Tom Landry, who was coach until 1989, the Cowboys reached the playoffs for eight years in a row from 1966 through 1973 to break their own NFL record. That string was broken in 1974 when the team finished 8-6. The Cowboys reached the Super Bowl again in the 1975 season, after beating Minnesota on Staubach's historic fifty-yard "Hail Mary" pass to Drew Pearson and destroying Los Angeles. However, they lost Super Bowl 10 to Pittsburgh 21-17. Dallas captured its second world championship by defeating the Denver Broncos 27-10 on January 15, 1978, with defensive linemen Harvey Martin and Randy White sharing the honor of most valuable player. It was also in 1978 that Bob Ryan, the editor in chief of NFL Films, tagged the Cowboys as "America's Team" because of their enormous appeal and popularity nationwide. The Cowboys' fourth appearance in the Super Bowl tied Minnesota for the most times ever, and their second win equaled the records of Green Bay, Miami, and Pittsburgh. Dallas reached the Super Bowl for a record-fifth time the next season, but dropped a 35-31 thriller to Pittsburgh.

In 1984 the Murchison family sold the Cowboys to an eleven-member limited partnership headed by Dallas banker H. R. "Bum" Bright. The following year Dallas running back Tony Dorsett became only the sixth player in NFL history to have a career record of 10,000 rushing yards. That season the Cowboys extended their NFL-record streak of consecutive winning seasons to twenty, the third longest in professional sports history, behind only the baseball New York Yankees (39 straight) and hockey Montreal Canadians (32). The Cowboys had difficulty in sustaining their winning power in the late 1980s. Despite Landry's career record of 250-162-6, the team went 3-13 in 1988. Arkansas oil-and-gas investor Jerry Jones purchased the club from Bright in 1989, fired Landry and hired his former Arkansas Razorback teammate Jimmy Johnson as head coach. Jones paid $65 million for the team and another $70 million for Texas Stadium. He also signed UCLA quarterback, Troy Aikman, for a rookie record six-year salary of $11.2 million. Despite the influx of cash and personnel, the Cowboys were 1-15 in the first year of new ownership and only 7-9 in the second. Jones and Johnson however were not discouraged and through tough training and shrewd draft picks they rebuilt the team. Along with Aikman, other outstanding players included Emmitt Smith, who earned his third straight NFL rushing title in 1993, Michael Irvin, Ken

Norton, Jr., and Charles Haley. The Cowboys won back-to-back Super bowls over the Buffalo Bills after the 1992 and 1993 seasons to become one of just three NFL teams to claim four world championships. Troy Aikman, most valuable player in Super Bowl 27, renegotiated his contract in 1993 for an NFL record of $50 million for eight years. Following Super Bowl 28 Johnson stepped down in March 1994 and was replaced as coach by Barry Switzer. The next season the Cowboys lost the NFC championship to their archrivals, the San Francisco 49ers. The executive offices of the team are at Valley Ranch in Irving.

BIBLIOGRAPHY: Skip Bayless, *God's Coach: The Hymns, Hype and Hypocrisy of Tom Landry's Cowboys* (New York: Simon and Schuster, 1990). Sam Blair, *Dallas Cowboys, Pro or Con?* (Garden City, New York: Doubleday, 1970). Donald E. Chipman, Randolph Campbell, and Robert Calvert, *The Dallas Cowboys and the NFL* (Norman: University of Oklahoma Press, 1970). *Dallas Cowboys Silver Season: 1960–1984* (Dallas, 1984). Tom Landry, *Tom Landry, An Autobiography* (Grand Rapids, Michigan: Zondervan Books, 1990). Carlton Stowers, *Dallas Cowboys: The First Twenty-Five Years* (Dallas: Taylor, 1984). Vertical Files, Barker Texas History Center, University of Texas at Austin. *Kirk Bohls*

DALLAS EXPRESS. The Dallas *Express,* a black newspaper, was published weekly at Dallas by W. E. King beginning in 1893. Carter W. Wesley,qv owner of the Houston *Informer* (*see* HOUSTON INFORMER AND TEXAS FREEMAN), purchased the paper around 1970, but plans to move it to Houston did not materialize, and publication ceased around November of that year.

BIBLIOGRAPHY: Louis Margot III, The *Dallas Express:* A Negro Newspaper, Its History, 1892–1971, and Its Point of View (M.A. thesis, East Texas State University, 1971). *Diana J. Kleiner*

DALLAS–FORT WORTH INTERNATIONAL AIRPORT. Dallas–Fort Worth International Airport received its current name in 1973, before which it had been known as Midway, Greater Fort Worth International, Amon G. Carter Field, and Greater Southwest International. As early as 1940 a regional airport for the Dallas and Fort Worth area was being considered. The Civil Aeronautics Administration approached the city of Arlington to sponsor an airport midway between the two larger cities. Both Dallas and Fort Worth were interested, since expansion of Meacham Field and Love Fieldqqv in Dallas would require extensive construction to accommodate increasing air traffic and larger aircraft. Arlington agreed, and with the support of American Airlines (*see* AMR CORPORATION) and Braniff Airways,qv which were to deed 1,000 acres of land, the CAA was to build the landing area; a seven-man board would control overall operation of the field. Construction began in 1942, but a disagreement over which way the terminal building should face, along with other considerations, caused the airport, then called Midway, to be turned over to the city of Arlington in 1943. It was operated during World War IIqv by the military as a training field and for test flights. In 1946 Fort Worth hired a firm to prepare an airport plan for the city. The next year it decided to develop Midway as its major airport and renamed it Greater Fort Worth International Airport. Dallas continued to develop Love Field. In 1948 the CAA National Airport Plan recommended that Greater Fort Worth International Airport be expanded into the major regional airport. Fort Worth annexed the site and continued to develop the airport with the support of American Airlines. Dallas continued its opposition. According to the Dallas *Morning News,*qv at one time the feud became so bitter that Fort Worth mayor Amon G. Carterqv refused to eat in Dallas restaurants and, when business made it necessary for him to be in Dallas, he carried a sack lunch. In 1950 the Fort Worth City Council renamed the airport Amon G. Carter Field. In September 1951 a bond election was held, and voters approved $28.9 million in bonds. Another election was held in May 1952 in which $1.5 million was approved for aviation improvements. This issue was part of the Love Field–Carter Field competition during the 1950s. The airport officially opened in April 1953.

During the 1950s two attempts were made by Fort Worth to convert Carter Field into a joint regional airport with Dallas participating as a full partner. Both efforts were rebuffed by Dallas, and expansion of Love Field continued. In May 1960 the airport, renamed Greater Southwest International Airport, was purchased by the city of Fort Worth in an effort to compete more successfully with Love Field, and a municipal board was established to supervise the city's airports.

From 1959 to 1965 the percentage of enplaning passengers from Greater Southwest declined from 6 percent of Texas air traffic to less than 1 percent, while Love Field increased from 40.3 percent to 49.0 percent. The result was the virtual abandonment of Greater Southwest International Airport and serious congestion at Love Field. Though Dallas and Fort Worth were archrivals, the Federal Aviation Administration (formerly the CAA) refused to put any more money into duplicate installations. In 1964 the Civil Aeronautics Board ordered the two cities to come up in less than 180 days with a voluntary agreement on the location of a new regional airport, or the federal government would do it for them. CAB examiner Ross I. Newmann served as a mediator between the two cities in an attempt to find a solution. Both cities appointed committees, and by 1965 plans were set for a Dallas–Fort Worth Board, which would consist of eleven members—seven from Dallas and four from Fort Worth. The board named Thomas M. Sullivan executive director of airport construction and operations. The site for an airport, originally called Dallas–Fort Worth Regional Airport, was chosen. The plan received broad support, and in December 1968 ground was broken at the intersection of the towns of Euless, Irving, and Grapevine. The new site included the old Greater Southwest International Airport.

The new airport, now known as the Dallas–Fort Worth International Airport, was dedicated in September 1973 and became operational on January 13, 1974, replacing Love Field. The first commercial flight that day, American Airlines Flight 341, flew from New York to Dallas via Memphis and Little Rock, touching down exactly on time. At the time of the opening of the airport nine airlines operated there. In addition, extensive facilities were in operation, including a 600-room hotel, a post office, and various shops and restaurants.

Dallas–Fort Worth International Airport is the fourth largest airport in the world. In 1988 42,000,000 passengers enplaned there on 635,000 flights. When designed, the airport occupied 17,500 acres, which equals more than twenty-seven square miles, an area larger than the island of Manhattan. The original plans provide for thirteen terminal buildings along a nine-mile International Parkway. In the original construction there were four pueblo-like terminals, each with a horse-shoe shape, along a linear central roadway. Each of the four terminals contains 790,000 square feet of covered space and can accommodate eighteen Boeing 747s. The grand design of thirteen terminals would provide 234 aircraft-boarding gates, up to eleven runways, and cargo-handling capability equal to the world's largest seaports, with expansion to take place as needed. The terminals are connected by the world's first automated transit system, called Airtrans. It is capable of moving 9,000 people, 6,000 bags, and 70,000 pounds of mail each hour.

Enough concrete and asphalt were used on the runways and roads to pave a four-lane expressway from Dallas to Oklahoma City. Air traffic is controlled from a 196-foot control tower with two separate control cabs for the two sets of parallel 11,400-foot runways. The eleven-sided tower cab is the only one of its kind in the world. For controlled aircraft approaches there are five instrument-landing systems. The airport was five years under construction at a cost of $700 million. From 1974 to 1988 an additional $600 million was spent on expansion and improvements. In 1988, under the threat of increased noise and reduced property values, the cities of Irving, Euless, and Grapevine began a legal battle against planned expansion of the airport. The Supreme Court sided with the airport in 1994. Dallas–Fort Worth contributes $5 billion annually to the local economy and provides 25,000 jobs.

BIBLIOGRAPHY: Dallas *Morning News,* January 8, 1989, December 6, 1994. Stanley H. Scott and Levi H. Davis, *A Giant in Texas* (Quanah, Texas: Nortex Press, 1974). *Texas Business Review,* April 1967. *Texas Parade,* June 1973. Vertical Files, Barker Texas History Center, University of Texas at Austin.

Art Leatherwood

DALLAS–FORT WORTH MINOR-LEAGUE BASEBALL.

Dallas entered a professional team named the Hams in the Texas League qv when it was formed in 1888. The team won the pennant that year, and minor-league baseball was tentatively established in Dallas. As was the case with many minor leagues in the late nineteenth and early twentieth centuries, the Texas League's early years were chaotic. Teams appeared and disappeared with great frequency. The Texas League failed to function in 1891, 1893, and 1894 and suspended play in 1898, at the outbreak of the Spanish-American War. In 1899 Dallas did not join the poorly reorganized Texas League when it resumed play. The league again faltered and did not reappear until 1902, when Dallas joined it and struggled to survive as the league warred with the newly formed South Texas League. Finally, in 1907, the stronger franchises of the Texas League and the South Texas League cooperated in forming a reorganized Texas League.

Throughout these years of difficulty, the Dallas franchise underwent a series of name changes. Fans cheered the Dallas Hams, the Dallas Submarines, or the Dallas Steers. Then, as the Texas League matured in the years immediately after World War I,qv the Dallas franchise became a bulwark in one of the stronger minor leagues in the United States. In 1922 a group of Dallas businessmen, including George and Julius Schepps,qv purchased the team. The 1920s were the golden age of baseball, and the Steers enjoyed enthusiastic fan support in a highly competitive league. In 1938, during the depths of the Great Depression,qv George Schepps bought controlling interest in the Steers for $150,000 and renamed them the Rebels. The Rebels did poorly at the ticket window but moderately well in the standings during Schepps's ownership, and in 1948 he sold the team to Richard Wesley Burnett qv for $550,000. Burnett, who also purchased the Steers' ballpark in Oak Cliff for an additional $265,000, promptly renamed the team the Eagles and the park Burnett Field. Under his brief leadership (he died in 1955), the Eagles flourished. They won three pennants and the Dixie Series, a best-of-seven-games contest between the champions of the Texas League and the Southern Association, in 1953. Burnett also integrated the Texas League in 1952, when he brought David Hoskins to the team and, using the Cotton Bowl qv as a baseball park, engineered an all-time attendance record of 53,578 for a Texas League game in 1950. Burnett upgraded Burnett Field into one of the best minor-league ballparks in the United States as he sought to bring major-league baseball to Dallas. After his death, his wife and daughters operated the team until 1959, when they sold it to J. W. Bateson and Amon G. Carter, Jr.qv The new owners transferred the team to the AAA American Association.

In 1960 the Dallas Eagles and their old archrival, the Fort Worth Cats, were combined into one team as the Dallas–Fort Worth Rangers and competed in the American Association. During its years in the association, the team split its home games between Burnett Field and LaGrave Field in Fort Worth. Then, when the American Association disbanded in 1962, the Rangers joined the Pacific Coast League. The Dallas–Fort Worth team competed in the Pacific Coast League in 1963. Fort Worth businessman Tommy Mercer bought the franchise and returned Fort Worth to the Texas League in 1964; Dallas remained in the Pacific Coast League.

During this time when the Dallas and Fort Worth clubs were switching from one league to another, major-league teams were moving to nearly all sections of the country, and expansion franchises were becoming an alternative to a third major league, the Continental League. Throughout this period minor-league baseball remained in the Dallas area, but it was apparent that it was stricken, as local leaders constantly maneuvered to bring major-league ball to the area. In 1965 the Dallas and Fort Worth teams were reunited into the Dallas–Fort Worth Spurs and competed in the Texas League. The Spurs played their games at the newly completed Turnpike Stadium in Arlington, with only mixed success but with good fan support. In 1971 the Spurs joined the AA Dixie Association, and when the Washington Senators moved to Arlington in 1972 to become the Texas Rangers,qv the Spurs were disbanded.

Minor league baseball thus began for Dallas and Fort Worth in 1888 and ended in 1972. The Dallas team won or shared twelve Texas League pennants, competed in the Dixie Series five times, and won it three times.

BIBLIOGRAPHY: Robert Obojski, *Bush League: A History of Minor League Baseball* (New York: Macmillan, 1975). Bill O'Neal, *The Texas League, 1888–1987: A Century of Baseball* (Austin: Eakin Press, 1987). William B. Ruggles, *The History of the Texas League of Professional Baseball Clubs* (Dallas: Texas Baseball League, 1932).

Larry G. Bowman

DALLAS GARMENT WORKERS' STRIKE.

In 1934, 100 Dallas dressmakers joined a grassroots "sewing club" shortly after the Supreme Court declared National Industrial Recovery Act codes stipulating minimum wages and maximum hours unconstitutional. Dallas garment workers who sewed cotton dresses were paid an average of $9.50 a week before October 1933, when the National Recovery Act codes went into effect. Highly skilled silk dress cutters, who earned weekly wages of $35 to $50 in other parts of the country, made as little as $10 to $15 in Dallas. The women of the "sewing club" sought advice from Larry Taylor, president of the Dallas Central Labor Council, who requested an organizer from the International Ladies' Garment Workers Union.qv Within four months of the arrival of New Yorker Meyer Perlstein, more than 400 of the almost 1,000 dressmakers in Dallas had joined the union. Local dress manufacturers immediately dismissed workers suspected of union activity, and picketing in support of fired union members began in early February of 1935. The walkout quickly spread to all fifteen Dallas factories owned by members of the Texas Dress Manufacturers' Association.

On February 12, as later, pickets attempting to keep strikebreakers from entering a dress factory clashed with Dallas police. Women blocking the doors to Donovan Manufacturing Company bit, kicked, and beat law officers and private guards who escorted scabs into the building. The Dallas *Morning News*qv and the *Evening Journal* supported the police. When, for instance, a law officer tore a union songsheet from a striker's hands and threw her to the pavement with such force that she was hospitalized with a hip injury, the *News* excused his actions, explaining that the police mistook the songsheet for a court-ordered injunction.

Despite the arrests of at least eighty-six women, the papers continued to print manufacturers' estimates that the strikers numbered no more than fifty. The ILGWU claimed it paid 150. Although depicted as easily led and relatively naive girls, almost half of the pickets arrested during the strike were or had been married.

On the morning of August 7 strikers entered the Morten-Davis and Lorch Manufacturing companies and stripped the clothing from ten female employees. Hundreds of spectators crowded the downtown streets and hung out of nearby office windows to witness the spectacle. "Strike stripping" in Dallas attracted international attention. An Italian artist's sketch of the August melee appeared in *La Tribuna Illustrata* of Rome. Accounts of the garment workers actions made the New York *Times* and papers as far away as Australia.

In October local pastors joined the state Industrial Commission's call for an arbitrated settlement. Still Dallas employers would not negotiate. A month later the dressmakers voted to end their walkout. Dallas's longest and most colorful strike ended almost without notice and completely without explanation in the daily newspapers. Despite the dressmakers' initial defeat, the ILGWU maintained its two Dallas locals. Perlstein made frequent trips to Dallas, and by 1936 five local dress plants operated as union shops.

BIBLIOGRAPHY: Patricia Evridge Hill, "Real Women and True Womanhood: Grassroots Organizing among Dallas Dressmakers in 1935," *Labor's Heritage,* Spring 1994. Patsy Putnam, The International Ladies' Garment Workers' Union in Dallas, 1933–35 (MS, University of Texas at Arlington Library, December 18, 1973). *Patricia Evridge Hill*

DALLAS AND GREENVILLE RAILWAY. The Dallas and Greenville Railway Company was chartered on February 15, 1886, to build a railroad and telegraph line from Greenville to Dallas. The initial capital was $800,000, and the business office was in Dallas. Members of the first board of directors included H. M. Hoxie, D. S. H. Smith, and George C. Smith, all of St. Louis; A. W. Hunter, Joseph Herrin, and G. J. Gooch, all of Palestine; and James A. Baker^qv of Houston. The road had its beginnings when the Missouri, Kansas and Texas Railroad Company, owned by Jay Gould,^qv decided to renew its program of construction in Texas. The Katy already served Dallas and Greenville, but these cities were not connected, and the "black belt" country between them was productive. Fifty-two miles of track connecting Dallas and Greenville were completed by December 2, 1886. On that date the line was sold to the Missouri, Kansas and Texas, and subsequently deeded to the Missouri, Kansas and Texas Railway Company of Texas on November 18, 1891. *S. G. Reed*

DALLAS *HERALD*. The Dallas *Herald* was established in 1849 by James W. Latimer^qv and William Wallace. The two purchased the Paris, Texas, *Times* that summer and moved it to Dallas in the fall. The paper may have originally been named the Dallas *Cedar Snag,* but by December it was the *Herald.* Wallace retired in 1850, and Latimer became the sole owner and editor. In 1854 John W. Swindells became co-owner and in 1859, upon Latimer's death, became owner and editor of the paper. On June 21, 1873, the paper was renamed Dallas *Weekly Herald* and published by J. W. Swindells and Company. Later that year the publisher was listed as the Dallas Herald Printing Company, with Swindells as president. In 1874 the company began publication of a daily edition called the Dallas *Daily Herald,* printed every morning except Monday and sold at an annual subscription rate of ten dollars. The rate for the weekly was two dollars annually. After March 8, 1877, J. L. Bartow was listed as head of the *Herald,* but Swindells continued as agent and correspondent. In 1879 the paper appeared under the new ownership of P. S. Pfouts, J. E. Elliott, and W. L. Hall, and that firm continued both the daily and weekly edition until December 3, 1885, when the paper was bought out and absorbed by the Dallas *Morning News.*^qv *See also* DALLAS TIMES HERALD.

BIBLIOGRAPHY: Sam Hanna Acheson, *35,000 Days in Texas: A History of the Dallas "News" and Its Forbears* (New York: Macmillan, 1938). Samuel P. Maranto, A History of Dallas Newspapers (M.A. thesis, North Texas State College, 1952). John William Rogers, *The Lusty Texans of Dallas* (New York: Dutton, 1951; enlarged ed. 1960; expanded ed., Dallas: Cokesbury Book Store, 1965). Ben C. Stuart, The History of Texas Newspapers (MS, Barker Texas History Center, University of Texas at Austin, 1917). WPA Historical Records Survey Program, *Texas Newspapers* (Houston: San Jacinto Museum of History Association, 1941).

DALLAS HISTORICAL SOCIETY. On March 31, 1922, George B. Dealey^qv and 100 other charter members founded the Dallas Historical Society. It was incorporated as an educational institution on August 10, 1922. Since its founding the society has focused on collecting, preserving, and interpreting materials relating to the history of Dallas, Dallas County, Texas, and the Southwest. The society originally operated out of the library of Southern Methodist University, but moved to the Hall of State^qv at Fair Park^qv in 1938. The society is a private nonprofit organization, and membership is open to the public. The society offers several educational programs. It provides school tours of the Hall of State to area school children studying Texas and United States history. The tours use the art, architecture, regional rooms, and statues of the Hall of State as teaching tools. The society also has outreach programs. An outreach specialist travels to area schools and uses artifact reproductions and slides to illustrate talks on Indians of Texas, African Americans,^qv pioneers, and cowboys. In addition, the society presents exhibits from its own archival and museum collections and hosts traveling exhibitions. Dallas Historical Society operates the George B. Dealey Library at the Hall of State, which is open to the public by appointment. The library's holdings include 2.5 million archival documents, 3,000 photographs, 14,000 books, and 3,000 periodicals. The collection contains rare books and manuscripts on the founding of the Republic of Texas,^qv Texas since 1845, and Dallas and North Texas. Large archival collections include the papers of local, state, and national leaders, such as pioneer attorney John C. McCoy, nineteenth century businesswoman Sarah Horton Cockrell, Congressman Hatton W. Sumners, Democratic party leader Thomas B. Love, George W. Briggs, Sam Acheson, Joseph W. Bailey, Jessie Daniels Ames,^qqv Dallas *Morning News* publisher George B. Dealey, "the Heroine of Tampico" Anne Chase, philanthropist Elmer Scott, P. Pacheco Martinez, Margaret Scruggs Caruth, John M. Moore, and the 1936 Texas Centennial Commission. The society's museum collection has over 15,000 items, including 3,500 costumes. The collection centers on the social, economic, and political history of Dallas and Texas. Rare items include the spurs of Antonio López de Santa Anna,^qv the watch of James W. Fannin,^qv and a sugar bowl made by a slave in Nacogdoches. In recent years the society has made strong efforts to acquire items documenting the different cultures living in Dallas and North Texas. The society's publications include *Dallas Rediscovered: A Photographic Chronicle of Urban Expansion. 1870–1925* (1978); *When Dallas Became a City: The Letters of John M. McCoy, 1870 to 1881* (1982); and *Legacies: A History Journal for Dallas and North Central Texas,* which is published with the Dallas County Heritage Society.

BIBLIOGRAPHY: *Dallas Historical Society* (Dallas: Dallas Historical Society, 1938). *Guy C. Vanderpool*

DALLAS *JOURNAL*. The Dallas *Journal,* a six-day afternoon newspaper, was established on April 1, 1914, by Alfred H. Belo^qv and Company, publishers of the Dallas *Morning News,*^qv with Tom Finty, Jr., as editor, Harry Clay Withers as city editor, and Hilton R. Greer^qqv as chief editorial writer. Its strong editorial page was later edited by Lynn W. Landrum.^qv Both in news coverage and editorial positions, this spritely journalistic enterprise was concerned mainly with local and state affairs, although it was an early advocate of a league of nations to promote world peace. It was sold on July 1, 1938, to Karl Hoblitzelle^qv and Alfred O. Andersson of Dallas, who consolidated it with the Dallas *Dispatch* under the name of *Dispatch-Journal.* The name reverted to Dallas *Dispatch* when the paper was sold on December 1, 1939, to James M. West^qv of Houston, whose heirs discontinued its publication in 1942.

BIBLIOGRAPHY: WPA Historical Records Survey Program, *Texas Newspapers* (Houston: San Jacinto Museum of History Association, 1941). *Sam Hanna Acheson*

DALLAS MALE AND FEMALE COLLEGE. Dallas Male and Female College was established by the Elm Fork Baptist Association in 1869, when the trustees of the Mount Calvary Seminary at Mount Calvary, Dallas County, offered to donate the property of that school to the association on condition that a college be located there. A board of trustees was appointed and authorized to make arrangements for the school and to employ a corps of teachers. John Hanna was elected principal. In 1870 the legal donation of the property was made with the provisions that the school remain there and that a quorum of the trustees be elected from the Mount Calvary church. The school operated until possibly 1873 or 1874 and expanded its plant a bit; but apparently it closed for want of patronage, for its supporters were later among the founders of Dallas College.

BIBLIOGRAPHY: Donald W. Whisenhunt, *The Encyclopedia of Texas Colleges and Universities* (Austin: Eakin, 1986). Carl Bassett Wilson, History of Baptist Educational Efforts in Texas, 1829–1900 (Ph.D. dissertation, University of Texas, 1934).

DALLAS MAVERICKS. The Dallas Mavericks, a professional basketball team, belong to the Midwest Division of the Western Conference of the National Basketball Association. The team officially became the twenty-third member of the NBA on May 1, 1980, when owner Donald Carter's Dallas National Basketball Association, Incorporated, was awarded a franchise by NBA commissioner Lawrence O'Brien. Norm Sonju, the club's first and only general manager, initiated the process of bringing professional basketball to Dallas in 1978, when he contacted Dallas mayor Bob Folsom. Together they put together a group of eight investors, headlined by the Carter family's Home Interiors and Gifts, Incorporated. Mayor Folsom and the city of Dallas also assisted by building the 17,007-seat Reunion Arena in downtown Dallas in 1979. Sonju hired Dick Motta, then the coach with the third highest number of wins in NBA history, as the team's first head coach. He was joined by assistant coach Bob Weiss. In the front office twenty-eight year old Rick Sund was hired as director of player personnel. Together, they built the first Mavericks team.

That first team had a record of fifteen wins and sixty-seven losses for the 1980–81 season. It had been feared that Dallas, with its rich football tradition, would not support the Mavericks; however, that first season the team finished a respectable eighteenth in the league in attendance. By the 1985–86 season the Mavericks had set an NBA record by filling Reunion Arena to 99.4 percent of its capacity. The next three seasons, the club increased its win total by thirteen, ten, and five wins, respectively. The 1983–84 season marked the first time that the club won more games than it lost, and it marked the team's first playoff appearance. The Mavericks won that first playoff series, known as Moody Madness, over the Seattle Supersonics in dramatic fashion. That same year Mark Aguirre became the first Maverick to ever play in the NBA All-Star game. The next two years the team finished with identical 44-38 season records, losing both years in the early rounds of the playoffs. The 1986–87 season marked the Mavericks' first and only Midwest Division championship. The team finished with a best ever record of 55-27 and was one of the premier franchises in the league. However, they lost their first round playoff series to the underdog Supersonics. After the season, another shock came as Dick Motta resigned as head coach. John MacLeod became the second coach and promptly took the Mavericks to the finals of the Western Conference playoffs. They even extended the defending champion Los Angeles Lakers to the seventh and deciding game of that series.

The Mavericks, however, slipped the next season and won only thirty-eight games, missing the playoffs for the first time in five years. The 1989–90 team lost in the first round of the playoffs. That marked the last time the Mavericks made the post-season playoffs. Richie Audobato took the reins from MacLeod during the next season, as the Mavericks entered a drastic decline. By the time he was replaced by Garfield Heard during the 1992–93 season, the Mavericks were the worst team in the NBA. They narrowly avoided being the worst team in league history by winning only eleven games. Quinn Buckner became the franchise's first head coach for the 1993–94 season. However, he won only thirteen games, and was fired after one year. The 1994–95 season marked the return of Dick Motta and a resurgence. The Mavericks won thirty-six games, one of the largest one-season improvements in NBA history, and young stars Jim Jackson, Jamal Mashburn, and Jason Kidd evoked memories of previous Mavericks heroes like Mark Aguirre and Rolando Blackman. Mavericks fans began to again turn out in large numbers to support their team, but they missed the playoffs once again.

BIBLIOGRAPHY: Steve Pate, *The Dallas Mavericks '87–'88* (Dallas: Taylor, 1987). Kevin Sullivan, *Dallas Mavericks 1986–87 Media Guide.*
Eric M. Pfeifle

DALLAS MEMORIAL CENTER FOR HOLOCAUST STUDIES. On April 15, 1984, the Dallas Memorial Center for Holocaust Studies opened its doors on the lower level of the Dallas Jewish Community Center. The purpose of the center is to keep the terrors of the Holocaust in the minds of present and future generations, so that they will never allow anything like it to occur again. Many individuals contributed to the establishment of the center, as did the Jewish Federation of Greater Dallas.

Visitors enter the center through an original boxcar used to transport Jews to concentration and death camps and a foyer containing Holocaust exhibits. Off the foyer is a library and research room. The display room is also connected to the foyer. In this room are photographs of the history of the Third Reich, of ghettos, concentration camps, and crematoriums, of atrocities and liberators. Artifacts of the Holocaust are exhibited in display cases, and films of the Holocaust are shown. The most imposing room connected to the foyer is the memorial room, in which is a large tabular "memorial stone" surrounded by twelve pillars inscribed with the names of concentration camps and connected by heavy barbed wire. With the monument is a bronze image by Ruth Litwin of a flame and hand, entitled *Grasping for Life*. In this room wall plaques commemorate the names of family members of survivors, names of survivors who have died since World War II,[qv] and names of non-Jews who tried to save Jews from the death camps.

The center is supported by donations, gifts, fund drives, and membership fees. An executive director is responsible for its operation and for maintaining a working relationship with schools, colleges, churches, and synagogues. In conjunction with Southern Methodist University, the center is involved in preserving the oral history of Holocaust survivors and liberators on videotape. A board composed partly of Holocaust survivors administers the center.

BIBLIOGRAPHY: *The Memorial Center for Holocaust Studies* (brochure, Dallas, n.d.).
Aaron Charles Yielding

DALLAS *MORNING NEWS*. The Dallas *Morning News* developed from the Galveston *News*,[qv] which was founded in 1842 by Samuel Bangs.[qv] By 1879 Alfred H. Belo,[qv] who had acquired control of the business, was investigating the possibility of establishing a sister paper in rapidly developing North Texas. When efforts to purchase the old Dallas *Herald*[qv] failed, Belo sent George Bannerman Dealey[qv] to launch a new paper, the Dallas *Morning News*, which began publication on October 1, 1885. Linked across 315 miles by telegraph, and sharing a network of correspondents across the state, the Dallas *Morning News* and the Galveston *News* were the first two newspapers in the country to publish simultaneous editions. From the outset the Dallas paper enjoyed the double advantage of strong financial support and an accumulation of journalistic experience. From its parent paper, the Dallas *News* inherited the concept of being a state paper and of refraining from becoming the organ of any political party. Beginning with a circulation of 5,000, the Dallas *News* soon absorbed its major competitor, the *Herald* (not to be confused with the Dallas *Times Herald*[qv]). It immediately leased a special train on the Texas and Pacific Railway to carry papers to Fort Worth, and in 1887 it engaged a special train on the Houston and Texas Central to deliver papers to McKinney, Sherman, and Denison on the morning they were printed. This expedient enabled the paper to meet the threat of the St. Louis newspapers, which in 1885 had a larger circulation in North Texas than did any state paper. By 1888 the *News* was printing an eight to twelve page edition daily and sixteen pages on Sunday. Its circulation reached 17,000 by 1895. In 1914 the *News* launched an evening paper, the Dallas *Journal,* which was sold in 1938. It also published the *Semi-Weekly Farm News* from 1885 until 1940.

During the 1890s the *News* stood firmly against the agrarian wing of the Democratic party,qv as represented in the state by James Stephen Hoggqv and by William Jennings Bryan in national politics. The paper supported both Grover Cleveland and William McKinley, especially as to hard-money views. Beginning about 1900 it avoided controversy and name-calling in political attack, with the exception of its vehement opposition to the reelection of Joseph Weldon Baileyqv as senator in 1906. In that year circulation climbed to 38,000. In a courageous move, the paper condemned the Ku Klux Klanqv in the early 1920s. Another step it took in the face of financial loss was its decision in 1920 not to accept any advertising for oil stock because of the difficulty of distinguishing between fraudulent and honest firms. Adolph Ochs of the New York *Times* stated in 1924, "I received my ideas and ideals from the Galveston *Daily News* and the Dallas *Morning News.*" By 1928 circulation had increased to 86,000.

The paper, which had initially supported Franklin D. Roosevelt and his New Deal, found itself disagreeing with Roosevelt's domestic policies as the president's tenure in office stretched to include a fourth term. However, it backed Roosevelt's foreign policies, including unreserved support of America's participation in World War IIqv after Pearl Harbor. The paper supported Republican Dwight D. Eisenhowerqv for president over Adlai Stevenson in 1952 and 1956, and Richard M. Nixon over John F. Kennedy in 1960. It was neutral in the contest between Lyndon B. Johnsonqv and Barry Goldwater in 1964, but endorsed Richard Nixon in 1968 and 1972, Gerald Ford in 1976, Ronald Reagan in 1980 and 1984, and George H. W. Bush in 1988 and 1992. The paper's circulation, which stood at 150,000 in 1950, grew to 276,000 (Sunday) and 346,273 (daily) by 1968. In 1994 the circulation of the *News* was 814,400 (Sunday) and 527,300 (daily).

Two long-time programs supported by the Dallas *Morning News* have been city planning for Dallas and encouragement of enlightened farming practices in North Texas. In addition, it has backed campaigns to clean up the city and make it more attractive, to build levees for flood control on the Trinity River, to construct a union railroad station, and to adopt first the commission form of government and later the city manager form. The *News* has published several special editions that have contributed to state and local history, including the Fiftieth Anniversary Edition of October 1, 1935; the Texas Centennialqv Edition of June 7, 1936; an edition of April 11, 1942, marking the 100th anniversary of its parent paper, the Galveston *News;* and the Texas Unlimited Edition of May 22, 1949. It subsequently published special editions celebrating its own 100th anniversary on October 1, 1985, and the 150th anniversary of the A. H. Belo Corporationqv on April 11, 1992. The Dallas *Morning News* received Pulitzer prizes in 1986, 1989, 1991, 1992, 1993, and 1994.

BIBLIOGRAPHY: *A. H. Belo Corporation: Commemorating 150 Years, 1842–1992* (Dallas, 1992). Steven Dwight Holley, The Dallas *Morning News* and *Times-Herald* and the Image of Dallas after the Kennedy Assassination (M.A. thesis, University of Texas at Austin, 1974). Ernest Sharpe, *G. B. Dealey of the Dallas News* (New York: Holt, 1955). Vertical Files, Barker Texas History Center, University of Texas at Austin.   *Judith M. Garrett and Michael V. Hazel*

DALLAS MUSEUM OF ART. The Dallas Museum of Art, formerly the Dallas Museum of Fine Arts, traces its beginnings to the Dallas Art Association, which was founded by a group of eighty citizens in 1903. Since its inception, the museum's facilities and most of its collections have been owned by the city of Dallas and operated and overseen by the board of trustees of the museum. The first museum facility opened in 1909 under the name Free Public Art Gallery of Dallas. It occupied a building in Fair Parkqv that was later damaged by a storm. Mrs. George K. Meyer was president of the Dallas Art Association and acting director of the gallery in the early years. Activity at the gallery accelerated with the appointment of artist and art historian John S. Ankeny as the museum's first professional director in 1929. Ankeny secured exhibitions of national importance, offered weekly lectures and art classes, and published a monthly newsletter. In 1932 the museum was renamed Dallas Museum of Fine Arts, and the next year it moved into the Dallas Power and Light Company building. In early 1934 Ankeny was succeeded by Lloyd LePage Rollins, under whom a $500,000 city bond issue was passed to build a new museum in Fair Park. The new facility, completed in 1936, opened with an exhibition of European and American art presented in conjunction with the Texas Centennialqv that attracted more than 154,000 visitors. Richard Foster Howard (1936–41) and Louise Britton McCraw (1942) succeeded Rollins as directors of the museum; McCraw was followed by Jerry Bywaters,qv a regionalist artist and critic who led the Dallas Museum of Fine Arts for twenty-one years.

Bywaters specialized in southwestern and Mexican art, and under his stewardship the museum focused primarily, though not exclusively, on regional art. The museum's commitment to education was manifested in the Museum School of Art, begun in 1941, which offered children and adult classes in sculpture and ceramics, lithography, painting, life drawing, and other subjects. Such prominent artists as Merritt T. Mauzey, Otis M. Dozier, Coreen M. Spellman,qqv Evaline C. Sellors, Octavio Medellín, Roger Winter, and David McManaway taught at the museum school until the mid-1960s, when the school was closed after a study committee determined that other institutions in Dallas were serving similar needs. Acquisitions under Bywaters's leadership focused on works by leading contemporary artists such as Rufino Tamayo, Alexandre Hogue,qv William Zorach, George Grosz, Thomas Hart Benton, Edward Hopper, Alexander Calder, and Jackson Pollock. During this period the museum's development was checked by cramped conditions at the building on the fairgrounds, which required that much of the permanent collection be kept in storage, and by a cultural climate in which hostility toward modern art was expressed in the "Red art" controversy of 1955–56. In March 1955 the Public Affairs Luncheon Club, a local women's group, charged the museum with exhibiting the work of artists with Communist affiliations and neglecting the work of Dallas artists. The museum temporarily removed works by Pablo Picasso, Diego Rivera, and other ideologically suspect artists from display. On December 7, 1955, the board of trustees issued a statement that they would "exhibit and acquire works of art only on the basis of their merit as works of art."

In 1963 the museum supplemented its permanent collection and increased its board of trustees to eighty-two members through a merger with the Dallas Museum of Contemporary Art. The following year the Foundation for the Arts was established as a holding agency for the former DMCA collection, with the power to solicit funds and acquire art objects to be placed at the disposal of the museum. Bywaters resigned in 1964 and was succeeded by Merrill C. Rueppel, who oversaw the opening in 1965 of a new two-story wing, financed by a city bond election, that nearly doubled the museum's exhibition space. Rueppel brought popular exhibitions such as the 1967 retrospective exhibition of Pablo Picasso's work to Dallas, strengthened the museum's holdings of contemporary painting and sculpture, and broadened the scope of the permanent collection through acquisitions of Japanese painting and Pre-Columbian and African art. Harry S. Parker III, director from 1974 to 1988, spearheaded the construction of the current museum building, which opened under a new name, Dallas Museum of Art, in January 1984. The $54 million facility is located on nine acres on the northern edge of the city's business district in what is now designated the Dallas Arts District. It was financed by a 1979 bond election in which Dallas voters pledged $24.8 million and by contributions from the private sector. Prominent New York architect Edward Larrabee Barnes designed the 195,000-square-foot building, which is dominated by a forty-foot barrel vault anchored by Claes Oldenburg's *Stake Hitch.* Other important pieces commissioned for the new building were Sol LeWitt's *Wall Drawing No. 398,* displayed on the eastern arch of the central barrel vault, and a large-scale steel work by Ellsworth Kelly that was installed in the museum's sculpture garden.

In November 1985 the museum opened a new decorative arts wing that houses more than 1,400 objects from the Wendy and Emery Reves's Collection in a replica of the Reves's Villa La Pausa in southern France, including an important collection of Impressionist and Post-Impressionist paintings and decorative art objects. The decorative arts collection was substantially augmented by the donation in 1986 of the Faith P. and Charles L. Bybee[qv] Collection of American Furniture, comprising American furniture from the eighteenth and nineteenth centuries, and the Hoblitzelle Foundation's[qv] donation in 1987 of a 550-piece collection of British silver that features outstanding works by such eighteenth-century silversmiths as Paul Lamerie. Other recent acquisitions include a granite bust of Pharaoh Seti I from the nineteenth dynasty (ca. 1303–1290 B.C.), Antonio Canaletto's *View Toward Murano* (ca. 1726–27), Barbara Hepworth's *Figure for Landscape* (1960), and Henry Moore's *Girl* (1932).

Holdings of eighteenth and nineteenth century and early modern European and American art were enriched by the donation in 1982 of thirty-eight Impressionist, Post-Impressionist, and contemporary American paintings and sculptures from the collection of Algur H. Meadows[qv] and his wife, Elizabeth. In 1991 the museum's collections were particularly strong in the areas of Pre-Columbian, African, and contemporary American art. The James H. and Lillian Clark Foundation has donated a number of works by Dutch abstractionist Piet Mondrian to the museum, which now has one of the broadest collections of this artist's work outside of Holland. The permanent collection has been built on community support, with endowment funds established by Trudie Munger, Margaret and Eugene B. McDermott,[qv] Virginia Lazenby O'Hara, Nancy and Jake L. Hamon,[qv] Roberta Coke Camp, and Edward S. and Betty Marcus. Other major benefactors include Wendy Reves, Joel T. Howard, Cecil and Ida Green, Stanley and Mary (Billie) Marcus, and Lupe and John Murchison.[qv]

Two longstanding objectives of the Dallas Museum of Art are education through exposure to art of the highest quality and the support of young regional artists. In order to accomplish these objectives, the museum offers a full and varied exhibition schedule. Traveling exhibitions from other institutions, such as the Museum of Modern Art's 1985 exhibition "Primitivism" in Twentieth Century Art: Affinity of the Tribal and the Modern, are presented, as well as exhibitions mounted by the DMA staff. The museum's Concentrations series highlights the works of living contemporary artists, and several traveling exhibitions organized by the museum, notably Lone Star Regionalism, the first official event of the Texas Sesquicentennial (1986), and Visions: James Surls, have focused attention on the quality and diversity of the work of Texas artists. The museum's interest in education is further evidenced by its Gateway Gallery, an entire wing devoted to education programming, with studios for art activities, interactive exhibits, and a children's library. A noncirculating research library is also available to the general public as well as to scholars, and a full schedule of activities is presented in the auditorium. Music, film, dance, and multimedia presentations are offered, as are more traditional lectures, gallery talks, and tours.

Since 1988 the museum staff has been particularly active in organizing exhibitions. By 1991 the staff numbered nearly 200 and was supplemented by the Dallas Museum of Art League, a source of volunteer support since its establishment as the Museum League in 1938. In 1991 a $30 million expansion was designed by Edward Larrabee Barnes. Construction began that same year, and the Nancy and Jake Hamon building was completed in 1993. With the addition of the new 140,000-square-foot wing, the museum underwent a restructuring. It now features minimuseums, with the old gallery housing the Museum of Africa and Asia, the Museum of Europe, and the Museum of Contemporary Art. The newly completed Hamon building houses the Museum of the Americas, which has art ranging from Pre-Columbian to the mid-1940s. The Hamon building also contains the Resource Center, where classrooms provide hands-on experience with objects of art. A computer system in the museum enables visitors to enter the name of an artist or period and find where the work is located in the museum.

BIBLIOGRAPHY: Anne R. Bromberg, *Dallas Museum of Art: Selected Works* (Dallas Museum of Art, 1983). Jerry Bywaters, *Seventy-Five Years of Art in Dallas: The History of the Dallas Art Association and the Dallas Museum of Fine Arts* (Dallas Museum of Fine Arts, 1978). Helen Dudar, "Down in Dallas, Art Has a New Home on the Range," *Smithsonian,* May 1984. Alfred Frankfurter, "Shame in Dallas," *Art News,* Summer 1955. *Texas Observer,* November 9, 1955, February 15, 1956.
Harry S. Parker III

DALLAS MUSEUM FOR CONTEMPORARY ARTS. Although the Dallas Museum for Contemporary Arts was short-lived, it was influential in developing an audience for modern art in Texas and set trends nationally. The museum developed from the Society of Contemporary Arts, which was organized in 1956, shortly after the "red art" controversy at the Dallas Museum of Fine Arts (later the Dallas Museum of Art[qv]) had been quelled by policy statements issued by the museum's board, backed by the support of the Dallas *Morning News.*[qv] However, the status of the Dallas Museum of Fine Arts as a city-owned organization rendered it vulnerable to ongoing pressure from protesters, some of whom equated abstract art with communism. As a private organization, the Society of Contemporary Arts provided a venue for contemporary art free from political pressures.

Begun by a group of fifteen that included artists, architects, theater directors, photographers, and critics, the Dallas Society for Contemporary Arts initially exhibited art in the lobby gallery of the Dallas Little Theater. Sculptor Heri Bert Bartscht served as director of the group, which by 1957 had attracted the support of such prominent patrons as Edward and Betty Marcus and John and Lupe Murchison. The society agreed that there was a growing need for a museum focused on contemporary art, and the Dallas Museum for Contemporary Arts subsequently opened to the public in November 1957 with the exhibition Abstract by Choice. The museum initially operated in a 1,600-square-foot rented store at 5966 West Northwest Highway and was funded by membership fees and underwriting by a number of business people. Edward S. Marcus served as the group's president, and exhibitions were organized and installed by members on a volunteer basis.

During the museum's first two years volunteers organized a number of ambitious exhibitions, such as The Fauves (1959), which featured works by Georges Braque, André Derain, Henri Matisse, Maurice Vlaminck, and others drawn from collections in Canada, England, and the United States. In 1959 five museum trustees purchased a building at 3415 Cedar Springs Boulevard that more than doubled the museum's exhibition area. An additional 10,000 square feet of space, which the trustees initially planned to rent out, was available for future expansion. The same year, the museum hired Douglas MacAgy, an experienced museum professional, to direct the museum.

Under MacAgy's guidance the Dallas Museum for Contemporary Arts organized a number of innovative exhibitions that attracted national attention, among them American Genius in Review: I (1960), which rediscovered five artists active in the early twentieth century whose work had been relegated to undeserved obscurity; René Magritte in America (1960), the first major museum exhibition of the

French Surrealist painter's work in the United States; and 1961 (1962), the first major museum exhibition of Pop art. The last prompted Claes Oldenburg's *Injun,* a performance-art piece that MacAgy claimed was the first museum-commissioned "happening." MacAgy also organized group exhibitions and included works by Texas artists Jim Love and David McManaway in the Museum of Modern Art's exhibition The Art of Assemblage when it traveled to Dallas in 1961.

The Dallas Museum for Contemporary Arts provided a supportive environment for a group of artists that included, in addition to Love and McManaway, Roy Fridge, Roger Winter, Herb Rogalla, Bill Komodore, Hal Pauley, and Charles T. Williams.qv Pauley, McManaway, Fridge, and Rogalla's wife, Jett, worked for the museum, and the others frequently helped install exhibitions. Over time the museum evolved into what MacAgy called an "artists' place," where they could meet, talk, and work with friends in an artistically stimulating milieu.

The Dallas Museum for Contemporary Arts supplemented exhibitions with public lectures, tours, and films. In 1960 the museum began offering children's art classes under the direction of Paul Rogers Harris. The public was further enriched by the museum's outstanding permanent collection of contemporary art, which included works by such artists as Paul Gauguin, Henri Matisse, Odilon Redon, Henry Moore, Francis Bacon, Joseph Stella, Gerald Murphy, and Joaquin Torres-Garcia.

The real estate demands of its new location and competition with an older, more established museum for financial support drained the museum's resources, and in 1962 the board sought a merger with the Dallas Museum of Fine Arts. In April 1963 the boards of both museums voted to merge the two institutions under the name Dallas Museum of Fine Arts. The trustees of the DMCA, still wary of community opposition to "red art," arranged for the formation of the Foundation for the Arts to serve as a holding agency for its collection, with the power to solicit funds and acquisitions. The foundation would manage funds and hold title to any acquisitions, although the Dallas Museum of Fine Arts retained possession of all works in the foundation's collection. A new board of directors was formed, with forty-one board representatives from each museum.

The Dallas Museum of Fine Arts was invigorated by the influx of new voices on its board of directors. It worked to enlarge its membership and pressed for more financial support from the city and from individual donors. Such former DMCA staffmembers as Paul Rogers Harris and Janet Kutner have played an active role in Texas art, and many of the artists associated with the Dallas Museum for Contemporary Arts have established national reputations. The DMCA's pioneering exhibitions and its relationship with local artists were celebrated in the 1971 exhibition One i at a Time, which was organized by MacAgy and took place at Meadows School of the Arts, Southern Methodist University.

BIBLIOGRAPHY: Files, Fine Arts Division, Dallas Public Library. Douglas MacAgey, *One i at a Time* (Dallas: Pollock Galleries, Southern Methodist University, 1971). *Time,* March 12, 1956.

Kendall Curlee

DALLAS NINE. The Dallas Nine, a group of painters, printmakers, and sculptors active in Dallas in the 1930s and early 1940s, turned to the land and people of the Southwest for artistic inspiration. "Nine" is somewhat misleading, as the group expanded and contracted at various points during the period it was active. The artists most closely identified with the name seem to have been the men who lobbied the Texas Centennialqv Commission unsuccessfully for the privilege of decorating the walls of the Hall of State,qv the main building of the Centennial Exposition in Dallas (1936). They were Jerry Bywaters, Thomas M. Stell, Jr., Harry P. Carnohan, Otis M. Dozier, Alexandre Hogue, William Lester,qqv Everett Spruce, John Douglass, and Perry Nichols. Other artists closely associated with the group were Charles T. Bowling, Russell Vernon Hunter, Merritt T. Mauzey, Florence McClung,qqv Don Brown, and Lloyd Goff. The sculptors Dorothy Austin, Michael G. Owen, Allie Victoria Tennant,qv and Octavio Medellín also participated in the Dallas Regionalist movement. The Dallas Nine flourished during a period when critics and theorists such as John Dewey, George Santayana, Constance Rourke, and Holger Cahill exhorted American artists to draw inspiration from their surroundings instead of following European trends. At the local level critics such as Henry Nash Smith, David R. Williams,qqv and Alexandre Hogue promoted the Regionalist aesthetic in the pages of the *Southwest Review.*qv In his role as art critic for the Dallas *Morning News*qv and editor of the short-lived *Southwestern Arts,* Bywaters emerged as the leading spokesman of Regionalism in Dallas. A number of changes and new organizations in Dallas stimulated the development of the Dallas Nine circle. John S. Ankeny's arrival in 1929 as the first professional director of the Dallas Art Association (later the Dallas Museum of Artqv) invigorated what had become a somewhat stodgy organization. Ankeny and his successor, Lloyd Rollins, presented exhibitions of early Italian painters, Mexican muralists, and contemporary American lithographers, all of which had a strong effect on the young artists in the area. The museum-sponsored annual competitive Allied Arts Exhibition functioned as an important source of encouragement and public recognition for the Regionalist artists. The Dallas Artists League,qv an informal discussion group active from 1932 to 1936, provided a forum for the exchange of ideas and heightened the public profile of its artist members with the popular annual Alice Street Art Carnivals. Organizations such as the Dallas Art Institute,qv the Highland Park Society of Arts, the Dallas University Club, the Klepper Sketch Club, the Lawrence Art Galleries, and the Joseph Sartor Galleries further stimulated the Dallas artistic climate by exhibiting young artists' work. Members of the Dallas Nine received much-needed financial support with the beginning in 1933 of the federal Public Works of Art Project, which awarded mural commissions to many Regionalist artists. New Deal patronage of artists continued into the early 1940s under the auspices of the Work Projects Administrationqv and the Treasury Section federal art project. The Centennial Exposition of 1936 was perhaps the most influential event in forging a group identity among the Dallas Regionalists. Although the Nine failed to secure the mural commissions for the Hall of State, they dominated the Texas section of the Dallas Museum of Fine Arts exhibition, and were praised in the national as well as the local press.

For the most part, the Dallas Regionalists eschewed the abstraction of School of Paris artists in favor of naturalistic representation. Most of the painters in the group used tight brushwork and an earthy palette, working in a hard-edged style that broke away from the misty Impressionism of the Bluebonnet School of painters that had dominated Texas art in the early part of the twentieth century. The Dallas Regionalists focused on the people, land, and wildlife of the Southwest as their principal subject matter. Positive evocations of the region can be seen in works such as Mauzey's *Neighbors* (1938) and McClung's *Squaw Creek Valley* (1937). More characteristic of the group was Hogue's grim *Drouth Stricken Era* (1934), in which parched brown earth threatens to engulf farm buildings, a derelict windmill, and a skeletal cow standing beside an empty water tub. Such contemporary Mexican painters as Diego Rivera and José Clemente Orozco were major influences on the Dallas Regionalists, particularly in their use of murals and inexpensive prints as populist tools to increase regional pride and political awareness. Italian primitive painting of the Quattrocento and American folk art also influenced the composition and draftsmanship of many of the Dallas Regionalists. Members of the Nine were familiar with the work of Thomas Hart Benton and other nationally known Regionalists, but they rejected the nativism of the American-scene movement led by Benton and critic Thomas Craven. Indeed, Harry Carnohan and several other members of the group traveled and studied in Europe and shared their experiences with their colleagues upon their return. A Surrealist influence can be detected in certain works by Carnohan, Dozier, Lester, Nichols, and Bywaters; Dozier also experimented with the contradictory perspective schemes of Cubism in his award-winning *Still Life With Striped Gourd* (1935).

Sculptors associated with the Dallas Regionalists experimented with direct carving, a modernist rejection of traditional processes that frequently required technical assistance, thus distancing the artist from his materials. Dorothy Austin, Michael Owens, and Allie Tennant worked in a blocky, robust style, although Tennant also produced such streamlined figures as the *Tejas Warrior* (1936), placed above the entrance to the Hall of State. Octavio Medellín developed a powerful style inspired in part by the art of the Maya and Toltec Indians, and exerted considerable influence over young artists through his teaching posts at the Witte Museum,[qv] North Texas State Teachers College, Southern Methodist University, and the Dallas Museum of Fine Arts.

In the later 1930s printmaking, particularly lithography, became an important medium for the Dallas Regionalists. Initially spurred by the establishment of the Dallas Print Society in 1934 and its Print Center, which opened in 1937, experimentation in that medium accelerated after Bywaters and other members of the Dallas Nine formed the Lone Star Printmakers in 1938. Approximately fifteen artists contributed prints to a traveling exhibition in which impressions were offered for sale. Hogue, Bywaters, and Dozier were the most experienced printmakers when the group was formed, but by the time of the last circuit in 1942 Bowling and Mauzey had emerged as the outstanding talents in the group. The Lone Star Printmakers prompted the establishment of the Printmakers Guild of Dallas,[qv] a group of printmakers originally limited to women, which operated a print circuit from 1940 to 1965.

The influx of European émigrés to the United States during World War II[qv] produced a ferment of art activity that culminated in the Abstract Expressionist movement of the late 1940s and early 1950s. Regionalism, sullied by its association with American Scene jingoism, became dated. Dozier, Spruce, Lester, and other Dallas artists injected new life into the Regionalist aesthetic by experimenting with a semiabstract style still rooted in Southwestern subject matter. Although the Dallas Nine ceased to operate as a group after its members scattered to pursue careers throughout the state and beyond, artists from that circle continued to do meaningful work and exerted a powerful influence over a new generation of artists through their positions as teachers and museum administrators. Their achievements as artists and teachers were celebrated in the Dallas Museum of Art's 1985 exhibition Lone Star Regionalism: The Dallas Nine and Their Circle.

BIBLIOGRAPHY: Jerry Bywaters, *Seventy-Five Years of Art in Dallas: The History of the Dallas Art Association and the Dallas Museum of fine Arts* (Dallas Museum of Fine Arts, 1978). Jerry Bywaters Collection on the Art of the Southwest, Southern Methodist University, Dallas. Rick Stewart, *Lone Star Regionalism: The Dallas Nine and Their Circle* (Austin: Texas Monthly Press, 1985). *Kendall Curlee*

DALLAS SYMPHONY ORCHESTRA. The Dallas Symphony Orchestra was founded in 1900; the first permanent orchestra played its inaugural concert under the direction of Hans Kreissig[qv] at Turner Hall on May 22 of that year. The thirty-two-member ensemble played music by Franz Joseph Haydn, Gioacchino Rossini, Richard Wagner, Pietro Mascagni, and Kreissig and continued sporadically with one or two concerts per season for the following ten years. In 1911 Walter J. Fried reorganized the Kreissig orchestra into the forty-member Beethoven Symphony Orchestra. Two years later Carl Venth[qv] moved to Dallas from the Kidd-Key Conservatory in Sherman and placed the Dallas Symphony Orchestra on a professional basis, with Fried as concertmaster. Economic reverses caused the orchestra to founder in its 1914–15 season, but Fried kept the group together and presented a four-concert series annually on a modest scale from 1918 to 1924.

Fried died in 1925. Just after his death the orchestra was expanded. Fried was succeeded by Paul van Katwijk, dean of music at Southern Methodist University, who conducted the orchestra until 1937. At that time the orchestra was taken over by Jacques Singer, whose spirited tenure ended in 1942, when he and a third of the orchestra's personnel entered military service.

Under Antal Dorati, who conducted the reconstituted DSO from 1945 to 1949, the orchestra rose to major status. Dorati was succeeded by Walter Hendl, who conducted the growing orchestra until 1958. At that time Paul Kletzki was hired and introduced a sense of Central European solidity to the programs. The Dallas Symphony engaged Georg Solti for the 1961–62 season, and the following year Donald Johanos, a young American conductor, was appointed music director. During his nine-year tenure, the Dallas Symphony received favorable national reviews and a recording contract. The 1970–73 tenure of Anshel Brusilow and the brief one-year appointments of Max Rudolf and Louis Lane were a period of waning community support, but the popularity of the orchestra was restored in 1977 when Eduardo Mata, a Mexican conductor, was hired as music director and Kurt Masur as principal guest conductor. The orchestra developed a brilliant image and prospered.

From the 1930s until 1989 the Dallas Symphony performed in the McFarlin Auditorium at Southern Methodist University and at the Fair Park Music Hall, which became its permanent home in 1973. A fund drive for a new hall was launched in 1982, and the new Morton H. Meyerson Symphony Center opened in September 1989. In 1985 the Dallas Symphony under Mata made its first European tour, to London, Paris, Berlin, Stuttgart, Frankfurt, Madrid, and Barcelona, performing to appreciative audiences and good reviews. The orchestra has made records with RCA Victor, which produced performances by Dorati, Hendl, and Mata; Turnabout-Candide, which produced the Johanos concerts; and both Telarc Records and Angel-EMI, which produced recordings of Eduardo Mata.

BIBLIOGRAPHY: Dallas *Morning News*, May 18, 1986. Robert Lincoln Marquis, The Development of the Symphony Orchestra in Texas (M.A. thesis, University of Texas, 1934). Hope Stoddard, *Symphony Conductors of the U.S.A.* (New York: Crowell, 1957).

Theodore Albrecht

DALLAS TERMINAL RAILWAY. The Dallas Terminal Railway and Union Depot Company was chartered on December 10, 1894, to build north from Dallas for twenty miles to a connection with the St. Louis Southwestern Railway Company of Texas between Plano and Fort Worth. The capital was $500,000, and the business office was in Dallas. Members of the first board of directors included Alexander Sanger, Royal A. Ferris,[qqv] W. C. Connor, J. C. O'Connor, E. M. Reardon, Barnett Gibbs, and J. E. Schneider, all of Dallas. Earlier businessmen of Dallas had offered the Cotton Belt, then operating as the Texas and St. Louis, cash, land, and right-of-way to extend its line from Mount Pleasant to Dallas by April 1, 1884. The Cotton Belt could not meet this deadline and, in fact, bypassed Dallas and built to Fort Worth. The Dallas Terminal Railway charter authorized it to build a belt line around Dallas and a connecting road to the Cotton Belt track in Fort Worth. For several years the company retained its charter but laid no track. Finally, between 1893 and 1896 it laid four miles of industrial track in Dallas. In 1899 the name of the company was changed to Dallas, Fort Worth and Gulf Railway Company, and the plan to build a line to Fort Worth was revived. Two miles of additional track was laid. In 1901 the company was purchased by the St. Louis Southwestern Railway to provide terminal facilities at Dallas for its Texas subsidiary. The charter was again amended when the company's original name was restored. A passenger depot was built in 1903, and track was laid connecting with all Dallas railroads. In 1916, when Union Depot opened, the Dallas Terminal passenger depot was closed. In 1953 the Interstate Commerce Commission authorized the St. Louis Southwestern Railway Company to lease and operate the company's properties, and Dallas Terminal Railway and Union Depot Company became a nonoperating lessor. In 1994 it was merged into the St. Louis Southwestern. *Cecil Harper, Jr.*

DALLAS TEXANS. In the late 1950s Lamar Hunt of Dallas sought to obtain a professional football franchise for that city. Hunt was told by the National Football League that there would be no expansion in the foreseeable future, so he set out to form a new league. He found other men to join him in this venture, and in 1959 Hunt formed the American Football League. Hunt named his team the Dallas Texans and hired Hank Stram, an assistant coach at the University of Miami, Florida, as his head coach. The American Football League made its professional debut in 1960. Hunt's Texans finished their first season with an eight-win and six-loss record, placing second in the AFL's Western Division. The 1960 Texans had the league's most exciting player, Abner Haynes, a rookie from North Texas State University, who won the league rushing title, was chosen the AFL's first "Player of the Year," and became the symbol of the dynamic new professional league. In 1961 the team slipped to a six-win and eight-loss record. Stram rewarded Hunt with his first championship in 1962, when the Texans, bolstered by the addition of quarterback Len Dawson and rookie fullback Curtis McClinton, swept to the Western Division title with a spectacular eleven-win and three-loss season. Stram was named "Coach of the Year," Dawson, "Player of the Year," and McClinton, "Rookie of the Year." The Texans' foe in the 1962 championship game was the Houston Oilers,[qv] who were bidding for a pro football record of three straight championships. Behind by seventeen points, Houston tied the score by the end of the regulation sixty minutes, and the stage was set for one of the most exciting endings in sports history. The Texans and Oilers struggled through a fifth fifteen-minute period and were two minutes and fifty-four seconds into a record-breaking "sixth quarter" when rookie Tommy Brooker kicked a twenty-five-yard field goal to give the Texans a 20 to 17 victory in the longest football game ever played. The Texans were champions, but all was not peace and tranquility in Dallas. The rival National Football League had placed a team, the Dallas Cowboys,[qv] there in 1960 to compete with the Texans. The fans were torn between two camps—the Texans and the Cowboys. In 1963 Lamar Hunt moved his team to Kansas City, Missouri.

BIBLIOGRAPHY: Harold Rosenthal, ed., *American Football League Official History, 1960–1969* (St. Louis: Sporting News, 1970).
Jim Schaaf

DALLAS THEOLOGICAL SEMINARY. Dallas Theological Seminary, a nondenominational Protestant school, is located on Swiss Avenue in eastern Dallas. The seminary opened in the fall of 1924 with twelve students who proposed to study with Bible teacher Lewis Sperry Chafer. The school was incorporated by the state on February 16, 1925, under the name Evangelical Theological College. Though denominationally unaffiliated, the seminary served those of like faith in evangelical Protestantism and welcomed qualified men in sympathy with their doctrine. In 1926 friends purchased the first portion of the present campus on Swiss Avenue. The following year memorial gifts provided for the construction of Lidie C. Davidson Hall and D. M. Stearns Memorial Hall. In 1929 George T. Besel of Philadelphia purchased an apartment house, thus adding to the Swiss Avenue frontage to complete the five-acre campus.

The seminary pioneered in offering a four-year course for the master of theology degree. The new curriculum incorporated essential theology courses offered in three-year programs and gave additional emphasis to systematic theology, Greek and New Testament exegesis, and English Bible exposition. Since 1935 courses in practical theology, missions, church history, and Christian education have been made available. In addition to the four-year Th.M. program for college graduates, the seminary program included a year of study leading to a S.T.M. for those having graduated from a three-year seminary course, as well as a three-year Th.D. for those having completed a Th.M.

The name of the school was changed to Dallas Theological Seminary and Graduate School of Theology in July 1936. The next major building, Lewis Sperry Chafer Chapel, was erected during 1952–53. Mosher Library, suitable for a student body of 500 and a collection of 125,000 volumes, was added in 1960. In the 1972–73 term the faculty numbered twenty-eight. Enrollment averaged 300 between 1950 and 1965, and in 1972–73 reached 543. In 1974–75 Academic centers I and II were built.

By 1976 the student body had increased to 1,000, making the seminary one of the five largest protestant seminaries in the world. A doctor of ministry degree program was begun in 1980, and programs of the seminary were instituted in Philadelphia and San Antonio. By 1992 Dallas Theological Seminary had a student body of 1,200 students, of which 200 were women and 160 were from forty foreign countries. The seminary had sixty faculty members and an endowment of $1.5 million. Lewis Sperry Chafer was president from 1924 to 1952, John F. Walvoord served from 1952 to 1986, and Donald K. Campbell subsequently assumed the post.

BIBLIOGRAPHY: Dallas *Morning News,* April 10, 1986, May 15, 1992. Dallas *Times Herald,* August 8, 1976. Vertical Files, Barker Texas History Center, University of Texas at Austin.

DALLAS *TIMES HERALD*. The Dallas *Times Herald* (formerly the Dallas *Daily Times-Herald*) was founded in 1888 after a merger of the Dallas *Daily Times* with the Dallas *Daily Herald.* The *Daily Times* was founded in 1879 by J. A. Adams, who later that year sold the paper to Edward C. McClure and William Greene Sterett.[qv] The *Daily Herald,* first published in 1873 by John Swindell, was published in 1886 by M. H. Claytor, who later that year sold the paper to L. L. Foster and Charles E. Gilbert. Gilbert, a prohibitionist, and Sterett, a prohibition[qv] opponent, were unlikely partners and had debated their differences in the editorial columns of their respective newspapers. However, when threatened by financial ruin they agreed to merge their papers and produce the Dallas *Daily Times-Herald,* the first issue of which came out on January 2, 1888. In July of that year Sterett sold his interest in the paper to Gilbert, who used the paper to fight for such causes as immigrants' rights and the development of Dallas. The paper also became the first in the city to use electricity. The Dallas *Daily Times-Herald* joined the Associated Press in 1890 and, as the decade progressed, continued its role as a Dallas booster. It advanced such causes as street paving, improved sanitation, and water facilities. In the gubernatorial election of 1892 it supported the reelection of James S. Hogg.[qv] During the depression of that year the paper suffered major financial setbacks, and Gilbert was forced to put it into receivership under the administration of Oliver P. Bowser.[qv]

During the next few years the *Daily Times-Herald* underwent a number of changes in ownership and editorial staff, as the editors were unable to reverse the paper's financial decline. In 1893 E. G. Myers bought the paper and James E. Simpson became the publisher. A year later the *Daily Times-Herald* was sold to John F. Elliot, who also served as the paper's editor-in-chief. By 1896 the paper was once again put up for sale. Edwin J. Kiest,[qv] a Chicago newspaperman and representative of the Western Newspaper Union, bought the *Daily Times-Herald* and retained Elliot as editor-in-chief until 1900, when he was replaced by the paper's city editor, Hugh K. Taylor. Under Kiest's direction the paper continued to boost Dallas, and the *Daily Times-Herald*'s fortune reversed. By 1903 the paper included sections on the arts, entertainment, agriculture, and sports. Seven years later its circulation reached 12,653. In 1926 Kiest bought KRLD radio. By 1929 the paper's circulation reached 64,063 for the daily edition and 62,846 for the Sunday edition. In that year the new headquarters at

Pacific, Griffin, and Patterson streets was completed, and the paper was moved into its new building without missing a single edition.

From 1931 to 1933 the circulation declined because of the Great Depression,[qv] but by 1941 it had rebounded to 95,432 for the daily edition and 96,682 for the Sunday edition. Kiest died that year and left the paper in the hands of Tom C. Gooch, who was president of the *Daily Times-Herald* until 1952, when John W. Runyon secured the office. In the first year of Gooch's tenure the paper's circulation increased to 140,489 for the daily edition and 139,892 for the Sunday edition. In 1954 the paper was redesigned and *Daily* was dropped from its name, which was henceforth unhyphenated.

In 1964 photographer Bob Jackson received a Pulitzer Prize for his photograph of the slaying of Lee Harvey Oswald.[qv] Three years later James F. Chambers, Jr., took over as publisher of the paper, which in 1969 was sold to the Los Angles based Times Mirror Company. The new owner expanded the paper's coverage of local news and began printing a morning edition as well as the regular afternoon edition. In 1973 W. Thomas Johnson became the executive editor and vice president, and two years later he replaced Chambers as publisher, a position he held from 1975 to 1977, when Lee Guitar succeeded him. Guitar served until 1981, when Thomas R. McCartin became publisher. Under the leadership of these last three publishers the paper reached the peak of its success. In 1975 *Newsweek* ranked it in the top five newspapers in the South, and in 1977 the Sunday edition of the *Times Herald* outsold the Dallas *Morning News*[qv] 322,093 newspapers to 321,167. In the decade following 1975 the paper won two more Pulitzer prizes, one going to photographer Erwin H. Hagler in 1980 and one to photographer Jay Dickman in 1983. The paper also had nine Pulitzer Prize finalists, four Picture of the Year awards, two George Polk awards, and two Overseas Press Club awards, in addition to a number of other awards. The *Times Herald* was known as a liberal publication, in contrast to the *Morning News*. The *Times Herald* claimed to have more blue-collar and minority readers. In 1986 William Dean Singleton and the Media News Group bought the paper from Times Mirror for $110 million. Two years later a majority of the *Times Herald's* stock was purchased from Media News Group by John H. Buzetta and the newly formed DTH Media, with MediaNews Group remaining as a minority stockholder.

By the late 1980s the *Times Herald* was in the middle of a decline that eventually ended in its demise. A number of factors contributed to the paper's decline. The paper, formerly an afternoon daily, began also issuing a morning edition in September 1977 as a result of the gradual demise of afternoon newspapers, which suffered from competition from evening television news broadcasts. In the late 1970s and early 1980s the owner, Times Mirror, failed to provide significant reinvestment in the paper, in contrast to an aggressive reorganization of activities at the *Morning News*. The *Times Mirror* also failed to recognize the growing trend away from city issues and towards suburban needs. There were also problems regarding suburban delivery routes; many subscribers failed to receive their papers. The paper's suburban circulation had fallen far behind that of the *Morning News*. A number of conflicts occurred within the *Times Herald's* management. The last blow came in 1989, when the rights to twenty-six Universal Press Syndicate features, which the *Times Herald* had been running, were bought by the A. H. Belo Corporation,[qv] publisher of the *Morning News*. In retaliation the *Times Herald* filed an antitrust lawsuit against Belo, but lost. The *Times Herald* appealed the decision and was denied again. On December 8, 1991, Belo bought the *Times Herald* for $55 million. The paper became another exemplar of the nationwide trend away from having competing papers in major cities, as large corporations bought out newspaper competitors. The Dallas *Times Herald* printed its final edition on December 9, 1991.

BIBLIOGRAPHY: Sam Hanna Acheson, *35,000 Days in Texas: A History of the Dallas "News" and Its Forbears* (New York: Macmillan, 1938). Austin *American-Statesman*, December 9, 10, 1991. Dallas *Times Herald*, December 9, 1991.
Matthew Hayes Nall

DALLAS AND WACO RAILWAY. The Dallas and Waco Railway Company was incorporated on December 22, 1886, when the Missouri, Kansas and Texas began building south from Dallas. By 1889 fifty-three miles of track had been built from Dallas to Milford, and the next year fourteen more miles had been added to extend the line to Hillsboro. There the road connected with another line of the MKT, which had been built from Fort Worth in 1882. The road was sold to the Missouri, Kansas and Texas on November 12, 1891, and consolidated with the Missouri, Kansas and Texas Railway Company of Texas on November 18, 1891.
S. G. Reed

DALLAS AND WICHITA RAILROAD. The Dallas and Wichita Railroad Company was chartered on December 2, 1871, by citizens of Dallas. The line was projected to be over 100 miles long and to penetrate the reputed mineral regions of the Wichita County area. John Neely Bryan[qv] broke ground for the road in 1872, but the panic of 1873 forced the construction to stop. Work was resumed in 1877, when Dallas citizens voted $100,000 in bonds for the project. By 1878 twenty miles of track had been built from Dallas north to Lewisville, but the road went into receivership the next year. In 1880 the line was bought by the Texas and Pacific Company, which completed the extension from Lewisville to Denton. The Dallas and Wichita was sold to the Missouri, Kansas and Texas Railway Company on December 15, 1881, and became part of the Missouri, Kansas and Texas Railway Company of Texas on November 18, 1891.
S. G. Reed

DALLMER, MARY (1852–1909). Mother Mary Joseph Dallmer, heroine of the Galveston hurricane of 1900,[qv] youngest child of Gregory and Mary Anne Dallmer, was born at Oberhausen, Baden, on March 19, 1852. Her mother immigrated with her children to Galveston, Texas, probably in 1858, at the invitation of her two older children there. Mary entered the Ursuline Academy[qv] in Galveston as a small child, graduated in 1869, and entered the Ursuline Sisters[qv] in the same year. Gifted intellectually and artistically, she was given responsibility in the school and community while very young. She was elected superior in 1891 and oversaw the construction of the new Ursuline Academy.

When the storm of September 8, 1900, struck Galveston, Mother Mary Joseph directed her community to open its buildings to more than a thousand refugees, black and white, to calm their terror and meet their needs. At the risk of their own lives the nuns pulled many persons from the floodwaters. Mother Mary Joseph ordered them to strip the convent of linens and give up their own wardrobes to clothe the refugees, and to share what food was spared by the tidal wave. For several weeks after the storm she kept the homeless in what was left of the convent buildings. The Houston *Post*[qv] stated at this time in a nationally reprinted story: "A fearful catastrophe like that of September 8 brings out all that there is in a human being . . . and when all the noblest attributes . . . are brought out in one individual, and that a woman, mere words become too weak . . . to do her proper honor. Such a woman is Mother Mary Joseph. She is the heroine of the storm."

In November 1900 she represented the Galveston Ursulines at an international gathering to form the Roman Union of the Order of St. Ursula. She was appointed the first provincial of the Ursuline convents in Texas and Illinois in the new union. In 1907, when she was elected American assistant to the mother general of the order, she moved to Rome. There she died on May 25, 1909. She is buried in Rome.

BIBLIOGRAPHY: Catholic Archives of Texas, Files, Austin. Stephen Morris Johnston, *A Light Shining* (New York: Benziger, 1937).
Sister Ignatius Miller, O.S.U.

DALRYMPLE, WILLIAM CORNELIUS (1814–1898). William Cornelius Dalrymple, soldier, politician, lawyer, and surveyor, was born in Moore County, North Carolina, on August 3, 1814, the son of

James and Rosanna (Dawd) Dalrymple. About 1835 he moved to Texas. He served on ranger scouting duties on the Brazos River in 1837 and in 1839 was stationed at Austin as a guard for the builders of the first government cabins. In 1840 he married Elizabeth Wilbarger and settled on a farm north of Austin. In 1842 he served under Gen. Edward Burleson[qv] in repelling the invasion of Rafael Vásquez.[qv]

In 1846 Dalrymple settled on the San Gabriel River, and in 1848 he was appointed one of the commissioners to determine the site of the Williamson county seat. He became the first assessor and collector of taxes when the county was organized and held that position until 1852. He also represented the county in the Sixth and Seventh legislatures. Although Dalrymple engaged primarily in farming, he reentered the ranger service in 1859 and was ordered to raise a company of rangers for service on the frontier; he commanded this company until June 1862. During the later part of the Civil War[qv] he served with the Confederate Army in Arkansas.

At the end of the war he returned to Williamson County and worked as a surveyor and attorney in Georgetown while pursuing various other activities. Between December 1866 and May 1867 Dalrymple and prospector Jacob Snively[qv] led two expeditions to investigate reports of gold in the Rio Grande country. The first group disbanded after Indians killed their horses and wounded Dalrymple and a number of others near Camp Colorado[qv] in Coleman County. A reorganized expedition set out in the spring and prospected unsuccessfully in the Rio Grande country. Dalrymple represented Williamson and Travis counties in the Constitutional Convention of 1866[qv] and in the Senate of the Eleventh Legislature. He was an outspoken opponent of black equality and suffrage and favored restricting blacks to "the station of 'hewers of wood and drawers of water'." In 1871 he assisted in the negotiations with the Methodist Church[qv] that brought Southwestern University to Georgetown. Dalrymple died at his home in Georgetown on March 29, 1898, and was buried in the city cemetery.

BIBLIOGRAPHY: *History of Texas, Together with a Biographical History of Milam, Williamson, Bastrop, Travis, Lee and Burleson Counties* (Chicago: Lewis, 1893). Clara Stearns Scarbrough, *Land of Good Water: A Williamson County History* (Georgetown, Texas: Williamson County Sun Publishers, 1973).
Carolyn Hyman

DALTON, TEXAS. Dalton is a lumbering and farming community 3½ miles northwest of Marietta on State Highway 77 in northwestern Cass County. The community, formed in the period following the Civil War,[qv] received a post office in 1875 and reached its peak around 1884, when it had three saw and flour mills, six churches, at least two schools, and a population of 200. Its post office was closed in 1887, then operated from 1897 until 1905, when it closed permanently. By 1940 a church, cemetery, and school were at the site; by 1983 only the church and cemetery remained there. The community still existed in 1990.
Cecil Harper, Jr.

DALTON GANG. The Dalton gang, a small band of outlaws who held up trains in the Missouri, Kansas, Oklahoma, and Texas region, was organized in February 1891, by Bob and Emmett Dalton, George Newcomb, Charley Bryant, and William McElhanie. In the winter of 1891–92 the gang had a hideout in Greer County,[qv] Texas (later Oklahoma). Bob, Grat, and Emmett Dalton, Bill Powers, and Dick Broadwell attempted to rob two Coffeyville, Kansas, banks on October 5, 1892, with the result that all were killed except Emmett Dalton.

BIBLIOGRAPHY: Emmett Dalton, *When the Daltons Rode* (Garden City, New York: Sun Dial Press, 1937). Emmett Dalton, *Beyond the Law* (New York: Ogilvie, 1918).
Carolyn Hyman

DALTON MOUNTAIN. Dalton Mountain, 6½ miles southeast of Gatesville within the boundaries of Fort Hood in Coryell County (at 31°21′ N, 97°42′ W), has an elevation of 1,358 feet above sea level. The surrounding terrain is sloping to hilly.
Sylvia Edwards

DALWORTHINGTON GARDENS, TEXAS. Dalworthington Gardens is off Interstate Highway 20 some twelve miles southeast of Fort Worth in east central Tarrant County. It was established after World War II,[qv] when the development of defense-related industrial plants in and around Fort Worth spurred rapid population and economic growth in the area. By the mid-1950s the population of Dalworthington Gardens stood at 267. In 1965 it was 630, and by 1976 it was 757. In 1988 Dalworthington Gardens reported a population of 1,281 and one manufacturing establishment. In 1990 the town had 1,758 residents.
Brian Hart

DALY'S, TEXAS. Daly's (Dalys), a farming community just off Farm Road 227 eight miles west of Grapeland in western Houston County, was established around 1850 and named for Thomas R. Dailey, an early settler. The Daly's Missionary Baptist Church was organized on July 1, 1853, and the community's first school was built a few years later. A post office operated at Daly's from 1876 until 1907. By 1885 the settlement had an estimated population of sixty, two steam gristmills and gins, and a general store, a church, and a district school. In the mid-1930s the community still had a church and a number of houses. After World War II[qv] many of its residents moved away, and by the mid-1960s only a church and a few widely scattered houses remained in the area. In the early 1990s Daly's was a dispersed rural community.

BIBLIOGRAPHY: Houston County Historical Commission, *History of Houston County, Texas, 1687–1979* (Tulsa, Oklahoma: Heritage, 1979).
Christopher Long

DAM B, TEXAS. Dam B is on U.S. Highway 190 and Farm Road 92, just east of B. A. Steinhagen Lake and north of Town Bluff, some twelve miles northeast of Woodville in northeastern Tyler County. The town was named in a plan to build several area dams, of which it was the second in a series of three. Dam B Wildlife Management Area is a mile north of the community. Dogwood Station and the Dogwood post office, a church, and several buildings were at the community's site in 1984. Its population was reported as fifty-six from 1968 to 1993. Dam B is a dispersed rural community with several campsites.
Diana J. Kleiner

DAMERON CITY, TEXAS. Dameron City, about 1½ miles from the old Midkiff post office in southeastern Midland County, was established in 1911. The townsite was promoted by two men named Willis and Kersner and may have been named after another promoter. Although some construction occurred there and a school was started, the community was abandoned two years later when its founders went broke. Workmen from Midland lumberyards salvaged much of the townsite's building material.

BIBLIOGRAPHY: Midland County Historical Society, *The Pioneer History of Midland County, Texas, 1880–1926* (Dallas: Taylor, 1984).
Charles G. Davis

DAMN BRANCH. Damn (Dam) Branch, a springfed intermittent stream formerly known as Spring Creek, rises a mile east of Hix in far northeastern Burleson County (at 30°42′ N, 96°39′ W) and runs east five miles to its mouth on the Brazos River, on the Brazos county line (at 30°41′ N, 96°35′ W). It traverses gently rolling to nearly level terrain surfaced by loamy and clayey soils that support post oak, blackjack oak, elm, and hackberry along its banks. Settlement in the area began in 1830 when the Mexican government constructed Fort Tenoxtitlán at the mouth of the creek where the Old San Antonio Road crossed the Brazos. Though the fort was abandoned a few years later, a trading post and settlement remained there until about 1860. Fraimville, later known as Hix, was founded a mile west of the headwaters of the creek about 1850. Rita was established on the south bank of the lower creek about 1890. Farm Road 1362 was constructed over the stream in the mid-1900s.

BIBLIOGRAPHY: Burleson County Historical Society, *Astride the Old San Antonio Road: A History of Burleson County, Texas* (Dallas: Taylor, 1980). Malcolm D. McLean, "Tenoxtitlán, Dream Capitol of Texas," *Southwestern Historical Quarterly* 70 (April 1967).

DAMON, SAMUEL (1808–1882). Samuel Damon, pioneer and participant in the Texas Revolution,qv was born in North Reading, Massachusetts, on May 7, 1808, the son of Daniel and Sally (Eaton) Damon. In 1831 he left his carpentry work in Massachusetts to settle in Texas. When his ship arrived at the mouth of the Brazos, he was told that Mexican officials would not allow any more Americans to enter Texas. Damon swam ashore undetected, made his way inland, and eventually found shelter in the home of Abraham Darst, one of Stephen F. Austin'sqv colonists. After working for Darst for several months helping him construct his home, Damon traveled to San Felipe and obtained permission from Mexican authorities to operate a freight line between Columbia and San Antonio. On September 18, 1834, he married Darst's eldest daughter, Lorena; the Damons had four sons and two daughters. Between 1834 and 1836 Damon built a home on a small rise known as Damon's Mound on a part of Darst's land. In the fall of 1835 he was assigned the duty of transporting military supplies to the Texas forces commanded by Edward Burlesonqv near San Antonio de Béxar. After delivering the supplies, Damon took part in the siege of Bexarqv and the capture of Gen. Martín Perfecto de Cos.qv As a soldier at the battle of San Jacintoqv he guarded the wagons, baggage, and wounded soldiers near Harrisburg. After Texas independence Damon supplied lumber and brick for construction in Galveston and the surrounding region. He operated a brick kiln and in 1840 built a sawmill. In the spring of 1842 he served as a private in the army sent to repel the Mexican invasion led by Gen. Rafael Vásquezqv and in the fall of the same year served as a captain of a company from Fort Bend against Adrián Woll.qv

In 1850 when construction began on the first Texas railroad, from Houston to Wharton, Damon received the contract to supply cedar ties. In order to buy additional equipment he mortgaged 5,000 acres of land to a New York bank. He also purchased $3,000 in railroad stock. The rail line was completed as far as Columbia when the Civil Warqv began, but it was never finished, and Damon lost all he had mortgaged. In 1860 the Brazoria County census listed him as a planter with landholdings valued at $15,500 and a personal estate of $15,150. He died at Damon's Mound (now in Damon) in Brazoria County on October 3, 1882, and is buried in the Damon Cemetery.

BIBLIOGRAPHY: Brazoria County Federation of Women's Clubs, *History of Brazoria County* (1940). Nanetta Key Burkholder, *The 1860 Census of Brazoria County* (Brazosport, Texas: Brazosport Genealogical Society, 1978). James A. Creighton, *A Narrative History of Brazoria County* (Angleton, Texas: Brazoria County Historical Commission, 1975). Sam Houston Dixon and Louis Wiltz Kemp, *The Heroes of San Jacinto* (Houston: Anson Jones, 1932). *John W. Damon II*

DAMON, TEXAS. Damon, originally known as Damon Mound or Damon's Mound, is at the junction of State Highway 36 and Farm Road 1462 in northwestern Brazoria County. The mound itself is a geological outcropping that rises seventy-five feet above the otherwise flat surrounding coastal plains. Samuel Damon,qv for whom the mound and town are named, moved into the area in 1831 and married Abraham Darst's eldest daughter Lorena; the couple built their home on the south side of the mound. By 1890 the community of Damon Mound had a population of 100, a post office that received mail every two weeks, a physician, a carpenter, a shoemaker, and a busy livestock industry. The community's post office had been discontinued by 1892, but three years later it reopened under the name Damon. By 1896 the settlement had a population of forty and a Baptist church. In 1906 Damon employed one schoolteacher to instruct forty children. In 1918 the Galveston, Harrisburg and San Antonio Railway built a twenty-one mile extension to Damon Mound, connecting the local sulfur, limestone, and other mineral extraction industries with Rosenberg. By 1925 Damon's population had risen to 300, and a Catholic parish had been started. Six years later Damon had a bank, an independent school district, fifteen businesses, and a population of 260. Although the bank had closed by 1939 and the Texas and New Orleans Railroad abandoned the track from Guy to Damon in 1944, the population of Damon was reported as almost 400 from the late 1940s through the 1980s. In 1989 the town had a population of 375 and sixteen businesses—including a quarry, feed stores, appliance shops, convenience stores, boot shops, cotton gins, and a taxidermists. It also had a Lion's Club and four churches: Church of Christ, Baptist, Lutheran, and Catholic. In the 1980s Damon was the site of the annual reunion of the Damon family, many of whom continued to live in close proximity to their pioneer home. *Chris Damon*

DAMON MOUND. Damon (Damon's) Mound, a limestone formation that rises 146 feet above the surrounding terrain, is just west of Damon and State Highway 36 in northwestern Brazoria County (at 29°17′ N, 95°45′ W). The mile-long mound runs east–west and is 600 to 800 yards wide; it covers 3,000 acres. Abraham Darst obtained a land grant for the area from the Mexican government. The mound was later part of the Damon estate for forty years (*see* DAMON, SAMUEL), after it was obtained through marriage with a member of the Darst family. Damon Mound has served as a source of limestone, and mineral springs at the site were once used for medicinal purposes.

BIBLIOGRAPHY: Clarence Wharton, *Wharton's History of Fort Bend County* (San Antonio: Naylor, 1939).

DAMSITE, TEXAS. Damsite was four miles east of what is now Lake Pauline and just north of Wanderers Creek on a north–south road that connected with what became Farm Road 2006 in east central Hardeman County. The community was part of a project to build a dam across Wanderers Creek to impound a reservoir that would irrigate 10,000 acres. Cecil A. Lyon,qv J. L. Elbert, and the Rice brothers of Houston bought several thousand acres of surrounding land in 1906, set up the Hardeman County Irrigation Company, and platted the town of Damsite in the middle of their holdings. Eventually a 6,000-foot dam was completed there at a cost of $75,000. The project proved successful until company general manager Cecil Lyon died in 1916. Later West Texas Utilities purchased the site and built a huge power plant there. The lake was known as Damsite until it was leased to Arlie Berry, who established a resort and renamed the reservoir after his daughter Pauline. By 1949 most of the irrigation company's land had been sold. The town was not shown on the 1980 county highway map.

BIBLIOGRAPHY: Bill Neal, *The Last Frontier: The Story of Hardeman County* (Quanah, Texas: Quanah *Tribune–Chief*, 1966). Quanah *Tribune–Chief*, July 19, 1906. *Charles G. Davis*

DAN, TEXAS. Dan, a farming community in northwestern Clay County, developed in the late 1890s when A. W. and George Byers established a settlement on the Wichita Valley rail line. The community remained small; one store and an estimated twenty-three residents were reported in 1940. Since that time no population estimates have been available. The community was not shown on the county highway maps. *David Minor*

DANA PEAK. Dana Peak is three miles south of Nolanville by the Lampasas River in western Bell County (at 31°02′ N, 97°36′ W). Its summit, with an elevation of 860 feet above sea level, rises some 300 feet above the river.

DANBURY, TEXAS. Danbury is on Spur 28 two miles off State Highway 35 and five miles northeast of Angleton in Brazoria County. Until the coming of the Missouri Pacific Railroad in 1905–06 this area was populated only by a few ranchers and farmers. The railroad gave access to hundreds of acres of rich farmland that had previously been almost inaccessible, and several towns grew up along the route. It is said the railroad construction workers gave the town its name in honor of D. J. "Uncle Dan" Moller, an area rancher who often entertained them at night with music and tall tales. Other sources say it was named for a Daniel T. Miller. Land promoters bought up large tracts and advertised in the North and Midwest. Settlers began to arrive, and a hotel was built to accommodate them. A demonstration farm garden was planted. Businesses began to open, including a general store, in which a post office was established in 1909.

Since most of the newcomers engaged in truck farming, docks were built on Austin Bayou, two miles southeast of Danbury, to ship produce by boat to Galveston. Watermelons, strawberries, cabbages, and onions went by train to Chicago, New York, and other cities in the north. When oil was found at nearby Hoskins Mound, it, too, was shipped by rail from Danbury. By 1916 most of the northerners had left, discouraged by freezes, floods, and storms; Czech farmers began to move into the area.

The first school in Danbury was held in a private home before 1909, when a one-room, frame school was built. More rooms were added in 1912 and 1917, and in 1920 the first brick school was constructed. The old frame building was divided in half and used for many years by the town's Protestants and Catholics. In 1990 both the Catholics and the Baptists had substantial buildings in Danbury, and major school-construction programs had provided modern facilities for the increasing number of students.

An airfield was located in Danbury during World War I.[qv] Planes from Ellington Field[qv] landed there, then flew on to West Columbia as part of the cross-country flight-training program. Danbury was incorporated in 1960, with a mayor and council form of government. In 1990 the chief industries of the area were rice farming and cattle ranching, both of which began long before the town sprang up, and declining oil production; a catfish farm was in operation. Danbury had a population of 1,447 in 1990.

BIBLIOGRAPHY: James Lewellyn Allhands, *Gringo Builders* (Joplin, Missouri, Dallas, Texas, 1931). Angleton *Times*, Sesquicentennial Edition, April 20, 1986. Brazoria County Federation of Women's Clubs, *History of Brazoria County* (1940). William Andrew Moller, *Memories of an Old Cow Hand* (Danbury, Texas, 1970).

Marie Beth Jones

DANCE BROTHERS. Civil War[qv] firearms manufactured by J. H. Dance and Company are among the most highly prized antique weapons, valued for their fine craftsmanship as well as their rarity. From July 1862 through May 1865 the company produced six-shot Colt-pattern revolvers in both .44 and .36 caliber; total output was fewer than 400. The Dance family, originally residents of North Carolina, moved to Daniels Prairie in Greene County, Alabama, around 1835. In 1848 James Henry Dance traveled to Brazoria County, Texas, and in 1853 he moved to Texas with most of his family, including father, brothers, cousins, and slaves. The family jointly purchased 450 acres of land in the Cedar Brake section, where they established a plantation. In 1858 they built a spacious home in the thriving riverport town of East Columbia, on the Brazos River. Across the street from their residence they opened a manufactory for metal and woodwork, named J. H. Dance and Company and operated by James Henry Dance and his brothers David Etheldred and George Perry. J. H. Dance and Company prospered before the Civil War[qv] manufacturing gristmills and cotton gins.

At the outbreak of the war James Dance enlisted in the Brazoria Volunteers; he later became first lieutenant in the Thirty-fifth Texas Cavalry. His brothers George, David, and Isaac enlisted, but because of their abilities and skills they were detailed to their steam factory at Columbia by early May 1862. Isaac died of measles in 1863. Initially the Dances' primary tasks were mounting cannons and repairing wagons for the Confederate Army and grinding cornmeal for Bates Company. In April 1862 George Dance wrote Governor F. R. Lubbock[qv] requesting an advance of $5,000. He claimed that this sum would enable the Dances to begin firearm production with an output of fifty revolvers a week. Evidently they received some aid, for on July 5, 1862, a letter written by George's cousin Mattie Duff states that "the boys think they will soon get some three or four of their pistols finished." While production may have been at a somewhat slower pace than originally anticipated, by October 2, 1862, the Dances were able to ship a dozen revolvers to the San Antonio Arsenal.[qv]

By November 1863 the Dances had decided to sell their business to the Confederate government. Cousin Mattie wrote that "the boys think it quite possible they will quit the shop soon" and added that George had left for Houston "to see if he could make a government affair of it." Further, "he thinks perhaps it will be done." Revolver production had come to an end in East Columbia by December 10, 1863, and Mattie wrote that she had been "in town all week helping the boys to leave."

The federal occupation of Matagorda Island, located just off the Texas coast near Brazoria County, prompted the belief that the county was about to be invaded. The Confederate government doubtless wanted to consolidate the Dances' skills farther inland and out of harm's way. The Dances relocated to a site three miles north of Anderson in Grimes County, and here the Confederate government built a powder mill and pistol factory. On February 7, 1864, Mattie Duff received word from Uncle Harrison that "they were not quite ready for making pistols but soon will." One of the last known shipments of Dance revolvers took place on April 18, 1865; a lot of twenty-five six-shot pistols was sent from Anderson to the Houston Depot of Supplies. At the end of the war the Dances returned to East Columbia and the manufacture of gristmills and cotton gins. *See also* COLT REVOLVERS.

BIBLIOGRAPHY: L. D. Satterlee and Arcadi Gluckman, *American Gun Makers* (Buffalo: Ulbrich, 1940; rev. ed., Harrisburg, Pennsylvania: Stackpole, 1953). Gary Wiggins, *Dance and Brothers: Texas Gunmakers of the Confederacy* (Orange, Virginia: Moss, 1986).

Gary Wiggins

DANCER, ASIEL (ca. 1795–ca. 1849). Asiel (Asahel) Dancer, a Baptist church elder and lay minister, was born, probably around 1795, in Tennessee. Around 1813 he married a woman named Mary, also of Tennessee, and the couple had eleven children. One of their sons, John Dancer, served with Capt. Nicholas M. Dawson[qv] and died on September 18, 1842. He is buried with the Dawson and Mier expedition[qv] soldiers on Monument Hill overlooking La Grange in Fayette County. Dancer and his wife moved to Texas around 1836, traveling from Tennessee and settling in Bastrop County. In 1839 church elders Dancer and R. G. Green were sent from the Providence Church in Bastrop County to help organize a church in Fayette County, the Plum Grove Baptist Church, often referred to as the Hopewell Church. In October 1839 Dancer, a strong antimissionary Baptist (*see* BAPTIST CHURCH), was chosen as its pastor. The church was affiliated with the Union Baptists of western Tennessee and evidently split over the missionary question shortly after its inception. In December 1841 Z. N. Morrell[qv] became its pastor. Asiel Dancer died in Bastrop County around 1849; his wife died in Bastrop County in 1853.

BIBLIOGRAPHY: James Milton Carroll, *A History of Texas Baptists* (Dallas: Baptist Standard, 1923). La Grange High School, *Fayette County: Past and Present* (La Grange, Texas, 1976). Houston Wade, comp., *The Dawson Men of Fayette County* (Houston, 1932). Leonie Rummel Weyand and Houston Wade, *An Early History of Fayette County* (La Grange, Texas: La Grange *Journal*, 1936).

Betty McCarty McAnelly

DANCER PEAK. Dancer Peak is an elevation in the Riley Mountains eight miles southeast of Llano in Llano County (at 30°40′ N, 98°36′ W). The Rev. Jonas Dancer, who died in 1859—perhaps the first white man killed by Indians in the county—established a Methodist church on nearby Honey Creek, which rises from several sources along the base of the mountain. The peak, with an elevation of 1,714 feet above sea level, rises some 600 feet above State Highway 71. The surrounding rolling to steep terrain is surfaced by soils that range from shallow and stony to sandy and clayey loams that support open stands of live oak, mesquite, and Ashe juniper.

BIBLIOGRAPHY: Wilburn Oatman, *Llano, Gem of the Hill Country: A History of Llano County* (Hereford, Texas: Pioneer, 1970). J. W. Wilbarger, *Indian Depredations in Texas* (Austin: Hutchings, 1889; rpt., Austin: State House, 1985).

DANCIGER, TEXAS. Danciger is on Farm Road 1301 near Dance Bayou and the Matagorda county line in extreme west central Brazoria County. The town was established in 1933 when the Danciger Oil and Refining Company opened the Pledger Dome gas field. The community had a post office by 1934 and reported a population of 150 and two businesses in 1939. Its residents numbered 314 from 1974 to 1990. In 1978 Danciger reported two businesses, and in the early 1990s, four.

Diana J. Kleiner

DANCY, JOHN WINFIELD SCOTT (1810–1866). John Winfield Scott Dancy, early legislator, farmer, and railroad promoter, was born to William and Percilla (Turner) Dancy in Greenville County, Virginia, on September 3, 1810. He was a descendant of Francis de Dance, a Castilian nobleman who fled persecution in France. Dancy had a sister and at least one brother, Charles, who spent time in Texas. General Winfield Scott was Dancy's cousin. After growing up in Decatur, Alabama, Dancy studied law, science, and languages and attended Nashville University. He received a law license in Tennessee from Judge John Catron, United States Supreme Court justice from 1837 to 1865. In July 1835 Dancy married Evalina Rhodes. After her death the following summer he decided to move to Texas. On December 28, 1836, he and Francis R. Lubbock[qv] arrived at Velasco on the schooner Corolla. Dancy became a citizen of Texas on January 13, 1837, before Judge Robert M. Williamson.[qv] He traveled throughout the republic and in 1838 purchased 640 acres in Fayette County. He introduced long-staple cotton to Texas and developed the first hydraulic ram in the state to provide irrigation for his plantation.

In 1841 he was elected Fayette County representative to the Sixth Congress of the Republic of Texas. He later served in the Senate of the Second and Fourth state legislatures (1847–48 and 1851–53) and in the House of the Sixth Legislature (1855–56). He was considered an eloquent but long-winded speaker. Dancy ran for governor as a Democrat in 1853 but placed last in a field of six candidates led by Elisha M. Pease.[qv] In February 1861 he was a delegate to the Secession Convention.[qv] His early advocacy of railroad development earned him the nickname "Father of Texas Railroads." During his first legislative term he advocated annexing California and constructing a railroad to connect the West Coast to Texas. He helped secure charters for the Harrisburg Railroad and Trading Company and the Buffalo Bayou, Brazos and Colorado Railway; he became a vice president of the latter and in 1866 transferred it to the Southern Pacific. In 1850 Dancy proposed using public lands to finance railroad construction.

He maintained a law practice in La Grange and was a developer of Colorado City, the site chosen by the legislature in 1838 for the new capital but vetoed by President Sam Houston.[qv] Dancy was a member of the Texas Monumental Committee, formed to raise funds for a monument to men killed during the Mier expedition and Dawson Massacre,[qv][qv] and edited the committee's newspaper, the *Texas Monument*, from July 1850 to June 1851. He was a founding trustee of Rutersville College. During the Mexican invasions of 1842,[qv] Dancy served in the First Regiment of Texas Mounted Volunteers under John Coffee Hays.[qv] From May to July 1847 he served as a private in a spy company of Texas mounted volunteers commanded by Benjamin McCulloch.[qv] He also fought in Indian skirmishes. He married Lucy Ann Nowlin of Austin on October 25, 1849. They had a son and five daughters. Dancy died in La Grange on February 13, 1866, and was buried in La Grange Cemetery.

BIBLIOGRAPHY: John Henry Brown, *Indian Wars and Pioneers of Texas* (Austin: Daniell, 1880; reprod., Easley, South Carolina: Southern Historical Press, 1978). Jon Winfield Scott Dancy Papers, Barker Texas History Center, University of Texas at Austin. Texas House of Representatives, *Biographical Directory of the Texan Conventions and Congresses, 1832–1845* (Austin: Book Exchange, 1941). Vertical Files, Barker Texas History Center, University of Texas at Austin.

Lawrence A. Landis

DANCY, OSCAR CROMWELL (1879–1971). Oscar C. Dancy, judge, was born in Wilkes County, North Carolina, on December 22, 1879. He achieved the equivalent of a high school education in a one-room schoolhouse there. At the age of seventeen he gained his first experience in politics by stumping for William Jennings Bryan in the presidential campaign of 1896. Soon thereafter Dancy attended Southern Normal University in Huntington, Tennessee, where he received his law degree in only four months. He then returned to North Carolina to teach in the common schools for a short time before leaving in 1898 to serve in the army as a private in the Spanish-American War. After returning to the United States he was mayor of North Wilkesboro, North Carolina, for a short time in 1908 before his wife's illness from typhoid fever caused him to resign.

For his wife's health, Dancy moved to Brownsville, Texas, in 1909. He was admitted to the bar the same year. He practiced law for several years before leaving for a short time "to attempt to help whip the Kaiser." In 1917 the county attorney was commissioned in the army, and Dancy was asked to fill the vacancy. Four years later he was elected county judge, a post he retained for the next fifty years, with the exception of one two-year term beginning in 1932. His forty-eight years of service, a state record for a county judge, eclipsed the old mark by twenty years. The hallmark of his judgeship was his effort to develop the county road system, which prompted him to claim that the "C" in his name stood for concrete. During his lengthy tenure he spent more than $10 million on paving roads in Cameron County. He was a believer in low local taxes, known for his ability to procure funds from the state and national governments to pay for programs that supported the family farm and provided flood control for the Rio Grande valley, as well as paying for many of the roads. His honest and straightforward nature won him many admirers in Austin and Washington. In 1948 Harry Truman, himself a former Missouri county judge, called Dancy "the county judge from Texas" when Dancy went to the Oval Office; Truman said he wanted "to meet a county judge who spent more money than I did." Despite all his work on behalf of good roads, Dancy never drove or owned a car.

He was a lifelong Democrat, Baptist, and member of various organizations, including the American Legion,[qv] the Masons, the Brownsville Chamber of Commerce, the Kiwanis Club, and the South Texas Judges and County Commissioners Association, of which he was president for a time. In 1900 he married Leva Jane Long, with whom he had three sons and two daughters. He stepped down from his post the year before his death, which occurred on January 10, 1971, shortly after his ninety-first birthday. In the days before his death he was quoted as saying, "If there is anything more I can do for my fellow man, let me know about it right now." Dancy was buried in Buena Vista Burial Park, Brownsville.

BIBLIOGRAPHY: Milo Kearney and Anthony Knopp, *Boom and Bust: The Historical Cycles of Matamoros and Brownsville* (Austin: Eakin Press, 1991). Vertical Files, Barker Texas History Center, University of Texas at Austin.

Brad Reagan

DANES. Danish immigration to Texas, like most European settlement in the Americas, was a result of stories of favorable conditions, actual or imaginary, put in contrast with real problems in a traditional homeland. In Denmark during the second half of the nineteenth century, population growth, low salaries, unemployment, and the difficulty of acquiring land joined with new legal freedom to bring about a large exodus from the country. The majority of Danish emigrants left between 1820 and 1920. Many discontented Danes saw Texas as a place for business opportunity and settlement.

Although colonial efforts were considered in the early years, the first Danish immigrants to Texas were individuals. The first known by name included sailors like Peter Johnson who, captaining his own ships along the Texas coast as early as 1832, first traded at, then settled near, Indianola. John Edward Henrichson, another seafarer, moved slightly inland and became a rancher near San Patricio. A Dane named Christian Hillebrandt moved his cattle from Louisiana into East Texas just after 1830, and one named Charles Zanco[qv] died at the battle of the Alamo[qv] in 1836. Some settlers wrote letters back to Denmark saying that Texas was the place to be.

By 1850 a sprinkling of Danes had arrived, some fifty individuals officially in that year's census, probably a low count that quickly grew. Until around 1950 the ratio of native-born Danes to the population of Texas was always fairly constant—about one to 3,000.

The early arrivals were mixed in skills and trades. They included Otto Kass, a soldier at Fort Worth; Thomas Moosewood, a Bexar County wagonmaster; Peter Hansen, a sailor in Galveston; George Henry Trube, former gardener and founder of a mercantile dynasty in Houston and Galveston; Peter Miller, a carpenter in the Rio Grande valley; Christian Dorbrandt, Texas Ranger and cotton-gin owner near Marble Falls; and Charles Grimur Thorkelin Lovenskiold,[qv] schoolmaster, lawyer, and colonel for the Confederacy from Corpus Christi. The Danes accepted most local spellings of their names and established lasting businesses and families.

But colonial efforts were not too far behind the first families. The first group resulted from a visit, just after the Civil War,[qv] of two Texans to Denmark. Travis Shaw and John Hester, whose wife was Danish, were promoting Central Texas as good farmland. The area they were selling was the part of Burleson County that went to make up Lee County in 1874. Initially, twenty families moved in, and others arrived before 1880. The group included Christian Moelbeck, a saddlemaker; Paul Paulsen, cabinetmaker; and Peter Jensen, blacksmith. The majority, the Sorensons, Rasmussens, Vittrups, and Olsens, were farmers. Here in the "Little Denmark" area of Lee County were enough families to preserve Danish customs for a time. They did not quickly lose their original foods, including *kartofler* (boiled potatoes) and *rodgrod* (fruit pudding), nor the custom of pastry and coffee every day at 10 A.M. and 3 P.M., nor the holiday observances. But the language and most of the customs of a European homeland thousands of miles away were quick to go. An immigrant is only a person who arrives after someone else, in the words of a later Danish arrival, Lloyd M. Bentsen, Sr.[qv]

Another settlement area was in Gillespie County, east of Fredericksburg around the Rocky Hill vicinity. Here, the choice of place seems to have been a matter of recommendation between families and friends. The fact that the county was already tolerably full of Germans, erstwhile Danish enemies, seemed to make no difference in Texas.

These arrivals coincided with the peak years of Danish emigration, 1885–95. But many more individuals came in these years than families, and many Danes moved directly into the young towns of Texas. H. P. N. Gammel[qv] arrived in Austin around 1878 and became state printer and one of the most notable book collectors, dealers, and bibliophiles of all times. Christian Mathisen moved into Fredericksburg as a blacksmith and subsequently invented an early wind-powered electric generator and innovative agricultural methods. Viggo Kohler was attracted to Beeville and Hebbronville, where he became a hotel owner and rancher.

Danevang, established in 1894, became the largest Danish settlement and still held on with a population of sixty-one in 1990. Land was contracted on the coastal plain south of El Campo by the Dansk Folkesamfund as a place for a church colony where Danish culture and language could be preserved. The society sold the land for nine dollars an acre and contacted potential colonists. The Danish Evangelical Lutheran Church, one of two synods resulting from a church dispute in Denmark, had the colony as a religious charge. Many of the initial colonists came from the north central United States, where thousands of Danes had first settled after their long move; others came directly from Denmark.

Until the turn of the century, the settlers had a rough time. The first crops, northern grains, failed. Carefully transported cattle died. The first homes were primitive, and the low coastal plain was easily flooded. One young wife admitted that she "cried nearly every evening." The initial land payments could not be made, but the president of the Texas Land and Cattle Company,[qv] after a visit to the colony, gave an immediate extension on the notes. It was evident that the Danes were there to stay. By 1901 they had survived hurricanes,[qv] crop failure, insects, and local depression. They had largely switched to cotton as a cash crop. Shortly thereafter, they established a Farmer's Cooperative Society for bulk purchases of supplies and sale of crops. Community members started schools, reading clubs, an insurance company, a telephone service, a grocery, a cotton gin, and a gasoline station—all on a cooperative basis. The schools taught biblical history, Danish history, and the Danish language—at least in the summers—along with the regular "American" curriculum, until incorporation and state laws took over the community schools.

Danish culture and language did survive for over a generation. The church was the formal sphere of spoken Danish, which was used for regular services until 1954 and by Den danske Kvindeforening, a women's church society, until 1971. Danish was commonly used in business through the 1930s, and today a few people still can speak "native Texas" Danish, a language retaining some nineteenth-century structure and vocabulary and of interest to contemporary linguists. The major holidays celebrated in the colony were joint Danish Constitution Day–United States Independence Day and Christmas. On these occasions the European circle dance around a community tree was maintained. One or two songs were always sung in Danish.

Danevang still attracts visitors from various Texas Scandinavian clubs, but today looks like, and mainly is, a small Texas country community. From a peak of nearly 200 Danish families, about twenty were in Danevang in the late 1980s. They very strongly remember where they are from. But the economics of large farmholdings destroyed the colony.

Danevang continued to attract a few Danish families until around 1920, but fewer came to the United States in the early twentieth century. And many of the arrivals, more often single men than not, headed for the cities rather than the country. Hans Guldmann, John Christensen, and Johan Rasmussen found in Galveston a place of opportunity and a warm climate. Here were opportunities for dealing in cotton products, automobiles, and vegetables. Steamship-company agents in Denmark were still willing to sell tickets after World War I,[qv] but soon the United States enacted quotas to limit European immigrants, including Danes. Yet, of those who came, most stayed. Only about 8 percent of the arrivals returned to their homeland. Danish culture was Nordic and similar to the English and other dominant European groups in Texas. Danes were rapidly assimilated in terms of learning English, marrying outside their own groups, and adopting local habits intentionally. Danish cultural groups outside of Danevang lasted but a short time. The Dallas group, nominally active in the early 1980s, was the longest in duration among groups from the Rio Grande valley, Houston, Austin, and other cities.

One of the last areas of Texas to attract a sprinkling of Danish families was the Panhandle.[qv] Typical of that area's settlers was the Sorrenson family, which moved to Swisher County to try farming. Not so typical was the fact that Harry Sorrenson was an amateur mathematician and photographer. He took so many glass-plate photographs that he was able to build a greenhouse using the plates as panes.

To the south, the influential Bentsen family started with the arrival of Peter Bentsen from South Dakota. The Bentsens allowed only English to be spoken in their home and attended churches other than the Danish Lutheran. They were not alone in taking definite moves to become American as soon as possible. Economically, in a dominantly English-speaking society, it was the only practical choice.

After the turn of the century, no colonial efforts were tried in Texas. John B. Christensen founded Kristenstad at De Cordova Bend on the Brazos River, but the cooperative effort was never a Danish colony. The group of about forty families, who quickly tired of the social experiment, included only a few Danes. Today, there are thousands of native Texans who are Danish in ancestry, although little remains of their heritage.

BIBLIOGRAPHY: John L. Davis, *The Danish Texans* (San Antonio: University of Texas Institute of Texan Cultures, 1979).

John L. Davis

DANEVANG, TEXAS. Danevang, on State Highway 71 in south Wharton County, started as a colonial effort in 1894. It is the most coherent, and only colonial, area of Danish settlement in the state. The first settlers, Danes who for the most part had spent some years in the north central United States, arrived following a land acquisition by the Dansk Folkesamfund (Danish People's Society). The Danish Evangelical Lutheran Church supported the settlement as a church colony—a place for the preservation of Danish culture. In the first year of the colony some seventy families arrived, some directly from Denmark. The area was soon named Danevang, "Danish Field," and a post office was established in 1895. The first years were so difficult, numerous families left and moved to California where they started a town "Solvang" (Sunny Fields). Currently it is a popular tourist attraction. After several difficult years, the Texas colony prospered as an agricultural center, depending initially upon cotton. The settlers established cultural institutions to preserve their heritage. The first public school opened in 1895, and for many years the children were taught Denmark's history and language. The town maintained its own lending library. In the early years Danish was the local language and was used in church and club meetings until 1971. Today, the Christmas observance and special church holidays are still noticeably Danish in origin. The inhabitants of Danevang maintained a Danish tradition of cooperation in their economic institutions. They established a fire insurance company in 1897 and their own telephone system in 1913. The Danish Farmer's Cooperative Society was formed in 1920 to facilitate cooperative buying, selling, and processing of supplies and farm products. In 1923 there were ninety-seven Danish families in the community, but four years later the population, then over 500, was declining. The 1967 population was 125. In 1980 Danevang had a population of sixty. In 1990 it had sixty-one residents. Danevang, widely known as a community of cooperatives, first used the word "cooperative" in 1896, when the United States Weather Bureau appointed L. Henningsen as a "Cooperative Observer." This weather station was the first in Wharton County and the first of its kind to be established between Sugar Land and Victoria. Danevang continues to keep records for the Weather Bureau. As of 1993 only seven persons have acted as recorder. All were men except one woman, Johanna Allenson, who was the recorder for thirty-one years. Rainfall and temperature are recorded each day, and all the past recordings have been kept on file and stored at the assembly hall. In 1994 the Danevang community and church celebrated their 100th anniversary, with festivities including Danish food, music, and dress and a display of the weather bureau records.

BIBLIOGRAPHY: Thomas P. Christensen, "Danevang, Texas," *Southwestern Historical Quarterly* 32 (July 1928). John L. Davis, *The Danish Texans* (San Antonio: University of Texas Institute of Texan Cultures, 1979; 2d ed., 1983). Grace Cone Grantham, The Danes in Wharton County (M.A. thesis, Texas College of Arts and Industry, 1947). Dennis Petersen, "Danevang," *Junior Historian*, January 1967.

John L. Davis

DANFORTH, GRACE (1849–1895). Grace Danforth, physician and suffragist, was born on February 21, 1849, in Southport, Kenosha County, Wisconsin, the daughter of David and Frances Howell (Coleman) Danforth. Her father followed several occupations, including that of music teacher, and the family moved often when Grace was a child. They lived in Eufaula, Barbour County, Alabama, in 1850; in Marshall, Texas, in 1853; in Clarksville, Texas, in the middle to late 1850s; in Boston, Texas, in 1858; and in Gilmer, Texas, in 1861. Grace taught school and music in various communities in Northeast Texas, including Daingerfield, Whitewright, Campbell, and Black Jack Grove (later Cumby). A newspaper account from the late 1870s or early 1880s noted that she had just finished a four-month stint of teaching music in Campbell and Black Jack Grove simultaneously, while commuting by train. The writer commented that Danforth was a "lady of remarkable energy, good education and extraordinary business qualities" and predicted that "the community that secures her services [after her attendance at a summer normal school in Sulphur Springs] will capture a prize indeed." Danforth later wrote that she decided to enter the medical field after finding "the confinement and nervous wear and tear of the schoolroom" injurious to her health. She said that she had considered bookkeeping and pharmacy as alternative occupations but rejected them in favor of medicine. She attended the Woman's Medical College of Chicago, where her training included work at Cook County Hospital and the Illinois Eye and Ear Infirmary. After graduating in 1886, she did her internship at the Chicago Hospital for Women and Children. During this time in Chicago, she said, she became a proponent of woman suffrage.[qv]

She began private practice in Dallas early in 1888 and was soon afterward admitted to membership in the Dallas County Medical Association. Upon being asked by the group "why a woman, and especially a southern woman, is desirous of a professional career," she responded that women who were "reaching out for a wider field of usefulness and freedom" were "simply obeying laws that underlie the march of civilization." She praised the medical profession as the most important force "contributing to the aid of woman on practical, commonsense grounds" because of the privileged view that doctors had of "domestic history." While in Dallas Danforth also joined the Woman's Christian Temperance Union,[qv] perhaps partly in hopes that the affiliation would help her practice. By July 1889, however, she had moved to Granger, where her brother Charles was also a physician. With the support of John Summerfield Griffith,[qv] she was appointed by Dr. David Richard Wallace[qv] as second assistant physician at the North Texas Hospital for the Insane (later Terrell State Hospital[qv]) on June 13, 1890. She served as a gynecologist and was the first woman doctor on the hospital staff. She apparently worked at the Terrell asylum until the following year, when a new superintendent brought in different personnel. By May of 1892 Danforth was living again in Granger. She returned to the Woman's Medical College of Chicago for postgraduate work in the winter of 1891–92 and again in 1893.

While endeavoring to establish a medical practice she attended meetings of the State Medical Association (*see* TEXAS MEDICAL ASSOCIATION) and wrote for professional journals. From 1888 through the early 1890s she contributed frequently to the *Texas Courier-Record of Medicine* and also published an article in the *Texas Sanitarian*. Her letters and articles included advice on the care of newborn infants and mothers in delivery, instruction on converting apothecaries' measurements into metric notation, and a rejoinder to another contributor's article, in which she argued that insanity was attributable to organic causes. Several pieces stressed the importance of educating girls and women in physiology and related subjects, arguing that such knowledge would improve women's health and happiness, make them better wives and mothers, and bring them into alliance with regular medicine (as opposed to homeopathy, spiritual cures, and quack medicine), thus putting the profession itself on a more secure footing.

In an appeal dated April 8, 1893, Danforth and nine other women urged supporters of woman suffrage to meet in Dallas to form a state suffrage organization. The convention, held in May, established the Texas Equal Rights Association.qv Danforth's mother and both of her sisters also attended the meeting and became charter members. Together with Ebenezer LaFayette Dohoney,qv Danforth drafted an eight-point plan of action that was adopted by the convention. The seventh point concerned "hygiene and dress improvement," a topic of intense interest to Danforth, who became head of a TERA department on "dress reform." During the next several years she was involved in suffrage work. In July 1893 she spoke at a meeting in Taylor that organized a local suffrage society. In the fall she was among those calling for a meeting in Granger to organize a similar group. When the Granger suffrage society was formed on November 4, she was elected vice president. In addition to speaking at suffrage meetings in Taylor and Granger, she sent letters to newspapers in the area to keep them abreast of suffrage activities and promote the cause. The *Washington* (D.C.) *Woman's Tribune*, a suffrage paper, published one of her articles, but the *Southern Mercury*,qv official journal of the Farmers' Allianceqv in Texas, declined it, saying that the text was too long and "too hot" to print. Later the *Southern Mercury* solicited succinct statements from her expressing the suffragists' positions on the "leading reform questions of monopoly, money, land and transportation." Danforth died the following month, however, and no response seems to have been published.

She upset some by criticizing the churches for their subordination of women. She viewed the suffrage effort as part of a general movement away from a society of force and competition toward one of justice and cooperation. At the same time, she appealed to the personal and regional interests of her audience. Stating that women would generally vote the interest of their region, she held forth the prospect of a block of women's votes reinforcing the "agricultural and mining interests of the west" against the "money power" of the East. In a letter addressed to the women of Granger, she linked the importance of the vote to their concern for the quality and administration of the public schools.

At the second annual meeting of the Texas Equal Rights Association in June 1894, Danforth was elected fourth vice president. When the discussion turned to the question of inviting Susan B. Anthony and Annie Shaw to lecture and organize in Texas, Danforth sided with those in favor. Opposition to the proposal included the president of TERA, Rebecca Henry Hayes. The issue of inviting Anthony was still a divisive one when the TERA executive committee met in September. Members favoring the proposal demanded that Hayes resign. When she refused, Danforth announced her own resignation as vice president in response. In November, however, Danforth was present at another meeting of the executive committee. With Hayes absent, committee members declared the office of president vacant and proceeded to invite Anthony to Texas, proposing lectures in thirteen towns. At the same meeting, Danforth was elected superintendent of press work.

She died in Granger on February 21, 1895, after having taken medicine for one of the severe headaches to which she was subject. According to one account, she had been "just emerging from a critical period of life," during which the state of her health had prevented her from doing much in her profession. She had, however, made arrangements to begin practice in Austin in a few weeks' time. Her survivors included her mother, two sisters, one brother, and a brother-in-law, Hamilton Biscoe Hillyer.qv She was buried in the Granger cemetery.

BIBLIOGRAPHY: Elizabeth Brooks, *Prominent Women of Texas* (Akron, Ohio: Werner, 1896). Clara Stearns Scarbrough, *Land of Good Water: A Williamson County History* (Georgetown, Texas: Williamson County Sun Publishers, 1973). A. Elizabeth Taylor, *Citizens at Last: The Woman Suffrage Movement in Texas* (Austin: Temple, 1987). *Texas Courier-Record of Medicine*, March, July 1888, September 1891, February 1895. Texas Equal Suffrage Association Scrapbook, Austin History Center. *Texas Medical Journal*, March 1895.

Mary M. Standifer

DANGERS, GOTTLIEB BURCHARD (1811–1869). Gottlieb Burchard Dangers, pioneer pastor and teacher, was born in Langenhagen, Hanover, on October 11, 1811. He left Europe on October 10, 1845, on the brig Johann Dethardt and arrived in Galveston on January 12, 1846. He conducted open-air religious services for German immigrants in Galveston and upon arriving in Indianola six weeks later founded a congregation of 700. After five months he moved on to New Braunfels, where he worked as a day laborer to earn money to reach Fredericksburg, his ultimate destination. At the end of 1846 he received additional money from relatives in Germany and bought land on the Guadalupe River. Dangers was married to Mathilda Max; their first child was born on March 16, 1848.

Dangers finally moved to Fredericksburg in 1849 and served as pastor of the Evangelical Protestant Church for the next twenty years. He became an American citizen on May 13, 1851, and was the third teacher at the Vereins Kircheqv school. He was succeeded by Heinrich Ochsqv on January 1, 1852. From February to March 1861 four of the Dangers' five children died of diphtheria; another daughter was born on April 3, 1861. During the Civil Warqv Dangers again taught school, and in 1867 he became one of the first ten teachers in Gillespie County to receive state teaching certificates. He also organized a male singing quartet and composed a number of unpublished musical scores. In 1869, while walking back to town from a wedding he had performed in the country, Dangers was caught in a sudden rainstorm; he developed pneumonia and died on November 12 of that year. He is buried in the Fredericksburg City Cemetery.

BIBLIOGRAPHY: Gillespie County Historical Society, *Pioneers in God's Hills* (2 vols., Austin: Von Boeckmann–Jones, 1960, 1974). Elise Kowert, *Old Homes and Buildings of Fredericksburg* (Fredericksburg, Texas: Fredericksburg Publishing, 1977).

Martin Donell Kohout

DANIEL, CHARLES DAVIS (1856–1939). Charles Davis Daniel, Baptist missionary, was born in Monroe County, Alabama, on March 17, 1856. At the end of the Civil Warqv his father took the family to Brazil. During their seven-year stay Daniel was educated by his mother and learned to speak Portuguese fluently. In 1872 he and his family moved to Navarro County, Texas. His father died three years later, and Daniel assumed responsibility as head of the household. In the summer of 1877 he joined the Bethesda Baptist Church of the Richland Association. He desired to teach but hesitated because of his lack of formal education and his responsibilities at home. He committed himself in 1880 to becoming a preacher and was licensed on July 31, 1881. In the fall of that year he entered Baylor University with the financial assistance of Baylor president R. C. Burleson.qv He studied Latin, Greek, and Spanish, in addition to the standard curriculum. While at Baylor Daniel met his future wife, Lena Kirk, and gained ministerial experience at the Dawson and Lorena Baptist churches. On November 4, 1883, he was ordained. He graduated from Baylor in June 1885 and was married in San Antonio in November.

After graduating he was appointed by the Foreign Mission Board of the Southern Baptist Convention as a missionary to Brazil. There he pastored several Baptist churches and edited the *Brazilian Baptist*, a newspaper. Two of his children were born during that time. He remained in Brazil until 1889, when his failing health necessitated his move back to the United States. For the next ten years he served churches in San Antonio and Mineola and did mission work among Mexican Americans.qv At the close of the Spanish-American War and the granting of Cuban independence by Spain in 1898, Daniel was appointed by the Home Mission Board to work as a missionary in Cuba. On the island he reorganized and revitalized Baptist work, which had deteriorated during the war. The four western provinces of Cuba were under his authority, including the city of Havana. Daniel remained in Cuba through 1905, when he returned to the United States due to ill health.

From 1906 to 1922 he was active in mission work among Hispanics in Texas. He spent the first few of these years in Gonzales and El Paso and later traveled around the state. In 1925 he returned to his former pastorate in Lorena, where he remained pastor as long as his health allowed. He was an active Mason for more than fifty years. On September 12, 1939, Daniel died in Waco after a long illness. He was survived by his wife, five children, three brothers, and nine grandchildren.

BIBLIOGRAPHY: *Encyclopedia of Southern Baptists* (4 vols., Nashville: Broadman, 1958–82).
Dale Wood Peterson

DANIEL, FERDINAND EUGENE (1839–1914). Ferdinand Eugene Daniel, physician and medical journalist, the son of R. W. T. and Hester Jordan (Adams) Daniel, was born in Emporia, Greenville County, Virginia, on July 18, 1839. He was educated at Vicksburg, Mississippi, where his family moved in 1845, and read law for a time before he turned to medicine at Jackson, Mississippi, where his family settled in 1852. He enlisted in the Confederate Army in May 1861 at Jackson as a private in Company K, Eighteenth Mississippi Infantry, Jones's Division, Beauregard's Corps, Army of Northern Virginia, and served at the first battle of Bull Run. He left the service under President Jefferson Davis'sqv order to release young men studying medicine, completed his medical degree at the New Orleans School of Medicine, and after graduation in 1862 was commissioned a major by Secretary of War George W. Randolph. During the war he participated as a surgeon in the battles of Perryville and Mumfordsville and was in charge of hospitals at Chattanooga, Tennessee; Marietta, Kingston, and Covington, Georgia; and Lauderdale, Mississippi.

He practiced medicine and surgery at Galveston, Texas, from 1866 to 1872 and in 1867–68 was professor of anatomy and surgery at Texas Medical College. He returned to his Mississippi plantation and practice at Jackson and in 1879 served as sanitary inspector for the National Board of Health in Mississippi. He stayed in Jackson for five years before returning to Texas in 1880 to live first at Sherman and then Fort Worth. In 1884 Daniel's wife died, and in 1885 he retired and founded first the *Texas Courier Record of Medicine* and then the *Texas Medical Journal*. From 1892 to 1898 he was secretary of the Texas quarantine department and in 1905–06 president of the American International Congress on Tuberculosis. Dr. Daniel served as secretary of the Texas State Medical Association (*see* TEXAS MEDICAL ASSOCIATION) from 1886 to 1892 and American secretary of the dermatology section of the Ninth International Medical Congress. He was a member of the American Public Health Association, the American Medical Association, the Association of American Medical Editors, and several state medical organizations. He wrote two books, *Recollections of a Rebel Surgeon* (1899) and *The Strange Case of Dr. Bruno* (1906). In "Castration of Sexual Perverts" (1893) he suggested a substitute for capital punishment in cases of rape related to mental illness. In 1897 he delivered a lecture on "Crime and Pauperism" and in 1898 published an article on "Criminal Responsibility of the Insane." He published other papers in the *Transactions* of the Mississippi State Medical Association.

Daniel married Minerva Patrick on July 5, 1863. They had one son before Minerva died with an infant daughter in the yellow fever epidemic of 1867. Daniel married Fanny Ragsdale Smith on October 10, 1872, and they had six children. In 1881 he moved to Sherman, Texas, where in 1884 his wife died. He subsequently moved to Austin and, on June 3, 1903, married Josephine Draper. Daniel died at his home in Austin on May 14, 1914.

BIBLIOGRAPHY: Ellis A. Davis and Edwin H. Grobe, comps., *The New Encyclopedia of Texas*, 4-vol. ed. *Who Was Who in America*, Vol. 2. Mamie Yeary, *Reminiscences of the Boys in Gray* (McGregor, Texas, 1912; rpt., Dayton, Ohio: Morningside, 1986).
Diana J. Kleiner

DANIEL, MARION PRICE, SR. (1910–1988). Price Daniel, governor of Texas, son of Marion Price and Nannie Blanch (Partlow) Daniel, was born on October 10, 1910, in Dayton, Texas. After earning a law degree from Baylor University in 1932 he opened a law practice in Liberty, Liberty County. He became known through his defense of two of the county's most infamous murder suspects, and used the popularity to win a seat in the Texas House of Representatives in 1939. As an outspoken member of the "Immortal 56," an alliance of state legislators adamantly opposed to a state sales tax, Daniel earned the respect of his colleagues and in early 1943 was unanimously elected speaker of the Texas House of Representatives. After serving one term in that office he enlisted in the army as a private and the following year graduated from officers' candidate school in Lexington, Virginia, as a judge advocate general. He was discharged from the army in May 1946 with the rank of captain, after having served in the Pacific and Japan. He returned to Texas and conducted a successful whirlwind campaign to become the youngest state attorney general in the United States. In his six-year tenure, Daniel disposed of more than 5,000 lawsuits, served on 25 state boards and agencies, composed more than 2,000 bills for the Texas legislature, and successfully defended more money and land claims than any previous attorney general.qv His three best-known crusades were the defense of the University of Texas law school in its refusal to admit Heman Marion Sweatt,qv a black postal clerk; the disbandment of a majority of the state's organized gambling operations; and the defense of Texas ownership of its tidelands against federal encroachment (*see* TIDELANDS CONTROVERSY). When the United States Supreme Court refused to allow Texas to retain the tidelands, valuable offshore lands rich in oil that Daniel argued belonged to Texas because of an agreement in the terms of the state's annexation,qv he defied the Democratic partyqv by endorsing the Republican, states'-rights candidate, Dwight D. Eisenhower.qv In 1952, Daniel was elected to the United States Senate on a "Texas Democrat" platform. He immediately drafted a tidelands bill similar to the one President Harry Truman had previously vetoed, and on May 22, 1953, Eisenhower signed it into law. As a result the Permanent School Fundqv has received an infusion of hundreds of millions of dollars. While in the Senate, Daniel directed a nationwide narcotics probe that eventually resulted in the most stringent narcotics regulation in United States history, and nearly succeeded in the passage of legislation designed to reform the electoral college.

Declaring that he would "rather be governor of Texas than President of the United States," Daniel returned home to run for governor and, upon his nomination in 1956, resigned from the Senate. He was reelected governor in 1958 and 1960. During his tenure 131 out of 151 of his major proposals were enacted into law. He was successful in pushing through a heavy legislative program that ranged from highways to prison reform, water conservation, higher teachers' salaries, and improved care for the mentally impaired. Being a devoted student of history, Daniel worked to establish the Texas State Libraryqv and Archives Building, which he virtually designed himself, to house many Texas papers and documents that had been subject to neglect. In 1961, despite his strident objections, he could only watch in his third term as the legislature approved a sales tax after two called special sessions. He allowed the tax to become law without his signature to keep the state from going broke. Much of the electorate blamed him for the sales tax, partly because store clerks developed the prac-

Price Daniel, Sr., and his family, during his 1952 campaign for the United States Senate. Price Daniel Papers, Sam Houston Regional Library and Research Center, Liberty.

tice of ringing up sales and then saying, "Now, let's have a penny for Price."

After losing a bid for an unprecedented fourth term in 1962, Daniel returned to his law practice and took cases in both Liberty and Austin. In 1967, President Lyndon Baines Johnson[qv] appointed him to head the Office of Emergency Preparedness in Washington, a post that gave him a position on the National Security Council. In addition, he served as the president's liaison to the governors of the fifty-three states and territories. Daniel was appointed to fill a vacancy on the Texas Supreme Court in 1971 by Governor Preston Smith. He was elected to the court in 1972 and 1979, then retired during his second term. In his eight years on the court, Daniel was most influential in the areas of groundwater law, as well as laws dealing with other minerals such as uranium, oil, and gas. He was a trustee of Baylor University and Baylor College of Medicine, and was awarded an honorary doctorate by his alma mater in 1951. He was president of International Christian Leadership (1956–57), and a leader of the Men's Bible Class of the First Baptist Church in Austin. He was a member of the Sons of the Republic of Texas, the Knights of the Order of San Jacinto, and the Philosophical Society of Texas.[qqv] In his later years he served as legal council for the Alabama Coushatta Indians[qv] and was appointed to the Texas State Library and Archives Commission.[qv] Daniel died on August 25, 1988, at which time he had held more offices of public trust than anyone else in Texas history. He was buried on his family ranch in Liberty and survived by his wife, the former Jean Houston Baldwin, a great-great-granddaughter of Sam Houston,[qv] and three children: Jean Houston Murph, Houston Lee, and John Baldwin. His eldest son, Marion Price Daniel, Jr.,[qv] had died on January 19, 1981.

BIBLIOGRAPHY: Dallas *Morning News,* August 26, 1988. Price Daniel Papers, Sam Houston Regional Library and Research Center, Liberty, Texas. Liberty *Vindicator,* August 28, 1988. *Presiding Officers of the Texas Legislature* (Austin: Texas Legislative Council, 1991). Texas Supreme Court, *Memorial Service for the Honorable Price Daniel, May 22, 1989* (Austin, 1989). Vertical Files, Barker Texas History Center, University of Texas at Austin.

Daniel Murph

DANIEL, MARION PRICE, JR. (1941–1981). Price Daniel, Jr., legislator, son of Jean Houston (Baldwin) and Price Daniel, Sr.,[qv] and a great-great-great grandson of Sam Houston,[qv] was born on June 8, 1941, in Austin, Texas. As a youth, he became interested in the political career of his father and, by the age of twelve, was making speeches on his behalf. He graduated from Stephen F. Austin High School in Austin in 1959, and then entered Baylor University in Waco. While in college Daniel owned and operated a mail-order book business and became a prominent seller of rare books about Texas history. He received his undergraduate and law degrees in 1964 and 1966. At twenty-five he opened a law practice in Liberty and was elected justice of the peace in Liberty County. In 1968 he ran successfully for the same seat in the Texas House of Representatives that his father had occupied nearly three decades earlier. His early years in the House were quiet and without fanfare. But in 1972, a major political upheaval brewed from a financial scandal in Houston, which led to the formation of the "Dirty Thirty,"qv a group that exposed the ill deeds of a large bloc of lawmakers in order to make state government more accountable. In that year's elections, much to the credit of the Dirty Thirty, turnover neared the 50 percent mark; seventy-six new state representatives and fifteen new senators were elected. During this period, largely because of his unscathed record, Daniel rose to the forefront. In January 1973 he was elected speaker of the House.

Under his leadership the Sixty-third Legislature passed new ethics and financial-disclosure laws pertaining to public officials and election campaigns, revised the existing open-meetings law, strengthened statutes related to the regulation of lobbyists, and passed a new open-records act. In addition, Daniel fought to allow no speaker to succeed himself and to make it illegal for a speaker or House member to offer favors or make threats in an attempt to secure votes. In 1973, *Texas Parade*qv magazine called Daniel the "man to watch" among the state's rising "political timber," and *Time* magazine recognized him as one of the nation's top 100 leaders. In addition, President Gerald Ford presented Daniel with the Legislative Leadership Award of the Citizens Conference on State Legislatures. Daniel was elected president of the Constitutional Convention of 1974.qv The House and Senate met in joint session from January to July to draft a new Texas Constitution that fell three votes short of passage. Many observers attributed the shortcomings of the convention to Daniel's attempts to be all things to all people. At first he had aligned with the progressives or liberals, then further opened his umbrella to embrace conservative opinion. During the convention he never succeeded in winning over the conservatives but only undermined his own political foundation. Believing the office of speaker of the Texas House of Representatives was too powerful to be held by a single legislator for more than one term, he did not seek reelection. In 1978 he was defeated in the Democratic primary for attorney general by Mark White, who later became governor.

Daniel resumed his law practice in Liberty and became involved in the real estate business. Intermittently, he taught law and government classes at Texas Southern University, the University of Houston, and South Texas College of Law. He died on January 19, 1981, as a result of a gunshot wound inflicted by his second wife, Vickie Loretha Carroll. He was survived by both parents, brothers Houston Lee and John Baldwin, sister Jean Houston Murph, and three sons, Thomas Houston (from his first marriage with Diane Ford Wommack), Franklin Baldwin, and Marion Price Daniel III.

BIBLIOGRAPHY: Liberty *Vindicator,* January 22, 1981. *Presiding Officers of the Texas Legislature* (Austin: Texas Legislative Council, 1991). Steve Salerno, *Deadly Blessing* (New York: Morrow, 1987). Vertical Files, Barker Texas History Center, University of Texas at Austin.

Daniel Murph

DANIEL, RUBY KATHRYN (ca. 1902–1978). Ruby Kathryn Daniel, eye surgeon, was born in Duncanville, Texas, around 1902, the daughter of Robert Harry and Beulah May (Fite) Daniel. After attending Southern Methodist University and the University of Texas, she enrolled in Baylor University College of Medicine in Dallas (now Baylor College of Medicine, Houston), where she graduated in 1928. She interned at Lane-Stanford Teaching Hospital in San Francisco and the University of Chicago and did her residency in Chicago. Before returning to Texas in 1939 she established herself as an eye surgeon; she was a fellow in ophthalmology at the Mayo Clinic in Rochester, Minnesota, from 1934 to 1936 and taught on the staff of the Union Medical College in Peking, China, in 1936–37. The following year she taught in Vellore, India, before returning to the Mayo Clinic in 1938 as a first assistant in ophthalmology. Also in 1938 she earned a master's degree from the University of Minnesota.

In 1939 she moved to Dallas and opened a private practice in ophthalmology. In conjunction with her practice, she served as chief medical consultant for the Lighthouse for the Blind and chief ophthalmologist for the Pilot School for the Deaf. She was a member of the staff at five Dallas-area hospitals and in 1943 joined the teaching staff of the Southwestern Medical Foundation in Dallas (now the University of Texas Southwestern Medical School) as assistant clinical professor of ophthalmology. During her career she founded two philanthropic organizations for rehabilitating and salvaging eyes and wrote several scholarly articles on the eye. She also delivered numerous papers on the science of the eye throughout the United States, Europe, and South and Central America.

Dr. Daniel was a diplomate of the American Board of Ophthalmology and a fellow of the American College of Surgeons. She belonged to the International College of Surgeons, the American Medical Association, and the American Association for the Advancement of Science. She was a president of the Dallas Academy of Ophthalmology and Otolaryngology and a member of the Dallas County Medical Society. She was a Methodist and was active in numerous civic and social clubs in Dallas. She died in Dallas on February 13, 1978, and was buried at Restland Memorial Park in Dallas.

BIBLIOGRAPHY: Dallas *Morning News,* February 14, 1978. *Texas Medicine,* July 1978, *Who's Who of American Women,* 1958–59.

Debbie Mauldin Cottrell

DANIEL, VARA FAYE MARTIN (1917–1987). Vara Faye Martin Daniel, civic leader and philanthropist, was born on June 17, 1917, in Hillsboro, Texas, one of three children of Will M. and Daisy (Beavers) Martin. Her father served in the Texas Senate, and one of her brothers, Crawford C. Martin,qv became attorney general of Texas. Because both of her brothers were in college in the 1930s, Vara forfeited her dream of attending Baylor University and saved money by studying at Hill Junior College in Hillsboro and Texas State College for Women (now Texas Woman's University) in Denton. In 1938 she graduated with honors from TSCW with a major in public school music. She moved to Liberty in 1938 to direct the music program for the public schools. In 1939 she married William Daniel, a lawyer from Liberty who later served three terms as a member of the Texas House of Representatives and became the governor of Guam. Vara Daniel devoted herself to numerous civic activities in and beyond Liberty. With her husband she established and endowed scholarships at Baylor University, the University of Texas, and the Methodist Boys Ranch in Waco. She served on several committees at Baylor and UT and was also a savings and loan director in Dayton and a member of the Daughters of the American Revolution.qv The Daniels served together as personal envoys to forty countries for presidents Dwight D. Eisenhower,qv John F. Kennedy, and Lyndon B. Johnson.qv Closer to home, they held annual parties for handicapped children at their Plantation Ranch, near Liberty. In 1985 they donated fifteen buildings from this ranch to Baylor University.

Because of her various civic endeavors, Vara Daniel was known as the "First Lady of Liberty." In 1985 the University of Texas at Austin established a professorship in her name. She also was honored by Hill Junior College, Baylor University, M. D. Anderson Hospital (*see* UNIVERSITY OF TEXAS SYSTEM CANCER CENTER), and the Texas Library Associationqv for her commitment to their causes. She was a Methodist. She died of cancer on February 7, 1987, in Liberty. Survivors included her husband, their four children, one brother, and several grandchildren. After her death, her family established the Vara Daniel Mammography Clinic at Baptist Hospital in Liberty and made low-cost mammogram testing available to any woman in Liberty County over age thirty-five.

BIBLIOGRAPHY: *Cattleman,* March 1987. Vertical Files, Barker Texas History Center, University of Texas at Austin.

Debbie Mauldin Cottrell

DANIEL, TEXAS. Daniel, a community east of Crockett in central Houston County, was apparently never more than a small collection of buildings. In 1880 Samuel M. Thompson established the Daniel School, which later merged with the Bellview School. A post office was established there in August 1887 and was discontinued in September 1906. Farming and ranching interests provided the livelihood for most residents. In 1936 and 1940 the community had fifty residents and two businesses. The Daniel community reported the same in 1948, the last year that statistics were available for it.

BIBLIOGRAPHY: Armistead Albert Aldrich, *The History of Houston County, Texas* (San Antonio: Naylor, 1943). Houston County Historical Commission, *History of Houston County, Texas, 1687–1979* (Tulsa, Oklahoma: Heritage, 1979).   *Eliza H. Bishop*

DANIEL BAKER COLLEGE. Daniel Baker College, in Brownwood, was founded in 1888 as a Presbyterian college and named after clergyman Daniel Baker,qv who had helped to organize both the first presbytery of his church in Texas in 1840 and Austin College in 1849 and had advocated a public school system for the state. The Coggin brothers, local residents, donated land for the campus in 1889, and in 1890 the college began to hold classes under the direction of Brainard Taylor McClelland,qv who served as president until his death eleven years later. The college opened with a faculty of seven, four of whom held M.A. degrees from eastern colleges, and with a student enrollment of 111, a figure that doubled in one year. In 1894 the enrollment had decreased to 95, and in 1899 to 62. Growth soon resumed, however, both in enrollment and in the physical plant; to the original main building were added a women's dormitory in 1911, a chapel in 1921, and a gymnasium in 1928. Nevertheless, financial difficulties plagued the college until, in 1929, the church released control and the institution became independent.

In 1942 John N. R. Scoreqv assumed the presidency of Southwestern University in Georgetown. Score, known as an expansionist, launched his "University of Small Colleges" plan under which, in 1946, Southwestern acquired Daniel Baker College. But the plan was unable to solve the smaller school's problems; enrollment once again was decreasing, accreditation was withheld, and finances were not improving. In 1949 the experiment was abandoned.

In 1950 the Episcopal Diocese of Dallas began operating the school, which had grown to comprise fourteen acres and eight buildings, as one of only two Episcopal senior colleges in the United States. Once again the college was accredited. It had an enrollment of 200 and a faculty of twenty-six, with eight Ph.D.'s; it offered B.A. and B.S. degrees and, beginning in September 1951, a program in church-work training with sixteen female students enrolled. Daniel Baker played basketball in the Big State Athletic Conference. Nevertheless, the college once again failed financially, and in 1953 it closed. Its campus was taken over by nearby Howard Payne College (now Howard Payne University), which remodeled the main Daniel Baker building for use as the Douglas MacArthur Academy of Freedom.

BIBLIOGRAPHY: *Dictionary of American Biography*. Ralph W. Jones, *Southwestern University, 1840–1861* (Austin: Jenkins, 1973). William Stuart Red, *A History of the Presbyterian Church in Texas* (Austin: Steck, 1936). Vertical Files, Barker Texas History Center, University of Texas at Austin.   *Louann Atkins Temple*

DANIEL CREEK. Daniel Creek rises two miles west of Murchison in north central Henderson County (at 32°17′ N, 95°48′ W) and runs northeast for five miles to its mouth on Kickapoo Creek, 1½ miles south of the Van Zandt county line (at 32°20′ N, 95°45′ W). It traverses flat to rolling terrain surfaced by sandy and clay loams that support water-tolerant hardwoods, conifers, and grasses.

DANIELS, BEBE VIRGINIA (1901–1971). Bebe Daniels, actress, scriptwriter, and producer, was born by chance in Dallas, Texas, on January 14, 1901, the only child of Danny and Phyllis (Griffin) Daniels. Her emigrant Scottish father had changed his name from Melville Daniel MacMeal to Danny Daniels when he founded his California-based traveling stock company. His wife and leading lady gave birth to Bebe as the troupe toured through Dallas. By age four Bebe was a frequent actor in her parents' company. She attended Sacred Heart Convent School in Los Angeles.

Her movie debut came in 1908 with *A Common Enemy* for Selig-Polyscope. At fifteen she played the leading lady to Harold Lloyd in Hal Roach's "Lonesome Luke" silent-film series. In four years with Lloyd and Snub Pollard, she made almost 200 comedies, in which she did all her own stunts. Cecil B. De Mille discovered her dancing in a restaurant and took her to his Paramount Studios at ten times her old salary. From 1919 to 1928 she worked for Paramount or its subsidiary, Realart, typically playing light leads for such comedies as *The Campus Flirt* (1926), *Miss Brewster's Millions* (1926) *Swim, Girl, Swim* (1927), and *She's A Sheik* (1928). The versatile actress also played in westerns such as *North of the Rio Grande* (1922) and *Señorita* (1927), melodramas such as *Volcano* (1926), and steamers like *Everywoman* (1919) and *The Affairs of Anatole* (1921), in which she portrayed vamp Satan Synne. Bebe Daniels spent ten days in jail for speeding in 1921 and capitalized on the publicity with the hastily written *The Speed Girl* (1921). Texas governor Pat. M. Neffqv asked that she use her growing popularity to aid growers who had lost heavily on their 1922 crops by wearing dresses made of Texas cotton.

Daniels was the only woman among twenty men on Paramount's "inner cabinet," where she headed her own unit for five years—controlling stories, casts, and budgets. Yet, with the advent of talkies, Paramount would not renew her contract. She signed instead with William LeBaron's RKO Studios and gained great fame with the lead in the lavish musical *Rio Rita* (1929), in which she proved that she could not only speak but sing as well. Her third talkie, *Alias French Gertie* (1930), also starred Ben Lyon, whom she married on June 14, 1930. They had a daughter of their own and adopted a son. After five pictures for RKO, Bebe Daniels signed a six-picture contract with Warner, where she starred in an early version of *The Maltese Falcon* (1931), *Silver Dollar* (1932), and *42nd Street* (1933).

After a return to the stage in Skeets Gallagher's *Hollywood Holiday* the Lyons moved to London and opened at the Palladium on June 29, 1936, with a long-running variety act. Despite World War II,qv in May 1940 they originated the lighthearted "High Gang!," a twelve-year radio and four-year television show. Daniels's war work included interviewing American wounded in Europe for the radio series "Stars and Stripes in Britain" (1941) and "Purple Heart Corner" (1944), which were broadcast in America; performing variety acts for the troops; and relaying battlefield reports fifteen days after D-Day as the first civilian woman back into Normandy. For her patriotism President Harry Truman awarded her the Medal of Freedom.

After the war the Lyons returned to America, where Bebe Daniels produced two films for Hal Roach, *Mr. Wilmer* (1947) and *The Fabulous Joe* (1948). She subsequently returned to London, where she wrote and produced the vastly popular *Life With the Lyons*, starring the whole Lyon family, including children Barbara and Richard. It played for twelve years on radio (1950–62), then inspired a thirty-two-episode television series and two movies, *Life with the Lyons* (1954) and *The Lyons in Paris* (1956). The Lyons played seven Royal Command Performances. On March 16, 1971, Bebe Daniels died in London of a cerebral hemorrhage.

BIBLIOGRAPHY: Jill Allgood, *Bebe and Ben* (London: Robert Hale, 1975). De Witt Bodeen, "Bebe Daniels," *Films in Review,* August–September 1964.   *Stacy A. Cordery*

DANIELS, GEORGE WASHINGTON (ca. 1840–1921). George Washington Daniels, author, was born into slaveryqv in Watertown, Texas, in 1840. During the Civil Warqv he was forced to serve the Confederate Army but managed to escape to the Union Army and serve there. Daniels described his life as a slave and his military adventures both North and South in a series of articles published in *Youth's Companion*. He died on May 13, 1921.

BIBLIOGRAPHY: Monroe N. Work, ed., *Negro Year Book: An Annual Encyclopedia of the Negro, 1921–1922* (Tuskegee Institute, Alabama: Negro Year Book Publishing Company, 1922).

Peggy Hardman

DANIELS, JOSEPH (1809–1886). Joseph Daniels, soldier and civil servant, was born in Boston, Massachusetts, on July 26, 1809. In 1830 he moved to New Orleans, Louisiana, where he raised and was elected first lieutenant of the Louisiana Greys. He and his company were detailed to serve as an honor guard for the arrival in New Orleans of the wounded Sam Houston qv after the battle of San Jacinto. qv This chance encounter grew into a close and lasting friendship. Daniels followed Houston to Texas in 1837 and settled at Houston. On November 9, 1838, he was elected captain of the Milam Guards, qv a militia company that he had organized and trained. In November 1838 he led his company, in cooperation with Maj. George W. Bonnell, qv against the Indians on the Little Brazos River above Nashville. On December 2 he was ordered to garrison and take command of Fort Houston, near the site of present-day Palestine, and to drive the Indians from that region. On January 8, 1839, he moved his company to the falls of the Brazos, near the site of present Waco, where he was to give "protection to the frontier against Indian depredations." "The destiny of the upper Brazos is in a measure committed to the custody of the Milam Guards," wrote Gen. Moseley Baker. qv Daniels returned to Houston at the end of the campaign and was commissioned a captain in the First Regiment of Infantry in the Army of the Republic of Texas qv on February 24, 1839. In Houston in October 1839 he married Ann Van Versal, a New Orleans widow with two children. The couple had five additional children, of whom three died in infancy.

Early in 1839 Daniels moved to Washington-on-the-Brazos, then the seat of the government, when he was appointed chief clerk of the General Land Office qv under Thomas W. Ward; qv he moved to Austin when the government moved there late in the same year. It was reported that during the so-called "Archive War" qv of December 30–31, 1842, Daniels was shot at several times by citizens attempting to keep the state papers in Austin. "What injury he sustained is unknown," reported Sam Houston. Daniels was later appointed acting postmaster general, then was elected captain of the Travis Guards and Rifles, qv and on December 5, 1844, became Governor Houston's aide-de-camp with the rank of colonel of cavalry. On June 26, 1846, when the Mexican War qv broke out, he was commissioned a captain in the United States Army and appointed assistant quartermaster on the staff of Gen. John A. Quitman. qv He served as Quitman's aide during Gen. Winfield Scott's Mexico City campaign and on August 20, 1847, was brevetted to major for "gallant and meritorious conduct" at the battles of Contreras and Churubusco. Daniels was discharged from federal service on October 15, 1848. After the war he moved to San Francisco, California, where he died on May 25, 1886.

BIBLIOGRAPHY: Francis B. Heitman, *Historical Register and Dictionary of the United States Army* (2 vols., Washington: GPO, 1903; rpt., Urbana: University of Illinois Press, 1965). Adele B. Looscan, "Capt. Joseph Daniels," *Quarterly of the Texas State Historical Association* 5 (July 1901). Amelia W. Williams and Eugene C. Barker, eds., *The Writings of Sam Houston, 1813–1863* (8 vols., Austin: University of Texas Press, 1938–43; rpt., Austin and New York: Pemberton Press, 1970).

Thomas W. Cutrer

DANIELS, VICTOR VALE (1869–1948). Victor Vale Daniels, journalist, was born on July 2, 1869, at Columbus, Texas, the son of J. M. Daniels, publisher of the *Colorado Citizen* (see COLORADO COUNTY CITIZEN). After learning journalism from his father and by working on the *Citizen*, he worked for newspapers in Bryan, Temple, and Austin. He published the *Angelina County Press*, but, on the basis of an attractive partnership offer from William Sydney Porter, qv sold out and moved to Austin. With Porter (better known as O. Henry) and Dr. Dixie Daniels, he published *Rolling Stone*, a weekly humor paper in Austin. Porter had obtained the printing plant from W. C. Brann's qv *Iconoclast* qv in Waco, and together he and Daniels wrote many essays and short stories.

Daniels moved to Corpus Christi in 1922 as managing editor of the Corpus Christi *Times* (see CORPUS CHRISTI CALLER-TIMES), where he published a serial history of Corpus Christi in May–July 1922. Under the close direction of W. E. Pope, the attorney who owned the *Times*, Daniels made sure that the paper followed the trial of Nueces county sheriff Frank Robinson for the murder of Fred Roberts, secretary of the local Ku Klux Klan. qv The trial, before Judge Mullally at Laredo in January 1923, was only perfunctorily covered by competitive news services. When the jury acquitted Sheriff Robinson at about 6:00 P.M. on Saturday, January 14, a competing paper was able to insert the story in its Sunday edition. Because the *Times* did not issue on Sundays, Daniels put a small card on his desk inscribed "Farewell Victory," which he considered the approximate English version of the name Victor Vale, and concerned himself with other news items. When the *Times* was sold to Houston Harte qv and Bernard Hanks, Daniels was permitted to remain in its employ until his retirement in 1935. He then worked as a pumper in nearby oilfields and operated a restaurant and bar. He died in Corpus Christi on March 14, 1948.

BIBLIOGRAPHY: Corpus Christi *Times*, March 27, 1936, March 15, 1948.

Frank Wagner

DANIELS, WILLIAMSON (1798–1872). Williamson Daniels, participant in the Texas Revolution, qv Republic of Texas qv congressman, and county official, was born in Somerset County, Pennsylvania, on January 28, 1798. In 1830 he came to Texas and settled in the San Augustine district. According to one report he was a missionary in Stephen F. Austin's qv second colony. He sold beef cattle, oxen, and other provisions to the Texas army in 1835 and early 1836. He enlisted in the San Augustine volunteers on April 1, 1836, and served as second lieutenant until July 22. He was elected justice of the peace for the Middle District of Colorado County on February 6, 1837; president of the board of land commissioners of Colorado County on May 7, 1838; member of the House of Representatives of the Sixth Congress (1841–42); and justice of the peace of Precinct 3, Colorado County, in February 1845. Daniels became chief justice of Colorado County on August 7, 1848, and in 1850 was a county commissioner. In 1851 he ran unsuccessfully for a House seat in the Fourth Legislature. In 1867 he helped to organize Florida Lodge No. 48 in Fayette County. He was married to Cynthia Alley. He died in 1872.

BIBLIOGRAPHY: Colorado County Historical Commission, *Colorado County Chronicles from the Beginning to 1923* (2 vols., Austin: Nortex, 1986). Daughters of the Republic of Texas, *Founders and Patriots of the Republic of Texas* (Austin, 1963–). *Telegraph and Texas Register*, June 6, 1851. Vertical Files, Barker Texas History Center, University of Texas at Austin.

DANIELS, TEXAS (Panola County). Daniels, on Farm Road 10 six miles southwest of Carthage in southern Panola County, was first settled after the Civil War. qv In the mid-1930s the community had a number of houses and a school, church, and store. After World War II qv its school was consolidated with the Carthage schools, and by the early 1970s only a store, a church, and a few houses remained in the area. In the early 1990s Daniels was a dispersed rural community.

Christopher Long

DANIELS, TEXAS (Washington County). Daniels is a farming community on Red Gully Creek near the intersection of Farm roads 1155 and 2447 in east central Washington County. The community was developed by 1960.

Carole E. Christian

DANIELS CREEK. Daniels Creek rises two miles northwest of McMahan in eastern Caldwell County (at 29°53′ N, 97°32′ W) and runs southwest for seven miles to its mouth on Tenney Creek, three miles west of Tilmon (at 29°48′ N, 97°34′ W). It traverses an area of rolling prairie surfaced by shallow clay loams that support mesquite, mixed hardwoods, and grasses. The stream may have been named for George Daniels, an early settler in the area.

DANT, TEXAS. Dant was a rural community on the east bank of Piney Creek three miles northwest of Bellville in central Austin County. Settlement in the vicinity began in the late 1830s, but the town itself was founded about 1846 on the John Wesley Kenney[qv] survey. The Bellville-Brenham spur of the Gulf, Colorado and Santa Fe Railway was extended through the township about 1880. The town appears to have declined rapidly in the early 1900s, and it was soon abandoned. The Ueckert cemetery east of the Atchison, Topeka and Santa Fe rail line marks the former townsite.

Charles Christopher Jackson

DANVILLE, TEXAS (Comal County). Danville, on Dry Comal Creek and the Old San Antonio Road some eight miles southwest of New Braunfels in southern Comal County, was settled in 1848 when William Bracken issued power of attorney to John James[qv] to sell land granted to Bracken in 1847. Several German families farmed the area. A post office opened in William Klaus's store in 1875 and operated until 1894, when a rural delivery route from New Braunfels was established. The Danville school opened in 1863 and operated until after World War II,[qv] when it was consolidated with other districts in southern Comal County to form the Comal elementary school.

BIBLIOGRAPHY: Oscar Haas, *History of New Braunfels and Comal County, Texas, 1844–1946* (Austin: Steck, 1968). *Oscar Haas*

DANVILLE, TEXAS (Gregg County). Danville, also known as New Danville and as Rabbit Creek, is a rural community off Farm Road 349 six miles southwest of Longview in south central Gregg County. It was established around 1847 and was reportedly named by S. Slade Barnett[qv] and his relatives for their former hometown, Danville, Kentucky. In 1848 the Gum Springs Presbyterian Church was organized in the community, and the New Danville Masonic Lodge was chartered in 1852. A post office opened in 1850 under the name Rabbit Creek; its name was changed to New Danville in 1852, and it remained in operation until 1873. At its height around the time of the Civil War[qv] New Danville had three or four stores, several saloons, a blacksmith shop, and a hand-fed gin powered by two mules. The community continued to prosper until the early 1870s, when the International–Great Northern Railroad bypassed it. Many of the town's residents and most of its businesses moved to Kilgore on the railroad. In the 1940s Danville, as it was later called, still had a church, a cemetery, and two stores. Later the stores closed, and in the early 1990s only a few scattered dwellings remained at the site.

BIBLIOGRAPHY: Marker Files, Texas Historical Commission, Austin. Eugene W. McWhorter, *Traditions of the Land: The History of Gregg County* (Longview, Texas: Gregg County Historical Foundation, 1989). *Christopher Long*

DANVILLE, TEXAS (Montgomery County). Danville, an East Texas settlement four miles west of New Waverly on the old Houston road in northern Montgomery County, was reported to be flourishing as early as 1838 and again in 1850. Danville was on the lower Coushatta Trace[qv] and was perhaps named by Samuel and Joseph Lindley,[qv] who moved their families to this area from Danville, Illinois, in 1830. At its height in the mid-1800s, the community had about 1,000 residents, 600 of whom were slaves. It had fourteen businesses, including two blacksmith shops, two mercantile stores, and an inn, as well as a cotton gin, general store, saloon, saddle shop, hotel, and grocery store. The town hosted Sam Houston[qv] at a barbecue on September 11, 1858. Most of Danville's businesses and many of its residents moved to the new railroad town of Willis in 1870. When the old Houston road (later U.S. Highway 75) was rerouted through New Waverly, the Danville economy was further damaged. This area of northern Montgomery County and southern Walker County was the scene of substantial Polish settlement in the late 1800s (*see* POLES). In 1872 Father Orzechowski led the effort to establish Sts. Peter and Paul Catholic Church in Danville. Though this church was abandoned in the 1920s, its site is commemorated by a bell and a historical marker in Danville, while the original church building serves as a hay barn on a nearby ranch. The loss of the church and highway led to the decline of Danville. In the 1980s it was a small, quiet, rural community.

BIBLIOGRAPHY: Robin Navarro Montgomery, *The History of Montgomery County* (Austin: Jenkins, 1975). *Gerald L. Holder*

DAPHNE, TEXAS. Daphne is on Farm Road 1896 eight miles northeast of Mount Vernon in northeastern Franklin County. This small, dispersed, lumbering and agricultural community was settled in the 1850s and received a post office in 1895, with mail delivered from Mount Vernon by special supply. Its post office was discontinued in 1906. By 1985 the community consisted of a community center and a few widely scattered houses.

BIBLIOGRAPHY: Billy Hicks and Doris Meek, comps., *Historical Records of Franklin County, Texas* (Mount Vernon, Texas: Franklin County Historical Survey Committee, 1972). *Cecil Harper, Jr.*

DAQUINATINO INDIANS. The Daquinatino Indians were reported by Henri Joutel[qv] in 1687 to be in northeast Texas. They were said to be allies of the Caddo Indians and were probably related linguistically.

BIBLIOGRAPHY: Frederick Webb Hodge, ed., *Handbook of American Indians North of Mexico* (2 vols., Washington: GPO, 1907, 1910; rpt., New York: Pageant, 1959). *Margery H. Krieger*

DAQUIO INDIANS. The Daquio Indians were a Caddo Indian[qv] group reported by Henri Joutel[qv] in northeast Texas in 1687. The name may be identified with the Daycao River (possibly the Trinity), the most westerly point reached by the Moscoso expedition[qv] of 1542.

BIBLIOGRAPHY: Frederick Webb Hodge, ed., *Handbook of American Indians North of Mexico* (2 vols., Washington: GPO, 1907, 1910; rpt., New York: Pageant, 1959). *Margery H. Krieger*

DARBY, TEXAS. Darby was near an old Indian trail and campground about four miles west of Moscow in central Polk County. The area was settled by Europeans before the Civil War;[qv] among the early settlers was an Irish family named Criswell, who arrived in 1835. The community was eventually named for Augustus Darby, a slaveowner who moved to the area during the 1850s. It is unique among Polk County settlements, as many of its early residents were from Ireland and Germany. Darby had a Catholic church and became a leather-tanning center for local hunters. A school was also established there. Residents formed the Darby Farmers Alliance, which met from at least 1886 to 1890. Darby was still a rural community during the 1930s, and in the 1940s it had the only Catholic cemetery in the county. Maps from the 1980s do not show the settlement.

BIBLIOGRAPHY: Emma Haynes, The History of Polk County (MS, Sam Houston Regional Library, Liberty, Texas, 1937; rev. ed. 1968). *A Pictorial History of Polk County, Texas, 1846–1910* (Livingston, Texas: Polk County Bicentennial Commission, 1976; rev. ed. 1978). *Robert Wooster*

DARCO, TEXAS. Darco is on State Highway 43 some nine miles southwest of Marshall in south central Harrison County. In the mid-

1930s the Darco mines employed some forty laborers to mine and ship lignite to the Darco Corporation of Marshall. There the lignite was used in the manufacture of "Darco," which was used in refining processes as a decolorizer and purifier. In 1937–38 the Darco district schools served some 100 white and seventy-six black pupils. In 1948 the Darco community had the mining operation, one other business, a school, and scattered dwellings. Its population was reported as ninety-five in 1964. In 1990 strip mining was still under way in the area, and Darco's population was eighty-five.

BIBLIOGRAPHY: Jerome McCown, Scraps of the Early History of Marshall and Harrison County (MS, Barker Texas History Center, University of Texas at Austin). *Mark Odintz*

DARDEN, FANNIE AMELIA DICKSON (1829–1890). Fannie (Fanny) Darden, early Texas writer and painter, the daughter of Eliza Ward (Pickett) and Moseley Baker,qv was born near Montgomery, Alabama, on September 13, 1829. Her second name is often given as Augusta and her third is often spelled Dixon. The Baker family arrived in Texas sometime between 1835 and 1837. From 1842 to 1846 Fannie attended school in Alabama. She started a novel, but destroyed the manuscript soon after her marriage on January 26, 1847, to William John Darden, an attorney from Norfolk, Virginia. She and her husband moved to Columbus, Texas, in 1852, where she began writing a series of poems that were published in the local newspaper, the *Colorado Citizen* (see COLORADO COUNTY CITIZEN). She also produced numerous novelettes, short stories, and paintings and taught art at Colorado College in Columbus after it opened in 1857. She established a reputation as an artist in Columbus, Dallas, Houston, Fort Worth, and other towns in Texas. Many of her paintings had religious themes; *The Good Shepherd,* for instance, hangs in the parish hall of St. John's Episcopal Church in Columbus.

Fannie's husband died in 1881. In November 1882 she underwent breast-cancer surgery in San Antonio. After returning to Columbus apparently fully recovered, she met Laura Jack Irvine, a correspondent for the *American Sketchbook,* when the latter was in Columbus researching an article. In March 1883, when Irvine resigned from the magazine, Darden took her position, apparently the only time she was employed as a professional writer. Some of her poetry was included in Sam Houston Dixon'sqv *The Poets and Poetry of Texas* (1885) and in Ella Hutchins Steuart's *Gems From a Texas Quarry* (1885). One of her poems, "Yokonah," was included in Davis Foute Eagleton'sqv *Texas Literature Reader* (1916). She was also published in the Houston *Telegraph, Texas Siftings*qv of Austin, and *Texas Prairie Flower* of Corsicana. Fannie Darden wrote about historical events and her own personal experiences; her best prose works are considered to be a short article called "Reminiscences of Early Childhood in Texas" (1921) and *Romances of the Texas Revolution* (n.d.). She was stricken with paralysis in December of 1889 and died in Columbus in October 1890.

BIBLIOGRAPHY: Evelyn M. Carrington, ed., *Women in Early Texas* (Austin: Pemberton Press, 1975). *Colorado Citizen,* November 9, 1882, March 8, 1883. Fannie A. D. Baker Darden, Narrative, 1870 (MS, Barker Texas History Center, University of Texas at Austin). Sam Houston Dixon and Louis Wiltz Kemp, *The Heroes of San Jacinto* (Houston: Anson Jones, 1932). Sam Houston Dixon, *The Poets and Poetry of Texas* (Austin: Dixon, 1885). Lee Quinn Nesbitt, Moseley Baker and His Daughter (MS, Nesbitt Memorial Library, Columbus, Texas). *Bill Stein*

DARDEN, IDA MERCEDES MUSE (1886–1980). Ida Darden, conservative dissident, was born on March 9, 1886, into the Muse family, evidently in Bosque County, Texas, but the family soon moved to Moran. She claimed that her family staunchly opposed reform governor James S. Hoggqv and that Senator Joseph W. Baileyqv was a frequent visitor to their farm home. After briefly taking courses at a business college and at the University of Texas, in 1904 she married Bert Darden, an employee of Swift and Companyqv in Fort Worth. The couple had a daughter, Helen, in 1905. Darden died in 1906, and Ida took up secretarial work. By the next decade she and her brother, Vance Muse,qv were employed by Bailey's friends, financier J. A. Arnold, for whom Ida worked, and lumber magnate John Henry Kirby,qv who employed Muse. They worked as publicists, fund-raisers, and lobbyists for a variety of conservative organizations, and the relationships lasted until the deaths of Kirby and Arnold in the 1940s. Ida was also employed Pauline K. Wellsqv as publicity director of the Texas Association Opposed to Woman Suffrageqv in 1916. The two ladies depicted woman suffrageqv as a socialist plot that would undermine white supremacy. Around 1920 Ida Darden married Fort Worth businessman Walter Myrick, who joined her and Muse in various projects. Their Southern Tariff Association, which lobbied for Arnold in the 1920s on behalf of higher tariffs for southern products, was investigated by Congress. Ida Darden denounced the Ku Klux Klanqv and voted for Al Smith in 1928. In 1932 she ran for congressman at large in the Democratic primary, believing the main issue to be stamping out prohibition,qv though she was personally dry. She published her first booklet in 1936, a gentle, tongue-in-cheek look at the Texas legislature, *Gentlemen of the House.*

By 1949, after decades of operating mostly behind the scenes, she was ready for a more public life. Financed largely by such Texas oilmen as George W. Armstrongqv and Arch Rowan, Darden launched her *Southern Conservative,* an eight-page newspaper, in Fort Worth in January 1950. Her major task was to take on the Communists, though she considered the fight nearly hopeless since she thought that Communist thinking had dominated all three branches of the government since 1933. Dwight D. Eisenhower,qv she thought, was as much a dupe of the Reds as Franklin Roosevelt. She considered the civil-rights movement,qv modern art, and modern movies all to be abominations perpetuated by inferior people. In 1959 she editorialized for the impeachment of all members of the United States Supreme Court. Darden was a Protestant, but she believed that the Protestant churches, having succumbed to the subversive social gospel, were increasingly atheistic. She alleged that all taxation was larceny and should be abolished, and that Edna Ferber's *Giant* was communist propaganda from cover to cover, with its depictions of children who repudiated their parents for accumulating property and humiliated their fathers by marrying down. Darden terminated the paper in December 1961 and moved to Houston. She published two more booklets around this time—*My Night* (1951), a witty parody of Eleanor Roosevelt's "My Day" newspaper column, and *Best of the Southern Conservative* (1963), selected articles from her paper. Though most contemporary observers in Fort Worth in the 1950s regarded Darden as a crackpot, she did not lack influence. In the 1950s the Minute Women of the U.S.A.qv took over the Houston school board and harassed and fired teachers and administrators for alleged communism. One of the two original organizers of the Minute Women was Darden's daughter, Helen Thomas, who was very close to her mother and was the resident intellectual and researcher in the organization. The *C.I.O. News* blamed the *Southern Conservative* for helping the Minute Women bar the annual United Nations essay contests in the Houston schools. A number of tumultuous events in Texas in the 1950s heartened ultraconservatives, and Ida Darden was with them every step of the way. Her columns were carried by or quoted favorably in daily papers in Dallas, Fort Worth, El Paso, and Lubbock. She died on March 24, 1980, in Holly Hall, New Hampshire, and is buried in Fort Worth.

BIBLIOGRAPHY: Vertical Files, Barker Texas History Center, University of Texas at Austin. *George N. Green*

DARDEN, STEPHEN HEARD (1816–1902). Stephen Heard Darden, public official and soldier, son of Washington Lee and Ann (Sharkey) Darden, was born in Fayette County, Mississippi, on November 19, 1816. He traveled to Texas in 1836 as a volunteer under Capt. David M. Fulton for service in the Texas Revolution.qv Darden served as clerk in the office of the comptroller in September 1836. He returned to Madison County, Mississippi, in the early 1840s but was back in Texas in 1841 and purchased land on the Guadalupe River in Gonzales County. He represented the county for two terms in the state House of Representatives and once in the state Senate. In 1861, as a state senator, he initially opposed secession qv but finally voted with the majority; at the coming of the Civil War qv he was elected first lieutenant of Company A of the Fourth Texas Infantry in Hood's Texas Brigade.qv He served under colonels Robert T. P. Allen, John Bell Hood, and John F. Marshall.qqv He was elected captain of his company on May 20, 1862, but after the battle of Antietam (Sharpsburg) that September he resigned due to ill health. Darden was the appointed colonel in command of the Fifth Infantry regiment of state troops on the Texas Gulf Coast in 1863 and, upon the death of John A. Wilcox,qv was elected to fill the unexpired term in the Second Confederate Congress, where he took his seat on November 21, 1864. As a Confederate congressman Darden served on the Naval Affairs Committee. As a firm states'-rights advocate he opposed the growth of the central government of the Confederate States of America and thus generally voted against the Jefferson Davis qv administration. While he supported higher taxation, a larger army, and a powerful commander-in-chief, he fought against taxation in kind, centralized control over transportation and production, and the confiscation of slaves for public works.

Darden was financially ruined by the war and apparently returned to his Gonzales County farm. When Reconstruction qv ended he was appointed comptroller of public accounts and served from 1873 to 1879. He recommended that the school money be invested in state bonds and thus raised the bonds to par. Although he retired from office in January 1881 because of his age, he accepted the chief clerkship in his old department. He was appointed superintendent of public buildings and grounds on February 9, 1884, and chief clerk of the comptroller's department in January 1887. He assisted in organizing the state Democratic party qv in 1871 and was secretary of the Texas Veterans Association qv from 1886 until his death. Darden was twice married, the second time to Catherine Mays on March 24, 1862; they had two children. He died at Wharton on May 16, 1902, and was buried in the State Cemetery,qv Austin.

BIBLIOGRAPHY: Lewis E. Daniell, *Personnel of the Texas State Government, with Sketches of Representative Men of Texas* (Austin: City Printing, 1887; 3d ed., San Antonio: Maverick, 1892). C. W. Raines, *Year Book for Texas* (2 vols., Austin: Gammel-Statesman, 1902, 1903). Jon L. Wakelyn, *Biographical Dictionary of the Confederacy* (Westport, Connecticut: Greenwood, 1977). Ezra J. Warner and W. Buck Yearns, *Biographical Register of the Confederate Congress* (Baton Rouge: Louisiana State University Press, 1975). Marcus J. Wright, comp., and Harold B. Simpson, ed., *Texas in the War, 1861–1865* (Hillsboro, Texas: Hill Junior College Press, 1965).
Thomas W. Cutrer

DARDEN, TEXAS (Bowie County). Darden, off U.S. Highway 67 fifteen miles southwest of Boston in southwestern Bowie County, lies in the low hills of the Sulphur Fork of the Red River. The settlement was called Brownstone, for Randolph H. Brown, when it was established on the St. Louis Southwestern Railway of Texas in the late 1890s. A post office was granted to the community in 1911. The office was renamed Darden in 1917, then discontinued in 1927. In 1940 Darden had a store and a population of ten; mail was delivered from Bassett, two miles to the northeast. In 1984 only scattered houses remained in the area.
Claudia Hazlewood

DARDEN, TEXAS (Polk County). Darden is on U.S. Highway 287 seventy-five miles northwest of Beaumont in northeastern Polk County. The area is in the densely forested regions of the Big Thicket.qv Darden was east of a Carter Lumber Company tram railroad that extended east from nearby Camden. In 1966 the largely black community had a population of seventy-five, most of whom were engaged in farming, ranching, and lumbering. The 1984 county highway map showed Darden with a church, cemetery, school, and business.

BIBLIOGRAPHY: *A Pictorial History of Polk County, Texas, 1846–1910* (Livingston, Texas: Polk County Bicentennial Commission, 1976; rev. ed. 1978).
Robert Wooster

DARDEN CANYON CREEK. Darden Canyon Creek rises about seven miles east of Roaring Springs in south central Motley County (at 33°54′ N, 100°44′ W) and runs southeast for about two miles to its mouth on the Tongue (or South Pease) River, two miles north of the Motley-Dickens county line (at 33°52′ N, 100°42′ W). The lower creek basin was noted as fine grazing land on early Matador Ranch qv maps. The creek traverses an area of gently rolling hills with moderately steep slopes, surfaced by shallow to moderately deep silt loam soils that support mesquite and grasses.

BIBLIOGRAPHY: Glenn A. Gray, *Gazetteer of Streams of Texas* (Washington: GPO, 1919).

DARDEN SPRINGS, TEXAS. Darden Springs (Darden Spring) was a farming community near the spring of the same name, sixteen miles northwest of Giddings in northwestern Lee County. A post office operated there from 1887 to 1899, and Dr. W. B. Darden, after whom the settlement was named, was postmaster. In 1891 the community had a cotton gin and gristmill. Its population in 1896 was estimated at twenty. By the mid-1930s the settlement was no longer shown on county highway maps.
Christopher Long

DARGAN, TEXAS. Dargan, a post office community seven miles northeast of DeBerry in northeastern Panola County near the Louisiana state line, was probably established in the early 1880s. A post office opened there in 1888, and in the early 1890s the settlement had a general store, a lumberyard, and an estimated population of fifty. Its post office closed in 1908, and local mail was sent to Bethany, Louisiana. By the mid-1930s Dargan was no longer shown on county highway maps.

BIBLIOGRAPHY: John Barnette Sanders, *Postoffices and Post Masters of Panola County, Texas, 1845–1930* (Center, Texas, 1964).
Christopher Long

DARK CANYON CREEK. Dark Canyon Creek rises about eleven miles east of Spur near the eastern limits of the Croton Creek oilfield in southeastern Dickens County (at 29°27′ N, 103°27′ W) and runs southwest through Dark Canyon for five miles to its confluence with Croton Creek, about five miles west of the Dickens-King county line (at 29°20′ N, 103°34′ W). The canyon was named for the profusion of trees that blocked sunlight from its course. The creek begins at an elevation of about 2,200 feet above sea level and descends more than 300 feet before reaching its mouth. The area is marked by dissected gullies and low hills with shallow soil and sparse vegetation.

BIBLIOGRAPHY: Dickens County Historical Commission, *Dickens County: Its Land and Its People* (Lubbock: Craftsman Printers, 1986).

DARK HOLLOW BRANCH. Dark Hollow Branch rises three miles southwest of Anson in south central Jones County (at 32°43′ N, 99°57′ W) and runs seven miles southeast to its mouth on the Clear Fork of the Brazos River, just east of Truby (at 32°39′ N, 99°54′ W). It crosses flat to gently sloping terrain surfaced by sandy loam that supports mesquite and grasses.

DARK VALLEY CREEK. Dark Valley Creek rises in northern Palo Pinto County (at 32°59′ N, 98°19′ W) and runs south for twelve miles to its mouth on the Brazos River, about ten miles east of Possum Kingdom Reservoir (at 32°52′ N, 98°18′ W). The creek crosses flat to rolling terrain with local deep and dense dissections, with generally shallow and stony soils that support oak, juniper, and some mesquite trees on the land near the stream.

DARLINGTON, JOHN WASHINGTON (1821–1915). John Washington Darlington, farmer and soldier, was born in Harrison County, Virginia, now Marion County, West Virginia, on February 5, 1821, the son of John W. and Henrietta Lang (Nazum) Darlington. His father, an Irishman, is said to have participated in the Lewis and Clark expedition and to have fought at the battle of New Orleans; he died while Darlington was still an infant, and the boy was apprenticed to a master with whom he did not agree. In consequence, Darlington ran away, intending to escape to Texas. En route he met and bound himself to John Webster, who took him to Texas in exchange for his labor. Webster and Darlington landed at Matagorda on January 14, 1838, and in May settled on Gilleland Creek some fourteen miles southeast of Austin in Travis County. In 1839–40 Darlington hauled freight between Houston and Bastrop.

When Webster was killed by Indians in the Webster Massacre[qv] in 1839, Darlington remained in Travis County and worked as a laborer on the first Texas capitol until January 1840. For the remainder of that year and part of the next he was a sharecropper in Travis County. In 1841 he took part in the battle of Plum Creek,[qv] and in 1842 he served with the volunteer forces that repulsed the raids of Rafael Vásquez and Adrián Woll.[qqv] In fall of 1842 Darlington rented land and took up farming in Rusk County, where, on October 19, 1843, he married Ellen J. Love. The couple had ten children. In 1844 he purchased the farm that he had been working, but the following year he returned to Travis County as a stock raiser on rented land. In 1849 he purchased a ranch in Travis County that was assessed in 1850 at $320. During the Civil War[qv] Darlington served as a private in the ranger company of a Captain Graham in Maj. George B. Erath's[qv] frontier defense battalion. He was stationed in Coryell County. In 1873 he purchased 520 acres near Hutto, where he ranched until 1884, when he moved to Taylor. Darlington was a Democrat, a Mason, a Presbyterian, and a member of the Texas Veterans Association.[qv] He died in Austin on September 12, 1915, and was buried at Manor.

BIBLIOGRAPHY: Austin *Statesman*, September 12, 1915. John Henry Brown, *Indian Wars and Pioneers of Texas* (Austin: Daniell, 1880; reprod., Easley, South Carolina: Southern Historical Press, 1978). Ellis A. Davis and Edwin H. Grobe, comps., *The New Encyclopedia of Texas* (2 vols., Dallas: Texas Development Bureau, 1925?; 4 vols. 1929?). *History of Texas, Together with a Biographical History of Milam, Williamson, Bastrop, Travis, Lee and Burleson Counties* (Chicago: Lewis, 1893). Vertical Files, Barker Texas History Center, University of Texas at Austin.
Thomas W. Cutrer

DARNELL, MONETTA ELOYSE (1923–1965). Monetta Darnell [pseud. Linda Darnell], film actress, one of six children of Calvin Roy and Margaret Pearl (Brown) Darnell, was born in Dallas, Texas, on October 16, 1923. She grew up in the Oak Cliff section of Dallas and attended Sunset High School, where she won local talent contests. As a teenager she modeled for Southwestern Style Shows, was a "Texanita" during the Texas Centennial,[qv] and won the regional Gateway to Hollywood contest. In 1938 talent scout Ivan Kahn arranged for her to have a screen test that led to an eventual contract with Twentieth Century–Fox studio. She starred in her first film, *Hotel for Women*, in 1939 and remained with Twentieth Century–Fox for thirteen years. Darryl Zanuck, the studio's production head, immediately cast her in a series of motion pictures opposite Tyrone Power, including *Daytime Wife* (1939), *Brigham Young—Frontiersman* (1940), *The Mark of Zorro* (1940), and *Blood and Sand* (1941).

In 1944 *Look* magazine selected Linda Darnell as one of the four most beautiful women in Hollywood. After reshaping her celluloid image from that of a sweet young thing into that of a sultry vixen, she reached international stature in the title role of the screen spectacle *Forever Amber* (1947) and further demonstrated her skill as an actress in such films as *Hangover Square* (1945), *Fallen Angel* (1945), *Unfaithfully Yours* (1948), *A Letter to Three Wives* (1948), *Slattery's Hurricane* (1949), and *No Way Out* (1950). Her contract with Twentieth Century–Fox came to an end in 1952, while the big-studio system was declining. She afterward made three pictures at RKO: *Blackbeard the Pirate* (1952), *Second Chance* (1953), and *This Is My Love* (1957); two in Italy; and low-budget productions for Paramount and Republic. Yet she never again equaled her earlier success.

Darnell made a Broadway debut in the unsuccessful *Harbor Lights* in 1956, appeared frequently in major television dramas, toured with tenor Thomas Hayward in a nightclub act, and performed regularly in regional theaters across the country in such plays as *Tea and Sympathy*, *A Roomful of Roses*, and *Janus*. She worked for numerous charities, including the National Kidney Foundation, and helped raise funds to preserve the battleship *Texas*[qv] as a public shrine.

She married Hollywood cameraman J. Peverell Marley, business tycoon Philip Liebmann, and airline pilot Merle Roy Robertson, but divorced all three. In 1948 she and Marley adopted a daughter, Charlotte Mildred (Lola). In later years the actress was overtaken by personal problems, in part stemming from her premature fame. She was visiting friends in Glenview, Illinois, in April 1965, when the townhouse in which she was staying caught fire, only hours after she and her hostess had watched one of her first movies on late television. She was severely burned and died on April 10 in the Koch Burn Center at Cook County Hospital.

BIBLIOGRAPHY: Ronald L. Davis, *Hollywood Beauty: Linda Darnell and the American Dream* (Norman: University of Oklahoma Press, 1991). New York *Times*, April 11, 1965. James Robert Parish, *The Fox Girls* (Secaucus, New Jersey: Castle, 1971). David Thomson, *A Biographical Dictionary of Film* (New York: William Morrow, 1976; 2d ed., rev., 1981). Evelyn Mack Truitt, *Who Was Who on Screen* (New York: Bowker, 1977).
Ronald L. Davis

DARNELL, NICHOLAS HENRY (1807–1885). Nicholas Henry Darnell, legislator and soldier, was born in Williamson County, Tennessee, on April 20, 1807, the youngest child of Nicholas and Nannie (Flewellen) Darnell. He was reared by his grandfather, William Flewellen. As candidate for the Tennessee legislature in 1835, Darnell was defeated by only eight votes. He was elected without opposition in 1837 but resigned in 1838 to move to Texas. He settled at San Augustine and was elected from that county to the Sixth and Seventh congresses. On November 24, 1842, he was elected speaker of the House. He was a member of the Convention of 1845[qv] and ran against Albert C. Horton[qv] for lieutenant governor that year. When the ballots were canvassed, Darnell was shown to be the winner by a few votes, but he declined to take the oath of office until all the votes had been returned. Horton was elected.

Darnell moved to Dallas in 1858. He was speaker of the House in the Ninth Legislature but resigned in 1862 to enter the Confederate Army as colonel of the Eighteenth Texas Cavalry. The flag of the regiment, made at his home, was placed in the Capitol[qv] at Austin. Darnell was assistant doorkeeper of the House of Representatives of the Fourteenth Legislature, 1874–75. He represented Dallas, Tarrant, and Ellis counties at the Constitutional Convention of 1875[qv] and returned to the House of Representatives of the Fifteenth Legislature in 1876 as the member from Tarrant County. He served as doorkeeper and assistant doorkeeper, respectively, in the Seventeenth and Eighteenth legislatures. Darnell helped to organize the Masonic lodge at San Augustine and held all offices of the Grand Lodge of Texas, including most worshipful grand master in 1844. He and his wife, the former Isabella Cozart, had seven children. Darnell died at Fort Worth in July 1885 and was buried in the Masonic Cemetery at Dallas.

BIBLIOGRAPHY: William S. Speer and John H. Brown, eds., *Encyclopedia of the New West* (Marshall, Texas: United States Biographical Publishing, 1881; rpt., Easley, South Carolina: Southern Historical Press, 1978). Texas House of Representatives, *Biographical Directory of the Texan Conventions and Congresses, 1832–1845* (Austin: Book Exchange, 1941).
L. W. Kemp

DARROUZETT, TEXAS. Darrouzett, on State Highway 15 in northern Lipscomb County, began as a station on the Panhandle and Santa Fe Railway in 1917. The town was platted at the junction of Plummer and Kiowa creeks and was originally named Lourwood after Opal Lourwood, the first child born there. Upon completion of the rail line in 1919–20, the town was renamed in honor of Texas legislator John Louis Darrouzett, who served as an attorney for the Santa Fe. Settlers and businesses moved south from the Sunset community in Oklahoma to be near the railroad. By 1920, when it was incorporated, Darrouzett had various businesses, two churches, a school, a post office, and a population of 425. The Darrouzett Cooperative Association was formed to make the town a grain-marketing center. A bank, a high school, and several grain elevators were added by 1930. During the 1940s and 1950s Darrouzett became "the best paved town per capita of the Panhandle," at a cost of some $80,000. In 1972 Darrouzett's leaders launched the Village Improvement Plan, under which recreational facilities were improved and expanded and cultural events like the annual Deutsches Fest were initiated. In 1984 Darrouzett reported twelve businesses and a population of 444. In 1990 its population was 343.

BIBLIOGRAPHY: *A History of Lipscomb County, Texas, 1876–1976* (Lipscomb, Texas: Lipscomb County Historical Survey Committee, 1976).
H. Allen Anderson

DARRS CREEK. Darrs Creek rises six miles northwest of Holland in southeastern Bell County (at 30°54′ N, 97°30′ W) and runs southeast for sixteen miles to its mouth on the Little River, near the Milam county line (at 30°52′ N, 97°17′ W). The two principal tributaries of the stream are Middle Darrs Creek, which empties into Darrs Creek just west of Holland (at 30°53′ N, 97°26′ W), and South Darrs Creek, which meets Darrs Creek just south of Holland (at 30°52′ N, 97°24′ W). Darrs Creek is lined with oak, mesquite, and juniper trees. It traverses gently sloping terrain that is surfaced by loamy and clayey soils and used predominantly for agriculture.

DARST, ABRAHAM (1786–1833). Abraham Darst (Durst), early settler, received a league and labor of land from the Mexican government in 1831. This property is the site of the present town of Damon in Brazoria County, named for Samuel Damon,qv who married Abraham's oldest daughter, Lorena; in early days the A. Darst league was in Fort Bend County. Darst was born in Woodford County, Kentucky, on May 14, 1786, the son of David Darst and Rosetta Holman. He was the brother of Jacob Darst,qv who died in the Alamo. The family moved to Missouri, and in 1810, in Saint Charles County, Abraham married Tabitha Callaway, the daughter of Flanders Callaway and Jemima Boone, and granddaughter of Daniel Boone and Rebecca Bryan. To this union, five children were born; when the fifth child was born in 1818 Tabitha died. According to legend, Abraham left the children with Daniel and Rebecca Boone for a time and married Jemima Brownfield in Fayette County, Illinois, about 1820. In the late 1820s, before railroad transportation was available, they moved to Texas with children from both marriages, coming down the Missouri River on a raft to the Mississippi, then on to New Orleans where they took a boat to Velasco at the mouth of the Brazos River. They stopped at Bailey's Landing on the Brazos River until they located their land. Abraham and Jemima Darst had five children. Abraham Darst and his sons were farmers and ranchers. Darst died on December 23, 1833, and is buried in Damon Cemetery. On his tombstone with his name is the following: "Emigrated to Texas from Missouri in 1827 as an Austin Colonist. Participated in the Battle of Velasco, 1832. Five of his sons were in the Army of Texas in 1836. Born May 14, 1786. Died in December, 1833."

BIBLIOGRAPHY: Houston *Post*, August 14, 1966. Andrew Jackson Sowell, *History of Fort Bend County* (Houston: Coyle, 1904; rpt, Richmond, Texas: Fort Bend County Historical Museum, 1974). Clarence Wharton, *Wharton's History of Fort Bend County* (San Antonio: Naylor, 1939).
Virginia Scarborough

DARST, JACOB C. (1793–1836). Jacob C. Darst, Alamo defender, son of David and Rosetta (Holman) Darst, was born in Woodford County, Kentucky, on December 22, 1793. He was a farmer. In 1813 he married Elizabeth Bryan in Charles County, Missouri. After her death in 1820, he married Margaret C. Hughs. Darst, his wife, and his two children left for Texas in 1830 and arrived in DeWitt's colonyqv on January 10, 1831. Darst registered for twenty-four labores of land on the Guadalupe River above Gonzales and also for one labor on a small creek that empties into the Lavaca. In September 1835 Darst was one of the original "Old Eighteen,"qv defenders of the Gonzales cannon. On February 23, 1836, he was mustered into service in the Gonzales Ranging Company of Mounted Volunteers. He entered the Alamo with this unit on March 3, 1836, and died in the battle of the Alamoqv three days later.

BIBLIOGRAPHY: Daughters of the American Revolution, *The Alamo Heroes and Their Revolutionary Ancestors* (San Antonio, 1976). Daughters of the Republic of Texas, *Muster Rolls of the Texas Revolution* (Austin, 1986). Bill Groneman, *Alamo Defenders* (Austin: Eakin, 1990). Ethel Zivley Rather, "DeWitt's Colony," *Quarterly of the Texas State Historical Association* 8 (October 1904).
Bill Groneman

DARST CREEK. Darst Creek rises about eleven miles east of Seguin in eastern Guadalupe County (at 29°36′ N, 97°47′ W) and runs south for 5½ miles to its mouth on the Guadalupe River, a mile south of U.S. Highway 90A (at 29°32′ N, 97°47′ W). It traverses an area of rolling prairie, surfaced by clay loam that supports primarily mesquite and grasses. Darst Creek was probably named for Jacob C. Darst,qv who received a grant for land on the stream from the Mexican government on April 24, 1831 (*see* MEXICAN TEXAS).

DARST CREEK OILFIELD. Darst Creek field was a linear-shaped oil-producing area on the Gulf Coastal Plain in eastern Guadalupe County. Its discovery was made by the Texas Company No. 1 Dallas Wilson on July 18, 1929. Its orderly development was primarily the work of Humble Oil and Refining Company (later Exxon Company, U.S.A.qv), Gulf Production Company, and Magnolia Petroleum Company,qv as well as the Texas Company (later Texacoqv). The original field produced from an average depth of 2,650 feet in a trap along a sealing fault in Edwards limestone of the Lower Cretaceous. The source of its primary recovery was a water drive. Its secondary recovery used water injection to maintain reservoir pressure. From its initial production until September 1, 1960, when Darst Creek field ceased to exist, it yielded almost 107 million barrels of oil. On that date two separate fields called Darst Creek–Edwards and Darst Creek–Buda were identified by the Railroad Commission.qv The original field was significant because it was the first to operate under proration in its region of Texas. Darst Creek field was named for the nearby watercourse. Before September 1928 A. B. Bauchman, an attorney and amateur geologist, found evidence of a subsurface fault structure in a gully near Darst Creek, five miles from the southwestern edge of the Luling oilfield.qv Bauchman told Dilworth S. Hager, a geologist, about his find. Shortly after the conversation with Bauchman, Hager and Robert Franks mapped the structure with alidade and plane table, finding it impressive. Hager, Bauchman, and their associates leased a large block of acreage around the structure and sold much of it to Humble and Texas, who agreed to drill a test. On

July 18, 1929, the Texas Company brought in the No. 1 Dallas Wilson with initial production of 1,000 barrels of oil per day.

Since most of the leases around the discovery well were held by major companies that saw no need to develop them quickly, the field was shut in for ninety days because overproduction in other fields had flooded the crude market. By November 1929 active drilling began with rotary rigs that needed only fifteen days to complete a well at the average cost of $22,500. Some short-lived wells were sunk into the cavities along the fault plane, finding prolific reserves. One well flowed nearly 42,000 barrels of oil the first day, illustrating the potential for overproduction in the field. To avoid the risks of unregulated production with its resulting loss of reservoir pressure, water encroachment, and cheap crude prices, operators installed voluntary proration in the field. H. H. Fitzpatrick, the appointed field umpire, arrived in the field on December 16, 1929, to prepare allowable schedules for the new year. At the end of 1929 Darst Creek field reported annual production of 243,000 barrels of oil. On January 1, 1930, Fitzpatrick placed the field on twenty-acre units and based allowables 50 percent on the unit and 50 percent on the potential of unit wells. Under regulation Darst Creek field produced only 15,369 barrels of oil per day. Fourteen operators drilled offsets to prove acreage from the northeastern end of the fault to the southwestern edge, an area of almost six miles in length and of less than a mile in width. By February forty-four wells were completed for a daily potential of 44,768 barrels of oil and by the end of the month operators were violating the voluntary proration. On March 17, 1930, the Railroad Commission held a hearing to consider problems in the field. By April 1 operators increased the number of productive wells to ninety-two with a daily potential of 135,014 barrels of oil. The commission raised the daily field allowable to 23,829 barrels on May 1, 1930, and operators stayed within that limit until late June. On July 12, 1930, the commission ordered operators to abide by their voluntary system of proration and to limit production to market demand. Not all companies accepted the latest order from the commission. Harrison and Abercrombie gained a temporary injunction against it and proration collapsed in the field, but other operators worked out a plan to reinstate controls on August 4, 1930. By late October, when 186 new wells were completed and daily potential climbed to 156,822 barrels of oil, the commission set the daily allowable at 30,000 barrels. Annual field production peaked in 1930 when 11,552,000 barrels of oil were brought to the surface. In the same year the field was defined in all directions, leaving only inside locations to be drilled. By the end of 1930 four pipeline companies—Gulf, Humble, Grayburg, and Texas—connected the field with refineries. Crude was shipped also in tank cars on the Southern Pacific Railroad.

In 1931 the commission responded to the slow national economy and to flush development in other Texas fields with a 10 percent reduction of allowables in all fields across the state, except the Panhandle field. Darst Creek daily allowable was restricted to 18,000 barrels of oil for the 1,670-acre field. The new allowable held annual yields to 8,196,000 barrels of oil. In 1932, as the economic depression deepened, the commission further reduced the daily allowable for the field to 14,000 barrels of oil. Yearly yields for 1932 declined to 6,084,000 barrels of oil. In August 1935 an uphole extension to Darst Creek was discovered in the Austin Chalk at a depth of 2,441 feet. However, the new production made little difference in the declining annual yields that continued throughout the decade, ending 1939 with 2,617,478 barrels of oil. In the 1940s annual productions in Darst Creek field maintained descending totals that hovered around 2.5 million barrels of oil. By August 1943 water encroachment became a problem in the field. In January 1951 the field was described as fully developed and in the advanced stages of depletion. The water-oil ratio in some wells reached as high as 90 percent water and 10 percent oil. On September 1, 1960, the commission dissolved the original Darst Creek field, listing its cumulative production as 106,918,612 barrels of oil. At that time, two separate fields at Darst Creek were formed by the commission. One was Darst Creek–Edwards, which appeared to include the original reservoir, producing by a water drive at an average depth of 2,650 feet on five-acre spacing. The other was Darst Creek–Buda, producing from a solution gas drive at an average depth of 2,395 feet on ten-acre spacing. During the 1960s water injection was initiated in the fields to maintain pressure. The waterfloods appeared successful in the Edwards field, but they managed limited results in the gas-driven Buda field. At the end of the 1960s Darst Creek–Edwards field reported annual yields of 1,385,611 barrels of oil and 16,980,000 cubic feet of casinghead gas. Darst Creek–Buda field reported 789,731 barrels of oil and 43,293,000 cubic feet of casinghead gas. Neither field produced dry gas. Production in both fields declined significantly in the 1970s and 1980s. By the end of 1993 the Edwards field annual production plummeted to 373,845 barrels of oil and 2,029,000 cubic feet of casinghead gas, and the Buda field production fell to 166,045 barrels of oil and 137,117,000 cubic feet of casinghead gas. During 1993 the fields reported a combined total of 750 producing wells. In the seventh decade after major companies recognized the need to preserve the reservoir by voluntary proration, the cumulative total from the original Darst Creek field combined with those of Darst Creek–Edwards field and Darst Creek–Buda field was 158,710,523 barrels of oil.

BIBLIOGRAPHY: William E. Galloway et al., *Atlas of Major Texas Oil Reservoirs* (Austin: University of Texas Bureau of Economic Geology, 1983). H. D. McCallum, "Darst Creek Oil Field, Guadalupe County, Texas," *Bulletin of the American Association of Petroleum Geologists* 17 (January 1933). *Oil and Gas Development, Year Book 1931* (Dallas: National Oil Scouts Association of America, 1931). Railroad Commission of Texas, *Annual Report of the Oil and Gas Division* (Austin, 1994). Charles Albert Warner, *Texas Oil and Gas Since 1543* (Houston: Gulf, 1939).
Julia Cauble Smith

DARWIN, TEXAS. Darwin was on Farm Road 1472 and Santo Tomas Creek near the bank of the Rio Grande in northwestern Webb County. It was named for David Darwin Davis, the superintendent of the Cannel Coal Company that began mining locally in 1882. The community had a post office from 1896 to 1915. In 1914 the population of Darwin was 800, and it was a station on the Rio Grande and Eagle Pass Railroad. At this time Thomas Worsham was the community postmaster, and H. H. Jefferies was a cattle breeder in the area. By 1920 the area mines had declined greatly; they closed in 1939. The Darwin population in 1936 had dropped to seventy-five, and there was one business. By 1983 all that remained at the site was a cemetery.
Karen Gratke

DASHIELL, JEREMIAH YELLOTT (1804–1888). Jeremiah Yellott Dashiell, physician, teacher, soldier, and editor, the son of George and Ester (Handy) Dashiell, was born on September 23, 1804, in Baltimore, Maryland, where his father was the first rector of St. Peter's Episcopal Church. He received his primary education in Newark, Delaware, and then studied medicine under his uncle, William Hardy, of Baltimore. He received his M.D. degree at the University of Baltimore at the age of nineteen and then established a practice in Louisville, Kentucky, where he became a founder of and professor at Louisville Medical College. He later practiced medicine at Princeton, Mississippi, and subsequently moved to New Orleans. From there he was appointed one of the delegates to escort Andrew Jackson and James K. Polk to the Chalmette battleground for the thirtieth anniversary of the battle of New Orleans.

On July 2, 1846, at the outbreak of the Mexican War,[qv] President Polk appointed Dashiell a paymaster in the United States Army. He was promoted to the rank of major on March 2, 1849, and the following month he traveled to San Antonio as paymaster on the staff of Gen. William Jenkins Worth.[qv] He was dismissed from service on July 10, 1858. In September 1862 Dashiell was appointed colonel, assistant adjutant general, and inspector general of state troops on the staff of Governor Francis R. Lubbock.qv After the Civil Warqv he became the editor of the San Antonio *Herald*.qv He held this position through the entire period of Reconstructionqv and is said to have done much for the cause of intersectional harmony. Dashiell first married a Miss Cottman. Upon her death he married Mildred Walker Hornsby of Kentucky, who died in October 1862. In 1866 he married Mrs. S. A. Ringold. Three daughters and three sons from these marriages grew to adulthood. Dashiell died on March 14, 1888. His papers are preserved at the Barker Texas History Center,qv University of Texas at Austin.

BIBLIOGRAPHY: Ellis A. Davis and Edwin H. Grobe, comps., *The New Encyclopedia of Texas,* 4-vol. ed. Francis B. Heitman, *Historical Register and Dictionary of the United States Army* (2 vols., Washington: GPO, 1903; rpt., Urbana: University of Illinois Press, 1965). Amelia W. Williams and Eugene C. Barker, eds., *The Writings of Sam Houston, 1813–1863* (8 vols., Austin: University of Texas Press, 1938–43; rpt., Austin and New York: Pemberton Press, 1970).

Thomas W. Cutrer

DASHIELL, L. TRAVIS (1869–1924). L. Travis Dashiell, lawyer and legislator, son of Benjamin D. and Julia A. Dashiell, was born at Chappell Hill, Texas, on April 30, 1869. From 1886 to 1890 he attended the University of Texas, where he was commencement orator of the Rusk Literary Society in 1889. He was admitted to the bar at Centerville in 1891 and appointed county attorney of Leon County in January 1892. He was a member of the Twenty-third through the Twenty-fifth legislatures, speaker of the House of the Twenty-fifth Legislature, and secretary of state from January 1907 to February 1908. He died on October 21, 1924, of a self-inflicted bullet wound and was buried at Jewett.

BIBLIOGRAPHY: Dallas *Morning News,* October 23, 1924. E. H. Loughery, *Texas State Government* (Austin: McLeod and Jackson, 1897). Vertical Files, Barker Texas History Center, University of Texas at Austin.

D'ASTI, BARTHOLOMEW (1827–1866). Bartholomew (Rev. Augustine) D'Asti, Franciscan missionary to the poor of Houston, was born at San Damiano D'Asti, Piedmont, in 1827. According to annals of the Franciscansqv he came from a noble and wealthy family. At sixteen he entered the reformed order of St. Francis to study for the priesthood, bringing with him a substantial sum of money. He spent the next thirteen years doing missionary work in Italy, as well as studying for doctorates in theology and philosophy at the University of Turin. He held the chair in philosophy at Turin when he decided to move to the United States in 1856. D'Asti and four Franciscan companions traveled to New York, where they established a house for their order. In addition they built a seminary, a convent for women of the minor order of St. Francis, and a college now known as St. Bonaventure University. When, in 1860, Bishop Jean M. Odinqv of Galveston, Texas, wrote to the friars in New York asking if some of them would be willing to move to his diocese to help reopen the missions left empty after the Texas Revolution,qv D'Asti responded to the call. He took two other Franciscan priests with him and arrived in Houston in May of the same year. Odin assigned D'Asti a pastorate at St. Vincent's Church in Houston, then located on Franklin Avenue between Caroline and San Jacinto streets. The Italian priest thus became the first Franciscan to work in Texas since the Spanish friars were forced to leave the area in 1832.

D'Asti's arrival in Texas coincided with the beginning of the Civil War,qv and the city of Houston already suffered from the poverty that spread throughout the South as a result of the war. D'Asti responded to the situation by selling all that he had and giving the proceeds to the poor. He then began a practice for which he became beloved among the citizens of Houston—that of walking the streets to beg funds from merchants and other wealthy people and giving the money to John Kennedy, owner of a local trading post, who distributed the donations to the needy while D'Asti tried to remain anonymous. In addition to endearing himself to his people by his works of charity, the pastor of St. Vincent's became a vibrant part of his community because of his loyalty to its cause. It is said that he blessed the Confederate flag that Lt. Richard W. Dowlingqv and his Jefferson Davis Guards took into the battle of Sabine Pass.qv

D'Asti died on March 12, 1866, at the age of thirty-nine. He was in poor health when he became pastor of St. Vincent's and seems to have been poisoned by water from a lead pipe. Most businesses in Houston closed for his funeral. His remains were to have been sent back to Allegheny, New York, for burial in the Franciscan cemetery there, but the people of Houston objected, and he was buried on the grounds beside St. Vincent's Church. His body was moved to St. Vincent's Cemetery on Navigation Boulevard in 1878 and again in 1915 to Holy Cross Cemetery, where the grave remained unmarked until a headstone was donated in 1953. D'Asti is now buried with eighteen other priests in Holy Cross mausoleum. Houston's St. Nicholas, as D'Asti has been called, has had a lasting impact on the Houston community, most notably through the D'Asti House, which bears his name. There, through the efforts of the Third Order of St. Francis, donated clothes are washed and mended by volunteers and distributed to the poor.

BIBLIOGRAPHY: Catholic Archives of Texas, Files, Austin. Robert C. Giles, *Changing Times: The Story of the Diocese of Galveston-Houston in Commemoration of Its Founding* (Houston, 1972).

Mary H. Ogilvie

DATANA INDIANS. The Datana Indians are known from a 1691 Spanish missionary report, which identifies them as a tribe living eighty leagues southwest of the Hasinai Indians of eastern Texas. The affiliations of the Datana Indians remain unknown.

BIBLIOGRAPHY: John R. Swanton, *Source Material on the History and Ethnology of the Caddo Indians* (Smithsonian Institution, Bureau of American Ethnology Bulletin 132, Washington: GPO, 1942).

Thomas N. Campbell

DATCHO INDIANS. The Datcho Indians were met by Henri Joutelqv in northeast Texas in 1687. He reported them as being enemies of the Caddo Indians.

BIBLIOGRAPHY: Frederick Webb Hodge, ed., *Handbook of American Indians North of Mexico* (2 vols., Washington: GPO, 1907, 1910; rpt., New York: Pageant, 1959).

Margery H. Krieger

DATURA, TEXAS. Datura, on Farm Road 1951 three miles south of Coolidge in northern Limestone County, appears to have formed in the late 1890s. A post office operated there from 1899 until sometime after 1930; Arthur C. Bayliss was the first postmaster. Datura became a shipping point for the Trinity and Brazos Valley Railway around 1900, and in 1902 the community had one store, operated by C. V. Reed. By 1914 the town reported a population of 100 and seven businesses. Its railroad line later became a part of the Burlington–Rock Island Railroad but was discontinued about 1935. In the mid-1940s Datura had a population of 100 and one business, and the 1948 county highway map showed two churches serving widely scattered rural residences in the area. In 1968 the Datura school was incorporated into the Mexia Independent School District, and by 1978 the community consisted of scattered dwellings and one business. Datura still existed in 1990.

BIBLIOGRAPHY: Ray A. Walter, *A History of Limestone County* (Austin: Von Boeckmann–Jones, 1959).

Stephanie Panus

DAUGHERTY, JACAMIAH SEAMAN (1849–1919). Jacamiah Seaman Daugherty, entrepreneur and land dealer, the son of Robert W.

and Lydia E. Seaman (Bryan) Daugherty, was born in Sullivan County, Missouri, on August 25, 1849. He attended the University of Kentucky for three years before moving to Texas in 1872. He taught school for a year at the Cedar Hill district school in Dallas and in 1873 opened a real estate office that expanded to become the firm of Daugherty, Connellee, and Ammerman, which had large holdings in Eastland County. The firm was instrumental in laying out Eastland and in making the new community the Eastland county seat in place of Merriman. In 1879 the Texas Trunk Railroad built a depot named for Daugherty on land he had purchased and improved in Kaufman County.

In 1888 Daugherty organized what may have been the first real estate association in Texas and the Texas Bureau of Immigration. He also obtained contracts to supply thirteen United States military posts in Texas with grain and hay obtained from Texas, Oklahoma, and Kansas. When the crop failed, financial reversals took him to Houston, where he developed mineral resources and real estate. In 1894 he acquired 6,000 acres in Harris County, provided a right-of-way and obtained a siding for the San Antonio and Aransas Pass Railway, founded Dairy (later Alief), and introduced the production of rice there.

Daugherty was active in the conflict over requiring Texas cattlemen to pay rent to the public school fund for school lands used in grazing cattle, the conflict that led to the formation of the Railroad Commission,qv and the effort to require banks to provide funds to protect depositors against loss. His Silver Day speech delivered at the Chicago World's Fair in 1893 became campaign literature for advocates of free silver. He is credited with the idea for the "business league" and served as chairman of the first league in Dallas from 1882 to 1888. From 1890 to 1895 he promoted efforts of the Good Roads Committee and by 1909 was chairman of the Harris County Drainage District and active in working for a deep-water harbor at Galveston. Daugherty married Margaret Cartmell Bryan on December 19, 1878; the couple had at least three children. He died in a railway-crossing accident at Fulton, Kentucky, on September 27, 1919.

BIBLIOGRAPHY: Ellis A. Davis and Edwin H. Grobe, comps., *The New Encyclopedia of Texas*, 2-vol. ed. Houston *Post*, September 28, 1919. Frank W. Johnson, *A History of Texas and Texans* (5 vols., ed. E. C. Barker and E. W. Winkler [Chicago and New York: American Historical Society, 1914; rpt. 1916]). Carolyne Lavinia Langston, *History of Eastland County* (Dallas: Aldridge 1904).   *Diana J. Kleiner*

DAUGHERTY, JAMES MONROE (1850–1942). James Monroe Daugherty, cattleman, the son of James M. and Eleanor (McGhee or McGehee) Daugherty, was born on February 27, 1850, in Texas County, Missouri. In 1851 he moved with his parents, five brothers, and one sister to Denton County, Texas. James M. Daugherty attended McKenzie College near Clarksville from 1861 to 1864. At the age of fourteen he joined the Confederate Army as an express rider delivering dispatches for Gen. Samuel Cooper's brigade. After the Civil Warqv Daugherty moved to San Antonio, where he hired on as a cowboy for cattle-raiser James Adams. In 1866, at the age of sixteen, Daugherty persuaded Adams to let him drive 500 head of cattle to the new market that was rumored to be opening in Missouri. Thus Daugherty, starting at Denton, Texas, participated in the fabled long drive of the open-range cattle business at its inception. Despite Daugherty's near death, and the loss of 150 head of cattle stolen by Jayhawkers, the drive was successful, with the herd being sold for thirty-five dollars a head at Fort Scott, Kansas. From 1867 to 1873 he drove cattle to Indian Territory for the government to feed the Indians. Sometime before 1872 he acquired a ranch near Trinidad, Colorado. After completing several contracts with the government, Daugherty started a ranch in Stonewall County, Texas, on the South Fork of the Brazos River, establishing his home in Abilene while pursuing a career in raising, buying, and marketing cattle on a large scale. In 1875 he married Sara Elizabeth (Bettie) Middleton, daughter of a pioneer cattleman; they had five children, born between 1880 and 1887. Daugherty became prominent in local civic affairs—as a member of the Progressive Committee of Abilene, as the first president of Abilene National Bank, and as secretary of the Abilene Cattle Association. In 1900 Daugherty moved to a portion of El Paso County, Texas, that later became Culberson County. He started the Figure 2 Ranch, the Black Mountain Cattle Company, and the community of Daugherty, where his ranch headquarters was located. He was one of the organizers of Culberson County, serving as an early commissioner. Daugherty was on the board of county commissioners when the first county courthouse was constructed in Van Horn, Texas. He was also the organizer of both the Van Horn State Bank and the Sierra Blanca State Bank. Daugherty was one of the first members of the Cattle Raisers Association of Texas (later the Texas and Southwestern Cattle Raisers Associationqv) and served twice as a delegate for that organization at the National Livestock Association Convention. He was a charter member of the Trail Drivers Association.qv James M. Daugherty's wife died on January 23, 1924, and he spent his remaining years on his ranch near Van Horn, Texas. He died on March 2, 1942, at the home of his daughter in Alpine, Texas. Some of Daugherty's papers, including account and tally books, are in the Barker Texas History Center at the University of Texas at Austin.

BIBLIOGRAPHY: *Abilene Remembered: Our Centennial Treasury Book, 1881–1981* (Abilene: Abilene *Reporter-News*, 1981). Abilene *Reporter-News*, March 29, 1884. James Cox, *Historical and Biographical Record of the Cattle Industry* (2 vols., St. Louis: Woodward and Tiernan Printing, 1894, 1895; rpt., with an introduction by J. Frank Dobie, New York: Antiquarian, 1959). J. Marvin Hunter, *Trail Drivers of Texas* (2 vols., San Antonio: Jackson Printing, 1920, 1923; 4th ed., Austin: University of Texas Press, 1985). Buckley B. Paddock, ed., *A Twentieth Century History and Biographical Record of North and West Texas* (Chicago: Lewis, 1906). Clarence R. Wharton, ed., *Texas under Many Flags* (5 vols., Chicago: American Historical Society, 1930).
Deborah Blank

DAUGHERTY, TEXAS (Culberson County). Daugherty, also known as the Figure Two Ranch, was a ranching community on State Highway 54 some thirty miles north of Van Horn in western Culberson County. In 1883 the R. P. (Perry) Bean family from Lampasas County settled at the site of what is now the Figure Two Ranch and established the B Ranch; they moved their headquarters in 1885. Several other ranches were established in the area in subsequent years, and in 1900 James M. Daughertyqv bought one of them, the Black Mountain Cattle Company, and changed its name to Figure Two Ranch. A local post office was established in 1912 with Daugherty as postmaster. Two years later the community had three cattle-breeding businesses: those of James M. Daugherty, F. X. Daugherty, and Young and Daugherty. Although the post office closed in 1927, the Figure Two Ranch survived for decades. In the mid-1970s maps of the area showed a barn and a handful of dwellings, and the ranch was still marked on maps in the late 1980s.   *Martin Donell Kohout*

DAUGHERTY, TEXAS (Rains County). Daugherty was at the junction of Farm roads 275 and 514, six miles north of Emory in northern Rains County. It was first settled around the time of the Civil War.qv During the 1930s the community had a church, a school, and two businesses. After World War IIqv its school and businesses closed, and in the early 1990s only the church and a community center remained in the area.   *Christopher Long*

DAUGHTERS OF THE AMERICAN COLONISTS. The Texas Society of the Daughters of the American Colonists, was organized in Washington, D.C., in March 30, 1930. Membership in June 1991 totaled 870 in twenty-one chapters located in various Texas cities. The National Society was organized in Washington, D.C., in April 1921 and in 1991 had over 10,000 members in fifty states and the District of Columbia. According to its bylaws, "The object of this society shall be patriotic, historical and educational; to make research as to the history and deeds of the American colonists and to record and publish the same; to commemorate deeds of colonial interest; to inculcate and foster love of America and its institutions by all its residents; to obey its laws and venerate its flag—the emblem of its power and civic righteousness." The Texas Society researches historical sites in Texas to be considered for markers. Its efforts have included Fort Bliss, Fort Crockett, and Nuestra Señora de Guadalupe de los Nacogdoches Mission.

BIBLIOGRAPHY: Vertical Files, Barker Texas History Center, University of Texas at Austin.

Josephine C. Kirby

DAUGHTERS OF THE AMERICAN REVOLUTION. The Texas Society of the Daughters of the American Revolution was organized in 1900 with five chapters. The membership in 1992 was 17,000 in 184 chapters. Each chapter has officers and committees to correspond to those on the state and national levels. To be eligible for membership a woman must be at least eighteen years of age and be descended from a man or woman who, with unfailing loyalty, rendered aid to the cause of American independence. The purpose of the society is to perpetuate the memory and spirit of the men and women who achieved American independence, to promote the general diffusion of knowledge, to cherish, maintain, and extend the institutions of American freedom, and to foster true patriotism and love of country. During the first half of the twentieth century the Texas Society contributed to national building projects, and during World War II[qv] it helped with plasma drives and fund-raising for the Red Cross and United Service Organization. Important state projects included marking the Old San Antonio Road[qv] with granite markers at five-mile intervals along 600 miles of the trail in 1920. The Texas Society was also active in the Texas Centennial[qv] and continues to emphasize preservation of historic monuments and landmarks. Outstanding among the many phases of the society are scholarships given to various schools and universities, the Junior American Citizen clubs, the Good Citizen program, the national defense material available from the National Society in Washington, D.C., and manuals for citizenship, written in eighteen different languages and used by foreigners in becoming citizens of the United States.

BIBLIOGRAPHY: *History of the Texas Society, National Society, Daughters of the American Revolution* (N.p.: Texas Society, DAR, 1975).

Marie B. Horn

DAUGHTERS OF CHARITY OF ST. VINCENT DE PAUL. In October 1869 the International Order of the Daughters of Charity, founded in 1633 by St. Vincent de Paul in Paris and in 1809 in the United States by Mother Elizabeth Bailey Seton, opened their first institution in Texas, an elementary school in Jefferson City. It took the six sisters assigned to teach in the school three weeks to travel the 800 miles from New Orleans. The school opened with five pupils, and by 1870 the enrollment had increased to fifteen. Within five years the population of Jefferson City had declined considerably as the railroad replaced the river trade, and so the sisters were withdrawn in 1875.

The second Texas institution opened by the order was in El Paso, a frontier town of only a few thousand residents when three Daughters of Charity arrived on February 3, 1892. The interested citizens of El Paso requested the nursing sisters to establish a hospital similar to Charity Hospital in New Orleans. The hospital rented space until the construction of the permanent building of the Hotel Dieu, named and modeled after the great hospital in Paris. The Hotel Dieu of El Paso remains on the site. Realizing the need for professionally trained personnel to care for the sick, the sisters established a school of nursing connected with the Hotel Dieu in 1898, and for the next seventy-seven years the majority of the hospital's nurses were educated in this school. In 1973 the institution closed, but nursing education continued through the auspices of the University of Texas System School of Nursing, which had established a baccalaureate program using the Hotel Dieu's facilities in 1972.

The expanding work of the Daughters of Charity took them to Dallas in 1895. There they took charge of St. Joseph's Orphanage in Oak Cliff and operated it for twelve years, despite great poverty and hardships. In 1896 Sister Stella located a suitable site in Dallas and made plans for a 110-bed hospital and clinic. St. Paul Hospital was established on June 15, 1898, with a staff of nine sisters. The first surgery was performed on June 17, 1898. In 1918, when the influenza epidemic was rampant, sixty-three tents were placed on the St. Paul Hospital grounds to take care of the overflow of critically ill and convalescent patients. The hospital, known today as St. Paul Medical Center, has expanded its facilities to include a cancer center, a patient-care tower, and a center for the elderly. The hospital is now affiliated with the University of Texas Southwestern Medical School.

Many important agencies, including hospitals, schools, a residential treatment center, and parish ministries, have been established by the Daughters of Charity in Texas since the turn of the century. Seton Medical Center, now a thriving facility known for its neonatal and cardiac units, was founded by the order in Austin in 1902. In Waco the sisters established Providence Hospital, which has been in operation since 1904. Holy Trinity Grade School and High School opened in Dallas in 1914, Our Lady of Victory Elementary School was founded in Beeville in 1983, and parish ministries have been begun by the order in Alpine, Cotulla, Odessa, Pampa, and San Antonio. In 1993 there were eighty Daughters of Charity serving in forty agencies located in fourteen towns or cities in Texas. On the occasion of the 350th anniversary of the Daughters of Charity and their 125th anniversary in Texas, the order received official congratulations from President Ronald Reagan, from the United States Congress, from the governor of Texas, and from many other civic and community leaders.

BIBLIOGRAPHY: Daughters of Charity Archives, West Central Province, Marillac Provincial House, St. Louis, Missouri. Catholic Archives of Texas, Files, Austin.

Sister Aloysius Williams, D.C.

DAUGHTERS OF THE REPUBLIC OF TEXAS. The Daughters of the Republic of Texas is the oldest patriotic women's organization in Texas and one of the oldest in the nation. In 1891 Betty Ballinger[qv] and Hally Bryan (later Hally Bryan Perry[qv]) formulated plans for an association to be composed of women who were direct descendants of the men and women who established the Republic of Texas.[qv] They were encouraged in their efforts by Hally Bryan's father, Guy M. Bryan,[qv] a member of the Texas Veterans Association.[qv] The organizational meeting was held on November 6, 1891, in the Houston home of Mary Jane Briscoe.[qv] Mary S. M. Jones,[qv] widow of the last president of the Republic of Texas, agreed to serve as president. The motto "Texas, One and Indivisible" was suggested by Colonel Bryan. The name first chosen for this group was Daughters of Female Descendants of the Heroes of '36; the association was renamed Daughters of the Lone Star Republic, then Daughters of the Republic of Texas at the first annual meeting in April 1892. The organization was planned as a companion to the Texas Veterans Association, and the two groups held joint meetings until the veterans disbanded in 1907.

The objectives of the association are to perpetuate the memory and spirit of the people who achieved and maintained the independence of Texas and to encourage historical research into the earliest records of Texas, especially those relating to the revolutionary and republic periods. The DRT encourages the preservation of documents and relics, the publication of historical records and narratives, and the celebration of important days in the state's history. It also encourages the teaching of Texas history in public schools and sponsors the placement of historical markers.

The Daughters hold an annual business meeting on or about May 14, the day on which the Treaties of Velasco[qv] were signed. Between the annual meetings the board of management, consisting of the president general and twenty-five officers general, oversees the association. Members are required to be women who can prove lineal descent from a man or woman who served Texas before annexation[qv] (1846). As of 1994 more than 6,500 members were organized into 108 chapters throughout the state. Local chapters also sponsor chapters of the Children of the Republic of Texas, a junior association organized in San Antonio in 1929. Members must be under the age of twenty-one and must prove the same lineal descent as DRT members.

One of the association's early projects was to persuade the Texas legislature to purchase the land on which the battle of San Jacinto[qv] was fought. The Daughters placed battlefield markers on the important sites pointed out by members of the Veterans Association. A more recent and continuing project is the placement of bronze medallions on the graves of citizens of the Republic of Texas. The Daughters were instrumental in the state's decision to purchase life-size statues of Stephen F. Austin and Sam Houston[qqv] sculpted by Elisabet Ney[qv] for the rotunda of the Capitol[qv] in Austin. The DRT also used its influence to place a monument at Washington-on-the-Brazos, where the Texas Declaration of Independence[qv] was signed.

In 1905, through the combined efforts of the association and two of its members, Clara Driscoll and Adina de Zavala,[qqv] the Daughters became custodians of the Alamo[qv] in San Antonio. In accordance with their agreement with the state, they have maintained the chapel and surrounding grounds and gardens without cost to taxpayers and with no admission charge. The Daughters of the Republic of Texas Library[qv] at the Alamo is open to all researchers. The original Long Barrack building has been restored and is currently being used as a museum. Additional buildings, including a museum and greenhouse, have been erected on the grounds.

In Austin the DRT maintains the French Legation,[qv] built in 1840 for the French diplomatic mission to the Republic of Texas. The sale of the property was finalized by the state of Texas on May 6, 1949, and the building was placed in the custody of the Daughters on August 25, 1949, who researched the legation with the help of historians and architects. The restored legation was opened to the public on April 15, 1956.

The DRT appealed to the legislature to save the Old Land Office Building[qv] on the southeast corner of the Capitol grounds in Austin, and in 1917 it was designated for use as a museum and headquarters for the association, which maintained a museum and business office on the top floor until 1989. The United Daughters of the Confederacy[qv] had a Confederate museum on the lower floor. The DRT purchased its own building in Austin to house the museum and headquarters, which they opened to the public on November 6, 1991. The DRT also owns and maintains the Cradle, a small building in Galveston where Betty Ballinger and Hally Bryan made plans to organize the association.

On August 11, 1961, the legislature adopted the Daughters' design for the reverse side of the Great Seal of Texas (*see* SEALS OF TEXAS). Sarah Roach Farnsworth of San Antonio produced the design, which incorporates the six flags of Texas, the Alamo, the Gonzales "Come and Take It" cannon,[qv] and Vince's Bridge,[qv] destroyed by Erastus (Deaf) Smith[qv] on orders from Gen. Sam Houston[qv] at the battle of San Jacinto. The original watercolor painting of the design, by Joy Harrell Carrington of Medina, hangs in the office of the Texas secretary of state.

In 1986 the Daughters buried a time capsule containing memorabilia of the Sesquicentennial celebration at the Cradle in Galveston. The capsule is to be opened during the Texas Bicentennial in the year 2036. On April 12, 1987, the DRT dedicated a bronze and marble plaque at the site where the original international boundary marker between the United States and the Republic of Texas still stands.

The DRT has sponsored the publication of several volumes of Texas history and biography and has published the lineages of its members in the multivolume *Founders and Patriots of the Republic of Texas* (1963–). Since 1928 the DRT has sponsored an annual fellowship, named for Clara Driscoll in 1930, awarded to a University of Texas student doing research on the state's history. In 1986 the association established the Texas Sesquicentennial Fellowship under the same guidelines.

BIBLIOGRAPHY: Daughters of the Republic of Texas, *Fifty Years of Achievement: History of the Daughters of the Republic of Texas* (Dallas: Banks, Upshaw, 1942). Daughters of the Republic of Texas, *Ninety Years of the Daughters: History of the Daughters of the Republic of Texas* (Waco: Texian, 1981). *Proceedings of the . . . Annual Convention of the Daughters of the Republic of Texas* (Austin, 1891–).

Mrs. Grady Rash, Jr.

DAUGHTERS OF THE REPUBLIC OF TEXAS LIBRARY. The Daughters of the Republic of Texas Library is a part of the historical complex of the Alamo[qv] in San Antonio. It is supported and maintained by the Daughters of the Republic of Texas[qv] and serves objectives included in their charter of 1895: encouraging research into early Texas records and preserving documents. The library operates under the direction of a library committee, which is responsible to the board of management of the Daughters of the Republic of Texas. It is open to researchers free of charge six days a week.

The DRT Library was established on October 12, 1945, in Alamo Hall, a building southeast of the Alamo, with opening ceremonies honoring Dr. William Eager Howard,[qv] who donated the nucleus of its collections. The forerunner of the library was the William E. Howard Library and Collection—over 2,000 Texas books, documents, manuscripts, and paintings—presented to the Daughters on June 10, 1943, and housed in Alamo Hall.

The present library building, built immediately west of Alamo Hall, was opened on December 2, 1950, and was constructed with funds donated by Sallie Ward Beretta[qv] honoring the memory of her husband, John King Beretta, who had been a friend of Howard's. An extension between the library building and Alamo Hall, for additional study and work space, was opened on February 6, 1964. An addition to the north side of the building, which contains a vault, a map room, study carrels, and storage, work, and office space, was dedicated on April 19, 1971, and on April 11, 1975, an addition of a meeting room and more work space to the south side of the building was dedicated.

The Daughters of the Republic of Texas Library is a noncirculating research library of Texas history, with particular emphasis on the republic period and on the Alamo and San Antonio history. The collections include books, newspapers and periodicals, family papers, genealogical records, documents, maps, architectural renderings, clipping files, fine arts, artifacts, and photographs—notably the Grandjean collection. Among primary source materials are Spanish royal and viceregal documents dating from the sixteenth century, the Bustillo, Cassiano-Perez, and John W. Smith[qv] manuscript collections, and the Gentilz art collection (*see* GENTILZ, JEAN L. T.). The library's materials are acquired through direct gifts and through purchases made from donated funds. Donors to the library have also established endowment and trust funds to support its operations.

The library has published a catalog of holdings and books and booklets on Texas historical subjects; it issues a periodic newsletter. The DRT Library is a member of the Council of Research and Academic Libraries and the Texas Archival Network. It also maintains memberships in national and regional historical, archival, and library associations.

When the library began its first year of operation, it was open three days a week and employed a single librarian. By 1984 its staff had increased to seven. Patrons during the 1980s approached 2,000 a year, and the library responded to approximately 350 written and 4,000 telephoned inquiries annually. In 1994 the library had five professional and three paraprofessional staff positions, and the size of the general collection had reached 17,500. Other library holdings include manuscript collections, maps, photographs, periodicals, newspapers, clippings, and sheet music.

The Daughters of the Republic of Texas Library was initially supervised by Mrs. Leita Small, custodian of the Alamo, and has been under the direction of librarians Cora Carleton Glassford, Marg-Riette Montgomery Hamlett, Carmen Perry, Catherine McDowell, Sharon Crutchfield, and Cathy Herpick.

BIBLIOGRAPHY: Catherine McDowell, comp., *A Guide to the Texana Holdings of the Texas History Library of the Daughters of the Republic of Texas* (San Antonio: DRT Library, 1978). *Proceedings of the ... Annual Convention of the Daughters of the Republic of Texas* (Austin, 1891–).
Martha D. Utterback

DAUPHIN, TEXAS. Dauphin was a flag stop on the St. Louis Southwestern Railway 5½ miles southwest of Athens in central Henderson County. A post office operated there from 1895 to 1904. After the railroad suspended service, most of the residents moved away, but as late as the mid-1930s a store and a church were in the area. In the early 1990s only a few scattered houses remained in the vicinity.
Christopher Long

DAVAGE, MATTHEW SIMPSON (1879–1976). Matthew S. Davage, black educator and Methodist churchman, the son of Rev. Samuel and Harriet (Lee) Davage, was born on June 16, 1879, in Shreveport, Louisiana. The family moved to New Orleans, where Davage attended New Orleans University (later called Dillard) and was the catcher and captain of the University Nine baseball team. He was eighteen years old and still a full-time student at New Orleans University when he began teaching school in the evening. Upon graduating from the Classical Department at New Orleans University in 1900, Davage began teaching mathematics and Latin and did postgraduate study at the University of Chicago and Columbia University. He married Alice Vera Armstead in 1904. He held the chair in math at New Orleans University and was business manager for the *Southwestern Christian Advocate* from 1905 to 1915. He presided over Methodist institutions of higher learning for most of his professional career. He served as president of George R. Smith College at Sedalia, Missouri, 1915–16; Haven Institute, Meridian, Mississippi, 1916–17; Samuel Huston College, Austin, Texas, 1917–20; Rust College, Holly Springs, Mississippi, 1920–24; and Clark University, Atlanta, Georgia, 1924–41.

Davage was a member of the board of trustees of eight colleges and secretary of the Department of Higher Education of the Methodist Board of Education for twelve years. From 1940 to 1952 he was director of all Methodist colleges for African Americans[qv] in the United States. He helped obtain accreditation for the colleges he served. He was also instrumental in building and stabilizing the finances of the colleges under his jurisdiction. He raised the combined operating budgets of these schools to more than $5.3 million. He was elected a member of the Methodist quadrennial General Council eleven times and served as a member of the Methodist ecumenical conferences from 1931 to 1951. He was also a member of the administrative board of the Commission on Christian Higher Education of the Association of American Colleges and held the record for the longest tenure on the Methodist Board of Publications. Davage led the movement to merge Samuel Huston and Tillotson colleges in Austin and became interim president of the new Huston-Tillotson College. He guided the transition period of the new college until his retirement in 1955. He died in a New Orleans hospital on September 20, 1976.

BIBLIOGRAPHY: Austin *American-Statesman*, September 22, 1976. James P. Brawley, *Two Centuries of Methodist Concern: Bondage, Freedom, and Education of Black People* (New York: Vantage, 1974). Nolan B. Harmon, ed., *The Encyclopedia of World Methodism* (2 vols., Nashville: United Methodist Publishing House, 1974). Vertical Files, Barker Texas History Center, University of Texas at Austin (Huston-Tillotson College, Matthew S. Davage).
Walter N. Vernon

DAVENPORT, HARBERT (1882–1957). Harbert Davenport, lawyer and historian, was born in Eastland, Texas, on October 19, 1882, the son of O. H. and Elizabeth (Merril) Davenport. In 1904 he married Elizabeth Pettit; they had two sons. After living in Rusk for two years, the family resided in Austin from 1906 to 1908, when Davenport received an LL.B. from the University of Texas. He practiced law in Anahuac until 1912, the year he established permanent residence in Brownsville, where he was a law associate of Judge James B. Wells, Jr.[qv] During World War I[qv] Davenport became a second lieutenant in the air corps. He was recognized as an authority on southwestern land and water law and on Spanish and Mexican law as it applied to Texas. Concerned with procuring needed water legislation for the Rio Grande valley, Davenport wrote "The Texas Law on Flowing Waters as Applied to Irrigation from the Lower Rio Grande." One of his important legal cases involved the disputed title to Padre Island.[qv] In 1944 the state Supreme Court decided the case in favor of the descendants of Padre Nicolás Ballí,[qv] who had received the original land grant from the Spanish government in 1800. As a historian, Davenport was particularly interested in early Spanish expeditions, personnel of the Goliad campaigns, and the history of the lower Rio Grande area. He contributed several articles to the *Southwestern Historical Quarterly*.[qv] From 1922 to 1955 he was a member of the executive council of the Texas State Historical Association,[qv] and from 1939 to 1942 he was president of the association. He also served as a member of the Brownsville school board from 1924 to 1932 and contributed to the American Legion[qv] and other civic organizations. He died on February 23, 1957, and was buried in Buena Vista Cemetery, Brownsville.

BIBLIOGRAPHY: Brownsville *Herald*, February 24, 25, 1957.
Wortham Davenport and Harbert Davenport, Jr.

DAVENPORT, JOHN G. (?–1838). John G. Davenport, newspaper publisher and judge, moved to Texas in the mid-1830s from Tuscaloosa, Alabama, where he had practiced law for some time. He settled in Matagorda County, where he served as chief justice and judge of probate in 1837–38. On June 28, 1838, he purchased the Matagorda *Bulletin*[qv] from John Warren J. Niles. Davenport edited the paper until his death in October 1838.

BIBLIOGRAPHY: Joe B. Frantz, Newspapers of the Republic of Texas (M.A. thesis, University of Texas, 1940). Matagorda *Bulletin*, October 4, 1838. Marilyn M. Sibley, *Lone Stars and State Gazettes: Texas Newspapers before the Civil War* (College Station: Texas A&M University Press, 1983).
Christopher Long

DAVENPORT, PETER SAMUEL (1764–1824). Peter Samuel Davenport, pioneer merchant and quartermaster to filibustering expeditions, son of William and Ann (Davidson) Davenport, was born on February 4, 1764, at Carlisle, Cumberland County, Pennsylvania. In 1780, after the death of his parents, he left Pennsylvania and traveled to Louisiana; he survived an Indian attack on the way. He settled near Natchitoches where he "engaged in commerce," working for well-known firms and for himself. In 1798 Davenport entered into partnership with William Barr,[qv] Luther Smith, and Edward Murphy under the name House of Barr and Davenport,[qv] and the firm soon secured a monopoly on trade with all Texas Indians from the Spanish government. Davenport became the local agent for the business and in time established his headquarters in the Old Stone Fort[qv] in Nacogdoches. In 1810, as the sole surviving partner, he continued to operate the enterprise on his own and became independently wealthy.

Davenport went back to Natchitoches Parish in 1802, where he married Marie Louise Gagnon. They had four children. A son, Juan

Benigno, married Jane Beall Edwards, daughter of empresario^{qv} Haden Edwards,^{qv} on November 12, 1829. When the Gutiérrez-Magee expedition^{qv} reached Nacogdoches in 1812, Davenport joined forces with the filibusters, furnished them with great quantities of arms and ammunition, assisted Capt. James Gaines^{qv} in raising a group of volunteers from east of the Trinity River, and marched with them toward San Antonio. Before reaching San Antonio, he became captain of a company of volunteers who participated in the capture of La Bahía,^{qv} whereupon he returned to Nacogdoches to obtain more supplies.

After the collapse of the Gutiérrez-Magee expedition in 1813, Davenport, now a fugitive from Spanish authorities with a price on his head, fled across the Sabine River into Natchitoches Parish, Louisiana. There he established himself on a luxurious plantation called Grand Ecore, where he remained until 1819, when he enlisted in James Long's^{qv} expedition into Texas. Before the failure of Long's filibustering effort, Davenport furnished supplies to the expedition's forces and served as a member of the governing council of Long's republic. He then returned to Grand Ecore. On a visit to Hot Springs, Arkansas, for his failing health, Davenport died, on October 19, 1824. His body was returned to Natchitoches Parish and buried in the Russell Cemetery at Grand Ecore. At his death he owned some 50,000 acres of land in eastern Texas and western Louisiana, forty-one slaves, and a great number of cattle, horses, and other livestock. His wife had died on February 27, 1812, in Nacogdoches and was buried there.

BIBLIOGRAPHY: J. Villasana Haggard, "The House of Barr and Davenport," *Southwestern Historical Quarterly* 45 (July 1945).

Joe E. Ericson

DAVENPORT, TEXAS (Anderson County). Davenport was just south of Farm Road 1137 and six miles east of Palestine in eastern Anderson County. In the 1930s the community had a church and the black school for the Swanson Spring school district. Its school served some sixty-six pupils in 1932, but by 1955 had been consolidated with the Palestine schools. In 1982 only a single dwelling was at the site, and in 1985 Davenport was no longer named on county highway maps.

BIBLIOGRAPHY: Thomas Paul Jones, The Reorganization of the Public Schools of Anderson County, Texas (M.Ed. thesis, University of Texas, 1934).

Mark Odintz

DAVENPORT, TEXAS (Coryell County). Davenport, fifteen miles from Gatesville in western Coryell County, was named for John A. Davenport, who became postmaster when the community's post office opened in 1879. It was discontinued in 1882, and mail for the community was sent to King. The community was not marked on county highway maps in the 1980s.

BIBLIOGRAPHY: Coryell County Genealogical Society, *Coryell County, Texas, Families, 1854–1985* (Dallas: Taylor, 1986). John J. Germann and Myron Janzen, *Texas Post Offices by County* (1986).

Vivian Elizabeth Smyrl

DAVENPORT, TEXAS (Red River County). Davenport is on a bend in the Red River eleven miles east of the Lamar county line in north central Red River County. When a community began to form there in the early 1880s, it was often called Jonesboro because it occupied the site of Jonesborough, one of the first settlements in the county. A post office opened in 1885 in James H. Johnson's store, and the community took the name Davenport. In 1890 its population was reported as fifty, but it fell to twenty-five by 1910. The community's post office was closed in 1922. In 1933 its population was estimated at forty-four. By 1984 Davenport consisted of a few widely scattered houses.

BIBLIOGRAPHY: Clarksville *Standard*, June 3, 1881, August 25, 1882.

Cecil Harper, Jr.

DAVENPORT BRANCH. Davenport Branch rises four miles northeast of Marysville in extreme north central Cooke County (at 33°49′ N, 97°18′ W) and runs south for 2½ miles to its mouth on North Fish Creek, three miles northeast of Marysville (at 33°47′ N, 97°17′ W). It traverses variable, often rolling, terrain with soils ranging from shallow and stony clay loams to shallow to deep expansive clays and clay loams. Local vegetation includes oak, juniper, chaparral, cacti, and grasses. The area has served as crop and range land.

DAVENPORT HILL. Davenport Hill is five miles southwest of Concan in north central Uvalde County (at 29°28′ N, 99°48′ W). Its summit, at an elevation of 1,785 feet above sea level, rises some 440 feet above the intersection of Farm Road 1051 and U.S. Highway 83.

DAVID CROCKETT. The *David Crockett* was a keelboat reported to be the first large craft to navigate the Colorado River. On April 11, 1838, it arrived at the head of "the raft on the Colorado," ten miles above the port of Matagorda in Matagorda County, after averaging more than sixty miles a day of daytime navigation. Cargoes of cotton were unloaded there and carried by wagon around the obstructing raft to Matagorda, where they were loaded on ocean-going vessels for shipment.

BIBLIOGRAPHY: William R. Hogan, *The Texas Republic: A Social and Economic History* (Norman: University of Oklahoma Press, 1946; rpt. 1969).

Jeff Carroll

DAVIDIANS AND BRANCH DAVIDIANS. Victor T. Houteff established the Davidians, a small Adventist reform movement, in 1929, and in 1955 Ben Roden organized the Branch Davidians. Both groups were formed to prepare for the second advent of Christ, and both movements survive in small but active communities in the 1990s. Houteff, a Bulgarian immigrant, left the Bulgarian Orthodox Church and accepted Seventh-day Adventist teaching in 1918. He led Sabbath classes in his Los Angeles church and began publishing a series of tracts called collectively *The Shepherd's Rod*. He embraced the Adventist teachings of Christ's imminent return, Saturday worship, dietary regulations and pacifism. But he criticized the General Conference of Seventh-day Adventists for compromise with worldly standards of behavior. The Shepherd's Rod movement called for reform of life. Houteff, like all Adventists, focused above all on the near return of Christ; this is the central idea of the movement. He taught that an elect group of 144,000 followers would form a truly reformed church and that the forming of his pure church was a prerequisite for Christ's return to earth.

When the Seventh-day Adventist Conference rejected his message, Houteff decided to settle in Texas. In 1935 he and thirty-seven followers moved to a site two miles from Waco, which they called Mount Carmel. The Davidians established a semicommunal organization. Because they wanted to avoid the corruptions of the world they settled beyond the city limits. Everyone worked and received pay. Together they farmed and built buildings on their property. But since one farm could not support an entire community, some Davidians worked in Waco and were encouraged by leaders to pay a double tithe. Despite the Great Depression^{qv} the community flourished, and by 1940 it had grown to sixty-four residents, ten buildings, and 375 acres. The members constructed water and sewage systems and added electricity and telephone services. Houteff had full authority in the community. He was viewed as a unique prophet: followers believed that only he could unravel Biblical secrets about the end of time.

Davidians worshipped on Saturday. They practiced vegetarianism and observed strict rules of conduct (no tobacco, dancing, or movies). Women used no cosmetics and wore distinctive long dresses. The group established its own press to print and distribute large numbers of Houteff's tracts. His writings were widely distributed, and Davidians converted scattered pockets of Adventists throughout the United States. Houteff changed the movement's name to Davidian Seventh-day Adventists in a successful effort to achieve conscientious-objector status for his followers. His death in 1955 shook but did not destroy the group, which survived under the leadership of his wife, Florence. By then Waco had grown too close to old Mount Carmel, and the Davidians sold their property for residential development. In 1957 the group bought a 941-acre farm, which they called New Mount Carmel, nine miles east of Waco, near Elk. The Davidians predicted the imminent establishment of God's kingdom. They called on members to gather at New Mount Carmel before April 22, 1959 (Passover). People from California, Wyoming, Canada, and elsewhere sold businesses, farms, and houses to move to Mount Carmel and await a sign from God. About 900 people gathered for this meeting, which began on April 18 and peaked on April 22. Hope soon faded when the sign did not appear, and the Davidians began to disperse rapidly. They sold all but seventy-seven acres of New Mount Carmel, and various Davidian splinters disputed ownership in court.

The most significant of the splinter groups to emerge after Houteff's death was the Branch Davidians, organized by Ben Roden. When the great gathering occurred in 1959, Roden appeared and announced that *he* was the sign the Davidians sought. The 1959 debacle discredited Florence Houteff, and a small following looked to Roden as their new prophet. The Roden faction laid claim to the property at New Mount Carmel. Roden embraced the central teachings of the Seventh-day Adventist church and also Houteff's message regarding the purified church. Roden's own thought centered on the significance of the restored state of Israel. This political fact was for him a key sign of preparation for Christ to return to earth. Roden not only visited Israel; he also established a small community of followers there. When he died in 1978, his wife, Lois, assumed leadership. Her distinctive teaching centered on the female character of the Holy Spirit and ordination for women. She devoted her short-lived journal, *Shekinah*, to women's issues. George Roden, son of Ben and Lois, assumed leadership of the Branch Davidians in 1985 and made messianic claims. Vernon Howell, a persuasive Bible teacher, led a rival faction that George Roden expelled at gunpoint. Howell and his followers moved to Palestine, Texas, but returned to New Mount Carmel in 1987 and exchanged gunfire with Roden. The rivals were taken to court. Roden was jailed, and the Howell faction secured control of New Mount Carmel by paying the back taxes.

Howell perpetuated the distinctive emphases of Davidian tradition—the authoritarian leader, communal life organized apart from society, and expectation of the imminent end of the world. He changed his name to David, suggesting his messianic task, and to Koresh, suggesting that his role was to destroy the enemies of God as King Cyrus had destroyed the Babylonians, enemies of Israel. However, whereas Adventists and Houteff had been pacifists, Koresh stockpiled weapons and ammunition. Finally, he believed that members of the New Kingdom should be children of the Messiah: DNA evidence gathered after his death indicated that he sired thirteen of the Davidian children by seven mothers.

The United States Bureau of Alcohol, Tobacco, and Firearms raided the Davidians on February 28, 1993, for possession of illegal arms. In a shootout both Davidians and ATF forces were killed. A fifty-one-day siege followed. On April 19, 1993, government forces used tanks to precipitate an end to the stand-off. Fire broke out, engulfing the building and killing eighty-one Branch Davidians. The event triggered heated debate over several issues relating to the nature of alternative religious groups, including their understanding of religious authority, arms accumulation, and the interpretation of apocalyptic Biblical images. Debate, including congressional hearings in 1995, also raged over government use of deadly force.

Davidians and Branch Davidians flourish in scattered communities in the United States and beyond. In 1991 Davidians purchased part of Old Mount Carmel, where they reestablished a press for reproducing Houteff's message. The Branch Davidians own New Mount Carmel. Though it has not been rebuilt, a small group meets there regularly for Sabbath study. The best known Davidian artifact is a clock, set in the floor of the central building of Old Mount Carmel, with the hands set near the eleventh hour, indicating that the end of time is near. This physical reminder of the end of time captures perfectly the essence of the Davidians and Branch Davidians. *See also* ADVENTIST CHURCHES.

BIBLIOGRAPHY: James R. Lewis, ed., *From the Ashes: Making Sense of Waco* (Lanham, Maryland: Rowman and Littlefield, 1994). Bill Pitts, "The Davidian Tradition," *Council of Societies for the Study of Religion Bulletin* 22 (November 1993). Bill Pitts, "The Mount Carmel Davidians: Adventist Reformers, 1935–1959," *Syzygy* 2 (1993). Stuart Wright, ed., *Armageddon in Waco* (University of Chicago Press, 1995).

William L. Pitts

DAVIDSON, ASBURY BASCOM (1855–1920). Asbury Bascom Davidson, lawyer and lieutenant governor of Texas, son of William and Cathrina (McBank) Davidson, was born on November 13, 1855, in Lincoln County, Tennessee. He moved to Williamson County, Texas, with his parents before 1870, was educated during the 1870s at Southwestern University in Georgetown, and then moved to Gonzales to study in a law office. After being admitted to the bar, he practiced for a time in Gonzales before moving in the early 1880s to Cuero, where he established his home and a law firm. There, in the late 1880s, he was elected district attorney for the Twenty-fourth Judicial District; he held that office for eight years, until he was elected state senator, a post he held for three years. Davidson was elected lieutenant governor of Texas for three consecutive terms, from 1906 to 1912; he was one of the few men to serve in that office for that many successive terms. He was also a member of the board of directors of the Agricultural and Mechanical College of Texas (now Texas A&M University). He served on the Texas executive committee for the Interstate Inland Waterway League of Louisiana and Texas after it was organized in 1905. Davidson was married to Minnie McClanahan in March 1890. He died on February 4, 1920, and was buried in Hillside Cemetery, Cuero.

BIBLIOGRAPHY: Niel John McArthur, *The Twenty-seventh Legislature and State Administration of Texas* (Austin: Ben C. Jones, 1901). *Proceedings of the Texas Bar Association*, 1921. Vertical Files, Barker Texas History Center, University of Texas at Austin.

Carolyn Hyman

DAVIDSON, CHARLES E. (1856–1944). Charles E. Davidson, lawyer, rancher, and county judge, was born on July 10, 1856, in Nicholas County, Kentucky, and spent his childhood on a farm in Iowa. After attending Cornell University and the University of Iowa, he received his law degree in 1882 from the Hasting School of Law, San Francisco, and went to work for a San Francisco law firm that dealt in Texas land and land scrip. His first case yielded him a fee of twenty-five sections of land in West Texas. He moved to Texas immediately and, with his brother Glen, opened a land and law office in San Angelo in 1883. The young lawyer and surveyor soon branched out into the cattle business and in 1891 moved to Ozona. That section of the state was then a part of Bexar County, but under Davidson's leadership the separate Crockett County was organized. Davidson was elected the first county judge and county school superintendent on July 7, 1891. His tenure as county judge is probably unparalleled in the United States: during his fifty-one years on the bench he never sought reelection. In 1893 Judge Davidson married Dixie R. Friend; they reared seven children. Davidson briefly published the Ozona

Stockman. He successfully combined the career of county judge with that of lawyer, rancher, surveyor, educator, publisher, businessman, and philosopher. His long service in behalf of his community earned him the nickname "Godfather of Crockett County." He was a Methodist and a Mason. Davidson died at his ranch home near Ozona on July 25, 1944.

BIBLIOGRAPHY: *Cattleman,* September 1944. Crockett County Historical Society, *History of Crockett County* (San Angelo: Anchor, 1976).

Gene Hollon

DAVIDSON, JAMES (1834–?). James Davidson, adjutant general of Texas, was born in Kelso, Roxburgh County, Scotland, in 1834. He received a common-school education and was proficient in reading and writing. When he immigrated to the United States in 1865 he claimed that after leaving school he had served in a cavalry regiment in the British army. In 1865 he settled in Maine. In March of that year he enlisted as a second lieutenant in an unassigned company of the Nineteenth Maine Infantry Volunteers. He was mustered out on May 23, 1865, at which time his commander described him as "zealous, energetic and competent." He joined the regular army the following June as a private in Company D, Corps of Engineers. He remained with the engineers until June 1867 and rose to the rank of first sergeant. In May 1867 he passed examinations allowing him to be appointed second lieutenant and was assigned to the Twenty-ninth Infantry. He transferred to the Eleventh Infantry on April 25, 1869.

In 1869 the Eleventh Infantry was headquartered at Jefferson, Texas. Davidson arrived in Clarksville and assumed the duties of military commissioner for Red River County on June 18. In this position he achieved a reputation for strict enforcement of military rule. He restricted the wearing of sixshooters and other weapons in town. He actively supported efforts by the local Freedmen's Bureau[qv] agent to educate and protect freedmen. During his service in northeastern Texas he became associated with prominent Republican politicians Amos Morrill and Albert H. Latimer.[qv]

Governor Edmund J. Davis[qv] nominated Davidson adjutant general of Texas with the rank of colonel on June 24, 1870. The Senate confirmed the nomination on July 6, and Davidson resigned from the United States Army with an honorable discharge. As adjutant general, Davidson was chief of the State Police,[qv] which he organized quickly. He also headed the state militia and was promoted to major general of it on March 15, 1871. His early priority in office was the suppression of outlaws and the Ku Klux Klan.[qv] He aggressively used the police and the militia in his efforts and personally headed militia operations following declarations of martial law in Madison, Hill, Walker, Limestone, and Freestone counties in 1870 and 1871. Under his leadership the State Police forcefully hunted down criminals and made 3,475 arrests in the first month of the organization's existence.

The State Police and the militia both were politically controversial institutions. Democrats charged that they were instruments of Republican tyranny. The fact that many members of both the police and militia were black further irritated whites. While both the militia and police received criticism, Davidson generally avoided personal attacks. In September 1871 a disgruntled state policeman accused him of malfeasance in procuring supplies for the police. Though the incident received attention in Democratic newspapers, the charges were never proved. Even among his political opponents Davidson earned a reputation for honesty and efficiency in operating the police and militia. When he readily complied with conservative efforts to cut back and reorganize the State Police after the spring of 1872 he received Democratic praise for being one of the better members of the Davis government.

On October 12, 1872, the local Republican executive committee at Austin nominated Davidson for state senator from the district embracing Travis County. He resigned his position as adjutant general on November 4 to run for the office on a platform that declared support for law and order and public education. He also broke with the Davis administration when he pledged to uphold the legislature's grant of state bonds to the International–Great Northern Railroad, a position opposed by the governor. In the election he faced Nathan G. Shelley,[qv] and although he received some praise in Democratic newspapers he still lost, in an election marred with charges of fraud. In December after the 1872 election, Davidson accompanied secretary of state James P. Newcomb[qv] to New York City, where Newcomb had gone to sell state bonds. In his absence, the new adjutant general, Frank L. Britton,[qv] discovered shortages in Davidson's accounts. Davidson had drawn warrants on the treasury for payment of State Police officers, which the comptroller allowed without vouchers filed showing legal services, and apparently pocketed the funds. The state immediately ceased payment on the warrants and attached Davidson's property to limit the potential loss. Later investigations placed the loss at $37,434.67, although what was recovered by the seizure of Davidson's property is not known. Governor Davis offered a reward for the former adjutant general's return and sent Capt. Leander H. McNelly[qv] of the State Police in pursuit. McNelly reported that Davidson probably had left the United States, although the policeman never determined the fugitive's location. He was later reported to have fled to Belgium but was never found and never returned to Texas.

BIBLIOGRAPHY: William T. Field, Jr., "The Texas State Police, 1870–1873," *Texas Military History* 5 (Fall 1965). Carl H. Moneyhon, *Republicanism in Reconstruction Texas* (Austin: University of Texas Press, 1980). William C. Nunn, *Texas Under the Carpetbaggers* (Austin: University of Texas Press, 1962). Otis Singletary, "The Texas Militia during Reconstruction," *Southwestern Historical Quarterly* 60 (July 1956).

Carl H. Moneyhon

DAVIDSON, JOHN WYNN (1825–1881). John Wynn Davidson, army officer and Indian fighter, the eldest of the four sons of William B. and Elizabeth Davidson, was born on August 14, 1825, in Fairfax County, Virginia. Davidson graduated from West Point in 1845 and saw frontier duty in Kansas and Wisconsin. During the Mexican War[qv] he was stationed in California and participated in the battles of San Pasqual and the San Gabriel. On June 18, 1851, he married Clara McGunnegle in St. Louis, Missouri. During the Civil War[qv] Davidson, served as a brigadier general in General McClellan's Army of the Potomac. He fought in the Peninsular Campaign and the Seven Days battles and throughout the rest of the war served in the Missouri, Arkansas, and Mississippi districts. In 1866 Davidson was commissioned lieutenant colonel of the Tenth United States Cavalry.[qv] Since the regiment consisted of black buffalo soldiers,[qv] he soon acquired the nickname "Black Jack." With the outbreak of the Red River War,[qv] Davidson, on September 10, 1874, led six companies of the Tenth Cavalry, three of the Eleventh Infantry, a section of mountain howitzers, Lt. Richard H. Pratt's[qv] Indian scouts, and forty-six supply wagons out of Fort Sill into the Texas Panhandle in search of Indians. Marching north to the Washita River, Davidson then turned west and for over a week toiled along the breaks of the Red River tributaries. By October fifty-eight horses and mules had been lost, and forage and rations were running low. Davidson's men surprised a band of Kiowas on October 2, but the remaining animals were too worn to carry out pursuit successfully. On October 24 he received the surrender of a Comanche band his troops had defeated on Elk Creek. With the onset of northers, sleet and snow in mid-November, about twenty-four troopers suffered from severe frostbite, food and supplies ran low, and 100 animals died during the "Wrinkled-hand Chase." However, Davidson and his subordinates destroyed several Indian camps and captured nearly 400 Indians and over 2,000 of their horses before returning to Fort Sill on November 29. In March 1875 Davidson relinquished regimental command to Benjamin H. Grierson[qv] and was transferred to Fort Griffin in Shackelford

County, Texas, where his duties were confined mainly to patrolling the nearby cattle trails and cow camps. In December 1876 Davidson became commander at Fort Richardson until its abandonment in 1878, then once more at Fort Sill. In January 1879 he was sent to command the garrison at Fort Elliott. There his humane policy toward transient Indians from the reservations brought him into sharp conflict with the Texas Ranger captain, George W. Arrington.qv Promoted to colonel of the Second Cavalry on June 25, Davidson took command of that regiment at Fort Custer, Montana. On February 8, 1881, Davidson was seriously injured during an inspection tour when his horse slipped on ice and fell on top of him. He died at St. Paul, Minnesota, on June 26, 1881. He was buried in the Bellefontaine Cemetery in St. Louis, and his remains were reinterred in Arlington National Cemetery in 1911.

BIBLIOGRAPHY: Homer K. Davidson, *Black Jack Davidson, a Cavalry Commander on the Western Frontier: The Life of General John W. Davidson* (Glendale, California: Arthur H. Clark, 1974). William H. Leckie, *The Buffalo Soldiers: A Narrative of the Negro Cavalry in the West* (Norman: University of Oklahoma Press, 1967).

H. Allen Anderson

DAVIDSON, ROBERT VANCE (1853–1925). Robert Vance Davidson, lawyer and legislator, son of Allen Turner and Elizabeth (Howell) Davidson, was born at Murphy, North Carolina, on July 23, 1853. He studied law in Asheville, North Carolina, and was admitted to the bar before he moved to Texas in 1874. He settled in Galveston, where he was elected city attorney in 1879 and served for fourteen years on the school board. He is one of the authors of the city charter granted after the Galveston hurricane of 1900.qv He served as state senator in 1902 and 1903 and as attorney general from 1904 until 1910, during which time he handled the Waters-Pierce case.qv He ran unsuccessfully for governor of Texas in 1910 on an antiprohibition platform. In January 1911 he went into private practice in Dallas. Davidson and his wife, the former Laura Harrison Jack, were the parents of four children. He died in Dallas on July 3, 1925, and was buried in Lake View Cemetery, Galveston.

BIBLIOGRAPHY: Dallas *Morning News*, July 4, 1925. Vertical Files, Barker Texas History Center, University of Texas at Austin.

Carolyn Hyman

DAVIDSON, SAMUEL (?–?). Samuel Davidson, one of Stephen F. Austin'sqv Old Three Hundredqv colonists, received the title to a sitioqv of land now in Brazos County on July 21, 1824. The grant is located on the Brazos River near Wellborn and includes Minter Springs. Although it is doubtful that he was the original colonist, a man named Samuel Davidson served in James Gillaspie'sqv company in the Mexican War.qv

BIBLIOGRAPHY: Lester G. Bugbee, "The Old Three Hundred: A List of Settlers in Austin's First Colony," *Quarterly of the Texas State Historical Association* 1 (October 1897). W. Broadus Smith, *Pioneers of Brazos County, Texas, 1800–1850* (Bryan, Texas, 1962).

DAVIDSON, THOMAS WHITFIELD (1876–1974). T. Whitfield (Whit) Davidson, jurist and politician, was born in the East Texas piney woods of Harrison County on September 23, 1876, to John Ransom and Sara Josephine (Daniels) Whitfield, who had moved to the area from Georgia in 1867. Davis attended the region's country schools, briefly went to East Texas State Normal College, and attended the University of Chicago and Columbia University. He subsequently taught for five years in the public schools of Marshall, during which time he read law; he was admitted to the state bar in 1903. In addition to practicing privately in Marshall and Dallas, he served as city attorney for Marshall from 1907 to 1914; Texas state senator, 1920 to 1922; lieutenant governor, 1923 to 1925; and general counsel for the Praeto-

rians, a Dallas insurance company, 1927 to 1936. In February 1936 he was appointed United States district judge, Northern District of Texas, Dallas. He retired in 1965 but remained involved in naturalization and citizenship activities.

Davidson was a member of the "Immortal Forty," the Texas delegation that supported Woodrow Wilson at the Democratic national convention in 1912. He organized and served as president of the Associated Roosevelt Clubs of Texas in 1932 and was again a national convention delegate. As lieutenant governor in 1923, he emphasized highway construction and penal reform and was a foe of the Ku Klux Klan.qv He was defeated in the nine-candidate Democratic gubernatorial primary in 1924 but subsequently endorsed and supported Miriam Amanda Fergusonqv in her successful runoff campaign against Felix Robertson,qv the Klan-backed candidate. Among the many cases Davidson heard on the federal bench, the most important was that dealing with public school integration in Dallas. Although reluctant to rule for integration, he issued the judgment in *Borders v. Rippy* that began the process of desegregation in Dallas in 1960.

Judge Davidson was active in various bar associations, the International Order of Odd Fellows, the Sons of the American Revolution, the Town and Gown Club of Dallas, and the Writers' Club of Dallas. He was president of the Texas Bar Association (see STATE BAR OF TEXAS) in 1927 and a past grand master of the Texas Odd Fellows. He wrote a memoir and seven books on law, history, folklore, and genealogy. He was an Episcopalian. He was married to Asenath Burkhart in 1902, Constance Key Wandel in 1936, and Beulah Rose in 1949. Davidson died on January 25, 1974, and was interred at Josephine Davidson Memorial Chapel in Diana, Texas, a chapel he built in 1955 in honor of his mother.

BIBLIOGRAPHY: *Who Was Who in America,* Vol. 6. Norman D. Brown, *Hood, Bonnet, and Little Brown Jug: Texas Politics, 1921–1928* (College Station: Texas A&M University Press, 1984). Vertical Files, Barker Texas History Center, University of Texas at Austin.

Robert S. La Forte

DAVIDSON, WILLIAM FRANCIS H. (1811–?). William Davidson, surgeon in the Texas army, was born in Tennessee. On January 14, 1836, he enlisted for six months in the Volunteer Auxiliary Corps at Nacogdoches and during the San Jacinto campaign served as surgeon of Col. Edward Burleson'sqv First Regiment, Texas Volunteers. During the battle of San Jacintoqv Davidson was detailed to remain with the sick at the army camp. Sam Houstonqv nominated Davidson as a surgeon, and his nomination was confirmed by the Senate of the Republic of Texasqv on May 22, 1837. He was married in 1845 and lived in Rusk County. He received a land warrant for 640 acres for his service at San Jacinto. In 1853 he received 320 acres and on June 4, 1857, he received 320 acres in Cooke County. In 1850 he was listed as J. F. Davidson, farmer, with a wife named Mary and one child. In 1860 he, his wife, and three children lived in Cooke County; his occupation was "M.D."

BIBLIOGRAPHY: Daughters of the Republic of Texas, *Muster Rolls of the Texas Revolution* (Austin, 1986). Sam Houston Dixon and Louis Wiltz Kemp, *The Heroes of San Jacinto* (Houston: Anson Jones, 1932). Thomas L. Miller, *Bounty and Donation Land Grants of Texas, 1835–1888* (Austin: University of Texas Press, 1967). Pat Ireland Nixon, *The Medical Story of Early Texas, 1528–1853* (Lancaster, Pennsylvania: Lupe Memorial Fund, 1946). E. W. Winkler, ed., *Secret Journals of the Senate, Republic of Texas* (Austin, 1911).

Thomas W. Cutrer

DAVIDSON, WILLIAM LEWIS (1845–1921). William Lewis Davidson, soldier, lawyer, and judge, was born in Grenada, Mississippi, on November 5, 1845, the son of Asbury and Mary (Fly) Davidson. His father, a Methodist circuit rider, moved his family to Texas in 1851. Davidson attended Gonzales College and Stonewall Institute.

He volunteered for the Confederate Army at age sixteen and served in Company B of the Thirty-second Texas Cavalry. In an autobiographical sketch written many years later, Davidson wrote that his company was an elite unit and the only one completely equipped with cavalry carbines, swords, and six-shooters west of the Mississippi. On his return from the war Davidson appears to have been involved in attacks on carpetbaggers and Reconstruction[qv] forces. One story claims that federal troops put a price on his head and that his mother smuggled food to him in a forest hideout for several months. In any case, he soon pursued a more staid career in the law and was admitted to the Texas bar in 1871. He married Susan B. Howard in Gonzales County in 1870, and they had seven children.

Davidson practiced law at Gonzales until he moved in January 1887 to Georgetown, partly if not wholly to send his children to Southwestern University. He was appointed assistant attorney general of Texas by Governor Lawrence S. Ross[qv] and served from 1887 to 1891, when he was appointed to the Court of Civil Appeals by Governor James S. Hogg.[qv] He was reelected to that position from 1892 to 1920. His legal philosophy, as presented in his autobiography, was characterized by a conservatively dim view of government interference, a concern for preserving the personal liberties of the individual, and an extreme aversion to paternalistic legal measures. Prohibitionists regarded him as an extremely influential opponent who consistently struck down their legislative efforts (*see* PROHIBITION). Davidson suffered a stroke of apoplexy while fishing in Austin and drowned on January 25, 1921. He was interred in the State Cemetery.[qv]

BIBLIOGRAPHY: Austin *American*, January 26, 27, 1921. Vertical Files, Barker Texas History Center, University of Texas at Austin.

Carolyn Hyman

DAVIDSON, TEXAS. Davidson, a farming community in southeastern Van Zandt County 8½ miles north of Brownsboro in Henderson County, had a post office from 1902 to 1916 and a general store in 1914. By 1905 seventy-three students were enrolled in the local school. In the 1980s county highway maps did not show the townsite location.

Diana J. Kleiner

DAVIDSON CANYON CREEK. Davidson Canyon Creek rises five miles north of U.S. Highway 82 and three miles west of the Dickens-King county line in east central Dickens County (at 33°41′ N, 100°34′ W) and runs south for six miles through Davidson Canyon to its mouth on the South Wichita River, near U.S. Highway 82 (at 33°36′ N, 100°32′ W). Both the creek and the canyon were named for a local family.

BIBLIOGRAPHY: Fred Arrington, *A History of Dickens County: Ranches and Rolling Plains* (Quanah, Texas: Nortex, 1971). Dickens County Historical Commission, *Dickens County: Its Land and Its People* (Lubbock: Craftsman Printers, 1986).

DAVIDSON CREEK (Crosby County). Davidson Creek rises twelve miles south of Crosbyton in the breaks of southeastern Crosby County (at 33°33′ N, 101°14′ W) and runs southeast twelve miles to its mouth on the White River (at 33°29′ N, 101°06′ W). It traverses generally flat terrain surfaced by moderately sandy soil that supports short grasses, vine mesquite, and yucca.

_____ (Milam County). Davidson Creek rises four miles southwest of Milano in southeastern Milam County (at 30°40′ N, 96°54′ W) and runs southeast for fifty miles to its mouth on Yegua Creek, on the Burleson-Washington county line two miles east of Somerville (at 30°21′ N, 96°27′ W). The creek, which is intermittent in its upper reaches, traverses low-rolling to flat terrain with local shallow depressions, surfaced by clay and sandy loams that support scrub brush, cacti, and grasses in the upper reaches of the creek and water-tolerant hardwoods and conifers in the middle and lower reaches. The stream was named for a settler who moved to Texas before 1829.

DAVIE, WILLIAM RICHARDSON (1843–1921). William Richardson (W. R.) Davie, state government official, was born in 1843. During the Civil War[qv] he served in the Army of Northern Virginia and achieved the rank of lieutenant colonel. After the war he lived in South Carolina and served in the state legislature. He married Henrietta C. on June 14, 1871, and they had at least two sons. They moved to Texas in 1900 and settled in Austin. Davie was Texas state tax commissioner under Governor Samuel W. T. Lanham[qv] and served as secretary of state under Governor Thomas M. Campbell[qv] from February 1908 to January 1909. After retiring he became a corporation agent. Davie died on October 8, 1921, and was buried in Mexia, Texas, next to his two sons.

BIBLIOGRAPHY: Austin *Statesman*, October 9, 1921.

Laurie E. Jasinski

DAVILLA, TEXAS. Davilla is on Farm Road 487 eighteen miles west of Cameron in western Milam County. It was settled in the 1860s and named for Miguel Davila, who had received the original grant for the land in 1833. A surveyor named Chamberlin purchased the site from the Davila estate and sold town lots with the restriction that alcoholic beverages should never be sold in the settlement. A post office was established there in 1871. Though the Gulf, Colorado and Santa Fe Railway bypassed the town by several miles in 1881, drawing away some of the population, Davilla continued to enjoy a measure of prosperity. In the mid-1880s the community had 350 residents, three churches, three gristmills and cotton gins, a steam sawmill, and a district school. In 1903 Davilla had a three-teacher school for 161 white students and a one-teacher school for thirty-eight black students. After serving many years as the center for a common school district, the Davilla schools were finally consolidated with the Bartlett district in Bell County in the early 1970s. Davilla's population level began a slow decline in the late 1890s, falling from 500 in 1896 to 400 in the 1920s to 300 in the mid-1940s. By the early 1970s only seventy-two residents were reported there. In the 1980s, however, this downward trend reversed. The 1988 county highway map showed five churches and several businesses in the area, and that year the community reported a population of 200. Davilla's population continued to be reported as 200 in the early 1990s.

BIBLIOGRAPHY: Lelia M. Batte, *History of Milam County, Texas* (San Antonio: Naylor, 1956). Milam County Heritage Preservation Society, *Matchless Milam: History of Milam County* (Dallas: Taylor, 1984).

Vivian Elizabeth Smyrl

DAVILLA INSTITUTE. In 1871–72 the Leon River and the Little River Baptist associations united to build a school for their territory, which consisted of Bell, Milam, Burleson, and parts of other counties. The institute, directed by R. L. Hood and his wife, Emma, was located at Davilla in northwestern Milam County. In 1873 the two associations chartered a joint-stock company. The charter provided that the trustees, required to be members of the Baptist Church,[qv] were to be appointed by both associations and that the school was to continue as long as it confined its goals to the advancement of the arts and sciences and the promotion of useful knowledge. George W. Baines, Sr.,[qv] became principal in 1874, and S. E. Woody succeeded him in 1875. The school lasted about five years.

BIBLIOGRAPHY: James Milton Carroll, *A History of Texas Baptists* (Dallas: Baptist Standard, 1923). Carl Bassett Wilson, History of Baptist Educational Efforts in Texas, 1829–1900 (Ph.D. dissertation, University of Texas, 1934).

Ida Jo Marshall

DAVIS, ANDREW (1827–1906). Andrew Davis, Methodist minister, the son of Nancy (McKelvey) and Daniel Davis,[qv] was born on March 10, 1827, in Jonesborough, in the area of present Red River County, Texas. He spent his early life in Tenaha, Shelby County, and at Fort Lyday near the site of present Honey Grove, Fannin County. He entered McKenzie College about 1841 and on October 12, 1844, was licensed to preach in the Methodist Church.^{qv} In December 1847 he married Maria S. Linn at Clarksville. He served in various circuits in Northeast Texas, later became a member of the Northwest Texas Conference, and about 1878 was appointed presiding elder of the Stephenville District. He was at one time a trustee of Southwestern University. Davis died on February 13, 1906, and was buried in Oakwood Cemetery, Corsicana.

BIBLIOGRAPHY: R. L. Jones, "Folk Life in Early Texas: The Autobiography of Andrew Davis," *Southwestern Historical Quarterly* 43 (October 1939, January 1940). Methodist Episcopal Church, South, *Journal of the Northwest Texas Conference*, 1906. *Carolyn Hyman*

DAVIS, BIRD B. (ca. 1827–?). Bird B. Davis, who represented Wharton County at the Constitutional Convention of 1875,^{qv} was born into slavery in North Carolina around 1827. He arrived in Texas in 1858 and was married at the time of the convention, where he was one of four black delegates.

BIBLIOGRAPHY: Merline Pitre, *Through Many Dangers, Toils and Snares: The Black Leadership of Texas, 1868–1900* (Austin: Eakin, 1985). *Walsh and Pilgrim's Directory of the Officers and Members of the Constitutional Convention of the State of Texas, A.D. 1875, and the State Officers of the State of Texas* (Austin: Democratic Statesman Office, 1875). *Paul M. Lucko*

DAVIS, CLARE OGDEN (1892–1970). Clare Ogden Davis, newspaperwoman and author, was born on November 26, 1892, in Kimball's Bend, Texas, the daughter of Charles Vance and Mary (Lawrence) Ogden. She entered Baylor College at Belton (now the University of Mary Hardin-Baylor) in 1913 and graduated there; afterwards she taught history in Bonham and Cleburne high schools. Her first newspaper job was as a reporter in the Fort Worth office of the Dallas *Morning News*.^{qv} There she was possibly the first Texas woman to cover police assignments. In Dallas in 1920 she married John Burton Davis,^{qv} with whom she later collaborated on seven novels under the pen name Lawrence Saunders. The Davises had no children. During the early 1920s Mrs. Davis became manager of the Houston bureau of several Texas newspapers. From 1923 to 1925 she was in Europe, reporting on various international events; while there she met writer Joseph Conrad and obtained the last interview he granted before his death. After returning to Texas, she worked as Governor Miriam A. Ferguson's^{qv} press secretary for a year before moving in 1926 to New York City, where she wrote a column on child psychology and reported on such important events as the Lindbergh baby kidnapping. In 1929 her novel about a woman governor of a southwestern state who was elected on an anti-Klan platform (Mrs. Ferguson had opposed the Klan), *The Woman of It,* was published. She also wrote a gardening book, *In Our Country Garden* (1938). Clare Davis was also a public relations counselor and press agent for a national seed company for twenty-five years; she took graduate studies in horticulture and landscape architecture at Columbia University. She returned to Texas in 1951 and, as garden editor for the Austin American,^{qv} wrote a column, "In My Texas Garden." She helped found the garden center in Zilker Park in Austin, and part of the center was named for her. She retired in 1965 when she suffered a stroke that left her paralyzed, and she died on May 17, 1970. She was buried in Odd Fellows Cemetery, Granger.

BIBLIOGRAPHY: Vertical Files, Barker Texas History Center, University of Texas at Austin.

DAVIS, DANIEL (?–1838). Daniel Davis, early settler, son of John Davis, was born and grew to manhood on the Duck River in Tennessee. He married Matilda Tidwell and moved to Missouri, where she died. Davis subsequently married Nancy McKelvey, probably of Ste. Genevieve, Missouri, on January 20, 1818. Later that year they moved to Pecan Point in what is now Red River County, Texas. The family was farming and raising livestock in the Liberty, Texas, area in 1826. At Pecan Point in 1832 Sam Houston^{qv} visited in the Davis home en route to Texas. Davis, a trapper and bear and buffalo hunter, hunted as far as the Wichita Mountains and the upper Red River. Late in 1832, after the death of his second wife, he again moved along Trammel's Trace^{qv} to Shelby County and settled on the Tenaha River. He took part in the battle of Nacogdoches^{qv} in July 1832 and by April 1836 was one of William Becknell's^{qv} mounted volunteers. Apparently he and several others moved north just before the battle of San Jacinto.^{qv} While living in East Texas Davis married his third wife, Mrs. Margaret Bascus. He moved back to the Red River country after the revolution and lived ten miles from Clarksville until late 1837, when he moved to his headright in the vicinity of Honey Grove in what is now Fannin County. Davis was killed by Indians in 1838.

BIBLIOGRAPHY: R. L. Jones, "Folk Life in Early Texas: The Autobiography of Andrew Davis," *Southwestern Historical Quarterly* 43 (October 1939, January 1940). Macum Phelan, *History of Early Methodism in Texas, 1817–1866* (Nashville: Cokesbury, 1924); *A History of the Expansion of Methodism in Texas, 1867–1902* (Dallas: Mathis, Van Nort, 1937).

DAVIS, EDGAR BYRAM (1873–1951). Edgar Byram Davis, oilman and philanthropist, was born on February 2, 1873, in Brockton, Massachusetts. With only a high school education, he began making his first million dollars in the shoe business in Massachusetts about 1905; later he made another fortune, about $3 million, as an early investor in foreign rubber plantations and as the largest individual stockholder in the United States Rubber Company. After thirteen years he sold his holdings and gave much of the proceeds away as gifts to friends and associates in New York. His brother Oscar invested in oil leases in Caldwell County, Texas, in 1919 and asked Edgar to manage his share of the oil leases. Edgar made his first visit to Luling that year. A deeply religious man, Edgar believed that he was directed by God to come to Texas and to deliver Luling and Caldwell County from the oppressive one-crop (cotton) economy that dominated the area. He believed he would do this by finding oil, though geologists claimed

Edgar B. Davis with his secretary, Inez Griffin. Luling, 1950. Courtesy Riley Froh, La Porte. When Edgar Davis sold his leases in the Luling Oilfield for $12 million in 1926, it was perhaps the biggest oil deal to date in Texas.

Edmund J. Davis. Courtesy Massachusetts Commandery, Military Order of the Loyal Legion, and the U.S. Army Military History Institute, Carlisle Barracks, Carlisle, Pennsylvania.

there was none there. In March 1921 Davis incorporated the United North and South Oil Company. After Oscar Davis died, Edgar purchased the oil leases from his estate. The first six wells were dry, and Davis's company was heavily in debt, but the seventh, Rafael Rios No. 1, gushed in on August 9, 1922. This well opened up a field near Stairtown that was twelve miles long and two miles wide. By December 1924 the field was producing 43,000 barrels of oil daily (*see* LULING OILFIELD). On June 11, 1926, Davis sold his leases to the Magnolia Petroleum Company qv for what may have been the biggest oil deal in Texas up to that time, $12 million (one-half in cash), and to celebrate gave a free barbecue for friends, associates, and employees; 15,000 to 35,000 people attended. In addition, to his employees he gave from 25 to 100 percent of their total salaries as bonuses. He also gave the citizens of Luling a golf course, an athletic clubhouse for local blacks, various other facilities, and endowments for each. He established the Luling Foundation qv there for the teaching of improved agricultural methods. In all, Davis donated at least $5 million to charity, as well as keeping a play, *The Ladder*, written by his friend James Francis Davis, qv running on Broadway for two years even though critics considered it one of Broadway's worst. Davis believed in the message of the play, which included the theme of reincarnation. Davis discovered two more oilfields in the area, Buckeye and Darst Creek, and again gave most of the cash away when they were sold. With the Great Depression qv he ran into financial problems again; by 1935 the development company was declared insolvent. He worked for twelve years paying off most of his indebtedness, always insisting that more oil could be found. Davis died in Galveston on October 14, 1951, and was buried in Luling at the site of one of his former homes. He never married. He belonged to no church but attended each church in Luling regularly. In 1966 the Edgar B. Davis Memorial Hospital was built on the site of his home in Luling; his gravesite is on the hospital grounds.

BIBLIOGRAPHY: Riley Froh, *Edgar B. Davis: Wildcatter Extraordinary* (Luling, Texas: Luling Foundation, 1984). Vertical Files, Barker Texas History Center, University of Texas at Austin.

DAVIS, EDMUND JACKSON (1827–1883). Edmund J. Davis, Union Army officer and Reconstruction qv governor of Texas, was born at St. Augustine, Florida, on October 2, 1827, the son of William Godwin and Mary Ann (Channer) Davis. His father, who came from South Carolina, was a land developer and attorney at St. Augustine. The young Davis received his education in Florida and moved with his family to Galveston, Texas, in January 1848. There he worked as a clerk in the post office and studied law. In mid-1849 he moved to Corpus Christi, where he worked in a store and read law. He was admitted to the bar in the fall of 1849. Between 1849 and 1853 he was an inspector and deputy collector of customs at Laredo. In 1853 he became district attorney of the Twelfth Judicial District at Brownsville. About 1856 Governor Elisha M. Pease qv named him judge of the same district, and Davis continued to serve as a state judge until 1861. As judge he accompanied the ranger unit of Capt. William G. Tobin, qv who was involved in the Cortina affair at Brownsville in 1859 (*see* CORTINA, JUAN NEPOMUCENO).

On April 6, 1858, Davis married Anne Elizabeth Britton, daughter of Forbes Britton, qv a state senator and friend of Sam Houston. qv The couple had two sons, Britton and Waters. Britton was born in 1860, attended West Point, and became an officer in the United States Army. Waters, born in 1862, attended the University of Michigan and became an attorney and merchant in El Paso.

Davis was a Whig until the mid-1850s. In 1855 he joined the Democratic party qv in a fusion against the American (Know-Nothing) party, qv and he remained a Democrat until after the Civil War. qv In later politics he supported Sam Houston and opposed secession qv in 1861, when he ran unsuccessfully to become a delegate to the Secession Convention. qv After secession Davis refused to take the oath of loyalty to the Confederacy, and the state vacated his judgeship on April 24.

As a result of his opposition to the Confederacy, he fled the state in May 1862. With John L. Haynes and William Alexander, qqv he went to New Orleans, then to Washington, where the men met with President Abraham Lincoln, who recommended providing arms to troops that they wanted to raise. On October 26, 1862, Davis received a colonel's commission and authorization to recruit the cavalry regiment that became the First Texas Cavalry (U.S.). qv

Davis and the First Texas saw extensive service during the remainder of the war. They were at Galveston on January 3, 1863, and barely escaped capture when Confederates took that city back from Union hands. On March 15, 1863, Confederate citizens and off-duty soldiers seized Davis in Matamoros, where he was attempting to take his family out of Texas and recruit men for his unit. This event precipitated diplomatic trouble between the Confederacy and Mexico that lasted until Gen. Hamilton P. Bee qv released Davis to appease Mexican governor Albino López. From November to December 1863 Davis was in Texas as a part of Gen. Nathaniel P. Banks's qv unsuccessful Rio Grande campaign. His unit marched to Rio Grande City and seized cotton and slaves in an effort to disrupt the border trade. On November 4, 1864, Davis was promoted to brigadier general. For the rest of the war he commanded Gen. Joseph J. Reynolds's qv cavalry in the Division of Western Mississippi. On June 2, 1865, he was among those who represented Gen. Edward R. S. Canby^qv at Gen. Edmund Kirby Smith's^qv surrender of Confederate forces in Texas.

Davis participated in state politics as a Unionist and Republican after the war. He served in the Constitutional Convention of 1866^qv and ran unsuccessfully for the state Senate from his old district in the 1866 general election. He represented the border district and was president of the Constitutional Convention of 1868–69.^qv In this period he consistently supported political programs that would have restricted the political rights of secessionists, expanded rights for blacks, and divided the state. He also favored the ab initio theory, which held that all laws passed since secession were null and void (*see* AB INITIO QUESTION).

In the election of 1869 Davis ran for governor against Andrew J. Hamilton,^qv another Republican, and won in a closely disputed race. His administration was a controversial one. Its program called for law and order backed by a State Police^qv and restored militia, public schools, internal improvements, bureaus of immigration and geology, and protection of the frontier. All of these measures encountered strong attacks from both Democratic and Republican opponents and added to the controversy surrounding Reconstruction in Texas. Davis ran for reelection in December 1873 and was defeated by Richard Coke^qv by a vote of two to one. Davis believed that the Republican national administration was partly responsible for his defeat, and relations between the governor and Washington were strained until he was removed from office by Democrats the following January in what is known as the Coke-Davis controversy.^qv

From 1875 until his death Davis, contemporarily described as a "tall, gaunt, cold-eyed, rather commanding figure," headed the Republican party^qv in Texas as chairman of the state executive committee. In 1880 he ran again for governor but was badly defeated by Oran M. Roberts.^qv In 1882 he ran for Congress in the Tenth District against John Hancock,^qv again unsuccessfully. He was nominated as collector of customs at Galveston in 1880 but refused the job because of his opposition to the administration of President Rutherford B. Hayes. Supporters recommended him for a cabinet position under President Chester A. Arthur, but he received no appointment. Davis died in Austin on February 7, 1883, and is buried there in the State Cemetery.^qv

BIBLIOGRAPHY: Ronald N. Gray, Edmund J. Davis: Radical Republican and Reconstruction Governor of Texas (Ph.D. dissertation, Texas Tech University, 1976). William C. Nunn, *Texas Under the Carpetbaggers* (Austin: University of Texas Press, 1962). Charles W. Ramsdell, *Reconstruction in Texas* (New York: Columbia University Press, 1910; rpt., Austin: Texas State Historical Association, 1970).

Carl H. Moneyhon

DAVIS, FANNIE BREEDLOVE (1833–1915). Fannie Breedlove Davis, Texas Woman's Missionary Union^qv leader, the daughter of Pleasant Ellis and Hannah (Crump) Breedlove, was born in Pittsylvania County, Virginia, on November 24, 1833. Her father was a plantation owner. After the family moved to Texas in 1847, Fannie studied in the Female Department of Baylor University. On January 4, 1855, she married George Bowen Davis; they had two daughters.

Mrs. Davis is most noted for her work with the Woman's Missionary Union. Women in the Southern Baptist Convention had become so involved in raising money for missions that in 1878 the convention recommended that the work of the women be coordinated through state central committees under the direction of the Foreign Mission Board and the Home Mission Board. In 1878 Fannie Davis was elected president of the Home Board Central Committee of Texas. The growing enthusiasm of women for both foreign and home missions inspired her and Anne E. Luther to lead the formation in October 1880 of the Texas Woman's Missionary Union. Mrs. Davis was elected its first president. A spirit of unification led, in 1886, to the merger of the WMU of Texas with the Ladies General Aid Society in order to ensure more effective support of missions. As the recognized leader of the women's missionary movement in Texas, Fannie Davis was elected president of the new Baptist Women Mission Workers. She continued in this capacity until 1895. She was one of the Texas representatives to the 1888 meeting of Southern Baptist women in Richmond, Virginia. When Annie Armstrong, in the face of some opposition, proposed the organization of a convention-wide women's missionary society, Mrs. Davis seconded and supported her. The result was the establishment, on May 11, 1888, of the Woman's Missionary Union as an auxiliary to the Southern Baptist Convention.

Fannie Davis launched the *Texas Baptist Worker* in 1889 in Houston, with her husband as business manager. The *Worker* provided information on missions for the women of Texas and served as one of the prototypes for the extensive WMU literature of today. Under her leadership, offerings for missions in Texas grew from $35 in 1880 to $23,193 in 1895. She retired as president of the Baptist Women Mission Workers in 1895. She was present, however, at the celebration of the silver anniversary in Waco in 1911. As a tribute to her early leadership, she was elected president emerita for life. Later the Fannie Breedlove Davis Memorial was established in her honor. She died in San Antonio on January 1, 1915.

BIBLIOGRAPHY: James Milton Carroll, *A History of Texas Baptists* (Dallas: Baptist Standard, 1923). Alma Hunt, *History of the Woman's Missionary Union* (Nashville: Convention Press, 1976). Mrs. W. J. J. Smith, *A Centennial History of the Baptist Women of Texas* (Dallas: Woman's Missionary Union of Texas, 1933).

Clyde M. DeLoach

DAVIS, FLETCHER (1874–1964). Fletcher Davis, editor and publisher, was born at Taska, a cotton farm near Mount Pleasant, in Marshall County, Mississippi, on February 1, 1874, one of thirteen children of Francis Marion and Mary (Lockhart) Davis II. Davis received a Mississippi teacher's certificate when he was quite young. His fragile health constrained him to go to Texas; he arrived in San Antonio, stayed for a brief time in 1895, and then moved on to Castroville in the spring of 1896. After receiving a Texas teacher's certificate, he taught for several years in the nearby schools.

When the Castroville *Anvil*, a weekly newspaper that had begun publishing in May 1886, was put up for sale in the spring of 1900, Davis—without any previous newspaper experience—bought it for $275. Meantime, the Hondo *Herald*, published in the new county seat, was also offered for sale. Davis bought it as well and combined the two papers, naming the new paper the *Anvil Herald*. He moved all operations to Hondo. The first issue came out on October 17, 1903, as a weekly; the paper has been published without interruption since that time. Davis sold the paper to William E. Berger in 1946, but continued to write a column for it for years afterward. The Centennial Edition of the Hondo *Anvil Herald* was published on December 25, 1986. Davis also owned and published the D'Hanis *Star* from 1914 to 1923.

From 1915 to 1921 he lectured at farmers' institutes for the Texas Department of Agriculture.^qv Later, he traveled over South Texas speaking to various farm groups about the beneficial applications of science to agriculture. He became editor of the monthly *Market Journal* for statewide mailings to farmers; and in 1921 he became editor of the *Monthly News Bulletin*, another publication devoted to agriculture. Davis returned to full-time editorship of the *Anvil Herald* in late 1921 or early 1922. From 1915 to 1921 Davis's wife, Roberta, was in effect both editor and publisher of the *Anvil Herald*. She made sure the paper reached its readers each week, edited and wrote copy, managed the bookkeeping and stock room, sold advertising, and oversaw the printing, while taking care of her home and four children.

In 1922 Davis started his *Fletcher's States' Rights Farming*, a monthly farm journal. It was discontinued in 1944 because of shortages attendant upon World War II.^qv Davis was a confirmed states' rightser and Democrat. He was also a strong believer in the power of the ballot; he emphasized in his papers that voting was not only a privilege but a duty. He spent his adult life working and writing for the conservation of natural resources, the preservation of the area's unique history, for a good educational system, and for the promotion of the wellbeing and progress of his hometown and county.

He was recognized by the South Texas Press Association in 1952 for his fifty years' service in the publishing industry. In 1953 the Hondo Chamber of Commerce named him Man of the Year for outstanding service since 1903. The board of trustees of Hondo schools honored him and a group of other former board members with a certificate and a banquet in 1954. The Masons presented him with the Fifty Year Pin in 1956. He was awarded a commendation by the Texas Election Bureau for his long years of tabulating and reporting the county's election returns. He was also cited as one of the 1909 charter members of the Hondo Volunteer Fire Department and for his years of service to it. On August 7, 1900, he and Roberta Octavia Hopp were married. Mrs. Davis was a Catholic. She died on March 28, 1956. Fletcher Davis was a Methodist and a Mason. He died on May 8, 1964. They both died in Hondo and are buried in Oakwood Cemetery there.

BIBLIOGRAPHY: Castro Colonies Heritage Association, *The History of Medina County, Texas* (Dallas: National Share Graphics, 1983). Hondo *Anvil Herald*, July 5, 1946, May 15, 1964, December 25, 1986. Charles E. Van Doren, ed., *Webster's American Biographies* (Springfield, Massachusetts: Merriam, 1975).
Martin O. Noonan

DAVIS, GEORGE ANDREW, JR. (1920–1952). George A. Davis, Jr., Medal of Honor recipient, was born in Dublin, Texas, on December 1, 1920, to Pearl and George Davis, Sr. He attended Morton High School at Morton and Harding College at Searcy, Arkansas. He joined the United States Army Air Corps as an aviation cadet at Lubbock on March 21, 1942. He completed flight training with Class 43-B and was commissioned second lieutenant at Lake Charles, Louisiana. After further training as a fighter pilot he was assigned to the 342nd Fighter Squadron, 348th Fighter Group, Fifth Fighter Command, in the Southwest Pacific. Around New Guinea he flew some of the first P-47 aircraft in the Pacific Theater. While in the Pacific during World War II,qv Davis became an "ace" with seven victories and was awarded the Silver Star, the Distinguished Flying Cross with one oak leaf cluster, and the Air Medal with seven clusters. He returned to the United States in 1945. During the Korean War, while leading a flight of four F-86 jet fighters near the Manchurian border, his element leader ran out of oxygen and with his wing man was forced to return to base. Major Davis and the other remaining F-86 continued the mission. The pilots sighted approximately twelve MIG-15 aircraft about to attack friendly fighter-bombers conducting low-level ground operations. Davis dove at the MIG formation and shot down two planes. While he was attacking a third, under continuous fire from enemy fighters, his aircraft received a direct hit, went out of control, and crashed into a mountain thirty miles south of the Yalu River. His bold attack permitted the friendly aircraft to complete their mission. For his "conspicuous gallantry and intrepidity at the risk of his life above and beyond the call of duty," Davis received the Medal of Honor posthumously. He had also been awarded the nation's second highest decoration, the Distinguished Service Cross, a ninth cluster to the Air Medal, a third cluster to the DFC, a second Silver Star, and the Korean WLCHI Medal. On his sixtieth combat mission in Korea, his final mission, he scored his thirteenth and fourteenth aerial victories and became America's leading jet ace at the time. Mrs. Doris Forgason Davis received the Medal of Honor at Reese Air Force Baseqv from air force chief of staff Gen. Nathan F. Twining. Also present were the three Davis children, Davis's parents, and Senator Lyndon B. Johnson.qv Davis's body was never recovered. A veteran's memorial was dedicated to him in the City of Lubbock Cemetery on November 16, 1990, and a Medal of Honor headstone was placed there by the United States Department of Veterans Affairs.

BIBLIOGRAPHY: Austin *American*, June 11, 1952. Dallas *Morning News*, May 15, 1954. Committee on Veterans' Affairs, United States Senate, *Medal of Honor Recipients, 1863–1973* (Washington: GPO, 1973). Vertical Files, Barker Texas History Center, University of Texas at Austin.
Art Leatherwood

DAVIS, GEORGE WASHINGTON (1797–1853). George Washington Davis, Texas patriot in the war for independence, son of Thomas and Ruth (Burk) Davis, was born near Philadelphia, Pennsylvania, on October 12, 1797. In 1800 the family moved to Richmond, Virginia, and after that to Alexandria, where George received his education and learned shoemaking. In 1808 the family moved back to Philadelphia, where Davis studied medicine. They moved to Pittsburg in September 1818 and on to Cincinnati, Ohio, in May 1819. On October 8, 1820, George married Rebecca Warfield Gaston, a widow with three children. They subsequently moved to Greenburg, Kentucky, where Davis established a shoemaking trade and began to study law. Failing health caused him to move on to Summersville, Kentucky, where he opened a tavern. A son was born there.

In 1830, having heard of the rich soil, fine climate, beautiful scenery, and abundance of cheap land in Texas, Davis determined to move again. He traveled by wagon to Louisville, put his family and possessions aboard a flatboat on the Ohio River, and undertook a six-weeks' journey to New Orleans. From there he traveled by schooner to Matagorda, Texas; he landed on February 12, 1831, at Cox's Point on Lavaca Bay, opposite the site of present Port Lavaca. Pressing inland, he ascended the Lavaca and Navidad rivers to Old Scotts, where he built a camp for his wife, who had become so severely stricken with rheumatism that she could walk only with the aid of crutches. A second son was born there. Davis left his family at Old Scotts, set out on foot toward his chosen destination, the Guadalupe River, and arrived at Gonzales in the colony of Green DeWitt.qv There he selected a league of land and was awarded title to it by a grant dated September 6, 1831.

After bringing his family to Gonzales, Davis became an active participant in the movement toward Texas independence. He was named a delegate to the Convention of 1833.qv He was appointed secretary of the committee of safety for Gonzales and in that capacity wrote a letter dated September 25, 1835, to John Henry Moore,qv asking for help in protecting the residents' cannon against the Mexican army. As a safety precaution, the cannon was temporarily buried in Davis's peach orchard. On October 2, 1835, as one of the original eighteen members of the Gonzales defense force, Davis took part in the first battle of the Texas Revolution,qv in which the cannon was successfully defended (*see* OLD EIGHTEEN and GONZALES "COME AND TAKE IT" CANNON).

On November 1, 1835, Governor Henry Smithqv commissioned Davis to install Andrew Pontonqv as first judge and Charles Lockhart as second judge of Gonzales Municipality. Davis was also appointed a delegate to the Consultationqv held at San Felipe de Austin in November 1835. On February 15, 1836, he was named subcontractor for the Texas army at Bexar, where he issued supplies to the army and to the families of the men who were in the army. This appointment was made by Mathew Caldwell,qv the prime contractor.

In February 1836 John E. Gaston,qv Mrs. Davis's son by her first marriage, was one of the thirty-two men from Gonzales who responded to the appeal for reinforcements at the Alamo. He and John Kellogg,qv her son-in-law, were among the men who died there in the battle of the Alamo.qv

When the first district court was organized in Gonzales in 1838, Davis was appointed county clerk under Judge James W. Robinson.qv On June 22, 1842, Davis was appointed postmaster of Cuero, which was then in Gonzales County. On November 10, 1846, the year after Texas was admitted to the Union, Governor J. Pinckney Hendersonqv appointed him notary public for DeWitt County.

Mrs. Davis died on December 29, 1846, and was buried under a spreading oak tree on a bluff overlooking the Guadalupe River. Davis died on January 30, 1853, and was buried beside her. The graves are marked and have been fenced off and maintained by the couple's descendants. A Texas historical marker dedicated to the Davises is located on Highway 183, seven miles north of Cuero and about two miles east of the gravesite.

BIBLIOGRAPHY: John Henry Brown, *History of Texas from 1685 to 1892* (2 vols., St. Louis: Daniell, 1893). Vertical Files, Barker Texas History Center, University of Texas at Austin.

W. Lamar Fly

DAVIS, GEORGE WASHINGTON (1817–1880). George Washington Davis, soldier in the Texas Revolution,qv son of Daniel and Elizabeth (Davidson) Davis, was born in Bedford County, Tennessee, on August 1, 1817. His father was a breeder of horses and was assisted in that occupation by his three sons and his daughter. In 1830 Davis and his family left Tennessee with their stock of fine-blooded horses, which became the basis of a family-operated Texas stud farm. On October 2, 1835, Davis participated in the battle of Gonzales,qv when the Gonzales "Come and Take It" cannonqv was successfully defended, and on October 28, 1835, he was with the Texas force at the battle of Concepción.qv He fought at the siege of Bexarqv in December 1835. In 1836 the Davises are said to have burned their homes and joined the Runaway Scrape,qv taking as many of their best-blooded horses as they could. A George Davis, possibly the subject of this article, joined Gen. Sam Houston'sqv volunteer army and fought with him in the battle of San Jacintoqv as a private in Company D of the First Regiment of Texas Volunteers. Davis was married on May 27, 1840, to Mary Caroline Pease, a widow. They had eight children. Mrs. Davis died between 1849 and 1854. On September 12, 1854, Davis married Elizabeth Ann McCullough, a widow. There were no children from the second marriage. Davis died on November 15, 1880, and was buried in the Davis Cemetery, which is on private property off Highway 766 northwest of Cuero, near the DeWitt-Gonzales county line.

BIBLIOGRAPHY: Gonzales County Historical Commission, *History of Gonzales County* (Dallas: Curtis, 1986). Louis J. Wortham, *A History of Texas* (5 vols., Fort Worth: Wortham-Molyneaux, 1924). Vertical Files, Barker Texas History Center, University of Texas at Austin.

W. Lamar Fly

DAVIS, GUSSIE NELL (1906–1993). Gussie Nell Davis, founder of the Kilgore Rangerettesqv (and therefore of the world-wide dance–drill team movement), daughter of Robert Augustus and Mattie Lavinia (Callaway) Davis, was born in Farmersville, Texas, on November 4, 1906. She attended public schools in Farmersville and, with the intention of becoming a concert pianist, entered the College of Industrial Arts (now Texas Woman's University), Denton, in 1923. She changed her major study to physical education and received a B.A. degree from CIA in 1927 and a M.A. from the University of Southern California in 1938.

Miss Davis began her professional career as instructor of physical education and pep-squad director at Greenville High School in 1928. Drawing on her combined experience in music, dance, and physical education, she trained the all-girl "Flaming Flashes" to use small wooden batons that she commissioned from a local furniture maker, as well as flags, various props, drums, and bugles in increasingly complex dance-drills and marches. Although there were several female drum and bugle corps or pep squads performing at football games, the Flaming Flashes were the first twirl-and-dance group. In 1939 when Davis was asked by B. E. Masters, president of Kilgore College, to "find a way to keep people in their seats at halftime" without using drums or bugles, she organized the Kilgore Rangerettes, a precision dance–drill team that performed for the first time in 1940. With the assistance of choreographer Denard Hayden, accompanist Hazel Stewart, long-time sponsor L. N. Crim, and assistants Peggy Coghlan, Barbara Harmon, and Deana Bolton, Miss Davis directed the Rangerettes until her retirement in 1979.

The Rangerettes performed for the Lions International Convention in 1940 and gave their first bowl-game appearance at the Little Rose Bowl in 1946. Subsequently, their performances at college and professional games, conventions, and other events have included the Cotton Bowlqv (annual since 1949, except for 1950), the Sugar Bowl (1950), the All-Star Game (1951–55), President Dwight D. Eisenhower'sqv Inauguration (1953), the International Rotary Convention (1959), the Pecan Bowlqv (1966), the Shrine Bowl (1966), Macy's Thanksgiving Day Parade (1967–69), the National Convention of Chambers of Commerce of Venezuela (1973), the American Fortnight in Hong Kong (1975), various engagements in Romania (1977), and the annual Rangerette Revels (since 1943). The Rangerettes have been cover girls on numerous publications, including *Esquire* (October 1950), *Look* (August 4, 1959), *Saturday Evening Post* (October 5, 1963), *Life* (numerous times), and *Newsweek* (December 12, 1977). They have been the subject of articles in such diverse publications as the *American Weekly* (November 22, 1953), the *Paris Match* (February 29, 1964), *Family Weekly* (December 27, 1964), *Southern Living* (January 1967), *Sports Illustrated* (December 16, 1974), *Texas Star* (November 14, 1971), *Texas Woman* (February 1979), and *Texas Highways*qv (January 1981). They have appeared on the "Ed Sullivan Show" (1952) and "60 Minutes" (1971), and in such movies as Cinerama's *Seven Wonders of the World* (1956). All-American and sportscaster Red Grange dubbed the Rangerettes "Sweethearts of the Nation's Gridirons" (1950). The Ice Capades designed a 1973 show around the young women, who wear white Western hats, belts, and boots, red tops, and "flippy" blue skirts, all parts of a copyrighted costume. The Contemporary Arts Museumqv in Houston spotlighted the group in 1977 as a "living art form."

With Irving Dreibrodt, retired director of the SMU Mustang Band, Davis founded American Drill Team Schools, Incorporated, which has provided instruction for drill teams across the United States. In addition to serving on the Kilgore College Staff (1939–79), Davis was a consultant to drill teams, a judge of drill-team competitions, a member of the National Drill Team Directors Association and Rangerettes Forever, and a member of the board of directors of Fiesta, International.

She and her Rangerettes did not escape controversy. Until the mid-1970's, there were no blacks in the Rangerette line. Davis said, however, that she would be receptive when a qualified black tried out. In response to an adaptation of Erwitt's film *Beauty Knows No Pain* (1971), titled after the Rangerette motto, feminists and other critics expressed dismay at the emphasis on physical attractiveness and rigorous and authoritarian training; the product, the critics charged, was a troupe of "sexist" and "mindless" "Barbie Dolls," and their activity was inappropriate for the college curriculum. Miss Davis countered that there is nothing wrong in learning self-confidence, discipline, cooperation, and the ability to perform precision dance, along with poise, etiquette, and personal grooming. Hard work, team work, and a "boss lady" were necessary ingredients, she stated, to produce a dance performance judged better than that of the professional Rockettes. She further argued that half-time and special-event performances by the Flaming Flashes or the Rangerettes gave girls a chance to experience acclaim previously open only to male athletes and the band. Although Davis admitted that she was "really a devil" in 1940 when she put the Rangerettes' skirts two inches above the knee, the young women, according to her, were always dressed modestly; sex appeal was never mentioned. The director of *Seven Wonders of the World*, Walter Thompson, said that all of America "should be proud" of the Rangerettes. Davis's numerous honors suggest that others share this view.

She was a member of the First Presbyterian Church, Kilgore. She was honored with Gussie Nell Day in Kilgore (1964) and in Farmersville (1970) and Gussie Nell Davis Day in Texas (1979). She was made Texas Woman of the Year by the Texas State Civitans (1969). Davis Hall, a dormitory at Kilgore College, is named in her honor (1969). She was named Women in Communications Headliner of the Year

(1973) and Outstanding Alumna of Texas Woman's University (1978), featured in the Rangerette-Showcase Museum (1979), enrolled in the Greenville High School Football Hall of Fame (1980) and the Texas Women's Hall of Fame as arts nominee (1990), and given numerous commendations. She died in Kilgore on December 20, 1993, of respiratory complications and was buried in Farmersville Cemetery.

BIBLIOGRAPHY: Dallas *Morning News,* December 21, 1993. *Notable Women of Texas, 1984–85* (Irving, Texas: Emerson Publishing, 1984). *Texas Star,* November 14, 1971. Vertical Files, Barker Texas History Center, University of Texas at Austin.   *Jeanie R. Stanley*

DAVIS, JAMES (1790–1859). James Davis, planter, soldier, and politician, was born in Virginia in July 1790. He was an officer during the War of 1812 and fought at the battle of New Orleans. He was appointed sheriff of Marian County, Alabama Territory, in 1818, became county judge of Franklin County, Alabama, in 1823, and was solicitor of the Fourth Judicial Court in that state in 1827. He was elected major general, Second Division, Alabama Militia, in 1833. Davis was appointed United States consul at Santa Fe in November 1831 and moved to Texas about 1834. He served on Gen. Sam Houston's qv staff in 1836 and was asked to help prevent attacks on the Alabama and Coushatta Indians in April 1842. As adjutant general of the Army of the Republic of Texas qv from May to July 1842, Davis and Capt. Ewen Cameron, qv leading what had been a mutinous, disorganized, ill-supplied command, defeated a Mexican force three times their size at the battle of Lipantitlán qv on July 7, 1842.

Having established the Lake Creek Plantation on the west bank of the Trinity River, Davis represented Liberty County in the Eighth Congress of the republic in 1843–44. He was a member of the Constitutional Convention of 1845 qv as well as a delegate to the national Democratic convention at Baltimore in 1848. He was elected state senator from Liberty, Jefferson, Tyler, and Polk counties and served in the Fourth Texas Legislature (1851–53). The 1850 census reported that Davis, one of the wealthiest men in East Texas, owned $50,000 in real property in Polk County and forty-seven slaves in Liberty and Polk counties. He was married to Anne Eliza Hill and had seven children. He supported homestead exemptions for property owners and gave land to help establish a Baptist church in 1848. He died on February 10, 1859, and was buried at Coldspring.

BIBLIOGRAPHY: James Davis Collection, Sam Houston Regional Library, Liberty, Texas. Amelia W. Williams and Eugene C. Barker, eds., *The Writings of Sam Houston, 1813–1863* (8 vols., Austin: University of Texas Press, 1938–43; rpt., Austin and New York: Pemberton Press, 1970).   *Robert Wooster*

DAVIS, JAMES FRANCIS (1870–1942). James Francis (J. Frank) Davis, newspaperman and author, was born on December 20, 1870, in New Bedford, Massachusetts, the son of James and Ann E. (Francis) Davis. He attended public schools in New Bedford and Brockton, Massachusetts. He married Clara Franklin Draper on October 7, 1896. From 1886 to 1904 he worked as a newspaperman, salesman, and publicity man. In 1904 Davis began working for the Boston *American* as dramatic editor and special writer. In 1907 he became managing editor of the Boston *Tribune;* by 1908 he was a special political writer for the Boston *Herald.* He was city editor of the Boston *Traveler* in 1908–09 and associate editor of that paper in 1910, when, because of an injury, he retired to San Antonio, Texas. From 1911 to 1914 he did advertising and publicity work in San Antonio, and about 1915 he began writing fiction. Davis published several books and plays; *Gold in the Hills* (1930) was one of his better-known plays. He wrote short stories and serials for many of the popular magazines of the day, such as *Collier's, Saturday Evening Post, Liberty, Scribner's, American,* and others. The setting of many of his stories was Texas, and he was made an honorary Texas Ranger for his vivid stories of early western life. In 1935 Davis became the state supervisor of the Texas Writers' Project qv of the Work Projects Administration, qv which published *Texas: A Guide to the Lone Star State* (1940) and guidebooks of San Antonio, Corpus Christi, Beaumont, Port Arthur, and Houston, all under Davis's direction. He died on April 6, 1942, in San Antonio and was buried in Mission Burial Park in that city.

BIBLIOGRAPHY: Sam Hanna Acheson, Herbert P. Gambrell, Mary Carter Toomey, and Alex M. Acheson, Jr., *Texian Who's Who,* Vol. 1 (Dallas: Texian, 1937). San Antonio *Express,* April 7, 1942. *Who Was Who in America,* Vol. 2.

DAVIS, JAMES HARVEY (1854–1940). James Harvey (Methodist Jim, Cyclone) Davis, political figure and Populist orator, son of William Barton and Salina (Moore) Davis, was born near Walhalla, South Carolina, on December 24, 1854. The family moved to Texas in 1857 and settled near Winnsboro in Titus (now Franklin) County. Davis's mother died in 1859. His father was a small-time planter who served briefly in the Confederate Army during the "Old Man's Call" of 1865. The Davis family was too poor to provide more than a common-school education for the children. James spent most of his adolescence working on the farm or in a sawmill. He was able to study under the tutelage of attorney John D. Templeton qv during his sixteenth year. He strenuously applied his native talents to academics at night and soon qualified for a teaching certificate. He married Belle Barton, a distant cousin, on December 25, 1878. The couple had four children.

Davis was elected Franklin county judge in 1878 on the Democratic ticket. At the time he was the youngest county judge in Texas. He passed the bar exam in 1879, after taking his seat on the bench. He was reelected in 1880 but declined nomination in 1882. That year he took to the campaign trail on behalf of his mentor, John D. Templeton, the successful Democratic candidate for attorney general of Texas. Davis purchased the Mount Vernon *Franklin Herald* and in 1882 became president of the Texas Press Association. qv

Although he was a passable writer, his real talent lay in oratory. He campaigned for John Ireland, qv who was elected governor in 1884, and became a lecturer for the state Farmers' Alliance qv that same year. Davis became one of the foremost attractions on the alliance speakers' circuit through his verbal assaults upon such opponents as banks and corporations. During the 1880s he was tagged "Methodist Jim" for the fervency of his address. He was neither a Methodist nor a preacher, but a lifelong member of the Disciples of Christ.

When Grover Cleveland blamed the Democratic party's qv support of the coinage of silver for his failure to win the presidency in 1888, Davis left the party. He also sold the *Franklin Herald* and in 1889 founded the Sulphur Springs *Alliance Vindicator.* He campaigned for Democrat James Stephen Hogg qv in his gubernatorial bid in 1890 because the Farmers' Alliance endorsed him. Thereafter, Davis cast his fortunes with the People's (or Populist) party. qv He was one of only five lawyers to participate in the founding convention of the People's party in Cincinnati in 1892, where he served on both the executive and platform committees. He reached the zenith of his career in the next five years, during which he delivered more than a thousand speeches in every important town west of Pennsylvania and south of Maryland for the Populist and prohibition qv causes.

He was one of the most electrifying speakers of his day. Standing nearly 6'3" tall and attired in a long Prince Albert coat, he could ascend a speaker's platform with the presence of a Biblical prophet. He received the nickname Cyclone from an 1894 debate with Kentucky attorney general Watt Hardin. According to an Associated Press reporter, Davis so demolished his opponent that only one sweep of the "Texas Cyclone" was sufficient cause for Hardin to cancel the remaining scheduled debates. With a vocabulary "almost every other word of which seemed drawn from the Gospels or the denunciatory Psalms," as one contemporary put it, Davis could speak for hours. He was said to be able to make his voice heard for blocks without any visible effort. He frequently punctuated his arguments with selections from the works of Jefferson, which he carried with him to the podium. He condemned the Democratic and Republican parties of his day as Hamiltonian in spirit and contended that "the crowd that take their politics from Alexander Hamilton is the crowd we have got to beat."

Davis was a delegate to the Populist national convention of 1892 and served on the committee that drafted the party's Omaha platform, the Bible of Populism. He claimed that every plank of the platform was based on Jeffersonian principles. Davis spoke at the Omaha convention as well as at the Populists' 1892 state convention at Dallas, which nominated him for attorney general. He came in third on election day, with the rest of the Populist ticket. The Populists nominated him for the United States Congress in 1894. He lost a close decision and contested his defeat, along with another Populist congressional candidate, but to no effect. Unlike most Texas Populists Davis favored fusion with the Democrats by 1896. He served as something of a moderating force at the third party's national convention, which nominated Democrat William Jennings Bryan for president and Populist Thomas E. Watson for vice president.

Davis worked to reconcile Populists to Bryan democracy in the declining years of the third party's existence and then joined the Prohibition party when conservatives displaced Bryan as the Democratic leader in 1904. He returned to the Democratic party in 1906 to support such Progressive candidates as Thomas M. Campbell,qv the heir to James Stephen Hogg's agrarian wing of the party (*see also* PROGRESSIVE ERA). Davis campaigned for Woodrow Wilson in 1912 and was elected congressman-at-large from Texas in 1914. He built a profarmer and prolabor record in the United States Congress. He opposed America's entry into World War Iqv and introduced a controversial bill to draft millionaires' money as well as men in time of war. He narrowly lost his bid for reelection in 1916.

Davis engaged in Chautauqua and prohibition work after 1916. He joined the second Ku Klux Klanqv in his later years. In 1932 he came out of political retirement to oppose Joseph W. Bailey, Jr.,qv for congressman-at-large in the Democratic primaries. The elder Joseph W. Baileyqv had been a vehement foe of Populism in the 1890s. Davis lost in the runoff primary. He legally changed his name to James Harvey Cyclone Davis in 1932. He remarried in 1935, after his first wife died, and moved to Kaufman, Texas. As late as 1939 he could be found haranguing the people of Dallas on the need to control Wall Street and the necessity for white supremacy. He died on January 31, 1940, and was buried at Sulphur Springs.

BIBLIOGRAPHY: Cyclone Davis, *Memoir* (Sherman, Texas: Courier, 1935). Frank W. Johnson, *A History of Texas and Texans* (5 vols., ed. E. C. Barker and E. W. Winkler [Chicago and New York: American Historical Society, 1914; rpt. 1916]). Roscoe C. Martin, *The People's Party in Texas* (Austin: University of Texas, 1933; rpt., University of Texas Press, 1970).   *Worth Robert Miller*

DAVIS, JEFFERSON (1808–1889). Jefferson Davis, representative and senator from Mississippi in the United States Congress and later president of the Confederate States of America, was born in Todd County, Kentucky, on June 3, 1808. He advocated the annexationqv of Texas to the United States in 1844. He was in Texas first in 1847, when as an officer in the United States Army he was with Zachary Taylor'sqv force on the Rio Grande. While Davis was United States secretary of war, he recommended in 1854 the Texas or thirty-second-parallel route for construction of a railroad to the Pacific Ocean and in 1856 sent camelsqv to Camp Verde in a project to use the animals for army supply and overland transportation. After Reconstructionqv a movement was launched in Dallas to purchase a homestead for Davis and invite him to move to Texas. On June 14, 1875, he was offered the presidency of the newly established Agricultural and Mechanical College of Texas. When he declined the appointment on July 8, 1875, he wrote of his hopes of revisiting Texas. He died in New Orleans on December 6, 1889. Davis is memorialized in Texas on three monuments placed by the Texas Centennialqv Commission and by the name of Jeff Davis County (formed in 1887).

BIBLIOGRAPHY: C. F. Arrowood, "The Election of Jefferson Davis to the Presidency of the Agricultural and Mechanical College of Texas," *Southwestern Historical Quarterly* 49 (October 1945). Mary Lois Blair, Jefferson Davis and His Interest in the West (M.A. thesis, University of Texas, 1929). Joseph E. Chance, *Jefferson Davis's Mexican War Regiment* (Jackson: University Press of Mississippi, 1991). Clement Eaton, *Jefferson Davis* (New York: Free Press, 1977). L. B. Leslie, "The Purchase and Importation of Camels by the United States Government, 1855–1857," *Southwestern Historical Quarterly* 33 (July 1929). S. S. McKay, "Texas and the Southern Pacific Railroad, 1845–1860, " *Southwestern Historical Quarterly* 35 (July 1931). Harold Schoen, comp., *Monuments Erected by the State of Texas to Commemorate the Centenary of Texas Independence* (Austin: Commission of Control for Texas Centennial Celebrations, 1938). Hudson Strode, *Jefferson Davis* (3 vols., New York: Harcourt Brace, 1955–64).   *Curtis Bishop*

DAVIS, JOHN (1811–1836). John Davis, Alamo defender, was born in Kentucky in 1811. He left his twin brother in Kentucky in his late teens and immigrated to Texas. On October 28, 1831, he received title to a quarter league of land on Lavaca Creek in DeWitt's colony,qv where he gained a reputation as an Indian fighter. On February 23, 1836, Davis was mustered into the Gonzales Ranging Company of Mounted Volunteers. With this unit he arrived at the Alamo on March 1, 1836. He died in the battle of the Alamoqv on March 6, 1836.

BIBLIOGRAPHY: Daughters of the American Revolution, *The Alamo Heroes and Their Revolutionary Ancestors* (San Antonio, 1976). Daughters of the Republic of Texas, *Muster Rolls of the Texas Revolution* (Austin, 1986). Bill Groneman, *Alamo Defenders* (Austin: Eakin, 1990). Texas General Land Office, *An Abstract of the Original Titles of Record in the General Land Office* (Houston: Niles, 1838; rpt., Austin: Pemberton Press, 1964).   *Bill Groneman*

DAVIS, JOHN BURTON (1893–1970). John Burton Davis, newspaperman, war correspondent, and writer, was born in Perryville, Missouri, on October 14, 1893, the son of John Brooks and Laurette (Saunders) Davis. He attended high school in Brownsville, Texas, and Western Military Academy near St Louis. In 1913 he entered the school of journalism at the University of Missouri but withdrew in 1914 due to illness and moved to Brownsville to convalesce. In 1915 he took his first newspaper job with the Brownsville *Daily Herald,* where he covered such events as the Mexican Revolutionqv and the activities of Francisco (Pancho) Villa.qv Davis acted as interpreter for Gen. John J. Pershing'sqv punitive forces in their efforts to capture Villa. From 1919 to 1925 he worked on newspapers in Houston, San Antonio, Fort Worth, and Dallas. He was drama editor for the New York *Morning Telegraph* in 1925–26 and drama critic in 1926–27; he also served as general press agent for Gene Buck in 1927 and associate agent for Florenz Ziegfeld in 1928–29. In World War Iqv Davis served with the American forces in France and Germany. In World War IIqv he was assigned by the Treasury Department to publicize war bonds, and he subsequently remained with the department for twenty years before retiring with honors in 1962 to return to Austin.

Davis married Clare Ogden (*see* DAVIS, CLARE OGDEN) in 1920 in Dallas. He assumed the pen name Lawrence Saunders in the several novels on which they collaborated; most of these were serialized in such popular magazines as *Liberty, Collier's, Ladies' Home Journal,* and *Saturday Evening Post* and later published as books. These included *The Columnist Murder* (1931), *The Devil's Den* (1933), and *Six Weeks* (1932). One of his stories, "Snowed Under," was adapted as a screenplay for Warner Brothers in 1935. Davis died in Austin on April 15, 1970.

BIBLIOGRAPHY: Austin *American-Statesman,* April 16, 1970.

DAVIS, LEWIS GARDNER (1827–1893). Lewis Gardner (L. G., Luke) Davis, legislator, son of William and Elizabeth Brown (Gardner) Davis, was born in Twiggs County, Georgia, on April 4, 1827. His father was a justice of the Inferior Court of Chattahoochee County, Georgia in 1860 and in January 1861 represented the county in the Secession Convention which met in Milledgeville, Georgia. The Davis family moved in the winter of 1835–36 to Russell County, Alabama, where L. G. Davis served one term as tax collector in 1855–56. In 1861 he enlisted in the Confederate States Army at Columbus, Georgia, in Company B, Twenty-eighth Battalion, Georgia Siege Artillery. Davis was promoted to First Lt., Company K, First Georgia Regulars in December 1864. He married Margaret Jane Aldredge on January 11, 1848, in Russell County, Alabama. They were the parents of four children. Davis moved his family in the winter of 1868–69 to Upshur County, Texas, where relatives had settled after the war. He farmed on his homestead, and after Camp County was organized from Upshur, he was elected county commissioner for Precinct No. 1 in 1878. Davis served in 1883–84 in the House of Representatives, where he was appointed to the Committee on Roads, Bridges, and Ferries. Davis died in Pittsburg, Camp County, on July 10, 1893.

BIBLIOGRAPHY: Laura J. D. Scarborough, *Southern Kith and Kin* (4 vols., Abilene, Texas, 1951–58). Texas Legislative Council, *Members of the Texas Legislature, 1846–1980* (Austin, 1980?). Texas Legislature, *House Journal*, 18th Leg., Reg. Sess., January 9, 1883.

Caroline B. Bass

DAVIS, MARY HILL (ca. 1860–1934). Mary Hill Davis, advocate of Baptist missions and denominational leader, was born in Greenville, Georgia, around 1860, the daughter of Waid Hampton and Margaret (Lawson) Hill. She descended from Huguenots who arrived in Virginia around 1700. In 1870 her parents moved to Dallas, Texas, where they joined the First Baptist Church.qv Her education came primarily from private tutors. When she was twenty years old she married F. S. Davis, a Dallas physician.

Mrs. Davis served as recording secretary of the Texas Woman's Missionary Unionqv from 1898 to 1906. She was elected president of the organization in 1906 and served for the next twenty-five years. Her first action as president was to organize the Young Women's Auxiliary in 1907 to educate young women for mission work. She organized the Royal Ambassadors in 1908 and the Girl's Auxiliary in 1913 for the same purpose. She also encouraged the WMU to support Baptist work among students on college campuses. Under her leadership the WMU grew from 350 mission societies in 1906 to 1,732 in 1931. To coordinate the union's work she helped introduce a district plan that organized the WMU into district unions. Although the organization grew, she stressed that the local missionary society was the most vital element of the WMU. She encouraged Baptists to support missions both spiritually and financially. During her tenure the WMU raised money to construct facilities for the Williford-Miller and Annie Jenkins Sallee schools in China, the Baptist Women's Missionary Training School in Fort Worth (a part of Southwestern Baptist Theological Seminary), and the Women's Memorial Dormitory at Baylor University. She also solicited WMU contributions to Buckner Orphans Home (see BUCKNER BAPTIST CHILDREN'S HOME). In 1910 the WMU set aside the last week in September as an annual time to stress financial and spiritual support for state missions.

In addition to her work with the WMU, Mrs. Davis served as chairman of the Advisory Board of the Women's Missionary Training School from 1911 to 1934 and as vice president of the Baptist Missionary Union, an auxiliary to the Southern Baptist Convention, for twenty-six years. As a vocal supporter of the involvement of women in denominational affairs, she also spoke publicly to promote the Seventy-five Million Campaign, a missionary offering. In 1935 the Texas Woman's Missionary Union named the annual offering for state missions the Mary Hill Davis Offering. Mary Davis died in Dallas on November 28, 1934.

BIBLIOGRAPHY: L. R. Elliott, ed., *Centennial Story of Texas Baptists* (Dallas: Baptist General Convention of Texas, 1936). *Encyclopedia of Southern Baptists* (4 vols., Nashville: Broadman, 1958–82). Mrs. W. J. J. Smith, *A Centennial History of the Baptist Women of Texas* (Dallas: Woman's Missionary Union of Texas, 1933).

Ricky Paris

DAVIS, MERVYN BATHURST (1844–1912). Mervyn Bathurst Davis, newspaper correspondent and conservationist, son of J. Lucius and Elizabeth H. Davis, was born in Henrico County, Virginia, on October 14, 1844. He was raised on his father's farm and attended Virginia Military Institute in Richmond. During the Civil Warqv he served in Company G, Tenth Virginia Cavalry, and Company E, Fifty-ninth Virginia Infantry, Army of Northern Virginia.

In 1873 he moved to Waco, Texas, where he worked on the staff of the Waco *Daily Reporter*. Between September 1877 and March 1878 he served two short periods as a Texas Ranger in the Frontier Battalion.qv In 1880 he was living in Bexar County and was employed as a journalist. By 1883 he was working in Fort Worth for the Dallas *Weekly Herald* (see DALLAS HERALD), but moved to Dallas the following year to join the Dallas *Morning News*.qv In 1885 he was placed on the staff of the Dallas *News* and in the following year was transferred to Waco as a correspondent, a position that he retained for the remainder of his life.

Davis was best known for his work in wildlife protection. In 1881, in association with Champe Carter McCulloch (McColluch in some sources) and Herman E. Ambolt of Waco, he formed the first Game Protective Association in Texas. As secretary of this association he conducted a campaign, chiefly through the press, to alert the public to the need for wildlife protection.

A chapter of the Audubon Society was formed in 1899 in Galveston, but most of its members were killed in the Galveston hurricane of 1900,qv and it was not until 1903 that an attempt was made to reestablish the society in Texas. From 1904 until his death in 1912, Davis was the secretary of the Texas Audubon societies. As such he had the responsibility of coordinating the formation of branch societies, implementing the educational campaign of the society, and reporting to the national organization. About 1906 Davis and state Audubon director Henry Philemon Attwaterqv organized a campaign through which they and other Audubon representatives lectured before local clubs and state organizations. In 1907 Davis, Attwater, and Oscar Charles Guessazqv served on the Game Law Committee that recommended not only the reenactment of the 1903 Model Game Law but also the requiring of licenses for both resident and nonresident hunters, with the revenue from licenses and fines to be used solely for game protection and propagation. In May 1910 Davis was elected an honorary life member of the Museum and Scientific Society of Houston in recognition of his work in conservation.

Davis was the author of numerous newspaper articles on the conservation and humane treatment of wildlife. He was instrumental in the formation of the Texas Humane Society in Waco during the early 1900s and for several years served as its secretary. In May 1912 he served on the Constitution and By-laws Committee of the Texas Game and Fish Protective Association, which was formed in Waco. He also collaborated with Attwater in the compilation of information for "Use and Value of Wild Birds to Texas Farmers and Stockmen and Fruit and Truck Growers," published in 1914 as Bulletin Number 37 of the Texas Department of Agriculture.

In 1888 Davis helped organize Pat Cleburne Camp in Waco. He was twice married and had two children, Constance and Mervyn Bathurst, Jr. He died on June 18, 1912, and is buried in Oakwood Cemetery, Waco.

BIBLIOGRAPHY: Dallas *Morning News*, June 19, 1912. M. B. Davis, "The Audubon Societies: News from Texas," *Bird Lore* 11 (1909). M. B. Davis, "State Audubon Reports: Texas," *Bird Lore* 11 (1909). "For Better Protection," *Texas Field and National Guardsman*, June 1912. Gilbert T. Pearson, "Some Audubon Workers: Captain M. B. Davis,"

Bird Lore 12 (1910). "Report of the Game Law Committee," *Texas Field and Sportsman,* February 1907.   Stanley D. Casto

DAVIS, MOLLIE EVELYN MOORE (1844–1909). Mollie Evelyn Moore Davis, poet and editor, daughter of John and Mary Ann (Crutchfield) Moore, was born Mary Evalina Moore on April 12, 1844, in Talladega, Alabama. The family moved to Texas in 1855 and lived at Manchaca, San Marcos, Garden Valley, Tyler, and Galveston. At the age of fourteen Mary Evalina Moore changed her name to Mollie Evelyn Moore. At the age of sixteen she began writing for Tyler newspapers, and her poems attracted the attention of Edward H. Cushing[qv] of the Houston *Telegraph.* During the next five years, which she spent in Tyler and Houston, she wrote most of her best poetry and gained a statewide reputation. In 1867, when her family moved to Galveston, her poems appeared in the Galveston *News*[qv] and her first collection, *Minding the Gap and Other Poems,* was published by Cushing. Enlarged editions appeared in 1869 and 1872. In 1874 she married Thomas E. Davis, who in 1879 joined the staff of the New Orleans *Times.* Mrs. Davis, already nationally recognized as a poet, became a leader in social and literary life in New Orleans as she had been during the previous five years in Houston. In a series of essays, "Kerenhappuch and I," in the *Picayune,* she described her experiences in learning the city. On visits to her brother's family in Comanche, Texas, she conquered tuberculosis and collected story material. By 1889, when she became editor of the *Picayune,* her home was a literary salon. Her works are divided between Texas and New Orleans backgrounds, between juvenile and adult literature, between poetry and prose, and between realism and romanticism. Although many of her poems are uncollected and some were never printed, she published twelve books in addition to the first volume of poetry: *In War Times at La Rose Blanche* (1888); *Under the Man–Fig* (1895), a novel of East Texas; *A Christmas Masque of Saint Roch* (1896); *Under Six Flags* (1897), a school history of Texas; *An Elephant's Track and Other Stories* (1897); *The Wire-Cutters* (1899), a novel of West Texas; *The Queen's Garden* (1900); *Jaconetta: Her Loves* (1901); *A Bunch of Roses and Other Parlor Plays* (1903); *The Little Chevalier* (1903); *The Price of Silence* (1907); and *The Moons of Balbanca* (1908). Selected Poems (1927) was published by friends years after her death on January 1, 1909. In 1955 a Japanese firm published her *Ships of Desire.*

BIBLIOGRAPHY: Mollie Evelyn Moore Davis Papers, Barker Texas History Center, University of Texas at Austin. *In Memoriam: Mary Evelyn Moore Davis* (New Orleans: Picayune Job Print, 1909?). Vertical Files, Barker Texas History Center, University of Texas at Austin. Clyde Winfield Wilkinson, The Broadening Stream: The Life and Literary Career of Mollie E. Moore Davis (Ph.D. dissertation, University of Illinois, 1951).   C. W. Wilkinson

DAVIS, MORGAN J. (1898–1979). Morgan J. Davis, petroleum geologist, son of John Wesley and Gabriella (Jones) Davis, was born at Anson, Texas, on November 18, 1898. He graduated from high school in Fort Worth in 1915 and enrolled in Texas Christian University in 1916. World War I[qv] interrupted his college studies, and he served briefly in the armed services. In 1918 he took a job as assistant engineer for Holway and Associates on the Spavinaw, Oklahoma, water supply project. He met Veta Clare Moore at Claremore, Oklahoma, and they were married in 1926.

In 1924–1925 he attended the University of Texas, where he earned a bachelor's degree in geology. At UT he came under the influence of Leonidas T. Barrow,[qv] who at that time was on the faculty. Barrow joined the Humble Oil and Refining Company (now Exxon Company, U.S.A.), and in 1925 Davis joined the company as a field geologist. In 1929 he took a position with the Nederlandsche Koloniale Petroleum Mattschappij as supervisor of geological exploration in Java and Sumatra. In 1934 he returned to the United States and rejoined Humble as geologist at Roswell, New Mexico. Later he rose successively to the posts of chief geologist, president, and chairman of the board. He retired from Humble in 1963 but continued his petroleum geology work in Houston as a consultant until his death.

He was president of the American Association of Petroleum Geologists in 1952–53 and president of the Geological Society of America in 1969–70. He received many honors, among them an honorary doctorate of engineering from the Colorado School of Mines and the Sidney Powers Memorial Medal (1979) from the American Association of Petroleum Geologists. He was a Mason. He died of cancer in Houston on December 31, 1979, and was buried from an Episcopalian church in Houston. Upon his death, the Houston *Post* eulogized him for "a life distinguished by vision and action for the common good."

BIBLIOGRAPHY: Wallace E. Pratt and Dean A. McGee, "Memorial to Morgan J. Davis," *American Association of Petroleum Geologists Bulletin* 65 (1981).   Samuel P. Ellison, Jr.

DAVIS, NATHANIEL HART (1815–1893). Nathaniel Hart Davis, pioneer and county official, third son of Nathaniel Bowe and Martha D. Davis, was born in Fayette County, Kentucky, on November 6, 1815. In 1817 his family moved to Alabama, where he received his early education. He attended Transylvania University and later taught at Marion Military Academy. He received a license to practice law in Alabama in 1837. In 1840 he moved to Montgomery, Texas. He served as county attorney, commissioner, and chief justice of Montgomery County, and as judge of the Thirteenth Judicial District from 1867 to 1870. As a member of the Somervell expedition[qv] he served under Col. Joseph L. Bennett,[qv] in whose home he had lived during his first years in Texas. In 1851 Davis married Sarah Elizabeth White, a native of South Carolina; they had seven children. He died on October 8, 1893, and was buried in Montgomery.

BIBLIOGRAPHY: Nathaniel Hart Davis Papers, Barker Texas History Center, University of Texas at Austin. Houston *Post,* October 10, 1893.
                Margaret Davis Cameron

DAVIS, NICHOLAS A. (1824–1894). Nicholas A. Davis, Presbyterian minister, the son of Mr. and Mrs. Nathaniel Davis, was born on August 8, 1824, in Limestone County, Alabama. His father served in the Alabama legislature from 1840 to 1851. Though he lacked college and seminary training, he studied theology with Robert Donnell of the Cumberland Presbyterian Church. After ordination he spent a decade in full-time ministry in northern Alabama communities, including White Plains, where he married Nancy Isabella Worthington on November 2, 1852. With their two small daughters the Davises moved to Bastrop, Texas, in November 1857. A son was born in the following year, but he and Mrs. Davis died before Davis departed for Virginia on August 16, 1861, as a chaplain in the Confederate Army.

Davis served in the Fourth Regiment of John B. Hood's[qv] Texas Brigade. Preaching sermons, visiting the sick and wounded, and performing funerals were among the chaplain's routine responsibilities. Davis, however, became dissatisfied with the dispersion of wounded Texas soldiers throughout Richmond and obtained permission to supervise the construction of a hospital ward for these soldiers, which became known as the Texas Hospital. His services also included alms and loans to the needy, and the personal items of some men found their way to him for safekeeping. Because he believed that General Hood's men had received insufficient praise, Davis wrote *Campaign from Texas to Maryland, with the Battle of Fredericksburg;* the book was published in Richmond in 1863, and a slightly revised edition appeared in Houston the same year.

Back in Texas and out of uniform, Davis married Eliza E. Coley Radford, widow of Robert W. Radford, on February 7, 1865. Radford's estate included property known as the Old John Smith Plantation, which amounted to more than 2,000 acres of Sabine County. To this second marriage were born four children. Davis continued to preach in various East Texas towns and to involve himself in diverse business interests. He established the first commercial orchard in Jacksonville, a peach orchard, and made that area noted for fruit growing. He served intermittently for nearly twenty years on the board of trustees of Trinity University and was highly influential, not only on young ministers but also on businessmen. He died in San Antonio on November 19, 1894, while on a visit to his daughter.

BIBLIOGRAPHY: Nicholas A. Davis, *Chaplain Davis and Hood's Texas Brigade*, ed. Donald E. Everett (San Antonio: Principia Press of Trinity University, 1962).

Donald E. Everett

DAVIS, ROY BENNETT (1900–1975). Roy Bennett Davis, cotton expert, was born on December 10, 1900, in McGregor, Texas, the second of ten children of Clifford L. and Jessie (Burson) Davis. In 1906 his father moved the family from the McLennan County farm to a farm near Lamesa, where they lived first in a dugout.qv There Davis began picking cotton at the age of six and attended a rural school when he could be spared from farm chores. He attended Lubbock High School and in 1923 became one of the school's first graduates of the vocational agricultural program. He enrolled at the Agricultural and Mechanical College of Texas (now Texas A&M University) and received a B.S. degree in animal husbandry in 1927. His first job was with the Texas Agricultural Extension Serviceqv as a county agent for Gaines, Hale, and Terry counties, a position he held from 1927 to 1932. He married Dennise Cobb on December 21, 1929. The couple had two children.

Davis next worked as manager of a butter and cheese plant, the Plains Co-Op, in Plainview. During his tenure there, he changed the cream-processing plant to a whole-milk operation and ultimately made it one of the largest of its kind in the Southwest. In 1935, as a result of his success during difficult economic times in his managership of the Plainview plant, Governor James Allredqv asked Davis to serve as a regent of Texas A&M.

From 1938 to 1943 Davis was secretary and vice president of the Houston Bank for Cooperatives. From 1943 to 1971 he was general manager of the Plains Cooperative Oil Mill in Plainview. Initially, under his leadership, four hydraulic presses of 1900 vintage were replaced, and in the early 1940s four more hydraulic presses were added. Later he added two screw presses. After World War IIqv the work was done by eight screw presses. In 1952 the mill was converted from the hydraulic and screw-press extraction method to that of a solvent operation, and its daily capacity increased to 800 tons. The mill capacity increased to 1,200 tons daily by the early 1960s. As a result of his work the Plains Cooperative Oil Mill became the largest in the world. Because he continuously sought international trade markets for United States cotton, Davis was the prime promoter in making Lubbock and the Texas South Plains the inland cotton capital of the world.

From 1951 to 1959 Davis served as director of the Texas Credit Administration; he was vice chairman for one term. In 1969 Governor Preston Smith appointed him chairman of the Texas Rural Development Commission. Later he was appointed a member of the Advisory Council for Technical Vocational Education in Texas, a position that pleased Davis because of his own high school training in vocational education. He shared his expertise in cotton importing and exporting for four years as a member of the Research Export Expansion Council under appointment by Secretary of Commerce A. B. Trowbridge. In the late 1940s and early 1950s he served on numerous industrial committees and the Department of Agriculture's cotton and cottonseed research and marketing advisory committee. He was one of the founders of Plains Cotton Growers in Lubbock. For eight years beginning in 1956 Davis was a delegate to the policy-making agency of the National Cotton Council of America. He served in various offices of the group, giving unusual advisory assistance as chairman of the special export committee.

He hosted an annual banquet for the Lubbock Eastern Little League baseball teams (including one team sponsored by his mill).

He was a member of the boards of directors of the Lubbock Chamber of Commerce and the United Fund. For many years he served as a member of the Texas Tech University Foundation Board. After retirement he served as an advisory director of the Textile Research Center at Texas Tech. In 1968 he was voted Distinguished Alumnus of the Year at Texas A&M, where in 1971 the Roy B. Davis Distinguished Professorship in Agricultural Cooperation was established. Davis was a Baptist and a Mason. He was a thirty-second degree Shriner. He died on August 25, 1975, in Lubbock and was buried at Resthaven Cemetery. *See also* COTTON CULTURE, COTTONSEED INDUSTRY.

BIBLIOGRAPHY: William N. Stokes, Jr., *Oil Mill on the Texas Plains* (College Station: Texas A&M University Press, 1979).

Jeanne F. Lively

DAVIS, SAMUEL BOYER (1827–1885). Samuel Boyer Davis, military officer, was born in 1827 in Louisiana; he attended the United States Military Academy for about six months. He served on the Texas border during the early part of the Mexican Warqv and later saw service as an officer of the Fourteenth Infantry under Col. Paul O. Hébert.qv He was brevetted first lieutenant at Churubusco, suffered a wound at Molino del Rey, and was in action at Chapultepec and Mexico City. After the war Davis resided in Texas until the Civil War.qv In mid-1861 he organized seven companies from Harris, Caldwell, Galveston, Leon, Montgomery, Washington, Liberty, and Fort Bend counties, formed them into Davis's Mounted Battalion, and became major of that unit. He also was assistant adjutant general at General Hébert's headquarters for the District of Texas. On December 7, 1861, Maj. Xavier B. DeBrayqv assumed command of the mounted battalion when Davis assumed full-time administrative functions under Hébert. In February 1862 three more companies from Montgomery, Grimes, and Harris counties were added to DeBray's command, which was reorganized as the Twenty-sixth Texas Cavalry. When Hébert appointed Davis colonel of the new unit, members of the regiment protested and claimed the right to elect their own officers. Davis then resigned from the unit, and DeBray was elected regimental commander. Davis was first married to Mary Minerva Monk Clark, with whom he had two sons; his wife and children died in 1854–55 during a yellow fever epidemic. On March 28, 1867, he married Rhoda Catherine Milby in Galveston; they had five daughters and three sons. After this marriage Davis lived in Houston and Galveston; he died in 1885 while visiting in New Orleans.

BIBLIOGRAPHY: Service Records, National Archives, Washington.

Allan C. Ashcraft

DAVIS, SAMUEL S. (1810–1859). Samuel S. Davis, soldier, legislator, and lawman, was born in Lincoln County, Georgia, in 1810. He emigrated to Texas in 1831 with his widowed mother, Mrs. Nancy Davis, and other family members. He served at the battle of Nacogdochesqv in 1832 and, in the Texas Revolution,qv served as a private in Capt. John M. Bradley'sqv company from April 30 to July 30, 1836. After the war he settled in San Augustine County, where he was reportedly a "great factor in promoting the general welfare and preserving the order" of the district. Davis was elected to the House of Representatives of the Fourth Congress of the Republic of Texas, where he represented San Augustine from November 11, 1839, until February 5, 1840. In 1843 he was elected sheriff of San Augustine—the second and last from the county during the period of the republic—and was subsequently reelected for several terms. Davis was said to have been an officer in the Mexican War;qv a Samuel Davis served as a second lieutenant in Company K of Col. George T. Wood'sqv Second Regiment, Texas Mounted Volunteers; since this company was recruited primarily at Milam in neighboring Sabine County, one may reasonably assume him to have been Samuel S. Davis. When Kenneth L. Andersonqv died in 1845, Davis purchased the Anderson estate on the southeast border of San Augustine County; he resided there for the rest of his life. Davis married Mary T. Price in San Augustine on February 21, 1845. They had four children. A land warrant was issued in October 1854 for Davis's military service. He died in November 1859, and is believed to be buried in the Davis-Sexton family cemetery in San Augustine.

BIBLIOGRAPHY: Daughters of the Republic of Texas, *Muster Rolls of the Texas Revolution* (Austin, 1986). John S. Ford, *Rip Ford's Texas*, ed. Stephen B. Oates (Austin: University of Texas Press, 1963). Texas House of Representatives, *Biographical Directory of the Texan Conventions and Congresses, 1832–1845* (Austin: Book Exchange, 1941).

Thomas W. Cutrer

DAVIS, THOMAS (?–?). Thomas Davis, farmer and public official, was a partner of David H. Milburn qv as one of Stephen F. Austin's qv Old Three Hundred qv families. They received title to a sitio qv now in Austin County on July 29, 1824. The census of 1826 classified Davis as a farmer, a single man aged between twenty-five and forty. He was elected regidor qv of the ayuntamiento qv of San Felipe de Austin in February 1828. At the January 1829 meeting of the ayuntamiento he proposed provisional organization of the colonial militia by election of company officers. On November 27, 1829, he was appointed to preside over an election to be held at the home of William Stafford.qv Davis's bill presented to the ayuntamiento in December 1830 for guarding and boarding two criminals was rejected on the grounds that he had aided Hiram Friley to escape. Davis was in San Felipe as late as 1834, but in 1838 he was proprietor of the Hamilton townsite, opposite Harrisburg. Austin County tax rolls for 1838 list Davis as the holder of 550 acres of land and ten cattle, an estate valued at $1,200.

BIBLIOGRAPHY: Eugene C. Barker, ed., *The Austin Papers* (3 vols., Washington: GPO, 1924–28). Eugene C. Barker, ed., "Minutes of the Ayuntamiento of San Felipe de Austin, 1828–1832," 12 parts, *Southwestern Historical Quarterly* 21–24 (January 1918–October 1920). Lester G. Bugbee, "The Old Three Hundred: A List of Settlers in Austin's First Colony," *Quarterly of the Texas State Historical Association* 1 (October 1897).

DAVIS, WATERS S. (1862–1935). Waters Davis, lawyer, sportsman, and reformer, was born on March 15, 1862, in Corpus Christi, the son of Anna (Britton) and republican governor Edmund Jackson Davis.qv He attended Texas public schools and the University of Michigan, where he received his law degree in 1885, the year he returned to Texas and married Mary Agnes Howard in San Antonio. The couple headed for the booming frontier town of El Paso, where Davis began a law firm. He was chosen president of the El Paso Republican Club in 1889 and headed the successful campaign to elect Adolf Krakauer qv mayor. It transpired, however, that Krakauer had not yet received his citizenship papers and was unqualified to serve. In 1892 Davis helped form the law firm of Davis, Hague, and Falvey.

He was a star of the El Paso Browns, the pioneer baseball team that had many of the town's leading citizens on its roster. He was credited with hitting the longest home run ever witnessed in pioneer El Paso. He helped to introduce golf in the city and was one of the organizers of the first El Paso Country Club. In 1895 Davis built a fine residence in what was then a choice section, at 1280 East San Antonio. Tillie Howard, one of the town's best known madames, had built a luxurious home across the street from Davis, who was already undertaking his first steps to reform the wide-open town. Even though the young city government had come to depend heavily on revenue from gambling and prostitution, Davis and Richard F. Burges qv established the Citizens Reform League in 1901 and were successful in curtailing gambling and prostitution in El Paso. Davis died on April 14, 1935.

BIBLIOGRAPHY: J. Morgan Broaddus, *The Legal Heritage of El Paso* (El Paso: Texas Western College Press, 1963). C. L. Sonnichsen, *Pass of the North: Four Centuries on the Rio Grande* (2 vols., El Paso: Texas Western Press, 1968, 1980). W. H. Timmons, *El Paso: A Borderlands History* (El Paso: Texas Western Press, 1990).

Conrey Bryson

DAVIS, WILLIAM (1805–?). William Davis was a prominent planter and slave owner in Burleson County. He was born in Georgia in 1805 and appears in the United States Census of 1860. He owned 121 slaves and held 900 acres of land on which he raised corn and cotton.

BIBLIOGRAPHY: Randolph B. Campbell, *An Empire for Slavery: The Peculiar Institution in Texas, 1821–1865* (Baton Rouge: Louisiana State University Press, 1989).

Art Leatherwood

DAVIS, WILLIAM KINCHEN (1822–1891). William Kinchen Davis, early Texas settler and Perote prisoner, son of Kinchen W. and Fannie (Pleasants) Davis, was born in Morgan County, Alabama, on November 11, 1822. The family moved to Texas in 1830 as members of Stephen F. Austin's qv colony and settled in what is now Fort Bend County. One source described Davis's early education as "meager." He served in a campaign against the Indians on the Brazos River in 1839 and in 1842 was with the Somervell expedition.qv When the command dissolved on the Rio Grande, he accompanied the Mier Expedition qv and was severely wounded at Mier. He was marched with other prisoners to Salado, escaped, and was recaptured and marched back to Salado, where he drew a white bean (see BLACK BEAN EPISODE). He was sent to Mexico City and put to hard labor, then held in Perote Prison qv until September 16, 1844, when he was given one dollar with which to make the trip back to Texas. In 1845 Davis married Jane Pickens. Five children were born to them. His first wife died in 1860, and he married Mrs. Jane Green of Richmond on March 5, 1865. He commanded a company for about six months during the Civil War.qv Davis was a Methodist and a member of the International Order of Odd Fellows. He died on August 2, 1891, and was buried in Morton Cemetery in Richmond.

BIBLIOGRAPHY: John Henry Brown, *Indian Wars and Pioneers of Texas* (Austin: Daniell, 1880; reprod., Easley, South Carolina: Southern Historical Press, 1978). Hugh Nugent Fitzgerald, ed., *Texans and Their State: A Newspaper Reference Work* (2 vols., Houston: Texas Biographical Association, 1918). Thomas J. Green, *Journal of the Texian Expedition Against Mier* (New York: Harper, 1845; rpt., Austin: Steck, 1935). Andrew Jackson Sowell, *History of Fort Bend County* (Houston: Coyle, 1904; rpt, Richmond, Texas: Fort Bend County Historical Museum, 1974). Clarence Wharton, *Wharton's History of Fort Bend County* (San Antonio: Naylor, 1939).

DAVIS, WILLIAM LEONARD (?–?). W. L. Davis, black newspaper editor and Houston civic leader, edited the *Western Star* newspaper until its demise in 1914. In August of that year Davis was elected president of the Teachers State Association of Texas.qv He later served as a trustee of Butler College, secretary of the State Sunday School Convention, vice president of the National Baptist Sunday School Congress, and superintendent of the Sunday school at Antioch Baptist Church. In 1918 he was secretary of the executive board of the Negro Division of the Federal Food Administration, and in 1920 he ran unsuccessfully for the state Senate. Davis was a coplaintiff with Charles N. Love,qv editor of the *Texas Freeman*, and others in filing for an injunction to test the validity of the white primary qv at Houston in 1921. Love and Davis retained R. D. Evans of Waco to handle the case, which eventually was decided in the United States Supreme Court against the plaintiffs.

BIBLIOGRAPHY: Alwyn Barr, *Black Texans: A History of Negroes in Texas, 1528–1971* (Austin: Jenkins, 1973). *Big Town, Big Money (The Business of Houston)* (Houston: Cordovan Press, 1973). Darlene Clark Hine, *Black Victory: The Rise and Fall of the White Primary in Texas* (Millwood, New York: KTO Press, 1979). Andrew Webster Jackson, *A Sure Foundation and a Sketch of Negro Life in Texas* (Houston, 1940).

Howard Jones, *The Red Diary: A Chronological History of Black Americans in Houston and Some Neighboring Harris County Communities—122 Years Later* (Austin: Nortex Press, 1991).

Diana J. Kleiner

DAVIS, TEXAS. Davis, also known as Davistown and as Davis Switch, is a farming community on State Highway 97 eight miles southwest of Charlotte in southwestern Atascosa County. It was named for M. M. Davis, a local rancher who gave land for the San Antonio, Uvalde and Gulf Railroad in 1914. From 1925 to 1929 the community was served by a post office officially named Daviston; Joe Key was the first postmaster. In the 1940s the community had a factory, two other businesses, and a few widely scattered dwellings. By the 1980s only a few dwellings remained at the site.

BIBLIOGRAPHY: *Atascosa County History* (Pleasanton, Texas: Atascosa History Committee, 1984). Margaret G. Clover, The Place Names of Atascosa County (M.A. thesis, University of Texas, 1952).

Linda Peterson

DAVIS COUNTY. Davis County existed under the Davis name between 1861 and 1871. It was originally named Cass County, for Senator Lewis Cass of Michigan. In 1861 the county was renamed in honor of Jefferson Davis.qv In 1871, reflecting the sentiments of the Reconstructionqv period, the name was changed back to Cass County.

BIBLIOGRAPHY: Hans Peter Nielsen Gammel, comp., *Laws of Texas, 1822–1897* (10 vols., Austin: Gammel, 1898).

Seymour V. Connor

DAVIS CREEK (Fannin County). Davis Creek, also known as Rock Creek, rises two miles north of Bailey in south central Fannin County (at 33°29′ N, 96°08′ W) and runs north for six miles to its mouth on Bois d'Arc Creek, just south of Bonham (at 33°33′ N, 96°10′ W). The creek traverses an area that varies from rolling prairie with locally steep slopes to flat terrain with occasional shallow depressions. Soils near the creek include sandy loams, as well as deep to shallow expansive clays and clay loams, that support oak, juniper, water-tolerant hardwoods, and grasses. The area has served as range and crop land.

_____ (Limestone County). Davis Creek rises three miles northeast of Thornton in southern Limestone County (at 31°27′ N, 96°33′ W) and runs southeast for twelve miles to its mouth on Steele Creek, four miles southwest of Oletha (at 31°20′ N, 96°29′ W). The stream descends from an elevation of 519 feet above sea level to 360 feet. Its tributaries include Brier Creek, Sand Branch, Wolf Hollow, and Keel Creek. Davis Creek first traverses rolling prairie with clayey soils, then passes into an eroded area with sandy loams and hardwood forests. Near the mouth of the creek its bed is broad and shallow. Davis Creek probably derives its name from the family of Brinkley Davis, who traveled from Indiana in the latter half of 1845 and received a land grant at the source of the creek. After serving in the Mexican War,qv Brinkley's two oldest sons, Eli and John, established farms of their own near their father's. The settlement was known as Davis Prairie.

BIBLIOGRAPHY: Hampton Steele, *A History of Limestone County, 1833–1860* (Mexia, Texas: Mexia News, n.d.). Ray A. Walter, *A History of Limestone County* (Austin: Von Boeckmann–Jones, 1959).

_____ (Newton County). Davis Creek rises about three miles south of Newton in central Newton County (at 30°49′ N, 93°46′ W) and runs southeast for just over fourteen miles to its mouth on the Sabine River, nearly two miles southeast of Belgrade (at 30°41′ N, 93°38′ W). The creek, which is particularly sluggish in its lower reaches, passes for the most part through deep loamy soil, although near its mouth the soil becomes more sandy. Davis Creek may have been named for Pleasant Davis, who received the original land grant for the area in which it rises.

DAVIS GUARDS. The Davis Guards, a Confederate Army unit named for Jefferson Davisqv and composed of forty-five enlisted men, one engineer, and one surgeon, all Irish and all in their twenties or younger, belonged to Company F, Texas Heavy Artillery, under Capt. Frederick H. Odlum. The recruits were hand-picked from the docks at Houston and Galveston and were known as the Fighting Irishmen. In August 1863 the unit, under command of Richard W. (Dick) Dowling,qv was ordered to man the guns at Fort Sabine,qv half a mile below Sabine City. They constructed an earthen-work fort large enough to hold their six guns. In the battle of Sabine Pass,qv September 8, 1863, in the space of forty minutes, they fired 137 shots without stopping to swab the guns. Although they captured 350 prisoners and killed 50 Union soldiers, the Davis Guards sustained no losses. Gen. John B. Magruderqv gave them a special citation and presented them with silver medals, said to be the only medals struck during the Confederacy. A benefit performance in Houston raised $3,000 for the Guards, and the Confederate States Congress passed a special resolution of thanks to the unit. The Guards spent the last two years of the Civil Warqv in comparative inactivity at Sabine Pass. A number of them, as well as Dick Dowling, are buried in St. Vincents Cemetery, Houston. The monument erected at Sabine Pass by the Texas Centennial Commission in 1937 bears the names of the Guards.

BIBLIOGRAPHY: V. G. Jackson, A History of Sabine Pass (M.A. thesis, University of Texas, 1930). Thomas Clarence Richardson, *East Texas: Its History and Its Makers* (4 vols., New York: Lewis Historical Publishing, 1940). Harold Schoen, comp., *Monuments Erected by the State of Texas to Commemorate the Centenary of Texas Independence* (Austin: Commission of Control for Texas Centennial Celebrations, 1938).

DAVIS HOLLOW. Davis Hollow, a valley in southeastern San Saba County, begins about 18½ miles southeast of San Saba (at 30°58′ N, 98°36′ W) and runs north for ten miles to its mouth on Cherokee Creek (at 31°02′ N, 98°35′ W). The valley crosses flat terrain with shallow to deep depressions, surfaced by clayey and sandy loam soils that support primarily live oak, Ashe juniper, mesquite, and grasses.

DAVIS MOUNTAINS. The Davis Mountains, the "Texas Alps," are the second highest range in Texas. They extend sixty miles in the shape of a V from north to west central Jeff Davis County, with the point to the southeast at Fort Davis; the approximate center of the range is ten miles northwest of Fort Davis (at 30°43′ N, 104°00′ W). The highest elevation in the Davis Mountains is 8,378-foot Mount Livermore, the fifth-highest peak in the state; several other peaks in the range rise to over 7,000 feet above sea level.

The Davis Mountains originated some thirty-five million years ago during a period of violent volcanic activity in western North America. They are composed of various horizontally bedded volcanic strata, formed from magma that erupted from two main volcanic centers—the Paisano Volcano, west of Alpine in Brewster County, and the Buckhorn Caldera, northwest of Fort Davis. The mountains are unique in West Texas in that they are the center of a circular area of higher rainfall; they receive up to eighteen inches of rain a year, while the rest of the Trans-Pecos generally receives only eight to twelve inches annually. This occurs because the mountains force westerly winds to rise; the flowing air is thus cooled, and the moisture it contains is condensed. Because of the rain, the Davis Mountains have temperate vegetation not found in the surrounding desert lowlands, such as yellow and limber pine, dwarf gray oak, Texas oak, and black cherry.

The mountains, once the domain of the Mescalero Apaches, were first visited by European explorers in August 1583, when friendly Jumano Indians showed Antonio de Espejo,qv who was returning to Mexico from Santa Fe, a shortcut through the area. In 1839 a Dr. Connelly traveled north with a group of Mexican freighters on the Old Salt Trail, which skirted the Davis Mountains. Not until the 1850s, however, when demand mounted for new routes from Central Texas to the west, did settlement of the area begin. In 1849 the first government reconnaissance party came to the Davis Mountains, and the following year Henry Skillman[qv] received a contract to carry the mail from San Antonio to El Paso and established four stagecoach stands in Jeff Davis County. Fort Davis was established in 1854 to provide protection for Skillman's coaches and others using the road to the west. The town of Fort Davis grew up around the military post in the late nineteenth century, and in the 1880s, after the Mescalero threat had been eliminated, the area attracted a number of cattle ranchers. The University of Texas McDonald Observatory[qv] was built on Mount Locke in 1932, and the Davis Mountains State Park[qv] was established two years later.

BIBLIOGRAPHY: Barry Scobee, *Old Fort Davis* (San Antonio: Naylor, 1947). Barry Scobee, *The Story of Fort Davis, Jeff Davis County and the Davis Mountains* (Fort Davis, Texas: Marvin Hunter, 1936). Darwin Spearing, *Roadside Geology of Texas* (Missoula, Montana: Mountain Press, 1991).

DAVIS MOUNTAINS STATE PARK. Davis Mountains State Park, which covers 1,321 acres in the Davis Mountains,[qv] is two miles west of Fort Davis in south central Jeff Davis County (its center is at 30°36′ N, 103°56′ W). The highest elevation in the park, on the western boundary, is 5,600 feet above sea level. The land was donated by private parties, most prominently local ranchers Jesse W. and Richard K. Merrill. The park was established in 1933. In addition to its panoramic views of the Davis Mountains, the park offers a four-mile hiking trail linking it to the Fort Davis National Historic Site,[qv] which abuts the park on the east, as well as camping facilities and an interpretive center, open during the afternoon from June to August. The interpretive center features plant and animal displays, both live and mounted; a bird observation window; and a wildlife watering station.

The most distinctive feature of the park is the fifteen-room, pueblo-style Indian Lodge, built by companies 879 and 881 of the Civilian Conservation Corps[qv] between June and November 1933. The adobe[qv] bricks used in constructing the lodge were made on-site, and the timber was cottonwood cut in Keesey Canyon. Authentic cedar furniture was made at Bastrop State Park,[qv] and the ceilings were of reeds gathered along the Rio Grande. In 1967 the lodge was renovated, and twenty-four rooms, a meeting facility, a heated swimming pool, and a restaurant were added. Each year the Indian Lodge hosts a Christmas open house. Special celebrations are held on several other holidays as well. Davis Mountains State Park attracts more than 155,000 visitors annually.

BIBLIOGRAPHY: Vertical Files, Barker Texas History Center, University of Texas at Austin. *Martin Donell Kohout*

DAVIS PRAIRIE, TEXAS. Davis Prairie is three miles east of Thornton in south central Limestone County. It was named for Eli Davis, who settled in the area in the 1840s. The community in the mid-1890s was the focus of a common school district that had two teachers and eighty-six students. The school, a business, and several scattered houses marked the community on county highway maps in the late 1940s. The Davis Prairie school was consolidated with the Thornton Independent School District in 1949. Little remained in the area in the 1980s.

BIBLIOGRAPHY: Ray A. Walter, *A History of Limestone County* (Austin: Von Boeckmann–Jones, 1959). *Vivian Elizabeth Smyrl*

DAVISVILLE, TEXAS. Davisville is on the Southern Pacific line and Farm Road 2021 where it crosses Mill Creek, about four miles northeast of Lufkin in northern Angelina County. It was named for W. J. and Sarah Davis, early settlers in the Lufkin area. The community consisted of a sawmill and a townsite in the early 1900s. It had a store, commissary, and mill, as well as a station on what was first the Houston, East and West Texas Railway (later the Texas and New Orleans). Taylor Clayton ran the commissary and a general store. The main lumbermill in Davisville was established by the Wright-Jones Lumber Company, although an additional smaller mill was run there by Joe Dunn and associates. In 1910 the population of Davisville was reported as 150. The community had a post office from 1908 to 1921, with William G. Herrington as postmaster in 1908, James S. Smith in 1909, and James H. Clayton from 1910 to 1921. Mail service was transferred to Lufkin in 1921. The community still existed in 1990.

BIBLIOGRAPHY: Angelina County Historical Survey Committee, *Land of the Little Angel: A History of Angelina County, Texas*, ed. Bob Bowman (Lufkin, Texas: Lufkin Printing, 1976). Archie Birdsong Mathews, The Economic Development of Angelina County (M.A. thesis, University of Texas, 1952). *Megan Biesele*

DAVY, TEXAS. Davy, a farming community in northwestern DeWitt County near the Karnes county line, developed its community focus with the 1886 establishment of the Davy school on Salt Creek, on land donated by Fred House in June 1885 for school and church purposes. At that time the House cemetery already existed nearby. The community's business district developed about 1½ miles north of this area. A Davy post office operated from 1895 until about 1938. By 1915 the settlement had 100 residents, two stores, and a blacksmith shop, and also had a telephone connection and a daily stage to Yorktown, the nearest banking and shipping point, eleven miles away. In the 1920s and early 1930s only about twenty people lived in Davy, though by 1940 some 125 residents and five businesses were reported there. The community declined after World War II,[qv] and by 1950 reported only twenty residents and one business, a tally that remained constant until the mid-1960s, after which no further population figures were reported. The Davy school closed in 1950. The 1984 county highway map designates the former Davy business district as Davy Community, and labels the settlement's original site, 1½ miles south (the former location of the Davy school), as New Davy. New Davy, located on State Highway 119 from Yorktown to Nixon, had one business in 1984. That year both the old and new sites also had a number of residences.

BIBLIOGRAPHY: Nellie Murphree, *A History of DeWitt County* (Victoria, Texas, 1962). *Craig H. Roell*

DAVY CROCKETT NATIONAL FOREST. The Davy Crockett National Forest is off U. S. Highway 69 west of Lufkin and east of Crockett. The preserve, which is administered by the United States Department of Agriculture Forest Service local headquarters in Lufkin, has a total of 161,842 acres, with 94,481 acres in Houston County and 67,361 acres in Trinity County. The national forests in Texas were established by an act of the Texas legislature in 1933 authorizing the purchase of lands for the national forest system. President Franklin D. Roosevelt proclaimed these purchases on October 15, 1936. The national forests are managed on a multiple-use philosophy and are used for lumbering, grazing, oil production, hunting, and recreation. In fiscal year 1994, 93.8 million board feet of timber was harvested from the national forests in Texas, providing 2,098 jobs and $73,108,000 in income to the surrounding Texas communities. In addition, Texas ranchers with special permits could graze their cattle in the national forests. At the Davy Crockett National Forest, 386 head of cattle grazed in fiscal year 1994. Davy Crockett National Forest, which is bordered on the northeast by the Neches River, includes the 45-acre Ratliff Lake. The area is pine-hardwood woodlands with flat to gently rolling terrain. Recreational facilities at this national forest include a bathhouse, camping and picnicking areas, boat ramps, and hiking trails.

BIBLIOGRAPHY: George Oxford Miller and Delena Tull, *Texas Parks and Campgrounds: North, East, and Coastal Texas* (Austin: Texas Monthly Press, 1984). *Christopher Long*

DAWN, TEXAS. Dawn, on U.S. Highway 60 in eastern Deaf Smith County, originated in 1887 when Jim Moore, ranch boss for the T Anchor Ranch,qv built a dugoutqv about six miles southwest of what is now the townsite. Two years later J. H. Parrish purchased the dugout and the filing rights for the surrounding lands and eventually opened a general store for area ranchers. The story goes that he labeled it "Dawn of a New Country," or "Dawn of Civilization"; when he applied for a post office, the first word of the phrase was chosen for its name. Another story relates that Parrish, upon seeing the land for the first time, exclaimed, "This is the dawn of a new day." James N. Askren, who had a broom factory in a barn at Dawn, opened the first school in the area in 1891. By the time Parrish sold his land holdings and moved to Oklahoma in 1893, the community of Dawn was thriving. Its survival was assured by the arrival of the Pecos Valley and Northeastern Railway, which established a depot at the site in 1898. During the next several years Dawn prospered as a shipping point for area ranchers, and several immigrant farmers were attracted to the area. By 1917 the town had a lumber company, a community church (later a Baptist church), and a hotel, in which a small band played. The advent of irrigation wells made wheat the town's economic mainstay. During the 1920s modern school facilities, among them the county's first school cafeteria, were built at the community. Henry Turner started a stone-ground grain industry, and in the 1940s David Rodgers began marketing from his elevator at Dawn his Deaf Smith corn meal, wheat berries, and stone-ground whole wheat flour. By then the town reported four stores and a population of 100. Paved roads and better transportation later took from Dawn some of its older businesses, including its hotel, bank, railroad depot, lumberyard, and flour mill. Its school district was consolidated with that of Hereford in 1963. Nevertheless several clubs built a new community center there in 1973. In 1984 Dawn reported a store, a post office, three elevators, and a population of ninety-four. In 1990 its population was still reported as ninety-four.

BIBLIOGRAPHY: *Deaf Smith County: The Land and Its People* (Hereford, Texas: Deaf Smith County Historical Society, 1982). Fred Tarpley, *1001 Texas Place Names* (Austin: University of Texas Press, 1980).

H. Allen Anderson

DAWSON, ALONZO N. (1854–1923). Alonzo N. Dawson, architect, was born in Hartford, Connecticut, on January 18, 1854. He married Carrie Rickard in 1878 in Paris, Texas, and they had two children. Dawson, who lived in Fort Worth and later in Houston, had a twenty-five-year career that covered the end of the Romanesque Revival period and the beginnings of new architectural styles such as the Neoclassical. He produced a number of significant churches and public buildings in which he demonstrated his competence with Romanesque Revival stonework and displayed a skillful eclecticism by including design elements from such other styles as Gothic and Norman.

Early in his career Dawson designed two buildings in Johnson County, the Cleburne Public School (1883) and the Johnson County Jail (1884). The two-story masonry jail was built on a T plan to house iron and steel cell blocks constructed elsewhere. From 1885 to 1900 Dawson lived and practiced in Fort Worth. He entered a brief partnership in 1885 with Marshall R. Sanguinet,qv a prominent Fort Worth architect, and helped plan Ann Waggoner Hall at Polytechnic College of the Methodist Episcopal Church (now Texas Wesleyan College), Fort Worth. Waggoner Hall, a three-story Queen Anne–style structure, housed all functions of the college except the men's dormitories. Later, working as supervising architect, Dawson directed construction of the First Baptist Church, Fort Worth (1887–89), a Gothic Revival structure designed by Illinois architects Bullard and Bullard. The Fort Worth church included rusticated limestone walls, rounded towers, and Gothic windows, features that Dawson incorporated later in churches in Beaumont and Houston.

He won design competitions for important buildings such as the Archer County Courthouse (1892–93), for which his plan was selected over twenty-five others. This building is constructed in the Romanesque Revival style, with limestone walls, rounded-arch openings, and convex roofs. In another competition Dawson defeated well known Texas architects J. Riely Gordonqv and Messer, Sanguinet, and Messer for design of the Fort Worth City Hall (1892–93), a massive three-story building with Romanesque stone walls, Spanish tile roofs, and a monumental tower rising to the height of seven stories.

In 1900 Dawson moved to Houston, where he lived for over twenty years and designed churches and residences. In 1902–03 he traveled to Beaumont to produce the First Baptist Church, a building in which he blended medieval styles—Romanesque stonework enriched with Norman stair towers and stained-glass Gothic windows. The church, adapted for use as a library, is known as Tyrell Historical Library.

In 1904 Dawson directed construction of the First Baptist Church in Houston, a structure reminiscent of the earlier Fort Worth church and bearing a close resemblance to the Beaumont church. The same year, also in Houston, he produced a neoclassical building for the Tuam Avenue Baptist Church. With its temple-like façade of Corinthian columns, pediment, and balustraded parapet, the extant Tuam Avenue structure was adapted in 1920 for use as a laundry and dry-cleaning establishment. Another Houston church designed by Dawson was the Cumberland Presbyterian. Constructed on the popular Akron floor plan, this frame church was cast in English country style and had square towers with battlements. Among the Houston residences designed by Dawson was one for T. F. Loftus, a two-story colonial structure with tall columns. Dawson died on April 27, 1923, of apoplexy, and was buried at Forest Park Cemetery, Fort Worth.

BIBLIOGRAPHY: Mary Anna Crary Anderson, "Tyrell Public Library: History of the Site and the Building," *Texas Gulf Historical and Biographical Record* 6 (November 1970). *Houston Architectural Survey* (6 vols., Houston: Southwest Center for Urban Research, 1980–81). Houston *Daily Post,* October 2, 1905, November 7, 1909. Willard B. Robinson, *Gone from Texas: Our Lost Architectural Heritage* (College Station: Texas A&M University Press, 1981). Willard B. Robinson, *The People's Architecture: Texas Courthouses, Jails, and Municipal Buildings* (Austin: Texas State Historical Association, 1983). Willard B. Robinson and Todd Webb, *Texas Public Buildings of the Nineteenth Century* (Austin: University of Texas Press, 1974).

Robert J. Robertson

DAWSON, HUBERT MCLEOD (1903–1995). Hubert McLeod Dawson, educator and civic leader, son of Emmett Beauregard and Sorintha Natalie (McLeod) Dawson, was born at Abbott, Hill County, Texas, April 24, 1903. He graduated from Abbott High School in 1918, but the school only had ten grades. Dawson went on to complete eleventh grade at Hillsboro High School and graduated in 1919. He earned his B.A. and M.S. from Baylor University in 1923 and 1956, respectively, and received an honorary LLD from the University of Mary Hardin-Baylor in 1965. In 1923 Dawson was the principal, a teacher, and a coach at Abbott High School. The following year he was a teacher and coach at Moody High School; in 1926 he left to serve as chairman of the modern language department at Meridian College. From 1927 to 1928 he was involved in graduate study at Southern Methodist University. In 1928 he was a language teacher at Temple High School and Temple Junior College as well as acting registrar at the college. In 1942 he entered the Air Corps, United States Army, as a private and was discharged as a captain. He served in the Military Intelligence Service for thirty-four months in the European theater of operations, in London, England; Paris, France; and Offenbach, Germany. Dawson returned to the United States and Temple Junior College as the associate dean and director of guidance in 1946; he became associate dean and registrar the following year. In 1953 he served as dean-registrar until he became president of the institution in 1959. He served in this capacity until 1973 when he retired and was made president emeritus. During Dawson's service to Temple Junior College, he was chiefly responsible for moving the college from four basement rooms in the old Temple High School to its own building on a thirty-two-acre campus in south Temple in 1957. Through his efforts this campus grew to include a total of 100 acres. He was largely instrumental in the separation of the college from the Temple public schools and the construction of nine modern buildings to house Temple Junior College. During his tenure of service the enrollment of the college increased from 82 to 1,250. Dawson belonged to numerous professional, civic, and social organizations. He was a life member of the Texas State Teachers Association.qv He served as president of the Texas Junior College Teachers Association and the Association of Texas Colleges and Universities.qv No other individual has served as president of both these organizations. Dawson also served as president of the Lone Star Chapter of the American Association of Teachers of Spanish, the Texas Junior College Speech Association, the Temple Public Schools Unit of the Texas State Teachers Association, and the Temple Kiwanis Club. He was a member of the First United Methodist Church of Temple, Texas, where he served as a member of the administrative board, the finance committee, and as teacher of an adult Sunday School class. He died in Temple on April 20, 1995, and was buried in Ridge Park Cemetery in Hillsboro, Texas.

Harry C. Farrell, Jr.

DAWSON, JOSEPH MARTIN (1879–1973). Joseph Martin Dawson, Baptist pastor, social activist, and writer, was born near Waxahachie, Texas, on June 21, 1879, to Martin Judy and Laura (Underwood) Dawson, Jr. As a youth he wrote for the Dallas *Morning News*qv and was torn between journalism and preaching as a career. In January 1899 he entered Baylor Academy to study for the ministry. While at Baylor he served as pastor for four country churches and became first editor of the Baylor student newspaper, the *Lariat*. He left school for a year and held a full-time pastorate at Albany (1902–03) before returning to graduate as class valedictorian in 1904. He then held a full-time pastorate at Lampasas (1905–06). This was followed by pastorates at the First Baptist Church, Hillsboro (1908–12), and the First Baptist Church, Temple (1912–15).

Though always outspoken on social issues, Dawson deepened his commitment to social justice in 1914 when he read the works of Walter Rauschenbusch in preparation for a series of articles for the *Baptist Standard*.qv These articles and the sermons they inspired dealt with social applications of the Gospel to such subjects as child labor, the exploitation of immigrants, and women's rights. The sermons were among the first to be preached by a Texas Baptist minister on social issues. Dawson continued his social activism when he became pastor of the First Baptist Church, Waco, in 1915. The following year he introduced a strong resolution to the Waco Pastors' Association condemning racial prejudice, and he frequently used the pulpit to denounce groups such as the Ku Klux Klan.qv

He also championed religious liberty and church-state separation. In 1945, as Baptist representative at the founding of the United Nations in San Francisco, he carried petitions with more than 100,000 signatures calling for the incorporation of a declaration of religious liberty in the United Nations charter. He took a leading role in organizing Protestants and Other Americans United for the Separation of Church and State (subsequently known as Americans United for Separation of Church and State) and served as its first executive secretary and acting director (1947–48). He opposed federal aid to church hospitals and parochial schools, as well as sectarian instruction in public schools. He also led an interdenominational campaign that defeated President Harry S. Truman's attempt to appoint an ambassador to the Vatican (1951).

Dawson's Waco pastorate, the longest in the church's history, lasted from 1915 to 1946 and brought church membership to over 2,000. Among his many denominational posts, he served as vice president of the Baptist General Convention of Texas (1922), chairman of the Southern Baptist Committee on World Peace (1945), chairman of the Executive Committee of the Southern Baptist Convention (1945–46), and first full-time executive director of the Baptist Joint Committee on Public Affairs (1946–53). He served on the boards of trustees of various religious, educational, and charitable institutions, including Baylor University, Mary Hardin-Baylor College (now the University of Mary Hardin-Baylor), Bishop College, Southwestern Baptist Theological Seminary, Southern Baptist Theological Seminary, Hillcrest Baptist Hospital (now Hillcrest Baptist Medical Center), Baylor Memorial Sanitarium (later called Baylor Hospital), and the Home Mission Board of the Southern Baptist Convention.

In addition to his other activities, Dawson served as editor of a number of publications, including the *Western Evangel* (1906), the *Baptist Standard* (1943–46), and *Report from the Capitol* (1946–53). He helped found the Texas Institute of Lettersqv and was elected a permanent fellow of the institute. He was a prolific writer, contributed articles and chapters to many publications, served as religious book editor of the Dallas *Morning News*, and wrote twelve books, among them *The Light That Grows* (1924), *The Spiritual Conquest of the Southwest* (1926), *A Century with Texas Baptists* (1947), *The Liberation of Life* (1950), *America's Way in Church, State and Society* (1953), *Baptists and the American Republic* (1956), *A Thousand Months to Remember: An Autobiography* (1964), and *José Antonio Navarro: Co-Creator of Texas* (1969).

Dawson married Willie Turner on June 3, 1908, and they had three sons and two daughters. He died in Corsicana on July 6, 1973, and was buried in Oakwood Cemetery, Waco.

BIBLIOGRAPHY: Joseph Martin Dawson, Oral Memoirs, Texas Collection, Baylor University. Joseph Martin Dawson Papers, J. M. Dawson Church-State Research Center, Baylor University. Joseph Martin Dawson, *A Thousand Months to Remember* (Waco: Baylor University Press, 1964). James M. Dunn, The Ethical Thought of Joseph Martin Dawson (Th.D. dissertation, Southwestern Baptist Theological Seminary, 1966). Travis L. Summerlin, Church-State Relations in the Thought of Joseph Martin Dawson (Ph.D. dissertation, Baylor University, 1984).

J. A. Reynolds

DAWSON, NICHOLAS MOSBY (1808–1848). Nicholas Mosby Dawson, hero of the Texas Revolution,qv was born in Woolford, Kentucky, in 1808. He later moved with his parents to White County, Tennessee, where he attended school. He moved to Texas in 1834 and settled in Fayette County near the home of a relative, William Mosby Eastland.qv Dawson enlisted in the revolutionary armyqv on January 24, 1836, and within a week was elected to the rank of second lieutenant of Company B, Texas Volunteers. He participated in the battle of San Jacinto.qv He served as captain of a militia company in 1840 during an Indian campaign in what is now Mitchell County. In August 1937 he was a lieutenant in Company C and in 1842 was captain of a company of volunteers under John H. Moore.qv He was residing in Fayette County when Adrián Wollqv invaded Texas in the fall of 1842. Dawson organized a small company of some fifteen men and left La Grange on September 16, 1842. Soon his company numbered fifty-three men, recruited from settlements in Fayette, Gonzales, and DeWitt counties. While attempting to join Texas forces under Mathew Caldwellqv on Salado Creek (*see* SALADO CREEK, BATTLE OF) near San Antonio, Dawson and his men were surrounded by a large number of Mexican cavalry on September 18. The following battle, known as the Dawson Massacre,qv resulted in the death or capture of nearly all the Texans. Dawson was among the casualties. On September 18, 1848, his remains and those of thirty-five other victims of the battle were buried along with casualties from the Mier expeditionqv in a vault on Monument Hill near La Grange. Dawson County is named for Nicholas Dawson.

BIBLIOGRAPHY: Sam Houston Dixon and Louis Wiltz Kemp, *The Heroes of San Jacinto* (Houston: Anson Jones, 1932). Zachary T. Fulmore, *History and Geography of Texas As Told in County Names* (Austin: Steck, 1915; facsimile, 1935). Houston Wade, comp., *The Dawson Men of Fayette County* (Houston, 1932).

Charles G. Davis

DAWSON, WILLIE EVELYN TURNER (1888–1963). Willie Dawson, Baptist teacher and lecturer, was born on September 9, 1888, in San Antonio, the daughter of Don F. and Alice (Evelyn) Turner. After her father, an accountant, was killed while attempting to stop a street brawl in Marble Falls, she and her mother made their home with relatives in Dallas. After graduation from Central High School (now Bryan Avenue High School) in Dallas, Willie Turner taught kindergarten and became prominent in the city's social circles. She was baptized by George W. Truett,qv and taught Sunday school in the First Baptist Church, Dallas,qv and later in the McKinney Avenue Baptist Church, while John Franklyn Norrisqv was pastor. At the Texas Baptist state convention at San Antonio in November 1907 she met Joseph Martin Dawson,qv who was then serving as editor of the *Baptist Standard*.qv They were married in Dallas on June 3, 1908, and had three daughters and two sons.

Mrs. Dawson was a gifted public speaker who addressed countless Baptist gatherings and taught the college women's Sunday school class throughout the years of Dawson's pastorate at First Baptist Church in Waco. She served as the Young Women's Auxiliary superintendent for the Baptist Women Mission Workers from 1913 to 1918. She also raised funds to help build the Women's Memorial Dormitory at Baylor University and the Women's Building at Southwestern Baptist Theological Seminary in Fort Worth. A public challenge that she issued to the Southern Baptist Convention in 1930 brought about a rapid rise in the Lottie Moon Christmas offering for foreign missions. Her services led her to be nominated for president of the Southern Baptist Convention. In 1935 Baylor University awarded her an honorary LL.D. degree and named a women's dormitory for her.

While her husband served as the first executive director of the Baptist Joint Committee on Public Affairs in Washington, D.C., from 1946 to 1953, Willie Dawson was active in teaching the Dawson Bible Class at the First Baptist Church in Washington. She delivered addresses to the Baptist World Alliance in 1947 and the Baptist World Congress in 1950. After their retirement in 1954 the Dawsons lived in Austin, and Mrs. Dawson was forced to curtail her activities by a long illness that left her an invalid during the last five years of her life. She died on April 18, 1963, and was buried in Oakwood Cemetery, Waco. The Southern Baptist Pastors' Wives Organization named her its "Ideal Preacher's Wife of 1963."

BIBLIOGRAPHY: Joseph Martin Dawson, *A Thousand Months to Remember* (Waco: Baylor University Press, 1964). *Encyclopedia of Southern Baptists* (4 vols., Nashville: Broadman, 1958–82). Vertical Files, Barker Texas History Center, University of Texas at Austin.

Travis L. Summerlin

DAWSON, TEXAS. Dawson is twenty-one miles southwest of Corsicana and fifty miles south of Dallas in southwestern Navarro County. The town was named for Britton Dawson, a cattle rancher and participant in the battle of San Jacinto,qv who arrived in the area from Alabama in 1847 searching for grass and water for his animals. He lived in the town until his death in 1903. The community began to grow after 1881, when the St. Louis Southwestern Railway built a narrow-gauge line from Corsicana to Waco. Dawson became a supply and shipping center for local farmers who grew cotton and other crops. A Dawson post office opened in 1882, and in 1883 the community had a lumberyard and a drugstore. Ike Hughes opened a photography studio not long after this but closed it in order to open a saloon. In 1887 the Dawson Masonic Institute occupied a two-story frame building; classes were held on the ground floor and Masonic lodge meetings on the second. In 1926 the town had four cotton gins, two banks, a bottling works, a telephone exchange, and a cottonseed oil mill (*see* COTTONSEED INDUSTRY); at that time the community also had three miles of pavement. Dawson reported a population of 500 by 1887 and was incorporated in 1908. Its population was reported as 950 from 1914 to the mid-1920s, peaked at 1,500 in 1928, and held steady at just over 1,100 from the early 1930s (when the community had some sixty-five businesses) through the mid-1950s. In the 1960s Dawson's population began to decrease and was reported as 789 in 1988, when the community had seven businesses and a post office. In 1990 its population was reported as 766.

BIBLIOGRAPHY: Annie Carpenter Love, *History of Navarro County* (Dallas: Southwestern, 1933). Wyvonne Putman, comp., *Navarro County History* (5 vols., Quanah, Texas: Nortex, 1975–84).

Julie G. Miller

DAWSON COUNTY. Dawson County (D-9) lies on the eastern edge of the Llano Estacadoqv on the southern High Plains. The center point of the county is at 32°45′ north latitude and 101°57′ west longitude, sixty miles south of Lubbock. The county comprises 902 square miles of rolling prairie, broken on the east. The land, surfaced with sandy and loam soils, drains to playas. The altitude ranges from 2,600 to 3,200 feet above mean sea level. The average annual rainfall is 16.09 inches. The average minimum temperature in January is 28° F; the maximum average in July is 94°. The growing season averages 212 days. The county is crossed by Sulphur Springs Draw, a natural trail used by the Indians since prehistoric times and by the first white men who entered the South Plains. The area was the summer home of Comanches and Kiowas, who moved from waterhole to waterhole in a region that white men supposed waterless. A portion of the future county was included in a Mexican grant issued to Dr. John Cameronqv on May 21, 1827. Cameron contracted to settle 100 families, but there is no record of any attempt to carry out the contract.

In the fall of 1875 the Twenty-fourth United States Infantry,qv commanded by Col. William Rufus Shafter,qv visited the area to prepare a report on the local Indians. On October 18, 1875, the company discovered an Indian encampment at Laguna Sabinas or Cedar Lake, the legendary birthplace of Quanah Parker;qv the band, however, escaped to the west. The Shafter party made the first wagon roads on the plains and reported favorably on grazing conditions, but the Indian menace remained too severe for immediate settlement. The Nolan expeditionqv of 1877 got lost in the area of the future Dawson and Lynn counties, and several members of the party of sixty died of thirst. Buffalo hunters, more than soldiers, were probably responsible for driving the Indians from the area. A surveying party for Texas and Pacific Railway lands in 1875 reported the presence of thousands of buffalo,qv and hunters moved in. As cattlemen learned that the grass on the Plains would produce fat cattle, ranchmen moved from the Lower Plains south of the Caprockqv to the new lands. By the mid-1880s four ranches, C. C. Slaughter'sqv Lazy S, the TJF, the Fish, and the Bartow, occupied most of the land in Dawson County. The Texas and Pacific reached Big Spring in neighboring Howard County in 1881, and that community served as the shipping point for the area. By 1890 there were 28,536 cattle reported in the county.

The first decade of the twentieth century was a time of dramatic growth for Dawson County, as the population jumped from thirty-seven people in 1900 to 2,320 in 1910, and the number of ranches and farms increased from four to 330. Between 1902 and 1905, as the grazing leases expired, Dawson County lands were filed on for settlement. Prospective settlers waited in line in Big Spring for as long as six weeks when choice pieces of land were released. In 1907 the first railroad land was sold at from three to five dollars an acre. One large ranch was not opened for settlers until 1946, when it sold for sixty-five dollars an acre. The first school in Dawson County began in one room of the Mullins ranchhouse in 1902. The first church was organized by the Baptists in Chicago in 1904, but the Methodists built the first church building in Lamesa in 1907; it was used alternately by four communions on successive Sundays. The first post office was north of Lamesa at the Bartow ranch headquarters, where residents produced a wagonload of mail to prove to postal authorities that a post office was needed. They were so impressed by the amount of their own handiwork that they humorously named their post office Chicago. That same year, the *Dawson County News* was begun by J. E. Garrison and the Dawson County Bank was organized. Dawson County, named for Nicholas Mosby Dawson,qv had been formed on August 21, 1876, but was attached to Howard County for judicial purposes until February 13, 1905, when separate organization was authorized. Dawson County's first election to choose officials and select the county seat was held on March 20, 1905. The contesting towns, Lamesa and Chicago, were only two miles apart. Lamesa won by five votes, but a movement was already afoot to consolidate the towns and all businesses and residences in Chicago were moved into Lamesa. After six years of effort to secure a railroad, the Santa Fe was built into Lamesa in 1911.

Although the first bale of cotton produced in the county was grown in 1903, cotton did not become a main crop until 1914 or 1915. During World War Iqv prices were good for the bumper crops produced. Settlers poured in, bought pieces of the newly partitioned ranches, and sent land prices soaring. More than 24,000 acres was planted in cotton by 1920; in 1930, 182,527 acres, well more than 60 percent of all county cropland harvested, was devoted to cotton production. The county population grew to 4,309 by 1920 and increased almost threefold during the 1920s to reach 13,373 in 1930. However, by 1930, under the impact of adverse farming conditions and prices, almost 70 percent of the county's 2,218 farms were worked by tenants. The Great Depressionqv caused many businesses to fail, but other industries that developed in the county during the 1930s partially offset these losses. The dairy industryqv prospered. A powdered-milk plant built in 1929 was closed by the depression but began seasonal operation in 1932 making powdered eggs. Oil development began in 1934. Twenty-eight wells were producing in the Welch community and two in the southeastern part of the county in 1946. Intermittent wildcatting has continued. In 1940 the county had a population of 15,367. Agriculture was more diversified, as county farmers grew sorghum on twice as much land as was planted with cotton. During World War IIqv Dawson County provided more men per capita for the armed services than did any other county in Texas. Despite critical farm-labor shortages, an organization of merchants, farmers, and the chamber of commerce met every agricultural quota set for the county. The egg-drying plant turned its entire facilities over to lend-lease production. Dawson County was one of the five counties in the state to win the coveted Army-Navy "E" award. Lamesa Field,qv an army airfield, was established in 1942 and deactivated two years later.

Irrigationqv was introduced into the county in the late 1940s, and cotton once again dominated the agricultural economy, with some 300,000 acres planted in 1950 and more than 180,000 in 1960. The county population reached 19,113 in 1950 and an all-time high of 19,185 in 1960, but declined thereafter to 16,604 in 1970 and 16,184 in 1980. New agricultural methods and the increasing use of farming technology saw the number of farms in the county shrink from a peak of more than 2,000 in 1930 to 841 in 1960 and 581 in 1980. The population of the county was predominantly white through the 1930s. In 1930 there were only 261 African Americansqv in the county, or some 2 percent of the population. The number of blacks increased to 537 in 1950 and 873, or 5 percent of the county population, in 1970. Thereafter the number of black residents began to decline. The Hispanic population of Dawson County began to increase dramatically in the mid-twentieth century. Almost 40 percent of the population was Hispanic in 1980 and more than 42 percent in 1990. Politically, the county held to the Democratic partyqv in national elections through 1964, with the exceptions of 1928, 1952, and 1960. From 1968 through 1992 Dawson County voters consistently supported Republican presidential candidates.

The mainstays of the county economy in the 1980s were agribusiness and oil. Dawson County was second in the state in cotton production in 1980, and through the 1980s cotton continued to be the most important agricultural product. Sorghum and wheat were also important crops, and cattle and hogs were raised. Between the first discovery of oil and 1990, oil production totaled 294,809,170 barrels. In 1990 the county population was 14,349. County towns included Lamesa (10,809), Ackerly (153 in Dawson County), O'Donnell (134 in Dawson County) and Los Ybanez (83).

BIBLIOGRAPHY: Dawson County Historical Commission, *Dawson County History* (Lubbock: Taylor, 1981). Matthew Clay Lindsey, *The Trail of Years in Dawson County* (Fort Worth: Wallace, 1958?).

Leona M. Gelin and Mark Odintz

DAWSON COUNTY. Another Dawson County, established by the Texas Legislature on February 1, 1858, was named for Nicholas Dawsonqv and included the western portion of what is now Kinney County and the eastern portion of Uvalde County. The act was never expressly repealed, but the territory was obliterated by acts dated September 29 and October 5, 1866. The area included no part of present Dawson County, established in 1876.

BIBLIOGRAPHY: R. L. Batts, "Defunct Counties of Texas," *Quarterly of the Texas State Historical Association* 1 (October 1897). Hans Peter Nielsen Gammel, comp., *Laws of Texas, 1822–1897* (10 vols., Austin: Gammel, 1898).

Seymour V. Connor

DAWSON CREEK. Dawson Creek rises just under a mile north of the park road between Panther Junction and the Maverick Ranger Station in Big Bend National Parkqv some nine miles east of Terlingua in southwestern Brewster County (at 29°19′ N, 103°29′ W) and runs southwest for five miles to its mouth on Terlingua Creek, just under five miles southeast of Terlingua (at 29°17′ N, 103°33′ W). It traverses an area of densely dissected terrain with gullies and low hills, with shallow or absent soils and little or no vegetation. The creek may have been named for an early prospector who camped on its banks.

DAWSON MASSACRE. After the capture of San Antonio on September 11, 1842, by Brig. Gen. Adrián Wollqv in the second of the Mexican invasions of 1842,qv Texan forces gathered on Salado Creek under Col. Mathew Caldwellqv to repel the raiders. While Texas arms were succeeding at the battle of Salado Creekqv on September 18, 1842, a calamity was occurring only a mile and a half away. In response to Caldwell's call for volunteers, Capt. Nicholas M. Dawsonqv had raised a fifty-three-man company, mostly from Fayette County, and marched down from La Grange. Believing Caldwell's forces to be in grave danger, Dawson's men chose not to wait for Capt. Jesse Billingsley'sqv company, which was following them, but to disregard the threat posed by numerous heavy Mexican cavalry patrols and to fight their way to the Salado. Near Caldwell's embattled line, between 3 and 4 P.M. on the eighteenth, the company was intercepted by a column of 500 irregular Mexican cavalry commanded by colonels Cayetano Montero, José María Carrasco, and Pedro Rangel and supported by a battery of two field pieces. According to the accounts of several survivors, the Mexican column was commanded by Juan Nepomuceno Seguín,qv but they were no doubt in error. Dawson dismounted his men in a mesquite thicket where Fort Sam Houston now stands and threatened to "shoot the first man who runs." The Texans were quickly surrounded but repulsed a spirited cavalry charge and inflicted a number of casualties on the enemy. The Mexicans then fell back out of rifle range and opened fire on the Texans with their artillery. Billingsley's company, which arrived while the fight was in progress, was too weak to go to Dawson's aid, and Caldwell's men on Salado Creek were heavily engaged throughout the afternoon. Montero once more ordered his cavalry, then dismounted, to charge. After a vigorous but futile resistance, the severely wounded Dawson sought to surrender. The Mexicans continued to fire, however, striking Dawson several more times. Seeing surrender to be impossible, he gasped out his dying words, "Let victory be purchased with blood." Alsey S. Miller took up the white mackinaw that Dawson had waved in token of surrender and rode with it toward the Mexican lines, only to be fired upon in his turn. Miller then galloped through the enemy toward the town of Seguin. Henry Gonzalvo Woods,[qv] after witnessing the death of his father and the mortal wounding of his brother Norman, also escaped. Some of the Texans continued to resist while others laid down their arms. Heroic in the fight was Griffin, a slave of Samuel A. Maverick,[qv] who, his rifle shattered, fought on with the limb of a mesquite tree until he was killed. By 5 P.M. the fight was over. Thirty-six Texans died on the field, fifteen were taken prisoner, and two escaped. The prisoners were marched away to Perote Prison[qv] in Mexico. Of these men, only nine survived to return to Texas. Thirty Mexicans were estimated to have been killed and between sixty and seventy wounded. Two days later the Mexican army retreated toward the Rio Grande, and the Dawson men were buried in shallow graves in the mesquite thicket where they fell.

BIBLIOGRAPHY: Joseph Milton Nance, *Attack and Counterattack: The Texas-Mexican Frontier, 1842* (Austin: University of Texas Press, 1964). Juan N. Seguin, *Personal Memoirs* (San Antonio, 1858). L. U. Spellmann, ed., "Letters of the 'Dawson Men' From Perote Prison, Mexico, 1842–1843," *Southwestern Historical Quarterly* 38 (April 1935). William P. Stapp, *The Prisoners of Perote: A Journal* (Philadelphia: Zieber, 1845). Leonie L. Weyand, Early History of Fayette County, 1822–1865 (M.A. thesis, University of Texas, 1932).

Thomas W. Cutrer

DAWSON-WATSON, DAWSON (1864–1939). Dawson Dawson-Watson, landscape artist, son of John and Jane (Edmondson) Dawson-Watson, was born on July 21, 1864, in London, England. His father was a popular illustrator. During childhood in St. John's Wood where his family lived, young Dawson became familiar with artists, actors, and men of letters. At age eight he was enrolled in the Diocesan Grammar School in Southsea, England, where he progressed rapidly in art. After returning home to continue his studies, he studied with Mark Fisher, an American artist living in England. When his family moved to Wales, Dawson-Watson first spent six months with the Royal Welsh Fusiliers, then returned to his art studies. His talent attracted the attention of Henry Boddington, who sent him to study in Paris with a small allowance. There he spent three years working under a number of artists including Carolus-Duran, portraitist, Aimé Morot and Léon Glaize, historical painters, and Luc Olivier-Merson and Raphaël Collin, decorators. With these mentors Dawson-Watson mastered a variety of media and skills. In spite of strictures on his allowance if he married, he met and on May 30, 1888, married Mary Hoyt Sellar, an American traveling in France with the Houston artist Emma Richardson Cherry.[qv] The couple went to Giverny, France, where they joined the American art colony and remained five years, until James Carroll Beckwith, an American artist, urged them to go to the United States. Within two weeks the Dawson-Watsons had moved to America. When they landed in New York in 1893, they had twenty-five dollars. Dawson-Watson painted enough pictures to enable them to move to Boston. From Boston they went to Hartford, Connecticut, where he directed the Hartford Art Society for four years. Then, having inherited a small sum of money, he returned to England, but found it difficult to earn a living. After reading of an art-school vacancy in Canada, he sold everything in England and went to Canada to apply, but failed to find the school. Still, he remained in Canada for three years, until an American artist, Birge Harrison, told him about a new artists' colony being established in the Catskills. He journeyed to New York and began teaching at Byrdcliffe in Woodstock. In 1904 he moved to St. Louis to accept a teaching position at the St. Louis School of Fine Arts at Washington University, where he remained the succeeding eleven years while spending the summers on sketching trips to Massachusetts.

After leaving his university position in 1915, Dawson-Watson began to divide his time between San Antonio, Texas, and St. Louis. He served as art director of the Missouri Centennial and the St. Louis Industrial Exhibition in 1920 and worked in theater design in St. Louis from 1920 to 1923. In 1918 and 1919 he also served as director of the San Antonio Art Guild and eventually was attracted to San Antonio as a permanent resident at the urging of Rolla Taylor, a San Antonio artist, and of Mrs. H. P. Drought and Mrs. John Herff, San Antonio art patrons, all of whom wanted him to enter the Edgar B. Davis[qv] Texas Wildflower competitions. In 1926 he made a $500 painting sale in Boston, left for San Antonio, and began to concentrate on painting Texas landscapes, particularly scenes with cacti.[qv] He painted seventy different canvases of cacti before completing the painting he entered. The following year, 1927, in the first Davis Competition, he won the $5,000 national award for his painting *Glory of the Morning*, a study of cacti. Two years later he was awarded both first and fifth prizes in the competitions. Dawson-Watson had numerous exhibitions in San Antonio, including three solo exhibitions at the Witte Museum[qv] (1928, 1932, and 1935). In 1934 he was one of eight local artists commissioned by the Civil Works Administration to execute murals in San Antonio. His canvas *Meditation* was installed in Jefferson Senior High School. A three-panel painting, *The Open Book of Nature*, was installed in the Wichita, Kansas, high school. Some of his easel paintings remain in the frames he hand-carved for them. He was a man of compassion as well as style, as demonstrated by his offering generous support to his adopted city when San Antonio suffered a devastating flood in 1921 and to the Witte Museum when it suffered a severe financial crisis in 1933. Dawson-Watson's work won prizes throughout the nation—in Portland, Oregon (1905), in Sedalia, Missouri, at the Illinois State Fair (1916), at the Texas State Fair in Austin (1926), and from the Nashville Art Association (1927), the Mississippi Art Association, and the Southern States Art League (1931). He was a member of numerous art organizations. He exhibited in the Paris Salon and the Exposition Universelle in Paris, at the Royal Academy, London, the Royal Canadian Academy, and the Royal Cambrian Academy, and in many exhibitions in this country. He is represented in permanent collections in St. Louis, Missouri, Springfield, Illinois, New Haven, Connecticut, Wichita, Kansas, New York City, Chicago, Oakland, California, the Archer M. Huntington Art Gallery[qv] at the University of Texas at Austin, the San Antonio Art League,[qv] the San Antonio Museum of Art,[qv] and the Daughters of the Republic of Texas Library[qv] at the Alamo.[qv] Though he is known to the public primarily for his cactus paintings, art historians recognize him as an important direct American link to French Impressionism. Dawson-Watson died in San Antonio on September 3, 1939, survived by his wife, a son, and a daughter.

BIBLIOGRAPHY: Cecilia Steinfeldt, *Art for History's Sake: The Texas Collection of the Witte Museum* (Austin: Texas State Historical Association for the Witte Museum of the San Antonio Museum Association, 1993). *Who Was Who in America*, Vol. 1.

Cecilia Steinfeldt

DAY, DONALD (1899–1991). Donald Day, writer, was born Horace Henry Day on May 11, 1899, at Millseat, Hays County, Texas, to Lillie (Saunders) and Edward Manning Day. A child of teachers, he was well educated in the San Marcos schools, where he graduated from high school; he then attended Southwest Texas State Normal College at San Marcos. He served in the United States Army during World

War I.qv In 1918 he received his bachelor's degree from Southwest Texas and in 1924 his master's from the University of Texas at Austin. On September 18, 1923, he was married to Nina Mae Starnes, and they had a daughter. From 1925 to 1927 Day taught economics at the University of South Dakota. He received his Ph.D. in English from the University of Chicago in 1940. He edited the *Southwest Review*qv at Southern Methodist University in Dallas (1943–45) and was a staff writer and roving editor for *Readers Digest* and a regional editor for *Southwest and West*. Donald Day was a prolific writer, and most of his works are biographical. Books that he wrote or contributed to include *Backwoods to Border* (edited with Mody C. Boatrightqv and published by the Texas Folklore Societyqv in 1942); *From Hell to Breakfast* (also edited with Boatright and published by the Texas Folklore Society around 1944); *Big Country Texas* (1947, edited by Erskine Caldwell); *The Autobiography of Will Rogers* (1949, edited by Day); *Franklin D. Roosevelt's Own Story* (1951, published concurrently in the United States and in Germany); *Will Rogers on How We Elect Our Presidents* (1952, selected and edited by Donald Day); *Woodrow Wilson's Own Story* (1952, selected and edited by Donald Day); *Uncle Sam's Uncle Josh* (1953); *The Autobiography of Sam Houston* (1954, edited by Donald Day and Harry Herbert Ullom); and *The Evolution of Love* (1954). Donald Day died on July 22, 1991, in a rest home at Westport, Connecticut. At his request he was cremated, and his ashes were scattered over Hartford, Connecticut, the place where the name of an ancestor, Robert Day, is engraved on a shaft as a founder of Hartford. Donald Day was married six times. He was survived by his wife, Klari Day.

BIBLIOGRAPHY: Vertical Files, Barker Texas History Center, University of Texas at Austin. *Dorothy Wimberley Kerbow*

DAY, FREEMAN H. K. (1806–1836). Freeman Day, Alamo defender, was born in 1806. He took part in the siege of Bexarqv and later served in the Alamo garrison as a member of Capt. Robert White'sqv Infantry company, the Bexar Guards. Day died in the battle of the Alamoqv on March 6, 1836.

BIBLIOGRAPHY: Daughters of the American Revolution, *The Alamo Heroes and Their Revolutionary Ancestors* (San Antonio, 1976). Daughters of the Republic of Texas, *Muster Rolls of the Texas Revolution* (Austin, 1986). Bill Groneman, *Alamo Defenders* (Austin: Eakin, 1990). John H. Jenkins, ed., *The Papers of the Texas Revolution, 1835–1836* (10 vols., Austin: Presidial Press, 1973). *Bill Groneman*

DAY, JAMES MONROE (ca. 1840–1904). James Monroe (Doc) Day, cattleman and drover, was born in Barry County, Missouri, around 1840, the son of Jesse and Sarah (Logan) Day. He was brought to Texas by his family in 1847 and eventually settled in Mountain City, Hays County. Before the Civil Warqv he engaged in stock raising with his father and brother William H. Day.qv In 1857, with William and Willis McCutcheon of Bastrop County, he pioneered in blazing a cattle trail to Sedalia, Missouri, and Quincy, Illinois. After the Civil War he owned a ranch in Denton County and drove cattle to Iowa and Kansas. He was a brother-in-law of Jesse L. Driskillqv and was associated for a time with the Driskill businesses in Austin. Day was ranching in New Mexico when he died at Roswell in 1904.

BIBLIOGRAPHY: Joseph G. McCoy, *Historic Sketches of the Cattle Trade of the West and Southwest* (Kansas City, Missouri: Ramsey, Millett, and Hudson, 1874; rpt., Philadelphia: Porcupine, 1974). James T. Padgitt, "Colonel William H. Day: Texas Ranchman," *Southwestern Historical Quarterly* 53 (April 1950). Vertical Files, Barker Texas History Center, University of Texas at Austin.

DAY, JERRY C. (1818–1836). Jerry C. Day, Alamo defender and son of Jeremiah Day, was born in Missouri in 1818. In 1836 he lived near Gonzales, Texas. He was a member of the Alamo garrison during the Texas Revolution,qv and his father served the Texas forces as a wagoner. Day died in the battle of the Alamoqv on March 6, 1836.

BIBLIOGRAPHY: Daughters of the American Revolution, *The Alamo Heroes and Their Revolutionary Ancestors* (San Antonio, 1976). Bill Groneman, *Alamo Defenders* (Austin: Eakin, 1990). *Bill Groneman*

DAY, WILLIAM H. (1833–1881). William H. Day, trail driver and livestock entrepreneur, son of Jesse and Sarah (Logan) Day, was born on May 8, 1833, in Cassville, Georgia. The family moved to Bastrop, Texas, in 1847. They later lived in San Antonio and then in Hays County. Day graduated from Cumberland University in 1858 with a degree in engineering. On his first cattle drive in 1860, his father drowned. Day and his brother James Monroe Dayqv attempted to drive the herd to Kansas City but were turned back by angry landowners. They nevertheless delivered the herd to St. Louis. Day continued in the cattle business after a brief tenure in the military in what is now Coleman County, Texas. In 1862 he drove herds to Louisiana markets, and after the Civil Warqv he was involved in the lumber business in East Texas. In 1868 or 1869 he drove a herd of cattle to Abilene, Kansas, in partnership with his brother-in-law, Jesse L. Driskill.qv In 1873 he was employed by the St. Louis livestock-commission firm of Hunter and Evans, and by 1875, after a brief return to the cattle business, he was the company's manager for Texas.

Day realized that the future of the cattle business depended on land ownership and fenced pastures, and he took steps to acquire thousands of acres from the school-land tracts of Brazoria and Fort Bend counties, which were situated at the confluence of the Concho and Colorado rivers south of Camp Colorado in Coleman County. In 1878 he bought a considerable plot in what was to become Coleman County and made several drives to Dodge City, Kansas. In the next year he married Mabel Doss (*see* LEA, MABEL D.) of Denison, and in the winter of 1880 their daughter Willie Mabel was born. Day died on June 14, 1881, from injuries sustained in a stampede and left his widow and infant child deeply in debt and burdened with a massive ranch operation. Mabel Doss Day turned misfortune into success, however, and during the 1880s became known as the "Cattle Queen of Texas" for her skillful management.

BIBLIOGRAPHY: James T. Padgitt, "Colonel William H. Day: Texas Ranchman," *Southwestern Historical Quarterly* 53 (April 1950). William S. Speer and John H. Brown, eds., *Encyclopedia of the New West* (Marshall, Texas: United States Biographical Publishing, 1881; rpt., Easley, South Carolina: Southern Historical Press, 1978).

John Allen Peterson

DAY, TEXAS. Day, a small agricultural settlement that was probably in central Washington County, obtained a post office in September 1858. The community was most likely named in honor of the county tax collector, John H. Day. In 1860 it had a population of about eighty, including a teacher. The growth of Brenham, Chappell Hill, and nearby Evergreen may have hastened the decline of the community. In November 1866 its post office was closed. No remains of this settlement existed in the 1980s. *Carole E. Christian*

DAYCAO RIVER. The Daycao River, mentioned as being ten days' travel beyond the most westerly point reached by the Moscoso expeditionqv in 1542, was possibly the Trinity. The name Daycao was said also to have designated an Indian province, possibly the home of the Hasinais in the area of the Trinity.

BIBLIOGRAPHY: Rex W. Strickland, "Moscoso's Journey through Texas," *Southwestern Historical Quarterly* 46 (October 1942). J. W. Williams, "Moscoso's Trail in Texas," *Southwestern Historical Quarterly* 46 (October 1942). Albert Woldert, "Expedition of Luis de Moscoso in Texas in 1542," *Southwestern Historical Quarterly* 46 (October 1942). *Margery H. Krieger*

DAY LAND AND CATTLE COMPANY. Day Land and Cattle Company, a private corporation with headquarters in Austin, was organized on March 24, 1884, by James Monroe Day, Charles E. Anderson,qqv Frank M. Maddox, John W. Maddox, and John W. Powers to buy, sell, and lease Texas land for grazing and breeding beef cattle. The company, chartered for fifty years with a capital stock of $510,000, bought 174,854 acres of donation and bounty land scrip and leased several thousand acres. On August 4, 1885, it leased 203,000 acres in Greer County.qv The loss of this property to Oklahoma was probably at least partly responsible for the firm's decline.

BIBLIOGRAPHY: Laura V. Hamner, *Short Grass and Longhorns* (Norman: University of Oklahoma Press, 1943). Joseph G. McCoy, *Historic Sketches of the Cattle Trade of the West and Southwest* (Kansas City, Missouri: Ramsey, Millett, and Hudson, 1874; rpt., Philadelphia: Porcupine, 1974).

DAYMON, SQUIRE (1808–1836). Squire Daymon, Alamo defender, was born at Tennessee in 1808. He was a resident of Gonzales, Texas, in 1836. After taking part in the siege of Bexar,qv he served in the Bexar garrison as a member of Capt. William R. Carey'sqv artillery company. Sometime after February 2, 1836, Daymon may have left Bexar for his home and then returned to the Alamo, possibly with the relief force from Gonzales on March 1, 1836. He died in the battle of the Alamoqv on March 6, 1836.

BIBLIOGRAPHY: Daughters of the American Revolution, *The Alamo Heroes and Their Revolutionary Ancestors* (San Antonio, 1976). Daughters of the Republic of Texas, *Muster Rolls of the Texas Revolution* (Austin, 1986). Bill Groneman, *Alamo Defenders* (Austin: Eakin, 1990).
Bill Groneman

DAYS CHAPEL, TEXAS. Days Chapel, also known as Day School, is near the intersection of Farm Road 1817 and a country road ten miles southeast of Palestine in southeastern Anderson County. In the 1930s the site had a number of dwellings, a church, and a district school for white students. The Day school served some sixty-two pupils in 1932. A school for black students was two miles to the east in the Union Hope Church community. The Day school had consolidated with that of Slocum by 1955, and by 1982 Days Chapel had a few scattered dwellings and a church. In 1985 the church was still standing.

BIBLIOGRAPHY: Thomas Paul Jones, The Reorganization of the Public Schools of Anderson County, Texas (M.Ed. thesis, University of Texas, 1934).
Mark Odintz

DAYTON. The 111-ton sidewheel steamship *Dayton* is chiefly remembered for the boiler explosions that caused it to sink in Corpus Christi Bay on September 12, 1845. The vessel was constructed in 1835 by Robert Beer of Pittsburgh, Pennsylvania, who also served as its master and sometime captain. The *Dayton* traded on the Ohio and down the Mississippi until about 1839, when its shallow draft provided an advantage in the Texas coastwide trade. In 1840 Galveston city recorder George F. Lawrence was killed during a fight aboard the *Dayton*. Augustus M. Tomkinsqv and his brother were charged with murder. When strong feelings in the community resulted in a change of venue to Houston, the *Dayton* carried the witnesses to Harris County. When the Mexican Warqv broke out, the United States Army quartermaster contracted the *Dayton* to transport men and goods from the depot on St. Joseph Island to the large army beach encampment at Corpus Christi. On July 23, 1845, Gen. Zachary Taylorqv and a party of the Third Regiment of Infantry made the trip.

The explosions on September 12 occurred after the *Dayton* left Corpus Christi on a return trip with a party of noncommissioned officers and enlisted men, among them Capt. George Hampton Crosman of the Sixth Regiment of Infantry, who was in charge of the transportation effort and who carried money and a letter of formal discharge from the contract. Near noon one of the boilers exploded off McGloin's Bluff. Two officers, Lt. Benjamin A. Berry of South Carolina and Lt. Thaddeus Higgins of Pennsylvania, were killed instantly. The second boiler exploded as the burning ship settled in the water before sinking. A small boat picked up the wounded in the water after the explosions, but six of the officers and crew of the *Dayton* were killed. Lt. Ulysses S. Grant had chosen at the last moment not to take the vessel, and wrote a graphic account of the matter to his fiancée, Julia Dent, on September 14 and October 10, 1845. Capt. E. Kirby Smithqv also wrote of the incident to his wife on September 18, 1845. The bodies of the dead officers and men were buried in a military cemetery northwest of camp. The burial ground, which commands a view of Nueces and Corpus Christi bays, is now called Old Bayview Cemetery.

BIBLIOGRAPHY: Charles Adams Gulick, Jr., Harriet Smither, et al., eds., *The Papers of Mirabeau Buonaparte Lamar* (6 vols., Austin: Texas State Library, 1920–27; rpt., Austin: Pemberton Press, 1968). Ethan Allen Hitchcock, *Fifty Years in Camp and Field: Diary of Major-General Ethan Allen Hitchcock, U.S.A*, ed. W. A. Croffut (New York: Putnam, 1909). Houston *Morning Star*, April 10, September 1, 10, October 3, November 2, 1840. William Gilman Lyford, *Western Address Directory for the Year 1837* (Baltimore: Robinson, 1837). John Y. Simon, ed., *Papers of Ulysses S. Grant* (12 vols., Carbondale: Southern Illinois University Press, 1967-). *Telegraph and Texas Register*, August 13, September 24, 1845. Austin *Texas Sentinel*, April 15, 22, May 9, 1840.
Frank Wagner

DAYTON, TEXAS. Dayton, on U.S. Highway 90 three miles west of Liberty in southwestern Liberty County, was first called West Liberty and was considered part of the original town of Liberty, founded in 1831. The Trinity River divided the two parts of the town: Liberty was on its east bank, and West Liberty was on a hill three miles west of the river. A new road and a ferry directly connected the two. Both parts of the town were located on the four-league Mexican land grant appropriated for the capital of the old municipality of Santísima Trinidad de la Libertad, which later became known as Liberty. The postmaster of West Liberty from March 25, 1839, through September 15, 1841, was A. Thouvenin, probably the same man as Arnold Thouvenin, who obtained a quarter-league Mexican land grant in Polk County in April 1835. The West Liberty post office was apparently discontinued after a few years. Land was designated for a school in 1847. The schoolhouse was accepted on December 31, 1853, by the board of trustees of the Corporation of the Town of Liberty. Also in 1853, A. N. B. Thompson was authorized to survey and plat the town of West Liberty. During the Civil Warqv thirty-three ladies of West Liberty wrote to Governor Francis R. Lubbockqv in January 1863, petitioning him to relieve Mr. Sol Andrews of his military duties so that he might continue his vocation of manufacturer of looms and spinning wheels, as cloth for clothing was desperately needed.

Sometime after 1854 West Liberty also became known as Day's Town, for I. C. Day, a wealthy landowner who resided just to the south of the town on the Munson league. The flag stop for the Texas and New Orleans Railroad, completed in 1860, was known variously as West Liberty, Days Station, and Dayton Station. The name Dayton was applied to the local post office in 1877, though the official name of the town remained West Liberty until the mid-1880s. In 1885 Dayton reported a population of sixty, and in 1890 a post office, a school, and two churches served its 239 residents. Lumbering and cattle raising were the chief industries until James E. Berry helped establish a drainage system to make rice a major crop. Texas governor Marion Price Daniel, Sr.,qv was born in Dayton on October 10, 1910; his brother Bill Daniel, governor of the United States Territory of Guam from 1961 through 1963, was born in Dayton on November 20, 1915. By 1910 the town had a bank, two cotton gins, a weekly newspaper, and 2,500 inhabitants. Dayton was recorded as an incorporated municipality on May 3, 1911. The mayor was W. M. Babcock, and aldermen were W. T. Jamison, J. H. Marshall, J. A. Coleman, and J. D. Spear. Town records indicate that the community was reincorporated in 1925. Oil development during the 1920s brought new industries. By 1940 Dayton reported 1,207 residents and seventy businesses and was listed as a railroad center. The population increased steadily from 3,367 in 1965 to 6,201 in 1988. In 1989 the largest school population in the county made the Dayton Independent School District the major employer in the city. At that time Dayton operated under a mayor-council form of city government.qv In 1990 Dayton had a population of 5,151.

BIBLIOGRAPHY: James M. Day, comp., *Post Office Papers of the Republic of Texas* (2 vols., Austin: Texas State Library, 1966–67). Frank W. Johnson, *A History of Texas and Texans* (5 vols., ed. E. C. Barker and E. W. Winkler [Chicago and New York: American Historical Society, 1914; rpt. 1916]). Miriam Partlow, *Liberty, Liberty County, and the Atascosito District* (Austin: Pemberton, 1974). Virginia H. Taylor, *The Spanish Archives of the General Land Office of Texas* (Austin: Lone Star, 1955).

Jean L. Epperson

DAYTON–GOOSE CREEK RAILWAY. The Dayton–Goose Creek Railway Company was incorporated on July 24, 1917, by Ross S. Sterling,qv who was later governor of Texas. The capital was $25,000. The members of the first board of directors were William S. Farish, Edgar E. Townes,qqv Walter W. Fondren, Ross Sterling, and F. P. Sterling, all of Houston, and A. E. Kerr and C. A. Brown, both of Dayton. Ross Sterling owned most of the shares in the railroad. The Dayton–Goose Creek constructed twenty-five miles of track at a cost of $632,738. Construction began at Dayton in 1917 and the railroad opened to Goose Creek in Liberty County on May 1, 1918. The extension to Baytown was completed in August 1919. The line was constructed to connect the newly discovered Goose Creek oilfieldqv and the Baytown refinery of Humble Oil and Refining Company (later Exxon Company, U.S.A.qv) with the Texas and New Orleans at Dayton. The line was profitable enough, primarily from moving petroleum products, to pay for itself in eight years. In 1926 it reported passenger earnings of $5,000 and freight earnings of $157,000. In 1926 Sterling sold the Dayton–Goose Creek to the Southern Pacific, which leased it to the Texas and New Orleans for operation. In 1934 the Dayton–Goose Creek, along with the other major Southern Pacific properties in Texas and Louisiana, was merged into the Texas and New Orleans. The Texas and New Orleans, in turn, was merged into the Southern Pacific in 1961, and the former Dayton–Goose Creek line is still operated as part of the Southern Pacific.

Barbara H. Fisher

DAYTON'S ROAD. Dayton's Road was built around 1834 and was the first road from Jonesborough to the Sulphur Fork prairies southeast of Clarksville.

BIBLIOGRAPHY: Sallie M. Lentz, "Highlights of Early Harrison County," *Southwestern Historical Quarterly* 61 (October 1957). Rex W. Strickland, Anglo-American Activities in Northeastern Texas, 1803–1845 (Ph.D. dissertation, University of Texas, 1937).

Carolyn Hyman

DEAD HORSE CREEK (Eastland County). Dead Horse Creek rises three miles east of Nimrod and twelve miles south of U.S. Highway 183 in west central Eastland County (at 32°16′ N, 99°00′ W) and runs northeast ten miles to its mouth on the South Fork of the Leon River, eight miles southeast of Eastland (at 32°19′ N, 98°54′ W). In the creek's upper reaches it traverses rolling hills surfaced by clay and sandy loams that support scrub brush, mesquite, cacti, live oak, juniper, and grasses; in its lower reaches, rugged hills and scarps are surfaced by shallow, stony, sandy loams that support post oak, grasses, and chaparral.

——— (Hill County). Dead Horse Creek rises four miles southeast of Whitney in west central Hill County (at 31°55′ N, 97°16′ W) and runs south for eight miles to its mouth on Aquilla Creek, just east of Aquilla (at 31°51′ N, 97°12′ W). It traverses flat to rolling terrain surfaced by sandy and clay loams that support scrub brush, cacti, and grasses. The creek was supposedly named for a large number of horses found dead at its banks. The area has been used as range and crop land.

DEADMAN CREEK (Callahan County). Deadman Creek rises about four miles northwest of Clyde in northwestern Callahan County (at 32°24′ N, 99°33′ W) and runs for a total of thirty miles, first northwest into Jones County, then north to parallel the Jones-Shackelford county line before reaching its mouth on the Clear Fork of the Brazos River, two miles south of U.S. Highway 180 (at 32°44′ N, 99°38′ W). The stream, previously known as Willow Creek, was renamed after an unidentified man was found dead at one of its crossings. Deadman Creek, which is dammed in Jones County to form a reservoir for municipal supply, traverses flat terrain with local shallow depressions, surfaced by clay and sandy loam soils that support water-tolerant hardwoods, conifers, and grasses.

DEAD MANS CANYON. Dead Mans Canyon, a valley with an intermittent stream, begins a mile northeast of Dead Mans Pass on State Highway 163 in central Val Verde County (at 29°49′ N, 101°08′ W) and runs southwest for seventeen miles to its mouth on the Pecos River, fourteen miles east of Langtry (at 29°47′ N, 101°21′ W). Faro Canyon joins Dead Mans Canyon two miles southeast of the Continental Ranch headquarters, and Crazy Canyon meets Dead Mans two miles north of the Southern Pacific tracks. The course of Dead Mans Canyon sharply dissects massive limestone that underlies flat to rolling prairies. It is a wide and deep canyon that ends on alluvial deposits of gravel, sand, clay, silt, and organic material. Soils in the area are generally dark, calcareous stony clays and clay loams that support oaks, junipers, grasses, and mesquites. The canyon was named for several skeletons, the remains of apparent victims of Indian attack, that were found there by early settlers about 1870. Dead Mans Canyon is a significant valley in the Pecos River drainage system.

DEADMAN'S (DEAD MANS) CREEK (Knox County). Deadman's Creek rises three miles southeast of Truscott in northwestern Knox County (at 33°44′ N, 99°46′ W) and runs northeast for six miles to its mouth on the North Wichita River, six miles northeast of Truscott (at 33°48′ N, 99°44′ W). It passes through an eroded area of densely dissected gullies and low hills, with little soil or vegetation. The creek is reportedly named for Dead Man's Mountain in the northern part of the county.

——— (Val Verde County). Dead Mans Creek rises 1½ miles southwest of Dead Mans Pass in south central Val Verde County (at 29°46′ N, 101°10′ W) and runs southeast for thirteen miles to its mouth on the Devils River, a mile south of Dark Canyon (at 29°44′ N, 101°01′ W). Its course sharply dissects massive limestone that underlies flat terrain, forming a deep and winding canyon. Soils in the area are generally dark, calcareous stony clays and clay loams that support oak, juniper, grasses, and mesquite. The creek was named for a traveling peddler who was robbed and killed by outlaws in a pass on the stream in the 1880s. Reportedly the outlaws openly sold the stolen cloth and kitchenware to workers building the Galveston, Harrisburg and San Antonio Railway, and Judge Roy Beanqv refused to hear the case because the robbery occurred east of the Pecos River and out of his jurisdiction.

DEAD MAN'S HOLE. Dead Man's Hole, in the W. L. Burnam pasture south of Marble Falls in southern Burnet County, is a deep, well-like hole probably caused by gas pressure. It was discovered in 1821 by entomologist Ferdinand Lueders while he was in the area to study night-flying insects. The cave achieved notoriety during the Civil War[qv] as a dumping place for the bodies of Union sympathizers. The remains of several bodies were recovered from the cave in the late 1860s, but the presence of gas prevented extensive exploration. The gas evidently dissipated over time, for in 1951 a group of spelunkers from the University of Texas successfully descended the hole. They reported that Dead Man's Hole was seven feet in diameter at the surface and about 160 feet deep; at its base, the hole split into two "arms," one extending straight back for about fifteen feet, and the other sloping downward at a 45° angle for about thirty feet.

BIBLIOGRAPHY: Houston *Chronicle*, September 9, 1951. Vertical Files, Barker Texas History Center, University of Texas at Austin (Marble Falls).

DEAD NEGRO DRAW. Dead Negro Draw, formerly known as Dead Nigger Creek, rises in southwestern Garza County just east of the Lynn county line (at 33°03′ N, 101°33′ W) and runs north for three miles to its mouth on the South Fork of the Double Mountain Fork of the Brazos River, twelve miles southwest of Post (at 33°05′ N, 101°33′ W). It traverses an area with moderately steep slopes and locally high relief, surfaced by highly erodible shallow to moderately deep silt loams that support mesquite and grasses.

DEADOSE INDIANS. The Deadose (Agdoza, Doxsa, Igodosa, Jacdoas, Judosa, Yacdossa) Indians are known to have existed only during the eighteenth century. It is now clear that they were closely related to the Bidais and spoke an Atakapan language. In the early eighteenth century they lived between the junction of the Angelina and Neches rivers and the upper end of Galveston Bay. Some time after 1720 the Deadoses moved westward to an area lying between the Brazos and Trinity rivers in the vicinity of present Leon, Madison, and Robertson counties. Between 1749 and 1751 the Deadose Indians, along with other Atakapan-speaking groups (Akokisas, Bidais, and Patiris), were represented at the short-lived San Ildefonso Mission near present Rockdale in Milam County. A few Deadose (Yacdossa) Indians entered San Antonio de Valero Mission shortly afterward. In the second half of the eighteenth century the Deadoses were at times closely associated with certain Tonkawan groups (Ervipiames, Mayeyes, and Yojuanes), and it was once thought that their language might have been Tonkawan. This view was abandoned because other evidence clearly indicated an Atakapan linguistic affiliation. The Deadose Indians suffered heavily from European-introduced diseases, especially measles and smallpox, and they eventually lost their ethnic identity in the latter part of the eighteenth century. Remnants of the Deadoses probably joined the Bidais, who survived into the nineteenth century, although some may have been absorbed by the Tonkawas. J. R. Swanton erred in identifying the Yacdossa of San Antonio de Valero Mission as Coahuiltecans.

BIBLIOGRAPHY: Herbert Eugene Bolton, ed. and trans., *Athanase de Mézières and the Louisiana-Texas Frontier, 1768–1780* (2 vols., Cleveland: Arthur H. Clark, 1914). Herbert Eugene Bolton, *Texas in the Middle Eighteenth Century* (Berkeley: University of California Press, 1915; rpt., Austin: University of Texas Press, 1970). Peter P. Forrestal, trans., *The Solís Diary of 1767*, ed. Paul J. Foik (Preliminary Studies of the Texas Catholic Historical Society 1.6 [March 1931]). Andre Sjoberg, The Bidai Indians of Southeastern Texas (M.A. thesis, University of Texas, 1951). J. R. Swanton, *Linguistic Material from the Tribes of Southern Texas and Northeastern Mexico* (Washington: Smithsonian Institution, 1940). John R. Swanton, *The Indians of the Southeastern United States* (Washington: GPO, 1946).
Thomas N. Campbell

DEADWOOD, TEXAS. Deadwood, previously known as Linus, is on Farm Road 2517 some ten miles east of Carthage in eastern Panola County. The area was first settled in 1837 by Adam LaGrone and his family, who built a homestead on Socogee Creek. Around 1860 LaGrone's son, H. C., built a mill and gin that became the nucleus of the later town. The small settlement was originally known as Linus, but when residents applied for a post office in 1882, another town already had that name, and the new name Deadwood was chosen at a town meeting. By 1885 Deadwood had an estimated population of fifty, two churches, a district school, and a steam cotton gin and gristmill. A hotel was built there around 1900 but went out of business a few years later; the local post office was discontinued in 1917. In the mid-1930s Deadwood had a church, a school, and two stores; its reported population in 1936 was 125. After World War II[qv] the community's school was consolidated with the Carthage district, and the remaining businesses at Deadwood closed. In 1990 Deadwood was a dispersed rural community with a reported population of 106.

BIBLIOGRAPHY: *History of Panola County.* (Carthage, Texas: Carthage Circulating Book Club, 1935?). Leila B. LaGrone, ed., *History of Panola County* (Carthage, Texas: Panola County Historical Commission, 1979). Marker Files, Texas Historical Commission, Austin. John Barnette Sanders, *Index to the Cemeteries of Panola County* (Center, Texas, 1964).
Christopher Long

DEAF SMITH COUNTY. Deaf Smith County (C-7), on the western edge of the Panhandle,[qv] is bounded on the west by New Mexico, on the north by Oldham County, on the east by Randall County, and on the south by Parmer and Castro counties. It was named for Erastus "Deaf" Smith,[qv] a famous scout of the Texas Revolution.[qv] The county's center point is at 102°30′ west longitude and 35°00′ north latitude. Deaf Smith County comprises approximately 1,497 square miles of level prairies and rolling plains on the western edge of the Llano Estacado.[qv] Its loam soils, ranging from deep chocolate to sandy, support abundant native grasses as well as numerous agricultural products. Elevations range from 3,200 to 4,200 feet above sea level; the minimum average temperature is 22° F in January, and the average annual maximum is 93° in July. The average annual rainfall is 17.37 inches, and the annual growing season averages 185 days. Tierra Blanca Creek flows intermittently across the southern part of the county, and Palo Duro and North Palo Duro creeks run across the northeastern portion of the county. These streams enter the Red River basin in or near Palo Duro Canyon, in Randall County.

The earliest prehistoric inhabitants of these prairies gave way to Plains Apaches, who in turn were forced out by the warlike Comanches and Kiowas. In 1787, and again in 1788, José Mares[qv] followed Tierra Blanca Creek in his search for a route from Santa Fe to San Antonio. The Indian wars of the 1870s, culminating in the Red River War[qv] of 1874–75, led to the nomadic red man's removal to the Indian Territory. Shortly thereafter ranchers began to appear in the area, and in 1876 the Texas legislature formed Deaf Smith County from the Bexar District. The census counted thirty-eight people in the county in 1880.

By the early 1880s the T Anchor Ranch,[qv] headquartered near the site of present Canyon, had spilled over into the eastern part of the county, and the LS Ranch[qv] extended over into its northeastern portion. Beginning in 1882, the western half of the county lay within the XIT Ranch,[qv] a real estate–cattle project of the Capitol Syndicate. One of the eight XIT division headquarters was established at Las Escarbadas, on Tierra Blanca Creek, in the southwestern corner of Deaf Smith County. The large ranches dominated the county; only a few small stock farms existed among them. By 1890 the county's population had increased to 179, and the census found seventeen farms or ranches in the area, seven of which were smaller than 500 acres. More than 28,600 cattle were counted in the county, while crop production occupied only a few acres: seventy-eight acres was planted in corn and eighty in cotton.

As the cattle industry in the county developed, the rising population created a need for local government. Accordingly, after an election on December 1, 1890, the county was organized with the new town of La Plata as county seat. Jerry R. Dean was elected the first county judge, and the colorful Jim Cook qv became the first county sheriff. In 1898 the Pecos and Northern Texas Railway, a subsidiary of the Santa Fe line, built tracks from Amarillo to the Texas–New Mexico border at Farwell. This railroad crossed the southeastern corner of Deaf Smith County and brought easy and economical transportation to the local ranchers. The coming of the railroad also brought forth a new town, Hereford, which quickly outstripped the other local hamlets. As a result Hereford became the county seat after an election on November 8, 1898, and La Plata soon faded into oblivion. By 1900 the county had ninety-seven ranches and farms and a population of 843.

Between 1900 and 1910 the large ranchers began to sell their lands, and land-company promotions brought a rush of settlers to the area. With them came significant changes in the local agricultural economy during the first half of the twentieth century. The number of farms and ranches in the county increased steadily during most of this period, rising to 361 in 1910, 382 in 1920, 605 in 1930, and 854 in 1940. The expansion of farming was responsible for most of this growth. In 1900, for example, little if any wheat was grown in the county; by 1920 more than 9,000 acres was planted in that grain, and by 1930 wheat acreage exceeded 26,000 acres. Sorghum became another important crop, and the production of corn also expanded. (See WHEAT CULTURE, SORGHUM CULTURE, CORN CULTURE.) Meanwhile, local farmers diversified into poultry production; qv in 1929 local chicken farms had more than 51,000 birds, and county farmers sold 208,023 dozen eggs. As the county's economy developed, its population grew to 3,942 in 1910, 3,747 in 1920, 5,979 in 1930, and 6,056 in 1940.

The county's transportation system evolved to meet its growing economic demands. As early as 1920 U.S. Highway 60 (then known as U.S. 366) ran from Canyon via Hereford to Farwell and Clovis. At the same time a roadway was graded from Hereford west to the New Mexico line, thus facilitating movement of crops from most of the county to the rail line; this road was later paved and designated a state farm-to-market road. Beginning in the late 1930s, U.S. 385 (originally State Highway 51) was built from Brownfield to Dalhart via Dimmitt, Hereford, Vega, and Channing. Throughout the 1940s and 1950s a full network of paved farm-to-market roads emerged, linking all parts of the county to either main highways or railroad lines. U.S. 66, which, with the Rock Island Railroad, cuts across the extreme northwestern corner of the county, gave rise to the border community of Glenrio, which declined after the completion of Interstate 40.

After World War II qv businesses were started in Deaf Smith County to process and ship local products. Vegetable production was introduced on a large scale, and processing and packing plants for onions, potatoes, and other perishable vegetables were also established. In 1964 the Holly Sugar Company opened its $20 million mill and refinery, having contracted with local farmers for the production of sugar beets (see SUGAR PRODUCTION).

Cattle feeding also began to flourish in the 1960s with the opening of several feedlots that used much locally grown grain. By the 1970s these lots were bringing 80 percent of the county's $230 million annual average income. In the late 1980s the county led the state in numbers of cattle fed; it often led the nation in this category. The establishment of feedlots brought commercial production of corn and the establishment of several meat-packing plants in the county. In 1982 Deaf Smith County produced more than 5.75 million bushels of sorghum, 4.75 million bushels of wheat, nearly 4 million bushels of corn, and 251,942 tons of sugar beets. Vegetable production occupied 2,153 acres, planted with carrots, onions, potatoes, and sweet corn.

The population grew steadily from World War II until the 1980s. The number of residents increased from 6,056 in 1940 to 9,111 in 1950, 13,187 in 1960, 18,999 in 1970, and 21,165 in 1980. Economic development brought other changes. The discovery and use of copious underground water in the Ogallala Aquifer in the 1930s led to large-scale irrigation qv in the 1950s, which further encouraged the expansion of farming. The labor needs of the farming economy drew large numbers of migrant laborers, mostly Hispanic, to the county's packing sheds. As this labor force grew, it became less migratory, and increasing numbers of Mexican Americans qv moved into the area permanently. By the 1980s, just over 40 percent of the county's population was of Hispanic descent.

Politically, after 1952 Deaf Smith County became more favorably disposed towards the Republican party qv than formerly, in both state and national elections. Its citizens voted Republican in eight of the nine presidential elections between 1956 and 1988; the county voted for Democrat Texan Lyndon B. Johnson qv in 1964 in his race against Republican Barry Goldwater.

For several decades the diversified agricultural economy of Deaf Smith County was a thriving, coordinated system. By the early 1980s, however, though farmers produced more on their land, they began realizing a smaller return than at any other time in history. The county population began to drop between 1980 and 1982; by 1992 it was estimated at 19,153, almost 10 percent less than only ten years earlier. Tight economic conditions, combined with a diminishing supply of groundwater, presented new problems. A search for innovations in farming methods intensified. Fearing contamination of the valuable aquifer, residents opposed attempts by the United States Department of Energy during the 1980s to make the county a nuclear-waste dump site.

Communities in Deaf Smith County include Dawn, Glenrio, and Westway. Hereford (1990 population 14,745) is the county's seat of government and only urban center; in the late 1980s the town had six public elementary schools, two junior highs, a large high school, a county library, and two museums (the Deaf Smith County Historical Museum, and the National Cowgirl Hall of Fame and Western Heritage Center qv). Every August the town conducts a Miss Hereford contest and hosts the Cowgirl Hall of Fame All-Girl Rodeo.

BIBLIOGRAPHY: Clois Truman Brown, The History of Deaf Smith County, Texas (M.A. thesis, West Texas State College, 1948). Deaf Smith County: The Land and Its People (Hereford, Texas: Deaf Smith County Historical Society, 1982). Sarah Ann Gilbert, The Origins of Modern Agribusiness: Deaf Smith County, Texas, 1930–1940 (M.A. thesis, Texas Tech University, 1981). J. Evetts Haley, The XIT Ranch of Texas and the Early Days of the Llano Estacado (Chicago: Lakeside, 1929; rpts., Norman: University of Oklahoma Press, 1953, 1967). Bessie Patterson, A History of Deaf Smith County (Hereford, Texas: Pioneer, 1964). Dulcie Sullivan, The LS Brand (Austin: University of Texas Press, 1968). *H. Allen Anderson*

DEAL, TEXAS. Deal, in northwestern Carson County, was established during the oil boom of the late 1920s as a flag stop on the Chicago, Rock Island and Gulf Railway. The name of the community was adapted from that of George Washington Deahl, who owned the ranchland near Antelope Peak on which the town was founded. A post office was established in 1926 but was discontinued two years later. A district school was opened in 1936. Although the population swelled to 200 soon after its inception, Deal failed to survive, as oil and gas development moved on north and east. Eventually the site returned to prairie land. By 1949 trains no longer stopped at Deal, and the school was closed.

BIBLIOGRAPHY: Jo Stewart Randel, ed., A Time to Purpose: A Chronicle of Carson County (4 vols., Hereford, Texas: Pioneer, 1966–72). Fred Tarpley, 1001 Texas Place Names (Austin: University of Texas Press, 1980). *H. Allen Anderson*

DEALEY, EDWARD MUSGROVE (1892–1969). Edward Musgrove (Ted) Dealey, journalist and publisher, was born to Olivia (Allen) and George Bannerman Dealey qv on October 5, 1892, in Dallas, Texas. He attended Dallas public schools and the Terrill School for Boys. He received a B.A. degree from the University of Texas in

1913 and an M.A. degree in philosophy from Harvard in 1914. In 1915 Dealey was studying business at Harvard when he was offered the job of secretary to Cesar Maurice Lombardi,^qv president of the A. H. Belo Corporation,^qv publisher of the Dallas *Morning News,* the Galveston *Daily News,* and the *Texas Almanac.*^qv He returned to Dallas to accept the position and later that year began his career with the Dallas *Morning News* as a reporter and thus a member of the fifth generation of his mother's family in the newspaper business. In 1920 he became a staff correspondent and lent his voice to the *News* crusade against the Ku Klux Klan.^qv In a memo dated August 5, 1924, to his father he insisted that the paper endorse Miriam A. Ferguson^qv against the 1924 Klan gubernatorial candidate. In 1924 Dealey became an editorial writer and editor of a Sunday magazine supplement. He began his executive rise in 1926 as a board member of the Belo Corporation and became assistant to the publisher in 1928, vice president in 1932, and president in 1940, succeeding his father, who had established the Dallas *Morning News* in 1885. At this time Dealey and the *News* campaigned editorially against courthouse corruption in Dallas County. In 1960 he became publisher and chairman of the board. He resigned the board chairmanship in 1964 but remained as publisher until 1968, when he became publisher emeritus.

Despite his administrative obligations, Dealey continued to write. During World War II^qv he served as staff correspondent of the *News* in the Far East and witnessed the Japanese surrender on the USS *Missouri.* His dispatches were later published by the *News* in *Sunset in the East* (1945). He also served as a major commanding the Twenty-ninth Battalion, Texas Defense Guard (1941–42), and as a major in the United States Army Specialist Corps (1942–43). In addition to accounts of his travels he published several short stories. His *Diaper Days of Dallas* (1966) was a reminiscence of early Dallas. Articles by Dealey also appeared in such popular magazines as the *Saturday Evening Post* and scholarly journals, including the *Southwestern Historical Quarterly.*^qv

Dealey was president of Dallas News Radio Corporation (owner of station WFAA), which acquired WFAA-TV in 1950. He was instrumental in founding Southland Paper Mills, which processed the first modern newsprint west of the Mississippi. He was also a member of the board of directors of the Texas Newspaper Publishers Association (president 1935–36, 1936–37), the Southern Newspaper Publishers Association (president 1937–38, chairman 1938–39), the Advertising Federation of America, and the American Newspaper Publishers Association. In 1948 he served as first vice president of the Associated Press. In 1961 Dealey made national news when he impugned President John F. Kennedy's leadership ability at a White House luncheon.

Among his civic activities Dealey served as a trustee of the Texas Research Foundation^qv and the Scottish Rite Hospital and director of the Dallas Historical Society and the State Fair of Texas.^qqv He was also a charter member of the Dallas Citizens Council. As organizer, president (1955), and then board chairman (1960) of the Dallas Zoological Society, he was responsible for extensive improvements at the Dallas Zoo, to which he donated his outdoor and sporting library of 2,000 volumes. For work such as this he was awarded the Poage Award from the Society for Animal Protection as Humanitarian of the Year in 1960. Another of his favorite concerns was the Southwest Diabetic Foundation in Gainesville, Texas.

On March 1, 1916, Dealey married Clara MacDonald, with whom he had three children. He married a second time on June 29, 1951, to Mrs. Trudie Kelley. Dealey was a thirty-third-degree Mason, a Presbyterian, and an independent Democrat. He was also an avid hunter and fisherman and was known nationally as a breeder of Airedale and Welsh terrier dogs. He died on November 27, 1969, of a heart attack at his home in Dallas.

BIBLIOGRAPHY: Dallas *Morning News,* November 27, 1969. *Who's Who in America,* 1960–61. Ernest Sharpe, *G. B. Dealey of the Dallas News* (New York: Holt, 1955).   *Joan Jenkins Perez*

DEALEY, GEORGE BANNERMAN (1859–1946). George Bannerman (G. B.) Dealey, publisher and civic planner, was born on September 18, 1859, in Manchester, England, to George and Mary Ann (Nellins) Dealey. In the mid-1860s the family moved to Liverpool, where he began his schooling and worked as a grocer's apprentice. In 1870 his family immigrated to Galveston, Texas, where he continued in public school and worked at various odd jobs. He took the position of office boy at the Galveston *News*^qv on October 12, 1874. He worked for this publishing concern the rest of his life.

Dealey took evening classes at the Island City Business College and rose steadily at the *News.* He became a traveling correspondent who sent news stories and business and circulation reports back to Galveston. When the Dallas *Morning News*^qv was founded in 1885 he was appointed business manager. By 1895 he became manager of the paper. He became a board member of both newspapers in 1902, vice president and general manager of the corporation in 1906, and president in 1919, upon the death of Cesar M. Lombardi.^qv In 1926 Dealey bought the Dallas *Morning News,* the *Journal* (an evening edition), the *Semi-Weekly Farm News,* and the *Texas Almanac*^qv from the heirs of Alfred H. Belo^qv and acquired the majority of the company stock.

Dealey was a principled journalist. The *News* was perpetually enlisted in the cause of civic planning. A Dealey campaign of 1899 led to the foundation of the Cleaner Dallas League, which became the Dallas Civic Improvement League in 1902. Dealey's efforts were instrumental in the adoption of the original plan to improve Dallas by city planner George E. Kessler^qv in 1910. Dealey refused advertising that he considered dishonest or immoral, including ads for hard liquor and even for oilfield promotions, since he could not determine sound from unsound petroleum ventures. The *News* also crusaded against the Ku Klux Klan's^qv influence in the 1920s.

Dealey's other business interests included the G. B. Dealey Land Company and the West Commerce Realty Company. He pioneered in newspaper-owned radio stations by opening WFAA in 1922. He helped establish Southern Methodist University and was instrumental in obtaining the Federal Reserve Bank of Dallas^qv for the city.

Dealey's personal involvement in civic activities included serving on the board of governors of the American City Planning Institute (1920–21), as vice president of the National Municipal League (1923–24), on the advisory council of the American Planning and Civic Association, and on the national committee of the Commission on Interracial Cooperation. He was a director of the Children's Hospital of Texas and was president of the Family Bureau, a pioneer Dallas social agency, from its inception in 1908. He was also president of the Philosophical Society of Texas,^qv a member of the Texas Press Association,^qv an honorary life member of the Texas State Historical Association,^qv founder (1922) and lifetime president (from 1933) of the Dallas Historical Society,^qv second vice president of the Associated Press (1923–24), an honorary national president of Sigma Delta Chi (1940–41), and an honorary member of Phi Beta Kappa (1943). He received honorary doctoral degrees from Southern Methodist University (1921), Austin College (1924), and the University of Missouri (1925), the last of which invited him to accept a gift to its school of journalism from the British Empire Press Union.

On April 9, 1884, Dealey married Olivia Allen; they had five children. Dealey was a Thirty-third-degree Scottish Rite Mason, Knight Templar, Shriner, and member of the Red Cross of Constantine. He was a Presbyterian and Democrat. Dealey Plaza in Dallas is named for him. The New York *Times* called him the dean of American publishers. He died at his home in Dallas on February 26, 1946, of a coronary occlusion.

BIBLIOGRAPHY: Sam Hanna Acheson, "George Bannerman Dealey," *Southwestern Historical Quarterly* 50 (January 1947). *Texas Almanac,* 1947–48. *Who's Who in America,* 1946–47. Ernest Sharpe, *G. B. Dealey of the Dallas News* (New York: Holt, 1955).   *Joan Jenkins Perez*

DEALEY, JAMES QUAYLE (1861–1937). James Quayle Dealey, professor and journalist, was born to George and Mary Ann (Nellins) Dealey on August 13, 1861, in Manchester, England. When he was nine, his family moved to Galveston, Texas, where he received some education in the local schools. At the age of seventeen, however, he joined his two brothers, Thomas W. and George B. Dealey,qv as an employee of the Galveston *News*.qv While working in a number of the newspaper's departments, including the business office, the mail room, and the circulation department, he developed an understanding of the industry. He also worked as a traveling salesman for various business firms operating from Galveston. In 1884 he left the Gulf Coast city and entered the Cook Academy of Montour Falls, New York, where he took courses in preparation for entering college. Apparently during the same year Dealey enrolled at Brown University, at Providence, Rhode Island, where he graduated in 1890 with a bachelor's degree in languages. Soon afterward, he returned to Texas as a teacher.

Dealey was appointed professor of ancient languages and history at Denton State Normal School (now the University of North Texas). He resigned after a year, however, to accept a teaching post in Latin at the Vermont Academy at Saxton's River. Dealey remained in Vermont for two years and in 1893 reentered Brown University, where he received the A.M. degree in Greek and German. The university hired him as a Latin instructor during the fall of that year.

He developed an interest in political and social science and completed a Ph.D. in these subjects in 1895. He was influenced in these relatively new fields by pioneer sociologist Lester F. Ward, one of his teachers at Brown. Dealey joined the faculty at Brown as an assistant professor of political sciences in 1895. In this position, often collaborating with Ward, he wrote a number of scholarly works, including *Spanish Sources of the Mexican Constitution of 1824* (1900), *Textbook of Sociology* (1905), *Development of the State* (1909), *The Family in Its Social Aspects* (1912), and *Sociology, Its Development and Applications* (1920). Dealey's publications, which also included contributions to both scholarly and popular periodicals, established his reputation as a leading academic and drew him into a number of professional organizations. He was a member of the Institut International de Sociologie and served as president of the American Sociological Society, vice president of the American Political Science Association, and president of the Southwestern Social Science Association.qv By 1905 he had risen to the rank of professor; by 1910 he had been appointed chairman of his department at Brown. In addition, he lectured periodically at the Naval War College at Newport, Rhode Island, from 1916 through 1928. In 1921 he was a visiting professor at Shanghai College, in China.

Dealey retired from the university in 1928. Soon afterward he returned to Texas to assume editorship of the Dallas *Morning News*,qv of which his brother G. B. was president. In 1930 Dealey, a Baptist, was awarded an honorary doctorate by Baylor University. Among the social organizations to which he belonged were the Critic, Town and Gown, the Faculty Club at Brown University, and the Author's Club of London. On August 7, 1890, Dealey married Clara Learned. The couple raised four children. Dealey died on January 22, 1937, at his desk at the *Morning News* offices in editorial conference with his brothers. He was buried at Restland Memorial Park in Dallas.

BIBLIOGRAPHY: Dallas *Morning News*, January 23, 1937. *National Cyclopaedia of American Biography* Vols. 27 and A.   *Wayne Gard*

DEALEY, JOSEPH MACDONALD (1919–1995). Joe M. Dealey, newspaperman, son of Clara MacDonald and E. M. (Ted) Dealey,qv was born in Dallas on July 18, 1919. Both his father and his grandfather, George Bannerman Dealey,qv were publishers of the Dallas *Morning News*.qv As a boy, Joe Dealey developed the firm conviction that he was destined to become a newspaperman. His natural instincts and intellectual curiosity, combined with family tradition, reinforced those early feelings. His career at the Dallas *Morning News* and A. H. Belo Corporationqv had its beginning in the mailroom of the Dallas *Journal*,qv where he worked in the spring of 1937 before he finished high school. He then prepared for a newspaper career at the University of Texas in Austin, studying English, history, and economics. Following that, at the Southwest School of Printing, he learned the mechanical side of the business. Dealey was drafted into the Army Air Corps in 1942, and following World War IIqv he returned to the *News*, renewing his career as a reporter in 1946. From that date, his service to Belo was uninterrupted until his death.

Dealey married Doris Carolyn Russell on January 18, 1947. They had four children. In 1950 he was named assistant secretary of Belo and became a key member of the management team at a crucial time as the company expanded into television, complementing its long-time newspaper and radio operations. In 1952 he was elected to the company's board of directors, along with three other grandsons of G. B. Dealey. With his cousins Al Dealey, Ben Decherd, and Jimmy Moroney, Dealey ushered in a third generation of family participation at Belo. Also in 1952, Dealey was one of the principal participants in the establishment of the G. B. Dealey Foundation, and with his leadership over four decades, the philanthropic foundation grew to almost $22 million in assets and made grants to 152 charitable organizations. In 1960 Dealey was named president and chief executive officer of Belo and the *News*, succeeding his father as head of the company. In assuming the role, he embarked on a career of unstinted civic involvement that continued throughout his life. His active participation with countless institutions, such as Children's Medical Center of Dallas,qv the United Way of Dallas, Scottish Rite Hospital, the Dallas Zoological Society, the State Fair of Texas,qv and the Dallas Historical Society,qv was recognized when he was presented the Linz Award in 1967.

During the 1960s and early 1970s he was also active in matters of importance to the newspaper industry. He served in various leadership roles with the Texas Daily Newspaper Association, the Southern Newspaper Publishers Association, and the American Newspaper Publishers Association, as well as United Press International. In 1980 he became chairman of the board of Belo and publisher of the Dallas *Morning News*. Teaming up with his cousins Jimmy Moroney and Robert Decherd, he held a steady course through the company's first public stock offering, which came in 1981. When Dealey stepped down as chairman in 1984, Belo had total assets of $692.4 million—sixty-six times the company's total assets when he became chief executive officer in 1960. After his retirement as chairman, Dealey continued his distinguished service as a director of Belo. He died on April 7, 1995.   *Judith M. Garrett*

DEALEY, SAMUEL DAVID (1906–1944). Samuel David Dealey, Medal of Honor winner, was born on September 13, 1906, to Samuel and Virgie Dealey in Dallas, Texas. He was a nephew of George B. Dealey and a cousin of Edward M. Dealey.qqv His father died in 1912, and his mother moved to Santa Monica, California, where Sam, Jr., began school. He returned to Dallas and graduated from Oak Cliff (now W. H. Adamson) High School. He then studied for two years at Southern Methodist University before entering the United States Naval Academy in the spring of 1925. He failed to maintain adequate grades that year but reentered in 1926 and graduated in the middle of the class of 1930. He subsequently married Edwina Vawter of Santa Monica. They had three children.

After serving on various battleships, destroyers, and submarines, in December 1942 Lieutenant Commander Dealey became the first and only commander of the newly commissioned submarine USS *Harder*. He took the ship in 1943 to the Pacific and made five highly successful patrols, but failed to return from a sixth. He was particularly noted for heading toward enemy destroyers and discharging the sub's forward tubes before making the standard maneuver of diving into silent running; this effective but dangerous maneuver, which

Dealey used by permission from the commander of the Pacific Fleet, sank five Japanese destroyers in four days. Dealey officially sank sixteen enemy vessels in all. He was Group Commander of a Submarine Wolf Pack consisting of the *Harder,* the *Hake,* and the *Hado* in waters off Luzon, Philippine. On August 24, 1944, the *Harder* was heavily and fatally depth-charged. Commander Dealey was declared missing in action and presumed dead on October 2, 1944.

During his command of the *Harder* in 1943 and 1944 he earned the Navy Cross with three gold stars, the army's Distinguished Service Cross (presented to him by Gen. Douglas MacArthur), two presidential unit citations, and a Purple Heart. He was commended for "sinking over 15,000 tons and damaging over 27,000 tons of enemy shipping," for "extraordinary heroism . . . in the presence of formidable concentrations of anti-submarine vessels," for rescuing an Allied pilot "from a rubber raft off a Japanese-held island despite harassing fire," and for many other acts of valor. The Medal of Honor was presented to Dealey's widow on August 28, 1945, for acts that attested "the valiant fighting spirit of Commander Dealey and his indomitable command." For the *Harder*'s sixth war patrol, Commander Dealey was awarded the Silver Star posthumously.

The United States Navy named a destroyer escort in his honor. Dealey Plaza, the site of the Kennedy assassination[qv] in Dallas, is also named for him. In 1994 a neglected plaque in his honor was moved from Seawolf Park in Galveston to the Science Place in Fair Park, Dallas, and dedicated in a ceremony.

BIBLIOGRAPHY: Committee on Veterans' Affairs, United States Senate, *Medal of Honor Recipients, 1863–1973* (Washington: GPO, 1973). Dallas *Morning News,* August 18, 1994. Charles A. Lockwood and Hans Christian Adamson, *Through Hell and Deep Water: The Stirring Story of the Navy's Deadly Submarine, the U.S.S. Harder, under the Command of Sam Dealey, Destroyer Killer!* (New York: Chilton, 1956). "Samuel David Dealey, Great WWII Submariner," *Medal of Honor Historical Notes,* October 1976. Vertical Files, Barker Texas History Center, University of Texas at Austin.　　　　　*Art Leatherwood*

DEAN, JAY HANNA (1910–1974). Jay Hanna (Dizzy) Dean, baseball player and sportscaster, claimed at various times that he had been born in Arkansas, Oklahoma, Mississippi, and Missouri and that his given name was Jay Hanna and Jerome Herman. In fact, he was apparently born in Lucas, Arkansas, on January 16, 1910, the second son of Albert Monroe and Alma (Nelson) Dean. He later boasted that his formal education ended after the second grade in Chickalah, Arkansas; as a teenager he pitched for a junior high school team in

Dizzy Dean (open coat), pitcher for the Chicago Cubs, at the Southern Pacific Railroad Station, San Antonio, April 6, 1939. San Antonio Light *Collection, ITC. The other men in this news photograph were Dean's army buddies and Cubs manager Gabby Hartnett. Dean started his baseball career as a recruit at Fort Sam Houston.*

Spaulding, Oklahoma, although he was not a student. Dean's mother died when he was eight, and from the age of ten to sixteen he worked with his two brothers and his father as an itinerant cotton picker. Though his father was a former semiprofessional baseball player and doubtless taught the boys something about the game, Dean later claimed that he and his younger brother Paul developed their pitching skills by throwing hickory nuts at squirrels. Dean joined the army at the age of sixteen and was stationed at Fort Sam Houston in San Antonio. He played on the post laundry baseball team until a sergeant recruited him for the Twelfth Field Artillery team. After his discharge in 1929 he joined the semiprofessional San Antonio Public Service Utilities team, for which he won sixteen games.

He was signed by a scout for the St. Louis Cardinals of the National League that fall and began his professional career the following year with their Western League farm team in St. Joseph, Missouri. Dean compiled a remarkable 17–8 record at St. Joseph before being promoted in August to the Houston Buffaloes of the Texas League,[qv] with whom he went 8–2. Dean was called up by the Cardinals in September and beat the Pittsburgh Pirates 3–1 on a three-hitter in his first major-league start. He began the 1931 season in St. Louis but did not appear in a game before being returned to Houston in May, reportedly because his boasting had irritated Cardinal manager Gabby Street. With Houston, Dean won twenty-six games, posted a remarkable 1.53 earned-run average, and struck out 303 batters, becoming the only pitcher ever to lead all minor leaguers in all three categories. He almost singlehandedly pitched the Buffaloes to the Texas League pennant, winning both games of a Sunday doubleheader against Fort Worth, then coming back after a day's rest and winning the last game of the season to give Houston the championship. He married Patricia Nash, a clerk at a Houston department store whom he had met in 1929, on June 15, 1931, and until the early 1960s he lived in the Lone Star State between baseball seasons.

Dean decisively made the major leagues in 1932 and quickly became one of the most colorful members of the Cardinals' celebrated "Gas House Gang." He remained an amusingly incorrigible braggart; one writer said that Dean's was "the strongest, best lubricated, and most frequently used voice apparatus the national pastime has ever known." But he had the talent to back up his bragging and became the dominant pitcher in the National League in the mid-1930s. In his first season with St. Louis, he compiled an 18–15 record, and in 1933 he won twenty games against eighteen losses and set a National League record when he struck out seventeen Chicago Cubs in a single game.

The Cardinals added Paul Dean, who Dizzy claimed was the hardest thrower in the family, to their pitching staff in 1934, and Dizzy brashly predicted that he and his brother would win forty-five games. In fact, this boast proved pessimistic; Paul won nineteen games, while Dizzy had his greatest season. He posted a 30–7 record and was named the most valuable player in the league; no National League pitcher has won thirty games in a season since. The brothers staged a one-day strike in June in an effort to win a $2,000 raise for Paul and were briefly suspended for refusing to accompany the team to Detroit for an exhibition game in August but returned to win twelve of the Cardinals' last eighteen games, as St. Louis won the National League pennant. In a September doubleheader against Brooklyn, Dean pitched a three-hit shutout in the first game, only to have Paul pitch a no-hitter in the nightcap. "I wished I'da known Paul was goin' to pitch a no-hitter," complained the irrepressible Dean afterward. "I'da pitched one too." The brothers had two wins apiece as the Cardinals beat the Detroit Tigers in the World Series. In the fourth game of that series Dean, who had been inserted into the game as a pinch-runner, was hit in the head by a throw while trying to break up a double play. He recovered to pitch on the following day, and the apocryphal headline "X-Ray of Dean's Head Reveals Nothing" became part of his legend. In 1935 Dean again led the league with twenty-eight wins, against twelve losses, and in 1936 he compiled a 24–13 record.

Dean was selected to play in the All-Star Game for four consecutive years, from 1934 to 1937. In the 1937 game in Washington, D.C., a line drive hit by Earl Averill of the Cleveland Indians broke a toe of Dean's left foot. He tried to pitch before the bone healed, changed his pitching motion, and consequently developed bursitis in his right shoulder. He finished the season with a 13–10 record, but his days as a dominant pitcher were over. The Cardinals traded him to the Cubs for three players and $185,000 in April 1938. He saw only limited action in 1938 but posted a 7–1 record, as Chicago won the National League pennant. He went 6–4 for the Cubs in 1939, then returned to the Texas League with the Tulsa Oilers in 1940. Despite his mediocre 8–8 record with Tulsa, the Cubs gave Dean one more chance. He posted a 3–3 record with Chicago after being recalled later in the 1940 season and retired after appearing in one game early in the 1941 season. He was briefly a coach for the Cubs but resigned in July 1941 to broadcast the home games of the Cardinals and the American League St. Louis Browns on the radio.

As a radio announcer, Dean earned a devoted following and some enemies. He broke into song, usually "The Wabash Cannonball," during dull games, and his neologisms and malapropisms, such as "He slud into third" and "The players returned to their respectable bases," became legendary. In 1946 two Missouri schoolteachers complained to the Federal Communications Commission that Dean's broadcasts were "replete with errors in grammar and syntax" and were "having a bad effect on their pupils." Norman Cousins of the *Saturday Review of Literature* was among those who rallied to Dean's defense, and Dizzy himself offered something of an apology. "Maybe I am butcherin' up the English language a little," he said. "Well, all I got to say is that when me and Paul and pa was pickin' cotton in Arkansas, we didn't have no chance to go to school much. But I'm glad that kids are gettin' that chance today."

Dean made two more appearances in uniform. In 1947, after frequent criticism of the team's pitching staff, Dean decided to show the hapless Browns how the game should be played. He came out of the broadcast booth to pitch four scoreless innings against the Chicago White Sox in the last game of the season. His final appearance on the pitcher's mound came in 1950, when the owner of the Dallas Eagles of the Texas League recruited Dean and an all-star team of former major leaguers, including Tris Speaker,[qv] to take the field against Tulsa for the first game of the season. After Dean walked the leadoff batter, the old-timers yielded to the Dallas regulars. Still, the stunt attracted a Texas League record—53,578 customers—to the Cotton Bowl.[qv]

Dean's countrified approach as an announcer seemed better suited to St. Louis, which until the mid-1950s was major league baseball's southernmost and westernmost frontier, than the metropolitan east, but in 1950 he signed to broadcast Yankee games on New York television station WABD for a salary of $40,000. No less an authority than the acerbic Walter Winchell said that Dean was one of his favorite sports announcers, but the Yankees let him go after the 1951 season, and he returned to St. Louis to become a part-time radio announcer for the Browns.

Dean apparently took his wife's advice on financial matters. He invested heavily in stocks and bonds, and besides a home in the Preston Hollow suburb of Dallas, he owned five office buildings and the 300-acre D. D. Ranch in Lancaster, where he raised registered Herefords. He also wrote a syndicated baseball column and earned money from the movie rights to his biography, which was filmed in 1952 as *The Pride of St. Louis*, with Dan Dailey in the title role. In 1953 Dean dropped his radio broadcasting to concentrate on the nationally televised "Game of the Week." As baseball's first national television broadcaster he made $100,000 a year, and he remained on the "Game of the Week" until 1965. In the early 1960s he and his wife left Texas and settled in her hometown of Bond, Mississippi. In 1967 there was some speculation that Dean might run for governor of Mississippi, but his wife's poor health precluded his seeking office.

In his eight years in the National League Dean compiled a record of 150 wins and 83 losses; he led the league in strikeouts four times and in complete games and innings pitched three times each. Despite his relatively brief major-league career, he was elected to the National Baseball Hall of Fame in 1953; at the induction ceremony, he said, "This is the greatest honor I ever received, and I wanna thank the Lord for givin' me a good right arm, a strong back, and a weak mind." He died on July 17, 1974, in Reno, Nevada, after suffering two heart attacks in five days, and was buried in Bond, Mississippi.

BIBLIOGRAPHY: *Current Biography*, 1951. Robert Gregory, *Diz: Dizzy Dean and Baseball during the Great Depression* (New York: Viking, 1992). John Thorn and Pete Palmer, *Total Baseball* (New York: Warner, 1989). Vertical Files, Barker Texas History Center, University of Texas at Austin. Martha E. War et al., *The Ballplayers: Baseball's Ultimate Biographical Reference* (Metuchen, New Jersey: Scarecrow Press, 1990).

Martin Donell Kohout

DEAN, JOHN M. (1852–1909). John M. Dean, early Presidio county attorney and land speculator, son of Dr. Y. S. and Martha (McCullough) Dean, was born in Forsythe County, Georgia, on May 13, 1852. When he was seven the family moved to North Carolina. During the Civil War[qv] Y. S. Dean served as a surgeon in Gen. Robert E. Lee's[qv] command. By 1874 John Dean was in Lee County, Texas, where he was admitted to the state bar. In 1878 he moved to Fort Davis, then in Presidio County. Since he had no money to open a law office, he drove an Overland stagecoach from Fort Davis to Van Horn Wells for three months.

In May 1878 Dean began his law practice in Fort Davis. He was appointed Presidio county attorney in 1879 but resigned a few months later. He was elected county attorney in 1880 and resigned in May 1882 to enter the cattle business with James B. Gillett[qv] and C. L. Nevill. In 1882 Dean was elected district attorney of the Twentieth Judicial District, a post to which he was reelected for 1884–90 and 1896–1902. From 1892 until 1896 he served a four-year term as state senator. From 1902 to 1909 he practiced law privately. Dean caused a controversy when he made Marfa the Presidio county seat without legal authority. In 1884 he bought the land around the Marfa railroad siding from the Galveston, Houston and San Antonio Railway Company. On October 9, 1885, he conveyed part of the section to four prominent citizens who supported making Marfa county seat. Dean and his four allies managed an election to legalize the action.

Dean was a Mason. He married Louise Haggart, and they lived first in Marfa. The couple moved to El Paso in 1889. Dean lived just over ten of his fifty-seven years in Presidio County. He died on August 20, 1909, in Chicago, Illinois, and was buried in El Paso. Fifty members of the bar and fifteen Chinese friends gathered on the Dean lawn during the Masonic funeral to pay him tribute.

BIBLIOGRAPHY: Frank W. Johnson, *A History of Texas and Texans* (5 vols., ed. E. C. Barker and E. W. Winkler [Chicago and New York: American Historical Society, 1914; rpt. 1916]). Virginia Madison and Hallie Stillwell, *How Come It's Called That? Place Names in the Big Bend Country* (Albuquerque: University of New Mexico Press, 1958). Niel John McArthur, *The Twenty-Seventh Legislature and State Administration of Texas* (Austin: Ben C. Jones, 1901). Buckley B. Paddock, ed., *A Twentieth Century History and Biographical Record of North and West Texas* (Chicago: Lewis, 1906). Cecilia Thompson, *History of Marfa and Presidio County, 1535–1946* (2 vols., Austin: Nortex, 1985).

Julia Cauble Smith

DEAN, JOHN M. (1859–1920). John M. Dean, legislator, banker, and teacher, the son of Robert B. and Amanda (Burress) Dean, was born in Anderson County, South Carolina, on November 17, 1859. His father was a planter. Dean came to Texas in 1881, farmed for a time, and then taught at towns in Smith County and at Ben Wheeler. In 1886 he graduated from Sam Houston Normal School (now Sam Houston State University) at Huntsville. In December of that year he married C. Ellis; they had nine children. Dean moved to Grand Saline in 1906 and in July 1907 aided in the founding of the Citizens National Bank, later incorporated as the First State Bank, which he served as first president. Dean was elected to the state legislature in 1898 and 1900. He served as a delegate to the state Democratic conventions of 1898 and 1914. He was a Mason and a Baptist. Sometime before 1920 he moved to Oklahoma, where he died.

BIBLIOGRAPHY: Frank W. Johnson, *A History of Texas and Texans* (5 vols., ed. E. C. Barker and E. W. Winkler [Chicago and New York: American Historical Society, 1914; rpt. 1916]). Niel John McArthur, *The Twenty-seventh Legislature and State Administration of Texas* (Austin: Ben C. Jones, 1901).

DEAN, TEXAS (Clay County). Dean is on State Highway 79 fifteen miles northwest of Henrietta in northwest Clay County. The settlement began as a cattle-shipping station when the Wichita Falls and Oklahoma Railway selected the site as a railroad switch in 1904–05. As a community developed the settlers named the location Dean in honor of Callaway Dean, one of the pioneer ranchers of the county. A little later the residents began to refer to the location as Dean-Dale in recognition of James E. Dale, the founder of the 13,000-acre Dale Ranch, established in 1896. The population of Dean climbed from a reported twenty-five in 1947 to 223 in 1988. In 1990 it was 277.

BIBLIOGRAPHY: William Charles Taylor, *A History of Clay County* (Austin: Jenkins, 1972).

David Minor

DEAN, TEXAS (Smith County). Dean, also known as Deanville, was five miles west of Tyler in central Smith County. The site was originally part of the E. D. Holland survey and was settled after the Civil War[qv] when Maj. John J. Dean, a Confederate veteran, returned to claim the land he had purchased in 1863. He built a large two-story house on the creek. In the 1870s the Cotton Belt Railroad built a line through the area, and in 1872 Major Dean used personal funds to construct a Baptist church. The cemetery was established soon after. In March 1874 the Deanville post office opened with Daniel L. Dean as postmaster. The facility closed after only nine months, and Dean never became an important railroad stop. Eight homes were in the vicinity in 1936, and the church and cemetery were still in use. By 1938 local students attended school in the Dixie Independent School District. In 1966 the community comprised the church and cemetery and a few homes. In 1969 children attended school in Tyler. In 1973 highway maps showed the church, the cemetery, and a scattered collection of dwellings on an unnamed paved road and two dirt roads. Dean no longer appeared on maps in 1981.

BIBLIOGRAPHY: Edward Clayton Curry, An Administrative Survey of the Schools of Smith County, Texas (M.Ed. thesis, University of Texas, 1938). "Major John Dean House (Dean)," *Chronicles of Smith County*, Spring 1967. "Post Offices and Postmasters of Smith County, Texas: 1847–1929," *Chronicles of Smith County*, Spring 1966. Smith County Historical Society, *Historical Atlas of Smith County* (Tyler, Texas: Tyler Print Shop, 1965). Donald W. Whisenhunt, comp., *Chronological History of Smith County* (Tyler, Texas: Smith County Historical Society, 1983). Albert Woldert, *A History of Tyler and Smith County* (San Antonio: Naylor, 1948).

Vista K. McCroskey

DEAN CREEK. Dean Creek, sometimes called Dillard or Boggy Creek, rises just south of Aiken in southwestern Shelby County (at 31°41′ N, 94°20′ W) and runs southwest for five miles to its mouth on Attoyac Bayou (at 31°38′ N, 94°22′ W). It traverses gently sloping to moderately steep terrain surfaced by deep, loamy, fine sand. The area is heavily wooded with pines and various hardwoods predominating.

DEANVILLE, TEXAS. Deanville is on Farm Road 60 four miles south of State Highway 21 in southwestern Burleson County. The first settler in the heavily wooded area was probably Horatio Chriesman,[qv] who moved there from Washington County in the late 1840s. The community that eventually developed in the vicinity was named for James L. Dean, who established a general store there in 1872. An arm of the Chisholm Trail^qv passed by Deanville, and cattlemen on their drives from Columbus, Texas, to Kansas often camped near the settlement. By 1884 the community had two churches, a steam engine, a cotton gin, a gristmill, and a population of about fifty. The first school in the area was called Chriesman Chapel School; Chriesman had it built, and it was also used by the local Methodist congregation. A public school was established at the community in the early 1880s and operated until 1973, when it was merged with the Caldwell Independent School District. The post office, located in Dean's Store, was opened in 1877 and was still operating in 1991. The Houston and Texas Central Railway reached Deanville in 1913. The First State Bank, organized in 1919, was still the financial hub of the community in 1991, when it operated as a branch of the Citizens State Bank of Somerville. In the early 1990s Deanville was the trading center for the southwestern part of the county. Cotton was the principal crop for many years; at one time, the town had two cotton gins and a cotton warehouse. Other businesses included two garages, a drugstore, a barbershop, a blacksmith shop, a cafe, and a large general merchandise store. By 1939 a produce house, a butcher's shop, a lumberyard, an icehouse, a machine welding shop, and a dry-goods store were operating in the community. In 1991 the town had the bank, the post office, two grocery stores, a cafe, and a welding and fabricating shop. The O. D. H. Lodge, established in 1916, still staged a Fourth of July celebration each year. The only church in the community was St. John's Lutheran Church, constructed in 1917. During the early 1990s the community was in an area with many feed, grain, and hay farms, as well as a large cattle ranch. Many oil wells had also been drilled in the area. The population of Deanville in 1990 was estimated at 130.

BIBLIOGRAPHY: Burleson County Historical Society, *Astride the Old San Antonio Road: A History of Burleson County, Texas* (Dallas: Taylor, 1980). S. G. Reed, *A History of the Texas Railroads* (Houston: St. Clair, 1941; rpt., New York: Arno, 1981). *Catherine G. Alford*

DEARBORN, TEXAS. Dearborn was on the Gulf, Colorado and Santa Fe Railway ten miles southeast of Votaw and thirty miles northwest of Beaumont in northwestern Hardin County. John A. McShane, president of McShane Lumber Company and partner in the Creighton-McShane Oil Company, had by the mid-1890s acquired considerable land in Hardin County. By 1905 McShane Lumber Company, with headquarters at Omaha, Nebraska, had begun logging in the area. Although the company owned or had timber rights to various tracts north of Saratoga and southwest of Hardin, operations centered around its sawmill and acreage at Dearborn. Tram lines extended from the company's rail station to logging camps in the surrounding forests. On August 25, 1913, a fire destroyed the company's planing-mill boilerhouse at Dearborn. The community's population subsequently declined, as the lumbering operations at Dearborn slowed and the company began to dispose of its Hardin County properties. The Dearborn post office had opened in 1904 and was discontinued in 1915. The Dearborn voting precinct was abolished the following year.

BIBLIOGRAPHY: W. T. Block, ed., *Emerald of the Neches: The Chronicles of Beaumont from Reconstruction to Spindletop* (Nederland, Texas: Nederland Publishing, 1980). *Robert Wooster*

DEARDUFF, WILLIAM (?–1836). William Dearduff, Alamo defender, was born in Tennessee. He immigrated to Texas and, on November 5, 1831, registered for a quarter league of land in DeWitt's colony.^qv He entered the Alamo with the relief force from Gonzales on March 1, 1836, and died in the battle of the Alamo^qv on March 6.

BIBLIOGRAPHY: Daughters of the American Revolution, *The Alamo Heroes and Their Revolutionary Ancestors* (San Antonio, 1976). Bill Groneman, *Alamo Defenders* (Austin: Eakin, 1990). Texas General Land Office, *An Abstract of the Original Titles of Record in the General Land Office* (Houston: Niles, 1838; rpt., Austin: Pemberton Press, 1964). *Bill Groneman*

DEATON DRAW. Deaton Draw, a valley also known as Deaton Canyon, rises 1½ miles southwest of the High Lonesome Ranch headquarters in central Val Verde County (at 30°05′ N, 100°59′ W) and runs northwest nine miles to its mouth on the Devils River, just west of State Highway 163 (at 30°07′ N, 101°06′ W). Its course sharply dissects massive limestone, forming a deep and winding canyon that continues through flat terrain and ends on wash deposits and caliche. Soils in the area are generally dark, calcareous stony clays and clay loams that support oaks, junipers, grasses, and mesquites.

DEAVER CREEK. Deaver Creek rises six miles northwest of Dorchester in central Grayson County (at 33°37′ N, 96°42′ W) and runs northwest for thirteen miles to its mouth on Big Mineral Creek, with which it forms a finger of Lake Texoma six miles northwest of Southmayd (at 33°42′ N, 96°47′ W). The stream, which is intermittent in its upper reaches, traverses flat to rolling prairie surfaced by dark, commonly calcareous clays that support mesquite, cacti, and various grasses. The area has served as crop and range land.

DE BERRY, ALFRED WESLEY (1829–1903). Alfred Wesley De Berry was born in Franklin, Kentucky, on February 11, 1829, to John Wesley and Patsy Ann Beezley (Lowe) De Berry. He moved to Texas in January 1850. After serving on the state Democratic committee from June 1853 to January 1854, he was admitted to the bar at Carthage in June 1855. In Panola County he organized and commanded Company C of Col. Horace Randal's^qv Twenty-eighth Texas Cavalry of Walker's Texas Division.^qv The company, locally known as the Texas Lancers, was called into service by Confederate secretary of war Judah P. Benjamin on May 12, 1862. Plagued by "chronic diarrhea of over ten months' duration," De Berry offered his resignation on July 3, 1863. His request was granted and his tenure of duty ended on August 27, 1863. He was a member of the House of the Tenth Legislature (1863–64) and served as secretary of state under Governor Richard Coke^qv from January 27, 1874, to December 7, 1876. He was a charter member of the Texas Bar Association (*see* STATE BAR OF TEXAS), organized at Galveston in 1882. De Berry married Elizabeth Hannah De Loach on December 13, 1860, in Panola County. They had three children. De Berry died on April 4, 1903, in his home in Aransas Pass and was buried in Prairie View Cemetery, Aransas Pass.

BIBLIOGRAPHY: H. L. Bentley and Thomas Pilgrim, *Texas Legal Directory for 1876–77* (Austin: Democratic Statesman Office, 1877). C. W. Raines, *Year Book for Texas* (2 vols., Austin: Gammel-Statesman, 1902, 1903). *Robbie Fort Sutlive*

DEBERRY, TEXAS. DeBerry is at the junction of U.S. Highway 79 and Farm roads 31 and 1794, fourteen miles northeast of Carthage in northeastern Panola County. A community, known as Evergreen, formed there before the Civil War,^qv after which the name of the town was changed to DeBerry, for Alfred Wesley De Berry,^qv a prominent local citizen and legislator. A post office opened in 1874, and by 1885 the community had a steam gristmill, two churches, three schools, eight general stores, and an estimated population of 150. Its population reached 300 by the early 1890s but dropped to fifty by 1914. In the 1920s oil was discovered in the area, and DeBerry enjoyed a brief boom. By 1929 its population reached 250. In the mid-1930s the community had a church, two schools, a post office, and eight rated businesses; in 1936 the reported population was 233. After World War II^qv the DeBerry schools were consolidated with those of Carthage. In 1990 DeBerry was a prosperous rural community with 191 inhabitants and eight businesses.

BIBLIOGRAPHY: *History of Panola County.* (Carthage, Texas: Carthage Circulating Book Club, 1935?). John Barnette Sanders, *Index to the Cemeteries of Panola County* (Center, Texas, 1964). John Barnette Sanders, *Postoffices and Post Masters of Panola County, Texas, 1845–1930* (Center, Texas, 1964).
Christopher Long

DEBOLDIN CREEK. Deboldin Creek rises three miles northeast of Marshall in north central Harrison County (at 32°40′ N, 94°20′ W) and runs northeast for twelve miles to its mouth on Haggerty Creek, three miles west of Karnack (at 32°41′ N, 94°14′ W). It traverses an area of gently undulating to hilly terrain surfaced by loamy and clayey soils that support dense patches of pine and hardwood trees. The land is used predominantly for agriculture.

DEBRAY, XAVIER BLANCHARD (1819–1895). Xavier Blanchard Debray, soldier, was born in Epinel, France, in 1819. He attended the French Military Academy at St. Cyr and served in the French diplomatic service until he immigrated to the United States via New York on September 25, 1848. He moved to Texas in 1852, settled in San Antonio, and was naturalized there on April 5, 1855. That same year he established a Spanish newspaper with A. A. Lewis called *El Bejareño*. Later he worked in the General Land Office qv as a translator. He also established an academy that prospered until the Civil War qv began.

He served as aide-de-camp to Governor Edward Clark qv and was major of the Second Texas Infantry.qv In December 1861 he was elected lieutenant colonel and commander of Debray's Texas Cavalry battalion and in March 1862 colonel of the Twenty-sixth Texas Cavalry. From January to June of 1862 he commanded on Galveston Island. In July he assumed command of the military subdistrict of Houston in the Department of Texas. He commanded some of the Confederate troops in the recapture of Galveston on January 1, 1863. On February 13, 1863, he was relieved of command of the eastern subdivision of Texas in the Trans-Mississippi Department, and on May 30 he took command of the troops on Galveston Island in the District of Texas, New Mexico, and Arizona. Although he was assigned temporary command of the eastern subdistrict of Texas in June 1863, by July 1 he had resumed his position on Galveston Island. Debray led his regiment in the Red River campaign qv in Louisiana during the spring of 1864. For his participation in the battles of Mansfield and Pleasant Hill, he was appointed brigadier general by General Edmund Kirby Smith qv on April 13, 1804, but this was never confirmed by President Jefferson Davis.qv Nevertheless, he commanded a brigade consisting of the Twenty-third, Twenty-sixth, and Thirty-second Texas Cavalry regiments. Debray discharged his men on March 24, 1865. After the war he moved to Houston and then to Galveston before eventually returning to his position as translator in the General Land Office. He died in Austin on January 6, 1895, and was buried in the State Cemetery.qv

BIBLIOGRAPHY: Xavier Blanchard Debray, *A Sketch of the History of Debray's (26th) Regiment of Texas Cavalry* (Austin: Von Boeckmann, 1884; rpt., Waco: Waco Village, 1961). *The War of the Rebellion: A Compilation of the Official Records of the Union and Confederate Armies.* Marcus J. Wright, comp., and Harold B. Simpson, ed., *Texas in the War, 1861–1865* (Hillsboro, Texas: Hill Junior College Press, 1965).
Anne J. Bailey

DEBRUHL, JOHN (?–?). John Debruhl, black Republican party qv leader during Reconstruction,qv was in Galveston by 1869 when the Union League qv nominated him for a seat in the United States House of Representatives. He failed to win election to Congress but served as a justice of the peace in Galveston from 1870 to 1873 and attended the Convention of Colored Men in July 1873. Debruhl attended the 1882 Republican state convention, where he criticized racially segregated public schools.

BIBLIOGRAPHY: Harrel Budd, The Negro in Politics in Texas, 1867–1898 (M.A. thesis, University of Texas, 1925). John H. Heller, *Galveston City Directory, 1872* (Galveston, 1872). Merline Pitre, *Through Many Dangers, Toils and Snares: The Black Leadership of Texas, 1868–1900* (Austin: Eakin, 1985).
Paul M. Lucko

DEBT OF THE REPUBLIC OF TEXAS. The Republic of Texas qv inherited from the provisional and ad interim governments qqv a debt estimated at $1.25 million. Of this, $100,000 was in the form of loans and the remainder in the form of claims for services and supplies. At the end of the republic the debt was officially estimated at $9,949,007. Postponement of the payment of the bulk of this debt was protracted over a period of eleven years, interest accumulating on it up to July 1, 1850. An official report on the debt in November 1851 reported the sum of claims filed at $6,480,748.58, interest due $3,166,504.56, and estimated unfiled claims with interest $2,789,738.20, or an estimated total debt of $12,436,991.34. The total debt included the revenue debt, for which the import duties levied by the republic had been pledged, and the nonrevenue debt of audited drafts and audited claims including an estimate of unfiled claims.

The republic authorized a loan of $5 million in 1836, but there were no takers. In May 1838 Congress passed another $5 million loan act, and commissioners were sent to the United States and Europe to market the 10 percent bonds with which the loan was to be made. The Pennsylvania Bank of the United States bought bonds amounting to $457,380. Before the final settlement of this obligation the principal and accrued interest on it amounted to $960,498. In the state rating of the items of debt based on what would have been the specie equivalent of each at the time of its issue, this particular item was rated at $.8745 on the dollar.

A second item, the naval debt (also called the Dawson and Holford debt) was in the form of 10 percent bonds of the $5 million loan act. The republic bought two vessels, the contract for each of which provided that if the amount was not paid at its maturity date of one year, the price would be doubled. Bonds at 10 percent in double the amount of the price were put up as security, and, as the debts were not paid at their maturity, the bonds were forfeited, the principal and interest on them finally amounting to $1,622,404.70. They were rated by the state at a valuation of fifty cents on the dollar.

In June 1837, 10 percent funding bonds were authorized, and a total of $837,500 was issued in 1837, 1838, and 1839, in exchange for audited drafts, claims, and land scrip. The principal and accrued interest of this debt item finally amounted to $1,687,094.80. Of this amount the state rated $29,291.47 at par and the remainder at seventy cents on the dollar.

The funding act of 1837 expired on January 1, 1840, and was succeeded on February 5, 1840, by an act funding the treasury notes issued by the republic. Notes presented before July 1, 1840, were fundable in 10 percent bonds ($813,800) and those after that date in 8 percent bonds ($27,080). The principal and accrued interest of these issues finally amounted to $1,674,380.42 and was rated by the state at thirty cents on the dollar.

The treasury notes, amounting to $3,945,500, were also a part of the debt. The earlier notes issued bore 10 percent interest, but the later ones, those called redbacks, were not interest-bearing. These were funded in bonds amounting to $792,880. By September 1, 1851, enough revenue had been collected to redeem and cancel $518,324 of the notes. The value of notes with accrued interest for which settlement was finally made was $2,716,645.29. Of this amount, $65,208.33 was rated at par, $451,708.32 at fifty cents on the dollar, and $2,199,728.64 (in redbacks) at twenty-five cents on the dollar.

In joining the United States, Texas retained her unappropriated lands with the idea that their first use should be to pay the debt of the republic. No action on the debt was taken by the First Legislature. In 1848 the Second Legislature instructed the state auditor qv and the comptroller of public accounts qv jointly to ascertain the amounts of the various items of the debt and to reduce their amounts to the "actual par value which may have been realized by the late Republic." This reduction, called rating or scaling, reduced the amount of liability from the face amount to what the amount would have been if there had been neither money nor credit risk on the obligation at the time it was incurred. This policy, called "the principle of equivalents," was in high favor in Texas at the time of annexation,qv but it was strenuously opposed by the holders of the debt. In the official state report of 1851 only $283,456.11 of the total estimated debt of $12,436,991.34 was rated at face value, and the total was scaled down to $6,827,278.64. By an act of February 11, 1850, Texas proposed to pay the scaled amount in land on the basis of fifty cents an acre. At the same time it was specified that interest on all liabilities would cease after July 1, 1850. The creditors, however, refused to accept this plan of payment.

The deadlock between the state and the creditors was solved by the settlement of the dispute over the northwestern boundary of Texas in the Compromise of 1850.qv The United States, in return for a cession of 67,000,000 acres of land, gave to Texas $10 million in 5 percent United States bonds, with the proviso that $5 million of the bonds should not be turned over to Texas "until the creditors of the State holding bonds of Texas for which duties on imports were specially pledged shall first file releases of all claims against the United States for or on account of said bonds." A controversy between the federal government and Texas over the interpretation of the proviso continued for more than 4½ years. It was finally settled by an act of Congress on February 28, 1855, which appropriated $7.75 million in cash to be prorated among the holders of the revenue debt. The basis of this amount was roughly the principal of the $5 million of the reserved bonds plus the accrued interest and the market premium on the bonds. In the general election of 1855 the people of Texas rejected the plan, but the congressional act had given the legislature the power of acceptance or rejection, and the legislature, by a narrow vote, accepted the plan, which was ratified on February 1, 1856. Opponents of the plan calculated the financial loss to the state at $6,082,244.

The revenue debt was interpreted by the federal government to include all the bond items and the paper money (*see* MONEY OF THE REPUBLIC OF TEXAS). It amounted to $10,078,703.21. Acceptance of the Texas rating of this amount would have reduced it to $4,467,756.41, or payment at the rate of 44.3 cents on the dollar. The $7.75 million prorated among the holders of the unscaled amount resulted in payment at the rate of 76.9 cents on the dollar.

Between 1852 and 1902 Texas paid out on the nonrevenue debt of the republic a net amount of $1,287,103.43, and between 1846 and 1860 the state received in the form of liabilities of the republic a net amount of $288,263.16 in payment of debts due the republic. A total, therefore, of $1,575,366.59 was what the state discharged of the debt of the republic, and this amount may be construed as a deduction from the $5 million of the United States bonds that had been turned over to the state in 1850.

The United States Treasury paid out of the $7.75 million all but $45,000, and this remainder was turned over to Texas in 1881. The total of the sums paid out by the federal government and the state was $9,280,366.59, which paid the republic's officially estimated debt of $12,436,991.34.

BIBLIOGRAPHY: Holman Hamilton, *Prologue to Conflict: The Crisis and Compromise of 1850* (Lexington: University of Kentucky Press, 1964). Abigail Curlee Holbrook, "Cotton Marketing in Antebellum Texas," *Southwestern Historical Quarterly* 73 (April 1970). Edmund Thornton Miller, *A Financial History of Texas* (University of Texas Bulletin 37, Austin, 1916). *Edmund Thornton Miller*

DECATUR, TEXAS. Decatur, the county seat of Wise County, is on U.S. highways 287 and 380 and the Burlington Northern Railway, forty miles northwest of Fort Worth at the approximate center of the county. It is near the western edge of the Grand Prairies, and overlooks the western Cross Timbers area. The Texas legislature established Wise County in 1856 and directed that a county seat named Taylorsville (in honor of Gen. Zachary Taylorqv) be founded within five miles of its center. The town was located and laid out by Absalom Bishop, an early settler in the region. Bishop, who was a member of the Texas Legislature, did not approve of Taylor's Whig partyqv affiliation, and in January 1858 he arranged to change the name of the town to Decatur in honor of the naval hero Stephen Decatur.

The new community prospered in the years before the Civil War.qv A post office was opened in 1857 in the store of Daniel Howell, the town's first merchant and postmaster. The first school was established in the fall of 1857, and a courthouse was erected in the early 1860s. The Butterfield Overland Mailqv line served the community for several years before the war. As an exposed settlement on the Texas frontier, Decatur and its area stagnated during the war years and continued to suffer from Indian raids until 1874. Perhaps the most dramatic event of the war for the inhabitants of Decatur was the trial of members of the Unionist Peace party in the town and the execution of five of them in 1862 (*see* PEACE PARTY CONSPIRACY).

The late 1860s saw the establishment of four stores and a hotel in Decatur, which served as a supplier and market for local ranchers. The eastern fork of the Chisholm Trailqv passed near Decatur in this period and is commemorated by the town's annual Chisholm Trail Barbecue. In 1882 the Fort Worth and Denver Railway reached Decatur, and the gambler's cant phrase "eighter from Decatur" was coined, according to local tradition, by a railway construction worker. In the 1880s and 1890s Decatur prospered as a shipping point and market for local farmers, a prosperity that was reflected in the establishment of Decatur Baptist College in 1892, the building of a new courthouse in 1896, and a population that grew from 579 in 1880 to 1,746 in 1890. The town continued to grow in the early twentieth century, from a population of 1,562 in 1904 to a peak of 3,200 in 1928. Between 1929 and 1960 Decatur fluctuated between 2,000 and 3,000 inhabitants and remained an important business center of some eighty to 150 establishments. Decatur Baptist College was moved to Dallas in 1965. A steady growth in population after the 1960s is attributable in part to the influx of people who commute to Fort Worth. In 1988 Decatur had 4,523 residents; it was a center for petroleum production, clothing and glass manufacture, and marketing and processing for Wise County agribusiness. The population in 1990 was 4,252.

BIBLIOGRAPHY: Jim Tom Barton, *Eighter from Decatur* (College Station: Texas A&M University Press, 1980). Cliff D. Cates, *Pioneer History of Wise County* (Decatur, Texas: Old Settlers Association, 1907). Rosalie Gregg, ed., *Wise County History* (Vol. 1, n.p: Nortex, 1975; Vol. 2, Austin: Eakin, 1982). *Jim Tom Barton*

DECKER, JAMES ERIC (1898–1970). James Eric (Bill) Decker, law officer, son of James A. and Cecille T. Decker, was born in Dallas, Texas, on August 31, 1898. He grew up there and attended local schools before dropping out to find work. On July 21, 1916, he married Clyde Ryals of Galveston. Four years later he became an elevator operator at the Dallas County Courthouse. In 1923 Decker joined Constable Murray Fisher's staff as deputy constable. In 1933 he was named chief deputy to Sheriff Richard A. (Smoot) Schmid, a position he held until Schmid lost the 1946 election. Decker resigned from his position as chief deputy and ran for sheriff in 1948, when he defeated incumbent Steve Guthrie. Decker was sheriff until his death in 1970. Throughout his twenty-two years as sheriff he never faced another opponent in an election.

Decker became somewhat of a legend as a Texas lawman. His relentless pursuit of Clyde Barrow and Bonnie Parkerqqv and his capture of hardened criminal Raymond Hamilton focused national attention on him in the 1930s. Even greater attention was focused on Sheriff Decker in November 1963, when President John F. Kennedy was assassinated in Dallas (*see* KENNEDY ASSASSINATION). During the trial of Jack Ruby,qv the killer of alleged Kennedy assassin Lee Harvey Oswald,qv five prisoners escaped from the county jail. Criticism was leveled on Dallas law enforcement as a result. Decker, in his typically calm manner, answered the critics, saying that "Dallas will survive all this, partner." As sheriff, he modernized and expanded the department and led his staff with a low-keyed dignity.

He and his wife had no children; they raised his cousin, William Tennant Decker. Decker received numerous awards during his lifetime but always maintained that he was no hero, just "a professional law-enforcement officer trying to do a job." He died on August 29, 1970, and was buried in Dallas.

BIBLIOGRAPHY: Dallas *Morning News,* August 25, 26, 1970, November 17, 1978. Vertical Files, Barker Texas History Center, University of Texas at Austin.
Gerald D. Saxon

DECKER, TEXAS (Nolan County). Decker was eight miles northwest of the site that became Blackwell in south central Nolan County. A post office, named for A. F. Decker, postmaster of the Sweetwater office, was established there in 1892 with Sarah A. Jones as postmistress; it was discontinued and moved to Maryneal in 1917. Little evidence of the settlement remained by 1947. County maps in 1980 showed a Decker Lane cemetery in the vicinity.

BIBLIOGRAPHY: Jim Wheat, *More Ghost Towns of Texas* (Garland, Texas: Lost and Found, 1971). E. L. Yeats and Hooper Shelton, *History of Nolan County* (Sweetwater, Texas: Shelton, 1975).
Charles G. Davis

DECKER, TEXAS (Travis County). Decker is three miles west of Manor in northeastern Travis County. A school opened there as early as 1882, and a Methodist church was established before 1900. In 1907 the Decker school had two teachers and sixty-one students; it was consolidated with the Manor Independent School District in 1943. A church, a cemetery, and several houses marked the community on county highway maps in the 1940s. In the 1980s Decker was the name of the junction of a branch line of the Southern Pacific on Walter E. Long Lake.

BIBLIOGRAPHY: Mary Starr Barkley, *History of Travis County and Austin, 1839–1899* (Waco: Texian Press, 1963).
Vivian Elizabeth Smyrl

DECKER CREEK. Decker Creek rises a mile east of Austin in eastern Travis County (at 30°19′ N, 97°38′ W) and runs southeast for ten miles to its mouth on Gilleland Creek, one mile south of Dunlap (at 30°15′ N, 97°33′ W). The creek was dammed in 1967 to form Decker Lake; the reservoir was renamed the Walter E. Long[qv] Lake in 1978. The local terrain is generally flat with local shallow depressions and is surfaced by clay and sandy loams that support water-tolerant hardwoods, conifers, and grasses.

DECKER HOLLOW. Decker Hollow, a valley, begins seven miles southeast of the Calf Creek community in southern McCulloch County (at 30°56′ N, 99°22′ W) and extends northeast for 1½ miles to a point six miles southwest of the Camp San Saba community (at 30°57′ N, 99°22′ W). The elevation of the local terrain varies from 1,700 feet above mean sea level at the beginning of the valley to 1,600 feet at the end. Decker Creek flows through Decker Hollow to its mouth on the San Saba River.

DECLARATION OF NOVEMBER 7, 1835. The Declaration of November 7, 1835, adopted by the Consultation[qv] at San Felipe, was a declaration of causes for taking up arms against Mexico preliminary to the Texas Declaration of Independence.[qv] Since hostilities had already begun and troops were marching against San Antonio, the Consultation had to justify the war. The peace party in Texas, however, feared that Mexican Federalists would interpret the movement as secession and unite with other Mexicans against them. The declaration had to be a strategic document, which would justify Texas action in the eyes of the rest of the world and at the same time convince the Federalists that the Texans desired only to preserve the Mexican Constitution of 1824.[qv] Consultation president Branch T. Archer[qv] called for a committee of twelve to draft a declaration and named John A. Wharton[qv] as chairman. Preliminary plans by Daniel Parker, Don Carlos Barrett, Robert M. Williamson, and Stephen F. Austin[qqv] were used in framing the declaration. As adopted, in eight parts, the document declared that the Texans had taken up arms in defense of their rights and liberties and the republican principles of the Constitution of 1824. It stated that Texas was no longer bound by the compact of union but that Texans offered their support to such members of the Mexican confederacy as would take up arms against military despotism, that they would not cease to carry on war against the centralist authorities while their troops were in Texas, that in the meantime they held it to be their right to establish an independent government, that Texas was responsible for the debts of her armies in the field and pledged to pay debts contracted by her agents, and that she would reward with lands and citizenship those who volunteered their services in the struggle. Despite serious discussion and expression of dissatisfaction, the ambiguous declaration was unanimously adopted, and 1,000 copies were ordered printed and distributed.

BIBLIOGRAPHY: Eugene C. Barker, "Declaration of Causes for Taking Up Arms against Mexico," *Southwestern Historical Quarterly* 15 (January 1912). Hans Peter Nielsen Gammel, comp., *Laws of Texas, 1822–1897* (10 vols., Austin: Gammel, 1898).

DE CORDOVA, JACOB RAPHAEL (1808–1868). Jacob Raphael De Cordova, Texas land agent and colonizer, was born in Spanish Town (near Kingston), Jamaica, on June 6, 1808, the youngest of three sons of Judith and Raphael De Cordova. Since his mother died at his birth, he was reared by an aunt in England. He was well educated and became proficient in English, French, Spanish, German, and Hebrew. His father, a Jewish Jamaican coffee grower and exporter, moved to Philadelphia, where he became president of Congregation Mikveh Israel in 1820. Jacob joined his father in Philadelphia, and there he married Rebecca Sterling about 1826 and learned the printing trade. His ancestors had supported themselves as printers for generations, beginning in the sixteenth century, when a De Cordova in Spain published Álvar Núñez Cabeza de Vaca's[qv] explorations in Texas. In 1834 Jacob moved back to Kingston, where he and his brother Joshua started a newspaper, the Kingston *Daily Gleaner,* which continued for more than 150 years. In early 1836 Jacob went to New Orleans, where he shipped cargoes of staples to Texas during its struggle for independence. At this time he served a term as Grand Master of the Odd Fellows. After the battle of San Jacinto[qv] he visited the Republic of Texas[qv] to install members in the Odd Fellows lodges, the first established outside the United States.

He settled in Texas in 1839 and lived in Galveston and later Houston, where he was elected a state representative to the Second Texas Legislature in 1847. He served for one term but lost the election in 1849. De Cordova traveled extensively through Texas, including the frontier western areas. Through scrip and direct purchase he acquired large amounts of land to sell to settlers; at one time he had a million acres in scrip or title. To attract settlers to Texas, he made speeches on Texas in New York, Philadelphia, and other cities, and even to the cotton-spinners association in Manchester, England. His lectures were published on both sides of the Atlantic and were widely read. His land agency, which he owned with his half-brother Phineas De Cordova,[qv] became one of the largest such agencies that ever operated in the Southwest. De Cordova and two other men laid out the town of Waco in 1848–49. Town lots of an acre sold for five dollars, and nearby farmland brought two to three dollars an acre. At the urging of his wife, De Cordova reserved free sites for schools, churches, and commons.

De Cordova and Robert Creuzbaur[qv] compiled the *Map of the State of Texas,* first published in 1849. Much subsequent Texas cartog-

Wanderer's Retreat. Residence of Mr. J. De Cordova. 5 miles from Seguin. By Sarah Ann Lillie Bumstead Hardinge Daniels, 1852. Watercolor, gouache, and graphite on paper. 6" × 9⅜". Courtesy Amon Carter Museum, Fort Worth; gift of Mrs. Natalie K. Shastid. De Cordova built this two-story house in 1851. He later added a large brick home to the site.

raphy (*see* MAPS) was based on this map, which was praised by Sam Houston^{qv} on the floor of the United States Senate. Books De Cordova wrote that were influential in attracting settlers included *The Texas Immigrant and Traveller's Guide Book* (1856), and *Texas, Her Resources and Her Public Men* (1858), the first attempt at an encyclopedia of Texas. Jacob and Phineas De Cordova published two early Texas newspapers, the *Texas Herald* (also known as *De Cordova's Herald and Immigrant's Guide*) out of Houston and the *Southwestern American* out of Austin. The latter was at the solicitation of Governor Peter H. Bell^{qv} and helped to pass the Compromise of 1850,^{qv} which resulted in a $10 million payment to Texas for adjusted boundaries after annexation.^{qv} In the 1850s De Cordova moved from Austin to Seguin, where five miles from town he built for his wife and five children a fine country home, which he called Wanderer's Retreat.^{qv} In the 1860s he tried to develop a power project on the Brazos River in Bosque County for textile mills to spin Texas cotton. The Civil War^{qv} brought financial reverses to De Cordova. When he died on January 26, 1868, he was buried in Kimball, but in 1935 his body and that of his wife were moved to the State Cemetery.^{qv} He was survived by five children. The De Cordova Bend Reservoir, south of Fort Worth near Lake Granbury, was named for him.

BIBLIOGRAPHY: Henry Cohen, "The Jews in Texas," *Publications of the American Jewish Historical Society* 4 (1896). James M. Day, *Jacob de Cordova: Land Merchant of Texas* (Waco: Heritage Society of Waco, 1962). John H. Jenkins, *Basic Texas Books: An Annotated Bibliography of Selected Works for a Research Library* (Austin: Texas State Historical Association, 1983; rpt. 1988). Natalie Ornish, *Pioneer Jewish Texans* (Dallas: Texas Heritage Press, 1989). Malcolm H. Stern, *First American Jewish Families: 600 Genealogies, 1654–1988*, 3d ed. (Baltimore: Ottenheimer, 1991). Vertical Files, Barker Texas History Center, University of Texas at Austin.   *Natalie Ornish*

DE CORDOVA, PHINEAS (1819–1903). Phineas De Cordova, early Austin newspaperman and land agent, was born in Philadelphia, Pennsylvania, on March 28, 1819, the son of Raphael and Leah De Cordova. He went to Jamaica as a young man and engaged in business. He married a Miss Delgado in 1847 and moved to Texas later that year, first to Galveston and Houston, then in 1848 to Austin to work with his half-brother, Jacob De Cordova,^{qv} on the *Texas Herald*. He also edited an Austin weekly called the *Southwestern American* for a time. In the 1850s he established a general land and agency business, which he operated with his son until poor health forced his retirement in the 1890s. De Cordova was a member of the Odd Fellows and of Temple Beth Israel of Austin. He died in Austin on May 8, 1903, and was buried in the Jewish section of Oakwood Cemetery. He was survived by one of his two children.

BIBLIOGRAPHY: Austin *Statesman*, May 9, 1903. Frank Brown, Annals of Travis County and the City of Austin (MS, Frank Brown Papers, Barker Texas History Center, University of Texas at Austin). James M. Day, *Jacob de Cordova: Land Merchant of Texas* (Waco: Heritage Society of Waco, 1962). Natalie Ornish, *Pioneer Jewish Texans* (Dallas: Texas Heritage, 1989).   *Carolyn Hyman*

DE CORDOVA BEND. De Cordova Bend is a bend in the Brazos River six miles southeast of Granbury in southern Hood and west central Johnson counties (at 32°22′ N, 97°39′ W). It is named for Jacob de Cordova,^qv an entrepreneur who attempted to develop water-powered manufacturing enterprises on the river in Hood County during the 1860s. The bend traverses flat to rolling terrain surfaced by moderately deep to deep sandy and clay loams that support hardwood trees and grasses. The area drained by the bend has served as a source of sand and gravel for local enterprises and has occasionally been the site of settlements.

DECOY, TEXAS. Decoy was off U.S. Highway 59 near the site later called Fern Lake, six miles south of Nacogdoches in southern Nacogdoches County. It began around 1900 as a flag station on the Houston, East and West Texas Railway and was known variously as Fern and Decoy. When a post office was established there in 1901, the name Decoy was chosen. By 1914 the community had the railway station, a general store, and a school. The settlement apparently declined after World War I,^qv and by the 1930s it no longer appeared on highway maps. In the early 1990s only a few scattered houses remained in the area.
Christopher Long

DECROS POINT, TEXAS. DeCros Point, also known as DeCrow's Point, Decros or DeCrow's Landing, Port Cavallo, Port Cabello, and Paso Cavallo, was an early coastal community on the western end of Matagorda Peninsula at Cavallo Pass in extreme southern Matagorda County. It was one of several settlements established on the peninsula before the region's recurring hurricanes persuaded the residents to leave. DeCrow's Point, which was probably named after Maine immigrant Daniel D. DeCrow,^qv one of Stephen F. Austin's^qv Old Three Hundred,^qv may have been inhabited as early as the 1820s by members of the seafaring DeCrow family, one of whom had a land grant there. Thomas DeCrow, who with his family settled in the area by 1837 and was a successful stock raiser there, constructed a wharf and also piloted vessels through Pass Cavallo into Matagorda Bay. Mary Ann (Adams) Maverick, who with her husband Samuel Augustus Maverick^qqv lived at DeCrow's Point, then also known as Paso Cavallo, from 1844 to 1847, includes her vivid accounts of life at DeCrow's Point and at the Mavericks' farm on the peninsula, Tiltona, in her *Memoirs of Mary A. Maverick* (1921). In 1847 Samuel Maverick traded several slaves for shares in the DeCrow townsite. A post office called Port Cavallo, or possibly Port Cabello, was established that year and remained open intermittently until 1853. Postal records suggest the site was part of Calhoun County between 1848 and 1852.

By 1854 the peninsula had two of the county's six school districts. From 1848 to the Civil War^qv Pass Cavallo saw its heaviest ship traffic, and in his autobiographical *A Texas Cow Boy* (first published 1885), peninsula-born Charles A. Siringo^qv writes of the early 1860s landing at "Deckrows Point" of "about five thousand Yankees" headed for the Confederate camp at the mouth of Caney Creek. When the hurricane of 1875, which also wiped out the nearby "German settlement," uprooted Thomas DeCrow's special storm-resistant house, thereby dooming some twenty-two people, it may well have ended the settlement, as no other information on it is available. In 1990 the site retained the name Decros Point.

BIBLIOGRAPHY: Rena Maverick Green, ed., *Samuel Maverick, Texan* (San Antonio, 1952). Rena Maverick Green, ed., *Memoirs of Mary A. Maverick* (San Antonio: Alamo Printing, 1921; rpt., Lincoln: University of Nebraska Press, 1989). Matagorda County Historical Commission, *Historic Matagorda County* (3 vols., Houston: Armstrong, 1986). Charles A. Siringo, *Texas Cowboy, or Fifteen Years on the Hurricane Deck of a Spanish Pony* (Chicago: Umbdenstock, 1885; rpt., Alexandria, Virginia: Time-Life, 1980).
Rachel Jenkins

DECROW, DANIEL D. (?–1837). Daniel D. DeCrow (Deckrow, Deckro, Decro), one of Stephen F. Austin's^qv Old Three Hundred^qv colonists, was one of at least seven children of Daniel D. DeCrow, Sr., of Lincolnville, Waldo County, Maine. He moved from Maine to Texas by 1823 or 1824, about eight years before five more of his brothers arrived. He and his partner, Thomas McCoy,^qv received title to a sitio^qv of land in what is now Matagorda County on July 24, 1824. In the 1820s one Captain DeCrow, probably Daniel DeCrow, operated a sloop between the Brazos River and San Jacinto Bay, often carrying mail and messages for the colonists and once rescuing Dr. Johnson Calhoun Hunter,^qv who had been wrecked in Galveston Bay. In October 1825 DeCrow was in the Cedar Lake area and reported on Karankawa Indian activities there. By 1829 he was among the soldiers stationed at a small fort built near the future site of Matagorda to protect incoming settlers. Later he was awarded a Matagorda town lot for making improvements to the land. In 1835 Samuel Rhoads Fisher^qv reported leaving some property salvaged from a shipwreck under Daniel DeCrow's care at Cavallo Pass. Though apparently neither served in the army, both Daniel and Thomas DeCrow transported supplies and soldiers for the Republic of Texas.^qv DeCrow died at Caney on January 20, 1837, and by August of that year Thomas DeCrow was made administrator of his estate. The Daniel DeCrow papers are housed at the Barker Texas History Center,^qv University of Texas at Austin. They have been reprinted in Volume 1 of *Historic Matagorda County* (1986). Decros Point, at the extreme western end of the Matagorda Peninsula by Cavallo Pass, is named for Daniel or Thomas DeCrow.

BIBLIOGRAPHY: Eugene C. Barker, ed., *The Austin Papers* (3 vols., Washington: GPO, 1924–28). Lester G. Bugbee, "The Old Three Hundred: A List of Settlers in Austin's First Colony," *Quarterly of the Texas State Historical Association* 1 (October 1897). Robert Hancock Hunter, *Narrative of Robert Hancock Hunter* (Austin: Cook Printing, 1936; 2d ed., Austin: Encino, 1966). John H. Jenkins, ed., *The Papers of the Texas Revolution, 1835–1836* (10 vols., Austin: Presidial Press, 1973). Matagorda County Historical Commission, *Historic Matagorda County* (3 vols., Houston: Armstrong, 1986). *Telegraph and Texas Register*, February 3, 1837.
Rachel Jenkins

DECUBADAO INDIANS. The Decubadao (Acubadao) Indians, an otherwise unidentified group mentioned by Álvar Núñez Cabeza de Vaca,^qv lived west of the Yguace Indians.

BIBLIOGRAPHY: Frederick Webb Hodge, ed., *Handbook of American Indians North of Mexico* (2 vols., Washington: GPO, 1907, 1910; rpt., New York: Pageant, 1959).
Margery H. Krieger

DEEN, CALLOWAY, SR. (1812–1892). Calloway Deen (Dean), soldier in the Texas Revolution^qv and public official, was born in Tennessee on January 11, 1812, to John and Mary (Mash) Deen. His grandfather Joshua Deen was a veteran of the American Revolution. Deen traveled to Texas in 1835 and enlisted in the Texas army on November 1 as sergeant in Henry W. Augustine's^qv company. He participated in the siege of Bexar^qv and was discharged on December 14. He enlisted in John M. Bradley's^qv company and served from June 25 to October 1, 1836. He settled in San Augustine County in 1837 and that year again served in the Texas army, in the First Regiment, First Brigade. He also served the republic as clerk of the district court at San Augustine. Deen married Mary C. Clark on August 10, 1837, in San Augustine County; they had seven children. On February 1, 1838, Deen received a bounty warrant of 640 acres for his service in the army, which he located in the area of present Smith County on August 25, 1840. In 1861 he represented San Augustine County in the state Secession Convention,^qv and later that year he moved to his headright in Smith County. At that time he possessed 800 acres and twenty-three slaves. He was a member of the Methodist Episcopal Church and was a Royal Arch Mason. Deen died on May 25, 1892, and was buried in the Starrville Cemetery in Smith County.

BIBLIOGRAPHY: Audited Military Claims, Republic of Texas, Texas

State Archives, Austin. Thomas L. Miller, *Bounty and Donation Land Grants of Texas, 1835–1888* (Austin: University of Texas Press, 1967). Thomas L. Miller, "Texas Land Grants to Veterans of the Revolution and Signers of the Declaration of Independence," *Southwestern Historical Quarterly* 64 (January 1961). Buckley B. Paddock, ed., *A Twentieth Century History and Biographical Record of North and West Texas* (Chicago: Lewis, 1906).

J. L. Bryan

DEEN, EDITH ALDERMAN (1905–1994). Edith Alderman Deen, newspaper columnist and best-selling author, was born in Weatherford, Texas, on February 28, 1905, to James and Sarah (Scheuber) Alderman. She graduated from Lufkin High School and attended Stephen F. Austin State Teachers College and Texas Christian University before beginning a newspaper career at the Fort Worth *Press* in 1925. She was women's editor and columnist for the Fort Worth *Press* from 1925 to 1954. Her first book, *All of the Women of the Bible,* was developed from a series of her columns on women in the Bible. Her husband, former Fort Worth mayor Edgar Deen, a retired Armour and Company executive, urged her to retire from the *Press* to write a book. *All of the Women of the Bible* was published in 1955 by Harper and Row. When the paperback edition was published in 1988, the book was in its third edition, fortieth printing. After her initial book, Mrs. Deen continued to write on biblical subjects. *Great Women of the Christian Faith* (1959), *Family Living in the Bible* (1963), *The Bible's Legacy for Womanhood* (1970), *All the Bible's Men of Hope* (1974), and *Wisdom from Women in the Bible* (1978) followed. Five of her books were Christian Herald Family Bookshelf selections, and sales of her six books, published in several editions and many languages, including German, Korean, and Japanese, exceeded two million copies. Jack Suggs, a biblical historian, theologian, and dean emeritus of Brite Divinity School at Texas Christian University, praised Edith Deen's work because it "excited interest in the contents of the Bible."

The former Edith Alderman was married twice. Her first husband, France Guedry, died less than two years after their marriage. She and Edgar Deen were married on December 30, 1945, and she moved her office into his North Side Fort Worth home and wrote her column from there until 1955. She was in her fifties when she entered Texas Woman's University to complete her degree in journalism. She continued her studies to receive her master's degree in 1960 from Texas Woman's University; *Family Living in the Bible* grew from her thesis. Mrs. Deen was not only a student at TWU, but a regent of the university for twelve years. In 1959 TWU gave her an honorary doctor of letters degree. Texas Christian University gave her an honorary doctorate in 1972. She was elected to the Fort Worth City Council in 1965, the third woman to serve on the council. She ran unsuccessfully for reelection in 1967 against a candidate who opposed an urban renewal plan Mrs. Deen favored. In 1963 she was named a National Headliner, the top award given by Theta Sigma Phi, now Women in Communications. She was a member of the Texas Institute of Letters[qv] and the first Texas Commission on the Status of Women, and was the Altrusa Club's First Lady of Fort Worth and the Zonta Club's executive woman of the year. The Women's Civic Club Council named her a distinguished senior citizen of Fort Worth. In 1960 she was presented the Brotherhood Citation by the National Conference of Christians and Jews. She was a member of the Disciples of Christ Church. Mrs. Deen lectured nationwide, speaking to such groups as the United States Conference of Mayors and the National Council of Churches. Her husband died on May 29, 1967. In 1982 Mrs. Deen donated the couple's 4,000-book library to the Texas Christian University Library and Archives. Included in the collection were twenty-nine years of her daily columns, book manuscripts, speeches, and personal correspondence with John F. Kennedy, Lady Bird and Lyndon B. Johnson,[qv] Hubert Humphrey, Jim Wright, and John B. Connally.[qv]

BIBLIOGRAPHY: Fort Worth *Star-Telegram,* January 4, 9, 1994. *Who's Who of American Women,* 1961–62.

Cissy Stewart Lale

DEEP CREEK (Baylor County). Deep Creek rises just south of Farm Road 422 and the Lively community center five miles east of Seymour in central Baylor County (at 33°36′ N, 99°11′ W) and runs south-southeast for fifteen miles to its mouth on the Brazos River, six miles southwest of Westover in southeastern Baylor County (at 33°28′ N, 99°05′ W). It crosses rolling hills with clay and sandy soils that support primarily scrub brush and grasses. One source of Deep Creek is Shawver Springs, named for Robert Shawver, who built a dugout near the spring in 1880. By 1979 the spring flow had nearly stopped.

BIBLIOGRAPHY: Gunnar Brune, *Springs of Texas,* Vol. 1 (Fort Worth: Branch-Smith, 1981).

——— (Callahan County). Deep Creek, also known as Asylum Creek, rises twelve miles southeast of Baird in east central Callahan County (at 32°15′ N, 99°18′ W) and runs north for fifty-five miles to its mouth on Hubbard Creek, in east central Shackelford County (at 32°40′ N, 99°11′ W). The stream, which is intermittent in Callahan County, traverses rolling hills surfaced by clay and sandy loams that support scrub brush, mesquite, cacti, and grasses.

——— (McCulloch County). Deep Creek rises three miles east of Rochelle in eastern McCulloch County (at 31°14′ N, 99°09′ W) and runs north for twenty-one miles to its mouth on the Colorado River, a mile northeast of Milburn in the northeast corner of the county (at 31°26′ N, 99°06′ W). It traverses generally flat terrain with local shallow depressions, surfaced by clay and sandy loams that support water-tolerant hardwoods, conifers, and grasses.

——— (San Saba County). Deep Creek rises in southwestern San Saba County at the convergence of East Deep Creek and Middle Deep Creek (at 31°05′ N, 99°00′ W) and runs north for 8½ miles to its mouth on the San Saba River (at 31°07′ N, 99°00′ W). A third branch is named West Deep Creek. Deep Creek crosses generally flat terrain with localized dissection, surfaced by stony and shallow clayey soil that supports Ashe juniper, mesquite, live oak, and grasses.

——— (Scurry County). Deep Creek begins near Farm Road 1269 four miles north of Fluvanna in northwest Scurry County (at 32°55′ N, 101°10′ W). The creekbed runs south-southeast for seventy miles to its mouth on the Colorado River, a mile south of the Mitchell county line in north central Mitchell County (at 32°31′ N, 100°55′ W). Elevation at its head is 2,820 feet above sea level, and the streambed gradually drops some 700 feet before joining the Colorado River. The creek passes through Snyder halfway along its course and becomes a flowing stream near the southern limits of the city. Indians, soldiers, and buffalo hunters commonly traveled the area after the Civil War.[qv] The stream was first known as Culver's Creek for United States army surgeon Ira Culver, who accompanied an expedition into the area in 1873. Buffalo hunter Josiah Wright Mooar[qv] later renamed it. Deep Creek offered good fishing for early settlers of Snyder, and residents later developed a park on its banks. The creek crosses primarily flat to rolling terrain with local escarpments. The area soils are deep, fine sandy loams that support brush and grasses.

BIBLIOGRAPHY: Ranch Headquarters Association. Snyder Unit, *Early Ranching and Water Sources in West Texas* (Snyder, Texas, 1972).

——— (Uvalde County). Deep Creek rises 4½ miles west of the junction of Farm Road 1051 and U.S. Highway 83 and four miles south of Reagan Wells in north central Uvalde County (at 29°29′ N, 99°51′ W) and runs southeast for ten miles to its mouth on the Dry Frio River, a quarter mile east of Highway 83 (at 29°25′ N, 99°45′ W). In its upper reaches the creek traverses flat terrain with locally deep and dense dissection, surfaced by shallow and stony clay and loam soils that support grasses, oak, juniper, and some mesquite. Toward the mouth of the creek the terrain becomes steep to gently sloping and the vegetation consists mostly of scrub brush and scattered grasses.

——— (Wise County). Deep Creek, named for its steep banks, rises five miles southeast of Decatur in southeastern Wise County (at 33°09′ N, 97°31′ W) and runs south for five miles to its mouth on the West Fork of the Trinity River, a mile east of Boyd (at 33°05′ N, 97°32′ W). It traverses undulating to hilly terrain with light to very dark loamy soils that have an accumulation of lime. Deep Creek was the site of the first house built in Wise County. Pioneer settler Sam Woody built a small house on the banks of the stream in 1854, and within a few years the Deep Creek community had developed in the area. By the mid-1980s a cemetery was the only reminder of the settlement.

BIBLIOGRAPHY: Cliff D. Cates, *Pioneer History of Wise County* (Decatur, Texas: Old Settlers Association, 1907).

DEEP DRAW. Deep Draw rises five miles northwest of St. Jo in northeast Montague County (at 33°41′ N, 97°37′ W) and runs north for four miles to its mouth on Farmers Creek, seven miles west of St. Jo (at 33°46′ N, 97°38′ W). It traverses flat to rolling terrain surfaced by deep, fine sandy loams that support brush and grasses. The Deep Draw area has been used as rangeland.

DEEP ELLUM. Deep Ellum is an entertainment and arts district on Elm Street east of downtown Dallas in Dallas County. The area was settled as a "freedmens' town" by former slaves after the Civil War;[qv] its location on Elm Street, just east of the Houston and Texas Central tracks near the depot, was too far from downtown Dallas to be desirable. The area was called Deep Elm or, as early residents pronounced it, "Deep Ellum." Because of the proximity of the railroad it was also called Central Track.

Several industries were located in Deep Ellum at one time. Robert S. Munger[qv] invented a new cotton gin in Mexia in 1883 that revolutionized the ginning industry. He built his first factory to manufacture the new gin in Deep Ellum in 1884. His company, Munger Improved Cotton Machine Company, merged with several smaller companies in 1899 to form the Continental Gin Company. In 1913 Henry Ford opened several regional assembly plants to supplement the manufacture of Model Ts at his Detroit plant. One was built in Deep Ellum and served as the Southwestern Ford Assembly Plant. The Grand Temple of the Black Knights of Pythias was designed in 1916 by William Sidney Pittman[qv] and constructed in Deep Ellum. In addition to serving as the state headquarters for the Knights, the building held offices of black doctors, dentists, and lawyers. It was therefore the first commercial building built for and by blacks in Dallas. An auditorium-ballroom on the top floor was used for dances, assemblies, and parties. At one time the Dallas *Express,* a weekly black newspaper, was published in the Temple, and the state and local headquarters of the YMCA were there.

By the 1920s the Deep Ellum area had become a retail and entertainment center for Dallas residents, primarily African Americans.[qv] Anything could be bought in the stores along Elm: new and used merchandise including furniture, clothing, shoes, and jewelry. Deep Ellum was famous for its "Pawnshop Row," where more than ten pawnshops operated until the 1950s. Entertainment was an important part of the business of Deep Ellum, which became a mecca for jazz and blues artists. In 1920 twelve nightclubs, cafes, and domino parlors were open in Deep Ellum, and by 1950 the number had grown to twenty. Many famous jazz and blues musicians played in the neighborhood at some time, including Blind Lemon Jefferson and Sam "Lightnin'" Hopkins.[qqv] Huddie "Leadbelly" Ledbetter[qv] began performing in 1920 in Deep Ellum, before he began his career in Greenwich Village in New York. Crap games in the back rooms of the domino parlors necessitated keeping an eye out for the police. Deep Ellum had a red-light district, and murders were not uncommon near the nightclubs and domino parlors.

Deep Ellum declined throughout the 1940s and 1950s. The Houston and Texas Central tracks and depot were removed. The growth of Dallas suburbs encouraged businesses in the area to move to shopping malls. As cars became more prevalent the pedestrian traffic decreased, and when the streetcar line was abandoned in 1956 it decreased still further. In 1954 the Uptown Improvement League was formed to improve business in Deep Ellum, including provision of off-street parking, but the area continued to decline. In 1969 the new elevation of Central Expressway bisected Deep Ellum and eliminated the 2400 block of Elm, the center of the community. By the 1970s and early 1980s few businesses remained.

In January 1983 the Near East Side Area Planning Study, or, as it was commonly called, the Deep Ellum Plan, was unveiled. This plan to redevelop the area called for Deep Ellum to be "downzoned" so as to keep the atmosphere on a small, artsy level. The height of buildings was to be limited, the streets would not be widened, and population would be kept down. While this was happening, artists were moving into the area, and art galleries and nightclubs were renovating the vacant buildings. By 1991 Deep Ellum had become popular as a nightspot for young urban dwellers and had fifty-seven bars and nightclubs. In addition, a plethora of avant-garde shops sold a variety of merchandise, including clothing, antiques, crafts, and art works.

BIBLIOGRAPHY: Denise M. Ford, Deep Ellum (MS, Dallas/Texas Collection, Dallas Public Library, 1985). Alan Govenar, "Them Deep Ellum Blues," *Legacies: A History Journal for Dallas and North Central Texas* 2 (Spring 1990). Virginia and Lee McAlester, *Discover Dallas–Fort Worth* (New York: Knopf, 1988). William L. McDonald, *Dallas Rediscovered: A Photographic Chronicle of Urban Expansion, 1870–1925* (Dallas: Dallas County Historical Society, 1978).

Lisa C. Maxwell

DEEP LAKE, TEXAS. Deep Lake, in northwestern Hall County, became the first post office in the county in November 1884, with Frederick S. Lord as postmaster. The office was moved ten miles northeast to the dugout[qv] of J. H. Lafferty, who acted as postmaster, and was renamed Ephraim for Ephraim H. Cone, an early settler, in August 1886. Mail was delivered to Lafferty from Clarendon by passing cowboys and later by W. R. Martin. This office was discontinued in May 1890, but Deep Lake again secured a post office in July 1909, with Rhoda Baker as postmistress. This office was closed in August 1911, and thereafter the community was served by rural free delivery from Lakeview. The Deep Lake area was the scene of the first ranching in the county, a fact that probably accounts for the early post office. It was named for a large lake that for many years was considered "bottomless." The site was a favorite campground for Indians, and stories were circulated that great treasures were buried near the lake. Although a few businesses were located there in 1909, only farms remained in the vicinity in the 1980s.

BIBLIOGRAPHY: Inez Baker, *Yesterday in Hall County* (Memphis, Texas, 1940). Arthur Hecht, comp., *Postal History in the Texas Panhandle* (Canyon, Texas: Panhandle-Plains Historical Society, 1960).

H. Allen Anderson

DEEPWATER, TEXAS. Deepwater, between Pasadena and Deerpark in southeastern Harris County, was named for its location on the Houston Ship Channel.[qv] The community, which developed around a station on the Galveston, Houston and Northern Railway, had a population of fifty in 1893. A local post office opened in 1894 and closed in 1921, when mail was delivered from Pasadena. By 1896 Deepwater had a population of 200, a sawmill, a blacksmith, a hotel, a church, a general store, and the weekly *Enterprise* newspaper. In 1905 the local white school had forty pupils and one teacher, and the local black school thirty-five students and one teacher. By 1914 the population had risen to 250, but the town had begun to decline, and the general store was its principal business. In the 1980s Deepwater was engulfed by Pasadena and was marked only by an abandoned railroad station at the former townsite.

Diana J. Kleiner

DEER CREEK (Bell County). Deer Creek rises just east of the southern tip of McLennan County in northeastern Bell County (at 31°16′ N, 97°16′ W) and runs east for twenty-four miles through Bell and Falls counties to its mouth on the Brazos River, four miles from Marlin in Falls County (at 31°17′ N, 96°58′ W). The creek, intermittent in its upper reaches, runs through nearly level to sloping terrain surfaced by clayey soils used predominantly for agriculture.

—— (Bell County). Deer Creek rises in two forks four miles north of Troy in northern Bell County (at 31°16′ N, 97°16′ W) and runs east for twenty-six miles to its mouth on the Brazos River, four miles southwest of Marlin in Falls County (at 31°17′ N, 96°58′ W). The East Fork rises three miles west of Bruceville-Eddy in southern McLennan County (at 31°18′ N, 97°18′ W) and runs southeast for 3½ miles to join the West Fork, which rises three miles east of Moody, also in McLennan County (at 31°18′ N, 97°19′ W), and runs southeast for four miles. Deer Creek traverses flat to rolling prairie with locally steep slopes and shallow depressions, surfaced by expansive clays and clay and sandy loams that support primarily oak, juniper, water-tolerant conifers, and grasses.

—— (Briscoe County). Deer Creek rises at the breaks of the Llano Estacado[qv] in northwestern Briscoe County (at 34°43′ N, 101°24′ W) and runs northeast three miles to join the Prairie Dog Town Fork of the Red River in Armstrong County (at 34°46′ N, 101°21′ W). The creek was in the old Tule division of the JA Ranch[qv] and is still partly within the JA properties. It crosses variable terrain surfaced by shallow to moderately deep silt loams that support primarily mesquite and grasses.

—— (Burnet County). Deer Creek rises nineteen miles northwest of Burnet in northwestern Burnet County (at 30°56′ N, 98°19′ W) and runs west for ten miles to its mouth on the Colorado River, a mile southeast of Indian Mountain (at 30°57′ N, 98°25′ W). The creek, intermittent in its upper reaches, traverses generally flat terrain with local deep dissections, surfaced by shallow, stony soil that supports oak, juniper, and mesquite.

—— (Clay County). Deer Creek rises five miles south of the Deer Creek community in southwestern Clay County (at 33°33′ N, 98°16′ W) and runs northwest for 12½ miles to its mouth on Lake Arrowhead, three miles west of the Deer Creek community (at 33°42′ N, 98°23′ W). It traverses flat terrain with local shallow depressions, surfaced by clay and sandy loams that support water-tolerant hardwood trees and conifers. The area has served as cropland and range.

—— (DeWitt County). Deer Creek rises eight miles west of Cuero in central DeWitt County (at 29°04′ N, 97°26′ W) and runs northeast for 7½ miles, passing through Blackwell Lake, to its mouth on Sandies Creek (at 29°07′ N, 97°21′ W). It traverses flat to rolling terrain surfaced by slowly permeable soil that supports water-tolerant hardwoods.

—— (Fort Bend County). Deer Creek rises about a mile southeast of Needville in southern Fort Bend County (at 29°22′ N, 95°49′ W) and runs northeast for seven miles to its mouth on Big Creek (at 29°25′ N, 95°43′ W). The vegetation along its banks consists mainly of mixed hardwoods interspersed with various prairie grasses. The stream traverses variable terrain surfaced variously by highly impermeable soil and calcareous clays.

—— (San Saba County). Deer Creek rises two miles south of Round Mountain in southwestern San Saba County (at 30°55′ N, 99°04′ W) and runs north for eleven miles to its mouth on the San Saba River (at 31°03′ N, 99°04′ W). The stream, intermittent for two-thirds of its course, crosses flat to rolling terrain with live oak, mesquite, Ashe juniper, and grasses growing in shallow sandy loam soil.

—— (Tarrant County). Deer Creek rises four miles north of Crowley in south central Tarrant County (at 32°35′ N, 97°24′ W) and runs east for 7½ miles to its mouth on Village Creek, seven miles northeast of Burleson (at 32°35′ N, 97°17′ W). It traverses flat to rolling terrain surfaced by dark, commonly calcareous clays that support mesquite trees, cacti, and various grasses. The area has served as cropland and range.

DEER CREEK, BATTLE OF. In August 1873 Thomas Phelps and his wife, who operated a ranch near Cypress Creek three miles south of Round Mountain in Blanco County, were killed by Indians. A group of Round Mountain residents pursued the Indians and sighted them a few days later. Ten men, spurred by the sight of an Indian scout on the crest of a small hill near Deer Creek, charged around the hill into an ambush. George Roberts was wounded in the first volley and carried out of the line of fire. Seven of the eight remaining men held their ground, while Dan W. Roberts[qv] maneuvered to catch the Indians in a crossfire. He was wounded in the leg, and his companions abandoned the fight to carry him to the Johnson farmhouse, some three miles distant. Texas Rangers[qv] led by Capt. Cicero R. (Rufe) Perry[qv] returned to the scene of the fight, but the Indians had fled. Scouts who tracked the band out of the county described it as a party of twenty-nine well-armed warriors and claimed to have found four hastily dug graves along the trail. The ten men who fought the battle of Deer Creek (also called the Deer Creek Fight) were recognized by the Texas legislature for "services rendered to the state" and presented with engraved 1873 Winchester rifles.

BIBLIOGRAPHY: Arthur E. Nall, "Old Rangers Visit Scene of Conflict," *Frontier Times,* September 1925. Daniel Webster Roberts, *Rangers and Sovereignty* (San Antonio, 1914; rpt., Austin: State House Press, 1987).
Susan Orr and H. D. Orr

DEER CREEK, TEXAS (Clay County). Deer Creek, named for a nearby stream, is on Farm Road 1883 fifteen miles southwest of Henrietta in southern Clay County. The area was settled shortly after 1900. During the mid-1930s Deer Creek had a population less than ten, but by the 1940s it had an estimated twenty-five residents, two churches, a school, and a business. The population continued to be reported at twenty-five until the mid-1960s.

BIBLIOGRAPHY: William Charles Taylor, *A History of Clay County* (Austin: Jenkins, 1972).
David Minor

DEER CREEK, TEXAS (Medina County). Deer Creek, named for the bountiful wild deer in the area, was near the junction of the East and West Squirrel creeks, nine miles west of Yancey in far southwestern Medina County. In 1907 seventeen students attended the one-teacher Deer Creek School. In the 1920s ranching was the principal means of livelihood for members of the community. The school and a few scattered dwellings were in the community as late as 1947 but were abandoned by 1970.

BIBLIOGRAPHY: Castro Colonies Heritage Association, *The History of Medina County, Texas* (Dallas: National Share Graphics, 1983). Houston B. Eggen, History of Public Education in Medina County, Texas, 1848–1928 (M.A. thesis, University of Texas, 1950).
Ruben E. Ochoa

DEER HOLLOW. Deer Hollow, a valley, begins two miles north of Fife in northern McCulloch County (at 31°25′ N, 99°22′ W) and runs northeast for less than a mile to a point near the confluence of Elm Creek and the Colorado River (at 31°25′ N, 99°20′ W). The elevation of the land falls from 1,400 feet above mean sea level at the beginning of the valley to 1,350 feet at its end.

DEER PARK, TEXAS. Deer Park, in the industrial section of central Harris County, was named for the private park for deer that formerly occupied the site. The subdivision was established in 1893 and was the site of a Galveston, Harrisburg and San Antonio Railway station by about 1894. A Deer Park post office was established in 1893, discontinued in 1919, and reestablished in 1930. In 1896 the community had a population of forty, a hotel, a general store, and three resident carpenters. In the 1930s an independent school district was established, but by 1940 the population had fallen to twenty-five. By 1946, however, the area began to flourish, as Deer Park became the site of refineries and toluol plants for the production of TNT. The local Shell plant alone produced ten million gallons of toluol annually. The 1940 census listed a Deer Park population of 100, and in 1948 the community was incorporated. During World War II[qv] the United States Maritime Commission contracted with the Houston Shipbuilding Corporation, a subsidiary of Todd Shipyards, to establish a $5 million yard at Irish Bend, near Deer Park. The town, governed by a city manager–council system, endorsed a plan to expand educational opportunities in 1961 and municipal recreational facilities in 1964. In conjunction with surrounding communities, Deer Park has supported San Jacinto Junior College since its opening in 1961. Industries include the manufacture of plastics, paper products, carbon, concrete products, and alkali materials. In 1970 the town reported eighty-six businesses. The population during the 1950s increased sixfold, from 736 in 1950 to 4,865 in 1960. The 1970 population of 12,773 represented a 162.5 percent increase over the previous decade, and from 1970 to 1990 the population continued a steady rise, reaching a high of 27,652 in 1990. The maximum number of businesses in the same period was 324 in 1986.

BIBLIOGRAPHY: David G. McComb, *Houston: The Bayou City* (Austin: University of Texas Press, 1969; rev. ed., *Houston: A History*, 1981).

Diana J. Kleiner

DEFALCO, LAWRENCE MICHAEL (1915–1979). Lawrence M. DeFalco, fifth bishop of the Catholic Diocese of Amarillo,[qv] was born on August 25, 1915, in McKeesport, Pennsylvania, to Rosario (Ross) and Margret (Desmone) DeFalco. His father was a streetcar-company foreman. While growing up, Lawrence worked for his father during summers as a laborer maintaining the tracks. He entered St. Vincent's College at Latrobe, Pennsylvania, in the fall of 1933. In the deprivation of the Great Depression,[qv] the Catholic Diocese of Pittsburgh decided that it could not support all its future priests, and the bishop dropped half of his seminarians, including DeFalco, who went to St. John's Home Mission Seminary in Little Rock, Arkansas, in 1935. He was ordained to the priesthood in June 1942 at St. Andrew's Cathedral in Little Rock. The same month, he received his first assignment, to St. Patrick's Church in Fort Worth. He was appointed vice chancellor of the Diocese of Dallas–Fort Worth in November 1952. He subsequently became associate pastor at Sacred Heart Cathedral in Dallas (January 1953), was sent by Bishop Thomas K. Gorman[qv] to study canon law at the Pontifical Gregorian University in Rome (September 1953), and returned in June 1955 to his diocese, where he became secretary of the diocesan marriage tribunal. In September 1955 he became administrator of St. Michael's parish in McKinney, where he commuted from Dallas. In April 1956 he was made the first pastor of Our Lady of Perpetual Help in Dallas. He was named papal chamberlain with the title of monsignor in February 1961. In January 1962 he became rector of St. Patrick Cathedral[qv] in Fort Worth. Upon his graduation from Gregorian University he became a licentiate of canon law and a doctor of divinity.

DeFalco was appointed fifth bishop of the Diocese of Amarillo by Pope John XXIII, to succeed John L. Morkovsky,[qv] who went to the Diocese of Galveston-Houston.[qv] He was consecrated by Bishop Gorman at St. Patrick Co-Cathedral in Fort Worth on May 30, 1963, and installed on June 13, 1963, at Sacred Heart Cathedral. Three months later, he went to Rome for the second session of the Second Vatican Council; he made subsequent visits there until Vatican II concluded in 1965. The documents of Vatican II fitted well with the bishop's attitudes, and he quickly established many consultative bodies in the diocese. These included pastoral councils and senates of priests, of nuns, and of deacons. In 1964 he and the other bishops of Texas collaborated in establishing the Texas Catholic Conference, the legislative and political arm of the Catholic Church[qv] in Texas. DeFalco's administration of the diocese began as the local economy was in decline following the post–World War II economic expansion. He canceled plans for further expansion, approved closings of schools and hospitals, and vastly reduced the diocesan debt. Exploratory surgery in July 1979 revealed advanced cancer of the pancreas, and DeFalco submitted his resignation on August 28. He died on September 22, after declaring to members of his family, "I am ready." He was buried in Llano Cemetery, Amarillo.

BIBLIOGRAPHY: Catholic Archives of Texas, Files, Austin. Vertical Files, Barker Texas History Center, University of Texas at Austin.

Jana E. Pellusch

DEFUNCT COUNTIES. At least thirty-two counties that were established by Texas law no longer exist. These defunct counties fall into five categories: (1) judicial counties; (2) counties established by declaration of the Constitutional Convention of 1868–69;[qv] (3) counties established by legislative act but never organized and later abolished by legislative act; (4) counties established outside the present boundaries of Texas; and (5) counties whose names have been changed. The so-called judicial counties had the same status as constitutional counties except that they were not represented in the Congress of the Republic of Texas.[qv] County seats were established; county courts were organized; county judges, surveyors, and land commissioners were appointed. At the spring 1842 term of the Texas Supreme Court, in the case of *Stockton v. Montgomery,* judicial counties were declared unconstitutional, principally because the Constitution of 1836 (see CONSTITUTION OF THE REPUBLIC OF TEXAS) specified that each county was entitled to at least one member in the House of Representatives. At its first session after the decision, the Republic of Texas Congress accepted the invalidity of the judicial counties but passed a law on July 18, 1842, that validated the acts of the surveyors and land commissioners of the defunct counties. The judicial counties were Burleson, Burnet, DeWitt, Guadalupe, Hamilton, La Baca, Madison, Menard, Neches, Panola, Paschal, Smith, Spring Creek, Trinity, Ward, and Waco.[qqv] The Constitutional Convention of 1868–69, by declaration, attempted to organize Delta, Richland, Webster, and Latimer counties. Probably because of Texas prejudice against the radical Republican convention (see RECONSTRUCTION and REPUBLICAN PARTY), the legislature never organized or legalized the counties, and three of them were never more than names. Delta County was reestablished by legislative act in 1870. The five counties authorized by the legislature but never organized were Buchel, Dawson, Encinal, Foley, and Wegefarth.[qqv] Counties established outside the present boundaries of Texas were Greer, Worth,[qqv] and Santa Fe, which were formed in areas that became parts of Oklahoma and New Mexico. Counties that were established under one name or functioned for a time under one name but have a different name at present include: Harrisburg County (changed to Harris County in 1839); Navasoto County (changed to Brazos County in 1842); Davis County (changed from Cass County in 1861 and back to Cass County in 1871); Buchanan County (changed to Stephens County in 1861); and Cibolo County (changed from Wilson to Cibolo and then back to Wilson County).

BIBLIOGRAPHY: R. L. Batts, "Defunct Counties of Texas," *Quarterly of the Texas State Historical Association* 1 (October 1897). James Wilmer Dallam, *A Digest of the Laws of Texas* (Baltimore: Toy, 1845). Hans Peter Nielsen Gammel, comp., *Laws of Texas, 1822–1897* (10 vols., Austin: Gammel, 1898).

DEGENER, EDWARD (1809–1890). Edward Degener, German settler and politician, was born in Brunswick, Germany, on October 20, 1809. He was twice a member of the legislative body in Anhalt-Dessay and was a member of the first German National Assembly at Frankfurt-am-Main in 1848. He immigrated to the United States in 1850 and settled at Sisterdale, Texas, where he farmed. During the Civil War[qv] Degener was court-martialed and imprisoned by the Confederate Army because of his devotion to the Union cause. After his release he engaged in the wholesale grocery business in San Antonio. He was a member of the Constitutional conventions of 1866 and 1868–69;[qqv] upon the readmission of Texas to representation in Congress he was elected as a Republican to the Forty-first Congress and served from March 4, 1870, to March 3, 1871. Degener was a member of the city council of San Antonio from 1872 until 1878. He died in San Antonio on September 11, 1890, and was buried in the City Cemetery.

BIBLIOGRAPHY: *Biographical Directory of the American Congress.*

Anne W. Hooker

DEGOLYER, EVERETTE LEE (1886–1956). Everette Lee DeGolyer, geophysicist and petroleum geologist, was born in a sod house near Greensburg, Kansas, on October 9, 1886, to John William and Narcissa Kagy (Huddle) DeGolyer. His father, interested in mineral prospecting, moved the family to the lead and zinc districts of Joplin, Missouri, where DeGolyer attended public schools. Attracted by the 1901 land openings in Oklahoma, they moved to Norman, where DeGolyer finished high school at the University of Oklahoma preparatory school. In 1906 he entered the university to study mining engineering. During the summers of 1906 through 1909 he worked first as a cook and then as a field assistant for the United States Geological Survey in Wyoming, Colorado, and Montana, and favorably impressed the chief geologist, C. Willard Hayes. In 1909, as chief geologist of the Mexican Eagle Oil Company (El Águila) in Tampico, Hayes hired DeGolyer to head the exploration staff, and the next year DeGolyer located the Potrero del Llano No. 4 well in the Mexican Golden Lane, one of the world's largest fields, which produced more than 110,000 barrels a day. DeGolyer returned to Oklahoma in 1910, married Nell Virginia Goodrich (*see* DEGOLYER, NELL VIRGINIA GOODRICH) on June 10 of that year, and received his B.A. from the University of Oklahoma in 1911. After another stint in Mexico, during which he located the second big Mexican field, Las Naranjas, he returned by 1914 to Oklahoma to run his own consulting office.

In 1916 DeGolyer moved his office to New York but maintained ties with El Águila and its owner, Lord Cowdray, as a consultant. He negotiated the sale of the company to the Royal Dutch Shell Company in 1918. Cowdray then commissioned him to organize the Amerada Petroleum Corporation for exploration in the United States and Canada and the Rycade Oil Company for exploration of salt-dome lands bordering the Gulf of Mexico. DeGolyer served as vice president and general manager of Amerada, then in 1926 became president and general manager of the corporation and its affiliates, Amerada Corporation and Amerada Refining Corporation. He was chairman of the board of all three companies from 1929 to 1932. With Rycade he served as vice president and general manager (1923–26) and president and general manager (1926–41). Through Rycade, he in 1922 instigated a torsion balance survey at the Spindletop oilfield,qv the first geophysical survey of an oilfield in the United States, and at Nash, Texas, Rycade in 1924 located what became the first oilfield discovered by geophysical methods. In May 1925 DeGolyer organized a subsidiary of Amerada, the Geophysical Research Corporation, which located a record eleven Gulf Coast salt domes in nine crew months and perfected a reflection seismograph that has become the principal tool for geophysical oil exploration worldwide. This technology inaugurated the modern age of oil exploration with the 1930 discovery of the Edwards oilfield in Oklahoma by reflection survey.

In 1932 DeGolyer resigned from all Amerada enterprises. He then moved to Dallas and initiated a number of prospecting concerns, such as Atlatl Royalty Corporation (1932, sold in 1950), the Felmont Corporation (1934), and, with John Clarence (Karch) Karcher and Eugene B. McDermott,qqv Geophysical Service, Incorporated, a seismic contracting company. He also established Core Laboratories, Incorporated (1932), and Isotopes, Incorporated (1956), to adapt radioactive isotopes to industrial use. He reorganized his consulting practice in 1936 with Lewis MacNaughton. DeGolyer served as a director of a number of companies, including Transwestern Oil Company, Texas Eastern Gas Transmission Corporation, Southern Pacific

Everette Lee DeGolyer (seated) and Leon Russ at the Potrero del Llano No. 4 oil well, near Tuxpan, Mexico, ca. 1915. Courtesy DeGolyer Library, Southern Methodist University; Ag83.283.2. DeGolyer located this well, one of the most famous in the history of the petroleum industry, when he was twenty-four.

Railroad Company, Dresser Industries,qv and the United States and Foreign Securities Corporation. During World War IIqv DeGolyer served as director of conservation in the Office of the Coordinator for National Defense (1941–42). He was also assistant deputy administrator of the Petroleum Administration for War (1942–43); he headed its mission to Mexico in 1942 and the Petroleum Reserve Corporation's mission to the Middle East in 1943–44. He was chief of the technical advisory commission to President Franklin D. Roosevelt at the Teheran Conference. His continued government service after the war included membership on the National Petroleum Council and the National Security Resources Board, and advisory functions for the Atomic Energy Commission and the International Scientific Conference on Conservation and Utilization of Resources.

DeGolyer was director of the American Petroleum Institute for more than twenty years and a founder of the American Association of Petroleum Geologists. He received the association's highest honor, the Sidney Powers Gold Medal, in 1950. He was also a fellow of the Geological Society of America, the American Association for the Advancement of Science, the British Institute of Petroleum, and other professional societies. He was an honorary member of the National Research Council, the National Academy of Sciences, the Society of Exploration Geophysicists, Sigma Xi, Phi Beta Kappa, the Texas Academy of Science,qv and the Texas Institute of Letters.qv He was also a trustee of the Texas Research Foundation.qv He became the first "oil man" president of the American Institute of Mining and Metallurgical Engineers (1927) and was awarded its Anthony F. Lucas (1941) and John Fritz (1942) medals. In 1939 he received the Distinguished Service Award of the Texas Mid-Continent Oil and Gas Association and, in 1948, the Distinguished Service Citation of the University of Oklahoma. He was inducted into the Oklahoma Hall of Fame in 1952.

DeGolyer contributed prolifically to the literature of his own science and assembled one of the world's best libraries for the history of science, which he donated to the University of Oklahoma. He was also associate editor of the *New Colophon* and the *Southwest Review*qv and chairman of the editorial board of the *Saturday Review of Literature,* of which he gained controlling interest in 1948. He was a student of the early Spanish exploration of the Southwest and wrote the 1930 *Encyclopaedia Britannica* biographical entry for Antonio López de Santa Anna.qv He donated his collection of first and rare editions of modern American and English writers to the University of Texas at Austin, where he served as distinguished professor of geology in 1940. His collection of works on oil and gas law and western and Mexican history makes up part of the DeGolyer Library holdings at Southern Methodist University.

DeGolyer was recognized as the "father" of American geophysics and was for a long time the world's leading oil consultant. His unorthodox acceptance of the European plastic-flow theory of the origin and nature of salt domes and his consequent development of the tools capable of subterranean prospecting revolutionized oil exploration, though he was convinced of the role of luck in his own success. Viewing science and technology as the key to wealth with its political ramifications, DeGolyer believed that the function of science was to serve the economy. He held seven honorary doctorates, lectured at the Massachusetts Institute of Technology and at Princeton, and was a regent of the Smithsonian Institution. DeGolyer was a Congregationalist and a Republican, a Mason, and the father of four children. After seven years' suffering from aplastic anemia, he took his own life at his office in Dallas, on December 14, 1956.

BIBLIOGRAPHY: Carl C. Branson, "E. L. DeGolyer, 1886–1956," *Oklahoma Geology Notes* 17 (January 1957). A. Rodger Denison, "Everette Lee DeGolyer," in *Biographical Memoirs, National Academy of Sciences,* Vol. 33 (New York: Columbia University Press, 1959). *Dictionary of Scientific Biography* (New York: Scribner, 1970). *National Cyclopaedia of American Biography,* Vol. 43. Lon Tinkle, *Mr. De: A Biography of Everette Lee DeGolyer* (Boston: Little, Brown, 1970). *Who Was Who in America,* Vol. 3.

Joan Jenkins Perez

DEGOLYER, NELL VIRGINIA GOODRICH (1886–1972). Nell Goodrich DeGolyer, civic leader and philanthropist, was born in New Florence, Missouri, on November 11, 1886, the daughter of Hugh Gideon and Emma Virginia (Hatton) Goodrich. Her father, a teacher and later a dentist, and her mother, a teacher, moved the family to Norman, Oklahoma, in 1900 to give the children access to the University of Oklahoma. Nell, the oldest child, enrolled in the university at age fifteen and studied music under Fredrik Holmberg. She received a music degree in 1906 and a bachelor of arts in 1907. While a student at the University of Oklahoma, she taught in the music department and served as a teaching assistant in the German department, where she met Everette Lee DeGolyer,qv an engineering student. Nell encouraged Everette to continue his college work, even though it was frequently interrupted by oil-exploration business. On June 10, 1910, they were married in the Goodriches' Norman home. The DeGolyers immediately moved to Tuxpan, Vera Cruz, Mexico, where Everette pursued a highly successful career as a geophysicist. They returned briefly to Norman in 1911 for him to complete his bachelor's degree, then moved to Tampico, Vera Cruz. There Mrs. DeGolyer became active in charity and mission work and served as president of a local club for American women living in Mexico. Her musical talents were also utilized, as she played for a Methodist mission and gave piano lessons in her home. She remained with her husband in Mexico until 1913, when, pregnant and suffering from malaria, she returned to Norman. The couple's first daughter was born there; Everette DeGolyer rejoined his family when political relations between the United States and Mexico deteriorated.

The DeGolyers traveled in Europe on the eve of World War I.qv Nell enjoyed observing the activities of militant suffragists in England at this time and was impressed with their commitment to civic involvement. Upon their return to the United States in 1916, the DeGolyers moved to Montclair, New Jersey, where three more children were born to them: two daughters and a son. While her husband pursued his oil interests in New York City, Nell became active in the League of Women Voters in New Jersey, but resigned from this nonpartisan group in 1928 to work for Herbert Hoover's presidential campaign. The DeGolyers remained in the Northeast until 1936, when they moved to Dallas to be closer to the East Texas oilfieldqv and Everette's other business interests.

In Dallas, Nell DeGolyer became as well known and respected as her successful husband for her civic activities. She supported the Dallas Symphony Orchestraqv and civic opera. Because of her earlier involvement in the League of Women Voters, she was asked to become a founding member and the first president of this league's Dallas chapter. She also became an organizer and member of the Dallas chapter of Planned Parenthood; she later served as national president of this organization. She served on the board of trustees for the Wadley Research Institute and Blood Bank and on the board of the Middle East Institute. She was an active Methodist. She shared with her husband a love of travel and books, and also maintained a lifelong devotion to music. Another abiding interest for her in Dallas was the family's forty-four-acre estate known as Rancho Encinal, which she and her husband built and decorated. The thirteen-room Spanish Colonial Revival structure on White Rock Lake in East Dallas, completed in 1940, reflected the DeGolyers' world travels, Everette's outstanding book collection, and Nell's expertise in gardening. Until her death Mrs. DeGolyer lived in this home; it was willed to Southern Methodist University after her death and several years later became the property of the city of Dallas. Into the 1990s the city used it, as the Dallas Arboretum and Botanical Society, to showcase the gardens planned and maintained by Nell DeGolyer. Nell and Everette DeGolyer also provided for establishment of the DeGolyer Foundation, which led to the foundation of the DeGolyer Library at SMU. After her husband's death in 1956, Nell DeGolyer served as president of the foundation's board. She died in Dallas on May 3, 1972. Her funeral was held in Dallas, and she was buried there in Hillcrest Memorial Park. She was survived by her son, two daughters, and numerous grandchildren.

BIBLIOGRAPHY: Dallas *Morning News,* February 11, 1947, February 2, 1949, May 6, 1972. Dallas *Daily Times Herald,* March 23, 1969, May 5, 1972, September 11, 1976, November 26, 1978. Nell Goodrich DeGolyer Papers, DeGolyer Library, Southern Methodist University. Lon Tinkle, *Mr. De: A Biography of Everette Lee DeGolyer* (Boston: Little, Brown 1970).

Debbie Mauldin Cottrell

DEGOLYER LIBRARY. The DeGolyer Foundation Library was established in 1957 as the result of a gift by Everette Lee and Nell V. DeGolyer,qqv and by a bequest under the will of Everette DeGolyer. In 1974 the collection was officially donated to Southern Methodist University, its name was changed to the DeGolyer Library, and it was moved into the Fondren Library West, where space was renovated with support from the Leland Fikes Foundation.qv The DeGolyer Library in 1995 consisted of more than 90,000 volumes on the history of the Trans-Mississippi West and the Spanish borderlands, as well as railroad history. A substantial collection of rare books on early voyages and travel is also housed in the Degolyer Library, helping to make its collection one of the finest in the world—especially for the history of Texas, New Mexico, Colorado, and California. Under Everett DeGolyer, Jr., the library's first director (1958–77), the library was transformed from a private collection to a public research library. The cataloging of materials was begun in 1960 by Dr. James Phillips. In addition to its printed materials, the DeGolyer Library has acquired by gift and by purchase a number of important groups of manuscripts. Chief among these are the papers of DeGolyer; the archives of Horton Foote; the personal and business papers of Stanley Marcus; the manuscripts and correspondence of Paul Horgan; the business papers of John Insley Blair, capitalist; the papers of Samuel M. Vauclain, longtime president of the Baldwin Locomotive Works; the specification records of the Baldwin Locomotive Works; the papers of the Muskogee Corporation, a railroad holding company; and the motive power files of the Burlington Railroad and the Fort Worth and Denver Railway. In recent years it has also formed the Archives of Women of the Southwest. The library also holds a photographic collection of more than 300,000 items on the West, Mexico, and railroads. A geology collection formed by Mr. DeGolyer is located in the Science Engineering Library of Southern Methodist University. Beginning in the 1980s, the catalog of printed books at De-Golyer was converted to machine-readable form, and in the 1990s it could be consulted on the Internet. Subject guides for nonbook materials have been published for library users, and beginning in the mid-1980s a series of interpretive exhibition catalogs were written and published, to make more widely known the results of two generations of private collectors in Texas.

BIBLIOGRAPHY: Vertical Files, Barker Texas History Center, University of Texas at Austin.

David Farmer

DE GRAFFENRIED, GAINES (1905–1991). Gaines De Graffenried, gun collector and museum curator, was born at Chilton, Texas, on August 10, 1905, the son of Fleming Taylor and Lillian (Gaines) De Graffenried. His father was a planter, cotton merchant, and banker. The family moved to Waco in 1920 but maintained the banking business in Chilton. De Graffenried attended Waco High School and after graduation worked as a cotton grader for Mason and Company. He married Ola Bradley in 1935. They had two sons. De Graffenried was trained in the business of cotton marketing but from his youth demonstrated a consuming interest in the study and collecting of antique and historic guns and weapons. He devoted the major portion of his life to this pursuit and eventually assembled one of the most extensive and valuable collections in the nation. De Graffenried was an organizer and exhibitor at some of Waco's early gun shows in the 1940s and 1950s. He was also a charter member of the Texas Gun Collectors Association. He displayed his collection at the Fort Fisher Museum in Waco. In 1973 he was a member of the commission appointed by Governor Dolph Briscoe to establish the Texas Ranger Hall of Fame and Museum qv at Waco. At the completion of this museum complex in 1975, he was invited to serve as its curator of exhibits, which post he occupied, without pay, until the time of his death in 1991. The city of Waco purchased a large part of his personal collection, which at one time was reported to include 700 guns, for the museum in 1989. De Graffenried died on March 21, 1991.

BIBLIOGRAPHY: Roger N. Conger, *Texas Collector: Gaines de Graffenried* (Waco: Texian Press, 1987). Dallas *Morning News*, March 23, 1991.

Roger N. Conger

DE GRAFFENRIED, REESE CALHOUN (1859–1902). Reese Calhoun (De, the Black Eagle of the Piney Woods) De Graffenried, lawyer and congressman, son of Gen. Matthew Fontaine and Martha (McLemore) De Graffenried, was born at Franklin, Tennessee, on May 7, 1859. He attended school in Franklin until the age of thirteen, when he matriculated at the University of Tennessee at Knoxville; he graduated at the age of nineteen. A year later he graduated from Cumberland Law School at Lebanon, Tennessee, and was admitted to the bar. For several years he practiced law in Franklin and Chattanooga, Tennessee, before moving to Texas sometime in late 1882. In 1882 and early 1883, after settling in Longview, he was temporarily employed by the Texas and Pacific Railway in various capacities, including assistant brakeman and fuel agent.

De Graffenried was elected county attorney of Gregg County in November 1882 but resigned after only two months to resume private law practice. On November 1, 1883, he married Annie Berry of Franklin, Tennessee. In 1888 he served as a Democratic elector in the general election. In 1890 he ran for the office of congressman for the Third District against C. B. "Buck" Kilgore and former governor Richard B. Hubbard qqv and was defeated. In 1896, however, he was elected congressman for the Fifty-fifth Congress from the Third Congressional District. Subsequently, he was reelected to the Fifty-sixth and Fifty-seventh congresses. A few months before his death he was defeated for the 1902 nomination for Congress by James Gordon Russell, qv who was subsequently elected his successor. De Graffenried died suddenly in Washington, D.C., on August 29, 1902. His funeral in Longview was attended by some 6,000 persons. He was buried with Masonic honors in Greenwood Cemetery.

BIBLIOGRAPHY: *Biographical Directory of the American Congress*. Dallas *Morning News*, August 30, 1902. Thomas P. DeGraffenried, *History of the DeGraffenried Family from 1191 A.D. to 1925* (Binghamton and New York: Vail-Ballou Press, 1925).

Suzanne Perry

DEGRESS, JACOB CARL MARIA (1842–1894). Jacob Carl DeGress, first Texas state superintendent of schools, was born to Carl Franz Wilhelm and Johanna Walburga (di Bramino) von Gress on April 23, 1842, in Cologne, Prussia. His father left Prussia because of political pressures, and by the time he died in 1856 he had moved his family to Cape Girardeau, Missouri. Jacob DeGress received eight years of formal education in Germany but did not continue school after his father died. He served as a cavalry commander in the Union Army during the Civil War. qv He fought at Vicksburg and in Louisiana and was wounded twice, promoted to major, and brevetted lieutenant colonel. He joined Gen. Joseph A. Mower's staff in 1864, as Mower moved with Gen. William T. Sherman's qv troops through Georgia.

DeGress entered Texas as General Mower's aide-de-camp in June 1865. He assumed the duties of assistant commissioner of the Freedmen's Bureau qv of the eastern division of the state. From 1865 to 1868, in positions at Galveston, Houston, and New Orleans (where he became secretary of civil affairs as well as inspector general of the Freedmen's Bureau), DeGress helped administer the bureau during the first years of radical Reconstruction. qv While working in Houston he married Bettie Buckner Young, the widow of a Confederate officer and daughter of a Castroville judge, on New Year's Day, 1867. The couple had seven children. In 1868 DeGress accepted a commission as captain in the regular army. He was assigned to the all-black Ninth United States Cavalry, qv located in West Texas, and on April 14, 1868, he reported to Fort Duncan at Eagle Pass. He commanded cavalry troops at the frontier post until December 1870, when he retired because of further trouble from his Civil War wounds.

After the passage of the 1871 public school law, Republican governor Edmund J. Davis qv appointed DeGress the state's first superintendent of public instruction. In this position DeGress attempted to institute a public school system with education for black children and compulsory attendance supported by a school tax. He traveled widely in order to promote and popularize public school reform, but he and public schools in general provoked strong opposition among Texans. Under constant attack, DeGress came to believe that Democrats "as a class" opposed tax-supported schools and only members of the Republican party qv should hold positions as school directors, a belief that cost him a Senate investigation. DeGress also protested the activities of the Ku Klux Klan, qv though he reassured the public that he too believed in segregation. In 1873 Democrats regained political power in Texas. Governor Richard Coke qv removed DeGress from his position in February 1874, and the idea of a public school system was made to wait.

DeGress was generally despised as a carpetbagger. Yet he remained in Texas after Reconstruction, made Austin his home, and continued to participate in political and community affairs. He was elected alderman from Austin's eighth ward in 1877 and became mayor that year. He was reelected in 1879, but a lawsuit challenging his eligibility was decided against him in August 1880, cutting short his second term. That summer DeGress's wife and two daughters died; he put his surviving daughter in St. Mary's Academy.[qv] On August 2, 1882, he married W. M. Johnston, a cousin of Gen. Joseph E. Johnston;[qv] they had three children.

DeGress was a delegate to state Republican conventions and served as treasurer and chairman of the state Republican executive committee. Republican presidents James A. Garfield and Benjamin Harrison appointed him postmaster of Austin, a position he filled from June 1881 to October 1885, and from October 1889 to December 1893. After another court ruling, he served again as alderman in 1887, and from 1885 to 1888 he was on various committees involved with the building and dedication of the Capitol.[qv] On March 19, 1894, DeGress died of complications from his war injuries; he was buried in Oakwood Cemetery, Austin. He was a Catholic.

BIBLIOGRAPHY: Walace Hawkins, Col. Jacob Carl DeGress (MS, Texas State Archives, Austin, 1949). History of Texas, Together with a Biographical History of Milam, Williamson, Bastrop, Travis, Lee and Burleson Counties (Chicago: Lewis, 1893). William C. Nunn, Texas Under the Carpetbaggers (Austin: University of Texas Press, 1962).

Michael E. McClellan

DEGÜELLO. The degüello, music played by the Mexican army bands on the morning of March 6, 1836, was the signal for Antonio López de Santa Anna's[qv] attack on the Alamo. The word *degüello* signifies the act of beheading or throat-cutting and in Spanish history became associated with the battle music, which, in different versions, meant complete destruction of the enemy without mercy.

BIBLIOGRAPHY: Amelia W. Williams, A Critical Study of the Siege of the Alamo and of the Personnel of Its Defenders (Ph.D. dissertation, University of Texas, 1931; rpt., *Southwestern Historical Quarterly* 36–37 [April 1933–April 1934]).

Degüello. Reproduced in Amelia Williams, "A Critical Study of the Siege of the Alamo," *Southwestern Historical Quarterly* 37 (January 1934), p. 183. The playing of this Mexican bugle call, announcing that no quarter would be given, signaled the final assault on the Alamo.

DEKALB, TEXAS. DeKalb is on the Missouri Pacific Railroad and U.S. Highway 82 twelve miles northwest of New Boston in western Bowie County. It was one of the earliest settlements in the county. According to some county histories a community had begun to take shape in the winter of 1835, when David Crockett[qv] visited the site on his way to the Alamo. These sources claim that when Crockett enquired about the name of the town, residents told him it had none and then asked him to name it. He suggested the name of the Prussian Baron de Kalb, a general of the American revolutionary army.

One purpose for founding the community was to establish a school. In fact, several of the early settlers were involved in the successful effort to get the Texas Congress to grant land for the establishment of DeKalb College in 1839. The school, however, seems to have been located several miles south of the community. Because DeKalb was supposed to serve as an educational focal point for surrounding farmers, the owners of the land attempted to restrict settlement to those they considered acceptable. As David Chisholm put it in 1837, "This town or village is situated on Browning's and my land, about one half mile from my house. This land is not to be sold to any Tom, Dick, or Harry to put up dram shops on, but for those who wish to have the river for health or the benefit of the school."

Despite the facts that DeKalb served as the first seat of Bowie County in 1841 and that it was on prime agricultural land, the town grew very slowly. One important cause was the lack of efficient, reliable transportation. When the Texas and Pacific Railway was built through the county in 1876, DeKalb became a station on the rail line and began to grow. By 1884 it had two churches, a school, a gin, a sawmill-gristmill, and a population of 200. By 1890 the town had a population of 500, a bank, and a weekly newspaper, the *Flag*, edited by L. A. Petit. Afterward, DeKalb grew slowly to a population of 1,023 by the 1930s.

In 1980 it had a population of 2,217. Agriculture remained of vital importance to the local economy, but, whereas cotton had been the dominant area crop during the nineteenth and early twentieth centuries, it had been replaced by vegetables, fruit, livestock, and hay. The town's businesses reflected that change. By the 1970s DeKalb was known for its cannery and its large shipments of tomatoes. Many of its residents were also employed at Red River Army Depot[qv] in eastern Bowie County. In 1990 the population was 1,976.

BIBLIOGRAPHY: Bowie County Scrapbook, Barker Texas History Center, University of Texas at Austin. Emma Lou Meadows, *DeKalb and Bowie County* (DeKalb, Texas: DeKalb News, 1968). Rex W. Strickland, Anglo-American Activities in Northeastern Texas, 1803–1845 (Ph.D. dissertation, University of Texas, 1937). *Cecil Harper, Jr.*

DEKALB AND RED RIVER RAILROAD. The DeKalb and Red River Railroad Company was chartered on November 27, 1891, with a capital stock of $50,000. Track was to be laid between DeKalb and the Red River to the north in Bowie County, a distance of ten miles. The members of the first board of directors included P. S. Ramsen, William Peters, and C. A. Skinner, all of DeKalb; and Benjamin Whitaker, J. H. Smelsen, J. C. Whitaker, G. B. Ellis, and Waverly Whitaker, all of Texarkana. In 1892 the line built eight miles between DeKalb and Lennox and 1½ miles between Muir and Mooresville. The railroad hauled logs for the DeKalb Lumber Company and owned only its road bed and ties. Rails, equipment, and fuel were provided by the lumber company. In 1895 the DeKalb and Red River reported total freight earnings of $5,000 and used one locomotive and sixteen freight cars. The company was dropped by the Railroad Commission[qv] by June 30, 1899, as the railroad had been abandoned and the rails removed.

Nancy Beck Young

DELAND DRAW. Deland Draw, a valley in southwestern McCulloch County, begins eleven miles south of Melvin (at 31°02′ N, 99°35′ W) and runs southeast for 8½ miles to a point three miles west of the Calf Creek community (at 30°58′ N, 99°30′ W). An intermittent stream runs through the valley, carrying water from an elevation of 2,070 feet above mean sea level to Calf Creek, which is at 1,780 feet. Deland Draw was named for the Deland family, who settled in the area in the 1870s.

BIBLIOGRAPHY: Wayne Spiller, comp., *Handbook of McCulloch County History* (Vol. 1, Seagraves, Texas: Pioneer, 1976; vol. 2, Canyon, Texas: Staked Plains Press, 1986).

DELANEY, JAMES JOSEPH (1879–1959). James Joseph Delaney, teacher and school administrator, son of Henry H. and Sarah (King) Delaney, was born on April 6, 1879, in Bristol, Virginia. He attended King College (B.A., 1900; M.A., 1918; honorary Litt.D., 1923), the University of Virginia, and Columbia University. He served as superintendent of schools at Marion, Virginia, and as president of Euharlee Institute, Georgia. He moved to Texas in 1904 as headmaster of Carlisle Military Academy (now the University of Texas at Arlington). He taught at Austin College in Sherman from 1908 until 1920, when he became headmaster of the University Training School in Dallas. In 1922 Delaney was chosen as the first president of Schreiner Institute (now Schreiner College), a position he held until retirement on July 14, 1950. His efforts resulted in Schreiner's becoming a fully accredited junior college.

Delaney was the first junior college representative to be chosen president of the Association of Texas Colleges. He was president of the Southern Association of Junior Colleges (1945–46) and a member of the Executive Committee for Secondary Schools of the Southern Association of Colleges (1939–47). He served as a member of accrediting committees of both the Southern Association and the Texas Education Agency. He represented the Southern Association of Colleges and Secondary Schools in evaluating the work of Mexican colleges seeking accreditation. He attempted to promote better relations with Mexico, Central America, and South America by helping young men from those areas to obtain an education in Texas.

Delaney served as president of the Kerrville Chamber of Commerce (1926–27), as a director of the West Texas Chamber of Commerce[qv] (1937–38), as a member of the board of directors, Texas Centennial[qv] of Statehood Commission (1946–47), and as a director of the Federal Building and Loan Association. He was a member of the Texas Academy of Science, the Texas State Historical Association, the Democratic party,[qv] Phi Gamma Mu, the International Rotary Club, and the Presbyterian Church.[qv] Delaney and Stella (Vineyard), whom he married on June 6, 1906, had two children. Delaney died in Kerrville on June 28, 1959.

BIBLIOGRAPHY: Sam Hanna Acheson, Herbert P. Gambrell, Mary Carter Toomey, and Alex M. Acheson, Jr., *Texian Who's Who*, Vol. 1 (Dallas: Texian, 1937). Bob Bennett, *Kerr County, Texas, 1856–1956* (San Antonio: Naylor, 1956; bicentennial ed., rev. by Clara Watkins: *Kerr County, Texas, 1856–1976*, Kerrville, Texas: Hill Country Preservation Society, 1975). *Presidents and Professors in American Colleges and Universities*, 1935. *Who's Who in the South and Southwest*, Vol. 2.

Joe R. Baulch

DELANEY, WILLIAM SHELBY (1825–1900). William Shelby Delaney, son of Henry Field and Rhoda (Prince) Delaney, was born in Union County, Kentucky, on September 18, 1825. He graduated from Cumberland College in July 1847 and taught Greek and Latin there from 1848 until 1851, while he studied law in his spare time. He was admitted to the bar in Caldwell County, Kentucky, where he married Gabriella R. Shropshire on July 14, 1850; after her death he married Mrs. Caroline Shropshire, on July 21, 1863. Delaney practiced law in Memphis and Nashville, Tennessee, from 1854 to 1860, when he moved to Columbus, Texas. He was colonel of a Colorado County regiment in the Confederate Army before he became district attorney of the Columbus district in 1862; he was removed from office as an alleged impediment to Reconstruction[qv] in 1865. In 1873 he was appointed to the bench of the Colorado County Court. He represented District Twenty-five in the House of the Fourteenth Legislature, 1874–75, where he served as chairman of the committee on finance. From 1881 to 1885 he sat as judge on the Colorado County Commission of Appeals. Delaney owned large tracts of land in Wharton, Colorado, and other counties and ranked as one of the leading stock raisers in the region. He served as vestryman and licensed lay reader in St. John's Episcopal Church at Columbus. He had five children with his first wife and two with his second. Delaney died at Austin on December 16, 1900, and was buried there in Oakwood Cemetery.

BIBLIOGRAPHY: Colorado County Historical Commission, *Colorado County Chronicles from the Beginning to 1923* (2 vols., Austin: Nortex, 1986). James D. Lynch, *The Bench and Bar of Texas* (St. Louis, 1885). *Memorial and Genealogical Record of Southwest Texas* (Chicago: Goodspeed, 1894; rpt., Easley, South Carolina: Southern Historical Press, 1978).

DE LA PORTA BROTHERS. Moses (Morin) and his younger brother Jao (Joseph) De la Porta financed the first settlement by Europeans on Galveston Island in 1816. The brothers were born in Portugal of Jewish parentage and found their way to Texas by a circuitous route. At a young age they moved to Paris, where they received their schooling. They later sailed to Brazil, to the British West Indies, and to New Orleans. The brothers financed the privateering venture of Louis Michel Aury[qv] and José Manuel de Herrera to San Luis Island, later called Galveston, in 1816. Aury set up a privateering camp on September 12 and was named military and civil governor of Texas and Galveston Island. Jao may have served as Aury's secretary of state. In December, Gen. Francisco Xavier Mina[qv] arrived and persuaded Aury to join him in invading Mexico. They lost the battle, and Moses lost heavily in the enterprise. He left the island and died soon after. Jao took over his brother's interests. While Aury was away, privateer Jean Laffite[qv] sailed down the Texas coast and set up camp in Matagorda Bay. Jao arrived at the camp and sold the De la Porta–Aury expedition's camp and supplies to Laffite. The Laffite commune took possession of the island on May 15, 1817, forcing Aury to abandon the Galveston camp. On May 15, 1818, Laffite appointed Jao supercargo for the Karankawa Indian trade. When Laffite left Galveston Island in 1820, Jao became a full-time trader. Many years later, Jao moved to New Orleans permanently, where he described his experiences with the buccaneer camps and the Karankawas to Gershom Kursheedt, a resident of New Orleans in 1835.

BIBLIOGRAPHY: Joseph O. Dyer, *The Early History of Galveston* (Galveston: Oscar Springer Print., 1916). Joseph Dyer, *Epitome of Important Events in Early Texas History* (Galveston *Daily News*, 1936).

Galveston Historical Collection of Rosenberg Library (Galveston: Rosenberg Library, 1929). Natalie Ornish, *Pioneer Jewish Texans* (Dallas: Texas Heritage, 1989). Vertical Files, Barker Texas History Center, University of Texas at Austin.

Natalie Ornish

DE LA ROSA, LUIS (ca. 1865–ca. 1930). Luis De la Rosa, revolutionary and follower of the Mexican anarchist Ricardo Flores Magón,qv was born around 1865. He believed in direct action to correct injustices done to Hispanics on both sides of the Rio Grande. One of his notices called for Mexicans to "unite with our brothers . . . in Texas . . . and take the same chances they are taking, for this is the solemn moment of the vindication of right and justice lost to us for so long a time." At various times he was a Cameron County deputy sheriff, a successful butcher in a small grocery store that he owned in Rio Hondo, and a cattleman east of San Benito. He suffered from consumption and had a deformed left arm and hand, with one or two fingers missing due to accidents. Confined to a bed most of the time, he read political ideology, especially Marxism and other revolutionary theory. He enjoyed reading *Regeneración*, which embodied Flores Magón's anarchist ideas. While writing his political reflections, now lost, De la Rosa fused his ideas with Flores Magón's views. As one newspaper noted in 1916, "De la Rosa, a large man in size, is said to have been the brains of what was known among Mexicans as the revolution of Mexicans in Texas." With Aniceto Pizaña qv he formed the Floresmagonista movement, which lasted from 1904 to 1919. By 1915 De la Rosa had split it into two groups, the combative Sediciosos and Pizaña's moderates. Shortly after Pizaña joined him, the two conducted raids from the Mexican side into South Texas. De la Rosa was in command of a force that took part in the Norias Ranch Raid,qv in which he was said to have "visited death and destruction upon the oppressors and left behind a bitter legacy." On October 18, 1915, he caused a train crash at Tandy's Station, eight miles north of Brownsville. He raised an army of 500 men whose raids and guerrilla fighting on the Mexican border of Texas became known as the Plan of San Diego,qv an effort to return the American Southwest to Mexico. In 1916 De la Rosa was known as the military commander of the PSD. Gen. Frederick Funston requested United States forces to respond, and army and federal investigators declared that the raids were part of PSD. Venustiano Carranza and his aids cooperated with American troops to stop the guerrilla raids along the lower Rio Grande by 1919. By June 1916 De la Rosa set out with a bodyguard for Monterrey to confirm his Mexican authority. En route a Mexican officer, Alfredo Ricaut, arrested him. Shortly after, he disappeared in Mexico, where he died of consumption about 1930.

BIBLIOGRAPHY: Brownsville *Herald*, September 23, 1915. Charles C. Cumberland, "Border Raids in the Lower Rio Grande Valley—1915," *Southwestern Historical Quarterly* 57 (January 1954). James Sandos, *Rebellion in the Borderlands: Anarchism and the Plan of San Diego, 1904–1923* (Norman: University of Oklahoma Press, 1992).

Carlos M. Larralde

DELAWARE BEND, TEXAS. Delaware Bend is near the banks of Lake Texoma seven miles north of Dexter in northeastern Cooke County. Settlement of the site occurred in the late 1870s, during the growth of the cattle industry. Delaware Bend had a post office, named for the bend of the Red River where the community was located, from 1872 to 1876. A school was operating there by 1884. Delaware Bend subsequently served as a church community for area farmers and ranchers. In 1936 it had a number of scattered dwellings. In the 1940s the community lost three-fourths of its land to Lake Texoma,qv and the school was consolidated with the Dexter school district. Throughout the 1940s and 1950s the population was estimated at twenty-five. In 1963 only a cemetery was shown on county maps for Delaware Bend, but by 1966 the population was estimated at fifty. In 1988 the town reported forty residents and no businesses.

BIBLIOGRAPHY: Gainesville *Daily Register*, Centennial Edition, August 30, 1948. A. Morton Smith, *The First 100 Years in Cooke County* (San Antonio: Naylor, 1955).

David Minor

DELAWARE CREEK. Delaware Creek rises two miles west of Burnet in central Burnet County (at 30°46′ N, 98°16′ W) and runs southeast for five miles to its mouth on Hamilton Creek, four miles south of Burnet (at 30°42′ N, 98°14′ W). It traverses generally flat terrain with local deep dissections, surfaced by shallow, stony soil that supports oak, juniper, and mesquite.

DELAWARE INDIANS. The Delaware Indians were one of many immigrant tribes from the United States who ventured into Texas in the late eighteenth and early nineteenth centuries. The Texas Delawares were remnants of a once-powerful people who had experienced more than 150 years of upheaval and relocation as they were pushed west by advancing Euro-American culture. The traditional home of the tribe was the Delaware River basin, an area that extends from what is now southern New York to Delaware Bay. The location on the Atlantic coast brought the tribe into early contact with English colonists, who called them Delawares because they lived on the bay named in honor of Lord de la Warr, governor of the English colony at Jamestown in 1610. The Delawares, members of the Algonquian linguistic family, called themselves Lenni Lenape, or "common people." The people called Delawares lived in small villages scattered along the numerous waterways of the region. Each village was an independent community with its own chieftains, who served as counselors and decision makers. Often residents of villages along the same stream constituted a band. The most influential village leader functioned as head of the band. The Delawares lived in one-room bark huts, called wigwams, with a single doorway and a smoke hole in the roof. When first contacted by Europeans, they had no metal tools, and their principal weapon was the bow and arrow. They grew corn, beans, pumpkins, squash, and tobacco, and supplemented their diet by hunting, fishing, and gathering. Their clothing was made of animal skins, feathers, and plant fibers, and both men and women often painted and tattooed their bodies.

The Dutch were the first Europeans to settle in Delaware territory. They arrived in the 1620s, interested primarily in the fur trade, and established the colony of New Netherlands. The Dutch negotiated the first land purchases from the Delawares in the late 1620s, followed by the Swedes in the 1630s, and the process was begun that ultimately removed the Delawares from their homeland. In 1664 the Dutch colony was taken over by the English, and the Delawares were subjected to yet another European power. The tribe fell victim to warfare, alcoholism, and epidemic diseases, and within a century none of the tribe remained in the valley of the Delaware River. The surviving Delawares began to drift west in the 1740s, first to the Susquehanna River valley, then across the Allegheny Mountains to the Ohio River, where they settled on land belonging to the Six Nations of the Iroquois. In 1768 the Iroquois ceded their land east of the Ohio River to the English, and the Delawares were forced to move west of the river into what is now Ohio. The American colonies declared independence from England in 1776, but the change of government did not alter the fate of the Delawares. Americans, driven by a pioneering spirit, continued to advance into Indian territory and claim land through warfare and treaty. Between 1778 and 1830 the Delawares were party to sixteen treaties that moved them from Ohio to Indiana, across Illinois, and into Missouri. The fact that they were compensated for land that they ceded and given new land on which to settle did not lessen the hardships involved in relocation. The main body of the Delawares lived on the White River in Missouri for nine years before government officials negotiated their move to the junction of the Kansas and Missouri Rivers in what is now Kansas. The tribe resided there from 1830 until their final relocation to Indian Territory in 1868, when they were settled on land purchased from the Cherokees in present northeastern Oklahoma. The location of the main body of the Delawares was dictated by the United States government from the late 1770s on, but small groups of the tribe often moved independently. In 1789 a group of Delawares received permission from Spanish officials to move into Missouri. They settled near Cape Girardeau, where they later became known as Absentee Delawares.

Remnants of that Missouri band drifted into Texas around 1820 and settled in the northeast corner of the Spanish province around the Red and Sabine Rivers. Those Delawares, along with other immigrant bands from the United States, shared East Texas with remnants of the Caddo Indians and a growing number of white settlers. After Mexico secured independence from Spain in 1821, the Delawares continued to have a peaceful relationship with Mexican officials, as well as with other immigrant tribes and Anglo-American colonists. When Gen. Manuel de Mier y Terán qv made an inspection of East Texas in 1828, he estimated that 150 to 200 Delaware families were living there. They petitioned the general to grant them land and send "teachers of reading and writing" to their villages. Mier was impressed with the level of acculturation that the Delawares had achieved and forwarded their request to Mexico City. The Mexican government, however, never granted the tribe legal title to any land. When Texans began their revolution against the Mexican government in 1835, they were anxious to win the immigrant tribes to their cause, or at least to ensure their neutrality. To accomplish that, the provisional government pledged to honor the land claims of twelve tribes living in East Texas, including the Delawares. In addition, government officials appointed three commissioners to negotiate a treaty with those groups. The resulting treaty, concluded in February 1836, delineated the boundaries of Indian land, but the agreement was never ratified by the Texas government.

When Texas became a republic in 1836, President Sam Houston qv sought peace with all Texas Indians. He enlisted the services of the friendly Delawares in protecting the frontier from hostile western tribes. In 1837 Delaware scouts accompanied several ranger corps as they patrolled the western line of settlement. Houston also worked to secure the land claims of the immigrant tribes, but without success. Houston's successor to the presidency, Mirabeau B. Lamar,qv considered the immigrant tribes to be unauthorized intruders who threatened public safety and illegally occupied Texas land. He ordered them to be expelled from Texas. His removal policy culminated in the Cherokee War qv (1839), a conflict that involved all the immigrant bands. As a result of the war, most of the immigrant Indians in the Republic of Texas,qv including the Delawares, were forced north of the Red River into Indian Territory. A few scattered Delawares remained in Texas after the war. When Houston was elected to a second term as president in late 1841, he immediately reinstated his peace policy. His emissaries negotiated a treaty with the Delawares and remnants of eight other tribes in 1843 at Fort Bird, near the site of present Fort Worth. Houston then elicited the aid of the Delawares in his attempts to make peace with the Comanches. He allowed a group of Delaware scouts and their families to settle along the Brazos and Bosque rivers, where they used their influence to induce the Comanches to come to council. Most prominent among those Delawares were John Conner, a mixed-blood chief, and Bill and Jim Shaw,qv brothers who had earned reputations as skilled traders and scouts. The Delawares' diplomacy helped to bring the Comanches to a treaty council in 1844.

After Texas was annexed to the United States in 1845, the Delawares continued to play important roles as scouts, diplomats, and interpreters for the United States Army and the Indian Bureau. John Conner helped guide the Chihuahua–El Paso expedition in 1848 and was compensated with a league of land, granted by special act of the Texas legislature in 1853. Jim Shaw helped John Meusebach qv settle his German community in the Hill Country qv in 1847 and continued to scout for military units on the West Texas frontier until his death in 1858. Black Beaver, a prominent Delaware chief, guided Randolph B. Marcy's qv map-making expeditions through West Texas in 1849, 1852, and 1854. In 1854 remnants of the Texas Delawares and other friendly tribes were moved to the Brazos Indian Reservation,qv established by the United States government on the Brazos River near the site of present Graham. But the Texas reservation system was short-lived. In 1859 the resident Indians were transplanted to a site on the Washita River in the vicinity of present Anadarko, Oklahoma. In 1874 the Anadarko Delawares decided to merge with the Caddos, while the main body of Delawares, transported to Indian Territory from Kansas in 1868, remained citizens of the Cherokee Nation. Both groups currently are represented by tribal business committees that meet respectively at Anadarko and Dewey, Oklahoma. Other significant groups of Delawares reside in Wisconsin, Kansas, and Ontario, Canada. The Delaware Nation, venerated by other American Indians as "the grandfather tribe," has survived a long journey.

BIBLIOGRAPHY: H. Allen Anderson, "The Delaware and Shawnee Indians and the Republic of Texas, 1820–1845," *Southwestern Historical Quarterly* 94 (October 1990). Rupert N. Richardson, "Jim Shaw the Delaware," West Texas Historical Association *Year Book* 3 (1927). C. A. Weslager, *The Delaware Indians: A History* (New Brunswick, New Jersey: Rutgers University Press, 1972). *Carol A. Lipscomb*

DELAWARE MOUNTAINS. The Delaware Mountains begin just south of Guadalupe Pass in northwestern Culberson County and stretch thirty-eight miles southeast (their center point is at 31°47′ N, 104°47′ W). The highest elevation in the Delawares is 5,632 feet above sea level. The mountains are characterized by long horizontal layers of sandstone, limestone, and shale, which were deposited in the sea at the edge of the Delaware Basin in Permian times, 250 million years ago. They and the Apache Mountains, to the south, are the uplifted eastern border of the salt flats in western Culberson County. The area's steep and rocky terrain is surfaced by shallow, stony soils that support live oak, piñon, juniper, and grasses. The mountains are named for the Delaware Indians.

DELAWARE RIVER. The Delaware River, also known as Delaware Creek, is an intermittent stream that rises in the Guadalupe Mountains National Park qv two miles west of Pine Springs and one mile east of Guadalupe Peak in northwestern Culberson County (at 31°54′ N, 104°51′ W) and runs northeast for seventy miles to its mouth on the Pecos River, just west of Red Bluff Reservoir in Eddy County, New Mexico (at 32°02′ N, 104°01′ W). Its tributaries include Wild Horse Draw. A number of early American explorers of Culberson County followed the Delaware River through the area, including Capt. Randolph Marcy in 1849 and John Russell Bartlett qqv in 1850. Beginning in 1858 the Butterfield Overland Mail qv followed the Delaware River across Culberson County en route to El Paso. The area is characterized by steep slopes surfaced by clay and sandy loams that support scrub brush and sparse grasses; some creosote bush and cacti occur along the river's lower reaches.

BIBLIOGRAPHY: Roscoe P. and Margaret B Conkling, *The Butterfield Overland Mail, 1857–1869* (3 vols., Glendale, California: Clark, 1947).

DELAWARE SPRINGS. Delaware Springs is a group of mineral springs located twenty miles east of the community of Pine Springs in northeastern Culberson County (at 31°52′ N, 104°29′ W). The surrounding terrain is mainly flat, with some locally steep slopes. Creosote bush, cacti, and sparse grasses grow in the shallow, stony soil of the area. These springs were of great importance to early travelers and were variously known as Head Springs, Five Springs, Ojo de San Martín, and La Cienega (the swamp). Capt. Francisco Amangual qv camped at the springs in 1808. Some of the springs are highly mineralized, and others are relatively fresh. In 1976 the springs produced sixteen liters per second.

BIBLIOGRAPHY: Gunnar Brune, *Springs of Texas,* Vol. 1 (Fort Worth: Branch-Smith, 1981).
Gunnar Brune

DELBA, TEXAS. Delba is on State Highway 78 five miles east of Leonard in southwestern Fannin County. It was formed in the mid-1870s when a Methodist church was established and a school opened. In 1879 postal service to the community began. By the mid-1880s Delba had fifty residents, a cotton gin, a steam flour mill, and nine businesses. Because of the decline in the community's population the post office closed in 1906. By the mid-1930s the population was reported at twenty-five, and by 1980 was reported at twenty, where it remained in 1990. In the early 1990s Delba served as a community center for area farmers.

BIBLIOGRAPHY: W. A. Carter, *History of Fannin County, Texas* (Bonham, Texas: Bonham *News,* 1885; rpt., Honey Grove, Texas: Fannin County Historical Society, 1975). *Fannin County Folks and Facts* (Dallas: Taylor, 1977).
David Minor

DE LEÓN, ALONSO (ca. 1639–1691). Alonso De León, the younger, Spanish explorer and governor, third son of Alonso De León and Josefa González, was born in Cadereyta, Nuevo León, in 1639 or 1640. At the age of ten he was sent to Spain, where he enrolled in school and prepared for a naval career. He joined the Spanish navy in 1657, but his service as a naval cadet was brief, for he had returned to Nuevo León by 1660. Over the next two decades he led a series of entradas that traversed the northeast coast of New Spain as well as the banks of the Río de San Juan. By the 1680s De León had become a seasoned outdoorsman and successful entrepreneur. In 1682 he petitioned the viceroy of New Spain for a franchise to work salt deposits along the Río de San Juan, open trade with neighboring settlements, and search for mines. Those efforts netted a fifteen year concession. When news that the French had founded a settlement on the northern Gulf Coast reached New Spain in the mid-1680s, De León was a logical choice to lead overland efforts aimed at finding the foreign interlopers and extirpating their colony.

In all, he led four expeditions between 1686 and 1689. His initial reconnaissance followed the Río de San Juan to its confluence with the Rio Grande. After striking the larger river, Don Alonso marched along the right bank to the coast and then turned southward toward the Río de las Palmas (the Río Soto la Marina). This effort yielded no conclusive evidence that Frenchmen had visited the region. His second expedition set out in February 1687. This entrada forded the Rio Grande, probably near the site of present Roma–Los Saenz, and followed the left bank to the coast. De León then marched up the Texas coast to the environs of Baffin Bay but again found no evidence of Frenchmen. The third expedition, launched in May 1688, was in response to news that a white man dwelled among Indians in a ranchería (temporary settlement) to the north of the Rio Grande. That effort resulted in the capture of Jean Jarry,qv a naked, aged, and confused Frenchman. The fourth expedition left Coahuila on March 27, 1689, with a force of 114 men, including chaplain Damián Massanet,qv soldiers, servants, muleteers, and the French prisoner, Jarry. On April 22 De León and his party discovered the ruins of the French settlement, Fort St. Louis,qv on the banks of Garcitas Creek.

In 1689 De León became governor of Coahuila. In the following year he and Massanet cooperated in founding the first Spanish mission in East Texas, San Francisco de los Tejas, at a site in the environs of present Augusta, Texas. De León, an honest soldier and an early pathfinder in Spanish Texas,qv left the future Lone Star State for the last time in July 1690. He is credited with being an early advocate for the establishment of missions along the frontier, and he blazed much of the Old San Antonio Roadqv on his expeditions. He returned to Coahuila and died there on March 20, 1691. His survivors included his wife, Agustina Cantú, four sons, and two daughters. His descendants still reside in the Mexican state of Nuevo León.

BIBLIOGRAPHY: Herbert Eugene Bolton, ed., *Spanish Exploration in the Southwest, 1542–1706* (New York: Scribner, 1908; rpt., New York: Barnes and Noble, 1959). Robert S. Weddle, *The French Thorn: Rival Explorers in the Spanish Sea, 1682–1762* (College Station: Texas A&M University Press, 1991). Robert S. Weddle, *Wilderness Manhunt: The Spanish Search for La Salle* (Austin: University of Texas Press, 1973).
Donald E. Chipman

DE LEÓN, FERNANDO (1798–1853). Fernando De León, colonization manager of De León's colonyqv and patriot leader in the Texas Revolution,qv the eldest child of Martín and Patricia De León,qqv was born on his father's ranch in Cruillas, Nuevo Santander (now Tamaulipas) in 1798; he was the only De León child born in Mexico. By the time Martín De León petitioned the Mexican government in 1824 to settle forty-one Mexican families on the lower Guadalupe River, Fernando had married María Antonia Galván and had a son. The government of Coahuila and Texasqv appointed him commissioner in charge of distributing land and issuing titles to the colonists introduced by his father; he employed as his secretary Plácido Benavides.qv De León was one of the ten principal citizens honored by the name of Guadalupe Victoria's main street, Calle de los Diez Amigos. He settled on his Rancho Escondido, located seven miles north of town on the Guadalupe River, on which were ruins of the presidio that once protected Nuestra Señora del Espíritu Santo de Zúñiga Mission. Legend tells of the padres hiding church valuables when Indians forced them to abandon the site; the treasure was *escondido* ("hidden"). Appropriately, De León's ranch was the hiding place of many colonists during Indian raids and of John J. Linn'sqv family during the Texas Revolution.qv María De León's death was the first in the colony, and her son also died while at college in Louisiana. Don Fernando later married Luz Escalera and adopted the two sons of his brother Silvestre De Leónqv when the latter was assassinated in 1842. Fernando assumed the responsibilities of his father upon the death of Martín De León in 1833.

Like other members of the De León family, Fernando took up the Texan cause against Antonio López de Santa Anna.qv In November 1835 he joined his brother-in-law José M. J. Carbajal and Austin colonist Peter Kerrqqv in driving to New Orleans a large herd of livestock, which they exchanged for $35,000 worth of munitions and provisions intended for the colony and the Texas army. The men chartered the schooner *Hanna Elizabeth* but were intercepted by a Mexican brig and arrested. De León and Carbajal were imprisoned at Brazos de Santiago and later Matamoros until they managed to escape. Although evidence suggests that the supplies still reached the Texans after the patriot ship *William Robbins* (*Liberty*qv) recaptured the *Hanna Elizabeth,* the three men were never recompensed for their loss.

After his return to Guadalupe Victoria, De León was appointed in February 1836 as aide-de-camp to acting governor James W. Robinson.qv He assumed command of the local militia as well as the responsibility for provisioning, arming, and "all other things necessary for the support of the army and the protection and the defense of Texas." Although he was ordered to Gonzales, De León was among the first arrested when Gen. José de Urreaqv occupied Guadalupe Victoria after the battle of Coleto.qv He was forced to reveal the location of stores of corn, beef, and horses hidden in a ravine at Dimitt's Landing,qv an act that underlay later charges of disloyalty to Texas. After the Texan victory at San Jacinto, Urrea released De León only upon his promise to expatriate himself and his brothers and return with the retreating army to Mexico, a promise soon renounced. De León was again arrested on charges of treason, however, when the Texas army under Gen. Thomas Jefferson Ruskqv liberated Guadalupe Victoria. While in custody he was wounded in an assassination attempt, an act reflecting the bitterness of many Anglo-Americans whose creed, according to John J. Linn, "was the total extermination of the Mexican race and the appropriation of their property to the individual use of the exterminators." Though released without trial De León was ostracized and forced to flee with the Carbajal, Benavides, and De León families to Louisiana, abandoning property and possessions valued at hundreds of thousands of dollars. They lived in poverty in New Orleans for about three years before moving to Mexico. Ironically, the De León family was cited as delinquent in paying their 1840 property taxes, over $1,820, to the Republic of Texas.qv

De León returned about 1844 to reclaim his property and was involved in lawsuits until his death. After recovering only a portion of his ranch and amassing but a few hundred head of cattle, he died at Rancho Escondido in 1853. Francisco Santiago De León, one of his adopted sons, who returned to Mexico about 1852, became the governor of Tamaulipas in 1862 and was assassinated.

BIBLIOGRAPHY: Joe Tom Davis, *Legendary Texians* (3 vols., Austin: Eakin Press, 1982–86). A. B. J. Hammett, *The Empresario Don Martín de León* (Waco: Texian Press, 1973). John J. Linn, *Reminiscences of Fifty Years in Texas* (New York: Sadlier, 1883; 2d ed., Austin: Steck, 1935; rpt., Austin: State House, 1986). Victor Marion Rose, *History of Victoria* (Laredo, 1883; rpt., Victoria, Texas: Book Mart, 1961).

Craig H. Roell

DE LEÓN, MARTÍN (1765–1833). Martín De León, the only Mexican empresarioqv to found a colony in Texas, was born in 1765 in Burgos, Nuevo Santander (now Tamaulipas), where his parents, Bernardo and María Galván De León, settled after moving from Burgos, Spain. The De Leóns were an aristocratic family of great wealth; members were educated in Madrid, Paris, and London and were acquainted with European rulers. Martín, however, declined his father's offer to complete his education in Monterrey and Europe, choosing instead to become a merchant and supplier of provisions to the miners of Real de San Nicolás. In 1790 he joined the Fieles de Burgos regiment, organized by Mexican viceroy Juan Vicente Guernes Pacheco as a defense against Indians in Nuevo Santander. De León was promoted to captain, thus achieving the highest rank available to a criollo.qv In 1795 he married Patricia de la Garza, daughter of Gen. Felipe de la Garza, commandant of the Eastern Internal Provinces. The couple settled in Cruillas, Nuevo Santander (now Tamaulipas), where they began ranching. An excursion to La Bahía, San Antonio, and Nacogdoches in 1805 induced De León to settle in Texas. He established a ranch between Chiltipin Creek and the Aransas River, stocked it with cattle, horses, mules, and goats that he brought from Mexico, and enclosed several leagues of land with a brush fence in an effort to corral and domesticate mustangs.qv

In 1807 De León petitioned the Spanish governor at San Antonio, Manuel María de Salcedo,qv to establish a colony in this vicinity. The government, however, denied this request as well as a second one in 1809, as a result of rising political troubles in Mexico and rumors that the De Leóns were not loyal to Spain. De León then established a new ranch on the east bank of the Nueces River near the site of present San Patricio, where he enclosed another pasture. He had by this time driven several herds of livestock to market at New Orleans, thus becoming one of the earliest traildrivers in Texas. Texas presidio garrisons were moved as a result of the uprising in September 1810 of Father Miguel Hidalgo y Costilla.qv Because the frontier then became vulnerable to hostile Lipans and Comanches, De León removed his family to the safety of San Antonio, where he joined the Republicans in resisting the Royalists under Joaquín de Arredondo and Ignacio Elizondo.qqv After a respite in Burgos in 1816 De León returned to his ranch and cattle, now numbering about 5,000 head. In 1823 he drove a large herd of livestock to New Orleans and became interested in settling a colony on the lower Guadalupe River.

Mexican independence from Spain brought a more open colonization policy. On April 8, 1824, De León petitioned the provincial delegation at San Fernando de Béxar to settle forty-one Mexican families on the lower Guadalupe and founded the town of Nuestra Señora Guadalupe de Jesús Victoria. The colonization grant was approved on April 13. Patricia De Leónqv contributed $9,800 and cows, horses, and mules valued at $300, which she inherited from her father. De León's colonyqv was the only predominantly Mexican colony in Texas, and as a Mexican citizen the empresario received legal preference in the numerous border disputes with American settlements encircling Guadalupe Victoria.

De León stood six feet tall and was skilled as a horseman and Indian fighter; Indians called him "Capitán Vacas Muchas" ("Captain Plenty of Cows") since he often placated raiding parties by feeding them beef. His five-league (22,140-acre) ranch was located on Garcitas Creek in what is now southeastern Victoria County and probably included the site of La Salle'sqv Fort St. Louis. His thousands of cattle carried the first brand in Texas, an E and J connected, signifying "Espíritu de Jesús." De León registered the historic brand in 1807; Jesuitsqv had used it for hundreds of years before the royal De León family in Spain adopted it. De León's ranchland, though considerably less extensive than that of later cattlemen, provided a foundation for one of the characteristic industries of Texas. As a devout Catholic, De León was planning to build a church without rival in Texas when he became a victim of the cholera epidemic of 1833 and died, leaving his widow, four sons, and six daughters an estate of over a half million dollars.

In addition to dominating Guadalupe Victoria, the family of Martín De León controlled the ayuntamientoqv of Goliad; sons-in-law José Miguel Aldrete and Rafael Mancholaqqv each served as alcalde,qv and Manchola was also commandant of the La Bahía garrison. The family was intimately involved with the Texas cause against Antonio López de Santa Annaqv as well. Gen. José M. J. Carbajal and Capt. Plácido Benavidesqqv were sons-in-law of De León. Martín's sons, Fernando, Silvestre,qqv Felix, and Agapito De León, contributed horses, mules, cattle, military equipment, and provisions to the Texas army and offered the safety of their ranches to colonists needing refuge. Not surprisingly, the Mexican army of occupation under Gen. José de Urreaqv singled out the De León family as traitors; Fernando and Silvestre were arrested.

After the Texas victory at San Jacinto, the De Leóns fell victim to the prejudice directed against Texans of Mexican descent. Agapito was murdered by Mabry B. (Mustang) Gray,qv who was rustling De León cattle. Fernando was wounded in a similar affray. The De León, Benavides, and Carbajal families were forced to abandon their lands, cattle, and most possessions and flee to Louisiana for their lives. The De Leóns remained in New Orleans for about three years before removing to Soto la Marina (now in Tamaulipas), the childhood home of Patricia de la Garza De León, where her daughter, Agustina De León Benavides, died in 1841. Soon thereafter, Patricia and her family returned to Texas to recover their property, but they were largely unsuccessful. In April 1972 the De Leóns were honored with Texas state historical markers in Evergreen Cemetery, Victoria. Among the dignitaries attending the dedication were Patricia De León, great-granddaughter of the empresario, and Dr. Ricardo Victoria of Mexico, great-grandson of President Guadalupe Victoria, for whom Victoria, Texas, is named.

BIBLIOGRAPHY: Joe Tom Davis, *Legendary Texians* (3 vols., Austin: Eakin Press, 1982–86). A. B. J. Hammett, *The Empresario Don Martín de León* (Waco: Texian Press, 1973). Victor Marion Rose, *History of Victoria* (Laredo, 1883; rpt., Victoria, Texas: Book Mart, 1961).

Craig H. Roell

DE LEÓN, PATRICIA DE LA GARZA (1775–1849). Patricia de la Garza De León, early settler, who with her husband, empresarioqv Martín De León,qv developed the city of Victoria, was born in Soto la Marina, Nuevo Santander (now Tamaulipas), Mexico, in 1775. Her father, Felipe de la Garza, served as commandant for the Spanish government. In 1795 Patricia and Martín were married, and they started a ranch near Cruillas, Nuevo Santander. Between 1798 and

1818 Doña De León gave birth to ten children. In 1805 the De Leóns moved to the east bank of the Aransas River, north of Corpus Christi. They moved several more times before 1824, when they were granted land by the newly independent Mexican government. Using money they had earned from the sale of livestock and the $9,800 Patricia inherited from her father, they established a colony on the bank of the Guadalupe River in Southwest Texas. Martín named the settlement Guadalupe Victoria in honor of the first president of Mexico; it was the only predominantly Mexican colony in Texas.

Life in frontier Texas was very different from the life Patricia had lived in Mexico. She was forty-seven years old when she settled in Victoria, where she lived in a house of hand-hewn logs with a dirt floor. Although her new home was simple, she placed fine furniture in it and kept servants. While Martín worked to bring financial success to the community, Patricia attempted to transplant to Texas some of the cultural traditions of Spain and Mexico. She saw that a school was established immediately after she arrived in Victoria. She also helped found a church, Nuestra Señora de Guadalupe, to which she donated money and furnishings. As the family's wealth increased she imported fine furniture and clothes and sent her children and grandchildren to Europe and Mexico to be educated. She and her daughters became known for their excellent embroidery skills and fine clothing. The De León home was described as among the most beautifully furnished in the area, and it became the center for community gatherings. Shortly before her death Madame De León donated the original homestead to the Catholic Church[qv] as the site for a new church building.

After Martín died of cholera in 1833, Patricia managed the family's property and continued to work for the community. She and her family supported the idea of an independent Texas and smuggled arms and ammunition from New Orleans to the Texans. Despite their support of the Texans, however, the De Leóns were victims of the anti-Mexican sentiment that swept through Texas after the Texas Revolution.[qv] Her youngest son was murdered by cattle thieves. The family fled to Louisiana, where they lived in poverty, and then to Soto la Marina. In 1837 Patricia sold 25,000 acres of Victoria County land on Garcitas Creek for $10,000. When she returned to Texas in 1844 she found her possessions scattered among newcomers, and she no longer held an influential position in the town. She resumed her work with the church and until her death lived as an ordinary parishioner. She died at Victoria in 1849, after devoting much time to the church her husband founded. Her homesite, donated to the parish at her death, is the site of the present St. Mary's Catholic Church, to which she also contributed altar vessels, including a gold monstrance. The state of Texas recognized the contributions of the De Leóns by dedicating historical grave markers to them in Evergreen Cemetery, Victoria, on April 8, 1972.

BIBLIOGRAPHY: Joe Tom Davis, *Legendary Texians* (3 vols., Austin: Eakin Press, 1982–86). A. B. J. Hammett, *The Empresario Don Martín de León* (Waco: Texian Press, 1973). Myrtle Murray, "Home Life on Early Ranches of Southwest Texas: Martín de León, Victoria County," *Cattleman*, June 1939. Victor Marion Rose, *History of Victoria* (Laredo, 1883; rpt., Victoria, Texas: Book Mart, 1961). Janelle D. Scott, Patricia de la Garza de León: Pioneer Woman from Mexico (MS, Blagg-Huey Library, Texas Woman's University).
Paula Stewart

DE LEÓN, SILVESTRE (1802–1842). Silvestre De León, one of the founders of De León's colony[qv] and the city of Guadalupe Victoria, was born in 1802 in Texas, the second son of Martín and Patricia De León.[qqv] He was a chief merchant in the colony and one of the ten principal citizens referred to by the name of the town's main street, Calle de los Diez Amigos. He served as third alcalde[qv] and with his brother-in-law Plácido Benavides[qv] was a captain of the militia defense against hostile Karankawas, Tonkawas, and Comanches. The first Christian births recorded in the colony were those of the children of Silvestre and Rosalie de la Garza De León. The couple settled on a league of land on the Guadalupe River near the site of present Nursery, Texas, and received their grant from the Mexican government on April 2, 1833.

Silvestre joined his brother Fernando De León,[qv] brothers-in-law Plácido Benavides and José M. J. Carbajal,[qqv] and John J. Linn[qv] in gathering local support for the Texas revolt against Antonio López de Santa Anna.[qv] De León contributed provisions, livestock, and military equipment to the Texas army and joined Benavides's company of thirty Mexican rancheros who participated in the siege of Bexar[qv] in December 1835. He also was elected with John J. Linn and Juan Antonio Padilla[qv] to the Consultation[qv] of 1835 but probably never arrived at either Columbia or San Felipe because of his service in the Texas army. Upon the occupation of Guadalupe Victoria by Gen. José de Urrea,[qv] De León was arrested by the Mexican army as a traitor; he was released after the Texan victory at San Jacinto but then fell victim to the severe prejudice directed against all Texans of Mexican descent. Forced to flee with the De León, Carbajal, and Benavides families to Louisiana, he lost his land, livestock, and most possessions to fortune hunters, though he later resettled in Victoria County. While returning from selling horses, mules, and cattle in Louisiana he was ambushed, murdered, and robbed in 1842 under still mysterious circumstances.

BIBLIOGRAPHY: Joe Tom Davis, *Legendary Texians* (3 vols., Austin: Eakin Press, 1982–86). Roy Grimes, ed., *300 Years in Victoria County* (Victoria, Texas: Victoria *Advocate*, 1968; rpt., Austin: Nortex, 1985). A. B. J. Hammett, *The Empresario Don Martín de León* (Waco: Texian Press, 1973). Texas House of Representatives, *Biographical Directory of the Texan Conventions and Congresses, 1832–1845* (Austin: Book Exchange, 1941).
Craig H. Roell

DE LEON, TEXAS. De Leon is at the intersection of State highways 6 and 16, in northeast Comanche County. The Leon River is three miles northeast of town and flows into the headwaters of Proctor Lake, a United States Corps of Engineers reservoir, which is a source of water supply and a center of recreation. In this part of the Western Cross Timbers the natural vegetation includes post oak, mesquite, and prairie grass. The first town lots in De Leon were sold on July 7, 1881, by officials of the Texas Central Railroad. The sale, conducted from a flatcar, was attended by about 100 people. The townsite in August of that year comprised thirty-three blocks covered with trees and brush. A post office was established in 1881 and named De Leon (pronounced "Dee Leeáhn" by residents). It was probably named for the Leon River, which was named by Spanish explorers in 1721 in honor of Alonso De León,[qv] who had established settlements in East Texas.

With the expansion of the railroad west from Waco came the settlers from several southern states. They came to grow cotton and raise cattle. A few businesses were opened, such as a general store and a commissary for the railroad. In May 1874 John Wesley Hardin[qv] shot and killed deputy sheriff Charlie Webb. This eventually led to Hardin's arrest and imprisonment. The first physician came in 1882, and the first newspaper, the De Leon *Messenger*, was published in 1882. In 1886 racial tension mounted, and after a young black man, Tom McNeal, was lynched for murdering a white women, Sally Stephens, a sign was posted in De Leon warning blacks to leave. As late as 1942 no blacks lived in Comanche County; in 1970 only two were reported. The first two people buried in the cemetery west of town were Rev. and Mrs. Cyrus Campbell. Reverend Campbell was paid five dollars by the Republic of Texas[qv] to construct the leg irons used on Antonio López de Santa Anna[qv] after his capture at San Jacinto.

In 1906 the boll weevil[qv] came to the area, and the primary cash crop changed from cotton to peanuts. One carload of peanuts was produced in 1907. By 1914 a peanut mill had been built, and 500 carloads brought sixty cents a bushel. By 1915 De Leon had a population of 1,015, two churches, two banks, four cotton gins, and numerous small businesses. In 1929 peanuts sold for $1.20 a bushel. The cultivation and marketing of peanuts changed when irrigation was introduced in 1949 and artificial drying started in 1950. The crop then could be handled in bulk rather than in sacks. Peanuts continue to be the leading crop, but pecans, peaches, and melons bring in a large agricultural income. The discovery of oil led to an oil plant with storage tanks and refinery equipment. There was also a nitroglycerin plant with its own railway siding called Torpedo Junction. Both plants died with the end of the oil boom.

An annual Peach and Melon Festival is held in De Leon the first week of August. The celebration started in 1914 and features a De Leon High School reunion, free melon slicing, and the crowning of a festival queen. The event was attended by 32,000 people in 1983. The railroad ceased operation in 1967. In 1990 the town had two peanut mills, a feed processing plant, and a pump manufacturing facility with a worldwide market. The population was 2,190.

BIBLIOGRAPHY: Comanche County Bicentennial Committee, *Patchwork of Memories: Historical Sketches of Comanche County, Texas* (Brownwood, Texas: Banner Printing, 1976). De Leon *Free Press,* June 28, 1929. Joe B. Frantz et al., *Texas and Its History* (Dallas: Pepper Jones Martinez, 1978). B. B. Lightfoot, "The Negro Exodus from Comanche County, Texas," *Southwestern Historical Quarterly* 56 (January 1953). *A Pictorial History of De Leon* (De Leon, Texas: De Leon *Free Press,* 1981). Eulalia Nabers Wells, *Blazing the Way: Tales of Comanche County Pioneers* (Blanket, Texas, 1942).

Frances Elizabeth Morris

DE LEÓN'S COLONY. De León's colony, the only predominantly Mexican colony in Texas, was established in 1824 by Martín De León,qv who petitioned the provincial delegation of San Fernando de Béxar on April 8, 1824, for permission to settle forty-one Mexican families "of good moral character" and to found the town of Nuestra Señora de Guadalupe de Jesús Victoria at an unspecified point on the lower Guadalupe River. As a prominent Mexican citizen, De León was given wider latitude than was allowed foreign empresarios. His settlement contract, approved on April 13, before the passage of restrictive colonization laws, specified neither time limitations, number of families, nor boundaries. His colonists were exempt for seven years from duties on everything except tobacco and from the customary excises and tithes on firstfruits for ten years. By October 1824 De León and twelve families had settled on the Guadalupe River at El Sabinal (Cypress Grove), thought to be the site where the river was discovered by Alonso De León,qv who had named the stream in 1689. The remaining twenty-nine families were delayed in what is now Tamaulipas, Mexico, by drought, then flood, but arrived the following spring. Not all the colonists were Mexicans. A few Anglo settlers such as Margaret R. Wrightqv were already living in the area, and a number of Irish immigrants, headed by John J. Linn,qv arrived soon thereafter, bringing to sixteen the number of non-Mexican families. Each settler received a town lot, plus one league (4,228 acres) of grazing land and one labor (177 acres) of arable land. The empresarioqv received five leagues upon the settlement of the forty-one families. The government issued these grants between 1833 and 1835.

De León named his settlement Guadalupe Victoria, after the first president of the Republic of Mexico. José M. J. Carbajal,qv De León's son-in-law and surveyor-engineer of the colony, platted the town, and the empresario designated the main street Calle de los Diez Amigos, implying the unity of the "Ten Friends" who, as principal citizens, were entrusted with the colony's welfare. Besides Martín De León, the first alcalde,qv the ten included three of his sons-in-law; Carbajal; Plácido Benavides,qv militia captain and second alcalde; and Rafael Manchola,qv attorney and commandant of La Bahía.qv Two of Martín De León's sons were also among the ten: first commissioner Fernando De León,qv who administered the colonization program, and his brother Silvestre De León,qv a chief merchant, militia captain, and third alcalde. The colonists settled on the Guadalupe and Lavaca rivers and Coleto, Garcitas, Arenosa, and Zorillo (Placido) creeks. The devout De León brought in priests alternately from La Bahía, Nacogdoches, and San Antonio until a church was established and a resident priest secured. A school and fort were soon built, a militia organized, and a courier service established with the Austin colony.

De León, a cultured Mexican aristocrat, was openly scornful of Americans. Clashes with bordering colonies were inevitable, especially since the De León colony boundaries were undefined, the empresario resented encirclement by Anglo-American colonists, and the colonization laws favored Mexicans. Also, De León had not yet notified authorities of exactly where he had established Guadalupe Victoria. Consequently, the legislature of Coahuila and Texasqv inadvertently included the De León colony within the boundaries of the grant made to Green DeWittqv in April 1825. A clash resulted when DeWitt's colony was established at Old Station,qv near the mouth of the Lavaca River, in 1825. As a Mexican citizen De León received preference in the ensuing legal battle, settled on October 6, 1825; DeWitt's contract required him to respect the rights of those already settled in his designated area. Relations further deteriorated in October 1826. The schooner *Escambia* arrived at the mouth of the Lavaca with merchandise for trade, which included contraband tobacco. Upon discovering the infraction the political chief at San Antonio ordered De León, with the aid of Manchola's La Bahía garrison, to seize the contraband. It was rumored that De León was allying with Indians to "cut off the white people as far as the Colorado," and that he intended also to cut off DeWitt's head and tie it to his saddle. With little incident, however, De León and Manchola seized the contraband along with the colonists' guns and removed DeWitt to La Bahía for trial. Apparently Stephen F. Austin'sqv intervention finally quieted the matter. In August 1827 the government ordered DeWitt to abandon Old Station because of its easy access to smuggled goods. Most colonists returned to Gonzales, while hatred increasingly characterized the De León–DeWitt relationship, despite an important treaty with the Karankawas negotiated in 1827 by De León, DeWitt, and Jacob Bettsqv of Austin's colony.

That same year the Mexican empresario petitioned the government to designate the boundaries of his colony, which were declared in 1828 to be Matagorda Bay on the south, Mission Valley on the north, the Lavaca River on the east, and Coleto Creek on the west. Yet, a border dispute erupted with the Power and Hewetson colonyqv to the south in 1828 and another with DeWitt in 1830. In 1829 De León had received permission to bring in an additional 150 families and to augment his territory. With the help of the ayuntamientoqv of Goliad he petitioned the government to annul the Power and Hewetson contract. The next year he forcibly tried to remove twenty-five DeWitt families from the newly designated area. This time, however, the government ruled that De León was encroaching, refused to nullify the Power-Hewetson contract, and annulled De León's boundary augmentation. In 1831, however, DeWitt's grant expired and extension was refused. De León was therefore free to colonize vacant lands in DeWitt's old grant. After much dispute the government ruled in May 1832 in favor of the De León colonists; preference was given to Mexicans wherever they occupied land. Although Martín De León died in the cholera epidemic of 1833, more than 100 titles were given to his colonists by July 1835, making him the only empresario besides Austin who completely fulfilled his contract. The De León colony comprised all of present Victoria and Calhoun counties and extended into Lavaca, Jackson, and DeWitt counties as well. Settlers farmed and raised horses and cattle. The estimated wealth of the colony at the empresario's death was over $1 million.

The De León family were ardent Federalists and supported the revolution against Antonio López de Santa Anna.qv Many citizens of Guadalupe Victoria, notably John J. Linn, Juan Antonio Padilla,qv José M. J. Carbajal, Plácido Benavides, and Fernando De León, participated in the Consultation of 1835 and the Convention of 1836,qqv served with the revolutionary army,qv or otherwise aided the Texas cause. Since most were Mexican citizens of Spanish descent, however, Santa Anna considered them traitors, and they suffered severely during the occupation by Gen. José de Urrea's qv forces after the battle of Coleto.qv After the Texas victory at San Jacinto they also suffered the ire of incoming Anglo-Americans, many of whom were fortune hunters and soldiers, who branded them as Mexican sympathizers. The De León family was particularly ostracized and forced to flee to Louisiana and Mexico, their lands and livestock taken by those Linn called "remorseless Gaels of the nineteenth century." The Mexican municipality of Guadalupe Victoria became an English-speaking town, with a new government under the Republic of Texas,qv and Linn, the last alcalde, was elected first mayor. A population of about 300 grew rapidly as American, German, and other immigrants settled in Victoria. Many descendants of the original colonists still live in the town or surrounding counties, some on portions of their forefathers' land grants.

BIBLIOGRAPHY: Joe Tom Davis, *Legendary Texians* (3 vols., Austin: Eakin Press, 1982–86). Roy Grimes, ed., *300 Years in Victoria County* (Victoria, Texas: Victoria *Advocate,* 1968; rpt., Austin: Nortex, 1985). A. B. J. Hammett, *The Empresario Don Martín de León* (Waco: Texian Press, 1973). Mary Virginia Henderson, "Minor Empresario Contracts for the Colonization of Texas, 1825–1834," *Southwestern Historical Quarterly* 31, 32 (April, July 1928).
Craig H. Roell

DELFINA, TEXAS. Delfina was on U.S. 281 thirty-six miles northeast of McAllen in northern Hidalgo County. Macedonia Vela operated a store in the community as early as 1900. By 1904 Delfina had a population of 121. In 1938 it had three houses and one business, and in 1941 the population was estimated at fifty. In 1947 the last recorded estimates for Delfina were twenty-five residents and one business. After 1948 the town did not appear on maps.
Alicia A. Garza

DELGADO, ANTONIO (?–?). Antonio Delgado, a lieutenant in the forces of the Gutiérrez-Magee expedition,qv removed Manuel María de Salcedo,qv Spanish governor of Texas, and members of his staff from prison under pretense of escorting them to Matagorda Bay, where they would be placed on board vessels bound for New Orleans. On April 5, 1813, a mile south of San Antonio Delgado and his troops murdered the prisoners. Delgado was brought to trial for the murder of the prisoners of war by the Anglo-American officers of the expedition and defended his action on the grounds that Salcedo had murdered his father for participation in the rebellion of 1811 and that he had acted with the permission of José Bernardo Gutiérrez de Lara.qv Delgado's actions resulted in the removal of Gutiérrez from command and the departure of many Anglo-Americans, among them Samuel Kemper,qv who had commanded the Americans after the death of Augustus W. Magee.qv

BIBLIOGRAPHY: Julia Kathryn Garrett, *Green Flag Over Texas: A Story of the Last Years of Spain in Texas* (Austin: Pemberton Press, 1939). George Pierce Garrison, *Texas: A Contest of Civilization* (Boston: Houghton Mifflin, 1903). Dudley Goodall Wooten, ed., *A Comprehensive History of Texas* (2 vols., Dallas: Scarff, 1898; rpt., Austin: Texas State Historical Association, 1986).

DELGADO, MIGUEL (ca. 1775–1835). Miguel Delgado, also known as José Miguel Delgado and as Miguel Moya y Delgado, early South Texas rancher, the son of Manuel Delgado and Angela de Arocha, was born around 1775 in San Fernando de Béxar (now San Antonio, Texas). He was a descendant of one of the Canary Islandersqv who helped found San Fernando de Béxar, and he lived there with his parents and brothers. During the early 1800s Delgado established the San Pedro Ranch in the Goliad jurisdiction, in an area where Antonio Montreal and others were living. By 1809 Delgado had petitioned the Spanish government for this land, stating that he had 1,066 head of beef, cattle, sheep, and horses, and needed four sitiosqv in the district known as Nombre de Dios, twenty-five leagues south of San Antonio de Béxar. He also stated that this parcel of land was bounded on the north by public lands, on the west by lands claimed by Antonio Montreal, on the south by the Nueces River, and on the east by lands of Martín De León.qv Later in 1809 Delgado is listed as married to María de Jesús de la Garza and living on his new Rancho de San Miguel de Buena Virtud on the banks of the Nueces River. According to a ranch report of November 10, 1810, Delgado's six children lived at the ranch, as well as his brothers, Francisco and Manuel, and their families. In 1810 or 1811, however, Delgado was reported as married to María Juana de la Garza and had moved his headquarters to a new location on the Nueces River in the jurisdiction of La Bahía del Espíritu Santo Presidio (Goliad, Texas). His new ranch, Delgado's Rancho, which was also known as San Miguel de Buena Vista, had grown from an original group of eleven people in 1809 to a group of twenty-four residents by 1811. He received title to the land as a "prominent and respected citizen" with his three sons, Juan, Pedro and Nepomuceno, under the McMullen and McGloin empresarioqv grant (*see* MCMULLEN-MCGLOIN COLONY) on November 26, 1831. By 1828 Delgado and his son Pedro had moved to Nacogdoches to live near his sister, Candida Delgado, wife of Encarnación Chirino, and her son, José María Chirino. On April 23, 1835, his sister Candida administered Delgado's will. Immediately after the Texas Revolutionqv Walter Henry obtained the four sitios of land, called the Delgado Grant. Henry in turn sold the four leagues of the Delgado survey for a dollar an acre to the Coleman, Mathis, Fulton Cattle Company (*see* COLEMAN-FULTON PASTURE COMPANY). The city of Mathis lies in the heart of this survey. In 1974, some of Delgado's descendents formed the Moya Association of Texas, a nonprofit family genealogical-historical association, honoring their ancestors' contributions to Texas history. Some Delgado descendents continued to live in the area in the early 1990s.

BIBLIOGRAPHY: Adán Benavides, Jr., comp. and ed., *The Béxar Archives, 1717–1836: A Name Guide* (Austin: University of Texas Press, 1989). Rachel Bluntzer Hébert, *The Forgotten Colony: San Patricio de Hibernia* (Burnet, Texas: Eakin Press, 1981). Jack Jackson, *Los Mesteños: Spanish Ranching in Texas, 1721–1821* (College Station: Texas A&M University Press, 1986). Nacogdoches Archives, Steen Library, Stephen F. Austin State University; Barker Texas History Center, University of Texas at Austin; Texas State Archives, Austin.
Gloria Candelaria Marsh

DELGADO V. BASTROP ISD. Until the late 1940s the public education system in Texas for Mexican Americans offered segregated campuses with often minimal facilities and a curriculum frequently limited to vocational training. The 1950 United States census showed that the median educational attainment for persons over twenty-five was 3.5 years for those with Spanish surnames and, by comparison, 10.3 years for other white Americans; about 27 percent of persons over twenty-five with Spanish surnames had received no schooling at all. No substantive legal suit had been initiated since *Del Rio ISD* v. *Salvatierra*qv (1930), in which Mexican Americans claimed they had been denied use of facilities used by "other white races" in the same school. In 1948 the League of United Latin American Citizens,qv joined by the American G.I. Forum of Texas,qv successfully challenged these inequities of the Texas public school system in *Delgado* v. *Bastrop ISD*.

In 1947 the Ninth Circuit Court in California found that separation "within one of the great races" without a specific state law requiring the separation was not permitted; therefore, segregation of Mexican-American children, who were considered Caucasian, was illegal. In Texas, following this ruling, the attorney general, in response to an inquiry by Gustavo C. (Gus) Garcia,qv a Mexican-American attorney, agreed that segregation of Mexican-American children in the public school system by national origin was unlawful and pedagogically justified only by scientific language tests applied to all students.

On June 15, 1948, LULAC (with Garcia as attorney) filed suit against the Bastrop Independent School District and three other districts. Representing Minerva Delgado and twenty other Mexican-American parents, the suit charged segregation of Mexican children from other white races without specific state law and in violation of the attorney general's opinion. In addition the suit accused these districts of depriving such children of equal facilities, services, and education instruction. Judge Ben H. Rice of the United States District Court, Western District of Texas, agreed and ordered the cessation of this separation by September 1949. However, the court did allow separate classes on the same campus, in the first grade only, for language-deficient or non-English-speaking students as identified by scientific and standardized tests applied to all.

The Delgado decision undermined the rigid segregation of Mexican Americans and began a ten-year struggle led by the American G.I. Forum and LULAC, which culminated in 1957 with the decision in *Herminca Hernandez et al. v. Driscoll Consolidated ISD,* which ended pedagogical and de jure segregation in the Texas public school system.

BIBLIOGRAPHY: Carl Allsup, *The American G.I. Forum: Origins and Evolution* (University of Texas Center for Mexican American Studies Monograph 6, Austin, 1982). Mario T. García, *Desert Immigrants: The Mexicans of El Paso, 1880–1920* (New Haven: Yale University Press, 1981). Joan Moore, *Mexican Americans* (Englewood Cliffs, New Jersey: Prentice Hall, 1970).
V. Carl Allsup

DELHI, TEXAS. Delhi is on Farm Road 304 nineteen miles southeast of Lockhart in eastern Caldwell County. The fine sandy loam soils in the area have made it ideal for agriculture and livestock raising. From 1873 to 1929 Delhi had a post office. In 1880 a Primitive Baptist church was established there and a year later a permanent cemetery. In 1884 Delhi reported a population of 150, two gristmills, two cotton gins, and a school. By 1890 the population had reached 200, but it had declined to thirty by 1925, when a general store was in operation in the community. County highway maps for 1936 showed scattered dwellings and a school, a church, a cemetery, and a business at the townsite. By 1940 the population of Delhi had dropped to twenty-five. In 1951 the community opened the Delhi Community Center, which was still in use in 1990. Legend has it that Delhi was named for a traveling medicine man who stayed in the area for several months in the late nineteenth century. It was not labeled on county highway maps in 1990, though a church, the cemetery, and the community hall still marked the site.

BIBLIOGRAPHY: Lennie White Baker, "Delhi," in Mark Withers Trail Drive Museum, *Historical Caldwell County: Where Roots Intertwine* (Dallas: Taylor, 1984).
Vanessa L. Davis

DELIA, TEXAS. Delia is on Farm Road 341 ten miles west of Coolidge in northwestern Limestone County. It was formed in the late 1870s and named for Delia Copeland, the daughter of an early settler. By the mid-1890s the settlement had a Baptist church, and by 1897 it had a one-teacher school with seventy-three pupils. A Delia post office operated from 1895 until sometime after 1930; James T. Thompson was the first postmaster. By 1914 the community had eight businesses and a population of 100, and during the 1920s and 1930s it reported four businesses and a population of 120. In 1947 Delia had a school, two churches, and three businesses. Its population was reported at forty in the late 1940s and twenty in the mid-1960s. In 1990 a church still met in the community.

BIBLIOGRAPHY: Ray A. Walter, *A History of Limestone County* (Austin: Von Boeckmann-Jones, 1959).
Stephanie Panus

DELLA PLAIN, TEXAS. Della Plain was five miles north of Floydada on Highway 207 near the center of Floyd County. It was the first community in what was to become Floyd County and was founded in 1887 by rancher Tom J. Braidfoot and cousins John R. and Jim S. McLain and named for Jim McLain's daughter, Della. A store was built there in 1887, and a post office operated from 1888 to 1893. In 1890 the Della Plain Male and Female Institute[qv] opened but moved to Floydada a year later. The Della Plain *Review* was published from 1889 to 1891, but the loss of the county seat election in 1890 and a poor local water supply finished the community. In 1894 its houses were moved to nearby Lockney, and in the early 1900s the site was planted in cotton. A roadside historical marker indicates the location of the former town.

BIBLIOGRAPHY: Ed Ellsworth Bartholomew, *The Encyclopedia of Texas Ghost Towns* (Fort Davis, Texas, 1982). Alma N. Holmes, *Favorite Stories about Floyd County* (Dallas: Vanguard Visuals, 1973).
Alma N. Holmes

DELLA PLAIN MALE AND FEMALE INSTITUTE. The idea for a school in Della Plain developed in 1890 with J. R. McLain, a founder and early citizen of this Floyd County community. McLain contacted Rev. B. F. Fronabager in Seymour, and Fronabager came to Della Plain and organized a board of directors for the proposed college. A sum of $500 was raised, and an administration building was built. The school was to provide instruction from elementary through college levels. Courses included English, history, mathematics, various languages, and art. Fronabager was to maintain the institute for five years. He initially hired C. W. Hutcheson and Anna Bedecarrax as assistants. Although the school opened in the fall of 1890, no additional money could be raised. After six months the institute closed and was sold for debts. In the 1890s the building was moved to Floydada on a special wagon that required sixteen oxen to pull. The journey took about seven days. In 1895 the building became a part of the Floydada public school.

BIBLIOGRAPHY: Floyd County Historical Museum, *History of Floyd County, 1876–1979* (Dallas: Taylor, 1979). Claude V. Hall, *Early History of Floyd County* (Canyon, Texas: Panhandle-Plains Historical Society, 1947).
Charles G. Davis

DELL CITY, TEXAS. Dell City is a farming town at the intersection of Farm roads 1437 and 2249, fifty-three miles northeast of Sierra Blanca in northeastern Hudspeth County. The area had been primarily devoted to sheep and goat ranching[qqv] until the discovery of large amounts of underground water. This discovery made possible the irrigation of some 40,000 acres and led to the founding of the town sometime before 1949, when a post office was established there with Dallas H. Thompson as postmaster. The estimated population of Dell City grew from 180 in the early 1950s to 360 in the mid-1950s. The number of residents had climbed to 950 by the early 1960s but dropped to 714 by the end of the decade. In the early 1970s the estimated population declined to 383 but rose by the late 1970s to 475. Dell City had four churches and a municipal airport during the mid-1980s. The community's estimated population was 569 in the early 1990s; at that time the town had around thirty businesses. Among the crops raised in the area were long-staple cotton, onions, and tomatoes.
Martin Donell Kohout

DELL COMPUTER CORPORATION. Dell Computer Corporation, originally known as PC's Limited, an international computer firm headquartered in Austin, Texas, designs, manufactures, sells, and services IBM-compatible personal computers. By 1993 the company was listed among the Fortune 500, owned fourteen international subsidiaries, employed more than 4,800 workers, sold computer products in more than seventy countries, generated sales of over $2 billion dollars, and was the world's fourth-largest computer maker. The company was founded in 1984 by Michael S. Dell, then an eighteen-year-old freshman at the University of Texas at Austin, during the early stages of the personal-computer industry. Intrigued by computers during his teens, Dell turned a hobby of building customized computers into a company that pioneered the marketing and sale of personal computer systems by telephone.

Dell was born in West Houston and applied for a high school equivalency diploma at age eight. He ran a mail order stamp-trading business at age thirteen and sold subscriptions to the Houston *Post*[qv] by telephone at sixteen. Within a year he was named salesman of the month and was earning $18,000 annually for a direct-mail campaign he had devised that targeted newlyweds. He turned to electronics in his late teens, when he began building customized personal computers by purchasing and assembling computer components from various manufacturers. According to Dell, his research on component manufacturers convinced him he could launch a business that would save users money, provide better support services, and make a profit.

In 1984 he purchased an Austin business license and incorporated a company he called PC's Limited. In 1985 the company introduced an IBM-compatible PC clone called the Turbo. By selling computer components and kits by telephone and advertising in trade magazines, Dell built a clientele of businesses and experienced computer users. His familiarity with the marketing potential of telephone sales gave Dell a competitive advantage over larger rivals IBM and Compaq, who, like the vast majority of computer makers, sold their products through high-markup retail outlets. Customers ordered Dell Computer products from computer-literate salespeople who directly provided information to customers. By building computers only to order, the company lowered inventory costs. By the end of the company's first fiscal year, sales totaled $6 million. Following a low-price leader strategy, PC's Limited grew exponentially. In fiscal year 1986 the company reported $34 million in sales, employed 100 workers, and expanded to a new 3,000-square-foot facility. Dell left college after his freshman year to focus on his business. By the end of 1986 sales had grown to $69.5 million, and manufacturing operations were moved to an 83,000-square-foot building in North Austin. In 1987 the company took its founder's name and became Dell Computer Corporation. Dell next opened its first sales office in Great Britain, printed its first catalog, began selling application software, and established a support center to handle customer inquiries. The company further differentiated itself from IBM, Compaq, and other mail-order rivals by introducing next day on-site service free for a period after purchase through such third-party service companies as Honeywell Bull, along with unlimited telephone technical support and a money-back guarantee. In fiscal year 1989 sales rose to almost $258 million. In 1988 Dell Computer Corporation made an initial public offering of common stock and subsequently opened wholly-owned subsidiaries in Canada and West Germany. By late 1989 the company had 1,600 employees worldwide, had introduced its first 316LT laptop computer, and had opened a French subsidiary. In 1990 the company announced an agreement with Soft Warehouse, Incorporated (Comp USA), then the largest computer superstore chain in the United States, to sell Dell products. In 1991 expansion continued, as the firm opened a manufacturing plant in Limerick, Ireland. As competitors began to imitate its telephone-sales strategy, Dell changed its image from that of a low-price leader to one offering quality and extensive service by becoming the first PC manufacturer to offer free installation of applications software with the purchase of a computer. In 1992 Dell entered into a third-party maintenance agreement with BancTec Service Corporation and announced Critical Care, a new and even more rapid response system for customer service problems. Michael Dell dedicated the Michael S. Dell Computer Lab at the University of Texas at Austin, was appointed to the board of directors of the Foundation for the National Technology Medal, and was named Man of the Year by *PC Magazine*. In 1992 the company was named to the Fortune 500 list of the country's largest manufacturers.

Despite its strong growth and status, the Dell Corporation's success was not assured as of mid-1993. Though the company introduced three new computer lines, had begun to sell computers by direct sale in Japan, and revenues in that year were expected to rise to $3 billion, company growth had begun to hinder its ability to manage its operations. Miscalculations of the pace of change in the notebook-computer market forced Dell to discontinue its notebook line. Losses associated with writeoff of the notebook line and falling personal-computer prices due to industry competition caused a decrease in company profits despite an 80 percent increase in revenues. Despite these setbacks, Dell Computer predicted a return to profitability in the third quarter of 1993 after an internal reorganization had addressed problems related to rapid growth. The company planned to consolidate its European operations and update its notebook computer business.

BIBLIOGRAPHY: *Business Week*, March 22, 1993. Claire Poole, "The Kid Who Turned Computers into Commodities," *Forbes*, October 21, 1991. Al Reinert, "Revenge of the Nerd," *Texas Monthly*, September 1992. Vertical Files, Barker Texas History Center, University of Texas at Austin (Michael Dell, Dell Computer Corporation).

Jon Kutner, Jr.

DELLSCHAU, CHARLES A. A. (1830–1923). C. A. A. Dellschau, inventor, scientist, and artist, was born on June 4, 1830, in Germany. Dellschau arrived in the United States in the 1850s and lived in Sonora and Columbia, California, among German scientists. He joined the Sonora Aero Club, a secret society of sixty-two members committed to designing and assembling aircraft, and served as their primary draftsman. In 1886 Dellschau moved to Houston, Texas. Although no clear evidence points to how Dellschau spent his years in between his time in California and Houston, there is some speculation that he may have served as a Civil War[qv] spy. Regardless, once in Houston, Dellschau worked for the Stelzig Saddlery Shop as a salesman until 1900, when he retired. Upon retirement Dellschau spent his time drawing imaginary airships, focusing on his interests in new inventions and aviation. Some of these drawings were his original inventions, while others were drawn from designs of his former colleagues. Dellschau collected extensive scrapbooks of his drawings. On April 20, 1923, he died, without recognition of his artistic contributions. Not until the 1960s were his scrapbooks discovered by art students in a Houston antique shop. The University of St. Thomas exhibited selections from Dellschau's work in a 1969 art show. The works rose in public prominence in 1977, when they were featured in a Rice University exhibition, and in 1979, when four of his scrapbooks were purchased by the San Antonio Museum Association.

BIBLIOGRAPHY: Cecilia Steinfeldt, *Texas Folk Art: One Hundred Fifty Years of the Southwestern Tradition* (Austin: Texas Monthly Press, 1981).

Jill S. Seeber

DEL MAR, TEXAS. Del Mar was on Boca Chica Island off State Highway 4 eight miles southeast of Port Isabel in southeastern Cameron County. The name means "of the sea." Spanish ranchers from Matamoros established summer homes and bathing beaches at the site before the Mexican revolution.[qv] A community was in existence by 1940, when it reported an estimated population of twenty. It had tourist facilities, a church, and supply houses for fishermen in 1948. Del Mar no longer existed in 1955, and by 1970 appeared on maps only as a triangulation point. In the early 1990s the site was part of the Brazos Island State Scenic Park.[qv]

Alicia A. Garza

DEL MAR COLLEGE. Del Mar College, originally named Corpus Christi Junior College, was established in 1935 under control of the board of trustees of the Corpus Christi Independent School District, although the junior college district and the CCISD taxes were collected separately. The superintendent of the school district, E. H. Hereford, also served as president of the junior college. The school's name was changed in 1948 to Del Mar College, and in 1951 the college became an independent political subdivision, legally the Corpus

Christi Junior College District, governed by a locally elected board of regents. In 1946 Del Mar College won accreditation from the Southern Association of Colleges and Schools.

In 1936 the institution had 154 students who attended evening classes at Roy Miller High School. A faculty of ten, four of whom had doctoral degrees, offered courses in business administration, education, English, foreign languages, mathematics, natural sciences, history, and government. In February 1942 the college moved to its East Campus on Baldwin Avenue, and a West Campus was opened in 1957 when additional land was acquired on Old Brownsville Road. Separate classes for black students were begun in 1948 on the campus of Solomon Coles High School and continued until the 1954 *Brown v. Board of Education of Topeka* decision, when the East Campus was integrated.

Though it was conceived as a liberal arts junior college, Del Mar became a two-year comprehensive community college. It offers an associate in arts degree for students completing a university-transfer course plan, an associate in applied science degree for those who complete a two-year technical-occupational degree plan, and a certificate for completion of a one-year occupational program. The college's full-time student body grew from the original 154 to 4,125 in 1969, 8,927 in 1986, and around 10,000 in 1990. The college budget was $28,000 in 1937. In 1969 it was $4,504,487 and in 1986, $27,648,220. The faculty increased from the initial ten to 247 in 1986, and since its first graduation ceremonies, the college has awarded 24,606 degrees and certificates.

When founded in 1935 Del Mar was intended to provide an opportunity for students affected by the Great Depression^{qv} to begin their college careers inexpensively. After World War II^{qv} the mission was broadened to provide vocational and technical training, and the college's name was changed to signal that the school was no longer a junior college in the traditional sense. In the decade of the 1960s the college also began to offer remedial courses to prepare students for entry into college-level programs.

BIBLIOGRAPHY: Nueces County Historical Society, *History of Nueces County* (Austin: Jenkins, 1972).

Richard Moore and Nancy H. Bowen

DEL MAR HEIGHTS, TEXAS. Del Mar Heights is a colonia^{qv} off State Highway 100 three miles east of Los Fresnos in east central Cameron County. It developed during the 1960s, and by 1976 it had forty-one dwellings and an estimated population of 186. At that time it did not have public water service, but by 1986 the area's forty-seven housing units were served by the Military Highway Water Supply Corporation, which provided water for an estimated population of 212.

BIBLIOGRAPHY: *Colonias in the Lower Rio Grande Valley of South Texas: A Summary Report* (Policy Research Project Report No. 18, Lyndon B. Johnson School of Public Affairs, University of Texas at Austin, 1977).

Alicia A. Garza

DELMITA, TEXAS. Delmita is four miles south and a mile east of San Isidro in northeast Starr County. Nicéforo G. Peña, Sr., founded the community in 1919 and named it Zaragosa. He moved his family there from Santa Theresa ranch, opened a general store, and soon started a post office. The mail carrier brought the mail by horseback from Linn three times a week; he exchanged horses in Zaragosa, continued his route to Rio Grande City, and brought more mail when he returned and got his own horse back. In 1931 Zaragosa had to change its name, because the mail was often confused with that of Saragosa in Reeves County. According to some records, on April 1, 1931, the name was changed to Delmita, a designation constructed from letters drawn by Peña's seven sons. The *Texas Almanac*,^{qv} however, listed Zaragosa as a separate community with a population and business figures distinct from those of Delmita from 1931 to 1948; thereafter, Zaragosa no longer appeared in the almanac.

The community is on a paved county road halfway between the old site of El Centro on Farm Road 2294 and La Reforma on Farm Road 1017. It had two stores and a population of twenty in 1940, when it was the leading community of northeastern Starr County. However, in the late 1940s the schools of the northeastern part of the county consolidated and placed their headquarters in San Isidro; later, when it grew time for the Delmita and San Isidro Catholic churches to rebuild, they also consolidated, and the new church was built at San Isidro, a community that continued to grow slowly while Delmita shrank to a few homes and a single store. A new post office opened in 1991, and one star rural route still ran from the community.

Dick D. Heller, Jr.

DEL NORTE GAP. The Del Norte Gap, or Paso del Norte, is a pass separating the Santiago Mountains to the south and the Del Norte Mountains to the north nineteen miles southwest of Marathon in central Brewster County (at 30°00′ N, 103°27′ W). With an elevation of 4,350 feet above sea level, the gap is 800 to 1,200 feet below the mountains on either side. The Del Norte Gap has been used for centuries. An unimproved road has traversed it at least since the 1940s. In the area, shallow, stony clay loams support juniper, oak, grasses, chaparral, and cacti.

DEL NORTE MOUNTAINS. The Del Norte Mountains, a range (centered at 30°13′ N, 103°28′ W), extend for twenty-six miles from a point eight miles east of Alpine in northwestern Brewster County to Del Norte Gap, nineteen miles southwest of Marathon in west central Brewster County. They form the northern part of a chain of mountains that runs northwest to southeast across central Brewster County. The highest peak in the Del Norte Mountains is Mount Ord, at an elevation of 6,803 feet above sea level; the average peak elevation in the range is 5,000 feet. The shallow, stony soils in the Del Norte Mountains support oak, juniper, and some mesquite.

DELOACH, WILLIAM GREEN (1880–1967). William Green DeLoach, farmer and diarist, son of Emmanuel P. and Elizabeth (Bowden) DeLoach, was born in Ellenville, Georgia, on February 1, 1880. The family moved in 1887 to Parker County, Texas, where William attended Post Oak School at Millsap. On January 14, 1903, he married Sallie Edna Newton in a dugout^{qv} near Duke, Oklahoma. Six children were born to them. During his early years DeLoach lived in numerous locations in northern Texas and Oklahoma, where he farmed or worked at odd jobs. He made two trips to the Texas plains before settling there permanently. In 1899 he worked as a cowpuncher on the Two-Buckle Ranch^{qv} in Crosby County, and in 1913 he moved his family in a covered wagon to Emma, also in Crosby County. After three years he moved on to other opportunities before settling on a farm near Sudan in 1925.

While farming in Crosby County DeLoach started a diary, on March 28, 1914. For the next fifty years he made lengthy daily entries that record the farming operations, weather, economic conditions, and family and community affairs of Emma, Ralls, and Sudan. When he was not at home he did his daily recording on a tablet and later transferred his writing verbatim to the diary. His last entry was March 28, 1964. This unique personal record is a history of the average farmer's everyday life in West Texas during the transition from ranching to farming and on into the era of modern agribusiness.

In 1914 DeLoach built perhaps the first cotton sled used in Crosby County, and in 1917 he built a sled for harvesting feed that was versatile enough to be adapted to tractor power in the 1940s. In 1936 he designed a collapsible chicken coop and took a model to Washington, D.C., seeking a patent, but lack of time and money prevented his obtaining it. He served as secretary-treasurer of Sudan Bull Circle No. 2, a group of farmers who in 1928 cooperatively purchased a registered bull to improve the bloodline of their cattle. When federal farm programs were implemented he was worried that only large farmers would benefit. In 1936 he agreed to serve on the Cotton Committee in Sudan with the single intent of protecting the interests of small farmers.

DeLoach was a lifelong Baptist; he helped organize the Friendship Union Church in 1928 and later served as secretary-treasurer. He was a Democrat and Mason and belonged to the Woodmen of the World. He retired from farming in 1952 and died on April 1, 1967; he was buried in Sudan. His diaries are now in the William G. DeLoach papers, housed in the Southwest Collection qv at Texas Tech University.

BIBLIOGRAPHY: Evalyn Parrott Scott, *A History of Lamb County* (Sudan, Texas: Lamb County Historical Commission, 1968). Nellie Witt Spikes and Temple Ann Ellis, *Through the Years: A History of Crosby County* (San Antonio: Naylor, 1952).

Janet M. Neugebauer

DELRAY, TEXAS. Delray, at the junction of Farm Road 1970 and U.S. Highway 79, six miles west of Carthage in western Panola County, was established around 1870. Its school, Walton School, began operating around 1878, and a post office was established in 1882. By 1885 the community had a steam saw and grist mill, two churches, a district school, and an estimated population of twenty-five. The post office closed in 1905, but in the mid-1930s Delray still had a school, a church, a cemetery, and a number of houses. After World War II qv the school was consolidated with the Carthage schools, and by the mid-1960s only a church, a cemetery, and a few scattered houses remained at the site. In 1990 Delray was a dispersed community with an estimated forty residents.

BIBLIOGRAPHY: Leila B. LaGrone, ed., *History of Panola County* (Carthage, Texas: Panola County Historical Commission, 1979). John Barnette Sanders, *Index to the Cemeteries of Panola County* (Center, Texas, 1964).

Christopher Long

DEL RIO, TEXAS. Del Rio, the county seat of Val Verde County, is on U.S. Highway 90 and the Southern Pacific Railroad near the confluence of the Rio Grande and San Felipe Creek, 154 miles west of San Antonio in the southern part of the county. The Spanish established a small presidial complex near the site of present Ciudad Acuña, the Mexican sister city of Del Rio, and some Spaniards settled on what became the United States side of the Rio Grande. The developments that led to the growth of Del Rio, however, took place after the Civil War.qv In the arid vastness of Southwest Texas, water was the key to survival; in the vicinity of Del Rio the San Felipe Springs qv provided millions of gallons. A number of developers acquired several thousand acres adjacent to San Felipe Creek and developed plans to sell small tracts of rich farmland to prospective buyers. These investors formed the San Felipe Agricultural, Manufacturing, and Irrigation Company in 1868. The organization soon constructed a network of irrigation qv canals, completed in 1871. Soon they began to sell small tracts of land to newly arriving settlers, who then established truck farms. Residents in the area referred to the slowly developing townsite as San Felipe del Rio. Local lore says that the name came from early Spanish explorers who offered a Mass at the site on St. Philip's Day, 1635. In 1883, after the first post office was opened, the United States Postal Department requested that the name be shortened to Del Rio to avoid confusion with San Felipe de Austin.

In 1885 Val Verde County was organized and Del Rio became the county seat. Early development was dependent on the railroad, the military, ranching and agriculture, government-related employment, and retail business. Other major economic activities were focused on tourism and ties with Mexico. From the mid-nineteenth century to the present the military has played a leading role in the fortunes of Del Rio. As soon as the Mexican War qv was over, military expeditions into the area began with patrols and the establishment of frontier military camps at Del Rio and Camp Hudson, to the west on the Devils River. Most military activities were controlled from Fort Clark, thirty miles east, near the site of present Brackettville. In the twentieth century the government continued to use the isolated Del Rio area for different types of military training. As World War II qv started, the army opened a base near Del Rio, Laughlin Field, for pilot training. Later the name was changed to Laughlin Air Force Base.qv Ranching and agriculture have always been an integral part of the economic scene of Del Rio. During the late nineteenth century sheep and goat raisers found the scrub terrain to be an ideal place for their livestock. For many years Del Rio served as a focal point for the wool and mohair industry.qv The development of the railroad in the 1880s served as an impetus to development of sheep and goat ranching.qv During that decade the Southern Pacific, which built a line from west to east, and the Galveston, Harrisburg and San Antonio, building west, linked up forty miles west of Del Rio. In 1990 the railroad still operated and served as a major employer in Del Rio. The town was incorporated on November 15, 1911.

The binational and bicultural population of Del Rio grew from fifty in 1880 to 2,000 by 1890. Thereafter, changes were slow until the 1970s, when the population grew by 40.8 percent. In 1990 Del Rio had a population of 30,705. Early Del Rio residences and businesses were close to San Felipe Creek. After the railroad developed, housing patterns began to move north of the rail line. By the 1960s the development of retail trade along U.S. Highway 90 brought growth north of the original townsite. In addition, Amistad Dam and Reservoir,qv built on the Rio Grande during the 1960s, also attracted housing.

Del Rio supports a council for the arts. The town's first school was established in 1874; in 1990 schools were administered by the San Felipe–Del Rio Consolidated Independent School District. Southwest Texas Junior College and Sul Ross State University have branch campuses in the community. The area also is host to a sizable winter Texan population. Del Rio has the council-manager form of city government.qv The United States Customs, the Border Patrol, and the National Park Service have had a significant impact on the region.

BIBLIOGRAPHY: Kathleen E. and Clifton R. St. Clair, eds., *Little Towns of Texas* (Jacksonville, Texas: Jayroe Graphic Arts, 1982). Vertical Files, Barker Texas History Center, University of Texas at Austin. Diana Sotelo Zertuche, *The Spirit of Val Verde* (Del Rio, Texas, 1985).

Robert C. Overfelt

DEL RIO ISD V. SALVATIERRA. The first case in which Texas courts reviewed the actions of local school districts regarding the education of children of Mexican descent was tried in Del Rio in 1930. Like many other communities in the state, Del Rio had for the first six decades of the twentieth century a tripartite segregation of students in its public school system. Article VII, Section 7, of the Constitution of 1876 qv provided for separate schools for white and black students. From 1902 to 1940, especially after 1920, Texas school districts opened segregated schools for Hispanic children. By 1942–43 these schools were operated in 122 districts in fifty-nine counties throughout the state. On January 7, 1930, the Del Rio School Board ordered an election to be held on February 1 to vote on a proposed expansion of school facilities, including elementary schools, one of which, a brick and tile building of two rooms, was already designated the "Mexican" or "West End" school. Five rooms were to be added. Jesús Salvatierra and several other parents hired lawyer John L. Dodson on March 21 to file a suit charging that students of Mexican descent were being deprived of the benefits afforded "other white races" in the previous year. In April El Popular, the Spanish-language newspaper of the League of United Latin American Citizens,qv published an essay by Vito Aguirre condemning segregationists, whom he called "enemies of Mexican children," and criticizing the Mexican consulate's complacency on the issue. Also that month, lawyer and

LULAC member M. C. Gonzales^{qv} consulted with Dodson and joined the case free of charge. By May Salvatierra had a support group, La Comité de Defensa, later known as Comité Pro-Defensa Escolar. On May 15 District Judge Joseph Jones heard the case, ruled in Salvatierra's favor, and granted an injunction. On June 10 the Court of Appeals of San Antonio heard the case. By June lawyers Alonso S. Perales and J. T. Canales^{qv} were also assisting Salvatierra; Dodson, Gonzales, and Canales served as the appeal attorneys. The case appeared before the Texas Court of Civil Appeals in San Antonio on October 29, and the injunction was voided. On December 24 a rehearing was denied.

LULAC provided the organizational and financial base for the movement against segregated schools, and Salvatierra's case spurred the growth of LULAC. According to George I. Sánchez^{qv} in 1964, the Salvatierra ruling legalized the segregation of children of Mexican descent in schools through the third grade. During the case the first chapters of LULAC were organized in West Texas at San Angelo, Ozona, Sonora, and Marfa. The case also highlighted the need for regular communication. In late 1930 LULAC sponsored bulletins in the columns of Spanish-language newspapers; *El Ciudadano*, *El Popular*, and *El Paladín* came to serve as LULAC's official organs; in 1931 the weekly *LULAC NOTES* was issued; and in August 1931 *LULAC News*, the official monthly magazine, began publication. Spanish-language newspapers^{qv} such as the Del Rio *El Popular*, *Las Noticias*, and *La Semana* followed the developments, and *La Prensa*^{qv} of San Antonio reached many other Tejano^{qv} communities. LULAC passed a resolution at its 1930 annual convention to assist the Del Rio chapter in its work on the case. In January 1931 Salvatierra asked LULAC chapters for contributions, and by April nine chapters had responded. In May LULAC elected Gonzales its president general, and in June he invited chapters to donate at least $5 each toward taking the case to the Supreme Court. Gonzales called a special convention in Kingsville on August 30, and by that date $493 had been raised. The convention's purpose was to convert the organization's monument fund for World War I^{qv} veterans to the School Defense Fund, and at that convention each council was required to raise $45 for Salvatierra. In spite of the Great Depression,^{qv} LULAC managed to raise more than $1,000. Councils in Corpus Christi, Brownsville, McAllen, Mission, La Grulla, Encino, Robstown, Edinburg, Falfurrias, San Diego, Del Rio, Eagle Pass, Rio Grande City, Roma, Hebbronville, Kingsville, Sarita, San Angelo, Ozona, and Sonora collected funds. San Antonio, the largest chapter, raised $230; even the small council of Sarita raised its $45 quota. Sociedades mutualistas,^{qv} Catholic groups, women's clubs, labor organizations, and Spanish-speaking PTAs^{qv} sponsored dances, baseball games, meetings, interviews, and benefits to raise money for the cause. Important individual and collective fund-raising was conducted by Paul C. Jones and Mr. and Mrs. Antonio Castanon in San Antonio, Adela Sloss and Zacarias Gonzalez in San Juan, and Mrs. Jose Stillman, Mrs. Ben Garza, Mrs. Louis Wilmot, and Ernesto Meza in Corpus Christi. On October 26 the Supreme Court refused to hear the Salvatierra case and another case in which Mexicans in Menard County were prevented from jury duty for lack of jurisdiction. LULAC called a special convention in San Antonio on November 29 to discuss strategy for bringing about school desegregation. The Del Rio Comité Pro-Defensa Escolar continued to exist at least until October 1932. In 1948 in *Delgado v. Bastrop Independent School District*,^{qv} the United States District Court, Western District of Texas, ruled that maintaining separate schools for Mexican descent children violated the Fourteenth Amendment of the United States Constitution. Nevertheless, failure to enforce this ruling resulted in continued legal challenges through the 1950s and 1960s; arguments first presented in the Salvatierra case were heard as late as 1971 in *Cisneros v. Corpus Christi ISD*.^{qv}

BIBLIOGRAPHY: Carlos M. Alcala and Jorge C. Rangel, "Project Report: De Jure Segregation of Chicanos in Texas Schools," *Harvard Civil Rights–Civil Liberties Law Review* 7 (March 1972). Arnoldo De León, *They Called Them Greasers: Anglo Attitudes Toward Mexicans in Texas, 1821–1900* (Austin: University of Texas Press, 1983). Guadalupe San Miguel, Jr., *"Let All of Them Take Heed": Mexican Americans and the Campaign for Educational Equality in Texas* (Austin: University of Texas Press, 1987).

Cynthia E. Orozco

DELROSE, TEXAS. Delrose, on U.S. Highway 271 three miles north of Gilmer in north central Upshur County, was established around 1885 as a stop on what later became the St. Louis Southwestern Railway of Texas. In the mid-1930s the settlement consisted of a church, a store, and a number of houses. After World War II^{qv} many of the residents moved away, and the school closed; by the mid-1960s Delrose was only a few scattered houses. In 1990 it was still a dispersed rural community.

Christopher Long

DELTA COUNTY. Delta County (B-20) is located in northeastern Texas seventy miles from the eastern and thirty miles from the northern state boundaries. It is bordered by the North Sulphur River on the north and the South Sulphur River on the south. The two waterways join to form the eastern boundary. Cooper, the largest town and the county seat, is in the center of the county (at 33°23′ N, 95°42′ W) at the intersection of State highways 24 and 154 with Farm roads 64, 128, 1528, and 1880. The Atchison, Topeka and Santa Fe Railway crosses the northwestern edge of the county by way of Pecan Gap and Ben Franklin. The county comprises 278 square miles of the Blackland Prairies. The terrain is undulating; soils vary from deep clay to clay covered with a dark loam. The elevation ranges from 400 to 500 feet above mean sea level. The vegetation along the streams consists primarily of hardwoods, particularly oak, elm, pecan, bois d'arc, and mesquite, while the prairie is covered with grasses including Texas grama, buffalo grass, and bunchgrass. Between 51 and 60 percent of the soil is prime farmland. The climate is warm and moist, with annual rainfall averaging forty-four inches. Temperatures range from an average low of 31° F in January to 95° in July. The first freeze in mid-November and the last late in March bracket a 233-day growing season.

The original inhabitants of Delta County were the Caddo Indians, an agricultural people with a highly developed society. The first European visitor was a Frenchman, François Hervey, who traveled through the area in 1750. Later in the eighteenth century, disease and threats from other tribes forced the Caddos to relocate. By 1820, however, scattered remnants of the Delawares, Quapaws, and Seminoles were hunting in the vicinity. During that decade, Hugh Castle settled near the future site of Ben Franklin, and, shortly thereafter a man known only as Blue built a pole hut in the Rattan area, probably to trade with the Indians. Other settlers soon began to arrive from Kentucky and Tennessee. The isolation caused by river boundaries on the north, south, and east, as well as the large Jernigan Thicket^{qv} on the west, also made the location attractive to horse thieves and other criminals who drifted down through Arkansas from Missouri. By 1830 an agent had moved into the area to report on local Indian activities, and in 1836 the government of the new Republic of Texas^{qv} recognized the land between the Sulphur rivers as part of Red River County. Without the restrictive regulations of the Spanish and Mexican governments, more settlers arrived, particularly from the South. By late in the 1830s, Dr. Moses Hogue and the Birdwell, Simmons, and Wilson families had established the little village of Ben Franklin. In 1840 the Congress of Texas formed Lamar County, which included present-day Delta County, from Red River County. In March 1846 the new state legislature organized Hopkins County, which absorbed the southern two-thirds of Delta County.

During the antebellum period, settlers mainly located on the North and South Sulphur rivers in order to be near the Hopkins and Lamar county seats, the most important local trade centers. Nat Corbet, a former resident of New York, established the first store in the county at Ben Franklin in 1845. The following year, a "Brigadier" DeSpain, his wife, Narcissa, and their three daughters claimed a land grant on the South Sulphur River along the Bonham-Jefferson Road, a major thoroughfare for cotton transportation that ran from Fannin County to Jefferson. The DeSpains built a bridge that was sturdy and high enough to escape flooding, thus facilitating trade in Hopkins County as well as at the Jefferson port. As the area began to prosper agriculturally, more settlers arrived. In 1847 pioneers from Shiloh, Tennessee, built a church and school named Shiloh just north of the South Sulphur River. The Lake Creek post office, originally called Odd's Creek, opened in 1848, but most pioneers continued to receive mail at Pin Hook (now called Paris) in Lamar County. In 1859 the residents of Giles, near Ben Franklin, established the Giles Academy, which became a respected school under the leadership of Thomas B. Hockaday. By 1860 the county had two Methodist Episcopal churches, one at Craig-Tranquil and another at Ben Franklin.

As the Civil War[qv] approached, some residents of the future county supported Governor Sam Houston's[qv] Unionist stand, a controversial one. Unionists were in the minority, however; most residents heartily endorsed the Confederate cause. In 1861 a militia was organized at Charleston, a small community near the fork of the rivers, and Gen. Sam Bell Maxey's[qv] Ninth Texas Infantry performed drilling exercises at Camp Rusk near Giles. The Confederacy also attempted to develop a saltworks on Lake Jordan, a few miles southeast of Klondike. In 1863 four Charleston men fighting on the Union side escaped capture in Arkansas by fleeing to Jernigan Thicket. Citizens apprehended three, who were summarily court-martialed and hanged. This was the only incidence of local violence, however, and the vicinity remained virtually untouched by the fighting.

At the end of the war the pioneers who had settled between the two rivers turned their attention to rebuilding an agricultural and herding economy. As the less-isolated county seats of Hopkins and Lamar Counties grew and developed, people from the river delta were forced to travel long distances over inadequate dirt roads and to cross waterways that were often flooded for long periods of time. In 1868 they petitioned the legislature to form a new county that would include parts of Hopkins, Lamar, Hunt, and Fannin counties. After much debate, Texas lawmakers granted their request on July 29, 1870, but only after excluding Hunt and Fannin counties because neither wished to be included. Governor Edmund J. Davis[qv] designated a five-man board of commissioners to organize the new district, to be called Delta County for its triangular shape. The county seat would be a new town named Cooper after Leroy Cooper, chairman of the House Committee on Counties and Boundaries, and situated directly between the North and South Sulphur rivers. Erastus Blackwell was appointed sheriff to supervise land sales. The first county election was held on October 6, 1870, to organize the municipal government, and Charles S. Nidever, John P. Boyd, J. F. Alexander, Alfred Allen, and J. M. Bledsoe were elected the first county commissioners. County organization, however, failed to settle continuing political divisions. In the election of 1872, Horace Greeley, the liberal Republican candidate endorsed by the Democrats, captured 50 percent of the vote, while Republican Ulysses S. Grant received 40 percent. Although the entire state became solidly Democratic after Governor Davis was defeated in 1873 by Democrat Richard Coke,[qv] the Republican party[qv] remained an important factor in Delta County politics. In 1876 local voters chose Democrat Samuel B. Tilden over Republican Rutherford B. Hayes, but only by a narrow margin of sixty-one votes.

The postwar years brought growth and, eventually, prosperity to the new county. Cooper soon became the center of local activities, and in 1873 Bob Michiel began publication of the first newspaper in the county, the *Delta Courier*. By 1880 the population had reached 5,597, including 598 African Americans.[qv] Fifty percent of the residents were native Texans. Education had become a more important issue during Reconstruction,[qv] and by 1880 the number of schools had increased from nine to almost thirty. These facilities operated 4½ months of each year and served a combined total of 998 students. Though the county had many small communities, the only towns were Cooper, Charleston, and Ben Franklin. Nine manufacturing establishments were in operation. The seven churches were predominantly Methodist. A new courthouse was constructed in Cooper, and Confederate and Union veterans planted pecan trees on the town square to symbolize the end of animosities. Development also extended to agricultural and herding pursuits. The fertility of the soil and natural pasturage made for more diversification than in other counties. Though only 32,120 or approximately 32 percent of the 102,086 acres in farms was improved, harvests were large. Local farmers ginned 4,911 bales of cotton, but this was not the most lucrative crop. The average corn yield was four bushels an acre, more than 130,000 bushels for the entire county, and one acre could produce nineteen bushels of oats. Sorghum was also grown on a large scale, and the county produced 11,345 gallons of sorghum molasses in 1880. The acreage not in use for planting was used for grazing. The county had 2,957 milk cows, mostly used for local needs, but other cattle amounted to 24 percent of the stock. Smaller numbers of horses, mules, and sheep also grazed on the open range. The number of hogs, most of them wild, had reached 10,994 and accounted for 43 percent of the animals raised in the county in 1880. The large numbers of cattlemen and the upsurge in farming resulted in fencing controversies that climaxed in 1883 with several fence-cutting[qv] incidents. The success of farming and herding was also complemented by a new interest in the lumber industry,[qv] and the wooded portions of Delta County became the sites of sawmills as well as shingle and furniture factories.

With the development of these industries, along with gristmills and cotton gins, crops and timber could be processed locally, but many county businessmen were interested in finding a method for shipping more goods to distant markets. In 1886 entrepreneurs J. M. Van Zandt and Joe C. Waller negotiated a contract with the Santa Fe Railway, and the following year a section of the line was built across the northwest corner of the county. Pecan Gap and Ben Franklin became stops on the new railroad, and many area people moved into the towns searching for jobs with the new company. By 1888 there were seven post offices in Delta County. The following year seven Baptist churches sent delegates to a meeting of the Delta County Baptist Association. The First National Bank, the only financial institution in the county, opened in 1889, as did East Texas Normal College. The school became very successful under the direction of William Leonidas Mayo,[qv] but it moved to Commerce after its only building burned in 1894.

The 1890s brought an even more impressive agricultural boom. Though the number of swine had decreased to 6,816 at the beginning of the decade and herds of other stock had grown only slightly, the amount of land in cotton, corn, and oats had increased sharply. Sixty-one percent of the acreage that made up the 1,188 farms was improved, and farms had doubled in value to $1,400 each. Cotton had boomed and was planted on 23,041 acres, as compared to 8,940 only ten years earlier. The census also reported 57,282 bushels of oats and 336,370 of corn. Sorghum acres had dropped to seventy-seven, but poultry production[qv] had begun to develop. Local growers produced 73,956 chickens in 1890. That year the Delta County population had increased to 9,117, including 728 black residents. While towns, especially those along the railroad, continued to grow, the majority of citizens still lived and worked in the country. The eighteen manufacturing establishments employed only thirty-three workers, who earned an average annual income of $208. The predominantly rural nature of the county was also reflected in political strife. The Populists won many local elections, and although Democrat Grover Cleveland won the county in the 1892 presidential election, third-party candidates captured 31 percent of the vote. Prohibition[qv] was also an important issue. Delta County remained dry throughout the Populist era.

At the beginning of the 1890s, there were eight Baptist churches in the Delta County Baptist Association and nine new Methodist churches. The lumber boom continued. In 1894 J. R. and W. H. Carson began a large lumber business at Pecan Gap. The following year the Texas Midland Railroad built a line through Cooper with stops at Enloe, Klondike, Horton, and Cooper, thus giving new life to those small towns. On February 21, 1897, Cooper was incorporated, and in 1898 a $40,000 bond issue passed to provide funds for the construction of a new brick courthouse. With the turn of the century, the county continued to prosper agriculturally. Most of the 15,249 citizens, including 967 blacks, preferred to remain on the farm. Though tenants and sharecroppers composed 60 percent of the farm labor force, huge outputs made theirs a profitable occupation. The number of farms had doubled over the past decade, and 73 percent of the farm acreage was improved. Sixty-nine percent of this cropland was planted in cotton, 25 percent in corn, and 4 percent in oats. Unimproved acreage was used primarily for open-range grazing. The number of swine had more than doubled to 15,413, and cattle numbered 10,943. Poultry remained an important source of income; growers reported 83,958 chickens and guineas and 2,599 turkeys. The poultry, livestock, and cotton were primarily shipped out of the area for sale, while corn and oats were used locally for human consumption and to feed cattle, hogs, and chickens. By 1910 the county population had increased to 14,566. Economically, most residents continued to rely on agriculture, but 66 percent of the 2,202 farmers were sharecroppers or tenant farmers who did not own land. In contrast to the rule in farm tenancy[qv] in other counties, only 3 percent (fifty-five) of this landless class was black because most of the 809 African Americans in the county worked for local manufacturers or on the railroad. The cultivation of cotton, corn, and oats remained lucrative, as did livestock and poultry raising. Fruits, particularly strawberries and peaches, were also being grown and shipped out of the county for sale. Local towns, particularly those along the railroad, continued to develop. Six new Methodist churches had been built since 1900, and the county had seventeen post offices. The First National Bank built a new building in 1909, but the most publicized county event of the decade occurred on May 19, 1910, when a 500-pound meteorite hit the earth near Charleston during the passage of Halley's Comet.

In 1920, 2,191 county residents were farming. The majority, 67 percent, were sharecroppers, and of these 1,469, eighty-two were black. That year county farmers produced more than 491,000 bushels of corn, 26,654 bales of cotton, and 9,047 bushels of oats. Potatoes had become the most important truck crop, although fruits were also marketed. The numbers of both cattle and swine had dropped considerably, however, and livestock production continued to decline throughout the decade because of a decrease in prices. In order to compensate for lost income, farmers began to produce even larger cotton crops.

By 1926, however, the prosperity of the early twentieth century was beginning to give way. That year the cotton crop failed, and citizens were forced to withdraw their savings from local banks. The First National Bank in Cooper closed in 1927, and even though it reopened two months later the economy of Delta County had been heavily damaged. Most citizens, relying on the income from the projected harvest, were deeply in debt. Bank capital had been drastically curtailed, making more loans almost impossible to obtain. By 1928 the Texas Midland Railroad sold out to the Southern Pacific Corporation. Although farmers grew more cotton in the hope of recouping their losses, prices continued to plummet. Lumber companies had exhausted much of the timber in the area, and the few that survived could not afford to continue through such hard times. It was as if Delta County had got the jump on the Great Depression.[qv] The population had decreased to 13,138 by 1930, as many people moved away in search of jobs. The number of black residents fell from 1,400 in the previous decade to 995. More people turned to sharecropping. Black tenancy doubled, and only 431 of 2,289 farmers actually owned their land. Corn production fell by 50 percent. The oat harvest dropped drastically. County farmer continued to produce more and more cotton. In the 1930 census county stockmen reported only 3,889 hogs and 4,739 cattle. Only four manufacturing establishments, employing thirty-six people, survived. In desperation, voters turned to the Democratic party[qv] for relief.

In the election of 1932 they supported Franklin D. Roosevelt with 96 percent of the vote, the largest Democratic margin of victory in county history. The First National Bank had closed again in 1933 as part of the national "Bank Holiday." It permanently reopened soon after. By the beginning of World War II,[qv] the local economy was fairly stable, and farming remained the prevalent occupation. Although the New Deal programs had lessened its production temporarily from 43,726 bales in 1931 to 11,421 in 1935, cotton remained the most important money crop. In 1932 300 farmers had formed a ginning cooperative, and by 1940 the county reported 26,789 ginned bales. Oats were no longer a cash crop, but 443,802 bushels of corn and large amounts of potatoes were grown, primarily for local use. Livestock were also consumed locally, and their numbers remained small. Schools and churches remained the centers of local activities as railroad towns declined with the decrease in trade. In 1931 there were thirteen Baptist churches in Delta County. The thirty-four common and six independent school districts employed 134 staff members and enrolled 4,000 children, who attended eight-month sessions. Enloe, Cooper, and Pecan Gap offered four-year high school programs. The small schools began to consolidate later in the decade with the help of state funding for transportation. In 1940 the Work Projects Administration[qv] built a new $110,450 four-story courthouse in Cooper and demolished the old one. While cotton was still the principal crop, alfalfa and hay were produced in larger amounts. Poultry and eggs as well as fruits, milk, and butter were shipped out in great numbers. Though stockmen produced good pork during this decade, the cattle industry never again attained its predepression success. At least one-fourth of all county farms were worked by tenants. By 1946 the county had 433 miles of roads, and 16 percent were graveled or paved. The WPA also constructed white rock roads so that school buses could travel more easily.

Many of the young people who left the area during the war chose not to return, and others moved to urban areas, particularly Dallas, in search of jobs. By 1950 the population of Delta County had decreased to 8,953, including 934 black residents, and by 1960 it had fallen to 5,860. Subsequently it hovered around 4,900. The number of farms was also in decline as mechanization made it easier for one farmer to work an area that might previously have supported several. Only 9 percent of the 1,413 farms were operated by black citizens, and all were tenants or sharecroppers. Although alfalfa, hay, and livestock had become the most lucrative products, cotton remained important to the local economy; growers produced 26,787 bales in 1950. In 1966 more than 50 percent of Delta County remained rural. Cooper was the largest town and the center of local activities. It had two elementary schools, a junior high, and a high school. Two small airfields were located nearby. Major employers included the schools, a battery and generator plant, five cotton gins, eight cottonseed cleaning and processing plants, a locker plant, the Lone Star Gas Company, Texas Power and Light, and two hospitals. The forty-acre Delta County Country Club, which included a ten-acre lake, had also been constructed. Seven Christian communions were represented in the county's thirty-two churches. Politically, the county was still overwhelmingly Democratic. Only 18 percent of the population had finished high school. Farming continued to decline through the 1960s. By 1969 the number of farms had decreased to 650; 136 of these operated under the share or tenant system. Only eighteen black families were involved in agriculture, and eleven of these were sharecroppers or tenants. Most farmers had abandoned even subsistence crops in favor of nursery products and hay, while 432 continued to grow cotton in smaller amounts than perviously. Almost one-third of all farmers worked off the farm for more than 200 days a year.

Although county residents had supported Democrat Hubert Humphrey by an overwhelming majority (1,037 to 370) in 1968, they gave Republican Richard Nixon 62 percent of the vote in 1972. Economic hardships, especially for farmers, led to this political upset. In 1976 Delta County residents again endorsed the Democratic candidate, James E. Carter, with 68 percent of their votes. They remained predominantly Democratic in their political affiliation throughout the 1980s. In 1982, 99 percent of county residents who voted did so in the Democratic primary. That year the county was still primarily rural, with 81 percent of the land in farms and ranches, although one-half of the population lived in Cooper. Wheat culture,qv which had recently been introduced into the area, was increasing in importance, but 73 percent of all farm income came from livestock and livestock products. There were sixty businesses and five manufacturing establishments. While these institutions employed 40 percent of the labor force, an additional 42 percent worked outside the county. The county supported three banks, two telephone companies, and a weekly newspaper, the Cooper *Review*. Two school districts had an average daily attendance of 993; 77 percent of the students were white, and 23 percent were black. Residents could attend any of twenty-seven churches, the largest being Southern Baptist, United Methodist, and Church of Christ. They also had access to the services of one doctor, one dentist, three attorneys, a police force of three, three sheriff's officers, and three volunteer fire departments. Cooper had a fifteen-acre municipal park and the Patterson Memorial County Library. Though eight communities maintained recreational centers, Cooper, with a population of 2,338, remained the largest town, followed by Pecan Gap (250) and Enloe (113). In 1987 there were 421 farming families in Delta County, but only 228 were involved in full-time agriculture. Cotton production had decreased to 1,710 bales, most of which was processed at local seed-cleaning plants. Grain had become the most important crop. Wheat was grown on more than 10,000 acres that produced 310,144 bushels. Large amounts of soybeans, sorghum, and corn were also harvested. The other successful county product was livestock. Herders raised more than 36,000 cattle and sold more than half of these. The population in 1990 was 4,857.

BIBLIOGRAPHY: Paul Garland Hervey, A History of Education in Delta County, Texas (M.A. thesis, University of Texas, 1951).

Vista K. McCroskey

DELTA DRILLING COMPANY. At its peak in 1981 the Delta Drilling Company, headquartered in Tyler, was one of the largest land-based, private, contract drilling firms in the world. It was founded in Longview on November 17, 1931, by four immigrants and a native Texan. Joseph Zeppa had immigrated from Italy to New York at the age of twelve in 1906 with no English. He rose to executive positions with Arkansas Natural Gas Company and McMillan Petroleum Company. Sam Gold (Simon Goldman), Sam Sklar, and Sam Y. Dorfman, all Jewish refugees from pogroms in czarist Russia, were partners in Louisiana Iron and Supply. Robert Stacy was born in Houston and experienced in sales. The ownership was originally divided into thirds—Zeppa, Dorfman-Gold-Sklar, and Stacy. The triangular Greek letter delta, used in the green company logo, symbolized the three-way ownership. "We formed this company without a dime," Joe Zeppa later recalled. The partners borrowed $22,000 in the depth of the Great Depressionqv to buy two junk drilling rigs and began drilling in the booming East Texas oilfield,qv one of the few economic bright spots in the entire United States at the time.

Gold died in 1936, and Dorfman and Sklar bought his share. When Stacy sold out in 1941, Zeppa acquired enough of his stock to become the majority stockholder. He held this position for the rest of his life and ran the firm as president and chairman of the board.

In the late 1930s and thereafter Delta branched out from East Texas, with operations in the Illinois basin, the Northeast (especially Pennsylvania and West Virginia), the Rocky Mountains, Louisiana, the Southeast, West Texas, and South Texas. It also accumulated oil and gas production in these regions and held interests in two gas plants, in Ozona and Chapel Hill, Texas. A major step in growth came in 1949 when Delta, under Zeppa's guidance, acquired twenty-two drilling rigs and substantial petroleum reserves from J. C. Hawkins, a colorful but creditor-plagued entrepreneur. The $3 million deal essentially doubled the size and assets of Delta. The Hawkins acquisition, operated as Delta Gulf for the next seven years until the assets were completely absorbed, covered properties in twelve states. Beginning in 1955 Delta operated an offshore drilling company, Delta Marine, in the Gulf of Mexico off the Louisiana coast, for about twenty years. Although Delta drilled briefly in Nova Scotia, Spain, Libya, Australia, the Philippines, and South West Africa (now Namibia) during the heyday of American overseas oil exploration, its main foreign operations were in Italy, Venezuela, Mexico, Argentina, and Brazil.

Delta achieved a number of distinctions over the years. It became the largest privately owned land-based drilling company in the world. It received publicity throughout the industry in 1972 when it hired Claudine Shapley as "the first lady roughneck in the Western world." It was one of the first companies to hire black drillers in this country.

Zeppa died in 1975 at the age of eighty-four. In 1984 the "accountant who headed West" was inducted into the Texas Business Hall of Fame. His son, Keating V. Zeppa, succeeded him as president and chairman of the board. A period of swift expansion followed in the next several years as the "energy crisis" brought in a petroleum boom. Revenues for 1981 reached a record $205.9 million; the following year reserves were valued at $235.7 million. A large bank debt helped fuel the expansion.

In 1981 the firm "went public" and began selling its stock over the counter. At its peak Delta operated fifty-nine domestic drilling rigs and six foreign onshore rigs. But as an industry-wide economic slump followed the erosion of the OPEC (Organization of Petroleum Exporting Countries) cartel, Delta entered a long trough. In 1984 the company became DeltaUS. The next year it sold its domestic oil and gas production and interests in two gas plants to Kerr-McGee Corporation for $140 million to pay off its bank debt.

In 1985, while Keating Zeppa remained chairman of the board, Donald L. Frankel became president. In 1988 DeltaUS sold 75 percent of its common stock outstanding to P.A.J.W. Corporation, wholly owned by Gordon P. Getty, for $7 million; Getty lent the firm $2.5 million as working capital. The following year Delta filed for Chapter 11 bankruptcy. Zeppa resigned as chairman and director after thirty years with the company. Delta emerged from bankruptcy in 1990, with Getty owning 100 percent of its stock. Delta Drilling Company again became the firm's name. It owned thirty-five land rigs in four regions—East Texas, South Texas, the Louisiana Gulf Coast, and the Appalachian region.

BIBLIOGRAPHY: James Presley, *Never in Doubt: A History of Delta Drilling Company* (Houston: Gulf, 1981). Tyler *Morning Telegraph*, February 2, 1989, January 13, 1990.

James Presley

DELTA KAPPA GAMMA SOCIETY. The Delta Kappa Gamma, an international honorary society for women in education, was founded by Annie Webb Blantonqv and eleven other Texas women on May 11, 1929, at the University Faculty Women's Club in Austin. The organization, originally called Kappa Gamma Delta, was chartered under its present name on August 15, 1929, after founders learned that the original name was being used by an aeronautics society. Exclusive rights to the name were not finally secured, however, until 1941. Blanton, a professor of rural education at the University of Texas, founded the society as a vehicle for its members to counter discrimination against women in education and to give recognition for excellence. Its purposes were also to provide women with a sense of unity and cooperation, to secure legislation supporting improvements in education, to help women gain equal representation in professional organizations, and to provide financial assistance for women preparing for careers in education. As Delta Kappa Gamma grew, it concentrated increasingly on providing intellectual and financial support for its members and on recognizing excellence.

Seventeen chapters were formed the first year; by 1987 the society had over 3,000 chapters in fifty states and thirteen countries. Nearly 300 of those chapters were in Texas. Blanton, the first president, decided that the society's name, symbols, and initiation ritual would remain secret to outsiders. Her invitations to potential members were signed with the pseudonymous initials KGD rather than with her own name. Initiates originally were required to have at least five years of experience in elementary, secondary, or postsecondary education; this was later changed to three years. Blanton hoped to attract members with a variety of experiences. Among the original twelve founders were an elementary teacher, three elementary principals, one mathematics and two history teachers, three college instructors (of physical education, elementary education, and psychology), and a dean of women.

Delta Kappa Gamma has chapter, state, regional, and international bodies, and its governance and operation are controlled by an executive board of 120 people. It holds biennial regional and international conventions. The society offers several awards and scholarships, including the annual International Achievement Award for leadership; the Educator's Award, given for the outstanding book on education by a woman; and more than twenty annual scholarships for members pursuing graduate study. It also makes several yearly awards through its World Fellowship Program to women from other countries studying at universities in the United States and Canada. The Delta Kappa Gamma Foundation was established in 1964 as a source of grants, scholarships, and fellowships and to support such educational projects as providing a reading teacher for the Navajo community college. The society publishes a quarterly *Bulletin,* a periodic newspaper called *News,* and numerous brochures and pamphlets. The group's collection of "pioneer figurines," dolls representing significant women in education, is displayed at its international headquarters in Austin. Its national headquarters are in Denton. Its membership grew from twelve in 1929 to 162,000 in 1987.

BIBLIOGRAPHY: Eunah Temple Holden, *Our Heritage in the Delta Kappa Gamma Society* (Austin: Delta Kappa Gamma Society, 1960; rpt. 1970).

Nancy Baker Jones

DELTA LAKE. Delta Lake, in the Nueces–Rio Grande basin four miles north of Monte Alto and twenty-four miles northeast of McAllen in Hidalgo County (at 26°25′ N, 97°56′ W), was previously called Monte Alto Reservoir and has also been called Mesteñas Reservoir and Willacy Reservoir. It is an off-channel storage reservoir to the Rio Grande. The project, constructed in 1939, is owned and operated by the Hidalgo-Willacy Counties Water Control and Improvement District No. 1. It has a capacity of 25,000 acre-feet and a surface area of 2,371 acres at the elevation of 56½ feet above mean sea level and consists of two units. Water is diverted from the Rio Grande in Cameron County by a gravity canal system. From this main canal water is diverted to another canal, known as Mesteñas Canal, for distribution to land during the irrigation qv season or to a pumping plant that lifts surplus water to the reservoir for storage. When needed for irrigation, the water is released and flows back to the Mesteñas Canal for distribution. Until the late 1970s the lakes formed by the reservoir were used as recreational facilities by area residents. After the water was discovered to be contaminated by an excess of microorganisms, it was closed to swimmers, and the park no longer attracted visitors.

Seth D. Breeding

DE LUXE SHOW. The De Luxe Show, one of the first racially integrated exhibitions of contemporary artists in the United States, occurred in the remodeled De Luxe movie theater in the Fifth Ward, Houston,qv from August 22 to September 29, 1971. The Menil Foundationqv sponsored the exhibition at a time of a nationwide controversy on opportunities for black artists. In 1968 the Black Emergency Cultural Coalition was formed to lobby for greater exposure of black artists and involvement of black expertise in curating exhibitions after the Metropolitan Museum of Art (New York) organized the exhibition Harlem on my Mind with only limited input from Harlem artists. In 1971 the coalition called for a boycott of the Whitney Museum's exhibition Contemporary Black Artists in America because black participation in its organization was limited. Fifteen of the seventy-five artists scheduled to participate subsequently withdrew, and critical response to the exhibition centered on black political reaction, with little discussion of the art itself. An increasing number of black artists thought that their work should be evaluated on the basis of aesthetics.

Two exhibitions organized by the Menil Foundation in 1971 for the Institute for the Arts at Rice University provided the immediate backdrop for the De Luxe Show. Some American History (February–April 1971), an exhibition on slaveryqv and black life in America, was criticized in the national press for focusing on the work of white artist Larry Rivers; the six black artists who assisted Rivers were dissatisfied with their role in the project. The controversy surrounding Some American History undoubtedly shaped the Menil Foundation's decision to call on black leaders to coordinate the De Luxe Show. For Children (May–August 1971), a popular exhibition that encouraged playful interaction with paintings and sculpture, prompted the idea of exhibiting black art in one of Houston's poor neighborhoods.

John De Menil,qv businessman and art patron, initially approached painter Peter Bradley, an associate director of the Perls Galleries in New York, with the idea of displaying black art in one of Houston's poor neighborhoods. Bradley, who had participated in Some American History, emphasized the need for an integrated exhibition, and agreed to curate the show after the decision was made to include artists of both races. De Menil also enlisted the aid of two instructors from Texas Southern University: Jefferee James, who publicized the show, and community leader Mickey Leland,qv who helped to select the site and coordinate the exhibition.

The De Luxe Theater, located at 3303 Lyons in the heart of the Fifth Ward, was a historically rich site for the event. The De Luxe had provided a safe, family-oriented alternative to other black neighborhood movie theaters when it opened in April 1941 and was described by Jefferee James as "THE PLACE for people to look forward to, particularly on weekends." The theater had fallen into decay after movie theaters were integrated and finally closed in 1969. With the help of experts from the Rice University Institute for the Arts, Jones and Bynam Construction Company transformed the old theater into an exhibition space in just three weeks. To emphasize the historical significance Bradley left the façade, lobby, and balcony intact. The balcony was walled off so that old westerns and horror movies could be shown there, and the rest of the interior was gutted, sheetrocked, and coated with two layers of white paint for an exhibition area measuring approximately fifty by eighty feet. Two rows of theater seats, the only other remnant of the past, were left in the center of the exhibition space to facilitate relaxed viewing. Photographs of the renovation were displayed in the lobby.

Bradley selected forty abstract works by nineteen contemporary artists, some well known and some new talents. Artists Sam Gilliam and Kenneth Noland, prominent critic Clement Greenberg, other community organizers and neighborhood members, and Institute for the Arts staff assisted Bradley. Huge posters depicted the exterior of the De Luxe in black and gray, and flyers, bumper stickers, and newspaper, radio, and television advertisements publicized the event as "hard art at the De Luxe Show." When the show opened on August 22, more than 1,000 people attended to view austere but colorful abstract works by such painters as Peter Bradley, Virginia Jaramillo, Ed Clark, Larry Poons, Jules Olitski, and William T. Williams. Sam Gilliam's sensuously draped canvas *Rather* (1970) and Alvin Loving's un-titled arrangement of brightly colored cubes vied with the minimalist constructions of Richard Hunt, Michael Stiener, and Anthony Caro for sculptural interest.

The audience's response to art that was quite challenging, and in some cases rather esoteric, was described by one critic as "somewhat skeptical but usually enthusiastic." Bradley conceded that children unhampered with preconceived notions about art appreciated the exhibition more than their elders. The exhibition was hailed by critic Eleanor Freed as a "challenging social and visual experiment" that brought painting and sculpture to a part of Houston "better known for urban decay than aesthetics." By the time the exhibition closed on September 29, more than 4,000 people had attended the De Luxe Show. The De Luxe Theater continued to serve the community after the exhibition closed. Outstanding examples of African art from the Menil collection[qv] were displayed there for three years. Until 1976 the theater also served as a gallery for the Black Arts Center, sponsored by Hope Development, Incorporated.

BIBLIOGRAPHY: Joseph James Akston, "Editorial," *Arts* 45 (May 1971). Maurice Berger, "Are Art Museums Racist?," *Art in America* 78 (September 1990). George Davis, "The DeLuxe Show," *Art and Artists* 6 (February 1972). *The De Luxe Show* (Houston: Menil Foundation, 1971). Houston *Post/Spotlight Magazine,* August 29, 1971. *Texas Observer,* September 24, 1941. Vertical Files, Barker Texas History Center, University of Texas at Austin (John and Dominique De Menil).

Kendall Curlee

DEL VALLE, SANTIAGO (?–?). Santiago Del Valle was an hacendado in the Monclova area of Coahuila. Del Valle, Texas, is named for him or for his grant of land, within which the town is situated. He served as president of the Congreso Constituyente of the state of Coahuila and Texas[qv] in 1825, as counselor to the governor, and as the arbitrator in a feud between the Sánchez Navarro and Elizondo families. He was associated with Thomas F. McKinney and Samuel May Williams[qqv] through the Banco de Comercio y Agricultura and the Galveston City Company. He received a ten-league grant, nine leagues of which he sold through Williams to Michel B. Menard[qv] and then to McKinney; the other league he sold to Bartlett Sims.[qv] Del Valle was a Catholic and a Federalist in Mexican politics and appears to have always resided in Coahuila.

BIBLIOGRAPHY: Charles H. Harris, *A Mexican Family Empire: The Latifundio of the Sánchez Navarros, 1765–1867* (Austin: University of Texas Press, 1975).

John W. Clark, Jr.

DEL VALLE, TEXAS. Del Valle is on the Colorado River seven miles southeast of Austin in southeastern Travis County. It was established in the mid-1870s and named for its location on Santiago Del Valle's[qv] land grant. A post office opened at Del Valle in 1878 with William Givens as postmaster. By the mid-1880s the community had three churches, a school, a steam gristmill, a general store, two cotton gins, and fifty residents; grain and cotton were the primary crops shipped by area farmers. By 1900 the population had grown to seventy-five. Del Valle was the focus of a common-school district, which in 1907 had a one-teacher school for nine white students and a one-teacher school for 108 black students. Del Valle was hurt by the onset of the Great Depression,[qv] as the population fell from an estimated 150 in 1927 to twenty-five in the early 1930s. Children from the area attended schools in the Colorado and Hornsby-Dunlap districts. However, the construction of Del Valle Army Air Field (later known as Bergstrom Air Force Base[qv]) in 1942 brought a small increase in population as new support services moved into the area. The community had 125 residents by the mid-1940s and 200 residents by the mid-1950s. The Colorado school district was renamed Del Valle in 1962, and the Del Valle community became the center of a large independent school district in 1963. Population estimates for Del Valle remained at 300 from the early 1970s through 1990, although the number of businesses in the community increased from twelve in 1970 to thirty-five in 1990.

BIBLIOGRAPHY: John J. Germann and Myron Janzen, *Texas Post Offices by County* (1986).

Vivian Elizabeth Smyrl

DELWIN, TEXAS. Delwin, in southwestern Cottle County, was named in the early 1900s for Delwin Drummond, the son of founders Tom and Ora Drummond. The Drummond ranch occupied a large part of the region. A school was established in the late 1890s. Delwin had a post office from 1916 until sometime after 1930. Its school was consolidated with that of Paducah in 1963. A cotton gin operated for many years, until it was destroyed by fire in the 1950s. The population was eighty-three in 1940 and seventy in 1980 and 1990.

BIBLIOGRAPHY: Carmen Taylor Bennett, *Our Roots Grow Deep: A History of Cottle County* (Floydada, Texas: Blanco Offset Printing, 1970).

William R. Hunt

DEMARET, JIMMIE NEWTON (1910–1983). Jimmie (Jimmy) Newton Demaret, golfer, was born on May 24, 1910, in Houston, Texas, the fourth of ten children of John O'Brien and Lila Mae (Winkler) Demaret. While in grade school he began golfing and caddying at the Camp Logan and Hermann Park courses in Houston. He then began a professional apprenticeship, attended North High School for two years, and at age fifteen became an assistant to Jack Burke, Sr., at River Oaks Country Club. In the late 1920s and 1930s Demaret was one of many financially strapped Texas professionals, including Ralph Guldahl, Ben Hogan, and Byron Nelson, who traveled the state playing in small tournaments, like those in oilfield towns west of Fort Worth. His first important title was the 1934 Texas Professional Golfers Association championship. He became professional at the municipal course in Galveston, where he secured backing for the winter tournament circuit, or "tour," from nightclub owner Sam Maceo. Victories in 1938 and 1939 earned him an invitation to the Masters Tournament, which he won in 1940 and twice subsequently; he was that tournament's first three-time winner.

After wartime service in the navy, Demaret was among the top ten in golf earnings from 1946 through 1950; in 1947 he was leading money winner, Vardon Trophy recipient, and holder of seven titles. He also played on victorious Ryder Cup (1947, 1949, 1951) and World Cup (1961) teams and was enrolled in the PGA Hall of Fame, the World Golf Hall of Fame, the Texas Sports Hall of Fame,[qv] and the Texas Golf Hall of Fame. In 1958 Demaret and Jack Burke, Jr., opened the Champions Golf Club in Houston. In the early 1970s he was a partner in the Onion Creek Club near Austin, where in 1978 he was instrumental in promoting the Legends of Golf Tournament, which inspired the Senior PGA Tour.

Well known in entertainment circles, he pioneered colorful dress on the professional tour and in the late 1960s hosted the popular television series "Shell's Wonderful World of Golf." Demaret was personable and witty, a goodwill ambassador for professional golf. His *My Partner, Ben Hogan* (1954) offers excellent insight into the emergence of today's big-purse tour. When he died of a heart attack on December 28, 1983, in Houston, his thirty-five titles made him the ninth all-time tournament winner. He was survived by his wife, Idella, and a daughter.

BIBLIOGRAPHY: Al Barkow, *The History of the PGA Tour* (New York: Doubleday, 1989). *Golf Digest,* March 1984, February 1992. Herb Graffis, *The PGA: The Official History of the Professional Golfers' Association of America* (New York: Crowell, 1975).

James A. Wilson

DEMENT, ADA BELL (1888–1945). Ada Bell DeMent, black educator and clubwoman, was born in 1888. She spent much of her life in Mineral Wells. Her early posts with the National Association of Colored Women's Clubs included chair of the peace and function committee and membership on the board of control. She served as senior state supervisor of girls before her election around 1933 as president of the Texas Association of Colored Women's Clubs (later the Texas Association of Women's Clubs qv). During her tenure, the Texas Association of Colored Women's Clubs activated a scholarship fund, promoted a training school for delinquent black girls, and cooperated with the (white) Texas Federation of Women's Clubs.qv DeMent was president of the National Association of Colored Women's Clubs from 1941 until her death. In this post she was instrumental in transferring the Frederick Douglass home in Washington, D.C., to the association. DeMent received an honorary doctorate from Bishop College in 1942. She was an active participant in the women's auxiliary to the National Baptist Convention and became secretary of its executive committee. She was the wife of the Rev. C. DeMent. She died on November 28, 1945, in Tarrant County.

BIBLIOGRAPHY: Andrew Webster Jackson, *A Sure Foundation and a Sketch of Negro Life in Texas* (Houston, 1940). Charles Harris Wesley, *The History of the National Association of Colored Women's Clubs* (Washington: National Association of Colored Women's Clubs, 1984).

Ruthe Winegarten

DEMENT, TEXAS. Dement was a dispersed rural community of black farmers fifteen miles south of Gonzales and about five miles west of U.S. Highway 183 in south central Gonzales County. The settlement had come into existence by about 1880 or 1890. In the 1920s it was a thriving community, with a one-room schoolhouse, Middlefork School, and directly across the street from the school a church, Mount Enon Baptist, which drew worshipers from Terrysville (Gonzales County) and Boyd Ranch (DeWitt County). The community had no store, however, and residents went to Cheapside, about four miles south of Dement, to shop. The school was discontinued sometime after 1936. Services continued to be held at the church until about 1985. Jones Cemetery (also known as Mount Enon Cemetery), about a mile north of the church, was established on land donated by Will Jones. Jennie Belle Covington qv grew up in Dement in the home of her uncle and aunt, Will and Jane Jones. In 1994 only the cemetery and the ruins of the church remained.

Mary M. Standifer

DEMIJOHN BEND, TEXAS. Demijohn Bend, eighteen miles northwest of New Braunfels in northern Comal County, was a German farming and ranching community that was settled in the 1850s by the Pantermuehl and Baetge families. The name derived from a demijohn-shaped bend in the Guadalupe River that formed a 400-acre peninsula that was nearly encircled by the stream. Much of the scenic bend has been submerged since Canyon Lake was filled in the mid-1960s.

BIBLIOGRAPHY: R. B. McDonald et al., *An Appraisal of Potential for Outdoor Recreational Developments in Comal County* (n.p.: Guadalupe-Blanco River Authority, 1967). Lillian Penshorn, A History of Comal County (M.A. thesis, Southwest Texas State Teachers College, 1950).

Daniel P. Greene

DEMOCRATIC NATIONAL CONVENTION OF 1928. In the winter of 1927 Jesse H. Jones qv traveled to Washington, D.C., with a certified check for $200,000 to enter Houston's bid for the Democratic National Convention to be held the following summer. In what is generally recognized as a conciliatory move, the national committee accepted the city's offer. Even then the nomination of Al Smith—the Catholic, Tammany Hall–backed New York governor who aggressively opposed prohibitionqv—seemed likely, and national party officials in the East felt the need to appease the Protestant, prohibitionist South, which had not hosted a national convention since the Civil War.qv Preparations in Houston began almost immediately; Sam Houston Hall, with a seating capacity of 16,000 and six acres of floor space, was built in sixty-four working days.

The convention opened on June 26, 1928. Al Smith remained in Albany but faced little competition from other candidates. Other names placed in nomination included Senator James Reed of Missouri, Representative Cordell Hull of Tennessee, and Jesse H. Jones of Texas. However, no contender provided a serious threat to Smith, and most candidates agreed to stand behind the party and support the convention's nominee. At the first roll call, Smith received 724⅔ votes, ten short of the number (two-thirds of the total) required for nomination. Ohio then switched its votes to Smith, and other states followed suit. Texas, the notable exception, cast its forty votes for Jones. State politicians had long opposed Smith's nomination. Former Texas governor Oscar B. Colquittqv publicly argued that Smith sought to nullify a provision of the Constitution only because it "happened to be out of harmony with his personal opinions," and that "to nullify this part of the organic law will bring contempt for other parts of it." Nevertheless, Smith easily won the nomination in Houston with 849⅔ votes. Although women's temperance groups and the local Baptist church held all-day and all-night prayer meetings near the convention hall and insisted that God would intervene to prevent the "catastrophe" of Smith's nomination, inside the hall the delegates saw Smith as their only hope of victory over the Republicans in the fall.

With Smith nominated, party officials looked to the vice-presidential slot and the official platform as means of ensuring harmony within the party. Many observers perceived the Texas delegation, in particular, as aloof and hostile towards Smith. Judge George W. Olvany, a Tammany Hall leader, therefore sent his and Jesse Jones's friend Col. Joseph M. Hartfield to offer Jones the nomination for vice president. Jones declined, and the Texas delegation considered supporting either Maj. Gen. Henry T. Allen,qv commander of the Nineteenth Division, or, a more likely possibility, Senator Alben Barkley of Kentucky. However, upon the prodding of one state delegate who insisted that the Texas delegation get "behind the ticket and [show] New York and the Democratic Party that Texans were true Democrats," the Texas delegates unanimously decided to support Smith's choice, Senator Joseph T. Robinson of Arkansas, the Democratic minority leader. Robinson supported prohibition and was the first southerner, apart from Woodrow Wilson, to have a place on the national ticket since the Civil War.

Harmony prevailed as well in the drafting of the party platform. The most heated controversy centered around prohibition and its enforcement. Texas governor Daniel J. Moody, Jr.,qv was expected to pursue a floor fight for a "bone-dry" plank on prohibition. However, when the proposed plank, which pledged "the party and its nominees to an honest effort to enforce the eighteenth amendment and all other provisions of the Federal Constitution and all laws enacted pursuant thereto," was accepted by such recognized prohibitionists as former secretary of the navy Josephus Daniels and Methodist bishop James Cannon, Moody decided to relinquish his fight.

The convention ended on June 29. During the final moments a telegram from Smith accepting the nomination was read to the delegates. Many of the dry delegates were stunned by the party's stand on prohibition and immediately questioned the appropriateness of their candidate. The nominee's message read, "It is well-known that I believe there should be fundamental changes in the present provisions for national prohibition. . . . I feel it to be the duty of the chosen leader of the people to point the way which, in his opinion, leads us to a sane, sensible solution of a condition which, I am convinced, is entirely unsatisfactory to the great mass of our people."

The candidate's remarks prompted many anti-Smith Democrats eventually to join forces with Republicans and elect Herbert Hoover in November 1928. In Texas the massive defection of Democrats was attributed both to Smith's antiprohibition views and his Catholicism. The state gave Hoover a majority, the first time in history that a Republican presidential candidate had carried Texas. The election had severely divided the Democrats and left them facing a struggle for control as the 1930s began.

BIBLIOGRAPHY: Norman D. Brown, *Hood, Bonnet, and Little Brown Jug: Texas Politics, 1921–1928* (College Station: Texas A&M University Press, 1984). David Burner, *The Politics of Provincialism: The Democratic Party in Transition, 1918–1932* (New York: Knopf, 1970). New York *Times*, June 29, 30, 1928. Roy V. Peel and Thomas C. Donnelly, *The 1928 Campaign* (New York: Richard R. Smith, 1931).

Ada Ferrer

DEMOCRATIC PARTY. State laws dictate the formal organization of the Democratic party in Texas and provide for both temporary and permanent organs. The temporary party organs consist of a series of regularly scheduled (biennial) conventions beginning at the precinct level and limited to persons who voted in the party primary. The chief function of the precinct convention is to choose delegates to the county convention or the senatorial district convention held on the second Saturday after the first primary. When a county has more than one senatorial district because of its large population, a separate senatorial district convention is held for each senate district in the county. The delegates who gather at the county and the senatorial district conventions are likewise chiefly concerned with choosing delegates to the state convention held biennially in June for the purpose of formally choosing the state executive committee, adopting a party platform, and officially certifying the party's candidates to be listed on the general election ballot. In presidential election years the state convention also chooses delegates to the national presidential nominating convention. Until 1984 two state conventions were held in gubernatorial years, one for state affairs in September and one for sending delegates to the national Democratic convention. The permanent organs of the party are largely independent of the temporary ones. Voters in the Democratic primary in each precinct elect for a two-year term of office a chairman or committee person who is formally the party's agent or spokesman in that precinct. A few of these precinct chairmen work diligently for the party and its nominees; some do very little. Normally the precinct chairman will be in charge of the conduct of the primary in his precinct, and, perhaps less assuredly, will serve as chairman of the precinct convention and of the delegation to the county convention. The party's county executive committee consists of the precinct chairmen plus a county chairman who is elected in the primary by the Democratic voters in the county as a whole. The county committee determines policy in such matters as the conduct and financing of the primary, and officially canvasses its results. It also serves as a focal point for party organizing and campaigning efforts.

The State Democratic Executive Committee includes one man and one woman from each of the thirty-one state senatorial districts, plus a chairman and a vice-chairman, formally chosen by the state convention but informally chosen by a caucus of the delegates from each senatorial district. Occasionally a governor and his advisers will decide that a caucus nominee is simply unacceptable and then will substitute his own choices. By law the state committee is responsible for overseeing the party primary and for canvassing the returns. It also undertakes fund-raising and campaign work for the party. Before Republican Bill Clements' election as governor in 1978, the committee's role was to serve as an adjunct of the governor's office, designed to help the governor as best as it could with political and policy problems. However, after Clements was elected, the party and its machinery developed a new degree of independence from the governor.

The Democratic party has played a central role in the political development of Texas since white Americans first settled the region. The majority of early settlers came from the American South and brought their past political allegiances with them. Texas Democrats evolved over the years from a very loose association into an organized party. This evolution was slow because the lack of a second party in Texas throughout much of the state's history caused Democrats to be less concerned with developing a unified, centralized party organization and more inclined to engage in factional strife. Throughout much of its existence, the Democratic party has been protective of the status quo.

The history of the party in Texas can be divided into two major periods. In the first period, from independence in 1836 through the presidential election of 1952, the Democratic party in Texas was the only viable party in the state. It dominated politics at all levels. In the second major period, after 1952, the party faced a growing challenge to its control of state affairs from the once ineffective Republican party.qv Both of the major periods, however, can be subdivided. The years 1836 through 1952 divide into six subsections: from independence in 1836 through the Civil War, Reconstruction,qqv the late 19th Century, the Progressive Era,qv the 1920s, and the New Deal–World War II era. The latter period divides into three subsections: the 1950s, the 1960s, and the 1970s and 1980s.

Several crucial events marked the years 1836 through 1865 in Texas political history, including the independent nationhood of the Republic of Texas,qv entrance into the Union, and secessionqv and the Civil War. During these years the Democratic party officially formed in Texas. As a result, the party in the state was both affected by these events and was a major actor in this period. Even before Texas gained its independence from Mexico the Democratic party in the United States influenced the politics of the region. As early as February 25, 1822, with the formation of the Texas Association in Russellville, Kentucky, individuals interested in land speculation came together to secure land grants in Texas. The Texas Association drew its membership from professionals—merchants, doctors, and lawyers—in Kentucky and Tennessee. Many of these men were also close friends of Andrew Jackson and had strong ties to the Democratic party. Likewise, most of the settlers in Texas were either from the Upper South or the Lower South and held strong allegiances to the Democratic party. Elections in the Republic of Texas demonstrated competition among rival factions or strong individuals. Despite sympathy for the Democratic party in the United States, as yet there was no strong party tradition in the Republic of Texas. Before 1848, elections in Texas were conducted without organized political parties. Personality was the dominant political force in the state. Contests between factions evolved into a more defined stage of competition with the development of the Democratic party in Texas as a formal organ of the electoral process during the 1848 presidential campaign. Even so, it was some time before Democrats adopted any sort of a statewide network or arranged for scheduled conventions.

Nevertheless, between annexationqv and 1861 partisanship developed slowly but steadily. Men who governed the state generally reflected the views of the burgeoning Democratic party. However, personal loyalty such as that found in the factions supporting and opposing Governor Sam Houstonqv (1859–61) still heavily influenced state politics. Competition for the Democrats came from various sources at different times and included first the Whig party, then the American (Know-Nothing) party,qqv and finally the Opposition or Constitutional Union party.qv The mid-1850s witnessed rapid growth of the formal mechanisms of party discipline. For example, delegations from twelve counties attended the state Democratic convention in 1855, yet the following year, with the Know-Nothing threat still seemingly viable, more than 90 percent of Texas counties were represented. During these years the convention system became the chief method of recruiting candidates for office in the Texas Democratic party. In the years after 1854 the ongoing upheaval in national politics influenced the party. In the process Texans moved away from an earlier identification with Jacksonian nationalism and became closely associated with the states'-rights goals of the lower South. Yet the election of Houston as governor in 1859 demonstrated the divisions within the state's political structure, since he represented the Opposition in the contest against the Texas Democratic party. During the Civil War, the Democratic party in Texas became closely associated with the extreme proslavery wing of the Democratic party in the Confederacy, and partisan activity came to a halt.

In the immediate aftermath of the Civil War, during the period of presidential Reconstruction, the split between Unionist and Secessionist Democrats reemerged. During the war the strongest Unionists had disappeared from the political scene or had moved north. Those who stayed active reluctantly supported the Confederacy. After the war the Unionists continued to support a more egalitarian distribution of power in the state, while working to reduce the influence of former planters. But they split also. Their positions on freedmen ranged from supporting full civil and political rights to opposing anything beyond emancipation. In part as a result of the split among Democrats but more as a result of congressional Reconstruction nationally, Republicans captured both the governor's office and the state legislature in 1869. By 1872 Democrats regrouped and overturned the Republican government in the Texas legislature, charging that the administration of Governor Edmund J. Davis^{qv} (1870–74) was corrupt and extravagant. Much of the money appropriated during Republican control had in fact gone to frontier defense, law enforcement, and education. Davis had two more years in office, but he could do little with a Democratic legislature pledged to austerity. In the gubernatorial election of 1873, the Democratic campaign theme included support for states' rights, loyalty to the Confederacy, and an attack on freedmen and Republicans. The final Democratic measure to overturn all Republican influence in Texas came with the passage of the Constitution of 1876,^{qv} which severely constrained the powers of the state government, cut back on state services and limited the amount of money that could be raised in taxes.

The Democrats' return to power at the end of the Reconstruction era did not mean an end to factional divisions within the state. Like the rest of the nation, Texas faced various third-party challenges during the Gilded Age, a fact that reflected a growing uncertainty about economic conditions. In 1876, however, the state Democratic party continued to focus its attention on the concerns of the Civil War era. In fact, the majority of the delegates to the state Democratic convention were Confederate veterans. Democratic voters were often white landowning agrarians, manufacturers, lumbermen, bankers, shippers and railroad men, and Protestants. Indeed the conservative political moods of the state through the late 1880s can be attributed to the growing cult of the Confederacy throughout the South. Against this backdrop a vote against the Democratic party became a vote against the cultural legacy of the "Lost Cause." Party organization also encouraged more Southern loyalist candidates through the convention process. After 1878 Texas Democrats had trouble adjusting to the various third-party challenges of the late nineteenth century, as demonstrated by conflicting responses to the Greenback movement (*see* GREENBACK PARTY). At times Democrats endorsed even more drastic inflationary measures, but at other times they bitterly attacked financial views that encouraged printing of additional paper money. In the end the Greenback challenge forced Texas Democrats to pay attention to the economic problems of the state. By the 1880s the issue of prohibition^{qv} also began to cause problems for Texas Democrats, who initially sought to dodge the question by calling for local-option elections. Nevertheless, prohibition politics evenly split the party and laid the ground for bigger battles in the early twentieth century.

In the 1880s and 1890s Texas Democrats faced an even bigger challenge, first from the Farmers' Alliance and then from the People's (Populist) party.^{qqv} Maintaining an official posture apart from organized politics, the Farmers' Alliance sometimes worked with the state Democratic party. By the late 1880s Texas Democrats recognized the agrarianists' demands and adopted a platform supporting the abolition of national banks, issuance of United States currency, and the regulation of freight rates and businesses. The election of James Stephen Hogg^{qv} as governor in 1890 temporarily allied the agrarian protest with the Democratic party. Hogg's efforts on behalf of the newly constituted Railroad Commission^{qv} divided the Democratic party into three factions: businessmen who sought to limit the commission's impact, leaders of the Farmers' Alliance who sought to dominate the commission, and farmers, businessmen, and politicians who supported Hogg. Alliancemen soon split further away from Hogg and the majority of Texas Democrats over the idea of subtreasuries. By the 1890s Texas Democrats had given their support to silver coinage. In the years after 1896 most Populists in Texas returned to the Democratic party because Democrats had incorporated portions of the Populist platform and economic conditions for farmers had improved, while segregationism discouraged economic cooperation with African Americans.^{qv}

In the first two decades of the twentieth century the party split into a progressive wing that increasingly identified with the demands of prohibitionists and a stand-pat wing opposed to progressivism. The reality of one-party politics in Texas and the South paved the way for factional splits, such as the one over the prohibition issue during the first third of the twentieth century. Personality also played a key role in the split in the Democratic party when the progressive forces within the party banded together to squelch the influence of United States senator Joseph Weldon Bailey^{qv} in state politics. The "Bailey question" became associated with the perceived evils of corporate power and swollen private interests in the public domain. Yet reforms during the 1890s and early 1900s had reduced the influence of railroads, out-of-state corporations, and insurance companies in state politics, leaving moral and cultural problems to consume the attention of Progressive Era reformers. During the presidential election of 1912 a common thread connecting the progressive Democrats supporting Woodrow Wilson and the advocates of prohibition became apparent. In the immediate aftermath of Wilson's election Texas Democrats—including Albert S. Burleson, Thomas Watt Gregory, Edward M. House, David F. Houston, and Morris Sheppard^{qqv}—established an important precedent for Texas Democrats by taking a significant role in national political affairs that continued throughout most of the twentieth century. In 1914 personality again ruptured the Democratic party in Texas with the election of James E. Ferguson^{qv} as governor. Ferguson sought to avoid the liquor question entirely, although his sympathies and his big contributors were wet. His official actions as governor, including an ongoing battle with the state's cultural and intellectual elite at the University of Texas, eventually united progressive Democrats in their opposition to him. After Ferguson was impeached, dry, progressive Democrats aligned with the new governor, William P. Hobby, Sr. (1917–21), and enacted their agenda of liquor reform, woman suffrage,^{qv} and reform of the election laws.^{qv}

For Texas Democrats the decade of the 1920s was a bridge between the ethnocultural issues of the Progressive Era and the economic concerns of the Great Depression^{qv} and the New Deal. During World War I,^{qv} Texas Democrats had addressed many issues of the Progressive Era and found legislative solutions, leaving Texans to argue over the results of prohibition for the next decade. But Texas Democrats, like their counterparts throughout the South, soon shifted their goals for reform away from a social and cultural agenda toward what can best be described as business progressivism, or an increased concern for expansion and efficiency in government. Yet they did not limit their attention to issues such as highway development,^{qv} economic growth, and education improvement, but also joined numerous intraparty battles revolving around the enforcement of prohibition, the Ku Klux Klan,^{qv} and "Fergusonism." Despite Pat Neff's^{qv} gubernatorial administration (1921–25) and its attention to the cause of business progressivism with such measures as government consolidation, prison reform, education reform, highway construction, and industrial expansion, the legislature was not willing to accept all of Neff's ideas. The result was a mixed record on business progressivism. The state elections in 1924 quickly evolved into a fight over the Klan issue. Furthermore, the presence of Ma (Miriam A.) Ferguson^{qv} as the leading anti-Klan candidate further weakened the progressive Democratic forces in the state. However, electing Mrs. Ferguson did have one ameliorative affect on Texas politics, namely the elimination of the Klan as a political force. The other major political development in Texas during the 1920s centered around the 1928 presidential election. In Texas, as in the rest of the nation, the contest served to heighten the tensions between wet and dry Democrats. In the fall of 1927 several young Democrats who opposed prohibition organized to fight the entrenched dry progressive wing of the state Democratic party and to work for an uninstructed delegation to the national convention that eventually endorsed Al Smith. They regarded Governor Dan (Daniel J.) Moody^{qv} (1927–31) as their leader. The selection of Houston as the host city for the Democratic national convention further enlivened Texas politics as Smith's backers and the bone-dry forces maneuvered for control of the state's delegation and Moody's support.

In the spring of 1928 the dry progressive Democrats formed the Texas Constitutional Democrats to gain control of the state's party machinery and to work for a presidential ticket that reflected their views. Governor Moody led a third group, the Democrats of Texas or the Harmony Democrats, that eventually organized to prevent a bitter feud between the warring factions of the party and to try to develop a common program. These factional divisions within the party resulted in a bitter division both among delegates at the Houston convention and within the state Democratic party. Some of the state's most ardent Democratic supporters of prohibition put principles above party and worked for the Republican nominee Herbert Hoover in the general election rather than support the Catholic wet candidate, Al Smith. The Klan faction of the Democratic party, although waning in influence, also informally supported Hoover. Dry voters in rural North and West Texas and urban voters influenced by the Klan and Republican prosperity in Harris, Dallas, and Tarrant counties account for most of the Democrats who went with Hoover. The Republicans also did well among fundamentalists. Hoover was the first Republican presidential nominee to carry Texas, but it was all for naught. The depression, the New Deal, and World War II^{qv} put Republican ascendancy in Texas on hold for twenty-four years.

Economic crisis followed by recovery dominated the period 1932–1952 in Texas politics. The early New Deal years yielded a period of political harmony within the state's Democratic party, but by the late 1930s conservative forces had regrouped and regained control of state politics. At the same time liberal factions began to exert pressures on the political process that did not subside for the remainder of the twentieth century. In the years immediately following the stock-market crash in 1929, controversies surrounding the oil and gas industry,^{qv} the agricultural depression, the return of Fergusonism, and the rapid passage of New Deal legislation that overshadowed state and local efforts to combat the depression paralyzed state government and the Democratic party in Texas. At the same time, Texas Democrats in Washington, including Jesse H. Jones, John Nance Garner, Tom (Thomas T.) Connally, Marvin Jones, James P. Buchanan, Hatton W. Sumners, J. W. Wright Patman, and Sam (Samuel T.) Rayburn,^{qqv} exerted significant influence after the election of Franklin D. Roosevelt. By the mid-1930s the depression became the single most important issue in state politics. As yet, little conservative opposition to New Deal reforms had coalesced in Texas. In 1934 Texas voters elected James Allred^{qv} governor. His administration attempted to deal with the impact of the depression on the state by reorganizing state law enforcement, putting a state tax on chain stores, increasing assistance to the elderly, starting a teachers' retirement system, and increasing funding to public schools. Allred's advocacy of these measures earned him the respect and admiration of the liberal wing of the state Democratic party.

By 1936 conservative reaction to the national Democratic party erupted in the formation of the Jeffersonian Democrats.^{qv} This national organization received significant aid from several prominent conservative Texas Democrats including John Henry Kirby, Joseph Weldon Bailey, Jr., and J. Evetts Haley.^{qqv} Though the Jeffersonian Democrats had little impact on the 1936 election, they did fore-

shadow political trends of the 1940s and 1950s. Indeed the election of W. Lee "Pappy" O'Daniel^{qv} as governor in 1938 signaled the return to power of the conservative wing of the Democratic party in Texas. Though O'Daniel's campaign rhetoric appealed to impoverished Texans still suffering the effects of the depression, his financial supporters and policy advisors were generally drawn from the state's business and financial leaders. The battle over a third term for Roosevelt also divided the party. When many Texas Democrats encouraged the unsuccessful presidential candidacy of Vice President John Nance Garner, the party split between Garner Democrats, including many of the old Jeffersonian Democrats, and the New Deal Democrats. The 1940 fissure remained throughout the coming decade as conservatives and liberals fought for control of the party. But attention to foreign policy during World War II temporarily slowed the battles between the warring factions.

The politics of race, however, renewed tensions within Texas when the Supreme Court overturned the state's white primary^{qv} law in the case of *Smith v. Allwright* (1944). The success of the white primary as a method of controlling access to the ballot box was closely tied to the fortunes of the Democratic party. The device went through several changes throughout its existence, but it relied heavily on a solid Democratic dominance that made a Democratic primary victory tantamount to election. In 1927 in *Nixon v. Herndon* the United States Supreme Court had struck down a Texas law preventing blacks from voting in the Democratic primary (*see* NIXON, LAWRENCE AARON). The Texas legislature then authorized the Democratic State Committee to exclude blacks, and, when the Supreme Court overturned this law in *Nixon v. Condon* in 1932, Texas repealed the law and left control of the primary entirely with the Democratic party. Since no state action was now involved in the committee's decision to exclude blacks from the Democratic primary, in 1935 the court held the new Texas arrangement valid in *Grovey v. Townsend* (*see* GROVEY, RICHARD RANDOLPH). Then came *Smith v. Allwright*. Though it initially opposed the decision, the Texas Democratic party came to rely on black voters.

More important at the time, however, the presidential election of 1944 heightened tensions between the Roosevelt and anti-Roosevelt wings of the party. FDR's renomination for a fourth term led conservative Texas Democrats to join with the American Democratic National Committee, an organization formed to defeat the president. Texas conservatives received support from the same individuals who had aided the Jeffersonian Democrats a decade earlier. Wealthy Texas conservatives with an interest in the increasingly powerful oil and gas industry funded the conservatives, who controlled about two-thirds of the delegates to the state Democratic convention in May 1944. National convention delegates from Texas thus supported the conservative anti–New Dealers, but angry liberals rejected the actions of the state convention and sent their own delegation to the national convention. The New Deal Democrats in Texas barely regained control of the state party's machinery at the governor's convention in September. However, conservative Texas Democrats organized into the Texas Regulars^{qv} and arranged for the placement on the November ballot of an independent slate of electors who would never vote for FDR. The Texas Regulars received less than 15 percent of the state vote; they and their conservative backers learned that a strong voice in state politics would not translate directly into influence on national politics. Despite the persistent loyalty of the majority of the state's voters to the Democratic party, the widening schism between the factions indicated that a growing number of Texans were receptive to more conservative politics both within and outside the traditional Democratic party. Indeed actions including the appointment of conservative businessmen to state boards and commissions and the passage of a right-to-work law that Texas governors, all Democrats, implemented during the 1940s reflected the dominant conservatism of the state.

The 1948 Senate race in Texas exemplified many of the tensions within the state party. Lyndon B. Johnson, who eventually defeated

Coke Stevenson qqv in an election fraught with charges of wrongdoing on both sides, represented the difficulties liberal New Dealers faced when they attempted to campaign statewide. To appeal to a conservative but Democratic electorate required pragmatic compromise. By the end of the 1940s the Democratic party in Texas had split at least three ways—into a conservative wing that usually controlled state politics, a liberal wing that had supported the New Deal and that later championed the rights of women, the working class, and ethnic minorities, and a group in the middle that shifted back and forth between the two extremes. By the middle twentieth century the Texas Democratic party was riven by factional strife. The liberal-conservative Democratic split also aided the development of a viable state Republican opposition. In the years after the 1952 presidential election a two-party system began to emerge. The gubernatorial administration of R. Allan Shivers qv (1949–57) and the efforts of the liberal opposition to reclaim power within both the state party machinery and the state government dominated state Democratic politics during the 1950s. During the 1950s Texas Democrats also wielded significant power in Washington with Sam Rayburn as speaker of the House and Lyndon Johnson as Senate majority leader. Texas Democrats Oveta Culp Hobby qv and Robert Anderson held cabinet appointments during the Eisenhower administration. After becoming governor, Shivers took control of the party machinery by instituting a purge of the State Democratic Executive Committee, an organization with two members from each state Senate district, and stacking its membership with his supporters. Shivers also engineered a change in the election laws that permitted cross-filing for both the Democratic and Republican primaries in the 1952 election. As a result of the change, conservative Democrats, termed "Shivercrats" because of their allegiance to the governor, also filed in the Republican primary, thus reducing the number of Republicans that ran for office.

The ongoing struggle with the federal government over control of the Texas Tidelands further complicated the 1952 election in the state. Though federal ownership of the submerged oil-rich lands would benefit Texas in terms of royalty payments, oil and gas interests in the state stood to profit more if the state retained possession of the Tidelands. Conservative Democrats took the lead in championing native interests, which were backed by most Texans as well. Liberal and moderate Democratic politicians, who had stronger ties to the administration of President Harry S. Truman and the national Democratic party, found themselves in a more precarious position and either carefully balanced their support for Texas ownership of the Tidelands with the larger national interests or opposed Texas ownership altogether (*see* TIDELANDS CONTROVERSY).

Following the triumphs of Eisenhower and Shivers in 1952, liberals in the Texas Democratic party decided to organize and increase their influence on party politics. In May 1953 the short-lived Texas Democratic Organizing Committee was formed. By January of 1954 this group became part of the newly constituted Democratic Advisory Council. The DAC participated in Texas politics for two years before the Democrats of Texas organized in 1956. The DOT, the most successful of the three groups, lasted through 1960 before disbanding. Each of these groups received support from the liberal weekly journal of political information, the *State Observer* and its 1954 successor, the *Texas Observer*.qv Each of these liberal organizations also received support from labor and a number of women activists. The goals of the groups focused on taking control of the official machinery of the Texas Democratic party away from the Shivers forces. In 1956 Johnson and Rayburn battled Shivers, the nominally Democratic governor who had helped deliver the state's votes to Dwight D. Eisenhower in 1952, for control of the Democratic party machinery. Three main groups—the Shivercrats or conservative Democrats, moderate Democratic backers of LBJ, and the liberals—engaged in this intraparty battle that featured mistrust, mudslinging, shifting alliances, and ultimately a deeper division within the party. The Republicans, with the help of Shivers, managed to carry Texas for Eisenhower again in 1956.

The following year liberal Democrats in Texas fought back against the strength of the Shivercrats, and Ralph Yarborough's narrow victory in the 1957 special United States Senate race gave the liberal wing of the Texas Democratic party a new elected voice in national politics.

Factional infighting in the Democratic party declined during the 1960s. First Johnson's presidential ambitions and then his presidency dominated Texas politics in that decade. In 1959 the state legislature authorized a measure moving the Democratic primary from July to May and permitting candidates to run simultaneously for two offices, thus allowing Johnson to run for the Senate and the presidency. (This measure, dubbed the LBJ law, also benefited Lloyd Bentsen's dual run for the vice-presidency and the Senate in 1988.) Despite efforts by the Democrats of Texas to secure the support of state convention delegates and power within the party machinery, conservative Democrats retained control. Through the work of LBJ and the Viva Kennedy–Viva Johnson clubs,qv the Democrats narrowly carried Texas in 1960, reversing the direction of the 1952 and 1956 presidential elections in Texas. Similarly, the 1961 special election to fill Johnson's Senate seat had a lasting effect on Democratic party organization in Texas. After Yarborough's unexpected victory in the 1957 special election, conservative Democrats in the state legislature amended the election laws to require a run-off in special elections when no candidate received at least 50 percent plus one vote. In 1961, within a field of seventy-two candidates, three individuals made a strong claim for the liberal vote, thus dividing liberal strength and opening the way for a runoff between William A. Blakley, the interim senator and a conservative Texas Democrat, and John G. Tower,qv the only viable Republican candidate in the race. Liberal Democrats thought Blakley as conservative as Tower and opted either to "go fishing" during the run-off or support Tower, thinking it would be easier to oust him in 1966 with a more liberal Democratic challenger. Tower, however, easily won his next two reelection bids and eked out a third in 1978. Liberals also hoped that a Republican victory would encourage the development of an effective Republican party in the state and allow moderates and liberals to gain control of the state Democratic party. Indeed, Texas Democrats statewide remained divided between liberals who supported Ralph Yarborough and moderates who backed LBJ. The two factions waged war over the gubernatorial contest in 1962, when John B. Connally,qv a moderate to conservative Democrat associated with the Johnson wing of the party, was elected. As governor, Connally concentrated his efforts on economic development but received criticism from liberals who thought he neglected minorities and the poor. The Kennedy assassinationqv on November 22, 1963, which traumatized the citizens of Texas, also deeply shook the state Democratic party since it propelled Johnson into the White House and created the need for a greater degree of accommodation between moderate and liberal Texas Democrats. In the 1964 presidential race Johnson carried his home state with ease. In the middle to late 1960s, however, Connally's iron rule of the State Democratic Executive Committee further weakened the liberal forces within the state Democratic party. The results of the 1968 presidential election in Texas also emphasized the sagging fortunes of the Democratic party in Texas, as Hubert Humphrey barely managed to carry the state.

Liberals in the Texas Democratic party reached a low point in 1970 with the defeat of their spiritual leader, Ralph Yarborough, in the Democratic primary by conservative Democrat Lloyd Bentsen, Jr. Bentsen successfully employed a strategy that conservative Democrats in Texas later used against the increasingly viable Republican party, namely, developing a base of support among middle to upper income voters in the primaries, then drawing from the traditional Democratic constituencies of lower income people, labor unions, and minorities in the general elections. The 1972 gubernatorial election marked the culmination of a gradual transition in Texas Democratic party politics from an era when elite leaders fighting behind closed doors over a conservative or liberal agenda dominated party politics to an era of moderation and greater toleration for diverse views. This contest took place against the backdrop of the Sharpstown Stock Fraud Scandal[qv] in the Texas state legislature. The scandal ended the political careers of Governor Preston Smith, Lieutenant Governor Ben Barnes, and Speaker of the House Gus Mutscher, all of whom were closely tied to the old Democratic establishment. The two front-runners in the race, Frances (Sissy) Farenthold and Dolph Briscoe, benefited from the public backlash against incumbents. The contest between Farenthold and Briscoe also reflected the nature of the transition at work in the Democratic party. Farenthold drew her strength from liberals and college students. But in his victory the politically conservative Briscoe effectively split the liberal coalition by securing the neutrality of organized labor. The trend was toward more moderate, establishment-backed Democratic candidates.

In the 1972 presidential election the GOP again demonstrated that it could carry Texas in national contests. In fact, from 1976 through 1992 Democratic presidential candidates failed to win Texas. Republicans also proved they could successfully challenge Democrats for control of state politics when Bill Clements won the governor's race in 1978. His victory further sparked the ascendancy of the moderates in the Democratic party, and in 1982 a new generation of Democrats came to power in Texas. The warchests of incumbent United States senator Lloyd Bentsen and incumbent lieutenant governor William P. Hobby, Jr., aided the election bids of challengers Mark White for governor, Jim Mattox for attorney general, Ann Richards for state treasurer, Gary Mauro for land commissioner, and Jim Hightower for agricultural commissioner, all of whom won in the general election. These candidates benefited from and represented the more moderate to liberal position of the state Democratic party.

In the 1970s and 1980s the Democratic party in Texas also appeared more open to the interests of women and minorities. Groups such as the Mexican American Democrats and Texas Democratic Women gained a greater voice in party affairs. Also, women and members of minorities could now be found in elected positions from the governor down. Nevertheless, the state GOP continued to gain strength into the early 1990s, demonstrating its ability to compete not only in gubernatorial and senatorial races but in such down-the-ballot offices as state treasurer, agriculture commissioner, state Supreme Court justice, and railroad commissioner, as well as in various county and local posts. By 1990 Republicans also held about a third of the seats in both houses of the state legislature.

In the early 1990s the GOP also successfully gained control of about a third of the Texas congressional delegation. Before the 1950s, Democrats had controlled the entire delegation. In 1993 the GOP held both United States Senate seats in Texas after Lloyd Bentsen became secretary of the treasury. The growing strength of the Republican party among the Texas delegation served to dilute the power of Texas Democrats in Washington. Compared with the 1950s, when Rayburn and Johnson controlled the House and Senate as speaker and majority leader, Texas Democrats in the 1980s and 1990s managed to retain only a few key chairmanships in Congress. However, after the election of William J. Clinton as president in 1992 Texas Democrats played a role in the executive branch, with Bentsen at the Treasury Department and Henry Cisneros as secretary of housing and urban development, despite the fact that Clinton did not carry Texas. Previously, Democrats had to win Texas in order to win the presidency; no Democrat had won the White House since Texas entered the Union in 1845 without carrying the state. But Clinton was elected, and Texas Democrats' political clout in Washington declined.

The Republican lock on about a third of the state's electorate by the early 1990s had a double impact on the Democratic party. It encouraged the development of a more moderate leadership for party machinery and pushed some individual Democratic candidates to try to appear more conservative than their Republican challengers. Thus, even though the fledgling GOP in the 1950s and 1960s developed on the political right, the hopes of liberal activists in the 1950s and 1960s for establishing a liberal Democratic party in Texas were at best only partially successful, since the revamped moderate Democratic party had difficulty retaining control of elected offices in the state. In 1994 Republicans regained the governor's office, retained the office of agricultural commissioner, gained all three seats on the Railroad Commission, and picked up two congressional seats.

See also LATE NINETEENTH-CENTURY TEXAS, TEXAS IN THE 1920S, TEXAS SINCE WORLD WAR II, *and* GOVERNORS.

BIBLIOGRAPHY: Alwyn Barr, *Reconstruction to Reform: Texas Politics, 1876–1906* (Austin: University of Texas Press, 1971). Norman D. Brown, *Hood, Bonnet, and Little Brown Jug: Texas Politics, 1921–1928* (College Station: Texas A&M University Press, 1984). Robert Dallek, *Lone Star Rising: Lyndon Johnson and His Times, 1908–1960* (New York and Oxford: Oxford University Press, 1991). Lewis L. Gould, *Progressives and Prohibitionists: Texas Democrats in the Wilson Era* (Austin: University of Texas Press, 1973; rpt., Austin: Texas State Historical Association, 1992). George N. Green, *The Establishment in Texas Politics* (Westport, Connecticut: Greenwood, 1979). Stanley Siegel, *A Political History of the Texas Republic* (Austin: University of Texas Press, 1956). Vertical Files, Barker Texas History Center, University of Texas at Austin.

Nancy Beck Young

DEMOCRATIC PROGRESSIVE VOTERS LEAGUE. The Democratic Progressive Voters League, organized in 1936 as the Progressive Voters League, is one of the oldest black political organizations in the state of Texas. It developed in an era in which the right to vote for black citizens was circumscribed by a white primary[qv] and a poll tax (see ELECTION LAWS). Both measures severely limited black political activity in the state; the Progressive Voters League emerged as an organization that allowed African Americans in Dallas to influence local politics and exercise their rights as citizens.

Blacks in Dallas began organizing a political base in 1934. In that year the Dallas graduate chapter of Alpha Phi Alpha fraternity held a week-long series of symposia on citizenship that stressed the importance of paying the poll tax and voting as an obligation of full citizenship. Speakers suggested that blacks in Dallas could solve the problems of poor housing, unemployment, overcrowded schools, and crime by voting and electing candidates sensitive to their needs. To act on the enthusiasm generated, such black leaders in Dallas as Antonio Maceo Smith[qv] and Rev. Maynard H. Jackson organized the Progressive Citizens League. The league was organized to encourage blacks to pay their poll taxes and to vote for candidates who would address the needs of Dallas blacks. In 1935 the organization's president, Ammon S. Wells, ran a strong campaign for the state legislature, placing sixth in a field of sixty candidates. This election demonstrated the potential power of the black electorate and prompted PCL leaders to organize another poll tax–payment campaign. The PCL was instrumental in securing federal funds to erect the Hall of Negro Life at the Texas Centennial.[qqv]

In 1936 the Progressive Citizens League was renamed the Progressive Voters League to reflect the organization's emphasis on paying the poll tax and voting as key objectives for achieving black citizenship rights in Dallas. In the same year the league coordinated the efforts of over 100 black organizations in Dallas in a massive poll tax–payment campaign. The league registered almost 7,000 voters and organized the black electorate into a voting bloc that carried the balance of power in the 1937 Dallas City Council elections. The league supported the Forward Dallas Association's slate of candidates over those of the Citizens Charter Association and assisted the former association in winning a majority of the seats on the Dallas City Council. The Citizens Charter Association had dominated Dallas city government since 1930 and did so again until 1970.

The 1937 election established the Progressive Voters League as a viable black political organization and set the tone for its activities for the next fifty years. The Forward Dallas Association rewarded the support provided by the league with a new black high school, more jobs for blacks in city government, and consideration of blacks for police jobs in the city. With this success, the league continued to register and organize black voters in the city, to endorse candidates in local elections, and to encourage black participation in the political process locally, statewide, and nationally.

After the National Association for the Advancement of Colored People won *Smith v. Allwright* in 1944 and eliminated the state's Democratic white primary, the Progressive Voters League attempted to become a statewide organization and align itself with the Democratic party.qv As early as 1940 Maynard Jackson, the league's first president, made attempts to expand statewide. As late as 1943 his efforts had proved futile. After 1944, however, the leaders of the league were successful in organizing statewide and even nationwide. But both the state and national organizations collapsed after 1950. After the victory in the *Smith* case, the league's leaders split over whether they should align with and accept funding from the Democratic party or remain nonpartisan. Those in opposition resisted joining the Democrats and maintained the league as a nonpartisan organization until 1948. In that year the league chartered itself in Dallas County as the Democratic Progressive Voters League, and since then it has supported the Democratic party locally and nationally.

In the late 1980s the Democratic Progressive Voters League of Dallas County primarily interviewed and endorsed candidates for local and state elections. Although it was no longer the mass organization that it was in the 1930s, 1940s, and 1950s, it maintained influence in local politics. In 1985 the league's president, John Wiley Price, used the organization as the political base for his successful campaign to become county commissioner. He became the first black to serve on the commissioners' court in Dallas County.

BIBLIOGRAPHY: Alwyn Barr and Robert A. Calvert, eds., *Black Leaders: Texans for Their Times* (Austin: Texas State Historical Association, 1981). J. Mason Brewer, *Negro Legislators of Texas and Their Descendants* (Dallas: Mathis, 1935; 2d ed., Austin: Jenkins, 1970). Conrey Bryson, *Dr. Lawrence A. Nixon and the White Primary* (El Paso: Texas Western Press, 1974). W. Marvin Dulaney, "The Progressive Voters League—A Political Voice for African Americans in Dallas," *Legacies: A History Journal for Dallas and North Central Texas,* Spring 1991. Michael L. Gillette, "The Rise of the NAACP in Texas," *Southwestern Historical Quarterly* 81 (April 1978). Darlene Clark Hine, *Black Victory: The Rise and Fall of the White Primary in Texas* (Millwood, New York: KTO Press, 1979). Darlene Clark Hine, "The Elusive Ballot: The Black Struggle Against the Texas Democratic White Primary, 1932–1945," *Southwestern Historical Quarterly* 81 (April 1978).

W. Marvin Dulaney

DEMONTEL, CHARLES S. (1812–1882). Charles DeMontel, colonizer, lawyer, engineer, soldier, and public servant, was born in Königsberg, Prussia, on October 24, 1812. He attended the University of Heidelberg, where he was a member of a student military guard unit. He probably first gained an interest in Texas while attending the Sorbonne at the University of Paris. Although most accounts of DeMontel's arrival in Texas indicate that he left Pennsylvania in 1837 for Indianola, there is some suggestion that he was present at San Jacinto in 1836, although not during the battle. During this time he changed his name from Scheidemontel to DeMontel. In 1837 he bought property and lived in Palacios before taking residence at the Lockmar Inn in San Antonio in 1839. There he met Henri Castro,qv who convinced him to join his colonization efforts as an aide, guide, and land surveyor.

DeMontel traveled to Indianola in the employ of Castro to help lead the original Castro colonists to San Antonio, where, on September 1, 1844, he and the colonists joined Castro's first trek to his land grant. DeMontel was present at the founding of Castroville on September 3, 1844. On November 13, 1845, he was married to Justine Pingenot, a daughter of one of the Castro colonists whom he had met late in 1844 at Port Lavaca and had romanced on their way to Castroville; seven children were born to the DeMontels.

In 1848, at the conclusion of the Mexican War,qv DeMontel commanded a company of Texas Rangersqv camped on Seco Creek near D'Hanis; in 1849 the site became Fort Lincoln. In 1853 he acquired 15,000 acres of land in the Hill Countryqv in partnership with John James,qv who had surveyed Castroville in 1844. Together the two men surveyed and plotted a townsite, constructed a commissary, sawmill, and cabins and helped to sponsor many of the Polish settlers in what soon became the town of Bandera. DeMontel subsequently returned to Castroville to continue farming and ranching. He had great success raising cotton and had earned the nickname Cotton Planter by 1858.

He was the first county clerk of Medina County and was one of the three petitioners in the move to establish the first public school in Castroville. He was the Medina County delegate to the Secession Conventionqv in 1861. Convention records indicate that DeMontel was forty-eight years of age, a lawyer, and the owner of nine slaves and slightly more than 30,000 acres.

He was appointed by Brig. Gen. Hamilton P. Beeqv to the position of provost marshal of Bandera, Uvalde, and Medina counties. By appointment of Governor Francis R. Lubbockqv he also served as captain of Company G (later changed to D), Mounted Rangers, for Bandera, Blanco, Medina, and Uvalde counties in the Frontier Regiment.qv He was discharged from service on February 9, 1863, and commissioned by Jefferson Davisqv on March 14, 1863, as commander of the steamer *Texas,* a privately owned vessel of the Confederate States.

After the Civil Warqv he traveled to the Mexican border to sell cotton and other farm products produced in part by Polish farmers. He frequently attended social and cultural functions in San Antonio and served as a master Mason of the Alamo Lodge. In 1871 in Medina County he organized the Charles DeMontel Company, which combined his business interests in real estate and lumber and shingle production. In the late 1870s DeMontel led the unsuccessful drive to bring the Southern Pacific Railroad through Castroville. His last act of public service was as Indian advisor to Company G of the Texas Volunteer Guards. The company, known as the Montel Guards, was organized at Montel, Texas, in August 1881. DeMontel died on August 3, 1882, at Castroville and was buried with Masonic rites in the family plot on the old Montel ranch north of Castroville.

BIBLIOGRAPHY: Castro Colonies Heritage Association, *The History of Medina County, Texas* (Dallas: National Share Graphics, 1983). Daughters of the Republic of Texas, *Founders and Patriots of the Republic of Texas* (Austin, 1963–). J. Marvin Hunter, *One Hundred Years in Bandera, 1853–1953* (Bandera, Texas: Hunter's Printing, 1953). Vertical Files, Barker Texas History Center, University of Texas at Austin. Bobby D. Weaver, *Castro's Colony: Empresario Development in Texas, 1842–1865* (College Station: Texas A&M University Press, 1985).

E. C. DeMontel

DEMORSE, CHARLES (1816–1887). Charles DeMorse (born Charles Denny Morse), editor, publisher, statesman, soldier, public official, lawyer, merchant, and farmer, was born in Leicester, Massachusetts, on January 31, 1816, the son of Aaron and Mary (Denny) Morse. He received a good academic education in New Haven and New York City and later studied law. In the autumn of 1835 he joined Maj. Edwin Morehouse'sqv volunteers to aid Texas. En route to Texas he was detained by the British at Nassau, and while there his name (Charles D. Morse) through error was enrolled as Charles DeMorse. He adopted the change, which was later approved by the Sixth Texas Congress. Upon his arrival in Texas, DeMorse accepted a commission in the Texas Navyqv but resigned in July 1836 to become a major in the army, where he received military training under Albert Sidney Johnston.qv When the army was disbanded in 1837 DeMorse entered law practice at Matagorda. In 1838 he married Lodiska C. Wooldridge; to them were born five children. DeMorse was stock commissioner, charged with refunding the public debt, under President Mirabeau B. Lamar,qv and at the same time he was reporter for the Texas House of Representatives. He founded the Clarksville *Northern Standard*qv in 1842 and continued as its publisher and editor until his death.

In 1862 he organized and became colonel of the Twenty-ninth Texas Cavalry, which saw service in Indian Territory and Arkansas. It bore the brunt of the fight at Elk Creek or Honey Springs in 1863. DeMorse was the commanding officer of the force at Poison Springs, near Camden, Arkansas, where an attempted federal advance into Texas from Little Rock was stopped.

Although not particularly ambitious for public office, DeMorse served in 1842 as first mayor of Clarksville and was congressman-elect at the time of annexation.qv He helped in the organization of the Democratic partyqv in Texas and advocated its principles so strongly that he was proclaimed the "Father of the Texas Democratic Press." He took a lead in attempting to get Texas to accept the results of the Civil Warqv and later worked to eliminate Radical Republican control of the state. He served as a delegate to the state and national Democratic conventions in 1872 and supported the Liberal Republicans as a temporary expedient. He was second to Richard Cokeqv in the nomination for governor in 1873; in 1886, against his wishes, he was again put forward as a candidate for that office.

DeMorse was an active member of the Grange,qv helped organize the Texas Veterans Associationqv in 1873, and in 1874 was named one of the directors of the Agricultural and Mechanical College of Texas (now Texas A&M University). He was one of the most influential framers of the Constitution of 1876,qv particularly of the judicial article. He spent his last years largely in championing the cause of the "nester." In 1873 the Texas Press and Editorial Association elected him president, and he has been called the "Father of Texas Journalism." DeMorse died on October 25, 1887.

BIBLIOGRAPHY: Randolph B. Campbell, *A Southern Community in Crisis: Harrison County, Texas, 1850–1880* (Austin: Texas State Historical Association, 1983). Marilyn M. Sibley, *Lone Stars and State Gazettes: Texas Newspapers before the Civil War* (College Station: Texas A&M University Press, 1983). Ernest Wallace, *Charles DeMorse* (Lubbock: Texas Tech Press, 1943; new ed., Paris, Texas: Wright, 1985).

Ernest Wallace

DEMOSS, CHARLES (?–1826). Charles DeMoss (DeMass, Demoss, Demos) was one of Stephen F. Austin'sqv Old Three Hundredqv colonists. He moved to Texas from Commerce, Missouri, with his wife, Martha, probably before April 20, 1824, when a Charles DeMass signed a petition for the appointment of the Baron de Bastropqv to serve as elector for the Austin colony. As one of the Old Three Hundred DeMoss received title to a sitioqv of land on Caney Creek in what is now Matagorda County, on August 3, 1824. The census of 1826 listed him as a farmer and stock raiser aged between forty and fifty, with a household that included his wife, two sons, and two daughters. Charles and Martha DeMoss apparently both died on December 18, 1826. They were survived by eight children, two of whom were minors. Their eldest son, Peter, was appointed guardian of one of the children.

BIBLIOGRAPHY: Eugene C. Barker, ed., *The Austin Papers* (3 vols., Washington: GPO, 1924–28). Lester G. Bugbee, "The Old Three Hundred: A List of Settlers in Austin's First Colony," *Quarterly of the Texas State Historical Association* 1 (October 1897). Matagorda County Historical Commission, *Historic Matagorda County* (3 vols., Houston: Armstrong, 1986).

DEMOSS, PETER (1796–?). Peter DeMoss, pioneer settler, was born in St. Charles, Missouri, in 1796. He married Susanah Bays, the daughter of Joseph L. Bays.qv As one of Stephen F. Austin'sqv Old Three Hundredqv settlers, DeMoss was granted a league of land now in Matagorda County on August 3, 1824. In 1824 he sold a labor of land to Silas Dinsmoreqv and A. J. Dalton. The 1825 census of the District of Colorado reported DeMoss as a farmer and stock raiser with a wife, a five-year-old son, and a three-year-old daughter, but the 1826 census of Austin's colony, which identified DeMoss as being between the ages of twenty-five and forty, stated that he had two male children between the ages of one and seven. A daughter named Susanah was born on November 4, 1830. In July of that year DeMoss had been named administrator of the estate of Charles DeMoss.qv DeMoss served in the company of James Collinsworthqv at the capture of Goliad and during the siege of Bexar.qv He was ill with scarlet fever and did not participate in the San Jacinto campaign. Lewis and William DeMoss, who had also received headrights in Matagorda County and were presumably Peter DeMoss's kinsmen, were under James W. Fannin'sqv command during the Texas Revolutionqv and were killed in the Goliad Massacre.qv DeMoss served as justice of the peace for Matagorda County's Third District in 1839 and was elected justice of the peace of Precinct 4 on February 6, 1843, and reelected on February 3, 1845. In 1860 he was living near the Goliad County community of Middleton with his wife and four dependent children, whose ages ranged from two to seventeen years; one or more of them may have been adopted. DeMoss's assets were $1,000 in real estate and $1,000 in personal property.

BIBLIOGRAPHY: Eugene C. Barker, ed., *The Austin Papers* (3 vols., Washington: GPO, 1924–28). Lester G. Bugbee, "The Old Three Hundred: A List of Settlers in Austin's First Colony," *Quarterly of the Texas State Historical Association* 1 (October 1897). *Compiled Index to Elected and Appointed Officials of the Republic of Texas, 1835–1846* (Austin: State Archives, Texas State Library, 1981). Daughters of the Republic of Texas, *Founders and Patriots of the Republic of Texas* (Austin, 1963–). *Texas State Gazette*, July 22, 1830. Vertical Files, Barker Texas History Center, University of Texas at Austin. Gifford E. White, *1830 Citizens of Texas* (Austin: Eakin, 1983).

Thomas W. Cutrer

DEMOSS, TEXAS. DeMoss, near Oyster Lake four miles south of Palacios across Tres Palacios Bay in southwestern Matagorda County, probably took its name from the Lewis DeMoss land grant on which it was located. The surrounding area produced cotton and cattle, but after several crop failures and a 1914 attack of charbon (anthrax) that devastated cattle in the region, many of the settlers who could afford to leave did so. Still, in 1914 a one-room DeMoss school opened and in 1917 served eight grades. The school also hosted community church services. In the early 1920s the DeMoss school added a second room; by the early 1930s it had been consolidated with Collegeport schools. Eventually the school building was moved to Collegeport, where for a time it was the property of the Mopac House Foundation. By the early 1920s the E. W. Turner Irrigation Company had moved a number of rice farmers into the area and started the settlement of Turnerville outside Collegeport. Though DeMoss was not named on the 1936 county highway map, at that time a few widely scattered dwellings remained in the area. The community did not appear on later maps.

BIBLIOGRAPHY: Matagorda County Historical Commission, *Historic Matagorda County* (3 vols., Houston: Armstrong, 1986).

Rachel Jenkins

DEMPSEY, TEXAS. Dempsey was seven miles east of Atlanta and twenty miles northeast of Linden in far eastern Cass County. A post office was established there in 1874 with Andrew J. Newton as postmaster. The office was discontinued the next year, reestablished in 1888, and permanently discontinued in 1901. By 1936 Dempsey had ceased to exist as a named community.

BIBLIOGRAPHY: Wright Patman, *History of Post Offices—First Congressional District of Texas* (Texarkana, Texas, 1946?).

Cecil Harper, Jr.

DENHAWKEN, TEXAS. Denhawken, at the junction of State Highway 119 and Farm Road 1347, fourteen miles east of Floresville in eastern Wilson County, was settled by German farmers between 1895 and 1898, when the San Antonio and Gulf Railroad was built to the area. By the mid-1930s the community had two stores and two mills. Children attended nearby Dillworth Ranch School. Ranching has been replaced by diversified farming as the mainstay of the local economy. The population of the rural community was seventy-five in 1947. In the 1980s Denhawken had two stores and a church. The population in 1990 was forty-six.
Claudia Hazlewood

DENISON, FRANKLIN LODOWICK (1831–1889). Franklin Lodowick Denison, lawyer, journalist, and Confederate Army officer, was born on April 7, 1831, in Stonington, Connecticut. When he was two years old the family moved to Ravenna, Ohio, where he was raised and educated. At age eighteen he moved to Aberdeen, Mississippi, where he published a newspaper and studied law. In 1854 he moved to Texas and established a legal practice at Waco. There, on October 10, 1856, he married Cornelia Anne Evans; she died in 1857. On August 11, 1859, he married Hannah Gibson Lambdin, the daughter of Rev. William M. Lambdin, president of Waco Female College. This couple had nine children. For five or six years Denison served as the state's prosecuting attorney. At the outbreak of the Civil War qv he helped to raise a company of infantry for service under Lt. Gen. Theophilus H. Holmes in Arkansas. Future governor Richard Coke qv was elected its captain and Denison its first lieutenant. Denison resigned from the army due to ill health and returned to Waco, where he was appointed tax collector for McLennan County.

After the war he established the *Register*. Because of continued ill health, however, he gave up the paper and traveled in Mexico for six months. After regaining his health he moved to Bryan and established the Millican *News-Teller*. In 1879 he moved to Belton and established the *Courier*. Its plant was destroyed by fire a few years later. He then founded the *Texas Farmer*, which he sold at a handsome profit. Finally he founded the Belton *Reporter*, which he edited until his death. He died on February 7, 1889, and is buried in the North Belton Cemetery. Denison and his wife were Methodists.

BIBLIOGRAPHY: Dayton Kelley, ed., *The Handbook of Waco and McLennan County, Texas* (Waco: Texian, 1972). *A Memorial and Biographical History of McLennan, Falls, Bell, and Coryell Counties* (Chicago: Lewis, 1893; rpt., St. Louis: Ingmire, 1984). Amelia W. Williams and Eugene C. Barker, eds., *The Writings of Sam Houston, 1813–1863* (8 vols., Austin: University of Texas Press, 1938–43; rpt., Austin and New York: Pemberton Press, 1970).
Thomas W. Cutrer

DENISON, GEORGE STANTON (1833–1866). George Stanton Denison, Unionist and United States Treasury official, the son of Eliza S. and Dr. Joseph A. Denison, Jr., was born at Royaltown, Vermont, on August 5, 1833. After his graduation from the University of Vermont in 1854, he moved to San Antonio, where for three years he taught in his uncle's private school. In 1857 he married Cornelia M. Forsyth, a Northerner with extensive holdings in land and slaves near Pensacola, Florida. A year later she died while giving birth to their only child, Willie. Denison sent the boy north, and spent the next three years reading law and administering his wife's estate. He himself hurried north after the secession qv of Texas in February 1861. During the Civil War qv his kinsman, Secretary of the Treasury Salmon P. Chase, appointed him special agent for the Treasury Department, and by May 1862 he was acting collector of customs for the recently captured port of New Orleans. Chase instructed Denison to write him personally about "all that relates to persons and things not proper for the subject of official communications." Denison's near-weekly reports to Chase included information and opinions on military matters, local politics, and social conditions.

He later became acting surveyor, acting collector of internal revenue for the district of New Orleans, and, for a few months after the war, supervising special agent for the Treasury Department for the state of Texas. He tried unsuccessfully to control the illegal cotton trade and worked behind the scenes of Louisiana's turbulent wartime politics. He promoted emancipating and arming slaves, and his insistence on a harsh Reconstruction qv led him to question the policies of Gen. Nathaniel Banks, qv the ranking Union general in Louisiana. Although at times he supported Radical Republican candidates, in the 1864 gubernatorial election he favored the more politically viable Michael Hahn, the victorious moderate. He and other Unionists founded the First National Bank and used the New Orleans *Times* to further their political interests. Denison clearly relished his role. "This is a great and glorious life," he wrote to his brother soon after his arrival. "Here is all the splendor and display of military government, with the triumphant consciousness of occupying the great stronghold of rebellion." Although his early years in Texas, from 1857 to 1861, made him remember the state as "the meanest country in the world," he apparently hoped to prosper in the postwar South. In June 1865 he wrote his uncle in Vermont that he and two partners were leasing three plantations and that he had been offered the presidency of an insurance company. En route to a visit with his family, he died of congestive fever on August 24, 1866, and was buried at sea.

BIBLIOGRAPHY: James A. Padgett, ed., "Some Letters of George Stanton Denison, 1854–1866," *Louisiana Historical Quarterly* 23 (October 1940).
James A. Marten

DENISON, JAMES (?–?). James Denison, attorney, traveled from New York to Texas in December 1839 and received a conditional land certificate on December 30. He went into partnership with attorney Henry P. Brewster qv in Matagorda in 1841. He interrupted his practice, however, to serve in the campaigns against Rafael Vásquez and Adrián Woll.qqv After representing Matagorda County in the Seventh Congress, in 1846 he went into a partnership with Alexander H. Phillips qv of Victoria and D. C. Van Derlip of Bexar. Denison was living at Indianola in January 1854.

BIBLIOGRAPHY: Texas House of Representatives, *Biographical Directory of the Texan Conventions and Congresses, 1832–1845* (Austin: Book Exchange, 1941).
Carolyn Hyman

DENISON, TEXAS. Denison is on U.S. highways 75 and 69 seven miles north of Sherman in northeastern Grayson County. In the early 1870s William Benjamin Munson, Sr.,qv and R. S. Stevens bought land in the area and prepared for the arrival of the Missouri, Kansas and Texas Railroad (the Katy). The townsite was laid out in the summer of 1872 and named for the vice president of the Katy, George Denison. The first train arrived on Christmas Eve. The town had over 3,000 residents by the summer of 1873, when it incorporated. Although Main Street appeared to be an orderly collection of businesses, the surrounding area consisted of a tent city, inhabited by bars, gambling halls, and houses of prostitution.

On February 6, 1873, Denison established the first free public school in Texas. The first Denison Independent Order of Odd Fellows was organized on February 19, 1873. Denison had the first women's club in Texas; the XXI club began in 1876. In 1886 a post office opened, and in 1889 the town had 5,000 residents. During the next ten years Denison established itself as a retail and shipping point for North Texas. In addition to the tracks of the MKT, the town also became a stop on the St. Louis, San Francisco and Texas and the Kansas, Oklahoma and Gulf railroads. Five additional rail lines that connected Denison with other communities in North Texas were chartered between the late 1870s and 1900, including the first interurban electric line between Denison and Sherman in 1896. By the end of the 1870s local businesses included two cotton compresses, a large flour mill, and a slaughterhouse capable of handling 700 cattle a day. In 1884 the town had an opera house that seated 1,200. In 1889 the Denison *Herald* began publication. During the twentieth century industrial and manufacturing plants provided a diversified economic base for the community. Electronic parts, clothes, furniture, and a variety of plastic goods are among the products manufactured in Denison.

In 1900 the population surpassed 10,000. By the mid-1920s Denison had just over 17,000 residents and 400 businesses, including four banks. It also had two high schools, nine grade schools, and numerous churches. In 1936 Denison had 13,850 residents and 460 businesses. By the end of World War II qv the number of residents was just short of 16,000. The population was 26,000 in 1966, when businesses numbered just under 600. In 1989 Denison had a reported 24,234 residents and 427 businesses. In 1990 the population was 21,505. Denison was the birthplace of the thirty-fourth president of the United States, Dwight David Eisenhower.qv The home he was born in in 1890 has been returned to its original appearance and sits in the Eisenhower Birthplace State Historic Site,qv a three-acre area that includes a museum.

BIBLIOGRAPHY: L. Tuffly Ellis, "The Revolutionizing of the Texas Cotton Trade," *Southwestern Historical Quarterly* 73 (April 1970). Graham Landrum and Allen Smith, *Grayson County* (Fort Worth, 1960; 2d ed., Fort Worth: Historical Publishers, 1967).

David Minor

DENISON, BONHAM AND NEW ORLEANS RAILROAD. The Denison, Bonham and New Orleans Railway Company was chartered on January 19, 1887, to connect Denison with Charleston in Delta County and a junction with the Marshall and Northwestern. "Nellie," as the Denison, Bonham and New Orleans Railway was nicknamed, originated as a project financed by a group of bankers and businessmen in Denison and Bonham. The capital was $200,000, and the principal place of business was Denison. Members of the first board of directors were W. B. Mumson, T. B. Harms, A. R. Collins, W. C. Tignor, and Saul Harma, all of Denison; and S. B. Allen, W. A. Nunnelee, John Sharger, and R. W. Campbell, all of Bonham. Although the promoters were able to begin construction, the project soon failed. A new company was incorporated as the Denison, Bonham and New Orleans Railroad Company on January 24, 1901. Capital stock was $100,000, and the projected route ran between Denison and Wolfe City. The Denison, Bonham and New Orleans Railroad Company acquired the partly graded roadbed of the Denison, Bonham and New Orleans Railway and in 1901 completed a twenty-four mile line between Bonham Junction and Bonham. Between Denison and Bonham Junction, the Denison, Bonham and New Orleans operated over the Missouri, Kansas and Texas Railway Company of Texas. The Katy operated the Denison, Bonham and New Orleans under contract and later leased the line. However, the Denison, Bonham and New Orleans was not included in the Katy reorganization of 1923. The company was operated by receivers from March 21, 1923, until February 6, 1925, when it was bought by several Bonham citizens. In 1926 the line reported passenger earnings of $300 and freight earnings of $45,000 and owned two locomotives and one car. Freight hauled included corn, cotton, cottonseed meal, watermelons, potatoes, and peanuts. In 1928 twelve employees received total pay of $15,500. Operations ceased on November 30, 1928, and the company was abandoned the following year.

Beverly M. J. Christian

DENISON AND PACIFIC RAILWAY. The Denison and Pacific Railway, originally organized as one of several projects of Col. Bob Stevens, John Scullin, and Ben Munson, was chartered on April 24, 1878, to build from Denison to Belknap, about 150 miles. The capital was $1.5 million, and the business office was in Denison. Members of the first board of directors included Scullin and R. S. Sterns of St. Louis; Henry D. Mirich of Hamilton, Missouri; and R. C. Fister, Edward Perry, William H. Sanford, and Alexander W. Achesonqv of Denison. In 1878–79 the company built 41.89 miles of track from Denison, the northern terminus, to Gainesville via Whitesboro. The line was abandoned in 1879, but on March 11, 1880, it was sold to the Denison and Southeastern Railway Company, which was renamed the Missouri, Kansas and Texas Extension Railway Company on March 23, 1880. Subsequent consolidation made what was once the Denison and Pacific one of the earliest acquisitions of the Katy in its intrastate expansion program.

Donna J. Kumler

DENISON AND PACIFIC SUBURBAN RAILWAY. The Denison and Pacific Suburban Railway Company, a subsidiary of the Texas and Pacific Railway Company, was chartered on April 18, 1895. The capital was $100,000. Members of the first board of directors included Alexander W. Acheson, William H. Abrams,qqv R. C. Shearman, Paul Naples, L. S. Thorne, B. S. Matheu, and T. J. Freeman, all of Texas. Seven miles of track was laid, connecting Denison with the Transcontinental Division of the Texas and Pacific in Sherman. Operations began on January 15, 1896. The company's office was in Denison until 1911, when it was transferred to Dallas. The line primarily shipped grain and coal; in the 1920s passenger service was discontinued. Abandonment of the Denison and Pacific Suburban was completed in September 1966.

Cecil Harper, Jr.

DENISON AND SOUTHEASTERN RAILWAY. The Denison and Southeastern Railway Company was chartered on July 27, 1877, by the citizens of Denison and Greenville to build a road along the fifty-mile stretch between the two communities. The company had an initial capital of $50,000, and the business office was in Denison. Members of the first board of directors included William Whitewright, William H. Appleton, Nathaniel L. McCready, Hezron A. Johnson, Edward R. Bell, George J. Forrest, Francis Skiddy, Horace M. Ruggles, all from New York, and Alexander W. Achesonqv of Denison. The Denison and Southeastern Railway completed twenty miles between Denison and Whitewright in early 1880 and acquired the seventy-one miles of the Denison and Pacific on March 11, 1880. On March 23 the name of the railroad was changed to the Missouri, Kansas and Texas Extension Railway Company, which completed the thirty-two miles from Whitewright to Greenville.

Chris Cravens

DENISON AND WASHITA VALLEY RAILWAY. The Denison and Washita Valley Railway Company was chartered on January 8, 1886. In that year five miles of track was built in Texas from Warner Junction to Ray, and in 1895 two more miles of yard and side tracks were added. A second division of the company operated fifteen miles from Atoka to Coalgate, Indian Territory. In 1895 the company owned one locomotive and 119 freight cars, and primarily served the coal mines in the Coalgate area. The road was owned by the Texas and Oklahoma Railroad Company, but was operated by the Missouri, Kansas and Texas until December 31, 1891. The Texas portion was then operated by the Missouri, Kansas and Texas Railway Company of Texas until it was sold to that company on May 13, 1903.

George C. Werner

DENMAN, LEROY GILBERT (1855–1916). Leroy Gilbert Denman, lawyer and Texas Supreme Court justice, was born in Guadalupe County, Texas, on October 31, 1855. He was educated principally by his father and subsequently taught school for four years before entering the law school of the University of Virginia, from which he graduated in 1880. He practiced law at New Braunfels for two years before he moved to San Antonio, where he had an active practice in both civil and criminal cases throughout Southwest Texas until 1894, when he was appointed associate justice of the state Supreme Court by Governor James S. Hogg.qv Denman was reelected to the position and remained on the bench until May 1899, when he resigned and returned to his practice in San Antonio. Among his important opinions was that in *Joske v. Irvin,* in which the Supreme Court of Texas refused to follow the scintilla-of-evidence rule previously announced by the United States Supreme Court; that in *Royal Insurance Company v. McIntyre,* in which the court defined for Texas the measure by which total losses in fires would be determined; and that in *Crawford v. MacDonald,* in which the court defined the difference between direct and collateral attacks on judgments. Denman was not noted for his forensic power, but he was a fluent speaker. He handed down 146 opinions—opinions marked by "brevity, simplicity of expression, and accuracy of legal conclusion." He was married in 1881 to Sue E. Carpenter. He died on September 14, 1916.

BIBLIOGRAPHY: Texas Supreme Court, *Texas Reports: Cases Adjudged in the Supreme Court,* Vol. 107 (1917). Leroy G. Denman

DENMAN CROSSROADS, TEXAS. Denman Crossroads, on Farm Road 1256 eight miles south of Canton in south central Van Zandt County, was probably named for J. Denman, who owned property in the area and was associated with the nearby community of China Grove. Nearby Morris Cemetery, on the farm of Elijah Newton Morris, dates to 1866. The community had a post office from 1891 until 1905. By 1892 it had three mills and gins, but 1936 county highway maps showed only a single business there. By 1981 only the cemetery and scattered dwellings marked the site. Denman Crossroads was still listed as a community in 1990.

BIBLIOGRAPHY: Van Zandt County History Book Committee, *History of Van Zandt County* (Dallas, 1984). Diana J. Kleiner

DENMARK, TEXAS. Denmark was a store and post office community on Beaver Creek fifteen miles northwest of Palestine and 6½ miles west of Montalba in northwestern Anderson County. It had a post office from 1905 to 1917. In 1914 C. L. Day was the postmaster, and Denmark had a population of twenty-five, two grocery stores, a blacksmith, a physician, and a poultry breeder. The community disappeared, probably sometime in the early twentieth century, as it was not named on state highway maps by the 1930s. Mark Odintz

DENNING, TEXAS. Denning is on Farm Road 3409 eight miles west of San Augustine in northwestern San Augustine County. A post office was opened there in 1891, and by 1896 Denning had an estimated fifty inhabitants, a Baptist church, three general stores, two gins, two sawmills, two flour mills, and two blacksmith shops. In 1904 the community had a one-teacher school for forty-seven white pupils and another for twenty-four black pupils. By 1914 Denning claimed to have 200 inhabitants. The post office was closed in the 1930s, and the population declined to seventy-five by 1939. In 1940 the community had two churches, a school, three businesses, and several dwellings. Residents numbered 361 in 1968. In 1990 the population was still 361. Mark Odintz

DENNIS, ISAAC N. (1829–1910). Isaac N. Dennis, lawyer, legislator, planter, and Confederate soldier, was born in the Dallas County, Alabama, community of Marian on June 25, 1829. He attended Richmond College in Dallas County, Alabama, and studied law in Cambridge, Massachusetts, before being admitted to the bar at Cahaba, Alabama, in December 1850. He moved to Texas from Marian and on January 2, 1853, settled at Wharton, where he established a legal partnership with Judge George Quinan.[qv] In August 1855 he was elected to represent Wharton and Matagorda counties in the Sixth Legislature; he was reelected in 1857 to serve in the Seventh and in 1859 to the Eighth Legislature. Dennis served as chairman of the Committee on State Affairs and of the Committee on Engrossed Bills and was a prominent candidate for attorney general at the time of secession.[qv]

During the Civil War[qv] he served on the staff of Brig. Gen. Paul Octave Hébert[qv] and saw duty in Texas, Arkansas, and Louisiana. At the end of the war he returned to Caney Creek in Texas and became a planter. A succession of poor crop years, however, forced him to return to the legal profession. In 1879 he was returned to the House of Representatives when Matagorda, Galveston, Brazoria, and Wharton counties elected him to the Eighteenth Legislature. In that session he chaired the Committee on Federal Relations.

On January 13, 1853, Dennis married Patience L. Texas Horton, the daughter of former lieutenant governor Albert C. Horton;[qv] they had one child. After her death in 1863 he married Sadie Hinton in 1865, and then, after her death in 1869, he married Maggie Knox; with Maggie he had five children. Maggie Dennis died in 1886, and Isaac Dennis on March 25, 1910. He was a Baptist, a Mason, an Odd Fellow, and a Democrat.

BIBLIOGRAPHY: H. L. Bentley and Thomas Pilgrim, *Texas Legal Directory for 1876–77* (Austin: Democratic Statesman Office, 1877). William DeRyee and R. E. Moore, *The Texas Album of the Eighth Legislature, 1860* (Austin: Miner, Lambert, and Perry, 1860). *Galveston Weekly Journal,* February 11, 1853. Frank W. Johnson, *A History of Texas and Texans* (5 vols., ed. E. C. Barker and E. W. Winkler [Chicago and New York: American Historical Society, 1914; rpt. 1916]). *Memorial and Genealogical Record of Southwest Texas* (Chicago: Goodspeed, 1894; rpt., Easley, South Carolina: Southern Historical Press, 1978). Thomas W. Cutrer

DENNIS, JOSEPH (1810–1894). Joseph (Uncle Joe) Dennis, early settler and Bell County official, was born in Warren County, Tennessee, on December 10, 1810, the son of Joseph and Ann (Bybee) Dennis. The elder Dennis was a farmer of Irish extraction. Dennis moved to Madison County, Arkansas, in 1839 and served in the state legislature from 1846 to 1848. He moved in 1849 to Milam County, Texas, where he became a herdsman in a ranching partnership with Judge Orville T. Tyler[qv] near Belton. At the 1850 Charter Oak election in newly established Bell County, Dennis was appointed chairman of a commission to locate the county seat at the site of Nolan Springs or present Belton, establish the county boundaries in Milam County territory, obtain the deed to the county seat from Mrs. Connell of Williamson County, plat the site, and advertise the lots for sale. He then served for eight years as first treasurer of Bell County. In 1854 he purchased more than 1,000 acres of land on Friar's Creek and the following year established a residence seven miles east of Belton. He subsequently purchased a larger farm on the Leon River, where he raised crops and livestock. But in 1861 he lost his house and possessions and returned to Friar's Creek to pursue a spinning and weaving business in addition to farming.

Dennis owned several tracts of land in Bell County; he operated a gristmill on Bird's Creek near the Midway Gravel Pit at Marietta and a lumberyard at Nolanville. When the Civil War[qv] began he was considered too old for active duty, so he remained at home aiding families whose men were in the army. He contributed to the outfitting of Capt. H. E. Bradford's Company from Bell County, served as a Democratic political leader, and was a member of the Primitive Baptist Church. After the war he sold his farm and mill on the Leon River, moved to new land on the Leon purchased in 1871, and in 1875 moved to 1,900 acres eighteen miles west of Belton, purchased from John Marshall. This site, known as Elmore Ranch, was continuously owned by his descendents until the 1970s. Dennis later divided his lands among his children, rented the farm, and moved to Temple, where he built three tenement houses. Sometime later he bought 600 acres in Callahan County and moved there.

Dennis married Isa (Ice) Seitze on March 15, 1836, and they had eleven children. In 1890 they broke up housekeeping and moved to California to be with their children. At his death on October 19, 1894, Dennis owned 870 acres of land in Bell, Callahan, and Eastland counties valued at over $7,000; he also had forty cattle and twenty-two horses. He died at the home of his daughter Margaret Neal near Temple and was buried in Hodge Cemetery there. His grave is marked by a Texas historical marker.

BIBLIOGRAPHY: *A Memorial and Biographical History of McLennan, Falls, Bell, and Coryell Counties* (Chicago: Lewis, 1893; rpt., St. Louis: Ingmire, 1984). *Texas State Gazette,* November 1, 1851.

Polly Peaks Elmore

DENNIS, THOMAS MASON (1807–1877). Thomas Mason Dennis, soldier and legislator, was born in Georgia on March 9, 1807, and moved to Texas in March 1835. He settled in Bastrop and in September joined Capt. Robert M. Coleman's qv company of volunteers that marched from Bastrop to the relief of Gonzales (see GONZALES, BATTLE OF). On December 20, 1835, he signed the Goliad Declaration of Independence.qv He enlisted in the Texas army on February 28, 1836, and at San Jacinto served in Capt. Jesse Billingsley's qv Company C—also known as the "Mina Volunteers"—of Col. Edward Burleson's qv First Regiment, Texas Volunteers. According to his obituary he was promoted to lieutenant, but no documentary evidence of this promotion has been located. He left the service on June 1.

After his discharge Dennis moved to Matagorda County, where he was elected clerk of the county court in February 1837. He was reelected on February 7, 1839. In 1841 he was elected to represent Matagorda County in the House of Representatives of the Sixth Congress of the republic. There he served on the Naval Affairs Committee. Dennis is said to have been elected captain of several volunteer companies that saw action against the Indians on the western frontier and to have served at the battle of Plum Creek,qv in the repulse of Rafael Vásquez and Adrián Woll,qqv and on the Somervell expedition.qv He served as a private in Capt. Albert C. Horton's qv company in Col. Clark L. Owen's qv regiment of volunteers from March 6 through April 13, 1842. On February 3, 1845, he was elected sheriff of Matagorda County. By 1850, in partnership with surveyor Joshua Threadgill, he was well known as a horse and general stock raiser; his property was valued at $5,000.

After leaving Matagorda County about 1852 he lived for a time in Gonzales County, where, on September 24, 1852, he was appointed to the county Democratic committee. He is said to have resided in Rockport for some twenty years before moving to Karnes and Wilson counties, where he was engaged in stock raising. By 1871 he was drawing a pension as a veteran of the Texas Revolution.qv In 1876 he was elected to the House of Representatives of the Fifteenth Legislature from the Seventy-eighth District. He resigned during the session but succeeded himself when he was reelected in the special election. He died the following year on October 15 at the Gonzales County community of Rancho. His will was signed on October 12, 1877, and opened for probate on November 6, 1877. Dennis never married. He was a Democrat and a member of the Texas Veterans Association.qv

BIBLIOGRAPHY: Austin *Daily Democratic Statesman,* November 21, 1877. *Compiled Index to Elected and Appointed Officials of the Republic of Texas, 1835–1846* (Austin: State Archives, Texas State Library, 1981). Daughters of the Republic of Texas, *Muster Rolls of the Texas Revolution* (Austin, 1986). Texas House of Representatives, *Biographical Directory of the Texan Conventions and Congresses, 1832–1845* (Austin: Book Exchange, 1941). *Texas State Gazette,* October 9, 1852.

Thomas W. Cutrer

DENNIS, TEXAS. Dennis is on Farm Road 1543 fifteen miles southwest of Weatherford in southwestern Parker County. In 1892, after a bridge was built across the Brazos River, Judge N. M. Dennis, a Parker County lawyer and farmer, developed the community to serve the farmers and ranchers of the area. A Dennis post office was established in 1895. Throughout its history the settlement has been a church and school community. The population surpassed 100 in the 1950s and 1960s. In 1980 and 1990 the community had eighty-six residents.

BIBLIOGRAPHY: John Clements, *Flying the Colors: Texas, a Comprehensive Look at Texas Today, County by County* (Dallas: Clements Research, 1984). Gustavus Adolphus Holland, *History of Parker County and the Double Log Cabin* (Weatherford, Texas: Herald, 1931; rpt. 1937). Kathleen E. and Clifton R. St. Clair, eds., *Little Towns of Texas* (Jacksonville, Texas: Jayroe Graphic Arts, 1982).

David Minor

DENNISON, STEPHEN (1812–1836). Stephen Dennison, Alamo defender, was born in either England or Ireland in 1812. He was a glazer and painter by trade. He traveled to Texas by way of New Orleans as a member of Capt. Thomas H. Breece's qv company of New Orleans Greys.qv He took part in the siege of Bexar qv and later served in the Alamo garrison as a member of Capt. William Blazeby's qv infantry company. Dennison died in the battle of the Alamo qv on March 6, 1836.

BIBLIOGRAPHY: Daughters of the American Revolution, *The Alamo Heroes and Their Revolutionary Ancestors* (San Antonio, 1976). Daughters of the Republic of Texas, *Muster Rolls of the Texas Revolution* (Austin, 1986). Bill Groneman, *Alamo Defenders* (Austin: Eakin, 1990).

Bill Groneman

DENNY, TEXAS. Denny was on the Houston and Texas Central Railway in the eastern corner of Falls County. Although Denny served primarily as a railroad siding, a small cluster of businesses and residences developed at the site. A post office was established there in 1899, and by 1914 a general store and a grocery were also in operation. The Denny post office was discontinued in 1917. County highway maps in the 1940s continued to show Denny as a railroad siding with several houses nearby, but by the 1980s the community was no longer marked on maps.

Vivian Elizabeth Smyrl

DENO, LOTTIE (1844–1934). Lottie Deno, known also at various times as Carlotta J. Thompkins, Charlotte Tompkins, and Charlotte Thurmond, was born on April 21, 1844, in Warsaw, Kentucky. She came from a wealthy family. Her father loved to gamble, raised racehorses, and traded in crops grown on the plantation. He took his eldest daughter, Lottie, with him abroad and entertained her at the finest gambling casinos of the world. After he was killed in the Civil War,qv Lottie's mother and sister were forced to manage the family plantation. To ensure their future security they sent Lottie to Detroit at the age of eighteen to find a husband of the right social standing. She was accompanied by her nanny, a seven-foot-tall black woman named Mary Poindexter. In Detroit Lottie met a jockey, Johnny Golden, who had ridden for her father. Johnny knew Lottie's skill at gambling and invited her to gamble with him. Soon they were doing well, and Johnny enticed her to gamble with him down the Ohio and Mississippi. Lottie's family, who had sponsored her education in Christian schools, was not happy with the news, however, because Johnny was Jewish. Lottie's mother disowned her. Lottie and Johnny, with Mary as companion, traveled the rivers during the height of the war. In 1863 the two split and were to meet in San Antonio, Texas. Lottie Thompkins and Mary Poindexter traveled to New Orleans and arrived in San Antonio in 1865, but Johnny did not show up for five years. During that time Lottie became a house gambler at the University Club, where she worked for the Thurmond family, from Georgia. She met and fell in love with Frank Thurmond. Lottie was known in San Antonio as the "Angel of San Antonio." Later in 1869 Johnny arrived claiming that Lottie was his wife, but Lottie denied the assertion. Frank went to West Texas after supposedly killing a man in an altercation during a game. Soon Lottie followed to find him, leaving behind Johnny and Mary. She gambled her way around West Texas—Fort Concho, Jacksboro, San Angelo, Denison, and Fort Worth—and eventually moved to Fort Griffin. Johnny Golden killed a man in San Antonio and became an outlaw.

In Fort Concho Lottie had been called Mystic Maud. It was in Fort Griffin that she began to call herself Lottie Deno. The name was supposedly derived from a card game where she was suspected of cheating; one player suggested she should call herself "Lotta Dinero."

Johnny Golden followed Lottie to Fort Griffin and was killed there within a day after locating her. Frank Thurmond was there under the alias Mike Fogerty. Lottie's gambling opponents included Doc Holliday and other well-known western figures. She left Griffin in May 1877 to join Frank in Kingston, New Mexico. There she and Frank ran a small gambling room on the rear of the Victorio Hotel. Later Lottie owned the Broadway Restaurant in Silver City. On December 2, 1880, in Silver City, New Mexico, Lottie and Frank were married. Carlotta J. Thompkins, the name that appears on the marriage register, is assumed to be her real name. From 1882 until Lottie's death the Thurmonds made their home in Deming, New Mexico, as upstanding and respected citizens. Frank became a miner, then dealt in land sales and eventually became vice president of the Deming National Bank. Lottie, who was always said to be a lady and had always worn the finest clothing and practiced the best manners, gave up gambling and became a founding member of St. Luke's Episcopal Church of Deming. She died on February 9, 1934, and is buried in Deming next to Frank. Frank and Lottie were immortalized as Faro Nell and Cherokee Hall in a series known as the *Wolfville* books, written by Alfred Henry Lewis. Lottie was also the prototype for Miss Kitty in the television series "Gunsmoke" and for Laura Denbo in Leon Oris's movie *Gunfight at the OK Corral* (Paramount, 1957).

BIBLIOGRAPHY: J. Marvin Hunter, *The Story of Lottie Deno, Her Life and Times* (Bandera, Texas, 1959). Cynthia Rose, *Lottie Deno: Gambling Queen of Hearts* (Santa Fe, New Mexico: Clear Light, 1994). Vertical Files, Barker Texas History Center, University of Texas at Austin.

Cynthia Rose

DENSON, TEXAS. Denson (also known as Densonville and Denison) was a scattered community on Willis Creek six miles northwest of Granger in northeastern Williamson County. The site was settled by members of the Denson family sometime before 1869. The community had, at different times, three different schools named Denson, a cotton gin, and a small store. In 1900 Denson's school served forty-eight pupils. By 1977 only the Denson family cemetery remained at the site.

BIBLIOGRAPHY: Clara Stearns Scarbrough, *Land of Good Water: A Williamson County History* (Georgetown, Texas: Williamson County Sun Publishers, 1973).

Mark Odintz

DENSON SPRINGS, TEXAS. Denson Springs is by Dream Lake on State Highway 294 eighteen miles southeast of Palestine in southeastern Anderson County. The site was settled before the Civil War qv and named for a Mrs. Denson, a member of the Bradshaw family that owned a land grant near the community site; the Bradshaws were among the early settlers in the area. An early school was located near the community on the land of a settler named Grayson and was called Grayson School. Before the Civil War the school was one of the largest in the county, and its building was also used as a Baptist church. In 1887 the school was moved to the site of present Denson Springs. Denson Springs post office operated from 1893 to 1918. In 1896 the community had a general store run by Wortham and Company, and in 1901 it had three businesses, a doctor's office, a gin and mill, a church, and the school. By 1914 the population was estimated at 100, and the community had two general stores and a cotton gin. In 1934 the Denson Springs school had forty-six pupils and two teachers, and in 1936 the school and several dwellings were still at the site. The school was consolidated with the Slocum schools by 1955, and by 1982 Denson Springs consisted only of a cemetery and several scattered dwellings.

BIBLIOGRAPHY: *Anderson County Herald*, July 5, 1901. Thomas Paul Jones, The Reorganization of the Public Schools of Anderson County, Texas (M.Ed. thesis, University of Texas, 1934).

Mark Odintz

DENTISTRY. Students of master surgeon Pierre Fauchard (1678–1761), the founder of modern dentistry, migrated from France to North America during the mid-to-late 1700s. Don Pedro Lartique, one of Fauchard's students, settled before 1783 in Louisiana, where he practiced for approximately twenty-four years before moving to Texas. On August 7, 1806, the ayuntamiento qv of San Antonio gave Lartique a license to practice dentistry in Texas. Other dental surgeons immigrated to the Republic of Texas.qv L. T. Carraway, N. Carson, and H. Marks moved to Houston from northeastern states in 1838. The United States census of 1850 listed 13 dentists in Texas; that of 1860 listed 65; that of 1870, 102. Some of these dentists had learned their craft as students of older, experienced dentists. Others had attended the earliest American dental schools, which were established in Maryland, Ohio, New York, and Pennsylvania between 1839 and 1852. As the last half of the nineteenth century evolved, an increasing number of formally trained dentists settled in the Lone Star State, many eager to improve the status of their profession. Between 1869 and 1881 they worked steadily to organize themselves into an effective state association. Although they adopted a constitution for the Texas Dental Association qv in 1869, the state legislature did not charter the group until May 17, 1871. The Austin Dental Association was consolidated with this state organization on May 5, 1881, when the members elected W. S. Carruthers of Galveston president. By 1931, nineteen city or regional societies had affiliated with the Texas Dental Association. Another important step in improving the character of the profession involved the appearance of the *Texas Dental Journal* in February 1883. It is the oldest dental periodical in the United States and the second oldest in the world. Licensure laws helped to elevate the image of dentistry. The Texas Dental Association established a Committee on Dental Law in May 1882. After seven years of discussion and negotiation, the Texas legislature adopted licensing regulations on March 27, 1889. These required an examination by three reputable dentists appointed by the presiding judge of a judicial district. The Board of Dental Examiners, one of many examining boards,qv has been composed of more than three dentists since 1905, all appointed by the governor.

Eager to train students "at home," enterprising dentists opened two proprietary schools in 1905: Texas Dental College in Houston and the State Dental College in Dallas. The State Dental College was affiliated with Baylor University in 1918. Texas Dental College became the University of Texas School of Dentistry in 1943 and was renamed the University of Texas Dental Branch in 1958. The new building for the latter school, constructed between 1952 and 1955, received the first educational-television license in the United States. In 1919, UTDB's curriculum expanded to four years. Most matriculants have earned bachelor's degrees, some master's and doctor's degrees. The percentage of female students increased from 3 percent to 48 percent between 1970 and 1994. Ancillary personnel, including dental assistants, dental hygienists, and dental laboratory technicians, have played important roles in the development of dentistry in Texas. The dental assistant, usually female, works directly with the dentist in providing treatment to patients. In 1971 Dean J. V. Olson established a program for training dental assistants at UTDB in Houston. After the legislature adopted a law that licensed dental hygienists to practice under the supervision of a dentist (1952), UTDB started the first academic training program for dental hygienists in Texas (1955). Baylor University also established its Caruth School of Dental Hygiene. Graduates of these schools are qualified to scale and polish teeth, take dental X rays, apply topical medications, apply pit and fissure sealants, make impressions for diagnostic models, and teach patients about proper oral-hygiene methods. The dental laboratory technician fabricates various dental prostheses and restorative appliances. The University of Texas Dental School in San Antonio sponsors a training program for technicians. The University of Texas Dental School in San Antonio, the third in Texas, opened for classes in 1971. Especially since the mid-1900s, dental specialties emerged. All three schools developed postgraduate programs in oral and maxillofacial surgery, orthodontics, endodontics, periodontics, pediatric dentistry, and prosthodontics. Specialists often associate in group practices, though solo practice is still quite prominent. During the mid-1970s the profession witnessed the emergence of dental clinics, which are not exactly like group practices. In group practices, each member of the group is an independent entity, while in a dental clinic each member is subservient to the owner or owners of the clinic. Health-insurance programs encouraged the formation of clinics. Many clinics advertise and are looked upon with disfavor by practitioners who do not advertise.

Changes in dental practice have occurred primarily through the development of new materials, equipment, and techniques. These include improved local anesthetics, the use of fluorides in drinking water, improved prosthetic materials, and high-speed handpieces. Fluoridation and the use of pit and fissure sealants (fluoridated plastics) to control dental caries have encouraged dental practitioners to practice preventive dentistry. Sumter S. Arnin, former professor and associate dean of graduate studies at UTDB, was a primary force in developing theories of preventive dentistry. The number of dentists licensed to practice in Texas increased from a mere thirteen in 1850 to 10,800 in 1994; Texas is third in the United States. Four dentists from Texas have been presidents of the American Dental Association: Walter H. Scherer, 1944–46; James P. Hollers, 1963–64; L. M. Kennedy, 1974–75; and Jack H. Harris, 1992–93.

BIBLIOGRAPHY: Ernest Beerstecher, Jr., *The Centennial of Dental Education in Texas* (University of Texas Dental Branch at Houston, 1972). Ernest Beerstecher, Jr., *The History of Dentistry in the Republic of Texas* (University of Texas Dental Branch at Houston, 1975). E. W. D'Anton, *Memories: A History of the University of Texas Dental Branch at Houston* (University of Texas Health Science Center at Houston–Dental Branch, 1991). Malvin E. Ring, *Dentistry: An Illustrated History* (New York: Abrams, 1985). Walter C. Stout, *The First Hundred Years: A History of Dentistry in Texas* (Dallas: Egan, 1969).

Erbert W. D'Anton

DENTON, JOHN BUNYAN (1806–1841). John B. Denton was born in Tennessee on July 28, 1806, and left an orphan at the age of eight. He was then adopted by a family named Wells, which shortly afterwards migrated to Arkansas Territory. Denton ran away from home when he was twelve years old and for a time worked as a deckhand on an Arkansas River flatboat. In 1824 he married Louisianan Mary Greenlee Stewart, who taught him to read and write. He underwent a conversion the following year, joined the Methodist Episcopal Church, and for ten years served in Arkansas and southern Missouri as an itinerant minister. In the fall of 1836 or early in 1837, in company with a fellow preacher, Littleton Fowler,qv Denton crossed the Red River into Texas. Because of the inadequate income afforded him and his growing family by the ministry, he began the study of law. Six months later he was licensed to practice and entered into partnership with John B. Craig at Clarksville.

He also served in the military, as a captain in a company commanded by Col. Edward H. Tarrant.qv On May 22, 1841, the unit attacked the Indians of Keechi Village in the battle of Village Creek,qv about six miles east of the site of Fort Worth. Denton, who, according to one account, was himself immediately in charge of the attacking force, was instantly killed by a bullet that hit his chest as he raised his rifle to fire. His body was brought back on horseback and buried in an unmarked grave on the east bank of Oliver Creek, near its confluence with a stream now called Denton Creek. Twenty years later John S. Chisumqv disinterred the remains and buried them in a wooden box in the corner of the yard of his home on Clear Creek, near Bolivar. In 1901 the Pioneer Association of Denton County, after diligent search and thorough identification, again removed the remains and buried them with appropriate ceremonies in the southeast corner of the Denton County Courthouse lawn.

BIBLIOGRAPHY: William Allen, *Capt. John B. Denton, Preacher, Lawyer, and Soldier: His Life and Times in Tennessee, Arkansas and Texas* (Chicago: Donnelly, 1905). Zachary T. Fulmore, *History and Geography of Texas As Told in County Names* (Austin: Steck, 1915; facsimile, 1935). Homer S. Thrall, *A Brief History of Methodism in Texas* (Nashville: Publishing House of the Methodist Episcopal Church, South, 1889; rpt., Greenwood, South Carolina: Attic, 1977). Vertical Files, Barker Texas History Center, University of Texas at Austin.

W. Stanley Hoole

DENTON, TEXAS (Callahan County). Denton, also known as Denton Community and Denton Valley Community, is on State Highway 36 twelve miles southwest of Baird in western Callahan County. The site was on open range until the middle 1860s. Land in the area was largely owned by the railroad and the state. G. W. Denton, the early settler after whom the town was named, became the largest private owner of land in the area; he patented his acreage in 1854. Denton had a school district petitioned for by Worth Williams and six other men in April 1899. By 1916 the community had a post office, blacksmith shop, gristmill, and cotton gin. Like many other small communities in West Texas, Denton began to decline in the 1920s. In 1933 it reported a population of fifteen and one business and in the mid-1940s a population of twenty-five. By the 1970s two churches, a business, and a cemetery remained at the site. Denton was still listed as a community in 1990.

BIBLIOGRAPHY: Callahan County Historical Commission, *I Remember Callahan: History of Callahan County, Texas* (Dallas: Taylor, 1986).

Julius A. Amin

DENTON, TEXAS (Denton County). Denton, the county seat of Denton County, is on Interstate Highway 35 where it forks to become 35E to Dallas and 35W to Fort Worth near the center of the county. Less than forty miles north of the cities, Denton has become closely associated with the Dallas–Fort Worth metropolitan area. The city was not an early settlement. It was founded in 1857 in order to become the county seat, because residents wanted one located near the center of the county. Hiram Cisco, William Woodruff, and William Loving donated 100 acres as the site for the town, which, like the county, was named in honor of John B. Denton.qv A commission composed of Otis G. Welch, sometimes known as the "Father of Denton," county surveyor Charles C. Lacy, and Joseph A. Carroll laid out the city. Although it was established in 1857 and a courthouse was built on the north side of the square, Denton was not incorporated until 1866. The charter provided for election of a mayor and five aldermen. J. B. Sawyer was elected the first mayor.

In its early years Denton grew slowly from 361 persons, thirty-two of whom were black, in 1870, to 1,194 in 1880. But in the decade of the 1880s the city experienced its largest percentage growth in any decade up to the 1980s. The population more than doubled, to 2,558 in 1890, as the Texas and Pacific Railway from Sherman to Fort Worth and the Missouri, Kansas and Texas to Dallas, both completed in 1881, gave the city a rail outlet. The Gulf, Colorado and Santa Fe, built in 1887 across western Denton County through Valley View, Krum, and Sanger, missed Denton and was not connected to it until about seventy years later. Since Denton had only north–south rail connections, the town did not develop as a manufacturing and wholesale center.

The city's growth in its first century depended on its position as the county seat, its role as a local agricultural trade center, and its function as a center for light agriculture-related manufacturing concerns, like flour mills and cottonseed oil mills, and small cottage industries, like pottery kilns and blacksmith shops. After 1890, however, Denton did have a feature to distinguish it from the seats of other agricultural counties. It became a college town when North Texas Normal College (now the University of North Texas) was established in 1890 and the Girls' Industrial College (now Texas

Woman's University) was established in 1903. Although the colleges' influence was slight for several years, they ultimately did more to establish the character of Denton than any other single influence. By the 1980s, with a total enrollment of almost 25,000 students, the two universities provided half the city's population and greatly influenced its cultural and economic life.

As in most other small towns in their early days, subscription schools in Denton were taught in churches and in the Masonic lodge building. But in 1884 the first public school, which was secondary as well as elementary, opened in a two-story building near downtown. Ten years later the public school received the equivalent of accreditation by becoming affiliated with the University of Texas. The earliest city newspaper, the Denton *Review,* which first appeared in 1864, was succeeded by the Denton *Monitor* in 1868. The *Monitor* was joined by several other short-lived papers in the 1890s, including the *Denton County Record,* and the Denton *Chronicle.* In 1899 the latter two combined as the Denton *Record and Chronicle,* which was still published in the 1990s as the only daily newspaper, the Denton *Record-Chronicle.*qv

The city's water supply depended entirely upon deep artesian wells up to the 1950s. In 1927, after Lake Dallas was constructed, Denton refused to make a contract with Dallas for water storage in that reservoir, but three decades later the picture had changed. Denton obtained water storage in Lewisville Lake qv after its dam was constructed in the 1950s. In the 1980s Denton contracted for water from a new reservoir, Lake Ray Roberts, under construction by the United States Army Corps of Engineers. Since 1905 both water and electric utilities have been owned by the city.

From 1914 to 1959 Denton was governed under a charter that provided for a mayor–city commission form of government, but a new charter adopted in the latter year provided for a council-manager form of government, which continued in existence into the 1980s. City politics were often enlivened by the fact that in the 1970s about 1,000 university professors resided in Denton. Most of the time, however, town-gown conflict has been minimal.

Because the Denton area was settled mostly by small subsistence farmers who owned few slaves and because it is far from the Mexican border and without large agricultural demand for hand labor, Denton has had relatively few black or Hispanic residents. By the 1980s, however, both universities enrolled a significant number of black students as well as about 2,000 international students.

Denton grew rapidly from 1960, when the population was 26,844, to 1980, when it was 48,063. Proximity to Dallas and Fort Worth, with good interstate highway connections, played a major role. Steady and at times rapid growth of enrollment at the two universities was important also. In 1960 the city gained a third large state institution when the Denton State School,qv a school for the mentally retarded, was established. By 1983 it had 1,014 students and several hundred employees. In 1954 the regional office of the Federal Civil Defense Administration moved from Dallas to Denton, and a few years later a large underground shelter was completed. For a time it was the only FCDA underground shelter and was designated as the place from which the president of the United States and other federal officials would direct the country in case of attack. After 1974 the city added many new residents as a result of the opening of Dallas–Fort Worth International Airport,qv which is closer to Denton than to many parts of Dallas and Fort Worth. Many airline employees and executives who traveled for major companies took up residence in southeast Denton, the most rapidly growing residential area of the city by the 1970s. Furthermore, such older manufacturing firms with significant employment as Moore's Business Forms and Morrison Milling Company were joined during the 1960s and 1970s by heavy manufacturing companies like Victor Equipment Company and Peterbilt, along with several additional light industrial concerns. All of them provided increased employment for local labor. The opening of Golden Triangle Shopping Mall in 1980 began drawing shoppers from surrounding areas. Agriculture, while proportionately declining in significance as an economic stimulus, nevertheless remained important to the city. The population in 1990 was 66,270.

BIBLIOGRAPHY: Edward Franklin Bates, *History and Reminiscences of Denton County* (Denton, Texas: McNitzky Printing, 1918; rpt., Denton: Terrill Wheeler Printing, 1976). C. A. Bridges, *History of Denton, Texas, from Its Beginning to 1960* (Waco: Texian Press, 1978).

E. Dale Odom

DENTON COUNTY. Denton County (G-16) covers 911 square miles in north central Texas. Its center point is at 33°12′ north latitude and 97°13′ west longitude. It borders Dallas and Tarrant counties on the south and Cooke and Grayson counties on the north; it is one county south of Oklahoma. The western half of the county is surfaced by the black soil of the Grand Prairie. An eastern sliver is on the western edge of the Blackland Prairie, where the rich black soil contrasts sharply with the sandy land of the Eastern Cross Timbers jutting down from Oklahoma through the central part of the county. Denton County ranges in elevation from 500 to 900 feet, has an annual average rainfall of about thirty-three inches, and a temperature average ranging from a minimum of 34° F in January to a maximum of 96° in July. With an average growing season of 226 days, it is a good area for general crop and livestock production. The Elm Fork of the Trinity River flows through the east central part of the county. It was dammed in the 1920s to form Lake Dallas, which has since been joined with Garza–Little Elm Reservoir to form Lewisville Lake,qv a moderately large reservoir. The western part of the county is cut by several major creeks. Clear Creek drains into the Elm Fork and Hickory Creek into Lewisville Lake. Denton Creek and its tributaries, in the southern part of the county, are sources of water for Grapevine Lake,qv which is partly in Denton County and partly in Tarrant County. In the Cross Timbers and the floodplains of the creeks black jack and post oak, pecan, white ash, sycamore, cottonwood, hackberry, elm, and willow trees predominate. Most of the rest of the county was originally covered by grasses. Some native pasture remained in the 1980s, but the bulk of county land not in cultivation was improved pasture, planted mainly with coastal Bermuda grass. The Trinity Sands underlie the area at about 700 to 1,200 feet, but in some parts of the county residents are able to reach artesian water at depths as shallow as 100 feet. Though Denton County is not abundant in natural resources, it has produced a modest but significant amount of oil (3,346,233 barrels by the end of 1990), mostly from the Bolivar field between the 1930s and the 1960s. Other natural resources are natural gas, sand and gravel, and some building stone—the stone courthouse on the square in Denton was built in 1896 from stone quarried a few miles north. Although archeological field surveys done under contract with the United States Army Corps of Engineers indicate some use of the area as early as the Middle Archaic Period (4,000 to 2,500 B.C.), only one county site, near Lewisville, has been deemed highly significant, and it is controversial. A Clovis point from the site was radiocarbon-dated at 37,000 B.C., but most other information contradicts the possibility that human beings inhabited the area that early. All other archeological work indicates nothing unique about prehistoric occupation of Denton County. There is no evidence that the county was the site of any large Indian villages in the Historic Period (1600–1800), although remains of many small transitory camps and small burial grounds have been found. Early Spanish and French explorers may also have trekked across the county, but documentation is lacking.

Anglo settlement began after William S. Peters,qv of Louisville, Kentucky, and several others, obtained a land grant from the Texas Congress in 1841. The land settled by their company, the Texian Land and Immigration Company, became known as the Peters colony.qv Their grant included all of the future Denton County, as well as parts or all of several other future counties. The earliest settlement in what became Denton County was in the southeastern section, near the site of present Hebron, and most of the early residents took up land in the Cross Timbers.

Although a few came from the lower South, most antebellum settlers in the area came from the upper South. In 1850, 40 percent gave Tennessee and Kentucky as their state of birth. Immigration from the upper South predominated because of the Kentucky-based Peters Company. The county was also limited to subsistence agriculture due to a lack of water transportation. Consequently, there were only 106 slaves in the county in 1850; in 1860, eighty-seven slaveholders owned 251 slaves.

In the 1840s Denton County was the site of the Icarian colony,[qv] a French utopian settlement north of the site of present Justin. The Icarians gave up and left after a few months of sickness and disappointment and made virtually no lasting mark on the county. The same cannot be said of the German community of Blue Mound, on the prairie a few miles northwest of Denton. Descendants of many of the German families that began settling there in the 1870s were still among the residents of the community a century later. Most were from Saxony, via Illinois or Missouri.

In 1846, the Texas legislature formed Denton County out of what had been a much larger Fannin County. It was named for John Bunyan Denton,[qv] an eastern Fannin County Methodist preacher and lawyer, who was killed in a raid against Indians in northern Tarrant County on May 22, 1841. A county seat, named Pinckneyville, was located near the center of the county, at a spot about a mile southeast of the present center of Denton. Although county officials were elected in 1846, no courthouse was built, and less than two years later a site named Alton, three or four miles to the southeast, was made county seat. Because water was not readily available, in 1850 the legislature allowed Alton to be moved about two miles south to Alexander Cannon's homestead near Hickory Creek. A log courthouse, the first in the county, was built there. Alton soon had stores, residences, and a hotel and was a regular stage stop. In the summer of 1856, however, county residents voted to establish a new county seat near the center of the county on a 100-acre tract donated by Hiram Cisco, William Loving, and William Woodruff. The new town, named Denton, was established the next year, but was not incorporated as a city until 1866.

Denton County grew slowly until after the Civil War.[qv] In 1860 it had 4,780 residents, slightly more than 10,000 acres of improved land, and a few more than 20,000 cattle, 6,000 of which belonged to John S. Chisum,[qv] who began ranching in the northwestern part of the county in 1854. Almost all residents were still engaged in subsistence agriculture. Cotton ginned that year totaled only two bales. Growth was rapid, however, in the decade of the 1870s, when the population grew from 7,251 to 18,143. Many new residents began farms, and in 1880 almost 50 percent of the county was in cultivation.

Railroads entered the county in the 1880s and had a great economic and demographic effect. Production of such subsistence crops as corn and vegetables declined, acreage in cotton and wheat increased rapidly, and the number of cattle grazing the prairies shrank substantially. Cotton acreage, 29,785 acres in 1880, peaked at 115,078 in 1920, but declined to insignificance in the 1980s. The Grand Prairie of Denton County was ideal for wheat culture,[qv] and between 1880 and 1900, wheat acreage increased by more than 80,000 acres. From 1890 to 1920 the county ranked either first or second in wheat production among the counties of the state, behind Collin County. Krum, a village near Denton, was reputed in 1900 to be the largest inland wheat market in the United States. Between 1880 and 1920 the number of beef cattle declined from 49,008 to 12,123, and 89 percent of county land was in cultivation at the latter date. Railroads also determined town location up to the 1970s, when only one town of any size was not on one of the railroad lines built in the 1880s.

Although Denton County's railroads made the county a significant agricultural producer, they did not make it an important commercial or manufacturing center. Consequently, population expansion in the twentieth century, slow in response to agriculture after 1900, depended to a great extent on other forms of transportation and on higher education. The county's population growth and its economic and cultural life were much influenced by the location in Denton of two large state-supported universities. The University of North Texas, established as Texas Normal College in 1890, had an enrollment of more than 20,000 in 1993. At the same time, Texas Woman's University, which originated in 1903 as Girls' Industrial College, had an enrollment of about 5,000 at the Denton campus.

Rubber-tired transportation and, perhaps to a lesser extent, the location of Dallas–Fort Worth International Airport,[qv] played a large part in the growth of Denton County after 1940. During World War II[qv] the county began to serve noticeably as a bedroom area for Dallas–Fort Worth. Completion of Interstate Highway 35 in the 1950s increased commuting, and in the 1980s Interstate highways 35E and 35W forked in Denton. All of the towns and cities of the county had a significant commuter element, but the southeastern portion, growing most rapidly, was virtually an extension of Dallas–Fort Worth. Lewisville, The Colony, and the part of Carrollton in Denton County were all population centers because they were suburbs of Dallas. The population of Denton had also grown because of the city's proximity to Dallas and because of the growth of the University of North Texas and Texas Woman's University.

The county population grew from 47,432 in 1960 to 143,126 in 1980. Many new rural residents owned small spreads, and mobile homes vied with expensive, sprawling ranchhouses for space. Large horse ranches were scattered through the county; in 1983 horses brought in $17,207,400, a significantly larger income than that from any other agricultural product (*see* HORSE AND MULE INDUSTRY). Newcomers and many older residents returned much of Denton County's rich cropland to pasture, and by the 1980s rural areas, almost depopulated by the rural-to-urban shift after World War II, had probably returned to their 1920s level in density of population.

Denton County voters supported Democratic candidates through 1948 with the exception of Herbert Hoover in 1928. From 1952 through 1992 they shifted their allegiance to the Republican party,[qv] again with only a single exception, Democrat Lyndon Baines Johnson[qv] in 1968. In 1990 the population of Denton County was 273,525. The largest towns were Denton (66,270) and Lewisville (45,966 in Denton County). Attractions included Lewisville and Grapevine lakes, the annual Jazzfest held in September, and the North Texas State Fair in August.

BIBLIOGRAPHY: Edward Franklin Bates, *History and Reminiscences of Denton County* (Denton, Texas: McNitzky Printing, 1918; rpt., Denton: Terrill Wheeler Printing, 1976). C. A. Bridges, *History of Denton, Texas, from Its Beginning to 1960* (Waco: Texian Press, 1978). Mary Jo Cowling, *Geography of Denton County* (Dallas: Banks, Upshaw, 1936). E. Dale Odom and Bullitt Lowry, *A Brief History of Denton County* (Denton, Texas, 1975).
E. Dale Odom

DENTON CREEK (Franklin County). Denton Creek rises a half mile south of Mount Vernon in central Franklin County (at 33°08' N, 95°14' W) and runs northwest for six miles to its mouth on Big Creek, two miles northeast of Saltillo in Hopkins County (at 33°12' N, 95°18' W). It traverses an area of gently undulating to rolling terrain surfaced by loamy soil with a clayey subsoil that supports dense woods, in which pines and various hardwoods predominate.

―――― (Gonzales County). Denton Creek rises in southern Gonzales County (at 29°23' N, 97°24' W) and runs southeast to its mouth on the Guadalupe River, a mile southwest of Hochheim in DeWitt County (at 29°17' N, 97°20' W). The stream was probably named for Abraham Denton, one of Green DeWitt's[qv] colonists, who acquired a quarter of a league of land in the area. Denton Creek passes through rolling to steep terrain surfaced by fine, sandy loams and clayey soils that support pines and a variety of grasses.

_____ (Gonzales County). Denton Creek rises two miles northeast of Gonzales in Gonzales County (at 29°38′ N, 97°24′ W) and runs southeast for ten miles to its mouth on Peach Creek (at 29°31′ N, 97°19′ W). The stream was also named for Abraham Denton, early DeWitt's colony^{qv} settler. The local flat to rolling blackland prairie supports mixed hardwoods and pines.

_____ (Montague County). Denton Creek rises four miles northeast of Bowie in central Montague County (at 33°36′ N, 97°49′ W) and runs southeast for thirty-two miles, through Wise and Denton counties, before emptying into Grapevine Reservoir (at 33°02′ N, 97°14′ W). The creek, named for John B. Denton,^{qv} is located in the Grand Prairie and Cross Timbers regions of north central Texas and is one of the major tributaries of the area, draining more than 520,000 acres.

DENTON FIELD. Denton Field, which was 2½ miles northeast of Denton, was the site of the North Texas civilian pilot-training program of the Civilian Aeronautics Authority from 1940 to 1945. The original purpose of the program, which began in 1939, was to aid in the proper instruction of private flyers, but after World War II^{qv} began, the program emphasized preparing young men for military flying. Colonel Ralph Devore, director of Region Four of the Civilian Aeronautics Authority, selected Denton as the site for the region's North Texas base, and construction was begun and completed during the summer of 1940. The program at Denton began on October 10, 1940, with Theron J. Fouts as director, C. S. Floyd, Jr., as flight instructor, and Fred Connell, Jr., as ground instructor. The program accepted young men between the ages of nineteen and twenty-six who had completed one year of college and could pass a medical examination. Each student received seventy-two hours of ground training and between thirty-five and forty-five hours of flying, half flown solo. In the fall of 1940 twenty students enrolled in the program. The following year that number increased to thirty-five. From 1942 to 1945 an average of thirty-three students graduated each academic year. At the end of the war the civilian pilot-training program ended and Denton Field was abandoned. The army later selected the field as the site of one of four Nike-Hercules missile batteries in the Dallas–Fort Worth area. The base was completed in 1959 and dismantled in the spring of 1964. Although not in use in the 1980s and early 1990s Denton Field remained the property of the federal government.

BIBLIOGRAPHY: *Campus Chat,* North Texas State University, July 20, 1941. Denton *Record-Chronicle,* September 27, 1940, September 8, 1959, May 12, 1964. James Lloyd Rogers, *The Story of North Texas* (Denton: North Texas State University, 1965). *David Minor*

DENTONIO, TEXAS. Dentonio, also known as Denton Colony, was real estate development sixteen miles southwest of Carrizo Springs in southwest Dimmit County. The settlement, named for its founder, Graham Denton, was among the largest of several similar attempts to profit from land in Dimmit County between 1910 and 1920. Denton divided his 32,000-acre site into tracts surrounding a townsite; those who bought at least $210 worth of farmland were to be given a free town lot. In 1910 Denton built a two-story schoolhouse on the site, established a railroad "bonus" fund in hopes of enticing a rail link to his town, and waged a national advertising campaign. By 1912 1,600 purchases of Dentonio land had been made, and the town had twenty-one buildings, including a school, a post office, and a hotel. An extended drought and inadequate supplies of cheap water made it difficult for family farms to survive. By 1920 Denton and his out-of-state investors were fighting in court over the railroad funds. The town rapidly diminished. By 1929 it had lost its post office, and by 1936 only seven dwellings and the school remained. In 1947 the school was consolidated with the Carrizo Springs Independent School District. In 1984 only a windmill stood on the site.

BIBLIOGRAPHY: Laura Knowlton Tidwell, *Dimmit County Mesquite Roots* (Austin: Wind River, 1984). *John Leffler*

DENTON *RECORD-CHRONICLE.* In 1899 William C. Edwards, son of James R. and Elizabeth (Cunningham) Edwards of Denton, purchased and consolidated the Denton *Chronicle* (founded in 1882) and the *Denton County Record* (1898) to form the weekly Denton *Record and Chronicle.* The paper published its first daily edition on August 3, 1903. Robert John Edwards joined his brother as part owner and editor in 1906. At one time five local newspapers were competing with the *Record and Chronicle,* but by 1912 the Edwardses' daily, delivered by carrier boys on ponies, survived as the only paper providing local and state news to Denton County residents.

The Edwards brothers were active in state politics and county affairs, and the *Record-Chronicle* (the *and* disappeared in 1915) reflected their political interests. William served one term in the state legislature (1922–24) and lost the Democratic nomination for lieutenant governor in a primary runoff in 1924. Robert was a member of the state Democratic executive committee and served a two-year term on the Texas Prison Board (*see* PRISON SYSTEM). The newspaper, reflecting the concerns of its owners, consistently supported Democratic candidates and policies and was a public booster for the city of Denton.

"Mr. Bob," as Robert Edwards was affectionately called by Denton residents, became publisher and managing editor in 1927 when his brother left Denton to work for the Hearst newspaper chain. In April 1945 Edwards sold the newspaper to Riley Cross, former publisher of the Marshall *News Messenger.* Few changes took place under the new owner. The thirty-nine-year-old Cross discontinued the Saturday edition and added a Sunday paper, but, in a new plant in Denton, the *Record-Chronicle* continued the tradition established by the Edwards family of focusing on local and state news, supporting Democratic politicians, and boosting the city of Denton. The paper benefited from Denton's growth. In 1945 it had 4,000 subscribers; by 1960 that number had increased to almost 11,000. During the twenty-five-year tenure of Riley Cross the newspaper received numerous awards from the Texas Press Association.^{qv} In the late 1950s the *Record-Chronicle* supported the racial integration of North Texas State University (now the University of North Texas), located in Denton. J. C. Matthews, president of the university, credited the peaceful integration in part to the editorials and reporting of the Denton *Record-Chronicle.*

After suffering a heart attack in 1957, Cross gradually withdrew from managing the daily publication of the newspaper. On March 11, 1970, he died. His wife, Vivian Griswold Cross, continued to own and publish the paper, as well as to oversee the operation of a local television cable station, until her death. In the early 1990s the Patterson family bought the paper. In 1994 the daily circulation was 18,000, and the Sunday circulation was 21,000.

BIBLIOGRAPHY: C. A. Bridges, *History of Denton, Texas, from Its Beginning to 1960* (Waco: Texian Press, 1978). Denton *Record-Chronicle,* July 28, 1963. *David Minor*

DENTON STATE SCHOOL. The Denton State School, in the early 1990s one of thirteen state facilities that provided care and treatment for the mentally retarded, operates under the management of the Texas Department of Mental Health and Mental Retardation.^{qv} The school is located on a 200-acre tract four miles south-southeast of Denton, and it serves twenty-two counties in northeast Texas. In 1957, after a vigorous lobbying effort by the Denton Chamber of Commerce, the Texas Department of Mental Health and Mental Retardation chose Denton as the site for the state school because of the city's proximity to Dallas and Fort Worth and because of its universities—Texas Woman's University, which at that time had the largest nursing program in the state, and North Texas State Teachers College (now the University of North Texas), which had the largest teacher-training facility in Texas. Another influence on the department's decision was the city's pledge to donate land for the school. In thirty-four days during November and December of 1957, 2,000 Denton residents contributed $102,000 to a Mental School Cash Campaign conducted by the city's chamber of commerce.

Construction of the school began on March 7, 1959, and was completed in July 1960. Originally, the school accepted only citizens of Texas between the ages of six and twenty-one who had IQs of seventy or below. By 1980, however, the age restriction had been removed. E. W. (Ed) Killian, a North Texas State graduate, was the school's first superintendent. During Killian's twenty-year tenure, the number of residents of the school increased, as did the number of facilities and programs designed for their care. In 1994 the school had more than sixty buildings—including residential facilities leased off-campus—and 2,000 employees serving 670 residents and a large number of off-campus clients. School programs included vocational services and early childhood intervention. The school also directed an outreach community service with facilities in twelve counties. In addition, Denton's foster grandparent program provides a means for senior citizens to give one-to-one attention to residents at the school. The Texas Department of Human Resources (now the Texas Department Of Human Services[qv]) and the Texas Education Agency[qv] provided funds to the school. Although well over 90 percent of the school's income came from the state, the school also received financial support from the United States departments of Health and Human Services, Agriculture, and Education. In 1994 Pat Jessee served as superintendent of the school.

BIBLIOGRAPHY: Denton *Record-Chronicle,* October 28, 1957, May 30, 1960.
David Minor

DENVER CITY, TEXAS. Denver City is on State Highway 83 on the Gaines county line, seventy miles southwest of Lubbock in south central Yoakum County. When the Wasson oil pool was developed in 1939, the town was founded and named by E. S. Ameen and Ben Eggink. Ameen selected the name because he had a close friend who was employed by Denver Productions near the townsite, and he added "City" to the name to show his faith in the town's future. Shortly after its founding the town was incorporated and had a refinery and a gas and water system. By 1940 Denver City had a population of 3,000 and 120 businesses.

In March 1939 W. J. Hale published the first Denver City newspaper at his plant in Plains. The paper, originally called the *Record,* went through several name changes before it was bought by a Mr. Watson, who changed the name to Denver City *Press.* Dr. D. K. Robinson established the Denver City Hospital and Clinic in a building at the rear of City Drug Store in 1942. By 1943 the initial boom had subsided; by 1944 the population had leveled to 2,000, and the number of businesses had dropped to fifty-five. In 1945 the population was estimated at 1,750, its level for the rest of the decade. Only thirty-eight businesses were in operation, but Denver City remained an important oilfield-supply point, in addition to its role as a principal retail center for area ranchers.

During the 1950s Denver City grew rapidly. In 1952 it reported 1,858 residents and ninety-five businesses, and by 1955 the number of residents was estimated at 3,800. In 1965 the town reported 4,854 residents and 163 businesses. As drilling activities in the area increased during the 1970s the town continued to grow. Denver City has a library, a county hospital, a radio station, and a semiweekly newspaper. In 1975 the town had 4,920 residents. Because Denver City is situated near the county line many of its businesses are able to serve two counties. Gas plants, cotton refineries, and cattle feedlots are among the local industries. Despite the fact that it has no railroad or airport the town continued to prosper until the 1990s, as the largest town in Yoakum County and headquarters for most of the county's oil-related business. In 1988 the population was estimated at 5,583. In 1990 it was 5,145.

BIBLIOGRAPHY: Ray Miller, *Eyes of Texas Travel Guide: Panhandle/Plains Edition* (Houston: Cordovan, 1982).
Leoti A. Bennett

DENWIDDIE BAYOU. Denwiddie Bayou rises 3½ miles north of Detroit in northwestern Red River County (at 33°43′ N, 95°16′ W) and runs northeast for 10½ miles to its mouth on Pecan Bayou, seven miles northeast of Bagwell (at 33°46′ N, 95°07′ W). The soils along the creek, which is intermittent in its upper and middle reaches, are loamy and clayey, and the area is heavily wooded, with pines and various hardwoods predominating.

DENWORTH, TEXAS. Denworth, near Farm Road 2857 three miles east of the Wheeler county line in eastern Gray County, was laid out in 1919 as a townsite for the Fort Worth and Denver Railway, for which it was named. Although it thrived for a time as an area shipping point during the oil boom days, its isolated location eventually caused the town to fail. A post office was opened in 1932 with Mrs. Ina Marshal as postmistress, and by 1939 the number of residents was estimated at fifty. Despite a reported population increase to 100 in 1945, the post office closed in March 1946. The completion of Interstate Highway 40 has subsequently caused the community to fall almost into oblivion. A pump station was still at the site in 1988.

BIBLIOGRAPHY: Arthur Hecht, comp., *Postal History in the Texas Panhandle* (Canyon, Texas: Panhandle-Plains Historical Society, 1960).
H. Allen Anderson

DEPARTMENT OF BANKING. State-chartered banks were not authorized in Texas until the Texas State Bank Law was enacted by the Twenty-ninth Legislature on August 14, 1905, an act that provided for the supervision of banks. After initially making the Commissioner of Agriculture, Insurance, Statistics, and History responsible for examining every corporation doing business under the act, the legislature the next year established a separate department for agriculture and changed the name of the other department to the Department of Insurance and Banking. In 1923 a separate banking department was established. The present department, established by the legislature in 1943, is supervised by the Finance Commission of Texas,[qv] which by the early 1990s was responsible for three agencies: the Department of Banking, the Savings and Loan Department,[qv] and the Office of Consumer Credit. The Finance Commission of Texas consists of a board with nine members, appointed by the governor for six-year terms. The board members appoint the banking commissioner as administrator of the Department of Banking. Two of the board members must be banking executives, two must be savings and loan executives, and the other five must be citizen members, one of whom must be a certified public accountant. There is also a three-member State Banking Board composed of the banking commissioner, the state treasurer, and an unsalaried member appointed by the governor for a two-year term. The responsibility of this board is approval or denial of bank and trust company charter applications, change of domicile, and conversion from national to state charters. By the end of 1992 the Department of Banking was responsible for 530 state-chartered banks with total assets of more than $45 billion. The major functions of the Department of Banking are to supervise and regulate all banks chartered by the state and to enforce the state laws pertaining to them. The deposits of such institutions are insured by the Federal Deposit Insurance Corporation. Additional responsibilities of the department include licensing and regulating prepaid-funeral-contract providers, perpetual-care cemeteries, currency-exchange activities, and sale of checks operations. In 1987 all trust companies came under the jurisdiction of the Department of Banking.
Dick Smith

DEPELCHIN, KEZIA PAYNE (1828–1893). Kezia Payne DePelchin, social worker, teacher, and nurse, was born in the Madeira Islands on July 23, 1828, the daughter of Abraham and Catherine Armstrong (Cartwright) Payne. She spent her early life in England. Sometime during the mid-1830s her mother died in her native Funchal, Madeira. The family went to New York in late 1836 and to Galveston, Texas, in 1837. In 1839 her father married their governess, Hannah Bainton. A yellow fever outbreak at Galveston left Kezia an orphan without financial resources; in 1839 she had contracted yellow fever as well but survived it. According to various sources, she arrived in Houston in 1841 accompanied by her widowed stepmother. Apparently Kezia raised a girl, Hannah Cordelia Buckner, for a time, in order to assist the child's widower father. In the 1840s she worked as a music teacher and also practiced charity work among the sick and destitute. With an acquired immunity to yellow fever, she nursed the sick in yellow fever epidemics in Houston. She operated a number of schools during the 1850s, including one in Bastrop (1850). She was married on August 23, 1862, to itinerant musician Adolph DePelchin. They had no children and soon parted company because of his financial recklessness. During the Civil War[qv] she joined a nursing corps in Houston. In 1875 she was employed by a German-English school, and in 1877, when the city's free public schools opened, she taught in the Fourth Ward, Houston.[qv] She nursed yellow fever victims in epidemics as far away as Memphis, Tennessee, and Seratobia, Mississippi. She was employed for a time at doctors Stuart and Boyle's sanitarium as a nurse. She was appointed head nurse of Houston's first City Charity Hospital, and in 1888 became the first woman matron of the Bayland Orphans' Home for Boys.[qv] In 1892, to help her meet the cost of renting two rooms over a store and hiring a woman to care for two homeless children, DePelchin founded Houston's first day-care center, charging only employed mothers who could pay ten cents a day. Kezia Payne DePelchin died on January 13, 1893, and was buried at public expense. Subsequently her work with the day nursery was carried on by her niece, Martha Payne.

The DePelchin Faith Home, a nonsectarian, community-supported institution for dependent children, was organized on January 20, 1893, by 100 Houston women to honor DePelchin after her death. The home was named in recognition of DePelchin's faith and her belief in the beneficence of the people of Houston. James A. Baker,[qv] founder of the law firm of Baker and Botts,[qv] drew up a charter and bylaws. The main building, modeled on an Italianate villa, was designed in 1912 by the architectural firm of Mauran & Russell of St. Louis, and was built on land donated in 1910 by Harriet Levy, wife of a Houston merchant. Harris County funding for the facility was first obtained in 1914. A twelve-acre site was purchased in 1927, and the institution was renamed the DePelchin Faith Home and Children's Bureau Association after it obtained a new charter in 1928. In 1934 a fifty-acre farm near Spring, Texas, was acquired for use as a summer camp, and in 1936 the institution absorbed the Florence Crittenden Home foster-home program and became involved in adoption and protection work. Nine new buildings were completed in 1937 with the help of the Works Progress Administration (*see* WORK PROJECTS ADMINISTRATION), as well as state and local funding. The DePelchin Home is considered the first Houston institution of its kind to serve black children (beginning in 1939). It was one of several founders of the city's Community Chest. In 1940 it provided services for a total of 1,087 children. By the 1950s, the institution included a hospital, a clinic, and a library, and was a member of the Child Welfare League of America and the Houston Council of Social Agencies. In the latter part of the twentieth century the home was called the DePelchin Children's Center. Its services expanded over the years. In 1978 the Cullen Bayou Place mental health program began, and during the 1980s the center opened satellite offices in nine locations. A new forty-bed psychiatric hospital began operation in 1991. At that time the Depelchin Children's Center offered programs in residential treatment, home therapy, parent education, and child-abuse prevention. A Texas Historical Commission[qv] marker was placed at the home in 1984.

BIBLIOGRAPHY: Mrs. Henry Fall, ed., and Mabel F. Smith, illust., *The Key to the City of Houston* (Houston: Federation of Women's Clubs, 1908). Harold Jackson Matthews, *Candle by Night* (Boston: B. Humphries, 1942). Marie Phelps McAshan, *A Houston Legacy: On the Corner of Main and Texas* (Houston: Gulf, 1985). David G. McComb, *Houston: The Bayou City* (Austin: University of Texas Press, 1969; rev. ed., *Houston: A History*, 1981). WPA Writers Program, *Houston* (Houston: Anson Jones, 1942).

Diana J. Kleiner

DEPORT, TEXAS. Deport is on Highway 271 at the Red River county line, eighteen miles southeast of Paris in southeast Lamar County. It was founded in the late 1800s by Col. Dee Thompson on Mustang Creek, supposedly so his horses would have a supply of water. A local post office was established in 1883 and named Deport in honor of Thompson. In 1890 the settlement had a population of 350 and two churches, four general stores, one gristmill and gin, and several other small businesses. It also supported a weekly paper called the Deport *Times*. By 1896 the population had grown to 600, and the number of businesses had increased to around twenty, a figure that included five physicians, three music teachers, a milliner, and a hotel keeper. In 1896 Deport had a school with three teachers for 149 students. The surrounding area produced cotton, corn, and high-grade livestock.

In 1911 Deport was incorporated, and the Paris and Mount Pleasant Railway was built through town. In 1914 the town had a population of 1,200 and forty businesses. In 1929 Deport suffered a disastrous fire that resulted in $30,000 damage to Main Street. In the 1930s the population of 819 supported fifty businesses. The railroad line was discontinued in 1956, however, and by 1961 the population had dropped to 639 and the number of businesses to twenty-eight. Deport had a population of 722, six churches, seventy stores, and a bank in 1982. The population was 746 in 1990.

BIBLIOGRAPHY: Deport *Times*, November 29, 1929, February 14, March 28, April 25, 1930. A. W. Neville, *The History of Lamar County, Texas* (Paris, Texas: North Texas, 1937; rpt. 1986). Kathleen E. and Clifton R. St. Clair, eds., *Little Towns of Texas* (Jacksonville, Texas: Jayroe Graphic Arts, 1982).

Sarah E. Calcote

DERBANNE, FRANÇOIS GUYON DES PRÉS (1671–1734). François Derbanne (d'Erbanne or d'Herbanne), a French Canadian who explored the upper Mississippi and Missouri rivers and was prominent in early Mobile and Natchitoches, is most often noted for his trek across Texas in 1717, of which he wrote an account. He was born at Quebec on February 6, 1671, and was with Le Sueur in his search for minerals on the upper Mississippi in 1698–99. He took part in the exploration of the upper Missouri in 1706. By 1710 he had moved to Dauphin Island, adjacent to Mobile Bay, where he had charge of Antoine Crozat's company warehouse. In 1716 he was at the forefront of Bienville's campaign against the Natchez Indians.

Later that year, when Louis Juchereau de Saint Denis[qv] returned to Mobile from his first journey to San Juan Bautista[qv] and Mexico City, Derbanne became his partner for contraband trade with the Spaniards. With merchandise from Crozat's storehouses, destined for sale in Nuevo León, the traders left Mobile in canoes on October 10, 1716, for the Natchitoches Indian villages on the Red River. They carried the merchandise thence on mules that had brought from Coahuila the effects of the six new Spanish missions of eastern Texas.

The traders spent two months among the Hasinai (Tejas) Indians, for whom the Spaniards were building missions. The journey from there to San Juan Bautista (Guerrero, Coahuila) extended from March 22 to April 21, 1717, on a route slightly at variance with the Spanish Camino Real (*see* OLD SAN ANTONIO ROAD). Derbanne's "Relation" is a valuable account of the country, the flora and fauna, and Indian demographics. It also reflects the geographical understanding of the time. From a commercial point of view, the trip was a disappointment, as Derbanne saw scant prospects for a lucrative trade because of the distance and Spanish opposition. He and the other partners left San Juan Bautista on September 1 and returned to Dauphin Island on October 26, 1717.

In January of that year Derbanne took up residence at Natchitoches, where he managed the Company of the West's warehouse, acquired land and slaves, and became the second wealthiest resident. He had married Jeanne de La Grand Terre, who is believed to have been a Natchitoches Indian. They had six children. After some years there Derbanne wrote his "Relation du poste des Natchitoches," dated June 12, 1724. He died in 1734 in New Orleans and presumably was buried there. His wife died two years later and was buried at Natchitoches.

BIBLIOGRAPHY: Katherine Bridges and Winston De Ville, trans. and eds., "Natchitoches and the Trail to the Rio Grande: Two Early Eighteenth Century Accounts by the Sieur Derbanne," *Louisiana History* 8 (Summer 1967). Jay Higginbotham, *Old Mobile: Fort Louis de la Louisiane, 1703–1711* (Mobile, Alabama: Museum of the City of Mobile, 1977).

Robert S. Weddle

DERBY, TEXAS. Derby is on the Missouri Pacific line at the intersection of Interstate Highway 35 and Farm Road 1583, nine miles southwest of Pearsall in south central Frio County. Englishman John Bennett, an engineer for the International–Great Northern Railroad, moved to the site in 1879 and helped manage the construction of the I–GN extension through Lenore from Melon to the Mexican border in 1882–83. In 1882 a post office called Lenore was established in the developing community. The post office and a rail depot at the site on lands owned by Bennett were eventually renamed Derby in honor of his English birthplace. In 1883 Bennett constructed a dam, known as Derby Dam, in the area, and shortly thereafter he had a town surveyed into lots, including lots for a church and a school. Sometime before 1885 he expanded the depot with a spur for loading vegetables and changed the name of the community to Otley, in honor of his wife's home in England. By 1906 the community was again called Derby and had several schools with a total of three teachers and fifty-five students. Derby was an emerging farming center in 1935. Eight large artesian wells in the community were used to irrigate fields of cotton, as well as onions, spinach, carrots, beets, and a variety of other vegetables. In 1936 the community had an estimated population of fifty, three businesses, and a church. No businesses were reported in Derby by 1971, though its population remained an estimated fifty. In the early 1990s its population was still reported as fifty and the Derby Cemetery was located southeast of the townsite.

BIBLIOGRAPHY: Pearsall *Leader*, May 24, 1935. Mrs. W. A. Roberts, "Frio County Has a Colorful History," *Frontier Times*, June 1936.

Ruben E. Ochoa

DERDEN, TEXAS. Derden, on a spur off Farm Road 2488 midway between Covington and Blum in northwestern Hill County, has served area farmers and ranchers as a school and church community throughout its history. The settlement began to form in the mid-1850s when the Ince brothers arrived in the area and built a cotton gin. In the following years the community gained an additional gin, as well as two merchandise stores, a drugstore, and a church. Later its settlers built a schoolhouse. The settlement was originally called Brushy Knob because of its location near a high wooded hill; it apparently adopted the name Derden sometime after the Civil War,qv supposedly in honor of a prominent citizen. Between 1875 and 1879 Derden had an active Grangeqv chapter. A post office operated in the community from 1881 to 1903. Derden was the home of an independent school district until 1919, when Derden, Oak Hill, and Old Union Hill consolidated under the name Union Hill. In 1970 a cemetery remained at the site.

BIBLIOGRAPHY: Hill County Historical Commission, *A History of Hill County, Texas, 1853–1980* (Waco: Texian, 1980).

David Minor

DERMOTT, TEXAS. Dermott, on U.S. Highway 84 in northwestern Scurry County, was named for Pete McDermott, who donated the land for the town and established a store there in the 1890s. A post office was granted in 1902 with William H. Smith as postmaster. Like many small Texas towns, Dermott literally followed the railroads. The town moved first to be near the Roscoe, Snyder and Pacific tracks; subsequently, although Dermott had no depot, the trains stopped to load cattle and cotton. Sometime before 1915 the town was moved to the Santa Fe tracks, where cattle-loading pens were built. With the Scurry County oil boom of 1949 the town's fortunes rose, but they fell with the bust in 1951. In 1990 Dermott still maintained a post office, though the population had fallen to five.

BIBLIOGRAPHY: Scurry County Historical Survey Committee, *Historical Markers in Scurry County* (Snyder, Texas, 1969).

Noel Wiggins

DERNAL, TEXAS. Dernal is just west of Farm Road 404 between Victoria and Bloomington in southern Victoria County. It was on the St. Louis, Brownsville and Mexico Railway. In 1947 it had a cotton gin and twenty-five residents, a population it also reported in 1961. Dernal was still listed as a community in 1990.

Melvin B. Jaschke

DERRETT CREEK. Derrett Creek rises just outside the city limits of Rhome in the southeastern corner of Wise County (at 33°03′ N, 97°28′ W) and runs southwest for 4½ miles. It flowed into the West Fork of the Trinity River until the early 1930s, when its course was diverted to empty into Eagle Mountain Lake, just outside of Newark (at 33°00′ N, 97°30′ W). The stream, which is intermittent in its upper reaches, traverses an area of undulating to hilly terrain with light to very dark, loamy soils that have an accumulation of lime.

DERYEE, CHARLES WILLIAM (1886–1917). Charles William DeRyee, writer, the son of Charles H. DeRyee, the discoverer of the boll weevilqv in Texas, was born in August 1886 in Corpus Christi. He was educated in public schools at Corpus Christi and by his father and grandfather. He wrote freelance pieces for Corpus Christi newspapers before going to San Francisco, where he was employed on the *Examiner*. After the death of Bret Harte, he became editor of the literary magazine *Overland Monthly* and wrote a novel, *Truth Unadorned* (1916). DeRyee also composed humorous verse. His brilliant conversation, broad knowledge of literature, and sparkling wit made him popular in the literary circles of San Francisco; Bret Harte, Douglas Fairbanks, and Jack London were particular friends. His novel *Coyote o' the Rio Grande* was made into a motion picture in 1917, produced by Fine Arts Film Company and featuring Bessie Love and Douglas Fairbanks. DeRyee married Mabel Carlson in 1914 in San Francisco. He died there of pneumonia on October 2, 1917.

BIBLIOGRAPHY: San Francisco *Examiner*, October 3, 1917.

Frank Wagner

DERYEE, WILLIAM (1825–1903). William DeRyee was born on May 15, 1825 in Würzburg, Bavaria, the son of Nicholas and Augusta Düry. He changed the spelling of his name when he emigrated to the United States. He was educated in the Gymnasium and Lateinschule in Würzburg. At the University of Munich, he studied with professor F. W. J. Schelling (philosophy), Karl F. P. von Martius (botany), John Lamont (meteorology), and Andreas Wagner (geology). He participated in the 1848 revolution against the king, and, after the Peoples Parliament named Archduke Johan of Austria administrator of the German Commonwealth, he went to the Netherlands, where he obtained passage to New York. DeRyee joined a group of German immigrants going to Tennessee. He met Ida Dorothea Mylius, from Themar, Saxony, and they were married on June 22, 1849, at Kingston, Tennessee; they had five children. That same year he built a cottonseed oil mill, and, with his brother-in-law, Henry Mylius, devised and constructed a cottonseed huller, which improved oil yield from cottonseed pressing. A Knoxville lawyer, W. Gibbs McAdoo, who represented the owners of several copper mines in Polk County, Tennessee, engaged DeRyee to explore the extent of the copper deposits. This job allowed DeRyee to travel in southeastern Tennessee and neighboring regions. In 1856 DeRyee came to New Braunfels, Texas and boarded with Wilhelm Thielepape,qv an inventor. While there, DeRyee experimented with photographic systems that did not use silver or mercury and developed a photographic system called homeography in 1857. The process used photography to make multiple copies of drawings and was used to print Texas Cotton Bonds during the Civil War.qv By 1858 DeRyee had moved to San Antonio; beginning a partnership with Carl G. von Iwonskiqv in 1859. DeRyee earned a living by photography and lantern-slide exhibitions. He exhibited photographic transparencies, which he produced on glass, at St. Louis, Cincinnati, and other cities. He made an album of photographs of the Eighth Texas Legislature, and two famous photographs of Governor Sam Houstonqv in Austin in 1860. With Ben McCulloch,qv he accompanied the Texas troops that secured the capitulation of San Antonio and recorded the surrender. At the beginning of the Civil War DeRyee was appointed state chemist and put in charge of the Texas Percussion Cap Manufactory in Austin by the Texas Military Board on January 11, 1862. He was the only chemist west of the Mississippi who knew how to make fulminate of mercury, and he personally prepared all that was produced from the Texas Military Board. Toward the end of the Civil War he was with the Confederate Nitre and Mining Bureau, and he developed several important sources of nitrates from the bat caves of Central Texas. As a part of developmental research, he worked out a procedure for making guncotton and demonstrated its value as an explosive in marine torpedoes, in admixture with nitroglycerin in forming a smokeless explosive, and in tracer bullets. Lacking well-trained chemists to carry out further development, Texas was unable to use DeRyee's inventions in the Civil War. He also helped incorporate the Texas Copper Manufacturing Company and was a prospector for that company in Archer County.

In December 1865 DeRyee went to New York and purchased a stock of hardware, chemicals, and other things in short supply and supervised their shipment to Corpus Christi. He opened a drugstore in Corpus Christi in January 1866. To raise money to finance this venture, he prepared a prospectus for some copper deposits in Archer, Baylor, and Seymour counties. Governor Throckmorton was president of the company, which benefited from DeRyee's analysis of the ore samples. DeRyee returned to Corpus Christi in 1867, during a yellow fever epidemic, which he ascribed to an unsanitary slaughterhouse. His son, Emil, died on August 12, 1867. DeRyee was called upon to treat the sick because all the physicians had died in the epidemic. He introduced the use of chlorine water with an alkaline solution of creosote as an antiseptic with some success. DeRyee was the Nueces County representative at the World Cotton Exposition in New Orleans in 1885. He was one of the original incorporators of the Corpus Christi National Bank. In 1888 he published a paper, "Economic Geology of Webb County" in the *Geological and Scientific Bulletin*. He bought a summer home at Topo Chico, near Monterrey, and another residence at Laredo. He maintained a lifelong interest in chemistry and mineralogy and gave private lessons to young men of the community. The DeRyee drugstore always had natural curiosities on display, and Dr. DeRyee was widely regarded as the most learned person in the city. His son, Charles DeRyee,qv first documented the presence of the boll weevilqv in Texas. DeRyee died on May 23, 1903, in Corpus Christi.

BIBLIOGRAPHY: S. W. Geiser, "Men of Science in Texas, 1820–1880," *Field and Laboratory* 26–27 (July–October 1958–October 1959). David Haynes, *Catching Shadows: A Directory of 19th-Century Texas Photographers* (Austin: Texas State Historical Association, 1993). James Patrick McGuire, *Iwonski in Texas* (San Antonio Museum Association, 1976). *Memorial and Genealogical Record of Southwest Texas* (Chicago: Goodspeed, 1894; rpt., Easley, South Carolina: Southern Historical Press, 1978). *Southwestern Historical Quarterly*, Texas Collection, October 1941. Cecilia Steinfeldt, *Art for History's Sake: The Texas Collection of the Witte Museum* (Austin: Texas State Historical Association for the Witte Museum of the San Antonio Museum Association, 1993).

Frank Wagner

DESAUQUE, FRANCIS L. (?–1836). Francis L. DeSauque, Alamo defender and victim of the Goliad Massacre,qv traveled to Texas from Philadelphia, Pennsylvania, in 1835 and settled in Matagorda County, where he made his living as a store owner. He was a married man. He entered the service of Texas on October 10, 1835, and served in the Texas Revolutionqv as a captain. He traveled to San Antonio de Béxar sometime before the siege of the Alamo began, probably with Capt. Philip Dimmitt.qv While in Bexar, DeSauque lent William B. Travisqv $200 for the garrison, charged against the account of the Texas government. He then left Bexar shortly before the arrival of the Mexican army and brought word of the Alamo's need for supplies to the Texan garrison at Goliad. DeSauque was returning to Bexar with Capt. John Chenowethqv and the much-needed supplies when he received a letter from Col. James W. Fannin, Jr.,qv at Goliad, describing the colonel's failed attempt to reach the Alamo and advising DeSauque and Chenoweth to return to Goliad or reach Gonzales and confer with any officers there. DeSauque returned to Goliad and rejoined Fannin's command. He was taken prisoner with this group by the Mexican army on March 20, 1836, and was killed in the Goliad executions on March 27, 1836. One week before his death, DeSauque's name began to appear on lists of Alamo casualties. His family received 1,920 acres of land for his service and death with Fannin. They later received 640 acres for his death at the Alamo. In 1853 DeSauque's wife, Ann, was killed in a railroad accident in Norwalk, Connecticut, leaving their daughter, Mary, and son-in-law, Samuel R. Keemle, as his only heirs. *See also* GOLIAD CAMPAIGN OF 1836.

BIBLIOGRAPHY: William Fairfax Gray, *From Virginia to Texas, 1835* (Houston: Fletcher Young, 1909, 1965). Bill Groneman, *Alamo Defenders* (Austin: Eakin, 1990). John H. Jenkins, ed., *The Papers of the Texas Revolution, 1835–1836* (10 vols., Austin: Presidial Press, 1973).

Bill Groneman

DESDEMONA, TEXAS. Desdemona, on State Highway 16 in the southeastern corner of Eastland County, is one of the oldest extant Texas settlements west of the Brazos River. Sometime around 1857 a group of settlers built a family fort for protection from the Indians on land owned by C. C. Blair. In 1873 the oldest organization of any kind in Eastland County, the Rockdale Baptist Church, was built nearby. Two years later William and Ben Funderburg acquired the old Fort Blair land, and a town began to develop. By 1877 the town had a post office, and although it was officially named Desdemona for the daughter of the town justice of the peace, for many years it was known as Hogtown for its location on Hog Creek. Some early sources refer to it as Desdemonia or Desdimonia. The main sources of revenue in early Desdemona were trade and agriculture, primarily peanut farming. Economic discontent in the early twentieth century spurred the growth of socialism, but political competition never grew more violent than a yearly picnic and baseball game pitting Socialists against Democrats. By 1892 the town was reported to have a population of 100, and by 1904 it had grown to 340.

The economic climate of Desdemona changed drastically in September 1918, when Tom Dees, director of the recently formed Hog Creek Oil Company, struck oil on land owned by Joe Duke. The discovery put Desdemona among the growing number of oil boomtowns in Eastland County. With speculators and workers flooding in, tents and shacks sprang up throughout the town, and the population may have reached 16,000 at one time. By 1919 the Desdemona field was probably the second largest in the oil belt, and the Hog Creek Oil Company's stockholders were able to sell their $100 shares for $10,250 each. As torrential rains broke an earlier drought, cases of influenza and typhoid reached epidemic proportions. Oil often overflowed tanks and dirtied streams or floated in clouds, making Desdemona an unpleasant place to live. Growing proportionately to the number of new wells was the number of gambling houses and brothels and violent crimes, and in April 1920 the Texas Rangers[qv] had to be called in to keep order. The Ku Klux Klan[qv] seems never to have garnered as much support in Desdemona as it did in Ranger, a neighboring boomtown, in the 1920s, but a Klan newsletter's reference to "three Kluckers from Desdemona" suggests that an organization did exist there.

Disappointment was probably not universal when oil production fell from 7,375,825 barrels in 1919 to 2,488,755 barrels in 1921, and an insignificant rise in 1922 suggested that the boom was over. The bust occasioned a decline in Desdemona much sharper than that experienced by other Eastland County boomtowns. In 1936 the city government dissolved itself. The twelve-grade school was closed in 1969. In 1976 ninety wells were still producing oil or gas in the Desdemona field, and a Mobil Oil Company plant was distilling butane. By 1980 Desdemona had an estimated population of 180 and three businesses. The population was still reported as 180 in 1990. *See also* RANGER, DESDEMONA, *AND* BRECKENRIDGE OILFIELDS.

BIBLIOGRAPHY: Edwin T. Cox, *History of Eastland County, Texas* (San Antonio: Naylor, 1950). Dallas *Morning News,* May 23, 1976.

Noel Wiggins

DESERT, TEXAS. Desert is on State Highway 160 in far northeast Collin County, within two miles of the intersection of the Grayson and Fannin county lines. The town, settled about 1890, has the same name as the creek that runs just outside it. A post office was established in 1893 but was discontinued in 1904. For most of its history Desert has served area farmers as a retail point, providing a general store, a school, a church, and a gristmill. The population of the community, never more than 100, was twenty-five from 1933 through 1990.

BIBLIOGRAPHY: Roy Franklin Hall and Helen Gibbard Hall, *Collin County: Pioneering in North Texas* (Quanah, Texas: Nortex, 1975).

David Minor

DESERT CREEK. Desert Creek rises a mile northeast of Desert in southern Grayson County (at 33°27′ N, 96°23′ W) and runs south through Grayson and Collin counties for twelve miles, passing under State highways 121 and 78 and bending around Blue Ridge, to its mouth on Pilot Grove Creek (at 33°17′ N, 96°24′ W). Collin County historians attribute the name to a branch of the Caddo Indians who camped on the stream banks and named them Desert. The creek, intermittent in its upper reaches, runs through gently rolling terrain surfaced by clayey soils that support oak, juniper, grasses, and row or cover crops. Unlike other streams in southern Collin County, Desert Creek in the 1980s remained untouched by urban or industrial growth.

BIBLIOGRAPHY: Roy Franklin Hall and Helen Gibbard Hall, *Collin County: Pioneering in North Texas* (Quanah, Texas: Nortex, 1975).

DESHIELDS, JAMES THOMAS (1861–1948). James Thomas DeShields, Texas historian, son of James Calvin and Drucilla (Chandler) DeShields, was born in Louisiana on May 3, 1861. About the end of the Civil War[qv] his parents moved to Texas and settled on a farm in Bell County. Between crops, young DeShields attended public schools, read avidly, and absorbed tales of frontier adventure. He attended Salado College and Baylor University. While working as a house-to-house book agent, he began, as a hobby, to collect manuscripts, books, and pictures relating to Texas history. This interest led him to write articles on frontier history, which he contributed to the Fort Worth *Gazette* and other newspapers and magazines. A collection, *Frontier Sketches,* appeared in 1883, and *Cynthia Ann Parker* was published in 1886. In 1886 DeShields married Ennola Lee Huddleston in Bell County. They had three daughters.

Over a long period, DeShields set down the stories of frontiersmen he knew and dug historical material from newspaper files and other sources. His *Border Wars of Texas* (1912) recounted many Indian engagements. In 1914 he moved to Dallas, set up a dry-goods business, and continued to write in his spare time. He wrote many articles on such subjects as Stephen F. Austin, Sam Houston, John Coffee (Jack) Hays,[qv] the battle of the Alamo,[qv] the story of the Texas Revolution,[qv] Texas border tales, riding and fighting with the Texas Rangers,[qv] and the lure of the frontier. His longer works were *The Fergusons: "Jim and Ma"* (1932), *Tall Men with Long Rifles* (1935), and *They Sat in High Places* (1940). He retired from business in 1935 but continued to write. He died in Dallas on February 8, 1948.

BIBLIOGRAPHY: Dallas *Morning News,* February 9, 1948.

Wayne Gard

DESHLER, JAMES (1833–1863). James Deshler, Confederate general, was born on February 18, 1833, in Tuscumbia, Alabama, of Pennsylvania parents. He was appointed to the United States Military Academy at West Point from Alabama on July 1, 1850, and graduated seventh of forty-six cadets in the class of 1854. Among his classmates was the famed Confederate cavalry officer James Ewell Brown (Jeb) Stuart. Deshler was commissioned a second lieutenant in the Third Artillery on July 1, 1854, transferred to the Tenth Infantry on March 3, 1855, and promoted to first lieutenant on September 17, 1858. During this time he saw service in California; at Carlisle Barracks, Pennsylvania; against the Sioux; and in the Utah expedition. In 1861 he was stationed at Fort Wise, Colorado Territory. He appears not to have resigned from the United States Army but to have been dropped on July 15, 1861, after overstaying a leave.

After appointment as a captain of artillery in the Confederate Army, Deshler reported to Gen. Henry R. Jackson in what is now West Virginia and served as brigade adjutant during the Cheat Mountain campaign. He was shot through both thighs at the battle of Allegheny Summit on December 13, 1861, and upon his recovery was promoted to colonel and assigned to North Carolina to serve on the staff of Gen. Theophilus H. Holmes. Deshler was Holmes's chief of artillery during the Seven Days' battles around Richmond in 1862 and later accompanied Holmes to the Trans-Mississippi Department. In October 1862 he was given command of a brigade of Texas infantry in the division of Brig. Gen. Henry E. McCulloch,[qv] then being organized at Camp Nelson, near Austin, Arkansas. His regiments were Col. Allison Nelson's[qv] Tenth Texas Infantry and Col. George H. Sweet's[qv] Fifteenth, Col. George Fleming Moore's[qv] Seventeenth, and Col. Nicholas H. Darnell's[qv] Eighteenth Texas Cavalry regiments, dismounted. The first three brigades of this division were to become known as Walker's Texas Division,[qv] but Deshler's brigade was detached to Arkansas Post soon after its organization.

Deshler was captured at the surrender of Arkansas Post in January 1863, then exchanged and promoted to brigadier general on July 28 of that year. His new brigade included the Tenth Texas Infantry regiment, a consolidation of the Fifth, Sixth, and Tenth Texas Infantry regiments; and the Seventeenth Texas Cavalry regiment (dismounted), a consolidation of the Seventeenth, Eighteenth, Twenty-fourth, and Twenty-fifth Texas Cavalry regiments, all dismounted. In Gen. Patrick R. Cleburne's division of the Army of Tennessee, Deshler was killed instantly by a federal artillery shell while inspecting his brigade before an attack during the battle of Chickamauga, Georgia, on September 20, 1863. His command was assumed by Roger Q. Mills.[qv] Deshler is buried in Oakwood Cemetery, Tuscumbia, Alabama.

BIBLIOGRAPHY: Francis B. Heitman, *Historical Register and Dictionary of the United States Army* (2 vols., Washington: GPO, 1903; rpt., Urbana: University of Illinois Press, 1965). Ezra J. Warner, *Generals in Gray* (Baton Rouge: Louisiana State University Press, 1959). Marcus J. Wright, comp., and Harold B. Simpson, ed., *Texas in the War, 1861–1865* (Hillsboro, Texas: Hill Junior College Press, 1965).

Thomas W. Cutrer

D'ESMANVILLE, ABBÉ (?–?). The Abbé d'Esmanville was one of three Sulpician priests who accompanied the La Salle expedition[qv] to the Gulf of Mexico and landed at Matagorda Bay in Texas in February 1685. The others were René Robert Cavelier, Sieur de La Salle's[qv] elder brother, the Abbé Jean Cavelier,[qv] and the Abbé Chefdeville. D'Esmanville, like the engineer Minet[qv] and several others, returned to France with Capt. Taneguy le Gallois de Beaujeu[qv] on the ship *Joly*, out of disillusionment with the enterprise. The abbé, like La Salle and many of his company, is said to have been from Rouen. His name, although most often written d'Esmanville, says Villiers du Terrage, perhaps should be d'Amonville, as a family living in Rouen in the twentieth century is so called.

D'Esmanville's brief sojourn on the Texas coast lasted only until the *Joly* sailed on March 12, 1685. Yet his writings comprise a valuable source on the expedition as a whole, since they relate events of the *Joly*'s round-trip voyage. A copy of d'Esmanville's journal, says Jean Delanglez, was obtained by Claude Delisle for use in preparation of the 1703 Delisle map, *Carte du Mexique et de la Floride.*

D'Esmanville himself explains his reason for returning to France in terms quite different from those of the expedition historian, Henri Joutel.[qv] La Salle, he said, confided to him after arriving on the Texas shore that he planned to send troops to conquer the Spaniards of Nueva Vizcaya. Protesting that the superior of missions, the Abbé Tronson, had sent him to make war on demons rather than Christians, he decided to abandon the colony.

BIBLIOGRAPHY: Pierre Margry, ed., *Découvertes et établissements des Français dans l'ouest et dans le sud de l'Amerique septentrionale, 1614–1754* (6 vols., Paris: Jouast, 1876–86). Marc de Villiers, *L'expédition de Cavelier de La Salle dans le Golfe du Mexique* (Paris: Adrien-Maisonneuve, 1931).
Robert S. Weddle

DE SOTO, LUIS (?–1543). Fray Luis De Soto left Spain with his kinsman, Hernando De Soto, on April 6, 1538. He followed the De Soto expedition through its many hardships in America and continued with Luis de Moscoso[qv] after Hernando De Soto's death in 1542. He died before Moscoso reached Pánuco on September 10, 1543.

BIBLIOGRAPHY: Carlos E. Castañeda, *Our Catholic Heritage in Texas* (7 vols., Austin: Von Boeckmann–Jones, 1936–58; rpt., New York: Arno, 1976).
Frank Goodwyn

DESOTO, TEXAS. DeSoto (De Soto) is twelve miles south of Dallas on Interstate highways 35 and 20, U.S. Highway 67, and Ten Mile Creek in southern Dallas County. It is bordered by Lancaster to the east, Glenn Heights to the south, Cedar Hill to the west, and the junction of the city limits of Duncanville and Dallas to the north. The community is located on the original land grants of W. Caldwell, Z. Heath, T. Rhodes, and C. Parks. It was founded in the 1840s by the Parks, Cheshier, Ramsey, and Johnson families. Parks is thought to be the first, and his land grant is the location around which the community developed. The Ramseys' daughter Mary, who was born in 1846, was reportedly the first white child born west of the Trinity. She eventually married another settler named F. M. Hamilton and lived in the area until she was ninety-four years old. In 1848 T. J. Johnson built the first general store in DeSoto at the junction of what became Belt Line and Hampton roads, and the place became known as the Store. In 1850 Otway B. Nance built a farm in DeSoto that eventually became a Texas historic landmark.

By the 1870s a community developed around Johnson's store. S. E. Judah built a harness shop in the 1870s, and his son built a general store in 1898. In 1884 a post office was established and named DeSoto, either after Hernando De Soto (*see* MOSCOSO EXPEDITION) or a local resident, Dr. Thomas Hernando DeSoto Stewart. By 1885 the community had a population of 120, a general store, and a cotton gin. By 1890 only the general store remained, and the population had decreased to forty-one. The post office remained in service until 1906. DeSoto had seven businesses and a population of ninety-seven in 1930. The town was incorporated in 1949 and by 1950 had a population of 300 and eight businesses. In 1960 DeSoto had a population of 1,969 and twenty businesses. As Dallas expanded southward, DeSoto continued to grow and became a city of commuters. An estimated 90 percent of DeSoto's workforce commuted to jobs in Dallas or Grand Prairie. By 1970 DeSoto had 6,617 residents and seventy-one businesses. This growth brought about improvements to the municipal infrastructure, including road and park construction and a new water and sewerage system. Industrial, commercial, and residential construction increased also. A newspaper, the DeSoto *News Advertiser*, has been published since 1977. In 1980 DeSoto had 168 businesses and a population of 15,538. By 1984 the number of businesses had increased to 360, and in 1991 the population was 30,544. This growth is supported by civic facilities that include a police station, three fire stations, thirty-seven public parks, one public library, and ten public schools.

BIBLIOGRAPHY: Dallas *Morning News*, August 30, 1960. Daniel Hardy, *Dallas County Historic Resource Survey* (Dallas: Dallas County Historical Commission, 1982). Kathleen E. and Clifton R. St. Clair, eds., *Little Towns of Texas* (Jacksonville, Texas: Jayroe Graphic Arts, 1982). Vertical Files, Barker Texas History Center, University of Texas at Austin.
Matthew Hayes Nall

DESPALLIER, CHARLES (1812–1836). Charles Despallier, Alamo defender, son of Caudida Despallier, was born in Louisiana in 1812 and lived in Rapides Parish. His older brother, Blaz Philippe Despallier, traveled to Texas and took part in the siege of Bexar[qv] but became ill and returned to Louisiana; soon thereafter Charles moved to Texas. He reached San Antonio de Béxar by mid-February 1836 and distinguished himself during the siege of the Alamo by sallying from the fort under fire to burn huts that were affording the Mexican army cover. His actions were praised by William B. Travis.[qv] Despallier left the Alamo sometime after February 25, 1836, as a courier. He returned with the Gonzales Ranging Company of Mounted Volunteers on March 1, 1836, and died in the battle of the Alamo[qv] on March 6, 1836.

BIBLIOGRAPHY: Daughters of the American Revolution, *The Alamo Heroes and Their Revolutionary Ancestors* (San Antonio, 1976). Bill Groneman, *Alamo Defenders* (Austin: Eakin, 1990). John H. Jenkins, ed., *The Papers of the Texas Revolution, 1835–1836* (10 vols., Austin: Presidial Press, 1973). Amelia W. Williams, A Critical Study of the Siege of the Alamo and of the Personnel of Its Defenders (Ph.D. dissertation, University of Texas, 1931; rpt., *Southwestern Historical Quarterly* 36–37 [April 1933–April 1934]).
Bill Groneman

DESPREZ, FRANK (1853–1916). Frank Desprez, playwright, essayist, and poet, the eldest of the eleven children of Charles Desprez, jeweler and silversmith, was born in Bristol, England, on February 9, 1853. The family was of French descent. After concluding his education at Cosham School, Wiltshire, Desprez was apprenticed to a Bristol copper-engraving firm. Because of trouble with his right eye, he gave up engraving and moved to Texas while he was still in his teens with his cousin Willie Pinder. For about three years Desprez worked on a Texas ranch, though its location is unknown. Shortly after his return to England, he became involved with the theater, a connection that lasted the remainder of his life. He was consecutively or concurrently theatrical secretary, playwright, drama critic, and editor of a theatrical newspaper. He wrote more than twenty dramatic productions, sometimes using a pseudonym. Many of these were short pieces presented as curtain raisers or afterpieces for the Gilbert and Sullivan operas produced by Richard D'Oyly Carte. Two of Desprez's supporting pieces contain references to his life in Texas.

Desprez was also an essayist and poet. Dozens of his pieces on travel, art, music, and famous personalities were published in English periodicals, most of them between 1905 and 1914. His best-known work, however, is a poem, "Lasca," about a Mexican girl and her cowboy sweetheart caught in a cattle stampede "in Texas down by the Rio Grande." The ballad-like poem, first published in a London magazine in 1882, has often been reprinted, usually with deletions and changes, and recited in many parts of the English-speaking world. Between 1873 and 1882 at least four other of Desprez's poems were published, two of which are about Texas. In 1883 Desprez married Jessie McQueen, the daughter of an officer in Her Majesty's dragoons; they had a son and two daughters. Desprez died in London on November 25 (or 22), 1916.

BIBLIOGRAPHY: Mabel Major, "The Man Who Wrote 'Lasca'," *Southwest Review* 36 (1951).   *Mabel Major*

DESSAU, TEXAS. Dessau, named for a town in Germany, is eleven miles northeast of Austin and two miles southwest of Pflugerville in northeastern Travis County. A post office was in operation there from 1886 to 1890 and from 1897 to 1901, at which time service was discontinued and mail rerouted to Austin. Dessau had a one-teacher school with forty students in 1907; the school was consolidated with the Pflugerville district in 1920. The population of Dessau was estimated at thirty in the late 1890s. It fell to ten by the early 1930s but by the late 1940s had risen to fifty, where it remained through the mid-1960s, after which population estimates were not available. Dessau was still listed as a community in 1990.

BIBLIOGRAPHY: John J. Germann and Myron Janzen, *Texas Post Offices by County* (1986).   *Vivian Elizabeth Smyrl*

DETMOLD, TEXAS. Detmold is near Farm Road 486 four miles north of Thorndale in western Milam County. Early settlers in the area were of German descent. Detmold had a one-teacher school with thirty-eight students in 1903. A church, a school, several businesses, and scattered houses marked the community on county highway maps in 1941. The Detmold school was consolidated with the Thorndale Independent School District in 1946. Detmold, which was named on county highway maps in the 1980s, was still listed as a community in 1990.

BIBLIOGRAPHY: Lelia M. Batte, *History of Milam County, Texas* (San Antonio: Naylor, 1956). Milam County Heritage Preservation Society, *Matchless Milam: History of Milam County* (Dallas: Taylor, 1984).
Vivian Elizabeth Smyrl

DETOBITI INDIANS. In 1683–84 Juan Domínguez de Mendoza[qv] led an exploratory expedition from El Paso as far eastward as the junction of the Concho and Colorado rivers east of present San Angelo. In his itinerary he listed the names of thirty-seven Indian groups, including the Detobiti (Tobite), from which he expected to receive delegations. Nothing further is known about the Detobiti, who seem to have been one of many Indian groups of north central Texas that were swept away by the southward thrust of the Lipan Apache and Comanche Indians in the eighteenth century.

BIBLIOGRAPHY: Herbert Eugene Bolton, ed., *Spanish Exploration in the Southwest, 1542–1706* (New York: Scribner, 1908; rpt., New York: Barnes and Noble, 1959). Charles W. Hackett, ed., *Pichardo's Treatise on the Limits of Louisiana and Texas* (4 vols., Austin: University of Texas Press, 1931–46).   *Thomas N. Campbell*

DETROIT, TEXAS. Detroit is on the Missouri Pacific Railroad and U.S. Highway 82, two miles from the Lamar county line in western Red River County. It developed around the proposed route of the Texas and Pacific Railway in the early 1870s. When the railroad was completed in 1876 the post office at nearby Starkesville was moved to the new town, which was named Bennett. In 1887 J. M. Stephens, the local railway agent, renamed the town Detroit for his former home in Michigan. Because of its location on the railroad the town soon became an important trading center and shipping point for area farmers. By 1884 the population had reached 200, and local institutions included two steam mills, two cotton gins, a church, and a district school. By 1890 the population had reached 750, and the town had a weekly newspaper, the *New Era*, published by S. B. Norwood. Two years later two hotels and a bank were in operation, and the population of Detroit was estimated at 900. By 1910 it had reached 1,500. During the years following 1910 the population of Detroit declined steadily, reaching a low of 425 by 1960. Then the town began to grow again, with populations of 726 and 805 reported in 1970 and 1980, respectively. In 1990 Detroit had 706 residents.

BIBLIOGRAPHY: Fred I. Massengill, *Texas Towns: Origin of Name and Location of Each of the 2,148 Post Offices in Texas* (Terrell, Texas, 1936).
Cecil Harper, Jr.

DEUELL, HENRIETTA ELEANOR GOODNOUGH (1889–1967). Henrietta Deuell [pseud. Peggy Hull], the first accredited woman war correspondent and a founding member of the Overseas Press Club (1939), daughter of Edwy and Minnie Eliza (Finn) Goodnough, was born on a farm near Bennington, Kansas, on December 30, 1889. She left school at sixteen, got her first newspaper job on the Junction City, Kansas, *Sentinel*, and between 1909 and 1916 worked for newspapers in Colorado, California, Hawaii, Minnesota, and Ohio. After Francisco (Pancho) Villa's[qv] forces made their notorious raid on Columbus, New Mexico (March 9, 1916), Peggy went to El Paso to report on the activities of national guard units sent to patrol the Texas-Mexico border while Brig. Gen. John J. Pershing[qv] and his troops pursued Villa in Mexico. She took up residence in the Paso del Norte Hotel, a hub of social activity for military personnel. Starting on the El Paso *Herald* and then moving to the El Paso *Morning Times*, she wrote a regular advertising column and reported on activities at Fort Bliss and Camp Pershing. A ubiquitous presence, she became popular with both the officers and enlisted men, and her work brought her to Pershing's attention. Her account in the *Morning Times* of Pershing's return with his troops is thought to be one of the most descriptive and accurate of the newspaper reports of the event.

In June 1917 Peggy persuaded the editor of the *Morning Times* to send her to France to report on World War I.[qv] She sailed for England, survived the submarine-infested Atlantic Ocean, and made her way to Paris—not an easy feat, since she was without benefit of War Department accreditation, which conferred a certain governmental blessing on and aid to war reporters. But no woman had ever been accredited, and it was War Department policy that none ever would be.

However, her acquaintance with Pershing was useful to her; he made it possible for her to spend six weeks at an American artillery-training camp, from where she sent reports to the El Paso *Morning Times* and the army edition of the Chicago *Tribune*. Other newspapers began to publish her articles as her popularity grew. Eventually, jealous male correspondents succeeded in getting her recalled to Paris, and, temporarily embittered, she sailed back to the United States. After returning to El Paso to a hero's welcome, Peggy resumed her job at the *Morning Times*. In the summer of 1918 she went to Washington, D.C., where, with the help of Gen. Peyton C. March, chief of staff of the army, whom she knew from both her El Paso and artillery-camp days, she finally got accreditation. She was authorized to join the American expeditionary force sent to Russia during the Siberian Intervention and was sponsored by the Newspaper Enterprise Association and the Cleveland (Ohio) *Press*.

After leaving Siberia and being divorced by her first husband, reporter George Hull, whom she had married in 1910, she worked on newspapers in Shanghai and in 1922 married English ship captain John Kinley. As a result of this marriage, she lost her United States citizenship. Her struggle to regain it played a part in changing United States law regarding the citizenship of married women. She was in Shanghai in January 1932 in the process of divorcing Kinley, when the Japanese attacked the city; ignoring personal danger, she reported on the carnage for the New York *Daily News.* In 1933 she married *Daily News* editor Harvey Deuell. He died of a heart attack in, 1939. During World War II^{qv} Peggy was accreditated once more, this time to the Pacific Theater of Operations. She reported first from Hawaii, then from Guam, Tarawa, Saipan, and other "pacified" islands until August 1945 for the North American Newspaper Alliance and the Cleveland *Plain Dealer.* For her service she was awarded a Navy Commendation.

In 1953 she moved to California, where she spent the last twelve years of her life in Carmel Valley. She was a long-time believer in astrology as well as the granddaughter of an Episcopalian missionary. She became Catholic 2½ years before her death. Peggy Hull's special contribution as a war correspondent was in her "little stories of war," which dealt with the ordinary soldier's hopes, fears, and day-to-day life. A GI wrote her in 1944, "You will never realize what those yarns of yours . . . did to this gang. . . . You made them know they weren't forgotten." She died of breast cancer on June 19, 1967.

BIBLIOGRAPHY: Haldeen Braddy, *Pershing's Mission in Mexico* (El Paso: Texas Western Press, 1972). Emmet Crozier, *American Reporters on the Western Front, 1914–1918* (New York: Oxford University Press, 1959). David Len Jones, And Peggy Hull Was There (M.A. thesis, University of Texas at Austin, 1980). Wilda M. Smith and Eleanor A. Bogart, *The Wars of Peggy Hull: The Life and Times of a War Correspondent* (El Paso: Texas Western Press, 1991).

Wilda M. Smith and Eleanor A. Bogart

DEUSSEN, ALEXANDER (1882–1959). Alexander Deussen, petroleum geologist, was born on January 19, 1882, in San Antonio, the son of Charles and Clotilda (Nordhaus) Deussen. Though his parents were natives of San Antonio, where his father was vice president at the Groos National Bank, his grandparents were of German and English descent. In his youth Deussen attended the German-English Grammar School, which gave instruction in both English and German. He then attended San Antonio High School before going on to the University of Texas at Austin, where he received his bachelor's degree in 1903 and master's degree in 1904. After receiving his M.A., Deussen took a position teaching geology at the University of Texas; he stayed there ten years. On August 23, 1905, he married Sue Burnett Campbell. Deussen had met her as a student in one of his classes, and she affectionately referred to her husband as "the Professor." Later in life they divided their time between their Houston home and their ranch, Deussendale, located on Elm Creek in northeastern Texas. They had one daughter. While teaching at the University of Texas, Deussen also held the position of assistant geologist in the United States Geological Survey from 1907 to 1915. At the end of this appointment he began work for the Guffey Petroleum Company, which would later be renamed Gulf Oil Corporation. In 1916 Deussen resigned his position with Guffey to work as an independent consulting geologist. Except for a brief interlude between 1924 and 1930, when Deussen served as vice president in charge of operations for the Gulf Coast Region for Marland Oil Company, he remained devoted to his private consulting practice for most of his life.

Deussen's study of the Gulf Coastal Plain is perhaps his most noteworthy contribution to the field of geology. In 1924 he directed the first seismographic survey of the Gulf. That year he was also instrumental in establishing one of the earliest laboratories devoted to the research and study of Gulf Coast sediments. His study, "Geology of the Coastal Plain of Texas West of the Brazos River" (first published by the United States Geological Survey in 1924 and again in 1930 by the University of Texas), is one of his more ambitious scholarly investigations into this area. Previously, in 1921, Deussen had discovered an oil well in the Mexia district, which was the first of the fault–controlled fields in East Texas (*see* WOODBINE FAULT-LINE FIELDS). His vanguard work in this area was a great contribution to the oil industry in Texas. Deussen was an active member in the American Association of Petroleum Geologists, serving as its second president in 1918–19. In 1947 he was awarded the Sidney Powers Memorial Medal by the American Association of Petroleum Geologists for his contributions to the field of petroleum geology. He was also director of the American Petroleum Institute from 1923 to 1925 and a member of a number of societies, including Phi Beta Kappa and Sigma Xi. Deussen was a Democrat and a Presbyterian. In 1954 he donated a 200-acre site on Lake Houston to Harris County. The site was converted into a public park and named the Alexander Deussen Park. Alexander Deussen died on September 5, 1959, in Flow Hospital in Denton, near Ponder, Texas, the site of his ranch home.

BIBLIOGRAPHY: Emory A. Bailey, *Who's Who in Texas* (Dallas: John B. McCraw Press, 1931). Wallace E. Pratt, "Alexander Deussen (1882–1959)," *Bulletin of the American Association of Petroleum Geologists* 44 (March 1960). Vertical Files, Barker Texas History Center, University of Texas at Austin.

Kris Ercums

DEVALL, LYDE WILLIFORD (1909–1986). Lyde Williford Devall, publisher and University of Texas regent, was born on December 14, 1909, in Dallas, the daughter of Herbert L. and Lyde Williford. She attended Highland Park High School and Southern Methodist University, where she received a B.A. in 1931 and an M.A. in 1932. She also did graduate work at the University of Texas (1935), the University of Southern California, and Oxford University. From 1933 to 1939 she taught at Highland Park High School. She married Charles K. Devall on July 15, 1939.

The Devalls owned several Northeast Texas newspapers, including the Kilgore *News Herald,* which they published from 1940 to 1979. From 1942 to 1946, while Charles was serving in the navy, Lyde served as acting publisher of the Kilgore *News Herald,* Mount Vernon *Optic-Herald, Morris County News,* and Hughes Springs *New Era.* Her weekly column, "Kilgoround," which she was still writing in 1955, won awards from the Texas Daily Newspaper Association.

In the 1940s or early 1950s Mrs. Devall was a member of the state Democratic executive committee. Following the 1952 national Democratic convention, to which she was a delegate, she served on the executive board of Democrats for Eisenhower. Governor Allan Shivers^{qv} appointed her to the first Texas Commission on Higher Education, in which she served from 1953 to 1955, and to the University of Texas Board of Regents, where she served from 1955 to 1961. She was also a member of the University of Texas Development Board from 1962 to 1968 and the University of Texas Centennial Commission.

Before her appointment as UT regent, she served as president of the Kilgore Garden Club, Kilgore Women's Club, and United Church Women of Kilgore. In 1953 she was selected "First Lady of Kilgore." In 1986 the Devalls donated to UT seven pieces of nineteenth-century oriental furniture, which were placed on exhibit in the Hoblitzelle Room of the Flawn Academic Center. Lyde Devall also helped to raise funds for the University of Texas M. D. Anderson Cancer Center^{qv} in Houston. She died on April 17, 1986, in a Tyler hospital after suffering a stroke. Services were held at the First Presbyterian Church in Kilgore, and burial was in the Kilgore City Cemetery. She was survived by her husband and a sister.

BIBLIOGRAPHY: Austin *American-Statesman,* October 4, 1986. *Daily Texan,* October 7, 1986. Dallas *Morning News,* July 16, 1939. Vertical Files, Barker Texas History Center, University of Texas at Austin (Charles K. Devall).

Mary M. Standifer

DEVEREUX, JULIEN SIDNEY (1805–1856). Julien Sidney Devereux, legislator and planter, son of John William and Sally (Griggs) Devereux, was born on July 23, 1805, at Montpelier, Hancock County, Georgia. He was a justice of the peace in Macon County, Alabama, in 1835 and was in federal military service during 1836 and 1837. In 1838 at Houston, Devereux declared his intention of becoming a citizen of the Republic of Texas,^{qv} and in 1841 he took up residence in Montgomery County, where he established Terrebonne Plantation. Five years later he moved to Rusk County and established his plantation home, Monte Verdi. Devereux became a successful planter and at one time owned 10,000 acres and eighty slaves. From 1848 to 1851 he served as a justice of the peace in Rusk County. In 1854 he was elected county commissioner, and in 1855 he represented Rusk County in the Sixth Texas Legislature. He married Adaline Rebecca Bradley on December 28, 1826. The couple's only child died in infancy. After their divorce in March 1843, Devereux married Sarah Ann Landrum, on June 27, 1843; they had four sons. He died on May 1, 1856, and was buried near Monte Verdi.

BIBLIOGRAPHY: Randolph B. Campbell, *An Empire for Slavery: The Peculiar Institution in Texas, 1821–1865* (Baton Rouge: Louisiana State University Press, 1989). Abigail Curlee, A Study of Texas Slave Plantations, 1822–1865 (Ph.D. dissertation, University of Texas, 1932). Devereux Family Papers, Barker Texas History Center, University of Texas at Austin. Dorman Winfrey, *Julien Sidney Devereux and His Monte Verdi Plantation* (Waco: Texian Press, 1962).

Dorman H. Winfrey

DEVERS, TEXAS. Devers is at the junction of U.S. Highway 90 and State Highway 61, thirty-two miles west of Beaumont in southeastern Liberty County. The earliest settlement at the site was called Carter Station, after Allen Carter's family. However, the community, settled by 1832, soon became better known as Dever's Woods, after Thomas Philip and John Dever. By the 1870s the town had become a station on the Texas and New Orleans Railroad, and in 1880 it reported a population of 100. The name of the Dever's Woods post office, established in 1874, was changed to Devers in 1892. The community had a sawmill and cotton gin. Rice culture qv was made possible after the construction of a series of irrigation qv canals. In 1920 the Northern Canal Company became the Devers Canal Company, which was in turn acquired by the Trinity River Authority qv in 1969. In 1872 voters agreed 86 to 37 to incorporate Devers. The population, estimated at 210 as late as the mid-1970s, had grown to 507 by the mid-1980s. Considerable discoveries of oil and natural gas were made at the Devers field in 1984. The town supported twelve businesses, two rice dryers, and a Trinity River Authority office in 1985. In 1990 the population was 318.

BIBLIOGRAPHY: Miriam Partlow, *Liberty, Liberty County, and the Atascosito District* (Austin: Pemberton, 1974).

Robert Wooster

DEVILBISS, JOHN WESLEY (1818–1885). John Wesley DeVilbiss, Methodist minister in the Republic of Texas,qv son of Alexander and Priscilla Devilbiss, was born in Graceham, Maryland, on August 18, 1818, and moved with his family to Licking County, Ohio. In 1833, while learning the saddler's trade in Tiffin, Ohio, he went to a Methodist camp meeting and had a conversion experience that turned him toward the ministry. After attending Methodist College in Augusta, Kentucky, he joined the Ohio Conference of the Methodist Episcopal Church in 1840 and received his ministerial training by riding the circuits as an assistant to experienced preachers. DeVilbiss (as he now wrote his name) was admitted into full connection and ordained a deacon by Bishop Thomas A. Morris in 1842, then recruited with five colleagues by Littleton Fowler qv as a missionary for Texas. The party left Cincinnati in November 1842, traveled by steamer to Natchitoches, Louisiana, and reached Texas in December. On his second appointment to the Gonzales circuit he organized a congregation in Seguin and reportedly preached the first Protestant sermon in San Antonio in 1844. He was ordained an elder in 1845 by Bishop E. S. Janes. Despite unrest caused by hostile Indians, DeVilbiss's circuit grew so rapidly that it was divided and the northern area assigned to him. In 1846 he was assigned to San Antonio to develop the ministry further there. During the following two years he organized a congregation and purchased a lot and a bell for a church on Villita Street. Because of his efforts the city was made the center of a new Methodist district in 1848.

DeVilbiss served on the Caldwell Colored Mission (1852–53); in the German District (1855–58); as an agent of the American Bible Society (1866–69); as presiding elder of districts (Helena, 1859; San Antonio, 1860–61, 1865; Corpus Christi, 1870–72); twelve years on circuits and stations including Rutersville, Franklin, Nashville, Caldwell, San Antonio, Goliad, Cibolo, and Clinton; as professor of Aranama College (1863–64); and as agent of Southwestern University (1875–76). He represented the West Texas Conference on the Board of Curators of Southwestern University from 1872 until his death and was president of that board in 1883. He was three times president of the Rio Grande Conference and was a delegate to the General Conference in 1866.

DeVilbiss married Talitha Ann Menefee, daughter of William Menefee,qv on February 11, 1845. After her death on August 15, 1846, he married Martha Lucinda Kerr of San Antonio, on September 28, 1847. In October 1880 he retired to his Palo Blanco ranch home near the Medina River at Oak Island, where he died on January 31, 1885; he was buried in Oak Hill Cemetery.

BIBLIOGRAPHY: H. A. Graves, comp., *Reminiscences and Events in the Ministerial Life of Rev. John Wesley DeVilbiss* (Galveston: Shaw, 1886). *Texas Christian Advocate*, May 24, August 2, 16, October 11, November 8, 1884. Vertical Files, Barker Texas History Center, University of Texas at Austin.

Norman W. Spellmann

DEVIL HOLLOW. Devil Hollow rises five miles southeast of Elm Grove in eastern Caldwell County (at 29°53′ N, 97°26′ W) and runs southwest for three miles to its mouth on Sandy Fork, two miles northwest of Delhi (at 29°50′ N, 97°26′ W). It traverses flat to rolling prairie with local escarpments, surfaced by fine, sandy loams that support hardwood forests.

DEVIL RIDGE. Devil Ridge begins four miles south of the Sierra Blanca in south central Hudspeth County and runs ten miles southeast (its center is at 31°03′ N, 105°16′ W). Its highest elevation is 5,294 feet above sea level, on Yucca Mesa, the northwestern end of the ridge. The system parallels the Quitman Mountains to the southwest; together the two chains form Red Light Draw, which runs southeast to the Rio Grande. The surrounding rolling terrain with local escarpments is surfaced by deep, fine sandy loams that support hardwood forest, brush, and grasses.

DEVIL'S BACKBONE (Comal County). The Devil's Backbone, a ridge in northeastern Comal County, is on the Hays county line thirteen miles north of New Braunfels (at 29°56′ N, 98°10′ W). The ridge runs east to west, rising to an elevation of 1,274 feet at a roadside park on State Highway 32. It lies in an area of the Balcones Escarpment characterized by flat to rolling terrain with locally deep and dense dissection and generally shallow to deep loamy soil with rock outcrops. Local vegetation consists mainly of live oak and Ashe juniper woods.

—— (Montague County). The Devil's Backbone is a narrow ridge five miles northwest of St. Jo in east central Montague County (at 33°44′ N, 97°30′ W). The ridge, with an elevation of 1,225 feet, was used between the 1850s and the mid-1870s by Comanches and Kiowas as a military lookout to monitor the movements of the Anglo-Americans who moved into the county and established the nearby settlements of St. Jo, Bonita, and Capps Corner.

BIBLIOGRAPHY: Jeff S. Henderson, ed., *100 Years in Montague County, Texas* (St. Jo, Texas: Ipta Printer, 1958).

DEVILS BAYOU. Devils Bayou rises three miles west of Wells in southern Cherokee County (at 31°31′ N, 94°58′ W) and runs southwest for eight miles to its mouth on the Neches River, two miles west of Emmanuel in northeastern Angelina County (at 31°25′ N, 94°59′ W).

The stream is intermittent in its upper reaches. It runs through flat to gently rolling country surfaced by clay and sandy loam that supports grasses and forests of mixed hardwoods and pines.

DEVIL'S COURTHOUSE PEAK. Devil's Courthouse Peak, west of the Atchison, Topeka and Santa Fe Railway line and twelve miles north of San Angelo in north central Tom Green County (at 31°36′ N, 100°23′ W), has an elevation of 2,315 feet. The surrounding rolling terrain is marked with gentle to moderately steep slopes, surfaced by shallow stony soils that support scrub brush, sparse grasses, creosote bush, and cacti.

DEVIL'S CREEK. Devil's Creek begins within the town limits of Tell in southwestern Childress County (at 34°23′ N, 100°24′ W) and runs southeast for eight miles to its mouth on the North Pease River, eight miles northeast of Cee Vee in northwestern Cottle County (at 34°17′ N, 100°21′ W). It traverses flat to gently sloping farm and ranch lands surfaced by moderately deep to shallow silt loam that supports mesquite and grasses. Garrison Springs, located southeast of Tell, was an early Indian campsite on the stream. By the 1980s however, irrigation pumping had reduced the spring to a small seep.

BIBLIOGRAPHY: Gunnar Brune, *Springs of Texas,* Vol. 1 (Fort Worth: Branch-Smith, 1981).

DEVILS DRAW. Devils Draw (also known as Devils River Canyon), a valley with an intermittent stream, begins in northern Val Verde County (at 30°14′ N, 101°20′ W) and runs southwest for fifteen miles to a point on Howard Draw, four miles east of the Pecos River (at 30°12′ N, 101°33′ W). Devils Draw is met by seven small tributaries—Flat Rock Draw, Mills Draw, Live Oak Draw, Divide Well Draw, New Well Canyon, Will Davis Canyon, and John Davis Canyon. The path of Devils Draw sharply dissects massive limestone that underlies flat terrain, forming a rugged and winding valley. Wash deposits of sand, gravel, and mud cover its floor. Soils of the area are generally dark, calcareous stony clays and clay loams that support oaks, junipers, grasses, and mesquites. The name of the draw reflects the interest early settlers of the area had for devil folklore. Gaspar Castaño de Sosa[qv] may have traversed Devils Draw in August 1590.

BIBLIOGRAPHY: Elton Miles, *Tales of the Big Bend* (College Station: Texas A&M University Press, 1976). Roy L. Swift and Leavitt Corning, Jr., *Three Roads to Chihuahua* (Austin: Eakin Press, 1988).

DEVIL'S FORD CREEK. Devil's Ford Creek, sometimes called Devil's Fork Creek, rises six miles southeast of Pineland in southwestern Sabine County (at 31°11′ N, 93°53′ W) and runs west for six miles to its mouth on Sam Rayburn Reservoir, three miles south of Pineland (at 31°11′ N, 94°57′ W). The area through which the creek runs is nearly level to steeply sloping and lies wholly within the Sabine National Forest.

DEVIL'S HILL. The Devil's Hill is twenty-one miles northwest of New Braunfels in western Comal County (at 29°49′ N, 98°27′ W). The peak, with an elevation of 1,520 feet above sea level, rises 280 feet above the junction of Ranch Road 475 and Lewis Creek. It lies in an area of the Balcones Escarpment characterized by flat to rolling terrain with locally deep and dense dissection, surfaced by generally shallow to deep loams, with rock outcrops, that support live oak and Ashe juniper woods, as well as mesquite and grasses.

DEVILS LAKE. Devils Lake, also called Lake Hamilton, a commercial reservoir built for power generation, was four miles above the Lake Walk[qv] dam on the lower Devils River and sixteen miles northwest of Del Rio in southeastern Val Verde County (at 29°34′ N, 100°59′ W). Its dam, a limestone masonry structure, was in the main channel of the river, and Rough Canyon fed into the lake from the east. The massive limestone around the lake was sharply dissected. Soils of the area are dark, calcareous stony clays and clay loams that support oak, juniper, grasses, and some mesquite. The lake was completed in December 1928 by Central Power and Light Company and used to generate electricity, as well as for fishing, boating, and swimming. Its capacity was 9,200 acre-feet, and its surface area was 406 acres. After the summer of 1968 Devils Lake and its dam were inundated by Amistad Reservoir.

BIBLIOGRAPHY: C. L. Dowell, *Dams and Reservoirs in Texas: History and Descriptive Information* (Texas Water Commission Bulletin 6408 [Austin, 1964]). Del Weniger, *The Explorers' Texas* (Austin: Eakin Press, 1984).

DEVIL'S MOUTH SITE. The Devil's Mouth Site is the desert twelve miles northwest of Del Rio in southern Val Verde County. It is directly northwest of the spot where the Devils River flows into the Rio Grande; the site has been covered by the waters of Amistad Reservoir. The site is made up of many layers of prehistoric camping debris within an alluvial terrace of the Rio Grande that was fifty feet above water level before the river was impounded. The terrace extends 150 feet southward from a high limestone cliff toward the Rio Grande and runs 1,000 feet along the edge of the river.

Scientific investigations at the site were carried out by the Texas Archeological Salvage Project (now the Texas Archeological Survey) of the University of Texas in 1959, 1961–62, and 1967. Controlled excavations into the terrace surface were made to recover prehistoric stone artifacts and flint (chert) chipping debris, soil samples with fossil pollen grains, and bone fragments from animals killed for food. Large cuts were also made with earth-moving equipment to expose and correlate deeply buried zones. The ancient vegetation and climate of the area were reconstructed by studies of fossil pollen and by analyses of alluvial sediments and buried erosional surfaces. At the end of the last, or Wisconsin, Ice Age, around 10,000 years ago, the Devil's Mouth site was a gravel bar and bedrock exposure only a few feet above river level. Periodic flooding gradually deposited layers of silt and sand, slowly raising the site's surface. The climate during this epoch was cooler and wetter than today, and piñon and grasses were more common in the surrounding desert than later.

Around 7000 B.C. the first prehistoric Indians camped at the site, leaving chert knives, scrapers, and long spear points of a type called Golondrina. A few points with a basal tang for attachment to the spear shaft were also made during this period. Lightweight spears with such points were propelled by throwing sticks (atlatls) rather than by hand and struck with great force. Deer, smaller animals, and some wild plants were apparently the main food items.

From 7000 until around 2300 B.C. the terrace continued to build upwards, while the climate gradually became drier and warmer. Successive soil layers contained short, barbed spear points in the lower zones and points of the Pandale type in the higher strata. The latter style is twisted longitudinally like an airplane propeller. A few milling stones (manos and metates) from these zones indicate that desert seeds were now being collected and ground into flour. Around 2300 B.C. heavy floods washed away part of the terrace on the southeast, nearest the junction of the two rivers. An arid climatic period with severe but infrequent rains and devastating runoff is thought to be responsible.

From 2300 B.C. onward the terrace gradually increased in height, while the climate apparently became slightly less arid, although the local vegetation was still typical of a desert. A brief return to cooler and moister conditions around 500 B.C. was followed by a warming and drying trend that continues today. The people who camped at the site after 2300 B.C. left behind layers of fire-cracked limestone from hearths used to bake such desert plants as sotol and lechuguilla. They also left a succession of many dart-point styles, from barbed and tanged forms called Shumla and Langtry to such later styles as Montell, Ensor, and Frio. Seed-grinding stones, as well as chert knives and scrapers, continued in use. Small chert arrow points and rare fragments of earthenware pots, both from after the time of Christ, appear in the topmost strata of the terrace.

The local artifact assemblage, with the possible exception of the early Golondrina material, belongs to the prehistoric desert cultures that stretched across the American Southwest, western Texas, and northern Mexico after the Ice Age. The Devil's Mouth Indians adapted their economy to hunting small game and gathering wild plants in an increasingly arid environment and lacked permanent housing or agriculture.

The Devil's Mouth Site is one of the first deep-well-stratified archeological sites to be excavated and reported in western Texas, as well as the first to yield a long record of vegetational and climatic change from pollen studies. Golondrina and early tanged and barbed projectile points were first found in a good stratigraphic context at this site. The artifacts and site records are housed at the Texas Archeological Research Laboratory of the University of Texas at Austin.

BIBLIOGRAPHY: Vaughn M. Bryant, Jr., and David H. Riskind, "The Paleoenvironmental Record for Northeastern Mexico: A Review of the Pollen Record," in *Papers on the Prehistory of Northeastern Mexico and Adjacent Texas,* ed. Jeremiah F. Epstein, Thomas R. Hester, and Carol Grimes (Special Report No. 9, Center for Archaeological Research, University of Texas at San Antonio, 1980). LeRoy Johnson, Jr., *The Devil's Mouth Site* (University of Texas Department of Anthropology Archaeology Series 6, Austin, 1964). LeRoy Johnson, Jr., "The Devil's Mouth Site: A River Terrace Midden, Diablo Reservoir, Texas," *Bulletin of the Texas Archeological Society* 30 (1959). William M. Sorrow, *The Devil's Mouth Site: The Third Season—1967* (Papers of the Texas Archaeological Salvage Project 14, Austin, 1968). Dee Ann Suhm et al., "An Introductory Handbook of Texas Archeology," *Bulletin of the Texas Archeological Society* 25 (1954).   LeRoy Johnson, Jr.

DEVIL'S POCKET. Devil's Pocket is seven miles north of Deweyville in the southeast part of Newton County (at 30°27′ N, 93°44′ W). It is a flat, pie-shaped area bounded on the west by Nichols Creek, which runs southeast into the Sabine River, the eastern boundary of Devil's Pocket. The northern boundary is Slaydon's Creek, which also runs into the Sabine. Settlers of East Texas were late in coming into the area, and in the nineteenth century it was known primarily for being the home of brush-loving longhorn cattle.[qv] Later it became a noted hunting reserve. This land between the creeks was a maze of hummocks and swamps, and the cattle that lived there were wild and hard to gather. Local residents have at least three explanations for the area's ominous name. One holds that early settlers, already plagued by bad luck and poor weather, saw a meteor hit the earth in the dense basin forest. This meteor's impact is said to have formed a depression that became a small lake. A second version holds that outlaws and other unsavory characters used the area as a hideout. Still a third account argues that the Devil's Pocket derived its name from the large numbers of water moccasins that inhabited the stagnant pools left there by a change in the course of the Sabine River. Solomon Alexander Wright, recalling the area as it was in the 1880s, said that "it would be hard to find a country more desolate." He described it at the time he was working stock there around 1900 as "swampy, brush country, with some open pinewoods" where the cattle grazed and bedded down. He said that during the roundup the cowboys always worked the Devil's Pocket first because it was the hardest drive and "the very devil to work"—yet another possible source for its name. This part of Southeast Texas is still referred to as the Devil's Pocket, or the Pocket. Most of its inhabitants now live on a loop at the terminal east end of Farm Road 253, which circles an island of relatively high ground. The poorly drained bottomland is now dominated by eastern cottonwood and sweet gum trees, with understory vegetation that includes pine-hill bluestem, switch cane, and sedge.   *Francis E. Abernethy*

DEVILS RIVER. Devils River, an intermittent stream, rises in southwestern Sutton County at the gathering of six watercourses, Dry Devils River, Granger Draw, House Draw, Jackson Draw, Flat Rock Draw, and Rough Canyon (at 30°20′ N, 100°57′ W) and runs southwest for ninety-four miles to its mouth on the northeastern shore of Amistad Reservoir in southern Val Verde County (at 29°28′ N, 101°04′ W). On its long route thirty-two tributaries disembogue into it, including Dolan Creek, where Dolan Falls is formed, Dark Canyon, Dead Mans Creek, and Satan Canyon. The path of Devils River sharply dissects massive limestone and traverses wash deposits of sand, gravel, and mud on flat terrain. The area's generally dark, calcareous, stony clays and clay loams support oak, juniper, grasses, mesquite, and water-tolerant hardwoods and conifers. In 1590 Gaspar Castaño de Sosa,[qv] a Spanish explorer, traveled along the river and called it Laxas, meaning "slack" or "feeble." Later travelers and settlers called the river San Pedro. In the 1840s Texas Ranger captain John Coffee (Jack) Hays[qv] asked the name of the river as he stood before one of its deep canyons. Upon hearing its name, he reportedly replied that it looked more like the Devil's river than Saint Peter's. The stream was well known to early travelers because it allowed access from north to south through rugged canyonland, and it offered water. East-west expeditions followed its banks as far as possible before striking out into the desert.

BIBLIOGRAPHY: Del Weniger, *The Explorers' Texas* (Austin: Eakin Press, 1984).

DEVILS RIVER, TEXAS. The community of Devils River was on the Southern Pacific Railroad and the lower Devils River near Devils Lake and Lake Walk,[qqv] near the Mexican border 1½ miles below Castle Canyon in southeastern Val Verde County. It was founded in 1882 as a siding and nonagency station on the Galveston, Harrisburg and San Antonio Railway. Prehistoric people had lived around the Devils River for 6,000 years and left artifacts in caves and rockshelters. After the coming of the railroad the small community prospered. At one time it reportedly had fifteen buildings and a population of fifty to sixty. During the 1940s twenty families lived there; breadwinners worked for the railroad or for the power company that operated plants at Devils Lake and Lake Walk. When Amistad Dam and Reservoir[qv] was built, the railroad station, the power plants, and the prehistoric relics were inundated.

BIBLIOGRAPHY: James Wright Steely, comp., *A Catalog of Texas Properties in the National Register of Historic Places* (Austin: Texas Historical Commission, 1984).   *Julia Cauble Smith*

DEVILS RUN. Devils Run rises in Bee County (at 28°18′ N, 97°26′ W) and runs southeast 10½ miles to its mouth on Sous Creek in Refugio County (at 28°13′ N, 97°21′ W). The creek, intermittent in its upper reaches, traverses flat to rolling terrain with scarps, surfaced by alkaline loam that supports hardwoods, pines, mesquite, and numerous prairie grasses.

DEVIL'S SINKHOLE. The Devil's Sinkhole, southeast of Rocksprings in Edwards County, was named in 1876 by the wives of Ammon Billings and other men who had discovered the entrance after an encounter with Indians. The earliest known explorer of the cave was H. S. Barber, whose name is carved in the cave with the date October 19, 1889. The pit entrance is sixty feet in diameter and expands downward into an oval room, 240 by 360 feet, that is partly filled with fallen rock. The cave is 310 feet deep. Cave explorers from all over the United States have been drawn to it because of its impressive size and rumors of lost bat rooms. Guano has been removed sporadically from the cave for use as fertilizer. The cave was added to the National Registry of Natural Landmarks in the early 1970s. It and the surrounding land are owned by the state of Texas.

BIBLIOGRAPHY: *Devil's Sinkhole Area: Headwaters of the Nueces River* (Division of Natural Resources and Environment, University of Texas at Austin, 1975). Tom Meador, "A Brief History of the Devil's Sinkhole," *Texas Caver,* April 1965. James R. Reddell and A. R. Smith, "The Caves of Edwards County," *Texas Speleological Survey* 2 (1965).

A. Richard Smith

DEVIL'S TOENAIL. The Devil's Toenail, an elevation, stands a mile west of Click in southern Llano County (at 30°33′ N, 98°37′ W). Its summit, at an elevation of 1,490 feet above sea level, rises 350 feet above Sandy Creek. A dramatic, 200-foot sandstone escarpment on its west face above the creek is the "toenail." The local terrain is flat to rolling, locally dissected, and surfaced by sandy and clay loam soils that support open stands of live oak and mesquite.

DEVINE, THOMAS JEFFERSON (1820–1890). Thomas Jefferson Devine, eminent Texas jurist and Confederate diplomat, son of Irish emigrants William and Katherine (Maxwell) Devine, was born in Halifax, Nova Scotia, on February 28, 1820. He worked for several firms in New York City and at age fifteen clerked for a clothing merchant in Tallahassee, Florida. He read law in Woodville, Mississippi, in 1838, then spent three years studying law at Transylvania University in Kentucky. After receiving his degree and license to practice law, Devine went to La Grange, Texas. He married Helen Elder there on October 31, 1844, and they moved to San Antonio the same year. They were the parents of several children, five of whom, three sons and two daughters, survived Devine.

Devine was appointed San Antonio city attorney and served until 1851, when he was elected district judge, a post he held for ten years. He was a member of the Secession Convention[qv] in 1861 and was appointed a member of the Committee of Public Safety that supervised the surrender of federal troops, supplies, and property in Texas (*see* COMMITTEES OF PUBLIC SAFETY). He was appointed judge of the Confederate Western District of Texas. In 1864 Judge Devine was appointed by Gen. Edmund Kirby Smith[qv] to go to Mexico to settle a dispute involving shipment of cotton from the Confederacy, a mission he accomplished successfully, thereby gaining fame as a diplomat.

At the close of the Civil War[qv] Devine returned to Mexico in order to avoid taking the oath of allegiance to the federal government and spent several months there. Upon his return to San Antonio he was arrested by federal officers and imprisoned in Fort Jackson Barracks, New Orleans. He suffered from pneumonia and was released on parole in January 1866 upon his promise that he would not leave the United States.

He was twice indicted for high treason and, with Jefferson Davis[qv] and Clement Clay, was one of the only three persons charged with treason during the war. He was pardoned without a trial, however, and his citizenship was restored on June 17, 1867.

He was appointed associate justice of the Texas Supreme Court in 1874 but resigned, partly because his wife was seriously ill, before the end of his term. He returned to the private practice of law. In his legal career he achieved a high reputation for intelligence and honesty. At the Texas Democratic convention of 1878, Devine was urged to permit his name to be placed in nomination for governor but declined. In 1881–82 he was a member of the board of regents of the proposed University of Texas.

Judge Devine died at his home in San Antonio on March 16, 1890. Funeral services were held at Saint Mary's Catholic Church, with interment in San Fernando Cemetery Number 1. The town of Devine was named in his honor.

BIBLIOGRAPHY: Sidney S. Johnson, *Texans Who Wore the Gray* (Tyler, Texas, 1907). Mary Owen Meredith, The Life and Works of Thomas Jefferson Devine (M.A. thesis, University of Texas, 1930). Jon L. Wakelyn, *Biographical Dictionary of the Confederacy* (Westport, Connecticut: Greenwood, 1977). San Antonio *Semi-Weekly Express,* March 19, 1890.

Yancey L. Russell

Thomas Jefferson Devine, ca. 1867. Courtesy Lawrence T. Jones III Collection, Austin.

DEVINE, TEXAS. Devine, on old U.S. Highway 81, Interstate Highway 35, and State Highway 173, thirty miles southeast of San Antonio in southeast Medina County, was established in 1881 when the rails of the International-Great Northern Railroad were extended from San Antonio to Laredo. It was named for Judge Thomas Jefferson Devine[qv] of San Antonio, an eminent Texas jurist and attorney for the railroad. Devine had a population of 504 when it was incorporated in 1904. It operates under the aldermanic form of government. The surrounding area was placed under irrigation in 1915 by Medina Irrigation Company, which furnishes gravity-flow irrigation from the waters of Medina Lake. Vegetables, corn, and small grains replaced cotton, which had been the principal crop until the advent of irrigation. The area is still noted for its production of white corn, which is milled and used in making tortillas. The town's population doubled to 1,000 when irrigation became possible, and it held steady until the early 1940s. During the 1920s natural gas and oil were discovered in the Devine area. Since the 1940s the community's proximity to San Antonio and the military installations in that area made it an ideal semirural alternative to city living. The population increased from 1,400 in 1941 to 4,016 in 1988. Rated businesses numbered ninety from 1961 to the mid-1980s. Devine has a municipal airport, a public library, a golf course, a public swimming pool, and two nursing homes. It is the site of the largest Spanish peanut shipping center in South Texas. Among its other prominent businesses are Texas Tire Test Fleet, Levans Manufacturing Company that makes women's undergarments, a bank, a farmer's co-op, two weekly newspapers, and two feedlots. The Devine Independent School District had an enrollment of 1,400 students, and Devine had a population of 3,928 in 1990.

BIBLIOGRAPHY: Greater Devine Chamber of Commerce, *Welcome to Devine, Texas* (Devine, 1982-83). Cyril Matthew Kuehne, S.M., *Ripples from Medina Lake* (San Antonio: Naylor, 1966).

Yancey L. Russell

DEVORE, CORNELIUS E. (1820–1885). Cornelius E. Devore, soldier at the battle of San Jacinto,qv son of Polly (Black) and Jesse Devore,qv was born in Louisiana in 1820. The Devore family moved to the Atascosito District of Texas in 1828. In 1836 Cornelius Devore served in Capt. William M. Logan'sqv company of the Second Regiment of Texas Volunteers at the decisive battle of San Jacinto.qv He was subsequently awarded 320 acres of land for his service from March 6 to June 6, 1836, and 640 acres for participating at San Jacinto. After the Texas Revolutionqv he became a prominent farmer and rancher in Liberty County. By 1862 his total estate, valued at almost $11,000, included 615 acres, three Liberty town lots, seven slaves, fifteen horses, forty cattle, and sixty sheep. Although a slaveowner himself, Devore reportedly lent assistance to a group of runaway slaves who organized a Baptist church in 1864 and called him Neil Devore. He later gave two acres for a church and school near Liberty. He was a Mason, and he apparently never married. He died on July 29, 1885.

BIBLIOGRAPHY: Miriam Partlow, *Liberty, Liberty County, and the Atascosito District* (Austin: Pemberton, 1974).

Robert Wooster

DEVORE, JESSE (1789–1849). Jesse Devore, early Texas settler of French descent, was born in New Jersey on January 16, 1789. He lived in Catahoula Parish, Louisiana, in 1809 and married his first wife, Polly Black, about 1811. The couple had two children, Hannah and Cornelius E. Devore.qv The family lived in Mississippi from 1814 to 1826 and moved to the Atascosito District of Texas in 1828. Devore married Rachel (Bohannon) Faulk on October 9, 1833; they had four children. Devore was one of six members of the Liberty Committee of Public Safety in 1835, the year he received his patent for lands in what later became Liberty County. By 1840 he had acquired a number of Liberty town lots and owned three slaves. Seven years later his total estate, which included twenty horses and 100 cattle, was assessed at $3,100. He was a member of the Liberty Masonic Lodge No. 3. Devore died at Liberty on January 24, 1849. Seven years after his death Rachel applied for bounty land as the widow of a veteran of the War of 1812.

BIBLIOGRAPHY: Jesse Devore, Genealogical Collection, Sam Houston Regional Library and Research Center, Liberty, Texas. Miriam Partlow, *Liberty, Liberty County, and the Atascosito District* (Austin: Pemberton, 1974).

Robert Wooster

DEW, TEXAS. Dew is at the junction of State Highway 75 and Farm Road 489, nine miles south of Fairfield in southern Freestone County. The area, originally known as Avant or Avant Prairie, was first settled in the 1850s by pioneers from Alabama. In 1870 the settlement's name was changed to Sunshine after the Sunshine Methodist Church moved there from Harrison Chapel. The town was renamed Dew in 1885, when a post office was established there. Locals requested the name Drew to honor a resident, but postal authorities misread the application. By 1891 Dew had three cotton gins, three general stores, a blacksmith, several churches, and a population of 150. Its post office was replaced with rural delivery in 1909. In 1947 the community had five stores, a school, and 195 inhabitants. By 1992 Dew had a reported population of seventy-one. Around 1912 a cemetery association was organized, and descendants and area residents still gather annually at the Dew cemetery. A historical marker was placed at the graveyard in 1977.

BIBLIOGRAPHY: Marker Files, Texas Historical Commission, Austin.

Christopher Long

DEWALL, LEWIS (1812–1836). Lewis Dewall, Alamo defender, son of John Dewall, a New York City mason, was born in New York in 1812. By 1832 he lived at 51 Lewis Street in Manhattan, where he worked as an East River boatman. He left New York at a time when abolitionist riots and cholera epidemics were sweeping the city and immigrated to Texas. On October 26, 1835, he registered for a league of land on Harmon's Creek in Joseph Vehlein'sqv colony; his name began to be recorded as Duel. His occupation in Texas is variously listed as blacksmith, plasterer, or mason. Dewall took part in the siege of Bexarqv and later served in the Alamo garrison as a member of Capt. Robert White'sqv infantry company, the Bexar Guards. Dewall died in the battle of the Alamoqv on March 6, 1836.

BIBLIOGRAPHY: Daughters of the American Revolution, *The Alamo Heroes and Their Revolutionary Ancestors* (San Antonio, 1976). Daughters of the Republic of Texas, *Muster Rolls of the Texas Revolution* (Austin, 1986). Bill Groneman, *Alamo Defenders* (Austin: Eakin, 1990). John H. Jenkins, ed., *The Papers of the Texas Revolution, 1835–1836* (10 vols., Austin: Presidial Press, 1973).

Bill Groneman

DEWALT, O. P. (ca. 1890–1931). O. P. DeWalt, civil-rights leader, the son of John and Caroline DeWalt, was born near Livingston, Polk County, Texas, probably around 1890. He attended a rural school in the area and entered Prairie View College in 1907. He graduated with high honors in 1910. DeWalt moved to Houston, where he worked as a real estate agent with T. M. Fairchild. In 1913 he married Maud Pernetter; they had one son. For a brief period DeWalt worked as principal of Independent Heights School before opening the Lincoln Theater, the first exclusively black theater in Houston. During the 1920s he was president of the Houston branch of the National Association for the Advancement of Colored People.qv During the time when the Ku Klux Klanqv experienced a resurgence in activity, DeWalt was heralded as an influential civil-rights leader who stood up to the KKK. He was involved in the white primaryqv fight in which the Democratic partyqv excluded black participation, and he also pushed for the establishment of a branch of the National Urban League in Houston. DeWalt remained NAACP president until his death. He was assassinated on April 24, 1931. Funeral services were held first in Houston and then in Livingston, where he was buried.

BIBLIOGRAPHY: Michael L. Gillette, The NAACP in Texas, 1937–1957 (Ph.D. dissertation, University of Texas at Austin, 1984). Darlene Clark Hine, *Black Victory: The Rise and Fall of the White Primary in Texas* (Millwood, New York: KTO Press, 1979). Houston *Informer and Texas Freeman*, May 2, 1931.

Laurie E. Jasinski

DEWALT, TEXAS. Dewalt is at the intersection of State Highway 6 and Farm Road 1092, fourteen miles east of Richmond in eastern Fort Bend County. In the 1850s the site was the plantation headquarters of Thomas Waters Dewalt. After the Civil Warqv the sugar plantation was divided into small blocks, and a predominantly black community grew up there. The town was granted a post office in 1898. The Sugar Land Railroad was built through the community in 1912, and by 1914 Dewalt had a population of 100, two general stores, and a sugar mill. The railroad was abandoned in the 1950s. Dewalt's population was estimated at twenty from 1925 to 1969, forty from 1970 to 1987, and twenty-five from 1988 to 1990. In 1980 the community had a church and a number of dwellings, and by 1990 the city limits of Missouri City had encompassed it.

BIBLIOGRAPHY: S. A. McMillan, comp., *The Book of Fort Bend County* (Richmond, Texas, 1926).
Mark Odintz

DEWBERRY BRANCH. Dewberry Branch, also known as Berry Creek, rises a mile southeast of Eagle Lake in southeastern Colorado County (at 29°35′ N, 96°17′ W) and runs southeast for over eight miles to its mouth on West Bernard Creek, just southeast of Lissie and sixteen miles north of Wharton in northeastern Wharton County (at 29°32′ N, 96°11′ W). The creek, intermittent in its upper reaches, traverses flat to rolling terrain with local escarpments, surfaced by deep fine sandy loam that supports hardwood forest, brush, and grasses.

DEWEES, JOHN OATMAN (1828–1899). John Oatman Dewees, cattleman, son of Thomas and America (Oatman) Dewees, was born in Putnam County, Illinois, on December 30, 1828. In 1849 he moved to Hallettsville, Texas, with his family and, in partnership with his father and brother Thomas, operated a stock farm near Bastrop. In 1854 he moved to Seguin and in 1857 to Live Oak County; he raised livestock in both places on free range. By the time of the Civil War[qv] he owned 1,600 cattle. In 1862 he joined Company B of Col. Peter C. Woods's[qv] Thirty-second Texas Cavalry, with which he served throughout the conflict; he reportedly participated in more than thirty skirmishes, including Blair's Landing and the battle of Yellow Bayou.

After he was paroled in 1865 Dewees returned to Texas and with borrowed money bought pastureland in Wilson County, on which he raised cattle. In 1871, in association with James F. Ellison, he drove 2,000 cattle to Kansas and sold them profitably. The two men soon thereafter formed a partnership: Dewees bought Texas cattle, and Ellison oversaw their delivery and marketing at northern railheads, ranges, and Indian reservations. By 1882, when the partnership was dissolved because of Ellison's financial reverses, the two had delivered more than 400,000 cattle to the northern market and ranked among the state's leading drovers. Afterward Dewees ranched on 60,000 acres that he partly owned and partly leased in Wilson, Karnes, and Atascosa counties. From 1876 to 1899 he lived in San Antonio and traded livestock there. Dewees was a Mason. He married Anna Irvin of Guadalupe County in 1873, and they had one daughter. When Dewees died in San Antonio on June 10, 1899, his estate was valued in excess of $300,000.

BIBLIOGRAPHY: John Henry Brown, *Indian Wars and Pioneers of Texas* (Austin: Daniell, 1880; reprod., Easley, South Carolina: Southern Historical Press, 1978). J. Marvin Hunter, *Trail Drivers of Texas* (2 vols., San Antonio: Jackson Printing, 1920, 1923; 4th ed., Austin: University of Texas Press, 1985). San Antonio *Daily Express*, June 11, 1899. San Antonio *Light*, June 11, 1899. Jimmy M. Skaggs, *The Cattle-Trailing Industry: Between Supply and Demand, 1866–1890* (Lawrence: University Press of Kansas, 1973).
Jimmy M. Skaggs

DEWEES, WILLIAM BLUFORD (1799–1878). William Bluford DeWees, pioneer settler and public official, was born in Virginia on September 8, 1799. He first visited Texas on a keelboat excursion up the Red River in 1819. In late 1821 he accompanied a group of four families from Arkansas to the Austin colony; the party arrived on the lower Brazos River on January 1, 1822. On August 3, 1824, DeWees and his partner, James Cook,[qv] who constituted one of the Austin colony's Old Three Hundred[qv] households, received title to a league of land on the Colorado River in the southern part of what is now Colorado County, about ten miles below Columbus. DeWees then obtained title to a second half league on the west bank of the river at the site of the Columbus township, on April 28, 1831. As property owner, developer, and early settler of the site he became known as a founder of Columbus. The census of 1825 listed him as a gunsmith, and he appears as a blacksmith in the census of 1826. In 1840 he held title to 1,207 acres, claimed another 887 acres under survey, and possessed a personal estate that included eleven slaves, thirty cattle, nine horses, and a carriage.

DeWees traveled in Mexico in 1826 and 1827, then took up residence in San Antonio, where he lived for almost two years before returning to his home on the Colorado. Beginning in 1837 he held a series of public offices in Colorado County, including justice of the peace, associate land commissioner, and associate justice of the county court. In 1865 he was again elected justice of the peace for Precinct 1 of Colorado County. Later that year he was appointed to a term as county treasurer by provisional governor A. J. Hamilton.[qv] But DeWees's political career and reputation were ruined in 1866 when he was charged by his successor with misappropriating $1,200 in county funds and was successfully sued for that amount in district court. His appeal of the decision was denied in 1870.

DeWees married a daughter of Austin colonist Benjamin Beeson,[qv] probably named Lydia, in 1823 and eventually became the father of two children. His wife apparently died before 1850, and DeWees probably married a German immigrant named Angelica. In the early 1850s he covertly collaborated with writer Emmaretta Cara Kimball Crawford[qv] in producing a journal of his pioneering experiences that purported to be a compilation of his letters to a Kentucky resident named Cara Cardelle; this volume of dictated reminiscences, actually written by Emmaretta Kimball, was published in 1852 under the title *Letters from an Early Settler of Texas to a Friend*. DeWees died in Colorado County on April 14, 1878.

BIBLIOGRAPHY: Colorado County Historical Commission, *Colorado County Chronicles from the Beginning to 1923* (2 vols., Austin: Nortex, 1986).
Charles Christopher Jackson

DEWEES, TEXAS (Waller County). Dewees (Dewess, Dewesse, De Weese) was a mile west of State Highway 6, a mile east of the Texas and New Orleans Railroad (later part of the Southern Pacific), and four miles north of Hempstead in northern Waller County. It was possibly named for Alfred Garrell Dewess, who settled in Waller County around 1900. A cemetery, a church, and a few houses were in the area in 1941. In 1979 Dewees remained only as a triangulation station on the Southern Pacific.

BIBLIOGRAPHY: Waller County Historical Survey Committee, *A History of Waller County, Texas* (Waco: Texian, 1973).
Paul M. Lucko

DEWEES, TEXAS (Wilson County). Dewees, at the junction of Farm roads 541 and 1344, eight miles south of Floresville in southwestern Wilson County, was named for Thomas DeWees, who settled in the area about 1870. A post office operated there from 1906 to 1911. In the mid-1930s the community had a store, a mill, and a school. As late as the 1960s a store, a gin, and a cemetery still remained. Subsequently, the businesses all closed, and in the early 1990s only a few scattered houses remained.
Claudia Hazlewood

DEWEESVILLE, TEXAS. Deweesville, on Farm Road 1344 ten miles southwest of Falls City in Karnes County, was named after John O. Dewees,[qv] a prominent rancher in the vicinity during traildriving days. In 1936 Deweesville had a school, cotton gin, and store. By 1948 maps show only scattered residences and a business at the site. The population at that time was thirty-six. After the discovery of uranium in Karnes County in 1954, the first uranium ore processing mill in Texas was built by the Susquehanna-Western Corporation in Deweesville in 1961. By 1958–59 the community had three businesses and ninety residents. Uranium mining and milling operations in the area lasted only a few years, and eventually the mill was dismantled. In 1990 extensive reclamation work was being done in the Deweesville area by the United States Department of Energy.

BIBLIOGRAPHY: Robert H. Thonhoff, *History of Karnes County* (M.A. thesis, Southwest Texas State College, 1963).

Robert H. Thonhoff

DEWEY, TEXAS. Dewey, on Farm Road 1749 twelve miles southeast of Montague in southeastern Montague County, was established in 1898 and named for Spanish-American war hero Adm. George Dewey. During the 1930s and 1940s the community reported a population of twenty-five and one business. In the 1990s Dewey served as a community center for area farmers and ranchers.

BIBLIOGRAPHY: John Clements, *Flying the Colors: Texas, a Comprehensive Look at Texas Today, County by County* (Dallas: Clements Research, 1984).

Brian Hart

DEWEY LAKE. Dewey Lake is on Thirty-six Draw near the intersection of State Highway 158 and Farm Road 1800 twelve miles west of Garden City in west central Glasscock County (at 31°55′ N, 102°41′ W). The natural lake, which has an estimated 100 surface acres, is surrounded by quartz sand and silt substrate with loose sandy soil. Scrub brush and grasses are found nearby.

DEWEYVILLE, TEXAS. Deweyville is on State Highway 12 and the west bank of the Sabine River thirty-five miles northeast of Beaumont in southeastern Newton County. The Sabine Tram Company built a sawmill at a site near an old ferry crossing on the Sabine known as Princeton, or Possum Bluff, in 1898. The new settlement was named after Adm. George Dewey, victor of the battle of Manila Bay of the same year. A post office was established in 1900. The Brotherhood of Timber Workers led an unsuccessful two-month strike against the Sabine Tram Company at Deweyville in 1910. The Peavy-Moore Lumber Company purchased lumber operations there in 1919. Deweyville was a typical sawmill town, where the general store, hotel, community house, and employee housing were owned by the company. The community depended for its livelihood on good railroad connections. The Texarkana and Fort Smith Railway established a line from the Sabine River to Beaumont in 1898, thus providing an outlet for Deweyville lumber products. A. J. Peavy also built a fifteen-mile line from Deweyville to Gist. With its headquarters in Deweyville this line, the Sabine and Neches Valley, linked the town with the longer Orange and Northwestern Railway. For a time Deweyville was the largest town in Newton County. However, it underwent a series of setbacks during the 1940s. A fire destroyed the Deweyville sawmill in 1943. The abandonment of the Sabine and Neches Valley line shortly thereafter also hurt the community, where the number of residents fell from an estimated 1,500 in 1936 to 800 in 1949. The population estimate remained at 800 until 1974, when it increased to 850. It was 850 in the mid-1980s. At that time a few local businesses and the nearby Hartsburg oilfield offered limited employment, and other workers found jobs at the industrial complexes in Orange and Beaumont. In 1990 the population of Deweyville was 1,218.

BIBLIOGRAPHY: Ruth Alice Allen, *East Texas Lumber Workers: An Economic and Social Picture, 1870–1950* (Austin: University of Texas Press, 1961). Newton County Historical Commission, *Glimpses of Newton County History* (Burnet, Texas: Nortex, 1982). Josephine Cochrum Peavy, A History of Newton County (M.A. thesis, University of Texas, 1942).

Robert Wooster

DEWITT, GREEN (1787–1835). Green DeWitt, empresario[qv] of DeWitt's colony,[qv] was born on February 12, 1787, in Lincoln County, Kentucky. While he was still an infant, his father moved the family to the Spanish-held territory of Missouri. Although little is known of his father's activities there, the family was prominent enough to educate Green beyond the normal rudimentary level, and when the boy turned eighteen he returned to Kentucky for two years to complete his education. He then returned to Missouri, where he married Sarah Seely of St. Louis in 1808. DeWitt enlisted in the Missouri state militia in the War of 1812 and achieved the rank of captain by the war's end. He then served for a time as sheriff of Ralls County. In 1821 he was inspired by Moses Austin's[qv] widely circulated success in obtaining a grant from the Mexican government to establish a colony in Texas. As early as 1822 he petitioned the Mexican authorities for his own empresario contract, but was unsuccessful. Having seen Texas and visited Austin, DeWitt journeyed in March 1825 to Saltillo, the capital of the Mexican state of Coahuila and Texas,[qv] where he petitioned the state government for a land grant. Aided by Austin and the Baron de Bastrop,[qv] he was awarded an empresario grant on April 15, 1825, to settle 400 Anglo-Americans on the Guadalupe River and was authorized to establish a colony adjacent to Stephen F. Austin's,[qv] subject to the Colonization Law of 1824 (*see* MEXICAN COLONIZATION LAWS). He was accused of having misappropriated public funds in Missouri by Peter Ellis Bean[qv] before the jefe político at San Antonio shortly after he received his grant, but was exonerated on October 16, 1825, after Stephen F. Austin[qv] investigated the matter.

Sara Seely DeWitt contributed to her husband's venture with the profits from the sale of her property in Missouri. By October 1825 Green DeWitt was inspecting the work already done in his colony by his surveyor, James Kerr.[qv] After a few weeks he returned to Missouri to promote the colony. By April 1826 he was bringing to Texas his wife, two sons, three of four daughters, and three other families. The group joined those already in the colony, who eventually settled at Gonzales. For almost the next decade DeWitt worked with Byrd Lockhart, José Antonio Navarro,[qqv] Charles Lockhart, Kerr, and others to develop the colony. As his contemporary, Noah Smithwick,[qv] later said of the empresario, he "was as enthusiastic in praise of the country as the most energetic real estate dealer of boom towns nowadays." Because the Mexican government had inadvertently included the earlier colony of Martín De León[qv] within DeWitt's grant, the two empresarios had numerous disputes involving boundaries and contraband trade, resulting in irreparable damage to their relationship.

DeWitt apparently did not have the degree of personal influence over his settlement that Austin exercised at San Felipe. Although he represented the District of Gonzales in the Convention of 1833,[qv] he never held an elected office in the colony's government. Despite his apparent success in establishing the colony, he was unable to fulfill his contract by the time it expired on April 15, 1831, and he failed to get it renewed. He spent his last years engaging in some limited commercial investments and improving his own land on the right bank of the Guadalupe River across from the Gonzales townsite, premium land given him as empresario. For the most part, however, his colony proved neither materially nor financially rewarding for him. He had apparently invested all his family's resources in his struggling colony, and as early as 1828 its problems compelled one visitor, though impressed with the empresario, to note that "dissipation [and] neglectful indolence have destroyed his energies." Indeed, DeWitt endorsed his wife's petition in December 1830 to the ayuntamiento[qv] of San Felipe de Austin asking for a special grant of a league of land in her maiden name "to protect herself and family from poverty to which they are exposed by the misfortunes of her husband." The Mexican government complied in April 1831. DeWitt colonists in general suffered similarly. Smithwick related that "money was as scarce as bread," and pelts were used as barter. DeWitt did issue money, what was essentially land scrip in denominations of five, ten, and twenty dollars, for his colonists to buy their lands; the handwritten currency was transferable and generally passed as a medium of exchange. Green DeWitt money is one of the earliest examples of Texas paper currency.

In an attempt to improve his economic position and to secure premium land for settling eighty families, DeWitt journeyed in 1835 to Monclova, where he hoped to buy unlocated eleven-league grants from the governor, who was attempting to raise money for defense through land sales. But he failed to acquire any land. While in Monclova DeWitt contracted a fatal illness, probably cholera. He died on May 18, 1835, and was buried there in an unmarked grave. Though he did not live to see the battle of Gonzales,qv which traditionally is considered the first skirmish of the Texas Revolution,qv his wife and daughter, Naomi, cut up Naomi's wedding dress to make the "Come and Take It" banner that his fellow colonists adopted as their battle flag (*see* FLAGS OF THE TEXAS REVOLUTION *and* GONZALES "COME AND TAKE IT" CANNON). Sara DeWitt, who was born in Brooke County, Virginia, on June 29, 1787, died in Gonzales on November 28, 1854. The Sara Seely grant was one of the few DeWitt colony land grants issued by the Mexican government to a woman. *See also* ANGLO-AMERICAN COLONIZATION.

BIBLIOGRAPHY: John Henry Brown, *History of Texas from 1685 to 1892* (2 vols., St. Louis: Daniell, 1893). Edward Albert Lukes, *De Witt Colony of Texas* (Austin: Jenkins, 1976). Ethel Zivley Rather, "DeWitt's Colony," *Quarterly of the Texas State Historical Association* 8 (October 1904). Noah Smithwick, *The Evolution of a State, or Recollections of Old Texas Days* (Austin: Gammel, 1900; rpt., Austin: University of Texas Press, 1983). William S. Speer and John H. Brown, eds., *Encyclopedia of the New West* (Marshall, Texas: United States Biographical Publishing, 1881; rpt., Easley, South Carolina: Southern Historical Press, 1978). Texas House of Representatives, *Biographical Directory of the Texan Conventions and Congresses, 1832–1845* (Austin: Book Exchange, 1941). Vertical Files, Barker Texas History Center, University of Texas at Austin.
Edward A. Lukes

DEWITT COUNTY. DeWitt County (N-17) is on the Gulf Coast Plain in southeastern Texas about forty-five miles inland from Copano Bay. It is bounded by Victoria, Goliad, Karnes, Gonzales, and Lavaca counties. Cuero, the county's largest town, serves as the county seat. The center point is at 29°05′ north latitude and 97°23′ west longitude. Although the present county was part of DeWitt's colonyqv and settlement dates to colonization in 1825, the county officially has two dates of origin. The first, DeWitt County (Judicial),qv was formed on February 2, 1842, but was declared unconstitutional along with other judicial counties later that autumn. The present DeWitt County was formed from Goliad, Gonzales, and Victoria counties in 1846 and named for empresarioqv Green DeWitt.qv It comprises 910 square miles, most of which is nearly level to sloping; the areas of greatest elevation are mostly in the northwest. The elevation ranges from about 150 feet above sea level in the east corner to more than 540 feet above sea level in the southwest. The eastern corner and an area along the Gonzales county line falls in the Post Oak Savannah belt, characterized by tall grasses and, along streams, oak, elm, and pecan trees. Most of the county is part of the South Texas Plains, surfaced primarily by dark calcareous clays and sandy and clay loams that support tall grasses, small trees, shrubs, and crops. The climate is humid-subtropical. The temperature ranges from an average high of 96° F in July to an average low of 44° in January; records of 2° and 110° were recorded in 1949 and 1954 respectively. The average length of the frost-free season is 270 days, from early March to late November. The annual precipitation averages 33.37 inches, commonly in the form of thundershowers. Most of the county is drained by the Guadalupe River and its tributaries, which include the various branches of Coleto Creek, and also Sandies, Salt, Smith, McCoy, Irish, Cuero, and Clear creeks. Small areas in the northern part of the county are drained by the Lavaca River, and a small area in the southern part by the San Antonio River. Typical mammals in the county include white-tail deer, bobcats, coyotes, opossums, squirrels, foxes, armadillos, skunks, bats, cottontail rabbits, raccoons, badgers, and the Plains pocket gopher, as well as numerous reptile, fish, and bird species.

Archeological digs within the present boundaries of DeWitt County show that human habitation dates from the Paleo-Indian period. The Guadalupe River was being a focal point of life for thousands of years. Later, Coahuiltecan-speaking tribes, most likely Aranamas and Tamiques, settled in the area, which was also visited frequently by Karankawas and Tonkawas and later by Apaches and Comanches, whose equestrian skills made them formidable raiders. The first European visitors to the area were probably the survivors of the Narváez expeditionqv of 1528, most notably Cabeza de Vaca.qv Additional European visitation involved Spanish attempts to find the French explorer René Robert Cavelier, Sieur de La Salle.qv Spanish missionsqv were later established within thirty-five miles of the present county boundaries, and the area was traveled via the La Bahía Road,qv but there is no evidence of Spanish settlement. Indeed, the territory remained largely unexplored until the period of Anglo-American colonization.qv

The development of DeWitt's colony brought the first white settlement to the county. In April 1825 empresario Green DeWitt was authorized by the Mexican government to settle 400 families between the Guadalupe and Lavaca rivers. These pioneers began landing at the mouth of the Lavaca, which became the site of the Old Stationqv settlement. Of the 179 people who took up the 199 DeWitt colony grants, 39 were located in what is now DeWitt County, almost all on farms along the Guadalupe River. In 1826 the Arthur Burns family established the first home in the county on Irish Creek near present Cuero. Irish Creek Settlement (*see* VERHELLE, TEXAS) became one of the two principal areas of growth, the other being Upper Cuero Creek Settlement,qv which was founded in 1827. Colonists who held grants now in the county include Byrd Lockhart, José Antonio Valdez, George W. Davis, Valentine Bennet, Churchill Fulshear, Joseph D. Clements,qqv John James Tumlinson, and Green DeWitt. With Charles Lockhart, Clements also served in the government of the Mexican municipality that encompassed the area after 1832 (*see* MEXICAN GOVERNMENT OF TEXAS). These settlers enjoyed relative peace. A treaty with the Karankawas was negotiated in 1827, Tonkawa raids were only occasional, and boundary disputes with nearby De León's colonyqv to the south were settled without bloodshed. The only towns in the area were Gonzales to the north, Guadalupe Victoria to the south, and Bexar, the seat of government, to the northwest. Between 1826 and 1831 the area was settled by people primarily from Tennessee, Kentucky, Missouri, and other Southern states. At the onset of the Texas Revolution,qv these colonists pledged loyalty to Mexico until late 1835, and although no important battle occurred in the future county, many area colonists, most notably Daniel Boone Friar, Thomas R. Miller, David Murphree, John York,qqv Bennet, Clements, and Davis were involved in the battle of Gonzales, the siege of Bexar, the battle of the Alamo, the Goliad Massacre, and the battle of San Jacinto.qqv

The 1840s were a particularly eventful decade. In 1846 Judge James McCulloch Bakerqv was appointed by Governor James Pinckney Hendersonqv to establish the temporary county government. In 1846–47 the county seat was Daniel Boone Friar's store at the junction of the La Bahía Road and the Gonzales–Victoria road. A courthouse was constructed at Cameron, but in the next four years the county had four new seats of government, each change being the result of an election, a recount of votes, an appeal, or a Supreme Court decision. On November 28, 1850, the county court met at Clinton near Chisholm's Ferry, and Clinton remained the center of county government until Cuero became county seat in 1876. The first post office was established at Friar's store in 1846 and named Cuero; it was one of the earliest United States post offices in Texas. Concrete and Price's Creek were also principal areas of settlement. In 1850 residents of the county numbered 1,716, of which 1,148 were white and 568 were black slaves; there were no free blacks reported. The population was significantly increased with the German immigrations of the 1840s and 1850s. By 1857 nearly half of the county's population were Germans.qv The main areas of early German settlement were Meyersville, Yorktown, Arneckeville, and Lateiner (later Five Mile). The census of 1860 recorded 5,108 people living in DeWitt County, of which 3,465 were white and 1,643 were slaves; again, no free blacks were reported. The male-to-female ratio of the population was about even.

In the antebellum years, grazing stock was the primary business; agriculture and industry were postwar developments. Nevertheless, a significant corn, cotton, and tobacco economy developed, assisted with slave labor. The 5,493 acres of improved farmland recorded in the 1850 census, valued at $173,233, jumped to 34,134 acres valued at $1.5 million before the Civil War.qv These figures hint at the increasing prosperity underway in Southeast Texas in the decade preceding the war, and some idea of its details can be gleaned from the increased production of principal farm crops and stock raising. While only 66,545 bushels of Indian corn and 547 bales of cotton were recorded in 1850, production increased to 167,652 bushels and 5,280 bales in 1860. The sweet potato crop also showed great gain, from 1,050 bushels to 11,306 bushels, primarily because the new German farmers preferred the sweet potato to the Irish potato (which, by comparison, was too small a crop to record in 1850 and amounted to only 2,604 bushels harvested in 1860). Entrepreneurial activity in the decade preceding the war accounted for an astounding rise in the tobacco crop, which was too small to record in 1850, but ten years later amounted to 1,400 pounds, ranking DeWitt County as twelfth in the state. In livestock raising, however, which was and remains the county's primary industry, the increasing prosperity was most notable. The total value of all livestock in 1850 was $160,055. It included 4,836 milk cows, 12,246 beef cattle, 872 working oxen, 2,443 horses, 192 mules, and 391 sheep. By 1860 the total value had jumped to $721,826, a figure that shows the county's early prominence in the cattle industry. The number of milk cows increased to 10,567, again a reflection of the German immigrations, while the number of cattle leaped to 47,085, ranking the county as sixteenth in the state. Indeed, the Chisholm Trail,qv a major cattle trail, originated near the site of present Cuero at a place called Cardwell's Flat. The first drive to northern markets on the Chisholm Trail occurred on April 1, 1866, and by the year's end 260,000 cattle had been driven up this route. The dramatic rise in crop cultivation is echoed in the growing number of animals used for transportation, trucking, and plowing: working oxen increased to 2,447, and mules and horses to 956 and 5,702 respectively. Pioneers in the county's wool industry were pleased that the 10,847 sheep recorded in 1860 produced 22,936 pounds of wool.

In 1861, with the election of Abraham Lincoln and the outbreak of secessionqv among the Southern states, DeWitt County joined the majority of organized Texas counties in voting to leave the Union. Several military units were raised in the county: Josiah Taylor's DeWitt Guerella [sic] Company, H. G. Wood's Shilo Home Guards, A. J. Scarborough's Davis Guards,qv Robert Kleberg'sqv Coleto Guards, Charles Eckhardt's York Town Hulan Reserve Companie, William R. Friend'sqv DeWitt Rifles, and M. G. Jacobs's Concrete Home Guards. Although citizens of Clinton protested the use of the county courthouse for military and hospital purposes, DeWitt County was not a center of conflict. Nevertheless, the ferries and roads were much used for shipping commerce, clothes, and supplies to the Confederate forces, since DeWitt county lay on the important route from Indianola to San Antonio. During Reconstruction,qv the county was placed in the Fifth Military Districtqv and was occupied by the Fourth Corps, based at Victoria. From April 1866 until December 1868 a subassistant commissioner of the Freedmen's Bureauqv served at Clinton. The notorious Sutton-Taylor Feud,qv the most bloody and longest in Texas history, originated in Clinton in December 1868 and ended in December 1875, and is traditionally attributed to the bad feelings generated during this period.

War and Reconstruction altered the county's wealth and economic base. The 1870 census showed the population had increased to 6,443, of which 4,686 were white and 1,757 were black. Germans made up almost 86 percent of the total foreign nativity. But the amount of land under cultivation had dropped to 22,884 acres, total farm value had plummeted from $1.5 million to $478,823, and the value of all livestock had fallen to $369,621. This depression is most notable in the decrease in the cotton harvest, which amounted to only 541 bales, a figure lower than that of twenty years earlier, and tobacco, which was not recorded at all. The corn crop was reduced to 107,896 bushels, the number of milk cows was only 5,547, working oxen, 1,555, and mules, 761; the census failed to record the total number of cattle, which no doubt also fell substantially. Not all the news was bad, however, during Reconstruction. By 1870 stockmen managed to increase the number of sheep to 17,232, which contributed 21,275 pounds of wool, slightly less than reported in the prewar census. The sweet potato harvest increased to 13,583 bushels (Irish potatoes were up to 4,402), and the numbers of hogs, swine, and horses remained relatively constant. For the first time the census recorded manufacturing in the county: thirty-nine establishments employing sixty-eight people, paying $5,651 in wages, and producing $93,850 worth of products.

Reconstruction also contributed to important transportation improvements in the county. The railroad from Victoria to Indianola was destroyed in 1863, but was rebuilt by the federal government in 1866. This line, the Gulf, Western Texas and Pacific, the first railroad to enter DeWitt County, was extended to San Antonio. It was responsible for the establishment of three towns: Cuero, which became the county seat in 1876, Thomaston, and Burns Station (present Verhelle). A second line, the San Antonio and Aransas Pass Railway, was extended through Cuero, Yorktown, and Nordheim to San Antonio in 1887–88, and led to the development of Yoakum and Edgar. In 1907 the Galveston, Harrisburg and San Antonio Railway also built through the county and connected Cuero to Stockdale through Lindenau. These three lines operated separately until January 1925, when they came under the control of the Southern Pacific lines and operated as the Texas and New Orleans Railroad. Passenger service continued until November 1950.

The railroad, however, was only the most recent transportation development in the county. The La Bahía Road, which dates to Spanish Texas,qv crossed DeWitt County from the northeast to the southwest. Wagon roads, however, developed only with increased travel resulting from Anglo-American settlement. Until the railroad opened from the coast to Victoria in 1861, all commerce was carried overland; thus freighting was also a profitable enterprise in the county and accounts for some of the increase in numbers of horses, mules, and working oxen. The Victoria-to-Gonzales road through the Price's Creek and Irish Creek settlements was in existence by 1841, and another road connected Indianola to San Antonio through Yorktown. About this time the county had three Guadalupe River crossings: Heard Ford near Sandies Creek, Cottingham Ford at Irish Creek, and Murphree Ford at Price's Creek. Richard Chisholm operated the first ferry in the county in 1838. The first road authorized by the DeWitt County commissioners was built in 1846 and connected Chisholm's Ferry to the La Bahía Road; a second project connected Hochheim with the Victoria–Gonzales road. Although Lip's Ferry was established at Hochheim in 1862, and Heard's Ferry south of Cuero in 1880, the first bridge appeared only in 1873, a wooden truss near Cuero. But by 1889 four iron bridges had been built near that town and another at Hochheim; the Thomaston iron bridge was erected in 1893.

The return to prosperity that Reconstruction initiated in some areas, coupled with the increasing wealth characteristic of Southeast Texas beginning in the late nineteenth century, is shown in the censuses of 1880, 1890, and 1900. The population steadily increased to 10,082 in 1880, 14,307 in 1890, and 21,311 in 1900. African Americansqv made up about 29 percent of the population throughout these years, and though Germans continued to dominate records of foreign nativity, they decreased to 54 percent by 1900 as Irish, English, Austrians, Poles, and especially Mexican Americansqqv increasingly settled in the county. Much of this new settlement resulted from the efforts of the DeWitt County Real Estate Exchange, chartered in the spring of 1887 to encourage settlement and advertise lands for sale.

The number of farms also steadily increased during the last

decades of the nineteenth century, from 1,181 in 1880 to 2,137 by 1900. Substantial crop production and stock raising contributed to the dramatic increase in farm value from $1.4 million to $6.8 million over the same period. The Indian corn, cotton, and sweet potato harvest regained pre–Civil War production records only by the 1890 census, which noted 460,270 bushels of corn, 13,101 bales of cotton, and 25,044 bushels of potatoes—all record amounts. Tobacco culture[qv] continued to decline, however, with the last recorded figure being only 170 pounds in 1890 (*see also* CORN CULTURE, COTTON CULTURE). The most dramatic indication of DeWitt County's increasing wealth was in stock raising, in which the total livestock value rose from the post–Civil War depressed figure of $369,621 in 1870 to $1.6 million by 1900. Sheep raisers managed to produce 197,924 pounds of wool from 70,524 sheep in 1880, a reflection of a statewide trend to establish a sizable sheep-raising industry in Texas during these years. The national market, however, soon bottomed out. In 1900 only 18,210 pounds of wool was delivered, from 3,291 sheep. The cattle industry offers quite a different tale. The number of DeWitt County cattle increased to 49,678 in 1890 (ranking the county seventeenth in the state), and to 50,790 by 1900. The extension of the railroad into the county made the cattle drives up the Chisholm Trail unnecessary, as shipping points for northern markets grew up around Cuero, Thomaston, and Yorktown. Perhaps the best known was Julia Pens, near Thomaston at the Victoria county line, named for Julia Rose Anderson, daughter of the historian Victor Marion Rose,[qv] who once owned the land. By 1900 the number of milk cows rose to 9,808, as the county's newly developing dairy industry[qv] grew, hogs and swine rose to 17,483, and chickens and turkeys increased to 99,544 and 10,252 respectively, showing the first real growth in what would become the county's second most important livestock-raising enterprise (*see also* CATTLE INDUSTRY, DAIRY INDUSTRY, POULTRY PRODUCTION).

This trend intensified in the early twentieth century, as the population of the county rose from 23,501 in 1910 to 27,941 in 1920. The population decreased slightly to 27,441 ten years later; black residents, who declined from 20.2 percent of the total population in 1910 to 16 percent in 1930, account for the change. Germans continued to make up the greatest percentage of foreign-born residents, although substantial numbers of Mexicans, Czechs,[qv] Poles, Austrians, English, and Syrians (*see* LEBANESE-SYRIANS) moved to the county. Although more than 75 percent of the population was rural in 1930, manufacturing increasingly became important in the county's economy. The ninety-four establishments recorded in 1900 fell to twenty-six by 1930, but the number of employees rose over the same period from 391 to 433, and wages grew from $198,944 to $310,942, while the total value of manufactured products increased from $681,808 to $3.5 million. Businesses included cotton gins, cottonseed oil mills (including Cuero Cotton Oil Manufacturing Company, one of the county's oldest large industries), Guadalupe Valley Cotton Mills (a cotton textile factory), Cuero Cotton Compress, a hydroelectric plant, railroad maintenance shops, Crescent Valley Creamery, and Texas Tanning and Manufacturing (Tex-Tan) of Yoakum. Tex-Tan, the county's largest industry in 1944, employed 700 leather workers and sold products to forty-eight states.

Nevertheless, agribusiness remained the county's primary industry. The number of farms steadily grew from 1,181 in 1880 to 3,548 in 1930, the year the census recorded that 88 percent of the county land was in farms, with 200,432 acres devoted to crops. Farm value reached a peak of $27.6 million in 1920, but decreased slightly to $20.3 million ten years later. Cotton, corn, and sweet potatoes continued to be the most economically important crops, while cattle and poultry remained the crucial livestock. By 1930, when the total value of all county livestock was $4.7 million, the number of cattle of all ages reached 58,933, making DeWitt County the ninth largest cattle-raising county in the state. The Cuero Livestock Commission Company, sellers of livestock from all over the county, state, and other states, was organized in 1940 and within ten years set several national price records. By 1950 DeWitt County ranked fourth in the state when it recorded 75,132 cattle. The construction of good roads and highways and the rise of the trucking industry combined to make the shipping of these cattle to market via railroad unnecessary. Rail traffic declined rail traffic, and the various shipping pens that had been operating since the late nineteenth century closed.

Growth in the county's turkey industry was even more spectacular. Only Gonzales County recorded more turkeys in 1930, when DeWitt County counted 107,255 birds and the Turkey Trot,[qv] held in Cuero since 1912, enjoyed record attendance and unprecedented international fame. Indeed, an estimated 40,000 people saw Governor James Allred[qv] and other state and federal officials lead the parade and celebrations in Cuero, the "Turkey Capitol of the World." By 1940 DeWitt County surpassed Gonzales County and became first in the state in numbers of turkeys raised; the 167,824 birds were almost 5 percent of the total state figure. Though in earlier years turkey flocks roamed expansive ranges, the industry by this time used scientific feeding programs and enclosed rangeland. Bigger species of birds were raised, such as the Beltsville white, Thompson broad white, and baby beef bronze, which could grow to thirty-five pounds. Nevertheless, by 1949 the broiler industry and the accompanying chicken-feed industry surpassed turkeys as the second largest source of livestock income. DeWitt County showed more continuous growth in poultry production than any other Texas county from 1945 to 1950. One of the leading new firms was Cudahy Packing Company, which distributed poultry, eggs, milk, and cream worldwide.

This increasing prosperity notwithstanding, DeWitt County also suffered during the Great Depression.[qv] In the decade from 1930 to 1940 the total farm value plummeted by almost half, from $20.3 million to $10.5 million, and although the numbers of cattle, chickens, turkeys, and other livestock increased, the total value of livestock decreased from $3.5 million to $2.5 million. This problem was echoed in manufacturing as well. The number of establishments increased from twenty-six to thirty, the number of employees from 433 to 636, the wages from $310,942 to $395,632 (representing an actual decrease of $96 per person in individual income), but the value of products manufactured decreased from $3.5 million to $2.9 million. Furthermore, retail sales, which rose phenomenally from $2.95 million to $9.1 million between 1920 and 1930, fell to $3.9 million in 1933. A trend to recovery was evident by 1940, when $6.4 million in retail sales was recorded.

World War II[qv] ended the doldrums. A fighter pilot flight school was established at Cuero Municipal Airport in 1941 and designated Cuero Field.[qv] Some idea of the postwar prosperity characterizing the county's economy is shown in crop and retail sales statistics for 1946. In that first postwar year the county was one of the state's largest tomato producers, shipped one-fifth of the state's total turkey crop, reaped great profits from egg sales and dairying, and saw an increase in retail sales to $9.1 million. By 1948 DeWitt County was third among Texas counties in horse raising. Retail sales reached $11.3 million that year and $20.8 million in 1953. The postwar era also brought significant changes in education. Education was not a priority in the county during the period of Anglo-American settlement; until 1840 the nearest school was located at Gonzales or Victoria. James Norman Smith[qv] established the first school in the county in 1840 at Upper Cuero Creek Settlement. Other tuition schools followed at Deer Creek, Meyersville, Irish Creek, and Price's Creek. A common-school system was organized in 1854 comprising thirteen districts; there were fifteen schools by 1862. During the Civil War years Viola Case's school was moved from Victoria to Clinton (*see* VICTORIA FEMALE ACADEMY), and Concrete College had a good reputation during its existence from 1856 to 1881. The county public school system, however, emerged only in the post–Civil War period, concurrent with the increasing population. Many new residents were the result of flight from Indianola after the hurricanes[qv] of 1875 and 1886. The rural school system was fully operating by the 1880s, and fourteen common districts were organized by 1884. Fifty-five public schools were noted in 1887, though by 1906 the figure was forty-five. At that time Yoakum had the only independent school district in the county. Cuero Independent School District was established in August 1911, Yorktown ISD in February 1921, and Nordheim ISD in October 1926. Most rural schools were closed in the 1940s and 1950s, when transportation improvements, requirements for specialized curriculum, and decreasing rural population brought consolidation and decline.

Horse racing, music, and dancing have long been common entertainments in the county, the brass bands and singing organizations of the German communities being particularly prominent (*see* GERMAN MUSIC). The Masonic Lodge was established in the county at Cameron in 1850, and Yorktown and Concrete organized charters in 1853 and 1855. The first Protestant ministers to enter the county were Cumberland Presbyterians, who came in 1839 and established the county's first church at Upper Cuero Creek Settlement in 1841. Methodist circuit riders appeared after 1841 at Upper Cuero Creek, and German Methodists organized at Hochheim in 1864. Although during the colonial period settlers were required by the Mexican government to profess the Catholic faith, Catholicism was not much practiced until the rise of the German and Polish settlements in Yorktown and the Meyersville area in the 1840s and 1850s. Baptists first organized at Hebron in 1855 and at Concrete in 1865. Lutheranism was particularly strong in the county both before and after the Civil War because of the large number of German Lutherans who settled at Meyersville, Yorktown, Arneckeville, Sasseville (Nopal), Cuero, and later Nordheim and Westhoff. The first Episcopal service was held in Cuero in 1873. Thus, the German influence was a crucial factor in the religious, social, and cultural development of DeWitt County. Indeed, Rudolph Kleberg's[qv] *Description of the Resources of DeWitt County, Texas,* a popular booster guidebook to the county published in 1887, was directed specifically at Germans. Even as late as 1972, 52 percent of the county's population was of German heritage; Hispanics numbered 22 percent. The total population of the county, however, declined after 1920, reaching 22,973 in 1950 and 18,660 in 1970. The black population fell from almost 19 percent to almost 14 percent between 1920 and 1960. Throughout most of the its history, however, the county has ranked as one of the highest in the state in percent of residents who are native Texans.

Despite the growth of its major towns and increasing industry, DeWitt County's economy remained agribusiness focused until after World War II. In 1930 more than 75 percent of the county's population was rural, and though this figure decreased to slightly over 55 percent by 1940, it was not until the 1950 census showed 34 percent of the population as rural that the county became predominantly urban. This rural-to-urban transition carried with it a number of changes. In 1930 more than 61 percent of the farms were operated by tenants; by 1950 only 32 percent were. Almost 22 percent of all farmers in 1940 reported income coming from off the farm, a presage of urbanization. In 1940 only 25 percent of the farms reported having a telephone and only 23 percent were lighted by electricity. By 1950, 43 percent had phones and 66 percent had electric lighting. County roads increasingly were hard-surfaced and graveled, so that rural areas became better connected with growing urban areas and markets. The decline of the rural school system and the concurrent rise of independent school districts and bussing were only a part of this change.

In the mid-1980s DeWitt County's economy was still primarily based on agribusiness, though there was a variety of other industry, such as wood, furniture, and leather-goods production, cotton weaving, and oil and gas production. About $43 million was generated in annual farm income, primarily from the county's traditional sources—beef cattle, dairy products, hogs, poultry, and such crops as sorghums, corn, oats, wheat, and pecans. Cotton was no longer planted. The county has retained its importance in the cattle industry. Though its tally of 110,000 cattle in 1982 was dwarfed by figures coming from those counties specializing in cattle feeding,[qv] DeWitt County ranked first among the neighboring Upper Coastal and Coastal Bend counties specializing in stock raising, a much more accurate measure of its significance in the regional industry. Many residents recognize at least the family names of the county's major pioneer ranchers, Jim Bell, Miles Bennet, William A. Blackwell, Robert E. Eckhardt, Caesar Eckhardt, Daniel Boone Friar, Alex Hamilton, Buck McCrabb, Henry Runge,[qv] John Milam Taylor, Joachim von Roeder, Vachel Weldon, John T. Wofford, and David Murphree.

Throughout most of its history DeWitt County has been a stronghold of the Democratic party,[qv] though significant Republican support grew during the 1872 presidential election, throughout the 1880s and until 1916, reflecting the national trend in politics. There was major support for the People's (Populist) party[qv] in 1892, but by 1896 county voters were about evenly divided between the Republican and Democratic loyalties. The first Republican majority occurred in the 1920 presidential election, a phenomenon almost repeated in 1928; but the Democrats regained the majority from 1932 to 1936, and overwhelmingly so in 1944. The Republican party[qv] gained support during the 1950s and reached a majority again in the 1960 election; this trend toward Republican loyalty for national candidates reemerged in 1968 and held through 1992. In elections for state office, however, the county has almost continuously supported Democratic candidates, though the Populists attracted considerable support from 1892 to 1900. The 1990 population of the county, 18,840, reflected a slight growth that perhaps halted the steady decrease between 1930 and 1970. Among the county's incorporated communities, Cuero remains the county seat and largest city; Yoakum, Yorktown, and Nordheim continue to be the principal towns. Except for the last, each publishes a weekly newspaper: the Cuero *Record,* the Yoakum *Herald Times,* the Yorktown *News,* and the Yorktown *DeWitt County View.* The unincorporated communities are Arneckeville, Clinton, Concrete, Edgar, Garfield, Gruenau, Hochheim, Lindenau, Meyersville, Nopal, Pearl City, Petersville, Stratton, Terryville, Thomaston, Upper Meyersville, Valley View, Verhelle, and Westhoff.

BIBLIOGRAPHY: Rudolph L. Biesele, *The History of the German Settlements in Texas, 1831–1861* (Austin: Von Boeckmann–Jones, 1930; rpt. 1964). Joseph L. Clark, *Texas Gulf Coast: Its History and Development* (4 vols., New York: Lewis Historical Publishing, 1955). Cuero *Record,* December 31, 1935, November 15, 1944, November 29, 1950, November 4, 1956. Cuero *Star,* October 1895, March 1906. DeWitt County Historical Commission, *History of DeWitt County, Texas* (Dallas: Curtis, 1991). Edward Albert Lukes, *De Witt Colony of Texas* (Austin: Jenkins, 1976). Nellie Murphree, *A History of DeWitt County* (Victoria, Texas, 1962). Ethel Zivley Rather, "DeWitt's Colony," *Quarterly of the Texas State Historical Association* 8 (October 1904). Dorothy House Young, The History of Education in DeWitt County (M.A. thesis, University of Texas, 1943). *Craig H. Roell*

DEWITT COUNTY (Judicial). DeWitt County was established for judicial and other purposes on February 2, 1842. It included the western half of what is now DeWitt County. The east boundary ran north and south through the site of present Cuero, and the southern boundary was Coleto Creek; Cuero was the county seat. The county was abolished by a Texas Supreme Court decision, *Stockton v. Montgomery* (1842), which declared judicial counties unconstitutional. Present DeWitt County was established in 1846.

BIBLIOGRAPHY: James Wilmer Dallam, *A Digest of the Laws of Texas* (Baltimore: Toy, 1845). Hans Peter Nielsen Gammel, comp., *Laws of Texas, 1822–1897* (10 vols., Austin: Gammel, 1898).

Seymour V. Connor

DEWITT'S COLONY. DeWitt's colony, one of the major colonies in the settlement of Texas, was established by Green DeWitt and

James Kerr[qqv] in 1825. Stirred by Stephen F. Austin's[qv] success, DeWitt petitioned the Mexican government to become an empresario[qv] as early as 1822, but was frustrated in his attempt. He was inspired to try again after the passage of the new federal colonization law of 1824 (*see* MEXICAN COLONIZATION LAWS) and after having met Austin, with whom he continued to have a close relationship. Austin's influence, together with Baron de Bastrop's,[qv] helped DeWitt to petition the Mexican government successfully on April 7, 1825, for an empresario contract to settle "four hundred industrious Catholic families . . . known to be respectable and industrious," and also any equally respectable families of Mexican nationals who "shall come to settle with us." The government approved the grant on April 15 in Saltillo, Coahuila. DeWitt's colony was to be adjacent to and southwest of Austin's grant. Its boundaries were vaguely defined on the basis of inaccurate maps as the right bank of the Arroyo de la Vaca (Lavaca River) beginning at a point ten leagues from the coast (the government forbade all colonization within ten leagues of the Gulf Coast), running up the river to the Bexar–Nacogdoches road (*see* OLD SAN ANTONIO ROAD) and then up the road to a point two leagues west of the Guadalupe River (approximately the divide between the Guadalupe and San Antonio rivers), then extending parallel to the Guadalupe River to the Paraje de las Mosquitos (a point again ten leagues from the coast), thence returning to the Lavaca River. DeWitt's six-year contract required him to respect the rights of ownership of those already settled in the area. He later found that these included all of De León's colony,[qv] which had been approved by the Mexican government more than a year earlier and settled successfully by October 1824 around the town of Guadalupe Victoria by the Mexican empresario Martín De León.[qv] Not surprisingly, DeWitt and De León had numerous disputes. The contract also required that all official correspondence be in Spanish and that the empresario establish schools with instruction in Spanish, organize and command a militia, and establish a Catholic church with a resident priest.

Even before his contract was approved, DeWitt had appointed James Kerr as surveyor general. Kerr's role was crucial to the success of the colony. In the summer of 1825 Kerr, along with Erastus (Deaf) Smith,[qv] Brazil Durbin, Geron Hinds, John Wightman, James Musick, and a Mr. Strickland, set out to select a site for the colony's capital. In August they chose the junction of the Guadalupe and San Marcos rivers and built crude cabins on what later became Kerr Creek. Despite being hampered by Indians, Kerr drew plans for the new town and named it Gonzales in honor of the provisional governor of Coahuila and Texas,[qv] Don Rafael Gonzales[qv] (this site was about a mile east of the present city). Some weeks after the party finished surveying and erecting cabins the Francis Berry family arrived, raising the population of Gonzales from August 1825 to July 1826 to fifteen; they were also visited by Henry S. Brown, Edwin Morehouse, Elijah Stapp, and Frost Thorn.[qqv] DeWitt arrived in October 1825 to inspect the site, then returned to Missouri, his home state, by year's end or by early 1826 to promote his colony. In July 1826 Indians attacked the budding settlement on a horse-stealing raid. Whiteman was killed and others fled to Austin's colony on the Colorado River. The vulnerability of Gonzales to Indian attack induced Kerr to find another site nearer the coast. He established "Old Station"[qv] near the mouth of the Lavaca River, about six miles inland on the river's west bank, as a landing point for the colonists. Although the *jefe político* in San Antonio, José Antonio Saucedo,[qv] granted permission to establish a port to receive colonists, he also stressed that Old Station could not become a permanent settlement since it lay within the ten-league coastal area forbidden to colonization. He did allow temporary settlement there until enough colonists gathered to ensure the safety of Gonzales, however.

In addition to his own finances, DeWitt used the profit from the sale of his wife's property in Missouri in the colonization scheme. Settlement of the colony was slow, though in 1826 DeWitt entered a four-year contract with the fifty-ton schooner *Dispatch* under captain William Jarvis Russell[qv] to bring in supplies and colonists. By April 1826 DeWitt and a small party of colonists set out for Texas: the Stephens, Locklands, and Reynolds families, along with DeWitt's wife, two sons, and three of four daughters. The party traveled from Missouri down the Mississippi River to New Orleans and arrived at the mouth of the Lavaca River by a schooner that, owing to the difficulty of navigating the Gulf, anchored only in July. DeWitt sent word to Kerr at Old Station for assistance and for protection against Indians. By October more colonists had arrived, bringing the population of Old Station to some forty people, who built cabins and planted crops. Although the Mexican government could issue no titles since the settlers were inside the forbidden zone, Saucedo did appoint James Norton[qv] as temporary alcalde.[qv] Kerr was made attorney for the colony in July 1827, thereby becoming DeWitt's official agent, a powerful position allowing him to administer the colony and freeing DeWitt to recruit more colonists.

DeWitt returned in September 1827 to find that the Mexican government had ordered the colonists to leave Old Station, a result of a boundary dispute with De León's colony. The edict resulted from the increasing suspicion that DeWitt's colonists were engaged in contraband trade and were permanently relocating the colony in an illegal place, as well as a growing distrust among Mexican officials of all foreigners. In October 1825 the Mexican government had granted preference to Martín De León in the legal battle over the boundary issue, which was inflamed by the Old Station settlement, on the grounds that De León's contract predated DeWitt's and DeWitt's contract required him to respect previous settlement. De León's status as an influential Mexican national no doubt played a role as well. Relations had deteriorated further in October 1826, when the schooner *Escambia* arrived at the mouth of the Lavaca with contraband tobacco belonging to Thomas Powell in its trade merchandise. Powell wished to settle in DeWitt's colony. Mexican officials discovered the infraction through a mysterious Doctor Oldivar (or Oliver), a fellow passenger purportedly of French origin but claiming to be a Mexican officer, who won Powell's confidence. The *jefe político* at San Antonio ordered De León, with the aid of the La Bahía[qv] garrison under command of Rafael A. Manchola[qv]—who happened to be De León's son-in-law—to seize the contraband. Fueled by Kerr's suspicions that Oldivar had been bribed by De León, rumors spread that De León and Manchola were out to kill Anglo-American settlers as far as the Colorado River and that the Mexican empresario would return with DeWitt's head tied to his saddle. With little incident, however, De León and Manchola seized the contraband, as well as the colonists' guns, and arrested DeWitt, whom they took to La Bahía for trial. Apparently Austin's intervention finally quieted the matter, but not without irreparable damage to the De León–DeWitt relationship.

Complicating the effects of the boundary dispute and the illegal trade controversies, the Mexican government's suspicion of foreign settlers increased after the Fredonian Rebellion[qv] in December 1826 at Nacogdoches. Although DeWitt colonists condemned the incident and drew up resolutions proclaiming their loyalty to Mexico, many Mexican officials made no distinction between the Anglo-Americans of DeWitt's colony and those of Haden Edwards's.[qv] Prompted no doubt by De León, who was also forbidden to settle within the ten-league coastal zone, the captain general of the Provincias Internas,[qv] Anastasio Bustamante,[qv] mindful of the possibility of recurrence of smuggling on the Lavaca River and suspicious that DeWitt was trying to relocate his colony, ordered Saucedo in San Antonio to remove DeWitt from Old Station in August 1827. Upon learning of the order, many colonists threatened to resettle in Austin's colony, so DeWitt applied for an extension, which was granted until December 1. Governor José María Viesca[qv] extended the date to June 1828. DeWitt probably was not intending to relocate his colony, since he had sent a party to Gonzales in January 1827 to build a fort, though the work had to be stopped because of Indian hostilities between the Comanches and their enemies, the Lipan Apaches and Tonkawas. Nevertheless, the fort was completed by April. By December DeWitt abandoned Old Station as ordered and took his forty colonists to Gonzales.

The official census of 1828 recorded an increase to seventy-five colonists—eleven families and twenty-seven single men. They were primarily from the Upper South, especially Missouri, Tennessee, and Kentucky, though some came from Louisiana, Alabama, Mississippi, Illinois, Indiana, Pennsylvania, and New York. One was from England. In time the population became more balanced with colonists from the Lower South. By mid-1829 the colony's population more than doubled to 158—thirty families and thirty-four single men, most apparently brought by Byrd Lockhart.qv By the year's end 186 colonists were recorded. The greatest increase in population occurred in 1830, when twenty-six families (160 people) and thirty-one single men joined the colony, bringing the total population to 377. The areas of settlement were primarily along the Guadalupe and San Marcos rivers, but also on the tributaries of the Lavaca River. Having reached the required minimum of 100 families, the colonists were allowed to receive land titles. To this end José Antonio Navarroqv was appointed land commissioner in January 1831, and with DeWitt and Kerr became one of the most important members of the colony. As his surveyor Navarro appointed Byrd Lockhart, who had acted as Kerr's deputy in Gonzales since 1827. Most of the surveying was done in 1831 and 1832; 189 titles were issued. The Colonization Law of March 24, 1825, allowed families a sitio and a laborqqv of land if they engaged in both stock raising and farming. A single person received only a fourth as much, though he could acquire the remainder upon marriage. Corn was the basic grain of the colony, water and game were plentiful, and colonists also raised hogs and cattle. Slaveryqv was not prevalent. Of the original colonists only Kerr had slaves, though a few later settlers apparently brought slaves with them. The colony had neither church nor priest, despite the stipulation in DeWitt's contract to supply them. Instead, religion was practiced within the family and the colony was occasionally visited by the Cumberland Presbyterian missionary Sumner Bacon.qv Green DeWitt himself performed marriages. The absence of church and priest hindered the development of formal education in the colony; indeed, until David Barnett Edwardqv arrived in 1831 and established "Gonzales Seminary," no institution existed.

Indians remained troublesome, but not serious. By 1827 a campaign against the Karankawas was launched by Austin's and De León's colonies, assisted by Mexican federal troops under General Bustamante, then in Texas to squelch the Fredonian Rebellion. The Karankawas were defeated and a peace treaty signed on May 13, 1827, in La Bahía by Bustamante, Martín and Fernando De León,qv Jacob Bettsqv for Austin, DeWitt, and Kerr, and by Father Miguel Miró and chief Antonito for the Indians. DeWitt colonists were also able to negotiate a peace with the Tonkawas. But they were still subject to Comanche raids, which were particularly bad in 1830. The Indians generally stole livestock from outlying settlements; Gonzales itself was probably never attacked after 1826. Despite DeWitt's prompting, the Mexican government was unable to send troops or establish a garrison at Gonzales because the few available soldiers were concentrated at La Bahía and San Antonio, which suffered raids more frequently. Only with the growth of contraband trade between San Antonio and San Felipe did the government order regular patrols of the area and deliver an artillery piece to DeWitt, in March 1831, though the troops were withdrawn to San Antonio in September after a defeat by the Comanches. Nevertheless, there was relative peace; from 1825 to 1836 only ninety-seven people were killed by Indians around San Antonio, La Bahía, and DeWitt's colony combined.

Gonzales remained the only town in the colony. In April 1831 the *jefe político* ordered Navarro to resurvey the town because Kerr, DeWitt's original surveyor, had not made provisions for public squares in 1825. By 1836 Gonzales had thirty-two structures, twenty of which were built before 1831. The colony's growth, however, was halted upon the passage of the Law of April 6, 1830,qv which prohibited further foreign immigration into Texas. Although DeWitt's colony was excluded from this ruling through Austin's influence, immigration was affected and finally ended anyway; no new arrivals were recorded after April 1, 1831, though immigration during the first three months of that year increased the colony's population to 531. DeWitt's contract expired on April 15, 1831, which also contributed to his failure to bring in the 400 families stipulated in his contract; he petitioned for an extension, but was unsuccessful. Since the greater portion of his grant was still unoccupied, the vacant lands reverted to the government to grant to any empresario it wished. Hence, grants were issued to Martín de León and another Mexican empresario, Juan Vicente Campos, though they too had to respect the rights of previous settlers. For the most part the colony was materially and financially a burden to DeWitt, and the citizens of Gonzales failed to make the town a commercial hub. Still, DeWitt's colony is generally considered after Austin's the most successful of the Anglo-American colonies in Texas.

DeWitt's personal influence in his settlement seems to have been comparatively weaker than Austin's was in the Austin colonies, and though he represented the Gonzales District in the Convention of 1833,qv he never held an elected office in the colony's government. While at Old Station the colony was too small to have its own ayuntamiento,qv so it fell under the direct supervision of the *jefe político* at San Antonio. From October 1828 to November 1832, the colony fell under the ayuntamiento of San Felipe (no one in the colony was proficient in the Spanish language) and known as the District of Gonzales. The only government official then living in the colony was the *comisario*qv of police, Fielding Porter and later James B. Patrick.qv In November 1832 Navarro called together a convention to elect the colony's own ayuntamiento. Ezekiel Williams was elected the first alcalde. A month later another election was held to comply with the Constitution of Coahuila and Texas;qv James B. Patrick was elected the new alcalde. One of the first acts of the new government was to establish a ferry on the Guadalupe River and set its rates. James C. Davis was elected alcalde in December 1833, and Andrew Pontonqv in December 1834. Also in 1834 the Mexican government divided Texas into three departments, and moved DeWitt's colony into the Department of the Brazos under the jurisdiction of the *jefe político* of San Felipe (rather than of San Antonio).

As dissatisfaction grew among many living in Texas toward the Mexican government, DeWitt's colony remained moderate in view, sympathetic with Austin's colony but loyal to Mexico, though delegates were sent to the Convention of 1832qv and the Convention of 1833. During the hostilities between Saltillo and Monclova over the location of the government of Coahuila and Texas, DeWitt was in Monclova, probably to buy land, which the Mexican government was fraudulently selling to speculators to raise money for defense. While in Monclova DeWitt died, probably from cholera, on May 18, 1835. Following Antonio López de Santa Anna'sqv suppression of Zacatecas and of the Coahuila and Texas legislature, DeWitt's colony, like other settlements in Texas, established a committee of safety and correspondence, though it professed loyalty to Mexico, especially after William B. Travis'sqv capture of Anahuac in June 1835 (*see* ANAHUAC DISTURBANCES). This incident, however, caused Gen. Domingo de Ugartecheaqv in San Antonio to fear armed rebellion in the various colonies, and provoked him to recover the cannon given the Gonzales residents for protection against the Indians. In an irony of history, DeWitt colonists, despite their professed loyalty to Mexico, defended their right to the Gonzales "come and take it" cannonqv in what became the first battle of the Texas Revolution,qv the battle of Gonzales.qv Since the jurisdiction over the colony had been moved in 1834 to the Department of the Brazos, alcalde Ponton argued additionally that the order to give up the cannon had to come from San Felipe, not San Antonio (though he knew that the *jefe político* of the Brazos department, James B. Miller,qv would have let the colonists keep the piece). As the revolution progressed, DeWitt colonists served the

Texas cause in every major engagement. Susanna W. Dickinson,^qv wife of colonist Almaron Dickinson,^qv verified rumors of the fall of the Alamo when she returned to Gonzales after surviving the battle of March 6, 1836. The news led Sam Houston^qv to order the town evacuated and burned. Its citizens and the growing number of volunteers gathered there to follow him east in the Runaway Scrape,^qv in order to regroup for the defense of Texas against Santa Anna. After the battle of San Jacinto^qv DeWitt colonists returned to their lands and rebuilt their capital. By the end of 1836 much of the colony was organized into Gonzales County. In 1846, after annexation,^qv DeWitt, Guadalupe, and Lavaca counties were also formed out of the old colony lands, as was Caldwell County in 1848. *See also* ANGLO-AMERICAN COLONIZATION.

BIBLIOGRAPHY: Eugene C. Barker, ed., *The Austin Papers* (3 vols., Washington: GPO, 1924–28). Eugene C. Barker, *The Life of Stephen F. Austin* (Nashville: Cokesbury Press, 1925; rpt., Austin: Texas State Historical Association, 1949; New York: AMS Press, 1970). Henry Putney Beers, *Spanish and Mexican Records of the American Southwest: A Bibliographic Guide to Archive and Manuscript Sources* (Tucson: University of Arizona Press, 1979). Bexar Archives, Barker Texas History Center, University of Texas at Austin. Carlos E. Castañeda, *Our Catholic Heritage in Texas* (7 vols., Austin: Von Boeckmann–Jones, 1936–58; rpt., New York: Arno, 1976). Edward Albert Lukes, *DeWitt Colony of Texas* (Austin: Jenkins, 1976). Ethel Zivley Rather, "DeWitt's Colony," *Quarterly of the Texas State Historical Association* 8 (October 1904). Texas General Land Office, *An Abstract of the Original Titles of Record in the General Land Office* (Houston: Niles, 1838; rpt., Austin: Pemberton Press, 1964). Vertical Files, Barker Texas History Center, University of Texas at Austin (Green C. DeWitt; Gonzales, Texas). David M. Vigness, *The Revolutionary Decades: The Saga of Texas, 1810–1836* (Austin: Steck-Vaughn, 1965).
Craig H. Roell

DEWITTY, VIRGIE CARRINGTON (ca. 1913–1980). Virgie Carrington DeWitty, music teacher and choir director, was born in Wetumka, Oklahoma, the daughter of William and Violet Carrington. The family moved to Austin when she was a small child and joined Ebenezer Baptist Church, where her mother sang in the choir for forty-eight years. Because of a strong musical influence and encouragement at home and at church, Virgie started playing the piano by ear at home. One Sunday when she was five, the Sunday school had no pianist. Her mother led her to the piano, where she played and sang her first solo, "Jesus Wants Me for a Sunbeam." From that time until her death she played for Ebenezer Third Baptist Church. She received her formal education from the Phillips White Private Academy, Austin Public Schools, and Tillotson (now Huston-Tillotson) College, where she earned a diploma in education and music. She received a bachelor of science degree in music from Prairie View A&M College (now Prairie View A&M University) and a bachelor of arts degree and teaching certificate in light opera from the American Conservatory of Music in Chicago, Illinois. She also studied in Boulder, Colorado, at Juilliard School of Music in New York City, and at the University of Texas at Austin. She married Arthur DeWitty, an Austin civic leader, in 1932; they had no children.

Virgie DeWitty directed the first commercially sponsored radio program over the Texas Quality Network, "The Bright and Early Choir," from 1938 to 1940. She composed more than 100 gospels, spirituals, and anthems. One of her most famous pieces was "Magnify the Lord." She taught music at Anderson High School in Austin and composed the school song. She also taught private classes in voice and piano for many years. Her specialty was writing four-part-harmony anthems and religious music for choirs.

Mrs. Dewitty was a charter member of the Alpha Kappa Zeta chapter of Zeta Phi Beta sorority and a member of the National Association for the Advancement of Colored People^qv and the Douglas Club. She received the 1957 Woman's Day Speaker award for Ebenezer Baptist Church. She was active in the Missionary Baptist General Convention of Texas and the National Baptist Convention of America. She died on August 11, 1980, at Holy Cross Hospital in Austin. In 1991 a fund for music students was established from her estate.

BIBLIOGRAPHY: Austin *American-Statesman,* August 28, 1980, June 21, 1992. Vertical Files, Barker Texas History Center, University of Texas at Austin.
Kharen Monsho

DEWVILLE, TEXAS. Dewville is at the intersection of a country road and Farm Road 1117, near the southwestern corner of Gonzales County twenty-five miles southwest of Gonzales. It is on the Old San Antonio Road^qv between the sites of two defunct communities, Albuquerque and Sandies Chapel. Dewville is named for two brothers, John Frank and Thomas M. Dew, who opened a steam-powered gin on the site in 1885. A Baptist church was organized there about 1890. The community was granted a post office in 1894, and in 1897 Sandies Chapel Methodist Church was moved to Dewville. A two-story school building was erected in the community in 1901, and Sandies Chapel School was consolidated with Dewville in 1907. In 1914 Dewville had a population of fifty, a gin, a general store, and telephone service. Its population was estimated at fifty-five from 1925 until the 1960s. At different times the community had a blacksmith shop, a meat market, and an Odd Fellows Hall. In 1940 Dewville comprised a post office, two churches, a school, a cemetery, and scattered dwellings. The post office closed in 1955. The community slowly lost population, as the nearby railroad community of Nixon prospered, and the population of Dewville dropped to forty in the 1960s and to fifteen by 1970. In 1990 the population was still estimated at fifteen, and the Methodist church and a cemetery were at the site.

BIBLIOGRAPHY: Gonzales County Historical Commission, *History of Gonzales County* (Dallas: Curtis, 1986).
Mark Odintz

DEXTER, HENRY L. (1823–1870?). Henry L. Dexter, El Paso settler, was born in Vandalia, Illinois, on September 2, 1823. Papers admitting him to the United States Military Academy were signed by O. N. McCurdy as guardian. He was admitted on July 1, 1842, and dismissed the following January 20 for deficiency in his studies. After leaving the academy he roamed the world as an able seaman until 1849, when he headed west with the gold rush. At Santa Fe, New Mexico, he changed his mind and turned toward the El Paso area, where he arrived in 1850. In 1855 he purchased the property known as Frontera, eight miles above El Paso del Norte; he served briefly as a customs inspector there and moved back to Ysleta later that year.

In his thirteen years on the border, mostly at Ysleta, Dexter held a number of appointive and elective offices, such as justice of the peace, postmaster, customs collector, tax assessor–collector, and county judge. He established a mercantile business, speculated in local grains, and served as a newspaper correspondent and town physician. He related his experiences on the border in a series of letters to his sister Mary Roundy, the only one in the family who would correspond with him. These letters, thirty in number, were returned to El Paso when a collateral relative, Charles J. Mapel, moved to the city, and they became the basis of a seventeen-part series published in the El Paso *Times.* One letter, written on the back of a rare edition of the Mesilla *Times* while Confederate forces controlled southern New Mexico, is now in the Museum of New Mexico.

In 1861 Dexter was appointed justice of the peace in Mesilla and became increasingly outspoken in his hatred of the policies of the federal government. He fled the El Paso area in 1862 with a price on his head, and some of his properties were eventually confiscated by the carpetbagger government after the war. He had married María Soledad Luján, a native of Mexico, on January 1, 1859, but abandoned her when he left the border region.

After the Civil War^qv Dexter lived in Guaymas and lower California, though he occasionally returned to the United States for brief visits. For a short time he lived in San Antonio. His last letter was written from the steamer *Continental* in the Gulf of California on December 27, 1869. He wrote that he expected to reach Guaymas the following day and that he planned to remain there, but he also said that he had become ill with a severe cold. He may not have recovered. A photograph of Dexter taken from a daguerreotype hangs in the El Paso County Courthouse, in a gallery of past county judges.

BIBLIOGRAPHY: William Wallace Mills, *Forty Years at El Paso* (El Paso?, 1901; 2d ed., El Paso: Hertzog, 1962). *The War of the Rebellion: A Compilation of the Official Records of the Union and Confederate Armies.*
Arthur H. Leibson

DEXTER, PETER BARTELLE (1799–1876). Peter Bartelle Dexter, soldier and civil servant, was born in Geneva, Ontario County, New York, on November 13, 1799. He moved from Tennessee to Texas in 1834. In 1835 he was elected secretary to the Consultation qv at San Felipe and later that year was elected secretary to the provisional government.qv On November 7, 1835, he became one of the signers of the Texas Declaration of Independence.qv When William B. Travis's qv final call for help went out from the Alamo,qv the citizens of San Felipe elected Joseph Baker qv to chair a meeting to determine their response. Baker appointed Moseley Baker, John A. Wharton, Alexander Somervell,qqv Dexter, and eight other men to draft a resolution. At the meeting on February 27, 1836, the committee reported that the colonists "must read and act in the same moment or Texas is lost."

Dexter enlisted as a private in Capt. Moseley Baker's company, but because of a quarrel with Baker soon after the retreat from Gonzales his name does not appear on the unit's muster roll. On April 10, 1836, Dexter reported to Baker from Camp Salvation near San Felipe that the enemy had evacuated the former Texas capital. Only a few days after the battle of San Jacinto qv Sam Houston qv appointed Dexter commander of a new company, made up of men newly volunteered for the army and attached to Col. Sidney Sherman's qv Second Regiment, Texas Volunteers. When the Army of the Republic of Texas qv was organized in 1838 Dexter was promoted to lieutenant colonel and given command of the Legion of Cavalry. He was also appointed as the army's commissary of subsistence. By August 3, 1839, he had been replaced by William Gordon Cooke.qv

On July 24, 1839, Dexter was nominated as assistant commissioner to the commission that was to determine the boundary between the United States and Texas. He went to New Orleans to meet with the American commissioners, but the Senate of the Republic of Texas qv refused to confirm his nomination. In 1840 Dexter was residing in Harris County, where his taxable assets amounted to one gold watch. In 1849 he left to search for gold in California, and there he remained. Dexter died in San Francisco on October 22, 1876, and was buried there in the Odd Fellows Rest cemetery.

BIBLIOGRAPHY: *Compiled Index to Elected and Appointed Officials of the Republic of Texas, 1835–1846* (Austin: State Archives, Texas State Library, 1981). John H. Jenkins, ed., *The Papers of the Texas Revolution, 1835–1836* (10 vols., Austin: Presidial Press, 1973). *Telegraph and Texas Register*, November 7, 14, 21, December 2, 1835. *Texas Almanac*, 1872.
Thomas W. Cutrer

DEXTER, TEXAS. Dexter is near the Red River twenty-five miles northeast of Gainesville in extreme northeastern Cooke County. It began as a town around 1870 with the arrival of the first settlers, Jesse Morris, S. E. and Dick Collum, and Bill Munday. The first choice for a townsite was Sugar Hill, three miles east of the final location, which was chosen because it had a natural spring that offered a stopping point for travelers. Morris is credited with the idea of naming the town after a famous racehorse of that time. By 1873 Dexter had its own post office, and by the early 1880s its population of 300 was served by at least thirty-seven businesses, including four blacksmith shops, three hotels, a district school, two steam gristmills and cotton gins, and four physicians. Dexter was expected to overtake Gainesville as the largest town in Cooke County when residents thought the Denison and Pacific Railway was going to pass through it, but when the rail line passed through Woodbine, a small town twenty miles south, Dexter began to decline. Many businesses and residents moved to other towns, mostly to Ardmore, Indian Territory. On February 28, 1885, residents of Dexter voted thirty to eighteen to incorporate. This incorporation did not stop the steady decline in population, although the city government remained in place until about 1900. From the late 1960s to 1987 seventy people lived in the general area. In 1988 the only institution remaining in Dexter was the Dexter Community Church. The community was still listed in 1990.

BIBLIOGRAPHY: A. Morton Smith, *The First 100 Years in Cooke County* (San Antonio: Naylor, 1955).
Robert Wayne McDaniel

DEXTRA, TEXAS. Dextra, just off Farm Road 1648 twenty-one miles northwest of Nacogdoches in northwestern Nacogdoches County, was settled before 1900. In the mid-1930s the community had a school, a church, and several stores. After World War II qv many of its residents moved away, but as late as the mid-1960s the community had a store and two churches. In the early 1990s Dextra was a dispersed farming community.
Christopher Long

DE YOUNG, HARRY ANTHONY (1893–1956). Harry Anthony De Young, artist, was born in Chicago, Illinois, on August 5, 1893. He studied at the Art Institute of Chicago, where he was an honor student, and at the University of Illinois under John W. Norton and Edward Lake. He served as a sergeant in the quartermaster corps in World War I.qv For a time he taught at the Academy of Art in Chicago and was the director of the Midwest Summer School of Art at Paw Paw Lake, Michigan. He also taught at Bailey's Harbor (Wisconsin) School of Art and was director of the Glen Wood School of Landscape Painting in Illinois. In Texas the artist founded and directed the De Young Painting Camp in the Davis Mountains. Recognition of his work in 1925 won him the Fine Arts Building Purchase Prize of $500 at the Art Institute of Chicago and honorable mention in landscape painting at the American Artists Exhibition of Chicago. In 1927 he received honorable mention at the Chicago Galleries Association. In the Edgar B. Davis qv Competitive Exhibition in San Antonio in 1928 he won the member prize of $200. A mural representing the *Basket Maker Indians of West Texas*, painted as a Public Works Administration project, is owned by the Witte Museum,qv San Antonio. *Cinchin' Up* is part of the San Antonio Art League qv collection. Among other pictures of Texas subjects are De Young's portraits of David Crockett and James Bonham,qqv which hang in the Alamo.qv Some of his other works are in the Chicago and Gary, Indiana, public schools, in Fort Davis, Texas, and in Brackenridge High School, in San Antonio. In 1942, at the height of his career, De Young suffered paralysis of his right side. He died in Waco on January 9, 1956, and was survived by his wife and daughter.

BIBLIOGRAPHY: Mantle Fielding, *Dictionary of American Painters, Sculptors and Engravers* (New York: Struck, 1945; rev. ed., ed. Glenn B. Opitz, Poughkeepsie: Apollo, 1983). Esse Forrester-O'Brien, *Art and Artists of Texas* (Dallas: Tardy, 1935). *Who's Who in American Art*, 1956–57. Witte Museum Files, San Antonio.
Caroline Remy

D'HANIS, TEXAS. D'Hanis is on Parkers Creek at the intersection of U.S. Highway 90, Farm roads 1796 and 2200, and the Southern Pacific Railroad, eight miles west of Hondo in western Medina County. The community is sometimes called New D'Hanis to distinguish it from the site of old D'Hanis one mile to the east. The original settlement was the third made by Henri Castro qv through his agent, Theodore Gentilz.qv When established in the spring of 1847 by twenty-nine Alsatian families, D'Hanis was the frontier settlement on the Old San Antonio Road.qv Castro named the village for William D'Hanis,

Antwerp manager of his colonization company. Jean Batot and his son Christian were the first settlers to arrive. Town lots and twenty-acre farms were surveyed and deeded to the first colonists.

With building materials in short supply, the early settlers built rough shelters of mesquite pickets and thatch, to be replaced eventually by the distinctive European-style rock homes of the settlement. Catholic services, conducted by priests from Castroville, were held in a small structure built in the middle of the village. The building of nearby Fort Lincoln in 1849 afforded the settlers employment and much-needed protection from Indian raids. By 1850 the settlement comprised twenty dwellings and had a schoolteacher. A post office was established in 1854, and the town became a stage stop on the San Antonio–Rio Grande road. St. Dominic's Church was built in 1869, and for a time in the early 1870s two nuns of the Sisters of Divine Providence[qv] taught school in D'Hanis.

In 1881, when the Galveston, Harrisburg and San Antonio Railway built across Medina County, it bypassed old D'Hanis, then the site of two stores, a dance hall, and sulfur-well baths. The new town grew up around the railroad loading depot 1½ miles west. Over the next few years the post office, the businesses, and the citizens moved to the railroad site, which was called New D'Hanis for a time and eventually became D'Hanis. The D'Hanis Brick and Tile Company was founded in 1883 and was still in operation in the 1980s. By 1890 the community contained four general stores, one saloon, and a flour and grist mill, and by 1896 two hotels served the community.

In 1900 the population numbered 266. St. Anthony's School was built in 1908, and Holy Cross Church was completed in 1914. The weekly D'Hanis *News* began publication in 1908, became the *Star* some years later, and was discontinued in 1923. A second brick factory, Seco Pressed Brick, opened in 1910, the year the D'Hanis Independent School District was formed. The town's first bank opened in 1916. A Catholic church, Our Lady Queen of Peace, was built in 1924 for the Mexican-Americans of the town. The population was an estimated 270 in 1930, 550 in the mid-1940s, and 500 to 550 from that decade through 1990, when it was 548. D'Hanis installed waterworks in 1955, street lights in 1957, and a sewer system in 1973. The town was flooded in 1894, 1919, and 1935, and Holy Cross Church was badly damaged by fire in 1963, though it was rebuilt the following year.

BIBLIOGRAPHY: Castro Colonies Heritage Association, *The History of Medina County, Texas* (Dallas: National Share Graphics, 1983).

Mark Odintz

DIAL, JOHN (1790–1844). John Dial, early settler and legislator, was born on January 19, 1790. In March 1837 he moved to what is now Shelby County, Texas, with his wife, Anna, whom he had married on June 16, 1816, and their eight children. In 1838 he was granted a conditional certificate for land in Shelby County, and in 1841 he received an unconditional certificate. He represented Shelby County in the House of Representatives of the Seventh Congress, 1842–43. In 1844 he furnished supplies to Capt. L. H. Mabbitt's company in Shelby County. The same year he represented the Moderators in the peace talks at the end of the Regulator-Moderator War.[qv] He was a member-elect of the Ninth Congress when he died in Shelby County on December 4, 1844.

BIBLIOGRAPHY: Marker Files, Texas Historical Commission, Austin. Texas House of Representatives, *Biographical Directory of the Texan Conventions and Congresses, 1832–1845* (Austin: Book Exchange, 1941).

Carolyn Hyman

DIAL, TEXAS (Fannin County). Dial is on Farm Road 824 twenty-five miles southeast of Bonham in southeastern Fannin County. The settlement was first called Bethel, when in 1837 the one-room Bethel school was established a mile from Fort Lyday.[qv] This nearby fort was named for Isaac Lyday, one of the first settlers in the area and the recipient of an original land grant from the Republic of Texas.[qv] The Dial Presbyterian Church (originally the Bethel Society) was founded in the mid-1840s and met in the log-cabin building of the Bethel school. The community was later called Lane, after Robert W. Lane, a teacher from Tennessee who founded Lane's Academy, the second school in the area. The Central National Road[qv] of the Republic of Texas passed through the settlement. When the post office opened in May 1880, the community was named Dial after another prominent citizen, James Dial. By 1890 the town had an estimated population of seventy-five. From 1903 to 1905 Sam Rayburn,[qv] the future speaker of the United States House of Representatives, taught in the Dial public school system. The community's post office closed in 1905. From 1900 through 1990 Dial's reported population never exceeded 100. In the 1930s it fell to twenty-nine but from the mid-1970s through 1990 was reported at seventy-six.

BIBLIOGRAPHY: *Fannin County Folks and Facts* (Dallas: Taylor, 1977).

David Minor

DIAL, TEXAS (Hutchinson County). Dial, also known as Gulf Dial, is on Farm Road 2277 southeast of Stinnett in central Hutchinson County. It was named for the Dial Ranch, on which it was established in 1925, when the Gulf Oil Company drilled its Dial No. 1 well, the first in the county north of the Canadian River. By 1926 a sizable oil town, complete with a post office, rose on the site. The improvement of highways and transportation facilities, however, which ended the oil subsidiary-camp system, led to the town's demise. By 1976 the post office had been discontinued. In the 1980s several wells at the site were still in production. Dial had a population estimated at eighty from 1968 to 1990.

BIBLIOGRAPHY: N. D. Bartlett, "Discovery of the Panhandle Oil and Gas Field," *Panhandle-Plains Historical Review* 12 (1939).

H. Allen Anderson

DIALECTS. When most Texans think of Texas dialects, they likely think of the speech of an elderly man sitting outside a country store at some rural Texas crossroads or that of some older relative living in a small Texas town. When non-Texans think about Texas dialects, they probably recall stereotypes based on movies or television programs in which actors or actresses speak with what passes for a Texas accent—at least in Hollywood. However, linguists see Texas dialects as a more complex picture. Because their goal is to describe how language is in fact used by speakers, they label any variety of language a dialect, and the term is used descriptively, not pejoratively. Hence, everyone has a dialect, or more accurately, a range of varieties he uses, depending on audience, topic, and context. Dialectologists, those linguists concerned with the regional distribution of speech forms, attempt to analyze settlement patterns and the ways in which those patterns have influenced language in an area. This work often samples speech forms across large geographic areas, especially rural areas, in hopes of gaining insight into how a language has changed over time. The result is a map dividing the area, in this case, the state, into dialect regions. With a slightly different focus, sociolinguists, who are concerned with how and why particular speech forms come to be associated with particular social groups, examine how speakers from different backgrounds use language to establish and reflect their identities as individuals and members of groups. Sociolinguists are likewise concerned with how language continues to change and how social forces might be influencing the courses of change. Although the dialects of Texas are less studied than those of some states and regions, research that has been conducted provides a basis for understanding the nature and significance of dialects in Texas, first, with regard to settlement history and its influence on the state's regional dialects and, second, with regard to social dialects.

No doubt many people—Texans and non-Texans—think of Texas dialects as dialects of English alone, but such a perspective is too narrow. Each group settling in the state has brought its language. If the language continues to be used over time, a local variety of speech develops. In some cases, because of the paucity of speakers, the language dies out locally within a generation or two. The Dutch spoken in some areas of Texas in the last century, for instance, represents such a language. Although a few speakers of Wendish survive in Central Texas, they soon will die, and the Wendish language will become extinct in Texas (*see* WENDS), though it continues to be spoken in parts of Germany. Such patterns of language extinction are quite common for languages other than English in this country. In fact, immigrant communities often exhibit a "three-generation" pattern with regard to language: grandparents who immigrated to the United States begin life as monolingual speakers of the language of the old country; parents grow up here bilingual, speaking the native language of their parents and English; and the grandchildren grow up speaking only English and perhaps a little of the grandparents' native language. In other cases, languages persist much longer. Even though they are on the decline, German and Czech, for example, continue to be spoken in parts of Texas and have persisted far longer than Dutch did or Wendish will. Texas Czech and Texas German differ in describable ways from the Czech spoken in the Czech Republic or the dialects of German spoken in Germany, Austria, or Switzerland because of their isolation from other communities where the language is used (a situation which gives rise to changes internal to the language), because of contact with English, and because of use in fewer and fewer contexts. Texas German, in particular, has been the subject of scholarly research.

The Spanish spoken in Texas represents a more complex case. Because of the state's history and the large number of speakers of Spanish who are native Texans, the state's proximity to Mexico, and the continuing number of Spanish-speaking immigrants, Spanish continues to be widely spoken in Texas. As dialectologists would expect, Texas Spanish is quite similar to the Spanish spoken in Northern Mexico. At the same time, as a result of prolonged contact with English, it, like other varieties of Spanish in the United States, shows influence of that contact. For example, the meaning of *levantar*, which means "to pick up, raise, get up," has been extended under the influence of the English figurative use of the verb to include the notion of "give someone a ride" ("Pick me up at eight"). Varieties of Spanish outside the United States would likely use the verb *recoger*, which means "to gather or collect" in this context. Similarly, varieties of Spanish in the United States have borrowed words like *troca* ("truck") and *parquear* ("to park") from English. But more than simply words has been borrowed. Research demonstrates that the verbal system of Spanish spoken in Texas and the United States in general is being influenced by that of English; new Spanish constructions have been produced in Texas and the United States based on English models. Thus, one hears *Hablame p'atrás* "Call me back" (literally: "Speak+to me to back"). Other varieties of Spanish do not have such phrasal or two-word verbs; instead, they would likely use *Llamame de nuevo*, literally "Call+to me again." Although purists decry such usages, they are just the sorts of borrowings linguists expect from prolonged language contact.

An especially interesting feature of Texas Spanish and Spanish in the United States is the extent to which its speakers codeswitch, or alternate between Spanish and English while speaking, often within a single utterance. Again, purists (and many speakers themselves) criticize this practice as "bad" Spanish. From a sociolinguistic point of view, however, codeswitching enables speakers to use all of the linguistic resources at their disposal to communicate effectively with a wide range of audiences. Research from around the world also demonstrates that when such codeswitching occurs (and it is common in many bilingual settings), speakers are demonstrating their membership in multiple communities and the complex nature of their identities. Because most non-Hispanic Texans do not speak Spanish and most Mexicans do not speak English, Texas Hispanics who speak Spanish and codeswitch thus use language to establish a unique identity for themselves as a group.

Ultimately, social factors govern the fate of languages, including minority languages. The number of speakers, their attachment to the language as part of their identity, the extent to which they marry within their community and reside in areas where the language is spoken, the functions the language serves in the community (e.g., religious, educational, interpersonal, business), the larger society's attitudes toward the language and its speakers, and the behaviors and laws to which these attitudes give rise influence whether a language survives in a given locale. Anti-German attitudes during the two world wars, for example, largely account for the rapid decline in the number of speakers of Texas German. German speakers were seen as suspect by the larger society, and laws limited the teaching of German and its use as a language of instruction. The future fate of Texas Spanish as well as the languages of recent groups of immigrants to this state from East and South Asia is, therefore, unclear.

Just as the Spanish spoken in Texas has been influenced by English, the English spoken here has been influenced by Spanish in at least two very different ways. First, some monolingual speakers of English, nearly all of whom are Hispanic, speak a variety of English that is clearly influenced by Spanish, especially at the level of phonology or accent. This variety of English, which is variously termed Spanish-influenced English or Chicano[qv] English by researchers, represents an ethnic variety of English. It is analogous to the speech of some Texans who speak varieties of English that sound "black" or "white" to various listeners. Further, all Texans who speak English use words borrowed from Spanish. Some, such as *tamale, bronco,* and *lariat,* have national currency. (*Lariat* is an interesting case because speakers of English borrowed both the Spanish article and the noun, *la riata* and collapsed them into one word.) Other borrowings, such as *arroyo, pilón,* and *llano,* are far less widely known and are in many cases limited to the English spoken in parts of the state where there has traditionally been a large Spanish-speaking population.

Such a distribution of words demonstrates the validity of the importance dialectologists have long attached to settlement history as a determinant of regional dialects. Thus the research of E. Bagby Atwood, the *Linguistic Atlas of the Gulf States,* and Craig Carver analyzes the regional distribution of linguistic forms, especially words. Carver offers detailed discussion of the settlement of the state and its influence on language in it. He notes the early Hispanic settlers in two distinct areas of the state and the waves of English-speaking settlers moving to Central Texas in the 1820s from what many dialectologists term the Midland dialect region (including the Appalachians and southern Ohio River valley). With the English-speaking populations and especially the settlement of East Texas came slavery[qv] and African Americans.[qv] The 1830s brought the beginning of European immigration to Central Texas and the Hill Country, as well as continued immigration from various parts of the Upper South and the Gulf South. West Texas was settled much later. Since the time of settlement, the demographics of these various regions has continued to shift. African Americans, for example, were once concentrated in East Texas. Although many continue to live in small towns and rural areas in that part of the state, far larger numbers live today in the state's largest cities. Carver uses the metaphor of layers to describe the changing regional dialects of Texas. Consequently, he illustrates the extent to which dialects of Texas English exhibit Southern dialect features that extend into East Texas and Midland dialect features that stretch to the central Eastern seaboard, on the one hand, as well as the dialects of English that stretch into the Southwest, on the other. These layers reflect the provenance and migration patterns of the various groups of English speakers who settled the state and those who continued moving westward. In addition, Carver delimits two dialect regions within the state itself: a South Texas layer that runs by-and-large along the Texas-Mexico border and reaches up to San Antonio, and a Central Texas region that includes the areas where large numbers of speakers of German and other European languages settled.

The work of sociolinguists complements work that divides dialect regions on the basis of lexical items (words). Sociolinguists often consider urban as well as rural varieties of speech and generally offer analyses of the quantitative differences between the speech patterns of various groups. For example, most Texas use *ain't* when speaking in certain contexts, but members of various social groups, whether defined by region, class, age, ethnicity, sex, or some combination of these, use it more frequently than others. Similar kinds of quantitative differences can be documented for the pronunciations of many sounds, such as the *i* in *might*, the *aw* in *hawk*, or the *r* in *forty*. Sociolinguistic research generally attempts to illuminate the changes in Texas speech brought about by social changes that have taken place in the state since World War II.qv These social changes include the great influx of non-Texans, the growing availability of education for the majority of Texans, and increasing urbanization. Some of the sociolinguistic correlates of these changes include the development of new urban varieties of speech. Although these are characterized by the loss of some features associated traditionally associated with Texas speech, especially the speech of rural Texans, they remain distinct from urban varieties of English in other parts of the country. Such changes are occurring in the speech of Anglos, Hispanics, and African Americans, with the speech of these ethnic groups converging in some respects but diverging in others. Thus, although Texas dialects of English continue to change, there is little chance that varieties identifiable as Texan will likely disappear. Texans are, with rare exception, proud of their identity as Texans, a fact that is reflected in their speech. Despite the fact that certain features of Texas dialects of English are sometimes stigmatized by speakers from other areas as hicky or "incorrect," Texans will continue to use them, partly because people who live in Texas wish to distinguish themselves from other Americans. Language is a particularly appropriate medium for marking this sort of difference. Such uses of language, clearly symbolic in nature, illustrate a basic fact about language and about dialects: Speakers use language to communicate information not only about the world but also about themselves and the groups to which they belong or do not belong. To use a particular dialect is to lay claim to an identity. Hence, even as Americans from other parts of the country and immigrants from around the world continue to move to Texas in large numbers, they become part of the development of dialects in Texas. Newcomers to the state inevitably pick up such traditional Southernisms as *y'all*. Those who are not already from the South sometimes begin saying *fixin' to* and *might could* as the natives do. In this way, language enables Texans, native or naturalized, to identify themselves as such.

See also CZECHS, GERMANS, MEXICAN AMERICANS, POLES, *and other articles on ethnic groups.*

BIBLIOGRAPHY: Elmer Bagby Atwood, *The Regional Vocabulary of Texas* (Austin: University of Texas Press, 1962). Guy Bailey, "Directions of Change in Texas English," *Journal of American Culture* 14 (1991). Craig M. Carver, *American Regional Dialects: A Word Geography* (Ann Arbor: University of Michigan Press, 1987). Glenn G. Gilbert, *Linguistic Atlas of Texas German* (Austin: University of Texas Press, 1972). Heinz Kloss, *The American Bilingual Tradition* (Rowley, Massachusetts: Newbury House, 1977). Lee Pederson et al., eds., *Linguistic Atlas of the Gulf States* (Athens: University of Georgia Press, 1986–). Joyce Penfield and Jacob L. Ornstein-Galicia, *Chicano English: An Ethnic Contact Dialect* (Amersterdam and Philadelphia: J. Benjamins, 1985). Keith Walters, "Dialectology," in *Language: The Socio-cultural Context,* ed. Frederick J. Newmeyer (Cambridge University Press, 1988).

Keith Walters

DIALVILLE, TEXAS. Dialville is on Farm Road 347 six miles northwest of Rusk in central Cherokee County. The area, which was part of the Beverly Pool three-league grant, was first settled in the late 1840s, but a community did not grow up until 1883, when John Dial established a store on the recently constructed Kansas and Gulf Short Line Railroad. The community was originally known as Dial or Dial's, but when a post office was established in 1885 the name was changed to Dialville because there was already a Dial in the state. The post office and store closed in 1886, and the place remained a flag stop on the railroad until 1897, when John Thomas Bailey opened a store and the post office was reopened. A Dialville school was established in 1899. Around 1900 C. D. Jarrett, one of the pioneers of the East Texas tomato industry, moved to Dialville and developed the town into a shipping point for tomatoes, peaches, and other produce. By 1915 the community had a population of 400, two churches, a school, a bank, and a weekly newspaper, the Dialville *News.* Around 1916 L. E. Scott opened a theater and published another newspaper, the Dialville *Reporter.* During the late 1920s the town began to decline; the population fell to 200 by the early 1930s, and many of the stores and other businesses were forced to close. The school was consolidated with the Jacksonville schools in 1959, and by the late 1980s only two churches and a single store remained at the site of Dialville.

BIBLIOGRAPHY: *Cherokee County History* (Jacksonville, Texas: Cherokee County Historical Commission, 1986). Hattie Joplin Roach, *A History of Cherokee County* (Dallas: Southwest, 1934). Marker Files, Texas Historical Commission, Austin.

Christopher Long

DIAMOND, GEORGE WASHINGTON (1835–1911). George Washington Diamond, journalist, Confederate soldier, and politician, one of six brothers who immigrated to Texas before the Civil War,qv was born on December 26, 1835, in De Kalb County, Georgia, son of James and Nancy Diamond. He moved to Texas shortly after receiving a law degree in 1857 from Albany (now New York) University. He settled first in Rusk County, where he became copublisher of the Henderson *Times.* When the Civil War began Diamond sold his interest in the newspaper and enlisted as a private on May 7, 1861, in Company B of Co. Elkanah Greer'sqv Third Texas Cavalry regiment.

Near the end of 1862 he took leave from his unit to visit his brother James J. Diamondqv at Gainesville. This was only a few weeks after the Great Hanging at Gainesville,qv in which James Diamond and other Confederate loyalists smashed an alleged "peace party conspiracy"qv in north central Texas by convening a "citizens' court" that tried, condemned, and hanged thirty-nine prisoners charged with conspiracy and insurrection against the Confederate state of Texas. George Diamond was asked to use the records of the court to prepare an official account of its work, a manuscript that he apparently completed before the end of 1876. It was not published during his lifetime, but was brought to light many years later by his granddaughter, Mrs. Harry Harlan of Dallas, and was published in 1963 by the Texas State Historical Association.qv

At Gainesville, Diamond transferred to the Eleventh Texas Cavalry, C.S.A., of which his brother James was colonel. He later raised a company of cavalry on the lower Brazos River and fought as a captain in the battles of Mansfield and Pleasant Hill (*see* RED RIVER CAMPAIGN) in 1864.

At the end of the Civil War he returned to Henderson, where he was elected state representative to the Eleventh Texas Legislature. Reconstructionqv prevented this legislature from convening until 1870. Meanwhile, Diamond had moved with his family to Whitesboro, where he spent the remainder of his life. Although he practiced law during Reconstructionqv in the Grayson county seat of Sherman and held several county offices at various times, he was chiefly interested in newspaper work and served for many years on the staff of the Whitesboro *News.* He died at Whitesboro on June 24, 1911, and was buried there.

BIBLIOGRAPHY: Sam Hanna Acheson and Julia Ann Hudson O'Connell, eds., *George Washington Diamond's Account of the Great Hanging at Gainesville, 1862* (Austin: Texas State Historical Association, 1963).

Sam Acheson

DIAMOND, JAMES J. (?–1867). James J. Diamond, secessionist politician and soldier, eldest of six sons born to James and Nancy Diamond in De Kalb County, Georgia, moved to Texas before the Civil War.qv He raised cotton in the Red River Valley and subsequently settled near Whitesboro in Grayson County. He became a leading spokesman for Southern rights and views. He was a delegate from Texas to the 1860 Democratic national convention in Charleston, South Carolina, and, after the nomination of Stephen A. Douglas for president, bolted the convention.

Upon the election of Abraham Lincoln in November 1860 Diamond helped call a public meeting of citizens from Cooke and Grayson counties. The gathering convened at Whitesboro on November 23 and named Diamond chairman of the committee that offered resolutions calling upon Governor Sam Houstonqv "to ascertain the will of the people . . . by convention, or otherwise" on the question of secession.qv As one of the two delegates from Cooke County, he voted with the majority at the Secession Conventionqv to sever the political ties of Texas with the Union. He was appointed a member of the convention's Committee of Public Safety, which served, in effect, as the interim government of Texas until March 2, 1861, when the referendum on the Ordinance of Secession was officially endorsed.

Diamond joined Col. William C. Young'sqv Eleventh Texas Cavalry, organized in July 1861, as a captain, was quickly promoted to lieutenant colonel, and later held the rank of colonel. He was one of the organizers and managers of the "citizens' court" formed in Gainesville in October 1862, which brought to trial and hanged thirty-nine persons accused of participating in the supposed "peace party conspiracy"qv (*see also* GREAT HANGING AT GAINESVILLE). He died in Houston during the yellow fever epidemic of 1867.

BIBLIOGRAPHY: Sam Hanna Acheson and Julia Ann Hudson O'Connell, eds., *George Washington Diamond's Account of the Great Hanging at Gainesville, 1862* (Austin: Texas State Historical Association, 1963). Graham Landrum and Allen Smith, *Grayson County* (Fort Worth, 1960; 2d ed., Fort Worth: Historical Publishers, 1967). Mattie D. Lucas and Mita H. Hall, *A History of Grayson County* (Sherman, Texas, 1936). A. Morton Smith, *The First 100 Years in Cooke County* (San Antonio: Naylor, 1955). E. W. Winkler, ed., *Journal of the Secession Convention of Texas* (Austin, 1912). Sam Acheson

DIAMOND, TEXAS. Diamond was not a town, but rather a group of oilfield buildings and houses located near a Diamond M refinery in southwest Scurry County. The refinery, originally owned by the Lyon Oil Company, in the mid-1970s was operating within the Diamond M oilfield, named for the nearby Diamond M Ranch. Although the oil area remains, no Diamond community appeared on 1980 county maps.

BIBLIOGRAPHY: Hooper Shelton, comp., *From Buffalo . . . to Oil: History of Scurry County, Texas* (Snyder, Texas?: Feather, 1973).
Charles G. Davis

DIAMOND BESSIE MURDER TRIAL. When a well-dressed man and woman calling themselves "A. Monroe and wife" got off the train and registered at the Brooks House in Jefferson on January 19, 1877, events were set in motion that led to the first big-name trial in Texas. A. Monroe was in reality Abraham Rothschild, the son of Meyer Rothschild, a Cincinnati jeweler. He was a traveling salesman for his father's jewelry business. During his travels he had met Bessie Moore at a brothel in Hot Springs, Arkansas, several years before the journey to Jefferson. Bessie was born Annie Stone to a successful shoe dealer in Syracuse, New York, in 1854. According to newspaper accounts, she became the mistress of a man whose last name was Moore when she was fifteen. Although the association did not last long, Bessie did keep the man's name. Articles written after her death alleged that she was a prostitute in Cincinnati, New Orleans, and Hot Springs before meeting Rothschild. Although they traveled together as husband and wife, there is no evidence that they ever married. On January 17, 1877, the couple arrived in Marshall by train and stayed in the Old Capital Hotel for two days, where they registered as A. Rothschild and wife. From Marshall, they rode the train to Jefferson and took a room at the Brooks House under the name Monroe. On the Sunday morning after their arrival, Abe Rothschild bought two lunches for a picnic from Henrique's Restaurant, and the couple were seen disappearing into the fog as they crossed the footbridge over Big Cypress Creek. Abe returned to town that afternoon by another path and was seen casually going about his affairs around town. When asked about his wife, he replied that she was in the country visiting friends and that she would meet him Tuesday morning to leave town. But on Tuesday morning the staff of the Brooks House found room 4 empty and "A. Monroe" gone. Witnesses later stated that Rothschild had left town alone on Tuesday morning on the eastbound train with the couple's luggage.

A week of snow and bad weather followed this, and after it began to warm up, Sarah King found the body of a well-dressed woman, without jewelry, near a twisted oak, while out looking for firewood. The remnants of a picnic lunch were also found near the tree. The coroner ruled that the woman died due to a gunshot wound in the head. The citizens of Jefferson took up a collection and buried the unidentified body at Oakwood Cemetery. An initial warrant was issued for the arrest of A. Monroe on suspicion of murder. After determining that Monroe had left on an eastbound train and that in Marshall he and Bessie had registered as A. Rothschild and wife from Cincinnati, Ohio, a new warrant was issued for Abraham Rothschild of Cincinnati, and the victim was identified as Bessie Moore. Meanwhile, in Cincinnati, Rothschild had been drinking heavily and swore someone was following him, after which he walked into the street and attempted to kill himself, but only succeeded in blinding his right eye. While he was in the hospital he was arrested, and Texas and Marion County officials were sent to Cincinnati in order to identify and extradite him. Rothschild's family put up a fight, but on March 19 extradition was approved.

The trial became very notorious. Most of the lawyers in East Texas tried to become involved either on the side of the state for prestige or on the defense for the money to be provided by the Rothschilds. The governor of Texas personally sent a letter to two attorneys, Campbell and Epperson, appealing for aid with the prosecution, and two Texas assistant attorney generals were involved. The defense had an impressive array of legal talent including a future governor of Texas, Charles A. Culberson,qv and a United States senator, David B. Culberson,qv among other legal minds who undoubtedly were paid very well for their efforts. With the lawyers in place a series of indictments, trials, and appeals set forth, and a legal battle began that took 2½ years to conclude. The first trial did not begin until December 1878 for several reasons: both sides filed a writ of habeas corpus, the lawyers were involved in state and national legislatures, and the defense moved for a change of venue. After three weeks of testimony with the closing arguments alone lasting three days, the jury found Rothschild guilty of murder in the first degree and sentenced him to death by hanging. Tradition says that during jury deliberation over the verdict, jury foreman C. R. Weathersby drew a noose on the wall, signed it, and stated that that was his verdict. After the sentencing, the defense appealed to the Seventh Texas Court of Appeals and Judge J. Clarke for reversal of the case on the grounds that the trial had been unfair. Clarke found that the trial had indeed been unfair and that the court had been in error in ignoring a motion by the defense and by accepting a potential juror after the man stated that he had an opinion in the case. The judge declared a mistrial.

The state issued another indictment against Rothschild on December 2, 1880, and the second trial began on December 14 in Jefferson. The jury was whittled down from the 156 men initially summoned to the requisite twelve, two of whom were black—an unusual occurrence in Texas at the time. The defense focused on the testimony of Isabelle Gouldy, one of the women who had prepared the body of the victim for burial, who claimed to have seen the victim in the company of a man who was not the defendant on Saturday, January 20, and on Thursday, January 25. Although the prosecution attacked Gouldy's credibility, the defense managed to plant a seed of doubt in the jurors' minds. Also, Rothschild's lawyers argued that the body was too well preserved to have been in the woods for fifteen days and that the murder must therefore have happened after their client left town. The strategy worked. On December 30, 1880, the jury found Rothschild not guilty.

There the actualities of the case ended and the rumors began. Many stories about the case and Rothschild circulated during and after the trial, and some of them became part of the folklore surrounding the trial. Several rumors concerning the jury were heard. It was said, for instance, that twelve $1,000 bills were lowered into the jury room during deliberations, and that all twelve jurors met violent deaths within a year of the trial. The rumor that a hack was waiting outside the door of the courthouse and that the verdict was not announced until after the train whistle blew has not been substantiated; nor has the rumor that Rothschild was later imprisoned on a twenty-year sentence for grand theft. The popular rumor that Bessie was pregnant when she died has also never been proved. In the 1890s a handsome, elderly man wearing a patch over his right eye asked to be shown the grave of Bessie Moore. Upon seeing it, he laid roses on it, knelt in prayer, commented on the goodness of the citizens to provide a decent burial, and gave the caretaker money for the care of the grave. Folklore asserts that this was a repentant Rothschild visiting the grave. In the 1930s a headstone mysteriously appeared on the grave where none had been before, and in the 1960s the Jessie Allen Wise Garden Club built an iron fence around the grave. In 1941, E. B. McDonald admitted putting up the headstone because it had not seemed right for Diamond Bessie to sleep in an unmarked grave. Thus ended at least one mystery surrounding the case. The case, still officially listed as unsolved, attracts many investigators and lawyers to this day. Furthermore, since 1955 a courtroom drama relating the story has been presented each spring as part of the Jefferson Historic Pilgrimage.

BIBLIOGRAPHY: Willie Mims Dean, *Jefferson, Texas: Queen of the Cypress* (Dallas: Mathis, Van Nort, 1953). Mrs. Arch McKay and Mrs. H. A. Spellings, *A History of Jefferson* (Jefferson, Texas, 1936). Traylor Russell, *The Diamond Bessie Murder and Rothschild Trials* (Waco: Texian Press, 1971). Fred Tarpley, *Jefferson: Riverport to the Southwest* (Austin: Eakin Press, 1983). Mahlon L. Walters, "Who Done It to Whom: Rothschild in Retrospective," *Texas Bar Journal*, February 1963.

Walter F. Pilcher

DIAMOND M MUSEUM. The Diamond M Museum, in Snyder, Scurry County, originated as the private collection of numerous paintings and other art pieces purchased by Evelyn L. and Clarence T. McLaughlin[qv] over the years, beginning with their honeymoon trip to Europe in 1921. The museum was essentially an outgrowth of their interest in art and their desire to share it with others. Evelyn McLaughlin in 1921 started collecting music boxes and crystal glasses, among other things. In 1936 she and her husband bought their first oil painting, *The Rancher's Daughter,* by Philip R. Goodwin. At that time they were not affluent and thus had no thought of assembling a collection, but over the ensuing years it became apparent that their home could not contain the growing number of valuable art treasures. Accordingly in 1949 the McLaughlins established the Diamond M Foundation, using oil royalties gleaned from their Diamond M Ranch properties. The foundation was to offer financial assistance in various charitable and philanthropic activities and was also to develop and support a museum to house their collection for viewing by the public.

On April 1, 1964, the Diamond M Museum, housed at McLaughlin's Diamond M Building in Snyder, was formally opened. Some 200 art enthusiasts and civic, business, and education leaders from various West Texas cities were on hand for the opening ceremonies. The guests of honor were artist Peter Hurd[qv] and his wife, Henrietta Wyeth Hurd. The Lubbock *Avalanche-Journal*[qv] hailed the museum as a cultural landmark that made it easier for people in remote West Texas areas to view prime examples of both eastern and western art and crafts. Initially the public exhibition galleries covered only the first floor of the Diamond M Building, but additional galleries were gradually added to the second floor beginning in June 1969. The museum saw a record number of visitors on March 12, 1967, when Peter Hurd's widely publicized portrait of President Lyndon B. Johnson,[qv] which Johnson had rejected, was shown just before it was moved to the Smithsonian Institution for permanent display.

The Diamond M Museum collection reflected the varied collecting interests of the McLaughlin family. Over the years they bought paintings by Frederic Remington, Charles M. Russell, W. H. D. Koerner, Peter Hurd, Manuel Acosta,[qv] and Frank B. Hoffman. One gallery displayed some seventeen works by N. C. Wyeth, Hurd's father-in-law and one of America's foremost impressionist artists and illustrators. The collection also included an original watercolor, *Winter Apples,* by Wyeth's son, Andrew. Other art treasures in the collection included prints by Currier & Ives, bronze sculptures by George Phippen, Charles M. Russell, Frederic Remington, and James Earle Fraser; carved ivory and jade; and soapstone pieces created by Eskimo artists in Canada. The museum also had changing exhibits by contemporary artists. During the 1960s McLaughlin often gave rising young artists opportunities to show at the museum and also bought works from them.

After the death of Evelyn McLaughlin in 1971 and that of her husband four years later, the foundation's responsibilities were carried on by its board of trustees, which included the McLaughlin heirs. In 1981 a contract was drawn up with Western Texas College to administer the museum through the Scurry County Museum, with funds provided by the foundation, which also continued to acquire art. The contract included provisions for professional staffing of the museum, which spurred a higher number of changing exhibitions. These temporary exhibitions, some organized by the staff and others borrowed from outside institutions, used themes reflecting the variety of the museum's collections and, along with the permanent exhibitions, provided opportunities for increased public education programs. In 1983 the museum initiated traveling exhibitions of its own works and circulated them to other museums and galleries throughout Texas. In 1992 the Diamond M Museum closed, and the collection was given to the Texas Tech Museum in Lubbock.

BIBLIOGRAPHY: Aline Parks, "C. T. (Mr. Mac) McLaughlin—Rancher, Oilman, Art Collector, and Philanthropist," ed. Ernest Wallace (Lubbock: Ranching Heritage Center, 1977). Scurry County Book Committee, *Footprints across Scurry County* (Lubbock: Specialty, 1984). Vertical Files, Barker Texas History Center, University of Texas at Austin.

H. Allen Anderson

DIAMOND SHAMROCK. Diamond Shamrock was one of the major oil-refining and marketing companies in Texas in 1993, with more than 6,000 employees and over $2.5 billion in revenue. It traces its origins back to three companies: Diamond Alkali, Shamrock Oil and Gas, and Sigmor Corporation. A group of glass manufacturers founded Diamond Alkali in Pittsburgh, Pennsylvania, in 1910 to produce soda ash, an important component in the glass industry. A large industrial plant was built at Painesville, Ohio, in 1912, and in the 1920s, under the leadership of T. R. Evans, Diamond Alkali developed into an important chemical company. It diversified into the production of calcium carbonates, coke, cement, chlorine, and a variety of other products. Under the presidency of T. R.'s son, Ray Evans, the company moved to decentralize after World War II.[qv] In 1946, in Deer Park, Houston, Texas, construction was started on a new plant to produce chlorine and caustic soda. Diamond Alkali changed its headquarters from Pittsburgh to Cleveland, Ohio, in 1948. A third plant was erected in Muscle Shoals, Alabama, in the 1950s, and Diamond Alkali further extended its range of products into plastics and agricultural chemicals. In the 1960s the company opened another facility in Delaware City, Delaware, and purchased several additional chemical companies, including the Chemical Process Company of Redwood City, California, and the Nopco Chemical Company of New Jersey. In spite of its growth, Diamond Alkali feared absorption by a larger chemical firm or by one of the major oil conglomerates, and in 1967 it merged with Shamrock Oil and Gas of Amarillo to increase its corporate strength.

The second progenitor of Diamond Shamrock, the Shamrock Oil and Gas Company, was founded on August 9, 1929, by John Sheerin, who named the company for a symbol of his native Ireland. The company was headquartered in Amarillo and financed by the Fownes family of Pennsylvania. In its early years Shamrock Oil and Gas lost some $9 million. Its first refinery was built in 1933 at Sunray, in Moore County, Texas, and that same year the company opened its first gas station, also at Sunray. In 1938 James Harold Dunn,qv a young engineer at the Lone Star Gas Corporation, joined Shamrock Oil and Gas as vice president and general manager, and the next year the company made its first small profit. In 1939–40 Shamrock and the Lone Star Gas Corporation jointly built a plant at Murchison in Henderson County to recycle natural gas. By 1941 there were 162 Shamrock service stations in the southwestern states. During the mid-1940s Shamrock became a major producer of natural gas. The company paid its first dividend in 1943, and was listed on the New York Stock Exchange in 1944. Dunn became company president in 1945 and served in that post for ten years; he was succeeded by C. A. Cash in 1955. In 1959 Shamrock opened its first catalytic cracking unit at the McKee complex at Sunray.

In 1960 Shamrock Oil and Gas increased the number of stations using its gasoline by purchasing much of the Sigmor chain of service stations—the third major component of the modern Diamond Shamrock Corporation. Sigfried (Sig) Moore operated the Midway chain of stations in the 1930s and 1940s. When, in 1943, Moore loaned one of his employees, Thomas E. Turner, the money to start up a business of his own, Turner adopted the name Sigmor for the chain of stores he built up in the 1940s and 1950s. Sigmor was incorporated in 1952, then restructured in 1959 so that each station could incorporate individually. Most of the Sigmor chain was purchased in 1960 by Shamrock, which then leased it back to Turner, who continued to run it. In the 1960s Shamrock expanded its production facilities at McKee and constructed pipelines throughout the Southwest.

In 1967 Shamrock Oil and Gas Company and Diamond Alkali merged to form the Diamond Shamrock Corporation. At the time of the merger, the products of the company were about 20 percent oil and gas and 80 percent chemical. The company expanded its oil and gas exploration efforts in the early 1970s and built several new chemical plants, including the Battleground plant in Houston. In 1978 the company headquarters were moved to Dallas. That same year Sigmor purchased its stations back from Diamond Shamrock, though it continued to market Diamond Shamrock products. In 1980 Diamond Shamrock employed some 12,400 people in thirty-seven countries and was a leader in energy, technology, and chemical markets.

In January 1983, Sigmor, by then one of the largest independent service-station chains in the country, merged with Diamond Shamrock. Diamond Shamrock acquired some 600 retail outlets by the merger, as well as the Three Rivers oil refinery, constructed by Sigmor in the mid-1970s in Live Oak County midway between San Antonio and Corpus Christi. In 1987 the Diamond Shamrock Refining and Marketing Company was separated from Diamond Shamrock Corporation, the parent company, and became an independent company headquartered in San Antonio. As part of the same reorganization, Diamond Shamrock Corporation changed its name to Maxus Energy Corporation, and severed all legal ties to Diamond Shamrock Refining and Marketing Company. In 1990 Diamond Shamrock Refining and Marketing Company, Incorporated, simplified its name to Diamond Shamrock, Incorporated. In 1993 Diamond Shamrock operated two major petroleum-refinery complexes: the Three Rivers plant and the McKee complex at Sunray. The two complexes had a combined capacity of nearly 200,000 barrels a day. An extensive network of some 4,400 miles of company-owned pipelines connected the refineries to supply points and markets in Texas, Colorado, New Mexico, and Oklahoma. Some 2,000 outlets carried the Diamond Shamrock brand, including 776 company-operated Corner Stores in Texas, Colorado, Louisiana, and New Mexico.

BIBLIOGRAPHY: J. Evetts Haley, *Story of the Shamrock* (Amarillo: Shamrock Oil and Gas Corporation, 1954).

Mark Odintz

DIAMOND TAIL RANCH. The Diamond Tail brand was first used in the late 1860s, when Mose Dameron of Jack County began running cattle on land now in De Baca and Roosevelt counties, New Mexico. In 1870, however, Dameron sold it, along with his herd, to the brothers Jim C. and William R. Curtisqv in Jack County. After securing a government contract to supply beef to the Fort Reno and Fort Sill Indian reservations, the Curtises were allowed to graze their herd along Cache Creek near Fort Sill. When the contract expired, the brothers established their first Diamond Tail headquarters, on the Big Wichita River in Clay County, near Cambridge. To this range they drove from the Indian Territory 13,000 cattle in one herd, the largest trail drive ever reported in Northwest Texas. Soon the range was crowded. After his brother's death Bill Curtis formed a new partnership with Tom J. Atkinson. In 1878 they moved the Diamond Tail herd north to Groesbeck Creek, near the site of what is now Quanah, and set up a headquarters built from native stone.

Even then, Curtis had already cast eyes on the Panhandleqv and its abundant grasslands; early in 1879 Dave Bowers drove the first of the Diamond Tail cattle to a new pasture in southeastern Childress County. A small rock-walled dugoutqv in the shelter of a bluff at the mouth of Gypsum Creek served as his headquarters, though it later became part of the Shoe Nail Ranch.qv A drift fence (*see* PANHANDLE DRIFT FENCES) was erected fifteen miles to the south and extended west to the site of Parnell, in Hall County. Later, Curtis moved his headquarters to Doe Creek in Collingsworth County, near the creek's junction with Buck Creek. There he and his men occupied a two-room shack with a kitchen nearby. They built dugouts and picket shacks as line camps on various sections of the Diamond Tail range, which at its peak covered portions of Childress, Collingsworth, Donley, Hall, and Greer counties. A supply store was maintained at the headquarters to sell to bullwhackers freighting north from Gainesville, and a stage stand was established there when a stage line from Wichita Falls to Mobeetie started. The Diamond Tail headquarters, at a site four miles north of the place where Memphis was later established, soon became known as Six-Shooter Camp or Pistol Palace, after one of the ranch employees, Scott (Six-Shooter) Ferguson. Bob Butterworth served as ranch bookkeeper, and other notable cowboys included John Dodson, Sam Bean, George Lewis (Tex) Rickard,qv Town (Timberleg) Embree, John Maddox, and Jim (Pie-Biter) Baker. Pat Wolfarth, Hall county sheriff, served also as foreman of the Diamond Tail until he shot Eugene de Bauerenfiend, publisher of the *Hall County Herald*, at Memphis on August 10, 1891. Wolfarth was later tried and given a fifteen-year prison sentence for second-degree murder, but Curtis subsequently obtained a pardon for him from Governor Charles A. Culberson.qv In the meantime, George Wilks succeeded Wolfarth as range boss.

Unlike many large Panhandle ranches, the Diamond Tail was never sold out to British capital during the height of the "Beef Bonanza." After the Fort Worth and Denver City Railway built through in 1887, the stage stand was discontinued, and the town of Giles became the Diamond Tail's leading shipping point and social center. In the lean years of the late 1880s, the ranch went bankrupt. It was then put into the hands of a receiver, Sam Lazarus, who within a few years put the enterprise back on a sound footing. The Diamond Tail herd was saved from the terrible blizzard of February 11, 1893, when Curtis cut his fences to let the cattle drift southward. To build up the blood of the Diamond Tail herd Curtis and Atkinson purchased fine cattle from Charles Goodnight[qv] of the JA Ranch.[qv] Throughout the peak years the partners branded from 10,000 to 15,000 calves and ran average herds of 60,000 head. From 1890 to 1895 nesters[qv] came to the ranch to claim school sections, with the result that the Diamond Tail reduced its operations, sold its cows, and operated as a steer ranch only. Curtis began moving his cattle to Chavez County, New Mexico, after 1895, keeping only 16,000 acres in Hall and Donley counties for blooded stock and a few fine bulls purchased from Charles W. Armour of Kansas City. Bill Curtis's oldest son, Jim, went with his bride to New Mexico to manage the Diamond Tails there; he gathered a large herd by buying out the DZ, the 9R, and other ranches. It took over two years to receive and brand all the cattle then belonging to the ranch. Jim Curtis and his brothers continued ranching in New Mexico for some time. Bill Curtis was accidentally killed in December 1901, and his heirs retained interest in twenty-five sections of Panhandle property until 1905, when they sold the land to John M. Browder. Browder, who continued the Diamond Tail brand, later divided the ranch among his children. In the 1970s his heirs were still using the brand.

BIBLIOGRAPHY: Virginia Browder, *Donley County: Land O' Promise* (Wichita Falls, Texas: Nortex, 1975). Gus L. Ford, ed., *Texas Cattle Brands* (Dallas: Cockrell, 1936). Laura V. Hamner, *Short Grass and Longhorns* (Norman: University of Oklahoma Press, 1943).

H. Allen Anderson

DIANA, TEXAS. Diana, also known as New Diana, is at the junction of State Highway 154 and U.S. Highway 259, eleven miles east of Gilmer in eastern Upshur County. New Diana was established in the 1930s by residents of Diana (also known as Old Diana) after oil was discovered three miles south of the old town. In the mid-1930s New Diana had a school, a church, a store, and a number of houses. The town continued to prosper after World War II,[qv] and by the mid-1960s, when it was generally referred to as Diana, it included two churches, a school, and three or four stores. In 1990 Diana was a commercial center for area farmers and ranchers; at that time it had an estimated 200 residents and a dozen or so businesses.

Christopher Long

DIAZ, RAFAELO (1883–1943). Rafaelo Diaz, operatic tenor, was born in San Antonio, Texas, on May 16, 1883, the son of Rafaelo and Rosa (Umscheid) Diaz. He was baptized Francisco Rafael Diaz but as an adult changed his name to Rafaelo Diaz. He received his early schooling at the German English School and the West Texas Military Academy.[qqv] Diaz showed musical talent at an early age and began his career as a pianist under the guidance of one of San Antonio's pioneer music teachers, Miss Amalia Hander. After his promising voice was discovered while he was studying at the Stern Conservatory in Berlin, he went on to Italy to study under famous Italian maestro Vincenzo Sabatini. He returned to America and made his debut in the Boston Opera Company's production of Giuseppe Verdi's *Otello*. In 1917 he joined the Metropolitan Opera Company and performed leading tenor roles in Jules Massenet's *Thaïs* and Nikolai Rimski-Korsakov's *Le Coq d'Or*. His stage presence and magnetic personality, along with his lyric tenor voice, kept him with the Metropolitan until 1936. He then toured the country with the Scotti Opera Company, making several stops in his home town of San Antonio along the way. In his spare time he made records for a leading phonograph company. He also conducted a series of concerts at the Waldorf–Astoria. Critics praised Diaz for his smooth performance, the depth and richness of his voice, the clarity of his enunciation, and the beauty of his phrasing. Diaz, who sang in English, French, Spanish, Italian, and German, was known as the "Lone Star Tenor of the Lone Star State." He never married. He died of a cerebral hemorrhage in New York on December 12, 1943.

BIBLIOGRAPHY: Vertical Files, Barker Texas History Center, University of Texas at Austin.

Jeremy Roberts

DÍAZ DE LEÓN, JOSÉ ANTONIO (1786/87–1834). José Antonio Díaz de León, the last Franciscan missionary in prerepublic Texas, was born in Mexico either in late 1786 or early 1787. He became a friar in 1811 and was admitted as a cleric in 1812 to the College of Nuestra Señora de Guadalupe de Zacatecas,[qv] which at the time administered all Franciscan missions in Texas. In 1815, after being ordained to the priesthood, Díaz de León began his missionary career in Nuevo Santander (present Tamaulipas). After being assigned to Texas in 1816 he took charge of Nuestra Señora del Refugio Mission in 1817. In 1818 he conducted a census at Refugio that showed 164 persons, not distinguished in the report by ethnic origin, living at the mission pueblo. This population was, however, soon decimated. In 1820 Díaz de León became resident minister of San José y San Miguel de Aguayo Mission in the outskirts of Bexar (San Antonio) and was appointed ad interim president of all the Texas missions. During his tenure at San José he took charge of the spiritual care of Indian and Spanish settlers at four partially secularized missions in the neighborhood of San Antonio. He also served briefly as chaplain of the presidio at Goliad and acted as assistant pastor of the church of San Fernando (later San Fernando de Béxar Cathedral[qv]) during the long absence of its parish priest, José Refugio de la Garza,[qv] who represented the province as a delegate in Mexico City.

Fray Miguel Muro succeeded Díaz de León at Refugio, where fierce Comanche attacks soon brought about the virtual disintegration of the mission. Díaz de León applied to Governor Antonio María Martínez[qv] for military protection for Refugio, or for permission to remove at least the sacred objects to La Bahía. After Mexican independence, the new governor, José Félix Trespalacios,[qv] donated fifty pesos to Refugio Mission and promised help, but the desperate situation did not change.

Unknown to Díaz de León, Father Garza recommended and obtained legislation for the final secularization of the Texas missions in 1823. Díaz de León, as acting president, received the order to transfer the missions but declined to comply without instructions from his superiors in Zacatecas. This was the first in a series of delays and requests for modification of the decree that Díaz de León presented to the government over the next seven years. While seeking exemptions for Espíritu Santo and Refugio missions on the basis that the mission Indians still needed protection, the Franciscan had to surrender the San Antonio missions to the Diocese of Monterrey, Nuevo León, on February 29, 1824.

Because of continuing Comanche depredations, Refugio Mission was officially abandoned that summer by order of the political chief, José Antonio Saucedo.[qv] But Díaz de León was determined to save the mission and did not give up. He also became the representative of twelve or thirteen Aranama Indian families who claimed right to the mission lands of Espíritu Santo, a move opposed by the ayuntamiento[qv] of La Bahía.[qv] By that time white colonists, who had been settling the coastal area traditionally considered Indian territory, were causing population displacements in the region. Indians from Refugio Mission, now roaming wild, apparently joined other coastal Indians in harassing the colonists. Armed confrontations ensued. Muro and Díaz de León secured a peace treaty between Stephen F. Austin[qv] and the Karankawas, but shortly afterwards hostility continued. The Mexican government became convinced that it was wise to support the rehabilitation of Refugio in order to keep the Indians out of trouble. Díaz de León used the opportunity to make a detailed analysis of the Indian situation in the area and listed the specific needs of Refugio Mission under such conditions. In 1825, while considering a request from the people of Nacogdoches to become their pastor, the missionary moved to Espíritu Santo. He did not wait for government help but set out with Muro to the wilderness in order to gather scattered mission Indians. Refugio was reestablished, and Muro resumed his ministry there, though without much success.

In 1826 Zacatecas officially named Díaz de León president of the Texas missions. The college also granted his request to trade a mission bell to the new town of Victoria for items useful to the Indians under his care at Espíritu Santo. The Franciscan—described by a contemporary French observer as "an industrious, disinterested man, adored by the indigenes"—continued against all odds, by pastoral visitations, to serve the spiritual needs of the whole region for three more years. The question of how to distribute the mission lands turned more complicated because settlers and empresarios coveted them. The town of Goliad (as La Bahía was renamed in 1829) obtained from the state government a new decree to enforce secularization of the missions on March 6, 1829. Díaz de León, upon receiving the order, went to San Antonio to argue once more for delays, conceding Espíritu Santo but requesting exemption at least for Refugio. Having finally lost the case of the Aranama families a few months before, he knew that secularization would result in depriving mission Indians of their land. He gathered a number of Aranamas, as well as some Karankawas and Cocos, and took them to El Oso, ten miles below Goliad on the San Antonio River. He tried to encourage them to farm in common there and live according to a modified mission routine. He took whatever he could from Espíritu Santo and gave it to them. But because the town protested the presence of the Indians in their neighborhood the experiment had to end. The Franciscan finally decided to comply with the secularization decree. He made an inventory and then, on February 8, 1830, surrendered the last remaining missions. The mission lands, as he had expected, were soon made available to colonists.

Under the jurisdiction of the see of Nuevo León the friar was assigned a parish post in Nacogdoches. The College of Zacatecas received an anonymous letter written in Latin by a Catholic empresario[qv] in Texas warning the superiors not to let missionaries move to Anglo settlements beyond the Colorado River because of danger to them. Díaz de León, refusing to believe the warning and showing no fear, accepted the risk and went to Nacogdoches. There he found the church being used as a barracks by the troops of Col. José de las Piedras,[qv] who had quartered them there since the Fredonian Rebellion[qv] of 1827. The friar rented a house as a temporary chapel but was eventually evicted when he could not pay. He organized a "piety board" (*junta de piedad*) intended to solicit private donations for the construction of a new church and school. Eager to help in civic activities, he became a member of the town's health board, established to combat smallpox. He also began signing the official reports of all births, baptisms, marriages, and deaths. Using Nacogdoches as home base, he undertook pastoral visitations throughout the whole district. He approached Indian, Hispanic, and Anglo alike. His English, however, was very poor, and he had little success with most Anglo colonists, who were willing to be only nominal Catholics in order to comply with the Mexican colonization law. The Anglos would have preferred someone like English-speaking Father Michael Muldoon,[qv] who had been performing token Catholic marriages in the Austin colony, thus producing scores of the nominal Catholics who came to be called "Muldoon Catholics." It was difficult to discern at the time who among the colonists was Catholic by conviction. A case in point is Sam Houston,[qv] baptized by Díaz de León at the house of Adolphus Sterne,[qv] a common friend, in 1833.

The Anglo-Hispanic polarity was reaching a dangerous level of tension in East Texas by 1834. Stephen F. Austin, who had been privately writing bitter condemnations of the Catholic Church in general and missionary friars in particular, was being held in jail without trial in Mexico, to the dismay of the colonists. After the Mexican government passed a national law of religious toleration that suddenly released Protestant colonists from their pretensions to Catholicism, the presence of Díaz de León, a pious and dedicated Mexican missionary, came to be resented in Nacogdoches. He received several death threats and learned that someone had been paid to assassinate him. After performing a marriage ceremony near Liberty (Liberty County), he wrote a moving farewell letter to friends and enemies, knowing that his end was near. On November 4, 1834, he was shot on his way back to Nacogdoches, in the vicinity of St. Augustine. At the moment of death he was kneeling, as if in prayer. He was the thirty-first, and last, Zacatecan missionary to die in Texas. Some Mexicans living in the area, convinced that Díaz de León and five other citizens had been murdered, sent a report to Gen. Martín Perfecto de Cos,[qv] who allocated 300 soldiers under Col. Domingo de Ugartechea[qv] to impose order in the Eastern District. Meanwhile, the official investigation of the Franciscan's death dragged for a few months until an inquiry concluded that the missionary had grown so frightened of being killed that he killed himself. Catholic historians regard this judgment as a calumny against a priest-martyr, whereas Protestant ones favor a verdict of suicide. It would at least have been impolitic for a court of inquiry staffed by colonists to return a verdict of murder. In 1926 a German, Robert Streit, published a historical novel on Díaz de León, *Der letzte Franziskaner von Texas*; the work remains untranslated. *See also* FRANCISCANS, CATHOLIC CHURCH, CATHOLIC DIOCESAN CHURCH OF SPANISH AND MEXICAN TEXAS.

BIBLIOGRAPHY: Jean Louis Berlandier, *Journey to Mexico during the Years 1826 to 1834* (Austin: Texas State Historical Association, 1980). Bexar Archives, Barker Texas History Center, University of Texas at Austin. Carlos E. Castañeda, *Our Catholic Heritage in Texas* (7 vols., Austin: Von Boeckmann–Jones, 1936–58; rpt., New York: Arno, 1976). Catholic Archives of Texas, Files, Austin. Marion A. Habig, "Mission San José y San Miguel de Aguayo," *Southwestern Historical Quarterly* 71 (April 1968). William H. Oberste, *History of Refugio Mission* (Refugio, Texas: Refugio Timely Remarks, 1942). William H. Oberste, *Our Lady Comes to Refugio* (Corpus Christi: Jones, 1944). Antonio López de Santa Anna et al., *The Mexican Side of the Texan Revolution*, trans. Carlos E. Castañeda (Dallas: Turner, 1928; 2d ed., Austin: Graphic Ideas, 1970). David J. Weber, *The Mexican Frontier, 1821–1846* (Albuquerque: University of New Mexico Press, 1982).

Aníbal A. González

DIBOLL, TEXAS. Diboll, on U.S. Highway 59 three miles north of the Neches River in southern Angelina County, was founded in 1894 when Thomas Lewis Latane Temple[qv] built a sawmill on the Houston, East and West Texas Railway. Temple came to East Texas in 1893, purchased 7,000 acres of pine timberland from J. C. Diboll, and began operation of his sawmill at Diboll in June 1894 under the name Southern Pine Lumber Company. By 1908 Temple had added a second sawmill at Diboll and enlarged his timberland holdings to 209,313 acres. In its early days Diboll was a company town. Many of its homes, built from lumber produced by the Southern Pine mills, were owned by the lumber company and rented to employees. Between the early 1900s and the 1950s the lumber company also maintained a large commissary, which included a drugstore, a post office, a grocery, and a feed store. Adjoining were doctors' offices, the railroad station, and lumber company offices. Diboll received a post office in 1897 with William P. Rutland as postmaster. The town's first school opened in 1894.

The Great Depression[qv] of the 1930s saw Southern Pine Lumber Company sell about 100,000 acres of its holdings to the United States government for less than three dollars an acre to keep its sawmill working. Many Diboll employees repaid the loyalty the company had shown them by lending Southern Pine small sums of money they had saved during good years. Diboll remained largely a typical sawmill settlement until 1948, when Arthur Temple, Jr., a grandson of T. L. L. Temple, arrived to become manager and vice president of Southern Pine Lumber Company. When his father died three years later, he became president of the company. Temple used his influence and wealth to sell many of the company-owned houses to the townspeople and encouraged the building of private homes. He provided Diboll with a medical clinic, ambulance service, improved streets, a new fire station, and new homes. A shopping center replaced the old town commissary in the 1950s, a new bank was opened, school improvements were made, a radio station began broadcasting, and later a library was built. In 1962 the town was incorporated, with Clyde Thompson as the first mayor. Temple's policies were based on his recognition that company and town are interdependent and that the health of both depends upon conservation of the forests.

In 1984 the population was 5,500. Diboll remained a community economically oriented toward forest products such as lumber, plywood, flooring, treated timber, handles, and resins. In 1973 the town became the corporate headquarters for Temple Eastex, Incorporated, one of the nation's largest forest-product companies and a descendant of the old Southern Pine Lumber Company operations. The population of Diboll in 1990 was 4,341. *See also* LUMBER INDUSTRY.

BIBLIOGRAPHY: Angelina County Historical Survey Committee, *Land of the Little Angel: A History of Angelina County, Texas,* ed. Bob Bowman (Lufkin, Texas, 1976). Megan Biesele, *The Cornbread Whistle* (Lufkin, Texas: Diboll Historical Society, 1987). Bob Bowman, *The Towns We Left Behind* (Diboll, Texas: Angelina Free Press, 1972). Paul Burka, "The King of the Forest," *Texas Monthly,* August 1982. Laurence C. Walker, *Axes, Oxen, and Men: A Pictorial History of the Southern Pine Lumber Company* (Diboll, Texas: Angelina Free Press, 1975).
Bob Bowman

DIBRELL, JOSEPH BURTON (1855–1934). Joseph Burton Dibrell, lawyer and politician, was born on December 1, 1855, in Whitley County, Kentucky, to J. B. and Margaret (Brawner) Dibrell. The family moved to Seguin, Texas, in December 1857. Dibrell attended the common schools of Guadalupe County before entering Emory and Henry College in Virginia, where he graduated in 1879. After returning to Seguin, he taught school for ten months and began studying law. He was admitted to the bar at Seguin in May 1882 and soon gained prominence as a lawyer and as a leader in the state Democratic party.qv Dibrell served as state senator from the Twenty-first District from 1894 to 1902. He was president pro tem of the Senate in 1897 and associate justice of the Texas Supreme Court from 1911 until 1913, when he resumed the practice of law in Seguin. He married Mollie E. Fennel of Seguin on June 21, 1882, and they had four children. After his first wife's death in 1898, he married Ella Peyton Dancy of Austin. They had three children before her death in 1920. Dibrell died at Seguin on April 11, 1934, and was buried in San Geronimo Cemetery.

BIBLIOGRAPHY: Austin *American,* April 12, 1934. Lewis E. Daniell, *Personnel of the Texas State Government, with Sketches of Representative Men of Texas* (Austin: City Printing, 1887; 3d ed., San Antonio: Maverick, 1892). E. H. Loughery, *Texas State Government* (Austin: McLeod and Jackson, 1897). Niel John McArthur, *The Twenty-seventh Legislature and State Administration of Texas* (Austin: Ben C. Jones, 1901).
W. W. White

DICEY, TEXAS. Dicey is on a spur off Farm Road 730 eight miles northeast of Weatherford in northeastern Parker County. The first settlers moved near the present site of Dicey in the mid to late 1850s. This group established one of the earliest churches in Parker County, and a community developed around it. Originally the settlement was called Power after Parson Power. Later the name Dicey was chosen in honor of the wife of pioneer settler W. G. Puryear. A post office was established there in 1891 and discontinued in 1929. Throughout its history Dicey served area farmers as a church and school community. The population of Dicey was reported at sixty-three from the mid-1920s through the mid-1940s, when it dropped to just over twenty. Dicey still existed in 1990.

BIBLIOGRAPHY: John Clements, *Flying the Colors: Texas, a Comprehensive Look at Texas Today, County by County* (Dallas: Clements Research, 1984).
David Minor

DICK THE DRUMMER (?–?). Dick the Drummer, one of two free blacks who participated in the battle of San Jacinto,qv was a musician. He was a member of the regular infantry who, with three fifers, constituted the Texas army's band. He is credited with confusing the Mexican troops at the battle. Dick served as a drummer during the Mexican War,qv at the battles of Monterrey and Buena Vista. He was described as an older man at a dinner honoring San Jacinto battle veterans in May 1850.

BIBLIOGRAPHY: Harold Schoen, "The Free Negro in the Republic of Texas," *Southwestern Historical Quarterly* 39–41 (April 1936–July 1937). Frank X. Tolbert, *The Day of San Jacinto* (New York: McGraw-Hill, 1959; 2d ed., Austin: Pemberton Press, 1969).
Diana J. Kleiner

DICKENS, TEXAS. Dickens, the county seat of Dickens County, is at the junction of U.S. Highway 82 and State Highway 70, eight miles below the Caprock of the Llano Estacadoqqv and sixty miles east of Lubbock, in the center of the county. It is named after the county. The site of Dickens served as a supply point for dugoutqv line camps used by cowboys from the Spur, Pitchfork, and Matador ranches.qqv In 1886 J. H. Edwards set up a camp in the vicinity and was followed by Charles O'Neal and J. A. Askins, who settled in the area in 1889. As others began moving in, a settlement developed near the springs east of the present townsite, and after the United States Postal Department located a post office there in 1892, the settlement officially became known as Dickens. On February 17, 1892, town lots were sold a half mile west of the previous settlement, and during the year Dickens replaced Espuela as the county seat. By 1893 Dickens had a school building, a wagonyard, a blacksmith shop, a saloon, a barbershop, a hotel, and two stores.

The town continued to thrive during the early 1900s; the population increased from 176 in 1900 to its maximum of 500 by 1927. The number of businesses in Dickens remained relatively stable at twenty-five during the 1930s and 1940s. In the 1950s, however, the town lost thirteen of its businesses as well as its school, which was torn down after the district was parceled out to Patton Springs, Spur, and McAdoo. The population, which had been slowly decreasing since the 1940 census, dropped to a low of 259 in 1975 but increased again to 409 in 1980, despite a reduction in the number of businesses. Dickens had nine businesses in 1980. The town remained a marketing center for the surrounding ranches, which include the Pitchfork and Four Sixes.qv The Dickens County Museum is located in the county courthouse. The nearby Croton Breaksqv region offers travelers a scenic view of colorful canyons, buttes, and creeks. In 1990 the population was 322.

BIBLIOGRAPHY: Fred Arrington, *A History of Dickens County: Ranches and Rolling Plains* (Quanah, Texas: Nortex, 1971). Kathleen E. and Clifton R. St. Clair, eds., *Little Towns of Texas* (Jacksonville, Texas: Jayroe Graphic Arts, 1982).
Edloe A. Jenkins

DICKENS COUNTY. Dickens County (B-11), in Northwest Texas, is bordered on the north by Motley County, on the west by Crosby County, on the south by Kent County, and on the east by King County; its center point is 33°38′ north latitude and 100°45′ west longitude fifty miles east of Lubbock. The county was named for J. Dickens, who died at the Alamo. The broken terrain is surfaced by sandy, chocolate, and red soils. Croton and Duck creeks drain the county. The flat northwest part of Dickens County is above the Caprock on the Llano Estacado,[qqv] and the rest, with rolling terrain, is below. The altitude over the county's 931 square miles varies from 2,000 to 3,000 feet. Trees include mesquite, hackberry, and cottonwood. Grasses are blue grama, sideoats, grama, white tidena, vine mesquite, and Indian grass. The average annual rainfall is 20.24 inches. The average minimum temperature in January is 28° F; in July the maximum is 95° F. The growing season is 217 days. Dickens County produces about $21.5 million worth of goods annually, mostly from beef cattle, horses, cotton, wheat, and sorghums. The county has no manufacturing and only a modest amount of oil. Oil production in 1982 was 93,179 barrels, valued at over $3 million. The road network includes U.S. Highway 82 (west to east) and State Highway 70 (north to south).

The Wanderers Who Make Bad Camps Band of the Comanches dominated the region before white settlement. The Comanches became fine horse-mounted warriors and hunters after they adapted their culture to the utilization of Spanish horses in the seventeenth century. The Comanche Indians hunted buffalo[qv] in summer and fall to provide most of their material needs. They met in an informal general assembly to decide the organization of their communal hunts, and war leaders made final decisions. A historian writes, "The buffalo was the lifeblood of Comanche culture; its near-extermination sounded the death knell for the kind of life Comanches had come to know." White hunters cleared the land of buffalo and wild horses in the 1870s, while Colonel Ranald S. MacKenzie's[qv] Fourth United States Cavalry[qv] subdued the Comanches in 1874 and 1875. MacKenzie's base of operations against the Indians was located at Anderson's Fort, also called Soldiers Mound, an army supply camp located near the site of present-day Spur. In 1876 the Texas state legislature formed Dickens County from land previously assigned to Bexar County.

Until the first years of the twentieth century, settlers shunned the area because of its remoteness and slight rainfall. Instead of farms, huge cattle ranches (the Spur, Pitchfork, and Matador[qqv]), took up most of the land. The Spur Ranch was started, for example, in 1878, with 1,900 head of cattle that Jim Hull drove from Refugio County. In 1880 only three homes, a schoolhouse, and twenty-eight people were in the county; most of the residents were apparently ranchhands.

The owners of the Spur, however, attempted to encourage settlement; in 1884, for example, S.W. Lomax, manager of the ranch, conducted an agricultural experiment on company lands. Cheap land—sold at two dollars an acre—inspired settlers like A. J. Hagins, who moved by covered wagon to Dickens County in 1889. Hagins joined other settlers such as W. L. (Bud) Browning, J. L. Gates, the Wilmores, and the Crawfords, and established a farm near old Fort Griffin. Hagins housed his wife and six children in a one-room dug-out.[qv] Wood and water were readily available, and the pioneers grew corn. In 1890 the census counted 295 residents in the county.

In 1890 Hagins planted the first cotton in Dickens County on school land obtained from the state for fifteen cents an acre and 5 percent of the valuation. To avoid the 100-mile haul he had to make to Jones County for ginning of his first crop, Hagins built a gin in 1891. That same year, the county was politically organized, with the town of Espuela (located on land belonging to the Espuela Land and Cattle Company, which now owned the Spur Ranch) initially designated as the county seat. Many of the settlers objected, however, because the Espuela Company refused to turn the townsite over to the county. Of course, the underlying issue was whether the county and its government would exist for the benefit of the company or the nesters who were moving into the area in increasing numbers. The nesters commanded more votes, however, and in 1892 successfully forced an election to challenge the company on the issue. Dickens was subsequently chosen as the county seat, and by 1893 the town had a courthouse, a hotel, two stores, and a wagonyard. By 1900, 197 farms and ranches had been established in the county, and the population had increased to 1,151. About 1,500 acres of county land was planted in corn, about 400 in cotton, and about 16 in wheat. Local farmers also raised poultry; 9,180 fowl of all kinds were counted in Dickens County that year by the United States agricultural census. Meanwhile, the cattle industry continued to dominate the local economy, as almost 58,750 cattle were counted in the county.

Growth in agriculture and population accelerated during the early twentieth century. In 1906 E. P. and S. A. Swenson headed a syndicate to purchase the Spur Ranch and encourage colonization. Under the administration of manager Charles A. Jones, the Spur sold excellent farm acreage to farmers at reasonable prices. The Stamford and Northwestern Railway initiated service in 1909, thus ending the county's isolation and encouraging marketing; that same year, Oran McClure began publishing the *Texas Spur* in Dickens for countywide subscribers. By 1910 there were 349 farms and ranches in Dickens County, and the population had increased to 3,092.

Windmills,[qv] a characteristic landscape feature throughout West Texas, provided water for thirsty livestock, cooling for various purposes, and irrigation for the garden. Several of Dickens County's windmills became well known to county residents, including the Poison, where a nester had apparently tried to poison a cowboy; the John's (1889), said to be the county's first; and the Courthouse Windmills, which dominated the courthouse square from 1890 to 1935. In 1910 Texas A&M established an agricultural experiment station on land donated by the Spur Ranch. The station came to contribute significantly to water and soil conservation, brush control, range management, and livestock production (*see* AGRICULTURAL EXPERIMENT STATION SYSTEM).

Between 1910 and 1930 the area developed rapidly, as thousands of new farmers moved into the county, encouraged by a cotton boom. Cotton farming took only 400 acres of county land in 1900, and only 5,481 as late as 1910; by 1920, however, a total of 35,494 acres was devoted to the crop, and by 1929 cotton cultivation in Dickens County had expanded to 95,525 acres. Production of cereal grains, especially sorghum, also increased during this period, and poultry production grew; in 1929 county farms raised more than 52,000 chickens and sold 158,773 dozen eggs. Meanwhile, the number of farms in the area steadily increased to 705 in 1920, to 967 in 1925, and to 1,228 in 1929; the population rose to 5,876 in 1920 and to 8,601 in 1930.

Many local farmers suffered devastating losses during the depression years of the 1930s, however, and their hardships were aggravated by the intense drought of 1934 and the failure of livestock feed crops. Farmers and cattlemen applied for federal aid to feed cattle and hogs, or accepted twelve dollars each for sickly animals that were destroyed as unfit for marketing. Meanwhile, the cotton boom collapsed; by 1940, cotton was raised on only 49,364 acres. Many farmers were driven out of business. By 1940 only 920 farms and ranches remained in Dickens County, and the county's population had dropped to 7,847.

Since the 1940s the mechanization of agriculture has combined with other factors (such as the severe droughts of the 1950s) to continue depopulating the area. After 1940 the county's population dropped to 7,177 by 1950; to 4,963 by 1960; to 3,737 by 1970; and to 3,539 in 1980; in 1992, an estimated 2,571 people lived in Dickens County.

Communities in Dickens County include Spur (1982 estimated population 1,690), site of the Texas A&M Research Station; Dickens (409); McAdoo (169), the only Dickens County community on the Great Plains; Afton (100); and Glenn (12). Dickens (1992 estimated population 332) is the county seat.

BIBLIOGRAPHY: Fred Arrington, *A History of Dickens County: Ranches and Rolling Plains* (Quanah, Texas: Nortex, 1971).

John J. Leffler

DICKERSON, SPENCER C. (1871–1948). Spencer C. Dickerson, physician and army officer, was born on December 1, 1871, to Patrick and Eliza Dickerson in Austin, Texas. He completed his early education in Austin and attended Tillotson (now Huston-Tillotson) College. After a stint of schoolteaching at Nashville, Tennessee, he entered the University of Chicago, where he excelled in both academics and sports. He worked with famed athletic director Alonzo Amos Stagg. Dickerson earned a B.S. in 1897, did graduate work at Northwestern University, and received the M.D. degree from Rush Medical College in Chicago in 1901. He interned at Freedmen's Hospital in Washington, D.C., in 1902 and began medical practice the same year at New Bedford, Massachusetts, where he remained for five years.

He subsequently returned to Chicago and became the first black pathologist at Provident Hospital. At this institution he was ophthalmologist and otolaryngologist, 1920–37; departmental chairman, 1930–37; chairman of the executive committee, 1943–46; and chairman emeritus, 1937–48. He also served as public school examining physician and as president of the Chicago Assembly, a medical organization. His awards included an honorary doctor of science degree from Lincoln University, Pennsylvania, in 1945; Distinguished Alumni Citation, University of Chicago, 1946; and Charles Victor Roman Medal for service in the John A. Andrew Clinical Society, Tuskegee, Alabama, 1946.

Dickerson enlisted in the lowest grade of the sanitary detachment, Eighth Illinois Infantry National Guard, in 1914. He was mustered into federal service for Mexican border duty in 1916 at the rank of first lieutenant. He reported for World War I[qv] service with the redesignated 370th Infantry in 1917 and received promotion to captain in the medical corps the following year. He garrisoned Camp Logan, Texas, prior to assignment to France. After returning from overseas in February 1919, Dickerson attained the federally recognized ranks of major in 1926, colonel in 1929, and commanding officer, Eighth Illinois Infantry, in 1929. He retired as brigadier general, Illinois National Guard, in 1934, the first black Texan to attain this rank. He died on February 25, 1948, at Billings Hospital, Chicago, of a heart ailment. He was survived by his wife, Daisy, two sisters, and a brother. Grace Presbyterian Church held a memorial service.

BIBLIOGRAPHY: Ocania Chalk, *Black College Sport* (New York: Dodd, Mead, 1976). U. G. Dailey, "Brig. General Spencer C. Dickerson, B.S., M.D., 1871–1948," *Journal of the National Medical Association* 40 (July 1948). Rayford W. Logan and Michael R. Winston, eds., *Dictionary of American Negro Biography* (New York: Norton, 1982).

Garna L. Christian

DICKEY, GEORGE E. (1840–19?). George E. Dickey, architect, was born in Wilmot, New Hampshire, on October 29, 1840, the son of James and Sebra Dickey. He received his academic education in Wilmot and New London, New Hampshire, and his professional training in Boston. From 1870 to 1872 he maintained a practice in Manchester, New Hampshire; he also listed himself as having practiced in Waltham, Massachusetts, in the late 1860s and early 1870s. Dickey moved to Toronto, Ontario, in 1873 and practiced there until 1878, when he moved to Houston, Texas.

He was the architect of numerous public, commercial, and residential buildings in Houston. His first major project there was the design of the five-story Capitol Hotel (1883, demolished), built on the site of the provisional capitol of the Republic of Texas.[qv] Of the retail and office buildings he designed, only the Sweeney, Coombs, and Fredericks Building (1889) remains standing in Houston. All three of his large Houston churches—Shearn Memorial Methodist Episcopal Church (1883), the First Baptist Church (1884), and the First Presbyterian Church (1894)—have been demolished, as have all but one (the Allen Paul house, 1899) of the large houses built to his designs in Houston. Dickey was the architect of Grand Central Depot (1887), the Houston Light Guard Armory (1891), Elysian Street School (later C. Anson Jones, 1893), and the third Houston City Hall and Market House (1904) in Market Square. None of these buildings is extant.

Outside Houston, Dickey was responsible for churches in Manchester, New Hampshire, and Bangor, Maine. In Texas he designed churches in Brenham, Bellville, Brownwood, and Hempstead; the Grand Opera House (1878) in Brenham; the Masonic Temple and Opera House (1880) in Sherman; a school in Angleton; county courthouses in Richmond and Centerville (1886); and a county jail in Liberty. The George Schneider (1886) and H. A. Landes (1887) houses still stand in Galveston, where Dickey also completed the interior of the extant First Presbyterian Church (1889).

During the course of his career, Dickey maintained short-lived partnerships with I. B. Samuels in Boston (1872) and in Texas with Henry J. Simpson (1884), S. A. Helmich (1886–87), J. Arthur Tempest (1894), Frank E. Rue (1896), and the Waco architect Glenn H. Allen[qv] (c. 1899–1902). Dickey was a charter member of the Texas State Association of Architects, organized in 1886, and a member of the American Institute of Architects. He also was a member of the First Presbyterian Church of Houston.

His personal history is obscure. He was married three times; first to Mary Messer of New London, New Hampshire, in 1862, then to Maria Watier of Montreal, Quebec, and finally to Georgia W. Dickey. With each of his first two wives Dickey had three children; with his third wife he had two children. As early as 1890 his eldest son, Dura Anderson Dickey, worked with him professionally. Between 1895 and 1899 Dickey and his son maintained an office in New Orleans, where Dickey lived from 1896 to 1899, the year he returned to Houston. He and all members of his family are last listed in the 1905–06 Houston city directory. Since no mention of his death can be found, it is presumed that he left Houston permanently before the next city directory was made.

Dickey's work followed prevailing trends in American architecture of the 1870s and 1880s, evident especially in his transition from the picturesque eclecticism of American High Victorian design to a fuller, more shapely approach to massing and a less exaggerated treatment of detail. His best buildings were the large houses he designed in Houston for S. K. Dick (1889), Charles Dillingham (1890), Alexander P. Root (1893), J. T. Campbell (1899), and Samuel F. Carter[qv] (1899).

BIBLIOGRAPHY: *History of Texas, Together with a Biographical History of the Cities of Houston and Galveston* (Chicago: Lewis, 1895). Houston *Post*, February 26, 1899.

Stephen Fox

DICKEY, JAMES LEE (1893–1959). James Lee Dickey, black physician, the son of John S. and Linnie A. (Sears) Dickey, was born in 1893 in Central Texas, probably near Waco. He attended Waco public schools from 1900 to 1912 and graduated from Tillotson College (now Huston-Tillotson College) in Austin in 1916. For a brief time he worked as an industrial-arts teacher in Marlin. Then he entered Meharry Medical College, Nashville, Tennessee, and graduated in 1921.

He planned to go north or east to a large city to practice. But just before graduation his father died in an accident, leaving his mother with eight other children. Dickey traveled to Taylor, Texas, to talk to Dr. J. Richard Moore, the black doctor there, but upon arrival found that Moore had moved to San Antonio. Dickey later said, "The hand of destiny guided me to Taylor, I came to stay a few years; I remained to do my life's work." He married Magnolia Fowler of Nashville, Tennessee, on November 29, 1922, and brought her to Taylor, where they worked together on many projects, including support of the African Methodist Episcopal Church.[qv]

At the time, Dickey was the only black practitioner in Williamson County and one of only 130 black doctors in Texas. In Central Texas he established a medical facility that began with a three-bedroom clinic and expanded to a fifteen-bed hospital with modern surgical and obstetrical facilities. There were no other provisions for blacks in any hospital in Williamson County except two beds in a building set apart from one hospital. Dickey discovered that there were no facilities for blacks in Bell, Lee, Milam, or Bastrop counties. He investigated health problems among the black population and discovered that the principle causes of death were typhoid fever, diarrhea among infants, convulsions and complications of childbirth, tuberculosis, pellagra, venereal diseases, and violence. He conducted health campaigns and established a prenatal clinic where all expectant mothers who were unable to pay could have free examinations and advice, and established a venereal-disease clinic to treat those unable to pay. Early in his career he also curbed a typhoid fever epidemic through a vigorous vaccination program.

His concerns extended to problems of segregation and emotional suppression of blacks. Because violence was the cause of numerous deaths, Dickey, along with others, developed recreational facilities for youth. He sought assistance from white physicians and got it. In 1940 the school board bought land for a park for African Americans,qv and with the help of black women in the community and donations from leading white citizens erected a building used as a community center. A major gain came when the Taylor Amusement Company opened a balcony where blacks could attend movies. Dickey observed that "it's hard to realize how much that meant. In earlier years, for example, one man had been whipped with a pistol for simply inquiring if seats were available for Negroes." There was no direct means of reaching the black school except by a "foot log" over Bull Branch, or over a railroad trestle. During high water children would fall off the log into the sewage-filled water and have to be rescued. Finally, through Dickey's intervention, a bridge was erected across the branch.

Dickey received many honors for his community service. He was named the year's most outstanding citizen of Taylor in 1953 by the chamber of commerce, the first time a black man had been so honored in the community. He was also named general practitioner of the year by the Lone Star Medical, Dental, and Pharmaceutical Associationqv in 1953. Honors were bestowed upon Dickey as he lent time and expertise to service at his alma mater, Tillotson College, where the Science Building is named for him and Theodore K. Lawless, a dermatologist, and where he served on the board of trustees from 1951 to his death. Dickey died in Williamson County on May 18, 1959.

BIBLIOGRAPHY: *Saturday Evening Post,* October 24, 1953. Vertical Files, Barker Texas History Center, University of Texas at Austin.

Olive Durden Brown

DICKEY CREEK. Dickey Creek rises three miles west of Berea in central Houston County (at 31°20′ N, 95°22′ W) and runs south for fourteen miles to its mouth on White Rock Creek, a mile east of the Smith Grove community (at 31°08′ N, 95°22′ W). The stream, which is intermittent in its upper reaches, traverses flat terrain surfaced by clay and sandy loam soils that support water-tolerant hardwoods, conifers, and grasses.

DICKIE, TEXAS. Dickie is at the intersection of Farm Road 2122 and a gravel road, between Mallory and Maxwell creeks a mile southwest of Ambia and five miles southwest of Paris in central Lamar County. A Dickie school opened before 1936, when it appeared on maps as part of an unidentified community that also included several dwellings and a church. By 1957 the school had been consolidated into the Roxton Independent School District. The Dickie cemetery still appeared on maps in 1984.

Vista K. McCroskey

DICKINSON, ALMARON (ca. 1800–1836). Almaron Dickinson, defender of the Alamo, was a Pennsylvanian who served as an artilleryman in the United States Army. He became a Mason in the area of Bolivar, Tennessee. On May 24, 1829, he eloped with Susanna Wilkerson (*see* DICKINSON, SUSANNA W.). The couple moved to Gonzales, Texas, in 1831 and had a daughter, Angelina Dickinson,qv in 1834. As a colonist in Green DeWitt'sqv colony, Dickinson received a league of land on the San Marcos River. He participated in the battle of Gonzalesqv on October 2, 1835, which began the Texas Revolution.qv At the siege of Bexarqv he distinguished himself as a lieutenant of artillery; at the battle of the Alamoqv he was the captain in charge of artillery. On the morning of March 6, 1836, as the troops of Gen. Antonio López de Santa Annaqv stormed the mission, Dickinson ran to his wife, reported that all was lost, and expressed hope that she could save herself and the child. Although he died at the Alamo, his wife and child survived.

BIBLIOGRAPHY: James T. DeShields, *Tall Men with Long Rifles* (San Antonio: Naylor, 1935). Gonzales County Historical Commission, *History of Gonzales County* (Dallas: Curtis, 1986). Edward Albert Lukes, *De Witt Colony of Texas* (Austin: Jenkins, 1976). Phil Rosenthal and Bill Groneman, *Roll Call at the Alamo* (Fort Collins, Colorado: Old Army, 1985). Vertical Files, Barker Texas History Center, University of Texas at Austin. Amelia W. Williams, A Critical Study of the Siege of the Alamo and of the Personnel of Its Defenders (Ph.D. dissertation, University of Texas, 1931; rpt., *Southwestern Historical Quarterly* 36–37 [April 1933–April 1934]).

Katherine L. Massey

DICKINSON, ANGELINA ELIZABETH (1834–1869). Angelina Dickinson, called the Babe of the Alamo, daughter of Almaron and Susanna (Wilkerson) Dickinson,qqv was born on December 14, 1834, in Gonzales, Texas. By early 1836 her family had moved to San Antonio. On February 23, as the forces of Gen. Antonio López de Santa Annaqv entered the city, Dickinson reportedly caught up his wife and daughter behind his saddle and galloped to the Alamo, just before the enemy started firing. In the Alamo, legend says William B. Travisqv tied his cat's-eye ring around Angelina's neck. Angelina and Susanna survived the final Mexican assault on March 6, 1836. Though Santa Anna wanted to adopt Angelina, her mother refused. A few days after the battle, mother and child were released as messengers to Gen. Sam Houston.qv

At the end of the revolution, Angelina and her mother moved to Houston. Between 1837 and 1847 Susanna Dickinson married three times. Angelina and her mother were not, however, left without resources. For their participation in the defense of the Alamo, they received a donation certificate for 640 acres of land in 1839 and a bounty warrant for 1,920 acres of land in Clay County in 1855. In 1849 a resolution by Representative Guy M. Bryanqv for the relief of "the orphan child of the Alamo" to provide funds for Angelina's support and education failed. At the age of seventeen, with her mother's encouragement, Angelina married John Maynard Griffith, a farmer from Montgomery County. Over the next six years, the Griffiths had three children, but the marriage ended in divorce. Leaving two of her children with her mother and one with an uncle, Angelina drifted to New Orleans. Rumors spread of her promiscuity.

Before the Civil Warqv she became associated in Galveston with Jim Britton, a railroad man from Tennessee who became a Confederate officer, and to whom she gave Travis's ring. She is believed to have married Oscar Holmes in 1864 and had a fourth child in 1865. Whether she ever married Britton is uncertain, but according to *Flake's Daily Bulletin,* Angelina died as "Em Britton" in 1869 of a uterine hemorrhage in Galveston, where she was a known courtesan.

BIBLIOGRAPHY: Clipping File, Library of the Daughters of the Republic of Texas, San Antonio (Historic Sites, Alamo, Alamo Defenders, Susanna Dickinson). C. Richard King, *Susanna Dickinson: Messenger of the Alamo* (Austin: Shoal Creek, 1976). Amelia W. Williams, A Critical Study of the Siege of the Alamo and of the Personnel of Its Defenders (Ph.D. dissertation, University of Texas, 1931; rpt., *Southwestern Historical Quarterly* 36–37 [April 1933–April 1934]).

Katherine L. Massey

DICKINSON, JOHN (?–?). John Dickinson, early Harris County settler and member of Stephen F. Austin'sqv Old Three Hundredqv colonists, received title to a sitioqv of land now in Galveston and Harris counties on August 19, 1824, and in that year paid twenty pesos for a strip of land a mile wide between League City and Galveston Bay. In

April 1825 he and John Sarver bought a league on the south side of Clear Creek from John K. Williams. In 1848 a John Dickinson testified as a witness at a trial to establish the rights of a free black in Harris County. The original colonist may be the John Dickinson who was a cotton factor and wholesale and retail merchant in Houston as late as 1853 and who accumulated a fortune of more than $100,000. According to some sources Dickinson's wife, whose maiden name was probably Andrews, toured England and Europe with at least three of her children after the Civil War,qv gave them French and dancing lessons, and visited her husband's relatives in Scotland, though she had to dip "into the principal" of her estate to do so.

BIBLIOGRAPHY: Eugene C. Barker, ed., *The Austin Papers* (3 vols., Washington: GPO, 1924–28). Lester G. Bugbee, "The Old Three Hundred: A List of Settlers in Austin's First Colony," *Quarterly of the Texas State Historical Association* 1 (October 1897). Marguerite Johnston, *Houston, The Unknown City, 1836–1946* (College Station: Texas A&M University Press, 1991). Louis Wiltz Kemp Papers, Texas State Archives, Austin. Andrew Forest Muir, "The Free Negro in Harris County, Texas," *Southwestern Historical Quarterly* 46 (January 1943). Andrew Forest Muir, "Railroads Come to Houston, 1857–1861," *Southwestern Historical Quarterly* 64 (July 1960). *Telegraph and Texas Register*, October 21, 1846. E. W. Winkler, ed., "Checklist of Texas Imprints, 1846–1876," *Southwestern Historical Quarterly* 47 (October 1943).

DICKINSON, SUSANNA WILKERSON (ca. 1814–1883). Susanna Wilkerson Dickinson (Dickenson), survivor of the Alamo, was born about 1814 in Tennessee, perhaps in Williamson County. Her first name has also been recorded as Susan, Susana, and Suzanna; her maiden name is sometimes given as Wilkinson. On May 24, 1829, she married Almaron Dickinsonqv before a justice of the peace in Bolivar, Hardeman County, Tennessee. The couple remained in the vicinity through the end of 1830. The Dickinsons arrived at Gonzales, Texas, on February 20, 1831, in company with fifty-four other settlers, after a trip by schooner from New Orleans. On May 5 Dickinson received a league of land from Green DeWitt,qv on the San Marcos River in what became Caldwell County. He received ten more lots in and around Gonzales in 1833 and 1834. The Dickinsons lived on a lot just above the town on the San Marcos River, where Susanna took in at least one boarder. A map of Gonzales in 1836 shows a Dickinson and Kimble hat factory in Gonzales. Susanna's only child, Angelina Elizabeth Dickinson,qv was born on December 14, 1834.

Susanna and her daughter may have joined other families hiding in the timber along the Guadalupe River in early October 1835, when Mexican troops from San Antonio demanded the return of an old cannon lent to Gonzales four years earlier. The resulting skirmish, the battle of Gonzales,qv was the first fight of the Texas Revolution.qv Susanna said goodbye to her husband on October 13 as the volunteers left for San Antonio under command of Stephen F. Austin.qv She remained in Gonzales through November, when newly arriving troops looted her home.

She joined Dickinson in San Antonio, probably in December 1835, and lodged in Ramón Músquiz'sqv home, where she opened her table to boarders (among them David Crockettqv) and did laundry. On February 23, 1836, the family moved into the Alamo. After the battle of the Alamoqv on March 6, Mexican soldiers found her—some accounts say in the powder magazine, others in the church—and took her and Angelina, along with the other women and children, to Músquiz's home. The women were later interviewed by Santa Anna, who gave each a blanket and two dollars in silver before releasing them. Legend says Susanna displayed her husband's Masonic apron to a Mexican general in a plea for help and that Santa Anna offered to take Angelina to Mexico.

Santa Anna sent Susanna and her daughter, accompanied by Juan N. Almonte'sqv servant Ben, to Sam Houstonqv with a letter of warning dated March 7. On the way, the pair met Joe,qv William B. Travis'sqv slave, who had been freed by Santa Anna. The party was discovered by Erastus (Deaf) Smith and Henry Wax Karnes.qv Smith guided them to Houston in Gonzales, where they arrived after dark about March 12.

Susanna Dickinson probably followed the army eastward in company with the other Gonzales women. Illiterate, without family, and only twenty-two years old, she petitioned the government meeting at Columbia in October 1836 for a donation, but the proposed $500 was not awarded. She needed a male protector, and by June 1837 she was cohabiting with John Williams, whom she married about November 27, 1837. He beat her and Angelina, and she petitioned in Harrisburg (later Harris) County for a divorce, which was granted on March 24, 1838—one of the first divorces in the county.

By 1839 Almaron Dickinson's heirs had received rights to 2,560 acres for his military service; they sold the land when Angelina reached twenty-one. Subsequent requests to the state legislature in November 1849 were turned down. Susanna tried matrimony three more times before settling into a stable relationship. She wed Francis P. Herring on December 20, 1838, in Houston. Herring, formerly from Georgia, had come to Texas after October 20, 1837. He died on September 15, 1843. On December 15, 1847, Susanna married Pennsylvania drayman Peter Bellows (also known as Bellis or Belles) before an Episcopalian minister. In 1850 the couple had sixteen-year-old Angelina living with them. But by 1854 Susanna had left Bellows, who charged her with adultery and prostitution when he filed for divorce in 1857. Susanna may have lived in the Mansion House Hotel of Pamelia Mann,qv which was known as a brothel, before marrying Bellows. The divorce petition accuses her of taking up residence in a "house of ill fame." Nevertheless, Susanna received praise from the Baptist minister Rufus C. Burlesonqv for her work nursing cholera victims in Houston, where he baptized her in Buffalo Bayou in 1849.

Susanna's fifth marriage was long-lasting. She married Joseph William Hannig (or Hannag), a native of Germany living in Lockhart, in 1857. They soon moved to Austin, where Hannig became prosperous with a cabinet shop and later a furniture store and undertaking parlor; he also owned a store in San Antonio. Susanna became ill in February 1883 and died on October 7 of that year. Hannig buried her in Oakwood Cemetery, and even though he married again, he was buried next to Susanna after his death in 1890.

BIBLIOGRAPHY: C. Richard King, *Susanna Dickinson: Messenger of the Alamo* (Austin: Shoal Creek, 1976). Margaret Swett Henson

DICKINSON, TEXAS. Dickinson is on State Highway 3 at the edge of the Galveston metropolitan area in the northwest corner of Galveston County. It was named after John Dickinson,qv who in 1824 received a Mexican grant for land just north of the community's present site. A settlement called Dickinson existed on Dickinson's Bayou shortly before 1850. The Galveston, Houston and Henderson Railroad, one of the earliest chartered in Texas, was built straight through Dickinson. In 1857 one of the railroad's directors, Ebenezer B. Nichols,qv built a summer estate on Dickinson Bayou. During the Civil Warqv Dickinson was a Confederate town. The Nolan home there served as a Confederate hospital, and Gen. John B. Magruderqv used the GH&H railroad for his successful retaking of Galveston in 1863. The town had a post office in 1890 registered under its current name.

In the 1890s Fred M. Nichols, the son of E. B., and eight other businessmen organized the Dickinson Land and Improvement Association to market unoccupied land in the Dickinson area. The primary attraction was the local soil's proven suitability for growing fruit, cane, berries, and potatoes. Nichols converted forty acres of his estate into a public park, the Dickinson Picnic Grounds. For the next three decades large groups came out from Galveston to picnic and holiday on the grounds. A Texas Coast Fair was organized there in 1896, and a harness racetrack (where the great harness champion Dan

Patch supposedly ran) was built to attract more people to Dickinson. By 1911 the Galveston and Houston Electric Railway Company had three stops in Dickinson, and prominent Galvestonians had established the Oleander Country Club and built homes there.

Another impetus for Dickinson's development came from Italian immigrants in 1900. A large group from Sicily who had settled in the Bryan area in 1894 were forced by a series of floods to seek resettlement help from the Italian consul in Galveston, Clemente Nicolini. He helped them resettle in the Galveston area, including Dickinson, where he was a property owner. In 1905 the Italian ambassador, Baron Mayor des Planches, in his efforts to find suitable places of settlement for the large number of newly arrived Italians qv living in overcrowded tenements in Eastern cities visited Dickinson. His welcome by an estimated 150 Italians at the train station helped convince him that Dickinson would be a good place to direct additional immigrants.

Industrialization and the growth of the oil industry in the Houston and Galveston area after both world wars contributed further to Dickinson's growth. More growth came with NASA's establishment in 1962 of the Lyndon B. Johnson Space Center qv in Webster just north of Dickinson. The fluctuating population figures of the town reflect these influences. Dickinson had a population of 149 in 1904. In 1914 the town had a population of 250, twelve businesses and a bank. After World War I qv the population had risen to 1,000; it dropped to 760 in 1931 but rose again to 1,000 in 1933; it remained stable through the rest of the Great Depression qv years. During World War II qv it rose to 1,500. By 1952 it was 3,500 and by 1961, 4,715. In 1970 the town's population peaked at 12,161. In 1977 Dickinson was incorporated with a population of about 11,000. In 1990 it had an estimated population of 9,497 and more than 150 businesses.

Dickinson has been an agricultural service center, a residential community, and the site of a mineral-oil processor. It once had a reputation as a strawberry capital. The Dickinson Railroad Museum testifies to the town's past as a commercial hub.

BIBLIOGRAPHY: Jim Hudson, *Dickinson: Taller Than the Pines* (Burnet, Texas: Nortex, 1979).

Pember W. Rocap

DICKINSON BAY. Dickinson Bay, a roughly circular bay just over a mile across at its widest point, is on the west side of Galveston Bay southwest of San Leon in north central Galveston County just south of the Chambers county line (at 29°28′ N, 94°56′ W). The bay is fed by Dickinson Bayou and formed by the extension of Cat Point, April Fool Point, and Shell Island into Galveston Bay.

DICKINSON BAYOU. Dickinson Bayou rises two miles northeast of Alvin in northwestern Galveston County (at 29°29′ N, 95°14′ W) and flows east for over twenty miles to its mouth on Dickinson Bay and Galveston Bay, just south of San Leon and a mile east of the Southern Pacific Railroad (at 29°28′ N, 94°57′ W). It traverses flat to rolling prairie surfaced by dark, commonly calcareous clays that support mesquite, grasses, and cacti. In the lower reaches of the bayou the soil changes to sandy and clay loams that support scrub brush, hardwoods, and pines.

DICKSON, DAVID CATCHINGS (1818–1880). David Catchings Dickson, physician, legislator, civil servant, Confederate soldier, and lieutenant governor of Texas, was born in Pike County, Mississippi, on February 25, 1818, and at the age of twelve moved with his family to the Copiah County community of Georgetown. There he married Sophronia L. Magee. In 1841, after graduating from medical school in Lexington, Kentucky, Dixon and his wife moved with a group to the area of Anderson, Texas, then in Montgomery County (now in Grimes County). He served for a time as a surgeon in the Army of the Republic of Texas.qv On June 4, 1845, he was elected justice of the peace of Precinct Two in Montgomery County.

Dickson was elected to the House of Representatives of the First Texas Legislature on August 25, 1849, was reelected to the Third Legislature, and in 1851 was elected to the state's Fourth Legislature, which he served as speaker of the House. He continued to serve in almost every session of the state legislature until secession.qv By 1850 his property was assessed at $1,500. He then had two children. During his terms in the house he continued his medical practice in Grimes County. On February 12, 1853, he announced his candidacy for lieutenant governor, with Elisha M. Peaseqv as the party's gubernatorial candidate. He and Pease were inaugurated on December 21, 1853. In 1855 Dickson ran for governor against Pease; he was endorsed by the American (Know-Nothing) party,qv though he was a staunch Democrat. Although defeated in his run for the statehouse, he was reelected to the House of Representatives on August 10, 1859, by a 175-vote majority. On November 16, 1859, when Dickson moved that Representative Basilio Benavidesqv of Webb County be allowed an interpreter, the Dallas *Herald* (*see* DALLAS TIMES HERALD) responded: "Don't you think it would be a good idea to allow an interpreter apiece to all the members who cannot speak Spanish? There is as much reason in one as in the other." Dickson chose not to run for reelection in 1861. By 1860 his real estate was valued at $50,000 and his personal property at $130,000. At that time he was married to Nancy Ann E. (Magee) and was the father of seven children.

During the Civil Warqv Dickson served as captain of a local militia company. On September 1, 1866, he was appointed financial agent of the Huntsville Penitentiary (*see* TEXAS STATE PENITENTIARY AT HUNTSVILLE). Governor James Webb Throckmortonqv praised Dickson's performance in that job, writing that he had "acted with much prudence in [his] purchases" and expressing himself "quite sure" that Dickson had "managed the whole affair better than it [had] ever been managed." In the penitentiary Dickson cared for convicts during a yellow fever epidemic.

After his service to the state penitentiary ended in 1867, when Throckmorton was removed from office as an "impediment to Reconstruction," Dixon retired to Grimes County, where he continued his medical practice. After his death he was buried in the family cemetery near his home at Anderson, on June 5, 1880. Dickson was a Mason. His papers are preserved at the Barker Texas History Center,qv University of Texas at Austin.

BIBLIOGRAPHY: Austin *Texas State Gazette*, August 25, February 12, June 18, December 27, 1853. *Compiled Index to Elected and Appointed Officials of the Republic of Texas, 1835–1846* (Austin: State Archives, Texas State Library, 1981). Dallas *Herald*, August 10, November 16, 1859, September 1, 1866. David Catchings Dickson Papers, Barker Texas History Center, University of Texas at Austin.

Thomas W. Cutrer

DICKSON, RAY ESTHER (1889–1950). Ray Esther Dickson, water and soil conservationist and agricultural scientist, son of Henry J. and Esther (Halliburton) Dickson, was born in Claude, Texas, on June 1, 1889. After high school in Greenville he graduated from the Agricultural and Mechanical College of Texas (now Texas A&M University) with a B.S. in agriculture, taught vocational agriculture in Cooper High School for a year, and in 1914 became superintendent of the Texas Agricultural Experiment Station at Spur (*see* AGRICULTURAL EXPERIMENT STATION SYSTEM), a position he filled until his death.

Dickson, a protégé of Arthur B. Conner,qv sought to discover and adapt agricultural principles to increase crop production in the semiarid area surrounding Spur. He pioneered in early feeding trials of grain sorghum with John McKinley Jonesqv and cotton and sorghum variety experiments with Robert E. Karperqv and John Roy Quinby (*see* COTTON AND COTTON CULTURE, SORGHUM AND SORGHUM CULTURE). Dickson's work on pasture improvement led to a mesquiteqv and brush control research program with principles that applied throughout Texas. His most significant contribution was in soil and water conservation.qv As a result of a Texas Agricultural Experiment Station project carried out with A. B. Conner and Daniel Scoates, Dickson developed the concept of "syrup-pan terraces," terraces that capture water during rains. Representative James Paul Buchananqv learned of Dickson's experiments, visited Spur, and, assisted by Dickson and Conner, wrote an amendment appropriating funds for soil-erosion investigation and regional soil-erosion experiment stations. With help from John Marvin Jonesqv the amendment passed and started a major federal program of soil and water conservation research and the Soil Conservation Service. In 1915 Dickson married Lillian Grace of Spur; they had two children. Dickson was a member of the First Christian Church. He died in Lubbock on June 26, 1950, and was buried in Spur Memorial Cemetery.

BIBLIOGRAPHY: Gladys L. Baker et al., *Century of Service: The First 100 Years of the U. S. Department of Agriculture* (Washington: GPO, 1963). Dallas *Morning News,* June 29, 1950. Irvin M. May, Jr., "Southwestern Agricultural Experiment Stations during the New Deal," in *Agriculture in the West,* ed. Edward L. and Frederick H. Schapsmeier (Manhattan, Kansas, 1980). *Irvin M. May, Jr.*

DICKSON GUN PLANT. The Dickson Gun Plant, operated during World War IIqv by the Hughes Tool Company of Houston, produced centrifugally cast gun tubes of various calibers. The plant occupied 124 acres on the north shore of Buffalo Bayou and was constructed between March 1 and December 20, 1942, at a cost of $28,779,133. Operation ended on August 14, 1945, when the chief of artillery production for the United States Army ordered the plant's general manager, John Teer, to stop production. All 1,350 employees were absorbed by the main plant of Hughes Tool Company, which had been seized by the government on September 6, 1944. The army relinquished control on August 29, 1945.

BIBLIOGRAPHY: Houston *Post,* December 18, 1942, August 14, 1945.

DICO INDIANS. The Dico Indians are known from a single 1691 Spanish missionary report that lists them among the groups that lived southeast of the Hasinai Indians. Since the distance was not given, it is impossible to tell whether the Dico area was in eastern Texas or western Louisiana. Their affiliations are unknown.

BIBLIOGRAPHY: John R. Swanton, *Source Material on the History and Ethnology of the Caddo Indians* (Smithsonian Institution, Bureau of American Ethnology Bulletin 132, Washington: GPO, 1942).

Thomas N. Campbell

DIELMANN, HENRY B., SR. (1892–1970). Henry B. Dielmann, Sr., the son of John C. Dielmann, was born in San Antonio in 1892. He attended St. Joseph's College and received a B.A. in German before entering Georgetown University in 1913. There he received an LL.B. degree in 1918. He was admitted to the bar and subsequently worked for the Law Library of Congress, the Law Library of the United States Supreme Court, and the Department of Labor. He returned to San Antonio in 1919, practiced law, and in 1923 formed a partnership with J. T. Gittinger, later Dielmann and Forster. Dielmann served as a member of the Texas State House of Representatives for three terms and was San Antonio assistant city attorney. He was the founder and first dean of St. Mary's University Law School, a member of the first board of directors of the Witte Museumqv in 1926, a director of the San Antonio Symphony Society, president of the Chamber Music Society and San Antonio Historical Association, and trustee of Our Lady of the Lake College. He was a member of the Beethoven Männerchor (*see* GERMAN MUSIC), St. Joseph's Society, the Order of Sons of Hermann,qv Siemering Lodge No. 32, and the San Antonio Bar Association. Dielmann married Betty Trester on June 26, 1919, and Edna Smith sometime later. He had four children. He was Catholic. He died at New Braunfels on April 20, 1970, and was interred at the St. Joseph's Society Cemetery.

BIBLIOGRAPHY: Horace Evans, *Bench and Bar* (Austin, 1937). San Antonio *News,* April 22, 1970. *Diana J. Kleiner*

DIELMANN, LEO MARIA JOSEPH (1881–1969). Leo Maria Joseph Dielmann, architect and civic leader, the son of John Charles and Maria (Gros) Dielmann, was born on August 14, 1881, in San Antonio. He graduated from St. Mary's College in 1898 and later studied architecture and engineering in Germany. He was appointed city building inspector of San Antonio in 1909 by Mayor Bryan V. Callaghan, Jr.,qv and held this position for three years. Dielmann served as an alderman in San Antonio for two years. Early in his career he was active in the building-materials firm of J. C. Dielmann. For the first five decades of the twentieth century he devoted himself entirely to architecture; he was especially noted as a church architect. Among the structures he designed are the Fort Sam Houston Post Chapel; the Conventual Chapel, the Science Hall, and other buildings at Our Lady of the Lake University in San Antonio; St. Mary's Catholic Church in Fredericksburg; and numerous churches, schools, civic buildings, and residences throughout Texas. Dielmann was a member of the Texas Society of Architects and of the board of trustees of the San Antonio Public Library, president of Harmonia Lodge of the Sons of Hermannqv in Texas, and committeeman for the Home for the Aged of the Sons of Hermann at Comfort. He belonged to the San Antonio Liederkranz, the Beethoven Männerchor, the Order of the Alhambra, and St. Joseph's Society. He was a member of the Democratic partyqv and St. Joseph's Catholic Church in San Antonio. Dielmann married Ella Marie Wagner on April 25, 1911. They had three children. He died on December 21, 1969, in San Antonio.

BIBLIOGRAPHY: Leo M. J. Dielmann Collection, Library of the Daughters of the Republic of Texas, San Antonio. *Southwest Texans* (San Antonio: Southwest Publications, 1952). *Who's Who in the South and Southwest,* 1950. *Bernice Strong*

DIENST, ALEXANDER, JR. (1870–1938). Alexander Dienst, Jr., dentist, historian, and antiquarian, was born in 1870 in St. Louis, Missouri, the son of Alexander and Augusta (Moller) Dienst. His father, who emigrated from Germany at age fourteen, was a doctor, dentist, and Union veteran of the Civil War.qv Young Alex attended Ozark College, Greenfield, Missouri, Ohio Wesleyan University, and Philadelphia Dental College. In 1889 he established himself as a dentist in Temple, Texas, where he practiced his profession intermittently until his death. He married Florrie Gooda at Temple on August 15, 1893; they had six children. He served as water commissioner at Temple, did volunteer work as a recruiting officer for the army and navy during World War I,qv and in 1917–18 was postmaster, under an appointment made by President Woodrow Wilson.

Dienst became an enthusiastic student of Texas history and a collector of books and source materials dealing particularly with the Texas Revolution.qv He found that his collection emphasized the history of the Texas Navy,qv and he determined to put in its proper light the important service of the navy in the establishment of the Republic of Texas.qv His study appeared in four numbers of the *Quarterly of the Texas State Historical Association,* beginning with the issue of January 1909 and later reprinted privately. In 1917 Dienst published in the *Southwestern Historical Quarterly*qv a significant collection of "Contemporary Poetry of the Texas Revolution," compiled mainly from Texas and New Orleans newspapers. For twenty years he was a member of the executive council of the Texas State Historical Associationqv and from 1932 to 1935 served as president of the organization. During his later years he gave much time to the promotion of his specialty in free public lectures on what he called "the grand theme of the pioneers of Texas." Much of his great collection of Texana became a part of the library of the University of Texas.

Dienst was a Democrat and was elected a delegate to state conventions from 1914 to 1924; he served as secretary of the Texas Democratic delegation to the national Democratic convention in St. Louis in 1916. Though he was a supporter of prohibition,^{qv} he was a close friend and supporter of Governor James Ferguson.^{qv} Dienst belonged to the Methodist Episcopal Church, South. He died of pneumonia at his home in Temple on May 6, 1938.

BIBLIOGRAPHY: Dallas *Morning News,* January 13, 1929. Clarence Wharton, *Wharton's History of Fort Bend County* (San Antonio: Naylor, 1939).

Eugene C. Barker

DIENTES ALAZANES INDIANS. The Dientes Alazanes (Spanish for "sorrel-colored teeth") are known only from a Spanish document of 1693, which lists them as one of fifty "nations" that lived north of the Rio Grande and "between Texas and New Mexico." This may be interpreted to mean the southern part of western Texas, since the document also mentions that the Apaches were at war with the groups named. Nothing further is known about the Dientes Alazanes. The name reference to stained teeth suggests that these Indians may have lived in the southern high plains of western Texas, since tooth-staining by minerals in the water of that area occurs today.

BIBLIOGRAPHY: Charles W. Hackett, ed., *Historical Documents Relating to New Mexico, Nueva Vizcaya, and Approaches Thereto, to 1773* (3 vols., Washington: Carnegie Institution, 1923–37).

Thomas N. Campbell

DIES, MARTIN (1870–1922). Martin Dies, congressman, son of David Warren and Sarah Jane (Pyburn) Dies, was born in Jackson Parish, Louisiana, on March 13, 1870. The family moved to Freestone County, Texas, in 1876. Dies attended public school in Texas, and some sources indicate that he graduated from law school at the University of Texas, although others claim that at the time in question he was working at various occupations in East Texas, including blacksmithing, railroading, teaching, and sawmilling. He was admitted to the of Texas bar about 1892 and practiced law at Woodville, Beaumont, Colorado City, and Kountze. He edited a newspaper in Freestone County and served as county marshall. He was elected county judge of Tyler County in 1894. Dies used his legal offices to secure land titles in the East Texas timber region until he moved south to Beaumont in 1897. During the Spanish-American War he joined the Beaumont Light Guards, which became Company D, Third Regiment, of the Texas Volunteers. After his return he was elected district attorney of the First Judicial District in 1898. Dies suffered a financial setback when he could not repay a debt to his friend John Henry Kirby.^{qv} As a result he moved his family to the West Texas town of Colorado City in 1899. In 1908 he defeated the incumbent, Samuel Bronson Cooper,^{qv} in his campaign for Congress. He represented the Second Texas Congressional District in the Sixty-first through Sixty-fifth United States Congresses (1909–19). During his tenure he opposed large military expenditures, American "imperialism," and high tariffs and supported an income tax. He was an outspoken nativist. Dies was opposed to woman suffrage^{qv} and in 1916 opposed Woodrow Wilson's preparedness program. He chose not to run for reelection in 1918. He married Mrs. Olive Cline Blackshear on May 15, 1892, and they had two daughters and one son, Martin Dies.^{qv} The marriage ended in divorce. Dies was a Democrat and a Methodist. He died in Kerrville on July 13, 1922, and is buried in Glenwood Cemetery, Houston.

BIBLIOGRAPHY: *Biographical Directory of the American Congress.* Dennis Kay McDaniel, Martin Dies of Un-American Activities: His Life and Times (Ph.D. dissertation, University of Houston, 1988). Vertical Files, Barker Texas History Center, University of Texas at Austin. *Who Was Who in America,* vol. 1.

Dennis K. McDaniel

DIES, MARTIN (1900–1972). Martin Dies, congressman, son of Olive M. (Cline) and Martin Dies,^{qv} was born on November 5, 1900, in Colorado City, Texas. He attended Cluster Springs (Virginia) Academy, graduated from Beaumont (Texas) High School, and earned a law degree from National University in Washington, D.C., in 1920. Dies soon joined his father's law firm in Orange and in 1930 was elected to Congress to represent the Second Congressional District, his father's old seat; he was the youngest member of Congress. In his early years he supported much of the New Deal but turned against it in 1937.

Dies achieved fame as the first chairman of the House Un-American Activities Committee, established in 1938 to investigate subversion. The Dies committee welcomed testimony against any suspected communists. The Texas Senate established a similar committee that attempted to ferret out communists at the University of Texas in 1941 but could not discover any. Dies ran unsuccessfully for the United States Senate in 1941, finishing last in a four-way race won by Lyndon B. Johnson.^{qv} During World War II^{qv} the Dies committee continued to oppose the New Deal and the Congress of Industrial Organizations, but in 1944 Dies announced his retirement after the CIO launched a vast voter-registration drive and found a candidate to oppose him.

In 1952 he won election to a new congressman-at-large seat, but he was not allowed to return to the HUAC, which believed that he had damaged the cause of anticommunism. When he ran for the Senate in the special election of 1957, state leaders such as Lyndon Johnson and Samuel T. (Sam) Rayburn,^{qv} believing that Dies was too conservative to defeat liberal challenger Ralph Yarborough, attempted to pressure him out of the race in favor of Lt. Gov. Ben Ramsey.^{qv} Their effort failed, however, and they turned to another tactic. They attempted to change the laws pertaining to special elections, which required only a plurality, and make a majority vote necessary. The Texas leaders were hoping the change would necessitate a runoff and make a win for Yarborough more difficult. This gambit failed also, and Dies finished second to Yarborough.

Dies married Myrtle M. Adams in 1920, and they had three sons. He practiced law in Lufkin between terms in Congress and after declining to run for reelection in 1958; he continued to warn that the United States was succumbing to communism. He wrote *Martin Dies' Story* (1963) and was the putative author of *The Trojan Horse in America* (1940), actually written by J. B. Matthews. From 1964 to 1967 Dies was a popular writer in *American Opinion* magazine. He died in Lufkin on November 14, 1972, and was buried there.

BIBLIOGRAPHY: Martin Dies, *Martin Dies' Story* (New York: Bookmailer, 1963). Martin Dies, *The Trojan Horse in America* (New York: Dodd, Mead 1940; rpt., New York: Arno Press, 1977). William Gellerman, *Martin Dies* (New York: Day, 1944; rpt., New York: De Capo, 1972). George N. Green, *The Establishment in Texas Politics* (Westport, Connecticut: Greenwood, 1979). Seth Shepard McKay, *W. Lee O'Daniel and Texas Politics, 1938–1942* (Lubbock: Texas Tech Press, 1944). August Raymond Ogden, *The Dies Committee* (Washington: Catholic University of America Press, 1945; rev. ed., Westport, Connecticut: Greenwood, 1984). Vertical Files, Barker Texas History Center, University of Texas at Austin.

George N. Green

DIES, TEXAS. Dies is near the junction of Farm roads 256 and 1632, seven miles northwest of Woodville in central Tyler County. The church and school set up by early settlers, originally called Cherokee for a Cherokee Indian village once located near the site, changed its name in 1915, when a post office was established and named for Martin Dies,^{qv} a congressman from Jasper. The area around Billums Creek and Colmesneil, where Dies is located, is surfaced by a band of blackland soil good for raising cotton. After 1835 Josiah Wheat, an early settler who donated land for the county seat at Woodville, cleared land south of Town Bluff for a farm but traded it soon afterward for land in Dies because he wanted to raise cotton there. Dies has been a dispersed farming community for most of its history. During the 1930s it had a post office. By 1941 it listed a population of twenty-five, but the post office had been discontinued. In 1978 the settlement had seventy-five residents and received its mail from Woodville. It was still listed as a community in 1990.

BIBLIOGRAPHY: *It's Dogwood Time in Tyler County* (Woodville, Texas), 1960, 1966. Robert Timbrook, The Geography of Tyler County (Research Paper, Stephen F. Austin State University, 1965).

Megan Biesele

DIETERICH, FRANCIS (1815–1860). Francis Dieterich, early settler and businessman, was born on February 2, 1815, in Cassel, Germany. He immigrated to Texas in 1834 and settled in Refugio, where he petitioned for and received several leagues of land. He also bought a lot there when the town was officially surveyed. In February 1836 he joined a company of militia that became part of a regiment commanded by Lt. Col. William Ward[qv] under Col. James W. Fannin, Jr.[qv] He participated in the defense of the mission at Refugio, where he was taken prisoner on March 14, 1836; his life was spared. He was again taken prisoner at Goliad but escaped the Goliad Massacre[qv] of March 27. After the war he applied for land and received two grants—640 acres of donation land in San Patricio County and 320 acres of bounty land in Comal County.

In 1839 Dieterich moved to Austin and, in that community's first year of real settlement, went into business as a meat dealer. Records of sales from November 29, 1839, to September 14, 1841, show that he sold about 25,900 pounds of beef preceding and during preparation by the government for the Texan Santa Fe expedition.[qv] He added to his landholdings by the purchase of three city lots in 1841. When the government of the republic was moved to Washington-on-the-Brazos in 1842, Dieterich moved there also to supply goods. On returning to Austin in 1845, he opened a store at the corner of Congress Avenue and Pecan Street (now Sixth Street) and joined in business with George D. Hancock,[qv] who bought the site from Alexander Russell. Later, Dieterich purchased lots on the east side of Congress Avenue, where he increased his trade by sales from his own storehouse. In 1846 he served as alderman of the city.

Dieterich was married three times: in 1834 or 1835 to Bessie Reed, by whom he had twins, one of whom survived; to Martha Ann Brown on March 12, 1845, Bessie having died sometime prior to 1845; and to Sarah Elizabeth Browning on June 17, 1847, Martha Ann having died in 1846. Francis and Sarah Dieterich were the parents of four children. Dieterich died in Austin on May 31, 1860, and was buried in Oakwood Cemetery.

BIBLIOGRAPHY: Dora Dieterich Bonham Papers, Barker Texas History Center, University of Texas at Austin. William H. Oberste, *Texas Irish Empresarios and Their Colonies* (Austin: Von Boeckmann–Jones, 1953; 2d ed. 1973).

Dora Dieterich Bonham

DIETERT, CHRISTIAN (1827–1902). Christian Dietert, a German master miller and millwright in the Hill Country[qv] and an early developer of Kerrville, was born on August 24, 1827 in Theessen, near Magdeburg, the son of Friedrich Dietert. Christian Dietert came to Texas on the *Franziska* in 1854 with his parents and four grown siblings and settled in the new township of Comfort, where in 1855 he married and where he and Nicolaus Zink[qv] were commissioned by Ernst Hermann Altgelt[qv] to build Perseverance Mill on the Cypress Creek, half a mile above the confluence with the Guadalupe River. This mill was destroyed almost immediately by a flood, and the replacement that Dietert rebuilt was thereafter idled by months of drought. A wiser Dietert later built another mill near Fredericksburg before he, his family, and a newly arrived assistant named Balthasar Lich removed to the new shingle-camp and settlement of Kerr(s)ville in 1857. At Kerrville, Dietert and Lich, also a German millwright, designed a mill, Dietert's fourth mill in Texas, high on a bluff over the Guadalupe; their low, diagonal dam across a wide part of the river that never went dry eliminated the need for a traditional millrace and thereby maximized the power attainable at the wheel from even low water levels. This grist and saw mill and the subsidiary businesses attached to it formed the mercantile backbone of the new town, along with Charles Schreiner's[qv] general store and bank and Lich's freighting operations that linked early Kerrville with San Angelo, San Antonio, and Mexico. Between 1867 and 1882 Dietert also served as the local postmaster and during part of Reconstruction[qv] as Kerr County judge; during this time, too, he helped his brother Wilhelm establish a water mill at Boerne. Dietert and his wife Rosalie Hess Dietert (1833–1929), the assistant postmistress, also contributed to the town's social development by holding dances. Local history credits them with having introduced the waltz and the Christmas tree to the town. The Kerrville mill was sold to Schreiner in 1880, and parts of the operation continued for nearly a century, never once idled by drought or damaged by frequent and violent floods. Dietert died on May 27, 1902, in Kerrville, survived by his wife and eleven children. He was interred in Glen Rest Cemetery in Kerrville. A state historical marker was erected in 1981, and the mill was commemorated in an historical painting entitled *Guadalupe Meditations* by Austin artist Bill Barrick in the same year.

BIBLIOGRAPHY: Francis Edward Abernethy, *Built in Texas*, Publications of the Texas Folklore Society 42 (Waco: E-Heart Press, 1979). Bob Bennett, *Kerr County, Texas, 1856–1956* (San Antonio: Naylor, 1956; bicentennial ed., rev. by Clara Watkins: *Kerr County, Texas, 1856–1976*, Kerrville, Texas: Hill Country Preservation Society, 1975). Guido E. Ransleben, *A Hundred Years of Comfort in Texas* (San Antonio: Naylor, 1954; rev. ed. 1974).

Glen E. Lich

DIETRICH, A. LOUISE (1878–1962). A. Louise Dietrich, nurse administrator, one of eleven children of Valentine and Mary Dietrich, was born on November 17, 1878, in Ossining, New York. She obtained her early education in Ossining and graduated from St. John's Riverside Hospital in Yonkers, New York, in 1899. Afterwards she worked as a private nurse in New York. She established residence in El Paso in 1902 and practiced nursing in that area. She worked at Providence Hospital as directress of nurses and then as superintendent of the hospital. In 1903 she established the El Paso Graduate Nurses Association, of which she was first president. For a time she left Texas and in 1907 became superintendent of St. Louis Skin and Cancer Hospital. Several years later she returned to El Paso and opened St. Marks Hospital, where she was superintendent until 1916. Miss Dietrich was chairman of the Red Cross Nursing Service Committee from 1912 to 1915 and during World War I[qv] remained active in that organization. In 1920 she was placed in charge of the El Paso Public Health Center. She became the first educational secretary for the Board of Nurse Examiners (*see* EXAMINING BOARDS) in 1923. As a strong advocate of better education in nursing, she helped pass the Nurses Compulsory Registration Bill in 1923. She was the first delegate sent from Texas to the American Nurses Association, and from 1928 to 1954 she was general secretary of the Texas Graduate Nurses Association. During World War II[qv] she worked to recruit nurses for the armed services. She was a member of St. Albans Episcopal Church in El Paso, the League of Woman Voters of Texas,[qv] and the Parent-Teachers Association. She never married. She died on January 22, 1962, and is buried in Roselawn Cemetery, El Paso.

BIBLIOGRAPHY: *American Journal of Nursing*, April 1962. *Who's Who of the Womanhood of Texas*, Vol. 1 (Fort Worth: Texas Federation of Women's Clubs, 1923–24).

Eleanor L. M. Crowder

DIETZ, TEXAS. Dietz was on State Highway 46 eight miles northwest of Seguin in Guadalupe County. The land was part of the 1831 Esnaurizar land grant of eleven leagues. Jacob de Cordova,[qv] land agent, author, and entrepreneur, settled in the area in 1851. His homestead was called Wanderer's Retreat because of the beauty of the land and the fertility of the soil. According to tradition, Cordova sold Wanderer's Retreat to nine young German bachelors who worked for him. Though this sale cannot be verified, Cordova did sell several parcels of land to Henry Bauer and August Dietz in 1849. Ferdinand Dietz bought adjoining land in 1853, and the area became known as the Dietz community. By 1854 Bauer had sold his land to the two Dietz brothers.

In the years preceding the Civil War^{qv} Dietz became a way station between Seguin and New Braunfels, on the "German Emigrant Road." After the war the community began to flourish. In 1861 Johann Phillip Stautzenberger bought land, and in 1871 Jacob Stautzenberger bought land from August Dietz. Phillip Stautzenberger built a home on a hill overlooking the dirt road to Clear Spring and New Braunfels. Near his residence he built a general store that still stood in the late 1980s. By the 1870s the citizens of Dietz had built a two-room schoolhouse and named it Frankfort School; the well close to the school site still stood on the east side of State Highway 46 in 1986. In 1886 Phillip Stautzenberger established a post office at Dietz; it was moved to Seguin in 1889. Frankfort School became the focal point for the community. At it was formed the Frohsinn Maennerchor, which still existed in 1986 as the Frohsinn Mixed Chorus of Clear Springs. The school was also the site of the founding of Frieden Church in 1895; the church is now three miles east of Dietz and has a state historical marker. By 1902 Dietz was served by rural free delivery mail. The Dietz community began to disperse in the early 1900s. Frankfort School was consolidated with the Clear Spring school in 1911. The choir moved to Clear Spring in 1916. By 1947 Dietz ceased to exist as a community.

BIBLIOGRAPHY: Claude W. Dooley, comp., *Why Stop?* (Odessa: Lone Star Legends, 1978; 2d ed., with Betty Dooley and the Texas Historical Commission, Houston: Lone Star, 1985). Willie Mae Weinert, *An Authentic History of Guadalupe County* (Seguin, Texas: Seguin *Enterprise*, 1951; rpt. 1976).
John Gesick

DIGA COLONY. The Diga colony was a self-help community established at San Antonio in 1932 by Maury Maverick.^{qv} It started as a relief effort by the city of San Antonio for destitute World War I^{qv} veterans, many of whom had returned from the unsuccessful Bonus March on Washington, D.C. As the tax collector of Bexar County, Maverick witnessed firsthand the ravages of the Great Depression.^{qv} He was especially concerned about veterans because he was a disabled veteran himself. He became involved in "Grocery Balls" and other efforts to provide relief for the destitute.

When the veterans moved into a municipal park in San Antonio, the city began to provide limited help. Maverick was appointed by the mayor as director of the War Veterans Relief Camp. Even though the veterans were moved to the fair grounds at Exposition Park, it soon became apparent that facilities in the city were neither large enough nor appropriate for the growing number of homeless people. Maverick secured land about five miles from the city from the Humble Oil Company (now Exxon Company, U.S.A.^{qv}) for a dollar a year. He was able to get discarded railroad boxcars from the Missouri Pacific Railroad; these he had moved to the site and remodeled into living quarters for the residents of the new community. The name of the colony—Diga—was Maverick's idea. He said it was an anagram made up from the words "Agricultural and Industrial Democracy."

Within a very short time the new site developed into a community organized along military lines with a commander, daily orders, and regular military-type reports. Residents numbered 171 in January 1933. R. R. Rogers, the camp commander, reported directly to Maverick, who did not live in the community. The Diga colony was organized along communal lines. Property was held in common, and people had to give up their possessions to join—a relatively small sacrifice, since few of them had anything to give up. Members were required to give a portion of their earnings from outside employment to the community treasury.

During the short existence of the community, Maverick did all he could to make it successful and well-known. He even had a medal struck to commemorate the venture. A library was set up, and various liberal and radical publications, some of which Maverick wrote, were made available to the residents. Maverick later bemoaned the fact that the residents were not really susceptible to radicalization. He said they were more concerned about jobs and food in their stomachs than about changing the world.

By late April 1933 Maverick's poor health forced him to give up his association with the community; he left the state for medical help. After President Franklin Roosevelt took office in 1933 and launched the New Deal, direct federal relief programs replaced some of the aid that people received through the community; Diga had received some government funds from the Reconstruction Finance Corporation. The exact date of the end of the experiment is not known. After Maverick's association ended, internal squabbling and bickering became more serious. Camp commander Rogers became very unpopular and a center of controversy. Records show that the community was still in existence in October 1933, but nothing beyond that date can be ascertained for certain.

BIBLIOGRAPHY: Richard B. Henderson, *Maury Maverick: A Political Biography* (Austin: University of Texas Press, 1970). Maury Maverick, *A Maverick American* (New York: Covici-Friede, 1937). Donald W. Whisenhunt, "Maury Maverick and the Diga Relief Colony," *Texana* 9 (1971).
Donald W. Whisenhunt

DIGNOWITY, ANTHONY MICHAEL (1810–1875). Anthony Michael Dignowity, Czech-American writer and public official, was born in the mining city of Kutná Hora, Bohemia, on January 16, 1810, the tenth and last child of Wenzeslas (Václav) and Catharine Dignowity. Like many other Czechs^{qv} who immigrated to the United States, he fled the Austrian conscription laws. He sailed from Hamburg for New York in 1832. In the United States he traveled from state to state, working at many different jobs.

After arriving in San Antonio with a group of Arkansas volunteers for the Mexican War,^{qv} he became a successful doctor and businessman, but in the 1850s his outspoken abolitionist views made him controversial. Possibly as a result of political persecution, he was convicted of a real estate swindle, briefly imprisoned until pardoned by his friend Governor Sam Houston,^{qv} and then charged with another swindle. In 1859 he published an autobiography in English, *Bohemia under Austrian Despotism*, to clear his name; he was one of the first Czech-born writers to publish in America. In his book Dignowity rails against the "tyranny" of American public opinion and criticizes the American legal system. Nevertheless, *Bohemia* is chiefly concerned with memories of his childhood and early adult life. He suffered from poverty in his youth, but his descriptions of family life and vignettes of the Bohemian countryside convey a strong sense of affection. His experiences as fugitive and rebel soldier, his boyhood occupations of pretzel vendor and birdcatcher, his stay in the Catholic Charity Hospital of Prague, and his conversion of a Hamburg prostitute to respectability are among the details that make the book interesting to a modern reader.

Dignowity's reputation as a Unionist and abolitionist continued to plague him, and in 1861 he narrowly escaped hanging in the San Antonio plaza. He traveled by horseback to Washington, D.C., where he was employed by the federal government. His property was confiscated, and two of his sons were conscripted into the Confederate Army. The sons later escaped to Mexico, however, and joined the Union Army.

After the war Dignowity returned to Texas. He was in poor health for the rest of his life and was never able to rebuild his fortune. During Reconstruction^{qv} he appealed to the Republican Congress for moderation on the behalf of the "loyal residents" of the South. Dignowity married Amanda J. McCann on February 9, 1843, in Little Rock, Arkansas. They had eight children, one of whom, František, was a founder of Del Rio, Texas. Dignowity died on April 22, 1875, in San Antonio.

BIBLIOGRAPHY: Estelle Hudson and Henry R. Maresh, *Czech Pioneers of the Southwest* (Dallas: South-West, 1934). Clinton Machann and James W. Mendl, *Krásná Amerika: A Study of the Texas Czechs, 1851–1939* (Austin: Eakin Press, 1983).   *Clinton Machann*

DIJU INDIANS. In 1683–84 Juan Domínguez de Mendoza[qv] led an exploratory expedition from El Paso as far eastward as the junction of the Concho and Colorado rivers east of the site of future San Angelo. In his itinerary he listed the names of thirty-seven Indian groups, including the Diju, from which he expected to receive delegations on the Colorado River. Nothing further is known about the Diju, who seem to have been one of many Indian groups of north-central Texas that were swept away by the southward thrust of the Lipan Apache and Comanche Indians in the eighteenth century.

BIBLIOGRAPHY: Herbert Eugene Bolton, ed., *Spanish Exploration in the Southwest, 1542–1706* (New York: Scribner, 1908; rpt., New York: Barnes and Noble, 1959). Charles W. Hackett, ed., *Pichardo's Treatise on the Limits of Louisiana and Texas* (4 vols., Austin: University of Texas Press, 1931–46).   *Thomas N. Campbell*

DIKE, TEXAS. Dike is on Farm Road 69 ten miles northeast of Sulphur Springs in northeastern Hopkins County. The site was first settled around 1850, when Michael and Elizabeth Miller built a mill and a small log schoolhouse; the mill, which became known as Smith Mill, continued to operate for some time after the Civil War[qv] but around 1887 was replaced by a gin and mill run by William Henry Moore and Bob Matthews. In 1888 Newton Rhodes opened the first store in the settlement, which during the 1870s and 1880s was known as Union Valley. In 1890 a post office was secured, and the name was changed to Dike at the suggestion of Bud Sheppard, a native of Dike, Iowa. A public school was in operation by 1905, when it had an enrollment of thirty-three. In 1914 Dike had six general stores, a blacksmith, and two physicians. The population reached 250 in 1925 but declined after World War II;[qv] in 1945 the town had 100 residents and two businesses. In 1948 Dike had two stores, two churches, a blacksmith shop, and a three-teacher school. In 1985 it comprised three churches, a post office, a business, a camp, and a population of 170. The population was the same in 1990.

BIBLIOGRAPHY: Sylvia M. Kibart and Rita M. Adams, eds., *Pioneers of Hopkins County, Texas*, Vol. 1 (Wolfe City, Texas: Henington, 1986).
J. E. Jennings

DIKES CREEK. Dikes Creek, a wet-weather draw fed by numerous seeps, rises a mile south of the Bateman Ranch headquarters in east central King County (at 33°33′ N, 100°08′ W) and runs northeast through remote ranch and oil lands for seven miles to its mouth on the South Wichita River, within the boundaries of the Bateman Ranch east oilfield, fifteen miles east of Guthrie (at 33°38′ N, 100°05′ W). It traverses rolling terrain with some steep slopes, surfaced by deep clay and sandy loams that support primarily juniper, cacti, and sparse grasses.

BIBLIOGRAPHY: Gunnar Brune, *Springs of Texas*, Vol. 1 (Fort Worth: Branch-Smith, 1981).

DILL, JAMES (ca. 1766–1825). James Dill, early Indian trader and alcalde,[qv] was born about 1766 at Lancaster, Pennsylvania. He was orphaned at age two. In 1785 he moved to New Orleans, where he stayed for two years before moving upriver to Arkansas Post and pursuing a hunter's life. He lived in Arkansas Territory for eleven years; there he married Helena Gimlech or Camiliech (Americanized as Kimble) on September 14, 1791; they eventually had four daughters and one son. The Dills moved to Natchitoches, Louisiana, in 1791 and later settled on Dill Creek in northern Nacogdoches County, where Dill farmed and, according to tradition, carried on a lucrative trade with the Indians and Spanish settlers. Two of the Dill children were baptized in Arkansas, and the rest were baptized in Texas; Maria Helena Dill, born on September 8, 1804, in Nacogdoches, was one of the earliest children born to English-speaking parents in Texas. The Dill family was living in Nacogdoches by 1799, and the family home was located at what is now the corner of North and Hospital streets.

While living in Nacogdoches in 1802 Dill applied for a grant of four leagues of land west of the Angelina River and north of El Camino Real (*see* OLD SAN ANTONIO ROAD). Not until July 1828, however, did his widow, Helena, obtain title to the land. The Dill family left Nacogdoches and moved to Fort Jesup, near Mansfield, Louisiana, in 1813 to avoid becoming embroiled in the Gutiérrez-Magee expedition[qv] and to send their children to the newly constructed school. After Erasmo Seguín[qv] invited Dill and others back to Nacogdoches in 1820, Dill became involved in local politics and the next year was elected alcalde for the Nacogdoches ayuntamiento[qv]—the first Anglo-American to be so honored. He was unable to read or write but exerted great influence. His lack of legal knowledge caused certain opposition to his holding elected office, however, and in 1823 a junto headed by Joseph Durst, alcalde Juan Seguín (Dill's opponent in the 1823 election), José Antonio Sepúlveda,[qqv] José Antonio Chirino, and Mariano Sanches ousted Dill. Juan Seguín replaced him on October 10, 1823. On May 18, 1825, Dill shot and killed Charles Duboys. Luis Procela, then alcalde of Nacogdoches, called upon other alcaldes of East Texas to sit with him in Dill's trial; a jury of twelve men found Dill not guilty, but José Antonio Saucedo,[qv] political chief in Bexar, later instructed Procela that Mexican law did not authorize jury trial. Procela was ordered to organize militia companies and rearrest Dill. In June 1825 Dill escaped to Natchitoches. On November 21, 1825, a fall from a horse led to his death.

BIBLIOGRAPHY: Robert Bruce Blake Research Collection, Steen Library, Stephen F. Austin State University; Barker Texas History Center, University of Texas at Austin; Texas State Archives, Austin; Houston Public Library, Houston. Carolyn Reeves Ericson, comp., *Citizens and Foreigners of the Nacogdoches District, 1809–1836* (2 vols., Nacogdoches, Texas: Ericson, 1981). Virginia H. Taylor, *The Spanish Archives of the General Land Office of Texas* (Austin: Lone Star, 1955). *Translation of Statistical Census Reports of Texas, 1782–1836, and Sources Documenting the Black Texan, 1603–1803* (microfilm, University of Texas Institute of Texan Cultures at San Antonio, 1984). Vertical Files, Barker Texas History Center, University of Texas at Austin.
Joe E. and Carolyn Reeves Ericson

DILLARD CREEK. Dillard Creek rises 2½ miles south of Avery in southeastern Red River County (at 33°31′ N, 94°48′ W) and runs south for 7½ miles to its mouth on Roden Creek, in southeastern Red River County 2½ miles west of the Bowie county line (at 33°25′ N, 94°47′ W). The soils along the creek are loamy, and the area is for the most part heavily wooded, with post and blackjack oaks predominating.

DILLARD, FRANK CLIFFORD (1854–1938). Frank Clifford Dillard, attorney, was born to George C. and Mary Frances (Williams) Dillard at Auburn, Alabama, in 1854. He graduated from Alabama Polytechnic Institute, located in his home town, and taught for some time at a woman's college in Kentucky. In 1897 he was admitted to the state bar of Kentucky, but rather than establish a practice in that state he moved to Grayson County, Texas, settling in Sherman. He quickly was admitted to the state bar and in 1883 established a partnership with David E. Bryant,qv who in 1890 became United States district judge for the eastern district of Texas. Dillard later was a partner in three other law firms in Sherman. He married Mary S. Rountree on July 10, 1894. His legal abilities combined with his location in the Sherman-Denison area, which was a rail center, apparently recommended him to rail magnate E. H. Harriman, who in 1907 hired Dillard. Dillard relocated to Chicago, hub of the Harriman railroad lines, where he oversaw legal work relating to interstate commerce. In 1912 Dillard became vice president and general counsel of the Chicago, Rock Island and Pacific Railway, a position that he held for two years. In April 1914 Dillard resigned his position with the railroad and returned to Sherman. He joined the firm of Head, Dillard, Maxey-Freeman, and McReynolds. Dillard was a member of the Democratic partyqv and the Methodist church. He died at his home in Sherman on September 25, 1938.

BIBLIOGRAPHY: *Who Was Who in America*, Vol. 1. Brian Hart

DILLARD, JAMES ELIZER (1830–1913). James Elizer Dillard, lawyer and judge, the son of David and Mahala (Durden) Dillard, was born in Houston County, Georgia, on September 26, 1830. He traveled to Texas in 1848 and lived in Liberty County, where he was a farmer and stockman. In 1853 he resettled in Cherokee County and studied law with the firm of Donnelly and Anderson. He began his own law practice in Rusk. From 1853 to 1857 Dillard was active in expelling Indians from white settlements. At the outset of the Civil Warqv he enlisted in the Confederacy as a private in Company K of the Third Texas Cavalry. He received severe wounds in the battle of Oak Hill but recovered and was promoted for his bravery. Later he served in the Fourth Texas Cavalry under Col. Walter P. Lane.qv

After the war Dillard resumed his law practice. He was elected county judge in Kaufman County and subsequently district judge in Ellis County. In 1870 voters elected him to the state Senate. Dillard's opposition to Reconstructionqv won him enemies. He was twice expelled from the Senate for making speeches against the bribery and corruption in the legislature, but his constituency sent him back each time. He served his district in the Twelfth, Thirteenth, and Fourteenth legislatures. During the turbulent term of Governor Edmund J. Davis,qv Dillard took an active part in opposing the "Carpetbag Constitution." By the end of the Coke-Davis controversy,qv he was a recognized leader in the destruction of misrule and the establishment of a Democratic state government. On January 19, 1874, Dillard and two others, armed with pistols, subdued the guards, stormed into the state capitol, and broke down the door of the governor's office. They removed state officials who refused to leave voluntarily. Dillard was often mentioned as a possible candidate for governor but instead chose to return to the practice of law.

He married Sarah Rosa Fallis Prather, a widow, on June 15, 1873, in Cherokee County. They had six children. In 1878 Dillard moved his family to Kaufman County, where he opened a successful law office. In 1882 voters elected him county judge and in 1893 district judge. He retired from office in 1906 but continued to practice law until his death, on December 8, 1913. *See also* CONSTITUTION OF 1866, CONSTITUTIONAL CONVENTION OF 1868–69.

BIBLIOGRAPHY: T. R. Fehrenbach, *Lone Star: A History of Texas and the Texans* (New York: Macmillan, 1968). Edna Davis Hawkins, et al., *History of Ellis County, Texas* (Waco: Texian, 1972). *Kaufman Sun*, March 20, 27, 1884. Kaufman County Historical Commission, *History of Kaufman County* (Dallas: Taylor, 1978). Randell G. Tarín

DILLARD, JOHN HENRY (1805–1836). John Henry Dillard, Alamo defender, son of William and Sarah Dillard, was born in Smith County, Tennessee, in 1805. He immigrated to Texas and settled at Nashville-on-the-Brazos. He served in the Alamo garrison and died in the battle of the Alamoqv on March 6, 1836.

BIBLIOGRAPHY: Daughters of the Republic of Texas, *Muster Rolls of the Texas Revolution* (Austin, 1986). Bill Groneman, *Alamo Defenders* (Austin: Eakin, 1990). Bill Groneman

DILLARD, NICHOLAS (?–?). Nicholas Dillard, one of Stephen F. Austin'sqv Old Three Hundredqv colonists, received title to a sitioqv of land now in Brazoria County on August 16, 1824. The census of 1826 listed him as a farmer, stock raiser, and single man between the ages of twenty-five and forty. He sold land on Cedar Lake to James Davis in January 1827 and later bought land on part of the original DeMoss grant as well as on Bay Prairie. Austin called Dillard captain, but whether the title is that of a military or a seafaring officer is not known. Dillard was apparently an importer or a merchant; in 1827 Austin owed him for clothing and sugar as well as other merchandise. In 1833 Dillard was involved in litigation relating to the legal practice of William B. Travis.qv

BIBLIOGRAPHY: Eugene C. Barker, ed., *The Austin Papers* (3 vols., Washington: GPO, 1924–28). Lester G. Bugbee, "The Old Three Hundred: A List of Settlers in Austin's First Colony," *Quarterly of the Texas State Historical Association* 1 (October 1897). William Barret Travis, *Diary*, ed. Robert E. Davis (Waco: Texian Press, 1966).

DILL CREEK. Dill Creek rises just east of Looneyville in northwestern Nacogdoches County (at 31°46′ N, 94°50′ W) and runs northeast for seven miles to its mouth on the East Fork of the Angelina River, just east of Farm Road 225 in southern Rusk County (at 31°51′ N, 94°49′ W). It traverses flat terrain with local shallow depressions, surfaced by clay and sandy loam that supports water-tolerant hardwoods, conifers, and grasses. The creek may have been named for James Dill,qv an early settler.

DILLEY, TEXAS. Dilley is on the Missouri Pacific Railroad and Interstate Highway 35 sixteen miles southwest of Pearsall in far southern Frio County. The community was originally called Darlington, after a local landowner who settled in the area in the mid-1860s. The settlement was established on the International–Great Northern Railroad from San Antonio to Mexico, completed during the early 1880s. At the time Darlington had a general store and several dwellings. The community was sometimes called Ford because of a nearby Frio River crossing of an old Spanish trail, known as Rocky Ford. The I–GN built its first railroad depot, siding, and stock pen near the crossing.

Paul and Alex Meersheidt of San Antonio purchased and platted land surrounding the railroad depot and laid out a town with the assistance of a local rancher, W. D. Harris. The name of the community was changed to Dilley in honor of George M. Dilley, an official of the railroad. There is also evidence to suggest that the name may have been derived from that of an early settler in the area named Dillahunty. A Darlington post office had been established in 1885. In 1890 Jim McAllister laid the first telegraph line in Frio County, from San Antonio to Darlington, which that year had an estimated population of fifty and a general store owned by J. N. Harris. The post office was named Darlington at least until 1892. By 1896 the community was officially called Dilley and had an estimated population of fifty. By 1900 the community supported two churches and a one-teacher school with fifty-five students. In 1906 the school had eighty-seven students and two teachers. Dilley was incorporated in 1912.

By 1914 the town had an estimated 1,000 residents, Baptist, Methodist, and Presbyterian churches, the Dilley State Bank, a weekly newspaper, a cotton gin, seven general stores, and two hotels. Dilley had become a shipping center for cattle, vegetables, and fruit. Editor James Howerton established the Dilley *Herald* in 1923. The second macadamized highway in Frio County was completed from Dilley to Eagle Pass in 1928. By 1929 Dilley had an estimated population of

1,600. The town had the county's sole surviving cotton gin sometime in the 1930s, after the destruction of the industry by boll weevil^{qv} and cotton fleahopper infestation. Although the population of the community had dropped to an estimated 929 in 1936, it rebounded by 1940 to an estimated 1,244.

Sometime in the late 1940s the Dilley Independent School District was consolidated with the Millett school district of La Salle County. As a result of the fund-raising efforts of Dilley State Bank president F. J. Avant and a nonprofit organization made up of more than 100 residents, a new hospital was constructed in 1950. In 1965 Dilley had a peanut-drying plant and a clinic and rest home, as well as a large statue of a watermelon. The population rose steadily during the 1950s and 1960s, to an estimated 2,318 by 1967. At that time Dilley was the county's second largest town and a commercial shipping point for peanuts, watermelons, and cattle. By 1987 Dilley had an estimated population of 2,773 and fifty-one business operations. Oil exploration in the region was encouraged by a horizontal-drilling technology developed in the late 1980s. In 1990 Dilley was chosen as the site for a new 1,000-bed state prison. The population in 1990 was 2,632.

BIBLIOGRAPHY: Data Compiled by the Texas History Class of 1936, Dilley High School (MS, Frio County Vertical File, Pearsall Municipal Library, Pearsall, Texas). *Frio County, Texas: A History* (Pearsall, Texas: Frio Pioneer Jail Museum Association, 1979). Will Harte, "Austin Chalk," *Texas Monthly*, February 1990. Frances Cox Wood, Using the Social and Historical Heritage of Pearsall, Texas, in Teaching Fourth Grade Children (M.A. thesis, Southwest Texas State Teachers College, 1953). *Ruben E. Ochoa*

DILLON, TEXAS. Dillon was four miles south of Saltillo in eastern Hopkins County. It was settled around 1900 and named for E. F. Dillon, who secured a post office in his store there in 1903. The post office was discontinued in 1906, and by the mid-1930s the community no longer appeared on highway maps. *J. E. Jennings*

DILWORTH, TEXAS (Gonzales County). Dilworth, on Farm Road 795 in northeastern Gonzales County, was established in 1889 when the San Antonio and Aransas Pass Railway ran a spur from Shiner to Luling. The town was named for G. N. Dilworth, a banker who was instrumental in the building of the railroad. Local citizens soon erected a railroad station, a section house, a cotton-shipping platform, and stock pens. The community acquired a post office in 1892 and by 1896 had a saloon, a physician, a dentist, a blacksmith, a Methodist church, a combination mill and gin, and 150 inhabitants. In 1915 Dilworth had two general stores, but the number of citizens had dropped to seventy-five; it remained at that level through the 1950s. The post office closed in the late 1930s. By 1950 Dilworth children were being bused eight miles to Gonzales to attend school. The population declined even more in the 1960s, and from 1970 through 1990 it was estimated at fifteen. *Stephen L. Hardin*

DILWORTH, TEXAS (Red River County). Dilworth is on Farm Road 1159 eight miles northeast of Clarksville in northeastern Red River County. The area was settled before 1900. A school was in operation there by 1907, when it had an enrollment of thirty-four. In the mid-1930s Dilworth had a church, a school, and a number of houses. Its school was closed around the time of World War II.^{qv} In the early 1990s Dilworth reported a population of twenty-two and had a church, a cemetery, and a few scattered dwellings. *Christopher Long*

DIME BOX, TEXAS. Dime Box is on Farm Road 141 twelve miles northeast of Giddings in eastern Lee County. It originated between 1869 and 1877, when a settler built a sawmill near what is now State Highway 21, three miles northwest of the site of the present community. Records suggest that the mill's builder was Joseph S. Brown, and the settlement of British-Americans, Czechs, Poles, Germans, and German-Wends which grew up around the mill was known as Brown's Mill (Browne's Mill, Brown's Mills). A Union School opened in January 1874. The school later housed the local Presbyterian church, which was one of the earliest of this denomination in the state. Until a government post office opened in 1877, settlers deposited outgoing mail and a dime in a small box inside Brown's office for a weekly delivery to Giddings. The Brown's Mill post office closed in December 1883. When it reopened the following Spring, frequent confusion of Brown's Mill with Brownsville had caused the town to be renamed Dime Box. In 1913, when the Southern Pacific Railroad built a line three miles southeast of Dime Box, the original settlement became Old Dime Box, and the new railroad station became Dime Box. The railroad encouraged growth, and the community's estimated population increased from 127 in 1904 to 500 in 1925. The number of residents remained between 300 and 500 throughout the middle years of the twentieth century and was estimated at 313 in 1972 and 1990. In the late 1970s oil was discovered in the Dime Box area.

BIBLIOGRAPHY: Julia Jones, *Lee County: Historical and Descriptive* (Houston, 1945). Lee County Historical Survey Committee, *A History of Lee County* (Quanah, Texas: Nortex, 1974). *Ray Spitzenberger*

DIMITT'S LANDING. Dimitt's Landing was a transshipment point between seagoing vessels and wagon trains to the interior on the west bank of the Lavaca River near its mouth at northeastern Lavaca Bay, now in Jackson County. It was founded in 1832 by Philip Dimmitt^{qv} and was basically a pier and a warehouse for handling imports. In March 1836 the remnants of William Ward's^{qv} Georgia Battalion,^{qv} after finding Victoria occupied by Mexican troops, marched to Dimitt's Landing in hopes of boarding a vessel to escape. On March 22 Ward's command halted within two miles of its destination to slaughter a beef and reconnoiter. There they were overtaken and forced to surrender by units of Mexican cavalry. Most were subsequently killed in the Goliad massacre^{qv} on March 27. After independence the site was used as a port until Dimmitt's death in 1841. *C. D. George*

DIMMIT COUNTY. Dimmit County (P-13), in southern Texas, is bordered by Zavala, La Salle, Webb, and Maverick counties. Carrizo Springs, the county's largest town and the county seat, is located in the northwestern part of the county at the intersection of U.S. Highways 83 and 277. The center point of the county is 28°25′ north latitude and 99°46′ west longitude. Dimmit County was named for Philip Dimmitt,^{qv} one of the framers of the Goliad Declaration of Independence;^{qv} his name was misspelled when the county was formed. The county comprises 1,307 square miles of generally flat to rolling terrain vegetated with mesquite^{qv} and small trees, scrub brush, cacti,^{qv} and grasses. The elevation of the county ranges from approximately 500 to 800 feet. Soils in the nearly level areas are loamy and sometimes poorly drained, while soils in the rolling south central part of the county are loamy to clayey. Most of Dimmit County is drained by the Nueces River, which flows across the northeastern quarter. In 1982 almost 90 percent of the county's land was devoted to ranching and farming. Two percent of the land was cultivated, largely with irrigation.^{qv} Dimmit County is known as part of the Winter Garden Region^{qv} for the vegetables grown there. Mineral resources include caliche, industrial sand, sand and gravel, oil, gas, and lignite coal. Oil and gas production is significant. Temperatures in Dimmit County range from an average high of 99° F in July to an average low of 40° in January, with average annual temperature of 72°. Rainfall averages twenty-two inches a year, and the growing season lasts for 290 days.

Indian artifacts dating from the Paleo-Indian period (9200 to 6000 B.C.) demonstrate that man has lived in the area of Dimmit County for about 11,000 years. The local Indian population seems to have increased during the Archaic period (6000 B.C. to A.D. 1000), when many groups of hunter-gatherers spent part or all of their time in the area. During this period the county's inhabitants subsisted mostly on game, wild fruits, seeds, and roots. They carved tools from wood and stone, wove baskets, and sewed rabbitskin robes. Their most effective weapon was the atlatl, a throwing stick that greatly increased the deadliness of their spears. The hunting and gathering life persisted into the Late Prehistoric period (A.D. 1000 to the arrival of the Spanish), though during this time the Indians in the area learned to make pottery and to hunt with bows and arrows. During the seventeenth and eighteenth centuries, the Coahuiltecan Indians native to Dimmit County were squeezed out by other Indian who were migrating into the area and by the Spanish, who were moving up from the south. Many of the Coahuiltecans were taken to San Juan Bautista,qv in Coahuila. Apaches and Comanches moved in to take their place.

No permanent Spanish settlement seems to have been established in the future Dimmit County. Beginning in the late 1600s, however, Spaniards passed through the area on the Old San Antonio Road,qv a *camino real*, to and from other Spanish settlements in Texas. In 1778 Juan Agustín Morfi,qv a Franciscan friar, for example, led a group through what later became southern Dimmit County and noted in his diary the Spanish names of various creeks and springs he saw. After the Mexican War of Independenceqv the Mexican government used land grants to encourage its citizens to settle in Texas. Perhaps as many as seven grants were made between 1832 and 1834 that included territory now in Dimmit County. None of the recipients seems to have made use of the land, however. By 1836, when Texas became independent from Mexico, the area remained populated almost solely by Indians.

Between the Texas Revolution and the Mexican Warqqv (1836–46), most of Dimmit County lay in the disputed area between the Rio Grande and the Nueces River. Since neither the Republic of Texasqv nor the Mexican government could establish control over this strip of contested land, known at the time as Wild Horse Desert or El Desierto Muerto (Dead Desert), it became a haven for desperate characters. This remained true for years after the Treaty of Guadalupe Hidalgoqv definitively assigned the Nueces Strip to Texas. In 1858, Dimmit County was officially formed from parts of Bexar, Webb, Maverick, and Uvalde Counties. Dangers posed by outlaws and unfriendly Indians, however, deterred settlement in the county until after the Civil War.qv Dimmit County as it was found by early settlers was much different than it is today. Grasslands punctuated by clumps of mesquite, oak, and ash trees supported an abundance of wildlife, including buffalo, deer, turkeys, wild horses, panthers, and javelinas. Springs, bubbling up from a vast reservoir of underground water, fed into running streams that harbored giant catfish, crawfish, and mussels. As one visitor described it, the place in the mid-nineteenth century was "a poor man's heaven." Before it was settled, the area became known to a number of men who went there on Indian patrols, to hunt mustangs,qv or to seek good places to feed and water their cattle.

According to local tradition, the first attempt to establish a settlement in the area occurred just before the Civil War, when a black man from Nacogdoches named John Townsend led a group of families to a site on Pendencia Creek. Harassed by Indians, this group soon moved on to Eagle Pass. A band of settlers from Milwaukee also attempted a settlement on San Lorenzo Creek near the Webb county line. The first permanent settlement in Dimmit County, Carrizo Springs, was founded in 1865 by a group of fifteen families from Atascosa County. These early settlers were led by Levi English,qv a cattleman and frontiersman who, like some of the other settlers, was already familiar with the area from earlier visits. A second group of settlers from Goliad arrived at Carrizo Springs about two years later. The first years of settlement were difficult. Most of the early residents of the county lived in primitive jacals or dugouts, and hostile Indians and outlaws often disturbed the peace. Indian attacks posed the greatest threat to isolated ranchers. Some of the earliest settlers were forced to abandon their lands and move closer to the Carrizo Springs settlement, which itself was sometimes endangered. But, hounded by patrols of Texas Rangersqv and local volunteers and with their numbers decimated by disease, the Indians were forced to leave Dimmit County by 1877. Banditry lasted well into the 1880s, partly because of the county's proximity to the Mexican border. Dimmit County residents filed many claims with the Mexican government for cattle stolen and driven across the Rio Grande by Mexican raiders. The Nueces Strip offered opportunities for cattle rustlers on both sides of the border; the Mexican government also registered protests about Mexican cattle taken to Carrizo Springs. Thanks in part to the sometimes extralegal efforts of John King Fisher,qv county marshall *cum* outlaw, banditry in Dimmit County was greatly reduced by the 1880s and the area became more domesticated.

The county was formally organized in 1880 with Carrizo Springs as county seat. That same year, Levi English donated land for a county courthouse, schools, and churches in the town. The Carrizo Springs *Javelin*, the county's only newspaper, was established in 1884. By 1885 the county seat was described as a "flourishing town" with two churches, a grocery, a livery stable, and a harness and boot shop. Unlike most frontier towns, Carrizo Springs had no saloon. County residents voted to outlaw the sale of alcohol in the early 1880s; and Marshall Fisher, himself a teetotaller, vigorously enforced this law. By 1892 the town also supported a steam gristmill-gin, two apothecaries, and a nursery. The growth of Carrizo Springs mirrored the development of the county as a whole between 1870 and 1890. Cattle ranchers firmly established themselves in the county during this period, especially after 1880, when barbed wireqv was introduced. According to the United States census, only sixteen farms and ranches existed in Dimmit County in 1870, and half of these were no larger than ten acres. By 1890 the county had ninety-six farms and ranches, and of these only five were ten acres or smaller. Twenty-three of the ranches in 1890 were larger than a thousand acres, and some considerably larger; the average size of all farms and ranches in Dimmit County that year was almost 4,100 acres. The number of cattle reported during this period almost tripled, rising from 15,575 in 1870 to 44,934 in 1890. Meanwhile, the county's population grew from 109 in 1870 to 665 in 1880 and 1,049 in 1890. Sheep ranchingqv was also an important part of the economy for a time. In 1870 there were only 300 sheep in the county, but in 1880, 36,714 were reported and 72,000 pounds of wool were produced. An intense drought in 1886 and 1887, however, helped to bring an end to this promising start. The dry weather killed many sheep outright and helped to wipe out much of the county's grassland, which was increasingly replaced by brush that harbored coyotes. As the forage decreased, the predators increased; by 1900 sheep raising was no longer profitable in Dimmit County, and the census for that year counted only 207 sheep left.

At the turn of the century cattle ranching completely dominated Dimmit County's economy and set the tone for its culture. There were 105 farms and ranches in the county in 1900, comprising 904,000 acres. Though some ranchers set aside a few acres for such crops as wheat, corn, oats, and peanuts, the vast majority of the land was devoted to raising cattle. No manufacturing establishments were reported. The population had grown to 1,049 by 1900, but many of its inhabitants lived on scattered ranches; the only real town in the county was still Carrizo Springs, which for all its growth was still a modest settlement. The county's demographic profile was also relatively homogeneous in 1900. The typical Dimmit County rancher at the end of the nineteenth century was a native white Protestant; many had Southern roots. Only thirty-seven of Dimmit County's 1,106 residents in 1900 were black. Mexican Americans,qv though growing in number, still constituted only a minority of the county's population, and though some of them owned their own land, the great majority had come to the county to work as shepherds or vaqueros. In the first decades of the twentieth century, however, the introduction of commercial agriculture made possible by the use of underground water brought an infusion of new settlers to the area and ushered in an era of optimism and prosperity. The early settlers who established ranches during the nineteenth century adapted their operations to the limited rainfall in Dimmit County. Even gardens were rare in the first years of the county's settlement. Though some experimented with irrigating small plots of land, few attempted to cultivate large fields. Of the county's 904,000 acres devoted to agriculture in 1900, "improved" land constituted only 3,100 acres. Only 163 acres was planted in corn, which was at that time the county's biggest crop. A gin built in the late 1880s or early 1890s in anticipation of a good cotton crop was left unused.

Water was the missing ingredient. The editor of the Carrizo Springs *Javelin* wrote in 1899, "Our soil only needs water to make it the most productive in the state." The first use of artesian water in Dimmit County is attributed to D. C. Frazier, who drilled a well near Carrizo Springs in 1884. Frazier's well spouted forty gallons of water a minute, which he used for his household and for a small irrigation project. "The water appears to have the same effect as rains," an 1890 report on Frazier's project noted. "Irrigation is necessary about three years out of five." Local ranchers were rather slow to appreciate the significance of Frazier's finding, though T. C. Nye proved the profitability of vegetable farming in the area in 1898, when his experimental patch of Bermuda onions brought him more than a thousand dollars an acre. By 1900 about twenty-five artesian wells were flowing in the Carrizo Springs area, but most of the water was wasted, and very little was used for irrigation. "Colonel" J. S. Taylor, an audacious land developer who had already helped to establish the town of Del Mar, California, was the first to use irrigation on a large scale in Dimmit County. In 1899, Taylor began construction of a thirty-foot dam across the Nueces River to irrigate 2,000 acres of farmland he hoped to sell in his Bermuda Colony development. To ensure a good water supply for his project, Taylor drilled a deep artesian well; he also introduced the planting of Bermuda onions and strawberries on a large scale. Local ranchers ridiculed the scheme at first, but when the Bermuda Colony proved to be a financial success it became a model for development. By 1910, Taylor's idea of changing dry rangeland into lucrative farmland was being imitated by a number of other developers. The remarkable land boom that ensued peaked between 1910 and 1916.

Artesian water, good soil, and the area's long growing season produced profitable results for the many farmers who began growing vegetables in Dimmit County. Perhaps 8,000 acres of county land was planted with onions as early as 1902. So many onions were produced in 1903 that, according to one estimate, the county's farmers would have had to use 100 wagons for six weeks to carry all of their produce to the nearest railroad. Forty-five carloads of onions was shipped in 1906. By 1909, water was flowing out of about 200 artesian wells in Dimmit County as more and more land was prepared for cultivation. Land values in the county rose dramatically after 1900 as a new influx of settlers moved in. "The man with the hoe has appeared on the horizon," the *Javelin* reported in 1902; "he is coming with his wife and children, and is coming prepared to stay." The real boom began about 1909, as developers laid out ambitious plans for entire new towns and "colonization" projects in anticipation of the county's first railroad connections. The towns of Palm, Dentonio, Valley Wells, Big Wells, and Winter Haven were all founded by developers during this period, as national advertising campaigns attracted settlers from states across the Union. About 1909 the town of Asherton was built by Asher Richardson, a prominent Dimmit County rancher. Apparently unhappy with the county government at Carrizo Springs, Richardson hoped Asherton would become the new county seat. His 40,000-acre development was the most successful of the projects begun in Dimmit County during the boom, largely because the Gulf and Asherton Railway, which Richardson built himself, began trips to the town in 1910. Richardson's hope that the railroad would help his settlement to eclipse Carrizo Springs failed, however, after the San Antonio, Uvalde and Gulf Railroad ran a spur into Carrizo Springs later that year in exchange for a bonus.

Irrigation and the long growing season transformed Dimmit County as it became known as part of the Texas Winter Garden Region, one of the most prolific vegetable-growing areas in the country. Though onions were the county's biggest cash crop, by 1920 farmers also planted spinach (called "green gold" by some of the farmers) and strawberries; meanwhile, orchards of figs, peaches, plums, and citrus fruits were also being harvested or planted. Improved acres in farms grew from 3,081 in 1900 to 8,053 in 1910, and then to 23,172 in 1920. Meanwhile, the average value of an acre of farmland jumped from $1.80 in 1900 (when much marginal ranchland seems to have been reported as farmland) to $24.60 in 1910, and then to more than $40 in 1920. The county's population grew rapidly in this period, too, rising from 1,106 in 1900 to 3,081 in 1910 and 5,296 in 1920. Many newcomers, attracted by the developers' nationwide advertising campaigns, were whites from midwestern or western states such as Ohio, California, and Oklahoma; a few came from Canada. More than a hundred Mennonites[qv] traveled from Ohio to settle at Palm, while many of those who settled at Valley Wells were from Oklahoma. Many began their farms with only limited financial resources. Some of them had never farmed before. Nevertheless, many of these new farmers brought with them a vested interest in the future of commercial agriculture that contrasted with the views of some of the ranchers in the county. As a contemporary writer put it, old ranchers doubted that anybody could "make a garden out of this country," but the new commercial farmer "was computing the number of acres he would plant to Bermuda onions and strawberries." Even as one wave of immigrants moved in from the North, another important source of the rise in Dimmit County's population during this period came from south of the border, as people moved into Dimmit County to clear land, to help build the railroads and towns, and to work on the new commercial farms. Perhaps 25 or 30 percent of the new Hispanic settlers came from other parts of Texas; when Big Wells was founded, for example, Mexican Americans[qv] from Cotulla were encouraged to move there. Many new workers, however, came from Mexico. Some were escaping the dislocations occasioned by the Mexican Revolution,[qv] which began in 1910; others were brought in by Mexican labor agents, who were sometimes paid a dollar for each worker they recruited.

These simultaneous influxes of new residents, one from the north, the other from the south, altered the social and political facts of Dimmit County life. Even as the new commercial farmers came to outnumber the old ranchers, the Mexican-American population grew more rapidly. By 1915, Mexican Americans constituted more than half of Dimmit County residents. As early as 1911 the editor of the Carrizo Springs *Javelin*, who seems to have sympathized with the interests of the new farmers, urged restricting the voting rights of Mexican Americans. Since the first days of settlement, Hispanics had never fully shared in the economic and political life of the county. But now they were also caught in the middle of the developing conflict between the old ranchers and the new commercial farmers. Some were suspected of sympathizing with the old ranchers rather than their employers, the new farmers. Small farmers feared that large ranchers would illegally obtain the votes of Mexican Americans to dominate county politics and perhaps inhibit development. These concerns, mixed with the sentiments evident in the *Javelin*'s editorials, contributed to the formation of the White Man's Primary Association in 1914. This organization helped to consolidate political power in the hands of the new farmers and effectively excluded Mexican Americans from any meaningful participation in county politics for almost fifty years thereafter (*see* WHITE PRIMARY). By 1930, Mexican Americans constituted almost two-thirds of the county population. In 1948, noting "segregation and discrimination" in virtually every aspect of Dimmit County life, one writer observed that Mexican Americans were considered to be "a class apart from the rest of the population."

A sharp drop in the price of onions, coinciding with an extended drought from 1916 to 1918, shook out many of the undercapitalized small farmers who came to Dimmit County between 1900 and 1916 and crippled Bermuda, Big Wells, and several other towns that had mushroomed during that time. The development spirit boomed again briefly during the 1920s. Dimmit County was hailed again as a "County of Miracles," where cow pastures were "transformed" into lucrative farms by the "abundance" of artesian water. During this period a wealthy and ambitious group of Kansas investors attempted to build another new town, Catarina, on the site of the old Taft-Catarina ranch; perhaps seven different "development propositions" were in operation by 1925, and the county's population rose to 8,828 by 1930. This boom failed, too, however, with the onset of the Great Depression[qv] and the end of the days of cheap and bountiful artesian water. Many of the county's farmers were forced to cut back their once-lucrative vegetable production during the depression, and fell back on raising poultry, hogs, and dairy cattle. Many farms failed or were abandoned. Only 11,666 acres of cropland was harvested in 1939, two-thirds of the 17,344 acres harvested in 1924. By 1940 the county's population had dropped to 8,542. Few had noticed when some of the original artesian wells stopped flowing between 1910 and 1912, since many wells continued to flow without mechanical aid. In the 1920s, however, most of the county's artesian wells had stopped flowing and many of the county's creeks and springs had gone dry. Farmers had to install pumps to get their water out of the ground, and the added expense, combined with the onset of the depression, drove many farms out of production during the late 1920s. The agricultural boomtown of Palm, for example, faded away after the irrigation pumps burned up, and the surrounding land was abandoned. In 1934 the United States Department of the Interior concluded, however, that the Carrizo sandstone appeared to contain enough water to supply Dimmit County farming at its new, lower level. But, noting the "persistent decline" in groundwater levels before 1929, the study concluded that the existing water supply would not support "substantial additional development."

The days of plentiful water were over. Nevertheless, after the hard days of the depression were over, irrigation enabled farmers to put more acres into production than ever before. In 1944 almost 15,000 acres was harvested in Dimmit County, nearly 30 percent more than in 1939; in 1950 almost 19,000 acres was harvested. By 1956, 40,000 acres was irrigated for crops, particularly vegetables. Onions, carrots, lettuce, and tomatoes were among the county's most important crops, along with cantaloupes, watermelons, squash, and radishes. Most of the produce was shipped to northern states during the winter and early spring. In the long run, however, these levels of production could not be sustained. A water survey conducted in 1955 demonstrated that water levels had dropped dramatically since the end of World War II.[qv] Farmers were taking two to three times more water out of the ground than annual recharge could replenish. Though Dimmit County continued to be an important source of the country's vegetable supply, production dropped over the ensuing decades. By 1965 only about 15,000 acres was being irrigated. Much of the land reverted to rangeland, as the cattle business again became more important to the county's economy. By 1969 about 60 percent of the county's farm income came from its crops, and most of the rest derived from beef cattle.

Meanwhile, oil and gas production had become the most important source of revenue. Trace amounts of oil were found in the county in 1903 by men drilling water wells, and the first systematic exploration efforts were conducted in 1915 near Las Vegas. The first producing well was not found until 1943, however, and relatively small amounts of oil were extracted until the late 1950s. Oil production in 1947 totaled only 973 barrels; the 1954 production was 56,947 barrels. But in 1958 more than 513,000 barrels of oil was taken from Dimmit County lands, and the rise in production continued through the 1960s and 1970s until oil and gas became the county's largest source of income. In 1972 more than 7,445,000 barrels of oil was produced in Dimmit County. Though production declined during the late 1970s and early 1980s, oil and gas remained an important part of the economy. In 1980, Dimmit County farmers earned about $20 million for their crops, while about $60 million in oil and gas was produced.

Since the county was organized in 1880, Dimmit County voters have regularly cast their ballots for Democrats. The county went Democratic in twenty-three of the twenty-seven presidential elections between 1884 and 1988. The only Republican presidential candidates to win majorities during this period were Herbert Hoover (1928), Dwight D. Eisenhower[qv] (1952 and 1956), and Richard Nixon (1972). Only in 1896, when the Populist ticket outpolled Republican William McKinley, and in 1912, when about 12 percent of the county's voters cast their ballots for Progressive candidate Theodore Roosevelt, have third parties played a significant role in county political history. In presidential elections since 1976, the Democrats have won large majorities in the county; in 1988, Michael Dukakis received 2,735 votes, while George H. W. Bush received only 900. In 1990, Dimmit County had a population of 10,433. Most of the towns that had appeared during the agricultural boom of the early twentieth century had severely declined or disappeared altogether, however, and the residents were increasingly concentrated in Asherton and Carrizo Springs. Reflecting this trend, the school districts regularly consolidated after 1940, so that by the early 1980s the county had only two, with a total of five elementary schools and two high schools. Carrizo Springs, with a population of 5,745 in 1990, continued to be the principal town and county seat, and was home to the county's general aviation airport, the Carrizo Springs *Javelin*, and the only radio station. In 1990 almost eighty percent of the county's inhabitants were of Mexican descent; most of the rest of the population was of English or Irish descent, while African Americans[qv] constituted less than 1 percent of the residents. *See also* AGRICULTURE, ONION CULTURE.

BIBLIOGRAPHY: Gunnar Brune, *Springs of Texas*, Vol. 1 (Fort Worth: Branch-Smith, 1981). David Montejano, *Anglos and Mexicans in the Making of Texas, 1836–1986* (Austin: University of Texas Press, 1987). Lura Rouse, A Study of Spanish-Speaking Children in Dimmit County, Texas (M.A. thesis, University of Texas, 1948). Paul S. Taylor, "Historical Note on Dimmit County, Texas," *Southwestern Historical Quarterly* 34 (October 1930). Laura Knowlton Tidwell, *Dimmit County Mesquite Roots* (Austin: Wind River, 1984).
John Leffler

DIMMITT, PHILIP (ca. 1801–1841). Philip Dimmitt, a pioneer Texas trader and merchant and major figure in the Texas Revolution,[qv] was born in Jefferson County, Kentucky, about 1801 and traveled to Texas about 1823 with a letter of introduction to Stephen F. Austin.[qv] He settled in La Villita[qv] at Bexar and for several years was commissary contractor to the Mexican garrison there. He married María Luisa Lazo, whose father was a De León colonist and kinsman of Martín De León,[qv] and by marriage received a three-league headright in De León's colony.[qv] The Dimmitts made their home on a ranch bordering the town of Guadalupe Victoria. Dimmitt, who was popular among his fellow Mexican citizens, maintained trading posts on the Guadalupe River near Victoria, at Goliad, and at Dimmitt's Landing[qv] on Lavaca Bay, where he established a wharf and warehouse. He accumulated "a large fortune by honest and judicious mercantile operations," according to a contemporary, the historian and statesman Henry Stuart Foote.[qv] Dimmitt also fought Indians on the Nueces River.

In 1835 he purchased land from an original member of the Power and Hewetson colony,[qv] but hostilities with Mexico interrupted his family's resettlement. When George M. Collinsworth's[qv] group of volunteers from Matagorda arrived at Guadalupe Victoria en route to capture Goliad, Plácido Benavides, Silvestre De León, José M. J. Carbajal,[qv] Dimmitt, and some thirty Mexican rancheros joined the expedition, though most did not sign the "Compact of Volunteers" drafted on October 9, 1835. While at Victoria Dimmitt received word from a contact at Goliad that Mexican general Martín Perfecto de Cos^qv had left La Bahía^qv with only a skeleton garrison and was en route to Bexar. Collinsworth's force then attacked and captured Goliad, and soon La Bahía was reinforced with additional volunteers, who elected Dimmitt captain (*see* GOLIAD CAMPAIGN OF 1835).

Dimmitt, a tough but respected disciplinarian whom Foote called "a very intelligent and chivalrous officer," commanded Goliad from about October 14, 1835, to about January 14, 1836. He was particularly well informed about activities in northern Mexico through various members of the De León family and his brother, who lived in Zacatecas. Though the capture of Goliad gave the Texas army needed provisions, Dimmitt supplied the army as well from his own warehouses. On October 21, 1835, he issued an "Appeal to the Inhabitants of Texas Residing East of the Guadalupe" for support. To show his allegiance to the Mexican Federalists, he designed the green-white-red tricolor flag that later became the traditionally recognized banner of the Texas force in the battle of the Alamo.^qv "I have had a flag made," he wrote Stephen F. Austin on October 27, 1835, "the colours, and their arrangement the same as the old one—with the words and figures, 'Constitution of 1824,' displayed on the white, in the centre." A peculiar feature of his Goliad commandancy was a permanent board of advisers, which included James Kerr, James Power, John J. Linn, Ira Ingram,^qqv Carbajal, Benavides, and others. Dimmitt's correspondence with Austin indicates his perception that La Bahía should be fortified to keep Cos from receiving seaborne reinforcements through Copano, and also to protect the municipalities of Refugio, Goliad, and Guadalupe Victoria, which had jeopardized themselves by pledging allegiance to the Constitution of 1824.^qv

In October 1835 Dimmitt sent Thomas G. Western,^qv James Kerr, and John Linn to negotiate a treaty of neutrality with menacing Karankawa Indians and then ordered an attack on the Mexican garrison at Fort Lipantitlán, which was successfully carried out by Ira Westover.^qv This significant victory freed the citizens of San Patricio Municipality to elect delegates to the Consultation^qv and organize a militia, supplied Goliad with additional cannons and provisions, eliminated the threat to Copano, and cut the Mexican line between Matamoros and Bexar. On the way back to Goliad, Westover's force encountered Governor Agustín Viesca,^qv recently escaped from prison, and brought him back to La Bahía. Dimmitt, though courteous and hospitable, refused to recognize Viesca's office, since his sentiment was changing towards preferring Texas independence from Mexico. This outraged Linn, Kerr, James Grant,^qv Westover, Viesca, and others still intensely loyal to Mexico, who launched a barrage of letters to Stephen F. Austin in protest. Austin, who wanted to restore the Constitution of 1824 and feared that Dimmitt's acts would alienate the Federalists of northern Mexico, removed Dimmitt from office without a hearing on November 18, 1835. The entire Goliad garrison immediately issued a series of protesting resolutions. The General Council,^qv which itself denied Governor Viesca's authority, refused to remove Dimmitt and instead recognized his commandancy.

About December 6, 1835, Dimmitt and a small force proceeded to Bexar and participated in the final assault against Cos (*see* BEXAR, SIEGE OF). Dimmitt may have taken the famed "Constitution of 1824" flag to Bexar at this time or in late January, when he hurried reinforcements to James C. Neill's^qv garrison at the Alamo. He returned to Goliad from Bexar about December 14 and designed what has been called the first flag of independence, depicting a bloody arm holding a bloody sword on a white field, which was raised on December 20, 1835, at La Bahía to commemorate the Goliad Declaration of Independence,^qv which he and Ingram framed.

Dimmitt's garrison belonged neither to the regular army nor to Austin's volunteer army, but was an independent command composed of volunteers who captured and garrisoned La Bahía. It received great praise from acting governor James W. Robinson^qv for gathering provisions, arms, and horses, which were supplied to the revolutionary army^qv and to refugees at Refugio, Goliad, and Victoria. When Francis W. Johnson^qv and James Grant arrived at Goliad with a force en route to capture Matamoros, in the Matamoros Expedition of 1835–36,^qv both men, being loyal to the Constitution of 1824 and antagonistic toward Dimmitt, and each thinking himself to be commander of the Texas army, demanded that the bloody-arm flag of independence be lowered and seized the garrison's transportation stock and many supplies. These actions induced Dimmitt to resign his command on or about January 10, 1836, and discharge his men, many of whom subsequently served with Francis W. Thornton,^qv who assumed command of Goliad.

Dimmitt arrived at Bexar about January 24 with about thirty volunteers to reinforce the Alamo and was appointed army storekeeper; his warehouse at Dimitt's Landing then served as a depot for government stores landed at Lavaca Bay. Though many of the volunteers returned home upon the arrival of William B. Travis^qv and his men on February 3, Dimmitt remained in San Antonio scouting for Travis and James Bowie^qv until February 24. He was with B. F. Nobles when the two were cut off by the arrival at Bexar of the Mexican army. Dimmitt retreated to the vicinity of Victoria, where until early March he operated a station to recruit volunteers to relieve the Alamo. On March 12, Sam Houston^qv ordered Dimmitt to join him at Gonzales, and though he had recruited but twenty-one volunteers, rumors spread that he headed a force of 200 to relieve Fannin at Goliad or Travis at Bexar. Dimmitt arrived at Gonzales to find it occupied by the Mexican army. After a fight on Kerr Creek, his force retreated down the Guadalupe River to Victoria. The men arrived on March 19 exhausted and without food and learned the next day of Fannin's surrender. Mexican general José de Urrea^qv entered Victoria on the twenty-first, and Dimmitt apparently helped with evacuations and joined the refugees in the Runaway Scrape.^qv After April 15 he arrived on Matagorda Island to bring recruits to General Houston's army, which was then moving to San Jacinto, and with John J. Linn he arrived on April 22, 1836, bringing the first supplies and reinforcements to Houston's victorious army after the battle of San Jacinto.^qv

After the revolution Dimmitt settled in Refugio, where he became a justice. In 1841 he bought part of the Aldrete family ranch on the Aransas River. In May he and a partner, James Gourley, Jr., began building a trading post near the site of present Calallen, about fifteen miles from the post of William P. Aubrey and Henry L. Kinney,^qv cofounders of Corpus Christi. Aubrey and Kinney had a monopoly on contraband traffic with the Mexican forces operating from Fort Lipantitlán, on the Nueces River. On July 4, 1841, Dimmitt and some comrades were captured by Mexican troops, who also looted merchandise valued at $6,000. Aubrey and Kinney's post, however, was bypassed. Dimmitt was taken to Matamoros. Various mass meetings were held at Aransas City, Lamar, Refugio, and Victoria, which demanded that the Texas government obtain the hero's release and threatened private retaliation. Some newspapers reported treason, asserting that Kinney utilized his friendship with Mexican general Pedro de Ampudia^qv to get the general to attack Dimmitt so as to eliminate trade competition. Aubrey and Kinney were eventually arrested and charged with treason but were acquitted on August 22, 1841, perhaps through the influence of President Mirabeau B. Lamar,^qv who depended on Kinney and his private force of about sixty men to hold the disputed Nueces region for Texas. In September Lamar sent Kinney to Mexico to petition for Dimmitt's release, but he was unsuccessful. The Centralist government in Mexico had issued a warrant for Dimmitt's arrest for his role in the Texas Revolution, particularly for the Goliad Declaration of Independence. Dimmitt and his comrades, together with nineteen other Texans, were put in irons and marched to Monterrey in August 1841 en route to prison in Mexico City. At Saltillo the Texans tried to escape by drugging their guards with alcohol laced with morphine. Eighteen escaped, but eleven were overtaken and shot, and the others were pursued into the mountains. Dimmitt, separately confined and unable to escape, overheard that he would be shot if the fugitives did not surrender. Facing either execution or interminable imprisonment, he chose to take his own life by morphine overdose, remarking: "I do not fear death but dread the idea of ending my life in a loathsome dungeon. Tell them I prefer a Roman's death to the ignominy of perpetual imprisonment, and that my last wish is for my country's welfare." Dimmitt's love for his country was evident even in his children's names, which included Antonio Alamo Dimmitt and Texas Philip Dimmitt. In 1858 Dimmit County was established and named in his honor. *See also* FLAGS OF THE TEXAS REVOLUTION.

BIBLIOGRAPHY: Eugene C. Barker, ed., *The Austin Papers* (3 vols., Washington: GPO, 1924–28). Philip Dimmitt Papers, Barker Texas History Center, University of Texas at Austin. Catherine George, The Life of Philip Dimmitt (M.A. thesis, University of Texas, 1937). Hobart Huson, *Captain Philip Dimmitt's Commandancy of Goliad, 1835–1836* (Austin: Von Boeckmann–Jones, 1974). Hobart Huson, *Refugio: A Comprehensive History of Refugio County from Aboriginal Times to 1953* (2 vols., Woodsboro, Texas: Rooke Foundation, 1953, 1955). John H. Jenkins, ed., *The Papers of the Texas Revolution, 1835–1836* (10 vols., Austin: Presidial Press, 1973). John J. Linn, *Reminiscences of Fifty Years in Texas* (New York: Sadlier, 1883; 2d ed., Austin: Steck, 1935; rpt., Austin: State House, 1986). Mary Agnes Mitchell, *The First Flag of Texas Independence* (Refugio, Texas, 1937). Joseph Milton Nance, *After San Jacinto: The Texas-Mexican Frontier, 1836–1841* (Austin: University of Texas Press, 1963). Kathryn Stoner O'Connor, *The Presidio La Bahía del Espíritu Santo de Zúñiga, 1721 to 1846* (Austin: Von Boeckmann–Jones, 1966). *Craig H. Roell*

DIMMITT, TEXAS. Dimmitt, the county seat of Castro County, is on U.S. Highway 385 thirty-one miles southwest of Amarillo in the central part of the county. In March 1890 the Bedford Town and Land Company, headquartered at Sherman, in Grayson County, bought a section of land near the center of the county and laid out a townsite. H. G. Bedford handled the sale of lots at the new site, which the promoters named for their colleague and Bedford's brother-in-law, Rev. W. C. Dimmitt. During 1890 other promoters, including Ira Aten and Lysius Gough,qqv sought to develop rival townsites as candidates to be county seat. But on December 18, 1891, Dimmitt was elected.

By that time Dimmitt had two stores, a post office, and a resident doctor. J. W. Carter, the county's first resident, established a hotel, and Miss Lou Belsher taught the first school. A Baptist church was established, and several different communions met in the schoolhouse. William Andrew (Uncle Buck) Tate established a lumber and wagon yard and later opened a second hotel. Aten waged unceasing war against cattle rustlers during his tenure as county sheriff. In 1892 a wooden frame courthouse was completed; it was used until 1906, when fire caused by lightning destroyed it. An elaborate brick structure replaced it in 1908. By then "Old Man" Callahan had started the *Plainsman,* the county's first newspaper, and C. E. McLean had opened the First State Bank of Dimmitt. A brick school building was completed in 1910. Although the town was for several years without a railroad and growth was relatively slow, it remained the county seat. In July 1928 the Fort Worth and Denver South Plains Railway was extended to Dimmitt. As a result the town of between 800 and 1,000 residents was incorporated, and the *Castro County News* succeeded the defunct *Plainsman.* During the 1930s a hospital and a county library were established. The present county courthouse replaced the earlier red-brick building in 1938. By 1940 Dimmitt was booming as the county's main trading point with a population of 943. The population increased to 1,441 by 1950.

Dimmitt, which had ninety-three businesses in the mid-1980s, depends upon the county's variety of agricultural products for most of its income. Amstar Corporation produces syrups and other corn products. Plants in Dimmitt process lettuce, onions, potatoes, and carrots. Cattle and sheep are fed in the county's numerous feedlots.

The Dimmitt Goodpasture Plant produces anhydrous ammonia and agricultural chemicals. Other industries include grain elevators and cotton gins and the manufacture of farming equipment. A federal youth corps project was located in Dimmitt in the 1970s. The city's resources include the Plains Memorial Hospital and Nursing Home, the Rhodes Memorial Library, the Castro County Country Club, a city park, and a radio station. Dimmitt Municipal Airport, just north of town, has facilities for both charter and agricultural services. The Castro County Historical Museum houses relics from the past in the Jeff Gilbreath farmstead, dating from 1909. It features craft exhibits and demonstrations during the county fair in September. Other annual events include a chamber of commerce banquet in January, a square dance and stock show in February, and a rodeo in June. Former state senator and United States congressman Kent Hance came from Dimmitt, which grew in population from 4,327 in 1971 to 5,019 in 1980. In 1990 the population was 4,408.

BIBLIOGRAPHY: Castro County Historical Commission, *Castro County, 1891–1981* (Dallas: Taylor, 1981). *H. Allen Anderson*

DIMPKINS, JAMES R. (?–1836). James R. Dimpkins, Alamo defender, was born in England and marched to Texas from New Orleans as a member of Capt. Thomas Breece'sqv company of New Orleans Greys.qv He took part in the siege of Bexarqv and later served in the Alamo garrison as a sergeant in Capt. William Blazeby'sqv infantry company. Dimpkins died in the battle of the Alamoqv on March 6, 1836.

BIBLIOGRAPHY: Daughters of the American Revolution, *The Alamo Heroes and Their Revolutionary Ancestors* (San Antonio, 1976). Daughters of the Republic of Texas, *Muster Rolls of the Texas Revolution* (Austin, 1986). Bill Groneman, *Alamo Defenders* (Austin: Eakin, 1990). *Bill Groneman*

DIMPLE, TEXAS. Dimple is six miles north of Clarksville in north central Red River County. It had a post office from 1901 until 1921. From 1914 through 1986 the estimated population of Dimple was reported as twenty-five. In 1990 it was sixty. *Cecil Harper, Jr.*

DINERO, TEXAS. Dinero is on Farm Road 534 some ten miles southeast of George West in southeastern Live Oak County. The town was first named Barlow's Ferry, after E. Barlow, who in 1846 ran ferries across the Nueces River for local ranchers. In 1872 the name was changed to Dinero ("money" in Spanish); there were rumors of a nearby silver mine hidden by Indians, and Mexican treasure-seekers favored the area. The community's name was probably changed, however, to reflect the area's profitable resources, which over the years have included cotton, dairy farms, and oil and gas wells. The community's first school opened in 1858 and closed in 1894. In 1885 Dinero was granted a post office, and George Wright's general store served a population of twenty. The community's population rose to seventy by 1892, and by 1906 Dinero had two schools with two teachers and a total enrollment of twenty-four. The population was thirty when the town moved a mile west in 1914 to be on the San Antonio, Uvalde and Gulf Railroad. Oil and gas discoveries in the 1920s failed to make Dinero a boomtown, and only a church, a school, several businesses, and scattered dwellings marked the community on the 1936 county highway map. The community's population reached fifty in 1943, and Dinero's separate schools for white and Mexican-American students were annexed to the George West Independent School District in 1949. From 1964 to 1990 Dinero reported thirty-five residents and three businesses.

BIBLIOGRAPHY: Live Oak County Centennial Association, *Live Oak County Centennial* (George West, Texas, 1956). Live Oak County Historical Commission, *The History of the People of Live Oak County*

(George West, Texas, 1982). Ervin L. Sparkman, *The People's History of Live Oak County* (Mesquite, Texas, 1981).

Brian Michael Todd Kryszewski

DING DONG, TEXAS. Ding Dong is on the Lampasas River eight miles south of Killeen in southwestern Bell County. In 1979 it had a church and several scattered dwellings, and in 1990 it had a population of twenty-two.

Mark Odintz

DINKINS, TEXAS. Dinkins was on White Switch Road, which runs north to south between Farm roads 2154 and 159, four miles west of Navasota in southern Brazos County. The area was included in Stephen F. Austin's^{qv} original colony, though it was not settled until the 1850s. The settlement developed as a stop on the International–Great Northern railroad when it built through Brazos County in the early 1900s. It had a post office from 1913 to 1931. G. W. Dunlap was postmaster and general-store owner, and the name submitted for the community was Dunlap; but through a mistake the name was recorded as Dinkins. The population in 1915 was twenty-five, where it remained until the train stopped running in the late 1940s. During that period Dinkins had a grocery store, the train stop, and a school, which was eventually absorbed by the Millican and Allen Farm schools. The International–Great Northern tracks were taken up in 1965–66. In 1990 the area was farmland.

BIBLIOGRAPHY: Fred Tarpley, *1001 Texas Place Names* (Austin: University of Texas Press, 1980).

Christina L. Gray

DINNER CREEK (Harris County). Dinner Creek rises a mile north of Settlers Village in northwest Harris County (at 29°54′ N, 95°44′ W) and runs southeast for four miles to its mouth on Langham Creek (at 29°52′ N, 95°41′ W). It traverses flat to rolling terrain with local escarpments and dissections, surfaced by shallow to deep sandy and clay loams that support native vegetation including mixed hardwoods and pines. In developed areas this vegetation has been replaced by cultivated row and cover crops.

_____ (Uvalde County). Dinner Creek rises a half mile east of the Frio River and seven miles north of Knippa in east central Uvalde County (at 29°24′ N, 99°38′ W) and runs southeast for nineteen miles to its mouth on Blanco Creek, fifteen miles east of Uvalde (at 29°13′ N, 99°32′ W). Scrub brush and various grasses predominate in the creek's upper reaches and give way to pecan, other hardwoods, and various grasses in the lower. The stream rises in steep to gently sloping terrain and runs into terrain with low relief surfaces. The soils throughout the length of the creek are deep, loamy, and clayey.

DINOSAUR VALLEY STATE PARK. Dinosaur Valley State Park, on Farm Road 205 four miles west of Glen Rose in north central Somervell County, was established by the Texas Parks and Wildlife Department^{qv} in 1969. The park derives its name from the 100-million-year-old dinosaur tracks found within its area. The tracks, which were likely made by three different types of dinosaurs—acrocanthosaurus, pleurocoelus, and an as yet unidentified species—range from twelve to thirty-six inches in length and nine to twenty-four inches in width and are found at seven locations in the park. Other dinosaur tracks from the vicinity of the park have been collected and displayed at the American Museum of Natural History in New York City and at the Texas Memorial Museum^{qv} in Austin. The park originally occupied 350 acres; in 1990 it covered 1,523 acres, mostly located within a large bend in the Paluxy River. Recreational facilities include nature and hiking trails, picnic areas, campgrounds, and five scenic overlooks. A herd of the state's longhorn cattle^{qv} lives in the park.

BIBLIOGRAPHY: George Oxford Miller and Delena Tull, *Texas Parks and Campgrounds: North, East, and Coastal Texas* (Austin: Texas Monthly Press, 1984). Vertical Files, Barker Texas History Center, University of Texas at Austin.

Brian Hart

DINSMORE, SILAS (ca. 1796–1846). Silas Dinsmore, state and county official, was born around 1796 and moved to Texas from Mobile, Alabama. In 1810–11 he was a government agent for the Choctaw Indian Reservation in Alabama and Tennessee. He represented Mina Municipality^{qv} at the Convention of 1832^{qv} and served on the 1833 Brazoria Committee of Safety, designed to protect citizens from Indians. Dinsmore was appointed by President Sam Houston^{qv} as first chief justice of Matagorda County in December 1836, reappointed by President Mirabeau B. Lamar^{qv} on January 23, 1839, and elected to the same office by the Fourth Congress in January 1840. He was also involved in establishing the Texas Navy.^{qv} He later moved to Austin, where he was involved in the real estate business and witnessed the survey of the Montopolis area. Dinsmore had a wife and daughter and was an Episcopalian vestryman in 1839. He died on September 13, 1846, and was buried at his plantation, Wells Point, ten miles west of Palacios.

BIBLIOGRAPHY: Lorraine Bruce Jeter, *Matagorda: Early History* (Baltimore: Gateway, 1974). Sam A. Shuler, "Stephen F. Austin and the City of Austin," *Southwestern Historical Quarterly* 69 (January 1966). Ralph W. Steen, "Analysis of the Work of the General Council, Provisional Government of Texas, 1835–1836," *Southwestern Historical Quarterly* 40–42 (April 1937, January–July 1938). Texas House of Representatives, *Biographical Directory of the Texan Conventions and Congresses, 1832–1845* (Austin: Book Exchange, 1941).

Diana J. Kleiner

DINSMORE, TEXAS. Dinsmore is on Farm Road 1301 and the Galveston, Harrisburg and San Antonio Railway two miles east of Wharton in Wharton County. It was established in John Dinsmore's quarter league by a black man, E. W. Roberts, for African Americans.^{qv} The plat was recorded in 1913, and the town was named Roberts; the residents, however, called the place Dinsmore, and the name Roberts appears only on the plats. The original plat had thirty-eight blocks, with nine avenues running east to west and six streets running north to south. One lot was designated for a school, with a park across the street. The streets and avenues had the names of local citizens. The lots were small but cheap, and gave descendants of former slaves, now working as tenant farmers, sharecroppers, or hired agricultural workers, a place to build and own their own homes. The site was near Burr, which had the largest black population in the county because the large plantations along the Caney Creek had been in that area.

After the railroad was built from Wharton to Van Vleck in 1900, white farmers moved in. E. W. Roberts, who owned and operated a brick two-story mercantile store on the east side of the courthouse square in Wharton, began selling lots in 1914. He eventually declared bankruptcy, sold all of his Wharton County holdings, and moved to Houston. A revised plat was recorded in 1920 that reduced the townsite to three avenues, four streets, and ten blocks containing twelve lots each. The school and park never materialized. In the early 1990s Dinsmore comprised fifty houses, an estimated 250 residents, and one business.

BIBLIOGRAPHY: Wharton County Historical Commission, *Wharton County Pictorial History: 1846–1946, Our First 100 Years* (Austin: Eakin Press, 1993).

Merle R. Hudgins

DIPLOMATIC RELATIONS OF THE REPUBLIC OF TEXAS. The diplomatic history of Texas began late in 1835 with the appointment of Stephen F. Austin, Branch T. Archer, and William H. Wharton^{qqv} as commissioners to the United States to get help to carry on the Texas Revolution.^{qv} After the battle of San Jacinto^{qv} and the establishment of constitutional government, the people of Texas voted by a large majority to seek annexation^{qv} to the United States of America. President Sam Houston^{qv} chose Wharton to take charge of negotiations. Recognition of independence and annexation to the United States were dealt with separately, because in the light of experience it was apparent that if recognition was gained as a preliminary step, membership in the Union might follow more easily. Meeting with congressmen, holding conferences with John Forsyth, secretary of state, and calling on President Andrew Jackson, Wharton finally secured the recognition of Texas independence. On March 3, 1837, Jackson appointed Alcee LeBranch as chargé d'affaires to the Republic of Texas.[qv] Recognition attained, Wharton withdrew, leaving Memucan Hunt[qv] to carry on. On August 4, 1837, the subject of annexation was formally presented to the United States. A considerable public opinion, expressed in memorials and petitions, favored annexation by the time Congress convened in December. Politicians declined to take action for months, however, and when the matter did come up, John Quincy Adams carried on an effective delaying action by speaking against it every day for three weeks. The session closed in the summer of 1838 without action. Houston instructed Anson Jones,[qv] who had replaced Hunt, to withdraw the Texas offer. This was done on October 2, 1838; the Texas Senate approved of the withdrawal on January 23, 1839. While the prospects for annexation were discouraging in the spring of 1837, the Texas authorities, convinced that they might have to carry on as an independent nation, decided to establish commercial relations with European powers and so strengthen their position. Accordingly, James Pinckney Henderson,[qv] secretary of state, was sent to London early in October 1837 to open negotiations with Lord Palmerston. The British were fearful that recognition would jeopardize their friendly standing with Mexico and declined to enter into formal relations; they did consent, however, to admit Texas commerce to British ports on their own terms. In France Henderson fared better. Dealing first with Count Mole, and later with his successor Marshal Soult, the Texas agent arranged a treaty by which France recognized the independence of Texas and admitted her commerce on a most favored nation basis. The treaty was signed on September 29, 1839, and Dubois de Saligny[qv] was appointed chargé d'affaires to the republic.

When Mirabeau B. Lamar[qv] became president, annexation was no longer agitated, and he was free to direct his efforts toward developing the republic into a strong, independent nation. It had become evident that European countries were not eager to enter into diplomatic or commercial relations with Texas while Mexico still asserted legal claims to the region; therefore Lamar's foreign policy centered about making peace with Mexico. In February 1839, seeing a favorable opportunity as a result of the French intervention in Mexico, Lamar instructed Barnard E. Bee[qv] to proceed to Mexico to arrange a formal peace. Bee was authorized, moreover, to spend up to five million dollars in getting the boundary of Texas established at the Rio Grande. He did not even get an official interview, however, and returned empty handed. Lamar tried again; he sent James Treat,[qv] a man of broad acquaintances in Mexico, as confidential agent. Treat worked long, gave promise of success, but accomplished nothing definite. Shortly before the failure of Treat, England promised assistance, and Lamar decided to make a third effort. He sent James Webb.[qv] Faring no better than his predecessors, Webb on his return urged the hostilities Lamar was considering. A military convention with the revolting Mexican state of Yucatan was then made, but this diplomatic threat was ineffective as Yucatan soon renewed its allegiance to Mexico. At the end of Lamar's administration, Texas–Mexican relations were actually more unfriendly than they had been at the beginning.

Financial needs often shaped foreign policies. Of all the agents employed to secure loans, none served with greater distinction than James Hamilton.[qv] Originally commissioned along with several others during the Houston administration to negotiate a $5,000,000 loan, Hamilton was retained by Lamar and spent the greater part of three years trying to place the loan in Europe. At times Hamilton's work was entirely diplomatic, as he was well aware that recognition by foreign powers would facilitate his financial work in those nations.

Given broad diplomatic powers, he negotiated with the governments of England, Netherlands, and Belgium, and his loan activities brought him in contact with influential men of many countries. His first success was in Holland, where on September 15, 1840, a treaty of commerce was signed. In London he drew up three treaties: one of commerce and navigation, a second providing for British mediation in the Texas–Mexico difficulties concerning peace, and a third calling for the suppression of slave trade. These were signed in November 1840, but because of various delays ratifications were not exchanged until July 28, 1842. A great deal of Hamilton's time was spent trying to conclude a treaty with the Belgians; he was unsuccessful, however, as were his successors. While Hamilton enjoyed some success in his diplomatic endeavors, he found it impossible to negotiate the loan; and when Houston reassumed the presidency and reversed most of Lamar's policies, especially the financial ones, Hamilton's services were terminated. Ashbel Smith[qv] was appointed and held conversations with Spanish officials relative to a treaty of commerce, by which Texas hoped to develop trade with Cuba, but no conclusion was reached. Smith's regular work as Texan envoy to London and Paris occupied so much of his time that he could not well extend the interests of Texas elsewhere. Houston commissioned William Henry Daingerfield[qv] as chargé d'affaires to the Netherlands and authorized him to negotiate treaty agreements with other continental powers. With Vincent Rumpff, representing the Hanse Towns of Hamburg, Lubeck, and Bremen, Daingerfield drew up a convention of amity, commerce, and navigation. Hamburg refused to ratify, and the Senate of Lubeck also declined, but Bremen approved and in anticipation of ratification, appointed a collector of customs for Galveston. When the treaty reached Texas, annexation was the all-engrossing topic and no action was taken, ratifications in fact were never exchanged. Meanwhile Daingerfield conferred with representatives of Prussia and other European powers but learned that they were not inclined to enter into any formal agreements, since the continued existence of Texas was doubtful in the face of renewed conversations on annexation.

Houston favored annexation although his actions did not always indicate it. In June 1843 he agreed to an armistice with Mexico. Charles Elliot,[qv] British chargé d'affaires to Texas, and Richard Pakenham, the British minister to Mexico, were in favor of the armistice and hoped it would mark the beginning of stronger British influence in Texas. Aware of the disadvantages that would result from a British foothold in Texas, President John Tyler authorized his secretary of state, Abel Upshur, to reopen the annexation question with Isaac Van Zandt,[qv] the Texas chargé. Houston agreed and sent James Pinckney Henderson to assist in the negotiations. A treaty proposing to admit Texas as a territory was drawn up but rejected by the United States Senate on June 8, 1844. The motives were varied, but undoubtedly most of the senators wanted to postpone the issue until after the national elections in November. The election of James K. Polk on an annexation platform was interpreted as a demand for immediate action and induced Tyler to renew his efforts. In December 1844 he submitted a proposition for the annexation of Texas by joint resolution. Passed late in February 1845 the joint resolution provided for the admission of Texas as a state instead of a territory, gave it the privilege of keeping its own public lands, thus providing a source of revenue with which to pay its debts, and extended the right to divide itself into as many as four additional states. Andrew J. Donelson[qv] brought the proposition to Texas and urged its immediate acceptance. The United States government had good reason to be solicitous, for both England and France, in the hope that Texas might be induced to reject annexation and remain independent, had been urging Mexico to agree to a treaty of peace. Anson Jones, president of Texas, consented to the preliminaries of a treaty with Mexico by which that country consented to recognize the independence of Texas on condition that Texas would not become annexed to the United States. Jones presented both propositions, annexation or Mexican recognition, to the Congress of the republic and to the people of Texas, who, by the

Convention of 1845,^{qv} accepted the terms of annexation. This action ended all diplomatic activity of the republic, although some time passed before the various foreign representatives of Texas returned.

BIBLIOGRAPHY: Nancy Nichols Barker, trans. and ed., *The French Legation in Texas,* Vol. 1: *Recognition, Rupture, and Reconciliation* (Austin: Texas State Historical Association, 1971); Vol. 2: *Mission Miscarried* (1973). Nancy Nichols Barker, "The Republic of Texas: A French View," *Southwestern Historical Quarterly* 71 (October 1967). Alma Howell Brown, "The Consular Service of the Republic of Texas," *Southwestern Historical Quarterly* 33 (January, April 1930). Mary Katherine Chase, *Négociations de la République du Texas en Europe, 1837–1845* (Paris: Champion, 1932). *Correspondence Relating to a Treaty of Peace between Mexico and Texas* (Washington: National Register Printing, 1845). Robert Emmet Cunningham, James Treat and His Mission to Mexico (M.A. thesis, University of Texas, 1950). *Diplomatic Correspondence of the Republic of Texas,* ed. George Pierce Garrison (3 parts, Washington: GPO, 1908–11). Herbert Rook Edwards, "Diplomatic Relations between France and the Republic of Texas, 1836–1845," *Southwestern Historical Quarterly* 20 (January 1917). Herbert Gambrell, *Anson Jones: The Last President of Texas* (Garden City, New York: Doubleday, 1948). Charles Adams Gulick, Jr., Harriet Smither, et al., eds., *The Papers of Mirabeau Buonaparte Lamar* (6 vols., Austin: Texas State Library, 1920–27; rpt., Austin: Pemberton Press, 1968). Anson Jones, *Memoranda and Official Correspondence Relating to the Republic of Texas* (New York: Appleton, 1859; rpt. 1966). Julia Luker, Diplomatic Relations between Texas and Mexico, 1836–1842 (M.A. thesis, University of Texas, 1920). Charles Louis Ternay Neu, The Foreign Relations of the Republic of Texas, 1836–1846 (thesis, University of California, 1925). Joseph William Schmitz, *Texan Statecraft, 1836–1845* (San Antonio: Naylor, 1941). Stanley Siegel, *A Political History of the Texas Republic* (Austin: University of Texas Press, 1956). Harriet Smither, The Diplomatic Service of Ashbel Smith to the Republic of Texas, 1842–1845 (M.A. thesis, University of Texas, 1922). Amelia W. Williams and Eugene C. Barker, eds., *The Writings of Sam Houston, 1813–1863* (8 vols., Austin: University of Texas Press, 1938–43; rpt., Austin and New York: Pemberton Press, 1970). J. L. Worley, "The Diplomatic Relations of England and the Republic of Texas," *Quarterly of the Texas State Historical Association* 9 (July 1905).

Joseph W. Schmitz

DIRECT, TEXAS. Direct is twenty-five miles northwest of Paris on Farm Road 79 in northwest Lamar County. According to local tradition, the town was named either for Indians who crossed the river "direct" to obtain whiskey or to a revivalist who believed the local people were going "direct" to hell. The local church was built with money donated by a converted saloonkeeper. A local post office operated from 1887 until after 1954. In 1896 mail was delivered twice weekly, and Direct had three general stores and a cotton gin. By 1914 the community had a population of 218, telephone service, four general stores, and two blacksmiths. State highway maps in 1936 showed numerous businesses and residences at the townsite. By 1945 the population was 250, but after 1949 it began to decline, and in 1983 only seventy residents, a single business, two churches, and scattered dwellings remained.

A. W. Neville

DIRGIN, TEXAS. Dirgin is on Farm Road 2658 fourteen miles northeast of Henderson in northeastern Rusk County. It received a post office in 1898 and in 1907 had a school with thirty-three white pupils and one teacher and another with ninety-two black pupils and one teacher. In 1914 Dirgin had an estimated 100 inhabitants, two general stores, and a sawmill. The post office closed in 1918, and by 1933 the community had declined to twenty-five inhabitants and a single business. In 1940 a church, a business, and a number of scattered dwellings were at the site. Dirgin's population grew to fifty in the 1940s and 1950s but had declined to twelve by the 1960s and was still estimated at twelve in 1990.

Mark Odintz

DIRKS, FRANCES GARRETT VALENTINE (ca. 1925–1991). Frances Garrett Valentine Dirks, leader in the Democratic party^{qv} in Texas, was born in Dallas around 1925, and for most of her life she lived on the same street in that city. She opened an apartment-cleaning business in Dallas after being employed briefly as a domestic worker. As a young woman she married Roosevelt Valentine, with whom she had three sons. Following Valentine's death, she married John Dirks, who also preceded her in death. In the 1960s Frances Dirks became interested in political and social issues, especially desegregation efforts in her hometown. As a result, she gave up her business and entered full-time political work. She was a member of the staff of several Texas Democratic politicians, including state senator Mike McKool and United States representative John Bryant, for whom she was working at the time of her death. She also served on the campaign staffs of Ron Kessler, Martin Frost, John Bryant, and Jim Mattox. She was an active participant in numerous Democratic state conventions and served as a delegate to the party's national conventions in 1976, 1980, 1984, and 1988. In 1974 she became the first black Texan to be elected to the state Democratic Executive Committee from her senatorial district. She was also a leader in the Democratic Progressive Voters League.^{qv} For her political activism and commitment to the Democratic party, Dirks was honored by the League of Educational Advancement, the Coalition of Black Democrats, the Lesbian-Gay Political Coalition of Dallas, and the Democratic Women of Dallas County. She died of cancer in Dallas on February 16, 1991. Her funeral services at Mount Horeb Missionary Baptist Church in Dallas were attended by numerous local, state, and national politicians. She is buried in Lincoln Memorial Cemetery in Dallas. Her survivors included her three sons, three brothers, one sister, and several grandchildren.

BIBLIOGRAPHY: Dallas *Morning News,* February 22, 24, 1991.

Debbie Mauldin Cottrell

DIRT FARMERS' CONGRESS. As a result of an invitation by the Texas legislature, Texas agricultural and livestock producers met in Austin in February 1939 to counsel the Forty-sixth Legislature on proposed legislation. This meeting, known as the "Dirt Farmers' Congress," was made up of representatives of more than 100 counties. A closer relationship between the producers and industries was stressed. The congress, under the guidance of its committee of resolutions, composed of C. H. Day and others, requested the legislature to consider such problems as insect and rodent control, conservation of forests and wildlife, soil erosion, and compulsory dog vaccination to prevent rabies. The Dirt Farmers' Congress met again with the House of Representatives on February 18, 1949. After that time no more references to it appeared in House journals.

BIBLIOGRAPHY: Ralph W. Steen, *Twentieth Century Texas: An Economic and Social History* (Austin: Steck, 1942).

J. C. Conradt

DIRTY THIRTY. "Dirty Thirty" was the name given to thirty members of the 1971 Texas House of Representatives who grouped against Speaker of the House Gus Mutscher and other Texas officials charged in a bribery-conspiracy investigation by the United States Securities and Exchange Commission. The coalition of thirty Democrats and Republicans, conservatives and liberals, has been given credit for keeping the Sharpstown Stock Fraud Scandal^{qv} alive as a political issue. One member called for a resolution to make Mutscher and his associates resign from leadership positions while the SEC investigation continued, but Mutscher was still favored by a majority in the House, and the measure failed. Another resolution, for the House to make itself a committee of the whole to study the SEC allegation, also failed. The criticism by the Dirty Thirty of Mutscher's system of controlling legislation led him, finally, to agree to an investigation. But he appointed five of his closest House allies, all chairmen of other committees he had appointed, to do the job. This blatant use of appointive power to clear himself actually helped the Dirty Thirty's cause. On the next-to-last day of the session, Mutscher attacked the group, accusing them of irresponsible and partisan politics. In return the group called Mutscher a dictator of state politics, more concerned with private than public interests. This began the electoral battle, which Mutscher lost.

In September 1971 a Travis County grand jury indicted Mutscher and two colleagues for conspiracy to accept a bribe and accepting a bribe. It also strongly recommended reform in the power of the speaker, although this recommendation was largely ignored; in 1993 minor reforms occurred. Mutscher was tried, found guilty, and sentenced to five years' probation. Although not brought to trial, Governor Preston Smith and Lieutenant Governor Ben Barnes saw their political careers effectively ended. The Dirty Thirty paid a price, also, for Mutscher blocked most of the legislation introduced by the members, and they found themselves isolated from other legislators.

BIBLIOGRAPHY: Sam Kinch, Jr., and Ben Procter, *Texas under a Cloud* (Austin: Jenkins, 1972). Vertical Files, Barker Texas History Center, University of Texas at Austin (John Hannah, Gus Mutscher). Tracy D. Wooten, "The Sharpstown Incident and Its Impact on the Political Careers of Preston Smith, Gus Mutscher and Ben Barnes," *Touchstone* 5 (1986).

John G. Johnson

DISABLED AMERICAN VETERANS. The Disabled American Veterans, World War, was organized in Cincinnati, Ohio, in 1920 by Robert S. Marks, who became its first national commander. In June 1921 the first Texas chapter, Harwood Davis Chapter Number One, was formed in Fort Worth. By July 1921 there were more than twenty-five chapters throughout Texas. In May 1923 the Department of Texas, Disabled American Veterans, World War, was organized at Kerrville, Texas. William Ellis Register was elected first department commander, a position which he held for two terms. Congress granted the organization a federal charter in 1932. This charter was amended in 1942 by the deletion of the words "World War." The purpose of the organization is to advance the interests of all wounded, gassed, injured, and disabled veterans of all wars. Laurence R. Melton of Dallas was the first state commander to be elected to the office of national commander, for the term 1941–43. During this term he was instrumental in securing an executive order from President Franklin D. Roosevelt for government agencies to cooperate in the hiring of the physically handicapped. This program became national in scope and was known as the President's Committee for the Hiring of the Handicapped. Larger chapters of the DAV offer scholarships to winners of essay contests held each year. In 1994 Texas had 155 chapters of the DAV, with 89,000 members in five regions throughout the state.

P. D. Jackson

DISCH, WILLIAM JOHN (1874–1953). William John (Billy) Disch, baseball coach, was born on October 20, 1874, in Benton County, Missouri. In 1886 the family moved to Milwaukee, Wisconsin, where Disch first attended public schools. His greatest interest was baseball, and in 1898 he began his coaching career at Sacred Heart College in Watertown, Wisconsin. On December 24, 1909, he married Anna Marie Kuck. Disch played professionally at Sioux Falls, South Dakota, from 1900 to 1902; at Fort Worth, Texas, in 1903 and 1904; and at Galveston from 1905 to 1907. He simultaneously coached at St. Edward's University in Austin from 1900 to 1910, and in 1911 he joined the staff of the University of Texas, where he compiled one of the nation's best coaching records. From 1911 until his retirement in 1940, Disch's teams won twenty-one out of a possible twenty-six baseball championships. He was called by some the "Grand Old Man" of Texas baseball and was noted for perfectionism and strict discipline. He played an important role in persuading the Southwest Conference qv to adopt baseball in 1915, and in 1947 "Uncle Billy" was honored at the opening of Disch Field in Austin, named for him; the later Disch-Falk field is named for him and Bibb A. Falk.qv Disch died on February 3, 1953. He was inducted into the Texas Sports Hall of Fame qv in 1954, into the Longhorn Hall of Honor in 1957, and the College Baseball Coaches Association Hall of Fame in 1965.

BIBLIOGRAPHY: Wilbur Evans and Bill Little, *Texas Longhorn Baseball: Kings of the Diamond* (Huntsville, Alabama: Strode, 1983). Austin *American*, February 4, 1953. Vertical Files, Barker Texas History Center, University of Texas at Austin.

DISTRICT ATTORNEY. The office of district attorney was first provided for in the Constitution of 1836.qv According to an 1840 law, the district attorney was to be appointed for a two-year term by the president of the Republic of Texas qv with the advice and consent of the Senate. The office was continued by the Constitution of 1845 qv and was made elective by law in 1850; the constitutions of 1866 and 1874 qqv likewise continued the office. A constitutional amendment in 1954 extended the term of office to four years. The district attorney is primarily an attorney for the state in district court. He may represent state agencies when the attorney general does not, and he may assist in the enforcement of state agency regulations.

BIBLIOGRAPHY: *Guide to Texas Laws for County Officials* (Austin: Texas Department of Community Affairs, 1988).

Vivian Elizabeth Smyrl

DITCH (Brewster County). The Ditch, an intermittent stream, rises five miles south of Mitchell Mesa and a half mile north of the point at which Duff Creek runs dry in west central Brewster County (at 29°53′ N, 103°41′ W) and runs south for fifteen miles to its mouth on Terlingua Creek, 2½ miles southeast of Straddlebug Mountain (at 29°45′ N, 103°41′ W). It traverses an area of rugged terrain characterized by numerous box canyons, with shallow, stony soils that support Mexican buckeye, walnut, persimmon, desert willow, scrub brush, and sparse grasses. On some maps the Ditch and Duff Creek are both labeled as the lower reaches of Goat Creek.

—— (Motley County). The Ditch rises twelve miles northeast of Matador in west central Motley County (at 100°42′ N, 34°09′ W) and runs east through isolated ranchland for eight miles to its mouth on the Middle Pease River, one mile north of the site of Tee Pee City (at 100°35′ N, 34°07′ W). An early Matador Ranch qv map indicated two creeks, Spring and Brush, in the area of the stream now called the Ditch. The Matador map stated that the region contained mostly high-quality grazing land.

DITTLINGER, TEXAS. Dittlinger, on the Missouri Pacific Railroad four miles southwest of New Braunfels in southeastern Comal County, originated in 1907 as a company town when H. Dittlinger established a lime kiln there. A rock-crushing plant was added to supply materials for highway construction. Dittlinger built low-rent homes for his employees and established a school. In 1934 the property was sold to the United States Gypsum Company. The population of Dittlinger grew from twenty-five at the end of World War II qv to a reported 171 in the 1980s.

Oscar Haas

DITTO, TEXAS. Ditto is on the Atascosa River five miles northwest of Poteet in northern Atascosa County. Before it got a post office the community went by the name of Agua Negra, which referred to the dark water that came out of a natural spring containing iron oxide. Records of settlement date back to the late 1700s, when the area was part of the San Jose Mission Ranch. The first post office in the area was called Mottomosa, from Spanish Mota Mosa ("beautiful grove"), and was discontinued in 1875. When the postmaster applied for a new post office in 1881, he wrote out the word *ditto* on the form to indicate that the office should have the same name as before, but his intention was misinterpreted and the town became Ditto.

In 1884 Ditto had a population of fifty, a steam gristmill and gin, a church, and a school that went by the name Agua Negra. In 1885 a petition to make Ditto the Atascosa county seat instead of Pleasanton would have passed except that the women signers were disqualified. In the 1890s the town's population decreased to twenty, but the number of businesses increased; at least two gins and one general store served area residents. In 1896, the last year for which population figures are available, the population of Ditto was listed at twenty.

In 1904 Ditto had one school with seventy-eight white students and two teachers and another with thirty-three black students and one teacher. In 1914 fifty-five white students and seventeen black students attended the two Agua Negra schools in Ditto. Thirty-four students and two teachers were recorded for Agua Negra School in 1934. In the late 1930s Ditto area students were transferred to Poteet. From the 1940s to the 1960s a few scattered dwellings stood at the site. Ditto does not appear on later maps.

BIBLIOGRAPHY: *Atascosa County History* (Pleasanton, Texas: Atascosa History Committee, 1984).
Linda Peterson

DIVERSEWORKS. DiverseWorks, a nonprofit organization dedicated to exhibiting and funding contemporary art, is located in a 10,000-square-foot red brick warehouse on East Freeway a few blocks north of downtown Houston. It was established in 1982 by a group of Houston artists led by Charles Gallagher, who desired exhibition and studio space during a period when local artists received minimal support from Houston's galleries and museums. Using New York City alternative spaces such as the Kitchen and P.S. 1 as models, the artists pooled their resources to establish a center in the historic Foley Building on Travis Street. Despite a flood that left the gallery a foot underwater, DiverseWorks opened in May 1983 with an exhibition of four East Texas artists and a performance by saxophone player Richard Landry.

During its first year DiverseWorks operated on an $8,000 budget drawn from the founders' private funds. Michael Peranteau joined Gallagher in 1984 as a programming director. The budget grew to $30,000 by 1984. In 1985 Gallagher and Peranteau were joined by Caroline Huber, who served as a second programming director. In 1987 Gallagher left the organization to pursue a career as an artist, and Huber and Peranteau became codirectors of DiverseWorks. Rather than building a permanent collection, the center has channeled available funds into an exhibition program dedicated to exhibiting emerging and recognized regional, national, and international artists. The organization mounted retrospectives of the work of local artists such as Mel Chin (1985), Jesse Lott (1987), and Dee Wolff (1989), and functioned as a venue for performances and installations that had limited commercial appeal. The organization's support of challenging work by local artists, especially those who were too young or controversial to be featured in the city's galleries and museums, contributed to Houston's emergence as a leading art center in the 1980s.

Exhibitions are frequently organized around political themes. Mothers of the Disappeared (1989) featured Houstonian Richard Lewis's photographs of members of Co-Madres, a group that provides support to relatives of those who have reportedly been arrested, kidnapped, or killed by Salvadoran "death squads." Perhaps the most successful exhibition to date was Project: Houston (1990), organized by Deborah Brauer, who invited over forty architects, artists, scientists, and engineers to collaborate on projects geared toward the future development of Houston. Outstanding among the various projects were proposals to restore historic Freedman's Town in the Fourth Ward,qv build an urban wetland featuring native plants in Buffalo Bayou Park, and turn a warehouse into a shelter for abused women and children. DiverseWorks has also participated in fund-raising efforts to benefit Amnesty International and Art Against AIDS.

In addition to mounting ten to thirteen exhibitions a year, DiverseWorks features film and video screenings and performances. The center has exhibited an ongoing commitment to placing local artists' work in public places; for example, it coordinated the renovation of Market Square Park in downtown Houston, where James Surls's sculpture was publicly installed in Houston for the first time. The organization also supports local artists with cash grants and offers studio space to artists-in-residence at its original location.

On February 9, 1989, a fire rendered the Travis Street location uninhabitable. The center subsequently found more spacious quarters in a 1920s cotton warehouse, which was remodeled with grants totaling $46,000 from the National Endowment for the Arts, the Cultural Arts Council of Houston, the Transco Energy Company, and individual pledges. The organization opened at its new location in the fall of 1990. In addition to gallery and performance areas, the new space includes DiverseBooks, an art bookstore, which sponsors PhoneWorks, a phone-in poetry-reading service.

DiverseWorks is governed by a board of directors responsible for fiscal and policy matters. An Artist Advisory Board, made up of artists representing a variety of artistic disciplines, works with the staff to determine programming. In 1991 the center had a staff of six and operated on a $425,000 budget. The organization is funded by membership dues, agencies such as the National Endowment for the Arts and the Houston Cultural Arts Council, and private foundations and individuals. The center has also won some support from corporate sponsors.

BIBLIOGRAPHY: Michael Ennis, "Alternative Cultures," *Domain*, January–February 1990. Jamey Gambrell, "Art Capital of the Third Coast," *Art in America* 75 (April 1987). Charlotte Moser, "Playing Cowboys and Artists in Houston," *Art News* 79 (December 1980).
Kendall Curlee

DIVERSION LAKE. Diversion Lake, a reservoir on the Medina River, is four miles below Medina Lake and eleven miles north of Castroville in northeastern Medina County (at 29°31′ N, 98°54′ W). The dam was completed in 1913 at a cost of $288,000. The lake, owned and operated by Bexar-Medina-Atascosa Counties Water Improvement District No. 1, has a normal capacity of 4,500 acre-feet and a maximum capacity of 16,199 acre-feet. It is used mainly to divert water for irrigation. The reservoir was constructed to avoid the expensive and difficult engineering required to build an irrigation-canal system through the rugged canyons of the Medina River immediately south of Medina Lake dam. Water impounded by the upper dam is released into Diversion Lake, which covers about 400 acres. The Diversion Lake dam in turn controls the flow and amount of water released into an extensive irrigation system. The solid concrete dam, fifty feet high and forty-four feet wide at the base, is 440 feet long.

BIBLIOGRAPHY: Castro Colonies Heritage Association, *The History of Medina County, Texas* (Dallas: National Share Graphics, 1983).

DIVIDE, TEXAS (Hopkins County). Divide, on Farm Road 3389 ten miles southwest of the community of Sulphur Springs in southwestern Hopkins County, first formed around 1880, when a post office was established there with James Webster as postmaster. By 1885 the town had a steam gristmill, two cotton gins, three churches, a district school, and a population of 130. By 1890 its population had dropped to twenty-five, and in 1899 the post office closed. A school was in operation there around 1900, and a Baptist church was established in 1905, but by the mid-1930s the community no longer appeared on highway maps. In the 1960s Divide had a church and a number of scattered dwellings. In the late 1980s the community still had a church.
Christopher Long

DIVIDE, TEXAS (Nolan County). Divide was on Farm Road 126 two miles northeast of the site that became Nolan in east central Nolan County. The Dora Methodist Church, presumably named for a nearby community, was established in Divide about 1889. In 1904 the Nolan community built Slater's Chapel Methodist Church and dedicated a cemetery near the Divide settlement. The church building was disassembled and moved to Nolan in 1939. Four rural schools, including the Dora and Nolan schools, combined in 1928 to form the Divide Rural School District, which operated through the 1970s. Nothing remained of the former settlement by the 1980s except the Slater's Chapel cemetery.

BIBLIOGRAPHY: E. L. Yeats and Hooper Shelton, *History of Nolan County* (Sweetwater, Texas: Shelton, 1975). *Charles G. Davis*

DIVISION OF PLANNING COORDINATION, GOVERNOR'S OFFICE. The Division of Planning Coordination, Governor's Office, was established by the Sixtieth Texas Legislature in 1967. The act designated the governor as the state's chief planning officer and specified the division as the focal point for coordination of state agency and regional planning activities. Among its responsibilities the division reviewed grant applications and state plans that required federal assistance, developed coordination of statewide transportation, identified Texas manpower needs, and was responsible for the Coastal Resources Management Program, which was a part of a total natural-resources program. The Interagency Councils,^qv set up by the same legislation in 1967, were given staff support by the division. The division and the Interagency Councils replaced the Planning Agency Council.^qv

The Division of Planning Coordination was also responsible for providing financial assistance and technical support to the twenty-four Texas regional councils of governments and also served as liaison between the state agencies and these regional councils. The division provided the coordination required between each state agency and the governor's office and also the administration of the Goals for Texas program. In addition, the Division of Planning Coordination worked with any special program or project that responded to state and federal legislation calling for the governor to take a more active role in Texas government. In 1976 the Division of Planning Coordination and the Governor's Budget Office were merged to form the Governor's Budget and Planning Office.

DIVISION OF TEXAS. The congressional joint resolution for the annexation^qv of Texas, passed on March 1, 1845, provided that new states, not to exceed four, could be carved out of Texas, the new states to be entitled to admission to the Union, with or without slavery^qv if south of the Missouri Compromise^qv line, and without slavery if north of that line. The gubernatorial campaign of 1847 centered around the division of Texas into East and West Texas—East Texas being a slave state and West Texas being a free state—but the death of Isaac Van Zandt,^qv chief proponent of division, ruined the hopes of the divisionists. In 1850 Senator Thomas Hart Benton of Missouri introduced a bill to reduce the size of Texas, and Senator Henry Stuart Foote^qv of Mississippi proposed a new state east of the Brazos River, to be called Jacinto, but the proposal received little consideration in the Senate. On February 16, 1852, a joint resolution was introduced into the Texas legislature proposing that Texas be divided into East Texas and West Texas, but the measure was defeated by a vote of 33 to 15.

With the end of the Civil War,^qv carpetbag administrations were keenly interested in the possibility of more carpetbag positions, which would result from the establishment of new states. The Constitutional Convention of 1866^qv gave much attention to the division of Texas. On March 6, 1866, a resolution was introduced providing for a state east of the Trinity River to embrace thirty-eight counties and be called East Texas. A countermove proposed that Texas sell to the United States all territory lying west of a line beginning at the mouth of the Pecos River, thence up the stream to Fort Lancaster, thence to the point where the 102d parallel crosses the Red River. These resolutions did not come to a vote.

In the Constitutional Convention of 1868–69,^qv Elisha M. Pease^qv proposed that the state sell to the United States all territory west of a line running from the mouth of the Pecos River to the northwest corner of Hardeman County. The question of division was referred to a special committee of fifteen. Later in the convention the so-called congressional plan of division was evolved. This plan called for division into three states: East Texas, Texas, and South Texas. As this plan grew in favor in the convention, two proposals were made to weaken the forces supporting it. William Wallace Mills^qv of El Paso proposed the sale of all West Texas to the United States, while Andrew J. Hamilton^qv proposed the division of the state into three parts, the Brazos River to be the boundary between East and West Texas, and the third state to be north of the thirty-second parallel. To complicate the matter further, James P. Newcomb^qv proposed a new plan of division that would have made the Colorado River the boundary line between two states. Over this maze of plans the members quarreled to the ignoble end of the convention without tangible results. The Texas radicals having failed to divide the state, a new plan emerged in Congress in 1869. This proposal, to divide Texas along the Colorado River, the part south and west to be designated the state of Lincoln, never emerged from the committee to which it was referred. On February 25, 1870, the Howard Bill, closely resembling earlier proposals in Congress, was introduced. It called for two territories, Jefferson east of the San Antonio River, and Matagorda west of the Colorado. The remaining portion of the state should retain the name Texas and be readmitted to the Union in accordance with Reconstruction^qv plans. The two territories were to be admitted when they were deemed ready to exercise the functions of statehood. In Texas itself, Edmund J. Davis's^qv regime came forth in 1871 with a proposal for a four-part division into western, northern, eastern, and southern. Congress failed to take final action, however, as did the Texas legislature.

The question of division continued to be discussed at intervals after Reconstruction. In 1906 it was proposed in Congress that Texas establish four independent legislatures, all functioning under one governor. According to the plan the state was to have eight senators, but the proposal met with only passing interest in Texas and no favorable action from Congress. In 1909, during the struggle over prohibition,^qv division was again discussed, but the talk failed to crystallize into party policy.

Failure to reapportion representation after the Thirteenth Census brought new agitation on the division question in 1914. The growth of the western part of the state made it necessary for more representation from that section, a need the legislature ignored. West Texans were also annoyed because few state institutions were established in their region. The result was the proposal in the Texas Senate for the state of Jefferson, to be composed of the Twenty-fifth, Twenty-sixth, Twenty-eighth, and Twenty-ninth senatorial districts. No more than six senators supported the measure, and other proposals to the Thirty-fourth Legislature were equally fruitless. In 1921 the veto of a bill calling for the location of an agricultural and mechanical college in West Texas revived the whole question. Mass meetings were held in West Texas, but the agitation died down quickly.

In the 1930s John Nance Garner^qv proposed a division that called for the maximum number of states permitted under the law, East Texas, West Texas, North Texas, South Texas, and Central Texas. Garner's arguments were familiar. Texas was too large, the sections of the state have contradictory interests, the West and South deserved increased representation in the Congress, candidates for office have too great a difficulty in carrying their program to all sections in an election campaign, and the people of the new states would be able to elect representatives more conversant with their needs. The Garner plan, like all others, came to naught.

After the 1930s division proposals were not taken seriously. In 1969 San Antonio Senator V. E. "Red" Berry proposed the formation of two states, North and South Texas. Senator Bob Gammage also proposed division in 1975. Generally, these later proposals sought the increase in political influence that multiple Texas states could stand to gain with two senators each in the federal government. In 1991 state representative David Swinford submitted a House bill to make the Panhandle into something called the state of Old Texas. The bill was not considered.

BIBLIOGRAPHY: Weston Joseph McConnell, *Social Cleavages in Texas* (New York: Columbia University, 1925). Donald W. Whisenhunt, *The Five States of Texas: An Immodest Proposal* (Austin: Eakin Press, 1987).

Claude Elliott

DIVOT, TEXAS. Divot is at the intersection of Farm roads 1581 and 117, nine miles northwest of Dilley in southwest Frio County. It was originally known as Leona Settlement because of its location near the Leona River. Evidence suggests that the earliest school in the area, Leona School, was a schoolhouse on wheels. Records from 1906 show eighty-nine students and three teachers there. J. J. King established a store at the site in 1908, and the name of the community was changed to Kingsville. Upon application for a post office in 1910, a new name had to be chosen, and Pivot was selected because the settlement was at a crossroads. But through a mistake, the name Divot was assigned.

By 1914 King owned a general store and was still postmaster. A cotton gin was constructed near the store around this time. The population of Divot remained steady at ten throughout the 1920s, and by 1929 the community comprised a school and scattered dwellings. In 1946 the population was estimated at thirty-five; the Leona school district had been annexed to the Dilley Independent School District. In 1948 two schools and three businesses were in operation in the community. In 1971 the population was twenty-eight. By 1974 Divot had two churches (one abandoned) and scattered buildings. In 1990 the community consisted of a well-kept Catholic Church, five family dwellings, and an abandoned red brick schoolhouse.

BIBLIOGRAPHY: *Frio County, Texas: A History* (Pearsall, Texas: Frio Pioneer Jail Museum Association, 1979). Pearsall *Leader*, May 24, 1935. Vertical Files, Pearsall Public Library, Pearsall, Texas (Frio County).

Ruben E. Ochoa

DIX, JOHN JAMES, SR. (1796–1870). John James Dix, Sr., businessman, judge, and Unionist, was born on April 12, 1796, at Littleton, Massachusetts. He ran away to sea in 1810 and served on an American privateer in the War of 1812. For a period he was engaged in cutting the English brig *Don Cossack* out of a California port. He made a voyage to the Sandwich Islands (Hawaii) from Mystic, Massachusetts, in 1820 and became interested in Pacific trading. In 1825 he was wrecked on the north island of New Zealand while trading between the Sandwich Islands and the islands of the South Pacific. On his return he married Mary Eliza Hayes, and they settled at Dixboro, a village he had surveyed in Washtenaw County, Michigan Territory. The town, just north of Ann Arbor, retains his name.

Dix moved his family to Texas in February 1834 and settled in Washington County. He was a part of the Texas force that took San Antonio in the siege of Bexar qv in 1835. He surveyed land that later became part of Coryell County but decided to live near the coast in 1849, when he moved to Corpus Christi. Upon arriving there, he and his sons constructed the Dix House, for many years one of the leading hotels of Corpus Christi. The Dix House was called the Seaside Hotel when Dix moved to Duval County. During the 1850s and 1860s his wife taught both black and white children regularly in the second-story meetingroom of the Dix House. As a strong Unionist, he opposed secession qv with vigor and reason. The last Confederate grand jury in Nueces County indicted him and several other prominent Unionists for treason but did not remain to prosecute the charge when the United States Army occupied the town. When he was appointed chief justice, these political indictments were quashed. Dix was appointed postmaster of Corpus Christi in 1869 but was able to serve only a short time.

In 1852 he helped organize the first Presbyterian church congregation in Corpus Christi. He introduced the idea of Sunday schools to the area and taught in them to the end of his life. Other churches in Corpus Christi followed his example and organized Sunday schools. Dix died of pneumonia in Corpus Christi on January 18, 1870, and was buried in the city cemetery. His son, John James Dix, Jr.,qv became county judge of Duval County and a state representative, and his other sons, William, Theodore, Benjamin, and Olwyn, were distinguished citizens of South Texas.

BIBLIOGRAPHY: Brownsville *Ranchero*, January 29, 1870.

Frank Wagner

DIX, JOHN JAMES, JR. (1826–1910). John James Dix, Jr., surveyor, soldier, and legislator, was born on March 27, 1826, in Washtenaw County, Michigan Territory. He was brought to Texas by his parents in the mid-1830s, and the family settled at Cole's Settlement, afterwards called Independence, in Washington County. He learned astronomical surveying, possibly from his father, John J. Dix, a sea captain, and was known throughout his life for meticulous care in his measurements. He moved to Corpus Christi in 1845 and was engaged in surveying land and managing horses for the United States and Texas troops. Capt. Thomas B. Ives put him in charge of a seventy-five-wagon freight train for the United States Army bringing American possessions out of Matamoros at the end of the Mexican War in 1848. Juan N. Cortina qv was second in command. When Dix left Cortina in charge of the train, near La Grange, Fayette County, a dispute arose between Cortina on behalf of his men and some of the American teamsters. Army officers sided with the American teamsters. Dix returned to the command and mediated the difficulties, giving Cortina credit for strict obedience to orders and faithful and effective discharge of his duties.

Dix married Cynthia Jemima McNeill at Fort Merrill in 1855 or 1856. He served under Col. John S. Ford and Santos Benavides qqv along the lower Rio Grande during the Civil War,qv and upon his return to Corpus Christi he calmed a potentially dangerous conflict between the civilian population and the occupying military forces. He moved to Duval County, where he served as deputy sheriff from 1872 to 1874 and as county surveyor and commissioner. He was a representative of the Eighty-third District in the Twenty-second Texas Legislature. A just and scrupulous man, he was an earnest believer in the economic and social philosophy of Thomas Jefferson; he differed sternly and warmly with younger, more conservative Democrats. During his latter years he often presided over meetings in South Texas to request help in driving off the bandits and Indians who disturbed the peace and robbed the citizenry. He was a member of the Democratic convention that nominated James Stephen Hogg qv for governor. Dix died in San Antonio in 1910.

BIBLIOGRAPHY: Lewis E. Daniell, *Personnel of the Texas State Government, with Sketches of Representative Men of Texas* (Austin: City Printing, 1887; 3d ed., San Antonio: Maverick, 1892). John S. Ford, *Rip Ford's Texas*, ed. Stephen B. Oates (Austin: University of Texas Press, 1963). Sue Watkins, ed., *One League to Each Wind: Accounts of Early Surveying in Texas* (Austin: Texas Surveyors Association Historical Committee, 1964?).

Frank Wagner

DIXIE, TEXAS (Grayson County). Dixie is on U.S. Highway 377 sixteen miles northwest of Sherman in west central Grayson County. The community developed shortly after the Civil War,qv when a group of Confederate veterans settled at the site and called it Theodore. It soon became a community center for area farmers. By 1886 the name had been changed to Dixie, and the community had acquired a post office, which it retained until 1902. In 1908 the settlement had three churches, a store, a gin, and a school. The school was consolidated with the Whitesboro district in the 1940s. A blacksmith shop continued in operation until about 1965. In the late 1970s the

Missionary Baptist and Primitive Baptist churches were still active in Dixie, which reported a population of fifty in 1933 and twenty-five from 1936 through 1990.

BIBLIOGRAPHY: *Twentieth Century Plat Book of Grayson County* (St. Joseph, Missouri: Jackson Map, 1908).

David Minor

DIXIE, TEXAS (Lamar County). Dixie was ten miles northwest of Brookston and sixteen northwest of Paris in northwestern Lamar County. The area was occupied by 1890 when a post office opened. In 1892 postmaster C. Stuckey reported that local businesses were a masonry, a blacksmith shop, and several flour mills. At that time mail was received by special delivery, and the community had one teacher, F. M. Walky. The Dixie school reported twenty-eight students and two teachers in 1896. The community's post office closed in 1905, and Dixie no longer appeared on maps by 1936.

Vista K. McCroskey

DIXIE, TEXAS (Panola County). Dixie was near the site of later Dotson fourteen miles southwest of Carthage in southwestern Panola County. It was probably established after the Civil War.qv A post office opened there in March 1880 with Ebenezer Sistrunk as postmaster; it closed the next year. In the early 1880s the settlement had a general store, a mill, and a number of houses. By 1900 it was no longer shown on maps.

BIBLIOGRAPHY: John Barnette Sanders, *Postoffices and Post Masters of Panola County, Texas, 1845–1930* (Center, Texas, 1964).

Christopher Long

DIXIE, TEXAS (Smith County). Dixie is off State Highway 64 just west of Tyler in central Smith County. The settlement had been established by 1906, when William C. Stallingsqv of Dixie became the first county agent in Texas. In 1923 the Dixie Independent School District was established when the Black Fork, Pleasant Retreat, and Enterprise schools were consolidated. From 1928, after their building burned down, until 1930, members of the Pleasant Retreat Methodist Church held services in the school auditorium. They completed a new structure adjoining the Dixie school in 1930, and the two communities shared the facilities. In 1936 the school had twelve teachers and 381 students. It offered classes for all twelve grades. While records also showed that 139 black children lived in the district, they were not enrolled. Dixie also had a church, a cemetery, two businesses, and a large cluster of dwellings.

In 1941 local residents established the Dixie (Southern) Baptist Church, and the following year they completed the church auditorium. In 1952 local students still attended the Dixie school. In 1966 the community had several dwellings and Beaird Cemetery, but the school had been consolidated with the Tyler district. Dayspring Preschool, sponsored by the Youth-Win-A-Mission organization, opened in the old Dixie Elementary facilities in April 1979. The following year the mission society established Christian Heritage School, also on the former school grounds. In 1981 Dixie had two businesses, Beaird Cemetery, Dixie School, and a residential area.

BIBLIOGRAPHY: Edward Clayton Curry, An Administrative Survey of the Schools of Smith County, Texas (M.Ed. thesis, University of Texas, 1938). "Pleasant Retreat Methodist Church," *Chronicles of Smith County*, Summer 1974. "School Sights," *Chronicles of Smith County*, Fall 1969. Smith County Historical Society, *Historical Atlas of Smith County* (Tyler, Texas: Tyler Print Shop, 1965). Donald W. Whisenhunt, comp., *Chronological History of Smith County* (Tyler, Texas: Smith County Historical Society, 1983).

Vista K. McCroskey

DIXON, OLIVE KING (1873–1956). Olive King Dixon was born on January 30, 1873, on Bent Mountain, eighteen miles southwest of Roanoke, Virginia, the eighth of ten children of Robert Woods and Mary Jane (Blankenship) King. The family estate had been given by the king of England to Gen. Andrew Lewis, Olive's great-grandfather, for his role in Lord Dunmore's War (1774) and was thus known as the Lewis grant. When Olive was seven her father, a Civil Warqv veteran, succumbed to an outbreak of smallpox. Olive and her sister Margaret were sent to Decatur, Alabama, to live with a cousin, Dora King Wade, and her husband Miles, who had two sons of their own. Olive remained at the Wade home and attended school in Decatur until she was sixteen, when she returned to Virginia.

In the meantime two of her brothers, Albert Richard and John Archie, had gone to the Texas Panhandle in the 1880s to work for the Seven K and Cresswell ranches.qqv Albert subsequently married and settled in Lipscomb County, and Archie settled in Roberts County; both were doing well as ranchers on their own. In 1893 Olive visited her brothers and spent most of her time at the home of Archie, who had married Sena Walstad on Christmas Eve, 1890, and now had an infant son, Woods. While Olive was there, James A. Whittenburgqv offered her the job of teaching at Garden Creek School, between Tallahone and Reynolds creeks, organized for the children of the Whittenburg and Newby families. She accepted, and soon afterward Olive met and was courted by the veteran plainsman William (Billy) Dixon.qv

Billy and Olive were married on October 18, 1894, at his Adobe Walls homestead on the Turkey Track Ranch.qv Rev. C. V. Bailey, a Methodist minister, came a hundred miles from Mobeetie to perform the ceremony. Later Olive stated that for three years after her marriage she was the only woman living in Hutchinson County. The Dixons lived at Adobe Walls until 1902, when they moved to Plemons. By then they had four children; three more were added after their move to Cimarron County, Oklahoma, in 1906. Before her husband's death on March 9, 1913, Olive carefully recorded his recollections of his younger years as a buffalo hunter and army scout. These she compiled and published as the *Life of Billy Dixon,* an important source of Panhandleqv history, in 1914. Frederick S. Barde, an Oklahoma western writer, helped her edit the manuscript.

Mrs. Dixon and her children moved briefly to Texline, then in 1915 to Canyon. They continued to farm the Cimarron County homestead until 1917, when they sold it and moved to Miami, in Roberts County. There she wrote sketches of Panhandle history for area newspapers, and several of her pieces also appeared in various magazines. In 1923 she made a memorable trip east to visit relatives and interview Gen. Nelson A. Milesqv and others who had known her husband and who attested to the truth of his exploits. As a charter member of the Panhandle-Plains Historical Society,qv Mrs. Dixon led the successful effort in 1924 to place historical markers at the Adobe Walls and Buffalo Wallow battle sites. In 1929 she moved to Amarillo and was hired as a part-time staff writer by the Amarillo *Globe-News.*qv She was made a salaried reporter in 1937 and was in charge of preparing the *Globe-News* Golden Anniversary Edition of August 14, 1938. She remained with the Amarillo newspapers until her death, on March 17, 1956. She was interred in Llano Cemetery, Amarillo. Dixon heirs live throughout much of West Texas, Eastern New Mexico, and the Pacific Northwest.

BIBLIOGRAPHY: Amarillo *Daily News,* March 19, 1956. Hutchinson County Historical Commission, *History of Hutchinson County, Texas* (Dallas: Taylor, 1980). John L. McCarty, *Adobe Walls Bride* (San Antonio: Naylor, 1955).

H. Allen Anderson

DIXON, SAMUEL HOUSTON (1855–1941). Samuel Houston Dixon, editor, author, and fruit grower, son of Shadrach and Judith (Covington) Dixon, was born on a farm in Hays County, Texas, on August 4, 1855. He attended Coronal Instituteqv in San Marcos and received his baccalaureate degree from Baylor University in 1878. He taught school for four years before joining the staff of the Galveston

*News.*qv In 1880 he married Baylor classmate Jennie Alice Wagner of Robertson County. They had five children. Between 1885 and 1888 Dixon served in a series of state appointments that included committee clerk for the state legislature from 1889 to 1891, journal clerk for the Twentieth Legislature, and chief clerk of the Department of Agriculture.

In 1889 he became the editor of the *Southern Mercury,*qv the official paper of the Farmers' Alliance,qv published in Dallas. During this period Jennie Dixon served as the secretary of the state Woman's Christian Temperance Unionqv and edited the Texas state temperance journal, the *White Ribbon.* Mrs. Dixon also managed the women's department of the *Southern Mercury.* The Farmers' Alliance ousted the Dixons from the Mercury when Sam supported Gov. James S. Hogg'sqv opposition to the subtreasury and an elected Railroad Commission.qv In 1891 the state House of Representatives elected Dixon chief clerk. After the legislative session he served as inspector of state penitentiaries and edited *Farmer's World,* an anti-subtreasury newspaper organized by the pro-Hogg faction of the Farmers' Alliance to oppose the alliance's drift toward the People's party.qv

In 1895 Dixon moved to a farm in Montgomery County. After four years he became an immigration agent for the Houston, East and West Texas Railway. Between 1903 and 1913 he held a series of state agricultural offices including horticultural representative to the St. Louis World's Fair, chief of the orchard and nursery inspection division, chief clerk of the agricultural department, and collaborator for the United States Department of Agriculture. In 1915 Dixon served in the state House of Representatives.

In 1906 he moved to Houston to edit *Texas Farm and Fireside.* In his career as an agricultural journalist he contributed to the development of the peach and citrus industry in Texas. His agricultural publications include *Money Crops* (1901), *Texas Fruits at the World's Fair, 1904* (1905), *A.B.C. of Truck Growing* (1909), and *A.B.C. of Fruit Growing* (1914). He was a prolific writer in other fields. In 1876 he published *Ten Nights with Big Foot Wallace,* which was followed by *Robert Warren, the Texas Refugee* (1879) and *Agnes Dale* (1882). In 1885 he produced an anthology of Texas verse, *Poets and Poetry of Texas.* In 1924 he published two historical works, *The Men Who Made Texas Free* and *Romance and Tragedy of Texas History.* In 1932 he and Louis Wiltz Kempqv coauthored *The Heroes of San Jacinto.*

Besides agricultural associations, Dixon belonged to the Houston Press Club, the Southern Benevolent Association, the Texas Progressive Club, the Knights of Pythias, the Loyal Order of Moose, and the Knights and Ladies of Honor. He died on October 23, 1941, and was buried in Houston. He was survived by two daughters and three sons.

BIBLIOGRAPHY: S. W. Geiser, *Horticulture and Horticulturists in Early Texas* (Dallas: University Press, 1945). *Houston Post,* October 24, 1941. Frank W. Johnson, *A History of Texas and Texans* (5 vols., ed. E. C. Barker and E. W. Winkler [Chicago and New York: American Historical Society, 1914; rpt. 1916]). *Memorial and Biographical History of Dallas County* (Chicago: Lewis, 1892; rpt., Dallas: Walsworth, 1976).

Keith L. King

DIXON, WILLIAM (1850–1913). William (Billy) Dixon, scout, plainsman, buffalo hunter, and Indian fighter, was born in Ohio County, West Virginia, on September 25, 1850. He was orphaned at twelve and lived with his uncle Thomas Dixon in Ray County, Missouri, until the fall of 1864, when he worked in woodcutters' camps along the Missouri River until he secured employment from government freight contractors in Kansas as a bullwhacker and muleskinner. Except for a year (1866) spent working on the McCall family's farm near Leavenworth, when he obtained some formal schooling, Dixon followed this occupation until the fall of 1869. He was a skilled marksman and occasionally scouted for eastern excursionists brought out by the railroads for buffalo hunting.qv In November 1869 he joined a venture in hunting and trapping on the Saline River northwest of Fort Hays. In 1870 buyers offered a dollar each for buffalo cow hides and two dollars for bull hides, and Dixon's marksmanship made hide hunting highly profitable. He invested in a road-ranch or supply store, a merchandising venture that was successful until 1871, when, during Dixon's absence, the store manager, Billy Reynolds, sold out and departed with the proceeds.

At one time Dixon probably had as many as four or five skinners in his employ. He had scouted Texas as far south as the Salt Fork of the Red River when the buffalo hunters moved into the Texas Panhandle in 1874. He and his group hunted along the Canadian River and its tributaries in the vicinity of the new Adobe Walls, the supply post established by businessmen and buffalo hunters near the South Canadian about a mile and a half from the remains of the old Adobe Walls trading post, built about 1843 by William Bent. It was said that after the spring migrations occurred, Dixon could shoot enough buffalo to keep ten skinners busy, and he found Adobe Walls a convenient place to store his wagonloads of hides hauled in from the field. He was one of the twenty-eight men who with one woman participated in the second battle of Adobe Wallsqv in 1874, fighting from inside James Hanrahan's saloon. The story of how he became a hero two days into the battle, when a bullet from his Sharps buffalo rifleqv knocked an Indian off his horse nearly a mile away, is perhaps exaggerated. Dixon himself never claimed credit for his "long shot."

Despite a partnership proposal from Hanrahan, Dixon did no more hide hunting after the battle. While he was in Dodge City early in August 1874, Gen. Nelson A. Milesqv enlisted his services as a scout in the detachment commanded by Lt. Frank D. Baldwin.qv In September the command was on McClellan Creek when Miles sent Dixon, Amos Chapman,qv and four enlisted men with dispatches to carry to Camp Supply. Near Gageby Creek on the second day out they encountered a large war party of Comanches and Kiowas, who surrounded them in the Buffalo Wallow Fight.qv Dixon was among the five survivors awarded the Medal of Honor for heroism in that engagement.

He was present at the rescue of the German sistersqv from the Cheyennes on McClellan Creek on November 8, 1874. He was with the party that selected the site of Fort Elliott in the spring of 1875 and was attached to that post for duty when he guided the Nolan expeditionqv in pursuit of the Comanches in August 1877. His knowledge of the country saved the command when he led the men to water at Double Lakes on the Llano Estacado.qv

Dixon returned to civilian life in 1883, worked on the Turkey Track Ranch,qv built a home near the site of the original Adobe Walls, planted an orchard and thirty acres of alfalfa that he irrigated from Bent's Creek, and became postmaster at Adobe Walls, a position he held for twenty years. In 1901 he was elected the first sheriff of the newly formed Hutchinson County but resigned in disgust at the political strife aroused in connection with the organization of the county. In addition, he served as a state land commissioner and justice of the peace for the area around Hutchinson, Gray, and Roberts counties. He and S. G. Carter operated a ranch-supply store at the house. On October 18, 1894, he married Olive King Dixonqv of Virginia, who for three years thereafter was the only woman living in Hutchinson County. They had seven children.

The family moved to Plemons in 1902 to provide schooling for their children. Small-town life proved irksome to the former scout, and in 1906 he went to homestead in the open spaces of Oklahoma. During his last years Dixon reportedly lived near poverty, and friends tried to obtain a pension for him. On March 9, 1913, he died of pneumonia at his Cimarron County homestead; he was buried in the cemetery at Texline by members of his Masonic lodge. On June 27, 1929, his remains were reinterred at the Adobe Walls site. Dixon Creek in southern Hutchinson County is named for him, as is the Billy Dixon Masonic Lodge in Fritch. Personal artifacts from his scouting days are housed in both the Hutchinson County Museum in Borger and the Panhandle-Plains Historical Museum^{qv} in Canyon.

BIBLIOGRAPHY: T. Lindsay Baker and Billy R. Harrison, *Adobe Walls: The History and Archaeology of the 1874 Trading Post* (College Station: Texas A&M University Press, 1986). Olive K. Dixon, *Life of "Billy" Dixon* (1914; rev. ed., Dallas: P. L. Turner Company, 1927; facsimile of original ed., Austin: State House, 1987). Hutchinson County Historical Commission, *History of Hutchinson County, Texas* (Dallas: Taylor, 1980). Mrs. Sam Isaacs, "Billy Dixon: Pioneer Plainsman," *Frontier Times,* June 1939. John L. McCarty, *Adobe Walls Bride* (San Antonio: Naylor, 1955). Vertical Files, Barker Texas History Center, University of Texas at Austin.
T. C. Richardson

DIXON, TEXAS. Dixon is on U.S. Highway 69 six miles from Greenville in southeastern Hunt County. It was established in 1880, apparently with the arrival of the Missouri, Kansas and Texas Railroad in the area, and had become a shipping point on the line by 1885. A post office began operations in Dixon in 1881, and by 1890 the settlement had a population of 180, a school, and two churches. The post office closed in 1924, and by 1933 the population had fallen to eighty-four and the businesses to two. Dixon had a population of fifty in 1952 and thirty-one from 1976 to 1990.
Brian Hart

DIXON CREEK (Carson County). Dixon Creek, sometimes known as Limestone Creek, rises in north central Carson County (at 35°34' N, 101°21' W) at the confluence of two of its three branches; the third branch joins it a mile south of the Hutchinson county line. The creek runs north for twelve miles to its mouth on the Canadian River, northeast of Borger and Phillips in southern Hutchinson County (at 35°45' N, 101°21' W). Dixon Creek is in the center of the Borger oilfield, where many of the early strikes that touched off the Panhandle^{qv} boom of the late 1920s were made. The stream traverses an area with deep sandy loams and was named for the frontier scout William (Billy) Dixon.^{qv} The headquarters of the Dixon Creek division of the Four Sixes Ranch^{qv} is located in Carson County near the middle branch of the creek.

_____ (Leon County). Dixon Creek rises fourteen miles east of Centerville in eastern Leon County (at 31°20' N, 95°48' W) and runs east two miles to its mouth on Beaver Dam Marsh (at 31°18' N, 95°46' W). It traverses gently sloping to nearly level terrain surfaced by clayey to sandy soils that support woods along the banks including intermittent loblolly pine, sweetgum, post oak, and black hickory. Settlement in the vicinity of the stream began in the latter half of the nineteenth century, but the area has remained sparsely populated.

DOAK BRANCH. Doak Branch rises a mile southeast of Charlotte in west central Atascosa County (at 28°50' N, 98°41' W) and runs south for seven miles to its mouth on Lagunillas Creek, six miles south of Charlotte (at 28°45' N, 98°42' W). In its upper reaches the creek crosses low-rolling to flat terrain surfaced by sandy and clay loams that support scrub brush, cacti, and grasses. Near the creek's mouth water-tolerant hardwoods and conifers grow in flat terrain with local shallow depressions. Some nearby land is irrigated for crops. Doak Branch was named for early settler Jonathon A. Doak, who moved to the area in 1856. The creek traversed his land.

BIBLIOGRAPHY: Margaret G. Clover, The Place Names of Atascosa County (M.A. thesis, University of Texas, 1952).

DOAK SPRINGS, TEXAS. Doak Springs is on Farm Road 3403 a half mile east of Leo in central Lee County. The small, black community centered around the Doak Springs school, which was organized in 1897. A Mr. Doak, of nearby Lexington, donated land for the school, which was officially known as Community School Number 49. The settlement was named after the springs running through Doak's land. In 1909 the community school was relocated to property owned by John Roberson. It was renamed Doak Springs District Number 33 and had thirty students. By 1919 its enrollment had grown to 120. In 1925 the Rosenwald Fund provided for a new school building with expanded facilities; student enrollment was around 150 into at least the 1950s. The Doak Springs school was consolidated with the Lexington school in 1967. In January 1936 Scott Phoenix, an early settler known as Uncle Scott, founded the Morning Star Baptist Church near the Doak Springs school. Church services were held in the schoolhouse until the congregation erected a church building around 1937. A larger church was built in 1951. There was still a church at the site until at least the early 1980s, and the community still existed in 1990.

BIBLIOGRAPHY: Lee County Historical Survey Committee, *A History of Lee County* (Quanah, Texas: Nortex, 1974).
Nolan Thompson

DOANS, TEXAS. Doans, also known as Doan's Store or Doan's Crossing, is at the junction of Farm roads 2916 and 924, a mile southwest of the Red River in north central Wilbarger County. Jonathan Doan and his nephew Corwin Doan established a trading post in 1878 to serve the cattle drivers who used the nearby Western Trail^{qv} to get their herds to market. A post office was established at the store in 1879 with Corwin Doan as postmaster. The cattle drives on the Western Trail reached their peak in 1881, when more than 300,000 head passed by Doans; between 1879 and 1895 six million head came through the settlement. By the mid-1880s Doans had a school, a hotel, a general store, a saloon, and a population estimated at 300. A wide variety of people came to the town to do business: cowboys, ranchers, Indians, buffalo hunters, peddlers, and itinerant preachers; among the more famous visitors were Quanah Parker^{qv} and A. J. Balfour, later prime minister of England, who impersonated a cowboy to help catch cattle rustlers on a ranch owned by the Francklyn Land and Cattle Company.^{qv}

In 1885, when the Fort Worth and Denver Railway bypassed Doans by several miles, the cattle drives that had been so important to the town's economy were rendered obsolete, and the town had no rail service to help replace the drives with new business. By the mid-1890s the population had fallen to seventy-five; it fell to thirty by 1914, and at that time only the general store remained. Postal service to Doans was discontinued in 1919, and by the 1930s the number of residents had dwindled to ten. The Doans school was consolidated in 1935 into the Northside school district. From the 1940s through the 1990s the population of Doans was reported at twenty. An annual picnic, a tradition that began in 1884, was held at Doans each May. In 1931 a historical marker was placed at Doans to commemorate the trail drives.

BIBLIOGRAPHY: T. Lindsay Baker, *Ghost Towns of Texas* (Norman: University of Oklahoma Press, 1986). Vertical Files, Barker Texas History Center, University of Texas at Austin. Wilbarger County Historical Commission, *Wilbarger County* (Lubbock, 1986).
Lea Anne Morrell

DOANS SPRINGS. The group of small springs known as Doans Springs is twelve miles north of Vernon near the Doans community in northern Wilbarger County (at 34°21' N, 99°15' W). Although it is uncertain whether Francisco Vázquez de Coronado^{qv} stopped at the site during his 1542 expedition, the springs have been frequented by travelers for hundreds of years. Doans Springs was a watering place for cattle along the Western Trail^{qv} and was known as Baldwin Springs on regional maps of the 1870s. In earlier times the springwater flow formed a mile-long creek. By the late 1970s, however, the springs had been reduced to wet-weather seeps. The surrounding steep to moderately sloping hills are surfaced with shallow, stony, clay and sandy loams that support oak, mesquite, and grasses.

BIBLIOGRAPHY: Gunnar Brune, *Springs of Texas,* Vol. 1 (Fort Worth: Branch-Smith, 1981).

DOBBIN, TEXAS. Dobbin is on Lake Creek at the junction of the Atchison, Topeka and Santa Fe, the Burlington Northern, and the Chicago, Rock Island and Pacific railroads, near the intersection of State Highway 105 and Farm Road 1486 in western Montgomery County. The earliest mention of the area comes from the French explorer René Robert Cavelier, Sieur de La Salle,qv who camped northwest of the site of Dobbin on February 14, 1687. One of the first families to settle in the area was that of Noah and Ester Wightman Griffith, natives of New York state, who received a Mexican land grant there in 1831.

In 1878 the Central and Montgomery Railway built a line through the area from Navasota to Montgomery. A post office was established in 1880 under the name Bobbin. In 1885 Bobbin was a shipping point for cotton and lumber and had daily mail service, four sawmills, a gristmill, a flour mill, a church, a district school, two general stores, a physician, and a population of 100. By the 1890s the settlement had a Baptist church, a cotton gin, W. G. Post's sawmill, J. M. Stinson's general store, two livestock dealers, one combination mill and gin, a blacksmith, and a population of 250. In 1903–04 the town had three one-teacher schools; one had thirty-seven white students, a second had eighteen white students, and the third had forty-three black students. By this time the population had declined to 168.

In 1906 or 1907 the Trinity and Brazos Valley Railway built through Bobbin on its way from Mexia to Houston, making the town a railroad junction. In 1909 the town's name was changed to Dobbin. By 1915 the population was 100, and local businesses included three general stores, two blacksmith shops, a drugstore, and a grocery. In 1926 Dobbin School was established. By the late 1940s the community had three churches, two schools, two sawmills, two factories, nine businesses, the railroad station, several dwellings, and a population of 175. In 1965 Dobbin had a post-peeling plant. In the late 1960s the population was 106, and in the early 1970s it was 170. In 1990 the town comprised Mock's Feed Store and Grocery, the post office, the Dobbin station of the Montgomery Fire Department, two churches, and a collection of dwellings; the population was estimated at 200.

BIBLIOGRAPHY: Robin Navarro Montgomery, *The History of Montgomery County* (Austin: Jenkins, 1975). Montgomery County Genealogical Society, *Montgomery County History* (Winston-Salem, North Carolina: Hunter, 1981).

Will Branch

DOBIE, BERTHA MCKEE (1890–1974). Bertha McKee Dobie, writer, daughter of Richard Alexander and Ray (Park) McKee, was born on July 8, 1890, on a farm in Susquehanna County (near Nicholson), Pennsylvania; at that time her parents had already established residence in Texas, but her mother had returned to Pennsylvania to have her first child. The family lived for short periods in the small Texas towns of Italy, Forreston, Coldspring, Waelder, and Aransas Pass before settling in Velasco when Bertha was seven years old. After graduation from high school she received a B.A. degree from Southwestern University in Georgetown (where she met her future husband) in 1910; she took a master's degree in English from the University of Texas in 1918. She taught English and mathematics in Dalhart, Galveston, and Alexander Collegiate Institute (now Lon Morris College) in Jacksonville.

Bertha McKee was married to J. Frank Dobieqv on September 20, 1916, and in later years she was credited by her husband as being his best literary critic and editor. She became a writer and contributed a series of articles on gardening to Texas newspapers; she also wrote for numerous periodicals, including *Nature Magazine*, *New York Herald Tribune Magazine*, *Garden Digest*, *Holland's Magazine*,qv *Publications of the Texas Folklore Society*, and *Southwest Review*.qv She was assistant editor of the Texas Folklore Societyqv Publications from 1923 to 1935. Occasionally she conducted classes at the University of Texas for her husband while he was away collecting materials for his books. She was well known for the flower garden at her home in Austin and was a guest lecturer on gardening at meetings throughout the state. Bertha Dobie was a member of the Audubon Society and helped formulate plans for Paisano Ranch,qv a Hill Countryqv retreat for Texas writers and artists. Upon the death of her husband, she edited his posthumous publications. She was named a distinguished alumna of Southwestern University on January 26, 1973. She died on December 18, 1974, and was buried alongside her husband in the State Cemeteryqv in Austin.

BIBLIOGRAPHY: Austin *American-Statesman*, May 3, 1987. Vertical Files, Barker Texas History Center, University of Texas at Austin.

Eldon S. Branda

DOBIE, DUDLEY RICHARD, SR. (1904–1982). Dudley Richard Dobie, Sr., antiquarian bookseller, was born on August 6, 1904, at old Lagarto in southern Live Oak County, Texas, to William Neville and Mary E. (Mills) Dobie, prominent South Texas ranchers. Family pioneers had first settled in Harris County in 1828. Dudley's branch moved to Live Oak County in the late 1860s. Dudley's first cousin, J. Frank Dobie,qv grew up on a nearby ranch, but their sixteen-year age difference inhibited the development of close friendship until Dudley reached maturity. He received his childhood education in the Lagarto school and graduated as valedictorian from Mathis High School in 1923. After a year of unsuccessful job seeking, he entered Southwest Texas State Teachers College, and from that time he considered San Marcos his home. He received his degree in history in May 1927 and that fall was named principal of Westover School on the west side of San Marcos. Two months later he married Deborah Galbreath, who became the mother of his three children. He later looked back on the winter of 1927–28 as the time he began to get serious about book collecting. In the summer of 1928 he embarked upon a graduate degree in history at the University of Texas, where he returned each summer for the next four years. Walter Prescott Webbqv supervised his thesis, A History of Hays County, Texas. In 1933 Dudley left teaching to become an educational advisor for the Civilian Conservation Corps.qv He had already begun free-lancing newspaper and magazine articles about historic persons, places, and events for sundry Texas publications.

He became a bookseller in 1935 and further supplemented his uncertain income by scouting artifacts for the Hall of State,qv which opened in Dallas the following year. Throughout the 1930s he systematically expanded his knowledge of books and his acquaintance among book people. He attended annual meetings of the Texas State Historical Association,qv the Old Trail Drivers Association, and on occasion the Texas and Southwestern Cattle Raisers Association.qv He also kept membership in the Texas Folklore Society,qv where his cousin J. Frank was the secretary-editor. In all of these groups, Dobie quickly identified the authors and collectors. During the winter of 1940–41 he helped the Texas State Historical Association organize its first book auction, now a traditional feature of its annual meeting. Following his debut as a bookseller, and while working for the Texas Centennialqv Commission, he was also running a mail-order book business out of his home. He would periodically load his car with books and head for San Antonio, Austin, or elsewhere, and collar potential customers in their homes or businesses. In 1941 he began a ten-year career at Southwest Texas State Teachers College as a non-tenured, part-time history instructor and part-time museum director. His status was such that he was able to continue his bookselling and, in 1947, issue his first printed catalogue, *Spirited Southwest: Roundup No. 1*. From 1949 to 1951 he served as a San Marcos city alderman.

Dobie's connection with the college ended in 1951. A year later he opened a bookstore in Austin on the site of what is now Dobie Center, near the University of Texas campus. Not achieving the hoped-for success, he closed his Austin store and later made an unsuccessful race for school superintendent in Hays County. In 1955 he opened a

J. Frank Dobie at a barbecue given by Austin writer and publisher Joe Small. Photograph by Russell Lee. Wimberley, ca. 1957. Russell Lee Photograph Collection, CAH; CN 03130.

bookshop and gift store in San Marcos, but again the time and place weren't right. At this time he unexpectedly received the opportunity to teach history and direct the Big Bend Memorial Museum (later the Museum of the Big Bend[qv]) at Sul Ross State Teachers College in Alpine. Except for the 1958–59 academic year, Dobie remained at Sul Ross until his retirement and return to San Marcos in 1966. For most of that time, however, he was affiliated with the library. From 1966 until his death, he sold books by mail order from his San Marcos home. He served a term as county Democratic chairman and was for ten years a member of the county historical commission. He made notes for the memoirs he always intended to write, but never did. He also regaled many a novice reporter with tales of frontier life that he knew not only from a wealth of reading, but from personal and family experience. Aside from various newspaper and magazine features, his publications include *A History of San Marcos and Hays County* (1948) and *Adventures in the Canyons, Mountains and Desert Country of the Big Bend of Texas and Mexico* (1952), both privately printed. He died of colon cancer on April 17, 1982.

BIBLIOGRAPHY: Al Lowman, *Remembering Dudley Dobie: The First Bookseller to Enrich My Life (and Empty My Pockets)* (Austin, Boerne, San Marcos, Texas: Lagarto Press, 1992). Vertical Files, Barker Texas History Center, University of Texas at Austin.   Al Lowman

DOBIE, JAMES FRANK (1888–1964). J. Frank Dobie, folklorist, was born on a ranch in Live Oak County, Texas, on September 26, 1888, the eldest of six children of Richard J. and Ella (Byler) Dobie. His ranching heritage became an early influence on his character and personality. His fundamentalist father read the Bible to Frank and the other five children, and his mother read them *Ivanhoe* and introduced them to *The Scottish Chiefs, Pilgrim's Progress,* and *Swiss Family Robinson.* He left the ranch when he was sixteen and moved to Alice, where he lived with his Dubose grandparents and finished high school. In 1906 he enrolled in Southwestern University in Georgetown, where he met Bertha McKee, whom he married in 1916, and Professor Albert Shipp Pegues, his English teacher, who introduced him to English poetry, particularly the Romantics, and encouraged him as a writer. Dobie's education as a teacher and writer continued after graduation in 1910. He worked two summers as a reporter, first for the San Antonio *Express* and then the Galveston *Tribune.* He got his first teaching job in 1910 in Alpine, where he was also the principal, play director, and editor of the school paper. He returned to Georgetown in 1911 and taught in the Southwestern University preparatory school until 1913, when he went to Columbia to work on his master's degree. With his new M.A. he joined the University of Texas faculty in 1914. At this time he also joined the Texas Folklore Society.[qv] Dobie left the university in 1917 and served for two years in the field artillery in World War I.[qv] His outfit was sent overseas right at the war's end, and he returned to be discharged in 1919. In 1919 he published his first articles. He resigned his position at the university in 1920 to manage his uncle Jim Dobie's ranch. During this year on the Rancho de Los Olmos with the vaqueros and the stock and the land that had been part of his formation, Dobie discovered his calling—to transmute all the richness of this life and land and culture into literature. The Texas Folklore Society was the main avenue for his new mission, and the University of Texas library with all its Texas resources was his vehicle.

Dobie returned to Austin and the university in 1921. The Texas Folklore Society had been formed in 1909 by Leonidas W. Payne[qv] and others, but had recessed during the war years. On April 1, 1922, Dobie became secretary of the society. He immediately began a publication program. *Legends of Texas* (1924) carried the seeds of many of his later publications. Dobie served as the society's secretary-editor for twenty-one years and built the society into a permanent professional organization. When the university would not promote him without a Ph.D., Dobie accepted the chairmanship of the English department at Oklahoma A&M, where he stayed from 1923 to 1925. During these two years he began writing for the *Country Gentleman.* With considerable help from his friends on the UT campus, he was able to return in 1925 with a token promotion. He began writing articles on Texas history, culture, and folklore for magazines and periodicals and soon started to work on his first book, *A Vaquero of the Brush Country.* Dobie's purpose in life from the time of his return to the university in 1921 was to show the people of Texas and the Southwest the richness of their culture and their traditions, particularly in their legends. John A. Lomax,[qv] another founder of the Texas Folklore Society, had done this with his collecting and publishing cowboy songs; Dobie intended to do this with the tales of old-time Texas and through the publications of the society and his own writing.

His *Vaquero of the Brush Country,* published in 1929, established him as a spokesman of Texas and southwestern culture. It was based on John Young the Vaquero's autobiographical notes and articulated the struggle of the individual against social forces, in this case the battle of the open-range vaquero against barbed wire.[qv] Two years later Dobie published *Coronado's Children* (1931), the tales of those free spirits who abandoned society in the search for gold, lost mines, and various other grails. It won the Literary Guild Award for 1931 and, combined with his continuing success as a popular writer in *Country Gentleman,* made Dobie a nationally known literary figure. He was also promoted in 1933 to the rank of full professor, the first Texan non-Ph.D. to be so honored at the university. In 1942 he published the *Guide to Life and Literature of the Southwest,* an annotated reading list. It was published again in 1952. As head of the Texas Folklore Society and author of *On the Open Range* (1931), *Tales of the Mustang* (1936), *The Flavor of Texas* (1936), *Apache Gold and Yaqui Silver* (1939), and *Tongues of the Monte* (1947), Dobie was the state's leading spokesman and literary and cultural figure during the Texas Centennial[qv] decade, the 1930s. His first period of writing ended with the publication of *The Longhorns* in 1941.

He spent World War II[qv] teaching American literature in Cambridge. After the war he returned to Europe to teach in England, Germany, and Austria. He said of his Cambridge experience in *A Texan in England* that it gave him a broader perspective, that it was his beginning of his acceptance of civilization, an enlightened civilization free of social and political rigidities and with full respect for individuality. In Texas the University of Texas regents, critical of the university's liberal professors, had fired President Homer P. Rainey[qv] in November 1944. Dobie, a liberal Democrat, was outraged and vociferous, and Governor Coke Stevenson[qv] said that he was a troublemaker and should be summarily dismissed. Dobie's request for a continuation of his leave of absence after his European tour in 1947 was denied by the regents, and he was dismissed from the UT faculty under what became known as the "Dobie rule," which restricted faculty leaves of absence to two years except in emergencies.

After this separation Dobie devoted all of his time to writing and anthologizing. The next decade saw the publication of *The Voice of the Coyote* (1949), *The Ben Lilly Legend* (1950), *The Mustangs* (1952), *Tales of Old Time Texas* (1955), *Up the Trail From Texas* (1955), and *I'll Tell You a Tale* (1960). Before he died he published *Cow People* (1964) and almost finished the manuscript for *Rattlesnakes,* which Bertha McKee Dobie[qv] later edited and published in 1965. Dobie began writing for the *Southwest Review*[qv] in 1919, when it was the *Texas Review,* and continued the association throughout his life. The *Southwest Review* published his *John C. Duval: First Texas Man of Letters* in 1939. Dobie wrote a Sunday newspaper column from 1939 until his death, and as an outspoken critic of the Texas scene he was a popular subject of newspaper stories. His most celebrated targets were professional educationists ("unctuous elaborators of the obvious"); state politicians ("When I get ready to explain homemade fascism in America, I can take my example from the state capitol of Texas"); Pompeo Coppini's[qv] Alamo cenotaph ("From a distance it looks like a grain elevator or one of those swimming pool slides"); and inappropriate architecture (a friend reports his saying that the University Tower, into which he refused to move, "looked like a toothpick in a pie, ought to be laid on its side and have galleries put around it"). His war against bragging Texans, political, social, and religious restraints on individual liberty, and the mechanized world's erosion of the human spirit was continual.

Dobie died on September 18, 1964. He had been feted by the Southwestern Writers and the Texas Folklore Society. Special editions of the *Texas Observer* and the Austin *American-Statesman*[qqv] had been devoted to his praise by his many admirers, and President Lyndon B. Johnson[qv] awarded him the nation's highest civil award, the Medal of Freedom, on September 14, 1964. His funeral was held in Hogg Auditorium on the UT campus, and he was buried in the State Cemetery.[qv] *See also* PAISANO RANCH.

BIBLIOGRAPHY: Francis Edward Abernethy, *J. Frank Dobie* (Austin: Steck-Vaughn, 1967). Winston Bode, *A Portrait of Pancho: The Life of a Great Texan, J. Frank Dobie* (Austin: Pemberton Press, 1965). *Texas Observer,* Special Issue, July 24, 1964. Lon Tinkle, *An American Original: The Life of J. Frank Dobie* (Boston: Little, Brown, 1978).

Francis E. Abernethy

DOBIE, JAMES MADISON (1856–1929). James Madison Dobie, rancher, son of Robert S. and Amanda (Hill) Dobie, was born on January 18, 1856, near Houston, Texas. He became a freighter before he moved to Live Oak County, where he ranched and raised horses to send to Dodge City, Kansas. After several years in Live Oak County, he moved to Indian Territory but returned to the area in 1895 almost broke. However, in San Antonio he managed to gather a herd of 25,000 cattle by year's end. He took this herd to Live Oak County and soon had one of the largest ranches in the area, with 30,000 acres in parts of Live Oak, McMullen, Webb, and La Salle counties. In 1905 he married Ida Mae Taylor.

According to his nephew, J. Frank Dobie,[qv] he claimed that one man was enough to handle the worst stampede of cattle and usually took control himself in such cases. Dobie not only had business interests in cattle, horses, and ranchland, but also owned real estate in San Antonio and at one time owned the Princess Theatre. He was active in shaping policies of the old Texas Cattle Raisers' Association and later the Texas and Southwestern Cattle Raisers Association.[qv] After establishing a permanent home with his wife in San Antonio in 1924, Dobie died there on May 21, 1929.

BIBLIOGRAPHY: Emory A. Bailey, *Who's Who in Texas* (Dallas: John B. McCraw Press, 1931). San Antonio *Express,* May 22, 1929.

Richard Allen Burns

DOBIE, WILLIAM (ca. 1777–1835). William Dobie [pseud. Dr. William Dobie Dunlap], early Texas colonist, was born in Sussex County, Virginia, about 1777, the son of Nathaniel Dobie. On April 21, 1803, he married Polly Chappel, with whom he had a son. He married Dolly Neblett on July 17, 1805, and they had seven children. By the early 1820s Dobie had acquired over 1,000 acres of land and nineteen slaves. He served as deputy surveyor of Sussex County from 1820 to 1826. But he then encountered financial difficulties, and in 1827 he disappeared. His eldest son was appointed to manage the family's affairs.

In 1828 Dobie, using the alias William Dunlap, was admitted to Austin's colony in Texas and employed as a clerk by John R. Harris[qv] in Harrisburg. At various times over the next two years, he served as Harrisburg agent for the *Texas Gazette,*[qv] as Harrisburg customs officer, and in several positions for the ayuntamiento[qv] of San Felipe. By 1831 he had become a merchant in Anahuac. That year he served briefly as customs officer in Brazoria. In 1832 he was granted a quarter league plus a labor of land on Middle Bayou in what is now southeastern Harris County; the certificate for this land is the only Texas record in which his name is given as Dobie rather than Dunlap. In July or August 1835 William Dobie died in Sussex County, Virginia, supposedly while in the process of moving his family to Texas.

Three of his sons, Nathaniel, Sterling, and Robert, immigrated to Harris County, Texas. Nathaniel set up a mercantile store in Harrisburg in 1834; he moved it to Houston in 1837. He served in several governmental positions. Along with his kinsman (probably uncle) Sterling Neblett, he played a part in the founding of Galveston. Nathaniel Dobie died in 1838. Sterling Neblett Dobie arrived in Texas in 1835 and Robert Neville Dobie by 1838; by the mid-1840s they were ranching on the William Dobie grant. Robert Dobie drowned in Middle Bayou in 1857. Soon afterwards, Sterling and his family moved to Live Oak County, Texas, where Robert's widow, Amanda, and children joined them in 1875. It was there that a grandson of Robert and Amanda, J. Frank Dobie,[qv] was born.

BIBLIOGRAPHY: Richard L. Gregg, "The William Dobie Survey," *Houston Archeological Society Newsletter,* March, August 1980, May, August, December 1981.

Richard L. Gregg

DOBROWOLSKI, TEXAS. Dobrowolski was on State Highway 97 six miles southwest of Jourdanton in west central Atascosa County. The settlement, originally called Tobey (Toby), had a post office from

1894 until 1919 and was still indicated on county maps as late as the 1940s. Tobey was named for Thomas Toby, a land speculator in the area around 1858; he was said to have managed a large ranch in New Orleans. In 1896 the population in Tobey was 200; that year the town had a general store, a gin, and a music teacher. In 1904 the school had thirty-eight students and one teacher. The number of students increased to sixty-five by 1913 and eighty-one in 1934, when the school had two teachers. The school was consolidated with the Charlotte school around 1936. The Tobey post office was closed in 1919.

A post office named Dobrowolski opened at the site in 1920 and operated until 1934. It was named for Alec Dobrowolski, who sold farm land in the area. In 1925 the population was listed as fifty. It dropped to twenty-five in the early 1930s, rose to a high of seventy-five in 1939, and dropped to fifteen in the 1960s. It was reported at ten in 1970 and 1990. By the 1980s only a few scattered dwellings remained at the site, which was no longer named on highway maps.

BIBLIOGRAPHY: *Atascosa County Centennial, 1856–1956* (Jourdanton, Texas: Atascosa County Centennial Association, n.d.). Margaret G. Clover, The Place Names of Atascosa County (M.A. thesis, University of Texas, 1952). Janie Foster, History of Education in Atascosa County (M.A. thesis, University of Texas, 1936).   *Linda Peterson*

DOBSKYVILLE, TEXAS. Dobskyville was three miles west of U.S. Highway 183 in northern Goliad County. Frederick and Agatha Dobsky, immigrants from Berlin, established a residence in the area in the 1850s. A grandson, Henry Dobsky, a rancher and farmer, opened a store in 1905 near the public road (now Farm Road 884) to serve neighboring farmers and ranchers. He enlarged the store and added a saloon in 1907. Two years later he built a dance hall. A local school was established in 1905. The area, which became known as Dobskyville, was a popular gathering place for celebrations, barbecues, dances, and political and sports events. Henry Dobsky operated the store until he retired in 1935; that same year the Dobskyville school was consolidated with the nearby Weesatche school. The dance hall was destroyed later by a hurricane. In 1986 the county highway map still designated the location as Dobskyville Community.

BIBLIOGRAPHY: Goliad County Historical Commission, *The History and Heritage of Goliad County*, ed. Jakie L. Pruett and Everett B. Cole (Austin: Eakin, 1983).   *Craig H. Roell*

DOBYVILLE, TEXAS. Dobyville was near U.S. Highway 281 twelve miles north of Burnet in northern Burnet County. Jacob and Adaline Wolf and Silas and Rebecca Shelburn were among the first settlers in the 1850s, soon after Burnet County was established. Mail was delivered to the community as early as 1858 through a post office called O'Hair's Hill; when that office was discontinued, the mail was routed through Naruna or Lampasas. The Dobyville post office was established in 1874 with Thomas S. Wolf as postmaster. It closed in 1884 but reopened under the name Pomona in 1889 and operated until 1900. Afterward, mail for the community was again sent to Naruna.

Lone Star School at Dobyville was established in 1878. By the mid-1880s the community had steam grist and syrup mills, a cotton gin, and thirty residents; cotton, livestock, and grain were the principal products shipped by area farmers. In the mid-1890s the school at Dobyville had one teacher and fifty-six students. The school building also served as a community center until 1911, when the structure burned. Lone Star School was consolidated with Lake Victor School in 1921. Dobyville's big annual entertainment was the spring rabbit drive, which took place on a Saturday in late March or early April; families would gather for a day of hunting and picnicking. A few scattered houses marked the community on county highway maps in the 1940s; only a cemetery remained by the 1980s.

BIBLIOGRAPHY: Darrell Debo, *Burnet County History* (2 vols., Burnet, Texas: Eakin, 1979).   *Vivian Elizabeth Smyrl*

DOCKUM CREEK. Dockum Creek rises by Farm Road 836 a mile from the Crosby-Dickens county line in east central Crosby County on the eastern edge of the Caprock (at 33°39′ N, 101°03′ W) and runs southeast for eighteen miles, forming the northern city limit of Spur before reaching its mouth on Duck Creek, in southwest Dickens County (at 33°29′ N, 100°50′ W). It traverses flat to moderately steep terrain surfaced by clay, sand, and silt loams that support grasses, scrub brush, mesquite, and cacti. This region was the first part of the county to be settled, when homesteaders moved to the area in the late 1870s. It was named for W. C. Dockum, a buffalo hunter who established a store and post office in the area.

BIBLIOGRAPHY: Fred Arrington, *A History of Dickens County: Ranches and Rolling Plains* (Quanah, Texas: Nortex, 1971).

DR PEPPER COMPANY. The Dr Pepper Company was officially incorporated on July 6, 1923, in Dallas. The company markets fountain syrups and sells soft-drink concentrates to independent franchised bottlers. These licensed bottlers then add sweeteners and carbonated water, package the result, and sell the finished product in the surrounding market. In the mid-1980s Dr Pepper's products were Dr Pepper, Sugar Free Dr Pepper, Sugar Free Pepper Free, Pepper Free, and Welch's soda flavors. Dr Pepper, with a 6.9 percent market share, was the nation's fourth largest soft drink company in 1983.

Dr Pepper was first made in Waco, Texas, in 1885. Wade B. Morrison, owner of Morrison's Old Corner Drug, employed a pharmacist named Charles Courtice Alderton, who, when not filling prescriptions, often served soft drinks to customers. Alderton enjoyed experimenting with various combinations of fruit extracts and sweeteners. One combination, later to become Dr Pepper, proved enormously popular with drugstore patrons. As the popularity of the beverage grew, the residents of Waco urged Morrison to name the drink. Morrison named the beverage after Dr. Charles T. Pepper, a physician and pharmacist for whom Morrison had worked in Rural Retreat, Virginia. The trademark employed a period after *Dr* until 1950.

As the consumption of Dr Pepper increased, Morrison's drugstore could no longer produce a sufficient quantity of the beverage. In an effort to satisfy the demand, Morrison, along with Waco beverage chemist Robert S. Lazenby, started the Artesian Manufacturing and Bottling Works in 1891. On September 8, 1898, the Southwestern Soda Fountain Company of Dallas purchased the rights to produce and sell Dr Pepper fountain syrups. On September 25, 1902, Southwestern Soda Fountain changed its name to Dr Pepper Company. Circle "A" Corporation, which purchased Artesian Manufacturing and Bottling Works in 1920, was the only bottler of Dr Pepper concentrate. On June 12, 1923, because of rising commodity prices and high bottling taxes, Circle "A" Corporation went bankrupt.

On July 6, 1923, in Dallas, the remnants of the old Dr Pepper Company and Circle "A" Corporation officially incorporated as the Dr Pepper Company. Lazenby's son-in-law, John B. O'Hara, was named general manager of the firm. In these early years, the struggling firm developed a small but loyal following in the South and Southwest.

An important 1963 district court ruling enabled Dr Pepper to expand when the United States Fifth District Court of Dallas declared that Dr Pepper was not a cola. This ruling allowed independent bottlers to carry Dr Pepper along with Pepsi-Cola or Coca-Cola, since bottlers could now carry Dr Pepper without violating their franchise contracts, which state that bottlers are not permitted to bottle competing brands. Through close personal contacts and cooperative promotional efforts, Dr Pepper aggressively courted independent bottlers. From 1968 to 1977, under the guidance of Chief Executive Officer Woodrow Wilson Clements, sales increased from $41.9 million to $226.8 million. In the same period net earnings jumped from $4.1 million to $20.3 million.

As the 1970s drew to a close, however, Dr Pepper's fortunes declined. First, the company incurred tremendous debts in its acquisition of bottling plants and purchase of Canada Dry in 1982. Second, as market growth leveled off, the soft drink industry became increasingly competitive. As much larger Coca-Cola, PepsiCo, and Seven-Up (the last owned by Phillip Morris) increased advertising expenditures, debt-ridden Dr Pepper struggled to hold its own. From 1980 to 1983 the Dr Pepper brand's market share declined from 5.5 percent to 4.9 percent. Third, the rapid brand proliferation, begun in 1982 by Seven-Up with Like Cola, pushed Dr Pepper off the grocer's shelves. Fourth, in an effort to meet other soft drink companies' advertising efforts, under President Chuck Jarvie Dr Pepper concentrated primarily on nationwide advertising and ignored independent bottlers' needs. Independent bottlers thus no longer pushed Dr Pepper with the same zeal. Though sales increased from $370.6 million in 1981 to $516 million in 1982, the increase was largely attributable to the purchase of Canada Dry. In 1982 earnings declined to $12.5 million, down from $29.9 million in 1981. The company reported earnings of $21.6 million in 1983, still below the 1981 figure. In late 1983 Dr Pepper began a search for a buyer, preferably a large conglomerate, to increase its competitiveness in the soft drink industry.

Because of the highly competitive nature of that industry and Dr Pepper's poor cash position, few companies showed interest in the firm. In late 1983 Forstmann and Little, a New York investment-banking firm, offered twenty-two dollars a share for Dr Pepper. This deal, using primarily borrowed funds, involved buying out existing shareholders, refinancing Dr Pepper's debt, and retaining the company's top management. At about the same time, another suitor entered the picture. Castle and Cooke, a large food producer based in Honolulu, wanted Dr Pepper. With Dr Pepper, Castle and Cooke would be able partially to offset volatile earnings swings caused by fluctuating commodity prices. Unable to obtain sufficient financial information from Dr Pepper, however, Castle and Cooke's investment group withdrew its offer of twenty-four dollars a share. On February 28, 1984, Dr Pepper shareholders accepted the Forstmann and Little offer, and the company went private.

Since the buyout, the company has sold a majority of its fixed assets. Canada Dry was sold for about $175 million to R. J. Reynolds Industries, Incorporated, in 1984. All ten company-owned bottling plants have also been sold. In 1984 the Dr Pepper brand slipped from fourth to fifth in soft drink popularity, while maintaining an approximate 5 percent share of the market. By 1985, however, it had climbed to the number three position in the market, moving ahead of Seven-Up. Dr Pepper closed out its centennial year in 1985 with a 7½ percent share of the market as the third largest soft drink. It was the biggest sales year in the company's 100-year history.

In 1986 Dr Pepper merged with the Seven-Up Company and soon thereafter moved its manufacturing operations to facilities in St. Louis, although the company's corporate headquarters remained in Dallas. In 1992 Dr Pepper/Seven-Up Companies, Inc., was the soft drink industry's third largest marketer, with a domestic market share of 11.1 percent. Its products included Dr Pepper, Diet Dr Pepper, 7UP, Diet 7UP, Cherry 7UP, Diet Cherry 7UP, Welch's, and IBC soft drinks. The company's net sales totaled more than $658 million in 1992. A collection of Dr Pepper memorabilia formed the core of the Dr Pepper Museum and Free Enterprise Institute, which opened in Waco in 1991. *See also* SOFT DRINK INDUSTRY.

BIBLIOGRAPHY: Dallas *Morning News*, May 11, 1991. Dr Pepper Company, *Annual Report*, 1977, 1982. Harry E. Ellis, *Dr Pepper—King of Beverages* (Dallas: Taylor, 1979). Ruth Miller Fitzgibbons, "The Dr Pepper Merger: So Misunderstood," *D Magazine*, April 1984. Charlene James, "Dr Pepper... Distinctively Different," *Texas Historian*, May 1981. Robert Lawrence Kuhn, "Taking Aim at the Giants," *Texas Business*, June 1982.
Patrick Farl

DOCTORS CREEK. Doctors Creek rises 1½ miles northeast of Pecan Gap and just southwest of the junction of Farm roads 128 and 1530 in northwestern Delta County (at 33°27′ N, 95°47′ W) and runs southeast for fifteen miles to its mouth on the South Sulphur River, just east of Harper's Crossing and two miles east of Liberty Grove (at 33°20′ N, 95°38′ W). Cannon Creek flows into Doctors Creek just south of Cooper. Near its origin Doctors Creek passes through rolling prairies surfaced by black clay that supports mesquite and grasses; the stream descends quickly into floodplains surfaced by sand, mud, and gravel that support water-tolerant hardwoods, conifers, and grasses. The creek may have been named for medicinal herbs which Indians gathered from the area or for a local physician whose horse and buggy became mired in a shallow crossing. The Doctors Creek community was located on the stream.

BIBLIOGRAPHY: Paul Garland Hervey, A History of Education in Delta County, Texas (M.A. thesis, University of Texas, 1951). Fred Tarpley, *1001 Texas Place Names* (Austin: University of Texas Press, 1980).

DOCTORS CREEK, TEXAS. Doctors Creek was a school community on Doctors Creek 1½ miles northwest of Cooper and just south of Price in central Delta County. The earliest settlers, including I. N. Gray, J. A. Good, Volney Rattan, B. F. Hunt, and J. M. Cannon, arrived in 1882 and soon established the one-room Doctors Creek School with Mrs. Cannon as the teacher. In 1905 the community school enrolled forty-four students and employed one teacher. Maps for 1936 did not name the community, but showed the school, a church, and a cluster of dwellings at the intersection of two dirt roads. The Doctors Creek school closed in 1949 when it was consolidated into the Cooper Independent School District. The settlement no longer appeared on maps in 1964.

BIBLIOGRAPHY: Paul Garland Hervey, A History of Education in Delta County, Texas (M.A. thesis, University of Texas, 1951). Wilma Ross and Billie Phillips, *Photos and Tales of Delta County* (1976).
Vista K. McCroskey

DODD, DAVID OWEN (1847–1864). David Owen Dodd, teenage Civil War[qv] spy, was born in Victoria, Texas, in 1847, the son of Andrew Marion Dodd. When he was twelve, his family moved to Benton, Arkansas. Dodd spent most of his life in Texas. In 1862 he moved with his parents and two sisters to Little Rock, Arkansas, where he attended St. John's College, then contracted malaria and withdrew from school. Instead of returning to college after his illness, he began working in the Little Rock telegraph office. During the summer of 1862 he and his father moved to Monroe, Louisiana, where Dodd worked in the local telegraph office, in which the lines were controlled by the Confederate Army. He remained there for four or five months, keeping in close contact with Confederate troop movement in Louisiana and Northern Mississippi. In January of 1863 he went to Granada, Mississippi, where for eight months he helped his father, a sutler for the Third Arkansas Regiment. In September of that year he returned to Little Rock to help his mother and two sisters get away and behind the Confederate lines because the federal troops had captured the city. He was not successful. After a few weeks Dodd began working in a sutler's store that aided federal troops. In December 1863 his father unexpectedly arrived in Little Rock to move his wife, son, and daughters to Camden, Arkansas, by wagon. Shortly thereafter, Dodd returned to Little Rock to help with his father's unsettled business.

He received a pass from Gen. James F. Fagan, a family friend, in exchange for information about the Union troops in Little Rock. Dodd was to report his findings to General Fagan when he returned to Camden. On his way to Little Rock, he met Frank Tomlinson of Pine Bluff, who was also a seventeen-year-old Confederate spy. Tomlinson, sent on a mission to find military information for Gen. John S. Marmaduke of Mississippi, succeeded in his endeavor. It was later believed that during the Christmas holidays Dodd visited Union headquarters and other military offices in Little Rock to gather strategic military information for General Fagan and wrote his notes in Morse Code. He left Little Rock on December 29 and safely passed by several federal pickets. At dusk he emerged from the woods to find a squad of the federal army and was arrested by Sergeant Miehr of Company B, First Missouri Cavalry, because he did not have his pass, which had been taken by a federal picket, Pvt. Daniel Olderburg. After he was escorted to the picket headquarters, it was confirmed that the pass had been taken. Before Dodd was to be released, he was searched for possession of contraband. He was found worthy of release until a member of one of the troops noticed he was wearing two different shoes. His shoes were inspected, and his small notebook was found in one of the soles. Lieutenant Stopral of the federal troops identified the Morse Code and could read enough to be skeptical. Dodd's papers were taken by Capt. George Hanna, and he was placed in the guardhouse. The next morning, December 30, he was turned over to Capt. John Baird, who took him to Little Rock to stand trial.

The trial, presided over by Brig. Gen. John M. Thayer, began the following day. In its six-day duration witnesses testified that they had seen Dodd at different functions during the holidays and did not notice any evidence of spying. Robert Clowery, assistant superintendent of the United States Military Telegraph and later president of the Western Union Telegraph Company, provided the deciding testimony. Clowery could read Dodd's Morse Code notes, which listed the manpower and weaponry of the Union forces. Dodd maintained his innocence, but on January 5, 1864, was found guilty and sentenced to hang. He then confessed that he had received orders from General Fagan to relay information about the federal troops in Little Rock and stated that he would not have been allowed to visit Little Rock unless he agreed to spy. Maj. Gen. Frederick Steele, who ordered Dodd's trial, believed a federal soldier had assisted Dodd and promised to drop the charges if Dodd would name the traitor. Dodd refused, and his sentence was confirmed. On January 8, 1864, at 3:00 P.M., he was executed by hanging on the grounds of St. John's College, his alma mater, before a crowd of 2,000 citizens and a 4,000-man military escort. Dodd, described by his mother as a "hot-headed Southern boy," may have been the youngest participant in the war who was hanged as a spy.

BIBLIOGRAPHY: Dwayne Holman and Henry Keatts, "The Coldest Day: The Activities and Execution of a Confederate Boy Spy, David O. Dodd," *Military History of Texas and the Southwest* 9 (1971). San Antonio *Express*, October 24, 1954.   *Laura House*

DODD, FREDERICA CHASE (ca. 1892–1972). Frederica Dodd, black teacher and social worker, was born in 1892 and lived most of her life in Dallas. After graduating in 1910 from what later became Booker T. Washington High School, she attended Howard University. With twenty-one other young women, she organized Delta Sigma Theta sorority there in 1913. When she returned to Dallas after earning her degree in 1914, she taught for a year at her old high school. After marrying physician John H. Dodd on June 10, 1920, she had to give up the post. She began her career in social work with the Dallas Family Bureau, or United Charities. Frederica Dodd was a leader in a successful effort to establish a YWCA branch for blacks. The organization, initially an after-school group for girls, expanded into the Maria Morgan Branch. She helped to organize a Dallas Alumnae chapter of Delta Sigma Theta and belonged to the Priscilla Art Club. She died on January 21, 1972, in Dallas County.

BIBLIOGRAPHY: Paula Giddings, *In Search of Sisterhood: Delta Sigma Theta and the Challenge of the Black Sorority Movement* (New York: Morrow, 1988). Julia K. Gibson Jordan and Charlie Mae Brown Smith, *Beauty and the Best: Frederica Chase Dodd, The Story of a Life of Love and Dedication* (Dallas: Dallas Alumnae Chapter of Delta Sigma Theta Sorority, 1985).   *Ruthe Winegarten*

DODD, JAMES ANDREW (1917–1984). James Andrew (Jimmie) Dodd, photographer, son of Earle Bartholomew and Ellen Belle (Horan) Dodd, was born in Houston, Texas, on July 20, 1917. After graduating from high school he worked as a mascot for the Missouri Pacific Railroad. He began photography as a hobby and in 1935, upon buying a used Auto Graphlex camera with a $250 loan from King Ranch[qv] president Robert Kleberg, Jr.,[qv] made it his profession.

For the next forty years Dodd worked as a photographer throughout South Texas while living in Kingsville. He photographed weddings, community pageants, school activities, political rallies, and other social and cultural events. He took many photographs on the King Ranch from 1935 to the early 1950s, a time when other photographers had difficulty getting access to the ranch. He photographed ranch life, as well as the Klebergs' public life and several of the famous personalities who visited there, including Will Rogers, Anne Baxter, and Nelson Rockefeller. For many years Dodd was the photographer for the Kingsville Police Department.

Other significant subjects that he photographed include the Texas City disaster[qv] in 1947, the opening of the Shamrock Hotel in Houston in 1948, Professional Golfers Association tour events in Texas in the 1940s and 1950s, and the Missouri Pacific Railroad in the Corpus Christi–Kingsville area. His professional memberships included the American Professional Photographers Association and the Texas Professional Photographers Association. Dodd belonged to Saint Gertrude's Catholic Church in Kingsville, was a charter member of the Kingsville Knights of Columbus, and was a member of the Confederate Air Force.[qv]

He moved to Kerrville in the early 1970s and continued working, despite health problems. He never married. Dodd died of heart failure on January 27, 1984, in Kerrville. In 1983 the Barker Texas History Center[qv] at the University of Texas at Austin acquired his negative files, which consisted of 23,000 negatives dating from 1937 to 1967.

BIBLIOGRAPHY: Jimmie A. Dodd Photograph Collection, Barker Texas History Center, University of Texas at Austin. Kerrville *Mountain Sun*, February 1, 1984. San Antonio *Express News*, October 24, 1982. Vertical Files, Barker Texas History Center, University of Texas at Austin.   *Lawrence A. Landis*

DODD, TEXAS. Dodd, on Farm Road 303 eighteen miles southwest of Dimmitt in the southwestern corner of Castro County, is named for a family that settled there in the early 1900s. Until 1945 students attended Big Square School, north of Dodd. After 1945, however, that school district was consolidated with the Springlake and Dimmitt schools. Dodd reported a store, a grain elevator, a gin, and a population of thirty-five through the 1970s and 1980s. In 1990 the population was still thirty-five.

BIBLIOGRAPHY: Castro County Historical Commission, *Castro County, 1891–1981* (Dallas: Taylor, 1981).   *H. Allen Anderson*

DODD BRANCH. Dodd Branch rises eight miles southeast of Purmela in central Coryell County (at 31°24′ N, 97°53′ W) and runs northeast for twelve miles to its mouth on the Leon River, within the city limits of Gatesville (at 31°26′ N, 97°46′ W). The stream traverses generally flat to rolling terrain surfaced by shallow clay and sandy loams that support primarily juniper, hardwoods, and grasses.

DODD CITY, TEXAS. Dodd City is at the intersection of U.S. Highway 82 and Farm Road 2077, five miles east of Bonham in central Fannin County. Settlement of the area occurred in 1839, when Maj. Edmund Hall Dodd and his wife, Elizabeth (Garnett), arrived from Kentucky. The couple built a log house that soon served area farmers and travelers as a trading center, post office, and stagecoach inn. From 1845 to 1865 a post office branch existed at the site under the name Licke. The post office was reestablished under the name Dodd from 1873 to 1902, when the name was changed to Dodd City.

Before the Civil War^{qv} several businesses were added to the growing community, including a two-story hotel. The war retarded growth, but over the next five years the community's population increased as Civil War veterans moved to Texas from the upper South. In 1873 the tracks of the Texas and Pacific Railway reached a community called Quincy, one mile west of Dodd. Quincy was included in the community when Dodd incorporated in 1879. During the next thirty years the town served as a retail center and shipping point for area farmers. By the mid-1880s its population surpassed 400, making it one of the largest communities in Fannin County, with twenty businesses, four churches, a school, a weekly newspaper, and a loan and exchange association. The population reached 500 by 1900, but economic growth leveled off by 1910. Dodd City had 400 residents, an estimated thirty businesses, and two banks in 1926. After 1930 the population steadily declined. At the end of World War II^{qv} the town had 308 residents and eight businesses. In 1950 the Texas and Pacific ended passenger service to the town, which had a population of 351 in 1990.

BIBLIOGRAPHY: *Fannin County Folks and Facts* (Dallas: Taylor, 1977). Floy Crandall Hodge, *A History of Fannin County* (Hereford, Texas: Pioneer, 1966).
David Minor

DODDRIDGE, PERRY (1832–1902). Perry Doddridge, merchant and banker, was born in Little Peach Tree, Alabama, on June 1, 1832. He was brought to Texas in 1840; his father died at Trinity, and a short time later his mother died in Galveston. He was employed as a clerk in Galveston. In 1852 he was working for M. Kenedy and Company, Brownsville. Major J. Durst appointed him deputy collector of customs at Roma in 1853. Doddridge then went into commerce on his own as a freighter and merchant at Mier, Tamaulipas. In 1865 he opened a merchandising business in Corpus Christi under the name Manuel Bustamente and Company and financed other enterprises. In partnership with Allen M. Davis, he purchased the exchange and commission business of H. F. Kirsteen in 1868. Doddridge and Davis established the first bank in Corpus Christi in 1871. Davis sold out to go to New York in 1885, leaving Doddridge and Company a sole proprietorship. The bank closed in February 1891 during a national monetary crisis and collapse of a local boom inspired by Col. Elihu H. Ropes.^{qv} Ropes had promoted schemes to build a deepwater port at Corpus Christi and a railroad from Corpus Christi through Brownsville to Panama, but was unable to marshal enough financial support to complete the works. Doddridge was unable to reopen the bank but obtained employment managing the local electric company.

He was instrumental in securing land for the public schools in Corpus Christi and served as president of the school board for twenty years. He was elected mayor in 1874 and later served on the county commissioners' court. He played a decisive role in the development of transportation in South Texas, particularly the ship channel into Corpus Christi Bay and various railway projects. His long-standing conflict with Norwick Gussett involved both their banking activities and shipping. He was a great friend and advisor to Richard King^{qv} and was named an executor of King's will.

Doddridge married Rachel Fullerton of Corpus Christi on June 12, 1862. He was a Presbyterian and a member of the Rio Grande Masonic lodge. He was a scholar and owned a library of a thousand volumes, including several rare editions that his widow was forced to sell to support herself. Doddridge died on June 11, 1902, and was buried in the family cemetery near his residence.

BIBLIOGRAPHY: Corpus Christi *Caller*, June 13, 1902. Tom Lea, *The King Ranch* (2 vols., Boston: Little, Brown, 1957).
Frank Wagner

DODDVILLE, TEXAS (Lee County). Doddville was a post office community in east central Lee County that existed around the time of the Civil War.^{qv} It is believed to have been somewhere between the sites of later Giddings and Dime Box, possibly near Old Evergreen. At one time the settlement had a school with T. N. Stead as the teacher. The town was apparently abandoned by 1900.

BIBLIOGRAPHY: Lee County Historical Survey Committee, *A History of Lee County* (Quanah, Texas: Nortex, 1974).
Christopher Long

DODDVILLE, TEXAS (Washington County). Doddville, also known as Dodd or Dodds, was probably on Yegua Creek fifteen miles north of Long Point in northern Washington County. It received its name from John Dodd, its first postmaster. In 1854 Doddville had a population of 287 whites and twenty-one black slaves. By 1856 the community had a school, and in September 1858 its post office opened. Doddville served as a center for an agricultural and stock-raising area. Its post office closed in June 1859, and by 1860 the population had decreased to 160, which included a teacher, a master mechanic, a well digger, and physician L. W. C. Lincecum, son of Gideon Lincecum,^{qv} famed physician and botanist. The community declined as more fertile areas of the county were opened to cultivation and the population moved nearer to the projected rail route in southern Washington County.
Carole E. Christian

DODGE, TEXAS (McCulloch County). Dodge, seven miles west of Brady in west central McCulloch County, was named for I. A. Dodge, who settled in the area in 1883. No evidence of the community appeared on county highway maps by the 1930s.

BIBLIOGRAPHY: Jessie Laurie Barfoot, History of McCulloch County, Texas (M.A. thesis, University of Texas, 1937).
Vivian Elizabeth Smyrl

DODGE, TEXAS (Walker County). Dodge, on Farm Road 405 a mile north of U.S. Highway 190 and ten miles east of Huntsville in eastern Walker County, was founded in 1872 on land granted to the Houston and Great Northern Railroad by William H. Parmer (Palmer); settlers had begun farming the land as early as 1825. Martin Parmer,^{qv} William's father, signed the Texas Declaration of Independence.^{qv} Other area pioneers included W. H. Baker, John Roark, Ed Farris, Haden Watts, and Ishom Green Webb. In 1853 several additional families moved to the area from Cincinnati to escape a yellow fever epidemic. Among the new arrivals were James Gillaspie^{qv} and Rev. William D. Shockley, who established a Methodist church known as Shockley's Chapel.

After the Civil War^{qv} the H&GN Railroad, constructed by the Phelps-Dodge Company, arrived in Walker County. A depot named Dodge Station was established and a town laid out in 1872. The town took its name from the construction company, although local legend has it that the name Dodge was chosen to indicate that the company "dodged" laying its tracks through Huntsville. In the 1870s the community had a Masonic lodge, a hotel, a vacant store, a school, and two general stores. When the post office was established in 1881 Dodge Station became Dodge, and the first postmaster was Russell Roark. By the mid-1890s the population was 150; by 1914 it was 500. The community prospered, adding two churches, a bank, cotton gins, two additional general stores, and two drugstores. The town was seriously damaged by a fire in 1924 and a second one the following year.

From 1901 until 1936 Dodge served as a junction for the Trinity Valley Southern and IGN railroads, which served the lumber industry^{qv} in the region. Dodge had three businesses, two churches, two schools, and numerous scattered dwellings in 1936. However, the Great Depression^{qv} years witnessed the phasing out of the lumber industry throughout the area, and the community began to falter. Several fires destroyed buildings over the next few years, and they were not rebuilt. In 1943 the town had a population of 150 and three businesses. In 1990 Dodge had two businesses, a church, a post office, and an estimated population of 150.

BIBLIOGRAPHY: D'Anne McAdams Crews, ed., *Huntsville and Walker County, Texas: A Bicentennial History* (Huntsville, Texas: Sam

Houston State University, 1976). Houston *Chronicle,* February 1, 1982. Walker County Genealogical Society and Walker County Historical Commission, *Walker County* (Dallas, 1986).

James L. Hailey

DODSON, ARCHELAUS BYNUM (1807–1898). Archelaus Dodson, participant in the Texas Revolution,qv son of Obadiah and Sarah (Garrison) Dodson, was born in North Carolina on December 31, 1807. He left for Texas in 1826, and was living in Harrisburg in 1827. He married Sarah Bradley there on May 17, 1835; they had six children. When the local committee of vigilance and safety learned of Gen. Martín Perfecto de Cos's qv planned invasion of Texas and sent out a call to arms on September 19, 1835, Dodson joined other Harrisburg volunteers in forming a company under Capt. Andrew Robinson.qv Dodson was elected first lieutenant.

Sarah Bradley Dodsonqv designed and, with help of other Harrisburg women, made the first tricolor Lone Star flag of Texas; when the company of Andrew Robinson, Jr., was mustered into the revolutionary armyqv in 1835, she presented it to the members (*see* FLAGS OF THE TEXAS REVOLUTION). The Robinson company participated in the siege of Bexarqv and did not return to East Texas until early 1836, still led by the Dodson flag. Dodson was among those detailed to ensure the safety of women and children beyond the Brazos River in the Runaway Scrape;qv he contracted measles from some of the sick children and was unable to participate in the battle of San Jacinto.qv

The Dodsons continued to live in Fort Bend County until 1844, when they claimed their headright in Grimes County. Sarah Dodson died in 1848, and Dodson married Katherine Maria McKnight McWhorter, a widow with several children, in 1850. He moved the family to Live Oak County in 1860 and became a rancher with his brother-in-law, Martin Culver, a cattleman. Dodson died on his ranch about five miles south of Alice on March 10, 1898, and was buried in the Old Collins Cemetery.

BIBLIOGRAPHY: Vertical Files, Barker Texas History Center, University of Texas at Austin.

Agnes G. Grimm

DODSON, SARAH RANDOLPH BRADLEY (1812–1848). Sarah Dodson, designer of an early lone-star Texas flag, was born on January 8, 1812, the daughter of Edward (or Edwin) R. and Elizabeth Bradley. In 1822 or 1823 her family moved from Kentucky to Texas as part of Stephen F. Austin'sqv Old Three Hundredqv and settled by the Brazos River on land now in Brazoria County. On May 17, 1835, Sarah married Archelaus Bynum Dodson.qv The couple moved to Harrisburg, where in September 1835 Dodson was elected first lieutenant of a volunteer company raised to resist the Mexican army. Sarah reportedly volunteered to make a flag for the company during a meeting of citizens at the home of William Plunkett Harris.qv Lacking silk or bunting, she made the flag out of three colored squares of cotton cloth. The square nearest the flagstaff was blue with a white star centered upon it. The middle square was white, and the outermost square was red. The flag was carried by the Harrisburg company to Gonzales, where an army of Texas colonists was assembling. Between October and December it went with the company through the battle of Concepción and the siege of Bexar,qqv though it is unclear whether the flag was actually carried in battle. The flag was reportedly taken back to Harrisburg when the company returned home, and it is said to have flown over the building where the Convention of 1836 qv met and declared independence from Mexico. The subsequent history of the flag is unknown. Mrs. Dodson's standard, made in September or October of 1835, thus predates the flag made by Johanna Troutman,qv which was brought to Texas by Georgia volunteers in December 1835.

Sarah Dodson and her husband took part in the Runaway Scrape,qv during which she had a daughter. Their home in Harrisburg was probably lost when Antonio López de Santa Annaqv burned the town. After the revolution they moved to Fort Bend County, and in 1844 they settled in the area of present Grimes County five miles northeast of Bedias, where Archelaus Dodson had located his headright league. There they helped organize a Presbyterian congregation and donated land for the Bethel Church and cemetery. Sarah Dodson and her husband were the parents of five children. Sarah died on October 9, 1848, and was buried in Bethel Cemetery. In September 1935, 100 years after she made her flag, her descendants placed a granite marker at her gravesite.

BIBLIOGRAPHY: Daughters of the Republic of Texas, *Founders and Patriots of the Republic of Texas* (Austin, 1963–). Louis Wiltz Kemp Papers, Barker Texas History Center, University of Texas at Austin. Adele B. Looscan, "Harris County, 1822–1845," *Southwestern Historical Quarterly* 18–19 (October 1914–July 1915). Vertical Files, Barker Texas History Center, University of Texas at Austin.

Mary M. Standifer

DODSON, VIOLA RUTH (1876–1963). Viola Ruth Dodson, folklorist and historian, was born on the Perdido Ranch in Nueces County, Texas, on September 3, 1876, the daughter of Milton and Susan Dodson. According to some sources, her great grandfather Bradley brought his family to Texas with the Old Three Hundred.qv Her early schooling took place on the family ranch and, for one year, in the public schools of Corpus Christi. She attended Lagarto College in 1883–84. Ruth learned to speak fluent Spanish from Mexican ranchhands, through whom she developed a lasting interest in Mexican culture. In 1935, at the insistence of J. Frank Dobie,qv to whose work she contributed stories and information, she wrote a volume of Southwest Texas folklore in Spanish, *Don Pedrito Jaramillo* (1934). Pedro Jaramilloqv was a faith healer and doctor, and the book contains many of his healing remedies. The library of the College of Physicians in Philadelphia acquired it as a reference book in the history of medicine, and it became a folklore classic. It was later published in 1951 as *The Healer of Los Olmos and Other Mexican Lore,* by the Texas Folklore Society,qv with a preface by Dobie. Dodson's other writings include an unpublished novel about migrant workers entitled *Cock Crows,* which won a prize at the Southwest Writers Conference in Corpus Christi. She also wrote pieces for the Texas Folklore Society, for which she was a counselor, that were published in the *Southwest Review* and *Frontier Times.*qqv Her aim was to present a true picture of the area between the Nueces and Rio Grande. Dodson lived at Alice, Texas, and on Catalina Island in California before moving to Mathis, Texas, when she was fifty. She died at Corpus Christi on July 19, 1963, and was buried in the Old Mathis Cemetery.

BIBLIOGRAPHY: Florence Elberta Barns, *Texas Writers of Today* (Dallas: Tardy, 1935). Agnes G. Grimm, *Llanos Mesteñas: Mustang Plains* (Waco: Texian Press, 1968). Lael Moore, "Ruth Dodson, South Texas Folklorist," *Texas Historian,* May 1971. Vertical Files, Barker Texas History Center, University of Texas at Austin.

Agnes G. Grimm

DODSON, TEXAS (Collingsworth County). Dodson (Dodsonville), a mile west of the Texas-Oklahoma state line in southeastern Collingsworth County, was founded in the spring of 1910 by Frank Kell,qv promoter of the Wellington branch of the Wichita Falls and Northwestern Railway, and named for Elmore Dodson, who contributed a 200-acre grant of land as a bonus for the railroad. A gala celebration, complete with a picnic, marked the town's formal opening on August 29, 1910, and was attended by a trainload of people from Oklahoma. N. L. Jones built the first residence and opened a cotton gin. The first store was operated by William T. McDowell, who was also the first postmaster. R. H. Miller established a hotel, and the town added a bank, a telephone exchange, and two churches. Three newspapers, all called the Dodsonville *News,* were published intermittently by three different men between January 1911 and December 1915. A fourth paper, the Dodsonville *Messenger,* was printed from 1928 until 1930. School was sometimes held in the churches until a permanent schoolhouse was completed in the fall of 1912; the previous school was located three miles northwest of town. Dodson was incorporated in the 1920s and by 1930 had twenty-five businesses and a population of 426. Public Works Administration appropriations enabled the town to install a $52,000 water system during the 1930s, and a volunteer fire department was organized. In 1947 a new consolidated high school served neighboring communities in Oklahoma as well as Dodson. The population dropped to 357 in 1940; this decline, attributed to decreased agricultural activity and a renewed interest in cattle raising, continued into the 1990s. In 1984 Dodson remained the county's second largest town, with a population of 185, one business, and four churches. In 1990 the population was 113.

BIBLIOGRAPHY: Clyde Chestnut Brown, A Survey History of Collingsworth County, Texas (M.A. thesis, University of Colorado, 1934). A History of Collingsworth County and Other Stories (Wellington, Texas: *Leader* Printing, 1925).   H. Allen Anderson

DODSON, TEXAS (Houston County). Dodson, five miles south of the site of later Hagerville in southeastern Houston County, was established in the mid-1880s. A post office opened there in 1887 with John M. Smith as postmaster. At its height in the mid-1890s the settlement had a two blacksmith shops, a gristmill and cotton gin, a sawmill, and a number of houses. Its post office closed in 1908, and by the mid-1930s Dodson no longer appeared on highway maps.

Christopher Long

DOE BRANCH. Doe Branch (also known as Doe Creek) rises two miles north of Bainville in southwestern Karnes County (at 28°45′ N, 97°58′ W) and runs northeast for eight miles to its mouth on Escondido Creek, two miles west of Kenedy (at 28°50′ N, 97°53′ W). It traverses flat to rolling terrain surfaced by clay and sandy loam that supports water-tolerant hardwoods and grasses.

DOE RUN CREEK. Doe Run Creek rises five miles west of Washington-on-the-Brazos in Washington County (at 30°19′ N, 96°15′ W) and runs southeast for ten miles to its mouth on the Brazos River, at the Waller county line (at 30°13′ N, 96°09′ W). The stream, intermittent in its upper reaches, traverses flat to rolling terrain surfaced by clay and sandy loams that support hardwood forests, conifers, mesquite, brush, and grasses.

DOGAN, MATTHEW WINFRED (1863–1947). Matthew Winfred Dogan, black college president, was born on December 21, 1863, at Pontotoc, Mississippi, the son of William and Jennie Dogan. He attended Rust College in Holly Spring, Mississippi, and, when he finished the preparatory courses, left school to teach in order to earn money for college. He later returned and graduated from the college at the head of his class in 1886. In the next fall term he was appointed to the faculty at Rust College. After five years he was hired as a mathematics instructor at Central Tennessee College in Nashville, which later became known as Walden College. In 1888 he married Fannie Forest Faulkner; they had seven children, two of whom died in infancy.

In 1896 Dogan left Walden to become president of Wiley College, Marshall, Texas, and during his administration Wiley developed into one of the best colleges for African Americans[qv] in the country. Dogan was also president of the Standard Mutual Fire Insurance Company, the National Association of Teachers in Colored Schools, and the Teachers State Association of Texas[qv] and was active in many Methodist Episcopal, fraternal, and civic organizations. Dogan voted Republican. He was awarded an honorary Ph.D by Rust College in 1904. New Orleans University conferred the doctor of divinity degree on him in 1910, and he received honorary degrees from Walden College and Howard University as well. Dogan retired in 1942 and died at his home in Marshall on June 17, 1947.

BIBLIOGRAPHY: *Journal of Negro History* October 1947. Clement Richardson, ed., *National Cyclopedia of the Colored Race* (Montgomery, Alabama: National, 1919). *Who's Who in Colored America,* 1941–44.   *Kharen Monsho*

DOG BRANCH. Dog Branch rises five miles northeast of Mason in central Mason County (at 30°49′ N, 99°11′ W) and runs southeast for 4½ miles to its mouth on East Willow Creek, 2½ miles northwest of Art (at 30°47′ N, 99°08′ W). The creek rises in the limestone hills on the eastern edge of the Edwards Plateau and crosses an area of the Llano basin characterized by flat to rolling terrain surfaced by deep to shallow sandy and clayey loams that support scrub brush, grasses, and open stands of live oak and mesquite.

DOG CANYON. Dog Canyon, which contains an intermittent stream, begins four miles east of Stairway Mountain in the Black Gap Wildlife Management Area in southeastern Brewster County (at 29°33′ N, 102°53′ W) and extends northeast for four miles to its mouth on Maravillas Creek, six miles west of the Rio Grande (at 29°35′ N, 102°52′ W). The surrounding steep to gentle slopes are surfaced by shallow to moderately deep clay and sandy loams that support scrub brush and grasses. Three variations of the source of the name are that a pack of wild dogs was discovered there, that a lost yoke of oxen guarded by a stray dog was found there, and that the canyon was named for an old rancher and trapper nicknamed "Dog" because he kept so many of them.

DOGIE MOUNTAIN. Dogie Mountain is four miles northeast of the Big Bend National Park[qv] Maverick Ranger Station in southwestern Brewster County (at 29°21′ N, 103°28′ W). With an elevation of 3,689 feet above sea level, it rises 940 feet above the ranger station. The mountain, which straddles the park's northwestern boundary, is a volcanic intrusion with shallow, stony soils that support live oak, piñon, juniper, and grasses.

DOG RIDGE, TEXAS. Dog Ridge is on U.S. Highway 190 three miles west of Belton in central Bell County. It is said to take its name from the dogs that settlers found running wild in the area after the Runaway Scrape[qv] in the 1830s. Dog Ridge School, or Mitchell School, was the focus of a common-school district by 1885 and had forty-two students in 1903; the school closed in 1918. The community grew after the completion of nearby Stillhouse Hollow Lake[qv] in the 1960s. Dog Ridge reported a population of 125 from the late 1960s through 1990.

BIBLIOGRAPHY: Bell County Historical Commission, *Story of Bell County, Texas* (2 vols., Austin: Eakin Press, 1988).

Vivian Elizabeth Smyrl

DOG-RUN HOUSES. The dog-run, dog-trot, or double log cabin was a common type of house in Texas at the middle of the nineteenth century. The building consisted of two cabins separated by a ten or fifteen foot passageway, with a continuous gabled roof covering both cabins and the passageway between them, or dog-run. Often a porch was built to extend across the entire front of the house, and lean-to shed rooms were constructed at the rear of each cabin for additional space. The walls were made of horizontally laid hand-hewn logs, with the openings between the logs chinked with sticks and clay. Later examples were often frame rather than logs. The floors were of either dirt, sawed boards, or split logs with the flat side up. There few windows in frontier cabins, and glass windows were rarely seen in pioneer times. Each cabin had a door opening onto the dog-run. Doors and shutters were hung on rawhide or wooden hinges. The roofs were made of overlapping oak clapboards held in place by weight poles. The chimney was constructed of sticks and a clay mixture, and the hearth was made of smooth rocks. Later dog-run houses often had fine brick chimneys and shingled roofs. The purpose of the dog-run was to cool the house by providing shade and catching the breeze.

The space served as a catch-all for farm and household articles and was the favorite sleeping place of the dogs. The structure was used on the frontier from Alabama to Ontario and has European antecedents.

BIBLIOGRAPHY: Louise Cezeaux, Social Life in the Republic of Texas, 1836–1845 (M.A. thesis, University of Texas, 1933). Herbert P. Gambrell and Lewis W. Newton, A Social and Political History of Texas (Dallas: Southwest Press, 1932). Terry G. Jordan, American Log Buildings: An Old World Heritage (Chapel Hill: University of North Carolina Press, 1985). Terry G. Jordan, Log Cabin Village: A History and Guide (Austin: Texas State Historical Association, 1980). Terry G. Jordan, Texas Log Buildings: A Folk Architecture (Austin: University of Texas Press, 1978).

W. W. White

DOGUENE INDIANS. The Doguenes (Aguenes, Deaguanes, Deguenes, Draguanes) were Indians of the Texas coast among whom Álvar Núñez Cabeza de Vaca[qv] lived for a time, presumably about 1528. Their precise location cannot be determined, but geographic details in the Cabeza de Vaca narrative seem to indicate the vicinity of Matagorda Bay. About 160 years later, when Europeans again visited this section of the coast, it was occupied by Karankawan groups. The Doguenes lived in the vicinity of San Antonio Bay.

BIBLIOGRAPHY: Adolph F. Bandelier, ed., The Journey of Álvar Núñez Cabeza de Vaca and His Companions from Florida to the Pacific, 1528–1536 (New York: Barnes, 1905). Frederick Webb Hodge, ed., Handbook of American Indians North of Mexico (2 vols., Washington: GPO, 1907, 1910; rpt., New York: Pageant, 1959).

Thomas N. Campbell

DOGWOOD BRANCH. Dogwood Branch rises three miles southeast of West Point in west central Fayette County (at 29°55′ N, 97°02′ W) and runs southeast for 3½ miles to its mouth on Buckners Creek (at 29°53′ N, 96°58′ W). It traverses an area characterized by soils with a sandy loam surface layer over a firm clay subsoil. This land is generally not used for agriculture except as unimproved pasture. Local vegetation is primarily a mixture of oaks and cedar with an understory of yaupon. The stream is named for the occasional dogwoods that grow nearby but are rare in surrounding areas.

DOGWOOD CREEK (Fayette County). Dogwood Creek rises in Colony on State Highway 95 between Cistern and Flatonia in southwestern Fayette County (at 29°47′ N, 97°10′ W) and runs northeast for 7½ miles to its mouth on Live Oak Creek, 2½ miles west of Muldoon (at 29°49′ N, 97°07′ W). Soils in the area have a fine sandy loam surface layer and a deep, firm clay subsoil. Although highly erosible, they are rated as fair for agriculture, and some farms in the area raise corn as well as hay; much of the land is used as pasture for cattle. Along the creek grow dense stands of mixed oak, cedar, and hackberry, with an understory of yaupon and a few dogwoods, for which the creek was named. Several locations along the upper reaches of the creek have been stripped to mine clay deposits.

_____ (Washington County). Dogwood Creek rises nine miles southwest of Brenham in southwestern Washington County (at 30°05′ N, 96°32′ W) and runs southeast for nine miles to its mouth on the East Fork of Mill Creek, 1½ miles north of Industry in Austin County (at 30°00′ N, 96°31′ W). It traverses an area of low-rolling hills and prairies, surfaced by clay and sandy loams that support grasses, mesquite, and occasional post oak.

DOHÄSAN (?–1866). Dohäsan, or Dohate, was a prominent Kiowa chief, the son of a chief named Dohá (Bluff). He was of the Kata or Arikara band of Kiowas, so named because of their close trading relationship with the Arikaras in the upper Missouri valley during the tribe's early history. Dohäsan's name, which was hereditary, has been variously translated as Little Mountain, Little Bluff, or Top-of-the-Mountain. Dohäsan became principal chief of the Kiowas in the spring of 1833, after the deposition of A'date, following the massacre of his village by Osages at Cutthroat Gap, near the head of Otter Creek in Indian Territory. That episode prompted the dragoon expedition of Col. Henry Dodge to Western Oklahoma in the summer of 1834. Dohäsan was among those on hand to greet the colonel and his retinue. George Catlin,[qv] who accompanied the expedition, sketched and painted the chief's portrait. In May 1837 Dohäsan was one of the principals who signed the Fort Gibson Treaty, by which the United States government sought to end intertribal warfare in Indian Territory.

Treaties, however, did little to stifle the Kiowas' frequent raids for horses and other booty. In their roamings Dohäsan and his followers frequented the Texas Panhandle, particularly the Canadian River valley. There, on September 17, 1845, he was entered in Lt. James W. Abert's[qv] watercolor portfolio. In the summer of 1851 Dohäsan led a war party against treacherous Pawnees near the head of Medicine Lodge Creek in Kansas, and in 1857 he successfully led his warriors out of an ambush by Mexican soldiers at Hueco Tanks near El Paso. In 1859, as a goodwill gesture, Maj. John Sedgwick's troops presented Dohäsan with an old army ambulance wagon. Unable to master the art of driving a team, the chief simply had a couple of Kiowa boys ride the harnessed horses as he sat in the driver's seat. Once, when federal authorities threatened to withhold annuity goods and send troops against the Kiowas if they did not cease their depredations, Dohäsan defiantly called the "white chief" a fool with the "heart of a woman." It was Dohäsan's camp that Col. Christopher H. (Kit) Carson's[qv] troops attacked and burned in the first battle of Adobe Walls[qv] on November 26, 1864; the old chief escaped to warn the villages farther down but had his horse shot from under him and lost his ambulance to the whites. In October 1865 Dohäsan signed the Little Arkansas Treaty, but he vigorously protested confinement to a reservation, declaring that the Kiowas owned all the land from the North Platte River to the upper Texas Panhandle and needed room to roam about. Shortly afterward, in early 1866, he died.

Although the principal chieftainship passed to Lone Wolf, the Kiowa tribe began to splinter into factions and never again was truly unified under one leader. A nephew of Dohäsan subsequently inherited his name. The younger Dohäsan took part in many important forays and battles staged by the Kiowas. He was part of the delegation to Washington in 1872 and participated in the Lost Valley[qv] Fight and the siege of Lyman's wagon train[qv] in 1874. He was among the last of the Kiowa leaders to surrender at the end of the Red River War[qv] in February 1875. Afterward, the younger Dohäsan lived with his family in peace on the reservation near Fort Sill until his death. In 1892 he gave his annual family calendar history, begun by his uncle, to Capt. Hugh L. Scott, who in turn donated it to the Smithsonian Institution. Dohäsan the younger died in 1893.

BIBLIOGRAPHY: Mildred P. Mayhall, The Kiowas (Norman: University of Oklahoma Press, 1962; 2d ed. 1971). James Mooney, Calendar History of the Kiowa Indians (Washington: GPO, 1898; rpt., Washington: Smithsonian Institution Press, 1979). Wilbur Sturtevant Nye, Plains Indian Raiders (Norman: University of Oklahoma Press, 1968). Frederick W. Rathjen, The Texas Panhandle Frontier (Austin: University of Texas Press, 1973).

H. Allen Anderson

DOHONEY, EBENEZER LAFAYETTE (1832–1919). Ebenezer LaFayette Dohoney, politician, son of Peyton and Mary (Hindman) Dohoney, was born on October 13, 1832, in Adair County, Kentucky. He graduated from Columbia College in 1854 as valedictorian of his class, received his law degree in 1857 from the University of Louisville, and practiced law for a short time in Kentucky before 1859, when he moved to Paris, Texas. His first appearance in politics took the form of canvassing Lamar County in opposition to secession.[qv] When the Civil War[qv] began he nevertheless joined the Confederate Army and eventually rose to the rank of captain of a Lamar County company. He served two active years but returned home because of poor health and did civil service for the remainder of the war. In 1862 Dohoney married Mary Johnson; the couple had eight children.

At the close of the war Dohoney resumed his private law practice and was appointed district attorney of the Eighth Judicial District by Governor A. J. Hamilton;qv he held that office in 1865–66. He considered Reconstructionqv a "military despotism" and believed that in itself it proved the South had been right in seceding. Dohoney was elected to the Twelfth and Thirteenth Texas legislatures as state senator. He is credited with originating the homestead law of 1871. He also supported a "six-shooter" act that prohibited carrying firearms in public places. While he was a legislator Dohoney made a committee report favoring woman suffrageqv and supported that issue nearly four decades before the Nineteenth Amendment to the United States Constitution gave women the vote. He also supported a return to the state's land-donation policy to encourage railroad building in 1871 and 1873. He was considered a leader in the Tax-Payers' Conventionqv of 1871. He claimed credit for putting together an effective school bill during the Thirteenth Legislature, but his program was repealed in the next session.

Dohoney is best known for his role in promoting prohibition.qv As a delegate to the state Constitutional Convention of 1875qv he authored a local-option clause—a clause authorizing citizens to decide by election whether alcoholic beverages will be sold in their communities—included in the Constitution of 1876.qv During the convention he also supported woman suffrage and a tuitionless school system. He became a Greenbacker in 1877 and published the *Greenback Advocate* for two years after the founding of the Greenback party.qv In 1882 he ran for Congress in the Fourth District but was defeated. He joined the new Prohibition party after the decline of the Greenbackers and in 1882 brought Woman's Christian Temperance Unionqv president Frances E. Willard to Paris for a speech.

Dohoney ran unsuccessfully for Texas governor in 1886 as the Prohibitionist candidate against Democratic nominee Lawrence Sullivan Ross.qv In September of that year he had served on the platform committee for the party convention, which produced a platform that characterized future governor Ross as "a saloon stump speaker." Dohoney considered himself a Democrat in the Jeffersonian mold; he claimed that the Democratic and Republican partiesqqv were in the hands of a few and that a new party was needed to address the issues of prohibition and labor. He also claimed to represent the interests of antimonopolists. But the Dohoney campaign garnered fewer than 20,000 votes.

In 1887 Dohoney joined B. H. Carroll, James B. Cranfill, William Poindexter, and William S. Herndonqqv as a speaker for the constitutional amendment for statewide prohibition, but the amendment lost. That year Dohoney purchased the Paris *Texas Tribune*. In 1891 he helped organize the People's partyqv in Texas. As chairman of its platform committee he induced the party to favor local option. As the party's candidate in 1894 for chief justice of the Court of Criminal Appeals, he polled almost 200,000 votes.

Dohoney was raised in the Cumberland Presbyterian Church but later served as an elder in the Paris Christian Church. He wrote six books, including *Man: His Origin, Nature and Destiny* (1884), *The Constitution of Man* (1903), and *Evolution of an Elder* (1916). His autobiography, *An Average American*, appeared in 1907. He was stricken with paralysis in 1917 and was an invalid until his death on March 29, 1919.

BIBLIOGRAPHY: Seth Shepard McKay, *Debates in the Texas Constitutional Convention of 1875* (Austin: University of Texas Press, 1930). A. W. Neville, *The History of Lamar County, Texas* (Paris, Texas: North Texas, 1937; rpt. 1986). E. W. Winkler, *Platforms of Political Parties in Texas* (Austin: University of Texas, 1916).

S. S. McKay and Doug Johnson

DOLAN CREEK. Dolan Creek rises three miles west of U.S. Highway 277 in northeastern Val Verde County (at 30°11′ N, 100°44′ W) and runs southwest for thirty-five miles to its mouth on the Devils River (at 29°53′ N, 101°00′ W), one mile northwest of Leon Spring. White Draw, Middle Dolan Creek, and West Dolan Creek are tributaries. Dolan Falls forms at the juncture of Dolan Creek and the Devils River. Dolan Creek dissects massive limestone that underlies flat terrain to form a rugged and winding valley. Wash deposits of sand, gravel, and mud cover the canyon floor. The area's generally dark, calcareous, stony clays and clay loams support water-tolerant oaks and junipers, grasses, and mesquites. The creek was named for Capt. Pat Dolan of the Texas Rangers,qv who, with Capt. Neal Coldwell, drove the outlaws from canyons of the area in the 1870s.

BIBLIOGRAPHY: Alice J. Shipman, *Taming of the Big Bend* (Austin: Von Boeckmann-Jones, 1926).

DOLAN FALLS. Dolan Falls is on the Devils River near its juncture with Dolan Creek in east central Val Verde County (at 29°53′ N, 101°00′ W). The falls are fed by a series of springs, mainly Dolan and Finegan. When the springs have strong flows, the falls are active. In droughts the falls fail. The surrounding flat terrain consists of massive limestone surfaced by dark, calcareous, stony clays and clay loams support water-tolerant conifers and oaks, junipers, grasses, and mesquites. The falls and Dolan Creek were named for Capt. Pat Dolan of the Texas Rangers.qv In 1873 an Indian fight occurred near the falls. The area around the falls and the springs was used by prehistoric people who left pictographs, mortar holes, middens, stone projectile points, and tools. Early travelers and explorers reported abundant grasses growing along the Devils River, but now overgrazing has destroyed the natural layer of organic mulch that covered the soils in the recharge areas. The bare ground allows rainwater to run off, rather than to recharge the springs. Decreased flow from the springs directly affects the activity of Dolan Falls.

BIBLIOGRAPHY: Gunnar Brune, *Springs of Texas,* Vol. 1 (Fort Worth: Branch-Smith, 1981).

DOLEN, TEXAS. Dolen is at the junction of Farm roads 787 and 223, sixty-eight miles northwest of Beaumont in northern Liberty County. The Dolen post office was established in 1903 and named for an early settler. The community was built on the Gulf, Colorado and Santa Fe Railway. Although its post office was discontinued in 1914, a voting precinct was set up at the Dolen schoolhouse the following year. Extensive gravel and sand pits southeast of the community provide the locale's most notable industry. In 1951 Dolen voters defeated an attempt to consolidate the Dolen Common School District with the Tarkington district by a 54-41 margin. Maps for the mid-1980s showed a number of buildings at the Dolen community, which still existed in 1990.

BIBLIOGRAPHY: Miriam Partlow, *Liberty, Liberty County, and the Atascosito District* (Austin: Pemberton, 1974). *Robert Wooster*

DOLORES, TEXAS. Dolores is on Farm Road 1472 and a private road called River Road, on the Rio Grande in southwestern Webb County. It originated before 1860 as a Mexican village called San José. In 1882 the Cannel Coal Company opened mines along the Rio Grande. Charles B. Wright, president of the company, built the Rio Grande and Eagle Pass Railroad to ship coal from the town and renamed the San José station for his daughter Dolores. The post office began service in 1913 and was discontinued after 1930. In 1914 Dolores reportedly had a population of 1,000 and a general store run by the coal company. Thomas Gardner, Jr., was a leading local cattle breeder. The mines had declined by 1920 and were closed in 1939. In 1936 Dolores had a school, a mine, one business, and a population of twenty. The population was reported as twenty from 1958 to 1990, and the populace supported two businesses. In 1983 Dolores had two cemeteries, an inactive mine, and a few houses. *Karen Gratke*

DOLORES CREEK. Dolores Creek rises three miles west of Callaghan in central Webb County (at 27°53′ N, 99°28′ W) and runs northeast for twenty-one miles to its mouth on Los Olmos Creek, just south of Ranch Road 863 (at 27°58′ N, 99°12′ W). The surrounding flat terrain is surfaced by sandy clays that support mesquite, cacti, and grasses.

A second Dolores Creek rises eight miles east of Laredo in southwestern Webb County (at 27°31′ N, 99°20′ W) and runs southwest for twenty-seven miles to its mouth on the Rio Grande, three miles south of Rancho San José in extreme northwest Zapata County (at 27°13′ N, 99°26′ W). It traverses flat to rolling terrain with locally active dune blowout areas, surfaced by sand that supports scattered oak mottes. The stream is dammed throughout its course to form tanks. Literally translated from the Spanish *dolores* means "pain," but in this usage probably refers to the nearby ruins of Nuestra Señora de los Dolores Hacienda.qv

DOLORES Y VIANA, MARIANO FRANCISCO DE LOS (?–?). Fray Mariano Francisco de Los Dolores y Viana, of the College of Santa Cruz de Querétaro,qv came to Texas in 1733 and by 1734 had made the acquaintance of all the principal Indian tribes along the Brazos River. In the summer of 1736 he participated in a controversy between priests and soldiers over the San Antonio River bridge, and in 1740 he addressed a strong representation to the viceroy against an order for the payment of tithes. As early as 1745 he was advocating the establishment of a mission on the San Xavier (San Gabriel) River and in 1746 began work at the site where San Francisco Xavier de Horcasitas Mission was formally established in 1748. Although Fray Mariano's actual assignment was that of minister of San Antonio de Valero Mission, he was active in the establishment of several missions, the San Xavier Missionsqv being his special interest. After the founding of the other two missions, Nuestra Señora de la Candelaria and San Ildefonso, and San Francisco Xavier de Gigedo Presidio, trouble between the soldiers and the Indians caused Fray Mariano to recommend the removal of the presidio and the establishment of a civil settlement. His defense of the missions, in spite of recommendations for their removal, caused trouble with Governor Pedro del Barrio Junco y Espriellaqv and his successor, Jacinto de Barrios y Jáuregui.qv After the murder of one of the friars, Pedro de Rábago y Teránqv ordered the removal of the missions to the San Marcos River; but he had no authority to do so, and the missions were shortly abandoned and the neophytes asked to join the San Antonio missions. For those who did not want to go to San Antonio, Fray Mariano established the mission of San Francisco Xavier in 1756. Dolores remained president of the four Queretaran missions until 1773, when they became the responsibility of the Zacatecan missionaries.

BIBLIOGRAPHY: Herbert Eugene Bolton, *Texas in the Middle Eighteenth Century: Studies in Spanish Colonial History and Administration* (Berkeley: University of California Press, 1915; rpt., Austin: University of Texas Press, 1970). Carlos E. Castañeda, *Our Catholic Heritage in Texas* (7 vols., Austin: Von Boeckmann–Jones, 1936–58; rpt., New York: Arno, 1976).
Frank Goodwyn

DOME HILL. Dome Hill, also known as Dome Mountain, is thirty miles northeast of Van Horn in south central Culberson County (at 31°22′ N, 104°29′ W). With an elevation of 4,638 feet above sea level, its summit rises 100 feet above Farm Road 2185, a quarter mile to the west.

DOME PEAK. Dome Peak is eleven miles northeast of the Sierra Blanca in east central Hudspeth County (at 31°14′ N, 105°11′ W). It rises 5,456 feet above sea level. Its surface of shallow, stony clay loams supports juniper, oak, grasses, chaparral, and cacti.

DOMENECH, EMMANUEL HENRI DIEUDONNÉ (1825–1903). Emmanuel Domenech, a Catholic priest, was born at or near Lyons, France, on November 6, 1825, to Gabriel and Jeanne (Fournier) Domenech. The elder Domenech was a bottle-top manufacturer. Emmanuel was recruited as a missionary by Bishop Jean Marie Odinqv and traveled to America in 1846 with Claude M. Dubuisqv and his companions. Upon finishing his theological studies at the Seminary of the Barrens in St. Louis, he was ordained in San Antonio on October 1, 1848; he may have been the first priest to be ordained in Texas. Although he worked in New Braunfels and Brownsville and traveled to surrounding communities, he was officially stationed first at Castroville, then at Eagle Pass. In 1852, because of his distaste for the hardships of missionary life and his continuing poor health, he returned to France, where he served as a priest and began a supplementary career as a travel writer and amateur ethnologist.

His *Journal d'un missionnaire au Texas et au Mexique*, published in Paris in 1857, was translated into English in 1858 as *Missionary Adventures in Texas and Mexico*. The book describes the trials of early Catholic missionaries and is filled with vivid sketches of the Texas frontier and anecdotes about its people. He found Houston "infested with Methodists and ants" and dismissed Austin, "the seat of the Texian legislature," as "a small dirty town" with "only one wretched hotel." Domenech's *Seven Years' Residence in the Great Deserts of North America* (London, 1860) contains much firsthand observation of Indian customs and archeological monuments in Texas and other border states. He published in the same year an anonymous collection of drawings of Indian pictographs from the holdings of the Bibliothèque de l'Arsenal in Paris. This collection he entitled *Manuscrit pictographique américain* (called *Livre des sauvages* in the Parisian library's records), a controversial work that, together with his *Seven Years' Residence in the Great Deserts*, is an important source of information on American Indians of the Southwest.

In 1864 Domenech accompanied French troops into Mexico as a chaplain; he later became press secretary to Emperor Maximilian. His three-volume *Histoire du Mexique* (Paris, 1868) is made up of extracts from hundreds of unedited letters and documents of the years 1848 to 1869, from both Mexico and Texas, to which he had access. He published many repetitious, exaggerated, and self-glorifying accounts of his experiences and travels, but his colorfully detailed narrative of the establishment of the Catholic hierarchy in Texas, amid the tensions of boundary disputes with Mexico and the devastation of an epidemic of cholera, has no counterpart. He died of apoplexy and was buried at Lyons, France, on September 9, 1903, with military honors.

BIBLIOGRAPHY: Catholic Archives of Texas, Files, Austin. E. H. D. Domenech, *Les Secrets de ma Valise* (Paris: Dentu, 1895).
Ann Lozano

DOMÍNGUEZ, CRISTÓBAL (?–1814). Cristóbal Domínguez, who briefly served as governor of Texas in 1813, came to the province probably from New Mexico. He was adjutant inspector of presidios for Coahuila and Texas,qv when he was ordered to Nacogdoches on November 26, 1810, by Governor Manuel María de Salcedo.qv With the outbreak of the Casas Revolt,qv José María Guadiana, military commandant at Nacogdoches, had Domínguez arrested because of his loyalty to the Spanish government. Domínguez escaped and fled to Natchitoches, Louisiana, where he remained until the overthrow of the Casas government in Béxar. He returned to Nacogdoches on May 1, 1811, arrested Guadiana, and took over the duties of lieutenant governor until September 20, when he returned to Béxar and served as inspector of presidios until the death of Salcedo during the Gutiérrez–Magee expedition.qv Joaquín de Arredondoqv appointed Domínguez the ad interim governor of Texas and on December 15, 1813, made him second in command. Domínguez died the following year in October.

BIBLIOGRAPHY: Bexar Archives, Barker Texas History Center, University of Texas at Austin. Julia Kathryn Garrett, *Green Flag Over*

Texas: A Story of the Last Years of Spain in Texas (Austin: Pemberton Press, 1939).

Robert Bruce Blake

DOMÍNGUEZ, SIMÓN G. (?–?). Simón G. Domínguez, school proprietor, salesman, and promoter of political unity of Texas Mexicans, lived in Laredo in the late nineteenth and early twentieth centuries. He married a woman named María, and they had four children. Domínguez was able to read and write in Spanish and English, and in 1908 he bought a typewriter. He founded and taught a private school or *escuelita* called Instituto Domínguez that operated from 1890 to at least 1913, with some interruption. María may have been a cofounder and teacher as well. Ninety-five students were enrolled in July 1911 and 150 in January 1912. The Instituto specialized in English and Spanish. It operated as both a day school for children and a night school for adults. The school had a telephone and may also have had a library with an encyclopedia. Domínguez also sold medicines, plants and seeds, and books that he obtained from companies across the United States. In 1904 he earned twenty-five dollars a month, with which he maintained a family of four.

He belonged to numerous *sociedades mutualistas*[qv] over several decades. In 1903 he belonged to the Sociedad Mutualista Hijos de Juárez, and in 1907 he was president. In 1912 he was a member of the Mexican Masonic lodge, the Knights of Pythias, the Woodmen of the World Lodge, and other minor lodges in Laredo. Around 1920 he was active in at least ten societies in Laredo. He corresponded with *mutualistas* in México, such as the Sociedad Mutualista Amigos del Trabajo and the Sociedad Unión de Jornaleros (Mutual-Aid Society of the Friends of Labor and Society of the Union of Day-Laborers).

As a delegate of the Hijos de Juárez, Domínguez addressed the first Congreso Mexicanista, the first known statewide political conference by *la Raza* (*see* RAZA UNIDA PARTY). In his speech on women's education, for which he was probably chosen because the Instituto permitted girls and women to enroll, he argued that education of women was indispensable not only for social position but also to mold the children.

Domínguez called for the merger of the six mutual-aid societies in Laredo, the merger of all *sociedades mutualistas* in the state, and the formation of a Congreso Masonico in each Texas town. He also proposed a night and day school of English and Spanish in each community, as he believed that both languages were needed for communication between Mexico and the United States. Domínguez also organized *fiestas patrias*.[qv] In 1910 he headed a commission to set up a Mexican Independence Centennial Celebration in Laredo and in 1914 helped initiate Cinco de Mayo. He was an acquaintance of the Idar family and may have written for *La Crónica*.[qv]

BIBLIOGRAPHY: Simón G. Domínguez Papers, Barker Texas History Center, University of Texas at Austin. José E. Limón, "El Primer Congreso Mexicanista de 1911," *Aztlán* 5 (Spring, Fall 1974). *Primer Congreso Mexicanista Verificado en Laredo, Texas* (Laredo: Idar, 1912).

Cynthia E. Orozco

DOMÍNGUEZ DE MENDOZA, JUAN (1631–?). Juan Domínguez de Mendoza was born in 1631 and went to New Mexico at age twelve. In 1654 he accompanied the expedition of Diego de Guadalajara[qv] from Santa Fe to the juncture of the three branches of the Concho River near the site of present San Angelo. Few details of the expedition are known. On expeditions from Santa Fe and El Paso del Norte[qv] in 1654 and 1683–84, Domínguez de Mendoza probably saw more of the Texas plains than any previous Spanish explorer.

As lieutenant general and *maestre de campo* in New Mexico, he played a prominent part in countering the Pueblo Indian revolt of 1680 (in New Mexico) before the Spaniards finally were forced to withdraw to the El Paso area. In 1681 a group of Indian chiefs led by the Jumano Juan Sabeata[qv] came to the Paso del Norte settlement requesting the Spaniards to establish missions among the Jumanos. Governor Domingo Jironza Petriz de Cruzate responded by sending Domínguez and Fray Nicolás López[qv] to Jumano country to explore, found missions, and establish trade.

The expedition left the El Paso area on December 15, 1683, to descend the Río Grande to La Junta de los Ríos,[qv] near the site of present Presidio, Texas. Leaving Fray Antonio de Acevedo in charge of new missions there, fathers López and Juan de Zavaleta continued with Domínguez de Mendoza on a journey that extended beyond the Pecos River to the Edwards Plateau.[qv] There, on a river that Domínguez called "the glorious San Clemente," the Spaniards spent six weeks. They built a bastion for protection against Apaches and hunted buffalo[qv] for the hides, as well as to feed the thousands of friendly natives who surrounded the camp. The two priests baptized many of the Indians.

Both the location of San Clemente and the route that Domínguez took to reach it have long been the subject of controversy. As early as 1908 Herbert Eugene Bolton[qv] theorized that the San Clemente encampment was on the Colorado River above the site of present Ballinger. Carlos E. Castañeda,[qv] reviewing the matter in 1936, conjectured a different route to place San Clemente at the juncture of the Concho and Colorado rivers. The Texas Centennial[qv] Commission in 1936 recognized Castañeda's choice with a historical marker. More recent studies have disagreed with both Bolton and Castañeda. Jesse W. Williams[qv] sought in 1962 to redefine the route but relied on Bolton's translation of the itinerary. He placed San Clemente on the South Llano River not far from the site of present Telegraph.

The various studies, while favoring divergent routes, agree that the expedition reached the point at which the three Conchos come together. The most recent version, inspired by the discovery of ruins thought possibly to be of the bastion that Domínguez built at San Clemente, is that of Seymour V. Connor (1969). Intrigued by the stone remains on the San Saba River eighteen miles west of Menard, Connor has made the most thorough, and evidently the most scientific, route study of all, alleging "serious errors" by each of the three previous interpreters. He claims to have spent "countless hours" poring over topographic maps; to have driven hundreds of miles "to view on the ground every conceivable point that might fit Mendoza's descriptions of the various campsites"; and to have surveyed the area from the air. After reaching the Pecos near Girvin, Connor suggests, the expedition traveled downstream some distance, traversed the corners of Crockett and Upton counties, and passed through Reagan and Irion counties, to reach the confluence of the Conchos in Tom Green County; thence southeast across the northeastern corner of Schleicher County to the place of the rock ruin on the San Saba River, six miles east of Fort McKavett in Menard County. The return route he describes proceeded southeast into Sutton County and thence west across Crockett County to the Pecos.

Excavation supervised by archeologists Earl Green and Curtis Tunnell failed to produce evidence to support Connor's conclusion—not even a buffalo bone. "Never in the experience of the archeologists on the dig," Connor admits, "have they seen a site of such obvious human construction so devoid of human remains and artifacts." He attributes the lack of artifacts to the shortness of the occupation.

Obviously, the huge rocks of the Menard County ruin indicate that the builder had a considerable labor force at his disposal. Domínguez de Mendoza, Connor points out, had such a force. But so did San Luis de las Amarillas Presidio[qv] (San Sabá), at the site of present Menard, which maintained a horse pasture "five leagues" west of the fort. Connor does not consider the possibility that the stone ruins may represent a bastion for the protection of soldiers sent to guard the horses.

Domínguez and López returned to Paso del Norte full of hope for establishing missions, and even a colony, among the Jumanos of the Texas plains. The spreading Indian revolt, however, continued to sap Governor Petriz de Cruzate's resources. Not easily discouraged, the explorers journeyed to Mexico City to urge the Jumano settlement as a barrier against the Apache onslaught. A combination of factors doomed their proposal: the revolt raging across the northern frontier and the invasion of Spanish territory by the Frenchman La Salle,qv who had landed at Matagorda Bay early in 1685. La Salle caused a shift of the missionary focus from western Texas to eastern.

BIBLIOGRAPHY: Herbert Eugene Bolton, ed., *Spanish Exploration in the Southwest, 1542–1706* (New York: Scribner, 1908; rpt., New York: Barnes and Noble, 1959). Carlos E. Castañeda, *Our Catholic Heritage in Texas* (7 vols., Austin: Von Boeckmann–Jones, 1936–58; rpt., New York: Arno, 1976). Seymour V. Connor, "The Mendoza-López Expedition and the Location of San Clemente," *West Texas Historical Association Yearbook* 45 (1969). Charles W. Hackett, ed., *Pichardo's Treatise on the Limits of Louisiana and Texas* (4 vols., Austin: University of Texas Press, 1931–46). J. W. Williams, "New Conclusions on the Route of Mendoza, 1683–1684," *West Texas Historical Association Year Book* 38 (1962).
Robert S. Weddle

DOMÍNGUEZ MEXICAN COMPANY. The Domínguez Mexican Company, also known as the Mexican Spy Company, was led by Manuel Domínguez, a weaver who was subjected to extortion by a Mexican officer and became an informant for the United States Army during the Mexican War.qv When the army arrived at Puebla in 1847, Domínguez made contact with Col. E. A. Hitchcock to offer his men to protect the lines of supply and communications. Their number rose to over 100, and some reliable authorities say they amounted to as many as 2,000 before the end of the war. On the day before the battle of Molino del Rey, Gen. Antonio López de Santa Annaqv sent Domínguez a commission as a colonel and a full and complete pardon to him and all his men. Domínguez turned it over immediately to his United States commander and resumed his position with the Americans.

Gen. William O. Butler suggested that Congress authorize enlisting the Mexicans into the army and paying them regular salaries, but the administration declined. Later General Butler recommended they be given a land bounty and three months' pay. Finally, each member of the company was given a gold double eagle and passage to Corpus Christi. Santa Anna offered the Mexican soldiers 1,000 acres of land and $300 each, but none accepted so far as is known. Some of the ships put in at New Orleans and some at Galveston. None apparently sailed to Corpus Christi, since that city had no port facilities for ocean-going vessels at that time. Sixty-two men with thirty dependents landed at New Orleans. It is not known how many landed at Galveston, though it was probably about the same. Domínguez went to Washington and was greeted by the president. American newspapers represented him as a traitor to his race and a bandit, even though he was allied with the United States Army. Nearly all the company settled in Cameron County, Texas. Part of Domínguez's family settled at Alexandria, Louisiana. Domínguez and several of his officers sought bounty land under the act of May 14, 1856, but their claims were rejected.

BIBLIOGRAPHY: Robert Anderson, *An Artillery Officer in the Mexican War, 1846–47* (New York and London: Putnam, 1911). Albert Gallatin Brackett, *General Lane's Brigade in Central Mexico* (Cincinnati and New York: Derby, 1854). Ethan Allen Hitchcock, *Fifty Years in Camp and Field: Diary of Major-General Ethan Allen Hitchcock, U.S.A*, ed. W. A. Croffut (New York: Putnam, 1909).
Frank Wagner

DOMÍNGUEZ Y VALDEZ, JUAN (1784–?). Juan Domínguez y Valdez, who planned a colony in Mexican Texasqv but did not bring it about, was born in Havana, Cuba, in 1784. He began military training as a cadet in 1795 and joined the Mexican army on October 9, 1813, when he landed at Veracruz. He was a lieutenant colonel in the Army of the Three Guarantees, in support of the Plan of Iguala, which proclaimed Mexican independence in March 1821. Domínguez retired in 1828 as a full colonel. He married Ignacia Quintanar, the niece of a general, in 1821, and by 1828 they had four daughters.

Domínguez was granted a colonization contract by the Texas government on July 6, 1829. By its terms he was to bring 200 American and European settlers to Texas within a period of six years, to be located in an area bounded as follows: beginning on the Arkansas River where the river is intersected by the twenty-third degree of longitude west of Washington, the boundary line between Mexico and the United States; thence south along this boundary line the distance of forty leagues; thence west twenty leagues; thence north on a line parallel with the twenty-third meridian to the Arkansas River; thence with the right bank of the Arkansas River to its intersection with the twenty-third meridian, the place of beginning.

Domínguez, who resided in Mexico, appointed Victor Blanco, lieutenant governor of Texas, to execute his contract. Domínguez brought no colonists to Texas, and the contract expired in 1835.

BIBLIOGRAPHY: Translations of Impresario Contracts, 1825–1835, Spanish Archives, General Land Office, Austin.
Virginia H. Taylor

DOMINICAN COLLEGE. Dominican College (Sacred Heart Dominican College) was founded in Houston, Texas, in 1945 by the Sisters of St. Dominic of the Congregation of the Sacred Heart (*see* DOMINICAN SISTERS), which Mother M. Agnes Magevneyqv founded in Galveston in 1882. The college was an outgrowth of the congregation's teacher-training school. In 1945 it was formally organized as a junior college and was affiliated with the Catholic University of America. The Texas State Department of Education approved the work of the college in June 1946. The Texas secretary of state granted the institution a charter to operate as a senior college in September 1946. Approval by the State Department of Education was received in 1948, and the first degrees were awarded by Bishop Christopher E. Byrneqv in May 1949.

In June 1947 St. Joseph's School of Nursing, conducted by the Sisters of Charity of the Incarnate Word,qv transferred its affiliation from the University of Houston to Dominican, and plans were initiated for an integrated four-year collegiate course leading to the bachelor of science degree in nursing. The programs of Dominican College focused on the modern woman. The general aim was to provide a climate in which the academic community could grow in Christian commitment through study, work, recreation, and prayer.

The college granted bachelor of arts and bachelor of science degrees, with majors in eighteen fields. Dominican was especially strong in art, music, elementary and secondary education, foreign languages, humanities, and nursing. In 1967 the Dominican Institute of Fine Arts in Florence, Italy, began to accept Dominican College art majors for their junior year abroad. Students in the Humanities Honor Program had the same opportunity. Dominican College also established the first competency-based bilingual teacher education degree in Houston.

The college was accredited by the Southern Association of Colleges and Schools and by the Texas Education Agency.qv The Department of Nursing was approved by the Texas State Board of Nursing and was accredited by the National League of Nursing. The Department of Medical Records Administration was accredited by the American Association of Medical Records Librarians. In addition, the college held membership in many state and national organizations. Dominican College closed in 1975.
Sister Antoinette Boykin, O.P.

DOMINICAN SISTERS. At the request of Bishop Nicholas A. Gallagher,qv third bishop of the Catholic Diocese of Galveston (*see* GALVESTON-HOUSTON, CATHOLIC DIOCESE OF), Mother Mary Agnes Magevneyqv brought the Sisters of St. Dominic of the Congregation of the Sacred Heart to Galveston in 1882 and opened Sacred Heart

Academy there. This congregation of twenty was the first group of Dominican Sisters (sisters of the Order of Preachers) to serve the Catholic Churchqv in Texas. Mother Agnes had at least one uncle who wore the Confederate uniform, yet she and her community experienced hostility because they were considered northerners by many of the people of Galveston. At Bishop Gallagher's request they opened Holy Rosary School, a free institution for black children in Galveston, in 1887, and antagonism towards them increased. Parents of the academy children threatened to withdraw their children unless the nuns closed Holy Rosary. The sisters refused, and both Holy Rosary and Sacred Heart Academy prospered. In 1893 the Dominicans opened a free school for the children of the cathedral parish.

Catherine (Mother Pauline) Gannon,qv who succeeded Mother Mary Agnes, carried the fledgling school system to Southeast and Central Texas and California, and in 1966 the sisters opened a school in Guatemala. Sixteen Dominican sisters attended the University of Texas in 1916; Sister Gertrude O'Brien, a transfer student from the Catholic University of America in Washington, D.C., was granted a bachelor of arts degree in June 1918. In her own words, Sister Gertrude "chanced to be the first nun to receive a degree from any college or university in Texas." The Dominican Sisters thus led the way for the education of numerous other religious women. In 1918 the opening of Newman Hall, the Dominican residence hall for women attending the University of Texas, furthered the educational program by providing housing for sisters from numerous congregations besides their own. The sisters established Sacred Heart Dominican College in Houston in 1945; the institution, the only women's college in Southeast Texas, continued to educate Dominicans until it closed in 1975.

Prompted by the storms that buffeted Galveston Island, the sisters transferred their motherhouse to Houston in 1926. In addition to teaching in parochial schools and parish religious-education classes, they taught the poor without pay. They took orphans into their boarding schools and academies and educated them free of charge. Between fifty and 100 poor people went daily to the convent in Houston for a hot meal. The order continues to help staff many educational institutions in Texas, California, and Guatemala, including a Montessori school, a school of environmental education, and individualized-instruction schools. The sisters also serve in health care and counseling centers, charitable and service organizations, leadership development programs, and legal professions.

BIBLIOGRAPHY: Catholic Archives of Texas, Files, Austin. Sheila Hackett, *Dominican Women in Texas: From Ohio to Galveston and Beyond* (Houston: Armstrong, 1986). *Sister Sheila Hackett, O.P.*

DOMINION, TEXAS. Dominion, on Wolf Creek in Lipscomb County near the Oklahoma state line, was one of two townsites that rivaled Lipscomb for the position of county seat. It was founded by two land agents, C. P. Walker and John Holzapfel, employees of the Interstate Town Company in Colony, Kansas. It was platted in February 1887 and named for the fact that its site was in the heart of the Dominion Cattle Company's holdings (*see* BOX T RANCH). The town's planners, anticipating the arrival of the Panhandle and Santa Fe Railway, reportedly sold $15,000 worth of land, in twenty-four sections. S. T. Gilbert erected a two-story hotel there. However, the railroad bypassed the site, Lipscomb was chosen county seat, and the Dominion townsite was abandoned within a matter of months. Gilbert's hotel was moved to Lipscomb under new ownership. Laura V. Hamnerqv commented that Dominion's advertising circulars "claimed 5,000 inhabitants. This claim could be substantiated since they had fully 5,000 prairie dogs as residents."

BIBLIOGRAPHY: *A History of Lipscomb County, Texas, 1876–1976* (Lipscomb, Texas: Lipscomb County Historical Survey Committee, 1976). *H. Allen Anderson*

DOMINO, TEXAS. Domino is on Farm Road 3129 ten miles northeast of Atlanta in northeastern Cass County. It was established in the late nineteenth century as a flag stop on the Texas and Pacific Railway. In the mid-1930s the town had two churches and a number of houses. The construction of nearby Wright Patman Lakeqv in the 1950s brought new growth. The community incorporated during the 1970s, and in 1990 had a population of 101. Many of the residents work in Atlanta or Queen City. *Christopher Long*

DONAHOE, TEXAS. Donahoe was on Donahoe Creek sixteen miles southeast of Belton in the southeastern corner of Bell County. It was named for the creek, which in turn was named for a merchant who explored the area as part of the Texan Santa Fe expeditionqv of 1841. Settlers acquired land along the creek in the late 1840s. Sometime after his arrival in 1854 Samuel Gibbs Leatherman opened the first general store there, and the 1860 census listed Howel Bass as the Donahoe blacksmith. Donahoe had a post office from 1888 to 1903. In 1896 it had a general store, the Science Hill School, a blacksmith shop, and a population of sixty. The Science Hill School had seventy-nine pupils and one teacher in 1903. A community called Dice, presumably named for John Dice, who owned a general store on the site in the mid-1800s, had a church, a school, and scattered dwellings on the same site in 1948. A Baptist church held services there into the 1950s, when it closed. On the 1963 topographical map the site is once again identified as Donahoe and shown to have two dwellings. By the late 1970s Donahoe had been abandoned, and only the cemetery remained. A Texas Historical Commissionqv marker was dedicated at the site in 1979.

BIBLIOGRAPHY: Bertha Atkinson, *The History of Bell County, Texas* (M.A. thesis, University of Texas, 1929). Clara Stearns Scarbrough, *Land of Good Water: A Williamson County History* (Georgetown, Texas: Williamson County Sun Publishers, 1973). *Mark Odintz*

DONAHOE CREEK (Waller County). Donahoe (Donaho) Creek rises two miles northeast of Howth in northern Waller County (at 30°11′ N, 96°02′ W) and runs northwest for 3½ miles and then southwest for 5½ miles to its mouth on the Brazos River, seven miles northwest of Howth (at 30°11′ N, 96°09′ W). It traverses an area of low-rolling hills and prairies surfaced by dark clay and sandy loam soils that support grasses and some mesquite and are suitable for agriculture. The creek was probably named for Mortimor Donaho, who received a land grant in the vicinity.

_____ (Williamson County). Donahoe Creek rises just east of Jarrell in north central Williamson County (at 30°49′ N, 97°36′ W) and runs east for thirty-four miles through northern Williamson County and southeastern Bell County to its mouth on the Little River, six miles west of Buckholts in western Milam County (at 30°50′ N, 97°12′ W). The Texan Santa Fe expeditionqv probably camped by the creek in 1841, though at that time they called it Deer Creek; the name Donahoe may derive from a merchant who participated in the expedition. The banks of the stream are heavily wooded in places with oak and mesquite, which were an important source of timber for early settlers in the area. The creek traverses gently sloping to gently rolling terrain with clayey soils used predominantly as cropland.

BIBLIOGRAPHY: Clara Stearns Scarbrough, *Land of Good Water: A Williamson County History* (Georgetown, Texas: Williamson County Sun Publishers, 1973).

DONALDSON MOUNTAIN. Donaldson Mountain is seven miles southeast of Hughes Springs in southwestern Cass County (at 32°59′ N, 94°30′ W). This small but generally steep peak, located in a relatively low marshy area just east of Black Cypress Creek, rises from an area 225 feet above mean sea level to 405 feet above mean sea level at its highest point. The soils in the area are sandy and loamy, and the land is heavily wooded, primarily with pines and various hardwoods.

DONALSON CREEK. Donalson Creek, a spring-fed stream that is intermittent in its upper reaches, rises a mile south of Knight Mountain and two miles southwest of U.S. Highway 190/183 in southwestern Lampasas County (at 31°09′ N, 98°21′ W) and runs southeast for nine miles to its mouth on Bean Creek, just below Reservoir Number 2 and 4½ miles west of Lampasas (at 31°04′ N, 98°15′ W). A mile downstream from its source the creek has been dammed to form Reservoir Number 1. It crosses an area of the Grand Prairie characterized by steep slopes and limestone benches that often give a stairstep appearance to the landscape. Soils in the area are generally shallow sandy and clay loams that support grasses and open stands of live oak, mesquite, and Ashe juniper.

DONELSON, ANDREW JACKSON (1799–1871). Andrew Jackson Donelson, diplomat, was born in Nashville, Tennessee, on August 25, 1799. He attended Cumberland College, Nashville, and graduated from the United States Military Academy in 1820. He spent two years as aide-de-camp to his uncle, Maj. Gen. Andrew Jackson, before resigning his commission in order to study law. In 1829 President Jackson appointed Donelson his private secretary; Donelson remained in Washington in that capacity until the expiration of his uncle's second term on March 4, 1837.

In 1844 President John Tyler appointed Donelson chargé d'affaires of the United States to the Republic of Texas.qv His duties were to present American propositions to President Anson Jonesqv and to further the cause of annexationqv of the republic to the United States. Donelson performed both tasks with skill and diplomacy. In March 1845, while he was temporarily in New Orleans, Congress passed a joint resolution admitting Texas to the Union, provided that the state adopt a republican form of government before July 1846. On April 12, 1845, Donelson interviewed President Jones, and on April 15 Jones called Congress to meet on June 16, 1845. Jones presented the proposition of the United States, and the offer was accepted unanimously. A convention was called to meet on July 4, 1845, and the ordinance accepting the terms outlined in the joint resolution of the United States Congress was passed the same day. Donelson was given a certified copy of the ordinance, which he forwarded to the secretary of state. He was subsequently minister to Prussia and in 1852 a candidate for the vice presidency of the United States. He died at Memphis, Tennessee, on June 26, 1871.

BIBLIOGRAPHY: George W. Cullum, *Biographical Register of the Officers and Graduates of the U.S. Military Academy at West Point, New York. Dictionary of American Biography*. Annie Middleton, "Donelson's Mission to Texas in Behalf of Annexation," *Southwestern Historical Quarterly* 24 (April 1921).
Hugo Ellis

DONELTON, TEXAS. Donelton, on Farm Road 1567 fifteen miles southeast of Greenville in extreme southeastern Hunt County, was probably established within ten years after the end of the Civil War,qv as a post office opened there in 1871. By 1885 the community had a gristmill and a cotton gin. Five years later it had a population of seventy-five, a school, and a church. The community reported no population or business statistics after 1900. Around 1970 a church still stood at Donelton.
Brian Hart

DONIE, TEXAS. Donie is on State Highway 164 eleven miles south of Teague in southwest Freestone County. The site was probably settled in the 1880s. The Dewey Prairie Baptist Church was organized in 1886, and in 1898 the residents applied for a post office under the name of Douie, which was misread in Washington as Donie. John W. Bond was the first postmaster. In 1907 the Trinity and Brazos Valley Railway built a line a couple of miles east of the town, so the townspeople all moved to the new location. In 1909 the name of the church was changed from Dewey Prairie to First Baptist Church of Donie, and by 1913 the building had been moved to the new location. In 1914 the town had a population of 600, seven businesses, and a blacksmith shop. It had a population of 400 in 1927 and by 1936 had two churches, two schools, and seven businesses. In 1969 the community comprised 230 people, seven businesses, three churches, and a school; the Donie Chair Company, in existence since 1902, was known for its colonial-style chairs, which were shipped throughout the Southwest. The population of Donie was somewhat more than 200 from 1972 to 1989. In 1990 it was 206.

BIBLIOGRAPHY: Freestone County Historical Commission, *History of Freestone County, Texas* (Fairfield, Texas, 1978).
Chris Cravens

DONLEY, STOCKTON P. (1821–1871). Stockton P. Donley, attorney, was born in Howard County, Missouri, on May 27, 1821. He attended Transylvania University in Lexington, Kentucky, and was admitted to the bar in that state before moving to Texas in 1846. He began his law practice at Clarksville and in 1847 moved to Rusk, where he became the partner of James M. Anderson.qv Donley soon distinguished himself as a skilled criminal lawyer. In 1853 he was elected district attorney of the Sixth Judicial District. His practical arguments and prodigious ability to unravel crimes were said to have been equal to those of such legendary lawyers as John Randolph and Patrick Henry. In 1854 he married Judith Evans of Marshall. Their son and only child, William S. Donley, later married Anna Reagan, a daughter of John H. Reagan,qv and became a prominent attorney.

In 1860 Donley moved his law office to Tyler. When the Civil Warqv broke out the following year he enlisted as a private in Col. John Gregg'sqv Seventh Regiment of Texas Volunteers. Soon after his promotion to a lieutenancy he was captured, along with the entire regiment, at the siege of Fort Donelson, Tennessee, in February 1862. Due to failing health after he was exchanged, he was assigned to post duty and continued in that capacity until the war's end, after which he resumed his practice at Tyler. He was elected to the Supreme Court of Texas in 1866 but removed from office by the Reconstructionqv military commandant on September 10, 1867. He then became the law partner of Oran M. Roberts, and later of John L. Henry.qqv His wife died, and in 1867 Donley married Mrs. Emma Slaughter, with whom he had a daughter. He died at Kaufman on February 17, 1871, and was interred at Tyler. Donley County, in the Texas Panhandle, was named for him.

BIBLIOGRAPHY: Zachary T. Fulmore, *History and Geography of Texas As Told in County Names* (Austin: Steck, 1915; facsimile, 1935). Sidney S. Johnson, *Texans Who Wore the Gray* (Tyler, Texas, 1907). James D. Lynch, *The Bench and Bar of Texas* (St. Louis, 1885). Ben H. Procter, *Not Without Honor: The Life of John H. Reagan* (Austin: University of Texas Press, 1962).
H. Allen Anderson

DONLEY COUNTY. Donley County (D-10), in the eastern Panhandleqv just east of the Llano Estacado,qv is bordered on the north by Gray County, on the west by Armstrong County, on the east by Collingsworth County, and on the south by Briscoe and Hall counties. It was named for Stockton P. Donley,qv a pioneer lawyer. The center of the county is at 30°00′ latitude and 100°50′ longitude. Clarendon, the county seat, is near the center of the county, seventy miles southeast of Amarillo. The county occupies 929 square miles of rolling prairie and broken rangeland. Its sandy clay, deep loam, and sandy loam support a variety of native grasses as well as cotton, grain sorghum, wheat, and corn. Oak, cottonwood, elm, mesquite, and other trees can be found near the rivers and streams in the county. The Salt Fork of the Red River rises to the west in Armstrong County, runs eastward across the center of Donley County, and is fed by Beckard, Allen, Carroll, Saddler's, and Whitefish creeks. Several tributaries, including Mulberry, McCullum, Hall, Big Sandy, Brush, West and East Bitter, Oaks, Indian, and Buck creeks, head in Donley County and flow southward toward the South Fork of the Red River.

Most of these streams are intermittent, and those that flow year-round do so in a trickle. Elevations in Donley County range from 2,200 to 3,200 feet above sea level, and the average annual rainfall is 20.74 inches. The average minimum temperature is 26° F in January, and the annual average maximum is 96° in July. The growing season averages 206 days per year.

The area that is now Donley County was part of the domain of the Plains Apaches until the eighteenth century, when Comanches and Kiowas entered the region. Several Spanish and American explorers came through the area; in 1787 Pedro Vial qv crossed the county, and in 1788 Santiago Fernández followed Vial's route. Americans did not enter the region until 1852, when captains Randolph B. Marcy and George B. McClellan qqv led their military surveying exploration of the Red River system into the area. The region remained the Indians' domain until the Red River War qv of 1874–75. On September 7, 1874, during Col. Nelson A. Miles's qv campaign, Lt. Frank D. Baldwin qv and a scout fought their way out of a Cheyenne ambush on Whitefish Creek in the northeastern section of what is now Donley County. The subsequent defeat of the Indians and their confinement to reservations in Indian Territory left the area open to white settlement. In 1876 the area was separated from the jurisdiction of the Bexar District, briefly assigned to Wegefarth County,qv and finally designated Donley County.

That same year Charles Goodnight and John Adair qqv established the huge JA Ranch qv in Palo Duro Canyon. The entire southwestern part of Donley County fell under the control of this operation, which covered all or part of six Panhandle counties. Soon other ranchers and settlers arrived to claim land. The first group of settlers, Methodists from the New York area, moved into Donley County intending to set up a colony. The colonists were sponsored and led by Lewis Henry Carhart,qv a young Methodist minister, who purchased 343 sections of the newly formed Donley County and established his colony at the junction of Carrol Creek and the Salt Fork of the Red River. The small settlement was organized in 1878 and named Clarendon, for Carhart's wife, Clara; it came to be called Saints' Roost by local cowboys, who disdained its prohibition qv regulations. Clarendon grew slowly. By the early 1880s it was one of only three towns in the Panhandle and was a small regional trade center. According to the census, seven ranches or farms had been established in Donley County by 1880, and 160 people lived there. No cattle were reported in the area that year, but the agricultural census did count 14,620 sheep and 7,592 horses. The county was politically organized in 1882, when residents formed a local government and chose Clarendon as the county seat. Ten other unorganized West Texas counties were attached to it for judicial purposes at one time.

Other ranchers followed the Methodist colonists into the county. The RO Ranch qv occupied much of the eastern part, while Carhart's Quarter Circle Heart Ranch qv filled a large area in the center. The Diamond Tail and Spade ranches,qqv headquartered elsewhere, owned large acreages in the central and southeastern parts of the county. Lesser ranches like the Morrison brothers' Doll Baby and Bill Koogle's Half Circle K,qv as well as stock farms, filled the gaps between larger cattle outfits.

The county remained largely unchanged until the arrival of the Fort Worth and Denver City Railway in 1887 as it built westward from Fort Worth to Colorado. As the railroad crossed the county, it passed five miles south of Clarendon, prompting that settlement's residents to move the town to a new site on the tracks in October 1887. By 1888 little remained of the old Clarendon; the site was later inundated by Greenbelt Reservoir. The relocated Clarendon was a division point on the railroad until 1902. Shops and offices were built there in 1887–88, and in 1887 Clarendon College, a Methodist School, was established.

By 1890, 1,056 people were living in Donley County, and the population increased to 2,756 by 1900. This growth can be attributed to the expansion of ranching, railroading, and, after 1890, farming. As early as 1890 fourteen farms existed in the county, but these were more stock farms than crop farms. By 1900, however, 188 farms and ranches were in operation in the county; "improved" land comprised 14,504 acres, with 1,716 acres devoted to corn production and much smaller areas planted in wheat and cotton. Farming became firmly established in the area between 1900 and 1910, when 601 farms and ranches could be found in the county, with almost 20,000 acres devoted to corn and almost 5,000 acres planted in cotton.

This trend continued for the next two decades, as the cultivation of cotton, forage crops, and fruit trees rapidly expanded in the area. By 1920 cotton was cultivated on 18,240 acres and various cereals on more than 68,000 acres; sorghum culture qv occupied 51,000 acres, and the county's new orchards were cultivating more than 30,000 fruit trees, mostly peach. Poultry was also rapidly becoming an important part of the county's economy; by 1920 local farms had 57,683 chickens and produced 262,431 dozen eggs. Cotton culture qv continued to expand rapidly in the 1920s, and by 1929 took up about 77,600 acres of county land. Meanwhile, cattle farming remained an important part of the county's economy: about 32,000 cattle were counted in the county in 1920, and almost 35,500 in 1930. The rise in the number of county farms between 1910 and 1930 clearly illustrates the trend: 601 farms had been established in the area by 1910, 810 by 1920 and 1,364 by 1930. Population trends followed the rise of the farmers' fortunes. The county had 5,284 residents by 1910 and 8,035 by 1920. The population peaked as the farming economy reached its zenith in 1930, when 10,262 residents were reported.

Many local farmers suffered devastating losses during the Great Depression,qv and their hardships were aggravated by the extended drought of the early 1930s. Cotton production dropped significantly during these years—by 1940 it occupied only about 38,500 acres—and many farmers were forced off their land. By 1940 only 877 farms and 7,487 residents remained in Donley County.

Since the 1940s the mechanization of agriculture has combined with other trends (such as the severe droughts of the 1950s) to continue depopulating the county. Small farming declined, and agribusiness replaced the small family farm. Between 1940 and 1970 the population dropped steadily, to 6,216 in 1950, 4,449 in 1960, and 3,641 in 1970. The population rose slightly during the 1970s to hit 4,075 by 1980, but then began to drop again: by 1992, an estimated 3,696 people lived in the county.

Since the early twentieth century Donley County has acquired a network of roads that has contributed to its development and made transportation more convenient for the area's residents. By the mid-1920s U.S. Highway 287 (originally U.S. 370) linked Fort Worth to Amarillo via Wichita Falls, Vernon, Childress, Memphis, and Clarendon. State Highway 70, from San Angelo to Perryton, runs north and south through the county and intersects U.S. 287 at Clarendon.

Educational and recreational facilities have also enhanced the county's economic and social life to a certain extent. Clarendon College, originally established in 1887, was placed under the supervision of the city of Clarendon in 1905. In 1927 the school closed, but local citizens reopened it in 1928 as a publicly funded junior college. Recreational facilities were built in 1966 when Greenbelt Reservoir, on the Salt Fork of the Red River, was completed. Although the principal use of the reservoir is to provide municipal and industrial water, recreation has developed as a major secondary use. Howardwick, a small resort settlement, was developed on the shores of this lake in the late 1970s and 1980s.

By the 1980s Donley County had become an agricultural center based on both cattle raising and farming, with supplemental income from the college, the lake, and some small distribution companies. The county produces a small amount of natural gas. In the 1980s agricultural income averaged around $28 million a year, of which 65 percent came from cattle, hog, and horse production. Cotton, corn, sorghum, wheat, and alfalfa revenues constituted the rest of the agricultural economy. The majority of the population lives in towns;

local communities include Ashtola, Hedley, Howardwick, and Lelia Lake. Clarendon is the county's largest town and its seat of government, and supports the Saint's Roost Museum.

BIBLIOGRAPHY: Virginia Browder, *Donley County: Land O' Promise* (Wichita Falls, Texas: Nortex, 1975). Harley True Burton, *A History of the JA Ranch* (Austin: Von Boeckmann–Jones, 1928; rpt., New York: Argonaut, 1966). Dalton Ford, History of Donley County, Texas (M.A. thesis, University of Colorado, 1932). Pauline D. and R. L. Robertson, *Cowman's Country: Fifty Frontier Ranches in the Texas Panhandle, 1876–1887* (Amarillo: Paramount, 1981).

Donald R. Abbe and H. Allen Anderson

DONNA, TEXAS. Donna is off U.S. Highway 83 and State Spur 374, fourteen miles northeast of McAllen in southeastern Hidalgo County. It is in territory that was granted to Lino Cabazos as part of the La Blanca land grant on May 19, 1834, by the Mexican state of Tamaulipas. The Cabazos family inhabited the area for at least twenty years after taking possession of the land, and their descendants continued to live in the area into the twentieth century. The first known Anglo-American settler was John F. Webber,qv who, accompanied by his wife Sylvia (Hector), a former slave, settled in the area in 1839. The Webbers moved to the area in order to escape persecution for their interracial marriage.

Several families from northern states, including the Ruthven, Champion, and Hooks families, settled the area. Thomas Jefferson Hooks arrived in the Lower Rio Grande valley in 1900 and the following year moved his family to Run in southeastern Hidalgo County. In May 1902 he helped to form the La Blanca Agricultural Company, which purchased 23,000 acres fronting the river two miles east and two miles west of the site of present Donna and extending north eighteen miles. He gave part of his purchase to his twenty-one-year-old daughter, Donna Hooks Fletcher, a divorcée. She settled in the area and established the Alameda (Grove) Ranch. Fletcher stocked the ranch with Jersey cattle purchased from the Lassater Ranch in Falfurrias and ran a successful butter business. The Hidalgo and San Miguel Extension (later called the Sam Fordyce Branch) of the St. Louis, Brownsville and Mexico Railway reached the site in July 1904, when the town was founded. In 1907 the town received a depot and was named Donna in honor of Donna Fletcher, who was postmistress when the Donna post office opened in 1908. That year the first store in west Donna was established by Ed Ruthven, and the community was recognized as the Texas station that shipped the most produce in a year. A 500-ton-capacity sugar mill was built in Donna that year. The Donna *Developer* was first printed on December 1, 1910, in Chapin. That year the Community Church was constructed and shared by the town's Protestant groups. The First Presbyterian Church was founded on July 10, and the First Baptist Church was organized on July 24, 1910. The telephone exchange was installed in 1911. Donna incorporated on April 13, 1911. By 1912 the town was divided into Donna and East Donna. East Donna, the Mexican side of town, had a post office named Beatriz, after Beatriz Hooks, from 1912 to 1916. Saint Joseph Catholic Church and a school for Mexican children were located there.

The first teacher in Donna was Paciana Guerra of Mier, Tamaulipas, hired in 1911 by Severiano Avila, Apolonio Ballí, and Bentura Bentiz to instruct their children. In 1913 the first graduating class of four graduated from Donna High School. At that time the Donna school district encompassed all of Weslaco and reached to the Mercedes corporate boundary.

A store was moved from Run to Donna in 1914 by Andrew Champion. In 1915 Donna had a population of 1,500, a bank, a hotel, four churches, two cotton gins, the sugar mill, and a weekly newspaper named the Donna *Dispatch*, published by B. L. Brooks. In 1916 the Donna Light and Power Company was incorporated by A. F. Hester, Sr., T. J. Hooks, Dr. J. B. Roberts, and twenty stockholders. The American Legionqv Hall, Donna Border Post No. 107, was dedicated in 1920. Donna had an estimated population of 1,579 in 1925. By 1936 it had a population of 4,103, a railroad stop, multiple dwellings, and 110 businesses.

The citizens of Donna first started using the motto "The City with a Heart in the Heart of the Rio Grande Valley" to promote the city in the 1940s. By 1945 the town had a population of 4,712 and seventy-eight businesses and continued to be a citrus and vegetable growing center. In 1953 Donna had three gins, three wholesale groceries, hardware and farm implements dealers, a wholesale distributor for feed mills, and the Donna *News*. The election of 1954 drew attention to Donna when Bob Jefferys, a newspaperman, requested that a special contingent of Texas Rangersqv be sent to the city by Governor Allan Shivers.qv He alleged that the election campaign was becoming violent because political bosses were physically threatening voters. The American Legion Hall was designated a historical landmark in 1964. In 1967 Donna reported 110 businesses (including eight manufacturers), ten churches, a bank, a library, and a newspaper.

From 1920 through the mid-1970s Donna had segregated schools. A third school for migrant students was in operation through the 1970s. The justification for its operation was that migrant children needed more attention because of their parents' work. It was opened to children in the third to eighth grade and had a separate campus. Donna had a population of 8,982 and 122 businesses in 1978. After the 1970s the economy in Donna continued to be based on fruits, vegetables, and the tourist trade. In 1990 Donna had an estimated population of 13,331 and eighty-nine businesses.

There are five colonias immediately south of the Donna city limits off Farm Road 493. Colonia Nueva is on Farm Road 493 two miles south of Donna; Colonia Algeria is on River Road and Eleventh Street next to the city dump; Colonia Tierra Prieta is on the east side of Farm Road 493; Colonia Salinas is south of Donna; and South Donna is a subdivision. Water is provided to the colonias by Colonia Nueva Water Distribution System, a privately owned enterprise that purchases water from the city of Donna and resells it to 400 coloniaqv domiciles. Tierra Prieta also receives water from North Alamo Water Supply Corporation; it had an estimated population of 180 in 1986.

BIBLIOGRAPHY: T. R. Fehrenbach et al., *A Shared Experience: The History, Architecture, and Historical Designations of the Lower Rio Grande Heritage Corridor* (Austin: Los Caminos del Rio Heritage Project and the Texas Historical Commission, 1991). Winnie Maddox, History of the Donna Community (M.A. thesis, Texas College of Arts and Industries, 1955).

Alicia A. Garza

DONNELLAN, THURSTON JOHN (1840–1908). Thurston John Donnellan, portrait painter, was born in Houston in 1840. His father was a violinist originally from Ireland and his mother was French, the daughter of General de Adendy of New Orleans. He studied art in Chicago and New Orleans under Oregon Wilson and began painting at the age of eighteen. In 1875 he married Jessamine Hawthorne. He painted portraits of several Confederate generals, including Robert E. Leeqv and Stonewall Jackson, but was best known for his portraits of Sam Houston,qv one of which is at Rice University, one at the Houston City Hall, and another in the Houston Public Library.qv Donnellan died in Houston in 1908.

BIBLIOGRAPHY: Vertical Files, Barker Texas History Center, University of Texas at Austin.

Julia L. Vivian

DONOGHUE, DAVID PATRICK (1891–1958). David Patrick Donoghue, geologist, was born on January 19, 1891, in San Antonio, the son of Patrick and Statia Madeline (Fitzgerald) Donoghue. He graduated in 1909 from St. Mary's University with a B.S. degree, and from 1909 to 1912 he studied mining engineering and geology at the University of Texas. He worked for the United States Geological Survey from 1911 to 1913. He was a scout, leaseman, and geologist for the

J. M. Guffey Petroleum Company from 1914 to 1918, and from 1919 to 1921 he was a geologist for Gulf Production Company. On June 30, 1914, Donoghue married Agnes M. Kennedy. He acted as a consulting geologist in Fort Worth and Houston from 1921 to 1924, when he became assistant to the vice president of Marland Oil Company. In 1925 he was made director of Texas Pacific Coal and Oil Company, and in 1929 he again became a consulting geologist. Donoghue became president of the Federal Royalties Company in 1933, a position he held until 1951. From 1952 to 1958 he served as president of Lasca, Incorporated. In addition to his regular duties, he acted as consultant for the Consejo Nacional de Petróleos in Colombia in 1948–49, and in 1948 he served as petroleum adviser for the United States mission in Libya.

Donoghue was active in numerous professional, religious, and civic organizations, including several southwestern historical societies. He served as vice president of the American Association of Petroleum Geologists from 1927 to 1929, and he was director and vice president of the Texas Independent Producers and Royalty Owners Association. He served as mayor of Westover Hills, Tarrant County, from 1946 to 1948 and was commissioner in 1948–49. Donoghue published many papers on petroleum appraisals, geology, engineering, and Texas history. He died on October 15, 1958, in Mexico City and was buried in Greenwood Cemetery in Fort Worth. He was a Catholic.

BIBLIOGRAPHY: Fort Worth *Star-Telegram*, October 18, 1958. Vertical Files, Barker Texas History Center, University of Texas at Austin.

DONOHO, TEXAS. Donoho was on the old Rusk–Lone Star road and just east of Mud Creek seven miles northeast of Rusk in east central Cherokee County. It was established around 1900 and named for the William Donoho^{qv} survey. The settlement flourished briefly but was abandoned in 1902, after the Texas and New Orleans Railroad bypassed it and the new town of Ponta was established one mile east of Mud Creek.

BIBLIOGRAPHY: *Cherokee County History* (Jacksonville, Texas: Cherokee County Historical Commission, 1986). *Christopher Long*

DONOVAN, TEXAS. Donovan was a logging camp and railway station east of Huntington in east central Angelina County. It was established by the Long Bell Lumber Company and was named for a lumberman. The town was active before 1915 and again around 1930. In 1900 the Texas and Louisiana Railroad completed 14½ miles of track to Donovan from Lufkin and in 1902 another 7½ miles from Donovan east to Monterey. In 1904 this railroad became part of the St. Louis Southwestern Railway of Texas. Donovan acquired a post office in 1927; the postmaster was Oma Wall. Postal service moved to Huntington in the early 1930s.

BIBLIOGRAPHY: Angelina County Historical Survey Committee, *Land of the Little Angel: A History of Angelina County, Texas,* ed. Bob Bowman (Lufkin, Texas: Lufkin Printing, 1976). *Megan Biesele*

DON AND SYBIL HARRINGTON FOUNDATION. The Don and Sybil Harrington Foundation was founded as a trust in Amarillo in 1951 by oilman Donald Harrington and his wife, Sybil Buckingham Harrington. It became a nonprofit corporation in 1971. It is a broad-purpose private foundation directed by a six-member board. Its interests include hospitals and health care agencies, cultural programs, higher education, youth agencies, social services, and civic affairs, and it concentrates its funds in Amarillo and the Panhandle.^{qv} In 1971 the capital fund of the foundation was a little more than $1 million. When Donald Harrington died in April 1974 most of his community-property estate went to the foundation. When the estate was closed in 1982 the value of the foundation was in excess of $54 million.

Notable contributions of the foundation to the Amarillo area have been to the Don and Sybil Harrington Cancer Center, the Harrington Petroleum Wing of the Panhandle-Plains Historical Museum^{qv} in Canyon, the Don Harrington Discovery Center, the Harrington Medical Library of Texas Tech Medical School in Amarillo, and the Harrington Library Consortium (a computerized network of the libraries of the city of Amarillo, Amarillo College, Texas Tech Medical School, and West Texas A&M University). Notable contributions outside the Amarillo area have been to the Harrington Arthritis Research Center in Phoenix, Arizona, and a substantial endowment to the Metropolitan Opera of New York City. The foundation was restructured as of January 1, 1988, from a private foundation to a public-support organization for the benefit and under the control of Amarillo Area Foundations, Incorporated. In 1989 the foundation had assets of $73,699,918, income of $7,392,832, and grants of $7,106,918, with the largest grant ($2,064,855) going to the Harrington Cancer Center.

BIBLIOGRAPHY: *The Hooper Directory of Texas Foundations* (San Antonio: Texas Foundations Research Center, 1976–). Harold M. Keele and Joseph C. Kiger, eds., *Foundations* (Westport, Connecticut: Greenwood, 1984). Vertical Files, Barker Texas History Center, University of Texas at Austin. *Richard D. Palmer*

DON TOL, TEXAS. Don Tol is a rural community on Caney Creek and Farm Road 1301, twelve miles southeast of Wharton in southeastern Wharton County. It is at the juncture of the Atchison, Topeka and Santa Fe tracks running east-west and the Southern Pacific tracks running north-south. A factory operated in the community in 1936, and in 1941 the local school became part of the Boling Independent School district. In 1989 the factory, a railroad station, and scattered dwellings remained at the site. *Diana J. Kleiner*

DOOLE, TEXAS. Doole is on Farm Road 503 a half mile east of the Concho county line and twenty-four miles northwest of Brady in northwestern McCulloch County. A ranching community called Gansel developed around Crossroads School, which had moved to the area from Fort Concho in 1908. Five stores and a cotton gin had been built there by 1910. Around 1911 residents decided to establish a post office and went to David Doole, Jr., the postmaster at Brady, for advice. The name Gansel was unacceptable to the postal service, so in appreciation for Doole's assistance the townspeople named their post office after him. The school was the dominant feature of the Doole community. In 1914 Doole reported a population of twenty-five. By the 1940s it had a population of 250, a school, a church, and ten businesses. After World War II^{qv} the settlement declined, mainly because of the consolidation of small family farms. The population declined to forty in the mid-1960s but was reported as seventy-four from 1970 to 1990.

BIBLIOGRAPHY: T. Lindsay Baker, *Ghost Towns of Texas* (Norman: University of Oklahoma Press, 1986). Jessie Laurie Barfoot, History of McCulloch County, Texas (M.A. thesis, University of Texas, 1937). *Vivian Elizabeth Smyrl*

DOOM, RANDOLPH COLUMBUS (1811–1881). Randolph C. Doom, judge, politician, and participant in the battle of San Jacinto,^{qv} was born in Caldwell County, Kentucky, on January 7, 1811, and arrived in Texas on May 18, 1836. He served as a volunteer in Capt. Henry Hubbe's company, Gen. Thomas J. Green's^{qv} division, of the Army of the Republic of Texas.^{qv} Doom, a violinist, may have been the musician whose tune accompanied the Texan charge at San Jacinto. He represented Jasper County in the Eighth Congress (1843–44) as a member of the House of Representatives. By 1846, when Texas became a state, he and his wife had extensive landholdings and owned four slaves. Doom, an attorney, was elected chief justice of Jasper County in 1850 and held that office for a year. In 1851 he was in Austin as a Jasper County representative at a railroad planning convention. He was a state representative from the district composed of Jasper, Sabine, and Newton counties in the Fourth Legislature, 1851–53. He also served in the Texas House of Representatives in the Seventh Legislature, 1857–58. The 1860 census listed him as a merchant with four slaves and more than $50,000 in personal property. After the Civil War,[qv] he resumed his law practice and in 1866 was elected state representative. Finally, he served as county judge of Jasper County from 1876 to 1880. Doom was married twice. The name of his first wife, by whom he had three daughters, is unknown. In 1847 he married Alta Zera Williams Everitt, widow of Stephen Hendrickson Everitt.[qv] Three children were born to this marriage. Doom died on December 5, 1881.

BIBLIOGRAPHY: Texas House of Representatives, *Biographical Directory of the Texan Conventions and Congresses, 1832–1845* (Austin: Book Exchange, 1941). Election Register, Texas State Archives, Austin.

Glenn Justice

DORA, TEXAS. Dora is near Elm Creek four miles east of Nolan in east central Nolan County. The community was established in 1877 and is said to have been the first in the county and the site of the first rural school. In 1888 it received a post office, which was named Dora after the daughter of the first postmaster, Edmond S. Collings. In 1891 the Dora school district was established, and by the early 1900s Dora had several churches, various stores, a gin, and a blacksmith shop. The community's population declined after its school merged with the Divide district in 1928. Many of Dora's citizens moved to Nolan. Its post office was discontinued on February 24, 1938, and by 1940 the population of Dora was fifteen. Dora was identified on the 1980 county highway map, which showed a cemetery at the site.

BIBLIOGRAPHY: Lelia Jeanette Wade, *Our Community: Organization and Development of Nolan County* (Sweetwater, Texas, 1960). E. L. Yeats and Hooper Shelton, *History of Nolan County* (Sweetwater, Texas: Shelton, 1975).

Charles G. Davis

DORANTES DE CARRANZA, ANDRÉS (ca. 1500–1550s). Andrés Dorantes de Carranza, early Spanish explorer, a native of the southwestern Castilian town of Gibraleón, was the son of Pablo Dorantes. Like many young Spaniards faced with bleak economic prospects in Spain, he sought his fortune in the New World. He enlisted in 1527 as a captain in the ill-starred expedition of Pánfilo de Narváez.[qv] After the expedition was compelled to travel along the Gulf Coast in crude barges, one boat was placed under the joint command of Dorantes and Alonso Castillo Maldonado.[qv] After a month at sea, disaster struck in early November on the Texas coast. The horsehide vessel bearing Dorantes ran aground and broke up on or near the western extremity of Galveston Island. Among the survivors were Dorantes, his slave Estevanico,[qv] Castillo, and Álvar Núñez Cabeza de Vaca.[qv] In March 1536, after considerable peregrination, the survivors contacted Spanish countrymen north of Culiacán. The governor of Nueva Galicia, Nuño de Guzmán, provided horses and clothing and dispatched his guests to Mexico City for an audience with Viceroy Antonio de Mendoza. The viceroy asked Dorantes to assist in a follow-up expedition; Dorantes declined, but did sell his slave, Estevanico, to Mendoza. Dorantes apparently hoped that he and Cabeza de Vaca would be granted a royal license to colonize Texas and New Mexico. His attempt to return to Spain miscarried when the ship's poor condition forced its return to Veracruz harbor. Perhaps viewing the experience as an ill omen, Dorantes remained in New Spain. He married the widow of Francisco de Valdés, María de la Torre, who controlled the *encomiendas* of Asala and Jalazintgo. After María's death, Dorantes married Paula Dorantes, widow of Antonio Gómez de Corona. He fathered more than fourteen children in New Spain. He died in the 1550s.

BIBLIOGRAPHY: Baltasar Dorantes de Carranza, *Sumaria relación de las cosas de Nueva España* (Mexico City: Imprenta del Museo Nacional, 1902). Harbert Davenport, ed., "'The Expedition of Pánfilo de Narváez,' by Gonzalo Fernández Oviedo y Valdez," *Southwestern Historical Quarterly* 27–28 (October 1923–October 1924). Robert S. Weddle, *Spanish Sea: The Gulf of Mexico in North American Discovery, 1500–1685* (College Station: Texas A&M University Press, 1985).

Donald E. Chipman

DORCHESTER, TEXAS. Dorchester is on Farm Road 902 eight miles southwest of Sherman in south central Grayson County. It was established in the late 1800s and named for C. B. Dorchester, a Sherman banker. The community was on the St. Louis, San Francisco and Texas Railway and quickly became a retail and community center for area farmers. In 1896 it received a post office, and over the next four decades Dorchester prospered. By the mid-1930s it had an estimated 400 residents and ten businesses. Later the population declined, and in 1989 the town had 222 residents and four rated businesses. In 1990 its population was 137.

David Minor

DORMAN, TEXAS. Dorman was on Farm Road 102 and the Atchison, Topeka and Santa Fe Railway two miles south of Egypt and eight miles north of Wharton in northeastern Wharton County. The 1936 county highway map showed a school, a church, and scattered dwellings near the townsite. In 1992 the railroad track, ties, and gravel bed were removed and the right-of-way returned to the contingent landowner.

Diana J. Kleiner

DORN, ANDREW JACKSON (1815–1889). Andrew Jackson Dorn, state treasurer and Confederate soldier, was born in Montgomery County, New York, on December 8, 1815. He graduated from the University of Vermont and in 1842 moved to St. Louis, Missouri. On June 19, 1846, with the outbreak of the Mexican War,[qv] he was elected first lieutenant and commander of a company of Lt. Col. Meriwether L. Clark's Missouri volunteer artillery battalion. This battalion served under Brig. Gen. Stephen Watts Kearny in New Mexico and California. By his own account, Dorn left the volunteer service on June 24, 1847, with the rank of major. After the war he remained in the regular United States Army as a second lieutenant of the Third Dragoons. Although he claimed to have achieved the rank of colonel and to have remained in the old army until the outbreak of the Civil War,[qv] he was in fact mustered out of federal service on July 31, 1848. When Missouri attempted to leave the Union in 1861 Dorn volunteered for service under his old Mexican War companion, Maj. Gen. Sterling Price, and was named paymaster of the pro-Confederate Missouri State Guard. In 1862 he transferred to the command of Maj. Gen. Samuel Bell Maxey[qv] in Indian Territory and was named commander of the Indian units allied with the Confederacy.

At the end of the Civil War Dorn moved to Bonham, Texas, where he went into the mercantile business with a Major Young. On August 6, 1872, he represented Fannin County at the Second Congressional District's Democratic convention held at McKinney, and in 1873, in what the Dallas *Herald* (*see* DALLAS TIMES HERALD) referred to as "one of those accidents that sometimes characterize nominating conventions," he was nominated as the Democratic candidate for Texas state treasurer "solely because he lived in north Texas." Although he was "an unknown man in Texas outside of two or three counties," Dorn was elected on Richard Coke's[qv] ticket, an apparent sectional concession to North Texas. When Dorn appointed his son, Thomas Jefferson Dorn, as chief clerk of the treasury, the *Herald*, which had supported his nomination and election, attacked him editorially on May 16, 1874, for nepotism, "one of the most odious of all political abuses." Although the paper retracted its attack on May 30, it came back with even stronger charges on June 13, accusing Dorn of "immodesty and violation of those delicate rules of propriety which should control all public officials" for putting out of office a poor old man with a family to make a place for his young and single son, a citizen of Nevada. The fault was compounded in the *Herald*'s sight, because Dorn had a second son who was a clerk in the General Land Office.qv Nevertheless, Dorn was reelected in February 1876, with the *Herald*'s endorsement, by a three-to-one majority. He remained in office until April 18, 1879.

Afterward he was unemployed and in 1883 went to Washington, D.C., seeking Maxey's aid in finding a government appointment. "He is the most helpless man I know," wrote Maxey of Dorn, "yet he is an honorable, good man but a fearfully and wonderfully made hanger-on for office." Dorn became one of seven applicants for one of the two assistant-doorkeeper appointments to which the Texas delegation was entitled, but when the appointments were decided by lot on January 3, 1884, he was not chosen. Unable to find a place for him, Maxey convinced Coke, then a senator, to split the cost of a train ticket back to Texas for Dorn "on the principle . . . that those who have done the most for him should continue in well doing." Coke and Maxey paid the fare "very cheerfully" because, Maxey wrote, it brought "the blessing of peace from the most persistent office seeker." On January 15, 1885, the destitute Dorn, with Maxey's influence, was elected on the fourth ballot as doorkeeper of the state Senate, a position he held from the Eighteenth through the Twenty-first legislatures. The Eighteenth Legislature sent Dorn to Washington to press a $700,000 claim of Texas against the federal government, but the claim was withdrawn. After his tenure as doorkeeper, Dorn remained in Austin "filling some minor positions in the state departments" until his death, on December 9, 1889.

Dorn was buried in the State Cemetery.qv He was survived by one child. He was a Mason and a member of the United Confederate Veterans,qv and as a member of the Veterans of the Mexican War Association he lobbied energetically for government pensions for Mexican War veterans.

BIBLIOGRAPHY: Dallas *Herald*, August 24, 1872, May 16, 30, June 13, 1874, January 8, 1876, January 3, 1884, January 15, 1885. Francis B. Heitman, *Historical Register and Dictionary of the United States Army* (2 vols., Washington: GPO, 1903; rpt., Urbana: University of Illinois Press, 1965). Louise Horton, *Samuel Bell Maxey: A Biography* (Austin: University of Texas Press, 1974). E. H. Loughery, *Texas State Government* (Austin: McLeod and Jackson, 1897). Thomas W. Cutrer

DORR, JOHN M. (?–?). John M. Dorr (Dor, Door), pioneer settler and Nacogdoches county official, moved to Red River County, Texas, in 1830 and served for a time as secretary to Benjamin Rush Milam.qv In 1834 he proceeded to Nacogdoches, where he became secretary of the ayuntamientoqv on January 1, 1835. He married Eliza Frisby in Nacogdoches on August 25. On January 1, 1836, he was elected a judge of the municipality and on August 30 issued a call for the organization of a local militia. Sam Houston'sqv appointment of Dorr, on November 8, 1836, as one of three commissioners to treat with the Indians was not confirmed by the Senate. On November 16, however, Dorr became primary judge of Nacogdoches. In 1837 he bought land there and purchased an interest in Travis, a landing on the Angelina River. On September 25, 1839, he made a deposition in Galveston concerning Vicente Córdova.qv Dorr died sometime between 1839 and 1845.

BIBLIOGRAPHY: Carolyn Reeves Ericson, *Nacogdoches, Gateway to Texas: A Biographical Directory* (2 vols., Fort Worth: Arrow-Curtis Printing, 1974, 1987). Charles Adams Gulick, Jr., Harriet Smither, et al., eds., *The Papers of Mirabeau Buonaparte Lamar* (6 vols., Austin: Texas State Library, 1920–27; rpt., Austin: Pemberton Press, 1968). Milam-McKinney Papers, Barker Texas History Center, University of Texas at Austin. Nacogdoches Committee of Vigilance and Safety Records, Barker Texas History Center, University of Texas at Austin. Amelia W. Williams and Eugene C. Barker, eds., *The Writings of Sam Houston, 1813–1863* (8 vols., Austin: University of Texas Press, 1938–43; rpt., Austin and New York: Pemberton Press, 1970). L. W. Kemp

DORR CREEK. Dorr Creek rises just east of the Nacogdoches city limits in central Nacogdoches County (at 31°36′ N, 94°37′ W) and runs southeast for ten miles to its mouth on Sam Rayburn Reservoir, a mile southeast of Saint's Rest (at 31°27′ N, 94°35′ W). Before its lower reaches were inundated by the lake in the mid-1960s, the creek's mouth was on the Angelina River, two miles southeast of Saint's Rest Church. The stream traverses flat terrain with local shallow depressions, surfaced by clay and sandy loam soils that support water-tolerant hardwoods, conifers, and grasses.

DORRAS, TEXAS. Dorras is on a local road seventeen miles southwest of Aspermont and three miles north of the Fisher county line in extreme southwestern Stonewall County. A Dorras post office, established in Fisher County in 1899 with James W. McWhirter as postmaster, became a Stonewall County post office in 1917. A Dorras school existed from 1914 to 1916 in northern Fisher County and was attended by residents of the Stonewall County settlement. In 1916 the Dorras school was consolidated with the Cactus Flat school in Stonewall County, and in 1927 the district was merged with Dowell in Fisher County. The Dorras post office was discontinued and moved to Rotan in 1928. Dorras reported a population of twenty-five and one business through the 1930s and 1940s. The 1984 county highway map indicated the community but showed no businesses at the site.

BIBLIOGRAPHY: Arthur Hecht, comp., *Postal History in the Texas Panhandle* (Canyon, Texas: Panhandle–Plains Historical Society, 1960). *A History of Stonewall County* (Aspermont, Texas: Stonewall County Historical Commission, 1979). Charles G. Davis

DORSEY, EMILY MILDRED (ca. 1894–1974). Emily Mildred Dorsey, teacher and children's-home founder, was born in Dallas around 1894, the daughter of Henry and Lula Dorsey. Her father ran a printing business in downtown Dallas, and her mother was a local leader in home missions and children's work in the Methodist Church.qv From childhood Emily participated in Methodist missionary work with her mother. She also showed a keen interest in teaching other children and convinced her parents to let her offer a summer school in their Oak Cliff home. Thirty children enrolled, and her father printed and distributed a primer Emily had written. She later started several informal schools in her neighborhood before she graduated from high school and left Dallas to enroll in the University of Texas in Austin. She completed three years of college before holding teaching jobs in Medina County and Dallas. She then enrolled for a two-year program at Scarritt Bible and Training School (now Scarritt College for Christian Workers) in Nashville, Tennessee, after which she taught in a Methodist children's home in Kansas City, Missouri, in 1922 and 1923. She was consecrated as a home missionary in 1924 and subsequently served three years as a teacher in London, Kentucky. She earned a master's degree from Scarritt in 1929.

Dorsey, who never married, adopted a four-month-old daughter upon finishing her degree. She later adopted a son. After teaching in Georgia, she returned to Dallas in 1933 and opened an institution for homeless girls, one of the earliest such efforts in Texas. In Oak Cliff she rented two buildings that became the Emily Dorsey Home for Little Girls. The home operated for fourteen years, during which care was provided for more than 800 children. In 1947 financial difficulties forced Dorsey to close the home and liquidate it. She continued her involvement in related social causes the rest of her life in the Methodist Church, the Woman's Missionary Society, and the Society for Christian Service. She died in Dallas on July 28, 1974, and was buried in Oak Cliff Cemetery. She was survived by her son, daughter, and sister.

BIBLIOGRAPHY: Dallas *Morning News*, July 29, 1974. Dallas *Times Herald*, July 29, 1974, April 27, 1980. *History of Woman's Work in the North Texas Conference of the Methodist Episcopal Church, South*

(Dallas: History Committee of the Woman's Missionary Society, 1929).
Debbie Mauldin Cottrell

DORSEY, TEXAS. Dorsey was near the junction of Dorsey and Ripley creeks, about nine miles northwest of Mount Pleasant in northwestern Titus County. The Dorsey post office was operated by Henry S. Summerlin at his mill and gin from 1891 to 1893. An abandoned public cemetery nearby containing between fifty and 100 graves suggests that there was an organized community at Dorsey at least for a brief period, but nothing further is known about the settlement.

BIBLIOGRAPHY: Wright Patman, *History of Post Offices—First Congressional District of Texas* (Texarkana, Texas, 1946?). Traylor Russell, *History of Titus County* (2 vols., Waco: Morrison, 1965, 1966; rpt., n.p.: Walsworth, 1975).
Cecil Harper, Jr.

DOSS, TEXAS (Cass County). Doss, on Farm Road 1399 some twelve miles northeast of Hughes Springs in northwestern Cass County, was probably named for the Doss family, early settlers in the area. In 1936 Doss consisted of a cemetery, a small business, and widely scattered houses. The 1983 county highway map showed scattered houses, a church, and a cemetery at the community.

BIBLIOGRAPHY: *Cass County Cemeteries: Texas Records* (Atlanta, Texas: Cass County Genealogical Society, 1976).
Cecil Harper, Jr.

DOSS, TEXAS (Gillespie County). Doss is on Mormon Creek nineteen miles northwest of Fredericksburg in northwestern Gillespie County. It was founded in 1849 by brothers John E. and Thomas C. Doss, who built a gristmill and distillery on Threadgill Creek in 1856 and later added a dam and sawmill. They sold the dam in 1864 to August Steiness, who tore down the distillery and expanded the gristmill's capabilities. A room he added onto the house served for many years as a mail delivery station for the community. After Steiness's death in 1866, his widow sold the mill to William F. Lange, a German immigrant, who built a larger dam. This dam, which was destroyed by a flood, was rebuilt between 1872 and 1875 by stonemason Philip Buchmeyer, and the mill came to be known as Lange's Mill. The Doss school was founded in 1884. A post office called Lange was opened in F. W. Lange's store in 1898, but in 1907 the name was changed to Doss, and the office was moved to what is now the Doss townsite, two miles south of the mill. The population of Doss was estimated at fifty in 1925, sixty in 1933, twenty-two in 1964, and seventy-five from 1972 to 1990. In the 1980s Lange's Mill, two miles north of Doss on Farm Road 783, still stood, along with the dam. In 1989 Doss was still a predominantly German community and included Lutheran and Baptist churches, a general store, a fire station, and a two-room schoolhouse, the last unconsolidated rural school in Gillespie County and one of only a few such schools remaining in the state. The school in 1989 served twenty-three children in eight grades.

BIBLIOGRAPHY: Austin *American-Statesman*, January 29, 1989. Fredericksburg *Radio-Post*, August 31, 1934.
Martin Donell Kohout

DOT, TEXAS. Dot is on Farm Road 1950 four miles southwest of Chilton in western Falls County. William B. Murphy applied for a post office and suggested that it be called Dot, his daughter's nickname; the post office was granted to the settlement in 1894. Two years later the community had two churches, a hotel, a cotton gin, and fifteen residents. Its post office was discontinued in 1905, and mail for Dot was sent to Chilton. Children from Dot attended nearby Liberty School, which in 1904 had one teacher and eighty-two students; by the mid-1930s it had forty-one students. The community appeared as a school, a church, and several residences on county highway maps in the late 1940s, when its population was twenty-five. The school was consolidated with the Chilton Independent School District in 1949. From 1964 to 1990 the population of Dot was reported as twenty-one.

BIBLIOGRAPHY: Lillian S. St. Romain, *Western Falls County, Texas* (Austin: Texas State Historical Association, 1951).
Vivian Elizabeth Smyrl

DOTCHETONNE INDIANS. The Dotchetonne Indians are known only from records of the La Salle expedition,[qv] which identify them as late seventeenth century allies of the Kadohadachos. Although some writers state that the Dotchetonnes lived in northeastern Texas, this has never been demonstrated. J. R. Swanton identified the Dotchetonne Indians as a Caddoan group that lived on Bayou Dauchite in the area of northwestern Louisiana, but he presented no argument for this identification.

BIBLIOGRAPHY: Frederick Webb Hodge, ed., *Handbook of American Indians North of Mexico* (2 vols., Washington: GPO, 1907, 1910; rpt., New York: Pageant, 1959). Pierre Margry, ed., *Découvertes et établissements des Français dans l'ouest et dans le sud de l'Amérique septentrionale, 1614–1754* (6 vols., Paris: Jouast, 1876–86). John R. Swanton, *Source Material on the History and Ethnology of the Caddo Indians* (Smithsonian Institution, Bureau of American Ethnology Bulletin 132, Washington: GPO, 1942).
Thomas N. Campbell

DOTHAN, TEXAS. Dothan, near the Callahan county line twelve miles west of Cisco in northwestern Eastland County, was established as Delmar when the Texas and Pacific Railway was built through the area in 1880. Delmar was moved to Red Gap a year later and became Cisco in 1882. A new community named Dothan sprang up at the site and gained a post office in 1902. A school was established soon afterward, and by 1915 Dothan reported a population of fifty. The community's school was closed in 1940, by which time the population had declined to twenty, a level it still retained in 1990.

BIBLIOGRAPHY: Homer Stephen, *The Frontier Postmasters* (Dublin, Texas: Dublin *Progress*, 1952).

DOTSON, TEXAS. Dotson, on Farm Road 1971 some fourteen miles southwest of Carthage in southwestern Panola County, is in a cotton and lumber producing area that was settled before the Civil War.[qv] A post office operated at the community from 1915 to 1921. In the mid-1930s Dotson had nine businesses, a school, a church, a number of houses, and an estimated population of twenty. Its reported population increased to fifty in the 1940s. After World War II[qv] the town declined, and by the early 1970s only a store and a few houses remained in the area. In the early 1990s Dotson was a dispersed rural community with about forty residents.

BIBLIOGRAPHY: Leila B. LaGrone, ed., *History of Panola County* (Carthage, Texas: Panola County Historical Commission, 1979). John Barnette Sanders, *Postoffices and Post Masters of Panola County, Texas, 1845–1930* (Center, Texas, 1964).
Christopher Long

DOTY, CHRISTOPHER COLUMBUS (1857–1944). Christopher Columbus Doty, pioneer sheepman and settler of Schleicher County, son of Mr. and Mrs. A. C. Doty, was born in Barry County, Missouri, on April 16, 1857. His formal education was limited to three months in a country school, but he continued studying at night. At the age of twenty-one he moved from Missouri to Uvalde, Texas, where his uncle, W. T. Moore, operated a sheep ranch. After gaining experience as a sheepman Doty purchased his uncle's sheep in 1882 and established his headquarters ten miles north of the site of present Eldorado, at the Ten-Mile Water Hole. He was the first settler in Schleicher County; he also drilled what was reputed to be the first windmill on the upper Edwards Plateau,[qv] a well that facilitated the future settlement of West Texas and the development of Schleicher County.

In 1884 prairie fires and a depressed wool market forced Doty to sell his sheep ranch and move to his family's farm in Fannin County. He was soon discontented with farm life and returned in 1886 to West Texas, where he worked sheep for various employers. He eventually went to work as a sheep boss for William L. Black,qv a prominent Menard County sheep rancher. By 1889 Doty had saved enough money to open a store on the South Concho River in Tom Green County, where he established a post office. He wanted to name his town Christobal, but the postal authorities erred and the town was named Christoval. Later that year a fire destroyed Doty's business. He took a job as manager of a 1,500-acre irrigated farm near Dove Creek, owned by Joseph Tweedy.qv Doty worked for Tweedy for two years and then entered the cattle business. From 1896 to 1902 he and a partner named Sheppard leased a nine-section ranch in Schleicher County. In 1901 Doty was elected Schleicher County's first tax assessor, an office he held until 1908. In 1909 and 1910 he worked as a bookkeeper for the First National Bank in Eldorado. After 1910 he remained active in ranching and served as justice of the peace in Eldorado for fifteen years. By 1925 he had sold his land and stock and purchased a leather-repair shop. Later that year he sold the shop and purchased a grocery store, which he still owned in 1930.

Doty married Alice Pancost on June 3, 1889, in Christoval. The couple had one daughter. Doty was a Mason and a devout Methodist who organized the first Sunday school between San Angelo and Del Rio. He died on October 16, 1944, in Ozona and was buried in Christoval. *See also* SHEEP RANCHING.

BIBLIOGRAPHY: Paul H. Carlson, *Texas Woolybacks: The Range Sheep and Goat Industry* (College Station: Texas A&M University Press, 1982). Roy D. Holt, ed., *Schleicher County, or Eighty Years of Development in Southwest Texas* (Eldorado, Texas: Eldorado *Success*, 1930).
Vanessa Brown

DOTY, TEXAS. Doty is on the Kansas City Southern Railway in central Orange County ten miles northeast of Beaumont. The community was established in 1897 and was one of the earliest sidings on the Texarkana and Fort Smith Railway between Beaumont and the Sabine River. The site was first known as Baer. Its name was subsequently changed to Stanford, but confusion with another locale, Stamford, led to the adoption of the name Adrian by 1905. A final revision, to Doty, came shortly thereafter. A small sawmill operated by G. W. Pearson was established at Doty during the first decade of the 1900s. Although the mill plant was soon dismantled, the section house at Doty was not removed until 1935. One estimate set the population of Doty at twenty-five in 1949. By the mid-1970s little more than a railroad siding remained there.
Robert Wooster

DOUAI, CARL DANIEL ADOLPH (1819–1888). Adolph Douai, educational reformer, abolitionist, newspaper editor, and labor leader, was born in Altenburg, Thuringia, on February 22, 1819, to Carl Eduard and Eleanora Douai. He attended elementary school and *gymnasium* in Altenburg and subsequently studied philology and history at the University of Leipzig. After receiving his doctorate in 1841 he embarked on an extended trip that eventually took him to Russia, where he worked as a private tutor. On September 26, 1843, in Königsberg, East Prussia, he married the baroness von Beust, with whom he eventually had ten children.

In 1846 Douai returned to Altenburg and founded an experimental private secondary school that emphasized the natural sciences and modern languages instead of the traditional classical curriculum. He participated in the uprisings of 1848 and wrote articles for various newspapers supporting revolutionary aims. For his role in the revolt Douai was arrested and eventually tried on five different occasions for high treason. Although acquitted of the more serious charges, he was convicted of several lesser offences and imprisoned for a year.

After his release he immigrated to America; he arrived in Texas in May 1852 and settled first in New Braunfels, where he founded a school. He moved the following year to San Antonio to serve as the editor of the newly founded San Antonio *Zeitung.*qv The *Zeitung* at first was educational and literary in tone, but within a short time Douai began to use it as a platform for abolitionist views. In a series of editorials he attacked the institution of slaveryqv as an evil incompatible with democratic government and called for a nation of "free tillers of their own soil." Douai's protest elicited a storm of controversy and fueled the growth of the American (Know-Nothing) partyqv in Texas. Sentiment against Douai and the newspaper reached such a pitch that members of the local German turnverein (*see* TURN-VEREIN MOVEMENT) volunteered to protect his offices against proslavery mobs. After the Texas State Convention of Germans in 1854, however, Douai's support within the German community began to erode. Several German towns passed resolutions condemning the paper's abolitionism, and many local German merchants withdrew their advertisements. The stockholders of the *Zeitung* decided to sell the newspaper, which Douai, with the help of northern abolitionists including Frederick Law Olmsted,qv purchased. Despite repeated threats, he continued to agitate for abolition and in the February 9, 1855, issue of the *Zeitung* called for a separate free state in western Texas. But in 1856, as revenues declined and ill-feeling grew, Douai was forced to sell his interest in the paper to Gustav Schleicherqv and leave the state.

He moved his family to Boston, where he established a kindergarten in 1859, reputedly the first in the United States, under the auspices of a German workingmen's association that he had organized. But controversy still followed him. Because of his public avowal of atheism he again met with opposition and left Boston in 1860. He moved first to Hoboken, New Jersey, where he became the director of a local German school and served as editor of the New York *Democrat.* In 1866 he moved to New York, where he continued to pioneer the kindergarten movement. He founded several schools and wrote a kindergarten manual and other education textbooks. From 1868 to 1870 he worked as the editor of a labor journal, the New York *Arbeiter-Union,* and from 1878 until his death he was the editor of the *Neu Yorker Volkszeitung*. In addition to his work as teacher and journalist, Douai was also a gifted musician and wrote over sixty compositions. Late in his life he wrote his autobiography, in which he described his years in Texas. He died in Brooklyn, New York, on January 21, 1888, and his body was cremated. *See also* GERMAN ATTITUDE TOWARD THE CIVIL WAR.

BIBLIOGRAPHY: Rudolph L. Biesele, *The History of the German Settlements in Texas, 1831–1861* (Austin: Von Boeckmann–Jones, 1930; rpt. 1964). Adolf Douai Papers, Barker Texas History Center, University of Texas at Austin. New Haven *Workmen's Advocate,* January 28, 1887. S. V. Pfeuffer, Scrapbook, Barker Texas History Center, University of Texas at Austin. Laura Wood Roper, "Frederick Law Olmsted and the West Texas Free-Soil Movement," *American Historical Review* 56 (October 1950). Marilyn M. Sibley, *Lone Stars and State Gazettes: Texas Newspapers before the Civil War* (College Station: Texas A&M University Press, 1983). Moritz Tiling, *History of the German Element in Texas* (Houston: Rein and Sons, 1913). Carl Wittke, *Refugees of Revolution: The German Forty-Eighters in America* (Philadelphia: University of Pennsylvania Press, 1952).
Marilyn M. Sibley

DOUAY, ANASTASE (?–?). Anastase Douay, a Recollect friar with the La Salle expeditionqv (1684), is said by Louis Hennepin to have been a native of Quesnoy, in the Hainaut region of northern France. Douay had never been to America until he accompanied La Salle on his voyage to the Gulf of Mexico. He was eyewitness to La Salle's murder, of which he tells in his often biased account of his two journeys from Fort St. Louis to eastern Texas in 1686 and 1687. Despite its flaws, Douay's narrative is the only account of La Salle's first eastern journey, which lasted from mid-April to late August 1686 and reached the habitations of the "Cenis" (Hasinai, or Tejas) Indians. It therefore is a valuable historical source, even if "not noted for strict adherence to the truth."

As one of the seventeen who set out again from the Texas Fort St. Louis in January 1687 hoping to reach Fort St. Louis of the Illinois, Douay continued his narrative. His account affords an interesting comparison to those of Jean Cavelier and Henri Joutel,qqv who were also on the journey. Douay claimed that his intention was to remain among the East Texas natives to begin a mission; he expected the other Recollects from the settlement on Lavaca Bay, Zénobe Membréqv and Maxime Le Clercq, to join him there later, with other clerics to be sent from France. The events that followed aborted such plans.

Among the more interesting passages of Douay's account are those telling of La Salle's last hours and of his death. The friar was the leader's only French companion as he started out to look for the long-overdue hunting party, unaware that three of his closest associates already had been slain. La Salle, he says, having confessed his sins before leaving the camp, was seized by a deep melancholy during their long walk. As La Salle lay dying in his arms, Douay gave him absolution, then, so he claims, buried him and erected a cross over the grave, a matter at odds with Joutel's account.

After La Salle's death, Douay and five others, including Jean Cavelier, returned to Canada and thence to France in 1688. Douay is said to have been vicar of the Recollects at Cambray, on the Scheidt River in northern France, in 1697. In September 1698 he sailed again for the New World, as chaplain of the Louisiana founding expedition of Pierre Le Moyne d'Iberville. He may have hoped to find his fellow Recollects, whom he believed had gone to the Hasinais expecting to join his mission. Douay celebrated Mass upon Iberville's discovery of the Mississippi, March 3, 1699. For Iberville, however, he was a source of aggravation, especially when he lost his journal and breviary and accused the Bayogoula Indians, who were hosts to the French, of having stolen them. When Iberville sailed for France, Douay chose to return to his monastery in Paris. Thus he fades from the record.

Yet he was to make one further contribution. His journals, including one of the Iberville expedition, are listed among the sources for Claude and Guillaume Delisle's 1703 map entitled *Carte du Mexique et de la Floride*. Douay, it seems, had either found his missing journal or reconstructed it. Unfortunately, it has since been lost again.

BIBLIOGRAPHY: John Gilmary Shea, *Discovery and Exploration of the Mississippi Valley* (New York: Redfield, 1852). Robert S. Weddle, *The French Thorn: Rival Explorers in the Spanish Sea, 1682–1762* (College Station: Texas A&M University Press, 1991). Robert S. Weddle et al., eds., *La Salle, the Mississippi, and the Gulf: Three Primary Documents* (College Station: Texas A&M University Press, 1987).

Robert S. Weddle

DOUBLE BAYOU, TEXAS. Double Bayou is between the two forks of the Double Bayou and just north of the junction of Farm roads 1985 and 562, fifty miles southwest of Beaumont in west central Chambers County. James Jackson settled the area in 1847, establishing a ranch of 26,000 acres. Though most operations of this type used the open range, the Jackson ranch was fenced at an early date. The local general store, established by John Jackson before 1900, served as the center for community life at Double Bayou. A sugar cane mill and cotton gin also provided gathering points for the widely scattered settlers of the region. The Double Bayou post office operated from 1860 to 1866 and from 1876 to 1919. Traveling on Double Bayou and Trinity Bay, boats remained the locale's primary means of communication with the outside world well into the twentieth century. The flooding that accompanied the hurricane of 1915 caused severe hardships for the people of Double Bayou, as it did for many residents of the upper coastal prairies of Texas. The largely black population of the isolated rural area was estimated at between 150 and 300 during the 1930s. Churches, a number of residences, and a school marked the Double Bayou community on maps in the mid-1970s. The port at Double Bayou handled 26,136 tons in 1981. The community's population in 1990 was reported as 400.

BIBLIOGRAPHY: Jewel Horace Harry, A History of Chambers County (M.A. thesis, University of Texas, 1940; rpt., Dallas: Taylor, 1981). Ralph Semmes Jackson, *Home on the Double Bayou: Memories of an East Texas Ranch* (Austin: University of Texas Press, 1961).

Robert Wooster

DOUBLE BRANCH. Double Branch rises four miles south of Indian Springs in south central Polk County (at 30°38′ N, 94°44′ W) and runs southeast for 2½ miles to its mouth on Big Sandy Creek, just within the Big Sandy Corridor of the Big Thicketqv National Preserve and three miles north of Segno (at 30°37′ N, 94°42′ W). The main stream is formed by the junction of the East and West forks of the Double Branch. Its East Fork rises about a mile south of Camp Ruby and runs south for three miles; its West Fork rises in the Indian Springs community and runs southeast for five miles. Both branches are intermittent and are dammed in their upper reaches to form small lakes, the larger of which, Wilson Lake, is formed from the East Fork.

DOUBLEDAY, ABNER (1819–1893). Abner Doubleday, military officer, son of Ulysses F. and Hester (Donnelly) Doubleday, was born at Ballston Spa, New York, on June 26, 1819. He attended school at Auburn and Cooperstown, where he prepared for a career in civil engineering. Tradition incorrectly has it that he originated the game of baseball, though he did popularize the sport when he laid out a diamond and explained his rules. He worked as a surveyor from 1836 to 1838 and graduated from the United States Military Academy in 1842. He served under Gen. Zachary Taylorqv in the Mexican War.qv In 1852 he married Mary Hewitt of Baltimore.

At the outbreak of the Civil War,qv Doubleday fired the first Union gun in defense of Fort Sumter, South Carolina, on April 12, 1861. He was promoted later to major general of volunteers and fought in many battles, including the second battle of Manassas, Sharpsburg, Chancellorsville, and Gettysburg, before a transfer took him to Washington, D.C. After the war he was promoted to colonel in the regular army and transferred to California, where he obtained the charter for the first San Francisco cable street railway. By December 1869, before any significant construction got under way, he had sold his interests and become colonel of the all-black Twenty-fourth United States Infantryqv regiment in Texas.

Doubleday did not assume his new duties until April 1871. At that time headquarters of the Twenty-fourth Infantry was at Fort McKavett, on the San Saba River in what is now Menard County. Regiments in Texas at the time rarely assembled but were scattered among the western frontier posts. In 1871 companies of Doubleday's Twenty-fourth were stationed in several of the more remote posts in West Texas, including forts Bliss, Clark, Davis, Duncan, McKavett, Quitman, and Stockton. They did little fighting, but Doubleday kept busy traveling between posts and overseeing general police duties. He ordered repairs, supervised the improvement of sanitary conditions, and inspected facilities. In August 1872, acting on orders, he transferred his headquarters to Fort Brown in the Rio Grande valley. From there he scattered his troops by companies among forts along the river.

After he became seriously ill of a stomach disorder Doubleday applied for and received an extended medical leave. He left Texas in June 1873, and because his condition did not improve, in December he retired from the army; he then made his home in Mendham, New Jersey. He died in 1893 and was buried in Arlington National Cemetery.

BIBLIOGRAPHY: Paul H. Carlson, "Baseball's Abner Doubleday on the Texas Frontier, 1871–1873," *Military History of Texas and the Southwest* 12 (1974).

Paul H. Carlson

DOUBLE HORN, TEXAS. Double Horn was at the headspring of Double Horn Creek, south of the Colorado River in Burnet County and fifty to sixty miles northwest of Austin. The town was formed in 1855 by Jesse Burnam[qv] (or Burnham), Levi Fowler, and others. The creek and town were reportedly named after an incident in which a pioneer found the remains of two bucks with interlocked antlers. The Francis Chapel or Frog Pond school, with William H. Holland as its first teacher, was located on the Colorado River; in 1855 among its students were the children of Noah Smithwick.[qv] The school, later known as the Double Horn School, was moved near Grid Iron Creek and then to Double Horn Creek. A post office was established for the community in October 1857, with Holland as the first postmaster. In 1884 Double Horn had a population of fifty along with the school, a cotton gin, and two churches. By 1896 its population had dropped to twenty-five, and a physician named Yett practiced there. The Double Horn post office was discontinued in 1911. The cotton gin and gristmill on Grid Iron Creek was later moved to the junction of Grid Iron and Double Horn creeks. A blacksmith shop and store were also nearby. The Double Horn school was still shown on the 1936 county highway map, but all traces of the community and school were gone by the second half of the twentieth century.

BIBLIOGRAPHY: Darrell Debo, *Burnet County History* (2 vols., Burnet, Texas: Eakin, 1979). Noah Smithwick, *The Evolution of a State, or Recollections of Old Texas Days* (Austin: Gammel, 1900; rpt., Austin: University of Texas Press, 1983).

Madolyn Frasier and Cyrus Tilloson

DOUBLE HORN CREEK. Double Horn Creek rises about 2½ miles east of the Round Mountain community in northeastern Blanco County (at 30°26′ N, 98°18′ W) and runs northeast for 12½ miles to its mouth on the Colorado River in what is now the upper end of Lake Travis, about eight miles from Marble Falls in southern Burnet County (at 30°32′ N, 98°11′ W). The stream traverses flat to rolling Hill Country[qv] terrain with clayey and loamy soils that support mixed vegetation, including Ashe juniper, live oak, mesquite, and grasses.

DOUBLE KNOBBS, TEXAS. Double Knobbs is on State Highway 29 some eight miles northwest of Mason in western Mason County. It was named for two nearby hills which lie on either side of the highway. The area was settled around 1890, when the Dodd and the Clark families arrived. The community's early development was focused around the establishment of a local school. Most of the area residents were farmers and ranchers. In the 1900s the local agricultural focus changed from cotton to peanut farming. The community's school was eventually closed. In the mid-1980s Double Knobbs was a dispersed farming community.

BIBLIOGRAPHY: Kathryn Burford Eilers, A History of Mason County, Texas (M.A. thesis, University of Texas, 1939).

Alice J. Rhoades

DOUBLE LAKES. The Double Lakes, two medium-sized natural lakes seven miles northwest of Tahoka in western Lynn County (at 33°13′ N, 101°55′ W), stand at approximately 3,100 feet above sea level. The sandy clay loam along the lakeshores supports a variety of tall grasses. Either Double Lakes or Twin Lakes, located five miles to the south in Lynn County, was the site of several skirmishes between Indians and Col. Ranald S. Mackenzie's[qv] troops in the early 1870s. One of these two lake groupings was also the site where Capt. Nicholas Nolan and the Nolan Expedition[qv] camped in 1877 after traveling eighty-six hours without water.

BIBLIOGRAPHY: H. Bailey Carroll, "Nolan's 'Lost Nigger' Expedition of 1877," *Southwestern Historical Quarterly* 44 (July 1940). W. C. Nunn, "Eighty-Six Hours without Water on the Texas Plains," *Southwestern Historical Quarterly* 43 (January 1940). Ernest Wallace, *Ranald S. Mackenzie on the Texas Frontier* (Lubbock: West Texas Museum Association, 1964).

DOUBLE MESA. Double Mesa is north of State Highway 25 in Archer County. A French fort or trading post operated there in the 1700s. Around 1772 Chief Nortends and several Pani-Maha and Wichita Indians built a trading village of mud to increase commerce in horses, mules, and slaves with the Europeans. French trader Jean Baptiste Lowasard traded at the post, and J. Gaignard of Opelousas, Louisiana, visited on February 16, 1774. The post stood three miles west of Archer City, in what is now the Harris Subdivision Club Ranch.

BIBLIOGRAPHY: Jack Loftin, *Trails Through Archer* (Burnet, Texas: Nortex, 1979).

DOUBLE MILLS. Double Mills, also known as Double Wells, is just south of Maravillas Creek and just east of U.S. Highway 385 some thirty-four miles south of Marathon in central Brewster County (at 29°45′ N, 103°10′ W). The site originally had a large natural waterhole, which was used by prehistoric peoples and later by Indians, Spaniards, and Mexicans. Sometime in the early 1900s the water table dropped and the spring dried up, due to the deepening of Maravillas Creek caused by overgrazing and other settlement activities. Rancher George Miller, who owned the land, dug two wells near the channel of Maravillas Creek and erected two windmills, so travelers and livestock could still find water there. Southern Brewster County ranchers driving cattle to the railhead at Marathon stopped at Double Mills, as did the wagon trains carrying ore and supplies to and from Boquillas. In October 1911 Edgar D. Lowe opened the first candelilla wax factory in Brewster County at Double Mills. The United States Army built the first concrete bridge in southern Brewster County at Double Mills during the early 1900s, when troops were stationed along the Rio Grande to guard against raids from Mexico. Parts of this bridge still stood decades later, although it had been replaced by a modern bridge just upstream on U.S. Highway 385.

DOUBLE MOUNTAIN (Stephens County). Double Mountain, about eleven miles south of Breckenridge in southern Stephens County (at 32°35′ N, 98°55′ W), has an elevation of 1,580 feet above sea level. It rises in an area of rolling hills surfaced by clay and sandy loams, and the vegetation on its slopes includes mesquite, scrub brush, cacti, and grasses. The mountain's name comes from the fact that at a distance it appears to be two mountains.

——— (Stonewall County). Double Mountain is the name of two separate hills located just north of the headwaters of Count Creek, thirteen miles southwest of Aspermont and eight miles south of Peacock in southwestern Stonewall County (at 33°08′ N, 100°25′ W). Both hills reach an elevation of about 2,000 feet above sea level and rise some 600 feet above the surrounding terrain. They have long been regional landmarks and in 1849 were cited by the surveying party of Randolph B. Marcy.[qv]

BIBLIOGRAPHY: *A History of Stonewall County* (Aspermont, Texas: Stonewall County Historical Commission, 1979).

DOUBLE MOUNTAIN, TEXAS. Double Mountain was on a local road a mile west of Farm Road 2211 and ten miles west of Aspermont in west central Stonewall County. The settlement, originally called Jackson by its first settlers in 1886, was renamed Double Mountain several months later. A post office was established there in June of that year, with John M. Lee as postmaster. By 1892 a sheriff, justice of the peace, and county commissioner were among the residents of the community. In 1905 its post office was moved from the Lee home to the Matthews home, which became a gathering place for area ranchers. Although locally known as Double Mountain, the post office name was formally changed to Lingo in 1905. It was discontinued in 1908 and moved to Aspermont. Double Mountain developed little beyond the post office and the Baptist and Methodist churches organized there in 1897 and 1898, respectively. A Double Mountain school was in existence by 1899; after it burned, classes were held in the Beulah Baptist Church until a new one-room school was built in 1914. The community had lost its identity long before the 1980s, when county highway maps indicated only a Double Mountain cemetery about two miles west of Stinking Creek.

BIBLIOGRAPHY: Arthur Hecht, comp., *Postal History in the Texas Panhandle* (Canyon, Texas: Panhandle–Plains Historical Society, 1960). *A History of Stonewall County* (Aspermont, Texas: Stonewall County Historical Commission, 1979). *Charles G. Davis*

DOUBLE MOUNTAIN FORK OF THE BRAZOS RIVER. The main stream of the Double Mountain Fork of the Brazos River rises in the break in the Caprock qv of the Llano Estacado qv known as Double Mountain Canyon in eastern Lynn County (at 33°05′ N, 101°39′ W) and runs east across southern Garza County, southern Kent County, northwestern Fisher County, southern Stonewall County, and western Haskell County, before turning back westward into eastern Stonewall County. It extends 165 miles to its mouth, on the Salt Fork of the Brazos near Old Glory oilfield, northeast of Aspermont (at 33°16′ N, 100°01′ W). At this confluence the Brazos River proper is formed. The North Fork of the Double Mountain Fork rises in Lubbock, central Lubbock County (at 33°36′ N, 101°50′ W), and runs roughly seventy-five miles through Crosby and Garza counties to its mouth, on the Double Mountain Fork of the Brazos River, southwest of Clairemont in western Kent County (at 33°06′ N, 101°00′ W). The Double Mountain Fork and its North Fork have been dammed to form Bell Springs Lake, Lake Ransom Canyon, Benson Lake, Blake Lake, Stewart Lake, and Clear Water Lake. The canyon is also known as Mooar's Draw, after John Wesley and Josiah Wright Mooar,qqv early buffalo hunters in the area.

DOUBLE OAK, TEXAS. Double Oak is on Farm Road 407 ten miles south of Denton in southern Denton County. The area had a school district as early as 1884, but Double Oak was not incorporated until the 1970s, when suburban sprawl from Dallas–Fort Worth arrived. Double Oak reported a population of 836 in 1980. Ten years later the residential community's population had nearly doubled, to 1,664. *Randolph B. Campbell*

DOUBLE TANKS, TEXAS. Double Tanks is on the Wood Ranch a half mile east of U.S. Highway 277 and ten miles southwest of Carta Valley in northeastern Val Verde County. It was founded in the early 1880s by R. L. Crouch, a rancher who constructed two tanks to supply water for his livestock and to offer water to travelers, emigrants, and temporary settlers. Many wayfarers stopped at Double Tanks to rest under the large oaks and to use the abundant water. In 1898 one of those visitors, Robert Kuntz of the Cherokee Strip in Oklahoma, decided to take advantage of the fertile black soil and lush grass around Double Tanks. Believing he had found the ideal site for homesteading, Kuntz sent news of it to his friend W. W. Riggs, who brought his family to Double Tanks in 1900. Several families had arrived earlier, among them the Galloways and the Carters. In 1901 the settlers established a school with Riggs as teacher, and by 1903 more than twelve new families had come to the settlement. The campsite at Double Tanks became a community of homesteaders, living in wagons, cabins, shacks, tents, and lean-tos. In 1905 Joseph Alexander Foster, a Methodist missionary, organized a church at Double Tanks. By 1908 many homesteaders had left Double Tanks for permanent homes in or near Carta Valley, in western Edwards County. By the late 1970s only two dirt tanks surrounded by tall oak trees remained at the site.

BIBLIOGRAPHY: Whitehead Memorial Museum et al., *La Hacienda* (Norman: University of Oklahoma Press, 1976). Diana Sotelo Zertuche, *The Spirit of Val Verde* (Del Rio, Texas, 1985).
Julia Cauble Smith

DOUCETTE, TEXAS. Doucette is on U.S. Highway 69 and the Southern Pacific Railroad three miles north of Woodville in central Tyler County. In 1834 Elijah Hanks received a land grant in the area. A community coalesced around a sawmill built in 1890 by Alva Carrolls and for a while was known as Carrolls' Switch. In 1891 Carrolls was bought out by William McCready, a Mr. Bodev, and Pete Doucette, for whom the community was renamed. A post office was established in 1893, and sawmill operator William McCready was the first postmaster. The sawmill was eventually bought by Samuel F. Carter qv and his brother, whose partnership firm was called the Emporia Lumber Company. Before Emporia ceased operating the mill in 1906, Doucette had become one of the leading towns in East Texas.

The Emporia Lumber Company was followed at Doucette by the Thompson Brothers Lumber Company (*see* THOMPSON TIMBER INTERESTS), which later sold out to Fidelity Lumber Company. Fidelity was succeeded in 1911 by Long-Bell Lumber Company and in 1956 by International Paper Company, which still maintains an office and yard in Doucette. However, the sawmill there has been closed down since 1944. During Long-Bell's ownership of the mill, Doucette prospered. The company had a commissary where everything "from bassinets to caskets" could be purchased. The town also had a drugstore, a doctor, a bank, a railroad station, and a post office. Civic and cultural aspects of the town included groups like the Masons, the Woodmen of the World, the Boy Scouts, and the PTA. There were traveling circuses and medicine shows, a little theater group, baseball, and church revivals and picnics. On the darker side, the Ku Klux Klan qv was active locally.

During the 1920s the population in Doucette reached its height at 1,800. In the 1930s it fell to around 500 people, served by about eight businesses. From 1943 to the late 1960s the population remained 250, and from 1970 to 1988 Doucette had 130 residents and four businesses. Though the heyday of lumber production at Doucette was during the early decades of the twentieth century, as late as 1946 the mills there were producing thirty cars of poles and piling each week. Doucette managed to retain a small amount of lumber and shipping business, which with the addition of newer sources of small business income kept it a small but viable community. In 1990 it had a population of 131.

BIBLIOGRAPHY: *It's Dogwood Time in Tyler County* (Woodville, Texas), 1962. Lou Ella Moseley, *Pioneer Days of Tyler County* (Fort Worth: Miran, 1975). *Megan Biesele*

DOUGHERTY, EDWARD (1819–1877?). Edward Dougherty, legislator, was born in County Caven, Ireland, on June 9, 1819. He immigrated to the United States in 1820 with his parents, James and Ann (Sheridan) Dougherty, and they settled in New York City, where Dougherty was raised. He traveled to Texas in July 1846 as a soldier in David Emanuel Twiggs's qv Second United States Dragoons during the Mexican War qv and participated in the first battles of that conflict at Palo Alto and Resaca de la Palma.qqv After his discharge he settled at the newly established town of Brownsville. Dougherty married Marcela García on November 13, 1847, and they were the parents of seven children.

Dougherty founded the trading town of Rudyville near Relampago in Hidalgo County about 1850. He acted as United States deputy collector at Rudyville in the 1850s. On November 29, 1852, he was admitted to the bar at Brownsville. He served as justice of the peace and county judge in the early days of Cameron County. In 1856 he was elected district attorney of the Twelfth Judicial District and held that office until 1863, being removed when the Union forces captured Brownsville during the Civil War.qv Dougherty also served in the Eighth State Legislature, having been elected without opposition in August 1859. He represented Hidalgo County in the Texas Secession Convention of 1861. On February 25, 1874, Dougherty was appointed commissioner for the extradition treaty between the United States and Mexico. He was a judge in two judicial districts: the twenty-fifth district at Laredo in 1874 and the fifteenth district at Brownsville in 1877.

BIBLIOGRAPHY: William DeRyee and R. E. Moore, *The Texas Album of the Eighth Legislature, 1860* (Austin: Miner, Lambert, and Perry, 1860). Valley By-Liners, *Roots by the River: A Story of Texas Tropical Borderland* (Mission, Texas: Border Kingdom Press, 1978).

J. L. Bryan

DOUGHERTY, JAMES ROBERT (1871–1950). James Robert Dougherty, attorney, oilman, and philanthropist, the son of Robert and Rachel (Sullivan) Dougherty, was born in San Patricio, Texas, on August 27, 1871. He was certified to teach at the age of sixteen and took a position in Webb County. Two years later he enrolled at Saint Louis University, after which he attended the University of Texas in Austin. He studied law in the offices of Lon C. Hill and James B. Wellsqv and was admitted to the bar on March 4, 1895. He went to Beeville to practice law, and later his brother, J. Chris Dougherty, joined him to form the law firm of Dougherty and Dougherty. James Dougherty helped to establish the legal precedent of private ownership of minerals in the beds of nonnavigable rivers.

He dealt in livestock all his life. He developed a silver mine in Durango, Mexico, in 1916. He was instrumental in discovering a number of South Texas oilfields, including the Tom O'Conner, Greta, Pettus, Flour Bluff, Refugio, Dougherty, and several others. With Dr. W. E. Hewit, he formed the oil company of Hewit and Dougherty, which operated over a wide area of South and West Texas. Dougherty spoke Spanish fluently and was a student of Latin, Greek, and French. He furnished capital to a publishing company in New York for translations from Latin and Greek. He was elected first lieutenant by a company of volunteers during the Spanish-American War. He married Genevieve Tarlton on April 24, 1911, and they had four children. He was a member of the board of regents of Texas A&I University at Kingsville for ten years and a member of the boards of regents of Incarnate Word and Our Lady of the Lake colleges in San Antonio. A decade before his death, he and his wife established the Dougherty Foundation as an aid to youths for obtaining an education.

Dougherty was a Catholic and a fourth-degree Knight of Columbus. He was made a knight of the Order of St. Gregory the Great (1947) and of the Order of Malta (1948), as well as of the Equestrian Order of the Holy Sepulchre (1948). In 1937 the Doughertys donated $12,000 to finance the construction of a new St. Joseph's School in Beeville. Later they built the James R. Dougherty, Jr., Recreation Center in memory of their son, who was killed in action during World War II.qv Dougherty died on July 8, 1950, in Corpus Christi and was buried in Beeville.

BIBLIOGRAPHY: Grace Bauer, *Bee County Centennial, 1858–1958* (Bee County Centennial, 1958). Grace Bauer (Lillian Grace Schoppe), The History of Bee County, Texas (M.A. thesis, University of Texas, 1939). Beeville *Bee-Picayune*, July 13, 1950. Fort Worth *Star-Telegram*, November 29, 1964.

Grace Bauer

DOUGHERTY, ROBERT FRANCIS (1827–1881). Robert Dougherty, teacher and local official, son of John and Catherine (McMahon) Dougherty, was born at Derrylaghan, County Donegal, Ireland, in 1827. He immigrated to the United States in 1847 and lived in New York and Kentucky. He taught at St. Mary's College in Bardstown, Kentucky, and was later an editor and poet for the Louisville *Courier-Journal*. He subsequently became a peddler of fancy dry goods, a job that took him to Mexico City. In 1860 he moved to Texas. He may have joined Capt. V. S. Rabb's company in the Confederate Army. On a mission to the Rio Grande he met Rachel Ann Schamp Sullivan from San Patricio, and they were married on November 14, 1864.

After the war Dougherty opened a store in San Diego. He returned to teaching at Hidalgo Seminary in Corpus Christi and in 1867 became principal. While running the seminary he served two terms as a city alderman and ran for mayor but was defeated. Ill health caused him to return to San Patricio, where he built St. Paul's Academy on fifty acres of land beside Round Lake; he purchased the site from Patrick McGloin with the help of a $6,000 loan from Nicholas Bluntzer. The school, which opened in 1877, answered a long-standing need in the area and was immediately filled by students. The Doughertys lived on the first floor, and the upstairs was used as a dormitory for the boys and classrooms. The building still stood in 1990. Robert ran the school, and Rachel cooked and ran a boarding house.

Dougherty is credited with having influenced many French priests who came to the Corpus Christi area between 1860 and 1880. He was elected San Patricio county judge in 1876 and again in 1880. He died in 1881 in Corpus Christi and was buried in the Old Cemetery on the Hill in San Patricio. When he died S. G. Bordenqv was appointed to fill the vacancy at the school. For a short time Mrs. Dougherty attempted to keep the school open but finally had to close it and devote her time to raising their three sons and four daughters.

BIBLIOGRAPHY: Keith Guthrie, *History of San Patricio County* (Austin: Nortex, 1986). Rachel Bluntzer Hébert, *The Forgotten Colony: San Patricio de Hibernia* (Burnet, Texas: Eakin Press, 1981). Vertical Files, Barker Texas History Center, University of Texas at Austin.

Keith Guthrie

DOUGHERTY, TEXAS. Dougherty, on the Fort Worth and Denver Railway and Farm Road 28 in southeastern Floyd County, was established in 1928 and named for F. M. Dougherty. Grace Garner was the first postmistress, and a school was built in 1929. For a time Dougherty prospered, but when U.S. Highway 62/70 bypassed the town by three miles, the community faltered. In 1948 Dougherty had a church, a post office, three businesses, and 150 people. Conditions remained similar in 1980, when the town had 135 people, a school, a post office, and four businesses. The population was 100 in 1990.

BIBLIOGRAPHY: Kathleen E. and Clifton R. St. Clair, eds., *Little Towns of Texas* (Jacksonville, Texas: Jayroe Graphic Arts, 1982).

William R. Hunt

DOUGHTY, WALTER FRANCIS (1873–1931). Walter Francis Doughty, school administrator and government education official, son of Daniel Milton and Sara Elizabeth (Ray) Doughty, was born in Emory, Mississippi, on July 22, 1873. He attended Arkansas public schools and Culberland College at Clarksville, then taught school in Arkansas. In 1895 he moved to Texas, where he taught at Mertens in east central Hill County. Two years later he married Ettie May Adler. The couple had two children. In 1898 Doughty became principal at nearby Brandon. The money he earned during this period financed his education at the University of Texas in Austin. In 1906 Doughty received his bachelor's degree and became superintendent of the Marlin School District. Subsequently, in addition to his duties as superintendent, he taught summer school at Baylor University (1908), served as president of the board of education of Falls County (1908–11), received his master of arts degree from the University of Chicago (1911), and taught summer classes at Southwest Texas State Normal School (now Southwest Texas State University) from 1911 to 1913.

Doughty was treasurer of the Texas State Teachers Association from 1908 to 1912 and president in 1912. Because of his experience as superintendent and involvement with the association, Governor Oscar B. Colquitt^{qv} appointed him state superintendent of public instruction on September 1, 1913. The following year he was elected to the position, which he held until 1919. During his tenure, Doughty lobbied to modernize the rural school system. He successfully campaigned for a $2 million appropriation package to aid poor school districts, for compulsory school attendance, for vocational education, and for the reorganization of rural school districts into a more efficient administrative system.

During World War I^{qv} he was in charge of supervising war training services for the federal government in the public schools of Texas. After the war he became district vocational officer for the Federal Board for Vocational Education. In this position he organized rehabilitation work in District Fourteen, which included the states of Arkansas, Oklahoma, and Texas. Between 1919 and 1923 he handled the claims of more than 30,000 disabled veterans.

In 1923 Doughty returned to Hill County to accept the presidency of Hillsboro Junior College (see HILL JUNIOR COLLEGE) and the position of superintendent of the Hillsboro schools. Under his leadership HJC became the first municipal junior college to be organized in the state. Doughty introduced the 5-4-4 plan: five years of elementary school (ages seven to eleven), four years of junior high school (ages eleven to fifteen), and four years of senior high school and junior college (ages fifteen to nineteen). In 1925 his duties increased as he became president of the board of education of Hill County. Doughty published a number of articles in educational journals. He was a Democrat, a Mason, and a Presbyterian. In the late 1920s his health failed, and after a long illness he died at Marlin on August 20, 1931.

BIBLIOGRAPHY: Ellis Bailey, *A History of Hill County, Texas, 1838–1965* (Waco: Texian Press, 1966). Vertical Files, Barker Texas History Center, University of Texas at Austin. *Who Was Who in America*, Vol. 2.

DOUGLAS, JAMES POSTELL (1836–1901). James Postell Douglas, Confederate artillery officer, the oldest son of Alexander and Margaret Tirzah (Cowsar) Douglas, was born near Lancaster, South Carolina, on January 7, 1836. He moved with his family to Talladega, Alabama, in 1838 and to Texas in 1847. In January 1848 the Douglas and Cowsar families settled at Tyler, where Douglas attended such public schools as were available. Generally, however, he was self-educated; he learned Latin with the aid of a neighbor in Talladega. Among his earliest jobs was delivery of the mail from Shreveport, Louisiana, to Nacogdoches, Texas. When his father died in 1854, the seventeen-year-old became head of the Douglas household, served as principal of the Tyler Male Academy by day, and read law at night. Although licensed to practice law, he purchased a half interest in and edited the Tyler *Reporter*, now the Tyler *Courier Times*, in 1859.

With the outbreak of the Civil War^{qv} Douglas was commissioned by Col. Elkanah Greer^{qv} to raise a fifty-man company in Smith County to man half a field artillery battery to be attached to Greer's Third Texas Cavalry. The other company was raised in Dallas County by John J. Good.^{qv} Douglas was commissioned first lieutenant and named second in command of the battery on June 13, 1861. He was promoted to captain and commander in July 1862. The battery, first commanded by Captain Good, was variously known as the First Texas Battery, the Dallas Light Artillery, the Good-Douglas Battery, and Douglas's Battery, and became the only unit of Texas artillery to serve east of the Mississippi River. It is said to have been the first Confederate unit to volunteer "for the duration of the war." After receiving its baptism of fire with Benjamin McCulloch's^{qv} Army of the West at the battle of Elkhorn Tavern in March 1862, the battery was transferred to Mississippi, where it saw action at the battle of Corinth. Thereafter it took part in all of the major battles of the Army of Tennessee—Murfreesboro, Chickamauga, Chattanooga, the battles for Atlanta, and John Bell Hood's^{qv} disastrous Tennessee campaign of 1864. Covering Hood's retreat from Nashville, the battery lost its guns when they bogged in the mud and were overrun by Union cavalry. Douglas barely escaped capture by riding away on the horse behind his younger brother. On February 16, 1864, the Confederate Congress offered a formal vote of thanks to the battery. Douglas's battery was paroled at Mobile, Alabama, on May 12, 1865, and Douglas returned to Tyler.

He resumed his work with the Tyler *Reporter* and in 1870 was elected to the Senate of the Twelfth Texas Legislature, where he was noted for his anti-Reconstruction attitude and activities. He was the organizer and first president of the Texas branch of the Cotton Belt Railroad, the so-called Tyler Tap, which was later sold to Jay Gould.^{qv} Douglas was also instrumental in the establishment of the Texas and St. Louis and the Kansas and Gulf Short Line railroads. He owned a chain of canning factories, the first in Tyler, to market produce from his farms. As a planter, he was greatly interested in agricultural experimentation and owned a large peach orchard, said to be the first in East Texas.

Douglas was married twice, first on March 24, 1864, to Sallie Susan White, who died on August 22, 1872, and subsequently to Alice Earle Smith, on July 7, 1874. Four children were born to the first marriage and six to the second. Douglas died on November 27, 1901, and was buried in Oakwood Cemetery at Tyler. His wife died on June 28, 1955, and is buried beside him.

BIBLIOGRAPHY: Alice Douglas, ed., "Recollections of a Centenarian," *Chronicles of Smith County*, Spring 1966. Lucia Rutherford Douglas, comp. and ed., *Douglas' Texas Battery, C.S.A.* (Tyler, Texas: Smith County Historical Society, 1966). Lester Newton Fitzhugh, ed., *Cannon Smoke: The Letters of Captain John J. Good* (Hillsboro: Hill Junior College Press, 1971). June P. Trop, ed., "An Update: The Douglas Letters," *Chronicles of Smith County*, Summer 1983. Marcus J. Wright, comp., and Harold B. Simpson, ed., *Texas in the War, 1861–1865* (Hillsboro, Texas: Hill Junior College Press, 1965).

Thomas W. Cutrer

DOUGLAS, TEXAS. Douglas is near Hope Pond, eleven miles east of Tyler and one mile south of State Highway 31 in eastern Smith County. The site was originally part of the Barns Clark survey; the Old Mound Indian Trail, or the old Jamestown-Tyler road, ran through the area. Maps for 1936 showed four school buildings and one nearby dwelling. That year the Douglas school employed five teachers and enrolled 130 black students in grades one through eleven. The community also contained sparsely scattered farms and a cemetery. By 1952 the Douglas school, along with other local rural schools, had been consolidated into the Arp Independent School District. In 1966 the community comprised one abandoned business, a church, and a number of dwellings scattered along dirt roads south of State Highway 31. By 1973 only a cluster of farms and a grain elevator remained. Douglas was still identified on maps in 1981.

BIBLIOGRAPHY: Edward Clayton Curry, An Administrative Survey of the Schools of Smith County, Texas (M.Ed. thesis, University of Texas, 1938). Smith County Historical Society, *Historical Atlas of Smith County* (Tyler, Texas: Tyler Print Shop, 1965).

Vista K. McCroskey

DOUGLAS CHAPEL, TEXAS. Douglas Chapel is just east of State Highway 43 and ten miles east of Jefferson in eastern Marion County. The Douglas Chapel school had twenty-six black pupils and one teacher in 1899. In 1938 the community had a one-room schoolhouse that accommodated twenty-seven black elementary students. The school was consolidated with the Jefferson schools by 1955, and in 1962 all that remained at the community site was a church, which was still identified on state highway maps in 1983.

BIBLIOGRAPHY: Jack Reed Harvey, Survey and Proposed Reorganization of the Marion County Schools (M.A. thesis, University of Texas, 1940).
Mark Odintz

DOUGLAS MOUNTAINS. The Douglas mountain range, four miles south of Killeen in southwestern Bell County (at 31°02′ N, 97°45′ W), runs southeast to northwest for two miles, with elevations ranging from 980 to 1,069 feet above sea level. At its highest elevation the range rises 150 feet above nearby State Highway 195.

DOUGLAS STORE, TEXAS. Douglas Store was on Farm Road 1861 twelve miles southeast of Canton in extreme south central Van Zandt County. In 1936 the settlement had numerous scattered dwellings, a business, a church, and a cemetery. The Mahagony school, church, and cemetery across Farm Road l861 was within half a mile. By 1987 the cemetery and church remained, but the community had disappeared.
Diana J. Kleiner

DOUGLASS, KELSEY HARRIS (?–1848). Kelsey Harris Douglass, Nacogdoches merchant and Republic of Texas qv congressman, came to Texas sometime before the Texas Revolution.qv In March 1836 he sold several large orders of apparel and dry goods to the Texas army. In 1837–38 he represented Nacogdoches County in the House of the Second Congress in Houston. He joined Col. Edward Burleson,qv who along with his volunteers from East Texas, succeeded in pushing the Cherokee Indians from Texas. Douglass was in command at the battle of the Neches.qv He was also a charter member of the Masonic Grand Lodge of Texas. He married Minerva Benton. He died in Nacogdoches on October 26, 1848, and is buried in Oak Grove Cemetery. The town of Douglass is named in his honor.

BIBLIOGRAPHY: Texas House of Representatives, *Biographical Directory of the Texan Conventions and Congresses, 1832–1845* (Austin: Book Exchange, 1941).
Kim Perkins

DOUGLASS, SAMUEL C. (1770?–?). Samuel C. Douglass, veteran of the War of 1812 and representative at the Convention of 1832,qv was probably born in the 1770s. He served in the War of 1812 in Captain Bacon's Company of Samuel Bayless's Fourth Regiment of the Tennessee Militia and arrived in Texas from Georgia between 1822 and 1832. He settled in Brazoria and farmed there until about 1845. He represented Mill Creek, Austin County, at the Convention of 1832. He was farming in Fort Bend County in 1850.

BIBLIOGRAPHY: *Southwestern Historical Quarterly*, Texas Collection, October 1954. Texas House of Representatives, *Biographical Directory of the Texan Conventions and Congresses, 1832–1845* (Austin: Book Exchange, 1941).
Carolyn Hyman

DOUGLASS, TEXAS. Douglass, on the Old San Antonio Roadqv four miles east of the Angelina River and fourteen miles west of Nacogdoches in Nacogdoches County, was originally settled about 1829. In 1836 Michael Costleyqv laid the town out around a square on an 800-acre tract purchased from John M. Durst.qv It was named for Gen. Kelsey Harris Douglass,qv a prominent early settler who established several businesses at the site. By 1836 Douglass had a stagecoach inn owned and operated by John R. Clute. At one time it supported numerous businesses, including a gristmill, a tannery, a sawmill, a brick kiln, and a cotton gin. Residents had a church, a school, and a Masonic lodge. Early in the twentieth century a teachers' school operated in Douglass for two years. By 1927 the town had a large community hall with electric lights. Two big fires, one in January 1943 and one in January 1954, occurred in Douglass. In 1980 and 1990 the town comprised a post office, two businesses, a school, and a population of seventy-five.

BIBLIOGRAPHY: Nugent E. Brown, comp., *The Book of Nacogdoches County, Texas* (Nacogdoches, 1927). Richard W. Haltom, *The History of Nacogdoches County, Texas* (Nacogdoches, 1880; rpt., Austin: Jenkins, 197-?).
Harold T. Purvis

DOUGLASSVILLE, TEXAS. Douglassville is at the junction of State highways 8 and 77, 12½ miles north of Linden in northern Cass County. The site was settled in the early 1850s and named for John Douglass, an early resident. Most of the early settlers came from Georgia and Alabama, and many established plantations along the Red River. A Douglassville post office was established in 1854 and continued to operate in 1990. After the Civil Warqv the town continued as a supply point and market for area farmers. In 1884 it had two churches, a district school, two gristmills, two cotton gins, and a population estimated at 150. In 1900 the population was 176. The community was incorporated in the 1950s. In 1980 it had four rated businesses and a population of 228. In 1990 the population was 192.

BIBLIOGRAPHY: Atlanta (Texas) *Citizens Journal*, 60th Anniversary Edition (1939).
Cecil Harper, Jr.

DOURO, TEXAS. Douro, ten miles southwest of Odessa in south central Ector County, was founded when the Texas and Pacific Railway built through the area in 1881. Original plans for the settlement set aside a city lot for a future courthouse. Although developers advertised the area and sold property, the community grew little beyond a station house. Development was stimulated by the establishment of the oil industry in the late 1920s, and by 1930 Douro reported a population of twenty-five and one business. In the early 1980s Douro remained a Missouri-Pacific railroad switch, just south of Interstate Highway 20.

BIBLIOGRAPHY: Finas Wade Horton, *A History of Ector County, Texas* (M.A. thesis, University of Texas, 1950).
Charles G. Davis

DOVE, TEXAS. Dove, just east of State Highway 114 in northeastern Tarrant County, was established during the 1870s. It developed as a loosely organized agricultural community surrounded by dairy and poultry farms. A post office operated there from 1894 to 1904. The community school registered ninety-seven students and employed one teacher during the 1896–97 term. A townsite reportedly was surveyed about 1900, but Dove was not developed further. Its school enrolled eighty-eight students during the 1905–06 term. A 1936 map shows a church, several farms, and a nearby school at the site. What was left of the settlement eventually became part of Southlake.

BIBLIOGRAPHY: *Historic Resources Survey: Selected Tarrant County Communities* (Fort Worth: Historic Preservation Council for Tarrant County, 1990).
Brian Hart

DOVE CREEK (King County). Dove Creek is formed by the joining of the West and East forks of Dove Creek. The West Fork rises twenty miles east of Spur in southeast Dickens County and flows southeast for three miles. The East Fork begins in King County just east of the Dickens county line and flows south for two miles. The confluence of these two branches occurs within a mile east of the county line and five miles west of Haystack Mountain (at 33°26′ N, 100°31′ W). The consolidated creek then winds southeast through ranch and oil lands in southwest King and northwest Stonewall counties for twelve miles. It flows over rolling to steep slopes surfaced by shallow to moderate silt, clayey, and sandy loams, locally stony. The surrounding vegetation includes mesquite and grasses, juniper, and cacti. Numerous salt springs and seeps along the creek have produced salt flats in the area. Dove Creek empties into Salt Croton Creek in northwest Stonewall County (at 33°23′ N, 100°26′ W).

____ (Schleicher County). Dove Creek rises thirteen miles northwest of Eldorado in western Schleicher County (at 30°56′ N, 100°48′ W) and runs northeast for thirty-four miles through Irion County to its mouth on Spring Creek, three miles southeast of Tankersley in Tom

Green County (at 31°20′ N, 100°36′ W). It traverses flat to rolling terrain with local shallow depressions, surfaced by clay and sandy loams that support water-tolerant hardwoods, conifers, and grasses.

DOVE CREEK, BATTLE OF. In the controversial battle of Dove Creek on January 8, 1865, about 160 Confederates and 325 state militiamen attacked a large encampment of migrating Kickapoo Indians some twenty miles southwest of the site of present San Angelo. The Texans were routed after a desperate fight. On December 9, 1864, Capt. N. M. Gillintine (Gillentine) and a militia scouting party of twenty-three, under command of the Second Frontier District, discovered an abandoned Indian camp. Gillintine reported that it had ninety-two wigwam sites and was located about thirty miles up the Clear Fork of the Brazos River from the ruins of old Fort Phantom Hill. A militia force of about 325 men from Bosque, Comanche, Coryell, Erath, and Johnson counties gathered under Capt. S. S. Totten (Totton). State Confederate troops of the Frontier Battalion were dispatched under Capt. Henry Fossett.

From the beginning the two forces neglected to cooperate fully or agree upon a unified command. After waiting two days at Fort Chadbourne for a rendezvous that never took place, Fossett impatiently set out on January 3 with 161 men and followed a broad trail to the North Concho River and beyond. Four days later his scouts found the Indians, whom they assumed to be hostile Comanches or Kiowas, encamped in timber along Dove Creek. As Fossett prepared to strike, Totten's delayed militia arrived early in the morning of January 8. Some historians have argued that by then the leader should have realized that the Indians were peaceful. Operating on the frontier assumption that all Indians were dangerous, however, the two commanders hastily formed a battle plan that was afterward criticized as inadequate and based on poor reconnaissance. The militia, on horses weary from a forced march, were to dismount and wade the creek for a frontal attack from the north. The Confederate troops were to circle southwestward, capture the grazing herd of horses, and attack from the lower side, thus cutting off an Indian retreat.

The attack went badly. Fossett later estimated the Indian fighting force at between 400 and 600. Totten said 600 and charged that Union jayhawkers were among them. The Indians' position in a heavy thicket was superior, for it gave the well-armed defenders cover, high ground, and a good field of fire. The militiamen were slowed by the creek, heavy briars, and brush. Participant I. D. Ferguson later recounted the fatal wounding of three officers, including Gillintine, and sixteen enlisted men in the opening minutes. The militia was soon routed and out of the battle.

Meanwhile, Fossett's mounted force quickly captured the Indian horses. He dispatched seventy-five troops under Lt. J. A. Brooks to hit the camp from the south, but they were repulsed by heavy fire that cost them twelve horses. The Confederate troops took positions in the timber and continued the fight; they were caught in a crossfire and separated into three groups as the Indians closed in under cover. An Indian counterattack early in the afternoon was repulsed, and the battle continued until almost dark before ending in disorder and confusion. The Indians recaptured their horses and inflicted additional casualties on the Confederates retreating toward Totten's militia, which was tending to the wounded three miles away on Spring Creek. The battered veterans spent a miserable night, drenched by chilling rain that turned to heavy snow. They remained the next day, cold and hungry, forced to eat some of the horses in order to survive. A casualty count showed twenty-two dead and nineteen wounded. An exact number was never known because many militiamen departed without leave.

Indian casualties were even less certain. Totten said they numbered more than a hundred. Fossett gave a body count of twenty-three. The Indians, after crossing the Rio Grande near Eagle Pass, said they had lost twelve in the fight and two more who died after arrival in Mexico.

Carrying their wounded on crude litters strapped between pairs of horses, the Texans retreated eastward on January 11, after retrieving their dead. They found shelter and food at John S. Chisum's[qv] ranch near the confluence of the Concho and the Colorado rivers.

The Kickapoos had been on their way to Mexico to escape the dissension and violence of the Civil War.[qv] The battle embittered this peaceful tribe and led to vengeful border raiding from the sanctuary given them by the Mexican government near Santa Rosa, Coahuila. White settlers along the Rio Grande paid heavily for the misjudgments that led to the Texans' defeat on Dove Creek. Col. Ranald S. Mackenzie[qv] finally led 377 men of the Fourth United States Cavalry[qv] from Fort Clark on a punitive expedition across the Rio Grande in May 1873. Hostilities declined thereafter.

BIBLIOGRAPHY: William C. Pool, "The Battle of Dove Creek," *Southwestern Historical Quarterly* 53 (April 1950). Ernest Wallace, *Ranald S. Mackenzie on the Texas Frontier* (Lubbock: West Texas Museum Association, 1964).
Elmer Kelton

DOVE MOUNTAIN. Dove Mountain is twenty miles northeast of the Persimmon Gap Ranger Station in east central Brewster County (at 29°45′ N, 102°51′ W). With an elevation of 3,792 feet above sea level, it rises 1,000 feet above Dove Mountain Road, three miles north. Its shallow, stony soils support scrub brush and grasses.

DOVER, TEXAS. Dover, northwest of Dawson in southwestern Navarro County, was established before 1900. By the early 1900s a two-teacher school was in operation there, and in 1906 it had an enrollment of seventy-nine. At its height before World War I[qv] the community had a church, the school, and a number of houses. The school was later consolidated with that of Dawson. By the mid-1930s Dover no longer appeared on highway maps.
Christopher Long

DOW, JAMES LORENZO (1878–1958). James Lorenzo Dow, pioneer journalist, was born on September 25, 1878, near Evant in Hamilton County, Texas, the third of five children of James and Margarete Goodall (Nisbet) Dow. His father, a retired sea captain, had immigrated to Texas from Scotland in 1871 and settled initially near McKinney. The family moved to Lampasas, then to Gail in Borden County, where Dow completed his elementary school education. He attended high school in Colorado City and there learned the printer's trade by working after hours and on weekends as an apprentice to his brother-in-law, C. W. Simpson, editor of the *Colorado Spokesman*. After graduating in 1897 he worked for the Stockman Publishing Company, which put out the *West Texas Stockman*, the first official mouthpiece of the Cattle Raisers' Association of Texas (*see* TEXAS AND SOUTHWESTERN CATTLE RAISERS ASSOCIATION). About 1900 Dow returned to Gail and edited his first newspaper, the *Borden Citizen*. On September 22, 1901, he married Leitha Smith, daughter of Charles (Scalper) Smith, an area surveyor and bounty hunter. Soon afterward, Dow sold the *Citizen* and moved with his bride back to Colorado City, but within four months Leitha died and was buried in the cemetery at Gail.

Dow conducted a weekly paper and commercial printing operation, initially with a partner, in Colorado City for a few years and then moved to Sweetwater, where he purchased the *Weekly Review*. After a fire destroyed that paper's plant, he worked as a journeyman printer for the papers in Merkel, Brownwood, and Stephenville. On May 1, 1904, he married Lila Dorn in Colorado City; they had three sons and a daughter.

With his savings Dow moved to Lubbock, then a tiny frontier settlement, in December 1905 and became foreman and associate editor of its weekly *Avalanche*. In 1909 he bought out the company and sought to increase the paper's size and circulation. By 1921 he had developed the Lubbock *Avalanche* from a one-man, five-column, four-page, hand-set weekly to a daily with modern, updated machinery and a staff of twenty. As editor of the *Avalanche,* Dow became an original booster of South Plains agriculture and of Lubbock as the area's industrial and distribution center. His advertisements served to bring in more railroad connections and attract more farmers and businessmen. He played in Lubbock's first brass band, served on the Lubbock school board, and was instrumental in organizing the annual Panhandle–South Plains Fair, one of the largest in the Southwest. He also served the Lubbock First Methodist Church as a board member and Sunday school superintendent. One of his last crusades was to secure the location of Texas Technological College (now Texas Tech University) in Lubbock in 1925. The town of Lorenzo in Crosby County was named for him.

In 1926 Dow sold the Lubbock *Avalanche* to a competing firm, the *Evening Journal,* which subsequently published it as the Lubbock *Avalanche-Journal.*qv Dow owned the Wink *Times-Telegram* until 1936 and then published the *Winkler County News* in Kermit before retiring from journalism in 1943. From 1943 to 1946 he served as manager of the Phillips-Dupre Hospital in Levelland. Afterward he moved to Seminole in Gaines County, where his father had moved in 1904. In Seminole, Dow managed the Gaines County Clinic and Hospital until his death, in 1958. He was buried in the City of Lubbock Cemetery.

BIBLIOGRAPHY: *Borden County, Texas: The First One Hundred Years* (Gail, Texas: Borden County Historical Commission, 1976). Gaines County Historical Survey Committee, *The Gaines County Story,* ed. Margaret Coward (Seagraves, Texas: Pioneer, 1974). Lubbock *Avalanche-Journal,* June 15, 1967. H. Allen Anderson

DOWDY CREEK. Dowdy Creek rises in a stock tank on land originally granted to Richard Dowdy four miles southeast of Weimar in western Colorado County (at 29°39′ N, 96°41′ W) and runs southeast for 4½ miles, passing through the Oak Grove community before reaching its mouth on Miller Creek (at 29°37′ N, 96°38′ W). It traverses a densely wooded area with deep, fine sandy loam soils, which, when cleared, are suitable for both pasture and agriculture. The stream skirts the northern edge of the Hamel oilfield. The generally flat land in the area is used primarily for oil production, unimproved pasture, and wildlife habitat.

DOWELL, BENJAMIN SHACKLETT (1818–1880). Benjamin Shacklett (Uncle Ben) Dowell, pioneer settler and first mayor of El Paso, son of James Board and Barbara (Shacklett) Dowell, was born in Meade County, Kentucky, on November 30, 1818. He served with Company G, First Regiment, Kentucky Cavalry, in the Mexican Warqv (1846–47), during which he was taken prisoner at La Encarnación. About 1850 he moved from Kentucky to Texas and was employed by Juan María Ponce De León,qv whose ranch occupied the site of present downtown El Paso. After a brief sojourn in Los Angeles (1854) he returned to El Paso, where his business interests came to include a saloon, general store, post office, stagecoach stand, billiard parlor, and hotel in the downtown area, plus an extensive ranch on the Rio Grande above the town.

After the incorporation of El Paso by the legislature in 1873, Dowell was elected the first mayor, in which office he supervised the water supply from the acequias fed by the Rio Grande and established a taxation system. After he lost his bid for reelection in 1875, the town government was dormant until 1880, when he was elected an alderman among a new group of officials. He also served as the town's third postmaster (1857–60) and as El Paso county commissioner (1878–80). He is reputed to have been the first El Pasoan to fly a Confederate flag. He served with the Confederate Army as a captain at San Antonio and Galveston and tried unsuccessfully to run the Union blockade with a shipment of cotton.

Dowell was among pioneer Masons of far West Texas; he served as worshipful master of El Paso Lodge No. 130 (1868–69) and as district deputy grand master for an area reaching to the Big Bend (1870–80). He was married in 1838 to a Kentucky neighbor, Melvina Stith, from whom he was divorced before moving to Texas. In El Paso County, about 1852, he married Juana Márquez, daughter of a Tigua Indian cacique of Ysleta. They had five children. Their daughter, Mary, who was married to Warner Phillips, became an early teacher in El Paso, and Dowell School, opened in 1959, was named in honor of her and her father. Dowell died at his ranch on November 8, 1880. His widow died in 1891.

BIBLIOGRAPHY: Nancy Hamilton, *Ben Dowell, El Paso's First Mayor* (El Paso: Texas Western Press, 1976). Nancy Hamilton

DOWELL, GREENSVILLE S. (1822–1881). Greensville S. Dowell, surgeon, teacher, and editor, son of James and Frances (Dalton) Dowell, was born in Albemarle County, Virginia, on September 22, 1822. The family moved to Panola County, Mississippi, in 1837. Before studying at the medical department of the University of Louisville in 1845–46, Dowell lived and studied medicine with his physician

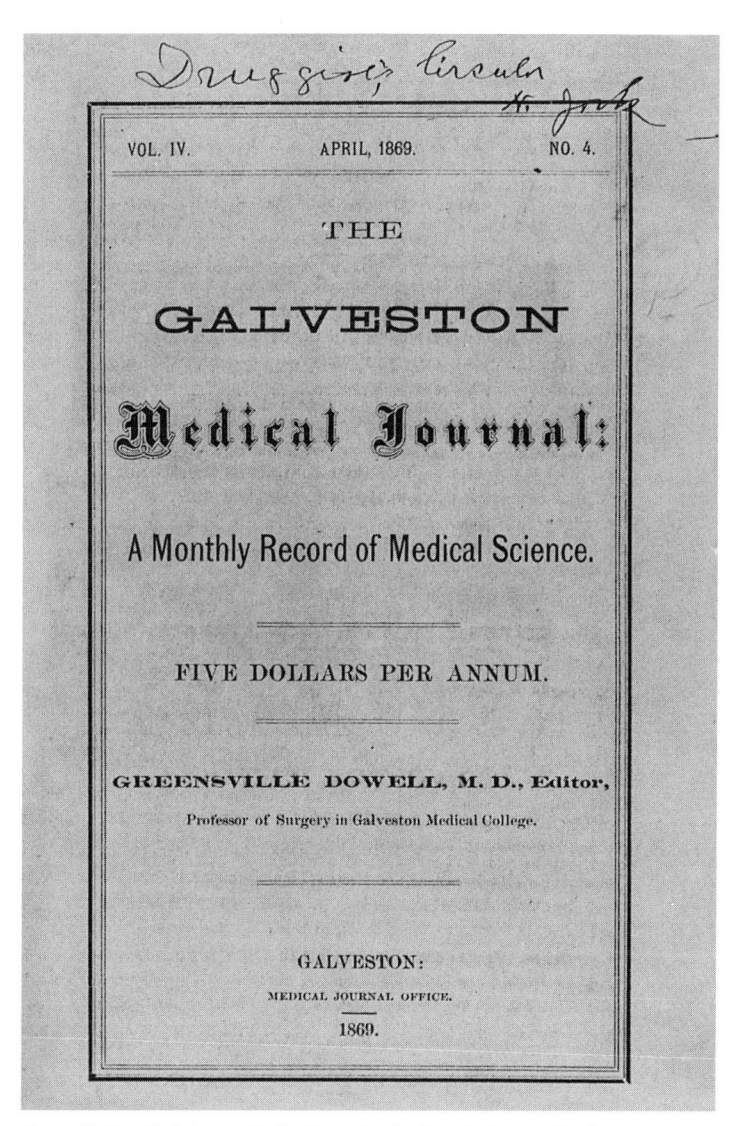

Greensville Dowell's Galveston Medical Journal *4 (April 1869). Courtesy Moody Medical Library, University of Texas Medical Branch at Galveston. Dowell's journal, which premiered in January 1866, was the first medical periodical published in Texas.*

brother, Alep Dowell, in Raleigh, Tennessee. He enrolled in Jefferson Medical College in Philadelphia and received his M.D. degree in 1847. He then set up practice in Como, Mississippi, where he lived until 1852. After a short practice in Memphis, Tennessee, he moved to Texas in September 1853 and settled in Sandy Point, Brazoria County. During the Civil War^{qv} he served as a surgeon with the Confederate States Army in Galveston.

On July 17, 1865, Dowell and a group of local physicians formed the Galveston Medical Society. In November Galveston Medical College, the first medical school in Texas, was organized by the trustees of Soule University,^{qv} and Dowell was appointed professor of anatomy. The same year Dowell began making plans to publish the first medical periodical in Texas, the *Galveston Medical Journal*, which began publication in January 1866.

In 1867 Dowell was appointed professor of surgery, and later that year he was elected dean of the college. When Soule University closed Galveston Medical College and moved to Louisiana in 1873, Dowell and J. M. Callaway founded Texas Medical College^{qv} and Hospital, where Dowell continued to teach surgery until his death.

In addition to his teaching and editing responsibilities, he published two books and about fifty articles. The surgical operation he devised for the cure of hernia by means of subcutaneous stitches was well known among his contemporaries; Dowell described the procedure in his monograph, *A Treatise on Hernia* (1876). He also designed several surgical instruments, including needles for repairing hernia and ligating varicose veins, and several kinds of forceps and specula. He was regarded as an authority on yellow fever, and he often traveled to epidemic-stricken cities to treat victims. His *Yellow Fever and Malarial Diseases* (1876) includes an account of his own experiences as well as reports written by other Texas physicians.

Dowell was a member of the American Medical Association, the Texas State Medical Association (*see* TEXAS MEDICAL ASSOCIATION), and the Galveston Medical Society; he was an honorary member of the Boston Gynecological Society and the New York State Medical Society. He married Sarah Zalinda White in 1849 at Como, Mississippi, and they had three children. In 1868, after his first wife's death, Dowell married Laura Baker Hutchinson of Galveston. He died in Galveston on June 9, 1881, and is buried in Evergreen Cemetery.

BIBLIOGRAPHY: Inci A. Bowman, "Beginnings of Medical Journalism in Texas," *Texas Medicine* 82 (February 1986). Greensville Dowell, *Yellow Fever and Malarial Diseases . . . in Texas* (Philadelphia: Medical Publications, 1876). *Texas Medical and Surgical Record,* July 1881.

Inci A. Bowman

DOWELL, TEXAS. Dowell, four miles northeast of Rotan in northern Fisher County, was established around 1885 and named for the Dowell family, early settlers in the area. E. H. Dowell moved there from Nebraska in 1886, opened a store in his home, and became postmaster when the post office opened in 1892. In 1896 the community reported a Baptist church and a population of eight, including J. F. Dowell, grocer. Most businesses moved to Rotan in 1907 when the railroad came to that town. Dowell's post office was also closed that year. The first school in Dowell was established before 1900 but was demolished before 1910; a new building was constructed and later replaced by a brick building that was used until students were transferred to Rotan when the schools were combined in 1946–47. After that time Dowell was abandoned. In the early 1980s the county highway map showed a cemetery at Dowell and the Highland Home Church a mile south.

BIBLIOGRAPHY: Fisher County Historical Commission, *History of Fisher County, Texas* (Rotan, Texas: Shelton, 1983). E. L. Yeats and E. H. Shelton, *History of Fisher County,* (n.p.: Feather, 1971).

Jeanne F. Lively

DOWLING, RICHARD WILLIAM (1838–1867). Richard William Dowling, businessman and Civil War^{qv} hero, son of William and Mary Dowling, was born in Tuam, Galway County, Ireland, in 1838. After 1846 the family migrated to the United States and settled in New Orleans. In the early 1850s, after the deaths of his parents, Dick Dowling worked his way to Texas and eventually settled in Houston.

The likeable, red-headed Irishman quickly made a reputation as an enterprising businessman. In October 1857 he opened the Shades, the first of his successful saloons. He probably received financial backing for this enterprise from Benjamin Digby Odlum,^{qv} whose daughter, Elizabeth Ann, Dowling married in November 1857. By 1860 he had sold his interest in the Shades and had purchased the popular Bank of Bacchus near the Harris County Courthouse. Still later he operated the Hudgpeth Bathing Saloon as well as a Galveston-based liquor-importing firm.

With the outbreak of the Civil War^{qv} Dowling joined the Jefferson Davis^{qv} Guards as first lieutenant. Capt. Frederick H. Odlum was commander. During the first part of 1861 Dowling and his associates raided United States Army outposts on the Texas-Mexico border. When the guards were designated Company F of the Third Texas Artillery Battalion in October 1861, Dowling's theater became the upper Texas Gulf Coast. By 1862 the battalion was upgraded to a full regiment, the First Texas Heavy Artillery, under the overall command of Col. J. J. Cook.

Dowling's early Civil War exploits were consistent but not spectacular. On January 1, 1863, he participated in Gen. John B. Magruder's^{qv} recapture of the port of Galveston (*see* GALVESTON, BATTLE OF).

Richard W. (Dick) Dowling. Albumen carte de visite by Harvey R. Marks. Houston, ca. 1865. Courtesy Lawrence T. Jones III Collection, Austin. For this portrait Major Dowling wore his Confederate uniform and the medal he was given for his victory at Sabine Pass on September 8, 1863.

Three weeks later, after the transfer of his company to Sabine Pass, which controlled access to the Sabine River, he earned his first individual praise. As artillery commander aboard the steamer *Josiah A. Bell,* he took part in a naval battle on January 21, 1863, with two United States vessels. In a two-hour engagement the Confederate forces achieved a victory, in part because of Dowling's accuracy with the eight-inch Columbiad gun, which he commanded. Not only was he singled out for making some of the "prettiest shots" but also for saving the *Bell's* magazine from flooding.

Throughout the spring and summer of 1863 Odlum, Dowling, and the guards manned defensive positions at Sabine Pass, including Fort Griffin, a nondescript post on the west side of the pass that controlled both the Texas and Louisiana channels of the river. By August 1863 Odlum was in charge of forces at nearby Sabine City, and Dowling commanded Company F, which consisted of forty-seven men armed with six cannons, at Fort Griffin. On September 8, 1863, the United States forces attacked the area in what became known as the battle of Sabine Pass.qv Dowling directed such intense and accurate fire from his guns that two of the United States gunboats, the *Clifton* and the *Sachem,*qqv were disabled, and the remaining United States vessels withdrew. As a result of federal ineptitude and Dowling's leadership, Dowling and his men captured two ships and 350 prisoners and routed the invasion without a single casualty.

The battle at Sabine Pass was the pinnacle of Dowling's career. During the remainder of the war he was a recruiting officer for the Confederacy, until his discharge with the rank of major in 1865. He returned to Houston, managed the businesses he had owned before the war, and acquired new businesses, including real estate, oil and gas leases, and an interest in a steamboat. His financial successes appeared to ensure a bright future, but he became ill with yellow fever and died on September 23, 1867. He was survived by his wife, a daughter, and a son and was buried in St. Vincent's Cemetery, Houston.

BIBLIOGRAPHY: Alwyn Barr, "Sabine Pass, September 1863," *Texas Military History* 2 (February 1962). Seymour V. Connor et al., *Battles of Texas* (Waco: Texian Press, 1967; 3d ed. 1980). Andrew Forest Muir, "Dick Dowling and the Battle of Sabine Pass," *Civil War History* 4 (December 1958). *Official Records of the Union and Confederate Navies* (Washington: Department of the Navy, 1894–1927). Frank X. Tolbert, *Dick Dowling at Sabine Pass* (New York: McGraw-Hill, 1962). James R. Ward, "Richard W. 'Dick' Dowling," in *Ten Texans in Gray,* ed. W. C. Nunn (Hillsboro, Texas: Hill Junior College Press, 1968).

James R. Ward

DOWNER, JAMES WALKER (1864–1932). James Walker Downer, classical scholar, was born in Orange County, Virginia, on June 23, 1864, the son of William Walker and Lucy Mary (Reynolds) Downer. He attended the University of Virginia, where he received the B.A. degree in 1895 and the M.A. in 1897. He taught for a year in high school in Charlottesville and was a teacher of Latin in Richmond College in 1898–99. After serving a year as principal of the high school at Clifton Forge, Virginia, and three years as teacher in the Marion (Alabama) Military Institute, Downer won a fellowship to the University of Pennsylvania, where he received his Ph.D. in Latin in 1905. For three years he taught in the Friends Central School in Philadelphia. In 1908 he moved to Texas to become head of the Latin department at Baylor University. He married Corneille Willingham of Richmond, Virginia, on December 28, 1909. Downer was the author of two works: *Metaphors and Word-Plays in Petronius* (1913), which is still a standard work in Petronian scholarship, and *A Plea for Latin* (1916). He was a Democrat and Baptist. From 1922 until his death he served as chairman of the graduate council of Baylor University. He died in Waco on March 19, 1932.

BIBLIOGRAPHY: *Baylor Daily Lariat,* March 22, 29, 1932. *Who Was Who in America,* Vol. 2.

J. D. Bragg

DOWNIE DRAW. Downie Draw, also called Downie Creek, a valley with an intermittent stream, rises a mile west of the Pecos county line in the low hills of northeastern Brewster County (at 30°14′ N, 102°51′ W) and runs east for fifty-nine miles, crossing the southwestern corner of Pecos County and meandering along the Pecos-Terrell county line, before reaching its mouth on Meyers Canyon, just north of State Highway 349 in central Terrell County (at 30°10′ N, 102°04′ W). Downie Draw is met by Javelina Draw 1½ miles east of Silver Lake in southwestern Pecos County and in western Terrell County is met by three other tributaries. Pyle Draw enters Downie on the southwestern edge of Two Top Mountain, and Fortyone Draw and Baker Draw meet Downie on the southern edge of the Wildcat Mountains. Downie Draw sharply dissects massive limestone that underlies flat to gently sloping terrain, forming a rugged and winding valley. Wash deposits of sand, gravel, and mud cover the floor of the canyon. Soils in the area are generally dark, calcareous stony clays and clay loams that support scrub brush, oaks, junipers, grasses, and mesquites. The draw was named for Charles A. Downie, who drove his sheep from Austin through San Antonio to the Trans-Pecos region, where he established a ranch in 1881. He was the first rancher to settle in the isolated Downie Draw area and was there at least a year before the railroad laid tracks through the area. More than twenty years earlier, on July 3, 1860, Lt. William H. Echols, with twenty soldiers and officers of the First Infantry, camped near the draw during their camel expedition to map the terrain and its waterholes for the United States Army.

BIBLIOGRAPHY: Terrell County Heritage Commission, *Terrell County, Texas* (San Angelo: Anchor, 1978).

DOWNING, TEXAS. Downing, on State Highway 16 ten miles northeast of Comanche in northern Comanche County, was founded in the early 1880s. At a meeting to name the town and apply for a post office Walter Henry Loudermilk suggested that the town be called Dawning because of the beautiful sunrise. The post office department in Washington made an error in the spelling, and the town was named Downing. William C. Davis was appointed the first postmaster on November 26, 1888. On May 11, 1911, the post office was consolidated with that of Comanche. The population of Downing was reported as 103 in 1940; subsequently, like other rural towns in the state, it began to decline. In 1980 and 1990 twenty residents remained in the community.

BIBLIOGRAPHY: Comanche County Bicentennial Committee, *Patchwork of Memories: Historical Sketches of Comanche County, Texas* (Brownwood, Texas: Banner Printing, 1976).

Tracey L. Compton

DOWNS, KARL EVERETTE (1912–1948). Karl E. Downs, black minister and college president, was born on June 2, 1912, in Abilene, the son of John Wesley and Lucretia (Hollis) Downs. He attended Moore High School in Waco and graduated in 1929. He received his A.B. degree from Samuel Huston College (now Huston-Tillotson College) in Austin in 1933, a B.D. degree from Gammon Theological Seminary in Atlanta, Georgia, in 1936, and a masters of sacred theology from Boston University in 1937. Downs, like his father, became a Methodist minister. After attending Boston University he traveled extensively for the Methodist Board of Foreign Missions recruiting college youth.

From about 1939 to 1943 he served as pastor of Scott Methodist Church in Pasadena, California. He established community services that gained widespread attention. Many of his efforts were designed to help children—the organization of a nursery, the building of a church recreational yard, and the provision of toys to poor children. Downs also helped organize the Interracial Fellowship Church, which met monthly and provided a forum for prominent speakers both black and white.

In 1943 he was named president of Samuel Huston College. Though he was only twenty-nine at the time, his leadership proved to be beneficial for the institution. In his 4½-year tenure enrollment increased from 174 to more than 600. The college's annual budget increased each year; several new buildings were added.

Downs published a number of religious articles and a book, *Meet the Negro* (1943). He was a member of Alpha Phi Alpha, the American Sociological Society, the National Association of College Presidents, and the National Association for the Advancement of Colored People.qv He married Marion Carroll Jackson, and they had one daughter. In 1945 he received an honorary doctor of divinity degree from Gammon Theological Seminary. At the time of his death he was a Ph.D. candidate at the University of Southern California. Downs died on February 26, 1948, in Austin, and was buried in Evergreen Cemetery.

BIBLIOGRAPHY: Vertical Files, Barker Texas History Center, University of Texas at Austin.
Ada C. Anderson

DOWNSVILLE, TEXAS. Downsville is on Farm Road 434 eight miles southeast of downtown Waco in southeastern McLennan County. William Woods Downs owned the land in the 1850s and used slaves to work it; after the Civil Warqv he gave each family a house and some adjacent land. Former slaves established the Mount Pleasant Missionary Baptist Church there in 1866. When the San Antonio and Aransas Pass Railway laid its track from Waco to Lott in the late 1880s, it passed through this community, where a post office called Price was established in April 1890 with William P. Sparks as postmaster. Later that year the community was renamed Downsville, in honor of Downs and his son, John Wesley. By 1892 Downsville had three flour mills, a general store, two grocery stores, and 100 residents. In 1896 the community had a one-teacher school with seventy-three white students. County school records also indicate the existence in the area of a school called Mount Pleasant, which had one teacher and 126 black students; although maps did not show it, it may have been located in Downsville and named after the church. The population of Downsville was estimated at 134 from 1900 to the late 1940s. The post office was discontinued in 1907, and mail for the community was sent to Waco. The number of residents fell to fifty by 1949 and to thirty-five by 1964. The Southern Pacific abandoned the track between Waco and Rosebud in 1967, thus depriving Downsville of rail service. In the 1980s county highway maps showed three churches, two cemeteries, and two or three businesses at the site. The population was still thirty-five in 1990.

BIBLIOGRAPHY: Dayton Kelley, ed., *The Handbook of Waco and McLennan County, Texas* (Waco: Texian, 1972). William Robert Poage, *McLennan County Before 1980* (Waco: Texian, 1981). Vertical File, Texas Collection, Baylor University.
Vivian Elizabeth Smyrl

DOYLE, TEXAS. Doyle, five miles northeast of Groesbeck in east central Limestone County, was known as Shady Grove when the Houston and Texas Central Railway established the town in 1871; when the post office opened in 1903, it was renamed Doyle, in honor of William Elliott Doyle, a former mayor of Mexia. In 1914 the community had a grocery store and a general store. The post office was discontinued in 1923, and mail for Doyle residents was sent to Groesbeck. County highway maps in the late 1940s showed a church, a business, and a number of residences at the site. Doyle reported a population of ten in 1990.

BIBLIOGRAPHY: John J. Germann and Myron Janzen, *Texas Post Offices by County* (1986). Ray A. Walter, *A History of Limestone County* (Austin: Von Boeckmann–Jones, 1959).
Vivian Elizabeth Smyrl

DOZIER, OTIS MARION (1904–1987). Otis Dozier, painter, printmaker, and teacher who first became prominent as a member of the Dallas Nine,qv a group of regionalist artists, was born on March 27, 1904, in Forney, Texas, one of four children of James M. and Valta (Farmer) Dozier. He was raised on a farm in nearby Mesquite and developed a love for wildlife and nature, which later became the primary subject matter of his art. In the early 1920s his family moved to Dallas, where Dozier received his earliest art training from Vivian Aunspaugh, Frank Reaugh,qqv and Cora Edge.

During the 1930s Dozier became involved with the circle of regionalist artists then active in Dallas. He was a charter member of the Dallas Artists League,qv exhibited his work in the Dallas Allied Arts exhibitions, and from 1936 to 1938 taught at the Dallas School of Creative Arts. During this period, while studying works by Matisse, Picasso, Léger, Derain, and other European artists reproduced in back issues of *Dial*, Dozier developed a style characterized by strong forms and brilliant colors. By the mid-1930s he had tightened up his brushwork and muted his palette to the earthy grays, beiges, greens, and browns favored by regionalist artists. Several of his major works from this era focused on the plight of farmers dispossessed by the Great Depression.qv In *Annual Move* (1936), for example, a family loads up the car with cherished possessions, ready to move on through the barren brown landscape; in *Grasshopper and Farmer* (1937), a baleful, outsized grasshopper pins a farmer to the ground. Dozier's continued interest in international trends was manifested in such works as *Grasshopper and Farmer and Jackrabbits* (1935), in which the exaggerated size of insects and animals suggests a Surrealist influence, and *Still Life With Striped Gourd* (1935), in which several conflicting perspective systems evidence the influence of Cubism on his work.

Local critics praised Dozier's work, and he won prizes in several Allied Arts exhibitions (1932, 1935, 1947) and Texas General exhibitions (1946, 1947). He executed murals at Forest Avenue High School and the Agricultural and Mechanical College of Texas (later Texas A&M University) and, under the auspices of the Public Works of Art Project, painted murals for post offices in Giddings (1937), Arlington (1941), and Fredericksburg (1942). He began establishing a national profile during the early 1930s, when he exhibited his work at the International Watercolor Exhibition, San Francisco (1932); the Museum of Modern Art, New York (1933); and the First National Exhibition, Rockefeller Center, New York (1936).

In the summer of 1938 Dozier won a scholarship to the Colorado Springs Fine Arts Center, where he studied with Boardman Robinson. The following year he became Robinson's assistant, a position he held until 1945. While in Colorado Dozier made hundreds of journeys into the Rocky Mountains and produced more than 3,000 sketches of mountains and ghost towns. Under Robinson's influence he developed a more spontaneous, fluid style, using implements such as paper dipped in ink, a burnt stick from a camp fire, or his thumb. He also developed expertise in the lithographic medium and participated in every circuit of the Lone Star Printmakers.

In 1945 Dozier returned to Dallas, where he taught life drawing at Southern Methodist University until 1948 and painting and drawing at the Dallas Museum of Fine Arts (now the Dallas Museum of Artqv) school until 1970. His work was featured in solo exhibitions at the Dallas Museum of Fine Arts (1944), the University of Texas, Austin (1944), and M. Knoedler and Company, New York City (1945), among others. A 1956 Dozier retrospective at the Dallas Museum of Fine Arts garnered a positive review of his work in the December 17, 1956, issue of *Time* magazine. He continued to exhibit his work nationally at such venues as the Whitney Museum of American Art (1946) and the Metropolitan Museum of Art (1951), both in New York City.

During the latter part of his career Dozier developed a semi-abstract style, using looser brushwork and more brilliant colors than he had during the Regionalist era. Although he moved away from the

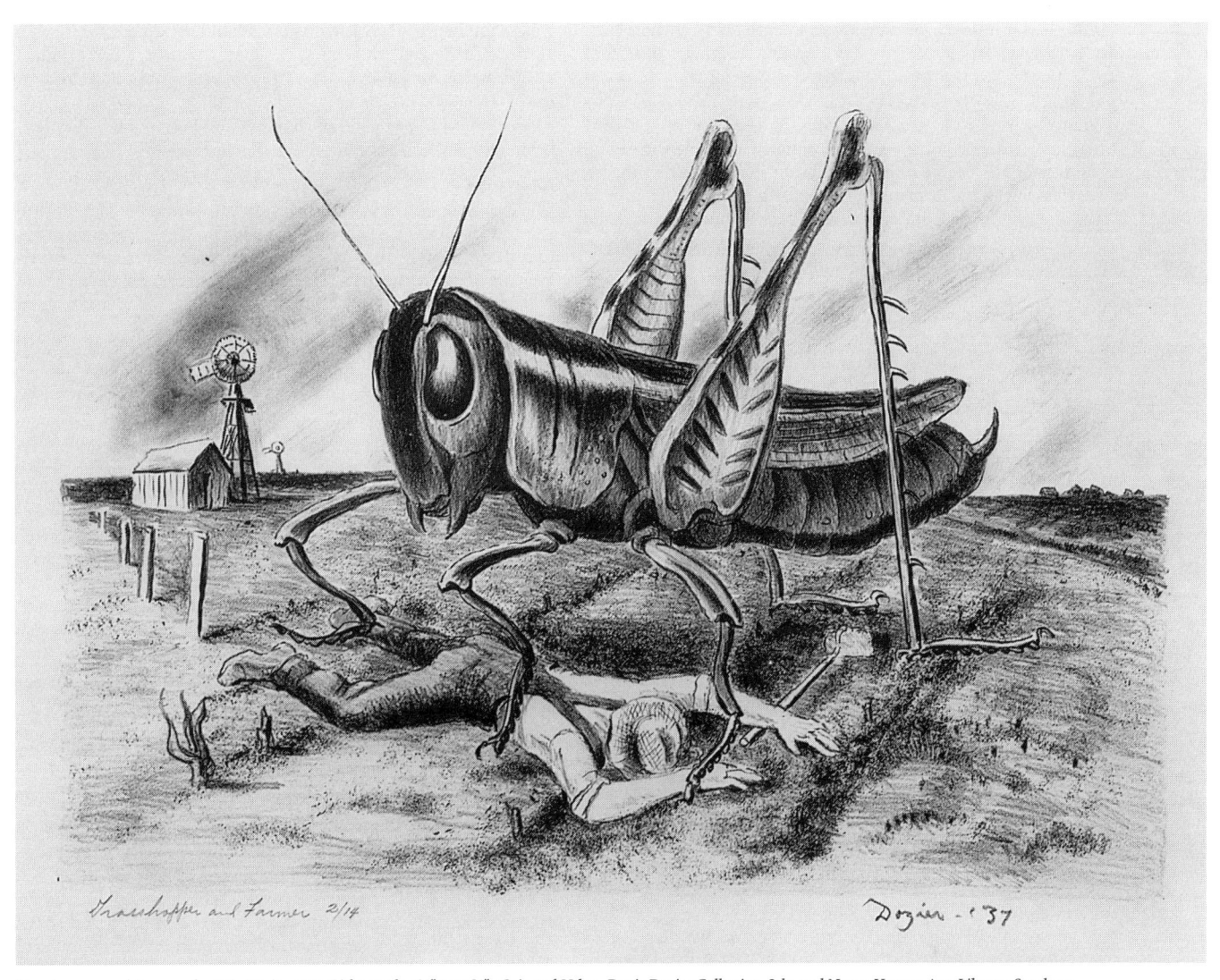

Grasshopper and Farmer, by Otis Dozier, 1937. Lithograph. 9⅝″ × 12⅞″. Otis and Velma Davis Dozier Collection, Jake and Nancy Hamon Arts Library, Southern Methodist University, Dallas, Texas.

anecdotal subject matter of his 1930s work, he continued to use natural forms as a source of inspiration, noting that "you've got to start from where you are and hope to get to the universal." He found fresh material for his work on sketching trips to the Big Bend and Gulf Coast areas of Texas, the swamps and bayous of Louisiana, and the Four Corners area of New Mexico, Arizona, Utah, and Colorado. During the 1950s and early 1960s he traveled to Italy, Spain, Turkey, India, Ceylon, Thailand, Japan, and Mexico. Examples of his later work were published in *Otis Dozier: A Portfolio of Six Paintings* (1960) and *Pecos to Rio Grande: Interpretations of Far West Texas by Eighteen Artists* (1983).

Dozier married Velma Davis, a jeweler and ceramist, in 1940. Their contributions to Dallas's cultural life were honored in the 1974 exhibition produced by the Dallas Museum of Fine Arts, A Salute to the Doziers of Dallas. Dozier died of heart failure on July 28, 1987, and was buried at Restland Memorial Park. His work is in the permanent collections of the Modern Art Museum of Fort Worth;qv the Museum of Fine Arts, Houston;qv the Witte Museum and the Marion Koogler McNay Art Museum,qqv both in San Antonio; the Archer M. Huntington Art Galleryqv at the University of Texas at Austin; the Longview Museum and Art Center; the Wichita Falls Museum and Art Center;qv the Panhandle-Plains Museumqv in Canyon; the Dallas Museum of Art; and Southern Methodist University, Dallas. He is also represented in the collections of the Colorado Springs Fine Arts Center; the Denver Art Museum; the Newark Museum, New Jersey; the Wadsworth Atheneum in Hartford, Connecticut; the Whitney Museum of American Art; and the Metropolitan Museum of Art.

BIBLIOGRAPHY: Jerry Bywaters, "Otis Dozier: Growth and Maturity of a Texas Artist," *Southwest Review* 42 (Winter 1957). Dallas *Times Herald,* July 29, 1987. Otis and Velma Davis Dozier Collection, Jerry Bywaters Special Collections Wing, Hamon Arts Library, Southern Methodist University. Rick Stewart, *Lone Star Regionalism* (Austin: Texas Monthly Press, 1985).
Kendall Curlee

DOZIER, VELMA DAVIS (1901–1988). Velma Davis Dozier, cofounder of the Dallas School of Creative Arts and the Craft Guild of Dallas and jeweler known for abstract designs in silver and gold, was born near Waco on April 17, 1901, the eldest of five children of Robert Edward and Elizabeth Eleanor (Harbour) Davis. She studied painting with Vivian L. Aunspaughqv in Dallas in 1920 and 1926 and from 1926 to 1927 attended Southern Methodist University. She then studied painting and printmaking at Texas State College for Women in Denton (later Texas Woman's University), earning a bachelor of science degree in 1932. The next year Davis attended Columbia University in New York City, where she was introduced to jewelrymaking. Her visits to museums in New York City stimulated a love for primitive art that became a major influence on her craft. By the time she earned her master of arts degree from Columbia in 1933, Davis had chosen jewelrymaking as her primary artistic medium. Upon her return to Dallas, she cofounded, with silversmith Esther Webb Houseman, the Dallas School of Creative Arts, at that time the only metalsmithing shop in the country outside of New York City. Davis taught metalsmithing at the school until it closed in 1940. One of the school's other teachers, painter Otis M. Dozier,qv became her husband in 1940. After their marriage in Dallas they moved to Colorado, where she attended the Colorado Springs Fine Arts Center, studying life drawing with Boardman Robinson and pottery with Eric Helman. The Doziers returned to Dallas in 1945. There she resumed her role as a leader in the art community, assisting in the organization of the Craft Guild of Dallas in 1948, and in 1956 becoming a charter member of Texas Designer Craftsmen. In 1950 Dozier participated in the National Design Exhibition at Texas Western College in El Paso, the first of many public exhibitions of her work. In the following years she traveled extensively in Mexico and visited Italy, Spain, Turkey, India, Ceylon, Thailand, and Japan.

Dozier's jewelry tended to be simple in effect, though each piece typically rewarded close examination with subtle flourishes such as textural variations, unexpected combinations of metals and beads, or an innovative clasp. Throughout her career she continued to learn new skills, mastering techniques such as casting, soldering, forging, riveting, hinging, fusing, granulation, tube drawing, enameling, stone cutting and setting, and patinating. She frequently combined several techniques in a single piece. Dozier exhibited a trend-setting interest in ethnic materials, using objects found on her travels for pieces, such as a copper and silver necklace set with a pre-Columbian ceramic head (1933) and a necklace with Cambodian burial beads (1964). Natural forms and materials were also an important source of inspiration. She preferred working with gold and after 1958 rarely used silver in her pieces. She won awards for work exhibited in crafts exhibitions at the Dallas Museum of Art;qv the Minnesota Museum of Art in St. Paul, Minnesota; the Everhart Museum in Scranton, Pennsylvania; and the Wichita Art Association in Wichita, Kansas, among others. Her work was featured with that of her husband in several dual exhibitions, notably A Salute to the Doziers of Dallas, mounted by the Dallas Museum of Art in 1974. Velma Davis Dozier died in Dallas on December 1, 1988, and was buried in Restland Memorial Park there. Examples of her work are in the collections of the Dallas Museum of Art and the Minnesota Museum of Art in St. Paul.

BIBLIOGRAPHY: Dallas *Morning News*, December 3, 1988. Otis and Velma Davis Dozier Collection, Jerry Bywaters Special Collections Wing, Hamon Arts Library, Southern Methodist University. *A Salute to the Doziers of Dallas* (Exhibition Catalogue, Dallas Museum of Fine Arts, 1974). Vertical Files, Barker Texas History Center, University of Texas at Austin.   Kendall Curlee

DOZIER, TEXAS. Dozier is near Dozier Creek and the Salt Fork of the Red River in northwestern Collingsworth County. The site was on the Rocking Chair Ranchqv until the ranch ceased to exist. After 1900 the community developed as a result of increased agricultural population in the northern part of the county. Early settlers included the families of C. H. Helvey, who built the first general store in 1904, and J. S. Caperton. Mrs. Caperton became the first postmistress in 1904. In 1909, when the Dozier school district was organized, a small schoolhouse was built a mile south of the present site. The location was changed several times before 1913, when school bonds were issued and a larger building was constructed. This building served Dozier until 1929, when a $6,000 brick building was erected. By 1930 Dozier had three general stores, two gins, a church, a barbershop, a garage, and a population of sixty. By 1940 the population had reached 100. Subsequently, economic change resulted in a population decrease. In 1984 Dozier had two churches, two businesses, and a population of thirty. The population was the same in 1990.

BIBLIOGRAPHY: Clyde Chestnut Brown, A Survey History of Collingsworth County, Texas (M.A. thesis, University of Colorado, 1934). *A History of Collingsworth County and Other Stories* (Wellington, Texas: *Leader* Printing, 1925). Estelle D. Tinkler, "Nobility's Ranche: A History of the Rocking Chair Ranche," *Panhandle-Plains Historical Review* 15 (1942).   H. Allen Anderson

DOZIER CREEK (Collingsworth County). Dozier Creek rises in northern Collingsworth County (at 35°09′ N, 100°21′ W) and runs south for six miles to its mouth on Big Sandy Creek (at 35°01′ N, 100°20′ W), which flows into the Salt Fork of the Red River in the northwestern part of the county. The stream, once part of the Rocking Chair Ranchqv properties, was named for a cowboy who had a line camp on its banks in the late 1880s. It traverses flat to gently rolling terrain surfaced by loose sand that supports scrub brush and grasses.

_____ (Cooke County). Dozier Creek rises seven miles northwest of Gainesville in north central Cooke County (at 33°43′ N, 97°13′ W) and runs southeast for seven miles to its mouth on the Elm Fork of the Trinity River, just west of Gainesville (at 33°38′ N, 97°10′ W). The creek was named for Adam Dozier, an original grantee of the land across which it runs. The local terrain is variable and surfaced by shallow stony clay loams that support oak and juniper trees, chaparral, cacti, and various grasses. The area has served as crop and range land.

DRAINAGE DISTRICTS. Drainage districts were first authorized by the Texas legislature in 1905; modifying laws followed in 1907, 1909, 1911, and 1945. The Canales Act of 1918 is also applicable. Drainage districts, which may be established upon a two-thirds vote of qualified resident property-tax payers in the proposed districts, are organized for the construction of canals, drains, ditches, and levees. The governing board is composed of three commissioners selected by the county commissioners' courtqv for four-year terms, although under certain conditions they may be elected. A civil engineer is appointed by the board. The board has the authority to examine levees, railroad culverts, ditches, and other drainage structures on land in or out of the district and can acquire right-of-ways for the purpose of surveying or drawing plans. The engineer makes a map of the district. The board can call for construction bids and awards contracts to the lowest bidders. Districts availing themselves of the Canales Act have no limitation on taxation or indebtedness; under the drainage acts indebtedness is limited to one-fourth of the assessed valuation of real property. Districts organized under the 1917 conservation amendment may use either the benefits or the ad valorem basis for taxation; other districts use ad valorem only. The county treasurerqv serves as the treasurer of the district, and the county tax assessorqv and collector handles the taxes, although county commissioners can appoint an assessor-collector specifically for the district through election approval. Many drainage districts are found along the Gulf Coast and in the irrigated sections of the state. In 1992, forty-six were registered with the Texas Water Commission.qv See also WATER LAW.

BIBLIOGRAPHY: Gwendolyn Lea Gilchrist, Texas Water Resources Management by Water Districts and River Authorities (M.A. thesis, University of Texas at Austin, 1992). *West's Texas Statutes and Codes*, Vol. 4 (St. Paul, Minnesota: West, 1984).   Dick Smith

DRANE, TEXAS. Drane, on Farm Road 744 six miles west of Corsicana in west central Navarro County, was founded in the early 1880s.

A post office opened there in 1883, and by 1892 the community had a population of forty. At its height in the 1890s Drane had a flour mill and cotton gin, Presbyterian, Methodist, and Baptist churches, and a number of houses. Its estimated population in 1896 was seventy-five. The Drane post office closed in 1906, but by the mid-1930s the community still had two stores, a church, a school, and several houses. After World War II,qv however, its businesses, church, and school all closed, and by the mid-1960s only a few widely scattered houses remained in the area. In 1990 Drane was a dispersed community with a reported population of sixteen.

Christopher Long

DRASCO, TEXAS. Drasco, in north central Runnels County, was once called County Line because of its proximity to the Taylor county line. The community had a post office from 1904 to 1911; its name was composed of letters taken from the various names submitted by residents but not accepted by the post office. The population of Drasco reportedly never exceeded thirty. By 1940 it had a population of fifteen and one store. The 1982 county highway map showed two churches and several businesses at Drasco, which was still listed as a community in 1990.

BIBLIOGRAPHY: Charlsie Poe, *Runnels Is My County* (San Antonio: Naylor, 1970).

William R. Hunt

DRAW, TEXAS. Draw is at the intersection of Farm roads 213 and 1054, seventeen miles southeast of Tahoka in southeastern Lynn County. It took its name from Mooar's Draw, a canyon to the northeast. The community had a school as early as 1904. Draw's population was reported as only twenty-five in 1933, but in 1940 its population was estimated at 100 and continued to be reported at that level through 1960. By 1970 the population had dropped to thirty-five. In 1974 Draw had a cotton gin and a store. In 1980 and 1990 its population was thirty-nine.

BIBLIOGRAPHY: Donald R. Abbe, The History of Lynn County (M.A. thesis, Texas Tech University, 1974).

Donald R. Abbe

DREAMLAND, TEXAS. Dreamland, on U.S. Highway 83 four miles east of Rio Grande City in southeastern Starr County, was an irrigated-farm project in the late 1920s. A local post office was granted in 1944 but replaced by rural delivery from Rio Grande City in 1945. The railroad station at Dreamland was named Santa Cruz. In 1940 the community had a population of ten, and in 1967 it listed two businesses and a cemetery. The settlement was subsequently absorbed by La Puerta and Santa Cruz and in 1991 was no longer identified on maps.

Dick D. Heller, Jr.

DREBEN, SAMUEL (1878–1925). Sam Dreben, a soldier of fortune who early in his career won the name of "Fighting Jew," was born in Poltava, Ukraine, on June 1, 1878. In 1896 he went to England and by January 1899 had immigrated to America, where he enlisted in the United States Army. He fought in the Spanish-American War, the Boxer Rebellion, and the Philippine Insurrection. In 1904 he made an unsuccessful attempt to enlist in the Japanese army to avenge Russian persecution of the Jews. He again enlisted in the United States Army and served three years at Fort Bliss. He fought with the rebels in Honduras, took part in the Madero Revolution in Mexico, and supplied ammunition to Francisco (Pancho) Villa.qv When Villa's forces raided Columbus, New Mexico, however, Dreben, loyal to his adopted country, volunteered to become Gen. John J. Pershing'sqv scout on the punitive expedition against the Villistas. When America entered World War I,qv Dreben, then a resident of El Paso, enlisted in Company A of the 141st Texas Infantry. As first sergeant of that company, he served with great bravery and was awarded the Distinguished Service Cross, the Croix de Guerre with palm, and the Médaille Militaire. General Pershing, who praised Dreben as "the finest soldier and one of the bravest men" he had ever known, chose him to be one of the honor guard at the funeral of the Unknown Soldier. Subsequently, Dreben was a successful insurance salesman until his death in Los Angeles on March 15, 1925.

BIBLIOGRAPHY: Martin Zielonka, "The Fighting Jew," *Publications of the American Jewish Historical Society* 31 (1928).

Jane Burges Perrenot

DREISSIGER. *Dreissiger* is a collective term for some of the intellectual refugees of the German liberal movements of the 1830s, which, in the wake of the French July Revolution of 1832, included the Hambacher Fest of 1832 and the Frankfurter Putsch of 1833. In opposition to official repression of academia and the media, some of the liberals subsequently known as the Dreissiger organized the Giessen Emigration Society under Paul Follenius and Friedrich Münch to direct German migration to a "new and free Germany in the great North American Republic." Others continued the resistance in Germany until the failure of the Frankfurter Putsch temporarily broke the liberal backbone. The exiles included several interesting early Texas personalities, among them Ferdinand J. Lindheimer,qv a New Braunfels botanist and editor, and Dr. J. E. F. Gustav Bunsen,qv a leader of the Frankfurter Putsch who, like Lindheimer, was a teacher in Frankfurt before his exile to the United States. Bunsen and Lindheimer first settled in 1834 at the "Latin" village of Belleville, St. Claire County, Illinois, across the river from St. Louis. From there, with others, they traveled to New Orleans and eventually to Texas. Bunsen fought under Sam Houstonqv and died at the battle of San Jacinto.qv Lindheimer, having missed the battle due to a storm at sea, remained in Texas as a botanical collector for George Engelmann and Asa Gray of Harvard; he also founded and edited the influential and often politically restrained *Neu-Braunfelser Zeitung* (later the New Braunfels *Herald-Zeitung*qv). Some primary accounts of the Dreissiger were written by later Forty-eighters, notably Friedrich Kapp. Secondary studies of the Forty-eighters, a numerically more significant group, often include overviews of the Dreissiger as predecessors of the later liberals. However, in general the Dreissiger were more tolerant and more circumspect and less doctrinaire than the later, and therefore often younger, Forty-eighters. The Dreissiger generally also saw themselves as heroic adventurers, while the Forty-eighters were more corporate in their thinking and actions.

BIBLIOGRAPHY: Rudolph L. Biesele, *The History of the German Settlements in Texas, 1831–1861* (Austin: Von Boeckmann–Jones, 1930; rpt. 1964). William Goetzmann, ed., *The American Hegelians: An Intellectual Episode in the History of Western America* (New York: Knopf, 1973). Minetta Altgelt Goyne, *A Life among the Texas Flora: Ferdinand Lindheimer's Letters to George Engelmann* (College Station: Texas A&M University Press, 1991). Glen E. Lich and Dona B. Reeves, eds., *German Culture in Texas* (Boston: Twayne, 1980). Carl Wittke, *Refugees of Revolution: The German Forty-Eighters in America* (Philadelphia: University of Pennsylvania Press, 1952).

Glen E. Lich

DREKA, TEXAS. Dreka, on Farm Road 2427 sixteen miles southeast of Center in southeastern Shelby County, was founded about 1890. A post office was established there in 1894 with Martin Shofner as postmaster; it closed in 1907. In 1933 Dreka had one business and a population estimated at twenty-five, and in 1946 it had several houses, a gin, a store, and a church. By 1988 only the church and widely scattered houses remained in the area. Dreka was still listed as a community in 1990.

Cecil Harper, Jr.

DRENNAN, LILLIE ELIZABETH McGEE (1897–1974). Lillie Elizabeth Drennan, the first licensed female truck driver and trucking-firm owner in Texas (and the United States), was born at John Sealy Hospitalqv in Galveston, Texas, probably in early January of 1897. Her mother, about whom little is known, gave her up for adoption; at three weeks of age Lillie became the foster daughter of Francis

Carolyn (Fannie, Grannie) Nichols McGee of Hempstead. Lillie married William Barney Jackson on December 18, 1912, when she was fifteen years old; the couple had a son but were divorced in June 1914. On July 17, 1917, Lillie married Willard Ernest Drennan; this couple, who had no children, were divorced in April 1929. Lillie married S. B. Boulware on October 31, 1931; they had no children and received a divorce in April 1943.

Lillie dropped out of school in the fifth grade. At the age of thirteen she obtained employment as a telephone operator; by the time she was twenty-two, however, she had lost most of her hearing ability, probably as the result of scarlet fever suffered some years earlier; she wore a hearing aid throughout most of her adult life. She and her second husband started a trucking business in March 1928, primarily to take advantage of an oil boom near Hempstead. They purchased their first truck, a used, open-cab Model-T Ford, which her husband drove. As their business rapidly prospered, they bought a second truck, a closed-cab Chevrolet driven by Lillie. Later they added other trucks and hired additional drivers. After their divorce in 1929, Lillie became the sole owner of the Drennan Truck Line and, until 1934, a soft-drink bottling plant in Hempstead that the couple had also acquired.

Lillie received her commercial truck-driver's license in 1929 after the Railroad Commission[qv] began supervising the motor-freight business in the state. Commission examiners appeared reluctant to grant her a license, contending that her hearing impairment would make her a safety risk. But Lillie perceived sex bias and effectively argued her case, based on her driving record: "If any man can beat my record I'll just get out of here."

She operated the Drennan Truck Line for nearly twenty-four years and withstood opposition from unfair competitors, dishonest shipping clerks, and others who believed that a woman lacked the fortitude to manage a trucking company. She and her drivers, most of whom were black men, hauled oilfield equipment, explosives, soft drinks, and general freight throughout East Texas, braving mud and ice. On occasions Lillie drove over forty-eight hour stretches with virtually no sleep or rest, but apparently she never had an accident. Joe Carrington, a well-known insurance carrier for Texas trucking companies, wrote in 1946 that he knew of "no other truck owner" who enjoyed a safety record comparable to Lillie's. Carrington also praised the excellent reputation of her other drivers. Lillie received safety awards from the Railroad Commission and the Texas Motor Transportation Association. She also demonstrated her driving skills as a guest participant on a Texas Motor Transport Association "Roadeo" obstacle course at the state fairgrounds in Dallas in September 1950.

Lillie Drennan achieved national fame for her colorful personality. Attired in her khaki pants and shirt, laced work boots, and a ten-gallon hat, she placed a loaded revolver by her side when she drove, although she never used it. She insisted upon training every driver she hired; she sometimes kicked her employees in the seat of their pants and threatened, in her foghorn voice, to "pistol-whip" or "brain them with an iron bar" for violating her rules. When criticized for her cursing, she responded, "Me and God have an understanding." During World War II[qv] the United States Army praised Lillie's success in its recruiting campaign to attract women truck drivers for the quartermaster corps.

During her long career Lillie received media attention in periodicals, newspapers, and radio broadcasts. In 1943 she visited Hollywood, where the Los Angeles *Times* hailed her as a "dry land Tugboat Annie." Although Lillie entered into negotiations for a movie based upon her life, the production apparently never occurred. On May 17, 1946, the Hempstead *News* dedicated a special oversized edition to Lillie, whom a trucking trade publication described as "a twentieth-century pioneer who has all the color of an Annie Oakley, and who lives the life of a hard-hitting frontiers-woman." The city of Hempstead, sometimes known as Six-Shooter Junction, honored Lillie with a banquet on Six-Shooter Junction Day, May 23, 1946; such luminaries as Texas Department of Public Safety[qv] director Homer Garrison[qv] and future governor Beauford Jester[qv] attended.

As an amateur horticulturist, Lillie wrote newspaper articles in the Hempstead *News* about flowers and their culture and became a member of the Texas Women's Press Association in 1939. She also was a member of the Texas Transportation Association and an honorary member of the Houston Freight Carriers Association. She delivered lectures to students at Prairie View A&M College (now Prairie View A&M University) about her experiences in trucking. She sold Drennan Truck Line in September 1952 and operated the Six Shooter Junction Novelty and Package Store on U.S. Highway 290 in Hempstead afterward. Lillie died in Hempstead on September 10, 1974, and was buried in the Hempstead Cemetery.

BIBLIOGRAPHY: Florence Guild Bruce, *Lillie of Six-Shooter Junction: The Amazing Story of Lillie Drennan and Hempstead, Texas* (San Antonio: Naylor, 1946). Joe C. Carrington Papers, Barker Texas History Center, University of Texas at Austin. Houston *Post*, September 11, 1974. Vertical Files, Barker Texas History Center, University of Texas at Austin.

Paul M. Lucko

DRESDEN, TEXAS. Dresden is at the junction of Farm roads 744 and 55, fifteen miles west of Corsicana in west central Navarro County. Jacob Hartzell had a trading post as early as 1836 near the present townsite. He traded mainly with the Indians. Ethan Melton moved to the area in the 1840s and established a general store where many of the early settlers received their mail. The early site was known as Spanky, but when the regular post office was established in 1846, the name was registered as Melton. It was the first post office in the county. In 1852 the name was changed to Dresden. Postal service was discontinued in 1907. Near the store there was a campground where settlers stayed until their houses were built. The first county elections were held there on July 13, 1846. A three-acre townsite was set aside in March 1847 with Jacob Hartzell, Ethan Melton, and Henry Cook as trustees. County records show the post office name as Richland in 1849; the office was moved to Hartzell's store in the new settlement. In the 1850s a Methodist church was established. In 1872 a two-story building was constructed a mile northeast of town to house Dresden College. In 1896 the community had a population of 200, a high school, a bank, a general store, a cotton gin, and a gristmill. In 1906 the school had two teachers and fifty-nine students. The decision in the late nineteenth century to run the railroad track through Corsicana ended Dresden's prominence in the county. In 1939 the population of the town was estimated to be 127. In 1959 and 1990 it was an estimated twenty-five.

BIBLIOGRAPHY: Annie Carpenter Love, *History of Navarro County* (Dallas: Southwestern, 1933). Wyvonne Putman, comp., *Navarro County History* (5 vols., Quanah, Texas: Nortex, 1975–84).

Brian Bruckner

DRESEL, GUSTAV (1818–1848). Gustav Dresel, writer, businessman, and first German consul in Texas, the son of Johann Dietrich and Maria (Morrien) Dresel, was born on January 26, 1818, at Geisenheim, Rheingau. He attended high school in Weilburg and later went to business school. After travel in Europe, he came to the United States in 1837 and, when plans for a sawmill or distillery failed to materialize, set out westward. Eventually, he gathered a stock of goods and moved to Houston, where he served as bookkeeper and salesman in a general store, managed a warehouse on Buffalo Bayou, and bought and sold dry goods, grain, and land. Between 1838 and 1841 he traveled in parts of Texas (particularly the area around Houston), Louisiana, and Mississippi, and was involved in a cotton-export business in New Orleans. From 1842 to 1846 Dresel helped in the family wine business in Europe. On his return, he served as business manager in Texas for the Adelsverein[qv] in Galveston.

He served as first German consul in Texas for Duke Adolph of

Nassau, from whose country many German immigrants came. He kept extensive accounts of his experiences and impressions in a diary called "Texanisches Tagebuch," first published in the 1920–21 yearbook of the German-American Historical Society of Illinois and published in translation in 1954 by the University of Texas Press[qv] as *Gustav Dresel's Houston Journal*. Dresel is credited with inspiring poet A. H. Hoffmann von Fallersleben's[qv] *Texanische Lieder*. While conducting business for the Adelsverein, he died of yellow fever on September 14, 1848, in Galveston.

BIBLIOGRAPHY: Vertical Files, Barker Texas History Center, University of Texas at Austin.

Max Freund

DRESSER, HENRY EELES (1838–1915). Henry Eeles Dresser, businessman and ornithologist, was born on May 9, 1838, at Thirsk, Yorkshire, England, the son of Henry and Eliza (Garbutt) Dresser. The elder Dresser was a timber merchant. The younger Dresser attended schools in Bromley, England, and Ahrensburg, Germany. In 1854 he was sent to Gefle and Uppsala to learn Swedish. From 1856 until 1863 he traveled extensively throughout Europe in the timber trade.

In early 1863 Dresser left England with a cargo for the Confederate government of Texas. He arrived on June 26, 1863, at Matamoros, Tamaulipas, and collected birds in the surrounding area for several weeks. In early September he traveled through San Patricio, Victoria, Yorktown, and Sutherland Springs to San Antonio, where he shared a house with a noted ornithological collector, Adolphus Lewis Heermann. From San Antonio, Dresser made collecting trips to the Medina and Atascosa rivers and to the Bandera region. In December he made a short trip to the upper Rio Grande and stayed shortly at Eagle Pass. In early 1864 he again went to Eagle Pass. He left San Antonio on May 15 and traveled to Austin and then Houston, whence he made two collecting trips to Galveston. He returned to San Antonio in June and in July traveled by way of Laredo to Matamoros, where he packed his specimens and boarded ship for the return to England.

Dresser spent thirteen months collecting in southern Texas and also received a collection made by Patrick Duffy, a hospital steward at Fort Stockton. He shipped about 400 birdskins to England. His travel account and observations on 272 species of Texas birds were published shortly after his return to England as "Notes on the Birds of Southern Texas" in the *Ibis* of 1865–66. The remnants of Dresser's collection of Texas birds, his extensive collection of European birdskins and eggs, his library, his notebooks, and his manuscripts are housed in the Manchester Museum at the University of Manchester. His published account greatly expanded upon the earlier observations made on the birds of the lower Rio Grande valley and, until the studies of James Cushing Merrill and George Burritt Sennett[qqv] in the late 1870s and early 1880s, was the definitive source of information on the birds of this area. Dresser's observations are also the first account of bird life in several of the other areas he visited during his travels in southern Texas.

He joined the British Ornithologists' Union in 1865 and served as the secretary of this organization from 1882 to 1888. He was also a member and fellow of the Linnaean and Zoological societies of London and an honorary fellow of the American Ornithologists' Union. He was an authority on the birds of Europe and the author of several important works, including *A History of the Birds of Europe* (1871–81), *Eggs of the Birds of Europe* (1910), and *Manual of Palaearctic Birds* (1902–03). After returning from Texas in 1864, Dresser entered business in London as an iron merchant. He was married on March 7, 1878, to Eleanor Walmisley Hodgson; a son and a daughter were born to them. Dresser died on November 28, 1915, at Monte Carlo, Monaco.

BIBLIOGRAPHY: S. W. Geiser, "Men of Science in Texas, 1820–1880," *Field and Laboratory* 26–27 (July–October 1958–October 1959).

Stanley D. Casto

DRESSER INDUSTRIES. Dresser Industries, Incorporated, a multinational corporation headquartered in Dallas, provides a wide range of technology, products, and services used for developing energy and natural resources. Its beginning goes back to the early oilfields of Pennsylvania and the mechanical enterprise of a Michigan-born man named Solomon Robert Dresser (1842–1911), who forsook the uncertainties of wildcatting to manufacture a product that he devised for drillers to keep oil and water separated underground. To do this Dresser constructed a "packer," using rubber for a tight fit, and after taking out a patent on May 11, 1880, he began advertising and selling his product, the Dresser Cap Packer, from his modest frame building in Bradford, Pennsylvania, in the heart of the oilfields. Dresser's packer was merely one of many available, and it was not that invention, but another, that converted his struggling company into one that was national in scope. This was a coupling that Dresser built in 1885 to join pipes together in such a way that they would not leak natural gas. This coupling also used rubber for a tight fit, and it was so successful that it permitted for the first time the long-range transmission of natural gas from the fields where it naturally occurred to faraway cities. The natural gas industry prospered and expanded after 1900, as more and more cities began preferring gas for heating and lighting, and Dresser's company grew as pipelines were built over great distances. By 1927 the company's annual sales had reached $3.7 million, and some 400 workers were required to keep up with the demand. Dresser's descendants, who had been operating the company since the founder's death, decided to sell it, and in 1928 the Wall Street investment-banking firm of W. A. Harriman and Company, Incorporated, converted the firm into a public company by issuing 300,000 shares of stock. H. Neil Mallon was selected as president and chief executive officer; he held that position until his retirement in 1962. Under Mallon, a Cincinnati native and Yale graduate whose earlier experience had been in the canning industry, Dresser took advantage of its strong cash position to launch a program of acquisitions designed to survive a new threat to its coupling business—the introduction of welding for joining pipes together. Between 1930 and the entry of the United States into World War II,[qv] Dresser acquired various companies that manufactured valves, heaters, pumps, and engines and compressors.

After the war, expansion continued, as the company diversified into such products as oil derricks, blowers, drill bits, refractories, and drilling mud. Dresser was energetic in following new oil and gas markets around the world, even behind the Iron Curtain. Future United States president George Bush worked for the company in several positions after the war. His father, Prescott Bush, had been a W. A. Harriman and Company executive who had been involved in the conversion of Dresser to a public company, and he served on the board of directors for twenty-two years. In 1950 the company headquarters were transferred to Dallas to be near the nation's major oil and gas fields and also to take advantage of the central location for managing what by then had become a far-flung empire. An aggressive acquisition program continued through the purchase of well-known companies involved in manufacturing such things as overhead cranes, gasoline-dispensing pumps, and heavy equipment for mining and construction. Many of these firms had themselves played pioneering roles in the nineteenth century with innovative products that had helped to develop the world's energy resources.

During the 1980s, as the oil industry began to decline, Dresser's chairman, John Murphy, began to streamline the organization of the company. Murphy ordered the elimination of the insurance, mining, and construction-equipment divisions. Beginning with a joint agreement with Komatsu of Japan in 1988 to manufacture construction equipment such as tractors, loaders, and hydraulic excavators, Dresser began to expand its operations once again. During the early 1990s the conglomerate purchased two European businesses. Dresser generated sales of more than $4 billion in 1992, and in 1993 it employed 31,800 people in fifty countries. At that time the company had three major divisions: Oil Field Products and Services, Industrial Operations, and Energy Processing and Conversion Equipment. In 1994 the company expanded through acquisitions of Wheatley TXT (a manufacturer of pumps, valves, and metering equipment) and the Baroid Corporation (a Houston-based oil-services firm that had competed directly with Dresser for customers). To comply with federal antitrust regulations, Dresser sold off its interest in M-I Drilling Fluids Company and Western Atlas International. Upon completion of the Baroid merger, Dresser became the third-largest oil-services company in the world.

BIBLIOGRAPHY: *Business Week,* February 22, 1988. *Forbes,* November 14, 1988, February 14, 1994. *Hoover's Handbook of American Business* (1993). Darwin Payne, *Initiative in Energy: The Story of Dresser Industries, 1880–1978* (New York: Simon and Schuster, 1979). Damon Robinson, "Tool Exporter Finds Key to Success," *Journal of Commerce and Commercial,* February 22, 1991.
Darwin Payne

DRESSY, TEXAS. Dressy, on the Little Pecan Bayou in southeastern Callahan County, was the center of a ranching area until the late 1870s. Samuel P. Long became the community's first postmaster on April 21, 1899. Dressy had a population of twenty-two in 1903. Its post office was discontinued on January 15, 1912. In 1940 the community reported a population of fifteen and two businesses, and in 1945 a population of fifty. The 1984 county highway map showed only a cemetery at Dressy.

BIBLIOGRAPHY: Brutus Clay Chrisman, *Early Days in Callahan County* (Abilene, Texas: Abilene Printing and Stationery, 1966).
Julius A. Amin

DREYER, MARGARET WEBB (1911–1976). Margaret Webb Dreyer, painter and gallery owner, was born in East St. Louis, Illinois, on September 29, 1911, the eldest of two daughters and a son born to Elmer E. and Eula Richey Webb. As a girl she moved with her family to Houston, Texas, where she lived most of her life. She exhibited an interest in art from an early age and took art courses at Westmoreland College, San Antonio; the University of Texas, Austin; the Museum of Fine Arts, Houston;qv and the Institute Allende in San Miguel de Allende, Mexico. She married Martin Dreyer, a newspaper columnist, on September 17, 1941, and they had a son named Thorne.

Throughout her career Margaret Dreyer experimented with such styles as Cubism, Surrealism, and Abstract Expressionism; her work was characterized by bold strokes and rich colors and textures. Her best-known series include *Blueprint for Survival,* a group of abstract works representing the artist's feelings about the Vietnam War, and *Maggie's Songs,* a series of large, nonobjective stained paintings on raw canvas that she completed shortly before her death. She exhibited her paintings in competitive exhibitions throughout Texas and won awards from the Texas Watercolor Society in 1970 and 1971 and from the Texas Fine Arts Associationqv in 1971. Her work was represented in the Eleventh Midwest Biennial at the Joslyn Art Museum in Omaha, Nebraska, and in traveling exhibitions sponsored by the Texas Fine Arts Association. Dreyer was a member of the Texas Watercolor Society, the Texas Fine Arts Association, and the Houston Art League.

In addition to painting and exhibiting her work, she taught art, first at Ripley House, then from 1950 to 1960 as director of the art program run by the Houston parks and recreation department. With a friend, Charlene Carpenter, she began a company that commissioned local artists to design and execute murals and mosaics for businesses and homes, thus providing jobs for leading artists in Houston. Dreyer had perhaps her greatest impact promoting the work of young artists in the Houston area. She ran Dreyer Galleries from her home on San Jacinto from 1961 to 1975, a period when few Houston galleries exhibited local artists. She showed particular support for African-American and young female artists. During the late 1960s she became involved in the human rights and peace movements and held meetings for various groups in her gallery. A group calling itself the Ku Klux Klanqv harassed her by riddling her home with bullets and throwing yellow paint on the side of her house; she responded by painting the whole wall yellow.

Margaret Dreyer died of cancer on December 17, 1976. She was eulogized for her contributions to the Houston art community in a service at the Rothko Chapel,qv and her last series, *Maggie's Songs,* was exhibited at the Contemporary Arts Museum, Houston,qv shortly after her death. In 1979 the University of St. Thomas mounted a retrospective of her paintings. Examples of Dreyer's work are in the permanent collections of the Institute of International Education in New York City; Abe Issa Interests in Kingston, Jamaica; and many private collections.

BIBLIOGRAPHY: Martin Dreyer, "Portrait of a Houston Artist: An Interview with Margaret Webb Dreyer," *Houston Review: History and Culture of the Gulf Coast* 5 (Winter 1983). Houston *Post,* December 19, 1976, April 8, 1979. *Who's Who in American Art,* 1973.
Kendall Curlee

DREYFOOS, TEXAS. Dreyfoos, in northern Hemphill County, was established in 1928, when the Cities Service Gas Company built a compressor station on land purchased from Dick Cann, a pioneer rancher. Between April and October 1929 a post office named Cann Station was located at the site. During the same time a two-year high school was built on land purchased from Ben Dreyfoos, and the community was called Dreyfoos, even though the official name was Patton. During this time the town had a population of about forty. The population had decreased to thirteen by 1966, when the inhabitants were ranchers, farmers, or employees of Cities Service Gas Company. In 1966 the school was still in use and had only one teacher. In 1970 the county school board voted to consolidate the Patton school with that of Canadian. Although the gas plant was still in operation in 1984, most of its employees lived then in Canadian.

BIBLIOGRAPHY: Sallie B. Harris, *Cowmen and Ladies: A History of Hemphill County* (Canyon, Texas: Staked Plains, 1977).
H. Allen Anderson

DREYFUSS, SOL (1885–1951). Sol Dreyfuss, merchant, was born on August 12, 1885, in Dallas, the son of Gerard and Julia (Hurst) Dreyfuss. His father, a native of France, owned several chains of stores before Sol's birth, including one with his wife's father founded in 1879 and called Hurst and Dreyfuss. Sol attended Bryan Street High School and Sachs Preparatory High School in New York. In the 1880s Hurst and Dreyfuss merged with E. M. Kahn and Company. In 1905 Dreyfuss began working at his father's clothing store and continued for several years until he joined Sanger Brothers (*see* SANGER, ALEXANDER). On August 11, 1910, the doors opened to the first Dreyfuss and Son clothing store, a one-story building on Main Street. By 1950, at the time of Dreyfuss's death, the store was a six-story building at Main and Ervay streets.

Dreyfuss owned the Dallas Baseball Club from 1928 to 1938, when the team was known as the Steers. He was a director of Hope Cottage. He was active in the Community Chest and Red Cross and was a member of the Salesmanship Club, the Citizens Charter Association, the Lakewood Country Club, the Columbian Club, and B'nai B'rith. He was also on the board of directors of both the Republic National Bank and the Pollock Paper Company. After the death of their parents, he and his sister, Hortense Pollock, turned their family home over to the Campfire Girls and the Visiting Nurses Association for its central offices. Dreyfuss was Jewish, but he called himself an unofficial member of all churches. His wife was Episcopalian; his daughter was raised Episcopalian and married a Methodist. Dreyfuss died on May 27, 1951, in Dallas and was buried at Emanu-El Cemetery.

BIBLIOGRAPHY: Dallas *Morning News*, May 28, 1951.

Lisa C. Maxwell

DRIFTWOOD, TEXAS. Driftwood, seventeen miles northwest of San Marcos in central Hays County, grew up in the 1880s as a supply center for neighboring ranches and farms. Pioneers settled in the area, then known as Liberty Hill, as early as 1850, but most settlers arrived in the early 1880s. The community grew rapidly in that decade, perhaps as a result of its access to the new rail terminals at Kyle and Buda. By 1890 Driftwood had a post office, a school, churches, a cotton gin, and a general store. From a low of ten in 1925, the population grew to nearly 100 during the middle years of the twentieth century, then dwindled to fewer than twenty-five by the 1970s. In 1945 Driftwood became part of the Buda school district. A century after its founding, the community remained a quiet Hill Country qv crossroads served by a general store and post office. In 1990 the population was twenty-one.

BIBLIOGRAPHY: Mary Starr Barkley, *A History of Central Texas* (Austin: Austin Printing, 1970).

Daniel P. Greene

DRINKING AND BEVERAGES IN NINETEENTH-CENTURY TEXAS. H. L. Mencken called the years between the American Revolution and the Civil War qv the "Gothic Age of American drinking," and Texas embodied the frontier excesses of the age. In 1840 British traveler Francis Sheridan remarked about Texas, "The passion for erecting grog shops supersedes the thirst of religious worship & Temples wherein to exercise it, for though we find every town plentifully supplied with Pot-Houses . . . we see neither a church or signs of building one." Many Texans came of hard-drinking Anglo-Saxon ancestors. They faced a life of rural hardship, tedium, and a diet of meats preserved by heavy salting. They also believed in the medicinal properties of alcohol. Moreover, people were often skeptical about drinking water, for in many cities and towns the water was often polluted. Selective readers of the scriptures "took their Bible straight, especially where it said: 'Give strong drink unto him that is ready to perish, and wine unto those that be of heavy hearts'" (Prov. 31.6). A traveler visiting Texas in 1837 claimed that the climate encouraged drinking. In 1838 Houston, one of the major "centers of vice," had forty-seven establishments for selling intoxicating drinks. The records at the clerk's office of Fort Bend County reveal that between 1838 and 1846 more licenses were issued for the sale of wines and liquors than for all other businesses combined. Many Texas frontier drinking establishments were elaborate, especially in the larger cities. Ferdinand von Roemer, qv a German traveler in Texas, described such a place in Houston in the early 1840s: "Upon passing through large folding doors, one stepped into a spacious room in which stood long rows of crystal bottles on a beautifully decorated bar. These were filled with divers kinds of firewater. Here also stood an experienced barkeeper in white-shirt sleeves, alert to serve to the patrons the various plain as well as mixed drinks." In contrast to fine establishments, a popular spot in Austin, Spicer's Tavern, was "made of logs covered with pine boards for the walls and rough-hewn pine planks for the floors." Drinking had its unwritten laws. One visitor noted, "Nothing was regarded as a greater violation of established etiquette than for one who was going to drink not to invite all within a reasonable distance to partake, so that Texians, being entirely a military people, not only fought but drank in platoons." Many women took pride in their homemade wines and cordials, but indulged with discretion. Most grogshops worked on a cash-only basis, and when times were hard they were forced to close.

The most common nineteenth-century drink was whiskey, sometimes called the "American wine." The liquor often took on the name of the region where it was produced; bourbon, easily the most popular, came from Bourbon County, Kentucky. In addition to bourbon, Texas stores advertised a wide variety of liquors. In 1838 A. G. Compton's store on Main Street in Houston was selling "cognac, champagne, brandy, gin, Jamaica and Santa Cruz rum, Irish, Scotch and rye whiskey, claret, port, Madeira wine, hock, Burgundy, gold and pale Sherry, and London brown stout." In the better hotels fancy drinks were available at twenty-five cents each, including many we would recognize today—mint julep, gin sling, apple toddy, and a cocktail described as "a stimulating liquor composed of spirits, sugar, water and bitters." Other drinking establishments offered very elaborate drinks with even more interesting names. According to British traveler William Bollaert qv the drinks offered by a Galveston hotel in the 1840s included "Tip and Ty, I.O.U., Moral Suasion, Pig and Whistle, Silver top, Poor man's punch, Jewett's fancy, Deacon, Stone Wall, Siphon, Smasher, Floater, Negus, and Mulled wines." In the early nineteenth century Texans also drank fermented home-brews such as persimmon beer and potato beer. Later, Germans qv introduced lager brewing, and by the 1860s the Menger Brewery, at the time San Antonio's largest industrial concern, employed ten skilled Germans and brewed 8,000 gallons of beer annually (*see* BREWING INDUSTRY).

Like their United States counterparts, Texans were ardent coffee drinkers, and coffee was probably the most indispensable nonalcoholic beverage in Texas. By 1838 Houston merchants were offering coffee at fifty cents a pound. When it was not available, a substitute was made of parched corn, wheat, or okra seeds. Tea was also consumed, although not as widely as coffee. Apparently chocolate drinks were also popular in Texas. Even with the availability of nonalcoholic beverages Texans were serious drinkers, and drunkenness was common. A Texas newspaper editorialized on the illness resulting from drinking and noted that "the graveyard held scores of young men who died from intemperance." Perhaps in response to this problem, in 1839 the first meeting of a Texas temperance society was held in Houston, and ninety-eight "drunkards" signed pledges. Whatever its goals and motivation, however, the temperance movement did not become a social and political force until the late nineteenth century, when prohibition qv was becoming a national movement that set the stage for increased moonshining qv and bootlegging.

BIBLIOGRAPHY: Ellen Garwood, "Early Texas Inns: A Study in Social Relationships," *Southwestern Historical Quarterly* 60 (October 1956). William R. Hogan, *The Texas Republic: A Social and Economic History* (Norman: University of Oklahoma Press, 1946; rpt. 1969). W. Eugene Hollon and Ruth L. Butler, eds., *William Bollaert's Texas* (Norman: University of Oklahoma Press, 1956). Andrew Forest Muir, *Texas in 1837* (Austin: University of Texas Press, 1958). Ferdinand von Roemer, *Texas* (Bonn: Marcus, 1849; trans., San Antonio: Standard, 1935; rpt., Waco: Texian Press, 1976). Francis C. Sheridan, *Galveston Island, or A Few Months off the Coast of Texas, 1839–1840,* ed. Willis W. Pratt (Austin: University of Texas Press, 1954). *Telegraph and Texas Register,* January 6, December 22, 1838, February 20, 1839. Kenneth W. Wheeler, *To Wear a City's Crown: The Beginnings of Urban Growth in Texas, 1836–1865* (Cambridge: Harvard University Press, 1968).

Ellen N. Murry

DRIPPING SPRINGS. Dripping Springs, a stream, rises just north of U.S. Highway 62/70 in west central Motley County (at 33°59' N, 100°55' W) and runs north for four miles to its mouth on Salt Creek, five miles west of Matador (at 34°01' N, 100°54' W). An early Matador Ranch qv map showed the creek to be in an area of high-quality grazing land. It runs through rolling terrain surfaced by moderately deep sandy loams that support brush and grasses.

DRIPPING SPRINGS, TEXAS. Dripping Springs, on U.S. Highway 290 twenty-five miles west of Austin in northern Hays County, emerged as a community center before the Civil War.^qv The first settler in the area is thought to have been a man named Fawcett, who arrived about 1849. Other families began farming the valleys of Little Barton and Onion creeks in the early 1850s, and in 1857 Dripping Springs opened what became a permanent post office. By 1884 the town supported several businesses, including a steam gristmill and cotton gin, and a population of 130. Education was provided by a public school and by the Dripping Springs Academy, which opened in 1881. The settlement's location on the Austin to Fredericksburg road made it a durable community center, and despite a population decline during the Great Depression,^qv Dripping Springs developed into the principal town in northern Hays County during the twentieth century. With only minor fluctuations, its population has grown slowly but steadily since World War II.^qv In the mid-1980s it reported twenty businesses and more than 600 residents. By 1990 its population had risen to over 1,000.

BIBLIOGRAPHY: Mary Starr Barkley, *A History of Central Texas* (Austin: Austin Printing, 1970). Dudley Richard Dobie, *A Brief History of Hays County and San Marcos, Texas* (San Marcos, 1948).

Daniel P. Greene

DRIPPING SPRINGS ACADEMY. Dripping Springs Academy, at Dripping Springs, was established in 1881 by W. M. Jordan, W. T. Chapman, and several other residents. The Pedernales Baptist Association managed it from 1882 until 1889, when dissatisfied local citizens caused the association to discharge the governing board and appoint a new one. The school reached a peak enrollment of 200 students, but when state-funded schools drew students away and local citizens demanded a public school, the association closed the academy. The campus consisted of a stone main building and two boarding houses. The main building served as a public schoolhouse from 1889 to 1949. In 1968 it was dedicated as a historic landmark.

BIBLIOGRAPHY: Tula Townsend Wyatt, *Historical Markers in Hays County* (San Marcos, Texas: Hays County Historical Commission, 1977).

Carolyn Hyman

DRISCOLL, CLARA (1881–1945). Clara Driscoll, businesswoman, philanthropist, and historic preservationist, was born on April 2, 1881, to Robert and Julia (Fox) Driscoll in St. Mary's, Texas, near the site of present Bayside. Her ancestors were among the Irish Catholic pioneers who had settled the area between the Nueces and Guadalupe rivers, and both of her grandfathers had fought in the Texas Revolution.^qv By 1890 her father had amassed a multimillion-dollar empire in ranching, banking, and commercial developments centered in the Corpus Christi area. For her education he sent his only daughter to private schools in Texas, New York City, and France.

Clara Driscoll, San Antonio, 1931. San Antonio Light Collection, ITC. Clara Driscoll Sevier, as she was then called, examines plans to beautify the Alamo plaza, almost thirty years after she helped save part of the Alamo property from commercialization.

After almost a decade of study and travel abroad, Clara Driscoll returned to Texas at the age of eighteen, imbued with an appreciation of the importance of preserving historic sites in Texas for the benefit of future generations. She was shocked to discover the disrepair of the three-acre plaza and barracks area adjoining San Antonio de Valero Mission, familiarly called the Alamo,qv and to learn that the property might soon be converted into a hotel. From 1903 to 1905 she worked with the Daughters of the Republic of Texas qv to acquire and preserve the Alamo by personally paying most of the purchase price. The attractive young philanthropist received extensive national publicity as the "Savior of the Alamo."

She then pursued a writing career. She wrote a novel, *The Girl of La Gloria* (1905), a collection of short stories, *In the Shadow of the Alamo* (1906), and a comic opera, *Mexicana,* the production of which she financed on Broadway in 1906. That same year she married Henry Hulme (Hal) Sevier qv at St. Patrick's Cathedral in New York City. The Seviers, who had met several years earlier in Austin, when Sevier was serving in the Texas legislature, remained in New York. Hal served as financial editor of the New York *Sun,* and Clara served as the president of the Texas Club and entertained extensively at their opulent villa on Long Island.

After Clara Sevier's father died in 1914, the Seviers returned to Austin to be near her family's financial interests. Sevier established a daily newspaper, the Austin *American* (*see* Austin *American-Statesman*), and his wife became active in the Austin Garden Club and Pan American Round Table and served as president of the Daughters of the Republic of Texas. She also directed construction of Laguna Gloria, a fine Italianate mansion located on the Colorado River near the city.

At the death of her brother, Robert Driscoll, Jr., in 1929, Mrs. Sevier closed Laguna Gloria and moved with her husband to her family's Palo Alto ranch headquarters to manage extensive land and petroleum properties and to serve as president of the Corpus Christi Bank and Trust Company. Under her astute leadership the financial dominion almost doubled in value. After a two-year residence in Santiago, Chile, while her husband served as the United States ambassador there, the Seviers returned to Texas in 1935 and shortly thereafter legally separated. When the childless, thirty-one-year marriage was dissolved, Clara legally resumed her maiden name and was thereafter officially known as Mrs. Clara Driscoll.

During the next decade much of her time, energy, and money were devoted to historic preservation, civic betterment, and club activity. She assisted the Texas Federation of Women's Clubs qv in liquidating the mortgage on its Austin clubhouse, served as vice chairman of the Texas Centennial qv Exposition executive board, and presented Laguna Gloria to the Texas Fine Arts Association qv to be used as a museum (*see* LAGUNA GLORIA ART MUSEUM). To memorialize her brother and to improve the economic life of Corpus Christi, she constructed the lavish twenty-story Hotel Robert Driscoll, where she occupied the large penthouse apartment. Colorful, outspoken, and independent-minded, Driscoll relished participation in the political arena. She was elected the Democratic party's qv national committeewoman from Texas in 1922 and served in that position for an unprecedented sixteen years. In 1939 she promoted the candidacy of her friend John Nance Garner qv for president. After Franklin D. Roosevelt was reelected for a third term, however, she remained loyal to what she considered the best interests of her party and supported Roosevelt's fourth-term efforts during a bitter battle at the 1944 state convention. Her political acumen and activity were acknowledged to be of national importance, and it was said that "political potentates and Texas voters knew her equally well."

Clara Driscoll was a Catholic. She died suddenly of a cerebral hemorrhage on July 17, 1945, in Corpus Christi. After her body had lain in state at the Alamo chapel, she was interred at the Masonic Cemetery in San Antonio. She bequeathed the bulk of her family fortune to establish the Driscoll Foundation Children's Hospital in Corpus Christi.

BIBLIOGRAPHY: Ann Fears Crawford and Crystal Sasse Ragsdale, *Women in Texas* (Burnet, Texas: Eakin Press, 1982). *Notable American Women: A Biographical Dictionary* (4 vols., Cambridge, Massachusetts: Harvard University Press, 1971–80). Martha Anne Turner, *Clara Driscoll* (Austin: Madrona, 1979). Dorothy D. DeMoss

DRISCOLL, ROBERT, JR. (1871–1929). Robert Driscoll, lawyer, banker, rancher, and early advocate for the port of Corpus Christi, was born near Victoria, Texas, on October 31, 1871, the son of Robert and Julia (Fox) Driscoll. He attended public school in Rockport and surrounding areas, and then went to Georgetown University before finishing a degree in 1893 at Princeton University. He maintained a private law practice in New York until 1903, when he accompanied his elderly mother to England for medical treatments. Upon her death in 1906, he returned to Texas. That year he began concerning himself with aggressive management of the Driscoll estate, of which he assumed control after his father's death in 1914. At their apex, the Driscoll holdings included 125,000 acres in Duval, Jim Wells, and Nueces counties.

Driscoll was extensively involved in banking and land speculations and in bringing farming to the lower Texas coastal plains. He was president of several large corporations, among them Corpus Christi National Bank, Corpus Christi Trust Company, Kingsville Producing and Milling Company, and the International Refining Company of San Antonio. He was also a director of the Frost National Bank in San Antonio, the San Antonio Joint Stock Land Bank, and the Guaranty Title Company of Corpus Christi. He was a coincorporator of the St. Louis, Brownsville and Mexico Railway. Driscoll was instrumental in developing the Rabb Pasture into farmlands and in founding the towns of Bishop and Robstown, the latter of which, along with the nearby town of Driscoll, was named after the Driscoll family. He was chairman of the port of Corpus Christi from 1926 until his death in 1929.

An earnest Catholic, Driscoll endowed and supported several church benevolences and was a member of the board of the Corpus Christi College-Academy, a Catholic institution, for a time. He died in San Antonio on July 7, 1929, from complications following the amputation of his leg. Driscoll was buried at the family mausoleum in the San Antonio City Cemetery. On the day of the funeral the mayor of Corpus Christi, P. G. Lovenskiold, requested all businesses to close for the hour of the burial. A memorial to Driscoll was erected at the port, and his sister and only survivor, Clara Driscoll,qv left, upon her death in 1945, the Robert Driscoll and Julia Driscoll and Robert Driscoll, Jr., Foundation, which included among its beneficiaries the Driscoll Foundation Children's Hospital in South Texas.

BIBLIOGRAPHY: Corpus Christi *Times,* July 8, 1929. Ellis A. Davis and Edwin H. Grobe, comps., *The New Encyclopedia of Texas,* 4-volume edition. The Driscolls: Benefactors of South Texas (MS, Kilgore Collection, Corpus Christi State University). San Antonio *Express,* July 9, 1929. Vertical Files, Barker Texas History Center, University of Texas at Austin (Robert Driscoll, Clara Driscoll, Driscoll Family). Frank Wagner

DRISCOLL, TEXAS. Driscoll, at the junction of U.S. Highway 77 and Farm Road 665, twenty-two miles southwest of Corpus Christi in south central Nueces County, was established in 1904, when the St. Louis, Brownsville and Mexico Railway built south from Robstown and located a station on ranchland belonging to Robert Driscoll, Jr.qv Driscoll named the site after himself, although there was already a town in the county bearing that name; the older town's name was changed to Alfred. By 1920 the new Driscoll had a population of 500; the population was 669 in 1960 and 626 in 1970. The town was incorporated in the early 1950s and had six businesses in 1970. In 1990 Driscoll reported 688 residents and four businesses.

BIBLIOGRAPHY: Nueces County Historical Society, *History of Nueces County* (Austin: Jenkins, 1972). Cyrus Tilloson

DRISKELL, TEXAS. Driskell was near the junction of Farm roads 2022 and 2423, eight miles northeast of Crockett in east central Houston County. It was first settled in the mid-1870s by families from Cherokee County. Around 1890 it had a cotton gin, a church, and a number of scattered houses. By the mid-1930s it was no longer shown on highway maps.

BIBLIOGRAPHY: Houston County Historical Commission, *History of Houston County, Texas, 1687–1979* (Tulsa, Oklahoma: Heritage, 1979).

Christopher Long

DRISKILL, JESSE LINCOLN (1824–1890). Jesse Lincoln Driskill, cattleman and builder of the Driskill Hotel^{qv} in Austin, was born on November 4, 1824, in White County, Tennessee. He is a descendant of the O'Driscoll family, originally of County Cork, Ireland. Six Driscoll brothers came to America in 1775 and settled in Virginia. At the age of twenty-three Jesse Driskill moved to Barry County, Missouri, where he married Nancy Elizabeth Jane Day, originally from Columbus, Georgia, on September 5, 1847. The couple lived in Missouri four years and then moved to Bastrop, Texas. Driskill went into the merchandising business, moving first to San Antonio and later to San Marcos and Bryan. In 1857 he entered the cattle business, and for three years during the Civil War^{qv} he furnished beef to the Confederate army and the Texas Rangers.^{qv} Driskill was paid for his efforts in Confederate dollars and by the end of the war, with no cattle and no money, had gone broke. He began to rebuild his herds. In the early days of the Chisholm Trail,^{qv} Driskill could be found driving cattle to northern markets with his brother-in-law, William H. Day.^{qv} Driskill was said to have been an adventurous drover and fearless ranchman, and through persistence he became successful once again in the early Southwestern cattle trade. Business fell off sharply after 1871, when permanent residents of Abilene, Kansas, the destination of many trail drives, became fed up with the cattle trade and the wranglers. In that year Driskill moved his wife, four daughters, and two sons to Austin, the westernmost metropolis in the state at that time. He also continued on in the cattle trade, establishing ranches in South Texas, Kansas, and the Dakota territories. In 1885 he purchased the site for his future hotel, an entire city block for $7,500. The Driskill Hotel opened on December 20, 1886. For many years it served as a social and political center in Texas society. The Driskill family lost their fortune in 1888, when a late spring freeze on the northern plains killed 3,000 cattle. Payments on the hotel could not be met, and Driskill was forced to sell to S. E. McIlhenny. Driskill died, some said a broken man, on May 3, 1890, of a stroke.

BIBLIOGRAPHY: Wayne Gard, "Retracing the Chisholm Trail," *Southwestern Historical Quarterly* 60 (July 1956). *Southwestern Historical Quarterly* (Texas Collection, January 1967). Vertical Files, Barker Texas History Center, University of Texas at Austin.

Mary Jayne Walsh

DRISKILL HOTEL. The four-story Driskill Hotel in Austin was built in the 1880s at the time that the Capitol^{qv} and the first building of the University of Texas were under construction. The hotel was one of the grandest in Texas, the meetingplace of legislators, lobbyists, and the social leaders of Austin, and was the site of inaugural balls, elaborate banquets, receptions, and university dances and ceremonies. The Driskill was also the headquarters for swarms of journalists and radio and TV reporters during the administration of Lyndon B. Johnson.^{qv}

In 1884 Jesse Lincoln Driskill,^{qv} a pioneer in the great cattle drives to northern railheads, purchased the half block bordered by Sixth, Seventh, and Brazos streets. Jasper N. Preston^{qv} and Sons of Austin designed the original cream-colored brick and limestone building, which was apparently inspired by H. H. Richardson's recently completed Ames Building in Boston. The Driskill's two-story porches with Romanesque Revival columns frame Richardsonian arched entrances, but the façade is more complicated than that of the prototype, and small balconies project from the canted corners of the Driskill building.

The hotel opened on December 20, 1886, but within a few months financial problems briefly forced its closing, as repeated changes of ownership began. Originally the hotel had sixty steam-heated guest rooms with four elaborate suites on the second floor. The skylit dining room was the most elegant restaurant in Austin for many years. The Driskill had additional dining rooms for ladies and children, a ladies' entrance on Seventh Street, and, for the men, a large billiard room, a bar, and a barbershop. The columned lobby was later modified by the addition of a ceiling at the mezzanine level. The utility rooms, kitchen, and servants' quarters were in a separate building.

In 1923 the large guest rooms were remodeled and subdivided into 125 rooms, and five years later a fifteen-story annex was begun to the north, which was completed in 1930. At that time eight mirrors once owned by Carlota, empress of Mexico, were installed in the Maximilian Banquet Room. In 1970, when the hotel was once again threatened with closing, the Heritage Society of Austin mounted a successful campaign to interest private investors to save and rehabilitate the building. Volunteers of the Austin Heritage Guild operate a popular luncheon restaurant, the 1886 Room, in the hotel. Though the Driskill continued to change hands during the 1970s, the effort to restore the hotel to its original grandeur has been steady.

BIBLIOGRAPHY: Joe B. Frantz, *The Driskill Hotel* (Austin: Encino, 1973).

Roxanne Williamson

DROP, TEXAS. Drop is on Farm Road 1384 four miles northwest of Justin in southwest Denton County. Legend has it that the rural community, originally part of the Denton Creek settlement established in 1854, petitioned postal authorities for a post office to be named Dewdrop. When the federal agency announced that Texas already had a town with that name, the residents simply decided to remove the first three letters and adopt the name of Drop. The Drop post office opened in 1886. Located in a wheat-producing area of Denton County, Drop acted as a supply point for area farmers. The railroad tracks, built near Justin in the late 1880s, attracted people and businesses from the surrounding rural communities. The post office at Drop was closed by 1910. In 1936 the population was estimated at thirty-eight. It was reported at fewer than thirty in 1963.

David Minor

DROSSAERTS, ARTHUR JEROME (1862–1940). Arthur Jerome Drossaerts, the first archbishop of the Catholic Archdiocese of San Antonio,^{qv} son of Cornelius and Sophie (de Fraiture) Drossaerts, was born in Breda, Holland, on September 11, 1862. He studied at a number of seminaries in Holland and was ordained by Bishop Adrian Godschalk of Bois le Duc on June 15, 1889. That same year Drossaerts traveled to the United States at the request of Archbishop Janssens of New Orleans, who immediately sent him to work in Lake Charles, Louisiana. He subsequently served as pastor at New Orleans, Broussard, and Baton Rouge, Louisiana.

On December 8, 1918, Drossaerts was consecrated bishop of San Antonio by Archbishop Giovanni Bonzano, apostolic delegate to the United States, in St. Louis Cathedral, New Orleans. As bishop, Drossaerts built more than sixty churches and fifty schools, the most significant of which was St. John's Seminary. The new building was dedicated on November 25, 1920. When the Diocese of San Antonio was made an archdiocese in 1926, Drossaerts became its first archbishop. He was consecrated in San Fernando de Béxar Cathedral^{qv} on February 16, 1927, and his new territory included that part of the New Orleans Province that was in Texas and Oklahoma. He continued to build churches and schools and fill speaking engagements. He kept the old Spanish missions alive and went without salary in order to assist poor parishes with expenses. During his tenure as archbishop, he dedicated about 134 churches and religious buildings.

On August 19, 1934, Pope Pius XI honored Drossaerts for his aid to those fleeing from religious persecution in Mexico; he had raised more than $21,000 for the victims during the years 1926–29. For his charitable works he was named assistant at the pontifical throne and papal count. Drossaerts died in Santa Rosa Hospital on September 8, 1940, and was buried in the priests' plot in San Fernando Archdiocesan Cemetery, San Antonio.

BIBLIOGRAPHY: Carlos E. Castañeda, *Our Catholic Heritage in Texas* (7 vols., Austin: Von Boeckmann–Jones, 1936–58; rpt., New York: Arno, 1976). Catholic Archives of Texas, Files, Austin.

Mary H. Ogilvie

DROUGHTS. Droughts have been recorded as a problem in Texas since Spaniards explored the area. Álvar Núñez Cabeza de Vaca,qv found a population of soil tillers near the site of present-day Presidio, where it had not rained for two years. Regarding the white man as a god, they begged him to tell the sky to rain. In 1720 a summer dry spell in Coahuila killed 3,500 of the 4,000 horses that the Marqués de Aguayo,qv governor of Texas, was prepared to bring to Texas. A drought in Central Texas dried up the San Gabriel River in 1756, forcing the abandonment of a settlement of missionaries and Indians. Stephen F. Austin'sqv first colonists also were hurt by drought. In 1822 their initial food crop of corn died from lack of moisture. Each decade since then has been marked by at least one period of severe drought. Associated with dry times are grasshopper plagues, brush and grass fires, sand and dust storms, crop failures and depression, livestock deaths, disease resulting from insufficient and impure drinking water, and migrations of citizens from parched territory. Information concerning pioneer-day droughts is sketchy because of the absence of official statistics; but data on some droughts, especially those during the nineteenth century, can be compiled from individual complaints recorded in newspapers, diaries, and memoirs. In 1883 Texas opened its western school lands, drawing thousands of immigrant farmers to the area. One of the worst droughts in Texas history occurred in 1884–86, causing most of the farmers to fail and to return to the East. In later years official detailed recordkeeping makes possible a better understanding of the geographical distribution of droughts. Drought occurs when an area receives, in a given year, less than 75 percent of its average rainfall. The number of drought years in each of ten geographical areas of Texas in the 100 years between 1892 and 1992 was as follows: Trans-Pecos,qv sixteen years; lower Rio Grande valley, seventeen; Edwards Plateau,qv seventeen; South Central, fifteen; Southern, fifteen; North Central, twelve; Upper Coast, thirteen; East Texas,qv ten; High Plains,qv ten; and Low Rolling Plains, eight. There has been at least one serious drought in some part of the state every decade of the twentieth century. The most catastrophic one affected every part of the state in the first two thirds of the 1950s. It began in the late spring of 1949 in the lower valley, affected the western portions of the state by fall, and covered nearly all Texas by the summer of 1951. By the end of 1952 the water shortage was critical; Lake Dallas for instance held only 11 percent of its capacity. Spring rains in 1953 gave some brief respite to Northeast Texas. In the Trans-Pecos, however, only eight inches of rain fell the entire year of 1953, and the drought grew worse from 1954 to 1956. Streams only trickled or dried up completely. The drought ended abruptly in the spring of 1956 throughout Texas with slow soaking rains. There were several less severe and shorter droughts in the 1970s. Most were ended by rain from tropical storms. A massive heat wave in 1980 started a severe drought that blistered most of Texas during the early 1980s. This gradually worsened until it reached extreme proportions in the Pecos River valley during 1983. Even mesquite trees withered. It was ended in the western half of the state by the residue of a north Pacific cyclone, which moved across Mexico. The drought shifted eastward in 1984, inflicting hardship on central and southern Texas; some towns ran out of water and others enforced rationing. On occasion, attempts to make rain artificially have been instituted by both private individuals and public organizations, but these have met with little success. Constant improvement in moisture conservation and utilization, however, has aided Texans in their struggle with drought.

BIBLIOGRAPHY: Roy Sylvan Dunn, "Drought in West Texas, 1890–1894," West Texas Historical Association *Year Book* 37 (1961). W. C. Holden, "West Texas Droughts," *Southwestern Historical Quarterly* 32 (October 1928). Vance Johnson, *Heaven's Tableland: The Dust Bowl Story* (New York: Farrar, Straus, 1947). Vertical Files, Barker Texas History Center, University of Texas at Austin. J. W. Williams, "A Statistical Study of the Drought of 1886," West Texas Historical Association *Year Book* 21 (1945).

Roy Sylvan Dunn

DRUMMOND, THOMAS (ca. 1790–1835). Thomas Drummond, naturalist, was born in Scotland, probably in the county of Perth, around 1790. Little is known of his formal study of botany; he was perhaps encouraged in his scientific interests by an older brother who at one time was director of the Botanical Gardens at Cork, Ireland. In 1825, upon the recommendation of the eminent botanist Sir William Jackson Hooker, Drummond accompanied Sir John Franklin's second overland expedition to Arctic America. As assistant naturalist, he was assigned to make botanical explorations of the mountains of western Canada, where for two years he collected bird and plant specimens. In 1830 he made a second trip to America, this time to collect specimens from the western and southern United States. While in Missouri he learned of the work Jean Louis Berlandierqv was doing in Texas, and in March 1833 he arrived at Velasco to begin his collecting work in that area. Despite the great floods of the spring and summer of 1833 and sickness from both cholera and diarrhea, Drummond spent twenty-one months working the area between Galveston Island and the Edwards Plateau,qqv especially along the Brazos, Colorado, and Guadalupe rivers. His collections were the first made in Texas that were extensively distributed among the museums and scientific institutions of the world. He collected 750 species of plants and 150 specimens of birds, a feat that stimulated the later studies of such botanical collectors as Ferdinand Jacob Lindheimer and Charles Wright.qqv Drummond had hoped to make a complete botanical survey of Texas, but he died in Havana, Cuba, in March 1835, while making a collecting tour of that island.

BIBLIOGRAPHY: S. W. Geiser, *Naturalists of the Frontier* (Dallas: Southern Methodist University, 1937; 2d ed. 1948).

DRUMMOND, TEXAS. Drummond was just west of the Brazos River and three miles southwest of the site of present Newcastle in west central Young County. The settlement evolved in the late nineteenth century across the river from the now-abandoned Belknap community and was named after the pioneer Drummond family, who owned a 5,000-acre local ranch. A post office was established in Drummond in 1895 with Virgil E. Curtis as postmaster; mail service was moved to Graham in 1909.

BIBLIOGRAPHY: Carrie J. Crouch, *Young County: History and Biography* (Dallas: Dealey and Love, 1937; rev. ed., *A History of Young County, Texas,* Austin: Texas State Historical Association, 1956). Jim Wheat, Postmasters and Post Offices of Texas, 1846–1930 (Microfilm, Grover C. Ramsey Papers, Barker Texas History Center, University of Texas at Austin).

Charles G. Davis

DRUMRIGHT, TEXAS. Drumright, near Lees west of U.S. Highway 87 in northeastern Glasscock County, was named for an Oklahoma oil boomtown because its founders expected this town to boom also. In 1925 the nearby Howard-Glasscock oilfield was brought in, and boom excitement seized the people of Drumright. Its population reportedly increased to 500. Two hotels, several businesses, and a school—which also housed a Sunday school and church services—were built in Drumright. However, no real boom came, and the community declined. In 1931 three businesses operated there, and by 1933 Drumright reported a population of fifty, served by two businesses. By 1934 the last business, a gas station, closed, and the building was moved to nearby Lees. Drumright was named on the 1984 county highway map, but no buildings were shown at the site. It was still listed as a community in 1990. *Julia Cauble Smith*

DRUMWRIGHT, HUBER LELLAND, JR. (1924–1981). Huber L. Drumwright, Baptist minister, educator, and author, son of Huber L. and Ruby Evalyn Drumwright, was born at Walters, Oklahoma, on February 1, 1924, and grew up in Dallas, Texas. He entered Baylor University in 1941, left to serve with the Seventh Fleet of the United States Navy during World War II,qv and graduated from Baylor in 1947. He received his B.D. degree in 1950 and his Th.D. degree in 1957 from Southwestern Baptist Theological Seminary and pursued postdoctoral studies at Princeton Theological Seminary and at the American School of Classical Studies in Athens, Greece. After a brief pastorate at the First Baptist Church of Ada, Oklahoma, he returned to Southwestern in 1960 with the rank of professor in the New Testament department. Drumwright was dean of the School of Theology at Southwestern from 1973 to 1980, when he resigned to become executive secretary-treasurer of the Arkansas Baptist State Convention.

He was much in demand as a preacher and lecturer and wrote numerous articles for a variety of theological and religious journals. In addition to his contributions to the *Wycliffe Bible Encyclopedia* and the *Zondervan Pictorial Encyclopedia*, he coedited *New Testament Studies: Essays in Honor of Ray Summers in His Sixty-fifth Year* (1975) and *Peloubet's Dictionary of the Bible—Revised* (1976). He also authored *Saints Alive: The Humble Heroes of the New Testament* (1972), *Prayer Rediscovered* (1978), and *An Introduction to New Testament Greek* (1980). Drumwright married Minette Williams in 1951. He died on November 2, 1981, in Little Rock, Arkansas. *W. R. Estep*

DRUSILLA, TEXAS. Drusilla was six miles southeast of Winnsboro and eight miles northeast of Quitman in northeastern Wood County. The community, which at one time had two Baptist churches, received a post office in 1895 and by 1896 had at least eleven businesses, including a sawmill, a gin and gristmill, a blacksmith, and a wagonmaker, as well as a drug and book store run by M. V. Morris, who also served as postmaster. The town also reported having a teacher, though official records for a Drusilla public school are not available for that time. Its post office closed in 1899. Drusilla does not appear on the 1936 county highway map. *Rachel Jenkins*

DRUSO, TEXAS. Druso, nine miles east of Ratcliff in eastern Houston County, was established around 1900 as a stop on the Houston, East and West Texas Railway. A post office opened there in 1902 with Mrs. E. F. Moore as postmaster. By 1914 Druso had a sorghum mill, two general stores, a cotton gin, and an estimated population of 100. The community began to decline in the early 1920s. Its post office closed in 1921, and by the mid-1930s the town was no longer shown on highway maps. In the early 1990s only a few widely scattered houses remained in the area. *Christopher Long*

DRY BAYOU. Dry Bayou rises seven miles northwest of Angleton in northwest Brazoria County, where the sources of the creek have been dammed to form Harris Reservoir (at 29°14′ N, 95°32′ W), and runs southwest for 14½ miles to a point where it is joined by Middle Bayou before running into the Brazos River, two miles north of Brazoria (at 29°05′ N, 95°35′ W). Dry Bayou, which parallels the Brazos River for most of its length, traverses flat terrain with local shallow depressions, surfaced by clay and sandy loam soils that support water-tolerant hardwoods, conifers, and grasses.

DRY BERRY CREEK. Dry Berry Creek rises five miles southwest of Jarrell in northwestern Williamson County (at 30°48′ N, 97°41′ W) and runs southeast for 9½ miles to its mouth on Berry Creek, three miles northeast of Georgetown (at 30°41′ N, 97°38′ W). The banks of the stream are heavily wooded in places with oak, mesquite, and juniper trees, and the creek traverses gently sloping terrain characterized by clayey soils used predominantly for agriculture.

DRY BLANKET CREEK. Dry Blanket Creek rises eight miles west of Comanche in southwestern Comanche County (at 31°51′ N, 98°44′ W) and runs south for twelve miles to its mouth on Blanket Creek, two miles east of Zephyr in southeastern Brown County (at 31°41′ N, 98°46′ W). It traverses variable terrain surfaced by shallow clay that supports post oak, vine mesquite, and grasses.

DRY BRANCH (Caldwell County). Dry Branch rises three miles north of Martindale in northwestern Caldwell County (at 29°55′ N, 97°48′ W) and runs southeast for 7½ miles to its mouth on the Clear Fork of Plum Creek, four miles southwest of Lockhart (at 29°52′ N, 97°43′ W). It traverses flat to rolling terrain with steep margins, surfaced by deep, sandy clay loams that support oak, juniper, elm, and grasses.

_____ (Hamilton County). Dry Branch rises fourteen miles southwest of Hamilton in south central Hamilton County (at 31°32′ N, 98°14′ W) and runs south for six miles, passing into Lampasas County before reaching its mouth on the Lampasas River (at 31°25′ N, 98°12′ W). It traverses flat terrain with local shallow depressions, surfaced by clay and sandy loams that support water-tolerant hardwoods, conifers, and grasses.

_____ (Stephens County). Dry Branch rises ten miles northwest of Breckenridge in northwest Stephens County (at 32°52′ N, 99°00′ W) and runs east for five miles to its mouth on Hubbard Creek, three miles southwest of Crystal Falls (at 32°52′ N, 98°56′ W). It first traverses rolling prairie surfaced by clay and sandy loam soils that support scrub brush, mesquite, cacti, and grasses. Near its mouth the terrain changes to flat with local shallow depressions, surfaced by clay and sandy loam that supports water-tolerant hardwoods, conifers, and grasses.

_____ (Stephens County). Dry Branch rises near the junction of U.S. Highway 183 and Farm Road 1481, eight miles northwest of Breckenridge in northwest Stephens County (at 32°44′ N, 98°58′ W) and runs northeast for four miles to its mouth on Hubbard Creek, two miles southwest of Crystal Falls (at 32°50′ N, 98°57′ W). It traverses flat terrain with local shallow depressions, surfaced by clay and sandy loam soils that support water-tolerant hardwoods, conifers, and grasses.

DRY BRUSHY CREEK. Dry Brushy Creek rises three miles southeast of Coupland in southeastern Williamson County (at 30°24′ N, 97°22′ W) and runs northeast for fourteen miles to its mouth on Brushy Creek, nine miles southeast of Taylor (at 30°32′ N, 97°16′ W). The banks of the stream are heavily wooded in places with post oak trees, and the creek traverses nearly level to gently rolling terrain surfaced by loamy and clayey soils used predominantly for agriculture.

DRYBURG, TEXAS. Dryburg was just across the road from Harrisburg to the east and 8½ miles northeast of Jasper in northeastern Jasper County. The Dryburg post office operated from 1912 to 1938 and served Harrisburg, as well as scattered rural inhabitants of northeast Jasper and northwest Newton counties. Dryburg was named by early settlers for the voting proclivities of its residents (who voted dry) and for its relative lack of rainfall. The 1971 county highway map showed no buildings at the site.

BIBLIOGRAPHY: Fred I. Massengill, *Texas Towns: Origin of Name and Location of Each of the 2,148 Post Offices in Texas* (Terrell, Texas, 1936). *Robert Wooster*

DRY CALIFORNIA CREEK. Dry California Creek rises just north of U.S. Highway 180 in extreme western Jones County (at 32°45′ N,

100°07′ W) and runs eleven miles north to its mouth on California Creek, just east of Hamlin in northwestern Jones County (at 32°54′ N, 100°05′ W). Dry California Creek is dammed in its middle reaches to form South Lake. It crosses flat to gently sloping terrain surfaced by quartz sand and silt that support scrub brush and grasses.

DRY CEDAR CREEK. Dry Cedar Creek rises ten miles southeast of Telegraph in south central Kimble County near the intersection of the Kimble, Edwards, and Kerr county lines (at 30°17′ N, 99°45′ W) and runs north for 14½ miles to its mouth on Cedar Creek, two miles south of Junction (at 30°27′ N, 99°45′ W). A spring keeps Dry Cedar Creek flowing for the first half mile above its mouth.

DRY CIBOLO CREEK. Dry Cibolo Creek rises sixteen miles east of Dilley in far southeastern Frio County (at 28°43′ N, 99°21′ W) and runs southeast for ten miles to its mouth on Cibolo Creek, near Woodward and five miles northeast of the intersection of Farm Road 469 and the Missouri Pacific in northwestern La Salle County (at 28°37′ N, 99°16′ W). *Cibolo* is Spanish for bison. The stream traverses flat terrain with locally shallow depressions, surfaced by expansive clays that support water-tolerant hardwoods, conifers, and grasses.

DRY COMAL CREEK. Dry Comal Creek, formerly Comal Creek, rises near the Valley View community in central Comal County (at 29°48′ N, 98°19′ W) and runs southeast for 34½ miles to its mouth on the Comal River at New Braunfels (at 29°42′ N, 98°08′ W). The West Fork of Dry Comal Creek, a tributary, rises near Smithson Valley in central Comal County (at 29°48′ N, 98°19′ W) and runs southeast for about seventeen miles to its mouth on Dry Comal Creek, 3½ miles northeast of Garden Ridge (at 29°40′ N, 98°16′ W). These creeks cross an area of the Balcones Escarpment characterized by steep slopes and limestone benches that give a stairstep appearance to the landscape along the creek. Soil in the area is generally dark, calcareous stony clay and clay loam with rock outcroppings, and vegetation consists primarily of live oak and Ashe juniper woods. The stream was the site of one of the first communities in Comal County, the Comal Creek settlement.

DRY CREEK (Armstrong County). Dry Creek rises at the breaks of the Llano Estacado qv in Palo Duro Canyon in western Armstrong County (at 35°00′ N, 101°32′ W) and runs southeast for nine miles to its mouth on the Prairie Dog Town Fork of the Red River (at 34°52′ N, 101°28′ W). It traverses an area of moderately steep slopes with locally high relief, surfaced by loamy soils that support rangeland grasses and mesquite. The creek was once part of the old JJ division of the JA Ranch,qv and cattle still graze along its banks.

____ (Brewster County). Dry Creek, which runs through Dry Valley Canyon, rises two miles north of U.S. Highway 90 and four miles north of the House Mountains in northeastern Brewster County (at 30°13′ N, 102°54′ W) and runs southeast for twenty-three miles to its mouth on Sanderson Canyon, a half mile south of U.S. Highway 90 and the Southern Pacific Railroad in extreme southern Pecos County (at 30°09′ N, 102°37′ W). It traverses an area of steep to gentle slopes surfaced by variable soils that support scrub brush and sparse grasses.

____ (Caldwell County). Dry Creek rises two miles west of the Lytton Springs community in northern Caldwell County (at 29°55′ N, 97°32′ W) and runs south for nine miles to its mouth on Plum Creek, three miles east of Lockhart (at 29°49′ N, 97°35′ W). It traverses flat to rolling prairie surfaced by shallow clay and sandy loams that support mesquite, mixed hardwoods, conifers, and grasses.

____ (Coke County). Dry Creek rises east of Hayrick in northeastern Coke County (at 32°00′ N, 100°21′ W) and runs southeast for four miles to its mouth on Kickapoo Creek (at 31°58′ N, 100°18′ W), which flows into the Colorado River. Dry Creek passes at first through steep-sloped terrain surfaced by shallow clay loams, then through an area of moderate slopes with shallow, stony clay and sandy loams. Local vegetation includes juniper, live oak, mesquite, and grasses.

____ (Coleman County). Dry Creek rises just northeast of Shield and fourteen miles south of Coleman in south central Coleman County (at 31°36′ N, 99°25′ W) and runs eight miles southeast to its mouth on Home Creek, two miles west of Farm Road 2633 (at 31°33′ N, 99°19′ W). It crosses flat, flood-prone terrain with local shallow depressions, surfaced by clay and sandy loams that support water-tolerant hardwoods, conifers, and grasses.

____ (Fort Bend County). Dry Creek, intermittent in its upper reaches, rises on the Brazos River just northeast of Rosenberg in central Fort Bend County (at 29°32′ N, 95°47′ W) and runs southeast for eleven miles to its mouth on Smithers Lake (at 29°30′ N, 95°40′ W). The vegetation along its banks consists mainly of mixed hardwoods interspersed with various prairie grasses. The variable terrain is surfaced by highly impermeable soil and calcareous clay.

____ (Hopkins County). Dry Creek rises a mile northwest of the Gamblin Cemetery in southeastern Hopkins County (at 33°04′ N, 95°31′ W) and runs southwest for five miles to its mouth on Running Creek, three miles west of the community of Reilly Springs (at 33°01′ N, 95°32′ W). The stream traverses flat to rolling terrain surfaced with clay loam and sandy loam soils that support water-tolerant hardwoods, conifers, and grasses.

____ (Kaufman County). Dry Creek rises a mile south of the Hunt county line in northern Kaufman County (at 32°49′ N, 96°15′ W) and runs northeast for five miles to its mouth on the South Fork of the Sabine River, five miles from the west shore of Lake Tawakoni in Hunt County (at 32°53′ N, 96°13′ W). The stream originates on a high point of ground that separates the watershed of the East Fork of the Trinity River and that of the Sabine River. The area soils are generally loamy. Hunt and Kaufman counties are both part of the Blackland Prairie, which is characterized by tall grass with oak, pecan, and elm trees along watercourses. Just south of the Hunt county line the creek is crossed by Farm Road 1565. At this site is the Dry Creek Cemetery, the burial ground for early settlers of the pioneer community of Turner's Point, which became Poetry, Texas, in the 1870s.

____ (McLennan County). Dry Creek rises near the southern city limits of Robinson in southern McLennan County (at 31°25′ N, 97°09′ W) and runs east for nine miles to its mouth on Bull Hide Creek, three miles northeast of Golinda in Falls County (at 31°23′ N, 97°02′ W). It traverses flat to rolling prairie with local shallow depressions, surfaced by clay and sandy loams that support mesquite, cacti, and grasses in the upper reaches of the creek, where the creek is intermittent, and water-tolerant hardwoods and conifers in the lower reaches.

____ (Menard County). Dry Creek rises fourteen miles north of the Fort McKavett community in northwestern Menard County (at 31°05′ N, 100°06′ W) and runs southeast for twenty-one miles to its mouth on the San Saba River, eight miles west of Menard (at 30°54′ N, 99°55′ W). It traverses flat terrain with local shallow depressions and deep dissections, surfaced by shallow and stony to moderately deep clay and sandy loams that support water-tolerant hardwoods, conifers, and grasses.

____ (Parker County). Dry Creek rises a mile northwest of Peaster in northwest Parker County (at 32°54′ N, 97°52′ W) and runs southwest for 11½ miles to its mouth on Rock Creek, just southeast of Mineral Wells (at 32°47′ N, 98°02′ W). The stream traverses undulating to gently rolling land surfaced by deep sandy and loamy soils that support grasses and hardwood timber. For most of the county's history the Dry Creek area has been used as rangeland and cropland.

____ (Rusk County). Dry Creek rises two miles west of New Prospect in north central Rusk County (at 32°12′ N, 94°45′ W) and runs north for five miles to its mouth on Mill Creek, two miles east of Craig (at 32°15′ N, 94°45′ W). The creek traverses flat to rolling terrain surfaced by sandy and clay loams that support water-tolerant hardwoods, conifers, and grasses.

____ (San Saba County). Dry Creek, intermittent in its upper reaches, rises 6½ miles southwest of Richland Springs in western San Saba County (at 31°12′ N, 99°00′ W) and runs east for 12½ miles to its mouth on the San Saba River (at 31°13′ N, 98°52′ W). It traverses flat to rolling uplands with live oak, mesquite, Ashe juniper, and grasses growing in clayey and sandy loam soils. The stream was originally named Jobe's (Job's, Jobs) Creek, for Abraham Jobe, who surveyed the area in 1847.

_____ (Schleicher County). Dry Creek rises eighteen miles northeast of Eldorado in northeastern Schleicher County (at 31°03′ N, 100°22′ W) and runs northwest for thirteen miles to its mouth on the South Concho River, three miles south of Christoval in Tom Green County (at 31°09′ N, 100°30′ W). It traverses an area of gentle to moderately steep slopes, surfaced by shallow stony soil that supports scrub brush, sparse grasses, and cacti.

_____ (Shackelford County). Dry Creek rises east of Farm Road 601 in east central Shackelford County (at 32°38′ N, 99°07′ W) and runs north for nine miles to its mouth on Hubbard Creek, just south of U.S. Highway 180 in extreme west central Stephens County (at 32°45′ N, 99°06′ W). The creek is dammed in its upper reaches to form De La Fosse Lake, an irrigation reservoir with a capacity of 773 acre-feet owned by Phillips Petroleum Company. The creek traverses an area of steeply to moderately sloping hills surfaced by shallow stony clay and sandy loams that support oak, mesquite, and grasses.

_____ (Sterling County). Dry Creek rises in the southeast corner of Sterling County (at 31°35′ N, 100°55′ W) and runs northeast for twelve miles, through the Water Valley oilfield in Tom Green County, to its mouth on the North Concho River (at 31°40′ N, 100°46′ W). The stream traverses flat to rolling lands with local escarpments and deep, fine, sandy loam soils that support brush, grasses, and cacti.

_____ (Terrell County). Dry Creek rises 3½ miles southwest of the Dry Creek Ranch headquarters in northwestern Terrell County (at 30°29′ N, 102°13′ W) and runs east for thirty miles to its mouth on Independence Creek, just east of State Highway 349 in the northeastern part of the county (at 30°27′ N, 101°49′ W). The path of the creek sharply dissects massive limestone underlying flat terrain, forming a deep and winding canyon. Wash deposits of sand, gravel, and mud cover the creekbed. Local soils are generally dark, calcareous stony clays and clay loams and support oaks, junipers, grasses, and mesquites. In 1860 Lt. William H. Echols and a camel expedition (*see* CAMELS) traveled along Dry Creek while mapping the area terrain and water sources and selecting a location for a fort near the trail used by Comanche war parties.

_____ (Travis County). Dry Creek rises four miles southeast of Manor in eastern Travis County (at 30°18′ N, 97°31′ W) and runs southeast for nine miles to its mouth on Wilbarger Creek, ten miles northwest of Bastrop in Bastrop County (at 30°15′ N, 97°26′ W). The area terrain is generally flat to rolling with steep margins, surfaced by clay and sandy loams that support hardwoods, mesquite, and grasses.

_____ (Travis County). Dry Creek rises three miles south of Austin in southern Travis County (at 30°07′ N, 97°45′ W) and runs northeast for twenty-five miles to its mouth on the Colorado River, ten miles northwest of Bastrop in Bastrop County (at 30°11′ N, 97°28′ W). The local terrain is generally flat to rolling with steep margins, surfaced by clay and sandy loam soils that support oak, juniper, elm, and grasses.

_____ (Uvalde County). Dry Creek rises five miles west of Montell in far northwestern Uvalde County (at 29°33′ N, 100°06′ W) and runs southeast for six miles to its mouth on the Nueces River, two miles southwest of Montell (at 29°31′ N, 100°02′ W). The local terrain is steep to gently sloping and is surfaced in the creek's upper reaches by shallow soils that are gravelly, stony, clayey, or loamy. Along the creek's lower streambed the soils are deep, loamy, and clayey. The vegetation along its course includes juniper, live oak, mesquite, scrub brush, and various grasses.

_____ (Van Zandt County). Dry Creek rises one mile northwest of Van in east central Van Zandt County (at 32°32′ N, 95°41′ W) and runs northeast for thirteen miles to its mouth on the Sabine River, southwest of West Mineola just across the county line in northwestern Smith County (at 32°40′ N, 95°34′ W). It crosses flat terrain with local shallow depressions surfaced by clay and sandy loam that supports water-tolerant hardwoods, conifers, and grasses.

_____ (Wise County). Dry Creek rises a mile northwest of Chico in northwestern Wise County (at 33°20′ N, 97°49′ W) and runs southeast for 11½ miles to its mouth on the West Fork of the Trinity River, a mile southeast of Bridgeport (at 33°12′ N, 97°43′ W). It traverses flat to rolling terrain surfaced by deep fine sandy loam. For most of the county's history the area has been used as range and cropland.

_____ (Wood County). Dry Creek rises six miles west of Winnsboro and two miles north of Farm Road 515 in north central Wood County (at 32°57′ N, 95°24′ W) and runs southwest for fifteen miles to its mouth on Lake Fork Creek, a mile south of Quitman (at 32°46′ N, 95°28′ W). Numerous small streams, including Little Dry Creek, empty into Dry Creek. It traverses generally flat to rolling terrain surfaced by deep, fine sandy loam that supports conifers and hardwoods. About three miles of Dry Creek's middle portion were inundated when the creek was dammed in 1962 to form Lake Quitman, four miles north of Quitman.

_____ (Young County). Dry Creek rises four miles southwest of Olney near the Olney Municipal Airport in northwestern Young County (at 33° 20′ N, 98°49′ W) and runs southeast for eight miles to its mouth on Salt Creek, six miles west of Jean (at 33°19′ N, 98°43′ W). As its name suggests, the creek consists primarily of a draw. It traverses flat terrain with local shallow depressions, surfaced by clay, mud, and sandy soils that support water-tolerant hardwoods and grasses. Herndon Springs, on Dry Creek near Orth, had stopped flowing by the 1930s. Much of the creek basin is within the Orth oilfield.

_____ (Young County). Dry Creek rises just south of the intersection of U.S. Highway 380 and Farm Road 2075 in southeastern Young County (at 33°09′ N, 98°27′ W) and runs southwest for twelve miles to its mouth on Salt Creek, two miles south of Graham (at 33°04′ N, 98°35′ W). It begins in an area of ledges and low cuestas with shallow stony soils and runs into steeply to moderately sloping hills with shallow stony clay and sandy loams. Local vegetation includes oak, juniper, live oak, mesquite, and grasses. The Center Ridge cemetery is a mile south of the creek in eastern Young County.

DRYDEN, WILLIAM G. (1807–1869). William G. Dryden, trader, adventurer, and politician, son of David H. Dryden, was born near Richmond, Kentucky, on February 11, 1807. After his mother's death he was left in the custody of relatives. In 1827 he became a Santa Fe trader and made numerous trips to Mexico during the following years. Although a foreigner, he was appointed captain of militia and engaged by Governor José Calve to build a military road in Chihuahua. On February 20, 1840, Dryden was shipwrecked off the Texas coast and made the most of the occasion by visiting President Mirabeau B. Lamar,[qv] who assigned him a confidential role in the projected Texan occupancy of New Mexico. Dryden returned to Santa Fe in September 1840 but left in 1841 before the Texan Santa Fe expedition[qv] reached San Miguel. Because of incriminating documents that fell into the hands of Governor Manuel Armijo, Dryden was arrested and kept in confinement at Chihuahua for thirteen months, being released on November 8, 1842. He filed a bill of damages for losses incurred because of his imprisonment, but he failed to perfect his claim. At the outbreak of the Mexican War,[qv] Dryden was living on the Texas side of the Rio Grande opposite Matamoros. He became identified with the federalist movement and was one of the editors of the bilingual *Republic of the Rio Grande*.[qv] During the American occupation of Matamoros he served as interpreter with the command of Col. David E. Twiggs.[qv]

In March 1850 Dryden joined a party traveling to California by way of Mazatlan. At Los Angeles he found opportunity for his talents in the field of local politics; he held the following offices: city clerk, 1850–60; city attorney, 1851–52; school commissioner, 1859–68; and city judge, 1856–69. He married twice in California, first to Dolores Nieto, with whom he had two daughters; and second to Anita

Domínguez in 1868. His death on September 10, 1869, closed a career in which mystery and adventure were strangely intermingled.

BIBLIOGRAPHY: William Campbell Binkley, *The Expansionist Movement in Texas, 1836–1850* (Berkeley: University of California Press, 1925). Carlos M. Bustamante, *El Gabinete Mexicano* (2 vols., Mexico: J. M. Lara, 1842). Charles Adams Gulick, Jr., Harriet Smither, et al., eds., *The Papers of Mirabeau Buonaparte Lamar* (6 vols., Austin: Texas State Library, 1920–27; rpt., Austin: Pemberton Press, 1968). Thomas B. Thorpe, *Our Army on the Rio Grande* (Philadelphia: Carey and Hart, 1846). *William E. Bard*

DRYDEN, TEXAS. Dryden is in Thurston Canyon on U.S. Highway 90, Farm Road 1217, and the Southern Pacific line, in south central Terrell County. In 1882 the Galveston, Harrisburg and San Antonio Railway built its tracks through Terrell County, and a section house was established at the new community, which was named Dryden for Chief Engineer Eugene E. Dryden. The Dryden community became the headquarters of the Pecos Land and Cattle Company[qv] in 1884. That company and several other open-range ranches shipped cattle from the Dryden station in the late 1800s and early 1900s. By 1886 W. W. Simonds, manager of the Pecos Land and Cattle Company, had built a large frame building for a post office and a store, which was operated by John Abney. The remaining rooms were used for storage and sleeping. The company built two adobe[qv] houses near Simonds's structure as residences for the Simonds family and for the family of ranch foreman Daniel Franks. The company drilled a plentiful water well, which supplied the town. Dryden received a post office in 1888. In 1889 Beverly Carter Farley came to work for the Pecos Land and Cattle Company, remaining there until the company was sold in 1895. Farley then took up eight sections of land in the Dryden area. By 1908 he had built the Dryden Hotel and a store, which he operated. In 1912 Farley bought the section of land that held the town and donated land for a school, which also served as a church and as a community center. From 1913 to 1917 the Mexican revolution[qv] and the possibility of border raids brought two units of United States Army troops to Dryden. Though the local citizens may have feared a border raid, they were accustomed to Mexican visitors. Mexican ranchers drove their cattle across the Rio Grande for shipment from Dryden to the San Antonio market. Several of those ranchers received mail and shopped for supplies in Dryden because it was more accessible than neighboring Mexican villages. In 1917 the Block Y Ranch also began shipping cattle from Dryden. The company settled several families there and built homes and headquarters offices. The 1920s brought new businesses to Dryden, and its population reached 100 by 1929. But in the 1930s, during the Great Depression,[qv] the railroad moved its crews and closed its depot. The large surrounding ranches broke up. The advent of the automobile and good roads allowed ranchers to travel to larger towns for supplies. By the early 1930s Dryden had fifty residents and three businesses. Its population grew again, however, reaching 100 by the end of the 1940s and staying at that level until the early 1960s, when the town still reported two businesses. From the mid-1960s to the early 1970s, Dryden had fifty residents and two or three businesses, which served a population including tourists and fishermen. From the mid-1970s through the mid-1980s the population was forty-five, and by 1988 it had dropped to thirteen. No businesses were reported at Dryden after 1985. In 1990 the community had a post office and an estimated population of thirteen.

BIBLIOGRAPHY: Terrell County Heritage Commission, *Terrell County, Texas* (San Angelo: Anchor, 1978). *Julia Cauble Smith*

DRY DEVILS RIVER (Edwards County). Dry Devils River rises at the Lantern community in extreme northwest Edwards County (at 30°13′ N, 100°31′ W) and runs forty-nine miles southwest to its mouth on Devils River, eight miles northeast of Comstock in southwest Val Verde County (at 29°47′ N, 100°59′ W). The surrounding terrain is flat with local shallow depressions and local deep and dense dissection. From the land surface of clay and sandy loams and shallow, stony soils grow water-tolerant hardwoods, conifers, grasses, oak, juniper, and mesquite.

_____ (Schleicher County). The Dry Devils River rises eight miles west of Eldorado in west central Schleicher County (at 30°54′ N, 100°44′ W) and runs southwest for sixty-three miles to its mouth on the Devils River, twenty-six miles southwest of Sonora in southwestern Sutton County (at 30°20′ N, 100°57′ W). It traverses flat terrain with local shallow depressions, surfaced by clay and sandy loams that support water-tolerant hardwoods, conifers, and grasses.

DRY DRAW. Dry Draw, through which flows an intermittent stream, rises at Rock Springs in central Edwards County (at 30°03′ N, 100°16′ W) and runs northeast for twenty-four miles to its mouth on the South Llano River, eight miles west of Rigsby Triangulation Station (at 30°14′ N, 100°01′ W). It crosses flat terrain with local shallow depressions and deep and dense dissection, surfaced by clay and sandy loams that support water-tolerant hardwoods, conifers, oak, juniper, mesquite, and grasses.

DRY DUCK CREEK. Dry Duck Creek, little more than a wet-weather ravine, heads seven miles northeast of Spur in south central Dickens County (at 33°29′ N, 100°43′ W). The streambed runs south for fifteen miles to its mouth on Duck Creek, in northeast Kent County three miles southeast of Gilpin (at 33°23′ N, 100°41′ W). The local terrain is flat to gently sloping, with sandy soil that supports scrub brush and grasses. Dry Duck Creek runs through the Croton Creek oilfield.

DRY ELM CREEK. Dry Elm Creek rises four miles northwest of Muenster in northwestern Cooke County (at 33°44′ N, 97°25′ W) and runs southeast for fourteen miles to its mouth on the Elm Fork of the Trinity River, five miles west of Gainesville (at 33°37′ N, 97°15′ W). The stream is dammed twice in its middle reaches and runs through the Muenster oilfield. Local terrain of flat to rolling prairie is surfaced by deep to shallow expansive clays, clay loams, and sandy loams that support water-tolerant hardwood, oak, juniper, conifers, and various grasses.

DRYER, TEXAS. Dryer (Dreyer), on Farm Road 443 in eastern Gonzales County, was named for Henry Dryer, one of a group of investors who in 1891 bought 6,568 acres from L. M. Kokernot and divided it into small farm lots. Dryer acquired a post office in 1897, but it closed in 1906. By 1936 the community had three businesses, two churches, and a school and was surrounded by scattered farms. In 1940 the settlement had 100 inhabitants and five businesses. Thereafter, it saw a period of sharp decline; by 1968 the population was forty. In 1988 and 1990 the community had twenty residents, two businesses, and a church. *Stephen L. Hardin*

DRY FRIO RIVER. The Dry Frio River is an intermittent, spring-fed stream that rises just south of Farm Road 337, which connects Camp Wood and Leakey, in Real County (at 29°47′ N, 99°51′ W) and runs south-southeast for sixty miles to its mouth on the main Frio, just below U.S. Highway 90 and southwest of Knippa in Uvalde County (at 29°17′ N, 99°39′ W). The stream descends the Balcones Escarpment in a winding course over a bed of limestone, gravel, and calcareous soil. Its course runs roughly parallel to that of the main Frio, and in Uvalde County Farm Road 1051 closely follows the stream. The surroundings of its upper reaches are typical of the heavily dissected canyonlands of the Balcones Escarpment on the southern edge of the Edwards Plateau, forested with open stands of live oak, mesquite, and Ashe juniper. In the lower elevations of the Dry Frio's southernmost reaches, immediately above its junction with the main Frio, the terrain levels off and is surfaced by the gravelly and loamy soils that support mesquite and blackbrush, characteristic of the South Texas plains.

DRY HOLLOW. Dry Hollow, which has an intermittent stream known as Dry Branch, begins eighteen miles southwest of Paint Rock in far east central Tom Green County (at 31°20′ N, 100°07′ W) and runs northeast for 15½ miles to its mouth on the Concho River, 5½ miles west of Paint Rock (at 31°31′ N, 100°01′ W). Local terrain of rolling prairie is surfaced by clay loams that support grasses, oaks, junipers, and mesquite.

DRY HOLLOW CREEK. Dry Hollow Creek rises a mile west of the Gellermann road in eastern Gillespie County (at 30°19′ N, 98°41′ W) and runs northeast for 6½ miles to its mouth on North Grape Creek, two miles west of the Blanco county line in eastern Gillespie County (at 30°22′ N, 98°37′ W). It rises in the hills of the eastern Edwards Plateau and crosses flat terrain broken by an area of steep slopes and limestone benches that give a stairstep appearance to the landscape. Shallow clayey and loamy soils support grasses and open stands of live oak, mesquite, and Ashe juniper.

DRY LIPAN CREEK. Dry Lipan Creek rises near Susan Peak oilfield in southeastern Tom Green County (at 31°14′ N, 100°19′ W) and runs northeast for twenty-three miles to its mouth on Lipan Creek, north of Mereta at Farm Road 1692 (at 31°28′ N, 100°08′ W). It crosses flat terrain with local shallow depressions surfaced by clay and sandy loam that supports water-tolerant hardwoods, conifers, and grasses.

DRY MORMON CREEK. Dry Mormon Creek, formerly known as Walnut Creek, rises four miles southeast of Doss in northwestern Gillespie County (at 30°24′ N, 99°05′ W) and runs northwest for six miles to its mouth on Mormon Creek, three-quarters of a mile northeast of Doss in northwestern Gillespie County (at 30°28′ N, 99°07′ W). The creek begins in the limestone hills on the eastern edge of the Edwards Plateau and crosses flat to rolling terrain surfaced by shallow to deep sandy and clayey loams that support brush and grasses, as well as open stands of live oak, Ashe juniper, and some mesquite.

DRY PRONG OF DEEP CREEK. The Dry Prong of Deep Creek, sometimes called the West Fork of Deep Creek, rises a mile northeast of Placid in northeastern McCulloch County (at 31°20′ N, 99°10′ W) and runs north for 7½ miles to its mouth on Deep Creek, a mile southeast of Milburn (at 31°25′ N, 99°07′ W). It traverses generally flat terrain with local shallow depressions, surfaced by clay and sandy loams that support water-tolerant hardwoods, conifers, and grasses.

DRY RUN. Dry Run rises in northwestern Gonzales County (at 29°38′ N, 97°27′ W) and runs northeast for four miles to its mouth on Sandy Fork (at 29°39′ N, 97°23′ W). It traverses flat to rolling prairie surfaced by sandy clay soil that supports mixed hardwoods and pines.

DRY SANDY CREEK. Dry Sandy Creek rises three miles southeast of Rockdale in southeastern Milam County (at 30°39′ N, 96°56′ W) and runs north for six miles to its mouth on Sandy Creek, three miles southeast of Minerva (at 30°44′ N, 96°57′ W). It traverses generally flat to rolling terrain surfaced by clay and sandy loams that support hardwoods, scrub brush, and grasses.

DRY SIMPSON CREEK. Dry Simpson Creek rises nine miles south of San Saba in southern San Saba County (at 31°05′ N, 98°47′ W) and runs northeast for 13½ miles to its mouth on Simpson Creek (at 31°11′ N, 98°41′ W). It traverses flat to rolling terrain surfaced by sandy and clayey loam soils that support live oak, Ashe juniper, mesquite, and grasses.

DUBBS, EMANUEL (1843–1932). Emanuel Dubbs, pioneer, minister, and county judge, was born on March 21, 1843, on a farm near New Franklin, Ohio, the youngest of the six children of Daniel and Elizabeth (Meckley) Dubbs. He attended Mount Union College and at the outbreak of the Civil War[qv] enlisted in Company I of the First Ohio Infantry. After the war he moved to Elkhart County, Indiana, and engaged in the lumber business with his brother. He married Angeline Freed in 1868. After a fire destroyed his sawmill in 1871, Dubbs and his wife moved to Kansas, where he worked for a time with railroad-construction crews and then engaged in buffalo hunting[qv] and dairy farming. He was said to have built the first house in Dodge City. In 1873 he opened a dairy farm and beer garden on Duck Creek about five miles from Dodge. He served beer and "milk punch" to passersby, and soon his "Buttermilk Ranch" became a favorite refreshment stop for travelers. In 1874 he accompanied A. C. Myers and Charles Rath[qv] to the Texas Panhandle and helped construct the buildings at the Adobe Walls trading post. He claimed to have taken part in the second battle of Adobe Walls, on June 27, 1874 (*see* RED RIVER WAR). The accounts of William (Billy) Dixon[qv] and others at Adobe Walls do not mention him, however, and the most reliable sources indicate that he was not present at the battle; Andy Johnson, an eyewitness of the battle, stated that Dubbs was at Dodge City at the time.

Dubbs continued hunting and reportedly had two more close brushes with Indians. He also rode in the posse that broke up "Dutch" Henry Born's[qv] horse-stealing ring. In 1875 Dubbs and his hunting party established a headquarters camp near the site of present Clarendon. His dairy cows all died of milk fever, but by 1877 he had accumulated about 400 longhorn cattle.[qv] Weary of a barkeeper's occupation, Dubbs sold his ranch and in the spring of 1878 moved his wife and three small sons to Sweetwater Creek in Wheeler County. Near Mobeetie he built a rock house with a dirt floor and roof and made money by selling meat and vegetables to the troops at Fort Elliott. Two more sons were added to the Dubbs family in Wheeler County.

When the county was organized in 1879, Dubbs was elected its first judge. Lacking practical experience in law, he often made decisions with little consideration for legal technicalities. He was shortly compelled to resign and go to Dallas to stand trial for ruling a series of arrests by a deputy United States marshall illegal and releasing the prisoners. He was acquitted, and in January 1880 was unanimously elected to serve again as county judge. He was subsequently reelected to that office in 1884, 1886, and 1888.

In 1890 he moved to a ranch northwest of Clarendon near his former buffalo-hunting campsite in Donley County. Having always been active in church work, Dubbs became a Disciples of Christ minister in 1896 and was placed in charge of that denomination's mission work in the Panhandle. In 1898 he was made pastor of the Christian church at Clarendon, where he made his home until 1922. Dubbs contributed several sketches, including his own reminiscences of his early years as a buffalo hunter, to the book *Pioneer Days in the Southwest*, published in 1909. His wife died in 1910, and after 1922 Dubbs moved to Amarillo to be near his sons. He died in July 1932 and was buried in Clarendon.

BIBLIOGRAPHY: T. Lindsay Baker and Billy R. Harrison, *Adobe Walls: The History and Archaeology of the 1874 Trading Post* (College Station: Texas A&M University Press, 1986). Virginia Browder, *Donley County: Land O' Promise* (Wichita Falls, Texas: Nortex, 1975). Seymour V. Connor et al., *Battles of Texas* (Waco: Texian Press, 1967; 3d ed. 1980). Millie Jones Porter, *Memory Cups of Panhandle Pioneers* (Clarendon, Texas: Clarendon Press, 1945).   H. Allen Anderson

DUBINA, TEXAS. Dubina, the first Czech settlement in Texas, is five miles east of Schulenburg in southern Fayette County. In November 1856 a group of Czech settlers found shelter from a strong north wind and hail under a grove of large oak trees in what is now Dubina. Among the group were Frank Marak, Joseph Kahlich, Ignac Sramek, Joseph Peter, Valentine Holub, Ignac Muzny, Valentine Haidušek, and Frank Kossa. The next day the settlers built a shelter and, as the months progressed, planted crops; they made a total of one bale of cotton the first year, but through perseverance and hard work, the community prospered.

When the Civil War[qv] broke out, many were unwilling to fight for a cause they didn't believe in, but most were drafted, among them Augustine Haidušek,[qv] who learned English during the war and became the first lawyer of Czech descent in the United States. He was also county judge of Fayette County, mayor of La Grange, state legislator, and publisher of a Czech-language newspaper called *Svoboda* (freedom). After the war members of the community built a gin, general store, saloon, meat market, blacksmith shop, hotel, mill, zoo, telegraph office, and post office, the last of which operated from 1885 to 1910. Most of the town's property was owned by Joseph Peter, who was elected state representative from Fayette and Lee counties.

The community was first called Navidad and later Bohemian Navidad. Augustine Haidušek renamed it Dubina, Czech for "oak grove." As favorable reports about Texas reached the old country, the number of Czech settlers entering Dubina increased greatly, and Dubina became the stopover place for Czechs entering Texas.

In 1876 a Catholic church, the first in Dubina, was built on land donated by Joseph Peter. Later a school was built on land donated by Ignac Muzny. In 1900 the church served a parish of more than 600 families. In 1909 a hurricane destroyed the first church, and in 1912 the building was replaced. Dubina's social life revolved around the church, and a number of Catholic social organizations were established, including a Katoliká jednota texaská (Czech Catholic Union of Texas) lodge in 1887, a St. Ann's Society (1889), and a Ceskorimská katolická podporující jednota zen texaskych (Czech–Roman Catholic Aid Union of Women in Texas) society (1900).

In 1873 the railroad bypassed Dubina, and in 1912 a fire caused extensive damage to the town; many settlers left the area. In the mid-1980s Dubina had a Catholic church, a community hall, a restaurant, several historical buildings, and many giant oak trees, one measuring twenty-six feet in circumference with a 110-foot spread. The population ranged from 160 to 500 in the late nineteenth century. The community was still listed in 1990.

BIBLIOGRAPHY: John Janacek, *St. Cyril and Methodius—Diamond Jubilee, 1877–1952, Dubina, Texas* (2d ed., Yorktown, Texas: *DeWitt County View*, 1979). La Grange High School, *Fayette County: Past and Present* (La Grange, Texas, 1976). Clinton Machann, ed., *The Czechs in Texas* (College Station: Texas A&M University Department of English, 1979).
Ed Janecka

DUBLIN, TEXAS. Dublin is on U.S. highways 67 and 377 in southwest Erath County. It was founded in 1854 by A. H. Dobkins and named in 1860, probably for the warning cry at Indian raids, "Double In," for the capital of Ireland, or for the double-log cabins used by early settlers. Growth increased in 1874 as Dublin acquired stagecoach service and a post office. In 1881 the Texas Central Railroad was built through to Mount Airy, a few miles from Dublin. J. D. Bishop laid out a townsite on the line four miles south of Mount Airy, which drew residents from old to new Dublin. Within a year the new Dublin had forty-five businesses and sixty-five homes, so the railroad moved its depot from Mount Airy to new Dublin. The town was incorporated on March 18, 1889. By 1890 the population was 2,025. It was 2,370 in 1900, 2,271 in 1930, 2,746 in 1950, 2,810 in 1970, 2,723 in 1980, and 3,190 in 1990. The town is a center for agriculture and industry, including oil and gas production, clothing factories, peanut shelling and drying plants, feed mills, milk processing, saddle and rope making, and metal stamping. Dublin has two city parks, the Lyon Museum, a public library, a hospital, and a nursing home. It also has an airport, two railroads, a golf course, and recreational facilities at Proctor Reservoir.[qv] The town was one of the first in the state to have streetcars. It is the birthplace of golfer Ben Hogan, home of a world-championship rodeo, and the former home of the annual Grand Army of the Republic reunion.

BIBLIOGRAPHY: Vallie Eoff, A History of Erath County, Texas (M.A. thesis, University of Texas, 1937). Ray Miller, *Eyes of Texas Travel Guide: Panhandle/Plains Edition* (Houston: Cordovan, 1982). Kathleen E. and Clifton R. St. Clair, eds., *Little Towns of Texas* (Jacksonville, Texas: Jayroe Graphic Arts, 1982).
William R. Hunt

DUBOIS, CHARLOTTE ESTELLE (1903–1982). Charlotte Estelle DuBois, music educator, daughter of Smith and Caroline (Lambert) DuBois, was born at Liberty, Indiana, on October 26, 1903. She earned a bachelor of arts degree at Western College in Oxford, Ohio, in 1925, an academic diploma in piano at the Cincinnati Conservatory of Music in 1927, and a master of arts degree at Teachers College, Columbia University, in 1936. Before coming to Texas she served in Louisiana as supervisor of music for the Shreveport and Caddo Parish schools. In 1940 she joined the music faculty at the University of Texas, where she remained until her retirement in August 1971. She took guest teaching assignments at the University of California at Los Angeles from January to August 1949, the University of Michigan from June to August 1952, and the University of British Columbia for the summer session of 1958.

She was the first woman to be named a full professor in the University of Texas Music Department. In the Music Educators National Conference she served as a member of the Education Research Council and as chairman of the National Committee on Music for the Elementary Teacher. She contributed articles to the *Music Educators Journal, The School Musician, Southwestern Musician,* and other publications. She wrote *Songs to Play* (1954) and *The Keyboard Way to Music* (1956); she was a coauthor of the elementary textbook series *This Is Music for Today* (1971), which is used throughout the country. She gave lectures and demonstrations at numerous colleges and universities and for conventions of such groups as the National Association of Schools of Music and the Music Educators National Conference. She was a member of All Saints Episcopal Church in Austin and a Republican.[qv]

DuBois was an honorary member of Sigma Alpha Iota, a national fraternity for women in music, and was awarded the fraternity's ring of excellence. She received a Teaching Excellence Award from the Students' Association of the University of Texas and in October 1971 the rarely given Citation of Service "in recognition of excellence and devotion to the music education profession" from the Texas Music Educators Association. Charlotte DuBois died on January 1, 1982, in Austin and was buried in Liberty, Indiana.

BIBLIOGRAPHY: Vertical Files, Barker Texas History Center, University of Texas at Austin. *Who's Who of American Women,* 1958–59.
Janet M. McGaughey

DUBOIS DE SALIGNY (1809–1888). Jean Pierre Isidore Alphonse Dubois, French diplomat in the Republic of Texas,[qv] son of Jean Baptiste Isidore and Marie Louise Rose (Bertrand) Dubois, was born on April 8, 1809, in Caen, Normandy, France. He entered on a diplomatic career in 1831 and became, successively, secretary of the French legations in Hanover, Greece, and the United States. While at this last post he was instructed by the French government to go to Texas to investigate the conditions and prospects of the new republic. During this mission in the spring of 1839 he visited Galveston, Houston, and

Jean Pierre Isidore Dubois de Saligny, ca. 1841. Lithograph. Ashbel Smith Papers, CAH; CN 01265. Dubois de Saligny inscribed a copy of this picture to Ashbel Smith, as a "token of esteem and friendship."

the coastal area as far west as Matagorda. His reports to the French foreign minister influenced the French government to recognize Texas in a treaty of friendship, navigation, and commerce.

Appointed to head the new legation with the rank of chargé d'affaires, Dubois, or "A. de Saligny," as he now signed himself (he was not in fact a member of the French nobility), returned to Texas in January 1840. He established his residence in Austin, then the capital of the republic, and lived successively in the inn of Richard Bullock (*see* BULLOCK HOUSE) and in a nearby house on West Pecan Street, where he entertained members of the Texas government. He bought twenty-one acres of land on the east side of town and began construction there of the house known today as the French Legation.qv As a strong supporter of the Catholic Church,qv he worked effectively in this period with John Timon and Jean Marie Odinqqv for the restoration of church property taken at the revolution. In acknowledgment of his efforts Pope Gregory XVI later awarded him the Order of Saint Gregory the Great. He was drawn into Texas politics and backed the controversial Franco-Texian Bill,qv became identified as a supporter of Sam Houston,qv and was a bitter enemy of the Mirabeau B. Lamarqv faction. His personal and political troubles culminated in the Pig Warqv with his landlord Richard Bullock and in his withdrawal in April 1841, without instructions from the French foreign minister, to Louisiana. Dubois had sold his still unfinished house and property to Odin, and he never again returned to Austin.

Although the French foreign minister criticized Dubois for leaving his post without permission, he stood behind the agent in his quarrel with the Texas government and insisted on receiving an appropriate apology and promises to bring Bullock to trial. Somewhat tardily, Anson Jones,qv secretary of state in the second Houston administration, fulfilled these requirements and paved the way for Dubois's return to Galveston in April 1842. Dubois resumed cordial relations with the Houston administration, but, his health failing, he departed for France in July. During his absence Viscount Jules de Cramayelqv served as chargé d'affaires ad interim.

Though he was disappointed in his hopes for promotion to a more prestigious post, Dubois returned in January 1844 to serve as the French representative until the annexationqv of Texas to the United States. During this last period of his mission he evinced a marked preference for Louisiana over Texas as a place of residence and traveled only infrequently and reluctantly to Galveston to fulfill his duties. With his British colleague, Capt. Charles Elliot,qv he tried to stave off annexation, but, constrained by his instructions to a position of reserve, he could offer only the good offices and moral support of France in seeking to obtain Mexican recognition of the Texas republic. Dubois withdrew to Louisiana in April 1845, where he remained until 1846.

In 1849–50 he served as French minister plenipotentiary to the Hague and in 1856 represented France on a commission to verify the Russo-Turkish border in Asia. Emperor Napoleon III appointed him plenipotentiary to Mexico in 1860. His dispatches from that post urging French intervention helped the emperor decide to undertake the military expedition that placed Maximilian and Carlota on their Mexican thrones. In 1862 Dubois was promoted to the rank of grand officer in the Legion of Honor. While in Mexico he married María de Ortiz de la Borbolla; they had one son. In 1864, after being accused of dishonest financial operations and too close an association with the clerical party in Mexico, Dubois was recalled in 1863 and returned to France in disgrace. Despite repeated attempts to vindicate himself, he was unable to obtain another assignment from the foreign ministry. He died in 1888 in his residence, known as Le Prieuré, in St. Martin du Vieux Bellême, a village in Normandy.

BIBLIOGRAPHY: Nancy Nichols Barker, "Devious Diplomat: Dubois de Saligny and the Republic of Texas," *Southwestern Historical Quarterly* 72 (January 1969). Nancy Nichols Barker, trans. and ed., *The French Legation in Texas*, Vol. 1: *Recognition, Rupture, and Reconciliation* (Austin: Texas State Historical Association, 1971); Vol. 2: *Mission Miscarried* (1973). Nancy Nichols Barker, "The Republic of Texas: A French View," *Southwestern Historical Quarterly* 71 (October 1967). Kenneth Hafertepe, *A History of the French Legation* (Austin: Texas State Historical Association, 1989). *Nancy N. Barker*

DUBOSE, TEXAS. Dubose was on the Texas-Mexican Railway fifteen miles southwest of Benavides in southern Duval County. A post office was established there in 1911 with John F. Dubose, after whom the community was named, as postmaster. In 1914 the community had a general store and cotton gin. Estimates of the Dubose population remained at twenty-five from the mid-1920s to the mid-1940s. Its post office was closed in 1929, and the community no longer appeared on maps of the area by the late 1940s.

Martin Donell Kohout

DUBUIS, CLAUDE MARIE (1817–1895). Claude Marie Dubuis, second Catholic bishop of Texas, son of François and Antoinette (Dubost) Dubuis, was born at Teche, France, on March 8, 1817. He was raised on his parents' farm and received his early instruction from his devout mother. When Dubuis was ten years old, he was sent to live with his maternal uncle, the abbé Dubost, a pastor in a nearby town. Though it was thought that the abbé would provide Dubuis with the knowledge he needed to enter the seminary, he actually used the boy as an assistant to run errands for him. In 1833, when the time came for Dubuis to enter L'Argentière, a preparatory seminary, he found that he was sadly lacking in educational background, notably Greek. Therefore, after six months of frustration, he gave up, withdrew from the seminary, and returned to his home in Teche, determined that he would acquire some skill that would see him through his life. He worked as a day laborer for a short time before he decided to become a missionary. His mother again suggested that he approach Dubost for help, and this time the abbé sent Dubuis to a tutor named Fouilland in a nearby village. Fouilland taught Dubuis Latin, Greek, and French grammar for eight months, after which the young man was given another chance at the seminary. He was sent first to St. Jodard, a minor seminary, where he passed all of his courses without difficulty. He then returned to L'Argentière and graduated with honors after two years. By 1840 he had entered the major seminary of St. Irenaeus at Lyons, and, in 1844, at the age of twenty-seven, he was ordained a priest.

His first assignment was at Lyons, where in 1846 he met Bishop Jean Marie Odin,qv vicar apostolic of Texas. Odin had returned to his homeland to recruit missionary priests and nuns for work in Texas. He did not gloss over the hardships his followers would have to endure, but this seemed to inspire more than to deter Dubuis, who, with a small group of fellow recruits, set sail from Le Havre in March of that year. The missionaries, sent first to the Barrens, a Vincentian Seminary in Perryville, Missouri, to learn English, did not arrive in Texas until the winter of 1847, about six months after Pope Pius IX elevated the state of Texas to a diocese with Odin as bishop. Dubuis's first assignment, in 1844, was a pastorate at Castroville, a relatively new settlement founded by the Texas entrepreneur Henri Castro.qv Dubuis's ministry there included the surrounding villages of D'Hanis, Vandenburg, Quihi, New Braunfels, and Fredericksburg, and he often had to ride on horseback through hostile Comanche territory in order to carry out his priestly duties. He was captured four times by Indians. When Dubuis left Castroville for San Antonio in 1851 he left behind him a healthy, growing St. Louis parish, as well as a church building and rectory built mainly by his own hands. He is credited with developing the architectural style distinctive to Castroville, which resembles that of Alsatian structures. He was given the pastorate at San Fernando in San Antonio (see SAN FERNANDO DE BÉXAR CATHEDRAL), a church that needed more religious to attend to its scattered members. Therefore, in 1852, he was sent to France for volunteers for the Texas missions. Fourteen students and priests responded to his appeal.

When he returned to Galveston, Dubuis was appointed vicar general and was again sent to San Antonio. There he completed work on the Ursuline convent, as well as the new St. Mary's Church (now St. Mary's Cathedralqv). When Odin was made archbishop of New Orleans, Dubuis was appointed bishop of Galveston. He was consecrated by Odin on November 23, 1862, in Lyons. In May 1863 he entered his episcopal city, where for the next seventeen years he worked for the Catholic Churchqv in Texas. During his tenure as bishop he brought sixty-six religious into the state, many of whom were members of the Sisters of Charity of the Incarnate Wordqv of Lyons. Dubuis was responsible for founding their order in the United States, with motherhouses in the Galveston-Houston and San Antonio dioceses.

Building upon the foundation laid during the colonial era of Texas by the Franciscansqv and during the 1840s and 1850s by the Vincentian Fathersqv and others, Dubuis was able not only to restore a church ravaged by the Civil War,qv but to leave to his successor a flourishing Catholic faith. As bishop he directed the building of hospitals, schools, and orphanages. By 1867 the Diocese of Galveston had fifty-five churches and chapels. By Dubuis's request Pope Pius established a second diocese in the state in 1874, that of San Antonio (see SAN ANTONIO, CATHOLIC ARCHDIOCESE OF).

By 1880 Dubuis was suffering from such poor health that he was forced to return to France, and Bishop Nicholas A. Gallagherqv took over the administration of the see of Galveston. Dubuis still remained ordinary of Galveston until he resigned in 1892. In that year Pope Leo XIII designated him titular archbishop of Arca, a title Dubuis held until his death at Vernaison, France, on May 21, 1895. He was buried in the parish churchyard at Coutouvre, France. In 1949 Bishop Lawrence J. FitzSimonqv visited the gravesite and discovered that Dubuis's name on the stone was unreadable and that his tenure as bishop of Texas was not mentioned. By 1951 FitzSimon had had the body removed to a crypt inside the parish church, where a suitable monument was erected.

BIBLIOGRAPHY: Catholic Archives of Texas, Files, Austin. Sister Mary Loyola Hegarty, C.C.V.I, *Serving with Gladness: The Origin and History of the Congregation of the Sisters of Charity of the Incarnate Word, Houston, Texas* (Milwaukee: Bruce, 1967).   *Patrick Foley*

DUCK CREEK (Clay County). Duck Creek rises just west of Lake Arrowhead in northwestern Clay County (at 33°55′ N, 98°22′ W) and runs southeast in its upper reaches, then east-northeast in its middle and lower reaches, for a total distance of fifteen miles before reaching its mouth on the Little Wichita River, a mile west of Henrietta in central Clay County (at 33°49′ N, 98°14′ W). The stream traverses generally flat terrain with local shallow depressions, surfaced by clay and sandy loams. The area drained by the stream, along which water-tolerant hardwoods and conifers are common, historically has served as crop and range land.

____ (Concho County). Duck Creek rises six miles northwest of Eden in central Concho County (at 31°17′ N, 99°53′ W) and runs twenty-nine miles north and then northeast to its mouth on the Concho River, nine miles east of Paint Rock (at 31°31′ N, 99°47′ W). It crosses steep slopes and benches surfaced by shallow clay loams that support grasses, live oaks, junipers, and mesquite.

____ (Cooke County). Duck Creek rises 11½ miles southwest of Gainesville in southwestern Cooke County (at 33°30′ N, 97°18′ W) and runs east for eighteen miles to its mouth on Clear Creek, two miles south of Sanger in Denton County (at 33°20′ N, 97°11′ W). The stream, located in the Grand Prairie region of north central Texas, traverses grasslands and croplands with clayey and loamy soils. Duck Creek was possibly the location of Denton County's first mill. Members of the Caddo Indian confederacy may have established settlements along its banks.

BIBLIOGRAPHY: C. A. Bridges, *History of Denton, Texas, from Its Beginning to 1960* (Waco: Texian Press, 1978).

____ (Dallas County). Duck Creek rises two miles east of the University of Texas at Dallas campus inside the Richardson city limits in northern Dallas County (at 32°58′ N, 96°43′ W) and runs southeast for 19½ miles to its mouth on the East Fork of the Trinity River, a half mile south of the Rockwell-Forney Dam and Lake Ray Hubbard in Kaufman County (at 32°48′ N, 96°31′ W). The terrain in the creek's watershed varies from rolling hills to flat and is surfaced by clay and clay loam. The creek is intermittent in its upper reaches and has some wooded areas in its lower. Settlement on Duck Creek began as early as 1851, and by the 1880s the communities of Duck Creek and Embree had developed there. In 1891 the two settlements voted to incorporate as Garland.

____ (Dickens County). Duck Creek rises seven miles northwest of Dickens on the eastern edge of the Caprock in northwest Dickens County (at 33°43′ N, 100°57′ W) and runs southeast for forty miles through southern Dickens and northern Kent counties to its mouth on the Salt Fork of the Brazos River, six miles northeast of Clairemont in east central Kent County (at 33°14′ N, 100°41′ W). Some of the first cotton in Dickens County was planted near the creek by Abel J. Hagins in 1889. Two years later Hagins built the first cotton gin in the county on Duck Creek. The stream, named for the numerous ducks that gathered at its water holes and small lakes, is the largest in

Dickens County. In its upper reaches it crosses a flat flood-prone area with local shallow depressions. Water-tolerant hardwoods, conifers, and grasses predominate in this area, which has clay loam and sandy loam soils. In its middle reaches the creek enters an area of moderately steep slopes and locally high relief, with shallow to moderately deep silt loams that support mesquite and grasses.

BIBLIOGRAPHY: Fred Arrington, *A History of Dickens County: Ranches and Rolling Plains* (Quanah, Texas: Nortex, 1971).

_____ (Grayson County). Duck Creek, which is intermittent in its upper reaches, rises just within the northern city limits of Denison in northern Grayson County (at 33°45′ N, 96°33′ W) and runs first northeast, then southeast for a total of just over four miles to its mouth on the Red River, 1½ miles northeast of Denison (at 33°47′ N, 96°30′ W). It traverses flat to slightly rolling terrain with local shallow depressions, surfaced by soils ranging from sandy and clay loams to shallow, stony, clay loams that support mixed hardwoods, pine, juniper, oak, conifers, chaparral, cacti, and various grasses.

_____ (Robertson County). Duck Creek rises on the Limestone-Robertson county line four miles north of Petteway (at 31°17′ N, 96°36′ W) and runs southeast for thirty-two miles to its mouth on the Navasota River, 3½ miles northeast of Camp Creek Lake (at 31°06′ N, 96°17′ W). It traverses nearly level terrain surfaced by sandy loams that support post oaks and grasses.

_____ (Smith County). Duck Creek rises two miles north of Carroll in northwestern Smith County (at 32°30′ N, 95°32′ W) and runs northeast for thirteen miles to its mouth on the Old Sabine River Channel, just south of the Sabine River and north of Lindale Club Lake (at 32°36′ N, 95°25′ W). It traverses flat to rolling terrain with some local steep slopes, descending into low-lying floodplains near its mouth. The area soil is a red clay covered by gravel, interspersed with a brown loamy fine sand; near the creek's mouth the soils change to poorly drained loams. In its upper and middle reaches grow pine and hardwood forests, while water-tolerant hardwoods, conifers, and grasses grow near its mouth. Bell Branch flows into the creek from the south. In 1929 the Duck Creek soil erosion project was established in the area to study erosion and to formulate effective methods to control it. In 1934 the watershed became the site of a demonstration project for testing erosion-control procedures. Landowners in the 25,000-acre area worked with federal officials to implement a conservation plan for each farm. A Civilian Conservation Corps^{qv} camp was transferred to nearby Lindale to provide a labor force for constructing dams and fences and planting trees and grass. The Duck Creek area thus became an important training ground for engineers, biologists, agronomists, foresters, and others. A Texas Historical Commission^{qv} marker was erected on the site of the Depression-era research station in 1984. A 1981 map showed the Duck Creek church, named for the stream, located in the area just northeast of Garden Valley.

BIBLIOGRAPHY: "Lindale CCC Camp Work on the Duck Creek Project Area Farms," *Chronicles of Smith County*, Summer 1978.

_____ (Van Zandt County). Duck Creek rises just over a mile east of Farm Road 2728 in extreme northwest Van Zandt County (at 32°46′ N, 96°07′ W) and runs north for seven miles before disemboguing into Duck Cove on Lake Tawakoni south of White Point (at 32°50′ N, 96°04′ W). The stream traverses flat terrain with local shallow depressions, surfaced with clayey and sandy loams that support water-tolerant hardwoods, conifers, and grasses.

DUCK CREEK, TEXAS. Duck Creek was the name of two communities, sometimes called Old Duck Creek and New Duck Creek, located in northeastern Dallas County; their site was within the present city limits of Garland, fifteen miles northeast of downtown Dallas. The first Duck Creek, at the present junction of Garland Road and Duck Creek, had its beginning as one of the original settlements of the Peters colony.^{qv} Early settlers were attracted to the area by the many springs along the creek. The first schoolhouse, a log structure built sometime after 1846, was replaced by a frame building in 1852. This second school also served as a meetingplace for the Baptist and Methodist congregations. In 1854 Duck Creek acquired a post office, which it retained until 1866. About 1868 the school was named Duck Creek Academy. Overcrowding caused the school to move into the Grange Hall at an unknown date and later into the Methodist Church. In 1880 a new one-room school was built on the site of the old school. The Masonic and Grange Hall was moved to the school and added onto it as a new wing. Permission to establish a Duck Creek Masonic lodge was granted on September 19, 1873, and a charter was issued on June 7, 1875. In 1874 a store was established on the west bank of the creek, and in 1876 a corn mill was built. Duck Creek acquired a post office again in 1877. By 1884 the community had a district school, three churches, two gristmills, three steam cotton gins, and three general stores. Its population of 100 included three physicians, two teachers, one carpenter and a carpenter-wagonmaker, one blacksmith, and one shoemaker. Two years later the town acquired a patent roller flour mill, which was built on the east side of the creek. The largest business in Duck Creek is said to have been the Grange^{qv} store, known as the Duck Creek Co-operative Association, which closed in March 1887.

In 1886, first the Gulf, Colorado and Santa Fe and then the Dallas and Greenville railroad bypassed Duck Creek. The Santa Fe built a depot about a mile to the east, while the Missouri, Kansas and Texas (which acquired the Dallas and Greenville later in 1886) established a depot less than a mile to the north. Both railroads bought land from William A. Tinsley and laid out towns adjacent to their depots. The community established by the Santa Fe was named Embree, after Kelley H. Embree, a physician, storekeeper, and Duck Creek postmaster. The community laid out by the MK&T took the name Duck Creek, and was also known as New Duck Creek. Thereafter, residents of Old Duck Creek moved to one or the other of the new communities. Sometime in 1886 or early 1887 the Duck Creek *Rustler* moved and became reincarnated as the Embree *Enterprise*. On February 1, 1887, the Duck Creek post office was moved to the Santa Fe depot at Embree.

The site of New Duck Creek is in Garland south of the Missouri, Kansas and Texas (later the Missouri Pacific) tracks and north of State Street. After the (Old) Duck Creek *Rustler* moved to Embree, John H. Cullum moved to Duck Creek at the urging of Thomas F. Nash, manager of the Grange store, and established the Duck Creek *News*, whose first issue appeared on April 8, 1887. Duck Creek remained a shipping point for area farmers. By late October 1887 it had shipped about 2,000 bales of cotton for the season and still had "a large quantity" on hand.

New Duck Creek and Embree engaged in an intense rivalry, with several attempts made by one town to take over the other. In April 1887, one or more Duck Creek partisans had a map recorded that gave the whole area the name of Duck Creek. The two towns also obtained injunctions to prevent each other from incorporating. In spite of this, Embree was incorporated on November 12, 1887. Two weeks earlier, on October 29, Congressman Joseph Abbott,^{qv} who was traveling to Washington for the opening of Congress, stopped at Duck Creek at the request of local residents to look at the situation. Shortly afterward he succeeded in having the post office moved to a site midway between the two depots. The new post office, established on December 9, 1887, was named Garland, after United States attorney general Augustus H. Garland, reportedly a friend of Nash's, Cullum's, and Abbott's. In 1891 Garland was incorporated and absorbed Duck Creek and Embree. That same year the Duck Creek *News* became the Garland *News*.

BIBLIOGRAPHY: Ruth Buchholz, "Our Garland (Lovely and Lively)," *Garland 1988 Magazine*. Dallas *Morning News*, March 7, 12, September 15, October 11, 30, 1887, August 4, October 4, 1953. Dallas *Times Herald*, August 5, 1962. Garland *Daily News and Times Reporter*, July 31, 1962. *Memorial and Biographical History of Dallas County*

(Chicago: Lewis, 1892; rpt., Dallas: Walsworth, 1976). David Switzer, *It's Our Dallas County* (Dallas: Switzer, 1954). Vertical Files, Barker Texas History Center, University of Texas at Austin (Garland, Texas).
Lisa C. Maxwell

DUCOS, ARMAND (?–?). Armand Ducos, in association with Alexander Bourgeois d'Orvanne,qv received two colonization contracts from the Republic of Texas.qv A contract of June 3, 1842, permitted the settlement of 1,200 families or single men in the region of the Uvalde, Frio, and upper Medina rivers, at least one-third of the colonists to be settled within eighteen months. The second contract, dated July 6, 1842, permitted the settlement of 500 families on the Rio Grande between the mouth of the river and Reynosa, Tamaulipas, but no evidence is extant that the grantees located any settlers on either grant.

BIBLIOGRAPHY: Rudolph L. Biesele, *The History of the German Settlements in Texas, 1831–1861* (Austin: Von Boeckmann-Jones, 1930; rpt. 1964). William Campbell Binkley, *The Expansionist Movement in Texas, 1836–1850* (Berkeley: University of California Press, 1925).
Rudolph L. Biesele

DUDE RANCHING. Dude ranching is a southwestern and western vacation industry in which paying guests of a ranch participate in ordinary ranch activities. Unlike resorts, where guests are free to do as they please, dude ranches combine social and recreational activity by requiring their visitors to interact with the owner's family or employees and to participate in the life of the ranch. Guests at dude ranches have traditionally included both men and women. The old stereotyped dude was a "tenderfoot," "greenhorn," or person with citified or outlandish clothes. He eventually came to be thought of as "someone from elsewhere" who came to take part in the ongoing activities of ranch life. Dudes have ranged from misfits who have left the East to live quietly in the West on remittance checks from home, to guests who park at Nevada dude ranches seeking privacy while their divorces go through. The phrase "dude ranching" did not come into common usage until the 1880s. The industry developed in the nineteenth century around stock ranches, mountain ranches or lodges, and hot-springs resorts or health spas located chiefly in the western and southwestern United States, but sometimes as far away as Hawaii. Dude ranching flourished in the early twentieth century at ranches in Wyoming, Montana, and Colorado, which offered summer fishing and hunting as well as ranch activities, and at their year-round counterparts in Arizona and New Mexico, more commonly known as "guest ranches." Others could be found in Idaho, Oregon, Texas, California, and Nevada. Because they are often located close to national forests or parks, dude ranches have been credited with a role in developing consciousness and support for conservation in the United States.

Dude ranching traces its beginnings to the period when the pursuit of a healthful climate and rugged life replaced an earlier preference of the wealthy for health spas and resorts. Buffalo Bill Cody, Capt. James Cook, and Howard Eaton, who led wilderness big-game hunting parties, made the first arrangements with ranchers to furnish guests with room, board, and the chance to hunt. Early clientele consisted largely of upper-class easterners and visitors from Europe, such as the Irish earl of Dunraven, who visited a dude ranch near Estes Park, Colorado, as early as the 1870s. Both Theodore Roosevelt and western fiction writer Owen Wister were first introduced to the West at dude ranches. In addition to cattle ranches, sheep ranches such as the Prade Ranch,qv which raised Angora goats, sheep, cattle, and horses in Real County, Texas, became dude ranches by promising a healthy environment and a chance to participate in the vigorous life of shepherds. Another type of dude ranch evolved in Nevada with the passage of a law in the 1920s permitting persons to obtain a divorce who had been in residence initially for only six months, a requirement eventually reduced to six weeks. With few good hotels in the area, dude ranches became popular places for celebrities to hide while waiting for divorces. On these ranches, the proprietor's wife often served as counselor to soon-to-be-separated individuals. Ranchers relied on guests to develop their clientele by word of mouth in New York, Boston, Philadelphia, and Chicago. Later, ranchers organized visits to the East to meet with prospective guests, and bought advertisements in national magazines and booklets. Writers who reported back to the East in novels with such romantic titles as Loraine Hornaday Fielding's *French Heels to Spurs* (1930) and Mary Roberts Rinehart's *Lost Ecstasy* (1927) popularized the industry by relating their ranch experience and celebrating the liberating qualities of ranch life, cowboy lore, and nature.

Declining cattle prices in the 1880s forced more ranch owners to take in guests, and World War Iqv fostered both American tourism and dude ranching as European travel declined. By the 1920s there were more than sixty dude ranches in Wyoming and Montana and numerous others elsewhere. A Dude Ranchers' Association was formed in 1926, and the industry gained support from railroads that advertised guest ranches in their brochures as a means of increasing passenger trade. In 1934 the University of Wyoming offered its first bachelor of science degree in "recreational ranching." By 1936 as many as 356 ranches were in operation.

In Texas, dude ranching began in Bandera County around 1920, when the Buck Ranch took in paying summer guests and the nearby Bruce Ranch began taking in overflow guests from its neighbor. By the 1930s, dude ranches were located at Alpine, Marfa, and Mitre Peakqv Park in Southwest Texas, in the Hill Countryqv at Comfort, Kerrville, Bandera, Hunt, Junction, Medina, and Wimberley, in north central Texas at Decatur, Mineral Wells, and Lancaster, and near Davis and San Antonio. Principal ranches such as the Gallagher Ranch near San Antonio, a cattle ranch of 10,000 acres, and those in the Bandera County area developed where land with limited agricultural value could be used for dude ranches and private youth camps.

Dude ranching declined during World War IIqv and failed to recover fully after the war as the population grew into sparsely peopled regions and altered the attitude toward nature and the West. Though cars made access to dude ranches easier, cheap gas and oil company promotions ultimately altered the habits of tourists and shortened the average length of stay of ranch visitors. Dude ranches in Colorado and New Mexico thrived after the war, but like many of those in Texas did so only through transformation into elaborate resorts. Since World War II, roughly twelve dude ranches have been continuously listed in Texas. The majority are near Bandera, the "Cowboy Capitol of the World." Dude ranches have become popular places for singles vacationing and, beginning with ranches outside of Dallas, have attracted company and club picnics and winter seminars of religious, business, and social groups as well as summer vacationers.

BIBLIOGRAPHY: Bandera County History Book Committee, *History of Bandera County, Texas* (Dallas: Curtis, 1986). Lawrence R. Borne, *Dude Ranching: A Complete History* (Albuquerque: University of New Mexico Press, 1983). *Dude Ranches Out West* (Chicago: Union Pacific Railroad, 1930). Texas Highway Department, *Texas Guest Ranches* (1930).
Diana J. Kleiner

DUDLEY, CHARLES ARTHUR, JR. (1894–1975). Charles A. (Doc) Dudley, black physician, civic leader, and civil-rights worker, son of Charles Arthur and Nancy Elizabeth Dudley, was born in Waskom, Texas, on January 10, 1894. He graduated from high school at nearby Marshall. After attending Bishop College in Dallas, where he excelled in football and baseball, he entered Meharry Medical College in Nashville, Tennessee. He financed his education by working as a Pullman porter and playing summer baseball in the Negro Professional League with such stars as Satchel Paige.

In 1923, upon completing his medical training, Dudley received a license to practice medicine in Texas. He moved to Victoria on January 1, 1924, and assumed the practice of his cousin, C. A. Whittier, who moved to San Antonio. Dudley long supported public education for black children in Victoria. Working with teachers at the black F. W. Gross High School, he helped furnish equipment not supplied by the school board. On January 17, 1940, he organized an athletic council that consisted primarily of black citizens. The council provided a fence, shrubs, grass, and cement walkways for the school. The school board later named an elementary school for Dudley.

He led a fund-raising drive to establish the George Washington Carver Civic Council, or Carver Center, for the recreational and cultural development of black youths. He was a member of the American Legion Citizens Committee, the Victoria Chapter of the State Progressive League, and the National Association for the Advancement of Colored People.qv During the struggle to secure voting rights for blacks, he worked closely with NAACP attorney Thurgood Marshall, a future United States Supreme Court associate justice. Dudley died on January 24, 1975.

BIBLIOGRAPHY: Biographical File, Victoria Public Library. Victoria *Advocate*, January 25, 1975.   *Agnes A. Jewett*

DUDLEY, RAY LOFTON (1891–1957). Ray Lofton Dudley, publisher, son of Nicholas Lee and Cordelia (Stover) Dudley, was born on August 8, 1891, at Stoverville, Denton County, Texas. He attended Lewisville Academy, Denton High School, and North Texas State Teachers College (now the University of North Texas), then taught in a rural school for three years. He entered Baylor University but did not stay to receive a degree. As a young man he held various newspaper positions in Dallas, Marshall, El Paso, Fort Worth, and Houston. His first connection with the oil industry was as oil editor of the Houston *Post*,qv a position he held briefly before becoming editor in 1918 of the *Gulf Coast Oil News* (later called the *Oil Weekly* and, still later, *World Oil*).

In 1918 he purchased the *Oil Weekly* and became president of Gulf Publishing Company, publisher of the magazine. In 1923 he became general manager for the Houston *Post Dispatch* in addition to presiding over Gulf Publishing. Sixteen months later he retired from daily newspaper work and thereafter devoted full time to his oil publications.

Under his leadership Gulf Publishing Company became the world's largest specialized publisher on oil subjects. *World Oil*, *Pipe Line Industry*, and *Hydrocarbon Processing* were its major publications. The company also published composite catalogs serving major branches of the oil industry. These publications became known as "oil industry Bibles."

Dudley was chairman of Gulf Printing Company, one of the largest printing firms in the South and Southwest, director of the American Petroleum Institute and Texas Mid-Continent Oil and Gas Association, and one of the founders of NOMADS, an organization made up of oilmen with international business experience. His civic activities included serving as trustee of Baylor University, board member of both Hermann Hospital and Texas Medical Center,qqv president of the Museum of Fine Arts, Houston,qv and board member of the Houston Symphony Orchestra.qv He was one of the founders of the Houston Livestock Show and for a number of years owned a large ranch at Rio Frio in the Uvalde area. He and his wife, the former Frederica Gross, had four children. He died on October 29, 1957, in Houston.

BIBLIOGRAPHY: Vertical Files, Barker Texas History Center, University of Texas at Austin.   *Silas B. Ragsdale*

DUDLEY, RICHARD M. (1862–1925). Richard M. Dudley, engineer and El Paso mayor, was born near Waco, Kentucky, on January 1, 1862, the son of a Baptist clergyman. He helped build the New York harbor and later directed construction of the Chihuahua and Pacific Railway and the Mexico and Northwestern Railway, while in a Mexican partnership. In New York he built up his own contracting business and in 1896 married Fannie Moore of Tarrytown, New York; the couple had no children. In 1912 Dudley permanently settled in El Paso, Texas, where he organized the Texas Bank and Trust Company, which was later merged into the First National Bank. He was twice elected as a Democrat to the state legislature and was in his second term when he became embroiled in a bitter city campaign. The Ku Klux Klanqv was making a strong resurgence in Texas and controlled the school board in El Paso. As the anti-Klan mayoral candidate, Dudley was elected with his entire aldermanic slate in an electoral setback from which the Klan never recovered. Dudley's administration was noteworthy for the construction of public buildings and recreational facilities, and he became the only mayor of El Paso to be elected without opposition when he ran for a second term. He was sworn in on April 16, 1925, but died in an El Paso hospital on May 1 of that year after undergoing ulcer surgery.

BIBLIOGRAPHY: Norman D. Brown, *Hood, Bonnet, and Little Brown Jug: Texas Politics, 1921–1928* (College Station: Texas A&M University Press, 1984). Richard M. Dudley Papers, El Paso Public Library.
    Arthur H. Leibson

DUDLEY, SHERMAN H. (ca. 1870–1940). Sherman H. Dudley, black vaudevillian and theater owner, was born in Dallas, Texas, around 1870. According to various sources he was involved in medicine shows and minstrel groups in his youth. One account reports that his Dudley Georgia Minstrels received a favorable review from the Galveston *News*qv in 1897. Most sources place him in P. T. Wright's Nashville Students and in the McCabe and Young Minstrels, where he was nicknamed either Happy or Hapsy. Dudley wrote a play, *The Smart Set*, first staged in 1896. In 1904 he appeared with Billy Kersands in *King Rastus*. Later that year, after Tom McIntosh's death, he took over McIntosh's lead role in *The Smart Set*. The same year he introduced his most famous stage act, a routine in which a mule dressed in overalls would nod his head as Dudley spoke, giving the impression that the mule understood. According to the obituary for Dudley in the Baltimore *Afro-American*, this number "never failed to convulse the house." Dudley introduced the mule act in *The Black Politician*, which he had written with S. B. Cassion. He also contributed material to *His Honor, the Barber*, produced in 1909–11, and, with Henry Troy, wrote *Dr. Beans from Boston*, which was staged in 1911–12.

Dudley reportedly organized the Colored Actors' Union, which was headquartered in Washington, D.C., and served as its general manager and treasurer. In 1911 he began buying theaters and organized S. H. Dudley Theatrical Enterprises. By 1913 this project had developed the first black theatrical circuit, which, in the beginning, included eight or nine theaters in Washington and Virginia, five or six of which were owned by Dudley. By 1916 more than twenty-eight theaters had joined the Dudley circuit, which extended into the East, South, and Midwest. The circuit enabled black entertainers for the first time to secure contracts for an eight-month season through one office.

Dudley retired from the stage after 1917 and devoted himself to producing black musicals. He regularly updated his *Smart Set* productions, which continued to be popular with black audiences. This show was one of a number of musicals written by blacks in the late nineteenth and early twentieth centuries that challenged the older minstrel pattern. Dudley was a pioneer in writing works about black life that included seriously considered plots and rounded characterization.

He was married to the actress Alberta (Bertie) Ormes. He was a friend of heavyweight boxing champion Jack Johnson, with whom he was once in business. Dudley sold his theaters after the onset of the

Great Depression^{qv} and retired to his farm near Oxon Hill, Maryland, where he raised thoroughbred cattle and racehorses. He died there on March 1, 1940, and was buried in Harmony Cemetery. He was survived by a son.

BIBLIOGRAPHY: Maud Cuney-Hare, *Negro Musicians and Their Music* (Washington: Associated Publishers, 1936). Tom Fletcher, *One Hundred Years of the Negro in Show Business: The Tom Fletcher Story* (New York: Burdge, 1954). James V. Hatch, *Black Image on the American Stage: A Bibliography of Plays and Musicals, 1770–1970* (New York: D.B.S. Publications, 1970). Rayford W. Logan and Michael R. Winston, eds., *Dictionary of American Negro Biography* (New York: Norton, 1982). Loften Mitchell, *Black Drama: The Story of the American Negro in the Theater* (New York: Hawthorn, 1967). New York *Age*, March 16, 1940. Henry T. Sampson, *Blacks in Blackface: A Source Book on Early Black Musical Shows* (Metuchen, New Jersey: Scarecrow Press, 1980).
Kharen Monsho

DUDLEY, TEXAS. Dudley, on Farm Road 1178 in western Callahan County, was founded in 1893 and named for its first postmaster and storekeeper, Nicholas M. Dudley. The community did grow and lost its post office in 1912. In 1940 it had thirty-five people, three stores, a church, and a school. In 1980 and 1990 the population was twenty-five.
William R. Hunt

DUDLEY'S CREEK. Dudley's (Dudley) Creek rises six miles southwest of Haskell in Haskell County (at 33°06′ N, 99°50′ W) and runs southeast for seven miles to its mouth on Paint Creek (at 33°01′ N, 99°46′ W). The area is surfaced by deep clay loam soils that support short grasses, scrub, and mesquite.

DUELING IN THE REPUBLIC OF TEXAS. The great Southern vogue in dueling reached its peak in Texas in 1837 and 1838. The practice, though strictly forbidden by regulations, was most popular among the officers of the Army of the Republic of Texas.^{qv} "We would opine," wrote the editor of the Austin *Texas Sentinel*^{qv} in the wake of one duel between army officers, "that there was fighting enough to be had on our frontier without resorting to private combats." The custom was enthusiastically cultivated, however, and the journalist, in common with most Texans of his day, concluded "not . . . to sermonize on the subject." According to a law approved by the Texas Congress on December 21, 1836, "Every person who shall kill another in a duel, shall be deemed guilty of murder, and on conviction thereof shall suffer death," and "Every person who shall be the bearer of any challenge for a duel, or shall in any way assist in any duel, shall, on conviction thereof, be fined and imprisoned at the discretion of the court before whom such conviction may be had."

Nevertheless, a strikingly high percentage of army officers and national officials were either killed or received debilitating wounds in duels. In June 1837, for example, army surgeon Chauncey Goodrich, "a truculent Mississippian," and Levy L. Laurens, reporter for the House of Representatives, faced each other with rifles at twenty yards after the former had falsely accused the later of the theft of a $1,000 bill. Laurens was mortally wounded. Col. James H. Milroy in Gen. Thomas Jefferson Green's^{qv} brigade frequently quarreled with his fellow officers and offered numerous challenges. In 1836 a Captain Graham killed a Captain Stanley on Galveston Island over the question of precedence in choosing cuts of beef for their respective companies. In 1837 a lieutenant killed a sergeant in a duel, and Maj. Stiles Leroy killed Maj. James W. Tinsley^{qv} in a dispute over a horse. In May 1840 "two heroes of San Jacinto," Col. Lysander Wells^{qv} of the First Cavalry, one of Sam Houston's^{qv} favorites, and Capt. William D. Redd^{qv} of the First Infantry, a protégé of Mirabeau B. Lamar,^{qv} both died after meeting on a field of honor at "Seguin's Ranch," a few miles below San Antonio. The difficulty, according to John J. Linn,^{qv} "was occasioned by some unimportant dispute, and the fiery spirits adjourned the matter to the 'code of honor.'" First fire was simultaneous from both pistols. Redd was shot through the heart as his bullet "went crashing through the brain" of Wells.

Albert Sidney Johnston,^{qv} as commanding general of the Texas army, prevented one duel by jerking the pistol from the hand of a "Major V____," and was unwittingly involved in another when one of his colonels called to ask the general to serve as a neutral judge in an affair of honor. Before Johnston could reply, the second principal arrived and opened fire on the colonel, leaving the commander a hapless bystander. The most famous duel fought between officers of the Texas army, however, involved Johnston as a principal. In December 1836 Felix Huston,^{qv} a swash-buckling Mississippi planter, slave trader, and soldier of fortune, was appointed junior brigadier of the army. He held the command of the army briefly, until superseded by Johnston in January 1837. Huston considered Johnston's appointment an attempt "to ruin my reputation and inflict a stigma on my character," and accordingly, on February 4, 1837, issued his new commander a challenge. Huston and Johnston met the following day on the Lavaca River. Huston, according to Linn, was "a most expert marksman," and Johnston "made no pretension at all in that line." After three exchanges of fire Johnston was seriously wounded by a ball passing through his hips. Although he lingered near death for several days and recovered only after months of suffering, Johnston never resented Huston's challenge or his wound, since he considered their meeting "a public duty" and believed that he could never have commanded the respect of the army if he had "shown the least hesitation in meeting General Huston's challenge."

Sam Houston was challenged by but refused to fight Commodore Edwin W. Moore, David G. Burnet,^{qqv} Mirabeau B. Lamar, Albert Sidney Johnston, and others. Most representative of these nonaffairs of honor is perhaps the controversy between Houston and Vice President Burnet. In 1841 each abused the other without stint in an acrimonious newspaper debate. Burnet called the hero of San Jacinto "Big Drunk," "Half Indian," and other insulting monikers, and Houston accused Burnet of being "an ex-*hog thief*." Thereupon Burnet despatched the speaker of the House of Representatives, Branch T. Archer,^{qv} with a "note." Houston refused to accept the challenge, which Archer returned to Burnet unopened, and the matter was allowed to drop.

Texas Rangers,^{qv} too, were affected by the dueling mania. When Ben McCulloch^{qv} ran for a seat in the House of Representatives of the republic against Alonzo B. Sweitzer,^{qv} Sweitzer accused McCulloch of "moral cowardice" for refusing to debate him during the election campaign. Three weeks after the election, Gonzales County was raided by Indians. Mathew Caldwell^{qv} called out the rangers in pursuit and dispatched McCulloch and Sweitzer to pick up the marauders' trail. Both claimed credit for discovering the route by which the Indians had left the county, and a bitter dispute arose between them. With what Victor M. Rose^{qv} characterized as "a base and slanderous charge," Sweitzer challenged McCulloch to a duel, but McCulloch declined, stating that personal quarrels while on campaign must be put aside in the face of community crises. McCulloch's unwillingness to fight Sweitzer while on campaign was a result neither of Houston's humane example nor of cowardice. Whether he had read the document or not, McCulloch was abiding by the *code duello* as set down in 1838 by former governor John Lyde Wilson of South Carolina. According to Wilson's rules, a gentleman, when insulted in public, must "never resent it there" if he has "self command enough to avoid noticing it" so as not to "offer an indignity to the company." He must, however, "let the time of demand" upon his adversary after the insult be as short as possible.

The issue between Sweitzer and McCulloch was dropped for the time as the rangers continued their pursuit of the raiders. The Indians outdistanced their pursuers, however, and the party turned back toward the settlements. As the company lay camped some nights later on the east bank of the Blanco River, Ben and Henry McCulloch^{qv}

approached Sweitzer's campfire. After joining the group around Caldwell's fire, Ben asked, "Captain, has your pursuit of the Indians ceased, and if so, do you have any reasonable expectation of a fight between this place and Gonzales?" When Caldwell replied that the expedition was at an end, Ben declared that the time had come to settle his grievance with Sweitzer and, rifle in hand, called upon him to defend himself. Sweitzer rose, leaving his rifle and pistols on the ground, claiming that he was not prepared to defend himself. McCulloch pointed out to him that his arms were within reach and promised him ample time to pick them up and use them. When Sweitzer declined the offer, McCulloch declared him "too base and cowardly to fight," except when drunk. In accordance with the *code duello,* since Sweitzer would not fight as a gentleman and since McCulloch could not afford to shoot him "like a dog," Ben contented himself by pronouncing his antagonist "a black-hearted, cowardly villain, in every respect beneath the notice of a gentleman."

Soon after the company returned to Gonzales, Reuben Ross,qv "a gallant but rash man," delivered a formal challenge to McCulloch from Sweitzer. McCulloch refused to recognize Ross's principal as a gentleman, he being, in Governor Wilson's terms, "one that has been posted, one that has been publicly disgraced without resenting it," and therefore declined to meet him. Ross was a man McCulloch respected, however, and as Sweitzer's second, he was bound by the code of honor to tender himself in his friend's stead. "The true reason of substitution," according to Wilson, "is the supposed insult of imputing the like inequality" charged upon a second's principal, and "when the contrary is declared, there should be no fight," for individuals were free to differ in their estimate of another individual's character and standing in society. Ben freely stated that he believed Ross a gentleman and his social equal. Nevertheless, on the next day, formal notes were exchanged between Ross and McCulloch and a meeting was arranged. On October 6, 1839, they faced each other with rifles at forty paces in a field two miles north of Gonzales. Ross, a trained duelist, fired at the word. His ball struck the under portion of McCulloch's right arm, passing from wrist to elbow, and causing him inadvertently to fire. Although McCulloch was severely wounded—some believed mortally—both men declared their honor satisfied, and Ross sent his personal surgeon to attend to McCulloch's wound. Ross told McCulloch that he regretted the circumstances that compelled him to "meet so brave a man in a private encounter," and expressed the hope that his wound was not serious, as he claimed to have never been McCulloch's enemy. "I assure you," Ross said, "that it would afford me great pleasure to henceforth claim you for a friend." The two shook hands. The force of the antidueling law is well illustrated by the fact that although McCulloch was indicted for "contriving and intending to break the peace of this Republic, setting at nought the quiet and good morals of this community" by "wickedly, willfully, and maliciously" accepting Ross's challenge, the district attorney choose not to prosecute, and the case was discharged.

BIBLIOGRAPHY: William R. Hogan, *The Texas Republic: A Social and Economic History* (Norman: University of Oklahoma Press, 1946; rpt. 1969). William Preston Johnston, *The Life of General Albert Sidney Johnston* (New York: Appleton, 1978). John J. Linn, *Reminiscences of Fifty Years in Texas* (New York: Sadlier, 1883; 2d ed., Austin: Steck, 1935; rpt., Austin: State House, 1986). Gerald S. Pierce, "A Minor Tragedy in the Texas Army: Lysander Wells and William D. Redd," *Texas Military History* 5 (Fall 1965). Victor Marion Rose, *The Life and Services of Gen. Ben McCulloch* (Philadelphia, 1888; rpt., Austin: Steck, 1958). *Thomas W. Cutrer*

DUFAL, PIERRE (1822–1898). Pierre Dufal, coadjutor bishop of the Catholic Diocese of Galveston (*see* GALVESTON-HOUSTON, CATHOLIC DIOCESE OF) son of Pierre and Françoise (Galey) Dufal, was born on November 8, 1822, at St. Gervais d'Auvergne, France. He entered the Congregation of Holy Crossqv on September 29, 1848. He was perpetually professed on August 5, 1852, and ordained to the priesthood at Blois on September 29, 1853. His early assignments were to Rome, where he taught and served as superior of his community, and to France, where he taught at the College of the Holy Cross in Mans and at the seminary in Orleans. He was sent to India in 1858 and made a titular bishop and vicar apostolic of Eastern Bengal on November 25, 1860. Bishop Dufal gave a solid foundation to this mission field of over 50,000 square miles. His order elected him superior general in 1866, and he spent his tenure in this office wrestling with personnel and financial problems. He resigned in 1868 to return to India. He attended the First Vatican Council (1869–70). The congregation recalled him to France in 1876.

Dufal was transferred on May 14, 1878, to Texas as coadjutor to Bishop Claude M. Dubuisqv of Galveston, whose poor health had led him to request help. Dufal had the right of succession, but Dubuis retained jurisdiction. In Texas Dufal encountered personnel problems like those he had faced as superior general, and the financial problems of the diocese extended to litigation. Contention about courses of action arose between Dufal and Dubuis. Dufal was overburdened with work, was said to know little English, and had great difficulty with the Texas climate. He resigned his Texas office in 1879. In Rome he held the office of procurator general of the Congregation of Holy Cross from 1883 to 1888. He was also able to advise the church on the missions in India and the United States because of his experience. He died in Paris on March 15, 1898.

BIBLIOGRAPHY: Catholic Archives of Texas, Files, Austin.
James F. Vanderholt

DUFF, JAMES (ca. 1828–?). James Duff, freighter and Confederate irregular, was born in Scotland about 1828. He had become a San Antonio merchant by 1856, when his wagons were used to transport a large meteorite (now known as the Wichita County Iron) to Austin; his wagons also were involved with the removal, directed by Robert S. Neighbors,qv of the Texas Comanches to Indian Territory in 1859. Duff served as commander of an irregular Texas Confederate military unit, Duff's Partisan Rangers. Unionism in the Hill Countryqv brought about his assignment to that area in May 1862. He left his duty station at San Antonio, camped on the Pedernales a few miles west of Fredericksburg, and declared martial law in several precincts of Kerr and Gillespie counties. He dismissed the Unionist enrolling officer, Jacob Kuechler,qv and began what many Hill Country people regarded as a reign of unjustified terror. Captain Duff learned of Fritz Tegener's battalion and its planned departure for Mexico and sent part of his troops in a pursuit that culminated in the battle of the Nuecesqv on August 10, 1862. One participant in the encounter testified to Duff's presence at the "massacre" and his refusal to provide medical assistance to the defeated Germans. Another story had Duff arriving there after the battle. Harassment of Unionists continued in the Fredericksburg area until Duff's return to San Antonio. Duff's command was later expanded into the Thirty-third Texas Cavalry; he served on the Texas coast throughout the remainder of the war.

BIBLIOGRAPHY: Don Hampton Biggers, *German Pioneers in Texas* (Fredericksburg, Texas: Fredericksburg Publishing, 1925). Kenneth F. Neighbours, *Robert Simpson Neighbors and the Texas Frontier, 1836–1859* (Waco: Texian Press, 1975). Guido E. Ransleben, *A Hundred Years of Comfort in Texas* (San Antonio: Naylor, 1954; rev. ed. 1974). Thomas C. Smith, *Here's Yer Mule: The Diary of Thomas C. Smith* (Waco: Little Texan, 1958). *The War of the Rebellion: A Compilation of the Official Records of the Union and Confederate Armies.* R. H. Williams, *With the Border Ruffians: Memories of the Far West, 1852–1868* (New York: Dutton, 1907; 2d ed., London: Murray, 1908).
Robert W. Shook

DUFF, TEXAS. Duff, eleven miles south of Center in south central Shelby County, was a flag stop on the Gulf, Colorado and Santa Fe

Railway and, for a brief period in 1907, the site of a post office. Residents of the area boarded the passenger train at Duff as it passed on its route from Longview to Beaumont. It was also a place where hoboes caught freight trains as they slowed to check for the signal to stop. By 1974 the flag stop had been abandoned.

BIBLIOGRAPHY: Charles E. Tatum, *Shelby County: In the East Texas Hills* (Austin: Eakin, 1984).
Cecil Harper, Jr.

DUFF CREEK. Duff Creek rises at the confluence of Goat Creek and Walnut Draw, 2½ miles east of Mitchell Mesa and just south of Black Canyon in west central Brewster County (at 29°59′ N, 103°41′ W), and runs south for nine miles before running dry at a point five miles south of Mitchell Mesa and a half mile south of the point where the Ditch rises (at 29°53′ N, 103°41′ W). Duff Creek is intermittent except for its first half mile and for a mile just past its midpoint, where it flows perennially. It traverses rugged terrain with numerous box canyons, surfaced by shallow, stony soils that support Mexican buckeye, walnut, persimmon, desert willow, scrub brush, and sparse grasses. On some maps Duff Creek and the Ditch are both labeled as the lower reaches of Goat Creek.

DUFFAU, FRANCIS T. (1808–1871). Francis T. Duffau, soldier and merchant, was born on July 10, 1808, in Albany, New York. After receiving a diploma from the Medical Society of Ostega County, Milford, New York, Duffau moved to Vicksburg, Mississippi, and early in April 1836 joined a volunteer cavalry company organized by John A. Quitman qv at Natchez, Mississippi, for service in the Texas Revolution.qv Duffau was a member of the Quitman company from April 5 to about May 15 and was among those who decided to remain in the Texas army after independence. After being honorably discharged on December 22, 1837, he settled in Houston, where he taught school, operated a grocery and baking business in partnership with J. T. Rendal, and practiced law. He moved to Austin in 1841 and worked in the General Land Office.qv He served as a private in the campaigns against Rafael Vásquez and Adrián Woll qqv in 1842 and afterward settled in Milam County, where he was county clerk from 1846 to 1850.

Duffau moved back to Austin, married Mary G. Davidson on December 17, 1850, and went into the drug business with George H. Gray, Jr., in February 1851. In April 1852 he acquired full ownership of the business. He was Austin city recorder during the greater part of the 1850s. Sam Houston qv appointed him a trustee of the Deaf and Dumb Institute (now the Texas School for the Deafqv) on December 29, 1859, and made him aide-de-camp to the commander of the Fourteenth Division, Texas Militia, on November 1, 1860. On September 12, 1863, Duffau was appointed to receive from the quartermaster the ammunition allotted to Travis County for home defense.

Duffau was affiliated with a wholesale drug firm in Galveston in 1866, but in early 1870 he was back in Austin in the drug business with Benjamin H. Thompson. He was a member of the Sons of Temperance in both Cameron and Austin, a charter member of the Independent Order of Good Samaritans, a charter vestryman of the Episcopal Church, and a Masonic officer. In 1871 he suffered from dropsy. He died in Bell County on December 14 of that year and was buried in Austin on December 16.

BIBLIOGRAPHY: Frank Brown Papers, Barker Texas History Center, University of Texas at Austin. Comptroller's Records, Texas State Archives, Austin. James H. McLendon, "John A. Quitman in the Texas Revolution," *Southwestern Historical Quarterly* 52 (October 1948). Thomas L. Miller, *Bounty and Donation Land Grants of Texas, 1835–1888* (Austin: University of Texas Press, 1967). Vertical Files, Barker Texas History Center, University of Texas at Austin.
James Hays McLendon

DUFFAU, TEXAS. Duffau is on Farm Road 1824 and Duffau Creek, fifteen miles southeast of Stephenville in Erath County. The town was named for Duffo, an Indian buried nearby. By 1860 a post office had been established at the community, and by the mid-1880s Duffau was a flourishing town of about 350 with steam flour mills and cotton gins, four churches, a hotel, a district school, three doctors, and two deputy sheriffs. Railroad routes bypassed Duffau, however, and by the mid-1890s it had begun to decline. In 1940 it was a small trading center with a post office, seven businesses, and 110 residents. By 1980 its population had declined to seventy-six. It was still reported at that level in 1990.
Susan Shaw

DUFFAU CREEK. Duffau Creek rises in southeastern Erath County (at 32°11′ N, 98°06′ W) and runs southeast for twenty-three miles, passing through Duffau before reaching its mouth on the North Bosque River, just west of Iredell in northwest Bosque County (at 31°59′ N, 97°53′ W). It traverses flat terrain with local shallow depressions, surfaced by clay and sandy loam soils that support water-tolerant hardwoods, conifers, and grasses.

DUFFY'S PEAK. Duffy's Peak is near State highway 207 eleven miles north of Post in northwestern Garza County (at 33°21′ N, 101°23′ W). It is composed of sand, clay, and sandstone and rises 2,710 feet above mean sea level and 100 feet above nearby State Highway 207. The local terrain is highly erodible, with moderately steep slopes and some high relief, surfaced by shallow to moderately deep silt loams that support mesquite and grasses. Duffy's Peak served as a landmark for peg-legged surveyor Jasper Hays, who in the late 1870s used it in marking off the boundaries of the Llano Ranch, one of the county's earliest settlements. Local tradition has it that the peak is named for a member of Hays's surveying team who died and was buried near it. Hays's notes, which he buried in mason jars on the peak, were later retrieved for use in further surveys, including that of 1906 for Charles William Post'sqv farm colony in Garza County. In 1969 the Texas Historical Commissionqv erected a historical marker for Duffy's Peak.

BIBLIOGRAPHY: Claude W. Dooley, comp., *Why Stop?* (Odessa: Lone Star Legends, 1978; 2d ed., with Betty Dooley and the Texas Historical Commission, Houston: Lone Star, 1985). Marker Files, Texas Historical Commission, Austin.

DUFLOT, JOSEPH LEO (1881–1957). Joseph Leo Duflot, sociology professor, was born on May 4, 1881, in Kentucky. He received a B.S. degree from Vanderbilt University and a B.A. degree from Western Kentucky University at Bowling Green, where he met Elizabeth Meloo, a fellow student, whom he married in 1908. That year Duflot began his teaching career, and in 1915 he became principal of Amarillo High School. He held that position until the fall of 1918, when he joined the faculty at West Texas State Teachers' College (now West Texas A&M University) in Canyon after doing graduate work at the University of Chicago. Duflot organized the college's sociology department and became its chairman. In 1929 he obtained his master's degree in sociology from the University of Chicago, where he worked as a Laura Spellman Rockefeller research assistant and completed residence requirements for the doctoral degree.

Duflot's philosophy, which he sought to pass on to his students, contrasted sharply with the conservative religious atmosphere prevalent in West Texas during the early decades of the twentieth century. Although he had joined the First Presbyterian Church in Canyon and begun teaching Sunday school shortly after his arrival in 1918, Duflot was dismissed by the church in July 1921 for allegedly mixing evolution with the Genesis account of creation and questioning the veracity of certain passages in the Bible. Wishing to maintain friendly relations with the denomination, he subsequently united with the Presbyterian congregation in Amarillo. From there Duflot's teachings eventually reached the ears of Jack L. Neville, a fundamentalist preacher whose show was known locally as the "Flying Parson of the Panhandle Church of the Air." When the Baptist State Convention met at Amarillo in November 1930, J. Franklyn Norris,qv Baptist pastor and editor of *The Fundamentalist,* arrived from Fort Worth to conduct a series of revivals, many of which were broadcast on Neville's radio program from Station KGRS.

Beginning the second week in December 1930, Norris instigated a series of personal attacks against Duflot and his "modernist" philosophy. Basically, the controversy involved two issues. For one thing, Norris had told a story he had heard from W. B. Riley, pastor of the Fundamentalist Baptist Church at Minneapolis, Minnesota, concerning a group of professors who had been tricked into believing that an abnormally large human tooth, recently extracted, was that of a prehistoric animal extinct for some six million years. Upon hearing that story, Duflot had asked his students to apply the principles of critical thinking he had taught them to the incident; the students concluded that the episode probably never happened. Norris considered that conclusion to be an attack against his honesty. Secondly, Duflot had circulated a questionnaire among his students on behalf of two seniors who were researching the behavior and characteristics of an only child. The professor had assured them that their responses were to be strictly voluntary, anonymous, and in private. Norris, who had somehow obtained a copy of the questionnaire, accused Duflot of trying to wrest lewd and improper information from his charges. The climax of the controversy occurred on December 12, when Norris staged a rally at the courthouse square in Canyon. Earlier, Norris had invited Duflot to meet him on that date in a debating session, which the professor had politely declined, preferring instead to play golf that day. At the rally Norris reiterated what he had broadcast over the airwaves, condemning Duflot as "an orangutang, God-denying, Bible-destroying, evolutionist professor" with atheistic tendencies and urging that he be dismissed from the West Texas State faculty. Although Duflot was called in for a hearing by the college's board of regents, he ably exonerated himself. Afterward, in reaction to Norris's printed speech in the December 19 issue of *The Fundamentalist,* Duflot wrote a forty-page manuscript in which he sought to clarify the issues involved and defend his belief in academic freedom.

Although his conflict with the fundamentalists was never entirely resolved, Duflot continued in his departmental chair at West Texas State. His students affectionately nicknamed him "Jumping Joe" because of his flashing eyes and expressive gestures that he used to get his points across. Duflot was a lifelong member of the Texas State Teachers' Associationqv and served as president of the Canyon organization of University of Chicago alumni from 1936 to 1940. He also was president of the Southwest Sociological Society in 1946–47 and was a member of the American Sociological Society. In 1951, after thirty-three years as department head, he retired from teaching.

Duflot was the father of three children by his first marriage. After his first wife's death he married Agnes Warriner, a former West Texas State student, in 1956. They moved to Houston, where Duflot died on February 21, 1957. He was buried in the Memory Gardens Cemetery at Canyon. His papers are in the Research Center of the Panhandle-Plains Historical Museum.qv

BIBLIOGRAPHY: James T. Hickman, "The Preacher and the Professor," *Panhandle-Plains Historical Review* 59 (1986). Ruth Lowes and W. Mitchell Jones, *We'll Remember Thee: An Informal History of West Texas State University* (Canyon: WTSU Alumni Association, 1984).

H. Allen Anderson

DUGAN CREEK. Dugan Creek rises three miles southwest of Oklaunion in north central Wilbarger County (at 34°06′ N, 99°11′ W) and runs northeast for ten miles, passing through Oklaunion before reaching its mouth on the Pease River, five miles northwest of Elliott and a mile south of the Oklahoma state line (at 34°11′ N, 99°08′ W). During the 1870s a spring located on the stream was known as Kilmartin or St. Andrews. It was once a substantial water source and an Indian campsite, but by the late 1970s it had diminished to a small seep. Dugan Creek traverses low to moderately rolling terrain. Its basin, which is composed largely of sand, supports sparse vegetation including grasses and nongrassy herbs.

DUGGAN, ARTHUR POPE (1876–1935). Arthur Pope Duggan, lawyer, West Texas promoter, and legislator, son of Alston and Eliza Permelia (Malone) Duggan, was born on September 21, 1876, in Hays County, Texas. In 1882 the family moved to San Saba, where Alston later served as county clerk. Arthur attended school in San Saba and college at the Agricultural and Mechanical College of Texas (now Texas A&M University), where he received a bachelor of civil engineering degree in 1895. He received a bachelor of laws degree in 1898 from the University of Texas. He subsequently worked in a law office in Galveston and in an abstract office in Cripple Creek, Colorado, before opening a law office in the new town of Stamford, Texas, in the fall of 1900. On June 18, 1902, in Austin, he married Sarah Elizabeth Harral, a niece of Maj. George W. Littlefield.qv Two children were born to the Duggans.

From 1904 to 1911 Duggan owned the Duggan Abstract Company in Denton. In the summer of 1912 he became sales manager of the Littlefield Lands Company, formed to sell the Yellow House Ranchqv in Lamb County to settlers and to develop the town of Littlefield, where Duggan became president of the school board, of the first bank, and of the chamber of commerce. In 1918 he resigned as sales manager and was commissioned a captain in the Texas National Guardqv for service in World War I;qv he was trained at Leon Springs.

After the war he returned to Littlefield, where he served as vice president and then president of the West Texas Chamber of Commerceqv (1925–27). Duggan worked untiringly for a university in West Texas. He helped organize the Littlefield Masonic Lodge and the Littlefield Rotary Club. He served as the Democratic senator from the Thirtieth District to the Forty-third Texas Legislature (1933–34) and to the Forty-fourth Legislature in 1935. He died of heart failure on September 6, 1935, in Gonzales. He and his wife were both Presbyterians, and both are buried in the State Cemeteryqv in Austin.

BIBLIOGRAPHY: Seymour V. Connor, ed., *Builders of the Southwest* (Lubbock: Southwest Collection, Texas Technological College, 1959). David B. Gracy II, *Littlefield Lands* (Austin: University of Texas Press, 1968). *Members of the Texas Legislature, 1846–1962* (Austin, 1962).

Alice Duggan Gracy

DUGGAN, EDMUND (1840–1911). Edmund Duggan son of Elizabeth (Berry) and Thomas Hinds Duggan,qv was born on September 19, 1840, in Travis County, Texas, but was reared in Guadalupe County. After attending school in Seguin, Edmund spent a term at Soule University in Chappell Hill, Washington County, before enlisting in May 1861 in what became Company D, Fourth Texas Infantry, Hood's Texas Brigade.qv He furnished his own horse and revolver; he was soon elected third lieutenant. In June the "Knights of Guadalupe County," as the company was called, were given a flag. At the close of the Civil Warqv Edmund was Captain Duggan. On November 21, 1867, Duggan married Julia E. Coorpender. The Duggans spent the years 1867–77 in Guadalupe County, farming and stock raising. In 1877 they moved to Austin, where Duggan was a bookkeeper in the State Treasurer's Department. He resigned in 1881 and moved to Tom Green County. He became county and district clerk of Tom Green County in 1888, serving until 1908, when he retired because of failing health. The Duggans had two sons. Duggan was a Democrat. He was active in the Masonic Lodge and had a Knight Templar Degree. Captain Duggan was reared in the Methodist Church; his wife helped organize in the mid-1880s the Emmanuel Episcopal Church in San Angelo. When she died on March 16, 1929, three stained glass windows were dedicated in her memory. Duggan died on April 22, 1911, in San Angelo. He and his wife are buried in Fairmont Cemetery beside their two sons.

BIBLIOGRAPHY: Alice Duggan Gracy, *Thomas Hinds Duggan, Descendant and Ancestor* (Austin, 1976). Joseph Benjamin Polley, *Hood's Texas Brigade* (New York: Neale, 1910; rpt., Dayton, Ohio: Morningside Bookshop, 1976). Willie Mae Weinert, *An Authentic History of Guadalupe County* (Seguin, Texas: Seguin *Enterprise*, 1951; rpt. 1976).

Alice Duggan Gracy

DUGGAN, THOMAS HINDS (1815–1865). Thomas Hinds Duggan, early settler, politician, and soldier, son of Edmund and Elizabeth (Alston) Duggan, was born in Jefferson County, Mississippi, on April 20, 1815. On May 20, 1834, he married Elizabeth Berry. From his mercantile store in Rodney, he outfitted parties leaving for Texas. Eventually he joined the migration and on September 16, 1835, applied to Joseph Vehlein qv for lands. In the fall of 1839 Duggan moved his family to Austin, where he was elected justice of the peace. Because of the Indian situation, he moved farther from the frontier and settled in 1845 five miles east of Seguin. He became the first county clerk of Guadalupe County and served as a senator in both the Fourth and the Eighth legislatures. In the latter he voted for secession.qv In 1861 he volunteered for the Texas militia. Duggan died on December 26, 1865, and was buried in Geronimo Cemetery in Seguin. He was survived by five children.

BIBLIOGRAPHY: Frank Brown, Annals of Travis County and the City of Austin (MS, Frank Brown Papers, Barker Texas History Center, University of Texas at Austin). Dunbar Rowland, *History of Mississippi, the Heart of the South* (2 vols., Chicago: Clarke, 1925).

Alice Duggan Gracy

DUGGER, TEXAS. Dugger is on State Highway 123 five miles south of Seguin in central Guadalupe County. The Dugger school was built in 1871; in 1904 it had one teacher and forty-eight students. In 1938 the Baptist church held services in the school. The school was consolidated with the Seguin Independent School District by the early 1950s. A cemetery, a business, and a few scattered houses were in the area in 1946; in 1990 the community had an estimated population of ten.

BIBLIOGRAPHY: Arwerd Max Moellering, A History of Guadalupe County, Texas (M.A. thesis, University of Texas, 1938). Vertical Files, Barker Texas History Center, University of Texas at Austin (Guadalupe County). Vertical File, Seguin-Guadalupe County Library, Seguin, Texas (Guadalupe County).

Vivian Elizabeth Smyrl

DUGGEYS LAKE. Duggeys Lake, also known as Old Salt Works Lake, is a natural lake six miles west of Palestine in southwestern Anderson County (at 31°44′ N, 95°44′ W). It drains into Wolf Creek near the junction of Wolf and Town creeks. The Palestine Salt Works qv were probably in the vicinity of the lake.

BIBLIOGRAPHY: Pauline Buck Hohes, *A Centennial History of Anderson County, Texas* (San Antonio: Naylor, 1936).

DUGOUT. A dugout is a rude shelter dug into the ground and roofed with sod or occasionally some other material. It was a most common shelter on the Texas plains and prairies, where timber for building was scarce. Dugouts were temporary and served as dwellings only until more sophisticated buildings could be erected. After houses were built, dugouts commonly became cellars or storage bins.

Like most primitive shelters, dugouts are difficult to document, but certainly they have been in use around the world for centuries. Evidently they were most common in regions with severe winters, where insulation against the bitter cold was essential to survival and where timber for building log cabins or picket-walled jacals was scarce. In addition to providing shelter with few manufactured materials, the dugout was made tolerably comfortable in both summer and winter by the temperature of the ground.

Dugouts belong to no particular historical period but rather to a phase of frontier development. On the Texas plains and prairies they were basic forms of shelter during early settlement and were particularly prominent on ranches and farms. Until a dugout could be completed, however, frequently families lived in wagons or tents, the latter of which were sometimes swept away by the winds.

On the plains, the dugout consisted of a rectangular pit, five to seven feet deep, eight or ten feet wide, and of variable length. If wood was available, short extensions of the walls above ground, about two feet high, were built around the pit, allowing the introduction of windows for light and ventilation; these were closed with either shutters or sashes. The roof was often fashioned from log beams that supported saplings or tree branches placed side by side and covered with grass, weeds, or tow sacks, all finally covered with dirt. In some instances the roofs were framed with sawed lumber, which was expensive to transport, and covered with shingles. Access to the dugout was down a stair dug into the ground. Dugouts were occasionally flooded.

Partial or half dugouts were favored in areas of broken terrain. A rectangular excavation was made into the side of a hill. This style provided improved drainage. Walls with doors and windows were placed at the open end of the pit and along the sides with the use of sod, stone, or logs. Openings also were sometimes made in the sides. Occasionally stone was used to line the sides of the excavation.

Regardless of the type of dugout, floors generally were tamped earth, although in some instances wooden flooring eventually was installed. Often rugs were placed over the earth floors. Walls were sometimes whitewashed or covered with domestics, and ceilings might be lined with canvas. Commonly, iron stoves were used in full dugouts, and occasionally fireplaces were built at the ends of partial dugouts, with flues dug through the earth.

Although dugouts provided vital shelter, they were not pleasant places of abode. Residents described problems with snakes, spiders, salamanders, and other pests, which infested the roofs. Evidently, on occasion an unwary cow stepped through the roof. Dirt constantly fell from the walls and roof onto dining tables and other furniture.

Examples of both types of dugouts are preserved at the Ranching Heritage Center qv on the Campus of Texas Tech University. Representative of the partial dugout is the building known as the Matador Half Dugout, a shelter with an excavation into the side of a hill lined with sandstone slabs, upper walls of cottonwood logs, and a framed roof covered with shingles; it originally was located south of Matador. The Two Story Dugout, originally located west of Levelland, represents the full dugout, although a wooden-framed second story eventually was added to it.

BIBLIOGRAPHY: Mondel Rogers, *Old Ranches of the Texas Plains* (College Station: Texas A&M University Press, 1976). Ruby L. Smith, "Early Development of Wilbarger County," West Texas Historical Association *Year Book* 14 (1938). Vertical File, Southwest Collection, Texas Tech University.

Willard B. Robinson

DUGOUT, TEXAS. Dugout, often called "The Dugout," was on the west side of Deep Creek just east of the site of what is now Milburn in northeastern McCulloch County. Settlers came to the Deep Creek area in the late 1860s, and the community that grew up along the creek supposedly took its name from the first store, a dugout qv in the side of a hill. The Dugout community had a saloon, a doctor, a blacksmith, and possibly a post office; it was said to have good schools and churches in 1877. The community declined in the early 1880s, and its remaining residents probably moved to nearby Milburn. The site in the late 1980s was overgrown with mesquite and prickly pear, and no evidence of Dugout was shown on county highway maps.

BIBLIOGRAPHY: Wayne Spiller, comp., *Handbook of McCulloch County History* (Vol. 1, Seagraves, Texas: Pioneer, 1976; vol. 2, Canyon, Texas: Staked Plains Press, 1986).

Vivian Elizabeth Smyrl

DUGOUT CREEK. Dugout Creek rises a half mile east of U.S. Highway 90 and three miles southwest of Cathedral Mountain in north central Brewster County (at 30°17′ N, 103°26′ W) and runs southeast for 21½ miles to its mouth in Rock House Gap on Maravillas Creek, four miles southeast of Black Peak (at 30°04′ N, 103°24′ W). It traverses an area of steep to gentle slopes, surfaced by variable soils that support scrub brush and sparse grasses. The creek is intermittent for all but the last 1½ miles of its length, where it flows perennially through steep, rocky land surfaced by shallow, stony soils that support Mexican buckeye, walnut, persimmon, desert willow, scrub brush, and grasses.

DUGOUT DRAW. Dugout Draw, which has an intermittent stream, rises a mile north of Nugent Mountain and four miles southeast of Panther Junction in Big Bend National Park[qv] in south central Brewster County (at 29°17′ N, 103°11′ W) and runs east for ten miles to its mouth on Tornillo Creek, 6½ miles southeast of Roys Peak (at 29°16′ N, 103°03′ W). In its upper reaches the creek traverses an area of steep to gentle slopes surfaced by variable soils that support scrub brush and sparse grasses. Its lower reaches are in flat to rolling terrain with local escarpments, surfaced by shallow to deep sandy loams that support pecan, willow, and grasses.

DUGOUT MOUNTAIN. Dugout Mountain is ten miles west of Marathon in north central Brewster County (at 30°13′ N, 103°24′ W). The peak, at an elevation of 5,175 feet above sea level, rises some 830 feet above the Southern Pacific tracks 4½ miles to the northeast. The soils on Dugout Mountain are shallow and stony and support oak, juniper, and some mesquite.

DUKE, CORDELIA JANE SLOAN (1877–1966). Cordelia (Cordia) Duke, rancher, writer, and game warden, was born near Belton, Missouri, on January 10, 1877, the daughter of A. R. C. and Belle (Wingert) Sloan. She attended school in Overbrook, Kansas, where her family moved shortly after her birth. She passed the teachers' examination at the age of sixteen and taught school for several years in the Cherokee Nation, Oklahoma Territory, before moving to Sherman County, Texas. In September 1906 she began teaching in a four-pupil school on a strip of Texas land between Oklahoma and the XIT Ranch.[qv] There she met Robert L. Duke, then foreman of the Buffalo Springs division of the XIT. The story goes that after returning with her charges from a late roundup near El Frio Springs, Cordia was warned by one young cowboy not to "fool with that Bob Duke," who had fired a cowhand for mistreating a horse. She took her chances anyway, and she and Duke were married on January 9, 1907; they eventually had three daughters. Duke became general manager of the XIT under Henry S. Boice,[qv] and when the ranch ceased its cattle operations in 1912, he was retained to oversee that portion of the range leased to the Shelton and Trigg partnership.

During her years as a ranch wife, Cordia Duke kept a diary in which she noted details of a rapidly vanishing way of life. She used these and reminiscences of the ranchhands in articles for such newspapers and magazines as the *Cattleman*.[qv] Later, excerpts from this diary were used as the basis for a book entitled *6,000 Miles of Fence*, which she coauthored with Joe B. Frantz.[qv] This book, published in 1961, was the first in the M. K. Brown[qv] Range Life Series of the University of Texas Press.[qv] In the 1920s, when the land around the Duke homestead was designated a wildlife sanctuary, Mrs. Duke was appointed game warden, the first woman to hold that job in Texas. She was warden for a number of years and became legendary for her rapport with the thousands of wild ducks that found refuge on the sanctuary during their annual migrations. After her husband's death in 1933, Cordia Duke moved to Dalhart, where she died on July 23, 1966, and was buried.

BIBLIOGRAPHY: Dorothy Nordyke, "Great Lady of the XIT," *Texas Parade*, May 1962.

DUKE, THOMAS MARSHALL (1795–1867). Thomas Marshall Duke, the first constitutional alcalde[qv] of Austin's colony and one of Stephen F. Austin's[qv] Old Three Hundred[qv] colonists, the son of Dr. Basil and Charlotte (Marshall) Duke, was born at Lexington, Kentucky, in 1795. His mother was a niece of Chief Justice John Marshall. Duke served in the War of 1812 under Gen. William Henry Harrison and was in the battle of the Thames, October 5, 1813. In 1818 he married Eliza J. Taylor of Newport, Kentucky. She died about six months after the marriage, and by 1819 Duke was in Natchitoches, Louisiana. In 1821 or 1822 he sailed to Texas on the schooner *Lively*[qv] to join Austin's colony. The 1823 census of the Colorado District listed him. On July 24, 1824, he received a sitio[qv] of land on Caney Creek in what is now Matagorda County. When the Baron de Bastrop[qv] arrived to organize the Austin colony, Duke acted as his secretary and accompanied him on the inspection tour. At one time Duke and Stephen Richardson[qv] were partners in a mercantile business at San Felipe. The census of 1826 listed a Thomas Duke as a single farmer and stock raiser, but sometime later that year or the next Duke married his second wife, Nancy Ashby of Lexington, Kentucky. They had one child. Around 1828 or 1830 Duke married his third wife, Jane McCormac (McCormic or McCormick; some sources have Jane Wilkins) at San Felipe; they eventually had six children. Duke and his third wife were active in Christ Church at Matagorda.

Like most of the colonists, Duke was a soldier and took part in numerous Indian fights. In 1827, while acting as alcalde of the Mina District, he drafted and signed the resolutions condemning the Fredonian Rebellion[qv] and attesting loyalty to Mexico. He was captain of one of the companies sent from Austin's colony to help in crushing the rebellion. Also in 1827 he became one of the proprietors of the townsite of Matagorda. In 1828 he was elected the first constitutional alcalde of the jurisdiction of Austin. He was secretary of an 1829 meeting of York Rite Masons at San Felipe and a charter member of the Masonic lodge in Matagorda. After serving as a member of the Convention of 1833,[qv] he was elected by the General Council[qv] in 1835 to be second judge of Matagorda Municipality. He apparently held that position until Gen. José de Urrea's[qv] advancing armies compelled him and his family to seek safety. Duke was collector at several ports, including Calhoun, Lavaca, and, by 1841, Cavallo Pass (*see* DECROS POINT, TEXAS). He was also at one time mayor of Matagorda. Around March 1842 he enrolled with the Matagorda volunteers under Clark L. Owen[qv] and went to the relief of Bexar when the Mexican army invaded. When Calhoun County was established in 1846, he was appointed one of the commissioners to locate the county seat. By July 1846 his third wife had died. During the late 1840s he moved from Matagorda to Refugio County, where he was one of the few resident slaveowners, and established a ranch in the vicinity of Hynes Bay. After an 1858 visit to Kentucky, he lived at Saluria before returning to his Hynes Bay ranch during the Civil War.[qv] As an ardent secessionist, he was a member of his precinct patrol; nearly all his sons served in the Confederate Army. Duke fell victim to the yellow fever epidemic of 1867 and was buried on his Hynes Bay Ranch in Refugio County.

BIBLIOGRAPHY: Eugene C. Barker, ed., *The Austin Papers* (3 vols., Washington: GPO, 1924–28). Lester G. Bugbee, "The Old Three Hundred: A List of Settlers in Austin's First Colony," *Quarterly of the Texas State Historical Association* 1 (October 1897). Hobart Huson, *Refugio: A Comprehensive History of Refugio County from Aboriginal Times to 1953* (2 vols., Woodsboro, Texas: Rooke Foundation, 1953, 1955). J. H. Kuykendall, "Reminiscences of Early Texans," *Quarterly of the Texas State Historical Association* 6–7 (January, April, July 1903). Matagorda County Historical Commission, *Historic Mata-*

gorda County (3 vols., 1986–88). Texas House of Representatives, *Biographical Directory of the Texan Conventions and Congresses, 1832–1845* (Austin: Book Exchange, 1941). *Hobart Huson*

DUKES HOLLOW. Dukes Hollow, a valley with an intermittent stream, begins at a point twelve miles southeast of Seguin in southeastern Guadalupe County (at 29°26′ N, 97°52′ W) and extends southeast for about two miles to a point two miles from the Guadalupe-Gonzales county line (at 29°25′ N, 97°51′ W). The stream empties into Sandies Creek, a mile west of Farm Road 1117.

DULANEY CREEK. Dulaney Creek rises at Ben Jones Spring, six miles northwest of Sweetwater in far northwestern Nolan County and a mile south of the Nolan-Fisher county line (at 32°30′ N, 100°30′ W), and runs northeast for six miles to its mouth on Kildoogan Creek, just north of the county line in far south central Fisher County (at 32°32′ N, 100°26′ W). It traverses flat terrain with locally shallow depressions, surfaced by expansive clays that support water-tolerant hardwoods, conifers, and grasses.

DULIN, TEXAS. Dulin was just off U.S. Highway 377 some two miles southeast of Brookesmith in Brown County. The farming and ranching community was named for Thomas S. Dulin, a teacher who served in the Civil War[qv] in Gager's Mounted Battalion. After Dulin received his discharge, he resumed teaching and married a schoolteacher. The couple purchased land, reportedly totaling twenty sections, and settled in the Clear Creek area. The first Dulin postmaster was Joseph J. Boyd, who was appointed in 1896. The Dulin post office was discontinued in 1903, when mail was rerouted through Brookesmith. Students attended a local school during the 1930s, but the school seems to have been consolidated, since the school board offered to sell the site on March 9, 1948. In the 1940s Dulin had two businesses and a population of fifty. Though no population figures are available after that time, the community continued to be shown on maps.

BIBLIOGRAPHY: Estill Allen, *Southwest Brown County, Texas* (Brookesmith, Texas: Brookesmith Volunteer Fire Department, 1984).
Jeanne F. Lively

DULL, TEXAS. Dull, also known as Nettaville, was 3½ miles southeast of Los Angeles on the San Antonio, Uvalde and Gulf Railroad in northeastern La Salle County. The community was named for the Dull Ranch, which had once encompassed a large part of La Salle County, including the townsite. Dull was established in 1912 and was granted a post office the next year. In 1915 the name of the post office was changed to Nettaville; it closed in 1919, but the community of Dull was shown on maps of La Salle County as late as 1965.

BIBLIOGRAPHY: Stanley D. Casto, *Settlement of the Cibolo–Nueces Strip: A Partial History of La Salle County* (Hillsboro, Texas: Hill Junior College Press, 1969). *John Leffler*

DULL'S RANCH, TEXAS. Dull's Ranch (Dulls Ranch or the Dull Ranch), formerly known as Waugh's Rancho and as Jahuey Ranch, was a ranching headquarters and rural post office fifteen miles northeast of Cotulla and just north of Cibolo Creek in north central La Salle County. The place was originally named for William A. Waugh, the first white settler of La Salle County and the original owner of the ranch. During the 1870s he maintained a large herd of cattle in the area between Cibolo Creek and the Frio River. Waugh's ranch headquarters, on the road between San Antonio and Laredo, became a stopping place for travelers. A store was established at the site, and the place became a center of activity in the area. In 1879 it was granted a post office called Waugh's Rancho. During the 1880s Waugh's land was apparently purchased by James J. and Andrew J. Dull, two wealthy brothers from Pittsburgh, Pennsylvania, who put together a vast ranching enterprise. In 1889 the name of the post office at Waugh's old ranching headquarters was changed to Dull's Ranch; in 1909 the post office closed. The Dull brothers sold their holdings in 1901, and by 1910 much of the land had been developed into towns such as Los Angeles and Fowlerton.

BIBLIOGRAPHY: Stanley D. Casto, *Settlement of the Cibolo–Nueces Strip: A Partial History of La Salle County* (Hillsboro, Texas: Hill Junior College Press, 1969). Annette Martin Ludeman, *La Salle: La Salle County* (Quanah, Texas: Nortex, 1975). *John Leffler*

DUMAS, TEXAS (Moore County). Dumas, the county seat of Moore County, is at the junction of U.S. highways 87 and 287 in the center of the county. It was named for Louis Dumas, president of the Panhandle Townsite Company in Sherman, who purchased railroad survey lands in the Panhandle.[qv] In January 1891 Dumas and his associates formed the Moore County Townsite Company and platted the town on a site some five miles south of South Palo Duro Creek. The first building housed the company office, a hotel, a general store, and the first post office. James C. Wilson served as first postmaster and was followed by John F. Patterson, who opened a general store later that year. The following year Moore County was organized, and Dumas was elected county seat. By then several lots had been sold and a courthouse erected. The first school was constructed in 1892 on the block west of the courthouse.

A plague of grasshoppers in the summer of 1893 and a severe winter during 1893–94 almost reduced Dumas to a ghost town. Even Louis Dumas gave up hope and moved back to Grayson County. At times during the next few years only one family was reported as inhabiting the townsite. In 1900 Arthur Nield's mercantile store was the sole business in operation. In 1904 Phillips and Son bought this establishment and started an enterprise that is still in operation. J. V. Mills opened a rival general store, and the first bank was opened in 1908. Since there was no railroad, supplies were hauled overland from Amarillo. A skating rink was opened, and the county's first newspaper, the *Moore County Pioneer*, began circulation in 1909. Two churches had been established, and by 1910 automobiles and telephones were in use. When the Enid, Ochiltree and Western Railroad announced plans to build through Dumas, the population increased from twenty-three in 1903 to over 100 by 1915. Though that railroad scheme fell through, Dumas grew to around 200 and had a blacksmith shop, a barbershop, a lumberyard, a drugstore, and other businesses serving area ranchers and wheat farmers. After cotton was introduced to the county in 1918, a gin was opened in Dumas.

The determination of the Dumas residents to stay in their windswept environment paid off when oil and natural gas were discovered in the county in 1926. The population grew rapidly as Shamrock Oil and Gas and other major companies moved into the vicinity. In 1931 the long-awaited hopes for a railroad were realized with the building of the North Plains and Santa Fe line from Amarillo to Boise City, Oklahoma. These new developments greatly boosted the town's economic, civic, and cultural growth. Streets were paved, a fire department was organized, a new courthouse was built, and a new newspaper, the *Moore County News*, replaced the defunct *Pioneer*. Despite the Dust Bowl,[qv] the population of Dumas grew to 2,500 by 1935. In 1936 a zinc-smelting plant was established in the vicinity, as were several carbon black plants that utilized the sour gas from the oilfields (*see* CARBON BLACK INDUSTRY). World War II[qv] further stimulated the area's petroleum industry, causing the population to increase from 2,117 in 1940 to 6,127 by 1950. On July 29, 1956, the county's worst disaster, a fire at the Shamrock-McKee plant near Dumas, killed nine plant employees and ten firemen. By 1965 deep-well irrigation and several petrochemical plants had further enhanced the town's economy. The population continued to grow, from 8,477 in 1960 to 12,194 in 1980, when Dumas had twenty-two churches, eight city parks, six public schools, two banks, a hospital, a nursing home, a library, two radio stations, a cable television company, and 257 businesses. In 1990 the population was 12,871.

Dumas is in the heart of one of the state's leading grain sorghum producing areas (see SORGHUM CULTURE). Moore County also produces large quantities of natural gas, as well as two-thirds of the nation's helium (see HELIUM PRODUCTION). Several feedlots, grain elevators, beef packers, and fertilizer plants, as well as a tannery, attest to the leadership in agribusiness. The Moore County Historical Museum, housed in a former hotel, features memorabilia and displays of local history, area wildlife, Indian artifacts, and changing exhibits. The major annual event, complete with parade and carnival, is called Dogie Days and occurs during the second weekend in June. Fall events are the Moore County Fair and the County Art Bazaar. Moore County Airport is west of the city. Dumas was made famous by the hit song "I'm a Ding Dong Daddy from Dumas," recorded by Phil Harris in the 1940s. The song was written by Phil Baxter of Navarro County after he had spent a night in Dumas on a trip to Denver. In 1982 Dumas was the home of the Arturo Toscanini Society, a national group dedicated to preserving the conductor's memory.

BIBLIOGRAPHY: Myrna Tryon Thomas, *The Windswept Land: A History of Moore City* (Dumas, Texas, 1967). H. Allen Anderson

DUMAS, TEXAS (Wood County). Dumas was on a soil-surfaced road a mile north of Hoard and six miles west of Mineola in south central Wood County. The community probably existed by at least 1881, which is the earliest recorded death date in the Dumas cemetery. By 1896 the Dumas school had one teacher and forty students; ten years later the school reported thirty-six students. Dumas was abandoned sometime after 1906 and does not appear on county highway maps for the 1930s, though the Dumas cemetery, also known locally as the Greer cemetery, is shown on a 1960 topographic map.

Rachel Jenkins

DUMBLE, EDWIN THEODORE (1852–1927). Edwin Theodore Dumble, geologist, the son of James F. and Mary A. Dumble, was born in Madison, Indiana, on March 28, 1852. Three months after his birth his family moved to Galveston. He was educated at Groce's plantation and the Houston Academy and attended Washington and Lee University, where his college education was interrupted when his father's cotton mills were destroyed by fire. He served as a bookkeeper for a lumber firm for two years and returned to school but was again forced to withdraw when the company failed. He eventually received a diploma in the School of Mathematics, Astronomy, and Chemistry and in 1912 a B.S. degree in mining engineering; in 1924 he received a doctorate of science from Washington and Lee.

Dumble returned to Houston and worked as a car accountant for the Houston and Texas Central Railway, devised a system for handling car records, and first considered the possibility of using lignite as a locomotive fuel. Eyestrain eventually forced him to retire to Llano, where he worked in a drugstore and assay office and developed his interest in geology. On June 15, 1876, he married Fanny Boswell Grey; the couple had two children. From 1874 to 1887 he assisted in his father's mercantile business in Houston as manager and buyer for glassware and china and served as consulting accountant for various firms. He also reported on water supplies for the city of Houston and conducted experiments at a small private chemistry laboratory on the use of Texas lignite as a cheap industrial fuel. Dumble served as Texas State Geologist from 1887 to 1897 and was responsible for directing the third Texas Geological Survey beginning in 1889. Beginning in 1897 he was a consulting geologist for the Southern Pacific lines. He was among the first to organize a department devoted to petroleum exploration and first applied micropaleontology in the search for subsurface structures. As a vice president of the Southern Pacific oil company subsidiaries, the Rio Bravo Oil Company and the East Coast Oil Company, he was active from South America to China and Alaska.

Dumble's first paper, "Nacogdoches Oil Field," appeared in the *Geological and Scientific Bulletin* of the Texas State Geological and Scientific Association qv of Houston, which he founded in 1884. He published some seventy scientific papers in all, and also wrote *Brown Coal and Lignite* (1891) and *The Geology of East Texas* (1920). He was a fellow of the Geological Society of America and the American Association for the Advancement of Science and was president of the Texas Academy of Science qv (1893–94). He was a member of the American Institute of Mining Engineers, the Mining and Metallurgical Society of America, the American Association of Petroleum Geologists, and the California Academy of Science. Dumble retired to Hanover County, Virginia, where by 1926 he had developed pernicious anemia. He died of leukemia on January 16, 1927, and was buried in the English cemetery at Nice.

BIBLIOGRAPHY: Lewis E. Daniell, *Personnel of the Texas State Government, with Sketches of Representative Men of Texas* (Austin: City Printing, 1887; 3d ed., San Antonio: Maverick, 1892). S. W. Geiser, "A Century of Scientific Exploration in Texas," *Field and Laboratory* 7 (January 1939). Houston Press Club, *Men of Affairs of Houston and Environs* (Houston: Coyle, 1913). Frederic William Simonds, "Memorial of Edwin Theodore Dumble," *Bulletin of the Geological Society of America* 39 (March 1928). Vertical Files, Barker Texas History Center, University of Texas at Austin. *Who Was Who in America*, Vol. 2.

Diana J. Kleiner

DUMONT, ARRIE ELLA ELGAR (1861–1943). Arrie Dumont, West Texas pioneer and sculptor, daughter of Lewis Steptoe and Elizabeth (Benson) Elgar, was born in Lee County, Mississippi, on July 3, 1861. She attended school in Johnson, Parker, and Young counties, Texas, from 1868 to 1877. She married James Thomas Bird, a Texas Ranger, on September 9, 1877, and the couple moved west to what is now King County to participate in the great buffalo qv hunt of the late 1870s. In 1881 they moved to adjoining Dickens County, where Bird became a line rider on the Pitchfork Ranch, qv and the following year they moved on to Cottle County to live on a line camp on the Ross Ranch. The couple had three children. One of them, Capp Jay Bird, later built the first telephone, phonograph, and radio in Cottle County.

Ella Bird began to model in clay as a child in 1867, an experience about which she later wrote, "this was the beginning of what my life career should have been, clay modeling, first step to sculpting." As an adult she worked with the porous gypsum plentiful in the area. She yearned for training to develop the talent further. She became known throughout the area as an expert seamstress of custom-made buckskin gloves, vests, and pants, for which she was paid. In her autobiography she expressed frustration at her inability to develop "a talent which would have been worth hundreds of thousands of dollars, as well as a world of pleasure to me." After the death of her husband, she remained a widow for nine years, living in several dugout qv homes with her children.

On December 29, 1895, she married Auguste Dumont, a Canadian immigrant, in the Paducah, Texas, First Baptist Church. The couple resided in Paducah and had two children. After a broken leg limited her mobility in 1907, Mrs. Dumont began making plaster casts of statues, busts, and smaller pieces—mainly floral decorations—for sale. She imported models from Los Angeles, and her business flourished, especially during the Christmas season. She once paid a doctor bill with a sculpted napkin ring decorated with flowers and topped by a squirrel holding an acorn. She carved the tombstone of her first husband, a five-foot-high, flower-filled model church building now in ruins in Quanah due to the effect of the elements on the porous "gyprock." She also sculpted a Bible (ca. 1887) as an heirloom for her children, but its location is unknown. A large vase, typically decorated in a floral motif, is the only work in gyprock that remains in the Dumont family. The remainder of her sculptures were either stolen or destroyed in a storm at the Bird home at Buck Creek near Paducah in 1895.

One of the Dumont children, Auguste Elgar (Frenchie) Dumont, was postmaster in Paducah for twenty years. The Dumonts supported the Republican party.qv Ella became a widow again in 1915. In 1927–28 she wrote her autobiography, which she attempted for the rest of her life to have published. She was active in the Order of the Eastern Star and in women's service clubs. She died and was buried in Paducah on April 10, 1943. The autobiography was finally published, along with documented research, by the University of Texas Pressqv in 1988.

BIBLIOGRAPHY: Vertical Files, Barker Texas History Center, University of Texas at Austin.

Tommy J. Boley

DUMONT, TEXAS. Dumont, on Farm Road 193 about 100 miles east of Lubbock in the northwestern corner of King County, was named after A. Dumont, the first postmaster at nearby Paducah. The first school at the community held classes in a dugoutqv on the farm of John Parker in 1891. The China Grove School was built in 1893, and the next year a community post office was established with Joel T. Saylers as postmaster. By 1896 Dumont had three churches and a population of fifty. In 1914 the schools of Union Corner, four miles to the north, and China Grove were combined to form the Dumont Independent School District Number 1. This district remained intact until 1959, when the Dumont school was moved to Guthrie. The region produces cotton, grain, and cattle. Ranching predominates, and numerous ranches have been nearby, including the Four Sixes, the SMS, and the Matador.qqv Though at one time Dumont had three grocery stores, three filling stations, a blacksmith shop, a barbershop, and a cotton gin, by 1980 it reported no rated businesses. The community's highest recorded population was 105 in the middle and late 1960s. Its population had fallen to ninety-five by 1980, but at that time Dumont was still the second largest town in King County. In the early 1990s Dumont was in both King and Dickens counties, and its population was reported as eighty-five, served by three businesses.

BIBLIOGRAPHY: Fred Arrington, *A History of Dickens County: Ranches and Rolling Plains* (Quanah, Texas: Nortex, 1971). King County Historical Society, *King County: Windmills and Barbed Wire* (Quanah, Texas: Nortex, 1976). Kathleen E. and Clifton R. St. Clair, eds., *Little Towns of Texas* (Jacksonville, Texas: Jayroe Graphic Arts, 1982).

Edloe A. Jenkins

DUNAGAN, JOHN CONRAD (1914–1995). Conrad Dunagan, businessman, philanthropist, and historian, was born in Midland, Texas, on December 31, 1914, to John Claiborne and Ada Lois (Hicks) Dunagan. After he graduated from Midland High School in 1931, he worked in the Midland Bottling Company until he entered the University of Texas in 1933. He married Kathlyn Cosper on August 21, 1933, and the couple moved to Monahans, where Dunagan managed the Coca-Cola Bottling Company until 1935. The couple returned to the university and continued their studies from 1935 to 1937, after which they moved back to Monahans. There they were both employed by First State Bank, where Conrad was an officer. The Dunagans' residence in Monahans was continuous for the remainder of their lives except for 1940–41, when Conrad worked as an assistant bank examiner for the Federal Reserve Bank of Dallas.qv He had a long career with the Coca-Cola Bottling Company, beginning as manager and ending as chairman of the board in 1983. Dunagan was highly active in bottling circles during most of his business career. He served on the executive committee of the National Soft Drink Association from 1961 to 1973, on the Standardization Committee of the Coca-Cola Bottlers Association, (U.S.A.), from 1960 to 1974, and as president of the Texas Bottlers Association in 1958. He was a cofounder of Southwest Canners, Incorporated, of Portales, New Mexico, in 1973. In the Permian Basin,qv he served as a director of the First State Bank, Monahans, from 1937 to 1995, and as chairman of the board from 1967 to 1984. He was also cofounder and chairman of the board of Texas Savings and Loan Association, Monahans, from 1965 to 1982, and an officer of Kermit (Texas) State Bank from 1944 to 1995. His other business activity included serving as president of Midessa TV, Incorporated (KMID), from 1954 until 1983.

In civic affairs, he served on the Monahans City Council in 1939, on the Good Neighbor Commissionqv from 1955 to 1961, and in the group that organized the Monahans Sandhills State Historic Park.qv From 1958 to 1961, Dunagan was president of the park association. He also supported the establishment of the Million Barrel Museum in Monahans and served on the board of the Historical Association of Ward County. He was an enthusiastic and generous supporter of educational and historical organizations. He served as president of the Texas State Historical Associationqv in 1986–87, of the West Texas Historical Associationqv in 1983–84, and of the Permian Historical Societyqv in 1962–63. He was an active member of the Texas Folklore Societyqv and of the Philosophical Society of Texas.qv In addition to significant gifts to the Permian Historical Society and the West Texas Historical Association, he established a research fellowship in Texas studies at the Texas State Historical Association to support the *New Handbook of Texas* project. He also endowed the J. Conrad Dunagan Professorship at the University of Texas of the Permian Basin.

He wrote the *New Handbook of Texas* entry on the soft-drink industryqv and two monographs, *Eugene Holman, a Texan of Distinction* (1989) and *The Holman Hotel: Its Owners and Early Monahans* (1988). Widely recognized in the Permian Basin region as an effective supporter of education, Dunagan was appointed to the President's Council on Education by President Dwight D. Eisenhowerqv in 1955. He played a key role in the establishment of the University of Texas of the Permian Basin in 1969, served on the university's development board from 1976 to 1995, and endowed merit scholarships at the institution. He also founded the Permian Honor Scholarship Foundation in 1976, headed the foundation until 1995, and, with his family, endowed numerous scholarships. By 1995 about 2,000 Permian Basin students had received awards from this foundation. Dunagan also served as a member of the Executive Committee of the University of Texas Systemqv Chancellor's Council.

Numerous organizations awarded honors to Dunagan, including the Monahans Chamber of Commerce (Outstanding Citizen Award, 1964), the Jaycees (Hall of Leadership, 1983), the Southwest Conference of Foundations (Founder Spirit Award, 1991), the Texas State Historical Association (Honorary Life Member of the Executive Council, 1988), the University of Texas of the Permian Basin (Distinguished Patron, 1991), the Permian Historical Society (Permian Academy of History, 1983), and the Heritage of Odessa Foundation (Community Statesman Award for Philanthropy, 1994). Dunagan died in a Dallas hospital on February 10, 1995. He was survived by his wife and five children.

BIBLIOGRAPHY: *Southwestern Historical Quarterly*, April 1995. Vertical Files, Barker Texas History Center, University of Texas at Austin.

Roger M. Olien

DUNAGAN, TEXAS. Dunagan (Dunagin) was seven miles east of what is now Lufkin and five miles northwest of what became Huntington near the center of Angelina County. It was named for Isaac Dunagan and was settled in the early 1840s before Angelina County was established. The county's first commissioners' court met at Isaac Dunagan's home in 1846. The Dunagan community, along with Moses Bluff, was up for consideration to be the county seat after the Texas legislature established Angelina County in April 1846. An election resulted in twenty-six votes for Moses Bluff and two for Dunagan. A second election, held to appease dissatisfied citizens, resulted in thirty-nine votes for Moses Bluff (designated as River Place for its location on the Angelina River) and again, only two for Dunagan (called Center for election purposes). The Dunagan community faded, and no further mention was made of it in local histories. In the mid-1980s a railroad siding in the vicinity was known as Dunagan.

BIBLIOGRAPHY: Archie Birdsong Mathews, The Economic Development of Angelina County (M.A. thesis, University of Texas, 1952).

Megan Biesele

DUNBAR, WILLIAM (ca. 1750–1810). William Dunbar, plantation owner, scientist, and explorer, son of Sir Archibald and Anne (Bayne) Dunbar, was born in Morayshire, Scotland, about 1750. In 1763 he attended King's College, Aberdeen, and graduated from there in 1767. Deciding to seek health and fortune in America, he arrived in Philadelphia in April 1771. In 1773 he formed a partnership with John Ross, a Scotch merchant in Philadelphia, and they established a plantation in West Florida. Dunbar opened another plantation called "The Forest" near Natchez, Mississippi, in 1792. Applying his knowledge of chemistry and mechanics to planting, he made a number of inventions and became sufficiently prosperous to retire and devote his time to scientific investigation. Dunbar invented a screw press and with its use introduced square cotton bales as a means of packing cotton. He was the first to suggest the manufacture of cottonseed oil. He was surveyor general in the Natchez area in 1798 and made the first meteorological observations in the Mississippi Valley in 1799. In 1804 he was appointed by President Thomas Jefferson to head an expedition with Dr. George Hunter. They were to explore the Ouachita River region and travel all the way to the source of the Red River. The Hunter-Dunbar expedition set out on October 16, 1804, traveling up the Ouachita River and on to the area of Hot Springs, Arkansas. Dunbar became the first man to give a scientific report of the hot springs, and his journal of the exploration was later published in *Documents Relating to the Purchase and Exploration of Louisiana* (1904). He made scientific reports on the Indian sign language, animal and plant life, fossils, and astronomical phenomena in the area. Dunbar never explored the Red River region and was never in Texan territory, however. He was later chief justice of the Mississippi Court of Quarter Sessions and a member of the Mississippi Territorial Legislature. He was a member of the American Philosophical Society. At some point in his life he married Dinah Clark. They had several children, although specific details are unknown. Dunbar died on October 16, 1810, in Mississippi.

BIBLIOGRAPHY: Isaac Joslin Cox, "The Louisiana-Texas Frontier," *Quarterly of the Texas State Historical Association* 10, 17 (July 1906, July, October 1913). Arthur H. DeRosier, Jr., "William Dunbar, Explorer," *Journal of Mississippi History* 25 (July 1963). Arthur H. DeRosier, Jr., "William Dunbar: A Product of the Eighteenth Century Scottish Renaissance," *Journal of Mississippi History* 28 (August 1966). *Dictionary of American Biography*. William Dunbar, *Life, Letters and Papers of William Dunbar*, comp. Mrs. Dunbar Rowland (Jackson: Press of the Mississippi Historical Society, 1930).

DUNBAR, TEXAS (Matagorda County). Dunbar was a farming community just west of the Tres Palacios River and a mile north of the Farm Road 521 bridge, six miles northeast of Palacios in southwestern Matagorda County. The community, named for early area landowners, in 1909 received a post office that was probably in postmaster Cora Ifland's store. For a time Dunbar had a two-room schoolhouse, but by at least 1917 the school had moved to nearby Prairie Center, where it served students in eight grades. By 1912 Dunbar had a one-room non-denominational church. Cattle and peaches were among the products Dunbar shipped. Its post office closed in 1913, and around that time Sydney Johnson Hill bought most of the land in the area and eventually moved into the store. Dunbar was not named on the 1936 county highway map.

BIBLIOGRAPHY: Matagorda County Historical Commission, *Historic Matagorda County* (3 vols., 1986–88).

Rachel Jenkins

DUNBAR, TEXAS (Rains County). Dunbar is just off State Highway 19 some five miles south of Emory in southern Rains County. The site was first settled in the 1890s and was originally known as Sabine Pass. A post office operated there from 1900 to 1904. The application for a post office required a different name, so Sam Aron, the first postmaster, chose Dunbar, probably for his former home, Dunbar, Tennessee. The first church in the community, organized by Al McKay, was called Zion Hill. Children attended school in nearby communities until 1904, when a second church building was used as a school. During the 1930s the settlement had a school, two churches, and two businesses. Its reported population in 1940 was fifty. After World War II[qv] the community's school and both of its businesses closed, and in the early 1990s only the church and a high school remained in the area. Dunbar's reported population in 1990 was forty.

Annie May Schrimsher

DUNBAR, TEXAS (Smith County). Dunbar was just south of Farm Road 2767 in extreme eastern Smith County. In 1936 the Dunbar school, apparently named for black poet Paul Lawrence Dunbar, had eight teachers and 178 black pupils. The twenty-four school-age white children in the area were not enrolled. The 1936 county highway map also showed a business and a scattered collection of dwellings at the site, while the Mount Zion church and cemetery were just to the east. By 1952 Dunbar's school had been consolidated into the Holts Independent School District. In 1966 Dunbar comprised a school building, the County Line church, and a few farms along four dirt roads. The Chapel Hill system had absorbed the Holts Independent School District by 1969. During the early 1970s the school building, church, and scattered dwellings remained at Dunbar. The community was no longer shown on the 1981 county highway map.

BIBLIOGRAPHY: Edward Clayton Curry, An Administrative Survey of the Schools of Smith County, Texas (M.Ed. thesis, University of Texas, 1938). "School Sights," *Chronicles of Smith County,* Fall 1969. Smith County Historical Society, *Historical Atlas of Smith County* (Tyler, Texas: Tyler Print Shop, 1965). Albert Woldert, *A History of Tyler and Smith County* (San Antonio: Naylor, 1948).

Vista K. McCroskey

DUNBAR DRAW. Dunbar Draw begins a mile south of the Hunt Ranch headquarters in south central Sutton County (at 30°27′ N, 100°30′ W) and runs west for about twelve miles to its mouth on Cusenbary Draw, about a half mile north of Galbreath Ranch (at 30°25′ N, 100°38′ W). The gully, located in the gently rolling limestone terrain of the western Edwards Plateau, runs through an area of shallow to deep loamy soils occasionally broken by rock outcrops. Local vegetation consists primarily of range grasses with scattered small stands of oak, juniper, and mesquite.

DUNCALF, FREDERICK (1882–1963). Frederick Duncalf, historian, was born in Lancaster, Wisconsin, on March 23, 1882. He attended Beloit College, where he received his B.A. in 1904, and the University of Wisconsin, where, as a student under Dana C. Munro, historian of the Crusades, he received his Ph.D. in 1914. He went to the University of Texas as a tutor in 1909; after two short intervals of teaching, at Bowdoin in 1910–11 and at the University of Illinois in 1913–14, he returned to the University of Texas as a professor of medieval history, a post he held until his retirement in 1950. During his tenure at UT Duncalf trained a group of medievalists who subsequently had distinguished careers at leading American universities. He also was instrumental in the inauguration of the university's Plan

II program in 1936, the earliest honors program at any major state university. He was married to Alma Rather in 1914.

After his retirement in 1950 he taught courses in church history at the Episcopal Seminary of the Southwest.[qv] He was a member of the council of the Medieval Academy of America and a fellow of the Royal Historical Society. His publications included *Parallel Source Problems in Medieval History* (1912), with August C. Krey; *A Brief History of the War* (1918); *Europe and Our Nation* (1932), with Eugene C. Barker;[qv] and *The Story of Civilization* (1938), with Carl Becker. His most important contribution to scholarship was the planning, with Krey, of a cooperative *American History of the Crusades,* the first volume of which appeared in 1955; to this volume he contributed an important chapter. Duncalf died on March 29, 1963.

BIBLIOGRAPHY: Vertical Files, Barker Texas History Center, University of Texas at Austin.

Archibald R. Lewis

DUNCAN, DONALD (1903–1987). Donald Duncan, professor of anatomy at the University of Texas Medical Branch at Galveston, was born in Marietta, Minnesota, on January 31, 1903, the oldest son of Henry and Clara (Olson) Duncan. He earned membership in Phi Beta Kappa and graduated from Carleton College in 1923. He received a master's degree (1927) and a Ph.D. degree (1929) in anatomy from the University of Minnesota School of Medicine. Duncan taught anatomy at the University of Utah (1929–30), the University of Buffalo (New York, 1930–32, 1942–43), Louisiana State University (1943–46), and the University of Texas Medical Branch (1932–41, 1946–68). He served as chairman of the UTMB Department of Anatomy for twenty-five years and associate dean of the Graduate School of Biomedical Sciences at UTMB for sixteen years (1952–69). From 1952 to 1968 he and M. Mason Guest[qv] represented UTMB at regular meetings of the Graduate Assembly at UT Austin. Their efforts were extremely important in the development of the school's graduate programs in the biomedical sciences. In 1968 the UT Board of Regents honored Duncan by designating him the Ashbel Smith[qv] Professor of Anatomy at UTMB.

Duncan was called "Daddy D" by admiring medical and graduate students, whom he encouraged to become involved in medical research. He published numerous research papers, especially in neuroanatomy, and served as editor of the *American Journal of Anatomy* for eight years (1960–68). He was a charter member of the Texas Society of Electron Microscopy. He served as president of the Texas Academy of Science[qv] (1962) and the American Association of Anatomists (1967); in 1971 the latter gave Duncan its highest honor, the Henry Gray Award. On September 18, 1924, he married Margaret Aileen Eberts. They had three daughters. Duncan was an Episcopalian. He died in Austin on February 17, 1987.

BIBLIOGRAPHY: Donald Duncan Papers, Truman G. Blocker, Jr., History of Medicine Collections, Moody Medical Library, University of Texas Medical Branch, Galveston. Galveston *Daily News,* February 19, 1987. *The University of Texas Medical Branch at Galveston: A Seventy-five Year History* (Austin: University of Texas Press, 1967). *Who's Who in America,* 1980–81.

Chester R. Burns

DUNCAN, JOHN MARTIN (1851–1917). John Martin Duncan, lawyer and statesman, son of Franklin and Caroline (McAnnelly) Duncan, was born in Lawrence County, Tennessee, on February 7, 1851. In 1858 the family moved to Marion County, Texas, where Duncan worked in Nash's Iron Foundry[qv] during the Civil War.[qv] He studied law and in 1872 was admitted to the bar at Jefferson, in the office of Judge John C. Stallcup. Duncan established his practice in Longview, where he was elected county attorney of Gregg County in 1876, the year he married Allie Davis. From 1878 to 1882 he represented Smith, Gregg, Upshur, and Camp counties in the Texas Senate. In January 1884 he moved to Tyler, where he formed a partnership with James S. Hogg.[qv] Duncan was elected county judge the same year. In February 1889 he was appointed general attorney with Horace Chilton[qv] for the receivers of the International–Great Northern Railroad. In 1896 he was a delegate to the national Democratic convention and a leader of the movement to swing votes to William Jennings Bryan. From 1905 to 1909 he was Smith County representative in the Texas legislature. At the close of his legislative service, Duncan moved to Houston, where he practiced for less than a year before ill health caused him to retire. He moved to San Antonio and died there on April 21, 1917; he was survived by his second wife, Edwina Louise (House), whom he had married in 1890 after the death of his first wife.

BIBLIOGRAPHY: Lewis E. Daniell, *Personnel of the Texas State Government, with Sketches of Representative Men of Texas* (Austin: City Printing, 1887; 3d ed., San Antonio: Maverick, 1892). Galveston *News,* January 21, 1917. Vertical Files, Barker Texas History Center, University of Texas at Austin.

Carolyn Hyman

DUNCAN, THOMAS ELMER (1911–1967). Thomas (Tommy) Elmer Duncan, singer and songwriter, was born on January 11, 1911, in Whitney, Texas, into a large and impoverished family of truck farmers. On the farm he worked with African Americans[qv] who indelibly marked his singing style and repertoire. He was further influenced, according to his sister, Corrine Andrews, "by the records of colored people and by the recordings of Jimmie Rodgers" (James Charles Rodgers[qv]). When he was seventeen he left home and moved in with a cousin near Hedley, where residents remembered that Duncan sang Jimmie Rodgers songs as he drove along in an "old stripped-down car." He evidently went broke on a farm he had leased in Hedley and in the early 1930s was still broke, out of work, and living in Fort Worth. The show-business bug had bitten him, and he was determined to have a career as a singer. Clifton "Sleepy" Johnson, an early member of the Light Crust Doughboys,[qv] recalled first seeing Duncan playing a little cheap guitar "about a foot and a half long" and singing at the Ace High root-beer stand for tips. In 1932 Duncan won an audition against sixty-six other singers to join bandleader James Robert (Bob) Wills[qv] as the vocalist for the Light Crust Doughboys.

He was versatile in his singing style and repertoire, had a fine voice and range, and was ideal for the kind of dance music Wills performed. In his earliest recording sessions for Wills, he sang everything from ballads and folk to pop, Tin Pan Alley, Broadway, and cowboy songs. Even in songs with sad lyrics he maintained a touch of fun. Like his black friends, he appeared to be completely detached from any sad mood or story in the lyrics. Duncan had "soul" in his singing like black blues singers, not the sentimentality of some country singers. His versatility was well-suited to the western swing music that he and Wills pioneered.

When Wills left the Light Crust Doughboys in August 1933 to form the Texas Playboys, Duncan went with him. Alton Stricklin,[qv] a member of the group, observed that Duncan remembered the lyrics to more than 4,000 songs and could learn the words to a new song within fifteen minutes. The song that made the Texas Playboys famous was a folk-rooted pop song that Irving Berlin heard Wills play as a fiddle instrumental and published in 1940. Since Berlin wanted lyrics for the selection, Wills asked Duncan and several other band members to help him write words for the fiddle tune. Wills called it "New San Antonio Rose." In 1940 Wills recorded it in Dallas. That recording, with the brilliant Duncan vocals, sold three million copies for Columbia Records (now CBS Records). Bing Crosby then recorded it and won his second gold record.

Tommy Duncan was the first member of Wills's band to volunteer for the armed services after the bombing of Pearl Harbor. He rejoined Wills in 1944 as the war neared its end and as Bob Wills was becoming even more famous in music and the movies. Duncan appeared with Wills in several movies, including *Bob Wills and His*

Texas Playboys (1944), *Rhythm Roundup* (1945), *Blazing the Western Trail* (1945), *Lawless Empire* (1945), and *Frontier Frolic* (1946). He became not only a movie star but the most famous singer in all of western swing. His voice matured in the middle to late 1940s, and he became a star in his own right, second only to Wills himself in the Texas Playboy band. Duncan, who could also play piano and guitar, joined Wills in writing several numbers, including "New Spanish Two Step" (1945), "Stay a Little Longer" (1945), "Cotton-Eyed Joe" (1946), and "Sally Goodin" (1947).

For various reasons—Wills's periodic drinking and Duncan's own ego and ambition to go on his own, for instance—Duncan left the Texas Playboys in 1948. He organized one of the best western swing bands ever assembled and called it Tommy Duncan and His Western All Stars. The band was technically perfect, and Duncan's singing was excellent, but the band lacked the spark that had made Wills's group exciting. The band had only minor success with such recordings as "Gambling Polka Dot Blues," "Sick, Sober, and Sorry," "There's Not a Cow In Texas," "Mississippi River Blues," and "Wrong Road Home Blues." Attendance at the Western All Stars' dances ranged from fair to poor, certainly not good enough to sustain a large band for very long. The band lasted less than two years. Duncan spent several years recording and entertaining on his own, but in 1959 returned to the Wills band. There was standing room only as they crisscrossed the country on national tours. In 1960–61 they made three albums that sold much better than either of their recordings had while they worked separately: "Together Again," "A Living Legend," and "Mr. Words and Mr. Music." In the early 1960s the two pioneers of western swing went their various ways, Wills to Oklahoma and Texas, and Duncan to California. Duncan never had a band of note after his All Stars disbanded in the late 1940s, although he continued to make personal appearances with various bands.

He never compromised his style in order to be more popular and commercial. He would never sing like vocalists of mainstream country and western or rock and roll or pop, though at times he appealed to almost all audiences. Among the singers who felt his influence were Elvis Presley, Ray Price, Willie Nelson, Waylon Jennings, John Denver, Merle Haggard, Ray Benson, Red Steagall, George Strait, Clint Black, Randy Travis, and Garth Brooks. Duncan died on July 25, 1967, in San Diego, after a performance at Imperial Beach.

BIBLIOGRAPHY: *The Illustrated Encyclopedia of Country Music* (New York: Harmony Books, 1977). Ruth Sheldon, *Hubbin' It: The Life of Bob Wills* (Kingsport, Tennessee: Kingsport Press, 1938). Al Stricklin and John McConal, *My Years with Bob Wills* (San Antonio: Naylor, 1976; 2d ed., Burnet, Texas: Eakin Press, 1980). Charles R. Townsend, *San Antonio Rose: The Life and Music of Bob Wills* (Urbana: University of Illinois Press, 1976). *Charles R. Townsend*

DUNCAN, WILLIAM (ca. 1786–1836). William Duncan, early settler in East Texas, was born in South Carolina about 1786. He apparently married and had at least one son in South Carolina. By 1818 he had moved to Louisiana, where two more children were born. Duncan married Jane Oden in St. Mary's Parish, Louisiana, on July 24, 1825. In 1826 Green DeWitt[qv] gave him and Col. Elijah Stapp[qv] letters of introduction informing fellow empresario[qv] Stephen F. Austin[qv] that the two men were bound for the San Marcos River or the Guadalupe to locate land "for a number of families." Duncan, however, decided to move his family to the Atascosito District. In 1827 he was one of a number of district residents who petitioned Anastasio Bustamante[qv] for recognition of their land claims. In 1831, unlike many other Americans in the area, Duncan received title to his land, which was on the west bank of the Trinity River. He also secured a town lot across from the courthouse square in Liberty. He remained loyal to Mexico during the early stages of the Texas Revolution,[qv] when he joined John A. Williams in opposing William B. Travis's[qv] armed attack on Mexican troops at Anahuac in 1835 (*see* ANAHUAC DISTURBANCES). Duncan died in late 1836; a Liberty County Bicentennial celebration group commemorated his prerepublic homesite with a marker in 1976.

BIBLIOGRAPHY: Eugene C. Barker, ed., *The Austin Papers* (3 vols., Washington: GPO, 1924–28). Miriam Partlow, *Liberty, Liberty County, and the Atascosito District* (Austin: Pemberton, 1974). C. Allen True, "John A. Williams, Champion of Mexico in the Early Days of the Texas Revolution," *Southwestern Historical Quarterly* 47 (1943). *Robert Wooster*

DUNCAN, TEXAS. Duncan, near Alligator Creek twelve miles northwest of Rockdale in western Milam County, was named for the Duncan family, who settled in the area in 1879. A school was built there in 1892 on land donated by George and Elizabeth Duncan. The school had two teachers and forty-six students in 1903. High school students from Duncan were sent to Sharp in the late 1920s, and the rest of the schools were consolidated with the Sharp district in the early 1930s. There was no evidence of the Duncan community on the 1941 county highway map.

BIBLIOGRAPHY: Milam County Heritage Preservation Society, *Matchless Milam: History of Milam County* (Dallas: Taylor, 1984). *Vivian Elizabeth Smyrl*

DUNCAN CREEK. Duncan Creek rises near Farm Road 1689 some five miles west of Comanche in west central Comanche County (at 31°54′ N, 98°41′ W) and runs northeast for fifteen miles to its mouth on Proctor Lake, near the Ivanhoe community (at 31°58′ N, 98°32′ W). The creek was named for settler John Duncan, who donated land for the town of Comanche in 1859. An early settlement of the same name was at a site three miles north of the county seat. The rural communities of Mount Pleasant and Fairview are near the creek. It crosses an area of mostly steep slopes with shallow, sandy soils that support oak and grasses.

BIBLIOGRAPHY: Comanche County Bicentennial Committee, *Patchwork of Memories: Historical Sketches of Comanche County, Texas* (Brownwood, Texas: Banner Printing, 1976).

DUNCAN FIELD. Duncan Field, in San Antonio, came into being at the end of World War I[qv] as a division of Kelly Field. It was named for Maj. Thomas Duncan, who was killed in an air crash in Washington, D.C., in 1923. Duncan Field was used as an aircraft-repair depot and was joined to Kelly Army Air Field in 1942 (*see* KELLY AIR FORCE BASE).

BIBLIOGRAPHY: Leah Carter Johnston, *San Antonio: St. Anthony's Town* (San Antonio: Librarians Council, 1947). Green Peyton [Wertenbacker], *San Antonio* (New York: McGraw-Hill, 1946). *Art Leatherwood*

DUNCAN'S WOODS, TEXAS. Duncan's (Duncans) Woods, also known as Duncan Woods and as Duncan's Wood, was on the nineteenth-century Beaumont and Orange Road in western Orange County. A scattered settlement was present there by 1854, when the Duncan's Woods post office was established. Though first designated as part of Jefferson County, the office was quickly switched to the new Orange County. Gilbert W. Stephenson served as its first postmaster. During the 1850s the Duncan's Woods area was considered one of the most valuable in the county, with higher land prices than for other Orange County sites. Several railroad contractors maintained camps there for workers building the Texas and New Orleans Railroad through Orange County in 1860. Yet the settlement was subsequently abandoned, and its post office was discontinued in 1866. By the mid-1980s the area was virtually treeless, with the North Port Neches and Bessie Heights oil and gas fields roughly marking the old townsite.

BIBLIOGRAPHY: W. T. Block, *A History of Jefferson County, Texas, from Wilderness to Reconstruction* (M.A. thesis, Lamar University, 1974; Nederland, Texas: Nederland Publishing, 1976). Jacob DeCordova, *Texas, Her Resources and Her Public Men* (Philadelphia: Crozet, 1858; rpt., Waco: Texian Press, 1969).
Robert Wooster

DUNCANVILLE, TEXAS. Duncanville is west of the intersection of Interstate Highway 20 and U.S. Highway 67 in southwestern Dallas County. The land on which the city lies originally belonged to the Peters Colony.qv Settlement began when Crawford Trees arrived from Illinois in 1845 and purchased several thousand acres south of Camp Dallas. Trees donated land in 1855 for the Little Bethel Male and Female School, which also served as a church building until 1881, when citizens constructed the Union Hall House. In 1880 the Chicago, Texas and Mexican Central Railway reached the area and built Duncan Switch, named for a line foreman. Charles P. Nance, the community's first postmaster, renamed the settlement Duncanville in 1882. The Gulf, Colorado and Santa Fe acquired the railroad in 1883 and erected telegraph poles and lines. Though a fire in 1884 destroyed most of the community's commercial buildings, by the late 1800s dry goods stores, a pharmacy, a domino parlor, and a school existed in Duncanville. The Farmers Gin and the Farmers Bank opened there in the early 1900s. Between 1904 and 1933 the population of Duncanville increased from 113 to more than 300. Fearing annexation by neighboring Dallas, Duncanville residents incorporated a 225-acre city on August 2, 1947. When the town's population reached 5,000 in 1962, citizens adopted a home-rule charter with council–manager city government.qv Duncanville has developed as a Dallas suburb. Its population increased from about 13,000 in 1970 to more than 31,000 in 1988. Local commerce, which formerly centered on Main Street, had by that time expanded to other sites in the town, most notably to shopping centers on the city's west side and along U.S. Highway 67 between Duncanville and Cedar Hill. In 1991 Duncanville reported 773 rated businesses and a population of 35,761.

BIBLIOGRAPHY: Duncanville Historical Commission, *The History of Duncanville, Texas* (Dallas: Taylor, 1976). Kathleen E. and Clifton R. St. Clair, eds., *Little Towns of Texas* (Jacksonville, Texas: Jayroe Graphic Arts, 1982).
Paula Stewart

DUNDEE, TEXAS. Dundee is on U.S. highways 82 and 277 twenty-seven miles southwest of Wichita Falls in northwestern Archer County. Several families were already living in the area when the town was laid out on the T Fork Ranch between 1886 and 1890. In 1890 the Wichita Valley Railway Company established a line between Wichita Falls and Seymour and constructed a three-story hotel at the station the railroad's president is said to have named for Dundee, Scotland. That year Amanda Giddens built the first post office and became postmistress. A school had begun by 1891, and in 1892 the town was described as a post office and station on the railway with a population of twenty-five. The railroad brought in more settlers. By 1896 the population was estimated at 199, and Dundee had two livestock dealers, a clothier, a general store, a hardware store, a seller of notions, and a Mr. Biffle who sold organs. The Methodists and Presbyterians organized in the late 1890s, and the Baptists in the early 1900s. Dundee prospered and became for a time the second largest town in Archer County. In 1909 a bank was established with Alex Albright as president. Albright later became well known as the owner of "probably the largest Karakul sheep ranch in the world," just outside Dundee.

By 1919 the town had added some businesses, and the population was about 165. In the 1920s the population was estimated at 400. The oldest of the county's federated study clubs was founded there in 1921. Lake Kemp was built during the 1920s fifteen miles west and Diversion Lake four miles north, as well as an irrigation system for the northern part of the county. Diversion Lake provided both irrigation and the site for a 141-acre fish hatchery, which was still in operation in 1990. In 1929 a tornado crippled Dundee, which rebuilt most of its businesses, but with the Great Depressionqv the town's growth was halted. The bank closed in 1933. The number of businesses dropped from ten in 1940 to five in 1946. By 1953 Dundee had an estimated population of 300 and three businesses. In the mid-1960s the population was seventy-five; by 1970 it was forty, and the town had lost its post office. In 1980 Dundee had no businesses, although the railroad still ran through and the population was forty. In 1990 the population was still forty.

BIBLIOGRAPHY: Jack Loftin, *Trails Through Archer* (Burnet, Texas: Nortex, 1979). Winnie D. Nance, A History of Archer County (M.A. thesis, University of Texas, 1927).
Monte Lewis

DUNLAP, RICHARD G. (?–1841). Richard G. Dunlap, diplomat and secretary of the treasury during the Lamar administration, the son of Hugh and Susannah (Gilham) Dunlap, was the first white child born in Knoxville, Tennessee. After serving in the War of 1812 and the Seminole campaign in Florida in 1817, he represented Knox and Anderson counties in the Tennessee legislature from 1829 to 1831. He moved to Texas in 1837 and was appointed secretary of the treasury by President Mirabeau B. Lamarqv on December 14, 1838. From March 13, 1839, until April 20, 1840, he served as minister from Texas to the United States. He married Mary Louisa Winnon on July 1, 1840. He died in New Orleans on June 24, 1841.

BIBLIOGRAPHY: Thomas Maitland Marshall, "Diplomatic Relations of Texas and the United States, 1839–1843," *Southwestern Historical Quarterly* 15 (April 1912).
Carolyn Hyman

DUNLAP, TEXAS (Cottle County). Dunlap, on U.S. Highway 83 eight miles north of Paducah in north central Cottle County, was settled in 1906, when OX Ranchqv owners Sam White and Doss Swearingen sold portions of the ranch to J. M. Abbott and W. B. Dunlap. In 1908 the community gained a post office, which operated until 1970. A cotton gin was also at Dunlap for some years. The community's population was reported as 100 in 1915 and as 113 in 1940 but declined to thirty by 1980. A school operated in Dunlap from 1908 until 1936, when local students were sent to Paducah. In the 1970s most Dunlap residents worshiped at the First Methodist Church or the Church of Christ. The community's population was still thirty in 1990.

BIBLIOGRAPHY: Carmen Taylor Bennett, *Our Roots Grow Deep: A History of Cottle County* (Floydada, Texas: Blanco Offset Printing, 1970).
William R. Hunt

DUNLAP, TEXAS (Travis County). Dunlap is on Farm Road 969 twelve miles east of Austin in eastern Travis County. It was named for William Dunlap Hunter, who became postmaster when the community was granted a post office in 1886. The post office was discontinued in 1901, and mail for the community was sent to Austin. In the early 1890s Dunlap had two stores and thirty residents. Its population increased to fifty by the early 1930s, and to 150 by the late 1940s. From the mid-1960s through 1990 Dunlap reported a population of eighty.

BIBLIOGRAPHY: John J. Germann and Myron Janzen, *Texas Post Offices by County* (1986).
Vivian Elizabeth Smyrl

DUNLAY, TEXAS. Dunlay, originally called Enterprise and also referred to as Enterprise Station, Interprise, Murray, Baldwin, Harper, and Summit, is on the Southern Pacific Railroad and Highway 90, six miles west of Castroville in Medina County. Enterprise developed on the Galveston, Harrisburg and San Antonio Railway around 1881 during a time of rapid rail expansion west through Medina County. A post office was established there in 1890 with Norval Seymour

Murray as postmaster. The community had a population of forty, a general store, a corn mill and gin, and a saloon by 1892. After May 10, 1895, the post office and town were called Dunlay, for Jerry Dunlay, a train conductor. A railroad spur line was laid from Dunlay to the Medina Dam construction site in 1911, and most materials for the dam project passed through Dunlay on this line. By 1914 Dunlay had 100 residents, a lumberyard, a general store, and a cotton gin. The community reported a population of 150 and six businesses by 1965. Its post office closed in 1974. In 1990 Dunlay reported a population of 119 and one business.

BIBLIOGRAPHY: Castro Colonies Heritage Association, *The History of Medina County, Texas* (Dallas: National Share Graphics, 1983). John J. Germann and Myron Janzen, *Texas Post Offices by County* (1986).
Ruben E. Ochoa

DUNN, JAMES HAROLD (1904–1987). James Harold Dunn, oilman, the son of Charles Allen and Charlotte (Webb) Dunn, was born on April 22, 1904, on a farm near Lancaster, in Dallas County. He and his brother spent their early years in Dallas, where he graduated from Oak Cliff (now Adamson) High School in 1921. After entering the Agricultural and Mechanical College of Texas (now Texas A&M University), he worked his way through college, then returned to Dallas, where he worked for the next thirteen years for the Lone Star Gas Corporation and became the company's chief production engineer. He married Louise McCallum of Garland in 1928, and they had a daughter.

In 1938, after receiving his master's degree in civil engineering at Texas A&M, Dunn joined the Shamrock Oil and Gas Corporation in Amarillo and was made manager. Under his leadership, Shamrock became a leading distributor of petroleum products and eventually was pulled out of the red. Dunn was concerned about the wasteful use of natural gas, particularly in the production of carbon black (*see* CARBON BLACK INDUSTRY), and often lobbied in Austin for the passage of needed conservation measures. He proposed the construction of the recycling plant in the Opelika Reservoir at Murchison, in Henderson County; the plant would strip gas of its liquid and return the dry residue gas to the ground to save it for a later date when its sale would be more profitable. Shamrock and Lone Star worked together to obtain the funds to design and build the facility, and on January 1, 1940, the plant began operation, with 6,000 barrels of motor fuel stripped from the processed gas the first day. This led to the advent of liquefied petroleum gas as a major product of Shamrock, and Dunn was instrumental in constructing the first LPG pipelines from the Panhandle field to other regions of Texas and the nation in association with the Phillips Petroleum Company. In 1945 Dunn was made president of the Shamrock Corporation, which by the 1960s emerged as one of the nation's most prosperous petroleum firms. At that time it was merged with the Diamond Alkali Company of Cleveland, Ohio, to form Diamond Shamrock, Incorporated. Dunn was elected chairman of the board of directors in 1960 and served as chairman of the executive committee. He was a member of the Independent Natural Gas Association of America, the Independent Petroleum Association of America, the Texas Mid-Continent Oil and Gas Association, and the Natural Gas Association, which he served as president from 1945 to 1954.

Dunn was an elder at the First Presbyterian Church in Amarillo, a Mason, and a member of the Khiva Shrine Temple. He served on the boards of the Amarillo Chamber of Commerce, the Tri-State Fair, and the YMCA, where he was president in 1955. He chaired the city's United Fund–Community Chest in 1950 and received the first Amarillo *Globe News*qv Annual Community Service Award that year. He also supported the Panhandle-Plains Historical Societyqv and was its president in 1955–56. As an A&M alumnus he was on the Texas A&M Research League, was president of the Amarillo chapter of the Association of Former Students of Texas A&M, and from 1953 to 1959 was on his alma mater's board of regents. In 1972 a new dormitory at Texas A&M was named for him. He was named to the First National Bank of Amarillo board of directions in 1977.

Dunn's association with Cal Farley's Boys Ranchqv began almost from its inception. He eagerly participated in its fund-raising campaigns and served on the board of directors from 1940 until his death. He supervised the construction of its first water tower and, with Phillips Petroleum and the Fulton construction firm, built the gas pipeline to the ranch facilities. He considered his work for Boys Ranch "the best investment in America," and in 1984 he donated his old hamburger stand from college days to the institution. He died in Amarillo on March 15, 1987, and was interred in Restland Cemetery in Dallas.

BIBLIOGRAPHY: Amarillo *Daily News,* March 16, 1987. Amarillo *Globe-Times,* March 16, 1987. Beth Feagles Day, *A Shirttail to Hang To: The Story of Cal Farley and His Boys Ranch* (New York: Holt, 1959). J. Evetts Haley, *Story of the Shamrock* (Amarillo: Shamrock Oil and Gas Corporation, 1954).
H. Allen Anderson

DUNN, JOHN (?–1853). John Dunn, first alcaldeqv of Refugio and soldier and government official of the Republic of Texas,qv was a native of Ireland who probably lived in the United States before 1829, when he came to Texas. Under the customary liberal interpretation of Mexican colonization laws, Dunn, who was single but had servants, was considered the head of a family and given the lands of such. He was one of the earliest members of the Power and Hewetson colony.qv He operated a store near Nuestra Señora del Refugio Mission before the arrival of the Irish colonists in 1834. He met James Powerqv and the colonists when they landed at El Cópano and carried to the *jefe político* at Bexar the official report of the arrival.

Upon the organization of the ayuntamientoqv of Refugio in 1834, Dunn became the first alcalde and was holding that office when Martín Perfecto de Cosqv and the Mexican army landed at El Cópano in September 1835. Having been notified by Power of Cos's expedition, Dunn dispatched messengers to the other colonies. He was a member of the committee of safety and correspondence of Refugio Municipality, was one of the party that accompanied Ira Westoverqv to Goliad to assist James Collinsworth,qv was a private in Capt. Philip Dimmitt'sqv garrison from October 10, 1835, to January 10, 1836, and was in the Lipantitlán Expedition.qv On November 28, 1835, Dunn was elected to the select committee for the purchase of supplies for the revolutionary army.qv He signed the Goliad Declaration of Independenceqv and was one of the committee of three that took the declaration to San Felipe de Austin.

In December 1836 Dunn was appointed first chief justice of Refugio County and entrusted with the political organization of the county. From his store's stocks he provided large quantities of dry goods and clothing to James W. Fannin'sqv command. Sometime around mid-February 1836 he seems to have sold his business and for a short time joined Fannin's force at Goliad.

Dunn was a member of the mounted spy company commanded by Ewen Cameron,qv a unit organized in May or June 1836. On several occasions during the period of the republic he was commissioned to reorganize Refugio County, largely depopulated by the Mexican advance earlier that year. He was later a senator in the First, Second, Third, and Fourth congresses and a representative in the House of the Ninth Congress from Refugio and San Patricio counties. He was chief justice of Refugio from 1845 to 1848 and was elected justice of the peace in 1850 but did not qualify for the place. He was in the mercantile business at Goliad and Refugio and was said to have taught school at one time. Dunn married about 1837 and was the father of three sons. He died on his ranch in Refugio County in January 1853.

BIBLIOGRAPHY: Hobart Huson, *Refugio: A Comprehensive History of Refugio County from Aboriginal Times to 1953* (2 vols., Woodsboro,

Texas: Rooke Foundation, 1953, 1955). Hobart Huson, *Souvenir Program, Refugio County Centennial Celebration* (Refugio: Refugio *Timely Remarks*, 1936?). Texas House of Representatives, *Biographical Directory of the Texan Conventions and Congresses, 1832–1845* (Austin: Book Exchange, 1941).
Hobart Huson

DUNN, ROBERT FRANKLIN (1855–1929). Robert Franklin Dunn, pioneer Methodist minister and circuit rider in West Texas, was born on March 11, 1855, near Charlottesville, Virginia. His father was a member of Gen. J. E. B. Stuart's cavalry during the Civil War, and one of Dunn's earliest recollections was keeping hogs off the corpses of dead soldiers after a nearby battle. Devastated by the war and Reconstruction,qv the Dunn family moved by covered wagon to Texas in 1873 and settled on a farm near Stephenville. Dunn attended Granbury College in Hood County, where he graduated in 1882 and was ordained a minister. On June 21, 1882, he married Luella Spruill. They had nine children.

At Sweetwater Dunn received his first assignment as a circuit rider for the Sweetwater District, which extended from Nolan County to Tascosa in the Panhandle.qv He was the first full-time circuit rider for this area, and he reportedly preached the first sermon in the region at a saloon, by invitation of its owner, in Colorado City, then the western terminus of the Texas and Pacific Railway. Dunn covered his circuit four times annually, riding a sorrel horse and preaching in dugouts and homesteads of isolated settlers, at ranches, and under brush arbors. Later, Rev. J. T. Bludworth took over the circuit in the Panhandle and Dunn rode only the southern half. At the first Methodist conference Dunn conducted, renegade Comanches from the reservation in Indian Territory stole the preachers' horses. As more settlers poured into West Texas, Dunn built and pastored the first churches in Sweetwater, Colorado City, Big Spring, and Snyder.

In 1890 he became vice president of and taught Greek at Granbury College, where he stayed for five years. After 1885 he continued his ministerial duties as a circuit rider and pastor until his retirement in 1926. In his later years the Dunn family moved to Lubbock. He died there on November 29, 1929, and was buried in the City of Lubbock Cemetery.

BIBLIOGRAPHY: Tanner Laine, *Cow Country* (Hereford, Texas: Pioneer, 1969). "The Peter Hurd Mural," *Museum Journal* 1 (1957).
H. Allen Anderson

DUNN, WILLIAM EDWARD (1888–1966). William Edward Dunn, history professor and foreign service official, was born in Sulphur Springs, Texas, on March 2, 1888, the son of James McMurry and Lucie (Ballinger) Dunn. He attended high school in Sulphur Springs and Austin. He was awarded a B.A. degree at the University of Texas in 1909, an M.A. at Stanford University in 1910, and a Ph.D. at Columbia University in 1917. He was a student of Herbert Eugene Boltonqv at the University of Texas and went with Bolton to Mexico City to assist in research work on the early history of the Spanish Southwest.

Dunn returned to Austin in 1913 as an instructor in history and then Latin-American history and economics; in 1915–16 he served as Spanish archives investigator for the Library of Congress. During World War Iqv he left the university faculty to serve in the naval intelligence service, in which he saw duty in various Latin-American countries. After the war he returned to the university to teach, then resigned to become Latin-American editor for the New York *Sun Herald*. From 1921 to 1924 he served as trade commissioner and commercial attaché in Lima, Peru, and from 1924 to 1927 as director general of internal revenue for the Republic of Haiti. In 1927 he resigned to enter private business in New York; in 1931 he retired from banking to become financial advisor to the Dominican government. From 1934 to 1937 he was assistant director for the Bureau of Foreign and Domestic Commerce, from 1937 to 1939 commercial attaché to Buenos Aires, Argentina, and from 1939 to 1941 commercial attaché in Guatemala City. After 1942 he worked for the State Department as counselor for economic affairs in Bogotá, Colombia, and Santiago, Chile. From 1947 to 1949 he was chief of coordination staff of the Office of Intelligence Research, and in 1949 a political advisor to the United States delegation at the United Nations. In 1950 he became a lecturer at the School of Advanced International Studies in Washington, D.C., and from 1953 on he was a director for the Inter-American Scholastic Service of the American Council on Education.

Dunn was the author of *Commercial and Industrial Handbook on Peru* (1925) and numerous monographs in the field of Latin-American history. He was a member of Phi Beta Kappa, Sigma Alpha Epsilon, and the Metropolitan and Cosmos clubs in Washington, D.C. He married Linda Tays, and they had two children. The family lived in Washington, D.C., and Dallas. Dunn died in Dallas on November 18, 1966, and was buried at Sulphur Springs.

BIBLIOGRAPHY: *Alcalde* (magazine of the Ex-Students' Association of the University of Texas), February 1915, February 1920, May 1921, February 1935, October 1937, June 1940, February 1950. *Who's Who in America*, 1923–53.
Richard T. Fleming

DUNN, TEXAS. Dunn, on State Highway 208 ten miles south of Snyder in south central Scurry County, was originally a watering hole for freighters carrying supplies from the Texas and Pacific Railway station at Colorado City north to Snyder and Lubbock. The town was founded by a man named Richardson and was named for Alonzo T. Dunn, who filed on land in the area in 1889. The Dunn home became a way station and mail drop for mail and passenger hacks, and Dunn became postmaster when a post office was granted to the community in 1890. That same year a school opened. Over the years the town grew into a trade center. A cotton gin opened there in 1930, and eight years later the old Dunn well was filled and covered to make way for State Highway 208. In 1980 and 1990 Dunn had a post office and reported a population of seventy-five.

BIBLIOGRAPHY: Lubbock *Avalanche–Journal*, June 27, 1966. Scurry County Historical Survey Committee, *Historical Markers in Scurry County* (Snyder, Texas, 1969).
Noel Wiggins

DUNN CREEK (Hunt County). Dunn Creek rises a mile northeast of Lone Oak in southeastern Hunt County (at 33°02′ N, 95°57′ W) and runs south for six miles, passing west of Lone Oak and east of Wind Point Park, before reaching its mouth on the Red Bird Cove of Lake Tawakoni (at 32°57′ N, 95°59′ W). The stream traverses an area of prairies and low-rolling hills, surfaced with clay and sandy loams that support mesquite, chaparral, and grasses. Throughout the county's history the Dunn Creek area has been used as crop and range land.

_____ (Robertson County). Dunn Creek rises eight miles southwest of Wheelock in southwestern Robertson County (at 30°52′ N, 96°27′ W) and runs southwest for six miles to its mouth on Spring Creek, two miles east of Sutton (at 30°49′ N, 96°30′ W). It traverses nearly level terrain surfaced by sandy loams that support post oaks and grasses. The creek was named for the Dunn family, early settlers of the area.

DUNNE, EDWARD JOSEPH (1848–1910). Edward Joseph Dunne, second Catholic bishop of Dallas, son of Richard and Judith (Cooke) Dunne, was born at Gertnahoe, Tipperary, Ireland, on April 23, 1848. He grew up in Chicago, where his parents had moved when he was less than two years old. Early in his life he showed a great interest in becoming a priest, and to that end he began his studies at St. Mary of the Lake School in Chicago, whence he went to St. Francis Seminary in Milwaukee and subsequently to St. Mary's Seminary in Baltimore. He was ordained to the priesthood in the cathedral of Baltimore by Bishop Thomas Andrew Becker of Wilmington, Delaware, on June 29, 1871. He returned to Chicago after his ordination to become assistant to Father P. W. Riordan, who was then the pastor of St. John's Church and later became archbishop of San Francisco. Dunne left this first assignment in December 1873 and worked at St. Mary's parish until the summer of 1875, when he was appointed pastor of the new parish of All Saints. At this time he was also appointed fiscal overseer of the Archdiocese of Chicago.

All Saints Parish grew out of a parochial school where Mass was celebrated on Sunday. Dunne's desire to emphasize good Catholic education prompted him to study the Chicago public schools and to try to make All Saints School superior to those in that system. Year after year children from All Saints passed the examinations given by the Public Board of Education of Chicago; the school's example brought about a much-improved Catholic educational system. Dunne received a congratulatory letter from the Chicago Public Board of Education that was displayed at the Chicago World's Fair in the Catholic Educational Exhibit.

Dunne finally managed to build All Saints Church in 1880. In that church he was consecrated bishop for the see of Dallas by Archbishop Patrick Augustine Feehan of Chicago on November 30, 1893. He had been appointed to the position the previous September. After working in the Chicago area for more than twenty years he moved to Texas, where he was installed in Dallas on January 17, 1894.

In Dallas Dunne continued his educational emphasis. During his tenure as bishop many new academies and schools sprang up all over the diocese. Perhaps his most important move for education was to invite the Vincentian Fathers,qv traditionally teachers, to return to Texas in 1905. The Vincentians established Holy Trinity parish in Oaklawn and shortly thereafter opened a parochial school. In 1907 they signed a twenty-year contract with the bishop stating that they would open and maintain Holy Trinity College, a Catholic college for boys, as Dallas was in great need of such an establishment at the time.

Dunne was also interested in improving health-care facilities in his diocese. As early as 1896, he invited a group of nuns to come to Dallas to establish a much-needed hospital. The Sisters of Charity of St. Vincent de Paul,qv whose motherhouse was in Emmitsburg, Maryland, responded to Dunne's call and arrived in Dallas in August of the same year. They began work on St. Paul's Hospital immediately, though it was not completed until 1898. Dunne also asked the Sisters of Charity of the Incarnate Wordqv to come from San Antonio to establish a hospital in Amarillo. As a result St. Anthony's Sanatorium, the first hospital in that area, was built around 1901.

The Catholic Diocese of Dallasqv made a great deal of progress during the sixteen years in which Dunne was at its helm. The number of churches increased from twenty-eight to ninety, and the Catholic population tripled. Dunne was given several thousand dollars by the priests and people of Chicago when he was consecrated bishop, and he gave the money to his new diocese when he arrived in Dallas. The Cathedral of the Sacred Heart (later renamed the Catedral Santuario de Guadalupe), which he built in Dallas, was paid for with money that he earned by making lecture tours of the North and East, and he chose to live in a small room in its rectory rather than to spend money on a lavish episcopal residence. On August 5, 1910, Dunne died of a heart attack while visiting a bishop friend at Green Bay, Wisconsin. At his brother's request, he was interred at Calvary Cemetery in Chicago.

BIBLIOGRAPHY: Catholic Archives of Texas, Files, Austin. Carlos E. Castañeda, *Our Catholic Heritage in Texas* (7 vols., Austin: Von Boeckmann–Jones, 1936–58; rpt., New York: Arno, 1976). *Southern Messenger*, October 30, 1902.
Mary H. Ogilvie

DUNSTAN, TEXAS. Dunstan, formerly known as Glenbelto and as Glenham, is just west of State Highway 95 near Big Sandy Creek and what was formerly the Missouri, Kansas and Texas Railroad five miles north of Bastrop in north central Bastrop County. The community, one of several company towns that sprang up with the growth in the lignite mining industry after 1900, served the needs of the Glenn Belto Coal Company, for which about fifty Mexican miners worked under the supervision of John Belto, who also served as the town's first postmaster. The community had a post office from 1901 to 1906. The coal enterprise was operated by Belto and his father-in-law, Martin Glenn, and was leased in 1904 to the Bastrop Coal Company. The town provided the miners' families with housing and a commissary; local children attended school in Bastrop. The area production of lignite peaked in the 1920s. In the depressed economy of the 1930s (*see* GREAT DEPRESSION), lignite produced through the shaft mining techniques characteristic of the mines at Glenham became increasingly uncompetitive compared to strip-mined coal and to petroleum. By the mid-1940s lignite mining in the county had ended. Glenham reported 100 residents from the mid-1930s through the late 1940s, when its population dropped to forty. Population estimates stayed at that level until the mid-1960s, after which no statistics were available. In the 1980s the townsite was uninhabited, although archaeologists had around that time shown considerable interest in it.

BIBLIOGRAPHY: H. Grady Jordan, *An Industrial Survey of Bastrop, Texas* (MS, Barker Texas History Center, University of Texas at Austin, 1947). Ray D. Kenmotsu, *Cultural Resource Investigations at the Powell Bend Prospect* (Texas Archeological Survey, University of Texas at Austin, 1982).
John J. Buder

DUPLEX, TEXAS. Duplex is on Farm Road 273 some fifteen miles north of Bonham and just east of Lake Fannin near the Caddo National Grassland in northeastern Fannin County. The community formed in the early 1880s. It was named to indicate that two families—whose names are not known—settled there in the 1850s. Duplex apparently served as a school community for area farmers and had two schools: Liberty, for white children, and Bethlehem, for black. From 1899 to 1909 the community had a post office. In 1936 the estimated population in Duplex was forty-two. In 1990 it was twenty-five.

BIBLIOGRAPHY: *Fannin County Folks and Facts* (Dallas: Taylor, 1977). Fred Tarpley, *1001 Texas Place Names* (Austin: University of Texas Press, 1980).
David Minor

DUPRE, MARCY MATHIAS (1866–1925). Marcy Mathias Dupre, teacher and school administrator, was born on September 4, 1866, near Winton, Gallia County, Ohio, to John and Nancy Sophia (Huntley) Dupre. He graduated from Ohio State University in 1886 and married Sallie Bell Naasson in 1887; to them were born ten children. Mrs. Dupre died in 1908, and Dupre subsequently married Zenobia Smith. He moved to Texas in 1888 to pursue a career of teaching and school administration in Shelbyville, Henderson, Troup, and Center; he became superintendent of schools in Lubbock in 1914. He was an early advocate of the University Interscholastic Leagueqv and was an active proponent of placing high school football on a state-championship basis, a development that came officially in 1921. He served on the committee of the West Texas Chamber of Commerceqv that successfully worked for the establishment of Texas Technological College (now Texas Tech University). He died on February 24, 1925, in Lubbock.

BIBLIOGRAPHY: Seymour V. Connor, ed., *Builders of the Southwest* (Lubbock: Southwest Collection, Texas Technological College, 1959).
David M. Vigness

DUPREE, ANNA JOHNSON (1891–1977). Anna Johnson Dupree, businesswoman and philanthropist, was born on November 27, 1891, in Carthage, Texas, the oldest of Lee and Eliza Johnson's six children. As the great-grandchild of a slaveholder and the grandchild of former slaves, she was moved by the stories of slaveryqv she heard from her grandparents to desire to improve the lives of blacks. As a child she lived in poverty in a two-room house and worked in the cotton fields with the rest of her family. In 1904, when she was thirteen, her mother moved the family to Galveston, where Anna worked as a nursemaid. In 1914 she married Clarence A. Dupree, a native of Plaquemine, Louisiana. Two years later the Duprees moved to Houston, where he worked as a porter at the Old Brazos Hotel and she became a beautician at the Ladies Beauty Shop. Eventually Anna Dupree was employed by a beauty salon in the exclusive white neighborhood of River Oaks and made personal calls to the homes of customers in both the River Oaks and Montrose districts of Houston. She earned enough making house calls to quit her salon job, but she and her black colleagues were eventually prevented from continuing their independent employment by the establishment of a white beauticians' protective organization.

Living simply and saving what income they could, the Duprees began to invest in real estate. In 1929 they opened the Pastime Theater on McKinney Street. In 1936 Anna built her own beauty shop, equipped with a Turkish bath, a sweatbox, and massage services. Then in 1939 the Duprees built the El Dorado Center, which included the El Dorado Ballroom, one of the first clubs for blacks in Houston and a showplace for black entertainment. By 1940 savings and profits from the Duprees' businesses allowed Anna to donate $20,000 toward the construction of an orphanage, the Anna Dupree Cottage of the Negro Child Center, on Solo Street in the Fifth Ward. In the mid-1940s, she donated property in Highland Heights and led a fund drive to build the Eliza Johnson Home for Aged Negroes; it opened in 1952 and was named for Anna's mother. The Duprees also donated their time to the home, cooking for its residents with food given by local groceries and businesses. They later donated the home to the city. In 1946 the Duprees donated $11,000 toward the construction of the first permanent building on the campus of Houston College for Negroes (now Texas Southern University).

The Duprees also sponsored Houston's first Little League baseball team for blacks and raised funds for the state's only Girl Scout camp for blacks, Camp Robinhood, at Willis. Anna Dupree had hoped her philanthropy would eventually result in the construction of what she called Welcome Acres, a development consisting of residential support services for unwed pregnant women, abandoned infants, and the mentally and physically disabled. But Welcome Acres never developed, and after C. A. Dupree died in 1959, Anna's health declined. She eventually moved into the Eliza Johnson Home, where she died on February 19, 1977. Her body was donated to medical research.

BIBLIOGRAPHY: Houston *Post*, December 3, 1972, February 22, 1977. Yvette Jones, "Seeds of Compassion," *Texas Historian*, November 1976.

Nancy Baker Jones

DUPREE, J. GOLDSTEEN (?–1873). J. Goldsteen Dupree, who represented Montgomery and Harris counties in the Twelfth Legislature in 1870, was probably born in Texas between 1822 and 1846. He was residing in Montgomery County when voters from the Fourteenth District elected him to the House of Representatives. He served on the State Affairs and the Public Buildings and Grounds committees and was one of twelve blacks in the House. Dupree, who only served a single term, became involved in a controversy over voter fraud after his term expired. He appeared before a legislative investigating committee and helped unseat two black legislators, Richard Allen and E. H. Anderson,[qv] by testifying that nonresidents of Harris and Montgomery counties had voted in the election of 1872. His critics charged that he had received money to testify against the two contested legislators. Dupree allegedly died at the hands of white vigilantes who opposed his campaigning for Governor Edmund J. Davis's[qv] reelection in 1873.

BIBLIOGRAPHY: Alwyn Barr, "Black Legislators of Reconstruction Texas," *Civil War History* 32 (December 1986).

Paul M. Lucko

DUPREE, TEXAS. Dupree (DuPree) was halfway between Hainesville and Mount Pisgah on what later became Farm Road 49 in southeastern Wood County. The community may have been settled as early as the 1860s. It was named for resident W. J. Dupree, a doctor whose practice, which served Pine Mills and Hainesville, was reportedly one of the first in that part of the county. From 1892 to 1893 the community had a post office called Dupree, which in early 1893 moved to Hainesville. The 1936 county highway map shows a sawmill and a number of dwellings in the area; Dupree is not shown on highway maps for the 1980s.

BIBLIOGRAPHY: Adele W. Vickery, *Chips of Wood County* (Mineola, Texas, 1969).

Rachel Jenkins

DURANGO. On March 22, 1836, the brig *Durango,* owned by James Reed and Company, a New Orleans mercantile house, and commanded by James C. Ryan, was seized by the Texas armed schooner *Liberty,*[qv] commanded by William S. Brown,[qv] somewhere in Matagorda Bay. The *Durango* was no stranger to the Texas trade. In fact, James Reed, the last recorded owner, purchased this vessel before July 9, 1835, while on a business trip to Texas. He obtained the *Durango* from Mexican authorities after the vessel was wrecked while attempting to cross the Brazos bar. He made repairs in Texas and sailed the vessel back to New Orleans, where the *Durango* was officially registered. He had several business connections with Texas and was sympathetic to the Texas cause.

Because of Reed's business interest in Texas, it seems unlikely that the *Durango* was carrying war contraband destined to assist Antonio López de Santa Anna's[qv] army. The documented and most logical reason why the *Durango* was seized is that Texas needed the supplies and the vessel, which was later used to transport troops and provisions along the Texas coast. Texas had issued orders to military leaders to press into service anything that could be used to support the war effort. The *Durango* fell victim to Texas impressment, despite the fact that it was displaying the Stars and Stripes on the day of its capture. Once the *Durango* was escorted into Matagorda, Texas marines were assigned to guard the vessel and cargo. Unable to reclaim his vessel, Ryan lodged a formal protest with Judge Charles Wilson before departing for the United States.

The *Durango* was taken to Galveston Island after impressment and kept there to avoid recapture by Santa Anna's advancing units. While it was there most of the supplies aboard the vessel were consumed by Texans; all that remained of the cargo recorded in an inventory conducted by William Lawrence,[qv] quartermaster for Galveston Island, on May 22, 1836, was forty-three barrels of damaged flour. The *Durango* disappeared from recorded history after the vessel was ordered to transport troops down the coast on September 16, 1836.

Texas was affected by the capture of the *Durango* in both a positive and negative way. The republic benefited because most of the cargo went to assist the army and aided some needy citizens who had hurriedly left behind all their possessions and fled for safety from the advance of Santa Anna's army. However, because of the Texas policy of attacking American merchant shipping, the *Durango* incident added to an already hostile attitude within the United States about attacks by both Mexico and Texas on United States vessels, which eventually led to the arrest of the crew of the *Invincible*[qv] after this vessel captured the United States merchant vessel *Pocket.*[qv]

A claim was later filed by the Sea Insurance Company of New York, the insurance carrier for the *Durango* and perhaps also the cargo. Added pressure by the United States Department of State compelled Texas into settling the claim for $8,050. However, Texas had no real objections to the settlement. The entire incident was closed officially on April 11, 1838, when a convention of indemnity was entered into by Texas and the United States. The total settlement, which also made provisions for the *Pocket* claims, was for $11,750 plus accrued interest.

BIBLIOGRAPHY: Robert W. Kesting, William Bryan and the Navy from Abroad (M.A. thesis, St. Mary's University, 1985).

Robert W. Kesting

DURANGO, TEXAS. Durango is on Farm Road 935 fifteen miles southwest of Marlin in western Falls County. The site was settled under the name West Falls by members of Robertson's colony,qv and a post office called West Falls operated there from 1871 to 1883. According to local lore, the community changed its name to Durango when a drunken cowboy, who had recently returned from Mexico, insisted that he was in Durango, Mexico. Postal records recorded the name change in 1883. By the mid-1880s Durango had a church, a district school, two gristmill–cotton gins, three general stores, several other businesses, and 200 residents. A public school was established in Durango in 1885. In the late 1880s J. T. Hedrick began publishing a weekly newspaper, the *Enterprise*. During the early 1890s the San Antonio and Aransas Pass Railway was built through five miles to the east of Durango, and some local residents and businesses moved to be closer to the railroad. Durango suffered a further setback in 1892, when a tornado killed several residents and destroyed a number of houses. The post office was discontinued in 1906, and mail for the community was sent to Lott. Population estimates for Durango remained around 200 for several decades, though the number of businesses decreased. The Durango school was consolidated with the Lott Independent School District in 1949. In the mid-1940s residents were reported to number 150; by the mid-1960s the population had fallen to fifty-four. Only a church and two businesses were shown at Durango on county highway maps in the 1980s. The reported population was still fifty-four in 1990.

BIBLIOGRAPHY: Lillian S. St. Romain, *Western Falls County, Texas* (Austin: Texas State Historical Association, 1951). Vertical File, Texas Collection, Baylor University.

Vivian Elizabeth Smyrl

DURANT, TEXAS. Durant, two miles northwest of Clawson in northwestern Angelina County, was the last sawmill town established in the county on the Cotton Belt line (officially known as the St. Louis Southwestern Railway). Around 1909 Louie G. Odum built a small mill at the site on the railway; Durant was often referred to as Odum's Town because Odum was not only a sawmill owner but also a county commissioner and the first postmaster at the community. The local post office opened in 1909 and was closed in 1915. Durant was named for the Durant Lumber Company, which at one time operated a mill there. From 1909 to 1915 the town served as a shipping point for lumber and farm goods. In 1912 Odum sold his sawmill to Arch Carraway, who moved a mill to a site near Durant from Nacogdoches County. Carraway went out of business when the area timber supply was exhausted, and the community subsequently declined. The population of Durant was listed as five in 1910 and twenty-five in 1920. In 1945 the settlement had one business and a population of twenty-five. The population was again reported as twenty-five in 1965. By the late 1980s Durant was an abandoned railroad station.

BIBLIOGRAPHY: Angelina County Historical Survey Committee, *Land of the Little Angel: A History of Angelina County, Texas*, ed. Bob Bowman (Lufkin, Texas: Lufkin Printing, 1976). Archie Birdsong Mathews, The Economic Development of Angelina County (M.A. thesis, University of Texas, 1952).

Megan Biesele

DURAZNO BAYOU. Durazno Bayou rises in the Angelina Nationalal Forestqv four miles northeast of Etoile in extreme southeastern Nacogdoches County (at 31°23′ N, 94°26′ W) and runs south for four miles to its mouth on Sam Rayburn Reservoir, a half mile north of Etoile (at 31°21′ N, 94°27′ W). It formerly ran southwest for 5½ miles to its mouth on the Angelina River, two miles southwest of Etoile. Since the construction of the Sam Rayburn Reservoir in the mid-1960s, the creek's lower reaches have been inundated. It traverses flat terrain with local shallow depressions, surfaced by clay and sandy loam soils that support water-tolerant hardwoods, conifers, and grasses. The creek's name is Spanish for peach tree.

DURDEN, MATTIE ELLA HOLMAN (1881–1972). Mattie Durden, black teacher and community leader, daughter of Silas and Eliza (Richardson) Holman, was born in Refugio, Texas, on July 18, 1881, the elder of two children. Her brother, Sidney, died in United States military service in 1906. Her education began in Refugio in a one-room, ungraded, one-teacher school, where the curriculum consisted of reading, writing, spelling, arithmetic, and a little history, with no provision for further training. At age fifteen she applied for admission to Tillotson Collegiate and Normal Institute in Austin and was accepted. Examinations for grade placement put her in the fifth grade, but through diligent study and reexamination she placed in the eighth grade. Financial difficulties necessitated her leaving Tillotson after two years. At age eighteen she took a county teachers' examination, passed, acquired a teaching certificate, and began teaching in Refugio County. After several years' teaching she returned to Tillotson to continue her education. There she met George Franklin Durden, a student from East Texas. They were married in 1902 in Corpus Christi, where her family had moved. They had two children. Both Durdens reentered Tillotson, and Mattie completed the normal course in 1909. By this time Tillotson had been chartered as a college. Mrs. Durden applied to the collegiate department and, because of her excellent record, became the first married woman to be admitted. She was also the first female graduate of the department. She pursued further education at Tillotson and Samuel Huston colleges (1926–27 and 1928–29), Tuskegee Institute (summer, 1930), and the University of California at Los Angeles (summer, 1946), as well as in short courses at other institutions.

Tillotson College employed her as matron and teacher of high school subjects and sewing from 1911 to 1917. She was subsequently employed by the Austin public schools as the first head of the home economics department at Anderson High School, on Pennsylvania Avenue. She was the first lunchroom supervisor for Anderson and later for Kealing Junior High. She organized the first New Homemakers of America chapter at the school. Mrs. Durden was an active figure in the organization of the Howson Nursery School and the operation of the first well-child clinic for black children at Rosewood Housing Project, which had begun at the Howson Community Center on Angelina Street and was called the Angelina Conference. Subsequently, it was named the M. E. Durden Well-Baby Conference by the Well-Baby Conferences of Austin, under the auspices of the Austin–Travis County Public Health Department. Mattie Durden was president of the board of trustees of the Community Welfare Association (1929–47), a committee member of the East Austin Young Women's Christian Association, a board member of the Central YWCA, and chairman of drives for the Red Cross and United Fund. She was also a member of the Austin Community Council and the Adult Services Council and director of summer vocational programs at various centers where black women could learn sewing, food preservation, and infant care. Her other affiliations included membership on the board of trustees of Tillotson College (1940–52), which she served as secretary for ten years. She signed the charter for the merger of Tillotson and Samuel Huston colleges into Huston-Tillotson College in 1952. She served also as a member of the Nursery School Board of Ebenezer Baptist Church. She was the "token" first representative of black involvement in many community affairs.

She retired as counselor and dean of girls from the Austin public schools on July 18, 1951, after which she became a member of the executive board of the Austin Retired Teachers Association. She died on October 18, 1972, in Austin. Her husband preceded her in death in 1951. Their daughter, Olive, became a teacher and a professional librarian and was employed by the St. Louis (Missouri) public schools (1930–41) as the first black professional librarian in the system.

She served as head librarian at Huston-Tillotson College from 1941 to 1975. The Union Building at Huston-Tillotson is named for Matthew S. Davage^{qv} and Mattie Durden.

Olive Durden Brown

DURHAM, EDDIE (1906–1987). Eddie Durham, one of the most important of the Swing Era's composer-arrangers, was born in San Marcos, Texas, on August 19, 1906, son of Joe Durham. His father played the fiddle at square dances, and his oldest brother, Joe, who played cello briefly with Nat King Cole, took correspondence lessons and in turn taught Eddie and his other brothers to read and notate music. Together with cousins Allen and Clyde Durham, Eddie and his brother Roosevelt formed the Durham Brothers Band around 1920. (In 1929 Allen recorded on trombone with Andy Kirk's Clouds of Joy.) They were later joined in Dallas by another cousin, Herschel Evans,^{qv} the great tenor saxophonist. According to his own account, Eddie began as a professional musician at age ten; at eighteen he was with the 101 Ranch Brass Band playing for circuses in the Southwest and traveling as far as New York City, where he performed in Yankee Stadium. He moved to New York in 1934.

Durham's early training in music theory led to his work during the 1930s and 1940s as a jazz composer-arranger for four important bands from Oklahoma, Missouri, and Tennessee: the Blue Devils, Bennie Moten, Count Basie, and Jimmie Lunceford. The tunes Durham composed or arranged for these bands include such classics as "Moten Swing," "Swinging the Blues," "Topsy," "John's Idea," "Time Out," "Out the Window," "Every Tub," "Sent for You Yesterday," "One O'Clock Jump," "Jumpin' at the Woodside," "Lunceford Special," "Harlem Shout," and "Pigeon Walk." In addition, he arranged music for Artie Shaw and Glenn Miller, among other white big bands of the Swing Era; Durham contributed to one of Miller's greatest hits, "In the Mood." He is primarily considered a key figure in working out arrangements in the famous Kansas City riff style.

As an instrumentalist, Durham was proficient on both guitar and trombone. The 1935 Lunceford recording of Durham's own arrangement of "Hittin' the Bottle" features Eddie as one of the first jazz musicians to perform on an amplified guitar. Durham later influenced fellow Texan Charles (Charlie) Christian,^{qv} probably the most important guitarist in jazz history. In 1938 Durham was the leader for a historic combo recording session with Lester Young, Count Basie's star tenor saxophonist. In the 1940s Durham organized his own band, directed an all-girl orchestra, and brought together a number of important Texas jazzmen from the Kansas City era, including Joe Keyes, Oran "Hot Lips" Page, and Buster Smith. During the 1950s and 1960s he performed less but still worked as an arranger for various groups. Durham and Smith appear in conversation on a 1979 video entitled *The Last of the Blue Devils*, on which Durham also plays

Eddie Durham recording with Lester Young and the Kansas City Six, 1940. Courtesy Alan Govenar, Dallas.

a trombone solo. In England albums were released under Eddie Durham's name in 1974 and 1981; on the latter he can be heard in impressive form at age seventy-five, in particular on "Honeysuckle Rose," where he plays single-string guitar solos in the southwestern style. In the 1980s Durham toured Europe with the Harlem Blues and Jazz Band. He died in New York City on March 6, 1987.

BIBLIOGRAPHY: Stanley Dance, *The World of Count Basie* (New York: Scribner, 1980). George Hoefer, "Held Notes: Eddie Durham," *Down Beat,* July 19, 1962. Barry Kernfeld, ed., *The New Grove Dictionary of Jazz* (London: Macmillan, 1988). Dave Oliphant, "Eddie Durham and the Texas Contribution to Jazz History," *Southwestern Historical Quarterly* 96 (April 1993).

Dave Oliphant

DURHAM, GEORGE JOHN (1820–1868). George John Durham, state official and writer, was born in Norwich, Norfolk, England, on May 12, 1820, the son of William and Ester (Bloomfield) Durham; he was a younger brother of William Davis Durham.qv He immigrated to the United States in 1835 and moved to Texas from New Jersey in 1837. The next year he became chief clerk in the comptroller's office, which was located in Houston at that time (*see* CAPITALS). He moved to Austin with the government in 1839. Durham was in Austin when surveyors laid out the site for the new capital in 1839 and purchased twenty-eight of the original lots. He served as an officer in the Travis Guards (*see* TRAVIS GUARDS AND RIFLES) in 1840, and in 1842 he resisted the moving of government documents from Austin during the Archive War.qv After annexationqv he was chief clerk in the comptroller's office under James B. Shaw and Clement R. Johns.qqv Durham was the auctioneer in Austin in December 1850, when the government sold town lots to raise money for the construction of a building for the land office. He married Cassandra Lincecum, the daughter of Gideon Lincecum,qv on December 23, 1852; they became the parents of seven children, three of whom lived to adulthood.

Durham was elected mayor of Austin in 1852. In 1854, while in that office, he shot and killed a man who had repeatedly threatened his life; he was acquitted. In 1861 he was a delegate to the Secession Convention.qv He served for a short time as an orderly sergeant in the Confederate Army but was recalled to act as state war-tax collector. In 1865, after the break-up of the Confederacy, he successfully resisted armed men who tried to remove funds from the comptroller's office. Durham ran for state treasurer on the ticket with James Webb Throckmortonqv in 1866 but was defeated. He served as secretary of the Democratic state convention in 1868.

He was also an ornithologist, an authority on Texas grapes, an excellent marksman, and a writer. Under the pen name De Los Llanos he contributed a series of hunting articles entitled "Shooting in Western Texas" to the *London Field* magazine. Durham was a correspondent of the Smithsonian Institution, and he wrote two articles on grape cultureqv and several articles on game in Texas published in the *Texas Almanac*qv of 1868–69. In 1867 he was elected a corresponding member of the Academy of Natural Science in Philadelphia. He died of typhoid in Austin on April 10, 1868, and was buried in the family plot at Oakwood Cemetery.

BIBLIOGRAPHY: Frank Brown, Annals of Travis County and the City of Austin (MS, Frank Brown Papers, Barker Texas History Center, University of Texas at Austin). Lois Wood Burkhalter, *Gideon Lincecum, 1793–1874: A Biography* (Austin: University of Texas Press, 1965). Marie Durham Cabler, "Unsung Hero: A Biography of George J. Durham," *East Texas Historical Journal* 10 (Spring 1972). *Dallas Herald,* April 24, 1869. S. W. Geiser, "Men of Science in Texas, 1820–1880," *Field and Laboratory* 26–27 (July-October 1958–October 1959). Amelia W. Williams and Eugene C. Barker, eds., *The Writings of Sam Houston, 1813–1863* (8 vols., Austin: University of Texas Press, 1938–43; rpt., Austin and New York: Pemberton Press, 1970).

Charles Durham Gouldie

DURHAM, JOSEPH IDELBERT (ca. 1854–1941). Joseph Idelbert Durham, known as A. D. Lloyd, "geologist" for the oil well Daisy Bradford No. 3., the discovery well for the East Texas oilfield,qv was probably born in 1854. He left studying medicine and clerking in a drugstore in Cincinnati to take a job as a chemist in the Idaho gold rush, where he analyzed ore for the government. Through work in the field and self-study, mostly from books from the United States Bureau of Mines, he became a mining engineer. After that he went to the Yukon and Mexico to hunt for gold. Then he peddled medicines he had made from oil and patented, in "Dr. Alonzo Durham's Great Medicine Show," which he took around the country. Around 1906 he appeared as A. D. Lloyd, a geologist who advised Columbus Marion Joinerqv on locations to drill in Oklahoma. The location Lloyd advised Joiner to drill later became the Seminole and Cement fields in Oklahoma—the oil was deeper than Joiner could afford to go. In 1927 Joiner and Durham moved to Rusk County to join Walter and Leota Tucker, who planned for them to find an oil well. Durham spent considerable time studying the Rusk County area. He mapped it out and on June 15, 1927, prepared a report, "Geological, Topographical and Petroliferous Survey, Portion of Rusk County, Texas, Made for C. M. Joiner by A. D. Lloyd, Geologist And Petroleum Engineer." The report described in scientific terms all the geologic features that supported the conclusion that oil would be found. It suggested that major companies had been buying in the area. It estimated the depth at which oil would be struck (3,500 feet). But nothing in the promotional study was true. None of the structures Durham described existed, and no companies were buying in the area. As it turned out, however, Durham's assertion that the field would be "of unusual importance" was true, and Daisy Bradford No. 3 did come in at 3,500 feet. Durham had tried to get Joiner to drill two miles to the west, which would have put the well in the thickest part of the area that became the great East Texas oilfield. Durham confessed to a few that he wasn't a geologist, "in that I didn't study prescribed courses in a recognized school to acquire a degree in geology. But I've studied the earth more, and know more about it, than any professional geologist now alive will ever know." Durham and two of his sons "spudded in" a well of their own with the accompaniment of a brass band for about 1,000 witnesses. But Durham soon disappeared. Apparently his picture in the papers had brought a number of women with children who were looking for him. He died in a hotel in Chicago in 1941.

BIBLIOGRAPHY: James Anthony Clark and Michel T. Halbouty, *The Last Boom* (New York: Random House, 1972).

Jerrell Dean Palmer

DURHAM, WILLIAM DAVIS (1815–1838). William Davis Durham, soldier, was born at Bardswell, Norfolk, England, on July 4, 1815, the eldest of seven children of William and Ester (Bloomfield) Durham; he was a brother of George J. Durham.qv The family immigrated to the United States in 1833 or 1835 and settled in New York. William enlisted in the New Orleans Greysqv on October 22, 1835, and landed at Velasco, Texas, three days later. As a member of that unit he participated in the siege of Bexar.qv When the Texas army split, Durham marched to the east and fought at the battle of San Jacinto.qv His name is engraved (incorrectly, as William Daniel Durham) on the face of the San Jacinto Monument. He died, a victim of a yellow fever epidemic, in Houston on August 27, 1838, and was buried in Old Founders Memorial Park. In 1936 the state placed a monument over his grave.

A man named William Durham received 1,280 acres from the Republic of Texasqv secretary of war on May 30, 1838, for his service from October 1835 to October 1836 and was awarded 1,280 acres in Goliad City on February 27, 1841.

BIBLIOGRAPHY: Daughters of the Republic of Texas, *Muster Rolls of the Texas Revolution* (Austin, 1986). Sam Houston Dixon and Louis

Wiltz Kemp, *The Heroes of San Jacinto* (Houston: Anson Jones, 1932). Louis Wiltz Kemp Papers, Barker Texas History Center, University of Texas at Austin. Thomas L. Miller, *Bounty and Donation Land Grants of Texas, 1835–1888* (Austin: University of Texas Press, 1967).

Charles Durham Gouldie

DURHAM, WILLIAM J. (1896–1970). William J. Durham, black civil-rights activist and attorney, was born on a farm near Sulphur Springs, Hopkins County, Texas, in 1896. After completing one semester at Emporia State College in Kansas, he served in the United States Army in France during World War I,qv after which he studied law in the office of Ben F. Gafford, a white attorney in Sherman, Texas. After passing the bar examination in 1926, Durham established his practice in Sherman and began taking on civil-rights cases, even though in the Sherman riot of 1930qv a lynch mob burned the black business district, including Durham's office. Though such lawsuits were rarely profitable, Durham had a lucrative practice as legal counsel to an insurance company and could therefore spend part of his time fighting for equal rights. By 1940 he was recognized as the leading black lawyer in Texas. Gasoline shortages during World War IIqv and his growing business ties and activities in the National Association for the Advancement of Colored Peopleqv in Dallas gave Durham enough reason to move in 1943 from Sherman to Dallas, where he became known not only as a civil-rights champion and the most effective black leader of the NAACP, but also for his effectiveness in court and pretrial strategy. He took part in more than forty civil-rights cases involving such causes as school integration, voting rights, and equalization of teachers' salaries. He and other attorneys fought successfully to enroll Heman M. Sweattqv at the University of Texas law school, to which Durham advised Sweatt to seek admission. Durham knew that there was no law school for African Americansqv in the state at that time and that UT would consequently be particularly vulnerable to a lawsuit if the school rejected Sweatt on the basis of race. Durham became best known for the school-integration cases in which he and his associates went to court to implement the 1954 Supreme Court rulings. Additionally, Durham was on the national board of the NAACP and assisted in directing its education and legal-defense fund. He also helped organize the Texas Council of Voters.

After living in Dallas and practicing law there for twenty-seven years, Durham died, on December 22, 1970. He was buried in Greenville Cemetery in Greenville, Hunt County. He was a trustee of Good Street Baptist Church.

BIBLIOGRAPHY: Dallas *News*, December 26, 1970. Michael L. Gillette, The NAACP in Texas, 1937–1957 (Ph.D. dissertation, University of Texas at Austin, 1984).

Richard Allen Burns

DURHAM, TEXAS. Durham was on Bull Creek ten miles southeast of what became Gail, three miles south of U.S. Highway 180, and two miles west of Farm Road 1610 in east central Borden County. Early members of the Durham community included the Waskom, Wicker, Calloway, Reeves, and Askin families. The first post office in Borden County was established in Durham on May 27, 1887, with Anthony Blum as postmaster. In the late 1800s Durham consisted of a trading post and stage stop on the Colorado City–Fort Sumner stage line. By 1910 the community had grown to include several houses and a general store, a church, and a school. A new school was built at Durham around 1911, but a severe drought in 1916 and 1917 resulted in the community's rapid decline. One store remained there for several years, but on October 25, 1925, the post office was discontinued and moved to Knapp in Scurry County. By the 1960s nothing remained at the site of Durham.

BIBLIOGRAPHY: *Borden County, Texas: The First One Hundred Years* (Gail, Texas: Borden County Historical Commission, 1976).

Charles G. Davis

DURNETT, SAMUEL J. (?–?). Samuel J. Durnett, a pioneer newspaperman, edited the San Luis *Advocate,* which was published by Tod Robinsonqv and Company and designed to promote the new city of San Luis on Galveston Island, beginning on August 31, 1840. Durnett was at Columbia in 1842 and 1843 publishing the *Planter's Gazette.*qv He worked on the *Brazos Planter*qv in 1845 and joined Hamilton Stuartqv in Galveston as an associate on the Galveston *Civilian*qv from 1847 to 1850 and from 1853 to 1855.

BIBLIOGRAPHY: Douglas C. McMurtrie, "Pioneer Printing in Texas," *Southwestern Historical Quarterly* 35 (January 1932). Marilyn M. Sibley, *Lone Stars and State Gazettes: Texas Newspapers before the Civil War* (College Station: Texas A&M University Press, 1983). Ben C. Stuart, "Hamilton Stuart: Pioneer Editor," *Southwestern Historical Quarterly* 21 (April 1918).

DURST, JOHN MARIE (1797–1851). John Marie Durst, early East Texas merchant and patriot, sometimes called the Paul Revere of the Texas Revolution,qv was born on February 4, 1797, at Arkansas Post, Arkansas, the son of Jacob and Anna Agnes (Schesser) Durst. Two years later his mother died, leaving Jacob Durst with eight children to raise. In 1803 the family moved to Natchitoches, Louisiana; then in 1806 Jacob and three of his sons, including John M., went to Texas. John, only nine years of age, was taken into the home of his godfather, P. Samuel Davenport,qv a prominent Nacogdoches merchant who was appointed his guardian after his father's death in 1814. Davenport taught Durst to manage a mercantile firm and to speak several languages, especially Spanish and Cherokee. After the Gutiérrez-Magee expedition,qv Durst accompanied his exiled godfather to Natchitoches. Soon thereafter, at the age of seventeen, he volunteered for military service in the Second Louisiana Division. He participated in the last years of the War of 1812 (1814–15) and returned to Natchitoches at its end. While living in Natchitoches, Durst became acquainted with Maj. John Jamison, the Indian agent at Fort Jesup, and on February 15, 1821, he married Jamison's young daughter, Harriet Matilda. They had twelve children, six of whom survived to adulthood. They employed John H. Reaganqv as a tutor for four years. In his will, dated 1824, Samuel Davenport bequeathed 10,000 acres of land in western Louisiana to Durst. In November 1829 as the result of an agreement with Davenport's son Juan Benigno, Durst acquired all Davenport's land titles west of the Sabine River in exchange for Durst's land titles east of the river. In April 1834 Durst received a Mexican land grant of five leagues in Houston, Nacogdoches, and Anderson counties. By 1837 the tax roll for Nacogdoches County listed him as the owner of 36,200 acres of Texas land.

By 1829 he had returned to Nacogdoches, where he established a mercantile business, became active in local politics, and was in great demand as an interpreter of Spanish, French, German, and a number of Indian languages. From 1829 until July 1834 he and his family lived in the Old Stone Fort.qv In 1832 he took part in the battle of Nacogdoches.qv Durst served as an interpreter for the Mexican government in its negotiations with the Indians. In 1834 he moved to his San Patricio grant on the Angelina River, where he laid out the town of Mount Sterling.

In 1835 Durst was serving as a Texas representative in the legislature of the Mexican state of Coahuila and Texas.qv While there he learned from Mexican friends of the impending movement into Texas of the forces of Antonio López de Santa Anna.qv Thereupon Durst rode 960 miles to warn the people of Texas. The ride earned him his Paul Revere sobriquet. During the revolution Durst commanded a company on the east bank of the Angelina River and reported the activities of Col. Galerno Cruz below Nacogdoches. Durst was also captain of a company operating with Thomas J. Ruskqv against the Kickapoo Indians and against Chief Bowlqv and the Cherokees. In 1844 he moved to Sterling C. Robertson'sqv colony in what later became Leon County, where he bought land near Leon Prairie. In 1846 he was an agent to receive government supplies for United States troops en route to Mexico. Durst died in Galveston on February 9, 1851, while attending a session of the Texas Supreme Court. He was buried in the family cemetery on his homestead near Leona in Leon County. His wife died in Leon County on September 23, 1885, and was also buried in the family cemetery. In 1936 the state of Texas erected a monument to John M. and Harriet Matilda Durst in the family cemetery in Leon County.

BIBLIOGRAPHY: Mary Smith Fay, *War of 1812 Veterans in Texas* (New Orleans: Polyanthos, 1979). Sanford Charles Gladden, *Durst and Darst Families of America* (Boulder, Colorado, 1969). Nacogdoches County Genealogical Society, *Nacogdoches County Families* (Dallas: Curtis, 1985). Harold Schoen, comp., *Monuments Erected by the State of Texas to Commemorate the Centenary of Texas Independence* (Austin: Commission of Control for Texas Centennial Celebrations, 1938). Vertical Files, Barker Texas History Center, University of Texas at Austin.
Joe E. and Carolyn Reeves Ericson

DURST, JOSEPH (1789–ca. 1843). Joseph Durst, pioneer and Nacogdoches official, was born on April 8, 1789, at Arkansas Post, Arkansas, the son of Jacob and Anna (Schesser) Durst. His mother died in 1799, leaving his father with eight children. In 1803 Jacob Durst moved his family to Natchitoches, Louisiana, and in 1806 he and his three sons, including Joseph and John Marie Durst,qv moved to Texas. In 1823 Joseph Durst was serving on the jury in Nacogdoches, where he became alcaldeqv in 1826. He was on the Nacogdoches Committee of Safety and Correspondence in 1835 and after the establishment of the Republic of Texasqv was active in Indian affairs. He went with Sam Houston and John Forbesqqv to Chief Bowl'sqv village and signed the Houston-Forbes Treaty in 1836. In 1842 he was appointed by Houston as one of a committee of four to treat with the Indians. Durst's wife, the former Delilah Dill, inherited the southeast league of the Helena Kimble grant, which borders the Angelina River on its west side and the Old San Antonio Roadqv on its north side. There Durst built Linwood, which later became the home of George Whitfield Terrell.qv Durst died before April 1, 1843.

BIBLIOGRAPHY: Robert Bruce Blake Research Collection, Steen Library, Stephen F. Austin State University; Barker Texas History Center, University of Texas at Austin; Texas State Archives, Austin; Houston Public Library, Houston. Carolyn Reeves Ericson, *Nacogdoches, Gateway to Texas: A Biographical Directory* (2 vols., Fort Worth: Arrow-Curtis Printing, 1974, 1987).
Carolyn Hyman

DUST BOWL. In the latter half of the 1930s the southern plains were devastated by drought, wind erosion, and great dust storms. Some of the storms rolled far eastward, darkening skies all the way to the Gulf and Atlantic coasts. The areas most severely affected were western Texas, eastern New Mexico, the Oklahoma Panhandle, western Kansas, and eastern Colorado. This ecological and economic disaster and the region where it happened came to be known as the Dust Bowl.

According to the federal Soil Conservation Service, the bowl covered 100 million acres in 1935. By 1940 the area had declined to twenty-two million acres. It disappeared in the forties. A prolonged drought, combined with unusually high temperatures and strong winds, caused the normally semiarid region to become for a while a veritable desert. During some growing seasons the soil was dry to a depth of three feet. Lack of rain plagued the northern plains states too, though less severely.

Droughts occur regularly on the plains; an extreme one comes roughly every twenty years, and milder ones every three or four. But in historic times there is no record of such wind erosion as accompanied the drought in the thirties. In 1932 there were 14 dust storms of regional extent; in 1933, thirty-eight; in 1934, twenty-two; in 1935, forty; in 1936, sixty-eight; in 1937, seventy-two; in 1938, sixty-one; in 1939, thirty; in 1940, seventeen; in 1941, seventeen. In Amarillo the worst year for storms was 1935, when they lasted a total of 908 hours. Seven times, from January to March, the visibility in Amarillo declined to zero; one of these complete blackouts lasted eleven hours. In another instance a single storm raged for 3½ days.

Some of the storms afflicting the plains were merely "sand blows," produced by the low sirocco-like winds that came from the Southwest and left the sandier soils drifted into dunes along fencerows and ditches. Less frequent but far more dramatic were the "black blizzards," which appeared with a sudden, violent turbulence, rising like a long wall of muddy water as high as 7,000 or 8,000 feet. The most notorious of these occurred on April 14, 1935. Like the winter blizzards to which they were compared, these storms were caused by the arrival of a polar continental air mass; the atmospheric electricity they generated lifted the dirt higher and higher in a cold boil, sometimes accompanied by thunder and lightning and at other times by an eerie silence. Such "dusters" were not only terrifying to observe but immensely destructive to the region's fine, dark soils.

Repeatedly in those years dirt and sand destroyed crops, property, and mental and physical health. The misery of the era was widely chronicled and eloquently captured in such books as John Steinbeck's *The Grapes of Wrath* (1939). People shoveled the dirt from their front yards and swept up bushel basketfuls inside their houses. Automobile and tractor engines were ruined by grit. The human costs were even harder to calculate and bear. Old people and babies were the most vulnerable to eye and lung damage, as were those with respiratory ailments like asthma. The medical remedies available to them were primitive and makeshift. The Red Cross furnished light gauze masks, and people stuffed rags around windows and door cracks. Domesticated and wild animals often suffocated or were blinded.

As the agricultural base of the region was buried under dust, extreme hardship loomed over the southern plains. In May 1934 dust fell from a massive storm on the Mall and the White House in Washington, D.C., and helped focus federal attention on the desperate situation. The Soil Erosion Service of the United States Department of Commerce established the Dalhart Wind Erosion Control Project in 1934 under the direction of Howard H. Finnell. That year $525 million was distributed to cattlemen for emergency feed loans and as payment for some of their starving stock; farmers were provided with public jobs such as building ponds and reservoirs or planting shelterbelts of trees. Seed loans were provided for new crops, and farmers were paid to plow lines of high ridges against the wind. In 1935 the Soil Conservation Service of the USDA replaced the Soil Erosion Service and opened the Region Six office in Amarillo. There Finnell supervised the conservation work for the entire Dust Bowl. With the cooperation of the Civilian Conservation Corps, the Work Projects Administration, the Agricultural Adjustment Administration,qqv the Resettlement Administration, the Farm Security Administration, state extension services, and other agencies, the Soil Conservation Service made efforts to limit the worst effects of wind erosion. Also in 1935 the Texas legislature established conservation districts for wind-erosion control in nine Panhandleqv counties, where local authorities were given power to force farmers to institute measures to halt blowing dust. Between 1935 and 1937 over 34 percent of the farmers in the area left.

The Dust Bowl was not only the result of bad weather but also of human actions that exacerbated the drought. Immediately before the thirties men had entered the plains fired with enthusiasm to make them yield abundant wealth, and, in a few short years, they had destroyed much of the native grass holding the dirt in place (*see* GRASSLANDS). Some of them had overstocked the land with cattle and reduced its ability to survive a time of severe drought. Others had come intent on transforming the area into row-crop agriculture. Both sorts of settler ignored the hard-won experience of their predecessors on the plains as well as available scientific data and thereby put at risk a vulnerable environment.

Dust storm in the Panhandle, April 14, 1935. Prints and Photographs Collection, Panhandle-sandstorm file, CAH; CN 02655. In 1935 the Dust Bowl covered 100 million acres across the western United States. Visibility in Amarillo that year dropped to zero seven times during the first three months, with one blackout lasting eleven hours.

In the boom years of the twenties, from 1925 to 1930, the time of what one writer has called "the great plow-up," farmers tore up the vegetation on millions of acres in the southern plains, an area nearly seven times the size of Rhode Island. They introduced new gasoline tractors, which allowed them to plow faster than ever before. Some "suitcase farmers" had no more responsible plan than speculating on a quick crop or two. More grandiosely, the movie mogul Hickman Price arrived in Plainview, Texas, in 1929 to establish a factory farm covering over fifty-four square miles in Swisher, Castro, and Deaf Smith counties. To every part of the region came similar pacesetters who fervently believed in the twenties' creed of unlimited, laissez-faire economic expansion and who were convinced that modern methods of industrial capitalism, so apparently successful elsewhere in the economy, were what the plains needed. Even traditional conservative agriculturists were induced to follow these entrepreneurs' lead and try to cash in on a period of good weather and high market demand. Most of the freshly plowed ground went into wheat, so that during the twenties wheat production jumped 300 percent, creating a severe glut by 1931. When the black blizzards began to roll, one-third of the Dust Bowl region—thirty-three million acres—lay ungrassed and open to the winds.

The origin of the Dust Bowl was therefore related to the near-simultaneous collapse of the American economy. Both catastrophes revealed the darker side of entrepreneurialism, its tendency to risk long-term social and ecological damage in the pursuit of short-term, private gain. The New Deal was elaborated partly to prevent such disasters in the future. Some argue that plains agriculture was chastened by the Dust Bowl years and has, with government help, reformed itself adequately so that the thirties nightmare will not recur. Others, less sanguine, point to the dust storms of the mid-1950s and 1970s as evidence that the old Dust Bowl can be reborn, if and when weather and market forces collide again. *See also* WEATHER.

BIBLIOGRAPHY: Paul Bonnifield, *The Dust Bowl: Men, Dirt, and Depression* (Albuquerque: University of New Mexico Press, 1979). R. Douglas Hurt, *The Dust Bowl: An Agricultural and Social History* (Chicago: Nelson-Hall, 1981). Donald Worster, *Dust Bowl* (New York: Oxford University Press, 1979). Donald Worster

DUSTER, TEXAS. Duster, at the junction of Farm roads 587 and 679 in north central Comanche County, was founded in the early 1880s. Local tradition has it that when early settlers met to determine a name for the post office, a man picked up a sheet of paper and blew the dust off it. He then suggested the name Duster and the others agreed. The community was first located at Polecat Pond, then with the coming of the Texas Central Railroad to the area, it was moved two miles north to be near the tracks. After the railroad ceased operations, the town moved back to its original location. The first postmistress there was Miss Belle Dukes. The post office was closed in 1927. The community's population was reported as fifty in 1940, but by 1980 no population statistics were reported. All that remained of the settlement in 1976 was a store.

BIBLIOGRAPHY: Comanche County Bicentennial Committee, *Patchwork of Memories: Historical Sketches of Comanche County, Texas* (Brownwood, Texas: Banner Printing, 1976).

Tracey L. Compton

DUTCH BRANCH. Dutch Branch rises five miles southeast of Aledo in southwestern Tarrant County (at 32°41′ N, 97°33′ W) and runs southeast for six miles to its mouth on Benbrook Lake, just west of the city limits of Benbrook (at 32°39′ N, 97°28′ W). It traverses flat to rolling terrain surfaced by dark, commonly calcareous clays that support mesquite, grasses, and cacti. For most of the county's history, the Dutch Branch area has been used as crop and range land.

DUTCHMAN CREEK (Knox County). Dutchman Creek rises six miles southwest of Benjamin in southwestern Knox County (at 33°33′ N, 99°53′ W) and runs east for ten miles to its mouth on the Brazos River, a mile east of Lake Catherine (at 33°33′ N, 99°43′ W). The stream is dammed to form lakes Catherine and Davis. It traverses flat terrain with local shallow depressions and steep to gentle slopes, surfaced by clay and sandy loams that support scrub brush and water-tolerant hardwoods, conifers, and grasses.

_____ (Motley County). Dutchman Creek rises twelve miles southwest of Matador on the eastern edge of the Caprock in extreme western Motley County (at 33°56′ N, 101°01′ W) and runs southeast for twenty miles to its mouth on the South Pease or Tongue River, about three miles southeast of Roaring Springs in south central Motley County (at 33°52′ N, 100°48′ W). When the area was originally settled, the stream was called Walnut Creek for the walnut trees that lined its banks. By 1877 it had been renamed for a settler who established a homestead in the area. The Matador Ranch[qv] later incorporated the region into its holdings and established the Dutchman line camp on the creek some six miles south of Matador. Campbell Lake, a small man-made reservoir, is on the creek about four miles east of its headwaters. The stream traverses rolling terrain surfaced by sandy loams that support brush and grasses.

BIBLIOGRAPHY: Harry H. Campbell, *The Early History of Motley County* (San Antonio: Naylor, 1958; 2d ed., Wichita Falls: Nortex, 1971). Eleanor Traweek, *Of Such as These: A History of Motley County and Its Families* (Quanah, Texas: Nortex, 1973).

DUTY, GEORGE (?–1837). George Duty, early Texas settler, was born in 1797 or 1799 to Solomon Duty. He was living with William Stephenson in Hampstead, Arkansas Territory, in October 1823, when he took a letter from Stephenson to Stephen F. Austin[qv] in Texas. Evidently Duty remained in Texas. As one of the Old Three Hundred[qv] settlers, he was granted title to a league of land now in Fayette County on July 19, 1824; Dutys Creek, a tributary to the Colorado River, is named in his honor. He participated in the alcalde[qv] election in 1825, and the census of that year listed him as a tanner. According to the census of March 1826 he was a partner of his brother, Joseph Duty,[qv] and was a single man, a farmer and stock raiser aged between twenty-five and forty. He was probably also a freighter, for in November 1831 he hauled brick to build a house for Anthony Butler.[qv] Duty moved to the Mina or Bastrop district before May 30, 1837, when he was appointed administrator of the estate of Matthew Duty. George Duty himself died later in 1837, and on January 22, 1838, William Duty was appointed administrator of George's estate.

BIBLIOGRAPHY: Eugene C. Barker, ed., *The Austin Papers* (3 vols., Washington: GPO, 1924–28). Lester G. Bugbee, "The Old Three Hundred: A List of Settlers in Austin's First Colony," *Quarterly of the Texas State Historical Association* 1 (October 1897). Worth Stickley Ray, *Austin Colony Pioneers* (Austin: Jenkins, 1949; 2d ed., Austin: Pemberton, 1970). Noah Smithwick, *The Evolution of a State, or Recollections of Old Texas Days* (Austin: Gammel, 1900; rpt., Austin: University of Texas Press, 1983). Vertical Files, Barker Texas History Center, University of Texas at Austin.

DUTY, JOSEPH (1801–1855). Joseph Duty was born in Tennessee on March 6, 1801. As one of Stephen F. Austin's[qv] Old Three Hundred[qv] settlers, he received title to a league of land on the east bank of the Colorado River near the northwest boundary of what is now Colorado County on July 19, 1824. The census of the Colorado District in 1825 classified him as a tanner, and the March 1826 census indicated that he was a single man, a farmer, and a stock raiser. In April 1829 he petitioned for land on the Colorado River between Winslow Turner's place and the Old San Antonio Road.[qv] Duty was granted a labor of land in Bastrop County and eventually settled with his wife, Louisa, his brother, George Duty,[qv] and three other brothers at Webberville, Travis County. He was a Travis County delegate to the Democratic state convention in October 1851. He recommended the establishment of Sevier Academy in July 1853. Duty died on September 11, 1855, and was buried in the Old Manor Cemetery at Webberville.

BIBLIOGRAPHY: Austin *Texas State Gazette*, August 27, 1853. Eugene C. Barker, ed., *The Austin Papers* (3 vols., Washington: GPO, 1924–28). Lester G. Bugbee, "The Old Three Hundred: A List of Settlers in Austin's First Colony," *Quarterly of the Texas State Historical Association* 1 (October 1897). Worth Stickley Ray, *Austin Colony Pioneers* (Austin: Jenkins, 1949; 2d ed., Austin: Pemberton, 1970). Noah Smithwick, *The Evolution of a State, or Recollections of Old Texas Days* (Austin: Gammel, 1900; rpt., Austin: University of Texas Press, 1983). Austin *Texas Sentinel*, August 22, 1840, August 12, 1841.

DUTYS CREEK. Dutys Creek rises two miles northeast of Ellinger in southeastern Fayette County (at 29°52′ N, 96°41′ W) and runs southwest for seven miles, crossing State Highway 71 before reaching its mouth on the Colorado River, near Horseshoe Bend and the Fayette county line in northwestern Colorado County (at 29°47′ N, 96°44′ W). It was named for George Duty.[qv] The surrounding flat terrain has local shallow depressions and is surfaced by clay and sandy loams that support water-tolerant hardwoods, conifers, and grasses.

DUVAL, BURR H. (1809–1836). Burr H. Duval, commander of the Kentucky Mustangs[qv] under James W. Fannin, Jr.,[qv] at Goliad, was born in Nelson County, Kentucky, in 1809, the son of Nancy (Hynes) and William Pope Duval.[qv] He was educated at St. Joseph's College in Bardstown, Kentucky, and was one of three brothers who aided the Texas struggle for independence from Mexico. He was elected captain of the company of Kentucky Riflemen that formed at Bardstown in November 1835. The group, which included Duval's brother, John Crittenden Duval,[qv] marched to Louisville, traveled by steamer to New Orleans, and on December 28, 1835, landed at Quintana, Texas, Velasco's rival town at the mouth of the Brazos River. The company reported to the provisional government[qv] two days later, when Duval requested that they be mustered as mounted rangers. The men served briefly, as John C. Duval recorded, as "a kind of marine corps" aboard the Texan vessel *Invincible*[qv] while it searched in vain for the Mexican privateer *Bravo* before returning to Quintana. About the middle of January 1836 the company sailed to Copano, then a principal Texas port on Aransas Bay, and marched to Refugio and then to Goliad, where the men became part of Fannin's Provisional Regiment of Volunteers. Fannin merged Duval's Kentucky Riflemen with Benjamin L. Lawrence's Tennessee volunteers and put Duval in command of the new company called the Kentucky Mustangs. This unit, along with Ira Westover's[qv] regulars, David N. Burke's[qv] Mobile Greys,[qv] Samuel Overton Pettus's[qv] San Antonio Greys, Benjamin F. Bradford's Alabama Greys, Amon B. King's[qv] Kentucky Volunteers, and John Shackelford's[qv] Red Rovers,[qv] formed the LaFayette Battalion, commanded by Benjamin C. Wallace.[qv]

In a letter to his father dated March 9, 1836, Duval wrote that, unlike himself, Fannin "is unpopular" and that only "the certainty of hard fighting, and that shortly, could have kept us together so long." He also wrote of his comrades that "no man ever thinks of retreat, or surrender, they must be exterminated to be whipped." During Fannin's attempted withdrawal from Goliad to Victoria on March 19 Duval joined Shackelford and Westover in protesting their commander's decision to rest the men and oxen on the open prairie before reaching the safety of the trees along Coleto Creek. In the ensuing battle of Coleto[qv] Duval's Mustangs were deployed along the rear of Fannin's square, which engaged the Mexican cavalry in close and bitter fighting. Duval was among the many wounded, but the square remained unbroken. After Fannin surrendered to José de Urrea,[qv] Duval was murdered with rest of Fannin's command in the Goliad Massacre,[qv] on March 27, 1836. His heirs received 3,840 acres of Texas land for his service and sacrifice. Duval County, established in 1858, was named for Burr H., John C., and Thomas H. Duval.[qv]

BIBLIOGRAPHY: William Corner, "John Crittenden Duval: The Last Survivor of the Goliad Massacre," *Quarterly of the Texas State Historical Association* 1 (July 1897). Harbert Davenport, "Men of Goliad," *Southwestern Historical Quarterly* 43 (July 1939). John Crittenden Duval, *Early Times in Texas, or the Adventures of Jack Dobell* (Austin: Gammel, 1892; new ed., Lincoln: University of Nebraska Press, 1986). Zachary T. Fulmore, *History and Geography of Texas As Told in County Names* (Austin: Steck, 1915; facsimile, 1935). Hobart Huson, *Refugio: A Comprehensive History of Refugio County from Aboriginal Times to 1953* (2 vols., Woodsboro, Texas: Rooke Foundation, 1953, 1955). Kathryn Stoner O'Connor, *The Presidio La Bahía del Espíritu Santo de Zúñiga, 1721 to 1846* (Austin: Von Boeckmann–Jones, 1966).

Craig H. Roell

DUVAL, ELLA MOSS (1843–1911). Ella Moss Duval, painter, daughter of Samuel and Isabel (Harris) Moss, was born in Pass Christian, Louisiana, in August 1843. When she was still in her teens, her mother took her to Dresden to escape the perils of the approaching Civil War[qv] and to give her the advantage of an uninterrupted education in Europe. After her stay there she was sent to the fashionable Düsseldorf School for art instruction and studied under August Wilhelm Sohn. In her last year at Düsseldorf, Ella was awarded a prize of a year's study in Rome, but she took money in lieu of the trip and returned with her mother to New York. There, in 1887, she established herself as an artist, with a studio in the Domestic Building, where she received several commissions for portraits, including one of the second wife of Cornelius Vanderbilt. She exhibited in the National Academy of Design in 1877 and 1878. Her naturalistic portrait style with its somber colors is representative of artists taught in Düsseldorf. In 1879 she married Burr G. Duval, and the couple went to Texas. In Austin she built a studio at home and was soon teaching art classes. Among her pupils was the portraitist Ida Weisselberg Hadra.[qv]

In the early 1880s the Duvals moved to San Antonio, where the artist taught first in the French Building and later in her home in Maverick Grove. Portraits she did at this time included those of Mrs. J. T. Woodhull, Dr. Ferdinand Herff,[qv] Phillipa G. Stevenson, and Duval West,[qv] the last of which now hangs in the courtroom of the United States District Court in Austin. While pursuing her art career Mrs. Duval constantly advocated the establishment of an academy of art in San Antonio. Until her death in 1911, in St. Louis, she made every effort to encourage San Antonio in its various art activities.

BIBLIOGRAPHY: Pauline A. Pinckney, *Painting in Texas: The Nineteenth Century* (Austin: University of Texas Press, 1967).

Pauline A. Pinckney

DUVAL, JOHN CRITTENDEN (1816–1897). John Crittenden (John C., Texas John) Duval, writer, son of Nancy (Hynes) and William Pope Duval,[qv] was born in Bardstown, Kentucky, on March 14, 1816, and grew up in Tallahassee after his father was appointed to a federal judgeship in what was then Florida Territory. Duval returned to Bardstown in 1831 with his mother to continue his education at St. Joseph College. Late in 1835 he left the college to join a small company organized by his brother Capt. Burr H. Duval[qv] to fight with the Texans against Mexico. The brothers were with James W. Fannin's[qv] army when it surrendered to the Mexican forces under José de Urrea.[qv] In the Goliad Massacre[qv] on Palm Sunday, 1836, Burr Duval was killed, but John escaped. Not long afterwards he entered the University of Virginia to study engineering. He returned to Texas by 1840 and became a land surveyor. In 1845 he was, alongside William A. A. (Bigfoot) Wallace,[qv] a member of John C. (Jack) Hays's[qv] company of Texas Rangers.[qv] Duval did not favor secession,[qv] but he joined the Confederate Army as a private, declining a commission. He was a captain by the war's end.

He liked to be out in wilderness places, to loiter and to read, write, and recollect. His writings justify his being called the first Texas man of letters. *Early Times in Texas* was published serially in *Burke's Weekly* at Macon, Georgia, in 1867, although it did not appear in book form (and then only as a pamphlet printed on rotten paper) until 1892. The story of Duval's remarkable escape from the Goliad Massacre and of his more remarkable adventures before he rejoined human society became a Texas classic. Of all personal adventures of old-time Texans it is perhaps the best written and the most interesting. *The Young Explorers* (189?), a narrative with a fictional thread, a book for boys, was published as a sequel to *Early Times in Texas*. Duval's most artistic and most important book is *The Adventures of Bigfoot Wallace, the Texas Ranger and Hunter* (1870). Always free and at home with himself, Bigfoot opened up to his old friend Duval with gusto, and Duval helped him stretch the blanket. He died in Fort Worth on January 15, 1897.

BIBLIOGRAPHY: William Corner, "John Crittenden Duval: The Last Survivor of the Goliad Massacre," *Quarterly of the Texas State Historical Association* 1 (July 1897). William Corner, *John Crittenden Duval: The Last Survivor of the Goliad Massacre* (Houston: Union National Bank, 1930). J. Frank Dobie, *John C. Duval: First Texas Man of Letters*, with Sketches by Tom Lea (Dallas: Southern Methodist University Press, 1939; 2d ed. 1965). John Crittenden Duval, *Early Times in Texas, or the Adventures of Jack Dobell* (Austin: Gammel, 1892; new ed., Lincoln: University of Nebraska Press, 1986). Vertical Files, Barker Texas History Center, University of Texas at Austin.

J. Frank Dobie

DUVAL, THOMAS HOWARD (1813–1880). Thomas Howard Duval, first United States judge for the Western District of Texas, the second son of Nancy (Hynes) and William Pope Duval[qv] was born in Buckingham County, Virginia, on November 4, 1813. He grew up in Bardstown, Kentucky, and received an A.B. degree from St. Joseph's College in 1833. He read law under Charles A. Wickliffe, postmaster general in President John Tyler's administration. After following his father to Florida in 1835, he was admitted to the Florida bar in 1837. In 1839 in Prince William County, Virginia, he married his first cousin, Laura Peyton Duval. The couple returned to Florida, where Duval began his career of public service as circuit clerk of Leon County, then became clerk ex officio of the court of appeals. In 1843 he was appointed secretary for Florida Territory.

His two brothers, Burr H. and John C. Duval,[qqv] had answered the call of the Texas Revolution[qv] in 1835. Thomas moved to Austin with his wife and two children in December 1845 to practice law. From 1846 to 1851 he served as a reporter for the state Supreme Court. In 1851 Governor Peter Hansborough Bell[qv] appointed him secretary of state. In 1855–56 he was judge of the Second Judicial District of Texas, and in 1857 President James Buchanan appointed him first United States judge for the new Western District of Texas, which extended from Tyler in East Texas to El Paso and Brownsville and included Waco, Austin, and San Antonio. Duval held this office until his death.

The outbreak of the Civil War^{qv} in 1861 caused suspension of the court's proceedings, but Judge Duval, intensely loyal to the Union cause, remained at his station in Austin. Between 1861 and 1863 he held two jobs there—one in the General Land Office,^{qv} which provided him with a small income, and another as deputy county surveyor, which provided no salary but protected him from conscription. So great was the respect he commanded that neither he nor his family suffered indignity under the Confederate government. Duval, however, found himself in an agonizing position: his son Burr G., perhaps hoping to protect his father and family, accepted a commission in the Confederate Army and went to the front. Duval, concerned for the boy's safety, and believing he had a plan for a just termination of the war, determined to go to Washington to present his plan to President Lincoln. He left his wife and younger children in Austin, made a precarious passage in October 1863 through the Confederate lines to Union-occupied Vicksburg, and traveled thence by boat and rail to Washington. Through the good offices of Secretary of State William H. Seward and other influential friends, Duval did gain a brief audience at the White House. His plan—to bring the war to an end by indemnifying each state as it returned to the Union for the value of its slaves—never materialized, but while in Washington he did secure payment for three years' back salary.

Duval made his way to New Orleans, then proceeded in early 1864 to Brownsville, where the Union Army had effected a beachhead in Texas. Disappointed eventually by the lack of progress in the invasion, he returned to New Orleans, went to New York, and traveled once more to Washington in an effort to stimulate recovery of Texas to the Union fold. In the winter of 1864–65 he returned to his family in New Orleans.

At the end of the war, upon opening court again in Austin, he accepted his son's oath of allegiance to the United States as condition for restoration of his citizenship. Duval, a moderate Republican, applied himself toward rebuilding acceptance and confidence in United States constitutional law. He pioneered in the opening of federal court sessions from Austin westward. An unsuccessful attempt to impeach him was launched by the radicals between 1872 and 1874, apparently because of his moderate stance within the Republican party^{qv} and the government jobs that he had taken during the war. After more than twenty-three years on the federal bench, Duval died on October 10, 1880, of an apparent attack of appendicitis at Fort Omaha, Nebraska. He is buried in Austin. He was survived by his wife and four of his five children, one of whom married Charles Shannon West.^{qv}

BIBLIOGRAPHY: Austin *Daily Statesman*, October 12, 1880. *The Charges against the Federal Court at Austin* (Austin: Tracy, Siemering, 1872). Duval Papers, Barker Texas History Center, University of Texas at Austin. Bessie Berry Grabowskii, *The DuVal Family of Virginia, 1701* (Richmond, Virginia: Dietz Printing, 1933). Andrew Jackson Hamilton Papers, Barker Texas History Center, University of Texas at Austin. James D. Lynch, *The Bench and Bar of Texas* (St. Louis, 1885).
Roy L. Swift

DUVAL, WILLIAM POPE (1784–1854). William Pope Duval, lawyer and congressman, the son of William and Anne (Pope) Duval, was born at Mount Comfort, Virginia, in 1784 and spent several years on the Kentucky frontier. In 1804 he was admitted to the bar and married Nancy Hynes. They had eight children. In 1812 Duval participated in Indian campaigns as a captain of mounted rangers. From 1813 to 1815 he represented Kentucky in the House of Representatives of the Thirteenth Congress, after which he resumed his law practice at Bardstown, Kentucky. President Monroe appointed Duval a United States judge in Florida Territory on May 18, 1821, and from 1822 to 1834 Duval served as civil governor there. In this post, he accomplished the removal of the Seminole Indians to South Florida. From 1839 to 1842 he was a senator in the Florida legislature. In 1845 he served as a commissioner to settle the disputed northern boundary of Florida. Duval was first grand master of the Masonic Grand Lodge of Florida. Two of his sons, Burr H. and John C. Duval,^{qqv} participated in the Texas Revolution.^{qv} Another son, Thomas H. Duval,^{qv} moved to Austin in 1845 or early 1846. William P. Duval followed his sons to Texas in 1848 and settled at Galveston to practice law. Sam Houston^{qv} was among his clients. Duval died in Washington, D.C., on March 19, 1854, while there on legal business. He was buried in the Congressional Cemetery.

BIBLIOGRAPHY: *Biographical Directory of the American Congress*, 1928. *Dictionary of American Biography. National Cyclopaedia of American Biography*, Vol. 11. Roy L. Swift, *Civilizers: The DuVals of Texas from Virginia through Kentucky and Florida* (Austin: Eakin Press, 1992). Amelia W. Williams and Eugene C. Barker, eds., *The Writings of Sam Houston, 1813–1863* (8 vols., Austin: University of Texas Press, 1938–43; rpt., Austin and New York: Pemberton Press, 1970).

DUVAL, TEXAS. Duval was a farming community on the International–Great Northern Railroad about ten miles north of Austin in northern Travis County. The site was settled in 1875 and was named for local storeowner Douglas Duval. A post office moved there in 1877 from Mount Juliet, and James A. Wright served as postmaster. By the mid-1880s the community had a district school, three churches, three stores, and seventy-five residents. Stone and cedar were the principal commodities shipped from the area. The population of Duval was estimated at fifty in 1890 and at thirty-five in 1899. The Duval post office was discontinued in 1902, and mail for the community was sent to McNeil. The area that made up the Duval community was annexed by the city of Austin in the mid-1970s.

BIBLIOGRAPHY: John J. Germann and Myron Janzen, *Texas Post Offices by County* (1986). *Vivian Elizabeth Smyrl*

DUVAL COUNTY. Duval County (Q-15) is in south central Texas about fifty miles inland from the Gulf of Mexico^{qv} and seventy-three miles north of the Rio Grande. It is bordered by Webb, La Salle, McMullen, Live Oak, Jim Wells, Brooks, and Jim Hogg counties. San Diego, the county seat and most populous town, is on the Texas Mexican Railroad at the intersection of State highways 44 and 359 and Farm road 1329, about fifty-two miles west of Corpus Christi and eighty miles east of Laredo. The county's center point is nine miles northwest of Benavides at 27°42′ north latitude and 98°30′ west longitude. State Highway 44 passes through the county from east to west, and State Highway 16 crosses from north to south. Two highways cross the county diagonally: U.S. Highway 59 and State Highway 359. The county comprises 1,795 square miles of nearly level to undulating terrain with an elevation ranging from 250 to 800 feet above sea level. The northern part of the county drains into the Nueces River, while the central and southern parts drain into the Laguna Madre through Baffin Bay.^{qqv} Northern Duval County is characterized by loamy cracking or crumbly clayey soils, deep to moderately deep, that overlie indurated caliche. Western Duval County is characterized by deep soils with loamy surface layers and loamy or clayey subsoils, and loamy soils with indurated caliche at shallow to moderate depths. Eastern Duval County is characterized by poorly drained loamy soils and well-drained dark soils with loamy surface layers and clayey subsoils. The vegetation consists of small trees, shrubs, and cacti,^{qv} with large areas of brush. The county's mineral resources include caliche, clay, salt domes, sandstone, uranium, oil, and gas. The climate is subtropical-subhumid. The average minimum temperature is 43° F in January, and the average maximum temperature is 98° in July. The growing season averages 298 days annually. The rainfall averages about twenty-four inches. Less than 1 percent of the land in Duval

County is considered prime farmland. Duval County's climate has likely remained unchanged for centuries, but beginning in the late nineteenth century cattle ranching, which was the county's main industry, and farming have had significant effects on the county's vegetation and water supply. Overgrazing led to the destruction of the watershed and clogged the springs that fed the county's streams, most of which are now intermittent, and, in combination with the suppression of grass fires, allowed mesquite^qv to become dominant.

Little is known of the prehistory of the future Duval County. The Venado Indians, a Coahuiltecan hunting and gathering group, roamed the area in the 1700s. The seminomadic Coahuiltecans hunted bison, deer, javelinas, and smaller mammals, as well as snakes, lizards, terrapins, and other reptiles. They also gathered wild fruits, nuts, berries, seeds, roots, leaves, and prickly pear tunas. They were disrupted by the Apache and Comanche incursions from the north and by the Spanish pushing north from Mexico. European exploration of the area apparently began in the eighteenth century, as the road between Mier and Goliad^qv passed through the area. The Marqués de Rubí^qv reportedly crossed the area upon his return from the Spanish frontier in 1767. In 1812 Julián Flores and his son Ventura received the deeds to the San Diego de Arriba and San Diego de Abajo grants, totaling eighty leagues, from the Spanish government; herdsmen in their employ may have been the first European settlers in the county. In 1848 Ventura Flores sold some land on San Diego Creek to Pablo Pérez.^qv The community Perez established there, called Perezville, was the precursor of San Diego. Also in 1848 Henry Lawrence Kinney and William Leslie Cazneau^qqv cut a road from Corpus Christi to Laredo that passed through San Diego.

In 1858 the Texas legislature formed Duval County, which originally embraced 1,887 square miles, from parts of Nueces, Live Oak, and Starr counties. County organization did not occur until eighteen years later. The county was named for Burr H. Duval,^qv who fought in the Texas Revolution and was killed in the Goliad Massacre.^qqv Duval County has always been somewhat off the beaten track of development. In 1867 Father Claude Jaillet^qv built a church in San Diego that became the only public place of worship between Corpus Christi and the Rio Grande. Despite this civilizing influence, however, Duval County could still be a wild and dangerous place. In 1873 the outlaw Alberto Garza^qv and some sixty followers made the county the center of their horse-stealing and cattle-skinning operations. They sent orders to the citizens of San Diego to bring enough money to buy the stolen hides or enough men to skin the hide-peelers. A party of Anglos chose the latter option, attacked the outlaw's camp, and scattered the rustlers. Five years later, in mid-April 1878, a band of forty Lipan Apache, Seminole, and Kickapoo Indians, reportedly led by a blond white man, cut a swath through Webb and Duval counties, murdering and pillaging several ranches before dispersing. The perpetrators of the so-called "Great Raid of '78" were never caught. A legend of more recent vintage holds that Francisco (Pancho) Villa^qv may have buried two saddlebags of silver in the area. The county was finally organized in 1876, and San Diego was selected as the county seat. James O. Luby,^qv the first county judge, dominated Duval County politics for most of the next three decades. When Luby defected from the Democratic to the Republican party,^qv he almost singlehandedly made the GOP an important factor in Duval County politics. The battles between the Botas and Guaraches^qv ("boots" and "sandals," or Republicans and Democrats) were often ferocious.

Luby was part of an influx of Anglos that also included Walter W. Meek, Sr., who had come to Duval County after the Civil War^qv and helped make it the sheep ranching^qv capital of Texas. The county at the time was described as "one extended pasture" and "a great sheep walk." The Corpus Christi, San Diego and Rio Grande Narrow Gauge Railroad reached the county in 1879, and in 1881, after being taken over by the Texas Mexican Railroad, built across the county and on to Laredo, in Webb County. The arrival of the railroad accelerated the sheep boom. Between 1873 and 1883 Duval County reportedly had more sheep than any other county in the United States. In 1880 county ranchers reported 196,684 sheep, up from 34,325 ten years before; a few years later the county reportedly had more than 400,000. The number of human beings rose with the sheep; in 1880 there were 5,732 people in the county, more than five times as many as in 1870, and Duval County seemed well on its way to lasting prosperity. But in the mid-1880s a mysterious plague began killing the sheep, and after Grover Cleveland was elected president in 1884 on a platform that included eliminating the tariff on foreign wool, the price of wool dropped from twenty-six cents a pound to seven cents a pound. The bottom fell out of the Duval County sheep. There were only 60,160 sheep in the county in 1890 and only 3,627 by 1900.

The white influx led to the county's most enduring characteristic: a vast Mexican-American majority held in thrall by a small but wealthy and influential white minority. In the late nineteenth century Anglos made up less than 10 percent of the county's population but controlled most of the county's trade and politics. Ironically, it was an Anglo, a former cowhand and schoolteacher named Archer Parr,^qv who turned this imbalance to his advantage by soliciting the Mexican Americans,^qv whom his fellow Anglo politicians had traditionally ignored. These people, many of whom were desperately poor, gave up their political autonomy in exchange for county jobs and occasional cash disbursements of questionable legality from the county treasury. This arrangement, which one Duval County official called "frankly corrupt but fully benevolent," allowed Parr, and later his son George B. Parr,^qv a free hand in running the affairs of the county, and became a way of life there. Parr was elected to the Duval County Commissioners Court in 1898, but he did not become the dominant figure in local politics until the assassination of the Duval County Democratic chieftain John Cleary in 1907. By the time Parr was elected to the state Senate in 1914, his control over the affairs of the county was virtually absolute. Yet his power did not go unchallenged. Duval County lost a portion of its land, including the town of Hebbronville, when Jim Hogg County was formed in 1913. Shortly thereafter, Parr made two additional attempts to divide Duval County. Through the establishment of Pat Dunn and Lanham counties he apparently hoped to increase the patronage jobs and tax revenue at his disposal, but he was foiled both times. Between 1912 and 1918 Ed C. Lasater,^qv a wealthy South Texas rancher, and C. W. Robinson, the Duval County Democratic chairman, both attempted to bring Parr down, but neither succeeded. In 1918 D. W. Glasscock, with the support of Governor William P. Hobby^qv and the Texas Rangers,^qv came close to ending Parr's political career. But Parr ultimately prevailed after his fellow senators decided not to examine too closely the irregularities that had characterized Parr's dubious electoral victory over Glasscock.

The Parrs found it expedient to keep the people of Duval County dependent on their largesse, and so placed little emphasis on the state of education in the county. Duval County's 25.3 percent illiteracy rate in 1930 was the sixth highest in the state. Oil was discovered in the county in 1905, but not until a wildcat well came in near Freer in October 1928 did a full-scale oil boom occur. By 1938 Duval County ranked third among the state's 254 counties in oil production, and by 1940 the population of the county reached an all-time high of 20,565. At that time, however, fewer than 7 percent of residents over the age of twenty-five had completed high school. George Parr, the "Duke of Duval," and his cronies became more deeply entrenched than ever, despite his imprisonment in 1936 for tax evasion. Duval County's reputation for political corruption peaked with Lyndon B. Johnson's^qv election to the United States Senate in 1948. The famous Box 13, which gave Johnson his eighty-seven-vote victory, was actually in Jim Wells County, but the manipulation of the returns was almost certainly directed by Parr. In the 1900 presidential election Duval County went Republican, but since that time, thanks largely to the efficiency of the Parr machine and the customary tendency of Hispanics to vote for Democrats, the county has delivered majorities to the Democratic party^qv on the order of 94 percent in 1916, 98 percent in 1932, 95 percent in 1936, 96 percent in 1940, 95 percent in 1944, 97 percent in 1948, and 93 percent in 1964. In fact, only once between 1916 and 1972 did the Democratic candidate receive less than 74 percent of the vote in Duval County; that year, 1956, a mere 68 percent voted Democratic. Even after the demise of the Parr machine in 1975 Democrats continued to dominate. In the 1988 and 1992 presidential elections 82 percent of the county's voters cast ballots for the Democratic candidate.

The oil boom in Duval County did not last. From its peak of 20,289,399 barrels in 1938, production dropped steadily. In 1946 county wells produced only 14,188,268 barrels, fourteenth in the state, and in 1958 the county's 10,167,303 barrels ranked twenty-eighth in Texas. By 1988 Duval County ranked fifty-third in the state, with 3,061,639 barrels. Paralleling the production of oil, the population declined in the second half of the twentieth century. In 1940, at the height of the oil boom, the county population was 20,565. Ten years later it had dropped to 15,643, and in 1960 to 13,398. By 1970 the population was 11,722, and in 1980 it had risen slightly to 12,517, 144th among Texas counties. At least part of the overall decline can be attributed to the problematic nature of the local economy. Farming and ranching in Duval County have never regained the importance they had during the late nineteenth century. That the county lacked the resources to become a major agricultural center was confirmed as far back as 1891 by Professor John T. Ellis of Oberlin College, who in October of that year chose the drought-ridden county as the site for an experimental attempt to produce rain by detonating explosives carried aloft by balloons. Ellis carried out his experiment about a mile and a half northeast of the San Diego railroad station. After several delays because of unsettled weather, a two-day bombardment of the sky apparently paid off with a downpour. But cynics said that Ellis had simply stalled until rain appeared inevitable, and doubts remained about the practicality of the technique.

In the late nineteenth century ranching was Duval County's most important industry. The county's 168 farms in 1880, 165 of which were operated by their owners, had an average size of 2,871 acres, and the county had 6,572 acres of improved farmland; ten years later, after the price of wool had dropped, the number of farms had declined to 102, all but one of which were operated by their owners, with an average size of 2,898 acres; the amount of improved farmland in the county had dropped to 4,331 acres. In the early twentieth century, when farming began to replace ranching as the county's most important agricultural pursuit, the trend was toward more and smaller farms and more tenant farming. In 1910 Duval County had 42,397 acres of improved farmland and 633 farms, 249 of which were operated by tenants, averaging 805 acres. In 1920 the amount of improved farmland rose to 52,232 acres and the number of farms to 754; 324 of these were operated by tenants, but the average size had declined to 584 acres. The trend peaked in 1930, when county farmers harvested 67,473 acres of cropland. In that year tenants operated 843 of the county's 1,241 farms, which averaged 579 acres. By 1950, however, the amount of harvested cropland and the number of farms had dropped to 50,675 acres and 711 respectively, but the average farm had grown to 1,632 acres. In subsequent decades the number of farms again increased, while the average size again decreased. In 1959, for example, there were 716 farms, averaging 1,056 acres; in 1969 there were 825 farms, averaging 1,198 acres; and in 1982 there were 1,074 farms, averaging 904 acres.

Mexican-American ranchers were growing cotton experimentally in Duval County in the 1880s, but by 1900 the county's production totaled only 638 bales. Production climbed to 3,570 bales by 1910 and 7,133 bales by 1920, however, and continued to climb for most of the next decade. In 1930, when 55,943 of the county's 67,473 acres of harvested cropland was devoted to cotton, 11,773 bales of Duval County cotton were ginned. In subsequent years cotton has diminished in importance to the county economy; only 4,159 bales were ginned in 1936, 1,656 in 1945, 1,124 in 1950, and a mere 571 in 1969. With the diminishing importance of cotton, other crops assumed prominence at various times. Duval County produced 351,999 pounds of peanuts in 1959 and 1,142,407 pounds in 1969, but by 1982 the local harvest had declined to insignificance. In 1940 Duval County farmers devoted 16,736 acres to sorghum culture;qv in 1959 that total had dropped slightly, to 15,701 acres, but by 1982 it had risen to 34,334 acres that yielded 1,447,319 bushels. In 1982, 2,519 acres, the fourth-highest total in the state, was devoted to watermelons, down from 2,778 acres in 1959. The amount of harvested cropland in Duval County declined for several decades, from 65,659 acres in 1940 to 50,675 in 1950 and 39,263 in 1969, but rose to 58,744 in 1982. In 1982 Duval County ranked ninth in the state in the production of peaches, with 9,500 bushels, and third in the state in the production of dry cowpeas and dry southern peas, with 24,460 bushels. The cattle industry had made something of a comeback. Duval County had 20,667 cattle, excluding milk cows, in 1920; in 1940 the total was 49,025, and in the mid-1950s the county was considered one of the state's leading beef producers. In the early 1980s Duval County had 80,795 cattle and calves, including 51,365 beef cows and 1,676 milk cows. The county's $28,372,000 in cash receipts from crops and livestock ranked 135th in the state.

At the peak of manufacturing in 1900 the county had only seven manufacturing establishments that together employed only twenty-eight people, and throughout most of the twentieth century the number of such establishments has ranged between two and six. In 1982 only 2 percent of the county's labor force was employed in manufacturing and the county had only three manufacturing establishments, each employing fewer than twenty people.

In 1982, 86 percent of Duval County's estimated population of 12,900 were of Hispanic origin, the eighth-highest percentage in the United States; 7 percent were of English descent, 5 percent of German descent, and 5 percent of Irish descent. The percentage of those over the age of twenty-five who had graduated from high school rose from 7.6 percent in 1950 to 11.3 percent in 1960 and 36.6 percent in 1980, but the latter figure still lagged well behind the state average of 62.2 percent. Twenty-three percent of the county's workers were employed in other counties, 31 percent in agriculture and mining, 21 percent in professional services, and 14 percent in wholesale or retail trade. Tourists, attracted by such spectacles as Freer's annual Rattlesnake Roundup in April and Old Fiddlers Contest in July, spent $3,519,000 in Duval County in 1982. In 1990 the population was 12,918. The largest communities were San Diego, with 4,109 in habitants in Duval County, and Freer, with 3,271 residents.

BIBLIOGRAPHY: Evan Anders, *Boss Rule in South Texas: The Progressive Era* (Austin: University of Texas Press, 1982). John Clements, *Flying the Colors: Texas, a Comprehensive Look at Texas Today, County by County* (Dallas: Clements Research, 1984). Arnoldo De León, *A Social History of Mexican Americans in Nineteenth Century Duval County* (San Diego, Texas: Duval County Commissioners Court, n.d.). Agnes G. Grimm, *Llanos Mesteñas: Mustang Plains* (Waco: Texian Press, 1968). Dudley Lynch, *The Duke of Duval: The Life and Times of George B. Parr* (Waco: Texian Press, 1976). Dorothy Abbott McCoy, *Oil, Mud, and Guts* (Brownsville, Texas, 1977). David Montejano, *Anglos and Mexicans in the Making of Texas, 1836–1986* (Austin: University of Texas Press, 1987).
Martin Donell Kohout

DUVALT, ANDREW (1804–1836). Andrew Duvalt, Alamo defender, was born in Ireland in 1804. He immigrated to Texas by way of Missouri and settled in Gonzales. He was a plasterer by trade. Duvalt took part in the siege of Bexar.qv Afterwards he remained in the town as a member of the Bexar Guards. Sometime after February 2, 1836, he returned to his home in Gonzales. He was mustered into the Gonzales Ranging Company of Mounted Volunteers by Byrd Lockhartqv on February 23, 1836. Duvalt returned to the Alamo, probably as a member of the relief force from Gonzales, on March 1, 1836. He died in the battle of the Alamoqv on March 6 of that year.

BIBLIOGRAPHY: Daughters of the American Revolution, *The Alamo Heroes and Their Revolutionary Ancestors* (San Antonio, 1976). Daughters of the Republic of Texas, *Muster Rolls of the Texas Revolution* (Austin, 1986). Bill Groneman, *Alamo Defenders* (Austin: Eakin, 1990).

Bill Groneman

DWIRE, TEXAS. Dwire was on a country road four miles northwest of San Augustine in northwestern San Augustine County. A post office opened in the community in 1904, and by 1914 Dwire had three grocery stores. The post office closed in 1920, and the community was no longer shown on county highway maps by the 1930s.

Mark Odintz

DWYER, EDWARD (?–1854). Edward Dwyer (Dyer), early San Antonio resident, a brother of Thomas Dwyer,qv was born in Ireland. He was a partner of William Elliottqv in San Antonio about 1839. In 1840, with George W. Blow and José Antonio Navarro,qqv he was appointed to investigate fraudulent land claims in the Bexar District. On July 18, 1843, he married Mrs. Mariana Rodríguez Ramón; they had four children. Dwyer was mayor of San Antonio in 1845 and owned a row of buildings facing the site of the present courthouse. He died in San Antonio in April 1854.

BIBLIOGRAPHY: Frank H. Bushick, *Glamorous Days* (San Antonio: Naylor, 1934). Frederick Charles Chabot, *With the Makers of San Antonio* (Yanaguana Society Publications 4, San Antonio, 1937). Amelia W. Williams and Eugene C. Barker, eds., *The Writings of Sam Houston, 1813–1863* (8 vols., Austin: University of Texas Press, 1938–43; rpt., Austin and New York: Pemberton Press, 1970).

DWYER, ELIZABETH AGNES (1866–?). Elizabeth Agnes (Bessie) Dwyer, writer, librarian, and reformer, the youngest child of Judge Thomas A. and Annie (Croker) Dwyer, was born on September 29, 1866, at Bonita, the family country home in Nueces County. Another daughter of Judge Dwyer's married Capt. Nicholas Nolan of the Nolan expedition.qv As a child, Bessie traveled abroad for five years, then studied under a family governess until her father's death, when she was sixteen. For the next six years she worked for the post office and for G. W. Baldwin and Company, the largest book and stationery house in West Texas. During this time she also began to write short stories and poems.

In 1868 she moved west and for three years lived in Arizona and New Mexico with a sister. When she returned to San Antonio she worked for the Galveston *News*, which published her stories "Mr. Moore of Albuquerque" and "A Daughter of Eve." Using the pen name Heliotrope, she published stories in the *Texas Baptist and Herald*qv and also served as a correspondent for several southern journals. In 1890 she graduated from a San Antonio business college and in November 1891 moved east to become a "congressional reporter" for the *National Economist*. Dwyer wrote articles for the National Farmers' Alliance newspaper on such issues as flexible currency, liquor laws, workmen's insurance, national politics, and political campaigns. Governor James Hoggqv appointed her a commissioner to the Chicago Exposition of 1893. In that year she became the first woman appointed to the Library of Congress, where she served as an assistant librarian until 1903. She lived in Manila, Philippines, for the purpose of establishing library service from 1909 to 1911 and last appeared in a portrait made in San Francisco and dated 1915.

BIBLIOGRAPHY: Elizabeth Brooks, *Prominent Women of Texas* (Akron, Ohio: Werner, 1896). Galveston *Daily News*, June 18, 1893. Robert C. McMath, Jr., *Populist Vanguard: A History of the Southern Farmers' Alliance* (Chapel Hill: University of North Carolina Press, 1975). Melissa Gilbert Wiedenfeld, Women in the Texas Farmers' Alliance (M.A. thesis, Texas Tech University, 1983). Frances E. Willard and Mary A. Livermore, eds., *American Women* (2 vols., New York: Mast, Crowell, and Kirkpatrick, 1897; rpt., Detroit: Gale Research, 1973–).

Melissa G. Wiedenfeld

DWYER, THOMAS B. (1819–1896). Thomas B. Dwyer, businessman and Republican partyqv leader, was born in Tipperary County, Ireland, on August 17, 1819. He was orphaned at age sixteen and immigrated to New Brunswick, Canada, worked in Maine logging camps, and arrived on February 8, 1845, in Texas, where his brother, Irish immigrant Joseph M. Dwyer, was a merchant and landowner. Thomas Dwyer operated a store in Brazoria in 1849 and then opened stores in Quintana and Columbia. By September 1853 he had formed the successful commission-merchant partnership of Clements and Dwyer. In 1858 he sold his property in Brazoria and moved to Brenham, where he resided until his death.

Dwyer was a Unionist and supporter of Gov. Sam Houston.qv During the Civil Warqv he operated a commission-merchant business, Dwyer, Randle, and Company, with partners John A. Randle and John V. Buster. In 1867 Dwyer's property was valued at $14,280. By 1868 he was operating retail and wholesale merchandising in the Dwyer-Healy partnership. In the postwar era he bought the Exchange Hotel in Brenham, made extensive real estate investments, reinvested his profits in his mercantile business, extended credit to customers, and made interest-bearing loans. These diversified business interests rapidly increased his wealth despite substantial losses in a fire in 1873. Dwyer's activities expanded to include agricultural enterprises and rural landholding. In 1896 he sold his business interests and retired with assets of about $1 million.

He became active in Texas Republican politics during the 1880s. Between 1888 and 1896 his sons, Thomas H. and William E., and his longtime political aid, Paul Fricke, held frequent Republican state and platform-committee memberships. Dwyer supported William McKinley and the gold standard. He was an opponent of fusion with the People's partyqv and in 1894 served as a liaison for the Republican "Lily White" faction in an unsuccessful attempt to conciliate Norris Wright Cuney'sqv predominantly black wing of the party. Dwyer's nephew, San Antonio mayor Joseph E. Dwyer, was state Democratic chairman pro tem.

In 1868 Dwyer became a charter member of the nonpartisan Sons of Texas, dedicated to preserving the state's heritage, and a member of the Literary Society of Brenham. In 1877 he founded the Dwyer Reading Room and Free Library Association, forerunner of the Brenham Public Library, one of the earliest libraries in the state. He was a Catholic and aided Catholic missionaries and Galveston bishop Claude Marie Dubuis'sqv establishment of St. Mary's parish in Brenham (1870). Before St. Mary's Church was constructed, Catholic services were held in Dwyer's home. Dwyer led a group of Brenham residents who opposed the 1880 school tax as unconstitutional; he obtained an injunction on its collection but lost in the case of *Hackworth* v. *Dwyer* (1882), his appeal to the state Supreme Court, which upheld the constitutionality of the tax.

Dwyer married Bridget Theresa Healy in 1854, and they had seven children. Bridget died on November 28, 1872. In 1874 Dwyer married Mrs. Sarah Diller. On January 29, 1896, he was murdered by four robbers at his office in Brenham. Local blacks held public meetings protesting the murder, and three of the murderers were executed. Dwyer's funeral was held at the Presbyterian church, and he was buried in Prairie Lea Cemetery in Brenham.

BIBLIOGRAPHY: Brenham *Banner Press*, Centennial edition, March 2, 1936. James A. Creighton, *A Narrative History of Brazoria County* (Angleton, Texas: Brazoria County Historical Commission, 1975). Thomas Dwyer Papers, Barker Texas History Center, University of Texas at Austin. Arthur A. Grusendorf, The Social and Philosophical Determinants of Education in Washington County, Texas, from 1835 to 1937 (Ph.D. dissertation, University of Texas, 1938). San Antonio *Express*, January 30, 31, 1896. Washington County Scrapbook, Barker

Texas History Center, University of Texas at Austin. E. W. Winkler, *Platforms of Political Parties in Texas* (Austin: University of Texas, 1916).
Carole E. Christian

DYE, TEXAS. Dye, also known as Dye Mound, is a farming community ten miles southeast of Montague on a spur off Farm Road 3206 in southeastern Montague County. Its settlement occurred in 1880, and the community developed around J. D. Bybee's general store. A post office branch operated at Dye from 1884 to 1905. Throughout its history Dye has functioned as a community center for area farmers. Its recorded population has never exceeded sixty, and since the late 1940s no population estimates have been available. In 1961 three dwellings and a church were in the vicinity. The 1983 county highway map showed a cemetery there.
David Minor

DYE CREEK. Dye Creek rises five miles southwest of St. Jo in east central Montague County (at 33°39′ N, 97°38′ W) and runs southeast for five miles to its mouth on Clear Creek, 6½ miles north of Forestburg (at 33°36′ N, 97°32′ W). It traverses generally flat terrain surfaced by clay and sandy loams that support water-tolerant hardwood trees, conifers, and grasses. The Dye Creek area has served as crop and range land.

DYER, CLEMENT C. (1799–1864). Clement C. Dyer, one of Stephen F. Austin's qv Old Three Hundred qv colonists, was born at Dyersburg, Tennessee, on January 29, 1799. He moved to Texas in 1822 and, on June 5, 1824, married Sarah Stafford, daughter of William Stafford.qv They had twelve children. On August 10, 1824, Dyer received title to a league of land in what is now Colorado County; on August 24 of that year he received title to 1½ labors of land in what is now Waller County. In 1825 Indians frightened Mrs. Dyer away from their home, and in April 1826 Dyer made affidavits concerning Indian hostilities. In 1833 he became the manager of the Stafford plantation. Soon afterward he was appointed to oversee the records of the Department of the Brazos. Sometime before March 28, 1835, he sold a half league to his father-in-law. On November 7, 1835, as a delegate to the Consultation qv from Harrisburg Municipality (*see* HARRISBURG COUNTY) he was one of the signers of the declaration that cited the causes for taking up arms against the Centralist forces of Antonio López de Santa Anna.qv After the Texas Revolution qv Dyer was justice of the peace in Harrisburg (later Harris) County. He moved to Fort Bend County in 1837 and from 1838 to 1841 was justice of the peace in the lower precinct of that county. He was also actively involved in the Methodist church organized in 1839 in Richmond. In 1843 he was elected county chief justice, a post he held until August 1856. On January 15, 1845, he was appointed to a committee that was to draft resolutions expressing the sentiments of Fort Bend County citizens regarding the annexation qv of Texas to the United States. The census of 1860 listed him as a wealthy planter with an estate worth $40,000. He died near Richmond in 1864.

BIBLIOGRAPHY: Eugene C. Barker, ed., *The Austin Papers* (3 vols., Washington: GPO, 1924–28). William Campbell Binkley, ed., *Official Correspondence of the Texan Revolution, 1835–1836* (2 vols., New York: Appleton-Century, 1936). Lester G. Bugbee, "The Old Three Hundred: A List of Settlers in Austin's First Colony," *Quarterly of the Texas State Historical Association* 1 (October 1897). John H. Jenkins, ed., *The Papers of the Texas Revolution, 1835–1836* (10 vols., Austin: Presidial Press, 1973). Andrew Jackson Sowell, *History of Fort Bend County* (Houston: Coyle, 1904; rpt, Richmond, Texas: Fort Bend County Historical Museum, 1974). Texas House of Representatives, *Biographical Directory of the Texan Conventions and Congresses, 1832–1845* (Austin: Book Exchange, 1941). Clarence Wharton, *Wharton's History of Fort Bend County* (San Antonio: Naylor, 1939).

DYER, EDWIN HAWLEY (1900–1964). Edwin Hawley Dyer, baseball player and manager, son of Joseph Dyer, was born in Morgan City, Louisiana, on October 11, 1900. After attending public schools there, he enrolled in Rice Institute, Houston, where he played football and baseball. He was a member of the class of 1924 but did not graduate until 1936, after playing with various minor-league baseball teams. As manager of the Houston club of the Texas League qv he won league championships in 1939, 1940, and 1941, and in 1942 he was named minor-league manager of the year for his direction of the Columbus, Ohio, team. Thereafter, he joined the St. Louis Cardinals and was manager of that club when it won the World Series in 1946 by beating the Boston Red Sox four games to three.

After twenty-three years as a player, manager, and coach, Dyer moved to Houston in 1948 and opened an insurance office. He relinquished managership of the Cardinals in 1950. On January 2, 1962, he suffered a stroke and on April 20, 1964, died of a heart attack. His survivors were his wife, the former Geraldine Jennings of Timpson, a son, and a daughter. Dyer was buried at the Garden of Gethsemane in Houston. He was described in the *Official Encyclopedia of Baseball* as a "slow-speaking and quick-thinking Texan" and was considered one of the best teachers and developers of young baseball talent. He discovered such men as Stan Musial, Howard Pollet, and Jeffre Cross. Pollet and Cross were associated with him in his Houston business.

BIBLIOGRAPHY: Houston *Post*, April 21, 22, 23, 1964. *Newsweek*, May 4, 1964. New York *Times*, April 21, 1964. *Official Encyclopedia of Baseball*, 1956.
Clay Bailey

DYER, ISADORE (1865–1920). Isadore Dyer, dermatologist and founder of a leprosy asylum in Louisiana, son of Isadore and Amelia Ann (Lewis) Dyer, was born on November 2, 1865, in Galveston. After receiving his bachelor of philosophy degree from Sheffield Scientific School at Yale University and his M.D. degree from Tulane, he interned and did graduate work at the New York Skin and Cancer Hospital from 1890 until 1892 and at the same time served as a lecturer at a New York postgraduate medical school. After studying in London and Paris in 1892, he lectured on diseases of the skin until 1905, when he went back to Tulane as associate professor of dermatology. He became dean of the school of medicine at Tulane in 1908. In addition to his work there, Dyer served as consultant at various hospitals and founded and became president of the first board of control of the Louisiana Leper Home. He joined the United States Medical Reserve in 1908 and served as president of the examining board of the medical reserve corps and as chairman of the medical section of the state committee of defense, 1917–18. He is best known for his essays, papers, and books on skin and tropical diseases. He married Mercedes Louise Percival on July 31, 1905, and died in New Orleans in October 12, 1920.

BIBLIOGRAPHY: *Dictionary of American Biography*. Vertical Files, Barker Texas History Center, University of Texas at Austin. *Who Was Who in America*, Vol. 2.
Carolyn Hyman

DYER, JOSEPH OSTERMAN (1856–1925). Joseph Osterman Dyer, physician, author, and historian, the son of Major and Mrs. Leon Dyer, was born in what is now Germany—in Mainz, Dessau, or Alzey—in 1856. In 1876 he moved to Galveston, Texas. He took a medical course in Louisville, Kentucky, and returned to Galveston in 1881 to start his medical practice. He wrote for the Galveston *News*qv and other papers, and his columns were read throughout the Southwest. They are preserved in "The Dyer Scrapbook" in the Rosenberg Library,qv Galveston. In New Orleans he met Gershom Kursheedt, who in 1835 had interviewed Jao de la Porta, a buccaneer from the Texas coast. After this contact Dyer wrote tales of surviving members of Jean Laffite'sqv commune on Galveston Island. He also wrote about Indians, especially the coastal Karankawas. He died of a heart ailment in Galveston at the home of his brother Alex on October 2, 1925. He also had a sister and a brother, John M. Dyer, who was a professor in England.

BIBLIOGRAPHY: Galveston *News,* October 3, 1925. Natalie Ornish, *Pioneer Jewish Texans* (Dallas: Texas Heritage, 1989).

Natalie Ornish

DYER, LEIGH RICHMOND (1849–1902). Leigh Richmond Dyer, Panhandle^{qv} pioneer and rancher, one of eight children of Henry Joel and Suzan (Miller) Dyer, was born in Dyersburg, Tennessee, in 1849. His father, former attorney general for the West District of Tennessee, moved his family in 1854 to Fort Belknap, Texas, and later to Fort Worth, where the elder Dyer resumed his law practice. After the death of both his parents in the mid-1860s, Leigh Dyer and his remaining two brothers were left in the care of their only sister, Molly (*see* GOODNIGHT, MARY ANN), who taught school at Weatherford. Dyer began working as a drover for Charles Goodnight^{qv} in 1867 and made several drives over the Goodnight-Loving Trail^{qv} to Fort Sumner, New Mexico, and beyond. In the fall of 1875, when Goodnight began moving his herd from Colorado to Palo Duro Canyon,^{qv} Dyer and his brothers Sam and Walter were among the drovers. When winter came, Goodnight left Dyer in charge of the herd. The following year the Dyers helped Goodnight and John George Adair^{qv} establish the JA Ranch.^{qv} In 1877 Leigh and Walter Dyer, in partnership with Samuel Coleman, filed on a 320-acre tract in Randall County near the site of present Canyon. Here the Dyers developed a quality herd of shorthorn cows, which they crossbred with registered bulls from the JA. Their brand was DY. In 1878 the Dyer ranch was sold to Jot Gunter, William B. Munson, and John S. Summerfield,^{qqv} as part of a vast spread they had bought. Dyer was hired as range boss by the GMS (later the T Anchor Ranch^{qv}). Later, Dyer and L. C. Coleman established what became the Shoe Bar Ranch^{qv} on the Red River in Hall County. When Dodge City opened as a cattle market, Dyer trailed the first JA herd there. When Donley County was organized in 1882, he was designated a commissioner. He was also active in the Panhandle Stock Association. After Goodnight bought the Quitaque (Lazy F) Ranch,^{qv} Dyer was appointed its manager. In 1883 he married Willimena Cantelou of Weatherford. A few years later he turned the management of the Quitaque over to Walter and established his own ranch on Mulberry Creek in Armstrong County. Dyer was known as a superb and humane breeder of horses. In the 1890s he and his wife sold the Mulberry Creek Ranch and, with Molly Goodnight, purchased several tracts west of the Goodnight community. The Dyers had two children. Dyer died on May 4, 1902, at his home near Goodnight and was buried at Goodnight. A log ranchhouse that he and his brother Walter built in 1877, later the T Anchor headquarters, is now on the grounds of the Panhandle-Plains Historical Museum^{qv} in Canyon. It is the oldest extant in the Panhandle.

BIBLIOGRAPHY: J. Evetts Haley, *Charles Goodnight* (Norman: University of Oklahoma Press, 1949). C. Boone McClure, "A Review of the T Anchor Ranch," *Panhandle-Plains Historical Review* 3 (1930). Pauline D. and R. L. Robertson, *Cowman's Country: Fifty Frontier Ranches in the Texas Panhandle, 1876–1887* (Amarillo: Paramount, 1981).

H. Allen Anderson

DYER, TEXAS. Dyer was a school community between Oyster Creek and Stafford in northeastern Fort Bend County. It was part of the original Oyster Creek settlement of Stephen F. Austin's^{qv} colony. The community was named for early settler and plantation-owner Clement C. Dyer,^{qv} the son-in-law of William Stafford,^{qv} whose plantation, cattle, and gin he managed. There is no record of the community ever having a post office; in 1884 mail was being routed via Richmond. About that same time the town served as a stop on the Gulf, Colorado and Santa Fe Railway. By 1936 Dyer was no longer shown on county maps.

Stephen L. Hardin

DYERSDALE, TEXAS. Dyersdale is on Farm Road 527 and the Missouri Pacific line (formerly the Beaumont, Sour Lake and Western Railway) six miles northeast of Houston in northeastern Harris County. It was named for Clement C. Dyer,^{qv} a colonist in Stephen F. Austin's^{qv} Old Three Hundred.^{qv} Dyersdale had a post office from 1913 to 1917. In 1914 the community had a lumber company and a population of 250. The 1936 county highway map showed the William G. Smiley school and scattered dwellings at the townsite. A local oilfield that opened in the mid-1930s was still in production in 1946. In the 1980s the area had a church, a trailer park, and an abandoned railroad station.

Claudia Hazlewood

DYESS, WILLIAM EDWIN (1916–1943). William Edwin Dyess, World War II^{qv} flier, was born on August 9, 1916, in Albany, Texas, the son of Judge Richard T. and Hallie (Graham) Dyess. He graduated from Albany High School and attended John Tarleton Agricultural College (now Tarleton State University) in Stephenville, where he graduated in 1936. After graduation he received pilot training at Randolph and Kelly fields in San Antonio and a second-lieutenant's commission. He was then assigned to Barksdale Field, Shreveport, Louisiana, and later promoted to first lieutenant and commander of the Twenty-first Pursuit Squadron at Hamilton Field, California. Dyess was sent to Nichols Field, Manila, Philippines, in October 1941.

After the Japanese attacked Pearl Harbor and began assaults on Bataan and Corregidor, Dyess was thrust into combat in the Asian Theater as commander of all flying squadrons on Bataan. On March 3, 1942, in Subic Bay he sank a Japanese ship and damaged shore installations. A New York *Times* reporter called him a "one man scourge of the Japs." As the enemy closed in, Dyess refused evacuation and remained with his men in the Philippines. On April 9, 1942, the American forces surrendered to the Japanese, and Dyess became a prisoner of war. He survived the horror of the Bataan Death March and imprisonment at camps O'Donnell and Cabanatuan and the Davao Penal Colony. At Davao, Dyess and several other prisoners escaped on April 4, 1943. They contacted Filipino guerillas who led them to the submarine *Trout* on July 23.

After evacuation to Australia and a hero's welcome in the United States, Dyess briefed the War Department on Japanese warfare and confirmed the enemy's brutality to POWs. After staying in an army general hospital in Virginia to regain his health, Dyess was promoted to lieutenant colonel and resumed flying on December 22, 1943. He was killed that day in Burbank, California, attempting an emergency landing and was buried in Albany. Dyess, a Presbyterian, was survived by his wife, Marajen (Stevick), and his parents. During his life he received the Distinguished Service Cross, the Legion of Merit, and the Silver Star. Soon after his death he was nominated for the Medal of Honor and was posthumously awarded the Soldier's Medal. Abilene Air Force Base was renamed Dyess Air Force Base^{qv} in his honor in December 1956.

BIBLIOGRAPHY: Vertical Files, Barker Texas History Center, University of Texas at Austin.

Martine Anderson

DYESS AIR FORCE BASE. Dyess Air Force Base, four miles west of Abilene, was named after William Edwin Dyess,^{qv} a distinguished World War II^{qv} pilot who died in 1943. The base was initially known as Tye Field when it was established in December 1942. It was deactivated at the end of the war, and in 1947 it was deeded to the city of Abilene as surplus and used as a municipal airport. The base was reactivated during the Korean War as Abilene Air Force Base, under the Strategic Air Command. In December 1946 it became Dyess Air Force Base. The 341st Bombardment Wing was the first SAC wing assigned to Dyess. It was equipped with B-47 aircraft, and they were supported by KC-97s. By 1961 the army had installed Nike Hercules missiles, and SAC had Atlas F ICBMs installed in nearby silos. Both missile units were deactivated by the mid-1960s. In 1965 Dyess AFB came under the control of the Second Air Force, which brought the Ninety-sixth Strategic Aerospace Wing, with its supporting units, to the base in

1967. The wing was equipped with B-52 aircraft and was supported by the 917th Air Refueling Squadron, using KC-135 aerial tankers. Between 1965 and 1973 both B-52s and KC-135s from Dyess were engaged in combat activities over Southeast Asia. The Ninety-sixth was reequipped with supersonic B-1B aircraft in June 1985. Through the years improvements and modernization have continued. The influence of the base on the Abilene area has been considerable; in 1989 Dyess contributed $239,229,745 and 1,563 off-base jobs to the local economy.

BIBLIOGRAPHY: *Abilene Remembered: Our Centennial Treasury Book, 1881–1981* (Abilene *Reporter-News,* 1981). John H. Hatcher, "The Founding of Dyess Air Force Base," West Texas Historical Association *Year Book* 39 (1963).

Art Leatherwood

E

E. O. SIECKE STATE FOREST. E. O. Siecke State Forest is on U.S. Highway 96 and Farm Road 82, five miles southeast of Kirbyville in Newton County (at 30°38′ N, 93°50′ W). It is a 1,722-acre forest established by the Texas legislature in 1924 and named for E. O. Siecke, Texas state forester from 1918 to 1942. A 100-acre adjunct area, two miles to the west, is leased for research and demonstration. Timber was harvested in the area before 1924, but the oldest plantation of slash pine in Texas, planted in 1926, remains just inside the entrance to the forest. Other pine plantations were established, and roads, bridges, buildings, and other improvements were constructed by the Civilian Conservation Corps[qv] during the mid-1930s. The forest provides swimming, picnic shelters, fishing, and fireplaces year-round.

BIBLIOGRAPHY: Newton County Historical Commission, *Glimpses of Newton County History* (Burnet, Texas: Nortex, 1982). *Texas State Travel Guide* (Austin: State Department of Highways and Public Transportation, 1990).

Diana J. Kleiner

EAGLE, JOE HENRY. (1870–1963). Joe Henry Eagle, congressman, was born in Tompkinsville, Kentucky, on January 23, 1870. After graduation from Burritt College at Spencer, Tennessee, in 1887 he moved to Texas, where he taught school at Vernon from 1887 to 1893, acting as superintendent of schools, 1889–91. After studying law at night and in his spare time, he was admitted to the bar in 1893 and was elected city attorney of Wichita Falls for 1894–95. Eagle moved to Houston in 1895 and ran unsuccessfully for Congress as a Populist in 1896. Later he served six terms in Congress as a Democrat, under Woodrow Wilson from 1913 to 1921 and under Franklin D. Roosevelt from 1933 to 1937. While in the House, he was a strong advocate of credit for farmers and of the resulting Federal Farm Loan Act of 1916. He also secured the establishment of Ellington Air Force Base in 1917 and an appropriation of $4,000,000 to deepen and widen the Houston Ship Channel[qv] in 1919. In the 1930s, as earlier, he advocated social security benefits and promoted the construction of several Work Projects Administration[qv] buildings in his district. In 1936 he ran unsuccessfully for the Democratic nomination for United States senator, then retired from Congress for a second time to practice law in Houston until 1957. He married Mary Hamman, daughter of William H. Hamman, and they had a son and a daughter. Eagle died on January 10, 1963.

BIBLIOGRAPHY: *Biographical Directory of the American Congress, 1744–1961* (1961). Galveston *Daily News,* August 9, 1896. Houston Metropolitan Research Center Files, Houston Public Library. Houston *Post,* January 11, 1963. Vertical Files, Barker Texas History Center, University of Texas at Austin. *Who's Who in America,* 1934–35.

Alwyn Barr

EAGLE, TEXAS. Eagle is east of Farm Road 563 between Oak Island and Double Bayou, forty-eight miles southwest of Beaumont in southern Chambers County. It derived its name from the eagle's nest built in a tall pine tree on the West (formerly North) Fork of Double Bayou. The community's post office, established in 1913, also served residents of Glen and Graydon when those post offices were discontinued in 1918 and 1919, respectively. At one time Eagle had a school and served as a voting precinct. In 1936 Eagle had two businesses, but none were reported after the early 1970s. The Eagle post office was discontinued in 1943. The scattered community reported a population of fifty-four in 1920 and fifty from the late 1940s through 1990.

BIBLIOGRAPHY: Jewel Horace Harry, *A History of Chambers County* (M.A. thesis, University of Texas, 1940; rpt., Dallas: Taylor, 1981).

Robert Wooster

EAGLE COVE, TEXAS. Eagle Cove was fifteen miles southwest of Baird in southwestern Callahan County. In 1875 Thomas Anderson planned a home there for his son-in-law, John Trent. Arthur Anderson built in the area what was one of the first homes in the county to have plank floors and glass windows. Episcopal Bishop Alexander C. Garrett[qv] of Dallas held services at the site in 1878, an occasion commemorated with a monument raised there in 1932. A post office was established at Eagle Cove in 1879 with David M. Thomas as postmaster. The community had thirty residents by the mid-1880s, and wool was the primary commodity produced by area ranchers. Eagle Cove began to fade around 1900 and was bypassed during the construction of the Abilene and Southern Railway in 1909. The community's post office was discontinued in 1913, and by the late 1930s only a few scattered houses remained in the area.

BIBLIOGRAPHY: Brutus Clay Chrisman, *Early Days in Callahan County* (Abilene, Texas: Abilene Printing and Stationery, 1966).

William R. Hunt

EAGLE CREEK (Hamilton County). Eagle Creek rises about a mile southeast of the Bethel cemetery in eastern Hamilton County (at 31°36′ N, 97°58′ W) and runs southeast for seven miles to its mouth on the Leon River, about four miles south of Jonesboro (at 31°34′ N, 97°54′ W). It traverses terrain characterized by steep slopes and benches, with shallow clay loams that support juniper, live oak, mesquite, and grasses.

——— (Harrison County). Eagle Creek rises five miles northwest of Harleton in northwestern Harrison County (at 32°42′ N, 94°39′ W) and runs south for five miles to its mouth on Little Cypress Bayou, three miles east of the Gregg county line (at 32°38′ N, 94°39′ W). The surrounding nearly level to hilly terrain is surfaced by loams and clays that support dense patches of pine and hardwood trees. The land is used predominantly for timber production.

——— (Nolan County). Eagle Creek rises four miles north of the Coke county line and ten miles northwest of Blackwell in southwestern Nolan County (at 32°09′ N, 100°31′ W) and runs southeast for sixteen miles to its mouth on Oak Creek, a mile southwest of Blackwell in far northeastern Coke County (at 32°04′ N, 100°20′ W). It traverses flat terrain with locally shallow depressions, surfaced by expansive clays that support water-tolerant hardwoods, conifers, and grasses.

——— (Palo Pinto County). Eagle Creek rises seven miles southwest of Palo Pinto in central Palo Pinto County (at 32°42′ N, 98°25′ W) and runs north for ten miles to its mouth on the Brazos River, four miles northwest of Palo Pinto (at 32°49′ N, 98°21′ W). The creek, which is intermittent in its upper reaches, traverses an area of rolling hills, surfaced by clay and sandy loams that support scrub brush, mesquite, cacti, and grasses.

_____ (Wilson County). Eagle Creek rises four miles northeast of Saspamco in western Wilson County (at 29°16′ N, 98°14′ W) and runs southwest for four miles to its mouth on Calaveras Creek, just north of Saspamco (at 29°14′ N, 98°15′ W). It crosses flat to rolling terrain surfaced by clay and sandy loams that support water-tolerant hardwoods and grasses.

EAGLE FORD, TEXAS. Eagle Ford was on the Missouri, Kansas and Texas Railroad and Loop 12 six miles west of downtown Dallas in western Dallas County. It was on the original land grants of H. Burnham and the Buffalo Bayou, Brazos and Colorado Railway. The area was first settled by the family of Enoch Horton, who moved there from Missouri in 1844 and established a home at a shallow part of the West Fork of the Trinity River, which became a fording spot for travelers. When Horton found an eagle's nest in the area, he named the crossing Eagle Ford. Several pioneer families from La Réunion[qv] settled in Eagle Ford. One source claims that another landowner was French marshall Achille François Bazaine, who was sent to Mexico by Napoleon III to help establish Austrian archduke Ferdinand Maximilian Joseph as emperor of Mexico in the 1860s. While in Mexico Bazaine reportedly acquired approximately 200 acres of land in the Eagle Ford area.

Eagle Ford had a post office from 1858 until 1866. The community did not begin to develop until the depression of 1873 halted construction of the Texas and Pacific Railway, which made Eagle Ford its western terminus until 1876. With the construction of cattle-holding facilities, the community soon became a cattle-shipping point to rival Dallas and Fort Worth as the major city of North Texas. Eagle Ford grew from a small community centered around a general store to a community with a population of several thousand people and fifty new businesses and homes, including a two-story hotel and a railway station. One year later W. W. Basaye began publishing the *Weekly Eaglet*, and the community secured another post office that operated until 1918.

By 1876 construction of the Texas and Pacific had resumed, and the line was completed to Fort Worth in 1878. The westward movement of the railroad decreased Eagle Ford's importance as a cattle-shipment center, but the community evolved into an agricultural shipping point for the surrounding region. By 1882 it had a population of 200, a cotton gin and a flour mill, two schools, and a general store. The community was primarily farmers, including the Santerre and Girard families, John Laupot, B. Lavois, Frank Horton, and Wesley Cockrell.

The Eagle Ford population decreased to fifty in the 1890s and stayed at that level well into the 1930s. By 1941 the population had increased to 150. After World War II[qv] Eagle Ford grew rapidly, when the return of war veterans spurred housing development in the area. The demand for housing was so great that by 1946 many of the residents in the town were living in temporary shelters until houses could be built. This construction was accompanied by industrial growth and infrastructure construction, which by 1947 included a steel-fabricating plant and new schools and roads. Eagle Ford was incorporated into Dallas in 1956, when it had a population of 4,679.

BIBLIOGRAPHY: Sam Hanna Acheson, *Dallas Yesterday*, ed. Lee Milazzo (Dallas: Southern Methodist University Press, 1977).

Matthew Hayes Nall

EAGLE HOLLOW. Eagle Hollow, also known as Eagle Arroyo, begins ten miles east of Clarendon in eastern Donley County (at 34°57′ N, 100°44′ W) and runs northeast for four miles to its mouth on the Salt Fork of the Red River, twelve miles southeast of Howardwick (at 34°59′ N, 100°43′ W). The area terrain varies from flat to gently sloping to rolling, with some local escarpments. Native vegetation includes mesquite shrubs and bushes and grasses in deep, fine, sandy loam and loose sand.

BIBLIOGRAPHY: Virginia Browder, *Donley County: Land O' Promise* (Wichita Falls, Texas: Nortex, 1975).

EAGLE ISLAND PLANTATION. Eagle Island Plantation was established in 1826 on part of five leagues of land given to Sarah Ann Groce by her father, Jared Ellison Groce,[qv] on the occasion of her marriage to William Harris Wharton.[qv] The plantation was on Oyster Creek twelve miles from the Gulf of Mexico in southeastern Brazoria County. At one time it included 16,000 acres of the richest alluvial soil in Texas. The cotton plantation was developed around 1826 and served as the Wharton home from 1828 to 1878. Wharton replaced the original log house with an elaborate frame structure built of imported timber, surrounded by landscaped grounds, and patterned after a home in Mobile, Alabama. It was capable of housing thirty guests. A brick sugar house, double kettles, and duplicate machinery to avoid delay in case of breakdowns made the plantation operations highly efficient.

According to the census, John Austin Wharton,[qv] Wharton's only child, owned the plantation in 1860, when it comprised 700 improved acres, used 133 slaves, and produced 7,000 bushels of corn, 100 bales of cotton, and 185 hogsheads of sugar. Wharton's real property in that year was valued at $113,000 and his personal property at $123,950. William Wharton Groce, a nephew of Wharton, owned the plantation after 1872, and in 1884 it was purchased by Harris Masterson. Two other plantations, the Evergreen plantation of Alexander Calvit[qv] and the Lake Plantation of Abner Jackson,[qv] were developed on Wharton land. Family members buried at the Eagle Island family cemetery include William H. and John A. Wharton and family friend Branch T. Archer.[qv]

BIBLIOGRAPHY: Randolph B. Campbell, *An Empire for Slavery: The Peculiar Institution in Texas, 1821–1865* (Baton Rouge: Louisiana State University Press, 1989). William Wharton Groce, "Major General John A. Wharton," *Southwestern Historical Quarterly* 19 (January 1916). Abner J. Strobel, *The Old Plantations and Their Owners of Brazoria County* (Houston, 1926; rev. ed., Houston: Bowman and Ross, 1930; rpt., Austin: Shelby, 1980).

Diana J. Kleiner

EAGLE LAKE. Eagle Lake, off-channel from the Colorado River near the town of Eagle Lake in eastern Colorado County (at 29°34′ N, 96°20′ W), is supposed to have been named from an Indian legend of a young girl who chose between two suitors by having them cross the lake, climb a tree, and return with a young eagle. The Eagle Lake project was first owned by William Dunovant, then by Rineyard-Walker and Company, and later by Eagle Lake Rice Irrigation Company, which became Lakeside Irrigation Company. The project was begun in 1899 and completed in 1900, with impoundment beginning in that year. Water was diverted for the irrigation season of 1900. Eagle Lake has a capacity of 9,600 acre-feet and a surface area of 1,200 acres at an elevation of 170 feet above mean sea level. The earthfill Eagle Lake Dam is 5,300 feet long. The lake stores water diverted from the Colorado River when excess flood flows occur. The early pumps were rope-driven by Corlis steam engines. They were later replaced by modern electric pumps that lift water from the Colorado River to a canal system that supplies water to the lake or directly to the land to be irrigated. The drainage area of the lake is twenty square miles, but the area is relatively unimportant as a water supply source.

BIBLIOGRAPHY: C. L. Dowell, *Dams and Reservoirs in Texas: History and Descriptive Information* (Texas Water Commission Bulletin 6408 [Austin, 1964]).

Seth D. Breeding

EAGLE LAKE, TEXAS. Eagle Lake is on Highway 90A east of the Colorado River and fifty miles southwest of Houston in southeast Colorado County. The town is beside a lake of some 1,400 acres, also known as Eagle Lake. Below the lake is the Lower Lake. Both lakes are privately owned and are leased for hunting and fishing. As early as 1835, Gideon Lincecum^{qv} studied the numerous fish in the lake and the fauna of the surrounding land; in 1990 snowy egrets, roseate spoonbills, great blue herons, white pelicans, coots, cormorants, and alligators were still common sights. North of the town is the Attwater Prairie Chicken National Wild Life Refuge.^{qv}

Eagle Lake is marked on early Texas maps. The name was probably given in 1821 by William W. Little and James Beard,^{qqv} two of Austin's scouts, when one of them killed an eagle on the lake and called the water Laguna del Águila. On March 22, 1838, Patrick Reels was granted 13½ labores of land (2,391 acres) on the shores of the lake, adjoining land grants owned by A. L. McLain and James McNair.^{qv} In 1848 this grant was patented to the heirs of P. Reels by the state. In 1856 Gamaliel Good purchased most of the land from the heirs of Patrick Reels. It was divided among Good and his sons. Good subsequently deeded half interest in 600 acres to DeWitt Clinton Harris,^{qv} a director of the Buffalo Bayou, Brazos and Colorado Railway. Together they planned the town to be a station on a new railroad between Harrisburg and Austin. The rails reached Eagle Lake in 1859. Later the Southern Pacific, the Cane Belt, the San Antonio and Aransas Pass, and the Santa Fe railroads all made Eagle Lake accessible for shipment of crops and, later, of gravel. In 1888 the town was incorporated, and Capt. J. W. McCarty was elected the first mayor.

After the Civil War,^{qv} Capt. William Dunovant started raising sugarcane and built a sugar mill at Lakeside, on the eastern shore of the lake. In 1913 the mill was sold and moved to Jamaica. Dunovant also introduced the cultivation of rice irrigated by lake water in 1896. John Linderholm of Chesterville expanded the rice industry, irrigated by wells, to the prairie north of Eagle Lake. Rice mills were also established in Eagle Lake. In the 1980s the mills were gone, though rice culture^{qv} was still one of the major local industries.

Huge sand and gravel deposits were mined west of the lake, leaving stretches of water for fishing and waterskiing and bringing the manufacture of concrete products to Eagle Lake. Numerous bones of ancient animals were found in the gravel mines. Production of both oil and natural gas in the area also contributed to the economy. In the 1960s Eagle Lake became a recreational center for hunting geese and ducks that wintered on the prairies in the rice stubble and around the lake. In the 1980s the planting and harvesting of hundreds of acres of wildflowers brought new interest to Eagle Lake. In 1990 the population of the town was 3,551.

BIBLIOGRAPHY: Lois Wood Burkhalter, *Gideon Lincecum, 1793–1874: A Biography* (Austin: University of Texas Press, 1965). Colorado County Historical Commission, *Colorado County Chronicles from the Beginning to 1923* (2 vols., Austin: Nortex, 1986). *Colorado County Sesquicentennial Commemorative Book* (La Grange, Texas: Hengst Printing, 1986). Eagle Lake Historical Committee, *A History of Eagle Lake* (Austin: Eakin Press, 1987).
Rosanne Harrison

EAGLE MILLS, TEXAS. Eagle Mills, three miles northeast of Joaquin in northeastern Shelby County, was a sawmill community founded about 1885 and named for an employee of the Hicks Mill. In 1903 it had a school for fifty students, and in 1938 the school served seventy-three. At one time the community had the school, a gin, a store, churches, and sawmills, but the town declined as the forest in the area was cut down. By 1946 Eagle Mills had lost its businesses and only one residence remained.
D. R. Taylor

EAGLE MOUNTAIN (Callahan County). Eagle Mountain is just north of State Highway 36 and five miles south of Eula in west central Callahan County (at 32°16′ N, 99°33′ W). Its peak, with an elevation of 2,204 feet above sea level, rises 204 feet above the highway.

_____ (Hudspeth County). Eagle Mountain is twenty-four miles southeast of Sierra Blanca in southeastern Hudspeth County (at 30°55′ N, 105°05′ W). With an elevation of 7,484 feet above sea level, it is the highest peak in the Eagle Mountain range. The surrounding rugged terrain is marked by numerous box canyons and high relief and is surfaced by shallow, stony soil that supports Douglas fir, aspen, Arizona cypress, maple, ponderosa pine, and madrone.

_____ (Tarrant County). Eagle Mountain is in the northwestern corner of Tarrant County (at 32°54′ N, 97°27′ W). It rises 150 feet above the surrounding terrain, and the Eagle Mountain School is located at its foot. The Eagle Mountain Dam has been built in sections separated by Eagle Mountain and Burgess Gap. Eagle Mountain Reservoir, in Tarrant and Wise counties, was named for the mountain.

EAGLE MOUNTAIN RESERVOIR. Eagle Mountain Reservoir, formerly Eagle Mountain Lake, is on the West Fork of the Trinity River just north of Lake Worth in northwestern Tarrant and southwestern Wise counties (at 32°53′ N, 97°28′ W). It is owned and operated by the Tarrant County Water Control and Improvement District No. 1 to supply water to Fort Worth for municipal and industrial uses and for irrigation and recreation. Construction of the dam began on January 23, 1930, and was completed October 24, 1932. Impoundment of water began on February 28, 1934. The dam is 85 feet high and 4,800 feet wide, with an original spillway width of 1,300 feet. The crest of the service spillway is at 649.1 feet above mean sea level. The reservoir has a normal capacity of 190,460 acre-feet and a maximum capacity of 680,335 acre-feet; its surface area at normal capacity is 9,200 acres and at maximum capacity, 19,050 acres. A new service spillway was added in 1971 at a cost of $2,565,679. The drainage area of the West Fork of the Trinity River at Eagle Mountain Dam is 1,970 square miles.
Seth D. Breeding

EAGLE NEST CREEK. Eagle Nest Creek, also known as Eagle Nest Canyon, rises a mile east of Farm Road 2083 in southern Val Verde County (at 29°53′ N, 101°33′ W) and runs south for five miles to its mouth on the Rio Grande, a half mile east of Langtry (at 29°49′ N, 101°33′ W). Eagle Nest Creek sharply dissects massive limestone that underlies flat terrain, forming a deep and winding canyon. The last mile of the streambed passes through the high vertical cliffs of One Mile Canyon. The area soils are generally dark, calcareous stony clays and clay loams and support oaks, junipers, grasses, and mesquites. Eagle Nest Creek was named for a landmark noted by travelers and settlers for over two centuries. It is an inaccessible, but highly visible, limestone cavern located near the top of a 300-foot vertical bluff on the course of the creek and just east of Langtry. At one time eagles nested on the ledge outside the cavern. On April 25, 1875, Lt. John L. Bullis^{qv} and his Black Seminole scouts^{qv} fought border Indians at Eagle's Nest Crossing, near the landmark. Three of the scouts won Medals of Honor for saving Bullis's life in the Eagle's Nest battle. In 1882 the Galveston, Harrisburg and San Antonio Railway established a grading camp near the crossing and named it Eagle's Nest.

BIBLIOGRAPHY: Robert Wooster, *Soldiers, Sutlers and Settlers: Garrison Life of the Texas Frontier* (College Station: Texas A&M University Press, 1987).

EAGLE NEST LAKE. Eagle Nest Lake is north of Mann Lake and three miles west of Angleton in west central Brazoria County (at 29°13′ N, 95°37′ W). The man-made lake is roughly two miles in diameter and is surrounded by freshwater marsh in which grasses and rushes stand on mud and sand bottoms.

EAGLE PASS, TEXAS. Eagle Pass, the county seat of Maverick County, is located on the Mexican border at the intersection of U.S.

highways 277 and 57, Farm Road 1021, and the Southern Pacific Railroad in the far western part of the county. During the Mexican War^qv a company of Texas Mounted Volunteers under the command of Capt. John A. Veatch^qv established an observation post on the Rio Grande opposite the mouth of the Mexican Río Escondido and beside an old smuggler's trail that crossed the river at this point. The crossing, known as El Paso del Águila, was so named because of frequent flights of Mexican eagles from the wooded grove along the Escondido. Though abandoned by the military at the conclusion of hostilities, the site remained a terminus and crossing point for trappers, frontiersmen, and traders. In 1849 Fort Duncan was established two miles upstream, and its proximity caused a rudimentary settlement to spring up at the crossing below the post. In 1850 San Antonio merchant James Campbell opened a trading post there, and he was soon joined by William Leslie Cazneau^qv and his bride, Jane Cazneau.^qv The village, named after the crossing on the Rio Grande, changed from El Paso del Águila to Eagle Pass as the Anglo presence grew. Concurrent with the growth of Eagle Pass below the fort, emigrants bound for the California gold fields (via Mazatlán) established a staging area above the post known as California Camp. The resulting trade and traffic brought a shift in the settlement of Eagle Pass from the old crossing downstream to its present location above the fort. John Twohig,^qv owner of the land, surveyed and laid out a townsite, which he named Eagle Pass. Friedrich W. C. Groos^qv contracted to haul supplies for the military and brought some seventy Mexican families to settle near the fort. A stage line between Eagle Pass and San Antonio was established in 1851. Our Lady of Refuge Catholic Church was constructed in 1852.

The early history of Eagle Pass was often characterized by violence. The settlement and adjoining fort were frequently attacked by the Lipan Apache and Comanche Indians. Piedras Negras, established in 1850 across from Eagle Pass in Mexico, became a haven for fugitive slaves, and both banks of the river were infested with outlaws. In 1855 James H. Callahan^qv crossed into Mexico at Eagle Pass with three companies of volunteer rangers in pursuit of Lipans and Kickapoos. After a fight with Mexican forces on the Escondido, he fell back on Piedras Negras and set the village afire as he crossed back into Eagle Pass. During the Civil War,^qv a party of renegades crossed from Piedras Negras and overran the Confederate garrison at Fort Duncan. The townsmen, fighting from behind a barricade of cotton bales, successfully drove off their assailants. Following federal occupation of Brownsville in 1863, Eagle Pass became an important shipment point for Confederate cotton. After the war the last Confederate force in the field, the Shelby expedition,^qv crossed the Rio Grande at Eagle Pass and in a ceremony buried in the river the last flag to fly over Confederate troops.

Maverick County, which had been formed from Kinney County in 1856, was finally organized in 1871, and Eagle Pass became the county seat. St. Joseph's Academy, a Catholic school for girls, was opened in 1872. By 1875 the population numbered 1,500 and consisted of Anglo-Americans, Germans, and mostly Mexicans. Their principal occupation was mercantile business and stock raising. Following the war years, bands of cattle thieves and fugitives led by John King Fisher^qv dominated Eagle Pass through the 1870s, notwithstanding the multiple interventions of the Texas Rangers.^qv Law and order was restored with the coming of the railroad in the next decade. In 1882 the Galveston, Harrisburg and San Antonio Railway built from Spofford to Eagle Pass, connecting the isolated community to the rest of the country. Rail construction was continued into Mexico at Piedras Negras as the Mexican National Railway, and the community became an important international center. By 1884 Eagle Pass had an estimated population of 2,000, and a new courthouse was erected the following year. An Episcopal church, the first Protestant church in the community, was completed in 1887.

Eagle Pass grew slowly in the early decades of the twentieth century, reaching 2,729 inhabitants in 1900 and 5,765 in 1920. The community served a diverse region of ranches, coal mines and farms. After falling slightly to 5,059 inhabitants in 1930, the population grew to 7,247 in 1950. Irrigated farming techniques strengthened the agricultural economy of the region in the 1930s and 1940s, and Eagle Pass Army Air Field^qv was constructed twelve miles north of Eagle Pass during World War II.^qv From the 1950s to the 1980s the town grew dramatically, reaching 12,094 inhabitants in 1960, 15,364 in 1970 and 21,407 in 1980. Always a town with a large Hispanic majority, Eagle Pass was 94 percent Hispanic in 1980. With the completion of Highway 57, Eagle Pass became a major gateway to Mexico, and the town, along with Piedras Negras, developed a substantial tourist trade. Retailers on both sides of the border served Mexican and American tourists and for years enjoyed a flourishing business. In the late 1960s the city embarked on a "Model Cities Program" to modernize city services. Government grants funded the construction of new water and sewer plants, new schools, and an industrial park. Several manufacturing concerns located in the area in the 1970s and 1980s, and significant oil finds boosted the local economy during those years. In 1982 the devaluation of the peso led to economic depression in Eagle Pass as Mexican shoppers stopped coming to the town. Later in the decade the local economy was given a boost from the establishment of maquiladoras^qv in the area. Five industrial plants were located in Eagle Pass and nineteen in Piedras Negras by 1987. Textile and arms manufacturing were the leading employers. In 1990 the population had dropped a bit to 20,651, but Eagle Pass remained a center for county government, tourism,^qv and varied manufacturing.

BIBLIOGRAPHY: Cora Montgomery, *Eagle Pass, or Life on the Border* (New York: Putnam, 1852; rpt., Austin: Pemberton Press, 1966). Ben E. Pingenot, *Historical Highlights of Eagle Pass and Maverick County* (Eagle Pass, Texas: Eagle Pass Chamber of Commerce, 1971). Ben E. Pingenot, ed., *Paso del Águila . . . Memoirs of Jesse Sumpter* (Austin: Encino, 1969).
Ben E. Pingenot

EAGLE PASS ARMY AIR FIELD. Eagle Pass Army Air Field, ten miles north of Eagle Pass in Maverick County, was an advanced single-engine flying school during World War II.^qv It was activated in 1942 and converted to a basic flying school in November 1944. All flight training at the field was discontinued in April 1945. During the Eisenhower administration an early-warning radar station was built on the site. It was later closed, and since then the facility has been used for county housing.

BIBLIOGRAPHY: Ben E. Pingenot, *Historical Highlights of Eagle Pass and Maverick County* (Eagle Pass, Texas: Eagle Pass Chamber of Commerce, 1971).
Art Leatherwood

EAGLE SPRING. Eagle Spring is at the northern edge of the Eagle Mountains and eight miles southwest of Allamoore in southeastern Hudspeth County (at 30°59′ N, 105°06′ W). The spring was well-known to nineteenth-century travelers. In 1849 Capt. Robert S. Neighbors^qv called the spring Puerto de la Cola del Águila, or Haven of the Eagle Tail. A year later Lt. S. G. French noted of the spring, "The water did not run, but merely oozed out of the ground, and was collected in numerous holes dug for that purpose." And in 1867 Maj. Edward Meyer described the spring as "a limited supply of not very good water." More important than the quality of its water was its strategic location. From 1854 to 1882 stagecoaches and wagon trains using the San Antonio–San Diego Mail Route^qv stopped at Eagle Spring for water. The spring was also popular with the Mescalero Apaches. In 1854 they stole the livestock of a wagon train camped at the springs, and in 1857 one wagon train passed the spring without stopping "on account of Indians whose regular stopping place it is reputed to be." In 1862, during the Civil War,^qv the Eagle Spring site was occupied by Union army troops, and in 1879 and 1880 a cavalry outpost was established there as part of the final campaign against the Mescalero chief Victorio.^qv A historical marker and the ruins of the stage station stand about half a mile north of the spring. The surrounding flat to rolling terrain with local escarpments is surfaced by deep, fine sandy loams that support hardwood forest, brush, and grasses. In 1972 the discharge from Eagle Spring was less than half a pint of fresh water per second. In 1976 the discharge of about a third of a pint per second disappeared into gravel about fifty yards downstream.

EAGLE SPRINGS, TEXAS. Eagle Springs was on Farm Road 107 sixteen miles southeast of Gatesville and two miles northwest of the site of Mother Neff State Park[qv] in the southeastern corner of Coryell County. The community supposedly received its name when the survey party at the site saw an eagle fly up from the spring. John McClain established a Baptist church there in 1858, and a post office opened at Eagle Springs in 1869. In 1882 the community's population was seventy-five, and two years later Eagle Springs reported having three general stores, two churches, a district school, and 200 residents. Area farmers shipped cotton and grain. The community began to decline in the 1890s, when its population fell to 100. The Eagle Springs post office was discontinued in 1901, and mail for the community was sent to Moody. The school was consolidated with a nearby school in 1936; the church was disbanded in 1948. Only a few scattered houses remained in the area in the 1980s.

BIBLIOGRAPHY: Coryell County Genealogical Society, *Coryell County, Texas, Families, 1854–1985* (Dallas: Taylor, 1986). Zelma Scott, *History of Coryell County* (Austin: Texas State Historical Association, 1965). *Vivian Elizabeth Smyrl*

EAGLETON, CLYDE (1891–1958). Clyde Eagleton, legal scholar and teacher, was born in Sherman, Texas, on May 13, 1891, the son of Addie Christian (Parker) and Davis Foute Eagleton.[qv] He attended the Sherman public schools and Austin College, where he received B.A. (1910) and M.A. (1911) degrees. As a Rhodes scholar he earned a second B.A. (1917) from Oxford University; he received a second M.A. (1928) from Princeton and a Ph.D. (1928) from Columbia University. Austin College gave him an honorary doctorate in 1941. Eagleton served on the faculty of New York University from 1923 to 1956, and at various times he taught at the University of Louisville, Southern Methodist University, Daniel Baker College, the University of Texas, the University of Chicago, Stanford, Yale, the University of Washington, and the Académie de Droit International (the Hague, Netherlands). He was a legal expert with the United States Department of State (1943–45) and served as assistant secretary of the Dumbarton Oaks Conference in 1944. In 1945 he was technical expert with the United States delegation to the Washington meeting of the Committee of Jurists and adviser to the United States delegation at the San Francisco Conference for the founding of the United Nations. He was director of the Institute for the Study of International Law at New York University, and at the time of his death he was studying legal aspects of the use of international rivers. He wrote many articles for professional journals and periodicals and several books, including *The Responsibilities of States in International Law* (1928), *International Government* (1932, 1948, 1957), and *The Forces That Shape Our Future* (1945). In addition, he was coeditor of seven volumes of the *Annual Review of United Nations Affairs* (1949–56), published by New York University Press. He was a Presbyterian, a member of numerous national and international associations and of the Texas State Historical Association,[qv] president of the American Branch of the International Law Association, and a consultant to United Nations bodies. He was married to Sara Virginia McKinney on September 15, 1917, and they had one son. Eagleton died on January 30, 1958.

BIBLIOGRAPHY: *New York Times*, January 31, 1958. *Who Was Who in America*, Vol. 3. Roger R. Wilson, "Clyde Eagleton: May 13, 1891–January 29, 1958," *American Journal of International Law* 52 (April 1958). *N. Ethie Eagleton*

EAGLETON, DAVIS FOUTE (1861–1916). Davis Foute Eagleton, teacher, school administrator, and author, was born on March 16, 1861, in Boon's Hill, Tennessee, the son of George Ewing and Mary Ethlinda (Foute) Eagleton. He was educated by his father, a Presbyterian minister, until 1879, when he attended Davidson College, North Carolina, for a short time. He followed his father as principal of Ouachita Seminary, Mount Holly, Arkansas, in 1879, and Magnolia Academy, Arkansas, in 1880. He subsequently returned to Davidson College and received a B.A. degree (1884), an M.A. (1894), and an honorary doctorate (1914). He was principal of Fannin College at Bonham, Texas (1884–86), principal of Ladonia Academy (1886–88), and professor of English at Austin College (1888–97). After resigning his position at Austin College, Eagleton opened Sherman Academy, which was later moved to Bonham as Bonham Academy. In 1898 he went to Calvert and conducted the public schools there until his return to Austin College in 1900. Eagleton was the compiler and editor of *Writers and Writing of Texas* (1913) and *Texas Literature Reader* (1916, 1922); he wrote several short works. In Sherman he was an elder of the College Park Presbyterian Church, which he had helped organize. He married Addie Christian Parker on June 19, 1890, at Mount Holly, Arkansas, and they had seven children. Eagleton died on June 9, 1916, and was buried in Sherman.

BIBLIOGRAPHY: *Alumni Monthly of Austin College*, July 1916. Sherman *Daily Democrat*, June 9, 1916. *N. Ethie Eagleton*

EAKER, IRA CLARENCE (1896–1987). Ira Clarence Eaker, aviation pioneer and United States Air Force general, was born on April 13, 1896, at Field Creek, Texas, the eldest of five boys born to Young Yancy and Dona Lee (Graham) Eaker. In 1906 the family moved to Concho County, where they spent three years in the rural community of Hills before moving to a farm a mile outside of Eden. They moved to southeastern Oklahoma in 1912 and returned to Eden ten years later. Ira attended public school at Hills, in Eden, and in Kenefic, Oklahoma. He graduated from Southeastern State Teachers College (now Southeastern Oklahoma State University) at Durant, Oklahoma, and entered the United States Army in 1917.

Eaker was commissioned a second lieutenant in the Infantry Section, Officers Reserve Corps, on August 15, 1917, and assigned to the Sixty-fourth Infantry at Fort Bliss, Texas. He received a similar commission in the regular army on October 26, 1917. His aviation experience began in March 1918, when he was directed to attend ground school at the University of Texas in Austin and flight training at Kelly Field at San Antonio. He received his pilot rating and a promotion to first lieutenant on July 17, 1918. After training, he was sent to Rockwell Field, California, where he met Col. H. H. "Hap" Arnold and Maj. Carl A. "Tooey" Spaatz, two men with whom he had a close military relationship for the rest of his life. In July 1919 he was appointed commander of the Second Aero Squadron and sent to the Philippines for a two-year tour. In 1920 he was reassigned as commander of the Third Aero Squadron and promoted to captain. Upon return to the United States in 1921 he was assigned to Mitchel Field, New York; while there, he attended Columbia Law School. He subsequently spent three years to the staff of Maj. Gen. Mason M. Patrick, chief of air service, in Washington, D.C.

Captain Eaker was one of ten pilots chosen to make the Pan American Goodwill Flight in 1926. During the flight both members of one crew died in a crash. Eaker and his copilot were the only team to complete the entire 23,000-mile itinerary, which included stops in twenty-three countries. The flight left San Antonio on December 21 and ended at Bolling Field, Washington, D.C., where President Calvin Coolidge presented the pilots with the Distinguished Flying Cross, a new award authorized by Congress just a few months earlier. In 1929 Eaker, with Tooey Spaatz and Elwood R. Quesada (both of whom were later generals), flew a Fokker tri-motor named the *Question Mark* for 150 hours, 40 minutes, and 15 seconds, shuttling between Los Angeles and San Diego, refueling with a hose lowered from a Douglas C-1. They set an endurance record that endured for many years. In 1930 Eaker flew the first transcontinental flight that depended solely on aerial refueling. Eaker was promoted to major in 1935. Beginning on June 2, 1936, he flew blind under a hood from Mitchel Field, New York, to March Field, Riverside, California. Maj. William E. Kepner (who also became a general) flew alongside in this experiment in instrument flight as a safety observer. He stated that Eaker "was under the hood and flying blind" the entire time except for eight take-offs and landings.

During the middle to late 1930s Eaker attended the Air Corps Tactical School at Maxwell Field, Alabama, and the Army Command and General Staff School at Fort Leavenworth, Kansas. He also served on the Air Staff in Washington. He was promoted to full colonel in December 1941 and to brigadier general in January 1942, when he was assigned to England to form and command the Eighth Bomber Command. He was instrumental in the development and application of daylight precision bombing in the European Theater. This tactic was a major factor in the defeat of the Germans. In December 1942 Eaker became commander of the Eighth Air Force in England. On September 13, 1943, he received promotion to lieutenant general, and on October 15, 1943, he assumed overall command of both American air forces in the United Kingdom, the Eighth and the Ninth. He took over as commander of the joint Mediterranean Allied Air Forces on January 15, 1944. With 321,429 officers and men and 12,598 aircraft, MAAF was the world's largest air force. On March 22, 1945, Eaker was transferred back to Washington to become deputy chief of the army air force under Gen. H. H. Arnold. In that position, representing the air force, he transmitted the command from President Harry Truman to General Spaatz, who was then commanding the Pacific Air Forces, to drop the atomic bomb on Japan. Eaker announced his plans to retire from the army in mid-June 1947, saying that he felt he could do more to provide security for the United States out of uniform.

After retirement he was associated with Hughes Aircraft from 1947 to 1957. In 1957 he became a corporate director of Douglas Aircraft Company, a post he held until 1961, when he returned to Hughes as a consultant, with the freedom to pursue a long-desired goal of being a journalist. He had already coauthored three books with H. H. Arnold: *This Flying Game* (1936), *Winged Warfare* (1941), and *Army Fliers* (1942). In 1964 he began a newspaper column in the San Angelo *Standard Times* that continued for eighteen years and was syndicated by Copley News Services in 700 newspapers. In 1974 he transferred to the Los Angeles Times Syndicate. He wrote from the point of view of a military man on security matters. Between 1957 and 1981, 329 of his articles appeared in military periodicals. In 1972 he became the founding president of the United States Strategic Institute.

Among his more than fifty decorations were the Congressional Gold Medal, the Distinguished Flying Cross with Oak Leaf Cluster, the Distinguished Service Medal with Oak Leaf Cluster, the Order of the Partisan Star (First Class), the Silver Star, and the Wright Trophy; he was also made a Knight of the British Empire. He was promoted from lieutenant general to general by an act of Congress in 1985.

Eaker married Leah Chase about 1930; the couple had no children, and the marriage ended in divorce the year it began. On November 23, 1931, he married Ruth Huff Apperson. General Eaker died on August 6, 1987, at Andrews Air Force Base, Maryland, and was buried at Arlington National Cemetery with full military honors. He was survived by his wife.

BIBLIOGRAPHY: Fort Worth *Star-Telegram,* August 6, 1987. James Parton, *"Air Force Spoken Here": General Ira Eaker and the Command of the Air* (Bethesda, Maryland: Adler and Adler, 1986). Vertical Files, Barker Texas History Center, University of Texas at Austin.

Art Leatherwood

EAKIN PUBLICATIONS, INCORPORATED. Eakin Publications, a trade-book publisher, was founded in 1979 and incorporated in 1980 in Burnet, Texas, by Edwin M. Eakin, who headed the company. He was previously copublisher of community newspapers in Quanah, Clarendon, Chillicothe, and Saginaw, Texas, and co-owner of newspapers in Iowa Park and Azle, Texas, and of Nortex Offset Publications, Incorporated, in Wichita Falls. In 1979 the company had some fifty books in print and added what became the principal imprint, Eakin Press, used for books marketed through the trade. Nortex Press was reserved for books the company's printing department printed for individuals, companies, and organizations. In February 1983 the firm moved into a new plant in southwest Austin. By 1985 Eakin Press had more than 250 books in print, including more than fifty juvenile titles, and marketed its books nationwide to schools and libraries and through bookstores. Although the press began by specializing in titles relating to Texas history, ethnic groups, folklore, and food, in 1984 editorial policy began to shift to include contemporary fiction and nonfiction of general interest. By the late 1980s Eakin Press was issuing some forty new titles each year.

BIBLIOGRAPHY: Eakin Press Records, Austin. *Edwin M. Eakin*

EARGLE, DOLAN HOYE (1905–1973). Dolan Hoye Eargle, stratigrapher and economic geologist, was born in Richland County, South Carolina, on December 8, 1905. He attended high school in Columbia, South Carolina, and in 1921 enrolled at the University of South Carolina. In 1926 he graduated with degrees in geology, music, and Greek. After spending one year each in South Carolina, Cincinnati, and Cornell studying in graduate school, he stopped his studies because of the Great Depression.qv Eargle took his first job in 1929 at Pittsburgh Gas and Electric Company in New York state, where he worked in reconnaissance geology. In 1930 he married a woman named Mayre, with whom he had two sons. He was employed as a micropaleontologist in Tulsa at the Skelly Oil Company until 1931. Afterwards he served as a teacher and superintendent in rural public schools in South Carolina for three years. In 1934 he accepted a temporary position with the United States Geological Survey and in 1935 worked for the Soil Conservation Service. In 1942 he accepted a full-time position with the United States Geographic Survey.

By this time he had returned to graduate school and in 1946 received his M.S. from the University of South Carolina. Subsequently he traveled throughout the country for the USGS, mapping out Cretaceous sections of various states and working on the Cross-Florida Barge Canal project. In 1954 Eargle began exploring the surface uranium deposits of South Texas. He and Alice Weeks worked out a description of the circumstances that brought about the radioactive minerals, and their work made it possible to locate hydrocarbon accumulations. Eargle's mapping of the Tatum salt dome in Lamar County, Mississippi, for the Atomic Energy Commission helped to ascertain how safe the area was by determining its explosive potential; it also helped the AEC to prevent the leakage of radioactive gas. Eargle belonged to the American Association of Petroleum Geologists and the Geological Society of America. He was an avid student of classical music and often played the piano at services sponsored by his church for inmates of Austin State Hospital.qv He died on March 11, 1973, in Austin from complications following surgery.

BIBLIOGRAPHY: Jules Braunstein, "D. Hoye Eargle (1905–1973)," *Bulletin of the American Association of Petroleum Geologists* 58 (March 1974). *Kris Ercums*

EARHART, JOSEPH BONAPARTE (1812–1869). Joseph Bonaparte Earhart, pioneer entrepreneur of North Texas, was born in Pennsylvania on April 15, 1812. He married Mary Ann Quesenbarry on January 18, 1843, and they had seven children. In 1843 Earhart was a trader at Fort Washita, Chickasaw Nation, and operated transport boats on the Red River. By 1847 he had moved into Texas and was operating a ferry at Rock Bluff. In 1849 he was employed to establish Colbert's Ferry^qv farther down the river on the Indian Territory side. After moving back to Texas around 1850, he built a steam mill on Iron Ore (now South Denison) Creek. He was active in the Hedgcoxe War,^qv a protest of settlers against the Peters colony.^qv Around 1855 he moved to Hog-eye Prairie, near Cundiff, Jack County, where he ranched and operated Earhart's Station on the Butterfield Overland Mail^qv route. Earhart was reported to be one of the first ranchers in Clay County. His headquarters was near the mouth of Post Oak Creek on the Little Wichita River near the site of present Henrietta. He died in Grayson County on February 28, 1869, of an illness that began on a northern cattle drive, and was buried in Knobs Cemetery, now in west Denison.

BIBLIOGRAPHY: Roscoe P. and Margaret B. Conkling, *The Butterfield Overland Mail, 1857–1869* (3 vols., Glendale, California: Clark, 1947). Seymour V. Connor, *The Peters Colony of Texas: A History and Biographical Sketches of the Early Settlers* (Austin: Texas State Historical Association, 1959). Rosalie Gregg, ed., *Wise County History* (Vol. 1, n.p: Nortex, 1975; Vol. 2, Austin: Eakin, 1982).
Morris L. Britton

EARL, TEXAS. Earl, also known as Earls and as Earl's Chapel, was a farming community off State Highway 110 some fourteen miles north of Rusk in northeastern Cherokee County. It was evidently first settled around the time of the Civil War^qv and was named for M. L. Earle, an early settler. A small church formed the nucleus of the community, which was called Earl's Chapel during its early history. A local post office operated briefly in 1874 under the name Earl, and a school, known as Earl's Chapel School, was in operation by 1896, when it had an enrollment of forty. In the mid-1930s the community comprised the church, the school, and a number of houses. The school later closed. In the early 1990s only the church, a cemetery, and a few scattered houses still remained.
Christopher Long

EARLE, HALLIE (1880–1963). Hallie Earle, physician, was born on September 27, 1880, on a ranch near Hewitt, Texas, daughter of Isham Harrison and Adaline (Graves) Earle, members of pioneer Waco families. She graduated from Baylor University in 1901, one of seven women in a class of seventeen. After she completed a master of science degree at Baylor in 1902, the administration honored her by placing a copy of her thesis in the cornerstone of the new Carroll Science Building. She taught school in Gainesville for three years before entering Baylor University Medical School in Dallas. She was the only woman in her class, and for many years her grade point average stood as the highest ever posted in the school. She received her M.D. degree in 1907, in a class of six graduates. She specialized in gynecology and did postgraduate work in Chicago, New Orleans, and New York; she interned at Belleville Hospital in New York. After graduation Dr. Earle practiced at Torbett Sanitarium in Marlin, Texas. In 1915 she established a private practice in Waco, where for many years she was the only practicing female physician. She retired in 1948 to the family ranch. Her father had begun keeping weather records in 1879; she shared his interest and continued the daily observation records after he retired in 1916. She was for years the only weather observer in Central Texas, and in 1960 the United States Weather Bureau presented her the John Campanius Holm Award in recognition of her work. She died on November 1, 1963, in Waco and was buried in Oakwood Cemetery.

BIBLIOGRAPHY: Graves-Earle Family Papers, Texas Collection, Baylor University.
M. Rebecca Sharpless

EARLE, THOMAS (?–?). Thomas Earle (Earl), one of Stephen F. Austin's^qv Old Three Hundred^qv colonists, received title on July 7, 1824, to a league and a labor of land in what became Harris County; in 1825 he settled on Buffalo Bayou near William Vince.^qv In March 1825 Earle wrote Austin requesting some timberland on Green's Bayou and asked also for land for his son James and for Alexander Kilpatrick. In September 1825 he got into difficulties for taking equipment from the schooner *Mary*. The census of 1826 classified Earle as a farmer and stock raiser aged between forty and fifty. His household included his wife, Jane, two sons, five daughters, and two servants. In April 1827 Earle arrived at the mouth of the Trinity River on the schooner *Augusta* with four or five families on board. In February 1834 he was defendant in a lawsuit. He was administrator for Luke Moore's^qv estate in 1837. In February 1838 Earle offered half his league on Buffalo Bayou for sale. He served on the grand jury in Houston in 1840 and was still living on Buffalo Bayou in 1845. That he was the Thomas Earl, aged sixty and a native of Ireland, who was living in Harris County in 1850 is doubtful. Sources indicate that Earle probably died before 1850.

BIBLIOGRAPHY: Eugene C. Barker, ed., *The Austin Papers* (3 vols., Washington: GPO, 1924–28). Lester G. Bugbee, "The Old Three Hundred: A List of Settlers in Austin's First Colony," *Quarterly of the Texas State Historical Association* 1 (October 1897). Adele B. Looscan, "Harris County, 1822–1845," *Southwestern Historical Quarterly* 18–19 (October 1914–July 1915). Marion Day Mullins, *First Census of Texas, 1829–1836, and Other Early Records of the Republic of Texas* (Washington: National Genealogical Society, 1959). *Telegraph and Texas Register*, February 10, 1838, May 6, 1840. William Barret Travis, *Diary*, ed. Robert E. Davis (Waco: Texian, 1966).

EARLE, TEXAS. Earle was on the San Antonio, Uvalde and Gulf Railroad twelve miles south of downtown San Antonio in southern Bexar County. A post office operated at the site from 1887 to 1904. In 1890 Earle had a blacksmith, a general store, a butcher, and a doctor. By the 1930s the site was no longer shown on maps.
Christopher Long

EARLY, TEXAS. Early is at the intersection of U.S. highways 67 and 84, on Pecan Bayou just east of Brownwood in central Brown County. The area was settled by farmer Welcome W. Chandler^qv in the early 1850s, and in 1856 the land was part of the site of Brownwood. In 1858 Brown County's first post office was established in Chandler's home. Around 1869 problems over the water supply and a disputed land title induced many citizens of Brownwood to move from the east to the west side of Pecan Bayou. Though people continued to live on the site, the east side of Pecan Bayou was not considered to be a separate community until the mid-twentieth century. In 1928 a new school district, named for Walter U. Early, an attorney who donated land for several school buildings, was formed on the site, and the Anderson, Ricker, Delaware, and Jenkin Spring schools consolidated with Early. In 1935 the Early school had 271 pupils and 9 teachers. The Early community began to grow around the school in the 1940s. A Baptist church was built across from the school in 1942, followed by a Church of Christ building in 1947. In 1948 the community had six businesses, two churches, and the school. Early incorporated on December 15, 1951, when it had an estimated 600 inhabitants. The Early Lions Club was organized in 1957. Early grew to 819 inhabitants by 1960 and to 1,097 by 1970. A Methodist church was built in 1979, and a second Baptist church in 1984. Heartland Mall, the first mall in the Brownwood area, opened there in 1980, when the community had 2,313 inhabitants. A city hall was built in 1982, and a post office was opened in 1985. In 1990 the community included four churches, the Early weekly *Press*, the Early Independent School District, and 2,380 inhabitants.

BIBLIOGRAPHY: Thomas Robert Havins, *Something about Brown: A History of Brown County, Texas* (Brownwood, Texas: Banner Printing, 1958).
Mark Odintz

EARLY AMUSEMENTS. The lusty spirit of frontier humor was quick to make the earliest settlers of Texas lighten their work with the good fellowship of their neighbors. All joined in house-raisings, log-rollings, rail-splittings, quilting^{qv} bees, bear hunts, and several other activities in which labor and fun were mixed. Dances were popular from the time of earliest settlement. On these occasions the frontiersman talked and laughed loudly and stamped his feet noisily while dancing. Other kinds of indoor parties were candy-pullings and candy-breakings, at which simple games were played. When local church members objected to dancing, the play party met favor, although it did not become prevalent in Texas until the 1840s. Most popular of all sports, however, was horse racing, with the chief racing centers located along the coast. The course at Velasco was talked of even in New Orleans. After the Texas Revolution,^{qv} dancing schools and theatrical organizations appeared. Patriotic occasions provided opportunities for barbecues, songs, oratory, and parades by military organizations. In 1844 the Fourth of July celebration at Clarksville featured the Montgolfier balloon and a fireworks display. At Christmas and New Year's the people enjoyed dances, torchlight processions, the decorated Christmas tree, and the practice of exchanging gifts. The polishing of entertainment had gone so far by 1848 as to cause Rutherford B. Hayes to observe in his diary that the social life in Texas was like that found elsewhere.

BIBLIOGRAPHY: Eugene C. Barker, *Readings in Texas History* (Dallas: Southwest Press, 1929). William R. Hogan, *The Texas Republic: A Social and Economic History* (Norman: University of Oklahoma Press, 1946; rpt. 1969).
Curtis Bishop

EARLYWINE, TEXAS. Earlywine is on Rocky Creek and State Highway 105, six miles from Brenham in east central Washington County. It was named for the Wren community's nineteenth-century postmaster, John W. Earlywine. The Harris Spring Church is in the Earlywine vicinity. The 1984 county highway map showed two businesses at Earlywine.
Carole E. Christian

EARP, JAMES (ca. 1798–1861). James Earp, farmer, merchant, and a founder of Earpville^{qv} (later part of Longview), was born about 1798 in Georgia, one of at least three children of Patsy (Robertson) and Cullin Earp. Cullin had been captain of a regiment in Washington County, North Carolina, in 1779. James Earp married Mary Sanders on June 20, 1818, in Lawrence County, Alabama. They were the parents of eleven children, the first eight of whom were born in Alabama. James Earp arrived in Texas along with his single brother, Benjamin, sometime before May 2, 1835, and James received a first-class headright certificate entitling him to 4,605 acres of land. After receiving his headright, James returned to Alabama and brought back his elderly father (who had apparently been widowed before moving to Texas), another brother, William, and his family. In 1846 James bought additional acreage. By the mid-1840s he had settled his large family just north of the Sabine River, in what is now Gregg County. At the time of the settlement it was in Upshur County, and the community that developed there was known as Earpville. The community, which had been laid out as a townsite as early as 1841, was a stopover for the stage from Louisiana. Many of the settlers moving west apparently found the rolling hills of East Texas^{qv} to their liking. James Earp, a gregarious fellow, sold seven pieces of his land between 1849 and 1860; by 1856 he was considered to be the most important citizen of Earpville. In 1861 Earpville included a store, a wagon shop, a blacksmith shop, a Methodist church, and a schoolhouse. In the early census, James Earp was listed as a farmer. But on February 29, 1856, he was appointed postmaster of Earpville, and by 1860 the census listed him as a merchant, indicating he was running a general store in Earpville. (It was common practice for the post office to be housed in a general store.) He was reappointed postmaster under the Confederacy in 1861, a post he held until his death on August 7, 1861. After he died, his daughter, Louisa (Earp) Glasco, sold 518½ acres of his estate to Ossamus Hitch Methvin, Sr.,^{qv} who in turn in 1870 sold 100 acres to the Southern Pacific line. Earpville was eventually subsumed into the new railroad town of Longview, and the last document showing the old town of Earpville was dated July 3, 1882. James Earp's final resting place has not been located. A historical marker on Highway 80, at 1107 E. Marshall Avenue, Longview, is the lone sentinel for this early pioneer.

BIBLIOGRAPHY: Longview Junior Chamber of Commerce, *The History of Gregg County* (Fort Worth, 1957). Longview *Morning Journal*, May 3, 1970. Jim Wheat, Postmasters and Post Offices of Texas, 1846–1930 (Microfilm, Grover C. Ramsey Papers, Barker Texas History Center, University of Texas at Austin).
Mary Glasco Hawkins

EARPVILLE, TEXAS. Earpville was on a site that is now within the city limits of Longview in Gregg County. It was founded by the James Earp family of Alabama in the 1840s and had a post office from 1850 to 1867. In 1848 James Earp and his son-in-law James Starkey purchased 1,031 acres of the Alexander Jordan headright bounded on the east by the Upshur-Harrison county line and on the west by the Hamilton McNutt survey. Earp purchased several adjoining tracts of land the following year and built his homestead near the Marshall-Tyler road at the base of the largest rock hill in the area, where Longview's water towers are now located. During the 1850s other members of the Earp family joined James in Upshur County, and the settlement became known as Earpville. The community was on the stagecoach line from Louisiana to San Antonio. Dr. Job Taylor, a physician and lay preacher, operated the stagecoach stop. In 1860 the population was 276, and the community had a saddler, three merchants, a carpenter, three blacksmiths, a wagonmaker, and a minister. A Methodist congregation met in a small log structure beginning in the mid-1800s. It moved to a new building in 1860 and in 1875 became the First Methodist Church of Longview, which still exists. Although there are no records of a school in Earpville, some evidence suggests that the children of the community received private instruction from the postmaster, who was also a teacher, in 1861. With the coming of the Southern Pacific Railroad in 1870 Longview was built, and Earpville ceased to exist as a separate settlement.

BIBLIOGRAPHY: Norman W. Black and Ellie Caston, comps., *Guide to Gregg County's Historical Markers* (Longview, Texas: Gregg County Historical Museum and Gregg County Historical Commission, 1988). John Dickson, History of Gregg County, Texas (M.A. thesis, University of Texas, 1957). Longview Junior Chamber of Commerce, *The History of Gregg County* (Fort Worth, 1957). Frank Waters, *The Earp Brothers of Tombstone: The Story of Mrs. Virgil Earp* (New York: Potter, 1960; rpt., Lincoln: University of Nebraska Press, 1976).
Charlotte Allgood

EARTH, TEXAS. Earth, on U.S. Highway 70 and Farm Road 1055 in northwestern Lamb County, was established in 1924 by William E. Halsell,^{qv} who also founded Amherst. Originally Halsell called the place Fairlawn or Fairleen, but it was renamed Earth, supposedly for a sandstorm blowing when storekeeper and first postmaster C. H. Reeves had to come up with a name acceptable to postal authorities in Washington. Another story is that Reeves described the storm in a letter to Washington and received the reply: "The earth seems to move in your country. You will call the post office Earth." Still another story is that Halsell was impressed with the region's fertile soil and wanted the name Good Earth, which the post office shortened. The population of the community was 350 in 1930 and 600 in 1940, when the town had sixteen businesses. Earth was incorporated in 1947. Its population was reported as 1,104 in 1960, as 1,152 in 1970, and as 1,512 in 1980. The community's population increases over these last few decades made it unusual among West Texas towns. Its growth can be attributed in part to the improved production of local farmlands since irrigation was developed and to the establishment of Plant X, Southwestern Public Service's generating plant, three miles south, which employs a number of residents. A medical clinic opened at Earth in 1957 and a swimming pool in 1959. Earth is a grain and cotton center. In 1990 its population was 1,228.

BIBLIOGRAPHY: Vincent Matthew Peterman, *Pioneer Days: A Half-Century of Life in Lamb County and Adjacent Communities* (Lubbock: Texas Tech Press, 1979). Evalyn Parrott Scott, *A History of Lamb County* (Sudan, Texas: Lamb County Historical Commission, 1968). Fred Tarpley, *1001 Texas Place Names* (Austin: University of Texas Press, 1980).

William R. Hunt

EARTHQUAKES. Between 1847 and 1994 there were more than 110 recorded earthquakes of magnitude three or greater in Texas. No Texas earthquake has exceeded a magnitude of 6.0, and most have been fairly small and caused little or no damage. Damage has occurred in at least twenty-five of the recorded earthquakes, however, and one death has been attributed to a Texas quake. Almost all of the earthquakes in Texas have been caused by one of two sources. The major source is relief of tectonic stress along fault lines. These are most common in the Rio Grande rift belt, the Panhandle,qv the Ouachita Belt, and the Coastal Plain.qv Small earthquakes have also been attributed to well injections associated with oil and gas field operations and occur in areas near large oil and gas fields. The largest earthquake in Texas occurred on August 16, 1931, near Valentine in Jeff Davis County; it measured about 6.0 on the Richter Scale. Many of the other West Texas earthquakes have occurred in El Paso, including the only Texas quake associated with a death; on March 7, 1923, in Ciudad Juárez, Chihuahua, a few kilometers from the quake's epicenter, an adobe house collapsed and suffocated the man inside. Some of the larger earthquakes in the Panhandle include the 1917, 1925, and 1936 Panhandle and Borger quakes and the 1948 Dalhart quake. No earthquake in the Panhandle has exceeded a magnitude of 5.0. Earthquakes in East and Central Texas have been fairly small. Some notable ones have occurred at Seguin (1847), Manor (1873), Paige (1887), Creedmore (1902), Mexia-Wortham (1932), and Trout Switch (1934). Other significant earthquakes have occurred in Wellborn (1857), Hempstead (1910), and Anderson (1914) in the Southeast and in Rusk (1891), Center (1981), and Jacksonville (1981) in the Northeast. In April 1993 an earthquake of magnitude 4.2 that took place in Atascosa County damaged homes and a gas pipeline.

BIBLIOGRAPHY: Scott Davis, Wayne D. Pennington, and Steven M. Carlson, *A Compendium of Earthquake Activity in Texas* (Bureau of Economic Geology, University of Texas at Austin, 1989). Wayne D. Pennington and Scott D. Davis, "Numerous Quakes Shake Texas," *Texas Almanac*, 1986–87. Vertical Files, Barker Texas History Center, University of Texas at Austin.

Erika Murr

EASLEY CHAPEL, TEXAS. Easley Chapel, a farming community on State Highway 21 two miles northeast of Weches in extreme northeastern Houston County, grew up around a church by that name built before 1900. In the mid-1930s the community had a church, a cemetery, and a number of houses. After World War IIqv most of its residents moved away, and by the mid-1960s only a cemetery and a few widely scattered houses remained in the area. In the early 1990s Easley Chapel was a dispersed rural community.

Christopher Long

EAST, JAMES H. (1853–1930). James H. East, cowboy, lawman, and author, was born on August 30, 1853, on a farm near Kaskaskia, Illinois. As a boy he heard many tales about Texas, and, after turning sixteen in 1869, he headed there, inspired by having read of Davy Crockett and the fall of the Alamo (*see* ALAMO, BATTLE OF THE). His first job was on the cattle ranges around Seguin, in the employ of John Files Tom.qv He participated in his first long cattle drive, to the New Orleans market, in 1870, and other drives soon followed. For the next ten years East, as a cowboy in South Texas, experienced occasional brushes with Indians and Mexican bandits, and in 1877 he made his first drive north over the Western Trailqv to Dodge City, Kansas. In 1880 East began work with the LX Ranchqv in the Panhandle,qv working in company with such men as W. C. (Outlaw Bill) Moore and Charles A. Siringo.qv He was a member of Patrick F. Garrett'sqv posse that trailed and captured Billy the Kid (*see* MCCARTY, HENRY) and killed Tom O'Folliard and Charlie Bowdre in November 1880. In 1882 East was elected sheriff of Oldham County, succeeding Caleb Berg (Cape) Willingham.qv In that position he aided Pat Garrett's Home Rangers and quickly restored order to Tascosa after the "Big Fight" on March 21, 1886, which left four men dead. East also owned the Equity Bar at Tascosa and later bought the Cattle Exchange Saloon. During this time he married Nettie Boulding of Virginia. After his tenure as sheriff, East was hired by Lucien B. Scott as range foreman of the LS Ranch.qv In this role he continued as a deputy sheriff. On May 13, 1889, he killed a gambler named Tom Clark in a shoot-out at Tascosa. One night Nettie East shot at what she thought was an outlaw waiting to ambush her husband, only to discover that she had killed the LS's prize bull. The Easts remained in the Panhandle until 1903, when they moved to Douglas, Arizona. There East served at various times as city marshal, chief of police, and police judge until his retirement in the late 1920s. In 1928 he collaborated with Viola Vivian in writing a play entitled *Billy the Kid*, which was presented at Tucson, Arizona. East died at Douglas on May 14, 1930, aged seventy-seven.

BIBLIOGRAPHY: J. Evetts Haley, "Jim East—Trail Hand and Cowboy," *Panhandle-Plains Historical Review* 4 (1931). Henry Hoyt, *A Frontier Doctor* (Chicago: Lakeside, 1979). John L. McCarty, *Maverick Town: The Story of Old Tascosa* (Norman: University of Oklahoma Press, 1946; enlarged ed. 1968). Charles A. Siringo, *Riata and Spurs* (Boston: Houghton Mifflin, 1927; 2d ed. 1931). Dulcie Sullivan, *The LS Brand* (Austin: University of Texas Press, 1968).

H. Allen Anderson

EAST, SARITA KENEDY (1889–1961). Sarita Kenedy East, South Texas rancher and philanthropist, daughter of John G. and Marie Stella (Turcotte) Kenedy, was born on September 19, 1889, in Corpus Christi, Texas. Her grandfather was Mifflin Kenedy,qv founder of the vast La Parra Ranch in what was then Cameron County (now Kenedy County). She spent much of her childhood at La Parra, and her father named the new town of Sarita, located on the Kenedy ranch, for his daughter upon the town's founding around 1904. Sarita attended Incarnate Word Academy in Corpus Christi and then H. Sophie Newcomb Memorial College in New Orleans. She also made her debut in New Orleans. She did not complete college, but instead returned to La Parra. On December 8, 1910, she married Arthur Lee East, a South Texas rancher. They did not have any children. After Arthur East died in 1944, Mrs East and her brother John G. Kenedy, Jr., were in charge of the 400,000-acre Kenedy ranch. Upon her brother's death in 1948, Sarita and her sister-in-law Elena Suess Kenedy became the sole heirs to the ranch. Sarita East also owned the San Pablo Ranch near Hebbronville and Twin Peaks Ranch in Colorado. She served as a county commissioner of Kenedy County and was on the board of directors of Alice National Bank. In addition to her business dealings she engaged in philanthropy especially to Catholic charities. In 1952 she received the Ecclesia et Pontifice medal and membership in the Ladies of the Holy Sepulchre of Jerusalem from Pope Pius XII for her service to the church. She was also named an honorary member of the Franciscans and the Oblates of Mary Immaculate.qqv In her 1948 will she bequeathed La Parra ranch headquarters and 10,000 acres of land to the Oblate fathers and 13,000 acres to the Diocese of Corpus Christi.qv The rest of her vast estate was divided among relatives and ranch kin.

In 1948 Mrs. East met Christopher Gregory, a Trappist monk who had taken the name Brother Leo. Two years earlier Brother Leo had been released from his vow of silence and assigned to raise funds for new Trappist monasteries. He was on a fund-raising trip through South Texas when he met Sarita East, and over the next few years he became her advisor and traveling companion. In the 1950s Mrs. East allowed oil and gas exploration on her ranch, which up to that time had largely been an untapped resource. During that time she gave money to the Trappist monks and visited monasteries throughout the world. In 1959, with other family members and Brother Leo, she went on a South American tour, one of several trips she made, and donated $300,000 to build a mission in Chile. That same year Brother Leo introduced her to J. Peter Grace, chairman of the board of W. R. Grace and Company, in New York. The three began the work of forming a charitable foundation. On January 21, 1960, they established the John G. and Marie Stella Kenedy Memorial Foundation, with Sarita Kenedy East as sole member. Mrs. East also wrote another will leaving the bulk of her estate to the foundation. Over the next few months she wrote a series of codicils to her will that increasingly gave more control of the foundation to Brother Leo and Grace. Just before her death she named Brother Leo sole member of the foundation. Sarita Kenedy East died of cancer on February 11, 1961, in New York City and was buried at La Parra Ranch.

Within months after her death a group of South Texans, including Elena Suess Kenedy, members of the Turcotte family, and the Diocese of Corpus Christi, filed a lawsuit disputing Brother Leo's control of the foundation, charging that Leo and Grace exerted undue influence over Mrs. East while she was disoriented by medication. Other relatives also contested her 1960 will and wished to reinstate her 1948 will dividing the estate among various beneficiaries. Over the course of the battle more than 200 people claimed to be legitimate heirs. In 1964 a settlement regarding the foundation resulted in the splitting of assets. Grace and the New York group relinquished control of the foundation over Brother Leo's objections. The bulk of the funds, approximately $100 million, went to the control of the South Texans, but Grace received oil royalties (not to exceed $14.4 million) from the estate and established a smaller foundation in New York, the Sarita Kenedy East Foundation, worth approximately $13 million. In 1966 Brother Leo filed an appeal against the decision; after a further series of appeals the Texas Supreme Court ruled against him. In June 1981 the United States Supreme Court refused to hear his appeal, thereby affirming the rights of the Texas relatives to retain control of the foundation. Through a series of court battles over the years the 1960 will was upheld over the 1948 will, and the assets of the foundation and most of the Kenedy estate remained intact. As Mrs. East wished, the ranch headquarters went to the Oblate fathers. The estate, which had been held in escrow by the Alice National Bank, was finally turned over to the foundation in 1982. In 1984, basically the first year that the foundation officially operated, it had $100 million in assets and was the largest charitable foundation in South Texas. It was stipulated that at least 10 percent of the income go to the Corpus Christi diocese, with a total of 90 percent of funds going for religious activities and the other 10 percent going to secular agencies.

BIBLIOGRAPHY: Corpus Christi *Caller-Times*, August 26–29, September 23–27, December 16–19, 1984. Stephan G. Michaud and Hugh Aynesworth, *If You Love Me You Will Do My Will* (New York: Norton, 1990). Vertical Files, Barker Texas History Center, University of Texas at Austin.
Laurie E. Jasinski

EAST AMARILLO CREEK. East Amarillo Creek, also known as Hedrio Creek, rises north of the Amarillo city limits in Potter County (at 35°13′ N, 101°50′ W) and runs north-northwest for about fifteen miles to its mouth on the Canadian River, a half mile from West Amarillo Creek, west of U.S. Highway 87 and almost directly north of Amarillo (at 35°27′ N, 101°52′ W). For most of the stream's length the flat terrain is surfaced by leveled sand dunes, with some low-rolling to flat, locally dissected areas surfaced by clay loam and sandy loam; at the stream's mouth the soil is loose sand. Vegetation along the creekbed includes scrub brush and grasses. The creek, once a favorite haunt of Indians and hide hunters, was later part of the LX Ranch[qv] range.

EAST BAY. East Bay, the southeast extension of Galveston Bay (centered at 29°31′ N, 94°40′ W), lies in southeastern Chambers County between the Bolivar Peninsula and the mainland. East Bay is twenty miles long, east to west, and five miles wide. Oyster Bayou is a tributary on East Bay.

EAST BAY BAYOU. East Bay Bayou rises four miles west of Stowell in eastern Chambers County (at 29°45′ N, 94°26′ W) and runs south until it merges with the Gulf Intracoastal Waterway[qv] in northern Galveston County. East Bay Bayou then follows this waterway to the southwest for five miles before emptying into East Bay (at 29°33′ N, 94°28′ W). The soil and wildlife vary along the seventeen-mile course of the bayou. The poor, impermeable, clay soil at the bayou's source and along its first few miles is good for grasses, legumes, herbaceous plants, hardwood trees, shrubs, and wetland vegetation such as smartweed, millet, rushes, and sedges; this habitat is suited for quail, rabbit, meadowlarks, deer, turkeys, and squirrels. The whole bayou is well suited for ducks, geese, cranes, mink, nutria, and muskrat.
Julianne Johnston

EAST BERNARD, TEXAS. East Bernard is on the west side of the San Bernard River at the intersection of State Highway 60 and U.S. Highway 90A, fifteen miles north of Wharton in northeast Wharton County. The community was originally on the east side of the river, where Jethro Spivi built the first residence around 1850; hence the name East Bernard. Settlement was slow until 1859 and the arrival of the Buffalo Bayou, Brazos and Colorado Railway. A bridge was built, and the depot, Bernard Station, though originally located on the east bank of the river, was moved by 1869 to the west side, to the site of East Bernard's future Main Street. The rest of the town grew up around the railway. The first post office was established in 1866, but the community was probably not officially named East Bernard until 1874. After the Civil War[qv] the community began to grow rapidly, as new settlers arrived with British surnames. Although Joseph Habermacher operated a store and saddle shop in Bernard Station some time before 1867, the main influx of German and Slavic immigrants came after the 1880s. In the mid-1890s the farming community had a population of 150, and businesses included a steam gin, a gristmill, a telegraph office, and two general stores. The first church in East Bernard was established in 1893, when German Methodist settlers dismantled their church in Content, three miles south of Weimar, and moved it by rail to East Bernard, where it was rebuilt in 1909. Catholic and Baptist congregations started holding services in private homes around 1900; their sanctuaries were completed between 1905 and 1907. The present Catholic church, built in 1925, has stained glass windows from Czechoslovakia, mosaics from Munich, a statue of St. Anthony from Italy, and statuary carved in the German Tyrol. An Assembly of God congregation began Pentecostal services in a private home in 1970 and moved into a new building by 1978. The first school building was erected around 1888 one mile north of the depot; by 1912 a brick high school had been built in town. Around 1916 East Bernard became an independent school district, and by 1956 nearby schools in Nottawa, Muldoon, Bernard Prairie, and Lissie were consolidated with the East Bernard school. A Texas historical marker now marks the site of the original school. East Bernard has had several newspapers, the first of which, the East Bernard Tribune, began in the 1920s. In the late 1980s the town was served by a weekly paper with the same name. Riverside Hall, built in 1927 on the east bank of the river, became a popular dance pavilion, where Paul Whiteman was once featured. In the early years of the settlement pioneer merchants H. P. Stockton and John G. Leveridge had operated a banking business in the back of Leveridge's General Store; by 1907 they had organized the Union State Bank. R. B. Boettcher purchased the controlling stock in 1911. In 1960 J. R. Peace, owner of a large furniture company, helped organize a chamber of commerce, which, since East Bernard is unincorporated, performs much of the duties of a city government. In the 1980s East Bernard's economy, though centered on agriculture, also included a gas pipeline company, a major kite-manufacturer, and several research corporations. In 1988 the population of 1,500 was served by sixty-three businesses. In 1990 the population was 1,544.

BIBLIOGRAPHY: Kathleen E. and Clifton R. St. Clair, eds., *Little Towns of Texas* (Jacksonville, Texas: Jayroe Graphic Arts, 1982). Annie Lee Williams, *A History of Wharton County* (Austin: Von Boeckmann-Jones, 1964).
Ray Spitzenberger

EAST BLACK HILLS. The East Black Hills are a mile east of the Black Hills and twenty miles northeast of the Persimmon Gap Ranger Station in east central Brewster County (centered at 29°49′ N, 102°57′ W). The hills, at an elevation of 3,365 feet above sea level, rise 525 feet above Dove Mountain Road a half mile to the south. Soils in the hills are generally shallow and stony and support oaks, juniper, and some mesquite.

EAST BOSQUE RIVER. The East Bosque River rises near the southeastern border of Erath County (at 32°08′ N, 97°56′ W) and runs southeast for seventeen miles to its mouth on the North Bosque River, in north central Bosque County (at 32°00′ N, 97°47′ W). It is dammed several times throughout its length to form lakes House, Big, Irrigation, and Ownsby. The surrounding terrain is flat with local shallow depressions and is surfaced by clay and sandy loams that support water-tolerant hardwoods, conifers, and grasses.

EAST BRANCH OF CEDAR CREEK. The East Branch of Cedar Creek rises about two miles west-northwest of the Byler Point Church in western Fayette County (at 29°54′ N, 97°07′ W) and runs northeast for about 3½ miles to its mouth on Cedar Creek (at 29°56′ N, 97°06′ W). It traverses an area of rolling terrain with a fine sandy loam surface layer and a very firm clay subsoil. The area is used mainly as unimproved pasture. Local vegetation varies from scattered to dense clumps of mixed oak and cedar with an understory of yaupon that provides good wildlife habitat.

EAST BUFFALO CREEK. East Buffalo Creek rises in southwestern Lipscomb County (at 36°10′ N, 100°27′ W) and runs north for seven miles to its mouth on Wolf Creek (at 36°14′ N, 100°25′ W). East Buffalo Creek was near the Jones and Plummer Trail[qv] and was part of the Seven K Ranch[qv] range. The area is flat with local shallow depressions; water-tolerant hardwoods, conifers, and grasses grow from clay and sandy loam soils.

BIBLIOGRAPHY: *A History of Lipscomb County, Texas, 1876–1976* (Lipscomb, Texas: Lipscomb County Historical Survey Committee, 1976). Clinton Leon Paine, The History of Lipscomb County (M.A. thesis, West Texas State College, 1941). Pauline D. and R. L. Robertson, *Cowman's Country: Fifty Frontier Ranches in the Texas Panhandle, 1876–1887* (Amarillo: Paramount, 1981).

EAST CADDO PEAK. East Caddo Peak is four miles northwest of Cross Plains and two miles east of West Caddo Peak in southeastern Callahan County (at 32°10′ N, 99°14′ W). Its peak, with an elevation of 2,029 feet above sea level, rises 230 feet above State Highway 36 to the immediate south.

EAST CANEY, TEXAS. East Caney, a farming community off Interstate Highway 30 and just west of East Caney Creek nine miles east of Sulphur Springs in eastern Hopkins County, was settled before 1900. In the mid-1930s East Caney had a church, a school, a cemetery, and a number of scattered houses. After World War II[qv] most of its residents moved away. Its school was consolidated with the Saltillo school district, and by the early 1960s only a church and two cemeteries remained in the area. In the early 1990s East Caney was a dispersed rural community.
Christopher Long

EAST CANEY CREEK. East Caney Creek rises just east of Como in southeastern Hopkins County (at 33°03′ N, 95°26′ W) and runs northeast for twelve miles to its mouth on White Oak Bayou, two miles northwest of Weaver (at 33°11′ N, 95°26′ W). It is intermittent in its upper reaches. The stream traverses flat to rolling terrain surfaced by clay and sandy loams that support water-tolerant hardwoods, conifers, and grasses.

EAST CARANCAHUA CREEK. East Carancahua Creek rises in southern Wharton County (at 29°06′ N, 96°19′ W) and runs southwest for thirty-two miles, through western Matagorda County and into southeastern Jackson County, to its junction with West Carancahua Creek at the head of Carancahua Bay (at 28°46′ N, 96°25′ W). Before 1939 the stream was known as Carancahua Creek. It is intermittent in its upper reaches. Upstream, it traverses flat to rolling prairie surfaced by dark, calcareous clay that supports mesquite, grasses, and cacti; the lower creek crosses flat terrain with local shallow depressions, surfaced by clay and sandy loam that supports water-tolerant hardwoods, conifers, and grasses.

EAST CENTER, TEXAS. East Center is on Farm Road 1652 eight miles northeast of Canton in northeastern Van Zandt County. The settlement had a school in 1890 that by 1904 had reached an enrollment of fifty-three and by the 1950s had been consolidated with the Grand Saline Independent School District. The 1936 county highway map showed a school and scattered residences at the townsite, but by 1981 only the church remained.
Diana J. Kleiner

EAST COLUMBIA, TEXAS. East Columbia, on the Brazos River nine miles west of Angleton in west central Brazoria County, was founded by Josiah Hughes Bell[qv] in 1823. Bell's plantation landing on the Brazos, which served as a supply depot for settlements on the river above, was first known as Bell's Landing, but in 1824 Bell laid out the new town and named it Marion. He advertised the sale of lots in 1829, but the promotion did not succeed. By 1831 the community had only two or three cabins, a country store, and the frame house of Bell's plantation. As large sugar and cotton plantations were established in the area, however, mercantile establishments, saloons, wharves, warehouses, and large homes grew up around the Bell home, and trading schooners carried goods from the riverport to New Orleans. Bell sold the townsite of what was to become East Columbia to Walter C. White[qv] on October 1, 1827, but the name "Bell's Landing" remained in use until at least 1840. By 1842, when Bell's settlement on the prairie was known as West Columbia, the community had been renamed East Columbia.

The town, situated near the head of navigation on the Brazos River, grew rapidly for a time after the capital of Texas was moved to Houston. The Houston Tap and Brazoria Railroad was built to East Columbia from Houston in 1859, but the Civil War[qv] caused the town to decline. In 1884 the community was on a division of the Missouri Pacific Railroad and had two hotels, steam-driven corn and saw mills, a cotton gin, and a population of 800. By 1890 the population had more than doubled to 1,500, and a weekly newspaper, the *Old Capitol*, was in publication. Planing and grist mills, special and general stores, a sugar mill, and several churches and schools were built between 1894 and 1914, though the population dwindled from 1,200 to 150. A post office, established in 1846 as Columbia, was renamed East

Columbia in 1927. The population grew from 200 in 1929 to 400 in 1933, but declined after World War II qv to a low of eighty-nine in 1972 and remained at ninety-five from 1974 to 1990.

BIBLIOGRAPHY: Eugene C. Barker, ed., *The Austin Papers* (3 vols., Washington: GPO, 1924–28). James A. Creighton, *A Narrative History of Brazoria County* (Angleton, Texas: Brazoria County Historical Commission, 1975). Mattie Austin Hatcher, *Letters of an Early American Traveller, Mary Austin Holley, 1784–1846* (Dallas: Southwest Press, 1933).
Merle Weir

EAST CORAZONES DRAW. East Corazones Draw originates on the northern slopes of the Christmas Mountains near the Corazones Peaks in south central Brewster County (at 29°30′ N, 103°21′ W) and passes to the south and east of the Corazones Peaks as it runs northeast along Rattlesnake Ridge and past Sombrero Peak for some 14½ miles to its mouth on Nine Point Draw, on the broad desert flats to the northwest of the Rosillos Mountains (at 29°33′ N, 103°19′ W), and three miles below the mouth of West Corazones Draw. East Corazones Draw runs over ancient stream deposits of volcanic materials laid down over limestone. The area at one time supported an arid grassland ecosystem, but heavy grazing virtually destroyed it. In the 1980s the area around East Corazones Draw was dominated by Chihuahuan Desert scrub, including lechuguilla, ocotillo, sotol, and creosote bush. Other local plants included catclaw, honey mesquite, and Mormon tea.

EAST DALLAS, TEXAS. East Dallas occupies an area in the city of Dallas bounded by Central Expressway to the west, Mockingbird Lane to the north, Loop 12 to the east, and Fair Park to the south. The Beeman family settled there in the 1860s, but only in 1872 did William H. Gaston qv begin promoting the forty-acre tract east of the city. Only four families settled there at the time, but with the coming of the railroads in 1872–73, a number of floaters came to work on the railroad and set up houses in the undeveloped area between Dallas and East Dallas. Gaston persuaded the railroads to go through East Dallas by giving them $5,000 and free right-of-way through his property. The Houston and Texas Central arrived at the Union Depot in East Dallas on July 16, 1872, and the Texas and Pacific on February 22, 1873. In the 1870s East Dallas became a popular recreation destination on the streetcar lines that ran from Dallas to the state fairs and the horse-racing track.

On September 9, 1882, East Dallas was incorporated on a site of 1,400 acres. Some residents believed the town should be called Gaston rather than East Dallas. The town had an aldermanic form of government. The next year it passed a tax ordinance that raised money for city services. East Dallas was considered the most luxurious place to live in Dallas County; 90 per cent of its houses had running water pumped from deep wells by 1889. The main thoroughfares were well maintained, and a speed limit of eighteen miles an hour was set to slow down swift horses. The first schools were built in 1883 for 400 white students and sixty black ones. In 1886 the first all-brick schoolhouse in Dallas County was built in East Dallas. In 1887 another boom occurred in East Dallas when the Texas State Fair and Dallas Exposition at Fair Park opened (*see* STATE FAIR OF TEXAS). In the late 1880s East Dallas reached a population of 6,000.

In 1889 state senator R. S. Kimbrough sponsored a bill to remove the charter of East Dallas so it could become part of Dallas. Some claimed that those who revoked the charter did so to make Dallas the largest town in Texas; according to the 1890 census, they were successful. Under the new charter of East Dallas, the city of Dallas took over all the debt of East Dallas in addition to its streets, schools, and public buildings. On December 31, 1889, the day before East Dallas officially became part of Dallas, the city council of East Dallas passed $45,000 in street improvements, which Dallas was forced to finance.

BIBLIOGRAPHY: Sam Hanna Acheson, *Dallas Yesterday*, ed. Lee Milazzo (Dallas: Southern Methodist University Press, 1977). Gerald D. Saxon, *Reminiscences: A Glimpse of Old East Dallas* (Dallas Public Library, 1983).
Lisa C. Maxwell

EAST DELTA, TEXAS. East Delta, on Farm Road 895 a mile northeast of Charleston in eastern Delta County, was established in 1939 as the site of the East Delta district school. This school was created by the consolidation of the Charleston, Vasco, Cleveland, and Long Ridge schools. By 1964 the facility had closed, but maps identified the East Delta church and cemetery and the Union Grove cemetery in the area. Local students attended school within the Cooper Independent School District by 1970. East Delta had a reported population of fifty in 1990.

BIBLIOGRAPHY: Paul Garland Hervey, A History of Education in Delta County, Texas (M.A. thesis, University of Texas, 1951).
Vista K. McCroskey

EAST DIRECT, TEXAS. East Direct is at the intersection of Farm roads 79 and 197, between Collard and Slough creeks 1½ miles east of Direct in extreme northwestern Lamar County. The settlement was shown on the 1936 county highway map as an unidentified collection of dwellings. In 1980 it had two businesses but remained unnamed on maps. The name East Direct first was shown on maps in 1983, when there was a grain elevator, one other business, and a small cluster of dwellings at the highway intersection.
Vista K. McCroskey

EAST ELM CREEK. East Elm Creek rises five miles northwest of D'Hanis in west central Medina County (at 29°23′ N, 99°21′ W) and runs southwest for twenty-two miles to its mouth on the Sabinal River, at a point where Farm Road 187 crosses the river 3½ miles west of Irishman Hill (at 29°10′ N, 99°28′ W). In its upper and middle reaches, the creek passes through an area of steep to gently sloping terrain surfaced by very shallow to shallow, gravelly loams that support scrub brush and grasses. In the creek's lower reaches the terrain changes to flat with local shallow depressions, surfaced by deep loamy and clayey soils that support water-tolerant hardwoods, conifers, and grasses.

EAST END HISTORIC DISTRICT. The East End Historic District comprises fifty-two blocks between the central business district and the University of Texas Medical Branch in central Galveston. The district, bounded by Broadway, Market, Eleventh, and Nineteenth streets, features 463 historic houses from the late nineteenth and early twentieth centuries, some of them the work of the city's most noted architects, including Nicholas J. Clayton, Alfred Muller, and George E. Dickey.qqv Architectural styles range from Greek Revival and Victorian eclectic to Colonial and Classical Revival. Among the most noteworthy structures in the district are the Smith-Chubb house (1859), the Gus Reymershoffer house (1887), the Bishop's Palace qv (1887–93), and Sacred Heart Church (1903; dome rebuilt 1915). The area was added to the National Register of Historic Places in 1975 and was declared a national historic landmark in 1976.

BIBLIOGRAPHY: James Wright Steely, comp., *A Catalog of Texas Properties in the National Register of Historic Places* (Austin: Texas Historical Commission, 1984).
Christopher Long

EASTER, TEXAS. Easter is on Farm Road 2397 two miles east of Farm Road 1055 in northwestern Castro County. It was named for William Frank Easter, who settled there in the early 1900s. In 1901 he donated the land on which a one-room schoolhouse was built. This school was disbanded in 1912 but then reopened in 1915. Church services and Sunday school classes were held there. A new two-room school was built across the road north of the first structure in 1919 and 1920 and was subsequently enlarged. After the building burned in 1940, the Easter school district was consolidated with the Dimmitt schools, twenty miles southeast. A combination church and community center was built on the site but was later moved away and remodeled into a private residence. During the 1950s a grain elevator, a fertilizer shop, and a cotton gin were built at the townsite. Community spirit was revived with the organization of the Easter Lion's Club in 1965; in 1967 the club built a new community building two miles west on Farm Road 1055. Since then the annual Easter "Oprey," along with other special events, has been held there. A grocery store near the gin also operated a hamburger stand. Mail was delivered to the community from Hereford. In 1984 and 1990 Easter reported a population of ninety-one.

BIBLIOGRAPHY: Castro County Historical Commission, *Castro County, 1891–1981* (Dallas: Taylor, 1981).   H. Allen Anderson

EASTER FIRES. On the Saturday evening preceding Easter, bonfires are lit atop as many as twenty-two specified hills flanking the Texas German town of Fredericksburg. At the appointed hour the church bells of the town toll, lights are extinguished, and the hilltops burst into flame. Elsewhere in the Hill Country,[qv] Easter Fires were reputedly once lit on heights such as the one at Kreutzberg, eight miles east of Boerne in Kendall County, but the Fredericksburg celebration is the only surviving one. In recent times the Easter Fires have become a tourist attraction, complete with a pageant at the fairgrounds, but the custom originally was part of the local German folk tradition. The fires, dating from the first Easter celebration in 1847, are almost as old as the town itself. According to local tradition, the custom originated when Comanche Indian scouts lit signal fires in the night to communicate with their chiefs, who were negotiating a treaty with German leader John O. Meusebach[qv] many miles to the north, beyond the Llano River. The scouts presumably were informing their chiefs concerning the movements of the town's inhabitants. According to this tradition, the signal fires terrified some German children in Fredericksburg, prompting one imaginative mother to tell her children that the Easter Rabbit and his helpers had lit the fires to cook eggs before decorating and distributing them among the children on Easter morning. Many Fredericksburgers, therefore, believe the Easter Fires are an indigenous custom linked to the founding of their town. In reality, the Easter Fires have a much more ancient history. The people of northwestern Germany, especially in the provinces of Westphalia and Lower Saxony, practice an identical custom of lighting Easter-eve fires on specified hills. The practice originated in preChristian times as part of a spring festival and, along with the rabbit and egg, represents pagan customs that passed intact into Teutonic Christianity. The German provinces where Easter Fires occur contributed almost half of the settlers who came to the Texas Hill Country. The most likely agents of diffusion were Hanoverians, one of the two largest groups in early Fredericksburg. A second point, equally damaging to the signal-fire story, is that the Meusebach-Comanche negotiations (*see* MEUSEBACH-COMANCHE TREATY) occurred on March 1 and 2, 1847, while Easter eve in that year fell on April 3. Perhaps these two major events in Fredericksburg's first spring later merged in the popular mind, or possibly the initial Easter Fires frightened German children from Hesse or some other southern province where the custom was unknown. In any case, the Old World origin of the fires is incontestable.

BIBLIOGRAPHY: Francis Edward Abernethy and Dan Beaty, eds., *The Folklore of Texan Cultures* (Austin: Encino, 1974). Irene M. King, *John O. Meusebach, German Colonizer in Texas* (Austin: University of Texas Press, 1967).   Terry G. Jordan

EASTERLY, TEXAS. Easterly is on U.S. Highway 79 between Franklin and the county line in Robertson County. It developed in the 1870s under the name Acorn. Settlers moved from old Lake Station to escape the frequent fever epidemics that plagued that locale on Duck Creek. The first post office in Acorn opened in 1881 with Dan Easterly, Sr., as its postmaster; it operated until 1891. When the International–Great Northern Railroad established a small depot in the community, local residents decided to change the town's name to Easterly, for twin brothers Dan J. and John Easterly. The new post office opened in 1894, and its postmaster was Dan J. Easterly. The community grew slowly. A school was built on Jim Davlin's farm, and he was the first teacher there. Eventually the local school district was consolidated with that of Franklin. Several businesses opened, and the Baptists had established a church in Easterly by 1890. The community's population was reported as 700 in 1914. After World War I[qv] the community declined; by 1930 it had a population of 250 and seven businesses. In the 1960s its population was 200, and in 1990 the town had a population of sixty-one and two businesses.

BIBLIOGRAPHY: J. W. Baker, *History of Robertson County, Texas* (Franklin, Texas: Robertson County Historical Survey Committee, 1970).   James L. Hailey

EASTERN TEXAS FEMALE COLLEGE. Eastern Texas Female College was at the corner of Fannin and Charnwood streets in Tyler. It was originally the female department of Tyler University, which was founded in 1853 by the Cherokee Baptist Association, and was under the direction of G. C. Baggerly and his wife in 1855. Two years later fire destroyed the main building, and only the women's classes were conducted that year. The female department was renamed Eastern Texas Female College and also known as Tyler Female Seminary; it was one of two Baptist female seminaries in Smith County. The college consisted of a sizable two-room frame building for regular classes and a separate large building in the schoolyard for music lessons and practice. J. T. Hand became president in 1860, when the enrollment reached eighty-seven. Mary Spear, Mollie Moore, and B. R. Lignoski taught piano, guitar, harp, drawing, oil painting, and French, as well as the basic courses. School began at eight in the morning and ended at dusk. No expensive clothing or jewelry was allowed. An unsuccessful attempt was made in 1861 to transfer the school to the Eastern Baptist Convention. Heavy debts and poor enrollment caused the college to operate at a loss. A fire destroyed much of the facility in 1862, and Hand conducted classes in his home for over two years. In 1865 the regents leased the building and equipment to Hand, who continued to operate the school as Charnwood Institute.[qv]

BIBLIOGRAPHY: Vicki Betts, *Smith County, Texas, in the Civil War* (Tyler, Texas: Smith County Historical Society, 1978). Alice Douglas, ed., "Recollections of a Centenarian," *Chronicles of Smith County*, Spring 1966. Donald W. Whisenhunt, comp., *Chronological History of Smith County* (Tyler, Texas: Smith County Historical Society, 1983).   Claudia Hazlewood

EASTERN TEXAS RAILROAD. The Eastern Texas Railroad Company, an antebellum line, originated as the Henderson and Burkeville Railroad Company, chartered in 1852 to connect Burkeville in Newton County with Henderson in Rusk County. In 1853 the charter was changed to provide that the line run from the Gulf through Nacogdoches and Mount Enterprise. The charter was again amended in 1856, when the name was changed to the Mexican Gulf and Henderson Railroad Company. Construction began at Pine Island Bayou north of Beaumont, and 30½ miles was graded before a new company took over the project. In January 1860 the Eastern Texas Railroad was chartered to run from Sabine Pass to Henderson along the line graded by the Mexican Gulf and Henderson. Slaves were used to build the road. According to tradition a change from cornbread to wheat bread caused an epidemic among the slaves and held up the work until the crewmen could recover from their change of diet. In 1861 the line was in operation for twenty-five miles between Beaumont and Sabine Pass, and grading had been done north from Beaumont. During the Civil War[qv] the equipment was moved to Beaumont as a precaution against capture by federal troops, and in September 1863 Richard W. Dowling[qv] used some of the rails to fortify Fort Sabine. That year the Eastern Texas was abandoned. An unsuccessful effort was made to revive the project after the Civil War.

EASTERN TEXAS RAILROAD. The later Eastern Texas Railroad Company was chartered on November 8, 1900, to connect Lufkin in Angelina County with Crockett in Houston County. The capital stock was $150,000, and the principal place of business was Kennard. The members of the first board of directors were W. H. Carson and W. H. Welch, both of Texarkana; David Alexander Nunn^{qv} and D. A. Nunn, Jr., both of Crockett; and R. H. Keith, J. C. Sherwood, and W. C. Perry, of Kansas City, Missouri. The railroad was built by the Texas-Louisiana Lumber Company to serve its mill at Ratcliff. This mill was one of the largest in the South at that time. During 1901–02 the railroad built twenty miles of track from Lufkin to Kennard. On November 1, 1906, the Eastern Texas was sold to the St. Louis Southwestern, but continued to operate as a separate railroad. In 1916 the Eastern Texas reported passenger earnings of $9,000 and freight earnings of $48,000 and owned one car. The mill closed in 1917, and the Eastern Texas discontinued service on May 1, 1921. However, the line was not abandoned until 1924, as the State of Texas appealed to the United States Supreme Court the Interstate Commerce Commission decision authorizing the closure.
Nancy Beck Young

EASTERWOOD, WILLIAM EDWARD, JR. (1883–1940). William Edward (Colonel) Easterwood, Jr., philanthropist and aviation enthusiast, was born on November 5, 1883, at Wills Point, Texas, to William Edward and Mollie (Busby) Easterwood. He attended the public schools at Wills Point, began his business career as a newsboy, and later worked as a traveling factory representative. During World War I^{qv} he served in the United States Marine Corps as a private, saw action in France, and was discharged a captain. He moved to Wichita Falls in September 1920 and organized and managed the Wichita Falls Cooperative Supply Company. Though he was born to wealth, he made his own fortune in the chewing-gum business and other enterprises in the late 1920s. During the depression years his chewing-gum company made $3 million annually.

Easterwood adopted Dallas as his hometown and provided valuable public-relations services. For several years he served as the city's official greeter, and his world travels and unofficial position of "goodwill ambassador" did much to spotlight Dallas and Texas. He offered a $25,000 prize for the first one-stop flight from Paris to New York to Dallas, which was collected in 1930 by the French flyers Coste and Bellonte. He also offered prizes for Rome–Dallas and Dallas–Hong Kong flights, but they were never claimed. Easterwood was a director of the Dallas National Bank, vice president of Vanette Hosiery Mills, manager and director of the Easterwood estate, and an advisory board member of Southern Methodist University; he also chaired the city's aviation committee from 1935 to 1937.

He was instrumental in developing airports in a number of cities in the Southwest. The Mineral Wells airport was named for him. In his booklet *What Aviation Means to This Country* (ca. 1930) Easterwood proposed that commercial aviation be developed to provide a basis for a national aviation defense. He was a member of the Aeronautical Society of Paris, the International Aeronautical Association, the National Aeronautical Association, and the national advisory board of the American Air Cadets, which recognized him as the American who had done the most for United States civil aviation.

Easterwood served in 1933 as national vice commander of the American Legion,^{qv} organized the American Legion departments of Great Britain, Belgium, and Greece, was awarded the French Legion of Honor, and, on a trip to Italy, made Benito Mussolini an honorary member of the American Legion. He later denounced Mussolini when the Italian dictator joined Hitler's war against Britain and France. Easterwood was for a time vice president of the United States Marine Corps League. He received an American Legion national citation for his work on Americanism, national defense, and aviation. In 1939 he was awarded a special diploma at the San Francisco International Exposition as ambassador of goodwill for the state of Texas. Several state governors on whose staffs Easterwood worked conferred the title of "Colonel" on him.

Easterwood is credited with bringing the first talking movie to Texas. His favorite charities included both the National and Texas societies for Crippled Children and annual dinners for needy Dallas children and veterans at the Baker Hotel. He was a Mason and a Methodist. He married Mae Coker in November 1928, and they had no children. Suffering from a heart ailment, Easterwood moved with his wife to California about 1938 for his health. He died at Santa Monica on August 25, 1940, of a heart attack; his body was brought back to Dallas for burial.

BIBLIOGRAPHY: Dallas *Daily Times Herald*, August 26, 1940. Dallas *Morning News*, August 26, 1940. *Who Was Who in America*, Vol. 1.
Joan Jenkins Perez

EAST FORK OF THE ANGELINA RIVER. The East Fork of the Angelina River rises at the junction of Ham Creek, Double Tree Branch, and several other small streams, three miles northwest of Mount Enterprise in southern Rusk County (at 31°57′ N, 94°44′ W), and runs southwest for nineteen miles to its mouth on the Angelina River, near the Nacogdoches county line two miles southeast of Reklaw (at 31°51′ N, 94°56′ W). It traverses flat to rolling terrain surfaced by sandy and clay loam that supports water-tolerant hardwoods, conifers, and grasses.

EAST FORK OF HOWARD DRAW. The East Fork of Howard Draw, a valley with an intermittent stream, rises in north central Crockett County (at 31°03′ N, 101°19′ W) and runs southwest for twelve miles to its mouth on Howard Draw, two miles north of U.S. Highway 190 (at 30°56′ N, 101°23′ W). It dissects massive limestone and crosses an area varying from steep to gentle slopes to flat terrain with wash deposits of sand, gravel, and mud. Soils in the area are generally dark, calcareous stony clays and clay loams and support oaks, junipers, grasses, mesquites, scrub brush, and water-tolerant hardwoods and conifers.

EAST FORK OF THE SAN JACINTO RIVER. The East Fork of the San Jacinto River rises near Dodge in extreme eastern Walker County (at 30°45′ N, 95°24′ W) and flows southeast for sixty-nine miles through western San Jacinto, northwestern Liberty, and southeastern Montgomery counties to northeastern Harris County, where it joins the West Fork of the San Jacinto River in Lake Houston (at 30°03′ N, 95°08′ W). Its upper course is in Sam Houston National Forest.^{qv} The river traverses gently rolling to nearly level terrain surfaced by sandy, loamy, and clayey soils. Loblolly pine, sweet gum, shortleaf pine, water oak, elm, pecan, willow oak, black gum, post oak, and black hickory trees mantle the riverbanks. Tributaries of the fork include Mill, McCombs, Johnson, Negro, Sand, and Miller creeks.

The San Jacinto River formed the eastern boundary of Stephen F. Austin's^{qv} colony. Settlement on the lower East Fork began in the mid-1820s and on the upper course in the mid-1830s. In 1844 Sam Houston^{qv} constructed a plantation home known as Raven Hill on the east bank of the upper river in San Jacinto County. Coldspring, originally called Coonskin, was founded on the east bank of the river's middle course in the late 1840s and became the seat of San Jacinto County in 1870. After the Civil War,^{qv} Dodge was established near the headwaters of the East Fork in Walker County. In 1880 Cleveland, on the east bank of the lower river in Liberty County, was founded as a station on a new line of the Houston, East and West Texas Railway; Cleveland soon became a lumber-shipping center. Williams and Plum Grove are long-established communities on the west bank of the river's lower course in Liberty County. The San Jacinto County communities of Laurel Hill, Spring Hill, and Magnolia are situated on the west bank of the middle course of the river; New Hope is on the east bank. East River lies on the west bank of the lower river in Harris County; River Terrace is on the east bank near the mouth. Limited flow in the East Fork renders it significantly narrower and shallower than the West Fork and restrict its recreational uses.

BIBLIOGRAPHY: *An Analysis of Texas Waterways* (Austin: Texas Parks and Wildlife Department, 1974). Gene Kirkley, *A Guide to Texas Rivers and Streams* (Houston: Lone Star, 1983). Miriam Partlow, *Liberty, Liberty County, and the Atascosito District* (Austin: Pemberton, 1974).

EAST FORK OF THE TRINITY RIVER. The East Fork of the Trinity River rises 1½ miles northwest of Dorchester in south central Grayson County (at 33°32′ N, 96°41′ W) and runs south for eighty-five miles, across parts of five northeast Texas counties, to its mouth on the Trinity River, five miles northeast of Bristol in western Kaufman County (at 32°29′ N, 96°30′ W). The stream is intermittent in its extreme upper reaches. It crosses into Collin County seven miles southeast of Gunter. In Collin County it passes just east of McKinney and enters Lavon Lake five miles southeast of McKinney. The East Fork exits the reservoir two miles west of Lavon and then enters Lake Ray Hubbard. As part of the lake, it enters Rockwall County three miles northwest of Rockwall and subsequently crosses into Kaufman County. The stream traverses flat to rolling prairie with occasional steep slopes, surfaced by clays and sandy and clay loams that support oak, juniper, water-tolerant hardwoods, conifers, and grasses. The region has served as range and cropland, although urban development and local mineral production were present by the late 1900s. The nine tributaries of the East Fork include Stanley Creek, Hurricane Creek, and Long Creek.

EAST FORK OF WHITE ROCK CREEK. The East Fork of White Rock Creek rises two miles southeast of Arbor Grove in east central Houston County (at 31°17′ N, 95°14′ W) and flows southwest for 6½ miles to its mouth on White Rock Creek, two miles southeast of Shady Grove (at 31°13′ N, 95°18′ W). The stream flows through flat terrain surfaced by clay and sandy loam that supports water-tolerant hardwoods, conifers, and grasses.

EAST FRIO RIVER. The East Frio River, a spring-fed stream that is intermittent for much of its course, rises in southwestern Kerr County just north of the intersection of the Real, Kerr, and Bandera county lines (at 29°56′ N, 99°36′ W) and descends into the Frio canyon, winding southwest over a bed of limestone, gravel, and calcareous soil for more than twenty-two miles to its mouth on the West Frio River, just northeast of Leakey in Real County (at 29°44′ N, 99°45′ W). The surroundings are characteristic of the heavily dissected canyonlands of the Balcones Escarpment on the southern edge of the Edwards Plateau, forested with open stands of live oak, mesquite, and Ashe juniper. In Real County U.S. Highway 83 closely follows the eastern bank of this stream.

EASTGATE, TEXAS. Eastgate is near the junction of Farm roads 1960 and 686, thirty-three miles northeast of Houston in western Liberty County. According to local tradition, the community was named for its location at the east gate of the fence crossing the Beaumont, Sour Lake and Western Railway. The town plat was drawn up by J. C. Perry in 1911, but it was not filed until two years later. The post office operated from 1912 to 1925. During the mid-1950s Eastgate had a peak estimated population of sixty and three businesses. Churches and scattered buildings remained dispersed in the area, and Eastgate was still listed as a community in 1990.

BIBLIOGRAPHY: Miriam Partlow, *Liberty, Liberty County, and the Atascosito District* (Austin: Pemberton, 1974). *Robert Wooster*

EAST HAMILTON, TEXAS. East Hamilton (Hamilton, Port Hamilton) is on Farm Road 2261 twenty-three miles southeast of Center in southeastern Shelby County. Local sources suggest that the community, which was originally called Hamilton, may have been named for Alexander Hamilton. Some of the earliest Anglo settlement in the county occurred in the area. The first burial in the cemetery there is said to have been in 1812. In 1837 William Brittain built a log cabin to serve as a community church and school, and in March 1847 the settlement received the second United States post office established in the county, with Charles H. Alexander as postmaster. In 1874 the post office name was changed to East Hamilton because there was another town in the vicinity known as Hamilton. The settlement, originally located on the banks of the Sabine River in an area now inundated by Toledo Bend Reservoir, was sometimes called Port Hamilton, because it served as a port of call for steamers plying the Sabine. During the antebellum period, when it was probably at its peak, the community had at least five stores and a warehouse. After the Civil War,[qv] it began to decline as other forms of transportation, in particular the railroad, replaced the steamers. In 1899 East Hamilton was still located on the banks of the Sabine River, but by 1946 the focus of the community had shifted to its location on Farm Road 2261. In 1884 East Hamilton's population was fifty, and by 1896 it had dropped to twenty-five, where it remained through the 1930s. Its post office had closed by 1936. In the late 1980s East Hamilton had a church, a store, and widely scattered houses.

BIBLIOGRAPHY: Center *Champion*, August 14, 1952. Charles E. Tatum, *Shelby County: In the East Texas Hills* (Austin: Eakin, 1984). Marker Files, Texas Historical Commission, Austin. *Cecil Harper, Jr.*

EAST JIM NED CREEK. East Jim Ned Creek rises ten miles south of Abilene in east central Taylor County (at 32°14′ N, 99°44′ W) and runs five miles southwest to its mouth on Jim Ned Creek, three miles southeast of Tuscola (at 32°11′ N, 99°45′ W). It traverses flat to gently sloping terrain surfaced by shallow to moderately deep silt loams that support mesquite and grasses.

EAST KICKAPOO CREEK. East Kickapoo Creek rises in east central Concho County six miles northwest of Eden (at 31°15′ N, 99°55′ W) and flows twelve miles northwest, joining Middle Kickapoo Creek 9½ miles southwest of Paint Rock (at 31°23′ N, 99°59′ W). The stream crosses a terrain marked by steep slopes and benches, where a soil of thin clay loams supports grasses, live oaks, junipers, and mesquite.

EASTLAND, TEXAS. Eastland, the county seat of Eastland County, is at the intersection of State highways 6 and 69, northwest of Interstate Highway 80 on the Missouri Pacific Railroad in the central part of the county. In 1875 Jacamiah S. Daugherty and Charles U. Connellee[qv] purchased land on the C. S. Betts survey and platted a townsite. County voters opted to move the county seat from Merriman to the newly platted site, as it was closer to the center of the county, and the new community was named Eastland. Connellee, Daugherty, J. B. Ammerman, and others built a stone courthouse, and the county commissioners court held its first session in the town in September of 1875. By January of 1876 the population was estimated at 250. The first public school was taught in the community in 1877, and Methodist, Baptist, and Christian churches were soon organized. The city's growth was assured when, in 1880, the Texas and Pacific Railway was given a number of town lots to build through the community. Eastland Independent School District was established in 1882, and a second courthouse of red stone was constructed in 1883. By 1884 Eastland had three churches, a school, a flouring mill, two cotton gins, and an estimated 500 inhabitants. Among the early newspapers in the town were the *Anchor* and the *Chronicle*. Eastland was incorporated for the first time on June 6, 1891, with W. Q. Connellee as the first mayor and for the second time on April 6, 1897, with June Kimble as mayor. The second courthouse was destroyed by fire in 1896, and a third courthouse was built the following year. A horned lizard,[qv] later to become famous as "Old Rip," was supposedly placed in the cornerstone. When the third and final courthouse was erected in 1928, the cornerstone was opened, and the toad was found to have miraculously survived. Though many doubted the toad's authenticity, he (and eventually his remains) got quite a bit of state and even national publicity and became an important part of town and county lore. Eastland grew slowly in the first decades of the twentieth century, reaching 596 inhabitants in 1900 and 855 in 1910. By 1914 the community had two banks, telephone service, and a public library. The local economy was heavily dependent on cotton. Eastland County experienced a dramatic oil boom from 1917 to 1922, and the city of Eastland grew rapidly, though not as rapidly as other communities in the county, notably Ranger and Desdemona. Eastland population increased four-fold between 1910 and 1920, reaching 3,368 in 1920, though some estimates claim that there were as many as 10,000 people in the town during the height of the boom in 1919. The town's prosperity in the 1920s helped fund city improvements like the new courthouse, a new high school, and the paving of city streets. The community reached its peak census population in 1930 with 4,648 inhabitants. Thereafter the city began a slow decline, falling to 3,849 inhabitants in 1940, 3,606 in 1950, and 3,178 in 1970. The community experienced some small scale growth in the 1970s, as the number of businesses increased from 78 in 1972 to 154 in 1982, and the population increased to 3,747 in 1980. In 1990 Eastland had a population of 3,690. The local economy depended on county government, agribusiness, printing, and several manufacturing plants.

BIBLIOGRAPHY: Ruby Pearl Ghormley, *Eastland County, Texas: A Historical and Biographical Survey* (Austin: Rupegy, 1969). *The History of Eastland County, 1873–1973.*   Mark Odintz

EASTLAND, JAMES (1827–1911). James Eastland, soldier and legislator, was born on November 1, 1827, in Madison County, Alabama, the son of Alfred and Eliza Wright (Petty) Eastland. The family lived in Tennessee. Around 1843 he moved to Scott County, Mississippi, where he worked as a clerk. In December 1846 he enlisted in an army company there. In January 1847, after mustering into service, he sailed from New Orleans and arrived at the mouth of the Rio Grande for service in the Mexican War.qv He was a sergeant in the Army of the Rio Grande under Gen. Zachary Taylorqv and was discharged at Vicksburg at the end of the war. Afterward, he worked as superintendent of construction on the Vicksburg and Meridian Railroad near Brandon, Mississippi. In 1849–50 he was a clerk in a store in Westville. In 1850–51 he was a trader with Indians for Barrington and McAllister in Washington County, Arkansas. On October 30, 1856, Eastland married Emily Butler, daughter of Landon Carter and Elizabeth (Byrn) Butler.

The couple moved to Texas in a train of 100 wagons, settled in Pert in 1856, farmed, raised cattle, and operated a corn mill. Eastland taught at Flinn's Schoolhouse for five months. The Eastlands established Clear Springs Academy for their children and others of the community. In 1862 Eastland was made captain of Company F, Sixteenth Cavalry, Walker's Texas Division.qv The unit saw action in Louisiana and Arkansas. Bad health forced Eastland to resign in the winter of 1863, and he was discharged at Alexandria, Louisiana. In 1872 he was elected representative of Anderson County. He served in the House of Representatives of the Thirteenth Legislature and was reelected to the Fourteenth Legislature. The Eastlands had ten children. Eastland died on January 13, 1911, and is buried at Olive Branch Cemetery at Brushy Creek, Texas.

BIBLIOGRAPHY: *Pioneer Families of Anderson County prior to 1900* (Palestine, Texas: Anderson County Genealogical Society, 1984).
Martha Jeanne Laumen Surles

EASTLAND, WILLIAM MOSBY (1806–1843). William Mosby Eastland, soldier, was born in Woodford County, Kentucky, on March 21, 1806, the son of Thomas B. and Nancy (Mosby) Eastland. As a child he moved with his family to Tennessee, where he was reared and educated. As a young man he entered the timber business and was persuaded by his friend and former neighbor Edward Burlesonqv to move to Texas in 1834. With his wife and children, two brothers, and a cousin, Nicholas Mosby Dawson,qv he settled near the site of present La Grange in Fayette County. From July 25 to September 15, 1835, Eastland served as first lieutenant of a volunteer company under Col. John H. Mooreqv against the Waco and Tawakoni Indians, and from March 1 to May 30, 1836, he served under Capt. Thomas V. Alley.qv

Eastland was elected second lieutenant of Capt. Thomas J. Rabb'sqv Company F of Col. Edward Burleson's First Regiment, Texas Volunteers, on April 3, 1836, and advanced to first lieutenant when Rabb left the company and 1st Lt. W. J. E. Heardqv moved up to captain. At the battle of San Jacinto,qv according to Robert Hancock Hunter,qv when Sam Houstonqv ordered that the killing of Mexican fugitives cease and that his men begin to take prisoners, Eastland responded, "Boys take prisners, you know how to take prisners, take them with the but of guns, club guns, & said remember the Alamo remember Laberde [La Bahía], & club guns, right & left, & nock there brains out."

Eastland enlisted in the Texas Rangersqv on September 5, 1836, and on December 14, 1836, succeeded Capt. M. Andrew as commander, but when he attempted to instill military discipline in their ranks the men "marched out, stacked their arms, told him to go to hell and they would go home." According to Walter P. Webb,qv however, Eastland yielded gracefully, maintained the rangers' respect, and continued to serve until as late as January 22, 1838. In 1839 he was elected captain of one of the three companies that campaigned against the Comanches on the upper Colorado River.

Eastland's wife, the former Florence Yellowly, died in September 1837, and in 1839 he married Louisa M. M. Smith, the daughter of Wilford B. Smith, a Methodist minister. By 1840 he owned 5,535 acres under survey in Bastrop County and four town lots in Bastrop. On January 31, 1840, Eastland was elected one of three land commissioners for Fayette County.

In response to the raid of Adrián Wollqv in 1842, Eastland raised a company that he led to San Antonio; but he arrived too late to take part in the battle of Salado Creek.qv He participated in the pursuit, however. His company was incorporated into Col. James R. Cook's First Regiment, Second Brigade, of Gen. Alexander Somervell'sqv Army of the South West for the subsequent Somervell expedition.qv Eastland, eager for revenge for the killing of his cousin Nicholas Mosby Dawson and his nephew Robert Moore Eastland by Woll's men (*see* DAWSON MASSACRE), chose to remain on the Rio Grande with William S. Fisher'sqv command when Somervell ordered his expedition to return to San Antonio. Eastland was elected captain of Company B for the Mier expedition.qv He was taken captive with his men after the battle of Mierqv on December 26, 1842, and marched to the interior of Mexico. There he participated in the Texans' abortive escape attempt and was the first of the Texans to draw a fatal black bean, the only officer of the expedition to do so (*see* BLACK BEAN EPISODE). In a brief private interview with Fenton M. Gibsonqv Eastland said, "For my country I have offered all my earthly aspiration and for it I now lay down my life. I never have feared death nor do I now. For my unjustifiable execution I wish no revenge, but die in full confidence of the Christian faith." After giving his money to his brother-in-law, Robert Smith (who responded with the joyous shout that he had "made a raise!"), and sending word to his wife that "I die in the faith in which I have lived," Eastland was shot to death, on March 25, 1843. Diarist Israel Canfield, to whom Eastland was handcuffed on the march to Salado, observed with some satisfaction that Robert Smith later died at Perote Prison.qv

On February 17, 1844, the Texas Congress passed a bill for the relief of Eastland's family. In 1848 Eastland's remains, together with those of the other Mier victims, were moved to Monument Hillqv near La Grange for reinterment. Eastland was a cousin of the famed Confederate partisan ranger Col. John Singleton Mosby. His nephew, Charles Cooper Eastland, a private in Capt. Jacob Roberts's Company F of Col. John Coffee Hays'sqv First Regiment, Texas Mounted Rifles, died in Mexico City on December 20, 1847, during the Mexican War.qv

Another nephew, William Mosby Eastland II, was born on March 15, 1843, ten days before the death of his uncle at Salado. Eastland County is named in Eastland's honor.

BIBLIOGRAPHY: Clarksville *Northern Standard*, February 10, 1844. *Compiled Index to Elected and Appointed Officials of the Republic of Texas, 1835–1846* (Austin: State Archives, Texas State Library, 1981). Daughters of the Republic of Texas, *Muster Rolls of the Texas Revolution* (Austin, 1986). James M. Day, *Black Beans and Goose Quills: Literature of the Texas Mier Expedition* (Waco: Texian Press, 1970). Sam Houston Dixon and Louis Wiltz Kemp, *The Heroes of San Jacinto* (Houston: Anson Jones, 1932). Nicholas W. Eastland Collection, Barker Texas History Center, University of Texas at Austin. Joseph Milton Nance, *Attack and Counterattack: The Texas-Mexican Frontier, 1842* (Austin: University of Texas Press, 1964). Walter Prescott Webb, *The Texas Rangers* (Boston: Houghton Mifflin, 1935; rpt., Austin: University of Texas Press, 1982).

Thomas W. Cutrer

EASTLAND COUNTY. Eastland County (E-15) is in Central Texas, bordered on the east by Erath County, on the north by Stephens and Palo Pinto counties, on the west by Callahan County, and on the south by Brown and Comanche counties. The county's center is at 32°20′ north latitude and 98°50′ west longitude. The county was named for Capt. William Mosby Eastland,qv who died in the Texas Revolution.qv Eastland County covers about 952 square miles of the West Cross Timbers region of Texas; its hilly, rolling terrain ranges from 1200 to 1800 feet above sea level. Eastland, the county seat, is located on Interstate Highway 20 in the north central part of the county, some ninety-five miles west of Fort Worth and fifty-five miles east of Abilene. Most of the county is drained by the Leon River and its tributaries, though other parts drain into Battle Creek and Sandy Creek in the northwest, Palo Pinto Creek in the northeast, the Sabana River in the south, and tributaries of the Colorado River in the southwest. Soils vary from sandy to loamy. Trees found in the county include post oak, shin oak, walnut, pecan, cedar, and ash. The average annual rainfall is 27.09 inches, and the average temperature ranges from 32° F in winter to 96° in summer. The growing season averages 229 days.

Comanche, Kiowa, and other plains Indians visited the area now known as Eastland County in the years before white settlement, though the region was too heavily wooded for the extensive migration of buffaloqv into the area. The area was part of the Department of Bexar during Mexican Texas.qv In 1822, much of it became a part of Robertson's colony,qv and in 1831 the area was part of the empresarial grant from Mexico to Stephen F. Austin and Samuel May Williams.qqv Part of the area was included in the Peters colonyqv during the republic era.

The first Anglo presence in the region cannot be positively documented, but in 1837 W. A. A. (Big Foot) Wallaceqv might have entered what later became Eastland County with a surveying expedition. Among the first settlers in the county was Frank Sánchez, a Mexican American who arrived in the area in the 1850s. By 1858 residents included the families of John Flannegan (or Flannagan) from Kentucky, W. H. Mansker from Arkansas, W. C. McGough and James Ellison from Georgia, J. M. Ellison from Texas, and the Gilbert boys from Alabama. That year the Texas legislature formed Eastland County from land formerly assigned to Bosque, Coryell, and Travis counties; the county was attached to Palo Pinto County for judicial purposes.

McGough Springs, the first community in the county, was established before the Civil War;qv another, Mansker Lake (later named Alameda), was founded around 1859. Blair's Fort was built by C. C. Blair about 1860 and used for protection against Indian raids. In 1860, the census counted ninety-nine people living in the county, and the area's agricultural economy had only begun to develop. While the agricultural census enumerated 330 sheep, 1,075 milk cows, and almost 2,550 other cattle in the county that year, "improved" land comprised only 650 acres. Settlers were growing small plots of corn, beans, and sweet potatoes.

Due in part to its isolation from other settled areas and frequent trouble from raiding Indians, the county remained sparsely settled until the 1870s. Conflict between settlers and Kiowa and Comanche Indians became serious enough during the 1860s that a company of minutemen was organized to guard the frontier; the largest fight occurred at Ellison Springs in August 1864. Due to the dangers of settlement in the area, the county's population actually declined during the 1860s; in 1870 the census found only seventy-seven people living in Eastland County. Agriculture had also declined since the beginning of the Civil War. There were only five farms in the county in 1870, all of them smaller than twenty acres in size; only sixteen acres of improved land existed in the entire county.

When Indian raids ceased to present a problem in the early 1870s, however, settlers moved into the area in increasingly larger numbers. In early 1874 the Flannagan's Ranch headquarters, also called Merriman, was designated as the county seat. Through the efforts of Charles U. Connelleeqv and other promoters, an election was held in 1875, and the new town of Eastland was designated the county seat. By 1880 there were 549 farms in the county encompassing about 100,800 acres of land, including 23,423 improved acres. Corn was planted on 5,867 acres that year, and cotton on 3,264. Meanwhile, cattle ranching was also becoming important to the local economy. In 1870, the agricultural census reported only sixteen cattle in the county; by 1880 there were 23,423 counted in the area. And the county's rising population reflected the area's economic development: by 1880, 4,855 people were living in Eastland County.

By 1881 the Texas and Pacific and the Texas Central railroads had reached the county. A new town was organized at the intersection of the two railways when residents of Red Gap, a mile away, moved and renamed their town Cisco. An intense rivalry grew between Eastland and Cisco, and in August 1881 a second county-seat election took place; Eastland won by 354 to 324.

The railroads encouraged immigration and helped to open the area to commercial farming and trade. During the last twenty years of the nineteenth century the number of farms in Eastland County increased from 549 to 2,510, and numerous settlements were established, among them Ranger, Rising Star, Ellison Springs, Pioneer, Red Gap, Rustler, Howard, Jewell, New Hope, Tiffin, Chaney, Delmar, Morton Valley, Okra, Olden, Staff, Romney, Nimrod, Cardon, Scranton, Kokomo, Mangum, and Shin Oak Springs. These new towns helped to diversify the local economy and provided opportunities for a variety of professions: dry goods stores, livery stables, saddleries, boardinghouses, drugstores, real estate agencies, and one nursery were advertising in local newspapers by 1890. The population of the county more than tripled between 1880 and 1900, rising to 17,971 by the turn of the century.

Agricultural development in the county continued almost uninterrupted into the teens, and much of the county's growth during the late nineteenth and early twentieth centuries can be attributed to a boom in cotton production during this period. Land devoted to cotton steadily increased from 3,264 acres in 1880 to 15,348 in 1890 and 57,305 in 1900. By 1910 cotton was raised on 87,441 acres in Eastland County, and by that year the number of farms in the area had increased to 2,981. Probably as a result of a boll weevilqv infestation that hit the county at about this time, however, cotton production dropped off abruptly sometime between 1910 and 1916, thus crippling the local agricultural economy. By 1916 only 6,265 bales of cotton were ginned in the county, and by 1920, the fiber was grown on only 23,600 acres. Total farm acres in the county dropped from 420,137 in 1910 to only 279,405 in 1920; meanwhile, the number of farms in the area decreased to 1,499.

In 1917, just as the cotton boom was disappearing, a major discovery of oil occurred at Ranger, on land leased from the Texas and Pacific Coal and Oil Company by William K. Gordon.qv The discovery touched off a spectacular oil boom that lasted into the 1920s.

The county produced twenty-two million barrels in 1919, the peak year. Thousands of expectant workers and investors flocked into the county, among them George L. (Tex) Rickard,qv the boxing promoter, Jess Willard, the heavyweight champion, and novelist Rex Beach, who set his novel *Flowing Gold* in Ranger. For a time conditions were chaotic as new arrivals threw up shacks and tents faster than community services could handle them. Population figures reflected the boom: in 1910, 23,421 people lived in the county, but by 1920 the census reported 58,508 residents, placing Eastland County in tenth place among Texas counties. The oil boom also had the effect of encouraging railroads to build into the area. Earnings of the Texas and Pacific grew from $94,000 to $2,350,000 in 1918 and 1919. Circus man John Ringling built the Eastland, Wichita Falls and Gulf Railroad from Mangum to Breckwalker, while Ardmore, Oklahoma, promoter Jake L. Hamonqv extended his Wichita Falls, Ranger and Fort Worth to compete for the Ranger trade (see also RANGER, DESDEMONA, AND BRECKENRIDGE OILFIELDS).

The boom faltered after oil production tapered off after 1922, but fortunately the agricultural sector began to recover at about that same time, driven in part by an increase in cattle production and a brief and limited resurgence of cotton production during the early 1920s. The number of cattle in the county almost doubled (from 11,085 to 20,174) between 1920 and 1930, and cotton production increased to 7,195 bales in 1926. By 1925 the number of farms and ranches in the county had increased to 2,012, more than 25 percent more than the number for 1910. By 1929, however, the figure had dropped to 1,990. County population figures for the time reflect the decline of the oil boom and declining number of farms. By 1930, only 34,156 people lived in Eastland County.

Many residents of the county suffered during the Great Depressionqv of the 1930s, and though the number of farms in the area actually increased to 2,332 by the end of the decade, the population of the county decreased during the same period, to 30,345 in 1940. Cotton production almost ceased entirely during the 1930s, and by 1940 occupied only 2,111 acres in the county.

From the 1940s to the 1970s the mechanization of agriculture combined with other factors to continue depopulating the county. County population dropped to 23,942 in 1950, to 19,526 in 1960, and to 18,092 in 1970. It rose slightly during the 1970s to reach 19,480 in 1980; in 1992 an estimated 18,488 people lived in Eastland County.

Though the county's petroleum industry has never returned to the levels of production of the boom years of the 1920s, oil has continued to be important to the area's economy. The county produced more than 985,000 barrels of crude in 1938, 728,218 in 1944, 865,979 in 1956, 631,969 in 1960, 880,731 in 1978, 2,487,169 in 1982, and 1,106,053 in 1990. By January 1991, 149,206,256 barrels had been taken from county lands since 1917.

Much of the present economy of Eastland County is centered around agriculture. In the 1980s the county had 498,000 of its 609,000 acres in farms and ranches; of this some 17,000 acres was irrigated. Cattle ranching was the most important sector of the economy, however; in 1982 about 52,000 cattle were reported in the county. That year the county also reported 3,925 hogs, 3,452 goats, and 1,575 sheep. In 1982 Eastland County ranked fifth in the state for the production of peanuts, with 29,533,617 pounds reported, or 8 percent of the total state production. That year the county produced 103,016 bushels of sorghum and 72,135 bushels of wheat; 102,848 bushels of pecans and 13,473 bushels of peaches were also reported. In 1982, 1,597 businesses were reported in the county, employing about 5,000 people for annual wages of $65 million. The most important of these were agribusinesses, petroleum industries, and manufacture of steel tanks, clothing, portable buildings, and oilfield equipment.

Politically, Eastland County has had a mixed history. Until the 1950s, county voters supported the Democratic partyqv except during the 1890s, when People's partyqv candidates won locally. During the 1950s the county began consistently to support Republican candidates for president; in statewide races for governor and United States senator, however, the Democrats almost always won except in 1986, when Republicans carried the county in the gubernatorial race, and in 1972 and 1984, when Republican candidates for senator won.

The county is well situated near the metropolitan areas of Dallas and Fort Worth and served by major highways, including Interstate 20 from east to west and U.S. 183 from north to south. State highways 6, 16, 36, 69, and 206 also pass though Eastland County along with a network of farm-to-market and county roads. Communities in the county include Eastland, Cisco, Ranger, Gorman, Rising Star, and Carbon.

Eastland County has a number of cultural assets, including Cisco Junior College and Ranger Junior College. It also has several lakes and smaller reservoirs, including lakes Leon and Cisco, which offer recreational opportunities. The Eastland County Fair and parade are held each October, and there is a permanent religious diorama and an annual Easter pageant at the Kendrick Religious Amphitheater, between Cisco and Eastland.

The story of "Old Rip" helped to draw attention to the county during the 1920s. Old Rip was a horned lizard,qv placed in the cornerstone of the old Eastland County courthouse in 1897, that supposedly emerged alive when the block was reopened in 1928. The toad became something of a national sensation, toured many U.S. cities, and received a formal audience with President Calvin Coolidge; he eventually returned home and died of pneumonia. Old Rip is now on display in a glass and marble case at the Eastland County Courthouse.

BIBLIOGRAPHY: Edwin T. Cox, *History of Eastland County, Texas* (San Antonio: Naylor, 1950). Ruby Pearl Ghormley, *Eastland County, Texas: A Historical and Biographical Survey* (Austin: Rupegy, 1969). *The History of Eastland County, 1873–1973.* Carolyne Lavinia Langston, *History of Eastland County* (Dallas: Aldridge, 1904). *John Leffler*

EASTLAND, WICHITA FALLS AND GULF RAILROAD. The Eastland, Wichita Falls and Gulf Railroad Company was chartered on December 12, 1918, to lay track from May in Brown County to Newcastle in Young County, a distance of ninety-six miles. The capital was $500,000, and the business office was in Eastland. Members of the first board of directors included William B. Munson, Sr.,qv of Grayson County, Oscar B. Colquittqv and J. E. Butler of Dallas County, B. S. Walker and Fred W. Frost of Stephens County, and Earl Conner, J. H. Cheatham, H. P. Brelsford, C. U. Conner, and R. E. Sikes, all of Eastland County. The line was financed by Richard T. Ringling, of circus fame, and was known for a time as the Ringling, Eastern and Gulf Railway. The road was constructed during the height of the Ranger oil boom and started at Mangum, where it connected with the Missouri, Kansas and Texas Railway. By November 1920 twenty-eight miles had been completed to Breckwalker, where the road linked up with the Wichita Falls, Ranger, and Fort Worth Railroad. A connection was also made with the Texas and Pacific at Eastland. The line was never extended to Newcastle or May. Between June 1921 and March 1922 the Eastland, Wichita Falls and Gulf was leased to the Wichita Falls, Ranger and Fort Worth, but afterward it was operated independently with headquarters at Eastland. In 1926 the Eastland was listed as a Class III road by the Railroad Commission;qv the company owned three locomotives and three passenger cars and earned $1,241 in passenger revenue, $55,214 in freight revenue, and $408 in other revenue. Earnings for 1931 were $41,558. In the early 1940s Samuel Butler served as president of the line, which was abandoned in 1944 due to diminishing profits. *H. Allen Anderson*

EAST LIBERTY, TEXAS. East Liberty is on State Highway 87 fourteen miles southeast of Center in southeastern Shelby County. The predominantly black community received its name in 1888 when the Rev. Jeff Goodwin organized the East Liberty Baptist Church there.

The church and school community, located in an area populated mainly by landowning black farmers, also periodically had a general store. The first school in the settlement was called Chinquapin for a huge chinquapin tree that grew in the schoolyard. In 1899 the community's school served twenty children, and by 1938 the school was operated by the Boles school district and had 137 students. In 1965 East Liberty had a twelve-room school with sixteen teachers and an enrollment of 337. By 1984 the school had been consolidated with the Shelbyville school district, and its building, which maps for the mid-1980s showed as the only structure at the site, stood vacant.

BIBLIOGRAPHY: Charles E. Tatum, *Shelby County: In the East Texas Hills* (Austin: Eakin, 1984). *Cecil Harper, Jr.*

EAST LINE AND RED RIVER RAILROAD. Jefferson, on Big Cypress Bayou, was the principal port for freight moving into and out of northeastern Texas. It was the largest river port in the state and by 1870 was second only to Galveston in volume of traffic. However, the number of railroads projected and under construction threatened to divert the traffic away from Jefferson, and the East Line and Red River Railroad Company was promoted by William M. Harris, Benjamin H. Epperson,qv and other local businessmen in an effort to protect the town's trade area. The company was chartered on March 22, 1871, to run from Jefferson to Sherman and from there to the western boundary of the state. The route was somewhat nebulous and seemed to depend on the financial incentives offered by towns along the projected line. The charter was amended twice, in 1873 to change the route to run via Greenville and in 1875 to again run via Sherman. Construction began in 1876, and the first twenty miles to Hickory Hill opened on December 5. The company reached Daingerfield on July 4, 1877, Leesburg in 1878, and Sulphur Springs in 1879. Track reached Greenville, 124 miles from Jefferson, in late 1880. The promoters of the East Line and Red River built the company as a narrow gauge railroad, which later necessitated a costly change to standard gauge. The railroad was acquired by Jay Gouldqv in June 1881, who sold it to the Missouri, Kansas and Texas Railway Company (Katy) on November 28, 1881. In May 1882 the thirty-one mile extension from Greenville to McKinney was completed. Katy's right to own property in Texas was challenged by Texas Attorney General James Stephen Hoggqv through legal proceedings involving the East Line and Red River. Hogg was successful in the lower courts, and the decree declaring the charter of the East Line and Red River forfeited was upheld by the Supreme Court of Texas on February 17, 1890. William M. Giles was appointed receiver for the road effective April 13, 1891. Hogg claimed that this was the first time in the United States that a railroad charter was forfeited and a receiver appointed on application of a state. In 1891 the company owned eleven locomotives, ten passenger cars, and 252 freight cars and earned $62,027 in passenger revenue, $158,471 in freight revenue, and $1,939 in other revenue. The company was sold on January 21, 1892, to Simon Sterne representing Henry V. Poor who was trustee for the bondholders. However, the court at Austin refused to confirm the sale and directed Giles to stay in office and to issue $400,000 in receiver's certificates to convert the Greenville to Jefferson section to standard gauge. The 124 miles were converted on September 13, 1892. The line between Greenville and McKinney had been converted in 1887. The East Line and Red River was again sold to Poor on January 31, 1893, and by him deeded to the Sherman, Shreveport and Southern Railway Company on March 8, 1893. *George C. Werner*

EASTMAN, SETH (1808–1875). Seth Eastman, artist and career military officer, was born in Brunswick, Maine, on January 24, 1808, the first child of Robert and Sarah Lee Eastman. In 1824 he entered the United States Military Academy at West Point. There he received his first lessons in technical draftsmanship from the French miniature painter and engraver Thomas Gimbrede and honed his skills in drawing landscape, topography, and the human figure. He graduated twenty-second in his class and received his commission on July 1, 1829. His first assignment was to Fort Crawford at Prairie du Chien, Wisconsin. In 1830 he was transferred to Fort Snelling, Minnesota, where he was assigned to topographical duty. He returned to West Point in 1833 and held the position of assistant teacher of drawing until 1840. His *Treatise on Topographical Drawing*, published in 1837, was used as a textbook at West Point. During this time he studied landscape painting under Charles Robert Leslie and Robert W. Weir and became known as a minor painter of the Hudson River School. His landscape drawings show the influence of the romantic landscape style of early nineteenth-century Europe. Between 1836 and 1841 he exhibited his work at the National Academy of Design and the Apollo Gallery in New York City, and in 1838 the NAD presented him a diploma as an "Honorary Member Amateur." While at West Point Eastman met Mary Henderson, daughter of the assistant surgeon at the academy. They married in 1835 and had four boys and a girl.

In 1840 Eastman participated in the Seminole War, and produced a number of sketches of the Seminole Indians. He returned to Fort Snelling in 1841 and remained there until 1848. His interest piqued by his contact with the Seminoles in Florida, he made hundreds of pencil and watercolor studies and oils of the Indians of the area (chiefly Dakotas and Chippewas). His straightforward representations of Indians engaged in everyday activities—chasing buffalo, gathering wild rice, preparing skins for lodges and clothes—established his reputation as a chronicler of Indian life. His wife shared his interest in Indians and wrote several books, many of them illustrated by her husband, that contained Indian legends and descriptions of scenes around the fort.

Against his wishes, Eastman was ordered to Texas in 1848 to protect settlers against Indian raids and to help establish a line of frontier forts. He kept a detailed sketchbook of his journey down the Mississippi River and his tour of duty in Texas. He also kept a journal and map that record a march in August 1849 from the Leona River to San Antonio and then on to the Nueces River. The sketchbook consists of nearly 150 drawings; more than seventy are scenes of his journey down the Mississippi, and sixty-five are Texas scenes. Five drawings record the approach to Matagorda Bay and the landing at Indian Point, and ten illustrate the journey up the river valley to Seguin and San Antonio. His nine drawings of San Antonio include the most detailed and accurate scenes of the Alamo;qv missions San José, Concepción, and San Juan; the old San Fernando Church (now San Fernando de Bexar Cathedralqv); and overall views of the city from that period. Although he was primarily an Indian painter, in Texas Eastman was captivated by the Hill Countryqv landscape. In the fifteen sketchbook views of the two-year-old settlement of Fredericksburg, live oaks and the activities of the German colonists predominate. Indians appear in these sketches only occasionally as background figures. Other sketches include views of the Leona and Frio rivers, military camps in those areas, and various landscape scenes from around San Antonio. In addition to the sixty-five scenes of Texas in his sketchbook, Eastman did a number of watercolor sketches and at least one oil painting.

In 1849 he was sent to Washington, D.C., where he was commissioned to do the illustrations for Henry Rowe Schoolcraft's *Historical and Statistical Information Respecting the History, Condition and Prospects of the Indian Tribes of the United States*, published in six volumes between 1852 and 1857. In 1855 he was sent back to Texas to command regiments at Fort Duncan and Fort Chadbourne. Eastman is not known to have done any drawings or paintings during his second stay in Texas. During the early part of the Civil Warqv he served as mustering and disbursing officer for Maine and New Hampshire, and he became the military governor of Cincinnati, Ohio, in 1863. Later that year he was retired from active duty at the rank of lieutenant colonel. He was brevetted brigadier general in 1866 and in 1867 served on modified assignment in Washington, D.C., where he was commissioned to paint scenes of American Indians and United States forts for the Capitol.

Eastman died in Washington on August 31, 1875. In 1947 his great-granddaughter, Anna Jayne Moebs, approached San Antonio businessman and collector Paul Adams with the intent of selling Eastman's sketchbook. Adams arranged for B. B. McGimsey, general manager of the San Antonio Brewing Association, to purchase the sketchbook and later discovered and bought the accompanying journal in a New York City bookstore. The sketchbook was donated to the Marion Koogler McNay Art Museum[qv] by the Pearl Brewing Company of San Antonio; the journal remained in the possession of Paul Adams. Eastman's work is also included in the collections of the Witte Museum[qv] in San Antonio, the Peabody Museum of Archeology and Ethnology, and the James Jerome Hill Reference Library in St. Paul, Minnesota.

BIBLIOGRAPHY: John Francis McDermott, *Seth Eastman, Pictorial Historian of the Indian* (Norman: University of Oklahoma Press, 1961). John Francis McDermott, *Seth Eastman's Mississippi* (Chicago: University of Illinois Press, 1973). San Antonio *Express*, June 5, 1949. *A Seth Eastman Sketchbook* (Austin: University of Texas Press, 1961).

Rebecca H. Green

EASTMAN, TEXAS. Eastman was on the Sabine and East Texas Railroad north of Village Creek and forty-two miles north of Beaumont in northern Hardin County. The locale was named for the Eastman-Hyatt Lumber Company, which owned land and sawmill facilities there. A post office was established at the site in 1907. A lawsuit over proper land title in 1907 probably ruined the lumber company; tax rolls list the property as unrendered in 1907 and 1909. The local post office was subsequently discontinued. The site is near what is now the Village Mills community. *Robert Wooster*

EAST MATAGORDA BAY. East Matagorda Bay, off Matagorda County on the Texas coast (at 28°43′ N, 95°49′ W), is enclosed by the Matagorda Peninsula and the tidal flats at the mouth of the Colorado River. Its only opening to the Gulf of Mexico is through Brown Cedar Cut, near the north end of the peninsula.

EAST MAYFIELD, TEXAS. East Mayfield was in what is now the southwestern portion of Hemphill in central Sabine County. The community, named for Earle B. Mayfield,[qv] formed around the large lumber mill built there in 1912 by Hiram Knox of the Knox Lumber Company. The town was incorporated in January 1919, and in 1922 the lumber company was sold to the Temple Lumber Company. By 1930 the town had a population of 1,179, with most of the adult residents working for the lumber company. The timber on the company's land was rapidly depleted, and when the mill burned in 1937, it was not rebuilt. In 1939 the town was disincorporated, and gradually its residents moved away. Many became part of the Hemphill community.

BIBLIOGRAPHY: Robert Cecil McDaniel, *Sabine County, Texas* (Waco: Texian, 1987). Edna McDaniel White and Blanche Findley Toole, *Sabine County Historical Sketches and Genealogical Records* (Beaumont, 1972). *Cecil Harper, Jr.*

EAST MESA. East Mesa, bordered by Interstate Highway 10 on the south and U.S. Highway 385 on the west, is ten miles east of Fort Stockton in central Pecos County. Its summit (at 30°56′ N, 102°39′ W) reaches an elevation of 3,120 feet above sea level. The area terrain varies from flat with deep, dense local dissection to rolling, and the shallow stony soil supports juniper, oak, sparse grasses, and cacti.

EAST MILL CREEK. East Mill Creek rises near the Antioch Church in the Sand Flat community in north central Smith County (at 32°29′ N, 95°17′ W) and runs east for a mile to Lake Clear, through the lake for one mile, and then northeast for four miles to its mouth on the Sabine River, four miles north of Winona (at 32°32′ N, 95°11′ W). It traverses flat to rolling terrain with some local steep slopes, descending into low-lying floodplains at the mouth. The area soil is a sandy clay loam, occasionally covered by gravel or a fine light-colored sand, that supports pines, hardwoods, and grasses near the creek's source and water-tolerant vegetation at its mouth.

EAST MOUNTAIN, TEXAS. East Mountain is on Farm Road 1845 eleven miles southeast of Gilmer in southeastern Upshur County. It was established in the 1870s near a small rise named East Mountain. A local school began operating in the mid-1870s, and a Primitive Baptist church was organized around the same time. Sam Slater settled in the area in the late 1870s and built a horse-powered cotton gin; a short time later Thomas Wells built a steam cotton gin and sawmill. A post office under the name Savannah was opened in 1902 with H. B. Jones as postmaster. It was closed in 1905, and the name of the town was changed to East Mountain a short time later. Oil was discovered in the 1930s, and a number of local families quickly became wealthy. At the height of the oil boom the school and all of the town's churches had producing wells. By the mid-1930s East Mountain had a three-teacher school, three churches, a store, and a number of houses. In 1940 the estimated population was seventy-five. In the mid-1960s East Mountain had five churches, a large district school, and two cemeteries. In the 1980s the town served as a commercial center for area farmers and ranchers and as a bedroom community for nearby Longview. The population in 1990 was 762.

BIBLIOGRAPHY: G. H. Baird, *A Brief History of Upshur County* (Gilmer, Texas: Gilmer *Mirror*, 1946). Doyal T. Loyd, *History of Upshur County* (Waco: Texian Press, 1987). *Christopher Long*

EAST NAVIDAD RIVER. The East Navidad River rises at an elevation of 455 feet above sea level in a series of tanks a mile south of O'Quinn in south central Fayette County (at 29°49′ N, 96°58′ W) and runs southeast for twenty-three miles to a point where it joins the West Navidad River to form the Navidad River, just above Oakland in Colorado County (at 29°36′ N, 96°50′ W). For a portion of its route before its confluence with the West Navidad River, it forms the boundary between Colorado and Lavaca counties. The area is flat with some low-rolling hills, surfaced by firm calcareous clay layers extending to a depth of some fifty inches. On uplands these soils are fair for agriculture and pasture. The low-lying areas are subject to frequent flooding. Vegetation along the stream is a mixture of oak, pecan, and sycamore with an understory of cedar, yaupon, and wild grape. It is an excellent area for wildlife.

EASTON, TEXAS. Easton is on Farm Road 2906 ten miles southeast of Longview in extreme southeastern Gregg County and northeastern Rusk County. Most of the site, first known as Walling's Ferry and then as Camden, is near a bluff on the south bank of the Sabine River. In 1885 the Texas, Sabine Valley and Northwestern Railway built a line through the area, and by the late 1880s a large sawmill was in operation there. In 1890 Easton reported the Buchanan and Company general store, a lumber and shingle plant, and a population of seventy-five. The community declined, and most of the remaining white inhabitants moved to Longview or other towns. By 1940 Easton was a predominantly black community with one business and a population of fifty. It revived in the 1940s with the development of oilfields in the area. In March 1949 a post office was again established, after which the town soon incorporated. The incorporated area straddled the Gregg-Rusk county line. Easton had 297 residents in 1970 and 401 in 1990.

BIBLIOGRAPHY: *Houston Chronicle Magazine*, July 13, 1952.

Norman W. Black

EAST PINEY CREEK. East Piney Creek, which is intermittent in its upper reaches, rises 4½ miles north of Mount Pleasant in central Titus County (at 33°14′ N, 95°00′ W) and runs north for seven miles to its mouth on White Oak Creek, three miles southwest of Wilkinson (at 33°18′ N, 94°59′ W). The stream passes through gently undulating to rolling terrain, surfaced by sandy soils along its upper reaches and loams through its middle and lower reaches. The area is heavily wooded, with pines and various hardwoods predominating.

EAST POINT, TEXAS. East Point is at the intersection of Farm roads 312 and 2088, eight miles east of Quitman in east central Wood County. The community, said to have been named for its place on the east point of an earlier settlement, was settled near Stout's Creek as early as the 1870s. In 1893 the East Point Missionary Baptist Church was organized with help from members of the nearby Little Hope church. By 1896 East Point's one-teacher school had eighty-six students; in 1905 that number had fallen to sixty. In 1932 the East Point school had 103 white students in ten grades and twenty black students in seven grades. By the mid-1930s the community had a church, a business, and twenty-five residents; the population was reported at that level until the mid-1940s, after which no figures are available. A 1988 map indicated a church and a business at the site. East Point still existed in 1990.

BIBLIOGRAPHY: Marker Files, Texas Historical Commission, Austin (Little Hope Missionary Baptist Church). *Rachel Jenkins*

EAST PRONG OF THE NUECES RIVER. The East Prong of the Nueces River, a spring-fed stream that is intermittent in its upper reaches, rises in eastern Edwards County on the southern edge of the Edwards Plateau (at 30°04′ N, 99°57′ W) and descends from the plateau into the sharply dissected canyonlands of the Balcones Escarpment, running 14½ miles over a bed of limestone, gravel, and calcareous soil to its mouth on Hackberry Creek (at 29°56′ N, 100°01′ W). The surroundings, forested with open stands of live oak, mesquite, and Ashe juniper, are typical of the escarpment. The East Prong of the Nueces crosses into Real County immediately below its source, eventually crossing back into Edwards County and joining Hackberry Creek just west of the county line. This stream flows on to join the West Nueces River to the south in Uvalde County, west of the city of Uvalde.

EAST SANDY CREEK (Colorado County). East Sandy Creek includes the East and West forks of East Sandy Creek, which join five miles northwest of Rock Island in southern Colorado County (at 29°30′ N, 96°48′ W). The creek runs south for 9½ miles to its mouth on Middle Sandy Creek, three miles southwest of Rock Island (at 29°26′ N, 96°50′ W). The stream traverses the Sheridan gas field and crosses Alternate U.S. Highway 90 in a heavily wooded area of mixed oak and yaupon known locally as "the post oaks." The area soils consist of deep layers of fine sandy loam overlying beds of mottled clay. The local terrain is generally flat to rolling, but the stream's banks are often quite steep and eroded, and its course is filled with deposits of finely washed sand. The area is used primarily for the production of oil and gas, as unimproved pasture for cattle, and as a wildlife habitat which attracts hunters from a wide area.

_____ (Eastland County). East Sandy Creek rises seven miles northeast of Cisco in northern Eastland County (at 32°27′ N, 98°53′ W) and runs northwest for eight miles to join Sandy Creek and form Big Sandy Creek, sixteen miles southwest of Breckenridge in southern Stephens County (at 32°32′ N, 98°57′ W). In its upper reaches it traverses an area of rolling hills, surfaced by clay and sandy loams that support scrub brush, mesquite, cacti, live oak, juniper, and grasses. In the creek's lower reaches a flat, flood-prone area with local shallow depressions is surfaced by clay and sandy loams that support water-tolerant hardwoods, conifers, and grasses.

_____ (Walker County). East Sandy Creek, a perennial stream, rises two miles north of New Waverly in southern Walker County (at 30°35′ N, 95°29′ W) and flows west for eleven miles to its mouth on Lake Conroe, near the Montgomery county line (at 30°33′ N, 95°37′ W). The stream lies within the boundary of the Sam Houston National Forest.[qv] It traverses gently rolling to sloping terrain surfaced by sandy and loamy soils that support woods of loblolly pine, shortleaf pine, sweetgum, water oak, elm, pecan, post oak, black hickory, willow oak, and blackgum along its banks. Settlement in the vicinity began in the early 1830s. The Moore's Grove and East Sandy communities were both established on the south bank of the middle creek during the 1850s.

EAST SWEDEN, TEXAS. East Sweden, also known as New Sweden or Sweden, is just off U.S. Highway 190 and 5½ miles northeast of Brady in east central McCulloch County. In the spring of 1885 Swen Leander Hurd, Carl August Johnson, and Daniel August Hurd of Round Rock inspected open land in McCulloch County, and each purchased a half section. In the fall of 1886 Swen L. Hurd moved his family to the new settlement, and in 1888 four other families arrived. Other immigrants came from Sweden in 1889, when the settlement had twelve households and about sixty-three residents. Homes were built with the help of A. M. Sanquest, a carpenter, and C. G. Thornbloom, a stonemason, of lumber brought from Brownwood by wagon. In the absence of a regular minister, Thornbloom held Lutheran Sunday services in homes and outside under the trees during summer. In 1890 J. A. Irvine, a Presbyterian minister from Mason, held services at Sweden once and sometimes twice a month. After discussion, the group decided to become Presbyterian, believing that no Lutheran minister would ever join the settlement, and in 1891 the Sweden Presbyterian Church was organized by Reverend Irvine and Dr. W. G. Little of Denison; Irvine became the full-time pastor. In 1892 landowners Swen Hurd, Carl C. Johanson, Carl Johnson, and C. G. Olson each donated an acre of land for a church school and the East Sweden Cemetery, where most early settlers were buried. Other settlers donated money and labor; the first church building was completed in 1892. In 1903 the St. Louis–San Francisco Railway built a track to the west of the settlement, and in 1912 the Santa Fe built to the east. Paul Junction was built at the intersection of the tracks.

In 1905 and 1906 Rev. Ernest Severin, a Swedish Methodist from Austin, started a Swedish settlement west of Brady where Rev. Abner Hanson organized a Swedish Methodist church and Hanson School was later founded. For a time both East and West Sweden settlements existed, but West Sweden eventually disappeared. The East Sweden church, destroyed by wind on June 14, 1916, was rebuilt in 1920. The three-room wooden school building was destroyed by fire in 1933 and rebuilt in 1934. The school was later consolidated with the Rochelle Independent School District. Cattle and sheep were raised locally, and two dairies operated in the community for a time, but cotton and later wheat and oats were the settlers' primary cash crops. A local cotton gin, owned by Swen L. Hurd, was later moved to Salt Gap. In 1936 state highway maps showed the church, a school, a cemetery, and scattered dwellings at the townsite. A monument listing the names of early Swedish settlers, dedicated on May 10, 1973, stands east of the schoolhouse, and in May 1976 residents buried a time capsule just south of the monument. A historical marker was placed at the East Sweden Presbyterian Church in 1989. The annual homecoming in August is attended by about 100 people. *See also* SWEDES.

BIBLIOGRAPHY: Wayne Spiller, comp., *Handbook of McCulloch County History* (Vol. 1, Seagraves, Texas: Pioneer, 1976; vol. 2, Canyon, Texas: Staked Plains Press, 1986). *Louise Hurd McWilliams*

EAST TAWAKONI, TEXAS. East Tawakoni is on State Highway 35 nine miles west of Emory in western Rains County. It was founded in the 1960s as a residential community on newly built Lake Tawakoni.

In 1970 the reported population was 278; by 1991 the settlement had grown to 433 residents.   *Christopher Long*

EAST TEMPE, TEXAS. East Tempe is on Farm Road 350 seventy-five miles north of Houston in west central Polk County. The settlement was named after East Tempe Creek, a stream that cuts through the area. Settlers were farming the surrounding lands by 1860; some twenty years later a sawmill had been erected. Further development came in 1908 at the completion of the Beaumont and Great Northern Railway, which connected East Tempe with Trinity to the north and Livingston to the southeast. East Tempe became a flag stop on the railroad. Although the railroad was abandoned in 1949, East Tempe remains an outlying community of Livingston. In 1990 the population was estimated at 100.

BIBLIOGRAPHY: *A Pictorial History of Polk County, Texas, 1846–1910* (Livingston, Texas: Polk County Bicentennial Commission, 1976; rev. ed. 1978). Charles P. Zlatkovich, *Texas Railroads* (Austin: University of Texas Bureau of Business Research, 1981).   *Robert Wooster*

EAST TEXAS. The East Texas area, which might be considered as the humid portion of the central dissected belt of the Coastal Plains of the United States, comprises the Sabine Uplift area, the East Texas basin, and the rolling plains southward as far as the coastal prairies. These areas may be separated from the rest of Texas roughly by a line extending from the Red River in north central Lamar County southwestward to east central Limestone County and then southeastward to Galveston Bay. Most of East Texas is forested, and except the post oak plains, the majority of the forests belong to the mixed type of shortleaf pine and hardwoods. Southward, however, along the southern margin of the dissected plains, a tongue of longleaf pines extends into Texas from Louisiana. The longleaf portion of East Texas is an area of deep sands underlain at a depth of several feet by well-drained sandy clays. Still farther south, extending into the edges of the flat coastal country east of Houston, is a forested area composed of an admixture of loblolly pines and water-tolerant oaks. The broad lowlands paralleling the larger streams that flow across East Texas are characterized by a heavy growth of hardwood forests (*see* LUMBER INDUSTRY). Most of the upland soils of the central dissected belt of East Texas are highly leached. The majority of the soils have yellow subsoils, the surface soils being grayish in aspect. Red soils occur in exceptional areas, such as on slopes underlain by calcareous materials; such soils may be red from the surface downward to the unoxidized parent materials. The Sabine Uplift district is a mixed forest area underlain by sandy clays. Geologically it is a domal area, and its structural relations are important to the accumulation of oil and gas. The large Panola gas field is situated in the Texas portion of the uplift. The East Texas basin overlies a syncline that is, in a structural sense, a complementary feature to the Sabine Uplift. This district comprises the redlands hilly country of East Texas lying west and north of the Sabine Uplift and the post oak plains district between the redlands hilly country and the black prairies. The post oak plains district is a dissected area underlain in part by glauconitic beds together with limy materials. The flat tops of the hills overlooking the wide intervening rolling lowlands apparently are remnants of a former plains surface, held up by a caprock of iron-ore beds that margin these hills, forming a layer resistant to erosion. The intervening lowlands are underlain by sandy clays. Where underlain by greensand marls, the soils are usually red in color, some of them being the deepest red of all soils found in the United States (*see* SOILS). One of the most important oil regions of the nation, the East Texas basin, includes the gigantic East Texas oilfield,qv the interior salt dome fields, of which the Van fieldqv is the largest, together with the fault line fields—the Mexia and Powell oilfields—on the western margin of the basin, as well as Talco and Sulphur Bluff along the northern margin of the basin. On the northern margin of the Sabine Uplift is the Rodessa oilfieldqv that continues northeastward through the corner of northwest Louisiana into southwestern Arkansas. The Hawkins pool in Wood County is also in the East Texas basin. All of the production in the East Texas basin is from the Cretaceous except for a small amount from the Jurassic near the Louisiana line. The large production, including that from the East Texas field and most of that from Van, is from the Woodbine sand, the basal beds of the Upper Cretaceous, which outcrop to the westward in the Eastern (or Lower) Cross Timbers.

BIBLIOGRAPHY: William Bollaert, *Observations on the Geography of Texas* (London, 1850). Zachary Taylor Fulmore, *The Geography of Texas* (n.p.: Rand, McNally, 1908). Terry Jordan, *Texas: A Geography* (Boulder, Colorado: Westview Press, 1984). Frederic William Simonds, *Geographic Influences in the Development of Texas* (Austin: Journal of Geography, 1912). H. D. Wang, "Ferrihydrite, Lepidocrocite, and Goethite in Coatings from East Texas Vertic Soils," *Soil Science Society of America* 57 (September–October 1993).
                                                                                    E. H. Johnson

EAST TEXAS BAPTIST INSTITUTE. East Texas Baptist Institute, at Rusk, was chartered on July 18, 1895, and opened in a three-story brick building on September 2, 1895, with seven teachers, 142 pupils, and a debt of $9,000. The institution had been discussed at the 1892 meeting of the Cherokee Baptist Association, but a provisional board was not formed until January 24, 1894. The association accepted the property donated by Mrs. Georgia Anna Bonner at its meeting in October 1894. J. H. Richardson was appointed the first president and J. H. Thorn the first business manager. Richardson resigned in 1897 due to illness and was succeeded by E. H. Wells, who served as president for the remainder of the school term and was succeeded by J. V. Vermillion. A disagreement arose between the Cherokee Association and the fourteen-member board of trustees in 1898 over action by the board to organize as an independent entity. The association named a new board and requested the previous board to return all titles to the association. At its meeting in 1899, the association failed to resolve the issue, with the result that East Texas Baptist Institute became a part of the Texas Baptist Correlated System and a new school, Jacksonville College, was organized by the Eastern Texas Educational Society.

Subsequently, East Texas Baptist Institute became Rusk Academy and in 1918 Rusk Junior College. When a new Cherokee Association of Baptist Churches organized on November 8, 1915, it supported the college as "the Baptist School for Southeast Texas." Between 1915 and 1928 the enrollment never exceeded 300, and deficits continued to accumulate. A succession of presidents was unable to rescue the failing institution. In 1927 the Baptist General Convention of Texas attempted to salvage the college by challenging the city of Rusk to raise $25,000 and offering to refinance the college debt and subsidize the office of the president for three years. The effort was to no avail, and in April 1928 President L. J. Mims announced to the executive board of the Baptist General Convention that Rusk Junior College would close at the end of the school term because of insurmountable debts.

BIBLIOGRAPHY: *Annual of the Baptist General Convention of Texas*, 1927, 1928. *Baptist Standard*, April 12, 26, 1928. James Milton Carroll, *A History of Texas Baptists* (Dallas: Baptist Standard, 1923).
                                                                                    C. Gwin Morris

EAST TEXAS BAPTIST UNIVERSITY. East Texas Baptist University originated as the College of Marshall, chartered in 1912 as a result of the work of W. T. Tardy. The charter was amended later to conform to requirements of the Education Board of the Baptist General Convention. In 1913 Thurman C. Gardner became the first president of the college. The first building was completed in 1916, and the institution opened as a junior college in the summer of 1917. By action of the board of trustees on January 31, 1944, the name was changed to East Texas Baptist College and the institution was reorganized as a four-year school. In 1945 the first eight baccalaureate degrees were granted. In 1949 the plant consisted of seven buildings on a campus of 100 acres. Enrollment was 643.

In 1972 the school received accreditation from the Southern Association of Colleges and Secondary Schools; it offered a program of teacher education as well as a four-year liberal-arts curriculum. Assets of the institution in 1965 stood at $5,388,664, which included $1,113,541 in endowment and annuity funds, in addition to a plant of eleven permanent buildings on a 100-acre campus. The operating budget was more than $900,000 in 1965. The library held more than 65,000 volumes in 1969. Student enrollment was 771 during the regular session of 1974–75. The Baptist General Convention approved organizing the college as a university in November 1982 and in 1984 renamed it East Texas Baptist University. ETBU is an undergraduate university with a background in liberal arts and Christian teaching.

In 1991 the school was accredited by the Association of Southern Baptist Colleges and Schools, the Association of Texas Colleges and Universities,qv the Independent Colleges and Universities of Texas, the National Association of Schools of Music, the Southern Association of Colleges and Schools, the Texas Association of Colleges for Teacher Education, the Texas Association of Music Schools, and the Texas Education Agency.qv It is affiliated with the Baptist General Convention of Texas and operated by a board of trustees. As of 1991 the school had had thirteen presidents, including Frank Shelby Groner qv (1928–42) and Harvey Daniel Bruce (1942–60), the two executives with the longest tenure. In 1991 ETBU offered nine associate and bachelor's degrees. The regular faculty numbered fifty-five and the adjunct faculty thirty-five. That year the campus was on a 193-acre site and had twenty-two buildings.

Nancy Beck Young

EAST TEXAS CHAMBER OF COMMERCE. The East Texas Chamber of Commerce, an organization of businessmen representing every type and size of business in East Texas, was founded in 1926 in Longview, where its home office is still located. The chamber is governed by a board of directors with a president elected annually. An executive vice president and a staff are employed to manage the business of the organization. The organization serves seventy-one East Texas counties as well as Caddo Parish, Louisiana, all located in the area between the Red River and the Gulf of Mexico and extending from Shreveport, Louisiana, in the east to Dallas, Austin, and Houston on its western edge. The region is divided into six districts and includes the metropolitan areas of Houston, Dallas, and Austin, as well as Shreveport, Louisiana. The East Texas Chamber of Commerce has long held the distinction of being the largest regional chamber of commerce in the South.

It was originally organized for the purpose of encouraging and aiding agricultural and industrial expansion, but later expanded its work to include various other programs. The agricultural program was effective in bringing about crop improvement and diversification, in developing industrial uses for crops, in encouraging dairying and poultry production, and in land utilization, soil conservation, and pasture improvement. The East Texas Chamber forestry program has included soil conservation through fire control, selective cutting, dedication of submarginal land to timber growing, and programs of replanting.

Industrial development has been a major program of the chamber, and for many years its industrial research centered on processing mineral wealth, forest products, and farm crops. However, the organization has directed much activity in the last twenty-five years to bringing new industries and businesses into the area. The chamber publishes an annual industrial guide, the *East Texas Story,* which is a comprehensive study of the region with valuable data for prospective businesses. The industrial emphasis has also included industrial-relations seminars and annual industrial tours that have been effective. A program to encourage international trade was initiated in 1953.

The East Texas Chamber of Commerce has taken an active part in keeping taxpayers informed of the facts of public finance, from national problems to those of local school districts, through a tax letter and other media. On both the state and national levels, the chamber has made efforts to aid communication between citizens and legislators through specially arranged meetings as well as published materials. The *Public Affairs Bulletin* was published until 1972, when it was replaced by a regular page in *East Texas,* the monthly magazine publication of the chamber. In addition to this, special legislative reports are distributed regularly so that recipients may keep up with the status of various bills.

One of the most active programs of the East Texas Chamber of Commerce is tourist development. This program, begun in 1963, has had a part in making tourism one of the thriving industries of East Texas through tourist conferences, exhibits, and publications. To promote the East Texas Heritage Trail and many other area attractions, the chamber publishes annually the *East Texas Vacation Guide and Fun Map.* A new program of marketing East Texas bus tours was begun in 1984.

The organization has also been actively involved in various programs that have benefited the communities of East Texas. The struggle for an adequate highway system paid for by the users instead of local property owners was an emphasis of the chamber, as were such activities as the malaria-control campaign, the drive for the Standard Milk Ordinance, and the fight for proration to conserve oil. The chamber has also helped communities by leading them to evaluate and develop their assets and by training their potential leaders. This organization also pioneered in citizenship and career conferences for young people and continues its emphasis on the need for education and business to work together for greater effectiveness. In the early 1980s the East Texas Chamber of Commerce took a leadership role in the East Texas 2000 Project, a part of the larger Texas 2000 Project commissioned by the governor in 1980 for the purpose of identifying and forecasting changes in the state's population, natural resources, economy, and service infrastructure over the next twenty years, developing and analyzing alternative state policy responses, and proposing solutions to long-range problems. As a result of the East Texas 2000 Project, the East Texas Chamber of Commerce published a comprehensive document made up of discussion papers dealing with population, transportation, agribusiness, economics, energy, government finance, relations with Mexico, research and development, and water. Participation in this project exemplifies the role that the East Texas Chamber of Commerce has maintained since its beginning.

BIBLIOGRAPHY: Betty C. Berry, An Updated History of the East Texas Chamber of Commerce (M.A. thesis, Stephen F. Austin State University, 1976). *East Texas 2000* (Longview, Texas: East Texas Chamber of Commerce Educational Foundation, n.d.). Howard Rosser, ed., *The First Fifty Years: A History of the East Texas Chamber of Commerce* (Longview, Texas: *East Texas Magazine,* 1976).

Betty C. Berry

EAST TEXAS AND GULF RAILWAY. The East Texas and Gulf Railway Company was chartered on August 1, 1917, to serve the interests of the Loderick Lumber Company. The capital was $20,000, and the principal office was in Hicksbaugh. The members of the first board of directors were S. B. Hicks and J. T. Wurtsbaugh, both of Shreveport, Louisiana: W. F. Johnson of Natchitoches, Louisiana; J. P. Wurtsbaugh, E. M. Lewis, and C. V. McGee, all of Dyersdale; and E. R. Campbell of Houston. In October 1917 the East Texas and Gulf completed 3.9 miles between Hyatt, where it connected with the Texas and New Orleans, to Hicksbaugh. The railroad also operated over the logging track of the Loderick Lumber Company from Hicksbaugh to Wurtsbaugh, while the lumber company also ran log trains over the East Texas and Gulf. In 1923 the physical valuation ascertained by the Railroad Commissionqv was $61,842. In 1926 the East

Texas and Gulf reported passenger earnings of $700 and freight earnings of $19,000 and owned two locomotives and two cars. The mill at Hicksbaugh closed in 1928, and the railroad was abandoned in 1934.

Megan Biesele

EAST TEXAS HISTORICAL ASSOCIATION. The first East Texas Historical Association began when W. F. Garner, chairman of the Department of History at Stephen F. Austin State Teachers College, invited members of his faculty and of the faculties at Sam Houston State Teachers College and East Texas State Teachers College to form an organization to promote the study of East Texas history. The group met in Nacogdoches from April 20 to 30, 1927, and annually thereafter on college campuses in Huntsville, Commerce, and Nacogdoches, until it disbanded because of the Great Depression[qv] in 1932. An annual issue of papers read at the meetings was also published. Historical papers were read at its meetings by such historians as Eugene C. Barker[qv] of the University of Texas, Martha Emmons of Nacogdoches High School and later Baylor College, and the Rev. George L. Crocket,[qv] who served as the first president of the association.

In 1962 a successor East Texas Historical Association came into being as a result of the work of Ralph W. Steen[qv] and C. K. Chamberlain, respectively president and history-department chairman at Stephen F. Austin State College, and attorneys F. I. Tucker of Nacogdoches and F. Lee Lawrence of Tyler. Lay and professional historians in East Texas received invitations to a meeting held on the SFA campus in Nacogdoches on September 29, 1962. They wrote a new constitution (revised in 1981), calling for an annual meeting each fall in Nacogdoches and a spring meeting elsewhere in East Texas; the publication of a semiannual publication, the *East Texas Historical Journal;* and the collection and deposit of archival material in the library at Stephen F. Austin State College. Lawrence served as the first president, and Chamberlain became editor of the journal, a post he held until 1971. Because charter membership was left open for many months, the association claims 425 charter members. Its officers are alternately lay and professional historians. In addition to a president, first and second vice presidents, and a secretary-treasurer, seven members serve alternating three-year terms on the board of directors; Stephen F. Austin State University appoints two ex officio members; in the early 1990s Lawrence was director emeritus.

Chamberlain was succeeded by Archie P. McDonald, who served as executive director, a position established in 1979, and editor of the journal and other association publications. The association meets on the campus of Stephen F. Austin State University in Nacogdoches and continues to publish two issues of its journal annually. Membership and attendance at meetings declined late in the 1960s, but subsequently rebounded; in 1991 it stood at 550, and registrations at meetings varied from 100 to 150, depending on the location of the spring meeting.

After 1971 the association established new programs to encourage the study of East Texas history and to honor those who do so. The C. K. Chamberlain Award is given for the year's best article in the *Journal;* up to fifteen fellows are honored for writings on the history of East Texas; the Ralph W. Steen Award honors those who have served the association primarily through activities other than writing; the Lucille Terry Historical Preservation Award, also sponsored by the Texas Forestry Museum, honors outstanding works of historical preservation; and the Ottis Lock Endowment supports awards for outstanding teaching, for the year's best book on East Texas, for an annual scholarship to a student attending an institution in East Texas, and for research grants in the study of East Texas history. In 1991 F. Lee Lawrence, with a generous donation to be matched by other members, challenged the membership to a fund-raising effort to establish a continuing endowment. The East Texas Historical Association also sponsors in-service workshops for teachers in conjunction with the Texas State Historical Association[qv] and provides a clearinghouse for information about the history of East Texas.

BIBLIOGRAPHY: Vertical Files, Barker Texas History Center, University of Texas at Austin.

Archie P. McDonald

EAST TEXAS OILFIELD. The East Texas oilfield, located in central Gregg, western Rusk, southern Upshur, southeastern Smith, and northeastern Cherokee counties in the east central part of the state, is the largest and most prolific oil reservoir in the contiguous United States. Since its discovery on October 5, 1930, some 30,340 wells have been drilled within its 140,000 acres to yield nearly 5.2 billion barrels of oil from a stratigraphic trap in the Eagle Ford–Woodbine group of the Cretaceous. The source of its primary recovery was a strong water drive. Because the field is so large geographically the first wells, located several miles apart, were originally regarded as discovery wells in separate fields. After the spaces between the first wells were drilled, it was revealed that all sectors drew oil from the same Woodbine sands. The giant field was named for its geographic region.

The first discovery in the East Texas field came in Rusk County. It was there in the summer of 1927 that Columbus Marion (Dad) Joiner,[qv] a sixty-seven-year-old promoter from Ardmore, Oklahoma, took mineral leases on several thousand acres of land with the intention of selling certificates of interest in a syndicate. Joiner presented a kind and gentle appearance, which belied his shrewd ability to use the labor, property, and money of others in his ventures. Joiner transferred 500 acres of mineral leases into the syndicate and offered a one-acre interest in the lease block and a pro-rata share in a drilling test for twenty-five dollars. He mailed copies of a misleading report, prepared by a nonprofessional geologist, to hundreds of names on his sucker list. The duplicitous report promised the existence of oil-productive geological structures in Rusk County and incorrectly claimed that major oil companies were actively leasing there. Joiner's real motivation, as evidenced by a later lawsuit, was the sale of his syndicate shares. Because he needed a drilling test to serve as a prop for impressing potential investors, Joiner commenced a lackadaisical poor-boy drilling operation with rusty, mismatched, and worn-out equipment. But, Joiner's unstable rig and his oil-rich promises appealed to the generosity and dreams of the hard-scrabble farmers and townspeople who donated their labor and traded supplies for syndicate certificates.

Joiner and driller Tom M. Jones spudded the Bradford No. 1 on an eighty-acre tract belonging to Daisy Bradford in the Juan Ximines Survey of Rusk County. After drilling for six months without finding a show of oil, the hole was lost to a stuck pipe. Joiner abandoned the well at a depth of 1,098 feet. By April 14, 1928, he formed a second syndicate from another lease block of 500 acres and sold certificates of interest through another mail promotion. A second well, the Bradford No. 2, was spudded by Joiner and driller Bill Osborne at a site 100 feet northwest of the original well. Joiner's certificates again were bartered for supplies and labor for the well, becoming an accepted medium of exchange in the poor economy of Rusk County. After eleven months of intermittent drilling, the Bradford No. 2 reached a depth of 2,518 feet, where the drill pipe twisted off and blocked the hole. Before abandoning the site, Osborne returned to test a shallower horizon at 1,437–1,460 feet where gas had been reported. When no evidence of production was found, the well was abandoned.

After abandoning the Bradford No. 2, Joiner formed a third syndicate and managed to oversell the shares of interest in a third test as he had in the first two. On May 8, 1929, driller Ed Laster skidded the rig to a new location, 375 feet from the second site, and spudded the Bradford No. 3. After two days of drilling, the well reached a depth of 1,200 feet, using the same rachitic rig, weary equipment, and farmers as rig hands. The boilers were fed green wood from the beginning and old automobile tires at the end. In late August Laster and farmer-rig hand, Jim Lambert, were seriously burned when the boiler exploded. The well was shut down until the driller recovered.

By January 1930 the well reached a depth of 1,530 feet, and drilling was suspended until the spring. Laster resumed work by late March, when Joiner sent word that he was bringing potential investors to the site and wanted Laster to take a core for their benefit. Drilling proceeded through the summer and into the fall. On September 5, 1930, after the well reached a depth of 3,592 feet in the Woodbine sand, it flowed live oil and gas on a drill stem test. Its initial production was 300 barrels of oil per day, and no one appeared more surprised that Joiner, who had oversold his shares. The well was completed on October 5, 1930.

In the month between the drill stem test and completion of the Bradford No. 3, both major company representatives and independent oil men rushed into Rusk County to take leases. But, it was the independents who drilled the first wells and led the early development of the field. The first of those independents to find oil was Deep Rock Oil Company when it completed the second well in the field, located one mile to the west of the Bradford No. 3 on the seventy-five-acre Ashby farm. It came in on December 4, 1930, flowing 3,000 barrels of oil per day.

On December 16, 1930, another independent, H. L. Hunt,qv brought in a small producer, yielding 100 barrels of oil per day. It was a puny well for East Texas, but it did not represent all of Hunt's interest in the field. On November 26, with Joiner's interest in Rusk County in receivership, Hunt bought his 5,000 acres of leases and the eighty-acre tract containing the Bradford No. 3 for $1,335,000, most of it to be paid in production payments. In late December 1930 Hunt formed a gathering system, Panola Pipeline Company, by linking his small well, the Bradford No. 3, and the Deep Rock well to a four-inch pipeline. Production from the three wells was pumped three miles to the Sinclair Oil and Refining Company loading rack at the Missouri-Pacific Railroad. The first oil leaving the field went in thirteen tank cars of 10,000 gallons each to the Sinclair refinery in Houston.

Later, in December 1930 Ed Bateman, a Fort Worth promoter who ran a poor-boy operation called Bateman Oil Company, completed a well ten miles to the northwest of the Bradford No. 3 in the E. G. Sevier Survey, Rusk County. It was the Lou Della Crim No. 1, and it flowed 22,000 barrels of oil per day from 3,653 feet. With four producing wells at the end of 1930, East Texas field reported a yearly production of 27,000 barrels of oil and no gas. On January 9, 1931, Humble Oil and Refining Company bought the Lou Della Crim No. 1 with 1,500 acres of leases for $1.5 million cash and a $600,000 production payment. And a week later, Humble announced plans to connect the field to its pipeline which ran from Van field in Van Zandt County to Louisiana.

A fourth important well came in on January 26, 1931, when John Farrell and his associates, W. A. Moncrief and Eddie Showers, completed their Lathrop No. 1, located twenty-five miles north of the Bradford No. 3. Its flow was choked through a half-inch valve and three-inch casing, but it flowed 320 barrels of oil per hour from a depth of 3,587 feet. Two weeks later, Farrell and his associates sold their interest in the Lathrop No. 1 and the surrounding acreage for $3,270,000 to Yount-Lee Oil Company of Beaumont.

By early spring of 1931 the widely-spaced discoveries revealed the vastness of the field as hundreds of small operators began its unconventional development. Unlike earlier fields, such as Big Lakeqv or Yates,qv which were controlled by one or a few operators who developed them by an orderly plan, East Texas field had no plan and no governor. Many landowners carved their holdings into small mineral leases that could be measured in feet, offering them to the highest bidder and realizing from $1,800 to $3,000 per acre. As the leasing frenzy seized the five counties of the field, Kilgore became the center of the boom. In that small town, wells were drilled in the yards of homes and derrick legs touched those of the next drilling unit. One city block in Kilgore contained forty-four wells.

Whether in town or on farms, independent operators were compelled to drill wells as quickly as possible to prevent neighboring producers from sucking up their oil. This principle, known as the rule of capture, guided the development of oilfields since the 1889 Pennsylvania Supreme Court decision gave ownership of oil to the one who captured it, even if part of that oil migrated from an adjoining lease.

However, rapid development of a field signaled its early decline, because it decreased field pressure and damaged its gas or water drive mechanism. As a result, wells in such fields stopped flowing and were placed on pump. Adequate depletion of a field after its drive and pressure were damaged was nearly impossible, but as the East Texas field faced this peril in the spring of 1931, its operators gave little attention to that fact.

Another ignored fact in East Texas field was the economic law of supply and demand. Crude sold for ninety-nine cents per barrel when the Bradford No. 3 began production, but the price was cut to forty-six cents in 1931. Oilmen responded to the lower price by increasing production, which sent prices even lower. No help came from the weak state regulatory agency, the Railroad Commission,qv because it had no authority to restrict production to the market demand. Rather, it was charged with the task of prohibiting physical waste and conserving oil and gas, making no connection in the early field between overproduction and field destruction. Although the commission established Rule Number 37, which dealt with well spacing, neither operators nor the commission worried about enforcement of that regulation. On April 4, 1931, the commission issued its first proration order for the field, restricting production to 50,000 barrels of oil per day from its current yield of over 200,000 barrels. Although the commission revised the allowable upward on April 22, and again on April 29, in consideration of newly-completed wells, it went into effect on May 1, 1931, to control the physical effects of overproduction.

In spite of the proration order, many operators disregarded well allowables and continued to produce their leases as they chose. By mid-summer of 1931 operators were producing approximately 900,000 barrels of oil per day from about 1,200 wells. Most of the 1931 production left the field through the seventeen pipelines or by the five railroads that served it. However, part of the crude was processed in the field, where six refineries worked. Although ninety-five refineries were eventually built, only seventy-six endured. They were profitable investments, costing only $10,000 to $25,000 to build and bringing in a profit of nearly $6,000 per month. Most of them were teapot refineries, where the owners skimmed gasoline from the high-quality crude, producing a low-octane fuel called Eastex, which was welcomed by the nation's depressed economy at eleven cents per gallon.

On July 14, 1931, when overproduction had driven the price of crude to thirteen cents per barrel, had reduced reservoir pressure by 130 pounds per square inch, and had made water encroachment a serious problem in the field, Governor Ross S. Sterlingqv called a special session of the legislature. A bill was introduced there to limit East Texas production to market demand, a measure to preserve the reservoir and to stabilize the price of crude. However, on July 28 a three-judge federal court ruled that the proration order of April 4, 1931, was invalid because it was an attempt to solve production glut and to fix prices. In compliance with the court decision, the legislature passed a law that prohibited the Railroad Commission from regulating production to meet the demand of the market. A group of hundreds in East Texas who wanted proration in the field appealed to the governor to declare martial law. On August 17, 1931, the governor ordered the Texas National Guard and Texas Rangersqqv into the ten-month-old field to shut in all of its 1,644 wells and to maintain order.

The field resumed production on September 5, 1931, under a new proration order that limited its production to 400,000 barrels of oil per day, permitting each well 225 barrels and giving no consideration to its potential or to the characteristics of the lease. New wells came on line, and by October allowables were reduced for each one to 165 barrels per day. Disgruntled operators filed lawsuits in protest. Others protested by shipping hot oil, or crude produced above the legal limit, out of the field. Because the military still maintained watch, hot-oil smuggling demanded creative maneuvers involving truckers as well as bribed railroad and pipeline employees. As 1931 ended, East Texas field reported its yearly legal production as 121,670,485 barrels of oil and 627,000,000 cubic feet of gas.

On February 2, 1932, a federal court ended martial law in the East

Texas field by ruling it illegal. Federal courts continued to dictate policy in the field throughout 1932, as they struck down each of the nineteen proration orders issued by the commission. However, the price of crude rebounded to nearly $1 per barrel in spite of continued hot-oil shipments. On November 12, 1932, Governor Sterling called a special session of the legislature, which passed a bill allowing for market-demand proration. At the end of December, as the state legislature made the producing of hot oil a felony, the field reported yearly production of 148,325,961 barrels of oil and 5,268,000,000 cubic feet of gas.

On April 6, 1933, the Railroad Commission again shut in East Texas. Before it reopened on April 24, the field allowable was set at 750,000 barrels of oil per day based on botton-hole pressure in individual wells. This excessively high allowable combined with illegally shipped oil, which was estimated to be hundred of thousands of barrels per year, forced crude prices down from seventy-five cents to ten cents and lower per barrel. With the East Texas field and the national oil industry facing economic collapse, on July 14, 1933, President Franklin D. Roosevelt signed an executive order to enforce the regulation of crude production. Secretary of Interior Harold L. Ickes, the enforcer of the order, sent investigators of the Federal Tender Board into the East Texas field to study refinery records, test oil gauges, inspect tanks, and even dig up pipelines to control the movement of crude from the field. With federal inspectors attempting to enforce proration at the end of 1933, the East Texas field reported its greatest production year, when 11,867 wells brought up 216,291,397 barrels of oil and 7,805,000,000 cubic feet of gas.

Throughout the early months of 1934 hot-oil production increased with state and federal authorities unable to eradicate it, but by November the Federal Tender Board had cracked down on producers and had reduced hot-oil shipments to about 10,000 barrels daily. However, in January 1935 the Supreme Court overturned the subsection of the National Industrial Recovery Act that outlawed hot oil. To maintain control of the interstate movement of crude, the United States Congress passed the Connally Hot Oil Act[qv] on February 22, 1935. The Texas legislature more narrowly defined the state's stand on May 11, by enacting the Texas Hot Oil Statute, which declared hot oil as contraband and allowed its confiscation and sale by the state.

With the hot-oil problem under legal control, the Railroad Commission turned its attention to reservoir conservation in East Texas. In June 1936 the commission reduced the allowable per well to 2.32 percent of potential but not less than twenty barrels daily. On November 15, 1937, the commission closed the field for four consecutive Sundays to study bottom hole conditions. This was the first regularly scheduled shutdown day order in Texas. Eventually there were fourteen shut-down days per month in the field.

As the first decade of the field's existence neared its end, many of the problems unique to the giant field had found solutions. Originally skeptic operators were convinced by 1938 that ultimate recovery of the field's production depended upon the conservation of its water-drive mechanism. They initiated a pressure maintenance program by reinjecting produced salt water into the aquifer, reducing the rate of pressure decline. Field operations throughout 1938 continued to be dominated by independents who controlled more than twice as many leases as the major oil companies. However, the reported yearly production of 151,881,842 barrels of oil was within the allowable, and the year ended with crude selling at $1.10 per barrel.

In the early 1940s, as the United States was drawn into World War II,[qv] the field became the original point on the largest pipeline ever laid to that time, the Big Inch (see BIG INCH AND LITTLE BIG INCH). The twenty-four-inch carrier was laid over 1,400 miles to transport East Texas crude to refineries in Philadelphia and on to New York and New Jersey, guaranteeing a dependable supply of crude for the nation. From the late 1940s and stretching into the 1960s, the field received national attention from a less impressive source when the slant-hole scandal was revealed. It was learned that operators had drilled slanted holes from barren acreage beyond the limits of the field back into the Woodbine formation, tapping into productive leases owned by major companies. During a series of investigations, inspectors found 380 deviated wells in East Texas field and shut them down. An estimated $100 million worth of oil was stolen over several decades from legal owners. Many of the oil pirates were leading citizens of East Texas communities. They built fortunes on stolen oil, but when they came to trial none was convicted. Although the state brought charges against them in civil suits, they suffered only public embarrassment and fines. Evidently, taking oil from major companies was not regarded as a serious crime in the communities of East Texas field.

In March 1972 the Railroad Commission set allowables at 100 percent, but the East Texas field and the Kelly-Synder were restricted to 86 percent. When reservoir engineers examined the field in 1983, they estimated that it would ultimately produce 5.6 billion barrels of oil or about 85 percent of the volume originally in place when the first discovery was made. This high productivity was credited to the strong water-drive mechanism, which has been preserved by reinjection of produced salt water, by early pressure maintenance regulated by the Railroad Commission through proration, and by successful polymer-augmented waterfloods established on a local basis in later years. At the end of 1990 the East Texas field completed its sixtieth year of operation and reported a yearly production of 35,559,769 barrels of oil. In January 1991, after a series of court hearings, the Railroad Commission calculated the East Texas field at 100 percent production factor. By January 1, 1993, cumulative production from East Texas field was reported as 5,145,562,000 barrels of oil.

BIBLIOGRAPHY: Robert O. Anderson, *Fundamentals of the Petroleum Industry* (Norman: University of Oklahoma Press, 1984). James A. Clark, *The Chronological History of the Petroleum and Natural Gas Industries* (Houston: Clark, 1963). James Anthony Clark and Michel T. Halbouty, *The Last Boom* (New York: Random House, 1972). William E. Galloway et al., *Atlas of Major Texas Oil Reservoirs* (Austin: University of Texas Bureau of Economic Geology, 1983). James S. Hudnall, "Geology and Economic Importance of the East Texas Field," *Oil Weekly*, July 31, 1931. Roger M. and Diana Davids Olien, *Wildcatters: Texas Independent Oilmen* (Austin: Texas Monthly Press, 1984). Edgar Wesley Owen, *Trek of the Oil Finders: A History of Exploration for Petroleum* (Tulsa: American Association for Petroleum Geologists, 1975). James Presley, *A Saga of Wealth: The Rise of the Texas Oilmen* (New York: Putnam, 1978; 2d ed., Austin: Texas Monthly Press, 1983). David F. Prindle, *Petroleum Politics and the Texas Railroad Commission* (Austin: University of Texas Press, 1981). Daniel Yergin, *The Prize: The Epic Quest for Oil, Money and Power* (New York: Simon and Schuster, 1991).
Julia Cauble Smith

EAST TEXAS RAILWAY. The East Texas Railway Company was chartered on April 29, 1880, to connect Sabine Pass with Troupe, in order to provide the Kountze interests of New York an outlet for their timber acreage in East Texas. The railroad had a capital stock of $4 million, and the principal place of business was Beaumont. The members of the first board of directors were Augustus Kountze, Erwine Davis, and Jacob Van Wagener, all of New York City; Thomas W. House,[qv] Josiah F. Crosby,[qv] and E. P. Hill, all of Houston; and B. D. Crary of Beaumont. The railroad built thirty miles of line from Sabine Pass to Beaumont in January 1881 and another twenty-four miles to Kountze in July. On August 3, 1881, the road was renamed the Sabine and East Texas Railway Company, which completed an extension to Rockland by March 1882 for a total of 103 miles of track. C. P. Huntington purchased the line and transferred it to the Texas and New Orleans Railroad on October 28, 1882.
Nancy Beck Young

EAST TEXAS STATE UNIVERSITY. East Texas State University was established by William L. Mayo[qv] at Cooper, Delta County, in 1889 and chartered in 1890 as Mayo or Mayo's College, a private institution where Mayo "could be at liberty to put into operation his idea of a democratic school of a college type." The school grew for five years, but the building burned in 1894; and since Cooper had no railroad at the time and Mayo was in financial straits, he proposed to move his school to the town offering the best incentives. Commerce put up land and $20,000 cash, so the college was rechartered there in 1894 as East Texas Normal College. It started with thirty-five pupils. The first session was held in a small business house, but soon a two-story administration building and two frame dormitories were erected. Mayo continued as president until his death in 1917. The school operated as an independent private college with no endowment or income except tuition and a small profit from its dormitories. Between 1889 and 1917 more than 30,000 students received their basic educational training in this school; records show that the college prepared more teachers for the public schools than any other college or university in Texas in the same period. The college had six degree programs.

Mayo wanted to perpetuate his school as a state teachers' college, and he started a move to place it under the authority of the board of regents of the state normal schools. After the Thirty-fifth Legislature passed an act to do this, the board of regents paid the Mayo estate $80,000 for the institution; Mayo died in March 1917, the same month that the state purchased the plant and fifty acres of land. Commerce donated $40,000 to renovate the buildings. The board of regents of the state teachers' colleges took over the plant and staff of East Texas Normal College, and its name became East Texas State Normal College. In 1923 the name was changed again to East Texas State Teachers College. Graduate courses were offered for the first time in 1935. Enrollment in 1947–48 was 1,593.

The educational scope of East Texas State Teachers College became much broader than teacher education, and consequently "Teachers" was dropped from the name in 1957. In 1962 the first doctoral program was initiated. University status was authorized by the legislature in 1965, and the name was changed to East Texas State University. ETSU was reorganized into three schools: graduate, education, and arts and sciences.

Buildings on the 150-acre main campus numbered eighty-seven in 1965, and twenty-five were on the 1,052-acre college farm. The value of the physical plant grew steadily from $175,000 in 1917 to $2,328,000 in 1947 and $19 million in 1965. The university operated on a $6 million budget in 1965, when sixty-nine undergraduate majors were offered in twenty-five academic departments and master's degrees were offered in thirty fields. Student enrollment in the regular 1974–75 term was 9,241.

In the 1990s the campus occupied 1,883 acres, and the physical plant was valued at $150 million. The main 140-acre campus was eight blocks southwest of the business district in Commerce. In 1994 the James G. Gee Library, built in 1959 and enlarged in 1969 and 1986, housed over 1,000,000 volumes, 2,000 periodicals, series of 68 newspapers, and 350,000 government documents. The McDowell Administration–Business Administration Building was constructed in 1970.

In 1990 ETSU was accredited by or belonged to the Association of Texas Colleges and Universities,qv the American Association of Colleges for Teacher Education, the American Association of State Colleges and Universities, the American Council on Education, the American Association of University Women, the National Commission on Accreditation, the Council of Graduate Students in the United States, the Association of Texas Graduate Schools, the Council of Colleges of Arts and Sciences, the Federation of North Texas Area Universities, the Inter-University Council of the North Texas Area, the National Association of Schools of Music, the American Assembly of Collegiate Schools of Business, the Texas Education Agency,qv the Southern Association of Colleges and Schools, the National Council for Accreditation of Teacher Education, the National Association of Schools of Music, and the Council on Social Work Education.

ETSU is a regional state university. In addition to the Commerce Campus, it has operated an upper-level institution in Texarkana since 1971 and maintains the ETSU Commuter Facility in Garland, a branch focused on graduate offerings. The university is divided into the College of Arts and Sciences, the College of Business and Technology, the College of Education, the Graduate School, and the Division of Continuing Education. In the fall of 1990 the faculty numbered 265; 7,900 students were enrolled in Commerce and 9,000 in the entire complex. ETSU offered more than 100 undergraduate and fifty graduate majors to students in twenty-six departments. Nine undergraduate degrees and seven graduate degrees were conferred. In cooperation with the Federation of North Texas Area Universities, ETSU offers a Ph.D. By 1988 the university had conferred 72,000 degrees. Presidents of ETSU have included Mayo, S. H. Whitley (1924–46), A. C. Ferguson (1946–47), James G. Gee (1947–66), and F. Henderson McDowell (1972–82).
Nancy Beck Young

EAST TEXAS STATE UNIVERSITY AT TEXARKANA. East Texas State University at Texarkana opened in 1971 as the East Texas State University Center at Texarkana with an enrollment of 323 students. By fall 1974 the enrollment had increased to 615. ETSUT holds accreditations and memberships with the Southern Association of Colleges and Schools and the Texas Education Agency,qv as well as numerous other professional associations. The school is on the campus of Texarkana College,qv the local community college. It was established to provide third and fourth year college instruction for people residing in an isolated region. Increased attention is given to adults and other nontraditional students. The majority of the student body is part-time female students with a median age of thirty-three. The school is a commuter-based campus. There are three academic divisions: arts and sciences, business administration, and teaching professions. The faculty numbers thirty-three full-time and thirty-five adjunct members. Eight undergraduate and five graduate degrees are conferred. John F. Moss became the school's president in 1971 and still held the job in 1991. In 1978 the A. M. and Welma Aikin Learning Center was constructed. A new library was built in 1983. In 1985 the university established a Center for Professional Development. Eighty percent of the school's graduates remain in the region. In June of 1991 a total of 4,976 people had received degrees ETSUT.
Nancy Beck Young

EASTVALE, TEXAS. Eastvale is on Farm Road 423 just east of Lewisville Lake in Denton County. It was incorporated during the 1970s and had a population of 503 by 1980. The town's growth slowed during the 1980s, however, and it disincorporated. In the early 1990s the population was estimated at 731.
Randolph B. Campbell

EAST WILLOW CREEK. East Willow Creek rises two miles southeast of Wagram in northeastern Mason County (at 30°52′ N, 99°06′ W) and runs south for seven miles to its mouth on Willow Creek, 1½ miles northwest of Art (at 30°48′ N, 99°07′ W). It rises in limestone hills on the eastern edge of the Edwards Plateau and crosses an area of the Llano basin characterized by flat to rolling terrain surfaced by deep to shallow sandy and clayey loams. Local vegetation includes scrub brush, grasses, and open stands of live oak and mesquite.

EAST YEGUA CREEK. East Yegua Creek, which is intermittent in its upper reaches, rises nine miles southwest of Rockdale in southern Milam County (at 30°33′ N, 97°06′ W) and runs southeast for forty-five miles to its mouth, where it joins Middle Yegua Creek to form Yegua Creek on the Burleson-Lee county line fifteen miles south of Caldwell (at 30°19′ N, 96°45′ W). It traverses generally flat terrain with local shallow depressions, surfaced by clay and sandy loams that support water-tolerant hardwoods, conifers, and grasses.

EATON, NICK T. (ca. 1839–ca. 1895). Nick T. Eaton, Panhandleqv rancher, was born about 1839 in Missouri and appeared in the Panhandle in 1878, when he brought a herd up from the vicinity of Fort Griffin. Among his hired trail drivers were George Finch, W. K. (Doc)

Franz, and James P. (Lengthy) Sutton, all of whom stayed to work on Eaton's new ranch, which he established twenty-five miles west of the site of present Wheeler. This ranch covered a third of Wheeler County and a third of Gray County. The headquarters, built out of cedar posts, was located on Hackberry Creek, a tributary of McClellan Creek, six miles northwest of the locale of present McLean near the North Fork of the Red River. On his range Eaton ran 3,000 head of cattle that carried his U Bar U brand. Finch served as the first wagon boss but became an invalid after a year and died in 1888. He was succeeded as wagon boss by Doc Franz, who as state surveyor for the Clay District had helped survey the Panhandle in 1869–73. Franz also served as range foreman. Thomas T. McGee,^{qv} later Hemphill county sheriff, was among those hired to drive U Bar U cattle to Dodge City.

Eaton was a charter member of the Panhandle Stock Association, formed in Mobeetie in 1880, and served consistently on the association's executive board. He was also on grand juries, county commissions, and school boards. Eaton and Henry Cresswell^{qv} became partners about 1880 in a cattle enterprise in which they used a Forked Lightning brand. Their cattle grazed on Eaton's U Bar U range until 1889, when the partners discontinued the brand, shipped out the cattle of that marking, and sold them. Marvin V. Sanders, later Wheeler county sheriff, who worked for Eaton, told of one episode in which Doc Franz and Lengthy Sutton discovered a band of reservation Indians slaughtering some Forked Lightning steers near the U Bar U headquarters. Sutton allegedly rode eighteen miles to Fort Elliott in forty minutes to alert the military. Troops came to escort the Indians back to their reservation, and the government later reimbursed Eaton and Cresswell for the cattle. In 1885 Eaton filed an injunction against Abner P. Blocker^{qv} to try to prevent him from driving the first XIT Ranch^{qv} herd across the U Bar U rangeland to Dallam County. However, the case was "dismissed at cost of plaintiff."

After 1889 Eaton, who was approaching fifty, ended his bachelorhood by marrying in Kansas City. There he maintained a palatial mansion for his bride and commuted to his Panhandle ranch during cattle-shipping times. He was known among the "cowpuncher element" as an expert "brand man," straightforward in all his dealing. Eaton reportedly turned the U Bar U's registry over to J. P. Sutton after 1892. Some accounts related that Eaton later committed suicide after going broke.

BIBLIOGRAPHY: Millie Jones Porter, *Memory Cups of Panhandle Pioneers* (Clarendon, Texas: Clarendon Press, 1945). Pauline D. and R. L. Robertson, *Cowman's Country: Fifty Frontier Ranches in the Texas Panhandle, 1876–1887* (Amarillo: Paramount, 1981).

H. Allen Anderson

EATON, TEXAS (Limestone County). Eaton was near Mills Creek two miles southwest of Thornton in southern Limestone County. It was named for Silas Eaton, who settled on Mill Creek in 1854. The community centered around a gristmill and a school. County highway maps of 1948 showed a few scattered houses at the site.

BIBLIOGRAPHY: Ray A. Walter, *A History of Limestone County* (Austin: Von Boeckmann–Jones, 1959). *Vivian Elizabeth Smyrl*

EATON, TEXAS (Robertson County). Eaton, just east of Farm Road 2446 and nine miles southeast of Franklin in central Robertson County, was named for D. C. Eaton, postmaster when a post office was granted in 1900. The office was discontinued in 1905. The community reported a population of fifty around 1910. In 1942 Eaton had a church, a school, and a few scattered dwellings. In the late 1980s scattered dwellings and a church remained at Eaton, which was still listed as a community in 1990. *Richard Allen Burns*

EBAHAMO INDIANS. Most writers who have studied the documents of the La Salle expedition^{qv} consider Bahamo, Bracamo, and Ebahamo (Hebahamo) as variants of the same name for a single Indian group. This is clearly supported by sound correspondences. However, close analysis of these documents leads to some doubt about this presumed synonymy. The journal of Henri Joutel^{qv} contains no names for the Indians who lived in the immediate vicinity of Fort St. Louis^{qv} (Matagorda Bay) and who gave the French colonists so much trouble. He does refer to the Ebahamos, but only in connection with La Salle's last trip to the Hasinai country. The geographic features described by Joutel indicate that the Ebahamo Indians were an inland group who lived in northern Jackson County or somewhere in that general vicinity. He does not identify the Ebahamos with the Indians who harassed Fort St. Louis. That they were not the same seems to be indicated by the fact that La Salle was curious about the Ebahamo language and is said to have recorded a few words. The Indians near the fort were called Bracamos by La Salle. Douay merely says that the neighboring Indian groups included the Quoaques (Cocos), Bahamos, and Quinets. A few years later, after the Spanish found Fort St. Louis abandoned, Alonso de León^{qv} reported that the Indians of the general vicinity were Bahamo and Quelanhubeche (Karankawa?). Thus the only Indians specifically linked with Fort St. Louis are the Bracamos. It seems safe to assume that Bracamo and Bahamo are variants of the same name and refer to the same people, but doubt remains as to whether Bahamo and Ebahamo are the same. Unless new documents become available, this situation may never be clarified. After 1690 the Spanish used other names for the Indian groups in this section of the Texas coast. These groups (Coapite, Cujane, and Karankawa) are all identifiable as Karankawan. Although they may not be strictly synonymous, it seems reasonable to conclude that Bracamo, Bahamo, and Ebahamo were French-derived names for two or more bands or tribes of Karankawan affiliation. This is supported by one bit of linguistic evidence: the word for "father" in Karankawan is *béhema*.

BIBLIOGRAPHY: Albert S. Gatschet, *The Karankawa Indians, the Coast People of Texas* (Cambridge, Massachusetts: Peabody Museum of American Archaeology and Ethnology, 1891). Charles W. Hackett, ed., *Pichardo's Treatise on the Limits of Louisiana and Texas* (4 vols., Austin: University of Texas Press, 1931–46). Henri Joutel, *Joutel's Journal of La Salle's Last Voyage* (London: Lintot, 1714; rpt., New York: Franklin, 1968). John Gilmary Shea, *Discovery and Exploration of the Mississippi Valley* (New York: Redfield, 1852).

Thomas N. Campbell

EBANITO CREEK. Ebanito Creek rises three miles northwest of Premont in southern Jim Wells County (at 27°23′ N, 98°09′ W) and runs east for twenty-nine miles to its mouth on Jaboncillos Creek, four miles southeast of Ricardo in southern Kleberg County (at 27°24′ N, 97°48′ W). The creek's name is from the Spanish word for "ebony." The stream traverses flat to rolling terrain with local escarpments, surfaced by deep, fine sandy loam and loose sand that support brush and grasses.

EBENEZER, TEXAS. Ebenezer is on Farm Road 557 five miles southeast of Pittsburg in southeastern Camp County. Settlement in the area began in the 1850s when Israel Braden Rape, Robert Devenport, and Thomas DeLaney (later shortened to Laney) brought their families and slaves from Georgia and established their homesteads on adjoining farms. Rape donated land for a cemetery and a building site for a school and church. From the beginning the building was often called Rape's Academy, and that served as the original name of the school district. The community consisted almost exclusively of farmers, and, with the exception of cotton gins and gristmills, there are no records of any commercial activity connected with the settlement. In 1897 the school district had forty-nine children of school age. The school was a one-room, one teacher, ungraded school. By 1935 improvements in transportation and the consolidation of common school districts had expanded the area served by the school at Ebenezer. That year six teachers taught ten grades to 180 white children. The school board also oversaw a ten-grade school, located two miles southwest, where five teachers taught 107 black children. By 1955 both schools had closed, and the district had been consolidated with the Pittsburg Independent School district. The population of Ebenezer was estimated at sixty in 1968. In 1983 Ebenezer had two churches, a cemetery, and a population estimated at fifty-five. The population estimate was still fifty-five in 1990.

BIBLIOGRAPHY: Artemesia L. B. Spencer, *The Camp County Story* (Fort Worth: Branch-Smith, 1974).

Cecil Harper, Jr.

EBERLE, EDWARD WALTER (1864–1929). Naval officer Edward Walter Eberle, the son of Joseph and Mary (Stemler) Eberle, was born in Denton, Texas, on August 17, 1864. He spent his childhood in Fort Smith, Arkansas, where his parents moved in 1865. He received an appointment to the United States Naval Academy at the age of eighteen and graduated in 1885. For the next forty-four years Eberle's career paralleled the evolution of the modern United States Navy. His first commission was aboard the USS *Albatross* off Cape Horn, Alaska. He was promoted to lieutenant, junior grade, in 1896 and sailed for three years on the USS *Oregon*. He served as commander of the forward turret during the battleship's famous race around the Horn in support of the attack on the port of Santiago during the Spanish-American War.

After the end of the war, Eberle became flag lieutenant and acting chief of staff under Adm. Albert S. Barker, commander-in-chief of the Asiatic station, headquartered in Manila. During this time he prepared what became the first modern manual of gun and torpedo drills for the United States Navy. From 1903 to 1905 he again served under Admiral Barker as a flag lieutenant, this time in the Atlantic Fleet. During this commission Eberle drew up the first codes for the navy's use of the wireless. In recognition of the two manuals he had prepared, he was sent to the War College, where his reputation as an administrator and technician resulted in his becoming commandant of the San Francisco Naval Training Station, a post he held from 1908 to 1910. For the next two years he commanded the USS *Wheeling* on a voyage around the world. After promotion to the rank of captain while commanding the Atlantic Torpedo Fleet, in 1912 Eberle developed the use of smoke screens to protect destroyers against attack. He was also a leading proponent of employing aircraft to sight and destroy submarines.

As a result of his administrative and sea experience, Eberle became superintendent of the Naval Academy in 1915. His orders were to restore the school's reputation after a series of scandals that threatened the institution's reputation. Eberle's success as administrator of the academy during the difficult years of 1915–18 resulted in his selection for the Distinguished Service Medal in 1918 and his promotion to rear admiral the following year. After leaving the Naval Academy, he commanded divisions of the Atlantic Fleet for two years and, from 1921 to 1923, divisions of the Pacific Fleet.

In 1923 he became chief of naval operations, the highest shore office the navy offered. His reputation for judicious command decisions and diplomatic skills with politicians resulted in the president's requesting his advice on matters that included disturbances then occurring in China and Nicaragua. In 1927 Eberle became chairman of the executive committee of the Navy General Board. The following year he reached the mandatory retirement age and on August 17, 1928, ended his forty-seven-year naval career.

He retired to Virginia, where he lived with his wife, Tazie (Harrison), whom he had married on October 24, 1899. They had one son. Eberle was an Episcopalian and a member of the Society of Foreign Wars, the Military Orders of the World War, and the Army and Navy Club. On July 6, 1929, he died in the Naval Hospital in Washington, D.C.; he was buried in Arlington National Cemetery.

BIBLIOGRAPHY: *Dictionary of American Biography*. Edward Walter Eberle, "The *Oregon* at Santiago," *Century Magazine*, May 1899. New York *Times*, July 7, 1929.

David Minor

EBERLY, ANGELINA BELLE PEYTON (1798–1860). Angelina Belle Peyton Eberly, innkeeper and Archive War[qv] cannoneer, was born in Sumner County, Tennessee, on July 2, 1798, the daughter of John and Margaret (Hamilton) Peyton. She married her first cousin, Jonathan C. Peyton, on July 2, 1818, and the couple left Tennessee for New Orleans. They boarded the *Good Intent* in June 1822 bound for Matagorda Bay. After living in Hawkins Camp and in Jesse Burnam's[qv] settlement, they located in San Felipe de Austin in 1825. With several slaves they operated an inn and tavern. The couple had three children. Jonathan died in June 1834, but Angelina continued to operate the hotel until the town was destroyed to prevent its falling into Mexican hands.

She was in Columbia after the Texas Revolution,[qv] and late in 1836 she met and married Jacob Eberly, a widower. They lived briefly in Bastrop and in 1839 settled in Austin, where she ran the Eberly House. On October 18, 1839, she served dinner to President Mirabeau B. Lamar[qv] and his cabinet; President Sam Houston[qv] chose to live in her house rather than occupy the president's home. Jacob Eberly died in 1841.

In December 1842 Thomas I. Smith and Eli Chandler[qqv] were ordered to return the public documents from Austin to Washington-on-the-Brazos. Mrs. Eberly, realizing that the symbols of federal government were being removed from the city, fired a six-pound gun that city officials kept loaded with grapeshot in case of Indian attack. Austinites, aroused by the cannon, became involved in what is known as the Archive War. Ultimately, the archives were returned to Austin permanently.

In April 1846 Angelina leased Edward Clegg's Tavern House in Lavaca (later Port Lavaca). By 1851 she was running a hotel in Indianola. She died in Indianola on August 15, 1860, and was buried in a cemetery outside the community. Peyton Bell Lytle, her grandson, was named sole heir to her estate, appraised at $50,000.

BIBLIOGRAPHY: Austin *American-Statesman*, July 11, 1937. Mary Austin Holley Papers, Barker Texas History Center, University of Texas at Austin. Louis Wiltz Kemp, "Mrs. Angelina B. Eberly," *Southwestern Historical Quarterly* 36 (January 1933). C. Richard King, *The Lady Cannoneer* (Burnet, Texas: Eakin Press, 1981). *The Peytons of Virginia* (Stafford, Virginia: Peytons of Virginia Society, 1976).

C. Richard King

EBONY, TEXAS. Ebony is twenty-three miles west of Goldthwaite in extreme western Mills County. The community, originally named Buffalo, was settled in the 1880s. In 1891, when residents applied for a post office, the name Buffalo was rejected. The town was then renamed Ebony, for Ebony Shaw, a local cowboy. Its post office opened on January 5, 1891, with Victoria Griffin as postmistress. Ebony grew to thirty-five residents by 1910 and to 113 by 1930, when the community had two businesses. By 1940, however, its population had declined to fifty; the post office was discontinued around 1945. By the late 1950s the community was virtually abandoned. Highway maps for the early 1980s show a cemetery and a community center at Ebony.

BIBLIOGRAPHY: Flora Gatlin Bowles, *A No Man's Land Becomes a County* (Austin: Steck, 1958). Fred Tarpley, *1001 Texas Place Names* (Austin: University of Texas Press, 1980).

Julius A. Amin

EBY, FREDERICK (1874–1968). Frederick Eby, Christian writer and teacher, was born in the rural community of Ebytown in Ontario, Canada, on October 26, 1874, the sixth of seven children of Aaron Eby, a physician. He was raised in the Mennonite community there, but at about age ten, he and most of his family converted to the

Baptist faith, and he remained a strong Baptist for the rest of his life. At age fourteen he entered the Stratford Institute and subsequently attended McMaster University in Hamilton, Ontario, with plans to become a minister. He received a B.A. from McMaster in 1895. He did graduate work at the University of Chicago and then in 1900 earned his Ph.D. from Clark University in Worcester, Massachusetts. Also in 1900, he married Elizabeth Newman, daughter of well-known church historian Albert Henry Newman.qv The couple had four children. Eby did postdoctoral study at the University of Berlin from 1905 to 1906; in 1921 he was awarded an honorary LL.D. from McMaster University. He taught at Morgan Park Academy in Chicago from 1897 to 1898, then at Baylor University in Texas from 1900 to 1908, before settling in at the University of Texas at Austin from 1909 until his retirement in 1957. At the University of Texas he served as professor and chairman of the department of history and philosophy of education. During his career he wrote seven books dealing with education and Christianity: *Christianity and Education* (1914), *Education in Texas: Source Materials* (1918), *Early Protestant Educators* (1931), *The Development of Modern Education* (1934), *The History and Philosophy of Education: Ancient and Medieval* (1940), *Albert Henry Newman: the Church Historian* (1946), and *Reorganizing American Education for World Leadership* (1958). While at the University of Chicago, Frederick Eby studied under philosopher and educator John Dewey; later, as a Christian, Eby came to oppose Dewey's secular and pragmatic ideas on public education. Some sources suggest that because of Eby's influence, Dewey's ideas and programs never became a strong part of the Texas educational system. Eby is best known for promoting a spiritual emphasis in education, for writing a history of Texas public education in celebration of its hundredth anniversary in 1954, and for helping shape the junior college system of Texas. He was often called the father of the Texas junior college movement,qv to which he replied, "Not the father, just the babysitter!" He died on February 10, 1968, and was buried in Austin Memorial Park in Austin.

BIBLIOGRAPHY: Austin *American-Statesman*, February 12, 1968. Vertical Files, Barker Texas History Center, University of Texas at Austin.

Jacqueline Jeffrey

ECAY MÚZQUIZ, JOSÉ ANTONIO DE (?–1738). The name of José (Joseph) Antonio de Ecay (Eca y) Múzquiz, Spanish soldier, first appears in witness to a document signed by Alonso De Leónqv in 1688. He was a criolloqv who served on the Coahuila-Texas frontier as soldier, governor, and presidial commander until his death in 1738. José Joaquín de Ecay Múzquizqv is believed to have been his son. On August 12, 1689, he witnessed the official founding of Santiago de la Monclova (present-day Monclova, Coahuila). During the terms of Francisco Cuerbo y Valdés (1698–1702) and Simón Padilla y Córdova (1708–1712) as governor of Coahuila, he several times pursued hostile Indians into the Sierra de Santa Rosa. Marching through barren, waterless country, he was frustrated in his objective by natives who took refuge on the mountain peaks and rolled rocks down upon his troops.

A fellow officer and close associate of Diego Ramón,qv Ecay Múzquiz led troops from the presidio of San Francisco de Coahuila on Ramón's 1707 march to the Nueces River in Texas. He signed the report of that expedition, purposes of which were to punish hostile natives and recruit neophytes for the San Juan Bautistaqv missions.

In 1717, when Fray Antonio de San Buenaventura y Olivaresqv was attempting to move San Francisco Solano Mission to San Antonio de Béxar,qv Ecay Múzquiz, as Coahuila governor ad interim, declined to furnish him an escort. Ecay Múzquiz was succeeded as governor by Martín de Alarcónqv on August 5, 1717. When Ramón died in 1724, Ecay Múzquiz succeeded him as commandant of Presidio de San Juan Bautista. In that capacity he helped José de Berroteránqv to organize his 1729 expedition that made an abortive attempt to reach La Junta de los Ríosqv by marching up the Rio Grande. In 1731 he provided an escort of San Juan Bautista troops to take the Canary Islandersqv on the last leg of their journey to San Antonio. In 1735 he joined Governor Blas María de la Garza Falcónqv in exploring up the Rio Grande to look for the site of a new presidio.

When Carlos Benites Franquis de Lugoqv was deposed as governor of Texas and brought to San Juan Bautista, it fell to the lot of Ecay Múzquiz to take testimony against him. With the Franquis affair at its zenith, he was called upon to officiate in lieu of Coahuila governor Clemente de la Garza Falcón in a new Coahuila mission, San Francisco Vizarrón. His life was winding down; yet it seemed administrative problems descended on him from every hand. In October 1737 he sat as judge in a hearing concerning allegations that the San Juan Bautista missions had been remiss in payment of tithes. He died in 1738 before the matter was resolved. He was succeeded as commandant by Joseph Hernández, formerly lieutenant of the garrison.

BIBLIOGRAPHY: Vito Alessio Robles, *Coahuila y Texas en la época colonial* (Mexico City: Editorial Cultura, 1938; 2d ed., Mexico City: Editorial Porrúa, 1978). Robert S. Weddle, *San Juan Bautista: Gateway to Spanish Texas* (Austin: University of Texas Press, 1968).

Robert S. Weddle

ECAY MÚZQUIZ, JOSÉ JOAQUÍN DE (?–?). José Joaquín de Ecay (Eca y) Múzquiz, a Spanish army lieutenant, probably the son of José Antonio de Ecay Múzquiz,qv was stationed at Presidio de Santa Rosa del Sacramento in February 1750, when he was appointed to investigate the site of the proposed San Francisco Xavier Presidio. He was instructed to take charge of the garrison at San Xavier, to measure the lands and water of the San Xavier (San Gabriel) River, to take a census of the mission Indians, and to do anything else pertinent to the determination of the necessity for a presidio. In June 1750 Ecay Múzquiz surveyed the San Xavier River, and his favorable report ended the doubt standing in the way of final consent to the establishment of the presidio. He turned the garrison over to the newly appointed presidial commander, Felipe Rábago y Terán,qv on December 13, 1751.

On January 16, 1753, Ecay Múzquiz was appointed by the viceroy to assist Capt. Miguel de la Garza Falcónqv in the official inquiry into the murder of Fray Juan José Ganzábalqv of Nuestra Señora de la Candelaria Mission. After the death of his chief in August 1753 Ecay Múzquiz commanded the garrison until he was relieved by the new inspector, Pedro de Rábago y Terán,qv on August 11, 1754.

In 1757 Ecay Múzquiz was assigned as lieutenant of the garrison of San Luis de las Amarillas Presidio (San Sabá). As official courier for the commandant, Diego Ortiz Parrilla,qv he carried dispatches, conducted a prisoner to Mexico City, and escorted a new parish priest from Presidio de Santa Rosa. By 1759 he had succeeded Toribio de Urrutiaqv as commandant of San Antonio de Béxar Presidio at San Antonio and was a member of the junta that recommended Ortiz Parrilla's campaign to punish the allied northern Indians responsible for the San Sabá Mission attack in March 1758. When Ortiz Parrilla departed for Mexico at the conclusion of that campaign, Ecay Múzquiz was the logical choice to fill the San Sabá post in his absence. An illness prevented his doing so. Consequently, Capt. Manuel Rodríguezqv of San Juan Bautistaqv Presidio took temporary command at San Sabá, where he remained until the arrival of Ortiz Parrilla's successor in 1761.

BIBLIOGRAPHY: Herbert Eugene Bolton, *Texas in the Middle Eighteenth Century: Studies in Spanish Colonial History and Administration* (Berkeley: University of California Press, 1915; rpt., Austin: University of Texas Press, 1970). Carlos E. Castañeda, *Our Catholic Heritage in Texas* (7 vols., Austin: Von Boeckmann–Jones, 1936–58; rpt., New York: Arno, 1976). Milam County Heritage Preservation Society, *Matchless Milam: History of Milam County* (Dallas: Taylor, 1984). Robert S. Weddle, *San Juan Bautista: Gateway to Spanish Texas*

(Austin: University of Texas Press, 1968). Elizabeth Howard West, trans., "Bonilla's Brief Compendium of the History of Texas, 1772," *Quarterly of the Texas State Historical Association* 8 (July 1904).

Herbert C. Taylor, Jr.

ECHANCOTE INDIANS. In 1683–1684 Juan Domínguez de Mendoza[qv] led an exploratory expedition from El Paso as far eastward as the junction of the Concho and Colorado rivers east of present San Angelo. In his itinerary he listed the names of thirty-seven Indian groups, including the Echancote (Enchacote) Indians, from which he expected to receive delegations on the Colorado River. Nothing further is known about the Echancotes, who seem to have been one of many Indian groups of north central Texas that were swept away by the southward thrust of the Lipan Apache and Comanche Indians in the eighteenth century. The name Echancote is not to be confused with Echuntica, which referred to the Kotsoteka band of Comanche in later times.

BIBLIOGRAPHY: Herbert Eugene Bolton, ed., *Spanish Exploration in the Southwest, 1542–1706* (New York: Scribner, 1908; rpt., New York: Barnes and Noble, 1959). Charles W. Hackett, ed., *Pichardo's Treatise on the Limits of Louisiana and Texas* (4 vols., Austin: University of Texas Press, 1931–46).

Thomas N. Campbell

ECHO, TEXAS (Bell County). Echo, formerly called Miller, was a post office and railroad station on the Missouri, Kansas and Texas Railroad two miles south of Temple in central Bell County. The site was known as Miller until about 1884, when the railroad established a branch line there, known as the Belton Railroad, and the community became a station at the intersection of the two lines. In 1884 a post office called Echo was granted to the community, which was known by that name through at least 1948. In 1890 Echo had a hotel, a railroad agent, and seven inhabitants. Its post office was discontinued in 1894. In 1948 Echo consisted of several scattered dwellings, and by 1988 the site of the community was within the Temple city limits.

BIBLIOGRAPHY: Bertha Atkinson, The History of Bell County, Texas (M.A. thesis, University of Texas, 1929).

Mark Odintz

ECHO, TEXAS (Coleman County). Echo, on State Highway 206 four miles northeast of Coleman in central Coleman County, developed around a store established in the 1870s. In 1881 William Dibrell bought the site as part of his purchase of the Miles and Gholson ranch and renamed it Echo for the echo that resounded on a cliff at Home Creek. The Echo post office opened in 1910. The population in 1940 was seventy-five, and the town had a post office and school. Since then both the school and the post office have closed. The population was sixteen from 1970 to 1990.

BIBLIOGRAPHY: Fred Tarpley, *1001 Texas Place Names* (Austin: University of Texas Press, 1980).

William R. Hunt

ECHO, TEXAS (Live Oak County). Echo (pronounced "Eeko"), also known as Mount Echo or the Point, was a stage depot and post office community a half mile north of Farm Road 888 and twenty-two miles southeast of the site of present Oakville in southeastern Live Oak County. The community was founded on land granted to Irish empresario[qv] James McGloin.[qv] McGloin himself never lived at the site, but a general store was established there by his daughter, Elizabeth, and her husband, Patrick J. Murphy. During the 1850s a house was built on the site by John Bernard Murphy and his wife, Margaret Mary Healy-Murphy.[qv] Perhaps as early as 1846, but certainly by the late 1850s, a one-room building near the Murphy's house became a stage stop on the road linking San Antonio with Corpus Christi and Mexico. In a building behind the stage stop, Patrick and Elizabeth Murphy ran an inn. A post office operated at the community from 1858 until 1879. In 1877 James G. Grover petitioned to establish a community school. Echo probably continued to serve as a stage stop until 1881. After Margaret Mary Murphy moved to San Antonio in the late 1880s and helped to found the Sisters of the Holy Spirit and Mary Immaculate,[qv] the Murphy Ranch at Echo was used as a retreat for nuns from 1893 to about 1906. The stagecoach depot building remained standing until 1970, when it was leveled by Hurricane Celia.

BIBLIOGRAPHY: Ervin L. Sparkman, *The People's History of Live Oak County* (Mesquite, Texas, 1981). Marker Files, Texas Historical Commission, Austin.

John Leffler

ECHO, TEXAS (Orange County). Echo is on the Southern Pacific Railroad three miles northeast of Orange in eastern Orange County. During the late 1870s the Texas and New Orleans Railroad began in earnest its long-awaited efforts to establish a direct rail link between Houston and New Orleans. The parent company chartered the Louisiana Western Extension Railroad in 1879 to complete the task. Finding the lands immediately east of Orange too swampy for construction, the company pushed the line to the north and east, thus crossing the Sabine River near a site that they named Echo because sounds reverberated in the nearby river swamp. A quarantine station was established there in 1880, but H. C. Schwaner's townsite plat was not filed until 1903. Although the quarantine station was later removed, Echo continued to be an important industrial site. In the mid-1930s Echo had fifteen dwellings. In 1964 shallow draft commerce on the Sabine River at Echo was 219,000 tons; much of that trade stemmed from the Alpha Portland Cement Company plant. Echo served as a freightyard for the Southern Pacific in 1981. Maps in the early 1980s showed a church and two businesses at the site, which by then was within the city limits of Orange. In 1990 Echo reported a population of twenty-five.

BIBLIOGRAPHY: Howard C. Williams, "'The End of the Line Station' of the Texas and New Orleans Railroad," *Las Sabinas: The Official Quarterly Publication of the Orange County Historical Society* 7 (October 1981).

Robert Wooster

ECHOLS, TEXAS. Echols was near Farm Road 2310 and U.S. Highway 84, eight miles west of Mexia in northern Limestone County. Two churches, a school, and several houses represented the community on county highway maps in the 1940s. The school was consolidated with the Mexia Independent School District in 1960. Only one church remained at Echols in the 1980s.

Vivian Elizabeth Smyrl

ECKERT, TEXAS. Eckert is 11½ miles northeast of Fredericksburg in northeastern Gillespie County. It was originally called Nebo, presumably after nearby Mount Nebo, and was founded in 1875 when eight Anglo-American families settled there and built a log church called Mount Zion. The town was officially renamed when local farmer and merchant Wilhelm Rudolph Eckert opened a post office in 1903. The population was estimated at 100 in 1925 but fell to fifteen in 1933 and to seven in 1964.

BIBLIOGRAPHY: Gillespie County Historical Society, *Pioneers in God's Hills* (2 vols., Austin: Von Boeckmann–Jones, 1960, 1974).

Martin Donell Kohout

ECLETO, TEXAS (Karnes County). Ecleto was at the crossing of the old road from Goliad to San Antonio and El Cleto Creek in northern Karnes County. The area evidently has long been the site of human habitation. John Charles Beales[qv] in his journal mentioned the remains of an Indian encampment there in 1834. In 1852 a post office called Cleto (a corruption of El Cleto) was opened at the site, and in 1854, when Karnes County was established, the community's name was officially changed to Ecleto. In the 1850s the settlement was a way station for stages between San Antonio and Victoria and was the location of Kelly's Stage Stand, operated by Riley A. Kelly. During the Civil War.^qv Ecleto was a mustering point for a company of Confederate soldiers under Capt. Thomas Rabb.^qv In 1871 the community's post office was moved to the new town of Riddleville (later Gillett) at the nearby intersection of the San Antonio–Victoria and Helena–Seguin roads. Shortly thereafter Ecleto was abandoned. The settlement is not to be confused with another Ecleto located nine miles southeast.

BIBLIOGRAPHY: Robert H. Thonhoff, History of Karnes County (M.A. thesis, Southwest Texas State College, 1963).

Robert H. Thonhoff

ECLETO, TEXAS (Karnes County). Ecleto is at the intersection of Farm Road 627 and Dry Ecleto Creek, about six miles southeast of Gillett in northern Karnes County. In 1921, Walter G. Riedel and others built a cooperative store and cotton gin there to serve the surrounding farm community. A post office opened in the store in 1921. The store closed in 1971, but the post office continued until June 30, 1987, when it was converted into a neighborhood delivery and collection-box unit. In 1990 Ecleto was a dispersed farming community with a population of about twenty-five.

BIBLIOGRAPHY: Robert H. Thonhoff, History of Karnes County (M.A. thesis, Southwest Texas State College, 1963).

Robert H. Thonhoff

ECLETO CREEK. Ecleto (Eclato) Creek rises nine miles south of Seguin in southern Guadalupe County (at 29°26′ N, 97°57′ W) and runs southeast for seventy-two miles to its mouth on the San Antonio River, two miles west of Runge in Karnes County (at 28°59′ N, 97°45′ W). The local terrain is generally flat to rolling with local escarpments, surfaced by clay and sandy loams that support vegetation ranging from scrub brush and cacti to water-tolerant hardwoods and conifers.

ECONOMY FURNITURE COMPANY STRIKE. The Economy Furniture Company strike by Local 456 of the Upholsters International Union started on November 27, 1968, in Austin, six months after company officials refused to recognize the 252–83 vote by the workers for union representation by the UIU in May 1968. Mexican Americans,^qv almost a quarter female, comprised 90 percent of the 400 workers. At the time Economy was the largest company in the furniture-making business in the three-state area of Texas, Arizona, and New Mexico. Milton T. Smith, the owner and operator of Economy, had been locally admired as a humanitarian for three decades. Yet many workers at his company earned only $1.75 an hour, even after more than fifteen years of service.

Following the vote to unionize, Smith refused to bargain with Local 456 and union officials asked the National Labor Relations Board to intervene. The NLRB ruled that Economy Furniture must negotiate with the union, but Smith rejected the board's order. Local 456 therefore called a strike against Economy Furniture. Smith appealed the NLRB decision to the United States Court of Appeals, Fifth Circuit. In his court brief the Economy owner castigated the strikers as misinformed and referred to them as "thugs."

The strike was jointly coordinated by Local 456 and the UIU national office. It lasted twenty-eight months, during which workers set up daily pickets outside the company headquarters, garnered the support of United Farm Workers Union^qv president César Chávez, and carried out boycotts against Economy Furniture products sold by local shops and Montgomery Ward, which was the largest chain store that carried a considerable amount of the company's furniture.

In January 1971 the appeals court handed down a ruling upholding the NLRB's certification of Local 456 as a legitimate union. It further ordered that the NLRB's judgment requiring Economy Furniture to enter into collective bargaining with Local 456 be enforced. In March of that year workers responded to the court's decision favorably by voting to end the strike. The following June two months of collective bargaining began on a new contract for workers. Six members of the union's negotiating team were Mexican American. The group agreed to a 3½-year contract, which was approved by a majority of Local 456 members in September 1971. It provided for wage increases each year, seniority, overtime, additional vacation, and other benefits.

BIBLIOGRAPHY: Economy Furniture Company Strike Collection, Benson Latin American Collection, University of Texas at Austin.

Teresa Palomo Acosta

ECTOR, MATHEW DUNCAN (1822–1879). Mathew Duncan Ector, Confederate general and judge, son of Hugh Walton and Dorothy (Duncan) Ector, was born in Putnam County, Georgia, on February 28, 1822, and raised in Merryweather County. He received his education at La Grange, Georgia, and Centre College in Danville, Kentucky. In 1841 he began studying law at Greenville, Georgia, under the supervision of Hiram B. Warner, a state Supreme Court justice, and was elected to one term in the state legislature. After marrying Louisa Phillips in 1842, Ector gave up the law and turned to farming for the next seven years. After his wife's death in 1848, he traveled to California for a brief period, returned briefly to his native state, and moved to Texas in 1850. He settled in Henderson and returned to the study of law under Judge William Wright Morris.^qv In 1851 he was admitted to the bar, opened a law office in Henderson, and married Letitia M. Graham. In 1855 he became the editor of the Henderson *Democrat* and was elected to represent Rusk County in the Sixth Texas Legislature. Ector's second wife died in 1859.

At the beginning of the Civil War^qv he enlisted as a private in the Third Texas Cavalry and was shortly elected first lieutenant and appointed adjutant to the brigade commander, Gen. James L. Hogg.^qv He saw combat with the Third Texas in the battles of Wilson's Creek, Missouri, Chustenahlah, Cherokee Nation, and Pea Ridge, Arkansas, before being promoted to colonel and command of the Fourteenth Texas Cavalry (dismounted). Ector was leading his men in the battle of Richmond, Kentucky, when he was promoted to brigadier general on August 23, 1862. He led his new command, known as Ector's Brigade, at Murfreesboro, Tennessee, before joining Joseph E. Johnston^qv in Mississippi in an attempt to relieve the Confederate garrison at Vicksburg. By September he had rejoined the Army of Tennessee in time to fight at Chickamauga, Georgia, where he received three slight wounds. His military career ended at Atlanta after he was wounded in the left leg on July 27, 1864, and the leg was amputated just below the knee. He was to have taken command of the Confederate forces at Mobile, Alabama, in 1865, but the war ended before he had recovered enough to assume those duties.

Ector married Sallie P. Chew of Mississippi in 1864 and in 1866 returned with her to Henderson, where he resumed his law practice and was elected district judge. He was removed in 1867 by Gen. Joseph J. Reynolds^qv for being a "Southern obstructionist." The following year he moved to Marshall and formed a law partnership with N. H. Wilson. He was appointed judge of the new Seventh District, and in 1875 he was elected to the Court of Appeals. The next year Ector's colleagues elected him presiding judge, a position he held until his death in Tyler on October 29, 1879. Ector was a member of the Methodist Church and is buried in Marshall. Ector County, established in 1874, was named in his honor.

BIBLIOGRAPHY: *Biographical Encyclopedia of Texas* (New York: Southern, 1880). Zachary T. Fulmore, *History and Geography of Texas As Told in County Names* (Austin: Steck, 1915; facsimile, 1935). Sidney S. Johnson, *Texans Who Wore the Gray* (Tyler, Texas, 1907). *Southern Home Magazine*, August 1897. Ezra J. Warner, *Generals in Gray* (Baton Rouge: Louisiana State University Press, 1959). Dorman H. Winfrey, *A History of Rusk County* (Waco: Texian, 1961).

David V. Stroud

ECTOR, TEXAS. Ector is at the intersection of Farm Road 898 and

U.S. Highway 82, six miles west of Bonham in central Fannin County. The community started in the late nineteenth century when farmers settled near Caney Creek. Residents named it Victor's Station but, when informed by postal authorities that a town of that name already existed, decided to honor one of the pioneer settlers of the area, Ector Owens. In 1886 postal service to the community began. The tracks of the Texas and Pacific Railway reached the site in 1892. The railroad quickly made Ector a shipping point for area farmers. In 1904 the town had 218 residents served by a church, a school, and a half dozen businesses, including a bank. The population reached 451 in 1926, when the businesses numbered twenty-five. In 1947 Ector had a reported 457 residents. Subsequently, the population steadily increased, reaching 650 in 1988. The number of businesses declined, however, from twelve in 1936 to three in 1988. By that time the majority of the residents were commuting to jobs in Sherman and Denison. The population of Ector in 1990 was 494.

BIBLIOGRAPHY: *Fannin County Folks and Facts* (Dallas: Taylor, 1977). *David Minor*

ECTOR COUNTY. Ector County (F-8) is in West Texas on the lower shelf of the Great Plains and on the northern border of the Edwards Plateau,qv bounded on the north by Andrews County, on the west by Winkler County, on the east by Midland County, and on the south by Crane and Ward counties. The county's midpoint is 30°53′ north latitude and 102°33′ west longitude, about thirty miles southwest of Midland. The county was named for Mathew D. Ector,qv a Confederate general and Texas jurist. It covers 907 square miles of level to rolling land with elevations that vary from 2,500 to 3,300 feet above sea level. The annual rainfall is 13.77 inches. The average minimum temperature in January is 30° F; the average maximum in July is 96°. The county has a growing season of 217 days, though less than 1 percent of the land is considered prime farmland. Ector County's geology is significant since the county is a major producer of petroleum products. Oil in the Permian Basinqv was formed in comparatively shallow reservoirs bound by Permian Age limestone. Above the oil a large gas cap formed, which in modern times provides the energy for producing the oil underneath, making the Permian Basin nearly ideal for oil and gas production. Over 35,897,000 barrels of oil were taken from Ector County lands in 1990; between 1926, when oil was first discovered in the county, and 1990 the county produced 2,726,524,140 barrels of petroleum, making it the second most productive oil county in Texas.

Impressive evidence of prehistoric Indian culture in the area that is now Ector County exists in the Blue Mountain pictographs, which depict various prehistoric hunting scenes. During the eighteenth and nineteenth centuries the area was within the range of Comanche hunters, but was not particularly attractive to them because of the region's limited water resources.

Ector County was marked off in 1887 from land previously assigned to Tom Green County, and was attached to Midland, Crane, and Upton counties for judicial purposes. As early as 1881 promoters of the Texas and Pacific Railway encouraged immigration by offering to haul farm machinery and household goods for prospective settlers at no charge; they ignored the limited rainfall and predicted a splendid agricultural potential for the area. Pointing to the county's supposed resemblance to the steppes of Russia, a railroad official named the first settlement in the county Odessa; in 1882 the town became one of nine stopping places on the railroad's route through West Texas. In 1886 the Odessa Land and Townsite Companyqv was formed in Zanesville, Ohio, to sell farmland in Ector County; the company's exaggerated promises and bi-monthly excursion trains failed to attract enough buyers, however, and by 1889 the company was bankrupt. In fact the region was most suitable for ranching, and for many years Ector County was known mainly for its fine Hereford cattle. Much of the land in the county was owned by the University of Texas.

But, as pioneer J. J. Amburgery later pointed out, the area did present one decided advantage to prospective farmers: "Land was pretty cheap out there. I bought seven sections of school land for $1 an acre." During the late 1880s and in the 1890s settlers began to trickle in. In 1890 the census enumerated 224 residents, and in 1891 Ector County was formally organized, with Odessa, the largest town, designated as the county seat. In the early 1890s Methodists established a small school, Odessa College, but it burned down in 1892. By 1900, there were twenty-five farms and ranches in the county, and the population had grown to 381.

Between 1900 and 1930, despite periodic droughts, farmers continued to move into the county in small numbers. A few farmers experimented with cotton production during this period. In 1908 about 800 bales of cotton were ginned in the county. In 1910 cotton was planted on 222 acres in the county; in 1920, when only about 80 acres in the entire county was devoted to cereal crops, cotton cultureqv occupied 363 acres; in 1930 cotton was produced on 1,326 acres of the 2,580 acres of cropland harvested. Local farmers also planted hundreds of fruit trees; by 1910, for example, 588 peach trees were growing in the county.

Local cattle ranchers continued to be noted for their registered Herefords during this period. Almost 24,000 cattle were counted in Ector County in 1910, and in 1914 Joe Graham and Charles Price shipped 15,000 yearlings from their ranch alone. In 1929, almost 16,000 cattle were counted in the area. Periodic droughts hindered the best efforts to establish farming in the county, however, and the number of farms subsequently fluctuated. In 1910 the United States Agricultural Census found 84 farms and ranches in Ector County, but only 55 in 1920; there were 107 in 1925, but only 69 in 1929. The county's population similarly fluctuated, rising to 1,178 in 1910, for example, before dropping to 760 in 1920. Farming virtually died in Ector County during the Great Depressionqv of the 1930s; in 1940 the 52 farms and ranches in the county harvested only 583 acres of land.

The great oil strike made in 1926 on W. E. Connell'sqv ranch, however, marked the beginning of a tremendous boom that fundamentally changed the character of the county's economy and society. After the Penn field was opened in 1929 and the Cowden field in 1930, Odessa became the shipping and oilfield supply center for the county's burgeoning petroleum boom. County lands produced almost 12,330,000 barrels of oil in 1938, and by the mid-1940s Ector County had over 2,000 producing wells, to rank as one of the leading oil-producing counties in the state. Almost 62,249,000 barrels of oil came from county lands in 1948; more than 57,132,000 barrels in 1956; almost 58,959,000 in 1960; almost 59,228,000 in 1978; and about 45,958,000 in 1982. In the mid-1960s the nation's largest petrochemical complex was established near Odessa.

The continuing oil and petrochemical boom induced thousands to move to the area in search of work and opportunity, and the population of the county rose almost continuously from the late 1920s into the 1990s. In 1930 3,958 people lived in Ector County; the population increased to 15,051 in 1940, 42,102 in 1950, 90,995 in 1960, 91,805 in 1970, and 115,374 in 1980. In 1992 the county's population was estimated at 118,934.

In politics Ector County has moved towards the Republican party,qv which locally won every presidential election from 1952 through 1988. In that same period the county went Republican in eleven of fourteen senatorial elections, and in six of fourteen gubernatorial races.

By 1982 the average annual income from agriculture in Ector County was $4.5 million, from beef cattle, poultry, pecans, and hay. According to the agricultural census the 214 farms and ranches in the county that year produced an income of $4.5 million; 1,752 farm acres were under irrigation.qv Although scanty rainfall and lack of irrigation continue to hinder agriculture in the area, Ector County reported 11,616 cattle in 1982, and 26,331 pounds of pecans were produced in the county that year (*see* PECAN INDUSTRY). Manufacturers earned $233 million, largely from petrochemical products. Oil income was almost $1.5 billion, from sales of 46 million barrels. By 1987 Ector County, with a total production of 2,572,304,080 barrels of crude since 1926, ranked second in the state behind Gregg County.

Ector County offers several cultural amenities to its inhabitants, including a replica of Shakespeare's Globe Theater where a seasonal festival is held, the Odessa College Museum, and the University of Texas of the Permian Basin. Residents and tourists in the county can also view the second largest crater in the United States, formed in some distant time when a meteor fell eight miles southwest of Odessa (*see* METEOR CRATER AT ODESSA).

Communities in the county include Goldsmith (1992 estimated population 297), Gardendale (1,103), and West Odessa (16,568). Odessa, with a population of 89,504 in Ector County (the city is partly in Midland County), is the county's largest city and seat of government. Major highways in Ector County include U.S. Highway 385 (north–south), U.S. Highway 80/Interstate 20 and State Highway 302 (west–east); the Missouri Pacific Railway also runs through the county from northeast to southwest. Commercial airline service is available at the Midland-Odessa airport.

BIBLIOGRAPHY: Finas Wade Horton, *A History of Ector County, Texas* (M.A. thesis, University of Texas, 1950).

John Leffler

ECTOR'S BRIGADE. Ector's Brigade was formed during the reorganization of Gen. Braxton Bragg's command in November 1862, which resulted in the Army of Tennessee. Gen. Mathew D. Ector[qv] was the original commander of this Civil War[qv] brigade and served until he was wounded in July 1864. Other commanders were Gen. William H. Young,[qv] Col. C. R. Earp, Col. David Coleman, and Col. Julius Andrews. The original units of the brigade were the Tenth, Eleventh, and Fourteenth Texas Dismounted Cavalry, and the Douglas Battery (*see* DOUGLAS, JAMES P.). The Fifteenth Texas Dismounted Cavalry (the Thirty-second Texas Cavalry) joined the brigade soon after it was formed. The Eleventh Texas Cavalry, commanded by Col. William C. Young,[qv] was remounted after the battle of Murfreesboro, and its place in line was taken by the Ninth Texas Infantry. The Douglas Battery also left the brigade in early 1863. The Twenty-ninth and Thirty-ninth North Carolina Infantry regiments were transferred to the brigade in August 1863 and May 1864 respectively and remained with it until the end of the war. Units that served briefly in the brigade were the Fortieth Alabama Sharpshooters, the Forty-third Mississippi Sharpshooters, and McNally's Arkansas Battery.

Ector's Brigade participated in the battle of Murfreesboro, Tennessee, and took part in the initial assault on the Union right on the morning of December 31, 1862. In one day of fighting the brigade suffered thirty-eight killed and 308 wounded. They did not take part in the fighting on January 2, 1863. The brigade marched to Mississippi and joined Gen. Joseph E. Johnston's[qv] forces in an attempt to relieve the besieged Confederates at Vicksburg. After the surrender of that city they participated in the siege of Jackson (July 10–17), before returning to the Army of Tennessee and fighting in the battle of Chickamauga, Georgia, on September 19–20, 1863. At this battle the brigade had fifty-nine killed, 239 wounded, and 138 missing.

In September 1863 Ector was again ordered to march his brigade to Mississippi, and after reaching General Johnston's army it joined Gen. Samuel French's division in the Army of Mississippi. After Johnston assumed command of the Army of Tennessee, Gen. Leonidas Polk took command of the Mississippi army and assembled his forces at Meridian to contest Gen. William T. Sherman's.[qv] When the federals moved, Polk transferred his troops to Demopolis, Alabama, where they remained until they joined the Army of Tennessee in Georgia in May 1864.

Ector's brigade reached Rome, Georgia, in time to defend the town from Union troops on May 16 before joining Johnston's army at Kingston, Georgia. It participated in the long retreat toward Atlanta, taking part in numerous skirmishes and being lightly engaged at Dallas (May 25–June 4) before seeing action at the Lattermoure House and then at Kennesaw Mountain on June 25 and Smyrna on July 2–5. After Gen. John Bell Hood[qv] took command of the Army of Tennessee on July 17, Ector's troops remained in their trenches at Atlanta until they were lightly engaged in the battle of Peach Tree Creek on July 20.

Once Hood had abandoned Atlanta, French's division was ordered to attack the federals at Allatoona, Georgia, where Ector's brigade saw heavy fighting. As a result of this action the brigade had forty-three killed, 147 wounded, and eleven missing out of about 400 troops and did not reach Hood's army until after the battle of Franklin on November 30, 1864.

Ector's brigade marched north with the Army of Tennessee and participated in the battle of Nashville (December 15–16) before retreating to Mississippi. During the retreat the brigade formed part of the rear guard that ambushed a federal force at Sugar Creek on Christmas Day.

After General Johnston resumed command of the Army of Tennessee, Ector's Brigade was detached and ordered to Mobile, Alabama, where it joined other Confederate soldiers defending Spanish Fort (March 27–April 8, 1865). It was forced to evacuate the city and finally surrendered at Meridian, Mississippi, on May 4, 1865.

BIBLIOGRAPHY: *The War of the Rebellion: A Compilation of the Official Records of the Union and Confederate Armies.*

David V. Stroud

EDCOUCH, TEXAS. Edcouch is at the intersection of State Highway 107 and Farm Road 1015, eighteen miles northeast of McAllen in southeastern Hidalgo County. The townsite was developed in 1927 and named for Edward Couch, landowner and banker. A post office and railroad stop on the San Antonio and Aransas Pass Railway were established at Edgeworth in 1927. By 1931 the town was shipping citrus fruits, vegetables, and cotton, had a weekly newspaper named the Edcouch *Enterprise*, and reported a population of 914. Edcouch was incorporated in 1933, when it had thirty-five businesses. The town grew slowly from an estimated population of 1,758 in 1941 to 2,925 in 1958. By 1963 Edcouch had a school, two churches, an estimated population of 2,814, and forty-two businesses. In 1990 the population was 2,878.

Alicia A. Garza

EDEL, ANDREW M. (1813–1891). Andrew Edel, pioneer Catholic educator, son of Andrew and Barbara (Dietrich) Edel, was born in Colmar, France, on February 2, 1813. In 1829 he became a brother of the Society of Mary (Marianists[qv]), a religious congregation dedicated to education. He was in the first colony of Marianists to arrive in America (November 27, 1849). The Marianists settled in Dayton, Ohio, and founded St. Mary's Institute; Edel joined its faculty as professor of botany, agriculture, and horticulture. In 1852 he was appointed head of a new educational institution to be founded by the Marianists in San Antonio at the request of Jean M. Odin,[qv] bishop of Texas. Edel set out for New Orleans, where he met his assigned coworkers, three Marianists newly arrived from France.

After a brief stay in Galveston the group sailed to Indianola and traveled from there by stagecoach to San Antonio. They rented an old livery stable on the southwest corner of Military Plaza and converted it into a temporary schoolhouse. St. Mary's Institute, a school for boys, officially opened on August 25, 1852. The "French School," as local people called it, was very well received in the city because of its multilingual academic approach, its acceptance of students of all faiths or national backgrounds, and its sliding-scale tuition. The enrollment grew from twelve to a hundred in just a few months, and the need for a larger building became evident. With some money raised by Bishop Odin, financial help and advice from John Twohig,[qv] and the support of Henri Castro's[qv] Alsatian colonists, Edel acquired a plot on the left bank of the San Antonio River and immediately undertook the construction of a simple, two-story stone structure, which still survives as part of the La Mansion Hotel.

The new building opened on March 1, 1853, and a rapid expansion ensued. Enrollment continued to increase, boarding students moved in, new teachers arrived, and additional quarters were hastily built. Making use of all the space available at the school site, Edel planted fruit trees between and around the buildings, as well as his famous French Gardens all along the riverfront. But the school was far from self-sufficient. Edel, trying to capitalize on his expertise as an agriculturist, decided to acquire some land for farming as a means of support for the school. The arrival in late 1854 of Brother Charles Francis,[qv] a capable teacher and administrator, gave Edel the opportunity to dedicate some of his own energy to a farming project. In 1855 he conditionally purchased the ninety-acre plot comprising Mission Concepción, which bordered the river 2½ miles from the city. The Marianists planted a vegetable garden at the mission, and Edel was soon able to provide food for boarders and teachers at the school. In 1859 Bishop Odin transferred the mission property to Edel, who set out to restore the old Spanish church and further improve the land. The church was solemnly reopened on May 28, 1861, and the mission complex became a training center for Marianist postulants and novices. But under Edel's administration, the mission property continued to be primarily a farm for the institute.

During the Civil War,[qv] despite shortages and inconveniences, the school remained in operation without much hardship, and by the end of the war there were 350 students enrolled, including thirty-three boarders. In 1865 Edel delegated the direction of the school to Charles Francis and sailed to France to present the Marianist superior general a list of recommendations for the activities of the society in Texas. He also asked to be relieved of his duties as director and requested more personnel for the school. He returned to San Antonio empty-handed, but a visit the following year to St. Mary's Institute by the Marianist American provincial from Ohio produced some positive results. Edel, finally replaced by Charles Francis, was transferred to the mission and officially charged with the cultivation of its land. The mission, no longer used as a novitiate, became the year-round residence of four hard-working monks and the summer residence of St. Mary's boarding students. While the school prospered under the competent management of Charles Francis, Edel, a hermit at heart, built a cabin and oratory at the mission site in a grove of trees near the river, where he could have a taste of nature, silence, and prayer.

In 1869, relieved of all responsibilities at the mission, he was given permission to retire. He returned to the Marianist motherhouse farm in Dayton, planted a garden, built a cabin in the woods for himself, and enjoyed for the rest of his life the solitude he had long desired. There he died on July 29, 1891. In 1954 Edel's name was enshrined in the Texas Hall of Remembrance, established by the Texas Heritage Foundation to honor the most important educators in the history of the state.

BIBLIOGRAPHY: Catholic Archives of Texas, Files, Austin. Pierre F. Parisot and C. J. Smith, *History of the Catholic Church in the Diocese of San Antonio* (San Antonio: Carrico and Bowen, 1897). Joseph William Schmitz, *The Society of Mary in Texas* (San Antonio: Naylor, 1951).
Aníbal A. González

EDEN, TEXAS (Concho County). Eden is on Harden Branch at the junction of U.S. highways 83 and 87 and Farm Road 2402, twenty-one miles southeast of Paint Rock in south central Concho County. The first settlers in the area were the family of Harvey and Louisa McCarty. The town was founded by Frederick Ede, who moved to Concho County with his family about 1881. In February 1882 Ede designated forty acres of his land as a townsite and donated land for the town square. When the settlement received a post office in 1883 it took the name of Eden, an adaptation of Ede's name. The first school in the community opened in 1884–85. By 1890 Eden had a Baptist church (organized in 1886), a general store, a saloon, a jeweler, and a population of 107. It acquired a bank in 1906 and telephone service about 1907, and by 1908 had a windmill and public well. Its early fraternal organizations included the Praetorians, the Woodmen of the World (organized in 1900), the Masons (1903), the Order of the Eastern Star (1907), and the International Order of Odd Fellows (by 1908).

Eden voted to incorporate on December 15, 1910, and formally incorporated on February 4, 1911. The following year it became the terminus of a Gulf, Colorado and Santa Fe Railway line built westward from Lometa. By 1914 the population had reached 600, and the community had a newspaper called the Eden *Echo*, Baptist and Methodist churches, a restaurant, two hotels, two general stores, two hardware stores, two lumber companies, and two cotton gins. The Eden Independent School District was approved in June 1920. As sheep ranching[qv] in the area increased after 1925, Eden became a trade center for wool and mohair. By 1940 the local ram sale was advertised nationwide. In addition to sheep, goats, and cattle, area ranchers also raised polo ponies for the eastern market. The population rose from 593 in 1925 to 1,603 in 1941, partly as a result of the increased use of tractors and the consequent displacement of tenants from farm to town. The population reached a high of 1,993 in 1954 and was 1,567 in 1990.

BIBLIOGRAPHY: *Concho Herald*, Golden Anniversary Edition, October 11, 1940. W. C. Montgomery, *Have You Ever Heard of the Great Concho Country?* (Ballinger, Texas, 1908). Emsy H. Swaim, *History of Eden* (Eden, Texas?, 1982).
Mary M. Standifer

EDEN, TEXAS (Guadalupe County). Eden, on what is now U.S. Highway 90A five miles east of Seguin in eastern Guadalupe County, was established in the late 1880s. In 1904 the settlement had a one-teacher school for forty-seven students. The school closed in 1943, and Eden became part of the Seguin Independent School District in 1949. As roads in the area were improved and more people acquired cars, its residents began attending church in Seguin. There were a few scattered houses and a cemetery in the area in 1946; by the mid-1980s only the cemetery marked the location of the community on county highway maps.

BIBLIOGRAPHY: Josephine S. Etlinger, *Sweetest You Can Find: Life in Eastern Guadalupe County, Texas, 1851–1951* (San Antonio: Watercress, 1987).
Vivian Elizabeth Smyrl

EDEN, TEXAS (Nacogdoches County). Eden, on Farm Road 225 some twelve miles west of Nacogdoches in western Nacogdoches County, had a small school and church in 1897. The school, known as Longview, was at a site on Dick Clevenger's farm and at one time had thirty-three students. In 1924 another building was established on the property of Tom Collins, but after 1940 the Eden school was consolidated with that of Douglass. A cemetery and a community center remained in the area in the 1980s.
Kim Perkins

EDENS, ROGER (1905–1970). Roger Edens, musician, composer, and producer, was born on November 9, 1905, in Hillsboro, Texas. He began his career in the early 1930s as a piano accompanist for ballroom dancers. He played piano in the orchestra pit for the musical *Girl Crazy* from 1930 to 1931. Afterward, he worked with Ethel Merman as accompanist and musical arranger. He also wrote songs for Judy Garland that she performed at the Palace Theater and in concert. Edens joined the staff at Metro Goldwyn Meyer as a musical supervisor and composer in 1935 and eventually became an associate producer. He worked on many noted films as musical supervisor or director, including *Born to Dance* (1936), *The Wizard of Oz* (1939), *Strike Up the Band* (1940), *Babes on Broadway* (1941), *Ziegfeld Follies* (1944), and *Meet Me in St. Louis* (1944). He received the Academy Award for *Easter Parade* in 1948 and *Annie Get Your Gun* in 1950. Some films he worked on as associate producer include *Show Boat*

(1951), *An American in Paris* (1951), *Funny Face* (1957), *The Unsinkable Molly Brown* (1964), and *Hello, Dolly* (1969). Edens helped produce many of the extravagant show numbers that have come to be associated with the great Hollywood musical. He died in Hollywood, California, on July 13, 1970.

BIBLIOGRAPHY: Roger D. Kinkle, *The Complete Encyclopedia of Popular Music and Jazz: 1900–1950* (4 vols., New Rochelle, New York: Arlington House, 1974). *The International Dictionary of Films and Filmmakers.*
Amanda Oren

EDGAR, TEXAS. Edgar is on U.S. Highway 77A about seven miles northeast of Cuero in northeastern DeWitt County. In 1853 James Edgar brought his family to the area and claimed the land granted to his son, Joseph Smith Edgar, for his service in the Texas Revolution.qv In 1887 the San Antonio and Aransas Pass Railway located a depot in the area and named it for these early settlers. The Grassbur school served the area in the 1880s. An Edgar school was established in 1888, and the Grassbur school was merged with it. The local post office was also established in 1888. In 1890 the community had daily mail delivered by rail, a general store, and a population of twenty-five, and by 1915 a reported 100 residents supported a Wells Fargo office, at least one store, the school, and a cotton gin; the community also had telephone service. A Cumberland Presbyterian church also served the community for some years. The local Baptist church operated until 1947. The Edgar post office was discontinued in 1940, and the school closed in 1951. Only fifty people were recorded as living in Edgar from the mid-1920s to the late 1940s; thereafter, no population figures are available, though in 1948 Edgar had a black Baptist church, a grocery, and a chicken hatchery. The 1983 county highway map indicated a church and a business at Edgar.

BIBLIOGRAPHY: Nellie Murphree, *A History of DeWitt County* (Victoria, Texas, 1962).
Craig H. Roell

EDGE, TEXAS. Edge is on Farm Road 974 near Caney Creek fourteen miles north of Bryan in northeast Brazos County. The community, named for Dr. John Edge, who founded it in the 1870s, was one of several Brazos County settlements near the Old San Antonio Road.qv A post office operated there from 1894 until after 1930. The first store was established by the three Edge brothers. By 1896–97 Edge had two churches, a post office, and eleven businesses. In 1900 W. H. McMichael opened a general store from which the post office was operated; that year a drugstore opened and the population was twenty-five. A cotton gin was added by J. M. Lawless in 1906. By 1910 the population had grown to fifty. Edge High School opened in 1912 and burned in 1940. The school district was consolidated with Kurten in 1946. Maps of 1948 indicate three churches and four businesses in and near Edge. By 1933 the population had reached 100, which was still the count in 1990.

BIBLIOGRAPHY: Glenna Fourman Brundidge, *Brazos County History: Rich Past—Bright Future* (Bryan, Texas: Family History Foundation, 1986).
Molly Kate McCaughey

EDGECLIFF, TEXAS. Edgecliff is an incorporated residential community on Farm Road 731 just south of the city limits of Fort Worth in south central Tarrant County. The establishment nearby of Carswell Air Force Baseqv in the 1940s and the manufacturing plants of defense contractor General Dynamics in the 1950s boosted the community's development. The population remained low until the 1950s, when it increased to 500; in the late 1980s it was reported at more than 3,000. In 1990 the population was 2,715.
David Minor

EDGEWOOD, TEXAS. Edgewood, on Farm roads 859 and 1504 and U.S. Highway 80 ten miles northwest of Canton in north central Van Zandt County, grew in three phases reflected in the community's three cemeteries. From 1840 to the 1870s settlers from eastern states founded a community two miles southeast of Edgewood close to the Dallas-Shreveport road and established the first cemetery. Barren Ridge, as this place was called, was the site of a post office opened in 1850. A second phase and second cemetery date roughly from 1870 to 1890; the railroad arrived, and in 1877 a county-seat war between Canton and Wills Point led to a decision to establish a new shipping point at Edgewood. District judge-elect John C. Robertson and his partner William S. Herndonqqv gave land for a railroad depot on the Texas and Pacific Railway. A sectionhouse and a freight and passenger depot were built at the edge of a wood and named Stevenson Switch. A town plat was filed on November 30, 1875; in 1877 a post office was established. Herndon employed John P. Groome to lay track from Canton to the new depot, and a dirt road was authorized. Before 1879 the Methodist minister from Canton held a meeting for the railroad men at Edgewood, thus assembling the first church congregation in town; a land grant on April 19, 1879, was obtained for a church that was built that year. By 1881 the Baxter House Hotel and a blacksmith shop were in operation in Edgewood, and the community was a stop on the Missouri Pacific. A third phase of development, reflected in Oak Hill Cemetery, is associated with the arrival of more settlers in 1890 and the start of many new businesses. Shortly after 1893 the original church was torn down and a second church was constructed east of Oak Hill Cemetery. A third, built in 1896, was sold to a black congregation. Northside Cemetery grew on land donated by John C. Robertson in 1896, but the deed was lost and burials declined. By 1890 Edgewood had a population of 650, a steam gristmill and gin, a church, a school, two general stores, and a hotel. The population reached 500 in 1914. The town had two banks, two cotton gins, a newspaper, a lumberyard, and an express office by 1919. In 1929 the population was 1,000; in 1931 it was 761. In 1988 Edgewood had twenty-two businesses. In 1990 the population was 1,284.

BIBLIOGRAPHY: Wentworth Manning, *Some History of Van Zandt County* (Des Moines, Iowa: Homestead, 1919; rpt., Winston-Salem, North Carolina: Hunter, 1977). Van Zandt County History Book Committee, *History of Van Zandt County* (Dallas, 1984).
Diana J. Kleiner

EDGEWOOD ISD V. KIRBY. In *Edgewood Independent School District et al. v. Kirby et al.*, a landmark case concerning public school finance, the Mexican American Legal Defense and Educational Fundqv filed suit against commissioner of education William Kirby on May 23, 1984, in Travis County on behalf of the Edgewood Independent School District, San Antonio, citing discrimination against students in poor school districts. The plaintiffs charged that the state's methods of funding public schools violated at least four principles of the state constitution, which obligated the state legislature to provide an efficient and free public school system. Initially, eight school districts and twenty-one parents were represented in the Edgewood case. Ultimately, however, sixty-seven other school districts as well as many other parents and students joined the original plaintiffs. The Edgewood lawsuit occurred after almost a decade of legal inertia on public school finance following the *Rodríguez v. San Antonio ISD*qv case of 1971, which asked the courts to address unfairness in public school aid. The Rodríguez plaintiffs ultimately lost in the United States Supreme Court in 1973. The plaintiffs in the Edgewood case contested the state's reliance on local property taxes to finance its system of public education, contending that this method was intrinsically unequal because property values varied greatly from district to district, thus creating an imbalance in funds available to educate students on an equal basis throughout the state. In its opinion deciding the case (1989), the Texas Supreme Court noted that the Edgewood ISD, among the poorest districts in the state, had $38,854 in property wealth per student, while the Alamo Heights ISD, which is in the same county, had $570,109 per student. In addition, property-poor districts had to set a tax rate that averaged 74.5 cents per $100 valuation to generate $2,987 per student, while richer districts, with a tax rate of half that much, could produce $7,233 per student. These differences produced disparities in the districts' abilities to hire good teachers, build appropriate facilities, offer a sound curriculum, and purchase such important equipment as computers. In its original 1984 brief, MALDEF had declared that such gaps amounted to the denial of equal opportunity in an "increasingly complex and technological society," and asserted that this was contrary to the intent of the constitution's Texas Education Clause.

On June 30, 1984, about a month after MALDEF filed its petition, the legislature passed a school-reform measure to increase state aid to poor schools. MALDEF challenged this law in 1985 by refiling an amended lawsuit that sought additional monetary reforms. MALDEF also deemed the legislature's bill "intolerably illegal." The court accepted the MALDEF petition and heard the Edgewood case in Austin between January 20 and April 8, 1987, with state district judge Harley Clark presiding. On April 29, 1987, Clark ruled in favor of the plaintiffs. He found that the state's public school financing structure was unconstitutional and ordered the legislature to formulate a more equitable one by September 1989. The state appealed his decision to the Third Court of Appeals. On December 14, 1988, the appeals court justices reversed the lower court by a two-to-one decision on the grounds that education was not a basic right. It further proclaimed that the present system of public school financing was constitutional. The plaintiffs appealed the decision, however, taking it to the Texas Supreme Court on July 5, 1989. On October 2 the court delivered a unanimous 9–0 decision that sided with the Edgewood plaintiffs and ordered the state legislature to implement an equitable system by the 1990–91 school year.

Following the court's order, the legislature met in four consecutive and often contentious special sessions to resolve the financing issue. On June 1, 1990, with the legislature still unable to pass a bill, a master appointed by the state Supreme Court offered an alternative plan to be implemented if the legislature failed in its mission. It called for a transfer of money from property-wealthy school districts to poor ones to equalize the amount each district spent to educate students. The press nicknamed this redistribution scheme, and similar proposals suggested later, the "Robin Hood" plan. On June 6, 1990, the legislature finally reached consensus and approved a funding bill that would increase state support to public schools by $528 million. Governor William Clements signed it into law the following day. The plaintiffs, however, were dissatisfied with the latest legislation and asked for another hearing in the Travis County District Court. A month later Judge Scott McCown, who replaced the retired Harley Clark, heard MALDEF's arguments against the constitutionality of the new law. Two months later, McCown agreed with the plaintiffs, affirming that the new legislation did not provide "substantially" equal access to public school funds. He instructed the legislators to organize a new financing system within a year. Dismayed with this challenge to the legislature, the governor promptly responded that the state would appeal McCown's ruling. The case was returned to the state Supreme Court, which, on January 22, 1991, once again asserted that the present system of public school funding was unconstitutional, arguing that the legislation approved had not fundamentally altered the state's unfair property-tax system. The court also suggested that one solution might lie in the consolidation of the state's 1,058 school districts. It gave the legislature slightly more than two months, by April 1, 1991, to come up with a final plan. The legislature entered a new round of debates to devise an acceptable finance plan. After McCown threatened to cut off state funds to schools and extended his deadline for a plan to April 15, the legislature approved a reform bill.

The legislature's new financing formula, taking the Supreme Court's advice, consolidated the 1,058 school districts into 188 County Education Districts to assure that public money spent per student would be equal. This would amount to $2,200 per student immediately and rise to $2,800 in four years, the result of setting a tax rate of 72 cents per $100 valuation, with an eventual increase to $1.00 per $100 valuation. Governor Ann Richards signed the bill into law on April 15, 1991. The lawyers for fifty-seven wealthy school districts, which would lose money under the new plan, appeared before McCown in June 1991 to argue against its legality. McCown, nonetheless, upheld the legislation. After continuous protest on the issue from property-wealthy districts, the Supreme Court heard more arguments challenging the latest method of school finance and concluded in a 7–2 decision on January 22, 1992, that the plan was illegal. It held that the legislature had acted improperly in setting up the County Education Districts because they were unlawful taxing units under the Constitution of 1876.[qv] The court ordered the legislature to devise a new plan by June 1, 1993, but in the meantime it allowed school funding to continue through the CEDs. On May 28, 1993, the legislature passed a multi-option plan for reforming school finance. Under the plan, each school district would help to equalize funding through one of five methods: (1) merging its tax base with a poorer district, (2) sending money to the state to help pay for students in poorer districts, (3) contracting to educate students in other districts, (4) consolidating voluntarily with one or more other districts, or (5) transferring some of its commercial taxable property to another district's tax rolls. If a district did not choose one of these options, the state would order the transfer of taxable property; if this measure failed to reduce the district's property wealth to $280,000 per student, the state would force a consolidation. This plan was signed into law by Governor Richards on May 31, 1993, and was accepted by Judge McCown. The action guaranteed that schools would receive funding for the 1993–94 academic year. Many poorer school districts still challenged the constitutionality of the new law, however, and Judge McCown set September 1, 1993, as the deadline for them to file their complaints. In January 1995 the Texas Supreme Court ruled that the options plan was constitutional but that the legislature still needed to work on equalizing and improving school facilities throughout the state.

BIBLIOGRAPHY: Austin *American-Statesman,* January 31, 1992, May 24, 1993, June 1, 1993. Dallas *Morning News,* January 31, 1993.

Teresa Palomo Acosta

EDGEWORTH, TEXAS. Edgeworth is on South Elm Creek and Farm Road 2184, fourteen miles southeast of Temple near the Milam county line in southeastern Bell County. A post office was established there in 1894, and in 1896 the community included a Baptist church, a drugstore, a doctor, and a blacksmith shop. The post office closed in 1904, and the population had declined to ten by 1933. In 1947 the community had revived somewhat and had two businesses and sixty inhabitants, but it had lost its business establishments and had declined to twenty inhabitants by 1964. In 1990 the population was still estimated at twenty.

Mark Odintz

EDHUBE, TEXAS. Edhube is near Farm Road 1629 seven miles south of Bonham in central Fannin County. It was originally called Bentonville, for Edmond Hugh Benton, a Confederate veteran who arrived in the area in 1867. Later the name was changed because a homonymous post office already existed; the name Edhube is concocted from Benton's names. Settlement of the community apparently occurred during the middle to late 1880s. Between 1894 and 1906 a post office served the forty residents of Edhube. In the 1990s Edhube remained a community center for area farmers. It had a reported twenty-five residents in 1990.

BIBLIOGRAPHY: *Fannin County Folks and Facts* (Dallas: Taylor, 1977). Floy Crandall Hodge, *A History of Fannin County* (Hereford, Texas: Pioneer, 1966).

David Minor

EDINBURG, TEXAS. Edinburg, the Hidalgo county seat, is on U.S. Highway 281 and State Highway 107 in the south central part of the county. It is part of the McAllen, Pharr, Edinburg metropolitan area. Hidalgo, on the Rio Grande, was the original county seat. John Closner[qv] and William Briggs, who had land-development projects in the vicinity of Chapin, seventeen miles north of Hidalgo, made Chapin county seat. The townsite was named after Dennis B. Chapin, another of its promoters. Chapin's involvement in a homicide caused a change of name in 1911 to Edinburg, in honor of the birthplace in Scotland of John McAllen and John Young. The town grew slowly to some 800 inhabitants by 1915 and remained unincorporated until 1919. During its early years it served a ranching community, but the arrival of irrigation[qv] in 1915 initiated an agricultural economy. Edinburg quickly became a center for buying and processing cotton, grain, and citrus produce. Other economic developments before World War II[qv] included vegetable, sorghum, corn, sugarcane, and poultry (eggs) industries. After the war the economy diversified further to include peach and melon production, food-processing plants, cabinetry, oilfield equipment, concrete products, agricultural chemicals, and corrugated boxes. In the 1970s tourism increased significantly.

The first railroad service in 1909 was a spur line of eight miles, extending from the one connecting Brownsville and San Juan. Seventeen years later the city received direct rail connections with Corpus Christi and San Antonio. After highways and trucks replaced rail service, Edinburg benefitted from its location on a major highway intersection. By the 1980s the city's trucking industry numbered six commercial freight lines and two bus lines. The city has been named the "gateway city" to the Rio Grande valley.

Edinburg's first radio station started in 1947 and by 1960 served both a Spanish and English listening audience. In the 1970s and 1980s three more stations were established. An influx of people from both Mexico and various parts of the United States has given the city an ethnic and religious mix. Hispanics constitute 80 percent of the population, and well over two-thirds of them are Catholic. The Protestant influx made its first appearance with the founding of the First Baptist Church in 1912. Other Protestant denominations arrived later and included the Disciples of Christ, Lutherans, Presbyterians, Methodists, Pentecostals, Christian Scientists, Seventh-day Adventists, and the First Foursquare Church. In 1946 the Rio Grande Bible Institute started its work of training Protestant ministers for Latin America. The first Catholic church, Sacred Heart church, did not open until around 1926. Two others were added later to serve the growing Catholic population.

By tradition, Edinburg is a Democratic stronghold that reflects county politics. The governing body consists of five commissioners, including the mayor, who administers through a city manager. State institutions and agency offices in Edinburg include the Texas Department of Human Services,[qv] a Texas National Guard[qv] company, the Evins Regional Juvenile Center, the Texas Employment Commission,[qv] and the Texas Rehabilitation Commission.[qv] In 1976 the city became the home of the South Texas Symphony Association, which sponsors the Valley Symphony Orchestra, the Valley Symphony Chorale, and the South Texas Chamber Orchestra. The University of Texas–Pan American, founded in 1927 as a junior college, is in Edinburg. It had an enrollment of some 12,200 students during the academic year 1990–91, and offers both undergraduate and graduate programs. Also located in the city are Region One Educational Service Center and Edinburg Consolidated Independent School District.

The major historical landmark of Edinburg is its city hall, erected in 1909 and located near the northwest corner of Hidalgo Plaza in front of the county courthouse. The plaza has a bust of the Mexican independence leader Padre Miguel Hidalgo y Costilla,[qv] after whom the county is named. The city hall, originally the county jail, has a trap door for hanging that has been used only once. Later the building became a city hall, and in 1989 it housed the county historical museum. During the late twentieth century Edinburg had an annual population growth of 3.4 percent. The 1990 population was 29,885.

BIBLIOGRAPHY: *Edinburg: A Story of a Town* (Edinburg, Texas: Edinburg Bicentennial Heritage Committee, 1976). Edinburg Chamber of Commerce, *A Comprehensive Community Audit* (Edinburg, Texas, 1965). Edinburg Chamber of Commerce, *1987 Community Profile: Edinburg* (Edinburg, Texas, 1987). Vertical Files, Barker Texas History Center, University of Texas at Austin.
Hubert J. Miller

EDISON, TEXAS. Edison was on the Holdsworth Ranch near Tortuga Creek 2½ miles west of Loma Vista in southeastern Zavala County. A schoolhouse, variously called Edison School, Tortuga School, and West Loma Vista School, was established in the eastern section of the Holdsworth Ranch around 1906. In 1907 nineteen students attended the one-teacher school; that same year a post office called Edison was established in a nearby store that was owned and operated by relatives of the Holdsworths, N. B. Simmons and his wife. By the mid-1920s the community had been abandoned.
Ruben E. Ochoa

EDITH, TEXAS. Edith was on what is now State Highway 158 south of E. V. Spence Reservoir nine miles west of Robert Lee in west central Coke County. The community began during the 1880s when cattlemen and stock-farming settlers came into the area, and it grew to include a store, gin, blacksmith shop, church, and lodge hall. A post office was established there on February 14, 1890, and named for Edith Bonsall of Ballinger. Three rural schools were located in the area. An early recreation spot near the community was Dripping Springs, where seeping springs along canyon walls produced a profusion of ferns. Economic changes in the twentieth century and the nearness of the county seat, Robert Lee, kept the community from growing. In the 1950s and 1960s the settlement reported one business and a population of twenty-five. Its post office closed in 1955. By the 1970s the town was abandoned. County maps for the 1980s show only the Edith cemetery near Salt Creek within a mile of E. V. Spence Reservoir.

BIBLIOGRAPHY: Jewell G. Pritchett, *From the Top of Old Hayrick: A Narrative History of Coke County* (Abilene, Texas: Pritchett, 1980).
Charles G. Davis

EDMOND, TEXAS. Edmond, six miles northeast of Grapeland in northwestern Houston County, was established in the early 1890s. A post office opened there in 1893 with J. N. Parker as postmaster. It operated until 1896. In the mid-1890s the settlement had a general store, a gristmill and cotton gin, and a number of houses. By the mid-1930s Edmond no longer appeared on highway maps.
Christopher Long

EDMONSON, TEXAS. Edmonson, originally known as Running Water, was platted by W. W. Edmonson in August 1929 at the Edmonson switch on the Fort Worth and Denver Railway twelve miles northwest of Plainview in south central Hale County. The town lies at the junction of State Highway 194 and Farm Road 1424. Running Water Draw was near the headquarters of the Morrison ranch, established in 1881 as the first ranch in the county. Later the land became part of C. C. Slaughter's[qv] extensive holdings. Settlers bought railroad lands in the area, and in 1890 a post office called Wadsworth was established. For promotional reasons the name was changed to Running Water in 1891. That year a school was built, and the town was platted. The railroad bypassed Running Water, and in 1928 the community's businesses were moved three miles north to the rail line. In 1935 the Running Water post office was moved to Edmonson and two years later was renamed Edmonson; Running Water was abandoned. In 1940 Edmonson had two grain elevators and 100 residents. It was incorporated in 1963 and in 1980 had four businesses and eighty-one residents. Its population in 1990 was reported as 107.

BIBLIOGRAPHY: Ed Ellsworth Bartholomew, *800 Texas Ghost Towns* (Fort Davis, Texas: Frontier, 1971). Kathleen E. and Clifton R. St. Clair, eds., *Little Towns of Texas* (Jacksonville, Texas: Jayroe Graphic Arts, 1982). Vera D. Wofford, ed., *Hale County Facts and Folklore* (Lubbock, 1978).

William R. Hunt

EDNA, TEXAS. Edna, the county seat of Jackson County, was established in 1882 when the New York, Texas and Mexican Railway line was built from Rosenberg to Victoria and bypassed Texana, then the county seat. Construction of the railroad began in September 1881. Edna was laid out on land owned by Mrs. Lucy Flournoy, who conveyed right-of-way and a half interest in the townsite to the railroad, which was promoted and built by Italian Count Joseph Telfener.^{qv} The town was named for a daughter of the count. The NYT&M, nicknamed the "Macaroni," was constructed by Italian laborers, most of whom were brought from Lombardy by Telfener (*see* ITALIANS). After completion of the road, the majority of the crew remained in the area and established homes. The first train arrived on July 4, 1882; the first merchant was Gideon Egg, who moved his general merchandise store from Texana in 1882, and the first child born in the new community was Edna Louise Traylor.

In an election of January 22, 1883, residents voted to make Edna the county seat in place of Texana. The contract for a new courthouse was awarded on February 11, 1884. A post office opened in 1886. The first church congregations in Edna were the Methodist and Presbyterian, whose memberships moved from Texana almost intact. The latter brought their 1859 sanctuary with them overland eight miles. It was also used by other denominations for worship services. The oldest public building remaining in the county, the Texana Presbyterian Church, has been restored and serves in Edna as an area cultural center. It is listed on the National Register of Historic Places and is a recorded Texas historic landmark. The first newspaper in Edna was the *Jackson County Progress*. The newspaper plant, along with a large part of the business district, was destroyed in 1906 in the town's second disastrous fire. Succeeding the *Progress* was the Edna *Herald*, first published on November 22, 1906.

Edna is the gateway to 11,000-acre Lake Texana, which covers the site of Texana. The city has a hospital, convalescent home, library, museum, city park with swimming pool, three banks, two savings and loan associations, a country club with a nine-hole golf course, and Oak Creek Village, a retirement community. It is the center of a prosperous agricultural area with petroleum and natural gas production and has an active chamber of commerce, oilfield service industries, and two grain elevators. Edna had a population of 1,000 in 1896. By 1929 residents numbered 2,500 and by 1958, an estimated 6,500. In 1990 the population was 5,343.

BIBLIOGRAPHY: Brownson Malsch, *Indianola—The Mother of Western Texas* (Austin: Shoal Creek, 1977). S. G. Reed, *A History of the Texas Railroads* (Houston: St. Clair, 1941; rpt., New York: Arno, 1981). Ira T. Taylor, *The Cavalcade of Jackson County* (San Antonio: Naylor, 1938). Vertical Files, Barker Texas History Center, University of Texas at Austin.

Brownson Malsch

EDNA HILL, TEXAS. Edna Hill is on Farm Road 1702 nine miles south of Dublin in the southwestern corner of Erath County. The area was settled in the 1850s. By 1900 Edna Hill School was in operation there, and a cotton gin was located in the community soon thereafter. The school had three teachers and eighty-five pupils in 1935. In 1940 Edna Hill had a school, two churches, and scattered dwellings. The school was consolidated with the Dublin schools in the 1940s. The population of the community was estimated at thirty-two in 1966, and in 1979 Edna Hill had a church and scattered dwellings. The population was still estimated at thirty-two in 1990.

BIBLIOGRAPHY: Henry Herbert Miller, A Proposed Consolidation Plan for the Schools of Erath County, Texas (M.A. thesis, University of Texas, 1938).

Mark Odintz

EDNAS CREEK. Ednas Creek rises a mile west of Bomarton in western Baylor County (at 33°30′ N, 99°27′ W) and runs six miles northeast to its mouth on the Brazos River, nine miles west of Seymour (at 33°34′ N, 99°25′ W). It traverses flat to rolling terrain with local escarpments, surfaced by deep, fine sandy loam that supports hardwoods, conifers, brush, and grasses. The creek was probably named for Mrs. Edna Duckworth, postmistress at Round Timber in 1910.

BIBLIOGRAPHY: Baylor County Historical Society, *Salt Pork to Sirloin*, Vol. 1: *The History of Baylor County, Texas, from 1879 to 1930* (Quanah, Texas: Nortex, 1972); Vol. 2: *The History of Baylor County, Texas, from 1878 to Present* (1977).

EDOM, TEXAS. Edom, at the crossing of Farm roads 279, 314, and 2339, sixteen miles southeast of Canton in southeast Van Zandt County, is the third oldest town in the county. It was first established several miles from its present site in 1849 and organized as a post office called Hamburg in 1852. In 1855 the post office moved one mile south of the present townsite. There it was renamed Edom for the name given to Esau in the book of Genesis. Local saloons filled with lumberjacks, freighters, and traders as the community became a stopover on the Porter's Bluff and Tyler Road. Sometime later the town was moved again to its present location. By 1860 it had a Baptist church, a Methodist church, a hotel, a Masonic lodge, a sawmill, a tanyard, a wagon factory, and a boot, shoe, and saddle shop. The Edom schools, which opened in 1866 with children of former Indian captive Cynthia Parker^{qv} in attendance, enrolled 130 pupils in 1904. By 1876 a Grange^{qv} was formed, and local farmers responded to worsening 1880s farm prices by forming a chapter of the Farmers' Alliance^{qv} at nearby Red Hill on November 20, 1885. By 1914 the town had a cotton gin and four general stores. Railroad service failed to reach Edom, yet its population grew from 150 in the 1890s to between 200 and 300, where it remained from the 1920s to the present. Edom was an independent school district until 1966, when it was consolidated with Van. Artisans in pottery, silver jewelry, glassware, macrame, and leather crafts who settled in the town in the 1960s began Edom's annual arts and crafts fair in 1972. The community was incorporated in 1966 with 300 residents but lost its post office in 1976. In 1988 Edom had three businesses, the frontier Red Hill cemetery at or near the townsite, and an estimated 277 inhabitants. The population was 300 in 1990.

BIBLIOGRAPHY: Claude W. Dooley, comp., *Why Stop?* (Odessa: Lone Star Legends, 1978; 2d ed., with Betty Dooley and the Texas Historical Commission, Houston: Lone Star, 1985). William Samuel Mills, *History of Van Zandt County* (Canton, Texas, 1950). Van Zandt County History Book Committee, *History of Van Zandt County* (Dallas, 1984).

Diana J. Kleiner

EDROY, TEXAS. Edroy is on Interstate Highway 37 in southwest San Patricio County. It was planned in 1913 by Ed Cubage and Roy Miller after the San Antonio, Uvalde and Gulf Railroad was built from San Antonio to Corpus Christi. It derived its name from the first names of the two developers, who bought the site from John J. Welder^{qv} and divided it up into farm lots for sale. The first settlers in the area were E. J. and William Heuermann, who bought land in 1900. In 1921 the Heuermann brothers bought land from Cubage and Miller, laid out the townsite of Edroy, and opened a store at the crossroads on the railroad. A depot and vegetable-packing sheds were built, and during the 1920s and 1930s Edroy was a major shipping point for vegetables. During that time thousands of Mexican laborers handgrubbed the land to prepare it for farming. Corded mesquite wood was shipped out of Edroy by the carloads. A local post office operated from 1914 until 1917. In 1950 it was reopened. The economy of Edroy has always depended on agriculture. Bob Tewes built the first cotton gin in 1916, and in 1988 a large co-op cotton gin and two grain elevators served a wide farming area. The population may have reached 500 in 1950, but by 1987 it was estimated at 200, where it remained in 1990.

BIBLIOGRAPHY: Keith Guthrie, *History of San Patricio County* (Austin: Nortex, 1986). *San Patricio County in 1976: A Bicentennial Perspective* (Sinton, Texas: Sinton Bicentennial Celebrations, 1976).

Keith Guthrie

EDS CREEK. Eds Creek, which is intermittent in its upper and middle reaches, rises about two miles southeast of Dalby Springs in southwestern Bowie County (at 33°21' N, 94°40' W), and runs southeast for 5½ miles to its mouth on Bassett Creek, two miles northwest of Bassett (at 33°19' N, 94°35' W). The soils through which the creek runs are loamy, and the surrounding pastures and fields are used to grow a wide variety of crops.

EDSON, TEXAS. Edson was a farming community on the south bank of the Leon River, five miles north of Hamilton in northern Hamilton County. It recevied mail from Hamilton. In the late 1980s the community was no longer shown on maps.

Claudia Hazlewood

EDUCATION. Education in Spanish Texas^{qv} was designed to Christianize and domesticate the Indians and to provide the rudiments of learning for the children of garrison troops and Spanish colonists. Mission schools were established for the Indians, the first being at San Francisco de los Tejas Mission in East Texas in 1690. The mission schools taught Christianity, the Spanish language, and practical arts, but they achieved few permanent results for many reasons, including the difficulty in getting supplies, illness, and indifference or hostility of some of the Indians. A nonmission school was in operation at San Fernando de Béxar (San Antonio) as early as the 1740s, but it, as well as all other schools started during the period, proved transitory. Legislative proclamations were issued as early as 1802 to compel parents to send their children to school. Settlements and military posts with large enough populations were called upon to provide salaries for teachers, but apparently the effort failed. Sometime after 1812 a public school was established at San Antonio. It was to be supported by public funds, but the school had a precarious existence and did not last. A private soldier, José Galán, taught school at La Bahía^{qv} in 1818. The military nature of the Texas colony, the frontier conditions, the sparseness of the population, the poverty of the people, and the failure of the central government to provide financial support contributed to the failure of the few attempts at general education in the Spanish period.

The Constitution of 1824,^{qv} ratified by the new Republic of Mexico, delegated control of education to the states. The Constitution of Coahuila and Texas^{qv} provided for the establishment of elementary schools and seminaries in the principal towns of the state but did not include any means of support. In 1829 action was taken to provide a plan for free instruction for pupils whose parents were unable to pay

Public School House, Teacher and Pupils, in Live Oak County, Texas, 1887. Photograph by Asa A. Brack. Courtesy Western History Collections, University of Oklahoma Library. Many rural schools remained small and primitive more than thirty years after the state initiated a public-school fund. Here a teacher meets fewer than a dozen pupils under a brush arbor.

tuition. The establishment of these "Lancastrian schools," which had arisen in England and were popular in the northern United States, was well received in other parts of Mexico, but none was established in Texas. In 1830 six primary schools were projected; at least one of these opened in Nacogdoches, but, overall, plans for education in Mexican Texas qv never materialized. Neither the towns nor the state had funds with which an educational system could be established. One of the grievances listed in the Texas Declaration of Independence qv was that Mexico had "failed to establish any public system of education." During the colonial period, however, several private schools operated, and some of them occasionally were subsidized by local funds. Among the Mexican towns, Bexar had the best school facilities. In 1828 the community established the Public Free Primary School, supported by private subscriptions and a municipal subsidy. Instruction was given in religion, morals, and the Three Rs. Plagued by lack of funds, supplies, and competent teachers, however, the school closed sometime during or after 1834. In the American settlements, the wealthier colonists sent their children to the United States for schooling. "Old field schools" and academies, similar to those in the South, sprang up as early as 1823. Largely because of Stephen F. Austin's qv interest, his colony retained educational leadership throughout the period. Thomas J. Pilgrim qv opened both an academy and a Sunday school in the colony around 1829. Frances Trask Thompson qv operated a boarding school at Coles Settlement as early as 1834, and by 1836 more than a score of private schools had been established among the Anglo-American colonists.

The Texas Declaration of Independence had condemned the Mexican regime for failing to establish a system of public education; the Constitution of the Republic of Texas qv therefore compelled Congress to provide such a system. During Sam Houston's qv administration several private schools were chartered, but problems demanding the attention of the new government prevented public education from receiving much consideration. The first definite action toward a system of public education was taken during the administration of Mirabeau B. Lamar, qv who requested Congress in 1838 to establish and endow an education system. As a result of his message, Congress passed bills in 1839 and 1840 that adopted a plan for a school system ranging from the primary to the university level, delegated control over this system to the counties, and granted 17,712 acres to each county for the support of schools. The plan failed to produce the desired results immediately because land prices were too low for this endowment to provide revenue. There was also some popular indifference on the county level to the establishment of schools, as evidenced by the fact that by 1855 thirty-eight counties had made no effort even to survey their school land. In spite of these setbacks, however, Lamar's vision later earned him the nickname "Father of Education in Texas." Private schools and academies of the type prevalent before the Texas Revolution qv continued to operate, and in the republic several institutions of higher education qv were chartered.

With the annexation qv of Texas to the United States, the state provided under the Constitution of 1845 qv for the establishment of free schools. The constitution further stipulated that it should be the duty of the legislature to set apart not less than one-tenth of the annual revenue of the state derived from taxation as a perpetual fund for the support of such schools. The actual foundation for the present Texas school system was laid in 1854 under a school law that called for the organization of common schools, provided a system for payment of tuition for indigent and orphaned children, allowed for the convertibility of private schools to common schools, and, perhaps most importantly, set aside $2 million of the $10 million received by Texas from the sale of lands to the United States as a school fund (*see* PERMANENT SCHOOL FUND). In 1858 New Braunfels was reported to be the first town in Texas where residents citizens voted for a tax to support a "free" school, New Braunfels Academy. qv After the Civil War qv the Constitution of 1866 qv incorporated most of the features of the Constitution of 1845 and further made provision for the education of

A. M. Aikin, Jr., 1941. Courtesy Aikin Regional Archives, Paris Junior College, Paris, Texas. As a state senator, Aikin helped to enact the Gilmer-Aikin laws of 1949, which established the Texas Education Agency and a multifaceted program to improve the quality of public education.

Heman Sweatt registering for courses at the University of Texas law school, Austin, 1950. Prints and Photographs Collection, Heman Sweatt file, CAH; CN 00323B. Sweatt won admission to the University of Texas law school as a result of Sweatt v. Painter, *which went to the United States Supreme Court.*

African Americans through taxation of their property. The Freedmen's Bureau brought in teachers from the American Missionary Association, primarily from the North, to teach in black schools. Later, some white Southerners and educated blacks taught, but the early African-American schools were often the subject of controversy and suffered discrimination and intimidation (*see* EDUCATION FOR AFRICAN AMERICANS). The Constitution of 1866 was soon supplanted by the Constitution of 1869, which eliminated the separation of taxation for the white and black populations and reaffirmed the provisions of the fund for public education. This constitution set compulsory school attendance at four months a year and provided that the legislature should set aside one-fourth of the general revenue for public schools, assess a poll tax of one dollar, and commit all money from the sale of public land to the school fund. In 1871 Governor Edmund J. Davis signed a bill initiating a public school system in the state. Its measures included the establishment of a state board of education consisting of the governor, attorney general, and superintendent of public education. The bill became the subject of partisan politics, however, as Democrats in their efforts to regain political power tried to discredit the actions of the Republican government.

During the latter half of the nineteenth century the educational system in Texas still operated on a sporadic and localized basis. Some Texans regarded education as a private matter and resented any state involvement. Private and church schools continued to play key roles in the educational development of Texas and in some areas offered the only choice of formal schooling. Schools short of funds often faced problems of low supplies, inadequate facilities, and poorly trained teachers. Since the days before the republic some government officials had called for guidelines specifying the qualifications of teachers. By the 1870s the Peabody Fund, established by wealthy New England merchant George Peabody, began to have some positive impact on schools in the state. The fund was to be used to establish tax-supported public schools. In Texas Peabody agents promoted city schools and teacher training, and instigated a campaign to enlighten the public about education and its benefits. The Constitution of 1876 provided that "all funds, lands, and other property heretofore set apart and appropriated for the support of public schools, all the alternate sections of land reserved by the state of grants heretofore made or that may hereafter be made to railroads or other corporations of any nature whatsoever, one-half of the public domain of the state, and all sums of money that may come to the state from the sale of any portion of the same shall constitute a perpetual public school fund" (*see* LAND APPROPRIATIONS FOR EDUCATION). The constitution allotted more than forty-two million acres of Texas public domain to school purposes and reestablished the separation of funding for white and black schools. It also provided for a poll tax of a dollar and a commitment of one-fourth of the occupation taxes for school support. Some legislators thought that one-fourth was too high, and later in a special session the amount was cut to one-sixth. Provision was further made for local taxation. Beginning in 1883 a constitutional amendment added a twenty-cent state ad valorem school tax. The rate was raised to thirty-five cents in 1918, when the state began supplying textbooks.

Around the turn of the century a growing movement in vocational education began, the result of increasing national awareness for the need to teach technical and trade skills to youth. Early training programs included courses in agriculture, carpentry, and industrial trades for both black and white boys and home economics for girls. Vocational education continued to evolve and play an important educational role throughout the twentieth century (*see also* INDUSTRIAL ARTS EDUCATION). In 1910 a scholastic census recorded 625,917 children attending school in country school districts. The numbers were broken down to 501,806 whites and 124,111 blacks. Many of the rural schools consisted of one-room schoolhouses with one teacher instructing a number of grade levels. That same year there were 342,552 children (272,075 whites and 70,277 blacks) attending school in independent school districts across the state. These districts included some 670 communities of all sizes. In 1920 Texas voters passed the Better Schools Amendment, which allowed the amount of local taxation for education to increase. The law was designed to ease the state's burden of school financing. The measure had some positive results, though some counties were slow to increase their school funding. The problem of financial inequality also contributed to inadequate funds and facilities for some schools. Sparsely settled counties, racial and linguistic differences presented by large percentages of African-American and Mexican-American students, and a wide variance in the distribution of natural resources made for considerable lack of uniformity in the state school system. In 1930 *Del Rio ISD v. Salvatierra* attempted to show the inferior quality of educational facilities for Mexican Americans and helped launch a movement against segregated schools, though the plaintiff, Jesús Salvatierra, lost. Advocates of desegregation gained some ground in the case of *Delgado v. Bastrop ISD* in 1948 when a district judge ruled against the segregation of Mexican-American children in the public school system. In 1949 the Fifty-first Legislature passed the Gilmer-Aikin Laws in an effort to raise the general level of school standards and to eliminate inequalities. Important measures of the bill included the increasing of teacher salaries, establishment of the foundation school program, and the establishment of the Texas Education Agency.

In the school year 1950–51 disbursements for the public education

President Lyndon Baines Johnson signs the Elementary and Secondary Education Act. Photograph by Yoichi R. Okamoto. Johnson City, April 11, 1965. Courtesy Lyndon Baines Johnson Library, Austin. Johnson's grade-school teacher, Kate Deadrich Loney, sat at his side as he signed this landmark legislation.

Summer English class for pre-school Spanish-speaking children, with teacher Iva Nelda Blohm. Austin Elementary School, Corpus Christi, 1959. E. E. Mireles Papers, Benson Latin American Collection, University of Texas at Austin. After a successful pilot project sponsored by the League of United Latin American Citizens, the state began offering English instruction to pre-school Spanish-speaking children in the 1959–60 school year.

system in Texas totaled $199,527,347. Of this amount $95,225,919 was provided from the available school fund, $59,056,428 from the foundation school program fund, $250,000 from vocational funds supplied by the federal government, and $44,500,000 from city and $495,000 from county funds. In 1950–51 the scholastic population numbered 1,566,610, and the state had 2,505 school districts. The ensuing two decades saw major changes in education in Texas. *Sweatt v. Painter*[qv] (1950) challenged the previous "separate but equal" doctrine of *Plessy v. Ferguson* (1896) and laid the groundwork for integration in schools. With the United States Supreme Court decision in *Brown v. Board of Education* in 1954, states were compelled to end school segregation for African Americans. San Antonio was one of the first districts to comply. School districts across the state began the implementation of integration, though some discriminatory practices continued well into the next decade. The 1954 decision was finally extended to Mexican Americans, for whom segregation had not been universal, in *Cisneros v. Corpus Christi ISD*[qv] in 1970. The federal government continued to enlarge its role in education in the 1960s. The Elementary and Secondary Education Act of 1965, signed by President Lyndon B. Johnson,[qv] offered government assistance to underfunded school districts. By 1965 approximately 98 percent of Texas public school teachers had college degrees and about 40 percent had graduate degrees. The Permanent School Fund totaled more than one-half billion dollars; annual earnings were used to defray current expenses of public schools. Earning power of the fund increased through legislative authorization permitting investment in corporate securities, in addition to investments previously authorized in federal, state, and municipal bonds. In the 1964–65 school year the state had 1,253 school districts with an enrollment of 2,535,381. Countywide day schools for the deaf and special classes for non-English-speaking preschool children, emotionally disturbed children, minimally brain-injured children, and the educable mentally retarded were initiated. In the middle 1960s a few schools in the state experimented with a longer school day and shorter school term in an attempt to educate the children of migratory workers.

By the 1970s some new major issues faced the Texas public school system. In 1970 in *United States v. Texas*[qv] a federal judge called for the integration of all Texas schools. Previous federal investigations

First grader on a school bus. Photograph by Mike Fluitt. Austin, 1974. Courtesy Austin History Center, Austin Public Library; photo no. PICA 10721. Continuing patterns of residential segregation hindered efforts to integrate schools in urban districts. To overcome that obstacle, desegregation plans often called for students to be bused to schools in neighborhoods other than their own.

had uncovered discriminatory practices in some Texas public school districts. The changing of school-district boundaries, reassessment of extracurricular activities, and increased busing of students to other schools were among some of the measures taken to enforce integration. Another issue that sparked controversy in the public school system was bilingual education.qv Throughout most of the twentieth century an English-only teaching requirement had been imposed. In 1973 the state legislature enacted the Bilingual Education and Training Act, which mandated bilingual instruction for all Texas elementary public schools that had twenty or more children with limited English-speaking skills. In the 1970s as the scholastic population and the cost of education increased, the number of school districts decreased. Small school districts in thickly populated areas were consolidated into larger units in order to effect a lower cost per pupil and to increase educational opportunities through providing better school facilities. Two factors then slowed the rate of consolidation. First, in many sparsely settled areas of Texas, further consolidation was difficult because of the time and distance involved in transporting children sometimes as far as 100 to 125 miles daily. Second, more than 100 small Texas schools joined forces to improve their educational programs through sharing resources and working together in a statewide small-schools project. A few schools built all or large parts of their plants underground to avoid noise, to reduce costs of construction and maintenance, and to provide less expensive, year-round climate control. Also in the 1970s much experimental work was underway in classrooms. More audiovisual aids were in use, and new approaches to learning enabled pupils to progress at their own rate of speed. Closed-circuit television, team teaching, nongraded schools, accelerated classes, and electronic laboratories were some of the innovations. School taxes were the subject of considerable controversy as school population increases necessitated more buildings, more supplies, more teachers, and more textbooks. In 1977 the state legislature formed the School Tax Assessment Practices Board to determine the property wealth of school districts. The state had 1,099 school districts and a scholastic population of 3,012,210 during the 1979–80 school year.

During the second half of the twentieth century church schools and other private schools also continued to play an important role in education. Some parents viewed them as attractive alternatives to the public school system, where classes were too big and standardized-test scores were declining. Many private schools focused more on academics and the teaching of deportment and moral discipline through religious courses than on extracurricular activities and peripheral matters. In the 1980s the Texas Education Agency examined the possibility of regulation for church and private schools—a move that some advocates of private schools saw as an infringement on religious freedom.

During the 1980s citizens, educators, and politicians raised concerns about declining test scores and literacy among public schoolchildren. This resulted in a call for major public school reform. Dallas billionaire H. Ross Perot was appointed to head a select committee to formulate school reform. In 1984 House Bill 72 placed stringent guidelines on teacher certification and initiated competency testing. Teachers' salaries were directly tied to performance. Stricter attendance rules were enacted, and the reforms also adopted the "no-pass, no-play" rule, which prohibited students who scored below 70 in any class from participating in any extracurricular activities. National norm testing was also implemented, as were equalization formulas for state financial aid. That same year the case of *Edgewood ISD v. Kirby*[qv] was filed. The plaintiffs charged that public school financing discriminated against students in poor school districts. The Mexican American Legal Defense and Educational Fund,[qv] which filed on behalf of the Edgewood ISD, came out against House Bill 72. For the next several years the case was involved in a series of appeals that ultimately led to a ruling for the Edgewood ISD. During this time the state legislature attempted to reach a plan for a more equitable system of school financing. In 1990 a "Robin Hood" plan was devised by which money from wealthy school districts would be redistributed to poorer ones. This measure was defeated by voters, but similar proposals were made in an effort to avoid court deadlines for an acceptable plan. Failure to find an equitable alternative plan would result in the loss of federal education money. In 1993 the state legislature passed another school financing plan, which gave school districts a number of options to choose from in order to distribute funding more equally. Afterward, various factions still argued that school financing needed more equalization.

Joshua at the Walls of Jericho High, by Bob Taylor. Original published in Dallas Times Herald, *October 18, 1984. Courtesy Bob Taylor, Auburn, California.* As chairman of a governor-appointed committee to study Texas schools, H. Ross Perot lobbied successfully for a measure known as "no pass–no play." This cartoon portrays Perot as Joshua, heralding the 3 R's and bringing down the walls of Tradition, within whose precincts individuals are worshipping a giant football.

In 1992–93 there were 1,060 school districts in Texas. In the 1990s a popular movement sought to increase the length of the school year or possibly to implement year-round school. A few school districts had already established the latter policy by 1995, when computers had become standard teaching tools in many classrooms. Parents continued to explore other educational options, including private and church schools, educational kindergartens, education vouchers, and home schooling.

See also ADVENTIST SCHOOLS, AGRICULTURAL EDUCATION, CATHOLIC EDUCATION, CHRISTIAN CHURCH EDUCATION, COMMISSIONER OF EDUCATION, GERMAN-ENGLISH SCHOOL, GOVERNMENT, JOB CORPS, MANSFIELD SCHOOL DESEGREGATION INCIDENT, METHODIST EDUCATION, MEXICAN AMERICANS AND EDUCATION, PRESBYTERIAN EDUCATION, PROTESTANT EPISCOPAL EDUCATION, SCHOOL IMPROVEMENT LEAGUE, TEACHER EDUCATION, TEACHERS STATE ASSOCIATION OF TEXAS, TEXAS ASSOCIATION OF SCHOOL BOARDS, TEXAS CONGRESS OF PARENTS AND TEACHERS, TEXAS STATE TEACHERS ASSOCIATION, UNIVERSITY INTERSCHOLASTIC LEAGUE, and WOMEN AND EDUCATION.

BIBLIOGRAPHY: Alwyn Barr, *Black Texans: A History of Negroes in Texas, 1528–1971* (Austin: Jenkins, 1973). Max Berger, "Stephen F. Austin and Education in Early Texas, 1821–1835," *Southwestern Historical Quarterly* 48 (January 1945). John Michael Bodi, Educational Equity in Texas: A Historical Case Study of the Policymakers (Ph.D. dissertation, University of Texas at Austin, 1994). *A Decade of Change: Public Education Reform in Texas, 1981–1992* (Austin: Lyndon B. Johnson School of Public Affairs, University of Texas at Austin and Texas Center for Educational Research, 1993). Frederick Eby, *The Development of Education in Texas* (New York: Macmillan, 1925). Frederick Eby, *Education in Texas: Source Materials* (Austin: University of Texas, 1918). Truman Harrison Etheridge, Education in the Republic of Texas (Ph.D. dissertation, University of Texas, 1942). *The Final Report and Recommendations of the Select Committee on Education* (2 vols., Austin, 1988). Charles W. Funkhouser, ed., *Education in Texas: Policies, Practices, and Perspectives*, 6th ed. (Scottsdale, Arizona: Gorsuch Scarisbrick, 1992). Hans Peter Nielsen Gammel, comp., *Laws of Texas, 1822–1897* (10 vols., Austin: Gammel, 1898). John Jay Lane, *History of Education in Texas* (Washington: U.S. Bureau of Education, 1903). William Franklin Ledlow, History of Protestant Education in Texas (Ph.D. dissertation, University of Texas, 1926). Charla Dean McCoy, The Education President: Lyndon Baines Johnson's Public Statements on Instruction and the Teaching Profession (Ph.D. dissertation, University of Texas at Austin, 1975). Carl H. Moneyhon, "Public Education and Texas Reconstruction Politics, 1871–1874," *Southwestern Historical Quarterly* 92 (January 1989). State Board of Education, *Quality, Equity, Accountability: Long-Range Plan for Public Education, 1991–1995* (Austin: Texas Education Agency, 1991). Rae Files Still, *The Gilmer-Aikin Bills* (Austin: Steck, 1950). *Texas Almanac, 1994–95.* Jose E. Vega, *Education, Politics, and Bilingualism in Texas* (Washington: University Press of America, 1983). James F. Veninga and Catherine Williams, eds., *Preparing for Texas in the 21st Century: Building a Future for the Children of Texas* (5 vols., Austin: Texas Committee for the Humanities, 1990). Vertical Files, Barker Texas History Center, University of Texas at Austin (Education—Private Nurseries, Private Schools).
Max Berger and Lee Wilborn

EDUCATION FOR AFRICAN AMERICANS. The education of African-American children during the late period of slavery,[qv] after 1800, was sporadic and unreliable in Texas as in other Southern states. Formal education was practically nonexistent for African Americans.[qv] Education most often consisted of on-the-job training in a variety of occupations. Before the Civil War[qv] most people believed education of African Americans would lead to discontent and rebellion. A few did support instruction and often volunteered their services. According to the census of 1850, 58,558 African Americans, representing 27.5 per cent of the population, lived in Texas. Fewer than 1 percent, or 397, were free, of which 217 were believed to be literate, 20 were in school, and 58 were illiterate adults. There are no actual statistics available on the 58,151 enslaved African Americans, but available data indicate that a portion of the slave population had been instructed in the basic rudiments of reading and writing.

In 1865 the United States Congress instituted the Freedmen's Bureau.[qv] The bureau's primary function was to supervise and coordinate a vast educational enterprise located in Texas, Maryland, Virginia, North Carolina, South Carolina, Georgia, Florida, Alabama, Mississippi, Louisiana, Arkansas, Kansas, Missouri, Kentucky, Tennessee, West Virginia, Delaware, and the District of Columbia. The bureau supervised schools offering classes from the elementary level through college. These schools provided a formal curriculum of arithmetic, reading, writing, history, and geography. In addition, a practical curriculum of civics, politics, home economics, and vocational training was provided. Most teachers were supplied by the American Missionary Association, with the majority initially coming from the Northern states. Soon thereafter, a few Southern whites and educated African Americans were recruited to teach in these schools. In January 1866, Texas began with ten day and six night schools for black children. There were ten teachers with a total enrollment of 1,041 students (many of whom were adults). Six months later, on July 1, 1866, the Freedmen's Bureau in Texas had ninety schools (including day, night, and Sabbath schools), forty-three teachers, and 4,590 students attending. John W. Alvord, the first and only inspector of schools and finances for the bureau, described Texas schools during this period as prosperous. He found that Texas freedmen's schools had needed only minimal assistance from Northern states and attributed this to what he perceived as the minimal impact of the Civil War upon the economic base of Texas. By the end of 1870 there were eighty-eight schools (both day and night) in Texas, eighty-five teachers of whom forty-four were African American, and 4,478 students. In addition, there were twenty-seven Sabbath schools with twenty-eight teachers (twenty-three were black) and 1,350 students.

The advent of schools staffed by Northern white missionaries was not acceptable to all the Southern white population. Some persons, alarmed by mandatory acceptance of African Americans in state politics, were vehemently opposed to the Freedmen's Bureau and exhibited their resentment by burning schools and intimidating the missionary teachers. This attitude was not universal in Texas. The Texas teachers' convention of 1866, for example, passed a resolution urging training for the newly freed African Americans of Texas. Divergences of opinion and fluctuating attitudes were most distinctly revealed in legislative enactments from 1866 to 1876. The Constitution of 1866[qv] provided that the "income derived from the Public School Fund be employed exclusively for the education of white scholastic inhabitants," and that the "legislature may provide for the levying of a tax for educational purposes." African Americans were taxed for "the maintenance of a system of public schools for Africans and their children." The Reconstruction[qv] legislature of 1870, by eliminating segregation, gave Texas a single educational system in which all children shared, but in 1873 and 1875 the state legislature repealed most of the laws of the Reconstruction period.

In 1871, Texas organized a public school system. The succeeding system, formed under the Constitution of 1876,[qv] reestablished the segregation of races but make impartial provision for each. Between 1873 and 1893 at black state conventions,[qv] African Americans from all sections of the state met to express their opinions, to delineate their needs, and to shape educational policies. Most significant were the Waco and Brenham conventions and the first meeting at Austin in 1884 of the Colored Teachers Association (*see* TEACHERS STATE ASSOCIATION OF TEXAS). The state Board of Education conducted its first survey of black schools in 1921. At that time 6,369 pupils were enrolled for secondary work, the majority being in city high schools. By 1925 there were 150 institutions in Texas offering one or more years of high school work for African Americans; included in this number

Members of the teacher-training class in trades and industries, Prairie View State Normal and Industrial College, Prairie View, summer, 1924. Courtesy Sam Houston Memorial Museum, Huntsville. Prairie View opened in 1885 as a coeducational school for training African-American teachers in trade and agricultural subjects.

were fourteen city high schools, six or more country high schools, and high school departments in every junior and senior college. In the 1920s to 1930s the average length of the school term for black children was only about four days shorter than that for white children. However, Texas spent an average of $3.39 or about a third less for the education of African-American students than for white students. During the same period, black teachers were paid significantly less than white teachers ($91.60 a month, compared with $121.03). In 1940 there were 222,715 black pupils in 116 accredited Texas high schools, twelve of which were rated by the Southern Association of Colleges and Secondary Schools. Approximately half of the 6,439 teachers had degrees.

The early 1950s marked several changes. These included improvements in school buildings and facilities, equalization of teachers' salaries, and an increase in funds for classroom instruction and libraries. The Texas Association of New Farmers of America, the African-American equivalent of Future Farmers of America, had chartered chapters in 178 high schools, with a membership of more than 9,000 high school boys studying vocational agriculture. The operating headquarters for the New Farmers of America program in Texas was at Prairie View A&M University. The NFA state adviser was also stationed at Prairie View, where the staff of the school of agriculture, in cooperation with the state staff in agricultural education, sponsored and planned jointly such activities as the annual state NFA convention and state livestock and poultry judging contests. They also participated in various fairs, shows, contests, and conventions at local, district, state, and national levels.

The United States Supreme Court decision in *Brown v. Board of Education* (1954) outlawed segregated education and consequently had tremendous influence on programs of education for African Americans. Texas was one of the leaders in desegregation throughout the South. Two black students had been admitted to previously all-white schools in Fiona, Texas, before the 1954 decision. Shortly after the 1954 decision, the San Antonio school district became one of the first districts nationwide to comply. San Antonio had the advantages of good race relations and an articulate policy statement. This desegregation process began in September of the 1955–56 school year. Though San Antonio's desegregation of its schools moved quite smoothly, other school districts, such as Houston's, were amazingly slow. In 1964 Texas accounted for about 60 percent of the desegregated school districts in the South and for more than half of all African-American students attending integrated schools in the South. The progress of civil-rights legislation and the process of school desegregation effected many changes in the education of black children in Texas. In 1965 the New Farmers of America was merged with the Future Farmers of America. The annual state conference of African-American teachers of vocational agriculture was discontinued. A similar change was made in the Four-H Club work of the Texas Agricultural Extension Service [qv] and in conferences of extension agents. Sponsorship of segregated participation in various fairs, shows, and contests was discontinued. By 1967, in the process of initial adjustment to the transition, the number of African Americans teaching vocational agriculture had declined 20 percent and the number in agricultural extension had declined 8 percent. This change was more than matched, however, by the increased employment of African Americans in professional positions that were formerly occupied almost exclusively by whites.

From Reconstruction to the present in Texas, conflicts have abounded on the subject of educating black children. the questions of what the schools should teach and who should control them have been foremost. Arguments persist about the effects of the quality of educational environments and resources on African-American students' achievements on standardized tests such as the Texas Assessment of Academic Skills. Although black students overall have greater difficulty than white students with the Texas Assessment of Academic Skills test, many educators attribute the problem to poverty and lack of educational resources. Legislation in the 1990s equalizing school financing may mitigate the problem. Another issue is that in many urban areas of Texas, resegregation appears to be occurring. In 1989, 63 percent of black students in Texas still attended predominantly black schools; this was exactly the national average (only ten states had higher percentages). It is impossible at the moment to assess the long-term consequences of this phenomenon. *See also* CIVIL-RIGHTS MOVEMENT, EDUCATION, HIGHER EDUCATION.

BIBLIOGRAPHY: John W. Alvord, *Freedmen's Schools and Textbooks: January 1866–July 1870* (New York: AMS Press, 1980). Alwyn Barr, *Black Texans: A History of Negroes in Texas, 1528–1971* (Austin: Jenkins, 1973). Henry A. Bullock, *A History of Negro Education in the South, from 1619 to the Present* (Cambridge: Harvard University Press, 1967). William R. Davis, *The Development and Present Status of Negro Education in East Texas* (New York: Teachers College Press, 1934). Vernon McDaniel, *History of the Teachers State Association of Texas* (Washington: National Education Association, 1977). Harry Morgan, *Historical Perspectives on the Education of Black Children* (Westport, Connecticut: Praeger, 1995). James Smallwood, *Time of Hope, Time of Despair: Black Texans during Reconstruction* (London: Kennikat, 1981). George Richard Urquhart, The Status of Secondary and Higher Education of Negroes in Texas (M.A. thesis, University of Texas, 1931). Ruthe Winegarten, *Black Texas Women: 150 Years of Trial and Triumph* (Austin: University of Texas Press, 1995).

Anna Victoria Wilson

EDWARD, DAVID BARNETT (1797–1870). David Barnett Edward, early Texas settler, teacher, and writer, was born in November 1797 in Forfarshire, Scotland. He emigrated from Scotland and lived in the West Indies and in Colombia for several years before moving to the United States in 1819. He taught at an academy in Alexandria, Louisiana, and in 1830, with a party of five persons, toured Texas. He subsequently moved his wife, Eliza, and three children to Gonzales, in Green DeWitt's qv colony, where he served as principal of a local academy, Gonzales Seminary. In 1834 he applied for a copyright for a book entitled *Observations on Texas, Embracing the Past, the Present, and the Future*, as having been published by the firm of Smith and McCoy in Alexandria, Louisiana. No copies, however, exist, and Texas bibliophile Thomas W. Streeter qv stated that it was unlikely that the book was ever published. While a citizen of Gonzales, Edward wrote *The History of Texas; or, the Emigrant's, Farmer's, and Politician's Guide to the Character, Climate, Soil, and Productions of That Country; Geographically Arranged from Personal Observation and Experience*, which was published in Cincinnati in 1836. Although Edward claimed to be objective, he was clearly pro-Mexican and anti-Texan in his reporting and was the subject of heated criticism. Stephen F. Austin qv branded the book "a slander on the people of Texas." Edward was also excoriated for plagiarizing entire passages from Mary Austin Holley's qv *Texas* (1833). He also made liberal use of several other published sources without giving credit to the authors.

Edward's book managed to offend almost everyone in Texas. Texas boosters, eager to present their country as a place of limitless opportunity, were aghast when Edward asserted, for instance, "There are no poor people here, if land makes rich; and none rich, if money is wealth." He alienated Houston and other supporters of President Andrew Jackson by proclaiming that the Mexican dictator was "a 'Jackson' of a fellow." Material for Edward's bitter condemnation of "shouting and howling" Texas Methodists may have come from experiences at Gonzales Seminary, which was operated by the Methodist Episcopal Church. He not only related scandalous anecdotes about several Methodist ministers, but also printed their names. As a leading spokesman for the Tory position, Edward maintained that American settlers had "by their perverse conduct, forfeited every claim to protection from the civil law; and therefore must either come under military control, or altogether be expelled from the [Mexican] Republic." Edward's suggestion that the martyrs of the Alamo and Goliad had been driven by the "wrong motives" and his praise of "enlightened" Mexican immigration policies was more than most Texans could abide.

Even so, Edward provided a valuable service in that he quoted the full texts or significant extracts from Mexican regulations relating to colonization, justice, and trade. Also reprinted are one of the first English translations of the Constitution of 1824, qv the full text of the proposed Constitution of 1833, and a note reporting the death of Benjamin R. Milam qv during the siege of Bexar. qv

The book's perspective generated such intense enmity in Texas that Edward found it advisable to take his family permanently out of the fledgling republic during or soon after the Texas Revolution. qv Thereafter, little is known about his activities. He died in Wheelersburg, Ohio, on March 18, 1870.

BIBLIOGRAPHY: John H. Jenkins, *Basic Texas Books: An Annotated Bibliography of Selected Works for a Research Library* (Austin: Texas State Historical Association, 1983; rpt. 1988).

Stephen L. Hardin

EDWARDS, BENJAMIN W. (ca. 1780–1837). Benjamin Edwards, pioneer settler and leader of the Fredonian Rebellion, qv was probably born in Bourbon County, Kentucky (then part of Virginia), around 1780, the son of John Edwards. Around 1820 he moved to the area of Jackson, Mississippi, where he and his brother Haden Edwards qv acquired a plantation. In 1825 he moved to Texas to Haden's colony. In May 1826, in the midst of difficulties with Mexican authorities, Haden Edwards went to the United States to secure financial aid for his Texas enterprise, and Benjamin took over the management of the Edwards colony qv upon his departure.

Benjamin Edwards and vice governor Victor Blanco qv had an exchange of letters in which Blanco stated that Haden Edwards had lost the confidence of the government and suggested that the empresario qv withdraw from the country and appeal to the national government for redress. Edwards, however, thought that the government was attempting to invalidate the claim. On November 22, 1826, some forty men captured Nacogdoches, arrested the alcalde, qv and seized his archives. On December 16, while the Mexican authorities and troops were advancing on Nacogdoches, Benjamin Edwards and about thirty men rode into Nacogdoches and proclaimed the Republic of Fredonia, thus instituting the attempted minor revolution known as the Fredonian Rebellion. qv On December 21 Edwards made an agreement with Richard Fields and Dr. John Dunn Hunter qqv by which, in return for their cooperation, the Cherokee Indians were to have the territory of Texas between the Red River and the Rio Grande west of the Old San Antonio Road, qv while the remainder of the territory should belong to the Republic of Fredonia. After the failure of the rebellion, Edwards retreated across the Sabine, on January 31, 1827.

During the Texas Revolution qv he presided at public meetings in Mississippi to raise money and men for the Texas cause. He had accepted a commission and was raising a regiment at the time of the battle of San Jacinto. qv In the summer of 1837 he ran for governor of Mississippi but died during the campaign.

BIBLIOGRAPHY: Eugene C. Barker, ed., *The Austin Papers* (3 vols., Washington: GPO, 1924–28). Eugene C. Barker, *The Life of Stephen F. Austin* (Nashville: Cokesbury Press, 1925; rpt., Austin: Texas State Historical Association, 1949; New York: AMS Press, 1970). Robert Bruce Blake Research Collection, Steen Library, Stephen F. Austin State University; Barker Texas History Center, University of Texas at

Austin; Texas State Archives, Austin; Houston Public Library, Houston. Archie P. McDonald, comp., Nacogdoches: Wilderness Outpost to Modern City, 1779–1979 (photocopy, Barker Texas History Center, University of Texas at Austin).

Curtis Bishop

EDWARDS, DANIEL R. (1888–1967). Daniel R. Edwards, Medal of Honor winner, was born at Mooreville, Texas, on April 9, 1888. He entered military service at Bruceville. He was nominated for the Medal of Honor twice for his exploits in World War I.qv Because the military preferred not to confer two such awards on an individual, his first award was changed to a Distinguished Service Cross, the second highest honor given. The action for which Edwards received the Distinguished Service Cross occurred on May 28, 1918, near Cantigny, France. He was serving as a private in Company C, Third Machine Gun Battalion, First Infantry Division, when he was part of a gun squad covering the retreat of the battalion. All the other members of the squad became casualties, and Edwards covered his battalion's retreat by himself, operating an eighty-pound weapon that he carried on his shoulder. As his battalion withdrew he repulsed several counterattacks from flame-throwers as well as other weaponry. He received bayonet wounds in the wrist and stomach but refused to quit until darkness fell. He was evacuated to a hospital, from where he was to be sent back to the United States.

The action that earned him the Medal of Honor took place some weeks later, during the battle of Soissons, on July 18, 1918. Edwards learned that his unit was preparing for another attack, left the hospital without permission, and hitchhiked to the front, where he rejoined his outfit. During the fighting he crawled into a German trench, his severely wounded right arm notwithstanding, and there killed four German soldiers and took four others prisoner. As he marched the group back to his own lines an artillery shell exploded nearby, killing one of the German soldiers and seriously injuring Edwards in his left leg.

After the war he became a celebrity. During the 1920 presidential election he served as a press aide to Warren G. Harding, who subsequently appointed him to a job helping war veterans. Later in his life Edwards worked as a fishing guide on Lake Ouachita in Arkansas. For a while he was also a popular speaker on the war. His exploits as he reported them approached the unbelievable, however, and doubts have been raised about some of them. Edwards married Mary Hanie in Georgia in June 1941, and they had four children. His life was chronicled in a book, *This Side of Hell: Dan Edwards, Adventurer* (1932), by Lowell Thomas. Edwards died on October 21, 1967, at the Veterans Administration Hospital in Little Rock, Arkansas, and was buried in Cunningham Cemetery, near Hot Springs, Arkansas.

BIBLIOGRAPHY: Thomas Turner, "Daniel Edwards—Hero or Hoax?," *The Annals: Official Publication of the Medal of Honor Historical Society* 12 (March 1990). Committee on Veterans' Affairs, United States Senate, *Medal of Honor Recipients, 1863–1973* (Washington: GPO, 1973). Waco *Tribune-Herald*, November 28, 1986.

Art Leatherwood

EDWARDS, EMILY (1888–1980). Emily Edwards, artist, art historian, teacher, and cofounder of the San Antonio Conservation Society,qv was born in San Antonio on October 7, 1888, the third of five children of Frank Mudge and Lillian (Brockway) Edwards. Her mother died in 1895. From 1898 to 1902 Emily and her three sisters boarded at the Ursuline Academy,qv where her talents as an artist were first manifested in sketches she made at an early age. She subsequently attended the San Antonio Female Institute for two years and studied drawing with sculptor Pompeo Coppini.qv

In 1905 she moved to Chicago, where she stayed with relatives and attended the Art Institute of Chicago; she studied with Enella Benedict, Ralph Clarkson, Harry Walcott, and John Vanderpoel. In her second year there she began working at the institute to pay her tuition. She also taught volunteer classes at Hull House, the settlement house established by Jane Addams, and taught at several girls' schools. From 1915 to 1917 she taught at the Francis Parker School, where the approach to learning through experience influenced her own teaching methods.

In 1917 Edwards returned to San Antonio to teach art at Brackenridge (now Wheatley) High School. In 1920 she taught at a mountain mission in Charles Town, West Virginia, then worked as a designer in a New York City theater for a short period of time, and subsequently made puppets and staged puppet shows in Provincetown, Massachusetts. She taught at Hull House again before returning to San Antonio in the early 1920s. In 1924 Emily Edwards and Rena Maverick Greenqv cofounded the San Antonio Conservation Society. As the first president (1924–26), Edwards led the society's crusade to prevent the river bend area from being paved over by the city. In 1926 she produced an annotated historical map of San Antonio to raise funds for the society and staged a puppet show for the city council, *The Goose that Lays the Golden Eggs*, in which the river represented the goose and each puppet was made in the likeness of one of the commissioners. The show was a hit, and the river was saved for posterity.

During the summers of 1925 and 1926 Emily Edwards traveled with a friend to Mexico, where she met the muralist Diego Rivera, who became a life-long friend. Her studies with Rivera stimulated an interest in Mexican murals, and Edwards subsequently spent ten years in Mexico, sketching in small villages and conducting research for a book on Mexican mural painting from the pre-Columbian era to modern times. She published a pamphlet, *The Frescoes by Diego Rivera in Cuernavaca* (1932), and a tourist guide, *Modern Mexican Frescoes* (1934), which was accompanied by a map to frescoes in the center of Mexico City. In 1932 she published a map of Mexico City, which was later reprinted and in the 1990s was displayed for sale at the San Antonio Museum of Art.qv During the 1930s Edwards established a modest reputation as an artist, exhibiting watercolors and color-block prints of landscapes, children, and Mexican subjects in Texas and New York. One of her prints was included in an International Exhibition of Prints in London, England. During her years in Mexico she was married to Librado de Cantabrana, with whom she had a child who died in infancy. She was divorced by the late 1930s, when she moved to Chicago to head the art program at Hull House.

In the late 1950s Edwards returned to San Antonio, where she remained until her death. In 1976 she received a special award from the Texas Society of Architectsqv for her "contributions to the quality of life in Texas." She wrote three books during this period: *Painted Walls of Mexico from Prehistoric Times Until Today* (1966); *Stones, Bells, Lighted Candles: Personal Memories of the Old Ursuline Academy in San Antonio at the Turn of the Century* (1981), a memoir; and *F. Giraud and San Antonio* (1985), a biography of François P. Giraud,qv an early San Antonio architect. The latter two books were published after Edwards's death on February 16, 1980. Examples of her work are included in the collection of the San Antonio Museum Association and the San Antonio Art League.qqv

BIBLIOGRAPHY: Frederick Charles Chabot, *With the Makers of San Antonio* (Yanaguana Society Publications 4, San Antonio, 1937). Emily Edwards, *The Story in Your Hand* (New York: Renard, 1925). Peter Haskins Falk, ed., *Who Was Who in American Art* (Madison, Connecticut: Sound View, 1985). Anne Leslie Fenstermaker, Conversation with Miss Emily Edwards, San Antonio, Texas (M.F.A. Research Project, University of Texas at San Antonio, 1978). Esse Forrester-O'Brien, *Art and Artists of Texas* (Dallas: Tardy, 1935). San Antonio *Light*, November 3, 1927.

Kendall Curlee

EDWARDS, GEORGE CLIFTON (1876–1961). George Clifton Edwards, attorney, one of five sons of William Mecklin and Elva (Gray) Edwards, was born in Dallas in 1876. He attended the Dallas public schools, the University of the South in Sewanee, Tennessee, and Harvard University, where he received a master's degree in English in 1899. In 1905 he married Octavia Nichols; the couple eventually had one son and three daughters, although two of the daughters died in infancy. Edwards returned to Dallas in 1901 and began teaching algebra and Latin at Oak Cliff High School. He became interested in socialism after being exposed to the plight of mill workers who lived in the slums of south Dallas. In 1902 he launched the Dallas Public Night School to educate illiterate adults. He soon became editor and publisher of the *Laborer,* the first official newspaper of the Texas State Federation of Labor qv and the Dallas Trades Assembly. In his editorials for the *Laborer* Edwards advocated equal rights for blacks, the abolition of child labor, compulsory education, the rights of workers to organize, a graduated income tax, public housing for low-income families, workmen's compensation, an eight-hour day, social security, and the abolition of capital punishment. In 1906 he was the Socialist candidate for governor of Texas. In 1907 he was elected to the Dallas City Charter Commission. In 1908, because of his politics, he was fired from his teaching job.

In 1910 Edwards was admitted to the bar, and he used his position as a lawyer to defend the causes he believed in. As an advocate of the poor and underprivileged he took cases involving landlord-tenant disputes, foreclosures, labor problems, and criminal charges against blacks and members of other minorities. In 1920 he became a charter member of the American Civil Liberties Union. He was an early activist in the National Association for the Advancement of Colored People.qv In 1939 Edwards left the Socialist partyqv because he thought its position of neutrality in World War IIqv in the face of Hitler's aggression was untenable. He later became a Democrat after seeing President Franklin D. Roosevelt's New Deal put into practice many of the reforms he had long advocated. Edwards's last major case was tried in 1956, when he successfully defended the NAACP's right to operate in Texas. He died on January 30, 1961, in East Lansing, Michigan.

BIBLIOGRAPHY: George Clifton Edwards, Jr., *Pioneer-At-Law* (New York: Norton, 1974). Vertical Files, Barker Texas History Center, University of Texas at Austin. *George Edwards*

EDWARDS, GUSTAVUS E. (?–?). Gustavus E. Edwards, member of the Old Three Hundredqv and an early Wharton County settler, came to Texas in 1822. He was a veteran of the War of 1812. His wife died en route to Stephen F. Austin'sqv colony. Edwards received title to a league of land now in Wharton County on August 19, 1824. In 1825 he was operating the Robinson ferry at the site of Washington-on-the-Brazos. He was postmaster at Piney in October 1836. His daughter, Mary Jane, married Robert McAlpin Williamsonqv in Austin County on April 21, 1837. In July 1837 Edwards sold his Austin County farm and moved to his league in Wharton County. He was living at Wharton in 1856, when Williamson died at his home.

BIBLIOGRAPHY: Lester G. Bugbee, "The Old Three Hundred: A List of Settlers in Austin's First Colony," *Quarterly of the Texas State Historical Association* 1 (October 1897). J. H. Kuykendall, "Reminiscences of Early Texans," *Quarterly of the Texas State Historical Association* 6–7 (January, April, July 1903). Duncan W. Robinson, *Judge Robert McAlpin Williamson* (Austin: Texas State Historical Association, 1948). *Telegraph and Texas Register,* October 1836, July 29, 1837. William Barret Travis, *Diary,* ed. Robert E. Davis (Waco: Texian, 1966).

EDWARDS, HADEN (1771–1849). Haden (or Hayden) Edwards, pioneer settler and land speculator, was born in Stafford County, Virginia, on August 12, 1771, the son of John Edwards. In 1780 the family moved to Bourbon County, Kentucky (at that time part of Virginia), where John Edwards acquired 23,000 acres of land, worked for statehood, and was elected to the United States Senate. Haden was educated for the law but like his father was more interested in land speculation. In 1820 he married Susanna Beall of Maryland, and they moved to the area of Jackson, Mississippi, where he and his brother Benjamin W. Edwardsqv acquired a plantation. He and Susanna eventually had thirteen children. In Mississippi the Edwardses first heard the news of Moses Austin'sqv plans for colonization in Texas. In 1823 Edwards traveled to Mexico City, where he joined Stephen F. Austin, Robert Leftwich,qqv and others in a three-year attempt to persuade various Mexican governments to authorize American settlement in Texas. Because of his wealth Edwards was often called upon to finance Austin. Their efforts resulted in the colonization law of 1824 in Mexico City and of 1825 in Saltillo, which allowed empresarios to introduce settlers to Texas (see MEXICAN COLONIZATION LAWS, 1821–30). Edwards suffered more than he profited from his relationship with Austin, at least in his own mind, since he believed that Austin claimed the best lands and tried to push his boundaries in every direction at the expense of other empresarios (*see* EMPRESARIO).

Edwards received a grant in the vicinity of Nacogdoches where he

Haden Edwards, ca. 1845. Daguerreotype. Courtesy East Texas Research Center, Ralph W. Steen Library, Stephen F. Austin State University.

could locate 800 families. Like other empresarios he agreed to honor preexisting grants and claims made by Spanish or Mexican officials. Of all empresarios, Edwards probably had the most such claims, some over a century old. In 1825 he posted notices to inform all potential claimants that they must come forward with proof of their claims or he would consider the land his, subject to sale to new settlers. This angered the older settlers, who opposed Edwards until he was expelled two years later. He also became involved in an election dispute between the representative of the older settlers, Samuel Norris,qv and Chichester Chaplin,qv Edwards's son-in-law. As empresario, Edwards certified the election of Chaplin. Norris then protested to Governor José Antonio Saucedoqv in San Antonio, and Saucedo upheld Norris's claim to office. However, Chaplin continued to hold the position until Norris requested aid from the local militia. Continued complaints from the area caused Edwards to come under suspicion, and his brother Benjamin, who handled business affairs while Haden was absent from Texas in 1826, addressed such strident correspondence to government officials that it resulted in the revocation of the Edwards grant in October of that year.

Edwards was shocked by this turn of events. He had invested more than $50,000 to secure and launch the grant, and he did not willingly surrender it. Additionally, the cancellation of his grant resulted in the forfeiture of the claims of all settlers who had moved onto his lands. Thus, when the events known as the Fredonian Rebellion,qv which the Edwards brothers eventually headed, began the following month, the Edwards grantees were most supportive. In November 1826 Edwards was arrested as a ruse. When no one appeared at his trial as an accuser he was freed, but Norris and militia chief José Antonio Sepúlveda were found guilty and judged deserving of the death sentence, which was commuted to banishment from office by this extralegal tribunal. News of the uprising reached the Mexican authorities, who dispatched Lt. Col. Mateo Ahumada to Nacogdoches. Learning that troops were on their way, Martin Parmerqv and Benjamin Edwards recruited the Ayish Bayou militia to come to town as well. They signed articles establishing the Fredonian Republic, with Haden Edwards as its leader. An alliance was also made with Cherokee Indians led by Richard Fields and John Dunn Hunter,qqv who also had grievances against the government. Before an armed clash occurred the Fredonians dispersed, in early February 1827, and Edwards fled to Louisiana for safety. He returned to Texas during the Texas Revolutionqv and made his home in Nacogdoches until his death, on August 14, 1849. Edwards was the first worshipful master of Milam Lodge No. 2 when it was organized in 1837, a fact that indicates his status in the Anglo leadership. Until his death he was engaged in the land business.

BIBLIOGRAPHY: Biographical Files, Special Collections, Steen Library, Stephen F. Austin State University. Archie P. McDonald, comp., Nacogdoches: Wilderness Outpost to Modern City, 1779–1979 (photocopy, Barker Texas History Center, University of Texas at Austin). Edward Morris Parsons, the Fredonian Rebellion," *Texana*, Spring 1967.
Archie P. McDonald

EDWARDS, HADEN HARRISON (1812–1865). Haden H. Edwards, soldier, merchant, and legislator, was one of the thirteen children of Susanna (Beall) and Haden Edwards,qv leader of the Fredonian Rebellion.qv He was born in Winchester, Virginia, in 1812 and traveled to Nacogdoches, Texas, with his father in 1825. By 1832 he had made three overland trips from Nacogdoches to Matamoros on stock-trading ventures, driving thousands of mules and cattle.

At the outbreak of the Texas Revolutionqv he was elected captain of a company of volunteers that served at the siege of Bexarqv in December 1835. After the revolution he fought in several Indian campaigns and attained the rank of brigadier general. In January 1844 President Sam Houstonqv sent Edwards on a trading mission among the Indians of the Clear Fork of the Brazos River. At the start of the Mexican Warqv Edwards enlisted as a private in Capt. William F. Sparks'sqv Company E of Col. George T. Wood'sqv Second Regiment, Texas Mounted Rifles, but left the service with a disability discharge on August 31, 1846.

Edwards was a founder and the first president of the Sabine Pass and East Texas Railway. Work on this railroad began in 1858 and was terminated by the outbreak of the Civil War.qv The rails are said to have been taken up and used in the fortification of Sabine Pass. Edwards represented the Nacogdoches district in the First Congress of the Republic of Texas, 1836–37, and in the First (1846) and Eighth (1859–61) legislatures of the state of Texas. He was also a member of the Secession Conventionqv in 1861. Edwards was married on October 22, 1843, to Sarah Forbes of Nacogdoches. The couple had eight children; their oldest was Peyton Forbes Edwards,qv a prominent politician known as the "Red Rooster of Nacogdoches." After the Civil War Edwards journeyed to Cincinnati to seek renewed funding for his railroad project and died there in August 1865.

BIBLIOGRAPHY: Frank W. Johnson, *A History of Texas and Texans* (5 vols., ed. E. C. Barker and E. W. Winkler [Chicago and New York: American Historical Society, 1914; rpt. 1916]). Charles D. Spurlin, comp., *Texas Veterans in the Mexican War: Muster Rolls of Texas Military Units* (Victoria, Texas, 1984). Texas House of Representatives, *Biographical Directory of the Texan Conventions and Congresses, 1832–1845* (Austin: Book Exchange, 1941). Amelia W. Williams and Eugene C. Barker, eds., *The Writings of Sam Houston, 1813–1863* (8 vols., Austin: University of Texas Press, 1938–43; rpt., Austin and New York: Pemberton Press, 1970).
Thomas W. Cutrer

EDWARDS, JAMES HENRY (1855–1925). James H. Edwards, legislator and county judge, the son of Dr. Augustus Lawson and Susan C. (Roquemore) Edwards, was born on December 24, 1855, in Butler, Georgia. His father served in the Confederate Army and after the war practiced medicine along the Rio Grande from Mier and Camargo, Tamaulipas, to Brownsville, Texas, until his death in 1909. In 1875 Jim Edwards moved to San Angelo and a year later to Rio Grande City, where he served first as deputy county clerk and then as Starr County district clerk. In 1880 he went into the abstract business with Judge J. H. Monroe in Starr County. He studied law under Judge James B. Wells, Jr.,qv of Brownsville, was admitted to the bar on October 19, 1888, and practiced law with Judge Wells for several years. Later he moved to Hidalgo and in 1896, on the Republican ticket, was elected state representative of District 85. He served on five legislative committees during his term. In Hidalgo he went into partnership with R. A. Marsh to establish the *Hidalgo County Advance*, an early newspaper. In 1898 Edwards held the post of internal revenue and customs collector for the federal government. Later he became an attorney for the Texas-Mexican Railway Company and lived in Monterrey, Saltillo, and Torreón, Coahuila. He and his family returned to the Valley in 1910, when the Mexican revolution broke out. Edwards became Hidalgo county judge on November 15, 1910, and served in that capacity until January 1914. He signed the order changing the name of the county seat from Chapin to Edinburg on February 14, 1911.

Edwards married Jane Elizabeth (Lizzie) Savage on June 2, 1898, in Travis Park Methodist Church, San Antonio. They had four children. Judge Edwards was instrumental in clearing land titles in Hidalgo County by securing data from old records and early settlers. Often he traveled into Mexico to find missing heirs to the Spanish land grants. In 1905 he went to the archives in San Carlos, Mexico, for that purpose. Deciderio Flores, Sr., acted as interpreter. Although Edwards could read and write Spanish, he never felt comfortable speaking the language. He practiced law and operated the abstract business with his wife until his death on March 3, 1925, in Edinburg.

BIBLIOGRAPHY: E. H. Loughery, *Texas State Government* (Austin: McLeod and Jackson, 1897). San Antonio *Express*, June 3, 1898.
Izora J. Tinkler Skinner

EDWARDS, LILBURN U. (?–?). Lilburn Edwards, early Texas legislator and public official, was in Texas serving as the clerk of the Board of Land Commissioners for Shelby County by 1838. In 1841 he served as clerk of the district court in Shelby County. From December 1843 until February 1844 he represented his county in the House of Representatives of the Eighth Congress of the republic, where he served on the Military Affairs and Public Lands committees.

BIBLIOGRAPHY: Texas House of Representatives, *Biographical Directory of the Texan Conventions and Congresses, 1832–1845* (Austin: Book Exchange, 1941). *Cecil Harper, Jr.*

EDWARDS, MARGARET ROYALTY (1895–1969). Margaret Royalty Edwards, poet laureate qv of Texas, the daughter of George William and Margaret (Jobe) Royalty, was born on October 31, 1895, in Gatesville. She wrote her first poem in 1912 to fulfill a graduation requirement from Gatesville High School. Later, as a student at Baylor University, she wrote for the *Baylor Lariat* and was associate editor of the 1916 *Baylor Round-Up*. She married Herbert R. Edwards in 1918; they had one son. Mrs. Edwards taught at the Baylor Academy and at West Junior High School in Waco and at the same time began to write for publication. She wrote articles for *Ten Men from Baylor* (1945), *Baylor's Generals* (1945), and the *Handbook of Texas* (1952). In 1947 she published a trilogy, *New Leaves, Quatrains, and Reflections on the Twenty-third Psalm*; and in 1959 the *Lure of the Road*. From 1957 to 1959 she was the thirteenth poet laureate of Texas. She compiled the 1966 *Poets Laureate of Texas*, in which she was included. She also wrote a column, "Think," for the Waco *Tribune-Herald*. She died on March 16, 1969.

BIBLIOGRAPHY: Dallas *Morning News*, March 18, 1969. Margaret Royalty Edwards, *Poets Laureate of Texas* (San Antonio: Naylor, 1956; rev. ed., 1966). *Patricia Ward Wallace*

EDWARDS, MARTIN LUTHER (1900–1970). Martin Luther Edwards, black physician, was born on January 1, 1900, in Columbus, Mississippi, to Simon and Jemima (Williams) Edwards. He attended Clark College in Atlanta, Georgia, and received a bachelor of science degree in 1926. He went on to get a master of science degree from Northwestern University at Evanston, Illinois, in 1927 and a doctor of medicine degree from Meharry Medical College at Nashville, Tennessee, in 1931. After interning at Prairie View A&M College Hospital in Prairie View, Texas, in 1931–32, he began practice in Hawkins, Texas. He was college physician at Jarvis Christian College at Hawkins, where he served without salary for more than fifteen years. During this time he started the school's first health program.

From sometime during World War II qv until April 1970, Dr. Edwards was a medical examiner for a local selective-service board. He was the first black physician to hold full staff privileges at the Medical Center Hospital in Tyler. He wrote several scientific articles. He was a member of the Smith County Medical Society, the Texas Medical Association, qv and the American Medical Association. He served as secretary and president of the Lone Star State Medical, Dental, and Pharmaceutical Association, qv president of the East Texas Medical, Dental, and Pharmaceutical Association, and vice president and member of the House of Delegates of the National Medical Association. He served as secretary to the board of Texas Southern University in Houston. In the late 1940s he was selected by Texas governor Beauford H. Jester qv as a member of the state's first biracial committee to seek solutions to various racial problems. Edwards was appointed to similar committees in the administrations of governors Allan Shivers and M. Price Daniel, Sr.qqv

He was a member of Bethlehem United Methodist Church, Jarvis Christian College Church, Eastern Star Masonic Lodge, and Omega Psi Phi fraternity. He received the Omega Achievement Award from Omega Psi Phi in 1955. Edwards and his wife, Arzelia (Jones), formerly of Kansas City, Kansas, had four children. He died on April 22, 1970, in Tyler.

BIBLIOGRAPHY: Houston *Chronicle*, April 26, 1970. *Texas Medicine*, July 1970. Vertical Files, Barker Texas History Center, University of Texas at Austin. *John S. Gray III*

EDWARDS, MONROE (ca. 1808–1847). Monroe Edwards, early Texas slave smuggler and forger, son of a once wealthy plantation owner, Moses Edwards, was born in Danville, Kentucky, about 1808. He moved to the Galveston Bay area of Texas about 1825 as a clerk for a prosperous merchant, James Morgan.qv Soon after his arrival, however, he found more lucrative, if less respectable, pursuits. He became involved in smuggling slaves to Brazil from Africa and soon made a profit of $50,000. Through his mistress's husband, a Mexican official, he obtained a large land grant in Brazoria County. He called his property Chenango Plantation (*see* CHENANGO, TEXAS) and used it as a base for continued slave smuggling to Texas from Cuba. His only claim to favorable historical recognition was his arrest and brief imprisonment, with others, by the Mexican garrison at Anahuac in 1832 (*see* ANAHUAC DISTURBANCES).

Christopher Dart, who later bought a half interest in Chenango, also joined Edwards in financing the smuggling of slaves. On March 2, 1836, Edwards took about 171 slaves up the Brazos River and drove them overland to Chenango, where they were to be kept for sale after the Texas Revolution qv ended. When Dart began pressuring him to sell the slaves and split the profits as they had agreed, Edwards conceived a different plan. He altered a letter signed by Dart so that it seemed to be a bill of sale to himself. Dart, of course, cried foul, and filed a civil suit. Although Edwards retained two distinguished lawyers, John C. Watrous and John W. Harris,qqv the forgery was discovered during the trial in Brazoria. Dart obtained judgment on April 2, 1840, for more than $89,000 plus interest and court costs. In addition, Edwards was indicted and jailed.

After making bond on the criminal charge, Edwards fled to Europe, where he posed as a wealthy veteran of San Jacinto and an abolitionist. He left Europe after a threat of exposure by the Texas envoy to England and returned to the United States, where he engaged in several large-scale forgeries. He was finally arrested and placed in the Tombs prison in New York. His trial was a celebrated one, with lengthy reports of each day's testimony printed in the New York *Daily Tribune* and other newspapers. Edwards again retained celebrated lawyers but was found guilty. He was sentenced to Sing Sing prison. After an escape attempt in 1847 he was severely beaten by prison authorities and died.

BIBLIOGRAPHY: *Life and Adventures of the Accomplished Forger and Swindler Colonel Monroe Edwards* (New York: Long, 1848). Edna Rowe, "The Disturbances at Anahuac in 1832," *Quarterly of the Texas State Historical Association* 6 (April 1903). *Texas Sentinel*, January 28, 1841. Homer S. Thrall, *A Pictorial History of Texas* (St. Louis: Thompson, 1879). *Marie Beth Jones*

EDWARDS, PEYTON FORBES (1844–1918). Peyton Forbes Edwards, Civil War qv combatant, lawyer, Nacogdoches county treasurer, Texas state senator, and district judge, was born on September 28, 1844, in Nacogdoches County, Texas, the eldest of eight children of Sarah M. (Forbes) and Haden Harrison Edwards.qv Sarah Edwards was the daughter of Col. John Forbes.qv Peyton Edwards was the grandson of Hayden Edwards,qv a leader of the Fredonian Rebellion.qv He volunteered as a private in August 1861 and served in the Confederate forces in the Fourth Texas Cavalry. He later served in Company A of the Seventeenth Texas Cavalry and became a brigade quartermaster.

Edwards was the clerk of his father's estate in 1866 and received a law degree from the University of Virginia in 1867, when he returned to Nacogdoches and practiced law. After serving as county treasurer, he represented the district in the state Senate of the Fifteenth and Sixteenth legislatures (1876 to 1879), during which time he was known as the "Red Rooster of Nacogdoches." He and Amory Reily Starr[qv] were friends and law partners in Nacogdoches until Starr moved to Marshall in 1873. In 1867 these two friends collected oil from Oil Springs Branch and sold it in Nacogdoches to soften leather. Edwards was judge of the Third Judicial District from 1874 to 1884. He was a Democratic party[qv] presidential elector in 1884. In 1886 he moved his family to El Paso.

He was married to Odelia Arnold, granddaughter of Hayden S. Arnold,[qv] on December 24, 1867. Their son Peyton F., Jr., was sheriff of El Paso County at the time of his father's death; they also had two daughters. Edwards later married Minnie Arnold, his wife's sister; he subsequently married Callie Myrna Stewart. He was a member of Sigma Chi, the Knights of Pythias, and United Confederate Veterans. He was a Freemason and an Episcopalian. He died in El Paso in 1918.

BIBLIOGRAPHY: W. B. Bates, "A Sketch History of Nacogdoches," *Southwestern Historical Quarterly* 59 (April 1956). H. L. Bentley and Thomas Pilgrim, *Texas Legal Directory for 1876–77* (Austin: Democratic Statesman Office, 1877). Daughters of the Republic of Texas, *Founders and Patriots of the Republic of Texas* (Austin, 1963–). Clement Anselm Evans, ed., *Confederate Military History* (Atlanta: Confederate Publishing, 1899; extended ed., Wilmington, North Carolina: Broadfoot, 1987–89). Frank W. Johnson, *A History of Texas and Texans* (5 vols., ed. E. C. Barker and E. W. Winkler [Chicago and New York: American Historical Society, 1914; rpt. 1916]). *Members of the Texas Legislature, 1846–1962* (Austin, 1962). Buckley B. Paddock, ed., *A Twentieth Century History and Biographical Record of North and West Texas* (Chicago: Lewis, 1906). E. W. Swindells, *A Legislative Manual for the State of Texas* (2 vols., Austin, 1879–83). Vertical Files, Barker Texas History Center, University of Texas at Austin.

Linda Sybert Hudson

EDWARDS, ROSS (1884–1978). Ross Edwards, West Texas merchant, inventor, musician, and mayor, was born on December 17, 1884, near Granbury, in Hood County. His father, a former buffalo hunter then farmer and small rancher, moved his growing family to Foard County in 1891 but by the following year severe winter weather had nearly wiped out the herd. Seven-year-old Ross received his first practical training as a cowboy during that move, and throughout his youth he attended school and worked part time at various ranching and farming tasks. He especially became adept at hunting and training wild game, an ability which often enabled him to earn extra income. Ross had four younger sisters, but was the only boy. Smitten with the wanderlust during his late teens, Ross Edwards worked as a cattle drover, camp cook, wheat harvester, railroad newsboy, and hotel clerk. In 1904, while accompanying a cattle shipment to St. Louis, Missouri, he attended the World's Fair. Afterward he worked as a teamster freighting supplies from El Paso south to Madera, Mexico, where he did carpentry work for the Chihuahua al Pacifico Railroad crews and prospected for a time in the Sierra Madre. On returning to Texas, Edwards became involved in the land rush to the Oklahoma Panhandle and worked briefly as an editor for the Texhoma *Weekly*. His various jobs, in addition to a tailor shop of which he became part-owner in Crowell, enabled him to attend Add-Ran College in Fort Worth. In addition to his hunting and trapping abilities, Edwards also came to be in demand throughout the West Texas ranches as a square dance fiddler. Inspired by his uncle, James Knox Polk Harris, he had taught himself to play the instrument as a boy. In 1907 he and a partner established a tailor shop in Lubbock. Two years later Edwards went to Spur, in Dickens County, and bought half-interest in a cleaning and pressing shop there; shortly afterward he and two other partners expanded the enterprise into a clothing goods store with merchandise from Sanger's in Dallas. Edwards also trapped and eradicated skunks, wolves, and other fur-bearing animals for the SMS ranches,[qv] shipping the pelts to St. Louis. After a few years he sold out his interest in the Spur store and moved to Post, in Garza County, where he established another tailor shop and sold men's furnishings, complete with his own delivery service. In 1913 he married Birta Wilson of Snyder; they had two daughters. Shortly thereafter they moved permanently to Lubbock, where he and various partners prospered in the dry goods business, owning at one time or another several downtown stores on Broadway, and later on College Avenue. He and his wife also opened a beauty salon, but she and their daughter Dorris Jeanne, died from the Spanish flu epidemic of 1918.

Edwards became involved in Lubbock's civic affairs. He helped organize the Lubbock Country Club and later started the city's first Sportsman Club, serving as its first president. In the summer of 1934 he and Charles A. Guy accompanied the anthropological expedition led by Dr. William Curry Holden[qv] to the Yaqui Indian villages in northern Mexico. Also that year Edwards ran for and was elected mayor of Lubbock, serving in that capacity for two terms. At the height of the Great Depression,[qv] his administration oversaw such projects as a massive street-paving operation funded by the Work Projects Administration[qv] to provide local men with jobs. In addition, his administration was responsible for adding 450 acres to the then seventy-five-acre Mackenzie Park and supported K. N. Clapp's unsuccessful efforts to establish that park's famous Prairie Dog Town. Toward the end of his second term in 1938, Edwards met and fell in love with Lula Barnett Simmons, a widow who had a daughter from her first marriage. They married in Seattle, Washington, and spent their honeymoon in Alaska, where he hunted and fished in its wilds. After returning to Lubbock he organized the "Ross Edwards Orchestra," a Western swing band that played at hotels and dances throughout much of Texas and neighboring states. Among the musicians who played in that organization during its twenty-year existence was Bill Harrod, who later started the Lubbock Symphony Orchestra. Edwards's fiddle-playing days ended when he lost two fingers in an accident with a table saw. In addition to his reputation as a sportsman and musician, Edwards was known for his inventiveness. During his earlier hunting days, he had perfected a device to trap, without injury, entire coveys of quail. Following his political career he bought a farm near New Deal, where in 1941 he and a partner, Jack Brogden, developed a new type of plow for the South Plains agricultural market. Known as the go-devils or "crustbuster," this plow contained a row of rotary hoes used to break the tough crust formed over seeds by heavy rains. The four-row device was patented in 1951 and subsequently manufactured and marketed under contract by H. V. Bigham and Sons. Throughout his multi-faceted career, Edwards often wrote cowboy poetry, which appeared on occasion in area newspapers. After moving permanently to Lubbock he was a member of its First Christian Church. In 1965 he published an autobiography, *Fiddle Dust*, which contains examples of his poetry and is laced with "down-home" humor. Plagued with ill health for the last two of his ninety-three years, Edwards died at Methodist Hospital on February 14, 1978, and was buried in the City of Lubbock cemetery.

BIBLIOGRAPHY: Lubbock *Avalanche-Journal*, February 15, 1978.

H. Allen Anderson

EDWARDS BRANCH. Edwards Branch (Edwards Creek) rises in northwestern Stephens County a mile east of the Shackelford county line (at 32°51′ N, 99°04′ W) and runs southeast for three miles to its mouth on Hubbard Creek Reservoir (at 32°49′ N, 99°02′ W). It traverses an area of rolling hills surfaced by clay and sandy loam soils that support mesquite, juniper, and live oak.

EDWARDS COLONY. The empresario[qv] grant of Haden Edwards,[qv] given in a contract on April 15, 1825, was bounded by a line that began at the intersection of the coast and border reservations (ten leagues from the sea and twenty leagues from the Sabine River) and ran north to fifteen leagues from Nacogdoches, thence west to the Navasota River, south in an irregular line along the Navasota, the Old San Antonio Road,qv and the San Jacinto River to the line of the coast reservation, and east to the point of beginning. Its bounds included Nacogdoches and touched the East Texas area where squatters had been settled for two generations without benefit of title. Conflicting land claims, a mixture of races, and assorted crimes and misdemeanors were characteristic of the area. Edwards had introduced some fifty families before May 22, 1826, when his difficulties with previously established settlers caused him to leave the province and led to the Fredonian Rebellion.qv

BIBLIOGRAPHY: Eugene C. Barker, ed., *The Austin Papers* (3 vols., Washington: GPO, 1924–28). Eugene C. Barker, *The Life of Stephen F. Austin* (Nashville: Cokesbury Press, 1925; rpt., Austin: Texas State Historical Association, 1949; New York: AMS Press, 1970). R. C. Donhano, The History of Nacogdoches and Haden Edwards Colony: A Study in the Spanish and Mexican Colonization in Texas (M.A. thesis, University of Oklahoma, 1929). Jordan Holt, The Edwards Empresarial Grant and the Fredonia Rebellion (M.A. thesis, Stephen F. Austin State University, 1977).

Curtis Bishop

EDWARDS COUNTY. Edwards County (L-12) is located in Southwest Texas east of the Big Bend country and 100 miles west of San Antonio. The center point of the county is 29°45′ north latitude, 100°16′ west longitude. The county encompasses 2,120 square miles of the Edwards Plateauqv region. The elevation varies from 1,500 feet to 2,410 feet. The average annual rainfall is twenty-two inches. The temperature ranges from 34° F to 62° in January and 71° to 97° in July; the growing season lasts 250 days, beginning in mid-March and ending in late November. The eastern section of the county has generally rolling terrain, with many hills and caves. The western region is typically flat. The county is situated upon a major limestone deposit surfaced with dark, calcareous stony clays and clay loams that principally support oak, juniper, mesquite, and cedar trees, as well as prairie grasses. Edwards County has more than fifteen natural springs that flow year-round; the headwaters of the Llano, Nueces, and West Nueces rivers are in the county. The vegetation, temperature, and abundant water supply make this an ideal area for many types of game animals, including white-tail deer, javelina, turkey, and quail. The area is rich in iron ore and sulfur and has some silver deposits, though these have not been mined or developed.

The region that became Edwards County was home to Lipan Apache Indians. Spain established the mission of San Lorenzo de la Santa Cruz in 1762 to help Christianize the Indians, but was otherwise unable to settle the area. White settlement in the region did not begin until the mid-1800s. In 1858 the county was formed from Bexar County; the first land was sold in 1876. Edwards County was not officially organized until 1883. It was named for Hayden Edwards,qv one of the first American settlers of Nacogdoches. The county seat was originally Bullhead, which subsequently changed its name to Vance. Rock Springs (now Rocksprings) became county seat in 1891. In 1913, Real County was taken from the eastern section of Edwards County, thus decreasing Edwards County to its present size.

The early settlers of this region soon realized that the area was not suitable for farming, but that it did supply ample natural food for sheep and angora goats. Ranching began to dominate the county as the demand for wool and mohair increased in the early twentieth century. The production of wool and mohair reached its apex in 1940, with 331,970 sheep and 376,322 angora goats being counted in the county, after which Rocksprings called itself the "Top-o-the-World" in mohair production. The number of animals declined to 43,293 sheep and 154,144 angora goats in 1987. Ranching continues to control the economy of the county, with most available land still used for raising sheep and goats. Less than 5 percent of the county is under cultivation.

The population of Edwards County increased from 266 in 1880 to 3,768 in 1910. The county saw a steady decline in population since that time, to 2,933 in 1940 and 2,033 in 1980. Between 1980 and 1990 the trend reversed toward moderate growth, with the 1990 population being 2,266. The county is 50 percent Anglo and 50 percent Hispanic. This equal split developed in the 1980s. Most young Anglos leave the county to look for education and employment elsewhere and do not return, whereas the Hispanics generally stay near their families. Other minority populations are nonexistent; the largest population of blacks, eleven, was recorded in 1900.

The number of high school graduates increased from 19 percent of the population aged twenty-five or older in 1950 to more than 50 percent in 1980. The county voted Republican in all elections after 1976, with the exception of the senatorial races of 1976 and 1988, which were won by Democrats. Before 1976 neither party consistently won a majority. More than 50 percent of the population in 1980 were registered voters.

Very little growth has taken place in the towns of this ranching county. Rocksprings, the largest population center, had 1,339 residents in 1990. Such transportation services as railroads have not entered the county. The closest railroad for transporting goods, the Southern Pacific, is twenty-five miles south of the county. The only reliable transportation came in the 1930s with the construction of the state and federal highway systems; State Highway 55 and U.S. 377 intersect in Rocksprings. The new roads enabled the county to expand the production of wool and mohair by giving ranchers greater access to markets. Perhaps the development of mineral resources has been prevented by inadequate transportation.

Edwards County is in a state of arrested economic growth. The demand for mohair has decreased, thus hurting the economy, though a small amount of oil has been produced. Oil was discovered in this region in 1946, and production increased from 1,066 barrels in 1958 to 8,254 barrels in 1978. Production had slowed to 4,371 barrels a year by 1990. The county has benefitted from tourism dollars spent by hunters and fishermen drawn to the area by the abundant game and wildlife. The revenue from these activities now constitutes 20 percent of the annual county income. Edwards County also benefitted when the state of Texas purchased the old hospital building in Rocksprings, turned it into the Sheriff Departments office, and built a new jail that houses both state and federal prisoners. The state has also purchased 40,000 acres of land around the Devil's Sinkhole, a cave that is home to thousands of Mexican freetail bats. The size and shape of this cave have kept it from being developed—the walls drop straight down 150 feet, and the mouth is about fifty feet wide. Plans for the area include creating a wildlife preserve, though no mention has been made of opening it to the general public. No other development has been discussed.

The county has a Fourth of July rodeo and parade each year. The Top-of-the-World festival, held annually in May, celebrates the wool and mohair industry.qv *See also* GOAT RANCHING, SHEEP RANCHING.

BIBLIOGRAPHY: Rocksprings Woman's Club Historical Committee, *A History of Edwards County* (San Angelo, Texas: Anchor, 1984)

James B. McCrain

EDWARDS PLATEAU. The Edwards Plateau, in South Central Texas east of the Pecos River and west of the Colorado, is the southernmost unit of the Great Plains. Physiographically, it is an erosional region with thin soil over beveled Comanchean limestone exposures that extend as limestone beds to constitute the underpinning of the High Plains, lying above the Permian and Triassic beds and beneath the more recent unconsolidated Pliocene and Pleistocene deposits, the latter forming the constructional surface of the High Plains. If any such loose cover ever mantled the Edwards Plateau, it has long since been carried away by erosion, although remnantal summit areas in the northwest portion of the plateau, in the transition zone adjacent to the High Plains, are characterized by a cover of unconsolidated silty materials. On such areas a deep black soil of the Chernozem type occurs. By and large, however, the Edwards Plateau is erosional with the margins of the region frayed rather deeply so that the plateau as a whole is perceptibly higher than adjacent areas.

Its distinctive physical features, especially its lack of deep soils suitable for farming, cause the Edwards Plateau to be an outstanding grazing region of Texas. Its cattle, sheep, and goat industries are of national importance. The distribution of livestock in the region serves to indicate the various types of the natural environment, particularly as reflected in the different kinds of natural vegetation. Cattle, for instance, are grazed on the typical mesquite-shrub, short-grass areas, characterized by deeper soils. Such areas are the best grazing lands of the region. The next best grazing areas support large numbers of sheep, while the poorest support large numbers of goats. Limited farming is carried on in the deeper soil areas along the broader valleys in the northeast quarter of the Edwards Plateau, as well as in the black-earth soil district on a remnantal summit area in the vicinity of Eldorado. Although some cotton is grown, much of the agriculture is devoted to grain sorghum production as an adjunct to the predominant livestock enterprises.

Along the northeastern edge of the plateau occurs a distinctive district unlike any other part of Texas. This is the Llano country, from which the radically dipping Comanchean limestones and older sedimentaries have been removed by erosion, thereby unroofing the pre-Cambrian rocks that form the central and higher portion of the area. The Llano country is a circumscribed basin, rimmed in by interior-facing escarpments, particularly of the Comanchean limestones. The inner portion is underlain by granitic and metamorphosed pre-Cambrian rocks; the outer portion, rimming the granitic outcrops, is underlain by Paleozoic sedimentaries that dip beneath the surrounding and geologically younger Comanchean limestones. Though structurally an uplifted area, the rough and broken Llano district is topographically a basin threaded by the Llano and Colorado rivers. It is timbered, but grasses are practically absent on the rougher portions of the granitic central section.

Historically, the Edwards Plateau as a whole, like the High Plains,qv is a region in which supplies of permanent surface water are sparse. Before modern transportation and the means of tapping underground supplies of water were developed, travel across the Edwards Plateau country was difficult. Even in 1950 no railway line crossed the entire region.

BIBLIOGRAPHY: William Bollaert, *Observations on the Geography of Texas* (London, 1850). Zachary Taylor Fulmore, *The Geography of Texas* (n.p.: Rand, McNally, 1908). Terry Jordan, *Texas: A Geography* (Boulder, Colorado: Westview Press, 1984). James A. Schmid, The Wild Landscape of the Edwards Plateau of South Central Texas (M.A. thesis, University of Chicago, 1969). Frederic William Simonds, *Geographic Influences in the Development of Texas* (Austin: Journal of Geography, 1912).
E. H. Johnson

EDWARDS UNDERGROUND WATER DISTRICT. The legislature established the Edwards Underground Water District in 1959 for the purpose of conserving, protecting, and recharging the waters of the Edwards Aquifer. Current programs of the EUWD include water quality investigations, water level monitoring programs, recharge enhancement activities, and water conservation projects. Since the mid-1970s the EUWD has constructed four recharge dams in Medina county, including the Middle Verde Creek Dam (1978), the San Geronimo Creek Dam (1978), the Seco Creek Dam (1982), and the Parker Creek Dam (1984). The district has also funded several studies concerning enhancing recharge to the Edwards Aquifer, including the Medina Lake Recharge Study and the Nueces Basin Recharge Study (funded in cooperation with the City of Corpus Christi, South Texas Water Authority, and the Texas Water Development Boardqv).

In 1987 the EUWD developed the state's first regionwide Drought Management Plan. Employees also worked in cooperation with the city of San Antonio in 1988 to develop the area's first Regional Water Study that later formed the basis of the Regional Water Plan. In 1989 the district launched the first regionwide municipal leak detection program in south central Texas. This service is available at no charge to cities and water distribution systems throughout the region. The district also maintains one of the most comprehensive data collection programs in Texas for an underground water supply. A network of over 100 monitoring wells, located throughout the Edwards Aquifer region, enables the district to maintain constant watch over water quality and quantity. Some of their most diligent conservation efforts in recent years have been in the monitoring and protection of the sensitive Edwards Aquifer Recharge Zone. In conjunction with the United States Geological Survey, the EUWD does annual calculations of recharge to the underground formation in the upper portions of the Nueces, San Antonio, and Guadalupe river basins, which are hydrologically connected by the underground reservoir. The average recharge in 1993 was 447,600 acre-feet of water. The original district included five counties: Uvalde, Medina, Bexar, Comal, and Hays. In 1989 Uvalde and Medina withdrew from the district. The EUWD in 1994 was governed by a board of directors elected by popular vote, representing the counties of Bexar, Comal, and Hays. A general manager oversaw three divisions: administration, field operations, and environmental management and planning. In 1989 the legislature revised their charter to give the EUWD authority to implement drought management plans. The district employed thirty-three people in 1994.
Tracé Etienne-Gray

EGAN, TEXAS. Egan is at the intersection of Farm roads 2280 and 917, eight miles northeast of Cleburne in north central Johnson County. The area was settled by M. J., J. P., and W. E. Miller during the Civil War.qv A townsite was surveyed in 1883, when the Missouri, Kansas and Texas Railroad extended its tracks through the area. A surveyor gave Egan its name. A post office began service there in 1883, and within two years the settlement had a population of fifty, a store, a school, and two churches. A winery operated in Egan during the early twentieth century, but was closed down during prohibition.qv The community had a population of 115 by the mid-1920s. Egan's post office closed sometime after 1930, and the population fell to fifty by the late 1940s. This estimate was reported consistently through the mid-1960s. In 1990 the population was twenty-one.

BIBLIOGRAPHY: Viola Block, *History of Johnson County and Surrounding Areas* (Waco: Texian Press, 1970). Johnson County History Book Committee, *History of Johnson County, Texas* (Dallas: Curtis Media, 1985).
Brian Hart

EGERTON, HENRY (?–?). Henry Egerton, a native of New York, was long a resident of Matamoros, Tamaulipas. In May 1832 James Prentissqv gave him a letter of introduction to Sam Houston.qv On January 1, 1834, Egerton and Fortunato Soto secured an empresarioqv grant to settle 800 families in Texas, but their contract was never fulfilled. In January 1844 Egerton and Soto were in correspondence with Benjamin Lundyqv concerning petitioning for land in northern Mexico. D. E. Egerton, an Englishman, was also a Texas empresario.

BIBLIOGRAPHY: Ephraim Douglass Adams, "British Correspondence Concerning Texas," *Southwestern Historical Quarterly* 19 (October 1915). Amelia W. Williams and Eugene C. Barker, eds., *The Writings of Sam Houston, 1813–1863* (8 vols., Austin: University of Texas Press, 1938–43; rpt., Austin and New York: Pemberton Press, 1970).

EGGERS, GEORGE WILLIAM NORDHOLTZ (1896–1963). George Eggers, orthopedist, was born to Emil E. F. and Gertrude (Mensman) Eggers on January 28, 1896, in Galveston. He attended

Ball High School from 1910 to 1913 and graduated from Rice Institute (now Rice University) in 1917. After two years with the 344th Field Artillery during World War I,qv he enrolled at the University of Texas Medical Branch, where he received his M.D. in 1923. He was instructor in anatomy at UTMB in 1923–24 and interned the next year at Charity Hospital in New Orleans. Upon returning to UTMB he became instructor in surgery (1925–29), assistant professor of surgery and orthopedic surgery (1929–31), associate professor of orthopedic surgery (1931–42), and clinical professor (1942). In 1943 he became UTMB's first professor of orthopedic surgery, chief of the newly established Division of Orthopedic Surgery, and medical director of physical therapy, a program he founded in 1937. He continued to serve in these positions until his death.

Eggers worked tirelessly to obtain funds for the construction of the State Hospital for Crippled and Deformed Children on the UTMB campus. When the hospital opened, he was given responsibility for its orthopedic services. Under his direction the residency program in orthopedic surgery at UTMB received accreditation by the American Medical Association Council on Medical Education and Hospitals in 1947.

Eggers published more than sixty articles in his field and designed numerous orthopedic appliances, including an internal splint that is named after him. He became a diplomate of the American Board of Orthopedic Surgery in 1937. Among many offices, he was president of the American Academy for Cerebral Palsy (1960–61), the American Board of Orthopedic Surgery (1960–62), and the Texas Surgical Society (1948). He was also president of the Texas Orthopedic Association, the Clinical Orthopedic Club, and the Texas Rheumatism Association. In 1962 Eggers was elected president of the American Orthopedic Association but died before his term was completed. He belonged to the American Medical Association, the Texas Medical Association,qv the Galveston County Medical Society, the American Association of University Professors, the American College of Surgeons, the International Society of Orthopedic Surgery and Traumatology, the Singleton Surgical Society, the Southern Medical Association, the Southern Surgical Association, the Orthopedic Research Society, and the Southwestern Surgical Congress, of which he was one of the founders. In addition to his elected offices Eggers was appointed chairman of the technical advisory committee of the Division of Crippled Children's Services of the state health department in 1948, a position he held for many years. He was also on the medical advisory committee of the Texas Rehabilitation Center at Gonzales and a member of the Executive Committee and the Board of Directors of the Texas Society for Crippled Children.

Eggers was an ardent hunter and fisherman, as well as a student of migratory birds. In 1923 he married Edith Sykes of Galveston. They had two children. On May 2, 1963, Eggers died in New York City, where he had been invited to attend the centennial celebration of the Hospital for Special Surgery as a guest of honor.

BIBLIOGRAPHY: "From the Editor," *American Journal of Orthopedics* 5 (June 1963). Galveston *Daily News*, May 3, 1963. Samuel Butler Graham and Ellen Newman, *Galveston Community Book: A Historical and Biographical Record of Galveston and Galveston County* (Galveston: Cawston, 1945). *Journal of Bone and Joint Surgery*, October 1963. *National Cyclopaedia of American Biography*, Vol. 52. *Texas State Journal of Medicine*, July 1963. *Who's Who in the South and Southwest*, Vol. 4.
Patricia L. Jakobi

EGYPT, TEXAS (Kaufman County). Egypt (Little Egypt), twelve miles southeast of Kaufman in eastern Kaufman County, formed sometime before the Civil War.qv This predominantly black community extended along Farm Road 1836 from Ayres Chapel on the west to the Cedar Hill church on the east. In the latter half of the 1800s it was a thriving community with a general store, blacksmith shop, and resident physician. A post office opened there in 1876 but closed in 1888. The community is not shown on county highway maps for the 1930s.

BIBLIOGRAPHY: Kaufman *Sun*, February 10, March 3, 1882, March 20, 1884, February 25, 1886.
Jack Stoltz

EGYPT, TEXAS (Wharton County). Egypt, on Farm Road 102 eleven miles northwest of Wharton, is the oldest community in Wharton County. John C. Clarkqv was there in 1822, and Egypt is located on his league. Robert Kuykendall'sqv land was below Egypt, and Thomas Rabb'sqv was above. These three men were among the first of the Austin colony settlers. The land along the Colorado River was the favorite hunting ground of the Karankawa Indians, and Clark, Kuykendall, and Rabb were noted Indian fighters. The area soon became safe enough for others to move into because of the efforts of these men. The original settlement was started in 1829, when Eli Mercerqv established a plantation and ferry on the Colorado River at the San Felipe–Texana crossing. The road from Matagorda to Columbus crossed the San Felipe–Texana road a mile or so from the river, and the community developed at this junction. The town was originally called Mercer's Crossing, but during a severe drought the area supplied corn to surrounding settlements, and people began to refer to it as Egypt.

In 1832 William J. E. Heardqv started Egypt Plantation on the 2,222 acres he purchased from John C. Clarkqv and built his home in what is now the center of Egypt; in 1992 it was still occupied by his family. The Republic of Texasqv opened a post office in November 1835 with Eli Mercer as postmaster. By 1840 four different Texas mail routes were passing through Egypt. The fertile soil has made Egypt an agricultural center since its beginning; Mercer produced some of the first sugarcane in Texas, and Heard had a cotton gin in 1836.

In February of that year Capt. Thomas Rabb recruited a company of men in the Egypt area. They became Company F of the First Regiment of Texas Volunteers. They were at Gonzales when Gen. Sam Houstonqv arrived, and they made the long retreat across Texas. Under Capt. W. J. E. Heard at San Jacinto, they formed the center of the Texas line and captured the Mexican cannons. During the Runaway Scrapeqv many of the people from west of the Colorado gathered in Egypt, hoping that Houston and the Texas army, which was camped just above Egypt, would keep the Mexicans from crossing the river. During the republic days many prominent Texans lived in Egypt, including William Menefee,qv who signed the Texas Declaration of Independence;qv Dr. John Sutherland,qv Alamo courier; and Eli Mercer's son-in-law, editor and inventor Gail Borden, Jr.qv Gen. Thomas J. Ruskqv and the Texas army established temporary headquarters at Egypt in May 1836 as they followed the retreating Mexican army. The republic opened Post Colorado at Egypt in 1837.

In 1839 a stagecoach line, operated by Andrew Northington, served Egypt. By 1840 a general store was well established. Egypt had originally been in Colorado County, but in 1846 it became part of newly established Wharton County. When the first election was held a general store was the polling place; in the 1990 primary election, the general store at Egypt was still the polling place.

In 1848 some enterprising people in Egypt built a railroad. The wooden rails were made of hard live oak, and the cars were pulled by horses. It operated between Egypt and Columbus. A school district was established in 1854 and operated until 1958, when it was consolidated with the Hungerford Independent School District. Just before the Civil Warqv Captain Heard's son-in-law Mentor Northington built a new cotton gin, which the family operated for over 100 years.

In 1881 George H. Northington and Green C. Duncan built a large general mercantile company in Egypt. The store became the business and social center for a large area of the county. It stocked everything from seeds, farm implements, clothes, and groceries to caskets. The post office moved to the new store when it was built and remained there until 1981, when a new brick building was constructed a block down the street. During the 1930s and until the beginning of World War II^{qv} a quarter horse^{qv} racetrack was in operation in Egypt. On race days large crowds of people from all over South Texas attended the races. The Cane Belt Railroad was built through Egypt in 1901. The line was sold to the Santa Fe in 1902, and in 1991 service was discontinued and the tracks were removed. The estimated population of Egypt in 1990 was twenty-six. In 1992, 300 registered voters lived in the area served by the Egypt post office.

BIBLIOGRAPHY: Colorado County Historical Commission, *Colorado County Chronicles from the Beginning to 1923* (2 vols., Austin: Nortex, 1986). Roy Grimes, ed., *300 Years in Victoria County* (Victoria, Texas: Victoria *Advocate*, 1968; rpt., Austin: Nortex, 1985). Ira T. Taylor, *The Cavalcade of Jackson County* (San Antonio: Naylor, 1938). Annie Lee Williams, *A History of Wharton County* (Austin: Von Boeckmann–Jones, 1964).

Barbara L. Young

EHRENBERG, HERMAN (1816?–1866). Herman Ehrenberg, surveyor and cartographer, survivor of the Goliad massacre,^{qv} writer, and engineer, was probably born in the village of Steuden, Prussia, where the birth of a Hermann Vollrath Ehrenberg was registered on October 17, 1816, at the Lutheran church. Sources differ as to the identity of his parents. He may have been the son of William von Ehrenberg, a Prussian royal official, or his parents may have been Johann and Sophie Ehrenberg. Many historians state that Ehrenberg was a Jew; if he was, the reason for registry of his name in a Lutheran church is not clear. He immigrated to New York in 1834, then in October 1835 joined the New Orleans Greys^{qv} at the encouragement of Nicholas Adolphus Sterne.^{qv} He went to Nacogdoches, fought in the siege of Bexar^{qv} in early December 1835, and, after spending the winter inside the Alamo^{qv} getting supplies for the army, set out from San Antonio toward Goliad with a number of men in the Greys. It was their goal to eventually march to Matamoros; however, the group ended up staying under James W. Fannin's^{qv} leadership. Ehrenberg recorded his account of Fannin's actions and the subsequent battle of Coleto,^{qv} where the Texan forces surrendered to Gen. José de Urrea.^{qv} The Mexicans offered all Germans the opportunity to join the Mexican cause, but Ehrenberg stated that he considered himself a Texan and refused the offer. A week later he was one of a few men who escaped the Goliad Massacre.^{qv} According to a translation of Ehrenberg's own account, after the command to kneel and the start of the shooting, he jumped up and, hidden by the gunsmoke, dashed for the San Antonio River. On the way a Mexican soldier slashed him in the head with his saber, but Ehrenberg managed to get by him and jumped in the river crying, "The Republic of Texas forever!" For several days he traveled through the prairies, finding shelter in a couple of abandoned plantation houses along the way, but finally he reasoned that the only way to survive would be to surrender to General Urrea. Ehrenberg posed as a Prussian traveler seeking protection, and Urrea, admiring the boy's daring action, took in the "little Prussian." Ehrenberg was taken with Urrea's troops to Matagorda, and after news of the battle of San Jacinto^{qv} he eventually reached freedom. He was discharged from the Texas army on June 2, 1836. He received a certificate for part of a league of land but never personally claimed it. In 1880 the land was awarded to his heirs from Teplitz, Bohemia.

Ehrenberg then returned to Germany and studied mining at Freiburg University. In the early 1840s he was an English teacher at Halle University. He came back to the United States in 1844 and traveled from St. Louis to Oregon with a fur-trapping party. In May 1845 he sailed from Oregon to Hawaii, where the government employed him to survey streets and draw a map of Honolulu. He also visited a number of Polynesian islands, including Tahiti. Ehrenberg was in California in time to join John C. Frémont and participate in the "Bear Flag Revolt" against Mexico in 1846. He helped rescue Americans held captive in lower California during the Mexican War.^{qv} He took part in the California gold rush in 1848–49. He traveled to the Gadsden Purchase in 1854 and made the first map of the purchase. In 1855 he surveyed and helped incorporate the town of Colorado City, Arizona. In 1856, with Charles Poston, Ehrenberg established the headquarters of the Sonora Exploring and Mining Company at Tubac, Arizona, and was appointed surveyor and mining engineer. Senator Barry Goldwater called Ehrenberg "one of the greatest surveyors and map makers ever to visit the Western United States." He was also an Indian agent for the Mojaves on the Colorado River Reservation from 1863 to 1866. The United States Board of Geographic Names gave the name Ehrenberg Peak to a summit in Grand Canyon National Park.

During his lifetime Ehrenberg compiled a number of maps including "Map of the Gadsden Purchase, Sonora, and portions of New Mexico, Chihuahua & California," in 1854. He wrote articles for *Mining Magazine and Journal of Geology* and *Arizona Weekly*. His other published works include an account of the battle of Coleto and the Goliad massacre. He named the first (1843) edition of his book *Texas und seine Revolution*. The 1844 edition was called *Der Freiheitskampf in Texas im Jahre 1836,* and the book was published again in 1845 as *Fahrten und Schicksale eines Deutschen in Texas*. In 1925 Edgar William Bartholomae translated the 1845 edition into English as a master's thesis at the University of Texas. In 1935 Henry Nash Smith^{qv} edited a translation by Charlotte Churchill for children entitled *With Milam and Fannin: Adventures of a German Boy in Texas' Revolution*. This version was reprinted in 1968. *Texas und Seine Revolution* is one of John H. Jenkins's^{qv} *Basic Texas Books.*

Ehrenberg never married. He was murdered by robbers on October 9, 1866, at Dos Palmas, near the site of present Palm Springs, California. Mineral City, Arizona, was renamed Ehrenberg in his honor through the efforts of Michael "Big Mike" Goldwater.

BIBLIOGRAPHY: Natalie Ornish, *Pioneer Jewish Texans* (Dallas: Texas Heritage, 1989). Diane M. T. Rose, "The Maps, Plans, and Sketches of Herman Ehrenberg," *Prologue: Journal of the National Archives* 9 (Fall 1977). Special Collection, Arizona Historical Foundation, Hayden Library, Arizona State University, Tempe. Vertical Files, Barker Texas History Center, University of Texas at Austin.

Natalie Ornish

EIGHTEEN CREEK. Eighteen Creek rises a mile north of the Motley-Dickens county line in extreme southeast Motley County (at 33°50′ N, 100°33′ W) and runs southeast for five miles, passing through the northeast corner of Dickens County, before reaching its mouth on the North Wichita River, a mile north of Dumont in King County and less than a mile east of the Dickens-King county line (at 33°49′ N, 100°30′ W). The stream crosses moderately sloping terrain with shallow silty loams that support mesquite and grasses.

EIGHTEENMILE CREEK. Eighteenmile Creek, also known as Eighteen Mile Coleto Creek, rises near the Emma Hayes oilfield in extreme northwestern Goliad County (at 28°54′ N, 97°31′ W) and runs southeast for fourteen miles to its mouth on Fifteenmile Creek, three miles east of Ander (at 28°51′ N, 97°18′ W). The creek traverses flat to rolling terrain surfaced by clay and sandy loam that supports water-tolerant hardwoods and grasses. It was named in 1850, when Clinton was the county seat of DeWitt County and the headstreams of Coleto Creek were given names determined by their distance from the courthouse door in Clinton.

EIGHTH TEXAS CAVALRY. The Eighth Texas Cavalry, a group of Texas volunteers for the Confederate Army popularly known as Terry's Texas Rangers, was assembled by Benjamin Franklin Terry^{qv} in August 1861. Each man was required to furnish a shotgun or carbine, a Colt revolver (*see* COLT REVOLVERS), a Bowie knife,^{qv} and a saddle, bridle, and blanket. The army would provide the mounts. The regiment was mustered into Confederate service at Houston on September 9, 1861. Terry was elected colonel, Thomas S. Lubbock^{qv} lieutenant colonel, and Thomas Harrison^{qv} major. With the death

Members of Company C, Eighth Texas Cavalry, also known as Terry's Texas Rangers (left to right: Pete Kendrum, William A. Lynch, Felix G. Kennedy, Thomas S. Burney, W. S. Wood), ca. 1861–65. Half-plate tintype. Courtesy Panhandle-Plains Historical Society, Canyon, Texas.

of Colonel Terry at the battle of Woodsonville, Kentucky, on December 8, 1861, Lubbock, then sick in a Bowling Green, Kentucky, hospital, was advanced to command of the regiment, but he died within a few days. Subsequently, John Austin Wharton[qv] was elected colonel and John G. Walker[qv] lieutenant colonel of the regiment. When Wharton was promoted to brigadier general in the fall of 1862, Harrison became the regimental commander; he served in that post until the end of the war.

Although the regiment had been promised duty in Virginia, it was diverted to Bowling Green, Kentucky, at the request of Gen. Albert Sidney Johnston,[qv] who was in command of the Confederate army headquartered there. The Terry Rangers distinguished themselves at the battles of Shiloh (April 6–8, 1862), Perryville (October 8, 1862), Murfreesboro (December 31, 1862–January 2, 1863), Chickamauga (September 19–20, 1863), and Chattanooga (November 24–25, 1863); in the Atlanta campaign (May 1–September 2, 1864); and as raiders in Kentucky and Tennessee under Lt. Gen. Nathan Bedford Forrest. The rangers were also part of the inadequate force under Gen. Joseph E. Johnston[qv] that attempted to slow Maj. Gen. William T. Sherman's[qv] inexorable "march to the sea" during the final months of the war. Terry's Rangers delivered what was probably the last charge of the Army of Tennessee at the battle of Bentonville (March 19–20, 1865). Rather than surrender with the rest of Johnston's army at Durham Station, North Carolina, on April 26, 1865, 158 of the reported 248 survivors of the regiment slipped through Union lines to join other Confederates yet in the field. With the total collapse of the Southern cause, however, the Terry Rangers drifted home as individuals and in small groups, having never officially surrendered. With the exception of Hood's Texas Brigade,[qv] the Eighth Texas Cavalry was probably the best-known Texas unit to serve in the Civil War.[qv] It earned a reputation that ranked it among the most effective mounted regiments in the western theater of operations.

BIBLIOGRAPHY: James Knox Polk Blackburn, *Reminiscences of Terry's Texas Rangers* (Austin: Littlefield Fund for Southern History, University of Texas, 1919; rpt., Austin: Ranger Press, 1979). Thomas W. Cutrer, ed., "'We Are Stern and Resolved': The Civil War Letters of John Wesley Rabb, Terry's Texas Rangers," *Southwestern Historical Quarterly* 91 (October 1987). William Andrew Fletcher, *Rebel Private, Front and Rear* (Austin: University of Texas Press, 1954). Leonidas B. Giles, *Terry's Texas Rangers* (Austin: Von Boeckmann–Jones, 1911). H. W. Graber, *The Life Record of H. W. Graber, A Terry Texas Ranger, 1861–1865* (1916; facsimile, *A Terry Texas Ranger*, Austin: State House, 1987).

Thomas W. Cutrer

EIGHTH TEXAS INFANTRY. The Eighth Texas Infantry battalion of the Confederate States Army was organized by Alfred Marmaduke Hobby[qv] in Refugio County on May 14, 1862. It later became known as Hobby's Eighth Texas Infantry regiment. It consisted of three companies under captains Robert E. Jones, William E. McCampbell, and P. H. Breeden. A fourth company under Edwin E. Hobby^{qv} was added on June 20, 1862, and a fifth, under José M. Peñaloza, completed the battalion. The battalion trained at Camp Charles Russell near Banquete until July 19, 1862, when it was ordered to defend Corpus Christi as a part of the Twenty-ninth Brigade. There it was joined by various other units of light artillery and mounted rifles and in February 1863 became the Eighth Texas Infantry regiment, with a staff including John Ireland, J. A. Throckmorton,^{qqv} Daniel D. Shea, and others.

As a battalion, the force prevented a federal invasion at Corpus Christi in August 1862 and in September captured J. W. Kittridge of the federal fleet. In 1863, after organization of the regiment, the Eighth guarded Fort Esperanza on Matagorda Island, kept a battery on Mustang Island, and in May drove Union troops off St. Joseph's Island. In the fall of 1863 superior Union forces under Nathaniel P. Banks^{qv} were able to force Hobby's troops back to the San Antonio River. After December 1863 they were ordered transferred to East Texas, but many entered Waul's Legion^{qv} instead. Part of the Eighth regiment was stationed on Galveston Island in the winter of 1863; other units in the area of Indianola and Lavaca engaged in skirmishes with the federals as late as February 1864. Most of the units fought under Thomas N. Waul^{qv} in the battles of Mansfield and Pleasant Hill (*see* RED RIVER CAMPAIGN) in April 1864 and from then to the end of the war were employed in coastal defense in Texas. The regiment was mustered out of service on May 22, 1865.

BIBLIOGRAPHY: Robert Underwood Johnson and Clarence Clough Buel, *Battles and Leaders of the Civil War* (4 vols., New York: Yoseloff, 1956). Coleman McCampbell, *Saga of a Frontier Seaport* (Dallas: South-West, 1934). Mary A. Sutherland, *The Story of Corpus Christi* (Corpus Christi Chapter, Daughters of the Confederacy, 1916). Dudley Goodall Wooten, ed., *A Comprehensive History of Texas* (2 vols., Dallas: Scarff, 1898; rpt., Austin: Texas State Historical Association, 1986).

Hobart Huson

EIGHTH UNITED STATES INFANTRY REGIMENT. In July 1838, Congress authorized formation of the Eighth Infantry regiment as part of a general army increase bill. After a brief tour of duty along the nation's northern border, the regiment was transferred to Florida, where it participated in the Second Seminole War. On the eve of the war against Mexico, the Eighth was transferred to Texas with Zachary Taylor's^{qv} army of occupation. The regiment fought with Taylor as he drove south from Corpus Christi to Monterrey, taking heavy losses but winning recognition for its role in eight engagements against Mexican troops. After the Treaty of Guadalupe Hidalgo,^{qv} the Eighth Infantry was deployed in Texas and New Mexico against various groups of Apache Indians. Organized into ten companies, it gradually assumed primary responsibility for protecting the trail between San Antonio and Santa Fe during the 1850s. Small detachments of the Eighth, occasionally riding borrowed horses, conducted numerous pursuits against Indians deemed hostile by the federal government, but long-range skirmishing rather than pitched battles usually characterized the decade's fighting. Routine duties in the army's scattered posts west of San Antonio, however, dominated the daily lives of most of the regiment's military personnel. The soldiers particularly detested fatigue and construction duty; desertion, a chronic problem among the antebellum army as a whole, also plagued the Eighth Infantry.

In February 1861, Gen. David E. Twiggs^{qv} surrendered federal posts in Texas to officials of the state Secession Convention.^{qv} According to these terms, the garrisons of West Texas posts, including much of the Eight Infantry regiment, were to march to the Texas coast, where they would be allowed safe passage to the North. Although several of the regiment's officers resigned their federal commissions and joined the Confederate Army, almost all of the enlisted personnel remained loyal to the Union. After the scattered garrisons had united and were marching toward San Antonio, news of the firing upon Fort Sumter, South Carolina, led Texas officials to reverse the earlier agreement. Nearly 400 Unionist Eighth Infantrymen under Bvt. Lt. Col. Isaac V. D. Reeve were forced to surrender to a much larger Texas force near San Lucas Springs. The Eighth's remaining officers were paroled the following year, but most of the enlisted personnel remained under guard in Texas until exchanged for Confederate prisoners in February 1863. During the Civil War,^{qv} elements of the old Eighth Infantry were reconstituted as part of the Fifteenth Infantry, which fought for the Union on the eastern front. Following postwar army reorganization, the Eighth Infantry fought in campaigns against the Indians in Montana (1872) and Arizona (1876, 1886). The regiment participated in the Santiago campaign during the war with Spain (1898), then fought in the Philippine Insurrection. As part of the Fourth Infantry Division, it participated in the Normandy invasion and conquest of Germany during the World War II.^{qv} The regiment later saw combat in Vietnam.

BIBLIOGRAPHY: John K. Mahon and Romana Danysh, *Army Lineage Series. Infantry, Part I: Regular Army* (Washington: Office of the Chief of Military History, U.S. Army, 1972). Francis Paul Prucha, *The Sword of the Republic: The United States Army on the Frontier, 1783–1846* (New York: Macmillan, 1969). Gregory J. W. Urwin, *The United States Infantry: An Illustrated History, 1775–1918* (London: Blandford Press, 1988). Robert M. Utley, *Frontier Regulars: The United States Army and the Indian, 1866–1891* (New York: Macmillan, 1973). Robert M. Utley, *Frontiersmen in Blue: The United States Army and the Indians, 1848–1865* (New York: Macmillan, 1967; rpt., Lincoln: University of Nebraska Press, 1981). Thomas Wilhelm, *History of the Eighth U.S. Infantry, from Its Organization in 1838* (2 vols., New York: Headquarters, Eighth Infantry, 1873). Robert Wooster, *History of Fort Davis, Texas*, Southwest Cultural Resources Center Professional Papers, No. 34 (Santa Fe: National Park Service, 1990).

Robert Wooster

EIGHT MILE CREEK. Eight Mile Creek rises just west of Scottsville in east central Harrison County (at 32°33′ N, 94°15′ W) and runs southwest for nineteen miles to its mouth on the Sabine River, just north of the Panola county line (at 32°20′ N, 94°21′ W). It passes through an area of nearly level to hilly terrain surfaced by loamy and clayey soils that support dense patches of pine and hardwood trees along its banks. The land is used predominantly for agriculture.

EIGHTMILE DRAW (Hudspeth County). Eightmile Draw rises a half mile north of Hueco Station in north central Hudspeth County (at 31°44′ N, 105°19′ W) and runs east for seventeen miles before drying out at a point four miles south of Linda Lake in the salt basin of northeastern Hudspeth County (at 31°44′ N, 105°08′ W). The stream is intermittent in the lower reaches. It traverses steep to gently sloping terrain surfaced by shallow, stony soils that support Mexican buckeye, walnut, persimmon, desert willow, scrub brush, and sparse grasses.

—— (Sutton County). Eightmile Draw begins two miles west of Farm Road 3130 in east central Sutton County (at 30°31′ N, 100°29′ W) and runs southeast for twenty-one miles to its mouth on Live Oak Draw, two miles south of Interstate Highway 10 (at 30°26′ N, 100°14′ W). The draw is located in the western Edwards Plateau, with gently rolling terrain surfaced by loamy soils, occasionally broken by limestone outcrops, that support range grasses with scattered small stands of oak, juniper, and mesquite.

EIGHT-SECTION ACT. The so-called Eight-Section Act of April 15, 1905, amended laws concerning the sale and lease of public free school, asylum, and public lands, especially the law of 1901, by permitting the purchase or lease of as much as eight sections of land in Bandera, Brewster, Crockett, El Paso, Jeff Davis, Loving, Pecos, Presidio, Sutton, and Val Verde counties. The sale or lease was directed by the General Land Office,qv and provisions of the law imposed restrictions on the area in which additional sections might be purchased, residence and improvement requirements, and a policy of preference to lessees. On May 16, 1907, Edwards, Kinney, and Terrell counties were added to the eight–section counties, and Bandera and Loving counties were excluded. The act was in effect as late as 1920 but was omitted in the *Civil Statutes of Texas* in 1925.

BIBLIOGRAPHY: *Complete Texas Statutes* (Kansas City, Missouri: Vernon Law Book Company, 1920). *General Laws of the State of Texas*, 1905.

Curtis Bishop

EISENHOWER, DWIGHT DAVID (1890–1969). Dwight David Eisenhower, general of the army and thirty-fourth president of the United States, was born in Denison, Texas, on October 14, 1890, to David J. and Ida (Stover) Eisenhower. His father, who had moved from Pennsylvania during the late nineteenth century, was employed on the Missouri, Kansas and Texas Railroad at the time. Shortly after his birth the family moved to Abilene, Kansas, from where Eisenhower was appointed to the United States Military Academy, West Point, in July 1911.

At West Point he was popular and gregarious, but no dedicated student. A promising football career ended with a broken knee in a game against Jim Thorpe's Carlisle Indians, after which the cadet coached the freshman team. His future leadership abilities were predicted by one superior who described him as "born to command." Another, however, advised that his first assignment, on graduation in 1915, should be under "a strict disciplinarian." Eisenhower graduated on June 12, 1915, at the top of the middle third of his class, which numbered 163. He was commissioned a second lieutenant and assigned to the Nineteenth Infantry at Fort Sam Houston, San Antonio, on September 13, 1915. He received promotion to first lieutenant on July 1, 1916, the day he married Mamie Geneva Doud. They had two sons.

Eisenhower's military career had an auspicious beginning when, during World War I,qv he commanded a heavy tank brigade at Gettysburg, Pennsylvania, and was awarded the Distinguished Service Medal. In 1926 he graduated number one in his class at the highly competitive Command and General Staff School, Fort Leavenworth. During the 1930s Eisenhower, as a major and lieutenant colonel, was assigned largely to staff positions. His years in the War Department (1929–35) and as chief of staff to Gen. Douglas MacArthur in the Philippines (1935–39) gave him an insight into governmental affairs, both military and civilian, that was denied most of his contemporaries.

On December 14, 1941, Eisenhower, then at Fort Sam Houston, was transferred to the War Plans Division, United States Army Staff, under Gen. George C. Marshall. From that time to 1961 he held one responsible position after another. As supreme commander, Allied Expeditionary Force, he gave the order that sent British and American troops into Normandy on June 6, 1944 (D-Day). Eleven months later (V-E Day) he accepted the surrender of Nazi representatives Wilhelm Keitel and Alfred Jodl.

In 1948 Eisenhower retired as army chief of staff to become president of Columbia University in New York. Though his tenure was short—and interrupted continuously by service in Washington—he was able, while there, to organize the American Assembly for the Study of War and Peace through a gift from W. Averell Harriman. In 1951 he was recalled to military duty to serve as supreme commander, Allied Powers in Europe, under NATO.

Though his name had often been mentioned in connection with the presidency, Eisenhower always demurred, insisting on an honest "draft" for that office. When he relented in 1952, however, he found himself bitterly opposed for the Republican nomination by Senator Robert A. Taft of Ohio. His nomination was achieved only by the seating of a pro-Eisenhower Republican delegation from Texas. By contrast, his election over Democrat Adlai E. Stevenson was remarkably free of acrimony.

As president, Eisenhower followed a moderate course, continuing most of the social reforms of Roosevelt's New Deal but insisting on fiscal responsibility in the federal government. His concern over the growing size of the Pentagon budget was reflected in his much-remembered farewell address, in which he warned of the "unwarranted influence of the military-industrial complex." His domestic achievements as president included, besides balancing the federal budget three times, the construction of the Interstate Highway System, passage of the first civil-rights law since the Civil War,qv and the dispatch of the 101st Airborne Division to enforce school integration in Little Rock, Arkansas (1957). Eisenhower cheerfully shared credit for these measures with fellow Texans Lyndon B. Johnson and Samuel T. (Sam) Rayburn.qqv Nevertheless, his major importance fell in the area for which he had been elected—national security. During the perilous early years of the nuclear age his will and patience did much to prevent the nuclear holocaust that did not happen.

Eisenhower left office in 1961 with his reputation still high among his countrymen. He died on March 28, 1969, at age seventy-eight, at Walter Reed Army Hospital outside Washington, D.C., survived by his widow, his son John, and four grandchildren. He is buried at the Place of Meditation, in Abilene, Kansas. Mamie Eisenhower died ten years later and was buried beside him. *See also* EISENHOWER BIRTHPLACE STATE HISTORICAL SITE.

BIBLIOGRAPHY: Stephen E. Ambrose, *Eisenhower* (2 vols., New York: Simon and Schuster, 1983). David Eisenhower, *Eisenhower at War, 1943–1945* (New York: Random House, 1986). Dwight D. Eisenhower, *At Ease: Stories I Tell to Friends* (New York: Doubleday, 1967). Dwight D. Eisenhower, *Crusade in Europe* (Garden City, New York: Doubleday, 1948). Dwight D. Eisenhower, *The White House Years* (2 vols., New York: Doubleday, 1963, 1965). John Eisenhower, *Strictly Personal* (Garden City, New York: Doubleday, 1974).

John S. D. Eisenhower

EISENHOWER BIRTHPLACE STATE HISTORICAL SITE. Eisenhower Birthplace State Historical Site is located just east of U.S. Highway 75 in Denison. Dwight D. Eisenhowerqv was born in the two-story frame home, which was acquired by a group of Denison residents and restored as a memorial to Eisenhower shortly after his election to the presidency in 1952. The home and the property were deeded to the Eisenhower Birthplace Foundation in 1953. This organization purchased and moved several houses to the site, landscaped the area, and added a parking lot. The site was deeded to the State Parks Board in 1958. In 1993, because of cuts in the state budget, Texas Rural Communities, Incorporated, a nonprofit organization, took over maintenance of the park.

The house contains furnishings typical of the 1890s, the decade in which Eisenhower was born. The only item in the house that actually belonged to the Eisenhower family, however, is a quilt in the room in which Eisenhower was born. An antique crank telephone in the home's entry hall greets visitors with a message that Eisenhower recorded in 1952.

BIBLIOGRAPHY: Ray Miller, *Texas Parks* (Austin: Cordovan, 1984).

Brian Hart

EISENHOWER STATE RECREATION PARK. Eisenhower State Recreation Park is five miles northwest of Denison near Farm Road 1310 in northern Grayson County. The Texas legislature voted in 1947 to honor World War IIqv hero Dwight D. Eisenhower,qv who was born in Denison, by establishing a state park on the south shore of the recently completed Lake Texoma. Not until 1954, however, when Eisenhower had been president of the United States for two years, did state officials purchase the 457-acre site from the United States Army and construct the park. Most of the park sits high above the lake, and its shoreline consists predominantly of cliffs, although part of it is a swimming beach. Lake Texoma is noted among fishing enthusiasts for bass, crappie, and catfish. Four fishing piers and a fish-cleaning shelter have been constructed in the park. In addition to fishing, waterskiing and sailing are popular activities among visitors to the park. Animal-watchers and bird-watchers are attracted to the wooded areas, which are home to white-tail deer, raccoons, grey foxes, and various birds. Eisenhower State Recreation Park maintains thirty-five screened shelters and forty-eight campsites for rent to park visitors.

BIBLIOGRAPHY: Mildred J. Little, *Camper's Guide to Texas Parks, Lakes, and Forests* (Houston: Pacesetter, 1978; 2d ed., Houston: Lone Star, 1983). Ray Miller, *Texas Parks* (Houston: Cordovan, 1984).

Brian Hart

EISENLOHR, EDWARD GUSTAV (1872–1961). Edward Eisenlohr, painter, lithographer, author, and lecturer, was born on November 9, 1872, in Cincinnati, Ohio, to Rudolph and Emma (Hellner) Eisenlohr. When he was two years old his family moved to Dallas as early settlers of Oak Cliff. He attended Temple Emanu-El[qv] School and Grove High School, where he displayed an early proclivity for art in his school-book sketches. In 1886 he won a first prize award in an exhibition at the State Fair of Texas[qv] for his pencil drawing of a map of Texas. Intent on providing their children with a broad and cultured education, the Eisenlohrs returned in 1887 to Europe; Edward studied in Zürich and Germany with the intention of becoming an artist. In 1888 business called his father back to Dallas, where the family followed him at the end of the 1889 school term.

Upon his return, Eisenlohr took a position as bookkeeper and teller at the American Exchange Bank, setting aside money from his income for his artistic ambitions. During the summers from 1889 to 1907 he studied with Robert J. Onderdonk and Frank Reaugh,[qqv] painters he later acknowledged as the most profound influences on his work. In 1907 Eisenlohr had one of his paintings accepted for an exhibition at the Cincinnati Museum of Fine Art. He then studied at the Art Students League Summer School in Woodstock, New York, with Birge Harrison and traveled to Europe. He was invited to join Gustave Schoenleber's class at the Grand-ducal Academy of Fine Arts in Karlsruhe, Germany, where he studied for two years (1907–08) and was introduced to "dark impressionism." He then returned to Dallas.

Between 1916 and 1926 Eisenlohr lived in Santa Fe, New Mexico, for six months out of each year. During this period he completed pencil, watercolor, and pastel drawings, as well as oil paintings, and exhibited at the Museum of Fine Art in Santa Fe. In New Mexico he developed a lighter palette and bolder brushwork; his works depicted sunlight, open land, and towering clouds. He started considering himself an American impressionist.

North Texas Pastoral, *by Edward Gustav Eisenlohr. Lithograph. Photograph by George Holmes. Courtesy Archer M. Huntington Art Gallery, University of Texas at Austin; gift of Charles and Dorothy Clark, 1982.*

Eisenlohr documented the early twentieth-century landscape of Dallas in over 1,000 drawings, watercolors, pastels, oil paintings, and lithographs. His earliest drawings and paintings recorded abandoned buildings on the edge of the city, as well as the emerging skyline of Dallas. He also painted fields, farms, and country churches around growing Dallas. Like other impressionists, he felt a responsibility to record the images of his surroundings. He produced more drawings and paintings of his local community and region than any other early Dallas artist and is considered one of the pioneer landscape painters of Texas.

His works have been exhibited at the Corcoran Gallery, Washington; the National Academy of Design and the Museum of Modern Art, New York; the Pan-American Exposition; the Albany Institute of the History of Art; the New York and San Francisco World's fairs; the St. Louis Museum; the Museum of New Mexico; and many one-man exhibitions. He is represented in the permanent collections of the Dallas Museum of Art, the Elisabet Ney Museum qv in Austin, the Delgado Museum of Art in New Orleans, the Witte Museum qv at San Antonio, and the art museums of Abilene, Houston, and Santa Fe. He won prizes from the Dallas Art Association (1931, 1932, 1948), the San Antonio Art League qv (1927, 1928), the Southern States Art League (1930), the Texas Federation of Women's Clubs qv (1931), and Dallas Allied Arts (1932).

Eisenlohr was one of the founding officers of the organization that became the Dallas Art Association. He was also a member of the Salmagundi Club, the Texas Fine Arts Association, qv the American Arts Professional League, the American Federation of Artists, the Southern States Art League, the New York Federation of Arts, and the New York Water Color Club. He was a printmaker and author of three books on art appreciation. He was also one of the founders and an active member of the First Unitarian Church of Dallas. He died after a long illness in a Dallas hospital on June 6, 1961, and was buried in Oak Cliff Cemetery.

BIBLIOGRAPHY: Diana Church, *Art and Accommodation in Dallas: Edward G. Eisenlohr* (M.A. thesis, University of Texas at Austin, 1987). Diana Church, "Edward G. Eisenlohr—Scenes of Santa Fe," *Southwest Art* 16 (November 1986). Diana Church, *Guide to Dallas Artists, 1890–1917* (Plano, Texas, 1987). Frances Battaile Fisk, *A History of Texas Artists and Sculptors* (Abilene, Texas, 1928; facsimile rpt., Austin: Morrison, 1986). Esse Forrester-O'Brien, *Art and Artists of Texas* (Dallas: Tardy, 1935). Vertical Files, Barker Texas History Center, University of Texas at Austin. Lucy Runnels Wright, "Edward G. Eisenlohr," *Texas Outlook* 21 (October 1937). *Diana Church*

ELAM, JOHN (?–?). John Elam, one of Stephen F. Austin's qv Old Three Hundred qv settlers, was in the Austin colony as early as April 20, 1824, when he voted for the Baron de Bastrop qv as deputy to the Constituent Congress of the eastern division of the Provincias Internas. qv Elam's title to a league of land was granted on August 7, 1824. The census of March 1826 listed him as a single man aged between twenty-five and forty. In October 1830 William Munson advertised lumber for sale on the land granted to Elam, and on December 15, 1830, the ayuntamiento qv of San Felipe de Austin declared the Elam league on the Brazos River vacant because he had abandoned the country without improving the land.

BIBLIOGRAPHY: Eugene C. Barker, ed., *The Austin Papers* (3 vols., Washington: GPO, 1924–28). Eugene C. Barker, ed., "Minutes of the Ayuntamiento of San Felipe de Austin, 1828–1832," 12 parts, *Southwestern Historical Quarterly* 21–24 (January 1918–October 1920). Lester G. Bugbee, "The Old Three Hundred: A List of Settlers in Austin's First Colony," *Quarterly of the Texas State Historical Association* 1 (October 1897). *Texas Gazette*, October 9, 1830.

ELAM, TEXAS. Elam was on the Elam grant eight miles southeast of Dallas in southeastern Dallas County. It was established by Jesse Elam in the early 1880s on the Texas Trunk line, which was constructed through the area in 1881. In 1884 the settlement secured a post office and became known as Elam Station. By 1890 it had a general store and a population of twenty-five. In 1899 the name was changed to Elam, and in 1904 the post office was discontinued. In 1933 Elam had six businesses and a population of fifty. From 1939 to 1963 the population was 150. After 1963 the community was no longer listed.

BIBLIOGRAPHY: Fred Tarpley, *Place Names of Northeast Texas* (Commerce: East Texas State University, 1969). *Matthew Hayes Nall*

ELAM CREEK. Elam Creek rises ten miles west of Medina in western Bandera County (at 29°49′ N, 99°25′ W) and runs southeast for 4½ miles through juniper and oak woodlands to its mouth on the West Prong of the Medina River, seven miles west of Medina (at 29°47′ N, 99°23′ W). The stream originates in an area with shallow, stony soils overlying flat terrain with localized dissection. In its lower reaches it crosses a region of steep slopes and limestone benches that give a stairstep appearance to the landscape.

ELAM SPRINGS, TEXAS. Elam Springs (Elam Spring), off Farm Road 1795 ten miles southwest of Gilmer in western Upshur County, was settled before 1900. By that year it had a school, which in 1906 had an enrollment of forty-nine black students. In the mid-1930s the community had a church and number of houses, and in the mid-1960s it had a church, a cemetery, and a few widely scattered houses. In 1990 Elam Springs was a dispersed rural community.
Christopher Long

ELAND ROUGH. Eland Rough is a small chain of hills located along the upper reaches of Pin Oak Creek, four miles southwest of Gause in eastern Milam County (centered at 30°46′ N, 96°47′ W). The hills have elevations as high as 515 feet above sea level and rise more than 100 feet above the surrounding countryside.

EL ATASCOSO, TEXAS. El Atascoso was an early Spanish settlement (*see* SPANISH TEXAS) on what is now State Highway 21 some eight miles east of Nacogdoches in eastern Nacogdoches County. The Rancho Atascoso, as it was sometimes known, was established by José Mora in 1778 after the Spanish withdrawal of 1772–73 and was located where El Camino Real crossed Atascoso Creek. The section of El Camino Real between Atascoso and Puenta Suelas creeks was the site of numerous such camps; others settled nearby, joining Mora for protection from the Indian inhabitants of the area. A Texas Historical Commission qv marker was established at the site in the 1970s.

BIBLIOGRAPHY: Marker Files, Texas Historical Commission, Austin.
Christopher Long

ELBA CREEK. Elba Creek rises four miles west of Sherman in central Grayson County (at 33°38′ N, 96°42′ W) and runs west for eight miles to its mouth on Deaver Creek, four miles east of Sadler (at 33°40′ N, 96°48′ W). It traverses an area of flat to rolling prairie surfaced by dark, commonly calcareous clays that support mesquite trees, various grasses, and cacti. The stream is intermittent in its lower reaches. The area has served as range and cropland.

EL BARROSA CREEK. El Barrosa Creek rises eight miles south of Carrizo Springs in western Dimmit County (at 28°24′ N, 99°55′ W) and runs northeast for thirteen miles to its mouth on Soldier Slough, 6½ miles east of Carrizo Springs and just west of the Thirteen oilfield in north central Dimmit County (at 28°30′ N, 99°45′ W). The stream rises in flat to rolling terrain with local escarpments, surfaced by deep, fine sandy loam that supports brush and grasses, and descends to a flat area with locally shallow depressions, surfaced by clay and sandy loam that supports water-tolerant hardwoods and grasses. *Barrosa* is Spanish for "muddy."

ELBERT, TEXAS (Polk County). Elbert was north of Dallardsville and about sixty miles northwest of Beaumont in extreme eastern Polk County. Elbert Harrison owned a store at the site. A post office, named Elbert in honor of the merchant, operated there from 1891 to 1896. The community was not shown on county highway maps for the early 1980s.

BIBLIOGRAPHY: *A Pictorial History of Polk County, Texas, 1846–1910* (Livingston, Texas: Polk County Bicentennial Commission, 1976; rev. ed. 1978).
Robert Wooster

ELBERT, TEXAS (Throckmorton County). Elbert, on State Highway 79 and Farm Road 1711 in eastern Throckmorton County, was established in the late nineteenth century to serve the needs of ranchers headquartered to the north on the Brazos River. By 1904 Elbert had a post office, and by 1915 it had thirty residents and a gin operated by W. F. Parsley. From 1940 until 1990 Elbert reported a population of 150.

ELBERTA, TEXAS. Elberta is just east of State Highway 110 a mile southeast of Tyler in central Smith County. The site was known as Douglas, when it became a station on the International–Great Northern Railroad in 1872. It was renamed Elberta for the Elberta peaches grown in the area. In 1936 Elberta had a church, a cemetery, and a small cluster of farms. Maps for 1973 showed a sizable community with a church, water tanks, and a water-tank substation.

BIBLIOGRAPHY: Smith County Historical Society, *Historical Atlas of Smith County* (Tyler, Texas: Tyler Print Shop, 1965). Donald W. Whisenhunt, comp., *Chronological History of Smith County* (Tyler, Texas: Smith County Historical Society, 1983). Albert Woldert, *A History of Tyler and Smith County* (San Antonio: Naylor, 1948).
Vista K. McCroskey

EL CALABOZ, TEXAS. El Calaboz is a dispersed colonia off U.S. Highway 281 and just north of the Mexican border, six miles south of San Benito in south central Cameron County. The site was settled in the late 1940s and by 1970 had fifty-three residences. In 1986 an estimated population of 162 lived in thirty-six homes. The name comes from Spanish *calabozo*, "calaboose" or "jailhouse."

BIBLIOGRAPHY: *Colonias in the Lower Rio Grande Valley of South Texas: A Summary Report* (Policy Research Project Report No. 18, Lyndon B. Johnson School of Public Affairs, University of Texas at Austin, 1977).
Alicia A. Garza

EL CAMINO DEL CABALLO. El Camino del Caballo (also known as Contraband Trace and Smugglers' Road) was a network of footpaths across the southern part of what is now Nacogdoches County, used for smuggling goods from Louisiana into Spanish Texas,qv particularly between 1800 and 1820. The main route left the Old San Antonio Roadqv near Arroyo Loco, west of Nacogdoches, crossed the lands of Nuestra Señora de Guadalupe de los Nacogdoches Mission, crossed Moral Creek near its junction with Alazan Creek, and then traversed lands granted to Nepomuceno de la Cerda and José María Mora. Near Carrizo Creek the trace joined another trail that came from the Saline Crossing of the Angelina River. From that juncture the smugglers returned to the Old San Antonio Road or went by Oil Springs, usually crossing Attoyac Bayou two miles below the site of the present State Highway 21 bridge. Efforts of José María Guadiana and other Spanish officials to prevent smuggling of contraband goods by way of the trace proved generally fruitless. The route continued to be used after Mexican independence, and segments remained in use until the 1890s, when fencing of the land cut off sections. Portions of the road could still be seen in 1991.

BIBLIOGRAPHY: Edward Blount, "Location of the Old Contraband Trace in Nacogdoches County," *Junior Historian*, December 1945. Herbert Eugene Bolton, *Texas in the Middle Eighteenth Century: Studies in Spanish Colonial History and Administration* (Berkeley: University of California Press, 1915; rpt., Austin: University of Texas Press, 1970). Nacogdoches County Genealogical Society, *Nacogdoches County Families* (Dallas: Curtis, 1985).

EL CAMPO, TEXAS. El Campo is on U.S. Highway 59 and State Highway 71, thirteen miles southwest of Wharton in south central Wharton County. The Lower Colorado River Authorityqv provides water, and several creeks flow near the city limits. In 1882 a railroad camp called Prairie Switch was situated where El Campo now stands and served as a switching point on New York, Texas and Mexican Railway. Cowboys called the camp "Pearl of the Prairies." Located in the midst of cattle country, the camp was used by Mexican cowboys who changed the name to El Campo in 1890. Ranching was the chief industry, and thousands of cattle were shipped yearly to San Antonio. Four large ranches surrounded the settlement: the Texas Land and Cattle Companyqv (KO Ranch) to the south, the Pierce Ranch to the east, the Herder Ranch to the west, and the Brown Ranch to the north.

For several years El Campo had no permanent structures except the section house and a switch serving the cattle-loading chute. In 1889 a general store was built. In 1890 a post office opened. In 1892 the community had an estimated population of twenty-five, a general store, a mill and gin, and a justice of the peace. Settlers began moving into the area and planted rice, cotton, and corn. Hay soon became one of the chief products, and in the early 1900s the town was the second largest hay-shipping center in the United States. The Farmers Union Warehouse Company was established in El Campo. A one-room schoolhouse was built in 1891, and in 1895 an independent school district was established. By 1901 it enrolled 177 students. Between 1890 and 1898 Swedish Lutheran, Baptist, Methodist, Presbyterian, Catholic, German Lutheran, and Swedish Methodist churches were organized.

In 1896 a fire destroyed the principal business section; by 1900, 130 businesses had been rebuilt. In 1901 another fire destroyed a large part of the town, and this time the residents built brick buildings. El Campo Brick and Tile Company provided building materials for many of the permanent structures. In 1901 a library was organized. In 1902 the first bank was established. On June 19, 1905, El Campo was incorporated. The El Campo Ice and Water Company was established in 1907. This plant lighted businesses, streets, and homes, and made enough ice to supply the city. The El Campo Rice Milling Company was established in 1903. By 1904 seventy rice farms and 126 pumping stations were in operation around El Campo. Broussard Rice Mills was established, and in 1914 the two rice mills consolidated under the name El Campo Rice Milling Company, now known as ELCO. At one time rice hulls were compressed into bricks used as an experimental building material.

The first doctor in El Campo arrived in 1890. By 1906 two funeral homes had been established. In 1910 there were 1,778 residents. The first hospital was established in 1912. The first newspaper was published in 1894. The El Campo *News* began in 1928 and has survived in the present El Campo *Leader News*. In 1931 a Czech-language paper, *Svoboda*, was published. It was later purchased by Culp Krueger and merged with the main newspaper. In the mid-1930s gas and oil were discovered in Wharton County and spawned the local petroleum and oil-service industries. The Texas Company (now Texaco, Incorporatedqv) established a branch office in El Campo. In 1930 the town had a population of 2,034 and 160 businesses. In 1941 the town had 3,906 residents and twenty-two businesses; the population was 6,216 in 1952, 7,700 in 1961, and 9,995 in 1970.

In 1990 agriculture and petroleum related businesses provided the base for local economy. Crops included milo, rice, corn, cotton, and soybeans. Three farm cooperatives were functioning. The area remained a major beef producer as well. Aquaculture products and pecans added to the diversity. Manufactured items included aluminum extrusion, children's clothing, nursery containers, foam cups and containers, and valves. El Campo also had a wholesale nursery. Much of the industrial development can be attributed to the work of the El Campo Economic Development Corporation, a nonprofit organization formed in 1959 to bring new industry and stimulate growth, and to the El Campo Chamber of Commerce and Agriculture. El Campo Independent School District covers 445 square miles and has an enrollment for grades prekindergarten through twelve of 3,600. In 1990 El Campo had a population of 10,511 and 294 businesses.

BIBLIOGRAPHY: El Campo *Citizen,* March 30, 1950. El Campo *Leader-News,* 75th Anniversary Edition, August 20, 1980. J. O. Graham, *The Book of Wharton County, Texas* (Wharton?: Philip Rich, 1926). Vertical Files, Barker Texas History Center, University of Texas at Austin. Annie Lee Williams, *A History of Wharton County* (Austin: Von Boeckmann–Jones, 1964).

Karen H. Meinardus and Arliss Treybig

EL CAPITAN. El Capitan, the southernmost promontory of the Guadalupe Mountains in the Guadalupe Mountains National Park,qv is three miles southwest of Pine Springs in northwestern Culberson County (at 31°53′ N, 104°51′ W). With an elevation of 8,085 feet above sea level, its rises 2,400 feet above Pine Springs. Its name, Spanish for "captain," signifies its commanding position.

EL CARO CREEK. El Caro Creek rises eleven miles north of Alice in northern Jim Wells County (at 27°56′ N, 98°07′ W) and runs southeast for ten miles to its mouth on Palo Hueco Creek, seven miles northeast of Alice (at 27°52′ N, 98°00′ W). Its name is apparently a misspelling of *carro,* Spanish for "cart." The stream traverses flat terrain with local shallow depressions, surfaced by clay and sandy loams and some dark clay in its upper reaches. Water-tolerant hardwoods, conifers, and grasses, as well as some mesquite, brush, and cacti, grow along the streambed.

EL CENTRO, TEXAS. El Centro (Centro) is a community of Spanish-speaking livestock raisers at the intersection of Farm Road 2294 and the Delmita cutoff, two miles south of San Isidro and one mile west of Delmita in northeastern Starr County. Residents included the Rojas, Valverdes, and Villarreal families. Some area land titles date from Spanish Texas.qv The community reported a population of twenty-five in 1940. Around that time it also had two businesses, four farm units, and two dwellings. In the mid-1960s it had three businesses and a cemetery. In 1991 only a few farmhouses were in the immediate vicinity, though more than fifty homes were on Farm Road 2294 between the intersection and San Isidro.

Dick D. Heller, Jr.

EL CORREO ATLÁNTICO. *El Correo Atlántico* was a newspaper first published in Mexico City by its owner and sole editor, Orazio de Attellis Santangelo.qv It was preceded by a prospectus published on April 1, 1835, and began publication on May 2. Numbers 1 to 16 were published in Mexico City from May 2 to June 24, 1835. Numbers 17 to 41 were published in New Orleans from February 29 to August 15, 1836. In Mexico City the newspaper came out twice a week, in Spanish. In New Orleans, it came out once a week, in Spanish and English.

In Mexico the *Correo* devoted itself to reporting the most significant events in the various states of the Mexican federation, as related by local newspapers, and in the world. Frequently the reporting was followed by a commentary. Politically, the *Correo* favored Federalist policies. Because of this and because of its defense of the Texas colonists, on June 24, 1835, its editor was expelled from Mexico. He settled in New Orleans, where he resumed the publication of the *Correo Atlántico* to counteract the propaganda of *La Estrella Mejicana,* a periodical first published in New Orleans on February 9, 1836, and subsidized by the Mexican government. The Mexican Federalists in exile in New Orleans committed themselves to the payment of all printing costs of the *Correo,* while Santangelo undertook the editing and paid for the administrative expenses. However, Santangelo lost their support when the *Correo* defended and upheld the Texans' decision to secede from Mexico in order to start an independent Republic of Texas.qv George Fisher and Thomas Tobyqqv helped him continue publication.

The last issue of the *Correo* appeared on August 15, 1836. In an editorial directed to subscribers, Santangelo stated that publication would be suspended for a few weeks but promised that it would be resumed in September with a better format. He was unable to keep his promise because of lack of funds. A complete run of *El Correo Atlántico* is housed at the American Antiquarian Society in Worcester, Massachusetts.

BIBLIOGRAPHY: Luciano G. Rusich, "Marquis of Sant'Angelo, Italian-American Patriot and Friend to Texas," *Italian Americana* 5 (Fall–Winter 1979). Orazio de Attellis Santangelo, *Statement of Facts Relating to the Claim of Orazio de Attellis Santangelo* (Washington: Force, 1841). Orazio de Attellis Santangelo, *The Texas Question, Reviewed by an Adopted Citizen* (New York, 1844).

Luciano G. Rusich

ELDER, ROBERT (?–1841). Robert Elder, one of Stephen F. Austin'sqv Old Three Hundredqv colonists, was in Texas before April 20, 1824, when he took part in the election of the Baron de Bastropqv as elector for the Austin colony. On August 24, 1824, he received title to a labor of land now in Waller County. He made his home on the east side of the Brazos River about three miles from San Felipe, where he took part in the alcaldeqv election in December 1824. He was killed in 1825 while serving in the militia under Capt. Andrew Robinson, his only kinsman in Texas. He had left his family in Kentucky. His property was probated in 1845 with John W. Hall, Robinson's son-in-law, as executor of his estate.

BIBLIOGRAPHY: Eugene C. Barker, ed., *The Austin Papers* (3 vols., Washington: GPO, 1924–28). Lester G. Bugbee, "The Old Three Hundred: A List of Settlers in Austin's First Colony," *Quarterly of the Texas State Historical Association* 1 (October 1897). *Telegraph and Texas Register,* April 19, 1841.

Mrs. W. A. Goodrich, Jr.

ELDERVILLE, TEXAS. Elderville is off State Highway 322 just west of the Gregg County Airport in southeastern Gregg County. It was established in the late 1840s and named for one Colonel Brown, an early settler. Portions of the extended community were known at various times as Brown's Settlement, Brown's Bluff, or the Colonel Brown Community. A post office called Brown's Bluff opened there in 1874. Around 1875 its name was changed to Iron Bridge and in 1887 to Elderville. By 1890 the community had a steam gristmill, a cotton gin, three churches, two schools, a general store, and an estimated population of 200. By the early 1920s Elderville reported ninety-six inhabitants and four businesses. After World War IIqv much of the area became part of the Gregg County Airport. In the early 1990s Elderville was a dispersed rural community.

BIBLIOGRAPHY: Eugene W. McWhorter, *Traditions of the Land: The History of Gregg County* (Longview, Texas: Gregg County Historical

Foundation, 1989). Marker Files, Texas Historical Commission, Austin.
Christopher Long

ELDORADO, TEXAS. Eldorado, the county seat of Schleicher County, is at the intersection of U.S. highways 190 and 277, forty-five miles south of San Angelo near the center of the county. The area was part of a grant made by the state of Texas to the Houston East and West Texas Railway Company in 1878, but the railroad laid no track there. In 1895 W. B. Silliman acquired half interest in one of the sections of land and formed a company with two other men to establish a new townsite. Silliman surveyed the site, named the new town Eldorado, opened a store, and attracted residents from nearby Verand by offering them free town lots if they would move to Eldorado. The post office at Verand was officially transferred to Eldorado in 1895, and by 1896 Eldorado had two general stores and 100 residents. The community's first school was established in 1897. When Schleicher County was organized in 1901, Eldorado was named county seat.

The town grew quickly as a result of the land rushes that took place in Schleicher County between 1901 and 1905, and it thrived as a commercial center for area ranchers. Residents hoped that a rail line would be extended to Eldorado from San Angelo, but the railroad company went into receivership in 1912. In 1914 Eldorado had three churches, a bank, a weekly newspaper, a variety of businesses, and a population of 500. Residents voted to incorporate in 1925 but revoked the ordinance two years later because they disliked the higher taxes and the fact that livestock within the city was required to be penned; the local Lions Club began to circulate a second petition for incorporation in January 1929, and in March of that year voters agreed, choosing a mayor-alderman form of city government. The Kansas City, Mexico and Orient Railway built a line between San Angelo and Sonora in 1930; the track passed through Eldorado and gave Schleicher County residents easy access to outside markets.

By the early 1930s Eldorado had grown to 1,404 residents and fifty-five businesses; the population rose to 1,530 by the 1940s and to 1,653 by the 1950s. West Texas Woolen Mills was established in 1941, and Eldorado became the region's principal wool-processing center. Population estimates for the town reached a high of 2,790 in the mid-1960s, but the residents numbered fewer than 1,400 by the mid-1970s. Improved highways lessened the community's dependence on rail service, and the Atchison, Topeka and Santa Fe Railroad abandoned its track through Eldorado in 1976. The population of Eldorado was estimated at 2,061 in 1982; in 1990 it was 2,019.

BIBLIOGRAPHY: Roy D. Holt, ed., *Schleicher County, or Eighty Years of Development in Southwest Texas* (Eldorado, Texas: Eldorado *Success*, 1930). Frederick W. Rathjen, Four Score Years of Ranching on the Edwards Plateau: The History of Schleicher County (M.A. thesis, University of Texas, 1956). Schleicher County Historical Society, *A History of Schleicher County* (San Angelo: Anchor, 1979).
Vivian Elizabeth Smyrl

ELDORADO CENTER, TEXAS. Eldorado Center, on Farm Road 638 twenty miles southwest of Corsicana in southwestern Navarro County, began as a settlement for workers on the large Eldorado Ranch. The area was first settled before the Civil War,qv but the first business, a grocery store, was not established until about 1910. A school was in operation at Eldorado by the early 1900s, and in 1906 it had an enrollment of forty-eight. At its height around the time of World War Iqv Eldorado Center had a number of houses, a church, a school, a cotton gin, and a store. By the mid-1930s only a store and a number of houses remained there. The community's estimated population in 1936 was fifty. The store closed after World War II,qv and in the mid-1960s only a few widely scattered houses remained in the area. In the early 1990s Eldorado Center was a dispersed rural community.

BIBLIOGRAPHY: Alva Taylor, *History and Photographs of Corsicana and Navarro County* (Corsicana, Texas, 1959; rev. ed., *Navarro County History and Photographs*, Corsicana, 1962).
Christopher Long

ELDRIDGE, JOSEPH C. (1818–1881). Joseph C. Eldridge, early Texas Indian commissioner and United States Navy officer, was born in New York City on May 8, 1818. He moved to Texas from Connecticut in 1837. During the ten years he lived in Texas, he served as commissioner; in 1843 he was head of the peace party that went into the Indian country. He was appointed assistant paymaster in the United States Navy on February 2, 1847, and served with several commands including that of Commodore Oliver Perry, which opened Japan to world trade. Eldridge also participated in the expeditions for laying the Atlantic telegraph cable. He retired from the navy in 1878 and died in New York on August 14, 1881.

BIBLIOGRAPHY: William S. Speer and John H. Brown, eds., *Encyclopedia of the New West* (Marshall, Texas: United States Biographical Publishing, 1881; rpt., Easley, South Carolina: Southern Historical Press, 1978).
L. W. Kemp

ELDRIDGE, WILLIAM THOMAS (1862–1932). William Thomas Eldridge, businessman, was born in Washington County, Texas, on September 8, 1862. He left home at the age of twelve and moved to Eagle Lake in the early 1880s. He served a term as city marshal, opened a hotel, and around 1900 helped build the Cane Belt Railroad. He built and operated two company towns (Bonus and Eldridge), as well as several businesses in Eagle Lake. After being acquitted of murder charges for killing two men who threatened his life, he moved to Sugar Land and, with the prominent Kempner family of Galveston, bought the Cunningham Sugar Refinery and its 20,000-acre plantation. The new owners organized as the Imperial Sugar Companyqv and named Eldridge manager. Under his control the company built a new refinery and developed a system of irrigationqv for the various crops. Tariff charges on sugar, however, prevented Texas cane from competing with Hawaiian and Cuban sugarcane, so Eldridge turned to other crops to diversify his farm. He then imported raw sugar from Cuba for refining, and in 1907 produced a half million pounds of sugar a day. His was the only sugar refinery operating in the Southwest. Imperial Sugar became one of the most important sugar companies in Texas history. Under Eldridge's control the partnership built a complete company town with 435 homes for permanent employees of the factory, the stores, and the farms at Sugar Land. On what had been the Cunningham plantation Eldridge grew sugarcane, cotton, feed grains, fruit crops, and such vegetables as cabbages, potatoes, yams, and corn. He acquired, improved, then sold seven more railroads of varying sizes, including the Sugar Land Railroad, the San Antonio, Uvalde and Gulf Railroad, the Asherton and Gulf Railway, and the Rio Grande City Railway. Most of these lines were sold to the Missouri Pacific. Eldridge contracted with the Sealy Mattress Company to manufacture mattresses at Sugar Land. He died on August 20, 1932.

BIBLIOGRAPHY: Robert M. Armstrong, *Sugar Land and the Imperial Sugar Company* (Sugar Land, Texas, 1991). Houston *Post*, August 22, 1932. S. G. Reed, *A History of the Texas Railroads* (Houston: St. Clair, 1941; rpt., New York: Arno, 1981).
Bill Stein

ELDRIDGE, TEXAS. Eldridge is near the junction of Farm roads 950 and 2614, between Garwood and Eagle Lake in southeastern Colorado County. In 1898 it was on the "Bonus Loop" of the Cane Belt Railroad and was named for William T. Eldridge,qv director of the railroad and part owner and general manager of the Imperial Sugar Company.qv In 1905 the Faber Planting Company purchased 1,140 acres of sugarcane and cotton land from Eldridge. Included in the purchase were several storage buildings and a gin. The Faber

Planting Company subdivided the acreage into forty to sixty acre tracts and built homes on each for tenant farmers, whose primary responsibility was to provide sugarcane for the Eldridge refinery, then known as Sugarland Industries. During harvest season convict labor was used to help the local residents. A post office was established in 1906 and continued in operation until 1942, when mail was delivered regularly from Eagle Lake. In 1914 Eldridge had a population estimated at 200, telephone and telegraph service, and a general store operated by the Faber company. In 1926 the community's population was 100. Mechanized equipment replaced the tenant farmers during the 1940s and 1950s, and, with the exception of some tenants who bought their homes, the population drifted away. In 1986 several of the original homes remained. In 1990 Eldridge was still listed as a community.

BIBLIOGRAPHY: *Colorado County Sesquicentennial Commemorative Book* (La Grange, Texas: Hengst Printing, 1986).   *Jeff Carroll*

ELECTION LAWS. The election statutes of Texas during most of the nineteenth century, like those of most other states, applied exclusively to general elections and were not voluminous. In 1895 and 1903 the first attempts were made to regulate the nominating procedure of political parties. With the enactment in 1905 of the Terrell Election Law, a statewide direct-primary system for all state, district, and county elective offices was established and made mandatory for all parties that had received as many as 100,000 votes in the previous election; the requirement was later altered to 200,000 votes and afterward to 20 percent of the vote in the last gubernatorial election. Though for decades, normally, only the Democratic party qv was affected, the Terrell law and its numerous amendments since 1905 constitute a large part of the extensive body of statutes governing Texas elections. When Texas was a one-party state and primaries of the Democratic party determined election to statewide, district, and county offices, the primary statutes were of prime importance and were subjected to frequent legislative alteration.

The party convention system, which grew up and operated under party rules before 1905, has been perpetuated under the primary laws. Small parties are free to use it for nomination purposes as the Democrats and Republicans do. The selection of the number of delegates for each candidate at national party conventions is now based on the number of votes candidates receive in the presidential primary of each party. The nomination of presidential electors of all parties still takes place in state party conventions held in presidential election years. In June (previously September) of each even-numbered year, following the runoff primary, a state convention is required by law to canvass the returns of the primary, enact party rules, adopt a platform, and select a state executive committee. In presidential election years, the convention also selects delegates to the national presidential nominating convention, elects members from Texas to serve on the party's national committee, and elects potential presidential electors to serve if the party's presidential candidate wins. The delegates to all state party conventions are chosen from county conventions made up of delegates previously elected in precinct conventions.

From 1905 to 1907 the state convention of the Democratic party was required to apportion votes received by primary candidates for statewide offices. This rule was abandoned in the later year, and a simple plurality rule for all primary nominations prevailed until 1913, when a second or runoff primary between the two most successful candidates for the United States Senate was required in case no candidate received an absolute majority in the first primary. The runoff became compulsory for all state and district offices in 1918 and for all county offices in 1947. After the latter year a first primary was held in July and the runoff in August of even-numbered years. In 1986 the legislature approved, beginning in 1988, primary elections to be held the second Tuesday ("Super Tuesday") in March to conform with primary elections in other Southern states. The intent was to give more weight in presidential election years to Southern primaries. The strategy has seemingly worked, as presidential candidates now spend more time campaigning in Texas and the rest of the South. Runoff elections are held the second Tuesday in April. The second primary had been generally adopted in the one-party states of the South in order to ensure majority elections, since final election in most cases was really determined in the primary and the general election in November amounted to little more than a formality. It should be added that, except for a short-lived presidential-preference primary adopted in 1913 (invalidated in 1916), the primaries in Texas were required by law to be administered and paid for by the party; most of the money came from filing fees. Candidates for statewide office, including the legislature, paid $1,000. Candidates filing for local office paid varying fees, usually $3,000 to $5,000 in heavily populated counties. In 1970 a federal court decided that the method used for filing fees was a violation of the Fourteenth Amendment. The legislature responded with a law modifying fees. The same court rejected this, and in *Carter v. Dies* (1972) the ruling was upheld by the United States Supreme Court. In 1973 the legislature passed a law calling for a combination of state and private funding. Filing fees in 1995 were $4,000 for the office of United States senator, $3,000 for other statewide elective offices, $2,500 for United States representative, $2,000 for certain members of the judiciary, and $1,200 for others. State senators paid $1,000 and state representatives $600. Fees for county offices ranged from $2,000 to $300. In 1995 the state paid up to 60 percent of costs of primary elections, and the rest came from filing fees.

The prospective candidacy of Senator Lyndon B. Johnson qv for the presidency in 1960 brought about special election laws enacted for his benefit in 1959. One law moved the dates of the primary elections from July and August to the first Saturdays in May and June. This law also dispensed with the second series of precinct and county conventions previously held in the summers of even-numbered years to choose delegates to the September state convention. Beginning in 1960 one set of precinct and county conventions elected delegates who served in both the presidential and gubernatorial state conventions, the precinct conventions to be held earlier on the moved-up day of the first primary. The earlier dates for the primaries allowed Johnson to be nominated for reelection to the United States Senate and simultaneously to have his name on the ballot as a presidential candidate. Opponents of Johnson resented these permanent changes in the primary arrangements, but the legislature has not repealed the law except for its specification of the time of the primary and runoff. The law has since been used to allow Lloyd Bentsen to run for vice president and senator (1988) and in 1996 can be used to allow Republican Phil Gramm to run for president and senator. Two other significant changes in the election law occurred in 1959. First, it was required that when a voter first voted in a party primary or attended a party convention, his poll-tax or exemption certificate (now registration certificate) be stamped with the name of the party in whose primary he was participating. During that year he could not participate in the primary or convention of any other party. The other requirement was that the county executive committee, after canvassing the votes of a primary election, had to file the results with the county clerk. Previously no official returns of primaries were required to be made except to party authorities.

The suffrage laws of Texas apply to primaries as well as to general elections and have changed over the years. Formerly all persons twenty-one years of age or above were generally qualified to vote in Texas if they met residence requirements, paid a poll tax if they were under sixty years old (adopted in 1902), and were free from certain disqualifications relating to mental condition, pauperism, conviction of crime, and connection with the armed services. Woman suffrage qv in primaries began in 1918 and general voting rights in 1920. In 1891 cities of 10,000 or more were permitted to set up voter registration; in 1949 a general registration law was enacted to become effective if the poll tax was repealed, but it was not. To participate in a primary the voter was supposed to subscribe to the pledge, required since 1907 to be printed at the top of the primary ballot, according to which he agreed in the following general election to support all candidates nominated in the primary. This pledge has been held by the courts to involve only a moral obligation on the part of the voter, since the law forbids his being barred from any primary for past political behavior; in some cases, however, violation of the pledge did prevent the names of bolters from going on the ballot as candidates in subsequent primary elections. In 1963 many minor changes and clarifications were made in election procedures. A voter registration system was set up to go into effect if the voters repealed the poll-tax requirement in the Constitution of 1876.[qv] A temporary registration system for voting for national officials was also established, to be applied in case the poll tax was repealed for federal elections by a pending amendment to the Constitution of the United States.

The election of 1964 was the first one in which no poll tax was required to vote in federal elections, though the tax still survived for state and local elections. The Twenty-fourth Amendment to the United States Constitution went into effect that year, abolishing the poll tax as a voting requirement for president, vice president, presidential electors, United States senators, and representatives in the United States Congress. Thus, in 1964 in Texas different ballots had to be provided for voters qualified for all elections and for those voting only in federal elections. Early in 1966 the poll tax was judicially invalidated for all elections. Senate Bill 1 of the first called session of 1966 of the Texas legislature required voters to register, in person or by mail, with the county tax assessor once each year between October 1 and the following January 31. Persons eligible to register and vote had to be twenty-one years of age, residents of the state for one year, and residents of the district or county for six months. Persons over sixty who did not live in a city of 10,000 or more, or who moved, could vote without registering, except in counties of 500,000 or more population, where the county commissioners could require all voters to register. A state constitutional amendment submitted on November 8, 1966, removed the poll tax from the state constitution and embodied a requirement for annual registration. Another proposed amendment was approved, removing the year's residence requirement for persons who qualified to vote in another state for presidential electors and who had lived in Texas at least thirty days, and allowing the legislature to provide for the reenfranchisement, under certain circumstance, of former Texas voters who had been away from the state for less than one year.

In 1971 the legislature eliminated the annual registration requirement and provided, instead, a continuing registration system, whereby voters were automatically registered after participating in primaries or elections. Passage of a statute effective August 27, 1973, by the Sixty-third Texas Legislature granted persons eighteen years of age all the privileges hitherto granted those twenty-one years of age. Neither the change in registration laws nor the vote for eighteen-year-olds came voluntarily. All changes in the election laws were fought bitterly by the Texas legislature and came only after United States Supreme Court decisions against the Texas position and amendments to the United States Constitution. In 1995, once a person was registered, he remained registered unless he moved and failed to notify the voting registrar. Registration in person or by mail is usually with the county tax assessor-collector.[qv] Once a family member is registered, that member can register for other family members. Registration is allowed anytime, but one must be registered thirty days before an election. For many years the Democratic party of Texas was successful in barring African Americans[qv] from its primaries. At first this was done by party rule of the county organizations. Between 1923 and 1944, statutory provisions, followed by rules of the Democratic state executive committee and finally of the Democratic state convention, were applied to accomplish this purpose. Each provision was attacked in turn in the United States Supreme Court. Except for sustaining the convention rule from 1935 to 1944, each successive device for keeping black citizens out of the Democratic primaries was struck down. Since *Smith v. Allwright* (1944) no white primary[qv] rule has functioned, and African Americans have been admitted to the Democratic primaries.

Absentee voting in Texas was provided for by Article 2956 of the Revised Civil Statutes of 1925, as amended by the Forty-third Legislature. Between three and twenty days before the date of an election a qualified voter could make application by affidavit for an absentee ballot. The application to the county clerk was accompanied by a statement why the voter could not appear on election day, his poll-tax receipt, and a fee for postage. The ballot had to be marked in the presence of a notary public or qualified official and returned to the county clerk at least three days before the election. Since 1987, however, early voting (no longer called "absentee") has been allowed beginning twenty days before a first primary or general election and ten days before a runoff primary election and ending four days before any election. There are no restrictions on cause, the voter may vote at the county clerk's office or any of several designated places in the county or by mail, and the notary public is no longer required. Since early voting began, the number of early voters has increased to as much as 40 percent of the total.

Additional past features of the Texas election laws are the Australian ballot adopted early in the present century and rendered more secret by the adoption of the detachable stub in 1949, the presidential short ballot, the extensive corrupt and illegal practices provisions particularly applying to the primary elections, and the acts of 1941 and 1949 which bar Fascists, Nazis, Communists, and other subversives from the ballot and exact loyalty oaths from all elected officials and other officeholders. The requirement of a loyalty oath was found to be unconstitutional, and the other provisions are no longer part of the election code. Texas long permitted aliens to vote but deprived them of the privilege in 1918. As of 1995 Texas had no standard ballot. Ballots varied by party in the primaries and by county in the general election. Forms included paper ballots to be marked with an X, punch cards in which the voter uses a metal punch to punch a hole beside the name of the person for whom he is voting, an optical-scanner system, and automatic voting machines. All have the option to vote a straight party slate at the top of the ballot. A new election code enacted in 1951 made few important changes in the law. It did, however, provide for listing of the candidates of one party by another in general elections. The election of 1952 saw its first and only use. In that year the Republican party[qv] cross-filed all but one of the Democratic party's candidates for statewide office to make it easier for Democrats to vote for Dwight D. Eisenhower,[qv] the Republican candidate for president. This action no doubt helped the general to carry the state and caused the Democrats to demand the repeal of the cross-filing privilege and to refuse in 1954 to allow their candidates to be cross-filed. The device was repealed in 1955. In that year a new provision for reports of campaign expenditures reduced the number required to one before and one after an election. A campaign-reporting law was passed in 1973 with the primary purpose of publicizing the names of large donors. The legislature subsequently refused to make any significant changes in campaign-finance laws, and there are still no limits on the amount any individual or political-action committee may give any candidate except for someone running for a federal office, covered by federal laws. In 1957 runoffs were provided for in special elections for United States senator and congressman-at-large between the two leaders in the initial election if no candidate received a majority. Special-election runoffs were later instituted for district congressmen.

BIBLIOGRAPHY: Richard H. Kraemer and Charldean Newell, *Texas Politics*, 5th ed. (Minneapolis: West, 1993). *Practicing Texas Politics* (Boston: Houghton Mifflin, 1971–). *O. Douglas Weeks*

ELECTRA, TEXAS. Electra is on U.S. Highway 477 fifteen miles northwest of Wichita Falls in northwestern Wichita County. Daniel

Waggoner^qv began ranching in the area in 1852. In the mid-1880s the tracks of the Fort Worth and Denver City Railway reached the area. Shortly thereafter Waggoner and his son William T. Waggoner^qv built loading pens and persuaded railroad officials to establish a switch at the site in 1885. The location was briefly called Waggoner, but with the construction of a depot and the opening of a post office in 1889, it was renamed Beaver, probably for Beaver Creek, beside which most of the original Waggoner ranchland was located. Within ten years Beaver provided businesses and a school for Waggoner employees. In 1902 residents selected the name Electra, in honor of W. T. Waggoner's daughter. In 1905 Waggoner sold the land to Fort Worth developer Solomon Williams.^qv He and his partners formed the Electra Land and Colonization Company, which extended the city limits, subdivided the town lots, and advertised in national publications to attract residents. The company was successful, and in 1907 the community incorporated with a commission form of government and 500 residents. The town grew to an estimated 1,000 people by 1910, when Electra had a newspaper, a bank, and a number of churches. The Electra Independent School District was established in 1911.

W. T. Waggoner had drilled unsuccessfully for water. But oil was a different matter. On April 1, 1911, Clayco No. 1 blew in a mile north of Electra. News of the gusher spread rapidly and a boom resulted. The town's population reached 5,000 within months. Because Electra was an established community and the oil land was already leased, the plague of tent cities and the chaos that accompanied the discovery of oil in other areas never materialized. Many who rushed to Electra seeking quick profits, however, just as quickly departed.

The Electra oilfield produced approximately ten million barrels between 1911 and the mid-1920s. In 1917 the population of Electra was 5,400; in 1926 it was 4,744, and the town had a high school, numerous churches, two newspapers, two banks, and over 100 businesses. In 1936 Electra had 6,712 residents and 170 businesses. Drilling operations declined, though, and the growing Dallas–Fort Worth metropolis attracted residents. In the mid-1960s the population in Electra decreased to just over 5,000. The community constructed a 100-acre park in hopes of attracting new industries, but the oil crisis of the 1970s assured decline. In 1982 the Electra Historical Museum was dedicated to celebrate the town's seventy-fifth anniversary. In 1988 the town had a population of 3,599 and seventy-seven businesses. In 1990 it had a population of 3,113 and forty-eight businesses. *See also* WICHITA COUNTY REGULAR FIELD.

BIBLIOGRAPHY: Louise Kelly, *Wichita County Beginnings* (Burnet, Texas: Eakin Press, 1982). *David Minor*

ELECTRICAL POWER. The first electric power plant in Texas was built at Galveston in the early 1880s, and thereafter industrial development was slow. By 1900 there were numerous small privately owned generating systems, some steam, some hydroelectric. The next decade brought a few larger developments, of which perhaps the best example was the hydroelectric plant established at a dam built across the Colorado in 1891–92 to serve the city of Austin. Thought expected to provide 14,000 horsepower, the system, it was found, would produce only 900 horsepower during the summer months of minimum flow. The dam was destroyed by flood in 1900. In 1912 a high-voltage transmission line was built from Waco to Fort Worth with a branch line from Hillsboro to Ferris, whence it branched north to Trinity Heights (near Dallas) and south to Corsicana. In 1920 the state consumed 679,000,000 kilowatt-hours, evidence of a marked expansion of the power industry. By 1925 consumption reached a total for the year of 1,268,000,000 kilowatt-hours, and in 1930 the total was 2,922,000,000. The only drop occurred in 1935, when only 2,538,000,000 kilowatt-hours was consumed. In 1945 more than 6,780,874,000 kilowatt-hours was sold to about a million customers. The average cost per kilowatt-hour to the consumer in 1945 was about one-half what it was in 1925.

Although rural electrification^qv began with the first cross-country transmission lines, it was not until the organization of rural electric cooperatives in 1936 under the Rural Electrification Administration that rural electrification began to be widespread. In 1946 seventy-one co-ops served 146,000 rural homes, and privately owned lines served approximately 118,000. By 1950 the transmission lines in Texas of all power-producers were coordinated into the Texas Grid System. By 1954 the total generating capacity of Texas power plants was 5,521,180 kilowatts, four times as much as in 1944. Of the 192 plants, seventy-two were powered by steam and produced 4,971,400 kilowatts; 101 were powered by internal combustion engines and produced 196,990 kilowatts; nineteen were hydroelectric and produced 352,790 kilowatts. By 1963 the 176 electrical power plants in Texas increased their total generating capability to 11,990,392 kilowatts, more than twice the 1954 figure. Although by 1970 the number of electric power plants had decreased to 171, their generating capability had risen to 25,117,928 kilowatts, almost five times the 1954 capacity. Of the total number of plants, eighty-two were steam-powered and had a capability of 23,955,741 kilowatts, sixty-eight were internal combustion engines or gas turbine-powered and had a capacity of 644,727 kilowatts, and twenty-one hydroelectric plants had a capability of 517,460 kilowatts. Seventy-seven distribution cooperatives of the Rural Electrification Administration served 97 percent of the total Texas farms in 1970.

In 1992 there were 132 electric power plants serving Texas (fourteen were not located in the state) with a combined capacity to generate 67,806 megawatts. Sixty-seven percent of the power plants were fueled by natural gas, 30 percent by coal and lignite, 7 percent by nuclear power, and 1 percent by water flow. Electric power in Texas was supplied by municipally owned systems, rural electric cooperates, federal and state financed projects, and ten investor-owner electric utility companies. In 1992 Texas electric utilities employed more 40,000 people and received $14 billion in revenues.

ELECTRIC CITY, TEXAS. Electric City was established on the south bank of the Canadian River in south central Hutchinson County. It began in July 1926 with the construction of the Panhandle Power and Light Company's Riverview Power Plant, three miles north of Borger. Men worked day and night until the plant was completed, so that electricity could be made available to neighboring oilfields as soon as possible. The plant's turbines began turning in November. Soon a subsidiary camp grew around the facility as the county's oil boom gained momentum. Within weeks, plant employees and oilfield workers had formed a sizable settlement, complete with dirt streets. With the improvement of local highways and transportation, however, employees no longer found it necessary to live next to the plant. By 1948 Electric City's population numbered only five. The plant was owned by Southwestern Public Service by the mid-1980s. At that time there was no longer a population at the site, since the plant was an easy commute from Borger.

BIBLIOGRAPHY: Bobby D. Weaver, ed., *Panhandle Petroleum* (Amarillo: Miller National Corporation, 1982). *H. Allen Anderson*

ELECTRIC FENCE. An electric fence was first used in Texas on the XIT Ranch^qv in 1888. D. H. Wilson of the United States Electric Fence Company contracted to fence a pasture and construct a thirty-mile telephone line. Electricity from a generator using an overshot wheel was to charge the top two wires of a four-wire fence. The device was supposed to eliminate the need for many fenceposts, to be less injurious to cattle than barbed wire,^qv and to enable the cowboys riding the fence line to communicate with the ranch headquarters by telephone. The LX Ranch^qv also experimented with the electric fence, but cowboys were skeptical about the invention, and the venture proved impractical. Ranchers revived the use of the electric fence in the modern era. Often solar-powered (*see* SOLAR ENERGY), such fences are used extensively in the Panhandle qv to prevent cattle from wandering onto farmlands.

BIBLIOGRAPHY: J. Evetts Haley, *The XIT Ranch of Texas and the Early Days of the Llano Estacado* (Chicago: Lakeside, 1929; rpts., Norman: University of Oklahoma Press, 1953, 1967). W. S. Mabry, *Some Memories* (Bandera, Texas: Frontier Times Print, 1927).

ELECTRIC INTERURBAN RAILWAYS. The electric interurban industry in Texas totaled nearly 500 miles, the second largest interurban mileage among the states west of the Mississippi River. Most of this mileage was in place by 1913, as the industry grew rapidly during the early 1900s to fill the need for frequent passenger service between urban centers that could not be met by existing steam-railroad service. About 70 percent of the mileage was in the Dallas–Fort Worth area, where electric lines connected Fort Worth and Cleburne, Fort Worth and Dallas, and Denison, Dallas, Corsicana, and Waco. Another 20 percent was in the Houston–Galveston and Beaumont–Port Arthur areas. The rest was scattered around the state. The decline in mileage was also swift, however, as the growth of improved highways and widespread private car ownership combined to siphon off most of the interurban ridership. By the end of 1941 only two lines, the Texas Electric and the Houston North Shore, a subsidiary of the Missouri Pacific, remained; they were both discontinued in 1948.

In 1901 the first interurban to be constructed in Texas, the Denison and Sherman Railway, ran ten miles between Denison and Sherman. The second, in 1902, was the Northern Texas Traction Company, which ran thirty-five miles between Dallas and Fort Worth. Operations ceased in 1934. The Belton-Temple Traction Company opened its thirteen miles between Belton and Temple in 1904. The company was reorganized in 1918 and the name changed to Southwestern Traction Company. Service terminated in 1926. The Texas Traction Company constructed a sixty-five-mile line from Dallas to Sherman in 1908. The company purchased the Denison and Sherman Railway in 1911. In 1912 the J. F. Strickland interests, which controlled the Texas Traction Company, purchased the twenty-eight-mile line built by the Dallas Southern Traction Company from Dallas to Waxahachie and named it the Southern Traction Company. In 1913 that railway was built on to Waco, and a fifty-six-mile line from Dallas to Corsicana was completed. In 1917 the Texas Traction Company and the Southern Traction Company merged to form the Texas Electric Railway Company, the largest interurban railway in the South, with more than 200 miles of track. The Dallas-Corsicana branch was discontinued in 1941 and the Dallas-Waco and Dallas-Denison branches in 1948.

Smaller systems operated around Texas. The Texas Interurban Railway Company had two lines, a twenty-nine-mile run between Dallas and Terrell from 1923 to 1932 and a thirty-eight-mile run from Dallas to Denton from 1924 to 1932. The Bryan and College Interurban Railway Company ran seven miles between Bryan and College Station. It began with gasoline-powered cars in 1910 and switched to electricity in 1915. In 1923 it was sold three times; after the third sale, to citizens in Bryan and College Station, it was operated as the Bryan-College Traction Company until 1930. The Galveston-Houston Electric Railway Company ran fifty miles between Galveston and Houston from 1911 to 1936. During 1925 and 1926 it won first place in the nation in an interurban speed contest. The Fort Worth Southern Traction Company opened thirty miles of track between Fort Worth and Cleburne in 1912. This company was reorganized in 1914 as the Tarrant County Traction Company, which was subsequently acquired by the Northern Texas Electric Company. The latter became the Northern Texas Traction Company, which closed the line in 1931. The Rio Grande Valley Traction Company ran twelve miles between El Paso and Ysleta from 1913 to 1925, when electric service between the Ascarate stop and Ysleta was replaced by bus service; electric service between El Paso and Ascarate was discontinued in early 1926. The Jefferson County Traction Company (subsequently the Eastern Texas Electric Company) ran twenty miles from Beaumont to Port Arthur from 1913 to 1932. The Roby and Northern Railroad, which began in 1915 and ran four miles between Roby and North Roby, was electrified in 1923 and operated until 1941. The last interurban railway to be built in the United States, the Houston North Shore Railway Company, built twenty-six miles from Houston through Baytown to Goose Creek in 1927. It operated until 1948. The line, no longer electric, is now an important industrial branch of the Union Pacific between Houston and Baytown and is virtually the only vestige of the Texas interurban network that remains.

BIBLIOGRAPHY: Margaret M. Gilson, A History of the Texas Electric Railway, 1917–1955 (M.A. thesis, North Texas State University, 1972). H. Roger Grant, "'Interurbans Are the Wave of the Future': Electric Railway Promotion in Texas," *Southwestern Historical Quarterly* 84 (July 1980). George W. Hilton and John F. Due, *The Electric Interurban Railways in America* (Stanford University Press, 1960). William D. Middleton, *The Interurban Era* (Milwaukee: Kalmbach, 1961). William D. Middleton, *Traction Classics: The Interurbans* (3 vols., San Marino, California: Golden West, 1983–85). Johnnie J. Myers, *Texas Electric Railway*, ed. LeRoy O. King (Chicago: Central Electric Railfans' Association, 1982). Rod Varney, *Texas Electric Album, Texas Electric Railway* (Glendale, California: Interurbans, 1975). Herb Woods, *Galveston-Houston Electric Railway* (Los Angeles: Electric Railway Publications, 1959). Andrew D. Young and Eugene F. Provenz, *The History of the St. Louis Car Company "Quality Shops"* (Berkeley: Howell-North, 1978).
Robert A. Rieder

ELECTRIC STREET RAILWAYS. Electric street railways played a central role in the development of thirty-three cities in Texas during a span of eighty-five years. The railway systems in Texas totaled more than 600 miles. The streetcar was a visible part of the urban scene, and during the age of electric traction no city seemed complete without it. Until the family automobile became commonplace, the streetcar was an important as transportation. During the first half of the twentieth century electric cars dominated the downtowns of the larger cities during rush hours. In some cities the extent of urban development was governed by the radius of operation of the street railway. Population growth followed the car lines. Commercial development and residential areas were built away from the downtown area. By providing fast and frequent transportation at a low fare the railway made growth in the size of cities possible. Distant points became a few minutes from downtown. The electric streetcar represented the most significant development in city transportation. This would continue as the most important vehicle in urban transit until the time of World War II.qv Texas had the largest number of cities with electric streetcar systems of any state west of the Mississippi River. In some of the larger cities of Texas the first day of operation of the street railway was front-page news in the local newspaper.
Robert A. Rieder

ELECTRONIC DATA SYSTEMS. Electronic Data Systems, headquartered in Dallas, is an independently operated and wholly owned subsidiary of General Motors Corporation that specializes in the management of information technology. EDS designs, installs, and operates data-processing systems for the automotive, communications, energy, financial, government, health-care, insurance, transportation, utility, and manufacturing industries, as well as for retail distributors. It owns and operates one of the world's largest private digital telecommunications networks, EDSNET, which reaches fifty states and twenty-seven countries. In the 1990s company subsidiaries included EDS Federal Corporation, EDS Financial Corporation, EDS Technical Products Corporation, National Heritage Insurance Company, and VideoStar Connections, Incorporated.

The firm was founded by H. Ross Perot and incorporated on June 27, 1962. Perot was born in 1930, attended public schools in Texarkana, and took a two-year prelaw course at Texarkana Junior

ELECTRIC STREET RAILWAYS

City	First Year of Operation	Last Year of Operation	Maximum Mileage	City	First Year of Operation	Last Year of Operation	Maximum Mileage
Abilene	1908	1931	6.0	Laredo	1889	1935	6.0
Amarillo	1908	1923	10.0	Longview	1912	1920	2.0
Austin	1891	1940	23.0	Marshall	1909	1925	4.6
Beaumont	1902	1937	15.6	McKinney	1907	1926	3.0
Bonham	1902	1913	3.0	Mineral Wells	1908	1920	7.0
Brownsville	1916	1926	3.0	Paris	1901	1927	5.5
Cleburne	1911	1917	8.5	Port Arthur	1910	1937	8.0
Corpus Christi	1910	1931	9.0	San Angelo	1908	1915	3.5
Corsicana	1903	1931	5.0	San Antonio	1890	1933	92.6
Dallas	1889	1956	110.6	Sherman	1891	1931	6.0
Denison	1898	1931	5.0	Texarkana	1903	1934	14.0
Denton	1908	1918	4.0	Texas City	1913	1918	2.5
El Paso	1902	1974	43.1	Tyler	1913	1916	7.0
Fort Worth	1889	1938	81.6	Waco	1891	1948	18.0
Galveston	1891	1938	38.4	Waxahachie	1912	1932	5.0
Greenville	1910	1918	10.0	Wichita Falls	1909	1933	15.5
Houston	1891	1940	91.0				

College. In 1949 he joined the United States Naval Academy and in 1953 was commissioned an ensign; he served on the aircraft carrier *Leyte*. When his tour of duty ended in 1957, Perot joined International Business Machines. Soon thereafter, the company set a maximum annual sales volume for him, which he reached by mid-January in 1962. Dissatisfied with his position as an IBM salesman, Perot decided to form EDS when he recognized that business personnel needed help in using electronic data-processing systems. When IBM showed no interest in pursuing his idea, Perot left the firm.

According to various sources, EDS offered data-processing and computing services, or "facilities management," at an economically attractive price, but profited from a nontraditional approach to the electronic data-systems market. While other companies' contracts often lasted only sixty to ninety days, EDS made five-year fixed-price contracts with its customers. This allowed company representatives to go into the customer's organization, set up a data-processing system, and then reassign employees to other jobs to save personnel costs, increase profits, and maintain a steady flow of business. From the beginning, Perot also held his employees to a strict corporate regimen that forbade alcohol consumption during business hours and required conservative dress along with loyalty and a sense of duty. Despite his almost militaristic management style, however, he developed a management team that listened to employee suggestions and was open to new ideas.

For his first customer, Collins Radio of Cedar Rapids, Iowa, Perot purchased computer time on an IBM computer at Southwestern Life Insurance in Dallas and sold this time at retail prices. By 1963 EDS had signed its first long-term commercial contract, with Herman Lay of the Frito Lay Corporation,[qv] and established a contract to process insurance data for Mercantile Security Life, the start of an interest that by 1990 made the firm the largest insurance data processor in the nation. Perot also took advantage of 1965 Medicare legislation that caused excessive paperwork by organizing claims-processing systems across the country, a business venture that by 1977 accounted for nearly 40 percent of sales.

In 1968 Perot made a public offering of 7 percent of the company, from which equal amounts went to himself and EDS. Company stock prices rose to a high of $160 in 1970 and dropped to a low of $15 in 1973. Perot served as the president of EDS until 1970, when former IBM salesman Milledge A. "Mitch" Hart took his place. After Hart resigned in 1977, Perot served as chief executive officer and chairman from 1977 to 1979. In 1979 former EDS vice president Morton H. Meyerson became president, and Perot resumed his position as chief executive officer.

After the firm's first financial institution, a Dallas bank, became a customer in 1968, EDS grew to become the world's largest provider of data-processing services for banks and savings and loan associations. In the early 1970s Perot also diversified into brokerage firms. With the support of the Nixon administration, he bought Wall Street Leasing, a subsidiary of retail stockbroker Dupont Glore Forgan, Incorporated, and invested $10 million in the firm. By 1973 he had put money into Walston and Company, another brokerage house, which he proposed to merge with Dupont Glore Forgan. However, losses at the latter put him $60 million behind. Furthermore, EDS was faced with a 1976 lawsuit by F. and M. Schaefer Company and F. and M. Brewing Company which alleged that EDS data-processing systems provided inadequate information. EDS countered that the companies simply wanted to avoid paying their $1.2 million tab for EDS services. An out-of-court settlement forced EDS to pay Schaefer $2.3 million, but Perot's company retained the $1.3 million Schaefer had already paid.

As in-house corporate data processing diminished business for outside service providers in the mid-1970s, EDS entered the sale of turnkey systems of hardware, software, and peripheral equipment geared to the needs of specific users such as individual hospitals or small businesses. It also diversified into data-processing services for some 3,000 credit unions nationwide. The firm became involved internationally in 1976, when EDS took as its clients King Abdulazziz University in Saudi Arabia and the government of Iran. The company suspended its services to the latter after the Iranian government became delinquent in its payments and, as the diplomatic situation worsened, Perot ordered all EDS employees out of the country. Eventually, Perot had assembled a rescue team led by Col. Arthur D. Simons, a Green Beret he had previously hired to look for missing servicemen in Vietnam, and managed to get his remaining executives out of the country in 1979.

After Meyerson became president, the company pursued federal government contracts, particularly a 1982 contract for Project Viable that streamlined and updated the United States Army's computerized administrative facilities and established a nationwide network. While EDS remained oriented to facilities management, the company began to offer customers systems integration—a service through which a company's telecommunications, computer, and software systems were all provided by EDS.

General Motors purchased EDS on June 27, 1984, for $2.5 billion, the largest price ever paid for a computer-services operation. The terms of the sale required GM to keep EDS as a separate corporate entity, retain some personnel, and issue performance stock based on EDS's performance rather than that of General Motors. Perot retained his managerial function and a position on the GM board of directors. Though his management ideas and those of GM chairman Robert Smith quickly clashed, Smith believed that Perot's management style would improve GM's huge data system, and EDS benefited from its new GM business. Revenues tripled in the first year after the GM acquisition, employee numbers increased, and the company entered the fields of telecommunications and factory automation.

Perot's involvement in the company ended in 1986, when GM management bought his special-performance shares for $700 million. Meyerson resigned, and Lester M. Alberthal, who joined the company as a systems engineer trainee in 1968, became president and chief executive officer; by 1989 he was also chairman of the board. Alberthal continued the diversification that Perot and Meyerson had instigated, moving into energy, transportation, communications, and manufacturing. He also developed a leadership council to replace the original EDS administration, thereby distributing daily operational powers throughout the EDS hierarchy.

In 1989 EDS opened an Information Management Center in Plano, Texas, to maintain its worldwide digital private-communications network, EDSNET. The center sends data, voice, and video to destinations across the globe and serves as operational headquarters for twenty-one similar information centers serving 7,200 customers worldwide.

EDS has been instrumental in supporting individual communities and national causes. Locally, the company supports education through its Education Outreach Programs and public school "adoptions." Beginning in 1989 it also sponsored Project JASON, which enabled 225,000 children to witness a Mediterranean Sea exploration. Within the firm, EDS funds a Systems Engineer Development program to provide ongoing training for its personnel. In 1992 Perot ran unsuccessfully for president of the United States.

BIBLIOGRAPHY: *The International Directory of Company Histories*. Vertical Files, Barker Texas History Center, University of Texas at Austin. *Damon Arhos*

ELECTRONICS INDUSTRY. The electronics industry expanded rapidly in Texas during the 1950s, when firms in the state ranged from small groups of research scientists in Austin to large corporations employing thousands of people in Dallas, Fort Worth, and Houston. Products ranged from high fidelity phonographs and television sets to defense microwave equipment and computers. Advantages of locating plants in Texas included proximity to markets, cheap labor, good living conditions, freedom from labor strikes, and a favorable tax structure. In the mid-1950s Houston became the home base for most electronics firms, most of which concentrated on geophysical instruments and automation systems. Total sales in that area in 1955 exceeded $10 million. The second major concentration of the electronics industry in the state at that time was in the Dallas–Fort Worth area. Texas Instruments,[qv] then the world's only source of high-temperature silicone transistors, reached $28 million in sales in 1955. In that year, TI supplied 85 percent of the transistors used in the newly developed transistor radios. Collins Radio maintained a $2 million plant near Richardson and was involved in the development of the microwave system of televising. Total 1955 sales for the Iowa-based company were $108 million. Texas Electronics became the only manufacturer of television picture tubes in the state and one of six such plants west of the Mississippi River. TI sales were $44 million in 1956 and $67 million the next year. The firm carried out eight mergers in the late 1950s, which boosted its sales by 1959 to $193 million. In the previous year Collins Radio, also of the Dallas area, was awarded a $3.3 million contract for the development of microwave-link installations.

Aided by government contracts, by 1963 Texas had 291 establishments producing electronic parts and equipment. In 1964 Texas Instruments boosted its total annual sales to $233 million. Texas manufacture of electronic navigation and guidance systems, radar, and communication equipment subsequently expanded at an ever-increasing rate. during the late 1960s more than 35,000 people were employed in large or small electronics plants in the Dallas metropolitan area alone. By 1966 Tracor,[qv] originally a small group of Austin scientists in the mid-1950s, had expanded its sales to $17 million and had branches in eight states; sales the following year reached $38 million. The war in Vietnam greatly stimulated the manufacture of military equipment at various Texas electronics firms. Developments included chaff-dispensing systems for the United States Navy, chaff units for the United States Air Force, and the development of a sophisticated missile penetration system. Analytical and medical instruments, as well as antisubmarine devices, were manufactured by Tracor.

In the late 1980s Texas became the fourth-largest employer in the American electronics industry. Electronic manufacturing firms employed 154,000 people, who accounted for 16.8 percent of jobs in Texas. The largest electronics industry in Texas was the manufacture of electronic components, followed by radio, TV broadcasting and communication devices. Dallas became the heart of the Texas electronics industry, with 39 percent of the electronic manufacturing firms in the state. Dallas was followed by Houston (19 percent), Austin (14 percent), and Fort Worth (12 percent). *See also* AERONAUTICS AND AEROSPACE INDUSTRY.

BIBLIOGRAPHY: Fred Young Phillips, *Directions for Manufacturing Education: A Survey of Texas Electronics Firms* (IC² Institute, University of Texas at Austin, 1989). *Charles Duval, Jr.*

ELEPHANT MOUNTAIN (Brewster County). Elephant Mountain is twenty-two miles southwest of Marathon in west central Brewster County (at 30°02′ N, 103°32′ W). The peak, at an elevation of 6,225 feet above sea level, rises 1,265 feet above State Highway 118, four miles west. Soils on the mountain are shallow and stony and support scrub brush and grasses. The mountain is capped by a flat sill of igneous trachyte and was named for its shape, which resembles an elephant's back. Burial places containing artifacts more than 5,000 years old have been discovered on Sheep Creek, just west of Elephant Mountain.

———— (Presidio County). Elephant Mountain, a summit also called Agua Adentro, is eight miles north of the Rio Grande between Tapado Canyon on its south and Bofecillos Canyon on its north in southern Presidio County (at 29°28′ N, 104°02′ W). The peak, at an elevation of 4,938 feet above sea level, rises 538 feet above the desert floor. Elephant Mountain is formed of conglomerate, sandstone, tuff, and basalt. It stands in the Bofecillos Mountains, an area of desert mountain terrain cut by rugged canyons and surfaced by loose rubble. Area vegetation includes sparse grasses, cacti, and desert shrubs.

ELEVATION, TEXAS. Elevation is near State Highway 36 four miles southeast of Milano in southeastern Milam County. It was built as a switch on the Gulf, Colorado and Santa Fe Railway, which was constructed through the area in 1881. The community is said to be named for the rise on which it is located. It had a population of twelve in 1990.

BIBLIOGRAPHY: Lelia M. Batte, *History of Milam County, Texas* (San Antonio: Naylor, 1956). *Vivian Elizabeth Smyrl*

ELEY, CHARLES NORMAN (1837–1894). Charles N. Eley, horticulturist, businessman, and public official, the son of James Norman and Anna (Strong) Eley, was born on April 6, 1837, in Hartford, Connecticut. Family tradition holds that he left home at the age of fifteen, after his father died. In Galveston on November 16, 1861, he enlisted in Company F of Xavier B. Debray's[qv] Twenty-sixth Regiment of Texas Cavalry. Eley served as the chief clerk of the Wharton cavalry corps. From 1867 to 1873 he worked in Galveston as a commission merchant and steamboat broker, primarily in the Trinity River trade. His 1893 recollections of that area, printed in the Dallas *News*, remain the primary resource for researchers interested in steamboating during that era.

Eley was married on January 22, 1868, in Double Bayou to Lettitia Laura Jackson of Chambers County. The couple moved to Smith Point, Chambers County, in 1873. Eley held a number of important public offices in Chambers County. He served as postmaster at Smith Point from May 8, 1876, when the post office was established, until his death. He served as county commissioner for Precinct No. 1 from 1876 to 1880 and county tax assessor in 1881–82. He was also a justice of the peace and a notary public. Eley is also listed as county coroner in some records. Shortly after settling at Smith Point he established the Smith Point Nursery and Nursery Agency, where he sold everything from trees and shrubs to flowers, grasses, chickens, and eggs. He also introduced the Marianna plum, evergreen grazing grasses, and the Plymouth Rock chicken to the area. He was an early member of the Texas State Horticultural Society and wrote extensively on horticultural subjects. He drowned in Galveston Bay on March 19, 1894, when a strong gust of wind capsized his boat. His body was never recovered. He was a Mason.

BIBLIOGRAPHY: Thomas H. Edgar, comp., *History of De Bray's (26th) Regiment of Texas Cavalry, Embracing Roster and Casualties* (Galveston: Finck, 1898). S. W. Geiser, *Horticulture and Horticulturists in Early Texas* (Dallas: University Press, 1945). Jewel Horace Harry, A History of Chambers County (M.A. thesis, University of Texas, 1940; rpt., Dallas: Taylor, 1981). Miriam Partlow, *Liberty, Liberty County, and the Atascosito District* (Austin: Pemberton, 1974).

Kevin Ladd

ELFCO, TEXAS. Elfco was on the Fort Worth and Denver City Railway three miles southeast of downtown Pampa in northwestern Gray County. It was the site of the Texas Elf Company carbon black plant, established during the 1930s. The company erected several houses near the plant for its employees. A county highway map for the 1940s shows Elfco as fourteen dwellings along dirt roads and the railway, on the edge of the Panhandle oilfield.[qv] The same map shows a second cluster of seventeen dwellings and one business, labeled "Texas Elf Company Settlement," a mile south of Elfco on a dirt road and a spur of the Fort Worth and Denver City Railway. Mail for Elfco was routed through Pampa. When local highways were improved, most of the plant employees were able to live in Pampa. After carbon black lost its importance in the petroleum industry during the late 1950s, the plant was abandoned and eventually dismantled (*see also* CARBON BLACK INDUSTRY). Almost nothing remained at the site in the 1980s.

H. Allen Anderson

EL FRIEDA, TEXAS. El Frieda was on the St. Louis, Brownsville and Mexico Railway near East Carancahua Creek four miles west of Blessing in northwestern Matagorda County. A townsite was platted for John W. Gaines in 1909, and though there is no record of any substantial construction at the site, a July 1917 Matagorda *County Tribune* reported El Frieda's population as ranging somewhere between fifty and 100. El Frieda is not named on the 1936 county highway map, but the map shows scattered farms in the area, concentrated along a network of graded and drained roads. The community does not appear on the 1989 county highway map.

BIBLIOGRAPHY: Matagorda County Historical Commission, *Historic Matagorda County* (3 vols., Houston: Armstrong, 1986).

Rachel Jenkins

EL GATO, TEXAS. El Gato, six miles east of Hidalgo in southern Hidalgo County, became a stop on the San Benito and Rio Grande Valley Railway when the Santa Maria (Kern) to Sammons segment was constructed in 1925–26. El Gato was named for the Spanish land grant, Porcion Agostadero del Gato, assigned to Juan José Treviño. A platform existed beside the railroad stop, but no settlement developed there beyond a modest cluster of houses for laborers on nearby farms. The surrounding area was served by mail routes out of nearby Alamo and Donna. The San Benito and Rio Grande Valley Railway was absorbed by the Missouri Pacific system in 1956, and the segment including El Gato was abandoned in 1957. The railroad right-of-way was absorbed by the adjoining farms, leaving no evidence of the former train stop. A small colonia bearing the name of El Gato exists two miles south of Texas Highway Loop 374 on El Gato Road. Although the two El Gatos both lie within the land grant of that name, they have no other relationship.

Robert E. Norton

ELGIN, JOHN EDWARD (1850–1938). John Edward (Jack) Elgin, surveyor and lawyer, was born in Austin on July 31, 1850, the son of John Edward and Mary Elizabeth (Mitchell) Elgin. He graduated from the engineering school of Waco University in 1871. He served as captain of the Waco Greys, a local militia unit that protected residents from Indians. He led a survey party from Coleman and Brownwood to the foot of Double Mountain in Stonewall County and also assisted in the survey of railroads from Brenham to Austin, from Bremond to Waco, and from Calvert to Dallas.

Elgin went to the University of Virginia to study law in 1876 and was admitted to the bar in 1882. In 1887 he bought the Waco *Examiner* and began an editorial campaign, particularly against prohibition.[qv] In 1888 he was a delegate to the Democratic convention in St. Louis, where he wrote the "heart of oak" plank in the party platform. He left the party as an independent at the time of the James Stephen Hogg–George Clark[qqv] campaign in 1892. On December 24, 1899, Elgin married Hedwig Schramm at Seguin. They lived at Rockport, where Elgin organized and promoted the first Intracoastal Canal Convention. He worked to secure federal aid for a deepwater port for Texas. He was also a member of the committee that consolidated Waco University with Baylor University in 1886 and served as secretary of the board of trustees of Baylor. In 1904 he moved to San Antonio and established a private practice. He was one of the first members of the Texas Bar Association and belonged to the Odd Fellows and the Knights of Pythias. Elgin died in San Antonio on September 22, 1938, and was buried in Oakwood Cemetery, Austin.

BIBLIOGRAPHY: Ellis A. Davis and Edwin H. Grobe, comps., *The New Encyclopedia of Texas*, 4-vol. ed. San Antonio *Express*, September 23, 24, 1938. Grace Miller White, "Captain John E. Elgin," *Frontier Times*, May 1944.

ELGIN, TEXAS. Elgin is at the intersection of U.S. Highway 290 and State Highway 95, fifteen miles north of Bastrop in north Bastrop County. In 1871 the Houston and Texas Central Railway built through the area and established a flag stop called Glasscock. The name was changed to Elgin, in honor of the railroad's land commissioner and surveyor, Robert Morris Elgin, on August 18, 1872, when the town was officially platted. Elgin was incorporated and received a post office the following year, and a Baptist Sunday school began meeting in a private home. Much of the community's early population was drawn from nearby Perryville, which the railroad had bypassed.

In 1879 Elgin was described as a "thriving depot town" of 400. It had a newspaper, a gin, and a gristmill. Three years later Methodists erected the first church building in town. In 1884 Elgin had five general stores, two druggists, three cotton gins, and a saloon; that year Thomas O'Conner started a brick-making enterprise that eventually led Elgin to adopt the epithet "Brick Capital of the Southwest." In 1886 the Missouri, Kansas and Texas Railroad came through, adding to Elgin's business as a shipping point for cotton, wool, and livestock.

By 1890 the community had a population of 1,100 and supported two hotels, a broom factory, two doctors, a dentist, and the Elgin *Courier.* The next year oil was discovered five miles southeast of town, but the strike was not large. Coal proved better for the economy, when the large coal belt nearby was mined in the early twentieth century.

Elgin grew slowly but steadily through the twentieth century, from 1,258 in 1904 to 4,846 in 1990. By 1940 it was not only the center of a farming community but the site of two big brick and tile plants. Elgin enterprise was stimulated during World War II qv by the proximity of the army training facility Camp Swift.qv A third brick company was established in the town in the mid-1950s, lured by the high-quality clay deposits in the area. In addition to the brick plants, a local sausage factory processed thousands of pounds of beef and pork a week; Elgin Hot Sausage continued to enjoy a widespread reputation. Other industries included cottonseed milling, feed and grain processing, and hydraulic press manufacturing. By the 1980s proximity to Austin had begun to attract commuters to Elgin. In the mid-1980s the Elgin *Courier* was still being published, the sausage had achieved wider fame, and two brick and tile plants were still in operation. Elgin was also the site of a furniture plant and a leather works.

BIBLIOGRAPHY: Bastrop *Advertiser*, April 20, 1972. Elgin Historical Committee, *Elgin: A History of Elgin, Texas, 1872–1972* (Austin: Von Boeckmann–Jones, 1972). Bill Moore, *Bastrop County, 1691–1900* (Wichita Falls: Nortex, 1977).   *Paula Mitchell Marks*

ELGIN-BUTLER BRICK COMPANY. The Elgin-Butler Brick Company, with central operations at a 1,000-acre site in Butler, five miles east of Elgin, and sales headquarters in Austin, is a fifth-generation family-owned business that ships bricks nationwide and internationally. In 1871 the Texas and New Orleans Railroad arrived at the site in Bastrop County, and the community that grew up came to be known as Butler, after an Irish immigrant bricklayer, Michael Butler, who was the first to make bricks from the nearby clay pits that he discovered by accident while digging holes on land then used for timber. The company was founded in 1873. Over the years Butler became a company town with a company store and brick houses for employees, who farmed on the side. By the 1940s the town population reached 150. The company also mined clay from a site now in the Zilker Park soccer fields in Austin and transported it in buckets, hung from mule-drawn lines, to kilns on the site of present Austin High School. Another plant was located farther down the lake at the site of the Zachary Scott qv Theatre. In 1912 the firm acquired the Austin Brick Company, and in 1965 it acquired its chief competitor, Elgin Standard Brick Company. The company supplied bricks for the Capitol,qv 80 percent of the brick structures at the University of Texas at Austin, fireplaces in many Austin residences, and many other brick buildings in Austin. Brick from the firm was also used for the façade of the United States Embassy in Mexico City.

In 1990 the company began using automation to mix the clay with water and to compress and extrude it into molds before baking. The company is noted for its innovative brick designs, produced to appeal to people living in different regions. In operating the firm, Butler was succeeded by members of his family, including a son who studied ceramic engineering at Ohio State University. In the 1990s Elgin-Butler employed 411 workers. At that time 15 percent of its business was from the Austin area and 30 percent from outside Texas. Sales in 1993 amounted to $18 million.

BIBLIOGRAPHY: Austin *American-Statesman*, September 10, 1990.
Diana J. Kleiner

ELGUÉZABAL, JUAN BAUTISTA (1741–1805). Juan Bautista Elguézabal, born in 1741, was appointed adjutant inspector of presidios of Coahuila and Texas qv in 1795 and made a detailed inspection of La Bahía qv in 1797. In 1796 he was appointed assistant to Governor Manuel Muñoz qv and became interim governor in August 1797. As acting governor when Louisiana was sold to the United States, Elguézabal received the flood of petitions of immigrants from Louisiana requesting to move to Texas. He was distressed with the deplorable condition of Texas and indirectly advocated a more liberal policy for its development. Under his administration the Alabama-Coushatta and Choctaw Indians were given permission to settle east of the Trinity River. José Irigoyen,qv appointed by the king to succeed Muñoz, never came to Texas to claim his governorship, and Elguézabal continued to serve as governor until his death in San Antonio on October 5, 1806. One of his four sons was Juan José Elguézabal.qv

BIBLIOGRAPHY: Archivo General de Indias, *Archivo General de Indias de Sevilla* (Madrid, 1958). Bexar Archives, Barker Texas History Center, University of Texas at Austin. Carlos E. Castañeda, *Our Catholic Heritage in Texas* (7 vols., Austin: Von Boeckmann–Jones, 1936–58; rpt., New York: Arno, 1976).

ELGUÉZABAL, JUAN JOSÉ (1781–1840). Juan José Elguézabal, the son of Juan Bautista Elguézabal qv and Maria Gertrudis Ximenes, was born in San Antonio de Béxar, Texas, in 1781. He spent most of his public career in Coahuila, where he was an army captain and commandant of the Presidio del Río Grande and, like his father, adjutant inspector of presidios of Coahuila and Texas.qv On August 30, 1834, during the controversy between the rival governments at Saltillo and Monclova, the ayuntamiento qv of Monclova appointed him governor ad interim of Texas. When the dispute was submitted to Antonio López de Santa Anna qv for solution, Elguézabal was kept in office until a new election could be called. He resigned on March 12, 1835, upon the election of Agustín Viesca.qv Elguézabal commanded the First Company of Tamaulipas, which reinforced Martin Perfecto de Cos qv during the siege of Bexar,qv was captured with Cos on December 10, 1835, and was sent back to Matamoros, where he died in 1840.

BIBLIOGRAPHY: Hubert Howe Bancroft, *History of the North Mexican States and Texas* (2 vols., San Francisco: History Company, 1886, 1889). Henderson K. Yoakum, *History of Texas from Its First Settlement in 1685 to Its Annexation to the United States in 1846* (2 vols., New York: Redfield, 1855).   *Robert Bruce Blake*

ELI, TEXAS. Eli, three miles southeast of Memphis in northeastern Hall County, was first known as Twin Buttes because of the twin hills nearby. John M. Gist, a wealthy businessman, purchased land in the vicinity and built a few houses and a store, a gin, a blacksmith shop, and a church at the foot of the hills. A one-room frame schoolhouse erected there in 1905 was later replaced by a four-room brick structure. In 1906 a post office was established and named Eli, in honor of Eli Melton Dennis, an early community leader. After fires and tornadoes destroyed some of the settlement's houses, it was rebuilt in the valley near the schoolhouse, which was west of the Twin Buttes site. Its post office was closed in December 1914, then restored under the name of Elite in November 1915 with Robert M. Craig as postmaster. This office was closed in August 1919, and mail was thereafter delivered from Memphis. In 1926 a Farmers' Union gin and two stores were built in the community. Although the name of the area reverted to Eli after 1919, a railroad station erected on the Fort Worth and Denver tracks southeast of Memphis near Twin Buttes was for many years labeled Elite. After the improvement of highway transportation in the 1940s, the community was abandoned, and in the mid-1980s only farms remained in the vicinity.

BIBLIOGRAPHY: Inez Baker, *Yesterday in Hall County* (Memphis, Texas, 1940). Virginia Browder, *Hall County Heritage Trails, 1890–1980* (2 vols., Canyon, Texas: Staked Plains, 1982, 1983). Fred Tarpley, *1001 Texas Place Names* (Austin: University of Texas Press, 1980).
H. Allen Anderson

ELIASVILLE, TEXAS. Eliasville is on the Clear Fork of the Brazos River near the intersection of Farm roads 1974, 3109, and 701, close to the Stephens county line in southwest Young County. The townsite was on the land of J. L. Dobbs, who settled there in the 1870s. In 1876 W. L. and F. T. Donnell established ranches in the area, and a few years later they built a flour mill that was a landmark until it was destroyed by fire in 1927. The town was named for Elias DeLong, who opened the first store in 1878. In 1881 the Presbyterian church was organized, and it has remained a strong force in the community. With the oil boom of 1921 Eliasville was incorporated, and the town grew rapidly for a few years. Banker W. T. Donnell was the first mayor. The number of residents declined as production slowed, however, and during World War II[qv] many moved to Fort Worth for defense work. The population was 400 in 1940, and although it had declined to 116 by 1980 the town still retained its post office. A city lake was completed in 1952. Eliasville is no longer incorporated. The population was still reported as 116 in 1990.

BIBLIOGRAPHY: Carrie J. Crouch, *Young County: History and Biography* (Dallas: Dealey and Love, 1937; rev. ed., *A History of Young County, Texas*, Austin: Texas State Historical Association, 1956). Kathleen E. and Clifton R. St. Clair, eds., *Little Towns of Texas* (Jacksonville, Texas: Jayroe Graphic Arts, 1982).
William R. Hunt

ELIGA, TEXAS. Eliga formed in 1900 around a popular swimming hole located at the junction of House Creek and Cowhouse Creek, fourteen miles south of Gatesville in southern Coryell County. It was first called Elijah and became known as Eliga in 1903 when a post office was granted with Leonard M. Layne as postmaster. The nearest school was five miles west of town, but at one time Eliga had two cotton gins, two general stores, two church buildings for three congregations, and a blacksmith shop. After 1912 the community's mail was rerouted through Killeen, and in the early 1940s Eliga's population was twenty-five. Eliga was enveloped by the expansion of the Fort Hood[qv] military reservation in 1942.

BIBLIOGRAPHY: Coryell County Genealogical Society, *Coryell County, Texas, Families, 1854–1985* (Dallas: Taylor, 1986).
Sylvia Edwards

EL INDIO, TEXAS. El Indio is two miles east of the Rio Grande and seventeen miles southeast of Eagle Pass in southwestern Maverick County. It is probably named for nearby Indio Creek. In the early 1850s William L. Cazneau[qv] established his ranch on the northern portion of the Antonio Rivas grant, where the town was later established. By 1880 the Cazneau Ranch had become the Indio Ranch; a post office called Indio was established that year ten miles south of the present site of El Indio. At this time the site was also known as Presidio or Indio Ranch. The post office at Indio, where Charles S. Murphy was postmaster, was discontinued in 1884; that year the community had an estimated thirty residents, weekly mail, and a general store owned by Humphries and Walker.

In 1902 the firm Goldfrank and Frank promoted colonization and irrigation to cultivate alfalfa and cotton at Indio Ranch. It is believed that Francisco Madero[qv] launched his revolution against the regime of Porfirio Díaz from the Indio Ranch sometime in 1910; incidents of cattle thievery, gun running, and military operations took place in and around the area throughout the Mexican Revolution.[qv] In 1928 the Indio Cattle Company, owners of the Indio Ranch, offered lots amounting to 20,000 acres of the ranch for sale. Advertising touted the farming potential that would be realized once the Maverick County Canal system reached the ranch. A highway, which was Farm Road 1021 in 1989, was constructed from Eagle Pass to Laredo in the early 1930s. It split the farming district of the ranch and paved the way for the development of El Indio at its present location. Irrigation waters via the county canal system reached the area in March 1938. A post office was established in El Indio in 1939 with Joseph Henry Ulery as postmaster. In 1941 the community had an estimated population of seventy-five and three businesses. The estimated population of the community remained steady throughout the 1940s and early 1950s; it rose to 370 in 1956 and 380 by 1964. In 1968 it was 148; the same figure was reported in 1990, when the community had a hotel, a school, a community center, a factory, and two businesses.

BIBLIOGRAPHY: John J. Germann and Myron Janzen, *Texas Post Offices by County* (1986). Ben E. Pingenot, *Historical Highlights of Eagle Pass and Maverick County* (Eagle Pass, Texas: Eagle Pass Chamber of Commerce, 1971). Ben E. Pingenot, ed., *Paso del Águila . . . Memoirs of Jesse Sumpter* (Austin: Encino, 1969). Vertical Files, Barker Texas History Center, University of Texas at Austin.
Ruben E. Ochoa

ELISABET NEY MUSEUM. After Elisabet Ney's[qv] death in 1907, her Austin studio, Formosa, was purchased in 1909 by Ella (Dancy) and Joseph B. Dibrell,[qv] who wished to preserve it as an art center in memory of Ney. They appointed a board of managers and opened the studio to the public for special exhibitions. On April 6, 1911, Mrs. Dibrell and other friends of Ney met in Ney's studio to found the Texas Fine Arts Association[qv] and the Elisabet Ney Museum. The museum was designated as the annual meeting place for the association and the gallery for its exhibitions; it thus functioned as one of the earliest centers for artistic development in Texas.

During the 1920s access to the museum was expanded with public visiting hours held once a week. In addition, the museum sponsored circulating exhibitions and programs, many of which focused on contemporary art. Ella Dibrell stipulated in her will that the studio be given to the Texas Fine Arts Association, but the organization was unable to maintain the property. In 1941 the city of Austin assumed ownership and has operated the museum as a component of the parks and recreation department. Management has rested with three people: Willie B. Rutland, 1927–67; May Diane Harris, 1967–77; and James D. Fisher, beginning in 1977. Willie R. Nunn served as museum attendant from 1946 to 1991. Curators have included Sarah D. Bolz, 1979–83; Lynn Lichtenfels, 1983–87; Martha George Withers, 1987–88; and Mary Collins Blackmon, 1989–.

In accordance with Elisabet Ney's wishes, her husband, Dr. Edmund Montgomery,[qv] gave the contents of the studio to the University of Texas, with the understanding that they were to remain in the building. These artworks and personal belongings comprise the core of the present collection. Besides furniture, tools, and personal effects, the museum has sculptures in bronze, marble, and plaster that include many of Ney's likenesses of contemporary political and literary figures: King Ludwig II, Otto von Bismarck, Giuseppe Garibaldi, Arthur Schopenhauer, and William Jennings Bryan. Also on display are her sculptures of Sam Houston, Stephen F. Austin, and Gen. Albert Sydney Johnston,[qqv] as well as the allegorical figure of Lady Macbeth, which Ney regarded as her masterpiece. The collection now includes over forty of the 100 statues, busts, and medallions executed by Elisabet Ney.

In 1891 the Board of Lady Managers of the Chicago World's Fair Association commissioned the Austin and Houston statues, providing the impetus for the construction of Ney's Austin studio. Construction delays caused her to miss the exhibition, but the statues were later recommissioned by the state of Texas. Formosa, completed in 1893 and enlarged in 1902, was the earliest art studio built in Texas and is one of four extant nineteenth-century art studios in the United States. Ney personally designed and supervised the construction of the studio, which is built of native limestone and employs an eclectic mélange of Classical and Gothic architectural elements. The property on which the studio is located originally encompassed seven acres; today the museum's grounds extend for a square block on East 44th Street in the Hyde Park section of Austin. The grounds are bisected by Waller Creek and include the dam that once impounded the private "Lake Ney." The large ground-level workrooms are now utilized as exhibition galleries. Other rooms house a small research library and provide space for cultural and educational activities such as concerts and classes in sculpture, life-drawing, and children's art.

Until 1973 the Ney museum emphasized the exhibition of contemporary art. After its designation as a national historic site in that year, the museum began a program to reconstruct the studio as it was used by Ney from 1892 to 1907. From July 1980 to November 1982 the museum was closed for a structural restoration and the installation of a climate-control system; the cost of $500,000 was raised from public and private sources. Afterward, attendance averaged about 35,000 people per year, fifteen times the earlier levels.

BIBLIOGRAPHY: *Daily Texan*, August 14, 1973, August 11, 1977. Files, Elisabet Ney Museum Archives, Austin. Elisabet Ney Papers, Ransom Humanities Research Center, University of Texas at Austin. Vertical Files, Barker Texas History Center, University of Texas at Austin.

James D. Fisher

ELISSA. The *Elissa* is a restored nineteenth-century full-rigged sailing ship that belongs to the Galveston Historical Foundation. She was designed as an iron-hulled, three-masted barque and built at the Clyde River shipyard of Alexander Hall and Company of Aberdeen, Scotland, for Henry Fowler Watt of Liverpool, England, and launched on October 27, 1877. Her overall length is 162 feet; her deck length is 152 feet. Her molded depth is sixteen feet, her beam twenty-eight. Her gross capacity is 430 tons. She carries nineteen sails made of 12,000 square feet of a synthetic material that resembles canvas. Her hull plates and forms are of iron, except where restored with welded steel. The fore and main masts (technically, the lower trunks) are welded steel, as are the lower yards and bowsprit. The upper yards and masts are made of Douglas fir, as are the decks. The interior woodwork is made of maple, teak, and pine. She carries 245 tons of ballast.

The *Elissa* began her career as a British merchantman on December 19, 1877, when she carried a cargo of Welsh coal to Pernambuco (now Recife), Brazil, where she arrived on January 28, 1878. For the next ninety years, she was steadily employed as a tramp freight carrier traveling all over the world. The main United States ports she stopped at were New York, Boston, Savannah, and Pensacola. She also stopped at Galveston in 1883 and 1886.

Although small sailing ships like the *Elissa* were soon replaced by the more efficient tramp steamers that were developed in the 1880s, the *Elissa* continued to serve her British owners until 1897, when she was badly damaged in a North Atlantic gale. In 1898 she was sold to the Norwegian firm of Bugge and Olsen, which changed her name to *Fjeld* and sailed her for another fourteen years. In 1912 she was bought by Carl Johansson of Sweden, and her name was again changed, this time to *Gustaf*. In 1918 she was cut down to a barkentine rig and an engine was installed. During the 1920s she operated primarily in Scandinavian waters handling lumber and general cargo. In 1930 she was bought by a Finnish firm, and her rig was cut down to that of a schooner. In 1936 a new engine was installed aft and her sailing ship bow was snubbed off.

The ship continued as a lumber and general cargo carrier in Scandinavian waters until 1960, when she was bought by a Greek firm and began operating in the Mediterranean. Her sailing rig had by now been completely removed, with her mizzen mast restepped as her main mast and used for cargo handling. She now sailed as the motor ship *Christophoros* and was used in the Greek coastal trade. In 1967 she was sold to new Greek owners, and her name was changed to *Achaios*. She was not, however, destined for the mundane coastal trade, but instead embarked on a career as a smuggler operating in the Adriatic.

In 1970 she was purchased again, this time the object being her restoration as a full-rigged sailing ship. She had been seen moored at Piraeus, the port of Athens, Greece, by Peter Throckmorton, curator at large for the National Maritime Historical Society. Throckmorton mortgaged his house to buy her from the Greek smugglers. While negotiations for the sale were in progress, her name was changed to *Pioneer*. When the purchase was completed, however, her name became again, for the first time in seventy-two years, *Elissa*. The next step in *Elissa*'s preservation was to find sponsors in the United States willing to underwrite such a project. In 1971 San Francisco expressed interest in obtaining the ship, but due to funding difficulties was unable to go forward. An offer then came from Vancouver, British Columbia, in 1972, but fell through upon the death of its sponsor. In 1974 the *Elissa* was at last purchased by the Galveston Historical Foundation, chaired by Peter Brink, as a restoration project to complement the Strand[qv] Historic District, the Victorian market center of the city. Galveston wanted the *Elissa* because of her old business connections in the port. She was also one of the few surviving square-riggers in the world and the oldest listed in the Lloyd's of London *Registry of Shipping*. For the next three years, she remained at Piraeus while civic groups in Galveston raised $40,000 to bring her across the Atlantic. In 1977 extensive hull repairs were undertaken in preparation for her transit, with the work being done largely by volunteers receiving minimal pay.

In the summer of 1978 the *Elissa* became the first item outside the United States to be placed on the National Register of Historic Places. In December 1978 the ship began the first leg of her long voyage to Galveston; she was towed to Gibraltar, where she passed the winter. On June 25, 1979, she was towed out of Gibraltar and set sail for Texas; she arrived off Galveston on July 20. A dockside celebration with flags and bunting and bands was held in Galveston on August 4 to honor the arrival.

In the next three years the *Elissa* underwent a complete restoration, under direction of David Brink, which included extensive hull repair and new masts, yards, rigging, and sails, as well as a new deck and new deck houses. Her cabins, saloon, and forecastle were restored. Restoration was largely complete by July 4, 1982, when she was formally opened as a tourist attraction. On Labor Day of that year, the *Elissa* also sailed again as a full-rigged ship on sea trials off Galveston in the Gulf of Mexico, and has sailed periodically since then.

The actual sailing of the *Elissa* was the capstone to her restoration and the climax of some twelve years' effort to save her, find her a home, and rehabilitate her. The total cost for the Galveston project was about $4.2 million. Money for this was obtained from individual donations and from grants from such organizations as the Moody Foundation[qv] of Galveston, supplemented by federal funding. In 1986 the *Elissa* went to New York Harbor to participate in the Fourth of July Statue of Liberty 100th birthday celebration. She again left Galveston in 1989 to sail along the southern coast visiting port towns, while construction began on the Texas Seaport Museum in Galveston. The museum, which showcases the *Elissa*, was open to the public in 1991 and includes 5,000 square feet of exhibit space and a theater where films on the restoration of the *Elissa* are shown. The *Elissa* is now berthed at Pier 21 in Galveston, just off the Strand, and is visited by approximately 60,000 to 70,000 tourists a year.

BIBLIOGRAPHY: *Sea History: Official Journal of the World Ship Trust*, Fall 1979.

William A. Ward

ELIZA, TEXAS. Eliza was on the Neches River five miles northeast of Augusta in northeastern Houston County. A post office opened there in 1859, and by the early 1870s the community had several stores and a number of houses. Its post office was discontinued in 1871. By the mid-1930s the community no longer appeared on highway maps.

Christopher Long

ELIZA RUSSELL AND LITTLE PENN CLAIMS. The *Eliza Russell* and the *Little Penn* claims of the British government against the Republic of Texas[qv] grew out of incidents of 1837, when ships of the Texas Navy[qv] seized cargoes of the two British vessels as prizes of war. When the *Little Penn*, carrying a cargo belonging to F. de Lizardi and

Company and destined for Tabasco, ran aground on a shoal, its cargo was saved by the Mexican vessels *Paz* and *Abispa*. The Texas warships *Brutus* and *Invincible*[qv] captured the *Abispa* and sent her to Matagorda, and then stripped the Little Penn of everything of value before wrecking the vessel. Lizardi and Company claimed, through the British foreign office, damages of over 3,640 pounds sterling, but Texas never recognized the claim. In January 1838 the British brought the claim to the attention of the Texas chargé, James Pinckney Henderson,[qv] but Texas claimed that Lizardi and Company were London agents for the Mexican government and that a prize court had already decided the case. In February 1845 the republic still refused to pay the claim.

The *Eliza Russell*, a schooner owned by Capt. Joseph Russell, was captured by Texas vessels off the Campeche coast on August 3, 1837, and was sent to Galveston, despite orders that ships carrying neutral flags were to be respected unless they were carrying contraband and bound for an enemy port. She was ordered released but was delayed and injured by storms in Galveston Bay, and Russell subsequently presented to the British government a claim for 865 pounds sterling because of the seizure and delay. The Texas government acknowledged its fault in the *Eliza Russell* case but postponed payment until September 1843.

The claims were relatively insignificant as to size and consequence, but they occupied much of the diplomatic correspondence of the republic and accounted for a brief period of unfriendliness between the two governments. At one time Lord Palmerston of the British Foreign Office threatened to send a British warship to take all action necessary to enforce payment of the claims. However, British representatives in Texas reported that Texas did not have resources to pay but intended to pay the claim for the *Eliza Russell*. The claim for the *Little Penn* was never vigorously pressed by the British. *See also* DIPLOMATIC RELATIONS OF THE REPUBLIC OF TEXAS.

BIBLIOGRAPHY: Ephraim Douglass Adams, "British Correspondence Concerning Texas, " *Southwestern Historical Quarterly* 19 (October 1915). Asa Kyrus Christian, *Mirabeau Buonaparte Lamar* (Austin: Von Boeckmann–Jones, 1922). Alex Dienst, "The Navy of the Republic of Texas," *Quarterly of the Texas State Historical Association* 12–13 (January–October 1909; rpt., Fort Collins, Colorado: Old Army Press, 1987). J. L. Worley, "The Diplomatic Relations of England and the Republic of Texas," *Quarterly of the Texas State Historical Association* 9 (July 1905).

ELIZABETH CREEK. Elizabeth Creek rises in southeastern Wise County (at 33°06′ N, 97°28′ W) and runs southeast for sixteen miles to its mouth on Denton Creek in Denton County (at 33°02′ N, 97°14′ W). The stream is named for a daughter of John B. Denton[qv] and is located in the Grand Prairie region of north central Texas. It traverses an area characterized by limestone and loamy mud soils that support grasses, primarily silver bluestem and Texas wintergrass, and crops.

ELIZABETHTOWN, TEXAS. Elizabethtown was on the north side of Elizabeth Creek, from which the town derived its name, in the southwest corner of the Shamblen survey, fifteen miles southwest of Denton in Denton County. The first settlers there, members of the Peters colony,[qv] arrived around 1850. The settlement served as a supply station in 1852 for cowboys driving their herds north to Kansas. The town's founders, the Harmonsons, built a church, homes, a business, and a school, which at one time had twenty-five students. In 1859 the town had six saloons, a hotel, and a post office. George Harper, the doctor, was postmaster; M. H. Smith, Newton Chance, and Amos Bullard were blacksmiths; Sewell Brown was a merchant, James Snyder a wagonmaker, and Robert Wright a carpenter. The Civil War[qv] left the frontier west of Denton County undefended against Indians, however, and many families moved east, though they later returned. As Elizabethtown grew, it acquired four general stores, a hotel and livery stable, Baptist and Methodist churches, and a Masonic lodge that functioned from 1873 to 1876. According to residents of nearby Justin, Elizabethtown was once nicknamed Bugtown, after bugs swarmed to the lights at a camp meeting one night in such numbers that it was necessary to stop the preaching. The 1880 tax roll is the last roll of Denton County in which Elizabethtown is mentioned. The Texas and Pacific Railway, built from Fort Worth through Denton County in 1881, bypassed Elizabethtown by two miles. When this happened, many residents moved two miles east to the new town of Roanoke with their businesses, churches, and lodge. The Elizabeth Cemetery, which is still in use, is all that remains of what was the first town in southwest Denton County.

BIBLIOGRAPHY: Edward Franklin Bates, *History and Reminiscences of Denton County* (Denton, Texas: McNitzky Printing, 1918; rpt., Denton: Terrill Wheeler Printing, 1976). C. A. Bridges, *History of Denton, Texas, from Its Beginning to 1960* (Waco: Texian Press, 1978). Seymour V. Connor, *The Peters Colony of Texas: A History and Biographical Sketches of the Early Settlers* (Austin: Texas State Historical Association, 1959). Denton *Record and Chronicle*, Bicentennial Issue, July 4, 1976. Grace Lee Parr, *The Justin Story* (Quanah, Texas: Nortex Press, 1976). Rodney J. Walter, The Economic History of Denton County, Texas, 1900–1950 (M.A. thesis, North Texas State University, 1969).

Jeannine Sellmeyer

ELIZONDO, IGNACIO (?–1813). Ignacio Elizondo, commander of a small force in the Casas Revolt[qv] in January 1811, was sent as prisoners the royalist governors, Manuel María de Salcedo of Texas and Simón de Herrera[qqv] of Nuevo León. The prisoners converted Elizondo to their side. On March 21 he captured Miguel Hidalgo y Costilla[qv] and other rebel leaders at Acatita de Baján, southeast of Monclova, for which he was rewarded with command of 1,050 troops, which he led into Texas on June 12, 1813, to reconnoiter the forces of José Bernardo Gutiérrez de Lara,[qv] who had captured San Antonio on April 1. Although Gen. Joaquín de Arredondo's[qv] had ordered not to engage in battle, Elizondo camped on Alazán Creek, half a league west of San Antonio, from which he demanded the surrender of the town. On June 20, 1813, Maj. Henry Perry[qv] led the republicans to recapture San Antonio from Elizondo, who retreated to the Rio Grande. In the meantime, General Arredondo, who was leading an army toward Texas to crush the rebellion, ordered Elizondo to join him. Then, with a force of 1,830 men under his command, Arredondo advanced toward San Antonio and defeated 1,400 republicans in the battle of Medina[qv] on August 18, 1813. Arredondo occupied San Antonio, and Elizondo pursued fugitive republicans as far as Nacogdoches. By September 3 he had caught and executed seventy-one rebels and held more than 100 as prisoners. On September 12, while resting at the Brazos River on his return trip to San Antonio, Elizondo was attacked and wounded severely by one of his officers. He died a few days later and was buried on the banks of the San Marcos River.

BIBLIOGRAPHY: Hubert Howe Bancroft, *History of the North Mexican States and Texas* (2 vols., San Francisco: History Company, 1886, 1889). Julia Kathryn Garrett, *Green Flag Over Texas: A Story of the Last Years of Spain in Texas* (Austin: Pemberton Press, 1939). Ted Schwarz and Robert H. Thonhoff, *Forgotten Battlefield of the First Texas Revolution: The Battle of Medina* (Austin: Eakin Press, 1985). Harris Gaylord Warren, *The Sword Was Their Passport: A History of American Filibustering in the Mexican Revolution* (Baton Rouge: Louisiana State University Press, 1943).

Robert H. Thonhoff

ELK, TEXAS. Elk, between U.S. Highway 84 and Farm Road 2957 four miles southeast of Axtell in eastern McLennan County, was formed in the 1880s, mainly by settlers of Czech and German descent.

An Elk post office was established in July 1894 with Martie Emma McKinley as postmistress. Elk had a general store in 1896 and a population of eighteen in 1900. Its post office was discontinued in 1906, and mail for the community was rerouted through Axtell. By the 1920s Elk had seventy-five residents, a cotton gin, two churches, a saloon, and a school. Its population fell to thirty-eight in the early 1930s but rose again to seventy-five by the end of the decade. A church, a few businesses, and several houses represented the community on county highway maps in the 1940s. The Elk common-school district was consolidated with the Axtell high school district in 1955. A church and a gas station were all that remained at Elk in the early 1980s. In 1990 it was a dispersed rural community.

BIBLIOGRAPHY: Dayton Kelley, ed., *The Handbook of Waco and McLennan County, Texas* (Waco: Texian, 1972). William Robert Poage, *McLennan County Before 1980* (Waco: Texian, 1981). Vertical File, Texas Collection, Baylor University.   *Vivian Elizabeth Smyrl*

ELKHART, TEXAS. Elkhart is at the intersection of State Highway 294 and U.S. Highway 287, eleven miles south of Palestine in southern Anderson County. In 1851 members of Daniel Parker's^qv Pilgrim community moved to land around Boxy Creek to take advantage of the new post office and a newly established railroad. With the efforts of a friendly Indian, the newcomers settled into a community that continued to survive. They named the town after the Indian. A nearby spa served many socialites with its excellent mineral waters.

The International-Great Northern Railroad ran both passenger and freight trains through Elkhart. The freight cars were loaded with tomatoes, cotton, and pulpwood from the local sawmills. The depot in Elkhart was a thriving center for both trains and trucks. One mile west of the Pilgrim Baptist Church established by Daniel Parker is a Methodist church with a historical marker pointing out the locale of its first building. The first Methodist sermon was preached by Rev. William Stevenson,^qv who came to Elkhart and met with members in their home until a church could be built about 1840.

In 1912 the downtown area was destroyed by fire. During the Great Depression^qv Elkhart continued to have both a bus stop and railroad station, but as the farming declined the services were gradually curtailed. In 1933 Elkhart's public school district enrolled 736 white and forty-three black students. In 1989 Elkhart had a bank and general store. Many area residents can trace their lineage to the town's first settlers. The population of Elkhart was 1,076 in 1990.

BIBLIOGRAPHY: Claude W. Dooley, comp., *Why Stop?* (Odessa: Lone Star Legends, 1978; 2d ed., with Betty Dooley and the Texas Historical Commission, Houston: Lone Star, 1985). Pauline Buck Hohes, *A Centennial History of Anderson County, Texas* (San Antonio: Naylor, 1936). Vertical Files, Barker Texas History Center, University of Texas at Austin.   *Dorothy K. Bridges*

ELKINS, JAMES ANDERSON (1879–1972). James Anderson (Judge) Elkins, attorney and banker, son of J. J. and Sarah (Sims) Elkins, was born at Huntsville, Texas, on September 25, 1879. His father, former sheriff of Walker County, died while Elkins was a youth, and his mother later operated a boardinghouse. Elkins attended the Huntsville public schools and Sam Houston Normal Institute (now Sam Houston State University) before transferring to the University of Texas. He received his LL.B. in 1901 and returned to Huntsville. From December 1903 until January 1905 he served as county judge of Walker County and practiced law.

Realizing the potential for growth of Houston, Elkins accepted the invitation of William Ashton Vinson^qv to come to Houston. On September 1, 1917, the two formed Vinson and Elkins for the practice of general civil law. Due largely to Elkins's leadership, the firm grew from three attorneys in 1917 to 158 attorneys in 1972. Elkins's interest in banking led in 1924 to his founding the Guaranty Trust Company.

Although the company started with little capital and no significant deposits, by 1972 it had become Houston's largest banking firm, First City National Bank.

Elkins's activities extended to business, educational, political and charitable endeavors. He served as a director of American General Insurance Company, Great Southern Life Insurance Company, the National Bank of Commerce, the District Federal Reserve Bank, Pure Oil Pipe Line Company, Humphreys' Carbon Company, Texas Gulf Producing Company, the Missouri, Kansas and Texas Railroad, R. G. LeTourneau,^qv Incorporated, and Longhorn Portland Cement Company. He was a member of the board of regents of the state normal schools, a regent of the University of Houston, and a member of the University of Texas Development Board. In 1962 Elkins received the University of Texas Distinguished Alumni Award.

He was a conservative Democrat who supported Lieutenant Governor Lynch Davidson, served on the legal-defense committee of the Texas Equal Suffrage Association, and chaired fund-raising drives for the University of Houston and St. Anthony's Home for the Aged. He was a member of the Texas Centennial^qv Commission in 1936 and actively participated in the Houston Chamber of Commerce, as well as other civic organizations. He belonged to several lodges and service organizations. He attended St. Paul Methodist Church of Houston. Professionally, Elkins was a member of the American Bar Association, the Harris County Bar Association, and the State Bar of Texas.^qv

He died in Houston on May 7, 1972, at the age of ninety-two. He was predeceased by his wife, Isabel (Mitchell) Elkins, to whom he was married on December 18, 1905, and survived by his two sons.

BIBLIOGRAPHY: Dana Blankenhorn, "James A. Elkins, Sr.: For Half a Century 'The Judge' Held Reigns of Houston Power," *Houston Business Journal*, March 12, 1979. Houston *Chronicle*, June 24, 1969, May 8, 1972.   *Irvin M. May, Jr.*

ELKINS, TEXAS (Brown County). Elkins, at the intersection of two country roads eight miles southeast of Brownwood in southeastern Brown County, developed on two early Comanche Indian trails. The community had a post office from 1901 to 1906, and in the early 1940s it had a church, a business, and a population of fifteen. By 1947 Elkins reported a business and a population of twenty-five, but by 1949 no population figures were available. A cemetery remained at the site in the 1980s.   *Rachel Jenkins*

ELKINS, TEXAS (Houston County). Elkins was on State Highway 19 three miles north of Lovelady in southern Houston County. It developed around 1900 near a lignite coal mine operated by the Houston County Coal Company. The community was named for William Eli Elkins, superintendent of the mine. At its height during the early 1900s the town had a store and a number of houses. In the early 1990s only a few widely scattered houses remained in the area.

BIBLIOGRAPHY: Houston County Historical Commission, *History of Houston County, Texas, 1687–1979* (Tulsa, Oklahoma: Heritage, 1979).   *Eliza H. Bishop*

ELKS LODGE. The Benevolent and Protective Order of Elks is a nationally chartered institution founded in 1865. Subordinate lodges are organized in countries that owe allegiance to the government of the United States and only in towns with 5,000 or more population. The Elks' fraternal activities include care for aged members, care for crippled children (regardless of their parents' connection or nonconnection with the order), educational assistance for those who need scholarships, and assistance to members who are called into the armed forces of the United States. Practically every eligible town in Texas has a subordinate lodge; these subordinate groups are coordinated in a state lodge. Texas has furnished two grand exalted rulers of the order—Judge William Hawley Atwell,^qv who was elected in 1925, and

Charles F. "Chuck" Williams, who was elected in 1993. The Benevolent and Protective Order of Elks sponsors many youth programs, including scholarships, scouting for boys and girls, and aid to the needy, as well as many other civic and community endeavors. The Elks formerly operated a hospital for crippled children at Ottine, Texas, coupled with an accredited school for regular classroom work. By 1988 the hospital had become a diagnostic center for children. The Elks also sponsor camps for disabled children. Their quarterly newsletter, *TESA News,* was edited in 1995 by Lonnie and Susan Hart. In 1994 the Texas Elks State Association had seventy-four lodges and 21,951 members, Dallas had the largest lodge in the state, and the president was Bill Hill.

BIBLIOGRAPHY: *TESA News,* Winter 1994–95.

ELKTON, TEXAS. Elkton, also known as Ashcraft, was on U.S. Highway 69 just south of Tyler in southwestern Smith County. It was originally part of the Don Thomas Quevado land survey and was called Ashcraft by its earliest settlers. In 1877 the settlement became a station on what later became the St. Louis Southwestern Railway, and in 1889 the community name was changed to Elkton. In 1936 Elkton had a business, a cemetery, and a few scattered farms near a bladed earth road. By 1973 it was no longer identified on county maps, though Cathedral Church was located in the area. In 1990 Elkton was a dispersed rural community.

BIBLIOGRAPHY: Donald W. Whisenhunt, comp., *Chronological History of Smith County* (Tyler, Texas: Smith County Historical Society, 1983). Albert Woldert, *A History of Tyler and Smith County* (San Antonio: Naylor, 1948).   Vista K. McCroskey

EL LAGO, TEXAS. El Lago is on Taylor Lake, Clear Lake, and Farm Road 328 in southeastern Harris County. The community was started in the 1950s, incorporated in 1964, and grew from a population of 750 in 1967 to 3,550 by 1975, as workers were drawn to the nearby Lyndon B. Johnson Space Center.qv The population declined briefly in the late 1970s and early 1980s; it was 3,269 in 1990.

Diana J. Kleiner

ELLEN, TEXAS. Ellen is on Farm Road 784 fifteen miles southeast of Plainview in eastern Hale County. Early residents in the area included the Churchwell, Beard, Whitney, Faytinger, Daugherty, Line, and Young families. The community was named for Ellen White, wife of Edward M. White, who started the town of Petersburg, Texas. An Ellen post office opened in May 1904 with Carl W. Richardson as postmaster; it closed in January 1923. A school was started at Ellen in 1905; in April 1917 the Ellen Common School District was established. The Ellen school was also used as a church and community center. The district was consolidated with that of Petersburg in the mid-1940s. In the mid-1980s Ellen still appeared on county maps, although no town landmarks were evident.

BIBLIOGRAPHY: Mary L. Cox, *History of Hale County, Texas* (Plainview, Texas, 1937). Jim Wheat, Postmasters and Post Offices of Texas, 1846–1930 (Microfilm, Grover C. Ramsey Papers, Barker Texas History Center, University of Texas at Austin).   Charles G. Davis

ELLERSLY PLANTATION. Ellersly (Ellersley, Ellerslie) Plantation was established by John Greenville McNeelqv on land granted to him and his brother, George W. McNeel,qv by the Mexican government under Stephen F. Austin'sqv first contract in 1824. It included one-half league on the Brazos River and one-half league on the San Bernard River. George died, and John Greenville built a prosperous sugar plantation in the area known as Gulf Prairie, on the San Bernard River eight miles from the Gulf of Mexico in Brazoria County. The plantation house was located in a grove of live oaks between two roads, and the entrance gates were flanked by hand-hewn oak posts topped by carved replicas of a spade, a diamond, a club, and a heart. The two-story house was constructed of slave-made bricks. It had twenty-one rooms, and galleries with pillars extended the length of the house on the west and south. The stairs and bannisters were made of mahogany, and the ceilings were plastered and decorated with intricate medallions. The fireplaces and mantels were made of marble, and the floors were carpeted. The furniture was either walnut or mahogany. Atop the house was a laboratory with a telescope. All in all, Ellersly was considered the finest home in Texas before the Civil War.qv

The plantation had an immense brick sugar mill that resembled a turreted castle and enclosed a double set of kettles. Outbuildings included a brick overseer's house, a cotton gin, a blacksmith's shop, and a hospital. The brick slave quarters lined a street leading off the main road; each consisted of two rooms with a double fireplace that accommodated two families.

Greenville and his family entertained often—dancing, fishing, hunting and riding. He had a stallion that cost $6,000. His brothers, Sterling McNeel, Pleasant McNeel,qqv and Leander McNeel, lived on neighboring plantations. Ellersly was prosperous; in 1852, for example, it produced 408 hogsheads or nearly 149,000 pounds of sugar. In 1860 the census appraised J. G. McNeel's real property at $100,000 and his personal property at $216,400. He owned 176 slaves. The 1870 census reflected his losses during Reconstruction,qv however, for he was listed with no property.

After his death in 1876 his heirs sold the plantation to James Marion Huntington, who was married to Greenville's niece. After her death Huntington remarried. The main house burned in the 1890s, and the family moved into the old brick hospital. It blew down in the Galveston hurricane of 1900,qv and they moved into the overseer's house. The descendants sold the house and property to the Phillips Petroleum Company in 1974. The overseer's house burned in 1983.

BIBLIOGRAPHY: Randolph B. Campbell, *An Empire for Slavery: The Peculiar Institution in Texas, 1821–1865* (Baton Rouge: Louisiana State University Press, 1989). Abigail Curlee, A Study of Texas Slave Plantations, 1822–1865 (Ph.D. dissertation, University of Texas, 1932). Abigail Curlee Holbrook, "A Glimpse of Life on Antebellum Slave Plantations in Texas," *Southwestern Historical Quarterly* 76 (April 1973). C. Richard King, ed., *Victorian Lady on the Texas Frontier: The Journal of Ann Raney Coleman* (Norman: University of Oklahoma Press, 1971). Allen Andrew Platter, Educational, Social, and Economic Characteristics of the Plantation Culture of Brazoria County, Texas (Ed.D. dissertation, University of Houston, 1961). Abner J. Strobel, *The Old Plantations and Their Owners of Brazoria County* (Houston, 1926; rev. ed., Houston: Bowman and Ross, 1930; rpt., Austin: Shelby, 1980). Vertical File, Brazoria County Historical Museum, Angleton, Texas. Ralph A. Wooster, "Wealthy Texans, 1860," *Southwestern Historical Quarterly* 71 (October 1967). Ralph A. Wooster, "Wealthy Texans, 1870," *Southwestern Historical Quarterly* 74 (July 1970).

René Harris

ELLES, NORMA BERTHA (1884–1959). Norma Bertha Elles, ophthalmologist and settlement-house organizer, was born in Evansville, Indiana, on June 30, 1884, to Jacob and Caroline Elles. After finishing high school in 1902 she attended the University of Michigan, where she received an A.B. and M.D. in 1906. Michigan later awarded her an honorary doctor of science degree in recognition of her work on diseases of the eye. After an internship at the Women's Hospital in Chicago, she entered general practice in Houston. With the encouragement of physicians in Houston and Chicago, she returned to Illinois for four years to complete a residency at the Illinois Eye and Ear Infirmary. After a further year of study in Vienna and at the Sorbonne in Paris, Dr. Elles returned to Houston in 1912 with a specialty in ophthalmology. She remained in Houston until her retirement in 1952 but spent many of her summers in Europe pursuing studies in her field. From 1943 to 1952 she also served as professor of ophthalmology at Baylor Medical School.

During one of her summer trips to London, Elles visited various settlement houses in that city. Upon her return to Houston, she helped establish a similar institution for the Ripley Foundation. She served for many years as one of the house's trustees. She was also a member of the Houston Settlement Association and a member of the board of directors of the Florence Crittenden Home in Houston.

In 1956 and 1957 Elles traveled to Haiti to assist in the organization of the Ophthalmologic Clinic at the Albert Schweitzer Memorial Hospital. Using her own photographs as illustrations, she described the hospital and its services in a 1958 issue of the *American Journal of Ophthalmology*. She was a member of the American Medical Women's Association and president of the Houston branch of that organization in 1945. She was elected an honorary member of the Texas State Medical Association (*see* TEXAS MEDICAL ASSOCIATION) in 1953. She was a member of the American Medical Association, the American Academy of Ophthalmology and Otolaryngology, and the American Ophthalmological Society. Upon her retirement she moved to Kalamazoo, Michigan, to be near her family. In 1959 she returned to Houston for a visit and had a heart attack. She died on January 12, 1959, in a Houston hospital.

BIBLIOGRAPHY: *Texas State Journal of Medicine*, March 1959.

Patricia L. Jakobi

ELLEY, GUSTAV (1816–1897). Gustav Elley, soldier and Methodist preacher, only son of Christine Wilhelmine Weisbach and Joachim Gustav Ferdinand von Elterlein, was born Gustavus von Elterlein on June 10, 1816, in Mittelschmiedeberg in the kingdom of Saxony. As far back as 1500 the family owned iron works in the Erzgebirge region. Elley was orphaned at an early age and reared by his grandparents and his uncle, Julius Weisbach, a mathemetician at Freiberg Academy of Mines. While still in his teens Elley immigrated to the United States. He traveled by way of New Orleans to Texas in 1836 with George H. Burroughs's qv Zanesville volunteers, Company G. Upon arrival he dropped his title of "baron" and anglicized his name to Elley, the name of his English governess. He was in the Army of the Republic of Texas qv from October 1, 1836, to December 21, 1837. He joined the Texas Navy qv in 1840 and was a fireman on the steamship *Zavala*.qv On June 1, 1842, he enlisted in Capt. John C. Hays's qv Texas Ranger Volunteer Spy Company, with headquarters in San Antonio. He was on special detail guarding the District Court as a member of Capt. Chauncey Johnson's company when he was captured by Gen. Adrián Woll's qv invading army on September 11, 1842. His occupation was listed as "miner." With his fellow prisoners he reached Perote Prison qv on December 22, after traveling a distance of more than 1,000 miles on foot. In July 1843 sixteen of the Perote prisoners escaped, Gen. Thomas J. Green qv and Elley among them, but Elley was recaptured and held until March 24, 1844, when he was released with all of the remaining San Antonio and Dawson Massacre qv prisoners to Waddy Thompson,qv United States minister to Mexico.

Elley returned to the vicinity of San Antonio and was influenced during this time by a Methodist missionary preacher, John Wesley DeVilbiss.qv Along with seven other people he and DeVilbiss began a church that eventually became Travis Park Methodist Church. In 1854 Elley was accepted on trial as a Methodist Episcopal minister and assigned to the New Braunfels and Castroville Circuit. In 1859 he was a charter member of the Rio Grande Methodist Episcopal Conference. He was appointed to the New Fountain and New Braunfels missions. In 1868 he transferred to the Methodist Episcopal Church (North) and was accepted as an elder. He was a charter member of the Southern German Conference and a pastor at Industry and Rabbs Creek. In 1870 he was presiding elder in the Guadalupe Circuit, which included Fredericksburg and Mason. He was subsequently appointed to San Antonio, where he organized the Little Church of La Villita, which is now included in the Aldersgate United Methodist Church. As a charter member of the Southern Conference of the Methodist Episcopal Church (North) in 1874, he supplied the La Grange mission. On January 31, 1847, Elley married Henriette Blumberg in New Braunfels. They had thirteen children who grew to adulthood. Upon his retirement he bought a farm near Seguin, where he was living at the time of his death, on November 13, 1897. He was buried in Guadalupe Valley Cemetery in Guadalupe County.

BIBLIOGRAPHY: Pearl Elley Bethune, *Forward to the Past!* (Austin, 1990). Rena Maverick Green, ed., *Samuel Maverick, Texan* (San Antonio, 1952). Thomas J. Green, *Journal of the Texian Expedition Against Mier* (New York: Harper, 1845; rpt., Austin: Steck, 1935).

Charlene Nash and Pearl Elley Bethune

ELLINGER, TEXAS. Ellinger is at the intersection of State Highway 71 and Farm Road 2503, eleven miles southeast of La Grange in eastern Fayette County. The town is on W. O. Burnham's league and was established as a point on the La Grange Tap spur of the Galveston, Harrisburg and San Antonio Railway. Its 200-acre site was donated by John H. Meyer and Henry Fordtran. Andreas Ondrey, a local resident, suggested the name in honor of Joseph Ehlinger, a veteran of the battle of San Jacinto qv who received a grant in the area and whose family settled there after his death. The first businesses in Ellinger were operated by the Hotmann, Meyer, Rosenberg, and Hill families. A post office was established in 1877, and by 1878 the community had a population of 100. Early farmers concentrated on the production of cotton, and the community prospered. By 1900 Ellinger had two churches, a school, four lodges, a public hall, fourteen stores, two gins, two blacksmith shops, and four saloons. During the 1890s the Missouri, Kansas and Texas Railroad passed through Fayetteville, four miles to the north, and much local trade moved there. Ellinger maintained its status as a business community, however, and by 1950 had eleven businesses and a population of 223. The decline of cotton reoriented the local economy to cattle ranching and the production of grain and pecans in the 1960s. During the 1970s the Lower Colorado River Authority qv began construction of its nearby Fayette County Power Project. In the 1980s Ellinger had an active chamber of commerce but only two rated businesses, serving a population of 200. In 1990 the population was still estimated at 200.

BIBLIOGRAPHY: Frank Lotto, *Fayette County: Her History and Her People* (Schulenburg, Texas: Sticker Steam Press, 1902; rpt., Austin: University of Texas Press, 1981). Leonie Rummel Weyand and Houston Wade, *An Early History of Fayette County* (La Grange, Texas: La Grange *Journal*, 1936).

Jeff Carroll

ELLINGTON FIELD. Ellington Field, an aircraft-landing field, was constructed in 1917 on 1,280 acres of Texas prairie eighteen miles east of Houston, now in Pasadena. The first aircraft flew from Ellington on November 27, 1917. Since that time almost every type of airplane in the Air Force inventory has flown from its runways. The base was named in honor of Lt. Eric L. Ellington, who was killed in an aircraft crash in San Diego, California, in 1913. It was originally established for pilot and bombardier training. By April 1918 training at Ellington included dropping live bombs. The base was closed in 1920, and by 1930 the only remains were the concrete water tower and some concrete slabs on which small hangars once stood. In 1940 Congress authorized a program to rebuild Ellington. The new base was occupied in the spring of 1941, and thousands of pilots, navigators, and bombardiers were trained there during World War II.qv The base was inactive from March 1946 until 1947, when it became Ellington Air Force Base, a navigator-training school. The navigator-training wing was phased out in 1958. From the 1950s through the 1970s the base was engaged in pilot and navigator training for air reservists, air guardsmen, and navy, marine, and foreign students. NASA became a tenant in 1962. In 1984 the base was turned over to the city of Houston to be operated as a municipal airport, once again named Ellington Field. It continued to provide support for military reserve and guard units, as well as NASA and the Grumman Corporation for its aerospace activities.

BIBLIOGRAPHY: *Houston Chronicle Magazine*, November 1, 1987. Mark L. Morgan, "Air Force Bases: 1946–1987," *AAHS Journal* 32 (Winter 1987). Drury M. Phillips, "Ellington Field, Houston, Texas," *Texaco Star* 6 (July 1919).   Art Leatherwood

ELLIOT, CHARLES (1801–1875). Charles Elliot, British knight, admiral, and chargé d'affaires in Texas, the son of Hugh and Margaret Elliot, was born in 1801, probably in Dresden, Saxony, where his father was serving as British minister. In 1815 he entered the Royal Navy for service in the East Indies and on the African coast. He retired from the navy in 1828 to enter the colonial service. In 1830 he was appointed protector of slaves in Guiana, where he became an abolitionist. In 1834 he became secretary to trade commissioners in China, and after 1835 was made trade superintendent and plenipotentiary at Canton. He was thus in charge of English trade relations at a time when Chinese authorities began efforts to stop the illegal opium traffic conducted by British merchants and was largely responsible for the outbreak of the Opium War in 1840. After attacking Chinese forts in January 1841 he and the Chinese plenipotentiary signed an agreement, the Convention of Chuenpee, that proved unacceptable to both governments. After being censured for inadequately representing British mercantile interests, Elliot was relieved of his duties by Henry Pottinger, but not before further hostilities and a threatened assault forced Chinese authorities to ransom the city of Canton. Elliot was reassigned and, on August 6, 1842, arrived at Galveston, Texas, as British chargé d'affaires of the Republic of Texas.qv In this post Elliot advocated the abolition of slaveryqv in Texas, worked for the establishment of free trade, and emphasized the importance of securing peace with Mexico. He became a personal and trusted friend of Sam Houston and Anson Jones.qqv Supposedly at the behest of Houston, he worked with the British minister in Mexico City for an armistice between Texas and Mexico in 1843 and was instrumental in securing the release of some of the prisoners of the Mier expedition.qv

Because of the advantage to Great Britain of a free and independent Texas, Elliot worked actively against the annexationqv of Texas to the United States. In 1845, with the approval of President Jones, he went to Mexico to secure a treaty guaranteeing Texas independence on condition that Texas not be annexed. He brought the treaty back to Texas, but Texans voted for annexation in preference to independence recognized by Mexico and guaranteed by England. Elliot, called "the man in the white hat" in the press, was the subject of much newspaper comment during the annexation controversy. He was ordered to return to England after the formalities of annexation were concluded.

He was governor of Bermuda from 1846 to 1854, of Trinidad from 1854 to 1856, and of St. Helena from 1863 to 1869. In 1856 he was nominated for a civil KCB, and his honorary promotions in the navy took him to the rank of admiral in September 1865. Elliot was married and had at least one child. He died at Witteycombe, Exeter, England, on September 9, 1875.

BIBLIOGRAPHY: Ephraim Douglass Adams, *British Interests and Activities in Texas, 1836–1846* (Baltimore: Johns Hopkins Press, 1910). Gertrude Clagette Blake, Charles Elliot, R.N. (Ph.D. dissertation, University of Texas, 1953). Gertrude Clagette Blake, *Charles Elliot, R.N., 1801–1875: A Servant of Britain Overseas* (London: Cleaver-Hume Press, 1960). *Dictionary of National Biography.* Herbert Gambrell, *Anson Jones: The Last President of Texas* (Garden City, New York: Doubleday, 1948). Frederick Merk, *Slavery and the Annexation of Texas* (New York: Knopf, 1972). Justin Harvey Smith, *The Annexation of Texas* (New York: Baker and Taylor, 1911; 2d ed., New York: Macmillan, 1919; 3d ed., New York: Barnes and Noble, 1941; 4th ed., New York: AMS Press, 1971). Amelia W. Williams and Eugene C. Barker, eds., *The Writings of Sam Houston, 1813–1863* (8 vols., Austin: University of Texas Press, 1938–43; rpt., Austin and New York: Pemberton Press, 1970).

ELLIOT, TEXAS. Elliot, on State Highway 19 six miles north of Trinity in western Trinity County, was first settled after the Civil War.qv A school was established there before 1884 and continued to operate until after 1900. In the 1930s the community had two stores and a number of houses. After World War IIqv Elliot's stores closed, and many of its residents moved away. In the early 1990s only a few scattered houses remained in the area.

BIBLIOGRAPHY: Patricia B. and Joseph W. Hensley, ed., *Trinity County Beginnings* (Groveton, Texas: Trinity County Book Committee, 1986).   Christopher Long

ELLIOT CREEK. Elliot Creek rises two miles northeast of Marietta in northwestern Cass County (at 33°13′ N, 94°31′ W) and runs west for three miles to its mouth on Mill Creek (at 33°13′ N, 94°34′ W). The creek traverses an area of gently undulating to low-rolling land surfaced by loamy soils that support native vegetation including water-tolerant hardwoods, conifers, and grasses. The area around the creek is flood-prone. The creek was named for James Elliott, the original grantee of land near its upper reaches.

ELLIOT'S FERRY, TEXAS. Elliot's Ferry, on the east bank of the Sabine River eight miles northeast of Carthage near the site of River Hill, was among the earliest settlements in Panola County. The community, located on the main road between Carthage and Shreveport, grew up around a ferry crossing operated by a man named Elliot. By 1850 the settlement had several stores and houses. Malaria and frequent floods drove most of the residents to River Hill on the bluff above the river, and the site was eventually abandoned.

BIBLIOGRAPHY: Leila B. LaGrone, ed., *History of Panola County* (Carthage, Texas: Panola County Historical Commission, 1979). Lawrence R. Sharp, History of Panola County, Texas, to 1860 (M.A. thesis, University of Texas, 1940).   Christopher Long

ELLIOTT, CLAUDE (1896–1958). Claude Elliott, teacher, writer, and historian, the son of Robert Mitchell and Martha (Smith) Elliott, was born at Cross Plains, Texas, on September 21, 1896. After attending Abilene Christian College, Simmons College (now Hardin-Simmons University), and West Texas State Teachers College, he began his teaching career at Sardis and Donna. He received his B.A. degree from Southwest Texas State Teachers College in 1923 and served as superintendent of the La Feria schools from 1923 to 1928. While at La Feria he pursued his graduate studies at the University of Texas, where he was awarded the M.A. degree in 1928 and the Ph.D. degree in 1934. He married Emma Edwin Moore at San Marcos on September 6, 1927, and joined the faculty of Southwest Texas State Teachers College in September 1929.

At UT, Elliott studied history under Eugene C. Barker, Charles W. Ramsdell, Walter P. Webb,qqv and others. As a faculty member at Southwest Texas State, he was a great influence in the growth and development of the school. Although classroom teaching was his primary interest, he found time to serve as registrar and, later, as graduate dean. He wrote *Leathercoat: The Life History of a Texas Patriot* (1938) and compiled and edited a checklist of theses and dissertations, *Theses on Texas History* (1955). He served on the advisory council of the *Handbook of Texas* and contributed articles to the Southwestern

Historical Quarterly,qv the *Georgia Historical Review*, the *Southwestern Social Science Quarterly* (now the *Social Science Quarterly*qv), and the *Journal of Southern History*. He was a fellow of the Texas State Historical Associationqv and served the organization as vice president (1947–52) and president (1953–55). He died in Houston on October 1, 1958, and was buried in San Marcos.

BIBLIOGRAPHY: *Who's Who in America*, 1952–53.

William C. Pool

ELLIOTT, GEORGE WASHINGTON (1830–1910). George Washington Elliott, physician and rancher, was born in Boone County, Missouri, in 1830, one of eight children of Reuben and Elizabeth (Wilhite) Elliott. He married Harriett E. McQuity in 1869, and they had three children. Although a physician by profession, in 1878 Elliott moved to Bexar County, Texas, where he established a 1,700-acre ranch a few miles northwest of San Antonio. Because of his interest in testing the endurance of Durham cattle in the Texas open range, he built the first pasture fence and the first artificial watering tanks in Bexar County for forty-five purebred Durhams that he bred to stocker cattle. He was one of the first ranchers to introduce pure-bred Durhams to Texas. He also cultivated hay to supply provender for the army post at San Antonio. In 1884 Elliott sold his ranch and stock, and two years later he established the 20,000-acre T Ranch in Upton County, on which he stocked 1,000 cattle. For his headquarters he built a two-room rock house across from the old Butterfield Overland Mailqv station. In 1890 Elliott sold the ranch to R. S. Benson and moved to Midland. He was elected chairman of the board for the organization of the First National Bank. In Midland he devoted full time to the practice of medicine and was credited with designing and patenting the Elliott saddlebag, known and appreciated by country physicians. The saddlebag was made and sold by A. D. Mollier and Son of St. Louis, Missouri. In 1900 Elliott moved to Fort Worth, where he died on May 12, 1910. He was buried in Oakwood Cemetery in Fort Worth.

BIBLIOGRAPHY: James Cox, *Historical and Biographical Record of the Cattle Industry* (2 vols., St. Louis: Woodward and Tiernan Printing, 1894, 1895; rpt., with an introduction by J. Frank Dobie, New York: Antiquarian, 1959). Wilson Gregg, *Alexander Gregg, First Bishop of Texas* (Sewanee: Tennessee University Press, 1912). Midland *Reporter-Telegram*, October 18, 1953.

N. Ethie Eagleton

ELLIOTT, LESLIE ROBINSON (1886–1966). Leslie Robinson Elliott, theological librarian, was born in Rosetta, Henderson County, Illinois, on September 30, 1886, the oldest son of Judson Andrew and Minnie Hortense (Robinson) Elliott. He moved with his family in 1897 to the Salt River valley of Arizona and attended high school in Phoenix. Following in his father's footsteps, he decided to become a Baptist minister and returned to the Midwest for his college and seminary education. He graduated from William Jewell College in Liberty, Missouri (B.A., 1910), and attended Southern Baptist Theological Seminary in Louisville, Kentucky, from 1910 to 1912, when illness compelled him to withdraw. He later completed his education at Southwestern Baptist Theological Seminary in Fort Worth (Th.M., 1921; Th.D., 1925). After he was ordained by the Immanuel Baptist Church of Louisville, Kentucky, in 1911, he served as pastor of churches in Butler, Missouri (1912–15), Denver, Colorado (1915–17), and Del Rey, California (1917–19). He married Mary Ethelyn Shearer of Unionville, Missouri, on May 31, 1911.

In 1919, when Elliott resumed his studies at Southwestern Baptist Seminary in Fort Worth, he intended to complete the basic theological degree as quickly as possible and enter the full-time ministry. Circumstances changed his course, however, and he remained in Fort Worth the rest of his life. Shortly after enrolling, he began working as an assistant in the seminary library. In 1922 he was appointed librarian and thus became one of the first full-time Protestant theological librarians in Texas. He served until his retirement in 1957 and developed at Southwestern an important theological library. Furthermore, he promoted a theory of the educational function of the library as a true partner with the classroom and made the seminary library a heavily used resource. He also taught New Testament Greek at the seminary (1925–42) and served as registrar from 1937 through 1943. Elliott's published writings include *A Comparative Lexicon of New Testament Greek* (1945) and *Syntax in Diagram* (1950). He edited *Centennial Story of Texas Baptists* (1936) and contributed to the *Encyclopedia of Southern Baptists* (1958).

He often felt isolated from the major theological libraries in the eastern and midwestern sections of the nation. His need for a closer professional relationship with other theological librarians led him to help in the establishment of the American Theological Library Association (1947). He served as president of that organization for the first two terms (1947–49), and in 1955 he represented it in the formation of the International Association of Theological Libraries in Brussels, Belgium. In 1957–58 Elliott served as acting librarian for the Midwestern Baptist Theological Seminary in Kansas City, Missouri. Also in 1957, William Jewell College awarded him an honorary doctorate.

On March 29, 1963, Elliott received a special citation at the fiftieth annual meeting of the Texas Library Associationqv in recognition of his contributions to professional librarianship and his work as a trustee of the Fort Worth Public Library. He died in Fort Worth on May 2, 1966.

BIBLIOGRAPHY: Stanley H. Benson, *Leslie Robinson Elliott: His Contributions to Theological Librarianship* (M.L.S. thesis, University of Texas, 1965).

Stanley Hugh Benson

ELLIOTT, ROBERT WOODWARD BARNWELL (1840–1887). Robert Elliott, Episcopal bishop, the son of Stephen and Charlotte Bull (Barnwell) Elliott, was born at Beaufort, South Carolina, on August 16, 1840. After graduating from South Carolina College in 1861, he entered the Confederate Army and became aide to Gen. A. R. Lawton. Elliott was wounded at the second battle of Manassas and was with Joseph E. Johnstonqv at the time of the general's surrender in May 1865. After the war Elliott entered a seminary to train for the Episcopal ministry and was ordained in 1868. He was rector at St. Philip's Church, Atlanta, Georgia, when he was elected by the House of Bishops to be the first missionary bishop of Western Texas; he was consecrated on November 15, 1874 and arrived in Texas the next month. He held his first service at Luling in a passenger coach of the Galveston, Harrisburg and San Antonio Railway. He found in his diocese six church buildings, three of which were unfinished and two without services; he left twenty-four churches, nine rectories, St. Mary's Hallqv in San Antonio, and Montgomery Institute in Seguin. Elliott married his third cousin, Caroline Elliott, on January 7, 1864, and they had five children. He had served as bishop for thirteen years when he died, on August 26, 1887, at Sewanee, Tennessee.

BIBLIOGRAPHY: Clara Childs MacKenzie, *Sarah Barnwell Elliott* (Boston: Twayne, 1980). *National Cyclopaedia of American Biography*, Vol. 13. William S. Speer and John H. Brown, eds., *Encyclopedia of the New West* (Marshall, Texas: United States Biographical Publishing, 1881; rpt., Easley, South Carolina: Southern Historical Press, 1978).

Seymour V. Connor

ELLIOTT, WILLIAM (1799–1847). William Elliott, merchant, was born in Ireland in 1799. He was apprenticed to a mercantile house in Dublin before he immigrated to America in 1820. He married Eleanor Connally in New Orleans in 1835, and they had three children. In 1836 he was interested in mining in Mexico and was a merchant in Matamoros. He may have been the William Elliott whom Adolphus Sterneqv reported as coming from San Antonio to Nacogdoches with $25,000 in specie in March 1839. In August 1839 Elliott moved to San Antonio and established a mercantile business in partnership with

Edward Dwyer.qv In 1843 he joined other San Antonio citizens to petition the government for better protection of the frontier. He died in New Orleans on May 12, 1847, while on a buying trip for his business.

BIBLIOGRAPHY: Frederick Charles Chabot, *With the Makers of San Antonio* (Yanaguana Society Publications 4, San Antonio, 1937). Amelia W. Williams and Eugene C. Barker, eds., *The Writings of Sam Houston, 1813–1863* (8 vols., Austin: University of Texas Press, 1938–43; rpt., Austin and New York: Pemberton Press, 1970).

ELLIOTT, TEXAS (Matagorda County). Elliott, also known as Elliott's Ferry and Elliott's and historically linked with Cayce's Ferry and Red Bluff, was on the Colorado River a few miles west of the future site of Bay City in north central Matagorda County. During Stephen F. Austin'sqv colonization of the area, the surrounding Bay Prairie was crossed by settlers traveling from Columbia (later West Columbia) or Brazoria to Texana and elsewhere, and very early a ferry is said to have operated across the Colorado there on the Thomas Cayce league. From late 1836 to early 1837 an army post of some thirty or forty soldiers, captained by Andrew Neill,qv was stationed at Cayce's Ferry. The post, known as First Colorado Station, Post Colorado, or Station Colorado, guarded the ferry, assisted official travelers, and facilitated communications between the temporary capital at Columbia and the military post near Texana. The army installation at Cayce's Ferry appears to have been dismantled by early 1837, when the Republic of Texasqv capital was moved from Columbia to Houston (*see* CAPITALS).

In 1839 English immigrant George Elliott bought land in the H. H. League survey to the north of the Thomas Cayce league, either at or near the site where Cayce's Ferry had operated, and settled in the area with his wife and son. He was working as a blacksmith in 1848, when he was joined by his nephews William and John Elliott. By the following year he had applied for a permit for a toll ferry across the Colorado. This ferry was an important link, especially before the Civil War,qv in the route used by shippers to move cotton to the then-navigable Wilson Creek and Tres Palacios River, which gave access to Matagorda Bay and ports such as Palacios Point (later Portsmouth). In 1863 Elliott's Ferry, as it was then called, hosted a Confederate encampment. Around 1869 a cemetery and a small log church located north of the ferry and known as Red Bluff served the Elliott's Ferry population. The Red Bluff church was the forerunner of Bay City's First United Methodist Church. In the early 1870s Dolph Phineas Moore built a general store at Red Bluff.

In 1872 the community at Elliott's Ferry received a post office called Elliott's. By 1884 Elliott's, which at that time shipped cotton and hides, had a population of fifty, a gristmill, a general store, two blacksmiths, a district school, and Methodist, Episcopalian, and Christian churches. The church and store at Red Bluff may have become part of the community of Elliott's when in 1885 the Elliott's post office was moved north from its site about two miles south of Red Bluff to Moore's general store at Red Bluff. Moore became postmaster and served until 1893.

By 1890 Elliott's reported a population of seventy-five, and two years later it had a population of ninety and at least seven businesses. In 1893 the post office changed its name to Elliott, and in 1896 it was moved to Bay City. Though the ferry probably continued to operate until at least 1898, by 1902 a contract had been awarded the New York–based American Bridge Company to construct a crossing over the Colorado about two miles northwest of Bay City; when completed, the bridge eliminated the need for a number of small ferries across the river, including the ferry at Elliott.

BIBLIOGRAPHY: Mary McAllister Ingram, *110 Years of Methodism: History of First United Methodist Church, Bay City* (Burnet, Texas: Nortex, 1980). Matagorda County Historical Commission, *Historic Matagorda County* (3 vols., 1986–88).
Rachel Jenkins

ELLIOTT, TEXAS (Robertson County). Elliott is at the intersection of U.S. Highway 79 and Farm Road 2549, five miles north of Hearne in western Robertson County. It was established in 1871 as a station on the International–Great Northern Railroad and named for the settler who gave land for the townsite. A post office named Una operated there from 1890 until 1892, when the community's population was thirty. In 1900 T. W. McNeil's general store marked the townsite. An Elliott post office operated from 1895 until 1916, when the population had decreased to twenty. In 1947 two churches, a school, a business, and scattered dwellings remained there. In 1988 Elliott still had a church and several dwellings, and in 1990 it was a dispersed rural community.
Richard Allen Burns

ELLIOTT, TEXAS (Wilbarger County). Elliott is at the intersection of Farm roads 1763 and 370, four miles south of the Oklahoma state line in northeast Wilbarger County. Cotton was the main crop of the region. Many of the first settlers in 1904 came from Williamson County to escape a boll weevilqv outbreak. These early farmers were successful, although they were told that cotton would not grow in the area. The settlement was first called Waggoner's Colony. In 1907 the name was changed to honor the first schoolteacher, probably Sarah Elizabeth Elliott, whose husband, J. W. Elliott, had donated the land for a school established in 1906. The community was also known as Bugscuffle. The Bethel Baptist Church was organized in 1906, and members erected a building the next year. The church remained active in 1986 and also served the communities of Oklaunion and Harrold. A Methodist church existed during the early twentieth century but closed sometime after 1937. In 1941 the school was consolidated with that of Oklaunion. Elliott was large enough during the 1920s to support a twenty-five-piece community band, and by 1940 perhaps 250 residents lived there. The town population, however, was consistently reported in census records from the 1930s through 1990 as around fifty. In 1986 the community had the Elliott Co-op Gin, a combination store and domino parlor, and the Baptist church. The Bugscuffle oilfield is four miles west.

BIBLIOGRAPHY: Wilbarger County Historical Commission, *Wilbarger County* (Lubbock, 1986).
Charles G. Davis

ELLIOTT CREEK (Bowie County). Elliott Creek, which is intermittent in its upper reaches, rises on the property of the Lone Star Army Ammunition Plantqv two miles south of Hooks in eastern Bowie County (at 33°27′ N, 94°16′ W). The stream originally ran southeast for seventeen miles to its mouth on the Sulphur River, five miles east of the Arkansas state line (at 33°18′ N, 94°08′ W). Wright Patman Lake, constructed between 1948 and 1957, subsumed a portion of Elliott Creek's middle reaches, leaving the stream in two segments. One segment runs south nine miles from the creek's headwaters to its mouth on Wright Patman Lake. This section runs for most of its course through the ammunition plant property, where it has been dammed to form Elliott Creek Reservoir. The other segment of the creek runs southeast for four miles from just east of Wright Patman Dam to the original creek mouth on the Sulphur River. The land along this part of the stream is heavily wooded, with pines and various hardwoods predominating.

_____ (Mills County). Elliott Creek rises in southern Mills County (at 31°22′ N, 98°30′ W) and runs south for ten miles to its mouth on the Colorado River (at 31°15′ N, 98°34′ W). The local terrain is flat with local shallow depressions and is surfaced by clay and sandy loams that support water-tolerant hardwoods, conifers, and grasses.

ELLIS, ALEXANDER CASWELL (1871–1948). A. Caswell Ellis, teacher and reformer, son of Orren Littleberry and Mary Louisa (McKnight) Ellis, was born on May 4, 1871, in Franklin County, North Carolina. He received his B.A. degree in classics at the University of North Carolina in 1894, attended Harvard in the summer of that year, and received his Ph.D. at Clark University in Worcester, Massachusetts, in 1897. He did advanced study at the University of Berlin in 1905.

Ellis joined the University of Texas faculty in 1897 as adjunct professor of pedagogy. From 1908 to 1926 he served as professor of educational philosophy, and he also directed the university's extension services in 1911–13 and 1914–16. In July 1917 he incurred the wrath of Governor James E. Ferguson,qv who directed the board of regents to fire him because he disapproved of Ellis's extension work. Ellis's dismissal was short-lived, however, as continuing differences with the university and other problems resulted in Ferguson's impeachment and resignation. Governor William P. Hobby qv reinstated Ellis in the fall of 1917.

Ellis was a Democrat and a leading spokesman for prohibition and woman suffrage qqv across the state. He worked closely with Texas suffrage leader Minnie Fisher Cunningham,qv and in 1918, when Texas women were allowed to vote in primaries for the first time, he assisted Cunningham and the Texas Equal Suffrage Association qv with financial and political planning in their successful endeavor to elect Annie Webb Blanton qv as state superintendent of public instruction. Ellis also worked in the 1919 campaign for a constitutional amendment to give Texas women full voting rights, by serving as editor of the *Texas Democrat,* a suffrage newspaper circulated during the effort.

In 1926 he moved to Ohio to become director of Cleveland College, a downtown adult-education facility of Case Western Reserve University. The college was started by former University of Texas president Robert E. Vinson,qv who was serving as Western Reserve president when Ellis was hired to run the adult school. Under Ellis's leadership Cleveland College grew from 1,400 students to approximately 7,000. In 1941 he resigned his position, was named director emeritus of the college, and returned to Texas.

In Austin he remained active as a lecturer and consultant. He was appointed adult-education counselor for the University of Texas in 1942, and in 1946 became director of the University Evening College. He also was active in the Texas Society for Mental Hygiene, and in 1946 served as president of the Austin–Travis County Mental Hygiene Society. Ellis was a fellow of the American Association for the Advancement of Science; president of the Association of Deans and Directors of University Evening Colleges in 1940–41; and a member of the Southern Educational Association, the Society for the Scientific Study of Education, the National Education Association, Kappa Alpha, and Phi Beta Kappa. He was author of a number of articles on education and was joint author with E. J. Kyle of *Fundamentals of Farming and Farm Life* (1912). He served as president of the Texas Pecan Association in 1947. He married Mary Heard (*see* ELLIS, MARY HEARD) in July 1901. He died in Austin on October 9, 1948, after suffering from heart disease, and was cremated. His wife established a mental health collection at the Austin Public Library in his memory.

BIBLIOGRAPHY: Austin *American-Statesman*, October 10, 1948. Roy Bedichek, "Dr. Alexander Caswell Ellis: Educator," *Texas Trends* 6 (Spring 1949). Minnie Fisher Cunningham Papers, Houston Metropolitan Research Center, Houston Public Library. Alexander Caswell Ellis Papers, Barker Texas History Center, University of Texas at Austin. Lewis L. Gould, *Progressives and Prohibitionists: Texas Democrats in the Wilson Era* (Austin: University of Texas Press, 1973; rpt., Austin: Texas State Historical Association, 1992). Lewis L. Gould, "The University Becomes Politicized: The War with Jim Ferguson," *Southwestern Historical Quarterly* 86 (October 1982). A. Elizabeth Taylor, *Citizens at Last: The Woman Suffrage Movement in Texas* (Austin: Temple, 1987). Vertical Files, Barker Texas History Center, University of Texas at Austin. *Who's Who in America,* 1946–47.

ELLIS, JOSEPH L. (?–?). Joseph L. Ellis, pioneer settler, was commissioned agent of the Alabama-Coushatta Indians by Sam Houston qv on August 1, 1844, and is known to have served in that capacity as late as 1860. It is believed that he came to Nacogdoches as early as 1835. He was a close friend of the Houston family.

BIBLIOGRAPHY: Nacogdoches Archives, Steen Library, Stephen F. Austin State University; Barker Texas History Center, University of Texas at Austin; Texas State Archives, Austin. Harriet Smither, "The Alabama Indians of Texas," *Southwestern Historical Quarterly* 36 (October 1932). Amelia W. Williams and Eugene C. Barker, eds., *The Writings of Sam Houston, 1813–1863* (8 vols., Austin: University of Texas Press, 1938–43; rpt., Austin and New York: Pemberton Press, 1970).

Jeanne Dibrell

ELLIS, MARY HEARD (1878–1961). Mary Heard Ellis, teacher and social reformer, one of four children of banker W. F. Heard, was born in December 1878 in Cleburne, Texas. She went at age sixteen to the University of Texas, where she received a degree in English. While at the university she met Alexander Caswell Ellis,qv a professor of education, whom she married in July 1901. The Ellises, who had no children, made Austin their home until they moved to Ohio in 1926.

Throughout her life, often working jointly with her husband, Mary Ellis advocated social causes that she believed enhanced individual dignity. She was active in the woman suffrage qv movement in Texas, and in 1918, after Texas women had received the right to vote in primaries, she was a major fund-raiser in Annie Webb Blanton's qv successful campaign for state superintendent of public instruction. In 1918–19 she served as president of the Austin Equal Suffrage Association. Later Mrs. Ellis was a member of the League of Women Voters.

She also taught in Austin public schools, at the University of Texas, and at Cleveland College, Ohio. The latter, the downtown branch of Case Western Reserve University, was an adult-education facility that her husband directed from 1926 to 1941. In addition to her teaching duties there, she was a dean in her husband's administration. In 1927 she received a master's degree from the University of Texas.

After retiring from Cleveland College in 1941, the Ellises returned to Texas. After Alexander's death in 1948, Mary continued the couple's longstanding commitment to mental-health programs by organizing a mental-health collection in Alexander Ellis's memory at the Austin Public Library. To establish the collection she contributed money she had received from the Hogg Foundation for Mental Health,qv as well as books and work. Within ten years the collection included more than 700 books and was widely used.

Mary Ellis served briefly on the Democratic State Executive Committee in 1950. She was also a member of the Travis County Democratic Women's Association, the Hogg Foundation, and the Texas Society for Mental Hygiene. She died in Austin on Nov. 21, 1961.

BIBLIOGRAPHY: Austin *American*, November 22, 1961. Austin *American-Statesman*, April 6, 1958. Vertical Files, Barker Texas History Center, University of Texas at Austin (Ellis, Alexander Caswell). Vertical Files, Austin History Center.

Debbie Mauldin Cottrell

ELLIS, OSCAR BYRON (1902–1961). Oscar Byron Ellis, prison administrator, was born in Oneonta, Alabama, on August 27, 1902, the son of school superintendent John Wesley Ellis. He lived at Cleveland, Alabama, during his youth and graduated from Birmingham Southern College with a B.S. degree in chemistry in 1924, the year he married Gertrude Tidwell. After graduating, Ellis worked as manager of a Florsheim shoe store in Memphis, Tennessee, for a brief period and later taught science and coached football at a high school there. By 1928 he was business manager of the Memphis schools. He was elected a commissioner of Shelby County, Tennessee, in 1937 and served as commission secretary and commissioner of the Shelby County Penal Farm and of county roads and bridges. He attracted national attention for his supervision of prisoners and his efficient man-

O. B. Ellis, late 1950s. Courtesy Mrs. Byron W. Frierson, Sugar Land. Appointed general manager of the Texas prisons in hopes that he could reform a system plagued by problems, Ellis traveled as many as 4,600 miles every month to visit prison facilities and did indeed enact some important reforms.

agement of the demonstration farm, designed to promote better agricultural practices for farmers in the region.

Ellis served in Texas as general manager of the prison system qv from January 1, 1948, until November 12, 1961. The Texas legislature enacted a law in 1957 that changed his title to director and the name of the state penal institution to Texas Department of Corrections. The Texas Prison Board recruited Ellis to reform an agency plagued by mismanagement, brutal disciplinary practices, harsh working conditions, poor living standards, and large numbers of escapes during World War II qv and afterward. From 1949 through 1961 Ellis, in cooperation with governors Beauford H. Jester, Allan Shivers, and Price Daniel, Sr.,qqv persuaded the legislature to appropriate $19 million for capital improvements. Using those funds, as well as revenues derived from the sale of prison agricultural and industrial products, the "Ellis Plan" resulted in new building projects at the Texas State Penitentiary at Huntsville qv and on the more than 73,000 acres of prison lands. During Ellis's administration the state constructed cell blocks to replace many of the prisoners' dormitories or "tanks" and built fences, picket towers, workshops, and other facilities at the eleven units of the prison system. Ellis reduced prison food and clothing purchases through reorganized agricultural and industrial methods that enabled prisoners to produce most of the food they consumed and most of the clothing they wore. Under the direction of Byron W. Frierson, assistant general manager for agriculture, the Ellis administration consolidated the various prison farms into a single unit, adopted modern drainage techniques for low-lying properties, placed thousands of acres in soil-conservation districts, improved the prison beef and dairy herds, and mechanized farming operations by replacing mules with tractors. With a labor force that increased from slightly fewer than 6,000 to nearly 12,000 prisoners between 1948 and 1961, Ellis held operating expenses well below the national average, as inmates performed agricultural, construction, and some industrial work.

He expanded educational, recreational, and religious programs and revamped prisoner-classification procedures in order to segregate individuals according to such factors as age, offense, and rehabilitation potential. His administration saw a sharp decline in escapes. Ellis virtually ended the practice of self-mutilation among inmates by refusing to transfer prisoners from the farms to hospitals when they intentionally injured themselves to avoid labor. He raised living standards through his building program and placed televisions in dormitories as a means of enhancing morale. He fired many brutal and corrupt prison employees and persuaded the legislature to raise guards' salaries. He also worked with members of the press to win support for his administration and avoid unfavorable publicity. His monthly automobile travel to prison facilities often totaled as much as 4,600 miles; "you can't run the prison system from a desk," he observed. Austin MacCormick, perhaps the most renowned penal expert in the United States, praised Ellis and commended him for elevating Texas prisons from among the nation's worst to among the best. The American Correctional Association elected Ellis president for the 1958–59 term; he was the first person from a state south of Virginia to occupy that position.

Though Ellis voiced his opposition to abusive treatment of prisoners by his employees, some criminal-justice scholars have characterized the supervisory methods of his administration as "repressive," "paternalistic," and "idiosyncratic." Those methods involved psychological and physical force exercised at the discretion of individual guards. Though Ellis criticized the use of inmates for the supervision of other prisoners, he allowed the practice to expand during his regime. Subsequent prison administrations continued the disciplinary tactics systematized during the Ellis years. In 1980, in the case of *Ruiz v. Estelle,* federal judge William Wayne Justice ordered the end of the inmate guard practice and issued other rulings intended to replace traditional control methods with more modern bureaucratic and legalistic procedures.

Ellis suffered critical injuries in an automobile crash in January 1957 but survived and returned to work six weeks later. Some observers believe, however, that he never completely regained his health. Ellis was a Methodist; he and his wife had one child, a son. Ellis died of a heart attack on November 12, 1961, in Houston, at a dinner on the eve of a scheduled prison-board meeting. He was buried in Huntsville. The state of Texas honored him by naming a new prison facility for him. The Ellis Unit, located north of Huntsville, opened in 1963.

BIBLIOGRAPHY: George John Beto Papers, Gresham Library, Sam Houston State University. Ronald Craig Copeland, The Evolution of the Texas Department of Corrections (M.A. thesis, Sam Houston State University, 1980). Ben M. Crouch and James W. Marquart, *An Appeal to Justice: Litigated Reform of Texas Prisons* (Austin: University of Texas Press, 1989). Price Daniel Papers, Sam Houston Regional Library and Research Center, Liberty, Texas. T. R. Havins Papers, Barker Texas History Center, University of Texas at Austin. Vertical Files, Barker Texas History Center, University of Texas at Austin.

Paul M. Lucko

ELLIS, RICHARD (1781–1846). Richard Ellis, planter, jurist, and legislator, son of Ambrose and Cecilia (Stokes) Ellis, was born in the

"Tidewater Section" (probably Lunenburg County) of Virginia, on February 14, 1781. After a common-school education he possibly attended college, but no record of attendance has survived. In any event, he studied law with the Richmond firm of Wirt and Wickham until 1806, when he was admitted to the Virginia bar and joined that law firm. Sometime between 1813 and 1817 Ellis left Virginia and settled at Huntsville, Madison County, and later at Tuscumbia, Franklin County, Alabama, where he established a plantation and continued the practice of law. Then, in 1818, he was elected one of two delegates to represent Franklin County at the Alabama Constitutional Convention. The next year saw him elected a judge of the Fourth Circuit Court of Alabama, an election that automatically made him an associate justice of the Alabama Supreme Court. During his tenure on the bench, Ellis had a reputation for firm administration and a rough manner that made him unpopular with the other members of the bar. In 1829 he helped to found and served on the first board of trustees of La Grange College in Franklin County, Alabama. The college had a Methodist connection, which may indicate that Ellis was a Methodist.

Ellis made his first trip to Texas in 1826 not as a colonist but in a futile effort to collect a debt from a Colonel Pettus. In December Stephen F. Austin qv induced him, along with James Kerr and James Cummings,qqv to go to Nacogdoches in an unsuccessful effort to persuade Haden Edwards qv to abandon his revolt against the Mexican government. It was not until February 22, 1834, that Ellis moved his family and more than twenty-five slaves to Pecan Point in the disputed territory claimed by Mexico as part of Old Red River County and by the United States as part of Miller County, Arkansas. Ellis's land grant of 4,428.4 acres (one league and one labor) was located near Spanish Bluff in what became Bowie County, Texas. He established a considerable cotton plantation there and entertained lavishly at his elegant home.

Late in 1835 he was chosen by Miller and Sevier counties as a delegate to the Arkansas constitutional convention scheduled to meet at Little Rock on January 4, 1836. Ill health forced him to decline, and he resigned his seat by January 21, 1836. Near the end of the month he was selected as one of five delegates from around Pecan Point to the Texas constitutional convention scheduled to meet at Washington-on-the-Brazos on March 1, 1836 (*see* CONVENTION OF 1836).

As the convention opened Ellis was unanimously elected president. On March 2, 1836, he signed the Texas Declaration of Independenceqv as president of the convention. Although some observers were critical of him as a presiding officer, the general verdict is that he had a good grasp of parliamentary procedure and that he presided with a remarkable degree of gentleness and urbanity. Most importantly, he held the convention together for the seventeen days needed to draft a constitution for the Republic of Texas.qv Between October 3, 1836, when he was first elected, and February 5, 1840, when he retired from public life, Ellis represented his district as a senator in the First, Second, Third, and Fourth congresses of the Republic of Texas.

On January 9, 1806, he married Mary West Dandridge, daughter of Nathaniel West and Sarah (Watson) Dandridge of Hanover County, Virginia. The bride was a second cousin of Martha Custis Washington and a first cousin of Dolly Madison. Richard and Mary Ellis had at least two children. An obituary printed in the Clarksville *Northern Standard* (*see* CLARKSVILLE STANDARD) reports that Ellis died at his home in Bowie County on December 20, 1846, at age sixty-five and states, "Judge Ellis came to his death suddenly by his clothes taking fire." He was buried in the family cemetery near New Boston, Texas, but in 1929 his remains and those of his wife, who died on October 20, 1837, were transferred to the State Cemeteryqv in Austin. A son, Nathaniel Dandridge Ellis, also settled in Old Red River County and was granted a league and labor of land as the head of a household. Ellis County, formed in 1849, most probably was named in Richard Ellis's honor.

BIBLIOGRAPHY: Sam Houston Dixon, *Men Who Made Texas Free* (Houston: Texas Historical Publishing, 1924). Louis Wiltz Kemp, *The Signers of the Texas Declaration of Independence* (Salado, Texas: Anson Jones, 1944; rpt. 1959). Rupert N. Richardson, "Framing the Constitution of the Republic of Texas," *Southwestern Historical Quarterly* 31 (January 1928). Gifford E. White, ed., *First Settlers of Red River County* (St. Louis: Ingmire, 1981).

Joe E. Ericson

ELLIS, WILLIAM H. (?–?) William H. Ellis was a San Antonio businessman who became active in the African-American emigration movement of the 1890s and early 1900s. He was well educated and spoke several languages. In 1889 he advocated the establishment of a black colony in Mexico with the object of raising cotton and coffee. In 1894, with the support of a group of Anglo and Mexican entrepreneurs, he received a grant from the Mexican government in which he promised to colonize as many as 10,000 black Americans in the area of Tlahualilo, Durango, Mexico. Previously in the nineteenth century, the predominant interest in the movement had centered around black nationalist Henry M. Turner, a bishop in the African Methodist Episcopal Churchqv who advocated emigration to Africa. At a national convention called by Bishop Turner in 1893, ostensibly to discuss African emigration, Ellis's Mexican colonization proposal gained support as a less expensive alternative. Ellis signed a contract with a well-known black Atlanta emigration agent, R. A. "Pegleg" Williams, to supply 5,000 black laborers by the end of 1895. In February 1895, concentrating their recruitment efforts in Alabama, Ellis and Williams transported the first and only consignments of 816 Alabama emigrants, including 145 families, to Mexico. Before further transfers could take place, the company decided to halt emigration for twelve months to determine if the colony would be profitable.

From the beginning, controversy, often encouraged by the Southern press, surrounded the colony. In early March, Williams returned to the United States and accused Ellis of not providing the housing, rations, and supplies promised the emigrants. The San Antonio *Express* reported on March 24, 1895, that several colonists, who had walked back across Mexico to the United States, reported that the colony was rapidly dissolving. Other newspapers in Alabama and Texas reported widespread mistreatment, starvation, and death of colonists. Ellis denied the criticism of the Southern press, refuted reports of deaths, and asked the State Department for an investigation. The investigation found the situation similar to that of Mexican workers, "but not as good as is received in [the emigrants'] own States." The report stated that Ellis had failed to provide the proper food and medical service required for the colony, but could not substantiate many of the accusations levied against him in the newspapers. The colony itself dissolved, and the United States paid for the colonists' return. Ellis, who went back to San Antonio, met with King Menelek of Ethiopia in 1903 in an effort to establish an Ethiopian emigrant colony.

BIBLIOGRAPHY: Edwin S. Redkey, *Black Exodus: Black Nationalist and Back-to-Africa Movements, 1890–1910* (New Haven: Yale University Press, 1969). Alfred W. Reynolds, "The Alabama Negro Colony in Mexico, 1894–1896," *Alabama Review* 5–6 (October 1952, January 1953).

Douglas Hales

ELLIS CHAPEL, TEXAS. Ellis Chapel was just south of Farm Road 1395 and twelve miles northwest of Canton in northwestern Van Zandt County. It had a school in 1890 that reached an enrollment of fifty-one in 1905. In 1917 Ellis Chapel merged with Woodall to form Elwood. A cemetery was still shown at the site on county highway maps in the late 1980s.

Diana J. Kleiner

ELLIS COUNTY. Ellis County (E–18) is located in north central Texas. Waxahachie, the largest town and county seat, is on Interstate Highway 35E thirty miles south of Dallas. The county is bounded by Dallas County to the north, Kaufman to the east, Navarro and Hill counties to the south, and Johnson county to the west. The center point of the county is at 32°21′ north latitude and 96°48′ west longitude. Ellis County comprises 939 square miles of the Blackland Prairie. Away from the streams it is almost treeless except for scattered mesquite, cacti, and shrubs. Native vegetation consists mainly of bunch and short grasses, including Indian, buffalo, grama, big and little bluestems, and three-awn. Such native trees as ash, cottonwood, pecan, hackberry, bois d'arc, oak, and elm grow along watercourses. The terrain is level to rolling, with an elevation ranging from 300 to 700 feet above sea level. The area lies in a southeastward-sloping plain and is well drained by many streams that flow into the Trinity River, which forms the eastern boundary of the county. Red Oak, Waxahachie, Mill, and Chambers creeks drain most of the county. The Austin Escarpment, a high chalk ridge, extends in a northeast–southwest direction and cuts off drainage to the southeast. Mountain Creek flows northeast and drains the northwestern part of the county. The soils—predominantly calcareous, marly and variegated clays and clay loams—have average to good moisture retention and are underlain by a water supply sufficient for livestock, irrigation, and domestic purposes. The alluvial soils are mainly clay. Mineral resources include gas, oil, stone, and clays valuable for brickmaking. Chalk and shale provide material for the manufacture of cement. Temperatures range from an average low of 35° F in January to an average high of 96° in July, rainfall averages slightly less than thirty-six inches a year, and the growing season extends for 245 days.

Tonkawa Indians were the earliest inhabitants of the future county, though parties of Wacos, Bidais, Anadarkos, and Kickapoos often hunted in the area. Spanish missionaries worked with the Tonkawas, and as the American settlers began to move into the region in the middle of the nineteenth century, the Indians offered little organized resistance. By 1859 the Tonkawas had been removed to Oklahoma. Before the Texas Revolution[qv] in 1836, the Mexican government granted land in what is now Ellis County to Thomas J. Chambers,[qv] Rafael Peña, and Alejandro de la Garza. In 1841 and 1842 the Republic of Texas[qv] granted land to William S. Peters[qv] in the northern half of the county, and Charles Fenton Mercer[qv] received a grant in 1843 in the southern part. One of the first settlers in the area was William R. Howe, who settled late in 1843 near the site of present Forreston. Howe immigrated under the Peters colony[qv] project and reportedly brought in a black woman thought to be the first slave in the county. The Southerland Mayfield family settled at Reagor Springs in February 1844, and the Billingsly family located near Ovilla later that year.

Acting on a bill sponsored by Gen. Edward H. Tarrant,[qv] the state legislature officially established Ellis County on December 20, 1849. It was drawn from Navarro County, organized in February of the following year, and probably named for Richard Ellis,[qv] president of the Convention of 1836.[qv] Waxahachie was named the county seat and established on land donated by E. W. Rogers in August 1850. William Hawkins was the first chief justice (county judge). Judge Oran Milo Roberts[qv] presided over the first term of the Ellis County district court during the fall of 1850. A boundary dispute with Johnson County was temporarily settled during Reconstruction,[qv] when Ellis County ceded nearly 100 square miles of land. The argument resurfaced in the late 1880s and was finally peaceably settled by a new survey of the line in 1939.

The early settlers of Ellis County came predominantly from the southern part of the United States, bringing their farming methods and their slaves. During the 1850s the slave population of the county increased more than twelvefold, to 1,104 in 1860, while the white population quadrupled to just more than 4,000. A number of Czechs[qv] (Bohemians), Hungarians, and Germans[qv] settled in the county during the 1850s. The most profitable business was cattle raising because of the mild climate and the native grasses covering the fertile prairies. The first settlers generally took land along the streams and raised some small grains to use at home or to trade for lumber in East Texas. Small amounts of cotton were raised and transported to Houston or Shreveport by ox teams.

Ellis County found itself deeply embroiled in the secession[qv] crisis. Waxahachie citizens formed a chapter of the Knights of the Golden Circle,[qv] and in the fall of 1860 rumors of slave insurrections[qv] in Waxahachie and in nearby communities led to the lynching[qv] of a number of blacks and allegedly antislavery whites. In January 1861 A. B. Bradshaw and T. C. Neel represented Ellis County at the state Secession Convention[qv] in Austin. The following month the citizens of the county overwhelmingly supported secession. When William H. Parsons[qv] was instructed to raise a cavalry regiment, volunteers from Ellis County formed companies E, F, and H of the Twelfth Texas Cavalry, Parsons's Brigade.[qv] When the Nineteenth Regiment of Texas Cavalry was formed, Ellis County men formed companies A and C. The Confederate government operated a powder mill in Waxahachie and a hat factory near the site of present Italy during the Civil War.[qv]

White residents deeply resented Reconstruction,[qv] which was marked by Union army occupation, emancipation and enfranchisement of blacks, and Republican politicians. Even before the Democratic party[qv] regained control of the political machinery of the state in 1874 Ellis County voted Democratic in national elections. The county voted solidly Democratic in all presidential elections from Reconstruction through the 1960s, though in 1948 the votes were too late to be counted. From 1972 through 1992, however, Ellis County returned Republican majorities in five out of six presidential races, with James E. Carter being the Democratic exception in 1976. Ellis County grew much in the 1870s. In 1868 J. W. Ferris and W. H. Getzendaner opened a bank that played a vital role in the development of the county's resources. The area began the change from a cattle range to an agricultural region in 1872 with the coming of the Houston and Texas Central Railroad. After the Panic of 1873 the heavy immigration from the Old South cotton areas prepared the country for its future leadership in cotton culture.[qv] The population almost tripled, growing from 7,514 in 1870 to 21,294 in 1880. Cotton production increased sixfold by the end of the decade, when it amounted to 18,956 bales. From 1855, when Rev. Michael Dickson organized the first county school at Milford, the residents of Ellis County were interested in education. During the postbellum period, most county schools were considered semiprivate because students paid some tuition in conjunction with a small supplement of state funds. Marvin College in Waxahachie opened in 1870 and made a significant contribution to the growth of the county.

Ellis County continued to be agricultural and rural from 1880 to 1930. The population grew quite rapidly in the closing decades of the nineteenth century, to 50,059 in 1900, and increased more slowly thereafter to 55,700 in 1920. A slow decline set in by 1930, when the population was 53,936. The black population grew more rapidly than the white, as African Americans[qv] increased to almost one-fourth of the county population in 1930. The number of farms in the county rose from 2,884 in 1880 to about 6,000 in 1900, and stayed at that level through 1930, when it reached an all-time high of 6,082. By 1900 the average farm included 87.5 acres, down more than thirty acres during the previous two decades. Cotton became the leading money crop as land was fenced with barbed wire,[qv] herds were sold or driven farther west, and small grains lost acreage to cotton. Ellis County produced 91,298 bales at the turn of the century and in the early twentieth century was recognized as one of the leading cotton-growing areas in the United States. Agricultural growth did not necessarily bring prosperity to county farmers, however, as the percentage of tenants increased to 70 percent by 1900 and almost 82 percent by 1930. Though Ellis County had better than average transportation facilities for north central Texas, its nonagricultural economy expanded slowly from 1880 to 1930. Seven railroad companies built track in the county before 1910, including the Missouri, Kansas and Texas, the Fort Worth and New Orleans, and the Trinity and Brazos. Two electric railway lines were also built by the Texas Electric Railway Company around the time of World War I.[qv] The two earliest roads were stage roads leading from Dallas to Waco and Dallas to Corsicana. By 1892, after some lobbying in the county seat, a substantial number of iron truss bridges were built over Ellis County creeks. Ellis County developed in other ways as well around the turn of the century. Texas Presbyterian College, a school for girls in Milford, served the county before it was consolidated with Austin College in 1929. Trinity University, founded at Tehuacana during Reconstruction, moved to Waxahachie in 1902. In 1887 Ellis County sponsored its first county fair, an event that was held intermittently until World War II. Southwestern Telephone Company introduced telephone service into Waxahachie by 1883. The first efforts to bring electricity to the county started in 1887. Waxahachie Electric Light Company was established in 1890 and provided limited service. In 1913 and 1914 Texas Power and Light Company constructed a high-voltage transmission line, with substations in six Ellis County towns. The county had 203 industrial establishments at the turn of the century, more than at any time before the mid-twentieth century.

The 1930s and 1940s marked the beginning of changes in Ellis County at least as important as those brought on by the Civil War and the coming of the railroad. The Great Depression[qv] drastically affected the county. There were more than 2,100 fewer farms in 1940 than in 1930, a trend that continued into the 1980s. In the same period the value of farm property fell 42 percent. Unemployment became a problem. In 1935, 3,054 workers were on government relief in Ellis County. The unemployment rate jumped from 6.9 percent to 16 percent between 1930 and 1940. In the latter year 1,026 workers were employed on public emergency works, and another 1,747 were looking for work. The number of pupils enrolled in the county public schools declined 18 percent during the decade. Farmers began to replace their farm animals with tractors, and the average farm size increased. The cotton crop was reduced by soil erosion and acreage controls. Increasing acreage was used for other crops, particularly small grains. Though World War II ended the depression, the trends begun in 1930 lasted for another forty years. County population fell to 47,753 in 1940 and to a twentieth-century low of 43,395 in 1960. In 1940 Ellis County was 48 percent urban after the decline of its farms in the previous decade. Two years later Trinity University moved from Waxahachie to San Antonio. A Southwestern Assemblies of God school did, however, move into Waxahachie in 1943. By 1950 more than half the county residents lived in urban areas.

As Ellis County suffered an agricultural decline and a population loss from 1930 into the 1960s, other developments indicated recovery. Since many of the area soils were damaged before World War II, soil-conservation districts were established in the 1940s to improve the agricultural output of the county. The automobile revolutionized transportation and necessitated improved roads. Ellis County had only 10,823 motor vehicles registered in 1938. By 1969 the total was 18,493. All major roads in the county were paved by 1948. By 1970 Interstate 45 and Interstate 35E were completed through the county. The Rural Electrification[qv] Administration brought electricity to the rural residences and farms in the county. The Brazos Electric Power Cooperative began its service in 1941. By 1954, 95 percent of the farms in the county had electricity. Educational advances were also evident. In 1950 only 21 percent of those aged twenty-five or older were high school graduates. By 1970 this figure had risen to 41 percent. Oil was discovered in 1953. Maize acreage overtook that of cotton, and ranches took the place of many small farms. Developments in Ellis County during the 1960s and 1970s suggested that the downward trend of the preceding decades was being halted or reversed. The county population began to increase again in the 1960s, reaching 46,638 in 1970, when the number of blacks had declined to 8,593, or some 18 percent of the whole. The population reached a new high of 59,743 in 1980, when black residents constituted 12 percent of the whole and Hispanics had risen to 10 percent. The decrease in the number of farms slowed, while agricultural property value rose to more than $275 million. All types of nonagricultural economic activities made gains. Establishments dealing in oil and gas, contract construction, manufacturing, transportation and public utilities, and wholesale trade more than doubled between 1970 and 1983. The growth of Waxahachie and the increasing development along Interstate 35E suggested a trend toward significant commercial county development. Educational advances continued; a majority of residents twenty-five or older were high school graduates in 1980.

In 1990 the Ellis County economy showed a balance between varied manufacturing, agribusiness, and commerce. The county population was 85,167. For the first time Hispanic residents formed a higher percentage (13.2) of the county population than blacks (10 percent). More than a third of the county's residents lived in the two largest communities, Waxahachie (18,168) and Ennis (13,883). Many county residents were employed in Dallas, and the growth of such communities as Midlothian (5,141), Red Oak (3,124), Ferris (2,212), and Ovilla (1,748 in Ellis County) demonstrated how county development had become tied to the Dallas–Fort Worth economy. Cultural events in the county included Scarbrough Faire, the National Polka Festival at Ennis, and the Gingerbread Trail homes tour, and the county continued to exhibit an extensive interest in historical preservation.

In 1989 Ellis County was chosen as the site for the Superconducting Supercollider, a planned fifty-mile tunnel in which electrically charged protons would be accelerated for collision experiments. Ellis County residents exulted at the prospect of a burst of prosperity. The Texas National Research Laboratory Commission[qv] oversaw the purchase of almost 17,000 acres of land and began to construct facilities west of Waxahachie. But opposition to the project in Congress, resulting from charges that it was "pork" for Texas and from uncertainty about the value to be derived from a supercollider, resulted in the defunding of "Super Clyde" in 1993. At that point some 20 percent of the project had been completed, including fourteen miles of tunnel, a magnet-development complex, the supercollider central facility, and the linear accelerator. At its peak the project had employed some 2,100 people at the Ellis County site. In the mid-1990s what to do with the existing facilities was still under discussion.

BIBLIOGRAPHY: Helen G. Goodlett, Settlement and Development of Ellis County, Texas, 1849–1860 (M.A. thesis, University of Colorado, 1933). Edna Davis Hawkins et al., *History of Ellis County, Texas* (Waco: Texian, 1972). *Memorial and Biographical History of Ellis County* (Chicago: Lewis, 1892; rpt., as *Ellis County History,* Fort Worth: Historical Publishers, 1972).
Robert J. Haaser

ELLISON CREEK RESERVOIR. Ellison Creek Reservoir is just west of Lone Star in southern Morris County (at 32°55′ N, 94°44′ W). Its dam is a rolled-earth structure 4,000 feet long, with a maximum height of 48½ feet. The impounded water comes primarily from Ellison Creek, also known as Brutons Creek. The surface area of the reservoir is 1,516 acres at the service spillway crest at elevation 268.1 feet above mean sea level. Its capacity is 24,700 acre-feet. The drainage area of the Ellison Creek watershed is thirty-seven square miles. The reservoir dam was constructed by the United States Defense Plant in 1942–43 and acquired by the Lone Star Steel Company in 1947. The company uses reservoir water for plant tasks such as ore washing. The reservoir is also the site of a power plant constructed and operated by the Southwest Gas and Electric Company.

BIBLIOGRAPHY: C. L. Dowell, *Dams and Reservoirs in Texas: History and Descriptive Information* (Texas Water Commission Bulletin 6408 [Austin, 1964]). Thomas C. Minter, A History of Morris County (M.A. thesis, East Texas State Teachers' College, 1952).
James R. Niendorff

ELLISON RIDGE, TEXAS. Ellison Ridge was near Farm Road 486 four miles northeast of Thorndale in southwestern Milam County. It was named for R. Ellison and had a one-teacher school with twenty-eight white students and a one-teacher school with forty-four black students in 1903. A school and a few scattered houses were shown at the site on county highway maps in 1941. The Ellison Ridge schools were consolidated with the Thorndale Independent School District in

1946. By 1988 no evidence of the community appeared on county highway maps.

BIBLIOGRAPHY: Lelia M. Batte, *History of Milam County, Texas* (San Antonio: Naylor, 1956). Milam County Heritage and Preservation Society, *Matchless Milam: History of Milam County* (Dallas: Taylor, 1984).
Vivian Elizabeth Smyrl

ELLISON SPRING BRANCH. Ellison Spring Branch rises two miles north of Gorman in southeastern Eastland County (at 32°14′ N, 98°40′ W) and runs east for six miles to its mouth on the Leon River, four miles northeast of Gorman (at 32°15′ N, 98°36′ W). In its upper reaches the stream traverses an area of steep-sloped terrain surfaced by shallow sandy soils that support juniper, grasses, and scattered oak. In its lower reaches it passes through steeply to moderately sloping hills, surfaced by shallow stony clay and sandy loams that support oak, mesquite, and grasses. It is probably named for J. M. Ellison, who had an early land grant in the area through which it flows. In 1864 the Ellison Springs Indian Fight took place near the headwaters of the creek.

ELLISON SPRINGS, TEXAS. Ellison Springs was off Farm Road 8 four miles northwest of Gorman in southeastern Eastland County. It was named for the perpetual springs that flowed from a nearby stone ledge, themselves named for the first settler on the site, James Madison Ellison, who built a cabin by the springs in 1858. In August 1864 Ellison and other ranchers fought a skirmish with Indian raiders near the site. Brush-arbor camp meetings were held by the springs in the 1870s, and about 1876 a Baptist church was built and a cemetery was begun in the community. The community had a number of scattered dwellings in 1940, but only the Ellison Springs Cemetery remained on the site by 1968.

BIBLIOGRAPHY: Edwin T. Cox, *History of Eastland County, Texas* (San Antonio: Naylor, 1950). Eastland County Historical Book Committee, *Gateway to the West: Eastland County History*, Vol. 1 (Eastland, Texas, 1989).
Mark Odintz

ELLISON SPRINGS INDIAN FIGHT. The Ellison Springs Indian Fight took place on August 9, 1864, near Ellison Springs in Eastland County, in Maj. George Bernard Erath's[qv] Second Frontier District. It was typical of the kind of small-unit actions that occurred on the frontier during the Civil War.[qv] Lt. Singleton Gilbert was in command of citizens of Eastland, Callahan, and Shackelford counties, who formed a company stationed at Nash Springs, three miles northwest of the site of present-day Gorman. On August 8, 1864, he sent out a squad of eight men, led by Cpl. James L. Head; they left camp for a ten-day scouting foray and the next morning came upon fresh Indian signs between the sites of future Cisco and Eastland. Moving southward, they followed a trail made by an estimated thirty to fifty Indians for more than twenty miles before overtaking the party at a ranch several miles west of Gorman, near Ellison Springs. Head promptly retreated to the Gilbert ranch, a few miles away, to where Gilbert brought recruits. Gilbert's arrival provided a force totaling twelve to sixteen troopers to face thirty to thirty-five Indians. Gilbert ordered a frontal assault against the Indians, a number of whom were on foot carrying blankets and bridles to be used on the horses they planned to steal. The charge fell back before a withering fire that killed Gilbert and two other Texans, wounded three more, and left no Indian casualties. The Indians left the field unimpeded by the Texans. This was the only unsuccessful Indian engagement of the summer for Erath's command. The Texans continued to trail the Indians, however, and managed to recover eighteen horses out of approximately fifty that the Indians stole near Stephenville. Several days after the Eastland County men ended their pursuit, Sgt. A. D. Miller, whose eight-man squad was due north of Eastland in Stephens County, came upon a party of at least twenty Indians northwest. These were probably the main body of the party attacked earlier by Gilbert's men. Miller followed the trail for fifteen miles, overtook the Indians, and attacked. In a one-hour battle, with no loss to themselves, Miller's men killed two Indians, wounded three, and captured seventy-three horses, seven saddles, and an assortment of bridles and blankets, thus bringing to a close the brief campaign that began in Eastland County.

BIBLIOGRAPHY: Charles Goodnight et al., eds., *Pioneer Days in the Southwest from 1850 to 1879* (2d ed., Guthrie, Oklahoma: State Capitol, 1909). Carolyne Lavinia Langston, *History of Eastland County* (Dallas: Aldridge 1904). Joseph Carroll McConnell, *West Texas Frontier* (Vol. 1, Jacksboro, Texas, 1933; Vol. 2, Palo Pinto, Texas, 1939).
David Paul Smith

ELLWOOD, ISAAC L. (1833–1910). Isaac L. Ellwood, rancher and barbed wire[qv] manufacturer, was born in Springfield Hollow, New York, on August 12, 1833. As a boy he exhibited the initiative and enterprise that made him one of America's great businessmen by selling sauerkraut to barge hands on the Erie Canal. In 1851 he followed the gold rush to California, from where he returned in 1855 with a capital of nearly $3,000, with which he opened a hardware and implement store in DeKalb, Illinois. There he married Harriet Augusta Miller on January 27, 1859. The couple had six children. Ellwood acquired several farm properties around DeKalb and after the Civil War[qv] began importing and breeding Percheron draft horses.

His interest in farming directed his attention to the need for a fencing material that would contain livestock. He patented a type of barbed wire but concluded that the wire patented by Joseph F. Glidden was more practical. With Glidden, Ellwood formed the I. L. Ellwood Manufacturing Company in 1873 and began producing a two-strand, twisted barbed wire in a back room of his hardware store. Success was almost immediate, for the Glidden-Ellwood wire fulfilled a practical need, especially for ranchers on the western plains. In 1881 the company expanded and reorganized as the Superior Barbed Wire Company, and in 1898 it merged into the American Steel and Wire Company, a predecessor of United States Steel.

In the meantime Ellwood became interested in ranching. He made a trip to Texas in 1889 and purchased the Renderbrook Ranch of some 130,000 acres in Mitchell County from John W. and Dudley H. Snyder,[qqv] for which Ellwood adopted the Spade brand. In 1891 he acquired an additional 128,000 acres northwest of Lubbock from the Snyder brothers. He added 45,000 acres in 1902 and additional acreage in 1906 to bring the total size of his ranch, which was known as the Spade Ranch,[qv] to 265,000 acres, thereby increasing his total Texas holdings to 395,000 acres. After the merger with American Steel and Wire, Ellwood focused on his Texas ranches, although his home remained in DeKalb, where he had other investments. He died in DeKalb, Illinois, on September 11, 1910.

BIBLIOGRAPHY: Seymour V. Connor, ed., *Builders of the Southwest* (Lubbock: Southwest Collection, Texas Technological College, 1959).
Seymour V. Connor

ELM, TEXAS (Karnes County). Elm, also called Seale's Chapel, in the extreme northeastern corner of Karnes County, was named for nearby Elm Creek. It had a post office from 1898 to 1911. Neal Bowen, father-in-law of John Wesley Hardin,[qv] ran a small grocery there, and the community also eventually had a cotton gin. The place declined after the Galveston, Harrisburg and San Antonio Railway was extended from Stockdale to Cuero in 1905, and Nixon was established in 1906. Highway maps in the early 1980s named Elm and showed a cemetery at the site.

BIBLIOGRAPHY: Robert H. Thonhoff, History of Karnes County (M.A. thesis, Southwest Texas State College, 1963).
Robert H. Thonhoff

ELM, TEXAS (Limestone County). Elm, in western Limestone County, was probably established in the late 1860s or early 1870s by former slaves from nearby farms. A small school served as the main focus of the community. No evidence of Elm appeared on county maps by the 1940s.

BIBLIOGRAPHY: Walter F. Cotton, *History of Negroes of Limestone County from 1860 to 1939* (Mexia, Texas: Chatman and Merriwether, 1939).
Vivian Elizabeth Smyrl

ELM, TEXAS (Rains County). Elm, on Farm Road 514 seven miles northeast of Emory in northeastern Rains County, was first formed around the time of the Civil War.qv It had a school that had an enrollment of twenty-nine in 1904. In the mid-1930s the settlement had a school, a church, and a number of scattered dwellings. After World War II qv the school closed, and in the early 1990s only a church and cemetery remained at the site.
Christopher Long

ELMATON, TEXAS. Elmaton is at the junction of Farm Road 1095 and the Missouri Pacific Railroad, twelve miles southwest of Bay City in western Matagorda County. By 1915 it had its own post office, which was still listed in 1929. In 1934 Elmaton became a stop on the St. Louis, Brownsville and Mexico Railway, which in 1956 became the Missouri Pacific. In 1936 the community had two businesses, a factory, twenty widely scattered dwellings, and a reported population of 150. From 1939 until 1943 Elmaton had seven businesses and a population of 150. By 1949 it had become part of the Tidehaven Independent School District in Tres Palacios. In 1988 and 1990 an estimated population of 165 was reported in Elmaton, but no businesses were registered.

BIBLIOGRAPHY: Matagorda County Historical Commission, *Historic Matagorda County* (3 vols., 1986–88).
Stephen L. Hardin

ELM BAYOU. Elm Bayou, which is intermittent in its upper reaches, rises five miles west of Stowell in eastern Chambers County (at 29°47′ N, 94°28′ W) and runs south for seventeen miles to its mouth on East Bay Bayou, four miles north of High Island (at 29°38′ N, 94°25′ W). Part of the lower third of Elm Bayou also forms Stanolind Reservoir. Most of the bayou's course is through prairie grassland, and its lower reaches serve as an important habitat for waterfowl of the upper Texas coast.

ELM CREEK (Atascosa County). Elm Creek, also known as Chiquihuitilla Creek, rises three miles east of Poteet in southeastern Atascosa County (at 29°03′ N, 98°33′ W) and runs southeast for 2½ miles to its mouth on the Atascosa River, just north of Pleasanton (at 29°01′ N, 98°31′ W). The local terrain, some of which serves as dry cropland, is flat to rolling with locally active dune blowout areas. Bunch grasses grow in the sand along the creek banks. *Chiquihuitilla*, the creek's original name, is Spanish for "very small."

BIBLIOGRAPHY: Margaret G. Clover, The Place Names of Atascosa County (M.A. thesis, University of Texas, 1952).

_____ (Atascosa County). Elm Creek rises eight miles northwest of Charlotte in western Atascosa County (at 28°59′ N, 98°48′ W) and runs south for three miles to its mouth on Lagunillas Creek, where the creek intersects with Farm Road 1549 (at 28°55′ N, 98°46′ W). The local terrain, some of which is used as dry cropland, is low-rolling to flat and surfaced by sandy and clay loams that support scrub brush, cacti, and grasses.

_____ (Bastrop County). Elm Creek rises where Upper and Lower Elm creeks meet, east of Bateman in southwestern Bastrop County (at 29°57′ N, 97°28′ W), and runs northeast for 4½ miles to its mouth on Walnut Creek (at 29°59′ N, 97°30′ W). It traverses an upland region with loamy surface soils and post oak woods.

_____ (Bastrop County). Elm Creek rises three miles north of Elgin in northern Bastrop County (at 30°23′ N, 97°22′ W) and runs southwest for seven miles to its mouth on Dry Creek, seven miles east of Manor in Travis County (at 30°20′ N, 97°26′ W). The stream traverses flat to rolling prairie surfaced by dark, calcareous clays that support mesquite, cacti, and grasses.

_____ (Bexar County). Elm Creek rises 2½ miles west of Atascosa in southwestern Bexar County (at 29°16′ N, 98°46′ W) and runs southeast for seventeen miles to its mouth on the Medina River, a mile east of State Highway 16 (at 29°15′ N, 98°34′ W). It traverses rolling terrain surfaced by clay loams and expansive clay soils that support mesquite and grasses.

_____ (Bee County). Elm Creek rises just west of Clareville in western Bee County (at 28°20′ N, 97°53′ W) and runs southeast for eight miles to its mouth on Aransas Creek, 1½ miles north of Skidmore (at 28°18′ N, 97°45′ W). It traverses flat to rolling terrain surfaced by clay and sandy loams that support water-tolerant hardwoods and grasses.

_____ (Brown County). Elm Creek rises just west of U.S. Highway 183 and three miles south of May in northeastern Brown County (at 31°55′ N, 98°54′ W) and runs southwest for fourteen miles to its mouth on Pecan Bayou, a few miles north of Brownwood (at 31°48′ N, 98°58′ W). The creek initially passes through steep-sloped terrain with shallow sandy soils, then traverses an area of resistant ledges and low cuestas qv with shallow stony soils. Along its upper reaches grow juniper, scattered oak, live oak, and grasses. In its middle reaches, rolling hills are surfaced by clay and sandy loams that support scrub brush, mesquite, cacti, live oak, and juniper. Near the creek's mouth the terrain becomes flat and flood-prone with local shallow depressions, surfaced by clay and sandy loams that support water-tolerant hardwoods, conifers, and grasses.

_____ (Coleman County). Elm Creek rises in southwestern Coleman County (at 31°50′ N, 99°40′ W) and runs south for twenty-six miles to its mouth on the Colorado River, on the Coleman-Concho county line (at 31°32′ N, 99°39′ W). The creek, which is used by fishermen, passes through steep-sloped terrain with shallow clay loam soils that support juniper, live oak, mesquite, and grasses.

_____ (Collin County). Elm Creek rises just east of Farmersville in east central Collin County (at 33°10′ N, 96°20′ W) and runs southwest for about eight miles, passing through gently rolling terrain with clayey soils. The stream ran into Sister Grove Creek until the early 1950s, when its course was diverted to empty in Lavon Lake (at 33°06′ N, 96°27′ W).

_____ (Collingsworth County). Elm Creek, also known as the Elm Fork of the Red River, rises in northern Collingsworth County near the Wheeler county line about six miles southwest of Shamrock (at 35°11′ N, 100°22′ W) and runs southeast across northeastern Collingsworth County and into Oklahoma, where it crosses southwestern Beckham County and central Greer County south of Granite before reaching its mouth on the North Fork of the Red River, near the Greer-Kiowa county line and just south of Altus Reservoir (at 35°03′ N, 99°57′ W). Two major tributaries, Hackberry and Long Dry creeks, originate in southern Wheeler County. Elm Creek traverses flat terrain with local shallow depressions, surfaced by clay and sandy loams that support water-tolerant hardwoods, conifers, and grasses. The creek, included in the disputed Greer County qv during the 1880s and 1890s, was used by various ranching outfits. Its upper portion in Collingsworth County was among the properties owned or leased by the Rocking Chair Ranch qv and later by the Mill Iron Ranch (*see* CONTINENTAL LAND AND CATTLE COMPANY) and the Crews brothers.

BIBLIOGRAPHY: Pauline D. and R. L. Robertson, *Cowman's Country: Fifty Frontier Ranches in the Texas Panhandle, 1876–1887* (Amarillo: Paramount, 1981). Estelle D. Tinkler, "Nobility's Ranche: A History of the Rocking Chair Ranche," *Panhandle–Plains Historical Review* 15 (1942).

_____ (Comal County). Elm Creek rises six miles south of Canyon Lake in south central Comal County (at 29°47′ N, 98°14′ W) and runs east for eight miles to its mouth on the Guadalupe River, four miles northwest of New Braunfels (at 29°46′ N, 98°08′ W). It traverses a flat area of the Edwards Plateau that is deeply dissected in places and surfaced by shallow to deep loams with rock outcrops. Local vegetation includes live oak and Ashe juniper. The area around the mouth of Elm Creek, once an Indian campground, became in the nineteenth century the site of the Waco Springs settlement and the first crossing on the Guadalupe River north of New Braunfels.

_____ (Eastland County). Elm Creek rises north of Rising Star in southwestern Eastland County (at 32°08′ N, 98°57′ W) and runs northeast for nine miles to its mouth on the Sabana River, near the Comanche county line (at 32°10′ N, 98°49′ W). It passes through rolling hills surfaced by sandy clay loams that support vegetation including tall grasses.

_____ (Guadalupe County). Elm Creek rises about five miles east of New Berlin in southern Guadalupe County (at 29°30′ N, 98°02′ W) and runs east for five miles to its mouth on Cottonwood Creek, five miles south of Seguin (at 29°30′ N, 97°58′ W). It passes through rolling prairie with clay loam soils that support mesquite and grasses.

_____ (Guadalupe County). Elm Creek rises about seven miles southwest of Seguin in southwestern Guadalupe County (at 29°30′ N, 98°05′ W) and runs south for fourteen miles to its mouth on Cibolo Creek, two miles east of La Vernia in Wilson County (at 29°21′ N, 98°05′ W). It traverses generally flat to rolling terrain with local shallow depressions, surfaced by clay and sandy loams that support water-tolerant hardwoods, conifers, and grasses.

_____ (Hays County). Elm Creek rises three miles north of Niederwald in the eastern corner of Hays County (at 30°04′ N, 97°45′ W) and runs southeast for fourteen miles, passing into Caldwell County before reaching its mouth on Plum Creek, a mile north of Lockhart (at 29°58′ N, 97°40′ W). The stream is intermittent in its upper reaches. Food and fiber crops grow in the clay and shale-based soils through which Elm Creek runs.

_____ (Hopkins County). Elm Creek rises two miles northwest of Shirley in southwestern Hopkins County (at 33°05′ N, 95°42′ W). It formerly ran fourteen miles southwest to disembogue in Lake Fork Creek about a mile west of Burke-Yandell in northeastern Rains County (at 32°56′ N, 95°43′ W). Since its lower streambed was inundated by the Lake Fork Reservoir in the late 1970s, the creek has flowed into the reservoir a mile north of the Elm Cemetery in northeastern Rains County. The stream traverses flat to rolling terrain with clay loam and sandy loam soils that support water-tolerant hardwoods, conifers, and grasses.

_____ (Hunt County). Elm Creek rises a mile northeast of Floyd in west central Hunt County (at 33°10′ N, 96°14′ W) and runs southeast thirteen miles to its mouth on West Caddo Creek, five miles northwest of Quinlan (at 33°00′ N, 96°10′ W). It traverses flat to rolling terrain surfaced by dark, commonly calcareous clays and clay and sandy loams that support mesquite, cacti, grasses, water-tolerant hardwoods, and conifers.

_____ (Kinney County). Elm Creek rises ten miles northeast of Brackettville in north central Kinney County (at 29°27′ N, 100°20′ W) and runs southwest for thirty-one miles to its mouth on Las Moras Creek, six miles northwest of Spofford (at 29°12′ N, 100°30′ W). Hardwoods, conifers, and various grasses grow along the creek, which runs through flat terrain with locally shallow depressions. Area soils consist of expansive clays.

_____ (La Salle County). Elm Creek rises 8½ miles southwest of Fowlerton in eastern La Salle County (at 28°20′N, 98°49′W) and flows northeast for 6½ miles to its mouth on Galinda Creek (at 28°24′ N, 98°45′W) about twelve miles southwest of Tilden in west central McMullen County. The creek traverses rolling to flat terrain surfaced by clay and sandy loams that support brush and grasses in its upper reaches and water-tolerant hardwoods and various grasses in its lower reaches.

_____ (Lee County). Elm Creek rises 5½ miles southeast of Manheim in western Lee County (at 30°13′ N, 96°04′ W) and runs northeast for eighteen miles to its mouth on West Yegua Creek, 2½ miles west of Lincoln (at 30°17′ N, 96°56′ W). The creek passes through an area of steep slopes and rolling hills with shallow to moderately deep clayey soils that support mixed hardwoods, pines, and grasses.

_____ (Limestone County). Elm Creek rises seven miles southeast of Prairie Hill in eastern Limestone County (at 31°35′ N, 96°43′ W) and runs south for ten miles to its mouth on Cottonwood Creek (at 31°29′ N, 96°45′ W). The creek traverses flat to rolling prairie with local shallow depressions, surfaced by dark, calcareous clays and sandy loams that support mesquite, cacti, and grasses in the upper reaches of the creek and water-tolerant hardwoods and conifers in its lower.

_____ (McCulloch County). Elm Creek is formed by the confluence of Big Elm and Little Elm creeks a mile southwest of Fife in north central McCulloch County (at 31°23′ N, 99°23′ W). Big Elm Creek in turn has west and east forks. Its west fork rises four miles southeast of Pear Valley (at 31°16′ N, 99°28′ W) and runs north for eight miles to its confluence with the East Fork of Big Elm Creek (at 31°21′ N, 99°27′ W). Its east fork rises in Cottonwood Canyon in the Brady Mountains (at 31°16′ N, 99°25′ W) and runs north for nine miles to join the west fork. From that point Big Elm Creek continues northeast for six miles to join Little Elm Creek. Little Elm Creek rises a mile southeast of Lohn (at 31°19′ N, 99°24′ W) and runs north for 7½ miles. From the confluence of Big and Little Elm creeks, Elm Creek proper runs northeast for five miles to its mouth on the Colorado River, two miles northeast of Fife (at 31°25′ N, 99°20′ W). The local terrain is flat to rolling with local shallow depressions, surfaced by clay and sandy loams that support water-tolerant hardwoods, conifers, and grasses.

_____ (McLennan County). Elm Creek rises a mile southwest of Wiggins in northern McLennan County (at 31°45′ N, 97°10′ W) and runs south for six miles to its mouth on Aquilla Creek, three miles southeast of Gholson (at 31°42′ N, 97°11′ W). It traverses low-rolling to flat terrain with local shallow depressions, surfaced by clay and sandy loams that support juniper, oak, and cacti in the creek's upper and middle reaches and water-tolerant hardwoods and conifers in its lower.

_____ (McMullen County). Elm Creek rises eleven miles northeast of Tilden in northeastern McMullen County (at 28°36′N, 98°27′W) and flows southeasterly for 7½ miles to it mouth on the Choke Canyon Reservoir (at 28°32′N, 98°24′W). The creek flows through rolling to flat terrain with clay and sandy loams which support grasses, mesquite, chaparral, and water-tolerant hardwoods.

_____ (McMullen County). Elm Creek rises ten miles northwest of Loma Alta in southern McMullen County (at 28°08′N, 98°34′W) and runs northwest for nine miles to its mouth on the Winn Lake Slue, fourteen miles southwest of Tilden (at 28°14′N, 98°39′W). It rises in low, rolling terrain, surfaced by clay and sandy loams that support grasses, mesquite, and chaparral, and descends to flat terrain with locally shallow depressions, surrounded by water-tolerant hardwoods and various grasses.

_____ (Mason County). Elm Creek rises about 2½ miles west of Bodie Peak in eastern Mason County (at 30°50′ N, 99°01′ W) and runs southeast for nine miles, passing through sandy beds during the last half of its course, to its mouth on the Llano River, 2½ miles east of Castell in Llano County (at 30°42′ N, 98°55′ W). The stream, which rises in the limestone hills on the eastern edge of the Edwards Plateau, crosses low-rolling to flat terrain in the Llano basin area, with deep to shallow clayey and loamy soils that support brush, grasses, and open stands of live oak and mesquite.

_____ (Medina County). Elm Creek rises between Verde and Main Quihi creeks eight miles west of Mico in northern Medina County (at 29°32′ N, 99°04′ W) and runs southeast for fourteen miles to its mouth on Quihi Creek in Quihi (at 29°24′ N, 99°01′ W). It traverses flat to rolling prairie surfaced by expansive clays that support mesquite and grasses.

_____ (Menard County). Elm Creek rises twelve miles south of Menard in southern Menard County (at 30°44′ N, 99°47′ W) and runs northeast for sixteen miles to its mouth on the San Saba River, eight miles east of Menard (at 30°53′ N, 99°39′ W). The surrounding flat to rolling prairie is surfaced by shallow, stony clay loams that support oak, juniper, mesquite, and grasses.

____ (Navarro County). Elm Creek rises in Retreat in central Navarro County (at 32°03′ N, 96°29′ W) and runs northeast for seven miles to its mouth on Post Oak Creek (at 32°05′ N, 96°24′ W). The stream, which is dammed in its lower reaches to form Lake Halbert, runs through low-rolling hills and prairies, surfaced by dark clays that support grasses and mesquite.

____ (Nolan County). Elm Creek rises three miles northeast of Nolan in far eastern Nolan County (at 32°17′ N, 100°11′ W) and runs northeast for thirty-seven miles to its mouth on the Clear Fork of the Brazos River, two miles southwest of Nugent in southeastern Jones County (at 32°40′ N, 99°41′ W). The stream is dammed to form Lake Fort Phantom Hill. Juniper, live oak, mesquite, and grasses grow beside the creek in its upper reaches; hardwoods, scrub brush, and grasses grow along its middle section; and water-tolerant hardwoods, conifers, and grasses grow near its mouth. The creek rises in steeply sloping terrain with benches, runs through flat to rolling land with local scarps, and ends in a flat area with locally shallow depressions and an expansive clay surface.

____ (Palo Pinto County). Elm Creek rises two miles northwest of Palo Pinto in central Palo Pinto County (at 32°47′ N, 98°15′ W) and runs northwest for ten miles to its mouth on the Brazos River, a mile east of Farm road 4 (at 32°52′ N, 98°17′ W). It traverses an area of rolling hills surfaced by clay and sandy loam soils that support mesquite, scrub brush, grasses, and cacti. Two other shorter Elm creeks also rise in Palo Pinto County.

____ (Red River County). Elm Creek rises about three miles southeast of Boxelder in southeastern Red River County (at 33°28′ N, 94°50′ W) and runs south for 7½ miles to its mouth on the Sulphur River (at 33°23′ N, 94°50′ W). The soil in the area is loamy and is used along the creek's upper reaches as pasture or for growing sorghum and small grains. The area near the mouth of the creek is heavily wooded, with pines and various hardwoods predominating.

____ (Stephens County). Elm Creek rises four miles southeast of Eliasville in extreme northern Stephens County (at 32°56′ N, 98°42′ W) and runs north for five miles to its mouth on the Clear Fork of the Brazos River, three miles southwest of South Bend in southern Young County (at 32°59′ N, 98°42′ W). The stream traverses an area of rolling hills with clay and sandy loam soils that support scrub brush, mesquite, cacti, and grasses. Much of the creek's lower drainage area is within the Maxey oilfield.

____ (Taylor County). Elm Creek rises in southeastern Taylor County (at 32°08′ N, 99°51′ W) and runs south for about twenty-seven miles to its mouth on the Colorado River, at Ballinger in central Runnels County (at 31°44′ N, 99°56′ W). The stream traverses flat to gently sloping terrain surfaced with moderately deep to shallow silt loams that support mesquite and grasses. The stream is dammed about a mile north of Ballinger to form an irrigation reservoir.

____ (Throckmorton County). Elm Creek rises seven miles southwest of Throckmorton in central Throckmorton County (at 33°08′ N, 99°15′ W) and runs east for a total of thirty miles, passing through the town of Throckmorton and into western Young County, then becoming a flowing stream when it passes near Proffitt, before reaching its mouth on the Brazos River, six miles west of Newcastle in west central Young County (at 33°12′ N, 98°50′ W). The stream passes through rolling hills surfaced by clay and sandy loams that support scrub brush, mesquite, cacti, grasses, live oak, and juniper. Elm Creek is the main source for Lake Throckmorton. Most of the stream's drainage area consists of isolated ranchlands and oilfields.

____ (Travis County). Elm Creek rises at the eastern edge of the Austin city limits in east central Travis County (at 30°17′ N, 97°37′ W) and runs southeast for nine miles to its mouth on Gilleland Creek, two miles south of the Dunlap community (at 30°14′ N, 97°33′ W). The local terrain is generally flat with local shallow depressions, surfaced by clay and sandy loams that support water-tolerant hardwoods, conifers, and grasses.

____ (Wilson County). Elm Creek rises just east of Pandor in eastern Wilson County (at 29°15′ N, 97°49′ W) and runs east twenty-five miles to its mouth on Sandies Creek, a mile west of Sample Cemetery in southern Gonzales County (at 29°15′ N, 97°32′ W). It is intermittent in its upper reaches. The stream traverses flat to rolling terrain surfaced by clay and sandy loam that supports water-tolerant hardwoods and grasses.

____ (Zavala County). Elm Creek rises ten miles northeast of Batesville in far northeastern Zavala County (at 29°05′ N, 99°33′ W) and runs southeast for twenty-five miles to its mouth on the Frio River, a mile northeast of the intersection of Farm roads 140 and 76 and seven miles southeast of Frio Town in northwestern Frio County (at 28°59′ N, 99°14′ W). It rises in steep to gently sloping terrain, then passes through flat terrain with locally shallow depressions. Along the creek's upper reaches grow sparse scrub brush and grasses; in its lower, water-tolerant hardwoods, conifers, and grasses.

ELM CREEK, TEXAS. Elm Creek was a school community on Farm Road 467 about six miles south of Seguin in southern Guadalupe County. In 1904 the community had two one-teacher schools for sixty-eight black students and two one-teacher schools for 104 white students. There were a few scattered houses and a cemetery in the area in 1946; by the mid-1980s only the cemetery marked the community on county highway maps.
Vivian Elizabeth Smyrl

ELM CREEK RAID. On October 13, 1864, in western Young County, several hundred Kiowa and Comanche Indians raided the Elm Creek valley northwest of Fort Belknap. Peter Harmonson[qv] and his son, after taking refuge in a thicket on nearby Rabbit Creek, shot and killed one of the Indian leaders. At the household of Elizabeth Ann FitzPatrick (*see* CLIFTON, ELIZABETH ANN), the Indians killed and scalped Mrs. FitzPatrick's daughter, Millie Durkin, and killed the son of Britt (Britton) Johnson,[qv] a black slave. Mrs. FitzPatrick, her son and two granddaughters, and Johnson's wife and children were taken captive. Farther upstream Dr. Thomas Wilson, Thomas Hamby, and his son Thornton K. Hamby, a Confederate soldier, rode to warn others in the area and then defended several families who had taken refuge in George Bragg's cabin. After charging the cabin several times, killing Wilson and wounding Bragg and Thomas Hamby, the Indians heard shots from a company of Confederate colonel James G. Bourland's[qv] Border Regiment and rode north with a herd of stolen cattle and horses. The company, under the command of a Second Lieutenant Carson, pursued the Indians but rode into an ambush, in which five soldiers were killed and several were wounded. Some sources claim that in March 1865 Britt Johnson went to live with the Comanches in order to find the captives and that he managed to pay a ransom and rescue his family and Mrs. FitzPatrick. Others regard Johnson's exploits as mere legend and credit friendly Comanches, namely Comanche chief Asa-Havey, with the rescue of Johnson's family in June 1865. Apparently, as a part of ongoing peace talks, Asa-Havey paid a ransom for the captives, rescued them, and took them to the Indian agent; eventually the family was delivered to Britt Johnson. United States troops rescued Mrs. FitzPatrick in November 1865.

BIBLIOGRAPHY: Carrie J. Crouch, *Young County: History and Biography* (Dallas: Dealey and Love, 1937; rev. ed., *A History of Young County, Texas*, Austin: Texas State Historical Association, 1956). Barbara Neal Ledbetter, *Fort Belknap Frontier Saga: Indians, Negroes and Anglo-Americans on the Texas Frontier* (Burnet, Texas: Eakin Press, 1982). Barbara Neal Ledbetter, comp., *The Fort Belknap of Yesterday and Today* (1963). Kenneth F. Neighbours, "Elm Creek Raid in Young County, 1864," West Texas Historical Association *Year Book* 40 (1964).
Kenneth F. Neighbours

ELMDALE, TEXAS. Elmdale was on the Missouri Pacific Railroad and Farm Road 18 in northeastern Taylor County. It began as a stop on the Texas and Pacific Railway in the early 1880s. According to some sources, early travelers saw a mirage of elm trees at the site and called it Elmdale; other sources claim there actually were elms there in the early years of settlement. A one-room school building was erected in Elmdale in 1895, and by 1902 the school had thirty-six pupils and one teacher. Baptist, Methodist, and Church of Christ congregations met in the school. A post office was opened in the community in 1905, and by 1914 Elmdale had a population of twenty, a grocery store, and a general store. In 1919 the old plank school was replaced by a new brick building. A Baptist church was built in 1924, and a larger building was constructed in the 1930s. The post office closed in 1927, and by 1940 the community consisted of the church, the school, one business, and a number of scattered dwellings. The school had closed by the 1950s. By the 1980s the site was within the Abilene city limits.

BIBLIOGRAPHY: Juanita Daniel Zachry, *A History of Rural Taylor County* (Burnet, Texas: Nortex, 1980). *Mark Odintz*

EL MEJICANO. *El Mejicano*, a bilingual imprint that may be called a newspaper, was a successor to the *Gaceta de Tejas*qv and was published in Natchitoches, Louisiana, by William Shaler and José Álvarez de Toledo y Duboisqqv in June 1813. The paper was published to attack José Bernardo Gutiérrez de Laraqv and was distributed in San Antonio de Béxar. The press, which was for a time set up in Nacogdoches, may have been returned to Texas and captured by Mexican forces under Joaquín de Arredondoqv at the battle of Medina.qv

BIBLIOGRAPHY: Julia Kathryn Garrett, "The First Newspaper of Texas: *Gaceta de Texas*," *Southwestern Historical Quarterly* 40 (January 1937). Ike H. Moore, "The Earliest Printing and First Newspaper in Texas," *Southwestern Historical Quarterly* 39 (October 1935). Marilyn M. Sibley, *Lone Stars and State Gazettes: Texas Newspapers before the Civil War* (College Station: Texas A&M University Press, 1983).

ELMENDORF, TEXAS. Elmendorf is at the junction of the Southern Pacific Railroad and Farm Road 327, some seventeen miles southeast of downtown San Antonio in southeastern Bexar County. The town was established in 1885 and named for Henry Elmendorf, former mayor of San Antonio and promoter of the first brick plant in the vicinity. W. F. Saenger discovered that the clay in the area was suitable for pottery, and that became an important local industry. A post office opened at the community in 1886, and by 1890 Elmendorf had a pottery, a general store, a hotel, and a population of fifty. The settlement grew rapidly after 1900, and by 1914 it had nine general stores, a cotton gin, a hotel, and a population of 300. The community's largest employer for many years was Star Clay Products, a firebrick factory. The population of Elmendorf was consistently reported as 300 until the 1950s. During the 1960s it fell to 200, but later it grew steadily, and in 1990 the town reported 568 residents and eighteen businesses. *Christopher Long*

ELMER, TEXAS. Elmer, seven miles south of Seguin in southern Guadalupe County, was established as early as 1854. A post office opened there in 1882, and by 1884 the community had a population of sixty and a church, district school, and general store. At that time local residents shipped cotton, cottonseed, and hides. The community's post office was discontinued in 1891, and the mail was sent to Seguin. By the 1940s no evidence of Elmer was shown on county highway maps. *Vivian Elizabeth Smyrl*

ELM FLAT, TEXAS. Elm Flat, on Farm Road 633 some nine miles southeast of Corsicana in southeastern Navarro County, first formed in the late 1870s. By 1906 it had two schools, one with forty white students and the other with fifty-three black students. At its height during the early 1930s, Elm Flat had a number of houses, several stores, two churches, a school, and a cemetery. In the mid-1960s the community had several houses, a district school, and a church. Elm Flat was a dispersed rural community in the early 1990s.

Christopher Long

ELM FORK OF THE TRINITY RIVER. The Elm Fork of the Trinity River rises just south of Saint Jo in eastern Montague County (at 33°42′ N, 97°33′ W) and runs southeast for eighty-five miles, through Cooke and Denton counties, to its confluence with the West Fork of the Trinity just west of downtown Dallas in central Dallas County (at 32°48′ N, 96°54′ W). In 1928 the stream was dammed in central Denton County to form Lake Dallas, which had a capacity of 194,000 acre-feet. In 1955 a new, considerably larger, dam was completed. The lake, originally known as the Garza–Little Elm Reservoir, was renamed Lewisville Reservoir in 1960. The stream traverses generally flat to rolling terrain surfaced by shallow, stony loams that support junipers, oaks, and grasses.

ELM GROVE, TEXAS (Caldwell County). Elm Grove is a mile southeast of the intersection of Farm roads 86 and 158 and four miles northeast of McMahan in northeastern Caldwell County. A post office operated there from 1874 until 1890, and in 1875 the settlement became the focus of a county school district. By the mid-1880s the community had steam saw and grist mills, three cotton gins, a church, and 150 residents. At that time area farmers shipped cotton and produce. By the 1920s most of the townsite was in ruins. The community's district school closed in the 1940s, and local students were sent to the McMahan, Dale, and Lockhart schools. Elm Grove's school building was made into a community center in 1953; it was used for community singing through the mid-1960s and was renovated in the 1980s. Improved roads and utilities in the area attracted new residents, many of whom commuted to work in nearby Lockhart or Luling.

BIBLIOGRAPHY: Mark Withers Trail Drive Museum, *Historical Caldwell County* (Dallas: Taylor, 1984). Carroll L. Mullins, History of the Schools of Caldwell County to 1900 (M.A. thesis, University of Texas, 1929). *Vivian Elizabeth Smyrl*

ELM GROVE, TEXAS (Cherokee County). Elm Grove, six miles northeast of Rusk on State Highway 110 in east central Cherokee County, was established before 1900. In the mid-1930s the community had several stores, three churches, a school, and a number of houses. Many of the residents subsequently left the area, but in the late 1980s the school, two stores, and three churches still remained.

BIBLIOGRAPHY: *Cherokee County History* (Jacksonville, Texas: Cherokee County Historical Commission, 1986). *Christopher Long*

ELM GROVE, TEXAS (Dallas County). Elm Grove was five miles northeast of Rowlett and four miles southeast of Sachse in northern Dallas County. It was in the original survey of J. Doen and F. T. Gaines and was settled in the late 1870s, when a local school and a church were named for their location in a grove of elms. In 1940 the community had two stores and a population of twenty-five. It received mail from Wylie. In the 1980s all that remained in the area was a church.

ELM GROVE, TEXAS (Hays County). Elm Grove, four miles west of Buda and sixteen miles northeast of San Marcos in northern Hays County, had a one-room school in 1871 on four acres donated by David William Crews. The Elm Grove school district was formed on October 21, 1876. Elm Grove was reportedly the largest public school community in the county in the late 1870s, when the school had some sixty-three students. In 1945 the Elm Grove school was consolidated with that of Buda. The Elm Grove school building was burned by vandals in the 1960s.

BIBLIOGRAPHY: Mary Starr Barkley, *A History of Central Texas* (Austin: Austin Printing, 1970). Dudley Richard Dobie, *A Brief History of Hays County and San Marcos, Texas* (San Marcos, 1948).

Henry C. Armbruster

ELM GROVE, TEXAS (Wharton County). Elm Grove is on Farm Road 2614 some sixteen miles northwest of Wharton in extreme north central Wharton County. A school for black children operated there in 1912. The 1936 county highway map showed a school and multiple dwellings at the townsite. In the 1980s two businesses, a church, a cemetery, and scattered dwellings remained.

Diana J. Kleiner

ELM GROVE CREEK. Elm Grove Creek rises five miles southeast of Navasota in southern Grimes County (at 30°19′ N, 95°59′ W) and runs south six miles to its mouth on Rocky Creek (at 30°16′ N, 96°01′ W), a tributary of Beason's Creek. Elm Grove Creek traverses gently sloping to nearly level terrain surfaced by clayey, loamy, and sandy soils that support long narrow lines of water oak, elm, and pecan woodland along the banks of the creek's lower course. Settlement in the vicinity began during the 1820s when the community of Lynn Grove, still extant in the 1980s, was established on the stream. During the 1870s and 1880s a school known as West Academy, which served western Wallace Prairie, operated on the upper creek.

BIBLIOGRAPHY: Grimes County Historical Commission, *History of Grimes County, Land of Heritage and Progress* (Dallas: Taylor, 1982).

ELMINA, TEXAS. Elmina was on U.S. Highway 75 some twelve miles southeast of Huntsville in Walker County. It is believed that the town was named for the El Mina Masonic Temple in Galveston. The settlement started out in 1870 as a sawmill owned by Kit Oliphant, a lumberman of East Texas. In 1902 the Oliphant mill was sold to the Walker County Lumber Company, a branch of the Foster Lumber Company. After this, the mill expanded significantly, and by the mid-1920s Elmina had more than 200 residents. A post office opened there in 1903 and closed sometime after 1930. An early map of the settlement shows seventy-four company-owned houses, a post office, mill, hotel, drugstore, company store, movie house, church, storehouse, schoolhouse, cemetery, and spur-line railroad. Also, hundreds of people lived in camps in forested areas around the mill. The mill used more than twenty-five miles of tram railroads, known as the Elmina and Eastern Transportation Company; many of the railroad beds were still visible half a century later. The Elmina mill also provided electricity from 6:00 P.M. to 10:00 P.M. for local residents. A company physician, Dr. Henry Robertson, lived at the mill. The community had an eight-grade school and an "all-religion" Protestant church that was shared mainly by Baptists and Methodists. The Polish cemetery on the eastern side of the settlement was the burial ground used by St. Joseph's Catholic Church in New Waverly. The cemetery's name was later changed to Elmina Cemetery; in it are buried some Italians as well as Poles who worked in the Elmina mill. By 1930 available timber nearby had been consumed, and the Great Depression[qv] was in full swing. On September 13, 1931, a fire raged through the millsite and destroyed the main mill. The fire, combined with worsening economic conditions, finished the town by 1935. Its structures were either torn down or sold and removed from the site.

BIBLIOGRAPHY: D'Anne McAdams Crews, ed., *Huntsville and Walker County, Texas: A Bicentennial History* (Huntsville, Texas: Sam Houston State University, 1976). Frances Scott, "A History of Elmina," *Junior Historian*, December 1965. *Gerald L. Holder*

ELMIR BRANCH. Elmir Branch rises four miles east of Morgan Mill in northeastern Erath County (at 32°24′ N, 98°05′ W) and runs southeast for four miles to its mouth on the North Paluxy River, 1½ miles west of Bluff Dale (at 32°21′ N, 98°02′ W). It traverses an area of steep slopes with shallow sandy soils that support juniper, scattered oak, and grasses.

ELM MOTT, TEXAS. Elm Mott is near the intersection of Interstate Highway 35 and Farm Road 308, eight miles north of Waco in northeast central McLennan County. The area was settled shortly after the Civil War[qv] by the Christian and Long families. A general store and a cotton gin served nearby farmers. The community was known as Geneva until residents applied for a post office in 1872; as there was already a Geneva, Texas, the name Elm Mott was chosen, for a nearby elm grove. The school that served the area was called Union Grove when it was established in 1876; its name was changed to Geneva in 1887 and to Elm Mott in 1897. When the Missouri, Kansas and Texas Railroad laid track from Hillsboro to Taylor in the early 1880s, it passed through Elm Mott, and the community began to grow. In the mid-1880s the settlement had a church, a school, and forty residents; by the early 1890s it had a hotel, a gristmill and gin, two general stores, two churches, and 150 residents. Its population grew to 247 by 1900 and to 300 by 1914. A private bank opened at Elm Mott in 1921, but a drought in 1925 made it impossible for area farmers to repay their loans; the bank was closed by state examiners in 1926. In spite of this setback and the Great Depression,[qv] Elm Mott maintained an estimated population of 247 and supported twelve businesses. County highway maps from the late 1940s showed a school, two churches, several businesses, and a number of residences at Elm Mott. The Elm Mott Independent School District was combined with the Lakeview Independent School District in 1951 to form the Connally Consolidated Independent School District. In the late 1950s, when plans were made for the renovation of U.S. Highway 81 and its upgrade to Interstate Highway status, some residents of Elm Mott were forced to move their homes away from the right-of-way, and several businesses were moved to sites along the new highway. The population of Elm Mott was reported at 275 in the 1950s, fell to 260 in the 1960s, and was stable at 190 from the 1970s to 1990.

BIBLIOGRAPHY: Charles Leroy Hinkle, *A History and Analysis of Rural Banking in McLennan County* (M.S. thesis, Baylor University, 1959). Vertical File, Texas Collection, Baylor University.

Vivian Elizabeth Smyrl

ELM MOUNTAIN (Bell County). Elm Mountain is two miles north of Killeen within the Fort Hood military reservation in southwestern Bell County near the Coryell county line (at 31°10′ N, 97°43′ W). Its summit, at an elevation of 1,020 feet above sea level, rises some 100 feet above the surrounding terrain.

_____ (Kinney County). Elm Mountain is seven miles east of Brackettville in east central Kinney County (at 29°20′ N, 100°18′ W). Its summit, at an elevation of 1,445 feet above sea level, rises some 360 feet above the nearby roadside park at the intersection of Elm Creek and Interstate Highway 90.

ELMO, TEXAS. Elmo is on U.S. Highway 80 some thirteen miles northeast of Kaufman in northeastern Kaufman County. When the Texas and Pacific Railway laid tracks through the area in the early 1870s, a community quickly developed around the railroad, and residents chose the name Elmo in honor of Elmo Scott, a wire engineer who surveyed and routed the T&P through the county. In 1873 a post office branch opened there. Within a decade Elmo had an estimated population of 900 and was a shipping point for cotton, corn, and wheat. The town had a flour mill, several cotton and grist mills, five churches, and a district school. By 1890 its population had dropped to 300, but the community still supported some fifteen businesses, four churches, one school, and several gins. For the first few decades of the twentieth century the population in Elmo remained at an estimated

400, but during the Great Depression^{qv} and World War II^{qv} its population declined. In 1945 the town had 150 residents, and over the next four decades that figure decreased. In 1990 Elmo had ninety residents and two businesses.

BIBLIOGRAPHY: Robert Richard Butler, History of Kaufman County, Texas (M.A. thesis, University of Texas, 1940). Mabel Covington Keller, History of Kaufman County, Texas (M.A. thesis, North Texas State College, 1950). *David Minor*

EL MOCHO (?–1784). El Mocho, or Tosche ("Left Hand"), was the head chief of the Tonkawa Indians from 1779 until 1784. During that period he organized an alliance of tribes that attempted to oust the Spaniards from Texas. Little is known about his early life, except that he was born in a Lipan Apache ranchería in Central Texas and was captured as a child by the Tonkawas, who adopted him. Beginning in the 1750s he rose to prominence as a warrior, and by 1758 he was one of the tribal war chiefs. In 1758 he helped organize the attack on San Sabá de la Santa Cruz Mission. This mission, organized in 1754 for the Apaches, had alarmed the Tonkawas, Wichitas, Bidais, and Comanches, who feared the Apaches would use it as a supply base from which they could attack other tribes.

After the destruction of the San Sabá mission, El Mocho frequently clashed with the Tonkawa peace chief, Neques, who favored an alliance with the Spaniards. El Mocho, who hoped to drive whites from Texas, persuaded most of his fellow chiefs to continue the war against Spain and the Apaches, until the last Apache missions were abandoned in 1769. Throughout the 1770s El Mocho resisted the overtures of Neques to the Spaniards and acquiesced in a general peace only after Spanish officials agreed to pay the Tonkawas for taking Osage and Apache scalps. He assumed the leadership of the Tonkawas in 1779 after a smallpox epidemic killed Neques and most of the other Tonkawa elders.

El Mocho, who had participated in several conferences with Spanish leaders, hurried to the Taovayas' village near the Red River and assured the Spanish Indian agent, Athanase de Mézières,^{qv} of his loyalty and friendship. Mézières escorted El Mocho to Bexar to visit the Spanish governor, Domingo Cabello y Robles.^{qv} El Mocho received gifts from the governor and was invested as the chief of the Tonkawas. But despite these overtures, he continued to press for an anti-Spanish alliance among Texas Indians. Hoping to free his people from Spanish control, he formed a loose confederacy of groups that included the Tonkawas, the Lipan Apaches (with whom he had made peace in 1781), and some Comanches and Caddoes. In January 1784 El Mocho began leading war parties against Spanish settlements, carrying off captives, and stealing horses. The Spaniards' Indian allies attempted to halt these attacks but were defeated by the Tonkawas. In July 1784 El Mocho was invited to a conference at the presidio of La Bahía,^{qv} and there he was assassinated.

BIBLIOGRAPHY: William E. Dunn, "The Apache Mission on the San Saba River: Its Founding and Failure," *Southwestern Historical Quarterly* 17 (April 1914). Elizabeth A. H. John, *Storms Brewed in Other Men's Worlds: The Confrontation of Indians, Spanish, and French in the Southwest, 1540–1795* (College Station: Texas A&M University Press, 1975). *Thomas F. Schilz*

ELMONT, TEXAS. Elmont is at the intersection of Farm roads 121 and 3356, some fourteen miles south of Sherman in extreme south central Grayson County. Settlers arrived in the late 1840s and called the site Cross Roads, since it was at the crossroads of north–south and east–west trade routes. Harry Campbell of Elmont, New York, established a general merchandise store there in 1845; this store was in continuous operation until its interior was destroyed by fire in 1964. The first church, the Elmont Baptist Church, was organized by Thomas B. McCombs in 1869. More extensive community development, however, did not take place until the late 1870s or early 1880s. In 1884 a post office opened at the community. By the mid-1890s Elmont had fifty residents, two general stores, a church, a school, and a cotton gin. The first public library north of Dallas was in Elmont, and at one time the Cross Roads Institute was considered one of the best schools in Texas. The community's population stabilized at between fifty and sixty residents, and in 1904 the local post office closed. By World War II^{qv} Elmont had only two businesses and a church that served an estimated fifty residents. In the 1980s Elmont had forty-one residents and the Elmont Baptist Church. *David Minor*

ELMORE, TEXAS. Elmore was established as a post office in extreme northwestern Hall County on May 4, 1891, with Andrew J. Jasper as postmaster. This office was discontinued on August 31, 1898, and mail sent to Clarendon in Donley County after the community failed to develop.

BIBLIOGRAPHY: Inez Baker, *Yesterday in Hall County* (Memphis, Texas, 1940). Arthur Hecht, comp., *Postal History in the Texas Panhandle* (Canyon, Texas: Panhandle–Plains Historical Society, 1960). *H. Allen Anderson*

EL MORITO CREEK. El Morito Creek rises ten miles southeast of Carrizo Springs in west central Dimmit County (at 28°23′ N, 99°56′ W) and runs northeast for 8½ miles to its mouth on El Moro Creek, two miles southwest of Asherton (at 28°25′ N, 99°47′ W). The stream rises in flat to rolling terrain with local escarpments and descends to flat terrain with locally shallow depressions. Brush and grasses grow in its upper reaches and water-tolerant hardwoods and grasses in its lower. The upstream land is surfaced with deep, fine sandy loam, and the downstream soils are predominantly clayey and sandy loams. *Morito* is Spanish for "little Moor."

EL MORO CREEK. El Moro Creek, also known as Moros Creek, rises fourteen miles southwest of Asherton in south central Dimmit County (at 28°19′ N, 99°57′ W) and runs northeast for twenty-one miles to its mouth on Soldier Slough, seven miles southeast of Carrizo Springs (at 28°29′ N, 99°43′ W). The creek is intermittent except for the last mile of its course. It traverses generally flat terrain with locally shallow depressions, surfaced by clay and sandy loams that support water-tolerant hardwoods and grasses. Before Soldier Slough was impounded in the early twentieth century, El Moro Creek flowed directly into the Nueces River, and the creek's mouth was an important border landmark. According to a royal cedula of 1805, the boundary of Spanish Texas^{qv} diverged from the Nueces River at the mouth of El Moro Creek and turned northeast toward the Medina River. *El Moro* is Spanish for "the Moor."

ELM RIDGE, TEXAS (Hopkins County). Elm Ridge, a farming community on State Highway 11 some six miles southeast of Sulphur Springs in southeastern Hopkins County, was established before the early 1900s, when a public school was operating nearby. In 1905 the school had thirty-seven students. During the mid-1930s Elm Ridge had a church, a school, and a number of scattered houses. After World War II^{qv} most of the community's residents moved away. Its school was consolidated with the Como school district, and by the early 1960s all that remained at the site was a church and a few houses. In the late 1980s Elm Ridge was a dispersed rural community. *Christopher Long*

ELM RIDGE, TEXAS (Milam County). Elm Ridge is on U.S. Highway 190 some four miles west of Cameron in central Milam County. It was probably established after the Gulf, Colorado and Santa Fe Railway built through the area in 1881. The community was named for Elm Creek. In 1903 the settlement had a school with two teachers and eighty students. The school and a few scattered houses were shown at the site on the 1941 county highway map. The community's population was reported as twenty-five in 1990.

BIBLIOGRAPHY: Lelia M. Batte, *History of Milam County, Texas* (San Antonio: Naylor, 1956).
Vivian Elizabeth Smyrl

ELMTOWN, TEXAS. Elmtown is at the intersection of a country road and Farm Road 315, nine miles north of Palestine in northern Anderson County. The community was named for the trees that lined nearby Mound Prairie Creek. Elmtown had a post office from 1901 to 1906. In 1933 the settlement comprised ten residents and two businesses, and by the late 1930s its population was estimated at fifty. During the 1940s there was a factory there. By the 1980s all that remained at the crossroads site was a cemetery, but the name Elmtown was still used on county highway maps to refer to the extended rural community.
Mark Odintz

EL MUERTO PEAK. El Muerto Peak is twenty-eight miles northwest of Fort Davis in west central Jeff Davis County (at 30°40′ N, 104°20′ W). It rises to an elevation of 5,900 feet above sea level, 500 feet above State Highway 166, four miles to the southeast. On the peak, shallow, stony soils support live oak, piñon, juniper, and grasses. The mountain is named for El Muerto ("Dead Man") Spring, on its north flank. Legend has it that a dead man was found near the spring in 1854 or 1855, when the first mail coaches between Santa Fe and San Antonio stopped there. Another story relates that around the same time, William A. A. (Bigfoot) Wallace[qv] was driving the San Antonio–El Paso mail coach and stopped at the spring to mend his buckskin breeches. Indians attacked him, and he escaped and supposedly made his way to El Paso with the mail but without his pants. Yet another legend holds that in 1879 twenty-nine bars of gold, along with silver, jewels, and other treasure, were buried in the area. The supposed treasure has never been found, despite much subsequent digging by trespassers.

ELMWOOD, TEXAS. Elmwood is at the intersection of a country road and Farm Road 315, eleven miles northeast of Palestine in northeastern Anderson County. The site was settled in the 1850s, and by 1881 the community had been named for the elm trees in the area. In 1901 Elmwood was mentioned in the Anderson County *Herald* as having a literary and debating society that met every two weeks. The community unsuccessfully applied for a post office that year. In the 1920s the town had two stores and a barbershop. The Elmwood school enrolled fifty-six white pupils and 112 black pupils in 1932. In 1933 the settlement had a population of ten and one business. The surrounding farms primarily produced cotton, poultry, and dairy products. From 1952 through 1987 the number of residents was estimated at twenty, and in 1985 Elmwood had a church.

BIBLIOGRAPHY: *Anderson County Herald*, April 19, May 31, 1901. Thomas Paul Jones, The Reorganization of the Public Schools of Anderson County, Texas (M.Ed. thesis, University of Texas, 1934).
Mark Odintz

ELMWOOD INSTITUTE. Elmwood Institute was a college-preparatory academy in Celeste, Hunt County. The catalyst for the school's establishment was the arrival of the Gulf, Colorado and Santa Fe Railway, which built through the area in 1886 to intersect the Missouri, Kansas and Texas. The intersection of the two lines transformed Celeste from a one-business rural community to a shipping point for area farmers. The town soon acquired the businesses that had operated at Kingston, three miles southeast. Kingston was the home of Calhoun College. As Kingston declined, the faculty of Calhoun joined the exodus. In 1890 C. C. Perrin established Perrin School. By 1897, however, it had changed hands and operated successively under the names Gladstone College and Hawthorne College. Unable to compete with the increasing number of schools offering college-level courses in the county, the residents of Celeste abandoned the idea of a college and in 1899 collected $10,000 towards the establishment of an academy. B. A. Stafford and C. F. Gibson owned and operated the college preparatory school called Elmwood Institute, located in an eight-room stone and brick building. The institute provided two dorms for girls and a curriculum designed to prepare students for college. Like the colleges that preceded it, Elmwood Institute failed to compete with the introduction of nearby academic institutions. The Celeste public high school enticed students from the private school, bringing declining enrollment, decreasing funds, and the decision in 1910 to close the academy for good.

BIBLIOGRAPHY: Ethel Cassles, A History of Hunt County (M.A. thesis, University of Texas, 1935). Jackson Massey, A History of College Education in Hunt County, Texas (M.A. thesis, University of Texas, 1928).
David Minor

ELOISE, TEXAS. Eloise is on Farm Road 1373 fourteen miles southeast of Marlin in southern Falls County. It was established as a post office in 1900 on the proposed route of the Calvert, Waco and Brazos Valley Railroad, which completed a section of track from Calvert Junction to Marlin the following year. The population was 20 in 1925, 75 in the late 1930s, and 100 in the mid-1940s. The post office at Eloise was discontinued in the early 1950s, and the population began to fall soon thereafter. By the mid-1960s the number of residents was reported at forty-seven. From 1970 through 1990 the reported population was forty-one.
Vivian Elizabeth Smyrl

EL ORCOQUISAC. El Orcoquisac, a Spanish outpost (1765–71), was located north of the site of present Wallisville and east of the Trinity River in what is now northern Chambers County. The settlement consisted of San Augustín de Ahumada Presidio and Nuestra Señora de la Luz Mission. The presence of Indians, primarily the Bidais and Orcoquizas, lured French traders into the surrounding region as early as the 1720s. Persistent rumors of Frenchmen operating out of the lower Trinity reached the ears of Governor Jacinto de Barrios y Jáuregui[qv] at Los Adaes.[qv] Alarmed over the French presence and the threat it posed to his own illegal trade monopoly with the Indians, the governor in 1754 dispatched Lt. Marcos Ruiz[qv] and a force of twenty-five soldiers to arrest the Frenchmen reputed to be operating near the mouth of the Trinity. Ruiz, after gaining the support of the Bidai and Orcoquiza villages nearby, arrested Joseph Blancpain[qv] of Natchitoches, four associates, and two blacks on October 10, 1754. Blancpain's log trading post was dismantled, and the lumber was given to the Orcoquizas. The prisoners were marched to Mexico City, where Blancpain died on February 6, 1756. After considerable discussion, Barrios decided to establish an outpost on the site of the French trading post. Ruiz marched to the Trinity with thirty-one men, 151 horses, guns, swords, saddles, supplies, and other military equipment in May 1756. He took possession of the site eleven days later. The presidio was named San Augustín de Ahumada in honor of the viceroy. Temporary structures were completed by July 12, 1756.

Two missionaries from the College of Nuestra Señora de Guadalupe de Zacatecas[qv] were assigned to the new Nuestra Señora de la Luz Mission, which was also constructed in temporary quarters on the site of the trading post. Fray Bruno Chavira and Fray Marcos Satarain arrived there in November–December 1756. Both priests quickly fell ill. Satarain, a young man, was ordered by the older Chavira to travel to Los Adaes for treatment. The elder priest became ill himself and died on June 27, 1757, alone and unattended in his hut. He was replaced by Fray José Francisco Caro.

By the time of Chavira's death the mission consisted of a wooden church plastered with clay and moss. By the fall of 1759 the mission had been moved to a hill a quarter league to the east of the presidio. The second mission was constructed of hewn timbers plastered with beaten clay mixed with moss. The entire structure was then whitewashed. Both missions appear to have been roofed with palmetto. The presidio consisted of a varying number of buildings that generally included barracks, a captain's quarters, a store, a presidial church, and a central plaza. The presidio covered approximately 8,000 square meters.

On November 23, 1763, Capt. Rafael Martínez Pacheco[qv] was appointed commander of the presidio. The previous command of Lt. Domingo del Río (1756–63) apparently left the garrison in an undisciplined and demoralized state. Although Martínez maintained cordial relations with the Franciscans[qv] and the Indians, the soldiers regarded his command as cruel and arrogant. All but five soldiers deserted by August 28, 1764, and fled to Natchitoches. Upon hearing of the grievances of the soldiers, Governor Ángel de Martos y Navarrete[qv] suspended Pacheco and ordered Lieutenant Ruiz and a small force to El Orcoquisac to arrest the commander and relieve him of his post. Refusing to surrender, Pacheco and a handful of his cohorts fortified themselves within his quarters. After three days of unsuccessful negotiations, Ruiz and his force of twenty men set fire to the presidio on October 11, 1764, in an effort to flush out Pacheco. A pitched battle ensued, in which Pacheco and his men killed one soldier and wounded two others. The wily commander slipped out of a secret passage located in the chimney of his quarters and fled with a companion to San Antonio.

Ruiz was briefly installed as commander of the outpost and served until his arrest in November 1765 on charges of burning a royal presidio. He was replaced by Melchor Afán de Rivera, the next commander at San Augustín de Ahumada. Ironically, the command of the presidio was restored to Pacheco, who returned there on September 28, 1769. The commander who had left the outpost under the most disgraceful of circumstances had been cleared of responsibility in the burning of the presidio. He served until the place was abandoned in 1771.

The mission and presidio were ravaged by hurricanes in 1762 and 1766. The presidio was moved to a low hill about a quarter league from its original location. The Marqués de Rubí[qv] and a capable engineer, Nicolás de Lafora,[qv] made a formal inspection of the outpost in 1767. Rubí concluded that the post was of little strategic importance to Spain. His report, along with a comedic series of attempts to relocate the outpost over the course of its history, led to its abandonment in 1771.

Two centuries later an amateur historian from Houston, John V. Clay, ended several years of investigations by discovering the actual site north of Wallisville in Chambers County. His discovery in 1965 was followed in 1966 by an archeological mission led by Curtis Tunnell, which verified the site. An area including the mission, presidio, Blancpain's trading post, and about 200 Indian sites, to be known as the El Orcoquisac Archeological District, was added to the National Register of Historic Places in Texas in 1972.

BIBLIOGRAPHY: Lawrence E. Aten, *Indians of the Upper Texas Coast* (New York: Academic Press, 1983). Bexar Archives, Barker Texas History Center, University of Texas at Austin. Herbert Eugene Bolton, *Texas in the Middle Eighteenth Century: Studies in Spanish Colonial History and Administration* (Berkeley: University of California Press, 1915; rpt., Austin: University of Texas Press, 1970). Carlos E. Castañeda, *Our Catholic Heritage in Texas* (7 vols., Austin: Von Boeckmann–Jones, 1936–58; rpt., New York: Arno, 1976). John V. Clay, *Spain, Mexico and the Lower Trinity: An Early History of the Texas Gulf Coast* (Baltimore: Gateway Press, 1987). Elizabeth A. H. John, *Storms Brewed in Other Men's Worlds: The Confrontation of Indians, Spanish, and French in the Southwest, 1540–1795* (College Station: Texas A&M University Press, 1975). Lawrence Kinnaird, *The Frontiers of New Spain: Nicolas de Lafora's Description* (Berkeley, California: Quivira Society, 1958). Jean-Baptiste Bénard de La Harpe, *The Historical Journal of the Establishment of the French in Louisiana*, trans. Joan Cain and Virginia Koenig (Lafayette: University of Southwestern Louisiana, 1971). Benedict Leutenegger and Marion A. Habig, *The Zacatecan Missionaries in Texas, 1716–1834* (Austin: Texas Historical Survey Committee, 1973). Thomas P. O'Rourke, The Franciscan Missions in Texas (Ph.D. dissertation, Catholic University of America, 1927; pub. as Vol. 5 of the Catholic University of America Studies in American Church History, New York: AMS Press, 1974). Curtis D. Tunnell and J. Richard Ambler, *Archeological Excavations at Presidio San Agustín de Ahumada* (Austin: State Building Commission, 1967).   *Kevin Ladd*

EL OSO, TEXAS. El Oso, on Farm Road 626 a mile north of Zunkerville in the southwestern corner of Karnes County, was the site of a general merchandise store and a cotton gin built in the 1920s to serve the surrounding farming community. Estimates of El Oso's population remained at fifty from the mid-1940s through the mid-1960s, after which no population figures were available. After the drought of the 1950s the nearby farms were abandoned, and El Oso's store and gin were closed. In 1971 a group of citizens from El Oso were instrumental in creating the El Oso Water Supply Corporation, which in 1990 furnished water for many residents of Karnes County.

BIBLIOGRAPHY: Robert H. Thonhoff, History of Karnes County (M.A. thesis, Southwest Texas State College, 1963).
Robert H. Thonhoff

ELOZÚA, ANTONIO (ca. 1783–1833). Antonio Elozúa (Elosúa), military officer of the Spanish and Mexican armies, the son of Bernardo Elozúa y Melo and Antonia Ximénez y Téllez, was born at San Carlos de Matanzas, Cuba, about 1783. On July 1, 1802, he enlisted in Havana as a cadet in the Infantry of Mexico City (Infantería de México). He was promoted to second lieutenant in 1811 and subsequently served in the Infantry of Vera Cruz (Regimiento Fijo de Veracruz). He was then appointed adjutant major of its Third Battalion and was later captain of the First Battalion from November 1812 to January 1817. Shortly after receiving orders on March 13, 1811, he was engaged in successful military campaigns under the command of Joaquín de Arredondo[qv] against insurgents in Nuevo Santander and San Luis Potosí. He accompanied Arredondo, now commandant general of the Eastern Interior Provinces, to Laredo in the spring of 1813, to prepare for the Texas campaign to avenge the Gutiérrez-Magee expedition[qv] and the executions of Governor Manuel Salcedo, Simón de Herrera,[qqv] and others. He participated in the battle of Medina[qv] (August 18, 1813), at which he was the highest ranking officer (brevet lieutenant colonel) of the Veteran Infantry; his valor earned a recommendation for a promotion. While in Texas he also was engaged in two Indian campaigns. In the spring of 1814 he journeyed with Arredondo from Bexar to Laredo and arrived in Monterrey in July of that year. From early 1815 through April 1816 he led the monthly convoys to Querétaro from San Luis Potosí and participated in military actions against rebels active in the provinces of San Luis Potosí, Zacatecas, and Guanajuato. He was transferred to the Eastern Provinces in early 1816 and garrisoned at Monterrey, where he was a member of the royalist forces sent to Soto la Marina in April 1817 to fight the expedition of Francisco Xavier Mina.[qv] On March 9, 1818, he was named adjutant inspector of Coahuila and Texas.[qv] He was appointed political and military governor of Coahuila on November 25, 1820, a position he had applied for unsuccessfully in 1816 and 1818.

As governor of Coahuila, on July 6, 1821, he proclaimed his support for Agustín de Iturbide's[qv] Plan de Iguala (February 24, 1821), which sought Mexican independence under a constitutional monarchy. Elozúa remained as governor until March 21, 1822, when he assumed the duties of deputy from Coahuila to the First Constituent Congress in Mexico City, which met through October 31, 1823. In October of the following year he was appointed colonel and military commandant of Coahuila and took office in Monclova in December 1824. He was appointed commander of the frontier defenses on January 10, 1826, and adjutant inspector of Coahuila and Texas when the position was reinstituted the following June. Subsequently, he was stationed at Río Grande (now Guerrero, Coahuila), Santa Rosa (now Músquiz, Coahuila), and Laredo. In September 1826 he also assumed command of the Tamaulipas presidios, and in March 1827 he functioned as interim commandant general of Coahuila, Nuevo León, and Tamaulipas, while the titular head, Anastasio Bustamante,qv was in Bexar. Elozúa's final commission was the principal command of the military troops of Texas, which he assumed on December 27, 1827, at Bexar. In this position he administered military posts in Texas, received reports from presidios in Coahuila, and reported directly to the commandant general of the eastern Mexican states. Ill health forced his retirement on September 15, 1833, after thirty-one years of military service. His correspondence as a military officer from the end of Spanish Texas through early Mexican Texasqqv (see also TEXAS IN TRANSITION, 1800–1821) remains principally in the Bexar Archives.qv These thousands of documents are a major source for the record of Coahuilan and Texan military affairs.

He married María Luisa de Urteaga on September 17, 1825. They had two sons, one daughter, and an adopted daughter. Shortly after his retirement Elozúa died at Bexar, on November 15, 1833, and was buried two days later in the chapel of the Alamo. After his widow's death at Presidio del Río Grande in 1841, an executor sold the real estate in San Antonio for the two surviving sons.

BIBLIOGRAPHY: Joaquín de Arredondo, "Report of the Battle of the Medina, August 18, 1813," trans. Mattie Austin Hatcher, *Quarterly of the Texas State Historical Association* 11 (January 1908). Adán Benavides, Jr., comp. and ed., *The Béxar Archives, 1717–1836: A Name Guide* (Austin: University of Texas Press, 1989). Adán Benavides, Jr., The Dispersion of the Commandancy General Archive of the Eastern Interior Provinces (Later, States), 1813–1836 (M.A. Report, University of Texas at Austin, 1983). Adán Benavides, Jr., "Loss by Division: The Commandancy General Archive of the Eastern Interior Provinces," *The Americas* 43 (October 1986). Bexar Archives, Barker Texas History Center, University of Texas at Austin.   *Adán Benavides, Jr.*

EL PASO, CATHOLIC DIOCESE OF. The area included in the Catholic Diocese of El Paso has belonged to as many as five dioceses. Until 1620 it formed part of the Diocese of Guadalajara, Mexico. From 1620 to 1872 it was part of the Diocese of Durango. From 1872 until 1890 it was assigned to the Vicariate of Tucson, Arizona. It became part of the Diocese of Dallas in 1890 and remained so for twenty-four years. In March 1914 the Diocese of El Paso was established. The first bishop was Rev. John J. Brown, S.J., who resigned before he was consecrated. Other bishops have been Anthony J. Schuler, another Jesuit,qv 1915–40; Sydney Matthew Metzger, 1940–78; Patrick F. Flores, 1978–80; and Raymundo F. Peña, installed in 1980. In 1926 the Diocese of Amarillo was formed from the northeast corner of the Diocese of El Paso. The Diocese of Las Cruces was established in 1982. It covers 44,483 square miles of southern New Mexico, the greater part of which was formerly in the Diocese of El Paso, which in 1990 consisted of 26,686 square miles. Two of the original missions in the Diocese of El Paso have continually been used since 1680. They have suffered greatly, however, due to the ravages of time and the Rio Grande. Some preservation efforts have begun restoration. San Elizario, the third mission still in use as a parish church, was founded in 1752 as San Elizario Presidio with its own chapel. In 1789 it was moved to its present site. Nuestra Señora de la Limpia Concepción del Socorro Mission contains the oldest extant original building materials: heavy beams from its first permanent mission of 1681. The old church was destroyed by floods, and the present building was started in 1843. Of interest is the cemetery in front of the church with *descansos* (resting places) at each of the four corners. These were once common, but those in El Paso are the only ones remaining on the Texas-Mexican border at this time.

San José de Concordia el Alto was erected in 1859 on the site of the present Concordia Cemetery. It was the nearest center of Catholic worship for El Paso residents at the time. From 1877 to 1887 the church of adobe,qv now called Our Lady of Mount Carmel, was built for the Spanish-speaking and Tigua and Piros Indians. It was originally called Ysleta del Sur to distinguish it from Isleta, New Mexico (see YSLETA, TEXAS). There was no church in El Paso proper before 1881. Catholics boarded a hand-pulled ferry to attend Mass at Our Lady of Guadalupe in Juárez. In 1882 under the Vicariate of Tucson, lots were purchased on North Oregon Street as a site for the first El Paso Church, known as St. Mary's or Holy Family, which was completed in November 1882; the first Mass was on Christmas Day. A year later two Masses were offered on Sundays in the Chapel, one for Anglos and one for Hispanics. Across the Rio Grande from El Paso del Norte, Mexico, was the small village of Franklin, Texas. In September 1888 the Mexican town changed its name officially to Juárez, and Franklin became El Paso, Texas. In 1892 the Rev. Carlos Pinto,qv S.J., vicar of the area when it was part of the Diocese of Durango, was named vicar of the Diocese of Dallas and superior of all the Jesuitsqv in the zone. In El Paso he was deputed to establish two parishes, one for the English-speaking and the other for the Spanish-speaking. After Pinto's efforts, Catholic parishes began to flourish in El Paso. His recommendations were responsible for Sacred Heart Church for the Spanish-speaking and Immaculate Conception Church, the pro-cathedral for the Anglo-Americans. St. Patrick's Cathedral was dedicated in 1915. That part of the Diocese of El Paso known as West Texas, east of El Paso, was in the jurisdiction of Dallas in its early stages of development. Missionaries from various orders commuted by horseback and early automobiles to serve the parishes in small villages. Most of this area is still part of the Catholic Diocese of El Paso. When S. M. Metzger became bishop in 1940, he found it necessary to ask for funds to revive the diocese. With the help of the Catholic Extension Society he traveled the United States, East and West, the first few years of his tenure, making his appeal from the pulpit. His success was evident in the continuing and establishing of Catholic ministries and institutions. He retired in 1978 and died in April 1986, greatly mourned.

The diocese established two Catholic Youth Organization camps in the New Mexico mountains. A retreat operated by Franciscans,qv Holy Cross Retreat, was established near Las Cruces. On the Mescalero Apache Indian Reservation, Franciscan father Albert Braun and the Indians built their large church in a mountain setting. In El Paso, St. Mary's School was opened for Catholic children in 1903. The earliest school of the Sisters of Loretto,qv Loretto Academy,qv dates from 1879 in San Elizario and, after moving to El Paso in 1892, continued to operate in the 1990s. Hotel Dieu, a hospital opened in 1892, operated for many decades. St. Charles Borromeo Seminary and Cathedral High School, opened in 1924, has grown with the population. The magnificent statue of Christ the King on a mountain above El Paso overlooks two countries, three counties, and three states; it was made possible by Monsignor Lourdes Costa and his parishioners. The Diocese of El Paso has had three diocesan newspapers (see CATHOLIC JOURNALISM). Two Mexican seminaries, St. Anthony's and Roger Bacon, are in El Paso. The diocese has been a unique mixture of two cultures that closely support each other. Bishop Peña, with the assistance of Ricardo Machado, Father Juventino Celino, and Sr. Noreen Creen, promoted Synod 85–86, a conference of priests, religious, and laity in which Anglo-American and Hispanic Catholics participated equally. A renovated Pastoral Center housed the offices and ministries of the diocese in 1990.

BIBLIOGRAPHY: El Paso *Times,* March 24, 1984.

Okla A. McKee

EL PASO, TEXAS. El Paso is at the far western tip of Texas, where New Mexico and the Mexican state of Chihuahua meet in a harsh desert environment around the slopes of Mount Franklin on the Rio Grande, which has often been compared to the Nile. As they approached the Rio Grande from the south, Spaniards in the sixteenth century viewed two mountain ranges rising out of the desert with a deep chasm between. This site they named El Paso del Norte (the Pass of the North), the future location of two border cities—Ciudad Juárez on the south or right bank of the Rio Grande, and El Paso, Texas, on the opposite side of the river. Since the sixteenth century the pass has been a continental crossroads; a north-south route along a historic *camino real* prevailed during the Spanish and Mexican periods, but traffic shifted to an east–west axis in the years following 1848, when the Rio Grande became an international boundary.

The El Paso area was inhabited for centuries by various Indian groups before the Spaniards came. The first Europeans in all probability were Álvar Núñez Cabeza de Vaca qv and his three companions, survivors of an unsuccessful Spanish expedition to Florida, who passed through the El Paso area in 1535 or 1536, although their exact route is debated by historians. Several years later, in 1540–42, an expedition under Francisco Vázquez de Coronado qv explored an enormous amount of territory now known as the American Southwest. The first party of Spaniards that certainly saw the Pass of the North was the Rodríguez-Sánchez expedition qv of 1581; its arrival marked the beginning of 400 years of history in the El Paso area. This was followed by the Espejo-Beltrán expedition (see ESPEJO, ANTONIO DE) of 1582 and the historic colonizing expedition under Juan de Oñate, qv who, on April 30, 1598, in a ceremony at a site near that of present San Elizario, took formal possession of the entire territory drained by the Río del Norte (the Rio Grande). This act, called La Toma, or "the claiming," brought Spanish civilization to the Pass of the North and laid the foundations of more than two centuries of Spanish rule over a vast area.

In the late 1650s Fray García founded the mission of Nuestra Señora de Guadalupe on the south bank of the Rio Grande; it still stands in downtown Ciudad Juárez. The Pueblo Indian Revolt of 1680 sent Spanish colonists and Tigua Indians of New Mexico fleeing southward to take refuge at the pass, transplanting the names of New Mexico river pueblos, including La Isleta and Socorro, to the El Paso area. On October 12, 1680, midway between the Spanish settlement of Santísimo Sacramento and the Indian settlement of San Antonio, the first Mass in Texas was celebrated at a site near that of present Ysleta, which was placed on what is now the Texas side by the shifting river in 1829; Ysleta thus has a claim to being the oldest town in Texas. By 1682 five settlements had been founded in a chain along the south bank of the Rio Grande—El Paso del Norte, San Lorenzo, Senecú, Ysleta, and Socorro.

By the middle of the eighteenth century about 5,000 people lived in the El Paso area—Spaniards, mestizos (*see* MESTIZO) and Indians—the largest complex of population on the Spanish northern frontier. A large dam and a series of acequias (irrigation ditches) made possible a flourishing agriculture. The large number of vineyards produced wine and brandy said to have ranked with the best in the realm. In 1789 the presidio of San Elizario was founded to help in the defense of the El Paso settlements against the Apaches.

With the establishment of Mexican independence from Spain in 1821 (*see* MEXICAN TEXAS), the El Paso area and what is now the American Southwest became a part of the Mexican nation. Agriculture, ranching, and commerce continued to flourish, but the Rio Grande frequently overflowed its banks, causing great damage to fields, crops, and adobe qv structures. In 1829 the unpredictable river flooded much of the lower Rio Grande valley and formed a new channel that ran south of the towns of Ysleta, Socorro, and San Elizario, thus placing them on an island some twenty miles in length and two to four miles in width. Of the various land grants made by the local officials in El Paso del Norte, the best known and most successful was given to Juan María Ponce De León, qv a Paseño aristocrat, in what is now the downtown business district of El Paso, Texas. By this time a number of Americans were engaged in the Chihuahua trade, two of whom—James W. Magoffin and Hugh Stephenson qqv—became El Paso pioneers at a later date.

After the outbreak of hostilities between the United States and Mexico in May 1846, Col. Alexander Doniphan and a force of American volunteers defeated the Mexicans at the battle of Brazito, entered El Paso del Norte, and invaded Chihuahua in December. The Treaty of Guadalupe Hidalgo qv (February 2, 1848), which officially ended the Mexican War, qv fixed the boundary between the two nations at the Rio Grande, the Gila River, and the Colorado River, thence westward to the Pacific. All territory north of that line, known as the Mexican Cession and comprising half of Mexico's national domain, became a part of the United States, which paid Mexico $15 million. Thus El Paso del Norte, the future Ciudad Juárez, became a border town.

By late 1849, aided by the gold rush to California, five settlements had been founded along the left bank of the Rio Grande. Northernmost was Frontera, established by T. Frank White; then the flour mill known as El Molino, founded by Simeon Hart qv the mercantile store of Benjamin Franklin Coons, qv located on the ranch which he purchased from Ponce de León; Magoffinsville, built by the veteran Chihuahua trader; and the property of Hugh Stephenson, later called Concordia, an estate that had belonged to his wife's family. In addition, the three Mexican towns of Ysleta, Socorro, and San Elizario were declared to be in the United States; thus by 1850 the bicultural, bilingual foundations of the future El Paso, Texas, were clearly established.

A number of important developments during the 1850s shaped the character of the area north of the river. A settlement on Coons' Rancho qv called Franklin became the nucleus of El Paso, Texas. El Paso County was established in March 1850, with San Elizario as the first county seat. The United States Senate fixed a boundary between Texas and New Mexico at the thirty-second parallel, thus largely ignoring history and topography. A military post called Fort Bliss qv was established in 1854, and the Butterfield Overland Mail qv arrived in 1858. A year later pioneer Anson Mills qv completed his plat of the town of El Paso, a name that resulted in endless confusion until the name of the town across the river, El Paso del Norte, was changed to Ciudad Juárez in 1888.

During the Civil War qv most of the El Paso pioneers were overwhelmingly sympathetic to the South. Although Confederate forces occupied Fort Bliss in 1861, the tide began to turn in favor of the Union cause the following year, and in August the Stars and Stripes was raised once again over Fort Bliss. The local Southern sympathizers eventually received presidential pardons, but some, such as Simeon Hart, battled for years before they recovered their properties.

In 1877 the region had its own civil war, the Salt War of San Elizario, qv a bloody racial conflict that had little to do with salt, but that set Texan against Mexican, strong man against strong man, faction against faction, and the United States against Mexico. Bad blood, personality conflicts, and intense personal rivalries characterized the affair, and mob violence, rape, robbery, and murder went unpunished with the breakdown of law enforcement. At length Fort Bliss, which had been shut down, was reestablished, and six months of bloodshed was brought to a halt.

Most authorities agree that the arrival of the railroads in 1881 and 1882 was the single most significant event in El Paso history, as it transformed a sleepy, dusty little adobe village of several hundred inhabitants into a flourishing frontier community that became the county seat in 1883 and reached a population of more than 10,000 by 1890. As El Paso became a western boomtown, it also became "Six Shooter Capital" and "Sin City," where scores of saloons, dance halls, gambling establishments, and houses of prostitution lined the main streets. At first the city fathers exploited the town's evil reputation by permitting vice for a price, but in time the more farsighted began to insist that El Paso's future might be in jeopardy if vice and crime were not brought under a measure of control. In the 1890s reform-minded citizens conducted a campaign to curb El Paso's most visible forms of vice and lawlessness, and in 1905 the city finally enacted ordinances closing houses of gambling and prostitution.

After 1900 El Paso began to shed its frontier image and develop as a modern municipality and significant industrial, commercial, and transportation center. The city grew from 15,906 in 1900 to 39,279 in 1910 and 77,560 in 1925. The exodus of refugees fleeing the disruption of the Mexican Revolution[qv] contributed heavily to the city's population growth during this period. Factors making this rapid development possible included El Paso's geographic location as a gateway to Mexico; its proximity to the mining areas of Mexico, New Mexico, and Arizona; its plentiful natural resources; and an abundant supply of cheap Mexican labor. The Kansas City Smelting and Refining Company constructed a large smelter at El Paso in 1887 and merged with several smaller companies in 1899 to become the American Smelting and Refining Company (ASARCO[qv]), which continued to be a major local employer into the 1980s. The completion of Elephant Butte Dam in 1916 in New Mexico ensured a steady water supply for agricultural development and helped cotton to become the predominant local crop. Standard Oil Company of Texas (now Chevron USA), Texaco,[qv] and Phelps Dodge located major refineries in El Paso in 1928 and 1929. Prohibition[qv] provided a boost to the local economy by stimulating a growing tourist trade with the drinking and gambling establishments across the border in Juárez.

For more than 130 years Fort Bliss has played a significant role in local, national, and international affairs, and the relationship between the city and the post has always been close. The military establishment was responsible for much of El Paso's growth during the 1940s and 1950s, when El Paso absorbed the town of Isleta and greatly increased its municipal area. In 1986 military personnel made up one-fourth of the city's population and accounted for one out of every five dollars flowing through El Paso's economy. Textiles, tourism, the manufacture of cement and building materials, the refining of metals and petroleum, and food processing were El Paso's major industries in 1980, with wholesale and retail tradespeople accounting for 23.3 percent of the local work force, professionals 20.8 percent, and government employees 20.9 percent. Prominent local brands included Tony Lama boots and Farah slacks (see TONY LAMA COMPANY and FARAH, INCORPORATED).

Public education in El Paso began with the establishment of an elementary school in 1884 and a high school in 1885. The State School of Mines and Metallurgy opened in 1914, held its first commencement in 1916, changed its name to Texas Western College in 1949, and became the University of Texas at El Paso in 1967. El Paso has had several junior colleges, beginning with the College of the City of El Paso, which held classes for two years starting in 1918 and was followed by El Paso Junior College from 1920 to 1927 and the current El Paso Community College, established in 1972. The El Paso Symphony Orchestra, one of the oldest in the state, traces its roots back to 1893. The El Paso Museum of Art,[qv] established in 1947 as El Paso International Museum, houses a collection of works by European Old Masters, including Botticelli, Filippo Lippi, Tintoretto, and Van Dyck. El Paso's two major newspapers, the *Times* and the *Herald Post,* date from the early 1880s, and the town has operated a public transportation system since 1882.

A major characteristic of border-town El Paso is its special relationship with Mexico in general and Ciudad Juárez in particular. In 1983 El Paso–Juárez was the largest binational urban area along the Mexican-American border. Historic developments such as the Taft-Díaz meeting[qv] of 1909; the taking of Ciudad Juárez by the revolutionary forces of Francisco I. Madero in 1911; the activities of Francisco (Pancho) Villa,[qv] particularly the raid on Columbus, New Mexico, followed by Gen. John J. Pershing's[qv] punitive expedition of 1916; the immigration of Mexican families, rich and poor, during and after the Mexican Revolution; the smuggling and bootlegging activities dur-

Parade in honor of President William McKinley, El Paso, May 6, 1901. Stereograph. Courtesy Lawrence T. Jones III Collection, Austin. El Paso welcomed McKinley with a parade and signs proclaiming the town's commitment to education. This view shows the parade as it passed Immaculate Conception Church.

ing the Prohibition era; the Chamizal dispute[qv] and its settlement in 1964; and the growing interdependence of the two cities—all attest to the unique relationship existing between El Paso and Ciudad Juárez.

The rapid growth that characterized El Paso during the first quarter of the twentieth century slowed somewhat during the 1930s. After reaching 102,421 in the 1930 census the population declined to 96,810 by the 1940 census. Postwar development brought the number of residents up to 130,003 in 1950. Fueled by rapid military and commercial expansion, El Paso's population more than doubled during the next ten years, reaching 276,687 in 1960. Slower but steady growth continued throughout the 1960s, with the population reaching 339,615 in 1970. Despite a period of sluggishness from 1971 to 1974, El Paso's population grew by 32 percent during the 1970s, to 425,259 in 1980. The population has always been predominantly Hispanic. In the 1870s a population of twenty-three Anglos and 150 Hispanics was reported. In 1980 the population was 62.5 percent Spanish-surnamed, and the interaction between the Spanish-Mexican North and the Anglo-American Southwest continued to be the dominant feature of El Paso's culture. As of 1980 other contributors to El Paso's rich ethnic mix included over 13,000 blacks, 3,315 Asians, and 1,484 Indians. El Paso is a colorful city with a distinctive blend of ethnic, border-town, military, Texan, and Southwestern elements. In 1990 the population was 515,342.

BIBLIOGRAPHY: Leon C. Metz, *City at the Pass: An Illustrated History of El Paso* (Woodland Hills, California: Windsor, 1980). C. L. Sonnichsen, *Pass of the North: Four Centuries on the Rio Grande* (2 vols., El Paso: Texas Western Press, 1968, 1980). W. H. Timmons, "American El Paso: The Formative Years, 1848–1854," *Southwestern Historical Quarterly* 87 (July 1983). W. H. Timmons, *El Paso: A Borderlands History* (El Paso: Texas Western Press, 1990). W. H. Timmons, "The El Paso Area in the Mexican Period, 1821–1848," *Southwestern Histor-*

Kohlberg Brothers cigar factory, El Paso, ca. 1915. Photograph by Otis Aultman. Otis A. Aultman Collection, A5747, El Paso Public Library. The International Cigar Factory, the first such factory in the Southwest, was founded by German immigrants Ernst and Moritz Kohlberg in 1886.

ical *Quarterly* 84 (July 1980). W. H. Timmons, ed., *Four Centuries at the Pass* (El Paso: Guynes Printing, 1980).   *W. H. Timmons*

EL PASO ARCHAEOLOGICAL SOCIETY. The El Paso Archaeological Society was founded in 1922, largely through the efforts of Elliott C. Prentiss and Maud D. Sullivan.[qv] Its purposes throughout the years have been the study and preservation of archeological resources and information. The society was granted nonprofit, tax-exempt status in 1964. It is open to all persons interested in archeology. It derives support from membership dues, contributions, publication sales, and fund-raising projects. Annual membership averages 200 family, individual, and institutional members.

During the 1920s and 1930s, the society's artifacts and archives were housed in the El Paso Public Library. After a short period of inactivity in the late 1930s, they were moved to the El Paso Centennial Museum.[qv] In 1976 the society contracted with the city of El Paso to become the support organization of the new Wilderness Park Museum.[qv] After completion of the museum, all properties were moved to the society's adjoining laboratory, print shop, and library.

The organization maintains an extensive library, including its own archives and many rare volumes. It also keeps a large study collection of ceramic and lithic samples from the region and a record of sites located in the western counties of Texas and southern counties of New Mexico. Site information is forwarded to the Texas Archeological Research Laboratory, the Texas Historical Commission,[qv] the El Paso Centennial Museum, and the New Mexico State Museum's Laboratory of Anthropology. The library, study collections, and site records are available for research use. Many of the society's artifacts are on loan to the Wilderness Park Museum.

The society publishes *The Artifact,* a quarterly journal, and *El Paso Archeology,* a monthly newsletter, and distributes them to members. Other ongoing projects include an education series, analysis of collections, surveys, salvage, volunteer assistance on professionally directed projects, and support of antiquities laws. Members also serve as docents for the museum. The society regularly hosts the annual meetings of the Texas Archaeological Society[qv] and the Archaeological Society of New Mexico, symposia of the Southwest Federation of Archaeological Societies, and the Jornada Mogollon Conference. The annual Awards of Distinction Banquet is held in the fall to recognize longtime contributors to archeological studies. The society also participates in Texas Archaeology Awareness Week every November 9–16 and provides a yearly scholarship of $500 to the study of archeology or a related field. In 1994 the El Paso Archaeological Society had a membership of 200.

BIBLIOGRAPHY: Nancy Hamilton et al., "Building a Museum: EPAS and the Wilderness Park," *The Artifact* 19 (Spring 1981). John A. Hedrick, "An Historical Review of the El Paso Archaeological Society, 1922–1972," *The Artifact* 10 (June 1972).   *Carrol Hedrick*

EL PASO CENTENNIAL MUSEUM. The El Paso Centennial Museum, on the campus of the University of Texas at El Paso, was one of several museums across the state established in 1936 as part of the celebration of the Texas Centennial.^qv It features exhibits pertaining to the human and natural history of El Paso, the American Southwest, and northern Mexico, including wooden tools, basketwork, and other items from prehistoric El Paso–area cave dwellers; pottery from Casas Grandes, Mexico; and colonial Spanish ironwork and textiles. Among the museum's special collections are the Ben Wittick Collection of nineteenth-century photographs, which is accessible to scholars but not on public display, and the Josephine Clardy-Fox Fine Art Collection.

BIBLIOGRAPHY: Paula and Ron Tyler, *Texas Museums: A Guidebook* (Austin: University of Texas Press, 1983). *Martin Donell Kohout*

EL PASO COMMUNITY COLLEGE. El Paso Community College was financed by a bond issue in June 1969 and was originally intended to accommodate 16,000 students. When the college opened in fall 1971, 901 students attended classes held at various locations around the city. By the following year, when the college leased a complex of buildings at Fort Bliss from the Department of the Army, enrollment had climbed to 3,501, and by 1974, under president Alfredo de los Santos, enrollment had more than doubled, to 7,443. In 1975 the college purchased a building complex in downtown El Paso that became the Rio Grande Center, where the college's allied health programs were housed. A second campus, the Valle Verde Campus in southeastern El Paso, opened in the fall of 1978, and a third campus, the Transmountain Campus in northeastern El Paso, opened a year later. The Rio Grande Campus was expanded and renovated in 1980. Among the special facilities at El Paso Community College are the Center for Educational Services to the Handicapped, the Women's Center, and the Center for Business Services. By the spring of 1992, under president Leonardo de la Garza, the enrollment had climbed to 17,326. The college is governed by a locally elected board of trustees and is fully accredited by state and regional educational agencies.

BIBLIOGRAPHY: W. H. Timmons, *El Paso: A Borderlands History* (El Paso: Texas Western Press, 1990). *Martin Donell Kohout*

EL PASO COMMUNITY FOUNDATION. The El Paso Community Foundation, established in 1977, is an independent, publicly supported, nonprofit philanthropic organization based in El Paso. As a community foundation, it manages a permanent collection of endowed funds for the benefit of its geographic area. In the early 1990s its assets stood at $23 million. In 1991 a bequest from media businessman Karl O. Wyler, Sr., gave a majority holding of stock in several television and radio stations to the Community Foundation's affiliated foundation, the Glyn Wyler and Karl O. Wyler, Sr., Foundation. The El Paso Community Foundation's fourteen-member board of trustees reflects the demographic makeup of the area, which is predominantly Hispanic; in 1992 six of the board members were Mexican nationals or Mexican Americans.^qv The foundation staff includes a president, two vice presidents, a development director, an accountant, a bookkeeper, and a secretary. The foundation is closely connected to Mexico: each year it receives substantial donations from Mexican citizens, and its trustees make grants to projects on both sides of the border. Janice Windle, foundation president during the early 1990s, held that its internationalism was inevitable in El Paso's geographic context. In the early 1990s foundation emphases included education and environmental protection. A major endeavor was the Lower Valley Water Authority Project. The project, implemented under the auspices of the foundation, five local banks, and the El Paso County Lower Valley Water District Authority, provides loans to residents of colonias^qv on the outskirts of El Paso to be spent on obtaining access to clean water. The foundation makes its grants "to protect and enhance the unique resources of El Paso—its diversity of race and culture, its richness of artistic creation and appreciation, and the beauty and quality of its desert: land, air and water, so that these resources may be enjoyed now and in the future."

EL PASO COUNTY. El Paso County (J-1) is the westernmost county of Texas. Its center point is 106°10′ west longitude and 31°40′ north latitude. Bounded on the southwest by the Rio Grande and Mexico, on the north and west by the state of New Mexico, and on the east by Hudspeth County, Texas, El Paso County is approximately 650 miles west of Dallas and 575 miles northwest of San Antonio. El Paso County and neighboring Hudspeth County are the only Texas counties on Mountain Time. The county comprises 1,057 square miles of desert and irrigated land that rises from an elevation of 3,500 feet at the Rio Grande to 7,000 feet at the summits of the Franklin Mountains.^qv The Rio Grande valley in this area has been irrigated since prehistoric times and produces bountiful harvests of cotton, pecans, and alfalfa, and lesser amounts of numerous vegetables and fruits. Agriculture depends entirely upon irrigation from the river; the average annual rainfall is only 7.77 inches. Desert flora and fauna abound away from the river, while fertile fields and gardens flourish under irrigation. Although summer temperatures usually rise above 100° F for brief periods and have reached a peak of 112, El Paso is not one of the nation's hot spots. A pleasant altitude and low humidity make most summer days agreeable. The average maximum temperature in July is 94° F. The average growing season lasts 248 days. Winters are pleasant, with occasional light snows, although such extremes as fourteen inches of snow and 8° below zero are on record. Some 240 square miles of the county is occupied by the city of El Paso (1992 population 515,342), the largest United States city on the Mexican border, the fourth largest in Texas, and twenty-eighth in the United States. Other El Paso County communities include Fabens, Tornillo, Clint, San Elizario, Socorro, Horizon City, Canutillo, and Anthony. Although a major industrial area, El Paso County has few natural resources other than abundant sunshine and bounteous agriculture. There is no oil production, although there are two oil refineries. There is little if any mineral production, although the county has long been a trade center for Southwest mining and contains a major smelter and a major copper refinery. The county is the only county in the United States to have mined, milled, and smelted tin. The source, deposits of cassiterite in the Franklin Mountains, was found insufficient for profitable operation.

The Spanish name El Paso del Norte denotes a historically important geographical point, the channel cut by the Rio Grande through the mountains to form a natural passageway for travelers to the north or south, east or west. The name El Paso appears in print as early as 1610, in the narrative of Gaspar Pérez de Villagrá, poet-historian of the Oñate expedition^qv of 1598. This large colonizing expedition claimed for the king of Spain all the vast territory of the upper Rio Grande. The way up the river had already been charted by the Rodríguez-Sánchez expedition^qv by 1582. The Oñate expedition, however, had sought a shortcut through the Chihuahuan Desert. Pérez de Villagrá wrote that without water, and almost without hope, the expedition continued on, seeking "el paso por las montañas." At the pass in 1598, on the banks of the river, Oñate and his followers staged a three-day celebration. One of his captains wrote and produced a drama for the occasion, perhaps the first drama presented on what is now American soil. Fish, ducks, and geese from the river supplied food for a great feast, to which Indians living in the area were invited guests, and gratitude was formally rendered to God for the safe arrival of the expedition. Should this be considered the first American Thanksgiving? The pass continued to serve as a way station for travelers between Spanish Mexico and its far-flung dominions to the north. In 1680 an Indian uprising drove the Spaniards out of New Mexico. Many of them found refuge in the El Paso valley, bringing with them members of two Indian tribes, the Tiguas and the Piros. For these were founded the missions of Corpus Christi de la Isleta in Ysleta and Nuestra Señora del Socorro in Socorro.

The people of El Paso had little involvement with the stirring events of 1836–45, the period of the Republic of Texas.^qv An old and valued part of the Republic of Mexico, the El Paso area went its own way. Then came the Mexican War,^qv and the resulting Treaty of Guadalupe Hidalgo qv in 1848, which made all of the area north of the Rio Grande a part of the United States. Suddenly the historic gateway at the pass became important to Texas, and the state almost immediately attempted to assert its right to the area. On March 15, 1848, the Texas legislature proclaimed Santa Fe County,qv which included the area of present-day El Paso County as well as other parts of west Texas and much of the present-day state of New Mexico. After heated protests by the citizens of the city of Santa Fe, Texas governor Peter H. Bellqv threatened to establish Texas authority over the area by force. Early in 1849 public meetings were held in Austin "to determine whether a practicable route could be had between Austin and El Paso," and two rugged frontiersmen, John Salmon (Rip) Ford and Col. Robert S. Neighbors,qqv were sent to the area to attempt to organize the territory. Ford and Neighbors almost failed to make it to El Paso—the explorers became lost many times and nearly starved—and were unable to obtain their political goal. That same year a military force under Maj. Jefferson Van Horneqv set out from San Antonio to establish a military post at El Paso. The company of 257 soldiers headed westward on June 1, with 275 wagons, 2,500 head of livestock, and a number of emigrants. It took 100 days for the group to reach El Paso, where they established the new post in the heart of the city. The post, later renamed Fort Bliss, has become one of the nation's major air-defense centers and is a strong influence in the El Paso County area.

In January 1850 the Texas legislature subdivided Santa Fe County into four smaller counties, one of which was named El Paso County; and in February 1850 Robert Neighbors arrived again in El Paso in another attempt to organize the area. This time his efforts were successful, and San Elizario, the ancient Spanish presidio town, was chosen to be the county seat. With its population of 1,200 San Elizario was at the time the county's largest town and possibly the largest settlement between San Antonio and the West Coast. Parts of the original county were subsequently stripped away from Texas as part of the Compromise of 1850,qv passed by the United States Congress in November of that year. In its resulting form the county also included the present Hudspeth and Culberson counties; Culberson was separated in 1912 and Hudspeth in 1917. By 1860 El Paso county had a population of 4,456 and a fairly extensive agricultural base; more than 12,300 acres in the county was planted in corn, and almost 17,000 acres was planted in wheat; the agricultural census for that year also found 7,253 sheep, 2,953 milk cows, and 2,049 other cattle in the county. Slaveryqv was an almost insignificant factor in El Paso County's agricultural economy, however, since there were only fifteen slaves in the area at that time.

Nevertheless, in February 1861 county citizens voted almost unanimously to support secession.qv Though the county was occupied by both Union and Confederate forces during the Civil War,qv it saw little actual combat. Fort Bliss was surrendered peacefully to the Confederates soon after secession; later that year an expedition under Confederate general Henry H. Sibleyqv marched from Fort Bliss, intent upon claiming all of New Mexico and Arizona for the Confederacy. The expedition failed, and when the Confederates returned to the pass they found that the California Column,qv commanded by Brig. Gen. James H. Carleton,qv was beginning to arrive to reclaim the area for the Union. It remained in Union hands for the remainder of the war. Despite its relative isolation during the Civil War, the county was economically disrupted during the conflict and for several years afterward. As late as 1870 the United States Agricultural Census found only one farm in the county, and crop production that year was insignificant. Gone, too, were the thousands of sheep that had ranged in the area before the war, and the census counted only two milk cows in the county. By 1880, however, the economy was recovering. The agricultural census for that year counted 279 farms and ranches encompassing almost 20,000 acres of land in the county; wheat was planted on more than 2,500 acres, and local farmers were also growing corn, barley, oats, and rye. Livestock were slowly being replenished; the census reported 613 sheep, 397 milk cows, and 844 cattle in the county, further evidence of economic revival.

Though the Republican partyqv dominated county politics until 1886, the county was convulsed during this period by political conflicts, such as the Salt War of San Elizarioqv of 1877. Although on the surface this was a struggle over rights to salt from the salt beds 100 miles to the east, it was primarily a conflict between political factions. It came to a bitter climax of riot and murder in the streets of San Elizario. One result of the conflict was that Fort Bliss, temporarily not in use, was quickly regarrisoned, to be a part of El Paso County life from that time forward. Postwar county politics also featured a protracted county-seat war. In 1866 the county's government was moved from San Elizario to Ysleta, one of the oldest settlements in the county. Then, in 1868, San Elizario again became county seat; it retained the role until 1873, when another election made Ysleta county seat. In 1883, after yet another hotly contested election, El Paso became the county seat.

The decision to make El Paso the seat of government reflected, in part, that city's growing importance as an international transportation hub during a period of rapid economic development in the county. In 1881 four railroads (the Santa Fe, the Texas and Pacific, the Southern Pacific, and the Galveston, Harrisburg and San Antonio) built their way into the county; the next year the tracks of the Mexican Central also reached the city. The arrival of the railroads helped El Paso County, already a crossroads of transportation, burgeon into a major metropolitan area. Its population of 3,845 in 1880 grew to 15,678 in 1890, to 24,886 in 1900, and to 101,877 in 1920. By opening the area to immigration and outside markets, the railroads also helped to stimulate farming and ranching in the county. After a brief downturn in the 1880s, a difficult decade for farmers throughout Texas and the Southwest, the agricultural sector of El Paso's economy grew steadily during the 1890s and the first years of the twentieth century. The number of farms in the area increased from 196 in 1890 to 318 in 1900, then to 669 in 1910. Cattle ranching became more important than ever for the county's economy during this period, as the number of cattle in the county increased from 1,631 in 1890 to almost 95,000 in 1910. Meanwhile, farmers grew increasingly large crops of sorghum and other feed grains; by 1910, for example, almost 10,000 acres of land in the county was planted in sorghum. Local farmers also planted tens of thousands of fruit trees during this period, including 9,970 pear trees. Poultry also began to be a significant part of the farming economy during this time; by 1910 birds raised for eggs or meat numbered more than 14,200 in El Paso County. The agricultural sector suffered a brief downturn in the that decade, but in the 1920s a cotton boom led to a significant increase in the number of farms in the county. Little if any cotton had been planted in the county in 1900, and only 1,548 acres was devoted to the crop as late as 1920. By 1929, however, cotton was raised on more than 46,300 acres win the county. Poultry productionqv similarly increased during the 1920s; in 1929, for example, county farms fed more than 57,300 chickens, and more than 377,000 dozen eggs were sold by farmers. Fruit production also accelerated, and by 1929 there were over 122,000 fruit trees in cultivation in the county. Meanwhile, the number of farms in El Paso County rose quickly to 1,035 by 1925 and to 1,263 by 1929.

The county's economy and its society diversified in other directions during this period, too. In 1880, the year before the arrival of the railroads, only 4 manufacturing establishments, employing 423 workers, were operating in El Paso County. By 1890 there were 73 manufacturers in the county; by 1900, there were 143; and by 1930, there were 160, which together employed 6,224 workers. The completion of Elephant Butte Dam on the Rio Grande in New Mexico in 1916 contributed to both farming and manufacturing, and brought electricity to thousands of residents. The enlargement of Fort Bliss during the World War Iqv also helped the area to prosper. The population of El Paso County grew from 15,678 in 1890 to 24,886 in 1900, 52,599 in 1910, and 131,957 in 1930. Manufacturers, farmers, and workers all suffered through the Great Depression^{qv} of the 1930s. Cotton production dropped more than 30 percent from 1929 to 1940, for example, and the number of farms in El Paso County decreased from 1,263 to 1,075. Meanwhile, the number of factories in the county declined from 160 in 1930 to 132 in 1940, throwing thousands of workers out of their jobs; in 1940 only 3,081 people worked for manufacturers in the county. The county's population as a whole also declined slightly during the depression, to 131,067. World War II,^{qv} and especially the considerable enlargement of Fort Bliss during the war, helped the area to recover and begin a new cycle of growth. After the 1940s the number of manufacturing establishments grew. In 1947, for example, there were 148 manufacturers in the county employing 6,167 workers; by 1963 the county had 251 manufacturing establishments employing 14,916 workers; and by 1982 there were 471 manufacturers in the county employing about 38,300 workers. Meanwhile, the county population increased to 194,968 by 1950, to 314,070 by 1969, to 359,291 in 1970, to 479,899 in 1980, and to an estimated 591,610 in 1992.

Modern El Paso County is fronted, just across the Rio Grande, with another metropolitan area, Ciudad Juárez, Chihuahua, the largest Mexican city on the border (estimated population in 1985: 750,000). The two populations shared the experiences of Civil War in the United States and of the Mexican Revolution.^{qv} The blending of two cultures is everywhere present on both sides of the border. More than 60 percent of the residents of El Paso County have Spanish surnames. In private life and in the public schools, there are constant efforts to make the population bilingual. Problems, of course, are many. Mexico, beset in the 1980s by inflation and unemployment, saw its citizens moving, legally and illegally, toward an anticipated better life in the United States. Thousands of aliens crossing the river without authorization were captured monthly and sent back to their own country, but a larger number succeeded in entering Texas. On the positive side, border commerce gives rich benefits to both countries. A relatively recent development is the "twin plants" concept, in which United States industries have twin operations in Mexico, where the labor-intensive part of the work is carried on (*see* MAQUILADORAS). A large supply of skilled and unskilled labor provides El Paso with a varied industrial base. The city is one of the nation's principal centers for the manufacture of outdoor clothing and boots. Smelting, copper and oil refining, railroad operations, and a large and varied retail trade join with government and military activities to provide an ever-changing variety of employment.

Educationally and culturally, El Paso County does much to substantiate its claim as "a land of better living." It is the site of the University of Texas at El Paso and El Paso Community College. Public museums include the El Paso Museum of Art, Wilderness Park Museum,^{qqv} and the El Paso Museum of History. The Texas Parks and Wildlife Department^{qv} operates Hueco Tanks State Historical Park,^{qv} a historic landmark with relics of the historic and prehistoric past. The National Park Service operates the Chamizal National Memorial,^{qv} an international cultural center. A professional symphony orchestra, a ballet company, and several theater companies provide a variety of entertainment. The annual musical and historical drama *Viva El Paso* is presented each summer in the McKelligon Canyon Amphitheater. A wide variety of sports is highlighted by Texas League^{qv} baseball, Western Athletic Conference competition, and the annual Sun Bowl,^{qv} one of the nation's oldest midwinter football games, with its attendant Sun Carnival attractions.

BIBLIOGRAPHY: Conrey Bryson, *The Land Where We Live: El Paso del Norte* (El Paso: Aniversario del Paso '73, 1973). Eugene O. Porter, *San Elizario* (Austin: Jenkins, 1973). C. L. Sonnichsen, *Pass of the North: Four Centuries on the Rio Grande* (2 vols., El Paso: Texas Western Press, 1968, 1980). W. H. Timmons, *El Paso: A Borderlands History* (El Paso: Texas Western Press, 1990).
Conrey Bryson

EL PASO COUNTY HISTORICAL SOCIETY. The El Paso County Historical Society was organized on March 18, 1954, as a project of the Civic Improvement Committee of the Women's Department, El Paso Chamber of Commerce, on the suggestion of historian Cleofas Calleros. Louise Schuessler was the organizing chairman, and Paul A. Heisig was elected the first president. The purpose of the society is to encourage and support research into the history, archeology, and natural history of El Paso and the region; the society publishes the results of research and preserves relics and monuments.

It had more than a hundred charter members and 750 members by 1956. It promoted community celebrations of the seventy-fifth anniversary of the coming of the railroads to El Paso in 1881 and the 100th anniversary of the Butterfield Overland Mail^{qv} in 1857. In 1973 it celebrated the centennial of the city by compiling a volume of articles entitled *El Paso: A Centennial Portrait*. The society, in its earliest years, presented to the city of El Paso three important historical relics: engine number one of the El Paso and Southwestern Railroad, an original mule car that provided El Paso's first streetcar service, and steam engine number 3420 of the Southern Pacific Railroad.

The society's quarterly, *Password*, began publication in the spring of 1956, with Eugene O. Porter of Texas Western College (now the University of Texas at El Paso) as its first editor. He was succeeded by Conrey Bryson in 1975, by Nancy Hamilton in 1980, and by Lillian Collingwood in 1983. The society offers an annual award for the best article published in *Password*. It also sponsors three annual essay prizes to encourage research by junior historians and three more for senior citizens in the annual historical memories contest.

In 1962 the society inaugurated the El Paso Hall of Honor, which annually honors two county residents, one living and one deceased, of "outstanding vision, courage and creative skill." Since its founding, the Hall of Honor has enrolled forty-two men and ten women. They are inducted at a community banquet, and their biographies are published in *Password*.

The society conducts an annual tour of historic homes in the El Paso area. It is also the operating agency for the El Paso Museum of History, which served as its headquarters until 1986. Since that date the offices have been at 603 West Yandell Boulevard, in a house willed to the society by Jane Burges Perrenot, a charter member.
Conrey Bryson

EL PASO ELECTRIC. El Paso Electric provides electric and nuclear power for much of the Southwest. It grew from the Brush Electric Light Company of El Paso, which was organized in the late 1880s by Mayor Joseph Magoffin^{qv} and the El Paso City Council at the urging of a group of local citizens. By 1890 El Paso pioneer Zach T. White^{qv} had taken over the electrical business and installed generating equipment to enable the use of incandescent lamps in the city. The current enterprise was founded when El Paso Electric Railway Company took over the Brush Electric plant on August 30, 1901, and originally incorporated as the El Paso Electric Railway Company to provide power solely within the El Paso area. Among early officers of the firm was El Paso businessman and journalist Felix Martinez,^{qv} who served as vice president.

In 1902 El Paso Electric Railway negotiated a management contract with Stone and Webster Management Consultants, a New England company that supplied contractual engineering and financial assistance to utilities nationwide, and accomplished its first objective of replacing mule-drawn streetcars with electric ones. Further expansion came in 1905, when the company purchased the International Light and Power Company, commissioned by the state in 1889 to supply power to El Paso and surrounding communities, and in 1914 acquired the electrical divisions of the El Paso Gas and Electric Company. By 1923 the new electric company had a generating capacity of 18,000 watts. Its name was changed to El Paso Electric Company in 1925, and later that year the organization was permitted to conduct business in New Mexico. By 1928 the communities of Hatch and Rincon in Texas had been added to the system.

As the company expanded, its ability to supply power to the citizens of El Paso and neighboring communities increased. The company's Rio Grande Power Station, built in the upper valley of El Paso in 1929, enabled the company to erect high-voltage lines to serve Sierra Blanca and Van Horn. A decade later El Paso Electric acquired the Mesilla Valley Electric Company, formed in 1924 in New Mexico to serve Las Cruces and its neighboring communities. Output capabilities increased with a 20,000-kilowatt unit at the same location in 1950 and a 50,000-kilowatt turbogenerator there in 1956. In 1950 customers of El Paso Electric grew from 4,844 to 54,108 in a single year, and by the end of 1956 a total of 75,747 customers belonged to the system. Meanwhile, El Paso Electric became an independent electric utility when it ended its relationship with Stone and Webster Management Consultants in 1947. A 90,000-kilowatt unit was under construction, and another was completed at Newman Power Station in Texas by 1960. In 1966 the station had a 115,000-kilowatt unit. The Santa Fe Power Station, built in 1901, was almost completely torn down in 1961, and the company purchased 7 percent interest in two of five units at Four Corners Generating Station in Farmington, New Mexico, completed in 1969. A more efficient unit, powered primarily by the Solar Photovoltaic Project, a joint venture of the company and New Mexico State University, was completed in 1975 at the Newman Power Station. In 1979, after sixty years headquartered in the Martin Building, the company ended the decade by moving to the Mills Building, originally constructed in 1912 and once one of the largest concrete buildings in the United States. By this time, the company was locally known for lighting a huge star on an El Paso mountain at Christmas.

In 1980 El Paso Electric completed its Copper Station, a turbine system built at El Paso to withstand the West Texas summer heat. The total cost of fuel used by the company grew from $882,257 in 1950 to $122.8 million in 1985. Faced by the energy crisis of the 1970s, El Paso Electric attempted to sign long-term fuel contracts, increase its research and development efforts, acquire new fuel-storage facilities, reconsider fuel-mix techniques, and increase its rates for the first time. In 1984 the company briefly opened downtown offices for customer convenience, which it subsequently closed in cost-cutting measures after the Public Utility Commission[qv] of Texas mandated rate reductions in 1984 and 1985. The reduced rates were discontinued in 1986. In 1983 the New Mexico Public Service Commission granted El Paso Electric a $5.9 million increase in base rates; in 1986 the commission granted a $7 million increase.

El Paso Electric has long been a leader in nuclear power, beginning with the formation of the Arizona Nuclear Power Project in 1972. Three units became operational at Palo Verde Nuclear Generating Station, near Phoenix, in 1988, making the plant the largest in the Western Hemisphere. The first unit was declared in "commercial operation" in 1985, thus allowing management to include its cost in the rate base for power. The second unit achieved a self-sustained nuclear chain reaction, was granted a full-power operating license, and declared in commercial operation in 1986. El Paso Electric subsequently sold part ownership of this unit to a group of investors and in the 1990s leased the unit back from the investor group, retaining partial responsibility for operation and maintenance costs in exchange for a 27½-year commitment and a renewal provision. The third unit obtained its commercial license in 1988, giving the plant an overall capacity of 3,810 megawatts. Another sale and lease-back transaction, also arranged in 1988, provided for the sale of 40 percent of this unit and its lease back to the company for a price of $250 million. The company used proceeds from the sale to retire debt and achieve other corporate objectives. By the 1990s El Paso Electric served more than 550,000 customers in a 10,000-square-mile area from New Caballo Dam, New Mexico, to Van Horn, Texas, a community 120 miles southeast of El Paso.

In the late 1980s, however, El Paso Electric was losing money, largely because of its investment in the Palo Verde Nuclear Generating Station, regulatory decisions that limited its ability to charge rates high enough to cover its costs, and failed attempts to diversify into such areas as real estate and furniture manufacture. In 1992, at which time it served 258,000 customers in El Paso, Las Cruces, New Mexico, and small farming communities along the Rio Grande, the company was forced to declare bankruptcy. Central and South West Corporation, a Dallas-based utility holding company, agreed to buy the firm in 1993 under a reorganization plan that would make it a wholly-owned subsidiary; the plan authorized the company to acquire 255,000 customers in the Rio Grande valley and southern New Mexico, to buy additional power, and to control all major electric interconnections along the border between the United States and Mexico, except one in San Diego. Central and South West, however, faced a takeover battle for the firm with the smaller Southwestern Public Service Company of Amarillo, which would likely increase rates to customers. Passage of the North American Free Trade Agreement, however, promised future success for the company, which was located on the border just across from Ciudad Juárez, Chihuahua, had long sold power to Mexico, and was in a strong position to expand.

BIBLIOGRAPHY: Dallas *Morning News,* May 5, 1993. New York *Times,* September 10, 1993. *Texas Monthly,* July 1989.   *Damon Arhos*

EL PASO MUSEUM OF ART. The El Paso Museum of Art, best known for its Samuel H. Kress collection of paintings and sculptures by Italian Renaissance and Spanish Baroque artists, is located at 1211 Montana Avenue. The museum is housed in Iva and William W. Turney's[qv] former home, a Neoclassical revival structure that was designed by Henry Charles Trost[qv] and completed in 1910. The idea for the museum originated in 1925, when Kate Moore Brown, then president of the woman's department of the chamber of commerce, purchased cases for the display of the Percival Henderson collection of books and tapestries, which had been left to the city of El Paso. The El Paso International Museum was granted a charter on February 17, 1930. Although the museum had no fixed location at that time, its collection continued to grow through bequests left to the city of El Paso. In the mid-1940s Iva Turney deeded her home to the El Paso Museum Board, and the International Museum subsequently opened to the public in the spring of 1947. In addition to furniture, clothing, decorative art objects, and paintings, the museum's permanent collection included the Casas Grandes Collection of pottery, the Wimber Collection of Guns, and Col. E. M. Barron's collection of southwestern and Mexican minerals. The museum's current emphasis on art developed from the close association between prominent El Paso citizens Evelyn Woods and Robert E. McKee[qv] and Rush Kress and Guy Emerson, president and art director, respectively, of the Samuel H. Kress Foundation. Samuel H. Kress (1863–1955), founder of the Kress stores chain, began collecting paintings and sculptures by old masters, with a focus on Italian artists, during the 1920s. He subsequently donated a substantial portion of his collection to the National Gallery and gave smaller groups of works to over forty museums and universities throughout the United States. In order to secure the donation of a portion of the Kress collection for the city of El Paso, the privately-owned International Museum became a public institution. This transition, necessary to raise funds for the required renovations, was facilitated by Mayor Raymond L. Telles, Jr., and Dan Ponder, then president of the museum association. Plans were drawn up in the late 1950s for a two-wing addition to the original museum structure, with interior spaces remodeled to provide additional exhibition galleries, an art classroom, an auditorium, offices, and maintenance and work rooms. After Emerson approved the plans, Ponder presented the deed for the International Museum to the city of El Paso, which agreed to maintain the museum with an annual appropriation. In 1959 the museum's name was changed to the El Paso Museum of Art, and the citizens of El Paso approved a $750,000 bond issue to remodel the facility. The museum was renovated in 1960 under the direction of the architectural firm Carroll and Daeuble and Associates, and in May 1961 the Kress collection was installed in three galleries of the museum's west wing.

The Kress collection at the El Paso Museum of Art consists of fifty-seven paintings and two sculptures that range in date from 1200 to 1800. The majority of the works are by Italian Renaissance painters, although there are some fine works by Spanish Baroque painters Juan De Borgoña, Jusepe de Ribera, Francisco de Zurburán, and Juan de Valdés Leal, among others. The collection also includes portraits by eighteenth-century French painters and a *Portrait of a Lady* (ca. 1618–20) by Flemish painter Anthony van Dyck. Highlights of the collection include a tondo of the Madonna and Child (ca. 1500–10) painted by a follower of Sandro Botticelli; a fine Venetian landscape, ca. 1730s, by Canaletto; and Bartolomé Esteban Murillo's *Ecce Homo* (ca. 1672–78). Other outstanding works in the collection are Filippino Lippi's *St. Jerome in His Study* (ca. 1490), Lorenzo Lotto's *Portrait of a Man with Allegorical Symbols* (ca. 1540s), and Artemisia Gentilleschi's *Saint Catherine of Alexandria* (ca. 1620s). In addition to the Kress collection, the museum has acquired collections of Pre-Columbian art, Mexican Colonial art, and graphics by Japanese, European, and American artists. Paintings by North American artists such as Gilbert Stuart, Rembrandt Peale, George Inness, Frederic Remington, Frank Duveneck, Childe Hassam, and Manuel G. Acosta[qv] are included in the museum's permanent collection. Since 1959 the city of El Paso has provided operating funds and salary support for the museum and has been the governing authority of the institution. A board of directors, consisting of fifteen members elected on a rotating basis for three-year terms, develops museum policies, guides acquisitions, and directs the activities of the El Paso Art Museum Association. The museum association, founded in 1960, uses membership dues and donations to finance museum services, programs, and acquisitions. Funds for acquisitions are raised by the Members Guild, a "working force" of dedicated volunteers drawn from the membership of the El Paso Art Museum Association. A full-time professional director implements plans and guides daily activities at the museum. Ann Butterfield Newman, director of the International Museum from 1947 until her death in 1959, was succeeded by Reginald Fisher (1959–63); interim directors Woody Crumbo and Clay Aldridge subsequently co-ordinated museum activities until Leonard Sipiora was hired in 1967. Sipiora was succeeded by interim director Peter de Wetter (1990–91). Becky Duval Reese has served as director since April 1991. The El Paso Museum of Art participates in approximately eight traveling exhibitions each year, hosts the annual El Paso Artists Association exhibition, and sponsors an annual art competition for high school students. The museum has organized exhibitions of the McKee collection (1968) and Anschutz collection (1976), both of which feature works by southwestern artists, and solo exhibitions of local artists such as Tom Lea (1963, 1971) and Manuel Acosta (1974, 1988). The museum's emphasis on southwestern art and history is also evident in the traveling exhibitions it has participated in, such as Texas Public Buildings of the 19th Century (1975), The Big Bend: a History of the Last Texas Frontier (1976), Raices Antiguas/Visiones Nuevas. Ancient Roots/New Visions (1978), and Dos Artistas Mexicanos: Benjamin Dominguez and Magali Lara (1991). Lectures, demonstrations, recitals, workshops, and film programs supplement the museum's exhibitions. Tours are offered to the public by trained volunteers from the Members Guild. Classes in oil painting, ceramics, print making, and other media are offered in the Junior Arts Center, which was established in 1960 by the Junior League of El Paso. Other facilities include a 500-volume library and a Sensorium. The Sensorium, a room filled with models of sculptures, originated as a place for the blind to appreciate art and has become a popular exhibit with many visitors to the museum. Additional monies for exhibitions and lecture series have been supplied by occasional grants from the Texas Commission for the Arts and the El Paso Community Foundation.

In the early 1970s Leonard Sipiora approached Mayor Fred Hervey with the suggestion that the museum extend its scope to encompass science and history. Sipiora subsequently worked with Hervey and the El Paso Heritage Foundation to establish two museums. The Cavalry Museum, now the El Paso Museum of History, is housed in a Spanish colonial building on Interstate Highway 10, East, and opened in July 1974. The museum features seven life-size dioramas representing events from El Paso's history; artifacts from the museum's permanent collection, such as tools, weapons, and quilts, are also displayed. The Wilderness Park Museum, located in a seventeen-acre park on Transmountain Road, opened to the public in October 1977. The museum uses dioramas and permanent exhibits to trace human development in the El Paso area. A mile-long nature trail in the park leads visitors past a pithouse, a kiva, and a replica of a Pueblo ruin, enriching the visitor's glimpse into the area's past. Changing exhibitions are also presented. Upon completion the new museums were deeded to the city of El Paso Museum Department for operation and maintenance. The El Paso Museum of Art director supervised the curatorial staff at both museums until December 1990, when the El Paso Museum of History hired its own director. The Museum of Art also provides maintenance staff for the Museum of History and the Wilderness Park Museum. In 1991 Reese led a staff of eighteen employees, seven of whom were full-time professionals. A $12 million fundraising campaign was underway to renovate a Greyhound building in downtown El Paso into a new facility for the El Paso Museum of Art. The El Paso Museum of Art is a member of the American Association of Museums, the Texas Association of Museums, and the Mountain Plains Museum Association.

BIBLIOGRAPHY: Thomas B. Hess, "Culture as the American Dream," *ARTnews*, December 1961. *The Samuel H. Kress Collection* (El Paso Museum of Art, 1961). Paula and Ron Tyler, *Texas Museums: A Guidebook* (Austin: University of Texas Press, 1983). Vertical Files, Barker Texas History Center, University of Texas at Austin.

Kendall Curlee

EL PASO NATURAL GAS COMPANY. El Paso Natural Gas Company, established just before the Great Depression,[qv] has withstood momentous regulatory, economic, and social changes in its nearly seven decades to emerge as one of the largest natural gas–transmission companies in the United States. In 1928 Paul Kayser, a Houston lawyer with a talent for business, discovered that El Paso was the only city of size in Texas without natural gas service and acquired a franchise from the El Paso city government. On June 19, 1929, deliveries of natural gas began to the largest community on the Texas-Mexico border. The gas flowed through a 204-mile, sixteen-inch-diameter pipeline from three wells drilled near Jal in southeastern New Mexico. In the company's first full year of operation, 1930, El Paso sold 5.5 million cubic feet of gas.

El Paso expanded even during the depression. Kayser took out construction loans to extend his company's pipelines to serve copper-refining companies in southern Arizona and northern Mexico in the early 1930s. El Paso next added the Tucson and Phoenix markets area, and by the end of the 1930s its pipelines extended to Ajo, Arizona. Further expansion was halted by the entrance of the United States into World War II.[qv] With the end of the war and the availability of steel pipe, El Paso Gas began service to California. The initial California contract was with the company that is now Southern California Gas Company. Deliveries began in November 1947, and additional contracts quickly followed, as El Paso sought to meet the state's burgeoning demand for energy.

Gas for El Paso's pipelines came from the Permian Basin[qv] of West Texas and southeastern New Mexico and included "casinghead" or residue gas, a by-product of oil production that previously had been burned ("flared") as a waste product. El Paso built the facilities necessary to treat the residue gas to make it suitable for pipeline transmission. El Paso's action in utilizing this natural resource was hailed as a major conservation step by the Railroad Commission.qv

El Paso Natural Gas Company acquired all of the California market in 1951 under a long-term pact with Pacific Gas and Electric Company, which serves central and northern California. Gas for this expansion came from a new supply source for El Paso, the San Juan Basin of northwestern New Mexico and Southwestern Colorado, in the Four Corners area. El Paso was the first major company in the San Juan Basin, which then and now, has large reserves of natural gas, bolstered in the late 1980s with the production of coal seam gas, largely methane extracted from the coal beds so prevalent in the San Juan Basin.

El Paso has been a pioneer and innovator in natural gas transmission. It was among the first to build high-pressure, long-distance pipelines and develop innovative pipeline-welding methods. With its first units in September 1952 it became the first company to use large gas-turbine-driven centrifugal compressors. They were still operating in 1990. El Paso perfected several methods of treating natural gas to remove impurities, and for many years it had more gas-treating capacity than all other interstate pipelines combined. El Paso joined with the United States Atomic Energy Commission and the Bureau of Mines of the Department of the Interior in 1967 to determine if a nuclear device could be used to "fracture" and thus increase production from a gas-bearing formation in the San Juan Basin. The experiment, Project Gasbuggy, was a technical success, but the procedure was not deemed commercially feasible.

During the 1970s El Paso Gas participated in large-scale importation of liquefied natural gas from Algeria. It contracted for a fleet of nine giant carriers that were to deliver sub-zero liquefied natural gas to specially constructed regasification terminals at Cove Point, Maryland, and Elba Island, Georgia. Initial shipments began in 1978 and eventually six of the LNG carriers were in operation. However, the project was short-lived. A pricing dispute between the Algerian and United States governments halted deliveries in early 1980. After months of fruitless negotiations, El Paso wrote off its $365 million investment in the project in early 1981.

Throughout its existence the company's pipelines have been the foundation of its success. In 1993 more than four billion cubic feet of natural gas flowed daily through the El Paso system to distribution companies and industries in West Texas, New Mexico, Arizona, Nevada, and California. El Paso's pipelines interconnect with lines moving gas into the Midwest, Gulf Coast, and East, and the company has begun deliveries to Mexico, a most promising market with major potential. However, most of the natural gas carried by El Paso is delivered to California. Since the mid-1970s El Paso has delivered more than half of all natural gas used in the nation's most populous state.

In addition to its own interstate system, El Paso Gas is a partner with Enron Corporation of Houston in the first interstate natural gas pipeline built in California. The Mojave Pipeline Project, which began service in February 1992, delivers natural gas to the enhanced oil-recovery and cogeneration facilities in central California. The gas is delivered into the Mojave system from the El Paso and Enron pipelines at a transfer line near Topock, Arizona.

El Paso once again became a publicly traded company in mid-1992, when it was spun off from Burlington Resources, a successor to Burlington Northern, Incorporated, which had acquired El Paso in 1983. In 1985 the Federal Energy Regulatory Commission made interstate pipelines open-access or common carriers. In essence, the new regulations moved El Paso from its traditional role as a merchant—producing or buying, treating, and selling gas—to that of a transporter. El Paso had a fully computerized system of 20,000 miles of pipeline and delivered 1.1 trillion cubic feet of gas in 1992.

BIBLIOGRAPHY: Frank Mangan, *The Pipeliners* (El Paso: Gaynes Press, 1977).
John H. McFall

EL PASO DEL NORTE. As they approached the Rio Grande from the south, Spanish explorers in the colonial period viewed two mountain ranges rising out of the desert with a deep chasm between. This site they named El Paso del Norte (the Pass of the North), and it became the location of two future border cities, Ciudad Juárez on the south or right bank of the Rio Grande and El Paso, Texas, on the opposite side of the river. The arrival of the first Spanish expedition at the Pass of the North in 1581 marked the beginning of more than 400 years of history in the El Paso area. It was followed in 1598 by the colonizing expedition under Juan de Oñate.qv On April 30, 1598, in a ceremony at a site near present San Elizario, Oñate took formal possession of the entire territory drained by the Rio Grande and brought Spanish civilization to the Pass of the North.

In 1659 Fray García de San Francisco founded Nuestra Señora de Guadalupe Mission, which still stands in downtown Ciudad Juárez, the oldest structure in the El Paso area. The Pueblo revolt of 1680 sent Spanish colonists and Tigua Indians of New Mexico fleeing southward to take refuge at the Pass. By 1682 five settlements were founded south of the river—El Paso del Norte, San Lorenzo, Senecú, Ysleta, and Socorro, thus providing the Pass with a concentration of population from that time to the present. A presidio was built in 1684. The area became a trade center on one of the historic *caminos reales*, or royal highways, and agriculture flourished, particularly the vineyards, producing wine and brandy that ranked in quality with the best in the realm.

When Mexico won its independence from Spain in 1821 the El Paso area and what is now the American Southwest became a part of the Mexican nation. The municipal council of El Paso del Norte granted land north of the Rio Grande to Juan María Ponce de León,qv and it became a thriving agricultural and ranching enterprise; his land is now the site of downtown El Paso. With the outbreak of hostilities between the United States and Mexico in May 1846, Col. Alexander Doniphan and his Missouri volunteers defeated the Mexicans at the battle of Brazito, entered El Paso del Norte, and occupied the city of Chihuahua in early 1847. The Treaty of Guadalupe Hidalgoqv of February 2, 1848, fixed the boundary between the two nations at the Rio Grande, and thus El Paso del Norte, the future Ciudad Juárez, became a bordertown.

By late 1849, aided by the gold rush to California, five settlements had been established by Anglo-Americans north of the river, one of them, known as Franklin, on the ranch of former proprietor, Ponce de León. In 1859, however, pioneer Anson Millsqv named this settlement El Paso, thus generating considerable confusion that lasted for almost thirty years.

During the period of the French intervention in Mexico the republican cause under the leadership of Benito Juárez took refuge in El Paso del Norte in August 1865 and remained there for almost a year. With the aid of American arms and munitions the tide began to turn in favor of the Juárez republicans, who returned to Mexico City in triumph in 1867. On September 16, 1888, El Paso del Norte was renamed Ciudad Juárez, and thus the historic name El Paso became the sole possession of the bustling little railroad town at the western tip of Texas.

BIBLIOGRAPHY: C. L. Sonnichsen, *Pass of the North: Four Centuries on the Rio Grande* (2 vols., El Paso: Texas Western Press, 1968, 1980). W. H. Timmons, *El Paso: A Borderlands History* (El Paso: Texas Western Press, 1990).
W. H. Timmons

EL PASO AND NORTHEASTERN RAILROAD. The El Paso and Northeastern Railroad Company was chartered on June 5, 1896. It was to connect El Paso with a point on the boundary line between

Texas and New Mexico twenty miles northeast of the city. According to an amendment to the original articles of incorporation the railroad had a capital stock of $300,000. Its principal place of business was El Paso, and its first board of directors comprised Charles B. Eddy and W. A. Hawkins of Eddy, New Mexico; J. C. Osgood of Denver, Colorado; and S. H. Buchanan, Charles F. Slack, C. C. Blodgett, and J. L. Bell of El Paso. On February 15, 1898, the railroad acquired the El Paso Northern Railway Company from Charles Eddy. Only slightly over four miles of this company was used; the balance of the El Paso Northern was abandoned and the material removed to be used elsewhere in the construction of the El Paso and Northeastern line. At the Texas–New Mexico border the company connected with the El Paso and Northeastern Railway Company. The two railroads formed a 164 mile route from El Paso to the coal fields near Capitan, New Mexico, which opened on January 1, 1899. All of the equipment was supplied by the El Paso and Northeastern Railway Company. Both the Texas and New Mexico companies were subsidiaries of the New Mexico Railway and Coal Company. In May 1905 Phelps, Dodge, and Company acquired the parent company, whereupon they dissolved that firm and established the El Paso and Northeastern Company to own and control the rail lines. The El Paso and Rock Island Railway Company opened a 128-mile line in February 1902 from Carrizozo to Santa Rosa, New Mexico. At Santa Rosa the line connected with a subsidiary of Chicago, Rock Island and Pacific Railway Company, giving El Paso another outlet to the east. The El Paso and Rock Island was acquired by the El Paso and Northeastern Company in May 1905. A reorganization of the Phelps, Dodge interests in 1908 resulted in the formation of the El Paso Southwestern Company to acquire and lease the properties of the El Paso and Northeastern Company. The Southern Pacific Company acquired the El Paso Southwestern Company on October 31, 1924, and operated the El Paso and Northeastern Railroad Company under lease until November 18, 1937. On that date the company was dissolved and the assets acquired by the El Paso and Southwestern Railroad Company of Texas.

Nancy Beck Young

EL PASO NORTHERN RAILWAY. The El Paso Northern Railway Company was chartered on September 13, 1894, to acquire the former Kansas City, El Paso and Mexican Railroad Company of Texas. The latter railroad, which had completed a ten-mile line from El Paso to Lanoria on December 1, 1888, had been bought by Jay Gould[qv] at foreclosure on April 28, 1892. Following Gould's death in December of that year, the executors of his estate conveyed the railroad to Charles Satterlee, who, in turn, conveyed it to the El Paso Northern. The initial capital was $300,000, and the business office was in El Paso. Members of the first board of directors included George J. Gould of Lakewood, New Jersey; Edwin Gould of New York; Satterlee of Brooklyn, New York; Charles R. Morehead[qv] of El Paso, and William H. Abrams,[qv] L. S. Thorne, and E. L. Sargent, all from Dallas. On November 16, 1897, the line was acquired by Charles B. Eddy in the interest of the El Paso and Northeastern Railroad Company.

Chris Cravens

EL PASO POLYCHROME POTTERY. El Paso polychrome pottery is a red, black, and brown ware produced by Indian workmen between A.D. 1200 and 1600. The type locality is the Hueco basin northeast of El Paso, Texas. Though common within a radius of 100 miles of El Paso, the pottery is most abundant in the type area and the southern portion of the adjacent Tularosa basin, New Mexico. The workmanship is crude both in the vessels and in the application of paint. The clay is grayish brown to black, sand-tempered, and friable. Sand, frequently quite coarse, may be visible on the surface. Vessels include ollas, jars, bowls, and, more rarely, ladles, zoomorphic forms, and erratically shaped pieces. The shoulders of ollas and jars are thin, remarkably so in some instances, with surface smoothing accomplished by wiping or rubbing. The brown to reddish base color is applied either by a thin wash or, more probably, by a float. The decoration on the brown background is red and black. The red paint varies from bright to dull and is thin on some pieces. Since the black is a carbon paint, it is more uniform in intensity, except when over-fired. Designs are geometric, made up of parallel lines and stepped elements with some use of circles, arcs, and massed colors. Ollas and jars are decorated on the shoulder, on the neck, and often on the inner lip. The interiors and rims of bowls and ladles are decorated, while odd-shaped vessels are painted in a manner consistent with their shape.

BIBLIOGRAPHY: W. S. Stallings, Jr., *El Paso Polychrome* (Santa Fe: Laboratory of Anthropology, 1931).

W. S. Strain

EL PASO SOUTHERN RAILWAY. The El Paso Southern Railway Company was chartered on March 14, 1897, with a capital stock of $100,000. The original stockholders and board of directors consisted of J. Ferguson Smith, Jonathan P. Ramsey, E. W. Mead, James W. Duke, James H. McHimmell, L. P. Atwood, Edwin B. Wynam, J. Douglas Matthew, L. D. Welch, and Max Weber, all of whom resided in El Paso. The line was originally to extend from the international bridge over the Rio Grande five miles north to Mount Franklin in El Paso County, but the company actually laid only two miles of track. The railroad handled cars between the Mexico North-Western Railway and the three American lines in El Paso and in 1937 was reclassified by the Railroad Commission[qv] as a terminal operation. The El Paso Southern was owned for most of its existence by the Mexico North-Western Railway Company (Compañia del Ferrocarril Nor-Oeste de Mexico). On December 13, 1954, all outstanding stock of the EPS was acquired by the El Paso and Southwestern Railroad Company of Texas, and the switching service contracted to the Southern Pacific. The El Paso Southern was merged into the Southern Pacific Company, and its corporate existence terminated at midnight, October 31, 1961.

Chris Cravens

EL PASO AND SOUTHWESTERN RAILROAD. The El Paso and Southwestern Railroad Company of Texas was chartered on June 6, 1902, to operate a railroad between the Texas–New Mexico border and El Paso. The initial capital was $2,000,000, and the business office was in El Paso. Members of the first board of directors included William G. Choate, Charles R. Morehead,[qv] N. S. Stewart, and Millard Patterson, all of El Paso, and James Douglas, William E. Dodge, and W. Willis James, all of New York City. The El Paso and Southwestern Railroad Company of Texas acquired the El Paso Terminal Company on February 9, 1903, and placed the line in service on March 1. The railroad ran from El Paso to the Texas and New Mexico boundary located at the center of the 1,692 foot bridge across the Rio Grande. At this point it connected with the El Paso and Southwestern Railroad Company. The Texas company was owned by and was operated as an integral part of the El Paso and Southwestern, which initially consisted of a route between El Paso and Tucson, Arizona. On November 18, 1937, the El Paso and Southwestern of Texas acquired the assets of the El Paso and Northeastern Railroad Company and bought the capital stock of the El Paso Southern Railway Company on December 13, 1954. In 1924 the Southern Pacific Company acquired control of the El Paso and Southwestern system. The El Paso and Southwestern of Texas was operated under lease until it was merged into the Southern Pacific Company on November 1, 1961.

Chris Cravens

EL PASO TERMINAL COMPANY. The El Paso Terminal Company was chartered on April 4, 1901, for the purpose of constructing a line nearly five miles long between El Paso and a connection with the El Paso and Southwestern Railroad Company at the Texas–New

Mexico border. This connection was made at the center of the 1,692 foot bridge over the Rio Grande. By February 9, 1903, when it was acquired by the El Paso and Southwestern Railroad Company of Texas, the El Paso Terminal had completed construction, but had not placed the line in service. The El Paso Terminal also owned yard tracks and an office building at El Paso.
George C. Werner

ELROY, TEXAS. Elroy is on Farm Road 812 some twelve miles south of Austin in southeastern Travis County. One local story has it that Antonio López de Santa Anna[qv] gave the land in the area to one of his officers, who in turn traded it for a horse and saddle to return to Mexico. The Elroy community, also known as Driskill, Dutch Waterhole, or Hume, was established in 1892 and was named by a local storeowner for his son Leroy. A post office opened in Elroy in 1899, with George L. Hume as postmaster. This post office was discontinued in 1902, and mail was sent to Del Valle. In 1907 Elroy had a two-teacher school for 107 white students and a one-teacher school for sixty-one black students. The Elroy schools were consolidated in 1961 with the Colorado district, which the next year became the Del Valle Independent School District. The population of Elroy grew from twenty-five in 1933 to 125 in 1947; its population was still reported as 125 in 1990.

BIBLIOGRAPHY: Mary Starr Barkley, *History of Travis County and Austin, 1839–1899* (Waco: Texian Press, 1963). John J. Germann and Myron Janzen, *Texas Post Offices by County* (1986).
Vivian Elizabeth Smyrl

ELSA, TEXAS. Elsa is at the intersection of State Highway 107 and Farm Road 88, some seventeen miles northeast of McAllen in east central Hidalgo County. It is on land that was a part of the Llano Grande land grant issued to Juan José Ynojosa de Ballí, and the area was settled by ranchers before 1800. The ranchers introduced cattle and sheep ranching and various crops to the area. After 1850 two ranches in the vicinity were Laguna Seca ("Dry Lagoon"), owned by Macedonio Vela, and La Bota ("the Boot"), owned by Miguel Fernández. Anglo-Americans did not settle in the area until the early 1900s, with the introduction of truck farming. The Elsa community was laid out on the Texas and New Orleans Railroad in 1927 and named for Elsa George, wife of a local landowner. By 1930 the town had a population of 400, sixteen businesses, three churches, and a school. In 1940 Elsa was incorporated, and its population was estimated at 1,006. By 1957 the community had the railroad stop, a school, a church, some sixty-five businesses, and an estimated population of 3,179. By 1978 its population was estimated at 5,174. In 1990 Elsa had an estimated population of 5,242 and shared a high school with its neighbor Edcouch.

BIBLIOGRAPHY: Emilia Schunior Ramirez, *Ranch Life in Hidalgo County after 1850* (Edinburg, Texas: New Santander, 1971).
Alicia A. Garza

EL SAUZ, TEXAS (Starr County). El Sauz is on Farm roads 3167 and 649, some sixteen miles north of Rio Grande City and thirteen miles north of Garceño in Starr County. It was one of the original 1753 settlements of José de Escandón's[qv] pioneers. Its name means weeping willow in Spanish; it may have been named after nearby El Sauz Creek, now known as Los Olmos Creek. In the early 1880s El Sauz was a ranch community on a rural mail route from Rio Grande City. During his flight to the Mexican border in 1901, Gregorio Cortez,[qv] renowned fugitive, was captured at El Sauz by Capt. John H. Rogers[qv] of the Texas Rangers.[qv] In the late 1940s the community had several farm units, a population of twenty-five, and a school. In 1991 it had two general stores and gas stations, Our Lady of Guadalupe Catholic Church, and a population of eighty-five; four miles east was a Southwest Tethered Aerostat System balloon, 233 feet long and 15,000 feet up in the air, which was visible over the entire county. The balloon supported a warning system that was designed to locate airplanes crossing the border between the Gulf of Mexico and Laredo for United States Customs, the Drug Enforcement Agency, and Immigration. It was one of six such balloons tethered along the southern United States border from El Sauz to Yuma, Arizona.

BIBLIOGRAPHY: Agnes G. Grimm, *Llanos Mesteñas: Mustang Plains* (Waco: Texian Press, 1968). Américo Paredes, *With His Pistol in His Hand: A Border Ballad and Its Hero* (Austin: University of Texas Press, 1958). Florence J. Scott, *Historical Heritage of the Lower Rio Grande* (San Antonio: Naylor, 1937; rev. ed., Waco: Texian, 1966; rpt., Rio Grande City, Texas: La Retama Press, 1970). J. Lee and Lillian J. Stambaugh, *The Lower Rio Grande Valley of Texas* (San Antonio: Naylor, 1954).
Dick D. Heller, Jr.

EL SAUZ, TEXAS (Willacy County). El Sauz is a ranching community and game preserve on Farm Road 497 some thirteen miles east of Raymondville in Willacy County. *Sauz* is a variant of *sauce*, Spanish for "willow." The ranch is on the San Juan de Carricitos land grant, which was given to José Narciso Cavazos in 1781 by the Spanish government (*see* SPANISH TEXAS). He took possession of the land and stocked it with 900 cattle. Richard King[qv] claimed to have come across a deserted ranch named El Sauz in that vicinity in 1852 while riding north from the Rio Grande. According to some sources, another community named El Sauz was established around 1852 on Redfish Bay, had a post office from 1870 to 1875, and was moved to the current site after the storm of 1882. In 1881 Richard King and Mifflin Kenedy[qv] took ownership of much of the land in the grant, including El Sauz, which became a subdivision of the King Ranch.[qv] The settlement was a stage stand between Alice and San Antonio, and a post office by the name of Sauz was in operation there from 1893 to 1915. The El Sauz school district was established on March 6, 1925. In the 1950s, when the ranch was owned by the Atwood branch of the King family, the ranch encompassed 100,000 acres. The school district was still in operation in the mid-1950s. During the early 1990s several dwellings were maintained on the ranch. El Sauz made national headlines in November 1936, when two residents of San Perlita, Luther Blanton and his son John, disappeared while hunting on the ranch. Some locals claimed that the two were murdered by King Ranch fence riders, and that the Kleberg family covered up the incident. Enough of the area's residents threatened to enter the ranch to destroy property that Governor James Allred[qv] ordered a company of Texas Rangers[qv] to the area. Capt. Bill McMurray found no evidence of foul play, however, thus confirming the previous findings of Willacy county sheriff Howard Cragg.

BIBLIOGRAPHY: Tom Lea, *The King Ranch* (2 vols., Boston: Little, Brown, 1957).
Alicia A. Garza

ELSER, FRANK BALL (1885–1935). Frank Elser, newspaperman, novelist, playwright, son of Elizabeth (Loving) and Maximilian Elser,[qv] was born in Fort Worth, Texas, on September 9, 1885. His parents were pioneer residents of the town, his mother a descendant of novelist Henry Fielding. Elser attended Mercersburg Academy, Pennsylvania, and graduated in 1902. He attended Cornell for two years and returned to Fort Worth in 1904 to write for the Fort Worth *Telegram* (*see* FORT WORTH STAR-TELEGRAM). There followed stints with newspapers in Arkansas, Oklahoma, and Missouri, and work as a publicist for some traveling circus acts. Elser began his New York journalistic career in 1906 as telegraph editor with the *Evening Sun* and moved to the Associated Press in 1908 as city editor. He served as correspondent with AP in London, where he covered the British in Belgium and the sinking of the *Lusitania* (1915). With the New York *Times,* he accompanied Gen. John J. Pershing[qv] on his punitive expedition against Francisco (Pancho) Villa[qv] in 1916 and was night city editor in 1916–17. Elser also contributed to *Century, Colliers,* and the *Saturday Evening Post.* He wrote one well-received novel, *The Keen Desire* (1926), based on his early newspaper experience in Fort Worth,

Little Rock, and New York. In theater, he adapted Liam O'Flaherty's novel *Mr. Gilhooley* for the Broadway stage in 1930. *Low Bridge* (1933) and *The Farmer Takes a Wife* (1934) were both adaptations of *Rome Haul*, Walter D. Edmonds's account of life on the Erie Canal around 1850 and the coming of the railroads. *The Farmer Takes a Wife*, coauthored by Marc Connelly and starring Henry Fonda, enjoyed a successful run and earned critical acclaim.

Elser was a member of the Authors' League, the Dramatists' Guild, and Zeta Psi Fraternity. He married Rebecca Elsbry Mix in 1910. They had one son, Robert Fielding, born in 1911. Elser was at work on "a folk drama of Texas and Oklahoma in the Nineties, 'a play about my own people,'" when he died, on January 31, 1935, at St. George, Grenada. He is buried in Cranford, New Jersey, where the Elsers lived for many years.

BIBLIOGRAPHY: Goldie Capers Smith, *The Creative Arts in Texas: A Handbook of Biography* (Nashville: Cokesbury, 1926). New York Times, November 11, 1934, January 6, February 2, 1935.

Douglas Martin Dawson

ELSER, MAXIMILIAN (1851–1933). Maximilian Elser, railroad superintendent, was born in Bath, New York, on July 29, 1851. In 1864 he began working as a telegraph operator in the office of the Erie Railroad at Coopers, New York. He had worked at several other locations in New York and at Shreveport, Louisiana, before he moved to Texas in 1872. His first work in Texas was as superintendent of the Texas and Pacific Railway track being constructed near Marshall. In 1874 as a private venture he and a partner built telegraph lines from Fort Worth to Eagle Ford to meet the Texas and Pacific telegraph lines. He later built lines to Cleburne and Denton before Western Union gained control. He also superintended the building of the telegraph line along the Texas and Pacific right-of-way from Fort Worth to El Paso and from Cleburne to Denton. He maintained his home in Fort Worth, where he was for many years cashier of the City National Bank. He became interested in the oil business about 1910 and spent most of the remainder of his life in and around Cisco. He was married to Elizabeth Loving. Elser died in Fort Worth at the home of his daughter on November 3, 1933, and was buried on November 6 in Oakwood Cemetery, Fort Worth, where services were conducted by the Knights of Pythias.

BIBLIOGRAPHY: Fort Worth *Star-Telegram*, November 5, 1933, October 30, 1949.

Carolyn Hyman

EL SORDO RANCH. El Sordo Ranch, off Highway 16 twelve miles southwest of Hebbronville in north central Jim Hogg County, was started in 1848. The land was part of the Agostadero del Sordo ("Summer Pasture of the Mute [or Deaf] One") grant from Mexico to Luis Vela. The present ranch known as El Sordo was part of the 23,400 acres purchased by William A. Waugh in 1883 from J. H. McLeary. The headquarters was on an additional 693 acres that Waugh bought from C. W. Earnest. Waugh was one of the first Anglo settlers in Jim Hogg County. He and his wife, Angelita María (Serña), had three daughters. In 1895 Florence, one of the daughters, and her husband, Henry C. Yeager, acquired the ranch headquarters and began raising red Durham cattle. Henry Yeager was known for refusing to foreclose on ranchers with delinquent loans. In 1906, at his death, part of the 14,000 acres of his land went to his daughter Martha Josephine Armstrong. Included in that bequest was El Sordo Ranch. Martha, with her husband, E. L. Armstrong, added 2,280 acres to their holdings and raised cotton, horses, and Hereford cattle. The ranch headquarters burned in 1934 and had to be completely rebuilt. The Armstrongs established a school for their children and the children of the ranchhands. Earnest Roberts Armstrong, who inherited the remaining 693 acres of the ranch, added improved pastures and watermelon fields to his cattle and horse raising. The original ranchhouse was remodeled in 1968 and continued in 1992 to be inhabited by the owners. El Sordo Ranch has served as ranch headquarters, post office, and way station for travelers.

BIBLIOGRAPHY: *Guide to Spanish and Mexican Land Grants in South Texas* (Austin: Texas General Land Office, 1988). *Jim Hogg County Enterprise*, Silver Anniversary, March 1939. David Montejano, *Anglos and Mexicans in the Making of Texas, 1836–1986* (Austin: University of Texas Press, 1987). *Texas Family Land Heritage Registry* (Austin: Texas Department of Agriculture, 1974–), Vol. 10. WPA Texas Historical Records Survey, Inventory of the County Archives of Texas (MS, Barker Texas History Center, University of Texas at Austin).

Alicia A. Garza

ELSTONE, TEXAS. Elstone was near Hondo Creek eight miles southeast of Hondo in south central Medina County. It was probably named after former resident Sarah Elstone Mercereau, a descendant of the Duke of Marlborough, although some believe that Elstone referred to the rocky hilltop bend of the community's main thoroughfare, which formed a perfect L. Elstone had a post office from 1910 until 1917, when mail was routed to Hondo. By 1914 Elstone had a population of fifty, a general store, telephone connections, and a cotton gin, which served the farming community well into the 1920s, when boll weevil[qv] infestations devastated area cotton fields. Though there may have been a business at the site as late as 1931, by 1936 Elstone appears to have been abandoned.

BIBLIOGRAPHY: Castro Colonies Heritage Association, *The History of Medina County, Texas* (Dallas: National Share Graphics, 1983). John J. Germann and Myron Janzen, *Texas Post Offices by County* (1986).

Ruben E. Ochoa

ELTON, TEXAS. Elton is on State Highway 70 some five miles north of Dickens in north central Dickens County. Among its early settlers was L. W. Stark, who came to the area in 1895. Large ranches dominated much of the surrounding land. A post office was granted to the community in 1925, with Lula Yantis as postmistress; the office was named for Elton Purcell, a local schoolteacher. In 1948 the community reported a store, a post office, and a population of fifty. Its post office lasted until 1954, when service was moved to Afton. The 1983 county highway map still indicated Elton, though it showed no businesses at the site.

BIBLIOGRAPHY: Arthur Hecht, comp., *Postal History in the Texas Panhandle* (Canyon, Texas: Panhandle–Plains Historical Society, 1960). Fred I. Massengill, *Texas Towns: Origin of Name and Location of Each of the 2,148 Post Offices in Texas* (Terrell, Texas, 1936).

Charles G. Davis

EL TORO, TEXAS. El Toro, at the junction of U. S. Highway 59 and Farm Road 234, four miles east of Edna in Jackson County, had a post office from 1899 to 1900. In 1948 the town had four businesses, and there were thirteen farms in the immediate area. By 1986 the community, located next to the Miller gas field and the Southern Pacific tracks, had a grain elevator and one other business. By the late 1980s El Toro consisted of a smattering of widely dispersed dwellings.

Stephen L. Hardin

EL TURCO (?–1541). El Turco (The Turk), so named by Spaniards because of his appearance, was a captive of Indians at Cicúique, an Indian town near the site of contemporary Pecos, New Mexico. He was presented to Capt. Hernando de Alvarado,[qv] an officer of Francisco Vázquez de Coronado,[qv] in 1540. In Spanish hands, the Turk described a region toward the east known as Quivira,[qv] which possessed much gold, silver, and rich fabrics. Coronado employed the Turk as a guide on his trek in 1541 from New Mexico into the Texas Panhandle and beyond to the area of present-day Kansas. Quivira, however, contained only buffaloes and the grass huts and cornfields of the Wichita Indians—not golden cities. Because the Turk had lied about the wealth of the land and conspired with the Quivirans to kill the Spaniards and their horses, Coronado reluctantly ordered him garroted prior to the return march to New Mexico.

BIBLIOGRAPHY: Herbert Eugene Bolton, *Coronado: Knight of Pueblos and Plains* (New York: Whittlesey; Albuquerque: University of New Mexico Press, 1949). Donald E. Chipman, *Spanish Texas, 1519–1821* (Austin: University of Texas Press, 1992).

Donald E. Chipman

EL VENADITO, TEXAS. El Venadito, also known as Venadito, is off U.S. Highway 281 twenty-one miles west of Brownsville in southwestern Cameron County. In the late 1940s the community had a few scattered farms, dwellings, and a cemetery. By 1970 the number of dwellings in the area had increased to sixty. The population of El Venadito was estimated at 207 in 1986, and the colonia encompassed three acres. *Venadito* means "little deer" in Spanish.

BIBLIOGRAPHY: *Colonias in the Lower Rio Grande Valley of South Texas: A Summary Report* (Policy Research Project Report No. 18, Lyndon B. Johnson School of Public Affairs, University of Texas at Austin, 1977).

Alicia A. Garza

ELWOOD, TEXAS (Fannin County). Elwood is on Farm Road 2554 fifteen miles north of Bonham in north central Fannin County near the Oklahoma border. The community formed in the late 1860s and early 1870s when James S. Baker, a Presbyterian minister, and his nephew, William R. Baker, established homesteads in the area. Elwood soon became a community center for area farmers. From 1871 to 1909 it had a post office, and in the 1930s it had a school, a church, a cemetery, at least one business, and a number of dwellings. From the 1930s through 1990 Elwood's population was reported at between thirty and forty. The 1987 county highway map showed only a cemetery at the site.

BIBLIOGRAPHY: *Fannin County Folks and Facts* (Dallas: Taylor, 1977).

David Minor

ELWOOD, TEXAS (Madison County). Elwood is on the Old San Antonio Road[qv] eight miles northeast of Madisonville in northeastern Madison County. Settlement in the vicinity seems to have begun in the early 1830s, when James Mitchell constructed a fort and a tavern on the Old San Antonio Road three miles west of the site of present Midway in what was then northern Montgomery County. In the mid-1830s Ransom Allphin settled on a one-league headright grant south of the road and established a gristmill. During the 1840s a Methodist church and Sunday school were organized in a log cabin built by James B. Durham about a mile north of the Old San Antonio Road and just west of the route of present Farm Road 1119. By the late 1940s William R. Barrett and his father were operating a general store in the settlement. In 1852 a post office was established in the community with the name Elwood, said to be refer to the abundant elms nearby. The post office was discontinued in 1860.

In 1874 the original log Methodist church, which had long doubled as a schoolhouse, was replaced with a frame structure also used as a school and community center, as well as a union church. The local school enrolled fifty-six pupils in 1896. By the late 1890s the town reported a population of 250. In 1899 William G. French, the proprietor of a country grocery near Elwood Cemetery, became postmaster of a revived post office designated French. However, in 1905 this post office too was closed and replaced with mail delivery over a rural route from Midway. In 1899 the Cobb Creek Baptist Church, now Elwood Baptist, constructed a building on the Old San Antonio Road southwest of the Elwood Cemetery.

During the early years of the twentieth century the town had a general store and a drugstore. In 1917 the old one-room school was replaced by a three-room schoolhouse on the Old San Antonio Road. In 1933 Elwood School and Cobb Creek School, two miles to the south, were joined; two years later the two segregated schools of the Elwood Consolidated School District enrolled 159 white and thirty-eight black pupils. In 1848 Elwood's schools were consolidated with the Midway Independent School District. In 1988 Elwood reported an estimated twenty-eight inhabitants. In the late 1980s it had two churches, two businesses, and a community center. In 1990 the population was still twenty-eight.

BIBLIOGRAPHY: Madison County Historical Commission, *A History of Madison County* (Dallas: Taylor, 1984). *Quarterly of the Texas State Historical Association*, Queries and Answers, April 1903. Hermann Wren, An Educational Survey of Madison County, Texas, With Plans for the Reorganization of Its Schools (M.A. thesis, University of Texas, 1936).

Charles Christopher Jackson

ELWOOD, TEXAS (Van Zandt County). Elwood is near Farm Road 47 thirteen miles northwest of Canton in northwestern Van Zandt County. Its Baptist church was started as early as 1898. The name Elwood was formed by a combination of the nearby Ellis Chapel and Woodall schools in 1917, when the local church moved and became known as the Elwood church. In 1904 the Ellis Chapel school enrollment had reached fifty and the Woodall school, forty-eight. In 1936 the Elwood community had the school, a cemetery, and scattered dwellings. Its school had been consolidated with the Edgewood Independent School District by the early 1950s. In 1981 scattered dwellings remained near the Woodall cemetery.

BIBLIOGRAPHY: Van Zandt County History Book Committee, *History of Van Zandt County* (Dallas, 1984).

Diana J. Kleiner

ELY, WALTER RALEIGH (1879–1978). Walter R. Ely, attorney, judge, and state highway commissioner, the youngest of ten children of Mr. and Mrs. Herod Ely, was born on April 3, 1879, in Somerset, Kentucky, during the family's move from Virginia to Texas. The Elys lived for a time in Denton and Mills counties before settling on a farm in Callahan County in 1895. Walter attended local schools before moving as a youth to Dallas to study law in the office of Judge Charles F. Clint and former lieutenant governor Barry Miller.[qv] After he was admitted to the bar in 1903 Ely returned to Callahan County, where he was elected county attorney in 1904. He was elected county judge in 1912 and served until 1918, when he resigned to go into the oil business. In 1919 Governor William P. Hobby[qv] appointed him to fill a vacant judgeship in the Forty-second District Court. Ely and his family moved from Baird to nearby Abilene during his tenure as judge. One of his notable cases was the Ross-Goode trial for the murder of cattle inspectors at Seminole in Gaines County.

Ely held the district judgeship until Governor Dan Moody[qv] named him to the Texas Highway Commission (*see* TEXAS DEPARTMENT OF TRANSPORTATION) in January 1927. The operation of the commission had been an issue in the bitter gubernatorial election of 1926, when Moody defeated Miriam A. Ferguson.[qv] Soon after the election the previous commission resigned, and Moody named Ross Sterling, Cone Johnson,[qqv] and Ely to the three-man board. Ely gave up his $4,500-a-year judgeship to take the commission post at an annual salary of $1,000. He served for eight years, half the time as member, half as chairman. The commission undertook a housecleaning, instituted competitive bidding, slashed construction costs, and revamped the financing program. A new road system began to emerge, with wider pavements and expanded rights-of-way. During this era Ely was named by President Calvin Coolidge to the Inter-American Highway Commission.

Subsequently, Ely returned to private law practice in Abilene. During World War II[qv] he served as chairman of the Taylor County gasoline and tire rationing board. He and his wife, the former Lucy McCoy of Callahan County, had two children. Ely was a Democrat and a Methodist. He died on January 31, 1978, two months before his 100th birthday, and was buried in Elmwood Memorial Park in Abilene.

BIBLIOGRAPHY: Abilene *Reporter-News*, April 8, 1956, February 3, 1978.
Katharyn Duff

ELY, TEXAS. Ely is on Farm Road 898 some ten miles southwest of Bonham in southwestern Fannin County. The community was established sometime in the 1890s, and from 1895 to 1906 it had a post office. Ely's reported population has never exceeded fifty, and in 1990 the community reported a population of fifteen.

BIBLIOGRAPHY: *Fannin County Folks and Facts* (Dallas: Taylor, 1977).
David Minor

ELYSIAN FIELDS, TEXAS. Elysian Fields is at the junction of Farm roads 31 and 451, a mile north of the Panola county line in Harrison County. The name of the town originated in a dinner conversation in New Orleans in 1817, in which Capt. Edward Smith, having lately ridden through what was then a Caddo Indian village known as Biff Springs, so vividly described the beauty of the area that one of his guests likened it to the Elysian Fields of Greek mythology. By the 1830s the Indians had moved west beyond advancing white settlement. Smith returned to Elysian Fields with his family in 1837 and established one of the first general stores in the area. By 1848 the town had a post office. The Golden Rule Presbyterian Church was organized on January 15, 1851, and was followed by the Bethel Methodist Church five miles from town, for more than fifty years the site of an annual camp meeting. Elysian Fields attained a population of sixty in 1884, and grew to 160 by 1896; that year the town had three churches and daily mail service at postmaster J. M. Furrh's general store. Cotton and lumber formed the economic base of the community. In 1910 the town was moved a mile west to take advantage of a newly laid stretch of the Marshall and East Texas Railway. Elysian Fields prospered for a time, growing to a population of 500 by 1929. The community reported fifteen businesses in 1931. Oil and gas became important to the town's economy in the 1950s, but later on residents came to rely mainly on cattle-raising and farming. In 1990 Elysian Fields had 300 residents, a bank, and at least three other businesses.

BIBLIOGRAPHY: "History of Harrison County, Texas," *American Sketch Book* 5 (1879). Marshall National Bank, *Historical Highlights of Harrison County* (Marshall, Texas, 1959). Fred I. Massengill, *Texas Towns: Origin of Name and Location of Each of the 2,148 Post Offices in Texas* (Terrell, Texas, 1936). W. C. Tenney, *History of Golden Rule Presbyterian Church* (Elysian Fields, Texas: Golden Rule Presbyterian Church, 1951?).
Pam Nordstrom

ELYSIUM, TEXAS. Elysium is near State Highway 71 some twelve miles west of Bastrop in western Bastrop County. It had a post office from 1896 to 1901. The community was still named on a 1981 county highway map, though no structures were shown at the site.
Paula Mitchell Marks

EMANUEL, ALBERT (1808–1851). Albert Emanuel (Emmanuel), early Jewish settler, merchant, and participant in the battle of San Jacinto,qv was born in 1808. He immigrated to Texas around 1834 and settled in Nacogdoches, where he established a mercantile business. In 1835 he joined the Texas army. He served as a private in Capt. William Kimbro'sqv Eighth Company, Second Regiment, Texas Volunteers, at the battle of San Jacinto. After the war Emanuel returned to his business in Nacogdoches. He evidently sold, or at least sought to sell, provisions to the Texas government. In a surviving letter to Sam Houstonqv dated August 1836 Emanuel requested Houston's aid in obtaining a contract to supply uniforms for the Texas army. He married Louisa Hart of New Orleans and continued to operate his business in Nacogdoches for the next four years. In 1840 he moved to New Orleans, where he established a legal practice and lived until his death in 1851.

BIBLIOGRAPHY: John H. Jenkins, ed., *The Papers of the Texas Revolution, 1835–1836* (10 vols., Austin: Presidial Press, 1973). Natalie Ornish, *Pioneer Jewish Texans* (Dallas: Texas Heritage, 1989).
Christopher Long

EMBERSON, JOHN (1798–1860). John Emberson, early settler and soldier in the Texas Revolution,qv was born in Virginia on May 22, 1798. He left a frontier school to join Andrew Jackson's army during the War of 1812 and took part in the battle of New Orleans in 1815. Afterward he joined Allen Carter of Arkansas in a trip to what is now Lamar County, Texas, and returned to that area to trap in 1816. On March 1, 1820, Emberson married Carter's daughter Matilda and settled in Arkansas. In 1824 he moved with his wife, a daughter, and two sons to the Lamar County site in Texas. Two other children were born in Texas. Emberson married Mrs. Kiz Martin on May 9, 1850; on October 8, 1856, he married Sarah J. Summer. The Embersons lived temporarily near Emberson Lake, then settled on Emberson Prairie, and finally located permanently in what is now Grayson County. About 1836 Emberson mustered a volunteer ranger company from Red River and Fannin counties and served under Daniel Montague.qv Tax rolls in 1842 showed that Emberson had 2,277 acres, fifteen horses, and 100 cattle. He died at Pilot Point on December 18, 1860.

BIBLIOGRAPHY: A. W. Neville, *The History of Lamar County, Texas* (Paris, Texas: North Texas, 1937; rpt. 1986). Paris *News*, December 16, 17, 1945. Ann Spencer, *Lamar County Marriage Records, 1841–1858* (Paris, Texas, 1977). Rex Wallace Strickland, "History of Fannin County, Texas, 1836–1843," *Southwestern Historical Quarterly* 33, 34 (April, July 1930).

EMBERSON, TEXAS. Emberson, a small farming community, is just north of the intersection of Farm roads 1499 and 1500 and seven miles northwest of Paris in north central Lamar County. It was named in honor of founder John Emberson,qv who arrived in the area in 1824. The community's post office was established in 1878. By 1884 the settlement had become important in cotton shipping and reported a population of 150, with three churches, a two-teacher district school, two physicians, a general store, a blacksmith shop, a cotton gin, and a gristmill. At that time John Goodgion served as postmaster, and mail arrived semiweekly. In 1889 the local school reported 148 students and four teachers. The community's population had increased to 175 by 1890, when there were also two new general stores. By 1892, however, the population was 100; that year residents reported a Baptist church, two new cotton gins, a new icehouse, another general store, and a drug emporium. The community's population was 133 in 1904, and the next year its post office closed. By 1931 the community had only four businesses. The 1936 county highway map showed four businesses (including a cotton gin), two churches, a school, a cemetery, and a cluster of dwellings at Emberson. In 1947 the community's population was fifty, and only one business was reported. By 1957 the school had been consolidated into the Central Independent School District. Emberson reported seventy-five residents in 1970 and eighty in 1975. In 1980 maps showed the community as a cluster of houses near the intersection of two dirt roads. Emberson reported eighty residents in 1990.

BIBLIOGRAPHY: Thomas S. Justiss, An Administrative Survey of the Schools of Lamar County with a Plan for Their Reorganization (M.A. thesis, University of Texas, 1937). A. W. Neville, *The History of Lamar County, Texas* (Paris, Texas: North Texas, 1937; rpt. 1986).
Vista K. McCroskey

EMBLEM, TEXAS. Emblem, a farming community on State Highway 71 some twelve miles northwest of Sulphur Springs in northwestern Hopkins County, was founded by G. D. Kennemore in 1876. A

Baptist church was organized at the settlement in 1883. T. J. Ross had a store and gin there and became postmaster when a post office was established in 1892. By 1905 the community had a school, which that year had an enrollment of forty-eight. The Emblem post office closed in 1906. By the mid-1930s the community had two churches, a school, and a number of scattered houses. The school was later closed, but in 1985 the community still had two churches and a cemetery. In 1990 Emblem reported a population of fifty-two. *Christopher Long*

EMBREE, TEXAS. Embree was at the intersection of State Highway 78 and the Santa Fe Railroad, at a site within the present city limits of Garland in northeastern Dallas County. It was established in 1886 when the Gulf, Colorado and Santa Fe Railway came through Dallas County a mile east of the old town of Duck Creek. Many Duck Creek residents moved to Embree, which was named for Dr. K. H. Embree, a physician and postmaster of Duck Creek. On February 1, 1887, the post office was moved from Duck Creek to Embree. The Embree *Enterprise* began in "Old" Duck Creek as the Duck Creek *Rustler;* the last issue appeared on October 18, 1888. Embree voted to incorporate on October 28, 1887. Because of a rivalry between Embree and the "New" Duck Creek, a mile west on the Missouri, Kansas and Texas Railroad, the post office was moved to a new location between the two communities and named Garland on December 9, 1887. Embree was disincorporated in 1891 so that it could be reincorporated, along with Duck Creek, as the town of Garland on March 31, 1891.

BIBLIOGRAPHY: Ruth Buchholz, "Our Garland, Texas (Lovely and Lively)," *Garland 1988 Magazine. Memorial and Biographical History of Dallas County* (Chicago: Lewis, 1892; rpt., Dallas: Walsworth, 1976). David S. Switzer, *It's Our Dallas County* (Dallas: Switzer, 1954). Vertical Files, Barker Texas History Center, University of Texas at Austin (Garland, Texas). *Lisa C. Maxwell*

EMERALD, TEXAS. Emerald was seven miles east of Ozona and eighty-five miles southeast of San Angelo in eastern Crockett County. The townsite was in a level divide at an elevation of 2,425 feet stretched between the hills of the Edwards Plateau.qv In 1888 a well-driller successfully tapped the aquifer 540 feet below the surface. T. A. Wilkinson of Tarrant County, an immigration commissioner for the Fort Worth and Rio Grande Railway Company, persuaded the company to equip the well with a windmill, a pump, a tank, a two-room schoolhouse, and a store. A townsite one mile square was established with 300 lots, one-fourth to be for business, and named Emerald Grove. Prospective clients came by railroad to San Angelo and were brought by buggy to view the townsite and the level land, available at a dollar an acre. Settlers came from Tarrant County, Texas, as well as Ohio, Minnesota, New Hampshire, and Iowa. Houses and buildings were constructed of lumber brought from San Angelo. The post office opened in 1890. A buckboard provided mail service and transportation from San Angelo.

But in 1890, when Crockett County was organized, Ozona became the county seat. Emerald was bypassed by the railroad, so the whole town moved to Ozona. The post office closed in 1891, and the school closed in 1893. In the fall of 1897 the school building, the last of the Emerald structures, was hauled to Ozona on four wagons. In Crockett County Memorial Park, Ozona, is preserved a home from Emerald.

BIBLIOGRAPHY: Crockett County Historical Society, *History of Crockett County* (San Angelo: Anchor, 1976). Ozona *Stockman,* July 31, 1941. San Angelo *Standard Times,* August 29, 1954. Marker Files, Texas Historical Commission, Austin. *Mary W. Clayton*

EMERGENCY MANAGEMENT. With the beginning of the nuclear arms race in the late 1940s, national and state civil defense acquired a greater urgency than it had had during World War II.qv Despite the founding of new federal bureaus in the 1950s, authority and responsibility for civil defense remained highly decentralized. Decentralization also characterized the state civil-defense program. In 1951 the Texas legislature unanimously passed the Civil Protection Act, establishing the governor as head of the Disaster Relief Council, which was composed of the directors of the various state agencies. The state program duplicated the national in that each agency retained responsibility for its respective relief function. The governor also appointed a state coordinator of defense and disaster relief, who operated at civil defense headquarters in Austin, served as a liaison among the state agencies, and took command during emergencies. William L. McGill served as state coordinator for the first eight years of the organization's existence.

Decentralization also characterized the local level, where mayors, county judges, or locally appointed civil-defense directors received responsibility for disaster planning in their cities, towns, or counties. In the 1980s the state channeled aid—in the form of funds and training—through sixteen state disaster districts coterminous with State Highway Patrol districts. Local civil-defense organizations provided manpower—chiefly volunteers—and implemented relief plans during disasters or practice drills.

In 1963 the Office of Defense and Disaster Relief was moved from the executive department to the Texas Department of Public Safety.qv The Texas Disaster Act of 1975 renamed the office the Division of Disaster Emergency Services, established the governor's Disaster Emergency Services Council, and provided for greater integration of state and local civil-defense functions. In August 1981 the division, while remaining within the DPS, became the Division of Emergency Management.

Division offices are at the State Emergency Operating Center, a 12,000-square-foot, concrete-reinforced facility located twenty-six feet beneath DPS headquarters in Austin. The director serves as chairman for the State Emergency Management Council, which is composed of representatives of twenty-seven state agencies and the American Red Cross. When a disaster occurs, DEM coordinates the resources and efforts of the council members to solve the problem or prevent the situation from deteriorating.

DEM maintains a duty officer twenty-four hours a day to alert state agencies of potential disasters and to coordinate responses. Heading the department on a daily basis is the state coordinator. DEM responds to a wide variety of disasters, both man-made and natural, such as hazardous material spills or severe weather. The division acts as the state search and rescue coordination center for missing airplanes in conjunction with the Civil Air Patrol and is the statewide coordinator for amateur emergency radio operators. The division also handles requests for federal aid—presidential, Small Business Administration, and Farmers Home Administration disaster declarations. DEM administers federal and state disaster-relief funds for eligible private and public damage in the event of a presidential declaration.

DEM personnel administer federal funds for thirteen programs, including Emergency Management Assistance, which provides matching funds for local-government emergency-management administrative expenses. DEM audits funds spent on both private and public disaster-recovery programs and administers three federal contracts: Nuclear Civil Protection, which includes population protection planning, shelters to help counter the threat of nuclear war, and all-hazard planning; the Flood Insurance Assistance Program, which assists local communities in floodplain management; and Hurricane Contingency Planning, which seeks to inform communities about actions to take to mitigate the effects of hurricanesqv as established by previously completed vulnerability analyses.

The primary function of the DEM through the years has been to aid victims of natural disasters. These range from the 1954 flood along the Rio Grande to the spring 1957 Panhandle blizzard to the 1979 Wichita Falls tornado, and include droughts, hailstorms, and hurricanes scattered in between. Perhaps the most impressive demonstration of Texas civil defense in action came during Hurricane Carla in September 1961, when the state organization mobilized to evacuate 530,000 residents of the Texas coast out of the path of the hurricane.

Refugee centers were rapidly opened and filled, in places as far away as Dallas and Texarkana. Local and state civil-defense officials, the Department of Public Safety and the Red Cross, local police departments, and the Texas National Guard,qv all cooperated. Their efforts limited to forty-five the number of deaths caused by Carla and helped Texans living along the coast to recover from a storm that inflicted well over $400 million worth of damage.

In order to fulfill its original purpose, protecting Texans during nuclear war, the Texas DEM participates in annual nuclear-alert exercises and disseminates information on fallout shelters and other aspects of civilian defense; it has also developed plans to evacuate and to shelter citizens in the event of a nuclear attack. Its bimonthly journal, *Texas Defense Digest,* has offered through the years about the same amount of information on nuclear as on natural disasters.

BIBLIOGRAPHY: Harry Estill Moore et al., *Before the Wind: A Study of the Response to Hurricane Carla* (Washington: National Academy of Sciences, 1963). *State of Texas Disaster Preparedness Manual* (Austin: Texas Department of Public Safety, 1977), Part 2. *Texas Defense Digest,* December 1951. Mattie E. Treadwell, "Civil Defense Planning in Texas," *Public Affairs Comment* 5 (November 1959). Mattie E. Treadwell, *Hurricane Carla* (Denton, Texas: Department of Defense Office of Civil Defense, Region 5, 1962).

James A. Marten

EMERSON COLLEGE. Emerson College, in Campbell, Hunt County, was established in September 1903 as a private, coeducational institution designed to offer a four-year college program. The school operated for three years. In April B. F. Holcomb, S. W. Miller, J. R. Johnson, and a number of Campbell residents purchased the old Henry College campus from Henry T. Bridges. In September 1903 they opened Emerson College, named for Ralph Waldo Emerson. The institution's facilities consisted of at least an administration-classroom building and dormitories. It maintained music, art, commercial, primary, and liberal arts departments aimed to "train the youth for duties incumbent upon them as citizens of the Republic, as factors of the social structure." Instruction was offered leading to four degrees: bachelor of arts, bachelor of science, bachelor of literature, and licentiate of instruction. Thirty-six courses were required for a degree. An unexpectedly large initial enrollment of 500 students almost overwhelmed the faculty, administration, and facilities of the new school. Such interest also encouraged the owners to borrow money with which to expand the college. On the heels of this beginning, however, drought and crop failure hit Northeast Texas in 1904 and 1905, ruining the area's economy, substantially reducing Emerson College's enrollment, and decreasing the tuition and fees collected. This reduction of income, which made repayment of the loans impossible, combined with the competition for students provided by such other Hunt County colleges as East Texas Normal College (now East Texas State University) at Commerce and Texas Holiness University at Peniel, forced the institution to close in June 1906.

BIBLIOGRAPHY: Jackson Massey, *A History of College Education in Hunt County, Texas* (M.A. thesis, University of Texas, 1928). Donald W. Whisenhunt, *The Encyclopedia of Texas Colleges and Universities* (Austin: Eakin, 1986).

Brian Hart

EMERSON LAKE. Emerson (Emberson) Lake is a natural lake on a former channel of the Red River sixteen miles northwest of Paris and a mile north of Razor in extreme northern Lamar County (at 33°53′ N, 95°39′ W). The small lake is named for John Emberson,qv who settled there in 1824. It is surrounded by flat terrain with local shallow depressions, surfaced by clay and sandy loams that support water-tolerant hardwoods, conifers, and grasses.

EMET INDIANS. In the late seventeenth century and during the first half of the eighteenth century the Emet (Emat, Emiti, Ymette) Indians lived on the coastal plain north of Matagorda Bay and between the Guadalupe and Colorado rivers. When encountered by Europeans they were usually occupying settlements jointly with other groups, particularly Cantonas, Cavas, Sanas, Tohos, and Tohahas. Between 1740 and 1750 some of the Emets entered San Antonio de Valero Mission at San Antonio. The linguistic and cultural affiliations of the Emet Indians are still debatable. Most writers have stated that the Emets were probably Tonkawan, but some have suggested a Karankawan affiliation.

BIBLIOGRAPHY: Herbert Eugene Bolton, ed., *Spanish Exploration in the Southwest, 1542–1706* (New York: Scribner, 1908; rpt., New York: Barnes and Noble, 1959). Frederick Webb Hodge, ed., *Handbook of American Indians North of Mexico* (2 vols., Washington: GPO, 1907, 1910; rpt., New York: Pageant, 1959). William W. Newcomb, *The Indians of Texas* (Austin: University of Texas Press, 1961). A. F. Sjoberg, "The Culture of the Tonkawa, A Texas Indian," *Texas Journal of Science* 5 (September 1953). John R. Swanton, *The Indian Tribes of North America* (Gross Pointe, Michigan: Scholarly Press, 1968).

Thomas N. Campbell

EMHOUSE, TEXAS. Emhouse, an incorporated farming town at the junction of three farm roads eight miles northwest of Corsicana in north central Navarro County, was laid out around 1906 after the Trinity and Brazos River Valley Railway purchased the right-of-way for a line between Waxahachie and Teague. The community was originally known as Lyford, but since there was already another Texas post office by that name, officials renamed the settlement Emhouse, after Col. Edward M. House,qv superintendent of the railroad. The town grew rapidly in its first few years. Lured by the prospect of being on the rail line, most residents of nearby Kelm and King Willow moved their houses and businesses to Emhouse. A post office was opened in 1908, and by 1914 the community had Baptist, Methodist Episcopal, and Methodist churches, a bank, two restaurants, five grocery stores, three general stores, three blacksmith shops, a weekly newspaper called the Emhouse *News,* and an estimated population of 500. In 1915 the town adopted the commission form of government. Emhouse continued to prosper during the 1920s, and as late as 1929 its population was still listed at 500. But the estimated population had fallen to 322 by 1936, when thirteen businesses were reported. The decline continued after World War II,qv and by the mid-1960s the number of residents had fallen to 150 and the businesses to five. In 1990 Emhouse was a rural community with several churches, a district school, a large number of houses, and an estimated population of 250.

BIBLIOGRAPHY: Annie Carpenter Love, *History of Navarro County* (Dallas: Southwestern, 1933). Wyvonne Putman, comp., *Navarro County History* (5 vols., Quanah, Texas: Nortex, 1975–84). Alva Taylor, *History and Photographs of Corsicana and Navarro County* (Corsicana, Texas, 1959; rev. ed., *Navarro County History and Photographs,* Corsicana, 1962).

Christopher Long

EMIGRANT AGENT ACTS. The Emigrant Agent Acts (sometimes called Emigrant Labor Agency Laws), a series of state laws passed from 1923 to 1929, sought to restrict the flow of Mexican-origin labor from Texas to other states. When industrial and agricultural employers in the Midwest and the North began utilizing Mexican-origin labor after quotas on European immigration were implemented by federal law in the early 1920s, Texas farmers feared for their labor supply. Throughout the 1920s sugar-beet companies annually recruited 10,000 Mexican workers to labor in the beet fields of Michigan and northern Ohio. State Representative A. P. Johnson from Carrizo Springs, Texas, introduced a bill in 1929 to charge out-of-state labor recruiters $7,500. It was negated by a federal court when a Michigan sugar-beet company petitioned the court. A later law levied a $1,000 charge on labor agents in Texas seeking workers for non-Texas jobs. In addition, there was a county surcharge of $100 to $300, the amount depending on the local labor market; each agent also had to purchase a ten-dollar license annually from each county in which he contracted. Another law required that labor agents post a $5,000 bond to ensure the return of recruited workers. A federal court ruled this law unconstitutional upon challenge by the beet companies. The beet companies furthermore utilized a loophole that exempted "private" agents, or those who worked for a single employer, from paying the tax.

The Emigrant Agent Acts received the endorsement of the American Federation of Labor, the South Texas Chamber of Commerce,qqv the Winter Garden Chamber of Commerce, and the West Texas Chamber of Commerce.qv But they did not prevent the migration of workers to other states. Mexican-origin workers were recruited surreptitiously and transported on isolated country roads in overcrowded canvas-covered trucks. Growers sometimes ran labor agents out of town or shot their tires. The Emigrant Agent Acts were enforced by the state commissioner of labor statistics and after 1934 by the Texas Farm Placement Service. However, according to T. Y. Collins of the Texas Bureau of Labor, by 1940 the state had not collected any occupational taxes.

BIBLIOGRAPHY: George Otis Coalson, *The Development of the Migratory Farm Labor System in Texas, 1900–1954* (San Francisco: R&E Research Associates, 1977). David Montejano, *Anglos and Mexicans in the Making of Texas, 1836–1986* (Austin: University of Texas Press, 1987). Mark Reisler, *By the Sweat of Their Brow: Mexican Immigrant Labor in the United States, 1900–1940* (Westport, Connecticut: Greenwood Press, 1976).
Cynthia E. Orozco

EMIGRANTS' GUIDES TO TEXAS. From the beginning of Anglo-American colonizationqv throughout the nineteenth century numerous books, almanacs, and pamphlets were written to induce Americans and Europeans to move to Texas. Many of the publications had misleading and incorrect information; others were accurate descriptions of Texas. Publications such as Mary Austin Holley'sqv *Texas in 1836*, the advertising pamphlets of the Galveston Bay and Texas Land Companyqv in the early 1830s, and *Texas in 1840 or the Emigrant's Guide to the New Republic* (author unknown) encouraged Americans to come to Texas. During the days of the republic Europeans were informed about Texas by such books as William Kennedy'sqv *Texas* (1841), Arthur Ikin'sqv *Texas* (1841), Prince Carl of Solms-Braunfels'qv *Texas, 1844–1845* (1846), Viktor Bracht'sqv *Texas Im Jahre 1848* (1848), and many others. In the period from 1845 to 1860 Ferdinand von Roemerqv published descriptive books and booklets in German about Texas. Don Egbert Bramanqv published *Braman's Information about Texas* in 1857; Jacob De Cordovaqv wrote *The Texas Immigrant and Traveller's Guide Book* in 1856; and almanacs (supported by commercial advertisements) such as Albert Hanford's *Texas State Register, 1856–1879*, and Willard Richardson'sqv *Texas Almanac and Emigrant's Guide to Texas, 1857–1873*, gave publicity to the growth of Texas and stimulated immigration. During the Reconstructionqv period the Republican administration in 1871 established the Texas Bureau of Immigration, which circulated almanacs and brochures to other states to foster immigration. When the Democrats regained control of the state, the bureau was discontinued, and official immigration agencies were prohibited. After the Civil Warqv land companies, railroads, and private enterprises published emigrants' guides such as the International and Great Northern Railroad's *The Lone Star Guide* (1877), *Burke's Texas Almanac and Immigrants, Handbook* (1875–85), the Union Pacific Railway Company's pamphlets in the early 1890s, the *Houston Post Almanac* (1895–97), and scores of others. As late as the 1920s land agencies such as those that settled the lower Rio Grande valley issued publications describing Texas potentialities to attract settlers to undeveloped regions.

BIBLIOGRAPHY: Terry G. Jordan, *Immigration to Texas* (Boston: American Press, 1980).

EMILEE, TEXAS. Emilee (Emille) was ten miles northeast of the site of present Woodville in eastern Tyler County. The community was named for Emilee McClendon, the wife of John B. McClendon, an early settler. Another early settler, Squire Cruse, moved there in 1833; Cruse Cemetery, where he is buried, is the oldest cemetery in the county. In 1892 Emilee had a population of 150, a gristmill–sawmill, a cotton gin, a store, and C. C. Dougherty's chair factory. By 1900 the population had fallen to fifty, the same figure cited in 1948 in the community's last available population count. The Emilee post office functioned from 1904 to 1946. In the 1930s the town had two businesses, and in the 1940s it had one business. After that the community disappeared, although it appeared on some maps (as Emille).

BIBLIOGRAPHY: Fred I. Massengill, *Texas Towns: Origin of Name and Location of Each of the 2,148 Post Offices in Texas* (Terrell, Texas, 1936). Thomas Clarence Richardson, *East Texas: Its History and Its Makers* (4 vols., New York: Lewis Historical Publishing, 1940).
Megan Biesele

EMINENCE, TEXAS. Eminence is west of Farm Road 563 and south of Interstate Highway 10, forty-six miles east of Houston in northern Chambers County. The Eminence post office operated from 1898 until 1909. By 1939 a filling station–general store, a school, and a church marked the site at Eminence. A sawmill, operated by J. E. Cline, opened in 1940. By the mid-1970s the Eminence church, several cemeteries, and widely scattered buildings were all that remained.

BIBLIOGRAPHY: Jewel Horace Harry, A History of Chambers County (M.A. thesis, University of Texas, 1940; rpt., Dallas: Taylor, 1981).
Robert Wooster

EMMA, TEXAS. A Texas historical marker on State Highway 207 twenty-five miles east of Lubbock is all that remains to mark the site of Emma, the once thriving county seat of Crosby County. In the fall of 1890 R. L. Stringfellow and H. E. Hume, owners of a general store in Estacado, purchased a section of land in the central part of the county. In 1890 a post office opened, and in 1891 Stringfellow and Hume laid out a town on this site and named it Emma, after the woman that one of them later married.

As settlers from Estacado and East Texas started moving into the area, residents of Emma called for a county-seat election, hoping to lure businesses to the new community. On October 14, 1891, the election was held, and Emma defeated Estacado by a vote of 109 to 103. Sometime after this the courthouse that had been built at Estacado in 1887 or 1888 was brought to Emma, where it was the most impressive building in town. Several businesses were also moved to Emma from Estacado, including the *Crosby County News*, edited by J. W. Murray, and the general store of Stringfellow and Hume, which was the largest business to be established in Emma. With new businesses moving in, Emma prospered, and by 1910 the town had several churches, a post office, a school, a bank, and an estimated population of 800.

Unfortunately, in 1910 the railroad came through the county and bypassed the town by five miles. On September, 17, 1910, Crosbyton defeated Emma in a new county seat election by a vote of 198 to 120. By October 1910 the majority of residents had moved from Emma to Crosbyton. Many of the business buildings and several residences were moved across the prairie to Crosbyton in a caravan consisting of four engines, thirty men, and twenty-two mules. The old courthouse was torn down and hauled to Cedric. In 1911 the post office was moved to Ralls, and Emma became a ghost town.

BIBLIOGRAPHY: Crosby County Pioneer Memorial Museum, *A History of Crosby County, 1876–1977* (Dallas: Taylor, 1978). Crosbyton Golden Jubilee, *Blanco Canyon Cavalcade: Official Souvenir Program* (Crosbyton, Texas, 1958). Nellie Witt Spikes and Temple Ann Ellis, *Through the Years: A History of Crosby County* (San Antonio: Naylor, 1952).
Mary L. Cox

EMMANUEL EPISCOPAL CHURCH, LOCKHART. Immanuel (later Emmanuel) Episcopal Church was organized by Rev. Joseph

Wood Dunn on his arrival in Lockhart in August 1853. Dunn delivered his first sermon in Lockhart to a large crowd on August 21, 1853, in a small schoolhouse borrowed for the occasion. In 1854, after he was informed that the school was no longer available for services, he set about raising funds for a church building. Four citizens, including Bingham Trigg, agreed to construct a roof and install windows if Dunn would arrange to have the walls built. The walls he had constructed extend under the surface two feet and are two feet thick. Hand-hewn cedar timbers form the ceiling beams, and the floor is made of limestone slabs, quarried locally and carefully cut and polished. Hand-carved native walnut is used in the window frames, the base of the font, the chancery rails, and the altar. The structure, completed in 1856, is the oldest known unaltered church building in use by Protestants in Texas.

After the Civil War,qv federal troops probably used the church as a stable. In 1899 the exterior walls were stuccoed to resemble stone. The same year a memorial stained-glass window was donated by the people of Lockhart in honor of "Grandma" Elizabeth Head. Since that time all the windows have been replaced with stained-glass memorials. In 1964 the church was listed as a Texas landmark, and in 1974 it was placed on the National Register of Historic Places. In 1976 an extensive restoration returned the building to its original state. Workers removed the wooden floor and repaired and finished the limestone slabs. Dunn's Bible and Prayer Book are displayed in a glass cubicle.

BIBLIOGRAPHY: Katherine Tally, "Lockhart's Little Church," *Texas Highways*, March 1978. Zona Adams Withers, comp., *Historical Lockhart* (2 vols., Lockhart, Texas: Mark Withers Trail Drive Museum, 1981).

Zona A. Withers

EMMETT, CHRISTOPHER (1886–1971). Christopher (Chris) Emmett, lawyer and historian, was born on the family ranch near Energy on June 30, 1886, the fourth of eleven children of Thomas Addis and Laura Frances (Pickett) Emmett. He grew up in Hamilton and attended the University of Texas, where he received an LL.B. degree in 1910. He practiced law in Hamilton until 1912, when he took a position with the legal department of the Southern Pacific Railway Lines, the company with which he was associated for over thirty years in San Antonio and Houston. On August 26, 1922, he married Margaret Craig.

The study and writing of history were his spare-time activity. He collected rare maps and drawings and presented papers to several regional historical societies. His contributions to the Texas State Historical Association,qv of which he was a member, were placed in the Eugene C. Barker Texas History Center,qv University of Texas at Austin. He was president of the San Antonio Historical Associationqv and helped organize the Harris County Historical Society. His book *Shanghai Pierce: A Fair Likeness* (1953), a biography of a cattle baron, won the 1953 Summerfield G. Roberts award of the Texas Institute of Lettersqv for the best book on the Republic of Texas.qv An earlier work, *Texas Camel Tales* (1932), was also widely acclaimed. Some of his other works were *Give 'Way to the Right* (1934), *Texas As It Was Then* (1935), *The General and the Poet* (1937), *In the Path of Events* (1959), and *Fort Union and the Winning of the Southwest* (1965). After his retirement from Southern Pacific, Emmett lived for a time in Santa Fe and devoted his attention to New Mexican history. He died in Dallas on October 20, 1971, and was buried in Hamilton.

BIBLIOGRAPHY: Sam Hanna Acheson, Herbert P. Gambrell, Mary Carter Toomey, and Alex M. Acheson, Jr., *Texian Who's Who*, Vol. 1 (Dallas: Texian Press, 1937). *A History of Hamilton County, Texas* (Hamilton, Texas: Hamilton County Historical Commission, 1979). Dallas *Morning News*, October 21, 1971.

EMMETT, TEXAS. Emmett, at the junction of Farm roads 639 and 744, twenty-one miles west of Corsicana in western Navarro County, was settled after the Civil Warqv by the Osburn and Goodson families. A post office opened there in 1888, and by 1890 the community had two combination corn mill-cotton gins, a grocery store, a school, a church, a blacksmith shop, and an estimated population of 250. After 1900 many of its residents moved to nearby Frost, which was on the railroad. The Emmett post office was closed in 1905, but the town remained a center for farmers. In the mid-1930s Emmett had an estimated population of 118, four businesses, a school, a church, a cemetery, and a number of houses. After World War IIqv the community's stores closed and its school was consolidated with that of Frost. In the late 1970s all that remained of Emmett was a church, a cemetery, and a number of houses. In 1990 Emmett was a dispersed rural community with an estimated population of 100.

BIBLIOGRAPHY: Annie Carpenter Love, *History of Navarro County* (Dallas: Southwestern, 1933). Wyvonne Putman, comp., *Navarro County History* (5 vols., Quanah, Texas: Nortex, 1975–84). Alva Taylor, *History and Photographs of Corsicana and Navarro County* (Corsicana, Texas, 1959; rev. ed., *Navarro County History and Photographs*, Corsicana, 1962).

Christopher Long

EMORY, TEXAS. Emory, the county seat and largest town of Rains County, is at the junction of U.S. Highway 69 and State Highway 19, at the center of the county. It was named for Emory Rains,qv who settled east of the townsite around 1848. The community was originally known as Springville, reportedly for the many springs in the area. A town plat was evidently prepared by the late 1840s, and by 1857 a store, a tannery, a gin, and a number of houses occupied the site. When Rains County was organized in 1870 Springville became the county seat, and the name was changed to Emory in honor of Rains, who had played an important role in the authorization of the county. A post office founded the same year has continued to operate to the present. A log house initially served as a temporary courthouse. In 1872 a two-room frame courthouse was built; it burned in 1879, along with all of the county records, and the county offices were again housed in the log house until 1884, when a brick courthouse was constructed. About 1880 the Denison and Southeastern Railway was built across the county, making Emory a shipping point for the surrounding lumber-producing area. In 1885 the town had two churches, two sawmills, two cotton gins, two saloons, two hotels, a weekly newspaper named the *Rains County Record*, and a population of 600. The town continued to prosper during the early years of the twentieth century. By 1914 it had three banks and 700 inhabitants, and in 1920 its independent school district was established.

The 1920s witnessed a period of unprecedented prosperity in Emory, and by 1929 the community, now incorporated, had a reported population of 1,000. The Great Depressionqv and the agricultural crisis of the early 1930s, however, began a decline that continued until the 1960s. By 1931 the population had fallen to 750, and by 1936 it had dwindled further to 447, as many inhabitants sought their fortunes in the larger cities. The early postwar period saw modest population growth, but it was not until the late 1950s, when nearby Lake Tawakoniqv was built and Rains County began attracting large numbers of retirees, that Emory began to see sizable increases in the number of inhabitants. After the mid-1960s the town grew steadily, from 578 in 1965 to 813 in 1985 and 1,012 in 1990. Over the same period the number of businesses increased from twenty to thirty-seven. Tourism and agriculture form the mainstays of the town's economy.

BIBLIOGRAPHY: William Oscar Hebison and Ambrose Fitzgerald, *Early Days in Texas and Rains County* (Emory, Texas: Leader Print, 1917; rpt., Garland, Texas: Lost and Found, 1977). *100th Anniversary of Rains County* (Emory, Texas: Hill, 1970).

Claudia Hazlewood

EMORY, WILLIAM HEMSLEY (1811–1887). William Hemsley Emory, United States Army officer and boundary surveyor of Texas, son of Thomas and Anna Maria (Hemsley) Emory, was born at Poplar Grove estate in Queen Anne's County, Maryland, on September 7, 1811. He attended the United States Military Academy, West

Point, New York, and graduated in 1831. He resigned from the army in 1836 to work as a civil engineer but returned to the service in 1838. That year he married the great-granddaughter of Benjamin Franklin, Matilda Wilkins Bache of Philadelphia; they had three children. In the coming years, as a lieutenant, captain, and major in the topographical engineers, Emory specialized in exploration and conducting boundary surveys along the Texas-Mexican border (1844), the United States–Canadian border (1844–46), the United States–Mexican border (1848–53), and the Gadsden Purchase (1854–57).

In 1844 Emory served on an expedition that produced a new map of Texas showing Texas claims westward to the Rio Grande. He came to public attention as the author of *Notes of a Military Reconnaissance from Fort Leavenworth in Missouri to San Diego in California,* published by the Thirtieth Congress in 1848. This report described terrain and rivers, cities and forts, pueblos and prehistoric ruins, animals and plants, and Indians and Mexicans, primarily in New Mexico, Arizona, and Southern California. It was then and later considered one of the important chronicles and descriptions of the Southwest, especially for its maps. Emory was a reliable cartographer and drew dozens of maps of the West. His accurate rendering of the topography usually made other maps obsolete. He acquired his greatest fame as supervisor of the United States–Mexican boundary survey between 1848 and 1853. That survey included an exploration of the Big Bend region of the Rio Grande River. Emory's maps and reports made him the foremost authority of the trans-Mississippi Southwest in the United States.

During the Mexican War[qv] (1846–48), Emory served in the Southwest and in California as chief engineer in the Army of the West under Gen. Stephen W. Kearny. At the outbreak of the Civil War[qv] in 1861 he was stationed with soldiers in Indian Territory and withdrew forces under his command to Fort Leavenworth. He served as a brigade commander in the Union's Army of the Potomac (1862). After transfer to the Western Theater, he commanded a division in the Port Hudson campaign and the Red River campaign[qv] in Louisiana (1863–64). He subsequently returned to the East as commander of the Nineteenth Corps, which performed badly in the Shenandoah Valley (1864), especially at the battle of Cedar Creek, where Emory was rescued by Gen. Philip Sheridan's[qv] arrival.

After the war Emory held a number of posts, most importantly commander of the Department of the Gulf (which included soldiers in Louisiana, Arkansas, and Mississippi)—a demanding and dangerous Reconstruction[qv] assignment. General Sheridan removed Emory from command and saw to it that he was retired in 1876. The Department of the Gulf was soon shifted to Sheridan's large Division of the Missouri, which included Texas. Emory died on December 1, 1887, in Washington, D.C.

BIBLIOGRAPHY: Joseph G. Dawson III, *Army Generals and Reconstruction: Louisiana, 1862–1877* (Baton Rouge: Louisiana State University Press, 1982). William Hemsley Emory, *Report on the United States and Mexican Boundary Survey* (2 vols., Washington: Nicholson, 1857, 1859; rpt., Austin: Texas State Historical Association, 1987). William Hemsley Emory, *Notes of a Military Reconnaissance* (Washington and New York, 1848; rpt., by the U.S. Army Corps of Topographical Engineers, as *Lieutenant Emory Reports*, with intro. and notes by Ross Calvin [Albuquerque: University of New Mexico Press, 1951]). W. H. Goetzmann, *Army Exploration in the American West, 1803–1863* (New Haven: Yale University Press, 1959; 2d ed., Lincoln: University of Nebraska Press, 1979; rpt., Austin: Texas State Historical Association, 1991). Robert L. Kerby, *Kirby Smith's Confederacy: The Trans-Mississippi South, 1863–1865* (New York: Columbia University Press, 1972).
Joseph G. Dawson III

EMORY PEAK. Emory Peak is in the Chisos Mountains within Big Bend National Park[qv] eight miles southwest of Panther Junction in southern Brewster County (at 29°15′ N, 103°18′ W). Its summit, at an elevation of 7,825 feet above sea level, is the highest peak in the county and the tenth highest in Texas, rising 2,425 feet above the Basin ranger station two miles northeast. Shallow, stony soils on the mountain support Douglas fir, aspen, Arizona cypress, maple, ponderosa pine, and madrone. The peak was named for William H. Emory,[qv] who led the United States-Mexican boundary survey after the Mexican War.[qv] It was named by M. T. W. Chandler, appointed by Emory in 1852 to survey the Big Bend area. In the early 1990s the summit of Emory Peak was the site of an antenna and other radio equipment used by the National Park Service.

EMPORIA, TEXAS. Emporia was a sawmill settlement on the Houston, East and West Texas Railway twelve miles south of Lufkin in southern Angelina County. In the 1890s lumberman Samuel Fain Carter[qv] built a saw and planing mill there. Around 1900 the mill had fifty employees and produced 40,000 board feet of lumber a day. A post office operated at the site from 1893 to 1907, when it merged with nearby Diboll. After the mill closed in 1906, most of the local residents left, and by the 1920s the site was abandoned.

BIBLIOGRAPHY: Angelina County Historical Survey Committee, *Land of the Little Angel: A History of Angelina County, Texas,* ed. Bob Bowman (Lufkin, Texas: Lufkin Printing, 1976).
Christopher Long

EMPORIA AND GULF RAILROAD. The Emporia and Gulf Railroad Company was chartered on August 18, 1900, to connect Emporia, Angelina County, with Prescott, twenty-five miles to the east. The capital stock was $100,000, and the principal place of business was Emporia. Members of the first board of directors were Samuel F. Carter,[qv] J. P. Carter, E. L. Crooker, L. Davidson, W. B. Banks, E. J. Mantooth, and E. W. Scott. In 1900 the railroad built fifteen miles of track between Emporia and Crooker, and the following year it was reclassified as a logging operation.
Nancy Beck Young

EMPRESARIO. An empresario was a land agent or land contractor. Under the system used by the Mexican government as a means of colonization (*see* MEXICAN COLONIZATION LAWS), outstanding Texas empresarios included Stephen F. Austin, Samuel May Williams, Green DeWitt, Martín De León, Haden Edwards, Sterling C. Robertson, James Power, James Hewetson, John McMullen, James McGloin, and Arthur G. Wavell.[qqv]

BIBLIOGRAPHY: Mary Virginia Henderson, "Minor Empresario Contracts for the Colonization of Texas, 1825–1834," *Southwestern Historical Quarterly* 31, 32 (April, July 1928).

ENCHANTED ROCK. Enchanted Rock is a spectacular granite pluton just west of State Highway 965 near the Gillespie-Llano county line in southern Llano County (at 30°30′N, 98°48′ W). The granite dome rises some 385 feet above the streambed of nearby Sandy Creek to a maximum elevation of 1,825 feet above mean sea level. This great granite monadnock is the second largest such mountain in the United States (the largest is Stone Mountain, Georgia). It is part of a rough, segmented ridge, which is in turn part of the surface expression of a large igneous batholith of middle Precambrian material intrusive into earlier metamorphic schists and gneiss. This intrusive granite was exposed after later sedimentary rock deposition and extensive erosion. In 1992 a University of Texas geophysics researcher, Ian W. D. Dalziel, linked Enchanted Rock geologically with granite peaks in Antarctica. The name Enchanted Rock derives from Spanish and Anglo-Texas interpretations of Indian legends and related folklore, which attribute magical and spiritual properties to the ancient landmark. According to one nineteenth-century writer, "the Indians had a great awe amounting almost to a reverence" for the rock (*see* ENCHANTED ROCK LEGENDS).

The first European to see Enchanted Rock was possibly Álvar Núñez Cabeza de Vaca,qv who traveled through this area before 1536. The rock was visited and described by many during the sixteenth, seventeenth, and eighteenth centuries. Capt. Henry S. Brown,qv who came from Green DeWitt'sqv colony on a punitive Indian expedition in 1829, appears to have been the first Anglo-Texan to visit the location. William B. DeWeesqv described the rock in 1834. Other writers describe an Indian encounter of Captain John (Jack) Coffee Haysqv at Enchanted Rock. The rock has also been the subject of paintings by such artists as Hermann Lungkwitz.qv Enchanted Rock was the subject of a natural-area survey published by the Lyndon Baines Johnson School of Public Affairsqv in 1979. The site was acquired by the Texas Parks and Wildlife Departmentqv in that year and was opened as Enchanted Rock State Park (see ENCHANTED ROCK STATE NATURAL AREA) in March of 1984.

BIBLIOGRAPHY: Steven M. Kotter and Linda A. Nance, *Archeological Assessments at...Enchanted Rock State Natural Area* (Austin: Prewitt and Associates, 1980). *Art Leatherwood*

ENCHANTED ROCK LEGENDS. Enchanted Rock,qv a granite dome in southwestern Llano County about twenty miles north of Fredericksburg, has long been the center of various legends. The local Comanche and Tonkawa Indians both feared and revered the rock, and were said to offer sacrifices at its base. One Indian tradition holds that a band of brave warriors, the last of their tribe, defended themselves on the rock from the attacks of other Indians. The warriors, however, were finally overcome and killed, and since then Enchanted Rock has been haunted by their ghosts. Another legend tells of an Indian princess who threw herself off the rock when she saw her people slaughtered by enemy Indians; now her spirit is said to haunt Enchanted Rock. Yet another tale tells of the spirit of an Indian chief who was doomed to walk the summit forever as punishment for sacrificing his daughter; the indentations on the rock's summit are his footprints. Finally, there is the story of a white woman who was kidnapped by Indians but escaped and lived on Enchanted Rock, where her screams were said to be audible at night. The Indian legends of the haunting of Enchanted Rock were probably bolstered by the way the rock glitters on clear nights after rain, and by the creaking noises reported on cool nights after warm days. Scientists have since theorized that the glittering is caused either by water trapped in indentations in the rock's surface or by the moon reflecting off wet feldspar, and the creaking noises by contraction of the rock's outer surface as it cools.

A number of stories involve rumors of great mineral wealth to be found at Enchanted Rock. Spanish explorers believed it was one large chunk of silver or iron. They also sought legendary gold and silver mines nearby, and some early Texans believed that the lost "Bowie Mines" were in the vicinity west of Enchanted Rock. Some gold has in fact been mined near Enchanted Rock, but not enough to be commercially profitable. According to an account written in 1834 the rock was once supposed to be of platinum.

One of the most enduring and romantic stories involving Enchanted Rock is that of a young Spanish soldier, Don Jesús Navarro, and his rescue of the Indian maiden Rosa. Navarro supposedly came from Monterrey to San José y San Miguel de Aguayo Mission in San Antonio in 1750. At the mission he met and fell in love with Rosa, the Christian daughter of the Indian chief Tehuan. But Rosa was kidnapped by a band of Comanches bent on sacrificing her to the spirits of Enchanted Rock. Her daring lover followed them there and managed to rescue her as she was about to be burned at the stake.

Another tale, given official credence when the state of Texas commemorated it with a plaque near the summit of Enchanted Rock in 1936, relates a heroic episode in the life of Capt. John Coffee Hays.qv Cut off by Comanche raiders from his company of Texas Rangersqv on a surveying trip in the fall of 1841, Hays took refuge on Enchanted Rock and singlehandedly held off the Indians in a three-hour battle that ended when the frustrated Indians fled, convinced even more firmly than before that Enchanted Rock was possessed by malevolent spirits.

BIBLIOGRAPHY: Samuel C. Reid, Jr., *The Scouting Expeditions of McCulloch's Texas Rangers* (Philadelphia: Zieber, 1847; rpt., Freeport, New York: Books for Libraries Press, 1970). Tillie Badu Moss Fry, A History of Llano County (M.A. thesis, University of Texas, 1943). Richard Zelade, *Hill Country* (Austin: Texas Monthly Press, 1983).
Martin Donell Kohout

ENCHANTED ROCK STATE NATURAL AREA. Enchanted Rock State Natural Area is on Sandy Creek and Ranch Road 965 at the Gillespie-Llano county line, eighteen miles north of Fredericksburg. The 1,643-acre park is roughly triangular, and Enchanted Rockqv is near its center. The first owners of this land were Anavato and María Martínez, to whom a headright certificate was issued on March 16, 1838. They sold it to James Robinson in 1841, and he in turn sold it to Samuel A. Maverickqv in 1844. Maverick, believing that Enchanted Rock might prove to be a source of mineral wealth, had part of the property surveyed in 1847, and it was patented to him by the state on September 22, 1851. Maverick's widow sold the property to N. P. P. Browne in 1880–81; on February 19, 1886, Browne sold it to John R. Moss, who sold it to J. D. Slator later that year. Two ranching brothers, C. T. and A. F. Moss, bought the property from Slator in 1895 and in November 1897 partitioned it between them, except for Enchanted Rock itself, which they held in common. Eventually C. T. Moss acquired his brother's holdings, and in 1927 C. T.'s son Tate inherited the property and opened it to the tourist trade. On October 26, 1946, he sold it to Albert Faltin, who later sold a half interest to Llano rancher Charles H. Moss, C. T.'s grandson. Charles and his wife, Ruth, managed and eventually acquired full title to the property but decided to sell it in 1978. Moss first offered it to the Texas Parks and Wildlife Department,qv but the agency could not pay his price. The Nature Conservancy, a private concern based in Arlington, Virginia, bought the property for $1.3 million on March 1, 1978, and agreed to act as interim owner until the state could take over, thus guaranteeing that the area would not be opened to private development. United States secretary of the interior Cecil Andrus told Governor Dolph Briscoe that a federal land and water conservation grant would be made available for purchase of the area when matched by state funds, and the Nature Conservancy deeded the land to the state on March 7, 1978, with the agreement that Moss would continue to operate it until June 1 of that year.

Besides Enchanted Rock itself, the Enchanted Rock State Natural Area includes Turkey Peak and Enchanted Rock Cave among its natural features, as well as a wide variety of native flora and fauna. Among the more than 400 species of plants in the park are live oak, Texas hickory, blackjack oak, cedar, American elm, honey mesquite, and pecan trees; lily yucca, prickly pear, barrel cactus, strawberry cactus, and pencil cactus; and about 100 species of mosses, lichens, and liverworts. Animals found in the park include white-tailed deer, armadillos, bobcats, raccoons, black rock squirrels, red foxes, cotton rats, four kinds of hawk, turkeys, great horned owls, turkey vultures, copperheads, diamondbacks, cottonmouths, bull snakes, checkered ribbon snakes, and spotted whiptails. The park also contains some 114 archeological sites, at which various Indian artifacts have been unearthed. The area has long been a favorite destination of hikers, campers, rock-climbers, hang-gliders, and other outdoor enthusiasts from around the state. In 1977 an estimated 50,000 people visited the area; the park drew 30,000 visitors in three months when it reopened in March 1984 after eighteen months of renovation. With $1.9 million in improvements made during those months, in 1986 the park had a new headquarters building, a visitors' center, fifty-two tent sites, sixty primitive campsites, forty picnic sites, and numerous hiking trails. Nearby places of interest include the towns of Fredericksburg and Llano and the Lyndon B. Johnson State Historic Park.qv

BIBLIOGRAPHY: *Enchanted Rock State Natural Area* (Austin: Texas Parks and Wildlife Department, 1983). Vertical Files, Barker Texas History Center, University of Texas at Austin.

Martin Donell Kohout

ENCINAL, TEXAS. Encinal is on Interstate Highway 35 twenty-seven miles south of Cotulla in southwestern La Salle County. Railroad officials reportedly named the spot the Spanish word for "oak grove." Before the International–Great Northern Railroad extended its tracks into the area, a small community called Ancaster already existed near, and possibly on, the site of present Encinal. It has been suggested that Encinal began as a settlement 1½ miles from the present site, which was moved to the railroad tracks when they were laid down in the early 1880s. An 1882 railroad map shows only a stop named Burro in the general location of present Encinal. In 1883, when a post office was granted under the name of Encinal, there were probably no more than two or three frame buildings on the site. But the town developed rather rapidly as a shipping center for sheep and cattle. In 1886 its first school was established, and by 1890 Encinal reportedly had a population of 900 and several businesses, including three general stores and a saloon. By 1896 the community had a school for sixty-one students, four general stores, the saloon, and an insurance agent.

Many of the early residents were of Mexican descent. A Catholic church was built in 1893. In 1908 a Presbyterian church was built; and by that year the town had two public schools, which enrolled 158 students. In 1931 the town had three public schools with a total of 363 students. In 1933 Encinal reported 800 residents and thirteen businesses; similar statistics were reported through the mid-1940s.

In 1947 the population of Encinal was 650, and by 1949 it was only 300; it was so reported until the 1980s. The number of businesses dropped from fourteen in 1949 to seven in 1974. That year the town had one school for its 203 elementary students; junior and senior high school students attended school in Cotulla. Natural gas wells had been discovered in the area by 1974, when businesses included two natural gas pumping stations, five cafes, a general store, and a drugstore, though ranching was still the primary business. In 1980 Encinal had twelve businesses and 300 residents. In 1990 the population was 620.

BIBLIOGRAPHY: Annette Martin Ludeman, *La Salle: La Salle County* (Quanah, Texas: Nortex, 1975).

John Leffler

ENCINAL COUNTY. Encinal County, as established on February 1, 1856, included the western part of present Webb County and was to have Encinal as county seat. The county was never organized and was abolished on March 12, 1899. The territory was incorporated into Webb County.

BIBLIOGRAPHY: Hans Peter Nielsen Gammel, comp., *Laws of Texas, 1822–1897* (10 vols., Austin: Gammel, 1898).

Seymour V. Connor

ENCINO, TEXAS. Encino is a rural community on U.S. Highway 281 eighteen miles south of Falfurrias in southern Brooks County. Its site is within Luciano Chapa's 1832 Mexican land grant, called La Encantada y Encina del Pozo ("Enchanted Place and Live Oak in a Hole"), a name reportedly derived from a large live oak at the site, around which a hole gradually developed as wind erosion and animals seeking the oak's shade wore down the surrounding land. The Encino community was established at the site in the early 1900s as a roundup point for cattle raised by Mexican cattlemen. The Texas and New Orleans Railroad was completed through Encino in 1904, and a post office was established there in 1914. The community's population in 1925 was fifty, and it remained at that level until 1939, when a population of 100 was reported. The population of Encino was estimated at 200 by 1941, but it dropped to 125 by 1945. In 1948 Encino had three schools, a church, and several dwellings. In 1970 the community's population was 110, and in 1976 it had eleven businesses. In 1982 Encino had a school, a church, three businesses, and several dwellings. During the early 1990s it was a dispersed community with nine businesses and 110 inhabitants.

Alicia A. Garza

ENDEMIC DISEASES. "Endemic disease" may denote a disease that repeatedly appears in small numbers of a population while the vast majority escape without evidence of illness. This type of endemicity, which most often results from human-to-human transfer of the agent of disease, is favored by crowding, extensive human contact, and the presence of widespread immunity in the population. Travel increases the chance of infection, and isolation reduces it. The incidence of such diseases has been causally related to changes in patterns of immigration, social mobility, urbanization, and transportation. In Texas, such endemic diseases have been similar to those encountered in other advanced nations of the world. The same diseases occur in Dallas or Houston as appear in New York, London, or Paris. Among these are tuberculosis, syphilis, gonorrhea, bacillary dysentery, influenza, and various types of pneumonia. Influenza, for example, attacked approximately one of a hundred Texans in 1984, while hepatitis of all types attacked 4,500 individuals.

The phrase may also refer to a disease that is peculiar to a region. Factors that favor endemicity of this type are isolation, rural occupations, distinctive geographic features, locally high concentrations of chemicals (fluorides, selenium, radioactive substances), climatic conditions, the presence of specific vectors of disease (mosquitoes, fleas, lice, and ticks), and reservoirs of infection in animals with intermittent transmission to humans. First among conditions in Texas arising from physical factors are those that result from prolonged exposure to intense sunlight. Nearly all places in the state receive from 60 to 70 percent sunshine out of all possible sunlit hours. The most common result is severe sunburn, sometimes requiring hospitalization. This condition is more common along the Gulf Coast, but it can occur anywhere in the state when human beings expose considerable parts of their bodies to direct rays. Additionally, the sustained heat of the Texas summer causes insolation, manifested as either heat exhaustion or sunstroke. While these conditions occur more commonly in the elderly and debilitated, a few instances of fatal heat stroke have occurred among young athletes, particularly in fall training programs for football. Texas also lies in that area of the United States sometimes referred to as "Tornado Alley." Violent storms are not uncommon, and injuries and fatalities occur intermittently (*see* TORNADOES). Similarly, the Gulf Coast has been a frequent site of hurricanesqv with attendant injuries and death.

A condition formerly common among Texans who were raised on the High Plains was mottled enamel of the teeth. Stains were caused by high concentration of fluorides in well water. With extension of city water supplies and reduction of fluorides, this condition has largely disappeared.

Infectious diseases of limited geographic distribution are those conveyed by vectors such as mosquitoes, those transmitted from animals to man, and those produced by agents that live in the soil. Since the initiation of effective mosquito-control programs, yellow fever and malaria have almost disappeared from Texas. In 1984 only seventy-five cases of yellow fever were reported to the Texas Department of Human Services.qv Relapsing fever, once prevalent in cattle, is transmitted to man through ticks. Though it was formerly more prevalent along the Mexican border, diseased cattle from that region were often driven north or mixed with other herds. In 1984 there were no reported cases of this disease.

Psittacosis (ornithosis) is transmitted from birds or domestic fowls to man. Since Texans operate a number of large turkey farms, episodes of this disease have been reported. During 1984, however, there were only seven reported cases. Parrots imported from South America also cause isolated cases of psittacosis. Tularemia occurs sporadically in Texas. Eight cases were reported in 1984. Humans are usually inoculated when skinning or cleaning infected rabbits. A febrile disease, originally designated Bullis fever, attacked a high proportion of military personnel stationed at Camp Bullis, near San Antonio, during World War II.qv Evidence accumulated that the disease was transmitted by tick bites. This disease appears very infrequently and is mostly limited to hunters or to individuals engaged in agricultural activities in the Camp Bullis area.

Rocky Mountain Spotted Fever appears in Texas as an occasional infection. The disease is transmitted by ticks. Occurrence is likely only in those who frequent wooded areas. Murine typhus, conveyed by fleas, has persisted in Texas for many years. At one time it was especially common along the Rio Grande, where it was known as "tabardillo," but control of rats, on which the fleas are parasitic, has reduced the incidence of this disease. During 1984, only thirty-five cases were reported. The condition appears sporadically throughout the state, and there is evidence that fleas from other rodents may be infectious.

Of organisms present in the soil and distributed by its disturbance, two fungi, *Histoplasma capsulatum* and *Coccidioides immitis*, are present in Texas. *Histoplasma capsulatum* may be encountered at any place where considerable accumulation of droppings from birds or bats occurs. Not infrequently, histoplasmosis occurs in subclinical forms and is not reported. Only eight cases were reported in 1984. These probably represent the most serious cases of chronic pulmonary histoplasmosis, which resembles tuberculosis. *Coccidioides immitis*, which infects desert rodents, is distributed by dust storms and by vehicles that have operated in contaminated areas. It also produces a mild, self-limited disease in humans. The organism is widely distributed throughout the lower western part of the state, along the Rio Grande, but it also appears as far upstate as Midland-Odessa, San Angelo, and south of San Antonio. First identified as San Joaquin valley fever in California, coccidioidomycosis occurs sporadically through the lower Sonoran Life Zone of the western United States and in adjacent states of Mexico.

Other mycobacteria occasionally produce disease in humans. The most virulent of these organisms, *Mycobacterium kansasii*, produces a significant number of pulmonary infections each year. Unquestionably a large number of people temporarily harbor the organism without resulting illness. The chief distribution of this organism is through the north central region of the state (Region 5 of the Texas Department of Human Services), but the infection also occurs in lower incidence in other states. *Mycobacterium avium-intracellulare* is prevalent throughout the Gulf Coast area. It is found chiefly in the eastern third of Texas. The organism appears to be closely linked to water, though certain types also appear in soil samples. It seems certain that although many people encounter and harbor the organism, only a small proportion become ill. This organism, along with *Mycobacterium Kansasii*, seems to account for as many as 10 percent of pulmonary infections originally thought from X-ray analysis to be tuberculosis.

BIBLIOGRAPHY: *Texas Preventable Disease News*, January 26, 1985.

John S. Chapman

ENDERLE, BENJAMIN LESTER (1889–1983). Benjamin Lester Enderle, peach grower, surveyor, and teacher, was born in Kerrville on February 28, 1889, to Albert and Amelia (Dietert) Enderle. His maternal grandparents were among the founders of Comfort, Texas. Enderle graduated from Tivy High School in Kerrville in 1906 and received a teaching certificate. For the next six years he taught school in several small towns around the state. On September 9, 1908, he married Louise Elizabeth Forres from Fayetteville. They had three children. In 1912 Enderle moved to Fredericksburg, where he was appointed Gillespie county surveyor, a position he held for the next sixty-three years. In 1913 he also accepted a post at Fredericksburg High School, where he was a math and science teacher and a coach until 1944.

In 1921 Enderle and his wife began planting peach trees on fourteen acres east of Fredericksburg as a means of paying off their land house. He worked to develop a durable species that would survive shipment, using Hale, Burbank, Elberta, and Stark clingstone varieties. By 1925 the Enderles were producing more from their several hundred trees than they could sell locally. Enderle's boyhood friendship with Howard E. Butt'sqv family provided an outlet for the sale of peaches outside the Fredericksburg area, the H-E-Bqv stores in Austin and San Antonio. In 1935 Enderle bought another 145 acres and soon had about 5,000 peach trees in production. He is regarded as the originator of the Hill Countryqv peach industry.

He was a charter member of the Gillespie County Peach Growers Association, the Gillespie County Historical Society, and the Hill Country Poultry Association. He was a member of the chamber of commerce and the Lions Club and was an elder at Memorial Presbyterian Church. He died on June 3, 1983, in Fredericksburg and was buried in Greenwood Cemetery. *See also* FRUITS OTHER THAN CITRUS.

BIBLIOGRAPHY: Fredericksburg *Standard* June 8, 1983. Lloyd Murphy, "B. L. Enderle: Father of the Hill Country Peach Industry," *Texas Hill Country View*, August 1981.

Lloyd Murphy

ENDSLEY, JANE JOHNSON (1848–1933). Jane Johnson Endsley, who was born a slave in Jefferson, Texas, in 1848, rose to a successful life as a businesswoman and community leader in Dallas. After spending her childhood on a plantation in Jefferson, she married Moses Calloway in 1862 in Jefferson. Moses had also been born a slave, in Tennessee. They moved to Rowlett, Texas, sometime between 1865 and 1868. The Calloways became sharecroppers but ultimately acquired their own 100-acre farm there. They had eleven children.

After her husband's death sometime in the late 1880s or early 1890s, Jane continued to manage their prosperous farm, which had been assessed at a value of $15,150 in 1882. She regularly delivered her own cotton to the local cotton gin. On one occasion, a white man attempted to steal her bale of cotton by grabbing it as it emerged from the gin. "Without thinking" Jane struck him with the cotton hook she was holding, splitting the man's skull. According to family accounts, a white man who witnessed the accident apparently took the blame for it, thus protecting her from prosecution.

In 1894 she married C. F. Franklin. After eleven years of marriage they divorced, and she married Alonzo Jones. That marriage also ended in divorce. She entered into her fourth and final marriage to H. E. Endsley, a tailor, in 1914.

Around that time she sold the family farm in Rowlett but kept the timber rights to the land and set up a railroad-yard coal and log business in the heart of Dallas. Jane Endsley ran the business with the assistance of her sons, Joe, Lube, and Emmett. The family company provided much-needed fuel for many Dallas residents and was considered the largest business of its kind in the city. The Endsleys acquired another portion of land close to the site of the present State Fair of Texas.qv Their wealth enabled them to build a fine home on Collins Street, with a veranda stretching the length of the house front, and to purchase a new Model T Ford.

With other friends, Jane Endsley founded the Macedonia Baptist Church, which later grew to a 5,000-member congregation known as the Good Street Baptist Church. In the 1920s she helped establish a women's lodge called the Household of Ruth, for which she rented a building. The lodge provided funeral insurance for African Americans,qv who could not acquire insurance from white companies at the time. The Household of Ruth also offered them a network of "trusted friends" in time of need.

Endsley had the only telephone in her neighborhood for a long

Jane Johnson Calloway Endsley. Courtesy Rita Calloway Mosley, Dallas. A successful businesswoman, Jane Endsley also founded the Dallas chapter of the Household of Ruth, a lodge for African-American women that sold funeral insurance and ministered to those in need. She is shown here in lodge attire.

time and welcomed her neighbors to use it. During the Great Depression,qv she and her youngest daughter, Maggie, worked to feed hungry, homeless people. She also spent time "ministering to the sick and elderly." Endsley never learned to read or write but apparently developed her own shorthand. In the 1990s her descendants still had regular family gatherings and maintained records of the family roots. She died at her home on Collins Street in 1933 and was buried in the family plot in Rowlett.

BIBLIOGRAPHY: Dallas *Morning News*, October 27, 1986.

Teresa Palomo Acosta

ENEPIAHE INDIANS. The Enepiahe (Exepiahohe) Indians are known only from records of the La Salle expedition,qv which indicate that in the late seventeenth century these Indians inhabited an area north or northeast of Matagorda Bay, probably between the Colorado and Brazos rivers. Their linguistic and cultural affiliations remain unknown. Attempts to identify the Enepiahes with the Ervipiames are not convincing. The Enepiahe Indians are known only from the late seventeenth century, at which time the Ervipiames were still living in the area around present Eagle Pass.

BIBLIOGRAPHY: Isaac Joslin Cox, ed., *The Journeys of René Robert Cavelier, Sieur de La Salle* (2 vols., New York: Barnes, 1905; 2d ed., New York: Allerton, 1922). Frederick Webb Hodge, ed., *Handbook of American Indians North of Mexico* (2 vols., Washington: GPO, 1907, 1910; rpt., New York: Pageant, 1959). Pierre Margry, ed., *Découvertes et établissements des Français dans l'ouest et dans le sud de l'Amérique septentrionale, 1614–1754* (6 vols., Paris: Jouast, 1876–86).

Thomas N. Campbell

ENERGY, TEXAS. Energy is on Farm Road 1702 sixteen miles southeast of Comanche in Comanche County. It was established around 1896 and was reportedly named for its energetic residents by Will and Charlie Baxter, store owners in the area. The community's post office opened about 1896, with John W. Moore as postmaster. The population of Energy was reported as sixty-seven in 1940 and sixty-five in 1990, when the post office was still in operation.

BIBLIOGRAPHY: Comanche County Bicentennial Committee, *Patchwork of Memories: Historical Sketches of Comanche County, Texas* (Brownwood, Texas: Banner Printing, 1976).

Tracey L. Compton

ENGELING WILDLIFE MANAGEMENT AREA. The 10,941-acre Gus Engeling Wildlife Management Area is on U.S. Highway 287 twenty miles northwest of Palestine in northwest Anderson County. The land, in the post oak savannah region of the state, was purchased by the Texas Game, Fish, and Oyster Commission (*see* TEXAS GAME AND FISH COMMISSION) between 1950 and 1960 for a state-owned and operated wildlife management area. Most of it was bought from W. L. Derden, and the area was originally named the Derden Wildlife Management Area. It was renamed in 1951, when Gus A. Engeling, the first biologist assigned to the area, was shot and killed by a poacher. Development was accomplished under the Federal Aid in Wildlife Restoration Act, approved on September 2, 1937, by the United States Congress. The Engeling Wildlife Management Area operates under the Wildlife Division of the Texas Parks and Wildlife Department.qv The staff consists of six permanent, full-time employees.

The EWMA has a well-defined drainage system that empties into Catfish Creek, a tributary of the Trinity River. The system covers 2,000 acres of bottomland. Abundant understory vegetation, fallen timber, beaver dams and ponds, and natural succession have altered and reduced the flow of Catfish Creek, thus aiding in the formation of sloughs and marshes. In 1990 more than eight miles of Catfish Creek provided a strong, continual water flow with abundant fish and other aquatic life. The United States Department of the Interior has named this section of Catfish Creek a national natural landmark, suitable for registering because it "possesses national significance in illustrating the natural heritage of the United States."

The purpose of the area is to provide consumptive and nonconsumptive use to the general public compatible with other programs and the resource itself. The principal goals are to plan experimental land-use and game-management programs for the area, to conduct vegetation and wildlife studies applicable to management of wildlife habitat resources in the post oak region of Texas, to establish sound management practices for wildlife and habitat resources, to document trends in wildlife population for use in setting open seasons and bag limits, to establish information on wildlife management practices and demonstrate the application of these practices, and to provide opportunities for education about natural resources. The Engeling Wildlife Management Area illustrates quality wildlife habitat and proper management, necessary attributes of proper land stewardship.

BIBLIOGRAPHY: *A Plan for Texas Wildlife, 1990–1995* (Austin: Texas Parks and Wildlife Department, 1990). Vertical Files, Barker Texas History Center, University of Texas at Austin.

John C. Jones

ENGERRAND, GEORGE CHARLES MARIUS (1877–1961). George Charles Engerrand, professor of anthropology at the University of Texas, was born on August 11, 1877, near Bordeaux, France, of French-Basque ancestry. He received his early education from private tutors, and at the age of eighteen he enrolled at the University of Bordeaux, where he received a licentiate in geology (1897) and a licentiate in botany (1898). At Bordeaux he was a student of the famed pioneer sociologist Émile Durkheim. In 1898 he went to Brussels, Belgium, where he had been invited to teach by the geographer Élisée Reclus. Between 1898 and 1907 Engerrand held numerous research and teaching positions, some of them concurrently, at several Belgian institutions.

From 1907 until the political revolution in 1917 made it impossible to continue, Engerrand lived in Mexico and was, for most of this period, professor of archeology in the Museo Nacional de Arqueología, Historia, y Etnología. He moved to Mississippi, where he taught geology until 1920, then to Austin, Texas, where he became adjunct professor of anthropology at the University of Texas. For the next forty-one years, until his retirement in 1961, Engerrand was a member of the UT anthropology department, from which he received a Ph.D. in 1935.

He wrote seventy-five articles and several books. He received many academic honors, including La Croix de Chevalier de l'Ordre des Palmes, a French decoration given for distinguished teaching and scholarly publication. In 1898 Engerrand married Alice Delsaute, from whom he separated in 1902; two sons were born of this marriage. In 1904 he married Jeanne Richard, and they had one son and two daughters. Engerrand died in Mexico City on September 2, 1961, and was buried in Austin.

BIBLIOGRAPHY: *American Anthropologist*, October 1962. A. P. Brogan, J. G. McAllister, and T. N. Campbell, "In Memoriam: George Charles Marius Engerrand," *Bulletin of the Texas Archeological Society* 32 (1961). John N. Graham, "George C. Engerrand in Mexico, 1907–1917," *Bulletin of the Texas Archeological Society* 32 (1961). William W. Newcomb, "George C. Engerrand in Europe, 1898–1907," *Bulletin of the Texas Archeological Society* 32 (1961). Vertical Files, Barker Texas History Center, University of Texas at Austin.   *Robert L. Wagner*

ENGLE, TEXAS. Engle is on U.S. Highway 90 and the Southern Pacific Railroad, five miles west of Schulenburg and five miles east of Flatonia in southern Fayette County. The area was thinly settled by Bohemian and Czech immigrants in the 1850s, but their community focus was at Praha to the southwest. During the late 1870s Engle was established as a point on the Galveston, Harrisburg and San Antonio Railway. The community was named for J. E. Engle, an engineer on that line. The land around Engle is drained to the south by Brushy Creek and to the north by Rocky Creek and is fair for agriculture. A post office was established at the community in 1888 and the first store in 1890. By 1900 Engle had three saloons, two stores, a blacksmith shop, a tinsmith shop, a lumberyard, and a photography studio. Sometime after 1930 its post office closed. By 1950 the community reported six businesses serving a population of 250. Most of the land that had been used for cotton reverted to pasture during the 1960s. In 1990 four businesses and 106 residents were reported at Engle.

BIBLIOGRAPHY: Frank Lotto, *Fayette County: Her History and Her People* (Schulenburg, Texas: Sticker Steam Press, 1902; rpt., Austin: University of Texas Press, 1981). Leonie Rummel Weyand and Houston Wade, *An Early History of Fayette County* (La Grange, Texas: La Grange Journal, 1936).   *Jeff Carroll*

ENGLISH. The first English in Texas, according to an early written account, were not settlers, but three seamen set ashore by John Hawkins in Mexico in the sixteenth century near Tampico, after a battle with the Spanish at Veracruz on Hawkins' third expedition to the Indies. The three seamen, David Ingram, Richard Twide, and Richard Browne, allegedly walked across lower Texas on their way north in 1568, and Ingram's brief account was included by the younger Richard Hakluyt in his publication in 1589 of *The Principall Navigations, Voiages and Discoveries of the English Nation* (though Hakluyt's doubts about the authenticity of the story caused its omission from subsequent editions). Scattered English farmers and businessmen may have settled in Texas by 1800. At least six Englishmen were awarded empresario[qv] contracts in the 1820s, though none was successful in bringing in families; in the 1830s attempts at colonization began on a much larger scale, though again with limited success. Beales's Rio Grande colony[qv] included a few English families, and the contract granted by the Republic of Texas[qv] to the Peters colony[qv] in 1841 eventually resulted in the scattered settlement of large areas in North Texas, covering parts of twenty-six future counties. William Kennedy[qv] failed to fulfill a contract to bring 600 families to Texas, but he did attract a good deal of attention with his book, *Texas: The Rise, Progress, and Prospects of the Republic of Texas* (1841); William Bollaert,[qv] who published some of his own accounts of traveling in Texas in English magazines, was attracted to the new republic by Kennedy's book. A later colonization attempt was made in Bosque County in 1850 (*see* COLONY OF KENT).

Ranching and land-investment interests in the Panhandle[qv] undoubtedly reflected the greatest intercourse between England and Texas, especially in the boom years of 1880–87. By the end of 1886 the English had invested about $25 million in western ranches and directly controlled more than twenty million acres of Panhandle land. The largest investor, the Capitol Freehold Land and Investment Company,[qv] showed nominal capital of £1,532,226 in 1885. Concerned that Texas lands were becoming monopolized by foreign control, many Texans sought protection from the large corporations. In 1891 Governor James S. Hogg[qv] approved the Alien Land Law,[qv] which prohibited aliens from holding lands unless they became United States citizens. Even though the law was later changed and did not prohibit land ownership by alien corporations, British investments declined in the following decades. The benefits that British investors and managers conferred upon the land and economy of Texas are not easily measured. They helped to introduce barbed wire,[qv] steel windmills, deep wells, and better breeds of cattle into the northwest part of the state, and they also made attempts to attract more settlers.

The considerable English influence upon the diplomacy and laws of Texas during its years as a republic resulted in several treaties and mediations (*see* ANGLO-TEXAN CONVENTION OF 1840, DIPLOMATIC RELATIONS OF THE REPUBLIC OF TEXAS, *and* LAW). English culture in Texas through the nineteenth and twentieth centuries, mostly mediated by the settlement of Anglo-Americans, became so pervasive that it is difficult to isolate various contributions. In the twentieth century the largest influx of English into the country occurred when soldiers returning home after World War II[qv] were accompanied by their English brides. In 1953 the Anglo-Texan Society[qv] was formed in London to foster the establishment of closer cultural ties; Graham Greene, the British novelist, served as the first president. In the latter part of the twentieth century, Renaissance festivals and the Texas Folklife Festival[qv] in San Antonio celebrated English culture. The 1990 census listed 2,024,001 persons of English descent in the state of Texas.

BIBLIOGRAPHY: E. D. Adams, *British Diplomatic Correspondence Concerning the Republic of Texas, 1836–1846* (Austin: Texas State Historical Association, 1918?). Seymour V. Connor, *The Peters Colony of Texas: A History and Biographical Sketches of the Early Settlers* (Austin: Texas State Historical Association, 1959). Thomas W. Cutrer, *The English Texans* (San Antonio: University of Texas Institute of Texan Cultures, 1985). W. Eugene Hollon and Ruth L. Butler, eds., *William*

Bollaert's Texas (Norman: University of Oklahoma Press, 1956). David Ingram, *Across Aboriginal America: Journeying through Texas in 1568*, ed. E. DeGolyer (1941). J. Fred Rippy, "British Investments in Texas Lands and Livestock," *Southwestern Historical Quarterly* 58 (January 1955). Lester Fields Sheffy, *The Francklyn Land & Cattle Company* (Austin: University of Texas Press, 1963). Vertical Files, University of Texas Institute of Texan Cultures, San Antonio.

John L. Davis and Phillip L. Fry

ENGLISH, CLARENCE T. (1902–1941). Clarence T. English, businessman, the son of Oscar Butcher and Sarah Jane (Mooney) English and great-grandson of Rev. James English,qv was born in Commerce, Texas, on April 17, 1902. Clarence lived with his family, which included twelve brothers and sisters, on a farm where cattle, cotton, and wheat were raised. He attended Overland School, near Brashear, and the University of Texas in Austin, where he earned a teaching certificate in 1920. He became a teacher and school principal when he was eighteen years old. Clarence married Myra Childress on July 14, 1929, in a Ford tri-motored monoplane flying over Dallas—an event well-covered by the local newspapers—before leaving on a honeymoon cruise to Havana.

He and his brothers Henry and Manzy were pioneers in the transportation industry in Texas. Clarence was the general manager of Red Ball Motor Coach Company and, in keeping with his love for all forms of transportation, had his own private plane. He owned a stock farm with horses and enjoyed leading the opening processions at rodeos on his favorite palomino, as well as hunting trips on horseback in Colorado and Wyoming. English was featured in "Men of Dallas in Pen and Ink" by Jack Moranz in the Dallas *Morning News*qv on January 20, 1937. He was a Mason, a Shriner, a Knight Templar, and a member of the Dallas Chamber of Commerce, the Community Chest, and Highland Park Presbyterian Church. He was president of the English Freight Company and secretary and treasurer of Air Line Motor Coaches, Incorporated, which operated buses in Texas and Louisiana. He started in his freight business in 1933 with one small truck and built it to a fleet of 108 trucks by 1937. He was in the bus business by 1926, when he organized the Southern Bus Owners Association, which arranged and scheduled passage, operations, and tickets. He began insuring operators in 1927. He was a member of the Common Carrier Motor Freight Association and the Southwestern Tariff Bureau. By 1939 his company had a fleet of 200 trucks operating in Texas, Oklahoma, New Mexico, Arizona, and California. English instituted fair labor practices with his workers, a measure that kept the company viable during difficult times and the freight delivered on time.

The Englishes had two daughters and a son. Clarence died in Dallas on April 24, 1941, after an automobile accident and was buried at Restland Cemetery in Dallas. In 1943 the English Freight Company hauled vital World War IIqv supplies under the direction of his widow, then company president. Mrs. English, who was born in McKinney, Texas, on December 28, 1900, died in Dallas in April 1959 and is buried at Restland beside Clarence.

Sarah Jane English

ENGLISH, GEORGE (1808–1876). George English, soldier and early sheriff, the son of Elizabeth (Tittle) and William English,qv was born in Warren County, Tennessee, in 1808. His parents were divorced when he was quite young, and evidently he moved to Texas many years after his father settled near Ayish Bayou. English became the first sheriff of the Ayish Bayou District under the Mexican government in 1827 and was serving in that office when San Augustine Municipality was organized in 1834. He was appointed a first lieutenant by the General Councilqv of the provisional governmentqv of Texas on November 29, 1835. He was subsequently promoted to captain and fought at the siege of Bexarqv in December 1835. He was president of the Board of Land Commissioners of Shelby County, Texas, in 1839. President Sam Houstonqv appointed him captain of a company of mounted gunmen for duty in Shelby County on May 31, 1837, and he continued to serve in this capacity through 1839. About 1843 he moved to Houston County. Soon he volunteered for military service in the Mexican War,qv in which he served as a first lieutenant under Capt. John Hall. Although he never married, English was the equivalent of a stepfather to the children of his uncle, Archibald English, who died in 1857. Though he was an avid opponent of secession,qv he organized a cavalry company, enrolled in the Confederate Army after the outbreak of the Civil War,qv and served until July 4, 1863. He died on October 12, 1876. His grave was marked with a Texas Centennialqv marker in 1936.

BIBLIOGRAPHY: Armistead Albert Aldrich, *The History of Houston County, Texas* (San Antonio: Naylor, 1943). George L. Crocket, *Two Centuries in East Texas* (Dallas: Southwest, 1932; facsimile reprod. 1962). Houston County Historical Commission, *History of Houston County, Texas, 1687–1979* (Tulsa, Oklahoma: Heritage, 1979). Gifford E. White, *Character Certificates in the General Land Office of Texas* (1985). Gifford E. White, *1830 Citizens of Texas* (Austin: Eakin, 1983).

Richard D. English

ENGLISH, JAMES (ca. 1755–1825). James English, frontiersman, was born about 1755, probably in Virginia. He spent his boyhood and youth in the New River area of Virginia and from 1780 to 1820 was an early settler successively in the frontiers of eastern Tennessee, western North Carolina, middle Tennessee, and western Tennessee. He married Elizabeth Denton, from whose family John B. Dentonqv came. They were the parents of William English, Rev. James English, John English, Joshua English,qqv and six other sons, as well as of Hannah English, the wife of Jonathan Anderson.qv Most of their children were living in Texas by the late 1820s. Among more than eighty grandchildren of James English was George English.qv James's descendants in late twentieth-century Texas numbered in the thousands. In 1825 English visited his children already living in Texas, among whom were William, James, John, and Thomas, and decided to join them in the Ayish Bayou District of Mexican Texas.qv Having returned for his wife and youngest son, Archibald, he died in Arkansas on the journey to Texas that year. His widow and son traveled on to Texas and were living in Tenehaw Municipalityqv in 1835.

BIBLIOGRAPHY: George L. Crocket, *Two Centuries in East Texas* (Dallas: Southwest, 1932; facsimile reprod. 1962). Houston County Historical Commission, *History of Houston County, Texas, 1687–1979* (Tulsa, Oklahoma: Heritage, 1979). Marion Day Mullins, *First Census of Texas, 1829–1836, and Other Early Records of the Republic of Texas* (Washington: National Genealogical Society, 1959). Gifford E. White, *Character Certificates in the General Land Office of Texas* (1985). Gifford E. White, *1830 Citizens of Texas* (Austin: Eakin, 1983).

Richard D. English

ENGLISH, JAMES (1788–1857). James English, early settler and minister, son of James and Elizabeth (Denton) English, was born in North Carolina or Tennessee in 1788. He was one of the earliest circuit-riding Methodist ministers in Texas. He settled in the future Shelby County in 1825 and was assistant judge for the municipality of Shelby in 1836. He was also a farmer and owned a blacksmith shop at Shelbyville. He preached at the McMahon Church, a few miles east of San Augustine in 1834, when it was established. It is one of the oldest Protestant churches in Texas in continuous operation. English was a trustee of the church in Shelbyville in 1843. He received a land grant from the Mexican government on October 17, 1835, located in what is now Newton County. Stephen F. Austinqv arrived in San Augustine on August 12, 1821, and spent the first night in the home of James English and his wife, Susan. The Englishes had eight children. English died in 1857.

BIBLIOGRAPHY: Joe V. Clouse, *The History of First Methodist Church, Established 1825, Shelbyville, Texas* (Shelbyville: First Methodist Church, 1964). Macum Phelan, *History of Early Methodism in Texas, 1817–1866* (Nashville: Cokesbury, 1924); *A History of the Expansion of Methodism in Texas, 1867–1902* (Dallas: Mathis, Van Nort, 1937). W. W. Sweet, *Religion on the American Frontier, 1783–1840* (Vol. 4, University of Chicago Press, 1946). Dudley Goodall Wooten, ed., *A Comprehensive History of Texas* (2 vols., Dallas: Scarff, 1898; rpt., Austin: Texas State Historical Association, 1986). *Sarah Jane English*

ENGLISH, JAMES N. (1837–?). James N. English, lawyer and legislator, the son of Campbell and Elizabeth English, was born in Red River County, Texas, on December 24, 1837. His family moved to Titus County, where he was educated. In the summer of 1861 he joined Company I of the Ninth Texas Cavalry of the Confederate Army, was elected captain, and served in the Trans-Mississippi Department until he resigned in 1862. He returned to Texas and entered the Texas frontier service, remaining in it until the close of the Civil War.qv In 1864 English married Marticia Stanfield in Johnson County. He went to Tennessee in 1866, but he returned to Texas in 1871 and entered a mercantile business at Cleburne. About 1873 he began to practice law and served as county attorney of Johnson County for two years. He represented the county in the House of the Sixteenth Legislature in 1879. In 1884 he was elected county attorney.

BIBLIOGRAPHY: *A Memorial and Biographical History of Johnson and Hill Counties* (Chicago: Lewis, 1892).

ENGLISH, JOHN (1793–1868). John English, a political leader in early Texas, the son of Elizabeth (Denton) and James English,qv was born on July 5, 1793, probably in North Carolina. He grew to manhood in Tennessee and in 1813 was drafted in Warren County, Tennessee, to serve as a private in Capt. James Cole's company of infantry against the Creek Indians. He was discharged in January 1814, volunteered again, and served in Capt. Bethell Allen's company of Mounted Volunteer Gunmen. English was a soldier at the battle of New Orleans under Gen. Andrew Jackson. He was taken prisoner on December 23, 1814, below New Orleans and held by the enemy for five weeks and six days, then exchanged. He married Elizabeth Choate, the daughter of Christopher Choate, in 1824 in Hardin (or McNairy) County, Tennessee, and they had eleven children. He moved to Texas immediately after his marriage, but was soon living in Louisiana, where the governor commissioned him a captain in the state militia. He moved again to Texas about 1828 and lived in the Tenehaw area. The Convention of 1832qv appointed him treasurer for Tenehaw Municipality.qv He was a delegate, with his brother William English,qv to the Convention of 1833.qv In 1835 he was appointed a captain in the revolutionary army.qv In 1837, when he was a resident of Shelby County, he served as a representative in the Congress of the Republic of Texas.qv In August 1838 he performed a special mission express to Clarksville in Red River County, at a time when, in the words of President Sam Houston,qv "it was almost impossible to obtain an express."

About 1851 English settled in Livingston, which had been founded by his brother-in-law. In the early 1850s he moved to the vicinity of Randolph in Houston County. He died on December 30, 1868. His grave, in the English-Hicks Cemetery, east of Crockett, was marked with a Texas Centennialqv marker in 1936. His son John Crockett English served in the Texas legislature in 1870–71 and as district clerk in Houston County thereafter.

BIBLIOGRAPHY: George L. Crocket, *Two Centuries in East Texas* (Dallas: Southwest, 1932; facsimile reprod. 1962). Houston County Historical Commission, *History of Houston County, Texas, 1687–1979* (Tulsa, Oklahoma: Heritage, 1979). Gifford E. White, *Character Certificates in the General Land Office of Texas* (1985). Gifford E. White, *1830 Citizens of Texas* (Austin: Eakin, 1983). *Richard D. English*

ENGLISH, JOSHUA (ca. 1807–1873). Joshua English, early Texas Ranger and soldier, was born about 1807 in Tennessee, the son of Elizabeth (Denton) and James English.qv He followed older brothers to Texas in the 1820s and settled in Tenehaw Municipality.qv Although a farmer most of his life, he fought in several military campaigns. He served from July 1835 to November 1835 in Capt. John English'sqv company and Col. Stephen F. Austin'sqv regiment, and was in the battle of Nacogdochesqv and at San Antonio before the siege of Bexarqv with his brother John. Joshua English fought in the Cherokee Warqv in 1837. He enlisted in one of the earliest companies of the Texas Rangersqv during the Republic of Texasqv and was part of the unit guarding the crossings of the Sabine River, the United States boundary. He also served with Capt. Alfred M. Truitt under Col. John C. Haysqv in the Mexican War.qv He married Candace Todd of Shelbyville, Texas, and they had ten children. He subsequently married Martha Ann Stephens, with whom he had three children. English died in Houston County on November 28, 1873. His grave was marked with a Texas Centennialqv marker in 1936.

BIBLIOGRAPHY: Houston County Historical Commission, *History of Houston County, Texas, 1687–1979* (Tulsa, Oklahoma: Heritage, 1979). Gifford E. White, *Character Certificates in the General Land Office of Texas* (1985). Gifford E. White, *1830 Citizens of Texas* (Austin: Eakin, 1983). *Richard D. English*

ENGLISH, LEVI (1817–1904). Levi English, pioneer, cattleman, and one of the first settlers of Dimmit County, was born in Little Rock, Arkansas, on August 25, 1817. His mother died while he was an infant, and he was brought up by his mother's sister and his uncle, Joel T. Walters. In 1824 his surrogate parents took him to Texas with them. English left home when he was about ten, and, according to his son Jake, lived for perhaps six months with a group of Comanche Indians.qv Family tradition says that English served as a scout for the Texas Rangersqv after leaving the Comanches and participated in several battles against Indians. According to his son, he also fought in the battle of San Jacinto,qv though no record of his service can be found. By the 1850s English had become a cattleman and a leader of a frontier community in Atascosa County, where he served as a county commissioner in 1856. In 1865 he led a group of fifteen families into what is now Dimmit County and established a settlement at Carrizo Springs. In 1880, when Dimmit County was organized and Carrizo Springs became the county seat, English donated land to the town for churches, schools, and a courthouse square. He married Matilda Burleson in 1838; the couple had at least one son, Jake, who was born in 1860. English died in Carrizo Springs on May 4, 1904.

BIBLIOGRAPHY: Daughters of the Republic of Texas, *Muster Rolls of the Texas Revolution* (Austin, 1986). Laura Knowlton Tidwell, *Dimmit County Mesquite Roots* (Austin: Wind River, 1984). Vertical Files, Barker Texas History Center, University of Texas at Austin. *John Leffler*

ENGLISH, WILLIAM (ca. 1786–ca. 1836). William English, early settler, was born in North Carolina or Tennessee, the son of Elizabeth (Denton) and James English.qv He married Elizabeth Tittle, daughter of George and Mary Cooper Tittle; they had three children, including George English.qv They separated about 1813 and were divorced by the Tennessee legislature. By 1818 English had married Myra Anderson, daughter of Wyatt and Nancy (McFadden) Anderson; they had ten children. In 1818 English moved to the Ayish Bayou District, presently the area of San Augustine, Texas. On February 18, 1821, he and fifteen other men swore their allegiance to Spain and became Spanish citizens. On July 16, 1821, Stephen F. Austinqv breakfasted at English's house on his first full day in Texas. During the 1820s eight brothers and one sister of William English settled in Texas. By 1826 he and his relatives had moved to the area near Shelbyville and Patroon Creek in what is now Shelby County. Among their neighbors were Jonas Harrison and Emory Rains.qqv English was a participant in the Fredonian Rebellion.qv When this insurrection had been put down by the Mexican government, he fled with his family to exile in Natchitoches, Louisiana, stayed for about a year, and returned to Texas. He was a delegate to the conventions of 1832 and 1833.qqv He was also perhaps a member of the legislature of Coahuila and Texasqv in 1835. He purchased many tracts of land, including the Pelham Humphries league in Jefferson County, where oil was discovered in 1901 (*see* SPINDLETOP OILFIELD). English died in the winter of 1836–37 in Shelby County.

BIBLIOGRAPHY: George L. Crocket, *Two Centuries in East Texas* (Dallas: Southwest, 1932; facsimile reprod. 1962). Houston County Historical Commission, *History of Houston County, Texas, 1687–1979* (Tulsa, Oklahoma: Heritage, 1979). Gifford E. White, *Character Certificates in the General Land Office of Texas* (1985). Gifford E. White, *1830 Citizens of Texas* (Austin: Eakin, 1983). Richard D. English

ENGLISH, TEXAS (Brazoria County). English, a farming community north of the Ramsey prison farm and twelve miles northwest of Angleton in northwestern Brazoria County, may have been named for the family of area resident "Buck" English. The town began as a station on the Columbia Tap line (*see* HOUSTON TAP AND BRAZORIA RAILROAD) 1½ miles north of what is now Farm Road 1462 on Oyster Creek. English had a cotton gin and a general store by 1917. A post office operated there from 1921 until 1924, when mail was transferred to Sandy Point. In 1980 area maps showed several abandoned buildings and scattered dwellings at the townsite.

BIBLIOGRAPHY: James A. Creighton, *A Narrative History of Brazoria County* (Angleton, Texas: Brazoria County Historical Commission, 1975). Diana J. Kleiner

ENGLISH, TEXAS (Red River County). English, eleven miles northeast of Clarksville in northeastern Red River County, was named for Oliver English, who in 1840 bought land that included what is now the English townsite, and Simeon English, his uncle, who brought three families and thirty slaves to establish plantations in the area in 1852. By 1860 the 2,000-acre English plantation, hedged by bois d'arc, had its own cotton gin and hauled the cotton to Jefferson for shipment. The gin burned in 1862. A post office, established with Thomas W. Anderson, Jr., as postmaster, operated at the community from 1890 to 1906, when it was replaced by rural delivery from Annona. English reported a population of 100 in 1910 and about ninety-two from 1920 through 1990. The Oliver English home has been restored.

Claudia Hazlewood

ENGLISH PRAIRIE, TEXAS. English Prairie was near the Houston county line between Friendship and Nogalus Prairie in northern Trinity County. It was established sometime in the 1870s or 1880s by John English and his wife and was also called English Town. A school operated there in the early 1900s, and church services were held in the schoolhouse.

BIBLIOGRAPHY: Patricia B. and Joseph W. Hensley, eds., *Trinity County Beginnings* (Groveton, Texas: Trinity County Book Committee, 1986). Joseph W. Hensley

ENID, OCHILTREE AND WESTERN RAILROAD. The Enid, Ochiltree and Western Railroad represents an unsuccessful attempt by the people of Ochiltree County to secure a railroad through the town of Ochiltree, then the county seat. Although three major lines crossed the Panhandleqv by 1908, none ran directly west from Oklahoma across the counties north of the Canadian River. The lack of rail service necessitated long trips by area farmers and ranchers to the nearest rail towns to market their produce.

Lynch Dodson, a farmer who lived near Ochiltree, met with state railroad commissioner O. B. Colquittqv at Austin in February 1908. Dodson then contacted A. E. Wiest, the chief promoter of the American Engineering Company of Indianapolis, Indiana, who agreed to come and inspect the terrain. Meanwhile, Dodson secured the backing of several influential local residents, including James H. Whippo, J. B. (Pop) Cartwright, and county judge George M. Perry. Wiest arrived on April 21, and for two months he and the Ochiltree County citizens worked to promote the railroad, secure stock certificates, and enlist potential subscribers. The Enid, Ochiltree and Western Railroad Company held its first meeting on June 11, with Judge Perry as president, Cartwright as secretary, W. B. Slaughter as treasurer, and Wiest as vice president and general manager. Hamlin Palmer, a freight agent for the Santa Fe line, was later recruited as assistant secretary. The citizens of Dalhart also agreed to help finance the project.

By the spring of 1909 the proposed route had been surveyed for 113 miles from Dalhart to Ochiltree, rights-of-way secured, and work begun on the roadbed. Proposed townsites such as Wilcoe, Orofino, Victor, and Jarvis were platted. On August 14 a building contract was signed with the Panhandle Construction Company. On September 23 W. D. Wagner, the mayor of Dalhart, drove the first spike during a gala celebration held at Dalhart. Soon, plans were made and permission secured to extend the proposed route via Enid to Oklahoma City. As construction progressed a small locomotive, piloted by J. M. (Johnny) McChord and dubbed Old Steamboat, was purchased from the Southern Iron and Equipment Company of Atlanta, Georgia.

When the EO&W failed to make its monthly payments to the Panhandle Construction Company in the summer of 1910, however, the Railway Audit and Inspection Company was brought in to inspect the books. Federal judgments were rendered against the EO&W properties for $9,000 and $14,000. Several factors contributed to the company's failure. Not all of the firm's $500,000 capital stock had been subscribed. Wiest had violated state law as well as the EO&W's own rules by signing over, endorsing, and selling promissory notes. And a prolonged drought in 1910–11 kept many well-intentioned farmers and small businessmen from fulfilling their subscriptions.

Consequently, on December 22, 1910, the EO&W went into the hands of Judge H. G. Hendricks, who had been designated receiver by the Eighth Judicial District Court at Dalhart. Wiest surrendered his power of attorney on February 11, 1911, and disappeared from the scene. Construction stopped with only the grade to Dumas completed and less than fourteen miles of track laid out of Dalhart. On June 11, 1912, C. A. Vawter and O. J. McKnight of Dalhart purchased the EO&W properties for $33,000; Old Steamboat was shipped back to Atlanta. Several lawsuits were filed against the EO&W, and in the fall of 1917 its properties were sold. The failure of the EO&W led to the eventual abandonment of the Ochiltree and Hansford townsites after Perryton and Spearman were founded on the North Texas and Santa Fe line in 1919. Dumas was left without a railroad connection until 1931. Remnants of the unfinished railroad may still be seen between Dumas and Dalhart.

BIBLIOGRAPHY: Carrie Whippo Correll and Spencer P. Whippo, "Enid, Ochiltree and Western Railroad," *Panhandle-Plains Historical Review* 33 (1960). *Wheatheart of the Plains: An Early History of Ochiltree County* (Perryton, Texas: Ochiltree County Historical Survey Committee, 1969). H. Allen Anderson

ENLOE, TEXAS. Enloe is at the junction of Farm roads 2949 and 198, three miles north of Cooper in north central Delta County. It is bordered on the southwest by Brushy Creek. The area was settled by 1888, when local residents established a Baptist Church. The town, however, remained unorganized until 1897, when J. A. Enloe donated the land to build a train stop on the Texas-Midland Railroad. That same year Jerry P. High opened the first Enloe post office and reported a population of about 100. The settlement began to develop around the railroad; the church was moved closer to the tracks. Town leaders obtained a school building from nearby Liberty and established the Enloe school district, which quickly absorbed the Mount Hebron, or Hagged, school. Records for 1897 reported one school, two teachers, and 104 students.

Enloe continued to grow and by 1904 had 273 inhabitants. In 1912 the Baptist congregation built a new church. In 1914 the population was 400. Residents could attend either the Baptist or Methodist Episcopal church and had access to a telephone exchange. Businesses included two banks, a telegraph office, a restaurant, two general stores, an apothecary, a seed store, and a bakery. The Carson Lumber Company was also headquartered in town. Cotton shipping was the major industry, and the community supported seven cotton buyers and two gins. In 1929 the town had 450 inhabitants. In 1936 the population was 265, and the town had a school, two factories, five businesses, a post office, two churches, and about forty homes. But with the onset of World War II,qv more residents moved away in search of jobs. By 1956 the population totaled 186. The Enloe school district had absorbed most of the nearby schools in 1959, but by 1964 only 150 people lived in town. Seven businesses and the two churches remained, and a hospital had been opened. Maps for 1970 showed that the school had been consolidated into the Cooper Independent School District, and citizens had access to a community center. In 1984 Enloe had three businesses, two churches, and a factory. A population of 113 was reported in 1990.

BIBLIOGRAPHY: John J. Germann and Myron Janzen, *Texas Post Offices by County* (1986). Paul Garland Hervey, A History of Education in Delta County, Texas (M.A. thesis, University of Texas, 1951). Wilma Ross and Billie Phillips, *Photos and Tales of Delta County* (1976).

Vista K. McCroskey

ENNIS, CORNELIUS (1813–1899). Cornelius Ennis, mayor of Houston, merchant, Confederate blockade runner, and railroad entrepreneur, was born on September 26, 1813, in Belleville, New Jersey. His father's family had come to New Jersey from Ireland in the latter part of the seventeenth century, and his mother was a descendant of the Doremus family, who were among the first settlers from Holland. After receiving a liberal education in New Jersey Ennis went in 1834 to New York City, where he worked in a drugstore. He moved to Houston, Texas, and opened a drugstore in 1839. After George W. Kimball became a partner, Ennis expanded into general merchandising. They sent the first shipment of cotton from Galveston to Boston in 1841.

His success in business allowed Ennis to marry Jeannette Ingals Kimball, his partner's sister, in 1841; they had four children. Ennis and his wife supported Christ Episcopal Church.

In 1842 Kimball sailed to New York with cotton and partnership funds to be invested, and was drowned with his family in a storm off the Florida coast. This serious setback did not hinder Ennis's cotton-export business for long. Realizing that improved transportation was necessary for expansion, he turned to railroads. He was an incorporator of the Houston and Texas Central Railway, which began in 1853; along with Paul Bremond, William M. Rice, Thomas W. House, William R. Baker, and William J. Hutchins,qqv Ennis served on the board of directors for many years. He was also the railroad's general superintendent and comptroller. For several years he had offices in New York, where he obtained loans and purchased supplies to complete the road. Ennis, Texas, an early terminus of the road, was named in his honor.

As mayor of Houston from July 1856 to December 1857, Ennis supervised the completion of the city-owned Houston Tap Railroad, begun in April 1856. This tap into the Buffalo Bayou, Brazos and Colorado Railway preserved the Brazos cotton trade with Houston. After the city sold the tap road in 1858, the new owners renamed it the Houston Tap and Brazoria. Ennis served on the board of directors of HT&B, which brought the first carload of sugar and molasses to Houston in 1859. He also succeeded in having arrested and sent to the penitentiary a band of robbers who had preyed for years on shippers and teamsters going to Houston.

During the Civil Warqv Ennis ran cotton through the Union blockade to Havana, Cuba, then to England via Mexico. At his own expense he purchased an ironclad steamer, the Jeannette, for $40,000 in gold. He used the ship to carry the rifles, gunpowder, percussion caps, clothing, and other equipment he bought in Havana for the Confederate government. His successful blockade running enabled him to expand his cotton-export business after the war, when he opened a branch office in Galveston with Frank Cargill and N. Anderson. He also invested heavily in the Galveston *News*qv and the Dallas *News* (see DALLAS MORNING NEWS). Alfred H. Belo,qv president of the *News*, married Ennis's oldest daughter, and Cargill married the second daughter. The youngest daughter married Cesar Lombardi,qv a Houston merchant and later president of the Dallas *News*.

Ennis also continued his interest in railways. The Houston Tap and Brazoria was sold to Houston businessmen in 1870, and three years later it was taken over by the International–Great Northern. Throughout these changes Ennis continued to serve on the board of directors. He promoted the Houston Ship Channel,qv street railways, and public utilities of all kinds. He lived in Houston sixty years and died on February 13, 1899, in his home. He was interred at Glenwood Cemetery in Houston.

BIBLIOGRAPHY: John Henry Brown, *Indian Wars and Pioneers of Texas* (Austin: Daniell, 1880; reprod., Easley, South Carolina: Southern Historical Press, 1978). Houston *Post*, February 14, 1899. Jesse A. Ziegler, *Wave of the Gulf* (San Antonio: Naylor, 1938).

Priscilla Myers Benham

ENNIS, TEXAS. Ennis is on the Southern Pacific Railroad and at the intersection of Interstate Highway 45, State highways 34, 75, and 287, and Farm roads 85, 879, 1183, 1722, and 3413, fourteen miles southeast of Waxahachie in southeastern Ellis County. Bardwell Lake, a popular recreational area, is less than a mile south of the city limits. The Houston and Texas Central Railway reached the area in 1871, and the community established there was named for an early railroad official, Col. Cornelius Ennis.qv The David Rose survey of 300 acres and the W. H. Bundy survey of 347 acres were purchased by the trustees of a land company in 1872. Capt. W. G. Veale selected the townsite in May, and Theo Kosse mapped it in August and laid out the streets and alleys. The first train ran through the community that year, on its way from Corsicana to Dallas. Citizens of Burnham, a small town to the south, responded violently to being bypassed and attacked the new community, killing one man and wounding several.

The Ennis post office opened in 1872 with J. M. Dickson as the postmaster and railroad agent. The first church in Ennis was the Cumberland Presbyterian Church, originally founded in Burnham, which moved to Ennis in 1872. As an incentive to settlement, the railroad offered free town lots to any Christian communion that would build a church. Ennis incorporated in November 1873 and held its first election in April 1874; Charles Pannil was elected the first mayor. The *Evening Argus* was founded in 1873, and the Temperance Council was established to provide an alternative to "drunken carousing." By 1874 the community had a population of 300 and rising land values. Ennis reached 3,000 by 1890, when it had two banks, a cotton compress, three cottonseed depositories, a cotton gin, a fruit-canning business, a brickyard, an opera house, and two weekly newspapers, the *Local* and the *Saturday Review*.

The Houston and Texas Central chose Ennis as its northern division headquarters in an agreement requiring that Ennis provide water for the railroad. The machine shops and roundhouse employed several hundred men. One condition of the agreement was that as long as Ennis was able to furnish water the shops could not be moved from the community. In 1891 the city of Ennis built the first of three lakes for this purpose, followed by another in 1895, and the last in

1940. This water was also used by the city for uses besides drinking, while wells were used for drinking water. Between 1910 and 1915 the railroad tried to move the shops, but the community was supported in the courts, and the shops remained in Ennis. In 1894 Ennis received its second railroad, the Texas Midland, which provided service from Paris, Texas, by 1897.

By 1914 Ennis had a population of 6,600, eleven churches, four banks, four cotton gins, a cottonseed oil mill and cotton compress, a mattress factory, an ice factory, a light and power plant, and two newspapers, the Ennis *Daily News* and the *Weekly Local*. In 1930 the community had a population of 7,069 and 205 businesses, including two ice companies, two printing companies, a cottonseed oil company, and a creamery. Ennis remained a predominantly agricultural community, as demonstrated in the chamber of commerce's slogan, "Where Railroads and Cotton Fields Meet." In 1934 the Texas and New Orleans Railroad acquired both the Texas Midland and the Houston and Texas Central. In 1942 the tracks between Ennis and Kaufman, which had been the Texas Midland, were abandoned because of frequent washouts in the Trinity River bottoms. From then on Ennis had only one railroad. In 1961 the Southern Pacific acquired the Texas and New Orleans.

In 1956 Ennis changed to a city manager government. New elections were held in 1957, and a comprehensive zoning ordinance was implemented in 1959. In 1964 a new hospital was built. Lake Bardwell was completed in 1965 and was used for flood control, storage, and recreation. In 1968 the Ennis Municipal Airport, the only airport in the county, was completed. By 1970 Ennis had a population of 11,550 and 250 businesses. The city had become an industrial community, where items including business forms, trophies, furniture, clothing, printing, novelties, and concrete were manufactured. Although agriculture had become less important, cotton was still grown, and cattle raising had become more prevalent.

By the 1990s Ennis was part of the Dallas–Fort Worth metropolitan area. In 1990 it had a population of 13,883 and fifty-three manufacturers. The community published three newspapers: the *Ellis County News*, founded in 1988 by a merger of the *Weekly Local* and the *Palmer Rustler*, both founded in 1891; the *Press*, founded in 1974; and the Ennis *Daily News*, founded in 1891. The Texas Motorplex, a professional and amateur racetrack founded in 1986, seated 26,000 and held races throughout the year. Two popular annual events are held in Ennis, the Bluebonnet Trails, begun in the 1930s and held in late April and early May when the bluebonnets are in bloom, and the Ennis Polka Festival, founded in 1967 and held every May, which brings thousands of visitors to the community to celebrate its Czech heritage.

BIBLIOGRAPHY: Edna Davis Hawkins et al., *History of Ellis County, Texas* (Waco: Texian, 1972). Lisa C. Maxwell

ENNIS CREEK. Ennis Creek rises thirteen miles northwest of Snyder in northwestern Scurry County (at 32°56′ N, 100°59′ W) and runs southeast for twenty-four miles to its mouth on Rough Creek, eleven miles northeast of Snyder (at 32°51′ N, 100°47′ W). It was named for John Ennis, an early settler on its banks. The creek traverses terrain ranging from flat to rolling with local escarpments to steep slopes with locally high relief. Local soils vary from deep, fine, sandy loams to shallow to moderately deep silt loams. Vegetation includes brush, grasses, and mesquite.

ENOCH, TEXAS. Enoch, on Farm Road 49 two miles west of Gilmer in central Upshur County, was established around 1912 by Mormons.qv Enoch and nearby Kelsey were founded as branches of the Mormon Church, and each was administered under the leadership of an appointed branch president who met weekly with the community to discuss spiritual and community affairs. By the mid-1930s Enoch had two churches, two stores, a school, and a number of houses. Its population in 1938 was reported as 250. The town's economy was largely agricultural, with dairying the most important industry. Cotton, grain, and truck-farming were also significant in the area. After World War IIqv the community began to decline. Its school was consolidated with the Gilmer Independent School District in 1951, and during the 1950s and early 1960s many of its young people moved away. In the mid-1960s Enoch still had a population of 125 and a church, cemetery, store, and service station. In 1990 Enoch was a dispersed rural community, with only the church, the cemetery, and a few scattered houses remaining in the area.

BIBLIOGRAPHY: *Dallas News*, May 8, 1938. Doyal T. Loyd, *History of Upshur County* (Waco: Texian Press, 1987). Christopher Long

ENOCHS, TEXAS. Enochs is at the junction of State Highway 214 and Farm Road 54, three miles from the Cochran county line in southern Bailey County. It developed as a trading center beginning in the 1920s and reached a peak reported population of 250 in 1940, when it had five stores. In 1980 and 1990 its population was estimated at 164, and the town had several businesses and a post office.

BIBLIOGRAPHY: LaVonne McKillip, ed., *Early Bailey County History* (Muleshoe, Texas, 1978).

ENON, TEXAS (Houston County). Enon, a farming community 2½ miles east of Grapeland on Farm Road 227 in north central Houston County, grew up around a school established there in 1883. In 1897 its school had an enrollment of fifty-one. By the mid-1930s Enon had two churches, a cemetery, and a number of houses. After World War IIqv most of its residents moved away, and by the mid-1960s the community was no longer shown on highway maps. In the early 1990s only a few scattered houses remained in the area.

BIBLIOGRAPHY: *Houston County Cemeteries* (Crockett, Texas: Houston County Historical Commission, 1977; 3d ed. 1987). Houston County Historical Commission, *History of Houston County, Texas, 1687–1979* (Tulsa, Oklahoma: Heritage, 1979). Christopher Long

ENON, TEXAS (Upshur County). Enon, also known as McPeek, is on Farm Road 852 six miles northwest of Gilmer in western Upshur County. The area was first settled in the late 1840s. The Enon Baptist Church, organized on May 13, 1848, was one of the earliest churches in the county. A school built across the road from the church began operating before 1900, and by 1906 there were two schools at Enon with a total enrollment of 203. A post office, named McPeek for one of the area's early settlers, opened there in 1903 but closed in 1905. In the mid-1930s the community had a number of scattered houses and a church, school, store, cemetery, and sawmill. After World War IIqv many of Enon's residents moved away, and its school was consolidated with that of Harmony. By the mid-1960s only the church, the cemetery, and a few houses remained in the area. In 1990 Enon was a dispersed rural community served by a church and cemetery.

BIBLIOGRAPHY: G. H. Baird, *A Brief History of Upshur County* (Gilmer, Texas: Gilmer *Mirror*, 1946). Doyal T. Loyd, *History of Upshur County* (Waco: Texian Press, 1987). Christopher Long

ENRÍQUEZ BARROTO, JUAN (ca. 1660–1693). Juan Enríquez Barroto, Spanish pilot, navigator, and explorer, was probably born in Mexico about 1660. He came to prominence while searching for the French colony of René Robert Cavelier, Sieur de La Salle.qv His maps and diaries, the source of many names for coastal features around the Gulf of Mexico, recorded the first detailed exploration of several Texas bays and river mouths. He studied mathematics and astronomy under the noted Mexican savant Carlos de Sigüenza y Góngora. By 1690 he was recognized as perhaps the foremost authority on Gulf navigation. As chief pilot or commanding officer, he was involved in three of the five Spanish sea voyages of the La Salle quest. When not at sea, he was often in consultation with the viceroy or his advisers concerning the search strategy.

When chosen in the fall of 1685 to conduct the first voyage to seek the French invaders, Enríquez Barroto was chief pilot of a frigate of the Armada de Barlovento,qv ported at Veracruz. He was known as "a person of recognized intelligence, adept at solar observations and coastal mapping." This initial voyage of the quest, begun on January 3, 1686, at Havana, reached the Mississippi River's North Pass after reconnoitering Pensacola and Mobile bays. Handicapped in this effort by his large ship, Enríquez recommended the building of two shallow-draft vessels called piraguas, carrying both oars and sail. These crafts built, he sailed as chief pilot in the voyage of captains Martín de Rivas and Pedro de Iriarte.qqv In his diary of the voyage, which began at Veracruz on Christmas Day 1686 and circumnavigated the Gulf, Enríquez relates the finding of the wreckage of La Salle's ships at Matagorda Bay. He also tells of the first known exploration of Galveston Bay, Sabine and Calcasieu passes, the Atchafalaya River, and the Mississippi passes, as well as encounters with Coahuiltecan, Karankawan, and Atákapan Indian groups.

Throughout the voyage Enríquez Barroto recorded latitudes from celestial observations and longitudes from dead reckoning, correcting previous charts. His place names from this diary were copied onto maps of diverse European mapmakers, including such notables as Claude and Guillaume Delisle. The toponyms pertaining to Texas, which were sometimes given an altered form or shifted about, include Río de San Joseph (Aransas Pass); Río de Flores (Cedar Bayou); Bahía de San Bernardo (Matagorda Bay) and its headlands, Punta de San Francisco and Punta de Culebras; Río Bajo (Galveston Bay); and Río Dulce (the Sabine River).

In 1688 Enríquez Barroto sailed as pilot under the command of Andrés de Pez y Malzárragaqv to explore Chandeleur and Breton sounds in response to rumors of a French settlement on the adjacent coast. Later the same year his maps served to guide a new voyage led by captains Rivas and Pez to explore the Soto la Marina River and the mouth of the Rio Grande. In 1691, as captain of a frigate of the Armada de Barlovento, he ferried troops and supplies to Matagorda Bay to support the expedition of Governor Domingo Terán de los Ríos.qv Terán, on leaving Texas early in 1692, boarded Enríquez's ship to seek passage into the Mississippi River as a possible means of access to the Caddoan tribes and the Texas missions. The effort was frustrated by a storm.

Enríquez Barroto, who from all accounts was a modest, retiring individual, freely shared his navigational data without expectation of reward. Consequently, he has stood in the shadow of his mentor, Sigüenza y Góngora, and Pez, who claimed Enríquez's discovery of Pensacola Bay as his own and used the pilot's other accomplishments to advance his own career. Enríquez Barroto furnished the information for the "Pez Memorial," describing the merits of Pensacola Bay and advocating its settlement, which Pez took to Spain and presented to the king as his own work.

While Pez pursued his star-crossed career, Enríquez Barroto perished at sea. On September 18, 1693, his ship was lost with all hands in a hurricane on the Carolina banks.

BIBLIOGRAPHY: William Edward Dunn, "The Spanish Search for La Salle's Colony on the Bay of Espíritu Santo, 1685–1689," *Southwestern Historical Quarterly* 19 (April 1916). Robert S. Weddle et al., eds., *La Salle, the Mississippi, and the Gulf: Three Primary Documents* (College Station: Texas A&M University Press, 1987). Robert S. Weddle, *Wilderness Manhunt: The Spanish Search for La Salle* (Austin: University of Texas Press, 1973).
Robert S. Weddle

ENSERCH CORPORATION. Enserch Corporation, with headquarters in Dallas, is a diversified energy company with interests in petroleum exploration and production, oilfield services, engineering design and construction, and natural gas transmission and distribution. The firm was founded under the name Lone Star Gas in 1909 as a utility company to transmit natural gas to Dallas and East Texas. Partners George W. Crawford and M. C. Treat, with the help of attorney L. B. Denning of Ohio, established the enterprise in Dallas as a pipeline company allied with Corsicana Refining. At the time, Crawford and Treat owned a drilling company in Marshall, Texas, and operated successful gas wells in several states as well as the Petrolia field, which was Lone Star's major source for gas east of Dallas. The company's first president was Henry Clay Edrington, a former fiscal agent for the Agricultural and Mechanical College of Texas and organizer of the Traders National Bank in Fort Worth.

By the end of 1909 Lone Star had begun the construction of what was then one of the world's longest pipelines, from Fort Worth–Dallas to Petrolia. The Petrolia field was not large enough to support the growing needs of Texas, however, so in 1916 Lone Star Gas expanded its business into southern Oklahoma. Between 1915 and 1924 the company confronted crises on three occasions when inability to deliver adequate gas supplies nearly forced it into receivership. In 1924 a technological breakthrough enabled the company to capture gas previously allowed to escape at the wellhead and revived the business. In 1927 Lone Star began to expand again with the purchase of the Dallas Gas Company, and by 1935 it had opened a new Dallas headquarters. In 1942 the company formed Lone Star Producing to develop oil and gas wells, and by 1968 it served a million customers through a network of pipelines across Texas and southern Oklahoma. In 1972, as part of the deep-well drilling projects in the Anadarko basin in southern Oklahoma, Lone Star Gas drilled a well 30,050 feet deep, the deepest ever completed at that time.

The company changed its name to Enserch in 1975 to reflect the change in its business, which now included not only natural gas distribution and transmission but also exploration, resource recovery, and other aspects of the industry. Diversification began in the 1970s, when the Justice Department pressed the Halliburton Corporation, of Houston, to divest itself of its utility-construction subsidiary Ebasco; Enserch purchased the division in 1976. The subsidiary specialized in construction and construction management for large power-station projects, including the Encogen Power Plant in South Texas and the South Texas Nuclear Project. By 1989 Ebasco had constructed over 1,000 plants around the world and had worldwide annual revenues of $2.9 billion. The company further diversified with the acquisition of Losinger AG, a Swiss construction firm founded in 1917, which in the 1980s employed 5,000 workers building dams, bridges, and tunnels. The company's oilfield-service subsidiaries included the Pool Company of Houston, which employed 6,000 workers at oil-rig operations statewide; Oiltools, which provided oilfield equipment worldwide from headquarters in London; Samson Ocean Systems, acquired in 1978, a provider of rope systems that succeeded Samson Cordage, founded in Boston in 1888; and Alaska International Constructors and Frank Moolin and Associates, both acquired in 1982, which did construction primarily for the oil and gas industry. In 1981 the company established Enserch Engineering and Construction at Houston, and in 1983 it acquired Humphrey and Glasgow, Limited, an international engineering firm founded in 1892, which designed and constructed processing plants throughout Europe. In the 1990s Enserch entered into a partnership with Tejas Gas Corporation known as Gulf Coast Natural Gas and continued to grow.

BIBLIOGRAPHY: *In Memory of L. B. Denning* (Dallas, 1940). Lone Star Gas Company, *The First Seventy-Five Years* (Dallas, 1984?).
Jeff Seidel

ENSIGN, TEXAS. Ensign was on Cummins Creek and Ensign Road four miles south of Ennis in southeastern Ellis County. About 1895 Albert N. Ellison built a small store in the area, and in 1896 a local post office opened, with Ellison as the postmaster. The store in which it was located changed owners and postmasters several times before the post office was discontinued in 1904. In 1899 a fifty-six member singing school was organized in the community's church. By the early 1900s Ensign had several blacksmith shops, a cotton gin, a Fraternal Union Lodge, and, a half mile north of the business district, the Antioch Baptist Church. In 1933 the community reported one business and an estimated population of twenty. From 1970 to 1990 Ensign's population was estimated at ten, and the community no longer reported a business.

BIBLIOGRAPHY: Edna Davis Hawkins, et al., *History of Ellis County, Texas* (Waco: Texian, 1972).   Lisa C. Maxwell

ENSWORTH, AUGUSTUS S. (?–?). Augustus Ensworth, soldier, land commissioner, and legislator, probably arrived in Texas during the Texas Revolution.qv He served in the Army of the Republic of Texasqv from November 3, 1836, until November 11, 1837, and settled at Goliad, where he was elected chief justice on January 1, 1840. He resigned to become commissioner to inspect the county land office on January 31, 1840. He later served in the House of the Fifth Congress of the republic, from November 2, 1840, to February 5, 1841. On February 24, 1851, he was issued an unconditional land certificate at Goliad. He was not listed in the 1850 Census.

BIBLIOGRAPHY: Texas House of Representatives, *Biographical Directory of the Texan Conventions and Congresses, 1832–1845* (Austin: Book Exchange, 1941).   Carolyn Hyman

ENTERPRISE, TEXAS. Enterprise is a farming community nineteen miles northwest of Canton and just west of Farm Road 2475 in extreme northwestern Van Zandt County. In 1906 the Enterprise school had an enrollment of seventy-five. By the mid-1930s the community had a school, a church, and scattered dwellings. The Enterprise school was consolidated with the Wills Point Independent School District in 1951, and by 1987 only the church remained at the townsite.   Diana J. Kleiner

ENVIRONMENTAL HEALTH. The environmental health of a country or state is essentially the sum of various categories: air pollution, water and soil pollution, and occupational health. Exposure to toxic chemicals plays a role in each of these categories. Air, water, and soil pollution result from industrial, vehicular, and natural sources, e.g., forest fires and volcanic eruptions, as well as domestic and agricultural sources. Air pollutants regulated by the Environmental Protection Agency, include sulfur oxides, carbon monoxide, nitrogen oxides, ozone (and oxidants), particulates (dust), and lead. The EPA has not formulated a policy, as yet, for regulating the so-called "toxic" emission of petrochemicals that contain carbon-hydrogen linkages (bonds). These toxic compounds are emitted from industrial stacks or are transferred to toxic-waste sites that may contaminate ground or surface water.

Some of the environmental health problems in Texas have occurred in other parts of the United States: asbestosis and lung cancer in Tyler, silicosis in Houston from exposure to silica among sand blasters, and water pollution in Galveston Bay. The petrochemical center of the nation is situated along the Gulf Coast of Texas and Louisiana. Petroleum is refined and converted into many toxic intermediates and end-products. Nearly 60 percent of American petrochemical capacity is located in Texas, lured primarily since the 1940s by low taxes, few environmental regulations, and good shipping facilities. The value of chemical shipments from Texas in 1986 exceeded $25 billion.

Texans have had an unfortunate familiarity with industrial accidents. Many still remember one of the earliest, the Texas City disaster.qv In March 1947, a ship loaded with ammonium nitrate, fertilizer with explosive properties, caught fire and then exploded. For two days other ships, wharves, and petrochemical facilities also burned and exploded. Almost 600 persons were killed, more than 3,000 injured, and 2,500 left homeless. Some fear that we are now in the midst of a more subtle, yet equally serious catastrophe. Some believe that Texans are exposed to higher levels of industrial chemicals than those living elsewhere and that these exposures may be having significant adverse effects. The United States Department of Health and Human Services, in its *Atlas of U.S. Cancer Mortality,* has noted that cancer death rates for white males along the Texas Gulf Coast are among the highest in the country. In addition, the death rates from cancer among whites are increasing faster in this area than in the rest of the United States. Studies at petrochemical facilities have indicated marked increases in cancers of the blood system, brain, prostate, and skin. In 1986 the U.S. Congress passed the Emergency Planning and Community Right to Know Act, which requires manufacturers to report annually their emissions of certain toxins. Texas and Louisiana have led the list every year to date. Moreover, according to the Toxic Release Inventory, of the more than 3,000 counties in the United States, Harris County is second in carcinogenic emissions, with nearly eleven million pounds released or transferred in 1988. Two other Texas counties (Brazoria and Jefferson) are among the top ten emitters of carcinogens.

In the summer of 1992 the Environmental Protection Agency's National Priorities List identified twenty-eight hazardous-waste sites in Texas that qualified for cleanup funds under the federal Superfund program. In Harris County alone, the EPA reported ten sites. These included Brio Refining, Crystal Chemical, Dixie Oil Processors, French Limited, Geneva Industries, Highlands Acid Pit, Industrial Transformers, North and South Cavalcade Street in Houston, and Sikes Disposal Pit. Other sites on the list are Bailey Waste Disposal (Orange County), Bio-Ecology (Dallas County), Crystal City Airport (Zavala County), Air Force Plant No. 4 (Tarrant County), Koppers (Bowie County), Lone Star Army Ammunition Plantqv (Bowie County), Longhorn Army Ammunition Plantqv (Harrison County), Motco (Galveston Bay), Odessa Chronium Sites I and II (Ector County), Pantex (Carson County), Pesses (Tarrant County), Petro Chemical (Liberty County), Sheridan (Waller County), Stewco (Harrison County), Tex Tin Corporation (Galveston County), Texarkana Wood Preserving (Bowie County), Triangle Chemical (Orange County), and United Creosoting (Montgomery County). Congenital anomalies, spontaneous abortions, low birth weight, respiratory and skin problems, infections, and neurological disorders are some of the conditions reported by residents near toxic waste disposal sites.

Beginning in the early 1970s, federal and state officials began to enact laws and establish agencies designed to address problems of environmental pollution. The EPA was established in 1970. In 1976 Congress enacted the Toxic Substances Control Act, which gave the EPA broad authority to control chemical risks. In 1976, Congress enacted the Resource Conservation and Recovery Act to control the disposal of hazardous wastes. It was followed by the Comprehensive Environmental Response, Compensation, and Liability Act, passed in 1980. This law, which established the Superfund, governs the cleaning of abandoned hazardous-waste sites. The Texas legislature has enacted various environmental laws and established new agencies or expanded the work of existing agencies. The Texas Water Commissionqv is responsible for hazardous and industrial solid-waste management, coordination of responses to spills of oil and hazardous waste, and cleanup of abandoned waste sites. Emissions of toxic substances into water are also addressed in the permitting process. Emissions into air are regulated by the Texas Air Control Board, which also maintains a statewide network for monitoring the air.

BIBLIOGRAPHY: S. A. Geschwind et al., "Risk of Congenital Malformation Associated with Proximity to Hazardous Waste Sites," *American Journal of Epidemiology* 135 (1992). Frank W. McKay, Margot R. Hanson, and Robert W. Miller, *Cancer Mortality in the United States, 1950–1977* (Bethesda, Maryland: National Cancer Institutes, 1982).

Norman M. Trieff, ed., *Environment and Health* (Ann Arbor: Ann Arbor Science Publishers, 1981).

Norman M. Trieff, Sabrina F. Strawn, and Marvin S. Legator

EOLA, TEXAS. Eola is at the junction of Farm roads 381 and 765, on Dry Hollow some thirteen miles southwest of Paint Rock in northwestern Concho County. The community has had a post office since 1901, when it was known as Jordan. In 1902 the name was changed to Eola, reportedly after a small local creek named for Aeolus, Greek god of the winds. In the middle to late 1890s public school lands in the county were put up for sale at fifty cents an acre. Spurred on by railroad promotion, a land boom resulted in the area of Lipan Flat, a section that stretched east from San Angelo to the Colorado River. Eola was one of the communities created during this boom, which included many immigrants from central and eastern Europe. In 1920 more than 100 people in the vicinity of Eola were reported to be of Czech descent. The first family to settle in the area was that of Asher L. and Lizzie Leona (Hollman) Lollar, who established themselves at a site 3½ miles southeast of Eola in 1898. By 1902, when the first local store was built, the community numbered four families. Within the next two years a Baptist church was erected. The first school was conducted in a church on the Will Stephenson ranch. A two-story, two-room schoolhouse was built in 1906. In 1908 the community had a windmill and an Odd Fellows lodge. By 1914 Eola had a drugstore, a general store, and a population of twenty-five. Its population rose from thirty-five in 1925 to 240 by 1931. In 1940 the community had a population of 250, five churches, three general stores, three filling stations, two gins, a drugstore, a barbershop, a beauty shop, a laundry, a shoe shop, and a wholesale oil concern. A nine-teacher school taught elementary and high school classes. By 1955, after consolidation, the Eola school district was one of four remaining in Concho County. In 1963 Eola had the school, one industrial concern, five other businesses, and five churches. The community's population reached a reported high of 350 in 1947; from 1974 to 1990 it was recorded as 218.

BIBLIOGRAPHY: Gus Clemens, Jr., *The Concho Country* (San Antonio: Mulberry Avenue, 1980). *Concho Herald*, Golden Anniversary Edition, October 11, 1940. Hazie LeFevre, *Concho County History: 1858–1958* (2 vols., Eden, Texas, 1959). Vernon Lee Rucker, A Proposed Reorganization of the Concho County, Texas, Public Schools (M.Ed. thesis, University of Texas, 1940). *Mary M. Standifer*

EOLIAN, TEXAS. Eolian, on Farm Road 576 eight miles southwest of Breckenridge in west central Stephens County, was settled by cattlemen in the 1860s and 1870s. In 1880 the town received a post office named by the post office department. S. S. Cook was the first postmaster. The population was fifty in 1910 and eighteen in 1920. In 1939 the post office was closed, but a store, a school, and a church remained in operation. Although population estimates rose to fifty in the mid-1960s, only nine residents remained in Eolian by 1980. In 1990 the reported population was still nine.

BIBLIOGRAPHY: Fred I. Massengill, *Texas Towns: Origin of Name and Location of Each of the 2,148 Post Offices in Texas* (Terrell, Texas, 1936).

EPIDEMIC DISEASES. Epidemic diseases may afflict large numbers of persons living in a particular geographical area. Symptoms of an epidemic disease also spread rather rapidly among many, but not all, persons in the same community. Epidemic diseases are frightening because of the number afflicted and because of the rapid spread of the disease. Some diseases, such as dengue fever and measles, disable victims for some days, but usually do not cause death. Others, such as cholera and yellow fever, cause a varying number of deaths. When particular groups have not been exposed to a disease vector, the outcome may be devastating, as appears to have been the case among the Plains Indians of Texas when they were exposed to the communicable diseases carried by the white settlers.

Texans experienced numerous epidemics during the nineteenth century. Cholera, yellow fever, smallpox, dengue fever, measles, influenza, diphtheria, and whooping cough afflicted Texans in different locales at different times. Though cholera appeared in 1833 and caused some deaths, it was far more destructive during an epidemic in 1849. Approximately 500 deaths from cholera had occurred in San Antonio by May of that year. During the early months of 1866 measles appeared "in nearly every house" in Galveston. In 1883 many residents of Galveston suffered with aches and pains of dengue fever. Galveston's doctors established a quarantine camp in 1899 to house some of the thirty-seven residents afflicted with smallpox.

Galvestonians experienced at least nine yellow fever epidemics between 1839 and 1867. The events of a yellow fever epidemic terrified everyone. A twenty-five-year-old man would be healthy one day and dead three days later, changing relentlessly from a state of debility, fever, and pains in the extremities and loins, to a stage of vomiting blood clots (called the black vomit), to jaundice and death. Doctors then did not understand the role of the mosquito in transmitting the yellow fever virus. Some thought that garbage heaps and stagnant ponds produced particles in the air (called miasmata) that caused the disease. To prevent their occurrence, doctors and town leaders advocated sanitary cleanups when epidemics appeared or threatened. Others believed that sick people transmitted the disease directly to others. During an epidemic in Galveston in 1839, Ashbel Smith[qv] tasted the "black vomit" of patients and did not become sick. He believed that yellow fever was not contagious and that Galvestonians should not quarantine incoming ships. Many disagreed with Smith and urged quarantines as ways to prevent the spread of this communicable disease.

Texans, like others, were confused because improved sanitation and enforced quarantine did not prevent epidemics from occurring or continuing. During a yellow fever epidemic in Galveston in 1853, approximately 60 percent of the 5,000 residents became sick and 523 persons died. There were 175 deaths from yellow fever in Houston during 1858. During Galveston's last yellow fever epidemic in 1867, thousands were afflicted and approximately 725 residents had died by early September. Improved sanitation and quarantines appeared ineffectual, though some argued that these reduced mortality and morbidity.

With dramatic improvements in sanitation and better control of the mosquitos that carry the yellow fever and dengue fever viruses, cholera, yellow fever, and dengue fever receded in importance. A few localized outbreaks of yellow fever occurred in Calvert, Brownsville, Laredo, and San Antonio between 1867 and 1903, and significant epidemics of dengue fever appeared in South Texas in 1907 and 1918.

Epidemics of other infectious diseases occurred during the twentieth century. The most prominent included influenza, polio, St. Louis encephalitis, and AIDS. During the fall of 1918 and the winter of 1919, an epidemic of Spanish influenza affected much of the civilized world. An estimated twenty-five million Americans experienced the disease; an estimated 550,000 died from the disease. During the fall months of 1918, many schools and businesses closed, and churches did not meet. In late October the Galveston schools closed for two weeks. By that time 5,000 cases had been reported in El Paso and 400 deaths had occurred. Since that time, various strains of influenza virus have afflicted Texans periodically. During the first week in January of 1944, for example, physicians reported 126,000 cases of influenza in the United States and 24,000 cases in Texas.

During the summer of 1943, 1,274 cases of poliomyelitis (infantile paralysis) were reported, the largest number ever recorded in the state. There were 168 deaths in this group. The total number of cases in 1943 more than doubled the cases reported in 1937. The epidemic in 1943 was most intense in the Panhandle.[qv] There were 996 cases confirmed for the entire state during 1945, and sixty-six counties reported 292 cases during the first six months of 1946. In Houston during 1948, 313 new cases were documented. Not yet fully understanding the etiology and transmission of the disease, physicians struggled desperately to avert the sad results of infantile paralysis. Polio receded with the advent and use of vaccines during the mid-1950s.

More than once, St. Louis encephalitis frightened Texans. An epidemic involving 114 persons occurred in Cameron County in 1957. The first epidemic of this arborvirus disease in Houston occurred during the summer of 1964. Of 149 adults admitted to Ben Taub Hospital with signs of brain infection, 119 had positive serological tests for antibodies to the arborvirus causing this disease. Among the fifty children admitted to Ben Taub with signs of meningoencephalitis, twenty-six tested positive for these antibodies. Severe brain damage occurred in some of these patients. During the summer and fall of 1966 this disease afflicted 172 residents of Dallas, with twenty deaths. The most likely vector for these epidemics were the *Culex* mosquitos that flourished after summer rains.

During recent years the most frightening epidemic involves those infected with the AIDS virus. By early 1992 officials at the Texas Department of Health knew of 14,782 Texans with full-blown AIDS but had no reliable data on the incidence of those testing HIV-positive. Six of 197 students at Rivercrest High School in Johntown reportedly tested HIV-positive. Between 1987 and early 1992, 357 Texas teenagers tested HIV-positive. This reality led some doctors and public health officials to believe that the AIDS epidemic might become one of the most devastating epidemics in human history.

BIBLIOGRAPHY: John P. Carrier, "Medicine in Texas: The Struggle with Yellow Fever, 1839–1903," *Texas Medicine* 82 (November 1986). Alfred W. Crosby, *Epidemic and Peace, 1918* (Westport, Connecticut: Greenwood Press, 1976). N. Joel Ehrenkrantz et al., "Pandemic Dengue in Caribbean Countries and the Southern United States: Past, Present and Potential Problems," *New England Journal of Medicine* 285 (December 23, 1971). John C. Ewers, "The Influence of Epidemics on the Indian Populations and Cultures of Texas," *Plains Anthropologist* 18 (May 1973). J. Villasana Haggard, "Epidemic Cholera in Texas, 1833–1834," *Southwestern Historical Quarterly* 40 (January 1937). Bradford Luckingham, *Epidemic in the Southwest, 1918–1919* (Southwestern Studies Monograph No. 72, El Paso: Texas Western Press, 1984). Ashbel Smith, *An Account of the Yellow Fever Which Appeared in the City of Galveston, Republic of Texas, in the Autumn of 1839, with Cases and Dissections* (Galveston: Hamilton Stuart; Houston: Cruger and Moore; Austin: J. W. Cruger, 1839; rpt., as *Yellow Fever in Galveston, Republic of Texas, 1839: An Account of the Great Epidemic, Together with a Biographical Sketch by Chauncey D. Leake, and Stories of the Men Who Conquered Yellow Fever*, Austin: University of Texas Press, 1951). Larry J. Wygant, "The Galveston Quarantine Stations, 1853–1950," *Texas Medicine* 82 (June 1986). *Chester R. Burns*

EPISCOPAL THEOLOGICAL SEMINARY OF THE SOUTHWEST. The Episcopal Theological Seminary of the Southwest was begun in Austin by John E. Hines, coadjutor bishop of the Diocese of Texas, because the established theological seminaries of the Protestant Episcopal Church^{qv} were unable to enroll all of the men volunteering for the ordained ministry in a period in which church growth was great. It was possible to make a beginning in Austin because the church had a lease on a residence near the University of Texas in which Bible classes were being taught by Rev. Gray M. Blandy, instructor at the Canterbury Bible Chair and chaplain of Episcopal students at the University of Texas. There were two other clergymen available to assist Blandy, Rev. Lawrence Brown, Bible Chair instructor at the Agricultural and Mechanical College of Texas (now Texas A&M University) at College Station, and Rev. John M. Holt, vicar of the mission church at Mexia. Classes began September 1, 1951, under the auspices of the Austin Presbyterian Seminary. Blandy, who lived in Austin, was appointed dean, and the other faculty members arranged to commute to teach their classes. All three were present for the weekly Eucharist, at which they alternated as celebrants and preachers, with students taking part as readers or servers.

Two gifts strengthened the infant seminary. First, it received a bequest from the estate of Ann Laird of Kilgore and was thus able to add to the faculty. Second, the library of the former De Lancy Divinity School of Buffalo, New York, was given to the seminary by Bishop Laurisand L. Scaife of the Diocese of Western New York. The De Lancy Divinity School was no longer active and its library no longer in use. It contained a collection of English sources now out of print and hard to replace.

The seminary received a charter from the state of Texas in 1951 and was recognized as an agency of the Diocese of Texas in January of 1952. At the same time it was recognized by two other dioceses in Texas, West Texas and Dallas, which had sent students to it and shared in its board of trustees. Its title, "of the Southwest," reflected this.

The need for a campus was met by the donation of an Austin family, Dr. and Mrs. Ernest Villavaso and Frederick Duncalf,^{qv} who, as a memorial for the Villavasos' son Ernest, donated a tract of five acres in the university neighborhood near Austin Presbyterian Seminary. The seminary retained the architectural firm Fehr and Granger to plan the campus. Of the proposed buildings two were begun in 1954, a two-story building with classrooms and faculty offices on one floor and the library on the second, and a dormitory for single students. The administration building, a connecting classroom and faculty office building, and the library were begun the next summer. Services were continued at nearby All Saints' Chapel at first, then space was set apart in the library for temporary use as a chapel. Christ Chapel was built in 1960.

After Bishop Hines was elected presiding bishop of the Episcopal Church and resigned as chairman of the trustees, he was succeeded by Bishop E. H. Jones of West Texas. The following priests have served as dean of the school: T. Hudnal Harvey, Lawrence Brown, Gordon T. Charlton, Jr., and Durstan R. McDonald. In 1990 the seminar had an enrollment of sixty students and a faculty of fourteen.

BIBLIOGRAPHY: Gray M. Blandy and Lawrence L. Brown, *The Story of the First Twenty-five Years of the Episcopal Theological Seminary of the Southwest* (Austin: Episcopal Theological Seminary of the Southwest, 1976). Robert Lee Shemwell, Redesign and Additions for the Campus of the Episcopal Theological Seminary of the Southwest (M. Arch. thesis, University of Texas at Austin, 1986). Vertical Files, Barker Texas History Center, University of Texas at Austin.
Lawrence L. Brown

EPPERSON, BENJAMIN HOLLAND (1826–1878). Benjamin Holland Epperson, East Texas lawyer, politician, and state legislator, was born in Amite County, Mississippi, in 1826. He attended Princeton University but did not graduate. He moved to Texas sometime before 1847 and settled in Clarksville, where he studied law and was admitted to the bar. He was immediately accepted as a community leader even though he was still quite young. After brief service as a county commissioner, he was elected to the Second Texas Legislature in 1847.

Epperson was a leader of the Whig party^{qv} in Texas during the early 1850s. He ran unsuccessfully for governor on the Whig ticket in 1851 and joined the new American (Know-Nothing) party^{qv} in the mid-1850s. He served as a delegate to the national American party convention in 1856. After the defeats suffered by that party, Epperson returned to his law practice and business. He became a director of the proposed Memphis, El Paso and Pacific Railroad and acquired a sawmill. By 1860 he was one of the wealthiest men in the state.

In 1859 he was elected to the state legislature, where he worked to preserve the Union. As a delegate to the national Constitutional Union party^{qv} convention he worked unsuccessfully to secure the presidential nomination for Sam Houston.^{qv} In the 1860 election

Epperson was a presidential elector for the Bell-Everett ticket. As a strong opponent of secession,qv he is said to have advised Governor Houston to accept Lincoln's offer to send troops to keep Texas in the Union.

After Texas seceded, however, Epperson pledged to support the Confederacy. He ran unsuccessfully for the Confederate Congress in the fall of 1861. Lameness in one leg kept him from military service, but he generously contributed funds and supplies to the war effort.

He returned to public life in the late spring of 1865. He traveled to Washington several times to represent the Memphis, El Paso and Pacific Railroad and in May 1866 was chosen president of the company. That same year he ran for the United States Senate and was defeated by Oran M. Robertsqv on the twenty-fourth ballot of the legislature. Later that year he was elected to the United States House of Representatives but was not seated by the Republican-controlled Congress.

From 1866 until 1870, when John C. Frémont replaced him as president, Epperson concentrated on managing the Memphis, El Paso and Pacific. In 1871 he moved to Jefferson, where the next year he built the House of the Seasons, an unusual structure in the style of an Italian villa with the seasons represented by the four colors of glass in its cupola. The house is listed in the National Register of Historic Places. Epperson represented Marion County in the Texas legislature in 1874–75. He continued to practice law and concern himself with railroad and party matters. Although only in his early fifties, he was forced to curtail his public activities in 1877 because of failing health. He died on September 6, 1878, from nervous prostration brought on by excessive work. He was twice married and was survived by a widow and five children.

BIBLIOGRAPHY: Claude Elliott, *Leathercoat: The Life History of a Texas Patriot* (San Antonio, 1938). James Smallwood, "Disaffection in Confederate Texas: The Great Hanging at Gainesville," *Civil War History* 22 (December 1976). Ralph A. Wooster, "Ben H. Epperson: East Texas Lawyer, Legislator, and Civic Leader," *East Texas Historical Journal* 5 (March 1967).
Ralph A. Wooster

EPPERSON'S FERRY. During its first session the First Congress of the Republic of Texas offered half a league of land to anyone who would operate a ferry across the Sulphur River. By April 1837 Mark Epperson had built a ferry on Trammel's Traceqv in Bowie County, almost due south of the location of present-day New Boston. Congress granted Epperson the half league, and the ferry was soon widely known as Epperson's Ferry. In December 1837 the legislature instructed the postmaster general to institute mail service from Nacogdoches to Epperson's Ferry, and from there to the county seat of Red River County. Although little is known about it, a small settlement apparently developed around the ferry in the early 1840s, which served as a gathering place for area settlers. The ferry was eventually replaced by a wooden bridge, and then by a bridge of more modern construction in 1924. In 1936 the Texas Centennialqv Commission erected a marker at the site of the old ferry.

BIBLIOGRAPHY: Rex W. Strickland, Anglo-American Activities in Northeastern Texas, 1803–1845 (Ph.D. dissertation, University of Texas, 1937). Austin *Texas Sentinel*, August 12, 1941.
Cecil Harper, Jr.

EPPS CREEK. Epps Creek rises a mile west of Farm Road 2597 in east central Sutton County (at 30°38′ N, 100°14′ W) and runs southeast for ten miles to its mouth on West Copperal Creek, in western Kimble County (at 30°34′ N, 100°06′ W). The stream, located in the gently rolling limestone terrain of the western Edwards Plateau, runs through an area surfaced by shallow to deep loamy soils occasionally broken by rock outcrops. Local vegetation includes range grasses with scattered small stands of oak, juniper, and mesquite.

EPWORTH, TEXAS. Epworth, which later split into Old and New Epworth, was established as a post office in central Hale County in June 1884 by Horatio Graves, a Methodist minister who reportedly was then the only resident of the county. Graves, who planned to found a colony of Methodists in the area, named the post office for the birthplace of John Wesley. A few settlers moved to the region, and mail was brought from Estacado on horseback and distributed in Graves's home, where he also kept a store to furnish supplies to settlers and to cowboys of the Yellow House Division of the XIT Ranch.qv In March 1891 Graves moved the Epworth post office to a site two miles from Hale City and organized the Hale County Townsite Company. By 1893 New Epworth had a school, general store, hotel, livery stable, and newspaper. A decline in settlement caused by a drought led the Epworth citizens to unite with those of Hale City, which had been established in 1891. The inhabitants abandoned the two settlements and moved to what is now the site of Hale Center, where the combined town took that name.

BIBLIOGRAPHY: Ed Ellsworth Bartholomew, *800 Texas Ghost Towns* (Fort Davis, Texas: Frontier, 1971). Vera D. Wofford, ed., *Hale County Facts and Folklore* (Lubbock, 1978).
Mary L. Cox

EPWORTH LEAGUE. For over half a century the Epworth League, the Methodist youth organization, was especially strong in Texas. The group was authorized in 1890 by the General Conference of the Methodist Episcopal Church, South, and local churches in Texas soon began organizing their youth in Epworth leagues. The purpose of the leagues was to develop young church members in their religious life and to provide training in churchmanship. It was parallel to the Sunday school and typically met on Sunday nights. The name Epworth came from the boyhood home in England of John Wesley, the founder of the Methodist movement.

A Texas State Epworth League was organized in 1892, and meetings across the state were attracting 10,000 members by 1896. In the early years there was a state league newspaper. In 1905 state encampment grounds were secured near Corpus Christi Bay and called Epworth-by-the-Sea; there, more than a thousand persons gathered annually until a tropical storm in 1915 led to the sale of the property.

Epworth leaguers of the state paid for a $13,000 boat, which they named the *Texas*, for use in Methodist mission work on the Congo River in Africa in 1920. By 1925 Texas had 40,000 league members. Some of these, especially the leaders, were young adults. The leagues provided many of the leaders, lay and clerical, in the years following for the Methodist Churchqv in Texas. Statewide meetings were later converted to regional annual conference meetings, and they reached even more youth. Olin W. Nailqv wrote, "Perhaps no other similar movement in Methodism influenced so many, at such a formative period of life, as [the Epworth League] did."

Texas Methodist youth were also introduced to unsegregated meetings at International Epworth League conventions; this was a foretaste of later unsegregated meetings after Texas Methodists merged in the United Methodist Church, in which were blacks, Indians, Asians, and Hispanics. Leaders and speakers at Epworth League rallies involved such prominent Texans as Robert S. Hyer, Bishop Seth Ward, George C. Rankin, Frank S. Onderdonk, and J. Morris Sheppard.qqv One well-known Texas Epworth League project was the Ruby Kendrick Memorial Fund. Ruby Kendrick volunteered as a missionary to Korea in 1907 but died in less than a year, and Texas leaguers ultimately raised nearly $120,000 in her memory as a mission project.

Several Texans served on the national staff of the Epworth League in Nashville, Tennessee. Horace M. DuBose, Texas pastor for several years, became the churchwide executive in Nashville in 1898; Gus W. Thomasson, called by some "Mr. Texas Leaguer," served a few years on the staff; Ina C. Brownqv served many years; and Walter Towner of the North Texas Conference guided the transition from the Epworth League organizations to the Methodist Youth Fellowship in the 1930s.

Walter N. Vernon became a frequent contributor to league publications about the same time and by 1938 went to Nashville as an editor of youth study resources. In more recent years Wallace Chappell from Texas was a staff member for youth ministry.

BIBLIOGRAPHY: Walter N. Vernon et al., *The Methodist Excitement in Texas* (Dallas: Texas United Methodist Historical Society, 1984).

Walter N. Vernon

EQUALITY, TEXAS. Equality was sixteen miles northwest of Marshall in northwestern Harrison County. It had a post office that served both Marion and Harrison county residents from 1882 to 1900. In 1884 Equality had a population of forty-five, two churches, a district school, and two steam gristmills and cotton gins and had become a cotton-shipping point. By 1890 it had a sawmill and a general store and by 1896 Baptist, Methodist, and Disciples of Christ churches. The community was not listed on the state highway map of 1948.

Mark Odintz

EQUESTRIA, TEXAS. Equestria was nine miles southwest of Cleburne in southwestern Johnson County. It grew up around a cotton gin in the late 1870s. From 1883 to 1896 Equestria had a post office. By 1884 it had a church, a steam cotton gin, and a population of ten. Stock raising was important in the area, but the community also shipped corn, cotton, wheat, and oats. In 1892 its population was estimated at nineteen. There is no evidence to suggest that the community survived to the twentieth century.

David Minor

ERA, TEXAS. Era is on Highway 51 twelve miles from Gainesville in southwestern Cooke County. It was named after Era Hargrave, the daughter of an early settler. Judge J. M. Lindsay's donation of six acres for a school in 1878 marked the beginning of the town, although settlers had been in the area since the early 1850s. The most notable person to be born in Era was Robert Ewing Thomason,qv speaker of the Texas House of Representatives, mayor of El Paso, member of Congress, and federal judge. In 1990 Era had 200 residents, several businesses and churches, a post office, its own schools, and a Masonic lodge.

BIBLIOGRAPHY: Gainesville *Daily Register*, August 30, 1948.

Robert Wayne McDaniel

ERATH, GEORGE BERNARD (1813–1891). George Bernard Erath, soldier, surveyor, and legislator, was born on January 1, 1813, in Vienna, Austria, and attended Vienna Polytechnic Institute, where he studied English and Spanish. He sailed for America after graduation and landed in New Orleans on July 8, 1832, then moved upriver to Cincinnati, where he established his home. On March 22, 1833, he moved to the Republic of Texas,qv where he became a surveyor in Tenoxtitlán, in Robertson's colony.qv In 1835 he joined John H. Moore'sqv ranger company to deal with marauding Indians, and on March 1, 1836, he enlisted as a private in Capt. Jesse Billingsley'sqv Company C of Col. Edward Burleson'sqv First Regiment, Texan Volunteers, for service in the Texas Revolution.qv After fighting in the battle of San Jacintoqv he joined Capt. William H. Hill'sqv ranger company and continued surveying. He platted the town of Caldwell in 1840. By 1841 he had become the captain of the Milam County minute company. In 1842 he participated in the botched Somervell and Mier expeditionsqqv but was on guard duty on the Rio Grande during the battle of Mier and thus escaped capture.

As a member of the House of Representatives of the Eighth and Ninth congresses of the republic, 1843–1845, Erath represented Milam County and was energetic and effective in his support of the annexationqv of Texas to the United States. After statehood, he was elected to the First Legislature. In 1846 he returned to surveying and laid out the towns of Waco and Stephenville. He was elected to the Senate of the Seventh Legislature in 1857 and subsequently reelected to the Eighth and Ninth. On January 20, 1858, Governor Hardin R. Runnelsqv was authorized to recruit a force of 100 Texas Rangersqv under Capt. John S. Fordqv for the protection of the frontier. According to the Austin *State Gazette*,qv "To the untiring exertions of Senator Erath, whose sympathies were warmly interested in the measure, are they more indebted than to any one else for the passage of this much needed act." In 1861 Erath resigned from the Senate in order to serve on a committee of two chosen to arbitrate disagreements between the state and its reservation Indians.

At the outbreak of the Civil Warqv Erath raised a company for Col. Joseph W. Speight'sqv Fifteenth Texas Infantry regiment, but was discharged due to ill health and returned to his home at Waco. In 1864, however, Governor Pendleton Murrahqv appointed him to the command of a regiment in the Second Frontier District with the rank of major. This regiment, recruited in Brown and Coryell counties, was responsible for the defense of its home region. Erath returned to the Senate for the final time in 1874, to represent the Nineteenth District in the Fourteenth Legislature.

He married Lucinda Chambers of New York in December 1845. He died on May 13, 1891, and was buried in Oakwood Cemetery, Waco. Erath County is named in his honor. Erath dictated his memoirs to his daughter Lucy in 1886; they were first published in 1923 in the *Southwestern Historical Quarterly*qv and later that year in an edition of about 100 copies by the Texas State Historical Association;qv they were reprinted in Waco in 1956. They provide one of the most important sources on the Texas Revolution and on pioneer days in the 1830s and 1840s. Although Erath was "seventy-three years of age, in very poor health and blind" at the time he dictated his memoirs, his daughter maintained that his mental vigor "was the same as it had always been."

BIBLIOGRAPHY: John S. Ford, *Rip Ford's Texas*, ed. Stephen B. Oates (Austin: University of Texas Press, 1963). John H. Jenkins, *Basic Texas Books: An Annotated Bibliography of Selected Works for a Research Library* (Austin: Texas State Historical Association, 1983; rpt. 1988).

Thomas W. Cutrer

ERATH, TEXAS. Erath was on Farm Road 1637 six miles northwest of downtown Waco in north central McLennan County. It was founded before 1860 and named for George Bernard Erath.qv By 1880 the settlement had a gristmill and a general store. At its peak, it also had two churches, a school, two cotton gins, and a blacksmith's shop. Erath had a post office from 1896 to 1907, when mail for the community was rerouted through Waco. The Erath school was consolidated with several others in 1917 to form the China Spring district. A few scattered houses marked the community's location on county highway maps in the 1940s. The population of Erath was reported at fifteen in 1900, forty-seven in 1911, twenty-four in 1931, and fifty in 1949 and from the 1960s through the mid-1980s. By the end of the 1980s, much of the area had been annexed by the city of Waco.

BIBLIOGRAPHY: Dayton Kelley, ed., *The Handbook of Waco and McLennan County, Texas* (Waco: Texian, 1972). William Robert Poage, *McLennan County Before 1980* (Waco: Texian, 1981). Vertical File, Texas Collection, Baylor University.

Vivian Elizabeth Smyrl

ERATH COUNTY. Erath County was marked off from Bosque and Coryell counties in 1856 and named for George B. Erath,qv one of the original surveyors of the area. The center of the county is near Stephenville, eighty miles southwest of Dallas (at 32°10′ N, 98°15′ W). The county comprises 1,983 square miles and is divided into two distinct regions. The Western Cross Timbers, dominated by such hardwoods as post oak and a soil surface of sandy and red clay, crosses the northwestern two-thirds of the county, while the Grand Prairie, with dark limy soils originally covered with little bluestem but now dotted with live oak groves, crosses the southeastern one-third. The northern part of the county, where Cretaceous sediment has eroded, is noted for deposits of bituminous coal, fireclay, oil, and natural gas. The sand of the southern part is of glass-making quality. The animal life of Erath County includes badgers, civet cats, grey foxes, minks, wolves, mockingbirds, woodpeckers, and quail. The county's altitude ranges from 900 to 1,750 feet; the rainfall averages twenty-nine inches a year; the average temperature ranges from a low of 34° F during January to 96° in July, and the growing season lasts 238 days. The two major streams, the Paluxy and Bosque rivers, are tributaries of the Brazos. Transportation in Erath County is provided by Interstate Highway 20, which crosses the northwest corner, and U.S. highways 67, 281 and 377. The Atchison, Topeka and Santa Fe and the Texas Central railroads cross the central and southwestern parts of the county.

The first attempts at settlement were made in 1854 by A. C. Dobkins and Will and Tom Holland near the site of present-day Dublin. In the following year a party of thirty pioneers was brought into the area by surveyors George Erath and Neil McLennan.qv Included in the group were John M. Stephen, his brother William F., and a black family. The Stephens moved to the 4,409 acres of the John Blair survey, and the black family may have been left alone in the post oak grove on the Bosque River, now the site of Stephenville, to establish relations with Caddo and Anadarko Indians, who still visited the area from their new reservation in what is now Young County. In 1856 John M. Stephen offered to donate land for a courthouse and townsite if the town was named Stephenville and made the county seat. The state of Texas agreed and formed Erath County that year.

Most of the early settlers were recent arrivals from southern states. Beginning in 1857, a series of incidents led to their alienation from the Caddos and Anadarkos, whom the newcomers called Comanches; but these Erath County Indians had discouraged raids by the real Comanches and campaigned against them alongside Texas Rangers.qv By 1860 the peaceful Caddo and Anadarko Indians were moved to Oklahoma by Robert S. Neighbors.qv Comanche raids continued until 1873. The Indian attacks, the Civil War,qv and raids by outlaw bands caused a decrease in population from 2,425 in 1860 to 1,801 by 1870. With the removal of the Comanches around 1873 the county grew rapidly, increasing to a population of 11,796 by 1880 and 30,000 by 1900. The county population reached a peak of 32,095 in 1910.

During the influx of settlers in the 1870s stock farming gave way to cotton farming, and cotton was the major crop from 1875 through 1915. In 1879 the Texas Central Railroad reached Dublin, and in 1889 the Fort Worth and Rio Grande was completed through Stephenville. This opened eastern markets for the county's cotton crops. The largest cotton production occurred in 1906.

As early as 1890 agricultural agents warned county growers of damage to the soil from lack of diversification. But investments in ginning equipment prevented changes until 1910. Eroding land, the boll weevil,qv and decreasing profits motivated the farmers to find alternatives. Dairy farms, fruit orchards, nurseries, production of peanuts and feed crops, and an extensive poultry industry that lasted until 1950 were instigated.

Mining and manufacturing have also played a roll in the Erath County economy. During the period from 1888 to 1921 the Texas Pacific Coal Company mined coal in the northwest corner of the county near Thurber. In 1918 the Thurber Brick Company was established in the same area to manufacture tile, sewer pipes, paving bricks, and stoneware. Small amounts of oil and natural gas were also mined.

Stephenville College was established in 1893 but faced financial difficulties within two years. John Tarleton,qv a local rancher, bequeathed funds from the sale of lands for the continuation of the school, and in 1899 the college was renamed for him. In 1916 the school was affiliated with the Agricultural and Mechanical College of Texas (now Texas A&M University), and the following year it was made a state college. Tarleton College began with an enrollment of 100 students and grew to 175 by 1900. In the fall of 1990 Tarleton State University enrolled 6,251 students.

The first newspaper in Erath County was the *Texas Pacific,* published first in 1871. It later took the name Stephenville *Empire* and went into competition with the Stephenville *Tribune,* which was founded in 1890. The two newspapers merged in 1930 to become the *Empire-Tribune.* Other county papers have been the Dublin *Enterprise,* begun in 1881, which became the present Dublin *Progress* in 1888; the *Texas Miner* in Thurber; and the Duffau *Progress.*

Two courthouses preceded the present building. The first, a wooden structure, burned in 1866, and with it burned many of the county's important records. The second, a stone building completed in 1877, needed renovation by 1891. The town of Dublin attempted to become county seat by offering to build the new courthouse, but Stephenville won the election, and architects J. Riely Gordonqv and D. E. Laub were hired to design the present Victorian structure. The building, started in 1891 and completed in 1893, was constructed of local white stone quarried on the Leon River and red granite brought from Pecos County. the building has a wrought-iron stairway, tessellated marble floors, and other elegant details. It was renovated in 1949.

After 1910 the population declined in Erath County, dropping to 28,385 in 1920 and 20,804 in 1930. Loss of cotton production drove farmers away. Railroads converted from coal to oil in 1921 and refused to negotiate with striking workers. The coal mines at Thurber were shut down, and the brick plant followed in 1933. Small farms were consolidated, and Erath County agriculture shifted from crop raising to ranching by 1945. The fruit industry was damaged when overgrazing allowed cedar trees to invade from the hills, bringing San Jose scale to the peach and apple trees.

Erath County's population rose to 18,434 in 1950 and fell to 16,236 in 1960, then grew to 18,141 by 1970 and 23,500 by 1983. In the 1970s small industries began to move in; however, 80 percent of the annual average county income of $70 million was still from dairy and beef cattle and other livestock. Erath County was the second leading county in Texas in milk production in the 1980s. Peanuts, sorghum, hay, and small grains continued to be important. *See also* COAL AND LIGNITE MINING.

BIBLIOGRAPHY: George B. Erath, "The Memoirs of George B. Erath, 1813–1891," *Southwestern Historical Quarterly* 26–27 (January–October 1923; rpts., Austin: Texas State Historical Association, 1923; Waco: Heritage Society of Waco, 1956). Kenneth F. Neighbours, *Robert Simpson Neighbors and the Texas Frontier, 1836–1859* (Waco: Texian Press, 1975). H. Grady Perry, *Grand Ol' Erath* (Stephenville, Texas, 1974).

Dan M. Young

ERDMAN, LOULA GRACE (1898–1976). Loula Grace Erdman, writer, daughter of August F. and Mollie (Maddox) Erdman, was born on June 8, 1898, near Alma, Lafayette County, Missouri. She attended Central Missouri State College (B.S., 1931) and Columbia University (M.A., 1941). She also studied at the University of Wisconsin, the University of Southern California, and West Texas State College. She subsequently moved to Texas and taught in the Amarillo public schools and at West Texas State College, where she eventually became novelist-in-residence and director of the Advanced Workshop in Creative Writing.

Erdman began writing in the 1930s, and by 1946 about fifty of her short stories and magazine articles had been published, as well as her first juvenile novel, *Separate Star* (1944), a book about career teaching. In 1946 she won the $10,000 Dodd, Mead–*Redbook* Award for *The Years of the Locust* (1947), a novel set in her native Missouri. In 1952 she received the *American Girl*–Dodd, Mead Award for *The Wind Blows Free* (1952), the first volume of a juvenile trilogy about a pioneer Panhandleqv family. She continued the story of the Pierce family in *The Wide Horizon* (1956) and *The Good Land* (1959). *Room to Grow* (1962), a novel about French immigrants who moved to the Panhandle via New Orleans, won her the Texas Institute of Lettersqv Juvenile Award. She received both the Texas Institute of Letters Award and the Steck-Vaughn Award for *A Bluebird Will Do* (1973).

Her other works include *A Wonderful Thing and Other Stories* (1940), *Fair Is the Morning* (1945), *Lonely Passage* (1948), *The Edge of Time* (1950), *Three at the Wedding* (1953), *My Sky Is Blue* (1953), *The Far Journey* (1955), *Short Summer* (1958), *Many a Voyage* (1960), *The Man Who Told the Truth* (1962), *Life Was Simpler Then* (1963), *Another Spring* (1966), *Bright Sky* (1969), *A Time to Write* (1969), and *Save Weeping for the Night* (1975).

Miss Erdman was a member of the Texas Institute of Letters, the Panhandle Penwomen, Delta Kappa Gamma, Kappa Delta Pi, and Phi Kappa Phi. As a career teacher who never considered abandoning teaching even after she gained recognition as a writer, she also belonged to the National Education Association and the Texas State Teachers Association.qv She attended Polk Street Methodist Church in Amarillo and died in that city on June 20, 1976.

BIBLIOGRAPHY: Ernestine P. Sewell, *Loula Grace Erdman* (Austin: Steck-Vaughn, 1970).

Sylvia Grider

ERHARD, CAYTON (1822–1884). Cayton Erhard, businessman and memoir writer, son of Ludwig and Laura Erhard, was born in Munich, Bavaria, on July 29, 1822. With his parents and younger brother, Adolph, he entered Texas at Galveston in 1839. The family made its way up the Colorado River to Bastrop. In January 1840 both parents died, and the boys were informally adopted by the family of James Nicholson,qv a local merchant.

In 1841 President Mirabeau B. Lamarqv issued a call for volunteers to undertake an expedition to trade with and secure the Santa Fe territory for the Republic of Texas. Motivated more by the possibility of trade than that of glory, Erhard and his cousin Antonio Erhard joined the expedition. Along with the others, Erhard was captured by Mexican troops and spent the next two years as a prisoner in Mexico (*see* TEXAN SANTA FE EXPEDITION).

In March 1843, after suffering cruel hardships, Erhard returned to Texas, where he rejoined the Nicholson family in Bastrop. Four years later, with his own savings and a loan from friends, he moved to San Marcos. There he was instrumental in organizing the Hays County government. He was elected the first county clerk and served as the first postmaster. In 1847 he opened a store in San Marcos that sold a large assortment of drugs and nostrums. This date marks it as the first drugstore in the state. During his eighteen years in San Marcos, Erhard prospered. He bought several lots of town property in San Marcos and Bastrop and several slaves.

His political convictions seemed solidly Democratic until the secessionqv of Texas in 1861. His papers indicate that his discontent resulted from the deterioration of business conditions and public order as Texas endured the ordeal of the Civil War.qv Although Erhard's formal education was limited, his writings, which contain frequent references to classical literature, point to considerable learning. When his business floundered in San Marcos, he moved his store to Bastrop, where he remained the rest of his life.

After the storm of Reconstruction,qv Erhard again began to prosper. His politics, decidedly conservative and nonradical, apparently attracted notice in Austin. In 1872 he was appointed a judge in municipal elections for Bastrop, a position of influence normally reserved for those who supported the politics of Radical Republican governor Edmund J. Davis.qv Erhard's political position became sufficiently acceptable to the citizens of Bastrop for him to be elected a delegate to the Constitutional Convention of 1875.qv There he remained relatively quiet during the debates but was apparently pleased enough with the new constitution to give it his endorsement.

During the next ten years, Erhard devoted himself to his many business interests. In the fall of 1882 he began to write reminiscences of the Texan Santa Fe expedition for a weekly publication in the San Marcos *Free Press*. The series ran from November 16, 1882, to July 24, 1884. Erhard was married to Harriet Smith in September 1851, and they had nine children, only three of whom lived to adulthood. Erhard died at his home in Bastrop on July 21, 1884, and was buried in the city cemetery.

BIBLIOGRAPHY: Ford Dixon, "Cayton Erhard's Reminiscences of the Texan Santa Fe Expedition, 1841," *Southwestern Historical Quarterly* 66 (April 1963). Cayton Erhard Collection, Barker Texas History Center, University of Texas at Austin. Thomas Falconer, *Expedition to Santa Fe* (New Orleans, 1842; rpt., as *Letters and Notes on the Texan Santa Fe Expedition, 1841–1842*, with intro. by Frederick Webb Hodges, New York: Dauber and Pine Bookshops, 1930). George Wilkins Kendall, *Narrative of the Texan Santa Fe Expedition* (2 vols., New York: Harper, 1844; rpts. Austin: Steck, 1935; n.p.: Readex, 1966).

Ford Dixon

ERIGOANNA INDIANS. This group is known only from brief mention in French documents that pertain to the La Salle expedition.qv In 1687 the Erigoanna Indians were enemies of the Ebahamos, a Karankawan group that lived in the vicinity of La Salle's Fort St. Louisqv near Matagorda Bay. A group of Ebahamo warriors told La Salle that their enemies lived farther inland to the northwest. Sound correspondences suggest that Erigoanna may be a French rendition of Aranama, the name of an early eighteenth-century Coahuiltecan group that lived within striking distance of the Ebahamos to the west and northwest, but this equivalence has yet to be demonstrated.

BIBLIOGRAPHY: Albert S. Gatschet, *The Karankawa Indians, the Coast People of Texas* (Cambridge, Massachusetts: Peabody Museum of American Archaeology and Ethnology, 1891). John Gilmary Shea, *Discovery and Exploration of the Mississippi Valley* (New York: Redfield, 1852).

Thomas N. Campbell

ERIN, TEXAS. Erin is on Walnut Creek at the intersection of Farm roads 252 and 1005, eleven miles south of Jasper in central Jasper County. Another Erin, also known as Richardson's, Jasper's Mills, and Evadale, was located on the Atchison, Topeka and Santa Fe Railway and the Neches River in southwestern Jasper County and had a post office from 1847 to 1862. Apparently this office was discontinued during the Civil War.qv The present Erin appeared in 1882. It has also been known as Faircloth, for its first postmaster, and Big Creek, a name for which application was made to postal officials. In 1885 the community had a population of 100, three churches, and two steam sawmill–cotton gins and shipped wool, hides, and cotton. By 1896 it had one general store and a population of fifty, which shrank to thirty-five by 1914; the post office was discontinued in 1923. The cotton gin was discontinued under the acreage-reduction program in 1935. State highway maps of 1936 showed a cemetery, a school, and scattered dwellings at the townsite. In 1934 Erin had a population of forty and a business. The population was estimated at fifty in 1949, but was no longer recorded after 1953. In 1984 Boyen Cemetery, two buildings, and scattered dwellings remained at the townsite.

Diana J. Kleiner

ERNA, TEXAS. Erna is just off U.S. Highway 377 twenty-one miles southeast of Menard in southeastern Menard County. The site is said to have been settled shortly after the Civil War,qv in part by German immigrants. J. N. Andrews operated the only store in the community in 1890. A post office was established there in 1915 with Amos Brewer as postmaster. The office was discontinued in 1919, and mail for the community was sent to Streeter in Mason County. Only a few scattered houses marked Erna on county highway maps in the 1940s. From the mid-1940s through the mid-1960s the population was reported at fifty. By the 1980s only the place name appeared on county maps.

Claudia Hazlewood

ERNEST L. RAINEY SITE. From May through December 1978 the Texas Highway Department excavated the Ernest L. Rainey Site, a natural sinkhole formation in limestone bedrock on the southeast side of a rocky hill in western Bandera County. The site is about 300 meters north of Mill Creek, a westward-flowing perennial tributary of the Sabinal River. The opening of the sinkhole measured 3.6 meters by 2.8 meters. Below the opening, the space expanded into a small underground chamber about eight meters in diameter; the sinkhole opening was located above the southwest side of the chamber. When the site was first recorded, fill material came within a meter of its ceiling. This material, which had washed in through the years, formed the culture-bearing deposits in the sinkhole. The deposits were excavated in their entirety. In addition, three hearths on the ground surface outside the sinkhole were excavated.

The deposits underneath the limestone ceiling were in nine distinct major strata. Zone 1 averaged thirty centimeters in thickness and contained both historic and prehistoric materials. Zone 2 averaged sixteen centimeters in thickness and consisted of coarse limestone spall material from the roof of the shelter. This layer was culturally sterile except for a minor occupation that took place at the bottom of the zone. Zone 3 averaged eight centimeters in thickness and appeared as a midden deposit. Artifacts included Perdiz arrowpoints; a bipointed, two-edged, beveled knife; and a mussel-shell pendant. Features consisted of an ash deposit containing charcoal, flint, and burned bone, and two fire pits. Faunal remains from Zone 3 comprise a wide variety of animals used as food, including bison. Zone 4, thirty centimeters thick, was subdivided into five major and several minor layers. It contained Perdiz arrowpoints, tools, and a mussel-shell pendant. The thirty-two features of the zone included two rock-lined hearths, a rock-lined pit, a burned-rock accumulation judged not to be a hearth, and other types of fire remnants. Faunal food remains from Zone 4 included bison. Separating Zone 4 from Zone 5 in the northern portion of the shelter was a sterile spall layer.

Zone 5 averaged twenty-five centimeters in thickness and was subdivided into three layers. It contained a dense midden deposit at the southern end. Edwards and Scallorn arrowpoints predominated. Other tools and a freshwater mussel-shell pendant were found. The zone had twenty features, including fire pits, rock-lined hearths, scattered hearths, and ash deposits. Zone 6, twenty centimeters thick, was subdivided into two major layers. It contained a predominance of Edwards and Sabinal arrowpoints. Its twelve features included basin-shaped burned areas filled with ash, accumulations of ash without underlying burned areas, a burned-rock accumulation, and rock-lined hearths. Zone 7 averaged thirty centimeters in thickness and was subdivided into seven minor layers in the northern portion of the shelter. In the central and southern portions of the shelter the zone was homogeneous. An Edwards arrowpoint and an untyped projectile point were among the artifacts recovered. The untyped specimen suggests a transitional phase of development between the manufacture of dart points and the manufacture of arrowpoints. The zone had ash deposits overlying burned, basin-shaped depressions and ash deposits from materials burned elsewhere.

Zone 8 was a homogeneous zone thirty centimeters thick. It produced only one diagnostic tool, a dart or arrow point similar to the untyped specimen in Zone 7. The two features in Zone 8 were a rock-lined, basin-shaped hearth and an ash deposit in a burned depression. Zone 9 was a homogeneous silty spall overlying bedrock. No diagnostics were recovered here, and only one feature, an ash deposit, was present.

The occupations at the Rainey Site represent the entire span of the Late Prehistoric Period in Central Texas. The number of artifacts and features in zones 3 and 4 suggests more intense utilization of the shelter during the Toyah Phase or Perdiz occupations than at other times. Exploitation of bison as a food source apparently arose during that time as well.

BIBLIOGRAPHY: Archeological Records Division, Texas State Department of Highways and Public Transportation, Austin.

Jerry Henderson

ERNEST WITTE SITE. The Ernest Witte Site, an aboriginal cemetery, is located on a bluff overlooking the Brazos River in Austin County, about forty miles west of Houston. A low sandy knoll marks its location. In the 1930s Ernest Witte and his brother, then young boys living on a nearby farm, began digging for a treasure that they believed an eccentric uncle had buried in the area. In a deep hole dug into the sandy knoll they found human bones. In 1974 Witte relayed this information to a team of field archeologists from the Texas Archeological Survey of the University of Texas at Austin, which was investigating prehistoric Indian sites on land where the Houston Lighting and Power Company proposed to build the Allens Creek Nuclear Generating Station. The Ernest Witte Site was therefore included in the investigation, which was sponsored by the company. The site is coincidentally located where engineers planned to place one of the reactors for the nuclear plant. Excavations began in 1974 and continued into 1975. The field crew was headed by Grant D. Hall and under the general supervision of David S. Dibble, director of the Texas Archeological Survey.

The site contained the skeletal remains of 238 people buried at various times over a period of more than 4,000 years, from 2700 B.C. to A.D. 1500. Reflecting the gradual accumulation of soil on the site and its periodic use as a burial ground by local prehistoric Indian populations, the burials occurred as four distinct, superimposed groups separated by layers of soil in a deposit with a maximum depth of about eight feet.

The group of skeletons buried deepest in the site, and hence the oldest, contained the remains of an estimated sixty-one people. Radiocarbon assays indicate that these earliest burials occurred between 2700 and 1600 B.C. These Group 1 burials, affiliated with the Middle Archaic Period, thus constitute the oldest human cemetery presently known in Texas. Artifacts were placed in the graves of seven people. A Pedernales dart point and some pencil-shaped bone implements represent the complete array of grave goods for these Middle Archaic burials.

Remains in the next layer were interred in the period from 600 B.C. to A.D. 300. This layer, designated Group 2, contained the skeletal remains of 145 people. Numerous interesting and significant artifacts were placed in the graves of these Late Archaic people. Seventy, or 48 percent, of the burials in Group 2 contained artifacts. Among these were dart points, marine-shell ornaments, corner-tang chert knives, boatstones, a ground-stone gorget, a graphite abrader, red jasper pebbles, ocher, biotite schist, various worked bone artifacts, and deer skulls and antlers. The rocks out of which some of the boatstones and the ground-stone gorget were made originated in the Ouachita Mountains of Arkansas. This fact suggests that the people represented by the Group 2 remains were participants in a far-reaching exchange network. Five of the people in Group 2 apparently died violently, as indicated by chert dart points stuck into their bones.

Above Group 2 was a third layer of burials consisting of ten individuals. Group 3 developed in the period from A.D. 550 to 950. Only one individual in this group had grave inclusions. Scattered about the chest of an adult male were seven chert projectile points.

The final use of the Ernest Witte Site as a cemetery was evidenced by a shallowly buried layer of the skeletons of thirteen people. These Group 4 burials, assigned to the Late Prehistoric Period, were probably interred well after A.D. 1000. No artifacts were found in any of these latest graves on the site.

Development of cemeteries in Middle and Late Archaic times at Allens Creek and elsewhere on the Texas coastal plain has been interpreted as evidence for substantial growth of human populations in the region. As these people were hunters and gatherers who lived off the natural products of the land, it may have become necessary to define territories containing adequate food supplies. Cemeteries may be one way the people had to legitimize their claim to a home range. The exotic artifacts and violent deaths evidenced in Group 2 may also be interpreted as signs of increased population densities in the period. With more people settled across the landscape, lines of communication were better, and material goods could pass from group to group, eventually being transported far from their natural origins. The boatstones, which came from Arkansas, and the marine-shell ornaments found with Group 2 burials at Allens Creek exemplify the results of such an exchange system. The violent deaths in Group 2 may also be symptomatic of more densely settled populations, the theory being that social organizations were not designed to cope with stresses produced as more people attempted to make a living from limited food resources. The greatly reduced body counts and the scarcity of grave inclusions in Groups 3 and 4 may indicate smaller, more mobile populations after A.D. 500.

The artifacts, skeletal remains, notes, photographs, and other data related to investigation of the Ernest Witte Site are curated at the Texas Archeological Research Laboratory, University of Texas at Austin.

BIBLIOGRAPHY: Grant D. Hall, *Allens Creek: A Study in the Cultural Prehistory of the Lower Brazos River Valley* (University of Texas at Austin, 1981).
Grant D. Hall

ERNST, JOHANN FRIEDRICH (1796–1848). Johann Friedrich Ernst, the first German to bring his family to Texas, was born Christian Friedrich Dirks, son of Meine and Sybille (Grimms) Dirks, on June 18, 1796, at Burg (Castle) Gödens near the village of Neustadtgödens, just north of Oldenburg in Lower Saxony. He began to use the name Ernst after his departure from Oldenburg. In 1800, after the death of his father, who was employed at Burg Gödens, Ernst moved with his mother to Varel in the Duchy of Oldenburg. In February 1814 he joined the Oldenburg Regiment of the Duke of Oldenburg, and he remained a soldier until June 1819. He reached the rank of quartermaster sergeant and received a medallion from the duke for his participation in the campaign against Napoleon. He married Louise Gesine Auguste Weber (*see* STOEHR, LOUISE W.) in Oldenburg on October 25, 1818; they had seven children. In June 1819 the duke appointed him clerk at the post office in Oldenburg.

In September 1829 Ernst, his wife, and their five surviving children fled Oldenburg; he was subsequently charged by the Duke of Oldenburg with embezzling a large amount of money from the post office. He and his family escaped by way of Bremen, Osnabrück, Münster, and Brussels and eventually sailed from Le Havre for New York, where they arrived in late 1829. For a time Ernst and his family ran a boardinghouse in New York. There he met Charles Fordtran,qv also a German. They became friends and decided to move together to Missouri. On the ship to New Orleans they read a prospectus about the favorable conditions in Austin's colony in Texas and changed their destination. The Ernst family and Fordtran sailed on the schooner *Saltillo* for Harrisburg and arrived before March 9, 1831; they were the first German family to arrive in Texas.

On April 16 Ernst obtained a league of land on the west bank of the west fork of Mill Creek in Austin's colony; Fordtran's grant was nearby. In February 1832 Ernst wrote a long letter to a friend in Germany describing Texas in glowing language. This letter appears to have been circulated widely in Germany and to have encouraged others to immigrate. Ernst became well known as a benefactor to new emigrants from his homeland: his house served as a hotel and a boardinghouse for travelers, and he even assisted new settlers financially. He acquired the nickname "father of the immigrants."

He became a justice of the peace in Austin County and sold lots from his league to new immigrants. The resulting settlement, Industry, was the first German town in Texas. Ernst became involved in a variety of other activities: cultivating tobacco, making cigars, recording rainfall and temperature data at his farm, establishing the Teutonic Order in Texas, and chartering a university, which never came into existence. He wrote several letters to the editor of the *Telegraph and Texas Register*qv regarding his tobacco enterprise and weather data. Also, he proposed to the Congress of Texas that the republic formally encourage German immigration. President Mirabeau B. Lamarqv at one time considered proposing Ernst as envoy to the Netherlands. Ernst died sometime between May 16 and July 10, 1848. *See also* GERMANS.

BIBLIOGRAPHY: Rudolph L. Biesele, "The First German Settlement in Texas," *Southwestern Historical Quarterly* 34 (April 1931). Rudolph L. Biesele, *The History of the German Settlements in Texas, 1831–1861* (Austin: Von Boeckmann–Jones, 1930; rpt. 1964). Detlef Dunt, *Reise nach Texas, nebst Nachrichten von diesem Lande, für Deutsche, welche nach Amerika zu gehen beabsichtigen* (Bremen: Wiehe, 1834). Ottilie Fuchs Goeth, *Was Grossmutter erzählt* (San Antonio: Passing Show Printing, 1915; trans. Irma Goeth Guenther as *Memoirs of a Texas Pioneer Grandmother*, Austin, 1969; rpt., Burnet, Texas: Eakin Press, 1982). Terry G. Jordan, *German Seed in Texas Soil: Immigrant Farmers in Nineteenth-Century Texas* (Austin: University of Texas Press, 1966). New Ulm *Enterprise*, January 2, 1986. Crystal Sasse Ragsdale, ed., *The Golden Free Land: The Reminiscences and Letters of Women on an American Frontier* (Austin: Landmark, 1976). Vertical Files, Barker Texas History Center, University of Texas at Austin. Miriam Korff York, *Friedrich Ernst of Industry* (Giddings, Texas, 1989).
Hugh E. Meredith

ERNST, JOHN FRIEDRICH MEINHARD (1820–1863). John (or Johann) Friedrich Meinhard (Fritz) Ernst was born on September 11, 1820, in Oldenburg, Lower Saxony, the son of Louise Gesine Auguste (Weber) and Johann Friedrich Ernst.qv He sailed to the United States in 1829 with his parents, among the first German settlers in Texas, and grew up in Austin's colony in what became the settlement of Industry. He married Maria Ann (Krumm) Brey, the widow of Ferdinand Brey, who died in the Mier expedition.qv They had four children. Fritz Ernst served as a guide and interpreter for Prince Carl of Solms-Braunfelsqv on his visit to Texas. He was a farmer and a justice of the peace as well as a soldier and pioneer. He served as a ranger for the Republic of Texasqv from July 20, 1836, to November 20, 1836. He also served in the Southwestern Army of the Republic of Texas, Company B, First Regiment, from October 3, 1842, to January 20, 1843. Although Ernst grew up at Industry, he later lived near Round Top and in 1861 served in the Round Top Guerrillas, a local militia group. During the Civil Warqv he helped a Captain Creuzbaur organize a company from Fayette County. He served as first lieutenant in Creuzbaur's company of light artillery, Texas Volunteers, from October 12, 1861, until he died in Waco in October 1863.

BIBLIOGRAPHY: Gilbert Giddings Benjamin, *The Germans in Texas: A Study in Immigration* (Austin: Jenkins, 1974). Rudolph L. Biesele, *The History of the German Settlements in Texas, 1831–1861* (Austin: Von Boeckmann–Jones, 1930; rpt. 1964). Paul C. Boethel, *The Big Guns of Fayette* (Austin: Von Boeckmann–Jones, 1965). Caroline Von Hinueber, "Life of German Pioneers in Early Texas," *Quarterly of the Texas State Historical Association* 2 (January 1899). Leonie Rummel Weyand and Houston Wade, *An Early History of Fayette County* (La Grange, Texas: La Grange *Journal*, 1936).
Miriam York

ERSKINE, ANDREW NELSON (1826–1862). Andrew Nelson Erskine, Texas Ranger, surveyor, and Confederate soldier, was born in Sweet Springs, Monroe County, Virginia, on March 12, 1826, the fifth of ten children born to Agnes D. (Haynes) and Michael H. Erskine.qv The family moved in 1831 to Kitchens Ranch near Huntsville, Alabama, and again in 1834 to Bolivar, Mississippi. In 1839 they settled on Arenosa Creek in Jackson County, Texas. Their home was attacked on August 6, 1840, by a Comanche scouting party on its way to Linnville (see LINNVILLE RAID OF 1840). Shortly thereafter the family moved west into what was to become Guadalupe County. By the time he was seventeen, Erskine had joined a company of Texas Rangersqv under John Coffee (Jack) Haysqv and fought in the battle of Salado

Creek.qv He returned to Seguin, became a surveyor under the tutorship of James P. Hector, and surveyed land for Hector and for Jacob de Cordova.qv In 1847, in company with his brother John P., he surveyed lands of Castro's colonyqv for the German Immigration Company of Hamburg.

On December 27, 1847, Erskine married Ann Theresa Johnson of Seguin; they had five sons. The couple first made their home on the ranch of Michael Erskine at the Capote Hills. In 1852 they moved to Mill Point on the Guadalupe River west of Seguin, where Erskine took over the management of a gristmill and ferry owned by his father-in-law, Joseph F. Johnson. In the succeeding years he built a sawmill and cotton gin and ran a stage stand and inn. This locality subsequently became known as Erskine's Ferry. In 1856 he was elected county clerk of Guadalupe County. In 1859 he served as lieutenant in the company of Andrew Herron under John S. Fordqv against the invasion of Juan N. Cortinaqv on the Rio Grande. Erskine enlisted in Hood's Texas Brigadeqv in 1862 for service to the Confederacy. In company with his brother Alexander M. he arrived at Richmond in time to take part in the Seven Days' Battle, June 26–July 2, 1862. He fought in the battle of Second Manassas and was killed at the battle of Sharpsburg (Antietam) on the morning of September 17, 1862.

BIBLIOGRAPHY: Andrew Nelson Erskine Papers, Barker Texas History Center, University of Texas at Austin. Vertical Files, Barker Texas History Center, University of Texas at Austin. Willie Mae Weinert, *An Authentic History of Guadalupe County* (Seguin, Texas: Seguin *Enterprise*, 1951; rpt. 1976).

L. J. FitzSimon

ERSKINE, MICHAEL H. (1794–1862). Michael H. Erskine, cattleman and diarist, son of Michael and Margaret (Paulee) Erskine, was born on January 9, 1794, near Union in what became West Virginia. On February 13, 1817, he married Agnes Davidson Haynes. In 1831 he moved to Huntsville, Alabama, and later to Mississippi, engaging in farming. He moved to Texas in 1839, first locating on Arenosa Creek ten miles from what is now the site of Port Lavaca. The Erskine family lived there during the Linnville Raid,qv and Michael Erskine defended the homestead against a Comanche scouting party. He moved in 1840 to Gonzales County, where he purchased the José de la Baume Ranch on the Guadalupe River near the Capote Hills, twelve miles southeast of Seguin. He took an active part in the development of early Seguin. When Guadalupe County was organized, he was elected chief justice. Erskine prospered in the cattle industry and from his Capote Ranch in 1854 drove a herd of cattle to California. On the drive he had the protection of an armed escort under the command of James J. Callahan. Erskine kept a detailed diary of his experiences on this drive (it was published in 1979). He became involved with several mining ventures, which were apparently failures. In 1859 he returned to Capote Ranch and resumed the raising of cattle. He drove a herd to New Orleans in 1861. During the return trip he died at New Iberia, Louisiana, on May 15, 1862. Michael Erskine had ten children, two of whom, Andrew Nelsonqv and Alexander Madison, were in the Confederate Army during the Civil War.qv

BIBLIOGRAPHY: Michael Erskine Papers, Barker Texas History Center, University of Texas at Austin. J. Evetts Haley, *The Diary of Michael Erskine* (Midland, Texas: Nita Stewart Haley Memorial Library, 1979).

L. J. FitzSimon

ERSKINE, TEXAS. Erskine, on a site originally known as Kickapoo Springs, was near Kickapoo Creek twenty-eight miles southwest of Paint Rock in southwestern Concho County. The settlement was established in 1883 and acquired a post office the same year. In 1884 Erskine had a hotel, a general store, and a population of seventy. Local employment centered on the shipment of livestock and wool. Erskine apparently declined after the post office was moved to the nearby community of Vigo in 1887.

BIBLIOGRAPHY: W. L. Nicholson, *Post Route Map of the State of Texas* (1886).

Mary M. Standifer

ERUDIA, TEXAS. Erudia, ten miles west of McKinney in extreme western Collin County, was probably named by settler William Allen, after a character in his *Erudia, the Foreign Missionary to Our World* (1890). Erudia got a post office in 1895; in 1902 it was closed and mail was routed through Frisco. After the early 1900s Erudia disappeared from county maps.

BIBLIOGRAPHY: J. Lee and Lillian J. Stambaugh, *A History of Collin County* (Austin: Texas State Historical Association, 1958).

Laurie E. Jasinski

ERVENDBERG, LOUIS CACHAND (1809–1863?). Louis Cachand (christened Christian Friedrich Ludwig Cachand) Ervendberg, minister, local official, naturalist, and teacher, was born on May 3, 1809, at Rhoden (near Paderborn), Westphalia. He said his father was a French refugee. Except for a church post held at Anklam, Pomerania, and a residency at Herford, Prussia, his European background is unknown. Shortly after immigrating to America in 1836–37, Ervendberg established congregations in northern Illinois. In September 1838 he married fellow German immigrant Maria Sophie Dorothea Luise Muench of Teuto, Illinois. After a son's death, the couple traveled to the Houston area, where Ervendberg purchased ground for market gardening and presumably first met Ferdinand Jacob Lindheimer,qv who was similarly engaged.

At Houston on December 22, 1839, Ervendberg held the first recorded church services among Germansqv in Texas. Historian R. L. Bieseleqv assumes Ervendberg officiated regularly during the year before he moved to Blumenthal, Colorado County. While pastor at Industry, Cat Spring, Biegel, La Grange, and Columbus, Ervendberg perhaps also taught briefly with Joseph Anton Fischer, with whom he helped to found the first synod of German Christian Churches in Texas. Ervendberg became the first signer of the document incorporating Hermann University. About the time an infant daughter died, Ervendberg was invited by Prince Carl of Solms-Braunfelsqv to minister to the Adelsvereinqv immigrants, whom he accompanied from Indianola to the site of present-day New Braunfels. There he joined his wife, his young daughter, and a short-lived son, whose impending birth had required the separation. The German Protestant congregation was incorporated on October 15, 1845. In 1851 Ervendberg, whom Ferdinand von Roemerqv had considered somewhat distracted by other duties from the ministry, lost his pulpit to a more single-minded pastor. Ervendberg's principal memorial, the Western Texas Orphan Asylum, was established in 1848. In 1850 it was supplemented by Western Texas University, where agriculture and, thanks to Mrs. Ervendberg, domestic skills were stressed. There was also a rudimentary open-air theater. Ervendberg called the site Neu Wied and there produced silk and experimented with exotic kinds of wheat. A public school he helped organize soon supplanted his "college." He was also first president of the Comal County agricultural and horticultural society, the state's first such organization, first probate judge of Comal County, and first president of the Demokratischer Verein, a club founded to foster political unity among German immigrants. In 1854 he worked for participation in the German-American Convention, a meeting of German Americans in St. Louis.

During the mid-1850s Ervendberg began an affair with Franzisca Lange, an orphan under his care. This behavior scandalized New Braunfels and severely damaged his reputation. Being reconciled with his wife, Ervendberg sent her north with their three daughters to make plans for a new start in another state. However, he apparently changed his mind and on October 1, 1855, took Franzisca, then seventeen, and his two sons to Mexico City. Whether he actually married Franzisca after his first wife obtained a divorce is unclear, but the couple had at least two daughters.

At Wartenberg, a lost settlement north of Veracruz, Ervendberg corresponded with and collected plants for Asa Gray from early 1857 to late 1860. He returned to Mexico City briefly, then settled at Pachuca, Hidalgo, where in February 1863 he was reportedly shot to death by plunderers of his experiment-station payroll. However, information published in 1982 reports that he was writing from Paris to a Texas friend four years later. Descendants of Mrs. Ervendberg's remarriage following her divorce in May 1859 still lived in the altered orphanage near Gruene in the late twentieth century.

BIBLIOGRAPHY: Rudolph L. Biesele, *The History of the German Settlements in Texas, 1831–1861* (Austin: Von Boeckmann–Jones, 1930; rpt. 1964). S. W. Geiser, *Naturalists of the Frontier* (Dallas: Southern Methodist University, 1937; 2d ed. 1948). *Minetta Altgelt Goyne*

ERVIPIAME INDIANS. The Ervipiame (Chivipane, Cibipane, Hierbipiane, Huvipane, Hyerbipiame, Yerbipiame, Yrbipia) Indians were first known in 1673, at which time they lived in northeastern Coahuila and were in close association with bands that have been identified as Coahuiltecan in speech. In 1675 they were encountered by the Bosque-Larios expedition[qv] north of the Rio Grande in the southwestern part of the Edwards Plateau,[qv] again with bands of Coahuiltecan affiliation. In 1698 some Ervipiames were in the missions of northeastern Coahuila. It was not until 1707 that the Ervipiame Indians appeared in central Texas and became the dominant group in the Ranchería Grande[qv] de los Ervipiames, a series of settlements made up principally of Coahuiltecan refugees from northeastern Coahuila and the adjoining part of Texas, but later augmented by refugees from various Spanish missions in Texas and Coahuila. In 1722 the San Francisco Xavier de Náxara Mission was founded at San Antonio for the Ervipiames of Ranchería Grande, and their village near the mission was known as the Ervipiame suburb. Nearly all of the groups associated with the Ervipiame Indians in this village were Coahuiltecans. Most of the evidence indicates that the Ervipiames were originally Coahuiltecans. After this the Ervipiame Indians who remained at Ranchería Grande, or who retired to it from San Antonio after their mission was merged with San Antonio de Valero Mission, were associated mainly with groups identified as Tonkawans— Tonkawas, Yojuanes, and Mayeyes. They were with these Tonkawans at San Francisco Xavier de Horcasitas Mission, founded about 1748 on the San Gabriel River near present Rockdale. In the latter part of the eighteenth century the name Ervipiame was rarely mentioned. It seems clear that they lost their identity among the various bands which in the nineteenth century came to be called Tonkawa. Although most modern writers have concluded that the Ervipiames were Tonkawans, the historical evidence suggests that the Ervipiame Indians were originally Coahuiltecans who later became so closely associated with Tonkawans that they were regarded as Tonkawan. Attempts to equate the Ervipiames with the Enepiahe Indians of the La Salle expedition[qv] documents are not convincing. The Enepiahes were known only in the late seventeenth century, at which time the Ervipiames were still in the vicinity of northeastern Coahuila.

BIBLIOGRAPHY: Herbert Eugene Bolton, ed. and trans., *Athanase de Mézières and the Louisiana-Texas Frontier, 1768–1780* (2 vols., Cleveland: Arthur H. Clark, 1914). Herbert Eugene Bolton, ed., *Spanish Exploration in the Southwest, 1542–1706* (New York: Scribner, 1908; rpt., New York: Barnes and Noble, 1959). Frederick Webb Hodge, ed., *Handbook of American Indians North of Mexico* (2 vols., Washington: GPO, 1907, 1910; rpt., New York: Pageant, 1959). William W. Newcomb, *The Indians of Texas* (Austin: University of Texas Press, 1961). A. F. Sjoberg, "The Culture of the Tonkawa, A Texas Indian," *Texas Journal of Science* 5 (September 1953). *Thomas N. Campbell*

ERWIN, FRANK CRAIG, JR. (1920–1980). Frank Craig Erwin, Jr., chairman of the University of Texas System[qv] Board of Regents, was born in Waxahachie, Texas, on January 24, 1920, one of two sons of Frank Craig and Margaret (Edwards) Erwin, Sr. He enrolled at the University of Texas in 1937 and graduated with a law degree in 1948, having interrupted his academic career in 1942 to serve in the navy during World War II.[qv] After a brief, successful legal career, Erwin entered the political arena in 1961, assisting Secretary of the Navy John B. Connally[qv] in his quest for the Texas governorship. Erwin quickly emerged as one of Connally's foremost advisors and developed friendships with many leading figures within the conservative faction of the Democratic party[qv] in Texas. He first made a statewide name for himself as chairman of the resolutions committee at the 1962 state Democratic convention. His hard work on behalf of the conservatives soon got him elected secretary (1962–63), and later chairman (1963–64), of the state Democratic Executive Committee. Later he served as Democratic national committeeman from Texas (1964–68), vice chairman of the Texas delegation to the 1964 Democratic National Convention, and Texas delegate and spokesman at the 1968 Democratic National Convention. His relationship with Connally led to a friendship with Lyndon B. Johnson,[qv] with whom Erwin worked closely for the development of the Lyndon Baines Johnson Library[qv] and Museum on the campus of the University of Texas at Austin. In 1972 Erwin was appointed to the board of directors of the LBJ Family Foundation, a position he retained until his death. In all circumstances Erwin was loyal to Connally's conservative group and was a major player in the struggles against the state's liberal Democratic wing.

Although politics was important to his life, Erwin's foremost passion was the University of Texas. From 1963 to 1975 he sat on the University of Texas System Board of Regents; he was chairman from 1966 to 1971. Working closely with his political allies in the state legislature, he increased university appropriations from $40.4 million in 1963–64 to $349.7 million in 1975–76. He further increased the system's available revenue by expanding the bonding capacity of the Permanent University Fund[qv] from 20 percent to 30 percent. Much of the money was allocated to expanding the university's physical plant, and the building contracts issued by the regents during Erwin's tenure totaled more than $762 million. This building program provided the University of Texas System with more than sixteen million square feet of new indoor space, of which the Austin branch received more than 6 million. The system's enrollment also increased rapidly, from 29,940 in 1963–64 to 77,437 in 1974–75. By the time Erwin stepped down, the University of Texas System, which he had helped form in 1967, comprised twelve component institutions and was one of the nation's leading state-supported systems of higher education.

In spite of these accomplishments, Erwin's career was marked by controversy. He firmly believed in his own authority to shape the university in the image he chose, and sought to ensure a system where the faculty taught, the students learned, and the regents made policy. This attitude clashed with that of a student protest movement that saw in Erwin an example of the societal elite who, in the student protesters' view, dominated America. Erwin first attracted notoriety in December 1964, when, on behalf of the regents, he fired the comptroller of the University of Texas at Austin. It was charged that this action enabled the regents to award building contracts to political allies rather than to contractors selected on the basis of merit; a major controversy arose when another regent publicly objected to the practice. Erwin's authority reached its zenith when he was appointed chairman of the board of regents in December 1966. With the support of most of the Texas legislature and of his fellow regents, Erwin often displayed an intolerance of opposing views, especially those of the left-leaning movements that were emerging on college campuses across the nation. Determined not to let the University of Texas become a voice of the counterculture, he began his stand in 1967, working behind the scenes to remove professors whose politics he considered unpatriotic. Later, in the hopes of stifling the growing Students for a Democratic Society and Young Socialist Alliance movements, he attempted to close campus facilities to nonstudents and to student organizations with nonstudent members. After the shootings at Kent State University in Ohio in May 1970, Erwin and the regents successfully fought student and faculty initiatives to cancel classes to protest the shootings and the Vietnam War. The next year Erwin led the regents to adopt a policy prohibiting administrators from negotiating with student demonstrators under any circumstances. Although such policies alienated many students, Erwin's firm control was widely praised in the conservative Texas legislature, which continued to increase university allocations.

Erwin had other problems with the student body and rarely tolerated student opposition. In October 1969 the board of regents decided to bulldoze several hundred feet of a local creek so they could expand the football stadium. In an attempt to stop the bulldozing, student protesters chained themselves to trees, and Erwin, complete with hard hat and bullhorn, personally oversaw their arrests. In another well-publicized incident, student protesters demonstrated against Lyndon Johnson, who was visiting the Austin campus. Erwin verbally chastised the protesters and then stood by as the police arrested the leaders. In 1974 Erwin, bluntly declaring, "we do not fund what we do not control," tried to cut funding for the student newspaper, the *Daily Texan*,qv because of its longstanding opposition to him. Time and time again students, student groups, and faculty called for his resignation but were ignored by Erwin and by the legislature, which reconfirmed him in 1969 with only three dissenting votes. Although Erwin was supported by most of the legislature, he had a tempestuous relationship with many members of the university faculty. His hands-on style of leadership led to conflicts with those professors who considered the academy to be their jurisdiction. The conflict culminated with the firing in July 1970 of Dean John Silber of the College of Arts and Sciences, who had led the opposition to a proposed splitting of his college into two. The dismissal was perceived by many as politically motivated, since Silber's growing popularity was often considered a threat to the regents' control of the university. After the dismissal, several notable professors fled the university.

After a stint as the official university lobbyist to the 1975 legislative session, Erwin left the University of Texas System and returned to the practice of law. In 1979 he was honored by the board of regents with a resolution expressing appreciation for all his years of hard work; later that year he was named a university distinguished alumnus. He died of a heart attack on October 1, 1980, in Galveston. Before the funeral, his body lay in state in the Great Hall of the Lyndon Baines Johnson Library, an honor previously granted only to Johnson himself. His funeral was held at the huge University Special Events Center (later renamed the Frank C. Erwin, Jr., Special Events Center), a fitting site for a ceremony honoring a man who had such a dramatic impact on Texas higher education. Jeff Sandefer, part-time UT business school lecturer and Houston businessman, organized the Frank Erwin History Project in 1993 to develop oral histories and archives on Erwin with the goal of writing a biography.

BIBLIOGRAPHY: *Austin Citizen*, November 23, 1974. Deborah Lynn Bay, The Influence of Frank Erwin on Texas Higher Education (Ph.D. dissertation, University of Texas at Austin, 1988). Dallas *Times Herald*, December 1, 1974. *On Campus*, October 13, 1980. Vertical Files, Barker Texas History Center, University of Texas at Austin.

Mitchell Lerner

ERWIN, SAMUEL AUGUSTUS (1786–1854). Samuel Augustus Erwin, early settler, was born in Virginia in 1789. He lived in Tennessee during his adult years before his arrival in Texas and was reportedly a friend of David Crockett.qv Crockett had once camped near the site of present Honey Grove and may have recommended the location to Erwin, who moved with his wife, Sallie (Crisp), and three children to the area that is now Fannin County in the late 1830s. They were the first permanent settlers in the east central part of the county. Following the arrival of additional settlers, Erwin helped found the community of Honey Grove in 1842. When the townsite was surveyed about 1850 and awarded a post office, Erwin was appointed the first postmaster. During his life in Honey Grove, he also worked as a surveyor and as a justice of the peace. He died in 1854.

BIBLIOGRAPHY: Floy Crandall Hodge, *A History of Fannin County* (Hereford, Texas: Pioneer, 1966).

Brian Hart

ERWIN, TEXAS. Erwin is on Farm Road 149 near the headwaters of Turkey Creek four miles west of Anderson in west central Grimes County. The area was first settled in the early 1830s, although it was not until the late 1800s that a community was established by local cotton farmers and cattle raisers. The area was originally known as Fuqua's Prairie, after the Ephraim Fuqua family, which settled there in 1832. A Methodist church known as Steele's Chapel was built a mile west of what was to become the townsite, and a Baptist congregation, the Fuqua Prairie Baptist Church, was organized in the area in 1877. A black congregation known as the Green Valley Church was established south of the settlement. During the 1890s Will H. and Simon Fuqua each operated a cotton gin in Erwin, and Will Fuqua ran a general store. The community had a post office from 1896 to 1923. In 1900 Erwin reported a population of ten. In 1936 its population remained ten, and the community had one business. The last available population estimate is from the late 1940s, when Erwin reported twenty-five residents and one business. In 1990 the community had a cemetery and a few scattered dwellings.

BIBLIOGRAPHY: Grimes County Historical Commission, *History of Grimes County, Land of Heritage and Progress* (Dallas: Taylor, 1982).

Charles Christopher Jackson

ESBON, TEXAS. Esbon, near San Fernando Creek in northwestern Llano County, was originally called Simpson's Bend for five Simpson brothers who settled at the site. The settlement was a post office as early as 1904, and Jeff Harlow, the postmaster, built a gin there by 1914. Esbon reported a store and a population of twenty-five from 1933 to the late 1940s; during the mid-1960s its population was estimated at thirty. In the early 1980s the Esbon community was named on county highway maps, but no buildings were shown at the site.

Alice Gray Upchurch

ESCAJEDA, JOSEFINA (1893–1981). Josefina Escajeda, teacher and folklorist, was from El Paso County, where she probably lived in Fabens, Clint, or San Elizario, or all three. She lived all her life in the area. She was one of several Mexican-descent women folklorists, such as Jovita González de Mirales and Fermina Guerra,qv who gained attention in the twentieth century. Josefina belonged to a prominent family, one of the oldest in El Paso County. She was considered a pioneer of Fabens, where she married J. M. "Joe" Escajeda, a local farmer, and raised a stepdaughter. Before her marriage she taught school in Clint for six years. Josefina Escajeda helped organize enchilada suppers, dances, and children's programs to raise funds for Our Lady at Mount Carmel Catholic Church (Old Mission). She also sang and played the organ there. She collected several stories for the Texas Folklore Society'sqv publication *Puro Mexicano*, edited by J. Frank Dobieqv in 1935. These included "The Witch of Cenecu," "Doña Carolina Learns a Lesson," "La Casa de la Labor," "Agapito Brings a Treat," and "A Hanged Man Sends Rain." Some of her stories were also used by Charles L. Sonnichsenqv in an article, "Mexican Spooks From El Paso," published in 1937 in *Straight Texas* and edited by Dobie and Mody C. Boatright.qv Josefina Escajeda died on March 8, 1981, and was buried at Mount Carmel Cemetery.

BIBLIOGRAPHY: El Paso *Times*, March 11, 1981.

Cynthia E. Orozco

ESCALANTE ALVARADO, GARCÍA DE (?–?). García de Escalante Alvarado was born in 1516 in Laredo, on the Bay of Biscay, to the licentiate Escalante (Christian name unknown) and Doña Beatriz Osorio. His father served twenty years in the court of Holy Roman Emperor Charles V (Charles I of Spain). Escalante Alvarado commanded a maritime expedition to salvage three treasure-laden Spanish cargo ships that wrecked on the Texas coast in 1554. He, like Luis de Moscoso Alvarado,^{qv} was a nephew of the renowned Pedro de Alvarado of the Mexican Conquest.

In 1538 Escalante sailed for the Spanish Indies to serve under Pedro de Alvarado, first in Guatemala, then in Nueva Galicia, where he put down the native uprising in which Alvarado was killed in 1541. In 1542 he embarked as a captain and royal factor in the voyage of Ruy López de Villalobos, nephew of Viceroy Antonio de Mendoza, to the Philippines and Moluccas. He wrote an account of that venture, which cost López his life. Only 144 of the 400 participants returned to Spain, almost seven years later, by way of India and Portugal.

Escalante returned to New Spain in the company of Viceroy Luis de Velasco in 1550. In 1552 he was serving as *alcalde mayor* of Vera Cruz (still at its second site, fifteen miles up the coast from present Veracruz). He wrote directly to the crown to urge that Viceroy Velasco be ordered to pursue the possibility of navigation to the Spice Islands and China, but not for another seven years was a new voyage undertaken. He saw to construction of port facilities on the mainland adjacent to the island fortress of San Juan de Ulúa while submitting for royal approval a comprehensive port-development plan. When a hurricane devastated San Juan de Ulúa and Vera Cruz on September 2, 1552, he urged removal of Vera Cruz to higher ground.

When word reached Vera Cruz early in June 1554 of the wreck of three ships on the Texas coast, Escalante was chosen to organize a salvage fleet of six vessels. The fleet operated in conjunction with Ángel de Villafañe,^{qv} who led a land march along the coast in search of survivors. Villafañe reached the wreck site on Padre Island first and began the salvage operations, which lasted until September 12. Escalante, who reached the site on Mary Magdalene's day, gave the Padre Island shore a name that appeared on various European maps for years to come: Médanos de Madalena—"Magdalene's Dunes." He kept a written account of the salvage operation, which contains a wealth of information.

Despite his part in the López de Villalobos voyage and the largely successful salvage effort, Escalante failed in his bid for a compensatory royal grant. Nothing more is heard of him after his account of the Padre Island treasure. *See also* PADRE ISLAND SPANISH SHIPWRECKS OF 1554.

BIBLIOGRAPHY: J. Barto Arnold III and Robert S. Weddle, *The Nautical Archeology of Padre Island: The Spanish Shipwrecks of 1554* (New York: Academic Press, 1978). David McDonald and J. Barto Arnold III, *Documentary Sources for the Wreck of the New Spain Fleet of 1554* (Austin: Texas Antiquities Committee, 1979).   Robert S. Weddle

ESCALONA PÉREZ, BEATRIZ (1903–1979). Beatriz Escalona Pérez (Noloesca, "La Chata"), Mexican-American comedienne, was born in San Antonio, Texas, on August 20, 1903, the daughter of a man named Escalona and Simona Pérez, both originally from Galeana, Nuevo León, Mexico. She was raised in San Antonio but spent much of her childhood in Monterrey, Nuevo León, with relatives. By the age of ten she was already drawn to the theater through frequent visits to the Teatro Independencia in Monterrey. Indeed, she was so entranced by theatrical entertainment that she sold bouquets to earn admission. In San Antonio she worked part-time as an usher at the Teatro Zaragoza (*see* CARLOS VILLALONGÍN DRAMATIC COMPANY *and* HERNÁNDEZ, CONCEPCIÓN). At the time, the Teatro Zaragoza, located in the heart of the Mexican-American community, was a showcase for entertainment in Spanish. By sixteen Beatriz had moved up to a position in the box office at the new Teatro Nacional. While working at the Nacional, she met a Cuban-born performer, José Areu, who was a member of the variety company Los Hermanos Areu. He invited her to travel with the company. Beatriz left San Antonio and studied singing and acting with the Areus. She made her first performance at the Teatro Colón in El Paso at the age of eighteen. At Areu's suggestion, she took the stage name Noloesca, an anagram of her last name. She married Areu. Her first and only child, Belia (who later also became a successful performer), was born in Mexico City on October 31, 1921.

Noloesca toured throughout Mexico and the Southwestern United States with Los Hermanos Areu. She performed in a variety of popular genres: risqué *bataclán* numbers (similar to burlesque), dramatic plays and comic sketches, and traditional and humorous Mexican songs. Although Noloesca had originally aspired to be a glamorous *vedette* (chorus girl), she discovered that she had a special gift for comedy and was encouraged by the Areus to develop her talent. She increasingly specialized in comic roles.

In 1930 she left the company, ended her marriage, and formed her own variety company, Atracciones Noloesca. Between 1930 and 1936 she managed and acted with her company and periodically contracted to perform with other companies. Most notably, she worked with Mexican entertainer Eusebio Pirrín, who was otherwise known by his stage name Don Catarino. Noloesca met and married her second husband, an immigration employee, José de la Torre, in Tijuana. Torre became her comic partner. In 1936 she returned to San Antonio, where she performed at the Teatro Nacional.

Probably in the late 1920s and early 1930s Noloesca developed the popular comic figure she maintained throughout the remainder of her career. She called the character "La Chata," an affectionate nickname that meant "button-nosed." She modeled the character on Mexican and Mexican-American maids. Trademarks of La Chata were a brightly printed, flounced cotton dress, perky little pigtails tied with big bows, and chunky men's shoes with boldly striped socks. Through her costume, gestures, and verbal wit Beatriz invented a character that was simultaneously innocent and savvy, sweet and strong-willed.

After the demise of her first company, Noloesca organized a second company, "Beatriz Noloesca 'La Chata' Compañía Mexicana," in San Antonio in 1938. She, her second husband, her daughter, and four hired San Antonio natives formed the troupe. Their fare varied but generally consisted of Mexican, Mexican-American, and American song and dance numbers and comedy sketches in which Noloesca starred. These sketches, performed by La Chata and a male partner, were the highlight of the productions. From the late 1930s to the 1950s Noloesca took her company on the road and performed to a range of Spanish-speaking audiences in the Southwest, Midwest, South, and Northeast, as well as Cuba. Significant cities on the tour included San Antonio, Chicago, Tampa, New York City, and Havana. By locating Spanish-speaking audiences beyond her native Southwest, Noloesca was able to sustain her company and her career through the 1940s. She was responsible for handling company finances, hiring and training performers, developing and directing the productions, and arranging contracts and tours. She was particularly successful in obtaining performance contracts and showed remarkable self-confidence in negotiating with theater managers. Her company performed at the Teatro Hispano in New York City in the 1940s.

In the early 1950s, after an extended tour in New York, Noloesca returned with her daughter to their home in San Antonio. She married her third husband, Rubén Escobedo, a San Antonio musician. She worked in radio and continued to do live performances, including many benefits, through the 1970s. In 1975 she was honored by the Mexican National Association of Actors in San Antonio. She died in San Antonio on April 4, 1979.

BIBLIOGRAPHY: Houston *Post*, February 7, 1982. Nicolás Kanellos, *A History of Hispanic Theatre in the United States: Origins to 1940* (Austin: University of Texas Press, 1990). Elizabeth C. Ramírez, *Foot-*

lights across the Border: A History of Spanish-Language Professional Theatre on the Texas Stage (New York: Lang, 1990). San Antonio *Express News*, December 4, 1977. Pamela A. Smith, Beatriz Noloesca, "La Chata": An Oral History (M.A. thesis, University of Texas at Austin, 1991). Tomás Ybarra-Frausto, "La Chata Noloesca: Figura del Donaire," in *Mexican American Theatre: Then and Now*, ed. N. Kanellos (Houston: Arte Público Press, 1983).

Pamela A. Smith and Elizabeth C. Ramírez

ESCANDÓN, JOSÉ DE (1700–1770). José de Escandón, South Texas colonizer, was born in Soto la Marina, Santander, Spain, on May 19, 1700, one of three sons of Juan de Escandón and Francisca de la Helguera. He is known as the colonizer and first governor of the colony of Nuevo Santander,qv which extended from the Pánuco River in Mexico to the Guadalupe River in Texas. He founded over twenty towns or villas and a number of missions in the colony, including Camargo, Reynosa, Mier, and Revilla south of the Rio Grande and Laredo and Nuestra Señora de los Dolores Haciendaqv north of the Rio Grande. For his colonization efforts Escandón is sometimes called the "father" of the lower Rio Grande valley.

Escandón received his early education in his native town. At the age of fifteen he arrived at Mérida, Yucatán, where he served as a cadet in the Mounted Encomenderos Company. In 1727 he subdued an Indian uprising in Celaya and received the rank of sergeant major of the regiment at Querétaro. In 1740 the viceroy of Mexico named him colonel of the military companies of Querétaro, since he had been successful in pacifying the Indians. In 1746 Escandón was commissioned to inspect the country between Tampico and the San Antonio River, later known as Nuevo Santander. In January 1747 he sent seven divisions into the area, and in October he presented a colonization plan. After delays by the Spanish bureaucracy, Escandón was made governor and captain general of Nuevo Santander on June 1, 1748. In 1749 he was made Count of Sierra Gorda and Knight of the Order of Santiago by Fernando VI, and he began establishing settlements along the Rio Grande. The first two were Camargo (founded on March 5) and Reynosa (March 14). On August 22, 1750, Escandón granted José Vázquez Borregoqv fifty sitios for the founding of Dolores, and on October 10 he sent Vicente Guerra to set up Revilla, twenty leagues northwest of Camargo. On March 6, 1753, Escandón founded the town of Mier, and in 1755 he granted permission to Tomás Sánchez de la Barrera y Garzaqv to found Laredo, the largest and most successful permanent Spanish settlement in Southwest Texas.

In 1724 Escandón married María Antonia de Ossio y Ocampo of Spain. Two children were born to this marriage: Ana María, who became a nun, and a son, José de Escandón y Ossio, who became a priest. María Antonia died in 1736, and in 1737 Escandón married María Josefa de Llera from Querétaro. They had seven children. After the appointment of a royal commission in 1767, the settlers of Nuevo Santander were assigned the land grants that Escandón had promised them. Grants were made to residents of the colonies of the Rio Grande, thus starting the colonization of South Texas from the Rio Grande to the San Antonio River. José de Escandón was accused by Diego Corrido of maladministration, and he had to leave for Mexico City to defend himself. He died during the trial, on September 10, 1770, and was buried in Mexico City. In 1773 his son Manuel Ignacio de Escandón y Llera petitioned the court for a settlement; a decision rendered by the court completely exonerated the count.

BIBLIOGRAPHY: Carlos E. Castañeda, *Our Catholic Heritage in Texas* (7 vols., Austin: Von Boeckmann–Jones, 1936–58; rpt., New York: Arno, 1976). *Estado General de las Fundaciones Hechas por D. José de Escandón en la Colonia del Nuevo Santander, Costa del Seno Mexicano*, 2 vols., Publicaciones del Archivo General de la Nación 14 and 15 (Mexico City: Talleres Gráficos de la Nación México, 1930). Joaquín Meade, *La Huasteca Tamaulipeca* (3 vols., Ciudad Victoria: Instituto de Investigaciones Históricas, Universidad Autónoma de Tamaulipas, 1977). Hubert J. Miller, *José de Escandón, Colonizer of Nuevo Santander* (Edinburg, Texas: Nuevo Santander Press, 1980). Florence J. Scott, *Historical Heritage of the Lower Rio Grande* (San Antonio: Naylor, 1937; rev. ed., Waco: Texian, 1966; rpt., Rio Grande City, Texas: La Retama Press, 1970).

Clotilde P. García

ESCANJAQUE INDIANS. The Escanjaque (Ercansaque, Escansaque, Escanxaque, Esquansaque, Excanjaque) Indians are known only from the seventeenth century, and their area remains in doubt. Some writers have interpreted the evidence as indicating that the Escanjaques lived in north central Texas; others have placed them in western Oklahoma. Early attempts to identify the Escanjaques with the Kansa Indians were not successful because it was found that the Kansa Indians lived elsewhere in the seventeenth century. It has been suggested that the Escanjaques were Apaches, but today most writers are inclined to identify them as a Wichita group, possibly the same as the Yscanis of the eighteenth century.

BIBLIOGRAPHY: Bancroft, *History of the North Mexican States and Texas* (2 vols., San Francisco: History Company, 1886, 1889). Herbert E. Bolton, "The Jumano Indians in Texas, 1650–1771," *Quarterly of the Texas State Historical Association* 15 (July 1911). George P. Hammond and Agapito Rey, eds., *Don Juan de Oñate: Colonizer of New Mexico, 1595–1628* (Santa Fe: Patalacio, 1927; rpt., Albuquerque: University of New Mexico Press, 1953). George E. Hyde, *The Pawnee Indians* (Denver: University of Denver Press, 1951; enlarged ed., Norman: University of Oklahoma Press, 1974). Albert H. Schroeder, "A Re-Analysis of the Routes of Coronado and Oñate into the Plains in 1541 and 1601," *Plains Anthropologist* 7 (February 1962). S. L. Tyler and H. D. Taylor, "The Report of Fray Alonso de Posadas in Relation to Quivira and Teguayo," *New Mexico Historical Review* 33 (October 1958).

Thomas N. Campbell

ESCOBAR, ELEUTERIO, JR. (1894–1970). Eleuterio Escobar, civil-rights activist, was born in Laredo, Texas, on September 11, 1894, to Eleuterio and Petra Martínez Escobar. The elder Escobar, a police officer, died in 1906, after which his wife worked as a cook. Escobar, Jr., married Cecilia Canales of Benavides in 1923. They had no children. He attended Laredo public schools and a Mexican school in Pearsall. His formal education ended with the sixth grade. As a child he sold milk, grubbed brush, picked onions, and worked as a farm and ranch hand. He established a bicycle repair and rental shop in Pearsall around 1912 and subsequently worked with Antonio Martínez as a traveling quilt and blanket salesman along the Mexican border. In 1918 he volunteered to join the army in World War I;qv he served in San Antonio and France and upon his return worked as a salesman for Fox Company in San Antonio.

In 1924 Escobar and Martínez set up the San Antonio Mercantile Company, which specialized in such products as blankets and quilts. Apparently Escobar sold the business to Martínez, and in 1924 he and Cecilia established the Escobar Furniture Company, the only furniture store owned by Mexican Americansqv in San Antonio at the time. They hired John C Solísqv as an employee. In 1926 Escobar invested in real estate. He donated land for a baseball field for boys (later known as Escobar Field) and helped organize the Hispano Americano League, a baseball association.

Around 1931 the Escobars sold Victrolas, records, Orthophonics, and Electrolas; Escobar was a songwriter and served as an agent for several local musicians from 1930 to 1934. In 1936 he formed the International Leather and Importing Company and the EECO Silver Craft Manufacture. Due to illness, he liquidated the leather business in 1943, but he kept the EECO until 1953. During World War IIqv his business recycled bottle caps. Escobar also worked as a real estate broker until 1970.

He participated in civil-rights organizational activities of the Mexican-descent community. He attended the first informal meeting of the Order of Sons of America[qv] and was familiar with the work of a similar group, the Order of Sons of Texas. He joined the Knights of America and served as a delegate at the Harlingen Convention of 1927.[qv] That year he joined other businessmen and professionals in founding the Mexican Casino, a social center. Along with Henry Guerra in 1932 he helped found the Association of Independent Voters, an organization that endorsed candidates sympathetic to Hispanic interests. In 1933 he organized precinct meetings to help elect Guerra park commissioner.

In 1934 Escobar served as chairman of the playground and school facilities committee in the League of United Latin American Citizens[qv] Council 16, and later he was selected as president of the Pro Schools Defense League,[qv] a coalition of fifty organizations representing 75,000 persons of Mexican descent in San Antonio. The league fought for better school facilities to avert overcrowding, prevent fires and eliminate health hazards, and foster education, especially through the building of playgrounds, classrooms, cafeterias, and auditoriums. Escobar helped reorganize the league as the School Improvement League in 1947 and subsequently neglected his business for three years. He worked with the group until 1954. LULAC honored him in 1949, and around 1959 Eleuterio Escobar School in San Antonio was named after him. He retired in the 1960s. He wrote an autobiography, which is unpublished. On May 10, 1970, he died of tuberculosis and was buried at San Fernando Archdiocesan Cemetery in San Antonio. His will was contested by Emma E. Elizondo, the daughter of Orfelina Elizondo and allegedly Escobar's daughter. Escobar papers are located at the Nettie Lee Benson Latin American Collection[qv] at the University of Texas at Austin.

BIBLIOGRAPHY: María G. Flores, comp., and Laura Gutiérrez-Witt, ed., *Mexican American Archives at the Benson Collection: A Guide for Users* (General Libraries, University of Texas at Austin, 1981). Mario T. Garcia, *Mexican Americans: Leadership, Ideology, and Identity, 1930–1960* (New Haven: Yale University Press, 1989).

Cynthia E. Orozco

ESCOBAR, ELIGIO ROQUE (1926–1994). Eligio Roque Escobar, musician, the fourth son and fifth child of Eleuterio and Andrea (Farías) Escobar, Sr., was born on December 1, 1926, and reared in Ben Bolt, Jim Wells County, Texas. He traced his family's origins to Escobares, a small town on the Rio Grande in Starr County. On September 24, 1944, he married Jesusa Koehler, with whom he had two daughters and two sons. He served in the United States Army of Occupation in Japan after World War II.[qv] For the first part of his life he worked principally as an oilfield truck driver around Alice. Through the influence of an uncle, Escobar learned to play guitar and sing as a child. He honed his skills as he grew to adulthood. He became a professional musician, however, after an automobile accident in 1960 injured his legs severely and rendered him unable to pursue his previous employment. He developed his Texas-Mexican conjunto[qv] music during his convalescence and thereafter launched his professional career. Beginning in 1962 Escobar recorded more than 250 songs. Although he sang in both English and Spanish, his voice became most familiar to Spanish-language radio[qv] listeners. Among his best-known songs were "Cuando Dos Almas," "Rosario Nocturno," and "El Gambler." Perhaps his most famous song, "El Veterano," spoke to the feelings of the Mexican-American veteran of the Second World War and endeared him to a sizable audience of postwar Hispanic music lovers. He likewise toured extensively with Spanish-language musicians in the United States and Mexico. Escobar helped launch the musical career of his daughter, Linda Escobar, who gained prominence as a singer and recording artist. After eventually moving in with his family in Corpus Christi, Escobar often used his music to benefit such civic organizations as the American G.I. Forum,[qv] of which he and his brothers were members. Firmly rooted in his South Texas culture, Escobar was an avid fisherman and hunter. Toward the end of his life, along with his music, he worked as a wildlife manager on South Texas ranches. He was revered by many for his generous spirit and easygoing manner as well as for his unique musical style. Escobar died of cancer on October 4, 1994, and is buried in Corpus Christi.

BIBLIOGRAPHY: Corpus Christi *Caller-Times,* October 10, 1994.

Thomas H. Kreneck

ESCOBARES, TEXAS. Escobares is between the Rio Grande and U.S. Highway 83 a mile east of Roma–Los Saenz in south central Starr County; it has expanded to fill the area between Roma and Garceño. The community is served by rural mail delivery from Roma. It is in the original Spanish land grants of the Mier jurisdiction given north of the Rio Grande to José de Escandón's[qv] colonists in the mid-eighteenth century. In 1899 Escobares had a public school that employed one teacher and had an enrollment of thirty-three. In 1940 the settlement comprised a store, a school, a church, and a population of ten. In 1990 it had 1,705 inhabitants, several stores, and a school. Sacred Heart Catholic Church, built in the early 1940s with seating for 188, was replaced in 1991 by a 500-seat Spanish Colonial–style church. The name Escobares is from a colloquial Spanish term that probably refers to fields of broomcorn.

BIBLIOGRAPHY: *Rio Grande Roundup: Story of Texas' Tropical Borderland* (Mission, Texas: Border Kingdom, 1980). Florence J. Scott, *Historical Heritage of the Lower Rio Grande* (San Antonio: Naylor, 1937; rev. ed., Waco: Texian, 1966; rpt., Rio Grande City, Texas: La Retama Press, 1970). J. Lee and Lillian J. Stambaugh, *The Lower Rio Grande Valley of Texas* (San Antonio: Naylor, 1954). Valley By-Liners, *Gift of the Rio* (Mission, Texas: Border Kingdom Press, 1975).

Dick D. Heller, Jr.

ESCOBAS, TEXAS. Escobas is on Escobas Creek and Farm Road 16 nineteen miles northeast of Zapata in Zapata County. The area, which was part of the José de Escandón[qv] colony of Nuevo Santander, was originally settled by Mexican rancheros in the mid-eighteenth century. They made no permanent settlement at the site but divided the region into large ranches. By 1897 a local school with one teacher and thirty students served the area. The Escobas townsite was called Laguna de Escobas before the late 1920s, when oil was discovered in the area; by the late 1930s the Texas Company (*see* TEXACO, INC.), the principal producer in the Escobas oilfield, had built the settlement of Escobas and provided a school there. The community had a post office and was a supply point for the local oil companies. Local students were bused to schools in Zapata after they reached the fifth grade. In 1940 the community reported one business and a population of twenty-five. In 1991 Escobas continued to report a population of twenty-five and had a few small homes and a combination general store and gas station. Oilfields and the Jacinteña and Los Mesquines ranches surround the site.

BIBLIOGRAPHY: Virgil N. Lott and Mercurio Martinez, *The Kingdom of Zapata* (San Antonio: Naylor, 1953). Florence J. Scott, *Historical Heritage of the Lower Rio Grande* (San Antonio: Naylor, 1937; rev. ed., Waco: Texian, 1966; rpt., Rio Grande City, Texas: La Retama Press, 1970).

Dick D. Heller, Jr.

ESCOBAS CREEK. Escobas Creek rises five miles west of Randado in northeastern Zapata County (at 27°05′ N, 98°57′ W) and runs southwest for sixteen miles to its mouth on Solomoneño Creek, eight miles west of Escobas (at 27°03′ N, 99°08′ W). The stream is dammed along its middle course to form tanks. It traverses an area of low-rolling hills and prairies surfaced by clay and sandy loams that support grasses and mesquite.

ESCONDIDO CREEK (Bexar County). Escondido Creek rises in eastern Bexar County (at 29°29′ N, 98°19′ W) and runs southeast for six miles to its mouth on Martinez Creek, a half mile east of Loop 1604 (at 29°26′ N, 98°15′ W). It traverses rolling terrain surfaced by clay loam and expansive clay soils that support mesquite and grasses.

_____ (Jim Wells County). Escondido Creek, also known as Sancito Creek, rises two miles south of Palito Blanco in western Jim Wells County (at 27°33′ N, 98°11′ W) and runs southeast for twenty-six miles to its mouth on Santa Gertrudis Creek, two miles south of Kingsville in central Kleberg County (at 27°28′ N, 97°51′ W). It traverses flat to rolling terrain with local shallow depressions and escarpments, surfaced by loose sand and clay and sandy loams that support water-tolerant hardwoods, conifers, scrub brush, and grasses.

_____ (Karnes County). Escondido Creek rises just west of the New Bremen Cemetery in western Karnes County (at 28°50′ N, 98°01′ W) and runs northeast for twelve miles to its mouth on the San Antonio River, three miles southwest of Runge (at 28°51′ N, 97°45′ W). It is intermittent in its upper reaches. The creek traverses flat to rolling terrain surfaced by clay and sandy loams that support water-tolerant hardwoods and grasses.

ESCOPETA. The escopeta or escopeda was a light, inexpensive, .69 caliber musket or shotgun, with a 38½″ barrel, popularized in the mid-seventeenth century by Spanish cavalry on the colonial frontier. This Spanish military weapon, designated as the standard shoulder arm for use by both regular light infantry and cavalry troops until the mid-eighteenth century, was considered too short and small of caliber for use against European infantry after that time. But when the mainline colonial regiments and militia in Mexico, Louisiana, and Florida were armed with 1752 and 1791 pattern regulation muskets, the mounted presidial forces and local militia units in Texas continued to use the escopeta, which was still considered acceptable for use against Indians as specified by the Royal Regulations of 1772. The escopeta was carried across the saddle bow in a soft leather sheath called a _funda_ or _ord_. John C. Duval[qv] wrote that the escopeta was a "a short bell-mouth, bull-doggish looking musket, carrying a very heavy ball, which is 'death by law' when it hits, but that is seldom, for they shoot with little accuracy. They are good for nothing except to make a noise."

The escopeta was by regulation, and to some degree in fact, replaced as the standard cavalry shoulder arm by the English-made .615 caliber Baker carbine after the Mexican war for independence in 1821. Nevertheless, it remained quite popular with mounted troops on the northern frontier. It was carried in great numbers by the troops of Gen. Antonio López de Santa Anna[qv] in Texas in 1836, although, according to Duval, "the Mexicans never place them on the shoulder, but hold them with both hands above their heads and fire at random, which accounts in a great measure for the little execution done by them." Duval, a survivor of the battle of Coleto,[qv] armed himself with an escopeta, which he described as "a short light 'blunderbuss' used by the Mexican cavalry," as well as with his rifle. He claims to have loaded the escopeta with "forty 'blue whistlers' and powder in proportion" in expectation of a cavalry charge against James W. Fannin's[qv] hollow infantry square at the battle of Coleto. On firing the gun, Duval went "heels over head" through the rank to his rear; so great was the recoil that he thought he had been shot by the enemy.

In fact, one reason that Texas forces were able to inflict such terrible casualties on their Mexican foes while themselves sustaining only light casualties—at the battle of Mier, for instance, the Texans killed and wounded an estimated 800 of the enemy while losing but thirty of their own—was the recoil of the escopeta. The Mexican soldier was a notoriously poor shot because he often closed his eyes and flinched while firing. This phenomenon was due to the fact that his cartridges contained twice as much powder as required in each charge, so that his weapon kicked brutally.

BIBLIOGRAPHY: Sidney B. Brinckerhoff and Pierce A. Chamberlain, _Spanish Military Weapons in Colonial America, 1700–1821_ (Harrisburg, Pennsylvania: Stackpole, 1972). John Crittenden Duval, _The Adventures of Big Foot Wallace, the Texas Ranger and Hunter_ (Macon, Georgia: Burke, 1870). John Crittenden Duval, _Early Times in Texas, or the Adventures of Jack Dobell_ (Austin: Gammel, 1892; new ed., Lincoln: University of Nebraska Press, 1986). John S. Ford, _Rip Ford's Texas_, ed. Stephen B. Oates (Austin: University of Texas Press, 1963). Angelina Nieto et al., eds., _The Mexican Soldier, 1837–1847: Organization, Dress, Equipment_ (Mexico City: Historical Documents, 1958).

Thomas W. Cutrer

ESCRIBANO. The escribano served as a combined clerk of court and notary public in a Spanish municipality. He acted as a member of the ayuntamiento,[qv] or town council, but did not have a vote. His duties included keeping minutes for the council and preparing legal documents for the city. Additionally, he maintained municipal records and kept the archives of the ayuntamiento. The _escribano_ had many other responsibilities beside those involving municipal affairs. Foremost among these was his role in the administration of justice. He worked along with the alguacil, or local judge, as an active part of the court. The _escribano_ took testimony from witnesses, served papers, and retained all evidence in pending cases. All documents, judicial records and decisions remained in his possession after a trial. Royal authorities intended that the position be more than that of a secretary, for the _escribano_ had to ensure that the legal affairs of a province remain within the law.

The law that established the position stated that only the Council of the Indies could appoint an _escribano_. He had to be at least twenty-five years old, have enough education to function in the office, and have served as apprentice to another _escribano_. No mulattoes or mestizos could be appointed. The _escribano_ received pay for his work based on a posted list of fees. The amounts were generally set by the Audiencia and were, for the most part, nominal. Indians were exempt from payment of the fees, unless they acted together as a community, in which case _escribanos_ could charge them half of the regular amount. The influx of Anglo-Americans into Texas after Mexican independence diminished the role of the _escribano_ in municipal affairs. The difficult task of finding settlers fluent in Spanish prevented the establishment of the position as a vital part of local government.

BIBLIOGRAPHY: Mattie Alice Austin, "The Municipal Government of San Fernando de Bexar," _Quarterly of the Texas State Historical Association_ 8 (April 1905). Eugene C. Barker, "The Government of Austin's Colony, 1821–1831," _Southwestern Historical Quarterly_ 21 (January 1918). Clarence H. Haring, _The Spanish Empire in America_ (New York: Oxford University Press, 1947; 2d ed., New York: Harcourt, 1963). O. Garfield Jones, "Local Government in the Spanish Colonies as Provided by the Recopilación de Leyes de los Reynos de las Indias," _Southwestern Historical Quarterly_ 19 (July 1915). John Preston Moore, _The Cabildo in Peru under the Bourbons_ (Durham: Duke University Press, 1966). John Preston Moore, _The Cabildo in Peru under the Hapsburgs_ (Durham: Duke University Press, 1954).

Geoffrey Pivateau

ESKOTA, TEXAS. Eskota, on Sweetwater Creek in southeastern Fisher County, in 1881 was a shipping point on the Texas and Pacific Railway for Dan and Riley Trent's ranch. The community's post office was established in 1888 and received its name after the "Eskota" rather than the "Trent" station marker sign was delivered. _Eskota_ is a word of Indian derivation. The settlement prospered for a time as the only railroad town in the county. Its two-story hotel served train crews and other travelers. In 1947 Eskota had fifty people, a church, a store, and a section house. By the early 1980s it had one business and was on the Missouri Pacific. The community still existed in 1990.

BIBLIOGRAPHY: Fred Tarpley, *1001 Texas Place Names* (Austin: University of Texas Press, 1980). E. L. Yeats and E. H. Shelton, *History of Fisher County*, (n.p.: Feather, 1971).

William R. Hunt

ESKRIDGE, CHARLES SANFORD, JR. (1937–1984). Charles Sanford Eskridge, Jr., activist in the cause of the handicapped, son of Charles Sanford and Olivee (Fortenberry) Eskridge, was born at Wink, Texas, on August 6, 1937. His father was assistant commissioner of education for special education and rehabilitation and director of community services for the Texas Department of Mental Health and Mental Retardation.qv Eskridge attended Garland and Austin public schools, East Texas State University, and the University of Texas, where he received the bachelor of journalism degree in 1962 and the master of journalism in 1965.

He was a journalist and public information consultant. He served with the Texas Education Agency,qv the Texas Department of Mental Health and Mental Retardation, the University of Texas Office of Personnel Services and Employee Relations, the National Endowment for the Arts, the National Center for a Barrier Free Environment, and the Austin Parks and Recreation Department. In 1974–76 he helped establish a city owned and operated transportation system for the handicapped. He helped draft the Employment Rights Protection Act. From 1969 to 1979 he helped write and pass numerous bills for the benefit of handicapped persons in Texas, including the expansion of the Architectural Barriers Act. Eskridge was a compliance consultant to many organizations for the Rehabilitation Act of 1973. In 1980 he was cofounder of MIGHT (Mobility Impaired Grappling Hurdles Together), a statewide organization dedicated to addressing all problems of the handicapped. Eskridge was a member of University Christian Church in Austin. In 1980 the Austin City Council named February 21 Charles S. Eskridge Day and passed a resolution of appreciation for his work. Eskridge died on August 5, 1984, in Austin and was buried in Austin Memorial Park.

BIBLIOGRAPHY: Austin *American-Statesman*, August 7, 1984.

Charles H. Cox

ESOM HILL, TEXAS. Esom Hill, also known as Wheeler's Hill, was near the site of what is now Nigton sixteen miles northeast of Groveton in eastern Trinity County. The area was first settled around the time of the Civil Warqv and was originally known as Wheeler's Hill, after Benjamin Wheeler who had a store there. From April through November 1871 a post office operated in Wheeler's store under the name Esom Hill. The community apparently declined thereafter, and by 1900 it no longer appeared on maps.

BIBLIOGRAPHY: Patricia B. and Joseph W. Hensley, eds., *Trinity County Beginnings* (Groveton, Texas: Trinity County Book Committee, 1986).

Christopher Long

ESPADA CREEK. Espada Creek rises thirty-two miles northwest of Callaghan in northwestern Webb County (at 28°07′ N, 99°54′ W) and runs south nineteen miles to its mouth on the Rio Grande, thirty-one miles northwest of Laredo (at 27°54′ N, 99°54′ W). It traverses flat terrain with locally shallow depressions, surfaced by expansive clays that support water-tolerant hardwoods, conifers, and grasses. *Espada* is Spanish for "sword."

ESPALIER, CARLOS (1819–1836). Carlos Espalier, Alamo defender, was born in Texas in 1819. He was said to be a protégé of James Bowie.qv He died in the battle of the Alamoqv on March 6, 1836, at age seventeen. Because of similarity in names the claim has been made that Carlos Espalier and Charles Despallierqv are the same person, but the claim is not accepted by most historians. Espalier's aunt, Doña Guardia de Luz, was his heir and was granted lands for his service.

BIBLIOGRAPHY: Daughters of the American Revolution, *The Alamo Heroes and Their Revolutionary Ancestors* (San Antonio, 1976). Bill Groneman, *Alamo Defenders* (Austin: Eakin, 1990). Amelia W. Williams, A Critical Study of the Siege of the Alamo and of the Personnel of Its Defenders (Ph.D. dissertation, University of Texas, 1931; rpt., *Southwestern Historical Quarterly* 36–37 [April 1933–April 1934]).

Bill Groneman

ESPANTOSA LAKE. Espantosa Lake, five miles northeast of Carrizo Springs in north central Dimmit County (at 28°35′ N, 99°49′ W), drains into Soldier Slough. The natural lake was once a campsite on the Old San Antonio Road. Perhaps because of a ghostly fog that frequently obscures the lake after dark, however, it was often avoided by travelers who feared its reputation as a haunted place of evil (*espantosa* is Spanish for "fearful," "horrid"). Many legends surround the place. Some center on wagonloads of gold and silver rumored to have been lost in the lake; others tell of apparitions of men said to have been murdered on its shores. One story says that the lake was once filled with alligators. In 1917 water from the Nueces River was diverted into the lake, and a dam was built to contain the flow for irrigation purposes. In 1990 the dam, operated by the Zavala-Dimmit County Water Control and Improvement District, impounded a reservoir with a capacity of 1,745 acre-feet. The lake covered 364 acres and was used for boating and fishing as well as irrigation.

BIBLIOGRAPHY: John Clements, *Flying the Colors: Texas, a Comprehensive Look at Texas Today, County by County* (Dallas: Clements Research, 1984). Marker Files, Texas Historical Commission, Austin. Laura Knowlton Tidwell, *Dimmit County Mesquite Roots* (Austin: Wind River, 1984).

ESPARZA, CARLOS (1828–1885). Carlos Esparza, South Texas separatist and supporter of Juan N. Cortina,qv was born in September 1828 in Matamoros, Tamaulipas, to Pedro and Felicidad (Villareal) Esparza. He was privately educated. With his father he managed a ranch twenty miles from Brownsville on the lower Rio Grande. On February 27, 1850, Esparza, his father, Enrique Sánchez, and other citizens of the area attempted to establish a territorial government and separate themselves from the rest of Texas. It was to be named the Territory of the Rio Grande and to be designed to protect the interests of Hispanics. The proposal became politically complicated and was dropped. Also in 1850 Esparza married Francisca García, daughter of Ramón García, who joined him as a guerilla strategist and spy against the Texas Rangersqv and other enemies of Cortina. Esparza chose his aids for their merit and strict discipline. With Cortina he managed to aid Union and Confederate forces against each other while promoting the Cortinista cause. From 1860 to 1876 he provided military supplies and funds for the Cortinistas. He was to all appearances an ordinary rancher, possessing neither Cortina's striking appearance nor leadership qualities. The eccentric, sharp-tongued Esparza remained Cortina's man in the shadows. Cortina gave him an honorary superintendent's position in Matamoros so that he would have access to city resources and information. In 1873 Esparza was appointed special deputy inspector of hides and animals in Cameron County. Texas Ranger Leander H. McNellyqv was probably referring to Esparza when he referred on January 24, 1876, to the Cortinistas' "organization ... called the 'rural police.' The chief man is owner of a ranch, or the superintendent ... He is a civil officer ... He sends an alarm to one ranch, and it is sent from ranch to ranch in every direction." After Cortina was arrested in 1876, Esparza retreated to his ranch. Except for his activities as a stockholder with the Rio Grande Railroad Company in Brownsville and other business matters, he became a recluse to avoid criminal charges for his controversial political activities. He also managed to save himself with his witty sayings and business talents. He died on September 28, 1885.

BIBLIOGRAPHY: Frank H. Dugan, "The 1850 Affair of the Brownsville Separatists," *Southwestern Historical Quarterly* 61 (October 1957). Carlos Larralde, *Carlos Esparza: A Chicano Chronicle* (San Francisco: R&E Research Associates, 1977).

Carlos M. Larralde

ESPARZA, ENRIQUE (1828–1917). Enrique Esparza, witness of the battle of the Alamo,qv son of Gregorio Esparza and Ana Salazar, was probably born in September 1828, although he claimed to have been born in 1824. His father was killed in the defense of the Alamo. In an interview with Charles Merritt Barnes,qv writer for the San Antonio *Express*,qv in 1907, Esparza begins his narration concerning his Alamo experience by saying, "All the others are dead. I alone live of they who were within the Alamo when it fell. There is none other left now to tell its story, and when I go to sleep my last slumber in the Campo de los Santos (cemetery), there will then be no one left to tell. You ask me do I remember it, I tell you, Yes. It is burned into my brain and indelibly seared there. Neither age nor infirmity could make me forget for the scene was one of such horror that it could never be forgotten." Esparza was married to Gertrudes Hernández. They had seven children. A daughter, María Josefa, was one of the first area women to be invested in the Sisters of Charity of the Incarnate Wordqv on January 4, 1871, when she became Sister Claude.

Esparza first farmed in the San Augustine community in Atascosa County, Texas. He moved to San Antonio and truck-farmed in the Nogalitos–South Flores area. He also transported merchandise to and from Indianola, Texas, in carts. So burdensome and dangerous was the trip, that on his return, the first place he visited was the church to give thanks for his safe return. Esparza died on December 20, 1917, and is buried in El Carmen Cemetery, Losoya.

BIBLIOGRAPHY: San Antonio *Express*, May 12, 19, 1907, December 21, 1917. San Antonio *Light*, December 21, 1917. Vertical Files, Barker Texas History Center, University of Texas at Austin.

Reynaldo J. Esparza

ESPARZA, FRANCISCA REYES (ca. 1901–ca. 1979). Francisca Reyes Esparza, early civil-rights activist, the daughter of Antonio and María (Reyes) Esparza and the granddaughter of Carlos Esparza,qv was born around 1901. By the 1920s she had become known for encouraging people to stand up for their rights. She worked with her friend Judge Dennis Bangs Chapin to establish the validity of Spanish and Mexican land grants that had been ignored or circumvented by landholders. From 1930 to 1937 Francisca Esparza worked as an aid to José T. Canalesqv in Brownsville. She acquired several properties there and owned a secondhand store where Canales and other lawyers gave free counsel. In Mexico she researched titles and other documents on Texas land grants. She formed the Alliance of Land Grants to help get land rights restored to the original owners, who were to have been protected under the Treaty of Guadalupe Hidalgo.qv She received funds from her followers for the alliance and support from Chapin, who also hired lawyers to help her pursue the issue. The effort received some attention in the press and courts during the 1940s, but by 1952 Chapin had died, and Francisca Esparza was accused of being a Communist and discredited. Her movement was destroyed, but others were inspired by her efforts, among them Reies López Tijerina, who became active in the restoration of New Mexico land grants. Francisca Esparza died around 1979.

BIBLIOGRAPHY: Corpus Christi *Caller*, April 3, 1953. Corpus Christi *Times*, June 7, 1946. Carlos Larralde, *Mexican-American Movements and Leaders* (Los Alamitos, California: Hwong, 1976).

Carlos M. Larralde

ESPARZA, JOSÉ (1856–1926). José Esparza, entrepreneur and political activist, son of Francisca (García) and Carlos Esparza,qv was born on July 8, 1856, at Rancho de San Juan el Encantado. His maternal grandfather, Ramón García, was one of Juan N. Cortina'sqv spies, and his father was a Cortinista activist. Esparza married Rufina Sayas, who died in a fire; he married Virginia Reyes on December 28, 1895. He used his position as a Cameron county commissioner from 1882 to 1885 to promote the railroad. In 1903 he invested in the Merchants and Planters Rice Milling Company in Brownsville. He later abandoned rice growing since it was "damaging the soil." Esparza donated money and land to the first San Benito public school in 1907. He also donated an acre of land along the military road in El Ranchito and expressed the wish that a school, La Encantada School, be built there. On November 23, 1970, the community built a memorial park to him at El Ranchito, not far from San Benito. Esparza aided militant Aniceto Pizañaqv during the turbulent era along the lower Rio Grande that began in 1915. He also encouraged the United States Army to station troops in the area. During the 1920s he invested $50,000 in the St. Louis, Brownsville and Mexico Railway Company, which built several branch lines in the area by 1926. He was checking records of his railroad investments when he had a stroke and died, on September 19, 1926.

Carlos M. Larralde

ESPARZA, JOSÉ MARÍA (1802–1836). José María Esparza, better known as Gregorio Esparza, defender of the Alamo, was born on February 25, 1802, in San Antonio de Béxar, the child of Juan Antonio and Maria Petra (Olivas) Esparza. He married Anna Salazar, who bore him a daughter and three sons, one of whom, Enrique, was an eyewitness to the siege of the Alamo. Esparza enlisted in Juan N. Seguín'sqv company in October 1835 and participated in the taking of the squares on the north side of the city during the siege of Bexar,qv December 5–9, 1835. He served until the capitulation of Gen. Martín Perfecto de Cosqv on December 10, 1835.

On the arrival of Gen. Antonio López de Santa Annaqv in February 1836, Esparza and his family were advised by John William Smithqv to take refuge in the Alamo, since they had been friendly with the Americans. They arrived at twilight and entered through a small window in the church of the compound. Although Col. William Barret Travis,qv through James Bowie'sqv influence, was allowing local citizens to leave if they so desired, Esparza elected to stay and fight, and his family to remain with him. He tended a cannon during the siege and died in the battle of the Alamoqv on March 6, 1836.

Francisco Esparza, Gregorio's brother, by his own admission a member of the local Mexican "presidial" company of the Alamo until the capitulation of Cos, requested and was granted permission to enter the Alamo and search for his brother's body after the siege. In company with his two brothers, he took the body and interred it in the Campo Santo on the west side of San Pedro Creek. Thus Gregorio Esparza received a Christian burial, unlike the others slain in the battle. Gregorio's heirs were instrumental in founding San Augustine, southeast of Pleasanton in Atascosa County.

BIBLIOGRAPHY: Enrique Esparza, Deposition, August 26, 1859 (Texas General Land Office, Austin). Manuel Flores, Deposition, December 13, 1858 (Texas General Land Office, Austin). Gregorio Hernández, Deposition, December 27, 1858 (Texas General Land Office, Austin). San Antonio *Daily Express*, May 12, 19, 1907.

Reynaldo J. Esparza

ESPEJO, ANTONIO DE (?–1585). Antonio de Espejo was born in Torre Milano, a suburb of Córdova, Spain. He went to Mexico in 1571 with Archbishop Moya y Contreras as an officer of the Inquisition and there became a cattleman. By 1580 he had several ranches in the districts of Querétaro and Celayo. After implication in the murder of one of his servants he was sentenced to pay a heavy fine, and to evade payment he fled to Nueva Vizcaya, where he met survivors of the Rodríguez-Sánchez expedition.qv After receiving permission to head and finance an expedition to assist Fray Bernardino Beltrán in searching for the friars, Espejo enlisted fourteen men as an escort and furnished 115 beasts of burden loaded with supplies.

The party left for New Mexico on November 10, 1582, and followed the Río Conchos to the Rio Grande, which Espejo named Río del Norte. They crossed the river and remained eight days in pueblos San Juan Evangelista and Santiago, near the site of present Presidio, before recrossing the Rio Grande. On the Mexican side they traveled to the pueblos of the Piro Indians, where they learned that the Franciscans[qv] Francisco López and Agustín Rodríguez[qv] had been killed by the Tiguex Indians. When they reached the Tiguex country on February 17, Beltrán proposed that the expedition return, but Espejo was determined to explore the area to the east. He reached the Pecos River about thirty miles southeast of Santa Fe and followed the river south to the site of present Pecos, Texas. From there the Jumano Indians guided him and his men along what is now Toyah Creek, through Balmorhea, and on up Limpia Canyon by the sites of present Fort Davis and Marfa and down Alamito Creek to the Rio Grande.

Espejo reached San Bartolomé on September 10, 1583. His discoveries probably did more to stimulate the settlement of New Mexico and the exploitation of its mineral resources than did those of any other of the early explorers. He started back to Spain to urge the settlement of New Mexico but became ill at Havana, Cuba, where he died in 1585.

BIBLIOGRAPHY: Carlos E. Castañeda, *Our Catholic Heritage in Texas* (7 vols., Austin: Von Boeckmann–Jones, 1936–58; rpt., New York: Arno, 1976). Charles W. Hackett, ed., *Pichardo's Treatise on the Limits of Louisiana and Texas* (4 vols., Austin: University of Texas Press, 1931–46). J. Lloyd Mecham, "Antonio de Espejo and His Journey to New Mexico," *Southwestern Historical Quarterly* 30 (October 1926). Vertical Files, Barker Texas History Center, University of Texas at Austin.
Robert Bruce Blake

ESPEJO-BELTRÁN EXPEDITION. The glowing accounts of the new discoveries made by the Rodríguez-Sánchez expedition[qv] of 1581–82 spread rapidly throughout the northern frontier of the viceroyalty of New Spain, fired imaginations, and stimulated activity. Moreover, in Santa Bárbara there was the greatest concern for the safety of Fray Agustín Rodríguez[qv] and Fray Francisco López, the two Franciscans[qv] who had remained in New Mexico to continue their missionary work. In Santa Bárbara a Franciscan named Bernardino Beltrán sought authority to send a rescue mission to New Mexico, and he began to search for a suitable leader to command the military escort. Residing in Santa Bárbara at this time was Antonio de Espejo,[qv] a wealthy fugitive from justice accused of murder, who had taken refuge on the frontier and was looking for an opportunity to exonerate himself. Espejo therefore offered his services to Fray Beltrán and agreed to join an expedition to rescue the two friars and to pay all expenses.

The Espejo-Beltrán expedition, consisting of fourteen soldiers, their servants, 115 horses and mules, arms, munitions, and provisions, left San Bartolomé, a mining outpost nine leagues north of Santa Bárbara, on November 10, 1582. A month later the expedition reached the juncture of the Río Conchos and the Rio Grande, which Espejo named the Río del Norte. Up the river was a nation Espejo called the Jumanos, who lived in large pueblos with flat roofs, gave the Spaniards food, and told them that some years before three Christians and a Negro had passed through the area. In January 1583 the expedition approached the El Paso area, inhabited by the Suma and Manso Indians. They followed the Río del Norte upstream, through a "mountain chain on each side of it, both of which were without timber," a possible reference to El Paso del Norte,[qv] as Spaniards later named it.

In late January 1583 Espejo and his companions reported "a large black rock," a possible reference to Elephant Butte, and on February 1 they arrived at the southernmost pueblos of New Mexico. Here they learned that both Rodríguez and López had been killed by the Indians. Beltrán therefore proposed that the expedition return since the fate of the two missionaries had been determined, but Espejo, whose leadership was unchallenged by this time, insisted on further explorations in the hope of finding riches. From March to July 1583 the party explored extensively in what is now Arizona. Although no riches were found, Espejo continued to be convinced that the reports of wealth were true. Meanwhile, Fray Beltrán and several others had left the expedition and returned to Santa Bárbara.

In June 1583 Espejo and his companions turned their attention eastward. They entered the Pecos valley, followed the Pecos River southward into the land of the Jumanos, and on August 22 reached the juncture of the Rio Grande and the Conchos. The little band finally arrived in San Bartolomé on September 10, 1583, after an absence of ten months.

Espejo's report of rich silver mines and natives of an advanced cultural level who would be receptive to conversion aroused widespread interest and a strong desire among Spanish officials to occupy and colonize the lands that he had visited. In the succeeding years there were numerous applicants, including Espejo, for the necessary official authorization to conquer and colonize New Mexico, but all were denied. Not until 1595 was a candidate found with the necessary qualifications to gain the approval of the Spanish crown for this important assignment. His name was Juan de Oñate.[qv]

BIBLIOGRAPHY: John Francis Bannon, *The Spanish Borderlands Frontier, 1513–1821* (New York: Holt, Rinehart, and Winston, 1970). Herbert Eugene Bolton, ed., *Spanish Exploration in the Southwest, 1542–1706* (New York: Scribner, 1908; rpt., New York: Barnes and Noble, 1959). George P. Hammond and Agapito Rey, *The Rediscovery of New Mexico, 1580–1594* (Albuquerque: University of New Mexico Press, 1966). Elizabeth A. H. John, *Storms Brewed in Other Men's Worlds: The Confrontation of Indians, Spanish, and French in the Southwest, 1540–1795* (College Station: Texas A&M University Press, 1975). Charles Kelly, "Report on Archeological Field Work in the Madera Valley Area," *West Texas Historical and Scientific Society Publications No. 5* (March 1933).
W. H. Timmons

ESPERANZA, TEXAS (Hudspeth County). Esperanza is near the Rio Grande on Farm Road 192, twenty-one miles southwest of Sierra Blanca in southwestern Hudspeth County. It was founded before 1935, when a post office was established there with Mrs. Bessie Greene McCoy as postmaster. The estimated population of Esperanza doubled from fifty in the late 1930s to 100 in the mid-1940s. It was 100 for two decades and then, by the late 1960s, dropped to seventy-five, where it remained in 1990. In the late 1980s Esperanza had scattered dwellings and a school. The town's name, which means "hope" in Spanish, was the name of a local farm.
Martin Donell Kohout

ESPERANZA, TEXAS (Montgomery County). Esperanza was on U.S. Highway 75 just east of Interstate Highway 45 seven miles north of Willis in northern Montgomery County. The town was founded around 1879 by William Spiller, who owned a tobacco farm in the area and wanted a post office address. When the railroad passed through the settlement the community was called Ada, after Lester Ada, who owned the general store. A post office called Ada operated there from 1893 to 1899. In 1899 Spiller changed its name to Esperanza, which means "hope" in Spanish. He hoped that the town would bring his tobacco business success, but it failed soon after, though the community continued to prosper. By 1915 Esperanza had a population of 100 and six businesses. Its post office was discontinued sometime after 1930. In the 1940s the community had two churches, two businesses, and eight dwellings. By 1965 the area was a part of the Willis Independent School District. In the 1960s a Texas Historical Commission[qv] marker was erected at the townsite.

BIBLIOGRAPHY: Montgomery County Genealogical Society, *Mont-*

gomery County History (Winston-Salem, North Carolina: Hunter, 1981).
Rebecca L. Borjas

ESPERANZA CREEK. Esperanza Creek rises sixteen miles east of Dilley in southeastern Frio County (at 28°42′ N, 98°54′ W) and runs southeast for twenty-four miles to its mouth on the Frio River, twelve miles west of Tilden in northwest McMullen County (at 28°28′ N, 98°44′ W). The stream traverses mostly flat terrain with local shallow depressions, and occasionally passes through low-rolling hills and prairie. The area is surfaced by expansive clays that support water-tolerant hardwoods, conifers, and grasses, interspersed with some mesquite and dwarf oaks.

ESPERSON, MELLIE KEENAN (ca. 1870–1945). Mellie Keenan Esperson, businesswoman and developer, was born in Manhattan, Kansas, around 1870, the daughter of Thomas and Hannah Marie (McFarland) Keenan. She moved to Oklahoma with her mother and stepfather, John Brown, as a young woman. While living there she met Niels Esperson, a native of Denmark who had become involved in real estate and other business dealings in Oklahoma. The couple were married in El Reno, Oklahoma, on December 20, 1893, and subsequently lived in Colorado and Kansas, where Niels pursued mining work and oil deals with limited success. In 1903 they moved to Houston, where Mellie learned the intricate dealings of the oil business while her husband became a pioneer developer of the Humble oilfield.qv Over the next decade the Espersons diversified their interests in Houston into real estate and other business efforts.

When Niels Esperson died in 1922, he left his wife substantial commercial wealth, including an oil-rich ranch in Liberty County, interest in the Reed Roller Bit Company in Houston, and large holdings in a tile plant in Kansas. Her first project was to construct the Majestic Theater. The theater, designed by Chicago architect John Eberson, opened in 1923 as film venue. It stood for almost fifty years before being demolished in 1971.

In 1924 Esperson initiated plans for an office building that her husband had envisioned for property he owned in downtown Houston. He had left no specific instructions for the building, so she traveled to Europe to gather ideas on materials and then again turned to architect Eberson to design what she intended as a memorial to her husband. The thirty-two story Niels Esperson Building at the corner of Travis and Rusk Avenue opened in 1927, the tallest structure in Texas at that time. The Italian Renaissance building features a gold-leaf tower topped by an elaborate six-story tiered monument. Inside, terra cotta urns, bronze elevator doors, arabesque obelisks, and extensive use of imported Roman marble convey the ornate sense that Esperson wanted. When completed the building reflected her forward-looking style, with an exercise area and adjacent parking garage included in its design. She had the structure air-conditioned in 1938.

Fourteen years after this building opened, Mellie Esperson turned to John Eberson and his brother Drew to design an adjoining structure. The Mellie Esperson Building on Walker Avenue was completed in 1941, a nineteen-story structure similar in style to its larger neighbor. The building bearing her name, which is separate from the first structure but adjoins it on most floors, was distinguished at its opening for being the largest office structure constructed in Houston during the Great Depressionqv and the first skyscraper in Houston to be built with central air-conditioning. The Esperson buildings remain a significant landmark in downtown Houston, where they provide offices for banks, oil companies, and other professional interests.

Apart from her downtown construction projects, Esperson planned and developed the Niels Esperson Industrial District and remained active in the oil business as a prospector and producer. She also acquired numerous substantial real estate holdings in Houston. The Houston Ship Channel,qv the development of which she supported, at one time crossed her property in four places. Her Liberty County interests included not only oil but rice farms. For some twenty years she oversaw all of these efforts from her suite of offices on the twenty-fifth floor of the Niels Esperson Building, taking great pride in her business judgment and ability to use wealth wisely. She was an active member of the Houston Chamber of Commerce and routinely made donations to the Museum of Fine Arts.qv She was also a large contributor to the Little Theatre and the Houston Symphony.qv During World War IIqv she donated office space for the local draft board and the Soldiers Service Bureau. She was a Christian Scientist and left her church in Houston a large cash bequest. She was also a member of the Business and Professional Women's club, the Downtown club, the French Club, and the city Federation of Women's Clubs.

In 1925 Mellie Esperson married Harry Ewing Stewart, a man some twenty years her junior, who subsequently established the Stewart Company, which in 1961 was considered the largest distributor of farm and industrial equipment in the United States. The couple were divorced in 1934.

Esperson received much recognition for her visionary business sense and good spirit, including an award in the 1930s from the Women's Advertising Club of Houston as the city's most successful businesswoman. In her later years she continued her business work even after losing her eyesight. She died in Houston on January 14, 1945, and was buried there in Forest Park Cemetery. The Espersons had no children; she was survived by her sister and numerous nieces and nephews.

BIBLIOGRAPHY: *Encyclopedia of American Biography.* Houston Metropolitan Research Center Files, Houston Public Library. *Houston Post,* January 15, 16, 1945.
Debbie Mauldin Cottrell

ESPERSON, TEXAS. Esperson was on Farm Road 1413 near the Esperson Dome oilfield thirty miles east of Houston in southwestern Liberty County. Rice farmers used the area extensively, and canals and irrigation ditches crisscrossed the countryside. Further growth was stimulated by the construction of the Dayton–Goose Creek Railroad in 1919. Exploration efforts were abandoned by the Union Exploration Company in 1928, but Harvey Smith drilled a producing oil well the following year. The Yount-Lee Oil Company quickly expanded into the Esperson Dome field, and twenty-five wells had been drilled by March 1934. Although no definable community center was noted on highway department or geological survey maps, the Esperson field had by 1984 produced a total of over fifty million barrels of crude oil.

BIBLIOGRAPHY: Rosalie Fincher, *History of Liberty County* (M.A. thesis, University of Texas, 1937).
Robert Wooster

ESPINOSA, ISIDRO FÉLIX DE (1679–1755). Isidro Félix de Espinosa was born in Querétaro on November 26, 1679. His parents, Isidro de Espinosa and Gertrudis de Miraelrío Tovar, had married in 1676, and had nine children, six of whom lived to adulthood. On March 18, 1696, Isidro Félix de Espinosa entered the Franciscan missionary College of Santa Cruz de Querétaroqv as a novice, and on March 19, 1697, made his profession. He accepted holy orders on December 17, 1700, and was ordained a priest on February 26, 1703. It seems likely that Espinosa was assigned to San Juan Bautistaqv Mission in late 1703 or shortly thereafter.

On April 5, 1709, Espinosa, accompanied by Father Antonio de San Buenaventura y Olivares, Capt. Pedro de Aguirre,qqv and fourteen soldiers, left San Juan Bautista and marched to the site of future San Antonio. There the padres were much impressed by the availability of water and the prospects for Spanish settlement. The Espinosa-Olivares-Aguirre expedition probed beyond the San Antonio River to the Colorado, where it hoped to make contact with the Tejas Indians who were rumored to have moved there. After finding no Tejas but learning that those Indians were still ill-disposed toward the Spanish, the expedition returned to San Juan Bautista on April 28, 1709.

Espinosa soon returned to Querétaro and remained there until he was named president of the new missions to be established in Texas by his missionary college. In 1716 he accompanied the expedition of Domingo Ramón,qv which established three Queretaran missions in East Texas: Nuestro Padre San Francisco de los Tejas, Nuestra Señora de la Purísima Concepción, and San José de los Nazonis.

Espinosa's missionary activities in Texas included participation in two more expeditions, those of Martín de Alarcón (1718) and the Marqués de San Miguel de Aguayo qqv (1721). His contributions as a chronicler of early Texas history are without peer. Dubbed "the Julius Caesar of the Faith in New Spain," because he worked by day and wrote all night, Espinosa left a remarkable body of literature. It includes a biography of his friend, Antonio Margil de Jesús,qv and his *Crónica de los colegios de propaganda fide de la Nueva España*, called "the most important contemporary account of the Franciscansqv in Texas"; the work was reprinted in 1964.

Espinosa was recalled from Texas in late 1721 to serve as guardian of his missionary college and never returned to the province. In 1733 he was named president of the future Hospicio de San Fernando in Mexico City. In late life he returned to the college of Santa Cruz in Querétaro, where he died on February 14, 1755.

BIBLIOGRAPHY: Donald E. Chipman, *Spanish Texas, 1519–1821* (Austin: University of Texas Press, 1992). Robert S. Weddle, *San Juan Bautista: Gateway to Spanish Texas* (Austin: University of Texas Press, 1968).

Donald E. Chipman

ESPINOSA-OLIVARES-AGUIRRE EXPEDITION. The expedition of Isidro Félix de Espinosa, Antonio de San Buenaventura y Olivares, and Pedro de Aguirreqqv of 1709 resulted from a combination of Spanish presence on the Rio Grande, international considerations, and continued interest in missionizing the Tejas Indians. In the early 1700s, a cluster of three missions and a presidio constituted the Spanish establishment west of the Rio Grande near modern Guerrero, Coahuila. San Juan Bautistaqv mission and presidio, destined to become the "Gateway to Spanish Texas," were the staging area for this early expedition into Texas.

During the summer of 1707, the viceroy of New Spain received intelligence that the French in Louisiana were intent upon establishing trade with Spanish dominions. A war council in Mexico City recommended that contacts be made with Indian nations in Texas, and that they be dissuaded from accepting goods of French origin. As it turned out, official concerns about contraband converged nicely with the missionary impulses of fathers Espinosa and Olivares.

At San Juan Bautista the two padres were joined by Capt. Pedro de Aguirre, and the expedition left the gateway settlements on April 5, 1709. With Espinosa and Olivares serving, respectively, as diarist and chaplain, the entrada traveled to the site of future San Antonio, where the party was much impressed with the land and availability of water. From the San Antonio River, the expedition pushed on to the Colorado, for it was rumored that Tejas Indians had moved settlements there in order to be closer to the Spaniards. That report proved unfounded, and in fact the Spaniards learned that the old Tejas chieftain, Bernardino, was still ill disposed toward them.

The expedition returned to San Juan Bautista on April 28, 1709. It had increased familiarity with Texas and lent a favorable impression of lands along the San Antonio River. But it seems likely that the immediate effect of this entrada was to delay the reestablishment of missions in East Texas, for it convincingly dispelled the notion that the Tejas were eager for renewed contacts with the Spanish.

BIBLIOGRAPHY: Carlos E. Castañeda, *Our Catholic Heritage in Texas* (7 vols., Austin: Von Boeckmann–Jones, 1936–58; rpt., New York: Arno, 1976). Donald E. Chipman, *Spanish Texas, 1519–1821* (Austin: University of Texas Press, 1992). Robert S. Weddle, *San Juan Bautista: Gateway to Spanish Texas* (Austin: University of Texas Press, 1968).

Donald E. Chipman

ESPIO CREEK. Espio Creek rises in the Big Wells oilfield in southeastern Zavala County (at 28°39′ N, 99°30′ W) and crosses through Dimmit County as it runs southeast for eighteen miles to its mouth on the Nueces River, seven miles west of Cotulla in west central La Salle County (at 28°27′ N, 99°22′ W). The creek rises in rolling prairie surfaced by shallow to moderately deep clay loams that support mesquite, grasses, and chaparral and descends to flat terrain with locally shallow depressions, surfaced by clayey and sandy loams that support water-tolerant hardwoods and grasses. The name of the creek is probably from Spanish *espión* ("spy").

ESPIRITU SANTO BAY. Espiritu Santo Bay, between San Antonio Bay and Matagorda Bay in extreme southern Calhoun County (at 28°21′ N, 96°32′ W), forms the barrier between Matagorda Island and the mainland. The bay is sixteen miles long and five miles wide. It is surrounded by low ridges and swales covered by grass and oaks, oyster reefs, and tidal flats of mixed mud, sand, and shell where blue-green algae predominate. The name, Spanish for "Holy Spirit," was applied by early Spaniards to several locations on the Gulf Coast, but in Texas it was most generally used to apply to the Matagorda Bay area, especially to what is now Lavaca Bay, which was also called San Bernardo Bay.

ESPOPOLAME INDIANS. The Espopolame (Isopopolame) Indians, who presumably spoke a Coahuiltecan language, lived in northeastern Coahuila during the latter part of the seventeenth century. Apparently they were never seen in Texas. However, documents of Coahuila indicate that the Espopolames were closely associated with the Pinanaca Indians, who in 1675 were encountered by the Bosque-Larios expeditionqv north of the Rio Grande near future Eagle Pass.

BIBLIOGRAPHY: Vito Alessio Robles, *Coahuila y Texas en la época colonial* (Mexico City: Editorial Cultura, 1938; 2d ed., Mexico City: Editorial Porrúa, 1978). Herbert Eugene Bolton, ed., *Spanish Exploration in the Southwest, 1542–1706* (New York: Scribner, 1908; rpt., New York: Barnes and Noble, 1959). Frederick Webb Hodge, ed., *Handbook of American Indians North of Mexico* (2 vols., Washington: GPO, 1907, 1910; rpt., New York: Pageant, 1959).

Thomas N. Campbell

ESQUIEN INDIANS. The Esquien Indians were a Karankawan group that entered Nuestra Señora de la Candelaria Mission on the San Gabriel River in 1750.

BIBLIOGRAPHY: Frederick Webb Hodge, ed., *Handbook of American Indians North of Mexico* (2 vols., Washington: GPO, 1907, 1910; rpt., New York: Pageant, 1959).

W. E. S. Dickerson

ESSEVILLE, TEXAS (Atascosa County). Esseville was five miles northeast of Pleasanton in northeastern Atascosa County. There is mention of an Esse family in the area in the 1960s. In the 1940s Esseville had one business and a reported population of twenty-five, which remained at that level until the mid-1970s. However, the community was not shown on county highway maps, and by the 1980s no trace of it remained.

BIBLIOGRAPHY: Pleasanton *Express*, Cowboy Homecoming Edition, September 3, 1969. Martin Stroble, Administrative Survey and Proposed Plan of Reorganization for the Public Schools of Atascosa County (M.Ed. thesis, University of Texas, 1936).

Linda Peterson

ESSEVILLE, TEXAS (Live Oak County). Esseville is on Farm Road 99 five miles northeast of Whitsett in northern Live Oak County. The area around Esseville was settled beginning around 1913, when ranchers in northern Live Oak County subdivided their large ranches into smaller sections for sale to farmers. In 1933 Willie Esse, Jr., built a store, a home, and a cotton gin in the area, and the site became known as Esseville. By 1936 the settlement included a dozen scattered residences, a business, and a school, which it shared with the nearby community of Nell and used for church services. By 1980 only the store was operating at the townsite. The community still existed in 1990.

BIBLIOGRAPHY: Ervin L. Sparkman, *The People's History of Live Oak County* (Mesquite, Texas, 1981). *John Leffler*

ESTACADO, TEXAS. Estacado, the first white agricultural settlement on the South Plains, is on Farm Road 1527 on the Crosby county line in northeast Lubbock County. It was established by Paris Cox[qv] in 1879. Looking for a suitable location to establish a Quaker colony, Cox had secured railroad land in western Crosby and eastern Lubbock counties in the late 1870s in exchange for his sawmill business in Indiana. In the fall of 1879 the first families (Cox, Stubbs, Spray, and Hayworth) arrived in the area in time to face a severe winter. Cox built a sod house for his family, but the other settlers spent the ordeal in tents and quit the colony the following spring, leaving only the Cox family in residence. After a successful crop was achieved, however, interest in the colony was renewed, and by 1882 ten families had been recruited. The community was named Marietta (or Maryetta) for Cox's wife Mary, but was renamed Estacado, from Llano Estacado,[qv] when the post office was established in 1884 with William Hunt as postmaster.

In 1886 Estacado became the county seat of Crosby County. The community provided some of the first organized education on the South Plains when Emma Hunt began teaching in a dugout[qv] classroom in 1882; by 1884 classes were being held in the Quaker meetinghouse. The Central Plains Academy, the first college on the Llano Estacado, was established in the community in 1890 and operated for two years. The town flourished for some years, and by 1890 the population was reported at 200. But in 1891 Emma became the county seat and Estacado began to decline. The town lacked leadership after Cox's death in 1888, and a grasshopper invasion and drought in 1892–93 all but finished it.

Favorable growing conditions attracted settlers to the region after 1900, however, and Estacado continued to exist, although the original Quaker colony had dissolved. The post office was closed in 1918, after which mail came through Petersburg. The population increased from sixty-eight in 1930 to eighty-five in 1940; it remained stable at eighty from 1970 through 1990. In the mid-1980s the town had a cotton gin and a few scattered residences.

BIBLIOGRAPHY: T. Lindsay Baker, *Ghost Towns of Texas* (Norman: University of Oklahoma Press, 1986). Roger Andrew Burgess, The History of Crosby County, Texas (M.A. thesis, University of Texas, 1927). Roger A. Burgess, "Pioneer Quaker Farmers of the South Plains," *Panhandle-Plains Historical Review* 1 (1928). Crosby County Pioneer Memorial Museum, *A History of Crosby County, 1876–1977* (Dallas: Taylor, 1978). Lawrence L. Graves, ed., *A History of Lubbock* (Lubbock: West Texas Museum Association, 1962). Mary Louise McDonald, The History of Lubbock County (M.A. thesis, University of Texas, 1942). *Charles G. Davis*

ESTACADO AND GULF RAILROAD. The Estacado and Gulf Railroad resulted from the initial attempt on the part of the citizens of Roby in Fisher County to get a railroad connection with their community. The line was chartered on June 4, 1908, and planned to build from Roby southeast to Coleman in Coleman County, for a distance of 100 miles. W. A. Butts, its promoter, requested that $50,000 be raised prior to construction. The people of Roby set out to do so through cash and pledges, and on April 1, 1910, construction started from McCaulley, which was on the Kansas City, Mexico and Orient line. The capital was $100,000. The principal place of business was Roby. The members of the first board of directors were William A. Butts and F. D. Jones, both of Fort Worth; W. B. Tate and T. H. Landon, both of Roby; Carl H. Jewell of Boston, Massachusetts; John T. Butts of Weatherford; James J. Jones of Tulsa, Oklahoma; W. C. Blanchett and D. H. Johnson, both of Stamford; and G. S. Mathews of Austin.

The original plan called for the Estacado and Gulf line to connect with the Orient in McCaulley, head west through Roby, which was some ten miles away, and go on to El Paso and eventually to the Gulf of California. By November 1, 1910, the roadbed had been completed to Roby, but the tracks had been laid only to the east bank of the Clear Fork of the Brazos near Pledger, about five miles away. At that time the officials held a picnic to celebrate their progress, and the train carried people from McCaulley to the railhead on a flatcar with cane-bottom chairs. But in spite of the picnic, the line was abandoned in 1911. The engine and other equipment lay for a few years where the tracks had stopped and was sold for scrap or salvaged to be used on the subsequent Roby and Northern Railway.

BIBLIOGRAPHY: B. W. Aston, "Roby Gets a Railroad," West Texas Historical Association *Year Book* 52 (1976). *H. Allen Anderson*

ESTELLE, TEXAS. Estelle was on Estelle Creek fourteen miles northwest of Dallas on the western border of Dallas County. It was on the original land grant of H. Burgoon. The site was settled in 1881 as a rural crossroads rest stop on the route between Farmers Branch and Bird's Fort (now Birdville) in Tarrant County. The community was named Estill in honor of an architect from Grapevine; the name was inaccurately recorded in Washington as Estelle. A local post office operated from 1881 until 1904. By 1885 the town had a population of seventy-five, a steam cotton gin, two churches, a school, a blacksmith, two doctors, a teacher, and a reverend. The community was a shipping point for cotton and grain on a stage route to Grapevine and Dallas. The stage ran three times a week. In 1890 Estelle had a population of fifty, a general store, a cotton gin, a physician, a blacksmith, and Presbyterian and Methodist ministers. It supported a school with one teacher and forty-one pupils in 1896–97. By 1930 the community had only one business and a population of thirty-eight, the figure it retained until 1948, the last year Estelle is listed in the *Texas Almanac*.

BIBLIOGRAPHY: Henry Gannett, *A Gazetteer of Texas* (U.S. Geological Survey Bulletin 190, Series F, Washington: GPO, 1902; 2d ed., U.S.G.S. Bulletin 224, 1904). Fred Tarpley, *Place Names of Northeast Texas* (Commerce: East Texas State University, 1969). *Matthew Hayes Nall*

ESTELLINE, TEXAS. Estelline, at the intersection of U.S. Highway 287 and State Highway 87, near the Red River in eastern Hall County, was established in 1892 by the brothers Elam and Math Wright. It was on the Fort Worth and Denver City Railway and was named for Estelle de Shields, daughter of an early settler. The area was originally part of the Diamond Tail Ranch.[qv] The Mill Iron range lay nearby, and after 1896 the Continental Land and Cattle Company[qv] moved its headquarters to a nearby bluff overlooking the Red River. A post office was opened in May 1892, and by 1894 Estelline had two hotels, a Methodist church, a cotton gin, a livery stable, and a one-room schoolhouse. Tom Macy opened the first store, and soon afterward T. R. Garrott established the Estelline Supply Company. In 1894 Math Wright obtained a depot and sidetrack for his town, and throughout the remainder of the decade Estelline was an important shipping point on the Fort Worth and Denver City line. Cattle from nearby Silverton and Paducah were driven there for shipment. In 1896 the Mill Iron Ranch bought the Estelline Supply Company and opened a large general merchandise store and lumberyard with R. L. Biggerstaff as manager. Two years later Biggerstaff established a private bank, which became the Estelline State Bank in 1905. The town had two newspapers, the Estelline *Star* (1894–96) and the Estelline *News* (1907–10). A two-story school was built in 1909. In 1912 the citizens of Estelline elected to incorporate with a mayor, a city marshal, and five aldermen. By then the town had attained a population of over 1,000.

The 1920s saw the erection of permanent brick school facilities, the emergence of a champion basketball team, and the organization of a town band conducted by Paul James. In 1927 the railroad began construction of a branch line out of Estelline to Plainview in Hale County. However, the Great Depression[qv] led to the closing of the bank and a decline in the population to 603 by 1940. That year two fires destroyed several businesses. Subsequent improvements in highway transportation led to an overall decline in Estelline's importance as a railroad junction town. The number of businesses dropped from fifteen in 1947 to four by 1980, when the population was 258. The town was still incorporated, and the post office remained open. In 1977 Estelline won notice as the home of Hot Idea, that year's All-American Futurity champion. In 1990 the population was 194.

BIBLIOGRAPHY: Inez Baker, *Yesterday in Hall County* (Memphis, Texas, 1940). Ray Miller, *Eyes of Texas Travel Guide: Panhandle/Plains Edition* (Houston: Cordovan, 1982). *H. Allen Anderson*

ESTELLINE SALT SPRINGS. Estelline Salt Springs is a group of brine springs less than a mile east of Estelline at the Childress county line in east central Hall County (at 34°33′ N, 100°25′ W). The springs are located on the floodplain of the Prairie Dog Town Fork of the Red River; they became active around the turn of the century when they washed out a funnel in the alluvium. They were used by servicemen stationed at Childress during World War II.[qv] In 1964 the United States Corps of Engineers built a dike around the springs to stop the flow and prevent the salt from entering the river. Since then the springwater has apparently grown more saline. Salt minnows or killifish swim in the milfoil growing there, and the surrounding flats support hardwoods and grasses. An endemic saltwater crab was known to live only at these springs, but may not have survived since the springs have been confined.

BIBLIOGRAPHY: Gunnar Brune, *Springs of Texas*, Vol. 1 (Fort Worth: Branch-Smith, 1981). *Gunnar Brune*

ESTEPISA INDIANS. The Estepisa Indians were a Karankawan group that entered Nuestra Señora de la Candelaria Mission on the San Gabriel River in 1750.

BIBLIOGRAPHY: Frederick Webb Hodge, ed., *Handbook of American Indians North of Mexico* (2 vols., Washington: GPO, 1907, 1910; rpt., New York: Pageant, 1959). *W. E. S. Dickerson*

ESTES, CARL LEWIS (1896–1967). Carl Lewis Estes, newspaper publisher and industrial leader, was born in New Market, Tennessee, on November 10, 1896, the son of Joseph Guinn and Della Marshall (Loy) Estes. He attended the public schools of Commerce and Denison and East Texas State Teachers College (now East Texas State University). As editor of his college newspaper, he became interested in journalism as a career, and he subsequently worked for the *Commerce Journal*, the Denison *Herald*, and the Tyler *Courier-Times*. As a foreign correspondent for the International News Service he spent 1927 in Paris and Stockholm. He founded the Tyler *Telegraph* in 1930 and four years later bought the Longview *Daily News* and the Longview *Morning Journal*. At Longview he also owned and published two weekly newspapers, the Longview *Lens* and the *Greggtonian*. During the 1930s Estes was publisher of the Van *Free Press*, the Carthage Panola *Watchman*, *East Texas Oil Magazine* (later the *Texas Oil Journal*), *East Texas Dairyman*, the *Wood County Record*, and the *Mineola Monitor*.

He served in the cavalry in World War I[qv] and was a lieutenant commander in the navy during World War II.[qv] He was a delegate to the national Democratic convention in Houston in 1928 and a delegate-at-large to the national Democratic convention in Chicago in 1932. He later served as confidential adviser to Arthur H. James, Republican governor of Pennsylvania. Estes was an originator of the Texas Rose Festival at Tyler, originator and first president of the East Texas Land and Royalty Owners Association, vice president and secretary of Van Oil Royalty Association, and an originator of the East Texas Dairy and Milk Products Association. Upon returning to Longview after World War II, he was effective in helping persuade a number of major industries to locate plants in the Longview area. As chairman of the Sabine Watershed Association, he was active in the development of the water resources of East Texas for industrial, recreational, and transportation uses.

Estes was a Mason and a Methodist. He married Margaret Virginia McLeod in Willow Grove, Pennsylvania, in 1943. He died at his vacation home in La Jolla, California, on May 29, 1967, and was buried in Memory Park, Longview, Texas.

BIBLIOGRAPHY: Sam Hanna Acheson, Herbert P. Gambrell, Mary Carter Toomey, and Alex M. Acheson, Jr., *Texian Who's Who*, Vol. 1 (Dallas: Texian, 1937). Dallas *Morning News*, May 31, June 1, 1967. *Texas Press Messenger*, June 1967. Vertical Files, Barker Texas History Center, University of Texas at Austin. *C. Richard King*

ESTES, WILLIAM LEE (1870–1930). William Lee Estes, lawyer and judge, the son of Benjamin Thomas and Jessie (Hicks) Estes, was born in Boston, Texas, on October 18, 1870. His father was a district judge and the founder of the Texarkana National Bank. Estes attended public school at Boston and Wytheville Military Academy at Wytheville, Virginia, where he graduated with honors in 1888. He received an A.B. degree with class honors at Hampden-Sydney College in 1891. He then entered law school at the University of Texas, where he received his LL.B. in 1894. He returned to Bowie County and opened a law office in Texarkana.

Estes was soon a prominent and successful attorney. In 1899, with Hiram Glass and John J. King,[qv] he founded the law firm Glass, Estes, and King. With the addition of A. L. Burford the firm was renamed Glass, Estes, King, and Burford. It became one of the best-known corporate law firms in the state and numbered among its clients some of the largest railroad corporations in Texas. On February 18, 1920, Estes was appointed United States district judge for the Eastern District of Texas, a position he held until his death.

He was also president of the Texarkana Board of Education and the state bar association, vice president of the Texarkana and Fort Smith Railway Company and the Port Arthur Channel and Dock Company, a director of the Texarkana National Bank, and a trustee of the William Buchanan[qv] Foundation. He was also a Mason and a Democrat. He attended the First Presbyterian Church of Texarkana, where he served as a deacon. On December 9, 1903, he married Annie Poindexter Dunn, the daughter of a prominent Arkansas congressman. The couple had three children, two of whom survived childhood. Estes died on June 14, 1930.

BIBLIOGRAPHY: Frank W. Johnson, *A History of Texas and Texans* (5 vols., ed. E. C. Barker and E. W. Winkler [Chicago and New York: American Historical Society, 1914; rpt. 1916]). Clarence R. Wharton, ed., *Texas under Many Flags* (5 vols., Chicago: American Historical Society, 1930). *Who Was Who in America*, Vol. 3.

Cecil Harper, Jr.

ESTES, WINSTON M. (1917–1982). Winston M. Estes, career Air Force officer, novelist, and short story writer, the son of Thomas Marvin and Grace (Newsom) Estes, was born at Quanah, Texas, on October 31, 1917. He graduated from Quanah High School in 1934, attended Texas Tech in 1938–39, and joined the Army Air Corps in 1941. He spent two years during World War II[qv] in the Pacific. He married Sarah Spears from Florence, South Carolina, in 1946, and afterwards served in San Antonio, Lubbock, and twice at the Pentagon in Washington. His first book, *Winston in Wonderland* (1956), is a spoof on Pentagon life.

Estes began to write seriously in 1960. He composed over seven book-length manuscripts and 120 short pieces, of which one collection of short stories and four novels have been published, all but one set in Texas. *Another Part of the House* (1970), a novel of the Panhandle[qv] in 1933–34 narrated by ten-year-old Larry Morrison, portrays the family of a small-town druggist confronting the Great Depression,[qv] drought, dust, and, especially, the death of Larry's fifteen-year-old brother. It became Estes's most successful novel and was reprinted in paperback. One critic lauded its concern with "the uncommon decencies over which neither want nor plenty can prevail."

A Streetful of People (1972), eight humorous short stories set in the Panhandle reveals Estes's wide range of comic techniques. In *A Simple Act of Kindness* (1973) he develops a theme of disillusionment as Pete Hamilton, Fort Worth salesman, attempts to help a wartime friend's widow. In *Andy Jessup* (1975) Estes enlarges the scope of his typical small-town settings, minimizes humor, and explores the theme of environmental determinism in an account of a forty-year relationship between outgoing Norman Stuart and enigmatic loner Andy Jessup. *Homefront* (1976), Estes's final and only non-Texas novel, is his least successful one, although it captures meticulously the effect of World War II upon Georgia citizens in small-town Bentley and bustling Atlanta. Though initiation, disillusionment, environmental determinism, and gentle social satire provide themes in Estes's fiction, he ultimately focuses on the affirmation of the best in humanity. He was a lieutenant colonel, an Episcopalian, and father of two children. He died in Camden, South Carolina, on September 13, 1982.

BIBLIOGRAPHY: *Contemporary Authors*, 1978. Bob J. Frye, "Humor and a Sense of Place in Winston Estes's *A Streetful of People*," *Concho River Review* 3 (Fall 1989). Bob J. Frye, *Winston M. Estes*, Western Writers Series, 103 (Boise State University Press, 1992). Bob J. Frye, "Winston Estes' Minor Classic: *Another Part of the House*," *Southwestern American Literature* 15 (Fall 1989). Quanah *Tribune-Chief*, April 2, 1970, September 16, 1982. *Bob J. Frye*

ESTEVANICO (?–1539). Estevanico, also known as Estevan, Esteban, Estebanico, Black Stephen, and Stephen the Moor, was a native of Azamor, on the Atlantic shore of Morocco. In Spain before 1527 he became the personal slave of Andrés Dorantes de Carranza.[qv] Though Estevanico is usually referred to as a Negro or African black, a Spaniard, Diego de Guzmán, who saw him in Sinaloa in 1536, described him as "brown." Estevanico accompanied his master as a member of the Narváez expedition, which landed in mid-April 1528 near what is now called Tampa Bay. Narváez, after a futile attempt at marching along the Gulf Coast, elected to slaughter the horses and to build five makeshift barges. The boat containing Estevanico was placed under the joint command of Dorantes and Alonso Castillo Maldonado.[qv] After a month at sea, the craft was wrecked on or near western Galveston Island. On foot Estevanico, Dorantes, and Castillo reached Matagorda Bay, the only survivors to do so. Their continued safety among hostile coastal Indians hinged on the success of faith healing, first introduced to them by Castillo Maldonado. After six years of precarious existence, a fourth survivor, Álvar Núñez Cabeza de Vaca,[qv] joined them. Subsequently, the castaways escaped to the interior of Texas.

Estevanico was the first African-born slave to traverse Texas. In the company of his master, he traveled a west-by-northwest route from the site of San Antonio to that of Pecos. In March 1536 the four survivors were reunited with their countrymen north of Culiacán in Nueva Galicia, where Dorantes sold Estevanico to Viceroy Antonio de Mendoza. The viceroy assigned the slave to a Franciscan, Fray Marcos de Niza.[qv] Niza had been ordered to Nueva Galicia, where he was to leave Culiacán in early March of 1539. On March 21, 1539, he and Estevanico arrived at the Río Mayo in what is now Sonora. There Estevanico, restless over the slow progress of the friar and his support party, was sent ahead as an advance scout. Separated by several days' travel from Niza, Esteban approached Cíbola, thought today to be the pueblo of Hawikuh, and announced his intentions to make peace and heal the sick. He told the villagers that he had been sent by white men who would soon arrive and instruct them in divine matters. The village elders, suspicious of his claims that he came from a land of white men because he was dark, and resentful of his demands for turquoise and women, killed him when he attempted to enter the village. Hawikuh, the southernmost of the seven pueblos known as the Seven Cities of Cíbola,[qv] was located fifteen miles southwest of the site of present Zuni, New Mexico.

BIBLIOGRAPHY: Carolyn Arrington, *Black Explorer in Spanish Texas: Estevanico* (Austin: Eakin Press, 1986). Stephen Clissold, *The Seven Cities of Cíbola* (London: Eyre and Spottiswood, 1961). Cyclone Covey, trans. and ed., *Cabeza de Vaca's Adventures in the Unknown Interior of America* (New York: Collier, 1961; rpt., Albuquerque: University of New Mexico Press, 1983). Harbert Davenport, ed., "'The Expedition of Pánfilo de Narváez,' by Gonzalo Fernández Oviedo y Valdez," *Southwestern Historical Quarterly* 27–28 (October 1923–October 1924). *Donald E. Chipman*

ESTILL, AMANDA JULIA (1882–1965). Amanda Julia Estill, educator, writer, and folklorist, daughter of James Thomas and Ellen Elizabeth (Wiley) Estill, was born in Fredericksburg, Texas, on October 27, 1882. She attended the University of Texas and received a B.S. in 1904 and an M.S. in 1905. She taught in the Fredericksburg schools in 1899–1900 and from 1905 to 1941; for eleven years she was high school principal. She was a teacher and elementary school principal in La Feria from 1947 until 1951 before returning to Fredericksburg.

She was a member of the Texas Folklore Society[qv] and served as its president in 1923–24; she contributed numerous articles to the society's publications. She was one of the first to write about the Sunday houses, Easter fires, Indian rock art,[qqv] and other landmarks in Gillespie County. She also contributed to the *American German Review*, wrote many historical pieces for the Fredericksburg Chamber of Commerce, and for twenty years was correspondent for the San Antonio *Express*. She served on the first board of directors of the Gillespie County Historical Society, and from 1943 to 1947 she was librarian at the Gillespie County Pioneer Museum and Library. She died on July 1, 1965, in Fredericksburg.

BIBLIOGRAPHY: Florence Elberta Barns, *Texas Writers of Today* (Dallas: Tardy, 1935). Fredericksburg *Standard*, July 7, 1965. Gillespie County Historical Society, *Pioneers in God's Hills* (2 vols., Austin: Von Boeckmann–Jones, 1960, 1974). Ella Amanda Gold, The History of Education in Gillespie County (M.A. thesis, University of Texas, 1945). *Esther L. Mueller*

ESTILL, HARRY FISHBURNE (1861–1942). Harry Fishburne Estill, teacher and college administrator, was born in Lexington, Virginia, on August 12, 1861, to Charles Patrick and Katherine (Fishburne) Estill. He was brought to Texas soon after the Civil War[qv] by his mother to join his father, who taught at Odd Fellows University in Bryan until 1881. Estill graduated in the first class at Sam Houston Normal Institute (later Sam Houston State Teachers University) in 1880. The next year his father moved to Huntsville to teach Latin at Sam Houston.

Estill taught in Grimes County until 1881 and was principal of the high school in Navasota for one year. He then succeeded his father in the Latin department at Sam Houston. He served as vice president of the college from 1898 to 1908, when he became president. He also taught at the State School of Methods in Austin in 1888 and conducted summer normal institutes in Orange, Jewett, Sulphur Springs, and Huntsville between 1890 and 1908.

Estill worked for the continuous improvement of Sam Houston State. He secured its change into a junior normal college in 1911 and into a state teachers' college in 1916 by expanding the curriculum and improving the physical plant. In 1898, in collaboration with Oscar Henry Cooper[qv] and Leonard Lemmon, he wrote a high school history text, *History of Our Country: A Textbook for Schools.* He published an elementary text, *Beginners' History of Our Country,* in 1901. Estill was a member of the Association of School Administrators, vice president of the college teachers' section of the National Education Association, president of the Texas State Teachers Association[qv] (1903), and a fellow of the Texas State Historical Association.[qv] In recognition of his authorship and cultural attainments Austin College conferred an honorary doctorate upon him in 1907. Estill became president emeritus in 1937 and continued his professorship in history until his death.

In 1892 he married Loulie Sharpe Sexton of Marshall; the couple had five children. Estill died in Huntsville on February 12, 1942. The Estill Library at Sam Houston State University is a tribute to his labors. He was a Democrat, a Presbyterian, a Mason, and a Rotarian.

BIBLIOGRAPHY: D'Anne McAdams Crews, ed., *Huntsville and Walker County, Texas: A Bicentennial History* (Huntsville, Texas: Sam Houston State University, 1976). *Leaders in Education,* 1941. Vertical Files, Barker Texas History Center, University of Texas at Austin. Walker County Genealogical Society and Walker County Historical Commission, *Walker County* (Dallas, 1986). *Who's Who in America,* 1938–39.

Mary S. Estill

ESTILL, MARY SEXTON (1901–1982). Mary Sexton Estill, teacher and author, was born on April 28, 1901, in Huntsville, Texas, to Loulie Sharpe (Sexton) and Harry Fishburne Estill.[qv] Her great-grandfather, Daniel L. Richardson,[qv] fought at San Jacinto. She received a B.A. degree from Columbia University, New York. After researching in London, she wrote a thesis comparing methods of public education in Great Britain and the United States, for which she received an M.A. degree from Columbia. She taught in Marshall, Trinity, Greenville, Huntsville, and other Texas towns, and on the college level at Stephen F. Austin State University, West Texas State University, and Sam Houston State University. In 1970 she wrote a history of Sam Houston State University, of which her father was fifth president. She preserved much Texas history with her writings, which included articles for several historical journals. She was active in many historic and educational organizations and was one of the earliest Presbyterian woman elders. She was a leader in integration in her area. She started the first interdenominational and interracial organization for improving housing for low-income citizens in Walker County. For her community service, the town named a street in her honor. She died on June 23, 1982, and is buried in Oakwood Cemetery, Huntsville.

BIBLIOGRAPHY: Walker County Genealogical Society and Walker County Historical Commission, *Walker County* (Dallas, 1986).

Natalie Ornish

ETHEL, TEXAS. Ethel is on Farm Road 902 fourteen miles southwest of Sherman in southwestern Grayson County. The community developed in the late 1850s as ranchers and lumbermen converged. John Dishman constructed a gin, and a school was built on the ranch of S. A. Schott. In 1885 a post office opened; the name Ethel was submitted by W. H. Burgin, who owned the general store and became the first postmaster. By 1900 the number of residents had increased to eighty-one. The post office closed in 1902. From 1930 until 1990 the population was estimated at twenty-five.

David Minor

ETHOLEN, TEXAS. Etholen was on the Southern Pacific Railroad four miles west of Sierra Blanca in south central Hudspeth County. According to one source a post office had been opened and closed there before 1884, although other sources hold that the community was not established until around 1885. Etholen seems to have been little more than a railroad station; in 1945 its population was fewer than twenty-five, and it no longer appeared on maps of the area by the mid-1960s. The community was reportedly named for the Etholen Knobs, a nearby cluster of buttes.

Martin Donell Kohout

ETNA, TEXAS. Etna was near the site of present Bullard thirty miles northwest of Rusk in northwestern Cherokee County. It was first settled by immigrants from the Old South around the time of the Civil War.[qv] A local post office opened in 1867, and by the early 1880s the community had a district school, a church, a steam gristmill, a blacksmith shop, several general stores, and a drygoods store. The settlement began to decline in the mid-1880s, after the Kansas and Gulf Short Line Railroad bypassed it. Most of the residents and businesses moved to Bullard. The post office was closed in 1883, and by 1900 Etna was a ghost town.

BIBLIOGRAPHY: *Cherokee County History* (Jacksonville, Texas: Cherokee County Historical Commission, 1986).

Christopher Long

ETOILE, TEXAS. Etoile is on State Highway 103 and Farm Road 226, between the Angelina and the Attoyac rivers twenty miles south of Nacogdoches and nineteen miles east of Lufkin in southeastern Nacogdoches County. In 1876 the Reverend James Sims, a Baptist minister, built a church at Macedonia Springs, and a town called Macedonia developed around the church. The community was sparsely settled in 1876. Roads were few and in very poor shape. Steamboats from Beaumont docked at Brown's Ferry on the Angelina River just outside the community until 1881. The town received its mail by horseback from nearby Cherino. By 1882 the community had grown a little, and that year residents applied for a post office, which they received in 1886 by paying for weekly deliveries of mail from Nacogdoches and by renaming the town. They chose the name Etoile, which means "star" in French. In 1897 Etoile had the Fisher and Crown General Store. By 1915 the town had a population of 300, telephone service, a post office, a gin, two general stores, and other businesses. By 1925 the community's population had dropped to 100, where it remained into the 1940s. The local rail line stopped serving the town in 1950, and the population dropped to a low of fifty. Between the late 1950s and 1965 the Sam Rayburn Dam and Reservoir was built in the area. During the 1980s Etoile comprised a population of seventy, a few stores, and several bait houses, marinas, boat stalls, and campgrounds. It was mainly a retirement community. Some residents raised beef cattle and chickens. In the early 1990s Etoile reported a population of seventy, with seven businesses and a post office.

BIBLIOGRAPHY: Nacogdoches County Genealogical Society, *Nacogdoches County Families* (Dallas: Curtis, 1985).

John Folsom

ETTER, TEXAS. Etter, on U.S. Highway 287 in northern Moore County, was established as a stop on the North Plains and Santa Fe Railroad in 1930 and was named for W. K. Etter, a vice president of the road. Later the Chicago, Rock Island and Gulf Railway intersected the Santa Fe at this point. In 1940 Etter comprised the railroad switch, three businesses, and a reported population of 150. When the Cactus industrial community was established to the north in 1942, Etter's businesses and many of its residents were absorbed into the new town. In 1980 and 1990 Etter reported a population of 160.

BIBLIOGRAPHY: Myrna Tryon Thomas, *The Windswept Land: A History of Moore City* (Dumas, Texas, 1967).

H. Allen Anderson

ETTLINGER, HYMAN JOSEPH (1889–1986). Hyman Joseph Ettlinger, mathematician and university teacher, was born on September 1, 1889, in St. Louis, Missouri, the second of six children of

Abraham and Pearl (Shucart) Ettlinger. He attended public schools in St. Louis and received his B.A. from Washington University, St. Louis, and his M.A. and Ph.D. from Harvard University. He was elected to Phi Beta Kappa in 1911. Ettlinger taught mathematics at the University of Texas from 1913 until 1969, when he was named professor emeritus. He taught courses at all levels from freshman to post-doctoral and supervised twenty-two doctoral dissertations and at least 105 master's theses. He wrote more than twenty technical papers and was coauthor of two textbooks and several technical reports. As a former star football player at Washington University, he was also the varsity line coach at UT for two years, freshman football coach for two years, and director of intercollegiate athletics from 1928 to 1930. For four decades he officiated at football games and track meets. Ettlinger served as secretary of Congregation Beth Israel in Austin for twenty-five years and chaired the building-fund committee for the University of Texas Hillel Foundation. For years he was a member of the executive committee of the National Conference of Christians and Jews, and he also served on the group's educational committee. He received the University of Texas Students' Association teaching award in 1959 and the distinguished service citation of the Texas section of the Mathematical Association of America in 1977. Ettlinger married Rosebud Segal in 1918; they had two children. He died in Austin on June 8, 1986.

BIBLIOGRAPHY: Vertical Files, Barker Texas History Center, University of Texas at Austin.

Robert E. Greenwood

EUDORA, TEXAS. Eudora was near Zavalla seventeen miles east of Lufkin in eastern Angelina County. The settlement was established sometime after the Civil War.qv A post office opened there in 1885, and by 1892 Eudora had a general store and a reported population of sixty. Its post office closed in 1903, and the mail was sent to Dunkin. In the early 1990s only a few scattered houses remained in the area.

BIBLIOGRAPHY: Angelina County Historical Survey Committee, *Land of the Little Angel: A History of Angelina County, Texas,* ed. Bob Bowman (Lufkin, Texas: Lufkin Printing, 1976).

Christopher Long

EUGENE MCDERMOTT FOUNDATION. The McDermott Foundation was established in 1955 by industrialist Eugene McDermott,qv cofounder of Geophysical Services, Incorporated (now Texas Instrumentsqv). The McDermott Foundation gives grants in support of educational, cultural, social-service, and other civic and community ventures. In 1994–95 the foundation had assets of over $43 million and made seventy-nine grants totaling $2,789,640. The foundation office was in Dallas, and Mary McDermott Cook was president.

Art Leatherwood

EULA, TEXAS. Eula is on Farm Road 603 some seven miles southwest of Clyde in western Callahan County. A post office was established there in 1889 with W. B. Ferguson as postmaster. In addition to Ferguson, early settlers included Wylie Miller, Ison Harris, Jules Janette, and Jim Massie, as well as the Merrick brothers and the Gardner and Farrar families. Eula's population was only seventeen in 1903, and in 1913 its post office was closed. The community, however, later revived somewhat, and by 1940 it reported seventy-five residents, three stores, three churches, and a school. In 1990 its population was estimated as 125.

BIBLIOGRAPHY: Brutus Clay Chrisman, *Early Days in Callahan County* (Abilene, Texas: Abilene Printing and Stationery, 1966).

EULESS, TEXAS. Euless is at the intersection of State highways 10 and 183, on the southwest side of the Dallas–Fort Worth Airport, north of the West Fork of the Trinity River in Tarrant County. Bird's Fort was established at a site just south of the present city limits in 1841. The community began by 1845, when a small party of pioneers led by Isham Crowley reached the confluence of Big Bear and Little Bear creeks. There on the eastern edge of the site of present Euless, on the current airport grounds, a post office was founded in 1857, named Estill's Station, and a school, a church, a store, and a cotton gin were established. The post office closed in 1868. It reopened, 1881–1904, under the name Estelle. Most of the community gradually dissipated and moved to present Euless and Irving. A mile or more to the southwest, around 1876, a community hall-church-school building was erected. In 1881 Elisha Adam and Julia Euless from Tennessee built a home and cotton gin nearby, and the community began to thrive. Local farmers decided to honor the young man whose presence seemed to coincide with better times, and the community was named for him. The Euless post office opened in 1886 and closed in 1910. Euless farmers usually journeyed to Dallas to buy supplies and sell produce and cotton.

In 1903 the Rock Island Railroad built a depot two miles south of Euless at Candon, whose name changed to Tarrant by 1905. Tarrant had a post office, 1905–23, and in the 1910s Tarrant may have had 100 people and Euless twenty-five. The Rock Island soon discontinued regular service, and the depot closed in the 1930s. By then Euless may have attained a population of 100, while Tarrant's was perhaps twenty-five. Tarrant gradually merged with Euless. From the early twentieth century to the mid-1930s Euless community life revolved around the general store run by the Fuller family, the Baptist and Methodist churches, and the Euless School, erected in 1913. The Tennessee Dairies receiving plant in Euless and the Fort Worth Sand and Gravel Company just south of town in the Trinity bottoms opened operations in the 1920s, aiding a number of local farm families in supplementing meager farm incomes. The brewing and sale of illegal whiskey during prohibition, 1919–33, was another economic stimulus in the area. Electricity arrived in 1929, and the school achieved high school status in 1934.

After the stimulus of World War IIqv there were perhaps 300 people in Euless and Tarrant by the end of the 1940s. The Euless post office reopened in 1949. A crisis moved the community to the edge of violence. In 1949 black parents in Mosier Valley refused to obey new orders from the Euless school superintendent, which called for the busing of their children outside their district to Fort Worth. There were closer schools in Euless, but they had always been for whites only. The Mosier Valley elementary school was a tattered branch of the Euless district. A district judge ruled that Texas law provided that students had a right to be educated in their own districts and that a district's schools were supposed to be funded impartially. Texas at the time had some 1,100 districts that bused blacks to other districts, and it appeared for some months as though segregation in Texas might stand or fall on the Euless case. Blacks entered the Euless school on September 4, 1950, in an attempt at enrollment, and the building was soon surrounded by a hostile crowd of some 150 whites. The school superintendent informed his black audience in the auditorium that he had to enforce the state's segregation laws. Blacks returned to the Mosier Valley school, which was quickly refurbished by white authorities. The village incorporated in 1951, disincorporated in 1952 over water and sewer taxes, and reincorporated in 1953. The Euless school district merged with Hurst in 1955 and was joined by Bedford in 1958. The HEB district desegregated in 1968.

Growth was enhanced in the early 1950s by the paving of old State Highway 183 and Farm Road 157 and the construction of Amon Carter (Air) Field on the eastern edge of Euless, which opened in 1953. The Euless Chamber of Commerce was established in 1952 and merged with that of Hurst in 1955. The Menasco Manufacturing Company, which made airplane parts, was an important local manufacturer. American Airlines began moving its installations to Euless in 1957. The population surged to over 4,200 in 1960.

In 1967 Euless voted 211 to 133 to merge with smaller Bedford, but an overwhelming majority in Bedford opposed it. Hurst, Euless, and

Bedford all approved the establishment of a joint hospital district in 1969. Euless's population climbed to 19,300 in 1970, but the completion of Airport Freeway and the Dallas–Fort Worth Airport drove land prices out of reach for most of the decade. The population increased only to 24,000 in 1980. The town is heavily committed to arboreal beautification, reflected dramatically in its annual Arbor Daze fair launched in 1989. The DFW Airport's announcement to expand a new west side runway in 1988 triggered an acrimonious conflict with Euless and a prolonged legal tussle. The town could lose $100,000,000 worth of property. Euless had a population of over 38,000 in 1990.

BIBLIOGRAPHY: Clippings File, Euless Public Library. *Historic Resources Survey: Selected Tarrant County Communities* (Fort Worth: Historic Preservation Council for Tarrant County, 1990). Janet L. Schmelzer, *Where the West Begins: Fort Worth and Tarrant County* (Northridge, California: Windsor, 1985).
George N. Green

EULOGY, TEXAS. Eulogy is near Farm Road 56 some nine miles northeast of Walnut Springs and fifty miles northwest of Waco in northern Bosque County. Charles Walker Smith founded the settlement when he moved his store there from Brazos Point; the store opened on July 11, 1884, and in 1885 a post office was established in it. The community originally applied for a post office under the name Smithville, in honor of a man called Uncle Billye Smith, but since there was already a Smithville in Texas, Smith's sister, Julia Smith Mickey, may have recommended the name Eulogy, based upon the idea that everyone eulogized Uncle Billye. This post office name was approved, and the office operated until 1912. In the 1890s Eulogy supported a school, at least three churches, a steam gristmill and gin, and several other retail and service businesses. Around 1900 a two-story wooden school building was erected at the community; the school's top floor served as a meeting hall for various associations. This building burned in 1929 and was later replaced by a brick structure. The school was eventually consolidated with those of Walnut Springs, after which the school building was used for community functions. The number of rated businesses at Eulogy had fallen to two by 1931, and after 1961 none were reported there. During the 1890s Eulogy's population was estimated at between 100 and 200, but in 1933 it fell to ninety-three and then by 1974 to forty-five, at which level it was still reported in 1990.

BIBLIOGRAPHY: Bosque County History Book Committee, *Bosque County, Land and People* (Dallas: Curtis Media, 1985). William C. Pool, *Bosque Territory* (Kyle, Texas: Chaparral, 1964).
Karen Yancy

EUNICE, TEXAS. Eunice is on State Highway 7 some fourteen miles east of Centerville in eastern Leon County. It was founded in the mid-1800s by John Morrison and was originally known as Morrison's Chapel. In 1907 a Eunice post office was established there in the store of Charles J. Hogan, who served as the first postmaster; the post office was named after his daughter. By 1914 the Eunice community had a population of 100, a livestock breeder, and a general store. In 1934 its post office was discontinued, and mail was rerouted through Nineveh. Eunice reported a population of twenty-five in 1940. A 1964 map shows about ten buildings and the Victory Church at the site. Eunice is labeled on the 1983 highway map, but no buildings are shown there.

BIBLIOGRAPHY: Leon County Historical Book Survey Committee, *History of Leon County* (Dallas: Curtis Media, 1986).
Dylan Wood

EUREKA, TEXAS (Franklin County). Eureka is twelve miles northwest of Mount Vernon in northwestern Franklin County. In 1896 it had a one-teacher, one-room school that served thirty-seven students. During the 1930s Eureka had a school, church, and business. By 1985 only widely scattered houses remained in the area.
Cecil Harper, Jr.

EUREKA, TEXAS (Navarro County). Eureka is at the junction of U.S. Highway 287 and Farm roads 637 and 3243, eleven miles southeast of Corsicana in southeastern Navarro County. The settlement developed around a log schoolhouse known as Dunn's School just before the Civil War.[qv] In 1870 residents applied for a post office, and at a Grange[qv] meeting decided on the name Eureka. That same year a post office was opened in the home of P. Anderson, and within a few years a small town grew up there. By 1885 Eureka reported several steam gristmills and cotton gins, two churches, a district school, and an estimated population of twenty-five. In 1914 its population was about 100. Three local schools were in operation by 1906—two for white students, with a total enrollment of eighty-five, and one for black students, with an enrollment of sixty-one. In the mid-1930s Eureka had a school and six businesses. The Eureka school was consolidated with that of Mildred after World War II.[qv] The community's population continued to be estimated at about 100 until the mid-1960s, when it was reported as 125. At that time two churches and several businesses still remained at Eureka. In the early 1990s Eureka was a dispersed rural community with an estimated population of 243.

BIBLIOGRAPHY: Annie Carpenter Love, *History of Navarro County* (Dallas: Southwestern, 1933). Wyvonne Putman, comp., *Navarro County History* (5 vols., Quanah, Texas: Nortex, 1975–84). Alva Taylor, *History and Photographs of Corsicana and Navarro County* (Corsicana, Texas, 1959; rev. ed., *Navarro County History and Photographs*, Corsicana, 1962).
Christopher Long

EUREKA MILLS, TEXAS. Eureka Mills, on the western edge of Houston in central Harris County, had a cotton factory in 1872 with about seventy-five operatives. A post office, established there in 1872, was discontinued in 1879, but was still listed on postal route maps in 1888, when the community was a stop on the Houston and Texas Central Railway. By the 1980s the site served as a major trainyard for the Missouri, Kansas and Texas line.
Diana J. Kleiner

EUSTACE, TEXAS. Eustace, on U.S. Highway 175 some ten miles northwest of Athens in northwestern Henderson County, was on the J. M. Beltram survey. In 1900, when the Texas and New Orleans Railroad extended its line eastward from Kemp to Athens, the area reportedly had only one inhabitant, who occupied a rented log cabin. Businessmen from nearby communities moved to be closer to the new railroad line. The town that developed was first called Moseley by W. L. Moseley, who had sold the railroad right-of-way across the Beltram survey and who had sold the first lots in the town. It was also called Jolo in honor of Joe L. Pickle, the town blacksmith. A post office for Jolo was established in 1900, but that same year the name was changed to Eustace, for Capt. W. T. Eustace, a popular Confederate Civil War[qv] veteran. Captain Eustace came to Henderson County from Virginia in 1867 and settled at the county seat, Athens, where he was active in local and county politics. By 1901 the name Eustace began to appear on deed records. The 1900 census reported a population of 150 at the community, and by 1904 the town had three churches, two general stores, a grocery store, a blacksmith, a restaurant, a saloon, and a cotton gin. Eustace was incorporated in 1926. Its population grew slowly, from 450 in 1940 to 541 in 1980 and to an estimated 662 in 1990. The early economy of the town was based primarily on cotton, but later its economy, along with that of other East Texas towns, gradually shifted to livestock raising and small-scale truck farming. During the 1970s and 1980s the local economy was given a boost by the discovery of oil and the production of petroleum products. In the late 1980s, however, these resources were being rapidly depleted. The town also benefited economically from nearby recreational areas, including Cedar Creek Lake (established 1964) five miles southwest, and Purtis Creek State Recreation Area^{qv} (established 1988), four miles north. In 1989 the town comprised twenty-six small businesses, five churches, and a school with a total enrollment of some 1,000 students (kindergarten through high school grades).

BIBLIOGRAPHY: Eustace Historical Committee, *A Brief History of Eustace, Texas* (Eustace, 1986). J. J. Faulk, *History of Henderson County* (Athens, Texas: Athens Review Printing, 1926). Winnie McGaughey Reynolds, The History of Henderson County (M.A. thesis, East Texas State Teachers College, 1952). *Rebecca Reynolds Gartrell*

EUTAW, TEXAS. Eutaw, two miles east of Kosse, was the most important town in southern Limestone County until the coming of the railroads after the Civil War.^{qv} The town formed in the early 1840s during the Republic of Texas^{qv} era and was said to have been named in honor of Eutaw, Alabama, birthplace of one of the new community's original settlers. The settlement's first church was the Salem Baptist Church, organized in 1855. Around the same time, L. E. Trevzant opened a local school. The town grew rapidly. By the eve of the Civil War it had four general stores, two churches, a tavern, a blacksmith shop, a stage depot, and a school. Adolph Harris, who later became famous as the owner of the A. Harris and Company department store in Dallas, opened his first store in Eutaw shortly after arriving there in the 1850s. A post office was opened at the community in 1856, and Nathan Gilbert was appointed its first postmaster. Eutaw's decline began shortly after the Civil War. In 1869 the Houston and Texas Central Railway established nearby Kosse as a terminus, and many residents of Eutaw, along with their businesses, moved to the new town. The Eutaw post office was closed in 1870, but the town itself continued to serve as the center for surrounding farms until after World War II.^{qv} The Eutaw school survived until 1949, when it was annexed by the Kosse Independent School District. The Salem Baptist Church had disbanded by the early 1980s, and in 1988 only the church building marked the site of the town. The old cemetery was nearby.

BIBLIOGRAPHY: Maggie Abercrombie, "Historical Sketch of Limestone County, Texas," *American Sketch Book* 6 (1878). Hampton Steele, *A History of Limestone County, 1833–1860* (Mexia, Texas: Mexia *News*, n.d.). Ray A. Walter, *A History of Limestone County* (Austin: Von Boeckmann–Jones, 1959). *Ray A. Walter*

EVA, TEXAS. Eva was near the site of what is now Palito Blanco off Farm Road 2295 thirteen miles south of San Diego in southwestern Jim Wells County. A post office called Eva was established there in 1904. By 1914 the community had two grocery stores and a cattle breeder and was described as a country post office. Eva's population reached twenty by 1925. Its post office was discontinued in 1928, and mail was sent to Palito Blanco. In 1938 the community had scattered dwellings and farm units, and by 1939 it reported a population of 100 and four businesses. Eva reported a population of 150 in 1947 but by 1963 all that remained of the dispersed community was a few dwellings. *Alicia A. Garza*

EVADALE, TEXAS. Evadale is at the junction of U.S. Highway 96 and Farm roads 105, 1131, and 2246, twenty-five miles northeast of Beaumont in southwestern Jasper County. During the 1830s and 1840s the site was called Richardson (Richardson's) Bluff, for early settler Benjamin Richardson, who operated a ferry on the Neches River and who also served as postmaster in 1839. Town lots for the area were listed in county tax rolls as early as 1859. After Richardson's death in 1849, the land was sold to John A., Philip U., and Charles T. Ford. At this time the site was often referred to as Ford's Bluff. Hoping to establish a sawmill, Philip Ford went to New Orleans to buy machinery but contracted yellow fever there and died shortly after returning to Jasper County. Nonetheless, Ford's Bluff became an important collection point for logs, which were floated down the river to Beaumont mills. In 1893 John Henry Kirby^{qv} chartered the Gulf, Beaumont and Kansas City Railway and rebuilt a tram line that already ran from Ford's Bluff to Buna as part of his larger common carrier project. Kirby renamed the site for Miss Eva Dale, a teacher at Jasper's Southeast Texas Male and Female College, and constructed a mill there by 1904, when the post office was established. By 1914 the Evadale plant, known as Mill U, included kilns, a circular sawmill, and a planing mill with a daily capacity of up to 70,000 board feet. Evadale had a population of 300 by 1920. The Kirby mill closed during the Great Depression,^{qv} and by the late 1940s the town's population had fallen to 100. Economic revitalization began in 1948, when the Champion Paper and Fiber Company acquired riverfront acreage for a pulp mill. By the 1970s the giant Temple-Eastex pulpwood and paper mill dominated the local economy. With the new activity, the population in Evadale reached 700 by the early 1960s. In 1984 the town had twenty-two businesses and an estimated 715 residents. In 1990 its population was 1,422.

BIBLIOGRAPHY: James M. McReynolds, A History of Jasper County, Texas, Prior to 1874 (M.A. thesis, Lamar State College of Technology, 1968). S. G. Reed, *A History of the Texas Railroads* (Houston: St. Clair, 1941; rpt., New York: Arno, 1981). Kathleen E. and Clifton R. St. Clair, eds., *Little Towns of Texas* (Jacksonville, Texas: Jayroe Graphic Arts, 1982). *Robert Wooster*

EVANGELICAL LUTHERAN COLLEGE. Evangelical Lutheran College was established in 1870 at Rutersville, Fayette County, where buildings were bought for $600 and Rev. H. Mertz became supervisor and instructor. The institution met with small success and in 1878 was forced to close. Another Evangelical Lutheran College was a predecessor of Texas Lutheran College.^{qv}

BIBLIOGRAPHY: Max Heinrich, comp., *History of the First Evangelical Lutheran Synod of Texas* (Waverly, Iowa: Wartburg, 1928).

EVANS, CECIL EUGENE (1871–1958). Cecil Eugene Evans, education advocate and university president, was born on January 21, 1871, at Bowdon, Georgia, the son of Hiram Martin and Georgia (Striplin) Evans. He was educated at Oxford College, Alabama, where he took a B.A. degree in 1888. He received an M.A. degree from the University of Texas in 1906, and in recognition of his work as an educator Southwestern University conferred on him an honorary LL.D. in 1923. Evans taught in Alabama schools from 1889 to 1893, then moved to Texas in 1894 to teach at Mexia. He was superintendent of the public school at Anson from 1895 to 1902, at Merkel from 1902 to 1905, and at Abilene from 1906 to 1908. From 1908 to 1911 he served as general agent for the Conference on Education in Texas, successfully conducting campaigns to secure three school amendments to the Texas Constitution. In addition, he was largely responsible for legislation designed to improve the public schools and teacher training. From 1917 to 1927 Evans served as a member of the Texas Textbook Board. His book *The Story of Texas Schools* (1955) is a volume on historical development of the public and private educational system of the state.

Evans went to Southwest Texas Normal School (now Southwest Texas State University) at San Marcos in 1911 as its second president. During his thirty-one years in this office, Southwest Texas added two years of college work to the curriculum, then a full college course accredited by the American Association of Colleges, and finally a graduate program awarding master's degrees. The college plant expanded from an original eleven acres to more than double that size, and from a three-building institution to fifteen classroom and administration buildings, eight dormitories and cooperative houses, a forty-acre farm, a swimming pool, and a park. Enrollment expanded from 600 to 1,600 students. Evans retired in 1942, at which time Lyndon Baines Johnson^{qv} (at one time secretary to Evans) came from Washington to speak at the ceremony.

Evans was a Democrat, a Methodist, a member of the National Education Association, and a trustee of Southwestern University. He was married to Allie Maxwell in Anson on May 18, 1899; they were the parents of one daughter. Evans died on August 23, 1958, and was buried at San Marcos.

BIBLIOGRAPHY: San Marcos *Record*, April 21, 1936. *Who's Who in America*, 1934–35.
Tula Townsend Wyatt

EVANS, HERSCHEL (1909–1939). Herschel Evans, black musician and composer, was born in Denton, Texas, in 1909 and spent some of his childhood in Kansas City, Kansas, where his cousin Eddie Durham qv was a trombonist and guitarist. Durham persuaded Evans to switch from alto to tenor sax, the instrument that ultimately established his reputation. After perfecting his craft in the famous jam sessions held in the jazz district between Twelfth and Eighteenth streets in Kansas City, Evans returned to Texas in the 1920s and joined the Troy Floyd orchestra in San Antonio in 1929. He stayed with the band until it dispersed in 1932. Evans performed for a time with Lionel Hampton and Buck Clayton in Los Angeles, but in the mid-1930s he returned to Kansas City to become a featured soloist in Count Basie's big band.

For the next three years Evans's reputation as a tenor saxophonist was at its peak. His musical duels with fellow band member Lester Young are considered jazz classics. Count Basie's popular "One O'Clock Jump" featured the contrasting styles of the two musicians and brought to each the praise of both critics and the general public. The composition displayed Evans's full-bodied, emotional timbre and Young's high-pitched, light, and buoyant tone, contrasting sounds that highlighted each other. Evans's greatest single success was his featured solo in Basie's hit "Blue and Sentimental."

Evans also made records with such notable jazz figures as Harry James, Theodore S. (Teddy) Wilson, qv and Lionel Hampton. Evans has been credited with influencing fellow tenorists Buddy Tate, Illinois Jacquet, and Arnett Cobb. qv Although not a prolific composer, Evans did write a number of popular works, including the hits "Texas Shuffle" and "Doggin' Around." On February 9, 1939, at the age of thirty, he died of heart disease in New York City.

BIBLIOGRAPHY: Frank Driggs and Harris Lewine, *Black Beauty, White Heat: A Pictorial History of Classic Jazz, 1920–1950* (New York: Morrow, 1982). Leonard G. Feather, *The Encyclopedia of Jazz* (New York: Horizon, 1955; rev. ed., New York: Bonanza, 1960). Len Lyons, *The 101 Best Jazz Albums* (New York: Morrow, 1980). Ross Russell, *Jazz Style in Kansas City and the Southwest* (Berkeley: University of California Press, 1971).
David Minor

EVANS, HIRAM WESLEY (1881–1966). Hiram Wesley Evans, "imperial wizard" of the Ku Klux Klan, qv son of Hiram Martin and Georgia (Striplin) Evans, was born on September 26, 1881, in Ashland, Alabama. While he was a youth his family moved to Texas, and he graduated from high school in Hubbard. He studied dentistry at Vanderbilt University but left before obtaining a degree. He received his dentistry license in 1900 and practiced in Dallas until 1920. On February 5, 1923, he married Bam Hill; they had three children.

In 1920 Evans joined the Ku Klux Klan and devoted most of his time to its support. By 1921 he had reached the rank of "exalted cyclops" and led a group of Klansmen who forcibly removed Alex Johnson, a black bellhop, from the Adolphus Hotel and wrote "K.K.K." on his forehead with acid. The next year Evans began his climb to power within the Klan. Early in 1922, when the "Realm of Texas" was organized, Evans became a "great titan" (district leader), and several months later he was appointed "imperial kligrapp," or national secretary, by the imperial wizard, William J. Simmons. Under his leadership the Klan became involved in state and local primary elections.

Evans was imperial wizard from 1922 until 1939. Shortly before his resignation he sold the Klan's Peachtree Street Palace to the Catholic Church. He wrote several books, including *The Menace of Modern Immigration* (1923), *The Klan of Tomorrow* (1924), *Alienism in the Democracy* (1927), and *The Rising Storm* (1929). While serving as imperial wizard he dealt in emulsified asphalt for highway construction in Atlanta. The state of Georgia brought a suit against him for violating the Sherman Antitrust Act, but the suit was eventually dropped. Evans died in September 1966 in Atlanta, Georgia. He was a Democrat, a Mason, and a member of the Christian Church and the Congressional Country Club.

BIBLIOGRAPHY: Charles C. Alexander, *The Ku Klux Klan in the Southwest* (Lexington: University of Kentucky Press, 1965). *Who Was Who in America*, Vol. 6.
Lisa C. Maxwell

EVANS, IRA HOBART (1844–1922). Ira Hobart Evans, soldier, legislator, and businessman, son of Ira and Emeline (Hobart) Evans, was born in Piermont, New Hampshire, on April 11, 1844. He attended public schools in Barre, Vermont, enlisted in the Vermont Volunteer Infantry in July 1862, and was commissioned first lieutenant in 1863 and captain in 1865. In March 1865 he attained the rank of brevet major and was appointed acting assistant adjutant general of the Twenty-fifth Army Corps, Army of the James. After Robert E. Lee's qv surrender at Appomattox, Evans was sent to Texas as a member of the occupation force of Maj. Gen. Philip Henry Sheridan. qv He held various administrative positions in the Brownsville area until he was transferred to New Orleans in September 1866. He received his discharge on January 31, 1867. In 1867 he settled in Texas north of Corpus Christi and began raising stock. He lost his investment there through the dishonesty of a partner.

Evans then joined the Freedmen's Bureau qv at Wharton but resigned on January 31, 1868, angered by his superiors in the bureau, whom he considered incompetent. He subsequently worked for the Internal Revenue Service, first in Eagle Pass and then in Corpus Christi. At the urging of Republican gubernatorial candidate Edmund Jackson Davis, qv in 1869 Evans ran for and won a seat in the Texas House, representing the Western District of Texas. He was elected speaker of the House in 1870; at age twenty-five he was the youngest person ever to hold this office. He took an active interest in all legislation, especially that relating to a railroad system.

In August 1870 an election law was passed that violated the Constitution of 1869 qv by postponing the date of the next election by one year to 1872. Evans strongly opposed this measure and was supported by all Democrats in both houses and by a few Republicans. He and his Republican supporters were called before a caucus of the Republican party qv and denounced, and afterward the caucus voted to remove Evans from the office of speaker. The next morning the office was declared vacant. Evans completed his extended term as representative, but when the Twelfth Legislature adjourned on December 2, 1871, he left political life.

He then pursued a business career. He was elected general manager of the Texas Land Company of Houston on January 16, 1872, and secretary of the Houston and Great Northern Railroad Company in 1873. After the merger of the International Railroad with the Houston and Great Northern, he was elected secretary of the consolidated International–Great Northern Railroad Company in 1874. He was director of this railroad from 1875 to 1908 and president of the New York and Texas Land Company, qv Limited, from 1880 to 1906. He was a cofounder of the Austin National Bank in 1890 and director of the bank from 1890 to 1922. He was appointed receiver of the Austin Rapid Transit Railway Company in 1897 and held that position for five years. He was president and director of the Austin Electric Railway Company in 1902–03.

Evans's lifelong interest in the advancement of southern blacks was manifest in his support for Tillotson College in Austin (*see* HUSTON-TILLOTSON COLLEGE). He was a member of the board of trustees of that college from 1881 to 1920 and president of the board from 1909 to

1920. He donated $10,000 to the college for use in training students in construction skills; as a result of this gift the college was able to construct a building that bears his name. Evans bequeathed an additional $10,000 to be used to build a residence for the president of the college.

He served as president of the American Missionary Society and the Sunday School Association. He was one of the organizers of the First Congregational Church in Palestine in 1881 and served that church prominently for many years. He was a member of the board of trustees of the First Presbyterian Church in Austin for twenty-two years and president of the board of trustees of the First Congregational Church of Austin for five years. He was also a member of numerous military, historical, scientific, and political organizations. His Austin home served as a meetingplace for a group that later became the Texas State Historical Association.qv Among the many honors conferred upon him was the Medal of Honor, which he was awarded for distinguished bravery at Hatcher's Run, Virginia, on April 2, 1865. He was selected as one of the officers of the honor guard to march in President Abraham Lincoln's funeral cortège.

Evans married Frances Abi Hurlbut of Upper Alton, Illinois, on July 13, 1871, and they had three sons. The marriage ended in divorce in 1917. He was married again, to Jessie M. Stewart, on October 14, 1920. He moved to San Diego, California, in 1921 and died on April 19, 1922. He was buried in the family plot in Montpelier, Vermont.

BIBLIOGRAPHY: Frank W. Johnson, *A History of Texas and Texans* (5 vols., ed. E. C. Barker and E. W. Winkler [Chicago and New York: American Historical Society, 1914; rpt. 1916]). San Diego *Union*, April 24, 1922. *Who Was Who in America*, Vol. 4.   *Hobart L. Evans*

EVANS, JOHN F. (1849–1935). John F. (Spade) Evans, pioneer cattleman, was born on May 1, 1849, near Chattanooga, Tennessee. About 1860 he moved with his family to Jefferson, in Marion County, Texas, and later to Parker County. After his father's death in 1861, John quit school and went to work to help support his family. He soon became one of the free-range cowmen of the Northwest Texas frontier. After the Civil Warqv he ran a supply store at Palo Pinto and later traveled for a saddlery house in St. Louis, Missouri. He became associated with such cattlemen as Charles Goodnight and William S. Ikard.qqv In 1872 Evans marketed his first herd at Wichita, Kansas.

In the 1870s he formed a corporation known as J. F. Evans and Company with Judson P. Warner, Joseph Glidden's co-agent for the sale of barbed wireqv in Texas. In the summer of 1880 they purchased twenty-three sections of land in Donley County from J. A. Reynolds. They then gathered a herd of cattle in Lamar County and moved them west to the Panhandle,qv along with necessary supplies. At the suggestion of a friend, Dave Cummings, Evans adopted a Spade brand in 1883 and was known thereafter by the nickname Spade. He erected a dugout on Glenwood Creek, but later built a log house on nearby Barton Creek, which he designated as permanent headquarters for his Spade Ranch.qv Although Evans had his business offices at Clarendon during the 1880s, his wife, Elizabeth (Lizzie), and four children remained at the family home in Sherman throughout the winter months and went out to Clarendon and the ranch during the summer. Furthermore, other business interests downstate took up much of his time, prompting Evans to turn the Spade operations over to resident managers.

Evans helped organize and write the bylaws for the Panhandle Stock Associationqv in 1881 and served as its first president for two years. He also chaired that organization's Protective and Detective Committee, composed of Hank Cresswell, Nick Eaton,qqv Goodnight, and Evans. Backed by the association, the committee was a vibrant force in maintaining law and order on the Panhandle frontier. In 1881 and again in 1883 Evans attended sessions of the Texas legislature in Austin as a lobbyist for the Panhandle cattlemen's interests.

Apparently J. F. Evans and Company was affected by the droughtsqv and blizzards of the late 1880s, for in December 1888 Evans sold his ranch and cattle to Isaac L. Ellwood,qv who subsequently developed the Renderbrook and Spade operations in the South Plains area. Afterward Evans ran a hardware store in Gainesville and bought cattle and real estate. He was a partner in the Smith, Reed, and Evans firm in Clay County. He also joined the Northwest Texas Cattle Breeders' Association and served, along with C. C. Slaughter, Samuel Burk Burnett, and John N. Simpson,qv on its twelve-man executive committee. His influence helped bring about cooperation between the Panhandle and Northwest Texas associations.

During the 1920s Evans lived for a time in Lubbock before retiring to a farm four miles east of Altus, Oklahoma, in 1929. On January 11, 1935, he was struck by a car on the highway near his home and apparently killed instantly; a passing motorist found his body and severed leg shortly afterward. He was buried in Altus. At the Texas Centennialqv celebration in Dallas in 1836, Evans was among the cattlemen portrayed in the Hall of Fame exhibition.

BIBLIOGRAPHY: Amarillo *Daily News*, January 12, 1935. Gus L. Ford, ed., *Texas Cattle Brands* (Dallas: Cockrell, 1936). Willie Newbury Lewis, *Between Sun and Sod* (Clarendon, Texas: Clarendon Press, 1938; rev. ed., College Station: Texas A&M University Press, 1976).
H. Allen Anderson

EVANS, JOHN S. (?–1841). John S. Evans edited the Galveston *Commercial Intelligencer*qv in May or June 1838. The paper was not a success, however, and lasted only a short time. He was also interested in starting another paper, the Galveston *National Intelligencer.*qv He wrote Mirabeau B. Lamarqv on June 29, 1839, asking for an appointment in Washington with the hope that this position would help him in establishing a paper. A newspaper called the *National Intelligencer* did appear in Galveston in July 1841, but Evans had died on April 22. Before his death he was an assistant editor of the Galveston *Morning Herald*.

BIBLIOGRAPHY: Charles Adams Gulick, Jr., Harriet Smither, et al., eds., *The Papers of Mirabeau Buonaparte Lamar* (6 vols., Austin: Texas State Library, 1920–27; rpt., Austin: Pemberton Press, 1968). Marilyn M. Sibley, *Lone Stars and State Gazettes: Texas Newspapers before the Civil War* (College Station: Texas A&M University Press, 1983). WPA Historical Records Survey Program, *Texas Newspapers* (Houston: San Jacinto Museum of History Association, 1941).

EVANS, JOSEPH WOOD (1877–1962). Joseph Wood Evans, cotton broker and civic leader, was born in Augusta, Kentucky, on October 17, 1877, son of Joseph Madison and Alice (Humphreys) Wood. After graduation from Hanover College in Madison, Indiana, and military service in the Spanish-American War, he moved to Houston, Texas, in 1901. He was married to Emily Scott on October 31, 1906; they had two daughters. He entered the cotton brokerage business and in 1908 organized a major cotton-exporting firm, Evans and Company. He was elected president of the Houston Cotton Exchange and Board of Tradeqv in 1918.

In his determination to bring Texas cotton producers improved transportation facilities, he took a key role in the development of Houston as a deepwater port. He served as chairman of the Houston Ship Channelqv Navigation Commission in Harris County from 1930 to 1945; during his tenure shipping tonnage doubled, and the port of Houston rose to third place in total tonnage and first place in cotton tonnage among the nation's deepwater ports.

Evans was chairman of the Houston War Work campaign and an official of the state Red Cross during World War I.qv Later he helped organize the Houston Community Chest and served on the state executive committee of the National Foundation for Infantile Paralysis. He was president of the Houston Chamber of Commerce in 1928. He was elected a director of the United States Chamber of Commerce in 1933 and named a vice president of that organization in 1935.

Evans was a trustee of Hanover College; in 1938 he was a member of the original building-fund campaign committee for the University of Houston. In recognition of his keen interest in higher education, after his death his widow and daughter, Alice Pratt, donated a substantial sum in his memory for the establishment of the Joseph W. Evans Collection of bibliographical references at the M. D. Anderson ᵠᵛ Library, University of Houston. Evans died in Houston on November 13, 1962.

BIBLIOGRAPHY: Houston *Post*, November 14, 1962. Max H. Jacobs and H. Dick Golding, *Houston and Cotton* (Houston Cotton Exchange and Board of Trade, 1949). *Who's Who in America*, 1952–53.

John O. King

EVANS, LEMUEL DALE (1810–1877). Lemuel Dale Evans, attorney, congressman, Unionist leader, and presiding judge of the Texas Supreme Court, was born in Tennessee on January 8, 1810. He was apparently educated in his native state, where he was admitted to the bar in 1840. In 1843, however, he moved to Fannin County, Texas, by way of Arkansas. He was an ardent supporter of annexation ᵠᵛ and represented Fannin County at the Convention of 1845,ᵠᵛ where he advocated the adoption of a system of citizens' tribunals rather than traditional courts to settle disputes between citizens. His suggestion apparently received very little support.

Sometime after 1845 Evans moved to Harrison County, where he practiced law and served as a district judge for a number of years. In 1852 he resigned from the bench to become a Democratic presidential elector. He sought the Democratic gubernatorial nomination the following year and campaigned strictly as an East Texas candidate. He emphasized intrastate sectional issues throughout the campaign, suggesting that East Texas provided the lion's share of the tax money collected by the state while West Texas unfairly managed to accrue the majority of the state's elective officials. He even went so far as to suggest that if a West Texas candidate won the election as governor, East Texas might renew agitation for division of the state. He finished in fourth place.

In 1855 Evans won election to the United States House of Representatives from the Eastern District of Texas as a member of the American (Know-Nothing) party.ᵠᵛ In 1857 he lost to John H. Reagan,ᵠᵛ a states'-rights Democrat. Evans became the leading Unionist in East Texas and a staunch supporter of Governor Sam Houston's ᵠᵛ antisecessionist views; he served as one of the four Texas delegates to the national convention of the Constitutional Union party,ᵠᵛ which met at Baltimore in 1860. His efforts to secure the party's presidential nomination for Houston failed, but he returned to Texas and campaigned for its nominee, John Bell. During October 1860 he delivered fifteen speeches in fifteen days in the Dallas area.

Unwilling to support the Confederate cause in the Civil War,ᵠᵛ Evans left the state. He apparently made his way to the national capital, where he wrote Secretary of State William Seward, suggesting means of isolating Texas so that it could not effectively contribute to the Confederate war effort. While these suggestions were largely ignored, Seward did award Evans a commission as a special agent and assigned him to monitor the movement of munitions and supplies into Texas from Mexico, an assignment necessitating Evans's relocation to the Mexican border. Evans's notoriety, combined with heavy Confederate activity along the routes into Texas, however, made it impossible for him to return safely to the state and engage in his undercover activities. His suggestion that he sail for Tampico, Veracruz, on a federal ship and return to Texas by way of Mexico was vetoed by Union commander George B. McClellan. Return to Texas thereby made an impossibility, Evans resigned his commission on March 3, 1862.

His activities during the remainder of the war are unknown. He returned to Texas after the war, reentered state politics, and attended the Constitutional Convention of 1868–69,ᵠᵛ where he generally voted as a moderate. In 1870 Maj. Gen. Philip H. Sheridan,ᵠᵛ Reconstruction ᵠᵛ commander of the district that included Texas and Louisiana, appointed Evans presiding judge (previously chief justice) of the state Supreme Court. He held this position on the much-ridiculed Semicolon Court,ᵠᵛ the derisive name given to the state's highest court during the years of Reconstruction, until 1871. Evans attempted unsuccessfully to win the gubernatorial election as a Republican in 1872, then received appointment to the post of United States marshal, stationed at Galveston, in 1875. He held this position until his death in Washington, D.C., on July 1, 1877. He was buried in the Congressional Cemetery.

BIBLIOGRAPHY: *Biographical Directory of the American Congress*. Harbert Davenport, *History of the Supreme Court of the State of Texas* (Austin: Southern Law Book Publishers, 1917). James D. Lynch, *The Bench and Bar of Texas* (St. Louis, 1885). James R. Norvell, "The Reconstruction Courts of Texas, 1867–1873," *Southwestern Historical Quarterly* 62 (1958). Thomas Schoonover, ed., "Documents Concerning Lemuel Dale Evans' Plan to Keep Texas in the Union in 1861," *East Texas Historical Journal* 12 (Spring 1974). Frank H. Smyrl, "Unionism in Texas, 1856–1861," *Southwestern Historical Quarterly* 68 (October 1964). Texas House of Representatives, *Biographical Directory of the Texan Conventions and Congresses, 1832–1845* (Austin: Book Exchange, 1941).

Brian Hart

EVANS, LUTHER HARRIS (1902–1981). Luther Evans, librarian of Congress and director general of the United Nations Educational, Scientific, and Cultural Organization, the son of George Washington and Lillie (Johnson) Evans, was born on October 13, 1902, in Sayersville, Texas. The University of Texas awarded him a B.A. in 1923 and an M.A. in 1924. Subsequently Evans went to Stanford University and received a Ph.D. in political science in 1927. He served as an instructor in citizenship at Stanford (1924–27), an instructor in government at New York University (1927–28), an assistant professor of political science at Dartmouth (1928–30), and an assistant professor of politics at Princeton (1930–35).

Evans began his association with the federal government in 1935, when he was named national director of the Historical Records Survey, a part of the Work Projects Administration ᵠᵛ that attempted to survey the archives of the nation. With the survey came organization and dissemination of information concerning the significant as well as the mundane documents and records of local, state, and public archives.

In 1939 Evans was brought to the Library of Congress by Archibald MacLeish, who had recently become librarian of Congress. Evans was the director of the Legislative Reference Service (1939–40) and chief assistant librarian (1940–45). He also served as director of the reference department. While MacLeish took a wartime assignment, Evans was the acting librarian of Congress in 1942–43. President Harry Truman nominated him for the post of librarian of Congress, and he was sworn in on June 30, 1945. In that post he increased the library's budget, acquired new manuscript collections, revamped the Legislative Reference Service, and in general led the postwar expansion of library holdings and services to both Congress and the public. He was active in resisting censorship of library materials during the McCarthy years and chaired a conference that issued a statement called Freedom to Read.

Evans resigned from the library in 1953 to become the director general of UNESCO. Before this, he had served as an advisor to the United States delegation when UNESCO was established and had served on the executive board from 1949 until he became director general. A major accomplishment of his tenure was the preparation of the Universal Copyright Convention.

After his departure from UNESCO in 1958, he directed a library project for the Brookings Institution and a study on the education implications of automation for the National Education Association. In 1962 he became director of the international and legal collections of the Columbia University Library. After retiring in 1971 he retained an active interest in many organizations concerned with international cooperation and affairs.

Evans was a Methodist and a Democrat. He was active in many professional organizations, including the American Library Association, the American Political Science Association, the Society of American Archivists, and the American Documentation Institute. He was given honorary degrees by several universities and was decorated by the governments of Brazil, France, Japan, Lebanon, and Peru. On September 12, 1925, he married Helen Murphy of Gainesville, Texas. They had one son. Evans died in San Antonio on December 23, 1981.

BIBLIOGRAPHY: *Current Biography*, 1945. William J. Sittig, "Luther Evans, Man for a New Age," in *Librarians of Congress, 1802–1974* (Washington: Library of Congress, 1977).   *Maurice G. Fortin*

EVANS, MOSES (1812–1853). Moses Evans, early Texas settler, soldier, and surveyor, was born in Kentucky in April 1812 and arrived in Texas before 1836. He lived at Washington-on-the-Brazos, where he was labeled the "wild man of the woods." He served in the Texas Revolution[qv] as a second lieutenant in Capt. Joseph Bell Chance's[qv] company of Maj. Robert McNutt's[qv] command. This company was left at the upper encampment to guard the sick and baggage during the battle of San Jacinto.[qv] Evans was awarded 320 acres for service from April 7, 1836, to May 30, 1836, and 640 acres for the baggage detail. About 1839 he joined the Mexican Federalist movement and was made captain of guerrilla forces. He was abandoned when he was wounded in the shin and unable to travel, but he managed to subsist. He joined the "spy" company of Benjamin McCulloch[qv] at the outbreak of the Mexican War[qv] and continued in service until hostilities ceased. Evans advertised his surveying service in various Texas newspapers, indicating his fee as from one-third to one-half of the land surveyed. Although he could not read or write he was able accurately to locate and describe the land surveyed and eventually owned a great deal of land. His name was associated with the so-called "wild woman of the Navidad," whom he pursued and caught only to find "she" was a runaway male slave. After his conversion to Methodism in 1847 he became an exhorter. His flaming red beard, unusual mannerisms, and striking costume combined to make him a picturesque figure on the frontier. Evans never married. He died on October 6, 1853, and was buried in Washington County Cemetery. When he died his estate was administered by William J. Evans, who advertised large tracts of land in Washington and other counties.

BIBLIOGRAPHY: *Colorado Tribune*, March 22, 1851. Daughters of the Republic of Texas, *Muster Rolls of the Texas Revolution* (Austin, 1986). Thomas L. Miller, *Bounty and Donation Land Grants of Texas, 1835–1888* (Austin: University of Texas Press, 1967). Worth Stickley Ray, *Austin Colony Pioneers* (Austin: Jenkins, 1949; 2d ed., Austin: Pemberton, 1970). Mrs. Jonnie Lockhart Wallis, *Sixty Years on the Brazos: The Life and Letters of Dr. John Washington Lockhart* (1930; rpt., New York, 1966).   *John G. Johnson*

EVANS, R. J. (1853–1921). R. J. Evans, black politician, was born a slave in Louisiana in 1853. He entered Texas in 1857 and became a schoolteacher after emancipation and before his election as city alderman of Navasota. In 1878 he was elected to the Sixteenth Legislature as a Republican from Grimes County. He won reelection as a Greenbacker in 1880 but ran as a Republican in 1882 and lost. Evans, seeking to obtain the rights of African Americans,[qv] became a skillful legislator. In the late 1870s he offered an amendment to the bill for regulation of railroad rates, which if passed would have made refusing to sell a black person a first-class ticket illegal. At the Colored Men's Convention of 1883 (*see* BLACK STATE CONVENTIONS) Evans and other black leaders rejected pleas from the governor not to denounce separate railroad accommodations. In 1879 Evans proposed legislation to do away with the convict lease system,[qv] especially as it led to mistreatment of black convicts. He also introduced a resolution to celebrate the anniversary of black emancipation in Texas, June 19, 1865 (Juneteenth[qv]). In an effort to prevent blacks from holding state office, the legislature under white leadership began a process of dismembering districts where blacks could be elected. Through proposed legislation Evans led the effort in the House to prevent this from happening; the white majority prevailed, however. As a former schoolteacher and member of the House education committee, Evans led the fight for better education facilities for blacks. In an address before the state Republican convention in 1882 he called for the establishment of a black state university, an important black aspiration for many years afterward. When a split developed in the 1884 Texas Republican convention, a splinter group, the Straight-Out Republicans, nominated Evans for General Land Office[qv] commissioner. After the 1884 campaign ended in defeat, he moved to Houston, where he remained active in the Republican party;[qv] he was a delegate to the national Republican convention in 1884. He died on September 27, 1921, in Harris County.

BIBLIOGRAPHY: Paul D. Casdorph, *A History of the Republican Party in Texas, 1865–1965* (Austin: Pemberton Press, 1965). Merline Pitre, *Through Many Dangers, Toils and Snares: The Black Leadership of Texas, 1868–1900* (Austin: Eakin, 1985).   *Douglas Hales*

EVANS, ROBERT (1800–1836). Robert Evans, ordnance chief of the Alamo garrison, was born in Ireland in 1800 and traveled to Texas from New York by way of New Orleans. After the siege of Bexar[qv] (December 1835) he served as master of ordnance of the Bexar garrison. Susanna W. Dickinson[qv] stated that during the final moments of the battle of the Alamo[qv] (March 6, 1836) Evans attempted to blow up the Texans' remaining supply of gunpowder with a torch. He was shot down before he could do so. Dickinson also described him as being black-haired, blue-eyed, nearly six feet tall, and always merry.

BIBLIOGRAPHY: Daughters of the American Revolution, *The Alamo Heroes and Their Revolutionary Ancestors* (San Antonio, 1976). Daughters of the Republic of Texas, *Muster Rolls of the Texas Revolution* (Austin, 1986). Bill Groneman, *Alamo Defenders* (Austin: Eakin, 1990). Walter Lord, *A Time to Stand* (New York: Harper, 1961; 2d ed., Lincoln: University of Nebraska Press, 1978).   *Bill Groneman*

EVANS, SAMUEL B. (1812–1836). Samuel B. Evans, Alamo defender, son of Musgrove and Abi (Brown) Evans, was born in Jefferson County, New York, on January 16, 1812. His grandfather, Samuel Evans, was a general in the colonial army during the American Revolution. His uncle, Gen. Jacob Brown, was at one time commander of the United States Army. Evans died in the battle of the Alamo[qv] on March 6, 1836.

BIBLIOGRAPHY: Daughters of the American Revolution, *The Alamo Heroes and Their Revolutionary Ancestors* (San Antonio, 1976). Bill Groneman, *Alamo Defenders* (Austin: Eakin, 1990). Reuben M. Potter, "The Fall of the Alamo," *Magazine of American History*, January 1878; rpt., Hillsdale, New Jersey: Otterden, 1977). Phil Rosenthal and Bill Groneman, *Roll Call at the Alamo* (Fort Collins, Colorado: Old Army, 1985). Amelia W. Williams, A Critical Study of the Siege of the Alamo and of the Personnel of Its Defenders (Ph.D. dissertation, University of Texas, 1931; rpt., *Southwestern Historical Quarterly* 36–37 [April 1933–April 1934]).   *Bill Groneman*

EVANS CREEK. Evans Creek, also known as Sells Creek, rises two miles southwest of Rattlesnake Gap and State Highway 163 in south central Val Verde County (at 29°46′ N, 101°10′ W) and runs southeast for twenty-four miles to its mouth on the north shore of Amistad Reservoir, a half mile east of the Southern Pacific line on the Mexican border (at 29°32′ N, 101°04′ W). The stream's course sharply dissects massive limestone as it crosses flat to rolling prairies; it ends on alluvial deposits of gravel, sand, clay, silt, and organic materials. The creek has formed a deep limestone canyon and several large caves. Soils in the area are generally dark, calcareous stony clays and clay loams that support oaks, junipers, mesquites, and grasses.

EVANS POINT, TEXAS. Evans Point was a railroad stop on the St. Louis Southwestern Railway twelve miles southeast of Sulphur Springs in southeastern Hopkins County. A post office opened there in 1887, and by 1890 the community had a population of fifty and a druggist, a grocer, a physician, a barber, a general store, and a blacksmith. In 1905 an Evans Point school had an enrollment of fifty. The community's post office closed in 1907. By the mid-1930s Evans Point no longer appeared on highway maps, and in 1948 no businesses remained.
Christopher Long

EVANSVILLE, TEXAS. Evansville was on the Houston and Texas Central Railway near Jewett and nineteen miles northwest of Centerville in northwestern Leon County. It had a post office from 1909 to 1931, and Howard Holleman was the first postmaster. When the post office closed, the mail was rerouted through Newby. Evansville was a coal-mining town and prospered until 1930, when the local supply of soft coal was depleted. From 1925 through the mid-1930s Evansville reported a population of 200, and in the 1930s it reported one business. The community was not shown on county highway maps in the 1930s.

BIBLIOGRAPHY: Leon County Historical Book Survey Committee, *History of Leon County* (Dallas: Curtis Media, 1986).
Dylan Wood

EVANT, TEXAS. Evant is on U.S. Highway 84 some twenty-five miles west of Gatesville in western Coryell County. It was first called Langford Cove, for Asa Langford, who in the 1850s built a sawmill and general store half a mile south of the present site. A post office called Cove was opened in 1876 with Langford as postmaster. In the late 1870s Evant Brooks moved to the area from Alabama and bought 160 acres of land. He donated sixty acres for a townsite in 1881, and in 1884 the name of the community was changed to Evant in his honor. By the 1890s Evant had three general stores, a hotel, a gristmill, a cotton gin, and 120 residents. The town grew over the next four decades, and its population stabilized at 500 during the 1930s and 1940s. It reported its peak population of 550 in the 1950s. When Evant was incorporated in 1976 it had a population of 540. In 1988 it reported nine businesses and 422 residents. In the early 1990s its population was reported as 438, served by twenty businesses. By that time the community had spread into Hamilton County.

BIBLIOGRAPHY: Coryell County Genealogical Society, *Coryell County, Texas, Families, 1854–1985* (Dallas: Taylor, 1986). John J. Germann and Myron Janzen, *Texas Post Offices by County* (1986).
Vivian Elizabeth Smyrl

EVE, JOSEPH (1784–1843). Joseph Eve, Kentucky legislator, judge, and chargé d'affaires of the United States to the Republic of Texas,[qv] was born in Culpeper County, Virginia, on July 17, 1784. By 1807 he had moved to Kentucky, where he received a grant of 300 acres on Spruce Creek in Knox County in 1808. Over the next fifteen years he acquired additional grants in Knox, Clay, Livingston, and Whitley counties. On November 11, 1811, he married Betsy Withers Ballinger of Garrard County, Kentucky. Eve and his wife had no children.

Eve was admitted to practice law in Knox County in 1807 and energetically entered county politics. He became a trustee, like his father-in-law, for the county seat of Barbourville in 1810. He also became a trustee for his church. The county elected him its representative in the Kentucky legislature in 1810, 1811, and 1815. During the War of 1812, he rose to the rank of colonel. After the war, from 1817 to 1821, he served as the Knox County state senator. In 1819 he was president of the Bank of Barbourville. From 1828 to 1836 he was a circuit judge in Kentucky. Often too generous for his own interests, Eve endorsed loans for some of his friends who went bankrupt, leaving him close to losing his own slaves and homestead.

Eve was a supporter of Henry Clay and advocated internal improvements by both state and national governments and high protective tariffs for United States industries; he reluctantly sponsored the national bank as well. As a National Republican and member of the Kentucky electoral college in 1833, he voted for Clay. He then campaigned on behalf of the Whigs and the election of William Henry Harrison to the presidency in 1840. As a reward for his diligent efforts, Eve was appointed chargé d'affaires to the Republic of Texas on April 15, 1841.

He greatly admired Sam Houston[qv] and sponsored the annexation[qv] of Texas. He toured Texas from Galveston to the new capital, Austin, and was favorably impressed with the productivity of the land. He was fully confident that Mexico could never reconquer Texas. Following Secretary of State Daniel Webster's instructions of June 14, 1841, Eve obtained the ratification of the boundary line surveyed by a joint commission of the Republic of Texas and the United States. Both parties agreed that the line was the Sabine River and, from near the southeast corner of what is now Panola County, the thirty-second parallel north to the Red River. Eve sought to negotiate a new commercial treaty with the Texas government, but disagreement over certain provisions of the convention prevented its acceptance by either side. Further negotiations were soon dropped with the renewal of American interest in the annexation of Texas.

Throughout 1842 Mexican attacks increased, and Texans encouraged Eve to lay the annexation issue before his government. Eve sympathized with the Texans' plight but regarded Houston's response to the attacks, the attempted naval blockade of Mexican ports, as ineffectual. He persuaded Houston to rescind his blockade proclamation since it adversely affected United States and British attempts to end current hostilities. Fearful that financial misery would cause Texas to depend upon some stronger nation, particularly Great Britain, Eve implored President John Tyler not to lose the opportunity to annex the republic. Although willing to acquire Texas, Tyler felt the timing was not right for passing annexation in the Senate. Instead, the president continued to offer the mediation of the United States government with Mexico on behalf of Texas.

Mediation failed, however, on September 11, 1842, when Mexican general Adrián Woll[qv] captured and held San Antonio for nine days. The Mexican incursions led Houston to remove the government from Austin to Houston, then to Washington-on-the-Brazos. While the republic had no permanent capital, Eve chose to move the legation archives to Galveston, where he could receive mail from the United States faster and where, he hoped, the sea air would help his tuberculosis.

William S. Murphy[qv] replaced Eve on April 3, 1843, as the United States diplomat in Texas. Assistant Secretary of State Fletcher Webster, an ardent antiannexationist, took the first opportunity to recall Eve for a slight infraction of the rules—Eve had violated his private instructions by drawing an advance upon his salary. During the past winter, Eve and his wife had suffered from bouts of fever. Eve died in Galveston in mid-June 1843 and was buried there. His wife returned to their home in Barbourville, Kentucky.

BIBLIOGRAPHY: William R. Manning, ed., *Diplomatic Correspondence of the United States* (12 vols., Washington: Carnegie Endowment for International Peace, 1932–39). Joseph Milton Nance, ed., "A Letter Book of Joseph Eve, United States Chargé d'Affaires to Texas," *Southwestern Historical Quarterly* 43–44 (October 1939–July 1940). James D. Richardson, ed., *A Compilation of the Messages and Papers of the Presidents, 1789–1897* (10 vols., Washington: GPO, 1896–99).
Priscilla Myers Benham

EVEA (?–?). Evea, a Comanche Indian chief, ratified a treaty at San Antonio with Governor Juan María Vicencio de Ripperdá^{qv} in June of 1772. While he was still chief, his son led a raid on Bucareli^{qv} in May 1778. Additional raids by the Comanches, probably under Evea, were partially responsible for forcing the people of Bucareli to move on east of the Trinity to the site of Nacogdoches, where they began to settle before April 30, 1779.

BIBLIOGRAPHY: Herbert Eugene Bolton, "The Spanish Abandonment and Re-occupation of East Texas, 1773–1779," *Quarterly of the Texas State Historical Association* 9 (October 1905). Frederick Webb Hodge, ed., *Handbook of American Indians North of Mexico* (2 vols., Washington: GPO, 1907, 1910; rpt., New York: Pageant, 1959).

EVENSVILLE PEAK. Evensville Peak, with an elevation of 1,435 feet above sea level, is 1½ miles southwest of Strawn in southwestern Palo Pinto County (at 32°32′ N, 98°31′ W). The local terrain is characterized by rolling hills, surfaced by clay and sandy loams that support scrub brush, mesquite, cacti, and grasses.

EVERETT, EDWARD (1818–1903). Edward Everett, artist and draftsman, was born in London, England, on March 13, 1818, the second son of Charles and Elizabeth Boyle Everett. His father was an American buyer and exporter. In 1840 the Everett family moved to the United States and settled in Quincy, Illinois, where his father operated a dry good, hardware, and grocery store. Edward was listed in 1841 as a machinist and engineer. In March 1843 he joined Capt. James D. Morgan's "Quincy Riflemen" Company and saw limited service in the 1845 Mormon War. Following a search patrol of Nauvoo, Everett wrote about and drew its Mormon temple. The company was disbanded in May 1846 but was quickly reorganized in June for service in the Mexican War.^{qv} On June 18 the company was mustered into the service of the United States as Company "A," First Illinois Volunteers, at a rendezvous held at Alton, Illinois. Everett served as the company clerk at the rank of sergeant. On July 30 the company arrived at Port Lavaca and marched as escort to a train of wagons bound for San Antonio. On the 22nd, the company arrived ahead of the main brigade at San Antonio, where it camped on the Alameda (now Commerce Street). Upon the arrival of the brigade on the 24th, the company was transferred to Camp Crockett at the headwaters of the San Antonio River. By special order of Col. John Hardin, Everett and two lieutenants were assigned to collect information respecting the history and customs of the area. Everett proceeded to make ink sketches of the Alamo and San José Mission. On September 11 Everett was on duty as sergeant of the provost. In the course of breaking up a disturbance, he was wounded just above the right knee by a pistol shot fired by a Texan named Hardy. While recuperating from his wound, the young soldier did numerous sketches of the San Antonio area and drew maps of the Texas frontier. His watercolors of the missions in San Antonio currently hang in the Amon Carter Museum in Fort Worth. Everett, owing to his wound, was offered a clerkship in the office of the assistant quartermaster, Capt. James Harvey Ralston.^{qv} He assisted Ralston in his plans to turn the ruins of the Alamo chapel and barracks into a depot for the United States Army's Quartermaster's Department. Everett's plan of the Alamo and estimates for placing the buildings into serviceable condition were forwarded to the Quartermaster General Thomas S. Jesup. Following the approval of the project, Everett helped supervise the remodeling of the Alamo "Long Barracks." The chapel, at this time, was merely cleared out of debris and retained as a historical relic. When Ralston was relieved of his duties in November 1848, Everett traveled with him to Washington, D.C. to turn over the account books to the quartermaster general. While in Washington, D.C., Everett did temporary work for the Topographical Engineers Department. This included the drawings of the Alamo and missions of San Antonio for Col. George W. Hughes's report on General Wool's expedition of January 20, 1849. Where Everett received his artistic training is not known. His landscape sketches resemble those produced by the Hudson River School artists. Despite definite artistic ability, Everett identified himself as a "mechanical engineer." Later in life, he wrote a lengthy review of his military career, including his travels to and in Texas. The manuscript was titled "A Narrative of Military Experience in Several Capacities;" it was published in 1906 by the Illinois State Historical Society. After his discharge, Everett lived three years in Washington, D.C., before returning to Illinois. On October 7, 1857, he married Mary A. Billings. During the Civil War^{qv} Everett served as an assistant quartermaster general at the rank of major to the State of Illinois. Everett later moved to Sing Sing, New York, before making his home at Roxbury, near Boston, Massachusetts. He died on July 24, 1903, and is buried in Boston's Forest Hills Cemetery.

BIBLIOGRAPHY: Richard E. Ahlborn, *The San Antonio Missions: Edward Everett and the American Occupation, 1847* (Fort Worth: Amon Carter Museum, 1985). George W. Hughes, *Memoir Descriptive of the March of a Division of the United States Army, under the Command of Brigadier General John E. Wool, from San Antonio de Bexar, in Texas, to Saltillo, in Mexico* (Sen. Exec. Doc. 32, 31st Cong., 1st sess., 1850).

Kevin R. Young

EVERETT CREEK. Everett Creek rises 11½ miles southeast of Jasper in east central Jasper County (at 30°53′ N, 93°57′ W) and runs south for fourteen miles to its mouth on Thickety Creek, five miles north of Kirbyville (at 30°44′ N, 93°52′ W). Everett Creek was probably named for Stephen H. Everitt,^{qv} an early Jasper County settler through whose land claim the stream travels. The creek cuts through the gently undulating terrain typical of central Jasper County, where deep loamy soils support a variety of pines and hardwoods.

EVERETTSVILLE, TEXAS. Everettsville, situated around a sulfur spring near what is now Roma–Los Saenz in Starr County, was established in 1847 by one of Gen. Zachary Taylor's^{qv} officers, Col. Jack Everett, as a health spa. Remoteness, bad roads, and a lack of transportation facilities crippled growth and led to the town's demise before 1900.

BIBLIOGRAPHY: Randy McMillon, "Vanished Towns of the Rio Grande Valley," *Junior Historian*, May 1955. *Dick D. Heller, Jr.*

EVERGREEN, TEXAS (San Jacinto County). Evergreen is at the junction of State Highway 150 and Farm Road 945, sixty-five miles north of Houston in central San Jacinto County. The community was named after the thick evergreen forest that surrounds it. The area was settled soon after San Jacinto County was established, and the community received a post office in 1880. Ben Ellis opened a store in 1884, and "Parson" Ellis owned and operated a small sawmill. Estimates of the rural community's population ranged from 112 in 1900 to 50 in 1925 to 150 in the early 1940s, when Evergreen reported five businesses. Its old schoolhouse was converted to a community center sometime after 1958. Evergreen's population fell to about fifty in the mid-1980s, when no businesses were reported at the community. The population was still recorded as fifty in 1990.

BIBLIOGRAPHY: Ruth Hansbro, History of San Jacinto County (M.A. thesis, Sam Houston State Teachers College, 1940).

Robert Wooster

EVERGREEN, TEXAS (Titus County). Evergreen was a black community between White Oak Creek and the Sulphur River, fourteen miles northwest of Mount Pleasant in northwestern Titus County. Until the 1940s the area between White Oak Creek and Sulphur River, known locally as simply "between the creeks," was an isolated, heavily wooded area generally considered inferior for farming. The roads into the locale were poor, and inhabitants had few contacts with other parts of the county. Evergreen had its origins in the mid-1870s when Green Logan homesteaded land in the area. He was soon joined by Mose Price, Abe Daughtry, and other blacks who were able to purchase land nearby. As a community began to emerge Logan conceived of it as an area where other less fortunate blacks could find shelter and refuge from persecution or hard times. He named the community Evergreen, taking the *green* from his first name and adding ever to symbolize the idea of permanence.

The community grew until, by the early years of the twentieth century, it had a church, a school, a gin, and a store. The settlement seems to have always been small, since most of the area's inhabitants lived on the farms they had cleared in the dense woods. By the 1920s Evergreen began to decline, as residents took advantage of opportunities elsewhere. The local school, which was operated by the trustees of the Wilkinson common school district, was still in operation in the 1940s but had closed by 1973. By the mid-1970s the site was a part of a large ranch, and only the Evergreen Cemetery remained to mark the spot.

BIBLIOGRAPHY: Deborah Brown and Katharine Gust, *Between the Creeks: Recollections of Northeast Texas* (Austin: Encino, 1976). John Marion Ellis II, *The Way It Was: A Personal Memoir of Family Life in East Texas* (Waco: Texian Press, 1983). Traylor Russell, *History of Titus County* (2 vols., Waco: Morrison, 1965, 1966; rpt., n.p.: Walsworth, 1975).
Cecil Harper, Jr.

EVERGREEN, TEXAS (Washington County). Evergreen was on the border of Washington and Lee counties. The area was first settled during the period of Stephen F. Austin's[qv] colony in what later became far western Washington County. In the early period of colonization the locality was called Waco Spring. In 1837 Waco Spring was the site of a famous battle between the Waco Indians and Tonkawa Indians, who had inhabited the central area of Washington County before Anglo settlement of the region. Evergreen had a post office between 1858 and 1877, and at one time had several stores, but they had closed by 1876. The exact site of the community is unknown, but it is probably covered by Somerville Lake.

BIBLIOGRAPHY: Ed Ellsworth Bartholomew, *The Encyclopedia of Texas Ghost Towns* (Fort Davis, Texas, 1982). W. O. Dietrich, *The Blazing Story of Washington County* (Brenham, Texas: Banner Press, 1950; rev. ed., Wichita Falls: Nortex, 1973). Mrs. R. E. Pennington, *History of Brenham and Washington County* (Houston, 1915). Charles F. Schmidt, *History of Washington County* (San Antonio: Naylor, 1949). Washington County Scrapbook, Barker Texas History Center, University of Texas at Austin.
Carole E. Christian

EVERGREEN PLANTATION. Evergreen Plantation, on Galveston Bay near Cedar Bayou, was bought by Ashbel Smith[qv] from Moseley Baker[qv] for $5,000 in early 1847. Corn, potatoes, and sugarcane were the major crops; some stock was raised. Upon his death Smith left part of the plantation to his adopted daughter; this portion later became a part of the Goose Creek oilfield.[qv]

BIBLIOGRAPHY: Abigail Curlee, A Study of Texas Slave Plantations, 1822–1865 (Ph.D. dissertation, University of Texas, 1932). Ashbel Smith Papers, Barker Texas History Center, University of Texas at Austin.

EVERHART, FORREST E. (1922–1986). Forrest E. Everhart, Medal of Honor recipient, was born in Bainbridge, Ohio, on August 28, 1922. He entered military service at Texas City, Texas. Technical Sergeant Everhart was assigned to Company H, 359th Infantry, Ninetieth Infantry Division, United States Army. On November 12, 1944, he was commanding a platoon near Kerling, France, which was bearing the brunt of a predawn attack. German tanks and self-propelled guns penetrated his left flank and infantry forces threatened to overrun his remaining machine gun. He ran 400 yards through enemy fire, joined the gunner, and directed fire. When the infantry advanced, he carried out a fifteen-minute grenade attack that forced the enemy to retreat, leaving thirty dead behind. After returning to his now threatened right flank, Everhart began a grenade duel that forced the enemy to withdraw and leave another twenty dead. The "gallantry and intrepidity" of Sergeant Everhart was instrumental in stopping an enemy attack on the American bridgehead across the Moselle River. Everhart was awarded the Medal of Honor for the action, and Congress credited his award to Texas, his state of residence at enlistment. Everhart died on August 30, 1986, in Philadelphia and is buried in Arlington National Cemetery near Washington, D.C.

BIBLIOGRAPHY: Committee on Veterans' Affairs, United States Senate, *Medal of Honor Recipients, 1863–1973* (Washington: GPO, 1973).
Art Leatherwood

EVERITT, STEPHEN HENDRICKSON (1806–1844). Stephen Hendrickson Everitt, politician, merchant, and speculator, was born in Poughkeepsie, New York, on November 26, 1806. He moved to Texas in 1834, acquired land now in Jasper County, and was elected a delegate from Bevil Municipality to the Consultation[qv] of 1835 and from Jasper Municipality to the Convention of 1836.[qv] He signed the Declaration of November 7, 1835, the Texas Declaration of Independence, and the Constitution of the Republic.[qqv] Everitt also served as one of three commissioners appointed to close the land offices in the Department of Nacogdoches and gained several mail contracts in Southeast Texas. Although apparently not a practicing physician, he was often referred to as Dr. Everitt. He married Alta Zera Williams, and they had four children. He was a strong supporter of Mirabeau B. Lamar[qv] and represented Jasper County as senator in the first five congresses of the Republic of Texas[qv] before resigning in December 1840. As a speculator he operated stores in Bevilport and on Sabine Pass and owned town lots in Bevil, Jasper, and Belgrade. He died in New Orleans on July 12, 1844. His home in Jasper County has been made a historical landmark.

BIBLIOGRAPHY: Louis Wiltz Kemp, *The Signers of the Texas Declaration of Independence* (Salado, Texas: Anson Jones, 1944; rpt. 1959). Madeleine Martin, *More Early Southeast Texas Families* (Quanah, Texas: Nortex, 1978). Texas House of Representatives, *Biographical Directory of the Texan Conventions and Congresses, 1832–1845* (Austin: Book Exchange, 1941).
Robert Wooster

EVERITT, TEXAS. Everitt was in a dense thicket nine miles southwest of Coldspring in southwestern San Jacinto County. It was named for W. N. Everitt, who moved to the area in the late 1880s. He also served as the first postmaster for the Everitt post office, established in 1890. Everitt had a peak population of 300 during the early twentieth century. As the Great Depression[qv] devastated San Jacinto County agriculture and lumbering, however, the population of Everitt fell rapidly. The post office was discontinued in 1929, and by the late 1940s Everitt no longer appeared on lists of Texas towns.

BIBLIOGRAPHY: Ruth Hansbro, History of San Jacinto County (M.A. thesis, Sam Houston State Teachers College, 1940).
Robert Wooster

EVERMAN, TEXAS. Everman is an incorporated residential community on the southern edge of Fort Worth near U.S. Highway 820 in southeastern Tarrant County. Members of the Kiowa-Apache and Wichita tribes inhabited the area until the arrival of Anglo-Americans in the early to middle 1850s. A hamlet named Oak Grove existed in the area for several years. Upon the arrival of the International–Great Northern Railroad in 1904, a more established community developed and was named for an engineer of the railroad, John W. Everman. In 1905 postal service to the settlement began, and in 1906 Everman established an independent school district. In 1917 the community was one of three sites selected to serve as a flight training school for the Canadian Royal Flying Corps and the United States Signal Corps, Aviation Section. Barron Field,qv just outside the city, stimulated the local economy and increased population growth. By the mid-1920s Everman had eight businesses and an estimated population of 138. In 1976 the Barron Munitions Building, which after the war had served as a schoolhouse for African-American schoolchildren, was awarded a Texas Historical Commissionqv marker. In the mid-1950s the community had a population of 450. After the nearby Dallas–Fort Worth International Airportqv was constructed, the number of residents at Everman increased to more than 5,000 by the mid-1970s. Everman adopted the council-manager form of city governmentqv in 1986. In the early 1990s the community had an estimated 5,701 residents.

David Minor

EVERTS, GUSTAVUS A. (1798–1884). Gustavus A. Everts, attorney and judge, was born in Ohio in 1798. He moved to Fannin County, Texas, in 1844 and served as a member of the Convention of 1845.qv He was a corresponding secretary at the organizational meeting of the Democratic partyqv of Texas on April 27, 1846. In 1850 he lived in Fannin County with his wife, Abigail, a native of New Hampshire. Judge John H. Reaganqv appointed him district attorney for Dallas County in 1855. By 1860 Everts had moved to a farm near Gainesville in Cooke County. As a Unionist who opposed secession,qv he felt threatened at the time of the Great Hanging at Gainesvilleqv in 1862 and fled the area; he spent the remaining years of the war in Navarro County. At the beginning of Reconstructionqv in August 1865, provisional governor Andrew J. Hamiltonqv appointed Everts judge of the Thirteenth Judicial District, but he held that position only until February 1866, when he resigned and moved to Sherman, Grayson County. There he was appointed county judge by Gen. Joseph J. Reynoldsqv in October 1868 and served until March 1870. After unsuccessfully seeking appointment by Governor Edmund J. Davisqv as a district judge in 1870, Everts held no other public offices. He died in January 1884.

BIBLIOGRAPHY: Texas House of Representatives, *Biographical Directory of the Texan Conventions and Congresses, 1832–1845* (Austin: Book Exchange, 1941).

Melanie F. Healy

EVIA, JOSÉ ANTONIO DE (1740–?). José Antonio de Evia was born in La Graña, Spain, in July 1740, the son of master mariner Simón de Evia and Felipa de Gantes y Pravio. He studied at the Royal Naval School of El Ferrol and on January 1, 1753, began serving on naval vessels as a pilot. After serving in the coast guard of Cartagena de Indias in 1760 he sailed around Spain's mare nostrum, the Gulf of Mexico. He made the round trip from Havana to New Orleans, Veracruz, and Mobile several times. In 1779 he commanded a launch at New Orleans and captured the English ship that tried to bring reinforcements and supplies to Manchak. He was shipwrecked in the *Volante* off Mobile in February 1780 but nevertheless captured the English ship and crew he was chasing. He also commanded the port of Mobile during its siege and capture by Bernardo de Gálvez.qv After convoying troop ships back to Havana, he served as courier between Gálvez, Gabriel de Aristízabal, and Juan Bautista Bonet. He served in the royal arsenal of Havana from March 1782 until May 1783, when he was assigned to the warship San Cristóbal. He was promoted to frigate ensign in 1783 and commissioned by Gálvez to draw up detailed plans of the entire Gulf Coast from West Florida to Tampico.

Evia made an unsuccessful attempt in 1783, then embarked again in 1785 to explore by lugger and canoe the rivers and inlets of Florida, Alabama, Mississippi, Louisiana, Texas, and Mexico—an arduous task that he completed at Tampico in September 1786. He explored San Bernardo Bay and named Galveston Bayqv for his patron after taking detailed soundings of it. Supported by Gálvez, he was rewarded on July 2, 1787, with the post of captain of the port and commander of the coast guard of New Orleans at an annual salary of $2,000. He left Havana with his wife, Francisca Ruiz Delgado, and his two sons for New Orleans, where he changed the spelling of his name to Hevia. In 1792 he was commissioned by Governor General Carondelet to capture William Augustus Bowles, who had used Seminole Indians to attack and take the post of San Marcos de Apalache. Upon the successful completion of the assignment, Evia returned to New Orleans, where he exercised the functions of port master throughout the Spanish occupation of Louisiana. His accurate and detailed charts, diaries, and descriptions of the Gulf area were the best by any navigator of the eighteenth century. They served as the basis of subsequent charts drawn by the Hydrographic Service of Spain, as well as key documents in the Spanish case against American claims to the Neutral Groundqv between Louisiana and Texas.

BIBLIOGRAPHY: José de Evia, *José de Evia y sus reconocimientos del Golfo de México, 1783–1796*, ed. Jack D. L. Holmes (Madrid: Porrúa Turanzas, 1968). Charles W. Hackett, ed., *Pichardo's Treatise on the Limits of Louisiana and Texas* (4 vols., Austin: University of Texas Press, 1931–46). Jack D. L. Holmes, "Gallegos notables en la Luisiana," *Cuadernos de Estudios Gallegos* 19 (1964). Lawrence Kinnaird, "The Significance of William Augustus Bowles' Seizure of Panton's Apalachee Store in 1792," *Florida Historical Society Quarterly* 9 (January 1931).

Jack D. L. Holmes

EWELL, TEXAS. Ewell, on Farm Road 593 ten miles north of Gilmer in northern Upshur County, was probably established soon after the Civil War.qv A post office opened in 1886, and by 1890 the community had two mills and a blacksmith shop. Ewell grew rapidly during the early 1890s; in 1896 it had two shingle mills, two sawmills, a cotton gin, two blacksmith shops, and Methodist, Baptist, and Primitive Baptist churches. After 1900, however, it began to decline. The post office closed in 1905, and by the mid-1930s the community had a church, two stores, a school, and a few houses. The population in 1940 was listed as 150. In the mid-1960s it dropped to 100, and only a community center, a church, and a few scattered houses remained. In 1990 Ewell was a dispersed community with an estimated population of 100.

BIBLIOGRAPHY: Doyal T. Loyd, *History of Upshur County* (Waco: Texian Press, 1987).

Christopher Long

EWING, ALEXANDER WRAY (1809–1853). Alexander Wray Ewing, early Texas doctor, was born in 1809 in Londonderry, Ireland. He studied medicine at Trinity College, Dublin, and at the College of Surgeons in Edinburgh. He moved to Pennsylvania and in 1834 to Texas. He lived briefly at San Felipe and acquired a quarter league now in Fayette County in 1835. He was appointed surgeon general of the Texas army on April 6, 1836, and treated Sam Houston'sqv wound at the battle of San Jacinto.qv Ewing incurred President David G. Burnet'sqv wrath by accompanying the wounded Houston to Galveston. He was dismissed by Burnet but was soon reinstated. The Texas Congress blocked President Houston's move to keep Ewing as chief medical officer in 1837, and he was succeeded in this post by Ashbel Smith.qv Ewing moved to Houston, where he became first president of that city's Medical and Surgical Society in 1838. He also was a member of a "committee of arrangements" for the proposed Houston and Brazos Rail Road Company. By 1842 Ewing was again serving in the army. He was married three times within a period of ten years—to Mrs. Susan Henrietta Smiley Reid, who died in 1842, to Elizabeth Tompkins, and to Elizabeth Graham, who died in 1904. Ewing had at least two children, and by 1850 owned real property valued at $6,000. He was a Mason. He died on November 1, 1853.

BIBLIOGRAPHY: Sam Houston Dixon and Louis Wiltz Kemp, *The Heroes of San Jacinto* (Houston: Anson Jones, 1932). Pat Ireland Nixon, *The Medical Story of Early Texas, 1528–1853* (Lancaster, Pennsylvania: Lupe Memorial Fund, 1946).

Robert Wooster

EWING, JAMES L. (1812–1836). James L. Ewing, Alamo defender, was born in Tennessee in 1812. He took part in the siege of Bexar[qv] as a member of Capt. William R. Carey's[qv] artillery company and later served as secretary to Lt. Col. James C. Neill,[qv] commander of the Texan forces occupying Bexar. Ewing died in the battle of the Alamo[qv] on March 6, 1836.

BIBLIOGRAPHY: Daughters of the American Revolution, *The Alamo Heroes and Their Revolutionary Ancestors* (San Antonio, 1976). Daughters of the Republic of Texas, *Muster Rolls of the Texas Revolution* (Austin, 1986). Bill Groneman, *Alamo Defenders* (Austin: Eakin, 1990).
Bill Groneman

EWING, PRESLEY KITTREGE (1860–1927). Presley Kittrege Ewing, lawyer and judge, son of Fayette and Eliza Josephine (Kittrege) Ewing, was born in La Fourche Parish, Louisiana, on July 21, 1860. He graduated in philosophy and law from the University of Mississippi in 1881. The next year he moved to Houston, Texas, where he was admitted to the bar and began practice. In May 1899 he successfully represented a plan for a deepwater Gulf outlet at Houston before the Trans-Mississippi Commercial Congress at Wichita, Kansas. Ewing served as president of the Texas Bar Association (*see* STATE BAR OF TEXAS) in 1899 and as chief justice of the Texas Supreme Court in 1905. He wrote several books and numerous legal treatises. He was a Mason, an Elk, a Democrat, and an Episcopalian. He married Mary Ellen Williams on February 10, 1885; they had two children. In 1919 his wife died, and on June 12, 1923, he married June Throckmorton. Ewing died on February 4, 1927.

BIBLIOGRAPHY: Emory A. Bailey, *Who's Who in Texas* (Dallas: John B. McCraw Press, 1931). Houston Press Club, *Men of Affairs of Houston and Environs* (Houston: Coyle, 1913).

EWING, WILLIAM MAURICE (1906–1974). William Maurice Ewing, geophysicist and oceanographer, was born on May 12, 1906, in Lockney, Texas, the son of Floyd Ford and Hope (Hamilton) Ewing. He received three degrees from Rice Institute (now Rice University)—a B.A. in 1926, an M.A. in 1927, and a Ph.D. in 1931. He taught physics at the University of Pittsburgh (1929–30); physics, geology, and geophysics at Lehigh University (1930–44); and geology at Columbia University (1944–72). While on leave from the latter two universities from 1940 to 1946, he was a research associate on national defense projects at Woods Hole (Massachusetts) Oceanographic Institute. Back at Columbia University in 1947, he became professor of geology, and in 1959 he was named Higgins Professor of Geology there. He was the first director of Columbia University's Lamont Geological Observatory (later Lamont-Doherty Geological Observatory), where he served from 1949 to 1972.

As a pioneer oceanographer Ewing led more than fifty expeditions to explore ocean bases. He made many contributions in the development of oceanographic instruments now in use for exploration of the oceans, including the development and use of the deep-sea camera and the piston cover. During the war he discovered the SOFAR Channel, a continuous layer in the deep ocean where sound energy is trapped by focusing, thus providing a mechanism for a long-range communications system. Over the years the vast collection of data that Ewing and his associates collected contributed enormously to the present concept of oceans as youthful features. His work in earthquake seismology confirmed the layered structure of oceans, which had been first demonstrated by his refraction studies. Ewing, perhaps more than any other single person, laid the foundation for the revolutionary concept known as plate tectonics.

In 1954 he discovered the Sigsbee knolls in the deep basin of the Gulf of Mexico, and he suggested that they might be salt domes. Fourteen years later he was the chief scientist aboard the oceanographic research ship *Glomar Challenger* when oil deposits were discovered beneath those salt domes.

Known worldwide for his contributions in geophysics and oceanography, Ewing was named head of the Division of Earth and Planetary Sciences in the Marine Biomedical Institute of the University of Texas Medical Branch at Galveston in June 1972; he was also named professor of geological sciences at the university. He published over 300 papers in scientific journals and was on the editorial boards of several publications. He was elected to the National Academy of Sciences and to the national academies of several other countries. He was also elected to foreign membership in the Royal Society of London. He served as president of the American Geophysical Union and of the Seismological Society of America. He received eleven honorary degrees from universities around the world. In addition to numerous medals and prizes awarded him during his lifetime, President Richard M. Nixon presented him the national Medal of Science. He was a member of the Philosophical Society of Texas[qv] for more than twenty-five years.

Ewing was married to Avarilla Hildenbrand on October 31, 1928; they had one son. He was married to Margaret Sloan Kidder on February 19, 1944; they had two sons and two daughters. Both marriages ended in divorce. Ewing was married a third time, on May 6, 1965, to Harriet Greene Bassett, who survived him. He died on May 4, 1974, at John Sealy Hospital[qv] in Galveston and was buried at Palisades, New York. He was awarded posthumously, in the fall of 1974, the Penrose Medal, highest honor of the Geological Society of America. In 1976 the Geophysics Laboratory of the University of Texas Marine Science Institute was renamed Maurice Ewing Hall.

BIBLIOGRAPHY: *Proceedings of the Philosophical Society of Texas*, 1973. Vertical Files, Barker Texas History Center, University of Texas at Austin. *Who's Who in America*, 1968–69.

EWING, TEXAS (Angelina County). Ewing was on the Angelina and Neches River Railroad ten miles southeast of Lufkin in northeastern Angelina County. It was the site of a hardwood lumbermill, active from 1920 to 1944. S. W. Henderson and H. G. Bohlssen formed a corporation called the H. G. Bohlssen Manufacturing Company and built a mill at a site near the Angelina River. The corporation was capitalized at $200,000, and stock was divided among thirty-five stockholders. Bohlssen died in the early 1920s, and after his widow sold out to Henderson the company name was changed to Angelina Hardwood Company.

James A. Ewing, one of the stockholders, gave his name to the post office granted to the community in 1920. The old Ewing plantation belonging to his family had had the largest number of slaves in Angelina County at the time of the Civil War.[qv] The first postmaster was John Bohlssen. Mail service was transferred to Huntington in 1944. At its largest, Ewing had nearly 1,000 inhabitants, several stores and churches, and many houses. The largest number of businesses listed for Ewing by the *Texas Almanac* was eight during the 1930s. The mill produced 40,000 feet of hardwood a day and employed 250 men. Around 1944 it was closed because the available timber was exhausted. In 1945 Ewing had only one business and a population of fifty, and shortly after that it was abandoned. The Texas Highway Department lists it as an abandoned railroad station.

During its two decades Ewing survived a large number of grave misfortunes. One of the founders of the hardwood mill, Bohlssen, was crushed to death by a falling stack of lumber about 1923. In 1924 a fire broke out in the plant and ravaged the town. From 1931 to 1933 the mill had to close because of the Great Depression.[qv] Not only the shortage of timber in the 1940s, but also the shortage of labor due to World War II,[qv] forced the closing of the mill. Moreover, while the operation was being dismantled, John Henderson, one of the co-owners, fell into a burning pile of sawdust and was killed. The spirit of the town, however, was kept alive in the late 1980s through yearly reunions of its former inhabitants, held each autumn in Lufkin.

BIBLIOGRAPHY: Angelina County Historical Survey Committee, *Land of the Little Angel: A History of Angelina County, Texas*, ed. Bob Bowman (Lufkin, Texas: Lufkin Printing, 1976). Bob Bowman, *This*

Was East Texas (Diboll, Texas: Angelina Free Press, 1967). Archie Birdsong Mathews, The Economic Development of Angelina County (M.A. thesis, University of Texas, 1952).
Megan Biesele

EWING, TEXAS (Coryell County). Ewing, six miles southeast of Gatesville in eastern Coryell County, may have been named for a railroad official. In 1910 the Temple-Northwestern Railway Company tried to build a railroad that would pass through Ewing on its way from Temple to Gatesville, but the line was never completed. The school at Ewing, which was formed by the consolidation of the Farmer's Branch, Branchville, and Pleasant Grove schools, became the focal point of the Ewing community. When the Fort Hood[qv] military reservation was established in the area during the early 1940s, Ewing residents were forced to relocate; an annual homecoming reunion is held in Gatesville.

BIBLIOGRAPHY: Coryell County Genealogical Society, *Coryell County, Texas, Families, 1854–1985* (Dallas: Taylor, 1986).
Vivian Elizabeth Smyrl

EWING COLLEGE. Ewing College, previously La Grange Collegiate Institute[qv] at La Grange, Fayette County, was chartered on February 11, 1860, under the Colorado Synod of the Cumberland Presbyterian Church. The school opened its first session in September 1860, with R. P. Decherd as president and three other faculty members. Tuition for a term of twenty weeks ranged from $12.50 to $20.00 in the preparatory department and from $20.00 to $25.00 in the collegiate department, with a $5.00 extra fee for Spanish, French, or German. In October 1860 the school was described as suitable for education of ministerial students. Fifty-five attended the second term, and a commercial science course was added. With the outbreak of the Civil War[qv] in the spring of 1861, the trustees suspended the college as a synodal school and allowed K. C. Decherd to use the building for a private school called La Grange Male Academy. In 1863 J. R. Casselman became Decherd's partner and advertised the school as La Grange Male and Female Academy. After the Civil War the school became Ewing Female College. A. H. Cross established a school in the college building in September 1867, but an outbreak of yellow fever ended it. The Colorado Synod retained its trustees in order to save the charter and the property. In 1868 James W. Smith and A. J. Adkisson were appointed to dispose of the property; they sold it in 1870 for $500 and turned the proceeds over to Trinity University.

BIBLIOGRAPHY: Johanna Caroline Walling, Early Education in Fayette County (M.A. thesis, University of Texas, 1941). Leonie L. Weyand, Early History of Fayette County, 1822–1865 (M.A. thesis, University of Texas, 1932).

EWING HALSELL FOUNDATION. The Ewing Halsell Foundation, based in San Antonio, is a private charitable trust dedicated to improving the quality of life for Texans by providing access to the arts, education, and quality health care, and by helping provide opportunities for the economically disadvantaged. The foundation, established in 1957 by Ewing Halsell[qv] and his wife, Lucile, has an endowment of $22 million and a grant-making level of $1.5 to $2 million a year. The endowment was built from the estates of the Halsells and from gifts from other family members such as Grace Rider, Lucile Halsell's sister. The foundation's trustees consist of Halsell family members and business associates. They are supported in their work by a grants administrator, a secretary-bookkeeper and a land manager. Ewing Halsell Foundation grants have included the first grant to establish the South Texas Medical Center and funding to rescue the Lone Star Brewery for reuse as the San Antonio Museum of Art.[qv] It has also made grants to underwrite the first Immigration Reform Study, and, more recently, to establish San Antonio's Botanical Gardens. The Ewing Halsell Foundation is a member of the Conference of Southwest Foundations.[qv]

EXALL, HENRY (1848–1913). Henry Exall, businessman and agriculturist, was born on August 30, 1848, in Richmond, Virginia, to Rev. George G. and Angeline (Pierce) Exall. His education at his father's academy was interrupted by the Civil War;[qv] Exall served in the Tenth Virginia Cavalry from the spring of 1863 until the end of the war. Thereafter he studied law, then switched to business. He moved to Kentucky in 1867 to work in merchandising and the manufacture of woolen goods. In 1869 he married Emma Warner. She and their three children had died by 1875. A business trip to Texas in 1877 informed Exall of the area's commercial potential, and he decided to make his home there.

After starting a cattle business near Fort Worth in 1876, Exall went to Lampasas in 1881 and worked in real estate. In Dallas on November 9, 1887, he married May Dickson (see EXALL, MAY DICKSON); they had one son. Exall soon became a leader in Dallas development, especially in real estate and banking. He helped organize the North Texas National Bank of Dallas in 1887 and served as its vice president. He was president of the State Fair of Texas[qv] and Dallas Exposition in 1889, built one of the city's first skyscrapers, and was instrumental in the development of Highland Park. In 1890 he constructed a dam on Turtle Creek to make Exall Lake, a popular resort spot of the time.

He represented Texas at numerous business and political conventions. In 1885 he was appointed vice president for Texas of the Cotton Centennial in New Orleans and colonel and quartermaster general of the Texas Volunteer Troops. He was elected vice president for Texas at the 1887 meeting of the American Bankers Association in Pittsburgh, Pennsylvania. President Benjamin Harrison appointed him one of the commissioners at large for the World's Columbian Exposition in 1893, and Exall served in a similar capacity at the Chicago Exposition that year. As president of the Texas Industrial Congress[qv] in 1910 he encouraged soil conservation and the study and application of farming methods that increased acreage yield by awarding $10,000 cash prizes to Texas farmers who achieved these ends. He was a member of the Democratic convention that nominated Grover Cleveland for president in 1884, and in the late 1880s he served as chairman of the state Democratic executive committee.

On his farms north of Dallas Exall pursued his agricultural interests and bred racehorses, one of which made him a fortune as a sire of trotting and harness racers. He was a member of the Sterling Price Camp, the United Confederate Veterans of Dallas, and the Dallas Chamber of Commerce; he was serving as president of the National Corn Exposition at his death. He was seriously ill for several weeks due to complications following an operation and died on December 29, 1913. The city of Dallas named Exall Park in his honor.

BIBLIOGRAPHY: Dallas *Morning News*, December 30, 1913. Frank W. Johnson, *A History of Texas and Texans* (5 vols., ed. E. C. Barker and E. W. Winkler [Chicago and New York: American Historical Society, 1914; rpt. 1916]). *Memorial and Biographical History of Dallas County* (Chicago: Lewis, 1892; rpt., Dallas: Walsworth, 1976).
Joan Jenkins Perez

EXALL, MAY DICKSON (1859–1936). May Dickson Exall, civic leader, was born on August 14, 1859, in McKinney, Texas, to Joseph J. and Sarah (Epperson) Dickson. She attended Vassar College and lived in various places in Texas, including Clarksville and Galveston, before moving to Dallas in 1883. She married Henry Exall on November 9, 1887; they had one son. Mrs. Exall was president of the Dallas Shakespeare Club, one of the state's first women's clubs, from its organization in 1886 until her death. In 1869 she organized the Dallas Federation of Women's Clubs to unite and direct the efforts of Dallas women towards the establishment of a public library. She was the first president (1898–99) of the federation, and she also served as president of the Dallas Library Association and of its board of trustees. Upon her entreaty Andrew Carnegie donated $50,000 to the fund-raising effort. In 1897 she helped form the Texas Federation of Women's Literary Clubs, which later became the Texas Federation of

Women's Clubs.qv She was instrumental in the formation of the Dallas Woman's Club in 1922 and served as its third president. She also helped organize and establish the Dallas Museum of Fine Arts (now the Dallas Museum of Artqv). She served on the committee for the Robert E. Leeqv memorial statue, unveiled in 1936 with President Franklin Roosevelt in attendance. She was a Presbyterian and a charter member of the YWCA. Upon the fiftieth anniversary of her presidency, the Dallas Shakespeare Club commissioned her portrait by Douglas G. Chandor.qv After a long illness, Mary Exall died at her home in Dallas on September 28, 1936.

BIBLIOGRAPHY: Biographical Files, Dallas Public Library. John William Leonard, *Women's Who's Who of America* (New York: American Commonwealth, 1914). *Joan Jenkins Perez*

EXAMINING BOARDS. There were almost forty separate examining boards in the Texas state government on January 1, 1994. In general these boards examine applicants and issue licenses for the practice of a particular profession or trade. The boards have the power to investigate and possibly revoke licenses. With a few exceptions, they are appointed by the governor. Members must have professional licenses and meet the requirement of at least five years' experience, though requirements do vary. Some other government agencies also administer licensing such as the Texas State Library and Archives Commission,qv 1909; Texas Education Agency,qv 1949; Texas Department of Aviation, 1989; State Board of Insurance,qv 1957; State Bar of Texas,qv 1936; and Texas Department of Health,qv 1879.

The examining boards, with their dates of establishment, are as follows:

Texas State Board of Acupuncture Examiners, 1993
Texas Appraiser Licensing and Certification Board, 1991
Texas Board of Architectural Examiners, 1937
State Board of Barber Examiners, 1929
Texas State Board of Chiropractic Examiners, 1949; an earlier board established in 1943 was declared unconstitutional in 1944
Texas Cosmetology Commission, 1971; replaced State Board of Hairdressers and Cosmetologists, 1935
Texas Court Reporters Certification Board, 1977
Texas State Board of Dental Examiners, 1919 (six-member), 1971 (nine-member), 1981 (twelve-member)
Texas State Board of Examiners of Dietitians, 1983
Texas Board of Examiners in the Fitting and Dispensing of Hearing Aids, 1969
Texas Funeral Service Commission, 1987; replaced State Board of Morticians
Texas Board of Irrigators, 1979
State Board of Law Examiners, 1919
Texas State Board of Marriage and Family Therapists, 1991
Texas State Board of Medical Examiners, 1907
State Board of Nurse Examiners, 1909
Texas Board of Licensure for Nursing Home Administrators, 1969
Texas Optometry Board, 1969; replaced Board of Examiners in Optometry, 1922
Texas State Board of Perfusion Examiners, 1994
Texas State Board of Pharmacy, 1907
Texas State Board of Physical and Occupational Therapy Examiners, 1993; included functions of Texas State Board of Physical Therapy Examiners
Texas State Board of Plumbing Examiners, 1947
Texas State Board of Podiatry Examiners, 1923; formerly known as the State Board of Chiropody Examiners
State of Texas Board of Polygraph Examiners, 1965
Board of Private Investigators and Private Security Agencies, 1969
Texas State Board of Examiners of Professional Counselors, 1981
State Board of Registration for Professional Engineers, 1937
Texas Board of Professional Land Surveying, 1979; replaced Board of Examiners of Land Surveyors, 1919, and State Board of Registration for Public Surveyors, 1955
Texas Board of Licensure for Professional Medical Physicists, 1991
Texas Board of Examiners of Psychologists, 1969
Texas State Board of Public Accountancy, 1945
Texas Real Estate Commission, 1949
Texas State Board of Examiners of Social Workers, 1993
State Committee of Examiners for Speech Pathology and Audiology, 1983
Texas Structural Pest Control Board, 1971
Board of Tax Professional Examiners, 1977
State Board of Veterinary Medical Examiners, 1911
State Board of Vocational Nurse Examiners, 1951   *Dick Smith*

EXCELSIOR, TEXAS. Excelsior was on the Houston, East and West Texas Railway fifty miles northeast of Houston in northern Liberty County. The Excelsior post office was established in 1912; in June of that year the town plat was drawn up at the direction of Minora Paxson Hinchliff. A large number of tram lines traversed the surrounding heavy forests, and George Hinchliff operated a sawmill at Excelsior. The post office, however, was discontinued in 1917, and the community was abandoned.

BIBLIOGRAPHY: Barbara Smith, comp., "Cleveland's History," *Cleveland Area Pioneer*, June 1978. *Robert Wooster*

EXELL, TEXAS. Exell, on the Moore-Potter county line just off U.S. Highway 287 in south central Moore County, derives its name from an inversion of the LX (*see* LX RANCH) cattle brand of the pioneer rancher Lee Bivins.qv It grew simultaneously with the Exell Helium Plant,qv which was built to produce helium for use as a lifting gas in semirigid and nonrigid airships and in observation and barrage balloons during World War II.qv As the town's sole industry, the plant began production in March 1943, only ten months after construction started. It was soon operating at 25 percent above its rated capacity. Railroad service was provided by the North Plains and Santa Fe Railroad, which furnished specially made cars to pick up the large cylindrical tanks of compressed helium for shipment. During construction housing was built for more than 1,000 plant employees. Through the mid-1980s the Exell plant was a leading producer of helium. With improved highways and transportation, however, the resident populace decreased. Mail for the plant's personnel comes through the post office at Masterson.

BIBLIOGRAPHY: M. D. Minor, The History of Moore County, Stressing Education (M.A. thesis, West Texas State College, 1949). *H. Allen Anderson*

EXELL HELIUM PLANT. The Exell Helium Plant, in southern Moore County near the Potter county line, was the first World War IIqv–vintage plant established in the Panhandleqv by the Federal Bureau of Mines. It came about as a result of the need for helium as a lifting gas in semirigid and nonrigid airships used to escort Allied shipping and in observation and barrage balloons. The plant began production on March 13, 1943, and was soon operating at 25 percent above its rated capacity. The facility, initially supervised by a few experienced operators from the bureau's Amarillo plant, became a model for efficiency. Housing was constructed nearby for over 1,000 employees. Railroad service was provided by the North Texas and Santa Fe line, which furnished specially made cars to pick up large cylinder tanks of compressed helium for shipment. Some of the helium extracted here figured prominently in the development of the first atomic bomb. Twice the Exell Plant was given the coveted Army-Navy "E" Award for excellence in the production of vital war materials. For several years a 125-foot guard tower, built out of an old oil derrick and containing a man-powered elevator, was a unique feature on the plant grounds.

Exell was the only bureau plant not to be temporarily deactivated immediately after the war. By 1953 it was a leader in the production of helium for intercontinental missiles and the embryonic space program. The plant's production capacity was expanded to about 240 million cubic feet in 1956–57 and to more than 300 million cubic feet annually in 1960. In 1968 a new separation unit, the largest of its type in any bureau plant, was added to recover more than 98 percent of the helium from the Colorado Interstate Gas Company's feed gas; as a result, an additional 40 million cubic feet per year could be extracted. Two more units, one of which raises the purity of helium-gas mixture stored for conservation from 70 to about 95 percent, were installed to recover helium extracted from the Cliffside gas field in 1970. In 1980 new cryogenic purification and liquefaction equipment and a pressure swing absorption unit were added to help supply the increased national demand. With about seventy full-time employees by 1986, the Exell Plant continued to be a major producer and supplier of both gaseous and liquefied helium for weather and medical research purposes and such federal government agencies as NASA. In 1994 the plant employed about 100 employees, and roughly 98 percent of all its production was for government use. Over the years equipment had been modernized for the purpose of meeting environmental standards, improving efficiency, and reducing operating costs. *See also* HELIUM PRODUCTION.

BIBLIOGRAPHY: Jay B. Funk and James C. Jarrett, *Moore County: Memories That Count* (Canyon, Texas: Staked Plains, 1986). M. D. Minor, The History of Moore County, Stressing Education (M.A. thesis, West Texas State College, 1949).
H. Allen Anderson

EXILE, TEXAS. Exile, named for its supposed distance from any settled area, was near the junction of Mare Creek and the Dry Frio River at the Uvalde-Edwards county line. A post office was established there in 1890 on the ranch of stock raiser W. C. Lee, who served as the first postmaster. In 1896 the one-teacher Exile school had an enrollment of fifty-six. The Exile Missionary Baptist Church, organized in 1906, held its services at the school. In 1915 this church changed its name to the Dry Frio Baptist Church and moved several miles south of Exile to the Heard community school. Exile appears to have been abandoned by 1946.

BIBLIOGRAPHY: *A Proud Heritage: A History of Uvalde County* (Uvalde, Texas: El Progreso Club, 1975).
Ruben E. Ochoa

EXODUS OF 1879. Beginning around 1875 a group of black Texas freedmen determined to move to Kansas, where a homestead act offered free land to settlers willing to meet occupancy and improvement qualifications. Between 1875 and 1880 Kansas became the "promised land" and "Kansas fever" spread, as black Texans left the Democratic South. The heaviest migration from Texas occurred in 1879–80. In 1879 African Americans[qv] from Washington, Burleson, Grimes, Nacogdoches, Walker, and Waller counties, tired of such harsh realities as share-cropping and limited political and economic influence under the Black Codes,[qv] boarded the Missouri, Kansas and Texas Railroad or traveled by wagon to Parsons, Kansas. So many arrived in Kansas that year that Kansans called them the "Texodusters." Their number can only be estimated, but it is known that around 1,000 left Texas in November of 1879 and 3,000 to 4,000 by March 1880. As many as 12,000 are estimated to have made the journey.

Before 1879 those leaving North Texas, only about 300 miles from Kansas, found the trip relatively easy. Benjamin "Pap" Singleton, a former Tennessee slave, promoted the migration, but as he inspired travelers, unscrupulous men began selling them bogus railway tickets and fictitious travel amenities. Richard Allen[qv] urged a planned, gradual movement out of the state. A convention held in Houston in 1879 to discuss leaving the state warned against any hasty move and against swindlers at both ends of the journey. As a result, later travelers enjoyed a greater measure of success in their new home. Although hardships abounded in Kansas, few Texodusters returned home. Most remained in Kansas and by 1900 found themselves improved economically and politically.

The exodus caused hardship for white Texas landowners. In some regions only a sparse labor force remained to work fields. In Washington County white farmers tried to retain black workers by offering not only the traditional one-year rentals on farms at five dollars an acre, but three-year terms at an annual reduction to three dollars an acre. Because these new contracts benefited workers choosing to remain, the exodus was generally beneficial for Texas blacks.

BIBLIOGRAPHY: Robert G. Athearn, *In Search of Canaan: Black Migration to Kansas, 1879–80* (Lawrence: Regents Press of Kansas, 1978). Nell Irvin Painter, *Exodusters: Black Migration to Kansas after Reconstruction* (New York: Knopf, 1976).
Peggy Hardman

EXOTICS. The terms *foreign, introduced,* and *exotic* have different connotations but are often used interchangeably to refer to foreign species introduced into new environments. Since colonization began, thousands of species of plants and animals have been brought to North America; many are now in Texas. The term *exotic* is commonly applied in Texas to foreign big game acquired by private landowners and released within fenced enclosures or allowed to range free.

Although exotics are not distributed statewide, several species have become prominent in certain regions. The most popular and numerous are species of deer, antelope, and sheep. Though less popular as a game animal, the European wild swine is among the most numerous introduced species.

Most of the more successful free-ranging exotic species in Texas come from the Asian continent. Axis deer, nilgai antelope,[qv] and blackbuck antelope were originally from India; the sika deer was imported from Southeast Asia. The mouflon sheep was from Sardinia and Corsica, the fallow deer from Asia Minor and southern Europe, and the European wild swine from Europe. The aoudad sheep was brought to Texas from North Africa.

Texans have acquired exotics to observe for pleasure, to substitute for extirpated native big game, to increase the variety of game for hunting, to increase production and income from rangelands by using combinations of animals that have varied food habits, and to sustain populations of species that are endangered on their native ranges. Most of the original exotic brood stock in Texas came from zoos. Subsequent stocking has been with animals mainly purchased from private landowners, zoos, and animal dealers. Exotics are not protected by the regulations that cover native game animals, and they are hunted at the prerogative of the landowner. Exceptions are the axis deer in Bexar and Kendall counties and aoudad sheep in counties contiguous to Palo Duro Canyon, where they are under state game regulations.

Perhaps the earliest releases of exotics were of nilgai antelope acquired by the King Ranch[qv] between 1930 and 1941 from the San Diego Zoo and stocked on the ranch's South Texas rangelands. During the same decade blackbuck antelope and axis (also called chital and spotted) deer, sika deer, and sambar deer were released. From the late 1930s through the 1950s mouflon sheep, eland antelope, red deer, swamp deer (barasingha), and other species were released.

Today, more species and greater numbers of exotic big game are in Texas than anywhere else in North America. The first statewide census of exotics by the Texas Parks and Wildlife Department[qv] in 1963 found thirteen species and 13,000 animals. The 1984 survey revealed about seventy-five species and 120,000 animals. Some species, such as the nilgai, are probably more numerous in Texas than they now are in their native habitats.

Exotics are found in about half of the 254 Texas counties; 55 percent are concentrated in the Edwards Plateau.[qv] South Texas has 18 percent, and most of the remaining number are in localized areas of North, central East, and far West Texas. About 70 percent are confined on pastures by game-proof fences. The remaining 30 percent range free. The most numerous species have developed substantial free-ranging populations.

Hybridization or intergradation has occurred between some species and subspecies through planned breeding and by chance; consequently, there are free-ranging individuals that are atypical of the species. Examples are mouflon that have crossed with Barbados and other breeds of domestic sheep, and crosses between swine and domestic feral swine.

Because exotic populations are localized and are found on private lands where their availability is limited, the general public is not aware of their numbers. Most exotics have been released without regard for their chances for survival, their compatibility with native biota, and their roles in the introduction and spread of diseases. Principal studies on exotics in Texas have been done by the Texas Parks and Wildlife Department, Texas A&M University, and Texas Tech University. The most studied species have been the axis, nilgai, blackbuck, sika, fallow, and aoudad; little is known about the ecology of other species.

Generally, though Texas exotics have fared well and ecological complications have been few, even successful free-ranging populations have occasionally had difficulty with their Texas habitat. Nilgai, blackbuck, and axis evolved in warm climates and are not physiologically adapted to withstand severe cold. Some have died during unusually cold winters. Aoudad have died from infestations of liver flukes, endoparasites for which the sheep are new hosts. Studies indicate that axis, sika, fallow, and nilgai are dominant competitors with native deer for food, and on some heavily populated ranges, native deer are declining as the exotics increase. A major need is proper control of their numbers where prolific free-ranging populations exist. Favorable economic methods of control are to harvest them by sport hunting and for meat. New management changes have begun to emphasize the husbandry of exotics, not just stocking and hunting. The new commercial enterprise involves the production of brood stock, meat, and body parts such as antlers (which are sold as aphrodisiacs in Asia). Exotic meat for human food is gaining attention in the United States, and exotic game dishes are becoming popular in restaurants. Because of the large number of foreign animals and the ecological backlashes they have often caused, many people are opposed to having exotics free-ranging in this country. In Texas, however, where large numbers of exotics are firmly established, the concern now is understanding their ecological roles and practicing sound management.

BIBLIOGRAPHY: W. E. Armstrong, and D. E. Harmel, *Exotic Animals Competing with Native Game*, (Austin: Texas Parks and Wildlife Department, 1981). Caesar Kleberg Research Program in Wildlife Ecology, *Symposium: Introduction of Exotic Animals—Ecological and Socioeconomic Considerations* (College Station: Texas Agricultural Experiment Station, Texas A&M University, 1968). D. E. Harmel, *Texas Big Game Investigations* (Austin: Texas Parks and Wildlife Department, 1980). Elizabeth Mungall and William J. Sheffield, *Exotics on the Range* (College Station: Texas A&M University Press, 1995). C. W. Ramsey, *Texotics* (Austin: Texas Parks and Wildlife Department, 1969). J. G. Teer, "Commercial Uses of Game Animals on Rangelands of Texas," *Journal of Animal Science* 40 (1975). John H. Wootters, *A Guide to Hunting in Texas* (Houston: Pacesetter, 1979).

William J. Sheffield

EX PARTE RODRIGUEZ. In the case of *Ex parte Rodriguez* (39 Tex. 705 [1874]), the Texas Supreme Court ruled invalid the state general election of December 2, 1873. The *Rodriguez* decision is often referred to as the Semicolon Case because of the importance of a semicolon in determining the court's ruling (*see* SEMICOLON COURT). *Ex parte Rodriguez* was greeted with hostility by Texas Democrats, who had ousted the administration of Republican governor Edmund J. Davis[qv] in the election. The court's findings produced severe criticism of that body and resulted in a tarnished reputation for the court for the entire period of Reconstruction.[qv]

Ex parte Rodriguez was one of several cases initiated by dissatisfied Republicans shortly after the December 2 election challenging its validity. Though Governor Davis refused to support these efforts, he did not restrain his supporters from pursuing this course. Because the nature of the *Rodriguez* case made it possible to obtain an early hearing in the Supreme Court, the case emerged as the focus of legal efforts to overturn the general election.

On December 16, 1873, presiding judge Wesley Ogden[qv] issued a writ of habeas corpus for the delivery of Joseph Rodríguez of Travis County to the court. Two prominent Republicans, former governor Andrew J. Hamilton and Chauncey B. Sabin,[qqv] represented Rodríguez, who had been arrested on December 15 on a warrant issued in Harris County. The warrant charged that the defendant had voted at Houston more than once in the general election. Hamilton and Sabin appealed for the writ on the grounds that Rodríguez was being held illegally because the election itself had not been legal.

The court began its hearings on December 22. Harris County district attorney Frank M. Spencer, acting in the absence of Attorney General William Alexander,[qv] represented the state. Prominent Democratic attorneys requested and received permission to assist Spencer because of the importance of the case to their party. These attorneys included Charles S. West, Thomas E. Sneed, George F. Moore, Alexander W. Terrell, party chairman William M. Walton,[qqv] and M. A. Long.

The state, influenced by its Democratic counsel, asked that the court dismiss the case. Spencer argued his point on the grounds that the case was fictitious, designed to "extort from this court" a ruling on the constitutionality of the election. Upon the testimony of a prominent Houston lawyer, George Goldthwaite,[qv] the state's attorneys asserted that the defeated Republican candidate for sheriff in Harris County, A. B. Hall, had hired Rodríguez to test the election law and was paying the expenses of Rodríguez's attorneys. Implying that the entire proceeding was political, M. A. Long threatened the court with impeachment if it involved itself in a political issue.

Hamilton and Sabin proceeded upon their contention that their client should be released despite the fact that he had voted twice because the election was unconstitutional and thus invalid. They argued that the legislative act of March 7, 1873, providing for the election conflicted with Article 3, Section 6, of the Constitution of 1869.[qv] The constitution provided that all elections "shall be held at the countyseats...until otherwise provided by law; and the polls shall be opened for four days." The legislature had established polling places at voting precincts outside the county seats and restricted the election to a single day. Rodríguez's attorneys argued that the semicolon in the constitution made the clause regarding the length of the polling period independent of the rest of the sentence, so that the legislature could not shorten an election.

The court decided against the state's petition for dismissal. Justice John D. McAdoo[qv] gave the majority opinion and noted that because Rodríguez's arrest appeared to be legal the court had no choice but to hear the facts of the case. At this point Spencer resigned, claiming that he could not prosecute a case that he believed had no basis in fact. The court replaced him with B. Trigg, Travis County district attorney. The Democratic attorneys already admitted to the proceedings were allowed to continue.

After dismissing a motion by Hamilton and Sabin to release Rodríguez, the court held a full hearing. Trigg and his associates pursued a course aimed at preventing the court from making a decision. They argued that Rodríguez had not voted twice and that there was no case for the court to decide. They contended that the court should remand the case to Harris County, where original jurisdiction resided. They argued that the court should not decide a constitutional question in a trial of a writ of habeas corpus. Finally, they argued that the court should not rule on a political question, especially one that determined the validity of the election affecting the succession in coordinate departments. Hamilton and Sabin denied all of the contentions of the state. On the political issue Hamilton argued that the requested ruling did not concern the results of the election but rather the validity of the electoral process.

The court announced a decision on January 6, 1874. The judges ruled against the state and concluded that Rodríguez should be released because the election had not been valid. The judges accepted Hamilton's arguments on the construction of relevant clauses in the constitution. The decision had no practical results, however, since it could not be enforced and Democrats chose to ignore it. Following the Coke-Davis controversy,^qv Democratic governor Richard Coke^qv seized office, thus achieving a practical political end to the issue raised by the case.

BIBLIOGRAPHY: James R. Norvell, "The Reconstruction Courts of Texas, 1867–1873," *Southwestern Historical Quarterly* 62 (1958). George E. Shelley, "The Semicolon Court of Texas," *Southwestern Historical Quarterly* 48 (1945).   *Carl H. Moneyhon*

EXPLORATION. Human exploration of the future Texas began during the Pleistocene, when lower sea levels exposed a land bridge between Siberia and Alaska and *Homo sapiens sapiens* migrated into what is now North America. The first explorers and perhaps colonizers possibly reached the continent during a convenient interglacial period, perhaps some 24,000 or more years ago. Other theories of Pre-Columbian exploration suggest that mariners from China, Africa, and the Mediterranean may have reached the New World by following favorable ocean currents. Numerous legends support the idea of transoceanic contacts, but the material evidence remains inconclusive. The first known explorers of Texas were the Clovis people of the Paleo-Indian Stage. An unmistakable presence of bone and stone evidence points to human exploratory and colonizing activity in Texas after 11,500 B.P. Clovis stone projectile points have been found in playas^qv and ancient springs in the far north (Blackwater Draw, the Lake Theo Site,^qqv Lubbock Lake, and Miami), and in rockshelters and stratigraphic layers in South and Central Texas (Aquarena Springs and the Levi Site^qqv). These points tell us of remarkable hunters and gatherers—men, women, and children whose daily existence was often tied to challenging exploration and later adaptation to a changing climate. For the Clovis and their probable Folsom and Plainview descendants, Pleistocene Texas was an extraordinary environment: full of dangerous species, paleosavannas noisy with game animals, high-quality lithic resources, plentiful rockshelters, and tremendous springlands. Though never numerous, perhaps a thousand or so on the great Llano mesa, the Clovis people explored Texas vigorously from a network of base camps, overlooks, kill sites, quarries, and hunting camps. Although the Paleo-Indians were likely more sedentary and vegetarian than the mammoth hunters of popular imagination, they ranged through and beyond the present state, widely exploited favored environmental niches at the end of the last Ice Age, and diffused flint from distant sources like the renowned Alibates Flint Quarries,^qv the "Paleolithic Pittsburgh" along the Canadian River outcroppings.

From the Clovis people forward the confederacy of peoples and ecosystems now called Texas has experienced most of the possible American discovery process. For 11,000 years or so each arriving human culture—Clovis, Pandale, Pedernales, Perdiz, Tonkawa, Coahuiltecan, Comanche, Spanish, French, English, Scots, Irish, African, and many others—has engaged in a spatial-environmental learning process of continual exploration and reexploration in Texas. The process was certainly vital to Archaic and Pre-Contact hunting and gathering peoples. Hunting, trading, climatic shifts, limited agriculture, transhumance, and sheer curiosity led to Archaic Stage exploration of the region that merged so conveniently the coast and mountain, plain and swamp. But even modern Texans must learn to explore and master a complicated world of satellite-city urbanization, internodal transportation, and ranching and agricultural enterprises. An important change in exploration over the past eleven millennia has been the means and ends of the ancient search. The Clovis Texans walked, hunted game trails, and used ordinary eyesight to open the secrets of a new continent; Texans at the Lyndon B. Johnson Space Center^qv in Houston or the University of Texas McDonald Observatory^qv travel by other means and use advanced technology to open the secrets of the universe.

European Discovery and Early Exploration. Because of its size and strategic location, Europeans encountered Texas early in their exploration of the New World. After the historical conquest, subjugation, and depopulation of the Greater Antilles, the Spanish turned their attention westward, where a new continent awaited. The discoveries of Florida and Mexico left a large gap between these two realms. Perhaps, they thought, this *terra incognita* also held the fabled Strait of Anian, the reputed open waterway in the New World that led straight to Asia. One of Cortés's rivals, the overextended governor of Jamaica, Francisco de Garay,^qv authorized an expedition in 1519 to explore the unknown country between the Río Pánuco of Mexico and the "island" of Florida. Lt. Alonso Álvarez de Pineda^qv set out with four ships and 270 men to explore the coast of the Gulf of Mexico^qv on behalf of Garay. He sailed to Florida, explored the western coast, and cast serious doubt on the theory that Florida was an island. The ships then turned and navigated along the mainland Gulf Coast from east to west, sailing into the sunset for weeks. Álvarez noted the mighty Mississippi River on June 2, and thereafter reached the low coast and barrier islands of Texas in late June and July of 1519, a land he called Amichel.^qv His journals and other records are lost, but a pilot's chart from the expedition, now in the Archivo General de Indias in Seville, Spain, provided a remarkable outline of the Gulf Coast, including the Texas portion. Indeed, Álvarez de Pineda's expedition discovered that the Gulf Coast was simply part of a vast contiguous mainland. Although there is no evidence that expedition members went ashore in Texas, it is possible that needs for water, fuel, and fresh food may have taken small parties ashore. Another and equally luckless rival of Cortés brought Spanish explorers back to the Texas coast in the fall of 1528. Pánfilo de Narváez's^qv expedition came to grief in the humid Gulf Coast of Florida, with the men reduced to eating their horses and employing their ingenuity in building a small flotilla of barges. These primitive vessels carried them westward along Álvarez de Pineda's newly discovered mainland coast back to the Spanish settlement at Pánuco.

Posterity is fortunate that the disintegration of the Narváez expedition along the Texas coast was recorded in considerable detail by the incomparable Álvar Núñez Cabeza de Vaca,^qv the greatest of the early discoverers. Cabeza de Vaca was not an explorer in the traditional or scientific sense. He had no specific royal charge, scientific mission, pilots, captains, instruments, writing utensils, or maps available to him in Texas. He was a lucky survivor, a castaway whose storm-tossed barge washed up on San Luis Island,^qv off the west end of Galveston Island,^qv on November 6, 1528. Cabeza de Vaca survived first as an abused captive and then as a small trader, living off the land and among the tribal peoples of the Texas coast. This experience was excellent preparation for exploration of the highest order, precisely because it involved the mental as well as the physical. Hitherto the Spanish had hugged the Texas coast, sending the occasional shore party to land perhaps, but ignoring the interior and its mysterious inhabitants. Now, without any choice in the matter, some eighty Spanish survivors were thrown into Texas from the coast to make their way home. Only "Four Ragged Castaways" managed to do so. For the four—Andrés Dorantes de Carranza, Alonso Castillo Maldonado, Dorantes's African slave Estevanico,^qqv and Cabeza de Vaca—daily life and survival involved not only an understanding of the physical and ecological realities of the Texas Gulf Coast, but a good deal of intuitive understanding of the Indians they encountered. Their sudden

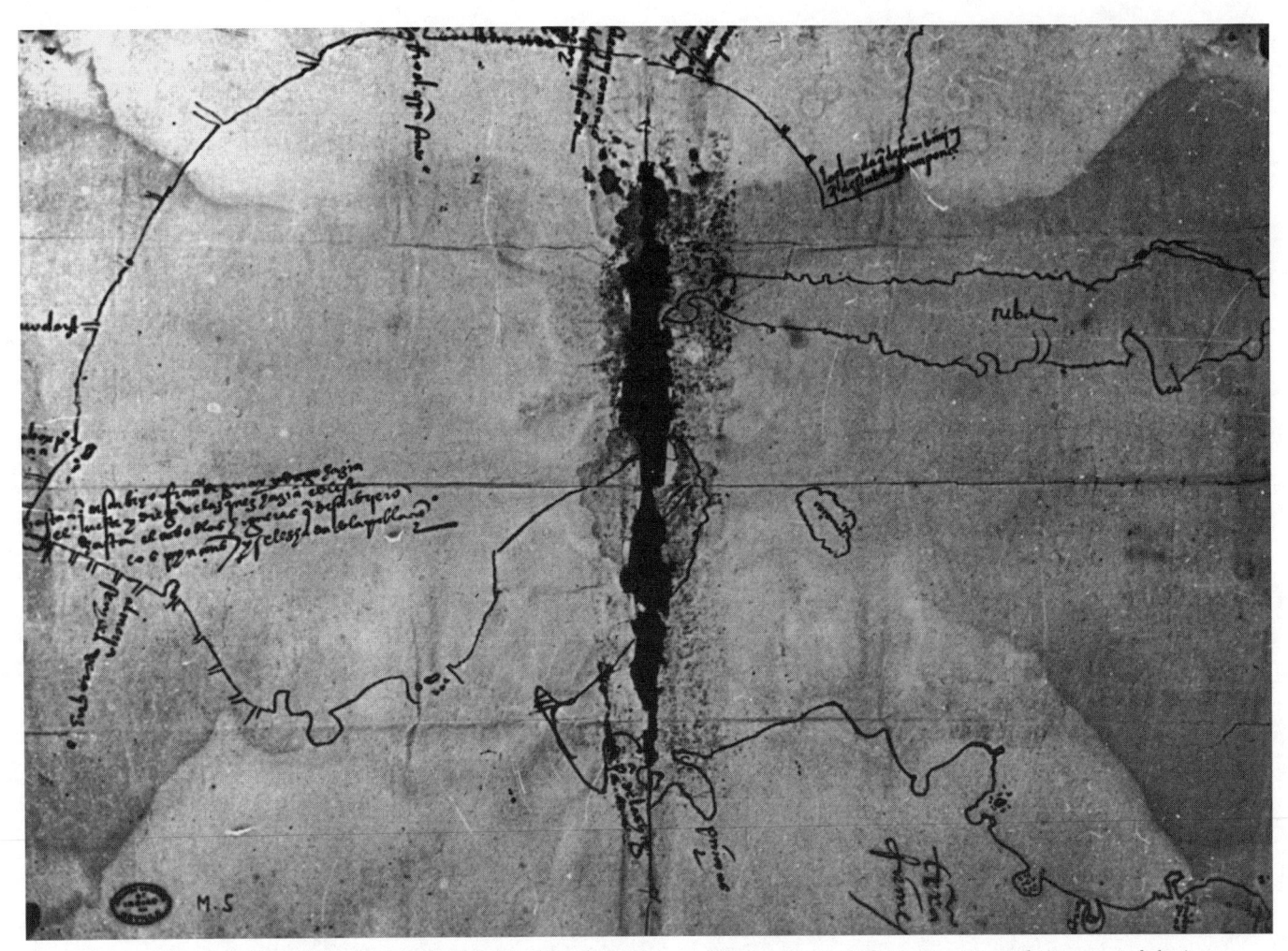

Map of the coast of the Gulf of Mexico, drawn by pilots of the Alonso Álvarez de Pineda expedition, 1519. Manuscript copy. Courtesy Archivo General de Indias, Seville; Mapas y Planos, México 5. Ms. copy in Grace Hesse Map Collection, CAH; CN 01335. This was the first European map to depict any part of what is now Texas, and the first portrayal of the entire Gulf Coast that was based on actual exploration.

and miraculous appearance in 1536 near Culiacán on the Pacific coast greatly excited the geographic imagination in New Spain. Such leaders as Melchor Díaz, Francisco Vázquez de Coronado,[qv] and the viceroy Antonio de Mendoza personally heard the survivors relate their adventures in the "northern mysteries." There were curiosities, including a buffalo[qv] robe, but it was the carefully considered hearsay reports of settlements, cultivated lands, and possible riches to be found deeper in the north that inspired Viceroy Mendoza to dispatch a reconnaissance under Fray Marcos de Niza[qv] and Estevanico. Marcos's subsequent glowing report of the Seven Cities of Cíbola[qv] launched an ambitious economic and military penetration of the Southwest from 1540 to 1542 under Mendoza's captain-general, Vázquez de Coronado. One of Coronado's conquistadors, Capt. Hernando de Alvarado,[qv] was first to penetrate the buffalo plains to the east. While on the plains in or near Texas, a captive known as El Turco[qv] related to Alvarado grand stories of a rich realm called Quivira.[qv] The Coronado expedition penetrated Texas from the west in 1541, while the survivors of Hernando De Soto's expedition, under the command of Luis de Moscoso[qv] after De Soto's death, penetrated Texas from the east in 1542.

Missionary Exploration of New Spain. The missionary exploration of Texas, which began in the west and then broadly swept the state, involved important personages for longer than a century and a half. The beginnings were humble enough. From the raw mining town of Santa Bárbara on the frontier of northern New Spain, a small party of friar-priests and soldiers entered Texas in the summer of 1581. Organized by Fray Agustín Rodríguez[qv] with soldiers under Francisco Sánchez[qv] (better known as Chamuscado), the party of three Franciscans,[qv] nine soldiers, and sixteen Indian servants followed the Conchos River of Chihuahua to its junction with the Rio Grande.[qv] From the rancherías at La Junta de los Ríos[qv] the Rodríguez-Sánchez expedition[qv] advanced up the Rio Grande through the Jumano country of Texas to reach the pueblos of New Mexico, where the friars elected to stay and proselytize. In November 1582 Antonio de Espejo[qv] led a relief expedition down the Conchos River. Diego Pérez de Luxán[qv] accompanied the party as chronicler, and Fray Bernardino Beltrán volunteered to search for the Franciscan order's remote brethren. At the junction of the rivers the Espejo-Beltrán expedition[qv] lingered for 2½ weeks before it too ascended the Rio Grande, passed the Jumano rancherías, and reached the Puebloan settlements. There the searchers learned of the martyrdom of the priests left behind. Espejo explored deeply to the west and then turned eastward to reconnoiter the buffalo plains. Once on the Pecos River, the expedition followed it downstream toward the Rio Grande. This course brought them into West Texas and the Trans-Pecos.[qv] Near the site of modern Pecos, Indians advised them of an overland shortcut to the Rio Grande, which they took, thereby passing through the scenic country where Toyah Creek, Balmorhea, Fort Davis, and Marfa are now located, before reaching the Rio Grande just above La Junta de los Ríos.

Two more unauthorized expeditions in the early 1590s completed the probe initiated by the Franciscans. Gaspar Castaño de Sosa qv led 170 people and their carts and stock across Coahuila in 1590. They started from Monclova,qv crossed the Rio Grande at an unknown location, advanced upstream, then turned up the Pecos River at its junction with the Rio Grande in what is now Val Verde County. Castaño de Sosa's carts thus rumbled through a long stretch of West Texas on their way to Pecos Pueblo. Eventually royal agents chased Castaño down, arrested him, and dispersed his party. The second unauthorized expedition, under Francisco Leyva de Bonilla and Antonio Gutiérrez de Humaña,qqv not only reached the Puebloans, but penetrated deep into the buffalo plains of Texas last seen by the martyred Fray Padilla and Coronado's men. Legends of a rich Quivira lured Leyva and Gutiérrez to the plains, where they were likely the first Spanish in half a century to explore the Canadian River valley of the Panhandle.qv The expedition disintegrated farther north on the Great Plains; Leyva was murdered in a quarrel, and the rest were killed or enslaved by hostile Indians.

Successful or not, the unauthorized explorers awakened official interest in the Pueblo country of New Mexico. In one giant leap that moved the frontier far to the north, the enterprising Juan de Oñate qv led a large and duly authorized entrada through the landmark El Paso del Norte qv to establish a new colony. From a far-flung outpost soon relocated to Santa Fe, Oñate dispatched his nephew, Vicente de Zaldívar,qv in the fall of 1599 to explore the buffalo plains to the east. One key to the success of the Spanish explorers was their ability to find Indian guides and utilize members of prior expeditions. Zaldívar made use of a Christianized Indian named Jusephe, who had survived the Leyva-Gutiérrez expedition eastward into the Texas Panhandle. Jusephe guided the group down the Canadian River valley until they encountered nomadic Plains tribes and large bison herds in the western Panhandle. Oñate himself had heard the Coronadoan legends of Quivira, and thither he launched an impressive expedition in 1601. With Jusephe guiding once more, Oñate, two Franciscans, seventy men, eight carts, and hundreds of draft animals entered the Canadian River valley of Texas in the summer of 1601. As the High Plains qv encompassed them, they observed the rocky outliers, "which the mountains of this land give off," and noted with favor the temperate climate, abundant plums, vast herds of buffalo, and the "springs of good water and groves of trees" found in the valley. A 1602 map of their route, prepared by a Portuguese mariner named Juan Rodríguez, prominently displays the "Río de Magdalena," or Canadian River. This map is said to be the earliest extant map of the American Trans-Mississippi West prepared by an actual observer.

With the gradual Spanish settlement and colonization in New Mexico, a second wave of missionary scouts soon continued the exploration of West Texas. In particular the Jumanos of the South Plains evinced great energy in attracting missionary attention to their rancherías. By this time horses, weapons, disease, and demographic and cultural upheavals were pressuring many tribes; perhaps the Jumanos sought Spanish religious and trade connections partly as a means to find new allies in the desperate wars and migrations. Catholic scholars still debate the claim of a mystical Franciscan nun, María de Jesús de Agreda,qv to bilocate miraculously while in a religious trance from her cell in Agreda, Spain, and appear before the Jumanos and other tribes of Texas; but accounts of appearances of the "Lady in Blue," a beautiful woman in a blue cloak who walked into remote rancherías and encampments to preach and exhort Texas Indians to seek conversion, circulated in church circles for a century. In any event the Jumanos sought missionaries, and Fray Alonso de Benavidesqv of New Mexico dispatched two friars, Juan de Salasqv and Diego León, into the southern High Plains of Texas in 1629. Led by Jumano guides, the priests struck out across the flat immensity of the plains to reach Jumano rancherías along the Middle Concho River of the Colorado River country. They were pleased by their reception, wrote favorably of the local pecans, and discovered that the mussels scooped from the river sometimes contained large freshwater pearls.

Fray Ascencio de Zárate and Fray Juan de Ortega returned to the same area in 1632 to proselytize and explore.

The Franciscan reports of pearls brought at least two commercial forays from New Mexico: the Martín-Castillo expedition (1650) and the expedition of Diego de Guadalajara (1654). These were large, well-financed operations that penetrated as far as the future Tom Green County. Indian allies were set to work harvesting pearls for many months, while Spanish scouting parties explored the surrounding country and looking for a reputed "Kingdom of the Teyas." In 1656 Fray Juan Pérez and Fray Juan Cabal started a small church near El Paso del Norte. From new bases in Coahuila and Nuevo León other small parties of Franciscans also penetrated beyond the Rio Grande into Texas. Fray Francisco Peñasco de Lozano and Fray Manuel de la Cruz ventured beyond the Rio Grande in 1674 on conversion missions in what later became Val Verde and Kinney counties. As Spanish pressure intensified toward the Rio Grande, several tribes attacked them, thus eliciting punitive expeditions from the Saltillo and Monterrey regions. In 1663 troops under Juan de la Garza attacked Cacaxtle Indians near the vicinity of modern Eagle Pass. It is possible that Juan de la Garza crossed the rio Grande and traveled as far as sixty-five miles north of the site of present-day Eagle pass. In 1665 Fernando de Azcuéqv definitely crossed the Rio Grande near the same site. At the head of a large company of soldiers and Indian allies, he eventually routed the Cacaxtles at a battle some sixty-five miles into Texas, possibly near the Nueces River. In 1675 a larger expedition under Fernando del Bosqueqv and the devout Franciscan Fray Juan Larios may have crossed the lower Rio Grande at Paso de Francia (see SAN ANTONIO CROSSING). The Bosque-Larios expeditionqv penetrated West Texas for many leagues, returned to the Rio Grande via the Pecos River, and made strong recommendations to establish more missions in the region. This sentiment was echoed by Juan Domínguez de Mendoza and Fray Nicolás Lópezqqv after their journey into the Edwards Plateauqv in 1683. Domínguez's prior experience with the Guadalajara pearling foray proved useful when he left El Paso del Norte in December of 1683. He descended the Rio Grande to La Junta, where Father López and another friar joined the expedition. The Mendoza-López party turned northeast, traversed a long stretch of what is now West Texas to reach the Pecos River, followed the river to the vicinity of Horsehead Crossing,qv then struck out east-northeast across the flat, featureless plains that intergrade the Edwards Plateau with the Southern High Plains. After returning to the Pecos River crossing by a new southern route, Mendoza and López retraced their prior route through the future Pecos, Brewster, and Presidio counties to reach La Junta.

By the latter seventeenth century, other distractions, problems, and opportunities diminished the Franciscan exploration impulse for West Texas. Nevertheless, the missionary pathfinders had blazed the essential trails across West Texas and into South Texas, trails that others now used for exploratory, commercial, punitive, and eventual colonization efforts to the north and east. Franciscan place names often endured. And after the various Spanish disasters along the inhospitable Gulf Coast, the plains and riverine corridors of the Rio Grande, the Pecos, the Canadian, the Concho, and the upper Colorado were now known and considered pleasant enough. With the Great Pueblo Revolt in New Mexico (1680), the exploration of Texas from the west or New Mexican side subsided. Many of the beleaguered Spanish survivors established themselves at El Paso del Norte (present-day Ciudad Juárez). But even as they lost the province of New Mexico, the northern frontier of New Spain had advanced to the Río Bravo or Rio Grande. Other far-flung outposts now superseded the mining district around Santa Bárbara as a staging area for exploration to the north and east. The new outposts of El Paso del Norte, La Junta de los Ríos, and the trail to Paso de Francia on the lower Rio Grande all laid the foundation for future endeavors.

French and Spanish Exploration. Shortly after the Pueblo Revolt, a feared European rival turned all Spanish attention to the Gulf Coast and coastal interior. The dramatic appearance of René Robert Cavelier, Sieur de La Salle,^qv at Matagorda Bay in 1685 spurred the Spanish into new rounds of military, economic, and religious exploration of coastal and East Texas in the latter 1600s. French rivalry with the Spanish proved a boon to exploration, however, as both sides fought for—and sometimes shared—information, trade, and control of the inhospitable intervening territory, the infamous *costa brava* of Texas, which most mariners feared as a relentlessly hostile environment. The French exploration of Texas was long-lasting and adaptive, but largely commercial. The Spanish reacted vigorously to the alarming disclosures of French presence accumulating from captured deserters, pirates, and Indian reports. From 1685 to 1689 they launched five maritime expeditions and a half dozen overland efforts to search for Fort St. Louis.^qv Further, newly arriving Franciscans such as Fray Damián Massanet and Fray Francisco Hidalgo^qqv now found their attention and missionary interest drawn eastward to the Tejas or Hasinai Confederacy of East Texas. Even a French expedition under Henri de Tonti^qv entered Texas to search for survivors of La Salle's coastal colony. The most important of the Spanish maritime expeditions in search of La Salle's fort was the Rivas-Iriarte expedition.^qv Two specially commissioned, shallow-draft ships, the *Rosario* and *Esperanza*, were placed under the command of captains Martín de Rivas and Pedro de Iriarte^qqv respectively. These so-called "Two Ladies" carried the explorers along the entire length of the Texas coast in the spring of 1687; indeed, Rivas and Iriarte circumnavigated the Gulf of Mexico. Using the accurate celestial navigation skills of Juan Enríquez Barroto,^qv the group prepared outstanding reports, maps, and records of coordinates for the entire Gulf coastline. Their voyage along the Texas coast was the most thorough and advanced to that date. Among other achievements, they accomplished a reasonably precise latitudinal fix of 25°55′ west latitude for the mouth of the Río Bravo (Rio Grande), a long sail past Padre Island^qv with Indians running along the dunes to observe them, a sounding of Aransas Pass,^qv a detour into Cedar Bayou, a reckoning of Cavallo Pass^qv into Matagorda Bay,^qv the discovery of the wrecked French ship *Belle*, a reconnaissance of Palacios Point^qv and Lavaca Bay,^qv a fix on Caney Creek, an important exploration—perhaps the first with any scientific basis—of Galveston Bay^qv on April 25, 1687, and finally a detailed study inside Sabine Pass,^qv to which they were led by the abundant discharge of freshwater into the sea. Even before the return of Rivas and Iriarte, nervous officials dispatched a further maritime expedition up the Texas coast. Two frigates under Francisco López de Gamarra and Andrés de Pez^qqv sailed in the summer of 1687 along the Texas coastline and sighted Corpus Christi Bay^qv and Galveston Bay. Tales, rumors, a deserter's hoax, and the failure to determine accurately the fate of Fort St. Louis led to the second dispatch of the *Rosario* and *Esperanza* to Texas waters in August of 1688 under captains Rivas and Pez. After anchoring their ships in the mouth of Rio Grande, they sent a number of canoes bearing armed Europeans up the river from September 3 to 7. After penetrating the riverine interior as far as Starr County, the canoes returned, and the "Two Ladies" sailed for Matagorda Bay. Once more they failed to find the fort on Garcitas Creek.

Although the Spanish maritime expeditions had charted the coast as never before, of necessity officials turned to a remarkable and experienced overland explorer to solve the French mystery. Alonso De León,^qv who bore the same name as his soldier-explorer father, had already explored the lower Rio Grande in the summer of 1686. The Marqués de Aguayo^qv dispatched him again in the spring of 1687 for a deeper reconnaissance. De León was named governor of Coahuila shortly after his return. After hearing ominous reports of a strange white war chief, very likely a Frenchman, living among the tribes to the north, he was off to Texas for the third time in March 1689. A small party under his leadership found the amazing deserter Jean Jarry^qv "tattooed like a Chichimeco" and living as a tribal chief in what is now Kinney County. Jarry willingly served as a guide. The expedition crossed into Texas at the Paso de Francia, by then a well-known ford, and subsequently followed the broad, grassy parallel of the outer Coastal Plain^qv to avoid the wetlands near the coast. On April 22, 1689, De León found the abandoned Fort St. Louis and the deserted rough dwellings of the colonists, with smashed, torn, and broken belongings strewn everywhere. There were three skeletons, including that of a murdered woman, still unburied. After gathering in two more Frenchmen hiding among the Indians, he returned at last with accurate news on the destruction of the French intruders. The result was De León's expedition of 1690. On April 2, 1690, De León, Massanet, and a large contingent of presidio soldiers crossed the Paso de Francia into Texas. They revisited the Fort St. Louis site; Massanet set fire to the depressing buildings, then De León blazed a trail northeast across the Colorado, Brazos, and Trinity rivers to reach the distant Neches River. There, among the agricultural Hasinai villages, the Spanish ransomed five French survivors who became adventurers themselves; among them was Pierre Talon, one of the Talon children.^qv The Spanish expedition organized the first East Texas barrier to French intrusion, San Francisco de los Tejas Mission. After its affairs seemed in order, De León and Massanet left the new mission with three priests and three soldiers.

At De León's death in March 1691, the process of exploration and expansion into Texas entered a new phase. The further travels and records of Domingo Terán de los Ríos^qv and Father Massanet in establishing additional missions extended Spanish presence and led to the exploration of the Caddoan villages of the Red River country in 1691. Preoccupied with internal affairs and frontier troubles, the Spanish launched fewer large expeditions into Texas from 1684 to 1714. Instead, both Spanish and French explorers concentrated on consolidating the approaches. Importantly, Diego Ramón^qv relocated the mission outpost of San Juan Bautista^qv to a more favorable site near the Paso de Francia in 1700. At this gateway on the south bank of the Rio Bravo, now thirty-five miles below the site of Eagle Pass, Texas, the mission settlement San Juan Bautista became the new staging area on the "Camino de Francia y de los Tejas." San Juan Bautista del Río Grande eventually grew to three missions and a presidio. Its occupants carried the seeds of destruction for many Coahuiltecans recruited for new missions, for a devastating outbreak of smallpox raged among the crowded camps and settlement in 1706 and spread north into Texas. From the missions and presidio a new generation of explorers also set out for Texas in the early 1700s. Though some of these were veterans of the De León or Terán expeditions, others were officers, adventurers, and the anonymous Indian explorers routinely used as spies on the French to the east. In 1709 the Espinosa-Olivares-Aguirre expedition^qv advanced inland from San Juan Bautista to the fabulous tributary springlands along the San Antonio River. Before pushing on to the Colorado River, Fray Espinosa and Fray Olivares explored San Pedro Springs^qv and Los Olmos Springs, finding the fountains and fertile lands sufficient for an entire city.

Spanish lethargy was shaken again in July 1714 with the unexpected arrival at San Juan Bautista of a brilliant Frenchman, Louis Juchereau de St. Denis,^qv a cousin of the French explorer Sieur d'Iberville. St. Denis had been charged by Governor Antoine de la Mothe Cadillac with opening trade connections to the east. After boldly crossing Texas, he was amiably arrested by Commandant Diego Ramón at San Juan Bautista, where he nevertheless charmed the Spanish entirely, married into the Ramón family, and eventually reemerged from Mexico City with a Spanish commission to help reestablish Spanish settlement in East Texas. Spanish exploration thus entered another reactive phase, a burst of activity leading directly this time to the settlement of interior Texas. From 1716 to 1790, more than a score of major expeditions, other reconnaissances and inspections, and an ambitious network of settlements and trails all gave the Spanish undeniable claims to the region. Inspired by St. Denis, supported by the missionary colleges of Zacatecas and Querétaro, and funded by the crown, Domingo Ramón's^qv entrada left San Juan Bautista and reached the Tejas tribes of East Texas in late June 1716. Fray Francisco Hidalgo and

Fray Antonio Margil de Jesús^{qv} supervised the establishment of four new missions, expanded a few months later with two more missions and a presidio. A new viceroy, the Marqués de Valero, authorized a second strategic way station in Texas with the entrada of Martín de Alarcón.^{qv} A feuding Alarcón and Fray Olivares crossed separately into Texas in April of 1718 and rendezvoused on the San Antonio River. On May 1, 1718, Alarcón gave possession of the projected San Antonio de Valero Mission (the Alamo^{qv}) to Olivares, who had just arrived. A small nearby fort, San Antonio de Béxar Presidio, provided a tenuous sense of security for the ten families or so making up the villa of San Fernando de Béxar.^{qv} Fear of a widespread French invasion, after a small French expedition under Philippe Blondel seized the new settlement at Los Adaes^{qv} in what became known as the "Chicken War,"^{qv} caused the Spanish to abandon East Texas to the French. The Spaniards withdrew to San Antonio under Fray Margil while awaiting further action.

The subsequent expeditions of the wealthy Marqués de San Miguel de Aguayo^{qv} in 1721 and 1722 displayed the increasing elaboration of Spanish exploration into settlement. The Spanish visionary and colonizer Col. José de Escandón^{qv} settled thousands of colonists from 1749 to 1755 in some twenty new towns, many on the Rio Grande frontier. Under his auspices the enduring Mexican borderland communities of Reynosa (1749), Camargo (1749), Revilla (Guerrero) (1750), and Mier (1753), as well as Roma (1751) and Laredo (1755), Texas, came into being. Escandón, the greatest of the eighteenth-century empresarios, laid the foundation for almost half the Texas borderland and much of South Texas.

By the 1740s three further areas of expansionary interest were the San Gabriel River, the lower Trinity basin, and the San Saba River country. Under Fray Mariano Francisco de los Dolores y Viana,^{qv} the short-lived San Xavier missions^{qv} were established in the San Gabriel River valley, which had been known to the Spanish since Ramón's visit in 1716. The missions were moved to the San Marcos River in 1755. Capt. Joaquín de Orobio y Basterra^{qv} of La Bahía^{qv} explored the lower Trinity basin in 1746. Small parties reconnoitered the San Saba River valley in the Hill Country^{qv} shortly after the founding of San Antonio de Béxar in 1718.

The contemporary French explorers of Texas were on the whole equally capable and intelligent, with an aptitude for scientific cartography and a ready supply of experienced traders and frontiersmen as pathfinders. Indeed French commercial forays into Texas were routine by the 1740s. Two remarkable French brothers and adventurers

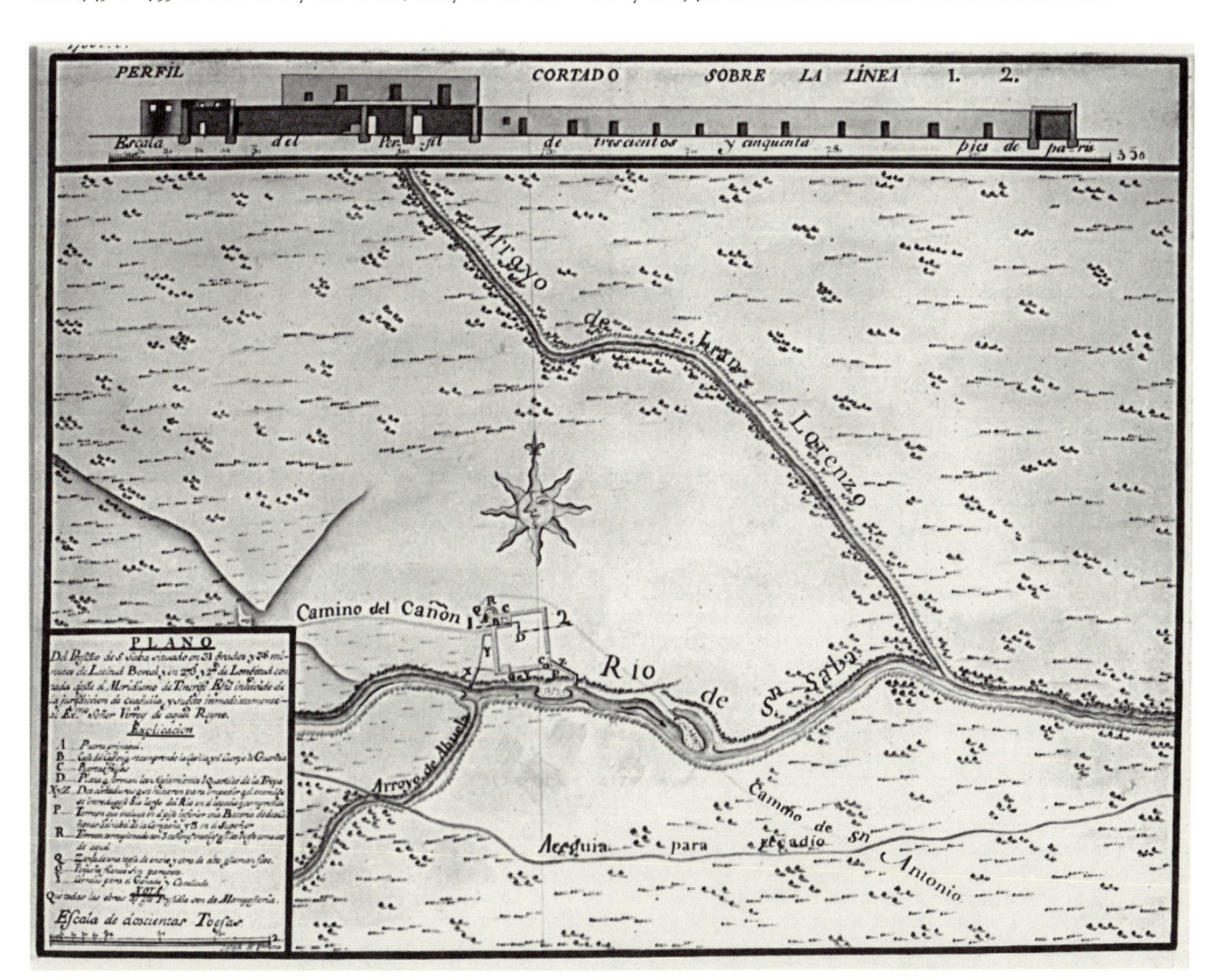

Plano del Presidio de S. Saba . . . , by Joseph de Urrutia, ca. 1767. By permission of the British Library; Add MS 17662 R: San Saba. When the Marqués de Rubí inspected the presidios of Texas in 1767, he was especially critical of the location and conditions at San Luis de las Amarillas on the San Saba River. Rubí recommended that the presidio be pulled back to the Rio Grande, and several years later it was moved to San Vicente Ford, opposite the Big Bend.

discovered a natural trade route between New Orleans and Santa Fe in 1739–40. After boldly crossing the Great Plains from the Missouri River, Pierre and Paul Mallet's qqv party of traders arrived in Santa Fe to the delight of settlers and the consternation of officials. The sheer bravado of the Mallets' feat inspired initial respect from the Spanish authorities, even if the desired commercial connection was denied owing to the usual mercantilist fears; indeed, the Spanish arrested the Mallets in 1751, when they had the audacity to show up again in Santa Fe. Some of the finest eighteenth-century explorers of Texas were undoubtedly the obscure *contrabandistas,* traders of mostly French extraction that roamed East Texas, the Red River country, the lower Trinity and Brazos River basins, and rarely the Canadian River valley in the far north. Culturally adept with local Indians, skilled at survival, and commercially prominent in the vital weapons, powder, and lead shot trade, *contrabandistas* often settled among the Texas tribes to trade, repair guns, hunt, and explore new lands.

With the 1763 Treaty of Paris, Spain dramatically acquired French Louisiana and its vast territory, as well as the unwelcome advances of more determined eastern rivals—the English initially, but steadily after 1776 an insurgent and growing nation known as the United States of America. After delay and confusion, Spanish officials reversed themselves and displayed a new interest in connecting New Orleans and Natchitoches, Louisiana, with Santa Fe and San Antonio. To aid in this task Spanish officials tolerated the services of an important generation of talented French explorers—Athanase de Mézières, Pedro Vial,qqv and Gaignard—for the east and north of Texas, while using its own explorers and inspectors for the critical west, central, and south regions of Texas. West and Central Texas suffered alarmingly from Apache and Comanche raids. The Marqués de Rubíqv finished a long inspection tour in 1767 by recommending that the appalling frontier presidios of Texas be closed. His recommendations, largely implemented in 1772, led once more to a forced retreat from East Texas. The journeys of Mézières in the 1770s and Vial in the 1780s epitomized the adaptive Spanish use of French explorer-diplomats and traders in the reorganization of the northern frontier during the 1780s. Mézières, a talented administrator, diplomat, and linguist, was born in Paris but began service with the Spanish in an expedition to the Red River (1770). He worked relentlessly to win the allegiance of the disturbed northern tribes—the Tawakonis, Tonkawas, and Taovayas—in 1778, while traveling between Natchitoches, the Taovaya villages on the Red River, Quiscat'sqv villages of the Tawakonis, and San Antonio. Perhaps the most colorful and unorthodox French explorer to serve the Spanish was the former French *contrabandista* Pierre (Pedro) Vial. Where a large force might have encountered difficulty in Comanche country, small parties under Vial and José Maresqv proved to be extraordinary trailblazers. After departing from San Antonio in 1786, Vial traveled up the Colorado River, turned to Quiscat's villages of the Waco Indians, and advanced to the Taovaya villages on the upper Red River. He made friends with the Comanches, including the great chief Ecuerocapa, then crossed the High Plains to the Canadian River, and rode thence to Santa Fe. In the search for an even shorter route authorities dispatched Mares, a retired corporal, who in 1787–88 blazed an admirable trail between San Antonio and Santa Fe across the High Plains, the Caprockqv canyonlands, the Rolling Plains, and Central Texas. Shortly after Mares's return, the New Mexican governor sent Vial and the diarists Fragoso and Fernández on a further journey, this time to find a direct route to Natchitoches, Louisiana. On his return voyage Vial traveled across the Llano Estacado,qv noted the playas, descended Palo Duro Canyonqv on July 4, 1788, and shortened the time and distance back to San Antonio. Vial and his companions returned to Santa Fe in 1789, exploring Blanco Canyonqv and crossing "el llano"—the vast flatland of the Southern High Plains. This area, the Llano Estacado, was increasingly the focus of eastward exploration by ciboleros and Comancherosqqv from New Mexico. The trails of Vial and Mares revealed the secrets of the Red River sources to the Spanish and promised to link New Mexico, Texas, and Louisiana together. The trade caravans never materialized, however, and new rivals appeared.

American Exploration. The American exploration of Texas begins with small streams of castaways, runaways, traders, and adventurers, then suddenly swells into a mighty current of colonizers and United States emigrants, officers and troops, diarists and scientists, hunters and farmers, all cascading across an insurgent province that won its independence as a republic in 1836. One of the first legendary travelers was John Rozée Peyton, who was captured in the Gulf of Mexico and marched with his Jamaican servant up the Rio Grande to Santa Fe. With the apparent help of the jailer's daughter, Peyton and two companions escaped Santa Fe in the winter of 1774 and made their way eastward across Texas and on to St. Louis. Spanish officials tolerated Americans like Moses Austin,qv who pioneered settlements in Missouri, as the price of peopling the land. But they widely feared expansionist Americans looking to build contraband trade with Spanish Texas. The most worrisome of the new Americans was Philip Nolan.qv This protégé of Gen. James Wilkinsonqv first traveled to Texas in 1791 at the age of twenty. After being relieved of his goods by Spanish officials, the youth wandered extensively among the Comanches and Taovayas, who proved as friendly to American *contrabandistas* as to French ones. Within a decade, Nolan's trading and mustanging activities had taken him to San Antonio, Nacogdoches, and Central Texas, and to many more remote camps of Comanches and Taovayas. He was one of the best informed Americans about Texas, and a decided expert on the strategic Red River country. His explorations provided key insights for the expansionist Americans. He has often been credited as the first American to map Texas, but no map of his has been found. His observations, however, were used to draw up a map of the Texas-Louisiana frontier around 1804. Operating from Natchez, Mississippi, Nolan was also a dedicated spy. His journey into Texas in late 1800 was a fatal mistake, for Spanish soldiers killed him somewhere in Central Texas in 1801.

For the United States the key to westward expansion toward Texas lay with European wars. Emperor Napoleon I reacquired Louisiana in 1800 for the French, plotted a projected colonial empire, and then broke all understandings with Spain by selling the territory in 1803 to the United States. With the stroke of a pen, the fortunate young nation acquired a new boundary, a new realm in which to exercise the Enlightenment passion for exploration, and a new course of empire. Under Thomas Jefferson's direction American explorers begin probing the new southwestern frontier. In 1804, at the urging of Jefferson, the scientists William Dunbar and George Hunter attempted an expedition up the mysterious Red River. They explored the Ouachita River area and the region near the site of present-day Hot Springs, Arkansas, but never explored the Red River region. Jefferson was more successful with the 1806 Red River expedition.qv The surveyor Thomas Freeman and the youthful naturalist Peter Custisqv assembled a flotilla of flatboats and canoes and ascended the Red River in the spring of 1806, bypassing the Great Raft. At Spanish Bluffqv a superior Spanish force under Francisco Vianaqv confronted and turned back the party, but Freeman and Custis had already studied and mapped more than 600 miles of the Red River.

Barely six weeks after Freeman and Custis were turned back, six American traders under John. S. Lewis and William C. Alexander slipped past Spanish patrols and followed the Red River to the plains. They delivered an American flag to the Taovaya villages and went mustanging with the Comanches. Indeed, despite Spanish protestations and patrols, American traders thoroughly penetrated the lower and upper Red River. "Captain" Anthony Glassqv entered Texas in 1808 at an Alabama-Coushatta village, followed the "Pani-Conchetta Trace" along the Sulphur River, hunted buffalo on the Blackland Prairie near the site of modern Paris, Texas, and reached the Taovaya villages on the upper Red River. Glass and several companions traveled deeper into the Rolling Plains, coveted a sacred meteorite near the site of modern Albany in Shackelford County, saw the Callahan

Divide,qv and descended the Colorado River before returning home. George Schamp, Ezra McCall, and other traders returned in 1809 to the middle Brazos River country to take the fantastic meteorite, which they supposed to be a valuable mass of platinum. American frontiersmen and squatters soon crossed to the south side of the Red River near the Great Bend. Worried authorities in the Provincias Internasqv correspondingly dispatched more Spanish military patrols and even an occasional large expedition. In 1808 Capt. Francisco Amangualqv led a 200-man force to reconnoiter the distant plains between San Antonio and Santa Fe. He and his men traveled north from San Antonio and the old San Luis de las Amarillas Presidio, parleyed with the Comanches, ascended the Llano Estacado at Blanco Canyon, and crossed the hot, dusty plains to reach the Canadian River and thence Santa Fe. Amangual laid out the shortest route from San Antonio to Santa Fe, then returned to San Antonio via El Paso.

A decade later Mexico won her independence, and a veritable tide of American settlers and squatters soon took advantage of the new nation's generosity with land grants. Geographic interest in the Red River boundary had accelerated after the conclusion of the Adams-Onís Treatyqv in 1819. The United States dispatched Maj. Stephen Harriman Longqv to the sources of the Red River in 1820, but Long bungled his assignment by following the Canadian River all the way through the Texas Panhandle. In noticeable contrast to the Spanish explorers' simple *diarios y derroteros,* secreted soon after the expeditions in the archives, Stephen Long's expedition narrative and scientific measurements were soon published for an eager eastern readership. The narrative was printed by a London publisher. American exploration thus opened a distinctive romantic horizon, where the explorer-hero narrated thrilling incidents in the West. Long employed a journalist-naturalist, Edwin James, and an artist, Samuel Seymour, to document the new visions. Long's vision of the High Plains led to the unfortunate label "Great American Desert," but for the day and time his expedition was a model of the new approach to exploration then spreading under Alexander von Humboldt's influence from Europe to Texas. In 1827 the Mexican government launched an expedition under the command of Manuel de Mier y Terán.qv The group, which included mineralogist Rafael Chovell and naturalist Jean L. Berlandier,qv was prevented from fulfilling one of its goals—a survey

Texas, by Fiorenzo Galli. Lithograph by Claudio Linati, 1826. Map Collection, CAH; CN 01593. This copy of the first printed map to focus entirely on Texas was probably carried on Manuel de Mier y Terán's scientific and boundary expedition of 1827–29. The margins are crowded with the commission's own observations and with a few corrections to the printed map: Stephen F. Austin's headquarters, for example, are noted as being on the right (west) bank of the Brazos, rather than on the left.

of the northeastern boundary of Texas—but succeeded in gathering significant collections of natural history material and taking various scientific measurements.

With the de facto independence of an American-dominated Texas in 1836, the exploration goals and process changed significantly between 1836 and 1845. The northern Indians were still friendly to such well-armed Americans with trade goods as Josiah Gregg,[qv] who explored a Canadian River trail to Santa Fe. Gregg's *Commerce of the Prairies* (1844) contained valuable botanical and geographical information about Texas, as did his map of the southern plains (1845). The pushy, slave-holding Texans to the south, however, were considered dangerous foes to the Indians. After Indian raids, counter-raids by Texas Rangers[qv] increased exploration and the acquisition of new land beyond the outermost farms, plantations, and towns. The Cross Timbers,[qv] the Canebrakes, the Hill Country, the Rolling Plains, the Big Thicket,[qv] the Rio Grande, and ultimately Comanchería itself became centers of contact and reexploration for hundreds of new Texans. What was largely old ground for Spanish and Mexican explorers was often a new world for American arrivals such as Albert Pike and William A. (Bigfoot) Wallace.[qqv] The country awaited their names, discoveries, trails, and towns. Many a Texan frontiersman, trailblazer, or peripatetic pioneer often saw himself as the "first white man" to discover a feature or place—an ethnocentric perception applied to the existing Indian and Spanish worlds. Two important Republic of Texas[qv] expeditions furthered the enmity between Mexico and Texans. The privateering Snively expedition[qv] set out across the interior plains in 1843 to waylay supposedly rich caravans, while the Texan Santa Fe expedition[qv] of 1841 disastrously sought to force Texan trade and control over Santa Fe. The great failure of the latter expedition underscored the problems of large groups with inadequate maps trying to make their way among hostile Indians across the unknown plains of Texas.

The annexation[qv] of Texas in 1845 and the subsequent Mexican War[qv] launched a fresh wave of less amateur exploration into the new state. Engineers under Zachary Taylor[qv] surveyed the Gulf Coast and mapped a victorious army's progress from Texas into Mexico. More importantly, a new generation of government-sponsored western explorers, often officers from the Corps of Topographical Engineers and civilian professionals, took to the field after the war. In a dozen years, a remarkable series of well-trained and experienced officer-explorers carried a transnational culture of science into Texas as they traversed, measured, plotted, observed, classified, and described much of the annexed state. Their expeditions provided vivid accounts, scientific data, information on natural history, important maps, and ethnographic studies of great worth. Moreover, advances in lithographic illustration added a strong visual component to the mid-nineteenth century exploration of Texas. Important new directions in Texas exploration involved surveying the Mexican boundary (William H. Emory and John R. Bartlett[qqv]), blazing westward trails (John S. Ford, Nathaniel Michler, William H. C. Whiting, Randolph Marcy,[qqv] and James H. Simpson), locating Indian reservations (Robert S. Neighbors[qv]), establishing frontier defense posts and patrols (Marcy), surveying potential routes for the projected transcontinental railroad (Amiel W. Whipple, John Pope, Andrew B. Gray[qqv]), and opening the remaining *terrae incognitae* (James W. Abert, George B. McClellan,[qv] and Marcy). The federal exploration of

West wild rose pass limpia valley, by John E. Weyss, October 22, [1854?]. J. Weyss Rio Grande Sketchbook, Eberstadt Collection, CAH; CN 08647. Weyss, an Austrian, made many of the topographical drawings that appeared in William H. Emory's Report on the United States and Mexican Boundary Survey *(3 vols., 1857–59). Wild Rose Pass, northeast of Fort Davis, was named by army engineer William H. C. Whiting in March 1849, while he was scouting a wagon road between San Antonio and El Paso.*

Camp of the Kioway Indians, *after Heinrich Balduin Möllhausen, ca. 1853–58. Colored lithograph by Hanhart. From Baldwin Möllhausen,* Diary of a Journey from the Mississippi to the Coast of the Pacific . . . , *trans. Mrs. Percy Sinnett (2 vols., London: Longman, Brown, Green, Longmans, & Roberts, 1858), I, facing p. 212. Photograph courtesy CAH; CN 08011. Möllhausen, who accompanied the 1853–54 Whipple expedition along the thirty-fifth parallel, sketched this scene in the Texas Panhandle.*

Texas began in earnest with the 1845 expedition of Lt. James William Abert, an offshoot of John C. Frémont's third expedition. Abert left Bent's Fort in August of 1845 to reconnoiter the Canadian River country. He encountered and sketched numerous Comanches in the Texas Panhandle. With the Treaty of Guadalupe Hidalgo qv in 1848, attention shifted to the sensitive Texas borderland and the strategic far West. Emory, Michler, and others overcame chaos and supply problems for years to survey the difficult Rio Grande. Emory rose to become chief astronomer of the Boundary Commission, then replaced the troubled Bartlett as commissioner. Some idea of the obstacles is gleaned from the adventures of W. M. T. Chandler's party, which surveyed the treacherous canyons of the Big Bend and passed the Comanche War Trail. One member of this hungry, ragged surveying crew, Charles Abbott, shot the rapids of Santa Elena Canyon qv in a rubber boat in order to draw a crude map of the area. The published and illustrated reports of the surveyors, particularly Emory's three-volume work *Report on the United States and Mexican Boundary Survey, made Under the Direction of the Secretary of the Interior* (1857–59) and John R. Bartlett's *Personal Narrative* (1854), stirred the Victorian interest in southwestern landscapes.

The discovery of gold in California brought an immediate military-commercial need for wagon roads and trails across Texas. Capt. Randolph Marcy and Lt. James H. Simpson of the Topographical Engineers opened the Fort Smith–Santa Fe Road in 1849, when they escorted a large wagontrain of gold seekers across the unsettled Panhandle. Marcy explored even farther on his return trek over the Trans-Pecos, across the Monahans Sandhills and lower Llano Estacado, through the Rolling Plains and Cross Timbers (where he noted new sites for frontier defense), and then back to Fort Smith. Marcy's travels proved invaluable in finding sites for new army forts. Such outposts as Fort Belknap, Fort Phantom Hill, and Fort Chadbourne not only provided a closing ring of staging areas for exploration and conquest, but also served as convenient way stations for the 1858 Butterfield Overland Mail qv route. Early civilian efforts to link San Antonio to El Paso began in 1848 when Texas Ranger John Coffee Hays and Capt. Samuel Highsmith qqv focused on opening a trail across West Texas. In 1850–52 Lt. Col. Joseph E. Johnston qv commanded a party of topographical engineers that surveyed and explored potential wagon roads and future railroad lines across Texas. Texas Ranger "Rip" Ford and Robert S. Neighbors blazed a northern route across the Edwards Plateau to the Horsehead Crossing on the Pecos River, a route resurveyed by Lt. Francis T. Bryan qv of the Topographical Engineers. A southern route to El Paso was first surveyed by topographical engineers under Lt. W. H. C. Whiting. The Topographical Engineers thus explored and surveyed the most important trails in West Texas, Central Texas, and the Trans-Pecos. In general the military exploration of Texas satisfied the complex political, economic, and scientific demands now made by an evolving national interest. The growing professionalism of exploration is evidenced in the "Great Reconnaissance" of the 1850s, when government teams of engineers, surveyors, soldiers, and scientists explored two of the four parallels for a projected transcontinental railroad within Texas. Captain Amiel Whipple conducted a masterly sweep across the thirty-fifth parallel. In the winter of 1853–54 surveying parties under John G. Parke and John Pope found excellent prospects for a railroad on the southern crossing of the thirty-second parallel. Andrew Belcher Gray,qv led a private expedition financed by the Texas Western Railroad into the field to tout the southern route as well. Sectional rivalry postponed any construction, but the voluminous reports of the Pacific Railroad stand as monuments to the national exploration impulse in Texas and elsewhere.

Head of Ke-Che-Ah-Que-Ho-No, or the Main Branch of Red River, ca. 1854. Lithograph by H. Lawrence. From Randolph B. Marcy and George B. McClellan, Exploration of the Red River of Louisiana, in the Year 1852 (Washington, D.C.: A. O. P. Nicholson, Public Printer, 1854), plate 10. Photograph courtesy CAH; CN 01833. This scene, sketched during Marcy's 1852 expedition, has been identified as the site of the spring in the Tule Canyon Narrows.

Two of the finest explorers of this period were Indian agent Robert S. Neighbors and Capt. Randolph Marcy. Authorized to find sites for Indian reservations, Neighbors and Marcy explored together the upper Brazos and Wichita River and much of Northwest Texas in 1854. As typical explorers of the age, they examined the geography, mapped the topography, collected specimens, parlayed with Penatekas and other Indians, inventoried resources, found routes for roads, reconnoitered new sites for forts and towns, and recorded climatic and ethnographic data. As stories of expeditions gained popularity, William B. Parker's *Through Unexplored Texas* (1856) narrated the Marcy expedition to a reading public. Marcy, already an author, earned national attention with his classic *Exploration of the Red River of Louisiana in the Year 1852* (1853). Americans were still uncertain of the sources of the Red River in 1851, although it was no secret to the Comanches, Wichitas, or comancheros. To penetrate this *terra incognita*, Marcy assembled in 1852 a model expedition of military and civilian professionals, including Capt. George B. McClellan, engineer and later presidential candidate against Abraham Lincoln, Black Beaver, a trusted and skilled Delaware guide, and Dr. George G. Shumard,qv a pioneer Texas geologist. In exploring the upper reaches of the Red River—Palo Duro Canyon, Tule Canyon, and the Prairie Dog Town and North forks—Marcy's men settled the mystery of the Red River while compiling a Wichita vocabulary, recording meteorological data, and collecting hundreds of plant, animal, and mineral specimens for examination by eastern scientists.

Many other naturalists and collectors were also busy exploring the Texas landscape. At a time when the scientific frontier coincided with the geographic frontier, Texas enjoyed a superabundance of naturalist-explorers. John James Audubon, Alexander Dallas Bache, Francis C. Baker, Viktor Friedrich Bracht,qqv Edwin James, Jules Marcou, and George Shumard labored to uncover the nature of the state. A long line of botanists, including Jean L. Berlandier, Thomas Drummond, Charles Wright, Julien Reverchon,qqv Frederick Adolphus Wislizenus, and John M. Bigelow, collected and classified many of the state's 5,000 wildflower species. German naturalists such as Ferdinand Lindheimer, Louis C. Ervendberg, and the distinguished explorer Ferdinand von Roemer qv roamed the Hill Country, identifying endemic species and collecting fossils. The frontiersman and doctor Gideon Lincecum qv traveled widely, collected voluminously, and became an outstanding naturalist who corresponded with Charles Darwin, among others.

By the time of the Civil War,qv Texas exploration was a multifaceted, often federally funded, military-commercial enterprise, a thrilling learning process that fielded teams of trained specialists to scan a romanticized landscape. Officers, scientists, engineers, artists, and Indian guides reexplored the entire state as new demands required. A national audience not only admired these heros, but also explored Texas vicariously through the well-illustrated reports and books. Though the Civil War retarded exploration, the return of federal soldiers after 1865 and their successful campaigns to defeat the hostile Texas tribes provided a new round of exploration activity. United States Army troops under Christopher (Kit) Carson qv had already penetrated the Panhandle in 1874. In fighting that year along the Canadian River the explorer-scout William (Billy) Dixon qv earned the Medal of Honor. Two army leaders who epitomized the exploration-conquest of North and West Texas were William R. (Pecos Bill) Shafter and Ranald S. Mackenzie,qqv who drove the last Comanches and Wichitas onto Oklahoma reservations in 1875, while vigorously traveling and exploring the landscapes, trails, and resources of the foe. Shafter's men conducted a systematic survey of the southern Llano Estacado and Big Bend region as Mackenzie's men did farther north. Their activities, trails, scouts, and geographic knowledge prepared the way for settlers. Follow-up expeditions like the Ruffner survey qv in Palo Duro Canyon also provided a wealth of natural-history data prior to pioneer settlement and railroad colonization.

In truth the Texas frontier was gone by 1890. The old, broad exploration impulse never died, however, but shifted into dozens of

Temple Canyon in the Big Bend, 1899. Courtesy U.S. Geological Survey, Denver; R. T. Hill #57. In the fall of 1899 Hill and a U.S. Geological Survey party filled in the last vacant section of the Texas map, the Rio Grande between Presidio and Langtry.

specialties in science and commerce over the following decades. The instrumentation grew more sophisticated and the terminology became more arcane, but the learning process itself continued with passion and precision. Texans began to explore the nether regions of the state after 1900, turning the age-old human search downward toward underground water, ancient fossils, Paleo-Indian artifacts, geological formations, and enough oil and gas reservoirs to fuel giant new industries. The modern spelunkers of karsts, the scuba divers in the coral gardens, and the petroleum engineers all continue exploration in the state. The search also led twentieth-century Texans to the heavens. A nation watched breathlessly in the 1960s and 1970s as NASA's Mission Control in Houston coordinated the exploration of outer space and the moon. Astronauts, astronomers, programmers, scientists, teachers, businessmen, technicians, and many other Texans are increasingly part of a vast global web of exploration activity at the beginning of the Third Millennium.

See also SPANISH TEXAS, MEXICAN TEXAS, MAPS, SPANISH MAPPING OF TEXAS, ANGLO-AMERICAN COLONIZATION, MAMMOTH HUNTING, MUSTANGS, and TEXAS IRON.

BIBLIOGRAPHY: Herbert Eugene Bolton, ed., *Spanish Exploration in the Southwest, 1542–1706* (New York: Scribner, 1908; rpt., New York: Barnes and Noble, 1959). Herbert Eugene Bolton, *Texas in the Middle Eighteenth Century* (Berkeley: University of California Press, 1915; rpt., Austin: University of Texas Press, 1970). Hodding Carter, *Doomed Road of Empire: The Spanish Trail of Conquest* (New York: McGraw-Hill, 1963). Carlos E. Castañeda, *Our Catholic Heritage in Texas* (7 vols., Austin: Von Boeckmann–Jones, 1936–58; rpt., New York: Arno, 1976). Donald E. Chipman, *Spanish Texas, 1519–1821* (Austin: University of Texas Press, 1992). John L. Davis, *Exploration in Texas* (San Antonio: University of Texas Institute of Texan Cultures, 1984). Dan L. Flores, ed., *Jefferson and Southwestern Exploration: The Freeman and Custis Accounts of the Red River Expedition of 1806* (Norman: University of Oklahoma Press, 1984). S. W. Geiser, *Naturalists of the Frontier* (Dallas: Southern Methodist University, 1937; 2d ed. 1948). William H. Goetzmann, *Exploration and Empire: The Explorer and the Scientist in the Winning of the American West* (New York: Knopf, 1966). William H. Goetzmann and Glyndwr Williams, *The Atlas of North American Exploration: From the Norse Voyages to the Race to the Pole* (New York: Prentice-Hall, 1992). Charles W. Hackett, ed., *Pichardo's Treatise on the Limits of Louisiana and Texas* (4 vols., Austin: University of Texas Press, 1931–46). Frederick Webb Hodge and Theodore H. Lewis, eds., *Spanish Explorers in the Southern United States, 1528–1543* (New York: Scribner, 1907; rpt., Austin: Texas State Historical Association, 1984). W. Eugene Hollon, *Beyond the Cross Timbers: The Travels of Randolph B. Marcy, 1812–1887* (Norman: University of Oklahoma Press, 1955). Elizabeth A. H. John, *Storms Brewed in Other Men's Worlds: The Confrontation of Indians, Spanish, and French in the Southwest, 1540–1795* (College Station: Texas A&M University Press, 1975). Noel M. Loomis and Abraham P. Nasatir, *Pedro Vial and the Roads to Santa Fe* (Norman: University of Oklahoma Press, 1967). Robert S. Weddle, *The French Thorn: Rival Explorers in the Spanish*

Sea, 1682–1762 (College Station: Texas A&M University Press, 1991). Robert S. Weddle, *San Juan Bautista: Gateway to Spanish Texas* (Austin: University of Texas Press, 1968). Robert S. Weddle, *Spanish Sea: The Gulf of Mexico in North American Discovery, 1500–1685* (College Station: Texas A&M University Press, 1985). Del Weniger, *The Explorers' Texas* (Austin: Eakin Press, 1984). *John Miller Morris*

EXRAY, TEXAS. Exray (X-Ray) is off State Highway 108 fourteen miles northwest of Stephenville in northern Erath County. The area was settled before the Civil War[qv] and named for its location at a crossroads. A settlement developed there about 1890, when coal mining was active at Thurber. In 1897 a post office was established at the community with George M. Shelby as postmaster. Postal service was discontinued in 1906, and the mail was sent to Stephenville. Exray was established primarily as a ranching community, but a cotton gin was built there and probably operated in the early 1900s. The Exray (or X-Ray) natural gas field was discovered in 1920 and kept the community active for a time. But by 1933 Exray had only a single business and a population of twenty-four. In the late 1980s the community had a church and cemetery and a few widely scattered dwellings.

BIBLIOGRAPHY: Ed Ellsworth Bartholomew, *800 Texas Ghost Towns* (Fort Davis, Texas: Frontier, 1971). H. Grady Perry, *Grand Ol' Erath* (Stephenville, Texas, 1974). Homer Stephen, *Fragments of History: Erath County* (Stephenville, Texas, 1966). Fred Tarpley, *1001 Texas Place Names* (Austin: University of Texas Press, 1980).

Jeanne F. Lively

EXTER, RICHARD (ca. 1791–1829). Richard Exter, merchant and land speculator, the son of John and Anna Exter of Pilton, Devonshire, England, was born about 1791. One of numerous British subjects who migrated to Mexico after its independence, he was a partner in the Mexico City firm of Exter, Graves, and Company, which had a business relationship with the General Pearl and Coral Association of London. He married María Dolores Soto y Saldaña on August 24, 1825. In November 1826 he purchased from Stephen Julian Wilson[qv] one-half interest in an empresario[qv] contract to settle 200 families on a vast tract of land in what is now eastern New Mexico, southwestern Kansas, southeastern Colorado, and the Texas and Oklahoma panhandles. Beginning at the intersection of the thirty-second parallel and the 102d meridian, the tract's boundaries extended west to the eastern boundary of New Mexico (not otherwise defined), thence north to a point twenty leagues south of the Arkansas River, thence southeast to the 102d meridian, thence south to the point of beginning. In acquiring his interest, Exter agreed to assume the obligation of paying the "expenses incurred, and . . . about to be incurred" in the development of the grant. These unspecified expenses undoubtedly were those Wilson previously had agreed to pay Alexander Le Grand[qv] to survey the grant and would have included the $10,000 Le Grand received before leaving Mexico City to begin the survey. Thereafter Le Grand dealt only with Exter, reporting to him from New Orleans and Missouri while organizing his expedition and from New Mexico after completing his survey in November 1827. Le Grand's exaggerated assessment of the productive potential of the lands he claimed to have surveyed undoubtedly influenced Exter and Wilson in 1828 to secure the twenty-league boundary-zone contract to settle the tract lying between their earlier grant and the Arkansas River and to apply for a monopoly over hunting and trapping in New Mexico and California.

While Le Grand's expedition was still on the High Plains, Exter began efforts to capitalize on his investment. In a letter of October 6, 1827, he broached the subject of the sale of land in his grants to Dennis A. Smith, a Baltimore speculator. Smith's initial response was an offer to purchase half interest in the lands. In the following year Smith and Exter concluded some type of agreement with regard to the lands. On the basis of this understanding, Smith organized a $400,000 stock company and, in a series of newspaper advertisements in July 1829, announced grandiose plans to develop the forty-eight million acres included in the grants made to Exter and Wilson. Whatever their extent, these plans were nullified before they were announced, for Exter had died at sea on June 18, 1829, en route from Veracruz to England. When news of his death reached Smith, Smith and his associates vainly tried to gain control over Exter's interests in the empresario contracts, which devolved upon his widow and his two-year-old daughter, Anita. Smith did not figure in subsequent plans to colonize the grants. Mrs. Exter's second husband, John Charles Beales,[qv] dealt only with New York speculators.

BIBLIOGRAPHY: Lucy Lee Dickson, Speculation of John Charles Beales in Texas Lands (M.A. thesis, University of Texas, 1941). Mary Virginia Henderson, "Minor Empresario Contracts for the Colonization of Texas, 1825–1834," *Southwestern Historical Quarterly* 31, 32 (April, July 1928). David J. Weber, *The Taos Trappers: The Fur Trade in the Far Southwest, 1540–1846* (Norman: University of Oklahoma Press, 1971).

Raymond Estep

EXXON COMPANY, U.S.A. Exxon Company, U.S.A., a division of Exxon Corporation, manages the corporation's oil and gas interests in the United States. Exxon U.S.A. traces its descent from the Humble Oil Company, which was chartered in Texas in February 1911 with a capital of $150,000 (raised to $300,000 in 1912). The company was reorganized in 1917 and incorporated on June 21 as the Humble Oil and Refining Company with a capitalization of $1 million based on 40,000 shares at $100 par value. The original company resulted from the collaboration of Ross S. Sterling and Walter William Fondren[qqv] with Robert L. Blaffer and William Stamps Farish[qv] and others. In the new organization were merged the Paraffine Oil Company, Blaffer and Farish, Schulz Oil Company, Ardmore Oil Company, and Globe Refining Company. In February 1919, Humble doubled the number of shares authorized and sold 50 percent of its stock to Standard Oil Company of New Jersey. This initiated Humble's long-term connection with the company that eventually absorbed it as Exxon Company, U.S.A. Standard Oil of New Jersey was identified as the particular target of antitrust enforcers in Texas in the early decades of the twentieth century, and the corporation found it much easier to do business in the state through Humble, its partially owned but autonomously directed affiliate. In 1948 Humble had issued a total of eighteen million shares with a total capitalization of $475 million; Standard Oil Company of New Jersey owned 72 percent of the stock.

In 1917 Humble had 217 wells and a daily crude oil production of about 9,000 barrels. The company's production was expanded steadily. It made large additions to its reserves in the 1930s and increased production during World War II[qv] in order to meet war needs. Humble became the largest domestic producer of crude oil during the war and continued in that position into the 1950s. In 1949 the company had a net production of 275,900 barrels daily of crude oil and 15,900 barrels daily of natural-gas liquids. At the end of 1949 the company was operating 9,928 wells. Among the important fields in which Humble has participated have been East Texas, Conroe,[qqv] Mexia, Powell (*see* WOODBINE FAULT-LINE FIELDS), Raccoon Bend, Sugarland, Thompsons, Friendswood, Tomball, Anahuac, Tomoconnor, Webster, Seeligson, and Hawkins, all in Texas. Humble established the first production of crude oil in Florida in 1943 and by 1949 had production in Louisiana, New Mexico, Mississippi, Alabama, and California. In 1917 Humble had three miles of gathering lines at Goose Creek. At the end of 1949 the Humble Pipe Line Company, a subsidiary, had 3,233 miles of gathering lines and 5,776 miles of trunk lines. These facilities served all important producing areas in Texas and southeastern New Mexico, and the Humble Pipe Line Company was the largest transporter of crude oil in the United States. In the postwar period, the company built a pipeline from Baytown to the Dallas–Fort Worth area and in June 1950 completed an eighteen-inch direct line from West Texas to the Gulf Coast.

When it was first organized, the company owned a small refinery at Humble, Texas. In 1919 construction was begun on the Baytown refinery, originally planned as a lubricant plant with a capacity of 260,000 barrels daily. In 1950 Humble's only other refinery was at San Antonio; the plant had a capacity of 7,000 barrels daily. In 1928 Humble constructed a refinery with a capacity of 12,000 barrels daily at Ingleside, near Corpus Christi. The Ingleside refinery was increased in capacity to 21,500 barrels daily by 1945. It was closed at the end of the war because the facilities could not make the quality products needed for the postwar period. Humble refineries during World War II produced high-octane aviation gasoline, toluene for explosives, Butyl rubber, and butadiene for synthetic rubber. The Baytown Ordnance Works produced nearly half of the toluene for explosives for World War II and was subsequently purchased by the company from the government. Humble continued to operate the government-owned butadiene and Butyl rubber plants at Baytown after the war. In the 1940s Humble products were retailed only in Texas, where retail sales had increased from seven million gallons of refined products in 1917 to 540 million gallons in 1949.

Humble's first home office, in Houston, was a nine-story office building at Main and Polk constructed in 1920–21. In 1934–35, a new fifteen-story building was added on the same block, and in 1940 a smaller addition was built on. Publications by the company included *The Humble Way, The Humble Bee, The Humble Sales Lubricator,* and the *Farm Family.* Early in 1963 the company moved into a new forty-five-story building, thus consolidating the work location of some 3,500 of its Houston employees. The building rose more than 600 feet above the city and at the time was the tallest building west of the Mississippi River. It is still a Houston landmark and is the headquarters office of Exxon Company, U.S.A.

In the 1950s Standard Oil of New Jersey began to reconsider its relationship with Humble Oil. In spite of the fact that Standard owned almost 88 percent of Humble's stock in 1954, Humble continued to maintain its autonomy for the rest of the decade. In 1958 Standard increased its holdings to some 98 percent of Humble's stock, and the following year Humble and Standard Oil of New Jersey consolidated domestic operations. In September 1959 Humble received a new charter from the state of Delaware. By the end of the year Esso Standard and the Carter Oil Company, other affiliates of Standard of New Jersey, were incorporated into Humble, and in 1960 they were joined by other affiliates including Enjay Chemical, Pate Oil, Globe Fuel Products, and Oklahoma Oil. The restructuring allowed the new Humble company to reduce duplication and costs and to coordinate all of its domestic activities more effectively. The Humble workforce dropped by a quarter in the first five years after the merger, while its profits doubled.

In the 1960s Humble had more than 21,000 square miles of land under lease in the United States. The company operated 24,000 producing wells in twenty-one states with a daily production of 600,000 barrels of crude oil. Humble-operated wells also produced 2.6 billion cubic feet of natural gas daily. Six Humble refineries and plants processed about 800,000 barrels of crude oil daily and produced from that volume a great variety of products. In 1960 Humble constructed one of the world's largest gas-processing systems near the King Ranch,qv with extensive storage facilities for natural gas. In 1961 Humble Pipe Line Company and Interstate Oil Pipe Line Company merged to form a wholly owned affiliate of Humble Oil and Refining Company with a combined network of more than 12,000 miles of gathering and trunk lines. Humble Pipe Line system received and delivered daily more than a million barrels of crude oil and petroleum products. The company operated about 10 percent of the nation's petroleum-transportation facilities. More than two million barrels of crude oil and oil products flowed daily through company lines or moved by tanker or barge. Aided by some chartered vessels, Humble's fleet of nineteen ocean-going tankers, ranging in capacity from 140,000 to 582,000 barrels, delivered approximately 400,000 barrels of crude oil and products to the eastern seaboard each day. Tows and barges of Humble's Inland Waterways system moved 300,000 barrels a day over the nation's rivers and other inland waterways. Humble began to increase its retailing outlets in the 1950s and 1960s. By 1961 it reached markets in some twenty-one states. Humble was the leading marketer of gasoline in Texas by 1951, and its share of the state market continued to increase through the decade, furthered by its creative marketing techniques. Humble was the first gasoline company to issue plastic gasoline credit cards in Texas. In 1961 the company began to sell its gasoline as Enco gas in nineteen states, but retained the old brand name Humble in Texas and Ohio. Esso, the brand name of Standard of New Jersey, continued to be used on the east coast. In 1964 the popular "Put A Tiger In Your Tank" advertising campaign was instituted.

In the 1960s Humble played a significant role in the development of Houston through its disposition of the West Ranch property. The company had purchased the West Ranch, located some twenty-two miles south of Houston, in 1938 and developed two oilfields there, Clear Creek and Friendswood. In 1958 Humble donated some of the land to Rice Institute for use as a geology laboratory. In 1961 the company donated a larger tract to Rice, which in turn gave or sold the land to NASA for use as the site of the new Manned Space Center (now the Lyndon B. Johnson Space Centerqv). In 1962, Humble joined forces with the Del E. Webb Corporation to develop 15,000 acres of the ranch for residential and industrial use. The Humble-Webb agreement led to formation of the Friendswood Development Company, which soon began development of the residential part of Clear Lake City on the ranch site. Humble became involved in a number of other Houston-area real estate developments, including Kingwood, a joint project of the Friendswood Development Company and the King Ranch located some twenty-five miles north of Houston.

In the 1960s and early 1970s the management of both Humble and Standard Oil of New Jersey had become increasingly concerned about the lack of a unified public corporate identity. At the same time, the other Standard Oil companies were raising objections to the use of the word Esso, derived from the first letters of the words *Standard Oil,* as the brand name for Humble and Standard of New Jersey gasoline products. In early 1972 Humble and Standard of New Jersey announced that their gasoline products were to be marketed as Exxon, that Standard of New Jersey was changing its name to Exxon Corporation, and that, as of January 1, 1973, Humble was changing its name to Exxon Company, U.S.A. The company, which operates only in the United States, is a division of Exxon Corporation, which operates also in foreign countries. Under its new name, it embarked on a renewed search for oil sources in the continental United States. By the mid-1970s most of Exxon's Middle Eastern oil suppliers had nationalized Exxon properties and, with the exception of Saudi Arabia, had become increasingly uncertain sources of crude oil. Exxon's attempts at increasing the domestic supply met with mixed success. In the early 1980s the company unsuccessfully attempted to develop shale oil from the Western Slope of Colorado as a significant source. In 1982, after losing over a billion dollars in the Colony Shale Oil Project, the company determined that shale oil could not yet economically compete with other energy sources and shelved the project. A more productive, though also more controversial, new source of oil for the company was the development of the Prudhoe Bay field in Alaska. Humble's interest in Alaskan oil dated back to the late 1950s, when the company joined with Shell Oil in a costly drilling attempt that ended in failure. In partnership with Arco, Humble resumed its drilling activities in Alaska in the 1960s and in 1968 discovered the extensive Prudhoe Bay field, the largest oilfield discovered in North America. Development of the field had to wait for nine years, as environmentalists fought the construction of an oil pipeline through Alaska to the port of Valdez. The pipeline was finally completed in 1977, and Exxon began shipping the oil by tanker from Valdez to world markets. By 1985 the Prudhoe Bay field had produced some 800 million barrels. In March 1989 the supertanker *Exxon Valdez* ran aground and spilled almost a quarter of a million barrels of oil in Prince William Sound, Alaska. Exxon organized a $2.5 billion cleanup and became involved in extended litigation over the damage caused by the spill. Exxon Company, U.S.A., was heavily involved in offshore drilling in the Gulf of Mexico[qv] from the 1950s and off the coast of Alaska and California from the late 1960s. It discovered and developed major gas reserves in Mobile Bay, Alabama, as well as an inland source of natural gas at LaBarge, Wyoming. Along with successive expansions of the Exxon refinery system at Baytown, new refineries were opened in Baton Rouge, Louisiana, Benecia, California, and Billings, Montana.

In 1990 Exxon Corporation moved its corporate headquarters from New York City to Irving, Texas. In 1994 Exxon had the largest hydrocarbon reserve base in the United States. Its domestic fields produced 562,000 barrels of oil and 2,021 million cubic feet of natural gas a day. Its annual income from exploration and production in the United States totaled some $852 million, some 30 percent of the corporate total, and its income from domestic refining and marketing was $243 million, 17 percent of the corporate total. The presidents of Humble were Ross S. Sterling (1917–22), William Stamps Farish (1922–33), Robert Lee Blaffer (1933–37), Harry Carothers Wiess (1937–48), Hines H. Baker, Sr.[qv] (1948–57), Morgan J. Davis[qv] (1957–63), Carl E. Reistle, Jr. (1963–1966), and Myron A. Wright (1966–73). The presidents of Exxon U.S.A. have been Myron A. Wright (1973–76), Randall Meyer (1976–88), William D. Stevens (1988–92), Harry J. Longwell (1992–94), and Ansel L. Condray (1995–).

BIBLIOGRAPHY: Henrietta M. Larson and Kenneth Wiggins Porter, *History of Humble Oil and Refining Company* (New York: Harper, 1959). Bennett H. Wall, *Growth in a Changing Environment: A History of Standard Oil Company* (New York: McGraw-Hill, 1988). Daniel Yergin, *The Prize: The Epic Quest for Oil, Money and Power* (New York: Simon and Schuster, 1991).

James A. Clark and Mark Odintz

"EYES OF TEXAS." "The Eyes of Texas," the official song of the University of Texas at Austin, considered by some a sort of unofficial state song, was first sung at a minstrel show to benefit the university track team at the Hancock Opera House in Austin on May 12, 1903. William L. Prather,[qv] an alumnus of Washington College (Lexington, Virginia) and president of UT from 1899 to 1905, had often in his student days heard Robert E. Lee,[qv] then president of Washington College, say to students, "The eyes of the South are upon you." Prather altered the saying for use at the University of Texas.

The best-documented version of the song's origin has Lewis Johnson, director of the band and the person in charge of the show, asking his roommate, John Lang Sinclair, to write the lyrics to a lively song. On the night before the show, Sinclair, recalling Prather's words, wrote lyrics fitted to the melody of "I've Been Working on the Railroad" on a piece of scrap paper. The glee club quartet performed the song repeatedly at the show to great applause, and the band paraded the campus playing and singing the song the next day. Two years later Prather's family requested that the song be sung at his funeral.

Sinclair later revised the words, and the chorus to the revised version is the song now in popular use. The song gradually became the students' favorite school song. It was translated into ten languages on order of university president Harry Y. Benedict[qv] in 1930. The UT Students' Association copyrighted the piece in 1936. In 1951 the association set up the John Lang Sinclair Eyes of Texas Scholarship Fund. Royalties were placed in the fund, and half went to the association and the other half to scholarships.

When the copyright expired in 1964, the Students' Association, with the assistance of the Ex-Students' Association and Congressman J. J. (Jake) Pickle, tried to renew the copyright, but the request was refused. Even so, "The Eyes of Texas" continued to be recognized as the official song of the University of Texas at Austin and at times was mistakenly identified as the state song.

UT students and administration were surprised in the late 1970s to hear that a man living in Oregon was claiming the ownership of the "Eyes of Texas" and collecting on his version of the composition. A former Fort Worth musician, Wylbert Brown, copyrighted the words in 1928 with the hope that the song would become the official state song during the Texas Centennial[qv] in 1936. In 1984 Arthur B. Gurwitz, president of Southern Music Company in San Antonio, set out to honor his son, who had died only five years after graduating from UT. Gurwitz negotiated with Brown, then ninety-one, who agreed to assign the copyright to UT Austin, provided he would continue to draw some royalty until his death. He died in February 1987. The copyright now belongs to UT Austin. Arthur Gurwitz was honored in a special salute on November 14, 1987, before a football game.

BIBLIOGRAPHY: *Alcalde* (magazine of the Ex-Students' Association of the University of Texas), February 1930, March 1936, January 1959. Austin *American-Statesman*, June 8, 1986. Margaret Catherine Berry, *UT Austin: Traditions and Nostalgia* (Austin: Shoal Creek, 1975). *On Campus*, November 9–15, 1987. T. U. Taylor, *Fifty Years on Forty Acres* (Austin: Alec, 1938).

Margaret C. Berry

EYLAU, TEXAS. Eylau, five miles southwest of Texarkana in the lumbering section of southeastern Bowie County, was established soon after the battle of San Jacinto[qv] by Collin M. Akin, who bought land along the river. A school on his land was consolidated with the Sylar school on the M. H. Jones survey in 1886. The community had a post office from 1885 to 1895. In 1890 the population of Eylau was estimated at thirty. By 1940 Eylau was no longer an organized settlement.

Claudia Hazlewood

EYTH, LOUIS (1838–1889?). Louis Eyth, portrait painter, was born in 1838 and moved to Galveston, Texas, with some of his family at the age of fourteen. His only known art training came in the years he spent with a firm of daguerreotypists and artists, Blessing Brothers.[qv] Eyth later applied for and received the commission of copying the early portrait of Stephen F. Austin[qv] (1873); his copy is now in the secretary of state's office in the Capitol.[qv] He went in 1878 to San Antonio, where he and other Texas artists were commissioned by historian James DeShields[qv] to provide illustrations for his books. Some of Eyth's paintings for DeShields remain only in photographic reproduction, works such as *Surrender of Geronimo* (1885) and *Death of Bowie: A Command from the Mexicans that He Be Killed* (ca. 1878). Though his pictures are rather two-dimensional and though he had some trouble with anatomical details, Eyth had an ability to represent the historic scene with spirit and accuracy. The artist probably died in San Antonio in 1889.

BIBLIOGRAPHY: Pauline A. Pinckney, *Painting in Texas: The Nineteenth Century* (Austin: University of Texas Press, 1967).

Pauline A. Pinckney

EZZELL, MARGARET MURPHY (1902–1987). Margaret Murphy Ezzell, civic leader and historic preservationist, was born on November 11, 1902, in Hillsboro, Texas, the daughter of Joshua Elmer and Linnie (Lovejoy) Murphy. She was active in civic affairs in Port Arthur, Beaumont, Nederland, and Port Neches. From 1962 to 1972 she was a member and vice chairwoman of the Jefferson County Historical Survey Committee. In 1962 she was coorganizer of the Port Arthur Historical Museum and chaired the building committee that oversaw construction of the first public library building in Port Neches. She was also actively involved in the planning and building of a clubhouse for the Nechesland Study Club. In 1972 she was the state coordinator of activities to commemorate the hundredth anniversary of the battle of Sabine Pass.[qv]

From 1961 to 1976 Ezzell served on the Battleship *Texas* Commission. During her tenure she gathered many of the historic items that were on the ship originally and opened a museum on the ship to house them. In 1966 she became a charter member of the Historic Naval Ships of North America, an organization of groups that maintain historic vessels, and in 1975 she was elected president. She also located and presented to the legislature the reverse side of the Great Seal of the state of Texas.

Margaret Ezzell was an active member of the Daughters of the American Revolution, the United Daughters of the Confederacy, and the Daughters of the Republic of Texas.qqv She served as president-general of the DRT from 1961 to 1963 and as registrar general from 1971 to 1973. From 1963 through 1969 she chaired the DRT projects committee. Under her leadership the Long Barrack of the Alamo, which is administered by the DRT, was restored and a museum established there. She raised funds for the restoration and directed the planning and completion of the museum. From 1965 to 1969 she served on the DRT Alamo committee.

In 1966 the Texas Historical Foundation honored Mrs. Ezzell for her work in historic preservation, and in 1970 the Texas State Genealogical Society recognized her for the preservation of historical documents. The Sons of the Republic of Texas qv awarded her a Medal of Appreciation in 1970 for her contributions to the preservation of American history.

Ezzell was married to Asa Murray Ezzell, an executive with the Texaco oil company. She died at her home in Port Neches on October 24, 1987, and was buried in Forest Park Lawndale Cemetery in Houston. Her large library of Texana was given to the Sam Houston Regional Library and Research Center qv at Liberty.

BIBLIOGRAPHY: Houston *Chronicle*, November 6, 1987.

John H. Murphy

EZZELL, TEXAS. Ezzell is on Farm Road 531 ten miles south of Hallettsville and two miles north of the Lavaca River in southern Lavaca County. It is the oldest settled area in the county. Families from Stephen F. Austin's qv colony settled at the site between 1830 and 1836 and traded at Petersburg, the old county seat, six miles to the north, until Sam and Ira Ezzell started a store during the Civil War.qv A private school taught by literate slaves operated at Ezzell. After the war, school was held in church buildings until 1883. In 1980 Ezzell had a population of fifty-five, a church, a school, and no businesses. The population was still reported as fifty-five in 1990.

BIBLIOGRAPHY: Paul C. Boethel, *The History of Lavaca County* (San Antonio: Naylor, 1936; rev. ed., Austin: Von Boeckmann–Jones, 1959).

Evelyn Turk

F

FABENS, TEXAS. Fabens is located on the Southern Pacific Railroad and State Highway 20 a mile southwest of Interstate Highway 10 and twenty-five miles southeast of downtown El Paso in southeastern El Paso County. The history of the town dates from the late nineteenth century, though in 1665 a mission branch known as San Francisco de los Sumas was established just southeast of the future site of Fabens, and a stagecoach station called San Felipe was in operation about three miles northeast of the site before 1870. In the 1870s Teodoro and Epitacia Álvarez owned a small farm on the actual site of Fabens, which was known as the Mezquital. In 1887 the townsite was sold to E. S. Newman by Sabas Grijalva and Diego Loya. The first permanent settler in what is now Fabens was Eugenio Pérez, who came from San Elizario around 1900. He owned a small farm and opened a small store shortly thereafter, when the Galveston, Harrisburg and San Antonio Railway built through the area and established a water-pumping station. In 1906 this store became the first Fabens post office. The town was named for George Fabens, an officer with the Southern Pacific.

Patrick O'Donnell, a native of Ireland working for the railroad, and his wife, Johanna, arrived in 1901 and lived in a section house. In 1910 Fabens had a few section houses and two stores, and in 1914 the estimated population was 100. The next few years brought to the area as many as 1,000 people fleeing the Mexican Revolution.[qv] The townsite was laid out in 1911, but development of Fabens did not begin in earnest until the Fabens Townsite and Improvement Company acquired it in 1915. The completion in 1916 of the Franklin Canal and the rise in cotton prices during World War I[qv] attracted a number of wealthy investors to the area. The estimated population rose from fifty in 1925 to 2,000 two years later, despite a major flood in 1925 or 1926. The price of cotton dropped during the Great Depression,[qv] and the estimated population of Fabens fell to 1,623 in the early 1930s, but it had risen to 1,800 by 1939 and continued to rise; it was 2,100 in the mid-1940s, 3,089 in the mid-1950s, 3,300 in the mid-1960s, 3,400 in the mid-1970s, and 5,599 in 1990.

In the summer of 1969 the University of Notre Dame sociology and anthropology department conducted a community study of Fabens. The study, published in 1970, called the town "basically unattractive," and noted that more than 40 percent of the families in Fabens were poor. Five-sixths of the local farms were owned by non-Hispanic whites, and virtually all the laborers on those farms were Hispanic.

BIBLIOGRAPHY: William V. D'Antonio and Irwin Press, *Fabens, Texas: A Community Study* (Notre Dame, Indiana: University of Notre Dame Department of Sociology and Anthropology, 1970).

Martin Donell Kohout

FABIUS, TEXAS. Fabius was a farming community eight miles northeast of Sulphur Springs and four miles southeast of Birthright in north central Hopkins County. A Fabius post office was established in 1902 with John Newberry as postmaster. At its height just after the turn of the century Fabius had a store and a gin. In 1903 its post office was closed and the mail rerouted through Birthright. By the early 1930s Fabius no longer appeared on highway maps.

BIBLIOGRAPHY: Florene Chapman Adams, *Hopkins County and Our Heritage*. (Sulphur Springs, Texas: 197–?).

Christopher Long

FACTOR, POMPEY (1849–1928). Pompey Factor, one of the Black Seminole scouts[qv] and Medal of Honor recipient, was born in Arkansas. He was cited for gallantry in action. Near the Pecos River on April 25, 1875, under the command of Lt. John Lapham Bullis,[qv] Twenty-fourth United States Infantry,[qv] Private Factor and two other scouts were pursuing a band of twenty-five or thirty Comanche Indians. The scouts dismounted, crept up on the Indians, and opened fire. They killed three, wounded another, and after three-quarters of an hour were in danger of being surrounded. They withdrew to the horses, where Bullis was unable to mount because his horse had broken away. The three scouts turned back into the face of hostile Indian fire, mounted Bullis behind them, and alternately carried him to safety. All three were awarded the Medal of Honor. Factor is buried in the Seminole-Negro Indian Scout cemetery at Brackettville, Texas.

BIBLIOGRAPHY: Bishop Powell, "Pioneering in the Concho Country: Rich Coffey," West Texas Historical Association *Year Book* 50 (1974). Frost Woodhull, "The Seminole Indian Scouts on the Border," *Frontier Times*, December 1937.

Art Leatherwood

FAILS, TEXAS. Fails is on State Highway 75 ten miles northwest of Huntsville in northwestern Walker County. The community developed around the Pine Creek Church. A school followed, constructed on property given by Joe Fails. The Pine Creek school offered six grades in 1911. In 1936 the community had scattered farm dwellings and one business.

BIBLIOGRAPHY: D'Anne McAdams Crews, ed., *Huntsville and Walker County, Texas: A Bicentennial History* (Huntsville, Texas: Sam Houston State University, 1976).

James L. Hailey

FAIRBANKS, TEXAS. Fairbanks is on U.S. Highway 290 and the Southern Pacific Railroad, inside the western city limit of Houston in central western Harris County. The town was established in 1893 and named for its founder, who bought 106 acres at a site previously called Gum Island by the Southern Pacific trainmen because of the gum trees growing between White Oak Bayou and Willow Creek. Fairbanks has had a post office since 1895. In 1914 the community reported a population of seventy-five, a general store–saloon, and a grocery store. The number of inhabitants dropped to twenty-five in the 1920s and 1930s but by 1940 rose to 800. In 1942 Fairbanks reported a population of 800 and thirty-five businesses in the vicinity. A decline to 350 people in the 1950s was followed by a period of rapid expansion; in 1962 the community reported 1,050 people and forty-five businesses. This report, however, came after Fairbanks was annexed by Houston in 1956 and reflects members in surrounding communities. In 1980 and 1990 the population was still reported as 1,050, although considerably more people lived in the surrounding area.

Timothy N. Smith

FAIRCHILD, MARGUERITE GIBSON SHEARER (1885–1974). Marguerite Gibson Shearer Fairchild, University of Texas regent, was born in Livingston, Texas, on February 4, 1885, the daughter of Robert Bruce and Mary Thomas (Palmer) Shearer. The family moved in 1887 to Lufkin, where Marguerite's father, a brickmaker and contractor, served as mayor from 1905 to 1907 and assisted in establishing the local Episcopalian church. Five children, in addition to Marguerite and her brother, were born to the Shearer family in Lufkin. Marguerite attended Hollins College in Hollins, Virginia, before marrying Lufkin lawyer I. D. Fairchild on August 8, 1906.

The Fairchilds lived in Lufkin but spent much time in Austin, where I. D. Fairchild represented Angelina and surrounding counties as a state representative and then state senator from 1915 until 1928. During this time Marguerite served on the County Board of Child Welfare and the Angelina County Chamber of Commerce. She helped establish the first library in Lufkin and was president of the Historical and Literary Club from 1914 to 1916; she did domestic volunteer work for the American Red Cross in World War I.[qv] The Fairchilds were strong supporters of governors James Edward and Miriam A. Ferguson.[qqv] They were also ardent supporters of the University of Texas, despite the controversy that James Ferguson had with this institution.

After the death of her husband in a car accident in 1928, Marguerite Fairchild withdrew from public life for several years. She returned to civic involvement in January 1935, when she was named to the nine-member University of Texas Board of Regents by outgoing governor Miriam Ferguson to fill an unexpired term. She was reappointed to a six-year term by Governor W. Lee (Pappy) O'Daniel[qv] in 1939 and served until February 1945. Although she began her term with some hesitancy, Fairchild quickly became an active and interested regent who regularly communicated with students, staff, and faculty. Her major accomplishments as a regent including serving on the building committee during a time of major expansion at the university; successfully promoting the College of Fine Arts; and casting the lone vote against firing university president Homer Price Rainey.[qv] In 1945, shortly before she left the board, she also cast the only vote against denying numerous petitions calling for Rainey's reinstatement. For her actions she was lauded by university faculty, alumni, and students.

Despite encouragement from these groups to accept appointment for a third term, she let it be known that she was not interested and was replaced on the board in February 1945. She was the second woman to serve on the board of regents (following Mary McClellan O'Hair[qv]), and at the time of her death six women had served as regents. She supported the efforts of the Black Citizens Chamber of Commerce to establish the first day-care center in Lufkin and was a generous contributor to the Lufkin Art League and other civic causes. She campaigned for Rainey's unsuccessful bid for governor in 1946.

In 1951 the university honored Marguerite Fairchild for her efforts in establishing the College of Fine Arts by dedicating its tenth annual Fine Arts Festival to her. She died on January 18, 1974, and was buried in the Garden of Memories Cemetery, Lufkin. She was survived by two sisters. In 1977 the I. D. and Marguerite Fairchild Foundation was established in Lufkin; the foundation contributes to Angelina County projects and the UT College of Fine Arts.

BIBLIOGRAPHY: Angelina County Historical Survey Committee, *Land of the Little Angel: A History of Angelina County, Texas*, ed. Bob Bowman (Lufkin, Texas: Lufkin Printing, 1976). Margaret Catherine Berry, *The University of Texas: A Pictorial Account of Its First Century* (Austin: University of Texas Press, 1980). Files, Office of the Board of Regents, University of Texas System, Austin. Vertical Files, Barker Texas History Center, University of Texas at Austin.

Debbie Mauldin Cottrell

FAIRCHILD, OLIVE ANN OATMAN (1839–1903). Olive Ann Fairchild, Indian captive and lecturer, daughter of Royse (Royce) and Mary Ann (Sperry) Oatman, was born in Illinois in September 1837 or 1839. In 1850 the family joined a wagon train bound for the part of the Colorado River now in southern California, but the train split several times until the Oatmans and their seven children were left to travel alone. On February 18, 1851, Apaches (some authorities say Yavapais) attacked them on the Gila River in Arizona. Olive and her sister Mary were captured, their brother Lorenzo left for dead, and the rest of the family massacred. The girls were held as slaves for a year at a village near the site of modern Congress, Arizona, then sold to a Mojave chief near Needles, California, after a march of several hundred miles. Olive and Mary's chins were marked with indelible blue cactus tattoos to proclaim their status as slaves, and they were forced to forage for their own food. In a subsequent year of drought, Mary died of starvation and abuse. Olive often feared death, for the Mojaves threatened her whenever whites were nearby or when the tribe went to war; they also made her watch other captives being tortured. In the winter of 1855–56, the army located her and began negotiations to free her. On February 28, 1856, wearing a bark skirt and able to speak only a little English, Olive was ransomed at Fort Yuma, Arizona, for a horse, blankets, and beads. There she was reunited with Lorenzo.

In 1857 Royal B. Stratton wrote their story. *Life Among the Indians* was wildly successful and sold out three editions in a year, for it was one of the few published accounts of such an event. Sales of the book paid for Lorenzo and Olive's education at the University of the Pacific. In 1858 the Oatmans moved to New York with Stratton, and Olive went on the lecture circuit to promote his book. These appearances were among the few occasions on which she appeared in public without a veil to cover her tattooed face.

She married cattleman John Brant Fairchild (1830–1907) in 1865; he is said to have burned all copies of Stratton's book that he could find. They lived in Detroit, Michigan, for seven years before moving to Sherman, Texas, where Fairchild was president of the City Bank. He made his fortune there in banking and real estate. In 1876 Olive and John adopted a daughter. Though shy and retiring, Olive interested herself in the plight of orphaned children but rarely discussed her own youth as an orphan and Indian captive. She always kept a jar of hazelnuts, a staple of Mojave food, as a reminder of those years. She died on March 20, 1903, and is buried in West Hill Cemetery, Sherman. A Texas historical marker was placed on her grave in 1969. *See also* INDIAN CAPTIVES.

BIBLIOGRAPHY: Denison *Daily Herald*, April 25, 1907. New York *Times*, May 4, 1858. Howard H. Peckham, *Captured by Indians: True Tales of Pioneer Survivors* (New Brunswick, New Jersey: Rutgers University Press, 1954). Edward J. Pettid, "The Oatman Story," *Arizona Highways*, November 1968.

Sherrie S. McLeRoy

FAIRCHILD, THORNTON MCNAIR (1875–19?). Thornton McNair Fairchild, black educator and businessman, was born in Houston, Texas, in December 1875. He received his early education in the Houston public schools and later attended Prairie View College (now Prairie View A&M University). He served for a time as principal of black high schools in Navasota and Hempstead and taught in the Houston public schools for a number of years. In 1899 he married a woman named Mary. Early in his business career Fairchild established a funeral home, which by the 1940s was recognized as one of the oldest and best-equipped black mortuaries in Texas. He also founded the Watchtower Life Insurance Company, which became one of the leading black insurance companies in Texas, and served as its president and major stockholder. Fairchild attended Trinity Methodist Episcopal Church in Houston and was a member of the National Association for the Advancement of Colored People[qv] and the Houston Negro Chamber of Commerce. After his death his wife gave a major donation to Houston College for Negroes (now Texas

Southern University), where the oldest building on campus was named in his honor.

BIBLIOGRAPHY: Andrew Webster Jackson, *A Sure Foundation and a Sketch of Negro Life in Texas* (Houston, 1940). *Diana J. Kleiner*

FAIRCHILDS, TEXAS. Fairchilds, on Farm Road 361 thirteen miles south of Richmond in southeastern Fort Bend County, is named for early settler Philo Fairchilds, who around 1840 built a home one mile south of the current site of the community. In 1890 Charles Blohm, August Bede, and Theo Aderholz established the initial settlement, which reportedly attracted Germans from other Texas counties. In 1896 a colony of northern Mennonites qv purchased a league on Big Creek that included the Fairchilds settlement. Fifty families established a community there with a road system, several stores, and separate schools for black and white students. An epidemic of mosquitoes and malaria drove away some of the settlers, and others abandoned the site after the Galveston hurricane of 1900 qv demolished many of the dwellings. Thereafter, only two or three Mennonite families remained. Fairchilds acquired a post office in 1912, but it closed in 1918. In 1914 the community had a single general store. In 1933 the town reported three businesses and twenty-five inhabitants, and by 1936 Fairchilds had four businesses (one with an adjacent factory), a school, and a number of widely scattered dwellings and farms. In 1940 it reported three businesses and seventy-five citizens, and by 1953, five businesses and a population of 125. In the 1960s the population was 110, and no businesses were recorded. In 1990 Fairchilds reported a population of 150 and had a general store, a feed store, a tire store, and a cafe. *Stephen L. Hardin*

FAIRCHILDS CREEK. Fairchilds Creek rises just north of Needville in south central Fort Bend County (at 29°25′ N, 95°51′ W) and runs northeast, then southeast, for a total of ten miles before reaching its mouth on Big Creek (at 29°25′ N, 95°43′ W). The stream was named for Philo Fairchilds, an original grantee of land in the area. The vegetation along the creek consists of mixed hardwoods interspersed with prairie grasses. The local terrain is surfaced by highly impermeable soils in some areas and in others by calcareous clay.

FAIRDALE, TEXAS. Fairdale was a lumbering and farming community fourteen miles southeast of Hemphill in southeastern Sabine County. Although the area was settled as early as the 1830s, little is known about Fairdale before it received a post office in 1902. A post office that operated under the name Oakdale from 1897 until 1899 may have been located in the same community. Fairdale had three stores and seventy-five residents in 1914. Its population had fallen to fifty by the 1920s and was reported at that level until the mid-1960s, after which no estimates are available. The Fairdale post office was closed in the early 1950s, and the last store in the community closed in 1959. By 1968 most of the area had been inundated by the waters of Toledo Bend Reservoir.qv

BIBLIOGRAPHY: Robert Cecil McDaniel, *Sabine County, Texas* (Waco: Texian, 1987). *Cecil Harper, Jr.*

FAIRFIELD, TEXAS. Fairfield, the county seat of Freestone County, is at the junction of Interstate Highway 45, U.S. highways 75 and 84, and Farm roads 27, 488, and 1580, in the center of the county. The site was originally called Mound Prairie, but the name was changed to Fairfield when the location was chosen for the county seat in 1850. The original townsite, 100 acres of the Redin Gainer league, was donated by David Hall Love. In 1851–52, 128 lots were auctioned off for prices ranging from six dollars to $101. Rich farmland, vast amounts of timber, clear springs, and proximity to the Trinity River for transportation attracted settlers from the eastern states. Fairfield acquired a post office in 1851 and by September 1852 had three dry-goods stores, two hotels, a grocery, and a jail. A Fairfield Masonic lodge chartered in 1853 was still active in 1989. The first of four courthouses, a small wooden building described as "no better than a pigsty," was built about 1852. New courthouses were built—in 1854–56, at a cost of $8,330; in 1891–92, at a cost of $22,120; and in 1919–21, at a cost of $125,000. In 1891 and 1918 the need for a new courthouse led to county-seat elections in which Fairfield defeated Wortham and Teague, respectively.

A weekly newspaper, the *Texas Pioneer*, was established at Fairfield in 1857. Subsequent newspapers included the *Ledger* (1869–72) and the *Recorder*, first published in 1876 and still in existence in the 1990s. In the fall of 1854 a school for girls opened in a new two-story building, the upper floor of which was used as a Masonic hall. A school for boys seems to have opened in a different building in 1856. The first session at Fairfield Female College was held in 1859 under the direction of Henry Lee Graves.qv The school offered preparatory and college curriculum and enrolled over 100 students in its first year. The college remained open during the Civil War,qv when its enrollment actually increased because of an influx of Southern refugees. Freestone County was one of four Texas counties in which martial law was declared during Reconstruction.qv On October 9, 1871, Governor Edmund J. Davisqv imposed martial law in the county in response to reports of coercion and fraudulent voting in Fairfield during the election of October 3–6. Martial law was lifted a month later, on November 10. By 1884 Fairfield reported a population of 500. The community had two hotels, four general stores, and five groceries and served as a shipping point for cotton and hides. By 1892 the town had a bank and Baptist, Methodist, and Cumberland Presbyterian churches.

The community experienced a series of reverses around 1900. A meningitis outbreak killed thirty-two people in 1890, a tornado heavily damaged the central area of town in 1902, the boll weevilqv scourge destroyed the cotton crop in 1903, and fire ravaged part of the business district in 1911. Nevertheless, the population advanced steadily, to 629 by 1904, 1,047 by 1940, 2,074 by 1970, and 4,093 by 1988. Fairfield never acquired a railroad. The Trinity and Brazos Valley bypassed the town by ten miles when it built its track through Freestone County in 1906–07. Although the lack of a railroad did not cause Fairfield to decline, it did deprive it of a strong economic stimulus. The town obtained water and sewer lines in 1933 and a public library in 1954.

From 1890 to 1931 and again in 1933, Fairfield was the site of an annual reunion of Confederate veterans, who held their three-day gathering on land donated by William Lewis Moodyqv and his brother Leroy. In 1951 the town held its centennial celebration on the old reunion campground. The success of the centennial led the townspeople to begin holding an annual rodeo-homecoming festival, which evolved into the county fair held each November. Other annual events include the Queen of the Trinity Star Pilgrimage in the spring, the National Coon Hunters Association meeting in the fall, and an arts and crafts fair in November. Local attractions and recreation facilities include the Freestone County Historical Museum (in Fairfield), and Fairfield Lake State Parkqv (completed in 1972). In 1989 industries in Fairfield included TU Electric, Dow Chemical, TXO Production Corporation, and Texas Utilities Mining Company. Major sources of income were oil, gas, and coal mining, as well as agribusiness. Noted Fairfield residents have included L. D. Bradley, a Texas legislator, district judge, and commander of Company B, Second Battalion, Waul's Legion;qv John Gregg;qv and William L. Moody. The population in 1990 was 3,234.

BIBLIOGRAPHY: John P. Carrier, *A Political History of Texas during Reconstruction, 1865–1874* (Ph.D. dissertation, Vanderbilt University, 1971). Dallas *News*, August 31, 1956. *Evidence of Lawlessness in Limestone and Freestone Counties Which Caused the Proclamation of Martial Law* (Austin: Tracy, Siemering, 1871). Fairfield *Recorder*, September 24, 1936, August 30, 1951. Freestone County Historical Commission, *History of Freestone County, Texas* (Fairfield, Texas, 1978).

William C. Nunn, *Texas Under the Carpetbaggers* (Austin: University of Texas Press, 1962). Vertical Files, Barker Texas History Center, University of Texas at Austin.
Helen Harrison Courtney

FAIRFIELD FEMALE COLLEGE. Fairfield Female College was located in Fairfield, Freestone County. On February 13, 1858, a group of town leaders incorporated as the Freestone County School Association "to put in operation and perpetuate a first class female institution of learning." The college was endorsed by the Baptist State Convention, but it was not an official Baptist institution. It may have opened in the bottom floor of the Masonic lodge in Fairfield. In November 1854 the Leon *Pioneer* reported, "The Masonic hall, quite imposing, is nearly complete. The lower room of the hall is occupied by Dr. Moore, who has under his charge a flourishing school composed of young ladies." W. B. Moore and principal (in 1856) H. V. Philpott were members of Fairfield Masonic Lodge No. 103.

Construction of a two-story building, located a mile southeast of the county courthouse, was completed in early 1859, and classes began in February 1859. About seventy girls were in attendance for the first session. The school was chartered on February 8, 1860, along with a male academy that failed. Henry L. Graves was selected president of the new college. Graves had previously served as president of Baylor University at Independence and of the Baptist State Convention. He taught ancient languages and moral and intellectual philosophy. Other courses offered included mathematics, English literature, music, and ornamental art. In addition to the college curriculum, a graded preparatory department was offered. The length of each session was twenty weeks, and tuition was fifteen to twenty dollars for prep school and twenty-five dollars for college classes. The students, faculty, and Graves and his family lived in the school building and were attended by nine slaves, who did maintenance, housework, cooking, and serving.

In February 1861, the same week that the Secession Convention [qv] in Austin passed the Ordinance of Secession, the college property was put on sale at public auction. Graves bought all the property, including ten acres of land on which the buildings were situated, for $5,000. Assisted by three women teachers, he operated the school until it closed. Attendance was good in 1861, and during the war a number of refugees descended on the area, bringing enrollment to its highest levels at about 200, but also causing a housing shortage. The war continued and attendance dropped. In December 1869 Graves and the other owners of the college and property sold their interest to Alice M. Adams for $1,500 and the assumption of $5,000 indebtedness against the school. In the following years the Fairfield Masons annually appointed a school committee to provide education for the children of deceased master Masons living in the jurisdiction of the lodge. The college was closed in 1889. In 1936 the state of Texas erected a marker at the site.

BIBLIOGRAPHY: James David Carter, *Education and Masonry in Texas, 1846 to 1861* (Waco: Grand Lodge of Texas, 1964). Freestone County Historical Commission, *History of Freestone County, Texas* (Fairfield, Texas, 1978). Donald W. Whisenhunt, *The Encyclopedia of Texas Colleges and Universities* (Austin: Eakin, 1986).
Douglas R. Shields

FAIRFIELD LAKE STATE PARK. Fairfield Lake State park is on Farm Road 3285 at the south end of Fairfield Lake, four miles northeast of Fairfield in eastern Freestone County. The park comprises 1,460 acres of woodland in which various types of oaks, as well as hickories, dogwoods, and cedars predominate. Indian grass, switchgrass, and other native Texas grasses are common there, as well as wildflowers. The lake contains a variety of fish including catfish, bass, sunfish, carp, and crappie. Shore and water birds such as herons, egrets, and geese frequent the area. The park has three campgrounds, a number of picnic sites, a swimming area, playgrounds, an amphitheater, two boat docks, and two hiking trails.

BIBLIOGRAPHY: Vertical Files, Barker Texas History Center, University of Texas at Austin.
Chris Cravens

FAIRLAND, TEXAS. Fairland is on Farm Road 1855 six miles north of Marble Falls in Burnet County. In the early 1850s a group of families from the eastern states settled on a strip of level land between Backbone Ridge and the Slaughter range, which they called "fair land." Early settlers were the R. S. Cates family in 1852 and the Lewis Thomas family. Others included John Harvey, a surveyor, Jefferson Barton, and the Atwoods, Grahams, Slaughters, Joys, Reeds, Alexanders, B. E. Fergusons, and Chessers. In 1859 Mrs. Senia Barton Harvey deeded land for a Methodist church and a school. The settlers soon began work on a stone building but were stopped by the Civil War,[qv] when many of the men left to fight. The building was not completed until 1870. Rev. Arter Crownover, a minister of the Methodist Episcopal Church, South, held the first service, and a school was begun. On July 13, 1872, the third quarterly Methodist conference for Lampasas, Bear Creek Circuit, named the house and lot Crownover Chapel. When the church was finished, the community had a picnic. An extra wooden room was subsequently added to the rock building and used for the school for many years.

In 1875 a Christian Church was built in Fairland. In 1887 a Church of Christ was built. The congregation eventually ceased to meet and in 1937 began to meet in homes. Eventually the members joined with a group in Marble Falls. The first local post office was opened in 1874 and called Backbone Valley. The post office named Fairland opened in 1890 and was discontinued in 1951, when a Marble Falls rural route served the community. In 1925 Fairland had an estimated population of 200. By 1939 the number of residents had dropped to fifty. The population was consistently estimated at fifty through the mid-1960s. The Fairland and Tobey schools were consolidated in 1937, and they joined the Marble Falls schools after 1943. The old rock church building was still maintained by the Fairland community and interested friends and used for community purposes in the late 1980s. The Fairland Cemetery located on the seven-acre plot with the building was also still in use. The earliest grave is dated 1857. Fairland was still listed as a community in 1990, but without population statistics.

BIBLIOGRAPHY: Darrell Debo, *Burnet County History* (2 vols., Burnet, Texas: Eakin, 1979).
Estelle Bryson

FAIRLIE, TEXAS. Fairlie is on State Highway 11 twelve miles northeast of Greenville in northeastern Hunt County. It received a post office in 1892 and was named for Fairlee Webster, apparently a resident. It grew to a population of 248 by 1904. In 1933 it had eight businesses, in 1952 six, and in 1964 four. The post office remained in operation until sometime after 1930, perhaps until as recently as 1964. From 1964 to 1990 Fairlie reported a population of eighty.
Brian Hart

FAIRMOUNT, TEXAS. Fairmount is on State Highway 87 in the Sabine National Forest[qv] twelve miles southeast of Hemphill in southeastern Sabine County. The community received a post office in 1854 and by 1884 had a population estimated at seventy and a gristmill, cotton gin, district school, blacksmith shop, and general store. In 1896 its one-teacher, one-room school had thirty-one pupils. By the 1920s Fairmount had ten residents and one rated business. Its post office closed in the late 1940s, when the county highway map showed a school and eleven dwellings at the site. The community was still listed in 1990, but without population statistics.
Cecil Harper, Jr.

FAIR OAKS, TEXAS. Fair Oaks is on Farm Road 39 a mile east of Lake Limestone at the eastern edge of Limestone County. In 1946 the community had a cemetery and a number of scattered dwellings. By 1966 Fair Oaks had two businesses, a church, and a number of scattered dwellings. The community was still listed in 1990, though population figures were unavailable.
Holly Marshall

FAIR PARK. Fair Park, the site of the State Fair of Texas,[qv] is located in east Dallas near the downtown business district. It is owned by the city of Dallas and is jointly operated by the Dallas Park and Recreation Department and the State Fair of Texas Association. In 1986 the 277-acre site was home to the State Fair, the Cotton Bowl, and five museums. Fair Park houses one of the greatest concentrations of early twentieth-century Art Deco exposition buildings in the United States.

The original eighty-acre site was purchased by Capt. William H. Gaston[qv] from the Thomas Lagow league and the John Grigsby league for $16,000 in 1886 and deeded to the newly chartered Dallas State Fair and Exposition Association. In return Gaston received 140 shares of stock, which he later donated to the fair organization. The Dallas Exposition opened its first fair on October 26, 1886.

A rival organization, the Texas State Fair, headed by C. A. Keating, opened its fair on October 25 of the same year on a section of John Cole's farm in north Dallas. Both fairs were successful and together drew over 35,000 people a day. Eventually, the two groups decided to merge and form the Texas State Fair and Dallas Exposition. The eighty acres in east Dallas were chosen as the site for future fairs of the new organization.

In 1899 the organization changed its name to Texas State Fair. The fair had financial difficulties even before 1902, when the exposition buildings burned. Furthermore, it lost its biggest source of income when the Texas legislature outlawed track gambling on horse racing. Still the directors refused an offer of $125,000 for the fairgrounds, which would have turned the site into a residential subdivision. Instead they offered the grounds to the city of Dallas as a park in 1904, in return for the payment of their outstanding debt and the agreement that the State Fair board would run the annual exhibition and pay the city a percentage. This arrangement worked well, and the Texas State Fair became one of the most successful in the country.

Fair Park was expanded in 1936 when it became the site of the Texas Centennial[qv] Exposition. At the persistence of a group of Dallas businessmen incorporated as the Texas Centennial Central Exposition Corporation, Dallas outbid San Antonio, Austin, and Houston for the celebration. Utilizing the grounds and buildings of the Texas State Fair, and obtaining additional land for expansion to 180 acres, Dallas also assured the Centennial Committee $5.5 million of public and private money.

Local architect George L. Dahl,[qv] of the firm of Greene, LaRoche, and Dahl, was selected as chief architect and technical director of the $25 million Texas Centennial Exposition, which opened on June 6, 1936. Construction began in October 1935, and in eight months an exposition site equivalent to a city was constructed. Twenty-one of the fifty buildings were permanent.

The main entry gate, which remained in the same location as for earlier fairs, opened onto an esplanade flanked by exhibit buildings. At the terminus of the esplanade was the magnificent Hall of State,[qv] built by the state of Texas. Other major exposition buildings still standing are the Agriculture Complex and the Civic Center, a museum complex built by the city of Dallas around a man-made lagoon. Ford Motor Company spent over $2 million on a temporary exhibit building and entertainment. Buildings constructed by Magnolia Oil Company, Lone Star Gas, and Continental Oil remain on the grounds. The United States government constructed a $1.5 million Federal Building and a Hall of Negro Life.[qv]

All construction plans had to meet the approval of George Dahl, who insisted that the entire plant follow his architectural theme. Building in the contemporary style later known as Art Deco, Dahl wanted to combine architecture and art. His design featured broad, low buildings with smooth expanses of sun-colored walls, brightened with murals in bold colors and accented by massive sculpture. Dahl dubbed his style "Texanic" and described it as "strong and bold, a quality possessed to an unusual degree by the majority of the residents of Texas."

After nearly fifty years of neglect the art and architecture of Fair Park was renovated. The city of Dallas initiated improvements in 1985, and Friends of Fair Park, a support group, was formed to ensure that restoration continued. In the fall of 1986 Fair Park was entered on the National Register of Historic Places as a national landmark. In 1993 the African American Museum was built and renovations were completed on the Cotton Bowl. In addition to the State Fair, Fair Park has also hosted other events, including the World Cup and the International Gold Cup Games.

BIBLIOGRAPHY: William L. McDonald, *Dallas Rediscovered: A Photographic Chronicle of Urban Expansion, 1870–1925* (Dallas: Dallas County Historical Society, 1978).

Sarah Hunter

FAIR PLAY, TEXAS. Fair Play, a farming community at the junction of U.S. Highway 79 and Farm roads 124 and 1251, eleven miles west of Carthage in western Panola County, is one of the oldest settlements in the area. The site occupies part of Immanuel Antonio Romero's land grant. The first settler there was John Allison,[qv] who operated a general store, boardinghouse, and blacksmith shop and became county judge when the county was organized in 1846. A post office was granted to the community in 1851. The site is said to have been named by a traveler who was impressed with the fair rates and treatment he had received at Allison's. A church, used by whites and blacks, was built on Allison's place, and buried in the churchyard were the Allison slaves and family, among them Thomas G. Allison, a member of the Constitutional Convention of 1875.[qv] By 1885 Fair Play had two schools, two churches, a sawmill, gristmills, a cotton gin, and an estimated population of 100. Its population dropped to fifty by 1890, and its post office was closed in 1904, when the mail was sent to Beckville. In the mid-1930s Fair Play had a reported population of ninety-five and a church, a school, a sawmill, and several stores. Its school was consolidated with the Carthage school in the 1940s, and after World War II[qv] many of the remaining residents moved away. In the mid-1960s the settlement still had three churches, a school, and a store. In 1990 Fair Play reported a population of eighty.

BIBLIOGRAPHY: *History of Panola County* (Carthage, Texas: Carthage Circulating Book Club, 1935?). Leila B. LaGrone, ed., *History of Panola County* (Carthage, Texas: Panola County Historical Commission, 1979). John Barnette Sanders, *Postoffices and Post Masters of Panola County, Texas, 1845–1930* (Center, Texas, 1964).

Claudia Hazlewood

FAIRVIEW, TEXAS (Armstrong County). Fairview is on Farm Road 1151 twelve miles west of Claude in western Armstrong County. A rural school was established in the area in 1892 and moved twice before being moved to the present site in 1912. One of the teachers was Sam Bratton, who later became a United States senator from New Mexico. Local Methodists used the church at Washburn until 1902, when they built their own wooden church. This building was utilized until 1948, when the congregation moved to the old school auditorium after the school district was consolidated with that of Claude. In 1953, when Fairview joined the Texas Rural Neighborhood Improvement program, a community center was constructed. Fairview was still listed as a community in 1990.

BIBLIOGRAPHY: Armstrong County Historical Association, *A Collection of Memories: A History of Armstrong County, 1876–1965* (Hereford, Texas: Pioneer, 1965).

H. Allen Anderson

FAIRVIEW, TEXAS (Bosque County). Fairview is near the Lake Whitney Dam 9½ miles northeast of Valley Mills and twenty-three miles northwest of Waco in southeastern Bosque County. A church was organized there in April 1889, probably on Coon Creek. In 1897 Gip Smith, who owned most of the land in Fairview, donated the grounds for a church and a school. A one-room school and church was erected in August 1897. A separate building for the church was built later that year. Local histories suggest that a post office was established in R. E. Conine's home, which also housed the general store. Outlaw Myra Shirley (Belle) Starr^{qv} owned 160 acres of land in the Fairview area that served as a hideout. The Fairview school was consolidated with the Valley Mills schools in 1949. The Fairview Baptist Church continued to serve the area in the late 1980s.

BIBLIOGRAPHY: Bosque County History Book Committee, *Bosque County, Land and People* (Dallas: Curtis Media, 1985).

Karen Yancy

FAIRVIEW, TEXAS (Collin County). Fairview is on Farm Road 1378 and State Highway 5, three miles south of McKinney and six miles northeast of Plano in central Collin County. The growth of nearby Plano as a business center of North Texas during the late 1960s stimulated the growth of Fairview, which doubled in population from 175 in 1960 to 325 in 1970. By 1981 the population had jumped to 893. In 1990 Fairview had 1,554 residents, many of which commuted to Plano or McKinney, the county seat.

David Minor

FAIRVIEW, TEXAS (Franklin County). Fairview is on Farm Road 71 in northwestern Franklin County. According to a count taken in 1972, a cemetery at the site comprises some 300 graves; the earliest marked one dates from 1881. By 1896 the settlement had a one-room, one-teacher school that served thirty-eight students. During the 1930s the community had a few widely scattered houses and a school, church, and store. By 1985 a church, a cemetery, and a few widely scattered houses remained at the site.

BIBLIOGRAPHY: Billy Hicks and Doris Meek, comps., *Historical Records of Franklin County, Texas* (Mount Vernon, Texas: Franklin County Historical Survey Committee, 1972).

Cecil Harper, Jr.

FAIRVIEW, TEXAS (Howard County). Fairview, on U.S. Highway 87 five miles northwest of Big Spring in central Howard County, was named for the view afforded by the flat land around it. In 1930 it had a population of fifteen and two commercially rated businesses. By 1940 its population had grown to fifty, and a school was located there. Between 1950 and 1960 the population was 100, but the last business had closed. In 1980 and 1990 the population was eighty-five.

Noel Wiggins

FAIRVIEW, TEXAS (Milam County). Fairview was a school community seven miles south of Thorndale in southern Milam County. The Fairview school district, which was formed in 1919, was consolidated with the Thorndale Independent School District in 1946.

BIBLIOGRAPHY: Lelia M. Batte, *History of Milam County, Texas* (San Antonio: Naylor, 1956). Milam County Heritage and Preservation Society, *Matchless Milam: History of Milam County* (Dallas: Taylor, 1984).

Vivian Elizabeth Smyrl

FAIRVIEW, TEXAS (Smith County). Fairview was on State Highway 110 a mile west of Mount Sylvan, Texas, in western Smith County. In 1936 there were a few farms in the area, and the Fairview School, a black elementary school with two teachers, had ninety students. By 1952 the school had been consolidated with the Dixie Independent School District. But the community continued to grow and by 1966 had two churches and a scattered collection of dwellings. Maps for 1973 showed a church, a business, and about thirty dwellings there. In 1981 the community was not shown on Smith County maps.

BIBLIOGRAPHY: Edward Clayton Curry, An Administrative Survey of the Schools of Smith County, Texas (M.Ed. thesis, University of Texas, 1938).

Vista K. McCroskey

FAIRVIEW, TEXAS (Tom Greene County). Fairview was on Lipan Flat west of U.S. Highway 87 four miles southeast of San Angelo in central Tom Greene County. In 1931 the local school had four teachers, and in 1933 it had fifty-nine students; a church and scattered dwellings were in the community. In the 1980s Fairview no longer appeared on state highway maps.

BIBLIOGRAPHY: Clarence George Parsons, Proposed Plan for the Reorganization of the Schools in Tom Green County, Texas (M.A. thesis, University of Texas, 1939).

Diana J. Kleiner

FAIRVIEW, TEXAS (Wilson County). Fairview is at the junction of Farm roads 536 and 2505, ten miles west of Floresville in western Wilson County. The town was established in the late 1850s, when German and Polish settlement began in the western portion of the county. Old Rock Church, a mile north, was the site of revival meetings and the scene of the trials of outlaws captured by the last of the local vigilante committees under Charles Westermann and Drake Gilliland. A Fairview post office opened in 1868, and by 1892 the town had four churches, three general stores, a drugstore, a barbershop, and a population of 100. A two-teacher school was in operation by 1896, when it had an enrollment of sixty-seven. The post office was closed in 1908 and the mail ordered to Floresville. The town declined during the 1920s and 1930s, and by 1947 it had two stores and a population of fifty. Fairview subsequently began to grow again and in 1990 had two churches, several businesses, and 322 inhabitants.

Claudia Hazlewood

FAIRVIEW, TEXAS (Wise County). Fairview is at the intersection of Farm roads 407 and 2264, southeast of Decatur in southeastern Wise County. In the 1930s highway maps showed a church and cemetery, a school, and scattered dwellings at the site. The community had a church and school for many years and was incorporated in 1973. The first population figure for Fairview was 180 in 1980. By the early 1990s the population was 206.

BIBLIOGRAPHY: Rosalie Gregg, ed., *Wise County History* (Vol. 1, n.p.: Nortex, 1975; Vol. 2, Austin: Eakin, 1982).

Lisa C. Maxwell

FAIRY, TEXAS. Fairy, at the junction of Farm roads 219 and 1602 in northern Hamilton County, was first known as Martin's Gap for James Martin, an early settler who took an oxcart through the mountain gap. The town was named for Fairy Fort, the daughter of Confederate Army captain Battle Fort, when the post office was established in 1884. Fairy had a cotton gin from 1900 to 1920 and schools, churches, and businesses serving the greater ranching and farming community. In 1947 Fairy had a post office, three churches, three businesses, and 150 people. The post office closed in 1957, and the Fairy school district was consolidated with the Hamilton schools in 1967. In 1980 and 1990 the population was thirty-one

BIBLIOGRAPHY: Hamilton County Historical Commission, *A History of Hamilton County, Texas* (Dallas: Taylor, 1979).

William R. Hunt

FAISON, NATHANIEL W. (ca. 1817–1870). Nathaniel W. Faison, Dawson and Perote prisoner, was born about 1817 in Tennessee. He immigrated to Texas sometime in the 1830s and arrived in La Grange in 1839 to work as a land surveyor. He purchased land there and seems to have been a merchant as well as a surveyor. Records show that he was given a license as a retailer of liquor by the drink in 1841, and most records of the prisoners of Perote kept by the prisoners themselves show him as a merchant. In the fall of 1842 a force of Mexicans under Gen. Adrián Woll^{qv} captured San Antonio, and all over the Republic of Texas^{qv} citizens heeded the call to battle. In Fayette County Capt. Nicholas Mosby Dawson^{qv} organized a company of volunteers under the live oak tree on the courthouse square in La Grange, and Faison was one of the first to join. Fewer than fifteen men joined Dawson at the square, but by the time they reached the edge of the county on their way to San Antonio, their number had risen to fifty-three. The company rode fast and hard and so were tired when they heard the sounds of battle. Faison and Alsey Miller were scouts for the group, and they rode ahead to check on the condition of the battle of Salado Creek^{qv} in progress between the Mexicans and the Texans. The two scouts misread the balance of the battle and believed the Texans badly needed help. Dawson gave his men the option of rest, but believing they were needed, they chose to join the main body of Texan forces. This proved to be a fatal mistake, as they advanced directly into General Woll's retreat. Faison was one of those captured in what came to be known as the Dawson massacre.^{qv} There is a story told by a fellow prisoner, Capt. Edward T. Manton,^{qv} of their capture and questioning by the Mexicans. The Mexicans asked the prisoners if they had any money, and Faison was the only one with any, having two dollars. He was also wearing a gold ring, which one of the Mexican soldiers was interested in. Faison acted as if the ring would not come off his finger, but when the Mexican guard drew a knife to cut it off, Faison slipped it right off and handed it over.

Those captured after the massacre were briefly imprisoned at San Antonio, where Faison had time to inscribe the names of the surviving prisoners on the walls. The Dawson prisoners were then forced to flee with the Mexican army as it retreated to Mexico. Along the way, the five Dawson prisoners who were injured were left at a small border town to heal their wounds, but Faison and the other nine continued on into the heart of Mexico. They were joined with another group of prisoners from Texas and forced to march on towards Mexico City. Faison and the other prisoners arrived at Perote prison^{qv} on December 22, 1842, and settled in for a stay that would prove to be much longer than any of them expected. It should be noted that local folklore at one time placed Faison and the Dawson prisoners as present at the black bean episode,^{qv} but this is not accurate. The story was that Faison had mixed a Mexican guard a cup of eggnog the morning of the drawing of the beans, and the guard had told him that the white beans were rough and the black beans were smooth, and he had thus been saved from execution by drawing a white bean. Faison was held at Perote prison until March 23, 1844, when Gen. Waddy Thompson^{qv} secured his release and that of the rest of the Bexar prisoners. Faison returned to La Grange and served as county clerk of Fayette County from 1846 to 1854. In 1848 Faison and Manton went with an expedition to bring back the bones of the Dawson men and others from the battle of Salado Creek to be interred at Monument Hill (*see* MONUMENT HILL–KREISCHE BREWERY STATE HISTORIC SITE). He bought a house a half mile from this monument in 1866. Faison died in June 1870. He had speculated on land all over Texas and at his death owned more than 50,000 acres in various parts of the state. He had never married, and his brother, Peter, and his family moved into his home after his death. This house, along with much of its original furniture, was purchased by the La Grange Garden Club in 1961 and restored to its original condition. It is registered with the Texas Historical Commission^{qv} and can be visited in La Grange.

BIBLIOGRAPHY: Houston *Chronicle*, May 5, 1963. Houston *Post*, April 28, 1963. Marker Files, Texas Historical Commission, Austin. Joseph Milton Nance, *Attack and Counterattack: The Texas-Mexican Frontier, 1842* (Austin: University of Texas Press, 1964). James L. Trueheart, *The Perote Prisoners; Being the Diary of James L. Trueheart* (San Antonio: Naylor, 1934). Houston Wade, comp., *The Dawson Men of Fayette County* (Houston, 1932). Leonie Rummel Weyand and Houston Wade, *An Early History of Fayette County* (La Grange, Texas: La Grange *Journal*, 1936).

Walter F. Pilcher

FALBA, TEXAS. Falba, a mile west of the intersection of Farm roads 2989 and 247 in extreme northwest Walker County, developed around the homestead of Christopher Columbus Edinburgh, who arrived in 1824. Edinburgh, reputed to be the first settler in what became Walker County, had fought in the battle of San Jacinto.^{qv} The community once supported a church and a school, and a post office was established in 1901. In 1911 the school offered six grades. In 1914 Falba had two doctors and a community store. In 1936 the community had scattered farm dwellings, two schools (one for white and one for black children), a church, and a cemetery. In 1990 all that remained was the Falba Cemetery.

BIBLIOGRAPHY: D'Anne McAdams Crews, ed., *Huntsville and Walker County, Texas: A Bicentennial History* (Huntsville, Texas: Sam Houston State University, 1976).

James L. Hailey

FALCON, TEXAS. Falcon is on U.S. Highway 83 two miles west of the Starr-Zapata county line. It was moved from an original Falcon at the junction of Medio Creek and the Rio Grande in southeast Zapata County during the flood in August 1953, which was caused by the completion of Falcon Dam in December 1952. Settlers had been brought to the area by Col. José de Escandón^{qv} in the 1750s. The Spanish crown set the land aside for the colonists of Revilla, known as Guerrero, after Mexican independence. In the mid-1700s the king of Spain granted 6,123 acres to José Clemente Gutiérrez, who later sold the land to José Clemente Ramírez. In 1780 Ramírez married Margarita de la Garza Falcón, thus uniting two of the area's most distinguished families, and moved to the old site of Falcón. The place was called Ramireño de Abajo. In the early 1900s Ildefonso Ramírez opened a general store there. In 1915 a post office was established, and the village changed its name to Falcon, in honor of the wife of the founder. This was done because there was already a post office a few miles away called Ramireño, at Ramireño de Arriba, and the post office needed a different name. Old Falcon had 4.01 acres in common riverfront and 12.27 acres in its town tract. The government offered to move the settlement of families to Zapata, the county seat, where good schools, parks, water, sewage disposal, and paved and curbed streets would be available; but the families, whose ancestors had come to the area, settled it and opted to keep their site. The government closed the dam before paying for the land and improvements, figuring they had several years before the water would rise—there had been six years of drought. But in August 1953 the rains came, and the 500-year floodplain was quickly reached. In a pouring rain, as the waters slowly swallowed up the village, the refugees fled, and some left behind their life's possessions. Rafaela Ramos de Serna marked off fifty acres of her nearby land into town lots, and sold them for $100 each to the villagers. Later, the government refused to pay them the full price for their homes and belongings because they were no longer usable.

The new Falcon has Santa Ana Catholic Church, an older community building, a new large community hall, three north-south paved and curbed streets, and three east-west curbed streets. It also has a combination general store with gas station, general supplies, a feed and seed store, a pool hall, and 500 residents. The government also picked out a common site for all of the local cemeteries, but all of the villages affected by Falcon Dam voted to buy their own separate sites. A total of 162 graves was moved from the old Falcon cemetery, only ten of them unidentified. The population of Falcon was recorded from 1960 to 1990 as fifty.

BIBLIOGRAPHY: Patsy Jeanne Byfield, *Falcon Dam and the Lost Towns of Zapata* (Austin: Texas Memorial Museum, 1971). Jean Y. Fish, *Zapata County Roots Revisited* (Edinburg, Texas: New Santander Press, 1990). Kathleen E. and Clifton R. St. Clair, eds., *Little Towns of Texas* (Jacksonville, Texas: Jayroe Graphic Arts, 1982).

Dick D. Heller

FALCONER, THOMAS (1805–1882). Thomas Falconer, jurist and adventurer, was born on June 25, 1805, in Bath, England, the second son of Rev. Thomas and Frances (Raitt) Falconer. His father was a physician, and his mother was a daughter of Lt. Col. Robert Raitt of the Second (or Queen's) Regiment of Foot. Falconer was admitted to Lincoln's Inn in 1823 and to the bar in 1830. After practicing for some years as an equity draftsman and conveyancer, he set about codifying the laws and statutes of England. From 1837 to 1840 he was the revising barrister of the London burroughs of Finsbury, Tower Hamlets, and Marylebone.

In 1840 he determined to immigrate to the Republic of Texas,qv where, according to a letter of introduction to President Mirabeau B. Lamar,qv "his services in its infant juris-prudence will be of no small value." He sailed from Liverpool for Boston on the Britannia on October 20 and arrived in Austin in May 1841, just as word of the intended Texan Santa Fe expeditionqv was on every tongue. Thinking the expedition into the wilderness a great opportunity for adventure, he sought and received Lamar's permission to accompany Hugh McLeod'sqv command as "historiographer" and scientific observer. In Lamar's words, "immense accessions" were to be gained by Falconer's "observations and labors to our knowledge of a Country, of which we are almost entirely ignorant." Before departing from San Antonio Falconer established a warm friendship with George Wilkins Kendallqv of the New Orleans *Picayune,* who was also to accompany the expedition as a chronicler. Kendall described Falconer as "a young gentleman of high literary and scientific attainments, mild and agreeable manners, and extremely sociable and companionable from the first." On the trail toward New Mexico Indians stole Falconer's horse, and a prairie fire singed off his hair and eyebrows. Although accustomed from birth to "the luxuries and good things of an English fireside," he endured the hardships of the journey across unexplored Texas well and even appointed himself camp cook for his circle of friends. When McLeod divided his command on the Pease River on August 31, Falconer, because he was now dismounted, was detailed to remain in camp. His diary of this period, published as an appendix to the 1856 edition of Kendall's Narrative of the Texan Santa Fe Expedition, is of special significance, since it provides the only record of attacks by the Kiowas on Falconer's party and their near starvation before McLeod's men returned on October 9 as prisoners of the Mexicans. The two halves of the expedition, now reunited, were marched to El Paso and then to Chihuahua, where Falconer was confined in the Salón de los Distinguidos of the Jesuit hospital at the presidio, the very room in which Father Miguel Hidalgo y Costillaqv had been held captive after the collapse of his revolt in 1811. The prisoners were removed to Zacatecas and allowed to roam at will until, because of a clerical error, Falconer was placed under arrest on New Year's night and remained so on the march to Mexico City. Upon arrival at the Mexican capital on February 3, 1842, however, he was immediately released at the demand of the British minister. He left the city a month later. Falconer's account of the Santa Fe expedition was published in New Orleans in 1842 as *Expedition to Santa Fé: An Account of Its Journey from Texas through Mexico, with Particulars of Its Capture.* This was supplemented by "Notes of a Journey through Texas and New Mexico, in the Years 1841 and 1842," published in the *Journal of the Royal Geographical Society of London* in 1844.

After returning from Texas Falconer chronicled his travels in such major works as *The Oregon Question; or a Statement of the British Claims to the Oregon Territory in Opposition to the Pretensions of the Government of the United States of America.* In 1848 he was offered, but declined, an appointment as private secretary to Sir Henry Barkley, governor of British Guiana. Late in 1850 he was appointed an arbitrator to determine the boundary between New Brunswick and Canada, and on July 29, 1851, he was nominated to, but declined to accept, the position of colonial secretary of Western Australia. On December 22, 1851, however, he accepted appointment as judge of the Welsh county courts of Glamorganshire and Brecknockshire and of the district of Rhayader in Radnorshire. As a judge he was described as "a laborious worker, a staunch liberal, an energetic opponent of abuses, and a strong advocate of prison reform." He was a fellow of the Royal Geographical Society and of the Geological Society. After thirty years on the bench Falconer retired, in December 1881. He died at Bath on August 28, 1882, as a result of a fall he had suffered the previous June.

BIBLIOGRAPHY: George Wilkins Kendall, *Narrative of the Texan Santa Fe Expedition* (2 vols., New York: Harper, 1844; rpts. Austin: Steck, 1935; n.p.: Readex, 1966).
Thomas W. Cutrer

FALCON HEIGHTS, TEXAS. Falcon Heights is near the dam that impounds International Falcon Reservoir on Farm Road 2098, three miles from U.S. Highway 83 in southwestern Starr County. It was founded in 1954 when Falcon Dam was completed, at the site of an active Catholic mission church, Holy Trinity. In 1990 the community had a post office, a population of 361, two motels, three trailer parks, a lumberyard, an automatic telephone center, a bar, a water company, and a Baptist church. The seventy-five-acre Starr County Recreation Park provided camping and picnicking facilities. Nearby Falcon State Parkqv offers fishing, boating, swimming, and camping. The predominantly Spanish-speaking residents, many of them descendants of settlers who came to the area nearly 300 years ago, provide services for tourists. More than 1,000 bird-watchers come every year to see the ferruginous pygmy owl, the brown jay, Audubon's oriole, and other birds.
Dick D. Heller, Jr.

FALCON STATE PARK. Falcon State Park is on the southeastern shore of International Falcon Reservoir,qv fifteen miles northwest of Rio Grande City in Starr and Zapata counties. It is accessible via U.S. Highway 83, Farm Road 2098, and Park Road 46. Falcon Dam, which impounds the sixty-mile-long reservoir, was dedicated by Mexican president Adolfo Ruiz Cortines and United States president Dwight D. Eisenhowerqv in October 1953. The dam was built for conservation, irrigation, power, flood-control, and recreation purposes. The park was leased from the International Boundary and Water Commissionqv in 1954 and opened to the public on May 16, 1965. Camping, picnicking, waterskiing, swimming, bird-watching, and fishing facilities are provided in the 572-acre park. A 3,000-foot lighted airstrip is also available there. Nearby points of interest are Nuevo Guerrero and Ciudad Mier in Mexico and Fort Ringgold in Rio Grande City. The surrounding terrain consists of gently rolling hills on which grow mesquite, huisache, ebony, wild olive, cactus, and native grasses.

BIBLIOGRAPHY: Vertical Files, Barker Texas History Center, University of Texas at Austin.
Alicia A. Garza

FALCON VILLAGE, TEXAS. Falcon Village is off State Highway 2098 at the southeast end of International Falcon Reservoir, four miles west of U.S. Highway 83 in southwestern Starr County. It is a restricted government town for federal employees, including personnel of the International Boundary and Water Commission,qv the Drug Enforcement Administration, and the Immigration and Naturalization Service. The homes, athletic areas, parks, and administration building were constructed by the federal government in 1949 when the dam was started. In 1990 Falcon Village had seventy-six inhabitants who lived in fifty homes with a beautiful view over Falcon State Park, Falcon Lake, and the Mexican mountains.
Dick D. Heller, Jr.

FALFURRIAS, TEXAS. Falfurrias, the county seat and principal trading center of Brooks County, is on State Highway 281 sixty miles southwest of Corpus Christi and ninety miles from Laredo in the northern part of the county. Its founding and development were largely the effort of Edward C. Lasater,qv pioneer Rio Grande valley rancher and land developer, who in 1895 started a cattle ranch in what was then northern Starr County; his spread came to be known as Falfurrias Ranch, after La Mota de Falfurrias, the grove of trees he chose as the site of his headquarters. To increase settlement in the area Lasater encouraged the San Antonio and Aransas Pass Railway to extend a line to his ranch in 1904. At the railway terminus four miles east of his ranchhouse he founded Falfurrias; he also changed the name of his ranch to La Mota. His Falfurrias Immigration Company set about attracting settlers by offering subdivided ranchland near the railroad at low prices and advertising extensively in the East and Midwest.

The name Falfurrias antedates Anglo association with the area, and its derivation is uncertain. Lasater claimed that it was a Lipan

Indian word meaning "the land of heart's delight"; others believed it was the Spanish name for a native desert flower known as the heart's delight. Less romantic is the theory that Falfurrias is a misspelling of one or another Spanish or French word. The word filfarrias, for example, Mexican slang for a filthy, untidy person, was long associated with an old shepherd in the region whom the locals referred to as Don Filfarrias. According to local tradition the shepherd's land came to be known as La Mota de Don Filfarrias (la mota meaning "a grove of trees"), which eventually evolved into La Mota de Don Falfurrias and was finally shortened to Falfurrias.

A post office under that name began operation in 1898. The Falfurrias *Facts* began publication in 1906. In 1911 the state granted a petition by local residents to form a new county, with Falfurrias as the county seat. Lasater established a creamery operation in 1909; he imported purebred Jersey dairy cattle to his ranch and eventually built what was said to be the largest Jersey herd in the world. Falfurrias butter is renowned. Irrigation, introduced during the late 1920s, brought in truck farming and the citrus fruit industry, with Falfurrias as the shipping center. The discovery of extensive oil and gas reserves around Falfurrias in the 1930s and 1940s added a new dimension to the town's growth and prosperity. Falfurrias had a population of 2,500 in 1925 and 7,500 by 1970. In the late 1980s the population was just over 6,500. Falfurrias continues to be a business center for the area's dairy, agricultural, and oil and gas industries. In 1990 the population was 5,788.

BIBLIOGRAPHY: *A Brief History of Falfurrias, The Land of Heart's Delight* (Falfurrias, Texas: Falfurrias Jersey Dairy, 1912). Dale Lasater, *Falfurrias: Ed C. Lasater and the Development of South Texas* (College Station: Texas A&M University Press, 1985). Dale Lasater

FALK, BIBB AUGUSTUS (1899–1989). Bibb Augustus (Jockey) Falk, major league baseball player and longtime baseball coach at the University of Texas at Austin, was born in Austin on January 27, 1899. As a boy he sold peanuts and worked as a batboy at the local Texas League qv ballpark. He graduated from high school in 1916 and enrolled at the University of Texas in 1917. He played football well enough to earn All–Southwest Conference honors as a tackle in 1919 but became even better known as a baseball player under William J. (Uncle Billy) Disch.qv Falk was undefeated as a pitcher and batted over .400 in all three of his varsity seasons, thus leading the Longhorns to a 57-14-1 record overall (29-3 in Southwest Conference play) and three conference championships.

In the summer of 1920 Falk signed with the Chicago White Sox, who gave him a $3,500 contract. The Sox, defending American League champions, offered to send him to the minor leagues, where he would be assured of playing regularly, but he elected to stay with the "big club" instead. He saw no action until just before the end of the season, in September, when the Black Sox scandal was revealed and eight Chicago players were banished for throwing games. Falk replaced the great Joe Jackson in left field and gave a hint of his batting prowess to come, by batting .294 in two games.

During the 1920s Falk became one of the best hitters in the American League, though he lacked the home-run power of contemporaries like Babe Ruth and Lou Gehrig. He also earned the nickname "Jockey" for the way he mercilessly "rode" opposing players. Falk became a regular in 1921 and batted .285 with eighty-two runs batted in; the next season he batted .298 with twelve home runs and seventy-nine runs batted in. After the 1922 season he accompanied a group of major league stars on a barnstorming tour of Japan, China, Korea, the Philippines, and Hawaii. In 1923 he batted .307, beginning a streak that saw him top the .300 mark in eight of his last nine major league seasons. In 1924 he finished third in the American League with a .352 batting average and after the season toured Europe with the White Sox and the New York Giants of the National League. Falk fell to a .301 mark in 1925, but drove in ninety-nine runs for the second year in a row; that season also marked the major league debut of his younger brother Chet, a pitcher who spent three mediocre seasons with the St. Louis Browns of the American League. Falk enjoyed his best statistical season in 1926, with a .345 batting average, eight home runs, and 108 runs batted in, and led American League outfielders in fielding percentage. He batted .327 in 1927, but in 1928 managed only a .290 average in ninety-eight games. Following that season the White Sox traded him to the Cleveland Indians for catcher Chick Autry. In 1929, his last year as a regular, Falk rebounded to bat .312 with a career-high thirteen home runs and ninety-three runs batted in. For the next two years he saw only parttime duty, but batted .325 and .304 and earned a reputation as the best pinch-hitter in the league.

In 1932 Falk served as player-manager for the Toledo Mud Hens of the American Association; as such he batted .321 as a part-timer. After the season he retired from active play. He spent the 1933 and 1934 seasons coaching for the Indians and for the Boston Red Sox, respectively, and in 1935 returned to Austin as a scout for the Red Sox.

In April 1940 he replaced Disch after the first conference game of the season, when a heart ailment forced Uncle Billy to step down as coach. Falk led the Longhorns to their twentieth conference championship in 1940 and to another pennant the following year; in 1942, however, Texas A&M University beat Texas in the last game of the season to win the Southwest Conference qv title.

Falk enlisted in the Army Air Corps in September 1942 and was stationed at Randolph Field in San Antonio, where he coached a service-league championship baseball team and served as trainer for the Randolph Ramblers football team, one of the best in the country. He returned to the University of Texas in 1946 and guided the Longhorns to three straight conference titles. In 1949 and 1950 Texas became the first college team to win back-to-back national championships.

Falk remained at Texas until 1967, compiling a 478-176 record (278-84 in the Southwest Conference). During his twenty-five years as coach the Longhorns won fifteen conference titles outright and tied for five more, and Falk's crusty demeanor and salty vocabulary became legendary. Once, when asked to assess the potential of a young player, Falk responded, "You can't make chicken salad out of chicken [bleep]." Several years later, after his retirement, Falk and his successor as Texas coach, Cliff Gustafson, were discussing the changes in the sport over the years. Gustafson asked Falk what he thought he would hit against modern pitching. Falk paused, then replied, "Oh, about .270 or .280." Gustafson, surprised by Falk's uncharacteristic modesty, asked, "There's that much difference?" "Hell, no," Falk answered. "But I'm seventy-five years old."

Falk was elected to the Longhorn Hall of Honor in 1962, the Helms Athletic Foundation College Hall of Fame in 1966, the College Baseball Hall of Fame in 1968, and the Texas Baseball Hall of Fame in 1988. In 1975 the University of Texas honored Falk and his former mentor by naming its new baseball stadium Disch-Falk Field. Falk was hospitalized with a heart ailment in May 1989 and died on June 8 of that year in Brackenridge Hospital, Austin.

BIBLIOGRAPHY: *Daily Texan*, August 13, 1948. Wilbur Evans and Bill Little, *Texas Longhorn Baseball: Kings of the Diamond* (Huntsville, Alabama: Strode, 1983). Bill Little, "The Bibb Falk Story," *Texas Longhorns Stampede*, March 1989. John Thorn and Pete Palmer, *Total Baseball* (New York: Warner, 1989). Vertical Files, Barker Texas History Center, University of Texas at Austin. Martin Donell Kohout

FALL BRANCH. Fall Branch rises a mile north of Interstate Highway 10 in the hills of the eastern Edwards Plateau qv in southwestern Gillespie County (at 30°12′ N, 99°16′ W) and runs south for about seven miles to its mouth on Johnson Creek, in north central Kerr County (at 30°07′ N, 99°17′ W). The stream, which is intermittent in its upper reaches, traverses flat terrain surfaced by shallow loamy and clayey soils that support grasses and open stands of live oak and Ashe juniper.

FALL CREEK (Blanco County). Fall Creek rises at the foot of Shovel Mountain, about four miles north of the Cypress Mill community in far northeastern Blanco County (at 30°27' N, 98°14' W), and runs east for 10½ miles through Hill Country^{qv} terrain to its mouth on the Pedernales River, in western Travis County (at 30°24' N, 98°07' W). The stream runs through scattered stands of live oak, mesquite, and Ashe juniper trees; the soil along its banks is loamy. Limestone and granitic outcroppings of the Llano Uplift mark the terrain.

_____ (Hamilton County). Fall Creek rises two miles north of Fairy in northeastern Hamilton County (at 31°52' N, 98°01' W) and runs northeast for seven miles to its mouth on the North Bosque River, in Bosque County just past the Hamilton county line (at 31°57' N, 97°57' W). It traverses flat to rolling terrain with local escarpments, surfaced by deep, fine sandy loam that supports hardwoods, brush, and grasses.

_____ (Hood County). Fall Creek rises about three miles west of Cresson in extreme northeastern Hood County (at 32°33' N, 97°41' W) and runs south for fifteen miles to its mouth on the Brazos River, at the North Arm of DeCordova Bend (at 32°23' N, 97°39' W). About half a mile north of the Brazos River, Fall Creek passes between Fall Creek Cemetery and the El Tesoro Campfire Girls Camp. The creek, intermittent at its source, runs through undulating terrain with shallow to moderately deep loamy soils. Stony and shallow soils limits the land's potential for farming and residential use, so it is used for range. Junipers, sumacs, and mesquites grow beside the creek, which runs mainly through open prairie.

_____ (San Saba County). Fall Creek rises about six miles southeast of Cherokee in southeastern San Saba County (at 30°55' N, 98°36' W) and meanders east along the San Saba-Llano county line for seventeen miles to its mouth on the northern end of Lake Buchanan (at 30°55' N, 98°27' W). The creek, which is intermittent in its upper reaches, traverses flat to rolling uplands with live oak, Ashe juniper, and grasses growing in shallow and stony clayey soils.

FALLON, TEXAS. Fallon, at the junction of Farm roads 39 and 1953, six miles northwest of Personville in eastern Limestone County, was established in the late 1870s when M. B. Cox opened a general store there. The community became a flag stop on the Texas and New Orleans Railroad in 1906, when the Mexia-Nelleva cutoff was built; the cutoff was discontinued in the 1930s. O. E. Williams opened a business at Fallon that became the community center in 1915. In 1933 Fallon had three businesses and fifty residents. By 1948 the community had one business and a number of scattered dwellings. Its population had dropped to forty by 1967, and the settlement was made part of the Mexia Independent School District in 1968. A 1983 map showed a church and cemetery at Prairie Grove, a mile southwest of Fallon, which was still listed as a community in 1990, though without census figures.
Stephanie Panus

FALLS CITY, TEXAS. Falls City, a mile southeast of the Wilson county line and seven miles northwest of Karnes City in northern Karnes County, owes its development to the railroad. Two earlier communities, Marcelina and Home Valley, had been located in the vicinity in the 1850s and 1860s, but people were not induced to settle the area until 1886, when the San Antonio and Aransas Pass Railway built a switch and depot called Brackenridge, named after railroad benefactor George W. Brackenridge.^{qv} To provide postal service for the settlement that developed, the post office of Skiles was established a mile west of the depot in 1887. On November 28, 1893, it was moved closer to the tracks on the east side of the river, where it was consolidated with Brackenridge and renamed Falls City, after several nearby natural waterfalls. On June 25, 1893, a train robbery at Brackenridge resulted in the only hanging at Karnes City, the new county seat. In 1895 Falls City had one general store, a post office, two saloons, a lumberyard, a hotel, a depot, two livery stables, and a steam mill and gin. The principal place of business was the Schulz Mercantile Company, which operated in a large brick building until it burned down in 1935. The site was later occupied by the Falls City National Bank.

A number of people from Panna Maria and Cestohowa moved to Falls City, where they could receive the benefits of a railroad. As a result Falls City became a predominantly Polish-American settlement. In 1902 Holy Trinity Catholic Church was erected; a parish school opened in 1911. In 1924 the Columbian Hall was built for the Knights of Columbus;^{qv} it was replaced by the Falls City Community Hall in 1983. In 1931 a new Catholic school, built for $4,000, enrolled 100 students. In 1938 a public school was built, and a high school was added in 1950. Polish-American farmers east and west of the town did most of their trading at Falls City, which incorporated on September 28, 1946. The discovery of oil helped the town to grow. After the discovery of uranium in 1958 near Tordilla Hill, ten miles west of Falls City, uranium mining and milling developed. In the mid-1970s the town was seriously divided over the uranium mines, which were said to contaminate the land and water. Businessmen wanted the mines to continue operation, but farmers did not. The conflict continued in the 1990s. By 1993 the uranium activity, except for a multimillion-dollar reclamation project by federal authorities, was all but over. In 1993 Falls City had a mayor-council form of government and a population of 478.

BIBLIOGRAPHY: Hedwig Krell Didear, *A History of Karnes County and Old Helena* (Austin: San Felipe, 1969). *Karnes County Centennial* (Karnes City, Texas, 1954). Robert H. Thonhoff, History of Karnes County (M.A. thesis, Southwest Texas State College, 1963). Vertical Files, Barker Texas History Center, University of Texas at Austin.
Robert H. Thonhoff

FALLS COUNTY. Falls County (H–18) is located in Central Texas and is surrounded by Limestone, Robertson, Milam, Bell, and McLennan counties. Marlin, the largest town and county seat, is 24 miles south of Waco and 121 miles south of Dallas. The county's center lies at 31°15' north latitude and 96°54' west longitude. Falls County covers 765 square miles in the Blackland Prairie region. The gently rolling terrain consists of broad flatlands, with elevations ranging from 300 to 500 feet, and the Brazos River bisects the county. Over 70 percent of the county contains upland clayey and loamy soil used primarily for pasture and cultivated crops. The rest of the area has deep loamy or sandy and loamy soil which is used for specialized crops such as tomatoes and watermelons. The main natural resource is the land, but there are a few oil and gas wells. Mineral artesian wells in Marlin have made it a health center. Temperatures range from an average high of 93° F in July to an average low of 39° in January. The average yearly rainfall is slightly less than thirty-four inches and the growing season lasts 257 days.

The falls of the Brazos River have long been an important fording and camping area for Indians and white settlers. The first Americans in the area were sent in 1819 by Dr. James Long to establish a trading house. Because of problems with the Mexican government they did not stay long. In 1825 the area was included in the empresario^{qv} grant to Robert Leftwich^{qv} of the Texas Association, a group from Nashville, Tennessee, which sought permission from the Mexican government to settle in Texas. Colonization did not take place at that time, however. Until 1829 the falls area did not have a permanent Indian settlement but served as hunting grounds for several tribes, including Wacos, Tawakonis, and Anadarkos, who were often attacked from the north by the stronger Comanches. The Cherokees arrived in the early 1830s, after the other Indians had been weakened by internal wars in 1829–30. The Cherokees were alone in the area until 1834–35, when Sterling C. Robertson^{qv} began bringing American settlers to his Nashville colony (later called Robertson's colony^{qv}). Although it was illegal under new laws passed by the Mexican government, nine families had settled in the area by 1830. In 1833 Robertson established the capital of his Nashville colony and called it Sarahville de Viesca.qv At this time problems with the Indians were exacerbated by clashes with the Mexicans, and in 1835 the settlers prepared for war with Mexico. The change of name from Fort Viesca to Fort Milam reflected the shift away from Mexico. In early 1836 all the settlers fled during the Runaway Scrape,qv giving Viesca the name of "the town that died overnight." After the battle of San Jacintoqv families returned to the area, but Fort Milam never reached its former importance except as the head of the Brazos military operations against the Indians. By 1837–38 the Marlin family returned to Bucksnort, near Fort Milam, along with the Morgan family. By this time Indians had become a constant threat. In June 1837 several men were attacked and one killed. On January 1, 1839, the women and children at Morgan Point, the home of the Morgans, were killed in what came to be called Morgan's Massacre. On January 10 the same group of Indians attacked Fort Marlin and were repulsed. Six days later the men from Bucksnort attacked the Indians; each side lost ten men, but the Indians won the encounter. Later that year the Texas legislature authorized men to patrol the region, and conflicts with Indians soon ceased. Peace was officially declared in 1845.

On January 28, 1850, the state legislature formed Falls County from Limestone and Milam counties. The falls of the Brazos gave the county its name. Since Falls County was established its boundaries have not changed. The legislature stipulated that Viesca would be the county seat, but the citizens petitioned for another location because most of the residents lived east of the Brazos River. The citizens voted 20–0 in favor of Adams, which officially became the county seat on January 30, 1851. Soon after, the town was renamed Marlin in honor of the Marlin family. The settlers of Falls County came from the slaveholding South, primarily Mississippi, Tennessee, and Alabama. By the census of 1860 the county had 1,716 slaves (47 percent of the total population) and 504 farms. Falls County relied less on cotton than other Texas counties, harvesting only 2,030 bales in 1860, and relied instead on a diverse agricultural economy. Wool was a major crop, with 17,500 pounds produced in 1860, the highest in Falls County history. Cattle was the most important livestock, with 26,310, a total not matched until 1900.

Falls County approved secessionqv almost unanimously in 1861. The only dissenters were two prominent slaveholders. Almost 600 men, twice the voting population, fought for the Confederacy, and many lost their lives. Because of the distance from the occupied areas of the Confederacy, many refugees fled to Falls County. Some paused only briefly on their way to Mexico. Between 1860 and 1870 the white population grew from 3,614 to 16,240 while the black population went from 1,716 to 4,681. At the same time the number of farms went down 35 percent. Reconstructionqv was not as painful in Falls County as in other areas. The only person who could be considered a carpetbaggerqv was District Judge J. W. Oliver, who was appointed by Governor Edmund J. Davis.qv During his tenure he called in black troops, which caused unrest in the county. George Elam, a Republican, was elected county judge in 1871 and 1873, perhaps with the help of the enfranchised freedmen. He could not be considered an outsider, however, since he fought in the Confederate army from Falls County. At the beginning of his term county taxes rose drastically. In 1876 Falls County was totally "redeemed" from Republican rule with the election of E. C. Stewart, a former slaveholder, who had owned thirty-nine slaves valued at $31,200 in 1864. After Reconstruction the county voted Democratic longer than most Texas counties. In 1872 the Republicans carried Falls County by only twenty-four votes, 50.7 percent of the total, due to the enfranchisement of blacks. After that, the county did not vote Republican in a presidential election for a century. The Democrats won 82 percent of the vote in the 1876 election. Falls County returned Democratic majorities in every election until Richard Nixon's victory over liberal Democrat George McGovern in 1972. The county then returned to its Democratic practices, voting overwhelmingly for Jimmy Carter in 1976 and 1980. County voters helped Republican Ronald Reagan win Texas in 1984 but returned to the Democratic party in 1988 and 1992.

Between 1880 and 1930 Falls County prospered, and its population gradually increased from 16,238 to 38,771. The economy remained primarily agricultural with diverse crops and livestock raising. The number of farms rose from 2,492 in 1880 to 6,014 in 1930. During this period cotton rose steadily from 12,495 to 61,989 bales, the largest crop ever. Five times as much poultry was raised by 1930, and corn rose from 376,555 to 1,110,376 bushels. The black population doubled during this fifty-year period but failed to keep pace with the white population. Blacks comprised 41 percent of the population in 1880 but only 32 percent by 1930. The black population and white population remained on good terms, and in 1882 a black county commissioner, Nelson Denson, was elected.

Transportation in Falls County relied on stagecoach lines and private transportation until the Reconstruction era. Until the middle 1880s cattle were driven up to the Waco area to connect with the Chisholm Trail.qv The Houston and Texas Central Railroad became the first railroad through the county around 1870. It passed through Marlin and led to the establishment of the towns of Reagan and Perry. Two other railroads eventually passed through the county. When the San Antonio and Aransas Pass Railway came through in 1890–92 it led to the founding of Rosebud, Travis, Lott, Chilton, and Satin, which in turn resulted in a shift of the county's population from east to west. In 1902 the Missouri Pacific passed through Marlin, and the towns of Eloise, Highbank, McClanahan, and Otto soon grew up along the line. The first automobile appeared in the county in 1904. By 1927 the road which eventually became U.S. Highway 77 became a state highway. In 1930 the other major road in the county became State Highway 7. In 1915 an airport shed was built to house three airplanes. Promoters put on an airshow near Marlin, but it was closed one year later when a female pilot was killed in a crash. Marlin was the largest town, with a population of 4,000, just over 10 percent of the county's total population. Most residents lived in rural areas or small towns. From 1880 to 1920 the number of manufacturing establishments increased from twelve to thirty-four employing 100 people. By 1930 the number dropped to eight establishments employing 118 people. Hot mineral springs were discovered in 1891 in Marlin, which became a major health resort in the early twentieth century.

The years of the Great Depression and World War IIqqv brought about significant changes in Falls County. The population dropped by 8 percent, the first decline since the formation of the county. The ratio of blacks to whites remained the same. The depression caused a 64 percent drop in the number of farms, and the value of the farms dropped 55 percent. Cotton dropped 57 percent, and corn dropped to less than 1 percent of its earlier high. Hog raising remained steady, while cattle and sheep raising increased 25 and 61 percent, respectively. Falls County continued to feel the effects of the depression and had a slow recovery from 1950 to 1982. The population decreased steadily until 1970, when it levelled off at 17,000. The county gained 646 people between 1970 and 1980, and the percentage of blacks dropped from the 32 percent level it had maintained for sixty years to 27 percent. In 1990 there were 17,712 county residents. The number of cattle reached its highest point of 106,807 in 1982, while the numbers of hogs and sheep dropped to an insignificant number. The decrease in farms continued until there were only 1,117 in 1982. Cotton became insignificant and corn returned almost to its predepression level, but wheat and grain sorghum became major crops, each with over a million bushels. Manufacturing establishments averaged around twelve during this period and employed the most people in 1967 before declining once again. Fertilizer, farming equipment, and supplies were the main manufactured goods. The mineral water in Marlin remained an important industry. Manufacturing went from 8 percent of employment in 1965 to 19 percent in 1986. Retail trade remained at around 35 percent and services around 29 percent during the same time period.

Although the automobile became an important mode of transportation, State Highway 6 was the only major highway built after 1930. In 1982 the total public road mileage was 1,179 miles. In 1974 Falls County had 6,944 registered vehicles and by 1982 there were 17,422. Marlin Oil Company installed the first electric generator in Marlin in the early 1890s, but it was only available to a few homes and businesses. Education improved drastically over three decades. In 1950 only 13 percent of those over twenty-five were high school graduates; by 1980 that number had risen to 42 percent. In 1982 an estimated 11,901 residents (65 percent) belonged to one of the fifty-three churches in the county, primarily Southern Baptist, Catholic, and Methodist. Marlin had two cab companies, an intercity bus service, and a municipal airport. The county had three newspapers, one radio station, two libraries, and nine parks containing 717 acres. Every spring Festival days are held in Marlin.

BIBLIOGRAPHY: Walter W. Brawn, The History of Falls County (M.A. thesis, Baylor University, 1938). Old Settlers and Veterans Association of Falls County, *History of Falls County, Texas* (Marlin?, Texas, 1947). Falls County Historical Commission, *Families of Falls County* (Austin: Eakin Press, 1987). Lillian S. St. Romain, *Western Falls County, Texas* (Austin: Texas State Historical Association, 1951).

Lisa C. Maxwell

FALLS CREEK (Garza County). Falls Creek rises a mile northeast of Pleasant Valley in northwestern Garza County (at 33°15′ N, 101°27′ W) and runs east for eight miles to its mouth on the North Fork of the Double Mountain Fork of the Brazos River (at 33°16′ N, 101°22′ W). The stream passes through moderately steep slopes with high local relief, surfaced by shallow to moderately deep silt loams that support mesquite and grasses.

FALLS PRONG. Falls Prong (Fall Creek) rises about 1½ miles east of the Gillespie-Kimble county line in western Gillespie County (at 30°21′ N, 99°16′ W) and runs northwest for ten miles to its mouth on the Little Devils River, six miles northeast of Noxville (at 30°25′ N, 99°21′ W). The creek is generally free-flowing for six miles, from Falls Prong Spring to its mouth. Once called Fall Creek, Falls Prong was probably named after a waterfall located 3½ miles upstream.

Anthony B. Gaxiola

FAMULINER, TEXAS. Famuliner, eight miles southeast of Morton in north central Cochran County, is named after an area ranch family. It was organized in the 1940s and by 1965 had a gin and a community center. Famuliner was listed as a community in 1990, but without census figures.

BIBLIOGRAPHY: Elvis Eugene Fleming, *Texas' Last Frontier: A History of Cochran County* (Morton, Texas: Cochran County Historical Society, 1965).

Melissa G. Wiedenfeld

FANCHER, TEXAS. Fancher, southwest of the site of what is now Seymour in western Baylor County, served as a stop for the Wichita Valley line after the train built through the area in 1908. A school was built in 1918 on land given by Alex Fancher, for whom the community was apparently named, and remained active until 1929. The community still functioned as a railroad station in the early 1950s, although 1980 county maps gave no evidence of its former location.

BIBLIOGRAPHY: Baylor County Historical Society, *Salt Pork to Sirloin*, Vol. 1: *The History of Baylor County, Texas, from 1879 to 1930* (Quanah, Texas: Nortex, 1972); Vol. 2: *The History of Baylor County, Texas, from 1878 to Present* (1977).

Charles G. Davis

FANDANGO CREEK. Fandango Creek rises half a mile southeast of Escobas Ranch in eastern Zapata County (at 27°02′ N, 98°59′ W) and runs southwest for six miles to its mouth on Arroyo Carrizales, half a mile southwest of La Cabrada Tank (at 26°57′ N, 99°03′ W). The stream traverses terrain that varies from low-rolling hills and prairies to flat land with locally active dune blowout areas. Local soils include clay and sandy loams and sands that support grasses, some mesquite, and chaparral.

FANNETT, TEXAS. Fannett is at the junction of State Highway 124 and Farm Road 365, fifteen miles southwest of Beaumont in western Jefferson County. It was named after B. J. (Frangel) Fannett, an early landowner. The nucleus of the community was formed when Fannett and Joe Dugal opened a general store on the Gulf and Interstate Railway during the mid-1890s. The two men secured a post office in 1899. Extensive irrigation and drainage networks were established to facilitate agricultural efforts in the area. The community served as a center for local rice farmers and ranchers, and the population was estimated to be seventy-five in 1925. Although Fannett lost its post office in 1928, the discovery of the Fannett oilfield to the south in 1927 and the Gilbert Ranch oilfield to the northwest in 1958 diversified the local economy. Nonetheless, the community's population has remained small, and the Fannett Independent School District was consolidated with the Hamshire district in 1961. Approximately 100 residents lived at Fannett during the mid-1980s. In 1990 the population was 105.

Robert Wooster

FANNIN, JAMES WALKER, JR. (1804–1836). James Walker Fannin, Jr., Texas revolutionary, was probably born on January 1, 1804, in Georgia, the son of Dr. Isham Fannin. He was adopted by his maternal grandfather, James W. Walker, and brought up on a plantation near Marion. He entered the United States Military Academy at West Point on July 1, 1819, under the name James F. Walker, but withdrew in November 1821. He returned to Georgia and several years later married Minerva Fort, with whom he had two daughters. In the autumn of 1834 he and his family moved to Texas and settled at Velasco, where he supposedly was a plantation owner. His letters affirm the fact that he was a slave trader.

Fannin became an agitator for the Texas Revolution[qv] and on August 20, 1835, was appointed by the Committee of Safety and Correspondence of Columbia to use his influence for the calling of the Consultation.[qv] On August 27 he wrote to a United States Army officer in Georgia requesting financial aid for the Texas cause and West Point officers to command the Texas army. In September Fannin became active in the volunteer army and subscribed money to an expedition to capture the *Veracruzana*, a Mexican ship at Copano; but the expedition did not materialize, and Fannin went to Gonzales, where, as captain of the Brazos Guards, he participated in the battle of Gonzales[qv] on October 2, 1835. On October 6 he was one of a committee urging Stephen F. Austin[qv] to bring all possible aid to Gonzales, and when Austin brought up the whole Texas army and moved toward Bexar, James Bowie[qv] and Fannin were sent as scouts to determine conditions between Gonzales and Bexar and to secure supplies. On October 27 Bowie and Fannin selected a campsite near Nuestra Señora de la Purísima Concepción de Acuña Mission and on October 28 led the Texas forces in the battle of Concepción.[qv]

On November 10 Fannin was ordered to cut a Mexican supply route between Laredo and San Antonio but returned to headquarters when he was not joined by a supporting force. On November 13 Sam Houston,[qv] commander in chief of the regular army, offered Fannin the position of inspector general, but Fannin received an honorable discharge from the volunteer army on November 22 and began an urgent campaign for a larger regular army. On December 5 the General Council,[qv] acting on Fannin's advice, established an auxiliary volunteer corps. Houston commissioned Fannin as a colonel in the regular army on December 7, and on December 10 the council ordered him to enlist reinforcements for the army and to contract for war supplies in the campaign against Bexar. Bexar had surrendered on December 9, so the accumulated supplies were used in the 1836 campaign.

Continuing as an agent of the provisional government,[qv] Fannin, on January 9, 1836, began recruiting volunteers for the Matamoros expedition.^qv After Houston withdrew from the expedition, Fannin was elected colonel of the Provisional Regiment of Volunteers at Goliad on February 7 and from February 12 to March 12 acted as commander in chief of the army. When he learned that the Mexicans under José de Urrea^qv had occupied Matamoros, Fannin went no further with plans for the expedition and fell back to strengthen defenses at Goliad. Other elements of the expedition, under James Grant and Francis W. Johnson,^qqv were destroyed by Urrea, who then proceeded to attack Goliad. On March 12 Fannin dispatched most of his force to aid Texans near Refugio. On March 14 he received Houston's order to retreat to Victoria, which rescinded a previous order to relieve the Alamo.^qv Waiting for the forces under Amon B. King and William Ward^qqv to return from Refugio, Fannin delayed retreating until he heard of their capture. On March 19 he began his retreat, but he and his men were surrounded and forced to surrender at the battle of Coleto.^qv The Texans were imprisoned by the Mexicans at Goliad and subsequently murdered by order of Antonio López de Santa Anna^qv on March 27, 1836. Fannin, because he was wounded, was shot separately at the mission on the same day.

In the months leading up to the Goliad Massacre,^qv Fannin had shown defects as a commander. Accustomed to the discipline of a regular army, he adapted poorly to his situation as head of volunteers. He scorned the idea of electing officers and was disturbed by the lack of a clearly established hierarchy among his forces. His arrogance and ambition earned him the contempt of many of the men under his command. One private, J. G. Ferguson, wrote in a letter to his brother: "I am sorry to say that the majority of the soldiers don't like [Fannin]. For what cause I don't know whether it is because they think he has not the interest of the country at heart or that he wishes to become great without taking the proper steps to attain greatness." In his final weeks, Fannin wrote repeatedly asking to be relieved of his command. Most historians now agree that Fannin made many serious mistakes as a commander. But despite his reluctance to carry on and his sometimes poor military judgment, he held out bravely until the end. Fannin County was named in his honor, as were the town of Fannin in Goliad County and Camp Fannin,^qv a United States Army installation. *See also* GOLIAD CAMPAIGN OF 1835, GOLIAD CAMPAIGN OF 1836.

BIBLIOGRAPHY: Harbert Davenport, "Men of Goliad," *Southwestern Historical Quarterly* 43 (July 1939). Harbert Davenport, Notes from an Unfinished Study of Fannin and His Men (MS, Harbert Davenport Collection, Texas State Library, Austin; Barker Texas History Center, University of Texas at Austin). Stephen L. Hardin, *Texian Iliad: A Military History of the Texas Revolution, 1835–1836* (Austin: University of Texas Press, 1994). Jeff Long, *Duel of Eagles: The Mexican and U.S. Fight for the Alamo* (New York: Morrow, 1990). Ruby C. Smith, "James W. Fannin, Jr., in the Texas Revolution," *Southwestern Historical Quarterly* 23 (October 1919, January, April 1920).
Clinton P. Hartmann

FANNIN, TEXAS. Fannin, on U.S. Highway 59 ten miles from Goliad in eastern Goliad County, is named for James W. Fannin, Jr.,^qv the controversial commander of Fort Defiance (La Bahía^qv) at Goliad in the Texas Revolution.^qv The settlement, on Perdido Creek near the site of Fannin's defeat in 1836 in the battle of Coleto,^qv was established sometime before 1852. The first post office, which operated from 1852 to 1856, was called Fanning's Defeat, "Fanning" being the common corruption of the commander's name. The town's name had been changed to Perdido, Spanish for "lost," by the time the second post office was established in 1873. Benson Goff, whose general store provided the community's focus, was postmaster. A combination steam gin and gristmill was built as cotton became important, and a school, a church, and daily stages to Victoria and Goliad served the fifty residents listed in 1884.

Although Perdido was on the Victoria-Goliad road, the Gulf, Western Texas and Pacific Railway was routed a mile to the south in 1889. The new depot was called Fannin. Cattle pens were built, and Perdido residents began moving to the railhead. Among them was Goff, whose new store housed Fannin's post office, established in 1890. The Goliad-Victoria road was rerouted through the new site as well. The town grew quickly, to 100 people in 1896, 200 in 1914, and 300 by 1925. A cotton gin, a flour mill, two saloons, a hotel, a dance hall, a jail, a blacksmith's shop, and a number of other businesses served the community, which in the early 1900s was an important livestock shipping center. A Methodist church was established in 1903; Catholic and black Baptist churches followed.

During a feud in which Taylor Drake and Ed Calliet opposed Frank Hall in 1911, a stray bullet punctured an oil cookstove in the saloon, thus igniting a fire that destroyed most of the town. Rebuilding was minimal. By 1933 the population had declined to about 100, a figure that remained constant for the next fifty years. The Fannin school closed in 1944, and students were bused to Goliad. The railroad stock pens were removed, as ranchers shipped by truck, and the cotton gin was torn down in the 1930s or 1940s. The Hanley Hotel operated continuously from 1890 to 1950, though in its later years it was known primarily for its restaurant. In 1986 the post office, located in the town's single store, served ninety-four residents. Fannin Battlefield State Park^qv is located less than a mile south of town. In 1990 the population of Fannin was 105.

BIBLIOGRAPHY: Goliad County Historical Commission, *The History and Heritage of Goliad County*, ed. Jakie L. Pruett and Everett B. Cole (Austin: Eakin Press, 1983).
Craig H. Roell

FANNIN BATTLEGROUND STATE HISTORIC SITE. Fannin Battleground State Historic Site, formerly called Fannin State Park, is located less than a mile south of U.S. Highway 59 at Fannin, Texas, in eastern Goliad County. The site encompasses the grounds of the battle of Coleto,^qv fought in 1836 during the Texas Revolution^qv between the Texan force under James W. Fannin, Jr.,^qv and the Mexican army under José de Urrea.^qv The defeated Texans surrendered at this site on March 20, 1836, and later were executed in the Goliad Massacre^qv (see also GOLIAD STATE HISTORIC PARK). The battlefield site was marked originally with a pile of rocks placed by William L. Hunter,^qv one of Fannin's men who survived the battle and escaped execution at Goliad. On October 15, 1891, Solomon Parks, Sr., of Goliad replaced the rocks with a massive iron screw from a cotton gin. Two yokes of oxen and a crew of men were necessary to transport and erect the new marker. In 1913 Mr. and Mrs. H. B. Hanley of Fannin donated the land for the park, which was established through the efforts of Leopold Morris of Victoria, then a member of the state legislature; Mrs. L. G. Kreisle and the Fannin chapter of the Daughters of the Republic of Texas;^qv and Goliad County officials. John Henry Kirby^qv of Houston joined Morris in introducing the bill in the legislature, and John H. Bailey of Cuero (later of Austin) secured passage in the state Senate. Governor O. B. Colquitt^qv signed the bill.

In 1914 the state built a rock wall around the park and set up a twenty-eight-foot grey-granite monument. Governor James Ferguson^qv attended the dedication of the park. In 1965 the thirteen-acre park was placed under the care of the Texas Parks and Wildlife Department^qv by act of the legislature. The gin screw now stands at the park entrance, and a small museum displays guns, implements, shot, and cannonballs exhumed at the site.

BIBLIOGRAPHY: Goliad County Historical Commission, *The History and Heritage of Goliad County*, ed. Jakie L. Pruett and Everett B. Cole (Austin: Eakin, 1983). Victoria *Advocate*, September 28, 1934.
Craig H. Roell

FANNIN COUNTY. Fannin County (B-19) is located in Northeast Texas on the Oklahoma border. Bonham, the county seat, is fifty-five miles northeast of Dallas. The center point of the county is at approximately 33°30′ north latitude and 96°10′ west longitude. Fannin County comprises 895 square miles of mainly blackland, with a claypan area in the north near the Red River. The topography has little variety, with ranges of moderately rolling hills throughout the county. Fannin County has an elevation ranging between 500 and 700 feet above sea level. The average annual rainfall is a little over forty-three inches. The land is drained by the Red River and Bois D'Arc Creek and is watered by numerous springs. The average minimum temperature in January is 33° F, and the average maximum in July is 94°. The growing season lasts 228 days. The natural flora consists of oak, hickory, ash, walnut, pecan, cottonwood, elm, cedar, and Bois D'Arc trees, as well as redbud, spicewood, dogwood, pawpaw, and dwarf buckeye. The main natural resource is timber; consequently, wood-product manufacture is important in the local economy.

When European explorers visited the region in 1687 they found it occupied by the Caddo Indians. By 1836, when white settlers first entered the area, no Indians inhabited the land. The Caddoes had joined a larger group known as the Cherokees and their Twelve Associated Bands. White settlers arrived by riverboat at Jonesboro in what is now Red River County. The pioneers crossed the river and established two early colonies. One, named Lexington, was located on the Red River and was headed by Dr. Daniel Rowlett.qv The other colony, begun by Daniel Slack, was on the east side of the middle Bois D'Arc Creek. Numerous other colonists quickly joined this initial band, and eighty-eight first-class land certificates had been granted before the Texas Declaration of Independence qv was signed in March 1836.

Because of rapid population growth, Rowlett presented a petition to the Texas Congress on October 5, 1837, requesting that a new county be formed from a section of Red River County west of Bois D'Arc Creek. The county was originally to be named Independence, but during the course of opening debates over the bill the name was changed to Fannin, in honor of James Walker Fannin, Jr.,qv a martyred hero of the Texas Revolution.qv The legislation, approved on December 14, 1837, designated the residence of Jacob Black the state house until a more suitable location could be found. The most significant act passed at Black's cabin was to approve the building of the first county road, from Rocky Ford Crossing to Daniel Montague'sqv plantation. The road passed through Fort Warren and bridged Bois D'Arc Creek. Other important legislation dealt with attempts to end Indian hostilities.

On November 28, 1839, another act was passed by Congress to define the boundaries of Fannin County, whcich at the time included land that later became Grayson, Collin, Cooke, Denton, Montague, Wise, Clay, Jack, Wichita, Archer, Young, Wilbarger, Baylor, Throckmorton, Hardeman, Foard, Knox, Haskell, Stonewall, King, Cottle, and Childress counties, as well as parts of Hunt and Collingsworth counties. The present-day boundaries were established and approved on March 14, 1846.

The development of Fannin County resulted from the efforts of several leaders. These included Bailey Inglish, John P. Simpson, Holland Coffee, Daniel Montague, Daniel Rowlett,qqv and Roswell W. Lee. The first successful center of commerce was Warren, a fort founded by Abel Warrenqv in 1836. The first courthouse, school, post office, and Masonic Lodge (Constantine No. 13) in Fannin County were in Warren. The first sermon delivered in Fannin County was preached in Warren by John B. Denton,qv a Methodist minister. The county government was moved from Black's cabin to Warren on January 8, 1840. The first district court for Fannin County was established at the same time. On April 27, 1840, Judge John M. Hansfordqv opened the first session in the new courthouse.

Bois D'Arc became county seat in turn on January 16, 1843, apparently for two reasons: the Indian threat at Warren, and a shift in political power that strengthened the Bois D'Arc community. Fort Warren no longer wielded significant influence on the development of the county after this move. In 1844 Bois D'Arc was renamed Bonham in honor of James Butler Bonham,qv a defender of the Alamo.

The inhabitants wanted the name to be changed to Bloomington, but the Texas legislature wanted to honor a war hero. Bonham has continued to be the major center of commerce for Fannin County.

The early settlers of Fannin County faced many difficulties with Indians, particularly with the Cherokees and their Twelve Associated Bands. The first skirmish took place on May 16, 1837, when settlers attacked a band of Indians made up of various groups. Tension had been mounting as the Indians grew less friendly with the rapid influx of white settlers and the resulting damage to hunting. The Indians retaliated with constant raids of their own in which settlers were killed and livestock stolen. Stories describe brutal attacks of Indians on cabins and travelers. Residents of Fannin County were infuriated particularly by the Indians' practice of mutilating dead bodies, and their indiscriminate killing of women and children. Skirmishes with the Indians continued over the next six years until the Treaty of Bird's Fort was signed by Edward H. Tarrant qv with the Tehuacanas, Keechis, Wacos, Caddoes, Anadarcos, and others. This treaty, for the most part, ended Indian hostilities.

Early settlers were predominantly from the South, particularly from Tennessee. The population of Fannin County grew to 9,217 by 1860; about 19 percent of the residents were black. The county depended upon agricultural products for its main means of support, with livestock, especially beef cattle, being the predominant product. Before the Civil Warqv the county had about 25,000 beef cattle; afterward the number was reduced by half.

The first church in the county was Rehobeth Chapel, built in 1850. Camp meetings had been held since 1840. Other early churches included the First United Methodist Church of Bonham (1844), Vineyard Grove Baptist Church (1847), and First Baptist Church of Bonham (1852). The county has remained overwhelmingly Protestant.

Numerous newspapers were started during the early years of the county. The Bonham *Sentinel*, the first to be published, began in July 1846. The *Northern Standard* was published in Bonham from a month later until April 1847 (*see* CLARKSVILLE STANDARD). Other early papers included the *Western Argus* (1847), the Bonham *Advertiser* (1849), the *Western Star* (1853), the Bonham *Independent* (1858), and the Bonham *Era* (1859).

The citizens of the county supported secession,qv despite a passionate speech for remaining in the Union given by state senator Robert H. Taylor.qv Fannin County supported the Confederate cause by raising several companies for the trans-Mississippi army. Taylor himself was elected colonel of a cavalry regiment. A Confederate commissary was located in Bonham, from where at least seven brigades drew supplies. A story has it that when a fire destroyed the commissary, which contained a large store of meat, the town turned out en masse to eat the accidental barbecue. More important than the commissary, the county hosted the military headquarters of the Northern Subdistrict of Texas, C.S.A., which was established by Gen. Henry E. McCulloughqv and located at the site of present-day Willow Wild Cemetery in Bonham. Finally, a Confederate hospital in Bonham housed many of the wounded soldiers during the war.

Fannin County grew steadily from the Civil War to the turn of the century. Agriculture remained the main source of income, with the number of farms increasing throughout the century, and crop production increasing as well. Cotton and corn were the two predominant crops. Numerous new businesses also were started after the war. Previously only five manufacturing establishments operated in the county; by 1870 factories numbered fifty-four, and new ones and continued to come into being. New newspapers included the Bonham *News* (1866), Honey Grove *Independent* (1873), Dodd City *Spectator* (1886), Bonham *Review* (1884), and Honey Grove *Simoon* (1884). The Fannin County Bank was chartered in 1872. The first railroad in the county, the Texas and Pacific, built an east–west track across the center of the county in 1873. Major communities received their first electricity in 1889. The first telephone exchange began in 1889.

Many schools and colleges were chartered during this time period.

The county school board, constituted in 1888, helped organize county efforts to school the children. Carlton College was established in 1867 in Bonham by Charles Carlton.qv Other schools included Ladonia Male and Female Instituteqv (1860), Paris District Honey Grove High School (1874), Savoy Male and Female Collegeqv (1876), Lone Pecan School for Boys and Girls (1879), Masonic Female Instituteqv (1881), and Fannin College (1883).

The population of Fannin County peaked in 1900 at 51,793 and slowly decreased afterward, with some fluctuations. Agriculture remained the main source of income. The chief crops were cotton and corn. Cotton production reached its highest level in 1920 with 65,154 bales. Corn production peaked in 1900 with 3,059,430 bushels. In 1900 the county had 7,202 farms, its highest number. Hogs and swine numbered 52,754 in 1900, also a record. Dairy farming had moderate success in the early part of the twentieth century. In 1920, the county fed 14,665 milk cows. The number of businesses in Fannin County peaked in 1900 also. In 1925 the Lone Star Gas company ran a gas main through the county, providing a new source of heat for residents. When aviation became practical, Fannin County residents raised money to build Jones Field near Bonham, in 1929. On December 31 of that year fire destroyed the bell tower of the county courthouse. Fortunately, no records were destroyed.

The Great Depressionqv in the 1930s caused economic hardship that lasted until World War II.qv In the 1920s and 1930s the population stabilized at around 41,000, but during the 1940s it dropped to 31,253. Businesses hit an all-time low of fifteen in 1947. The number employed in manufacturing dipped to 310 in 1929 and slowly recovered to 630 in 1947. Product value dropped dramatically in 1929 but then slowly increased. Agriculture was hit hard. The depression forced the average farm value to plummet 46 percent below its value in 1920. The number of milk cows dropped sharply in the 1920s, and an effort was made to prime the market in 1929 with financial benefits raised by local businesses. In 1934 the Kraft-Phoenix Cheese Company moved to Bonham and provided a market. By 1940 the number of milk cows had risen to 10,279, but during the 1940s the number began to decrease dramatically. The only livestock to show promise during this time were beef cattle. The number of cattle increased considerably in the 1930s and continued to increase slowly during the rest of the century.

The population dropped dramatically in the 1950s and continued a slow decline in the 1960s. Fannin County had only 22,705 people in 1970, fewer than its population in the 1880s. The county subsequently began a slow population increase, reaching 24,804 in the 1990 census. The educational level of the county gradually increased. In 1950 only 17 percent of residents had high school diplomas. In 1980, 45 percent were high school graduates.

Cotton production took a sharp decline during the 1950s, dropping by half to 24,928 bales in 1959. In 1987 only 337 bales were produced in the county. Corn steadily declined to only 496,557 bushels in 1987. Wheat, the only major agricultural product to increase in the late twentieth century in Fannin County, peaked in 1982 at 1,997,530 bushels. Peanuts and sorghum also increased production in the latter part of the twentieth century.

The number of farms steadily decreased after 1920, to only 1,533 in 1987. Stock farming moved from hogs and milk cattle to beef cattle. Swine production slowly declined in the twentieth century to only a little over a thousand hogs in the 1980s. By 1987, Fannin County had nearly 65,000 beef cattle but only a few thousand producing milk cows.

The number of manufacturing establishments increased from fifteen in 1947 to twenty-nine in 1958 and thirty-seven in 1987. the main commodities were in lumber and wood products. Banking and service businesses slowly increased from 1950 to 1990. Retail, wholesale, transportation, utilities, and construction businesses remained fairly stable during this time period. Overall product value peaked in 1982 at 58.5 million.

The citizens of Fannin County have remained strongly Democratic throughout their voting history, favoring this party in all the elections except three. County loyalty to the party in the twentieth century may be due in part to the influence and prestige of Samuel T. (Sam) Rayburn,qv a resident of Bonham who served as speaker of the House from 1940 to 1961. Bonham claims Rayburn as a favorite son. The county voted for Democrat Jimmy Carter instead of Ronald Reagan in 1980. The rare votes for other parties included a large Populist vote in 1892. Republicans gained victories in 1972, when a good majority voted for Richard Nixon and in 1984, when Ronald Reagan barely won a majority; but the county voted for Democratic candidates in 1988 and 1992.

Fannin County has remained rural and predominantly white. The racial proportions have been relatively stable, with blacks constituting between 10 and 20 percent of the population over the years of the county's history. The black population peaked in 1920 at 5,968 and afterward decreased to 1,633 by 1990. Bonham, the largest city in Fannin County, maintained a fairly constant population of about 7,000 in the twentieth century. Honey Grove, the next largest, remained stable in population at around two thousand.

BIBLIOGRAPHY: W. A. Carter, *History of Fannin County, Texas* (Bonham, Texas: Bonham *News*, 1885; rpt., Honey Grove, Texas: Fannin County Historical Society, 1975). *Fannin County Folks and Facts* (Dallas: Taylor, 1977). Floy Crandall Hodge, *A History of Fannin County* (Hereford, Texas: Pioneer, 1966). Tom Scott, *Fannin County: The Early Years* (Bonham, Texas: *Fannin County Genealogical Quarterly*, 1982). Rex Wallace Strickland, "History of Fannin County, Texas, 1836–1843," *Southwestern Historical Quarterly* 33, 34 (April, July 1930).

Kelly Pigott

FANNIN CREEK. Fannin Creek rises four miles southeast of Greenville in south central Hunt County (at 33°01′ N, 96°05′ W) and runs southeast for about 5½ miles to its mouth on Hickory Cove, part of Lake Tawakoni (at 32°58′ N, 96°02′ W). The stream traverses flat to rolling terrain surfaced with moderately deep to deep sandy and clay loams that support hardwood and grasses. For most of the county's history the Fannin Creek area has been used as crop and range land.

FANNIN-MIMS PLANTATION. The Fannin-Mims Plantation was located on the west bank of the San Bernard River four miles west of Brazoria, near the present Sportsman Span bridge in southwest Brazoria County. The plantation was jointly owned by Col. James Fannin, Jr., and Joseph Mimsqqv from 1834 until Fannin's death at Goliad in 1836. Fannin, who engaged in slave trading, provided slaves for the enterprise. After completing a five-year partnership contract, Mims acquired Fannin's portion of the property, built a mansion, and raised cotton. Mims's estate at his death in 1844 comprised 3,000 acres, thirty-nine slaves, sixty cattle, and 220 bales of cotton but was heavily encumbered with debt. After Mims's death, his widow, Sarah (Weekly), converted the plantation from cotton to sugar production. Between 1852 and 1858 she harvested five sugar crops, 368 hogsheads in 1852 alone. The estate continued to expand, and by 1860 had 700 improved acres and 103 slaves. In 1860 Sarah Mims reported real property assessed at $73,480 and personal property valued at $96,030, and the plantation produced 700 bushels of corn, 105 bales of cotton, and 65 hogsheads of sugar. The plantation's activities ceased with the Civil War.qv

BIBLIOGRAPHY: Randolph B. Campbell, *An Empire for Slavery: The Peculiar Institution in Texas, 1821–1865* (Baton Rouge: Louisiana State University Press, 1989).

Diana J. Kleiner

FANNIN STATE BATTLEGROUND COMMISSION. The Fannin State Battleground Commission, established in 1947, was composed of three members appointed by the governor for six-year overlapping terms; its responsibility was to advise the state Board of

Control qv about the care of the Fannin State Battleground. The commission was reorganized in 1965 as the Fannin State Park Advisory Commission, and control of the battleground was given to the Parks and Wildlife Commission. By the early 1980s the commission was defunct. *See* TEXAS PARKS AND WILDLIFE DEPARTMENT.

FANT, DILLARD RUCKER (1841–1908). Dillard Rucker Fant, Texas trail driver pioneer, was born on July 27, 1841, in the Anderson district of South Carolina, the son of W. N. and Mary (Burriss) Fant. In 1852 the family moved to Texas and settled at Goliad, where W. N. Fant established himself as a merchant and served as county judge. Dillard Rucker Fant began his career freighting with ox teams between Indianola, Goliad, and San Antonio. During the Civil War qv he enlisted in Col. George Washington Carver's qv Twenty-first Texas Cavalry and served in the Trans-Mississippi Department, seeing duty in Texas, Arkansas, and Louisiana and achieving the rank of orderly sergeant. After the war "Colonel" Fant returned to Goliad, where he married Lucy A. Hodges on October 15, 1865, and became a farmer and rancher. From 1867 to 1869 he drove cattle to Rockport, Texas, and sold them to packeries. Upon learning that some North Texas cattlemen drove small herds of cattle through Indian Territory to Kansas at good profit, he decided to redouble the effort by taking a large herd from Southwest Texas. He first went "up the trail" in 1869 and was so successful that others followed suite. In 1874 he began improving his cattle with Durham and Hereford stock. For fourteen years he held government contracts to supply thousands of beeves to various military posts and agencies in Dakota and Indian Territory and wintered herds on pastures in Nebraska, Wyoming, and Idaho. During the fifteen years he was in business he took between 175,000 and 200,000 cattle up the trail, reportedly never losing more than 3 percent. So extensive were his operations that he had several tremendous herds on the trail in a single season. In 1884 he employed 200 cowboys to drive one of the largest herds on record—42,000 cattle and requiring 1,200 saddle horses—to Kansas, Nebraska, and Wyoming. Though these cattle cost him from twelve to twenty dollars a head, he sold the stock for almost $1 million. He was still driving cattle as late as 1889, long after rail service had been extended northward from the Texas interior. Fant is credited with extending the Chisholm Trail qv to Corpus Christi and financing the construction of Texas public schools and railroads. By the 1890s his extensive Texas ranch holdings totalled 700,000 acres in Goliad, Refugio, Frio, Live Oak, Tarrant, and other counties and included the 225,000 Santa Rosa Ranch in Hidalgo County. Many cattlemen, such as George W. Saunders qv apprenticed with him and then became operators themsevles. Fant disposed of his cattle and land upon his retirement in April 1901 and moved to San Antonio's King William District. He is described as a large man of 262 pounds, "vigorous and healthy, with those special qualities that make the domestic circle delightful and happy." Fant died on January 15, 1908, while visiting in Goliad. Lucy Fant, his widow, died at her home in San Antonio in March 1909. During her lifetime she dispensed probably $200,000 in charity and devoted much work towards educating Mexicans.

BIBLIOGRAPHY: James Cox, *Historical and Biographical Record of the Cattle Industry* (2 vols., St. Louis: Woodward and Tiernan Printing, 1894, 1895; rpt., with an introduction by J. Frank Dobie, New York: Antiquarian, 1959). J. Marvin Hunter, *Trail Drivers of Texas* (2 vols., San Antonio: Jackson Printing, 1920, 1923; 4th ed., Austin: University of Texas Press, 1985). Hobart Huson, *Refugio: A Comprehensive History of Refugio County from Aboriginal Times to 1953* (2 vols., Woodsboro, Texas: Rooke Foundation, 1953, 1955). "Dillard R. Fant," *Pioneer*, September 1922.

Craig H. Roell

FANT, TEXAS. Fant, four miles south of Linden in southern Cass County, was probably named for James C. Fant, who ran the post office, which was established in 1894 and discontinued in 1901. The community was likely at its largest in 1896, when it had an estimated population of 100 and a Baptist church, flour mill, gin, and general store. Fant was connected to Linden by a triweekly mail stage that ran through Kildare and charged a fare of seventy-five cents. The reasons for the decline of Fant are unknown, but by 1936 the town had ceased to exist as a named community.

BIBLIOGRAPHY: Wright Patman, *History of Post Offices—First Congressional District of Texas* (Texarkana, Texas, 1946?).

Cecil Harper, Jr.

FANTHORP, HENRY (ca. 1790–1867). Henry Fanthorp, merchant, innkeeper, and land speculator, was born in Lincolnshire, England, about 1790. He sailed for America in search of a livelihood and arrived at Washington-on-the-Brazos in 1832. When later that year he applied for land in the Stephen F. Austin and Samuel M. Williams qqv colony, he testified that he was a widower and had left a son in England. In 1833 Fanthorp purchased from Francis Holland qv a tract of 1,100 acres on the west bank of upper Holland Creek in what is now central Grimes County. At once he began trading in agricultural commodities and built a small log house on his property. In the spring of 1834 he built for his bride, Rachel (Kennard), a much larger house near the intersection of stage roads from Houston to Springfield and Nacogdoches to San Felipe de Austin; he soon established the Fanthorp Inn qv at the new residence. In December 1835 Fanthorp was appointed postmaster of Grimes County's first post office. In 1837, with his brother-in-law Mike Kennard and Abraham Womack, he opened a general store at the inn, perhaps the first such establishment in Grimes County. In 1839 he purchased a second tract of land, surveyed a townsite, and began to sell lots. The community that grew up near the inn was known as Alta Mira until 1846, when its name was changed to Anderson. In 1851 Fanthorp was agent for the United States mail coaches operating between Houston and Austin. The Fanthorps had a son and two daughters. Both Rachel and Henry Fanthorp died in Grimes County in 1867 and were buried in the family cemetery near the Fanthorp Inn.

BIBLIOGRAPHY: E. L. Blair, *Early History of Grimes County* (Austin, 1930). Grimes County Historical Commission, *History of Grimes County, Land of Heritage and Progress* (Dallas: Taylor, 1982).

Charles Christopher Jackson

FANTHORP INN. The Fanthorp Inn, a well-known hotel of the period of the Republic of Texas, qv was located in what became Anderson, in central Grimes County. The original structure was built by Henry Fanthorp qv in 1834 as a home for himself and his wife Rachel (Kennard) at the crossing of the mail routes between Houston and Springfield and Nacogdoches and San Felipe de Austin. Fanthorp soon enlarged the original two-room log building into a hotel, and in 1835 it became the first post office and store in the area. Kenneth Lewis Anderson, qv vice president of the republic, died at the inn on July 3, 1845. The inn served as a community center between 1850 and 1865. After Fanthorp died in 1867 it was operated for another year and then closed. The house continued to be used by the family as a private home until 1976. In 1977 the house and adjoining property were purchased by the Texas Parks and Wildlife Department qv to serve as a historical exhibit. The inn and the Fanthorp family cemetery were restored, and a new building was constructed to house a small exhibit on transportation of the period. In 1974 the inn and a portion of the surrounding Anderson downtown area became part of the Anderson Historic District.

BIBLIOGRAPHY: Irene Taylor Allen, *Saga of Anderson—The Proud Story of a Historic Texas Community* (New York: Greenwich, 1957). Texas Historical Commission, National Register Files. Vertical Files, Barker Texas History Center, University of Texas at Austin.

Christopher Long

FANTHORP INN STATE HISTORIC SITE. Fanthorp Inn State Historic Site is on Fanthorp Street in central Anderson, Grimes County. The 1.4-acre site features the historic Fanthorp Inn, built by Henry Fanthorp[qqv] in 1834 and extensively remodeled in 1850. The log structure, now clad with clapboard, is the only authentically restored stagecoach inn of the 1850s in the state. Among the inn's many important guests were Sam Houston, Anson Jones, and Robert E. Lee.[qqv] The state acquired the site from Edward Buffington in 1977 for $100,000 and opened it to the public in the mid-1980s. Much of the surrounding area is part of the Anderson Historic District.

BIBLIOGRAPHY: Ray Miller, *Texas Parks* (Houston: Cordovan, 1984).
Christopher Long

FARABEE, HELEN JANE REHBEIN (1934–1988). Helen Jane Rehbein Farabee, mental health and human services advocate, was born in Appleton, Wisconsin, on November 12, 1934, the daughter of Wilmer C. and Myra Rehbein. She graduated in 1957 from the University of Wisconsin, where she was the first woman elected student-body president at a Big Ten school. Through her student government work she met Ray Farabee, a native of Wichita Falls, Texas, and president of the University of Texas student body. They were married on December 6, 1958, and while he served in the air force she worked for the Dallas *Times-Herald*[qv] and *Better Homes and Gardens*. She also served as assistant dean of women at the University of Texas and worked with the Hogg Foundation for Mental Health[qv] while her husband completed his law degree. The couple later had two sons.

In 1961 the Farabees moved to Wichita Falls, where Helen's voluntary activities included work with the local mental health and mental retardation board and the Wichita Falls State Hospital. By 1965 she had broadened her activities to a statewide focus and worked with future lieutenant governor William P. Hobby, Jr., in encouraging the state legislature to establish the Texas Department of Mental Health and Mental Retardation.[qv] Mrs. Farabee later served as president of the Texas Mental Health Association (1972–74, 1985) and director at large of the National Association of Mental Health. She also was appointed to the Public Committee on Mental Health by first lady Rosalyn Carter. Helen Farabee served on numerous special commissions and planning groups for human services in Texas. She chaired the State Mental Health Code Task Force (1981–83), which culminated its work in the revision of the 1957 Texas mental health code. The revised code was signed by Governor Mark White and became effective in 1983.

In addition to her work in mental health, she served on the Texas Juvenile Probation Commission, worked for improved child care, and addressed better services for the elderly through the Special Senate Committee on the Delivery of Human Services. Her work on the Governor's Task Force on Indigent Health Care (1983–85) resulted in landmark state legislation in 1985 that expanded medical care for the poor. She also served on the Governor's Commission for Women and was inducted into the Texas Women's Hall of Fame in 1985 for her contributions to volunteerism.

Mrs. Farabee's voluntary work was a tandem effort with her husband, who represented the Thirtieth District in the Texas Senate from 1974 to 1988 and shared her advocacy of improved human services for all Texans. Upon his resignation in the spring of 1988 to become general counsel for the University of Texas, she entered the special election to succeed him in the Senate. However, when a committee of Democratic county leaders in the district did not select her as the candidate for the fall general election, she withdrew from the race.

After this brief foray into politics, she continued her part-time work for the Benedictine Health Resource Center in Austin. In June 1988 she was hospitalized for complications from phlebitis and was diagnosed as having lung cancer. She died in Austin on July 28, 1988, and was survived by her husband, two sons, one brother, and her parents. Helen Farabee's funeral was held at the First Presbyterian Church of Wichita Falls; a memorial service was also conducted at Covenant Presbyterian Church in Austin. She received numerous awards for her voluntary work during her lifetime, and after her death several special memorials were established. These included the Helen Farabee Patient Education Scholarship at the Austin State Hospital,[qv] the Helen J. Farabee Public Policy Fellowships for graduate students, offered by the Texas Mental Health Association, and the Helen Farabee Award of the United Way. In February 1989 the Texas Senate sponsored a tribute in her honor.

BIBLIOGRAPHY: Claudia Dee Seligman, *Texas Women* (Dallas: Hendrick-Long, 1989). Vertical Files, Barker Texas History Center, University of Texas at Austin.
Debbie Mauldin Cottrell

FARAH, INCORPORATED. Apparel manufacturer Farah, Incorporated, was founded in 1920 by Lebanese immigrants Mansour and Hana (Abihider) Farah. After studying shirt design and manufacturing in New York City, Farah returned to El Paso and set up operations in October 1920 in a tiny (1,250-square-foot) shop on San Francisco Street. The couple employed a handful of Mexican seamstresses and limited production to blue chambray work shirts sold under the Apache (Legion) label for thirty-five cents each. As business increased, the plant was moved in 1924 to South Oregon Street and again in 1930 to a 5,000-square-foot plant at 104 Leon Street. At that time the Farahs employed twelve to fifteen women on the stitching line. Two Farah sons also assisted with the business. During the 1930s Farah found himself in direct competition with the federal government when United States prison authorities began using convict labor to produce work shirts. From this point on adaptability became the key to his success. The plant was refitted for the production of blue denim work pants, and production reached sixty to eighty pairs daily. In 1935 matched khaki shirts and pants were added to the Farah line. Farah leased a section of a multilevel building at 208 San Francisco Street (the old *Times* building) in 1936; he expanded a few years later to fill the entire 65,000 square feet. He purchased the building in 1939 and remained at this location for the next fourteen years. On May 11, 1937, Farah died at the age of fifty-two. James Farah, then twenty-one, stepped into his father's role as head of Farah Manufacturing.

During World War II[qv] the company's production was converted from civilian garments to army khaki combat pants, fatigues, jungle wear, and uniforms. While William Farah[qv] served as a B–26 pilot in Europe, James remained in charge of the business, which now employed 140 workers. Hana Farah still supervised the sewing room. The plant production record of 359,000 consecutive pairs of pants without a rejection and five consecutive work weeks without an absence earned Farah the Army-Navy "E" flag, awarded on November 3, 1944. Farah was the first clothing plant west of the Mississippi to earn this award.

In 1953 a 116,000-square-foot single-level Farah plant was completed at East Third and Cotton streets. It produced 2,000 dozen pairs of pants daily. Half of the production was sold to J. C. Penney, Sears and Roebuck, and Montgomery Ward, and the other half was sold under the gold Farah label. By 1960 the company's entire production was marketed under its own label. James Farah died at work on January 30, 1964, and William Farah, then forty-five, succeeded him as president. In 1967 Farah Manufacturing made the transition from a family-owned business to a public corporation listed on the New York Stock Exchange. The company employed more than 7,000 workers, but emphasis remained on purchasing strictly United States-manufactured supplies, employing only United States citizens in a nonunion shop, and limiting the sale of Farah products to the United States. The Farah, Incorporated, of 1970 had seven domestic manufacturing facilities, five in El Paso and one each in San Antonio and Las Cruces, New Mexico. Combined, they comprised 1,837,000 square feet of manufacturing space and employed 9,500 workers. The company had also expanded to include operations in Belgium and Hong Kong. At this, its peak, Farah was the second largest employer in El Paso. Sales for 1971 were a record $164 million. Unique in the garment industry, Farah offered its workers on-site health care, cafeteria benefits, and a generous wage. However, the large capital expenditures required to meet growth necessitated strict control on production and increasing pressure on workers to meet higher quotas. As relations between management and workers grew less personal, union activists began to agitate for better working conditions. By 1974, 3,000 workers were on strike and a sixty-city boycott of Farah products was in effect (*see* FARAH STRIKE). A settlement was reached in 1977, but not before sales had dropped 40 percent, 5,000 employees had been laid off, and all domestic plants outside El Paso had been closed. Poor management decisions such as the opening in 1974 of a textile division in El Paso (closed in 1977) and major miscalculations in production and marketing also contributed to a $24.4-million operating loss in 1976. William Farah had been removed as president in March of that year, and William C. Leone assumed the position. Two others, William Conroy and Andrew Galef, held the office in the ensuing year.

Early in 1978 William Farah made his bid to regain control of the company. In April, amid bitter controversy, stockholders restored him to his former position, a move that stabilized operations for a time. In July company matriarch Hana Farah died at the age of eighty. The main Paisano Street plant (a 285,000-square-foot facility completed in 1963) was reopened, and by 1979 annual reports showed a profit for the first time in three years. Farah added a line of women's wear in the early 1980s and acquired Generra Sportswear, an upscale brand of clothing, in August 1984. The renewed prosperity was short-lived, however. From 1985 to 1990 the company posted annual loses. Contributing factors were the shifting of consumer demand to jeans away from casual dress clothing and poor inventory controls. During 1987 and 1988, in an effort to regain a competitive edge, Farah purchased two manufacturing plants in Torreón, Coahuila. The main Farah plant at Gateway East was sold and leased back to the company, and Generra Sportswear was sold back to its founders. On July 11, 1989, William Farah retired as president and CEO of the company, which he had led for more than a quarter of a century. He was succeeded by Richard C. Allendar. Farah remained active as chairman of the board and also held a consulting contract with the firm. Fiscal 1989 ended with an $11.6 million loss, and by mid-1990 William Farah again filed suit to gain control. However, on August 10, 1990, stockholders not only defeated his bid to oust six board members, including Allendar, but they also removed Farah as chairman of the board, thus denying him any further active role in company operations. In 1990 Farah, Incorporated, placed renewed emphasis on product quality. The company, which had led the way in fabric innovation in 1963 with polyester permanent-press slacks, developed an antiwrinkle garment finishing technique known as Process 2000, designed expressly for use with its 100 percent cotton line of casual men's wear. In 1994 Farah lines included Farah, Savane, and John Henry brands for men and Farah Savane for the Boys' and Kids' Division. Richard C. Allendar was chairman and CEO, and Mike Mitchell was president. Farah employed 3,000 workers in El Paso and 5,500 on a worldwide basis.

BIBLIOGRAPHY: Evan Haywood Antone, *William Farah, Industrialist* (El Paso: Carl Hertzog, 1969). Laurie Coyle et al., *Women at Farah: An Unfinished Story* (Oakland, California, 1979). Leon C. Metz, *City at the Pass: An Illustrated History of El Paso* (Woodland Hills, California: Windsor, 1980). Vertical Files, Barker Texas History Center, University of Texas at Austin.
Myrna Zanetell

FARAH STRIKE. In May 1972, 4,000 garment workers at Farah Manufacturing Company (*see* FARAH, INCORPORATED) in El Paso went out on strike for the right to be represented by a union. The strikers were virtually all Hispanic; 85 percent were women. Their labor action, which lasted until they won union representation in March 1974, grew to encompass a national boycott of Farah pants. Before the strike Farah was the second largest employer in El Paso. Low wages, minimal benefits, pressure to meet high production quotas, and tensions between workers and supervisors produced a dissatisfied work force.

In 1969 male workers from the cutting room voted to affiliate with the Amalgamated Clothing Workers of America. Organizing soon spread to the rest of Farah's five El Paso plants. When workers at Farah's San Antonio plant were fired for joining a union-sponsored march in El Paso, more than 500 of them walked out; El Paso workers followed on May 9, 1972. The strike was quickly declared an unfair-labor-practice strike, and a month later a national boycott of Farah products was begun, endorsed by the AFL-CIO. The strike exacerbated ethnic tensions between Anglos and Hispanics, and split the Hispanic community as well. Striking workers were quickly replaced by workers from El Paso and Ciudad Juárez. But union relief funds, the national boycott, and the Catholic Church all provided important sources of support for the strikers. Strikers acquired skills such as public speaking and organizing activities that brought new groups of people together. The company, its sales badly damaged by the national boycott, was ordered by the National Labor Relations Board in January 1974 to offer reinstatement to the strikers and to permit union organizing. In February Willie Farah recognized the ACWA as the bargaining agent for the Farah employees. The 1974 union contract included pay increases, job security and seniority rights, and a grievance procedure. But a national recession and company mistakes in production and marketing left Farah in a serious financial predicament. Layoffs, plant closures, and high turnover of the work force followed, thus inhibiting the growth of a strong union. Subsequent contracts removed many of the benefits won by the strike.

BIBLIOGRAPHY: Laurie Coyle et al., *Women at Farah: An Unfinished Story* (Oakland, California, 1979). Magdalena Mora and Adelaida R. del Castillo, *Mexican Women in the United States* (Los Angeles: Chicano Studies Research Center, University of California, 1980). Allen Pusey, "Clothes Made the Man," *Texas Monthly*, June 1977.
Laurie Coyle, Gail Hershatter, and Emily Honig

FARGO, TEXAS. Fargo is on Farm Road 924 ten miles north of Vernon in northern Wilbarger County. It was established on a stage line from Wichita Falls to Mobeetie about 1883. A school known as Richland was built there in 1889, and a post office was added on April 15, 1894. By 1900 the town had grown to include a store and post office, a gin, and several church groups. Although the post office was moved to Tolbert in 1915, the population reached 200 during the 1940s, where it remained through the 1960s. Northside School replaced the Fargo district in 1935. In 1986 the town had a Northside Oil Company office and a pump station, the Fargo Church of Christ (founded in 1889), the Fargo Methodist Church (1887), the Fargo Baptist Church (1904), and the Northside School. The population was estimated at 161 in 1986 and 1990.

BIBLIOGRAPHY: Wilbarger County Historical Commission, *Wilbarger County* (Lubbock, 1986).
Charles G. Davis

FARIS, WILLIS A. (?–?). Willis A. Faris, legislator and postmaster, was living in Vicksburg, Mississippi, as early as January 1832. He moved to Texas in December 1834. He was secretary pro tem of the Convention of 1836[qv] and after the Texas Revolution[qv] was appointed postmaster of Columbia. He was elected clerk pro tem of the House of Representatives of the First Congress of the republic on October 6, 1836.

BIBLIOGRAPHY: Brazoria County Federation of Women's Clubs, *History of Brazoria County* (1940). Louis Wiltz Kemp, *The Signers of the Texas Declaration of Independence* (Salado, Texas: Anson Jones, 1944; rpt. 1959).
L. W. Kemp

FARISH, WILLIAM STAMPS (1881–1942). William Stamps Farish, pioneer in East Texas oilfield development, was born in Mayersville, Mississippi, on February 23, 1881, the grandnephew of Jefferson

Davis^qv and son of William Stamps and Katherine (Power) Farish. He attended school at St. Thomas Hall, an Episcopal preparatory school at Holly Springs, Mississippi. After receiving a law degree from the University of Mississippi in 1900, he practiced law for three months at Clarksdale, Mississippi, before moving to Beaumont, Texas, when oil was discovered at the Spindletop oilfield.^qv He became supervisor of wells for Texas Oil Fields, Limited, an English syndicate. The next year he organized the Brown-Farish Oil Company, which did contract drilling and traded in oil. The firm became bankrupt at Brown's death, but Farish succeeded in borrowing money to pay creditors. By 1904 Farish and Robert Lee Blaffer had formed a partnership to do contract drilling and lease trading. The next year Blaffer and Farish moved to Houston to be nearer the Humble field. In 1915 Farish became president of the Gulf Coast Producers Association and subsequently was named president of the Texas-Louisiana Oil and Gas Association. In March 1917 he and others organized the Humble Oil and Refining Company (later Exxon Company, U.S.A.^qv). Farish served as vice president for five years and in 1922 became president. In 1933 he became chairman of the board of Standard Oil Company of New Jersey, which held substantial stock interest in Humble, and in 1937 he became president of Standard. He was one of the founders of the American Petroleum Institute and served as its president in 1926. At the beginning of World War II^qv Farish was a member of the National Petroleum Industry War Council. He was married to Libbie Randon Rice in Houston on June 1, 1911; they had a son and a daughter. Farish died on November 29, 1942, in Millbrook, New York, while visiting friends; he was buried in Houston.

BIBLIOGRAPHY: Dallas *Morning News*, November 30, 1942. Henrietta M. Larson and Kenneth Wiggins Porter, *History of Humble Oil and Refining Company* (New York: Harper, 1959). *Who's Who in America*, 1934–35.

Karen S. Collins

FARLEY, CAL (1895–1967). Cal Farley was born on December 25, 1895, at Saxton, Iowa. He and his twin sister, Zaida, were the youngest of six children of Frank and Jennie Farley, who later moved to a small farm near Elmore, Minnesota. The product of a loveless marriage which ultimately ended in separation, Cal learned early how to fend for himself. He found an escape in baseball and other sports and soon revealed a remarkable athletic prowess. At the age of sixteen he left home and began playing semiprofessional baseball. In 1917 he enlisted in the army and was sent to Europe for combat in World War I^qv with Company C, Sixth Engineers, Third Army Division. During the postwar occupation, the American Expeditionary Forces and Inter-Allied Games athletic programs were held in Paris, France, where Farley was a member of the American team. In welterweight wrestling he defeated Walter O'Connor for the AEF championship and George Bridges of Australia for the Inter-Allied Games title. Farley continued in professional wrestling after the war. His relationship with Dutch Mantell,^qv a wrestler from Luxembourg, remains a sports legend. He also played baseball in the minor leagues.

In 1923 Farley settled in Amarillo, Texas, where he acquired a defunct tire shop and built it into a $750,000-a-year business. He also pioneered department-store merchandising in Amarillo and for fifteen years broadcast a daily radio program. Mantell and comedian Cecil Hunter, known as "Stuttering Sam," were among the star performers in Farley's show. In 1924 Farley married Mabel (Mimi) Fincher. Their daughter and only child, Gene, born in 1926, was named after Farley's longtime friend, boxer Gene Tunney.

In January 1934 Farley, along with others, started the Maverick Club, an organized program of athletics designed to keep boys constructively occupied. By 1966 Kids Incorporated, an outgrowth of the Maverick Club, was helping over 10,000 boys aged six to sixteen years to become involved in athletics; the boys were supervised by more than 1,500 adult volunteers. Some boys, however, could not be helped by the Maverick Club because of their lack of supervision and encouragement at home. For these boys, which he called "the lower 10 percent of our nation's youth," Farley founded Cal Farley's Boys Ranch^qv in 1939. His work became more widely known, and he received requests to take boys from all over the country. In 1947 he sold his business so that he and his wife could devote their lives to helping homeless and delinquent boys. The famous professional wrestler Dorrance (Dory) Funk^qv was among those who served on Farley's staff. Jack Dempsey, J. Edgar Hoover, and Roy Rogers were among Farley's staunchest friends and supporters.

For his career as an athlete, businessman, and humanitarian, Farley was honored many times. He was a district governor of Rotary International and is in the Panhandle Sports Hall of Fame. For his work with boys he was named Outstanding Citizen of Texas and given the Veterans of Foreign Wars Silver Citizenship Medal, the Bronze Keystone Award of the Boys Clubs of America, an honorary doctor of humanities degree from Texas Technological College (now Texas Tech University) in 1963, and the Democracy in Action Award in 1966 by students at Long Beach, California. On February 19, 1967, he died suddenly while attending chapel services with the boys at the ranch. Mrs. Farley died on March 19, 1967, at Hermann Hospital^qv in Houston. They were both buried at the Llano Cemetery in Amarillo.

BIBLIOGRAPHY: Beth Feagles Day, *A Shirttail to Hang To: The Story of Cal Farley and His Boys Ranch* (New York: Holt, 1959). Louie Hendricks, *No Rules or Guidelines* (Amarillo: Cal Farley's Boys Ranch, 1971). John L. McCarty, *Maverick Town: The Story of Old Tascosa* (Norman: University of Oklahoma Press, 1946; enlarged ed. 1968).

Louie Hendricks

FARMER, ALEXANDER (1794–1878). Alexander Farmer, artisan, soldier, civil servant, and cattle rancher, was born in Argyllshire, Scotland, in 1794. After reserve service in the British navy, he immigrated to Texas, probably from Louisiana, in February 1828 or in 1829; he took the oath of allegiance to the Republic of Mexico on March 27, 1830. In his petition to Juan Antonio Padilla,^qv commissioner general of Coahuila, for a league of land he described himself as "a carpenter . . . instructed in all matters pertaining to steam engines," citing "the one I have erected in this Colony to produce boards, etc. over the waters of Galveston Bay [for] Messieurs Harris and Wilson." Advertisements in Farmer's name appeared in the *Texas Gazette*,^qv while extant bills of sale show that Samuel May Williams^qv bought lumber from Farmer in July 1830. On November 23, 1831, Farmer received title to a league of land on Dickinson Bayou, thus joining Stephen F. Austin's^qv coast (or fourth) colony.

In 1831 Farmer married Edith Little (Lytle), daughter of John W. Little (whose own league of land, located at the mouth of Dickinson Bay, was granted on January 23, 1832); they had seven children. At the convention held in San Felipe from April 1 to 13, 1833, Farmer represented the Mina District. For an undetermined period he was among several guards Austin engaged for his protection. On June 22, 1835, Farmer joined John W. Moore^qv and others in the "San Felipe Pledge," which led to the expedition against Anahuac that month (part of the Anahuac Disturbances^qv). On September 16 he entered the volunteer army of Texas as a second lieutenant of artillery in Col. James W. Fannin's^qv regiment, which was in the unit commanded by Lt. Col. James C. Neill;^qv Neill personally signed Farmer's certificate of honorable discharge on December 16, 1836. These documents support the family tradition that Farmer fought in the battle of San Jacinto.^qv

After Texas independence, Farmer settled in Galveston, where in 1841 he was elected justice of the peace for Precinct 5, a post to which he was reelected for over ten years. On November 15, 1856, he purchased from Harvey N. Little 458 acres in the William P. Kerr survey and moved from Galveston to what was to become the community of Paige in Bastrop County. The log house he built on this property in 1858 still stands. By 1860 he was in the cattle business; a letter to John Grant Tod, Sr.,^qv on September 11 offers 200 "first class cattle" for sale to the Tod beef-packing establishment at Dickinson, with the addendum that "a good many more" cattle were available.

After the death of Edith Farmer in 1867, Alexander divided his estate, including over 1,000 cattle and from 75 to 100 horses, all "running in the range at Bastrop." Farmer died in 1878 and was buried beside his wife in the family graveyard two miles east of Paige. On July 22, 1871, the Farmers initiated a pension claim based on their father's service in the revolutionary army[qv] of Texas. On March 31, 1887, in "An Act for the Relief of the Heirs of Alexander Farmer, Deceased," the Texas legislature acknowledged Alexander Farmer's contributions to Texas by awarding his heirs certificates for one headright, one donation, and one bounty in three separate counties for a total of two-thirds of a league, one full labor,[qv] and more than 1,300 additional acres of land. House Bill No. 463 was the last such act passed by the legislature of Texas.

BIBLIOGRAPHY: John H. Jenkins, ed., *The Papers of the Texas Revolution, 1835–1836* (10 vols., Austin: Presidial Press, 1973). Doris Goerner Laake, *The History of Paige, Texas and Vicinity* (Austin: Eakin Press, 1983). Virginia H. Taylor, *The Spanish Archives of the General Land Office of Texas* (Austin: Lone Star, 1955). Texas House of Representatives, *Biographical Directory of the Texan Conventions and Congresses, 1832–1845* (Austin: Book Exchange, 1941). Villamae Williams, *Stephen F. Austin's Register of Families* (Nacogdoches, Texas: Ericson, 1984).

Norman Kittrell Farmer, Jr.

FARMER, EDWARD DISNEY (1849–1924). Edward Disney Farmer, real estate developer and philanthropist, was born in 1849 at Ballybrophy, Ireland, the son of an Episcopal minister. After a public school education in England he immigrated to Minnesota and worked in a flour mill until 1875, when he moved to Fort Worth, Texas. He spent the next few years employed as a construction worker for $1.50 a day. Although his income was meager, Farmer managed to save money and invest it in cattle ranching. He moved from Fort Worth to Aledo, a small community in southeast Parker County, to oversee his new investment. Within a few years he had established large spreads in both Parker and Tarrant counties. Using the profits from his cattle business, he began to invest in real estate, which gradually became his main interest. He accumulated large holdings in Fort Worth and in Vancouver, British Columbia, where his nephew had settled. In the early 1920s Farmer returned to Fort Worth, where he lived in the Texas Hotel, a building he helped to finance. By 1920 the value of his real estate holdings in Fort Worth was estimated at $1 million. Farmer was a quiet, soft-spoken bachelor who avoided publicity and preferred to make his extensive charitable donations anonymously. Not until after his death was it revealed that he had given thousands of dollars annually to religious, patriotic, educational, and social-welfare organizations. Both Weatherford College and the University of Texas received sizable sums from his estate. UT established the E. D. Farmer International Scholarship Fund to support an exchange of students between Mexico and Texas. Farmer died on May 29, 1924, of complications following surgery at the Mayo Clinic in Rochester, Minnesota. He was buried in Weatherford, Texas.

BIBLIOGRAPHY: Dallas *Morning News*, May 31, 1924. Gustavus Adolphus Holland, *History of Parker County and the Double Log Cabin* (Weatherford, Texas: Herald, 1931; rpt. 1937). Malcolm D. McLean, comp. and ed., *Papers Concerning Robertson's Colony in Texas* (19 vols., Fort Worth: Texas Christian University Press, 1974–76; Arlington: University of Texas at Arlington Press, 1977–92).

David Minor

FARMER, JAMES LEONARD (1886–1961). James Leonard Farmer, evidently the first black man in Texas to have a Ph.D., was born on June 12, 1886, in Kingstree, South Carolina, the son of Carolina and Lorena (Wilson) Farmer. His parents were former slaves. He attended grade school in Pearson, Georgia, and then studied at Cockman Institute in Daytona Beach, Florida, before going to Boston University, where he received B.A. and S.T.B. degrees. He received the Ph.D from Boston University in 1918. He also studied at Harvard in 1916–17 and received an honorary doctorate in 1929 from Gammon Theological Seminary, Atlanta, Georgia.

Farmer was a deacon in the Methodist Episcopal Church in 1917 and after college served as pastor of black churches in Texarkana and Galveston. He taught philosophy and religion and also served in administrative capacities at Wiley College in Marshall, Texas (1919–20, 1933–38); Rust College, Holly Springs, Mississippi (1920–25); Samuel Huston (now Huston-Tillotson) College, Austin, Texas (1925–30, 1946–56); Gammon Theological Seminary (1930–33); and Howard University, Washington, D.C. (1938–46). From 1932 to 1956 he was also dean of Gulfside Summer School of Ministerial Training in Mississippi. He was versed in Greek, Hebrew, Aramaic, Latin, French, and German; he was a poet and the author of two books, *The Coming of Peace and the Prince of Peace* (1943) and *John and Jesus in Their Day and Ours* (1956). He wrote biblical criticism, articles for secular magazines, and Sunday school lessons for the *Southwestern Christian Advocate* (see UNITED METHODIST REPORTER) and contributed several sermons to a book, *Pulpit Eloquence* (1939).

Farmer married Pearl Marion Houston on September 2, 1917. They had three children. One, James Leonard Farmer, Jr., became a civil rights leader and founder of the Congress of Racial Equality. Farmer was a Mason, a Republican, and a member of Omega Psi Phi. He died in Washington, D.C., on May 14, 1961.

BIBLIOGRAPHY: *National Cyclopaedia of American Biography*, Vol. 48. James Farmer, *Lay Bare the Heart: An Autobiography of the Civil Rights Movement* (New York: Arbor House, 1985).

Gail K. Beil

FARMER, WILLIAM CARLTON (1866–1944). William Carlton Farmer, tuberculosis specialist, was born on December 6, 1866, in Bloomington, Indiana, the son of Joel and Emma Farmer. When he was ten his family moved to Texas. After receiving much of his early education in Lamar County schools, he obtained his medical education at the Hospital College of Medicine in Louisville, Kentucky, where he graduated in 1891. For the next fourteen years he practiced medicine in Bowling Green, Kentucky, and Paris, Texas. In 1905, four years after he began to limit his practice to diseases of the lungs, he moved to San Antonio, where he stayed for the rest of his life. On January 1, 1906, he established the San Antonio Tent Colony, an open-air colony for the treatment of tuberculosis. Farmer pioneered the use of X ray for diagnosis of tuberculosis; during his experiments he received the X-ray burns that are believed to be the cause of the carcinoma from which he died. He continued his education with postgraduate studies at clinical centers in Rochester (Minnesota), Philadelphia, New York City, Baltimore, Asheville (North Carolina), and Hamburg (Germany).

Farmer was a member of the Bexar County Medical Society, the Texas State Medical Association (see TEXAS MEDICAL ASSOCIATION), and the American Medical Association. He served as director of the National Tuberculosis Association from 1931 to 1934 and was a member of the Southern Tuberculosis Association, the International Union Against Tuberculosis, and the American College of Chest Physicians. He married Ellen Cook of San Antonio in 1934. They had one child. Farmer was a thirty-third-degree Scottish Rite Mason and a Methodist. He died in San Antonio on April 5, 1944.

BIBLIOGRAPHY: *Texas State Journal of Medicine*, July 1944. *A Twentieth Century History of Southwest Texas* (2 vols., Chicago: Lewis, 1907).

Patricia L. Jakobi

FARMER, TEXAS (Crosby County). Farmer is on Farm Road 193 thirty-two miles northeast of Lubbock in northwestern Crosby County, in the center of a cotton-growing region. Acting on a petition by S. D. Thornton, in 1893 the Crosby county court established Sonora School District Number Eight in the area. The name Sonora was not legally changed to Farmer until 1913, but the district was always referred to as Farmer, after a pioneer, W. W. Farmer. In 1893 the community built its first schoolhouse, a one-room building financed by donations. By 1951 three other school buildings had been constructed, and the Farmer school district had grown to an area of twenty-seven square miles. The school built in 1951 was razed in 1974–75, after the Farmer district was consolidated with the Lorenzo Independent School District. In 1925 J. A. Zeh constructed a country store, which was in operation until 1965; a gin built by the Murray Company in 1929 remained in operation through the 1975 ginning season. Farmer had seventy-five residents in 1940, recorded a population of forty-nine in 1980, and did not appear on the 1990 census list.

BIBLIOGRAPHY: Crosby County Pioneer Memorial Museum, *A History of Crosby County, 1876–1977* (Dallas: Taylor, 1978).

Edloe A. Jenkins

FARMER, TEXAS (Young County). Farmer is near the junction of Farm roads 1769 and 2652, eight miles northwest of Loving and sixteen miles east of Olney in northeast Young County. The community, originally called Brush, was renamed in honor of Rev. William H. Farmer, who settled in the area in 1877. He built a store there, and a post office was opened in it on August 7, 1878. John Casey, a former ferry operator, added a second store, and a large Methodist church was built at the settlement in 1889. By 1892 Farmer had 125 residents and challenged Graham for area prominence. Businesses in the community included the Farmer general store and two blacksmith shops, as well as a hotel, barbershop, drugstore, meat market, and weekly newspaper, the Farmer *Headlight*. The town also had Methodist, Baptist, and Presbyterian congregations and a town band. Farmer declined quickly when the Gulf, Texas and Western Railroad, running from Jacksboro to Olney in the early 1900s, bypassed the town to the south. The Farmer post office was moved to Jean on January 15, 1921. During the 1930s and 1940s Farmer had about fifty residents. County maps for the 1980s showed only a rural settlement and nearby cemetery at the site.

BIBLIOGRAPHY: Carrie J. Crouch, *Young County: History and Biography* (Dallas: Dealey and Love, 1937; rev. ed., *A History of Young County, Texas*, Austin: Texas State Historical Association, 1956).

Charles G. Davis

FARMERS' ALLIANCE. The years after the Civil War^{qv} brought hardship to Southern farmers as their economic mainstay, cotton, steadily dropped in price. In September 1877 farmers gathered in Lampasas County, Texas, to discuss their grievances. This gathering began the National Farmers' Alliance and Industrial Union, more commonly referred to as the Southern Farmers' Alliance. This organization eventually claimed a membership of almost three million, one of the largest protest organizations in American history.

The initial growth of the alliance in Texas was slow, and its membership rather inactive. To the state alliance convention in August 1883 only thirty of the almost 100 local alliances sent representatives. Alliance president W. L. Garvin appointed S. O. Daws a full-time, salaried lecturer and ordered him to revitalize the alliance. Daws accompanied his discussion of possible relief strategies with a protest ideology that blamed the agrarian crisis on "the capitalist [who] holds your confidence in one hand, while with the other he rifles your pocket." Daws's influence was considerable. More than 600 delegates attended the 1885 state alliance convention.

The economic strategies subsequently implemented were of two types. First, farmers looked at their plight in terms of the purchasing system, stressing the excessive prices on supplies. Second, they focused on the marketing system, stressing the falling price of cotton and the absorption of much of the profit of cotton production by middlemen.

The first attempt to address problems in the purchasing system was the trade-agreement strategy. Each county alliance appointed a committee to ask merchants for the lowest prices in return for a guarantee of the alliance members' cash business. Though trade agreements did marginally improve purchasing conditions for hundreds of alliance farmers, at least temporarily, they had major limitations. Indebted farmers, forced to buy goods on credit, could not participate in the cash terms of the trade agreements. Trade agreements were also vulnerable to violation. They stipulated a certain charge above wholesale, but farmers were suspicious of reported wholesale costs. Finally, the trade-agreement strategy suffered from wholesalers' hostility. A trade agreement with one merchant meant lost business to nearby merchants. Since most retail merchants were in debt to wholesalers, the latter had a stake in retail profits. When trade agreements began affecting those profits, wholesalers pressured merchants cooperating with the alliance to renege on the trade agreements by threatening delays in delivery of supplies or by refusing to extend credit for supply purchases.

Another economic strategy was alliance-owned cooperative stores, which reported annual sales ranging from $5,000 to $36,000. Many claimed to sell goods at 20 to 30 percent below regular retail price. However, the stores suffered from several problems. Not only did they face the hostility of wholesalers, but retailers often lowered prices temporarily below those of the cooperatives, hoping to draw away enough customers to close the stores. In addition, to obtain adequate capitalization, most of the cooperatives had to entice the farmer's investment with the promise of dividends. Dividend payments added to the cost of supplies, and consequently prices were not reduced as much as farmers had hoped.

Cooperative flour, cottonseed oil, and corn mills, as well as cotton gins, were also established. Though the importance of savings from these mills and gins, as well as from the trade agreement and cooperative stores, should not be considered trivial, these strategies did not directly address the problem of declining cotton prices. Nor did they help the poor farmer who did not have the ready cash to participate.

Consequently, some alliance farmers demanded political action to address their economic problems. Tensions between political insurgents and political conservatives within the alliance climaxed at the August 1886 alliance convention in Cleburne. The insurgents scored a major victory with the passage of a series of political demands. Several of these related to labor issues highlighted by the 1886 Great Southwest Strike^{qv} by the Knights of Labor,^{qv} governmental land policy, and railroad regulation. The most controversial demands, however, related to monetary reform. Believing that significant relief from declining crop prices required the expansion of the currency supply, alliance farmers demanded that the government immediately use silver in addition to gold as legal tender in order to ease the contracted currency supply. They argued, however, that significant relief required a more radical revamping of the existing monetary system than entailed by "free silver"—the establishment of a fiat currency system wherein the government would issue "greenbacks" based on a predetermined per capita circulation volume, rather than on an inflexible metallic standard.

Political conservatives within the alliance condemned the Cleburne demands and maneuvered to establish a rival alliance that would be strictly a business organization dedicated to economic self-help. Andrew Dunlap, a "strictly business" advocate, resigned from the alliance presidency. The chairman of the state executive committee, Charles William Macune,^{qv} assumed the powers of president pro tem and called a special convention in January 1887. In his opening address to this convention, he proposed a central, statewide alliance exchange to coordinate the marketing of the cotton crop of the state membership and to act as a central purchasing house. He also called for the mobilization of the entire cotton belt under the alliance banner and set forth plans for a nationwide organizing effort. The "strictly business" advocates were pacified by the scope of his plans, and unity once more prevailed.

In its attack on the purchasing system, the alliance exchange attempted to bypass both retail and wholesale merchants. Purchasing was direct from the manufacturer whenever possible. Most importantly, a cooperative credit program was established as an alternative to the existing crop-lien credit system. Under crop-lien financing, the merchant advanced credit—not by lending money but by advancing supplies and goods in return for a lien on the growing crop. In addition to the interest, the rate of which ranged from 20 to 200 percent, the farmer was charged "time prices" on his purchases; the typical markup was at least 25 percent above the "cash price." The alliance credit program entailed no time prices, and the interest rate was only 1 percent a month from the date of supply shipment until the date of payment.

In its attack on the cotton-marketing system, the exchange plan instituted statewide bulking of cotton. Each county alliance bulked its members' cotton and sent bale samples to exchange headquarters in Dallas. There they were displayed in a sample room, where textile manufacturers examined them. Having eliminated the middlemen, alliance members received a larger proportion of the profit from cotton production and trade.

The enthusiasm for the exchange plan among farmers was evident in the dramatic growth of the alliance from 75,000 in early 1887 to 150,000 by the following year. But by May 1888 the exchange was in a serious financial struggle, and in 1889 creditors foreclosed. A significant decline in state membership ensued; active, dues-paying members dropped from an alleged high in early 1888 of 225,000–260,000 to 142,000 by 1889. Furthermore, a national organizing campaign had begun, and organizers had planned to export the Texas exchange's credit strategy to other states.

The crisis was abated momentarily by a boycott on jute bagging. Jute bagging, which held together cotton bales, dramatically jumped in price in 1888 because of a price-fixing agreement among eight American companies. Such alliance leaders as Texas state alliance president Evan Jones[qv] called for a boycott on jute bagging and the use of a newly developed cotton-bagging product. The boycott reduced the price of jute. Alliance leaders, however, continued the boycott because they wanted to kill any chance of a resurgence of the jute trust by promoting cotton bagging. But there was too much cotton and there were too many cotton mills for a cotton-bagging trust ever to form. Despite their efforts, the development and use of cotton bagging encountered a number of major obstacles, and the jute boycott faltered.

In 1889 a major redirection of alliance strategies was provided by Macune. In his presidential address to the national alliance convention in 1889, he argued that the root cause of the agricultural depression was an insufficient currency supply, thus echoing the analysis found earlier in the controversial Cleburne demands. A committee was appointed to formulate a solution to the currency supply problem. This committee, in which Macune played a major part, proposed the "subtreasury plan," which entailed a governmental commodity-loan program and later a land-loan program. Under this plan, federal warehouses would be established for storage of nonperishable crops to wait for higher crop prices, and farmers would be allowed to borrow up to 80 percent of the local market price on the products deposited. The annual interest rate on these loans would be 2 percent, with additional nominal charges for handling, storage, and insurance. The program would be funded with newly printed money until the volume of circulating currency reached fifty dollars per capita, a volume associated with the prosperous war years.

In Texas, a subtreasury educational campaign was begun. The Southern Mercury,[qv] the state alliance's newspaper, routinely included educational articles on the subtreasury. Scores of lecturers visited local alliances to explain the subtreasury. Grand alliance encampments were centered around the idea of the subtreasury. The shift toward political action was decisive. In Texas the alliance played a major role in the 1890 victory of gubernatorial nominee James Stephen Hogg,[qv] a reform Democrat, who was a strong advocate of an intrastate Railroad Commission.[qv] However, neither Hogg nor the state Democratic party[qv] platform had supported the subtreasury plan. Delegates to the 1890 state alliance convention voted to make future support of the Democratic party contingent on its support of the subtreasury.

Some loyal Democrats in the alliance were alarmed and attempted to mobilize an anti-subtreasury faction. In March 1891 they issued their "Austin Manifesto," which claimed that the subtreasury plan was merely a scheme of third-partyites trying to undermine the Democratic party. The manifesto was signed by eleven alliance members, eight of whom were state legislators. It caused tempers to flare; one of its signers got in a fist fight in the corridors of the Capitol[qv] with a prominent subtreasuryite. A special alliance convention was called to discuss the manifesto, and a resolution denouncing it passed easily.

In May 1891 a third party became a reality with the establishment of the People's party,[qv] whose platform was identical to the national platform of the alliance. Democratic leaders began drawing battle lines. In October 1891 the Democratic Executive Committee of Dallas demanded the resignation of one of its members, an alliance subtreasuryite, W. R. Cole. The state Democratic Executive Committee followed suit with its ruling that subtreasury advocates could neither hold leadership positions in the Democratic party nor vote in Democratic primaries. This stand prompted Texas alliance leaders to begin campaigning for the People's party; the national alliance organization formally endorsed that party in February 1892.

Thereafter, the fate of the alliance was intricately linked with that of the People's party. The party's betrayal of alliance principles in 1896, in particular its abandonment of the subtreasury, was assailed by Texas alliance activists. However, by 1896 the alliance was a faint shadow of itself. Since the People's party had endorsed the alliance platform in 1891, most alliance members saw no further need to continue paying alliance dues and attending alliance meetings. Consequently, the monetary resources of the alliance were not sufficient to fight the People's party betrayal of its cherished principles.

BIBLIOGRAPHY: Donna A. Barnes, *Farmers in Rebellion: The Rise and Fall of the Southern Farmers Alliance and People's Party in Texas* (Austin: University of Texas Press, 1984). Dallas *Morning News*, April 22, 1891. W. L. Garvin and J. O. Daws, *History of the National Farmers Alliance and Cooperative Union of America* (Jacksboro, Texas: Rogers, 1887). Lawrence Goodwyn, *Democratic Promise: The Populist Moment in America* (New York: Oxford University Press, 1976). Robert C. McMath, Jr., *Populist Vanguard: A History of the Southern Farmers' Alliance* (Chapel Hill: University of North Carolina Press, 1975).

Donna A. Barnes

FARMERS' ALLIANCE EXCHANGE OF TEXAS. The Farmers' Alliance Exchange of Texas, the central state cooperative exchange of the Farmers' Alliance,[qv] opened for business in Dallas in September 1887. The idea had been outlined at the alliance's January 1887 meeting by Charles William Macune.[qv] The proposed exchange would help the farmer sell his crop at higher prices and purchase supplies at lower prices. Macune was subsequently elected state business agent of the alliance and in August set forth detailed plans for the exchange. It was to be based on a capitalization of $500,000, raised by a two-dollar assessment on each member. Dallas was chosen as the site for the venture when the city offered a $3,500 cash bonus and a 100-by-150-foot lot in the business section.

In order to bring the individual farmer closer to the prices being paid for cotton on the world market, a system of weighing, numbering, and grading cotton by local alliance agents was devised. Only samples of the cotton were sent to Dallas. Buyers from all over the world could then bid on the cotton on the basis of the samples, with the exchange guaranteeing the weights and samples.

Initially the exchange also supplied goods at a discount on a strictly cash basis. Most of the members were unable to take advantage of the system because they had no cash and were locked in the crop-lien system. In an effort to make the exchange more useful and break this system, the directors of the exchange announced the joint-note plan. The exchange would provide goods to farmers on credit and would accept notes signed jointly by poorer farmers and their more prosperous landowning neighbors as collateral. To pay suppliers, the directors planned to borrow money from area banks with the joint notes as collateral. By March 1888 over $200,000 in joint notes had been forwarded to the exchange, and the exchange began issuing supplies.

As the joint-note program began, the directors of the exchange began construction of a building on the lot Dallas had given the organization. Although Macune opposed it, the directors decided to build a massive and elaborate four-story structure at a cost of $45,000. As the joint notes continued to pour in, Macune made unsuccessful efforts to find banks that would advance money on them. Furthermore, although original plans for the Alliance called for a capitalization of $500,000, the paid-in capital of the exchange was only slightly more than $20,000. By May 1888 creditors were demanding payment, and the exchange faced bankruptcy. June 9 was designated a day for mass meetings, and in 200 counties across Texas, farmers gathered to pool their meager resources in an effort to save the exchange. From the pledges received that day, the exchange eventually realized a little over $80,000. That was enough to prevent immediate collapse, but the exchange was forced to curtail its activities, since bankers and suppliers alike continued to refuse to accept joint notes as collateral. Indebtedness and a lack of patronage after the failure of the joint-note plan forced the liquidation of the exchange in December 1889.

BIBLIOGRAPHY: Lawrence Goodwyn, *Democratic Promise: The Populist Moment in America* (New York: Oxford University Press, 1976; abridged ed., *The Populist Moment: A Short History of the Agrarian Revolt in America*, 1978). Robert C. McMath, Jr., *Populist Vanguard: A History of the Southern Farmers' Alliance* (Chapel Hill: University of North Carolina Press, 1975).   *Cecil Harper, Jr.*

FARMERS BRANCH. Farmers Branch rises just south of Addison Airport in northwestern Dallas County (at 32°57′ N, 96°50′ W) and runs southwest for 6½ miles to its mouth on the Elm Fork of the Trinity River, in the town of Farmers Branch a quarter mile north of the Dallas city limits (at 32°54′ N, 96°55′ W). Rawhide Creek is the stream's major tributary. The land around Farmers Branch was first settled in 1841 by Thomas Keenan, who called the creek Mustang Branch. By 1845 a number of other families had settled in the area, which was so productive that the creek's name was changed to Farmers Branch. By the 1980s the creek lay wholly within the cities of Addison and Farmers Branch. Most of the area around the stream has been developed for commercial or residential use. The local terrain is flat to rolling, and near the stream's mouth grasses and mesquite grow in dark calcareous clay soils.

FARMERS BRANCH, TEXAS. Farmers Branch is on Interstate Highway 35 and State Highway 77 twelve miles north of downtown Dallas in northeastern Dallas County. The Burlington Northern and Missouri, Kansas and Texas railroads serve the city. Farmers Branch was the location in 1845 of the first office of the Texan Land and Emigration Company, or the Peters colony.[qv] It was the most well-known Dallas County town during the 1840s because of its advertising throughout Europe and the United States. Thomas Keenan, Isaac B. Webb,[qv] and William Cochran all arrived in 1842 and received original land grants in the area that became the site of Farmers Branch. By 1843 settlers had established a community called Mustang Branch, named for the Mustang grapes that grew along the creek. Cochran later changed the name to Farmers Branch because of the area's rich farmland.

On May 5, 1845, Isaac Webb established the first formal church in Dallas County, called Webb or Webb's Chapel. This Methodist church originally met in a log cabin, which went through several buildings but still existed as a congregation in the 1990s. A school was started in the church in 1846. Webb became the first postmaster of Farmers Branch when the post office was established there on January 5, 1848. The post office functioned until 1866, was closed, and was reinstated in 1875. The first blacksmith shop in Dallas County was built at Farmers Branch in 1845 by William Bowles, a Baptist preacher, and his slave Jordan, who worked as the blacksmith. In the same year the first Dallas County gristmill was built there; it used rawhide belts that could be used only when the weather was dry because they stretched when wet. The first local cotton gin was built in 1849 by James A. Smith.

In 1878 the Dallas and Wichita Railway was completed from Dallas to Lewisville and passed through Farmers Branch. The road went into receivership and became part of the Missouri, Kansas and Texas in 1881. By 1890 Farmers Branch had a population of 100, a district school, three general stores, two blacksmith shops, and two physicians. By World War I[qv] the population was 300, and the area was a center for grain and cotton shipments. The community had a large number of new stores, including a millinery, a lumberyard, a grocery, and the Riddle Banking Company. Telephone connections and telegraph service were available. In 1916 the first brick school building was constructed.

The population of Farmers Branch remained stable until after World War II.[qv] In April 1946 the community was incorporated and began to implement improved city services. In the next several years a new artesian well was drilled, a water tower constructed, and new water mains were laid throughout the city. A city hall and community house were built. Three industries were located in the town—a bag factory, a tile plant, and a woodworking and planing mill. The first fire station in the community was built and manned by twenty volunteer firemen. In 1956 Farmers Branch received a home-rule charter that provides for a city council–manager form of government. At that time an estimated 80 percent of the 800 residents commuted to work in Dallas.

Proximity to Dallas contributed to rapid growth. The population of Farmers Branch reached 28,550 by the mid-1970s, when a variety of manufacturers were located there. Thirty-four firms produced many items, including steel products, tile, cement, asphalt, drugs, cosmetics, machine parts, and food products. Students in Farmers Branch attended school in either the Carrollton–Farmers Branch Independent School District or the Dallas Independent School District. Areas for recreation proliferated—fifteen parks, three golf courses, seventeen tennis courts, three youth centers, two indoor theaters, and a swimming pool. Brookhaven Medical Center was completed. The Farmers Branch *Times Chronicle* had been published since 1956, and the *Metrocrest News* had been established in 1960. In the 1990s Farmers Branch had a population of 24,250, sixty Fortune 500 companies, and fifty-two manufacturers, most recently including printing and publishing firms. Brookhaven Community College and Brookhaven Country Club were within the city limits. The Farmers Branch Historical Park comprised twenty-two acres and five historic buildings.

BIBLIOGRAPHY: John H. Cochran, *Dallas County: A Record of Its Pioneers and Progress* (Dallas: Mathis, 1928). Dallas *Times Herald*, August 22, 1948. Georgia Myers Ogle, comp., *Elm Fork Settlements: Farmers Branch and Carrollton* (Quanah, Texas?: Nortex, 1977). Vertical Files, Barker Texas History Center, University of Texas at Austin.
                                                                              Lisa C. Maxwell

FARMERS CANAL COMPANY. The Farmers Canal Company, also known as the Hankamer-Stowell Canal Company, was the first canal company to irrigate rice farms in Chambers County. Digging began in 1899, and the canal opened the following year. Water was pumped from Turtle Bay (now Lake Anahuac) into the canal, which traversed northern Chambers County to Stowell, where the company maintained its offices. The first president was F. W. Schwettman. By 1902 the canal watered some 10,000 acres of rice fields. Acreage increased until salt water began infesting Turtle Bay and seeping into the canal. Poor crops, declining markets, the continued problem of salt water, and the devastating 1915 hurricane (*see* HURRICANES) further hampered operations. After several temporary shutdowns, the Farmers Canal Company closed in 1925. The Devers Canal Company purchased most of the channels in 1927.

BIBLIOGRAPHY: Jewel Horace Harry, A History of Chambers County (M.A. thesis, University of Texas, 1940; rpt., Dallas: Taylor, 1981).
Robert Wooster

FARMERS CREEK. Farmers Creek rises at State Highway 59 west of St. Jo in northeastern Montague County (at 33°41′ N, 97°34′ W) and runs for twenty-five miles west and north through Lake Nocona, or Farmers Creek Reservoir, to its mouth on the Red River, southeast of Spanish Fort at the Montague county line (at 33°54′ N, 97°35′ W). It crosses flat terrain with local shallow depressions surfaced by clay and sandy loam that supports water-tolerant hardwoods, conifers, and grasses.

FARMERS' HOME IMPROVEMENT SOCIETY. The Farmers' Home Improvement Society (also known as the Farmers' Improvement Society) was founded in 1890 by Robert Lloyd Smith[qv] at Oakland, Colorado County, as a farmers' association for African Americans.[qv] The purposes of the society were to abolish the sharecropping and credit system that ensnared poor farmers, encourage self-sufficiency, promote home and farm ownership, promote crop diversification and use of improved farming methods, foster cooperative buying and selling, provide sickness and health benefits, and encourage the social and moral elevation of members. By 1898 the society claimed 1,800 members; by 1900 it had grown to eighty-six branches and 2,340 members; and by 1909 it had 21,000 members spread over Texas, Oklahoma, and Arkansas. In 1909 its cooperative business was estimated at $50,000 a year. In 1912 the membership owned 75,000 acres of land valued at considerably over $1 million. The society sponsored agricultural fairs to demonstrate the effectiveness of its programs. In addition to the cooperative business, it established the Farmers' Improvement Agricultural College at Wolfe City in 1906 and, to implement the overall program, the Farmers' Bank at Waco in 1911. During the late teens and early 1920s the society gradually declined, but for more than twenty years it contributed more than any other organization to elevating the status of blacks in Texas.

BIBLIOGRAPHY: Robert Carroll, Robert Lloyd Smith and the Farmers' Improvement Society of Texas (M.A. thesis, Baylor University, 1974).
Lawrence D. Rice

FARMERS' AND LABORERS' PROTECTIVE ASSOCIATION. The Farmers' and Laborers' Protective Association of America, organized in 1915 for the advancement of farming and laboring men and for the cooperative purchase of various kinds of supplies, enlisted several thousand members in north central and northwestern Texas. Members were required to take a binding oath of secrecy under threat of death. Lodge emblems included a strap, which stood for slavery, and a dirk and pistol, emblems of the laborer's self-defense against the capitalist. Evidence indicates that the FLPA was inactive before late 1916 and that its cooperative program never was significant.

Little was known about the FLPA in Texas before mid-1917. In May and June, however, just after the entry of the United States into World War I,[qv] more than fifty members of the FLPA were arrested, indicted, and charged with seditious conspiracy to prevent conscription. At least one man was killed during the roundup. Trial followed in September in the United States district court at Abilene. The prosecution charged that leaders urged forcible opposition to conscription, since members were advised to obtain rifles and ammunition, to blow up railroad bridges, to tear up tracks, and to cut telephone and telegraph wires; that the organization denounced the president and Congress; and that FLPA leaders sought amalgamation with the Industrial Workers of the World and the Working Class Union of Oklahoma. Although witnesses subsequently verified that some of the defendants had made intemperate statements, the conspiracy charges were unsubstantiated. Testimony revealed that most FLPA members were of good character and reputation, that most believed the organization was simply a marketing and purchasing cooperative, that in fact the association had a store in operation, that only the organizer, G. T. Bryant, had connections to the International Workers of the World, and that before the passage of conscription legislation, seditious acts were limited to resolutions like the one proposed by Haskell County locals and considered in convention. This resolution, which was not entered into association minutes, declared that the members were peace-loving and opposed to militarism, that they would refuse to invade a foreign country or to shoot another human being at the command of the "capitalist class," and that if war was declared, all who wanted war and every American official, from the president down to the constable, should resign and be forced to fight and leave the American people in peace. Testimony indicated also that the purchase of rifles by the Rotan and Snyder lodges was more the result of hysteria following disclosure of the Plan of San Diego[qv] than of FLPA activity. Although the trial was given wide press coverage and the general public believed the FLPA was disloyal, the jury acquitted all defendants except the lodge president, secretary, and organizer.

BIBLIOGRAPHY: William Hawley Atwell, *Autobiography* (Dallas: Warlick Law Printing, 1935). Jim Feagin, *Forty Years Under the Bench in Texas* (San Antonio: Naylor, 1950). E. F. Smith, *A Saga of Texas Law* (San Antonio: Naylor, 1940).
Joe R. Baulch

FARMERS UNION. The Farmers Union was formed as the Farmers' Educational and Cooperative Union in the Rains County town of Point. The organization was the basis for the National Farmers Union, which has been active in agricultural and rural public policies since it was first incorporated in 1902 by Isaac Newton Gresham,[qv] a small newspaper editor in Point. Because of the failure of the Farmers' Alliance and the People's Party[qqv] to maintain a sustained movement and organization on behalf of farmers, Gresham was well aware of the political problems facing another organization. Therefore, the first ten charter members brought a variety of backgrounds and political persuasions when the Farmers Union was officially incorporated by the Texas secretary of state on August 28, 1902. The founders included a newspaperman, a county clerk, a physician, a teacher, and six farmers. Politically, there were three populists, one Socialist, one Independent, and five Democrats.

The first local was organized at Smyrna, southwest of Emory in Rains County. At first the organization was confined to Rains County, but success there in collective bargaining over cotton sales led to rapid expansion into the South, the Midwest, and the far West. Many of the new local unions were formed from still-existing community branches of the defunct Farmers' Alliance. Like the alliance and the Grange,[qv] which preceded it, the Farmers' Union grew rapidly while joining was a novelty and large benefits from organization were anticipated. In 1910 the membership was 121,800, with the greatest strength in the Gulf states. In 1919 the union had 140,000 members, but by 1930 membership had fallen to 91,109. Many of the organizers were, like Gresham, former members of the alliance or the Grange. However, by 1906, internal dissention had already developed within the organization over the qualification of members who were not full-time farmers. This included Gresham and many of the charter members, who lost power after the Texas state convention in 1905.

In the beginning, the union's major objective was to gain control of cotton marketing. Cotton prices had dropped steadily since 1890, when cotton sold for ten cents a pound, to less than six cents by 1898. The Spanish-American War caused an upsurge in the market, and by 1907 cotton reached twelve cents a pound. However, prices again declined for the next five years, while production increased. The local and state unions worked to establish farmer-owned cooperative warehouses where producers could store their cotton and receive certificates of deposit that could be used as loan collateral. In this system, farmers could hold their crops off the market during the usual period of low harvest-time prices. Although many warehouses were founded in Texas, however, they could not prevent cotton prices from dropping to six cents a pound again after the panic of 1907. Efforts by the union leadership to withhold cotton from the market in order to increase the price also failed to have a significant effect before World War I.[qv]

In addition to emphasizing the importance of cooperatives and political involvement, the Farmers Union advocated many other reforms that eventually occurred. Some of these included better education for rural children, improved roads, diversified production, and better farm-management training for farmers. Although membership in the Farmers Union declined from a high of 100,000 in Texas in 1908, the organization continued to expand among the grain farmers of the Midwest. Unlike its predecessors, the organization did not attempt to form its own political party.

Although the union all but disappeared from other southern states after the 1920s, the Texas Farmers Union remained a part of the National Farmers Union in 1990, when it had 10,000 members. The organization is governed by an executive board of nine members elected from designated districts. The president and vice president are selected from the membership at large. County presidents serve on the full board of directors. All officers are elected for a term of two years, and the organization holds annual conventions at various cities around the state. The Texas Farmers Union has maintained an active program consistent with the philosophies of its founding members. It has worked at the state level for programs to increase agricultural education and marketing of commodities through such measures as loan programs. Also, rural health programs, improved public school funding, education, and transportation remain priorities. The Texas Farmers Union sponsors the Senior Texans Employment Program, the first program of its type in the United States when it was instigated by the Texas legislature in 1973. STEP enables retired persons in rural areas to work with nonprofit groups and government agencies for improvements. At the national level, the union supports supply-management programs for commodities in an effort to ensure a sufficient food supply for domestic and export needs while also providing for a strategic reserve. The Texas Farmers Union has its headquarters in Waco and legislative offices in Austin and Washington, D.C.

BIBLIOGRAPHY: Gilbert C. Fite, *Cotton Fields No More: Southern Agriculture, 1865–1980* (Lexington: University Press of Kentucky, 1984). Robert Lee Hunt, *A History of Farmer Movements in the Southwest, 1873–1925* (College Station: Texas A&M University Press, 1935?). C. Richard King, "Dave J. Neill and the Farmers' Union," West Texas Historical Association *Year Book* 40 (1964). Carl C. Taylor, *The Farmers Movement, 1620–1920* (New York: American, 1953).

Patrick Cox

FARMERS VALLEY, TEXAS. Farmers Valley is at the intersection of Farm roads 925 and 392, nine miles west of Vernon and one mile east of the Hardeman county line in west central Wilbarger County. A small community had been established in the area when a school was built in 1887. By the early 1900s it had grown to include a Methodist congregation established in 1881, a cotton gin, and a combination grocery store and service station. The Methodists built their church building about 1922. The school was renamed Wells Chapel in 1924 and served the area until it was consolidated with the Chillicothe school in 1946. The Farmers Valley population was reported at twenty-five during the 1930s and 1940s and fifty in later records. The Methodist church dissolved in the late 1970s, and the gin closed in 1982. The reported population was fifty in 1990.

BIBLIOGRAPHY: Wilbarger County Historical Commission, *Wilbarger County* (Lubbock, 1986).

Charles G. Davis

FARMERSVILLE, TEXAS. Farmersville, at the intersection of U.S. Highway 380 and State Highway 78 in east Collin County, was founded about 1849 by settlers who named the community after their principal occupation. An earlier settlement known as Sugar Hill had been started in 1845 by the John Yeary family two miles northeast of the site of present-day Farmersville but was abandoned when its residents moved to Farmersville in 1854. The post office was established in 1857, with Thomas E. Sherwood as its first postmaster. William Gotcher donated the site of the present town square in 1859, and John S. Rike became the first mayor when the town was incorporated in 1873. The Little Flock Primitive Baptist Church was organized in 1855, the First Methodist Church in 1856, and the First Baptist Church in 1865. There were private schools in Farmersville as early as the 1860s. The public school system was established around 1890, and in 1988 the Farmersville Independent School District had over 900 students on three campuses. Both the First National Bank at Farmersville and the Farmersville *Times*, a weekly newspaper, were founded in 1885 and were still in operation in 1988, when First Bank was the oldest independent bank remaining in Collin County and one of the oldest in the state. Farmersville began as a trading center for the farmers who were rapidly settling the area. In the early days the settlement was a major railroad shipping point for cattle and bois d'arc posts. In later years cotton, corn, and maize became major crops, along with onions and cantaloupes. A number of dairies were established. In the late 1980s most agricultural production was in wheat, maize, and beef cattle. Many residents commuted to jobs in neighboring cities. Beginning in 1935 an Onion Festival was held each year in Farmersville until it was suspended during World War II.[qv] In the fall of 1980 began the annual celebration of an Old Time Saturday, a day that commemorates the pretelevision days when "the country went to town" every Saturday all over Texas. Audie Murphy[qv] was born near Kingston, not far from Farmersville. He lived and worked in Farmersville for a time before his entry into the United States Army and used his sister's address in Farmersville as his own while he was overseas. Farmersville is a charter member city of the North Texas Municipal Water District and owner of its own electrical system. In 1988 the community of 2,900, although growing steadily as a part of rapidly expanding Collin County, still retained much of its rural flavor. In 1990 the population was 2,640.

BIBLIOGRAPHY: Roy Franklin Hall and Helen Gibbard Hall, *Collin County: Pioneering in North Texas* (Quanah, Texas: Nortex, 1975). J. Lee and Lillian J. Stambaugh, *A History of Collin County* (Austin: Texas State Historical Association, 1958).

Edward E. Stuart

FARMINGTON, TEXAS (Grayson County). Farmington is on Farm Road 1417 ten miles south of Sherman in south central Grayson County. The first settlers arrived in the area in the mid-1840s. Community development occurred through the efforts of William L. Wheat, Henry Campbell, and Samuel C. Watson. A post office opened in 1861. By the end of the Civil War[qv] Farmington had established itself as a school and church community for area farmers. By 1885 it had three churches, a school, a general store, a cotton gin, and a gristmill. The population slowly increased over the next two decades, to peak of 171 in 1904. That year postal service ended, and over the next few decades the number of residents steadily declined. By the end of World War II[qv] Farmington had fifty residents, a church, a school, and a general store. The population was estimated at twenty from 1940 to 1990.

BIBLIOGRAPHY: Grayson County Frontier Village, *History of Grayson County, Texas* (2 vols., Winston-Salem, North Carolina: Hunter, 1979, 1981).

David Minor

FARMINGTON, TEXAS (La Salle County). Farmington, 2½ miles northwest of Artesia Wells in west central La Salle County, was one of many new settlements that grew up in the county during the early 1900s when irrigation opened additional land to farming. The community was established in 1909, and a post office operated there from 1910 to 1911. Farmington was still shown on county maps in 1948.

BIBLIOGRAPHY: Annette Martin Ludeman, *La Salle: La Salle County* (Quanah, Texas: Nortex, 1975).

John Leffler

FARM PLACEMENT SERVICE OF TEXAS. The Farm Placement Service of Texas, which started in the mid-1930s, was an outgrowth of the federal government's Farm Placement Service, which had been set up in Fort Worth in 1919. Though the federal Farm Placement Service operated for only forty-five days during its initial year to oversee the hiring of farm workers for the state's wheat harvest, it continued to function in Texas for the next several decades, eventually passing its role to the state. The Farm Placement Service helped stabilize the farmers' search for workers and the workers' search for employment. Before the establishment of the federal Farm Placement Service, both groups had operated through labor agents, whose major interest was financial. In 1916, even before the national government moved in to regulate the agricultural labor market, the state's commissioner of labor had recommended that Texas manage the market to eliminate waste and promote better hiring practices. The Farm Placement Service was principally concerned with finding workers for the cotton harvest, though it covered vegetable and fruit crops as well. By 1925 it had set up farm-labor recruitment offices in Brownsville, Houston, Lubbock, and other cities. To accomplish its work, the Farm Placement Service sent staff members out to survey crop-harvest needs and to determine available housing for the workers. Many businesses assisted it, and chambers of commerce provided it with free telephone service. After congressional passage in 1933 of the Wagner-Payser Act, which reorganized the country's employment services, the federal government discontinued its direct operation of the Farm Placement Service, and in 1935 the program was subsumed under the newly organized Employment Service of Texas.

Once under the state's jurisdiction, the Farm Placement Service coordinated the pool of agricultural workers through a system of local offices that directed strategies for meeting regional needs. Each district supervisor maintained a calendar of seasonal labor requirements for harvesting various crops. In 1939 the Farm Placement Service could boast that it had placed just over half a million workers throughout the state in that year alone. The service also joined forces with the Federal Farm Security Administration to set up labor camps for agricultural workers in Raymondville, Robstown, Sinton, Weslaco, and other Texas towns. By June 1945 forty-one towns in the state had established these camps, which were also known as "reception centers." The camps generally provided wood, water, and toilets for workers during the harvest. Other camps offered other features. For example, at the Robstown site, which could serve up to 1,200 individuals, two types of shelters were available. One-room apartments that accommodated five people rented for $1.25 a week, and occupants were provided with community showers, baths, toilets, and a laundry room. In the same camp a small number of four-room houses with private baths were available for larger families at a cost of $2.25 a week. Some of the camps were still in operation under a different guise in the 1990s. The one at Weslaco, for instance, had been transformed into an apartment complex for farmworkers under the control of the Farmer Home Administration, a program of the United States Department of Agriculture. In the mid-1970s, after some thirty-five years as a separate program, the Farm Placement Service was disbanded, and its services were integrated into the regular job-placement programs of the Texas Employment Commission.qv In the early 1990s the agency reported placing agricultural workers both in Texas and out of state at an annual rate of 25 to 28 percent.

BIBLIOGRAPHY: Everett Ross Clinchy, Jr., *Equality of Opportunity for Latin-Americans in Texas* (New York: Arno Press, 1974). George Otis Coalson, *The Development of the Migratory Farm Labor System in Texas, 1900–1954* (San Francisco: R&E Research Associates, 1977). Pauline Rochester Kibbe, *Latin Americans in Texas* (Albuquerque: University of New Mexico Press, 1946).

Teresa Palomo Acosta

FARM AND RANCH. *Farm and Ranch*, an agricultural journal, was first published by Franklin Pierce Hollandqv in Austin in 1883. The paper, originally known as *Texas Farm and Ranch*, failed to profit in its early years of operation, and in 1885 Holland moved the magazine to Dallas at the encouragement of local businessmen, convinced that agriculture would eventually surpass livestock raising in the region. The journal's circulation increased, and in 1899 its title was shortened to *Farm and Ranch*. It was issued in Upper South, Lower South, and Southwestern editions and appeared either weekly or monthly. John H. Connell became editor in 1902, when the paper moved to a new building. Holland promoted agriculture and improvements in the quality of farmers' lives, including experimental farms in Ellis County and near Corpus Christi. He also sponsored farmers' institutes in Texas, Louisiana, and Oklahoma, which were the forerunners of the Texas Agricultural Extension Service,qv and agricultural clubs for Texas farm children before the founding of 4-H Clubs. Holland organized the Texas Swine Growers Association in 1891 and the Texas Corn Growers Association in 1906, lobbied in support of legislation in the farmers' interest, and championed the cause of education for farmers. In 1949 *Farm and Ranch* absorbed the *Southern Agriculturist* and continued its volume numbering as *Farm and Ranch with Southern Agriculturist*. Its last issue was published in November 1963.

BIBLIOGRAPHY: Tom Mann, "A Record of Forty Years of Progress," *Farm and Ranch*, February 5, 1921. *National Cyclopaedia of American Biography*, Vol. 33.

Diana J. Kleiner

FARM TENANCY. Since the colonial period, there have always been some Texas farmers who rented the land they farmed rather than owning it. Although no statistical information was collected until 1880, when United States census officials began to include that information in their returns, it is clear from letters, court cases, and newspaper advertisements that tenants rented land for a variety of reasons and paid in a variety of ways. Some farmers who possessed the resources to buy land rented until they were more familiar with Texas before making a permanent commitment to a specific location, while others rented because they lacked the resources necessary to obtain land of their own. Some tenants, sharecroppers, paid for rented land by promising a share of the crop or labor, while others paid in cash. In antebellum Texasqv most farm tenants probably lived outside the plantation areas of the state, since most plantations involved in the production of commercial crops utilized slaves. Precise figures are impossible to obtain, but it seems clear that only a relatively small percentage of farmers were tenants. Thus they are rarely if ever mentioned in newspapers or descriptions of the state.

The end of the Civil Warqv and the demise of slaveryqv brought a need for new labor arrangements in the production of commercial crops. Texas plantation owners, like others in the South, had little or no cash, and they wanted to assure themselves of a stable labor supply throughout the growing and harvesting season. A system of tenant farming evolved that met these needs. The most common arrangement after the Civil War was a share tenant or sharecropping arrangement. Since the crop would not be split until after the harvest, tenants could only receive payment for their labor after the crops were in. Most tenants in the period just after the Civil War were black, and the Freedmen's Bureau^{qv} supervised the signing and implementation of tenant-farming agreements in areas where it had local agents until it closed its local offices in December 1868. Although the agents sometimes complained that black women did not want to work as long in the fields as they had before the war and that many blacks did not want to work as many hours as they had as slaves, they generally reported that African Americans^{qv} worked well as tenants when treated fairly. Blacks and, later, whites seem to have preferred tenancy arrangements over other forms of agricultural labor because tenancy gave them greater independence and flexibility than wage labor. It also directly rewarded them for their hard work with better crops. They seem to have viewed tenancy as an agricultural ladder that could lead to farm ownership under the right conditions.

As tenant farming became more common, it also became more systematic. In Texas, as in other Southern states, a hierarchy of tenant farmers developed, according to what tenants provided for themselves. At the top were share and cash tenants who supplied the mules, plows, seed, feed, and other supplies needed. Share tenants typically paid the landlord a third of the cotton crop and a fourth of the grain. At the bottom were sharecroppers who supplied only their labor. They typically received half the crops. The differences were critical, not only because share tenants received a larger portion of the crops, but also because they were considered the owners of the crops. Sharecroppers were generally considered laborers whose wages were paid with a share of the crops, which were owned by the landlord. A sharecropping arrangement gave owners greater control over how their land was worked. By 1880, when the first systematic data were collected, approximately 38 percent of all farmers were tenants. More than 80 percent of these rented for a share of the crops. Although statistics on farm tenure by race were not collected until 1900, blacks comprised a much higher proportion of the total number of tenant farmers than their proportion of the population. The highest percentages of tenant farmers were in counties with black majorities. In Fort Bend, Harrison, and Marion counties, for example, tenant farmers comprised 74, 60, and 51 percent of all farmers, respectively. Census returns did not differentiate between sharecroppers and share tenants until 1920, so it is impossible to determine what percentage of the group listed as share tenants were actually sharecroppers.

In addition to paying out a portion of the crop as rent, many tenants also mortgaged their share of the cotton crop to a furnishing merchant or their landlord for food and other supplies. Because the crops were of an uncertain size, and the price of cotton at harvest was unknown, cotton crops were risky collateral for the lender. Consequently, the interest on the loans was quite high, sometimes as high as 150 percent. Once forced to make a crop lien, many tenants could never get away from the system, as they found themselves just breaking even or owing more than the total received for their crops. One economist estimated that by 1914 half the tenants borrowed 100 percent of their income. As the population of the state grew and the state's vast lands were claimed, acquiring ownership of a farm became more difficult. This led to a corresponding increase in the proportion of tenants. By 1900, half of all Texas farmers were tenants. Again as in 1880, more than 80 percent of these were either share tenants or sharecroppers. The biggest proportional increase was probably the increase in white tenants. In 1900, 47 percent of all white farmers and 69 percent of all black farmers were tenants.

The conditions under which tenant farmers lived and worked became political issues with the rise of the People's party^{qv} in the 1890s and became even more prominent when James E. Ferguson^{qv} used them as part of his successful campaign for governor in 1914. Despite the rhetoric, except for the temporary prosperity the high cotton prices of World War I^{qv} brought, conditions for tenant farmers did not materially change, and the number of tenants continued to rise. Each census recorded a larger proportion of tenants among Texas farmers.

The census of 1930 recorded the highest percentage of tenants ever reported in the state. That year, almost 61 percent of all Texas farmers were tenant farmers, and one third of these were sharecroppers. In terms of the population as a whole, in 1930, nearly one quarter of all Texans lived on tenant farms. With the coming of the New Deal, however, the number of tenant farmers began to fall. Although Franklin D. Roosevelt saw tenant farming as evidence of economic problems and supported programs designed to make tenants into owners, the programs that had the highest impact on tenants were those that paid farmers to restrict crop acreage. These programs reduced the need for labor and caused many owners to push sharecroppers off the land. By 1935, the proportion of tenant farmers in Texas had dropped to 57 percent. This drop was due to a much larger decrease in the number of sharecroppers, as the number of other types of tenants rose slightly. The changes brought on by the New Deal signaled the beginning of a rapid drop in the proportion of Texas farmers who rented their land rather than owned it and a dramatic change in the types of farmers who were tenants. By the time of the 1945 census, the pull of the job market and the armed services in World War II^{qv} had accelerated the changes already begun by the Great Depression^{qv} and New Deal programs. The proportion of farmers who were tenants fell from almost 61 percent in 1930 to a little over 37½ percent by 1945. The number of sharecroppers fell from more than a third to 16 percent of all tenant farmers. By 1987 tenants comprised just under 12 percent of all farmers.

As the numbers fell, the very nature of tenant farming also changed. The most striking changes came in the number of part owners listed in the census. Part owners—that is, farmers who owned some of the land they farmed and rented the rest—comprised less than 10 percent of all Texas farmers until 1940, when they accounted for 11 percent of all farmers. By 1978 part owners made up almost 30 percent of all farm operators. During this same period, Texas farming became more highly mechanized. In 1929, for example, fewer than 10 percent of all Texas farms had tractors. By 1960, Texas had more tractors than farms. As farming became more mechanized and thus more capital-intensive, viable economic units became too large for one family to own enough farmland and provide machinery and working capital at the same time. Therefore, many of the larger operations were run by part owners or by tenants who owned no land at all. In 1987 full owners comprised 56 percent of all farmers but farmed only a quarter of all harvested cropland. Tenants, who comprised just 12 percent of all farmers, also farmed approximately a fourth of all harvested cropland. Part owners made up about 32 percent of all farmers and harvested a little over half of all harvested cropland. *See also* AGRICULTURE.

BIBLIOGRAPHY: Barry A. Crouch, *The Freedmen's Bureau and Black Texans* (Austin: University of Texas Press, 1992). James Edward Ferguson, *The Need of Outside Capital for Turning Landless Men of Texas into Home Owning Farmers* (Temple, Texas: Telegram Print, 1915). Louis Ferleger, "Sharecropping Contracts in the Late Nineteenth Century South," *Agricultural History* 67 (Summer 1993). Neil F. Foley, The New South in the Southwest: Anglos, Blacks and Mexicans in Central Texas, 1880–1930 (Ph.D. dissertation, University of Michigan, 1990). Cecil Harper, Jr., Farming Someone Else's Land: Farm Tenancy in the Texas Brazos River Valley, 1850–1880 (Ph.D. dissertation, University of North Texas, 1988). Virgil Lee, *Farm Mortgage Financing in Texas* (College Station: Texas Agricultural Experiment Station, 1925). Richard G. Lowe and Randolph B. Campbell, *Planters and Plain Folk: Agriculture in Antebellum Texas* (Dallas: Southern Methodist University Press, 1987). *Studies in Farm Tenancy in Texas* (Austin: Division of Public Welfare, Department of Extension, 1915). *Texas Historic Crop Statistics, 1866–1975* (Austin: Texas Crop and Livestock Reporting Service, 1976). Harold D. Woodman, *King Cotton and His Retainers: Financing and Marketing the Cotton Crop of the South, 1800–1925* (Columbia: University of South Carolina Press, 1990).

Robert Yantis, *Farm Acreage, Values, Ownership and Tenancy* (Austin: Texas Department of Agriculture, 1927).

Cecil Harper, Jr., and E. Dale Odom

FARNESE, COUNT CHARLES DE (?–?). Charles, Count de Farnese, traveled to Texas in July 1837 and offered "his fortune and personal influence to the glorious Texas cause." He proposed to Sam Houston[qv] that a separate Catholic bishopric be established in Texas to insure peace with Mexico and Texan independence. According to his plan, the Congress of the Republic of Texas[qv] was to grant 1,280 acres to the parishes and their schools and the Vatican was to decide upon the structure of the system. When Count de Farnese returned to Rome, his idea was rejected, and the plan was never completed.

BIBLIOGRAPHY: Ralph Francis Bayard, *Lone-Star Vanguard: The Catholic Re-Occupation of Texas, 1838–1848* (St. Louis: Vincentian Press, 1945). Amelia W. Williams and Eugene C. Barker, eds., *The Writings of Sam Houston, 1813–1863* (8 vols., Austin: University of Texas Press, 1938–43; rpt., Austin and New York: Pemberton Press, 1970). Henderson K. Yoakum, *History of Texas from Its First Settlement in 1685 to Its Annexation to the United States in 1846* (2 vols., New York: Redfield, 1855).

FARNSWORTH, JOSEPH EASTMAN (1862–?). Joseph Eastman Farnsworth, telephone executive, was born to Simeon Dow and Jennie Ambrose (Eastman) Farnsworth on January 31, 1862, at Manchester, New Hampshire. As both of his parents died before he was six years of age, he was raised by a guardian in Lowell, Massachusetts, where he attended public schools and graduated from high school in 1880. Two years later he moved to San Antonio, Texas, where he entered the newspaper business as a reporter. He soon moved to Austin and became a reporter for the Austin *Statesman* while working as the legislative correspondent for the San Antonio *Express* and Waco *Examiner*. In addition, he operated a printing business.

In 1885 he was hired as an auditor by the Southwestern Telephone and Telegraph Company in Austin. Within two years he had risen to the position of general auditor of the company. He remained in this post until 1896, when he was promoted to superintendent of the organization's North Texas division and moved to Dallas. He continued his progress in the company when he was made general superintendent and general manager of the division; in 1902 he became general manager of the company. In 1905 Farnsworth also became vice president of the Bell Telephone Company, the parent corporation of Southwestern Telephone and Telegraph. He retired from his position as general manager in 1912, but maintained the vice presidency. In 1919 he became president of the Dallas Telephone Company. His success as an executive brought him appointment to the boards of directors of a number of local businesses, including the Texas Employees Accident Insurance Company and the Liberty Building and Loan Association, both of which he served as vice president. Farnsworth was an Episcopalian, Democrat, Freemason, and Elk. He married Laura Maas of Austin on October 30, 1890. The couple raised one child.

BIBLIOGRAPHY: Frank W. Johnson, *A History of Texas and Texans* (5 vols., ed. E. C. Barker and E. W. Winkler [Chicago and New York: American Historical Society, 1914; rpt. 1916]). *Who Was Who in America*, Vol. 4.

Brian Hart

FARNSWORTH, TEXAS. Farnsworth, on State Highway 15 ten miles southwest of Perryton in west central Ochiltree County, was established in 1919 when the Panhandle and Santa Fe Railway arrived. Ranchers had begun settling this area in the early 1880s, and by 1900 had established a school and community called Olds. A post office was established at the site in 1905 and initially named Nogal, but in November 1906 the name was changed to Rogerstown. The present post office dates from 1920 and was named for H. W. Farnsworth, director of the railroad. Population estimates have fluctuated between a low of twenty, first recorded in 1925, and a high of 200 in 1949. In 1947 Farnsworth had five businesses, two churches, and two schools. In 1984 the community had six businesses and an estimated population of 149, which was still the population figure reported in 1990.

BIBLIOGRAPHY: *Wheatheart of the Plains: An Early History of Ochiltree County* (Perryton, Texas: Ochiltree County Historical Survey Committee, 1969).

H. Allen Anderson

FARR, LOUIS LEE, SR. (1865–1930). Louis Farr, county surveyor, rancher, banker, and businessman, the third of six children of James and Laurena Finney (Stevens) Farr, was born in Greenville, Texas, on August 19, 1865. He attended schools in Greenville and then went to Add-Ran College (now Texas Christian University). In 1884 he moved to San Angelo, where he surveyed for C. D. Foote. The San Angelo *Standard* subsequently employed him as a typesetter, after which he worked in the county clerk's office and for Frank Lerch's land firm. When Edgar P. Sawyer came to Texas to seek land for his family's firm Farr helped him secure acreage to start the Bar S Ranch, which eventually grew to 269 sections.

In 1889 Farr became San Angelo's first city engineer. He was twice elected county tax assessor but declined to run a third time. In 1905 he and others purchased the buildings and surrounding land at Fort Concho and started a corporation called Fort Concho Realty Company. That year Farr helped raise $50,000 for the Kansas City, Mexico and Orient Railway to bring its main line through San Angelo. In 1906 he was elected mayor. In 1907 he was vice president of the Park Land and Cattle Company, the townsite company that developed the Mertzon area. The cornerstone of the new First Christian Church building names him chairman of the finance committee. He became chairman of the church board.

Farr served as director and vice president of the Wool Grower's Central Exchange Storage Company, which he had helped organize in 1909. He was secretary-treasurer of Eldorado Townsite Company and a partner in Broome, Farr, and Lee Real Estate and Insurance. He managed the Sawyer Cattle Company's Bar S Ranch in Irion and Reagan counties and became a director and secretary in the firm. With the 1919 Central National–Western National Bank merger, Farr was named Central National Bank vice president; he became board chairman in 1927. On October 29, 1926, one of the largest oil strikes in the nation was made at the Yates oilfield.[qv] Ira Yates chose Farr as his business manager and attorney. The two had been business partners and friends since 1885.

Farr was a member of the Masonic Lodge, the Rotary Club, and the San Angelo Country Club. He enjoyed spectator sports and card-playing and almost never missed the Southwestern Exposition and Fat Stock Show in Fort Worth. He married Ellen Osmer (Nellie) Johnson on March 7, 1887. They had three sons and a daughter. Nellie died on February 17, 1907, and Farr married Mattie C. Pistole on August 23, 1907. He was working at the warehouse of Wool Grower's when he became ill. His doctor and friend Ira Yates took him to a Temple hospital, where he died on June 10, 1930. He was buried in Fairmount Cemetery, San Angelo. Many memorials honored Farr, including the donation of land and construction of a building near Mertzon for the Boy Scouts called Camp Louis Farr.

BIBLIOGRAPHY: Fort Worth *Star-Telegram*, June 10, 1930. Joe A. Gibson, *Old Angelo* (San Angelo: Educator, 1971). San Angelo *Standard Times*, June 10, 1930.

Nonie Green

FARR, THENA MAE (1927–1985). Thena Mae Farr, champion cowgirl, rodeo producer, and cofounder of the Women's Professional Rodeo Association,[qv] daughter of Tom and Lula Farr, was born on December 16, 1927, in Baylor County, Texas, where she lived all of her life. Both her parents were Baylor County natives, and they raised three children on their ranch near Seymour. A typical ranch youngster, Thena Mae learned to ride at a very young age and became a noted equestrienne as well as outstanding all-around athlete. At Seymour High School, where she graduated in 1944, she was class secretary and basketball captain in 1942–43. But her equestrian skills and outgoing personality earned her greater honors in the community. In her four terms as "Miss Seymour" she represented the town at rodeos and horse shows throughout the Southwest. She earned many honors in amateur "sponsor contests," combination beauty and equestrian contests that during the early 1940s were the only rodeo events open to women.

She attended Texas State College for Women in 1944–45 before returning home to become a full-time rancher. However, her interest in rodeo remained strong, and she dreamed of the chance to compete in real, rough, stock and roping contests like the cowboys. She and her close friend Nancy Binford of Wildorado, Texas, often discussed their frustration at being shut out of rodeo competition. In September 1947 they solved the problem by producing an all-girl rodeo at the Tri-State Fair in Amarillo. Their successful venture broke all fair attendance records and motivated the participants to form the Girl's Rodeo Association (now the Women's Professional Rodeo Association) the following year.

Farr served on the original board of directors of the GRA and followed Binford in the presidency in 1951. In addition, the two incorporated their production company as the Tri-State All Girl Rodeo and for the next five years produced all-girl rodeos in Texas, Colorado, and Mississippi, thus providing women opportunities they had long lacked. Farr also continued competing, winning saddles, trailers, and prize money in cutting, bareback bronc riding, barrel racing, and flag racing. By the time she and Nancy Binford decided to dissolve their company in 1953, all-girl rodeos were well established in many states, and the GRA had become accepted as the sole governing body for women's contests in American rodeo. The two, confident that they had achieved their goals, left the business having broken even but never having shown a profit.

Farr then turned her attention to ranching and community activities. She served as an adult leader for the 4-H Club and belonged to the Texas and Southwestern Cattle Raisers Association, West Texas Chamber of Commerce,qv American Cattle Raisers Association, Seymour Remuda Club, Seymour Chamber of Commerce, Baylor County Farm Bureau, and American Quarter Horse Association. She was a lifelong Democrat and active in the Seymour First United Methodist Church, to which she donated several items in memory of her parents. For her many contributions to women's rodeo through her all-girl rodeos and charter membership in the GRA, Thena Mae Farr was inducted into the National Cowgirl Hall of Fameqv in June 1985. She died after a short illness in October of that year and was buried at Westover Cemetery, near Seymour. Professional rodeo is today a lucrative full-time career for women.

BIBLIOGRAPHY: *Cattleman*, January 1986. Files, National Cowgirl Hall of Fame and Western Heritage Center, Hereford, Texas.

Mary Lou LeCompte

FARR, TEXAS. Farr was near Hog Creek six miles northeast of Crawford in northwestern McLennan County. A post office operated there from 1892 to 1902, when mail was sent to Crawford. Sarah J. Walker was Farr's first postmaster. In 1896 the community had a general store operated by F. S. Ewing. Farr became the focus of a common school district in 1901 but was consolidated with the Walnut Grove district in 1905. The settlement was not shown on county highway maps in the 1940s.

BIBLIOGRAPHY: Martin Luther Bannister, The Historical Development of the Public School System of McLennan County (M.A. thesis, Baylor University, 1945). Dayton Kelley, ed., *The Handbook of Waco and McLennan County, Texas* (Waco: Texian, 1972).

Vivian Elizabeth Smyrl

FARRAR, LOCHLIN JOHNSON (1837–1901). Lochlin Johnson Farrar, lawyer, legislator, and Confederate soldier, was born on December 27, 1837, in DeKalb County, Georgia, the son of Jesse C. and Nancy (Johnson) Farrar. He was educated in Atlanta and moved in 1858 to Austin, where he read law in the office of George W. Paschal.qv He was admitted to the bar on January 4, 1859. On February 14 of that year he moved to Limestone County and established a practice in Springfield. Joseph Abbottqv read law in Farrar's office and subsequently became his partner for a time. In 1860 Farrar, who was living in a hotel, owned no land and had only $300 in personal property.

In 1861, with the outbreak of the Civil War,qv Farrar raised the first company from Limestone County, the "Limestone County Volunteers," and joined Col. William H. Parsons'sqv Twelfth Texas Cavalry regiment. The sixty-two-man company soon became restive and abandoned its camp of instruction after only three weeks in the army. Farrar remained with Parsons, however, as a private; he soon rose to sergeant major and then in 1862 to major, at Little Rock, Arkansas. After service in Arkansas and in the Red River campaignqv in Louisiana in 1864, Farrar was paroled in Hempstead in 1865.

With the close of the war Farrar taught school in Limestone County through the latter months of 1865 and into 1866, when he was elected district attorney for the Fifteenth Judicial District. He was removed from office in 1867, however, by Maj. Gen. Gordon Granger,qv who considered him "an impediment to Reconstruction." Farrar returned to the practice of law in Groesbeck in partnership with A. C. Prendergastqv until he was elected as a Democrat to the House of Representatives of the Fourteenth Legislature. In July 1869 Farrar married Mattie Starley; they had two children. In 1882 he was elected to the Senate of the Nineteenth Texas Legislature. He served as chairman of the Committee on State Asylums. His term expired in November 1886, after which he helped to organize and became the first president of the First National Bank of Groesbeck. Farrar was elected one of the vice presidents of the Parsons's Texas Cavalry Brigade Association at its first meeting in Corsicana on August 8, 1881. He delivered the principal addresses to the annual reunion at Alvarado on August 2, 1883, and at Cleburne on August 5, 1885. He died in 1901.

BIBLIOGRAPHY: Anne J. Bailey, *Between the Enemy and Texas: Parsons's Texas Cavalry in the Civil War* (Fort Worth: Texas Christian University Press, 1989). H. L. Bentley and Thomas Pilgrim, *Texas Legal Directory for 1876–77* (Austin: Democratic Statesman Office, 1877). Dallas *Herald*, August 11, 1881, August 2, 1883, July 30, 1885. Lewis E. Daniell, *Personnel of the Texas State Government, with Sketches of Representative Men of Texas* (Austin: City Printing, 1887; 3d ed., San Antonio: Maverick, 1892). Clement Anselm Evans, ed., *Confederate Military History* (Atlanta: Confederate Publishing, 1899; extended ed., Wilmington, North Carolina: Broadfoot, 1987–89). E. W. Swindells, *A Legislative Manual for the State of Texas* (2 vols., Austin, 1879–83).

Thomas W. Cutrer

FARRAR, ROY MONTGOMERY (1870–1943). Roy Montgomery Farrar, banker and civic leader, son of John H. and Sarah (Rose) Farrar, was born in St. Louis, Missouri, on December 16, 1870. After attending public schools in St. Louis he moved to Houston, Texas, in 1885, to Dallas in 1888, and back to Houston in 1896. He was connected with many lumber companies in Houston, including the South Texas Lumber Company, which he established with Jesse H. Jonesqv in 1902, and the Farrar Lumber Company, which he established in 1912. Farrar was president of the National Bank of Commerce of Houston from 1915 to 1921 and became the president of the Union National Bank in 1924. He was a member of the Houston Port Commission from 1914 to 1925, president of the Houston Chamber of Commerce in 1916–17 and from 1925 to 1926, and chairman of the Houston Housing Authority. He married Margaret Campbell on April 30, 1906; they had three children. Farrar died on August 17, 1943.

BIBLIOGRAPHY: Emory A. Bailey, *Who's Who in Texas* (Dallas: John

B. McCraw Press, 1931). Houston *Post*, August 18, 1943. *Southwestern Historical Quarterly*, Texas Collection, October 1943.

Carolyn Hyman

FARRAR, TEXAS. Farrar is on State Highway 39 eighteen miles south of Mexia in southeastern Limestone County. The area was first settled in the 1850s, but no community developed there until the 1880s. The settlement was named in honor of Lochlin Johnson Farrar,qv who moved to Limestone County in 1859. In 1883 the community received a post office with John Bishop, who owned the first mercantile business, as postmaster. By 1884 Farrar had a population of twenty-five and a steam gristmill and cotton gin. By 1914 the town had ten businesses and a population of seventy-five. In 1940 the population was estimated to be 150. Houston Lighting and Power Company opened a lignite plant near Farrar in 1986. In 1990 the town had a population of fifty-one and two businesses.

BIBLIOGRAPHY: Ray A. Walter, *A History of Limestone County* (Austin: Von Boeckmann–Jones, 1959).

Stephanie Panus

FARRER CREEK. Farrer Creek rises in north central King County (at 33°48′ N, 100°17′ W) and runs east for fifteen miles to its mouth on the Middle Fork of the Wichita River, two miles west of Lowrance Mountain in northeast King County (at 33°48′ N, 100°04′ W). The stream passes through remote ranch and oil lands with rolling to steep-sloped terrain. Its headwaters are near the Tom B oilfield, and its mouth is within the Juniper gas field. Local soils of shallow clay and sandy loams, occasionally rocky, support juniper, cacti, and sparse grasses. Farrer Spring, slightly active in 1979, is located near the mouth of the creek; Indians once camped beside it.

BIBLIOGRAPHY: Gunnar Brune, *Springs of Texas*, Vol. 1 (Fort Worth: Branch-Smith, 1981).

FARRIS, TEXAS. Farris, on what is now Ranch Road 2690 thirteen miles north of Uvalde, was named for Charles Jefferson Farris, who moved to the area with his brother and a nephew in 1891. Farris subsequently bought the other two men out and expanded the original holding of 1,500 acres to 5,000 acres. Most of his prosperity was from cotton, but he also raised cattle, horses, and mules. He married Ida Rutland in 1893 and took her to live at the ranch in 1894. The couple had six children. In 1907 or 1908 Farris replaced his original four-room home with a two-story, ten-room house made of concrete blocks manufactured on the site. He built a barn and silos of the same material. The community of Farris grew up on land that Farris sold. In the first decade of the 1900s he donated an acre for the establishment of a school, which was named after him. The one-room schoolhouse also served as a community center and as a meetingplace for the Church of Christ, of which the Farrises and many of their neighbors were members. For summer revivals held under the nearby brush arbor, preachers and song leaders would come from as far away as Austin and would get their room and board at the Farris home. In 1935 the school closed, and students were bused to Uvalde. As paved roads entered the area and the means of transportation improved, residents moved away, and the community disappeared. Only the lower story of the Farris ranchhouse was still standing in 1990.

BIBLIOGRAPHY: *A Proud Heritage: A History of Uvalde County* (Uvalde, Texas: El Progreso Club, 1975). Uvalde *Leader-News*, March 23, 1969, April 2, 1987.

Jane A. Knapik

FARRIS CHAPEL, TEXAS. Farris Chapel is on Farm Road 1791 two miles north of the Montgomery county line in southwestern Walker County. Among the earliest settlers in the area were Hezekiah Farris and his brother William, former residents of Franklin County, Tennessee, who arrived in 1835 and were soon joined by other Tennesseans. In 1841 Farris and his neighbors built a church on the north bank of West Sandy Creek. Services were conducted by Methodists, Baptists, and Presbyterians in the building. However, after the Civil Warqv the Baptists built their own building, and residents of the area supported a school based in the Methodist church. In 1880 a new church building was erected to replace the old structure. In 1990 Farris Chapel Methodist Church remained a place of worship for the community, and the cemetery was still used.

BIBLIOGRAPHY: D'Anne McAdams Crews, ed., *Huntsville and Walker County, Texas: A Bicentennial History* (Huntsville, Texas: Sam Houston State University, 1976). Walker County Genealogical Society and Walker County Historical Commission, *Walker County* (Dallas, 1986).

James L. Hailey

FARRIS CREEK. Farris Creek rises five miles east of Walnut Springs and 4½ miles northwest of Morgan in northern Bosque County (at 32°05′ N, 97°39′ W) and runs south for four miles to its mouth on Steele Creek (at 32°02′ N, 97°39′ W).

FARRSVILLE, TEXAS. Farrsville is on State Highway 63 fifty miles north of Beaumont in northwestern Newton County. Settlers arrived in the area in the 1840s or early 1850s and named their community for Alfred E. Farr, a wealthy farmer and Methodist minister. Census returns show that Farr, who was born in Mississippi, had amassed a total estate of just under $50,000 in Newton County by 1860. The community, originally called Farr's Mill, had a sawmill, water mill, gristmill, and cotton gin. It was on the military road used by Confederate troops during the Civil Warqv and was also on a stage route running from Alexandria, Louisiana, to Beaumont, Texas. A post office opened in Farrsville in 1875. By 1884 the community had a population of 150. The sawmill closed in 1918, when the huge mills at Wiergate began to operate. The gristmill closed seventeen years later. Farrsville maintained a population of seventy-five through most of the first half of the twentieth century and had a post office as late as 1948. In the mid-1960s the population rose to 150, a level it maintained through 1990.

BIBLIOGRAPHY: Newton County Historical Commission, *Glimpses of Newton County History* (Burnet, Texas: Nortex, 1982).

Robert Wooster

FARWELL, JOHN VILLIERS (1825–1908). John V. Farwell, wholesale dry goods merchant and member of the Capitol Syndicate, was born at Painted Post in Steuben County, New York, on July 29, 1825. He was the third of five children born to Henry and Nancy (Jackson) Farwell, who made their living by farming and shipping lumber. In 1838, when John was thirteen, the family moved to Ogle County, Illinois, and settled in the Rock River valley near the town of Oregon. There John spent the remainder of his youth; he and his brothers helped build the family home, which often served as a local meeting house on Sundays. In 1845, after graduating from Mount Morris Seminary, John went to Chicago, where his older brother had moved the year before. After working briefly for the city, he became a bookkeeper for the Hamilton and Day dry goods firm, with which he remained for four years. On April 16, 1849, he married Abigail Gates Taylor. She died on May 9, 1851, a month after giving birth to their daughter. In the meantime, Farwell had joined the firm of Wadsworth and Phelps (later Cooley, Wadsworth, and Company), of which he was made general manager. In 1854 he married Emeret Cooley, a sister of a business associate; they had three sons and a daughter. In 1862 the firm became known as Cooley, Farwell, and Company, then in 1865, after he took it over, John V. Farwell and Company. Marshall Field, Potter Palmer, Levi Z. Leiter, and S. N. Kellogg were numbered among Farwell's partners at one time or another, and the Farwell Company was for many years Chicago's leading dry goods store.

Unlike his brother and partner Charles, who helped form the Republican party and later served in both houses of Congress, John

Farwell rarely participated in politics; however, he was an elector for Abraham Lincoln in 1860. In 1869 he was appointed a commissioner for Indian Affairs by President Ulysses S. Grant. He was a devout Methodist who headed the Chicago branch of the United States Christian Commission during the Civil War^{qv} and was a leading friend and supporter of Dwight L. Moody's ministry. Farwell helped build the First Methodist Church in Chicago and was also a zealous supporter of the Young Men's Christian Association; he donated land in downtown Chicago for the first YMCA building.

Farwell entered the Texas cattle-ranching scene in 1882, when, as a leading member of the Capitol Syndicate, he helped finance the building of the new Capitol^{qv} in Austin. Both he and Charles were directors of the Capitol Freehold Land and Investment Company,^{qv} organized in London in 1885 to handle the land that became the XIT Ranch.^{qv} In addition, he was for a time managing director of the XIT. In that position, Farwell spent some time at the ranch, where he occasionally held church services for the employees; his nephew Walter erected a summer residence near Channing that served as the new XIT headquarters.

Farwell died on August 20, 1908, and was interred in Chicago. Even after ceasing cattle operations in 1912, the Farwell estate continued ownership of XIT properties in the form of a trust known as the Capitol Reservation Lands, organized in 1915. This trust remained in existence until the last of the Panhandle^{qv} properties was sold. The family also maintained the dry goods business in Chicago until 1926, when it was sold to Carson, Pirie, and Company. Two towns in Texas were named for Farwell.

BIBLIOGRAPHY: Cordia Sloan Duke and Joe B. Frantz, *6,000 Miles of Fence: Life on the XIT Ranch of Texas* (Austin: University of Texas Press, 1961). Abby Farwell Ferry, *Reminiscences of John V. Farwell* (Chicago: Seymour, 1928). J. Evetts Haley, *The XIT Ranch of Texas and the Early Days of the Llano Estacado* (Chicago: Lakeside, 1929; rpts., Norman: University of Oklahoma Press, 1953, 1967). James D. Hamlin, *The Flamboyant Judge: As Told to J. Evetts Haley and William Curry Holden* (Canyon, Texas: Palo Duro, 1972). Parmer County Historical Society, *A History of Parmer County* (Quanah, Texas: Nortex, 1974).

David B. Gracy

FARWELL, TEXAS (Hansford County). Farwell, in the center of Hansford County about three miles east of what later became Gruver, was established in 1880 by the Canott family of Illinois and was the first town in the county. Water was supplied to the settlement by a hand-dug well 200 feet deep. Like Farwell in Parmer County, the Hansford County community was named for John V. Farwell,^{qv} a Chicago merchant and a principal in the Capitol Syndicate, which built the present Capitol^{qv} building in Austin. The county's first newspaper, the Farwell *Graphic*, was established in Farwell, which at one time also had a livery stable, store, hotel, saloon, and butcher shop. A post office was established there in 1887 but was moved to Hansford in 1894. Farwell rapidly fell into oblivion after 1889, when it lost a county seat election to Hansford.

BIBLIOGRAPHY: Hansford County Historical Commission, *Hansford County, Texas* (2 vols., Dallas: Taylor, 1980?). Dotty Jones, *A Search for Opportunity: A History of Hansford County* (Gruver, Texas: Jones, 1965).

H. Allen Anderson

FARWELL, TEXAS (Parmer County). Farwell, the county seat of Parmer County, is at the junction of U.S. highways 60 and 84, on the New Mexico state line in the southwestern part of the county. The townsite was located at the point where the Pecos Valley and Northern Texas Railway entered New Mexico, on land originally part of the XIT Ranch.^{qv} R. H. Kemp established a lumber company nearby in 1904. The site, named for the brothers Charles B. and John V. Farwell,^{qv} who headed the Capitol Syndicate, was surveyed in 1905. Farwell was made headquarters for the company's resident representative, James D. Hamlin,^{qv} and its land commissioner, F. W. Wilsey. Almost immediately several substantial buildings were constructed: a large brick warehouse for R. C. Hopping and the Robertson brothers, who operated a grocery store in Texico; a group of brick stores and offices known as the "Hamlin Brick"; and later the Farwell Inn, a three-story brick hotel. A Congregational church built in 1907 doubled as a public school until separate facilities were built in 1910. A post office was established in 1906. Farwell supplanted Parmerton as county seat when Parmer County was organized in 1907; Hamlin was elected county judge. In 1908 the First National Bank of Farwell was chartered, and the Santa Fe Railroad established a freight depot, warehouse, and coalyard on the Texas side. B. F. Fears started publication of the State Line Tribune by 1910, when Farwell's population had grown to more than 800 and the town had begun to rival Texico and Clovis, New Mexico, as a railroad shipping center. The citizens had voted to incorporate in 1907, but Farwell was disincorporated and the bank closed in 1910 when city funds became badly depleted. The bank was rechartered in 1912 as the Texas State Bank of Farwell.

Farwell grew while real estate developers continued to parcel off XIT lands and attract more settlers. A permanent courthouse was erected in 1917. That year C. A. Roberson sought to establish an automobile and tire manufacturing plant, but that scheme folded when he was jailed for selling fraudulent stock. By the mid-1920s the town had modern utilities, and further improvements were made on the waterworks by 1930. In 1950, with a population of 1,250, the town voted once again to incorporate and established a mayor-commission government. A medical clinic was built in 1955, and a year later a volunteer fire department was organized. The last thirty-nine acres of XIT Ranch land in Farwell was sold in 1963.

The industries that serve modern agriculture in Farwell include a fertilizer plant, an irrigation pipe plant, several feedlot operations, and four grain elevators with a total storage capacity of more than six million bushels. The town has five churches. By 1960 the population was just over 1,000, and by 1967 Farwell supported more than ninety businesses. The annual Border Town Days is held the last weekend in July. The population in Farwell increased from 1,185 in 1970 to 1,354 by 1985 and 1,373 by 1990.

BIBLIOGRAPHY: James D. Hamlin, *The Flamboyant Judge: As Told to J. Evetts Haley and William Curry Holden* (Canyon, Texas: Palo Duro, 1972). Parmer County Historical Commission, *Prairie Progress* (Dallas: Taylor, 1981). Parmer County Historical Society, *A History of Parmer County* (Quanah, Texas: Nortex, 1974).

H. Allen Anderson

FASHING, TEXAS. Fashing is at the junction of Farm roads 2924 and 99, twenty-nine miles southeast of Jourdanton in southeastern Atascosa County. In 1916 the 5,500-acre Hickok Ranch was subdivided into farms. The surrounding area had been settled as early as the 1850s by ranching families along the San Patricio Trail.^{qv} O. F. C. Henke was the first to purchase a small tract of land from the Warnecke and Stieren Land Company, the promoters responsible for subdividing the Hickok Ranch. The settlement was first called Hickok, then Hindenburg; the name Fashing, from "Fashion" brand tobacco and German *Fasching* ("carnival" or "Shrovetide"), was approved for the community post office in 1920. Albert Schroeder was the first postmaster. Before 1920 residents constructed a one-circuit phone list. Fashing did not have electricity until the 1930s, when the Karnes Electric Cooperative was constructed.

Most of the residents of this farming community have been of German descent and have maintained many German traditions. Oil, gas, and uranium have added to the economy. In the 1930s Fashing had a population of twenty-five and five businesses. From 1939 until 1964 it had 125 residents and four businesses. In 1968 it had ninety residents and no businesses. From 1970 to 1990 the population was recorded at fifty. In 1972 Fashing was proclaimed the "Grand Champion Rural Community of Texas" for its efforts in community improvement. Its first school, built in 1917, was replaced by later buildings in 1921 and 1952. In 1930 a separate school for Hispanic children was constructed. This building was used until the two schools were combined in 1947. The Fashing Common School District was consolidated with the Karnes City Independent School District in 1958. After 1980 the seventh and eighth grades were bused to Karnes City. Grades one through six remained in Fashing until the school was closed in 1988. Over the years, Methodist, Catholic, and Lutheran churches were built in Fashing. The post office was discontinued in 1988.

BIBLIOGRAPHY: *Atascosa County History* (Pleasanton, Texas: Atascosa History Committee, 1984). Vertical Files, Barker Texas History Center, University of Texas at Austin.   *Robert H. Thonhoff*

FASKEN, TEXAS. Fasken, in east central Andrews County, was established in 1917 by the Midland Farms Company as a speculative enterprise. Since the site was on the newly built Midland and Northwestern Railway, it was hoped that substantial numbers of settlers would move there. The community soon had a depot, store, hotel, barbershop, school, and zoo, and many town lots were sold, but few buyers actually took up residence. In 1923 heavy rains destroyed much of the track, and the railroad was abandoned. Fasken rapidly declined and had completely vanished by the early 1930s.

BIBLIOGRAPHY: *Andrews County History, 1876–1978* (Andrews, Texas: Andrews County Heritage Committee, 1978). Ed Ellsworth Bartholomew, *The Encyclopedia of Texas Ghost Towns* (Fort Davis, Texas, 1982).   *Charles G. Davis*

FASTRILL, TEXAS. Fastrill, on the Neches River twelve miles south of Rusk in western Cherokee County, was established in 1922 by the Southern Pine Lumber Company as a base for its logging operations in that county. The name Fastrill is derived from a combination of three names: that of a former Diboll postmaster, F. F. Farington; that of P. H. Straus, lumberman; and that of Will Hill, lumberman. At its height Fastrill had a barbershop, a cleaning and pressing shop, a drugstore, a commissary, the Southern Pine office, a two-story hotel for single male workers, a wooden superintendent's office, a four-teacher school, two churches, a post office, the Barrel House, and an approximate population of 600 people. The community was a voting precinct. Located southwest of the town on a railroad spur were a blacksmith shop, an engine shed, a water tank, a bathhouse, and an underground crude-oil tank. All houses were constructed of clapboards and consisted of four rooms with a front and back porch. Each house had an outdoor privy. One light plant supplied electricity at specified hours for the entire town. The company supplied farmland and equipment so that its employees could raise produce, and a cannery so that they could preserve it for their use. Four steam engines transported logs to Diboll and Maydelle from the town, and also carried loggers to and from the woods, where they worked a ten-hour day. Fastrill had water piped directly from what is known as the pump hole on the Neches River and stored in a wooden tank built on stilts. The untreated water was used by the steam engines as well as the people and was considered unpolluted because of the absence of industry up the river. A celebration occurred annually on the Fourth of July, when people from neighboring communities would come to a dance sponsored by Southern Pine. A similar celebration for blacks occurred on Juneteenth.[qv] Other recreation included baseball, home dances, and Sunday afternoon trips to the Rock Hole, the best swimming hole on the Neches River.

By 1941, when most of the Southern Pine timber was depleted, employees gradually vacated, and the post office, school, and voting precinct were closed. Shortly thereafter the town was totally evacuated. In the 1980s the Arthur Temple Research Area on Farm Road 23 south of Rusk occupied the site of old Fastrill. An old railroad tram and a bridge across the Neches River is known to area residents as the Fastrill Bridge. Annually, on the second Sunday in June, at a park near the old Fastrill site, the former residents of Fastrill gather together for a reunion and drink "good ole river coffee."

BIBLIOGRAPHY: Bob Bowman, *This Was East Texas* (Diboll, Texas: Angelina Free Press, 1967). Hattie Joplin Roach, *The Hills of Cherokee* (1952; rpt., Fort Worth, 1976).   *Phylena Helm*

FATE, TEXAS. Fate is on State Highway 66 and the Missouri, Kansas and Texas line four miles northeast of Rockwall in northern Rockwall County. The community's name derives from the nickname, "Fate," given to Lafayette Brown, one of the area's early settlers, by his wife. A post office was established in the community in July 1880. By the mid-1880s Fate had a school, a cotton gin, two general stores, and a population of seventy-five. In 1886, in anticipation of the arrival of the Missouri, Kansas and Texas, Dr. Wylie T. Barnes platted a new community on his land about a half mile northeast of Fate, calling the new community Barnes City. The railroad built through later that year, and the residents and businesses of Fate moved to the new community. Seeking to avoid having to apply for a new post office, the residents of Barnes City changed their community's name to Fate in February 1887. By 1890 the community had fifteen businesses, a two-room school, two churches, and a population of 100. In 1899 the first rural mail route in Texas began operation from Fate. The population of the community continued to grow steadily through the 1890s and the first decades of the twentieth century, reaching 299 by 1920. The business community witnessed a similar growth, and Fate's first bank opened in 1907. Fate was incorporated in 1908. The federal highway reached the town after World War I.[qv]

During the 1920s and 1930s the small community began to decline. While agriculture remained the area's major occupation, better roads and automobiles took trade from local merchants to those in larger towns. Nonetheless, a bank, a drugstore, and a number of stores remained in business at Fate. Fate's school eventually dropped its high school grades, and the community's population declined to 194 by 1930 and 127 by 1940. During the 1940s and 1950s Fate lost businesses and residents to the growing cities of Dallas and Fort Worth. The number of businesses operating in Fate declined from fifteen to six during the 1940s. Since 1950, however, the population of Fate has increased, rising to 475 by 1990. In the 1990s many of the town's residents held jobs in the Dallas area, but Fate was still able to support four businesses.

BIBLIOGRAPHY: Rockwall County Historical Foundation, *Rockwall County History* (Dallas: Taylor, 1984). O. L. Steger, Sr., *History of Rockwall County* (Wolfe City, Texas: Henington, 1969).
   Brian Hart

FATE BELL SHELTER. Fate Bell Shelter is located in Seminole Canyon State Historical Park[qv] about thirty miles west of Comstock on U.S. Highway 90. The site is approximately 150 yards long, and its greatest depth is forty feet. The shelter, which is a state archeological landmark, was named after Mrs. Fate Bell, who owned the land that the shelter occupies. Fate Bell Shelter is a deeply stratified rock shelter containing evidence of over 8,000 years of occupation, from the Archaic Period to the Late Prehistoric Period (ca. 7000 B.C. to A.D. 1500). Dating the recovered artifacts and rock art in Fate Bell Shelter and in Seminole Canyon in general has been difficult because of the extreme damage done to many sites, including Fate Bell, by looters.

The site was first excavated by the University of Texas between October 20 and November 18, 1932, by a crew of five men led by James E. Pearce[qv] and A. T. Jackson. The site was chosen by Pearce out of eight sites they located because it was the largest and least disturbed. The 1932 expedition was the only major excavation of the shelter. A smaller excavation was carried out by Mark Parsons in 1963 as part of the salvage operations prior to the construction of Amistad Dam.

Various projects since then have documented the Indian rock art[qv] extant in Fate Bell Shelter and in the surrounding area.

The initial excavations revealed much material culture, including engraved shells, painted pebbles, fiber sandals (complete and in various stages of manufacture), baskets, manos, and metates. Ceramics of any type are conspicuously absent. Also found were various types of projectile points. These are normally diagnostic of a particular time period and can be used to determine time of occupation when found in context. Unfortunately, some of each point type were found at all levels. The most probable explanation is that the site had been previously disturbed, either by looters or by natural process. The Pearce expedition also noted the existence of sotol pits—circular depressions used to cook the yucca-like sotol plant. Eight burials were found. Three of these had no skeletal remains; presumably they had not been preserved. One was a group burial and contained the skeletons of five individuals. Found within many of the burials were traces of matting made from either sotol or agave.

Fate Bell Shelter is best known for its pictographs, which are among the best documented and best preserved of the Pecos River style. This style, which may date between three and four thousand years before the present, is generally considered the oldest of the types found in the Lower Pecos area. This would place the art in the middle Archaic period. The Pecos River style is a polychrome style that is considered a manifestation of the shaman cult. The central characters of the pictographs are faceless anthropomorphic figures, elaborately dressed and often holding a variety of accessories such as atlatls, darts, and fending sticks. The figures are often depicted with their arms outstretched, and in later pictographs the shamans' arms are increasingly stylized and seem to be more akin to wings than arms. At one end of the shelter there are also examples of Red Linear figures—a Late Archaic Period style characterized by very small stick figures engaged in various activities.

Although the pictographs of Fate Bell Shelter were noticed by the Jackson expedition, they were not mentioned in his 1933 publication. He did, however, include illustrations from the shelter in his 1938 publication *Picture Writing of the Texas Indians*. The first real attempt to make a systematic and permanent record of the pictographs was undertaken by Lula and Olea Forrest Kirkland[qv] during the 1930s. The Kirkland expedition produced beautiful watercolors of the Fate Bell pictographs, but the public did not see much of this work until *The Rock Art of Texas Indians*, by Kirkland and W. W. Newcomb, Jr., was published in 1967. When acquired by the Texas Parks and Wildlife Department,[qv] the rock art was documented in detail using stereo-photogrammetric methods, regular photography, and artistic renderings. These and Kirkland's original drawings are now maintained at the Texas Memorial Museum[qv] in Austin. As part of Seminole Canyon State Historical Park, the site is open to the public on a limited basis.

BIBLIOGRAPHY: Mark L. Parsons, *1963 Test Excavation at Fate Bell Shelter, Amistad Reservoir, Val Verde County, Texas* (Texas Archeological Salvage Project, Miscellaneous Papers No. 4, Austin: University of Texas, 1965). James Edwin Pearce and A. T. Jackson, *A Prehistoric Rockshelter in Val Verde County, Texas* (University of Texas Bulletin 3327, Anthropological Papers 1.3, Bureau of Research in the Social Sciences, July 15, 1933). Harry Shafer and Jim Zintgraff, *Ancient Texans: Rock Art and Lifeways along the Lower Pecos* (Austin: Texas Monthly Press, 1986). Solveig A. Turpin, *Seminole Canyon* (Texas Archaeological Survey Report 83, University of Texas at Austin, 1982).

Arturo René Muñoz

FAUBION, TEXAS. Faubion, twelve miles southeast of Burnet in southeastern Burnet County, was named for William J. Faubion, its first postmaster. A post office was established there in 1886 and discontinued in 1888, when mail for the settlement was sent to Smithwick. No evidence of the community appeared on county highway maps by the 1940s.

BIBLIOGRAPHY: Darrell Debo, *Burnet County History* (2 vols., Burnet, Texas: Eakin, 1979).

Vivian Elizabeth Smyrl

FAUGHT, TEXAS. Faught is at the intersection of Farm roads 195 and 196, eight miles northeast of Paris in northeast Lamar County. In 1893 the community acquired a post office named for its first postmaster, Dr. Robert Faught. At the time the settlement had two businesses, a corn mill, and a population of twenty. The post office was discontinued in 1905, but 1936 state highway maps showed two churches and a cemetery, a school, two businesses, and multiple dwellings at the townsite. The World War II[qv] period brought an increase in population to 100, but from 1949 until the mid-1970s the population remained at twenty. Faught recorded twenty-five residents from 1974 to 1990, when the community had one business, a church, and a town hall.

Jana Jordan

FAULK, JOHN HENRY (1913–1990). John Henry Faulk, humorist and author, fourth of five children of Henry and Martha (Downs) Faulk, was born in Austin, Texas, on August 21, 1913. His parents were staunch yet freethinking Methodists who taught him to detest racism. He entered the University of Texas in 1932. Under the guidance of J. Frank Dobie, Walter P. Webb, and Roy Bedichek,[qqv] he developed his considerable abilities as a collector of folklore. For his master's degree thesis, Faulk recorded and analyzed ten African-American sermons from churches in Travis and Bexar counties. His research convinced him that members of minorities, particularly African Americans,[qv] faced grave limitations of their civil rights. Between 1940 and 1942, Faulk taught an English I course at the University, using mimicry and storytelling to illustrate the best and worst of Texas societal customs. Often made to feel inferior at faculty gatherings, Faulk increasingly told unbelievable tales and bawdy jokes. His ability both to parody and to praise human behavior led to his entertainment and literary career. Early in World War II[qv] the army refused to admit him because of a bad eye. In 1942 he joined the United States Merchant Marine for a year of trans-Atlantic duty, followed by a year with the Red Cross in Cairo, Egypt. By 1944 relaxed standards allowed the army to admit him for limited duty as a medic; he served the rest of the war at Camp Swift, Texas.

Radio provided Faulk the audience he, as a storyteller, craved. Through his friend Alan Lomax, who worked at the CBS network in New York, Faulk became acquainted with industry officials. During Christmas 1945, Lomax hosted a series of parties to showcase Faulk's yarn-spinning abilities. When discharged from the army in April 1946, CBS gave Faulk his own weekly radio program, entitled "Johnny's Front Porch"; it lasted a year. Faulk began a new program on suburban station WOV in 1947 and the next year moved to another New Jersey station, WPAT, where he established himself as a raconteur while hosting "Hi-Neighbor," "Keep 'em Smiling," and "North New Jersey Datebook." WCBS Radio debuted the "John Henry Faulk Show" on December 17, 1951. The program, which featured music, political humor, and listener participation, ran for six years.

Faulk's radio career ended in 1957, a victim of the Cold War and the blacklisting of the 1950s. Inspired by Wisconsin Senator Joseph McCarthy, AWARE, Incorporated, a New York-based, for-profit corporation, offered "clearance" services to major media advertisers and radio and television networks. For a fee, AWARE would investigate the backgrounds of entertainers for signs of Communist sympathy or affiliation. In 1955 Faulk earned the enmity of the blacklist organization when he and other members wrested control of their union, the American Federation of Television and Radio Artists, from officers under the aegis of AWARE. In retaliation, AWARE branded Faulk a Communist. When he discovered that the AWARE bulletin prevented a radio station from making him an employment offer, Faulk sought redress. Several prominent radio personalities and CBS News vice president Edward R. Murrow supported Faulk's effort to end blacklisting. With financial backing from Murrow, Faulk engaged New York

John Henry Faulk, New York City, 1947. John Henry Faulk Papers, CAH; CN 05869.

attorney Louis Nizer. Attorneys for AWARE, including McCarthy-committee counsel Roy Cohn, managed to stall the suit, which was originally filed in 1957, for five years. When the trial finally concluded in a New York courtroom, the jury had determined that Faulk should receive more compensation than he sought in his original petition. On June 28, 1962, the jury awarded him the largest libel judgment in history to that date—$3.5 million. An appeals court subsequently reduced the amount to $500,000. Legal fees and accumulated debts erased the balance of the award.

Despite his vindication, CBS did not rehire Faulk—indeed, years passed before he worked again as a media entertainer. He returned to Austin in 1968. From 1975 to 1980 he appeared as a homespun character on the television program "Hee-Haw." During the 1980s he wrote and produced two one-man plays. In both *Deep in the Heart* (1986) and *Pear Orchard, Texas,* he portrayed characters imbued with the best of human instincts and the worst of cultural prejudices. The year 1974 proved pivotal for Faulk. CBS Television broadcast its movie version of *Fear on Trial,* Faulk's 1963 book that described his battle against AWARE. Also in 1974, Faulk read the dossier that the FBI had maintained on his activities since the 1940s. Disillusioned and desirous of a return to the country, Faulk moved to Madisonville, Texas. He returned to Austin in 1981. In 1983 he campaigned for the congressional seat abdicated by Democrat-turned-Republican Phil Gramm. Although he lost the three-way race, the humorist had spoken his mind. During the 1980s he traveled the nation urging university students to be ever vigilant of their constitutional rights and to take advantage of the freedoms guaranteed by the First Amendment. The Center for American History qv at the University of Texas at Austin sponsors the John Henry Faulk Conference on the First Amendment.

In 1940 Faulk wed one of his students at the University of Texas, Hally Wood. They had a daughter. After he and Hally were divorced, Faulk married Lynne Smith, whom he met at a New York City rally for presidential candidate Henry Wallace in the spring of 1948. Born of their marriage were two daughters and a son. After his divorce from Lynne, Faulk married Elizabeth Peake in 1965: they had a son. Faulk died in Austin of cancer on April 9, 1990. The city of Austin named the downtown branch of the public library in his honor.

BIBLIOGRAPHY: Austin *American-Statesman*, April 10, 1990. Michael C. Burton, *John Henry Faulk: The Making of a Liberated Mind* (Austin: Eakin Press, 1993). John Henry Faulk Papers, Barker Texas History Center, University of Texas at Austin. Andie Tucher, ed., *Bill Moyers, A World of Ideas II: Public Opinions from Private Citizens* (New York: Doubleday, 1990). Vertical Files, Barker Texas History Center, University of Texas at Austin. *Page S. Foshee*

FAULKENBERRY CREEK. Faulkenberry Creek is formed by the confluence of Frost and Rocky creeks, two miles southeast of Groesbeck in southeast Limestone County (at 31°29′ N, 96°31′ W). It runs east for 6½ miles to its mouth on the old channel of the Navasota River (at 31°30′ N, 96°27′ W). The stream traverses rolling prairie surfaced by sand and mud that supports grasses and mesquite. Faulkenberry Creek is probably named for David Faulkenberry, who settled in the area in 1835 as part of Sterling C. Robertson's qv colony. David and Evan Faulkenberry reportedly helped repel the Indian attack on Fort Parker on May 19, 1836, but arrived too late to save Cynthia Ann Parker qv and four others from being taken captive.

BIBLIOGRAPHY: Ray A. Walter, *A History of Limestone County* (Austin: Von Boeckmann–Jones, 1959). *Don Allon Hinton*

FAULKEY GULLY. Faulkey Gully rises in the Willow Flats area of northwest Harris County (at 30°01′ N, 95°39′ W) and runs southeast for six miles to its mouth on Cypress Creek, near the intersection of Grant and Jones roads (at 29°59′ N, 95°35′ W). The stream traverses an area where the coastal prairie begins to yield to woodlands, primarily pine and oak. Area soils are primarily sandy and clay loams. In the post–Civil War qv years, black freedmen settled along Faulkey Gully in an area known locally as "the Bottoms." The community's cemetery remained 100 years later as the only reminder of the early settlement in an area of rapidly expanding urban development.

BIBLIOGRAPHY: *The Heritage of North Harris County* (n.p: North Harris County Branch, American Association of University Women, 1977).

FAULKNER, TEXAS. Faulkner was at a site on what is now Farm Road 906 nine miles east of Arthur City and nineteen miles northeast of Paris in northeastern Lamar County. It was probably established in the early twentieth century and was named for Ira Faulkner, owner of a local store and sawmill. The 1936 county highway map shows farmhouses lining the road at Faulkner and a factory on the outskirts, but no sawmill. By 1951 the factory and some of the farmhouses had disappeared, and other farmhouses had been abandoned. By 1980 the name of the community no longer appeared on the county highway map. The name Faulkner has also sometimes been applied to the community of Pin Hook, 3½ miles to the southeast.

BIBLIOGRAPHY: A. W. Neville, *The History of Lamar County, Texas* (Paris, Texas: North Texas, 1937; rpt. 1986). William A. Owens, *This Stubborn Soil* (New York: Scribner, 1966). Fred Tarpley, *Place Names of Northeast Texas* (Commerce: East Texas State University, 1969). *Robert M. Towle*

FAUNA, TEXAS. Fauna, on U.S. Highway 90 at the southern end of Sheldon Reservoir, five miles northeast of Houston in east central Harris County, began as a station on the Texas and New Orleans Railroad. A post office was established there in 1903 and was probably discontinued in the 1930s. By the 1980s the Beaumont Place subdivision had been developed west of the former townsite, of which only an abandoned railroad station and scattered dwellings remained. *Diana J. Kleiner*

FAUNT LE ROY, FREDERICK WILES (1818–1900). Frederick Wiles Faunt Le Roy, lawyer, judge, and early settler, was born in Greenville, Virginia, on February 7, 1818, the son of Joseph and Emily

Faunt Le Roy. He was reared at New Harmony, Indiana, where he clerked, read law, and was admitted to the bar in 1841. In 1842 he raised a company of volunteers and traveled to Texas to assist against the Mexican invasion of Adrián Woll.^qv He participated in Indian campaigns and was in the ranger service from 1843 to 1845, when he raised a company of Mississippi Rifles, which he headed throughout the Mexican War.^qv In 1855 he married Mary Ann Trotter of Cameron. They had four children. In 1856 the family settled at Belton but soon moved to Gatesville, where Faunt Le Roy was the only resident attorney when the first term of district court was held. In March 1860 Governor Sam Houston^qv addressed to him and chief justices of various counties a circular instructing them to return to their homes to raise companies of volunteers for protection of the frontier. In February 1864 Faunt Le Roy enrolled in G. W. Haley's company under George B. Erath.^qv In the late 1860s he was clerk and master in chancery of the district court at Brownsville and served for a time as district attorney. From 1882 to 1884 he was county judge of Coryell County. Faunt Le Roy was an Odd Fellow and a Methodist. He died at Gatesville on September 24, 1900.

BIBLIOGRAPHY: *A Memorial and Biographical History of McLennan, Falls, Bell, and Coryell Counties* (Chicago: Lewis, 1893; rpt., St. Louis: Ingmire, 1984). Zelma Scott, *History of Coryell County* (Austin: Texas State Historical Association, 1965).

FAUNTLEROY, WILLIAM H. (1814–1836). William H. Fauntleroy, Alamo defender, was born in Logan County, Kentucky, in 1814. He traveled to Texas with Peter J. Bailey, Daniel W. Cloud, Joseph G. Washington, and B. Archer M. Thomas^qqv in late 1835. On January 14, 1836, he and his companions took the oath of allegiance to Texas and were mustered into the Volunteer Auxiliary Corps at Nacogdoches. Fauntleroy traveled to the Alamo as a member of Capt. William B. Harrison's^qv company, which included David Crockett.^qv He arrived on or about February 9, 1836, and died in the battle of the Alamo^qv on March 6 of that year. His name is often misspelled as Fontleroy or Furtleroy.

BIBLIOGRAPHY: Daughters of the American Revolution, *The Alamo Heroes and Their Revolutionary Ancestors* (San Antonio, 1976). Daughters of the Republic of Texas, *Muster Rolls of the Texas Revolution* (Austin, 1986). Bill Groneman, *Alamo Defenders* (Austin: Eakin, 1990). Phil Rosenthal and Bill Groneman, *Roll Call at the Alamo* (Fort Collins, Colorado: Old Army, 1985). *Bill Groneman*

FAVER, MILTON (ca. 1822–1889). Milton Faver (Don Melitón), first cattle baron of Presidio County, was born in Virginia about 1822. Nothing is known about his family and childhood. As a young man he fought a duel in Missouri and, believing he had killed his opponent, fled to Mexico. By 1840 Faver worked for Francisco De León in a flour mill in Meoqui, Mexico, 100 miles south of Ojinaga, then called Presidio del Norte.^qv In Mexico Faver met Francisca Ramírez, whom he soon married. Faver became a freighter between Meoqui and Ojinaga, and when the business became profitable he expanded it to freight goods over the Chihuahua Trail and the Santa Fe Trail.^qv He made many hazardous trips with his men and once was severely wounded in an Indian attack. Sometime between 1855 and 1857 Faver's freighting business became so well established that he left it with employees and moved his family from Meoqui to Ojinaga, where he opened a general store. In 1857 Faver, his wife, and their only child, Juan, left Ojinaga and settled on the frontier in the Chinati Mountains of Presidio County, Texas, twenty-five miles north of the Rio Grande. Beginning in January 1858 Faver bought small tracts of land around three springs—Cibolo, Cienega, and La Morita—to secure a water supply for cattle and sheep. He established cattle ranches near Big Springs Cibolo and Cienega Spring and a sheep ranch at La Morita Spring. Faver made Cibolo his headquarters and built a 100-square-foot adobe block compound with circular defense towers at the north and south corners to protect the inhabitants from Indian attack. At Cienega he built an eighty-nine-foot stockade with defense towers at the northeast and southwest corners. Morita Ranch was unfortified and later suffered loss of life in a raid by Apache Indians.

Faver's prime market for cattle was the military at Fort Davis before and after the Civil War.^qv During the war Fort Davis was abandoned, and without military protection cattlemen in the area suffered from Indian raids. Most of Faver's herd of 300 cattle was stolen. Left with only thirty-two corralled calves, he began to rebuild, and eventually his herd exceeded 10,000 cattle. Although he registered an F-shaped brand, most of his herd ran unbranded and wild in inaccessible mountain canyons. By 1883 Faver owned only 2,880 acres of land, but he used the open range and cheap Mexican labor to build his self-sufficient ranches. He paid the ranch hands 12½ cents per day to tend cattle, goats, and sheep and cultivate vegetables and fruits in gardens and orchards near the springs. Faver traded for anything he or the workers needed but could not grow or make themselves. Like other early area ranchers, he made homegrown peach brandy, which was a popular barter item. Faver was an autocrat and individualist; he made the law on his ranches and meted out his own justice. His ideas about money and cattle sales were eccentric. He accepted only hard money, and when he sold cattle he stood by the gate and received the coins for each animal as it passed.

In 1886 the aging Faver decided to get out of ranching. He offered D. G. Knight the use of his land, cattle, horses, and equipment for three years. Faver would pay the operating expenses for the first year. For his work, Knight would receive every third calf branded and every eighth steer on the range. Due to low market prices and underweight cattle, however, the contract proved unprofitable for Knight. At the expiration of the contract in 1889, Faver sold his remaining cattle to Joe Humphreys. Milton Faver died of natural causes on December 23, 1889, in Presidio County. He was buried on Chinati Peak above Big Springs Cibolo as he requested. The site is now overgrown and secret.

BIBLIOGRAPHY: Leavitt Corning, Jr., *Baronial Forts of the Big Bend* (Austin: Trinity University Press, 1967). John Ernest Gregg, History of Presidio County (M.A. thesis, University of Texas, 1933). Virginia Madison, *The Big Bend Country of Texas* (Albuquerque: University of New Mexico Press, 1955; rev. ed., New York: October House, 1968). Carlysle Graham Raht, *The Romance of the Davis Mountains and Big Bend Country* (Odessa, Texas: Rahtbooks, 1963). Roy L. Swift and Leavitt Corning, Jr., *Three Roads to Chihuahua* (Austin: Eakin Press, 1988). Cecilia Thompson, *History of Marfa and Presidio County, 1535–1946* (2 vols., Austin: Nortex, 1985). Ronnie C. Tyler, *The Big Bend* (Washington: National Park Service, 1975). Robert M. Utley, "The Range Cattle Industry in the Big Bend of Texas," *Southwestern Historical Quarterly* 69 (April 1966). Vertical Files, Barker Texas History Center, University of Texas at Austin. *Julia Cauble Smith*

FAWIL, TEXAS. Fawil is on Farm Road 363 five miles west of Bon Wier and fifty-five miles northeast of Beaumont in central Newton County. Land grants in the area date from 1836, although dense forests and red clay made early agriculture difficult. By 1903 Tom Hughes had established a small-scale lumbering operation near what was once known as Davis Community. Hughes hauled cut trees to Belgrade, then floated them down the Sabine River to awaiting mills. Fonzo A. Wilson, a native Georgian who had come to Texas in the early 1890s, built a sawmill at the site that would eventually be called Fawil in 1905. Local lore holds that in painting a sign on his mill, Wilson had room for only his initials, *F. A.*, and the first three letters of his last name, Wil. When the Jasper and Eastern Railway came through the region to link the forested areas with outlets at Kirbyville, Texas, and Oakdale, Louisiana, the stop was named Fawil, after Wilson's sign. Wilson subsequently sold his mill to Will E. Gray, and ownership eventually passed to John Ramsey and Joe Kinnear. Nearby lumbering operations continued to offer employment to community residents. During the early 1970s the Kirby Lumber Company built a new plywood plant at Fawil, thus revitalizing the little community. It was still listed as a community in 1990.

BIBLIOGRAPHY: Thomas A. Wilson, *Some Early Southeast Texas Families* (Houston: Lone Star, 1965). Newton County Historical Commission, *Glimpses of Newton County History* (Burnet, Texas: Nortex, 1982).

Robert Wooster

FAY, ALBERT BEL (1913–1992). Albert Bel Fay, businessman, Republican party[qv] leader, and United States ambassador, was born on February 26, 1913, in New Orleans, the son of Charles Spencer and Marie Dorothy (Bel) Fay. He was the nephew of Edwin Whitfield Fay[qv] and the cousin of Charles Hemphill Fay.[qv] His father was vice president and traffic manager of the Southern Pacific Railroad. The family moved to Houston in 1928, and Fay graduated from the old San Jacinto High School there. In 1936 he earned a B.S. in geology from Yale University and received a commission as an ensign in the United States Naval Reserve. During World War II[qv] he commanded a submarine chaser in the Gulf of Mexico and the Atlantic. He next served on the staff of the Submarine Chaser Training Center in Miami and then as first lieutenant on the USS *Yokes* at Okinawa.

In 1938 Fay and his brother Ernest founded the Seabrook Shipyard, which built submarine chasers and rescue boats during World War II. Fay was also founder and vice president of Eagle Lake Rice Dryer (Texas); founder of Lake Arthur Rice Dryer (Louisiana); cofounder, vice president, and director of the family-owned Bel Oil Corporation (Louisiana); a vice president and director of the Lacassane Company; a partner of Quatre Parish Company (Louisiana); a director of Gates Learjet Corporation; and a member of Lloyd's of London. In 1972 his petroleum interests included holdings in Texas, Louisiana, and several other states, as well as in Canada and New Zealand. He also had real estate interests in Nicaragua and the Little Cayman Islands in the Caribbean. In 1992 his business interests included ranching, timber, marinas, and banking.

Fay's work with the Republican party began at the precinct level in 1952, during the presidential campaign of Dwight D. Eisenhower.[qv] By 1960 he had become a Republican national committeeman. In 1962 and 1966 he was the Republican nominee for Texas land commissioner. In the latter race he won the endorsement of the AFL-CIO executive board and the Political Association of Spanish-Speaking Organizations.[qv] He lost both races to Jerry Sadler. One of the issues on which Fay distinguished himself from Sadler was in his support for national parks in Texas. He supported the movement for a park on Padre Island in 1962 and in the Guadalupe Mountains in 1966 (*see* PADRE ISLAND NATIONAL SEASHORE *and* GUADALUPE MOUNTAINS NATIONAL PARK).

In 1969 Fay was ousted as national committeeman. Three years later he ran against five other candidates for the Republican gubernatorial nomination. He made it into the primary runoff but lost in that election to Henry C. Grover, who was defeated in the general election by Dolph Briscoe. In the primary campaign Fay argued for a national park in the Big Thicket,[qv] a state park on Mustang Island,[qv] and a recreational area along Armand Bayou.[qv] He also urged the development of a comprehensive water plan and advocated reducing property taxes on the homes of the elderly. He served as chairman of the state Republican finance committee, a member of the national Republican finance committee (1968–76), a member of the state Republican executive committee, and a member of the executive committee of the Republican national committee. He was a delegate to the Republican national conventions of 1960, 1964, and 1968; he served as cochairman of the state delegation in 1960 and vice chairman of the state delegation in 1964. In October 1969 President Richard M. Nixon appointed him to the thirteen-member board of governors overseeing the Panama Canal Company. He retained that position until 1976, when President Gerald R. Ford named him ambassador to Trinidad and Tobago. He served in that capacity until 1977.

Fay was a director and president of the Houston Museum of Natural Science,[qv] a director of the American Brahman Breeders Association, a vice president of the Houston Branch of the English Speaking Union, and a member of the Yale alumni board. He was also a licensed pilot and a yachtsman. He won the 5.5-meter world championship in Hankø, Norway, in 1983, defeating twenty-five other helmsmen from around the world. He was also a three-time winner of the Scandinavian Gold Cup and the United States Nationals. Fay served on the United States Olympic Yachting Committee, the United States Naval Academy Sailing Advisory Council, and the board of trustees of the Yale University Sailing Association. He married Homoiselle Randall Haden on February 3, 1935, and they became the parents of three children. He was a Presbyterian. Fay died in Cuernavaca, Morelos, Mexico, on February 29, 1992, and was buried in Glenwood Cemetery, Houston.

BIBLIOGRAPHY: John R. Knaggs, *Two-Party Texas: The John Tower Era, 1961–1984* (Austin: Eakin Press, 1986). Roger M. Olien, *From Token to Triumph: The Texas Republicans since 1920* (Dallas: Southern Methodist University Press, 1982). Vertical Files, Barker Texas History Center, University of Texas at Austin. *Who's Who in America*, 1980–81.

Mary Smith Fay

FAY, CHARLES HEMPHILL (1910–1987). Charles Hemphill Fay, physicist, was born on January 29, 1910, in Austin, Texas, to Edwin Whitfield Fay[qv] and Lucy Belle (Hemphill) Fay. He attended the Whitis School, a private school in Austin, until he completed the sixth grade, at which time the Whitis school closed. He then attended and graduated from John T. Allen Junior High School and Austin High School. He majored in physics at the University of Texas at Austin and was a Junior-5, one of only five juniors elected to Phi Beta Kappa in his junior year. He graduated in 1930 with highest honors and in 1931 earned his master's degree, also at the University of Texas. On May 17, 1931, in Austin, Fay married Dorothy Louise Wild, who had received the masters degree that year in clothing from the home economics department of the University of Texas; they had two children. Fay was a Whiting Fellow at Harvard University (1932–34) and a Thayer Scholar (1934–35); in 1936 he received his Ph.D. in theoretical physics from Harvard. He remained at Harvard as an assistant from 1936 to 1937, then moved to the University of Tulsa, Oklahoma, where he was an instructor (1937–38) and an assistant professor and the head of the physics department (1938–41). He was elected to the Society of Sigma Xi in 1938. Fay joined the Geophysical Laboratory of Shell Oil Company in Houston in 1941 and remained with Shell until his retirement from the Exploration and Production Research Laboratory in February 1969. At that time his title was Consultant, Physics. His specialty was the design of seismometers, seismic amplifiers, and well instruments. He is named on twenty-one United States Patents and is the sole inventor on eleven of these. He was a member of the American Association for the Advancement of Science, the American Association of Physics Teachers, the American Geophysical Union, the American Physical Society, the Society of Exploration Geophysicists, and the Society of Petroleum Engineers. He was also a member of the Texas Academy of Science,[qv] the Houston Philosophical Society, and the St. Bartholomew Chapter of the Huguenot Society of Texas. After the death of his first wife, Fay married Mary Smith on September 4, 1969, at St. Stephen's Episcopal Church in Houston. Fay died on December 16, 1987, and was buried at the Oakwood Cemetery in Austin.

BIBLIOGRAPHY: *American Men of Science*, 1949. *Geophysics: The Leading Edge of Exploration*, February 1989. Houston *Post*, December 17, 1987.

Mary Smith Fay

FAY, EDWIN WHITFIELD (1865–1920). Edwin Whitfield Fay, philologist, was born on January 1, 1865, in Minden, Louisiana, to Edwin Hedge and Sarah Elizabeth (Shields) Fay. He entered Southwestern Presbyterian University in Clarksville, Tennessee, at the age of fourteen and was awarded an M.A. degree in 1883. Following his father's example, he became a teacher and taught successively at Jackson, Mississippi, in 1883–84; Bonham, Texas, 1884–85; and Beaumont, Texas, 1885–86. He entered Johns Hopkins University and studied Sanskrit, comparative philology, Greek, and Latin for four years, then received his Ph.D. in 1890 with Phi Beta Kappa honors. He was an instructor in Sanskrit and the classics at the University of Michigan for a year before traveling in Europe and studying at the University of Leipzig. For the session of 1892–93 he was acting associate professor of Latin at the University of Texas. From 1893 through the spring of 1899 he was professor of Latin at Washington and Lee University. He returned to the University of Texas as professor of Latin in 1899 and held this position until his death. Fay was married to Lucy Belle Hemphill on December 20, 1904, in Louisville, Kentucky. They had two children.

Fay published 103 works, including three books: *A History of Education in Louisiana* (1898), *The Treatment of Rig-Veda Mantras in the Yrhya Sutras* (1899), and *T. Macci Planti Mostellaria* (1902). He had an extraordinary interest in modern literature, was an earnest student of the Bible, wrote creditable verse, and was a skillful pianist and tennis player. While in Pittsburgh, Pennsylvania, visiting his sister, he contracted pneumonia. He died on February 17, 1920. His body was brought to Austin and buried in Oakwood Cemetery.

BIBLIOGRAPHY: Morgan Callaway, Jr., *In Memoriam: Edwin Whitfield Fay* (University of Texas Bulletin 2425, 1924). Vertical Files, Barker Texas History Center, University of Texas at Austin.

William James Battle

FAYETTE COUNTY. Fayette County (L-18) is on Interstate Highway 10 sixty miles southeast of Austin in the Blackland Prairies region of south central Texas. The center of the county lies at 29°55′ north latitude and 96°55′ west longitude. La Grange is the county seat and largest community. In addition to Interstate 10, transportation needs are served by U.S. highways 77, 90, and 290 and State highways 71, 95, 159, and 237. The county's terrain varies from level land to steep slopes, with altitude ranging from 200 to 600 feet. The Colorado River, which bisects the county from northwest to southeast, is fed by several major creeks: Rabb's, Cedar, and Baylor on the east and Buckner's and Williams on the west. Cummins Creek flows through the eastern part of the county and the East and West Navidad rivers through the southern part. Potable groundwater is readily available from the Carrizo-Wilcox and Catahoula-Oakville aquifers at relatively shallow depths. The county covers 950 square miles and is composed of three land resource areas—Blackland Prairies (63 percent), the Post Oak Belt (30 percent), and the Colorado river bottom (7 percent). Within the Blackland Prairie on the uplands are the clayey blacklands and loamy claypen areas. The bottomlands contain dark loamy and clayey soils. The Post Oak Belt contains the Texas Claypan Area with uplands of gray, slightly acid sandy loam and sandy to clayey bottomland soils. Scattered outcrops of the Willis Formation form gravelly ridges along the Colorado River and large areas of gravelly soils in the northern half of the county. The vegetation is a mixture of the post oak savannah and Blackland Prairie region, with tall grasses, oak, and elms predominating. Also commonly found are eastern red cedars, pecans, cottonwoods, and sycamores. Some hickory, walnut, mesquite, and yaupon grow in diverse areas. The north central section is forested by loblolly pine, a continuation of the Lost Pine Forest qv of neighboring Bastrop County. White-tail deer are native to the area, especially in the timbered areas, and raccoon, beaver, and possum live along the many creeks. Coyotes are so numerous that a control program has been instigated. Game species found in this district include squirrel, quail, dove, and water fowl. Southern bald eagles traverse the county, particularly along the Colorado River. Natural resources include timber, lignite, sand, gravel, bleaching clays, volcanic ash, oil, and gas. The climate is subtropical humid, with hot summers and mild winters. The average annual precipitation is thirty-six inches. Temperatures range from an average low of 41° F in January to an average high of 96° F in July, and the average growing season is 277 days. Flooding is common along the Colorado River; major floods in 1869, 1870, 1900, 1938, and 1992 caused considerable damage to crops and property.

Prior to European settlement Lipan Apaches and Tonkawa Indians inhabited parts of what is now Fayette County. Many Indian artifacts have been found, especially along the Colorado River and near Round Top. A few miles north of the Colorado River, above Little Pin Oak Creek, a stratified multicomponent campsite was found, with Clovis, Plainview, and other later artifacts. In the early eighteenth century Spanish explorers passed through the area. La Bahía Road,qv which ran southwest to northeast and crossed the river at the site of present La Grange, was the major route for travel during the Mexican period. The area was part of Stephen F. Austin'sqv first colony, but the earliest known white settlers, Aylett C. Buckner and Peter Powell,qqv arrived earlier and lived on La Bahía Road west of La Grange, where they ran a trading post. Formal settlement began in 1822 with the arrival of the Austin colonists. From 1824 to 1828 ten members of the Old Three Hundredqv received title to their land grants in the fertile Colorado River valley; William Rabbqv received four leagues in order to build a mill. A total of ninety-two Mexican land grants were granted in the area that is now Fayette County. The earliest settlers gathered at Wood's Fort, Moore's Fort (La Grange), the James Ross home, and Jesse Burnam'sqv blockhouse, twelve miles below La Grange. Burnam's Ferryqv on the Colorado River provided a cutoff route from La Bahía Road to San Felipe. Prior to Texas independence, the area above La Bahía Road was in the Mina Municipalityqv and the area below in the Municipality of Colorado. Gotier's Trace,qv the Wilbarger Trace, and the La Grange–San Felipe road intersected La Bahía Road. Ferries were used to cross the Colorado River until the first bridge was built at La Grange by private subscription in 1883. On December 14, 1837, upon petition of the citizens, the Congress of the Republic of Texas qv established the county of Fayette, named in honor of the Marquis de Lafayette. La Grange, the name of the chateau to which Lafayette retired, was designated the county seat. The citizens organized the county government on January 18, 1838, and the southwestern boundary of the county was extended westward on May 3, 1838. The county lost territory in the south to Lavaca County in 1854 and in the north to Lee County in 1874.

The early settlers' life revolved around their plantations, but problems with Indians occupied much of their time. Sometimes the settlers felt so threatened that they moved down to the lower Colorado River area. At other times they grouped together, sometimes aided by Lipan Apache and Tonkawa Indians who were friendly to the settlers, to resist marauding bands of Comanches, Wacos, and Kichais. Fayette County men were prominent in the Texas Revolution;qv more than fifty men participated in the battle of San Jacinto,qv including Joel C. Robinson, one of the captors of Antonio López de Santa Anna.qv The Somervell, Mier,qqv and Dawson expeditions were composed mostly of Fayette County men. In 1848 the remains of the men killed in the Dawson Massacreqv and in Perote Prisonqv were returned to Fayette County and interred on Monument Hill; in 1933 a granite tomb was dedicated there (see MONUMENT HILL–KREISCHE BREWERY STATE HISTORIC SITE). The historic Muster Oak, still standing on the square, has been a rallying site since the early settlement. William Menefee,qv a signer of the Texas Declaration of Independence,qv was from Fayette County. A proposal to permanently locate the state capital in Fayette County was approved on April 11, 1838, by an overwhelming majority of the Second Congress. Local citizens arranged for the purchase of the Eblin league on the east side of the Colorado River near La Grange, reserving all vacant lands within a nine-mile radius. The measure was vetoed by Sam Houston,qv however, and the capital was located upriver in what later became Austin.

The first private schools opened in the county as early as 1834. Academies and institutes were operated in La Grange, Fayetteville, and Round Top in the 1840s. The Methodists founded Rutersville College,qv one of the first colleges in Texas, in 1840; it consolidated with the Texas Military Institute, Galveston,qv in 1856. The earliest churches organized in the county were Methodist (1838), Baptist (1839), Presbyterian (1841), and Episcopal (1852). Most of the early settlers were from the Old South, but the Austin Colony also included a few German immigrants. In 1832 Joseph Biegel received title to a league in the area and developed the first German community in the county, Biegel Settlement. In the 1840s many more German immigrants settled in Fayette County. The Adelsvereinqv purchased a league in 1843 and established a plantation called Nassau Farm.qv During the mid-1850s sizable numbers of Bohemian Czechs also began moving into the county. In the 1856 the first Bohemian settlement in Texas, Dubina, was founded in Fayette County. The county's population grew rapidly, especially after Texas joined the Union; already by 1850 it had 3,756 residents. During the early years the economy was based largely on subsistence farming, but during the late 1840s and 1850s a thriving plantation economy emerged. In the early 1850s plantations were producing impressive quantities of corn and shipping tobacco, wool, and cotton to outside markets. To clear land, harvest crops, and perform other forms of labor, planters brought in increasing numbers of African-American slaves. Between 1840 and 1850 the slave population grew from 206 to 820, and by 1855 the number had reached 2,072. On the eve of the Civil Warqv Fayette County was among the most well-developed areas in the state, with nearly 1,000 farms containing 75,463 improved acres. In 1859 farmers produced 12,683 bales of cotton and 320,580 bushels of corn, placing Fayette County among the state's leaders in both categories. The population of 11,604 was more than three times what it had been only a decade before; the number of slaves alone (3,786) in 1860 exceeded the entire population for 1850. Despite the county's large slave population, however, voters narrowly rejected secessionqv by a margin of forty-six votes (626 against, 528 for), primarily due to the area's numerous German and Bohemian residents, who generally opposed slavery.qv Despite the result, after the war broke out three volunteer companies were immediately organized, and before the war's end a total of about 800 men had served in the Confederate army.

The Civil War and its aftermath brought profound changes to the county. Although it made only a small material contribution to the war effort, the lack of markets and wild fluctuations in Confederate currency caused hardships for many. The end of the war brought wrenching changes in the economy. For many whites the abolitionqv of slavery meant devastating economic loss. Before the war slaves had constituted more than a third of all taxable property in the county, and their loss coupled with a sharp decline in property values caused a profound disruption for most planters. The county's African Americansqv fared no better. Although most of the county's black residents remained, many left the farms owned by their former masters to seek better working conditions. For the vast majority, the change brought only marginal improvement in their living and working conditions; most ended up working on the land on shares, receiving one-third or one-half of the crop for their labors.

During Reconstructionqv Fayette County received little attention from federal political or military authorities. Federal troops were stationed there only briefly, and there was little of the violence that many other areas experienced. The economy began to recover in the late 1860s, and by 1870 production levels neared or exceeded the 1860 figures. During the next three decades the county experienced a long period of growth, fueled in large measure by a surge of new German and Slavic residents. Many of the early plantation owners, hard-pressed to make ends meet without their bondsmen, sold their lands to German, Bohemian, or Wendish settlers, who in turn sold portions of it to others. As a result the large plantations that had dominated antebellum Texasqv were gradually replaced by smaller, more numerous farms. This trend is reflected in the agricultural census of the late nineteenth century, which shows the number of farms increasing from 1,483 in 1870 to 5,189 in 1900. The number of acres under cultivation also grew dramatically during this period, rising from 76,401 to 287,853. Although the new farms were smaller, they tended to be much more productive because of intensive cultivation by the Germans and Bohemians. Most of these small farmers grew cabbages, tomatoes, potatoes, beans, peas, turnips, and peaches, but the leading cash crops remained cotton and corn. In 1880 farmers produced 24,766 bales of cotton and 694,833 bushels of corn; by 1890 cotton output had grown to 37,559 bales, and corn production topped 912,000 bushels.

The influx of Germans, Czechs, and Wendsqqv after the Civil War also gradually altered the cultural face of the county. Although some of the new settlers moved in from other counties, including most of the Wends, many of the settler were new immigrants who brought their own distinct culture with them. The tide of immigration was particularly strong in the 1880s, as numerous additional German and Bohemian settlers arrived. By 1890 nearly one-fourth of the county's residents (7,856 of 31,481) were foreign-born, with the largest contingents from Germany (3,667) and Austria-Hungary (3,224). As a result, by the late nineteenth century many of the leading businesses and civic organizations were dominated by Germans and Czechs. During the late nineteenth and early twentieth centuries La Grange had two foreign-language newspapers, the *Svoboda*qv (Czech) and the La Grange *Zeitung* (German). The Germans and Czechs formed shooting clubs, poetry groups, and fraternal and religious organizations. The KJT (Czech Catholic Union), the SPJST (a Czech benevolent society), and the Round Top Rifle Association, founded in the nineteenth century, still existed in the early 1990s. Public education in the late nineteenth and early twentieth century was supplemented by private and parochial schools, which were often taught in German and Czech. Despite the increasing number of white residents, African Americans continued to form a large segment of the population. In 1870 the black population was 5,901, and as late as 1900 blacks still represented about one-third of the population; in spite of these numbers, however, African Americans had little political power. While Fayette County citizens rejected the white primaryqv—largely due to German and populist sentiment against it—African-American voters were often excluded from voting and had little say in the local political structure.

During the early decades of the twentieth century Fayette County continued to grow and prosper. Corn remained an important crop, with cattle and dairy products also providing significant sources of income. But it was cotton which emerged as the single largest cash crop. Cotton production averaged more than 30,000 bales annually between 1900 and 1930, and by 1929 more than half of all of the cropland (118,256 of 196,847 acres) was devoted to cotton. The growth of cotton in turn fueled a steady rise in farm tenancy.qv By 1920 nearly half of all farmers (2,195 of 4,728) were tenants. During the years of the Great Depression,qv when nearly all farmers suffered, these tenants found themselves particularly hard pressed. Overproduction, droughts,qv and boll weevilqv infestations combined to drive down prices and reduce the crop size. Between 1930 and 1940 the amount of land planted in cotton fell by more than 50 percent (from 118,858 to 50,858 acres), and production was barely a third of what had been during the peak years of the 1920s. After World War IIqv the agricultural emphasis changed. Cotton continued to be grown on a much smaller scale through the early 1950s, but farmers also turned increasingly to cattle raising. By 1987 there were 2,235 milk cows and 110,511 head of cattle in the county, and cotton was no longer being grown. Due to rich soils and abundant surface and ground water, Fayette County remains an important agricultural county. In the late 1980s it ranked among the top three counties in the state in cow and calf production. In 1989 there were 2,476 producers. Leading crops included corn, grain sorghums, peanuts, and pecans. The estimated gross agricultural income for 1988 was $42,427,000—beef cattle 57 percent, grain

10 percent, poultry (eggs) 8 percent, swine 8 percent, hay 8 percent, dairy products 7 percent, pecans 1 percent, and miscellaneous 1 percent. Of the 2,750 farm operators, about half held additional jobs.

During the 1980s and 1990s the economic development of the county was largely dependent on its natural resources. Construction gravel and sand, grinding pebbles, clays, and fuller's earth were mined. Oil, first discovered in 1943, was an important source of income. Due to new horizontal drilling techniques Fayette County experienced a dramatic rise in oil and gas production in the early 1990s. As a highly active part of the Giddings oilfield of the Austin Chalk trend, the county produced 14,044,733 barrels of oil and 72,469,984 million cubic feet of gas in 1992. Timber is selectively cut for commercial purposes from 28,200 acres of privately owned woodlands. Agribusiness plays a major role in the economy. Light industry includes shops, a cabinet factory, plastic recycling, gas processing, and other manufacturing. The Lower Colorado River Authority[qv] Fayette Power Project is the largest employer in the county, with around 500 workers. Other sources of employment are banking, services, retail sales, trucking, government, schools, and drilling and pipeline management.

Beginning in 1872, the development of the railroad system caused the decline of many rural communities and the development of the new towns of Schulenburg and Flatonia. In the 1990s three railroad lines crossed the county—the Missouri, Kansas and Texas from east to west and two branches of the Southern Pacific, one from north to south and the other along the southern boundary. A public airport for light planes was located in La Grange. Fayette County has published English-language newspapers since 1843. Three were published in the early 1990s—the *Fayette County Record*, the Flatonia *Argus*, and the Schulenburg *Sticker*. In the early 1990s there were five independent school districts, one Catholic high school, and two Catholic schools through eighth grade. Although Father Michael Muldoon[qv] visited the county under Mexican rule, followed by other visiting priests and Lutheran pastors, the Catholic and Lutheran churches did not flourish until the second half of the nineteenth century under German, Czech, and Wendish influence. In the 1990s there were sixty churches and one Jewish temple; Lutheran and Catholic churches accounted for half the total.

Historically, the majority of county voters have been Democratic or independent, and Democratic candidates have typically received the majority of the county's votes. Populist, Greenback,[qqv] and other third-party candidates fared well during the late nineteenth and early twentieth centuries. In recent years, however, Republicans have been making strong inroads, particularly in presidential and statewide races. Republican presidential candidates won every election between 1968 and 1992, with the exception of 1976, when Democrat Jimmy Carter eked out a narrow victory. Democratic officials, however, continued to maintain control of most county offices, and as late as 1982, 97 percent of voters in the primary voted Democratic. The population of Fayette County reached an all-time high of 36,542 in 1900 but has been gradually declining. The population was 29,796 in 1910, 29,965 in 1920, 30,708 in 1930, 29,246 in 1940, 24,176 in 1950, 20,384 in 1960, 17,650 in 1970, and 18,832 in 1980. In 1990 the county recorded a small gain, rising to 20,095. The largest communities were La Grange (3,951), Schulenberg (2,455), Flatonia (1,291), and Fayetteville (283). The largest minority groups were African Americans (8.4 percent) and Hispanics (8.5 percent). Most of the residents (80 percent) live in small communities or rural areas. Tourism and recreation are a growing economic resource for Fayette County. The cooling pond of the Fayette Power Project has been developed into a stocked fishing lake of 2,400 surface acres, averaging a depth of thirty feet. It is open to the public and has become especially popular with bass fishermen. Monument Hill–Kreische Brewery State Historic Site, the historic Henkel Square in Round Top, and Winedale Historical Center[qv] draw visitors year round. Antique fairs, the International Festival-Institute at Round Top,[qv] ethnic and town festivals, and the County Fair are popular special events. The "painted churches" at Dubina, Praha, Ammansville, and High Hill offer popular historic-preservation tours, and each of the four major towns has a museum actively preserving county history.

BIBLIOGRAPHY: Frank Lotto, *Fayette County: Her History and Her People* (Schulenburg, Texas: Sticker Steam Press, 1902; rpt., Austin: University of Texas Press, 1981). Worth Stickley Ray, *Austin Colony Pioneers* (Austin: Jenkins, 1949; 2d ed., Austin: Pemberton, 1970). Julia Lee Sinks, *Chronicles of Fayette* (La Grange, Texas, Bicentennial Commission, 1975). Julia Lee Sinks, "Editors and Newspapers of Fayette County," *Quarterly of the Texas State Historical Association* 1 (July 1897). Houston Wade, comp., *The Dawson Men of Fayette County* (Houston, 1932). Leonie Rummel Weyand and Houston Wade, *An Early History of Fayette County* (La Grange, Texas: La Grange *Journal*, 1936).
Daphne Dalton Garrett

FAYETTEVILLE, TEXAS (Fayette County). Fayetteville is on State Highway 159 and Farm roads 955 and 1291, twelve miles east of La Grange in eastern Fayette County. It developed from a settlement formed by three families of Stephen F. Austin's[qv] Old Three Hundred[qv]—those of John Crier, James Cummins, and James J. Ross.[qqv] The surrounding area was known as Ross Prairie, after Ross. The developing settlement was on the Old San Felipe to Bastrop road and was a stagecoach stop. In 1834 the Breeding family established nearby the first school in what would become Fayette County; some of James J. Ross's children attended classes there. The settlement was called Wadis Post Office in 1835. Jesse Burnam's[qv] ferry across the Colorado River was nearby, and during the Texas Revolution[qv] Sam Houston[qv] and his army used this ferry and then burned it on their march to San Jacinto. From the area came nine men who fought in the Texas Revolution, among them Jerome B. Alexander;[qv] the community was for a time called Alexander's Voting Place after him. It was also known as Lick Skillet (Lickskillet), supposedly for the fact that latecomers to the numerous community festivals who complained that all the food was gone were told to lick the skillet. By the 1830s some German immigrant settlers were arriving in the area. The Congress of the Republic of Texas[qv] established Fayette County in 1837, and the community of Fayetteville was officially founded shortly thereafter. It was named Fayetteville in 1844, for the birthplace of Philip J. Shaver of Fayetteville, North Carolina. Shaver surveyed the community, named the streets, and donated lots for the Fayetteville Academy and the multidenominational Union Church. Fayetteville had a post office and postmaster during the Republic of Texas,[qv] and as of the early 1990s the town had had continuous postal service since 1850.

In 1853 the first group of Czechs[qv] entered Fayette County, and that year Tom Batla settled in Fayetteville, becoming its first permanent Czech resident. This group of immigrants was made up of Protestants, and the first Czech Protestant service in the state of Texas was held near Fayetteville in 1856. In 1856 a second group, this time Czech-Moravians, arrived in Fayette County; these were primarily Catholics who, like the Czech Protestants, had left their homeland because of the Austro-Hungarian Empire's occupation of their land. Fayetteville is known as the "cradle of Czech immigration to Texas" because after the Civil War[qv] most Czech immigrants to Texas went to Fayetteville first. By the 1870s nearly all of the Anglo settlers and their families had left Fayetteville, which at that time had a large Czech-Moravian population but no Czech-speaking priest. On December 25, 1872, the first Czech Catholic service there spoken in Czech was held by the first Moravian Catholic priest in Texas, Father Josef Chromčik.[qv] By the 1880s the population of Fayetteville was predominantly Czech and German. Its citizens were instrumental in the formation of two of the first Czech insurance and fraternal organizations in the state and in the nation—the the KJT (Katolická jednota texaská) and the SPJST (Slovanská podporující jednota statu Texas, known in English as the Slavic Benevolent Order of the State of Texas). Fayetteville was also the site of the organization of the first

Czech band in Texas, organized in 1892 and known as the Baca Family Band.

Fayetteville was incorporated on March 2, 1882. In October 1887 the Taylor, Bastrop and Houston Railway built a line through the town. A fire consumed one side of the town square in 1893, prompting the installation of a city waterworks and the establishment of a fire department. The Schumacher Bank opened in 1900; it eventually merged with another bank to form the Fayetteville Bank. The population of Fayetteville was 356 in the early 1980s, when most local residents were involved in raising beef cattle, corn, grain sorghums, or wheat. In 1986 the community had the post office, five churches, and more than thirty businesses, including a bank and a savings and loan. Fayetteville reported a population of 283 in 1990. The Lickskillet Festival is held there each October. During the early 1990s the town had a number of restaurants, hotels, antique stores, and other specialty stores.

BIBLIOGRAPHY: Frank Lotto, *Fayette County: Her History and Her People* (Schulenburg, Texas: Sticker Steam Press, 1902; rpt., Austin: University of Texas Press, 1981). Leonie Rummel Weyand and Houston Wade, *An Early History of Fayette County* (La Grange, Texas: La Grange *Journal*, 1936). *Louis J. Polansky and David S. Walkup*

FAYETTEVILLE, TEXAS (Fort Bend County). Fayetteville was on the east side of the Brazos River within the Isaacks/Whitehead Survey six miles from Fort Bend (now Richmond) in northeastern Fort Bend County. Jesse H. Cartwright,qv advertised the town as early as June 1836 and proposed that it be made the county seat. The site received only twenty votes in the county seat election, and the town project was abandoned. *Leonie Weyand*

FAYETTEVILLE ACADEMY. Fayetteville Academy opened at Fayetteville, Fayette County, in 1849 in quarters built for a church and school by the citizens of Ross's Prairie in 1848. The school was chartered on November 26, 1860, as Fayette Academy, but advertisements called it Fayetteville Academy. The school was nonsectarian; P. B. Chandler, a Baptist minister, was in charge for two terms, and W. P. Smith, a Methodist minister, conducted the institution for four sessions. The student body numbered between thirty and forty in 1851. Practical instruction was stressed. The public examination in 1852 covered two days, presented sixty pupils, and included a barbecue dinner and entertainment by German musicians. The school operated at least until 1858.

BIBLIOGRAPHY: Johanna Caroline Walling, Early Education in Fayette County (M.A. thesis, University of Texas, 1941). Leonie L. Weyand, Early History of Fayette County, 1822–1865 (M.A. thesis, University of Texas, 1932).

FAYETTEVILLE MALE AND FEMALE ACADEMY. The Fayetteville Male and Female Academy opened on February 6, 1860, as a successor to the Fayetteville Academy; it was housed on the lower floor of the Masonic lodge building in Fayetteville, Fayette County. R. A. Williams and his wife and Mary Haswell offered music classes and primary, secondary, and advanced classes in other subjects; tuition ranged from ten to fifteen dollars and twenty dollars for music. Out-of-town students paid ten dollars a month for board. The school had eighty-eight students in the summer of 1860. In 1861 the forty male students organized a military company and drilled at noon and recess. The Civil Warqv probably brought an end to the school.

BIBLIOGRAPHY: Johanna Caroline Walling, Early Education in Fayette County (M.A. thesis, University of Texas, 1941).

FAYSVILLE, TEXAS. Faysville is off state Highway 281 sixteen miles northeast of McAllen in central Hidalgo County. In 1926 the St. Louis, Brownsville and Mexico Railway built a line from Faysville to Edinburg. The former was named for Fay Devine, wife of P. S. Devine, who laid out the townsite about 1920. In 1933 the town had a population estimated at ten and one business. In 1947 Faysville received its mail from Edinburg and reported one store and a population of twenty-five. By 1963 the town's population had increased to fifty, and it had two churches and several dwellings. During the 1970s a colonia (*see* COLONIAS) formed outside Faysville; by 1986 it had 200 dwellings and an estimated population of 900. During the same period Faysville proper had an estimated population of 300, which remained constant through 1990. *Alicia A. Garza*

FAZENDA, TEXAS. Fazenda was a farming community on Farm Road 2796 ten miles north of Gilmer in northern Upshur County. The settlement, on the postal route between LaFayette and Coffeeville, was probably established in the early 1890s. A Fazenda school was in operation by the mid-1890s, and in 1896 it had an enrollment of twenty-two. A post office opened in the community in 1899 and closed in 1905. By the mid-1930s Fazenda was no longer shown on county highway maps. Its population was reported as twenty from 1933 through 1945 and not reported thereafter.

Christopher Long

FEDERAL CORRECTIONAL INSTITUTION. The Federal Correctional Institution at La Tuna (now part of Anthony) in northwestern El Paso County is a medium-security prison for men. It was formally opened on May 1, 1932, and designated to house offenders from Texas, New Mexico, Arizona, Colorado, Wyoming, and southern Utah; its Spanish-mission architecture was designed to reflect the Southwestern environment. A minimum-security Federal Prison Camp was added in 1978. In 1992 the inmate population was 890 at the Federal Correctional Institution and 324 at the Federal Prison Camp; the staff numbered 359. Thomas P. White, who served from the facility's opening in 1932 until 1951, had the longest tenure of any warden. During White's service some 300 of the institution's 630 acres was irrigated, and inmates were trained in farming and dairying. Agricultural activities were discontinued in subsequent years but resumed in 1992, with the aim of supplying vegetables and some fruits for the facility and for other federal prisons. The FCI offers a variety of educational and vocational programs, including studies for the general-equivalency diploma, English as a second language, computer literacy, continuing-education courses, and training in automobile repair, building trades, and horticulture. The institution formerly served as a detention center for aliens held by the United States Immigration Service. *Martin Donell Kohout*

FEDERAL JUDICIARY. Texas is one of only two states (the other being New York) to be divided into four judicial districts, the North, South, East and West, for purposes of federal trial-level courts. Appeals from decisions of these courts are heard by the United States Court of Appeals for the Fifth Circuit, headquartered in New Orleans, with jurisdiction over federal courts in Texas, Louisiana, and Mississippi. Federal courts in Texas, as elsewhere, are courts of limited jurisdiction. Before the Civil War,qv the bulk of the docket was comprised of "diversity" cases, that is, cases involving citizens from two different states or lawsuits between an American citizen and a foreign national. During the Reconstructionqv period, partly due to fear that Southern state courts would not vigorously enforce federal law, federal courts in Texas, and elsewhere also, were given authority to decide "federal questions," that is, lawsuits arising under or hinging on a determination of federal law. At all times, however, Texas state courts have continued to hear a substantial number of federal issues, except for situations in which the United States Constitution or a statute grants exclusive jurisdiction to federal courts—such as copyright, admiralty, and bankruptcy matters. It should be noted that Texas is unique among the states in that, as a functioning independent sovereign during the period of the Republic of Texas,qv Texas courts handled such exclusively "federal" matters as admiralty cases.

In the late twentieth century, a marked legislative trend developed toward increasing the orientation of federal courts toward questions of federal law, and decreasing the availability of federal courts as fora for matters of state law in which the only claim to federal jurisdiction was diverse citizenship. A common reason given for this trend is that, as American society becomes more mobile, there is less fear that an out-of-state defendant will be "home-towned" by a state judge and jury.

When Texas was annexed to the United States in 1846, the entire state constituted one federal judicial district. John C. Watrous^{qv} was appointed the first United States District Judge for Texas. His tenure was marred by strident complaints of partiality arising from his involvement in land speculation, including four separate impeachment attempts. In 1857, keeping pace with the state's rapid expansion in population, the state was divided into two judicial districts. Judge Watrous continued as judge of the Eastern District and Thomas Howard Duval^{qv} was appointed judge of the Western District. When Texas seceded, judges Watrous and Duvall were the only Southern district judges to opt for the Union. In consequence, William Pinckney Hill and Thomas J. Devine^{qqv} were appointed by the Confederate government as judges of the Confederate Eastern and Western District Courts, respectively. Virtually no business was conducted by the courts, however, except that which related to the conduct of hostilities and the sequestration of "alien" property. After the war Watrous and Duvall returned to their former positions and to an enormous backlog of legal business. In 1879 the Northern District was established from counties carved out of the two older districts; Andrew P. McCormick[qv] was appointed judge. In 1902 the Southern District similarly was established; Waller T. Burns[qv] was the first judge.

Geographically, the Northern District of Texas includes such population centers as Dallas, Fort Worth, Abilene, San Angelo, Amarillo, Wichita Falls, and Lubbock; the Southern includes Houston, Galveston, Laredo, Brownsville, Victoria, and Corpus Christi; the Eastern includes Tyler, Beaumont, Sherman, and Texarkana; and the Western includes Waco, Austin, San Antonio, El Paso, Del Rio, and Pecos. The growth and relative workload of federal courts in Texas reflects changes in business development and population patterns of the state as a whole. In 1949 the Northern District had three judges, the Southern and Western Districts had two, and the Eastern District still had only one. By contrast, 1995 figures reflect the explosion of federal litigation during the latter half of the twentieth century, as well as the movement of population to newer districts. The Southern District led the state with sixteen active district judges, the Northern District had eleven, the Western District ten, and the Eastern District—the successor to the original District of Texas—had only five active judges. The Southern District is particularly notable, over the long term, for its heavy workload. In 1931 it had the largest single-judge federal caseload in the nation; in 1961 it ranked in the top ten on workload; and in 1990 it ranked among the four busiest. While the four federal district courts are the most visible signs of a federal judicial presence in Texas, the state also is home to other members of the federal judiciary. Since passage of the Bankruptcy Act of 1867, federal bankruptcy judges have decided cases in this major area of federal law. The heavy workload in federal courts also led in 1968 to the formation of positions for federal magistrates, now "magistrate judges," who assist the federal district judges in the performance of their duties. Unlike federal district and appellate judges, neither bankruptcy judges nor magistrate judges enjoy life tenure.

BIBLIOGRAPHY: Charles L. Zelden, *Justice Lies in the District: The U.S. District Court, Southern District of Texas, 1902–1960* (College Station: Texas A&M University Press, 1993).   James W. Paulsen

FEDERAL MUSIC PROJECT. Before the Great Depression,[qv] radio and sound movies had forced thousands of musicians into unemployment; music was being delivered electronically rather than by live musicians. The economic collapse intensified their situation, causing by 1934 a 60 percent displacement (an estimated 20,000 to 70,000 people), compared to a national unemployment rate of 25 percent. Early relief was administered inefficiently under the New Deal's Civil Works Administration and Federal Emergency Relief Administration, forerunners of the Work Projects Administration, until, in mid-1935 the Federal Music Project was organized as an agency of the WPA. The FMP was directed by Nikolai Sokoloff. It sought to employ professional musicians, to give free concerts, and to educate the public about music. Soon musicians were taken from manual labor and reassigned to work better suited for their talents. The project's relief efforts focused on New York City, Chicago, Los Angeles, San Francisco, and Boston, traditional centers for musical activity. A third of federal relief was divided among the forty-four remaining states. Texas was in Region 8 with Oklahoma, Arkansas, and Louisiana, and received the careful administration of Lucil M. Lyons[qv] of Fort Worth, who was well known in Texas musical activities. Although she was appointed by and technically under Sokoloff, she was administratively responsible to the state WPA administrator, H. P. Drought, in San Antonio. Under Mrs. Lyons's direction, city councils, school boards, chambers of commerce, universities, locals of the musicians' union, and especially the Texas Federation of Music Clubs[qv] coordinated relief programs with the national office.

Employment in the project peaked in spring 1936. During Sokoloff's tenure (1936–39), Texas FMP units gave 4,077 performances attracting 2,784,823 listeners. Though WPA activity occurred statewide, four centers were San Antonio, Fort Worth, Dallas, and El Paso. The San Antonio Symphony Orchestra[qv] began as a WPA unit. The FMP also launched the career of the symphony's illustrious future conductor, Victor Alessandro,[qv] a native Texan. Although Texas lacked a composer's forum, state copyists and arrangers transcribed vernacular folk songs. San Antonio units recorded examples of Mexican, Spanish, and Cuban music and early Texas plains songs for the Library of Congress, thus saving a wealth of folk music.

Although Texas had no assigned FMP opera units, WPA workers in Fort Worth performed operettas and choruses under the direction of Walker Moore. The highlight of the 1936 season was the "Texas under Six Flags" folk festival at Texas Christian University stadium; a chorus of 1,500 voices sang historic songs in celebration of the Texas Centennial.[qv] The FMP also encouraged music appreciation in the schools. Moore divided the Fort Worth WPA orchestra into teams to teach school children all over the city and county. Similar projects by educational units reached two-thirds of the rural areas having no prior musical instruction.

Not only did WPA orchestras train hundreds of musicians; their programs emphasized American compositions. Texans also heard works by their own, such as David Wendell Guion and Oscar Julius Fox.[qqv] Most important, the FMP lifted the nation's morale and awakened pride in native music.

Major reorganization followed Sokoloff's resignation in May 1939. Partly because of the uneven distribution of funds under Sokoloff, under Dr. Earl Vincent Moore the FMP lost its charter as a federal agency; this shifted the sponsorship of projects to the state and local level, where it had been in Texas virtually all along. The state thus autonomously preserved the beneficial effects of the FMP. The public activities of the project ended in 1941.

BIBLIOGRAPHY: Cornelius B. Canon, The Federal Music Project of the Works Progress Administration: Music in a Democracy (Ph.D. dissertation, University of Minnesota, 1963). Earl Vincent Moore, *Final Report of the Federal Music Project, October 10, 1939* (Washington, D.C.: Government Printing Office, 1939). Nikolai Sokoloff, *The Federal Music Project* (Washington, D.C.: Government Printing Office, 1936). Texas Reports, Record Group 69, WPA-FMP Files, National Archives, Washington, D.C. Janelle J. Warren, Of Tears and Need: The Federal Music Project, 1935–1943 (Ph.D. dissertation, George Washington University, 1973).   Craig H. Roell

FEDERAL RESERVE BANK OF DALLAS. The Federal Reserve System was established by the United States Congress in December 1913. Its primary purpose is to provide a flow of credit that will foster economic stability and growth, a high level of employment, stability in the purchasing power of the dollar, and a reasonable balance in transactions with foreign countries. The Federal Reserve Bank of Dallas, one of the twelve regional Federal Reserve Banks, serves the Eleventh Federal Reserve District. The district covers approximately 350,000 square miles and includes Texas, northern Louisiana, and southern New Mexico. Branch offices are located in El Paso, Houston, and San Antonio. The site of the Federal Reserve Bank of Dallas building was purchased in 1918, and the structure has been occupied since March 1921. The Dallas Fed, built by architects Graham, Anderson, Probost, and White of Chicago in the Neoclassical style of the Beaux Arts School, was designated a historic landmark by the city of Dallas on May 10, 1979.

At the Dallas Fed a nine-member board of directors oversees operations under the general supervision of the board of governors in Washington, D.C. Each of the branch offices has a seven-member board of directors, who work closely with the reserve bank president to provide regional input on management of monetary policies. Like the other reserve banks, the Dallas branch is primarily a "banker's bank." It serves as a bank for financial institutions in basically the same way commercial banks and thrift institutions serve the public. Financial institutions send their excess currency and coin to the Fed, where the money is verified, sorted, and stored until it is needed to fill new orders.

One function of the Dallas Fed is to ensure that currency in circulation is in good physical condition. Bills, processed through high-speed machines, are checked for denomination and fitness. If a bill is suspected of being a counterfeit, it is rejected by the machine and visually inspected. Bogus bills are then sent to the United States Secret Service for investigation. Worn or damaged bills are destroyed. Bills in good condition are bundled and sorted for redistribution to institutions in the Eleventh District. To replace currency withdrawn from circulation, the Dallas Fed uses newly printed currency from the Bureau of Engraving and Printing and coins from United States mints in Denver, Philadelphia, and San Francisco.

Since so many dollars spent in the United States are in the form of checks, perhaps the largest operation at the Fed is its check-clearing service. The check departments at the Dallas Fed and its branches operate twenty-four hours a day, five days a week, and process millions of checks daily. Other functions include operation of the payments mechanism system, which includes the automated clearinghouse and electronic fund transfer services; a reserve maintenance division, which maintains reserves of members; and a supervision and regulation department, which conducts regular bank examinations. As fiscal agent for the United States Treasury, the Dallas Fed sells and redeems United States government securities. Though the Fed is a governmental agency that reports to Congress, it is not civil service but a self-funding organization that generates earnings mainly from interest on its holdings of securities.

Monthly and quarterly publications released by the Dallas Fed include articles on economic trends, financial-institution news, and agricultural, energy, and district highlights. It makes available pamphlets on such topics as the Federal Reserve System, savings bonds, government securities, automated clearinghouse, electronic funds transfer, and consumer credit. Films on economics and banking are also available through the Public Affairs Department. Bulletins, regulations, and circulars (which publicize any amendments or special announcements) can also be obtained from the Public Affairs Department. An economic education program is also sponsored by the Public Affairs Department to assist Eleventh District public schools and universities in teaching economics and banking.

BIBLIOGRAPHY: *Federal Reserve Bank of Dallas: Historic Landmark* (Dallas: Federal Reserve Bank, n.d.) *Federal Reserve Bank of Dallas: Past and Present* (Dallas: Federal Reserve Bank, n.d.) *The Federal Reserve System: Purposes and Functions* (Washington: Board of Governors of the Federal Reserve System, 1939; 7th ed. 1984).

Dione Anteau

FEDOR, TEXAS. Fedor, also known as Moab, West Yegua, and Long Prairie, is eight miles north of Manheim in north central Lee County. It was settled in the late 1850s by a group of Wends[qv] from Serbin, Texas, who organized Trinity Lutheran Church in 1870. A post office was established in 1880 and called Fedor in honor of Fedor Soder, a local merchant. In 1884 Fedor had an estimated population of 130 and a steam saw, a gristmill, a cotton gin, and a school. By 1900 many of Fedor's residents had moved to Thorndale, and in 1905 the post office was discontinued. Since the 1930s the population in Fedor has remained relatively stable, with eighty-six residents reported in 1936 and seventy-six in 1990.

BIBLIOGRAPHY: Lee County Historical Survey Committee, *A History of Lee County* (Quanah, Texas: Nortex, 1974). Ray Spitzenberger

FEILD, JULIAN (1825–1897). Julian Feild, civic leader of Fort Worth and founder of Mansfield, was born in Mecklenburg County, Virginia, on August 14, 1825, the son of Robert and Frances Feild. In 1838 he moved with his family to Harrison County, Texas, but went to Tennessee to live with relatives after he was orphaned in 1840. Feild married Henrietta Roberta Boisseau on November 29, 1843. They had seven children. He returned to Harrison County about 1844 and stayed there for eight years. He owned a large tract of farmland worth $4,400.

Feild moved west to Fort Worth about 1854, just after the fort closed. He purchased a log cabin from an officer, at what is now the corner of Belknap and Throckmorton streets. When the first Masonic lodge in Fort Worth was organized by ten Masons in April of 1854, Feild was elected worshipful master. The lodge hall, a two-story structure at East Belknap and Grove, was constructed under Feild's supervision in 1857. Masons met on the second floor, and the lower floor was used for church services, a school, and social events. Feild also served as a trustee for the public schools in 1856. The Dallas-based firm of Gold and Donaldson provided financial assistance and sent a representative in the person of W. J. Masten, a Methodist minister, to help Feild build a stone general store on the future Belknap and Taylor streets. Feild brought coffee and sugar from Shreveport, salt from Grand Saline, and other supplies from Houston. He sold merchandise to local citizens and traded with the Indians. The store also served as a post office, and Feild was commissioned as the first postmaster, a position he held from February 1856 until February 1857. In 1856, with the help of Ralph S. Man[qv] and David Mauck, Feild built the first gristmill in town at the confluence of the Clear Fork and West Fork of the Trinity River. He was one of thirty-eight men who signed a bond guarantee for the construction of the first courthouse in Fort Worth, part of an effort to make Fort Worth the county seat instead of Birdville. Unfortunately, the spot Feild selected for his original mill had inadequate running water, and two years of drought hurt the mill's business.

Feild sold his nineteen slaves in 1857 and purchased 2,500 acres of land on the Clear Fork and the West Fork of the Trinity, and Walnut and Bear creeks. In 1857, with the help of his friend R. S. Man, he relocated south of Fort Worth in the oak groves of Walnut Creek. He rebuilt the mill in 1858 as a three-story brick structure. The new location and steam-powered mill had a readily available supply of water, fuel, and grain from local farmers. The mill expanded and added production of lumber. As the Civil War[qv] began, Feild owned thirteen slaves and had property valued at $22,000. Because his mill proved invaluable to the Confederacy, he was exempted from military service. The mill shipped grain south as far as the Rio Grande and north to Jefferson City, Missouri. Feild entered into a lucrative contract with the federal government in 1867 to supply meal and flour to such army bases as Fort Belknap and Fort Griffin. In 1871 Kiowa Indians intercepted a shipment in what became known as the Warren Wagontrain Raid.qv The town that evolved around the successful mill ultimately became known as Mansfield, a derivative of the names of R. S. Man and Julian Feild. Feild platted the townsite and donated the land from the original Hanks survey. In 1868 he donated land for the Walnut Creek Congregational Church and Man donated land for the cemetery.

In 1875 Feild returned to Fort Worth. In 1880 he accompanied his friend Col. Olin Wellborn qv on a western campaign tour in his bid for Congress. On December 27, 1881, a fire destroyed Feild's home and stable. Three mules and five horses were lost to a blaze that probably originated from roman candles. In 1884 Feild was elected alderman of Fort Worth. He again served as postmaster, beginning on October 19, 1885. In 1890 he left Texas for the last time and moved to California. He died on September 9, 1897, and was buried in San Diego. Several of his sons remained in Fort Worth and continued the process of building a town begun by their father. Julian T. Feild became a prominent doctor in town after graduating from Louisville Medical School in 1868. He had the first telephone in town. W. Henry Feild studied law and became a bill collector for the firm of Feild and Durlager. Jeff D. Feild became a local druggist.

BIBLIOGRAPHY: Dallas *Morning News*, September 11, 1897. Mansfield *News-Mirror*, December 6, 1984. Buckley B. Paddock, *History of Texas: Fort Worth and the Texas Northwest Edition* (4 vols., Chicago: Lewis, 1922).

Kenneth E. Austin

FELDER, GABRIEL (1797–1868). Gabriel Felder, judge, was born in Orangeburg, South Carolina, on January 29, 1797, the son of Samuel and Ann (Horger) Felder. He was a justice of the peace in his young manhood and thereafter was known as Judge. He moved first to Mississippi, where he married. In the spring of 1851 he moved to Texas with his wife, Ann, and two sons. He settled in Washington County and between 1852 and 1856 purchased several tracts of land totaling 2,418 acres on the banks of New Year Creek, at a cost of more than $19,000, to be paid as he received money from his property in South Carolina. He had inherited a fourth of the estate of his brother, John M. Felder, of Orangeburg, South Carolina, amounting to $100,000, which included $48,830 in "Negro property," or ninety-five slaves, and $51,000 in money, mules, and horses. Jesse Y. Felder, a relative, was employed to bring the slaves from South Carolina to Texas. They arrived about June 20, 1854, too late to make a crop that year. Felder was a cotton planter, but since most of the land he purchased in Texas was heavily timbered, time and money were required to bring it into cultivation. By the time of his death only about 250 acres had been plowed. He made a trip back to South Carolina almost every year and always returned with sufficient money to satisfy his debts. He constructed his home, together with the millhouse, cotton gin, slave cabins, and other outbuildings, using the labor force from his own plantation; he was aided in building the mill and gin by an experienced mechanic.

At the Methodist Conference of 1855 he was appointed to the first board of trustees of Soule University, in Chappell Hill. He served as president of the board from June 29, 1858, until his death. In 1854 he endowed the Chair of Ancient and Modern Languages at Soule, called the Felder Professorship, in the amount of $25,000. In 1853 he provided the pews and finished the belfry of the new brick Methodist church at Washington-on-the-Brazos. After the death of his first wife on October 19, 1863, he married Mrs. Mildred S. Oliver, on April 28, 1864. The ceremony was performed by his friend James W. Shipman, an elder in the Methodist Episcopal Church, South. The census of 1860 listed Felder as owning 130 slaves; he was thus the largest slaveholder in Washington County.

Felder died on March 10, 1868. His will provided a 200-acre homestead for his widow, which included the residence, household furniture, carriage, and two carriage horses. To Mattie Alexander, an orphan raised by Felder, he left "a sum sufficient for her maintenance and support and to give her a good English education." His son Adlai D. (who was non compos mentis) and grandson, Gabriel S. Felder (son of Rufus H. Felder, who preceded Gabriel Felder in death) shared equally in the remainder of the estate.

BIBLIOGRAPHY: Macum Phelan, *History of Early Methodism in Texas, 1817–1866* (Nashville: Cokesbury, 1924); *A History of the Expansion of Methodism in Texas, 1867–1902* (Dallas: Mathis, Van Nort, 1937). Homer S. Thrall, *History of Methodism in Texas* (Houston: Cushing, 1872; rpt., n.p.: Walsworth, 1976). Ralph A. Wooster, "Notes on Texas' Largest Slaveholders, 1860," *Southwestern Historical Quarterly* 65 (July 1961).

Nath and Judy Winfield

FELDER, TEXAS. Felder, twelve miles northeast of Brenham in eastern Washington County, received a post office in February 1890 with Samuel Buchanan as postmaster. In 1892 the community had a general store, cotton mill, and gin. Wilson C. Hogan served as Felder's postmaster from December 1900 until the post office closed in September 1907. The mail for the community was then sent to Chappell Hill. Felder is not labeled on the 1942 county highway map.

BIBLIOGRAPHY: Henry Gannett, *A Gazetteer of Texas* (U.S. Geological Survey Bulletin 190, Series F, Washington: GPO, 1902; 2d ed., U.S.G.S. Bulletin 224, 1904).

Carole E. Christian

FELICIA, TEXAS. Felicia, at the junction of U.S. Highway 90 and Farm Road 1009, in southeastern Liberty County thirty-eight miles west of Beaumont, was the center of a scattered rice and ranching community. It became a stop on the Texas and New Orleans Railroad during the 1890s. From 1916 to 1921 Felicia also had a post office. After that date mail was sent to Nome in Jefferson County. By 1986 only a grain elevator marked the former townsite.

BIBLIOGRAPHY: Miriam Partlow, *Liberty, Liberty County, and the Atascosito District* (Austin: Pemberton, 1974).

Robert Wooster

FELIX LONGORIA AFFAIR. The controversy surrounding the burial of Felix Longoria provided a successful case for the American G. I. Forum,qv a civil rights organization for Mexican Americans, to fight racial discrimination with political pressure. In 1948 the remains of Private Felix Longoria of Three Rivers, Texas, were recovered from the Philippines, where he had been killed on a volunteer mission during the last days of World War II. His body was shipped home for burial in the Three Rivers cemetery, where the "Mexican" section was separated by barbed wire. The director of the funeral home would not allow the use of the chapel because of alleged disturbances at previous Mexican-American services and because "the whites would not like it." Longoria's widow and her sister discussed the refusal with Dr. Hector Garcia, the founder of the American G. I. Forum. He, in turn, contacted the funeral director and received the same refusal and rationale. On January 11, 1949, Garcia called a meeting of the Corpus Christi Forum, which he had organized as the first G. I. Forum chapter in March 1948; he also sent many telegrams and letters to Texas congressmen. Senator Lyndon B. Johnson qv responded immediately with support and an offer to arrange the burial at Arlington National Cemetery. The funeral took place on February 16, 1949, at the Arlington National Cemetery; with the Longoria family were Senator Johnson and a personal representative of the president of the United States.

After the funeral, the Texas House of Representatives authorized a five-member committee to investigate the Felix Longoria incident. The committee held open hearings at the Three Rivers Chamber of Commerce and, after recriminations and exculpatory arguments, concluded that there was no discrimination on the part of the funeral director and that he had acted in anger but had apologized. Four of the committeemen signed the report. Frank Oltorf, the fifth member, stated that the funeral director's words "appear to be discriminatory." Another member withdrew his name from the majority report and filed his own account, which stated that the actions of the director were on "the fine line of discrimination." The report was never filed. The Felix Longoria Affair provided Mexican Americans an example to unify and expand their struggle for civil rights in the coming decades.

BIBLIOGRAPHY: Carl Allsup, *The American G.I. Forum: Origins and Evolution* (University of Texas Center for Mexican American Studies Monograph 6, Austin, 1982).
V. Carl Allsup

FELTIN, LOUISE (1830–1905). Louise (Mother St. Andrew) Feltin, foundress of the Sisters of Divine Providence^qv in Texas, was born to Jean Claude and Marie (Seiter) Feltin of Alsace on December 27, 1830, and educated in the villages of Geispolsheim and La Walk. At nineteen she entered the convent of St. Jean de Bassel, situated in a Lorraine village of the same name; this convent was the home of the Sisters of Divine Providence, founded by Jean Martin Moye in 1762. Sister St. Andrew taught in several schools in Lorraine after her formation.

Meanwhile, in Texas, Bishop Claude Marie Dubuis^qv needed parish schools for his huge diocese, the whole of Texas (*see* CATHOLIC CHURCH). He went to his native country for religious teachers and recruited two sisters at St. Jean de Bassel, Sister St. Andrew Feltin and Sister Alphonse Boegler. Besides the incentive to be a missionary, Sister St. Andrew was motivated by reports from her brother, Father Nicholas Feltin, a prominent San Antonio and Austin priest. Bishop Dubuis sent the two sisters to Austin to establish the first parish school in Texas.

This school opened in the spring of 1867. By this time two native Texans had entered the Austin convent. The following year, however, Bishop Dubuis decided to establish in Austin the Holy Cross Fathers and Sisters (*see* CONGREGATION OF HOLY CROSS, HOLY CROSS SISTERS) from Notre Dame, Indiana. He asked Mother St. Andrew to move to Castroville, a village of Alsatians. She requested that the establishment in Castroville be permanent, and so she and Dubuis signed a contract on September 8, 1868.

In Castroville the parish priest, Father Peter Richard, moved into the sacristy of the church and gave the priests' residence to the sisters. By October a school was opened for the children of Castroville. In 1870 only three teaching sisters were in Castroville: Mother St. Andrew, Sister Mary Agnes Wolf, and Sister Mary Theresa Schultz. By August of the same year, however, the number of Sisters of Divine Providence in Texas had increased to nine, enabling Mother St. Andrew to open schools in D'Hanis, Fredericksburg, and New Braunfels.

From 1870 to 1878, as the number of religious grew, more schools were opened in Texas towns, and because the need for teachers increased, Mother St. Andrew returned for help to Lorraine, which was now part of Germany. The Sisters of Divine Providence at St. Jean de Bassel were uncomfortable under German rule and were looking to Texas for a settlement. Consequently, Mother St. Andrew returned to Texas with ten subjects. She visited St. Jean de Bassel three more times, bringing at least sixty-nine and perhaps as many as ninety-two religious back to the Castroville convent.

The latter part of her service in Texas was clouded by a long conflict with Jean Claude Neraz,^qv bishop of the new Diocese of San Antonio. Neraz wanted to separate the Texas Sisters of Divine Providence from the motherhouse in Lorraine, a separation that Mother St. Andrew refused to countenance. Bishop Neraz consequently tried to rid Castroville of Mother St. Andrew and supported Sister Florence Walter as her successor. Mother St. Andrew resigned as mother superior in 1886 and, after further conflict with Neraz, moved in 1887 to California to live with her motherless nieces and nephews. When Bishop Neraz died, she put on her religious habit and returned to the Castroville convent. There she lived in retirement until her death in February 1905. She was praised at her burial Mass for undergoing "hardships, trials, and humiliations . . . known to Him alone for whose sake they were borne so generously."

BIBLIOGRAPHY: Sister Mary Generosa Callahan, C.D.P., *The History of the Sisters of Divine Providence, San Antonio, Texas* (Milwaukee: Bruce, 1955). Catholic Archives of Texas, Files, Austin. University Archives, Our Lady of the Lake University, San Antonio.
Sister Mary Generosa Callahan, C.D.P.

FENCE CUTTING. Fence cutting in Texas in the summer and fall of 1883 was a part of the conflict between landless cattlemen who wanted to retain practices of the open range and those who bought barbed wire^qv to fence the land to establish themselves on permanent ranches. The fence war was precipitated by the drought of 1883, which made it all the harder for the cowman without land of his own to find the grass and water necessary for his herds.

Most of the ranchmen owned or leased the land they fenced, but some of them enclosed public land when they enclosed their own, and others strung their wire about farms and small ranches belonging to other persons. Often the fences blocked public roads; in some instances they cut off schools and churches and interfered with the delivery of mail. This unwarranted fencing led some men whose land was not actually fenced in to join in the nipping. As the cutting continued, it became less discriminate and attracted rougher elements; soon no ranchman's fence was safe.

Wrecking of fences was reported from more than half the Texas counties and was most common in a belt extending north and south through the center of the state, the ranchman's frontier of 1883. Much of the cutting was done at night by armed bands who called themselves such names as Owls, Javelinas, or Blue Devils. Often those who destroyed fences left warnings against rebuilding, but these were usually disregarded. In some instances, pastures of the fencers were burned. Some owners defended their property, and at least three men were killed in clashes between fence cutters and ranchmen.

Texas newspapers generally condemned the cutting but indicated that not all the fencers were free of blame. Few attempts were made to reconcile the embittered groups, but at Henrietta spokesmen for the fence cutters met with Clay County ranchmen, and the two groups agreed that fences would be removed from across public roads and land not owned or leased by the fence builders, that gates would be provided for farmers' use, and that wire-cutting would end.

By the fall of 1883 damage from wrecking of fences in Texas was estimated at $20 million—at more than $1 million in Brown County alone. The Fort Worth *Gazette* asserted that fence troubles had caused tax valuations to decline $30 million. The clashes discouraged farming and scared away some prospective settlers. Politicians shied from the explosive issue, but on October 15 Governor John Ireland^qv called a special session of the legislature to meet on January 8, 1884. After a deluge of petitions and heated debates, the legislature made fence cutting a felony punishable by one to five years in prison. The penalty for malicious pasture-burning was two to five years in prison. Fencing of public lands or lands belonging to others knowingly and without permission was made a misdemeanor, and builders of such fences were to remove them within six months. Ranchers who built fences across public roads were required to place a gate every three miles and to keep the gates in repair.

These measures ended most of the fence troubles, although sporadic outbreaks of nipping continued for a decade, especially during droughts. Texas Rangers^qv were sent after fence cutters in Navarro County in 1888, and for several years the rangers had occasional fence cases in West Texas.

BIBLIOGRAPHY: Hans Peter Nielsen Gammel, comp., *Laws of Texas, 1822–1897* (10 vols., Austin: Gammel, 1898). Wayne Gard, "The Fence-Cutters," *Southwestern Historical Quarterly* 51 (July 1947). Roy D.

Holt, "The Introduction of Barbed Wire into Texas and the Fence Cutting War," *West Texas Historical Association Year Book* 6 (1930). Henry D. McCallum, "Barbed Wire in Texas," *Southwestern Historical Quarterly* 61 (October 1957). Henry D. and Frances T. McCallum, *The Wire That Fenced the West* (Norman: University of Oklahoma Press, 1965). Vertical Files, Barker Texas History Center, University of Texas at Austin (Barbed Wire).

Wayne Gard

FENCED-IN VILLAGE. Fenced-in Village ranked second in importance among the settlements established by the Alabama Indian tribe in the Big Thicket^{qv} region. The center of this village was on a hill of the Kisatchie Wold^{qv} or ridge five miles southeast of Peach Tree Village^{qv} in northwestern Tyler County. The Fenced-In Village site is on present County Road 135 of the Tyler County road system, midway between Mount Zion Church and Bethany Church. The location of this village is shown on a map included with the surveyor's field notes for a Republic of Texas^{qv} two-league grant of land for the Alabama tribe in 1840. Also, it is shown on a map of Liberty County (which included Tyler County during the years of the Republic of Texas) drawn by H. L. Upshur in 1841. This village and the surrounding territory were included in a survey of land patented to Harmon Frazier. The Alabamas usually demonstrated considerable skill in trailblazing and in selecting advantageous sites for their villages. The choice of the Fenced-In Village site is a good example. The hilltop location provided drainage, and the existence of nearby springs and the headwaters of several creeks assured an adequate water supply. The Liberty-Nacogdoches Road^{qv} passed through this Indian community, which developed into a significant trading center. Typically an Alabama Indian village, such as Fenced-In, was actually a community in which cabins were located in a succession of neighborhoods scattered through the woods and along streams and connected by a network of trails. Cabins were usually grouped in family or clan units, with adequate land around each cabin for cultivating vegetables and growing fruit trees. Near the center of each community was a square ground used for a variety of governmental, social, entertainment, and religious activities. Thus, a village would usually be a scattering of homesites extending for miles around a square ground. The identification of this village as "Fenced-In" may suggest a number of Indian cabins enclosed by a rail fence, but this name refers only to a tract of land in the village site designated for agricultural use by village residents. A rail fence was constructed around this community gardening or farming area to provide at least partial protection for the Alabama Indians' vegetable crops and fruit trees. Incoming white settlers saw the desirable agricultural land in the surrounding area, and the land around Fenced-In Village was soon surveyed and claimed by these newcomers. Also, the Alabamas' rights to hunting grounds in the area were disputed and restricted. In 1840 the Fourth Congress of Texas had passed an act granting two leagues of land, including the village, for the Alabamas. Apparently, when surveyors arrived in the area, the remaining Alabamas left, believing that the men had come to secure the land for white settlers. They abandoned at least 200 acres of fenced-in agricultural land and moved south along Big Cypress Creek.

BIBLIOGRAPHY: Gustav Dresel, *Houston Journal: Adventures in North America and Texas, 1837–1841*, trans. and ed. Max Freund (Austin: University of Texas Press, 1954). Howard N. Martin, "Polk County Indians: Alabamas, Coushattas, Pakana Muskogees," *East Texas Historical Journal* 17 (1979). Harriet Smither, "The Alabama Indians of Texas," *Southwestern Historical Quarterly* 36 (October 1932). Dorman H. Winfrey and James M. Day, eds., *Texas Indian Papers* (4 vols., Austin: Texas State Library, 1959–61; rpt, 5 vols., Austin: Pemberton Press, 1966).

Howard N. Martin

FENELLA, TEXAS. Fenella was twelve miles northeast of Hempstead in northern Waller County. It was probably on what is today Howell Road slightly north of the Fields Store community and west of Farm Road 362. In 1897 Jackson Bush opened a post office in his general store there to serve nearly 200 residents from the surrounding area. The post office closed in 1899, and the office at Gladish, four miles southwest of Fenella, handled local mail service. By 1941 Fenella was not shown on county highway maps.

BIBLIOGRAPHY: Mildred W. Abshier et al., *Former Post Offices of Waller County* (Hempstead, Texas: Waller County Historical Society, 1977).

Paul M. Lucko

FENN, JOHN RUTHERFORD (1824–1904). John Rutherford Fenn, early Texas soldier and settler, was born in Lawrence County, Mississippi, on October 11, 1824, the son of Eli and Sarah (Fitzgerald) Fenn. On June 7, 1833, the family arrived at the area that later became Fort Bend County, Texas. During the Texas Revolution^{qv} young Fenn was captured by Mexican soldiers but escaped to be reunited with his mother and brother at the William W. Little^{qv} camp in the Brazos riverbottom. In 1842 Fenn served in William Ryon's company under Alexander Somervell^{qv} but did not continue on the Mier expedition.^{qv} He served as a second lieutenant in the Confederate Army during the Civil War.^{qv} In 1852 he married Rebecca M. Williams; the couple had four children. The Fenns settled on a plantation they called Duke on Oyster Creek, where they lived until 1872, when they moved to Houston. There they observed their fiftieth wedding anniversary in 1902. Fenn was first vice president of the Texas Veterans Association^{qv} and a Democrat. He died at Houston on November 23, 1904, and was buried in the family cemetery at Duke.

BIBLIOGRAPHY: John Henry Brown, *Indian Wars and Pioneers of Texas* (Austin: Daniell, 1880; reprod., Easley, South Carolina: Southern Historical Press, 1978). Adele B. Looscan, "John R. Fenn," *Southwestern Historical Quarterly* 8 (January 1905). Andrew Jackson Sowell, *History of Fort Bend County* (Houston: Coyle, 1904; rpt, Richmond, Texas: Fort Bend County Historical Museum, 1974). Vertical Files, Barker Texas History Center, University of Texas at Austin.

FENTER, DAVID (1794?–1858). David Fenter (Fenton), one of Stephen F. Austin's^{qv} Old Three Hundred^{qv} colonists, was born in Pennsylvania, the son of German immigrant Christian Fenter. He was a Methodist and a Whig and fought in the United States Army during the War of 1812. He received title to a sitio^{qv} of land in what is now Matagorda County on July 29, 1824. The census of March 1826 classified him, under the name Fenton, as a farmer and stock raiser aged between twenty-five and forty. His household included his wife, Martha (Fisher), aged between sixteen and twenty-five, and two sons. The couple eventually had a total of twelve children. A family genealogy claims that Fenter was en route to the Alamo but became ill and dropped out, thus escaping the impending massacre. Muster rolls for 1836 show one "David Fluter (Fenter)" enlisted in Capt. B. F. Ravill's company of Texas volunteers in July of that year. Fenter, a wheelwright as well as a farmer, lived in Texas for about thirteen years before returning to Arkansas, where he settled on a farm. In 1858 he died in Fenter Township, in what later became Grant County, Arkansas.

BIBLIOGRAPHY: Lester G. Bugbee, "The Old Three Hundred: A List of Settlers in Austin's First Colony," *Quarterly of the Texas State Historical Association* 1 (October 1897). Matagorda County Historical Commission, *Historic Matagorda County* (3 vols., Houston: Armstrong, 1986). Vertical Files, Barker Texas History Center, University of Texas at Austin.

Rachel Jenkins

FENTRESS, TEXAS. Fentress is on the San Marcos River at the southwestern edge of Caldwell County. A settlement, first called Riverside, began developing there in the vicinity of a Cumberland Presbyterian church established in 1869. A horse-powered cotton gin was built in the vicinity about 1870 by the partnership of Cullen R. Smith and Joseph D. Smith. The enterprise was moved to the riverfront and converted to waterpower in 1879; it was operated by family members until it closed in 1968. In 1892 the community was renamed Fentress in honor of James Fentress, its first doctor; he was also a large landholder and a participant in the battle of Plum Creek.qv A year later a post office was established in W. A. Wilson's general store, with Wilson as postmaster. The community was then on the daily mail route between Luling and San Marcos. A one-room school, which operated for three months each year, opened in 1895. An 1896 business directory lists a doctor, a blacksmith, and a population of 150 in Fentress. The Fentress Waterworks was established in 1898 and a lighting system in 1902. The Fentress Telephone Company was formed soon after 1900, and around 1904 the community had its own newspaper, the Fentress *Indicator*. In 1905 a Methodist congregation was organized, and four years later they built their own church. In 1907 the one-room school was replaced with a two-room structure that served until 1922, when a two-story, five-room facility with an auditorium was completed. A 1915 business directory lists Fentress with 300 residents, three general stores, a mercantile company, a meat market, a confectionery, a pharmacy. a gin, and a blacksmith shop.

In 1915 Josh Merritt and his partner C. E. Tolhurst created a resort with a swimming and camping facility that offered bathhouses, a water slide, and screened tents with wooden floors. Two years later Merritt and Tolhurst sold the resort to the partnership of J. C. Dauchy, W. R. Smith, and J. M. Dauchy. The new owners added a maple-floored skating rink, where, on alternating nights, dancing was permitted. This move aroused controversy among church members in surrounding communities. In 1918 the six-year-old Fentress water tower collapsed onto the town's only bank; cashier J. W. Lipscomb saved his life by dashing into the vault. This high water mark in Fentress history was viewed by some as divine judgment. For four decades, beginning in the 1920s, nearby oilfield activity was significant in the local economy, and Fentress grew to a peak of 500 residents in 1929. By 1940, however, the population had slipped to 250. The local school was closed in a merger with the Prairie Lea school district in the 1940s. By the early 1990s most of the businesses had disappeared. Even the Fentress Hog Farm, once noted for supplying the performing pigs at Aquarena Springs,qv no longer existed. In 1990 another riverside recreation facility attracted campers and tubers. A nearby landing strip provided an operating base for area skydivers. Otherwise, two businesses, two churches, and a post office were all that remained. Fentress reported a population of eighty-five in 1990.

BIBLIOGRAPHY: Mark Withers Trail Drive Museum, *Historical Caldwell County* (Dallas: Taylor, 1984). *Plum Creek Almanac*, Fall 1983.

Barbara Stock

FENWICK, MARIN B. (ca. 1860–1928). Marin B. Fenwick, writer, suffragist, and civic leader, was born in Highland County, Ohio, around 1860, the daughter of James and Marinda (Sloan) Fenwick. She earned a degree at Rockford Female Seminary (later Rockford College) in Illinois, where she was a classmate of Jane Addams and Julia Lathrop. She lived in the Midwest for a while and then moved to San Antonio in 1891. The next year she took a job with the San Antonio *Express*,qv thus beginning a newspaper career that continued until shortly before her death. Fenwick served as editor of the society page until 1911, when she began a column entitled "Facts and Fancies." In addition to this column she began a second one, "Just Among Ourselves," for the San Antonio *Evening News*qv in 1918. She also edited and published *Who's Who Among the Women of San Antonio and Southwest Texas* in 1917. Fenwick was active in women's club work in San Antonio and held positions of leadership in the Woman's Club, Wednesday Luncheon Club, and Young Women's Christian Association. Her other memberships included the San Antonio History Club. She was an ardent advocate of voting rights for women and was involved in local and state suffrage organizations. Through this effort she became a close friend of San Antonio suffragist Mary Eleanor Brackenridge.qv In 1905 Fenwick sailed around the world with Eleanor and her brother George Brackenridgeqv and met woman suffrageqv leaders in other countries along the way. Highlights from this trip were chronicled in the San Antonio *Express*. In 1924 Governor Pat Neffqv and San Antonio leaders honored Fenwick for her lengthy service to the local press. Marin Fenwick, a Presbyterian, died after a brief illness on June 27, 1928, in San Antonio and was buried in Mission Burial Park.

BIBLIOGRAPHY: San Antonio *Express*, June 28, 1928. *Who's Who among the Women of San Antonio and Southwest Texas* (San Antonio: Fenwick, 1917).

Debbie Mauldin Cottrell

FERBER, EDNA (1887–1968). Edna Ferber, novelist, was born on August 15, 1887, in Kalamazoo, Michigan, to Jacob Charles and Julia (Neumann) Ferber. Her father was a Jewish immigrant from Hungary. The family left Kalamazoo when Edna was three years old to live in Chicago for a year. Afterward, they spent seven years in Ottumwa, Iowa, and finally settled in Appleton, Wisconsin, where she graduated from Ryan High School. She became the first female reporter for the Appleton *Crescent*, although she had no desire to be a writer. Her work on the high school newspaper and her publication of a feature article on the confirmation service at Temple Emanu-El in Appleton had impressed the *Crescent*'s editor. After she was fired by a new editor who did not care for her style of writing, Ferber was offered a job with the Milwaukee *Journal*. She took a leave from her duties at the *Journal* due to illness and returned to her family's home in Appleton to recuperate. There she started writing and selling her short stories and began work on her first novel, *Dawn O'Hara, The Girl Who Laughed* (1911). Although she later covered such political events as the Democratic and Republican national conventions on special assignment, she never again worked as a full-time newspaper reporter. *So Big* (1924), the first of four western novels, won the Pulitzer Prize. *Giant* (1952), another western novel, was set on a fictitious South Texas ranch. Ferber wove into the story themes of the exploitation of human labor and land by arrogant landowners. *Giant* was viewed with dismay by some Texans upon its publication. Despite some bad reviews, the book became a best-seller, as did many other of Ferber's works. In fact, the film rights to nine of her books were sold to Hollywood. In 1955 the movie *Giant*, starring Elizabeth Taylor and Rock Hudson, was filmed on a ranch near Marfa. The movie was a box-office success and has been rereleased on several occasions and shown on network television. Edna Ferber wrote several other novels, eleven short-story collections, nine plays, two autobiographies, and one screenplay. She died on April 16, 1968, a few months before her eighty-first birthday. At her funeral service in New York City, she was eulogized as "a gallant, dauntless, irrepressible champion" of "great causes." Her body was cremated.

BIBLIOGRAPHY: Edna Ferber, *A Peculiar Treasure* (New York: Doubleday, Doran, 1939). Julie Goldsmith Gilbert, *Ferber, A Biography* (Garden City, New York: Doubleday, 1978). Mary Rose Shaughnessy, *Women and Success in American Society in the Works of Edna Ferber* (New York: Gordon Press, 1977). *Twentieth-Century Western Writers* (Detroit: Gale Research, 1982; 2d ed., Chicago: St. James Press, 1991). Vertical Files, Barker Texas History Center, University of Texas at Austin.

Teresa Palomo Acosta

FERGUSON, ALANSON (1791–1851). Alanson Ferguson, chief justice and legislator, was born in 1791 and moved to Texas sometime before 1840, when he was chief justice of San Patricio County, a position that he resigned on September 1, 1841. He was elected to represent the county in the House of the Sixth Congress of the Republic of Texas,qv but he lost a contest on the election. Ferguson died at Corpus Christi on December 31, 1851.

BIBLIOGRAPHY: Texas House of Representatives, *Biographical Direc-*

tory of the Texan Conventions and Congresses, 1832–1845 (Austin: Book Exchange, 1941).

FERGUSON, CHARLES M. (ca. 1860–1906). Charles M. Ferguson, political leader, county official, and civil servant, was born in Houston, Texas, about 1860 of mixed racial ancestry; he was probably born a slave. He graduated from Fisk University at Nashville, Tennessee, in 1880. He then moved to Fort Bend County and with his brother, Henry Clay Ferguson,qv began a career of government service. Ferguson was living in Richmond and owned a 1,500-acre plantation on Jones Creek when he won election to the position of clerk of the district court in Fort Bend County in 1882, 1884, and 1886. He did not complete the final year of his last term. On September 6, 1888, white members of a political association known as the Jaybirds ordered Ferguson and several other black political leaders to leave the county. Facing threats upon his life and detested by many white residents for his efforts aimed at organizing African Americans, Ferguson moved temporarily to Nashville. He and James D. Davis, another exiled black political leader, filed a civil rights suit against the Jaybirds in a federal court at Galveston in 1889. In an out-of-court settlement Ferguson received a $13,000 payment for his damages. His involvement in the political and racial controversies of Fort Bend county were a part of the infamous Jaybird-Woodpecker War.qv

Ferguson returned to Texas permanently in 1889 and represented the state on the executive committee of the Bureau of Relief, which met in Washington, D.C., in 1889. He had served as a delegate to the national Republican partyqv convention in 1888 and did so again in 1892, 1896, 1900, and 1904. Ferguson frequently opposed Norris Wright Cuneyqv in intraparty battles and successfully fought Robert Lloyd Smith'sqv appointment to the United States Treasury Department. Although Ferguson occasionally cooperated with the People's partyqv during the 1890s, he always retained his Republican affiliation and was rewarded with appointments to federal government positions. He reportedly refused an appointment to a South American consulate, but by 1892 he began a period of service as clerk of the Federal District Court in Paris, Texas. President William McKinley named him deputy collector of customs in San Antonio in 1900; Ferguson remained at that position for the rest of his life. San Antonio newspapers described him as "uniformly courteous" and "respected by the whites as well as the negroes" in the performance of his duties. On his deathbed he answered correspondence pertaining to his job until an hour before his passing. He was a Methodist and a leader of the Grand Order of the Odd Fellows. He was married and the father of two children. He died in San Antonio on July 21, 1906, after a short illness resulting from complications relating to Bright's Disease. He was buried in Houston.

BIBLIOGRAPHY: San Antonio *Daily Express*, July 22, 1906. Pauline Yelderman, *The Jay Bird Democratic Association of Fort Bend County* (Waco: Texian Press, 1979).
Paul M. Lucko

FERGUSON, DANIEL (1891–1963). Daniel Ferguson, lawyer and book collector, was born at Chireno, Texas, on December 8, 1891, son of Richard Oliver and Minnie Jane (Pate) Ferguson. He attended Nacogdoches public schools and graduated from the University of Texas with an LL.B. degree in 1916. He interrupted his Dallas law practice during World War Iqv for service as a second lieutenant in the army air corps. For forty years Ferguson was an attorney with the Magnolia Petroleum Company.qv During that time he built a remarkable private library on Texas and the Southwest; he used this collection to study the relationships of early churches and education in Texas, about which he published several articles. In 1956 he presented his library of 5,500 volumes and his collection of presidential signatures to the Bridwell Libraryqv of Southern Methodist University. A catalogue of the collection was published in 1960. Ferguson was a trustee and member of the board of Oak Lawn Methodist Church, Dallas, and a member of the Texas State Historical Association.qv He was a Mason and a member of the State Bar of Texas.qv He married Lucile Harding on June 27, 1923, and they had three children. After Lucile died in 1932, he married Ten Tower, on June 2, 1935. He was the uncle of Senator John Tower.qv Ferguson died on December 17, 1963, and was buried at Grove Hill Cemetery, Dallas.

BIBLIOGRAPHY: Dallas *Times Herald*, December 18, 1963. Vertical Files, Barker Texas History Center, University of Texas at Austin.
Decherd Turner

FERGUSON, HENRY CLAY (1847–1923). Henry Clay Ferguson, county official and Republican partyqv chairman, was born in Texas in 1847, probably into slavery.qv He moved to Houston and became secretary of the Harris County school board. He later served with distinction in the State Police.qv In 1870, after the disbanding of this force, he moved to Fort Bend County, one of the few Texas counties with a black majority (5,510 black residents and 1,604 white ones). A contemporary who knew Ferguson described him as "a man of great dignity, [who] never talked loud in conversation, and looked one in the face when he talked." Ferguson succeeded another African American, Walter M. Burton,qv as sheriff, an office in which he took an even-handed approach that gained the respect of many whites. With their support he easily obtained the surety bond, required at the time, to run for public office. In 1876 he was elected county tax assessor, a position he held until 1888. His brother Charles M. Ferguson,qv whom Henry supported at Fisk University, returned to Fort Bend County and was elected district clerk in 1882. In 1888, in an effort to eliminate black Republican control of the county, a number of young white men formed the Young Men's Democratic Club, which became known as the Jaybirds. Black Republicans and their white supporters became known as the Woodpeckers. In the hostilities that developed two white men were killed. The Jaybirds blamed black leaders for the deaths, even though no African Americansqv were formally charged. The Jaybirds demanded that six prominent black leaders leave the county. Though the club banished Charles, it allowed Henry to remain. Ferguson later gave up his tax-assessor position, sold his property, and left for Houston (*see* JAYBIRD-WOODPECKER WAR).

After leaving Fort Bend County, Ferguson obtained a concession from Mexico and proposed to colonize 10,000 blacks to grow cotton. Even though the plan fell through, he gained a position on the committee for permanent organization at the national Republican convention in 1888. His growing prominence in the Texas Republican party and his support for William McKinley led to his election over Norris Wright Cuneyqv as temporary state party chairman in 1896. Ferguson defeated William Madison McDonaldqv to become permanent chairman at the 1898 state Republican convention, but the split that developed between the Ferguson and McDonald factions weakened black influence within the Republican party. Ferguson died on January 6, 1923, in Ellis County.

BIBLIOGRAPHY: Alwyn Barr, *Black Texans: A History of Negroes in Texas, 1528–1971* (Austin: Jenkins, 1973). Paul D. Casdorph, *A History of the Republican Party in Texas, 1865–1965* (Austin: Pemberton Press, 1965). Lawrence D. Rice, *The Negro in Texas, 1874–1900* (Baton Rouge: Louisiana State University Press, 1971). Clarence Wharton, *Wharton's History of Fort Bend County* (San Antonio: Naylor, 1939). Pauline Yelderman, *The Jay Bird Democratic Association of Fort Bend County* (Waco: Texian Press, 1979).
Douglas Hales

FERGUSON, JAMES EDWARD (1871–1944). James Edward (Pa) Ferguson, Texas governor, son of James Edward and Fannie (Fitzpatrick) Ferguson, was born on August 31, 1871, near Salado, Bell County, Texas. When he was four years old, his father died. His mother continued to live on the farm, and he began working in the fields as a young boy. He entered Salado College, a local preparatory school, at age twelve but was eventually expelled for disobedience. He left home at sixteen and wandered for two years through the states of the Far

West, where he lived by accepting any employment offered. After returning to Bell County, he farmed and worked with a railroad-bridge gang until, after a brief study of law, he was admitted to the bar in 1897 and began the practice of law in Belton. On December 31, 1899, he married Miriam A. Wallace (see FERGUSON, MIRIAM A. W.); they had two children. His law practice did not require all of his time, so Ferguson expanded his interests to include real estate and insurance and later turned his attention to banking. He was associated with the Farmers State Bank of Belton for several years and was a member of the Texas Bankers Association.qv He moved to Temple and in 1907 joined with others in establishing the Temple State Bank. Throughout his years in banking he took an active interest in county and local politics.

Although he had never held office, he was not a stranger to political problems; he had done much work in keeping local-option prohibition qv from Bell County, had been one of the Bell County managers in the campaign of Robert L. Henryqv for Congress in 1902, had helped carry Bell County for Cone Johnsonqv in his contest with Joseph Weldon Baileyqv in 1908, had served as a campaign manager for Robert V. Davidsonqv in 1910, and had aided Oscar B. Colquittqv in his successful gubernatorial campaign (1912). Prohibition was a major issue in the campaign of 1914, with several aspirants for the governorship on both sides of the question. The prohibitionists held an elimination convention and pledged their support to Thomas H. Ballqv of Houston. The antiprohibitionists attempted to have a similar convention, but Ferguson, whose statements and Bell County record identified him as an antiprohibitionist, refused to submit his name to it. As a result it was impossible for the convention to eliminate him and obviously unwise to divide the vote by naming a rival candidate. The convention did not endorse Ferguson, but the other antiprohibition candidates withdrew from the race. Ferguson won the nomination by a majority of about 40,000 votes.

The campaign proved him to be a man of considerable native ability and the possessor of a captivating personality. As a political speaker he had few equals. The most discussed plank in his platform, which appealed especially to tenant farmers, proposed a law that would limit the rent charged by landlords and prevent the collection of bonuses. Landowners were assured, however, that they need not be alarmed by the proposal, as it would benefit all concerned. During Ferguson's first term, the legislature passed several measures of major importance. The tenant law was passed but remained on the statute books only a short time before being declared unconstitutional. The policy of state aid to rural schools was begun, and a rather timid law requiring compulsory school attendance was passed. Three new normal schools were authorized. Provision was made for the establishment of the Austin State School.qv Needed buildings were provided at other eleemosynary institutions. The colleges were permitted to begin building programs, and the educational appropriation bills were more generous than usual. As a result of these and other expenditures, the ad valorem tax rate for state purposes advanced from 12½ to 30 cents. The landholdings of the prison systemqv were greatly increased, and because of the rising price of farm commodities, the system became self-sustaining; during the years of war prosperity, it showed a profit.

In 1916 Ferguson's reelection seemed certain. The prohibitionists passed over their better-known leaders and gave their support to Charles H. Morris of Winnsboro, a political unknown. The issues were prohibition, the tax rate, and certain unpalatable rumors concerning the Ferguson administration. Ferguson was reelected by a majority of about 60,000 votes, but opposition was sufficient to show that many Texans, including a number who were not prohibitionists, were displeased with his stewardship. Aside from the act instituting the highway department, the second Ferguson administration was marked by little in the way of important legislation. The legislature passed generous appropriation bills, and the ad valorem tax rate reached the constitutional maximum of thirty-five cents. Early in his second term the governor became involved in a serious quarrel with the University of Texas. The controversy grew out of the refusal of the board of regents to remove certain faculty members whom the governor found objectionable. When Ferguson found that he could not have his way, he vetoed practically the entire appropriation for the university. The excitement that greeted the veto was soon overshadowed by the greater excitement that surrounded the impeachment trial. While the campaign of 1916 was in progress, the Ferguson administration had been charged with a number of irregularities. Preliminary investigations failed to uncover any charge that would merit impeachment, and for a time the incident seemed closed. The Ferguson controversy with the university brought renewed interest in the old charges, however, and at about the same time a number of new charges were made. On July 21, 1917, in the midst of the excitement, Ferguson appeared before the Travis County grand jury, and several days later it was announced that he had been indicted on nine charges. Seven of the charges related to misapplication of public funds, one to embezzlement, and one to the diversion of a special fund. Ferguson made bond of $13,000 and announced his candidacy for a third term as governor.

As a result of these developments, the speaker of the House called a special session to consider charges of impeachment against the governor. This call was of doubtful legality, but Ferguson removed all question by calling the legislature to meet for the purpose of making appropriations for the University of Texas. The House immediately turned its attention to the numerous charges against the governor and, after a lengthy investigation, prepared twenty-one articles of impeachment. The Senate, sitting as a High Court of Impeachment, spent three weeks considering the charges and finally convicted the governor on ten of them. Five of the articles sustained by the Senate charged Ferguson with the misapplication of public funds, three related to his quarrel with the University, one declared that he had failed properly to respect and enforce the banking laws of the state, and one charged that he had received $156,500 in currency from a source that he refused to reveal. Nine of the charges can be described as violations of the law, while the obtaining of $156,500 from a secret source was certainly not in keeping with good policy. The Court of Impeachment, by a vote of twenty-five to three, removed Ferguson from office and made him ineligible to hold any office of honor, trust, or profit under the state of Texas. Ferguson declared that the legislature constituted little more than a "kangaroo court," but only a few months before, both the House and the Senate had refused to sustain charges against him, and his removal from office was far from certain when the legislature convened in special session. He resigned his office the day before the judgment was announced and contended that it did not apply to him. The question was eventually carried into the courts, where the judgment of the Court of Impeachment was sustained. But the mere fact that Ferguson had been impeached and made ineligible to hold any office of trust or profit under the state did not in any sense remove him from the field of Texas politics. In 1918 he sought the Democratic partyqv nomination for the governorship but was defeated by William P. Hobby.qv In 1920 he was an unsuccessful candidate for President on his own American party ticket. In 1922 he was an unsuccessful candidate for the United States Senate.

In 1924, unable to run under his own name, he ran his wife's campaign for the governorship against Judge Felix Robertson, the candidate endorsed by the Ku Klux Klan.qv The Fergusons beat Robertson and went to the Governor's Mansionqv for a third time. Two years later they lost a reelection bid amid new scandals concerning excessive pardons and political patronage abuses. In 1928, for the first time since 1914, Ferguson was not an active participant in a political campaign, but even then he took some interest in the race for the governorship and gave his support to Louis J. Wardlaw. In 1930 he conducted the unsuccessful campaign of his wife for the governorship, and in 1932 he conducted her successful campaign for the same office. In 1940 Mrs. Ferguson again sought the governorship, and for the last

Governor Miriam Ferguson signs the Ferguson amnesty bill, with former governor James E. Ferguson (second from right) looking on. Austin, March 31, 1925. Photograph by Jordan Co., Austin. Courtesy Austin History Center, Austin Public Library; photo no. CO2898. When Governor James Ferguson was convicted on impeachment charges in 1917, he was barred from holding state political office. His wife signed a bill removing that disability in 1925, but the legislature repealed the amnesty measure two years later.

time "Farmer Jim" appealed to the voters of Texas. He was by this time an old man. He made only a few speeches and must have known long before the votes were cast that Mrs. Ferguson had no chance to win. James Ferguson died on September 21, 1944, and was buried in the State Cemetery qv in Austin.

BIBLIOGRAPHY: Norman D. Brown, *Hood, Bonnet, and Little Brown Jug: Texas Politics, 1921–1928* (College Station: Texas A&M University Press, 1984). James T. DeShields, *They Sat in High Places: The Presidents and Governors of Texas* (San Antonio: Naylor, 1940). James Edward Ferguson Collection, Barker Texas History Center, University of Texas at Austin. Lewis L. Gould, *Progressives and Prohibitionists: Texas Democrats in the Wilson Era* (Austin: University of Texas Press, 1973; rpt., Austin: Texas State Historical Association, 1992). W. V. Howerton, ed., *Facts on Ferguson: A Review of the Impeachment and a Reply to Charges Made by Ex-Governor Ferguson* (Austin, 1918). Norman Kittrell, *Governors Who Have Been and Other Public Men of Texas* (Houston: Dealy-Adey-Elgin, 1921). Ouida Ferguson Nalle, *The Fergusons of Texas, or "Two Governors for the Price of One": A Biography of James Edward Ferguson and His Wife* (San Antonio: Naylor, 1946). Ross Phares, *The Governors of Texas* (Gretna, Louisiana: Pelican, 1976). Bruce Rutherford, *The Impeachment of Jim Ferguson* (Austin: Eakin Press, 1983).

Ralph W. Steen

FERGUSON, MIRIAM AMANDA WALLACE (1875–1961). Miriam Amanda (Ma) Ferguson, first woman governor of Texas, daughter of Joseph L. and Eliza (Garrison) Wallace, was born in Bell County, Texas, on June 13, 1875. She attended Salado College and Baylor Female College at Belton. In 1899, at the age of twenty-four, she married James Edward Ferguson,qv also of Bell County. Mrs. Ferguson served as the first lady of Texas during the gubernatorial terms of her husband (1915–17), who was impeached during his second administration. When James Ferguson failed to get his name on the ballot in 1924, Miriam entered the race for the Texas governorship. Before announcing for office, she had devoted her energies almost exclusively to her husband and two daughters. This fact, and the combination of her first and middle initials, led her supporters to call her "Ma" Ferguson. She quickly assured Texans that if elected she would follow the advice of her husband and that Texas thus would gain "two governors for the price of one." Her campaign sought vindication for the Ferguson name, promised extensive cuts in state appropriations, condemned the Ku Klux Klan,qv and opposed passing new liquor legislation. After trailing the Klan-supported prohibitionist candidate, Felix D. Robertson,qv in the July primary, she easily defeated him in the August run-off to become the Democratic gubernatorial candidate. In November 1924 she handily defeated the Republican nominee, George C. Butte,qv a former dean of the University of Texas law school. Inaugurated fifteen days after Wyoming's Nellie Ross, Miriam Ferguson became the second woman governor in United States history.

Political strife and controversy characterized her first administration. Although she did fulfill a campaign promise to secure an antimask law against the Ku Klux Klan, the courts overturned it. State expenditures were slightly increased, despite a campaign pledge to cut the budget by $15 million. The focal point of discontent centered upon irregularities both in the granting of pardons and paroles and in the letting of road contracts by the state highway department. Ma Ferguson pardoned an average of 100 convicts a month, and she and "Pa" were accused by critics of accepting bribes of land and cash payments. Critics also charged that the Ferguson-appointed state highway commission granted road contracts to Ferguson friends and political supporters in return for lucrative kickbacks. Though a threat to impeach Miriam Ferguson failed, these controversies helped Attorney General Daniel James Moodyqv defeat Mrs. Ferguson for renomination in 1926 and win the governorship.

Miriam Ferguson did not seek office in 1928. However, after the Texas Supreme Court again rejected her husband's petition to place his name on the ballot in 1930, she entered the gubernatorial race. In the May primary she led Ross Sterling,qv who then defeated her in the August runoff. Her defeat proved fortuitous politically because Sterling, rather than she, was blamed by the voters when Texas began to feel the full impact of the Great Depression.qv In February 1932 she again declared for the governorship; she promised to lower taxes and cut state expenditures, and condemned alleged waste, graft, and political favoritism by the Sterling-controlled highway commission. After leading Sterling in the May primary by over 100,000 votes, Ma Ferguson narrowly won the Democratic nomination in the August primary. She then defeated the Republican nominee, Orville Bullington,qv in November to secure her second term as governor. Her second administration did not engender as much controversy as the first, despite dire predictions to the contrary by her political opponents. The fiscally conservative governor held the line on state expenditures and even advocated a state sales tax and corporate income tax, although the state legislature did not act on these proposals. Mrs. Ferguson continued her liberal pardoning and parole policies, but even that action did not stir as much controversy as in her first administration since every convict paroled or pardoned represented that much less fiscal strain on the state during the depression.

In 1934 the Fergusons temporarily retired from direct involvement in politics and also refused to seek office in 1936 and 1938. However, Ma Ferguson did declare for governor once again in 1940. Although sixty-five years old, she alleged that she could not resist a "popular draft" for the nomination and joined a field of prominent Democrats that included incumbent governor W. Lee O'Daniel.qv Ma's platform advocated a 25 percent cut in state appropriations, a gross-receipts tax of .5 percent to raise social security funds for the elderly, support for organized labor, and liberal funding for secondary and higher education.qv O'Daniel proved to be too popular to unseat, but the Ferguson name was still strong enough to poll more than 100,000 votes. After her husband's death in 1944, Miriam Ferguson retired to private life in Austin. She died of heart failure on June 25, 1961, and was buried alongside her husband in the State Cemeteryqv in Austin.

BIBLIOGRAPHY: Norman D. Brown, *Hood, Bonnet, and Little Brown Jug: Texas Politics, 1921–1928* (College Station: Texas A&M University Press, 1984). James Edward Ferguson Collection, Barker Texas History Center, University of Texas at Austin. Ouida Ferguson Nalle, *The Fergusons of Texas, or "Two Governors for the Price of One": A Biography of James Edward Ferguson and His Wife* (San Antonio: Naylor, 1946). *Notable American Women: A Biographical Dictionary* (4 vols., Cambridge, Massachusetts: Harvard University Press, 1971–80). *Women of Texas* (Waco: Texian Press, 1972).

John D. Huddleston

FERGUSON, THOMAS JEFFERSON (1877–?). Thomas Jefferson Ferguson, black business executive, was born on January 3, 1877, in Richmond, Texas, the son of Sylvia (Johnson) and Henry Clay Ferguson.qv He was educated at the Gregory Institute in Houston before moving on to Prairie View College (now Prairie View A&M University). During his studies at Gregory Institute from 1890 to 1893 he served as assistant clerk of the District Court in Richmond, Texas. He also attended Columbia University as well as the University of Chicago. On July 21, 1903, he married Gertrude May Scott. From 1907 to 1920 Ferguson was assistant to the treasurer at Tuskegee Institute in Alabama, from 1920 to 1927 the treasurer of Standard Life Insurance, and from 1921 to 1926 the director and vice president of the Citizens Trust Company in Atlanta, Georgia. He was the registrar for the National Negro Business League from 1923 at least through 1932 and served as director of the Atlanta Building and Loan Association beginning in 1925. In 1931 he founded Pioneer Savings Association in Atlanta. Ferguson belonged to a number of civic, business, and fraternal organizations including the NAACP, the YMCA, the Masons, the Elks, and Alpha Phi Alpha. He voted as a Republican and was a Methodist.

BIBLIOGRAPHY: *Who's Who in Colored America*, 1930–32.

Kharen Monsho

FERGUSON, TEXAS. Ferguson, south of Turpentine in northwestern Jasper County, was established in 1928 as a postal stop for the nearby lumber camp at New Blox and named for W. A. Ferguson, its first postmaster. The population at Ferguson grew to about fifty before New Blox was abandoned by the loggers in the mid-1930s. The Ferguson post office was removed in 1933. By 1949 Ferguson was no longer listed in the *Texas Almanac*'sqv list of towns and post office villages.

BIBLIOGRAPHY: Jasper County Scrapbook, Barker Texas History Center, University of Texas at Austin.

Robert Wooster

FERGUSON FORUM. The Ferguson Forum, a weekly political newspaper, was the organ of James E. Fergusonqv throughout eighteen years of his political life. He considered it necessary because Texas newspapers had "submarined the truth" concerning his impeachment. The *Forum* began publication in Temple on November 8, 1917. It was published there, except for a five-month period in 1923 when Ferguson moved it to Dallas, until October 6, 1927, and thereafter in Austin. The Fergusons used the paper to generate campaign funds as well as to present their views to the public. During Miriam Amanda (Ma) Ferguson'sqv first term as governor in the 1920s, her administration was criticized for awarding lucrative highway contracts to firms that purchased expensive advertising space in the *Forum*. The paper continued publication until April 11, 1935. The Texas State Archivesqv possesses a good run of the newspaper.

BIBLIOGRAPHY: Norman D. Brown, *Hood, Bonnet, and Little Brown Jug: Texas Politics, 1921–1928* (College Station: Texas A&M University Press, 1984).

FERNÁNDEZ, BERNARDO (?–?). On November 21, 1794, Bernardo Fernández was put in charge of the Spanish garrison at Nacogdoches. In September of the following year he was relieved of his duties and sent as interpreter by Manuel Muñoz,qv governor of Texas, to urge the Ais and other East Texas Indians to come to San Antonio. On April 9, 1797, Fernández was appointed captain of the garrison at La Bahía.qv

BIBLIOGRAPHY: Carlos E. Castañeda, *Our Catholic Heritage in Texas* (7 vols., Austin: Von Boeckmann-Jones, 1936-58; rpt., New York: Arno, 1976).

Frank Goodwyn

FERNÁNDEZ, EUGENIO (?–?). Eugenio Fernández, soldier and explorer, was part of an expedition led by Col. Diego Ortiz Parrillaqv that left San Juan Bautistaqv on September 13, 1766, to explore the Texas coast from La Bahíaqv to the mouth of the Rio Grande, especially the island known as Isla de San Carlos de los Malaguitas or Isla Blanca (Padre Island). Fernández was sent with José Antonio de la Garza Falcónqv and Mateo Martínez, twenty-six soldiers, and nine Indians to explore the island, which they traversed from near the site of present Aransas Pass to the Rio Grande before reporting it uninhabited and waterless. Fernández was subsequently alferez at Santa Rosa María del Sacramento Presidio in Coahuila. In 1768 he served in campaigns against the Mescalero Apaches with Manuel Rodríguez,qv acting commandant of Coahuila. He also accompanied Rodríguez to La Junta de los Ríosqv and El Paso in 1769, and he was sent to Chihuahua to locate Lope de Cuellar. In 1772 Fernández was appointed to serve under Vicente Rodríguezqv as lieutenant of San Juan Bautista. Though Rodríguez and the governor of Coahuila supported the appointment, San Juan Bautista soldiers protested it and took their complaints to the Mexican viceroy, but apparently to no avail.

BIBLIOGRAPHY: Carlos E. Castañeda, *Our Catholic Heritage in Texas* (7 vols., Austin: Von Boeckmann–Jones, 1936–1958; rpt., New York: Arno Press, 1976), Robert S. Weddle, *San Juan Bautista: Gateway to Spanish Texas* (Austin: University of Texas Press, 1968).

John G. Johnson

FERNÁNDEZ, RAMÓN (1900?–1988). Ramón (Raymond) Fernández, Houston community leader and president of the Club Cultural Recreativo México Bello and the local Comité Patriótico Mexicano,qqv was born in Camargo, Chihuahua, Mexico, in 1900. His parents owned land in Camargo, where the family raised cattle, horses, and mules for sale in Mexico and the United States. The family also operated an import-export business in Juárez. Ramón's father became an important political leader in Mexico, and served as mayor of Camargo and secretary of state of Chihuahua. After the Mexican Revolutionqv of 1910, he served as governor of Chihuahua until he was forced to go into exile in the United States. He remained in Texas for the rest of his life, first in Gonzales and later Houston, where he worked for the Southern Pacific Railroad. He also wrote articles and editorials for the influential San Antonio newspaper *La Prensa*.qv He attended schools in Camargo, Torreón, and Monterrey, and attended the Universidad Nacional Autónoma in Mexico City. During his youth Ramón accompanied his father on business trips to Texas, which took them as far away as Presidio, Marfa, and Alpine. As a young man, he also competed as a boxer in various cities in Texas, New Mexico, and Arizona. His numerous injuries, however, cut his boxing career short. After his graduation from the university in 1922, he joined his family in Houston and settled in the Fifth Ward,qv in the small but growing Mexican-American neighborhood known as the Northside. Thanks to his father's connections, he found employment at the Southern Pacific Railroad. He started in the machine shop and eventually moved to the drawing room, where he worked as a drafter, and later to the lay-out room, where he transferred the details of his drawings to the actual materials. He occupied several different positions during his forty-six-year tenure with the SP and supervised the work of dozens of employees. He retired in 1968.

Fernández was an early member of the Club Cultural Recreativo México Bello, an organization that sponsored social, cultural, and recreational activities for Houston Hispanics. He served as president of the club from 1926 to 1936, the longest term of any president in the club's history. As president, he played an important role in breaking down barriers of discrimination by getting local restaurants and banquet halls to rent to Mexican Americans.qv In 1926, Fernández founded the Houston Comité Patriótico Mexicano, a coalition of local social, cultural, civic, and political organizations that, together with the Mexican consul in Houston, organized activities for Mexican Americans that instilled pride in their cultural heritage. These included the annual celebration of *fiestas patrias*qv in the City Auditorium. Fernández served as Comité president from 1926 to 1936. He was also active in the Asamblea Mexicana and Council No. 60 of the League of United Latin American Citizens.qv He dropped out of the latter, however, because he refused to renounce his Mexican citizenship. He joined Council No. 2333 of the Woodmen of the World, also known as El Campo Laurel, and became the second Mexican American to be accepted in the local chapter of the Elks Lodge.qv

Fernández married his first wife, Helen, in 1934. She developed cancer early in their marriage, and in order to meet the medical expenses, Fernández took an additional job in the evenings working at Foley's Department Store downtown. After years of medical treatments and hospitalizations, Helen died in 1942. Fernández married his second wife, Alice, in 1951. He was a parishioner at various times of Our Lady of Guadalupe Catholic Church, Holy Name Church, and St. Ambrose. He never became naturalized. He maintained property in Camargo during his lifetime and frequently visited family and friends there. He died in 1988.

BIBLIOGRAPHY: Ramón Fernández, Oral History Interview by Thomas D. Kreneck, July 5, 1979, Houston Metropolitan Research Collection, Houston Public Library.
María-Cristina García

FERNÁNDEZ CARRASCO, PEDRO (?–?). Pedro Fernández Carrasco was a pilot in the Armada de Barloventoqv and diarist of the Rivas-Pez expedition, sent from Veracruz in 1688 to search for René Robert Cavalier, Sieur de La Salle.qv Fernández relates in detail the ascent of the Soto la Marina River of Tamaulipas and the Rio Grande, a distance of "thirty-six leagues." He also chronicles the reconnaissance of Matagorda Bay, where the Rivas-Iriarte expedition had seen wreckage of La Salle's ships the year before.

BIBLIOGRAPHY: Robert S. Weddle, *Wilderness Manhunt: The Spanish Search for La Salle* (Austin: University of Texas Press, 1973).
Robert S. Weddle

FERNÁNDEZ CASTRILLÓN, MANUEL (?–1836). Manuel Fernández Castrillón, major general in the Mexican army and trusted companion of Gen. Antonio López de Santa Anna,qv was originally from either Cuba or Spain. His association with Santa Anna dated back to 1822, when he served as the general's agent in a campaign against a combined force of loyalist and Spanish soldiers near Veracruz. While fighting under the command of Santa Anna in 1832, Fernández was captured by government troops and imprisoned. After his release, he again served with the general and was involved in quelling various rebellions in Mexico.

During the campaign in Texas, however, Fernández frequently protested the actions of Santa Anna. He was one of the few officers who opposed an immediate assault on the Alamo;qv nonetheless, when the attack occurred he led a column of troops credited as the first to reach the fortress walls. As a staunch advocate for the humane and honorable treatment of prisoners, he interceded on behalf of a small group of captured Texans that may have included David Crockett.qv Though he pleaded for their lives, the prisoners were executed. He also protested the execution of captured Texans at Goliad (*see* GOLIAD MASSACRE).

Fernández Castrillón again found himself in opposition to Santa Anna's commands at San Jacinto, and when the battle began he was one of the few officers to stand and fight. Gen. Thomas J. Ruskqv of the Texas army reported that Fernández was attempting to rally his troops while standing fully exposed to enemy fire on an ammunition crate. After the panicked soldiers failed to respond, he slowly turned and walked away from the oncoming Texans. He was shot and later died on the battlefield. Santa Anna maintained that Fernández was not a hero but that his incompetence greatly contributed to the Mexican defeat at San Jacinto. Several days after the battle Lorenzo de Zavala,qv an old friend, recovered his body. Fernández was interred on Zavala's plantation across the bayou from the battlefield.

BIBLIOGRAPHY: C. M. Bustamante, *Continuación del Cuadro Histórico de la Revolución Mexicana*, Vol. 4 (Mexico City: Instituto Nacional de Antropología e Historia, 1963). Henry Stuart Foote, *Texas and the Texans* (2 vols., Philadelphia: Cowperthwait, 1841; rpt., Austin: Steck, 1935). Jeff Long, *Duel of Eagles: The Mexican and U.S. Fight for the Alamo* (New York: Morrow, 1990). José Enrique de la Peña, *With Santa Anna in Texas* (College Station: Texas A&M University Press, 1975). Antonio López de Santa Anna et al., *The Mexican Side of the Texan Revolution*, trans. Carlos E. Castañeda (Dallas: Turner, 1928; 2d ed., Austin: Graphic Ideas, 1970). Frank X. Tolbert, *The Day of San Jacinto* (New York: McGraw-Hill, 1959; 2d ed., Austin: Pemberton Press, 1969).
David L. Fisher

FERNÁNDEZ DE JÁUREGUI URRUTIA, JOSEPH ANTONIO (?–?). From 1732 to 1741 Joseph Antonio Fernández de Jáuregui Urrutia served as governor of Nuevo León. In 1735 he wrote a report to the viceroy on conditions in his province. The document focused on the need to curb the hostile natives who inhabited the adjacent coastal region later incorporated into the province of Nuevo Santander.qv Although Fernández failed to offer a comprehensive plan for conquering the coastal strip, his report initiated a series of efforts to solve problems stemming from the region's hostile natives. When the viceroy failed to respond, Fernández forwarded his report with a map and supporting documents to the Crown, but King Felipe V took little notice. On July 11, 1737, the Nuevo León governor was given an additional assignment as governor extraordinary and *visitador* of Texas; he was to investigate the administration of ousted Texas governor Carlos Benites Franquis de Lugo.qv Not until 1738 was he able to renew his appeal on behalf of Nuevo León settlers. In the meantime, other plans, largely self-serving, emerged, leading ultimately to the choice of José de Escandónqv to subdue and colonize the Costa del Seno Mexicano (Gulf of Mexico Coast). Upon completion of the Franquis investigation, Fernández returned to Monterrey to serve out his term as Nuevo León governor. Prudencio de Orobio y Basterraqv was named governor *ad interim* of Texas.

BIBLIOGRAPHY: Carlos E. Castañeda, *Our Catholic Heritage in Texas* (7 vols., Austin: Von Boeckmann–Jones, 1936–58; rpt., New York: Arno, 1976). Joseph Antonio Fernández de Jáuregui Urrutia, *Description of Nuevo León, Mexico (1735–1740)*, ed. Malcolm D. McLean and Eugenio del Hoyo (Monterrey: Instituto Tecnológico de Estudios Superiores, 1964). Robert S. Weddle, *The French Thorn: Rival Explorers in the Spanish Sea, 1682–1762* (College Station: Texas A&M University Press, 1991).
Robert S. Weddle

FERNÁNDEZ DE RETANA, JUAN (1652–1708). Juan Fernández de Retana, Spanish military commander on the frontier of northern New Spain and son of Juan Fernández de Retana and María Martínez de Mendivil, was born in the village of Nanclares de Gamboa in the province of Alava in northern Spain, where he was baptized on February 27, 1652. His parents were poor Basque pastoralists who apparently did not have much of an estate. Fernández married María Ruiz Lucuriaga in Nanclares in 1670. According to baptismal registers there, the couple had two sons and four daughters between 1672 and 1683, which would have been unremarkable if Fernández had not migrated to the viceroyalty of New Spain sometime before May 1676, when his signature appears in Mexico City records. Between 1676 and 1684 he was a merchant-freighter hauling goods between Mexico City and the northern silver-mining communities of Zacatecas and Parral. In New Spain he always claimed he was single and had no family, and there is no record of his returning to Spain before his wife's death in 1684.

By 1678 Fernández was living in Parral, the most important mining center in the province of Nueva Vizcaya and the unofficial residence of the governors of Nueva Vizcaya in the seventeenth century. He had established ties with the merchant-freighting Urrutia family of Mexico City, who loaned him money to go into freighting himself. Fernández also engaged in mining and became an influential citizen, holding the positions of *diputado de minería* (mining deputy) and *alcalde mayor* (chief executive officer) of Parral. By 1681 he was being addressed as *capitán* and was apparently protecting supply trains as well. Three years later the merchants' guild of Parral petitioned the governor of Nueva Vizcaya to make the title official and appoint Fernández a regular military officer in charge of a squad of soldiers escorting wagon trains on the road between Parral and the mining center of Cuencamé to the southeast. Governor José de Neyra y Quiroga did so in 1684, thus paving the way for Fernández's appointment as captain of the new presidio of San Francisco de Conchos in 1685. Before that appointment Fernández campaigned against the Conchos and Julime Indians in 1684.

He remained captain of the strategic frontier garrison of Conchos, located in a beautiful valley of the Conchos River northeast of Parral, until his death. As commander of fifty soldiers, he campaigned against the numerous Indian groups in the region, including the Tobosos, Chizos, and Cocoyames of Chihuahua and Coahuila. In 1689 Fernández also led an expedition to the region of La Junta de los Ríos,qv where the Conchos flows into the Rio Grande, to investigate reports of the Sieur de La Salle'sqv men and other French traders and soldiers among the Hasinai Indians in East Texas. He subsequently embarked on a journey eastward toward Espíritu Santo Bay in search of La Salle, but turned back at the Pecos River upon meeting Indians returning from a trading expedition with the Hasinais, who brought news of the Fort St. Louis massacre. Fernández won his greatest notoriety suppressing the rebellions of the Tarahumara Indians of the Sierra Madre in 1690 and 1697–98. After the last revolt, the largest in the history of the Tarahumaras, he carried out the orders of Governor Gabriel de Castillo and executed more than thirty Tarahumara leaders by arquebus firing squads. He was consequently accused of cruelty and mistreatment of the Indians, and Carlos II, the aging last Hapsburg king of Spain, ordered the viceroy to remove him from office and banish him from New Spain.

Fernández acknowledged the order but refused to comply. For the next five years he remained captain of the presidio while pleading his case, arguing that he was just carrying out orders and that the harsh punishments were merited. It was a time of great political confusion; Carlos II died in 1700, and the Bourbon dynasty of France acceded to the Spanish throne. Finally, after mustering support from fellow military commanders, Jesuit missionaries, loyal Tarahumara leaders, and influential miners, Fernández was absolved of the charges against him by King Felipe V in 1704. He was also appointed *teniente de gobernador* (lieutenant governor) of Nueva Vizcaya (1704) and *alcalde mayor* (1708) of the new mining community of Santa Eulalia, fifteen miles east of another mining community that developed into the city of Chihuahua. When he died at Conchos on February 24, 1708, he left most of his estate to the Jesuit college of Parral, claiming, once again, to be single and heirless. *See also* SPANISH TEXAS.

BIBLIOGRAPHY: Oakah L. Jones, *Nueva Vizcaya: Heartland of the Spanish Frontier* (Albuquerque: University of New Mexico Press, 1988). Thomas H. Naylor and Charles W. Polzer, comps. and eds., *Pedro de Rivera and the Military Regulations for Northern New Spain, 1724–1729* (Tucson: University of Arizona Press, 1988). Thomas H. Naylor and Charles W. Polzer, S.J., *The Presidio and Militia on the Northern Frontier of New Spain, 1570–1700* (Tucson: University of Arizona Press, 1986).
Thomas E. Sheridan and Thomas H. Naylor

FERNÁNDEZ DE SANTA ANA, BENITO (1707–1761). Father Fernández de Santa Ana was born Benito Fernández y Rana at Berán, in the province of Orense, Spain, on June 4, 1707. He entered the Franciscan order and was ordained a priest, probably in Spain; shortly afterward he was sent, in 1731, as a member of the College of Santa Cruz de Querétaro,qv to San Antonio de Valero Mission in Texas. Between the Rio Grande and Mission San Antonio on June 25, 1731, a band of Apache Indians robbed him and Brother Estevan Zaes Monge of all their baggage and horses and killed two of the five soldiers who accompanied them. Three years later, at the age of twenty-seven, Fernández succeeded Father Gabriel de Vergaraqv as president of the Texas missions of the College of Querétaro and the principal missionary at Nuestra Señora de la Purísima Concepción de Acuña Mission in San Antonio.

In 1739 the Canary Islandersqv in the villa of San Fernando obtained from viceroy archbishop Juan Antonio de Vizarrón y Equirreta a decree permitting them to hire mission Indians on their farms. Father Fernández wrote a memorial in which he refuted false statements and accusations made in the petition of the Canary Islanders, and as a result in 1741 the viceroy Duque de la Conquista revoked the decree of 1739. However, in 1743–44 two agents sent to Mexico by the cabildoqv of Villa de San Fernando succeeded in having a second decree, similar to the one of 1739, issued by Viceroy Conde de Fuenclara. Fernández then appeared in person before this viceroy in January of 1745 and persuaded him to rescind the decree of 1744.

After a severe epidemic in 1739, Fernández began the construction of permanent buildings of stone and mortar at Concepción Mission, including the twin-tower church that is still standing. To Father Mariano de los Dolores y Viana'sqv project of founding three new missions, with a presidio, on the San Xavier (San Gabriel) River, Father

Fernández gave his full support, despite persistent objections by the governors and presidio commanders in Texas (see SAN XAVIER MISSIONS). After Dolores y Viana had officially founded Mission San Francisco Xavier in 1748, Fernández personally founded San Ildefonso and Nuestra Señora de la Candelaria missions in 1749. To correct the misstatements in a report of Governor Pedro del Barrio Junco y Espriella,qv Fernández made a second trip to Mexico City and successfully presented to Viceroy Conde de Revillagigedo a long memorial, of fifty-nine sections, on November 11, 1749. In February of the following year he also presented his plans for the establishment of Apache missions on the Pedernales River, which included the transfer of San Antonio de Béxar Presidio to this river. Though his plans were not accepted, they led to an investigation that culminated in the choice of the San Saba River for an Apache mission with a new presidio.

Like his predecessor, Vergara, Fernández had always disapproved of military punitive campaigns against the Apaches as a means of putting an end to their raids. He believed that, like the other Indian groups, the Apaches could be induced to settle in missions, and that this would be a more effective means of establishing peace in Texas. He deplored the enslavement of Apaches who were taken prisoner in Capt. José de Urrutia'sqv campaign in 1739, and after the campaign in 1745, in which he accompanied Capt. Toribio de Urrutia,qv he asked the viceroy to turn the Apache prisoners over to him, "so that they can help me to win the others." Though the fear of their enemies, the Comanches, was one reason why the Apaches finally agreed to a peace treaty with the Spaniards on November 28, 1749, this achievement was due in great measure to the consistent conciliatory policy of Father Fernández.

Shortly after February 1750 Fernández became ill and had to retire to the college in Querétaro, and Father Dolores was appointed his successor as president of the Texas missions. Fernández died at the college in late March or early April 1761. News of his demise was received at the College of Nuestra Señora de Guadalupe de Zacatecasqv on April 12, 1761. See also FRANCISCANS, SPANISH MISSION SYSTEM.

BIBLIOGRAPHY: Herbert Eugene Bolton, *Texas in the Middle Eighteenth Century* (Berkeley: University of California Press, 1915; rpt., Austin: University of Texas Press, 1970). Benedict Leutenegger, trans. and ed., *Letters and Memorials of the Father Presidente Fray Benito Fernández de Santa Ana*, (San Antonio: Old Spanish Missions Historical Research Library at Our Lady of the Lake University, 1981).
Marion A. Habig, O.F.M.

FERNANDO, TEXAS. Fernando was in the vicinity of Fernando East Road and Farm Road 2925 ten miles northeast of Combes and U.S. Highway 77 in north central Cameron County. The area was first settled in the early 1800s by Mexican ranchers who found the land around the Arroyo Colorado suitable for raising herds of cattle and small patches of corn and melons. The settlement, originally called San Fernando, became a station on the San Benito and Rio Grande Valley Railway in 1913. The railroad was discontinued in 1928, and the site was consequently deserted. In 1948 the mail for the remaining dispersed community of citrus-fruit growers and irrigated farms was routed through Rio Hondo. By 1970 only the Fernando East Road remained in the area.
Alicia A. Garza

FERNDALE LAKE. Ferndale Lake, once known as Ferndale Club Lake, is located in the Cypress River basin seven miles southwest of Pittsburg in southwestern Camp County (its center is at 32°57′ N, 95°04′ W). The lake was built in 1909 with the construction of the earthen Ferndale Lake Dam on North Lilly Creek and serves recreational purposes. It has a normal capacity of 1,414 acre-feet and a maximum capacity of 2,800 acre-feet. The surrounding flat to rolling terrain is surfaced by sandy and clay loams that support water-tolerant hardwoods, conifers, and grasses.

FERNS, TEXAS. Ferns, beside Caddo Lake twelve miles northeast of Marshall and eight miles north of Scottsville in northeastern Harrison County, was founded before 1888, when a post office was opened there. The settlement had twenty-five inhabitants, two general stores, and five cotton gins in 1890. By 1896 it had grown to fifty residents and had a voting box and Methodist and Baptist churches. The Ferns school served twenty-eight students in 1897. The community's post office was moved to Hailey in 1900. Ferns was not shown on county highway maps by 1948.

BIBLIOGRAPHY: Jerome McCown, Scraps of the Early History of Marshall and Harrison County (MS, Barker Texas History Center, University of Texas at Austin).
Mark Odintz

FERREE, FRANK ELLIS (1894–1983). Frank Ellis Ferree, faith healer and freelance social worker, son of Josiah Benjamin and Isabel E. (Kenyon) Ferree, was born on August 6, 1894, in a village on the Platte River near Omaha, Nebraska. At the time of his birth, his father ran a small weekly newspaper, the *Valley Enterprise*. When Ferree was fifteen and in the eighth grade, the family moved to northwestern Nebraska to homestead. With the move, his public schooling ceased. As a child he frequently heard a voice calling from the sky. Although he was not enamored of the hard labor associated with homesteading, he did love animals and the vast expanses of prairie, where he frequently wandered alone communing with nature. In 1915 he left home for a year and did odd jobs, including working for Northwestern Bell Telephone Company.

In an effort to see the world, Ferree enlisted in the army in 1918. He was assigned to the signal corps and sent to the front lines in the Argonne Forest in France just as World War Iqv was ending. At the battlefront he was greatly shocked by the many wounded and dead soldiers he saw. He returned to his homestead in Nebraska and for ten years worked as a rural mail carrier, first on horseback and later in a Model-T Ford. He also built and repaired telephone lines. When his father died in the early 1930s he and his mother moved to Colorado and filed for a homestead near Denver. By 1937 he had increased their landholdings from eighty to 3,000 acres. In Colorado he became interested in the writings of faith healer Amie S. McPherson and in numerology.

At his mother's death in 1937 he traded the Colorado land for 800 acres of timberland in Wisconsin, but he was dissatisfied with it. Within a year, part of which he spent in California, he had sold that land, bought twenty-three acres of land near Harlingen in the Rio Grande valley, and moved to Texas. In addition to working at various jobs, Ferree started giving healing massages. He also began to be haunted by the poverty, hunger, and frequent sickness of the many border Mexicans he encountered in the Valley.

Although he did not belong to a church, he was an extremely religious and contemplative man. By the 1940s the Bible had become his source book, and he began to pattern his daily life after the examples of Jesus. He started to help the poor and the sick in an extemporaneous and understaffed organization that he called Volunteer Border Relief. It was headquartered in a ramshackle house in Harlingen.

A tall, gaunt man with pendulous ears and a bulbous nose, Ferree always dressed in tire-tread sandals and ragtag clothes. Thus attired, he canvassed the alleys of Harlingen, virtually begging restaurateurs and grocers to give him the food or goods that they were discarding, so that in turn he could give these things to the poor. The Valley citizenry was at first taken aback by his behavior. But many merchants, newsmen, doctors, and wealthy individuals, both in the United States and northern Mexico, were won over by his kindness and persistence and began to champion his cause. He established two distribution and clinic sites, one in Matamoros and the other in Reynosa, where he went weekly to dispense food, second-hand clothes, and medicines. Because he could perform medical procedures legally in Mexico, he frequently gave injections at these clinics. He arranged for doctors to perform countless free operations on afflicted people, especially children with cleft palates.

Because the Volunteer Border Relief was loosely organized and not top-heavy with management—it consisted of Ferree and a few Mexican men and women and their children, who were his surrogate family—it could respond quickly in times of need. In 1955 when hurricane Hilda hit the isolated coast of Tampico, Mexico, Ferree was able to mobilize a relief mission that employed daily cargo flights from Harlingen Air Force Base carrying food, blankets, and other necessities.

He was known in the Valley as "El Amigo" and the "Border Angel." He was twice nominated for the Nobel Peace Prize. In 1960 he was invited by President Dwight D. Eisenhower[qv] to a black-tie dinner in Washington, for which he had to borrow a tuxedo, and in 1982 he received a letter of commendation from President Ronald Reagan. Ferree died on March 10, 1983, at the age of eighty-nine and was buried on his land in north Harlingen.

BIBLIOGRAPHY: Austin *American-Statesman*, January 3, 1982, March 14, 1983. Fort Worth *Star-Telegram*, March 16, 1983. Bill Starr, *Border Angel* (New York: Vantage, 1979). Suzanne Winckler, "Friends in Deed," *Texas Monthly*, March 1983.   *Suzanne Winckler*

FERRIES. Before modern bridges were constructed to span Texas rivers, ferries were maintained at most points where roads crossed streams or rivers that were not fordable. From the beginning, ferries were subject to regulation by the community they served, and as early as July 1824 Stephen F. Austin and Baron de Bastrop[qv] issued a license to John McFarlan,[qv] giving him the exclusive privilege of operating a ferry at San Felipe de Austin[qv] but stipulating certain duties he must fulfill to retain the charter. On December 20, 1836, one of the first acts of the Congress of the Republic of Texas[qv] regulated ferries, delineated their responsibilities to the public, and required that they be chartered by the county in which they operated. Many early immigrants entered Texas by way of Gaines Ferry[qv] on the Old San Antonio Road[qv] crossing of the Sabine River. Ferries that played a sufficient part in the life of the republic and the state to be marked by the Texas Centennial[qv] Commission in 1936 were Burnam's Ferry, Colbert's Ferry, Epperson's Ferry, Groce's Ferry, Lynch's Ferry, Robbins's Ferry, Stephenson's Ferry, and Thompson's Ferry.[qqv] Ferries had various styles of construction, but perhaps the most common type was a flat raft-like barge onto which a wagon or cart could be driven from the inclined stream banks. These banks were required by the ferry charters to be kept graded by the ferrymen. Many ferrymen stretched a bank-to-bank cable for a guide. Fares, which were supposed to be posted, averaged one to two dollars for light and heavy wagons, twenty-five cents for one man and horse, 6¼ to 12½ cents for a man on foot, four to six cents a head for cattle, and lesser amounts for smaller animals. Ferrymen were allowed to raise their fares for crossings at night or in bad weather. In 1850 and 1854 the state legislature passed laws relating to ferries and their responsibility to the community as public conveyors.

In 1949 two ferries were in operation on the state-maintained highway system, one on State Highway 87 between Galveston and Port Bolivar with a twenty-five cent fee, and one on State Highway 146 at Morgan's Point, with no fee. The Morgan's Point Ferry closed in 1952. Around that time the privately owned Harbor Island Causeway and ferry between Aransas Pass and Port Aransas charged a nominal fee. In 1995 the state operated a free ferry service at Galveston and Port Aransas. One of the last ferry services to operate in Texas on the Rio Grande was the Los Ebanos, owned by the Reyna family. Located eighteen miles out of Rio Grande City off U.S. Highway 83, the ferry began service in 1950. It provided the residents of several border towns with cheap transportation across the river. The ferry, reminiscent of its nineteenth-century predecessors, was a hand-drawn flatboat, with a capacity of only three cars. In 1975 a Texas Historical Commission[qv] marker was placed at the site, commemorating the point of crossing as the trail taken by José de Escandon's[qv] expedition. In 1991 the ferry was closed and replaced with a bridge.

BIBLIOGRAPHY: Eugene C. Barker, ed., *The Austin Papers* (3 vols., Washington: GPO, 1924–28). Eugene C. Barker, ed., "Minutes of the Ayuntamiento of San Felipe de Austin, 1828–1832," 12 parts, *Southwestern Historical Quarterly* 21–24 (January 1918–October 1920). Hans Peter Nielsen Gammel, comp., *Laws of Texas, 1822–1897* (10 vols., Austin: Gammel, 1898). William R. Hogan, *The Texas Republic: A Social and Economic History* (Norman: University of Oklahoma Press, 1946; rpt. 1969). Harold Schoen, comp., *Monuments Erected by the State of Texas to Commemorate the Centenary of Texas Independence* (Austin: Commission of Control for Texas Centennial Celebrations, 1938). Vertical Files, Barker Texas History Center, University of Texas at Austin.

FERRIS, CHARLES DRAKE (1812–1850). Charles Drake Ferris, soldier, surveyor, and newspaperman, was born at Pittsfield, New York, on December 5, 1812, the son of Angus and Sarah (Gray) Ferriss and younger brother of Warren Angus Ferris.[qv] He spent his boyhood and youth in Buffalo, New York. In later years he dropped the final letter of the family name. In November 1835 Ferris left Buffalo for Texas, with letters to Sam Houston and Lorenzo de Zavala.[qqv] Intending to join the army, he proceeded to headquarters at San Antonio. Although his family believed that he fought at the battle of San Jacinto,[qv] it was never proved. He may have been the "Col. Ferris" that James W. Fannin[qv] dispatched to Lt. Gov. James W. Robinson[qv] on February 28, 1836, with the information that Fannin's troops had made an unsuccessful attempt to reach Bexar and had returned to Goliad (see GOLIAD CAMPAIGN OF 1836). On April 10, 1836, Ferris, acting as a spy for Moseley Baker,[qv] sent a message to Baker informing him of Mexican troop movements. Robinson, in camp at Harrisburg in May 1836, gave to Ferris a letter of introduction to Gen. Thomas J. Rusk,[qv] then in command of the Army of the Republic of Texas.[qv] The letter referred to Ferris as a colonel and a young man of classical education, moral habits, and tried valor. Shortly thereafter Ferris joined the command of Maj. Isaac Watts Burton,[qv] a force later known as the Horse Marines.[qv]

He returned to Buffalo on leave in the summer of 1836 and assisted his brother Warren in editing the latter's journal, *Life in the Rocky Mountains*. In October 1836 Texas president David G. Burnet[qv] described Ferris as an "agent to receive donations for Texas." Ferris returned to Texas and was reported on the Trinity River locating land in February 1837. He resigned from the army in April and joined his brother as a surveyor; at this time he was also associated with Isaac W. Burton[qv] as surveyor and as editor of the Nacogdoches *Texas Chronicle*.[qv]

Ferris again returned to Buffalo in August 1837, intending to take his family to Texas. Financial difficulties intervened, however, and he turned to the study of law. Later he engaged in newspaper work and in writing. In May 1834 he married Hester Ann Bivins; they had five children. He never realized his desire to move with his family to Texas. He left home in ill health in 1849 and is believed to have died at sea in December 1850. By special act of the Texas legislature in 1860, his heirs were granted 960 acres of land in Denton County, in recognition of his military service to the republic.

BIBLIOGRAPHY: Dallas *Herald*, October 14, 1871. Daughters of the Republic of Texas, *Muster Rolls of the Texas Revolution* (Austin, 1986). Warren Angus Ferris, *Life in the Rocky Mountains* (*Western Literary Messenger*, July 13, 1842–May 4, 1844; rpt., ed. Paul C. Phillips, Denver: Old West, 1940). John H. Jenkins, ed., *The Papers of the Texas Revolution, 1835–1836* (10 vols., Austin: Presidial Press, 1973). Louis Wiltz Kemp Papers, Texas State Archives, Austin.   *Walter McCausland*

FERRIS, JUSTUS WESLEY (1823–1899). Justus Wesley Ferris, lawyer and judge, the son of Rev. Philo Ferris, was born in Hudson, New York, on March 23 or 26, 1823. He lived there through early childhood and the first years of his public schooling, then in Cazenovia, where he attended high school and the Oneida Conference Seminary. After his graduation he taught school at Christiansburg, Shelby County, Kentucky. He graduated from Transylvania University in 1845 and left Kentucky in 1846 to study law with a Judge Brent at Alexandria, Louisiana. Brent, however, suddenly died. On the advice of friends Ferris left Alexandria for Jefferson, Texas, now in Marion County, in 1847. He was admitted to the bar in 1847 and began a law practice with M. D. Rogers of Jefferson. The partners practiced both civil and criminal law. In 1850 Ferris married Mattie J. Crow of Floydsburg, Kentucky. The couple had two sons.

Ferris, a Democrat, commented on the political activities of Texans in 1852 as editor of the Jefferson Herald. That same year he was elected to represent Titus and Cass counties in the Fifth State Legislature. Although he served only one term, he made a lasting contribution to Texas as the author of the common school law. Ill health forced him to retire from politics. In 1854 he moved to Waxahachie, where he opened a law office with E. P. Nicholson of Dallas in 1858. The men also established exchange offices in the two cities.

Improved health allowed Ferris to return to politics. In 1861 he was selected judge of the Sixteenth Judicial District. He served in this capacity until the end of the Civil War,[qv] when he returned to private practice. He established partnerships with W. H. Getzendaner and Anson Rainey.[qv] With Getzendaner, Ferris opened a bank at Waxahachie that later became the Citizens National Bank. As a member of the Constitutional Convention of 1875,[qv] Ferris served as chairman of the Committee on Railroads. He also was one of five commissioners appointed by Governor Richard Coke[qv] to revise the statutes of Texas. The governor enlisted his legal services in 1876, when he asked Ferris to serve as a special judge on the Texas Supreme Court to hear the case of *International Railroad Company vs. A. Bledsoe, Comptroller.*

For the next ten years Ferris concentrated his efforts on his private law practice and conducted the affairs of the Citizens National Bank, of which he was president for two years. His interest in politics remained, however, and in 1884 he attended the Democratic national convention as a delegate from Texas. He also contributed political commentary in a number of articles published in a variety of newspapers in North Texas.

On April 26, 1899, Ferris died at his home in Waxahachie. He was a member of the Methodist Episcopal Church, South. He was buried in the Methodist Cemetery at Waxahachie. The town of Ferris was named in his honor. His papers are housed at the Dallas Historical Society.[qv]

BIBLIOGRAPHY: John Henry Brown, *Indian Wars and Pioneers of Texas* (Austin: Daniell, 1880; reprod., Easley, South Carolina: Southern Historical Press, 1978). Justus Wesley Ferris Papers, Dallas Historical Society, Dallas. *Memorial and Biographical History of Ellis County* (Chicago: Lewis, 1892; rpt., as *Ellis County History*, Fort Worth: Historical Publishers, 1972).

David Minor

FERRIS, ROYAL ANDREW (1851–1929). Royal Andrew Ferris, banker and railroad entrepreneur, was born to Martha J. (Crow or Crowe) and Justus W. Ferris[qv] on August 8, 1851, at Jefferson, Texas. After the family moved to Waxahachie in 1854, he was educated in the local public schools and later at Kentucky Military Institute, Farmdale, Kentucky. He was trained for the banking profession by his father—who, after a successful career as an attorney, a state district court judge, and a member of the state legislature, established the private banking firm of Ferris and Getzendaner at Waxahachie—Ferris entered his father's company as a clerk on July 1, 1870. Four years later he became a partner in the firm, which was renamed Getzendaner and Ferris. On December 13, 1882, he married Lula Brown in Waxahachie. She died some eight months later. In 1884 Ferris's private bank was reorganized as Citizens National Bank, and Ferris became a shareholder in the corporation. He and Jeremiah Reardon helped finance the Waxahachie Tap Railroad, which was chartered in 1875 and completed in 1879. The road gave Waxahachie access to Fort Worth and Houston by connecting with the Houston and Texas Central Railway near Ennis. Ferris also played a part in organizing the Waxahachie Real Estate and Building Association, and he served one term as a city alderman.

He moved to Dallas in March 1884 and became cashier of the Exchange Bank of Dallas, the firm where he spent the remainder of his career. Shortly after his arrival he purchased a controlling interest in the local street-railway system. He financed the modernization and electrification of the previously horse-drawn system and sold it, although he continued to serve as president of the Dallas Consolidated Electric Street Railway Company for a number of years. When the Exchange Bank was reorganized as the Exchange National Bank in February 1887, Ferris was elected a vice president. He was a stockholder, director, and officer until his retirement. He became president in 1897, and continued in that position when the bank merged with American National Bank to form American Exchange National Bank of Dallas in 1905. Ferris retired from the bank's presidency in 1918 but remained chairman of the board of directors until 1920.

He married Mary A. Brown at Weatherford on October 3, 1894 (or 1895). He was a member of the Democratic party,[qv] the Knights of Pythias, and the Odd Fellows. He served as president of the Commercial Bank and Trust Company of Dallas and the Dallas Telephone Company, vice president of Hughes Brothers Manufacturing Company, and director of Southwestern Bell Telephone Company, Southwestern Life Insurance Company, Texas Power and Light Company, and Republic Insurance Company. He was also active in the Dallas Chamber of Commerce and the State Fair of Texas,[qv] which he served as president for two terms and as a stockholder and director for a number of years. Ferris donated over $50,000 to Southern Methodist University and endowed a student loan fund at the University of Texas. He died on March 2, 1929. His funeral service was held at the First Presbyterian Church, and burial was in Grove Hill Cemetery, Dallas.

BIBLIOGRAPHY: Dallas *Morning News*, March 3, 1929. Frank W. Johnson, *A History of Texas and Texans* (5 vols., ed. E. C. Barker and E. W. Winkler [Chicago and New York: American Historical Society, 1914; rpt. 1916]).

Brian Hart

FERRIS, WARREN ANGUS (1810–1873). Warren Angus Ferris (Ferriss), surveyor and early settler of Dallas County, was born on December 26, 1810, in Glen Falls, New York, the son of Angus and Sarah (Gray) Ferriss. As a youth he lived in Buffalo, New York. He left home in 1828 and reached St. Louis in 1829, where he joined the American Fur Company. He mapped the Yellowstone country and kept a journal of his five adventurous years in the West, first serialized in the *Western Literary Messenger* from January 11, 1843, to May 4, 1844, and later published as a book, *Life in the Rocky Mountains* (1940).

Ferris came to Texas with his younger brother, Charles, a veteran of the Texas Revolution,[qv] and in 1837 was elected surveyor of Nacogdoches County, which then stretched west to the Trinity River. Between 1839 and 1841 Ferris led a series of daring surveying expeditions into northeastern Texas, which was occupied by Indians. He also surveyed for William P. King's[qv] Southern Land Company, for whom he began to found a town, Warwick, at the Three Forks of the Trinity River. At King's death in 1841 the townsite was taken by John Neely Bryan[qv] of Dallas. Parts of what became Dallas, Kaufman, Hunt, Van Zandt, Collin, Denton, and Henderson counties were surveyed by Ferris and his deputy, John H. Reagan.[qv] In 1841 the surveyors scouted for Gen. James Smith's[qv] military expedition against the Indians at Village Creek (Arlington).

Surveyors were prohibited from speculation, so Ferris filed personal land claims in the name of his half brother, Clarence A. (Joshua) Lovejoy. Sections along White Rock Creek in Dallas were later ceded to Ferris's first wife, Melinda G. Cook of Crockett. Ferris's surveys of

Dallas County dictated the peculiar slant of grants east of the Trinity River, and his Lagow and Grigsby surveys determined the directions of Dallas city streets.

After the death of his first wife, Ferris married Frances Moore of Palestine and in 1847 settled on his land on White Rock Creek. He fathered twelve children, cultivated eighty-five acres of his extensive holdings, surveyed for the Peters colony,qv supervised road building, and in 1850 surveyed the boundaries for Dallas County. Ferris played no active role in the Civil War,qv although his sympathies ran with the Democratic partyqv and the Confederacy. When Frances Ferris died in childbirth in 1869, Warren was left a widower with young children to raise. He taught surveying and wrote his reminiscences for the Dallas Herald (see DALLAS TIMES HERALD). He died on February 8, 1873, and was buried in a community cemetery in what is now the Forest Hills addition of Dallas, near White Rock Lake.

BIBLIOGRAPHY: Vertical Files, Barker Texas History Center, University of Texas at Austin. *Susanne Starling*

FERRIS, TEXAS. Ferris is on Interstate Highway 45, U.S. Highway 75, and Farm roads 660, 664, and 983 fifteen miles northeast of Waxahachie in northeastern Ellis County. It was named for Judge Justus W. Ferrisqv of Waxahachie, a county business and civic leader. The community's establishment was associated with the construction of the Houston and Texas Central Railway in 1874. Railroad employees surveyed and laid out the settlement on land donated by the McKenzie family, pioneers who had arrived in the early 1850s. Attracted by the region's fertile soil and the commercial possibilities offered by the railroad, settlers began moving into Ferris at once. A general store and a post office began operation in 1874. Within ten years the town had a population of 300, gristmills, cotton gins, four churches, and schools. In 1892 Ferris was incorporated, and its 350 residents supported some twenty businesses in addition to a number of cotton gins and hotels.

Ferris grew until the 1920s. In 1904 it had a population of 901 and in 1910, 1,233. Before World War Iqv the Ferris Brick Company and various other brick-manufacturing firms took advantage of the mineral clays found in the soils of the area and provided Ferris with a lasting industry. By 1914 some fifty business establishments, including six brick plants, a broom factory, and a weekly newspaper operated in Ferris. The town's population stood at 1,586 in 1925.

During the 1930s and 1940s, no doubt due to the dislocations resulting from the Great Depression and World War II,qqv Ferris declined slightly, to 1,436 people and thirty businesses by 1945. Its population rose from 1,734 in 1952 to 1,807 in 1964; the number of operating businesses decreased from sixty-eight to forty-six. Known locally as the "brick capital of the nation," Ferris had four brick plants during the 1950s. The population grew in the 1980s from 2,180 to 2,228, although businesses continued to decrease in number. Agriculture and brickmaking continued to dominate the local economy. No doubt the town's proximity to the Dallas metropolitan area played some part in its growth. In 1990 the population was 2,212.

BIBLIOGRAPHY: Edna Davis Hawkins et al., *History of Ellis County, Texas* (Waco: Texian, 1972). *Memorial and Biographical History of Ellis County* (Chicago: Lewis, 1892; rpt., as *Ellis County History*, Fort Worth: Historical Publishers, 1972). *Brian Hart*

FERRY LAKE. Ferry (Fairy) Lake was a natural lake in Harrison and Marion counties (at 94°14′ N, 32°46′ W). Before the Red Riverqv raft was cleared in 1873 below Shreveport, Louisiana, water was backed up into the Cypress Bayou system in southeastern Marion County and northeastern Harrison County and formed a series of natural lakes. Others besides Ferry Lake were Shirt (Shift) Tail Lake, Black Lake, and Sodo (Soda) Lake. Over time, after the raft was cleared, water levels fell an estimated six to fifteen feet, and navigation in the system ended. The various lakes drained, silted up, or merged into Caddo Lake.qv A United States Army Corps of Engineers map dated as late as 1908 gave Caddo Lake as a secondary name of Ferry Lake.

BIBLIOGRAPHY: Vertical Files, Barker Texas History Center, University of Texas at Austin. *Max S. Lale*

FETZER, TEXAS. Fetzer (Fetzer Switch), in far northeast Waller County near the Montgomery and Grimes county lines, developed as a switching yard on the International–Great Northern Railroad (later the Missouri Pacific, which in the 1980s paralleled Farm Road 1774). Sometime before 1913 Laura Fetzer gave a one-mile stretch of land for the railroad switch and later mysteriously departed from the community that bears her name. Farmers, stock raisers, and sawmill workers made up the early population. A post office located on land provided by J. M. Allan operated there from 1913 until 1940. By 1914 an estimated 150 persons lived at Fetzer; perhaps as many as twelve sawmills operated within a twenty-mile radius of the community. When the timber in the area was depleted the sawmills closed and Fetzer declined. During the 1920s the population dropped to seventy-five; in the 1930s it was only about twenty-five. The railroad switch ceased operations, but a few homes still existed in the area in the late 1970s. Fetzer was listed as a community in 1990, but without census figures.

BIBLIOGRAPHY: Mildred W. Abshier, et al., *Former Post Offices of Waller County* (Hempstead, Texas: Waller County Historical Society, 1977). *Paul M. Lucko*

FEUDS. Although the feuds of Texas have received far less general attention and publicity than have the Kentucky variety, they were probably even more numerous and bitter. Half a dozen of the worst ones have become fairly well known, but dozens of others, big and little, have raged in practically every county in the state. Only one important feud broke out in Texas before the Civil War:qv the Regulator-Moderator War,qv which flourished in Shelby County and adjacent regions from 1839 to 1844, involved several hundred men on each side, and caused much bloodshed and violence. Like many of the later feuds, this trouble was at first a contest between organized outlaws and a group of vigilantes. Typically, the Regulators went to such extremes in their attempts to break up the outlaws that a group of countervigilantes came into existence to "moderate" the Regulators. Typically also, both sides drew in friends, relatives, and sympathizers from many miles away, and a war of extermination would have been the inevitable result if Sam Houstonqv and the militia had not marched in.

Great outbursts of the feuding spirit were part of the aftermath of the Civil War.qv Feeling against Union authorities and their local supporters touched off several explosions in the 1860s. An example of this type of disturbance was the Early-Hasley feud which occurred in Bell County from 1865 to 1869. John Early, a member of the Home Guard, abused an old man named Drew Hasley. When Hasley's son, Sam, came home after service in the Confederate Army, he took the matter up. Early had become a supporter of the Yankee officials, and they backed him. Hasley soon became the head of a party of friends and relatives, including, notably, Jim McRae, a fearless and possibly a desperate man. Early and his crowd accused the Hasley party of all sorts of thievery and depredation and brought in soldiers to clean them out. On July 30, 1869, McRae was ambushed and killed. The Hasley party broke up after that, though one of them pursued Dr. Calvin Clark, an Early supporter, into Arkansas and killed him shortly thereafter. The Lee-Peacock feud, which flourished from 1867 to 1871 in the contiguous corners of Fannin, Grayson, Collin, and Hunt counties, followed the same pattern. Bob Lee, a former Confederate officer, fell out with the Union authorities and aroused the enmity of Lewis Peacock, one of their supporters. There was killing on both sides, and Lee was waylaid and killed in 1869. A systematic hunt for his friends and supporters was then begun, and several were killed. Peacock himself was shot on June 13, 1871, bringing the feud to an end. The Sutton-Taylor feud,^qv the biggest of the feuds rooted in the war, began in 1869 and continued to cause litigation until 1899, though most of the bloodshed was over by 1876.

The 1870s saw more lawlessness and more feuding than did any other period in Texas history. Most of the disturbances were the result of depredations by outlaw bands, and the typical pattern of vigilantes and countervigilantes was repeated many times. The war had left Texas comparatively undamaged, and this fact attracted many settlers from ruined communities in the older states, while the frontier offered a refuge to lawless characters. Many good people moved to Texas at this time, but the bad ones, combining forces with home-grown scoundrels, caused an outbreak of desperadoism that was hard to put down. Capt. Leander H. McNelly's^qv special force of Texas Rangers^qv and Maj. John B. Jones's^qv Frontier Battalion^qv gradually got the situation in hand, but large groups of outraged citizens felt obliged to take the law into their own hands until life and property were comparatively safe. Many of the cattle feuds of this period occurred in such frontier outposts as Mason, Lampasas, and Shackelford counties. The Horrell-Higgins feud^qv in Lampasas County in 1877, the Hoodoo War or Mason County War^qv of 1875, and the trouble over the Shackelford County mob are typical. Cattle and horse stealing in Shackelford County led to the forming of a secret vigilante society that was responsible for several midnight lynchings.^qv Former sheriff John M. Larn^qv and his henchman John Selman^qv eventually incurred the suspicion of this "mob," and great enmity grew up between them and some of their neighbors. Larn was surprised and arrested, but in June 1878 his enemies broke into the jail and shot him before he could be tried. Organized highway robbery and cattle theft brought on a lynching feud in Bastrop County. Not long after the Civil War a gang of thieves had gotten a foothold in the county, and by 1874 a vigilante organization was at work. There were fights and extralegal executions in 1876. On June 27, 1877, four of the supposed outlaws were taken from a dance and hanged. This did not stop the gang from killing and robbing their opponents, and on Christmas Eve, 1883, three more men thought to be in sympathy with the thieves were escorted from a store at McDade, taken out into the woods, and lynched. Friends and relatives of the dead men came to town on Christmas Day and staged a battle in the main street of McDade that resulted in three more deaths. The hanging of Pete Allen in 1884 and of Frank Renault in 1886 are supposed to have been the final acts in this feud.

The Salt War of San Elizario^qv in El Paso County in 1877, a different sort of disturbance, involved bitter political divisions and was complicated by a desire to exploit the salt deposits at the foot of Guadalupe Peak. Unusual also was the Mitchell-Truitt trouble caused by a land dispute, which began at Granbury in Hood County in 1874. The two parties fought along the highway after their case had been called in court. Two of the Truitts were killed, and as a result white-bearded Nelson (Cooney) Mitchell, the patriarch of the clan, was hanged at Granbury on October 9, 1875. His son Bill held a grudge against James Truitt, a young minister whose testimony had sent the elder Mitchell to his death. On July 20, 1886, Truitt was shot in his home in Timpson. Mitchell was hunted for years as the killer and captured in New Mexico in 1905, but no conviction against him was obtained until 1910. He did not go to the penitentiary until 1912, and even then the state could not hold him, for he escaped after serving a little more than two years. He was not heard of again.

By the mid-1880s the worst of the feuding was over, and only a handful of fresh disturbances occurred. One of these was the trouble at Graham, Young County, in 1888. A family of brothers named Marlow was accused of mishandling cattle and horses, though the brothers contended that they were victims of the desire of the big cattlemen to own everything. They killed Sheriff Marion D. Wallace when he tried to arrest them. Boone Marlow got away, but Alfred, George, Epp, and Charley were jailed. They broke jail once, were recaptured, and stood off an attempt by a local mob to kill them in their cell. The mob tried again the next day when the prisoners were being moved to Weatherford. The Marlows, though chained, seized guns from their guards and killed three of the mob before the others ran away. Alf and Epp Marlow were killed; Charley and George, each chained to a dead brother, cut off the feet of the corpses with pocketknives and got away. Boone Marlow was later killed in Oklahoma, and the feud subsided into litigation, which was finally dropped. Mob trouble was also at the root of the killings in San Saba County, where organized stealing became unbearable in the late 1880s. A vigilante group led by some religious people began to function, and there were hangings and ambushings. In 1893 a young man named Jim Brown was killed by a mob as he was going home from church. In 1896 there were two more mob executions. Public sentiment turned against this sort of Klan-like work, and District Attorney Linden joined forces with ranger sergeant W. J. L. Sullivan to work up a case that broke the power of the mob and sent its leaders into exile, though the last suits were not dismissed until 1903. The worst of the troubles of the period was the Jaybird-Woodpecker War^qv of 1889 at Richmond, Fort Bend County. The control of the black vote was the main issue. Family divisions helped to bring on a terrible fight in front of the courthouse on August 16. In the 1950s the Jaybird Democratic Association still existed. Another political feud was the clash between the Botas and Guaraches^qv at Laredo, which ended in a street riot on April 7, 1886, during which the Guaraches used an old cannon, the only documented case in which Texas feudists made use of artillery.

During the 1890s feuds again grew numerous, but they were neither so big nor so bloody as the feuds of the 1870s. The killing of Sheriff Andrew Jackson Royal^qv at Fort Stockton on November 21, 1894, was the result of a small but bitter feud. Jim Miller and Sheriff Bud Frazer fell out at Pecos, and several people lost their lives. Frazer was shot in a saloon at Toyah on September 13, 1896. Somewhat bigger than these disturbances was the Broocks-Border-Wall feud in San Augustine just before and after 1900. The Wall boys were enemies from boyhood of Curg (Lycurgus) Border, a relative of the powerful Broocks family. The Walls themselves had numerous kin with plenty of backbone. In April 1900 Border shot and killed Sheriff George Wall on the streets of San Augustine. Eugene Wall retaliated by killing Ben Broocks on June 2. On June 4 a battle around the courthouse resulted in the deaths of Sid and Felix Roberts. Later two more of the Wall boys were ambushed, and many of their friends and supporters left the country. The feud was not really ended until Sheriff Sneed Nobles killed Curg Border. As bitter as any other were the feuds at Columbus, Colorado County. Two great clans of cattlemen, the Staffords and the Townsends, had trouble that culminated in the killing of R. E. and John Stafford in front of a Columbus saloon on July 7, 1888. Larkin and Marion Hope were accused of the deed. In the 1890s the Townsend family divided against itself. Former Sheriff Sam Reese, who had married a Townsend, grew bitter against the local political machine led by lawyer Marcus Townsend and Sheriff Lite Townsend. On August 3, 1894, Marcus Townsend's follower Larkin Hope was murdered. Reese himself was assassinated in a street battle on March 16, 1899. Numerous engagements and killings followed, the last being another general shooting on June 30, 1906.

Probably a hundred smaller feuds could be listed. A book could be written on the political feuds in the lower Rio Grande valley between the Reds and Blues^qv in such places as Brownsville and Rio Grande City. There were three small feuds at Hallettsville in the 1890s. The death of William Cowper Brann,^qv the "Great Iconoclast," at Waco in 1898 was the result of a feud-like action. Even after 1900 feuding went on. Trouble between a ranger detachment and the Mexican-American population of Brownsville in 1902 assumed the proportions of a feud. In 1905 two flare-ups over prohibition,^qv one at Groveton and the other at Hempstead, brought feud motives into play. The Black, Johnson, and Echols families feuded at Coahoma in 1910. The Boyce-Sneed feud^qv at Amarillo in 1912 and the Johnson-Sims unpleasantness at Snyder in 1916 were brief but bloody feuds. As late as the 1940s Texas papers carried items that reminded one of episodes that cropped up more frequently fifty years before.

BIBLIOGRAPHY: C. L. Douglas, *Famous Texas Feuds* (Dallas: Turner, 1936). James B. Gillett, *Six Years with the Texas Rangers, 1875 to 1881* (Austin: Von Boeckmann-Jones, 1921; rpt., Lincoln: University of Nebraska Press, 1976). Albert Bigelow Paine, *Captain Bill McDonald, Texas Ranger* (New York: Little and Ives, 1909). C. L. Sonnichsen, *I'll Die Before I'll Run—The Story of the Great Feuds of Texas* (New York: Harper, 1951; 2d. ed, New York: Devin-Adair, 1962). Vertical Files, Barker Texas History Center, University of Texas at Austin. Walter Prescott Webb, *The Texas Rangers* (Boston: Houghton Mifflin, 1935; rpt., Austin: University of Texas Press, 1982).

C. L. Sonnichsen

FEWEL, WILLIAM JOHNSON (1846–1921). William Johnson Fewel, soldier and businessman, son of Robert William and Louisa Marion (Crawford) Fewel, was born at Greensboro, North Carolina, on August 7, 1846. At age sixteen he left Princeton College and enlisted in the North Carolina infantry during the Civil War.[qv] He fought with distinction and was granted a captaincy, though the commission was never confirmed because of Gen. Robert E. Lee's[qv] surrender. After the war, Fewel moved to Missouri and served as a major on the staff of Gen. Perry Catron of the United Confederate Veterans. There he married Euphemia Carrie Catron, cousin to Senator Thomas B. Catron of New Mexico. They had three children. Fewel arrived in El Paso a few months ahead of the railroad in 1881 and soon became one of its most active citizens. He organized the El Paso Coke and Gas Company, the first plant to supply the town with lights. He then organized the town's first volunteer fire-fighting company, built the first brick office building, built a structure to house the State National Bank (the oldest financial institution in El Paso), and organized the town's first streetcar company (mule drawn). From 1905 to 1907 Fewel served as a city councilman; he was instrumental in initiating the first street-paving program in El Paso. He died in that city on December 13, 1921. A street in Sunset Heights, a historic residential area in El Paso, memorializes his name.

BIBLIOGRAPHY: C. L. Sonnichsen, *Pass of the North: Four Centuries on the Rio Grande* (2 vols., El Paso: Texas Western Press, 1968, 1980). Owen P. White, *Out of the Desert: The Historical Romance of El Paso* (El Paso: McMath, 1924).

Herb Marsh, Jr.

FICKLIN, BENJAMIN FRANKLIN (1827–1871). Ben Ficklin, Civil War[qv] blockade runner and stage operator, son of Benjamin and Ellen (Slaughter) Ficklin, was born in Albemarle County, Virginia, on December 18, 1827. He entered Virginia Military Institute on July 7, 1845, and even though he was temporarily kicked out for breaking rules and playing pranks, he graduated on July 4, 1849, after stopping to serve in the Mexican War[qv] as a corporal in 1846–47. He subsequently taught school for a time and then began operating stage lines. In 1857, under the command of Albert Sidney Johnston,[qv] he traveled on an expedition to Utah to settle trouble with the Mormons.[qv] In 1859 he helped organize and became general superintendent of the Central and Overland California and Pike's Peak Express Company. In this role he became known as the originator of the Pony Express.

Ficklin returned to Virginia to become state quartermaster general in April 1861. In 1861–62 he served in the Virginia campaign and was a staff officer at the battle of Malvern Hill. Later in 1862 he was sent west of the Mississippi River to control the Indians and lawless whites. He assisted in the organization of the John B. Floyd Brigade and until the end of the war, as a Confederate purchasing agent, bought supplies in Europe for the Confederate government, including a steamer for running the blockade to carry cotton overseas. Ficklin was arrested for suspicion of complicity in Abraham Lincoln's assassination but was released a few months afterward, thanks to the efforts of a friend, Senator Orville Browning, from Illinois.

After the war Ficklin received a government contract for a weekly mail service from Fort Smith, Arkansas, to San Antonio, Texas, with a branch line to El Paso. He established the Concho Mail Station, headquarters for his stage operations, near the site of Fort Concho, in what is now Tom Green County. The stage stand grew into the community of Ben Ficklin, the county seat of Tom Green County in 1874. Ficklin died in Georgetown, D.C., on March 10, 1871, and was buried with Masonic honors in Maplewood Cemetery, Charlottesville, Virginia.

BIBLIOGRAPHY: Julia Grace Bitner, The History of Tom Green County, Texas (M.A. thesis, University of Texas, 1931). James Evetts Haley, "Ben Ficklin, Pioneer Mail Man," *The Shamrock*, Spring 1959. Theodore Calvin Pease and James Garfield Randall, *The Diary of Orville Hickman Browning* (2 vols., Springfield, Illinois: Trustees of the Illinois State Historical Survey, 1925, 1933). Vertical Files, Barker Texas History Center, University of Texas at Austin. John Wilkinson, *The Narrative of a Blockade-Runner* (New York: Sheldon, 1877).

Susan Miles and Mary Bain Spence

FIDELITY UNION LIFE INSURANCE. Fidelity Union Life Insurance, headquartered in the twenty-six-story Allianz Financial Center in Dallas, Texas, grew from Texas roots to become part of a worldwide network of diversified insurance organizations and in the 1990s ranked in the ninety largest stock life-insurance companies in the nation. Carr P. Collins[qv] and William Morriss founded the company in 1927, beginning with four employees who sold insurance in Texas and Alabama. Collins previously served as secretary to the Texas Employers Insurance Association and established and ran Fidelity Union Fire and Casualty, a forerunner of the present firm, with B. P. Bailey until 1931. Earl B. Smyth, a local bank president, served as vice president, and E. F. White as agency director after Morriss left the firm. Despite the onset of the Great Depression[qv] Collins and White's promotion of a "life insurance plus stock-option" plan gave the firm $30 million of life insurance in force by 1931. Collins became increasingly involved with his Crazy Water Crystals business in Mineral Wells and removed himself for a time from active management of the firm to become chairman of the board in 1932. He later returned and was succeeded by his son, James Mitchell Collins, as president in 1954. After Smyth died in 1943, Collins developed a new "market concept" approach to insurance, an idea that developed from his original business selling only to cottonseed-oil mills and cotton ginners. The new plan moved away from standardization and classified members by "markets" with common insurance needs, such as school teachers, college graduates, and "total abstainers," a group modeled on plans used in Europe. Individual markets were targeted with advertising. By 1953 the firm employed 341 agents and 175 home office workers and had the largest life-insurance headquarters building in the South. Jim Collins, who became a United States Congressman, was succeeded by his son, Michael James Collins, in 1972.

In 1979 Allianz Versicherungs A.G., a Munich-headquartered insurance company founded in 1896, acquired Fidelity Union. It was merged with North American Life and Casualty Company in 1993. By the 1990s Allianz had 225,000 employees in forty countries worldwide, more than $120 billion in assets, and more than $34 billion in premium income, along with three other United States affiliates. Fidelity Union had over $10 billion of life insurance in force and almost $1 billion in assets. The German parent company had become the world's sixth largest insurer and twenty-third among the world's largest public companies of all industries.

BIBLIOGRAPHY: Dorothy Neville, *Carr P. Collins* (Dallas: Park, 1963).

John Ftacek

FIELD, JOSEPH E. (?–1882). Joseph E. Field, physician, reached Texas in 1833 and lived near Brazoria and Matagorda for two years. Late in 1835, when the Texas Revolution[qv] broke out, he was at Gonzales, on his way to Mexico, and he and the four other doctors in the area volunteered their services. Field marched with the army to San Antonio and during and after the siege of Bexar[qv] served as both doctor and soldier. On his way from San Antonio he met Sam Houston,[qv] with whom he traveled as far as Nacogdoches. At the Mexican armed incursion in the spring of 1836, Field joined the command of James Walker Fannin, Jr.,[qv] fought at the battle of Coleto,[qv] and was made a prisoner along with Fannin's other men. He and the other doctors were spared from the Goliad Massacre[qv] so that they could treat wounded Mexicans. After two weeks Field made his escape and heard the news of the battle of San Jacinto.[qv] After the revolution he made a visit to Massachusetts, where, in September 1836, he published *Three Years in Texas*. On his return to Texas late that year he joined the army. After a year of service he practiced medicine, first at Brazoria, and then, as late as 1874, at Corpus Christi. He experienced extreme poverty in his later life. A small pension granted him in 1858 was subsequently withdrawn, and efforts were being made for its reinstatement when Field, then blind and forgotten, died in Clear Water Harbor, Florida, in 1882.

BIBLIOGRAPHY: William Campbell Binkley, ed., *Official Correspondence of the Texan Revolution, 1835–1836* (2 vols., New York: Appleton-Century, 1936). Pat Ireland Nixon, *The Medical Story of Early Texas, 1528–1853* (Lancaster, Pennsylvania: Lupe Memorial Fund, 1946). Noah Smithwick, *The Evolution of a State, or Recollections of Old Texas Days* (Austin: Gammel, 1900; rpt., Austin: University of Texas Press, 1983).
Pat Ireland Nixon

FIELD, SCOTT (1847–1931). Scott Field, politician, was born in Canton, Mississippi, on January 26, 1847, the son of Henry and Jane (Bates) Field. During the Civil War[qv] he enlisted in Harvey's Scouts, and his unit was attached to Jackson's command under Gen. Nathan B. Forrest. In the Georgia campaign, he saw action with Joseph E. Johnston,[qv] and he also fought in the Tennessee theater under John B. Hood.[qv] After the war Field attended the University of Virginia, from which he graduated in 1868. He returned to Mississippi, taught school for two years while he studied law, and was admitted to the Mississippi bar in 1871. He moved in 1872 to Calvert, Texas, where he established a private practice. Field served two terms as county attorney in Robertson County between 1878 and 1882 and was elected to the Texas Senate for two terms, 1887 through 1891. While in the Senate he was credited with the act that forbade convict leasing (*see* CONVICT LEASE SYSTEM). He was a delegate to the Democratic national convention at Chicago in 1892. He represented the Sixth Congressional District as a Democrat from 1903 to 1906. His law practice prospered, and he became a substantial landholder. Field was married three times. His first wife, Victoria Luckey of Mississippi, died after two years of marriage. He then wed Lucy Randolph of Calvert. They had three sons. After Lucy's death Field married a widow, Maude Green, of Calvert. He died in Robertson County on December 20, 1931.

BIBLIOGRAPHY: *Biographical Directory of the American Congress*. Richard Denny Parker, *Historical Recollections of Robertson County, Texas* (Salado, Texas: Anson Jones, 1955).
James L. Hailey

FIELD, THOMAS WILLIAM (1847–?). Thomas William Field, pioneer real estate developer and builder of the first opera house in Dallas, was born in September 1847 in Missouri. He arrived in Dallas in 1872, the same year as the first railroad, the Houston and Texas Central, and immediately took an interest in business. He supported the Texas and Pacific Railway and aided in its arrival. He controlled large plots of land in what later became downtown Dallas, dealt in grain, and opened the first opera house in Dallas in the 1870s on the south side of Main Street. In 1872 he married Florence Peak, a woman from a prominent Dallas family; they had two children. They built a house that encompassed an entire block. In the late 1880s and early 1890s Field's firm, Field and Field Real Estate and Financial Agents, developed much of the Dallas area with little planning and no zoning, a lack that led to premature deterioration. Field began his largest project in 1893, the "most elegant hotel east of the Mississippi." The $500,000 Oriental Hotel, at the corner of Akard and Commerce, with 150 guest rooms and many lobbies, bars, and dining rooms, was finished entirely with Italian marble and mahogany and had fully electrified rooms and elevators. Often called "Field's Folly" because of its enormous cost, the Oriental was sold to a group of St. Louis businessmen when Field went bankrupt. He was also forced to sell his house. In 1900 he was living in the Oriental Hotel with his wife and daughter. They later moved to Oak Lawn, where he remained for the rest of his life. Field Street in downtown Dallas was named in his honor.

BIBLIOGRAPHY: Sam Hanna Acheson, *Dallas Yesterday*, ed. Lee Milazzo (Dallas: Southern Methodist University Press, 1977). William L. McDonald, *Dallas Rediscovered: A Photographic Chronicle of Urban Expansion, 1870–1925* (Dallas: Dallas County Historical Society, 1978).
Lisa C. Maxwell

FIELD, TEXAS. Field, a farming community off Farm Road 90 twelve miles west of Canton in extreme western Van Zandt County, had a school in 1890 and a church by 1936. State highway maps showed the church, a cemetery, and scattered dwellings at the townsite in 1987.
Diana J. Kleiner

FIELD CREEK. Field Creek, a free-flowing stream, rises 1½ miles northeast of the location where the Mason, Llano, and San Saba county lines meet in southwestern San Saba County (at 30°57′ N, 98°58′ W) and flows southeast for eight miles to its mouth on San Fernando Creek in Llano County (at 30°52′ N, 98°56′ W). The stream crosses an area of flat to rolling uplands with live oak, mesquite, Ashe juniper, and grasses growing in shallow to moderately deep sandy and clayey loam soils.

FIELD CREEK, TEXAS. Field Creek is on State Highway 71 twenty miles northwest of Llano in the northwest corner of Llano County. The area was first settled in the late 1850s, and a store was built at the site on Trout Creek in 1877. The creek was renamed Field Creek at this time, and the town was named for it. A post office was established there in 1878 with Moses Fisher as postmaster. Field Creek had two cotton gins before 1900. From World War II[qv] to the 1980s the population was thirty. The post office was closed in 1976.

BIBLIOGRAPHY: Tillie Badu Moss Fry, *A History of Llano County* (M.A. thesis, University of Texas, 1943). Wilburn Oatman, *Llano, Gem of the Hill Country: A History of Llano County* (Hereford, Texas: Pioneer, 1970).
James B. Heckert-Greene

FIELDER MUSEUM. The Fielder Museum is located at the corner of Fielder and Abram streets in Arlington. The two-story building, a community landmark, was built in 1914 as the home of James Park and Mattie (Barnes) Fielder, Sr. Fielder was a successful lawyer, banker, farmer, and philanthropist, who had come to Texas from Tennessee in 1884. The Fielder House was one of the earliest brick homes in Arlington. It had electrical lighting, central heating, a hot-water system, and indoor plumbing. It crowned a 215-acre hilltop farm and became known as the "Home on the Hill." It was surrounded by large oaks and reportedly had one of the finest fruit orchards and vegetable gardens in the county.

In 1977–78 a group of Arlington citizens successfully campaigned for the preservation and restoration of the Fielder home. It was opened in April 1980 as the Fielder Museum. The purpose of the museum is the collection, preservation, and interpretation of local and county historical materials. The museum houses a permanent display of local artifacts including the extensive J. W. Dunlop collection of over 200 early local photographs. One permanent classroom has been furnished, and two galleries provided for changing exhibits.

Annual events at the museum include the Community Christmas Tree Lighting, the Arlington Art Association Annual Juried Show, and a Fall Fest. Museum classes are scheduled throughout the year for youths and adults on a variety of subjects. The museum's education outreach program is designed to aid the public schools in their study of local and state history. Historical programs are also given to the community and organizations upon request. The museum administrator and staff publish a monthly newsletter and calendar of events, *The Field World*. Eight to ten exhibits are displayed at the museum per year. The Fielder House is a creative historical learning center and is designed to be a working museum. It has two state historical markers, a subject marker for James Fielder, and a building marker for the home itself. Both were placed in 1979 and dedicated on April 20, 1980, at the opening of the museum.

BIBLIOGRAPHY: Dallas *Morning News*, April 18, 1982. Fielder House and Museum Scrapbooks, Fielder House Reference Library, Arlington, Texas. Fort Worth *Star-Telegram*, March 1, 1980. Rene Harris and Arista Joyner, *Arlington, A Pictorial History* (Norfolk, Virginia: Donning, 1982).

Gayla Weems Shannon

FIELDS, JAMES H. (ca. 1921–1970). James H. Fields, Medal of Honor recipient, was born at Caddo, Texas, in 1920 or 1921, the son of Mr. and Mrs. R. B. Fields. He graduated from Lamar High School in Houston and was drafted into the army in 1942. He was a member of the Tenth Armored Infantry, Fourth Armored Division, United States Army. First Lt. Fields was cited for "conspicuous gallantry and intrepidity at risk of life above and beyond the call of duty" on September 27, 1944, at Réchicourt, France. He led his depleted platoon in a counterattack on an enemy position and exposed himself to enemy fire while attending to one of his wounded men. He himself was wounded in the face by a bursting shell. Badly injured and rendered speechless he continued to direct his platoon in the attack by hand signals. Two enemy machine-guns had the platoon in a deadly crossfire. Fields left his foxhole, picked up a light machine gun, and, firing from the hip, knocked out both the enemy positions. His action inspired his men to increase the pressure of the attack. Only when the enemy was scattered did Fields allow himself to be evacuated to the command post. There he refused further evacuation until he could brief the battalion commander. Only eleven of the fifty-five men in his platoon survived the day's engagement. Fields's heroism was largely responsible for the repulse of the enemy forces and was an inspiration to the entire command. After the war he became an independent oil operator. He died at the Veterans Administration Hospital in Houston (now the Veterans Affairs Medical Center, Houston qv) on June 17, 1970, and was survived by his wife, Mathilde, and three children. He was buried in the VA Houston National Cemetery.

BIBLIOGRAPHY: Dallas *Morning News*, August 16, 1945. Houston *Post*, June 18, 1970.

Art Leatherwood

FIELDS, JOHN F. (?–?). John F. Fields, one of Stephen F. Austin's qv Old Three Hundred qv colonists, received title to a labor of land in Brazoria County on August 24, 1824. The colonial census of 1826 listed him as a single man aged between forty and fifty. Fields was likely the same person who captained the Rob Roy and sailed between New Orleans and Texas ports carrying freight, passengers, and mail. The fact that he was a seaman and probably had little desire to farm or ranch possibly accounts for the relatively small size of his grant. He may also have been the John Fields, born in South Carolina about 1785, who lived in Harrison County in 1850.

BIBLIOGRAPHY: Eugene C. Barker, ed., *The Austin Papers* (3 vols., Washington: GPO, 1924–28). Lester G. Bugbee, "The Old Three Hundred: A List of Settlers in Austin's First Colony," *Quarterly of the Texas State Historical Association* 1 (October 1897). Texas General Land Office, First Census of Austin's Colony, 1826 (MS, Barker Texas History Center, University of Texas at Austin).

FIELDS, RICHARD (ca. 1780–1827). Richard Fields, one-eighth Cherokee, was diplomatic chief of his tribe in Texas, sharing leadership with Chief Bowl.qv Fields was born around 1780 and was first noted in 1801 as an emissary of the Cherokee council to United States agents in Tennessee. He appeared as an interpreter on September 19, 1812, at the Council House treaty council in the Chickasaw country. In 1814, during the War of 1812, he served as captain of a unit of Cherokee auxiliaries attached to Gen. Andrew Jackson's army. Fields appeared in Texas around 1820, at about the time Chief Bowl brought the Cherokees into the region; he was leader of one of several Cherokee villages in East Texas.qv Because of his skill and experience in diplomacy, Fields was chosen by the Cherokee intervillage council to negotiate a Spanish land grant for his people. In late 1822 he led a delegation to San Antonio de Béxar to present the Cherokee request to Governor José Félix Trespalacios.qv Trespalacios and Fields agreed that the Cherokees would provide patrols to guard the Sabine against American incursions and against smuggling; in return, the Cherokees could remain on their East Texas land, and Fields's delegation was permitted to travel to Mexico City to petition the viceroy. Fields's mission was to secure a grant of territory for the Cherokees, but Agustín de Iturbide'sqv overthrow of the Spanish government and the resulting political turmoil in Mexico City spoiled that opportunity. Later, after Emperor Iturbide's abdication in March 1823, Fields unsuccessfully petitioned the new congress for assistance. The Cherokee delegation left Mexico City without having secured a grant. After his return to Texas, Richard Fields continued to serve as diplomatic chief of the Cherokees. In 1824 Fields became involved with trying to unite the Texas Indian tribes into a grand alliance and encouraging other nomadic tribes to settle in Texas. These efforts alarmed the Mexican government and hampered land negotiations. In 1826, despairing of ever receiving an official grant of territory from the Mexican government, Fields sought other means of obtaining land for his people. He and John Dunn Hunter,qv an American residing among the Cherokees and serving as a political advisor of sorts, began negotiations with Martin Parmer, Benjamin W. Edwards,qv and other Anglo-Americans living around Nacogdoches. The allies formed a Fredonian Republic that divided Texas between the Indians and the Anglo-Americans. The Mexican government moved quickly to quash the impending uprising, however, and the Cherokee council reversed course and refused to take part in the Fredonian Rebellion.qv After trial by the Cherokee council, Richard Fields and John Dunn Hunter fled; they were captured separately and were executed in early February 1827.

BIBLIOGRAPHY: Eugene C. Barker, ed., *The Austin Papers* (3 vols., Washington: GPO, 1924–28). Richard Drinnon, *White Savage: The Case of John Dunn Hunter* (New York: Schocken, 1972). Dianna Everett, *The Texas Cherokees: A People between Two Fires, 1819–1840* (Norman: University of Oklahoma Press, 1990). Edmund Morris Parsons, "The Fredonian Rebellion," *Texana* 5 (Spring 1967). Emmet Starr, *History of the Cherokee Indians and Their Legends and Folklore* (Oklahoma City: Warden, 1921).

Dianna Everett

FIELDS, SMALLWOOD S. B. (?–1846). Smallwood S. B. (Steamboat) Fields, lawyer and editor, moved to Fayette County, Texas, when the county was organized in 1838. From January 21 to February 25, 1839, he campaigned with John Henry Mooreqv against the Comanches. He practiced law in La Grange in 1839, was elected county tax assessor in 1840, and served until 1849. In 1842–43 he also represented Fayette County in the Texas House of Representatives during the Seventh Congress. Although he was a member of the La Grange Company under William M. Eastland,qv he did not participate in the Mier expedition.qv With the departure of William P. Bradburn, Fields became editor of the La Grange *Intelligencer*qv in March 1844 and promised that each issue would be devoted to "Politics, the Sciences, Agriculture, Religion, Foreign Affairs, Miscellaneous Items, [and] Domestic Matter." Until 1845 the paper presented a flamboyant and often cynical view of life in Texas and maintained a critical rivalry with the *National Vindicator*,[qv] edited by Thomas Johnson[qv] of Washington-on-the-Brazos. The September 12, 1845, issue of the *Intelligencer* reported "Hard times! Hard times! and the scarcity of money is wrung upon us at every turn and corner of life." The following week the La Grange *Intelligencer* suspended publication. Seven months later, in April 1846, Fields died in Austin.

BIBLIOGRAPHY: Frank Lotto, *Fayette County: Her History and Her People* (Schulenburg, Texas: Sticker Steam Press, 1902; rpt., Austin: University of Texas Press, 1981). Leonie Rummel Weyand and Houston Wade, *An Early History of Fayette County* (La Grange, Texas: La Grange *Journal*, 1936).
Jeff Carroll

FIELDS, WILLIAM (ca. 1810–1858). William Fields, author and legislator, was born in North Carolina about 1810. He moved to Tennessee and published the first edition of *Fields' Scrap Book,* a collection of literary efforts, anecdotes, and sketches, before moving to the Lone Star State in 1837. After living briefly in Liberty County he moved to Galveston County but returned to Liberty in 1842. He was elected to represent Polk and Liberty counties in the first of four consecutive terms in the state legislature in 1847. While in the Texas House, Fields opposed the legislature's hurried call for delegates to the Nashville Convention[qv] of 1850. He also opposed any measure asserting the state's supposed claim to Santa Fe that might lead to war with the United States. For most of the period he engaged in a heated newspaper quarrel with his bitter rival Thomas Jefferson Chambers.[qv] In 1855 the American (Know-Nothing) party[qv] chose Fields as its candidate for land commissioner. Claiming that he had been and would remain a Democrat, Fields mounted an unsuccessful campaign for the position in the Democratic primary. Despite the defeat, he was named state engineer in 1856.

Fields revised his *Scrap Book* in 1851; new editions appeared in 1854, 1856, 1860, 1872, 1884, and 1890. He accumulated little property in Liberty County; the 1854 county tax rolls assessed his estate (including one slave, four horses, thirty cattle, and a watch) at less than $1,200. Fields was married to a native of Tennessee and had at least five children. He died at Hempstead on September 9, 1858, and was interred at Galveston.

BIBLIOGRAPHY: Randolph B. Campbell, "Texas and the Nashville Convention of 1850," *Southwestern Historical Quarterly* 76 (July 1972).
Robert Wooster

FIELDS STORE, TEXAS. Fields (Field's) Store is at the junction of Farm roads 1488 and 362, ten miles northeast of Hempstead in northeast Waller County. It existed as early as 1872 and received its name from Andrew Field and his son Druey Holland Field, the first of several Field family members to operate a general store in the area. By 1874 the community had a post office called Field's Store operated by Isaac Newton Jones, Druey's son-in-law. In 1895 the post office dropped the apostrophe from the name. Thirty residents lived in the community during the 1880s; in the next decade the town had a population of 150, three general stores, at least one church, and a physician. In 1905 Fields Store School enrolled 179 students who were instructed by four teachers. A local Masonic lodge existed during the same period, and by 1907 a Woodman of the World chapter had received its charter. A cotton gin also served local farmers.

Fields Store declined when the neighboring communities of Myrtle Grove and Joseph developed gins and opened post offices. The Fields Store post office closed in 1909, and most residents began receiving mail from Waller. During the 1930s sixty-nine students attended primary school at Fields Store; high school students rode the bus to Waller. In 1953 the Fields Store school was consolidated with the Waller schools, where area children still attended school in 1990. The old Fields Store school building, completed in 1923, served as the Fields Store Community House in 1990. Pleasant Hill Masonic Lodge No. 380 still met at the meeting hall in Fields Store, and an active cemetery association continued to raise money from July 4 picnics and an annual rodeo. The picnics served as community reunions. New Hope United Methodist Church continued to hold services in 1973. The Texas Historical Commission[qv] has placed markers at the site of the old store and at the cemetery.

BIBLIOGRAPHY: Mildred W. Abshier, et al., *Former Post Offices of Waller County* (Hempstead, Texas: Waller County Historical Society, 1977). James Henry Goettee, Administrative Survey of the Public Schools of Waller County, Texas (M.Ed. thesis, University of Texas, 1937). Waller County Historical Survey Committee, *A History of Waller County, Texas* (Waco: Texian, 1973).
Paul M. Lucko

FIELDTON, TEXAS. Fieldton, at the intersection of Farm roads 37 and 1072, on the Double Mountain Fork of the Brazos River in eastern Lamb County, was named for its location midway between Littlefield and Olton. It was originally called Jaun Dell by Jim Pickrell, the first merchant on the site, which was purchased from the Halsell Land Company in 1924 by Jess Mitchell, its promoter. Pickrell named the place after his two granddaughters, but Mitchell requested that the name be changed to Fieldton. Fieldton received a post office in 1930. The first church, built in 1926, was shared by the Baptists, Methodists, and Church of Christ. A cotton gin started operation at Fieldton in 1931. By 1940 the settlement had a school, four businesses, and 175 people. In 1966 it had eight businesses, including two gins. The population was 126 in 1980 and 1990.

BIBLIOGRAPHY: Evalyn Parrott Scott, *A History of Lamb County* (Sudan, Texas: Lamb County Historical Commission, 1968).
Claudia Hazlewood

FIESTA SAN ANTONIO. Fiesta San Antonio, previously called Fiesta San Jacinto, is a ten-day festival held every spring in San Antonio. It originated in the 1891 flower parade conceived by Ellen Maury Slayden,[qv] wife of Congressman James L. Slayden,[qv] as an April 21 salute to the heroes of the battles of the Alamo and San Jacinto.[qqv] A group of San Antonio women formed the Battle of Flowers Association. The first parade was moved a day ahead to accommodate the schedule of visiting President Benjamin Harrison, but it was then delayed for four days by bad weather. With the arrival of fair weather, participants in carriages pelted one another with flowers as they rounded Alamo Plaza. By 1895 an elaborate weeklong celebration surrounded the Battle of Flowers Parade, and the first queen was chosen. In 1909 the Order of the Alamo was organized, with John B. Carrington as president, to oversee some features of the carnival, including the election of the queen and her coronation. The Battle of Flowers Association continued to coordinate the parade, as well as a children's fete and a band competition, the forerunner of today's Band Festival. The parade tradition lapsed briefly during World War I,[qv] but another tradition was started—the Pilgrimage to the Alamo. By the 1980s the Daughters of the Republic of Texas[qv] were sponsoring this event, in which participants march from the city's Municipal Auditorium to the Alamo to hear the names of Texas men who died in the battle of the Alamo. The fiesta was not very old before the crowning of a king was added to the week's activities. Before a King Antonio line was established in 1916, kings were chosen by the Spring Carnival Association, the Downtown Business Club, and the Chamber of Commerce. Early monarchs were dubbed Selamat (*tamales* spelled backward), Omala (*Alamo* backward), King Cotton, Zeus, and Rex. In 1926, when the Texas Cavaliers were organized by Carrington, the king began to be named from their ranks. In the same year Mrs. Alfred Ward of the Battle of Flowers Association founded the Oratorical Contest for college students, to encourage writing on some phase of Texas history.

The celebration continued to grow, and by 1945 the San Antonio Conservation Society[qv] was playing a substantial role with its popular

Float for the Battle of Flowers Parade, San Antonio, ca. 1916–17. Courtesy Jean Herff Henderson, San Antonio. The Battle of Flowers parade, now part of Fiesta San Antonio, originated in 1891 as a salute to those who fought at the battles of the Alamo and San Jacinto.

Night in Old San Antonio, held in picturesque La Villita.qv In the mid-1980s the Night in Old San Antonio, held on four successive evenings, continued to be one of the most popular and highly successful additions to the gala week. It is an authentically costumed recreation of San Antonio's early life under six flags, held in La Villita, an internationally recognized historic restoration of the little village that existed at the site before the time of the Alamo. By 1959 Fiesta Week had grown to the point that the San Antonio Chamber of Commerce formed a coordinating agency called the Fiesta San Antonio Commission, and the event became officially known as Fiesta San Antonio. In 1980 Fiesta royalty was expanded when the League of United Latin American Citizensqv Council No. 2 began the Paseo del Rey Feo (Ugly King Parade). By the mid-1980s the Fiesta San Antonio Committee was underwriting some twenty-five events, including the four major parades. The Battle of Flowers Parade continued to be the only major parade in the United States that was conceived, organized, and presented by a women's group. The Texas Cavaliers sponsored the annual River Parade, and their King Antonio attended nearly 120 Fiesta-related functions. Fiesta activities included art shows, sports tournaments, and tours of local historical areas and military bases. The final event of the festival had become the Fiesta Night Parade or "Fiesta Flambeau," sponsored by the San Antonio Jaycees and lit by torchlight and fireworks. In the early 1990s some 50,000 volunteers from the military, the general public, and more than eighty nonprofit organizations helped to put on the Fiesta events, which were estimated by organizers to generate more than $100 million for the community each year.

BIBLIOGRAPHY: Marlene Gordon, "Fiesta," *San Antonio*, April 1984. *Humble Way* (publication of the Humble Oil and Refining Company, Houston), May–June 1946. Ann Moore, "The Fiesta de San Antonio," *Junior Historian*, May 1959. Tommie Pinkard, "Fiesta," *Texas Highways*, April 1985.

Mrs. Willard E. Simpson, Jr.

FIESTAS PATRIAS. In Texas and throughout the Southwest, Mexican Americansqv annually celebrate two Mexican national holidays referred to as the *fiestas patrias*. These celebrations originated in Mexico in the nineteenth century. The first one, Cinco de Mayo (May 5), commemorates Gen. Ignacio Zaragoza'sqv victory on May 5, 1862, over the French expeditionary forces at Puebla, Mexico. The second, Diez y Seis de Septiembre (September 16), commemorates Father Miguel Hidalgo y Costilla'sqv *grito de Dolores* ("cry of Dolores") on September 16, 1810, at the village of Dolores, near Guanajuato. Hidalgo called for the end of Spanish rule in Mexico. Diez y Seis de Septiembre has been celebrated in San Antonio for more than 167 years and in Goliad for 160 years. On September 16, 1825, the Republic of Mexico officially declared Diez y Seis de Septiembre its national Independence Day.

At the time of the Texas Revolutionqv of 1836, which ended Mexican Texas,qv Hispanic peoples in Texas possessed a unique cultural heritage, enriched by a combination of Spanish and Indian customs. This biculturation enabled Mexican Americans to adapt and join the mainstream Anglo-American culture while maintaining in group relationships and family structures their valued ethnic traditions. Mexican Americans began celebrating *fiestas patrias* to reinforce their cultural links with each other and with Mexico. The first *fiestas patrias* were held in Texas in the early 1820s. They included festivities that involved special music, songs, dances, native cuisine, costumes, and homage to folk heroes. In these celebrations Tejanos displayed and preserved their ethnicity. Diez y Seis celebrations persisted in Texas from 1825 through the period of the republic and into the post–Civil War years. They spread to such towns along the border as Brownsville, Laredo, Eagle Pass, and El Paso, and to centrally located cities. Many eventually were held at county fair grounds and drew large crowds.

At the turn of the century San Antonio held elaborate three-day *fiestas patrias* on September 15 through 17 that typified events elsewhere in Texas. A committee called the Junta Patriótica (Patriotic Board), aided by local benevolent societies, planned the program and chose a site in or near a Mexican barrio for the event. Additional committees decorated booths and bandstands with bunting, flags and flowers. A grand marshal and aides were appointed to lead a parade. On September 15 marchers bearing the colors of the United States and Mexico, accompanied by military bands, headed the procession. Next came the carriages with city and county officials and dignitaries from Mexico and the United States. A line of decorated floats with costumed characters representing prominent figures in Mexican history followed. Then came local societies, which included, for example, the Mutualista Benevolencia, Sociedad Unión, Sociedad Benito Juárez, Sociedad Hidalgo, Sociedad Zaragoza, Círculo de Obreros, and other groups (*see* SOCIEDADES MUTUALISTAS). At the rear were carriages carrying people of prominence, the *fiestas patrias* committee, invited associations, and individuals. The procession followed a designated route to the fairgrounds or some other location. The crowd surged by decorated booths to a speakers' stage, and at exactly 11 P.M. the traditional *grito de Dolores* was made. The Mexican Declaration of Independence was read, and cries of "*Viva la independencia!*" filled the air. A United States artillery battery fired a twenty-one-gun salute. The program often included singing the Mexican national hymn, the coronation of lovely señoritas, orations, eulogies, and the singing of such patriotic songs as "El Cinco de Mayo." As the ceremonies concluded, the crowd participated in social games, watched historic plays, flooded food and drink concessions, and danced. On the evening of September 17 the *fiestas patrias* officially closed with fireworks.

The Cinco de Mayo festival was next in importance. This event recalled the Mexican defeat of the French forces in Mexico in 1862. Disgruntled, exiled Mexican conservatives had invited Napoleon III of France to send the Hapsburg Maximilian and his wife, Carlota, to rule Mexico, in opposition to the reform movement led by Benito Juárez. Cinco de Mayo also celebrated the cultural ties that the *raza* (the "race" or "clan," i.e., Mexican Americans) shared with each other and with Mexico. Sporting costumes and banners, the people gathered to hear speeches, sing patriotic songs, and eat and dance. Sponsoring societies might include Sociedad Benevolencia Mexicana, Sociedad de la Unión, Sociedad Benito Juárez de Señoras y Señoritas, Sociedad Morelos, and others.

San Angelo has a long tradition of *fiestas patrias* celebrations. In 1910 the *raza* held a grand centennial parade of 300 people, with floats and buggies, and two-day festival at the Lake Concho Pavilion. People from miles around came to see the paintings of Mexican heroes and listen to a Mexican string band. By the 1920s the *fiestas patrias* in San Angelo followed a regular pattern. Every year the Mexican government called upon a Comisión Honorífica Mexicana[qv] to convene the Mexican-American people, who appointed a Comité Patriótico Mexicano[qv] to organize the *fiestas patrias* that year. They chose a location convenient to the barrio and large enough to accommodate the affair. Early *fiestas patrias* were held on the north side of San Angelo, near the Mexican-American neighborhood, but in the late 1920s the population shifted to a barrio on the south side. The program expanded to included more sporting events, such as baseball games, and school band concerts, oratory, and children's recitations. Radios, loudspeakers, public-address systems, and automobiles often complicated the event. Locations changed during the Great Depression.[qv] In 1946, Estanislado Sedeno, an active celebrant since 1932 and a member of the Comisión Honorífica and the Comité Patriótico Mexicano, was named Comisión president. He opened the 1946 *fiestas patrias* celebration in his front yard at 113 W. Avenue N, and Sedeno Plaza was subsequently the site of the *fiestas patrias* in San Angelo for twenty-seven years. On September 5, 1972, Estanislado Sedena returned to Sedeno Plaza, and Mayor C. S. "Chic" Conrad proclaimed the date Estanislado Sedeno Day.

Other Texas cities developed a *fiestas patrias* tradition. In Houston the celebrations began in the 1920s, when the Hispanic population grew large enough to require a Mexican consulate. The earliest celebrations included historic dramas at Teatro Azteca, Houston's first Hispanic theater, founded in 1927. The dramas included *Maximiliano*, a nineteenth-century play depicting Mexico's armed resistance to French imperialism. Later, such civic-minded groups as the Hispanic Club Familias Unidas, established in 1947, sponsored dances. The popular Baile Ranchero began in 1950, with participants wearing costumes representing different regions of Mexico and performing native dances. From the mid-twenties, *fiestas patrias* were held at the City Auditorium, following a parade through the downtown business district. The Mexican consul or his official representative frequently opened the Diez y Seis celebration on the night of September 15 by delivering a *grito de Dolores*. During the late 1960s, Juan Coronado was instrumental in making the annual parade down Houston's Main Street on September 16 a permanent event. The success of the "16th" festivities was ensured in 1971, when the Houston *Fiestas Patrias* organization, led by Rita and Armando Rodriguez, A. John Castillo, Johnny Mata and Rita Villanueva, obtained a charter.

Although primarily held to maintain Mexican-American cultural life and customs, *fiestas patrias* occasionally rendered a political service. In 1973 Mexican-American leaders clashed with the Mexican consul in declaring that the true function of their *fiestas patrias* was to promote their own unique Mexican-American heritage and lifestyle, and not that of Mexico. In 1977 and 1978 the Cinco de Mayo celebration in Houston evolved into political protests against police brutality and discrimination against the Hispanic population. In 1979 and 1980 *fiestas patrias* organizers used the celebration to honor prominent Hispanic citizens and civic leaders, and to give a Distinguished Mexican-American of the Year award. The *fiestas patrias*, like Juneteenth,[qv] are traditional celebrations rooted in historic events and devoted to preserving the multiethnic life of Texas.

BIBLIOGRAPHY: Charles A. Arnold, *Folklore, Manners and Customs of the Mexicans in San Antonio, Texas* (Austin: University of Texas Press, 1928). Arnoldo De León, *Ethnicity in the Sunbelt: A History of Mexican-Americans in Houston* (University of Houston Mexican American Studies Program, 1989). Arnoldo De León, *Las Fiestas Patrias: Biographic Notes on the Hispanic Presence in San Angelo, Texas* (San Antonio: Caravel Press, 1978). Arnoldo De León, *The Tejano Community, 1836–1900* (Albuquerque: University of New Mexico Press, 1982). Thomas H. Kreneck, *Del Pueblo: A Pictorial History of Houston's Hispanic Community* (Houston: Houston International University, 1989).

Rebeca Anne Todd Koenig

FIFE, TEXAS. Fife is on Elm Creek at the intersection of U.S. Highway 283 and Farm Road 765, eighteen miles north of Brady in northern McCulloch County. Robert Kay Finlay's mother named the site in 1882 in remembrance of her native Fifeshire, Scotland. A school was established at Fife in 1890 with Henry H. Smith as teacher. A post office opened in 1902. In 1914 Fife had two general stores, a cotton gin, and 200 residents. By the late 1940s the population had fallen to fifty, and the school had been consolidated with the Lohn district. The population was thirty-two in 1990.

BIBLIOGRAPHY: Jessie Laurie Barfoot, History of McCulloch County, Texas (M.A. thesis, University of Texas, 1937). Wayne Spiller, comp., *Handbook of McCulloch County History* (Vol. 1, Seagraves, Texas: Pioneer, 1976; vol. 2, Canyon, Texas: Staked Plains Press, 1986).

Vivian Elizabeth Smyrl

FIFTEEN-MILE COLETO CREEK. Fifteen-Mile Coleto Creek, also known simply as Fifteenmile Creek, rises a mile northeast of Yorktown in west central DeWitt County (at 29°04′ N, 97°34′ W) and runs southeast for forty miles to its mouth on the Guadalupe River, six miles south of Victoria in central Victoria County (at 29°00′ N, 97°31′ W). It forms portions of the DeWitt-Goliad and Goliad-Victoria county lines, as it flows through flat to rolling terrain surfaced by clay and sandy loam that supports mixed hardwoods and pines. The stream was known as Coleto Creek as early as 1836, but in 1850, when Clinton became the county seat of DeWitt County, the head streams were named Three-Mile Coleto, Five-Mile Coleto, Twelve-Mile Coleto, Fifteen-Mile Coleto, and Eighteen-Mile Coleto. The names signified the distance from the streams to the courthouse door at Clinton. Below the junction of Twelve-Mile Coleto with Fifteen-Mile Coleto in northwestern Victoria County, the stream is known simply as Coleto Creek.

FIFTH CREEK (Lipscomb County). Fifth Creek rises eight miles south of Darrouzett in central Lipscomb County (at 36°22′ N, 100°20′ W) and runs south for seven miles to its mouth on Wolf Creek, three miles west of Lipscomb (at 36°14′ N, 100°19′ W). It was once within the Seven K Ranch[qv] range. The stream traverses flat to rolling terrain with some local escarpments, surfaced by thick, fine sandy loams that support mesquite and grasses.

BIBLIOGRAPHY: Clinton Leon Paine, The History of Lipscomb County (M.A. thesis, West Texas State College, 1941).

FIFTH FERRYING GROUP. In October 1941 the ferrying of planes, training of personnel, and movement of air freight began on a limited scale at Hensley Field, fifteen miles west of Dallas (*see* NAVAL AIR STATION, DALLAS). On May 26, 1942, the Midwest Sector of the Air Corps Ferrying Command became the Fifth Ferrying Group, and on September 28 activities were transferred to Love Field[qv] in Dallas. Fewer than a hundred enlisted men formed the original cadre, and a local recruiting program was initiated. The group had its basic training and indoctrination camp at White Rock Lake, in eastern Dallas.

The primary mission was the ferrying of military planes from factory areas to domestic stations and fighting fronts. Functions in addition to ferrying included training, transport, servicing, and post maintenance. A complete training program for the crew of pilots, navigators, flight engineers, radio operators, and weather observers was formulated to qualify the crews to fly "anything, anywhere, anytime." The first important course was for B-24s. Later courses included A-20s, B-25s, C-47s, and B-29s. Because of its proximity to several great aircraft factories, the Fifth Ferrying Group became a dispatching system for strategic domestic and foreign ferrying routes, and its headquarters became a stopover and servicing point for planes being ferried by other groups of the Ferrying Division. In February 1943 the Fifth Ferry Group assumed supervision of nine subordinate units and service stations of the First Army Airway Communication System Wing, located in Texas, New Mexico, and Oklahoma. In the summer of 1944 the group assumed responsibility for the newly established Military Air Transport, which was to transport war supplies and materials, move personnel to and from assignments, and evacuate war wounded from coastal ports of entry to general hospitals.

The personnel of the group comprised both men and women, civilian and military. The Women's Airforce Service Pilots^{qv} were civilians, and the Women's Army Corps were military. At the end of World War II^{qv} the Fifth Ferrying Group was discontinued.

BIBLIOGRAPHY: *The Flying V* (Dallas: Love Field Post Exchange), September 24, October 8, 1943, September 23, 1945, May 7, 1946.

Albert B. Luckey

FIFTH MILITARY DISTRICT. By the First Reconstruction Act of March 2, 1867, the United States Congress divided the defeated South, already restored under presidential Reconstruction,^{qv} into five military districts, of which Louisiana and Texas, under Gen. Philip Henry Sheridan^{qv} at New Orleans, constituted the Fifth Military District. For readmission to the Union under the congressional plan, each unreconstructed state was required to ratify the Fourteenth Amendment and elect by universal manhood suffrage (excluding prewar officeholders who had served the Confederacy) a convention to write a constitution acceptable both to the state's voters and the Congress. A Second Reconstruction Act of March 23 added procedural details, particularly regarding voter registration, and required that a majority of a state's voters approve the holding of a convention. And a Third Reconstruction Act of July 19 further clarified procedure and empowered district commanders such as Sheridan to remove state officials impeding Reconstruction. These acts of 1867—representing to some extent a collusion of Republican congressional leaders and the War Department—plus other influences such as violence and racial hostility provided the context within which the commanders of the Fifth Military District and other districts operated.

Sheridan and his subordinate, Gen. Charles Griffin,^{qv} who headed military affairs in Texas, immediately interpreted the first two Reconstruction acts in such a manner as to proceed with what would be clearly authorized only in the third act. Sheridan relieved Louisiana officials in March; and in April Griffin initiated a county-by-county cataloging of acceptable potential Texas officeholders. On July 30 Sheridan replaced Texas governor James W. Throckmorton^{qv} with Elisha Marshall Pease,^{qv} who only recently had helped found the state's Republican party.^{qv} But before the generals could institute a mass purge, Griffin died of yellow fever in Galveston and President Andrew Johnson replaced Sheridan with General Winfield Scott Hancock,^{qv} a Democrat.

Because Hancock did not assume his command in New Orleans until late November the district stayed under the senior officer there, Gen. Joseph A. Mower,^{qv} an aggressive Reconstructionist, who busied himself in Louisiana. Meanwhile Griffin's successor, Gen. Joseph J. Reynolds,^{qv} a close friend of army general in chief Ulysses S. Grant, rushed to replace several hundred officeholders with Republicans. When Hancock subsequently protested, Grant advised against reversing Reynolds's decision. Although Hancock became an instant favorite of the district's conservatives, he allowed the election of the Constitutional Convention of 1868–69^{qv} under a registration that had been controlled by Reynolds, despite allegations that the military-appointed local registration boards had acted illegally and unfairly in disfranchising about 10,000 former Confederates. In March 1868, after serving only four months, Hancock was granted a transfer, and Gen. Robert C. Buchanan, the senior officer in Louisiana, succeeded him.

In June, after fulfilling the conditions of the congressional Reconstruction acts, Louisiana gained readmission to the Union, leaving only Texas in the Fifth Military District under Reynolds. Reynolds served until Grant was elected president in November, when Johnson replaced him with Gen. Edward R. S. Canby,^{qv} whom in turn Grant replaced with Reynolds upon Grant's inauguration in March 1869. Reynolds, opposing further disfranchisement or division of the state, initially favored moderate Texas Republicans, who supported the election of former provisional governor Andrew Jackson Hamilton^{qv} for governor. By midsummer, however, Reynolds turned on the moderates, either for personal reasons because of their failure to back him for a United States Senate seat, or because of the moderate Republicans' flirtation with white Democrats, whom they needed due to the Radical Republican control of the black vote. At Reynolds's suggestion, Grant set the gubernatorial election late in 1869, allowing Radical Republicans an extended period to organize, and he purged the Hamilton-Pease federal officeholders, replacing them with radicals, who supported the candidacy of Edmund Jackson Davis,^{qv} recently president of the constitutional convention.

President Grant's action, plus that of Reynolds in purging state and local officeholders who backed the Hamilton-Pease faction, caused Governor Pease to resign on September 30. Reynolds declined to fill the position before the November election, in which Davis, with Reynolds's aid, won by a small margin. Reynolds called a session of the provisional legislature in February 1870 to apply for the readmission of Texas to the Union, a session that also elected the state's United States senators. He was a candidate for a short time before withdrawing his name. In April Texas was readmitted to the Union, and the Fifth Military District ceased to exist.

BIBLIOGRAPHY: Charles W. Ramsdell, *Reconstruction in Texas* (New York: Columbia University Press, 1910; rpt., Austin: Texas State Historical Association, 1970). Robert W. Shook, Federal Occupation and Administration of Texas, 1865–1870 (Ph.D. dissertation, North Texas State University, 1970).

James Alex Baggett

FIFTH WARD, HOUSTON. The Fifth Ward, east of downtown Houston, is bounded by Buffalo Bayou on the south, Lockwood Drive on the east, Liberty Road on the north, and Jensen Drive on the west. The site was sparsely inhabited before the Civil War.^{qv} It was subsequently settled by freedmen and became known as the Fifth Ward in 1866, when an alderman was elected to represent the community in the Houston city government. At the time, half the population was black and half white. By 1870 the population of the ward comprised 561 white and 578 black residents. Two schools, one black and one white, corresponded to the roughly equal segments of the ward's population in 1876. Mount Vernon United Methodist Church, founded in 1865 by former slave Rev. Toby Gregg, is the oldest institution in the ward. Five other churches are over 100 years old: Pleasant Grove Baptist, Mount Pleasant Baptist, Sloan Memorial United Methodist, Payne Chapel Methodist, and First Shiloh Baptist. The Fifth Ward was also the site of a saloon named for Carry Nation,^{qv} which, after considerable damage resulting from a dispute with the owner over the name, was subsequently known as the "Carnation." In the 1880s the ward enjoyed a boom following the construction of repair shops for the newly built Southern Pacific Railroad. Growth was interrupted by a fire in 1891 at the Phoenix Lumber Mill and another in 1912 that burned 119 houses, 116 boxcars, nine oil tanks, thirteen plants, and St. Patrick's Catholic Church and school.

Eventually, the Fifth Ward population became predominantly black. At Frenchtown,^{qv} a four-square-block neighborhood in the ward, 500 blacks of French and Spanish descent from Louisiana organized a community in 1922. Black-owned businesses, including a pharmacy, a dentist's office, an undertaking parlor, a theater, and several barbershops, operated after 1900 on Lyons Avenue and numbered forty by 1925. Working-class blacks were primarily employed within walking distance of the ward; many worked for the Southern Pacific Railroad or at the Houston Ship Channel.^{qv} Others commuted across town to work as domestics and servants for wealthy Houstonians. By 1927 Phillis Wheatley High School in the ward, with 2,600 students and sixty teachers, was one of the largest black high schools in America. Other new businesses developed in the 1930s, including printing plants, photography studios, and the Club Matinee, which came to be known as the Cotton Club of the South. Local businessman Grand Duke Crawford organized the Fifth Ward Civic Club.

Houston's second housing project for African Americans,qv the Kelly Court Housing Project, opened after World War II.qv Early community activists included Lonnie Smithqv and Lilly Portley. Peacock Records, a black-owned recording company, started in the ward, as did C. F. Smith Electric Company, one of the state's early licensed electrical-contracting companies. Finnigan Park, the second public park for blacks in Houston, opened in the community in the postwar years, and the Julia C. Hester House, a black community center, began service. Nat Q. Henderson, long-time principal of Bruce Elementary School, was the mayor of the Fifth Ward and became known for his leadership.

With passage of integration laws in the 1960s, however, many residents left the community seeking wider opportunities. The Fifth Ward is noted for training many prominent athletes. Musicians from the ward include Arnett Cobb,qv Milton Larkin, and Illinois Jacquet. Barbara Jordan and Mickey Leland, members of Congress, graduated from Wheatley High School. In the 1990s efforts were being made to preserve the Houston Place, a seventy-five-year-old gathering center.

BIBLIOGRAPHY: Marie Phelps McAshan, *A Houston Legacy: On the Corner of Main and Texas* (Houston: Gulf, 1985). David G. McComb, *Houston: The Bayou City* (Austin: University of Texas Press, 1969; rev. ed., *Houston: A History*, 1981). WPA Writers Program, *Houston* (Houston: Anson Jones, 1942).
Diana J. Kleiner

FIFTY CENT ACT. The Fifty Cent Act, advocated by Governor Oran M. Robertsqv and approved by the Texas legislature on July 14, 1879, provided for selling Texas public lands at fifty cents an acre, one-half the proceeds to be used to pay the public debt and the other half to establish a permanent school fund. The act opened to settlement about fifty-two West Texas counties, out of which the state sold 3,201,283 acres for $1,600,641.55. On January 22, 1883, the Fifty Cent Act was repealed as a public necessity resulting from fraudulent speculation in the land.

BIBLIOGRAPHY: Hans Peter Nielsen Gammel, comp., *Laws of Texas, 1822–1897* (10 vols., Austin: Gammel, 1898). Texas Legislature, *House Journal*, 16th Leg., extra sess., 1879.
Alice Gray Upchurch

FILES VALLEY, TEXAS. Files Valley, or Files, was on Farm Road 66 and Valley Branch fourteen miles northeast of Hillsboro in northeastern Hill County. Originally the community was called Eureka Valley, but it was renamed on November 19, 1879, for David Sidney Files, who built the first house at the site in 1846. Many artesian wells in the area supplied soft but slightly sulfurous water. The community received a post office with the name Files in 1880 and by 1890 had a population of fifty, a church, a district school, a general store, a steam cotton gin, blacksmiths, carpenters, and physicians. In 1905 the school had sixty-one pupils. The railroads bypassed the community, however. In 1906 the Southwestern Home and School for Orphans was founded in Files. It remained into the 1980s, when it was known as the Presbyterian Children's Home. In 1907 the post office was withdrawn from the community. In the 1930s Files had a population of 100 and three businesses. The population remained at this level until the 1970s, when it dropped to fifty and no businesses remained. Afterward the community has been called Files Valley rather than Files. In 1990 Files Valley remained on maps as a community, and the population was still fifty. A cemetery, a church, and the Presbyterian Children's Home remained there.

BIBLIOGRAPHY: Hill County Historical Commission, *A History of Hill County, Texas, 1853-1980* (Waco: Texian, 1980).
Lisa C. Maxwell

FILIBUSTER CREEK. Filibuster Creek, formerly known as Caddo Creek, rises in the southeast corner of Young County (at 33°03′ N, 98°26′ W) and runs south for about 3½ miles to its mouth on the Brazos River (at 32°59′ N, 98°27′ W). The stream, fed by Caddo Springs, traverses an area of rolling hills where clay and sandy loams support scrub brush, mesquite, cacti, and grasses. Caddo Indian villages existed in the area in the mid-1800s; hence the early name of the stream.

BIBLIOGRAPHY: Gunnar Brune, *Springs of Texas*, Vol. 1 (Fort Worth: Branch-Smith, 1981).

FILIGONIA, TEXAS. Filigonia was at the junction of the Missouri Pacific Railroad and Farm Road 490 on the Hidalgo-Willacy county line, 1½ miles northeast of Hargill. The town was built by the Missouri Texas Land and Irrigation Company in an effort to develop the area. The company dug a well and erected a clubhouse to entertain and lodge prospective buyers. The clubhouse was located on what is now Farm Road 490 just north of the county line in Willacy County. A town began to spring up around the clubhouse and well, and in 1915 a post office was opened with Anna Richards as postmistress. The town is said to have been named after Filigonio Cuellar, a prominent resident. During its peak period the community supported a school, a dairy, two stores, and a garage. However, shortly after its founding the area experienced a serious drought and attacks by bandits. Among the victims killed by the bandits was Cuellar. Soldiers were stationed in the area to protect the townspeople, but the majority of residents left rather than face further hardships. The post office was closed in 1926 and moved to Hargill, and the settlement was apparently abandoned.
William E. Richards

FILISOLA, VICENTE 1789–1850). Vicente Filisola, military officer, was born in Ravello, Italy, in 1789 and went to Spain quite early, presumably with his family. He joined the Spanish army on March 17, 1804, and was in the military for the rest of his life. Because of his dedication, six years later he became a second lieutenant. He went to Mexico or New Spain in 1811, the year after Miguel Hidalgo y Costilla'sqv proclamation of independence in the famous "*Grito de Dolores*" of September 10, 1810. Filisola, a loyalist devoted to the Spanish cause, was made captain of artillery in 1813 and the next year captain of grenadiers. He won the confidence and friendship of Agustín de Iturbide,qv and through this association became a leading military figure in Mexico. Supportive of Iturbide in his Plan de Iguala and his declaration as emperor of Mexico, and in command of the Trigarante ("Three Guarantees") army, Filisola was promoted to brigadier general and ordered to Central America to bring that region into Iturbide's empire. Filisola gained control of Central America only to have to relinquish it once Iturbide fell from power.

Despite his support of Iturbide, Filisola held a number of important posts in the Republic of Mexico during the 1820s, and in January 1833 he was named commander of the Eastern Provincias Internas. Because of a desperate illness he relinquished his command for a time, but was later able to resume his duties. As a minor empresario,qv Filisola, on October 12, 1831, received a grant to settle in Texas 600 families who were not Anglo-Americans. The area of his grant in East Texas included part of the land granted to the Cherokee Indians in 1823. Filisola failed to fulfill his contract with the government. When Antonio López de Santa Annaqv organized his campaign against Texas, he commissioned Filisola as second in command of his army. Thus, with the capture of Santa Anna at the battle of San Jacinto,qv he was faced with the formidable task of withdrawing the Mexican forces from Texas. Despite considerable opposition from other officers, Filisola carried out Santa Anna's orders and began to retreat. By the time he received instructions from the Mexican government on May 28, he had already ordered the evacuation of San Antonio and had ratified the public treaty of Velasco, and his army had crossed the Nueces.

Upon receiving the government's order to preserve conquests already made, he offered to countermarch, but because of the condition of the Mexican troops the retreat continued to Matamoros. On June 12, José de Urrea[qv] replaced Filisola in general command; Filisola resigned his own command to Juan José Andrade[qv] and retired to Saltillo. Filisola was accused of being a coward and a traitor in overseeing the withdrawal of the Mexican troops, and he faced formal charges upon his return to Mexico. The general successfully defended himself before the court-martial and was exonerated in June 1841. Upon his return to Mexico in 1836, Filisola published a defense of his conduct in Texas. It was translated into English and published by the Republic of Texas[qv] in 1837. During the Mexican War[qv] Filisola commanded one of three divisions of the Mexican army. In 1928 Carlos E. Castañeda[qv] published a translation of Filisola's account in *The Mexican Side of the Texas Revolution*. Filisola's most complete account of the Texas Revolution[qv] is his *Memoirs for the History of the War in Texas*, which was not published in English translation until 1985. Filisola died on July 23, 1850, in Mexico City during a cholera epidemic.

BIBLIOGRAPHY: Hubert Howe Bancroft, *History of the North Mexican States and Texas* (2 vols., San Francisco: History Company, 1886, 1889). Eugene C. Barker, ed., *The Austin Papers* (3 vols., Washington: GPO, 1924–28). Valentine J. Belfiglio, *The Italian Experience in Texas* (Austin: Eakin Press, 1983). Vertical Files, Barker Texas History Center, University of Texas at Austin.   A. Wallace Woolsey

FILM INDUSTRY. The origins of the film industry date to the first public demonstrations in 1891 of Thomas Edison's Kinetoscope, a "peep" cabinet in which the viewer saw moving images generated from a continuous roll of celluloid film. Three years later the industry began in Texas. In its earliest stages the activity of making films in Texas was not so much an industry as an entrepreneurial phenomenon. Individuals and small companies were involved in introducing a new medium to an audience unfamiliar with cinema. One of the state's first Kinetoscope parlors opened in Austin on November 10, 1894. Between that date and 1900, technical improvements made possible the projection of film onto a screen or wall, transforming it into a mass medium. Interest in the new medium spread quickly; the first public screenings of projected film in the southern United States were held in Virginia and Atlanta, Georgia, in 1895 and in New Orleans in 1896. Although the fact cannot be definitively established, public demonstrations of Thomas Edison's Vitascope in Dallas on February 1 and 2, 1897, were probably the first instances of projected film in Texas. The program at the Dallas Opera House consisted of scenes of a Mexican duel, a lynching, a fire rescue, and Niagara Falls. In Austin, projected film debuted at a tent show on January 10, 1900.

The first motion pictures made in Texas did not tell stories, but documented events and simple activities. The earliest documented and extant moving film shot in Texas is of the aftermath of the Galveston hurricane of 1900.[qv] Cameraman G. W. "Billy" Bitzer of the New York–based Biograph Company arrived at Texas City on September 13, and in the following days shot eight scenes of the destruction. Other short scenes made in Texas at that time, probably by Bitzer, include a passing train and oil wells at Beaumont. Excluding entities that did not apply for incorporation through the office of the Texas secretary of state, the earliest documentable company established in Texas for the purposes of making and distributing motion pictures was the Wheelan-Loper Film Company of Dallas and San Antonio, incorporated on July 18, 1908, as the J. D. Wheelan Film Company. The enterprise was started by John D. Wheelan, exclusive Texas representative of the monopolistic Motion Picture Patents Company, and, later, the General Film Company and the Mutual Film Corporation of Texas. Although the enterprise was formed primarily to distribute the films of a number of domestic and foreign companies, part of the capital stock is listed in the company's charter records in terms of equipment and supplies, including cameras, lighting apparatus, and reels of unexposed film stock. The Wheelan-Loper Film Company ceased doing business after the teens and was declared inactive and dissolved on May 19, 1950. Another early film production company, and the earliest non-Texas production company to operate in Texas, was Star-Film, established in early 1910 in San Antonio and operated by Gaston Méliès, brother of pioneer French filmmaker Georges Méliès. Méliès's choice of Texas, based upon its favorable climate, variety of geographical settings, and history, is an early example of outside interest in the state's unique qualities for filmmaking. At the Star Film Ranch, Méliès made approximately seventy titles before moving operations to California in May 1911. Also in 1910, brothers Paul W. and Wesley Hope Tilley[qv] started the Satex Film Company in San Antonio. The business was moved to Austin in 1911 and produced several features and shorts, some released nationally. Production ceased in July 1913.

Other studios operated briefly in the San Antonio area. Patrick Sylvester McGeeney (lawman, Western genre novelist, and actor) organized the Lone Star Company on September 2, 1915, and produced several films. The company was abandoned briefly, then reorganized in May 1917 as the Shamrock Photoplay Corporation. It produced numerous feature films and serials, many of which achieved national distribution. Its production facilities were also leased to out-of-state companies conducting on-location shoots in San Antonio. Production ceased in early fall 1923. Also operating for a brief period in San Antonio were the Neal Hart Production Company (1921–22) and the Sunset Corporation, a studio and processing laboratory branch of a New York–based company. Other attempts at establishing studios in Texas included one by character actor and San Antonio native Maclyn Arbuckle,[qv] financed by William Clifford Hogg,[qv] and National Pictures' Kier-Phillips Productions, which produced numerous features between 1926 and 1956. The Jamieson Film Company was founded in Dallas in 1916 and became an established film-production company in the Southwest. In 1972 the company was absorbed into the Masters Film Company of Houston. Sack Amusement Enterprises, of San Antonio and later Dallas, was formed in 1920 by Alfred N. Sack. The business, a combination theater chain and production company, was a major producer and distributor of features and short subjects starring and produced for African Americans[qv] between 1937 and 1945. Sack Amusement Enterprises was declared an inactive corporation in 1979 (see BLACK FILMMAKING).

Despite fitful but encouraging beginnings, Texas could not compete as a base of film production with the East and West coasts. By the middle teens, centers of film production had become firmly established in the Hollywood–Los Angeles area in California, and in the New York–New Jersey area on the East Coast, thus lessening the likelihood of studios establishing permanent residence in Texas. Instead, the film industry of the state for many years consisted of Hollywood and East Coast–based companies using various Texas locales for location shootings. This trend began in Spring 1918, when Samuel Goldwyn filmed *Heart of the Sunset* in the San Antonio area for the Rex Beach Pictures Company of New York. Much more publicized was a larger production in November 1923, when the Fox Film Company shot exteriors for *The Warrens of Virginia*, also in San Antonio. Clever use of existing sites and structures, natural surroundings, and local extras reduced production costs for the studios and encouraged several to film in the state. The army and air force bases of the San Antonio area, for example, provided locations for *The Big Parade* (1925), *The Rough Riders* (1927), *Wings* (1927), which won the first Oscar award for best picture, *West Point of the Air* (1934), *I Wanted Wings* (1940), and *Air Cadet* (1951). Film production in Texas was sporadic from the 1920s through the 1960s. A true industry did not begin to mature in the state until the 1970s. Approximately five major productions were shot in Texas during the 1920s, only five in the 1930s, fourteen in the 1940s, nine in the 1950s, and eleven in the 1960s. Although Texas would seem a logical place to make movies in the popular Western movie genre, only a handful were shot on location within the state. Authentic Texas landscapes provided the backdrop for several notable Westerns, such as *North of 36* (1924), the progenitor of cattle drive-movies, which was filmed at a ranch near Houston; one of its two remakes, *The Texans* (1938), was filmed in South Texas. Other noteworthy Westerns of this period shot in Texas included *Sundown* (1924) and *The Big Show* (1936). In a smaller but vastly popular genre, the story of the battle of the Alamo qv has been filmed ten times in Texas, beginning with Gaston Mélies's *The Immortal Alamo* (1911), which was shot in San Antonio. Several versions, including *The Alamo* (1959), *Seguin* (1981), *Lone Star* (1984), *The Alamo: Thirteen Days to Glory* (1986), and *Alamo . . . The Price of Freedom* (1988), have made use of a historically accurate replica of the chapel-fortress in Brackettville.

The turning point in on-location filming in Texas occurred during the 1950s and after, when the major motion picture projects *Viva Zapata!* (1952), *Giant* (1956), John Wayne's *The Alamo* (1959), *Hud* (1962), and *Bonnie and Clyde* (1967) attracted national attention and cultivated an interest that has not waned. By the 1970s the film industry outside the state coordinated location shooting within the state through the Texas Film Commission,qv an office established in 1971 by Governor Preston Smith. More than 100 movie projects were filmed in the state during the 1970s; in the 1980s the number more than doubled to 247. In 1992, 28 film projects were shot in Texas. A boom in Texas filmmaking occurred in the late 1970s and 1980s and carried over into the 1990s as a number of Hollywood-established Texans, especially writers and directors, reintroduced Texas as a shooting location. L. M. "Kit" Carson, Horton Foote, Warren E. Skaaren,qv William Whitliff, and others, responsible for *Barbarosa* and *Raggedy Man* (1980), *Places in the Heart* (1983), and *Lonesome Dove* (1988), helped attract film and video crews that bring many millions of dollars in revenue to the state. Other movies shot in Texas include *Arrowhead* (1952), *State Fair* (1962), *The Last Picture Show* (1971), *Leatherface: Texas Chainsaw Massacre* (1974), *Outlaw Blues* (1977), *The Best Little Whorehouse in Texas* (1981), *Silkwood* (1984), and *JFK* (1991). In 1992, total gross budgets were estimated at $143,207,800. Foreign and independent directors have also capitalized on Texas. Their films include Louis Malle's *Alamo Bay* (1984), Wim Wenders's *Paris, Texas* (1983), Paul Verhoven's *Robocop* (1987), and Richard Linklater's cult film *Slacker* (1990).

Because an estimated 50 percent of a production's budget is spent in the location filming area, filmmaking boosts local economies. Film production puts money in circulation as film and tape professionals, local talent, properties, sound stages, rentals, and facilities are utilized. Dollar figures reflecting the impact of film production in Texas before the mid-1970s are elusive and not readily available. In 1977 at least $40 million was spent on film and videotape-related goods and services in the state, and the following year the figure increased by about $20 million. More complete records are available for the 1980s, based on gross sales and gross receipts as reported by the Texas comptroller of public accounts. Film and tape-related goods and services are defined by a classification scheme known as the Standard Industrial Code. In 1984 gross sales reached just over $128.8 million; four years later in 1988, they totaled over $244 million. During the first two quarters of 1992 more than $151 million was earned in gross sales for film and tape-related businesses in the state.

BIBLIOGRAPHY: Austin *Statesman,* November 10, 1894. James R. Buchanan, "A Look at the Texas Film Industry," *Texas Business Review* 46 (January 1972). Dallas *Morning News,* March 19, 1978. Don Graham, *Cowboys and Cadillacs: How Hollywood Looks at Texas* (Austin: Texas Monthly Press, 1983). Joseph North, *Early Development of the Motion Picture* (New York: Arno Press, 1973). *Texas Production Manual* (Austin: Texas Film Commission, 1993). Frank Thompson, *Alamo Movies* (East Berlin, Pennsylvania: Old Mill Books, 1991).

John H. Slate

FINANCE COMMISSION OF TEXAS. The Finance Commission of Texas was established in 1943 to act as the supervisor and policy maker for the state Banking Department, Savings and Loan Department, and Office of the Consumer Credit Commissioner. A nine-member board, consisting of two banking executives, two savings and loan executives, and five business representatives, is appointed by the governor for overlapping six-year terms. The commission appoints the executive directors of the three agencies and conducts examinations of their financial activities to submit an annual report to the governor. The board also approves departmental budgets and reports to legislative committees about financial issues. The commission is generally responsible for determining regulation policies for the state financial industries. The agencies of the Banking and Savings and Loan departments and the Consumer Credit Commissionerqv furnish support services and operating funds to the Finance Commission. Almost thirty employees worked for the commission in 1991.

Laurie E. Jasinski

FINANCES OF THE TEXAS REVOLUTION. The public financial administration of Texas before the Texas Revolutionqv is vaguely understood. Colonists were required to pay the state a small fee for land, and titles had to be written on stamped paper. Receipts from these sources were collected by local municipal officers and in due time, no doubt, were paid into the state treasury. The colonists were exempt from federal tariff duties until 1830, and thereafter the tariff administration was intermittent. When the revolution began, there was no accumulation of federal funds in Texas, and only negligible state fees were held by local collectors.

The provisional governmentqv passed through several stages during the revolution and at each stage faced the duty of providing supplies for military forces in the field. Briefly, the government used the receipts from stamped paper and land fees; obtained some goods on credit from local merchants, chiefly from the firm of Thomas F. McKinney and Samuel M. Williamsqqv and accepted some subscriptions and donations from citizens. It passed a tariff act and took steps to collect tonnage and ad valorem duties, with little or no effect. It authorized a loan for $1 million and appointed a commission consisting of Stephen F. Austin, William I. Wharton, and Branch T. Archerqqv to solicit loans and aid in the United States. In the meantime individuals and mass meetings made cash and commodity contributions in the United States.

Austin, Archer, and Wharton arranged two loans in New Orleans, one for $200,000 and the other for $50,000, on which they received a total down payment of possibly $60,000. The lenders had the option of taking repayment in land at the rate of fifty cents an acre, but the provisional government did not ratify the contract, and further installments were withheld by the lenders. Volunteers received land bounties as an inducement to enlistment, and ultimately most of the cost of the revolution, estimated at $1.25 million, was borne by the public lands.

BIBLIOGRAPHY: Eugene C. Barker, "Finances of the Texas Revolution," *Political Science Quarterly* 19 (October 1904). Edmund Thornton Miller, *A Financial History of Texas* (Bulletin No. 37, Austin: University of Texas, 1916).

Eugene C. Barker

FINCASTLE, TEXAS. Fincastle, on Farm Road 315 four miles north of Poyner in southeastern Henderson County, was settled in 1848. A post office was established there on March 6, 1855, with Daniel R. McRae as postmaster. Apparently McRae proposed the name Fincastle, after a town in Scotland. Seven years later a town plat was drawn up by John and Mary Tindel for a site that the Tindels purchased from Dr. P. P. Adams in 1851. Through the years the town saw a succession of general stores, a drugstore from which several doctors practiced medicine, a blacksmith shop, a cotton gin and gristmill, and a well and wagonyard where farmers could park their wagons.

Some stores sold whiskey, although the Tindels stipulated in a deed to Thomas Hendon on March 22, 1862, that "if he sold any spiritous liquors to the injury of the schools and church" the title to the lots would be void.

The first school was begun by the Tindels in a small log building on their property. It was followed by one established by Dr. P. P. Adams. Then Tindel put up a larger building for use both as a school and church. The land for both the church and a large cemetery across the road was later formally deeded to the town by Lydia Frances Tindel Parmer from her inheritance from John and Mary Tindel. The church building was used by various congregations on alternate Sundays and as a school until the 1930s. It was used in 1980 for elections and for such community meetings as the annual memorial on the first Sunday in August. In the early 1990s burials continued to occur in the Fincastle Cemetery.

The Confederate flag was raised in Fincastle in 1861, and the first Confederate company in the county was organized there in May 1861. During the Civil War,[qv] the Confederate government built a quartermaster storage depot on Lot 1, Fincastle. At this time, the vicinity was reputed to be the most prosperous part of the county. As the war progressed, several planters from Louisiana and Arkansas moved their slaves to the Fincastle area to keep them out of reach of the Union Army.

By 1884 Fincastle had three steam cotton gins, three churches, and a population of 100. Cotton was the principal shipment out of the area. By 1896 a local sawmill had been established and the population had risen to 150. Fincastle's decline came when the Texas and New Orleans Railroad built south of the town in 1900–01 and diverted commerce to other centers. Many Fincastle residents moved to Athens or Poyner, both of which had rail connections. The post office was discontinued in 1907. In 1929 Fincastle had a store, a school, a church, and two families. The reported population stood at 100 in 1939 and at forty from 1949 to 1969, the last year for which a figure was available. In 1985 the Fincastle Cemetery and church received a Texas historical marker. In 1989 the name was still preserved in Fincastle Lake and Fincastle Nursery and Farms. Fincastle was listed as a community in 1990, but without census figures.

BIBLIOGRAPHY: J. J. Faulk, *History of Henderson County* (Athens, Texas: Athens Review Printing, 1926). Winnie McGaughey Reynolds, *The History of Henderson County* (M.A. thesis, East Texas State Teachers College, 1952).
Kathryn Brown

FINCH, JOSEPH HENEAGE (1849–1885). Joseph Heneage Finch, English nobleman and sportsman, was born in Middlesex, England, to Heneage and Jane (Wightwick) Finch on February 21, 1849. Heneage was the sixth earl of Aylesford; Joseph, the seventh earl, was a minor but legendary figure on the West Texas frontier. He married Edith Williams, the daughter of a member of Parliament, in 1871. They had two daughters. In late 1874 Finch lavishly entertained the prince of Wales, the future Edward VII, at his estate, Packington Hall, outside London. Finch quickly became a member of the prince's inner circle of raucous intimates, infamous for their materialistic, extravagant lives.

The prince invited Finch to accompany him on a seventeen-week goodwill tour of India in 1875–76. Though he arranged the sporting events and served as his sponsor's personal hunting guide, Finch abruptly returned home in early 1876 to confront his unfaithful wife and her lover. The divorce suit that followed involved the highest members of English society and resulted in Finch's being exiled, in effect, by Queen Victoria herself.

No longer welcome in polite company in England, he dropped out of sight, but in late summer 1883 he arrived at the West Texas cattle town of Big Spring. There he bought a 2,500-acre ranch north of town and a $40,000 herd of cattle on "range delivery," or sight unseen. Because the rustic boomtown had few conveniences, in quick succession Finch bought a hotel and a bar, the former, at least, at an inflated price. He also built a meat market.

Though initially unable to gain the acceptance of the local cowboy-cattleman fraternity, the earl won them over in time by his generosity with his liquor, by his being introduced formally at roundup by a prominent cattleman, and by his pleasant personality. He spent his waking hours partying, drinking, and hunting, to the neglect of his ranch and stock. Although mysterious and remote, he became a valued and respected member of the community, for the frontiersmen did not pry into one's personal life. On January 13, 1885, after hosting a two-week party that was spoken of in awe for years, he unexpectedly died. His hard drinking had apparently caught up with him.

Finch's significance, however, does not lie in his self-destructive antics but rather in his being a classic example of a little-publicized but stock frontier character who, along with the buffalo hunter, Indian fighter, and cowboy, helped settle the frontier West—the remittance man. Few in number, perhaps never more than a few hundred, remittance men were typically wealthy Europeans, mostly Englishmen, who for various reasons were exiled to reform or to perish, to the remote regions of the world, where they regularly received money (remittances) from home. On the United States frontier, where men were expected to be rugged individualists, these outcasts were generally not admired. Finch was an exception.

BIBLIOGRAPHY: James I. Fenton, "Big Spring's Amazing Tenderfoot: The Earl of Aylesford," West Texas Historical Association *Year Book* 55 (1979).
James I. Fenton

FINCH, TEXAS. Finch, a farming community off Farm Road 1129 fourteen miles northeast of Corsicana in northern Navarro County, was established before 1900. By the early 1900s a school was in operation there, and in 1906 it had an enrollment of thirty-six. At its height in the mid-1930s Finch had four churches, two schools, a cemetery, and a number of houses. Many residents moved away after World War II,[qv] and by the mid-1960s only a school, two churches, a cemetery, and a few scattered houses remained at the site. In the early 1990s Finch was a dispersed rural community.
Christopher Long

FINGER, GEORGE W. (1857–1899). George W. Finger, attorney and land commissioner, was born on June 21, 1857, in Tarrant County, Texas, the son of Louis and Christena (Pless) Finger. He entered Mansfield College at age seventeen and graduated three years later. He then studied law in several Fort Worth law offices and was admitted to the bar in 1878. On December 19, 1880, he married Jessie L. Butler; they had at least three children. Finger spent the next several years in Arlington, during which time he was elected the first mayor of the town. He then moved to Fort Worth and practiced law in the firm of Stedman, Ayres, and Finger until 1891. He served as reading clerk for the Eighteenth, Nineteenth, Twentieth, and Twenty-second legislatures. He was chief clerk in the Twenty-third Legislature and temporarily presided over the House of the Twenty-fourth Legislature. In 1894 he became legal examiner for the General Land Office and on January 16, 1899, began his duties as land commissioner. Finger's brief service as commissioner did not allow time for any major changes in the land office. He preferred landless buyers as recipients of state lands. He died on May 4, 1899, at Marlin, Texas, and was buried at Arlington.

BIBLIOGRAPHY: E. H. Loughery, *Personnel of the Texas State Government for 1885* (Austin: Snyder, 1885). Garry Mauro, *Land Commissioners of Texas* (Austin: Texas General Land Office, 1986). C. W. Raines, *Year Book for Texas* (2 vols., Austin: Gammel-Statesman, 1902, 1903).
William N. Todd IV and Gerald Knape

FINGER, JOSEPH (1887–1953). Joseph Finger, architect, was born on March 7, 1887, in Bielitz, Austria, the son of Hani (Steifter) and Henri Finger. Finger received his primary, secondary, and technical education in Bielitz. Immigrating to the United States in 1905, Finger settled initially in New Orleans. He moved to Houston in 1908, where he worked in the branch office of the Dallas architect C. D. Hill and Company. In 1912 Finger became the junior partner of Houston architect Lewis Sterling Green. Between 1914 and 1919 he was in partnership with James Ruskin Bailey and from 1920 to 1923 with Lamar Q. Cato. From 1923 to 1944 Finger practiced under his own name. From 1944 until his death he was in partnership with George W. Rustay. From the beginning of his first partnership, Finger was identified with the design of office, hotel, retail, and industrial buildings. He was responsible for the American National Insurance Company[qv] Building in Galveston (1913, demolished); the Ricou-Brewster Building in Shreveport, Louisiana (1924, with Seymour Van Os); the De George (1913), Plaza (1925), Ben Milam (1925), Auditorium (1926), and Texas State hotels in Houston (1929); the Vaughn Hotel, Port Arthur (1929); the Charlton Hotel, Lake Charles, Louisiana (1929); and the McCartney Hotel, Texarkana (1930). Finger designed retail stores for Everitt-Buelow (1926, altered), Levy's (1930, altered), and Battelstein's (1923, 1936, 1950) in Houston, and numerous auto showrooms in Houston during the 1920s. He was architect of the Model Laundry, Galveston (ca. 1913); and the Cheek-Neal Coffee Company (1917), Texas Packing Company (1924), H. M. Tennison Manufacturing Company (1925), and Truscon Steel Company (1941) buildings in Houston.

As the city's foremost Jewish architect from the 1910s through the 1940s, Finger designed many Jewish institutional buildings, as well as buildings for individual Jewish clients. Among these were Congregation Beth Israel[qv] Temple (1925), Congregation Beth Israel Mausoleum (1935), and Congregation Beth Yeshurun Synagogue (1949), as well as the Concordia Club (1915, demolished) and the Wolff Memorial Home (1930, demolished). During the 1930s Finger was responsible for such major public buildings as the Montgomery County Courthouse, Conroe (1935, altered); Jefferson Davis Hospital (1937, with Alfred C. Finn[qv]); Houston City Hall (1939); and the Houston Municipal Airport Terminal and Hangar (1940). At the time of his death, Finger and Rustay's Harris County Courthouse (1953) was under construction in Houston. Finger was best known for his exuberant modernistic designs. These included the Art Deco–style Houston Turn-Verein (1929, demolished), the A. C. Burton Company auto showroom (1929, demolished), and the Barker Brothers Studio (1930). Finger's office produced the Clarke and Courts printing plant (1936) and the Carnation Company creamery (1946–47, demolished) in the streamlined modernistic style. Finger's public buildings of the 1930s and 1940s were also designed in the modernistic style. Among the prominent clients for whom Finger designed multiple buildings, for both personal and business use, were the industrialist Henry M. Tennison, the confectioner W. H. Irvin, the merchant Philip Battelstein and his sons, the grocer Joseph Weingarten[qv] and his brothers, and the oil operator James M. West and his sons and business associates.

Finger married Gertrude Levy of Houston on June 18, 1913. They were the parents of one son, Joseph Seifter Finger, a landscape architect and golf course designer. Finger was a member of the American Institute of Architects. He was also a member of Congregation Beth Israel, the Independent Order of B'nai Brith, the Houston Turn-Verein, the Westwood Country Club, Chamber of Commerce, and the Benevolent and Protective Order of Elks. Joseph Finger died on February 6, 1953, in Houston. He is buried in Beth Israel Mausoleum in Beth Israel Cemetery, Houston.

BIBLIOGRAPHY: Emory A. Bailey, *Who's Who in Texas* (Dallas: John B. McCraw Press, 1931). Ellis A. Davis and Edwin H. Grobe, comps., *The New Encyclopedia of Texas* (2 vols., 1925?; 4 vols., 1929?). Houston *Post*, February 7, 1953. Natalie Ornish, *Pioneer Jewish Texans* (Dallas: Texas Heritage, 1989). Yolita Schmidt, *The Moderne Style in Architecture: A Houston Guide* (Houston Public Library, 1978).

Stephen Fox

FINHIOVEN (?–?). Finhioven was a chief or "gran casique" of the Caddo Indians. He led the Wichita Indians from the upper Red River to Natchitoches, Louisiana, to witness the treaty between the Wichitas and the Spanish governors of Louisiana and Texas on October 27, 1771.

BIBLIOGRAPHY: Frederick Webb Hodge, ed., *Handbook of American Indians North of Mexico* (2 vols., Washington: GPO, 1907, 1910; rpt., New York: Pageant, 1959).

FINIELS, NICOLÁS DE (ca. 1767–?). Nicolás de Finiels was born in France about 1767. He traveled to America with the French expeditionary force and served as a captain of engineers during the American Revolution. In 1797, armed with a passport from the Spanish minister to the United States, he went from Philadelphia to St. Louis to help with fortifications of upper Louisiana during the period when Spain feared a British attack from Canada. Despite jurisdictional disputes with the Flemish engineer, Luis de Vandembenden, and Col. Carlos Howard, Finiels drew several plans of the Missouri River and environs. Ordered to leave Louisiana and the Spanish service in 1798 by the minister of war in Spain, he went to New Orleans, where his patron, Governor-general Manuel Gayoso de Lemos,[qv] continued to employ him as an engineer and draftsman in drawing plans of Baton Rouge and New Orleans. A royal order of June 19, 1799, reinstated Finiels in the service. He was a valuable member of the staff of the governor-general, the Marqués de Casa Calvo.[qv] In addition to his skill in cartography, Finiels was an inventor of surveying instruments. Casa Calvo chose him as chief surveyor of the 1805 expedition to western Louisiana and Texas.

The party left New Orleans in October, ascended by canoe up the Bayou de La Fourche de Chetimachas, descended the Atchafalaya River, and followed the coast toward Texas. They charted the Gulf Coast and in particular the Mermentau, Calcasieu, Sabine, and Trinity rivers. The expedition employed the galiot *Vigilante* to explore San Bernardo Bay, from which point they trekked overland to Atascosito, near the Trinity River, and thence to San Antonio and Nacogdoches. After three weeks of examining mission records to determine the location of the mission and presidio of San Miguel de Linares de los Adaes, the expedition examined the region toward Arroyo Hondo, some 2½ leagues west of Natchitoches and the boundary between Louisiana and Texas. Upon the return of the expedition to New Orleans in 1806, Finiels and other Spanish officers were expelled from Louisiana by Governor William C. C. Claiborne. Lt. Col. Finiels was attached to the Pensacola garrison, where he soon became engineer in chief of West Florida, a post he held until 1819. He supervised fortifications at Pensacola, San Carlos de Barrancas, and Mobile, and in 1818, as a member of the Security and Vigilance Committee, was wounded when Andrew Jackson captured Pensacola. Finiels was twice married. He and his second wife, Mariana (Rivier), a native of Pensacola, had four sons, all of whom served in the Spanish army.

BIBLIOGRAPHY: Jack D. L. Holmes, *Documentos inéditos para la historia de la Luisiana, 1782–1810* (Madrid: Porrúa Turanzas, 1963). Jack D. L. Holmes, "The Marqués de Casa-Calvo, Nicolás de Finiels, and the 1805 Spanish Expedition through East Texas and Louisiana," *Southwestern Historical Quarterly* 69 (January 1966). Jack D. L. Holmes, "Some French Engineers in Spanish Louisiana," in *The French in the Mississippi Valley*, ed. John Francis McDermott (Urbana: University of Illinois Press, 1965).

Jack D. L. Holmes

FINIS, TEXAS. Finis was along Rock Creek near the intersection of the Young, Jack, and Palo Pinto county lines in far southwestern Jack County. Finis was founded about 1880 at a natural crossing of the creek; the community name was derived from that of an early-day cattleman and merchant, Finis Marshall. The community was granted a post office in 1881, and served as a stage stand along the old Fort Belknap–Weatherford road. By 1884 Finis had a general store, a steam gristmill and cotton gin, and an estimated population of fifty. In 1889 the celebrated shootout between the Marlow brothers and a lynch mob (see FEUDS) took place near the Rock Creek Crossing, and two of the Marlows were buried in Finis Cemetery after the fight. This incident was later the subject of the John Wayne film *The Sons of Katie Elder*. By 1896 the town had an estimated 100 inhabitants, served by Methodist and Christian churches, three general stores, and a blacksmith shop. The community had a school in the early 1900s. The Finis post office closed in 1920, the school closed around the same time, and the community disappeared in the 1920s, leaving only the Finis Cemetery. *Mark Odintz*

FINK, TEXAS. Fink is a farming community just off Farm Road 120 twelve miles northeast of Sherman in north central Grayson County. The community began to form in the late 1850s when farm families from Mississippi settled in the area. The settlement was named for Fred Fink, a member of this group. No established community center developed there until the late 1860s or early 1870s, when W. J. Bilderback opened a general store. From 1897 to 1903 the settlement had postal service. The community's population has never exceeded fifty; in 1936 it was estimated at fifteen. Fink's population was estimated at twenty-five for most of the period from the mid-1940s to the mid-1970s, after which no figures were available. The community is labeled on the 1984 county highway map, but no buildings are shown at the site. The Sixty-sixth Texas Legislature designated every fourth Friday in June as Fink Day in Texas, in recognition of the "National Fink Week" celebration held by Finks, during which the roads to Fink "are overflowing with Finks and Fink well-wishers." The event has drawn national attention.

BIBLIOGRAPHY: Grayson County Frontier Village, *History of Grayson County, Texas* (2 vols., Winston-Salem, North Carolina: Hunter, 1979, 1981). *David Minor*

FINLAY, GEORGE PRESTON (1829–1911). George Preston Finlay, lawyer, legislator, and Confederate soldier, was born in Augusta, Perry County, Mississippi, on November 16, 1829, the son of James and Cada (Lewis) Finlay. Later that year his family moved to a farm some two miles south of Brandon, Mississippi, and there Finlay was reared and educated. During the Mexican War[qv] he served as a private in Col. Jefferson Davis's[qv] famed First Mississippi Rifles but was discharged at Camargo in 1846 due to ill health. He graduated from Brandon College in 1849 and then read law in the office of local attorney E. H. Lombardin. He served briefly as postmaster at Brandon in 1851 and then, in October, entered law school at the University of Louisville, Kentucky. He graduated in March 1852 and was admitted to the bar at Brandon. John Henry Brown[qv] observed that Finlay "inherited nothing except a stainless name," so for nine months he taught school in Hinds County, Mississippi, while saving for passage to Texas. He moved in November 1853 to the Calhoun County community of Lavaca. There, on November 16, 1854, he married Carrie Rea. The couple had three children.

In 1854–55 Finlay edited the Lavaca *Register*. He established a partnership with J. J. Holt in 1857 and was appointed notary public in 1858. He served as a state senator in the Ninth Legislature (1860–61). At the end of the session he raised and was elected captain of an infantry company for Confederate service in Victoria County that was attached to Col. Robert R. Garland's Sixth Texas Infantry. When the regiment was captured at Fort Hindman at Arkansas Post, Arkansas, on January 11, 1863, Finlay was imprisoned first at Camp Chase, Ohio, and then at Fort Delaware before being exchanged at City Point, Virginia, on May 6, 1863. Thereafter he and the remainder of the regiment were consolidated with Col. Roger Q. Mills's[qv] Tenth Texas Infantry and saw action at the battle of Chickamauga before Finlay was transferred to the Trans-Mississippi Department to serve as judge advocate on the staff of generals John B. Magruder and John George Walker[qqv] with the rank of colonel.

In 1866 he made an unsuccessful run for Congress from the Fourth District, but in November 1872 he was elected to represent the Twenty-fourth Senatorial District in the State Senate of the Thirteenth Legislature. The campaign was characterized as "one of the bitterest and most hotly contested campaigns ever witnessed in the State." Finlay served as chairman of the judiciary committee and the committee on military affairs but declined renomination in order to move to Galveston, where he established a partnership, George P. Finlay and Brother, with his younger brother, Oscar E. Finlay. Finlay represented the Thirty-fifth Congressional District in the House of Representatives of the Sixteenth Legislature in 1879 and was reelected to the Seventeenth Legislature in 1881. In both of these terms he served as chairman of the judiciary committee and in 1881 came in second to George R. Reeves[qv] in balloting for speaker of the House. In 1882 he ran unsuccessfully against Thomas P. Ochiltree[qv] for the United States House of Representatives from the Seventh Congressional District. Finlay was nicknamed the "Father of the Public Schools" in Galveston, for organizing the public school system and serving on its board of trustees from 1881 to 1887. On July 10, 1883, his accusation that a former superintendent named Gwyn had behaved "with boorish uncouthness, partiality, favoritism and conduct unbecoming a gentleman toward lady teachers and applicants" produced a major controversy in the school system and provided a "profound sensation" for the community. He also served as city attorney in 1878 and from 1885 until 1889, although his nomination in 1885 was initially rejected by a city council at odds with the mayor. In 1893 Finlay was appointed collector of customs for the port of Galveston.

In his prime Finlay stood six feet, four inches tall and was known as "Tall Sycamore." He was an ardent Democrat who attended every state convention from 1865 until at least 1881, a Mason, a Knight Templar, and an Episcopalian. He died in Houston on March 24, 1911, and was buried in Austin.

BIBLIOGRAPHY: H. L. Bentley and Thomas Pilgrim, *Texas Legal Directory for 1876–77* (Austin: Democratic Statesman Office, 1877). *Biographical Encyclopedia of Texas* (New York: Southern, 1880). Dallas *Herald*, October 6, 1866, November 23, 1872, November 15, 1873, April 24, 1875, January 22, 1876, January 31, 1881, May 11, 1882, July 12, 1883, May 28, 1885. Lewis E. Daniell, *Personnel of the Texas State Government, with Sketches of Representative Men of Texas* (Austin: City Printing, 1887; 3d ed., San Antonio: Maverick, 1892). *History of Texas, Together with a Biographical History of the Cities of Houston and Galveston* (Chicago: Lewis, 1895). E. W. Swindells, *A Legislative Manual for the State of Texas* (2 vols., Austin, 1879–83). Homer S. Thrall, *People's Illustrated Almanac: Texas Handbook and Immigrants Guide for 1880* (St. Louis: Thompson, 1880). *Thomas W. Cutrer*

FINLAY, TEXAS. Finlay was on the Southern Pacific Railroad seventeen miles northwest of Sierra Blanca in southwestern Hudspeth County. It was named for pioneer settler J. R. Finlay, who also gave his name to the mountain range northwest of the town. A local post office was established in 1890 but never officially opened. A second one was established in 1903, with Arthur S. Dowler as postmaster. In 1914 Finlay was described as "a rural post office on the Galveston, Harrisburg & San Antonio Railway," and grocer George W. Norsworthy had a store there. In the mid-1930s the estimated population of Finlay was twenty-five; by the late 1930s it had grown to seventy-five. The last available population estimates for Finlay date from the mid-1940s, when the town had about 100 inhabitants. By the early 1970s Finlay was only a stop on the railroad. *Martin Donell Kohout*

FINLAY MOUNTAINS. The Finlay Mountains begin five miles north of Finlay in south central Hudspeth County and extend seven miles to the east (their center is at 31°21′ N, 105°35′ W). The highest elevation in the Finlays is 5,710 feet above sea level. The area's shallow, stony sandy and clay loams support live oak, piñon, juniper, and grasses. The mountains were named for J. R. Finlay, an early settler in the area.

FINLEY, NEWTON WEBSTER (1854–1909). Newton Webster Finley, lawyer and judge, son of Rev. Robert S. and Mary H. (Cole) Finley, was born in Lauderdale County, Mississippi, on July 31, 1854, and his family moved to Texas later that year. Finley had four brothers, one of whom was Richard Watson Finley,qv and three sisters. He was educated in the common schools of Marshall, Jefferson, and Daingerfield and heard law lectures from Gen. Thomas J. Jenningsqv in Tyler. In June 1876 Finley was admitted to the bar by district judge William H. Bonner at Quitman. He entered practice at Tyler that year. Until 1885 he worked in a partnership, Chilton, Robertson, and Finley, in Smith County. Afterwards he formed a partnership with Marsh and Butler that lasted until he moved to Dallas in 1893.

Finley served as a Democratic presidential elector in 1884. He was chosen state chairman of the Democratic partyqv of Texas in 1888 and was reelected to that position in 1891. He organized the Car Stable Convention,qv which renominated James Stephen Hoggqv for governor. Governor Hogg appointed Finley associate justice of the new Court of Civil Appeals of the Fifth Supreme District in Dallas in 1893. The Democrats nominated Finley for the same position in 1894, and he was elected. Governor Charles A. Culbersonqv appointed him chief justice of the same court in 1897. He was elected to that position the following year and retained it until April 1900, when he resigned to practice law in Dallas. He was head of Finley, Harris, Ethridge, and Knight, a firm that later became Finley, Knight, and Harris. In 1907 Governor Thomas M. Campbellqv appointed Judge Finley a member of the board of regents of the University of Texas, a position he held until his death.

Finley was a member of the Masons, the International Order of Odd Fellows, and the Knights of Pythias. He was also a member of the Trinity Methodist Church in Dallas. He was chairman of the board of stewards of the church and president of the Methodist Laymen's Council of Dallas from its inception. He was active in the building of Trinity Church. In June 1877 he married Alma Louise Woldert of Tyler. They had two daughters. After Mrs. Finley died in 1883, he married Minnie Lee Simms of Fort Worth in 1886. They had four children. Finley died of pneumonia on September 23, 1909, in his home in Dallas and was buried in Greenwood Cemetery.

BIBLIOGRAPHY: John Henry Brown, *Indian Wars and Pioneers of Texas* (Austin: Daniell, 1880; reprod., Easley, South Carolina: Southern Historical Press, 1978). Dallas *Morning News*, September 24, 1909. *Biographical Souvenir of the State of Texas* (Chicago: Battey, 1889; rpt., Easley, South Carolina: Southern Historical Press, 1978). Lewis E. Daniell, *Texas—The Country and Its Men* (Austin?, 1924?). *A History of Greater Dallas and Vicinity*, Vol. 1., by Philip Lindsley; Vol. 2., *Selected Biography and Memoirs*, ed. L. B. Hill (Chicago: Lewis, 1909).

Kelly A. Woestman

FINLEY, RICHARD WATSON (1851–1937). Richard Watson Finley, politician and businessman, the son of Rev. Robert S. and Mary H. (Cole) Finley, was born on November 9, 1851, in Lauderdale County, Mississippi. He was brought to Texas as a small child by his Methodist parents, who settled first in Anderson County. He was educated in Texas common schools and Marshall College, then moved to Jefferson, where he became a store clerk. He later moved to Queen City and began a successful cotton commission and warehouse business and served as a justice of the peace. In 1883 Finley moved to Austin, where he became a clerk in the office of the comptroller of public accounts.qv He worked there for eight years and eventually became the chief bookkeeper.

Finley was a consistent Democrat and, like his brother, Newton Webster Finley,qv a friend and loyal supporter of James Stephen Hogg.qv When Hogg became governor in 1891 he appointed Finley the financial agent for the Texas penitentiaries, at the time one of the most important gubernatorial appointments. In that post Finley labored successfully to make the state penitentiaries self-sustaining, a stated goal of the Hogg administration. In 1894 he was nominated by the Democratic partyqv and then elected comptroller. He was reelected in 1896 and retired at the end of that term, when he entered private business in Austin as representative of the United States Cast Iron Pipe and Foundry Company and as an insurance commissioner for Southwestern Bell Telephone Company. He was a founder of the Southwestern Water Works Association and a director of the Austin National Bank.

Finley married Texana Blalock on July 16, 1873, and the couple had eight children. He died in Austin on December 12, 1937. He was an Elk, a Mason, an Odd Fellow, and a member of the Methodist Episcopal Church, South.

BIBLIOGRAPHY: Austin *American-Statesman*, December 13, 1937. Lewis E. Daniell, *Personnel of the Texas State Government, with Sketches of Representative Men of Texas* (Austin: City Printing, 1887; 3d ed., San Antonio: Maverick, 1892). E. H. Loughery, *Texas State Government* (Austin: McLeod and Jackson, 1897).

Cecil Harper, Jr.

FINN, ALFRED CHARLES (1883–1964). Alfred Charles Finn, architect, was born in Bellville, Texas, on July 2, 1883, the son of Edwin E. and Bertha (Rogge) Finn. He grew up in Hempstead, where he attended public schools. In 1900 he moved to Houston and worked for the Southern Pacific Railroad as a carpenter, then as a draftsman. Between 1904 and 1913 Finn was employed by the architects Sanguinet and Staats, first in Dallas (1904–07), then in the firm's head office in Fort Worth (1907–12), and finally in its Houston office (1912–13). Finn began independent practice in Houston in 1913. His first job was to supervise construction of the Rice Hotel, designed by the St. Louis architects Mauran, Russell, and Crowell for the Houston entrepreneur, Jesse H. Jones.qv This began his life-long association with Jones, Houston's foremost real estate developer and builder. During the first years of his practice Finn designed a variety of building types. These included the ten-story Foster Building (1914), for newspaper publisher Marcellus E. Foster,qv and the adjoining Rusk Building (1916), for Jesse Jones; large houses for Sid Westheimer (1920) and Walter W. Fondren (1923) in Montrose, Earl K. Wharton in Shadyside (1920), and Sarah Brashear Jones in Courtlandt Place (1921); the Humble Oil and Refining Company's first retail service station (1918, demolished); the Melba Theater in Dallas (with W. Scott Dunne, 1921, demolished) for Jesse H. Jones and John T. Jones, and buildings in Shreveport, Wharton, Bellville, and Sealy. By the mid-1920s Finn had become Houston's leading commercial architect, producing skyscraper office buildings, hotels, retail stores, and theaters in the downtown business district. For Jones he designed a seventeen-story addition to the Rice Hotel (1926), the sixteen-story Lamar Hotel and adjoining Metropolitan Theater (1926; demolished), the Loew's State Theater (1927; demolished), and the tallest building constructed in Texas in the 1920s, the thirty-seven-story Gulf Buildingqv (1929, with Kenneth Franzheimqv and J. E. R. Carpenter). Finn's office produced the eleven-story Kirby Building (1927) for John H. Kirby;qv large houses for William L. Moody III in Galveston (1927) and Ross S. Sterlingqv at Bay Ridge (1928), and such institutional buildings as the Houston Light Guard Armory (1925), the Pilgrim Building (c. 1928, demolished), and St. Paul's Methodist Church (1930). His firm collaborated with the Fort Worth architect Wyatt C. Hedrickqv on the Worth Hotel and Worth Theater (1928), the eighteen-story Electric Building and Hollywood Theater (1929), and the nineteen-story Fair Building (1930) in downtown Forth Worth. Finn's office designed major buildings in Galveston and Brenham. During the early years of the Great Depression,qv Finn was able to secure such substantial commissions as the Forest Hill Abbey mausoleum in Kansas City, Missouri, (1931) and the fifteen-story Peoples National Bank Building in Tyler (1932).

Coinciding with Jesse Jones's move from business into government in the 1930s, Finn obtained some of the most prominent publicly financed building commissions in Texas. Under the auspices of the Public Works Administration, his office designed the Sam Houston Coliseum and Music Hall (1937), the twelve-story Jefferson Davis Hospital (1937, with Joseph Finger qv), the United States Post Office, Courthouse, and Customhouse in Galveston (1937, with Andrew Fraser), a twelve-building dormitory complex at Texas A&M College (1940), and the 570-foot tall San Jacinto Monument (1939). He was appointed to the board of Reconstruction Finance Corporation and went on to serve as FRA's secretary of commerce from 1940 to 1945. Subsequently, Finn became an architectural supervisor for the Federal Housing Administration. During World War II qv Finn designed the 1,000-bed, 37-building U.S. Naval Hospital complex in Houston (1945, subsequently the Veterans Administration Hospital, demolished). Finn's office participated in the postwar building boom that occurred in Houston, designing the twenty-four-story City National Bank Building for Judge James A. Elkins qv (1947), the Ezekiel W. Cullen Building at the University of Houston (1950), the downtown specialty store of Sakowitz Brothers (1951), and the suburban headquarters building of the Great Southern Life Insurance Company (1952). It also produced the ten-story First National Bank Building in Longview (1956). Finn designed two hospitals in the Texas Medical Center, qv the Arabia Temple Crippled Children's Hospital (1952) and Ben Taub qv Hospital (1963, with H. E. Maddox and C. A. Johnson). Controversy in 1953 over an earlier version of what became Ben Taub Hospital led to serious financial reversals for Finn, after he was unable to collect fees for preparing a full set of construction documents. This was followed by a stroke he suffered in December 1953 that left him partially paralyzed. Finn maintained his practice until his death, but his participation in its day-to-day operations was limited.

Finn's architecture was stylistically conservative. It was abreast of current trends, but never at the forefront. After the late 1910s Finn seems to have delegated design responsibility to his associates, notably H. Jordan MacKenzie, who had a significant independent career in New Orleans between 1904 and 1916. MacKenzie worked with Finn between 1920 and 1940. Victor E. Johnson, who was with Finn between 1928 and 1952, also did design work, as did Robert C. Smallwood, who was in the office between 1923 and 1928. Other longtime associates were Milton R. Scholl, J. Russ Baty, and Ernest L. Shult. Finn's eldest son, Alfred C. Finn, Jr., joined the firm in 1934. Finn served twice as a trustee of the Houston Independent School District. He was also a member of the first City of Houston Planning Commission. Finn belonged to the Gray Lodge No. 329, the York and Scottish Rite bodies, the Arabia Temple Shrine, the Rotary Club, and the Houston Club. He joined the American Institute of Architects in 1920 and was elected to fellowship in the institute in 1949. Finn was a member of St. Paul's Methodist Church. In 1909 he married Mary Elizabeth Riley. They were the parents of two sons. Alfred C. Finn died in Houston on June 26, 1964, and is buried in Forest Park Cemetery. His papers are deposited at the Houston Metropolitan Research Center of the Houston Public Library.

BIBLIOGRAPHY: Jay C. Henry, *Architecture in Texas, 1895–1945* (Austin: University of Texas Press, 1993). Houston *Post*, June 27, 1964. Michael E. Wilson, *Alfred C. Finn, Builder of Houston* (Houston Public Library, 1983).
Stephen Fox

FINNEY, TEXAS (Hale County). Finney, at the junction of Farm Road 788 and Interstate Highway 27 in northeast Hale County, developed around a switch on the Santa Fe Railroad after 1907. In 1945 it had two residences, an elevator, a store, and a gas station. In 1980 and 1990 the population was fifteen.

BIBLIOGRAPHY: Mary L. Cox, *History of Hale County, Texas* (Plainview, Texas, 1937).

FINNEY, TEXAS (King County). Finney is on Farm Road 193 100 miles northeast of Lubbock in King County. The community is in the fertile, rolling country between Grow and Dumont and derives its name from Finney Springs. Settlers in the area during the early 1900s had to send their children several miles to school until about 1912, when the Finney school district was organized and a school building was constructed on land donated by John F. Gibson. The number of residents reached a record of 120 in 1969 but then declined. In the early 1970s the Finney school was consolidated with the Guthrie district. Finney had a population of seventy from 1970 to 1990 but did not have a rated business in 1980.

BIBLIOGRAPHY: King County Historical Society, *King County: Windmills and Barbed Wire* (Quanah, Texas: Nortex, 1976).
Edloe A. Jenkins

FINNIGAN, ANNETTE (1873–1940). Annette Finnigan, suffragist and art patron, was born into the family of John Finnigan in West Columbia, Texas, in 1873. When she was three years old her family moved to Houston, where her father developed business and real estate interests. She attended Houston public schools and received a diploma from Tilden Seminary in West Lebanon, New Hampshire. In 1889 she entered Wellesley College, Wellesley, Massachusetts, where she developed skills in fine arts and athletics and graduated in 1894. She then studied philosophy at Columbia University and worked as an administrative assistant to her father. She also began a long-term practice of travel in the United States and abroad.

By 1903 Annette Finnigan had returned to Houston, where she collaborated with her sisters, Elizabeth Finnigan and Katherine Finnigan Anderson, in launching equal-suffrage leagues in Houston and Galveston—the first twentieth-century woman suffrage qv efforts in Texas. In the next three years the sisters organized statewide, helping to establish the State Woman Suffrage Association. Annette served as its president from 1904 to 1906. The Finnigans left Texas by 1908, however, and the association disintegrated in their absence. When her father died in 1909 Finnigan assumed management of his businesses and began dividing her time between Houston and New York. In 1913 she revived the Houston suffrage league and for the next two years shared leadership of the renewed Texas Woman Suffrage Association with San Antonian Mary Eleanor Brackenridge. qv Finnigan corresponded with state legislators in 1914, requesting a voters' referendum for a constitutional amendment to authorize woman suffrage. In January 1915 she moved to Austin to lobby the legislature for this resolution. Though it received a majority vote in the House, the Senate did not consider it. Still, suffragists had gained increased publicity for their cause.

In 1916 Finnigan contracted a paralysis, which permanently debilitated her right arm and required her to use a cane. She not only retired from business and athletic activities but also discontinued political organizing. After moving to New York, she generally made winter sojourns to Houston, where she joined the local art league. She devoted the remainder of her career to traveling and cultural philanthropy. She had interests in European, Oriental, and Near Eastern antiquities and rare books. She frequently consulted with the curator of the Museum of Fine Arts, Houston, qv before embarking on tours, and returned with prized art objects to donate to the museum. These included Mediterranean vases and jewelry, Oriental and Near Eastern textiles, Spanish sculpture, and a lace collection. Like her father, who had endowed the Houston Carnegie Library fund, Finnigan also favored the Houston Public Library qv in her giving. She conducted research in Europe to collect illuminated manuscripts and sixteenth-century literary classics for the library. Also, she donated early Texas books and maps. Months before her death, she gave eighteen acres of Northside land to the city of Houston for use as a park, intending it particularly to benefit black residents.

In 1940 Finnigan's health declined, and she spent the last two months of her life in treatment for cancer at Memorial Hospital, New York. She died there on July 17, 1940. Her cremated remains were sent to Houston for burial at Glenwood Cemetery. Her will provided for a $25,000 grant to Wellesley College, as well as large contributions to the American Foundation for the Blind and the American Commission for Mental Hygiene.

BIBLIOGRAPHY: Houston *Chronicle*, July 18, 1940. Jane Y. McCallum, "Activities of Women in Texas Politics," in *Texas Democracy*, ed. Frank Carter Adams (Austin: Democratic Historical Association, 1937).

Sherilyn Brandenstein

FINTY, TOM, JR. (1867–1929). Tom Finty, Jr., lawyer, newspaper editor, public servant, and writer, son of John and Honora (Dollin) Finty, was born on October 1, 1867, in Xenia, Illinois. He attended public schools and worked as clerk and bookkeeper in a general store from 1880 to 1885. From 1885 to 1889 he was employed by various railroads as telegraph operator, station agent, and business solicitor. About 1889 he came to Texas as an employee of the Cotton Belt (St. Louis Southwestern) Railway. Later, working as accountant in a Rusk bank, he ventured into journalism as the Rusk correspondent of the Galveston *News*,qv a part-time job that could have taken hardly more than thirty minutes a week. From 1892 to 1894 Finty did double duty as a court stenographer and law student, and in 1894 he was admitted to the bar. In that year he became associated with the Galveston *Tribune*, first as reporter and then as city editor. In 1897 he moved to the Galveston *News* as city editor; from 1901 to 1914 he was political editor of the Galveston *News* and Dallas *Morning News*,qv with headquarters at Dallas. When the Dallas *News* decided to establish the *Evening Journal* in 1914, Finty was chosen editor. He also became legal counsel and editorial executive of the A. H. Beloqv Corporation, publisher of the Dallas *News* and associated enterprises. He was made a director of the corporation in 1919.

Finty's genius for making friends gave him a statewide acquaintance probably not rivaled by that of anyone else outside of public office. He organized and for some years directed the activities of what became the Texas Election Bureau. He spent months making several studies of public concerns, including city planning and public education. He became the secretary of the Texas Educational Survey Commission in 1923. His professional associations included the Texas Press Association,qv the Texas Editorial Association, the Southwestern Political and Social Science Association (*see* SOCIAL SCIENCE QUARTERLY), and the Texas Newspaper Association, for which he served as chairman of the libel committee. He was a Democrat, a Knight of Pythias, and a member of the University, Writers, and Lions clubs. His publications include *Penitentiary System of Texas* (1909), *Anti-Trust Legislation in Texas* (1915), and *Texas Homestead Exemption Law* (1918).

Finty married Georgie Bonner of Rusk on September 14, 1892; they had one daughter. He died in Dallas on April 25, 1929, and was buried there.

BIBLIOGRAPHY: Sam Hanna Acheson, *35,000 Days in Texas: A History of the Dallas "News" and Its Forbears* (New York: Macmillan, 1938). Tom Finty Papers, Barker Texas History Center, University of Texas at Austin. *Who's Who in America*, 1928–29.

Alonzo Wasson

FIREMEN'S TRAINING SCHOOL ADVISORY BOARD. The Firemen's Training School Advisory Board, first established in 1931, has nine members, who represent the industrial sector, Texas A&M University, the Texas Forest Service, and the State Firemen's and Fire Marshals' Association of Texas. The board, an adjunct of the Firemen's Training School, has advisory duties only; they are concerned with the type and quality of training in the annual firemen's training courses and in the year-round training services offered at Texas A&M University. *See also* TEXAS COMMISSION ON FIRE PROTECTION.

Annette Finnigan. Photograph by C. W. Hearn, Boston. 1894. Courtesy Houston Metropolitan Research Center, Houston Public Library.

FIRES, AMOS J. (1860–1941). Amos J. Fires, lawyer, judge, and civic leader, son of Thomas J. and Emeline Fires, was born on June 16, 1860, on a farm in Clay County, Indiana. In May 1886 he received his law degree from the University of Louisville, Kentucky. After accompanying an attorney to San Antonio, Fires decided to move to Texas. On July 15, 1886, he joined the law firm of Matthews and Wood at Lampasas, but a severe drought caused him to move north to Vernon later that year. Hearing that Childress County was going to be organized, Fires and a companion named Upfold drove a covered wagon to the new townsite of Childress City, where they arrived on November 10, 1886, during a heavy snowstorm.

Over the next few months Fires built up acquaintances by doing odd jobs for various farmers and ranchers. On April 11, 1887, he was elected the first county judge. During this time he led the fight to elect Childress City county seat. His satirical letters to Robert E. Montgomery, agent for the Forth Worth and Denver City Railway, reflect his combined humor and earnestness in his attempts to get the line to build through the town. In the end Fires and his partisans accepted the railroad's compromise proposal to move their homes and businesses to the nearby depot town of Henry in September 1887, and Henry was renamed Childress.

When Fires was first elected county judge, he boarded at a dugout and slept in his courthouse office. After the town moved in 1887 he entered private law practice and filed on a section of land northwest of Childress, on which the town of Carey was later located. Here he was said to have sown the first wheat in the county. From the time of his initial arrival in Texas, Fires kept in touch with his sweetheart, Margaret Warwick, in Bloomfield, Indiana. They were married in Kansas City on May 15, 1889. Afterward they settled on a section southeast of Childress, where Fires built a three-room house; they had a daughter and two sons.

During his long career as the leading Panhandle[qv] trial lawyer, Fires defended 123 persons charged with murder and lost only four cases. People came from miles around to hear his trials; many camped out in the court towns. Temple Houston[qv] worked with him in several cases. Fires helped establish the county's first public school, organized the first bank, built the first brick business house, helped dig the first grave in Childress Cemetery, and did legal work to secure the railroad shops for the city. He also helped to organize Collingsworth, Cottle, Motley, and Floyd counties by preparing their petitions and representing them before the commissioners' court.

In 1927 Fires retired as attorney for the FW&D and accepted appointment by Governor Dan Moody[qv] as district judge of the 100th Judicial District. He was elected to that office in 1928 and again in 1932. He strongly opposed the Ku Klux Klan[qv] as being un-American and became involved in a bitter feud with that organization. Throughout his later years Fires was looked upon as a one-man university by many aspiring young lawyers. In 1936 he retired from active public life to live quietly at his home in Childress. After a lengthy illness he was taken to the home of his daughter, Callie, in Wichita Falls, where he died on April 13, 1941. During his funeral in Childress, the entire town flew flags at half-mast.

BIBLIOGRAPHY: Billy Mitchell, "Judge A. J. Fires, Childress Pioneer," *Panhandle-Plains Historical Review* 19 (1946). LeRoy Reeves, The History of Childress County (M.A. thesis, West Texas State College, 1951). Glenn Shirley, *Temple Houston* (Norman: University of Oklahoma Press, 1980).
H. Allen Anderson

FIRST BAPTIST CHURCH, DALLAS. The First Baptist Church of Dallas was organized on July 30, 1868. Its founding marked the fourth attempt at organized Baptist work in the city. The first two churches had disbanded by 1860, while the third moved out of Dallas and changed its name to Pleasant View Baptist Church. First Baptist was organized with eleven charter members on the first floor of the Masonic Hall, on Lamar Street near the intersection of Ross Avenue. Some believe that it was actually a split from the Pleasant View church; however, there is no evidence to support this belief. W. W. Harris was called as pastor in 1868 and served until 1870. Other pastors have included George W. Truett[qv] and W. A. Criswell.

Under Truett the church increased its membership from 797 to 7,804. The growth continued under Criswell, and in 1991, with a membership of more than 28,000, First Baptist was the largest church in the United States. Many well-known figures of American Christianity have been members of First Baptist, including Billy Graham.

In 1897, under the leadership of Truett, First Baptist established the first known training class for Sunday school teachers. During the late 1800s the church was involved in numerous controversies with one of its members, Samuel A. Hayden.[qv] The ultimate resolution to these controversies came after Hayden left the church and, in 1900, helped form a new Baptist denomination known as the Baptist Missionary Association.

Throughout its history First Baptist has pioneered ministries in Dallas. In 1919 it began one of the earliest ministries to the deaf in Texas. The services of First Baptist were broadcast on radio in 1921, and by 1926 three radio stations were broadcasting its programs. Its first televised service occurred on January 7, 1951. In 1970 First Baptist established a biblical institute named for Criswell, which in 1985 became Criswell College. During the controversy that occurred in the Southern Baptist Convention in the 1980s, many saw First Baptist as a leader in the conservative resurgence because of Criswell's commitment to the inerrancy of scripture and conservative theology.

First Baptist has remained in downtown Dallas throughout its history. In 1991 the physical plant of the church comprised twelve buildings covering five city blocks. In 1990 the church collected over $13 million to help support its work, including thirty-seven inner-city missions.

BIBLIOGRAPHY: Church History Files, Roberts Library, Southwestern Baptist Theological Seminary, Fort Worth. H. Leon McBeth, *The First Baptist Church of Dallas: Centennial History* (Grand Rapids, Michigan: Zondervan, 1968). W. A. Criswell, Baptist Biography File, Roberts Library, Southwestern Baptist Theological Seminary, Fort Worth.
Alan J. Lefever

FIRST BAPTIST CHURCH, FORT WORTH. The earliest congregation of the Baptist Church[qv] in Fort Worth was organized in 1867 by W. W. Mitchell, missionary of the West Fork Baptist Association (established 1855) and A. Fitzgerald, who became its first pastor and served from 1868 to 1871. Its succeeding pastors, Meredith D. Neal (1871), D. Dennis Swindall (1872), and T. F. Lockett (1873), witnessed periods of growth, struggle, and the eventual demise of the congregation.

On September 12, 1873, two Baptist ministers, J. R. Masters and W. M. Gough, organized a new church with twenty-seven charter members. They took the name First Baptist Church, Fort Worth. Masters served as pastor from October 1873 to October 1874, during which time the congregation met in the Masonic Hall. Under Gough the church held services in the Tarrant County Courthouse until it burned in the spring of 1876. Later that year the church built a new brick meetinghouse on Jennings Avenue. John Smith Gillespie came in January 1878 as pastor of the seventy-five-member congregation, located just one block from the infamous "Hell's Half Acre."[qv] By the end of his five-year pastorate the church had added 199 members. In 1882 a portion of this congregation broke away to form the Southside Baptist Church (now Broadway Baptist Church). John Decatur Murphy pastored the congregation in 1883–84, and Walter E. Tynes served from 1884 until 1886. Under the leadership of J. Morgan Wells, 1886–96, the church grew to 541 members, built a new 1,100-seat building on Taylor and Third streets, and hosted the Tarrant County Baptist Association organizational meeting on October 14, 1886, and the national Southern Baptist Convention in May 1890. After Wells died in 1896, the church was led by pastors A. W. McGaha (1897–99), Luther Little (1900–04), and Charles Daniel (1905–08).

A new, long chapter in the church's history began when it called as pastor John Franklyn Norris,[qv] owner-editor of the *Baptist Standard*[qv] from 1907 to 1909. Norris accepted the pastorate in 1909 and remained at First Baptist for the rest of his life. The church lost at least 600 members in 1911 after a division, and the following year lost its building and pastor's home by fire. Though Norris was indicted for arson, he was acquitted after a month-long trial. During his long tenure, the church's personality became inseparably entwined with that of its pastor. It aligned with the prohibition[qv] movement, sponsored an interdenominational Bible school, and became the leader of the World's Christian Fundamentals Conference in 1919. That year the church built a 5,000-seat auditorium, and four years later it helped to form the Baptist Bible Union of America. Because of Norris's continued open criticism of the Southern Baptist Convention, his decision to discard SBC literature, his attacks on SBC schools (particularly Baylor University, which he charged with teaching "evolution and infidelity"), and his spirit of noncooperation, the Tarrant County Baptist Association withdrew fellowship from the church in 1922. The Baptist General Convention of Texas refused Norris a seat at the state convention in 1923 and permanently excluded him in 1924.

On July 18, 1926, Norris shot and killed a Fort Worth lumberman, Dexter Elliot Chipps, in the church office. He was charged with murder but was acquitted on a ruling of self-defense at his trial in Austin. Two years later the church and parsonage were burned again. By 1931 the church reported 12,000 members, with 6,000 attending Sunday school, and property valued at $1.5 million. Throughout the next two decades Norris and the First Baptist Church stood solidly against Modernism, Communism, liberalism, evolution, ecclesiasticism, and organized crime. The growing congregation gained notoriety for extreme independence, a controversial and pugilistic attitude, and a flare for sensationalism.

In July 1931 the First Baptist Church established the Premillennium Baptist Missionary Fellowship, which in subsequent years splintered into the World, Bible, Southwide, and Independent Baptist Fellowship groups, each of which acts as an independent organization. Norris's church papers, *The Searchlight* and *The Fundamentalist*, provided platforms for his views. An institute (1931, 1939), renamed the Bible Baptist Seminary in 1946, was begun under his leadership as well. In 1935 Norris accepted a second pastorate in addition to his Fort Worth church—the Temple Baptist Church in Detroit, Michigan—thus broadening his influence. Discord and internal rivalry surfaced in 1945, when Norris's son George became pastor of a dissenting party that split from the First Baptist Church. Norris's health began to fail in 1948, and the Premillennium Fellowship fractured in May 1950, the same month Norris was dismissed by the church in Detroit.

Norris died on August 20, 1952, and the First Baptist Church called Homer Ritchie as pastor four days later. Ritchie served in that capacity until October 11, 1981, much of that time with his twin brother Omer serving as his co-pastor. The church underwent numerous upheavals in these decades, with attendance dwindling as the older congregation gave way to an emphasis on children and youth. During the mid-1960s the church moved its location to Fifth and Pennsylvania streets and built a 2,000-seat auditorium. In 1974 this facility was sold to Calvary Temple, and the First Baptist Church met in the Tandy School building. In 1981 the First Baptist Church, Fort Worth, and the Rolling Hills Baptist Church merged and moved to Haltom City. The new church retained the name First Baptist Church, Fort Worth. When the merger occurred, Homer and Omer Ritchie resigned as pastors, and Johnny Ramsey became pastor.

Bill Ramsey succeeded his father as pastor in 1984 and still served in that role in 1992. Following his mediating leadership, the First Baptist Church petitioned the Tarrant Baptist Association for membership on October 8, 1990, and was received under a "Watchcare" program for one year. Under this provision, the church was encouraged to participate in all association activities and responsibilities, and special efforts were made to help the congregation better understand the work of the Southern Baptist Convention. After almost seventy years, on October 14, 1991, the First Baptist Church, Fort Worth, was fully readmitted into the Tarrant Baptist Association as a member in good standing with the Baptist General Convention of Texas. In 1993 the First Baptist Church had 2,500 members.

BIBLIOGRAPHY: James E. Carter, *Cowboys, Cowtown and Crosses: A Centennial History of the Tarrant Baptist Association* (Fort Worth: Tarrant Baptist Association, 1986). Roy Emerson Falls, *A Biography of J. Frank Norris, 1877–1952* (Euless, Texas, 1975). James Leo Garrett, *Living Stones: The Centennial History of Broadway Baptist Church, Fort Worth, Texas, 1882–1982* (2 vols., Fort Worth: Broadway Baptist Church, 1984). J. Frank Norris, *Inside History of First Baptist Church, Fort Worth, and Temple Baptist Church, Detroit* (Fort Worth, 1938). C. Allyn Russell, "J. Frank Norris: Violent Fundamentalist," *Southwestern Historical Quarterly* 75 (January 1972).

Karen O'Dell Bullock

FIRST BAPTIST CHURCH, WACO. The First Baptist Church of Waco was organized on May 31, 1851, with four charter members, who extended a call to Noah T. Byars[qv] to become their pastor on June 1. After Byars retired at the end of 1853, S. G. O'Bryan became pastor and served from 1854 to 1860. Other pastors have included Rufus C. Burleson (1862–63, 1865–67, 1870), Benajah H. Carroll (1871–99), James M. Carroll (1901–02), Joseph Martin Dawson,[qqv] (1915–46), and John Wood (1981–91).

During the early years of the church, the congregation met in the Methodist meetinghouse, but in 1857 they moved into a brick building of their own at Fourth and Mary streets, where they met until 1877, when it was destroyed by fire. A program to construct a larger building was immediately launched. The new structure was finished in 1883 and served until 1907. During the pastorate of B. H. Carroll, First Baptist hosted the annual meeting of the Baptist General Convention of Texas twice. In 1906 a new building was built at Fifth and Webster streets, with a auditorium that could seat 3,000; it was still in use in the 1990s and is considered one of the most beautiful churches in Texas.

By 1854 separate Sunday afternoon services were being held for slaves who were members of the church. Black deacons were ordained, and eventually several black preachers were licensed. African Americans[qv] in the church numbered sixty-three in 1860 and seventy-six in 1864. In May 1866 letters of dismission were granted to 105 black members, who organized their own church the following month. In 1856 members of First Baptist were involved in the founding of Trinity River Male High School, later known as Waco Classical School. This institution was absorbed into Waco University when the latter was established in 1861. Waco University merged with Baylor University when Baylor was moved to Waco in 1886. In 1873 B. H. Carroll began teaching ministers in his office; their meetings led to the establishment of a Bible department at Baylor in 1893, with Carroll as chairman. Fifteen years later this department separated from the university and became Southwestern Baptist Theological Seminary, though it remained on the Baylor campus until moving to its own campus in Fort Worth in 1910. In 1899 Carroll resigned as pastor of First Baptist to devote more time to Baylor University. First Baptist was also involved in establishing in Waco in 1919 a Baptist hospital, today known as Hillcrest Baptist Medical Center. Noted members of the church have included former governor Pat Neff[qv] and Confederate generals James E. Harrison, Thomas Harrison, Joseph W. Speight, and Allison Nelson.[qqv]

Throughout its existence First Baptist, Waco, has emphasized mission work. Many members have become missionaries, including the well-known couple Anne and William B. Bagby.[qv] Although First Baptist is not as prominent as it once was, it remains an influential member of the Baptist General Convention of Texas. In 1992 its members numbered 5,585 and its annual budget was almost $2 million.

BIBLIOGRAPHY: Frank E. Burkhalter, *A World-Visioned Church: Story of the First Baptist Church, Waco, Texas* (Nashville: Broadman Press, 1946). Church History Files, Roberts Library, Southwestern Baptist Theological Seminary, Fort Worth. Alan J. Lefever, The Life and Work of B. H. Carroll (Ph.D. dissertation, Southwestern Baptist Theological Seminary, 1992). Waco *Tribune-Herald*, May 2, 1976.

Alan J. Lefever

FIRST CREEK. First Creek rises a mile from the Ochiltree-Lipscomb county line in southeastern Ochiltree County (at 36°21′ N, 100°34′ W) and runs southeast for eight miles to its mouth on Wolf Creek in Lipscomb County (at 36°15′ N, 100°27′ W). The stream was on the route of the Jones and Plummer Trail[qv] and on the range of the Seven K Ranch.[qv] First Creek traverses flat to rolling terrain with some local escarpments, surfaced by thick, fine sandy loam that supports mesquite brush and grasses.

BIBLIOGRAPHY: Pauline D. and R. L. Robertson, *Cowman's Country: Fifty Frontier Ranches in the Texas Panhandle, 1876–1887* (Amarillo: Paramount, 1981).

FIRST ELM CREEK. First Elm Creek rises four miles northwest of Artesia Wells in western La Salle County (at 28°20′ N, 99°20′ W) and runs southeast for five miles to its mouth on Las Raices Creek, a half mile south of Artesia Wells (at 28°16′ N, 99°17′ W). It traverses low-rolling to flat terrain with some locally shallow depressions, surfaced by clay and sandy loams that support grasses, mesquite, and chaparral in the creek's upper reaches and water-tolerant hardwoods and grasses in its lower.

FIRST REGIMENT, TEXAS MOUNTED RIFLEMEN. The First Regiment, Texas Mounted Riflemen, was the first regiment in Texas to be mustered into Confederate service in 1861. On March 4, 1861, Confederate secretary of war Leroy Pope Walker directed Benjamin McCulloch*qv* to raise a regiment of ten companies of mounted riflemen to protect the Texas frontier between the Red River and the Rio Grande. McCulloch, hoping for a command east of the Mississippi River, turned the colonel's commission over to his brother, Henry Eustace McCulloch,*qv* who, on February 5, 1861, had been appointed to the rank of colonel by the state Committee of Public Safety and already had five under-strength companies along the state's northwestern frontier to replace the United States troops withdrawn after secession.*qv*

In mid-March Henry McCulloch arrived in Austin, where he recruited men for five additional companies for the new regiment. By the early part of April he had his regiment organized with men recruited from Bexar, Travis, Gonzales, Bell, Comanche, Bosque, Rusk, Burleson, and Lamar counties. The men already on the frontier who wished to join the new regiment had to be mustered out of state service and into Confederate service. By mid-April McCulloch's new regiment entered Confederate service as the First Regiment, Texas Mounted Riflemen, also known as the First Texas Mounted Rifles. This was not only the first regiment in the state organized for Confederate service, but the original commission to Ben McCulloch was one of the first in the Confederacy.

At San Antonio Henry McCulloch was elected colonel, Thomas C. Frost*qv* lieutenant colonel, and Edward Burleson, Jr.,*qv* major. By the following month the ten companies of the regiment occupied a line of forts from Camp Jackson, at the confluence of the Red River and the Big Wichita, southwestward to Fort Belknap, Camp Cooper, Fort Phantom Hill, Fort Chadbourne, Camp Colorado, Camp Concho (at present-day San Angelo), Fort McKavett, and Fort Mason.

McCulloch's patrols covered the regiment's 400-mile line, to which were added regular expeditions of two to three weeks into suspected haunts of hostile Indians northwest of the line of forts. The summer and fall of 1861 saw diminished Indian activity compared to the years before the war, and no major incursions of Indians into the settlements. McCulloch returned to San Antonio in September to take temporary command of the Department of Texas, and in December he accepted command of the Western Military District of Texas. As his attention turned to defense of the Texas coast his regiment on the Indian frontier was commanded for a time by his adjutant and senior officers.

The enlistment for the regiment was to run out in the spring of 1862; rumors spread that Confederate officials planned to remove it from the frontier. The regiment mustered out in mid-April 1862 at Fort Mason, and the state-financed Frontier Regiment*qv* replaced it on the frontier. Some of the men returned to frontier service, but most enlisted in the Eighth Texas Cavalry Battalion, which later became part of the First Texas Cavalry Regiment.

BIBLIOGRAPHY: Harry M. Henderson, *Texas in the Confederacy* (San Antonio: Naylor, 1955). Frances Richard Lubbock, *Six Decades in Texas* (Austin: Ben C. Jones, 1900; rpt., Austin: Pemberton, 1968). David Paul Smith, Frontier Defense in Texas, 1861–1865 (Ph.D. dissertation, North Texas State University, 1987). *The War of the Rebellion: A Compilation of the Official Records of the Union and Confederate Armies.*
David Paul Smith

FIRST TEXAS CAVALRY, USA. During the Civil War*qv* Texas contributed two regiments and two battalions of cavalry to the federal army. A total of 1,915 men from Texas served the Union; of these 141 died, 12 in action. One source states that "the strength of the Texas Federal Regiments consisted primarily of Mexicans, Germans, and Irishmen." While it is true that the regiment had a high proportion of Spanish-speaking Texans and first-generation immigrants, among them German Unionists from the Hill Country,*qv* the officer cadre was mostly mainstream southern in background. The larger of the two Texas units was the First Texas Cavalry Regiment. It was organized at New Orleans, Louisiana, on November 6, 1862, under the command of Edmund J. Davis,*qv* who, before the war's end, became a brigadier general. The unit was composed of eight companies. Until September 1863 the First Texas Cavalry was assigned to the defense of New Orleans. During that time two companies were sent to Galveston but did not land due to the Confederate capture of that city in January 1863. While in Louisiana, the regiment saw its initial action on the Amite River in May 1863 and participated in operations around Morgan City. In September 1863 the First Texas Cavalry sailed from New Orleans as part of the Sabine Pass expedition but was not in action. Returning to Louisiana, the regiment was engaged in the Western Louisiana (Têche) Campaign from October 3 through October 17, 1863. The regiment was moved back to New Orleans at the end of this assignment and embarked on October 23 as part of the Rio Grande expedition, landing on the south Texas coast on November 2 and occupying Brownsville four days later. Within a month the First Texas Cavalry, which had reached Texas with a strength of 16 officers and 205 enlisted men, grew by slightly over 50 percent. During this time the Second Texas Cavalry Regiment was formed at Brownsville. Both regiments left Texas in July 1864 for Louisiana. Two companies, however, of the First Texas Cavalry remained at Brownsville and did not rejoin their parent regiment until six months later. In September 1864 the First Texas Cavalry was involved in some minor actions near Morganza, Louisiana. On November 1, 1864, the two regiments were merged into one twelve company regiment (normally a regiment at this time had ten companies). The new command was called the First Texas Volunteer Cavalry. Ordered to Baton Rouge on November 19, 1864, the First Texas Volunteers engaged in patrolling and reconnaissance duties until the end of the Civil War. In May and June 1865 the regiment was at Vidalia, Louisiana. On June 29, 1865, the Volunteers were ordered to Texas and mustered out of service on November 4, 1865.

BIBLIOGRAPHY: Frederick H. Dyer, *A Compendium of the War of the Rebellion* (3 vols., 1908; rpt., Dayton, Ohio: National Historical Society, 1979). Frank H. Smyrl, "Texans in the Union Army, 1861–1865," *Southwestern Historical Quarterly* 65 (October 1961). *The War of the Rebellion: A Compilation of the Official Records of the Union and Confederate Armies.* Marcus J. Wright, comp., and Harold B. Simpson, ed., *Texas in the War, 1861–1865* (Hillsboro, Texas: Hill Junior College Press, 1965).
Eugene M. Ott, Jr., and Glen E. Lich

FIRST UNITED STATES VOLUNTEER CAVALRY. The advent of the Spanish-American War in 1898 saw the regular United States Army and the state militias inadequately staffed to support operations overseas. Under a law passed on April 22, three regiments of volunteer cavalry were raised in the western states and territories to augment the regular defense establishment. President William McKinley was to appoint all commanding officers, who in turn selected their own staff and line officers. Recruiting began late in April. The most famous of these units—in fact, the only one to serve in combat—was the First United States Volunteer Cavalry, better known as the "Rough Riders" but also called "Teddy's Terrors" and the "Rocky Mountain Rustlers." The unit was nominally commanded by Col. Leonard Wood, an army surgeon who had won the Medal of Honor for an Indian fight ten years before, but in fact was led by Lt. Col. Theodore Roosevelt. This legendary aggregation of cowboys, Indian fighters, outlaws, Eastern aristocrats, and Ivy League athletes took part in the attack on Santiago de Cuba and wrote a gallant and bloody record during its brief existence. "We drew a great many recruits from Texas," wrote Roosevelt, "and from nowhere did we get a higher average, for many of them had served in that famous body of frontier fighters, the Texas Rangers. Of course, these rangers needed no teaching. They were trained to obey and to take responsibility. They were splendid shots, horsemen, and trailers. They were accustomed to living in the open, to enduring great fatigue and hardship, and to encountering all kinds of danger." Near the end of June Colonel Wood was promoted to command of the cavalry division's second brigade, and Roosevelt became in fact commander of the regiment. "We rendezvoused at San Antonio," one of the men wrote in later years, "Twelve hundred as separate, varied, mixed, distinct, grotesque, and peculiar types of men as perhaps were ever assembled in one bunch in all the history of man . . . and one—possibly two—Democrats." Roosevelt joined his regiment in San Antonio on May 16. There, encamped in what is now Roosevelt Park, it learned drill and discipline. The men, their lieutenant colonel wrote, were pleased to have been organized and trained "in the city where the Alamo commemorates the death fight of Crockett, Bowie, and their famous band of frontier heroes." The regiment also purchased its horses In Texas. These animals "were not showy," Roosevelt wrote, "but they were tough and hardy" and made excellent cavalry mounts.

On May 30 Lt. Gen. Nelson A. Miles ordered the Rough Riders to Tampa, Florida, where the troop was assigned to Maj. Gen. Joseph Wheeler's cavalry division of Lt. Gen. William R. Shafter's qv Fifth Corps for the forthcoming invasion of Cuba. As no transports could be found to move the division's horses to Cuba, however, the cavalry fought through the campaign as infantry. The Rough Riders were the first United States troops to land in Cuba. They raised their regimental flag over a blockhouse swiftly taken from the Spaniards. The regiment's baptism of fire came at Las Guasimas on June 24, when Roosevelt's men, well-armed with Krag-Jörgensen carbines, mauled a detachment of the Spanish army impeding the invasion force's penetration to the interior of the island. The Spaniards then fell back to and fortified San Juan Hill, which Shafter's corps assaulted on July 1. In this battle the First United States Volunteer Cavalry, with elements of the Ninth and Tenth United States Cavalry qqv regiments, made the famed charge on San Juan (actually Kettle) Hill, seizing the Spanish fortifications and pushing the defenders back into Santiago de Cuba. The attack cost 1,000 American casualties and induced Roosevelt to write to his friend Senator Henry Cabot Lodge, "We have won so far at a heavy cost; but the Spaniards fight very hard and charging these entrenchments against modern rifles is terrible. We are within measurable distance of a terrible disaster." Fearful of further unacceptable casualties, Shafter entrenched his corps to besiege the city. "The boys are simply exhausted," wrote one Rough Rider officer, "having to work all night and lie in the sun all day in the trenches. We have to build our own fortifications, but we are getting along alright." On August 7, following the capitulation of Santiago de Cuba, the regiment, suffering from malaria and yellow fever, was evacuated from Cuba with the rest of Shafter's Fifth Corps.

The fame of the Rough Riders catapulted Theodore Roosevelt into the vice presidency and later the presidency of the United States. In San Antonio, in addition to Roosevelt Park, Roosevelt Street and the Roosevelt Bar of the Menger Hotel,qv a favorite watering place of the regiment, are named in memory of their sojourn in Texas.

BIBLIOGRAPHY: Graham A. Cosmas, *An Army for Empire: The United States Army in the Spanish American War* (Columbia: University of Missouri Press, 1971). Walter Millis, *The Martial Spirit: A Study of Our War with Spain* (New York: Literary Guild, 1931). Theodore Roosevelt, *The Rough Riders* (New York: Scribner, 1899). David F. Trask, *The War with Spain in 1898* (New York: Macmillan, 1981).

Thomas W. Cutrer

FISCHER, TEXAS. Fischer, twenty miles northwest of New Braunfels in the Hill Countryqv of northern Comal County, developed in the 1850s as a supply center on the Devil's Backbone section of the road between San Marcos and Blanco. The site, settled by Hermann Fischer in 1853, became known as Fischer's Store when Fischer built a log trading post to serve the frontier community. Potters Creek School opened for local children in 1875, and a year later the Fischer's Store post office was established. Fischer Store School replaced Potters Creek in 1888, and after World War IIqv Fischer became the center of a school district for northern Comal County. At the request of postal officials the community's name has changed twice: in 1894 Fischer's Store became Fischer Store, and in 1950 the name was shortened to Fischer. Sources in the 1960s reported that the Fischer family had held the local postmastership continuously since 1876. Fischer recorded a population of forty or fifty for most of the twentieth century but fell to twenty in the mid-1960s as Canyon Lake, four miles to the south, began filling. In 1967 Fischer was described just as it might have been a hundred years earlier—a country store and post office at a rural crossroads. Its population was listed as twenty from 1967 through 1990.

BIBLIOGRAPHY: Oscar Haas, *History of New Braunfels and Comal County, Texas, 1844–1946* (Austin: Steck, 1968).

Daniel P. Greene

FISHBAUGH, WILLIAM (?–1836). William Fishbaugh (Fishback), Alamo defender, was a resident of Gonzales. He was mustered into the Gonzales Ranging Company of Mounted Volunteers by Byrd Lockhartqv on February 23, 1836. He rode to the Alamo with this unit and arrived on March 1, 1836. Fishbaugh died in the battle of the Alamoqv on March 6, 1836.

BIBLIOGRAPHY: Daughters of the American Revolution, *The Alamo Heroes and Their Revolutionary Ancestors* (San Antonio, 1976). Daughters of the Republic of Texas, *Muster Rolls of the Texas Revolution* (Austin, 1986). Bill Groneman, *Alamo Defenders* (Austin: Eakin, 1990).

Bill Groneman

FISH BRANCH, TEXAS. Fish Branch, on the Houston, East and West Texas Railway, probably near where the line crosses the Fish Branch of Mussel Shoals Creek, was within the R. W. Wilburn tract between Shepherd and Urbana in eastern San Jacinto County. The locale was listed as a stop on a 1918 railroad map of Texas. It was also shown on a late-1920s map of San Jacinto County. Although not labeled on more recent maps, the site was still marked by a few buildings and a church in the mid-1980s.

Robert Wooster

FISH CREEK (Cooke County). Fish Creek originates from the confluence of North Fish Creek and South Fish Creek at the dam of Moss Lake in north central Cooke County (at 33°46′ N, 97°13′ W) and winds east, then northwest, southeast, and finally south for a total of three miles to its mouth on the Red River, five miles southeast of Sivells Bend (at 33°46′ N, 97°11′ W). It traverses an area of flat to rolling terrain surfaced by deep, fine sandy loam that supports brush and various grasses.

―――― (Falls County). Fish Creek rises eight miles southeast of Marlin in eastern Falls County (at 31°17′ N, 96°46′ W) and runs south for twelve miles to its mouth on the Little Brazos River, two miles east of Highbank (at 31°09′ N, 96°47′ W). The stream, which is intermittent in its upper reaches, traverses low-rolling to flat prairie surfaced by clay and sandy loams that support scrub brush, mesquite, cacti, and grasses.

―――― (Nolan County). Fish Creek rises a half mile southwest of State Highway 153 and nine miles northeast of Blackwell in southeast Nolan County (at 32°12′ N, 100°15′ W) and runs southeast for twenty-four miles to its mouth on Valley Creek, a half mile southwest of State Highway 53 and 2½ miles southeast of Wingate in northwest Runnels County (at 32°01′ N, 100°06′ W). It traverses flat terrain with locally shallow depressions, surfaced by expansive clays that support water-tolerant hardwoods, conifers, and grasses.

―――― (Shackelford County). Fish Creek rises eight miles northwest of Albany in north central Shackelford County (at 32°48′ N, 99°24′ W) and runs northwest for fourteen miles to its mouth on the Clear Fork of the Brazos River, near the Hendrick Ranch in northwest Shackelford County (at 32°54′ N, 99°31′ W). The creek, which is dammed in its upper reaches, traverses an area of steep slopes and benches surfaced by shallow clay loams that support juniper, live oak, mesquite, and grasses.

_____ (Tarrant County). Fish Creek rises just south of Arlington in eastern Tarrant County (at 32°40′ N, 97°07′ W) and runs northeast for twelve miles to its mouth on Mountain Creek Lake, five miles south of Lakeview (at 32°42′ N, 96°58′ W). It traverses flat to rolling terrain surfaced by dark, commonly calcareous clays that support mesquite, grasses, and cacti.

_____ (Young County). Fish Creek rises two miles north of the Stephens county line in extreme southwest Young County (at 33°04′ N, 98°57′ W) and runs east for sixteen miles to its mouth on the Brazos River, four miles north of South Bend (at 33°03′ N, 98°43′ W). It is joined by the North Fork of Fish Creek, which rises in western Young County (at 33°05′ N, 98°50′ W) and runs southeast eight miles to empty into Fish Creek (at 33°03′ N, 98°50′ W), and by Salt Branch, which rises in south central Young County (at 33°01′ N, 98°45′ W) and runs three miles to its mouth on Fish Creek (at 33°02′ N, 98°44′ W). The main stream traverses an area of steep to rolling hills surfaced by shallow to moderately deep clay and sandy loams that support mesquite, oak, scrub brush, cacti, grasses, live oak, and juniper.

FISHER, GEORGE (1795–1873). George Fisher, early settler, was born in Székésfehérvór, Hungary, in April 1795 and named Djordje Ribar by his Serbian parents. After his father died, he was sent to the Serbian Orthodox Church School at Karlovci, seat of the Serbian metropolitan in Vojvodina, to study for the priesthood. He left in 1813 to join the Slavonic Legion during the Serbian Revolution. When the legion was disbanded in 1814, he sailed for America as a redemptioner. Upon arriving, because of his lack of money, he was held by the ship's owners to redeem his contract. He and two companions escaped in the ship's boat and landed above Philadelphia, where they were later mistaken by suspicious onlookers for fishermen. Here Ribar assumed the English version of his name, George Fisher.

Fisher settled in Mississippi before 1819, when he tentatively planned to go to Texas with the James Long[qv] expedition. In 1825 he went to Mexico, where he was active in establishing the first York Rite Masonic lodge in that country. After failing to secure an empresario[qv] contract in 1827, he took out Mexican naturalization papers in 1829 and, as a Mexican citizen, contracted to settle five hundred families on lands formerly held by Haden Edwards.[qv] Fisher was appointed collector of customs at Galveston in 1829 but failed to receive his credentials; in 1830 he was recognized as administrator of the port of Galveston. After Manuel de Mier y Terán[qv] ordered the port suspended in July 1830, Fisher became secretary of the ayuntamiento[qv] at San Felipe but was discharged when he was suspected of acting as secret agent for Vicente Ramón Guerrero.[qv] Having been reinstated by Terán, Fisher set up the customhouse at Anahuac on Galveston Bay in November 1831. He decreed that all ships leaving Brazoria and certain other ports had to be cleared through Anahuac. To secure these clearances some shippers had to journey 200 miles overland. Some shipmasters expressed their dissatisfaction by running past the fort on the lower Brazos. During one encounter a Mexican soldier was wounded. As the result of the Anahuac Disturbances,[qv] threats by the Texas colonists caused Fisher to return to Matamoros, where, from 1832 to 1835, he published *Mercurio del Puerto de Matamoros*. The paper was too liberal for the taste of Mexican officials and caused his dismissal from Mexico. In October 1835 Fisher was in New Orleans acting as commissary general and secretary for the Tampico expedition.[qv]

In 1837 he went into business as a commission agent in Houston. He served as justice of the peace in 1839, was admitted to the bar in 1840, and was a member of the Houston city council in 1840. He was also president of the German Union, a philanthropic society founded in 1840. In 1843 he was major of the Second Brigade of the Texas militia. He went to Panama in 1850 and to California in 1851. In 1856 he presented his library, papers, and correspondence to the state of Texas. He served in civic posts in San Francisco from 1860 to 1870, when he became consul to Greece. When the Harris County Historical Society was organized in 1870, Fisher sent its president, Ashbel Smith,[qv] a record of his activities in Texas.

Fisher was married four times: first to Elizabeth Davis of Mississippi in 1815, with whom he had three sons and from whom he was divorced in 1839; second, to Mrs. M. C. Page in Galveston on July 20, 1840; third, to Mrs. Mary Caroline Fleming, in Galveston on April 13, 1848; and fourth, to Mrs. Caroline H. Fisher. Fisher died in San Francisco on June 11, 1873. Flags at all consulates flew at half-mast as a mark of respect.

BIBLIOGRAPHY: George Fisher Papers, Barker Texas History Center, University of Texas at Austin. George Fisher: Secretary and Translator to the California Land Commission (MS, Barker Texas History Center, University of Texas, 185-?). Bessie Lucille Letts, George Fisher (M.A. thesis, University of Texas, 1928). *Memorials of George Fisher* (Houston: Telegraph Office, 1840). Ohland Morton, *Terán and Texas: A Chapter in Texas Mexican Relations* (Austin: Texas State Historical Association, 1948). Vertical Files, Barker Texas History Center, University of Texas at Austin.
Claudia Hazlewood

FISHER, HENRY FRANCIS (1805–1867). Henry Francis Fisher, colonizer, son of Henry Francis Fisher, was born in Kassel, Hesse, in 1805. He left Europe late in 1833 and spent a year each in London and New York and two years in New Orleans. In 1837 or early 1838 he came to Houston, Texas, where he was consul for the Hanseatic League (modern-day Germany). He became interested in the exploration and colonization of the San Saba area and in 1839 was acting treasurer of the San Saba Company, which was later reorganized as the San Saba Colonization Company. In 1841 Fisher married Mrs. Mary E. Kessler. In a contract made on June 7, 1842, and renewed on September 1, 1843, he and Burchard Miller[qv] received the Fisher-Miller Land Grant.[qv]

Sam Houston[qv] appointed Fisher the Texas consul to Bremen in December 1843, and in March 1844 Fisher left for that city, where he hoped to serve the interests of Texas as well as his own and his partners' colonization interests. On June 26, 1844, he associated himself with the Adelsverein.[qv] The society bought an interest in the Fisher-Miller grant and placed Fisher on its colonial committee. He returned to Texas in August 1844 to make preparations for transporting the prospective settlers to the grant and for providing supplies for them. Prince Carl of Solms-Braunfels,[qv] the society's commissioner general, charged Fisher with negligence and was generally dissatisfied with his activities. On December 30, 1845, by means of an indenture with John O. Meusebach,[qv] the society's second commissioner general, Fisher and Miller assigned their rights in the colonization contract to the society for $5,000. Fisher died on October 23, 1867, in Wiesbaden, Germany, and was survived by his wife and four children.

BIBLIOGRAPHY: Rudolph L. Biesele, *The History of the German Settlements in Texas, 1831–1861* (Austin: Von Boeckmann-Jones, 1930; rpt. 1964). Rudolph L. Biesele, "Prince Solms's Trip to Texas, 1844–1845," *Southwestern Historical Quarterly* 40 (July 1936). Rudolph L. Biesele, "San Saba Colonization Company," *Southwestern Historical Quarterly* 33 (January 1930). Don Hampton Biggers, *German Pioneers in Texas* (Fredericksburg, Texas: Fredericksburg Publishing, 1925). Henry Francis Fisher Papers, Texas State Library, Austin; Barker Texas History Center, University of Texas at Austin. Hans Peter Nielsen Gammel, comp., *Laws of Texas, 1822–1897* (10 vols., Austin: Gammel, 1898). *History of Texas, Together with a Biographical History of the*

Cities of Houston and Galveston (Chicago: Lewis, 1895). Republic of Texas Colonization Papers, Texas State Library, Austin.

Rudolph L. Biesele

FISHER, JAMES (ca. 1780–ca. 1854). James Fisher, pioneer farmer, was born in North Carolina about 1780. As one of Stephen F. Austin's^{qv} Old Three Hundred^{qv} colonists he received title to a league of land on the west bank of the Brazos River in what is now southeastern Burleson County, on July 19, 1824. The census of March 1826 described him as a farmer and stock raiser between forty and fifty years of age. His household then consisted of a wife, Jenny (or Jane), and six children. On January 1, 1830, Fisher married Sarah (or Sally) Hensley; they had ten children. He lived in Burleson County in 1850 and died sometime before 1854.

Another James Fisher, aged twenty-eight, his wife, Bethany, and their three children came from Hinds County, Mississippi, to Sterling C. Robertson's^{qv} colony in Texas in December 1834.

BIBLIOGRAPHY: Lester G. Bugbee, "The Old Three Hundred: A List of Settlers in Austin's First Colony," *Quarterly of the Texas State Historical Association* 1 (October 1897). Malcolm D. McLean, comp. and ed., *Papers Concerning Robertson's Colony in Texas* (19 vols., Fort Worth: Texas Christian University Press, 1974–76; Arlington: University of Texas at Arlington Press, 1977–92).

FISHER, JOHN. (1800–1865). John Fisher, early settler, public official, and signer of the Texas Declaration of Independence,^{qv} was born in Richmond, Virginia, on January 18, 1800, the son of James and Margaret (Nimmo) Fisher. In 1832 he traveled to Texas with his family and settled in Gonzales in Green DeWitt's^{qv} colony. His brother, William S. Fisher,^{qv} led a company at the battle of San Jacinto^{qv} and was also the commander of the Mier expedition.^{qv} Another brother, Henry Fisher, was purser on the Texas ship *Liberty*^{qv} in 1835.

In 1835 John Fisher served as secretary of the committee of safety for Gonzales Municipality; in that capacity he wrote Stephen F. Austin^{qv} on November 3, 1835, protesting the abuses of San Augustine volunteers who, according to Fisher, robbed "money clothing and every thing that they could lay their hands on." At the Convention of 1836^{qv} in Washington-on-the-Brazos, Fisher represented Gonzales. On March 2, 1836, he signed the Texas Declaration of Independence. On November 17, 1837, he petitioned President Sam Houston^{qv} for a appointment as notary public for the port of Velasco. He apparently did not receive the post, for soon afterward he assigned to Peter W. Grayson^{qv} his rights to a headright certificate for a league and a labor of land and returned to Virginia, where he married Margaret Connor McKim. The couple had two children, one of whom died in infancy.

By 1860 Fisher was listed as a tobacconist in Richmond, Virginia. In February of 1860 he wrote Sam Houston that he had petitioned the Texas legislature to grant him a league of land, but that his application had been rejected by the Senate. The letter requested that the governor use his influence to "get the Senate to reconsider their vote," but there is no evidence that Houston ever did so. Fisher died on August 13, 1865, in Charlotte, North Carolina. He was buried in Hollywood Cemetery, Richmond.

BIBLIOGRAPHY: Louis Wiltz Kemp, *The Signers of the Texas Declaration of Independence* (Salado, Texas: Anson Jones, 1944; rpt. 1959).

L. W. Kemp

FISHER, JOHN KING (1854–1884). King Fisher, rancher, outlaw, and lawman, was born in Collin County in 1854, the son of Joby and Lucinda (Warren) Fisher. Just before the Civil War^{qv} the family moved to Florence, Williamson County. In 1869 Fisher was accused of stealing a horse after he borrowed it without telling the owner. He was arrested by a posse but reportedly escaped with the help of the horse's owner, who had decided not to press charges. Fisher made his way to Goliad, where he was arrested again, this time for housebreaking, and sent to prison. After being pardoned four months later, he moved to Dimmit County and established a ranch on Pendencia Creek. The region, known as the Nueces Strip, was a lawless area, where cattle rustling was the major industry. Fisher, relying on both patronage and intimidation, quickly established himself as one of the leaders of the Strip, and his ranch became a haven for drifters, criminals, and rustlers in the region. He was an imposing figure, once described by Texas Ranger N. A. Jennings^{qv} as wearing an ornamented Mexican sombrero, a black Mexican jacket embroidered with gold, a crimson sash, and boots, with two silver-plated, ivory-handled revolvers swinging from his belt. In the section where he reigned, Fisher was feared and respected. A certain road branch bore the sign: "This is King Fisher's road. Take the other." Fisher reportedly placed the sign to distinguish between his private road and the public road, but many at the time viewed it as evidence of the extent of Fisher's power and control.

In addition to operating his ranch, Fisher was evidently engaged in cattle rustling in Texas and Mexico, and his escapades led more than once to violence. He was arrested at various times by the famous Texas Ranger captain Leander McNelly^{qv} and his successor Lee Hall. Charged with murder and horse and cattle theft, he managed to avoid conviction, but his legal ordeals took their toll, and Fisher decided to live a quieter life. He married in April 1876 and later bought a ranch near Eagle Pass. In 1881 he was appointed deputy sheriff of Uvalde County. He became acting sheriff in 1883 after the sheriff was indicted. He turned out to be an efficient and popular lawman and made plans to run for the office in 1884. But on the night of March 11, 1884, in the Vaudeville Variety Theater in San Antonio, Fisher and his companion, noted gunman Ben Thompson,^{qv} were involved in a shootout brought on by a quarrel between Thompson and the theater's owners. Both Fisher and Thompson were killed in the melee.

BIBLIOGRAPHY: George Durham, *Taming the Nueces Strip: The Story of McNelly's Rangers* (Austin: University of Texas Press, 1962). Ovie Clark Fisher and Jeff C. Davis, *King Fisher: His Life and Times* (Norman: University of Oklahoma Press, 1966).

Paul Adams

FISHER, ORCENETH (1803–1880). Orceneth Fisher, Methodist minister and author, the son of Davis and Britannia (Chase) Fisher, was born in Chester, Vermont, on November 5, 1803. Before 1821 he moved to Indiana Territory, where he joined the Methodist Church,^{qv} in which he became a pioneer minister. After admission on trial to the Missouri Conference in 1823, he was assigned to various Illinois circuits. In 1839 he visited Texas for his health and preached at Brazoria. He returned to Springfield, Illinois, where he published *Sketches of Texas* in 1840.

Fisher moved to Texas in 1841 and served in Washington and Brazoria. In 1844 and 1845 he was chaplain of the Congress of the Republic of Texas.^{qv} He resumed the ministry in Houston in 1846, served the Houston African Mission in 1848, and edited the *Texas Wesleyan Banner* and later the *Texas Christian Advocate* (*see* UNITED METHODIST REPORTER). He was transferred to the East Texas Conference, where he served as pastor at Marshall and presiding elder for the Nacogdoches, Palestine, and San Augustine district. During this period he published several tracts: *Baptismal Catechism* (Houston, 1849), *The Christian Sacraments* (Nacogdoches, 1851), and *History of Immersion as a Religious Rite* (Rusk, 1852).

After being transferred to the Pacific Conference in 1855, Fisher was pastor in San Francisco and Stockton, California, and presiding elder of several districts. His most noteworthy western accomplishment was the opening of the work of Southern Methodism in Oregon, including the establishment of Corvallis College in 1861. He was first editor of the *Pacific Methodist* (1856–57) and president of the trustees of Pacific Methodist College at Vacaville, California. He published further editions of *The Christian Sacraments* at San Francisco (1858) and St. Louis (1870).

After serving as a delegate to the General Conference of the

Methodist Episcopal Church, South, at Memphis, Tennessee, in 1870, Fisher returned to Texas and served as Sunday school agent, as presiding elder, and as minister at Austin, Chappell Hill, Bellville, Belton, Georgetown, Round Rock, and West Point.

He married Elizabeth Watts in St. Clair, Illinois, on September 25, 1825. His second wife was Rebecca J. (Gilleland) Fisher,qv whom he married on May 15, 1848. He died in Austin, Texas, on August 28, 1880.

BIBLIOGRAPHY: Robert Edgar Ledbetter, Jr., Orceneth Fisher, Pioneer Methodist Preacher of Texas and the Pacific Coast (M.A. thesis, University of Texas, 1938). W. W. Sweet, Religion on the American Frontier, 1783–1840 (Vol. 4, University of Chicago Press, 1946).

Robert Edgar Ledbetter, Jr.

FISHER, REBECCA JANE GILLELAND (1831–1926). Rebecca Jane Gilleland Fisher, preservationist, was born in Philadelphia on August 31, 1831, the daughter of Mary (Barbour) and Johnson Gilleland.qv Around 1837 the family arrived in Texas and settled in Refugio County near the Don Carlos Ranch. In 1840 Comanches attacked the home, killed the parents, and captured Rebecca and her brother William. The children were rescued by Albert Sidney Johnstonqv and a detachment of Texas soldiers and taken to Victoria, where they stayed with William C. Blairqv until they could be sent to live with Jane Trimble, an aunt in Galveston. Rebecca Gilleland attended Rutersville College from about 1845 to 1848, when she married Orceneth Fisher,qv a Methodist minister. The couple had six children. In 1855 the Fishers left Texas for the Pacific coast, where for nearly sixteen years Fisher served as a pastor in California and Oregon. They returned to Texas about 1871 and eventually established a home in Austin, where Fisher died in 1880.

Mrs. Fisher was a charter member of the Daughters of the Republic of Texasqv and served as its state president for eighteen years. She was also president of the Austin chapter. She delivered an oration at the unveiling of the Sam Houstonqv monument at Huntsville and aided Clara Driscollqv in saving the Alamo from destruction. For several years she gave the opening prayer when the Texas legislature convened. She was the only woman elected to the Texas Veterans Associationqv and was its last surviving member. Her portrait was the first of a woman to be hung in the Senate chamber at the Capitol.qv She died in Austin on March 21, 1926. Her body lay in state in the Senate chamber, where funeral services were held. The Senate unanimously adopted a resolution in her memory and draped her portrait in mourning cloth. Honorary pallbearers included the two United States senators from Texas and four former governors. She was buried in Oakwood Cemetery, Austin.

BIBLIOGRAPHY: Elizabeth Brooks, Prominent Women of Texas (Akron, Ohio: Werner, 1896). Rebecca J. Gilleland Fisher, "Capture and Rescue of Mrs. Rebecca J. Fisher, née Gilleland," Quarterly of the Texas State Historical Association 3 (January 1900). Annie Doom Pickrell, Pioneer Women in Texas (Austin: Steck, 1929).

FISHER, SAMUEL RHOADS (1794–1876). Samuel Rhoads Fisher, secretary of the Texas Navyqv during the republic era, was born in Pennsylvania on December 31, 1794. Before 1819 he married Ann Pleasants; they had four children. Fisher came to Texas in 1830 and settled at Matagorda. He represented Matagorda Municipality in the Convention of 1836qv at Washington-on-the-Brazos and there signed the Texas Declaration of Independence.qv Fisher's nomination by President Sam Houstonqv as secretary of the Texas Navy was confirmed by the Senate on October 28, 1836. In October 1837 Houston suspended Fisher from office, supposedly to secure harmony and efficiency, but the Senate resented the suspension and ordered Fisher's reinstatement on October 18, 1837. Fisher died on March 14, 1839, and was buried at Matagorda. Fisher County, established in 1876, was named for him.

BIBLIOGRAPHY: Linda Ericson Devereaux, The Texas Navy (Nacogdoches, Texas, 1983). Jim Dan Hill, The Texas Navy (New York: Barnes, 1962). Louis Wiltz Kemp, The Signers of the Texas Declaration of Independence (Salado, Texas: Anson Jones, 1944; rpt. 1959).

L. W. Kemp

FISHER, WILLIAM S. (?–1845). William S. Fisher, soldier and secretary of war of Texas, son of James and Margaret (Nimmo) Fisher, moved to Texas from Virginia in 1834 and settled in Green DeWitt'sqv colony at Gonzales. Fisher represented the municipality of Gonzales at the Consultationqv at San Felipe in 1835. On March 10, 1836, he joined the Texas army and on March 26 reinforced Sam Houston'sqv army with the company that he had raised, Company I, First Regiment of Texas Volunteers, and participated in the battle of San Jacinto.qv He remained in the army until June 10, 1836, and served again from June 27 to September 27, 1836. Appointed secretary of war of the Republic of Texas,qv he served from December 21, 1836, to November 13, 1837, but his was a recess appointment and was not confirmed when the Senate met because of the change to the Mirabeau B. Lamarqv administration. On January 23, 1837, Lamar appointed Fisher lieutenant colonel of a frontier cavalry regiment. On March 19, 1840, he was in command of two companies of regulars at San Antonio at the time of the Council House Fight.qv Later in 1840 he was attracted to the Republic of the Rio Grandeqv and led 200 men to join the army of that organization at San Patricio. Returning to Texas after a few months of unsuccessful campaigning, he joined the Somervell expeditionqv in 1842 and was elected captain. With Alexander Somervell'sqv abandonment of the enterprise, Fisher was elected leader of those members of the expedition who continued on into Mexico on the Mier expedition.qv During the attack on Mier, Fisher was wounded. Imprisoned with his men by the Mexican general Pedro de Ampudia,qv Fisher was marched to Perote Prison.qv He was released in 1843 and returned to Texas, where he died at his home in Jackson County in 1845.

BIBLIOGRAPHY: Sam Houston Dixon and Louis Wiltz Kemp, The Heroes of San Jacinto (Houston: Anson Jones, 1932). Sam W. Haynes, Soldiers of Misfortune: The Somervell and Mier Expeditions (Austin: University of Texas Press, 1990). Dudley Goodall Wooten, ed., A Comprehensive History of Texas (2 vols., Dallas: Scarff, 1898; rpt., Austin: Texas State Historical Association, 1986).

David M. Vigness

FISHER COUNTY. Fisher County (H–11) is on U.S. Highway 180 west of Abilene in the Rolling Plains region of central West Texas. The county is bordered on the north by Kent and Stonewall counties, on the east by Jones County, on the south by Nolan County, and on the west by Scurry County. Its center point is 32°45′ north latitude and 100°23′ west longitude. Roby is the county seat; Rotan, the county's largest town, is 225 miles west of Dallas, 65 miles northwest of Abilene and 125 miles southeast of Lubbock. In addition to U.S. 180 the county's transportation needs are served by State highways 70 and 92. Fisher County covers 897 square miles of grassy, rolling prairies. The elevation ranges from 1,800 to 2,400 feet. The northern third of the county is drained by the Double Mountain Fork of the Brazos River, and the southern two-thirds is drained by the Clear Fork of the Brazos. Soils range from red to brown, with loamy surface layers and clayey or loamy subsoils. Between 51 percent and 60 percent of the land in the county is considered prime farmland. The vegetation, typical of the Rolling Prairies, features medium-height to tall grasses, mesquite, and cacti. Cedar, cottonwood, and pecan trees also grow along streams. Many species of wildflowers bloom in the spring and early summer, including daisies, buttercups, tallow weed, Indian blanket, baby's breath, prairie lace, wild verbena, belladonna, and hollyhock. Texas bluebells thrive in low places. The climate is subtropical and subhumid, with cool winters and hot summers. Temperatures range in January from an average low of 28° F to an average high of 56°, and in July from 70° to 96°. The average annual rainfall measures twenty-two inches, and the average relative humidity is 73 percent at 6 A.M. and 40 percent at 6 P.M. The average annual snowfall is five inches. The growing season averages 222 days, with the last freeze in early April and the first freeze in early November.

Fisher County comprises a region that has been the site of human habitation for several thousand years. Archeological artifacts recovered in the area suggest that the earliest human inhabitants arrived around 10,000 to 12,000 years ago, and evidence of Paleo, Archaic, and Historic cultures have been found in the county. Following these earliest inhabitants were the Lipan Apaches, who had settled in the region by the sixteenth century; later, around 1700, Comanches and Kiowas drifted in from the north, and Pawnees, Wichita, and Wacos occasionally hunted along the upper Brazos valley. The Old Indian Trial, which crossed the county, was used by various Indians to travel between the Plains region and Central Texas. Spanish explorer Francisco Vázquez de Coronado qv traversed the general region in 1541, and José Mares qv crossed it in 1788 while searching for a more direct route from Santa Fe to San Antonio. In the spring of 1847 Robert B. Marcy qv traveled along the Old Indian Trial through Fisher County on his way to El Paso; he camped for two days near the site of present-day Rotan. In the early summer of 1856 Robert E. Lee qv explored the county while leading a punitive expedition against the Indians.

A few buffalo qv hunters passed through the area in the early 1870s, but not until 1876, when the legislature separated the county from Bexar County, did the first permanent settlers arrive. The new county, named for Samuel Rhoads Fisher, qv a signer of the Texas Declaration of Independence, qv however, remained sparsely populated and was not organized until 1886. Most of the early residents were cattle ranchers, who were attracted to the area by its abundant grasslands and available water. The census of 1880 reported 136 inhabitants. Only four of those who responded listed their occupation as farmer; the remainder were connected with the livestock industry. Cattle, in fact, greatly outnumbered people in the county's early years; by 1880, 24,164 cattle were reported. Among the early residents was a colony of Swedes qv from Travis and Williamson counties, who settled in the northeastern portion of Fisher County near the site of present-day McCaulley. Other early settlers came from East and North Texas. The first post office, Newman, was established in 1881. The first townsites registered were Fisher, now North Roby, on November 11, 1885, and Roby on April 16, 1886. There was a bitter county-seat struggle between Roby and Fisher. Roby eventually won the election, but many questioned its legality, and it was later discovered that one of the voters, a Mr. Bill Purp, was actually a dog whose owner lived near Roby.

Railway construction began in 1881, when the Texas and Pacific Railway routed an east-west branch through Eskota in the southeastern corner of the county. Cheap land, and improved access to markets made possible by the new railroad connection, lured many new settlers to the county. Between 1880 and 1890 the population grew more than twentyfold, from 135 to 2,996, and by 1910 the number of inhabitants had more than quadrupled again, increasing to 12,596. Many of the new settlers were farmers, who began plowing and fencing the prairie. In 1880 there were only three farms in the entire county; in 1890s that figure had grown to 332; and by 1910 the county had 1,839 farms. One result of the dramatic rise of the farming economy was the gradual decline of ranching. The number of cattle in the county was nearly 70,000 in 1890, but by the turn of the century only about one-third of that number remained. Although ranching continued to be a mainstay of the economy, it never again dominated the scene as it had in the county's early years. The earliest farmers in the county planted such subsistence crops as corn and wheat. But in the 1880s cotton was introduced, and by the early 1890s corn, oats, and wheat were being grown commercially. In 1900 Fisher County farmers produced 113,640 bushels of corn, 41,290 bushels of oats, 7,320 bushels of wheat, and 1,280 bales of cotton. After 1910 wheat and cotton increasingly took center stage, and by 1920 the county was among the state's leaders in wheat production. High prices for cotton, however, persuaded many farmers to dedicate ever-increasing acreage to cotton culture qv in the 1920s. In 1926 more than 48,000 bales were ginned in the county, and production levels continued to be high through the end of the 1920s. Falling prices, droughts, and boll weevil qv infestations, however, combined to drive down cotton production in the 1930s. Although the amount of land planted in cotton continued to be quite high—as much as 165,000 acres in 1930—both yields and profits dropped significantly, especially after 1932. In 1930 Fisher County farmers produced only 17,937 bales, half the peak figure of the mid-1920s.

Because of the rapidly growing population, land prices showed a marked increase between 1910 and 1930, and many new farmers found it impossible to buy land. The number of tenants grew rapidly, particularly in the 1920s, and by 1930 more than half of all farmers in the county—1,326 of 2,088—were working someone else's land. In contrast to many other areas of the state, the overwhelming majority of the tenants were white, but the practice nonetheless had serious results during the Great Depression qv of the 1930s. As a result of the poor yields and the reluctance of banks to extend credit to financially strapped farmers, many of those who made a living from the land, particularly tenants, found themselves in a precarious position. Numerous farmers were forced to give up their livelihoods and seek work elsewhere. The population of the county as a whole fell from 13,563 in 1930 to 12,932 in 1940. Oil, discovered in 1928, helped some poor farmers to settle long-standing debts and survive the depression years, but the farming economy did not fully recover until after World War II.qv Cotton was the chief money crop in the years after 1945, with grain sorghum, wheat, hay, corn, and watermelons providing a significant source of income. Cattle, sheep, and poultry were also raised commercially. Large-scale irrigated farming was introduced during the 1950s, and by 1964 the county had 4,140 acres under irrigation.qv The percentage of proceeds from livestock grew in the 1950s and 1960s; by the early 1970s the county's average annual farm income evenly divided between livestock and crops. In 1982, 94 percent of the land in the county was in farms and ranches, with 27 percent of the land under cultivation and 2 percent irrigated. Fisher County ranked 102d in the state in the highest agricultural receipts, with 73 percent coming from crops. Primary crops were cotton, wheat, sorghum, hay, and oats; cantaloupes, tomatoes, watermelons, peaches, and pecans were also grown in sizable quantities. The leading livestock products were cattle, milk, and hogs.

The total number of businesses in the county in the early 1980s was ninety-seven. In 1980, 23 percent of the laborers were self-employed; 18 percent were employed in professional or related services, 13 percent in manufacturing, 13 percent in wholesale and retail trade, and 31 percent in agriculture, forestry, fishing, and mining; 23 percent worked in other counties; 727 retired workers lived in the county. Nonfarm earnings in 1981 totaled $45,908,000. Gypsum, discovered in Fisher County around the turn of the century, is mined in large quantities and processed in plants in Nolan County and at the National Gypsum Company facility in Rotan (see MINERAL RESOURCES AND MINING). Oil also continues to be produced in sizable amounts. Production in 1990 was 2,265,676 barrels. Between 1944 and January 1, 1990, 230,887,287 barrels was pumped from the county's wells.

Wood's Chapel, built in 1883, was the first church and school building in the county. In the early 1980s Fisher County had four school districts, with four elementary, one middle, and three high schools. The average daily attendance was 968 in 1981–82, when expenditures per pupil were $2,785. Seventy percent of the seventy-seven high school graduates that year planned to attend college. In 1983, 55 percent of the school graduates were white, 37 percent Hispanic, 8 percent black, 0.1 percent Asian, and 0.1 percent American Indian. The first churches in Fisher County were established shortly after county organization. In the mid-1980s the county had twenty-three churches with a estimated combined membership of 5,379. The largest denominations were Southern Baptist, Catholic, and United Methodist.

Fisher County has generally been staunchly Democratic, although Republicans have made some inroads. In elections since World War II[qv] the only Republican candidate to win a majority of votes was Richard Nixon in 1972. Democratic officials have also continued to maintain control of county offices. In the 1982 primary 100 percent voted Democratic, with a total of 1,986 votes cast. The population of Fisher County fell steadily after World War II, as residents moved away to find jobs. The number of residents was 11,023 in 1950, 7,865 in 1960, 6,344 in 1970, 5,891 in 1980, and 4,842 in 1990. In 1990, nearly half of the population (2,284) lived in Rotan. Other communities include Roby, Busby, Claytonville, Eskota, Hobbs, Longworth, McCaulley, Palava, Royston, and Sylvester. In 1990, 91.8 percent of the population was white, 3.9 percent black, 0.4 percent American Indian, and 0.3 percent Asian. The largest ancestry groups are English, Irish, and Hispanic. Moore, West Moore, and Plasterco lakes and the Brazos River are popular with fishermen, and the county also attracts numerous dove and quail hunters. A stock show and a fair in October are among the prime tourist attractions.

BIBLIOGRAPHY: R. C. Crane, "Early Days in Fisher County," *West Texas Historical Association Year Book* 6 (1930). Fisher County Historical Commission, *History of Fisher County, Texas* (Rotan, Texas: Shelton, 1983). E. L. Yeats and E. H. Shelton, *History of Fisher County*, (n.p.: Feather, 1971).

Hooper Shelton

FISHER-MILLER LAND GRANT. The Fisher-Miller Land Grant, made by the Republic of Texas[qv] on June 7, 1842, and renewed on September 1, 1843, resulted from a petition made by Henry Francis Fisher, Burchard Miller, and Joseph Baker[qqv] on February 8, 1842, to be permitted to settle 1,000 immigrant families of German, Dutch, Swiss, Danish, Swedish, and Norwegian ancestry in Texas under the auspices of the San Saba Colonization Company. The grant included more than three million acres between the Llano and Colorado rivers. The original contract allowed the introduction of 600 families and single men. Fisher and Miller did not succeed in colonizing the grant within the allotted time and took advantage of a legislative amendment passed on January 6, 1844, which extended the deadline. The amendment also increased the number of settlers to 6,000 families and single men. After seeking and obtaining the title of Texas consul to Bremen, Fisher went to Germany to promote colonization. On June 26, 1844, he sold an interest in the contract to the Adelsverein[qv] (the Society for the Protection of German Immigrants in Texas). On December 30, 1845, Fisher and Miller sold their rights in the grant to the society. As a stipulation of the sale Fisher was appointed to the society's colonial committee. Along with the rights to the grant, the society had the responsibility to settle the area and take over any expenses accrued by the San Saba Colonization Company. The grant actually received few colonists from the society, which made only five small settlements; of the five, only Castell survived. Many of the settlers moved to New Braunfels or Fredericksburg and subsequently sold the grants they had received in the Fisher-Miller tract.

BIBLIOGRAPHY: Rudolph L. Biesele, *The History of the German Settlements in Texas, 1831–1861* (Austin: Von Boeckmann–Jones, 1930; rpt. 1964). Solon Ollie Loving, A History of the Fisher-Miller Land Grant from 1842–1860 (M.A. thesis, University of Texas, 1934).

Rudolph L. Biesele

FISHES OF THE GULF OF MEXICO. There are probably more than 600 species of Texas marine fishes, counting all habitats from the estuaries to the ocean depths of the abyssal zone 150 miles off the barrier islands. This is more than all the different kinds of Texas freshwater fishes, reptiles, amphibians, and mammals put together. At least 120 families of marine fishes live along the Texas coast. Getting an exact count is difficult because there are few effective barriers in the ocean, and it is large and difficult to explore; secretive species therefore often go unnoticed.

Most abundant in numbers are the schooling fishes, including the herrings or shads (*Clupeidae*); the commercial Gulf menhaden (*Brevoortia patronus*); the anchovies (*Engraulidae*), of which the most common is the bay anchovy (*Anchoa mitchilli*) which abounds in brackish water and spawns anytime water temperatures exceed 20° C; and the striped mullet (*Mugil cephalus*), most notable in its lazy jumping, but swift when chased by predators such as trout, jacks, or another of the many species that depend on it for food. The most diverse family is the sea bass (*Serranidae*), with nearly forty species, but the gobies (*Gobiidae*), jacks (*Carangidae*), drums or croakers (*Sciaenidae*), and flounders (*Bothidae*) all have around twenty each. More species have ranges that extend farther north than south, allowing the coastal fishes to be characterized as warm temperate, but many are tropical, especially offshore.

Many species are found closer inshore when young and move offshore as they grow. This movement is frequently associated with seasonal changes, and large movements are especially stimulated by northers. Recent extensive collections have verified and extended observations of the zoning of certain species. For example, in the bays and northern Gulf near-to-shore, croakers are the common bottom fishes. These are replaced on the continental shelf by sea robins (*Triglidae*), on the middle shelf by small sea basses, and with snappers (*Lutjanidae*) and porgies (*Sparidae*), especially the longspine porgy (*Stenotomus caprinus*), on the outer edge.

The state of Texas has had practice in freshwater stocking and is pioneering the stocking of selected marine species. The first to be stocked was red drum (*Sciaenops ocellata*). Stocking was not possible in salt water until recent breakthroughs in spawning red drum and other species allowed the raising of large numbers of fingerlings. Stocking is based on the premise that reproduction is the controlling factor in numbers of fish and has been used in fresh water where reproduction was inadequate or absent. Stocking effects in salt water are yet unknown, and stocking does not seem to alleviate the problem, since scarcity of saltwater species is often a consequence of port development, which removes the critical shallow habitat needed by the young to grow toward maturity.

Popular sport fishes include the sea trouts (*Cynoscion*), red drum, and southern flounder (*Paralichthys lethostigma*) inshore, and the billfishes, including sailfish (*Istiophorus*) and marlins (*Makaira, Tetrapturus*), mackerel (*Scomberomorus*), and red snapper (*Lutjanus campechanus*) offshore. Inshore commercial fishing has been legally restricted and includes mostly black drum (*Pogonias cromis*), southern flounder (*Paralichthys lethostigma*), and menhaden. The latter is a very large fishery limited to the upper coast.

Two especially interesting habitats are the offshore reefs formed on top of protruding salt domes and the Laguna Madre, where salinities frequently exceed that of seawater. The offshore reefs, although poor versions of tropical coral reefs, contain an impressive assembly of fishes. Some of these, such as the beautiful spotfin butterfly fish (*Chaetodon ocellatus*), drift inshore as larvae to spend their first summer on the similar habitat of the inlet jetties.

Though there are areas on the upper Texas coast where freshwater fishes actually intrude into the bays, the shallow Laguna Madre, on the driest part of the coast, has historically exhibited salinities double or even triple that of normal seawater strength during dry years, causing many fish to die. The completion of the Gulf Intracoastal Waterway[qv] to Port Isabel in 1949 provided sufficient circulation to prevent recurrences, but the shallow lagoon still suffers very large mortalities from killing freezes such as the Christmas freeze of 1983. The freezes are worse here because the lagoon is shallow, the distances to deeper and warmer water are great, and the cold fronts strike with great rapidity (*see* BLUE NORTHER).

Coastal fishes have provided much sport and essential food from the time of early settlement to the present. As early as 1685 people were known to eat fish killed by freezes. Fishing and fish watching with snorkel or scuba are large industries on the coast. Threats to fish populations include development, pollution, and lack of sufficient freshwater in the bays.

BIBLIOGRAPHY: A. C. Becker, *Fishing the Texas Coast: Inshore and Offshore* (Houston: Cordovan Corporation, 1975). Gordon Gunter, *Studies on Marine Fishes of Texas* (Austin: University of Texas Institute of Marine Science, 1945). H. Dickson Hoese and Richard H. Moore, *Fishes of the Gulf of Mexico: Texas, Louisiana, and Adjacent Waters* (College Station: Texas A&M University Press, 1977).

H. Dickson Hoese

FISHHOLE CREEK. Fishhole (Fishole) Creek, also known as Jackson Branch, rises three miles north of Afton in extreme north central Dickens county (at 33°49′ N, 100°48′ W) and runs northeast for five miles to its mouth on the South Pease (or Tongue) River, in south central Motley County a mile north of the Dickens-Motley county line (at 33°51′ N, 100°46′ W). The local terrain is characterized by moderately steep slopes with locally high relief, surfaced by shallow to moderately deep silt loams that support mesquite and grasses.

FISH SPRING BRANCH. Fish Spring Branch rises four miles northeast of Alvarado in east central Johnson County (at 32°25′ N, 97°10′ W) and runs northeast for 2½ miles to its mouth on Mountain Creek, seven miles northeast of Alvarado (at 32°28′ N, 97°09′ W). It traverses flat to rolling prairie surfaced by dark, commonly calcareous clays that support mesquite trees, cacti, and grasses. The area has served as crop and range land.

FISK, GREENLEAF (1807–1888). Greenleaf Fisk, Brown County pioneer, was born in Albany, New York, on May 19, 1807, to English immigrants. He served in the Texas army at the battle of San Jacinto qv and as a member of the House of Representatives of the Republic of Texas qv from Bastrop. One of many children, Fisk began earning his own living at the age of twelve when he worked on a dairy farm in New Jersey. Despite the need to work for a living he managed to get a good general education and, at the age of twenty, entered Lane's Theological Seminary in Cincinnati, Ohio, to prepare for the Presbyterian ministry. He later attended Hanover College at Hanover, Indiana.

For some reason he gave up his plans to enter the ministry and moved to Texas in 1834. He settled at or near Mina (now Bastrop) shortly before Texas independence was declared. There he married Mary A. Manlove before joining the Mina Volunteers under Capt. Jesse Billingsley qv and participating in the battle of San Jacinto. After the war he and his wife and their first son returned to Bastrop, where he served as clerk of the district court (1827) before he was elected to the House of Representatives (1838–39). In 1841 he served as chief justice of Bastrop County. His wife bore him seven children before her death, after which he moved to Williamson County, where he married Mary Hawkins, who bore him eight children.

In 1860 Fisk moved his family to Brown County, portions of which he had surveyed in 1846. He had been granted title to 1,280 acres of land, called the Marcus Hulen survey, in Brown County on December 8, 1846, by J. Pinckney Henderson qv for his service to the Republic of Texas.qv In Brown County, between 1862 and the mid-1870s, Fisk served variously as county judge, justice of the peace, county surveyor, district clerk, county clerk, and county treasurer. Because of his service in these offices he was known as Judge Fisk.

His first home in Brown County was a log house on a slough east of the site of present downtown Brownwood. He later built a two-story stone home and a stone gristmill, doing the masonry work himself. The gristmill has since been converted into a private residence and is still standing in Brownwood. Fisk also taught what was perhaps the first school in Brown County, and a Brownwood school that existed as late as 1876 was named for him. When a drought left the main settlement without water and a problem with the title of an alternate townsite developed after a few years, Fisk donated sixty acres near his own home for a townsite and an additional 100 acres for county use. The deed of this transaction was burned in the courthouse in 1880, but the move was made sometime between 1867 and 1879. In a replacement deed filed in 1880 Fisk described the deed of the townsite as made by him "about ten years ago." As a teacher and father of fifteen children, Fisk wanted enough settlers to move to the new townsite to provide students for a school in Brownwood. He sold T. D. Harriss 800 acres of land adjoining the townsite at a good price, on the condition that Harriss move his family of many children to the new town. In 1877 Brownwood was incorporated.

At Fisk's death on January 26, 1888, the entire town closed in honor of its founder, whose funeral was conducted in the old First Presbyterian Church in Brownwood. He was buried in Brownwood in Greenleaf Cemetery, for which he had earlier donated the land.

BIBLIOGRAPHY: Thomas Robert Havins, *Something about Brown: A History of Brown County, Texas* (Brownwood, Texas: Banner Printing, 1958). Tevis Clyde Smith, *Frontier's Generation* (Brownwood, Texas, 1931; 2d ed. 1980). Texas House of Representatives, *Biographical Directory of the Texan Conventions and Congresses, 1832–1845* (Austin: Book Exchange, 1941). James C. White, *The Promised Land: A History of Brown County* (Brownwood, Texas: Brownwood *Banner*, 1941).

Charlotte Laughlin

FISK, TEXAS. Fisk, on Farm Road 1026 in south central Coleman County, grew up near the headquarters of the Adam T. Brown ranch after it was broken up for sale to farmers in 1904. John Terry and others built the first gin and store. The town had three businesses and seventy people in 1940. By 1980 the population had declined to forty, where it remained in 1990.

William R. Hunt

FISKVILLE, TEXAS. Fiskville was on Little Walnut Creek and old U.S. Highway 81 (now North Lamar Boulevard) six miles north of Austin in north central Travis County. It was founded in the early 1870s and named for pioneer settlers George Greenleaf Fisk and Josiah Fisk. A Fiskville post office was established in 1873 with Edward Zimmerman as postmaster. The population of the community that year was estimated between 150 and 200. By the mid-1880s Fiskville had a steam flour mill and cotton gin, a general store, a union church, and a district school to serve a population of sixty. A dairy had been added by the early 1890s, and the population had grown to 120. Continued growth, however, was curtailed by the opportunities available in nearby Austin, and after the turn of the century Fiskville began to decline. The post office was discontinued in 1901. By the early 1930s the number of residents had fallen to fifty. The Fiskville county school district was consolidated with the Summitt county school district in 1953 and with the Austin Independent School District in 1959. Fiskville retained its identity as a separate community until the mid-1960s, at which time it was annexed to Austin.

BIBLIOGRAPHY: John J. Germann and Myron Janzen, *Texas Post Offices by County* (1986).

Vivian Elizabeth Smyrl

FITZE, TEXAS. Fitze, on the Southern Pacific Railroad four miles southeast of Garrison in northeastern Nacogdoches County, was settled after the Civil War.qv In 1883 the Houston, East and West Texas Railway was constructed as far as Fitze; in 1885 the railroad completed a line from there to the Louisiana border. During the 1930s the community had a flag station and a number of houses; several stores and a gin were also located in the area. After World War II qv many of the residents moved away, but as late as the mid-1960s there were still two sawmills and two churches in the area.

Christopher Long

FITZGERALD, ALICE MARTHA PARSONS (1860–1910). Alice Fitzgerald, journalist, was born in Washington County, Iowa, in February 1860, the daughter of Robert and Lucy (Draper) Parsons. Her father was a physician. Alice was educated in Iowa schools, then attended college in New York. She was married briefly to a man named Wood; the couple had a daughter before his death. In 1879 she married Hugh Nugent Fitzgerald,^qv a news reporter. Through her husband, who eventually became managing editor of both the Dallas *Morning News* and the Dallas *Times Herald*,^qqv Mrs. Fitzgerald developed her own interest in journalism. When the family moved to Dallas in 1889 she began regular contributions to several local newspapers and other publications. She later became society editor of both major Dallas papers.

In 1895 Alice Fitzgerald founded *Beau Monde*,^qv a weekly society tabloid. As editor and publisher she used her paper to increase the level of sophistication in Dallas society by relating the news and interests of its socially elite women. Although the publication could be arbitrary, flowery, and flamboyant, it was considered to contain strong and accurate reporting and was later seen as one of the city's best printed historical records from the turn-of-the-century era. In addition to standard society news, the paper included editorial comments on national and international events, largely written by Hugh Fitzgerald, and a directory advertising when socialites would be at home for callers. Mrs. Fitzgerald occasionally wandered into other areas such as sports with mixed results, as when she reported on a golf tournament that featured a socialite "gracefully swinging her caddy" on the links. She also used her paper to discourage improper behavior, including spitting tobacco on sidewalks and streetcars, which she believed deserving of punishment by imprisonment. Her paper lasted until 1913 and successfully contributed to Dallas society.

Alice Fitzgerald was a member of the Episcopal Church. She died after a sudden illness in Dallas on December 13, 1910, and was survived by her husband, one daughter from her first marriage, one daughter and one son from her marriage to Fitzgerald, and several siblings. She is buried in Oakland Cemetery in Dallas. She died a wealthy woman and left her property to her husband and children; many years later, after the death of her eldest daughter, a suit was filed over her estate, which was valued at $750,000 and included several downtown Dallas properties.

BIBLIOGRAPHY: Dallas *Morning News*, December 14, 1910. Dallas *Times Herald*, June 14, 1950, November 25, 1951, March 30, 1969. Vertical Files, Barker Texas History Center, University of Texas at Austin.

Debbie Mauldin Cottrell

FITZGERALD, DAVID (?–1832). David Fitzgerald, Old Three Hundred^qv settler, came to Texas as a widower aged over fifty, probably from Georgia, late in 1821. With his son John and two slaves, he paddled a canoe up the Brazos River in search of Stephen F. Austin's^qv colony in January 1822 and settled on the east bank of the river three miles below the site of present Richmond. On October 20, 1823, Austin wrote Luciano García^qv that he had been compelled to cause five men and their families, including David Fitzgerald, to leave the colony because they were fugitives from justice in the United States. Apparently Austin reconsidered because Fitzgerald, as one of the Old Three Hundred^qv settlers, received title to a league of land now in Fort Bend County on July 10, 1824, and raised crops there in 1825 and 1826. He died in 1832, and his plantation became the property of his daughter, Sarah, who had married Eli Fenn in Georgia before the Fitzgerald and Fenn families moved to Texas.

BIBLIOGRAPHY: Eugene C. Barker, ed., *The Austin Papers* (3 vols., Washington: GPO, 1924–28). Lester G. Bugbee, "The Old Three Hundred: A List of Settlers in Austin's First Colony," *Quarterly of the Texas State Historical Association* 1 (October 1897). Clarence Wharton, *Wharton's History of Fort Bend County* (San Antonio: Naylor, 1939).

FITZGERALD, EDWARD (?–1850). Edward Fitzgerald, pioneer settler of Refugio County, represented the county in the House of the Fourth Congress of the Republic of Texas, 1838–40. He moved to Texas before March 2, 1835, as a single man. On January 29, 1840, he advertised a law partnership in Aransas City with James W. Robinson.^qv He served as tax assessor that year and was a member of the Refugio County Minute Men, a ranger company, in 1841–42. He died at Corpus Christi on September 17, 1850.

BIBLIOGRAPHY: Texas House of Representatives, *Biographical Directory of the Texan Conventions and Congresses, 1832–1845* (Austin: Book Exchange, 1941).

Stephen L. Hardin

FITZGERALD, HUGH NUGENT (ca. 1857–1936). Hugh Nugent Fitzgerald, journalist, son of William Laurens Fitzgerald, was born in Charleston, South Carolina, probably in 1857. He attended Jesuit College in Ireland. Upon returning to North America he traveled throughout the United States, Mexico, and Canada, working in mining camps and at various occupations. He married Alice Parsons Wood in 1879 in South Carolina. They had two children. The family moved to Texas in 1889, where Fitzgerald began newspaper work, first as a sports writer and later as a political commentator. He became managing editor and staff correspondent on the Dallas *Morning News*,^qv with which he was associated for fourteen years. In the early 1900s he was employed as editor of the Dallas *Times Herald*^qv for ten years. He later edited the Fort Worth *Record* (see FORT WORTH STAR-TELEGRAM) and was owner, publisher, and editor of the Wichita Falls *Record News*, before he joined the Marsh-Fentress interests and established his home in Austin in 1921; there he was chief editorial writer for the Austin *American*, the Austin *Statesman* (see AUSTIN AMERICAN-STATESMAN), and allied newspapers for more than ten years.

Fitzgerald managed the gubernatorial campaigns of Charles A. Culberson and Oscar B. Colquitt,^qqv served two terms as a member of the Texas Historical and Library Commission, and was for twelve years a member of the board of regents of the College of Industrial Arts (now Texas Woman's University). From 1925 until 1933 he was president of the board; one of the residence halls at the university is named in his honor. Fitzgerald wrote almost exclusively for newspapers. His other works include *Texans and Their State* (1918), which he edited with other Texas newspapermen, and *Governors I have Known* (1927). In February 1931 he was honored by the Texas Senate for his service in journalism, and his portrait was hung on the Senate wall.

Fitzgerald's first wife died in 1910. On April 30, 1921, he married Donna Roberts. He was a Catholic. He died in Austin on May 6, 1936, and was buried in Dallas.

BIBLIOGRAPHY: Austin *Statesman*, May 6, 7, 1936. Hugh Nugent Fitzgerald, ed., *Texans and Their State: A Newspaper Reference Work* (2 vols., Houston: Texas Biographical Association, 1918). San Antonio *Express*, May 7, 1936.

Edward Crane

FITZGERALD, TEXAS. Fitzgerald, on Mound Prairie Creek eleven miles north of Palestine in northern Anderson County, was probably named for W. A. Fitzgerald, who settled in the area in the 1850s and who was the oldest resident of Fitzgerald in 1901. The settlement had a post office from 1888 to 1905. In 1896 C. D. Kelley was the postmaster, and Fitzgerald had two general stores and a flour mill and gin. The community was probably abandoned in the early 1900s, as it was not labeled on state highway maps by the 1930s.

BIBLIOGRAPHY: *Anderson County Herald*, July 12, 1901.

Mark Odintz

FITZGERALD CREEK. Fitzgerald Creek rises fourteen miles northwest of Menard in northwestern Menard County (at 31°03′ N,

99°56′ W) and runs northeast for twelve miles to its mouth on Brady Creek, two miles south of Eden in Concho County (at 31°11′ N, 99°51′ W). The stream crosses flat to rolling terrain where the soil, in some places shallow and stony and in others composed of clay loams, supports grasses, oaks, junipers, and mesquite.

FITZHUGH, JOHN T. P. (1815–?). John T. P. Fitzhugh, physician and soldier at San Jacinto, was born in Prince William County, Virginia, in 1815 and immigrated to Texas in 1835. At Nacogdoches on January 14, 1836, he enrolled for six months as a private in the Volunteer Auxiliary Corps. Later he served as assistant surgeon under William Francis H. Davidson^{qv} on the staff of Col. Edward Burleson,^{qv} commander of the First Regiment, Texas Volunteers. At the battle of San Jacinto,^{qv} having received no orders, Fitzhugh and the other medical officers advanced with the Texas troops, ready to treat the wounded or take part in the fighting as need be. Fitzhugh entered the fight at the center of the Mexican line.

His brother Wesley was a private in Capt. Gustavus A. Parker's^{qv} company of Georgia volunteers and later a "surgeon dentist" in Brig. Gen. Thomas J. Green's^{qv} Second Brigade of the Army of the Republic of Texas.^{qv} Wesley Fitzhugh died on September 11, 1836. After leaving the army John Fitzhugh practiced medicine in Bastrop County for five years. He was in Bastrop as late as January 22, 1840, when he made application to become administrator of his brother's estate; both he and his brother had received bounty donations in Van Zandt County. By 1858 he had returned to Prince Edward County, Virginia, and the following year was living in Canton, Mississippi. He was still living there in 1874, when he became a member of the Texas Veterans Association,^{qv} but by October 1877 he had moved to Warren County, Mississippi.

BIBLIOGRAPHY: Daughters of the Republic of Texas, *Muster Rolls of the Texas Revolution* (Austin, 1986). Sam Houston Dixon and Louis Wiltz Kemp, *The Heroes of San Jacinto* (Houston: Anson Jones, 1932). Thomas L. Miller, *Bounty and Donation Land Grants of Texas, 1835–1888* (Austin: University of Texas Press, 1967). Pat Ireland Nixon, *The Medical Story of Early Texas, 1528–1853* (Lancaster, Pennsylvania: Lupe Memorial Fund, 1946). *Telegraph and Texas Register*, September 28, 1836.

Thomas W. Cutrer

FITZHUGH, WILLIAM F. (1818–1883). William F. Fitzhugh, soldier, Texas Ranger, and farmer, the son of John and Sarah (Shelton) Fitzhugh, was born in Kentucky in 1818. As a child he moved with his parents to Missouri, and at the age of seventeen he volunteered for service in the Seminole War in Florida. After returning to Missouri he participated in the campaign to expel the Mormons^{qv} from that state. In 1845 he moved to Texas with his parents and settled just south of the site of present Melissa. He married Mary Rattan and received a 640-acre headright. During the Mexican War^{qv} he served in the First Regiment, Texas Mounted Volunteers, commanded by Col. John Coffee (Jack) Hays.^{qv} Fitzhugh returned to Collin County after the war and divided his time between farming and serving with the Texas Rangers^{qv} on the Indian frontier. In March 1862 he entered Confederate service as first colonel of the Sixteenth Texas Cavalry, a regiment that served in the Trans-Mississippi Department. After the war Fitzhugh resumed farming at Melissa. He served as doorkeeper for the Constitutional Convention of 1875^{qv} and as Senate doorkeeper for the Fifteenth through the Eighteenth legislatures. On October 23, 1883, he was killed when he was thrown from a wagon. He was first buried in Forest Grove Cemetery near McKinney but was subsequently reinterred in Fairview Cemetery in Denison. He was survived by seven children.

BIBLIOGRAPHY: J. Lee and Lillian J. Stambaugh, *A History of Collin County* (Austin: Texas State Historical Association, 1958).

Lester Newton Fitzhugh

FITZHUGH, TEXAS. Fitzhugh was on the border of Hays and Travis counties twenty miles west of Austin. It grew up at the Barton Creek crossing on the old road between Austin and Fredericksburg after the Civil War.^{qv} In the years of the cattle drives the road through Fitzhugh was the primary trail from western counties to Austin. The community, originally known as Barton Creek Settlement, took the name of another creek in the vicinity when a post office opened in 1898. Fitzhugh was the site of a small public school in the 1880s, and for an unknown period of time George W. Brackenridge^{qv} of San Antonio made his home there. The community declined in the early twentieth century; the post office closed in 1914, and soon thereafter the population dropped below twenty-five; it was last recorded as twenty-five in the late 1960s.

BIBLIOGRAPHY: Dudley Richard Dobie, *A Brief History of Hays County and San Marcos, Texas* (San Marcos, 1948). Hays County Scrapbook, Barker Texas History Center, University of Texas at Austin.

Daniel P. Greene

FITZSIMON, LAURENCE JULIUS (1895–1958). Laurence Julius FitzSimon, Catholic bishop and historian, was born in San Antonio, Texas, on January 31, 1895, son of John Thomas and Theodora (Okelmann) FitzSimon. The family moved the following year to Castroville, where John FitzSimon practiced medicine until his death in 1924. At the age of twelve, Laurence was sent to St. Anthony's College in San Antonio. In 1911 he was sent by the Diocese of San Antonio to Rome to complete his studies for the priesthood. Ill health forced him to return to Texas in 1916. After recuperating for a few months, he joined the United States Navy and was assigned to the minesweeper Heron during World War I^{qv} as a pharmacist's mate.

FitzSimon resumed his theological studies in 1919 at St. Meinrad's Seminary, Indiana, and was ordained on May 17, 1921. After teaching for four years at St. John's Seminary, San Antonio, and then serving as pastor at Runge, Karnes City, and Kenedy for seven years, he was transferred to Seguin in 1932. While there he directed the activities celebrating the founding of Seguin and wrote a history of Seguin and a pageant on the city's founding.

In 1941, when Bishop Robert E. Lucey^{qv} of Amarillo was made archbishop of San Antonio, he appointed Father FitzSimon chancellor of the archdiocese. It was a short assignment, however, for on August 5, 1941, the chancellor was named bishop of the Catholic Diocese of Amarillo.^{qv} He was consecrated on October 22 and installed on November 4. During his administration the number of churches, priests, schools, and institutions in the diocese more than doubled.

FitzSimon was a scholar and historian. His Texana collection ranked among the best private historical libraries. During his custodianship of the Catholic Archives of Texas,^{qv} he made frequent trips to France and Rome to gather materials on bishops and priests who had labored in Texas during the colonial period. For his research on pioneer French priests of Texas, he was awarded the title of Chanoine d'Honneur de la Primatiale in 1951 by the cardinal bishop of Lyons, the first American to be so honored.

FitzSimon suffered a stroke in May 1954 and never fully recovered, though he continued the work of his diocese and historical collecting. He died on July 2, 1958, at St. Anthony's Hospital in Amarillo and was buried in Llano Cemetery. In 1976 the bishop's personal library was donated to the Amarillo Public Library as the Bush-FitzSimon Collection. In 1989 the Texas Catholic Historical Society^{qv} established the Laurence J. FitzSimon Award to honor Catholic archivists in Texas.

BIBLIOGRAPHY: Catholic Archives of Texas, Files, Austin. Texas Catholic Historical Society *Newsletter*, March 1989. Vertical Files, Barker Texas History Center, University of Texas at Austin. *Who's Who in America*, 1950–51.

Sister M. Claude Lane, O.P.

FIVEMILE (FIVE MILE) CREEK (Dallas County). Fivemile Creek rises in Duncanville about two miles from Redbird Airport in southwestern Dallas County (at 32°40′ N, 96°54′ W) and runs north-northeast for 3½ miles, then south-southeast, for a total length of about fifteen miles, before reaching its mouth on the Trinity River, a quarter mile north of Interstate Highway 20 (at 32°41′ N, 96°42′ W). The stream originally emptied into the Trinity about three miles south of its present mouth, but was diverted to feed what is now the Pin and Feather Club Lake, then later channeled into the Trinity at its present location when Interstate 20 was constructed. The stream passes through five city parks—Pecan Grove, Kiest, Glendale, Arden Terrace, and College. Where it has not been diverted into man-made channels, layers of Austin chalk and Eagle Ford shale lie under its basin. The soil in its drainage area consists of calcareous and clayey surface layers over chalky subsoils. Originally there were three vegetative zones within the creek's drainage basin: cedar brakes along the stream course and hillsides, riparian woodlands on the floodplains, and tall grasses on the upland prairies. Black bear, cougar, bobcat, white-tailed deer, and bison roamed the area. By the mid-1980s, most of the nearby terrain had been extensively developed for commercial and residential use, though the area around the creek's upper reaches remained relatively untouched.
BIBLIOGRAPHY: Dallas Dept. of Public Works, *Flood Plain Management of Five Mile Creek* (Dallas, 1976).

____ (DeWitt County). Fivemile Creek, formerly known as Five-Mile Coleto Creek, rises three miles southeast of Blackwell Lake in central DeWitt County (at 29°02′ N, 97°23′ W) and runs southeast for seven miles to its mouth on Twelvemile Creek (formerly Twelve-Mile Coleto Creek), two miles east of Meyersville (at 28°56′ N, 97°16′ W). It traverses an area of low-rolling hills and prairies surfaced by moderately to highly expansive clay soil that supports prairie grasses and some mesquite. The creek was named in 1850, when the DeWitt county seat was located in Clinton. The five-mile designation signified the distance from the creek's headwaters to the courthouse door.

____ (Gonzales County). Five Mile Creek rises slightly south of Cost in central Gonzales County (at 29°23′ N, 97°31′ W) and runs south for about nineteen miles to its mouth on Sandies Creek, about 1½ miles northeast of Westhoff in DeWitt County (at 29°14′ N, 97°26′ W). The stream traverses flat terrain with shallow depressions and fine sandy loams that support hardwoods, conifers, and grasses.

____ (Menard County). Fivemile Creek rises six miles north of Saline in southeastern Menard County (at 30°48′ N, 99°33′ W) and runs north for ten miles to its mouth on the San Saba River, two miles north of Hext (at 30°54′ N, 99°32′ W). It traverses rolling prairie surfaced by shallow to moderately deep clay loams that support oak, juniper, mesquite, and grasses.

____ (Upton County). Fivemile Creek rises at the intersection of China Draw and Rankin Draw, near King Mountain in Upton County (at 31°12′ N, 102°00′ W), and runs south across south Upton and northwest Crockett counties for a total of 15½ miles to its mouth on the Pecos River, between State Highway 349 and Farm Road 308 (at 30°59′ N, 102°02′ W). The stream crosses an area of sand, gravel, and mud substrate with variable soils. Flooding along the creek is very sudden and severe, although infrequent. Scrub brush and sparse grasses grow along the steep to gentle slopes beside the stream.

FIVEMILE DRAW. Fivemile Draw begins eight miles northeast of Carta Valley in southwestern Edwards County (at 29°51′ N, 100°33′ W) and runs east for eleven miles to its mouth on the West Nueces River, at State Highway 674 (at 29°51′ N, 100°25′ W). It traverses flat terrain with local deep and dense dissection, surfaced by shallow, stony soils that support oak, juniper, and mesquite.

FIVE MILE HOLLOW. Five Mile Hollow, a valley, begins five miles from Brady in south central McCulloch County (at 31°05′ N, 99°23′ W) and extends northwest for a little more than a mile to a point two miles south of Brady Reservoir (at 31°06′ N, 99°24′ W). The elevation falls from 1,880 feet above mean sea level at the beginning of the valley to 1,780 feet at its end. An intermittent stream runs through Five Mile Hollow to join Little Bear Creek.

FIVE MILE MESA. Five Mile Mesa, five miles southeast of Fort Stockton in central Pecos County, is flanked by Interstate Highway 10 on the north and U.S. Highway 285 on the west (at 30°52′ N, 102°49′ W). The summit of Five Mile Mesa has an elevation of 3,358 feet above sea level. The mesa stands in an area characterized by flat terrain with local deep and dense dissection and shallow, stony soils that support stands of oak, juniper, and some mesquite. Five Mile Mesa was named for its distance from Fort Stockton.

FLACCO. Flacco the Elder and Flacco the Younger, Lipan-Apache chiefs, were both friends of the Texas settlers and were frequently used as scouts and guides against the Comanche Indians and the Mexicans. The older man, principal chief of the Lipans, and his father, Castro, were asked by Sam Houston,[qv] in a letter dated September 1, 1842, to send some of their people with doctors Tower and Cottle to other Apache tribes and to supply them with horses if needed. Presents were promised to any Lipans who went with the doctors. The younger Flacco, born about 1818, accompanied the John H. Moore[qv] expeditions of 1838 and 1839, served under John Coffee (Jack) Hays[qv] in 1840 and 1841, and in 1842 went with the Somervell expedition[qv] to the Rio Grande. He was returning with horses he had rounded up when he was murdered near San Antonio in the winter of 1842. Several different accounts of the murder exist; one of the most accepted is that he was killed by Mexican bandits who took the horses to Louisiana. Another account had it that the bodies of six Cherokees were found next to him, implying that he was killed by the Cherokees. His father and others of the tribe who searched for him believed that he was killed by whites. In March 1843 the elder Flacco wrote Houston of his grief and said that he wished to change his name to Señor Yawney. Houston replied with a poem to the Lipans in memory of the murdered Flacco. One writer suggests that the murder of Flacco and the fact that his killers were not caught and punished is the reason for the constant warfare with the Apaches after the murder.
BIBLIOGRAPHY: Sterling B. Hendricks, "The Somervell Expedition To The Rio Grande, 1842," *Southwestern Historical Quarterly* 23 (October 1919). Adele B. Looscan, "Capt. Joseph Daniels," *Quarterly of the Texas State Historical Association* 5 (July 1901). William S. Speer and John H. Brown, eds., *Encyclopedia of the New West* (Marshall, Texas: United States Biographical Publishing, 1881; rpt., Easley, South Carolina: Southern Historical Press, 1978). *Telegraph and Texas Register*, March 29, 1843. *Texas Sentinel*, October 28, 1841. Amelia W. Williams and Eugene C. Barker, eds., *The Writings of Sam Houston, 1813–1863* (8 vols., Austin: University of Texas Press, 1938–43; rpt., Austin and New York: Pemberton Press, 1970).

FLACCUS, TEXAS. Flaccus, five miles east of Helena in Karnes County, was the center of a colony of blacks who lived along McTennel Creek. The settlement dates back to Reconstruction,[qv] when area slaveholders released their slaves, many of whom retained the surnames of their former masters. The name Flaccus was chosen for a post office established there in 1903 with Lorenzo Perryman as postmaster. The post office was discontinued, and its records were moved to Runge in 1906. A school, referred to as Brieger school in the 1930s, was built there. In 1990 only a few wooden houses and some graves remained at the site.
BIBLIOGRAPHY: Robert H. Thonhoff, History of Karnes County (M.A. thesis, Southwest Texas State College, 1963).

Robert H. Thonhoff

FLACHMEIER, WILLIAM AUGUST (1900–1979). William August Flachmeier, Lutheran minister, was born in Pflugerville, Texas, on August 20, 1900, the son of Wilhelm Heinrich Gottlob and Emilie (Pautz) Flachmeier. He received a B.D. degree from the Wartburg Theological Seminary, Dubuque, Iowa, in the spring of 1923 and was ordained by his father in Fredericksburg, Texas, in July of that year. With the Columbus Mission parish he worked in small communities in Colorado and Austin counties from 1923 to 1942. He married Jeanette Hastedt of Columbus on December 2, 1933, and they had a daughter. During World War II[qv] Flachmeier served in the Pacific Theater as a chaplain in the United States Army. After the war he moved to a ministry in La Marque, but after discovering that the climate was bad for his wife's health he requested another assignment. He went back to school and earned an M.A. from the University of Texas in 1948 and a Ph.D. in 1955. Flachmeier served as director of parish education for the Texas District of the American Lutheran Church from 1948 to 1961. In the 1960s and 1970s he wrote a column on the church's audiovisual collection and a column entitled "Into All the World" for the *Southern Lutheran.* In the early 1970s church officials asked him to write a history of Lutherans in Texas; the result was *Lutherans of Texas in Confluence* (1972). Flachmeier died in Austin on December 21, 1979, and was buried at the Odd Fellows Rest Cemetery in Columbus.

BIBLIOGRAPHY: Flachmeier Family Papers, Barker Texas History Center, University of Texas at Austin. Vertical Files, Austin History Center. Vertical Files, Barker Texas History Center, University of Texas at Austin. *Vivian Elizabeth Smyrl*

FLAG BRANCH (Erath County). Flag Branch rises five miles southeast of Duffau in extreme southeastern Erath County (at 32°06′ N, 97°57′ W) and runs southeast for eight miles to its mouth on the East Bosque River, east of Big Lake in northeastern Bosque County (at 32°04′ N, 97°50′ W). The creek, which is dammed at one point to form Flag Branch Lake, traverses variable terrain surfaced by shallow, stony clay loams that support juniper, oak, grasses, chaparral, and cacti.

—— (Jones County). Flag Branch rises in the BMW oilfield west of Lueders in east central Jones County (at 32°49′ N, 99°42′ W) and runs northeast for eight miles to its mouth on California Creek, five miles northeast of Avoca (at 32°54′ N, 99°40′ W). It crosses flat to gently sloping terrain surfaced by shallow silt loam that supports mesquite and grasses into flat terrain with local shallow depressions surfaced by clay and sandy loam that supports water-tolerant hardwoods, conifers, and grasses.

FLAG CREEK (Gillespie County). Flag Creek rises three miles north of the Old Harper Road in western Gillespie County in the hills of the eastern Edwards Plateau (at 30°21′ N, 99°10′ W) and runs south for 8½ miles to its mouth on the Pedernales River, a mile south of Ranch Road 2093 (at 30°15′ N, 99°09′ W). The stream crosses flat terrain surfaced by shallow clayey and loamy soils that support open stands of live oak, Ashe juniper, mesquite, and grasses.

—— (Llano County). Flag Creek rises four miles northwest of Oxford in central Llano County (at 30°39′ N, 98°44′ W) and runs north for ten miles to its mouth on City Lake, on the western side of Llano (at 30°45′ N, 98°41′ W). The stream traverses an area of the Llano basin with terrain varying from flat, to rolling, to steep and surfaced by soils ranging from deep, fine, sandy loams to shallow and stony. Local vegetation includes open stands of live oak and mesquite.

FLAGG, TEXAS. Flagg, at the intersection of Farm roads 1055 and 1524 in southwestern Castro County, was originally part of the 52,000-acre 7-UP Ranch established in 1884 by James W. Carter,[qv] the county's first resident. C. T. Herring bought the property in 1904 and named it Flag (Flagg) Ranch because the layout of the land resembled a flag. In 1925 Herring decided to subdivide the land into 160-acre blocks and sell them as farms. He and his associates erected a two-story hotel, in which a post office was opened, and laid out a townsite. Interested buyers came, some from great distances, to select their allotments. By the end of the year Flagg had two stores, a land office, a blacksmith shop, a lumberyard, and a one-room school that was also used as a union church. The Flagg school district was formally organized in 1929, and a four-room brick building was completed the following year. However, this small agricultural retail center on Running Water Draw was short-lived, mainly because of improved highways and the proximity to Dimmitt. In the early 1930s its population was about ten. In 1945 the school district was consolidated with the Dimmitt schools, and the post office was discontinued two years later. Such local clubs as the Ladies' Aid Society likewise merged with those of Dimmitt. Although the original townsite has been abandoned, a fertilizer company, a grain elevator, and a cotton gin are located two miles west on Farm Road 1055. From 1940 to 1990 Flagg recorded a population of fifty.

BIBLIOGRAPHY: Castro County Historical Commission, *Castro County, 1891–1981* (Dallas: Taylor, 1981). Fred Tarpley, *1001 Texas Place Names* (Austin: University of Texas Press, 1980).

H. Allen Anderson

FLAG MOUNTAIN. Flag Mountain is six miles southeast of Utopia in far northeastern Uvalde County (at 29°33′ N, 99°28′ W). Its summit, at an elevation of 1,955 feet above sea level, rises 750 feet above nearby Farm Road 187.

FLAG SPRINGS. Flag Springs is a popular spring-fed watering hole and cow camp on the Fort Worth–Fort Belknap road and an unnamed tributary of Salt Creek, ten miles east of Fort Belknap and three miles north of Graham in central Young County. A large pool at the spring, twelve feet in diameter, is fed by a constant flow out of Cisco sandstone. A smaller pool, four feet by two feet and thirty inches deep, has long provided water to wayfarers. Plains Indians camped by the watering hole as they ranged through the northern end of the Cross Timbers[qv] hunting deer and following buffalo[qv] down from the Great Plains. The remains of a bedrock metate and evidence of paleolithic campsites may still be seen at the spring.

After an attack by Indians on Company G of the Frontier Regiment[qv] on Salt Creek Prairie on September 13, 1864, Lt. William R. Peveler sought refuge at the small settlement by the springs, bearing some seventeen wounds. The nearest physician, summoned from Palo Pinto, performed surgery with implements forged at the springs. On Monday, April 10, 1865, as the Young County government began to falter, the commissioners' court voted to remove the county records and papers from the courthouse at Belknap and place them for safekeeping at the stone stable at Flag Springs. Whether the records were ever actually hidden there is unclear. During the roundup in July 1870 J. B. "Blue" Terrell and eleven other cowboys camped at the springs were attacked by Indians. Some ten days before, the same group had lost forty-five horses to the Indians at Lost Valley Pens on Salt Creek Prairie. This time the cowboys were better prepared and recovered ten to twelve horses from the Indians. In August 1878 horse fanciers in the area organized a jockey club in Graham and built a racetrack east of the springs. The springs were used to keep the refreshments cool. Races were held on regular occasions, with prize purses as high as $400 and occasional sweepstakes. The last race on the original track was held in 1905. In the 1920s oil-exploration and road crews blasted out much of the natural dam at the springs, lowering the water level to three feet in the large pool.

This spring is not to be confused with Flag Springs in Archer County, visited by Randolph B. Marcy[qv] during his 1849 expedition.

BIBLIOGRAPHY: Gunnar Brune, *Springs of Texas*, Vol. 1 (Fort Worth: Branch-Smith, 1981). Benjamin Capps, *The Warren Wagontrain Raid*

(New York: Dial, 1974). Carrie J. Crouch, *Young County: History and Biography* (Dallas: Dealey and Love, 1937; rev. ed., *A History of Young County, Texas*, Austin: Texas State Historical Association, 1956). Joseph Carroll McConnell, *West Texas Frontier* (Vol. 1, Jacksboro, Texas, 1933; Vol. 2, Palo Pinto, Texas, 1939). J. W. Wilbarger, *Indian Depredations in Texas* (Austin: Hutchings, 1889; rpt., Austin: State House, 1985).
Steve M. King

FLAGS OF TEXAS. The strong Texas interest in flags is shown in public and private displays of the "Six Flags Over Texas," i.e., the flags of the six countries that have ruled over Texas: the Kingdom of France, the Kingdom of Spain, the Mexican Federal Republic, the Republic of Texas,[qv] the Confederate States of America, and the United States of America. Spain has had four significant flags during its occupation of the New World. The royal banner of Castile and León, bearing two lions and two castles, was used as a state flag and ensign from around 1230 to around 1516. From 1516 to May 28, 1785, Spain used a state flag and ensign consisting of a modified red saltire on white to signify the house of Burgundy. A variant of the state flag and ensign 1580 to 1640 depicted the complete Spanish coat of arms on a white field. King Charles III established the familiar Spanish flag, with horizontal stripes of red-gold-red and the simple arms of Castile and León as the Spanish ensign, effective on May 28, 1785, and as the Spanish state flag on land, effective March 8, 1793. These flags were used until April 27, 1931.

The flag of France that was allegedly carried by René Robert Cavelier, Sieur de La Salle,[qv] was probably a plain white flag strewn with fleurs-de-lys. This flag (circa 1643 to October 31, 1790) was a simplified version of the French state flag and ensign that bore the entire arms of France on the field of fleurs-de-lys. Another French flag frequently displayed in Texas today contains three or more fleurs-de-lys on a blue field; this was the French state flag and ensign from about 1370 to about 1600.

In April 1823, Mexico adopted its first republican flag, which was used until 1863. This flag is similar to the current Mexican flag, with vertical stripes of green-white-red, representing the "Three Guarantees" of religion, independence, and union. Both flags show an eagle holding a serpent in its mouth and standing on a nopal, or cactus, but the current Mexican flag depicts a stylized Aztec eagle rather than the more natural eagle in the 1823 flag. The eagle and serpent represent the tradition that the Aztecs were to make their permanent settlement where they saw a snake being eaten by an eagle standing on a nopal growing from a rock in the middle of water. Legend has it that the Aztecs saw this omen at Lake Tenochtitlán, the site of the future Mexico City.

Texas has had three official national or state flags during its existence: the 1836 national standard, the 1836 national flag for the naval service, and the 1839 national flag, which became the state flag. Stephen F. Austin[qv] designed a proposed Texas flag that was never adopted, and some authorities also claim that Lorenzo de Zavala[qv] designed a Republic of Texas flag. Austin designed his flag in New Orleans between December 1835 and January 1836, while he was serving as a commissioner to the United States. The design apparently used sixteen green and white stripes, a red and white English jack in the canton, and a red and white star in the fly. This design was modified with assistance from other commissioners, Branch T. Archer and William H. Wharton.[qv] The changes apparently resulted in a flag with thirteen blue and white stripes, a red and white English jack in the canton, and a sun with the head of Washington surrounded by the words "Lux Libertatis" or "Light of Liberty" in the fly. The "Zavala flag" was allegedly adopted in Convention of 1836[qv] at Washington-on-the-Brazos. It is usually portrayed as a blue field with a white star of five points central and with the letters "TEXAS," one letter at each star point. This description of the flag, however, is inconsistent with the journal entries of the convention for March 3, 1836, and March 12, 1836, which do not indicate that the convention accepted Zavala's design. In addition, the actual configuration of the flag is unknown because the journal does not describe Zavala's proposal of March 11, 1836, though it does state that William B. Scates's[qv] motion to add a "Rainbow and star of five points above the western horizon; and a star of six points sinking below" was accepted. Finally, the journal reflects that Charles Stanfield Taylor,[qv] not Zavala, suggested that the letters "TEXAS" be placed around the star. Although several books claim that the "Zavala flag" is the first official Texas flag, the historical record does not support this assertion.

The first official flag, the "National Standard of Texas," was passed by the Congress of the republic and approved by President Sam Houston[qv] on December 10, 1836. It consisted of an azure ground with a large golden star central. This flag, known as David G. Burnet's[qv] flag, served as the national flag until January 25, 1839, and the war flag from January 25, 1839, to December 29, 1845. President Burnet proposed the national standard, as well as the 1836 national flag for the naval service, in a letter of October 11, 1836, to Congress. The second official flag was the 1836 national flag for the naval service, or war ensign. This was the same flag Burnet adopted for the navy at Harrisburg on April 9, 1836. It was similar to the United States flag and showed thirteen stripes and a blue canton with a single white star. It was passed by Congress and approved by Houston on December 10, 1836, and remained in use until January 25, 1839.

The Lone Star Flag was adopted by the Texas Congress in 1839: "[T]he national flag of Texas shall consist of a blue perpendicular stripe of the width of one third of the whole length of the flag, with a white star of five points in the centre thereof, and two horizontal stripes of equal breadth, the upper stripe white, the lower red, of the length of two thirds of the whole length of the flag." Senator William H. Wharton introduced a bill on December 28, 1838, containing the flag's design, and the bill was referred to a committee consisting of Senator Oliver Jones[qv] and two unnamed senators. This committee reported a substitute bill embodying the flag design introduced by Wharton, and the substitute bill was passed by the Congress on January 21, 1839 and approved by President Mirabeau B. Lamar[qv] on January 25, 1839. Official art for the Lone Star Flag was drawn by Peter Krag and approved by President Lamar. The actual designer of the Lone Star Flag is unknown, but it could have been Wharton. The Lone Star Flag was the legal national and state flag from January 25, 1839, to September 1, 1879, and the de facto state flag from September 1, 1879, to August 31, 1933. The Lone Star Flag was also the legal national ensign from January 25, 1839, to December 29, 1845. The Sixteenth Legislature promulgated the Revised Civil Statutes of 1879 and provided that "all civil statutes, of a general nature, in force when the Revised Statutes take effect, and which are not included herein, or which are not hereby expressly continued in force, are hereby repealed." Since the 1879 revised statutes neither included legislation concerning the flag nor expressly continued in force the 1839 flag law, the 1839 law was repealed. Texas therefore had no legal flag from the date of the repeal, September 1, 1879, to the effective date of the 1933 flag act, August 31, 1933. The Mexican National Museum of Artillery has two revolutionary Lone Star flags, one dating from 1836 and the other from 1835 to 1837. Both of these flags display the red stripe over the white stripe, but otherwise resemble the 1839 national flag.

The 1933 description of the flag was extremely detailed and included precise instructions for the design and location of the Lone Star. The colors of the stripes, blood red, azure blue, and white, were said to impart the "lessons of the Flag: bravery, loyalty, and purity." Despite these specifications, there was no standard reference to define what constituted "blood red" and "azure blue," and few Texas flags were manufactured in the official proportions (hoist to fly) of two to three. In 1993 the legislature revised the description of the flag: "The state flag consists of a rectangle with a width to length ratio of two to three containing: (1) a blue vertical stripe one-third the entire length of the flag wide, and two equal horizontal stripes, the upper stripe white, the lower red, each two-thirds the entire length of the flag long; and (2) a white, regular five-pointed star in the center of the blue stripe, oriented so that one point faces upward, and of such a size that the diameter of a circle passing through the five points of the star is equal to three-fourths the width of the blue stripe." The 1993 law stipulates that the red and blue colors of the state flag are the same colors used in the United States flag, the so-called "Old Glory Red" and "Old Glory Blue." The red and blue colors are specifically defined by the *Standard Color Reference of America,* a standard textile-industry reference work. The 1993 law specifies that the finial for the state flag should be a lone star or a spearhead, and gives the governor the authority to adopt a governor's flag. The 1993 law also contains a complete revision of the Texas Flag Code, which was first adopted in 1933.

In addition to the three national and state flags, Texas has recognized five other official flags: the 1835 flag for registered civil vessels and vessels sailing under letters of marque and reprisal, the 1839 pilot flag, the 1839 revenue service flag, the 1839 coasting trader flag, and the 1985 county sesquicentennial flag. The flag for registered civil vessels and vessels sailing under letters of marque and reprisal was an ensign adopted by the provisional government[qv] on November 29, 1835. It consisted of the Mexican flag with "1824" replacing the eagle and signifying loyalty to the Mexican federal Constitution of 1824.[qv] This flag disappeared from use after the adoption of the 1836 national standard and the 1836 national flag for the naval service. The revenue service, pilot, and coasting trader flags were auxiliary naval flags authorized by the 1839 act that gave specifications for the Lone Star Flag. Official art for these flags was drawn by Peter Krag. The revenue service flag consisted of a white star on a blue square surrounded by white and red borders, the pilot flag consisted of a white star on a blue stripe with a white stripe above and a red stripe below, and the coasting trader flag consisted of a white star on a vertical blue stripe with swallowtail white and red horizontal stripes. These flags were probably used from January 25, 1839, to December 29, 1845. The pilot flag has been portrayed erroneously at times as the Texas national flag at sea, civil ensign, or merchant flag.

Certainly the most unusual Texas flag is the official county flag for the Texas sesquicentennial, celebrated in 1986. This flag was designed by Mrs. Joydelle G. Wolfram for Falls County and subsequently recognized by the legislature on February 28, 1985, for use by counties. It shows the county's name, date of formation, and a large white star on a royal blue field, surrounded by two white arcs and 254 gold, red, blue, and green stars. The use of this flag is optional.

The Confederate States of America had three principal flag designs during its existence. The first, known as the Stars and Bars, was chosen by the provisional government as the national flag and ensign and was raised over the Capitol in Montgomery, Alabama, on March 4, 1861. Its specifications were "a red field with a white space extending horizontally through the center, and equal in width to one-third the width of the flag. The red space above and below to be the same as the white. The union blue extending down through the white space and stopping at the lower red space. In the center of the union a circle of white stars corresponding to the number with the States in the Confederacy." The Stars and Bars was never officially adopted by legislation, but served as the Confederate flag for more than two years. Many of the Stars and Bars flags flown in Texas during this period featured unions with a single star surrounded by a circle of stars. Because of the flag's similarity to the United States flag, it was unsatisfactory for use as a battle flag or regimental flag. The most commonly known Confederate battle flag was the flag used by the Army of Northern Virginia. It was a square having a red ground with a blue saltire bordered with white and emblazoned with white five-pointed stars corresponding in number to that of the Confederate States. Texan and other Confederate soldiers fought under a wide variety of battle flags because the Confederate Army never adopted a single battle flag for use by all troops. In 1906 the United Confederate Veterans designated the battle flag of the Army of Northern Virginia the standard battle flag for use by Confederate veterans related organizations. This decision has unintentionally encouraged the popular misconception that a standard battle flag existed.

The design of the battle flag of the Army of Northern Virginia was also used in the second national flag of the Confederacy, the Stainless Banner. This flag flew from May 1, 1863, to March 4, 1865, and consisted of a white field with the battle flag in the canton. The Confederate Navy shortened the length of the Stainless Banner and authorized its use as the national ensign on May 26, 1863. The Stainless Banner was revised on March 4, 1865, in part because naval officers objected that the flag looked both like a flag of truce and the British White Ensign. The revision added a vertical red stripe to the flag's fly. The Confederate Navy apparently did not authorize the revised Stainless Banner's use as the national ensign. The third national flag was short-lived, as the Confederacy surrendered the month after it was adopted. Another Confederate flag that is sometimes displayed in Texas today is a rectangular version of the square battle flag of the Army of Northern Virginia. This flag was the Confederate naval jack as it appeared after May 26, 1863, and was similar to the battle flag issued to the Army of Tennessee in 1864. The Confederate naval jack was used in the design for the reverse of the Texas state seal from August 26, 1961, to June 14, 1991 (*see* SEALS OF TEXAS).

The last of the "Six Flags" to fly over Texas is the flag of the United States. Texas entered the Union on December 29, 1845, as the twenty-eighth state. The twenty-seven-star United States flag was first raised in Texas on February 19, 1846, when the state government was organized in Austin. The twenty-eight-star United States flag flew only from July 4, 1846, to July 3, 1847, after which Iowa's admission to the Union necessitated the addition of another star. In 1915 the legislature declared Texas Independence Day, March 2, as Texas Flag Day. In 1933 the legislature passed a law establishing rules for the proper display of the flag and providing for a pledge to the flag: "Honor the Texas Flag of 1836; I pledge allegiance to thee, Texas, one and indivisible." The pledge erroneously referred to the 1836 national flag, known as David G. Burnet's flag, instead of the Lone Star Flag. Senator Searcy Bracewell introduced a bill to correct this error in 1951, but the legislature did not delete the words "of 1836" until 1965. In 1989 the legislature celebrated the sesquicentennial of the Lone Star Flag by incorrectly recognizing Dr. Charles B. Stewart[qv] as the flag's designer and also incorrectly recognizing Thomas Barnett, Sterling C. Robertson, Thomas J. Gazley, and Richard Ellis,[qq] Lorenzo de Zavala, and William B. Scates, the 1836 flag committee, as the 1839 committee that approved the design for the Lone Star Flag. The legislature corrected these mistakes in 1992 by acknowledging that the actual designer of the Lone Star Flag is unknown and by recognizing Senator Wharton and Senator Jones for their efforts in adopting the flag.

BIBLIOGRAPHY: Devereaux D. Cannon, Jr., *Flags of the Confederacy: An Illustrated History* (Memphis, Tennessee: St. Lukes Press, 1988). George Pierce Garrison, "Another Texas Flag," *Quarterly of the Texas State Historical Association* 3 (January 1900). Museo Nacional de Historia, *Banderas: Catálogo de la Colección de Banderas* (Mexico City: Secretaría de Gobernación, 1990). Whitney Smith, *The Flag Book of the United States* (New York: Morrow, 1975). Whitney Smith, *Flags through the Ages and across the World* (New York: McGraw-Hill, 1975). Charles A. Spain, Jr., "The Flags and Seals of Texas," *South Texas Law Review* 33 (February 1992). Alan K. Sumrall, *Battle Flags of Texans in the Confederacy* (Austin: Eakin Press, 1994). *Charles A. Spain, Jr.*

FLAGS OF THE TEXAS REVOLUTION. Many groups designed and flew flags during the Texas Revolution.[qv] Other sporadic, short-lived revolutionary movements also produced flags. With the exception of the flag of the New Orleans Greys[qv] and some of the flags flown at the battle of San Jacinto,[qv] however, none of these flags still exist. Descriptions of them are therefore based on historical accounts that have varying degrees of reliability. Several revolutionary movements predated the revolution. The Gutiérrez-Magee expedition[qv] is said to have displayed a green flag. In 1816, Louis Michel Aury's[qv] three Galveston Island pirate ships are said to have flown a flag consisting of a white field bordered in red, which in the center displayed a blue sword and olive branch surmounted by a green wreath. Aury is also said to have displayed the 1815-1821 Mexican privateer ensign. Jean Laffite's[qv] pirate ships, also based on Galveston Island, are said to have flown the flag of the Republic of Cartagena, which contained a white eight-pointed star on a green rectangle surrounded by yellow and red borders. This flag is sometimes mistakenly identified as the Venezuelan flag. Laffite is also said to have flown the 1815-21 Mexican privateer ensign. He may also have flown a simple red flag and Colonel Long's flag. Two other revolutionary movements that had flags were the Long expedition and the Fredonian Rebellion.[qq,qv] Col. James Long's[qv] expedition is said to have carried a red-fringed flag similar to the United States flag, showing thirteen alternating red and white stripes and a red union with a white "lone star." Long's flag is possibly the first Texas lone star flag. Haden Edwards's[qv] Fredonian Rebellion flag was raised on December 16, 1826, and is said to have consisted of two horizontal white and red stripes with the words "INDEPENDENCE FREEDOM AND JUSTICE" displayed on the white stripe.

From the battle of Gonzales,[qv] the first episode in the revolution, to the Texas Declaration of Independence,[qv] Texans fought under at least eight flags: Gonzales, Dodson, Scott, Dimmitt, Brown, Red Rovers, Troutman, and Baker. The Gonzales or "Come and Take It" flag was designed and painted by Cynthia Burns and Evaline DeWitt and was allegedly used at the battle of Gonzales in October 1835. The flag may have been carried by Stephen F. Austin's[qv] volunteer army to the siege of Bexar.[qv] In his book *The Evolution of a State or Recollections of Old Texas Days* (1900), Noah Smithwick[qv] described this flag as "a breadth of white cotton cloth about six feet long, in the center of which was painted in black a picture of the old cannon, above it a lone star and beneath it the words 'Come and take it.'" Charles Mason,[qv] who participated in the battle of Gonzales and later married Evaline DeWitt, described the flag as "a white ground with a black cannon in the center, and the motto 'Come and take it!' above and below." The Gonzales flag, with or without a lone star, apparently was the first flag used in the Texas Revolution. Sarah (Bradley) Dodson's[qv] flag was made about September 1835 and possibly antedated the "Come and Take It" flag. She made the flag at Harrisburg, where her husband, Archelaus Bynum Dodson,[qv] assisted in forming a company of soldiers. The flag apparently consisted of three horizontal squares of blue, white, and red, with a white lone star centered in the blue square. Some illustrations of the Dodson flag suggest that the term "square" was not meant to be taken literally and that the squares were actually three vertical rectangles similar to the bars in the Mexican flag. The white star allegedly symbolized that Texas was the only Mexican state in which the star of liberty was rising. The Dodson flag and the 1839 national flag of the Republic of Texas[qv] are very similar; in the latter the white and red squares are altered into a white stripe over a red stripe. James Ferguson carried the Dodson flag as far as Cibolo Creek, and it may have been carried at the battle of Concepción[qv] and the siege of Bexar. There are also reports that the Dodson flag was flown, along with a bloody-arm flag (possibly either the Dimmitt or Brown flag), over the cabin where the Convention of 1836[qv] met. If the reports are true, it is possible that the Dodson flag was the flag Lorenzo de Zavala[qv] proposed for adoption as the national flag. Another lone star flag that may have been at the siege of Bexar is the William Scott[qv] flag. It was made in Lynchburg in the fall of 1835 by Charles Lanco with the assistance of Mrs. Joseph Lynch. It is said to have consisted of four yards of blue silk donated by Scott with a painted white star and the word "INDEPENDENCE." The flag was supposedly raised in Lynchburg over the protest of conservative elements that considered the word "independence" premature. James L. McGahey took the flag to the battle of Concepción where he gave it to Thomas B. Bell,[qv] who may have also participated in the siege of Bexar.

A flag made by Philip Dimmitt[qv] is said by some to have been the first flag of Texas independence, a claim based on the fact that the other 1835 flags were symbols of a separate Mexican state still maintaining allegiance to the Constitution of 1824.[qv] According to Nicholas Fagan, the Dimmitt flag measured six feet by three feet and was made of cotton. It is said to have displayed in its center a sinewy arm and hand grasping a bloody sword. This flag was raised at Goliad on December 20, 1835, on the occasion of the Goliad Declaration of Independence.[qv] It was taken from Goliad to Velasco, and according to some reports it was allegedly unfurled with and above the Troutman flag on January 8, 1836. Another bloody-arm flag was supposedly designed by William S. Brown[qv] of Velasco. The Brown flag is said to have consisted of thirteen alternating red and white stripes like those in the United States flag, with the word "INDEPENDENCE" written on one white stripe. The flag had a blue union with a sinewy arm and hand grasping a bloody sword. It is not known when the flag was made. One story is that after Brown took part in the siege of Bexar, he took the flag to Goliad, where it was unfurled on December 20, 1835. Brown reportedly then took the flag to Velasco, where it—not the Dimmitt flag—was displayed with and above the Troutman flag on January 8, 1836, over the American Hotel. The Red Rovers,[qv] themselves dressed in red, brought to Texas a small, square, red battle flag that was reportedly captured at Goliad and taken to Mexico City.

In November 1835, Johanna Troutman[qv] made a lone star flag in Crawford County, Georgia. The Troutman flag is said to have consisted of white silk displaying a blue embroidered lone star and the words "LIBERTY OR DEATH" on one side and on the reverse the motto "UBI LIBERTAS HABITAT, IBI NOSTRA PATRIA EST" ("where liberty resides, there is our homeland"). Troutman presented her flag to William Ward's[qv] Georgia Battalion,[qv] which carried the flag to Texas and unfurled it at Velasco on January 8, 1836, over the American Hotel. The flag was later carried to Goliad, where James W. Fannin[qv] raised it on March 8, 1836, to celebrate the news of the Texas Declaration of Independence. The Troutman flag was reportedly destroyed by the wind during the Goliad Campaign of 1836[qv] when it got caught in its halyard. The flag of the San Felipe Company under Moseley Baker[qv] also bore a lone star. Gail Borden, Jr.,[qv] presented it to the company on March 2, 1836. It is said to have consisted of thirteen alternating red and white stripes with the words "OUR COUNTRY'S RIGHTS OR DEATH" written on the white stripes. The Baker flag had a blue and white British jack in the union, and below the union a white star on a green square. This flag closely resembled Stephen F. Austin's proposed national flag, and it may have been designed on the basis of Austin's letter of January 18, 1836, to Borden.

Five flags are associated with the siege and fall of the Alamo[qv]: San Fernando de Béxar, Crockett, Coahuila and Texas,[qv] 1824, and New Orleans Greys. On February 23, 1836, Santa Anna raised a red flag over the tower of San Fernando de Béxar Church (now San Fernando de Béxar Cathedral[qv]) to proclaim to the defenders of the Alamo that no quarter would be given. There are several theories about what flag was flown by the Texans during the siege of the Alamo. According to David Crockett's[qv] journal entry for February 23, 1836, the Alamo defenders flew a national flag "composed of thirteen stripes, red and white alternately on a blue ground with a large white star of five points in the center, and between the points the letters 'TEXAS.'" On the same day, Col. Juan N. Almonte[qv] wrote in his journal that the Texans hoisted a tricolored flag with two stars, designed to represent Coahuila and Texas. Some writers maintain that this flag was the Mexican red, white, and green tricolor with two blue or gold stars on the white stripe. Others are of the opinion that the Alamo flag was the Mexican tricolor with the numerals "1824" on the white bar, representing allegiance to the Constitution of 1824. The only flag still in existence that allegedly flew at the Alamo is the flag of the first company of the New Orleans Greys, a guidon presented to the Greys by a group of East Texas ladies. It is a blue silk banner displaying an eagle and sunburst with the inscription "FIRST COMPANY OF TEXAN VOLUNTEERS! FROM NEW-ORLEANS." The eagle carries in its beak a banner with the motto "GOD & LIBERTY." After the siege of Bexar, the Greys apparently left their flag at San Antonio when they went on to Goliad and Refugio. It is believed to have been captured by Antonio López de Santa Anna[qv] after the fall of the Alamo. On March 6, 1836, Santa Anna wrote his secretary of war and navy, Gen. José María Tornel, "The bearer takes with him one of the flags of the enemy's battalion captured today. The inspection of it will show plainly the true intention of the treacherous colonists and of their abettors who come from parts of the United States of the North." Most historians believe that Santa Anna was referring to the Greys flag rather than the Crockett flag or the various flags based on the Mexican tricolor.

In 1933, former Texas attorney general John A. Keeling "found" the Greys flag in the National Museum of History at Chapultepec Castle in Mexico City. That same year members of the Texas Highway Commission made an unsuccessful attempt to persuade Mexico to return it to Texas. In 1965 the legislature passed a concurrent resolution sponsored by Representative W. H. Miller that authorized a committee to seek the return of the Greys flag from Mexico. Governor John B. Connally[qv] refused to sign the resolution for fear of interfering with United States–Mexico foreign relations. In response, the United States Congress in 1965 passed a resolution sponsored by Senator John G. Tower[qv] that urged the Department of State to assist Texas in seeking the flag's return. A third attempt to retrieve the flag began in April 1985, when the Texas congressional delegation sent a request to Mexican President Miguel de la Madrid in connection with the Texas Sesquicentennial. Finally, the legislature in 1991 passed a concurrent resolution sponsored by Representative Ralph R. Wallace III requesting Mexican President Carlos Salinas de Gortari to return or lend the Greys flag to Texas. Like Governor Connally, Governor Ann W. Richards refused to sign the resolution. In a warming of relations between Texas and Mexico, partly due to the passage of the North American Free Trade Agreement, Senator Carlos Truan began discussions with Mexican officials in July 1994 about the return of the Greys flag in exchange for the return of the Toluca, Matamoros, and Guerrero battalion flags to Mexico. In response in part to rumors of a 1985 reward offered to anyone who returned the flag to Texas, Mexican officials removed the Greys flag from public display. Arriaga Ochoa, former director of the National Museum of History in Mexico City, stated in 1965 that Mexico seized several flags besides the Greys flag during the Texas Revolution, but these flags were burned or discarded when the old Museum of Artillery was dismantled in 1917. A search of a 1990 Mexican catalog of flags, however, shows that Mexico has at least two revolutionary lone star flags in addition to the Greys flag. Both of these flags display the red stripe over the white stripe, but otherwise resemble the 1839 national flag. One was seized by Santa Anna in 1836 and the other by General Bravo in 1837 at Brazos Santiago.

At least four flags flew at the battle of San Jacinto—one Texan and three Mexican. The San Jacinto battle flag, brought to Texas by Sidney Sherman,[qv] was allegedly painted by James H. Beard and presented to the Newport (Kentucky) Rifle Company by Katherine Isabelle (Cox) Sherman, Sherman's wife. The flag is made of white silk with the painted figure of a partially bare-breasted woman grasping in one hand a sword over which is draped a streamer with the words "LIBERTY OR DEATH." The flag was probably based on Eugène Delacroix's painting *Liberty Leading the People;* the woman in the flag is said to symbolize Liberty. On August 5, 1836, Texas presented the flag to Mrs. Sherman, and it was kept in the family until 1896, when it was presented to the state by the daughters of Isabelle and Sidney Sherman, Lucy Craig, Belle Kendall, and Carrie Menard. In 1925 the flag was lent to the Daughters of the Republic of Texas,[qv] who worked with Representative Preston L. Anderson to have it restored in 1932 for $500. The restored flag was presented to the state on April 21, 1933, and placed in the House of Representatives chamber behind the speaker's rostrum. It was removed for further restoration costing $18,000 in November 1989. It was then determined that the flag's reverse was better preserved, so the flag was reversed. The restored flag was returned to the House chamber on April 19, 1990. Gen. Sam Houston[qv] wrote shortly after the battle of San Jacinto that Texas troops had seized vast amounts of Mexican property, including three general standards of the Mexican army. At least two of these flags are still in the state's custody, the Toluca battalion flag (inscribed "Batallon Activa de Toluca") and the Matamoros battalion flag (inscribed "Batallon Matamoros Permanente"). The state has one other Mexican battle flag, the Guerrero battalion flag (inscribed "Pe. Batallon Guerrero"), which may have been the third flag captured at San Jacinto. The three flags are green, white, and red tricolors bearing the names of their respective battalions and differing versions of the Mexican coat of arms. The Guerrero flag was restored in 1932, but the banner was finished on the wrong side so that the inscription reads backwards. The Toluca flag was restored in 1966. In 1967 the legislature authorized the Texas State Library and Historical Commission to give temporary custody of the Toluca flag to the San Jacinto Monument and Museum,[qv] where it is now displayed. In 1969 the legislature unsuccessfully offered to exchange the Toluca flag for the New Orleans Greys flag. The Guerrero and Matamoros flags are stored in the Texas State Archives. It is periodically discussed whether Texas should retain the three Mexican flags as legitimate spoils of war or return them to Mexico as a display of friendship and goodwill.

Finally, there were three flags that flew after the revolution—the Morgan flag, the Burroughs flag, and the flag of the Republic of the Rio Grande.[qv] In September 1836, Thomas Jefferson Morgan organized a company of soldiers in Washington, Pennsylvania. He had a flag made that is said to have consisted of a lone star and the words "LIBERTY OR DEATH." The flag was flown in front of the courthouse, where it angered some that were not sympathetic with the Texas cause. Militia officers ordered Morgan to remove the flag, but he refused and threatened to have anyone shot that disturbed the colors. A compromise was reached in which Morgan displayed the flag in front of his residence. The flag was brought to Texas in December 1836 when the company reported to Camp Independence. Capt. George H. Burroughs's[qv] company of cavalry arrived in Texas in September 1836 carrying a flag presented by Mary Love of Zanesville, Ohio. The Burroughs flag is said to have been light blue with a white border and the words "ZANESVILLE, OHIO" on the bottom. It was fringed with gold, and in the center it displayed a dark blue rectangle with a gold star and the letters "TEXAS" between the points of the star. Above the dark blue rectangle was a golden eagle holding a streamer bearing the words "HERO OF SAN JACINTO"— apparently referring to Sidney Sherman. In December 1874 the flag was said to be in the possession of the Austin *Statesman*, but its current location is unknown. The central design of the Burroughs flag, a dark blue rectangle with a gold star and letters "TEXAS," may be the origin of the mythical "Zavala flag" that is often described in books. The flag of the short-lived Republic of the Rio Grande[qv] was adopted in January 1840 and supposedly consisted of two horizontal stripes, white over black or possibly blue, and a red vertical stripe at the hoist bearing three white stars to represent the three Mexican states that declared independence: Coahuila, Nuevo León, and Tamaulipas. The Republic of the Rio Grande Museum in Laredo flies a reconstruction of this flag. *See also* FLAGS OF TEXAS, GOLIAD CAMPAIGN OF 1835.

BIBLIOGRAPHY: Austin *American-Statesman*, April 15, 1990. Mamie Wynne Cox, *The Romantic Flags of Texas* (Dallas: Banks Upshaw, 1936). Fort Worth *Star-Telegram*, July 16, 1994. John H. Gámez, "The

Controversy over the Alamo Battle Flag," *Raven: A Journal of Vexillology* 1 (1994). Charles E. Gilbert, Jr., *Flags of Texas* (Gretna, Louisiana: Pelican, 1989). Museo Nacional de Historia, *Banderas: Catálogo de la Colección de Banderas* (Mexico City: Secretaría de Gobernación, 1990). David Ott, "Nine Months along the Texas-Mexico Border: The Rio Grande Flag," *Flag Bulletin*, March–April 1981. Whitney Smith, "What Flag Was Flown by the Pirate Jean Laffite?," *Flag Bulletin*, July–August 1994. Waco *Tribune-Herald*, December 26, 1965. Dudley Goodall Wooten, ed., *A Comprehensive History of Texas* (2 vols., Dallas: Scarff, 1898; rpt., Austin: Texas State Historical Association, 1986).

Charles A. Spain, Jr.

FLAKE, FERDINAND (?–1872). Ferdinand Flake, publisher of both German and English language newspapers, was born in Göttingen, Germany, the son of a Lutheran minister, Rev. Henry Flake. Both of his parents died during his adolescence, and he raised his younger brother and sister. After the small family inheritance was depleted, Flake emigrated to Texas, a popular destination for young Germans of the 1840s. After a few years inland he settled in Galveston, where he operated a profitable seed business and brought his younger siblings, Adolph and Lina Flake, to his new home.

In 1855 Flake brought *Die Union*, a German-language newspaper that F. Muhr had started in 1855. Flake, acting as both editor and publisher, brought out the paper three times a week, and soon it had the largest circulation in Galveston. But this success was undermined by Flake's unpopular strong criticism of secession[qv] and the slave trade; "the odor of the slave trade was too strong for my nostrils," he wrote. In 1860 he wrote an editorial condemning the secession of South Carolina, and in response a mob destroyed his offices. Undaunted by this violence, Flake used type that he had hidden at home to produce the next issue of the paper. Even local political opponents defended him and condemned the actions of the mob, which was said to be composed mostly of German Americans. One of Flake's defenders, James P. Newcomb[qv] of the Alamo *Express*, asserted, "Mr. Flake is an old Texan, a slave holder, and a better Southern man than any editors of the *Herald*. Mr. Flake's crime was a devotion to the Union."

Flake remained staunchly Unionist throughout the war, and only his strategic friendships with local Confederate leaders prevented further violence. After 1861 he discontinued his German-language paper in favor of a newspaper called *Flake's Bulletin*. It appeared in any color paper that Flake could obtain, white being unavailable due to the war, and was set on a small Washington handpress by an inexperienced compositor. Flake printed all the news he could receive from Shreveport by pony express and wire. After the war he produced the *Bulletin* with the aid of his son-in-law, Selim Rinker, and also restarted *Die Union*. Supported by the local businessmen, Flake's paper became increasingly popular in the late 1860s. On March 22, 1872, he transferred his interest in the paper to the Bulletin Publishing Company, of which he became president. That summer he went East for new printing material. He died in a New York hotel of a chronic kidney ailment on July 19, 1872. *Die Union* and *Flake's Bulletin* soon ceased publication. Flake was survived by his wife of twenty-five years, Anna Margaret (Olichslager) Flake Buchholtz, who died in 1878, as well as by six children.

BIBLIOGRAPHY: *History of Texas, Together with a Biographical History of the Cities of Houston and Galveston* (Chicago: Lewis, 1895). C. Richard King, "Horace Greeley in Texas," *Southwestern Historical Quarterly* 64 (January 1961). Marilyn M. Sibley, *The Port of Houston* (Austin: University of Texas Press, 1968). *Randolph Lewis*

FLAKEMOORE CANYON CREEK. Flakemoore (Flakemore) Canyon Creek rises eleven miles northeast of Gilpin in southeastern Dickens County (at 33°31′ N, 100°34′ W) and runs east through isolated ranchland for three miles before reaching its mouth on North Croton Creek, less than a mile west of the Dickens-King county line (at 33°31′ N, 100°32′ W). The creek and canyon are within the Croton Breaks,[qv] an area of moderately steep slopes and locally high relief, with an elevation of 2,140 feet above sea level, surfaced by shallow to moderately deep silt loams that support mesquite and grasses.

FLANAGAN, DAVID WEBSTER (1832–1924). David Webster Flanagan, Republican leader, was born in Cloverport, Breckinridge County, Kentucky, on January 9, 1832, the son of Polly (Miller) and James Winwright Flanagan.[qv] When he was eleven the family moved to Henderson, Texas. Flanagan attended local private schools and Henderson College and read law in the office of his father. Though the Flanagans, father and son, were opposed to secession,[qv] David served in the Confederate Army. During Reconstruction[qv] both Flanagans took a prominent part in Texas politics as members of the moderate wing of the Republican party.[qv] David Flanagan was a Texas senator and member of the Constitutional Convention of 1875.[qv] He served as collector of internal revenue from 1897 to 1913 and was a prominent figure in Republican national conventions for many decades. He also took an active part in the civic affairs of his hometown and helped to promote the building of the Henderson and Overton Branch Railroad, of which he was president. His love of fine cattle and horses led to great improvement in livestock breeding in Rusk County. Flanagan was twice married, first to Elizabeth Graham, who died in 1872, and later to Sallie Ware. He died at Henderson on May 5, 1924, and was buried in the nearby family cemetery.

BIBLIOGRAPHY: *Dictionary of American Biography*. Seth Shepard McKay, *Making the Texas Constitution of 1876* (Philadelphia: University of Pennsylvania, 1924). *Myrtis Watkins*

FLANAGAN, JAMES WAINWRIGHT (1872–1950). James Wainwright Flanagan, banker and petroleum engineer, son of Robert Buck and Anna Bell (Cornelius) Flanagan, was born on October 26, 1872, at Henderson, Texas. He was a nephew of Gen. Webster Flanagan and great-nephew of United States senator James Winwright Flanagan.[qv] Flanagan left Henderson at an early age and engaged in railroad work and mining in Cuba, Mexico, and the United States from 1888 to 1912. He became president of the Royal Bank of Canada in 1913 and in 1919 organized a corporation to build 615 miles of petroleum pipeline from Cartagena to Barrancabermeja, Colombia. For this work the Colombian government erected a monument to Flanagan in 1949.

Flanagan was a lieutenant colonel in the Cuban army in 1896 and was awarded the Medal of Military Merit, served on the staff of Brig. Gen. W. W. Gordon in 1898, and held an honorary commission as lieutenant colonel in the First and Second battalions of the Irish Regiment of Canada in 1940. He was given many awards by South American and European countries, and in 1926 he was decorated by Pope Pius XI as a commander in the Order of St. Gregory. He was a member of the Texas State Historical Association and the Sons of the Republic of Texas.[qqv] In 1933 he translated Theodore Wolf's *Geography and Geology of Equador*.

For many years Flanagan lived in Toronto, Ontario, and served as vice president of Standard Oil Company of New Jersey. In 1946 he retired from public life and moved to Houston, Texas. He was married twice: to Panchita G. Love in 1902 and to Hazel B. Brown in 1913. He had two children. Flanagan died in Houston on July 24, 1950.

BIBLIOGRAPHY: James Wainwright Flanagan Collection, Barker Texas History Center, University of Texas at Austin. Houston *Chronicle*, July 25, 1950. *Who's Who in America*, 1947–48.

FLANAGAN, JAMES WINWRIGHT (1805–1887). James Winwright Flanagan, Texas lieutenant governor and United States senator, was born in Gordonsville, Albemarle County, Virginia, on September 7, 1805, the son of Charles and Elizabeth (Saunders) Flanagan. In 1815 the family moved to Boonesboro, Kentucky, where James received a rudimentary education. As a young man he traded in horses and mules in eastern Kentucky and western Virginia before entering the mercantile trade at Cloverport, Kentucky. He was successful enough that he soon owned a flotilla of flatboats that he sent down the Ohio and Mississippi rivers as far as New Orleans to sell local produce. In 1826 at Cloverport he married Polly Miller Moorman. The couple had five children, including David Webster Flanagan,qv who became a prominent Republican politician in Reconstructionqv Texas. Flanagan served for twelve years as justice of the peace at Cloverport and in 1833–34 was a member of the circuit court of Breckenridge County.

In 1843 he moved to Texas and settled in a community called Slabtown, near the Louisiana border, where he established himself as a farmer and merchant. On August 9, 1844, he moved to Henderson, where he opened a store, farmed, speculated in land, and practiced law. His wife, Polly, died in 1844 at Henderson, and sometime after 1850 Flanagan married a widow named Elizabeth Ware. By 1850 he had amassed $14,856 worth of real estate.

A Whig in the 1830s and 1840s and thereafter a staunch Republican, Flanagan was a close friend and supporter of Sam Houston.qv In 1851–52 he served in the Texas House of Representatives and in 1855–58 in the Texas Senate. While in the state legislature he was a strong advocate of a state asylum for the insane and favored such causes as government-supported railroads. In 1856 he was a presidential elector, and in 1860 he was elected a delegate to the Peace Conference called by Houston. During the Civil Warqv Flanagan, ever a strong Unionist, retired to his farm and produced leather on contract for the Confederate States Army.

He was a delegate to the Constitutional Convention of 1866,qv but the document produced by this convention was rejected by the federal government, and congressional Reconstruction was instead imposed upon the state. Flanagan was a delegate to the Texas Constitutional Convention of 1868–69,qv this time with his son, Webster. When the new constitution was approved by the federal government, Flanagan was elected lieutenant governor in 1869 under Edmund J. Davis,qv and his son was elected to the state Senate. When the elder Flanagan vacated the position later that year, having been elected by the legislature to the United States House of Representatives as an at-large representative, his son replaced him as president pro tem of the Senate. The next year the legislature sent Flanagan to the United States Senate, where he served from March 30, 1870, until March 3, 1875, when he was succeeded by Samuel Bell Maxey.qv In Congress and in the Senate Flanagan supported Ulysses S. Grant and his administration. He was appointed chairman of the Committee on Post Offices and Roads, the Committee on Education, and the Committee on Labor. On March 7, 1872, he delivered a speech to the Senate in support of his proposal to alienate to the federal government all of Texas north and west of a line drawn from the northwest corner of Hardeman County to the mouth of the Pecos River. This land, more than a third of the state, was to be designated an Indian reservation.

Upon leaving the Senate, Flanagan retired to his farm at Longview. His third marriage was to Elizabeth Lane. He had a total of eleven children. He died at Longview on September 19, 1887, and is buried in Henderson beside his first wife. He was a Baptist and an Odd Fellow. Some of his papers are preserved in the James Wainwright Flanaganqv collection Barker Texas History Center,qv University of Texas at Austin.

BIBLIOGRAPHY: James Wainwright Flanagan Collection, Barker Texas History Center, University of Texas at Austin. Frank W. Johnson, *A History of Texas and Texans* (5 vols., ed. E. C. Barker and E. W. Winkler [Chicago and New York: American Historical Society, 1914; rpt. 1916]). William S. Speer and John H. Brown, eds., *Encyclopedia of the New West* (Marshall, Texas: United States Biographical Publishing, 1881; rpt., Easley, South Carolina: Southern Historical Press, 1978).
Thomas W. Cutrer

FLANAGAN, MINNIE A. (1902–1987). Minnie Flanagan, black civil-rights leader, was born in 1902 in Chandler, Texas. She moved to Dallas in 1918 and immediately became active in the civic affairs of the city. She and her husband, Pat Lee Flanagan, a native Texan and locker-room manager at the Dallas Country Club, had one son. From 1937 to 1949 Minnie Flanagan was active in the Democratic Progressive Voters League;qv she became one of two women on the league's executive committee. She served also on the National Metropolitan Council of Negro Women and with the Dallas Negro Chamber of Commerce. In the 1950s, with her husband, she opened the Oak Cliff Youth Center in their home, thus providing a place for Dallas teenagers to meet on weekends. By day the center functioned as a day nursery for working black mothers. In 1953 she was named Zeta Phi Beta sorority's Woman of the Year. Aside from her civil-rights activities, the sorority recognized Minnie Flanagan's tireless efforts on behalf of the Maria Morgan Branch of the YWCA and her presidency of the Daughters of Smith Chapel, AME Church, as well as of the American Democratic Association. Throughout the 1950s and 1960s her interest in civil rights increased. She worked to organize and participated in demonstrations against segregated cafeterias and public facilities in Dallas. She served as president of the Dallas NAACP from 1959 to 1961. In 1986 her achievements were recognized by the bestowal of the NAACP Heritage award. In her last years she gave dedicated service to the American Cancer Association. She died in May 1987.

BIBLIOGRAPHY: Dallas *Morning News*, December 19, 1969, May 15, 1987. W. Marvin Dulaney, "The Progressive Voters League—A Political Voice for African Americans in Dallas," *Legacies: A History Journal for Dallas and North Central Texas*, Spring 1991. Minnie Flanagan Papers, Dallas Historical Society.
Peggy Hardman

FLANAGAN, TEXAS. Flanagan, four miles northwest of Tatum and twenty-one miles northeast of Henderson in northeastern Rusk County, was named for David Webster Flanagan,qv Confederate soldier and Republican politician. The community was established in 1882 as a station on the Longview and Sabine Valley Railway. John Kroeger was postmaster when a post office opened there in 1900. That year the population was recorded as fifty, and the community was known as a shipping point for lumber. Although population estimates for the community reached 200 by 1914, its post office was discontinued in 1916. As of 1950 the town had a predominantly black population. The community was not labeled on the 1982 county highway map.

BIBLIOGRAPHY: Dorman H. Winfrey, *A History of Rusk County* (Waco: Texian, 1961).
Megan Biesele

FLANAKIN, ISAIAH (?–?). Isaiah Flanakin, one of Stephen F. Austin'sqv Old Three Hundredqv colonists, received title to two labores of land on the west bank of the Brazos River four miles north of the site of old San Felipe de Austin, in the area of present eastern Austin County, on July 19, 1824.

BIBLIOGRAPHY: Lester G. Bugbee, "The Old Three Hundred: A List of Settlers in Austin's First Colony," *Quarterly of the Texas State Historical Association* 1 (October 1897). Texas General Land Office, *General Land Map of Austin County* (Austin, 1943).

FLANDERS, JOHN (1800–1836). John Flanders, Alamo defender, son of Levi and Mary (Sargent) Flanders, was born in Salisbury, Massachusetts, in 1800. He was in business with his father in Massachusetts until they argued over foreclosing on a mortgage held by a widow. Flanders left for Texas and never communicated with his family again. He settled in Gonzales and was part of the force from that town that rode to the relief of the Alamo. He entered the Alamo on March 1, 1836, with this company and died in the battle of the Alamoqv on March 6, 1836.

BIBLIOGRAPHY: Daughters of the American Revolution, *The Alamo Heroes and Their Revolutionary Ancestors* (San Antonio, 1976). Bill Groneman, *Alamo Defenders* (Austin: Eakin, 1990). Walter Lord, *A Time to Stand* (New York: Harper, 1961; 2d ed., Lincoln: University of Nebraska Press, 1978). Phil Rosenthal and Bill Groneman, *Roll Call at the Alamo* (Fort Collins, Colorado: Old Army, 1985).

Bill Groneman

FLASH. The *Flash*, a privateer, was fitted out for Texas in the spring of 1836; the crew was sworn in and Luke A. Falvel was commissioned captain on March 12, 1836. With the cannons known as the "Twin Sisters"qv on board, the ship was ordered to proceed to the Brazos River to pick up victims of the Runaway Scrape,qv take them to Morgan's Point, and defend that place in case of a Mexican attack. At Morgan's Point the "Twin Sisters" were sent to Harrisburg on the *Opie*, and the *Flash* picked up members of the ad interim governmentqv and took them to Galveston Island. She proceeded to Fort Point on April 20, 1836, and on April 26 was prepared to sail for New Orleans when news was received of the battle of San Jacinto.qv The vessel was stranded on shore in May 1837, when her pilot mistook San Luis Pass for the entrance to Galveston harbor, and lost. The Tenth Texas Legislature made an appropriation to pay Falvel for his services as sailing master in the Texas Navy.qv

BIBLIOGRAPHY: Alex Dienst, "The Navy of the Republic of Texas," *Quarterly of the Texas State Historical Association* 12–13 (January–October 1909; rpt., Fort Collins, Colorado: Old Army Press, 1987).

A. L. Weinberger

FLAT, TEXAS. Flat is at the intersection of State Highway 36 and Farm Road 931, ten miles southeast of Gatesville in southeastern Coryell County. The name Mesquite Flat was originally chosen because of the local terrain and vegetation, but when residents applied for a post office in the 1890s, the postal department rejected the name. They then submitted the name Flat, and in 1897 were granted a post office by that name. Flat had a cotton gin, three general stores, and 100 residents in 1914. Population estimates fell to twenty-five in the mid-1920s but rose again to 125 by the late 1930s. Farming was the primary occupation of area residents until the 1940s, when much of the farm acreage was taken over by the establishment of Fort Hood. In the 1950s and 1960s Flat became home to military and civilian personnel associated with Fort Hood as well as to people who commuted to work in Gatesville or Temple. The population of the community was estimated at 200 in 1960 and 210 in 1970. The school at Flat was consolidated with the Gatesville Independent School District in 1963, and in the early 1980s residents converted the old school building to a community center. Population estimates for Flat remained at 210 through 1990.

BIBLIOGRAPHY: Clyde and Mabel Bailey, *Vignettes of Coryell County* (Gatesville, Texas: Gatesville Printing, 1976). Coryell County Genealogical Society, *Coryell County, Texas, Families, 1854–1985* (Dallas: Taylor, 1986).

Vivian Elizabeth Smyrl

FLAT CREEK (Blanco County). Flat Creek rises 2½ miles west-southwest of Henly in far eastern Blanco County (at 30°11′ N, 98°15′ W) and runs north-northeast for 13½ miles to its mouth on the Pedernales River, 6½ miles below the lower end of Pedernales Falls (at 30°19′ N, 98°13′ W). It runs through an area of the Edwards Plateau characterized by loamy, clayey soils with rock outcroppings that support grasslands and stands of live oak, mesquite, and juniper. Flat Creek is intermittent in its upper reaches but mostly free-flowing for its lower nine miles.

——— (Cass County). Flat Creek rises in the Cusseta Mountains four miles east of Marietta in northwestern Cass County (at 33°11′ N, 94°29′ W) and runs south for nineteen miles to its mouth on Black Cypress Creek, six miles southwest of Linden (at 32°58′ N, 94°29′ W). The stream, which is intermittent in its upper and middle reaches, runs first through a hilly area, then through terrain that is gently undulating to gently rolling and surfaced by fine sandy loam. The area is flood-prone, and native vegetation includes water-tolerant hardwoods, conifers, and grasses.

——— (Cherokee County). Flat Creek rises just west of Bullard in extreme northern Cherokee County (at 32°09′ N, 95°20′ W) and runs southwest for nine miles to its mouth on the Neches River, in the northwestern corner of Cuney (at 32°03′ N, 95°25′ W). The stream is intermittent in its upper reaches. It crosses flat to gently rolling terrain surfaced by clayey and sandy loam that supports grasses and mixed hardwoods and pines.

——— (Cooke County). Flat Creek rises a half mile southeast of Hood in southwestern Cooke County (at 33°34′ N, 97°20′ W) and runs southeast for 8½ miles, passing through the Ellenburger oilfield in its upper reaches before reaching its mouth on Grasshopper Creek, in extreme north central Denton County (at 33°24′ N, 97°19′ W). The stream, which is dammed in its lower reaches, traverses variable terrain surfaced by expansive clays and moderately deep to shallow stony clay loams that support oak, juniper, chaparral, cacti, and grasses.

——— (Edwards County). Flat Creek rises west of Ellis Peak in Edwards County (at 29°46′ N, 100°29′ W) and runs seven miles northeast to its mouth, on the West Nueces River a mile north of the Kickapoo Springs community on Farm Road 674 (at 29°47′ N, 100°25′ W). The local Edwards Plateauqv region is flat, deeply dissected, and surfaced by dark, calcareous, stony clays and clay loams that support scrub oaks, juniper, grasses, and some mesquite. The creek runs parallel to Farm Road 674 for part of its distance and is crossed by several unimproved roads and trails.

——— (Erath County). Flat Creek rises two miles north of Farm Road 8 in extreme western Erath County virtually on the Eastland-Erath county line (at 32°18′ N, 98°29′ W) and runs south for fifteen miles to its mouth on the Leon River, five miles north of De Leon in Comanche County (at 32°10′ N, 98°31′ W). A Flat Creek community is located several miles west of the stream. The creek runs through an area of steep slopes and sand that support brush and grasses.

——— (Henderson County). Flat Creek rises a mile west of Ash Cemetery in north central Henderson County (at 32°16′ N, 95°47′ W). It formerly flowed southeast for twenty-one miles to its mouth on the Neches River, just west of Cape Tranquility (at 32°10′ N, 95°30′ W). With the construction of Lake Palestineqv in the early 1960s the lower seven miles of the creek were inundated, and the creek now enters the lake 1½ miles west of the Farm Road 314 bridge. The creek is dammed in its upper reaches to form Lake Athens. Flat Creek traverses flat to rolling terrain surfaced by sandy and clay loams that support water-tolerant hardwoods, conifers, and grasses.

——— (McLennan County). Flat Creek rises within the western city limits of Hewitt in south central McLennan County (at 31°29′ N, 97°13′ W) and runs east for twelve miles to its mouth on the Brazos River, four miles east of Robinson (at 31°30′ N, 97°03′ W). The stream, which is intermittent in its upper reaches, traverses flat to rolling prairie with locally steep slopes, surfaced by expansive clays and clay loams that support juniper, oak, mesquite, and grasses in the creek's upper and middle reaches and water-tolerant hardwoods and conifers in its lower.

FLAT FORK, TEXAS. Flat Fork is on State Highway 96 and the Atchison, Topeka and Santa Fe Railway seven miles north of Center in northern Shelby County. It was founded around 1904. A post office was in operation there from 1909 until 1911 with Daniel D. Parker as postmaster. From 1933 through 1964 the community reported a population of ten. In 1946 it had a cotton gin, a sawmill, and a store. In 1988 Flat Fork had a store and widely scattered houses. It was still listed as a community in 1990.

Cecil Harper, Jr.

FLAT FORK CREEK. Flat Fork Creek rises a mile north of Timpson in northwestern Shelby County (at 31°55′ N, 94°25′ W) and runs southeast for thirty-two miles to its mouth on Toledo Bend Reservoir (at 31°51′ N, 93°57′ W). It traverses level to moderately steep terrain surfaced by soils that vary from sand to clayey and loamy. The area is heavily wooded, with pines and various hardwoods predominating.

FLATIRON BUILDING. The Flatiron Building in Fort Worth, designed by Sanguinet and Staats[qv] in 1907, was one of the earliest skyscrapers in the Southwest, and at the time of its construction was one of the tallest buildings in North Texas. The 2,755 square-foot seven-story reinforced concrete and steel structure, the first of its kind in Fort Worth, was erected as a professional office building for Bacon Saunders,[qv] pioneer of medicine in Texas and dean of Fort Worth Medical College. It is situated at the corner of Ninth and Houston streets. The wedge-shaped site dictated the building's unusual triangular plan, similar to the famed Flatiron Building designed by Daniel Burnham in New York in 1902, from which it derived its name. The building's composition, a two-story base and a five-story body capped by a large cornice with sixteen terra-cotta lions' heads, echoed Chicago architect Louis Sullivan's practice of dividing high-rise structures into a base, shaft, and crown. The ornamentation, which is vaguely Sullivanesque, also suggests links with the contemporary Chicago School. The building became a state historical landmark in 1969 and was listed on the National Register of Historic Places in 1971; it is the only flatiron building in Texas and one of five on the National Register.

BIBLIOGRAPHY: Fort Worth *Star-Telegram*, February 11, 1971. Sanguinet and Staats–Hedrick Collection, Architecture and Planning Library, University of Texas at Austin. Ruby Schmidt, ed., *Fort Worth and Tarrant County* (Fort Worth: Texas Christian University Press, 1984). *Tarrant County Historic Resources Survey: Principal Findings and Resource Characteristics* (Fort Worth: Historic Preservation Council for Tarrant County, 1982).

Betty B. Ambrose

FLATONIA, TEXAS. Flatonia is on Interstate Highway 10, U.S. Highway 90, and the main line of the Southern Pacific Railroad twelve miles west of Schulenburg in southwestern Fayette County. It was established on April 8, 1874, on land acquired from William Alexander Faries (Ferris, Farris) by the Galveston, Harrisburg and San Antonio Railway and named for pioneer merchant F. W. Flato. At that time residents of the original Flatonia settlement, one mile southeast, and Oso, three miles northeast, loaded their homes and businesses on wagons and moved to the new location on the tracks. The post office that had been established at old Flatonia in 1870 was moved to the new town without changing its name. Flatonia was incorporated on November 10, 1875, and its first election was held the following December 6. By 1878 the town had a population of 800, and the economy depended equally on cattle and cotton.

The original settlers in the area were primarily Anglo-American. Opportunities provided by the railroad and inexpensive real estate, which sold for one to fifteen dollars an acre for uncultivated land and five to thirty-five dollars per acre for cultivated, brought successive waves of German, Bohemian, Greek, Arabian, and Italian immigrants. In the mid-1880s the Waco branch of the San Antonio and Aransas Pass Railway completed a north-south line through Flatonia and brought new settlements, Muldoon on the north and Moulton on the south. This competition for business plus the agricultural depression of the time caused a decline in the town's economy and by 1900 occasioned a substantial loss in population.

During the first half of the twentieth century the prospects of Flatonia rose and fell in response to the national economy and the markets for cotton and cattle. In 1950 the town had forty businesses, a population of 1,024, and a wide service area of farms and ranches. Cotton ceased to be a factor in the local economy during the 1960s, and many farms were converted to cattle ranching. The population remained between 1,000 and 1,500, and the number of businesses rose to sixty-nine by 1985. The completion of I-10 during the 1970s caused tourist-oriented businesses to move away from Highway 90 and the railroad to the new highway, a mile north. Each year a weeklong "Czhilispiel," a festival named by Czechs[qv] who like chili, attracts visitors from a wide area of Central Texas. In 1990 the population of Flatonia was 1,295.

BIBLIOGRAPHY: Frank Lotto, *Fayette County: Her History and Her People* (Schulenburg, Texas: Sticker Steam Press, 1902; rpt., Austin: University of Texas Press, 1981). James L. Rock and W. I. Smith, *Southern and Western Texas Guide for 1878* (St. Louis: Granger, 1878).

Jeff Carroll

FLAT PAINT CREEK. Flat Paint Creek rises a mile east of Stamford in north central Jones County (at 32°56′ N, 99°46′ W) and runs northeast seven miles to its mouth on Paint Creek, five miles northeast of Stamford in south central Haskell County (at 33°00′ N, 99°41′ W). It traverses an area of densely dissected gullies and low hills, with shallow or absent soils and sparse plants.

FLAT PRAIRIE, TEXAS (Trinity County). Flat Prairie is just off Farm Road 2781 ten miles northwest of Groveton in north central Trinity County. A school was established there before 1899, and the Flat Prairie Congregational Methodist Church was organized in 1912. The community school was later consolidated with that of Pennington. In the mid-1930s Flat Prairie had the church, a cemetery, and a number of houses. In the early 1990s Flat Prairie was still a dispersed rural community with an active church.

BIBLIOGRAPHY: Patricia B. and Joseph W. Hensley, eds., *Trinity County Beginnings* (Groveton, Texas: Trinity County Book Committee, 1986).

Christopher Long

FLAT PRAIRIE, TEXAS (Washington County). Flat Prairie (Flatprairie) is on Farm Road 594 a mile south of Somerville Lake in northwestern Washington County. On April 9, 1913, a United States post office was established there with Eugene E. Williams as postmaster. William Thomas was in charge of the community's post office when it closed on November 30, 1914, and mail was rerouted through Burton. The 1984 county highway map showed only a church and cemetery at the site.

Carole E. Christian

FLATROCK (FLAT ROCK) CREEK (Blanco County). Flatrock Creek rises in the Hill Country[qv] two miles northeast of the Round Mountain community in northern Blanco County (at 30°26′ N, 98°19′ W) and runs northeast for eleven miles to its mouth on the Colorado River, just below Marble Falls at the Max Starcke dam in southern Burnet County (at 30°33′ N, 98°15′ W). Little Flatrock Creek, a tributary, rises near the Blanco-Burnet county line (at 30°28′ N, 98°20′ W) and runs northeast for six miles to its mouth on Flatrock Creek (at 30°32′ N, 98°17′ W). Both streams traverse flat to rolling terrain surfaced by clay and loamy soils that support live oak, Ashe juniper, mesquite, and grasses.

——— (Bosque County). Flat Rock Creek, originally known as Rock Creek, rises three miles south of Eulogy in northern Bosque County (at 32°08′ N, 97°39′ W). It runs northeast for five miles to its mouth on the Brazos River, near Brazos Point (at 32°11′ N, 97°36′ W).

——— (Edwards County). Flat Rock Creek rises two miles northwest of the Dobbs triangulation station in southwestern Edwards County in the Edwards Plateau (at 29°42′ N, 100°31′ W) and runs south for seventeen miles to its mouth on the East Fork of Sycamore Creek, three miles southeast of Horn Ranch in northwestern Kinney County (at 29°31′ N, 100°34′ W). It traverses flat terrain with local deep and dense dissection, surfaced by shallow, stony soils that support oak, juniper, and mesquite.

——— (Kendall County). Flat Rock Creek rises seven miles north of

Comfort in northwestern Kendall County (at 30°04′ N, 98°54′ W) and runs southeast for nine miles to its mouth on the Guadalupe River, two miles east of Comfort (at 29°58′ N, 98°52′ W). It traverses terrain characterized by steep slopes and benches and surfaced by clay loams that support juniper, live oak, mesquite, and grasses.

____ (Lee County). Flat Rock Creek rises six miles north of Ledbetter in southeastern Lee County (at 30°10′ N, 96°49′ W) and runs north for 2½ miles to its mouth on Pin Oak Creek (at 30°13′ N, 96°48′ W). The stream, which is intermittent in its upper reaches, runs through low to moderately rolling terrain surfaced by shallow to deep clay and sandy loam that supports hardwoods, mesquite, and grasses.

____ (Stephens County). Flat Rock Creek rises ten miles southeast of Caddo in southeastern Stephens County (at 32°35′ N, 98°38′ W) and runs east for five miles to its mouth on Palo Pinto Creek, in extreme southeastern Stephens County (at 32°32′ N, 98°36′ W). It traverses an area of rolling hills surfaced by clay and sandy loams that support scrub brush, mesquite, cacti, grass, live oak, and juniper.

____ (Throckmorton County). Flat Rock Creek rises two miles south of the Upshur Triangulation Station in northwest Throckmorton County (at 33°18′ N, 99°19′ W) and runs southeast for ten miles to its mouth on Elm Creek, four miles northwest of Throckmorton (at 33°15′ N, 99°14′ W). There are several small reservoirs along its course. The streambed crosses variable terrain with a sandy and clayey loam surface in which grow juniper, live oak, mesquite, and grasses.

____ (Young County). Flatrock (Flat Rock) Creek rises four miles east of Graham in southeast Young County (at 33°04′ N, 98°35′ W) and runs southwest for six miles to its mouth on the Brazos River, near Farm Road 1287 three miles south of Graham (at 33°04′ N, 98°30′ W). The source of the creek is Agency Springs in Dark Canyon. These springs, which provided water for the Brazos Indian Agency (*see* BRAZOS INDIAN RESERVATION), remained slightly active in 1980, though much below their former flow. Flatrock Creek runs through a ranching area with hilly terrain surfaced by shallow, stony clay and sandy loam soils that support oak, grasses, and mesquite.

FLATS, TEXAS. Flats is at the junction of State Highway 47 and Farm Road 514, seven miles southwest of Emory in southwestern Rains County. The site was settled around the time of the Civil War.[qv] In the mid-1930s the settlement had a school, two stores, and a number of scattered dwellings. After World War II[qv] the school closed, but in the early 1990s a church and two stores remained. In 1990 the reported population was 100. *Christopher Long*

FLATT, TEXAS. Flatt, on the Colorado River ten miles northwest of Austin in west central Travis County, took its name from Cameron Flatt, the name of the surrounding region. The community had a store and a blacksmith shop in 1892. That same year a post office opened there with Wiley H. Milam as postmaster, but it was discontinued the following year, and the community's mail was sent to Bee Caves. Flatt was not marked on county highway maps in the 1940s. *Vivian Elizabeth Smyrl*

FLAT TOP, TEXAS. Flat Top was on Elm Creek and Farm Road 2134 four miles southwest of Voss and twenty miles southwest of Coleman in southwestern Coleman County. It was founded about 1862 when Richard Coffey,[qv] one of the earliest white settlers in southwestern Coleman County, started ranching at the site. Coffey built a number of cabins to house his cowboys and enclosed the settlement with a picket fence as a defence against Indian raids. The community was known as Flat Top because of a flat-roofed building that stood on the site in its early years. As a result of their exposed frontier location, Coffey's ranch and the neighboring ranches suffered Indian raids several times in the early 1870s, and the last victim of such raids in the county was killed near Flat Top in 1875. At the same time, the community profited from its location on the road that paralleled the telegraph line between forts Concho and Belknap. Local ranchers supplied the army posts with cattle, and Flat Top became a change station on the Fort Concho–Brownwood stage line. In the 1870s a series of rock corrals, still standing in the mid-twentieth century, were built to hold the stage horses. The community had a post office from 1879 to 1881. Flat Top declined thereafter and was no longer listed on county maps by the 1930s.

BIBLIOGRAPHY: Coleman County Historical Commission, *History of Coleman County and Its People* (2 vols., San Angelo: Anchor, 1985). *Mark Odintz*

FLAT TOP HILL (Stephens County). Flat Top Hill is on the Shackelford county line in northwestern Stephens County (at 32°51′ N, 99°06′ W). The hill, at an elevation of 1,380 feet above sea level, rises fifty feet above the surrounding terrain, which consists of rolling hills surfaced by clay and sandy loam soils that support scrub brush, mesquite, cacti, and grasses.

FLAT TOP MOUNTAIN (Bosque County). Flat Top Mountain is between the North and East forks of the Bosque River four miles west of Walnut Springs in northwestern Bosque County (at 32°03′ N, 97°49′ W). The elevation of its summit is 1,176 feet above sea level. It lies in an area of the Grand Prairie region characterized by flat to rolling terrain with local escarpments. Local vegetation includes juniper, oak, grasses, chaparral, cacti, and some mesquite, growing in deep, fine sandy loam and shallow, stony clay loam soils.

____ (Eastland County). The level ridge of Flat Top Mountain stands seven miles northeast of Cisco in northern Eastland County (at 32°29′ N, 98°54′ W). Its elevation is 1,560 feet above sea level, eighty feet above the surrounding area. The moderately deep clay on its slopes supports numerous short grasses.

FLAT TOP PEAK. Flat Top Peak is seven miles northwest of Lampasas in south central Lampasas County (at 31°09′ N, 98°15′ W). Its summit, at an elevation of 1,531 feet above sea level, rises 200 feet above nearby Lucy Creek. The peak stands in an area of the Grand Prairie region characterized by shallow clay loam soils and steep slopes and limestone benches that often give a stairstep appearance to the surrounding landscape. Local vegetation includes grasses and open stands of live oak, mesquite, and Ashe juniper.

FLATWOOD, TEXAS. Flatwood, on Farm Road 279 seventeen miles southeast of Canton in southeast Van Zandt County, had several businesses and scattered dwellings in the mid-1930s. By the late 1980s the community church alone remained to mark the townsite. *Diana J. Kleiner*

FLAT WOODS, TEXAS (Nacogdoches County). Flat Woods is off Farm Road 225 a mile west of Redland Cemetery in northwestern Nacogdoches County. The site was settled in the 1850s. A school known as Plank House opened there before the Civil War,[qv] and the settlement was known for many years as Plank House or Pine Grove. Around 1880 the name Flat Woods came into use. At its height around 1900 the community had a school, several churches, and a sawmill. After World War II[qv] the school closed, and many of the residents moved away. In the early 1990s only a few scattered houses remained in the area.

BIBLIOGRAPHY: Nacogdoches County Genealogical Society, *Nacogdoches County Families* (Dallas: Curtis, 1985). *Christopher Long*

FLECHAS CHIQUITAS INDIANS. In 1683–84 Juan Domínguez de Mendoza[qv] led an exploratory expedition from El Paso as far eastward as the junction of the Concho and Colorado rivers, east of the site of future San Angelo. In his itinerary he listed the names of thirty-seven Indian groups, including the Flechas Chiquitas, from whom he expected to receive delegations. Nothing further is known about the Flechas Chiquitas (Spanish for "little arrows"), who seem to have been one of many Indian groups of north-central Texas that were swept into oblivion by the southward thrust of the Lipan-Apache and Comanche Indians in the eighteenth century.

BIBLIOGRAPHY: Herbert Eugene Bolton, ed., *Spanish Exploration in the Southwest, 1542–1706* (New York: Scribner, 1908; rpt., New York: Barnes and Noble, 1959). Charles W. Hackett, ed., *Pichardo's Treatise on the Limits of Louisiana and Texas* (4 vols., Austin: University of Texas Press, 1931–46). *Thomas N. Campbell*

FLECHAS FEAS INDIANS. The Flechas Feas ("ugly arrows") Indians are known from a Spanish document of 1683 that does not clearly identify their area. They seem to have lived east of the Pecos in west central Texas. Their affiliations are unknown.

BIBLIOGRAPHY: Charles W. Hackett, ed., *Pichardo's Treatise on the Limits of Louisiana and Texas* (4 vols., Austin: University of Texas Press, 1931–46). *Thomas N. Campbell*

FLECHAZOS VILLAGE. Flechazos was the name given by Spanish explorers in the eighteenth century to the upper of two Tawakoni Indian settlements located on the west side of the Brazos River near what is now Waco (*see* WICHITA CONFEDERACY).

BIBLIOGRAPHY: Frederick Webb Hodge, ed., *Handbook of American Indians North of Mexico* (2 vols., Washington: GPO, 1907, 1910; rpt., New York: Pageant, 1959). *Margery H. Krieger*

FLEESON, ISAAC NEVILLE (1815–1848). Isaac Neville Fleeson, journalist, was born in 1815 at Woodville, Mississippi, and learned the printer's trade at Pittsburg, Pennsylvania. He worked on various newspapers until April 1842, when he joined Capt. Jack R. Everett's Company B of the Mobile Greys[qv] for six months' service on the Texas frontier. Fleeson was elected second corporal of the company, and his brother W. B. was elected fourth corporal. Fleeson was discharged on October 2, 1842.

From January 1 until April 2, 1846, he was associated with the Corpus Christi *Gazette*, a newspaper founded by Samuel Bangs[qv] to promote the interests of the United States army in the area. When Maj. Gen. Zachary Taylor[qv] moved his troops into Mexico after the battles of Palo Alto and Resaca de la Palma,[qqv] Fleeson accompanied the army to Matamoros, where, on June 1, 1846, in partnership with Hugh McLeod and William G. Dryden,[qqv] he began publication of the *Republic of the Rio Grande*, a semiweekly bilingual newspaper that strongly advocated the separation of the states of northern Mexico from the mother country. The paper's outspoken editorial policy led to its demise, and when McLeod and then Dryden dropped out of the project, Fleeson reorganized the paper as the *American Flag*. John H. Peoples and later John R. Palmer, printers who had come to Mexico with a Louisiana infantry company that mustered out at Matamoros, became his partners. The *Flag*, one of the longest running and most important of the war papers, continued under Fleeson and Palmer until the end of the Mexican War.[qv]

Fleeson died of tuberculosis on July 26, 1848, and was buried at Fort Brown.[qv] The *Flag* was removed to Brownsville on October 9, 1848, and in 1849 was purchased by Edwin B. Scarborough, who ran it for ten years. In 1850 Scarborough incurred much official displeasure when he used the *Flag* to advocate a separate territorial government for the so-called "Nueces Strip" between the Nueces River and the Rio Grande. *See also* REPUBLIC OF THE RIO GRANDE.

BIBLIOGRAPHY: Frederick Charles Chabot, *Texas Expeditions of 1842* (San Antonio: Artes Gráficas, 1942). Joseph Milton Nance, *Attack and Counterattack: The Texas-Mexican Frontier, 1842* (Austin: University of Texas Press, 1964). Marilyn M. Sibley, *Lone Stars and State Gazettes: Texas Newspapers before the Civil War* (College Station: Texas A&M University Press, 1983). Justin H. Smith, "La República de Río Grande," *American Historical Review* 25 (July 1920). Lota M. Spell, "Anglo-Saxon Press in Mexico, 1846–1848," *American Historical Review* 38 (October 1932). *William E. Bard*

FLEMING, ARIZONA (1884–1976). Arizona Fleming, black civil-rights activist, was born on March 23, 1884, in Richmond, Texas, the daughter of Beauregard (Bully) and Laura Fleming. She attended segregated schools through the twelfth grade, then entered Guadalupe College, an all-black school in Seguin. After college she worked for four years as a bookkeeper for Seagul Laundry in Houston, then later returned to Richmond and became a leading seamstress in the county. Little is known of her personal life. Some unverified sources suggest that she married F. A. Hicks on October 21, 1903, and Robert Simmons on January 10, 1912. In 1927 she and several others founded the Fort Bend Fraternal Undertaking Company in Richmond; Fleming served as secretary and manager. During the Great Depression[qv] she received financial assistance from her uncle, C. H. D. Fleming of Beaumont, who helped her establish a good credit rating. After several years with the undertaking company, Fleming rose to the position of sole proprietor. She also eventually owned her own house. In the early 1950s she became involved in reestablishing the African-American vote in Fort Bend County.

After the Civil War[qv] the balance of political power shifted in the county. In 1870 the census reported 5,510 blacks and 2,007 whites in Fort Bend County. During Reconstruction[qv] African Americans[qv] could vote and hold office. Black officeholders generally were Republican freedmen. In 1886 local whites formed the Young Men's Democratic Club of Fort Bend County, and three years later they changed the name to the Jay Bird Democratic Association. The group soon controlled who could nominate and run in the Democratic primaries. Texas was a state dominated by the Democratic party[qv] and the Jay Bird Democratic primaries determined who won the county elections. African Americans, Hispanics, and Jews were excluded from the political process.

In 1950 Willie Melton, a prosperous black farmer from the Kendleton area, sought to participate in the Fort Bend County Democratic primaries. A black victory there might also bring the end of white domination in neighboring counties. Melton had William J. Durham,[qv] an attorney for the National Association for the Advancement of Colored People,[qv] inform the Jay Birds that blacks in the county wanted to vote in their primaries. He cited violations of rights on account of race or color in applicable federal statutes. The Jay Birds responded that they were a private club and could hold private primaries. Melton gathered a group of supporters that included Arizona Fleming, who became an ardent worker. Her name regularly appeared in the records of civil-rights efforts to end local voter discrimination. Melton asked Attorney General Marion Price Daniel, Sr.,[qv] whether they could take legal action against the Jay Birds. The assistant attorney general responded, declining involvement in the matter. Next, Melton, on the advice of J. Edwin Smith of the Houston firm of Allen, Smith, Neal and Lehmann, sought people to attach their names as plaintiffs in a legal action. Fears of retribution made the search more difficult until several people over age sixty agreed to step forth. One was John Terry, age seventy-seven, of Beasley, who remarked, "I am an old man, use my name, they can no longer hurt me." Terry's name headed a petition filed against A. J. Adams, president, Jay Bird Democratic Association, and other officers. Wealthy black Houstonians, church groups, and the NAACP assisted in court costs, but Melton and Fleming bore much of the financial burden.

On May 1, 1950, the United States District Court for the Southern District ruled in favor of Melton's group. The Fort Bend Civic Club was organized to get out the black vote in the upcoming elections; Melton was president and Fleming, secretary. They went house to house, encouraging African Americans to vote. Of 550 eligible black voters in the county, 400 voted. Though many were fearful of retribution, the sheriff reported no incidents at the polls. The Jay Birds then appealed the decision, and won on January 11, 1952. Melton now proposed taking their case to the United States Supreme Court. The Fort Bend Civic Club solicited funds from the Fort Bend black churches and sponsored a Freedom Ball fund-raiser. Black business leaders in Houston, Dallas, and other towns contributed. The club raised some $6,000. Melton and Fleming were the only African Americans to attend the Supreme Court session. The high court on May 4, 1953, ruled in favor of the appellants in the case *John Terry et al., Petitioners, v. A. J. Adams, et al., Repentant.* The work of Melton, Fleming, and others had firmly secured for Fort Bend County blacks the right to vote.

During the campaign to obtain the vote for African Americans in Fort Bend County, Arizona Fleming made substantial financial and emotional contributions to the cause. It was said that her personal finances were depleted in the fight and that she died penniless. However, she said "I'd do it all over again." She died on January 18, 1976, in Richmond and was buried in the Mount Carmel Baptist Church cemetery. In 1994 the Fort Bend Independent School District opened the Arizona Fleming Elementary School in the Providence subdivision located off State Highway 6 South in Houston. *See also* CIVIL-RIGHTS MOVEMENT.

BIBLIOGRAPHY: *Fort Bend Sun*, June 28, 1994. Neal Tannahill, *Texas Government Policy and Politics* (1993). *Texas Coaster*, December 20, 1951. Pauline Yelderman, *The Jay Bird Democratic Association of Fort Bend County* (Waco: Texian Press, 1979). Bonni C. Hayes

FLEMING, JAMES RICHARD (1848–ca. 1904). James Richard Fleming, attorney, businessman, and public official, was born in Feliciana, Groves County, Kentucky, on September 10, 1848, the son of William Carpenter and Arlette (Davis) Fleming. His family soon moved to Tennessee, where Fleming attended school until August 17, 1861, when he entered the Confederate service under Gen. Nathan Bedford Forrest. In 1867 he moved to Columbus, Texas, where he purchased the Columbus *Times* and published it for one year. He was admitted to the bar on March 16, 1870, and the following November 1 he married Mrs. Mary McLeary Grace. They moved to Comanche County, where Fleming engaged in law, merchandising, and banking. After serving as a delegate to the Constitutional Convention of 1875,qv he was elected judge of the twelfth judicial district. He resigned from the bench in 1880 and moved to Cisco. He was elected to represent the Twenty-ninth District in the Senate of the Eighteenth Legislature, 1883–84. In August 1883 Fleming, who was then living at Albany, was appointed commissioner to represent Texas at the Southern Agricultural and Cotton Exposition at Louisville, Kentucky. In 1889 he moved to San Antonio, where he was appointed master of chancery for the San Antonio and Aransas Pass Railway Company. He was delegate and temporary chairman at the state Democratic convention at Dallas in 1894 and the same year was delegate to the national Democratic convention in Cleveland, Ohio. He moved to Houston in 1894 and in 1896 to Spokane, Washington, where he died about 1904 at the age of fifty-five. Fleming was a thirty-second-degree Mason and a Methodist.

BIBLIOGRAPHY: *Members of the Legislature of the State of Texas from 1846 to 1939* (Austin: Texas Legislature, 1939).

FLEMING, LAMAR, JR. (1892–1964). Lamar Fleming, Jr., merchant and civic leader, was born in Augusta, Georgia, on August 13, 1892, the son of L. L. Fleming, a prominent cotton merchant of that city and later of New York City. He was educated in the public schools and attended Harvard University until his junior year in 1911, when, for family financial reasons, he left school to join Anderson, Clayton and Companyqv in Oklahoma City. He became the firm's representative in Holland and Germany in 1914, and from 1915 to 1922 he directed its operations in Italy under the name Lamar Fleming and Company. In recognition of his continuing interest in Italy, the Italian government awarded him the Italian Solidarity Star in 1962, the highest honor it can bestow upon the citizen of another country. From 1922 to 1924 Fleming lived in Liverpool, England, where his firm acted in partnership with D. F. Pennefather and Company.

Fleming became a resident of Texas in 1924. He retired from Anderson, Clayton and Company in 1960, having served as president from 1939 to 1953 and chairman of the board from 1953 to 1960. He helped his firm evolve from a copartnership trading only in American-grown cotton into a publicly owned corporation that dealt also in foreign cotton and coffee, grain, and vegetable oils. During the last decade of his business career, Fleming directed the firm into the food-products field.

He served on the governing boards of the University of Houston and Rice University, as well as the Kinkaid Schoolqv in Houston. He was a board member of Texas Children's Hospitalqv and Baylor University Medical Foundation. He was vice chairman of President Dwight D. Eisenhower'sqv Commission on Foreign Economic Policy and was an adviser to the ninth session of the General Agreement on Tariffs and Trade conference in Geneva. He served on the board of directors of the Federal Reserve Bank of Dallas.qv Although never a candidate for public office, he exercised a strong influence in local and state politics.

On February 7, 1920, Fleming married Clare Evelyn Knowles of England. They became the parents of four children. Fleming died in Houston on July 5, 1964.

BIBLIOGRAPHY: Lamar Fleming, Jr., *Growth of the Business of Anderson, Clayton and Company*, ed. James A. Tinsley (Houston: Texas Gulf Coast Historical Association, 1966). Vertical Files, Barker Texas History Center, University of Texas at Austin. *Who's Who in America*, 1960–61. James A. Tinsley

FLEMING, RICHARD TUDOR (1890–1973). Richard Tudor Fleming, business executive and collector, was born in Temple, Texas, on April 12, 1890, the son of Richard Tudor and Edna (Griffin) Fleming. After graduation from Temple High School he attended the University of Texas, where he lettered as a pole vaulter for the track team, was editor of the yearbook, *Cactus,* and was one of three originators of the infamous *Blunderbuss,* an underground newspaper first published on April Fool's Day, 1913, and then published for sixteen years. He received a B.A. degree in 1912 and an LL.B. in 1915.

Fleming began his legal career in Houston, where he practiced from 1915 to 1928, with the exception of the years 1917 to 1919, when he served in the United States Army; he rose to the rank of major. Back in Houston after World War I,qv he became president of the Houston Bar Association, executive secretary of the State Democratic Executive Committee, and one of the leaders in the fight against the Ku Klux Klan.qv He was married to Harriet H. Jameson on March 10, 1928, and they had one son. In 1928 Fleming moved to New York as an attorney for Texas Gulf Sulphur Company. He advanced in the company through the years as assistant secretary, secretary and general counsel, and finally vice president and general counsel from 1951 until his retirement a decade later.

His retirement from business opened a new career. A collector since his student days, he had particularly gathered all sorts of writings, paintings, photographs, and even sheet music and phonograph records by former University of Texas students and faculty. He offered his collection to the university, which installed the Richard T. Fleming Library of Texas Writers, with Fleming as volunteer founder, collector, and curator. For eleven years, until his death, he worked as an unpaid employee of the University of Texas in Austin, continuing to gather one of the most nearly complete collections of its kind in any major university. Wherever he went, Fleming was outspoken and always gathered controversy. Short of stature, but with tremendous vitality, he made both a powerful advocate and adversary. He died on March 12, 1973, and was cremated.

BIBLIOGRAPHY: Vertical Files, Barker Texas History Center, University of Texas at Austin.   *Joe B. Frantz*

FLETCHER, HERBERT HERRICK (1892–1968). Herbert Herrick Fletcher, bookseller and publisher, son of William Herbert and Bernita Tyler (Herrick) Fletcher, was born at Waverly, New York, on June 6, 1892. He attended public school in Philadelphia and attended the University of Pennsylvania, where he studied the liberal arts and excelled on the track team. He was employed by Wanamaker's store and was honor graduate of the Wanamaker Institute and head of the rare book department. Among his customers were Woodrow Wilson and Shakespearean actor George Arlis. In 1914 Fletcher moved briefly to Cleveland, Ohio, and within a year founded a bookstore in Akron, Ohio, which became the gathering place for author-poet Hart Crane and his friends.

In 1925 Fletcher moved to Texas, where he met and married Thelma Rawls, a San Antonio bookseller. He moved to Houston and established Fletcher's Book Store at the corner of San Jacinto and Rusk streets. In 1929 he began the Anson Jones Press to publish books about Texas. By 1936 he had edited and published *Interwoven*, a classic chronicle of pioneer life in Texas. During the twenties and early thirties he wrote a column, "In the Offing," for the avant-garde Houston *Gargoyle*. He later was rare book editor in the "Bibliomania" column of the Dallas *Times Herald*.qv An article by Fletcher, "Life, Liberty and the Pursuit of Texiana" was published in the *Southwestern Historical Quarterly*qv in July 1950.

In 1954 Fletcher closed his business in Houston and moved to Salado, where he and his wife continued the Anson Jones Press and the sale of rare and fine books. He had an acid wit and was an advocate of the little known in Texas history; he served as vice president and editor of the Harris County Historical Society, revitalized the Bell County Historical Society and served as its president, and was editor and publisher for the Texas Academy of Science.qv He was a lifelong Episcopalian, a member of the American Legionqv and the Sons of the American Revolution, a life member of the Texas State Historical Association,qv and the father of two children. He died on March 8, 1968, and was eulogized in a Texas State Senate resolution dated June 28, 1968. He is buried in the Salado cemetery.

BIBLIOGRAPHY: Michel Cadoret and Sibylle de L'Epine, *Houston* (Houston, 1949). George Fuermann, *Houston: Land of the Big Rich* (Garden City, New York: Doubleday, 1951). Vertical Files, Barker Texas History Center, University of Texas at Austin. Brom Weber, *Hart Crane* (New York: Bodley, 1948).   *Tyler Herrick Fletcher*

FLETCHER, WILLIAM ANDREW (1839–1915). William Andrew Fletcher, lumberman and Civil Warqv soldier, the son of Thomas and Eliza (Miller) Fletcher, was born in St. Landry parish, Louisiana, on April 23, 1839. In 1856 the family moved to Texas, where they settled first at Wiess's Bluff in Jasper County and in 1859 at Beaumont. In 1861 Fletcher joined Company F, Fifth Texas Regiment, Hood's Texas Brigade,qv at Richmond, Virginia. He fought at Chickahominy, Seven Pines, and around Richmond, served as the commanding general's scout at the battle of Gaines' Mill, and was wounded at the second battle of Manassas. He returned to the front, took part in the battle of Fredericksburg, and was made a temporary corporal. In 1863 he fought with Robert E. Lee'sqv army and with James Longstreet's corps at the Round Tops and at Gettysburg. Under Joseph E. Johnstonqv he was wounded again at Chickamauga. In 1864 he joined Company E of the Eighth Texas Cavalryqv (Terry's Texas Rangers) and accompanied the unit on campaigns in Tennessee and Georgia. He was captured briefly but escaped near Murfreesboro, Tennessee, and last served with Johnston's army near Bentonville, North Carolina. Fletcher recounts his experience in his book *Rebel Private, Front and Rear*, first published by the Greer Press at Beaumont (1908); much of the original edition was burned in 1924, and the book was reprinted by the University of Texas Pressqv in 1955.

After Lee surrendered, Fletcher returned to Texas. In 1866 he married Julia Long, with whom he had five children. He opened a general repair shop in 1867 and went to work for his wife's brother James M. Long in 1869. Long and F. L. Carroll were involved in a steam sawmill operation built by John R. Ross and James R. Alexander, originally known as Long and Company and later as the Beaumont Lumber Company. Fletcher subsequently entered into the partnership in the Village Mills Company, later the Texas Tram and Lumber Company, which specialized in yellow pine. In 1901 he sold his part of the business to John Henry Kirbyqv and retired to his farm. Fletcher at one time owned 1,000 acres of timber in Orange County, in addition to other property interests. He invented a steam log skidder to load timber, was a director of the Keith Lumber Company and the Neches Iron works, and promoted highways and canals in the region. He died on January 5, 1915.

BIBLIOGRAPHY: W. T. Block, *A History of Jefferson County, Texas, from Wilderness to Reconstruction* (M.A. thesis, Lamar University, 1974; Nederland, Texas: Nederland Publishing, 1976). Dermont H. Hardy and Ingham S. Roberts, eds., *Historical Review of South-East Texas* (2 vols., Chicago: Lewis, 1910). Judith Walker Linsley and Ellen Walker Rienstra, *Beaumont: A Chronicle of Promise* (Woodland Hills, California: Windsor, 1982).   *Diana J. Kleiner*

FLETCHER, TEXAS. Fletcher is between U.S. highways 69/287 and 96, fifteen miles north of the center of Beaumont in southeastern Hardin County. Its site is that of a nineteenth-century ferry across Village Creek. The community was founded when the Gulf, Beaumont and Kansas City Railway was built through the area in 1894 and was probably named for the Fletcher family of Beaumont, which operated a sand pit north of Village Creek as well as several sawmills in northern Hardin County. The post office at Lumberton, a railroad stop in the early 1900s, was transferred to Fletcher in 1914. In the mid-1920s the sawmill at Fletcher was dismantled, and its post office was discontinued in 1926. Although the site of Fletcher, on a sandy bluff overlooking Village Creek, remained a popular recreation area, the community's population declined from an estimated 450 before the mill closed to about fifty by 1945. No population figures have been reported for Fletcher since 1947, although the area remains populated as Beaumont and Lumberton expand to the north.

BIBLIOGRAPHY: Mary Lou Proctor, *A History of Hardin County* (M.A. thesis, University of Texas, 1950).   *Robert Wooster*

FLEWELLEN, ROBERT TURNER (1821–1899). Robert Turner Flewellen, Texas legislator and professor of medicine, son of James and Elizabeth (Parson) Flewellen, was born in October 1821 in Tuscaloosa, Alabama. After his father died in 1829 his mother moved to Culloden, Georgia, where Flewellen attended school. He read medicine in a private office, then attended a course of lectures in the Medical College of Charleston, South Carolina, and one in the medical department of the University of New York, from which he graduated in 1845. He married Carrie Bivins in 1848. She died in 1854, and in 1860 Flewellen married Eugenia Andrews.

He moved from Georgia to California in 1850 and to Washington County, Texas, in 1853. He served two terms in the legislature from Washington County and one term from Harris County. He introduced and secured passage of legislation chartering a medical college in Texas and advocated a high standard of professional ethics and protection by law of the practice of medicine. He was professor of anatomy and a trustee of Texas Medical College in Galveston. In 1870 Flewellen became a charter member of the Texas Historical Society, and in 1872 he was elected president of the Texas State Medical

Association (later the Texas Medical Association^{qv}). He died in January 1899.

BIBLIOGRAPHY: Lewis E. Daniell, *Types of Successful Men in Texas* (Austin: Von Boeckmann, 1890). Ralph W. Jones, "The First Roots of the University of Texas Medical Branch at Galveston," *Southwestern Historical Quarterly* 65 (April 1962). George Plunkett [Mrs. S. C.] Red, *The Medicine Man in Texas* (Houston, 1930).
L. W. Kemp

FLEWELLEN, TEXAS. Flewellen, near the intersection of Farm roads 359, 1093, and 1463, twelve miles northwest of Richmond in northwestern Fort Bend County, appears to have been named after an early settler. The community sits on land that was originally included in the eastern part of Stephen F. Austin's^{qv} colony. Following the Civil War a gristmill served the surrounding farms. In the mid-1930s Flewellen reported fifty inhabitants and one business and was served by a metal-surfaced road and the Texas and New Orleans Railroad. The town still had fifty citizens and one business in 1948, but that year is the last for which population statistics are available. In the 1980s Flewellen still was shown on county highway maps.
Stephen L. Hardin

FLICKWIR, A. H. (1879–1939). A. H. Flickwir, physician and city health officer, was born on April 28, 1879, in Beardstown, Illinois, the son of David Henry and Catherine Rebecca (Norbury) Flickwir. He attended public schools in Illinois and the University of Illinois. He earned a medical degree from the University of Pennsylvania in 1901 and took postgraduate training at Howard Hospital (Philadelphia), Southside Hospital (Pittsburgh), and Maplewood Sanatorium (Jacksonville, Illinois), where he also served as a resident physician. Before World War I^{qv} he practiced at Detroit, Michigan; Buda, Illinois; and Lyford, Blessing, and Houston, Texas. He served in the Medical Corps of the United States Navy during the war. He was health officer for the city of Houston (1920–27) and director of public health and welfare for the city of Fort Worth (1929–39).

He served as president of the Harris County Medical Society, vice president of the Texas State Medical Association (*see* TEXAS MEDICAL ASSOCIATION), first president of the Texas Public Health Association (1922), and a vice president of the American Public Health Association. At the time of his death Flickwir was president of District No. 2 of the Texas Public Health Association, a member of the Executive Committee of the Fort Worth Council of Social Agencies, a member of the Public Relations Committee of the Tarrant County Medical Society, and secretary of the public health section of the Texas State Medical Association. He was a Legionnaire, a Mason, an Episcopalian, and a member of the Military Order of Foreign Wars. He and his wife had two daughters. He died in Fort Worth on July 26, 1939.

BIBLIOGRAPHY: Fort Worth *Star-Telegram*, July 27, 1939. *Texas State Journal of Medicine*, October 1939.
Chester R. Burns

FLINT, TEXAS. Flint, at the junction of Farm roads 2868, 346, and 2493, four miles north of Bullard in Smith County, was originally part of the Tomás Quevedo survey. The site, named for local landowner Robert P. Flynt, became a stop on the Kansas and Gulf Short Line Railroad in 1882. The post office began operations in 1887 as Flint, when postmaster Charles B. Brown misspelled the name on application forms. Robert Flynt succeeded him the next year. In 1890 the settlement had a general store, three cotton gins, a physician, and a population of twenty-five. In 1892 the Etna Methodist Church was moved there. By 1902 some 100 local families were engaged in truck farming. That year they shipped eighty-five railroad cars of tomatoes, as well as large amounts of cabbage, cantaloupes, and peaches. The town supported a blacksmith shop, a telephone exchange, a telegraph service, and the C. B. Rather and A. M. Campbell mercantile companies. The local gin and gristmill shipped 750 to 1,000 bales of cotton each year. Flint also had Methodist and Baptist churches. Records for 1903 showed two schools, one with three teachers and 147 white students and the other with two teachers and eighty-one black students.

By 1914 local farmers shipped record amounts of nursery stock, fruit, and tomatoes from Flint. That year the population peaked at 450. The town had six general stores, a bank, and a newspaper, the Flint *Weekly Reader*. During the 1920s the original frame school building was torn down and replaced with a two-story brick structure where six teachers taught grades one through ten. There were five businesses, a physician, and a justice of the peace court. By 1925 the population had stabilized at 200.

In 1936 a Flint school with seven teachers had 203 white pupils, and a two-teacher facility had fifty-one black students. The Great Depression^{qv} greatly injured the business of the area. After 1950 the population remained around 150. By 1952 the Flint Independent School District had been established, but it was later consolidated into the Bullard Independent School District; Flint students still attended school in Bullard in 1969. Maps showed two churches and a cemetery at Flint in 1973, when the old school was in use as a community center. In 1989 an incredible thirty-seven businesses and a post office were reported. In 1990 the population was still recorded as 150.

BIBLIOGRAPHY: Edward Clayton Curry, An Administrative Survey of the Schools of Smith County, Texas (M.Ed. thesis, University of Texas, 1938). Sammie Morgan, "Flint in the 1920s," *Chronicles of Smith County*, Spring 1966. "Post Offices and Postmasters of Smith County, Texas: 1847–1929," *Chronicles of Smith County*, Spring 1966. "School Sights," *Chronicles of Smith County*, Fall 1969. Smith County Historical Society, *Historical Atlas of Smith County* (Tyler, Texas: Tyler Print Shop, 1965). "The Southland," October 1902 (facsimile in *Chronicles of Smith County*, Fall 1969). Donald W. Whisenhunt, comp., *Chronological History of Smith County* (Tyler, Texas: Smith County Historical Society, 1983). Albert Woldert, *A History of Tyler and Smith County* (San Antonio: Naylor, 1948).
Vista K. McCroskey

FLINT CREEK (Coryell County). Flint Creek rises four miles east of Flat in eastern Coryell County (at 31°18′ N, 97°34′ W) and runs southeast for seven miles to its mouth on Owl Creek, eleven miles north of Belton in Bell County (at 31°14′ N, 97°31′ W). Since the completion of Belton Lake in 1954, the lower reaches of Flint Creek have been subject to flooding. It traverses an area of rolling prairie with some steep slopes, surfaced by clay loams that support oak, juniper, and grasses.

——— (Young County). Flint Creek rises two miles southeast of Loving in west central Young County (at 33°14′ N, 98°30′ W) and runs southwest for twelve miles to its mouth on Salt Creek, two miles northwest of Graham (at 33°10′ N, 98°35′ W). The headwaters of Flint Creek are known as Baylor Springs; they were a stop along an early stage route from Fort Richardson to Fort Belknap.^{qqv} In its upper reaches the stream is an intermittent draw that runs through private ranchland and the Knox oilfield. After meeting with Turtle Hole Creek, however, Flint Creek becomes the main source of Lake Eddleman, a municipally owned reservoir that supplies water, electrical power, and recreational facilities to the Graham area. The creek runs through terrain of resistant ledges and low cuestas, where shallow, stony soils support live oaks, juniper, and grasses.

——— (Young County). Flint Creek rises three miles southeast of Loving in eastern Young County (at 33°14′ N, 98°30′ W) and runs southwest for ten miles to its mouth on Lake Eddleman, northwest of Graham (at 33°10′ N, 98°35′ W). The stream is dammed to form the lake. It traverses steeply to moderately sloping hills and flat terrain with local deep and dense dissection, surfaced by stony clay and sandy loams that support mesquite, oak, juniper, and grasses.

FLINT HILL, TEXAS. Flint Hill is at the intersection of two country roads two miles southeast of Neches and eleven miles northeast of Palestine in eastern Anderson County. In 1932 Flint Hill High School enrolled 257 black pupils; the poverty of the area at the time is indicated by the fact that the Flint Hill school district had the lowest assessed valuation per student in the county. In the 1930s the community comprised the school, a church, a lodge, and several scattered dwellings. The church and the school were still at the site in 1985.

BIBLIOGRAPHY: Thomas Paul Jones, The Reorganization of the Public Schools of Anderson County, Texas (M.Ed. thesis, University of Texas, 1934).

Mark Odintz

FLINTOFF, THOMAS (ca. 1809–1891). Thomas Flintoff, an itinerant portrait painter who worked in Texas in the mid-nineteenth century, was born in Newcastle-upon-Tyne, England, in 1809 and moved to the United States around 1850. Though little is known of his early life, the fact that he had received some training is evident in his work, for his paintings show that he had at least been exposed to the elements of English romantic style. However, his work is somewhat primitive, showing a lack of skill in rendering depth and painting detail. He arrived in Galveston, Texas, in the spring of 1851. There he painted several portraits, including those of Pryor M. Bryan and his wife, Mary Angelica, Thomas Jefferson Chambers^{qv} and his wife, Abbie, and a group portrait of William J. Jones's^{qv} children. In late 1851 Flintoff went to Austin, where he was commissioned by the legislature to restore its portrait of Stephen F. Austin.^{qv} One of his portraits of Austin was donated to Austin College at Sherman in 1855. Other commissions followed, and Flintoff completed portraits of Gen. Edward Burleson, Guy Morrison Bryan, and George Washington Smyth.^{qqv}

In the spring of 1852 he visited Houston, Corpus Christi, Indianola, and Matagorda. He recorded his impressions of these towns in a series of watercolor sketches that are invaluable to historians. Many of them represent municipal buildings and churches that were demolished later in the nineteenth century and would otherwise have been known only by written descriptions. The muddy streets, luxuriant vegetation, and livestock included in Flintoff's sketches evoke the rustic flavor of early Texas towns.

Flintoff disappeared from the scene in 1852 just as mysteriously as he had earlier appeared. He eventually went to Melbourne, Australia, where he died in 1891. His portraits of Texans are in the collections of the state Capitol, the Texas State Archives, the Barker Texas History Center,^{qqv} the San Jacinto Museum of History (*see* SAN JACINTO MONUMENT AND MUSEUM), and Austin College. His landscape sketches are included in the Houston Metropolitan Research Center^{qv} and a private collection.

BIBLIOGRAPHY: Pauline A. Pinckney, *Painting in Texas: The Nineteenth Century* (Austin: University of Texas Press, 1967). Michael E. Wilson, "Thomas Flintoff Visits Houston," *Houston Review* 8 (1986).

Pauline A. Pinckney

FLINTROCK, TEXAS. Flintrock (Flintrock Hill), eighteen miles northwest of Austin near what is now the Lakeway community in western Travis County, was named for the abundance of flint in the area. A post office opened there in 1875 with Paul Renke as postmaster. The post office was discontinued in 1882, and mail for the community was sent to Bee Caves. Flintrock was not labeled on the 1946 county highway map.

BIBLIOGRAPHY: John J. Germann and Myron Janzen, *Texas Post Offices by County* (1986).

Vivian Elizabeth Smyrl

FLIPPER, HENRY OSSIAN (1856–1940). Henry Ossian Flipper, engineer, the first black graduate of West Point, the eldest of five sons of Festus and Isabella Flipper, was born a slave at Thomasville, Georgia, on March 21, 1856. He attended school at the American Missionary Association, and in 1873, as a freshman at Atlanta University, he was appointed to the United States Military Academy. Although

Henry O. Flipper, ca. 1878. Courtesy Texas Memorial Museum; acc. 160-2.

Flipper was the fifth black accepted to West Point, he was the first to graduate. At West Point he was often ostracized and had little social interaction with white cadets beyond official activities. He graduated fiftieth in a class of seventy-six on June 14, 1877, and accepted a commission as a second lieutenant. Flipper described his successful struggle against ostracism and prejudice in *The Colored Cadet at West Point* (1878). In January 1878 he was assigned to Company A of the Tenth United States Cavalry.^{qv}

As an officer in the Tenth Cavalry, Flipper served at forts Elliott, Concho, Quitman, and Davis, Texas, and at Fort Sill, Indian Territory. He first reached Texas on his way to Fort Sill, where he supervised the drainage of malarial ponds. Flipper's Ditch is now a national historic landmark. He later constructed a road from Gainesville to Fort Sill after a troop of the Fourth United States Cavalry^{qv} got drunk and deserted the lieutenant assigned to do the job. Flipper also installed a telegraph line from Fort Elliott to Fort Supply, Indian Territory, scouted on the Llano Estacado,^{qv} and assisted in the return of Quanah Parker's^{qv} band from Palo Duro Canyon^{qv} to the Fort Sill reservation in the winter of 1878–79. During the Victorio^{qv} campaign of 1880 he fought in two battles at Eagle Springs, Texas. For his service in the field Flipper was made acting assistant quartermaster, post quartermaster, and acting commissary of subsistence at Fort Davis,

Jeff Davis County. The positions placed him in charge of the fort's supplies and physical plant.

When Col. William Rufus Shafter[qv] became commanding officer of Fort Davis in 1881, he immediately relieved Flipper as quartermaster and planned to relieve him as commissary as soon as he found a replacement. Flipper suspected what he later called a systematic plan of persecution, and is said to have been warned by civilians at the post of a plot by white officers to force him from the army. The following year, when he discovered post funds missing from his quarters, he attempted to conceal the loss until he could find or replace the money. When Shafter learned of the discrepancy, he immediately filed charges against him. A divided court-martial acquitted Flipper of charges of embezzlement but pronounced him guilty of "conduct unbecoming an officer and a gentleman." He was dismissed from the service on June 30, 1882. (Accounts of the court-martial proceedings may be found in the San Antonio *Express,* November 2–December 14, 1881.) President Chester A. Arthur made a final confirmation of the verdict on June 24, 1882. Flipper maintained his innocence until his death and waged a lifelong battle for reinstatement in the army.

He went to El Paso after his dismissal and remained there until 1883, when he went to work as an assistant engineer for a surveying company composed of former Confederate officers. He assisted the company in surveying public lands in Mexico and helped run a boundary line between the states of Coahuila and Chihuahua in 1883. Between 1883 and 1891 he worked in Chihuahua and Sonora as a surveyor for several other American land companies. In 1887 he opened a civil and mining engineering office in Nogales, Arizona. In 1891 the community of Nogales employed Flipper to prepare the Nogales de Elias land grant case (1893), a dispute over title to the San Juan de las Boquillas y Nogales Mexican land grant in Cochise County, Arizona. Flipper served as the government's only witness, and his testimony resulted in the grant's being declared invalid. The ruling saved the property of hundreds of landowners. Flipper's activity in the community led to his appointment as a special agent for the United States Court of Private Land Claims. In that position he worked on court materials, served as an expert on penmanship, and surveyed land grants in southern Arizona. In 1892, before the Nogales case, he compiled and translated *Mining Law of the United States of Mexico and the Law on the Federal Property Tax on Mines.* In 1895 the United States government published his translation of *Spanish and Mexican Land Laws: New Spain and Mexico.* Flipper also briefly edited the Nogales *Sunday Herald* and published articles in *Old Santa Fe,* which later became the *New Mexico Historical Review.* He became a member of the Association of Arizona Civil Engineers, the National Geographic Society, and the Southwest Society of the Archaeological Institute of America. He offered to serve in the Spanish-American War in 1898, but bills in the United States House of Representatives and in the Senate to restore his rank both died in committee. He served in the court of private land claims until 1901.

Beginning in 1901 Flipper spent eleven years in northern Mexico as an engineer and legal assistant to mining companies. He joined the Balvanera Mining Company in 1901 and remained as keeper of the company's property when it folded in 1903. William C. Greene bought the company in 1905, renamed it the Gold-Silver Company, and placed Flipper in the legal department, where he handled land claims and sales and kept mining crews out of trouble with the local authorities. Greene, who had learned earlier of Flipper's research on the Lost Tayopa Mine, sent him to Spain to do more investigation. The story of Flipper and the Lost Tayopa Mine appears in J. Frank Dobie's[qv] *Apache Gold and Yaqui Silver.* In 1908 Albert B. Fall bought out William C. Greene to form the Sierra Mining Company and retained Flipper in the legal department. In 1912 Flipper moved to El Paso, and in 1913 he began supplying information on conditions in revolutionary Mexico to Senator Fall's subcommittee on Mexican internal affairs. Flipper drew national attention when he was reported to be in league with Francisco (Pancho) Villa[qv] and denied the rumor in a letter to the Washington *Eagle* dated May 4, 1916. Flipper published an article, "Early History of El Paso," and also reputedly wrote a pamphlet entitled *Did a Negro Discover Arizona and New Mexico?,* which concerned itself with Estevanico's[qv] role in the Marcos de Niza[qv] expedition in 1539. In 1916 Flipper wrote a memoir of his life in the Southwest, which was published posthumously as *Negro Frontiersman: The Western Memoirs of Henry O. Flipper* (1963).

In 1919 Senator Fall called Flipper to Washington, D.C., as a translator and interpreter for his subcommittee. Upon his appointment as secretary of the interior in 1921, Fall appointed Flipper assistant to the secretary of the interior. In that position Flipper became involved with the Alaskan Engineering Commission. He served in the Department of the Interior until 1923, when he went to work as an engineer for William F. Buckley's[qv] Pantepec Petroleum Company in Venezuela. In 1925 the Pantepec Petroleum Company published Flipper's translation of *Venezuela's Law on Hydrocarbons and other Combustible Minerals.*

Flipper worked in Venezuela until 1930 and retired in 1931. He lived out his life at the Atlanta home of his brother, Joseph S. Flipper, a bishop of the African Methodist Episcopal Church. Henry Flipper died of a heart attack on May 3, 1940. In December 1976, when a bust of him was unveiled at West Point, the Department of the Army granted Flipper an honorable discharge, dated June 30, 1882. Two years later his remains were removed from Atlanta and reinterred at Thomasville, Georgia. An annual West Point award in honor of Flipper is presented to the graduate who best exemplifies "the highest qualities of leadership, self-discipline, and perseverance in the face of unusual difficulties while a cadet."

BIBLIOGRAPHY: Bruce J. Dinges, "The Court-Martial of Lieutenant Henry O. Flipper," *American West,* January 1972. Henry Ossian Flipper, *The Colored Cadet at West Point* (New York: Lee, 1878; rpt., New York: Arno Press and New York *Times,* 1969). Theodore D. Harris, ed., *Negro Frontiersman: The Western Memoirs of Henry O. Flipper* (El Paso: Texas Western College Press, 1963). Steve Wilson, "A Black Lieutenant in the Ranks," *American History Illustrated,* December 1983.
Bruce J. Dinges

FLO, TEXAS. Flo, also known as Kidd's Mill, Wheelock, Bethlehem, Oneta, New Hope, Oden(s), and Midway, is on Farm roads 1151 and 831 and Wheelock Creek twelve miles northeast of Centerville in central Leon County. There Thaddeus O. Kidd built a combined grist and saw mill and received a post office named Kidd's Mill in 1855; this post office closed in 1868. In 1880 a post office operated briefly as Odens. Another one operated as Oden from 1885 until 1891, when it was given its final name of Flo, after the postmaster's dog. The post office closed sometime after 1930.

The first school in Kidd's Mill was opened before the Civil War.[qv] In 1927 a consolidated school was established at Flo. In 1940 a rock-walled school building, called "Flo's Folly" by some, was named Lone Star School and served students all the way from the Midway-Russel area, until it burned and was replaced by a brick building. The remnants of the rock school could still be seen in 1990. As of 1986 the children of Flo were being bussed to Oakwood.

In 1896 the Flo area had a gin and mill, two general stores, a breeder, and one physician. In 1914 the population was sixty, and the town had a gristmill. The community had forty-six residents in 1968–69 and twenty in the mid-1970s. A 1989 map indicates one church and one business. The population in 1991 was still twenty.

BIBLIOGRAPHY: Leon County Historical Book Survey Committee, *History of Leon County* (Dallas: Curtis Media, 1986).
Dylan Wood

FLOMOT, TEXAS. Flomot is on Farm roads 97 and 599 between the North Pease River and Quitaque Creek in northeast Motley

County. Its name combines those of Floyd and Motley counties, since the original post office, opened in 1902, was built on the county line. The town developed with a school and store in the early 1890s. Early residents included A. J. Hudson, Clarence and Marvin Washington, Leonard Crowell, and H. D. Gilbert. In 1915 the post office was moved to W. R. Welch's home. In 1940 the town had ten stores and 200 residents. The population was 181 in 1980 and 1990.

BIBLIOGRAPHY: Arthur Hecht, comp., *Postal History in the Texas Panhandle* (Canyon, Texas: Panhandle-Plains Historical Society, 1960). Eleanor Traweek, *Of Such as These: A History of Motley County and Its Families* (Quanah, Texas: Nortex, 1973).

FLORA, TEXAS (Fort Bend County). Flora was a farming community and rail stop on U.S. Highway 59 (now 90A) about a mile northeast of Richmond in north central Fort Bend County. The community seems to have been established after 1894 and may have been named for J. C. Florea, who taught the first school in nearby Missouri City in 1894 and afterward became a county judge. According to other sources it was named for Flora Emmich, the wife of railroad employee Leon Emmich. Flora never had a post office; its mail was delivered through Richmond. By 1936 the site was apparently a stop on the Texas and New Orleans Railroad. By 1987 all reference to Flora had disappeared from county maps.

BIBLIOGRAPHY: Clarence Wharton, *Wharton's History of Fort Bend County* (San Antonio: Naylor, 1939). *Stephen L. Hardin*

FLORA, TEXAS (Hopkins County). Flora, on Farm Road 69 thirteen miles northeast of Sulphur Springs in northeastern Hopkins County, is said to have been named for the many wildflowers on the surrounding prairie. A. F. and H. F. Conner settled in the area in the early 1860s. A tannery established there furnished leather for shoes and harnesses. A post office opened at the site in 1902 but closed in 1905. By the mid-1930s Flora had a school, a business, and a number of scattered dwellings. In 1940 its population was twenty-five. After World War II[qv] the school was consolidated with that of Sulphur Bluff, and by the mid-1980s the community had one business and a number of scattered houses. *J. E. Jennings*

FLORENCE, FRED FARREL (1891–1960). Fred Farrel Florence, banker and civic leader, was born in New York City on November 5, 1891, to Lithuanian immigrants Mose and Celia (Freedman) Fromowitz. His family moved in 1892 to New Birmingham, Texas, then two years later to Rusk, where he attended public school through the tenth grade, worked in the family store, sold newspapers, and, like his brothers and sister, legally changed his name to Florence. At age fifteen he began his life's work at the First National Bank in Rusk. He advanced to assistant cashier by 1911 and moved on to positions as bookkeeper at the American Exchange Bank in Dallas (1911), cashier at the First State Bank in Ratcliff (1912), and vice president (1912), then president (1915) of the Alto State Bank.

Florence enlisted in the Signal Corps Aviation School of the United States Army with the rank of corporal in 1918 and was discharged later that year as a second lieutenant. He then returned to his bank presidency in Alto and later served as a town alderman, then mayor (1919). In 1920 he became first vice president of the Guaranty Bank and Trust Company, which became Republic National Bank and Trust Company in 1922 and was renamed Republic National Bank of Dallas in 1937. Florence was president from 1929 until 1957, when he became chairman of the executive committee with the duties of chief executive officer.

He took a lead in commodity financing, especially of cotton and oil reserves; he supplanted many northern credit facilities and made his bank one of the first Texas banks to extend loans on oil reserves and natural-gas production. Under his direction deposits at his bank increased from $1 million to almost $900 million. Florence was also a director of several other Texas banks and businesses, including Lone Star Steel (where he also served as board chairman), Bond Stores, Wyatt Industries, the MKT Railroad Company, Dallas Power and Light, the Austin Bridge Company, the Hotel Baker, Sanger Brothers,[qv] and Neiman-Marcus.[qv] He was a member of the executive committee and vice president of the Dallas Joint Stock Land Bank. He was active in the American Bankers Association in 1934, served on the National Defense and War Loan committee (1941–44), chaired the Credit Policy Commission of the American Bankers Association (1951–54), and was elected vice president (1954) and president (1955) of the American Bankers Association. He was president of the Texas Bankers Association (1956) and a director of the Texas Mid-Continent Oil and Gas Association.

In addition to his banking interests, Florence was appointed by governors Ross S. Sterling and Miriam A. Ferguson[qqv] and President Franklin Roosevelt to serve on various recovery and relief boards during the Great Depression.[qv] He was president of the Texas Centennial[qv] Central Exposition in 1936 and of the Greater Texas and Pan-American Exposition the following year. He was a board member of the State Fair of Texas[qv] and also served the Dallas Civic Federation, Citizens Council, Clearing House, and Chamber of Commerce, as well as the city's art, opera, symphony, and historical organizations. He was a member of the executive committees of Southern Methodist University, where a building is named for him, and the Southwestern Medical Foundation, of which he was also a trustee; a director of the National Merit Scholarship Corporation, the Southwest Research Institute,[qv] and the Research and Educational Foundation; and a trustee of Hebrew Union College and St. Mark's School of Texas.[qv] He was also vice president, treasurer, and a member of the executive and endowment committees of the Texas Research Foundation.[qv] He served on the boards of Dallas United Charities and other welfare organizations from the 1920s to his death and was life chairman of the Dallas County chapter of the National Foundation for Infantile Paralysis, treasurer of the American Cancer Society's Texas division, and campaign chairman for the March of Dimes. He was a director of Temple Emanu-El in Dallas and vice president and president of the Jewish Federation for Social Service, chairman of the United Palestine Fund for Dallas and Texas (1924), and national chairman of the Combined Campaign for American Reform Judaism (1960–61). He was national director of the Camp Fire Girls and vice president and a director of the Boy Scouts of America. In 1956 President Dwight D. Eisenhower[qv] named him chairman of the banking committee of the People to People program, which promoted international understanding and friendship. Florence established the Florence Foundation in December 1956 to support charitable, religious, educational, scientific, and recreational projects "for the benefit of humanity."

He received the Linz Award (1944) for civic contributions to Dallas, the Dallas Distinguished Salesman Award (1954), and the Kudos College award of the Dallas Advertising League (1955). He was named Headliner of the Year for 1956 by the Dallas Press Club and presented the Distinguished Civic Service Award in 1960 by the Greater Dallas Planning Council. He received honorary doctorates from Westminster College at Fulton, Missouri (1955), Oklahoma City University (1956), and Texas Technological College (1960), and, in 1959, was given the Catholic Benemerenti Medal for his work as general chairman of the building campaign for St. Paul Hospital, of which he was later board chairman and trustee. Florence was a thirty-second-degree Mason, a Shriner, and a Democrat. On February 21, 1928, he married Helen Lefkowitz; they adopted two children. He died in a Dallas hospital of hepatitis on December 25, 1960.

BIBLIOGRAPHY: Sam Hanna Acheson, Herbert P. Gambrell, Mary Carter Toomey, and Alex M. Acheson, Jr., *Texian Who's Who*, Vol. 1 (Dallas: Texian, 1937). *Current Biography*, 1956. Dallas *Morning News*, December 26, 1960. *Who Was Who in America*, Vol. 4. H. Harold

Wineburgh, *The Texas Banker: The Life and Times of Fred Farrel Florence* (Dallas, 1981).
Joan Jenkins Perez

FLORENCE, TEXAS. Florence is on Farm Road 195 thirty-four miles north of Austin in northwestern Williamson County. The site was settled in the early 1850s and briefly called Brooksville but had become known as Florence by 1857, when its first post office was established. The origin of this name is uncertain: it may have derived from Florence, Alabama, an early home of the first postmaster, or it may refer to Florence Brooks, the daughter of the town's first merchant. A successful cattle industry developed around Florence after the Civil War,qv when wheat and cotton were significant local crops. In the 1890s Florence had a number of retail stores, mills, churches, schools, lodges, hotels, doctors, and photographers, and a stone quarry, a bank, and a cheese factory. Florence College opened around 1895 under the direction of W. S. Holden and offered classes for about eight years. Beginning with the Florence *Flower* in 1890, the town had four newspapers, the last of which ceased publication in 1955. The Bartlett and Western Railway (originally chartered in 1909 as the Bartlett and Florence Railway Company) served the town from 1912 until the line was abandoned in 1935. Florence grew steadily from an estimated population of 350 in 1900 to a high of 1,000 recorded from 1927 to 1929. By 1931 its estimated population had dropped to 421, where it remained for eight years before beginning a slow but steady growth that reached an estimated 672 by 1976. In 1978 its reported population was 837, and in 1982 it was 744. In 1986 Florence had twenty retail businesses, a post office, a bank, and a medical clinic. In 1990 the population was 829.

BIBLIOGRAPHY: Eleanor Adeline Caskey, *One Hundred Years in Florence, Texas* (Georgetown, Texas: Roberts Printing, 1963; 2d ed., Georgetown: Heritage Printing, 1970). Clara Stearns Scarbrough, *Land of Good Water: A Williamson County History* (Georgetown, Texas: Williamson County Sun Publishers, 1973).
Clara Stearns Scarbrough

FLORENCE HILL, TEXAS. Florence Hill was a mile north of the shores of Joe Pool Lake, six miles south of Grand Prairie, and six miles west of Duncanville in southwestern Dallas County. The site of Florence Hill was in the original land grant of Thomas J. Tone.qv According to one account, the community received its name from the hilly terrain and from David W. Florence, an Alabama native who moved there from Van Zandt County in 1871. Another story relates that the community was named for Florence, who donated land for a school in the 1890s, and for Billy Hill. In the 1896–97 school year the Florence Hill school had one teacher and an enrollment of sixty-eight. Around 1940 Florence Hill's population was twenty, and the community comprised several houses, an athletic field, a general store, a school, and a church. At that time the surrounding farms raised alfalfa, corn, oats, wheat, and milo maize. During the 1940s the establishment of military and industrial facilities in nearby Grand Prairie led to enormous population growth in the area. In 1952 the Florence Hill common school district received funds under a federal program to help schools overburdened from increased population due to new federal projects and installations. By 1964, the last year that Florence Hill was listed in the *Texas Almanac*,qv the community's population was 150. Afterward Florence Hill eventually became part of Grand Prairie.

BIBLIOGRAPHY: Dallas *Daily Times Herald*, August 28, 1949. WPA Texas Writers' Project, *Dallas: Guide and History* (1940).
Lisa C. Maxwell

FLORES, JUAN JOSÉ (1743–1790). Juan José Flores the younger was born in Saltillo in 1743, the son of Juan José Flores de Abrego y Valdés and Nicolasa de Ávila. After the death of his wife the elder Flores moved to San Antonio de Béxar. On February 3, 1750, he married Leonor Delgado, the widow of Bernardo Leal. Around 1756 they started a ranch near San Bartolo on the lower Cibolo Creek, one of the earliest in the vicinity. Flores the younger, his three brothers, and his sister eventually left Saltillo and joined their father in Texas. In 1777 Flores, his wife, and two children were residents of Presidio del Río Grande, the old San Juan Bautista.qv The family kept close ties with their native city, however. When the elder Flores died in 1779, all the children but one were mentioned in his will, along with his three children by Leonor Delgado. Flores soon petitioned the estate for 900 pesos owed to Francisco de Yermo, an administrator of tithes in northern Coahuila. This sum was apparently owed in connection with the annual tithe that the elder Flores had collected in Texas. Flores began driving herds of livestock, branded and unbranded, to the Rio Grande to fulfill his father's obligation to Yermo.

In so doing he soon ran afoul of Governor Domingo Cabello y Robles,qv who had the thankless job of taxing unbranded livestock— decreed the property of the king—taken from the province. By mid-1784 Flores had fled Texas, carrying petitions against the cattle tax directly to the commandant general. He remained in Chihuahua during Cabello's term of office, little more than a fugitive from justice, and continued working for the stockmen's interests. Because of these labors the ranchers were granted additional time to gather and brand their "stray" stock, thereby avoiding the tax.

After Rafael Martínez Pachecoqv replaced Cabello as governor, Flores returned to Texas and acted as the private raisers' agent in negotiating a roundup agreement with the missions of San Antonio de Béxar and La Bahía in 1787. He probably authored the "San Fernando Memorial," one of the most comprehensive stock-raising documents of eighteenth-century Texas. In the early years of Martínez Pacheco's administration several cattle drives were made to Coahuila by the citizens of Bexar in order to pay Flores for his defense of their rights.

Unfortunately, the cattlemen's attorney did not live to see his protests bear fruit. He was killed at his ranch by Apaches in March 1790, leaving a widow, Manuela de Aguilar, their three children, and a large debt owed to San José y San Miguel de Aguayo Mission. Flores's legal efforts were not entirely in vain, however. Five years after his death the viceroy and a council of the Royal Treasury canceled all debts owed the king's Mustang Fund; nevertheless, they ordered the old detested fees on wild livestock to be collected after a final roundup extension of one year. *See also* RANCHING IN SPANISH TEXAS.

BIBLIOGRAPHY: Bexar Archives, Barker Texas History Center, University of Texas at Austin. Jack Jackson, *Los Mesteños: Spanish Ranching in Texas, 1721–1821* (College Station: Texas A&M University Press, 1986). Nacogdoches Archives, Steen Library, Stephen F. Austin State University; Barker Texas History Center, University of Texas at Austin; Texas State Archives, Austin.
Jack Jackson

FLORES, MANUEL (?–1839). Manuel Flores, trader and Mexican agent, lived before the Texas Revolutionqv in Natchitoches Parish, Louisiana, where he illicitly traded with the Caddo Indians who lived in the vicinity. In 1835 he failed in an attempt to keep the Caddos from making a treaty with the United States that called for the removal of the Indians from Louisiana. The next year, during the Texas Revolution, he unsuccessfully tried to recruit these Indians to the side of Mexico. He eluded United States military units and presumably fled to Mexico; by 1838 he was associated with the Mexican authorities at Matamoros as an emissary with the task of convincing the Texas Indians that they should overthrow the Republic of Texas.qv In the spring of 1839, under orders from Valentín Canalizo, he led an expedition from Matamoros that carried war supplies to the Indians in Texas whom the Mexicans were trying to organize. After killing four members of a party of surveyors between Seguin and San Antonio on May 14, the Flores group was trailed by a company of Texas Rangerqv for two days, and a part of the ranger company, led by Lt. James O. Rice,qv confronted the Mexican group on the North San Gabriel

River on May 17, 1839. Flores's band was routed, and Flores was reported among the dead. In the baggage removed after the skirmish the Texans found several documents that seemed to link the Cherokee Indians with a Mexican plot to conquer Texas. These documents prompted President Mirabeau B. Lamar^{qv} to demand that the Cherokees leave Texas, and this precipitated the Cherokee War.^{qv} In 1936 a marker was placed near the site of the Rice–Flores engagement. Flores has often been confused with another Manuel Flores.^{qv} *See also* SAN GABRIELS, BATTLE OF THE.

BIBLIOGRAPHY: William L. Mann, "James O. Rice, Hero of the Battle on the San Gabriels," *Southwestern Historical Quarterly* 55 (July 1951). Joseph Milton Nance, *Attack and Counterattack: The Texas-Mexican Frontier, 1842* (Austin: University of Texas Press, 1964). J. W. Wilbarger, *Indian Depredations in Texas* (Austin: Hutchings, 1889; rpt., Austin: State House, 1985).

Roderick B. Patten

FLORES, MANUEL (ca. 1801–1868). Manuel Flores, participant in the Texas Revolution,^{qv} was born in San Antonio around 1801 (possibly as early as 1799), the son of José Antonio Flores de Abrego and María Antonia Rodríguez. He was a widower for the second time before he married María Josefa Courbiere in 1835. In the fall of 1835 he became a member of the volunteer company organized by his brother-in-law, Juan N. Seguín.^{qv} This company was composed of San Antonio–area Mexicans who were sympathetic to the Texas colonists' stand against Antonio López de Santa Anna,^{qv} president of Mexico. Flores participated in the expulsion of Gen. Martín Perfecto de Cos^{qv} at the siege of Bexar^{qv} in December 1835. The company disbanded but was reorganized in Gonzales during the first week of March 1836, and Flores became Captain Seguin's first sergeant. He fought in this capacity at the battle of San Jacinto.^{qv}

In 1838 Flores and his wife established a ranch on the south side of the Guadalupe River across from Seguin, Texas. In the spring of 1842 he again took up arms in defense of Texas; he was a member of the party that pursued the army of Rafael Vásquez^{qv} after the brief invasion of San Antonio by the Mexicans. In 1853 he sold his ranch and established a new one in Atascosa County. His wife died the next year, and about 1858 he married Margarita Garza. He was a Mason in Alamo Lodge No. 44. Flores died on December 3, 1868. He has often been confused with the Mexican emissary Manuel Flores,^{qv} who was killed at the battle of the San Gabriels.^{qv}

BIBLIOGRAPHY: Antonio Menchaca, *Memoirs* (San Antonio: Yanaguana Society, 1937). Thomas L. Miller, *Bounty and Donation Land Grants of Texas, 1835–1888* (Austin: University of Texas Press, 1967). Juan N. Seguin, *Personal Memoirs* (San Antonio, 1858).

Roderick B. Patten

FLORES, VITAL (1791–1886). Vital Flores, early Nacogdoches official, was born on April 28, 1791, at Rancho Tortuga in Nacogdoches County, the son of José Flores and Anna María Gertrudis Mora. His father and grandfather had come with Antonio Gil Ibarvo^{qv} in 1779 and rebuilt the town of Nacogdoches. Flores was considered well-educated. He was elected alcalde^{qv} of Nacogdoches for 1834 and was acting political chief of the Department of Nacogdoches during the long period that Henry Rueg,^{qv} the regular political chief, was absent. Flores died on January 23, 1886, at Rancho Tortuga.

BIBLIOGRAPHY: Robert Bruce Blake Research Collection, Steen Library, Stephen F. Austin State University; Barker Texas History Center, University of Texas at Austin; Texas State Archives, Austin; Houston Public Library, Houston. Carolyn Reeves Ericson, *Nacogdoches, Gateway to Texas: A Biographical Directory* (2 vols., Fort Worth: Arrow-Curtis Printing, 1974, 1987). Nacogdoches Archives, Steen Library, Stephen F. Austin State University; Barker Texas History Center, University of Texas at Austin; Texas State Archives, Austin.

Robert Bruce Blake

FLORES, TEXAS. Flores, a farming and ranching community a mile west of Farm Road 1333 and eight miles west of Poteet in west central Atascosa County, may have derived its name from that of the Flores family, who before 1900 had a large land grant in the area. During the 1940s the area had a church, business, and cemetery, but by the 1960s only the cemetery remained there. In the 1980s Flores had a business and a cemetery.

Linda Peterson

FLORES DE ABREGO, JOSÉ GASPAR MARÍA (1781–1836). Gaspar Flores de Abrego, land commissioner and ally of the Austin colonists, was born in San Antonio de Béxar on January 5, 1781, to Vicente Flores and María Antonia de las Fuentes Fernandes. In Bexar he was elected alcalde^{qv} in 1819, 1824, 1829, and 1834. At a meeting on October 13, 1834, described as the "first strictly revolutionary meeting in Texas," anti-Centralists of Bexar, worried by the dictatorial actions of President Antonio López de Santa Anna,^{qv} called on all Texans to join them in convention on November 15. Among the thirty-five signers of the memorial were Erasmo and Juan N. Seguín,^{qqv} Gaspar Flores and his son Nicolás, and Luciano and José Antonio Navarro.^{qv}

By 1835 Santa Anna had dissolved Congress and was dispersing state governments, including that of Coahuila and Texas.^{qv} The crisis reached Bexar with the arrival of troops under Col. Domingo de Ugartechea.^{qv} Flores, at that time serving as administrator of the Revenue Department, refused to obey the colonel's demand for his official documents, writing that "the military have no right to interfere." Santa Anna next sent Gen. Martín Perfecto de Cos^{qv} to Bexar with additional troops, but Texas volunteers drove them out of Bexar and out of Texas. A small group of the volunteers remained in Bexar, headquartered in the Alamo with neither money nor supplies. Gaspar Flores offered them all his "goods, Groceries and Beeves." When the soldiers met with citizens in January 1836 Flores served on a committee that included James Bonham, James Bowie,^{qqv} and Juan Seguín, to draft resolutions for the consideration of the committee.

February 1 was voting day for Texas towns, each to select four delegates to the March 1 convention that would decide the future of Texas. Bexar elected Antonio Navarro, José Francisco Ruiz,^{qv} Erasmo Seguín, and Gaspar Flores. Two weeks later Tejano spies brought word that Santa Anna was crossing the Rio Grande with thousands of troops for the purpose of capturing Bexar. As the younger men joined the Texas army or rode as couriers, Flores and Seguín took charge of gathering their own and other families and with loaded oxcarts and 3,000 sheep hurried to the safety of East Texas.

After the battle of San Jacinto^{qv} Juan Seguín found them in Nacogdoches struck down by a fever that took a number of lives. Flores died on September 6, 1836, having gone as far as the home of George Huff,^{qv} a few miles east of San Felipe. His second wife, Petra Zambrano, his son Nicolás, and his two sons-in-law accepted his estate as inventoried on February 11, 1837.

BIBLIOGRAPHY: Eugene C. Barker, ed., *The Austin Papers* (3 vols., Washington: GPO, 1924–28). Eugene C. Barker, *The Life of Stephen F. Austin* (Nashville: Cokesbury Press, 1925; rpts., Austin: Texas State Historical Association, 1949; New York: AMS Press, 1970). Bexar Archives, Barker Texas History Center, University of Texas at Austin. Bexar County Archives, San Antonio. Frederick Charles Chabot, *With the Makers of San Antonio* (Yanaguana Society Publications 4, San Antonio, 1937). John H. Jenkins, ed., *The Papers of the Texas Revolution, 1835–1836* (10 vols., Austin: Presidial Press, 1973). Louis Wiltz Kemp, *The Signers of the Texas Declaration of Independence* (Salado, Texas: Anson Jones, 1944; rpt. 1959). Antonio Menchaca, *Memoirs* (San Antonio: Yanaguana Society, 1937). José María Rodríguez, *Rodríguez's Memoirs of Early Texas* (San Antonio, 1913; 2d ed. 1961). Juan N. Seguin, *Personal Memoirs* (San Antonio, 1858). *Texas Republican*, November 1, 1834. Louis J. Wortham, *A History of Texas* (5 vols., Fort Worth: Wortham-Molyneaux, 1924). Henderson K. Yoakum, *History of Texas from Its First Settlement in 1685 to Its Annexation to the United States in 1846* (2 vols., New York: Redfield, 1855).

Camilla Campbell

FLORES DE ANDRADE (?–?). Señora Flores de Andrade, early Mexican activist, was born in the state of Chihuahua, where she spent her early years on the estate of her grandparents. The family was relatively well off, and the girl was given an education and encouraged in such sports as bareback horse riding. Her grandparents died when she was thirteen, leaving her a good inheritance. To her family's displeasure, she immediately "gave absolute liberty" to all the peasants who had worked on the estate and supplied them with tools and animals to continue to work the land as long as they wished. She married a man of German origin, with whom she had six children. He died twelve years after the marriage, and she moved with her children to Chihuahua City, where she began to work with a political group known as the Daughters of Cuauhtémoc, who were involved with the Partido Liberal Mexicano.qv Her work with the group caused even further dissension within her family, and she became quite impoverished and ultimately moved with her children and Pedro Mendoza, a member of the party, to El Paso in 1906, in hope of improving her economic situation.

There she lived and worked with Mendoza organizing the local Mexican community for the PLM; she was apparently forced by the American authorities to marry him because they lived together. The marriage was an unhappy one, and Flores de Andrade ultimately separated from Mendoza, accusing him of infidelity and abuse. Three years after her arrival in El Paso, she joined another women's group, which also worked with Mexican revolutionaries. In addition, she allied herself with Francisco I. Madero,qv a Mexican revolutionary who later became president of Mexico. Her oral history, as recounted to Mexican anthropologist Manuel Gamio, has provided insights into the political activism of women among Mexican political refugees in Texas in the early twentieth century. Like Mexican-born Texans Sara Estela Ramírezqv and Teresa and Andrea Villarreal, Flores de Andrade sought a democratic society for Mexico.

BIBLIOGRAPHY: Manuel Gamio, *The Life Story of the Mexican Immigrant: Autobiographical Documents* (New York: Dover, 1971).

Teresa Palomo Acosta

FLORES DE BARKER, JOSEFA AUGUSTINA (?–?). Josefa Augustina Flores de Barker, donor of the site of Floresville, was born to José María Flores and María Leonides Flores probably in the early 1800s. She grew up on the family's extensive lands and, in San Antonio on April 17, 1854, married Samuel Williams Barker, who became the first sheriff of Wilson County. When her father died, Josefa inherited a portion of his estate, 200 acres of which she donated to establish the town of Floresville in 1833, with the request that the settlement be named in honor of her great-great-grandfather, Francisco Flores de Abrego,qv whose hacienda was six miles from the site of the present town. Many of her descendants have continued to live in the community and surrounding areas, and in 1990 some still owned the land that was handed down to them through five generations of the Flores de Abrego family.

BIBLIOGRAPHY: Louise Stadler, ed., *Wilson County History* (Dallas: Taylor, 1990).

Teresa Palomo Acosta

FLORES BAYOU. Flores Bayou rises 6½ miles north of Angleton in central Brazoria County (at 29°16' N, 95°26' W) and runs southeast for twelve miles, passing along the western edge of Danbury and across the Missouri Pacific tracks before reaching its mouth on Austin Bayou, six miles east of Angleton (at 29°11' N, 95°19' W). The stream, which is intermittent in its upper reaches, is dammed to form in its middle reaches the Bieri Lakes and other reservoirs. The bayou traverses flat terrain with local shallow depressions, surfaced by clay and sandy loams that support water-tolerant hardwoods, conifers, and grasses.

FLORES MAGÓN, RICARDO (1873–1922). Ricardo Flores Magón, revolutionist, journalist, and dramatist, son of D. Teodoro Flores and Margarita Magón, was born in San Antonio Eloxochitlán, Oaxaca, September 16, 1873. His father, an Indian, was a veteran of the War of the Reform and the French Intervention; his mother, a mestiza, provided him with the simple life of rural Oaxaca, including elements of communal living. His younger brother, Enrique, born in 1877, was a lifetime supporter of Ricardo. Due to his mother's influence, Ricardo studied in the nation's capital, first at the Escuela Nacional Superior, and then at the Escuela Nacional Preparatoria. In 1893 he began the study of law in the Escuela Nacional de Jurisprudencia, and although he remained there for three years he never completed law school. On August 7, 1900, with his brother Jesús, he founded the newspaper *Regeneración,* an "independent organ of combat" to oppose the centralism and autocracy of the government of Porfirio Díaz. Later, at the Liberal Congress held in San Luis Potosí in 1901, he publicly denounced the Díaz administration as "a den of bandits." After being arrested on May 22, 1901, Jesús and Ricardo were held at Belén prison without a trial until April 30, 1902, when, with the suppression of *Regeneración,* he became a writer for Daniel Cabrera's *El Hijo del Ahuizote,* a position he held until the paper's demise in February 1903. He was arrested again, imprisoned in Belén until October 1903, and prohibited from publishing in Mexico. In January 1904 he and his brother Enrique crossed the border into Laredo, Texas, and went to San Antonio, where they renewed the publication of *Regeneración* on November 5, 1904. At this time Flores Magón met Tejanos such as Aniceto Pizañaqv who later conducted border raids during the Mexican Revolution.qv *Regeneración* fueled a "Floresmagonista" movement in Texas. At the same time other anti-Díaz publications, such as *1810* and *El Mensajaro,* were begun at Del Rio. After a local incident led to the arrest of Enrique, the Floresmagonistas set up shop in St. Louis, Missouri, in 1905–06. Sometime in September 1906 Ricardo traveled back to Texas and met with Mexican Liberal party factions in El Paso to coordinate an uprising in Mexico. Persecutions forced the brothers to abandon St. Louis and in 1907 the Liberal party established its publication in Los Angeles. Flores Magón was arrested again in August 1907, held in the Los Angeles County Jail for several months, and then transferred to Tombstone, Arizona, where he was found guilty of conspiracy to violate the neutrality laws and sentenced to eighteen months in the territorial prison. While he was incarcerated, his newspaper was published under the name *Revolución.* After his release from the Florence penitentiary in August 1910, Flores Magón ushered in *Regeneración*'s third epoch and started plans for a Baja California revolt and an anarchist manifesto. The Baja revolt led to his formal separation from Francisco I. Maderoqv and the Maderista movement, and he was once again arrested in 1911. When World War Iqv erupted in 1914, Flores Magón, as an anarcho-communist and pacifist, was its foremost critic in the United States. Ironically, though his writings had a direct influence on Texas border troubles and the Plan of San Diego,qv he had no personal involvement in the struggles. He thought that the Plan of San Diego was a "bourgeois" invention and denied the existence of any Texas-Mexican conspiracy. He largely ignored the border raids and viewed them not as anarchist uprisings but acts of self-defense against Anglo exploiters. Flores Magón was arrested on March 22, 1918, on a charge of sedition and eventually found guilty of violations of the Espionage Act of 1917. Under that act he was accused of conspiracy to write and publish false statements that tended to interfere with the operation of the military and naval forces of the United States. He was sentenced to twenty years at McNeil Island (Washington state) and transferred in November 1919 to Leavenworth penitentiary. Throughout his career he had been aided by his lifetime companion and common-law wife, María Talavera. In 1907 she was instrumental in developing socialist support for Floresmagonistas in the Los Angeles County Jail, and in 1918 she too was tried by a federal court in Los Angeles for violations of the Espionage Act. On the morning of November 21, 1922, Flores Magón died at Leavenworth. Although several radical scholars claim that he was murdered, he probably died of natural causes, likely of a heart attack. On May 1, 1945, his remains were reburied in Dolores Cemetery in Mexico city.

BIBLIOGRAPHY: Ward S. Albro III, *Ricardo Flores Magón and the Liberal Party: An Inquiry into the Origins of the Revolution of 1910* (Ph.D. dissertation, University of Arizona, 1967). Roderic A. Camp, *Mexican Political Biographies, 1884–1935* (Austin: University of Texas Press, 1991). *Diccionario Histórico y Biográfico de la Revolución Mexicana* (Mexico City: Instituto Nacional de Estudios Históricos de la Revolución, 1990–). W. Dirk Raat, *Revoltosos: Mexico's Rebels in the United States, 1903–1923* (College Station: Texas A&M University Press, 1981). James Sandos, *Rebellion in the Borderlands: Anarchism and the Plan of San Diego, 1904–1923* (Norman: University of Oklahoma Press, 1992).

W. Dirk Raat

FLORES DE VALDÉS, NICOLÁS (?–1731). Nicolás Flores de Valdés joined a supply expedition organized in 1693 by Governor Gregorio de Salinas Varona[qv] for the missions in Texas. In 1701, when the garrison of San Juan Bautista[qv] was established, Flores was the first to enlist. He continued to serve there for fourteen years, first as a private, then as a sergeant, and later as alferez. He married Nicolasa Ximenes y Baldés on May 3, 1707, in Monclova. He joined the Aguayo expedition[qv] in 1719 and at the Marqués de Aguayo's[qv] request took soldiers from San Antonio de Béxar to help suppress an Indian revolt at Santa Rosa de Nadadores in 1700. He also acted as scout for the expedition and was of great assistance in securing supplies from San Antonio. When Aguayo went to La Bahía[qv] del Espíritu Santo, Flores was left in charge of rebuilding the presidio of San Antonio de Béxar, where he remained as captain. He was an able Indian fighter and kept Apache raids at a minimum. With the exception of one interruption in 1724–25, caused by a misunderstanding with the friars of San Antonio de Valero Mission, he retained his command until his death on June 6, 1731.

BIBLIOGRAPHY: Carlos E. Castañeda, *Our Catholic Heritage in Texas* (7 vols., Austin: Von Boeckmann–Jones, 1936–58; rpt., New York: Arno, 1976). William Edward Dunn, "Apache Relations in Texas, 1718–1750," *Quarterly of the Texas State Historical Association* 14 (January 1911).

FLORESVILLE, TEXAS. Floresville, the county seat of Wilson County, is at the junction of U.S. Highway 181 and State Highway 97, thirty miles southeast of San Antonio in the central portion of the county. The area was settled by Canary Island immigrant Don Francisco Flores de Abrego, who established a ranch headquarters six miles northwest of the site of present Floresville in the eighteenth century. In 1833 the nucleus of the present town included the Flores home, a chapel, and a graveyard. The community was called Lodi and served as the county seat when Wilson county was established in 1867. That year Floresville, named for the Flores family, was founded; its site included part of the area known as Lodi. In the early 1870s a townsite was surveyed and laid out. At that time a prominent citizen, Andrew G. Pickett, who owned a ranch with an irrigation system, started raising peanuts. A Floresville post office was established in 1872. In the 1870s Floresville Academy offered several levels of education. Development accelerated in 1883, when the San Antonio and Aransas Pass Railway announced plans to construct a line through the town. Floresville replaced Lodi as county seat. By 1885 Floresville had two hotels, several stores, a weekly newspaper named the *Chronicle*, two steam cotton gin–gristmills, and a population of 400. The town was incorporated in 1890, when the reported population was 1,500. A five-teacher school was in operation by 1896, when it had an enrollment of 206.

The town continued to grow during the early years of the twentieth century, supported by both the cotton and livestock industry, and by 1910 it had two banks and a population of 1,800. Peanuts were developed as a cash crop in the surrounding region around 1915 and in later years residents nicknamed Floresville the "Peanut Capital of Texas." Between 1930 and 1970 the town grew steadily, from 1,581 residents in 1931 to 1,935 in 1952 and 2,980 in 1965. In 1990 the population was 5,414. The number of businesses reached a peak in the early 1950s at 112, but in 1990 was seventy-five. The town serves a market center for area peanut, small grain, and cattle producers. Many residents now commute to work in San Antonio. Floresville is best known for its annual Peanut Festival, which attracts 10,000 to 15,000 visitors each year.

BIBLIOGRAPHY: Louise Stadler, ed., *Wilson County History* (Dallas: Taylor, 1990).

Claudia Hazlewood

FLOREY, TEXAS. Florey, on U.S. Highway 385 twelve miles north of Andrews in northwestern Andrews County, was named for A. J. Florey, a pioneer rancher who settled in the area in 1908. The community, originally called Smackover, was first formed around 1903 by Pete Hollebeke, Willis Howell, Bob Hill, and the Jimerson families. When a post office began operation there in 1909, Lee N. Smith was postmaster. That same year the community's first school was built through donations, and Miss Edna McCorkle was appointed the first teacher. On December 15, 1938, the Florey school was incorporated into the Andrews Independent School District. A camp for the Humble Oil Company (later Exxon Company, U.S.A) was established in Florey in 1934 but was abandoned in 1956. In 1940 the community had one store and a population of fifty. In 1978 Florey consisted mainly of a county park. The community reported a population of twenty-five in 1990.

BIBLIOGRAPHY: *Andrews County History, 1876–1978* (Andrews, Texas: Andrews County Heritage Committee, 1978).

Tracey L. Compton

FLOURNOY, GEORGE M. (1832–1889). George M. Flournoy, state official and Confederate officer, was born in Louisville, Georgia, on November 30, 1832, the son of Marcus A. and Margaret (Shelman) Flournoy. He attended the University of Georgia and graduated from law school at Tuskegee, Alabama, in 1853. He and his bride, Eugenia (Haralson), moved to Austin, Texas, the following year, and Flournoy opened a law practice there. After Eugenia died, Flournoy married Virginia L. Holman in 1858. He was attorney general for the state of Texas in 1860 and a delegate to the 1860 Democratic nominating convention in Galveston. At a mass meeting in Austin on September 22, 1860, he asked the audience, "What will you do if Lincoln is elected? That, I know, is what you want to hear about. I say, secede from the Union." With Oran M. Roberts, Guy M. Bryan, W. S. Oldham, and John Marshall,[qqv] Flournoy helped call a Secession Convention[qv] at Austin on December 3. He sat as a delegate to the convention from January 28 through February 4, 1861, and served as a coauthor of the declaration of causes for secession.[qv] He resigned the following year to organize the Sixteenth Texas Infantry regiment of Walker's Texas Division.[qv] He served as the colonel of the regiment throughout the war. After the fall of the Confederate government he fled to Mexico, where he served for a while with Maximilian's forces. After his return to Texas, Flournoy practiced law at Galveston for a few years. He was a member of the Constitutional Convention of 1875[qv] and moved to California the following year. He died in San Francisco on September 18, 1889.

BIBLIOGRAPHY: Dudley Goodall Wooten, ed., *A Comprehensive History of Texas* (2 vols., Dallas: Scarff, 1898; rpt., Austin: Texas State

Historical Association, 1986). Marcus J. Wright, comp., and Harold B. Simpson, ed., *Texas in the War, 1861–1865* (Hillsboro, Texas: Hill Junior College Press, 1965).
Thomas W. Cutrer

FLOURNOY, SAMUEL MARTIN (1799–1878). Samuel Martin Flournoy, early settler in the Republic of Texas,qv one of twin sons of Samuel Flournoy and Nancy Ann Martin, was born in 1799 in Scott County, Kentucky. As young men the brothers, Samuel and John, traveled by flatboat to New Orleans. When John died unexpectedly on the return trip, Samuel chose not to return to Kentucky. He traveled instead to Madison County, Mississippi, and settled near Canton. In 1831 he was elected sheriff of Madison County and that year also married Minerva Ann Waddlington. They had ten children.

Flournoy prospered and in 1836 sent an overseer with 100 slaves to build a home in Chireno, Nacogdoches County. When he received word that the party had mistakenly gone to Sabine County to the South, he traveled to Texas and personally guided them to Chireno. On his arrival he bought additional lands in what are now Smith, Rains, and Wood counties. In 1840 he donated land for the Chireno Presbyterian Church and its nearby cemetery. He completed his home by 1841 and returned to Mississippi for his family.

The Flournoy home was a large, two-story, log and clapboard structure located midway between San Augustine and Nacogdoches on the Old San Antonio Road.qv The home, which still stood in 1991, evolved into a popular stagecoach stop called the Halfway Inn. Among early Texas immigrants and notables frequenting the inn were Sam Houston, Thomas J. Rusk, and James Pinckney Henderson.qqv In 1843 Flournoy established the first post office in Chireno and served as its postmaster. He served for six months in the Mexican War,qv from May 15 until September 15, 1846. By the summer of 1850 he had selected a new homesite a mile southeast of Quitman in Wood County. He sent his oldest son, Warner Mitchell Flournoy, to supervise a large group of slaves in the home's construction. The family occupied the new home by late 1851.

From the beginning Flournoy was active in public affairs. In 1852, as commissioner of the Second Precinct in Wood County, he, with two associates, used slave labor to build a road from Quitman to the Upshur county line. They met another crew who had constructed a similar road from Jefferson. The Jefferson Road, as it was called, was the first of its kind in Northeast Texas. Flournoy helped organize Presbyterian churches in Chireno and Quitman. He helped gain the charter for the Flora Masonic Lodge of Quitman in 1855. He was sixty-one years old when Texas joined the Confederacy in March 1861. The Texas governor commissioned him brigadier general and commander of the Texas Militia, Twelfth Brigade. Flournoy provided the land for Camp Flournoy from his property holdings just southeast of his home. In October 1861 he enlisted at Camp Flournoy in the Third Texas Confederate Cavalry. He served with this unit for one year as a teamster, with his own team and wagon. Flournoy retired from public service after the war. He died in his Quitman home in 1878.

BIBLIOGRAPHY: Kathryn Turner Carter, *Stagecoach Inns of Texas* (Waco: Texian Press, 1972). Carolyn Reeves Ericson, *People of Nacogdoches in the Civil War* (Lufkin, Texas: Piney Woods Printing, 1980). Archie P. McDonald, ed., *Hurrah for Texas: The Diary of Adolphus Sterne* (Waco: Texian Press, 1969; rpt., Austin: Eakin Press, 1986). Adele W. Vickery, *A Transcript of Centennial Edition, 1850–1950, Wood County Democrat* (Mineola, Texas, 1974). *Wood County, 1850–1900* (Quitman, Texas: Wood County Historical Society, 1976).
Randell G. Tarín

FLOWELLA, TEXAS. Flowella, at the intersection of Farm Road 2191 and State Highway 285, four miles east of Falfurrias in northeastern Brooks County, was founded in 1909 by promoters Burton and Danforth. The community was planned so that at its center would be a flowing well. A post office operated there from 1910 until 1923, with R. M. Calahan as the first postmaster. In 1914 the estimated population of Flowella was sixty, and the town had a hotel and a general store. In 1948 there were several dwellings, a school, and paved roads at the site. In 1991, though no population estimates were available for Flowella, the settlement continued to exist as a dispersed rural community.
Alicia A. Garza

FLOWER GROVE, TEXAS. Flower Grove, on Farm Road 2002 in the northeastern corner of Martin County, was named for an early settler, Hardy Flowers. A rural school district was established there in 1920 and an independent school district in 1928. During the 1930s and 1940s five neighboring schools were consolidated with Flower Grove. The town also had the Flower Grove Missionary Baptist Church, the Bethel Assembly of God Church, and the Farmer's Co-op Gin. The community still existed in the early 1980s.

BIBLIOGRAPHY: Vernen Liles, *Pioneering on the Plains: The History of Martin County, Texas* (M.A. thesis, University of Texas, 1953). Martin County Historical Commission, *Martin County, Texas* (Dallas: Taylor, 1979).
Noel Wiggins

FLOWER HILL, TEXAS. Flower Hill is three miles southeast of Smithville in southeastern Bastrop County. In 1907 it had a one-teacher school for fifty-four black students; the school was probably absorbed by the Smithville Independent School District shortly after the district's creation in 1921. In the 1940s a church and a few scattered houses marked the Flower Hill community on county highway maps, but by the 1980s only a cemetery remained there.
Vivian Elizabeth Smyrl

FLOWER MOUND, TEXAS. Flower Mound, south of Denton and northwest of Dallas in south central Denton County, is a residential suburban community of 20,000 acres on the shore of Grapevine Lake. It was established soon after Sam Houstonqv settled a tribal dispute in 1844 and Indian raids in the area ceased. Permanent settlers moved in, attracted by the quality of the soil, which was suitable for raising cotton, corn, and wheat. The Peters colonyqv named the town for a fifty-foot-high mound covered with Indian paintbrush; the mound was once used by Indians as a holy place. Unlike many pioneer settlements in Denton County that were bypassed by the railroads in the late nineteenth century or unable to survive the Great Depression,qv Flower Mound maintained a steady population throughout the first four decades of the twentieth century and became a substantial farming and cattle-raising community.

In the mid-1950s the town began to grow. The increase in the number of residents was a result of the construction by the United States Corps of Engineers of Grapevine Lake, which was completed on July 2, 1953. The lake stimulated the economy of the community and attracted workers who preferred to live outside the central Dallas area. Flower Mound was incorporated on February 27, 1961. The town had an estimated population of 275 in 1966 and 664 in 1968.

Flower Mound was chosen one of thirteen communities to be affected by the 1968 New Communities Act (Housing and Urban Development Title IV) as the site of a new planned community that would offer model social and environmental conditions to residents. The act, amended in 1970, provided $18 million of a total $294 million in federal loan guarantees for new towns, for developers Raymond D. Nasher, former UN General Assembly delegate, and Edward S. Marcus, chairman of Neiman-Marcus,qv to set up four village centers or neighborhoods, each with schools, parks, and shopping and recreational facilities, on 6,156 acres on the north shore of Grapevine Lake. Flower Mound New Town, designed as a satellite town to limit the growing urban sprawl of Dallas and Fort Worth, was expected to house some 60,000 to 70,000 persons comprising a mixture of racial and income groups, and to provide such services as cable television, rapid transit to the new Dallas–Fort Worth International Airport, and environmental protection for the area. Residents of the original town of Flower Mound, however, fought tax increases proposed to accommodate the new development. The dispute resulted in replacement of the city's five aldermen with two city commissioners.

The population of Flower Mound was 1,685 in 1970. Construction began on the new town in 1972, but federal red tape, the 1973–75 economic recession, slow land sales, changing federal policy, and the relative isolation of the site brought failure of the project, despite an additional HUD grant of $170,000. In the spring of 1974 Nasher sold out to Marcus, who in turn sold his half interest to Tinnie Mercantile Company, owned by Robert Anderson, chairman of Atlantic-Richfield. By September 1976, with other new towns failing and Flower Mound experiencing financial difficulty, HUD foreclosed on its model Texas experiment in public-private cooperation. The development, which by then numbered 300 persons and 100 homes, subsequently attracted builders and was renamed Timber Creek Community. In 1980 the town's population was 4,402. In 1990 Flower Mound reported a population of 15,527.

BIBLIOGRAPHY: C. A. Bridges, *History of Denton, Texas, from Its Beginning to 1960* (Waco: Texian Press, 1978). Denton *Record-Chronicle*, February 28, 1961. Scott W. Mellon, "The Only New Town That Worked," *Muse Air Monthly*, June 1985. Rodney J. Walter, The Economic History of Denton County, Texas, 1900–1950 (M.A. thesis, North Texas State University, 1969).

David Minor

FLOWERS, ALLEN GILBERT (1869–1935). Allen Gilbert Flowers, lawyer, teacher, and college administrator, was born in Sumter, South Carolina, on December 31, 1869, the son of Thomas Evans and Matilda Anne (Mack) Flowers. He worked for more than a quarter of a century as a printer, first in Sumter and after 1900 in the Government Printing Office in Washington, D.C. He attended the YMCA night school and received LL.B and LL.M. degrees at George Washington University in 1906 and 1907. In 1908 he was admitted to the bar and on November 8 of that year married Sue Duncan Hall of Meredithville, Virginia. In 1911 Flowers moved to Fayetteville, Arkansas, to publish the Arkansas Sentinel. From 1912 to 1919 he served as deputy prosecuting attorney of Washington County, Arkansas. He was a lecturer in economics at the University of Arkansas in 1916 and during World War I[qv] served as a major in the home guards and as a representative of the adjutant general of Arkansas to advise selective service boards. In 1920 Flowers helped to establish the law school at Baylor University and was named its dean, a position he held until his death. He was a Democrat, a Mason, and a Baptist. He died in Waco on May 11, 1935.

BIBLIOGRAPHY: Dallas *Morning News*, May 12, 1935. *Who's Who in America*, 1942–43.

J. D. Bragg

FLOWERS, ELISHA (?–?). Elisha Flowers, one of Stephen F. Austin's[qv] Old Three Hundred[qv] settlers, was the son of Edward and Rebekkah Flowers of Kentucky. He probably arrived in Texas by 1822. He married Polly Smalley, also of Kentucky, and by around 1823 they had a son. They eventually had at least two children. Flowers received title to a sitio[qv] of land in what is now Matagorda County and a labor of land now part of Colorado County on July 19, 1824. On December 26, 1826, he wrote Stephen F. Austin[qv] from Bay Prairie that he had had a labor of land in front of his half league surveyed and was plowing it. In the winter of 1826–27, when the Flowers and nearby Charles Cavanah families were living on Liveoak Bayou, Polly Flowers and Cavanah's wife and three daughters were killed by Karankawa Indians. Flowers and his son Romulus returned to Kentucky, where Elisha married Mrs. Susannah Baker, with whom he had at least one more child. Romulus Flowers eventually returned to Matagorda County, where he married Elizabeth DeMoss, daughter of Susan (or Susanna) and Peter DeMoss.[qv]

BIBLIOGRAPHY: Eugene C. Barker, ed., *The Austin Papers* (3 vols., Washington: GPO, 1924–28). Lester G. Bugbee, "The Old Three Hundred: A List of Settlers in Austin's First Colony," *Quarterly of the Texas State Historical Association* 1 (October 1897). Matagorda County Historical Commission, *Historic Matagorda County* (3 vols., 1986–88).

Rachel Jenkins

FLOWERS, JOHN GARLAND (1895–1965). John Garland Flowers, college president and education promoter, was born at San Antonio, Texas, on October 17, 1895, the son of Richard Morton and Mary Frances (Butts) Flowers. He attended Southwest Texas State College (now Southwest Texas State University) from 1911 to 1913, received a B.A. degree from East Texas State College (now East Texas State University) in 1924, and earned an M.A. in 1925 and a Ph.D. in 1932 at Columbia University. He married Lora Hogan in 1916, and they had two children.

After teaching in the public schools of Texas from 1912 to 1917, Flowers was principal of the demonstration school and later director of teacher education at East Texas State College (1921–28), professor of education at New Jersey State Teachers College (1928–37), and president of Pennsylvania State College at Lock Haven (1937–42). In September 1942 he became the third president of Southwest Texas State College, a position he held for twenty-two years. He assumed a role of educational leadership at both the state and national levels. He served as a member and later as chairman of the standards committee of the American Association of Colleges for Teacher Education and was president of the association in 1950–51. He was a member of the interim committee that founded the National Council for Accreditation of Teacher Education. In 1949 he was a special consultant to the educational branch of the American military government of occupied Germany, where he assisted in establishing a teacher-training program for Germany. In 1959 he was chairman of a committee appointed by the council of presidents of state-supported institutions of higher learning to study library needs in Texas colleges and universities.

Flowers was a director of the Texas Society for Crippled Children for three years, vice president for a term, and president from 1949 to 1951. He was also governor of Rotary District 584 in 1957–58. He retired on August 31, 1964, and died on February 23, 1965, in Harlingen.

BIBLIOGRAPHY: Vertical Files, Barker Texas History Center, University of Texas at Austin.

L. E. Derrick

FLOWERY MOUNTAIN. Flowery (Flower) Mountain, formerly known as Brewer's Mountain, is near Nat, Looneyville, and Flat Woods in northwestern Nacogdoches County (at 31°46′ N, 94°49′ W). The mountain, a mesa-like area of six square miles with an elevation of 250 feet above the surrounding terrain, was named Flowery for the wildflowers there. It rises from a rolling prairie with clay loam soils that support mesquite, grasses, and mixed hardwood and pine forests. The Flowery Mountain community was located on the mountain.

Marthea Turnage

FLOWERY MOUNTAIN, TEXAS. The Flowery Mountain community was on the elevated expanse of land in northwestern Nacogdoches County known as Flowery Mountain.[qv] On January 13, 1835, this land was granted to Henry Brewer, who with his wife and their six children traveled from Ohio to settle in Texas. Rev. Washington Wiggins Albritton moved to Texas in 1869 and was one of the first preachers at the Redland Baptist Church on Flowery Mountain. The mountain was first called Brewer's Mountain, but Albritton renamed it for the wildflowers—including wild plum, dogwood, redbud, black and red haw, granddaddy greybeard, and others—that grew around his church, The church also doubled as a school, which in 1897 had thirty-six students. The school was closed around 1898–99. In 1862 Rufus McClain and Andrew Hayter developed an iron foundry to process iron ore from Flowery Mountain, but the business was abandoned with the outbreak of the Civil War.qv The population at Flowery Mountain peaked about 1936. After World War II qv its inhabitants began to move to the cities for jobs.

BIBLIOGRAPHY: Dallas *Morning News*, April 25, 1966. Carolyn Reeves Ericson, *Nacogdoches, Gateway to Texas: A Biographical Directory* (2 vols., Fort Worth: Arrow–Curtis Printing, 1974, 1987). Nacogdoches *Daily Sentinel*, June 2, 1972.   *Marthea Turnage*

FLOY, TEXAS. Floy, a switch and siding on the Southern Pacific line, is on Farm Road 154 2½ miles southwest of Muldoon between West Point and Flatonia in southwestern Fayette County. The switch was built before 1900 on the Waco branch of the San Antonio and Aransas Pass Railway at the request of E. A. Arnim and was named for Arnim's daughter. The railroad switch was designed as a loading point for firewood cut from the abundant oaks in the area. Because of the proximity of Muldoon, Floy never developed a business community but did have a school that operated until local consolidation. Floy residents both voted and received mail at Muldoon. Floy is located within the heart of the Muldoon oilfield, and during the 1980s a charcoal manufacturing plant remained in the area to take advantage of the abundantly available firewood that aided the foundation of the community.

BIBLIOGRAPHY: Frank Lotto, *Fayette County: Her History and Her People* (Schulenburg, Texas: Sticker Steam Press, 1902; rpt., Austin: University of Texas Press, 1981).   *Jeff Carroll*

FLOYD, DOLPHIN WARD (1804–1836). Dolphin Ward Floyd, Alamo defender, son of Thomas Penuel and Mary (Beckwith) Floyd, was born in Nash County, North Carolina, on March 6, 1804. He immigrated to Texas and settled in Gonzales, where he made his living as a farmer. On April 26, 1832, he married Ester Berry House. Floyd joined the relief force from Gonzales and rode to the besieged Alamo, where he arrived on March 1, 1836. He died in the battle of the Alamo qv on his thirty-second birthday, March 6, 1836. Floyd County is named in his honor.

BIBLIOGRAPHY: Daughters of the American Revolution, *The Alamo Heroes and Their Revolutionary Ancestors* (San Antonio, 1976). Bill Groneman, *Alamo Defenders* (Austin: Eakin, 1990). Ethel Zivley Rather, "DeWitt's Colony," *Quarterly of the Texas State Historical Association* 8 (October 1904).   *Bill Groneman*

FLOYD, TEXAS (Denton County). Floyd, in Denton County, was named for K. S. and Charles S. Floyd, who operated a store there in 1877. The community had probably ceased to exist before 1900.
Brian Hart

FLOYD, TEXAS (Hunt County). Floyd is on U.S. Highway 380 eight miles west of Greenville in west central Hunt County. The settlement that became Floyd was established in 1882, when the East Line and Red River Railroad extended its tracks westward from Greenville to McKinney in Collin County. Railroad officials originally named the new settlement Oliverea, in honor of one of their owners, whose last name was Oliver. A post office opened in the new community during its first year. Residents were unhappy with the name, however, and requested that postal officials change it to Foster. Since a post office with that name already existed in the state, residents agreed upon Floyd, perhaps after Joseph Floyd, a dispatch bearer in Sam Houston's qv army. The Floyd post office opened in 1887. The community's population reached 231 in 1904 and 300 in 1933, when the town had some seven businesses, including two banks, two dry-goods stores, a cotton gin, a blacksmith shop, and a gristmill. The arrival in Hunt County of good roads and automobiles during the first half of the twentieth century, however, facilitated travel to Greenville, the county's major town, and contributed to Floyd's decline. Its post office closed sometime after 1930. By 1946 Floyd's population had fallen to 150, with three reported businesses. In 1948 Floyd combined its school with that of nearby Merit to form the Bland school district. Under this arrangement, which remained in effect in 1989, Floyd maintained the elementary school and Merit, the high school. Floyd reported a population of seventy from 1952 until the mid-1970s, and from then until 1990 a population of 220.

BIBLIOGRAPHY: W. Walworth Harrison, *History of Greenville and Hunt County, Texas* (Waco: Texian, 1976).   *Brian Hart*

FLOYDADA, TEXAS. Floydada, the county seat of Floyd County, is at the junction of U.S. highways 62 and 70, State Highway 207, and Farm roads 784 and 1958, on the Fort Worth and Denver Railway in the south central part of the county. The town, originally named Floyd City, was established in 1890 by M. C. Williams on 640 acres donated by James B. and Caroline Price of Jefferson City, Missouri. The community won the county seat election after a bitter contest with supporters of Della Plain. When a post office was opened, the town's name was changed to Floydada to prevent confusion with Floyd in Hunt County. Some claim the new name was meant to be Floydalia and was garbled in transmission to Washington; others say it was a combination of the county name and that of donor James Price's mother, Ada; still another version is that it was named for Caroline Price's parents, Floyd and Ada. The town's rate of growth was slow in early years, when immediate expectations of a railroad were disappointed. The Santa Fe built through in 1910. The town was rebuilt after a devastating fire in 1911 and boomed for several years. A newspaper, the *Texas Kicker,* was published briefly in 1890, and beginning in 1896 Claude V. Hall published the *Floyd County Hesperian.*

Aside from setbacks in 1918, when the flu epidemic caused more than fifty deaths, and during the Great Depression,qv Floydada has shown a steadier prosperity than many West Texas towns. In 1950 it had ninety-two businesses and a population of 3,214. The population was 3,769 in 1960 and reached 4,109 in 1970, when the town had 118 businesses, a hospital, an expanded school system, twenty-two churches, a library, and three parks. The population was 4,193 in 1980 and 3,896 in 1990. Much of Floydada's commerce derives from cotton, wheat, vegetables, soybeans, corn, and sunflowers, as well as livestock. Industries include the manufacture of race-cars, sheet metal goods, and oilfield equipment. The Texas A&M Engineering Extension Service is located in Floydada.

BIBLIOGRAPHY: Floyd County Historical Museum, *History of Floyd County, 1876–1979* (Dallas: Taylor, 1979). Claude V. Hall, *Early History of Floyd County* (Canyon, Texas: Panhandle-Plains Historical Society, 1947). Alma N. Holmes, *Favorite Stories about Floyd County* (Dallas: Vanguard Visuals, 1973). Fred Tarpley, *1001 Texas Place Names* (Austin: University of Texas Press, 1980).   *William R. Hunt*

FLOYD COUNTY. Floyd County (E-9) is on U.S. Highway 70 northeast of Lubbock in the High Plains region of the Panhandle.qv The county is bordered on the north by Swisher and Briscoe counties, on the east by Motley County, on the south by Crosby County, and on the west by Hale County. The center of the county lies at 34°05′ north latitude and 101°20′ west longitude. Floydada is the county seat and largest town. In addition to U.S. Highway 70 the county's transportation needs are served by U.S. Highway 62, State Highway 207, and the Fort Worth and Denver, the Atchison, Topeka and Santa Fe, and the Quanah, Acme and Pacific railroads.

Floyd County covers 992 square miles. The mostly flat land is broken on the east by the Caprockqv and Rolling Plains and on the south by the White River and Blanco Canyon. The elevation ranges from 2,600 to 3,300 feet. The northeast corner has level to undulating soils, with some clayey subsoils. The remainder of the county has nearly flat terrain and alkaline soils with dark loamy surfaces and clayey subsoils. Vegetation is typical of the High Plains, with moderately short to tall grasses and plenty of mesquite.qv Between 71 and 80 percent of the land in the county is considered prime farmland; about 500,000 acres is considered arable.

The climate is arid and mild, with cool winters and hot summers. Temperatures range in January from an average low of 24° to an average high of 53°, and in July from 67° to 94°. The average annual rainfall is nineteen inches, and the average relative humidity is 73 percent at 6 A.M. and 39 percent at 6 P.M. The average annual snowfall is eleven inches. The growing season averages 213 days per year, with the last freeze in early April and the first freeze in early November.

Evidence of prehistoric hunters has been found in Floyd County, which was part of the vast domain of the Plains Apaches and later of the Comanches. Spanish explorer Francisco Vázquez de Coronadoqv is believed to have come through the area in 1541. Quitaque Peak was a familiar landmark to José P. Tafoyaqv and other Comancherosqv who came from New Mexico to trade with the warlike "Mongols of the West"; indeed, it marked the southern boundary of the notorious Valley of Tears,qv so named because white captives were separated among various Indian bands or ransomed there by Comancheros. In August 1841 the Texan–Santa Fe expeditionqv members established Camp Resolution near the junction of Quitaque and Los Lingos creeks, in the county's northeastern part, and there made the fateful decision to split into two groups in a desperate bid to reach their objective.

In 1871 and again in 1874 Col. Ranald S. Mackenzie'sqv Fourth United States Cavalryqv came through Floyd County in pursuit of the hostile Quahadi Comanches. In their wake came hide hunters operating out of Fort Griffin and Charles Rath'sqv Teepee City. With the Indians and buffaloqv gone, ranchers entered the area with their free-range cattle outfits. The Baker brothers and O. J. Wiren established the headquarters of the Quitaque (Lazy F) Ranch,qv later owned by Charles Goodnightqv and for a time part of the JA Ranch,qv on the banks of Quitaque Creek. The firm of Owens, Marseilles and Duncan grazed both cattle and sheep on its H Bar L (later the TM Bar) Ranch in Blanco Canyon. Other pioneer ranches that had land in Floyd County included the Two-Buckle and the Matador.qqv

On August 21, 1876, the Texas legislature formed Floyd County, named for the Alamo martyr Dolphin Ward Floyd,qv as one of the fifty-four counties established from the Bexar and Young territories. In 1884 Arthur B. Duncan and his family became the county's first settlers when they located in Blanco Canyon a short distance above Henry Clay (Hank) Smith'sqv ranch in Crosby County. Since Floyd County at that time was attached to Donley County for administrative purposes, the Duncans and other settlers who soon followed had to go to Clarendon to file on state lands for homes. In the spring of 1887, Thomas J. Braidfoot and his family located on a section of school land that afterward was platted as the town of Della Plain. There the county's first school was begun late in 1888.

The move to organize Floyd County produced heated rivalry among its developing communities for the honor of being the county seat. Lockney, which became Della Plain's chief rival, was founded in 1889. In the spring of 1890 J. K. Gwynn appeared on the scene as a representative of Carolina V. Price, a Missouri native who owned numerous patented sections in Floyd County. Gwynn had one of the prize sections platted as Floyd City, another candidate for county seat. Lockney combined with Floyd City, and in the organization election on May 28, 1890, Floyd City won by a vote of 55 to 33. The election was subsequently contested in the district court and later in the Supreme Court, but its validity was sustained; Floyd City, renamed Floydada in 1892, remained the seat of local government, with A. B. Duncan serving as the first county judge.

Although Floyd County had a population of 529 by 1890, droughts, financial panics, and grasshopper plagues caused many settlers to vacate the region during the next decade. Some of the communities, including Della Plain and Mayshaw, were abandoned, but Lockney was revived in 1894 with the establishment of Lockney Christian College,

which lasted until 1917. A gradual influx of population resulted in a movement to choose a new county seat and build a new courthouse, but in the election of 1912 Floydada was again victorious by a small majority. After that, town and sectional rivalries waned.

The first railroad to build into the county was the Santa Fe, which in 1910 built a branch line from Plainview to Lockney and Floydada. In 1928 the Quanah, Acme and Pacific Railway extended its tracks from McBain, thus connecting Floydada directly with points east and north. At the same time, the Fort Worth and Denver constructed its South Plains line from Estelline and Quitaque to Lockney via Sterley and South Plains. This line, later taken over by Burlington Northern, is noted for the Quitaque Tunnel, a remarkable engineering feat that is now the state's only functioning railway tunnel, located in northeastern Floyd County.

The construction of the railroads brought numerous new settlers to the area. Between 1900 and 1930 the population increased six-fold, growing from 2,020 to 12,409. Many of the new settlers were farmers, lured to the area by abundant land, and during the first three decades of the twentieth century the number of farms in the county grew rapidly. In 1900 there were only 286; by 1930 that figure had grown to 1,671. Corn was the most important crop in the early years, but after 1900 wheat and cotton were both introduced on a commercial scale. By 1930 Floyd County farmers were harvesting more than two million bushels of wheat annually, making the county one of the leaders in the state in wheat culture.qv Cotton cultureqv also saw impressive growth, particularly after 1920. By 1930 nearly one-fifth of the improved land in the county—71,184 of 490,731 acres—was devoted to cotton. Production increased from 430 bales in 1910 to 42,801 bales in 1926, one of the peak years of the cotton boom.

The 1920s and 1930s saw other important improvements. Tractors began to be used on a large scale, and numerous new roads were laid out and graded. In 1937 paved highways came to Floyd County with the completion of State Highway 28 (now U.S. 70) through Floydada.

During the early 1930s cotton was the leading cash crop. Falling prices, droughts, and boll weevilqv infestations, however, combined to drive down cotton production in the 1930s. Although the amount of land planted in cotton continued to be quite high, both yields and profits dropped significantly, especially after 1932. In 1936 Floyd County farmers produced only 11,137 bales, only slightly more than a quarter of the peak figure for the mid-1920s.

Because of the rapidly growing population, land prices showed a marked increase during the second and third decade of the twentieth century, and many new farmers found land impossible to buy. The number of tenants and share croppers grew rapidly, particularly in the 1920s, and by 1930 more than half of county farmers—923 of 1,691—were working someone else's land. In contrast to those in many other areas of the state, the overwhelming majority of the tenants were white. The high rate of tenancy had serious results during the Great Depressionqv of the 1930s. As a result of the poor yields and the reluctance of banks to extend credit to financially strained farmers, many of those who made a living from the land, particularly tenants, found themselves displaced. Numerous farmers were forced to give up their livelihoods and seek work elsewhere. The population of the county as a whole fell from 12,409 in 1930 to 10,659 in 1940.

During the late 1940s agricultural prices began to rebound, but the farming economy did not fully recover until after World War II.qv Oil, discovered in the county in 1952, helped some cash-strapped farmers to settle long-standing debts, but oil production in Floyd County has been modest compared with that of other counties in the region; between 1952 and 1990 only 123,510 barrels were produced, with an annual production in the late 1980s of around 3,000 barrels.

Since World War II Floyd County has remained a leader in agricultural production. In the years after the war, wheat production continued to grow and cotton made a strong recovery. In 1950 Floyd County farmers grew 2,758,000 bushels of wheat, and 47,332 bales of cotton. Alfalfa, corn, popcorn, and sorghum were also raised in large quantities. Large-scale irrigation[qv] was introduced after the war, and by the early 1950s some 150,000 acres were irrigated. Subsequently, agricultural production continued to grow. In the early 1990s more than 220,000 acres was under irrigation and the county's farmers were earning an average $75 million a year. Most of the receipts came from cotton, wheat, vegetables, soybeans, corn, sunflowers, beef cattle, and hogs. Floyd County remained a leading cotton-producing area; twenty-one cotton gins operated in the county in 1990. Additional sources of income included the production of farm machinery and race cars, meat and vegetable processing, and other agribusinesses. Floydada is the site of the Texas A&M Engineering Extension Service. In 1982, 98 percent of the land in the county was in farms and ranches, with 70 percent of the land under cultivation and 59 percent irrigated. Floyd County ranked twenty-first in the state in agricultural receipts, with 75 percent coming from crops. Primary crops were soybeans, sunflowers, cotton, wheat, sorghum, and corn; onions, bell peppers, cucumbers, and pecans were also grown in sizable quantities. The leading livestock products were cattle, milk, and hogs.

The total number of businesses in the county in the early 1980s was 189. In 1980, 24 percent of the labor force was self-employed, 19 percent was employed in professional or related services, 6 percent in manufacturing, 19 percent in wholesale and retail trade, 34 percent in agriculture, forestry, fishing, and mining, and 9 percent in other counties; 894 retired workers lived in the county. Nonfarm earnings in 1981 totaled $68,652,000.

In the early 1980s Floyd County had four school districts, with five elementary, two middle, and two high schools. The average daily attendance in 1981–82 was 2,057, with expenditures per pupil of $2,494. Twenty-two percent of the 127 high school graduates planned to attend college. In 1983, 41 percent of the school graduates were white, 55 percent Hispanic, 5 percent black, and 0.3 percent Asian.

The first churches in Floyd County were established shortly after the organization of the county. In the mid-1980s the county had twenty-eight organized churches, with a estimated combined membership of 8,997. The largest denominations were Baptist, Catholic, and United Methodist. Historically Floyd County has been staunchly Democratic, although Republicans made strong inroads after 1960, particularly in presidential elections and some statewide races. Between 1960 and 1988 Republican presidential candidates received the majority of votes in every race except for Lyndon B. Johnson[qv] in 1968 and Jimmy Carter in 1976. Democratic officials, however, continued to maintain control of most county offices.

The population of Floyd County grew between 1950 and 1960 from 10,535 to 12,369, but afterward fell steadily as residents gradually moved away to find jobs. The population was 11,044 in 1970, 9,834 in 1980, and 8,497 in 1990. In 1990, nearly half of the population lived in Floydada (4,193). Other communities included Lockney, Aiken, Barwise, Cedar Hill, Dougherty, Lakeview, Lone Star, McCoy, Mickey, Muncy, Sandhill, South Plains, and Sterley. In 1990, 65 percent of the population was white, 3.8 percent black, 39.8 percent Hispanic, and 0.2 percent Asian. The largest ancestry groups are English, Hispanic, and Irish.

The area is popular with hunters and fishermen, particularly in the fall and winter. The Old Settlers Day Reunion held in Floydada and the Floyd County Fair in Lockney are among the main tourist attractions.

BIBLIOGRAPHY: Floyd County Historical Museum, *History of Floyd County, 1876–1979* (Dallas: Taylor, 1979). Claude V. Hall, *Early History of Floyd County* (Canyon, Texas: Panhandle-Plains Historical Society, 1947). Pauline D. and R. L. Robertson, *Cowman's Country: Fifty Frontier Ranches in the Texas Panhandle, 1876–1887* (Amarillo: Paramount, 1981).   *H. Allen Anderson and Christopher Long*

FLOYD HILL, TEXAS. Floyd Hill is on Farm Road 2345 between State Highway 77 and Farm Road 995, some five miles southwest of Douglassville in Cass County. On October 9, 1854, four acres of a land grant in Cass County made to John Stiles was deeded to the Missionary Baptist Church by Killis S. Floyd. The church was to be known as Floyd's Hill Church. Worship services were held in the Frifogle House, former home of a pioneer family, until a log church was built in 1855. About 1858 this log building was replaced by a large one-room structure built of virgin timber on a rock foundation with the help of slave labor. The slaves worshipped in Floyd's Hill Church with their masters until Floyd donated land for their church, Floyd Valley Church. The Floyd's Hill Cemetery, which comprises 200 known graves, was still in use in 1989. The community's site was on pioneer routes to Texas from Georgia and Alabama during and after the Civil War.[qv] Mail to the Floyd Hill community was routed through the Cusseta post office. The farming community declined after World War I,[qv] and regular church services ended in 1926. In 1932 a storm damaged the church, and the structure was dismantled. On the same rock foundation Henry Grady Riddlespurger built a smaller structure that still stood in 1989. The Floyd's Hill Church Cemetery Association, established in 1948, sponsors an annual homecoming on the second Sunday of September for the descendants of early families. The Riddlespurger family reunion is held there each year on the second Sunday in November. These celebrations include having worship services in the church, decorating the graves in the cemetery, holding business meetings, and having lunch under the oak trees on the grounds.   *Martha Spurger Moore*

FLURY, GODFREY (1864–1936). Godfrey Flury, decorative painter and commercial artist, was born in Oensingen, Switzerland, on July 6, 1864, the son of Josef and Zäzilia Flury. He was educated by priests in Solothurn, but instead of entering the church, at age sixteen he immigrated to the United States with his family. He found work in New York City as a painter and decorator and stayed in the United States when his family returned to Switzerland in 1886. He and his sister moved to Buffalo, New York, where their father had acquired some land; sometime thereafter Flury moved to Kansas City, where he established himself as a decorator. On April 14, 1887, he married Margaret Elnettie Shafer in Buffalo, New York; they had one son. A year after their move to San Antonio in 1891, Flury divorced Margaret.

In 1892 he moved to Moulton, where he painted the interiors and exteriors of homes and churches. In 1895 he was commissioned to paint the interior of St. Mary's Church of Praha, a work that proved to be the most important of his career. He painted the ceiling of tongue-and-groove planks a cool sky-blue and emphasized the church's classic vault with trompe l'oeil ribs that mimicked medieval stone vaulting; He adorned the wooden columns with painted Gothic capitals. The ceiling he divided into panels ornamented with painted vines, flowers, curving gold scrolls, and symbols such as a chalice, a star, and an eye within a radiant triangle. Above the altar Flury commemorated Praha's Czechoslovakian heritage by depicting the main cathedral in Prague and an important convent nearby. At the highest point above the altar he painted three angels around a jeweled cross. The church was a great success and won Flury other commissions, notably one to paint the pressed steel ceilings of the Lavaca County Courthouse (since repainted). Sketches indicate that he also painted the interior of St. John's (near Schulenburg), and the interior of the church in Cestohowa has been attributed to his hand, but there is not enough original work remaining in either church to support an attribution. The painted ceilings in the C. Cockrill and Kellough Faires homes in Flatonia have both been attributed to Flury.

On April 16, 1895, Flury married Agnes Valchar in the Praha church; they had two daughters and three sons. In 1902 the Flurys moved to San Antonio, where Godfrey worked primarily as a commercial artist after an unsuccessful attempt at chicken farming. His second marriage ended in divorce in 1911, and he moved to Austin that year. In 1911 Flury established a sign-painting business at 502 Colorado Street. At this time he ceased to paint the interiors of buildings and immersed himself in business, real estate, and civic activities. He transferred his Masonic membership from Moulton to Austin and joined the Shriners, the Scottish Rite Temple, the Austin branch of the Knights Templars, and the Austin Saengerrunde Society. On November 11, 1911, he married Alvine Glismann. This marriage, a happy one, lasted until Flury's death. They had one daughter and one son. In 1918 Flury became a naturalized citizen.

His most notable artistic efforts during his Austin years were the preparation of elaborate floats for parades and various civic displays. Following the sale of his advertising company in 1929 he spent the remainder of his years traveling, dabbling in real estate, and painting scenic views of the Hill Country^{qv} and wildflowers and Austin landmarks such as Barton Springs.^{qv} In 1934 he temporarily resumed control of his faltering advertising business, which he resold to a San Antonio company, and entered the University of Texas as a freshman to study mechanical engineering. He died at home on October 28, 1936. His friends subsequently organized a memorial exhibition of his work at the Elisabet Ney Museum.^{qv} The interior of St. Mary's Church in Praha was attributed to him in 1972, his work authenticated by preliminary sketches and notes that correspond to the church's interior. These sketches were exhibited at the University of Texas Institute of Texan Cultures^{qv} in San Antonio in April 1972.

BIBLIOGRAPHY: Austin *American-Statesman*, October 30, 1936. Dorothy Agnes Flury, *Our Father Godfrey: A Biography* (Austin: Hart Graphics, 1976). Godfrey Flury Collection, Barker Texas History Center, University of Texas at Austin. Richard Pierce, "Maticka Praha," *Texas Highways*, December 1974. Connie Sherley, "In Praise of Painted Churches," *Texas Highways*, October 1989.   *Kendall Curlee*

FLUVANNA, TEXAS. Fluvanna is at the junction of Farm roads 612, 1267, and 2350, sixty-six miles southeast of Lubbock in northwestern Scurry County. Named for a surveyor's home county in Virginia, Fluvanna was established by realty promoters who knew that the Roscoe, Snyder and Pacific Railway would terminate at its site. By the time the railroad arrived in 1908, the townsite had already been staked off and lots put on sale. It boomed briefly and by 1911 had two real estate offices, a thirty-room hotel, a lumberyard, a cotton gin, and other businesses. The community's population in 1915 was estimated at 500, and in 1920 and 1940, at 375. Fluvanna's importance lessened when major highways bypassed the area, and when the Roscoe, Snyder and Pacific closed the Fluvanna station in 1941, the town's days as a shipping center were over. In 1980 Fluvanna had a post office, an estimated population of 180, and at least four businesses. Its population in 1990 was still reported as 180.

BIBLIOGRAPHY: Scurry County Historical Survey Committee, *Historical Markers in Scurry County* (Snyder, Texas, 1969).
Noel Wiggins

FLUVANNA MERCANTILE COMPANY. The Fluvanna Mercantile Company, a pioneer general store at Fluvanna, Scurry County, sold clothing, fabrics, groceries, hardware, millinery, patent medicines, seeds, and shoes. It also sold quantities of flour, block salt, and other staples. The enterprise was founded in 1915 by D. A. Jones and John A. Stavely, who first settled in dugout^{qv} homes after they arrived in the area just after 1900. The Jones and Stavely families helped to build the community's first Presbyterian church, a school, and a bank. Original shareholders included J. E. Park, S. P. Smith, and W. R. Craft. Jones was the firm's first president, and Stavely was vice president. The company freighted in its stock on the Roscoe, Snyder and Pacific Railway, which also shipped cattle, and received flour and feed by rail from Sherman. After the tracks were removed in 1942, supplies were delivered by truck. During the Great Depression^{qv} the company reverted to barter, allowing local people to trade cream and eggs for store-bought goods. In 1958 the owners sold the firm to J. D. Patterson, who renamed it the Patterson General Store and took up residence on the store's balcony. Its third owner, Clyde A. Smith, who bought the enterprise in 1966, restored its original name, converted it to a grocery store, and with his family also lived in the building. In the 1990s the store continued in operation. Examples of merchandise sold there in frontier days are on display at the Texas Museum in Canyon. An official Texas historical marker was placed at the site in 1970.

BIBLIOGRAPHY: Charles Anderson, *Reflections: An Album of West Texas History* (Snyder, Texas: Snyder Publishing Company,, 1990). Marker Files, Texas Historical Commission, Austin.
Diana J. Kleiner

FLY, ASHLEY WILSON (1855–1919). Ashley Wilson Fly, Galveston surgeon and mayor, was born in Waters Valley, Yalobusha County, Mississippi, on August 27, 1855, the son of Anderson B. and Margaret Jane (Giles) Fly. He received his medical degree from Louisville Medical College in 1875, and in the course of his studies he won prizes for his work in anatomy and surgical anatomy. After practicing in Bryan, Texas, for a short time, he moved to Galveston in 1876. Fly taught anatomy and surgery at Texas Medical College and Hospital (1877–81, 1888–91), attended patients at Galveston City Hospital and St. Mary's Infirmary (later St. Mary's Hospital^{qv}), and served as member and president of the Galveston Board of Health (1881–84). He was mayor of Galveston from 1893 to 1899, during which time he helped pass measures to clean up financial corruption in the city. He was president of the Galveston County Medical Society in 1914. In July 1913 Governor Oscar B. Colquitt^{qv} appointed Fly to the University of Texas Board of Regents, a post he held until 1917. On March 28, 1878, Fly married Kate R. Wilson, who died in 1905. On June 23, 1915, he married Frances E. S. Brand; they had a son. Fly died in Galveston on January 24, 1919.

BIBLIOGRAPHY: Galveston *Daily News*, January 25, 1919. *History of Texas, Together with a Biographical History of the Cities of Houston and Galveston* (Chicago: Lewis, 1895). Frank W. Johnson, *A History of Texas and Texans* (5 vols., ed. E. C. Barker and E. W. Winkler [Chicago and New York: American Historical Society, 1914; rpt. 1916]). Vertical Files, Barker Texas History Center, University of Texas at Austin.
Chester R. Burns

FLY, FRANK MERRIMAN (1866–1962). Frank M. Fly, Gonzales County sheriff and banker, son of Callie (Bell) and George Washington Lafayette Fly,^{qv} was born at Big Hill in Gonzales County, Texas, on June 12, 1866. After a brief schooling and a short employment with the Peck and Fly store in Gonzales, he became a deputy under Sheriff Richard M. Glover and later under Capt. W. E. Jones. On June 14, 1901, Sheriff Glover was killed by the notorious Gregorio Cortez,^{qv} and on June 17 Fly was appointed sheriff.

After a search described as "one of the greatest manhunts ever pulled off in South Texas," Cortez was apprehended near Laredo and returned to the county jail at Gonzales, where he was indicted for murder, tried and found guilty, and sentenced to fifty years in the state penitentiary. After receiving a tip that a lynch mob was forming to take Cortez, Fly locked himself in the jail with the Mexican. At midnight the mob first attempted to pick the lock and then began ramming the door with a telephone pole. Fly saved Cortez's life by confronting the crowd with drawn pistol through a barred window and convincing them that he would defend the prisoner to death; he took Cortez to the railroad station the next day and conducted him safely to San Antonio. Fly was also a personal acquaintance of the notorious John Wesley Hardin^{qv} during Hardin's attempt to establish a law practice in Gonzales after his release from the penitentiary.

Fly joined the staff of the Gonzales State Bank in 1909 and served as its president during the Great Depression.^{qv} From 1946 to 1962 he was justice of the peace. He was a member of the Selective Service Board, the Red Cross, the County Fair Association, the Chamber of Commerce, the Good Roads Commission, the Gonzales School Board, and other bodies. He described himself as "a Methodist, a Mason, and a Democrat." He married Stella Miller of Waelder in 1908, and they had five children. He died on July 13, 1962, at the age of ninety-six, and was buried in the Gonzales Masonic Cemetery.

BIBLIOGRAPHY: Gonzales *Inquirer*, September 28, 1961. Houston *Post*, July 17, 1962. Vertical Files, Barker Texas History Center, University of Texas at Austin.
W. Lamar Fly

FLY, GEORGE WASHINGTON LAFAYETTE (1835–1905). George Washington Lafayette Fly, Confederate Army officer and Texas legislator, the youngest of ten children of William and Mary (Mitchell) Fly, was born on June 2, 1835, in Yalobusha County, Mississippi; in 1846 the family moved to Sharon, Madison County. Fly enrolled at the University of Mississippi in 1851 but after one term went to Madison College, where he graduated in 1853. He then traveled to Texas to join his parents, who had settled on Oyster Creek in Brazoria County earlier that year. At the death of his father in 1855 he moved with his mother to Big Hill Prairie in Gonzales County. There he became a planter.

Fly was a staunch supporter of states' rights and a regionally noted orator. He favored the Breckinridge-Lane ticket in 1860. During the Civil War[qv] G. W., as he was called, was a seasoned commander in the Second Texas Infantry[qv] and commandant of Galveston. In 1861 he gathered a small group of volunteers in Gonzales County who elected him their captain. These men were mustered into Confederate service as Company I, Second Texas Infantry, known as the Gonzales Invincibles, and later joined the Wilson Rifles to form a complete infantry company. Though designated the second, this unit was really the first infantry regiment organized in the state. Its colonel was John Creed Moore.[qv] With his regiment Fly saw action in the battles of Shiloh in April 1862 and Iuka in September; he was reported killed at Corinth in October. His family mourned at least three weeks before learning that he had been captured, exchanged, and returned to his command. He was promoted to major before the siege of Vicksburg, where his regiment served. He was again captured upon the surrender of Vicksburg on July 4, 1863, and again paroled and exchanged. He was ordered briefly to Demopolis, Alabama, and Enterprise, Mississippi, but in November was told to return to Texas to take command of and reorganize the regiment. With the forces he raised, Fly joined the expeditionary forces under Col. John S. Ford.[qv] In August 1864 he was made commandant of the post at Galveston, which he defended until the war's end. At that time he returned to his family in Gonzales County.

From 1866 to 1870 Fly ran an independent boarding school named Stonewall Institute (after Confederate general Thomas J. "Stonewall" Jackson), about six miles from Gonzales at Big Hill. He also took up the practice of law and was admitted to the Texas bar at Gonzales in February 1871. From 1873 to 1875 he served as president of Gonzales College. He was elected to the Seventeenth Texas Legislature in 1880 but refused to run for reelection despite his popularity. About 1885 he moved with his family to Victoria, where he continued his law practice and was a charter member of the William R. Scurry[qv] Camp, United Confederate Veterans. He was also a promoter of the Pan-American Railway Company. Fly long served as a lay member of the West Texas Annual Conference of the Methodist Episcopal Church, South. His original law partnership with lieutenant governor Asbury Bascom Davidson and civil appeals judge William Lewis Davidson,[qqv] known as Fly, Davidson, and Davidson, dissolved in 1889, and Fly formed a new partnership with his son-in-law, J. L. Hill.

On April 4, 1857, he married Mary Caroline Bell of Madison County, Mississippi; the couple had four sons and one daughter. Fly died at his law office in Victoria on January 27, 1905, and was buried in the Masonic Cemetery at Victoria. A son, Ben W. Fly, was county judge of Victoria County and city attorney of Victoria; another son, William M. Fly of Gonzales, was a state legislator.

BIBLIOGRAPHY: H. L. Bentley and Thomas Pilgrim, *Texas Legal Directory for 1876–77* (Austin: Democratic Statesman Office, 1877). Joseph E. Chance, *The Second Texas Infantry: From Shiloh to Vicksburg* (Austin: Eakin Press, 1984). Roy Grimes, ed., *300 Years in Victoria County* (Victoria, Texas: Victoria *Advocate*, 1968; rpt., Austin: Nortex, 1985). Methodist Episcopal Church, South, *Journal of the West Texas Conference*, 1905. Vertical Files, Barker Texas History Center, University of Texas at Austin. *The War of the Rebellion: A Compilation of the Official Records of the Union and Confederate Armies.* Theora H. Whitaker, comp., *Victoria* (Victoria, Texas: Victoria *Advocate*, 1941). Dudley Goodall Wooten, ed., *A Comprehensive History of Texas* (2 vols., Dallas: Scarff, 1898; rpt., Austin: Texas State Historical Association, 1986).
Betty D. Fly and Craig H. Roell

FLY, WILLIAM SEAT (1851–1934). William Seat Fly, drover, Democratic leader, and jurist, son of Elijah Madden and Nancy Edmondson (McKie) Fly, was born in Madison County, Mississippi, on October 29, 1851. In November 1855 the family moved to Gonzales County, Texas. In 1869 Fly worked in a hide and tallow factory in Rockport and in 1870 drove a herd of horses to Mississippi, where he studied anatomy and physiology and got some practical experience as a clerk in a drugstore. He changed the course of his study, however, and in October 1873 was admitted to the bar at Gonzales, Texas. He became a prominent lawyer and a leader in the Democratic party;[qv] he was one of the electors on the Grover Cleveland ticket in 1888, presided over the state convention in 1890, and was chairman of the convention in 1892. He was appointed associate justice of the Court of Civil Appeals of the Fourth Supreme Judicial District in San Antonio in 1893 and was elected chief justice in 1912. He married Cayloma Pilgrim on November 16, 1876; they had one daughter. Fly died on June 1, 1934.

BIBLIOGRAPHY: San Antonio *Express*, June 2, 1934. Clarence R. Wharton, ed., *Texas under Many Flags* (5 vols., Chicago: American Historical Society, 1930).

FLY, TEXAS. Fly was on Farm Road 462 a mile west of Hondo Creek and four miles northwest of Hondo in central Medina County. Two teachers taught eighty-seven black students and twenty-nine white students at the Fly school in 1907. By the mid-1920s most of the landowners around the Fly community were living in Hondo while Mexican tenant farmers cultivated their lands. Though in 1947 Fly had the school and numerous homesites, it was abandoned by 1982.

BIBLIOGRAPHY: Houston B. Eggen, History of Public Education in Medina County, Texas, 1848–1928 (M.A. thesis, University of Texas, 1950).
Ruben E. Ochoa

FLY GAP, TEXAS. Fly Gap is a half mile west of Ranch Road 1900 and twelve miles northeast of Mason in northeastern Mason County. According to legend, the community got its name from an incident involving a band of settlers who were pursuing some Indians as they retreated from a raid somewhere south of the Llano River. The settlers hid in ambush in a gap in the Kothmann Mountains and tied their horses in a nearby thicket. The outcome of the ambush is unknown, but when the men returned to their mounts, they found that the horses had been badly bitten by horseflies, and the spot was consequently named Fly Gap. By May 1883 about a dozen families were already in the area. In October 1884 Samuel L. Fleming and Diedrich Kothmann deeded a parcel of land for a combination church and school, which was built at a site supposedly two miles southwest of where the posse had waited for the Indians. Miss Belle Starkey was the first teacher there. This first building burned in the spring of 1917, and a new school was subsequently built. In October 1884 a post office was established in the Fleming home west of the school, and Sam Fleming was the first postmaster. This office was discontinued in 1898. Jacob Oehler opened one of the community's first stores in 1895.

In the late 1970s the Fly Gap Community Club, organized in 1932, had been using the old school as a community center for a number of years. In 1980 a town cemetery and school building were at the site.

BIBLIOGRAPHY: *Mason County News*, Centennial Edition, June 19, 1958. Stella Gipson Polk, *Mason and Mason County: A History* (Austin: Pemberton Press, 1966; rev. ed., Burnet, Texas: Eakin Press, 1980).

Alice J. Rhoades

FLYNN, TEXAS. Flynn is on Farm roads 977 and 39, twelve miles southwest of Centerville in Leon County. When the Trinity and Brazos Valley Railway arrived in the area around 1906, Flynn developed by the line. Its post office was established in 1909. The community was first known as Conner but was renamed Flynn, after railroad official Edward J. Flynn. The town's unofficial name was "Bugs Scuffle" after a tavern there. Until 1910, when a two-story school was built, classes were held in the local Baptist church. In 1912 the Houston and Texas Central Railway built track into the town. By 1920 Flynn had two churches and a high school, as well as a cotton gin and gristmill, a two-story hotel, a leather shop, a lumberyard, a chair factory, a phone office, a café, and an icehouse. In 1930 a new school was built, with seven classrooms, a gymnasium, an auditorium, and an agriculture and homemaking building. By 1948 Flynn had a population of 150. In 1972 the community had a population of eighty-one and at least three businesses. A 1989 map indicates three churches and one business at the site. In 1990 Flynn's population was still reported as eighty-one, with two businesses.

BIBLIOGRAPHY: Leon County Historical Book Survey Committee, *History of Leon County* (Dallas: Curtis Media, 1986).

Dylan Wood

FOARD, ROBERT LEVI (1831–1898). Robert Levi Foard, attorney and soldier, was born in Cecil County, Maryland, on January 18, 1831. He graduated from Princeton College and was admitted to the bar at Elkton, Maryland, in 1852. He moved to Texas the same year and established a practice at Columbus. He married Georgiana Sherrill, probably in 1855, and by 1860 they had two small children, neither of whom lived to adulthood. Foard later adopted his nephew, age four, whom he renamed Robert Levi Foard, Jr. His wife died on September 28, 1886, and Robert, Jr., was killed in 1897. At the outbreak of the Civil War[qv] Foard enlisted as a first lieutenant in the Colorado County Militia. He later served with Col. Joseph Bates's[qv] Thirteenth Texas Infantry and reached the rank of major on November 11, 1863. This regiment was organized in the fall of 1861 and spent practically the entire war in Texas guarding the coast between Galveston and Matagorda. After the war Foard returned to his law practice; he also raised stock and was a principal moneylender until the establishment of banks in Columbus. In 1891 Foard County was named in his honor at the request of his law partner, Marcus H. Townsend, a member of the Texas Senate. Foard died in Columbus on November 8, 1898.

BIBLIOGRAPHY: Colorado County Historical Commission, *Colorado County Chronicles from the Beginning to 1923* (2 vols., Austin: Nortex, 1986). Vertical Files, Barker Texas History Center, University of Texas at Austin.

Charles Christopher Jackson

FOARD CITY, TEXAS. Foard City, on Farm Road 263 and the Atchison, Topeka and Santa Fe tracks nine miles south of Crowell in south central Foard County, was established after the Kansas City, Mexico and Orient Railway was built through the county in 1908. In 1910 F. R. Lefevre donated land for a school and a cemetery, and a one-room schoolhouse was moved a short distance from what had been known as Harrisonville. Eventually Foard City had both elementary and secondary schools, but in 1939 its schools closed. The community's post office, dating from 1907, closed in 1955, as did its only store, leaving a grain elevator, a church, and a few residents. In 1968 the church disbanded, and most of the remaining residents moved their houses to Crowell. The population of Foard City was reported as ten in 1980 and 1990.

BIBLIOGRAPHY: Bailey Phelps, *They Loved the Land: Foard County History* (Quanah, Texas: Quanah *Tribune-Chief*, 1969).

William R. Hunt

FOARD COUNTY. Foard County (A-13), in north central Texas on the rolling plains east of the base of the Panhandle,[qv] is bounded on the north by Hardeman County, on the west by Cottle County, on the south by Knox County, and on the east by Wilbarger and Baylor Counties. The county's center lies at 33°58′ north latitude and 99°45′ west longitude. The county, named for Robert L. Foard,[qv] a lawyer and former Confederate officer, covers an area of 703 square miles ranging from 1,400 to 1,700 feet in altitude. The Wichita River forms part of the southern boundary of the county, and the Pease River forms part of the northern border. Soils vary from deep sand in the east and along the Pease River in the north, to rich loam in the central section, and to rough pasture land in the south and west; the diversity of soils makes possible an unusual diversification in agriculture. The annual rainfall averages 23.93 inches, temperatures range from 28° F average minimum in January to 98° average maximum in July, and the growing season lasts an average of 219 days.

Evidences of prehistoric animals and primitive man have been unearthed in Foard County. In the eighteenth and nineteenth centuries, the abundance of wild fruits and herbs made this area a favorite haunt of Comanche and Kiowa bands, who frequently camped there during the winter as they followed the migrating buffalo[qv] herds. Pedro Vial[qv] is thought to have come through the area in 1786. The Comanche chief Peta Nocona[qv] staged several raids on white settlements from a favorite winter campground on the Pease River near its junction with Mule Creek; he paid the price on December 18, 1860, when Capt. Lawrence S. (Sul) Ross[qv] and his Texas Rangers[qv] attacked his camp and captured his wife, the white captive Cynthia Ann Parker,[qv] and her infant daughter. As Indian power was being broken during the 1870s, hide hunters came into the region on the "Buffalo Road" from Henrietta and points east and killed off the great herds that once roamed the region.

With the Indians and buffalo gone, ranchers began moving their cattle herds into the area that is now Foard County. In 1880, for example, the large Clay County ranch owned by William B. Worsham[qv] and J. R. Stevens extended its holdings into the area; meanwhile, Dick Forsyth grazed his OX Ranch[qv] herd on the banks of the Pease River, and J.G. Witherspoon established a ranch. The first post office in the area was established at Pease City in May 1880. Later in the decade the discovery of copper deposits in the northwestern section of the county resulted in attempts to establish a mine there; Gen. George B. McClellan[qv] led an expedition to the site in 1877. One ore shipment was made, but the venture was abandoned in 1887, mainly because of the lack of water, fuel, and transportation (*see* COPPER PRODUCTION). By 1890 at least three country schools had been established in the area.

In 1891, Foard County was marked off from lands previously assigned to Cottle, King, Knox, and Hardeman County. Witherspoon had circulated a petition for the county's organization and presented it to the state legislature. Although Beaver County was the original name proposed, the county was named for Robert Foard because he was the law partner of an influential member of the committee that reported on the bill to establish the county. Shortly after the county was authorized on March 3, 1891, the new townsites of Foard City and Crowell vied to become the county seat; a third townsite, Sandrock, was also a contender for a brief time. Crowell was chosen after an election on April 27, 1891. J. C. Roberts was elected county judge, G. W. Thompson county clerk, and S. J. Moore sheriff. Nine school districts were established.

By that time, barbed wire[qv] fences had closed the cattle ranges, and farmers had begun to move into the county. In 1900 the United States census counted 1,568 residents in Foard County, which had 210 farms and ranches; according to the agricultural census, cotton culture qv occupied 1,982 acres in the county, corn culture qv 2,712 acres, and wheat culture qv 2,060 acres. Almost 38,000 cattle were counted in Foard County that year. The county's development accelerated after 1908, when the Kansas, Mexico and Orient Railway built tracks from Knox City and Benjamin through Foard County to Chillicothe and established depots at Foard City, Crowell, and Margaret. By 1910, 718 farms and ranches had been established in Foard County, and the county's population had risen to 5,726. More than 21,300 acres in the county was planted in cotton that year, 9,100 acres in corn, and almost 6,700 acres in wheat. Meanwhile, local farmers were also establishing orchards; by 1910 more than 10,000 fruit trees (mostly peach) were cultivated in the county. Cattle ranching continued to be a significant part of the local economy, but since 1900 had declined in importance in both real and relative terms; in 1910, only about 16,000 cattle were counted in the county.

Droughts and other adversities reduced crop production and drove some farmers off their lands in the second decade of the twentieth century; by 1920 the number of farms in Foard County county had dropped to 629, and the population had declined to 4,724. Thanks to an increase in cotton production during the 1920s, the county recovered somewhat during that decade. Cotton acreage expanded to more than 58,500 acres by 1929, and by that year the number of farms in the county had again increased to 720; by 1930 Foard County had a population of 6,315.

Agriculture suffered serious setbacks during the 1930s, however, because of the Great Depression qv and the concurrent Dust Bowl. qv Cotton production plunged by more than 50 percent, and by 1940 only 24,098 acres of Foard county was planted in the fiber; wheat production also dropped from about 33,400 acres in 1929 to about 24,100 acres in 1940. More than 15 percent of the county's farmers were forced out of business during this period, and by 1940 only 561 farms remained. County population also dropped by more than 15 per cent during the 1930s; by 1940, 5,237 people were left. The thirties would have been even more difficult for the county, but oil production helped to reduce some of the depression's worst effects.

Although oil leases in Foard County had been sold as early as 1901, no actual discoveries were made until 1925, when the Thalia field was first drilled; the boom there started in 1929, when the Shell Petroleum Company struck a pool that yielded 500 barrels a day. Beginning in 1933 the Texas Company (Texaco qv) discovered the county's largest oil and gas field twenty miles west of Crowell. In March 1934 a $150,000 natural gas stripping plant was built at the field, with a three-inch pipeline laid from there to the railroad tracks at Foard City. Another pipeline was built to transport natural gas about thirty miles to the West Texas Utilities plant east of Quanah. The Gamble-Dickerson field northeast of Crowell produced several wells beginning in 1940, but gas pressure and shallow oil depths later led to its abandonment. In 1938 county oil production reached 240,742 barrels, but by 1944 production had declined to 59,408 barrels; by 1948 it had dropped to 22,012 barrels, and by 1956 only 769 barrels of petroleum were produced in the county. A resurgence occurred in the late 1950s, when the Lucerne Corporation opened the Rasberry field nine miles northwest of Crowell. In 1960 the county produced 850,330 barrels of crude; in 1978, almost 191,000 barrels; and in 1982, 493,234 barrels. In 1990 production was more than 347,000 barrels. Cumulatively, by the beginning of 1991, 20,816,157 barrels of crude had been produced in Foard County since 1929.

After the 1940s the mechanization of agriculture combined with other factors, such as the severe droughts of the 1950s, to depopulate the area steadily. The county's population dropped to 4,216 in 1950, 3,125 in 1960, 2,211 in 1970, and 2,158 in 1980. In 1992, an estimated 1,794 people lived in Foard County. The shrinking population has remained generally loyal to the Democratic party. qv In presidential elections from 1952 to 1988 the county voted only twice for Republican candidates: in 1972 for Richard Nixon, and in 1984 for Ronald Reagan. Even in those years, the county supported Democratic candidates in gubernatorial and senatorial elections.

Alongside oil and cattle, agriculture has remained a leading industry of Foard County, of which more than 4,000 acres are irrigated. Cotton, wheat, and other grains are the chief crops, while irrigation qv and subirrigation, beginning in the 1940s, made possible the limited commercial production of fruits and vegetables, especially onions and sweet potatoes, in the eastern part of the county. Poultry and other livestock also add to the area's farm income, which averaged $11.5 million annually during the 1980s. The county's gins handled some 4,000 bales of cotton during harvest, while its grain elevators contained more than 350,000 bushels. According to the United States agricultural census for 1982, Foard County produced 1,162,749 bushels of wheat, 14,623 bushels of sorghum, and 7,748 bales of cotton that year; 14,771 cattle were also reported. In the 1980s the county had one bank with assets of nearly $21 million.

U.S. Highway 70 intersects State Highway 6 at Crowell, and several farm and ranch roads provide access to outlying communities. Crowell (1992 estimated population: 1,230) is the county's largest town and the county seat. Although the town was devastated by a tornado on April 27, 1942, it recovered quickly and remains the center of the county's agribusiness and oil economy; Foard County's sole newspaper, the *Foard County News*, is published in the town. Other communities include Margaret, Vivian, Foard City, and Rayland.

BIBLIOGRAPHY: Bailey Phelps, *They Loved the Land: Foard County History* (Quanah, Texas: Quanah *Tribune-Chief*, 1969).

John Leffler

FODICE, TEXAS. Fodice, a farming community off U.S. Highway 287 four miles west of Pennington in southern Houston County, was established after the Civil War. qv Some sources maintain that the town's name came from "four dice," a favorite game of the early inhabitants. Other sources suggest that the first settlers came from the Arkansas community of Fordyce, from which "Fodice" was derived. In 1875 a Methodist church was founded there, and around 1886 a public school began operating. The community had a post office from 1902 to 1966. By 1914 Fodice had two general stores, a cotton gin, a gristmill, and a Masonic hall. During the 1920s and the mid-1930s it had a church, cemetery, and school. Its estimated population in 1936 was twenty-five. After World War II qv the Fodice school was closed, but by the mid-1970s the community's population increased to nearly fifty. In the early 1990s Fodice was a dispersed rural community with a church, a cemetery, and a number of scattered houses. Most of the area's residents were black. The community's reported population in 1990 was forty-nine.

BIBLIOGRAPHY: Houston County Historical Commission, *History of Houston County, Texas, 1687–1979* (Tulsa, Oklahoma: Heritage, 1979). *Houston County Cemeteries* (Crockett, Texas: Houston County Historical Commission, 1977; 3d ed. 1987).

Sabra D. Berry and Christopher Long

FOIK, PAUL JOSEPH (1880–1941). Paul Joseph Foik, priest, librarian, and Texas historian, son of John and Joana (Dameck) Foik, was born in Stratford, Ontario, Canada, on August 14, 1880. He immigrated to the United States to pursue religious and academic studies. He received the Ph.B. degree from the University of Notre Dame in 1907, completed theological studies at Holy Cross College, and was ordained a priest in 1911. In 1912 he completed a Ph.D. in history at Catholic University of America, and was assigned by his order, the Congregation of Holy Cross, qv to serve as librarian of Notre Dame. He held this position until 1924, when he was transferred to Austin, Texas, to become librarian at St. Edward's College (now St. Edward's University).

Foik made unique contributions to librarianship in the United States. He was one of the founders of the Catholic Library Association and was instrumental in the initiation of the Catholic Periodical Index. His most outstanding contribution to Texas history was as editor of Carlos E. Castañeda's qv *Our Catholic Heritage in Texas, 1519–1936* (1936–58). Father Foik labored to collect the archival documents used in the writing of this definitive source. The documents, many of which were microfilmed in Mexican archives, became part of the Catholic Archives of Texas.qv Foik served with J. Frank Dobie and Louis Wiltz Kemp qqv on the Texas Centennial qv committee named to select Texas historical sites for designation by markers in observance of the centennial. He was a fellow of the Texas State Historical Association qv (elected in 1931). He was also a charter member of the Texas Geographic Society qv and a corresponding member of the Sociedad Mexicana de Geografía. He died in Austin on March 1, 1941, and is buried in the Holy Cross congregation cemetery at Notre Dame, Indiana.

BIBLIOGRAPHY: Mayellen Bresie, Paul J. Foik, C.S.C., Librarian and Historian (M.A. thesis, University of Texas, 1964). Catholic Archives of Texas, Files, Austin. St. Edward's University Archives, Austin. Vertical Files, Barker Texas History Center, University of Texas at Austin.

Mayellen Bresie

FOLEY, WASHINGTON GREEN LEE (1780–1874). Washington Foley, Lavaca County pioneer, immigrated to Texas in 1838 with his wife, Sarah, two sons, a daughter, and a large number of slaves. He established a plantation at a site on Nixon Creek in Colorado County (now in Lavaca County). The mill, gin, blacksmith shop, and cluster of slave huts were listed on Ferdinand von Roemer's qv map of Texas as Foley's Settlement and were described by William Bollaert qv in 1843 as "a very fine settlement and good cotton and corn plantation." Foley was wealthy and made extensive loans to settlers and merchants in the area, including one for $1,000 to Gail Borden qv to finance his "meat biscuit." In 1851, on the tax roll for Lavaca County, Foley is listed as owning ninety-five slaves and over 12,000 acres. He had five sons and two daughters. Sarah Foley died in 1863; W. G. L. Foley died on January 23, 1874. His funeral was attended by seventy of his former slaves.

BIBLIOGRAPHY: Paul C. Boethel, *Colonel Amasa Turner, the Gentleman from Lavaca, and Other Captains at San Jacinto* (Austin: Von Boeckmann–Jones, 1963). Paul C. Boethel, *Ole Foley: The Story of W. G. L. Foley* (Houston: Armstrong, 1981). W. Eugene Hollon and Ruth L. Butler, eds., *William Bollaert's Texas* (Norman: University of Oklahoma Press, 1956).

Paul G. Boethel

FOLEY BRANCH. Foley Branch rises a mile northwest of Ezzell in south central Lavaca County (at 29°17' N, 96°55' W) and runs east for 2½ miles through wooded rangeland to its mouth on the Lavaca River, at the bottom of Tiger Bend (at 29°17' N, 96°53' W). The creek traverses gently sloping terrain surfaced by deep clay loam soils. Though the area is usually well-drained, it is subject to flooding. Local vegetation ranges from scattered oak clusters on the prairie to grape-hung thickets of oak, pecan, sycamore, and yaupon near the mouth of the stream. Foley Branch is named for the pioneer Foley family, whose members included Mason B. and H. S. Foley, who fought with John Coffee Hays's qv company during the Texas Revolution.qv

BIBLIOGRAPHY: Paul C. Boethel, *On the Headwaters of the Lavaca and the Navidad* (Austin: Von Boeckmann–Jones, 1967).

FOLEY COUNTY. The Texas legislature passed an act that created Foley, Buchel, and Jeff Davis counties out of part of Presidio County on March 15, 1887, shortly after passing a similar act making Brewster County from Presidio County. The original Brewster County occupied the northwestern portion of what is now Brewster County, and Foley County occupied most of the southern part. Foley and Buchel counties were not organized, however, and on March 22, 1889, the legislature passed an act attaching them to Brewster County for surveying purposes. Foley County had only twenty-five residents in 1890; thus it was one of the most sparsely settled counties in Texas. Seven years later the legislature passed a bill abolishing Foley and Buchel counties and attaching their territory to Brewster County; this bill was presented to Governor Charles A. Culberson qv on April 9, 1897, but he neither signed it nor returned it with his objections to the Senate within the constitutional time limit, so it became law without his signature. With the addition of the territory of Foley and Buchel counties, Brewster County became the largest county in Texas.

BIBLIOGRAPHY: Hans Peter Nielsen Gammel, comp., *Laws of Texas, 1822–1897* (10 vols., Austin: Gammel, 1898).

Martin Donell Kohout

FOLK ARTS AND CRAFTS. The craft is the skill required in the making of a thing that will function as intended. The art is decoration of the object. Both the craft and the art are "folk" if they have been

Comanches, by Lino Sánchez y Tapia after Jean Louis Berlandier, ca. 1828–31. Watercolor. 10″ × 8″. Courtesy Gilcrease Museum, Tulsa; acc. no. 4016.336 plate II. *This painting depicts two men in war dress—a war leader (mounted) with long feather headdress and a shield apparently covered with feathers, and a member of a lower-status, informal warrior group (denoted by the buffalo-scalp bonnet), whose rawhide shield bears paintings, and possibly dried specimens, of his sacred paraphernalia. Both carry lances decorated with feathers and tipped with long, sharp metal heads that may be sabers.*

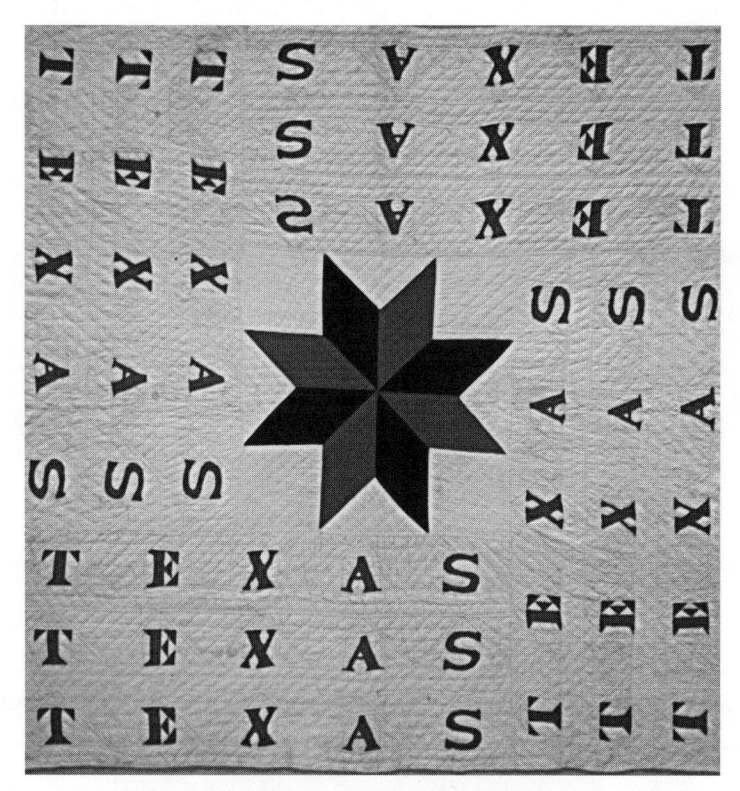

"Texas Quilt, ca. 1886" by Nancy Rebecca Dickson Callan, from Lone Stars: A Legacy of Texas Quilts *by Karoline Patterson Bresenhan and Nancy O'Bryant Puentes, Copyright (c) 1986. Courtesy of the authors and the University of Texas Press. The reversed S in this pieced red, white, and teal blue quilt may have been a deliberate error, such as those introduced by many American quiltmakers. To include a mistake was considered a mark of humility, an acknowledgment that only God was perfect.*

passed down orally or by demonstration. The number of folk craftsmen has diminished since the Industrial Revolution. Most remaining craftsmen are hobbyists who make quilts, furniture,^qv belts, or pots for their own amusement—or profit, if they can find a market that appreciates and can afford fine craftsmanship. Some craftsmen, such as wheelwrights and wainwrights, remain to supply the needs of limited markets, and some crafts—basketry, for instance—defy machine production.

The earliest Texas traditional artisans were Indians, who crafted the needs of their cultures from available materials and decorated their artifacts and themselves with symbols of their cultures. Though the wandering Coahuiltecans of South Texas left few artifacts, they wove mats, tanned hides, and crafted simple tools and weapons. Their Karankawa neighbors, also hunters and gatherers, made a wide assortment of distinctive pottery that was coated inside with natural asphalt for waterproofing and decorated on the outside with asphalt designs. Their main recorded artistry was applied to their bodies in the form of tattoos, bamboo splints pierced through men's lips and breasts, symbolic scarification, and elaborate face-painting. The Comanches wove fabrics of many textures and colors, painted their lances red, and feathered and colored their war shields as well as their horses. The agrarian Caddos of East Texas built palisade log houses and were skilled tool and weapon makers, potters, basketmakers, and artists who decorated artifacts and themselves. They tattooed their bodies, practiced cranial decoration, and crafted body ornaments of shells, bones, feathers, and stones. Besides the crafting and decoration of their artifacts and themselves, Texas Indians developed an art form in their petroglyphs and pictographs. Some of these forms might have functioned in imitative magic, but many seem to represent the nonutilitarian urge to capture in pictures the beautiful animal or protective spirits. The Indians pecked wavy, circular, and zigzag lines on rocks. In the shelter caves along the Pecos River, the Jumanos painted on ceilings and walls in bright yellow, orange, red, white, and black. They drew deer and cougars, fish and snakes, hands, and shapes whose meaning we can only guess at.

The Spanish, who in the sixteenth century began crossing into what is now Texas, brought glass beads, woven cloths, and silver ornaments and added a dimension to this area's arts and crafts. When they began seriously settling Texas in the eighteenth century they brought wheels, screws, metal tools, and religious sculptures and artifacts, as well as such artificers as gunsmiths and wheelwrights. The European settlers of the nineteenth century came with all sorts of skills and as many concepts of art as ethnic groups. As they adapted to their new environment they crafted what they could, used what was available, and learned from each other. The craftsmen who came into Texas from the East fashioned tight log houses out of straight pine logs, hewn and laid horizontally and often secured with half-dovetail corner joints. Germans who arrived at Indianola and went up the Colorado to the rocky Hill Country^qv quarried limestone and built strong rock houses. Later settlers who went further west, where there was neither rock nor timber, mixed mud with grass and made houses of adobe.^qv When these settlers and their descendents finally prospered, they artistically coated their rock or adobe houses with plaster and painted them white, or nailed sawed boards over their log houses. Some painted the interiors of their houses with all manner of scrolls and curlicues and flowers.

Settlers who came to Texas brought, bought, or made spinning wheels, looms, cotton carders, and other tools of the textile craft. They separated themselves from the weavers of skin by their skills in making fabrics of wool, cotton, and flax. They spotted and stripped, colored and shaded the materials according to their artistic tastes. Selected black slaves were trained early in the textile crafts and were widely known for the quality of their beautiful patterns, called, for instance, World's Wonder, Love's Knot, and Blooming Leaf of Mexico. Used material was later cut up and used again in quilt patterns called Texas Star, Double Wedding Ring, the Primrose, and Henry Clay's Choice. Or it was cut into strips to be crocheted into rag rugs or hooked into burlap backing. Linens were embroidered, cross-stitched, and hemmed with delicate tatting. Wool was spun into yarn to be knitted into socks and sweaters. Textile craftsmen, mostly hobbyists, still abound, and the products of quilting^qv frames and knitting needles sell dearly at craft fairs.

Metal crafts, especially blacksmithing, came to Texas with the Spaniards, and with great difficulty because of the weight of iron. Knives, window grates, and andirons were made first for simple utility. Artistry, usually in the form of a simple twist or scroll or incised design, was spare. With the opening of the Texas frontier and the Gulf ports, iron became more plentiful and the blacksmith became the most necessary craftsman in the farming community. Blacksmiths entering Texas as slaves were extremely valuable to their owners, particularly since they made most of the tools other craftsmen required in their work. Other slaves afforded these ironworkers high status and looked upon them as leaders. Aspects of their technology still existed in the 1980s in rural East Texas.^qv Farmers became blacksmiths who forged and forever patched their plows and farm tools and shod their horses and mules. Artists in iron, who made fancy bridle bits, gal-leg spurs, and decorative iron gates, were found among both professionals and amateurs.

Three different types of traditional utilitarian pottery were made in early Texas: Indian, Spanish-Mexican, and Anglo-American. Among the many Indian groups in Texas that made pottery, the Caddos may have been the most aesthetically developed in the potter's art. They stacked coiled clay and formed and decorated their pots without benefit of a wheel. They fired pots but did not glaze them. They often colored the clay in the working stage and made decorative incisions and applications. The Spanish and Mexicans used the wheel rarely, if it all, but did lead-glaze some of their pots and pitchers. The Anglos brought with them the potter's wheel and the use of alkaline and salt glazes and established commercial kilns wherever they went, particularly in those areas where Wilcox Formation clay was accessible. They made jugs of all forms, preserving and storage jars, bowls, pitchers, churns, and chamberpots. Some African Americans[qv] worked clay as slaves and established their own potteries as freedmen. The art and craft of pottery making still thrives, and contemporary potters are continually experimenting with new forms, colors, glazes, and techniques.

The Europeans who came to Texas brought a long tradition of woodcrafting—of ship and house building, of shaping weapons and tools, plows and wagons, axe and hammer handles, of treenware and furniture crafting. Because they brought little furniture with them they began their new lives on the frontier with the roughest tables and chairs and bedsteads. Factories in the northern states began manufacturing furniture in the 1830s, but handcraftsmen flourished long after that in Texas because of transportation problems. Black carpenters in antebellum Texas[qv] also crafted log cribs, barns, log cabins, wagons, benches and stools, beds, spinning wheels, and looms. Cabinetmakers prospered first in East Texas because that was the first area of settlement and because of the easy availability of wood. The artistic form of early Texas furniture was Southern Classical Revival, with pillars and scrolls. Spring-pole lathes were common, as were mortising machines, but simple hand tools, such as planes, chisels, and augers, were most often used. German cabinetmakers who had been apprenticed in Europe became the leading artisans in the Hill Country and southeastern bottomlands. They introduced Texans to furniture in the Gothic and Renaissance styles. And, of course, each craftsman had his own individual style. The craft declined with the improvement of transportation and the availability of cheaper, manufactured furniture in the 1870s; makers became assemblers of prefabricated furniture, and finally merchants. Modern cabinetmakers are usually weekenders who love wood grain and the pleasure of crafting.

Round Top in Fayette County illustrates in miniature the evolution of folk arts and crafts. In 1860 the settlement was the center of a cotton community not yet ten years old, but its small population included a gunsmith, a shoemaker, three blacksmiths, three wagonmakers, a saddler, a chairmaker, a tinner, a cigarmaker, a bookbinder, a shinglemaker, a mechanic, and an engineer. Few of these crafts survived industrialization as necessities. The twentieth-century Round Top consists almost exclusively of a self-conscious artist community. There, restored early buildings and musical and theatrical productions are the most prominent features of the community. For the most part the availability of all kinds of manufactured items eliminated the role of the craftsman. In the twentieth century there is almost nothing the artist can make that cannot be purchased more inexpensively, although the item will not be unique. It is the motivation for individual expression that attracts modern craftsmen. Craft fairs accompany almost all forms of outdoor entertainment. Towns of any size at all feature at least one or two annual events that encourage the sale of arts and crafts. And larger cities support a variety of craft shops interspersed with other commercial endeavors. *See also* ARCHITECTURE, MEXICAN-AMERICAN ARTS AND CRAFTS, POTTERY.

BIBLIOGRAPHY: Francis E. Abernethy, *Folk Art in Texas,* Publications of the Texas Folklore Society 45 (Dallas: Southern Methodist University Press, 1985). Richard Burns, Afro-American Blacksmithing in East Texas (Master's report, University of Texas at Austin, 1984). Sherry B. Humphreys and Johnell L. Schmidt, *Texas Pottery: Caddo Indian to Contemporary* (Washington, Texas: Star of the Republic Museum, 1976). Joyce Ann Ice, Quilting and the Pattern of Relationships in Community Life (Ph.D. dissertation, University of Texas at Austin, 1984). Terry G. Jordan, *Texas Log Buildings: A Folk Architecture* (Austin: University of Texas Press, 1978). Cecilia Steinfeldt, *Texas Folk Art: One Hundred Fifty Years of the Southwestern Tradition* (Austin: Texas Monthly Press, 1981). Lonn W. Taylor, *Texas Furniture: The Cabinet Makers and Their Work* (Austin: University of Texas Press, 1975). *Texana II: Cultural Heritage of the Plantation South* (Austin: Texas Historical Commission, 1984). John Michael Vlach, "Afro-American Folk Crafts in Nineteenth Century Texas," *Western Folklore* 40 (April 1981).

Francis E. Abernethy

Storage jars, made by Hiram, James, or Wallace Wilson (left) and by H. Wilson and Company (right), Capote, Guadalupe County, ca. 1872–74. Large jar, 23¾" high; small jar, 16" high. Courtesy Witte Museum, San Antonio, Texas. The Wilson potteries of Capote, operated and staffed by both black and white potters, supplied stoneware throughout much of Central Texas in the latter half of the nineteenth century.

FOLK BELIEF. Folk beliefs in Texas, like many other elements of folk culture, came with the various groups who entered and settled the state. Though some may have been adapted to their new locale, few if any are unique to the state. Folklorists divide folk beliefs—ideas that are accepted as true without hard evidence and passed down through generations without the sanction of official institutions—into two broad categories, magical and empirical. Magical beliefs are based on supernatural or mysterious elements and include omens, taboos, and good-luck charms. Empirical beliefs, based on experience and observation, include lore about the weather and other natural phenomena. Though many folk beliefs are unique to some ethnic group, most cross ethnic boundaries.

Texas folk beliefs analyze the weather, usually in an attempt to predict it. The more important weather is to a group, the more likely there will be an abundance of weather beliefs. For Gulf Coast fishermen, for instance, a circle around the moon means bad weather. A well-known proverb expresses a common belief: "Red sky at morning, sailor take warning; red sky at night, sailor's delight." Bad weather and other "bad luck" can be caused by whistling on board ship, by shaving on board, or by bringing a black suitcase aboard. Good luck, including good weather, can be ensured by a silver dollar or fifty-cent piece under the ship's mast. Some Hispanic Texans predict the coming year's weather on the basis of the first twelve days of January. Other beliefs about the weather are shared by many in the state. When ducks migrate early in the fall a difficult winter can be expected. When wasps, flies, or spiders come into the house, rain is coming. When cattle run about with their tails up in the air, a storm is coming. An ax stuck in the ground can "split the cloud" to prevent an unwanted storm.

The moon is important in the Texas folklore. Among some representatives of almost every ethnic group in rural Texas, the moon is believed to pertain to birthing, weaning, breeding, planting, harvesting, canning, castrating, and egg hatching. Sleeping in moonlight will make one crazy. Looking at a new moon over the left shoulder will bring bad luck. Many serious fishermen pay attention to the signs of the moon. Some gardeners believe that tubers or root vegetables should be planted in the dark of the moon and leafy and above-ground vegetables in the light of the moon. Hogs butchered in the dark of the moon produce firm meat and abundant lard; soap made between the full moon and the last quarter will be firm. Wood cut during the right quarter of the moon will not snap when burned. Timbers cut in the last quarter of the moon will last longer. Some Mexican Americans[qv] of South Texas believe that the mesquite[qv] used to build jacals will not rot if cut during the full moon. Some East Texans believe that a tree cut in the dark of the moon in August will not sprout back, and its stump will rot within a year.

Several of the most fascinating Texas folk beliefs center around creatures common to the state. Snakes, particularly, play an important role in the folk beliefs of most ethnic groups. Many of these beliefs are shared, though some are unique to specific groups. A common belief is that snakes charm their victims—birds, small animals, or even people—and exert a strange power over them to make them helpless against attack. A "snake doctor" (dragonfly) can supposedly cure an injured snake if the snake's head isn't chopped off; snakes mortally injured during the day will not die until sundown; a rattlesnake hung with its belly to the sun will bring rain; and horsehairs put into rainwater will turn into snakes. Specific kinds of snakes enjoy their own fanciful reputations. The hoop snake forms a hoop, rolls downhill, and stabs its prey with its tail as it hurls itself, spearlike, after uncoiling. If the barbed tail strikes its victim, the poison kills. Kill a copperhead, and its mate will seek revenge. The coachwhip whips its victims with its body. The red racer chases people. The milk snake sucks cows' teats and makes their milk bloody. Killing a "witch snake" (chicken snake) brings permanent bad luck; it makes cows give bloody milk and causes children to die. A king snake crushes other snakes with blows of its tail, then eats them. "Joint" snakes, when struck or frightened, break into numerous pieces and then reassemble after the danger is past.

Rattlesnakes[qv] are believed to swallow their young and to live in peace with prairie dogs[qv] in prairie dog holes. A common cowboy belief was that a horsehair rope coiled around a camp bed would keep rattlesnakes out. The snake's mortal enemy, the roadrunner or paisano (see BIRDS), is said to kill it by building a corral of thorns or prickly pears around it and forcing it to starve to death or bite itself in frustration. A victim of rattlesnake bite can cure himself by biting off the head of the offending reptile or by splitting the snake open and laying it on the bite. A chicken, split open while alive, is better. Other reptiles[qv] have their own accretions of folk belief. When snapping turtles bite, they do not let go until it thunders. Even with their heads cut off, they attempt to get back to the water. Horned lizards[qv] ("horned toads") are believed to spit blood from their eyes, and killing one will cause a person's milk cows to go dry or give bloody milk. Some believe that a salamander can get into one's body through conjuring or from wet grass through bare feet. The "mountain boomer" lizard, found in West Texas, is falsely believed to be poisonous. It is said to bite with its teeth, sting with its tail, and bark loudly.

Other creatures are also the subject of folk beliefs in Texas. Birds of ill omen, particularly nightjars (also called goatsuckers because of their reputation for sucking milk from goats), whippoorwills, nighthawks, and owls, foretell death or other misfortune. When a redheaded woodpecker pecks on the roof, a member of the family will die. If a buzzard's shadow crosses one's path, he will surely have bad luck. Killing a wren or disturbing a kildeer's nest will bring bad luck. The owl and sometimes the turkey are ominous to Hispanic Texans, for witches often take these forms, as well as that of a cat. On the other hand, a fairly common belief among older rural Mexican Americans is that roadrunner broth, prepared correctly, has strong curative properties. No birds are supposed to be poisonous. Tarantulas, however, are thought to be deadly, and some believe that if a centipede walks across any part of you, that part will rot to the bone and fall off. Folk beliefs about domestic animals are also common. Feeding hens red pepper supposedly increases egg production. Hispanics' beliefs about horse color affect their choice of mounts. Sorrel horses are thought to have thin hides and therefore to be poor brush-country horses; darker horses are better. Andy Adams[qv] noted a similar Caucasian preference for dark horses in Log of a Cowboy.

A number of folk beliefs have to do with social relationships. Most predict future events. A dropped dishrag, an itchy nose, or a rooster crowing through a door or window indicates that company is coming. An itching right hand will soon shake the hand of a stranger. A person whose palm itches or whose ears ring is being talked about. Many beliefs deal with love and marriage. Hold a burning match upright, and the flame will point toward where your sweetheart lives. If four persons cross each others' arms to shake hands, one of them is soon to marry. When an empty bottle is set inside a circle of girls and spun, the open end will point out the one who will marry first.

Most omens and taboos are based on magical beliefs and give a sense of control over one's "fate" by assigning causes and providing counterremedies to ward off ill fortune. Omens of death in the family are myriad: a run-away mule, a dog howling at midnight, a hen crowing like a rooster, taking off a wedding ring, dreaming of losing all one's teeth, carrying a hoe in one door and out another, not cleaning one's shoes before returning from a funeral—all of these portend a death in the family. Taboos include opening an umbrella indoors, leaving a rake on the ground with tines pointing up, dropping a knife, breaking a mirror, allowing a bird to fly into the house, telling a bad dream before breakfast, moving on Friday, carrying an ax through a house, and many others. If one drops scissors and they stick upright, bad luck is coming. Giving a knife or scissors to a friend will sever the friendship; to ward off the evil, one must exchange gifts or buy the knife or scissors for at least a penny. Giving a friend or family member a new empty wallet will cause him to go broke. If one spills salt, he can prevent bad luck by throwing a pinch of it over the right shoulder. If one puts a stocking on backwards in the morning, he can prevent bad luck by wearing it all day. If two people say the same thing at the same time, they can prevent bad luck by saying, "Jinx, you owe me a Coke."

On the other hand, there are a number of ways to make sure that one gets good luck. A horseshoe on a post or over the door brings good luck. If one finds a horseshoe, he should spit on it and throw it over his shoulder; if he doesn't see where it lands, he will have good luck. Carrying a rabbit's foot ensures good luck. If a person finds a pin with the point toward him, he should pick it up for good luck. A wish made before a falling star disappears will come true. Some good luck is portended by happenings that do not take effort on the recipient's part. A dress turned up at the hem promises a new dress. Toads in the garden or chirping crickets bring good luck. If a butterfly sits on one's hat, he will get a new hat.

BIBLIOGRAPHY: E. R. Bogusch, "Superstitions of Bexar County," ed. J. Frank Dobie, in Publications of the Texas Folklore Society 5 (Austin: Texas Folklore Society, 1926). Bill Brett, "Plantin' by the Moon," in *Paisanos: A Folklore Miscellany*, ed. Francis Edward Abernethy, Publications of the Texas Folklore Society 41 (Austin: Encino, 1978). J. Frank Dobie, *Coffee in the Gourd* (1935). Patrick B. Mullen, *I Heard the Old Fisherman Say: Folklore of the Texas Gulf Coast* (Austin: University of Texas Press, 1978). John K. Strecker, "Folk-Lore Relating to Texas Birds," in *Follow de Drinkin' Gou'd* (Austin: Texas Folklore Society, 1928). John K. Strecker, "Reptiles of the South and Southwest in Folklore," in Publications of the Texas Folklore Society 5 (Austin: Texas Folklore Society, 1926). Tressa Turner, "The Human Comedy in Folk Superstitions," in *Straight Texas*, ed. J. Frank Dobie and Mody C. Boatright (Austin: Texas Folklore Society, 1937).

Joe S. Graham

FOLK BUILDING. Each cultural group that inhabits Texas brought its own ideas of proper forms, materials, and styles for buildings, and many cultures flow together in Texas, as the HemisFair '68 qv theme proclaimed. Anglos—here meaning English, Scots-Irish, and assimilated Germans—moved into the state from cultural regions centered in the Upper South and the Tidewater region. Most Hispanics came from Mexico. Germans, Czechs, Poles, Norwegians, and Swedes qqv settlers came directly from Europe, and Europeans of all sorts came who had first sojourned elsewhere in North American. French qv came both from Louisiana and directly from Europe. Chinese, Japanese, qqv and Africans came, the last mostly as slaves, to round out the nineteenth-century cultural confluence. These groups brought building customs with them but often changed their traditions as a result of the new physical environment, of the influence of new neighbors, and of changing styles in formal architecture. In the hot climate of Texas, where there was little snow, settlers from Central and Northern Europe soon lowered their rooflines and enlarged the number and size of windows. They derived the idea of porches from Anglo neighbors. Hispanic building customs did not change so much. Greek Revival and Victorian styles led in time to folk versions. The interchange of materials, methods, and styles resulted in a degree of sameness, but usually enough difference remained that the buildings could be traced to a particular group or tradition.

Both square and rectangular houses in eastern Texas were usually built of logs in the beginning. If the house was to be only a temporary structure until the "big house" was built, or if the builder lacked woodworking skills or time, the logs were either not squared or at best squared only for the inside wall. Four major notch types, derived from the eastern United States and German Central Europe, found their way to Texas: the half-dovetail, saddle, V, and square. The corner notches on the logs were also reflections of skills and available time as well as of cultural traditions. Settlers from the Upper South, the first to arrive in Texas, generally used the half-dovetail and V notch on hewn logs. Texas Germans also used the V notch, and may have learned it from Upper Southerners in their vicinity. Lower Southerners, who arrived later when log-working skills were beginning to deteriorate in the eastern United States, generally used the simpler square-and-saddle notch. These types also were used extensively for outbuildings, even when dwellings had more complicated forms. When Anglo settlers moved west of the forested region of Texas, they used sod blocks to build their houses or constructed half dugouts with or without upper walls of logs (*see* DUGOUT). Most of the pioneer settlers in western Texas, however, did not arrive until after sawmills became widespread in the 1880s and therefore built their homes of sawn lumber, as did the later settlers in forested East Texas. Both cultural traditions and availability of building materials led the Germans of Central Texas to build their houses of *Fachwerk*, or half-timbering, or of mortared stone (*see* GERMAN VERNACULAR ARCHITECTURE). Hispanics used either stone or adobe, qv and a few buildings of palisado construction still stand.

Shotgun houses in the Freedmen's Town Historic District, Fourth Ward, Houston. Built ca. 1907–24. Photograph by Kenneth Breisch, 1984. Courtesy Texas Historical Commission. The one-room-wide shotgun house was erected on countless narrow urban lots and was also a common type in certain rural areas.

The simplest and most universal folk house in Texas, English in origin, consisted of a square usually about sixteen feet on a side, usually enclosing a single pen or room but sometimes two rooms. In East Texas the single-room dwelling was often used for slave housing. The dimensions could vary with the materials available, especially for log buildings, and rectangular structures occurred. The square, single-pen house was brought to Texas by settlers from both the Upper and Lower South, and also from Mexico and Germany. The Germans contributed the two-room square house. It was usually constructed of logs when built by Anglos and of adobe or mortared stone when built by the Hispanics of South Texas. Anglos left their walls bare in the earlier days of settlement, but Hispanics and Germans usually plastered theirs both inside and out. Later, the Anglos sometimes covered the inside walls with sawn boards and the outside ones with weatherboarding, thereby improving both appearance and durability. A second square room added to the side of a house containing the fireplace and chimney made a saddlebag house. This house form, possibly with Swedish roots, was introduced to Texas by Upper Southerners. Replacing the massive fireplace with a flue enlarged the living space and was characteristic of later saddlebag houses and the similar Creole house from Louisiana. The second room added to the wall opposite the chimney yielded a double-pen or Cumberland house, perhaps the most widespread form in the part of the state settled by Anglos. Most of the double-pens in Texas are of the Cumberland type. The basic plan of the Cumberland house was often modified by the addition of shed or lean-to porches in front and back or of one or more rooms across the back. In both the saddlebag and Cumberland houses, each room usually had its own outside entrance. Sometimes a hall separated the two rooms of a rectangular house. If the central hallway was enclosed and contained the only entrance to the house, the dwelling was a central-hall house. This type was brought to Texas especially from the Upper South. If the hallway was left open and entrances to the two rooms were either on the front wall or in the hallway, the house was what is now usually called a dogtrot house, a type particularly associated with settlers from the Lower South. When the long axis of the house was oriented perpendicularly to the roadway rather than parallel as in the rectangular house, the shotgun was the result. Although the basic form had African roots, and in some parts of Texas was associated with blacks, it proved to be very popular and was used by other groups. Sections of some cities, housing for sawmill and other industrial workers of many cultural derivations, and even some of the twentieth-century pioneer houses in Panhandle qv cities were constructed on the shotgun form. The Fourth Ward qv in Houston contained several shotgun houses in the 1980s, as did the old bottomland plantation district between the Brazos and the Little Brazos rivers in Robertson County. A house consisting of two shotgun units with a common central wall and roof yielded a bungalow house. Sometimes this type had two front doors, a feature that suggested evolution from the Cumberland house, and sometimes only one. The bungalow form became the first all-wood house built in much of West Texas.

All of these house forms were one or 1½ stories high. The single-story structure was by far more common. One form of taller dwelling has come to be called the I (pronounced "eye") house. With variation in details, it was introduced to Texas by settlers from both the Upper and Lower South. Regardless of the source, however, the I house was the preferred dwelling of the well-to-do in both rural and urban settings. The placement of stairways in houses of 1½ and two stories varied with region and culture. In Anglo-built houses the stairway generally rose from the central hall or dogtrot, whereas in German houses it was usually on the outside of the house. All of these houses were customarily topped with pitched roofs containing simple gable ends, through one of which projected a chimney or flue. The roof ridge usually paralleled the road except in the shotgun and bungalow types. When one or more rooms were added to the back of the single-room or rectangular house, the roofline could be carried with little or no break in angle over the rear room, thus forming a saltbox or catslide house. Hispanic homes, particularly in the drier parts of the state, were usually topped by flat roofs consisting of poles and brush covered with clay and plaster. In the lower Rio Grande valley area, however, are Hispanic houses with side walls that extend one to two feet above the pitched roof. This distinctive type of parapet roof is perhaps derived from Irish influence. Houses built by Hispanics and Central Europeans generally had casement windows, and Anglos' houses had sash windows. The Anglos did not usually use shutters, but Hispanics and Central Europeans did. Various porches embellished the basic house forms. The enclosed porch was made by carrying the front roofline out over the porch space without a change in angle. This type, often erroneously attributed to Louisiana, came from the Tidewater region. Although structurally and aesthetically more unified because it did not appear to be so much an afterthought as a shed porch, the enclosed porch cost more to build.

Folk housing also varies by region and culture in the relation of house to ground surface. Hispanic and German houses usually sat firmly on the ground, whereas Anglo houses, particularly those from the Lower South, were generally elevated on piers made of tree-trunk sections, piled native stones, or bricks. Traceable to the Tidewater region is the custom of raising some houses above the ground by a half or full story. *See also* AFRICAN AMERICANS, ARCHITECTURE.

BIBLIOGRAPHY: Francis Edward Abernethy, *Built in Texas,* Publications of the Texas Folklore Society 42 (Waco: E-Heart Press, 1979). Drury Blakeley Alexander and (photographs) Todd Webb, *Texas Homes of the Nineteenth Century* (Austin: University of Texas Press, 1966). Henry Glassie, *Pattern in the Material Folk Culture of the Eastern United States* (Philadelphia: University of Pennsylvania Press, 1968; rpt. 1980). Clovis Heimsath, *Pioneer Texas Buildings: A Geometry Lesson* (Austin: University of Texas Press, 1968). Terry G. Jordan, "German Folk Houses in the Texas Hill Country," in *German Culture in Texas,* ed. Glen E. Lich and Dona B. Reeves (Boston: Twayne, 1980). Terry G. Jordan, *Texas Log Buildings: A Folk Architecture* (Austin: University of Texas Press, 1978). Fred B. Kniffen, "Folk Housing: Key to Diffusion," *Annals of the Association of American Geographers* 55 (1965). Lonn W. Taylor, "Fachwerk and Brettstuhl: The Rejection of Traditional Folk Culture," in *Perspectives on American Folk Art,* ed. Ian M. G. Quimby and Scott T. Swank (New York: Norton, 1980). John Michael Vlach, "The Shotgun House: An African Architectural Legacy," *Pioneer America* 8 (1976).   G. Loyd Collier

FOLK DANCE. The background of Texas folk dancing is rich and varied. All the steps and choreography were introduced into the state by settlers and visitors. The resulting dances have consistently reflected the potpourri of ethnic and social backgrounds of the people, the changing dance styles and clothing fashions, the setting, and the type of music available. Through the years a definite traditional Texas folk style of dancing has developed.

Society-minded colonists took lessons from dancing masters and stepped out in refined ballroom style. The immigrant pioneers copied them, and in some cases revived the traditional folk dances of their homeland. During the early 1800s aristocratic Spanish and Mexican officials held formal balls at the Spanish Governor's Palace[qv] in San Antonio. Other Mexican settlers danced on the public square or in adobe huts with dirt floors. While the upper class attended formal balls that included dance repertoire from Europe, the most popular entertainment to attract revelers from all parts of the Hispanic community was the fandango, a dance of Spanish derivation. Since the colonial period the term had come to refer to a kind of diversion, usually a festive gathering marked by music, dancing, gambling, drinking, and eating. Fandangos were held in the streets, in makeshift dance halls, or in fandango houses throughout the year. Violins and guitars at these functions played the equivalent of "Turkey in the Straw" while couples danced a polka or bolero. The fandangos were outlawed by the 1870s, though they still lingered inconspicuously until the end of the century (*see also* FORT GRIFFIN FANDANGLE). *Bailes* (occasions for dances), which included the *baile de regalo* (regional dances) served as less rowdy get-togethers for families, friends, relatives, and lovers.

The colonists who came later held elegant public dances in the populated areas. For example, in 1832, Anglo citizens of Brazoria gave "a Public Dinner and Ball . . . honoring General Santa Ana" (Antonio López de Santa Anna[qv]), who later became the archenemy of Texas independence. The upper stratum issued satin-bound invitations and dance cards for posh balls. At formal affairs, after a ceremonial grand march, the dancers postured and bowed in imitation of the stately elegance of European court dances, choreographed for both group and couple participation. Many of the steps had been adapted from peasant folk dances such as Bohemian polkas and Irish reels, then set to classical music by dancing masters for the enjoyment of European royalty. Group dances included structured, many-figured cotillions (one called a "german"), four-couple French quadrilles (some called "lancers"), lively reels and longways dances, and measured minuets. Among the dances for couples were Viennese turning waltzes, polkas, schottisches, galops, gavottes, and redowas. Less sophisticated settlers not inclined toward formal dance training romped off to "all invited, none slighted" shindigs, where a manager kept a list of dance partners. The people exuberantly polkaed the splinters off of split-log floors and schottisched across wagon sheets spread on the ground. They copied the refined forms of the old-time folk dances, improvising when necessary to complete a half-remembered sequence or when the proper music was not available.

Due to the large number of single men on the Texas frontier, the state became known as the Bachelor Republic. Two men frequently danced as partners, the one taking the lady's part "heifer branded" by wearing an apron or a handkerchief tied around one arm. Finding suitable dance music was a problem. If no one had ox-carted a piano to the site or brought a fiddle or accordion, the dancers improvised. At times, to make rhythm, someone banged on a clevis with a piece of iron, scraped a file across a hoe blade, "blew a tune" on a peach leaf, or rhythmically slapped his legs in a maneuver called "patting juba." Both formal and informal dance socials were called balls, hops, cotillions, or germans. Clubs were named Cotillion or German after the type of dances they did, and the names continued to be used long after those dance forms had been replaced. The San Antonio German Club, for example, founded in 1880, was still active in the 1980s. At early-day informal dances, in Texas and elsewhere, the multifigured quadrilles were simplified. Reminders describing the simpler figures were shouted out to the dancers, usually by the musician. As time went on, the one shouting became known as a "caller." Callers added

Square dancing on a wagon sheet (John Selmon, fiddler). Photograph by Ray Rector. SMS Flat Top Ranch, Jones County, ca. 1930. Courtesy Margaret Rector, Austin. Photograph courtesy HRHRC. The dancers have spread the wagon sheet out to keep the dust from rising.

rhyming lines between the actual directions. Their patter reflected the setting and the occupation, and from it grew the unique, free-wheeling Western square dance, the only folk dance wholly configured to extemporaneous calls.

The pioneers danced at forts and on ranches. One year, all-night dances were held throughout the Christmas holidays at the Mobeetie courthouse. Many large balls were held in Houston. In 1835, at the Brazoria boarding house formerly operated by Jane Long,^{qv} 1,000 colonists attended a ball honoring Stephen F. Austin.^{qv} In 1837 settlers gathered for a San Jacinto Victory Ball. General Sam Houston,^{qv} president of the new Republic of Texas,^{qv} led the grand march, thus setting a precedent for later inaugural balls. Opening balls traditionally started off the season (September to June) in Austin after the city became the capital in 1840. At the 1883 inaugural ball for Governor John Ireland,^{qv} over 2,500 people thronged the hall. In 1887 Austin newspapers reported a number of German Club dances. The University of Texas, established in 1883, held frequent dances, including a 6:30 A.M. "morning German" held on the riverboat *Ben Hur*. Before 1900 the climax of commencement week was always a dance held at the Driskill Hotel.^{qv} In December 1885 M. G. Rhodes held a ball at the Star Hotel in the little cowtown of Anson; the Cowboys' Christmas Ball^{qv} later became an annual affair and was still going strong in the 1980s.

Some religious leaders denounced the practice of dancing. They objected to the close embrace in polkas and waltzes and believed the fiddle to be an instrument of the devil. As a result, some dancers turned to "play-party games." These were modified square, circle, and reel dances "played" (danced) to rhythm provided by clapping and singing (*see also* FOLK MUSIC). Around the turn of the century modern developments—radios, telephones, automobiles, and electricity—expanded contact with the outside world, and people lost interest in the traditional dances. A 1913 Elks Club dance card showed a monotonous alternation of waltzes and two-steps. Some versions of pioneer dances were preserved in scattered pockets in the hills and on the prairies of the state by people dedicated to enjoying the dances that were authentic witnesses to the lives of early Texans. In the late 1920s Texas fiddle player James Robert (Bob) Wills^{qv} introduced his infectious "hot Texas rhythms," designed specifically for dancing. Soon afterward the big-band era swept the dancers of Texas and the nation back to the dance floors. The Charleston, swing, jitterbug, and fox-trot became popular.

After World War II^{qv} a revival of interest drew dancers back to the traditional squares, schottisches, and polkas. Public-address systems made it possible for one caller to be heard by a large groups of dancers, and an increase to some 4,000 newly choreographed calls led to standardization of terminology and choreography. Square dance and round (couple) dance enthusiasts organized into clubs, and in June 1987 some 4,000 dancers met in Dallas to celebrate the twenty-fifth anniversary of the Texas State Federation of Square and Round Dancers. A spin-off from the revival of square dancing was an increased interest in foreign folk dances. In 1949 the Texas Folk Dance Camp (later named Texas International Folk Dancers) met and organized to promote performances of an assortment of international folk dances. The organization was still active in 1987. Other groups formed to present specific ethnic dances—Czech, Polish, Irish, and German—at the 1936 State Fair of Texas,^{qv} HemisFair '68,^{qv} and the Texas Folklife Festival^{qv} sponsored by the University of Texas Institute of Texan Cultures.^{qv} Some thirty-one different folk dance groups were on the 1987 roster.

While square dancers confined themselves to club dancing and proliferated, in the 1960s the general public took to the twist, the frug, the funky chicken, disco, and other nontouching couple dances. The

Cast of Los Pastores. *Photograph by John G. Bourke. San Antonio, 1893. From M. R. Cole, "Los Pastores," Memoirs of the American Folklore Society 9 (1907), facing p. 12. The entire cast appears here in full costume, except that the devils (center) do not have their masks.*

1970s saw national interest in country-and-western music and movies bring the traditional couple dances back to the dance floors under a new name—country dancing. Some dances had new Texas styling. The hippety-hop Bohemian couple-polka had evolved into the popular Cotton-eyed Joe performed by nonpartner lines of dancers. Selected versions of schottisches and waltzes also adopted the spoke-line form to accommodate the singles who flooded the dance floors. A fox-trot step for couples evolved into a dance known around the world as the Texas two-step. A 1981 article in *Redbook* magazine stated, "the whole damn country is going Texas."

BIBLIOGRAPHY: Jan Harold Brunvand, *The Study of American Folklore: An Introduction,* 2d ed. (1978). Betty Casey, *Dance Across Texas* (Austin: University of Texas Press, 1985). Joann Wheeler Kealiinohomoku, "Folk Dance," in *Folklore and Folklife: An Introduction,* ed. Richard M. Dorson (University of Chicago Press, 1972). Gertrude P. Kurath, "Dance: Folk and Primitive," in *Funk and Wagnalls Standard Dictionary of Folklore, Mythology, and Legend* (New York: Harper and Row, 1972). José E. Limón, "Texas-Mexican Popular Music and Dancing: Some Notes on History and Symbolic Process," *Latin American Music Review* 4 (Fall–Winter 1983). William A. Owens, *Swing and Turn: Texas Play-Party Games* (Dallas: Tardy, 1936). Manuel H. Peña, "Ritual Structure in a Chicano Dance," *Latin American Music Review,* Spring 1980. Irma Saldívar Vela, *Bailes a Colores, Dances to Colors* (Austin: American Universal Art Forms, 1972). Betty Casey

FOLK DRAMA. Although folk drama—drama performed by an ethnic or folk group that has developed traditional rules for time, place, and manner of performance—is relatively rare in the United States, some folk dramas have endured in Texas. They come from Old World religious drama and are staged as a part of the Hispanic Christmas celebration, especially along the Rio Grande border. In contrast to the static scripts of literary dramas, the dialogue and actions represented in these plays maintain a certain fluidity, especially when the "same" play is performed in two different communities. Variation is the rule rather than the exception in folk theater. Nevertheless, in Texas only two general plots produce the various texts. Both recount events surrounding the birth of Christ. The more elaborate of these plays, in terms of dramatic development, is usually referred to as the *Pastorela,* or *Los Pastores.* As the title suggests, the plot is drawn from scriptural accounts of the shepherds' adoration of the Christ in the New Testament. The core of the drama portrays the journey of a group of shepherds to the birthplace of the Messiah and the efforts of Satan and related forces of evil to block his coming. The action is confined to an informal stage, usually a patio. Costuming and masks are used. Dialogue is interspersed with song. As in European medieval drama that reenacts sacred episodes, broad comedy remains integral to the performance. In one text, for example, during the shepherds' journey to Bethlehem, Lucifer attempts to discover from a clownish member of the group whether the Christ child has been born. This shepherd drives Lucifer into a rage of frustration by his foolish prattle, which results from his misunderstanding of simple questions. The action of the play is usually localized, the stock characters are given common local names, and the props and costumes anachronistically reflect the area's Mexican-American culture and Spanish ancestry.

The second folk drama, *Las Posadas,* is an expansion upon St. Luke's account of Joseph and Mary's search for shelter. *Las Posadas* is less elaborate than the *Pastorela,* however. It incorporates no comedy, and all the dialogue is sung. Whereas the action of *Los Pastores* is restricted to a comparatively limited performing area, *Las Posadas* combines the features of procession and drama. On the nine nights from December 16 through December 24, a group bearing images of St. Joseph and the holy Virgin reenact the couple's search for lodging. They go from house to house in the neighborhood and are refused until they arrive at a predetermined last dwelling, where they finally are invited to enter. Rejoicing, more prayer, and more song follow, then refreshments, piñatas, and sometimes social dancing. The dialogue in the play consists of entreaties for admittance sung by the group carrying the images of the holy couple and responses sung by persons portraying the innkeeper and others inside the homes visited. On the ninth and final night the participants celebrate the birth of Christ. Compared to *Los Pastores, Las Posadas* appears stylized, but a realistic enactment of the sacred event is not a particular goal of the performance.

Numerous Spanish nativity plays featuring shepherds and the holy family have been preserved from the sixteenth and seventeenth centuries, although evidence suggests that the tradition was far older. Some writers speculate that these plays were introduced into the New World by Spanish clerics during the early period of colonization. There are reports of *Pastorelas* and *Posadas* in San Antonio in the mid-1800s and texts and documented performances of *Pastorelas* from the 1890s. Fewer performances of these folks plays have been reported in recent years than earlier in the twentieth century. The decline results in part from urbanization, increasing secularity, and the mobility of contemporary society. Urbanization has brought in outsiders who are unfamiliar with and perhaps even hostile to local traditions. Nor do the dangers and complexities of an urban environment encourage the casual, middle-of-the-street procession vital to the performance of *Las Posadas*. The loss of members of the group— older ones through death, younger ones through departure—has caused an unavoidable decline in this dramatic folk tradition. Nevertheless, the Christmas plays have not disappeared entirely. In fact, there has been an effort in some Hispanic communities to revive them. The performances are not "folk" in the strictest sense of the term; the literary sources of scripts and the frequent lack of folk modifications violate the principles of traditional performance. But efforts to reintroduce dramatic elements into Christmas festivities may eventually lead to a genuine revival of this Hispanic holiday tradition. *See also* MEXICAN-AMERICAN THEATER.

BIBLIOGRAPHY: Roger Abrahams, "Folk Drama," in *Folklore and Folklife,* ed. Richard M. Dorson (University of Chicago Press, 1972). M. R. Cole, *Los Pastores: A Mexican Play of the Nativity, Memoirs of the American Folklore Society* 9 (Boston: Houghton Mifflin, 1907). Richard Reyes Flores, "Los Pastores": Performance, Poetics, and Politics in Folk Drama (Ph.D. dissertation, University of Texas at Austin, 1989). Thomas A. Green, "Introduction," *Journal of American Folklore* 94 (1981). Thomas A. Green, "Toward a Definition of Folk Drama," *Journal of American Folklore* 91 (1978). Juan Bautista Rael, *The Sources and Diffusion of the Mexican Shepherds' Plays* (Guadalajara: Librería La Joyita, 1965). Frances Toor, *A Treasury of Mexican Folkways* (New York: Crown, 1947).

Thomas A. Green

FOLK FESTIVALS. Festivals in Texas reflect a tradition of community cooperation and celebration that began at least as early as the arrival of permanent settlers. Early European Texans of all faiths, occupations, and ethnic backgrounds brought their traditions with them. Texas festivals reflect this diversity of cultural identity and also demonstrate the wide range of occupations, agricultural products, and historical events that characterize the state. The origins of some celebrations reach far back into history in other lands; others originated in twentieth-century Texas. In frontier Texas full-scale festivals were sometimes impossible, but groups still gathered frequently to celebrate special occasions with music, dance, and food. Older traditional festivals are rarely called that. Instead, they derive their names from what they celebrate—a saint such as St. Anthony, for instance, or an object that is celebrated, as in the Luling Watermelon Thump. Those festivals that were brought to Texas usually incorporate features from life in the state, especially a heightened awareness of ethnicity. Traditional festivals based solely on experience in Texas are associated with particular towns, regions, or historical events. The major symbol of these celebrations is often a natural product, such as watermelons, cattle, or trees. All festivals foster the concept of identity based on shared experience. A second group of festivals of more recent origin do use the term *festival* in their names. These have not developed out of a community or ethnic group and are typically sponsored by an institution or an individual. Such festivals are designed to attract masses of people for performance and the display of traditions. The range and variety of festivals in Texas make a listing impossible. The editors of *Texas Highways*[qv] keep a file of community events for the year and publish a monthly list of events in the magazine. At any festival an event may be added or removed at any time, and dates can be altered from year to year.

For early settlers traditional festivals celebrated in the country of origin often took on even greater significance in Texas. In the latter half of the nineteenth century Mexican Americans[qv] celebrated the full round of religious fiestas throughout the year, with special emphasis on the December holidays. In San Antonio the Feast of Our Lady of Guadalupe (December 12) was observed as early as the 1840s with an elaborate procession. Twelve girls dressed in white carried the image of the Virgin Mary, and fiddlers accompanied the procession to San Fernando de Bexar Cathedral[qv] on the Main Plaza. After Mass people attended all-night dances in their homes. During the Christmas season the Texas-Mexican population, especially in San Antonio, performed the Spanish medieval drama *Los Pastores* and enacted *posadas,* rituals commemorating Joseph and Mary's search for shelter in Bethlehem (see FOLK DRAMA). Hispanic Catholics all over the state have continued to celebrate the various saints days in the twentieth century. Additionally, El Cinco de Mayo, a secular holiday, is celebrated with parades, floats, folk dancing, and an all-night ball in some parts of Texas (see FIESTAS PATRIAS).

Germans[qv] brought unique celebrations to their new homes in Central Texas. Immigrants came in large numbers between 1845 and 1850 and organized singing societies in most of the German Texas communities. Singers and families assembled on Saturday morning for a *Sängerfest* (singers' festival), at which they sang and ate sausage, sauerkraut, and potato salad and drank beer. The festivals began with parades, included dancing, and concluded with grand finales of song. An older tradition among the Germans are the *Schützenfeste,* or marksmen's festivals. These originated as archery contests in Europe several hundred years ago. They developed into shooting fairs and then folk festivals. In Texas a festival of shooting clubs includes an opening parade, competitive shooting, music, dancing, and feasting. The largest current German festival is the Wurstfest of New Braunfels, held in October and featuring German food and music.

To Czechs[qv] the Feast of the Assumption of the Virgin on August 15 has historical, religious, and ethnic value. Czechs from Moravia and Bohemia immigrated to Texas in the 1850s and established the town of Praha, where in 1890 they built a church that became the mother parish for surrounding communities. When Czechs from Central Texas gather in Praha on August 15, Mass is celebrated in the historic church, which is Czech in architectural style, Czech food is served, and Texas Czech bands play music for dancing throughout the evening.

For Italians[qv] near Bryan, St. Joseph's Day (March 19) is an annual event to honor the saint and bring Italians together. The Italian feast is primarily a domestic celebration with roots in Sicily, but in Texas it

Turkey Trot, Cuero, ca. 1912. Parks Photo, Port Lavaca. Louis Lenz Collection, CAH; CN 08007. The Turkey Trot was organized in 1912 to promote the area turkey industry, a principal source of revenue in DeWitt County throughout most of the twentieth century.

is associated with a miraculous cure in a particular family, which occurred in 1938 and is attributed to San Giuseppe.

A date of great importance to African Americans[qv] in Texas is June 19, popularly known as Juneteenth,[qv] the anniversary of the day in 1865 when Gen. Gordon Granger[qv] officially announced in Texas that slavery[qv] was ended. This day has been celebrated ever since in Texas, western Louisiana, southern Oklahoma, and southwestern Arkansas by black communities with parades, picnics, music, and sports events, especially baseball. Since 1979 Juneteenth has been an official Texas holiday. Among blacks the occasion is important for reunions and homecomings. Since it is the only specifically black festival in Texas, it serves multiple purposes and may exhibit wide variation.

On June 13 the Tigua Indians of Ysleta del Sur Pueblo, located in the mission lands of El Paso, honor their patron saint, San Antonio, in the Fiesta de San Antonio. The Tiguas built their city in the 1680s, when they moved south from their original home on the Rio Grande in northern New Mexico. On June 11 and 12, the two days preceding the fiesta, the reservation becomes the scene for intertribal Indian dances, and the pueblo holds an Indian market. The day of the fiesta is celebrated with processions, feasting, traditional dances, and a Mass, all in honor of San Antonio, whom the Tiguas associate with gods of their indigenous religion.

Among the most popular festivals based on the Texas experience are cowboy festivals—events of several days' duration that feature rodeos,[qv] barbecue, and fiddle music. In Stamford the Fourth of July is celebrated with three days of rodeo and reunion, known as the Texas Cowboy Reunion.[qv] Many individuals hold family or class reunions at the same time as the Cowboy Reunion. Festivals often honor the fruits of the land and the experience of living on the land. The Luling Watermelon Thump, a popular festival of this type, lasts several days in July and includes a watermelon auction and coronation of a queen. In deep East Texas the town of Winnsboro holds an October festival called Autumn Trails that includes trail rides, gospel singing, and evening dances.

Audiences who attend large so-called folk festivals are frequently unfamiliar with the traditions displayed or have consciously learned the music or acquainted themselves with the food of another culture. Among the most popular of the contemporary festivals is the Kerrville Folk Festival,[qv] where visitors can hear country, folk, bluegrass, and gospel music. Amateur banjo players, guitar pickers, and fiddlers are judged in competition at the Bluegrass Festival, and the winners are offered the opportunity to perform the following year. Every year the University of Texas Institute of Texan Cultures[qv] in San Antonio hosts the Texas Folklife Festival,[qv] which celebrates the many ethnic groups of Texas. Visitors can try ethnic foods such as Cajun boudin, Jewish bagels, or Czechoslovakian kolaches. Costumed musicians and dancers perform tunes and steps from Lebanon, Germany, and other nations. Other traditions demonstrated at the festival reflect pioneer life, and under a large shade tree yarn spinners captivate audiences. In the fall the Chamizal National Memorial[qv] in El Paso hosts the Border Folk Festival. Sponsored by the National Park Service, the National Council for the Traditional Arts, and the El Paso Friends of Folk Music, the festival specializes in music and dance of folk traditions around the world and presents performances on three stages.

BIBLIOGRAPHY: Richard Bauman and Roger D. Abrahams, eds.,

"*And Other Neighborly Names*": *Social Process and Cultural Image in Texas Folklore* (Austin: University of Texas Press, 1981). J. Frank Dobie, ed., *Coffee in the Gourd*, Publications of the Texas Folklore Society 2 (Dallas: Southern Methodist University, 1923). Richard Dorson, ed., *Handbook of American Folklore* (Bloomington: Indiana University Press, 1982). Victor Turner, ed., *Celebration* (Washington: Smithsonian Institution, 1982).

Beverly J. Stoeltje

FOLK GAMES. The variety and range of games played by children and young adults in Texas today and in the past reflect the familiar cultural migration patterns of Texas history as well as the creative imaginations of children. The games played by prehistoric and historic Indians are now faint outlines like the fading images of Indian rock art.[qv] The games brought by the children of the first Spanish settlers reflected a Western European culture that was later blended into mestizo culture. These games found counterparts in the games played by nineteenth-century European immigrants who came to Texas directly by sea and those who came to Texas after first stopping for a few generations on the Atlantic seaboard and in the inland Southern states. Finally, the games played by African-American children are only now being fully recognized for their unique blend of the European and the African. Games defined generally are those forms of individual or team competition, played to a decision according to agreed upon rules. They are voluntary and nonproductive and are played outside everyday reality, in their own territories by their own characters. "Folk" games are those traditional games passed along informally from one group to another. The folk games of Texas children, like the games of today, had the same functions that games have had from the beginnings of the human race: they amused, instructed, and inspired. They reflected the values and beliefs of their parent cultures. Games help small minds and imaginations mature, providing children with a chance to act out roles, make choices, and experience the thrill of winning and the disappointment of losing.

A form of hockey and "spear the hoop" were popular games among the Caddos in East Texas, as well as elsewhere. Games that developed toughness and physical endurance were especially favored by the boys. In the nineteenth century, Plains Indian boys were observed staging mock buffalo[qv] hunts, in which some of the little boys went out on stick horses to hunt other little boys who were the "buffaloes." The "buffaloes" defended themselves with prickly-pear leaves mounted on sticks. Indians played many forms of ballgames. Kickball and a simple form of field hockey were played by Plains Indian girls, and a game the French named Lacrosse was played throughout the Indian world. Indians especially loved guessing games and gambling games and developed a large number of these, which both children and adults played.

By the Middle Ages Europe and the British Isles were bound together by a set of common cultural ties, among them the games that children played. Many of these—tops, marble games, and jacks, for instance—can be traced to Greek and Roman times. Some of these games are played with rhymed formulas, often set to song, which have been handed down from generation to generation. Many are grounded in superstition, religious belief, historical events, or celebrations tied to specific times of the year. They exhibit such themes as courtship, warfare, stolen children, and the magic of numbers and prophecy. They are often built around the joys of motion and jest. They exist in numerous variations. Successive waves of immigrants from throughout Europe brought these games to the North American continent. In Texas the first European children arrived in significant numbers in the early part of the eighteenth century, when Spain began to attempt to colonize the East Texas frontier, the Rio Grande valley, and the San Antonio area. Games played by Mexican-American children in the early part of the twentieth century are a good illustration of pan-European culture. La Puerta Esta Quebrada ("The Door is Broken") is a variant of the well-known London Bridge. In both games, two children form an archway with their hands; the other children file through as a song is sung. As the song ends, the last child to file through is caught in the arch and must pay a penalty or choose between joining the side of good or evil, represented by the two arch makers. Often, after every child has been caught by the arch and has joined one side or the other, a tug-of-war ensues to determine the victor. The Germans[qv] also brought this game to Texas when they began to establish their colonies around such places as Fredericksburg. There it was called Zieh Durch. London Bridge has been traced in recognizable form to the year 1553, when it occurred simultaneously in such countries as England, Italy, and Germany. Some think it had its beginnings in an early belief that a bridge would be opposed by evil spirits and that a human sacrifice would be required to keep it from falling down. Another consistent theme in the pan-European games was the stealing of children by the devil or an old witch or a buzzard. The children of Anglo pioneers in Texas played Chickamee Craney Crow, German children played Kluck mit Heunkel ("Hen with Chickens"), and Mexican-American children played Colores, a game in which the children were assigned colors and the devil had to pay a forfeit to win the color or child desired. Variations of the familiar Hide-and-Seek (or I Spy) and Blindman's Buff were also played by Anglo, German, and Mexican-American children in Texas. These very old games were described by Julius Pollux, a Greek lexicographer, in the second century and played throughout Europe. In Fredericksburg the variation of Blindman's Buff was Blinde euch, ich Fuehre dich. Special games for certain seasons of the year were notably played by both German and Mexican-American children. Mexican Americans inherited a particular love for wordplay, with riddles, sayings, or *dichos*, as well as animal fables, favored by young and old alike.

The theme of courtship is a perennial favorite with children as well as young adults. A ring game with courtship implications played in South Texas in the early twentieth century was introduced into that area directly from Mexico. It thus illustrates the continual cultural interchange between the two areas that has taken place. In María Blanca (called Doña Blanca in Mexico), the children form a ring. A girl is chosen to represent María Blanca, who stands in the center of the circle; a toy called Jicotillo ("the Hornet") is outside the circle. The game ends with Jicotillo chasing María Blanca until he catches her. In German Fredericksburg, the girls pretend to be little birds and flutter inside a circle drawn on the ground; the boys are "buyers" and must bid for the girl they desire by handclaps. This game is called Vögel zu verkaufen ("Birds for Sale"). Jump-rope games became very popular in Texas in the first half of the twentieth century. These often have courtship themes, linked to prophecy through numbers, the numbers being functions of the number of times a girl could jump the rope without missing. Some of the rhymes are adapted from familiar verses, like the button-counting rhyme "Rich man, poor man, beggar man, thief." Newer verses expressing romantic themes include "Cinderella Dressed in Yellow" and "Ice Cream Soda, Delaware Punch." A particular favorite on the Gulf Coast was the rhyme that began "Down by the Ocean, Down by the Sea."

Very popular in frontier Texas, where strict religious precepts sometimes forbade dancing, were the ring and longways games played at play-parties, or Josey parties, a uniquely American development. Many of the songs sung at play-parties had their origins in Europe, but the words were distinctly and peculiarly American. Many of the songs have words that could have come only out of the West and South: "Shoot the Buffalo," "Wish I Was a Cowboy," and "Raise Big 'Taters in Sandy Land."

Blacks came with Southerners to Texas, mostly as slaves, occasionally as free people. They brought with them their own cultural mixture, a blend of the European with the African, developed within the conditions of slavery[qv] and rural life. Black children played and sang games from the Anglo tradition, like Chickamee Craney Crow and Lil' Liza Jane. As to be expected, many of their game songs, like those of Anglo children from the South, exhibited regional flavor, referring to raccoons in persimmon trees, collard greens, and even hangings. Although most of the black games seem to be European in origin, it is now increasingly recognized that they have been significantly modified by the strong oral traditions and the love of rhythm originating in Africa. The handclap games of black children, such as Mary Mack, Mack, Mack, exhibit more syncopated rhythms than do handclap games of white or Hispanic children, and black children show a greater willingness to experiment with sounds for their own sake. The ring games and the line games played by black children, such as Little Sally Walker, are really primarily performance games, in which the child in the middle of the ring actually puts on a dance or a mime. In this the games also reflect the heritage of African dances.

The folk games played by children in Texas have an important role to play in the development of the children. Through game playing, children act out the war between good and evil and learn moral lessons. Games instruct children in the folklore of a culture as well as in the mental and physical skills required of them as adults. They teach children about courtship and marriage, and about power and cunning and luck. They help them learn about humor. They show them how to think by solving riddles and how to make choices. And finally they are a child's outlet for often secret hopes and fears and dreams.

BIBLIOGRAPHY: Francis E. Abernethy, ed., *Texas Toys and Games* (Dallas: Southern Methodist University Press, 1989). J. Frank Dobie, Mody C. Boatright, and Harry H. Ransom, eds., *Texian Stomping Grounds* (Austin: Texas Folklore Society, 1941). Julia Estill, "Children's Games in Fredericksburg," in *Texas Folk and Folklore*, ed. Mody Boatright et al. (Dallas: Southern Methodist University Press, 1954). Rosalinda Gonzales, "Work and Play on a Border Ranch," in *The Golden Log*, ed. Mody Boatright et al. (Dallas: Southern Methodist University Press, 1962).

Martha Hartzog

FOLKLORE AND FOLKLIFE. Folklore is, in one workable and rememberable definition, the traditional knowledge of a culture. More inclusively, it is the traditional customs and beliefs, speech patterns, stories, and songs that a culture passes along informally from one group or generation to another. It must be old enough to have separated itself from its origins and must be plastic enough to be moulded by each generation to suit its needs and attitudes. The term *folklife* falls within the definition of folklore but is mainly concerned with arts and crafts, customs and traditions. The folklore of Texas is Texas folklore only because it passed through the state during the course of its eternal ramblings. Texas folklore is the heir of many cultures. Paleo–Americans and then Indians were the first to come within the state's boundaries with their cultures. The Indians' culture shock when they met the Spanish in the sixteenth century could not have been greater had the conquistadors been from another planet. In the following centuries of settlement people continued to come, with new ways of talking and believing and doing things, with their own folklore. Spanish and Mexican folklore set the patterns south of the Nueces and along the Rio Grande. Anglos crossed the Sabine and the Red rivers, bringing their ways of life from the British Isles through the Tidewater to the South and to East Texas[qv] and beyond. African Americans,[qv] brought to work the big plantations on the Brazos and Trinity bottoms, carried songs and stories and beliefs that still bore traces of Africa in them. Germans[qv] came directly from the Old World and carried their lore up the Colorado and Guadalupe rivers to the Hill Country.[qv] The Cajuns brought theirs from France to Nova Scotia, then to Louisiana and on into the Coastal Plain[qv] of Southeast Texas. The Dutch went to Nederland, the Danes[qv] to Danevang, the Poles[qv] to Panna Maria, the Czechs[qv] to Praha, the Norwegians[qv] to Norse—and they all took their own ways of life, their folklore, that had bound them together in durable communities.

This imported folklore that became Texas folklore is distinguished by five characteristics. First, folklore is passed along by word of mouth, by demonstration, or by a combination of the two. The creation myths of the Alabama-Coushatta Indians, the legends of Gregorio Cortez Lira,[qv] and the lyrics to "Weevily Wheat" were transmitted orally. The craft of quilting[qv] in the Texas Star pattern was passed along by demonstration. Learning to dance the Cotton-Eyed Joe requires both. Second, folklore is traditional. It is passed from one particular people, place, or time to another in a fixed form that maintains cultural continuity. Some East Texas deer hunters still hunt with dogs and blow horn signals that can be traced back to the Middle Ages; they blood a hunter on his first kill and cut off his shirttail (a castration substitute) when he misses an easy shot. Cowboys follow many dress and work customs of the vaquero,[qv] who was working cattle 300 years before the post–Civil War Texas cowboy was born. Third, folklore is variable and is continually being changed by those who use it. That classical "Texas" cowboy song, "Streets of Laredo," changed many times before it got to that Rio Grande town. The song had its beginning in the latter part of the eighteenth century as a broadside ballad. It was originally about an English soldier who was dying of syphilis at St. James Infirmary in London. The title of the broadside was "The Unfortunate Rake." It changed setting, characters, and cause of death in its long journey to Texas. Jack Thorp in his 1908 edition of *Songs of the Cowboys* set the song in Galveston. John A. Lomax[qv] published it in 1910 as "The Cowboy's Lament" and set it in Laredo. "The Unfortunate Rake," following another path to Texas, evolved into the classical blues song, "St. James Infirmary." Fourth, folklore is anonymous because it is passed along by those who are continually remaking it to suit their moods and needs, and authorship is lost in transmission. No one knows who invented the first dog–run houses[qv] or who first set down the words to "Shoot the Buffalo" or "Sally Goodin." And fifth, folklore is formularized, or set in traditional patterns. The pattern of threes is widespread; we read about the Three Bears, Three Little Pigs, Three Billy Goats Gruff, and the Christian and Hindu Trinities. Seven is a traditional formulaic number, as illustrated by the Seven Sisters, the days of the week, and Snow White's dwarfs. Stories are still sung to the medieval ballad stanza of "Barbara Allen" and told with a "once-upon-a-time" beginning and the youngest-is-best Cinderella theme.

Folklore is not restricted to studies of antiquities and rural life, but includes modern lore. As much folklore is promulgated by modern journalism, on college campuses, and in businesses as was by West Texas cowboys. Folklore is timeless and is as much a part of the present as it is of the past. All of the academic disciplines were at one time a part of the lore of the folk, passed along orally, traditionally, anonymously, and continually changing to fit a culture's contemporary occasions and attitudes. In mathematics the manipulation of numbers was once a priestly exercise. All of the fine arts—music, painting, sculpture—were preceded by folk arts. Drama began as imitative magic. History and literature began as stories told and handed down. Meteorology began with Zeuses and Thors and Jehovahs who controlled the below from the above. The knowledge of wheels, screws, and inclined planes became physics; and the study of the four basic elements—earth, air, fire, and water—led the way to the valence tables in chemistry. Geology was simpler when the world was flat, twice as long as it was wide, and created in 4004 B.C. Medicine began with folk cures. And anthropology, archeology, and all the social studies are studies of folklore because they deal with customs, traditions, religions, tools, and tales that the folk use together to bind themselves together in surviving communities and cultures.

Folklore is generally classified under four basic groupings: oral literature, material culture, folk custom, and performing folk arts. Oral literature includes the traditional prose narrative forms: myth, legend, and folktale. Folk songs and ballads are also in oral literature, as are riddles and proverbs. In children's folklore counting-out rhymes, jump-rope rhymes, and other game chants are in oral folk literature. Texas folk speech falls under this heading and includes three major American dialects—Southern Mountain, Deep South, and Southwestern—as well as folk naming and regional vocabularies. This does not take into account the speech and vocabularies of blacks, Hispanics, and two dozen (at least) other ethnic groups. Material culture includes Texas arts and crafts: the pots the Caddos made, Spanish ironwork, Mexican horsehair bridles and lariats, and furniture styles brought from the Old World and modified in the New. Texas material culture includes children's toys, yard art and distinctive mail boxes, clothes made out of the materials at hand, and foods cooked from what was in the pantry or the garden. Material culture includes all the log, rock, and adobe[qv] houses that Texans built, the rugs they crocheted, and the bowls that they carved. Folk social customs include group activities that are performed usually to bind a group together. Celebrating Texas Independence Day and all the other specially observed days of the year keeps us surviving as one people. Modern berry picking, fox hunting, and trot lining apply the social cement to the participating group as did old-time barn raising, log rolling, or corn husking. The games that children play—One-eyed Cat, Wolf Over the River, marbles, tops, and knife games—are traditional. The formalities of religions—marriages, christenings, rites of passage from one religious or age state to another, funerals—are the traditions that tie groups and generations together. Dogwood, Black-Eyed Pea, Rose festivals; the Texas Folklife Festival;[qv] *Schützenfeste*, Juneteenth,[qv] and Cinco de Mayo: these are a few of the folk social customs that hold groups together. Folk performing arts include those activities that people do for their own and others' entertainment. Folk songs, the words of which are part of oral literature, becomes performed folk art when they are sung for the satisfaction of an audience or for personal pleasure. Square dances, Josey parties, and all the forms of round dancing are kinds of performed art. Folk drama[qv] is performed for an audience; religious folk drama is performed for the church and God and an audience. Often the categories overlap. Folk drama—the *Matachines*,[qv] for example—is a performed art using oral literature, with material-cultural masks and costumes, and acted out as a periodic social custom. Most folklore, when in use, becomes a natural part of life, rather than a classified part of folklore. Classification is for purposes of study.

The study of folklore in Texas was begun when travelers such as Frederick Law Olmsted[qv] and Nat Taylor commented incidentally on their observations of Texas life. Reminiscences of early Texas by Noah Smithwick and John C. Duval[qqv] are invaluable carriers of accounts of Texas folklore. Serious academic preservation and publication of Texas folklore began with the founding of the Texas Folklore Society[qv] in 1909. The Center for Intercultural Studies in Folklore and Ethnomusicology at the University of Texas, founded in 1967, now offers degrees in folklore. And the University of Texas Institute of Texan Cultures[qv] at San Antonio, founded in 1968, provides a museum of Texas folklore and culture and an annual Texas Folklife Festival, which is a celebration of the folklore of the many ethnic groups that settled Texas. The folklore of this land is rich with the variety of its people. All colors, shades, and kinds have mingled with the flow and have made their languages, customs, and cultures into the state we call Texas. *See also other articles beginning with* FOLK, *articles on ethnic and Indian groups, and* ARCHITECTURE, CURANDERISMO, DIALECTS, FIESTAS PATRIAS, LITERATURE, MEXICAN-AMERICAN FOLK ARTS AND CRAFTS, *and* TEX-MEX FOODS.

BIBLIOGRAPHY: Francis Edward Abernethy and Dan Beaty, eds., *The Folklore of Texan Cultures* (Austin: Encino, 1974). Francis E. Abernethy, "The Universality of Folklore," in *Introduction to Folklore* (Nacogdoches: Stephen F. Austin State University Press, 1983). James T. Bratcher, *Analytical Index to Publications of the Texas Folklore Society, Volumes 1–36* (Dallas: Southern Methodist University, 1973). Jan Harold Brunvand, *The Study of American Folklore: An Introduction*, 2d ed. (1978). Richard M. Dorson, ed., *Folklore and Folklife: An Introduction* (Chicago: University of Chicago Press, 1972).

Francis E. Abernethy

FOLK MEDICINE. Folk medical beliefs and practices differ from culture to culture in Texas but have in common the process by which they are passed on—from person to person and generation to generation by word of mouth and imitation. Though most Texans have come to rely almost entirely on official medicine, others have continued to rely to a greater or lesser degree on folk medicine. These have maintained their beliefs and practices as a coherent system, rather than a seemingly unrelated collection of remedies, cures, and preventives.

Though Indian concepts of illness and cure varied from group to group, most ascribed some serious illnesses to deities, tribal enemies, or the maleficence of spirits. Tonkawas, for example, believed that spirits of the dead, particularly if not properly buried, would haunt those responsible and bring illnesses and other misfortunes upon them. One entering an area haunted by such spirits would soon die, and if a dead relative called to you in a dream, your days were numbered. By wearing small bags of herbs and roots next to the body, one could ward off bad spirits, which often took the form of owls or wolves, and the illnesses they could cause. This category of illness required the services of the medicine man, or shaman, whose office seems to have existed in every Indian group. The medicine man, an important man in the tribe, used divination and trances in diagnosing illnesses and relied on exorcisms, chanting, religious ceremonies, and supernatural powers in treating them. He also administered herbal remedies, sweat baths, and suction to remove objects thought to be supernaturally injected into his patients. The Apaches, who attributed much illness to malevolent spirits, used singing, drumming, applying amulets, the laying on of hands, and incantations to placate or expel these powerful forces. Texas Indians also used nonsupernatural remedies. The Comanches, for example, had knowledge of the tourniquet and simple surgery and were quite effective in treating such injuries as broken bones and gunshot wounds. They gave a wide assortment of herbs and other medicines to treat illnesses. Herbal remedies included castor oil and euphorbia as purgatives, sassafras for pleurisy, and alder bark as a dressing for wounds. The Apaches used jalap, cinchona, guaiacum, peyote, and lobelia. Natchez Indian remedies included the red seed of the magnolia as a febrifuge, the wood of acacia for toothache, and *Chaparrola margosa* for amebic dysentery. Comanche snakebite remedies included oral suction, poultices of such plants as snakeroot, alder bark, and peyote, and the application of a piece of the biting snake to the snakebite.

Most cures and remedies in Anglo-Texan folk medicine reveal the practitioners as pragmatic folk who relied on whatever was available at hand to treat illnesses. Their home remedies included common household items—soda, coal oil, kerosene, sugar, whiskey, vinegar, turpentine, soot from wood stoves—to supplement the meager pharmacopoeia of paregoric, sulfur, alum, Epsom salt, camphor, asafetida, and medicinal plants like mullein, pennyroyal, anise, oregano, horehound, senna, sassafras, and other native roots, barks, and leaves. Mud plasters soothed and relieved the pain of insect bites and stings; vinegar soothed sunburn. A number of white Texans' medical beliefs and practices are survivals or vestiges of a more primitive European past. For example, they used sympathetic or contagious magic to transfer illness to another person, to animals, to plants, or even to objects. One might get rid of a crick in the neck by rubbing the afflicted neck where a hog had rubbed its neck. Most wart remedies involve sympathetic magic: rub a wart with a slice of potato or stolen dishrag, bury the object, and as it rots the wart will disappear. Asthma may be cured by keeping a "Mexican hairless" Chihuahua dog in the house—the dog gets the asthma. Rattlesnake bites may be treated by killing a chicken and wrapping the warm body around the bite to draw the poison out. Magical words, formulae, incantations, and amulets were thought to be curative. Styes could be removed by recitation of the rhyme "Sty, sty, leave my eye; catch the first one passing by." Rubbing them with a gold wedding band would also work. Copper bracelets were worn as a cure for

Curandera (Faith Healer), by Carmen Lomas Garza. Oil on linen mounted on wood. 24″ × 32″. Photograph by Wolfgang Dietze. Collection of the Mexican Museum, San Francisco, California. Courtesy Carmen Lomas Garza. This portrayal of a curandera *draws on the artist's South Texas childhood and includes a can with copal incense at the foot of the bed and a home altar with a figurine that may be Don Pedrito Jaramillo, a legendary South Texas* curandero.

rheumatism. A lead fishing sinker was worn on a string around the neck to cure nosebleeds. An ax was put under the bed to "cut" labor pains. Folk healers played an important role in such folk medicine. Certain people—particularly seventh sons of seventh sons—were presumed to have power to cure warts, to stop bleeding, to relieve burns, and treat other maladies. Usually, the healer touched or rubbed the afflicted spot while uttering a secret verse or reading a passage from the Bible, and the afflicted person was cured. Another important folk practitioner in early Texan culture was the midwife, who received her training and knowledge through the traditional folk process of apprenticeship. Midwives are still used by some people and are gaining acceptance as part of the medical establishment.

Texas-Mexican folk beliefs and practices constitute a coherent, logically consistent system in which theories of etiology and treatment correspond with social and religious beliefs. Illnesses may be divided into two major classes, *mal natural* (natural illness) and *mal puesto* (illness caused by Satanic powers under the control of witches). Natural illnesses may be the result of sin, of excess indulgence, or of excess anger or admiration. Many Mexican Americans[qv] rely on the intercession of the Virgin Mary and the saints to cure natural illnesses and control the devil's powers. Folk illnesses include *susto*, fright or terror usually treated by "sweeping" with "brooms" made of special plants and herbs; and *empacho*, timidity or incapacity ascribed to blockage of the digestive tract and treated with massages and herbal potions. *Mal de ojo* is a syndrome associated with the English term "evil eye." It occurs when someone looks at a weaker person with excess admiration, and its treatment includes prayers and rubbing with a chicken egg. *Caída de la mollera*, sinking of a baby's fontanel or soft spot, an often fatal illness, is treated by such practices as holding the child upside down over a container of water or rubbing the roof of its mouth. Many less serious illnesses such as nosebleed, headache, and stomach ache are treated with household remedies, often made from herbs. They number in the hundreds and include such remedies as *yerba buena* tea for stomachaches, aloe vera for burns, and a number of other illnesses. Folk medicine for minor ailments is usually in the charge of the mother, grandmother, or aunt in an extended family. More serious illnesses, including those noted above, are usually treated by a semiprofessional medical practitioner, usually called simply *la señora*. Midwives remain popular in many areas and often become local neighborhood healers. *Sobadores* (massagers or folk chiropractors) treat bruises and sprains and set broken bones. The healer par excellence in the culture is the *curandero*, who receives power to heal as a sacred gift from God and is the sole source of treatment for *brujería* (witchcraft), though the local priest might also be consulted. Attitudes vary toward the two competing medical systems. Even in the same family some members favor institutionalized medicine, and others stick more with the folk system.

Black folk medical beliefs and practices in Texas, derived from

African and European folk medicine, consist of home remedies, herbal remedies prescribed by root doctors, and treatments administered by conjurers. Home remedies, the most common form of folk medicine today, were once used to treat the majority of illnesses not likely to be fatal. Many of the remedies reveal the practicality of rural African Americans,[qv] who used what was at hand to treat their maladies. The cures included catnip tea for colic, garlic, Epsom salt, and vinegar for high blood pressure, corn-shuck tea and ice water for measles, tallow on a flannel cloth warmed and put on the chest to relieve congestion, redroot tea for stomach pain, honey and apple cider for arthritis, and honey and alum for coughs. Bee stings were treated with snuff to ease pain and draw out the poison, bleeding from cuts was stopped with soot from the stove, snakebites were soaked in kerosene. Some remedies required faith, since the logic of the treatment was not apparent: placing a broomstraw on top of a baby's head cured the hiccups; in case of nail puncture, the nail was driven into the chimney to keep down soreness and prevent lockjaw; a dime under the upper lip, or scissors or keys hung down the back of the neck, stopped a nosebleed; tea made from dirtdauber nests helped to induce labor; carrying a buckeye in the pocket helped rheumatism. Another important concept of illness—particularly life-threatening illness—was inherited from African ancestors and mixed with popular beliefs of whites. Some blacks of earlier days attributed sudden deaths, especially those accompanied by delirium, to witchcraft or voodoo. Death was often thought of in terms of the soul leaving the body, and many taboos surrounded the treatment of dying or dead people. If offended, the spirits of the dead might return to cause great mischief. One took special care to avoid contact with ghosts, using both disguise and such propitiations as gifts or flattery. Proper burial procedures, however, would prevent the restless dead from haunting the living. Witchcraft, the use of spiritual power for evil purposes, was thought to be responsible for a great number of life-threatening illnesses. Witches, having sold their souls to Satan, were believed to inherit a number of supernatural powers with which they could plague man. The most serious illnesses, particularly those thought to be of supernatural origin, were treated by all-powerful "root doctors" or conjurers, descendants of the African medicine man with his supernatural powers. Such painful and bothersome but usually nonfatal illnesses as boils and constipation, as well as such maladies as insanity, ill luck in courting, and sudden or unexplainable calamity, were sometimes thought to be a result of witchcraft. One could get protection from witchcraft through charms and through the ministrations of conjurers. *See also* CURANDERISMO.

BIBLIOGRAPHY: John Q. Anderson, *Texas Folk Medicine* (Austin: Encino, 1970). Joe S. Graham, "Folk Medicine and Intracultural Diversity among West Texas Mexican Americans," *Western Folklore* 44 (1985). Newbell Niles Puckett, *Folk Beliefs of the Southern Negro* (Chapel Hill: University of North Carolina Press, 1926). Eliseo Torres, *Green Medicine: Traditional Mexican-American Herbal Remedies* (Kingsville, Texas: Nieves Press, 1983). Virgil J. Vogel, *American Indian Medicine* (Norman: University of Oklahoma Press, 1970).

Joe S. Graham

FOLK MUSIC. Folk music is tunes, beats, and songs that usually originated in the forgotten or dimly remembered past and have been passed from one generation to the next down to the present. It exists in the forms of tunes, songs, and ballads. Folk tunes are traditional melodies such as those played by fiddlers. Folk songs are melodies with accompanying verses. Ballads are folk songs that tell stories. Some folk music is utilitarian; that is, it accompanies an activity such as work, worship, or dance. Other folk music exists just for the stories it tells or the feelings it expresses. Texas folk music is "Texas" only because it passed through the state during the course of its transmission. Its traditional nature means that it was played or sung long before being brought to Texas.

John Lomax. John Avery Lomax Family Papers, CAH; CN 00343. Raised on a branch of the Chisholm Trail, Lomax began collecting cowboy and other folksongs in his youth and published his first compilation in 1910. He later helped establish the Archive of Folksong at the Library of Congress.

There are as many varieties of folk music in Texas as there are cultures that came to Texas. Anglo-Texan folk music, the dominant strain, has taken the forms of tunes, songs, and ballads. Much of the history of Texas is accompanied by folk music. "Shoot the Buffalo" and "Texas Boys" describe early attitudes toward settling Texas. "The Greer County Bachelor" and "Little Old Sod Shanty" tell of life on the Texas frontier. "Buffalo Skinners" is the story of the rigors of a buffalo hunt in the 1870s, and "The Old Chisholm Trail" describes the life of the Texas trail-driving cowboy of the same period. According to tradition, Texans marched into battle at San Jacinto to the tune of "Will You Come to the Bower?" They fought the Mexicans again in 1846, to the sweet strains of "Green Grow the Lilacs." Fifteen years later Hood's Texas Brigade[qv] marched off to the Civil War[qv] to the "Yellow Rose of Texas." "Texas Rangers" was a song about one of that heroic group's early adventurers, and "Sam Bass" was a ballad about the other side of the law. Later events such as the Galveston hurricane of 1900,[qv] the Dust Bowl and Great Depression,[qqv] and the Kennedy assassination[qv] were memorialized in folk songs. Now, however, topical folk songs have generally lost out to news media and copyrighted popular music.

In Texas, as elsewhere, children's songs fall into two categories, songs sung to children and songs sung by children. The first song a child usually hears is a lullaby like "Babes in the Woods," sung to the child to put it to sleep. Then children are patty-caked, bounced, and counted to in chants and songs whose purpose is to entertain. These simple songs and later more complicated traditional songs, such as "Froggie Went a-Courtin'" and "Fox Is on the Town," are sung to children. The songs sung by children are simple and basic. They begin with simple game songs like "London Bridge," grow to elaborate jump-rope chants and songs, and conclude with such crudities as "The Monkey Wrapped His Tail Around the Flagpole." Perhaps the last realization of children's songs is the fraternity-party song.

Love has spawned a world of songs and ballads that have made their ways into the Texas repertoire. The most venerable of these were Child's ballads, so called after Francis James Child's *English and Scottish Popular Ballads* (1882–98). Two of the best known of these in Texas were "Barbara Allen" and "Fair Eleanor." Both of these ballads told stories of love affairs that ended in death. Many other English ballads not blessed with the stamp of Child's approval came to Texas. These included "My Horses Ain't Hungry," "Roving Gambler," and "Little Sparrow." Most Anglo-Saxon love songs, including "Wildwood Flower," "Fond Affection," and "Columbus Stockade Blues," relate in some way to the Old World. "Careless Love" is an Anglo response to the black blues tradition. Such love ballads as "Rosewood Casket" and "Bury Me Beneath the Willow" filtered down into the folk idiom from Tin Pan Alley. Though these late-nineteenth-century weepers were not authentic folk music, they became a much-loved part of the singing traditions of Texas.

One of the most popular forms of folk music on the Texas frontier was square-dance music with a lead fiddle. The tunes played were old jigs and reels and hornpipes that were ancient in the British Isles when the settlers first came to the New World. Many of the tunes, like "Irish Washerwoman," "The Campbells are Coming," and "Sailor's Hornpipe," stayed close to their originals. Most underwent subtle and gradual changes as they were passed along from one fiddler and generation and area to another, and now only a hint of their Old World ancestry remains. Most of the early dancing was group dancing, for which a leader called the steps and patterns while the music was being played. Sometimes fiddle tunes became songs when lyrics were thrown in between calls. In the evolution of some fiddle-dance songs—"Sally Goodin," "Cindy," "Cotton-Eyed Joe," and "Old Joe Clark," for instance—the calls were dropped and the words became almost as important as the tunes. Fiddlers took their tunes and songs from everywhere, but their richest source during the nineteenth century was black minstrelsy, where they found the classic "Arkansas Traveler," "Turkey in the Straw," "Buffalo Gals," and "Old Dan Tucker." The purest of old-time fiddle music can best be found nowadays at fiddle contests held all over Texas, for instance at the annual Crockett World's Champion Fiddlers' Contests held on the second Friday of June. Some of the favorite tunes played there and at other Texas contests are "Billy in the Low Ground," "Sally Johnson," "Durang's Hornpipe," "Devil's Dream," and "Tom and Jerry." Such fiddling dance music as that played by Bob (James Robert) Wills[qv] and Milton Brown in the 1930s became modern country and western music.

Another folk song-and-dance tradition is the play party. Many early Texas settlers were fundamentalists who believed that dancing and fiddle music were sinful. They satisfied the universal urge to move to music with the play party, which was song-accompanied dance that allowed no instruments. They called their rhythmical group movements "marches" or "games," they danced in rings or in longways formations but never in squares, and they swung each other by hand, never by the waist. They used many popular dance tunes—"Old Clark," "Old Dan Tucker," "The Gal I Left Behind Me," "Willis Ballroom"—but because of the lack of instrumental music, the words became all-important. Play-party songs have preserved many stanzas that were lost in the fiddle-dance tradition. A play party usually began with a choosing game such as "Needle's Eye" or "Hog Drovers," then progressed to ring-game songs like "Saro Jane" or "Coffee Grows on White Oak Trees," and in full swing went into longways dances like "Weevily Wheat," "Little Brass Wagon," and "Baltimore." Play parties were not only popular among fundamentalists; they were necessary when no musician was around. In spite of the reservations laid on the players by their elders, play-party songs and formations were just as joyful and exuberant as their sinful fiddling square-dance counterparts.

One of the richest veins in Texas folk music is its religious strain, and the particular kind to which the state owes the most is Sacred Harp music,[qv] named after B. F. White's 1844 songbook, *Sacred Harp*. The tunes and words in this book, still much used in Texas, go back to the Great Revival on the southern frontier at the turn of the nineteenth century, then beyond to the British Isles. Southern preachers found themselves with vast congregations and no songs, so they took familiar popular tunes and put religious words to them. A ballad about Captain Kidd the pirate became "Wondrous Love," and "Auld Lang Syne" became "Hark! From the Tomb." Music in this tradition also employed easily remembered single lines and repeated refrains, in which substitutions of words prolonged the song and increased its intensity. "We Have Fathers Over Yonder," with its simple refrain "Over yonder ocean," could continue as long as substitutions could be made for "fathers." The same was true with the song that began, "You [or "Father," "Mother," "Jesus," etc.] got to walk that lonesome valley." A final influence on Sacred Harp singing was the eighteenth-century singing schools that taught shaped notation. Because it is written in the shaped notes called, since medieval times, fa, sol, la, etc., Sacred Harp music is also called fasola music. The fasola tradition and the "fuguing tunes," whose counterpoint and joyful play of rounds was popular with early singing masters, lost their popularity in the East but became a vehicle for religious enthusiasm in the South and an integral part of Sacred Harp singing, which often lasted all day and was accompanied with "dinner on the grounds." A modern outgrowth of early Sacred Harp is Gospel music.[qv] It is livelier than Sacred Harp, more concerned with the play of tune and tempo, and more optimistic in tone. It started to develop at the beginning of the twentieth century and culminated in 1926 with the founding in Dallas of the Stamps-Baxter Music Company. Stamps-Baxter music used the idioms of jazz[qv] and popular music and incorporated most modern instrumentation. All-day gospel singing can be found in just about any county in Texas on any weekend. It is a religious folk-music form that is still growing.

Though cowboy songs were sung all across the cow-country frontier of the United Sates, these folk songs and ballads are still most closely associated with Texas. The Texas cowboy originated in the 1860s and 1870s, when cattlemen began trailing herds to the newly established railheads in Kansas. His skills were derived from the vaquero,[qv] his Spanish and Mexican forbear, who had been working large herds for 300 years. The cowboys' mores were Southern. Many men left their Southern homes after the surrender at Appomattox to start again in Texas, and they brought with them the hymns, minstrel songs, and sentimental ballads that were their tradition. Some of the old songs were rewritten to fit the new way of life. "Little Old Log Cabin" furnished the tune for "Little Joe the Wrangler." An old song about a dying English soldier became "The Streets of Laredo." The sad tale of a sailor buried at sea became "Bury Me Not on the Lone Prairie," and "My Bonnie Lies Over the Ocean" furnished the tune for "The Cowboy's Dream." Some cowboy songs exist in differing versions, one traditional and one written. D. J. O'Malley claimed "When the Work's All Done This Fall," and Jack Thorp wrote "Little Joe the Wrangler." Both men put their lyrics to tunes already traditionally circulating. In the 1930s, cowboy songs and the cowboy mystique formed the basis for western swing, which was the primary antecedent of modern country-and-western music.

Country-and-western music, the modern heir to traditional Texas folk music, incorporates both the earthy themes of traditional music and the elemental three-chord sounds. Country-and-western bands also regularly include such folk classics as "Cotton-Eyed Joe," "Wildwood Flower," and "Careless Love" in their repertoires. Commercial country music, which developed in the 1920s, combined Anglo folk music, old-time religion, and elements of nineteenth-century show business. *See also* AFRICAN AMERICANS, CZECHS, GERMAN MUSIC, BLUES, *CORRIDOS*, MUSICA NORTEÑA, FOLK FESTIVALS, MILTON BROWN AND HIS MUSICAL BROWNIES, *and* FUNDAMENTALISM.

BIBLIOGRAPHY: Francis Edward Abernethy, *Singin' Texas* (Dallas: E-Heart Press, 1983). John A. and Alan Lomax, *Cowboy Songs and Other Frontier Ballads* (New York: Sturgis and Walton, 1910; rev. ed., New York: Macmillan, 1945). Bill C. Malone, *Country Music U.S.A.* (Austin: University of Texas Press, 1968). William A. Owens, *Swing and Turn: Texas Play-Party Games* (Dallas: Tardy, 1936). William A. Owens, *Tell Me a Story, Sing Me a Song* (Austin: University of Texas Press, 1983). William A. Owens, *Texas Folk Songs,* Publications of the Texas Folklore Society 23 (Austin: Texas Folklore Society, 1950; 2d ed., Dallas: Southern Methodist University Press, 1976).

Francis E. Abernethy

FOLK NARRATIVE. In the range of Texas folk prose narrative, *myth, legend,* and *tale* keep the same meanings they have in worldwide folklore studies. In their natural state, examples of these genres are communicated mainly by word of mouth in differing versions within groups of people. They might be quite long or as brief as a single anecdote. True myths, rare in American folklore except among the Indians, are prose narratives of supernatural or religious content meant often to explain the origin of life, geographical features, or natural phenomena. The mythology of the Lipan Apaches of the Texas South Plains includes a culture hero, Killer-of-Enemies. During his stay among the mortals, he killed men's foes, created deer, horses, and other animals, and taught Lipans all they knew, including warfare and raiding. Among Caucasian Americans a few spurious Indian myths circulate, such as the explanation of how Twin Sisters, a mountain near Alpine, came to be. Two Indian girls quarreled and the Great Spirit turned them into a mountain as punishment. Mythic elements are sometimes present in legends and in tales such as the story of how God, having created the world, took dominion over most of it but gave Texas to the devil.

A legend purports to be a historical account of events and persons in the remote or recent past. Regardless of its content, it is told as truth or believable rumor. Many legends include supernatural details, and most Texas communities, like communities everywhere, have their own accounts of local people caught up in eerie doings at a nearby haunted house or graveyard. Witchcraft may be involved, as in the Waco legend of a cotton-gin worker who cut off the head of an attacking cat, only to return home and find his wife decapitated. Often such a story becomes a localized legend. A very common one of these tells of a farmer or rancher "just a few miles from here" who died of a rattlesnake bite. Afterward, one or more of his sons died because the snake's fangs were left in the inherited boots. A more recent urban legend states that Houston sewers are infested with alligators that breed after being flushed down toilets and live on white marijuana that grows in the dark. Sometimes this legend is used to warn children not to play in storm drains. Personal legends include anecdotes of local persons or the teller's own family. They may tell, for instance, of a local simpleton or skinflint such as the dying rancher who arranged to have a telephone installed in his coffin so that he could carry on his business. Some books are devoted to Texas folk place names with their legends, others to legends of treasures and lost mines from the Gulf Coast to the Panhandle.[qv] Historical legends about actual persons and events claim to relate regional history, sometimes that of a great white buffalo, an oil strike, a killing, or an outlaw, and often with violent contests for revenge or ownership of property. These sometimes evolve into lengthy cycles of legends, or sagas, about the same persons and general theme. One cycle is about the supposed quarter-century conflict over the ownership of the Fort Leaton trading post and other lands near Presidio. One legend in the cycle says that in the late 1840s Ben Leaton lured a large number of Indians to a barbecue in the fort, then massacred them with a concealed cannon. This legend seems an alteration of an actual event of 1837, when Leaton was in New Mexico with a scalp-hunting party led by John Johnson, who perpetrated a massacre. In a newly settled country, historical records help folklorists observe the vernacular legend-building process. Additionally, historical legends give the historian clues to follow in searching for facts.

A tale for entertainment is not usually meant to convey facts, though it is sometimes told to dupe the listener. Texas folk narrative is replete with such animal tales as that about the hunting dog that drives quail into a prairie-dog hole and releases them one at a time with a forepaw; with fables and magic tales for children, especially in the Mexican-American tradition; with Aggie jokes, simpleton tales adapted to students and professors of Texas A&M University; with stories about oil-rich "shirt-sleeve millionaires"; with stories in dialect, especially that of blacks, Mexicans, or European immigrants ("Throw dot hoss over der fence some hay"); or with punning jokes about white Texan speech: "She's some doll." "Yeah, a crocodoll."

The tall tale has been the special object of serious study by Texas folklorists James Frank Dobie and Mody Coggin Boatright.[qv] As Dobie observes, the Texas tall tale has changed in nature since 1940. Earlier Texas humor "bragged on the worst." Instead of cutting out a longhorn from the thick brush of South Texas, for instance, a cowboy gave up and rode away when he saw a rattlesnake try to crawl into the brush and have to back out. "Now," says Dobie, "we are veering rapidly to the California style of bragging," as "so many Texans... have felt called upon to justify their Texan pride." The Texan of Dobie's time modestly explains to a New York friend that though his forty acres is not a ranch and has no brand or name, "some people call it downtown Houston." Boatright calls "tall lying" an art. The tall tale is made up of authentic details rather than generalized exaggeration, and these details are ludicrous in their combination. It includes such circumstantial detail as names, places, and tangential facts. In structure, "it begins plausibly and builds carefully to a climax, and the narrative must not topple until the climax is reached." One tall tale relates that at his noon break on a hot autumn day of knocking cornstalks, a farmer went for a swim in the creek. As he dived in, the southwest wind dried up all the water. Before he crashed on the rocks, a flash flood filled the creek up again. Before he could come up, he was trapped as a sudden blue norther[qv] froze the surface. But he didn't drown because the sun came out to melt the ice, and the farmer climbed onto the bank with no injury besides a sunburn.

BIBLIOGRAPHY: Richard Bauman and Roger D. Abrahams, eds., *"And Other Neighborly Names": Social Process and Cultural Image in Texas Folklore* (Austin: University of Texas Press, 1981). Mody C. Boatright, *Folk Laughter on the American Frontier* (1961). James T. Bratcher, *Analytical Index to Publications of the Texas Folklore Society, Volumes 1–36* (Dallas: Southern Methodist University, 1973). John Mason Brewer, *Dog Ghosts and Other Negro Folktales* (Austin: University of Texas Press, 1957). John Mason Brewer, *The Word on the Brazos: Negro Preacher Tales from the Brazos Bottoms of Texas* (Austin: University of Texas Press, 1953). Jan Harold Brunvand, *The Study of American Folklore: An Introduction,* 2d ed. (1978). J. Frank Dobie, *The Longhorns* (Boston: Little, Brown, 1941; rpt., Austin: University of Texas Press, 1980). Wayland D. Hand, *American Folk Legend: A Symposium* (Berkeley: University of California Press, 1971). Stan Hoig, *The Humor of the American Cowboy* (1958). Elton Miles, *Tales of the Big Bend* (College Station: Texas A&M University Press, 1976). Patrick B. Mullen, *I Heard the Old Fisherman Say: Folklore of the Texas Gulf Coast* (Austin: University of Texas Press, 1978). William W. Newcomb, *The Indians of Texas* (Austin: University of Texas Press, 1961). Américo Paredes, *With His Pistol in His Hand: A Border Ballad and Its Hero* (Austin: University of Texas Press, 1958). University of Texas

Folklore Archives, Barker Texas History Center, University of Texas at Austin. *Elton Miles*

FOLLETS ISLAND. Follets Island, a peninsula, is across San Luis Pass to the southwest of Galveston Island in southern Brazoria County (at 29°03′ N, 95°10′ W). The peninsula is bordered by the Gulf of Mexico to the east and Christmas Bay to the west. It was formerly known as the Velasco Peninsula, and the north end has been joined with what was formerly San Luis Island. Follets Island protects Christmas Bay and Mud and Moodys islands from the storms and tides of the Gulf of Mexico.

FOLLETT, WILLIAM W. (1856–1915). William W. Follett, engineer, the son of William T. and Julia Merrill Follett, was born at New Sharon, Maine, on September 22, 1856. He graduated in civil engineering from the University of Michigan in 1881 and received his masters in engineering there in 1914. From 1897 to 1900 and again from 1902 to 1914 he served as construction engineer for the International Boundary Commission (*see* INTERNATIONAL BOUNDARY AND WATER COMMISSION) of the United States and Mexico. From 1906 to 1914 he was a construction engineer with the United States Reclamation Service in the drainage of the Rio Grande. Follett was also construction engineer for several private irrigation qv projects. He married Helen Jordan on June 13, 1888. He made his home in El Paso, where he died on December 28, 1915.

BIBLIOGRAPHY: *Who Was Who in America*, Vol. 1.

FOLLETT, TEXAS. Follett, on State Highway 15 in northeastern Lipscomb County, was established in 1917 by Santa Fe railroad official Thomas C. Spearman as a townsite on the North Texas and Santa Fe Railway. It was named for Horace Follett, a locating engineer for the line. The town boomed almost overnight, as the citizens of Ivanhoe, Oklahoma, moved their homes and businesses across the state line to the new railroad. In 1917 Follett acquired a post office, and by 1920, when the town was incorporated, its population had grown to 550. The Farmer's Grain Cooperative soon made Follett a wheat and grain sorghum storage and distribution center and helped give rise to its nickname, "Gateway to the Golden Spread." By 1940 the town reported thirty businesses and a population of 431. During the 1980s the area produced grain and cattle. Beginning in the 1950s it also produced oil and gas. Modern irrigation techniques aided agriculture. In 1980 Follett reported thirty-seven businesses and a population of 547. In 1990 its population was estimated at 441.

BIBLIOGRAPHY: *A History of Lipscomb County, Texas, 1876–1976* (Lipscomb, Texas: Lipscomb County Historical Survey Committee, 1976). *H. Allen Anderson*

FOLSOM, MARIANA THOMPSON (1845–1910). Mariana Folsom, Universalist minister, lecturer, and reform activist, was born on July 30, 1845, in Pennsylvania, probably in the Borough of Sunbury, Northumberland County, the daughter of merchant S. N. and Susan O. Thompson. The family moved to Mount Pleasant, Iowa, sometime between 1857 and 1860. After her high school education in Mount Pleasant, Mariana received a degree from St. Lawrence University in Canton, New York. Although of Quaker background, she became a Universalist minister. In 1871 she married Allan Perez Folsom, who listed himself as a crockery merchant in 1880, an abstracter in 1898, and a lawyer in 1900. By 1879 Mariana was a state lecturer of the Iowa Woman Suffrage Association, living in Marshalltown, Iowa. The family moved to Texas in 1881 following a lecture tour there; the Folsoms lived in San Antonio and Edna before settling in Austin between 1898 and 1900. They had four children. Mariana Folsom was a leader in the National American Woman Suffrage Association and asked Lucy Stone in 1885 for assistance in establishing a state suffrage society. The resulting Texas Equal Rights Association qv was established in 1893. Mrs. Folsom also corresponded with Susan B. Anthony and Elisabet Ney; qv she arranged for the latter to appear before a Texas House of Representatives committee and request the ballot for women. She was also a member of the Universal Peace Union and the state Woman's Christian Temperance Union. qv She died before March 26, 1910.

BIBLIOGRAPHY: Austin *American-Statesman*, January 1, 1968. A. Elizabeth Taylor, *Citizens at Last: The Woman Suffrage Movement in Texas* (Austin: Temple, 1987). *Tony Black*

FOLSOM CHAPEL, TEXAS. Folsom Chapel, also known as Folsom, is on Farm Road 2026 six miles northwest of Center in northwestern Shelby County. It was established around 1880 and named for a pioneer family. In 1903 it had a one-room, one-teacher school for thirty-three white students. By 1938 the community school had expanded to include four teachers and 115 students. The local district also operated a school nearby for thirty-three black students. By 1946 both schools had closed. In the late 1980s Folsom Chapel had widely scattered residences and a church, a cemetery, and a business.
Cecil Harper, Jr.

FOLSOM, ALFRED IVERSON (1883–1946). Alfred I. Folsom, pioneer urologist, son of Dr. Alfred Iverson and Mary Frances (Powell) Folsom, was born on May 9, 1883, in McGregor, Texas. After his preliminary education in McGregor and Waxahachie, he obtained a bachelor of arts degree from Southwestern University in Georgetown, followed by a degree in medicine from Southwestern Medical College (now the University of Texas Southwestern Medical School at Dallas) in 1908. The first two years after medical school, he practiced general medicine in Alba, Texas. Subsequently, he acquired specialty training at the Mayo Clinic in New York in what was then the new surgical specialty of urology under the guidance of the eminent surgeon William F. Braasch.

In 1913 Folsom began a practice in urology that became busy enough to require the services of numerous assistants. After training with Dr. Folsom, many of these assistants became distinguished urologists throughout the Southwest. Folsom held numerous clinical appointments, including professor of urology at Baylor University College of Medicine in Dallas. He was also chief of the Department of Urology at Parkland Hospital in Dallas, where he was on the staff for thirty years.

In 1916 Folsom was listed in the membership of the Texas Surgical Society as the state's only urologist. He founded the Dallas Southern Clinical Society in 1919 and is credited with starting the first urology training program in Texas, at Southwestern Medical College. He was also one of the nine organizers of the American Board of Urology, which oversees the board certification of all urologists in the United States. As a result of his dynamic and exciting lectures, Folsom was frequently sought as a guest speaker. His role was pivotal in altering urology from the undeveloped genitourinary surgery of the early twentieth century into an independent surgical specialty.

On October 3, 1946, after becoming the only Texan to hold the office of president of the American Urological Association, Folsom was killed in an automobile accident outside Dallas. He was survived by his wife, Erma, and three children. Folsom was a Methodist.

BIBLIOGRAPHY: Dallas *Morning News*, October 4, 1946. *Texas State Journal of Medicine*, December 1946. *William D. Steers*

FONCINE, TEXAS. Foncine is near Farm Road 720 five miles west of McKinney in west central Collin County. The community was named for Foncine Fisher, the daughter of R. C. Fisher, the owner of the community's gristmill, gin, grain elevator, and general store. The community was settled in the early 1890s and had a post office from 1895 to 1901, when the mail sent to McKinney. In 1900 Foncine had 100 residents, a blacksmith, a cotton gin, a general store, and an insurance agent. From 1940 to 1990 its population was reported as twenty.

BIBLIOGRAPHY: Roy Franklin Hall and Helen Gibbard Hall, *Collin County: Pioneering in North Texas* (Quanah, Texas: Nortex, 1975). J. Lee and Lillian J. Stambaugh, *A History of Collin County* (Austin: Texas State Historical Association, 1958).

David Minor

FONDREN, ELLA FLORENCE (1880–1982). Ella Florence Fondren, philanthropist, was born on June 1, 1880, the third child and elder daughter of Allen Cathy and Mary (Pogue) Cochrum of Hazel, Kentucky. When Ella was about six, the family moved to Corsicana, Texas. Her father died in 1895, and she quit school to help care for her family with six siblings. As a teenager she worked in her family's boardinghouse. There she met Walter W. Fondren,qv her future husband, who worked as a driller. Fondren remained in Corsicana only a few years, leaving in 1901 to take drilling jobs in the Gulf Coast oilfields. He continued to stay in contact with Ella, however, and returned to marry her on February 14, 1904. They had three children. Walter Fondren continued running operations in oilfields along the Gulf Coast but increasingly concentrated his drilling in the Humble oilfieldqv northeast of Houston. He credited Ella with determining some of his oil acquisitions. In 1911 he became the major stockholder in the new Humble Oil Company (now Exxon Company, U.S.A.qv).

The Fondrens established the Fondren Lectures in Religious Thought at Southern Methodist University in 1919. They gave major financial support for the construction of a new building at St. Paul's Methodist Church in 1929. In 1938 they donated nearly half a million dollars to SMU to build the Fondren Library. Walter Fondren also made large contributions to the Methodist Home for Orphans at Waco. Walter Fondren died in January 1939 while attending a Methodist conference. Ella Fondren carried on his philanthropic interests and assumed some of his directorial posts. She replaced him at Southern Methodist University, thereby becoming the first woman to serve on SMU's board of trustees and governors. In 1940 she succeeded him on the board of directors of the Methodist Home for Orphans at Waco and on the Methodist Board of Homes and Hospitals, retaining her position on the latter board for twenty years. In 1946 Ella Fondren and her children provided $1 million for the Fondren Libraryqv at Rice Institute.

The Fondren Foundation,qv established by Ella Fondren in 1948, made major grants to assist the expansion of Methodist Hospital in 1950 and 1976 and to launch the Fondren and Brown Cardiovascular and Orthopedic Research Center, completed in 1964. Fondren also ensured that the original Methodist Hospital operations remained solvent until a modern structure was completed in 1951. She served on the board of directors for Methodist Hospital for more than thirty years and on the board of Baylor University as well. Her foundation supported the growth of Baylor University College of Medicine and of St. Luke's Episcopal Hospital. The Institute for Religion at the Texas Medical Center was launched with her support. She regularly visited the institutions her family had assisted, evaluated their facilities, and insisted that the buildings she funded be large and the equipment state-of-the-art. The Fondren family provided major support for science buildings at Southwestern University in Georgetown and at Southern Methodist University. The foundation also established the Fondren Scholarships and the Fondren Lectureships there. Scarritt College in Nashville, Tennessee, named an education building for Ella Fondren in appreciation of her grant to construct the facility. When Rice University sought funds to add a research wing onto the Fondren Library in 1968, the Fondrens responded with another large grant. Ella Fondren left the Southern Methodist University board of trustees and governors in 1969 but continued serving on several other boards, especially that of Methodist Hospital. She outlived her children and spent her last five years at that facility, which provided both social opportunities and nursing care. She died there on May 3, 1982, shortly before her 102d birthday, and was buried at Forest Park Cemetery in Houston.

BIBLIOGRAPHY: Nolan B. Harmon, ed., *The Encyclopedia of World Methodism* (2 vols., Nashville: United Methodist Publishing House, 1974). Houston *Post,* May 4, 1982. Virginia Kirkland Innis, "Walter and Ella Fondren: Benefactors and Builders," *The Flyleaf: Friends of the Fondren Library,* Winter–Spring 1982. Marilyn McAdams Sibley, *The Methodist Hospital of Houston: Serving the World* (Austin: Texas State Historical Association, 1989).

Sherilyn Brandenstein

FONDREN, WALTER WILLIAM (1877–1939). Walter William Fondren, oil operator and philanthropist, was born in Union City, Tennessee, on June 6, 1877, the son of Thomas R. and Susannah (Fondren) Fondren. His parents were first cousins. His father, a Civil Warqv veteran, died in the early 1880s, and when Walter was six he and his family moved to Arkansas in search of more productive farmland. Here he learned how to drill water wells, a skill he later adapted for drilling for oil. He was orphaned at age ten and worked on farms and in sawmills until age sixteen, when he went to Texas and became a farm laborer. In 1897 he gave up farming to work as a roughneck in the Corsicana oilfield,qv and by 1901 he was a skilled rotary driller, an expert on drilling equipment, and an independent operator in the newly discovered Spindletop oilfield.qv Fondren moved from field to field as new oil pools were discovered, and by 1905 he was operating under his own name and through a dozen companies and partnerships. On February 14, 1904, at Corsicana, Fondren married Ella Florence Cochrum (*see* FONDREN, ELLA F.), with whom he had three children. Fondren was aided by his wife throughout his career, beginning shortly after their marriage, when she settled the family in Houston and used money left over to purchase stock in the firm that became Texaco, Incorporated,qv an investment that was eventually worth millions. To avoid dependence on others for transportation and marketing, Fondren became vice president of the Coleman Oil Company, a marketeer of crude oil. In 1911, with Ross Sterlingqv and others, he organized the Humble Oil Company, which became Humble Oil and Refining Company in 1917 and later Exxon Company, U.S.A.qv Fondren served as director of the firm and as vice president in charge of drilling and production in the Gulf Coast division from 1913 until his retirement in 1933. From its beginnings in the Humble oilfield,qv the company was highly successful. Company activities included acquiring, exploring, and developing oilfields in Texas, Oklahoma, Louisiana, and Arkansas; the company also refined oil, transported crude oil, and distributed refined products. Its properties included a number of refineries, more than 1,000 producing wells, and 1,200 miles of pipeline.

After his retirement Fondren established the Fondren Oil Company. In 1934 he accepted the post of district director of the Houston office of the Federal Housing Administration. With his wife, he gave the Fondren Library to Southern Methodist University and also gave the university endowment funds to support the Fondren Lectures In Religious Thought and a scholarship. Fondren was a Methodist and served as a trustee and member of the executive committee of Southern Methodist University; he was also a member of the general missionary council of the Methodist Episcopal Church, South. For many years he was a director of the Houston YMCA, and at the time of his death he was vice president of the National Bank of Commerce in Houston. Fondren died in San Antonio on January 5, 1939. He was buried in Glenwood Cemetery and later moved to Forest Park Cemetery. The Fondren Foundation,qv established by the family in 1948, was largely administered by his wife. In an effort to implement their combined wish to benefit institutions of higher learning, she established the Fondren Libraryqv at Rice University, which opened in 1949, and bestowed major gifts on the Methodist Hospital of Houston,qv Southwestern University, Scarritt College in Nashville, Tennessee, and other health and education facilities.

BIBLIOGRAPHY: Houston Metropolitan Research Center Files, Houston Public Library. Marguerite Johnston, *Houston, The Unknown City, 1836–1946* (College Station: Texas A&M University Press, 1991). Henrietta M. Larson and Kenneth Wiggins Porter, *History of Humble Oil and Refining Company* (New York: Harper, 1959). Vertical Files, Barker Texas History Center, University of Texas at Austin.

Diana J. Kleiner

FONDREN FOUNDATION. The Fondren Foundation was established in 1948 by Ella Florence Fondren,qv the widow of Walter W. Fondren,qv one of the founders of Humble Oil and Refining Company (later Exxon Company, U.S.A.qv). The foundation supports agencies for education, health, and human services, and the chair of the board of governors rotates among family members. In 1995 foundation assets exceeded $100 million, and the foundation office was located in Houston.

Art Leatherwood

FONDREN LIBRARY, RICE UNIVERSITY. The Fondren Library of Rice University, on the Rice campus three miles southwest of downtown Houston, serves as the research library for the university and a public library. It was founded and endowed as the Rice Institute Library by William Marsh Riceqv in 1891. It has always been privately funded from the university endowment. Rice opened in 1912 but did not get a librarian until 1914, when Alice Dean, of the Rice class of 1916, became acting librarian. The institute library was originally located on the second floor of the administration building (now Lovett Hall), but careful and extensive purchasing increased holdings until they overflowed two additional floors and expanded to several departmental libraries in other buildings. By 1946, when Dean officially became the librarian, plans were underway for a central library.

The Fondren Library, made possible in part by a gift from the Walter W. Fondren family, was built in 1947–48. Under librarian William Dix, appointed in 1948 after Alice Dean's retirement, the collections were moved into the new building, which officially opened in November 1949. The new facility held the entire collection and provided reading space and study carrels for faculty. In 1953 Dix was succeeded by Hardin Craig, Jr., a member of the history faculty. The collections continued to grow, and toward the end of Craig's tenure the library was again experiencing space problems. With the help of a grant through the Higher Education Facilities Act and a gift from the Fondren Foundation, a new wing for the library was planned to include additional stack space, over 200 study carrels for students and faculty, and a center for rare books and manuscripts. The Graduate Research Wing of Fondren Library, containing the Woodson Research Center, was completed in 1968, the year Richard O'Keefe became university librarian.

Fondren has continued expanding in size and services. Since 1967 the Regional Information and Communication Exchange, established by grant to provide information to area businesses, has become a complete fee-based information and document-delivery service for corporations in the Southwest. In 1979, when Samuel M. Carrington, Jr., became university librarian, the Fondren Library celebrated not only its thirtieth anniversary, but also the addition of its millionth volume, a milestone in the life of any library.

By 1985 the Fondren Library collections consisted of over 1.2 million volumes, 11,000 serial subscriptions, and over 1.6 million microforms, including newspaper and periodical backfiles, as well as research collections. A staff of thirty-eight professional librarians and ninety-eight paraprofessionals maintained these resources for the university. Among the special collections in the library are the papers of Julian S. Huxley, an early member of the Rice Institute faculty; documents pertaining to the reign of Maximilian and Carlota in Mexico; the Masterson collection of Texana; and the papers of Texas entrepreneurs such as W. H. Hamman, W. B. Sharp,qqv J. L. Autrey, H. W. Masterson, and W. W. Fondren. Also, the Fondren Library now houses the archives of NASA space programs, from the Mercury flights through the Skylab projects (*see* LYNDON B. JOHNSON SPACE CENTER), and is the general repository for the university archives. The general collections are strong in the scientific and engineering disciplines but also include special art and music libraries, as well as the O'Connor Center for Business Information. The Fondren Library has been a federal depository for government documents since 1968 and is a patent depository as well, with holdings from 1961. The Friends of Fondren Library, a support group of 1,200 members, publishes *Flyleaf,* a magazine reporting Fondren's major activities, major collection additions, and other items of interest to library supporters.

BIBLIOGRAPHY: Fredericka Meiners, *A History of Rice University: The Institute Years, 1907–1963* (Houston: Rice University Studies, 1982).

Kay Flowers

FONTAINE, EDWARD (1814–1884). Edward Fontaine, early minister and amateur naturalist, was born in Greenwood, Virginia, on August 5, 1814, the son of Patrick Henry and Nancy (Dabney) Fontaine and great-grandson of Patrick Henry. He was admitted to the United States Military Academy, West Point, in July 1830 but was discharged in July 1832 because of a deficiency in math. He was admitted to the bar on February 28, 1835. That year he worked in Pontotoc, Mississippi, as a draftsman on the survey of Chickasaw lands acquired by the federal government.

He became active in the Methodist Episcopal Church, was admitted to the ministry in 1838, and served in Texas at Houston and Galveston by 1840, but later that year he relinquished his ministry. He married Mary Ann Swisher in November 1840, and they had three sons. From May to October 1841 he was private secretary to President Mirabeau B. Lamar.qv There being no clergyman of any denomination in Austin, Fontaine resolved to do what he could for the religious welfare of his fellow citizens. He organized a Sunday school and preached to all comers, black and white, at informal services in the Capitol or outside in an oak grove. When the seat of government was moved away from Austin and Lamar's term had ended, Fontaine taught school in Independence and Gay Hill in 1842–43. He may have participated in the Somervell expeditionqv in the fall of 1842. About 1843 he went to Mississippi, where he entered the Episcopal Church and was ordained to the ministry on May 14, 1848. In 1851 he returned to Austin as rector of the Church of the Epiphany. He supervised the building of a church, completed and consecrated in May 1855, that became part of the present St. David's Church, Austin. Fontaine's wife died in 1855. In 1859 he married Mrs. Susan Taylor Britton. They had several children, but only two lived to maturity. In Austin Fontaine was active as a clergyman, politician, and amateur naturalist. He traveled widely, served as chaplain of the Texas Senate in 1857–58, and advocated establishment of a state university and a geological survey.

The church suffered in antebellum Texasqv because of a division in the membership on questions of slavery and secession.qqv Fontaine resigned his charge in Austin and moved to Mississippi in 1859. He was captain of Company H, Eighteenth Regiment, Mississippi Volunteers, and chief of ordnance of the Mississippi Army during the Civil War.qv He served subsequently as rector at St. Mark's, Mississippi, and at Plaquemines Parish, Louisiana. He was a member of the New York Historical Society, the Maryland Academy of Science, and the New Orleans Academy of Science. He delivered addresses and wrote papers about his various scientific interests. His lectures included "How the World Was Peopled" (1872), which contained information on the natural history of Texas, "Winds of the Gulf States" (1873), and "A Lecture on the Peculiarities of the Physical Geography of the Mississippi River and its Delta" (1874). He died at Belvidere, Mississippi, on January 19, 1884.

BIBLIOGRAPHY: Austin History Center Files. Edward Fontaine Papers, Barker Texas History Center, University of Texas at Austin. Louis Wiltz Kemp Papers, Barker Texas History Center, University of Texas at Austin. *Southwestern Historical Quarterly,* Texas Collection, Octo-

ber 1943. Daisy Barrett Tanner, *The History and Treasures of St. David's Church* (Austin, 1976). Work Projects Administration Writers' Program, *St. David's through the Years* (Austin: St. David's Episcopal Church, 1942).
DuBose Murphy

FONTAINE, JACOB (1808–1898). Jacob (Jake) Fontaine, Baptist preacher, political and civic leader, and newspaper publisher in Austin, was born into slavery^qv in Arkansas in 1808. His several owners included the Tuttle and Isaacs families, but his best known and most influential master was Rev. Edward Fontaine,^qv a great-grandson of Patrick Henry, who moved to Austin, Texas, in 1839 as the personal secretary of Texas president Mirabeau B. Lamar.^qv

Jacob was Edward Fontaine's sexton at St. David's Episcopal Church in Austin in 1855, but in 1860 he was attending the First Baptist Church, which Sam Houston^qv attended. While serving as Edward Fontaine's sexton, he would preach in the afternoons to blacks in the basement of the old Methodist church at Brazos and Tenth streets. Jacob Fontaine and other members of the black congregation began to meet secretly in 1864 to organize a break from the white church. In 1867, after emancipation, Jacob founded the First (Colored) Baptist Church in Austin. He was a janitor in the old Land Office Building, became active in Republican and Greenback party^qqv politics during Reconstruction^qv in Travis County, operated a grocery, laundry, book, and medicine store, and in 1876 established the *Gold Dollar*,^qv one of the first black weekly newspapers in the South and the first newspaper under black ownership in Austin.

In 1867 Fontaine helped to found the St. John Regular Missionary Baptist Association, originally known as the Travis County Association, and was elected its first moderator. He also founded five churches in addition to the First (Colored) Baptist Church: Mount Zion (Williamson Creek), 1873; Good Hope (Round Rock), 1874; Sweet Home (Clarksville), 1877; New Hope (Wheatsville), 1887; and St. Stephen's (Waters Park), 1887. He and his minister son Israel Jacob Fontaine II later founded a local chapter of the Colored Brothers of the Eastern Star.

The Fontaine family lived on the Woodlawn plantation near the Austin home of ex-governor Elisha M. Pease.^qv Jacob's wife Melvina (Viney) was a housekeeper there and had cooked at the Governor's Mansion,^qv where their daughter Melissa married a custodian, Joe Gordon, on March 18, 1870. They had two other daughters. From 1875 to 1898 the Fontaines lived in a two-story structure at twenty-fourth and Orange (San Gabriel), now an Austin landmark. Fontaine started his newspaper there, with sixty dollars he earned from the investment of a gold dollar given to him in 1872 by his sister, Nelly Miller, when they were reunited in Mississippi after a separation caused twenty years before by slavery. In 1881–82 Fontaine emerged as Austin's leading black advocate for the establishment of the University of Texas in Austin. He traveled to San Antonio, Seguin, and Marlin to secure the black vote for his cause. Fontaine's work in the church and in newspaper publishing was continued by his son George, a depot porter in Austin, who published the *Silver Messenger* in 1897–98. George's son, Rev. Israel Jacob Fontaine III, founded the Fontaine Memorial Baptist Church in 1962 and published the Austin *Express* and the Fort Worth *Community News* before taking up advertising and insurance work in Austin.

BIBLIOGRAPHY: Jacob Fontaine III and Gene Burd, *Jacob Fontaine* (Austin: Eakin Press, 1983). Charles William Grose, Black Newspapers in Texas, 1868–1970 (Ph.D. dissertation, University of Texas at Austin, 1972).
Gene A. Burd

FONTAINE, WILLIAM WINSTON (1834–?). William Winston Fontaine, school administrator and founder, son of William Spotswood Fontaine, was born at Montville, Virginia, on November 27, 1834. He was the great-grandson of Patrick Henry. He attended Rumford Male Academy and the University of Virginia, where he graduated in 1859, and then taught mathematics and Latin at Pegram School in Richmond. He married Mary Burroughs on April 2, 1861; they had six children. During the Civil War^qv Fontaine was a colonel in the Richmond Artillery, served at Seven Pines and at Richmond, was captured scouting behind enemy lines in 1864, and was released on parole in June 1865. The Fontaine plantation, Fontainebleau, was destroyed during the war, and Fontaine moved to Fredericksburg, Virginia, where he established Spotswood Female Institute. In 1870 he moved to Texas to teach at Port Sullivan College in Milam County. He was president of Baylor Female Institute from 1871 to 1875, when he organized the Texas Female Institute at Austin. He was in charge of a boarding school for girls in Louisville, Kentucky, from 1880 to 1886, when he helped organize William Carey Crane College, at Independence, Texas; he taught there until 1889.

BIBLIOGRAPHY: *Biographical Souvenir of the State of Texas* (Chicago: Battey, 1889; rpt., Easley, South Carolina: Southern Historical Press, 1978). William S. Speer and John H. Brown, eds., *Encyclopedia of the New West* (Marshall, Texas: United States Biographical Publishing, 1881; rpt., Easley, South Carolina: Southern Historical Press, 1978).

FOOD PROCESSING. Before the Civil War,^qv food processing in Texas was restricted chiefly to local and regional markets. Milling^qv for a local market was the first food-processing industry in the state and has continued to be one of the most important overall industries, with the market expanding considerably. Milling was the first-ranking of all Texas industries in 1850, 1860, and 1880; it ranked second in 1890 and 1910, third in 1900, and fourth in 1920, 1930, and 1940. The baking industry did not become prominent in Texas until the 1850s, and until about 1900 bakeries were operated in conjunction with confectioneries. Extensive marketing of bakery goods was limited by transportation facilities. The industry was characterized by small, local plants until the development of a good highway system. By 1940 baking had become the sixth-ranking industry in the state. Dehydration of fruits and vegetables was perhaps the earliest method of food preservation practiced in Texas. In 1836 Mary Austin Holley^qv judged dried foods an important article of produce, but because of their supposed unappetizing appearance and taste, extensive production of them has been limited to times of stress, particularly wartime. The dehydration industry expanded temporarily during World War I and again during World War II,^qqv but generally other methods of food preservation have been preferred on the competitive market. During the first decade of the twentieth century the canning industry moved into areas of the state where fruits and vegetables were produced in significant quantities, especially the lower Rio Grande valley. Commercial quick freezing was added to industrial canning after World War II. Both canning and freezing are periodic industries that support migrant workers. The development of the quick-freezing process and the rapid expansion of the freezing industry was accompanied by the opening of hundreds of cold-storage locker plants throughout the state and a large sale of home freezer units (*see* REFRIGERATION).

After the Civil War and the rise of the cattle trade, meat packing^qv grew sharply into prominence. By 1900 it was the sixth-ranking industry in the state and the second-ranking food-processing industry. In 1910 it became the state's most important industry and has remained significant among food industries. Meat packing has become specialized along several major lines: custom slaughtering, wholesale meat packing, poultry dressing and packing, and the manufacture of sausages and other prepared foods. One of the earliest prominent processing industries was the making of liquors and malts. As early as the 1850s Texans were producing not inconsiderable amounts of whiskey, peach and grape brandy, and rum to be sold at local groceries. The making of liquors and malts was the sixth-ranking industry in Texas in 1860. Mustang grape wine became a specialty in some areas of the state, and by 1885 a Texan had patented a beer cooler for use in saloons and hotels, although most of the beer consumed in Texas was then imported. By 1890 Anhaeuser-Busch had opened a brewery in Houston and two breweries had been established in San Antonio. The brewing industry[qv] expanded until the prohibition[qv] fight and eventually was closed by law on June 25, 1918. With the repeal of prohibition, breweries again became an important Texas industry. In 1948 the industries classified by the United States Bureau of the Census as Food and Kindred Products were the second-ranking industrial group in the state. Of the Food and Kindred Products, grain-mill products, including flour and meal, prepared animal feeds, and white rice, ranked first according to value added by manufacture. Meat (including poultry) products ranked second. Bakery products ranked third and beverages, including soft drinks, fourth. The food-processing industry employing the largest number of persons was wholesale meat packing; bakeries were second. There were in 1948 a total of 2,029 establishments engaged in some phase of food processing, employing a yearly average of 57,784 persons at a total annual salary of $130,543,000. These plants added by manufacture $387,558,000 to Texas agricultural products.

General food processing and associated industries as a whole in 1953 employed the greatest number of Texas workers among Texas industries. Employing 59,209 people, this industry had a value added by manufacture of $498,226,000. Throughout the 1950s the industry remained the least mechanized and the largest industrial employer in the state. Subsequent expansion of Texas food-processing plants and associated industries ranged from new breweries to rice-packaging plants. Expansion in the beverage industry was particularly great; by the mid-1960s Texas ranked among the leading states in the production of beer and canned soft drinks. Four nationwide companies operated breweries in Texas in 1965. In 1995, there were five nationally owned breweries and one Texas owned, Spoetzl Brewery[qv] in Shiner, in operation. Overall, beverage production in the state grossed $2.5 billion in gross sales in 1993. By the early 1960s meat-packing plants generally decentralized and built new, small plants far from their traditional centers and close to their raw materials. High wage rates and obsolescence in old centers, as well as abundant labor in small rural communities, influenced this relocation. In 1993, Texas had seventy-one producers of meat products, which generated more than $3 billion in sales. A $20 million sugar-processing plant with a capacity of 600 tons of beets a day was constructed in Hereford. In 1964 beet sugar was made in Texas for the first time. By 1990 Texans planted more than 41,000 acres of sugar beets with a total production of 1,013,000 tons. Deaf Smith, Castro, Parmer, and Swisher counties were the leading producers. In 1964 the food-processing and associated industries employed more than eighty thousand workers, or approximately 13.2 percent of the state's total workforce. Value added by manufacture totaled $923,362,000, and capital investment in the industry as a whole amounted to more than $500 million. A 1965 survey indicated that the industry had expanded 15 percent over the previous year because of population growth, larger family incomes, and greater agricultural production. Many nonindustrial towns benefited from this expansion. The Paris soup cannery, the Corsicana potato-chip plant, and the Plainview castor-bean processing facility were all examples of the expansion and decentralization of the food-processing and associated industries. By 1973, 85,000 Texans were employed in food processing, more than in any other manufacturing industry. Nearly $5 billion worth of food products was being shipped annually. In the 1990s the industry continued to be a leading employer, with over 97,000 Texans holding jobs in food processing and kindred fields in 1994. *See also* AGRICULTURE, SOFT-DRINK INDUSTRY, SUGAR PRODUCTION.

BIBLIOGRAPHY: Leo C. Haynes, Manufacturing in Texas: A Statistical Story (M.B.A. thesis, University of Texas, 1929). William R. Hogan, *The Texas Republic: A Social and Economic History* (Norman: University of Oklahoma Press, 1946; rpt. 1969). Mary Austin Holley, *Texas* (Lexington, Kentucky: J. Clarke and Company, 1836; rpts., Austin: Steck, 1935; Texas State Historical Association, 1985). Ashley Wood Spaight, *The Resources, Soil and Climate of Texas* (Galveston: Belo, 1882). Ralph W. Steen, *Twentieth Century Texas: An Economic and Social History* (Austin: Steck, 1942).

FOOSHEE, MARION FRESENIUS (1888–1956). Marion Fresenius Fooshee, architect, was born on July 27, 1888, in Weatherford, Texas, the only child of Francis Marion and Margaret Christine (Fresenius) Fooshee. The family moved to Corpus Christi, where his father died when he was seven. In 1898 he and his mother moved to Dallas, where she established a boarding house at the corner of Live Oak Street and Haskell Avenue. Fooshee spent his youth here and attended nearby Bryan High School, but did not attend a college.

About 1911 he secured a position with H. B. Thompson designing eclectic houses for the Dallas elite. Much of his work was in such established enclaves as Munjer Place (now a listed historic district), where Fooshee worked on the Aldredge House (5500 Swiss Ave., 1917), and houses for other prominent Dallasites, including Judge George C. Greer and Charles Sanger. Fooshee was a tall Southern gentleman whose easygoing, friendly demeanor made him well suited to serve Thompson's clientele—so well in fact, that several projects, including the majestic residence of Orville Thorp in Highland Park (4908 Lakeside, ca. 1915), are generally credited to the partners.

Fooshee entered officers' training camp at the outbreak of World War I[qv] and eventually was sent to the Bethlehem Ship Yards in San Francisco, where he performed architectural work for the navy. After his discharge in 1918 he began independent practice in Dallas. James B. Cheek,[qv] whom he met in Thompson's office about 1914, joined him soon after. At one point, the firm was apparently located in Wichita Falls. In Dallas, Fooshee and Cheek solidified their reputation for designing large houses for the wealthy. The two usually worked independently on their residential commissions; Fooshee is credited with the house at 3606 Cornell (Highland Park, ca. 1923). They also built apartment buildings and duplexes, including much of the 4400 block of Westway in Dallas, where both men lived. Fooshee was appointed architect for the Dallas Park Board in 1920, and the firm's practice expanded to include civic and commercial buildings. Among these is Highland Park Village[qv] (ca. 1930–35), the first self-contained shopping center in the United States, though this project is generally credited to Cheek. Fooshee and Cheek was one of eleven firms involved in the design and construction of the Hall of State[qv] at the Texas Centennial[qv] Exposition in Fair Park[qv] (1936). They were also involved in the design of the aquarium, and Cheek designed the United States Federal Exhibits Building. The firm designed a variety of gas stations, motels (some of which, including the Parkway Hotel, were partially owned by Fooshee), and several of the state's first radio and television stations. Fooshee is credited with designing the Grand Court Tourist Lodge (1931) and a Magnolia Service Station in Dallas. His firm was noted for its Spanish Colonial designs. Interestingly, mausoleums were considered a specialty of the firm.

In June 1927 Fooshee married Annie Linda Atkins of St. Louis; they had a daughter. Annie died in 1931, and Fooshee married Peggy Montague Neale in June 1940; they also had a daughter. Fooshee was a member of the Dallas Country Club and president of the Idlewild Club. He helped organize St. Michael and All Angels Episcopal Church and designed its first building. His civic activities included membership in the Dallas City Plan Commission, the American Institute of Architects, and the Junior Chamber of Commerce, as well as a key role in the attempt to remodel historic Union Station in Dallas. Fooshee continued his practice with Cheek until he suffered a heart attack and died on January 4, 1956. He is buried at Hillcrest Memorial Park in Dallas, the site of his most noted mausoleum.

BIBLIOGRAPHY: Dallas *Morning News*, January 5, 1956. Jay C. Henry, *Architecture in Texas, 1895–1945* (Austin: University of Texas Press,

1993). *Texas Architect*, November–December 1989. Vertical Files, Barker Texas History Center, University of Texas at Austin.

Duncan T. Fulton III

FOOT, TEXAS. Foot, near Farm Road 2478 about six miles west of McKinney in central Collin County, was named in honor of one of the first settlers in the area, Dr. Gerald (or Gerard) Alexander Foote. Foote was born in Virginia and moved to Texas from Arkansas in the late 1840s. In 1848 he received a Peters colony[qv] land certificate for 640 acres. Within forty years his holdings had increased to 2,000 acres and included the Foote settlement, which was a farming and lumbering community. By 1900 it had a store, and on January 16 of the next year it received a post office. In 1903 Foot's post office was discontinued. The community reported a population of fifty from the late 1930s to the late 1940s, when the number dropped to twenty; its population continued to be reported at that level through 1990.

BIBLIOGRAPHY: Seymour V. Connor, *The Peters Colony of Texas: A History and Biographical Sketches of the Early Settlers* (Austin: Texas State Historical Association, 1959). Roy Franklin Hall and Helen Gibbard Hall, *Collin County: Pioneering in North Texas* (Quanah, Texas: Nortex, 1975). J. Lee and Lillian J. Stambaugh, *A History of Collin County* (Austin: Texas State Historical Association, 1958).

David Minor

FOOTE, HENRY STUART (1804–1880). Henry Stuart Foote, politician and historian, the son of Richard Helm and Catherine (Stuart) Foote, was born in Fauquier County, Virginia, on February 28, 1804. He attended Georgetown College and Washington University, studied law at Warrenton, Virginia, and was admitted to the bar in 1823. As a lawyer and newspaper editor he lived in Tuscumbia, Alabama, and in Jackson, Natchez, Vicksburg, and Raymond, Mississippi. In 1839, while a member of the House of the Mississippi legislature, he visited Texas and subsequently wrote his first book, *Texas and the Texans* (2 volumes, 1841). As a member of the United States Senate, Foote defended the Compromise of 1850.[qv] In 1851 he defeated Jefferson Davis[qv] for the governorship of Mississippi on a Unionist ticket. He resigned the governorship five days before the end of his term and moved to California. In 1858 he returned to Mississippi, but his Unionist sympathies caused him to move on to Tennessee. He became a member of the House of the Confederate States Congress but resigned when that group rejected Abraham Lincoln's peace proposals. He was in Europe during the Civil War.[qv] His *War of the Rebellion* (1866) was an effort to justify his part in the war. He also wrote *Casket of Reminiscences* (1874) and *Bench and Bar in the South and Southwest* (1876). Foote married Elizabeth Winters in Tuscumbia, Alabama. After her death he married Mrs. Rachel D. Smiley of Nashville, Tennessee. He died in Nashville on May 20, 1880.

BIBLIOGRAPHY: *Dictionary of American Biography*. Mary Sexton Estill, ed., "Diary of a Confederate Congressman," *Southwestern Historical Quarterly* 38, 39 (April, July 1935).

FOOTES, TEXAS. Footes, a farming community four miles southwest of Longview in east central Gregg County, was established before 1900 as a station on the International–Great Northern Railroad. In the mid-1930s the community had two stores and a number of houses. By the early 1990s Footes was a dispersed rural community, and many of the area's residents worked in nearby Longview.

BIBLIOGRAPHY: Eugene W. McWhorter, *Traditions of the Land: The History of Gregg County* (Longview, Texas: Gregg County Historical Foundation, 1989).

Christopher Long

FORBES, ANDREW ALEXANDER (1862–1921). Andrew Alexander Forbes, photographer, was born in Ottawa Township, Waukesha County, Wisconsin, on April 18, 1862, the fifth child of James McLaren and Lucinda P. (Sanders) Forbes. Although little is known about him, his photographs are important historical documents that present the often tedious reality of life on the range. In the late 1880s Forbes began traveling on seasonal circuits through Texas and Oklahoma, visiting isolated spreads to photograph cowboys. He used glass plates, probably commercially prepared, to take his pictures. Ranchhands would pay fifty cents to a dollar for his photographs, and they gave him free bed and board. In addition to the expected shots of cowboys roping, branding, and dipping cattle, Forbes photographed cowhands engaged in more prosaic activities such as cooking, eating, smoking, and packing their gear.

Guns, chaps, boots, and other accoutrements of Hollywood legend are relatively scarce in Forbes's photographs, although most of the cowpunchers wear broad-brimmed hats and are shown close to their horses. In some of Forbes's photographs the cowhands were obviously posing for the "folks back home," as in a roping scene labeled *Branding*, in which no fire or irons are visible. Forbes's inclusion of rocky outcrops, mesas, vast expanses of space, and other landscape details provide a more romantic air in some of his shots; however, a photograph of cowboys in long coats, braced against a bitterly cold, dreary day, is more characteristic of his unvarnished approach to his subject matter. Forbes also photographed other aspects of western settlement, such as the April 1889 land rush in Oklahoma's unassigned lands, pioneers posed by their sod homes, Sac and Fox Indian children and teachers at a mission school in Indian Territory, and buffalo[qv] and other animals on the ranch of Charles Goodnight.[qv]

In 1909 Forbes moved to Bishop, California, where he married Mary R. Prutsman on June 30, 1909; they had one child. As a pioneer photographer in that area, Forbes specialized in mining and commercial work. He died in Lampoc, California, on March 21, 1921. His photographs are included in the collections of the University of Oklahoma Library in Norman, Oklahoma; the Library of Congress; and the Smithsonian Institution National Anthropological Archives, Washington, D.C.

BIBLIOGRAPHY: Karen and William R. Current, *Photography and the Old West* (New York: Abrams, 1978). Owen Ulph, "No Trade for Heroes," *American West*, July 1968.

Kendall Curlee

FORBES, JOHN (1797–1880). John Forbes, lawyer, judge, and military man of the Texan army during the Texas Revolution,[qv] was born to Scottish parents on February 26, 1797, in Cork, Ireland. His family moved when he was two to England, where he remained until 1817. That year Forbes immigrated to Cincinnati, Ohio, where he engaged in business. While in Ohio he married Emily Sophia Sisson. They moved to Nacogdoches, Texas, in 1835. There, Forbes was appointed chairman of the Committee of Vigilance and Public Safety, and according to one account he wrote to President Andrew Jackson, protesting that various Indian chiefs of the Creek Nation were contracting with Archibald Hotchkiss[qv] and Benjamin Hawkins to enter and settle a vast tract of land in East Texas, to which 5,000 Creeks would migrate. When the General Council[qv] of the provisional government passed an act providing the council authority to elect two judges, Forbes was elected first judge of Nacogdoches Municipality on November 26, 1835. In December Gen. Sam Houston, John Cameron,[qqv] and Forbes were appointed commissioners by provisional governor Henry Smith[qv] and the Consultation[qv] to secure a treaty with the Cherokees who were living near Nacogdoches. This treaty was signed by Chief Bowl,[qv] Sam Houston, and Forbes after a three-day conference with the Indians; the treaty bound the Cherokees to strict neutrality. Forbes also administered the oath of allegiance to army recruits, including David Crockett,[qv] as they passed through Nacogdoches. Forbes was then given the rank of major and appointed aide-de-camp to Sam Houston. He also served as commissary general under Houston during the campaigns at Anahuac and San Jacinto.

According to the accounts of Nicholas D. Labadie,qv Forbes murdered one or two Mexican women, took prisoners without justification, and reportedly took a gold snuffbox from the dead body of a Mexican colonel. After the defeat of the Mexican forces under Antonio López de Santa Anna,qv Forbes was placed in charge of the spoils of war and acquired Santa Anna's sword. Eventually his reputation was restored, after he filed a libel suit in a Nacogdoches court against Labadie, a suit that was on the civil agenda from 1859 to 1867. Forbes was cleared of all charges. He was discharged on November 17, 1836, from military duty. On his return to Nacogdoches, he served as principal judge of the Municipality of Nacogdoches, in which office he administered the oath of allegiance to many of the new Texans who arrived after the revolution. In 1856 he ran for mayor of Nacogdoches and won. He served in that capacity for several years. In 1876 he was appointed lieutenant colonel on the staff of Richard Coke.qv Forbes died on February 10, 1880, in Nacogdoches, and was survived by two daughters, who buried him beside his wife in the Oak Grove Cemetery.

BIBLIOGRAPHY: Robert Bruce Blake Research Collection, Steen Library, Stephen F. Austin State University; Barker Texas History Center, University of Texas at Austin; Texas State Archives, Austin; Houston Public Library, Houston. James M. Day, comp., *Texas Almanac, 1857–1873: A Compendium of Texas History* (Waco: Texian Press, 1967). Pauline Shirley Murrie, *Early Records of Nacogdoches County* (Waco, 1965). Vertical Files, Barker Texas History Center, University of Texas at Austin.

Eileen Nicholas

FORBES, ROBERT MITCHELL (1809–?). Robert Mitchell Forbes, merchant and state representative, son of William and Fanny Forbes, was born in Kinsale, Westmoreland County, Virginia, on September 22, 1809. He attended the University of Virginia and traveled in 1828 to Pensacola, Florida, where he embarked upon a business career. He was elected to represent Escambia County in the Florida legislature in 1832 and served one term. Having heard of the Texas Revolutionqv in the autumn of 1835, he set out for Texas aboard the steamer Comanche and arrived at the mouth of the Brazos River on February 18, 1836. He settled in Columbia, where he became a prominent merchant. He was elected to a seat in the House of Representatives of the Sixth Congress from Brazoria County in 1841 and served through the special, or war, session of 1842. Three years later he was elected delegate to the Convention of 1845.qv After the outbreak of the Mexican Warqv in 1846, Forbes transferred his business west to Port Lavaca. Although bankrupted by the Civil War,qv he remained there until 1873, when he moved to Cuero. In 1880 he moved to Dallas and in 1881 to Galveston. Forbes married Mary James Reed on December 20, 1848, and they became the parents of eleven children, of whom six survived to adulthood.

BIBLIOGRAPHY: William S. Speer and John H. Brown, eds., *Encyclopedia of the New West* (Marshall, Texas: United States Biographical Publishing, 1881; rpt., Easley, South Carolina: Southern Historical Press, 1978). Texas House of Representatives, *Biographical Directory of the Texan Conventions and Congresses, 1832–1845* (Austin: Book Exchange, 1941).

Charles Christopher Jackson

FORD, HAMILTON FAITH (1908–1990). Hamilton Faith Ford, psychiatrist and professor at the University of Texas Medical Branch, was born on October 24, 1908, in Goldthwaite, Texas, the son of Walter and Barbara (Scarborough) Ford. He graduated from Sonora High School in 1924, from the University of Texas in 1927, and from UTMB in 1931. He was the first resident to finish the three-year program in psychiatry. Ford completed postgraduate training at Charity Hospital in New Orleans, John Sealy Hospitalqv and the Galveston State Psychopathic Hospital in Galveston, and the Mayo Clinic in Rochester, Minnesota.

He joined the UTMB faculty in 1935 and was promoted to professor in 1946. He was chairman of the Department of Neurology and Psychiatry from 1963 to 1973 and chairman of the Department of Psychiatry in 1973–74. In 1972 he received the Ashbel Smithqv Distinguished Alumnus Award and in 1974 was selected as the first Ashbel Smith professor of psychiatry.

Ford wrote more than forty scientific publications and served as editor of *Diseases of the Nervous System* from 1968 to 1976. He was a member of the board of editors of *Psychiatry Digest* from 1963 to 1971. He served as president of the Texas Society for Mental Health (1950), the Galveston County Medical Society (1951), the Central Neuropsychiatric Association (1959), the Texas District Branch of the American Psychiatric Association (1959), the Texas Association for Mental Health (1963), the Southern Psychiatric Association (1969), and the American College of Psychiatrists (1974). In 1969 he was elected vice president of the American Psychiatric Association.

In 1934 he married Josephine Evangeline Dean, who also graduated from UTMB, worked in the Department of Neurology and Psychiatry, was president of the Women's Auxiliary of the Texas State Medical Association (*see* TEXAS MEDICAL ASSOCIATION), and was chairman of the Mental Health Division of the National Auxiliary Organization. The Fords had three daughters. Ford died in Texas City on July 21, 1990.

BIBLIOGRAPHY: Galveston *Daily News*, July 22, 1990. *The University of Texas Medical Branch at Galveston: Past, Present, Future* (Galveston: University of Texas Medical Branch at Galveston, 1966). Vertical Files, Barker Texas History Center, University of Texas at Austin.

Chester R. Burns

FORD, HENRY (1845–1910). Henry Ford, banker and business writer, was born in Ohio County, West Virginia, on January 28, 1845. He moved to Texas at the age of seventeen and worked for a time on a ranch in Brown County before he moved into Brownwood, where he became prominent as a private banker. He also served at various times as county clerk, mayor of Brownwood, treasurer of Brown County, city school trustee, and chairman of the Central County Committee. The firm of Coggin, Ford, and Martin, with which he was associated, published several business-aid booklets. A series of articles called "Dawn of Brown County" written by Ford appeared in *Banking Made Plain* (1904), *Pocket Cotton Calculator* (1905), *Pocket Cotton, Cotton Seed*, and *Cotton Picking Calculator* (1906), and *Wheat, Oats, Corn, and Hay Pocket Calculator* (1907). Although the last sketch was "To be continued," no Brown County material was included in *Six Hundred Business Law Points* (1909). Brown married Josephine Jones on September 13, 1871; they had six children. His second wife was Collie Couch, with whom he had three children; his third wife was Eloise Porter. He died on March 6, 1910, and was buried in Greenleaf Cemetery, Brownwood. It was rumored that he was in actuality the notorious outlaw Jesse James.

BIBLIOGRAPHY: Frank W. Johnson, *A History of Texas and Texans* (5 vols., ed. E. C. Barker and E. W. Winkler [Chicago and New York: American Historical Society, 1914; rpt. 1916]). James C. White, *The Promised Land: A History of Brown County* (Brownwood, Texas: Brownwood *Banner*, 1941).

FORD, JOHN SALMON (1815–1897). John Salmon (Rip) Ford, soldier, elected official, and newspaper editor, son of William and Harriet (Salmon) Ford, was born in Greenville District, South Carolina, on May 26, 1815. He moved to Texas in June 1836 and served in the Texas army until 1838, rising to the rank of first lieutenant under John Coffee (Jack) Hays.qv Ford settled in San Augustine and practiced medicine there until 1844, when he was elected to the House of the Ninth Congress, where he introduced the resolution to accept the terms of annexationqv to the United States. In 1845 he moved to Austin and became editor of the Austin *Texas Democrat;*qv he was later in partnership with Michael Cronican.qv

During the Mexican War Ford was adjutant of Hays's regiment and in command of a spy company; he was commended for gallant service by Gen. Joseph Lane. While serving as adjutant, Ford acquired the lasting nickname "Rip." When officially sending out notices of deaths he kindly included at the first of the message, "Rest in Peace"; later, under the exigencies of battle conditions, this message was shortened to "R.I.P."

In 1849, with Robert S. Neighbors, Ford made an exploration of the country between San Antonio and El Paso and published a report and map of the route, which came to be known as the Ford and Neighbors Trail. Later in 1849 he was made captain in the Texas Rangers and was stationed between the Nueces and the Rio Grande, where he had numerous Indian fights during 1850 and 1851.

In 1852 he was elected to the Texas Senate; again he became an editor and, in partnership with Capt. Joe Walker, established the *State Times*, which was published in Austin until 1857. Early in 1858 he accepted a commission in the state troops and defeated the Indians in two major battles on the Canadian River. Late in 1859 he was sent to the Rio Grande, where he commanded operations against Juan N. Cortina. In 1861 Ford served as a member of the Secession Convention, commanded an expedition to Brazos Santiago, initiated a trade agreement between Mexico and the Confederacy, and was elected colonel of the Second Texas Cavalry, with a command in the Rio Grande district. Between 1862 and 1865 he discharged with tactful moderation the duties of commandant of conscripts, while at various times he was engaged on border operations protecting Confederate-Mexican trade. In May 1865 he led Confederate forces in the battle of Palmito Ranch, the last battle of the Civil War.

In 1868 Ford moved to Brownsville to edit the Brownsville *Sentinel*. In 1872 he was a delegate to the Democratic convention in Baltimore. He was a special sergeant-at-arms when Richard Coke was inaugurated as governor in 1873 and quelled a riot of Austin citizens who were aroused against the radicals and Edmund J. Davis. In 1873 Ford served as a cattle and hide inspector of Cameron County, and in 1874 he was mayor of Brownsville. He was a member of the Constitutional Convention of 1875 and served in the Texas Senate from 1876 to 1879, when he was appointed superintendent of the Deaf and Dumb School (later the Texas School for the Deaf). While in the Senate he urged the promotion of immigration to Texas and popular education, supported in part from the sale of public lands.

Ford spent his later years writing reminiscences and historical articles and promoting an interest in Texas history. As a charter member of the Texas State Historical Association, he contributed one of the first articles published in its *Quarterly*. He died in San Antonio on November 3, 1897.

BIBLIOGRAPHY: *Biographical Souvenir of the State of Texas* (Chicago: Battey, 1889; rpt., Easley, South Carolina: Southern Historical Press, 1978). John S. Ford, Memoirs (MS, John Salmon Ford Papers, Barker Texas History Center, University of Texas at Austin). John S. Ford, *Rip Ford's Texas*, ed. Stephen B. Oates (Austin: University of Texas Press, 1963). William J. Hughes, *Rebellious Ranger: Rip Ford and the Old Southwest* (Norman: University of Oklahoma Press, 1964). Texas House of Representatives, *Biographical Directory of the Texan Conventions and Congresses, 1832–1845* (Austin: Book Exchange, 1941).

Seymour V. Connor

FORD, LYNN (1908–1978). Lynn Ford, a craftsman, cabinetmaker, builder, and teacher who frequently collaborated with his brother, architect O'Neil Ford, was born in Sherman, Texas, on February 20, 1908, the second son of Leonides Bertram and Lula Belle (Sinclair) Ford. In addition to his brother, Lynn had a younger sister, Authella. Bert Ford, a railroad worker, introduced Lynn to the art of wood carving and fostered his childrens' creativity by bringing home discarded ink pencils from the railroad dispatch office, grocery sacks for drawing paper, and scrap lumber. The elder Ford died in a train acci-

Col. John Salmon (Rip) Ford. Carte de visite by Louis de Planque, Brownsville, Texas, and Matamoros, Mexico. Ca. 1865. Courtesy Lawrence T. Jones III Collection, Austin.

dent in 1918, and the family moved to Denton, where Belle Ford took in boarders and sewed.

In both Sherman and Denton the Fords built backyard workshops where Lynn, O'Neil, and occasionally Authella built toys, miniature furniture, and makeshift vehicles. By the age of eighteen Lynn was able to sell furniture, sculpture, and copper items. In 1928–29 he attended North Texas State College in Denton (now the University of North Texas) with the intention of becoming a coach and woodworking teacher. Although he supported himself by working as an architectural draftsman, he still found time to be art editor of the annual and president of the sophomore class. He enrolled in architectural drafting courses at the University of Texas in the fall of 1930 but was forced to drop out in December due to financial problems. During this period he temporarily lost his eyesight due to eyestrain; eye problems periodically troubled him for the rest of his life.

In the early 1930s Ford moved to Dallas, where he lived with his brother and converted an old stable on Maple Avenue into a shop.

There he produced furniture, wood carvings, rugs, and copper light fixtures for about ten years, assisted by his mother, who had taught herself to weave, and friends, neighbors, and students eager to learn his methods. The regionalist fervor of Dallas's art scene during this era provided a congenial atmosphere for Ford's craft production. He taught at the Dallas Art Institute[qv] and participated in government-sponsored art programs. In 1932 he supervised a woodworking shop in the government resettlement town of Woodlake; four years later he executed wood sculptures for the Hall of State,[qv] assisted by a group of National Youth Administration workers. In 1937–38 Ford supervised Texas Womens' College (now Texas Woman's University) students in making doors, furniture, light fixtures, and decorative carvings for the Little Chapel in the Woods in Denton, which was built by NYA students under the direction of O'Neil Ford and Arch Swank.

From 1938 to 1953 Ford collaborated with his brother in building homes for prominent Texans. Generally he worked with unskilled laborers to lay bricks, set tile, and make furniture, doors, mantels, beams, and other carpentry work. He temporarily left this activity for service in the army during World War II,[qv] for which he won several medals. Afterward he moved to San Antonio and built his Willow Way shop, where he and his assistants produced decorative pieces for homes, frequently commissioned by architects. Ford stopped building homes in 1953, apparently for health reasons, but continued to operate the Willow Way shop until he retired in 1973.

At the shop he produced doors, screens, walls, light fixtures, containers, and other items in wood, copper, and brass. He also taught himself to work with ceramics, lead, and cast babbitt (a lead alloy). Ford found inspiration for his designs by reading about topics ranging from African primitive art to Mexican and Swedish folk art. His characteristic style was to fill the surface of an object with a pattern formed by the repetition of simple geometric motifs such as triangles, squares, or circles. Occasionally he alternated plain panels with carved motifs for elegantly simple designs, as in the shutters he crafted for the McNay Art Institute (1970) (*see* MARION KOOGLER MCNAY ART MUSEUM). In other works, such as his wall of carved basswood sticks for the Denton Public Library (1967), he combined a variety of motifs for a tapestry effect. He also combined materials to effect a rich interplay of color and texture; his wooden doors for the Lone Star Steel Company in Dallas, which feature panels of lead and copper hammered into star and circle shapes, are an outstanding example of this technique.

Ford designed his work with an awareness of the way light falls across surfaces. In many of his carved pieces, traces of chisel marks lend a stippled effect that activates the surface of the object. He preferred natural colors and used unorthodox materials, such as shoe polish, baby oil, and car wax, to achieve and maintain a desired color. A spirit of self-reliance and innovation frequently shaped Ford's technique: for example, when he made six ceramic plaques representing the six flags of Texas (1958) for the Villita Assembly Building in San Antonio, he carved the patterns into dry clay, an unusual method that suited his wood-carving skills. Ford used both hand and machine tools, and frequently invented his own when standard tools were not available. He usually drew patterns directly onto an object, a habit formed when paper was scarce.

During the 1960s he completed a number of private and public commissions, often working on projects with his brother. In 1964–65 he made several decorative objects for the Chapman Graduate Center and the Marguerite B. Parker Chapel, both on the Trinity University campus in San Antonio. He carved the wooden screen wall for the federal courthouse in San Antonio (1968) and the wooden entry doors for the post office in Johnson City (1969). Between 1963 and 1975 he completed a carved wooden wall, doors, a light fixture, and a sign for Skidmore College in Saratoga Springs, New York. Although Ford avoided art competitions and public recognition, he nevertheless received an award for "outstanding craftswork" from the San Antonio Conservation Society[qv] in 1962. He also received an award for "excellence in craftsmanship" from the San Antonio chapter of the American Institute of Architects in the 1960s and again, posthumously, in 1983. In the 1960s his work was honored in an exhibition at Trinity University and featured in a regional craft exhibition sponsored by the San Antonio Craft Guild at the Witte Memorial Museum.[qv]

Ford never married, but his life was filled with companionship provided by his close family, assistants in his shop, and a diverse group of friends. He constantly attracted new apprentices, who were drawn by his sense of design, his philosophy that one learned by doing, and his gift for spinning yarns. In the 1970s he informally adopted a young woman named Denise Kocourek and paid for her education at Texas A&M. He suffered heart attacks in 1965 and 1970, and in 1973 he decided to retire. He continued to produce work in a shop that he set up in a barn on Pyron Street until he died, on January 1, 1978. At the time of his death he had produced work for over 100 clients throughout Texas and also had fulfilled commissions in Colorado, California, and New York. The San Antonio Conservation Society has awarded an annual Lynn Ford Memorial Craftsmanship Award in his honor since 1978.

BIBLIOGRAPHY: Michael Ennis, "Doing What Comes Naturally," *Texas Monthly*, June 1978. Mary Lance, *Lynn Ford: Texas Artist and Craftsman* (San Antonio: Trinity University Press, 1978). San Antonio *Express-News*, January 2, 1978. *Kendall Curlee*

FORD, O'NEIL (1905–1982). O'Neil Ford, architect, son of Bert and Lula Belle (Sinclair) Ford, was born at Pink Hill, near Sherman, Texas, on December 3, 1905. His creative bent was nurtured by his parents, who sought educational opportunities for their children. He attended a progressive elementary school in Sherman, where drawing was incorporated into every phase of the curriculum. After Bert Ford died in a railroad accident, Mrs. Ford moved her family to the university town of Denton. Neil assumed the responsibilities of breadwinner at twelve. He developed a flair for persuasive showmanship to obtain jobs for himself and his younger brother, Lynn Ford,[qv] who gained fame as a wood-carver and cabinetmaker, and sister Authella (Mrs. Roland Hersh), skilled in working with copper. He perfected this technique throughout his lifetime to bring in jobs for his architectural firm or to lobby for favorite environmental or political causes. During his high school years Ford haunted the library at the nearby college, where the librarian encouraged his passion for reading. He entered North Texas State (now the University of North Texas) in 1924, but economic pressures forced him to abandon his efforts to get a formal education after two years. Ford subsequently enrolled in an architecture course from the International Correspondence Schools of Scranton, Pennsylvania. His lack of university training became part of his mystique. In 1924 he and an uncle traveled through the Alsatian and German communities of Castroville, Brackettville, and Fredericksburg. Ford was deeply impressed by the simplicity and beauty of the German vernacular architecture,[qv] and the experience decisively influenced his later work.

In 1926 Ford entered the office of Dallas architect David R. Williams,[qv] a leading spokesman for Texas vernacular architecture, where he served his apprenticeship. Flamboyant, extravagant, and often outrageous, Williams became Ford's role model. He responded to Ford's abilities as a designer, and together they produced a number of fine regional houses of native brick, wood, and stone in north central Texas. Ford was deeply influenced by the tradition of the English Arts and Crafts Movement and the works of Greene and Greene in California, especially their attempt to synthesize architecture and visual arts. In an attempt to carry on this tradition he enlisted the help of his brother, Lynn, to carve doors, mantels, and beams; artists Jerry Bywaters and Thomas M. Stell, Jr.,[qqv] also collaborated on many projects, stenciling walls and making mosaics. During the Great Depression[qv] the young architect worked on WPA projects and with the

Texas Instruments Semi-Conductor Building during construction, Dallas, ca. 1958. O'Neil Ford, architect. Photograph by N. Bleeker Green. Reprinted by permission of Texas Instruments. This structure united manufacturing, labs, and offices under one roof, and provided interior courtyards to facilitate collegial exchange.

Rural Resettlement Administration. Ford formed his first partnership in 1937 with Arch Swank in Dallas. Their major job was the Little Chapel in the Woods on the campus of Texas Woman's University, Denton, constructed by National Youth Administration[qv] trainees with interior craft elements by college art students. The restoration of La Villita[qv] by the Work Projects Administration[qv] precipitated Ford's move to San Antonio, where he took Jerry Rogers as his partner (1939–53). Their research into building systems including the Youtz–Slick lift slab and stressed concrete was put to the test in 1949, when they received the commission to design a new campus for Trinity University in San Antonio, along with Bartlett Cocke and Harvey P. Smith.[qqv] From 1953 to 1965 O'Neil Ford and Associates did a number of projects for burgeoning Texas Instruments,[qv] both in Texas and abroad. Among the firm's best-known works for TI was the Semiconductor Building in Dallas (1958), which made use of a new structural system made of thin concrete shells known as hyperbolic paraboloids, developed by Mexican architect Félix Candela. In 1967 Ford formed a partnership with Boone Powell and Chris Carson. Bright young people fresh out of architecture schools were eager to work in this innovative office, and Ford's best work was accomplished in collaboration with talented youth. Campuses for Skidmore College in New York and the first phase of the University of Texas at San Antonio are notable examples of the firm's work during Ford's final years.

O'Neil Ford devoted much energy to serving causes outside his profession. During World War II[qv] he was a flight instructor in the United States Army Air Force. In later years he was often called upon for advice on historic preservation, the environment, aesthetics, and quality education. In 1968 he was appointed by President Lyndon B. Johnson[qv] to the National Council on the Arts. David Rockefeller, Jr., invited him to serve on the American Council for the Arts in Education (1975). Ford was a member of numerous professional, civic, and social organizations. He was a liberal Democrat. Honors garnered in his later years included election in 1960 to the College of Fellows, American Institute of Architects, and honorary doctoral degrees awarded by Trinity University of San Antonio (1967), Southern Methodist University (1973), the University of Dallas (1976), and Skidmore College, New York. The first endowed chair in the School of Architecture at the University of Texas at Austin was named for Ford. Ford married Wanda Graham in 1940; the couple had four children. Wanda Ford served as president of the San Antonio Conservation Society[qv] (1955–57) and played a prominent role in the community. O'Neil Ford died on July 20, 1982, in San Antonio.

BIBLIOGRAPHY: Carole Cable, *O'Neil Ford, Architect* (Monticello, Illinois: Vance Bibliographies, 1981). Dallas *Morning News,* July 25, 1982. David Dillon, *Dallas Architecture, 1936–1986* (Austin: Texas Monthly Press, 1985). Mary Carolyn Hollers George, *O'Neil Ford, Architect* (College Station: Texas A&M University Press, 1992). Vertical Files, Barker Texas History Center, University of Texas at Austin.

Mary Carolyn Hollers George

FORD, TEXAS. Ford is at the intersection of U.S. Highway 385 and Farm Road 2587 in northeastern Deaf Smith County. It is named for J. W. (John) Ford, who brought his family to his homestead in November 1901 and later served as county assessor. Several more homesteaders followed, and by 1905 a school had been established there.

The school building also served as an interdenominational church and as a community center. After the school district was consolidated with that of Hereford in 1940, the building was seldom used until the 1950s, when the county bought it and remodeled it as a shop for maintaining road equipment. The local 4-H Club and Extension Homemakers also use it, and elections are held there as well. The 1983 county highway map showed three businesses at Ford.

BIBLIOGRAPHY: *Deaf Smith County: The Land and Its People* (Hereford, Texas: Deaf Smith County Historical Society, 1982).

H. Allen Anderson

FORD CREEK. Ford Creek rises about 1½ miles northeast of Kanawha in northwestern Red River County (at 33°53′ N, 95°14′ W) and runs first north, then east, for a total of eight miles before reaching its mouth on the Red River (at 33°57′ N, 95°10′ W). The stream, which is intermittent in its upper reaches, initially traverses an area with loamy soils, changing to clayey near its mouth. The area to the east and south of the stream is generally wooded with pines and hardwoods. On the other side of its lower reaches, however, the land is primarily used to grow sorghum, grain, or cotton.

FORD AND NEIGHBORS TRAIL. The Ford and Neighbors Trail was a route between Austin and El Paso laid out in the spring and summer of 1849 by Robert S. Neighbors and John S. Ford,qqv who were accompanied by D. C. Sullivan, A. D. Neal, and various Indian guides and interpreters. The outward route taken by the party to El Paso was declared impractical, but the return route, well watered and easily followed, was recommended and marked for general travel. As used by numbers of California-bound emigrants, the route followed several trails from Austin to the head of Brady Creek in what is now Concho County, an overland distance of 160 miles. From Brady Creek the trail went seventy-five miles west to Blue River, or the Middle Concho, a site now in the northwest corner of Irion County, thence southwest forty-five miles to Flat Rock water hole in the area of present Upton County, thence west thirty-five miles to a point on the Pecos River, probably near the mouth of Comanche Creek in present Crane County, thence up the Pecos 110 miles into New Mexico, thence northwest for forty miles, and thence southwest for 115 miles to El Paso. The total distance between Austin and El Paso was 580 miles, and the trip could be made in twenty days on horseback.

BIBLIOGRAPHY: C. L. Greenwood, "Opening Routes to El Paso, 1894," *Southwestern Historical Quarterly* 48 (October 1944). William J. Hughes, *Rebellious Ranger: Rip Ford and the Old Southwest* (Norman: University of Oklahoma Press, 1964). Kenneth F. Neighbours, *Robert Simpson Neighbors and the Texas Frontier, 1836–1859* (Waco: Texian Press, 1975).

FORDTRAN, CHARLES (1801–1900). Charles Fordtran, early settler and surveyor, son of John H. Fordtran, was born in Minden, Westphalia, on May 7, 1801. He immigrated to America in 1830 and in January 1831 joined Friedrich Ernstqv to move to Texas, where they began the settlement that developed into the town of Industry. Fordtran surveyed Ernst's grant in Stephen F. Austin'sqv colony for one-fourth of the land. He marked the boundaries of Samuel M. Williams'sqv land. Fordtran was in poor health and spent some time with Henry Austinqv at Bolivar Point and some time in Mississippi before he purchased a half headright now in Austin County in 1833. He made a contract to secure 800 families for Austin's colony but became discouraged and gave up the idea. In 1835 and 1836 he was a member of Capt. James Bird's company of Spy Rangers and, as such, helped move Texas families out of reach of the Mexicans and protected the communities from Indian attacks. Fordtran married Almeida Brookfield on July 4, 1834, and they had nine children. The family home was in Austin County, where Fordtran died on November 1, 1900.

BIBLIOGRAPHY: *History of Texas, Together with a Biographical History of the Cities of Houston and Galveston* (Chicago: Lewis, 1895). Frank W. Johnson, *A History of Texas and Texans* (5 vols., ed. E. C. Barker and E. W. Winkler [Chicago and New York: American Historical Society, 1914; rpt. 1916]).

Carolyn Hyman

FORDTRAN, TEXAS. Fordtran, just west of U.S. Highway 77 and twenty miles north of Victoria in Victoria County, was named for Henry Fordtran, a Galveston real estate agent responsible for bringing settlers to the site from Tennessee and the Midwest in 1898. The area was once part of the 44 Ranch, which in 1844 covered parts of DeWitt, Victoria, and Goliad counties. By 1899 most of the ranch had been sold to developers. One factor in the location of the community may have been the promise of the Guadalupe Valley Railroad, which was to have run through the site on its way from Port O'Connor to Yoakum and Austin. Though the roadbed was built from the coast to Hallettsville by 1898, the line was never completed because funds ran out. Nevertheless, by 1900 the settlement was thriving. It had a post office from 1898 to about 1930. The Fordtran Oil Company was established in 1915. A rural common school was built at the community, and by 1920 Fordtran's population had risen to seventy-five. By the 1950s, however, the town was in decline. The Fordtran school was discontinued, after which area students attended classes within the Victoria Independent School District. Fordtran's population was reported as eighteen from 1974 to 1990.

BIBLIOGRAPHY: Roy Grimes, ed., *300 Years in Victoria County* (Victoria, Texas: Victoria *Advocate*, 1968; rpt., Austin: Nortex, 1985). Victoria *Advocate*, Progress Edition, March 10, 1963.

Craig H. Roell

FORE, SAM JR. (1891–1966). Sam Fore, Jr., newspaperman, the son of Samuel Lane and Letitia (Chenault) Fore, was born in Cuero, Texas, on May 3, 1891. His family moved to Stockdale, in Wilson County, and finally in 1903 to Floresville. But even at Stockdale, before he was twelve, the boy had smelled printer's ink, at Charles Hanson's *Enterprise*, and he prevailed upon the old editor to make him the printer's devil. There, for six months, he learned to set type by hand from wooden cases in the tiny plant. When the family moved to Floresville, Sam soon was nominally on the payroll of the *Chronicle*, a semiweekly owned by Dr. John V. Blake, a local physician. Here, before and after school and on Saturdays, Fore learned to set type at the rate of two galleys an hour, as well as to pump the old-fashioned press and to handle job printing. When he finished the eighth grade, he began full-time employment with Blake and was soon getting into the editorial side of country newspaper work. In 1910 he was promoted to society editor and in 1911 to assistant editor.

On July 11, 1911, Fore married Elma Teas, daughter of C. S. Teas, a family friend. Later that year, when H. C. Thompson, editor of the *Chronicle*, died, Blake concluded that Fore was the man to take over as editor. Sam was barely twenty. Two years later Blake proposed that the young couple (Elma was working in the front office) should buy the paper. The purchase became official at year's end, 1912.

Sam and Elma Fore devoted the next forty-nine years toward making the Floresville *Chronicle Journal* an effective instrument for community improvement. The new editor made a point of traveling throughout the county to meet his public. He did not neglect Floresville itself. In February of his first year as publisher he organized a civic club; it soon had thirty-five members, and Fore was its secretary. The first business of the new club was to organize a city "Clean Up Campaign," which Fore backed with full publicity. During those same months he ran for city clerk in the April election and won, 169 to 52. It was the only political office he ever held, and he held it for fifty years.

In 1919, five years after he first attended the annual convention of the Texas Press Association,qv he was elected vice president. A year later he was president—the youngest president ever elected. In the

1920s he helped organize the South Texas Press Association to serve the special interests of that region. He continued active in both groups for the rest of his life.

His hometown paper was always the base of his operations. In the 1960s a budding journalist, Emily Lamon, was chosen by a foundation to find and celebrate an ideal country editor. She found Sam Fore and wrote a little book about him. In her preface she says: "He believes in what he calls the mission of the press. 'If I couldn't say things good, I wouldn't say anything,' he says. 'I didn't try to step up strife and discord. It is as important to know what to leave out as what to put in. I never put anything sensational into the paper. That's not good for this town.' His ideas are strong— he never voted against a bond issue, never voted for liquor, and never scratched a Democrat on an election ticket. Yet his paper is not a campaign sheet for anything but community improvement. Sam Fore comes close to being THE country editor—and for his community he is."

Fore worked hard to establish the Wilson County Fair. The advent of World War I^qv got him into fund-raising; by the end of the war he was county chairman of the Great United War Work Campaign. In the 1920s he began to advocate the diversification of farm crops rather than total dependence on King Cotton. He began also to diversify his own business interests; he bought from the Chamber of Commerce in Robstown its newspaper, the Robstown *Record*. Operating under a succession of editors, the paper augmented the Fore family's income and extended Sam's influence. In May of 1929 Governor Dan Moody^qv appointed Fore a regent at the Texas College of Arts and Industries in Kingsville (now Texas A&M University at Kingsville), adjacent to the King Ranch.^qv His served two six-year terms.

In the 1930s Floresville was in the Nineteenth Congressional District, which ran all the way from San Antonio south to the coast, including Floresville and the King Ranch. Richard M. Kleberg,^qv was the congressman for that district, and Sam Fore was his enthusiastic supporter. When Kleberg appointed a young unknown, Lyndon B. Johnson,^qv to his staff, he told Johnson to go by Floresville and visit Sam Fore before reporting for duty. Johnson made such an impression on Sam and Elma Fore that Sam told Elma next morning, as they watched him drive away: "That boy is going to be President of the U.S.A., and I'm going to be at his inauguration." This was the beginning of a close relationship between the small-town editor and the rising young politician.

The country was by now in the depths of the Great Depression,^qv and Floresville and all South Texas was suffering. Fore worked through Johnson and Kleberg to get all possible relief measures from the burgeoning New Deal programs. He had become Democratic executive committeeman for the Nineteenth Senatorial District. His efforts in behalf of this constituency won him the appellation "Mr. Democrat of South Texas."

Sam and Elma Fore had two daughters. When the family attended the Democratic Convention in Philadelphia in 1936, Governor James Allred^qv appointed one of the daughters Texas Sweetheart at the Convention. To the delight of all Texas Democrats, Marion Fore was chosen "Queen" of the entire convention. Sam Fore attended his last Democratic Convention at Atlantic City in 1964. He and Elma had operated the *Chronicle Journal* for a full half century. They were past seventy, and Sam's health was failing. They sold the paper on September 1, 1963, to Mr. and Mrs. Joe H. Fietsam.

Fore died at home in Floresville on December 24, 1966. President and Mrs. Johnson headed those who joined the Fores' neighbors at the Methodist church on December 26 to pay their last respects. He was survived by his wife, his two daughters, four grandchildren, and one great-grandchild.

BIBLIOGRAPHY: Emily Lamon, *Sam Fore, Jr., Community Newspaper Editor* (Austin: Department of Journalism Development Program, University of Texas, 1966). Vertical Files, Barker Texas History Center, University of Texas at Austin.

Roy L. Swift

FOREMAN, PERCY EUGENE (1902–1988). Percy Eugene Foreman, criminal-defense lawyer, the son of Ransom Parson and William Pinckney (Rogers) Foreman, a Polk County sheriff, was born on June 21, 1902, in a log cabin near Cold Springs, Texas. He was one of eight children. At the age of six he was a shoeshine boy in Livingston. At fifteen he left school to pursue a variety of enterprises; these included shoeshine stands, newspaper routes, a laundry, a bill-collection agency, and a contract to load bales of cotton on freight trains—for which he eventually hired laborers to do the work for eight cents a bale. By the end of World War I^qv Foreman had accumulated significant savings. After finishing a correspondence course in Houston and spending a year at the Staunton Military Academy in Virginia, he joined a chautauqua circuit and toured small towns giving humorous lectures on topics including "how to get the most out of life" and "the high mission of women." In 1927 he graduated from the University of Texas law school, where he had typed manuscripts for extra money. He was admitted to the State Bar of Texas^qv and spent several years as a county prosecutor and assistant district attorney before entering private practice as a junior partner in the Houston law firm of Lockett and Foreman. Foreman, who was known for his unconventional trial strategies, handled society divorces, and in sixty years of practice defended more than 1,000 accused murderers, only one of whom was executed. Among his most famous clients were James Earl Ray, whom he persuaded to plead guilty to the assassination of Martin Luther King, Jr., in exchange for a life sentence; socialite Candace Mossler's nephew Melvin Lane Powers, acquitted of a murder charge; Alvin Lee King, who killed five people in a Baptist church and committed suicide before his trial; and Charles Harrelson, sentenced to fifteen years for a contract killing and involved in the assassination of a federal judge in San Antonio. Foreman preferred cash as payment for his services, but if a client didn't have any, he would take property instead, including jewelry, real estate, boats, automobiles, furniture, and artwork. He became a multimillionaire. Foreman served as president of the National Association of Defense Lawyers. He was twice married; he and his first wife adopted a son. On April 21, 1957, he married German-born Marguerite Obert, with whom he had one child. Foreman died on August 25, 1988, and was buried at Forest Park Westheimer.

BIBLIOGRAPHY: *Alcalde* (magazine of the Ex-Students' Association of the University of Texas), June 1926. Houston Metropolitan Research Center Files, Houston Public Library. Vertical Files, Barker Texas History Center, University of Texas at Austin.

Diana J. Kleiner

FORENSIC MEDICINE. Broadly, the term *forensic medicine* can be applied to medicine generally or can denote the forensic aspects of the several specialties of medicine either collectively or individually. Hence the designations forensic psychiatry, forensic pediatrics, forensic pathology, and so on. In the narrow sense the term denotes forensic pathology, which may be defined as the application of the medical specialty of pathology to problems of law. Traditionally, this linkage between law and pathology—the use of a body of knowledge dealing with the reaction of the body to disease and injury to resolve legal questions—has been the province of the medicolegal investigator of death, whether he be a pathologist to the coroner or a medical examiner. It is the task of the pathologist to examine the body of the victim of the homicidal attack, of the suicidal venture, or of the accident, as well as to examine the mortal remains of those who have died under unusual circumstances, or where the cause of death is unknown or questioned.

In Texas there are no coroners. The duties and the responsibilities of the coroner's office are delegated to the justices of the peace. The justices derive their death-investigation powers from the portion of the Texas Code of Criminal Procedure loosely designated as the "Inquest Law." This segment of the code is old and was originally intended to provide for the detection of homicide. It has been modified many times and in the process has been extended so as to include the authority of the justice to investigate suicidal deaths, deaths due to accident, and other deaths. It is not known when a justice of the peace, in the exercise of his duties, first ordered a physician to undertake an autopsy to determine the cause of death. Certainly this was an uncommon practice, not only in frontier days, but also and more recently in the more remote and sparsely settled counties. There is no record of how many times a quick examination of a body was carried out in funeral homes or at graveside by physicians whose primary interest was the treatment of patients, not the performance of autopsies to determine the cause of death. Certainly such examinations were conducted, but no central repository of records exists, and with 254 counties, each maintaining records of its own (sometimes very incomplete), no coherent picture of this phase of the forensic examination of bodies emerges. Physicians who conducted these examinations most probably considered such activity as public service and responded to the order of the justice of the peace as one way of bringing their area of expertise to aid in the administration of justice.

Lost also in the records of numberless court cases and files of the justices of the peace are records of early instances of the employment of pathologists to perform autopsies in the interests of justice. Most certainly this first occurred in Galveston County, where the first medical school in Texas was opened, or in the other populous counties such as Harris County, where pathologists were most likely to be located. These pathologists, whoever they may have been, served not only to bring their expertise to the better administration of justice, but also as a nidus of agitation for the passage of a medical-examiner law in the state. In the late 1940s and early 1950s a coalition of physicians (both pathologists and others), attorneys, and others pushed for legislative action to permit heavily populated counties to establish positions for appointed medical examiners. These were to be physicians skilled in autopsies, that is, pathologists. The so-called Baker Bill was proposed at the 1955 session of the Texas legislature and with some modification was enacted into law and thus became part of the Code of Criminal Procedure. The new law provided that counties with a population of more than 500,000 were required to establish a medical-examiner system, with the proviso that if such a county had within its boundaries a medical school the system was not required. Bexar County (without a medical school) was thereby required to establish a system. Harris and Dallas counties (each with a medical school) were not required to establish a system; the former opted for a medical-examiner system, the latter chose not to establish one. Dr. Gared E. Clarke was appointed the medical examiner for Harris County in 1957. That same year Dr. Joseph A. Jachimczyk began serving as the forensic pathologist to the medical examiner and, upon Dr. Clarke's retirement in 1960, was appointed medical examiner, and held the position in the late 1980s. For many years he worked under very difficult conditions in inadequate facilities. After nearly thirty years of continuous service to the county and several false starts, Jachimczyk was provided a fine new building designated as the Dr. Joseph A. Jachimczyk Forensic Center of Harris County. This was public recognition of long and faithful public forensic service in the interests of justice. The Bexar County Commissioners Court appointed Dr. Robert Hausmann medical examiner in 1956. His office and laboratory were situated in the county hospital and, like that in Harris County, were inadequate for the task. A modern building housing office and laboratory was constructed in 1971. Dr. Vincent J. M. DiMaio assumed office in 1981.

Over the years there were a few changes in the basic law, some of which eventually made it possible for any county to adopt the medical-examiner law. As of 1986 the following counties had adopted the law and appointed medical examiners: Bexar, Collin, Dallas, El Paso, Galveston, Harris, Johnson, Nueces, Tarrant, Travis, and Wichita. Other counties were contemplating such action. It should be noted that once a county has adopted the medical-examiner law, all duties and responsibilities of the justices of the peace with regard to death investigation devolve upon the medical examiner; further, there does not appear to be any "escape clause"—having adopted the law, the county must keep the medical examiner's office in operation.

Some of the Texas county medical examiner systems are first class; others are hampered by lack of adequate facilities and support. Also, the personalities of the medical examiners have influenced the advance of forensic pathology, for better or worse. Dallas County, reluctant at first to develop a medical-examiner system, finally adopted the law in 1969. Harris and Bexar counties had at that time operated systems for more than ten years. But when Dallas County did establish a system, it did so with characteristic energy and great foresight. A modern facility in which to house the medical examiner's activities was constructed as rapidly as possible. In addition, a unique arrangement was set up whereby the criminal investigation laboratory (the "crime lab") and the medical examiner's office were combined in the new facility and placed under the same administrative head. This combined enterprise, named the Southwestern Institute of Forensic Sciences, has since been expanded to include other forensic activities such as the examination of rape victims and the functions of the Rape Crisis and Child Sexual Abuse Center. Bexar and Tarrant counties subsequently adopted similar arrangements. An integral part of an adequate medical examiner's facility is the provision of a reasonable forensic toxicology laboratory. Harris, Dallas, and Bexar counties have established these, and others are building them. By the 1980s forensic toxicology had become a complex activity requiring academic education, trained technologists, and highly sophisticated equipment so as to detect, identify, and measure very small amounts of drugs and poison diluted in the tissues of the body. One of the interesting spinoffs of the county medical examiners' offices is their use by other counties. Several of the larger and better equipped medical examiners provide an autopsy service for the justices of the peace of counties still operating under the old Inquest Law. Thus the larger offices are serving, to a degree, as regional forensic centers and provide a service sorely needed for reasonable death investigation.

From time to time there have been some efforts to establish a statewide medical-examiner system. The cost of establishing and maintaining such a system, however, is not inconsiderable, and the legislature has been reluctant to support such proposals. Other concepts, such as the "regional forensic center" plan, have been advanced. With the anticipated shortfall in revenues, it would appear that either a statewide system or a state regional system will be slow in developing. Education is an activity of medical examiners sometimes not recognized, especially when a medical school is located in a county where a strong and active medical-examiner system operates. Because the medical-examiner law mandates that all "unnatural" deaths be investigated by the office, instances of death as a result of all manner of traumas are not available for teaching of medical students and young physicians in residency training. The medical examiner must provide such teaching, especially since trauma is frequently a cause of death in our society.

The medical examiner or justice of the peace also supplies transplantable tissues and organs. In 1977 a law was passed enabling the medical examiner or justice of the peace to remove corneas for transplant. Many thousands of Texans have had their sight restored as a result of this forward-looking legislative action. In 1985 attempts were made to broaden the law; time will tell how effective this new legislation will be. The provision of tissues and organs for transplantation is a predictable extension of forensic medicine, for medical examiners investigate deaths from injuries, frequently of younger people without disease. Perhaps in the long run, this newer activity will be the lever to promulgate better scientific death investigation in Texas.

BIBLIOGRAPHY: William J. Curran, A. Louis McGarry, and Charles S. Petty, *Modern Legal Medicine: Psychiatry and Forensic Science* (Philadelphia: Davis, 1980).

Charles S. Petty

FOREST, JOHN ANTHONY (1838–1911). John Anthony Forest, third Catholic bishop of San Antonio, son of Jean and Marie (Thollet) Forest, was born at St. Martin-la-Sauvete, Loire, France, on December 26, 1838. He was educated at the Petit seminaries of St. Jodard, Loire, and L'Argentière, Rhône, and at the Grande Seminary of St. Irénée, Lyons. He was subdeacon at Lyons when he responded to the call issued by the newly consecrated Bishop Claude Marie Dubuis[qv] of Galveston for seminarians to come to Texas as missionaries. Forest and about fifty of his fellow students sailed for New Orleans on January 3, 1863. They were refused admittance to the port when they arrived, however, since Gen. Ben Butler suspected that they might be allies of the Confederacy. He finally allowed them ashore when he had been convinced that they were only missionaries. They entered the seminary at Bouligny, New Orleans, where Forest was ordained by Bishop Dubuis on April 17, 1863. Shortly thereafter, he and two companions were sent to San Antonio, Texas, to begin their apostolates. They traveled on foot and by oxcart by way of Mexico because of the raging Civil War[qv] and arrived at their destination about three weeks later. Forest stayed in San Antonio only a month before he was assigned to work as assistant to Father Charles Padey, pastor of St. Mary's Church at Smothers Creek in Lavaca County. He eventually became pastor of St. Mary's and later of Sacred Heart Church in Hallettsville, which was about four miles away. During his thirty-two years in that area, he built many new churches and schools and made improvements in many others. He did much of the labor required for these tasks with his own hands. When he arrived at St. Mary's he knew little English and no Czech. Within three months he had mastered a practical vocabulary in both languages and had won the admiration of his parishioners.

Forest remained in Hallettsville until 1895, when he was appointed successor to Bishop John C. Neraz[qv] of San Antonio. He was consecrated on October 28 of that year in San Fernando de Béxar Cathedral[qv] by Archbishop Francis Janssens of New Orleans. His tenure as bishop, like that of Neraz, was marked by tremendous growth of the diocese. Many new parishes came into being, and many of the old ones built larger churches and schools. The religious orders in the area were also establishing new convents and schools. During Forest's first year as bishop, the Sisters of Divine Providence[qv] opened the Academy of Our Lady of the Lake (now Our Lady of the Lake University). In the years that followed, the Sisters of Charity of the Incarnate Word[qv] opened Incarnate Word Academy, and the Sisters of Our Lady of Charity of Refuge came to San Antonio at the request of the bishop and founded Our Lady of Victory School, a rehabilitation center for delinquent and neglected girls. In 1899 the Ursuline Sisters,[qv] who had been in the city since 1851, established a new academy; and in 1902 Forest invited the Claretians to take charge of San Fernando Cathedral to work with the Spanish-speaking population.

He continued to bring in religious orders and to develop the educational facilities in the diocese. Though this work was important, it was something of an outgrowth of the work of previous bishops. Forest's most striking achievement was his fostering of the establishment of more and better charitable institutions. The Incarnate Word nuns bought St. Mary's Sanatorium in Boerne in 1896 to work exclusively with tubercular patients, and Forest established the Home for the Colored Poor in San Antonio in 1901. He put Father John A. Dumoulin in charge of the home, which became the nucleus of Holy Redeemer Parish, associated with St. Peter Claver Parish. In 1906 St. Francis Home for the Aged was completed, and in 1910 the doors of St. John's Sanitarium (named for Forest) in San Angelo were opened.

Forest continued his building projects, but as the Catholic population grew, he also sought to improve the administration of the diocese. He expanded the number of officials from about four to about eighteen in the sixteen years he held office, and in 1906 he called the first diocesan synod at St. Louis College (now St. Mary's University). Also during his tenure San Antonio was honored by the visits of two apostolic delegates to the United States. The first delegate, Francesco Cardinal Satolli, visited on February 24, 1896, and in 1903 Archbishop Diomede Falconio came to San Antonio to bless the cornerstone of the new Oblate Seminary (now the Oblate School of Theology).

Forest's health began to fail around 1910, and he asked for an assistant to help with the affairs of the diocese. Father John William Shaw[qv] of Mobile, Alabama, was appointed coadjutor with the right of succession on February 7, 1910. The bishop formally welcomed him in a ceremony held at San Fernando Cathedral on May 18 and shortly thereafter retired to Santa Rosa Infirmary (now Santa Rosa Hospital). He suffered a stroke in February and died on March 11, 1911, thus ending an era in the history of the Catholic Church[qv] in Texas. Forest was the last of the great missionaries, the "Apostles from Lyons," who came to evangelize the Southwest. Bishop Shaw and Bishop John B. Morris of Little Rock, Arkansas, celebrated a pontifical Mass for him on March 15, 1911, in San Fernando Cathedral. Forest was buried in San Fernando Cemetery.

BIBLIOGRAPHY: *Archdiocese of San Antonio: Diamond Jubilee, 1874–1949* (San Antonio, 1949). Carlos E. Castañeda, *Our Catholic Heritage in Texas* (7 vols., Austin: Von Boeckmann–Jones, 1936–1958; rpt., New York: Arno, 1976). Catholic Archives of Texas, Files, Austin. Pierre F. Parisot and C. J. Smith, *History of the Catholic Church in the Diocese of San Antonio* (San Antonio: Carrico and Bowen, 1897). Alexander C. Wangler, ed., *Archdiocese of San Antonio, 1874–1974* (San Antonio, 1974).

Mary H. Ogilvie

FOREST, TEXAS. Forest is on the Old Jim Hogg Highway, better known as Farm Road 1911, ten miles south of Alto in southeastern Cherokee County. The community was established when Wiley Thompson opened the first business—a store, saloon, watermill, gristmill, and cotton gin—on Larrison Creek. The name Forest is said to have come from a traveler who was resting under a tree and who, when asked why he was there, replied, "For rest." In March 1879 Wiley Thompson was appointed the first postmaster at the community. The mail was transferred to Wells in 1887 but was routed back to Forest the same year. The post office was permanently transferred to Wells in 1980. During the 1920s and 1930s the Forest area produced tomatoes, and two tomato packing sheds were built beside the Cotton Belt Railroad (officially known as the St. Louis Southwestern Railway of Texas). The Forest Baptist Church was established in 1888 with a pastor named Rushing. In the 1980s Forest was mainly a cattle-raising community, and its only store was in and out of business. During the first half of the twentieth century, Forest's population was reported as around 100. It was reported as 120 from the 1950s to the 1970s and as eighty-five in 1990.

BIBLIOGRAPHY: *Cherokee County History* (Jacksonville, Texas: Cherokee County Historical Commission, 1986). Hattie Joplin Roach, *A History of Cherokee County* (Dallas: Southwest, 1934).

Phyllis Aswell

FOREST ACADEMY, TEXAS. Forest Academy, a farming community just off State Highway 11 and eight miles southeast of Sulphur Springs in southeastern Hopkins County, developed in the early 1850s around a combination church and school at a site in a dense forest. Each summer until the early 1900s the community, which was made up almost exclusively of Methodist families, held revival meetings in a large open-air church there. Around 1900 Forest Academy had a public school, which in 1905 had an enrollment of sixty. By the early 1930s the community had a church, a cemetery, and a few houses, and by the early 1960s only the church and cemetery remained at the site. Forest Academy was a dispersed rural community in the late 1980s.

BIBLIOGRAPHY: Florene Chapman Adams, *Hopkins County and Our Heritage.* (Sulphur Springs, Texas: 197–?).

Christopher Long

FORESTBURG, TEXAS. Forestburg is at the intersection of Farm roads 455, 1655, 922, and 677, some fifteen miles southeast of Montague in southeastern Montague County. It was settled in the early 1850s by cattlemen including Austin Perryman, Wash Williams, and Bob Clark, and remained largely undeveloped, due to frequent Indian raids, until the 1870s. The county's first school was established near the settlement in 1858. It was originally known as Horn Hill, but the name was changed soon after its founding to Forest Hill because of its location in a grove of live oak trees. When its post office application was rejected because there was already a Forest Hill in Texas, the community was renamed Forestburg. A post office began operations locally in 1876. By 1885 Forestburg had a population of 200 and a number of businesses, including sawmills and cotton gins. By 1900 its population had reached 372, and a telephone system had been established there. The community's population declined from 212 in the mid-1920s to 100 by the mid-1950s, when eight businesses were operating there. From the mid-1970s through the early 1990s Forestburg reported a population of 200. In the early 1990s it also had eight businesses and the post office.

BIBLIOGRAPHY: Guy Renfro Donnell, The History of Montague County, Texas (M.A. thesis, University of Texas, 1940). Jeff S. Henderson, ed., *One Hundred Years in Montague County, Texas* (St. Jo, Texas: Ipta Printer, 1978).
Brian Hart

FOREST CHAPEL, TEXAS. Forest Chapel is a church community at the intersection of Farm roads 197 and 1500, just north of Pat Mayse State Park and two miles southwest of Chicota in extreme northern Lamar County. The area was settled by 1896, when the Forest Chapel school reported fifty-six students and two teachers. Though the settlement was not named on the 1936 county highway map, it was shown with two churches, two cemeteries, a cotton gin, and a cluster of dwellings at the crossroads. By that time the Forest Chapel school had closed, and local children attended the nearby Forest Grove school. Throughout the 1940s the Forest Chapel community reported one business and twenty-five residents. By 1957 the Forest Grove school had been consolidated into the Chicota Independent School District, which had become part of the North Lamar system by 1970. In 1980 the community had the Forest Chapel Church and cemetery as well as a few scattered dwellings. County highway maps identified one business at the site in 1984.
Vista K. McCroskey

FOREST CREEK. Forest Creek, formerly considered part of Chrystal Creek, rises twenty miles northwest of Sterling City in northwestern Sterling County (at 32°02′ N, 101°14′ W) and runs northeast for fifteen miles, passing into southwestern Mitchell County, where it reaches its mouth on Mustang Creek, fourteen miles south of Westbrook (at 32°09′ N, 101°04′ W). The stream traverses generally flat terrain with local shallow depressions, surfaced by clay and sandy loams that support water-tolerant hardwoods and grasses.

FOREST GLADE, TEXAS. Forest Glade is on U.S. Highway 14 and Farm Road 1633, three miles west of the Southern Pacific tracks, eight miles north of Groesbeck, and two miles south of Mexia in northern Limestone County. The site is on a mail route from Mexia and was temporarily settled in the late 1840s. W. A. Brown built a house there in 1861 and put the first local farm under cultivation. A school operated in the community as early as 1872, and in 1896 one teacher taught forty-five white students. In the late 1920s a store was established, and in 1933 the community had one business and a population of ten. The 1936 county highway map indicated a number of businesses and residences on State Highway 14, the only highway to Forest Glade at the time. The community's population had jumped to 450 by 1966, when the town had a cemetery and a drive-in movie theater. Forest Glade developed with the growth of its neighbor, Mexia. Oil deposits in the area stimulated regional growth. Also, the Southern Pacific line that ran three miles east of Forest Glade aided the development of the area. A Methodist church met for a time at Forest Glade. The town grew as people working in nearby Mexia and Groesbeck established homes in Forest Glade. In 1990 the community reported a population of 340.

BIBLIOGRAPHY: Groesbeck *Journal*, May 15, 1936.
Holly Marshall

FOREST GROVE, TEXAS (Collin County). Forest Grove is on Farm Road 1378 six miles south of McKinney in south central Collin County. It was settled about 1858 on White Rock Creek and served as a church and school community for area farmers. Its population was reported as twenty in 1990.

BIBLIOGRAPHY: Roy Franklin Hall and Helen Gibbard Hall, *Collin County: Pioneering in North Texas* (Quanah, Texas: Nortex, 1975).
David Minor

FOREST GROVE, TEXAS (Henderson County). Forest Grove was on the north side of Caney Creek, a tributary of Cedar Creek (now Cedar Creek Reservoir) about ten miles from Athens and just west of Malakoff in Henderson County. The diffuse rural settlement began about 1890 and covered about six square miles. At its peak it consisted of at least thirty-three residences, two stores, and a cemetery. By 1910 it was a prosperous farming community using some of the best farmlands in the county. Virtually all of the upland oak and hickory forest had been cleared by then. Most of the residents were white, though a few blacks lived as sharecropping tenants along the north side of Caney Creek in the bottomlands. The focal point of the community was the school, a one-room plank building with a shingled roof and a potbellied stove. After 1900, attendance averaged forty to fifty students. In 1913 the Hickory Grove and Forest Grove schools were consolidated, and a three-room brick structure was built at Stockard. The 1918–19 enrollment records showed 137 students at the Stockard school. The area was served by the Methodist and Baptist churches in Stockard and Pickens. Payne Cemetery, on the edge of the community, began in the 1840s as a burial plot for the Payne family, early settlers of the area, and was enlarged to become a central burial place. Two stores, the Davis and Taylor stores, were located in Forest Grove. Neither endured long, however, as most trade was conducted in the larger towns of Athens and Eustace. A post office was housed in a private residence. Forest Grove's economy centered on diversified agriculture. Cotton was the most important cash crop, while peaches, corn, peas, melons, and ribbon cane were also grown. This agricultural diversification allowed the community to survive the Great Depression.qv With mechanization, however, and the shift to larger farms in the late 1930s, Forest Grove began to decline. By 1948 the United States Geological Survey recorded only ten standing structures in the area that had been Forest Grove. Most of these were farm and ranch outbuildings. By 1985 the entire area was owned by Texas Power and Light Company (later renamed TU Electric).

BIBLIOGRAPHY: Thomas H. Guderjan, "Forest Grove: A Dispersed Farming Community in East Texas, Circa 1900," *East Texas Historical Journal* 20 (1982).
Thomas H. Guderjan

FOREST GROVE, TEXAS (Milam County). Forest Grove is a rural church community on U.S. Highway 77 some seven miles south of Rockdale in southern Milam County. Its population was reported as forty in 1966 and as sixty in 1990.
Vivian Elizabeth Smyrl

FOREST GROVE, TEXAS (Titus County). Forest Grove, often called Damascus by local residents, was about four miles northwest of Mount Pleasant in northwestern Titus County. Its first building was a log house that served as a church and school. Although the land had been donated for that purpose in 1868, the building was not constructed until sometime around 1880. The structure was called Damascus Church, and Damascus seems to have been the earliest name for the community. The only business known to have operated in the settlement was a country store owned and run by Jess Chapman. The school, which by 1910 was called Forest Grove, was maintained until 1956, when it was consolidated with the Mount Pleasant Independent School District. By 1971 the only building left in the community was a church that held no regular services but that was maintained to provide funeral services for those to be buried in the local cemetery.

BIBLIOGRAPHY: Quasqui Centennial Committee, *Titus County Celebrates 125 Years* (Mount Pleasant, Texas, 1971). *Cecil Harper, Jr.*

FOREST HILL, TEXAS (Lamar County). Forest Hill is a church community on Farm Road 38 three miles north of Petty in extreme western Lamar County. It had been established by 1936, when maps showed a church, a cemetery, a school, and a collection of dwellings there. The next year the community had a total of three teachers, who taught sixty-eight elementary school students and seventeen high school students. By 1957 the secondary school had been consolidated into the West Lamar system. In the early 1980s maps showed a Forest Hill Community Center, a church and cemetery, and a few scattered dwellings at the site.

BIBLIOGRAPHY: Thomas S. Justiss, An Administrative Survey of the Schools of Lamar County with a Plan for Their Reorganization (M.A. thesis, University of Texas, 1937). *Vista K. McCroskey*

FOREST HILL, TEXAS (Tarrant County). Forest Hill is at the intersection of Interstate Highway 20/820 and State Highway 496, eight miles southeast of Fort Worth in south central Tarrant County. It was established as a residential suburb of Fort Worth by 1896, when its segregated schools registered fifteen black students and ninety-one white students and employed three teachers. By 1905 Forest Hill operated no school for black students and two schools for white; the schools had 226 students and four teachers. In 1911 the community was designated a stop on the Fort Worth Southern Traction Company's electric interurban rail line between Fort Worth and Cleburne. By 1925 Forest Hill reported a population of twenty-five and two businesses. In the late 1940s the population was ninety; it increased to 1,519 by the mid-1950s. By this time Forest Hill had incorporated. Forest Hill continued to grow as a result of its proximity to Fort Worth: in 1967 its population was 3,800; in 1976 it was 19,250, and in 1990 it was 11,482.

BIBLIOGRAPHY: *Historic Resources Survey: Selected Tarrant County Communities* (Fort Worth: Historic Preservation Council for Tarrant County, 1990). *Brian Hart*

FOREST HILL, TEXAS (Upshur County). Forest Hill, a farming community on the old Cherokee Trace just south of Farm Road 2088 and six miles northwest of Gilmer in northern Upshur County, was probably established before 1900. A school began operating there around 1900 and was later consolidated with that of Union Hill. By the mid-1930s Forest Hill was no longer shown on county highway maps.

BIBLIOGRAPHY: Doyal T. Loyd, *History of Upshur County* (Waco: Texian Press, 1987). *Christopher Long*

FOREST HILL, TEXAS (Wood County). Forest Hill is on State Highway 37 three miles northeast of Quitman in north central Wood County. The area was probably settled as early as 1860. Local lore has it that in its early days the Forest Hill school was also known as Ratscuffle, after the many large rats that roamed the schoolhouse during Saturday night spelling bees. During the 1930s the community had a number of dwellings, a schoolhouse, a Baptist church, and at least one business. In 1949 Morris Coats discovered the Coats oilfield just to the south of Forest Hill, but this apparently had no lasting effect on the community. By 1980 Forest Hill had gained a second church, and county highway maps for the late 1980s show a church and a business at the site.

BIBLIOGRAPHY: *Wood County Democrat*, October 29, 1936. *Rachel Jenkins*

FOREST HILL PLANTATION. Forest Hill, off Farm Road 241 3½ miles northeast of Alto in south central Cherokee County, was the antebellum plantation of Capt. Henry and Helena (Dill) Berryman.[qv] Berryman, a career officer in the United States Army, resigned his commission in 1843, and in 1847 the couple settled on a league of land that Mrs. Berryman had inherited from her mother, Helena Kimble Dill. The property was part of the original grant for which James Dill,[qv] first alcalde[qv] of Nacogdoches, had petitioned the Spanish government in 1802. Shortly after their arrival Berryman put his slaves to work to clear the land for a cattle ranch and to construct a large two-story log house, which he intended to serve as a temporary home for his family while a replica of his Virginia home, Whitehall, could be built of native stone. Berryman died before work began on the stone house, however, and the log house became the family's permanent home. Among the illustrious guests who visited the house were Zachary Taylor and Joseph Lewis Hogg.[qqv]

After Helena Berryman's death in 1888, the property passed to her oldest son, Henry Waters Berryman. The property was later divided among various members of the family, but the house remained in the Berryman family until 1957. A state historical marker was placed at the site in 1962. In the early 1990s the house was still standing, though the original slave quarters and other outbuildings were not.

BIBLIOGRAPHY: *Cherokee County History* (Jacksonville, Texas: Cherokee County Historical Commission, 1986). Hattie Joplin Roach, *A History of Cherokee County* (Dallas: Southwest, 1934). Marker Files, Texas Historical Commission, Austin. *Gary Winfree*

FOREST HOME, TEXAS. Forest Home is on a soil-surfaced road 1½ miles north of Farm Road 515 and four miles west of Winnsboro in northern Wood County. In 1859 John R. Wright traveled from South Carolina and settled in the area; he donated an acre of land for a community project, probably a school. Locals established a Forest Home school district in 1884, and in 1896 it served forty-seven students. By 1905 it served sixty-two. During the 1930s the community had a number of farms, a church, and a school, which in 1932 had forty-three students in eight grades. By the late 1940s the school was gone, and in 1960 the Forest Home church served widely scattered farms in the area. Though Forest Home is not labeled on the 1988 county highway map, a church is still shown at the site. *Rachel Jenkins*

FORESTS. To early explorers and settlers, the forests of East Texas[qv] must have been an awesome sight. On dry hills in Southeast Texas, longleaf pines towered to 150 feet and had bases four to five feet in diameter. The woods were open and easily accessible. Mesic uplands and creekbottoms in other parts of eastern Texas also contained large trees. Magnificent open forests of white oak, beech, elm, water oak, and magnolia occurred in creekbottoms, as did thick clumps of switch cane. In bottomlands, tree trunks stood far apart and sometimes were so big that three men could not touch hands around them. Giant cypress trees were encountered in swamps and sloughs. The pristine forest was a beautiful sight. As settlers increased in numbers, they cut trees for houses, barns, and furniture and cleared forests for farmland. Thus the numbers of large trees began to decline. By 1830 sawmills began to dot the East Texas landscape. As the mills increased in size and were modernized, and as more people settled in East Texas, the primeval forest was manipulated until few remnants of the original forest, if any, remained. Therefore, most forests in East Texas are in youngers stages of plant succession. In addition many are still being managed for the production of pine. Pine plantations are commonplace over the East Texas landscape. On the other hand, several sites in eastern Texas contain old-growth stands that remind us of how the primitive forest might have looked. Such forests can be found, for example, in Caddo Lake State Park and Turkey Hill Wilderness Area.qqv

A forest is a large area containing closely spaced trees. Texas has approximately 22,032,000 acres of forest. There are five principal forest and woodland regions in the state: pine-hardwood, located essentially in East Texas in the Pine Belt or "Piney Woods"; post oak, associated primarily with the Lost Pine Forestqv in Bastrop County; the Eastern and Western Cross Timbers, centered around the northern part of the state near the Red River; cedar brakes, found primarily on the Edwards Plateau;qv and scattered coastal forests, found near the Gulf of Mexico.qv There are four national forests in Texas: Angelinaqv (153,176 acres), in Angelina, Jasper, Nacogdoches, and San Augustine counties; Davy Crockettqv (161,841 acres), in Houston and Trinity counties; Sabineqv (160,609 acres), in Jasper, Newton, Sabine, San Augustine, and Shelby counties; and Sam Houstonqv (161,508 acres), in Montgomery, San Jacinto, and Walker counties. The five Texas state forests are the E. O. Siecke State Forest, I. D. Fairchild State Forest, W. Goodrich Jones State Forest, John Henry Kirby State Forest, and Paul N. Masterson Memorial Forest.qqv All the state and national forests are located in East Texas, the primary and most important forest area in Texas. The East Texas Pine Belt extends over forty-three counties and accounts for almost all the state's commercial timber. Also, East Texas forests are a part of the Eastern Deciduous Forest Formation, and although positioned on the western edge, display an affinity to those forests eastward.

General descriptions of the forests of East Texas were initiated by William L. Bray in 1906 and by Benjamin C. Tharpqqv in 1939. They found that the great variation in topography in East Texas resulted in accompanying vegetational change. For example, dry upland, creekbottom, riverbottom, and swamp forest communities are each quite different in species composition. Until 1970 only a smattering of additional information was provided to aid in our understanding of these communities. Since then, mainly through the efforts of E. S. Nixon, P. A. Harcombe and C. A. McLeod and their graduate students, forest stands have been analyzed in greater detail, and thus there is presently a better understanding of forest structure and composition.

FORMBY, MARSHALL CLINTON, JR. (1911–1984). Marshall Clinton Formby, Jr., public official and writer, was born on April 12, 1911, near Como, Hopkins County, Texas, the son of Marshall Clinton and Rosa Mae Formby. When he was five years old his family moved to McAdoo in Dickens County. There he attended public school through the junior year in high school. He obtained his diploma at Spur High School in 1928 and he enrolled in Texas Technological College (now Texas Tech University), where he received the bachelor of arts degree in 1932. He received his master's degree in journalism from the University of Texas in 1937.

His long career in public service began in 1936, when he was elected county judge of Dickens County, a position he held until 1940. He was elected to the Texas Senate and represented District Thirty (Lubbock) for a four-year term, although service in the United States Army (1942–46) precluded constant participation in Austin matters during World War II.qv On September 8, 1946, he married Sharleen Wells in Seale, Alabama. They had two children.

In 1948 Formby moved to Plainview, where he sold the *Plainview Tribune,* a weekly newspaper that he had purchased in 1941, and began to devote his time to the operation of a number of West Texas radio stations. His nephew, Clint Formby, served as manager and partner. After a year of study at the Baylor University School of Law, Formby was admitted to the state bar on December 4, 1952. He returned to Plainview, where, in 1953, he joined the law firm of a longtime friend, Judge Harold LaFont. In 1953 Governor Allan Shiversqv appointed him to the Texas Highway Commission, and he served as chairman of that body during the last two years (1957–59) of his tenure. The period of his membership on the commission was marked by an acceleration in the farm-to-market paved road program and by the construction of the Texas Turnpike, the tollway between Dallas and Fort Worth.

In 1962 Formby made an unsuccessful bid to be the Democratic nominee for governor of Texas. That same year saw the publication of his historical novel, *These Are My People.* He pursued his favorite hobby, travel, with vigor. In 1955 he visited Russia with a group of newspaper and radio editors. In 1960 he traveled to South and Central America and in 1968 took his family around the world. He went to China in 1979. Formby was named to the board of directors of Texas Tech University in 1967; he served in that capacity until 1971 when he was appointed to the Coordinating Board, Texas College and University System, (now the Texas Higher Education Coordinating Boardqv), a position he held for two six-year terms.

After a lengthy illness, probably from uremic poisoning, Formby died on December 27, 1984, at his home in Plainview. His funeral was held at the First Baptist Church there, and he was buried at McAdoo.

BIBLIOGRAPHY: Austin *American-Statesman,* December 28, 1984. Dickens County Historical Commission, *Dickens County: Its Land and Its People* (Lubbock: Craftsman Printers, 1986). Vera D. Wofford, ed., *Hale County Facts and Folklore* (Lubbock, 1978).

William M. Pearce

FORNELL, EARL WESLEY (1915?–1969). Earl Wesley Fornell, government professor and author, son of Oscar and Theresa (Larson) Fornell, was born on November 12 in Laketown, Wisconsin; the year of his birth is variously given as 1908, 1911, and 1915. He served in the United States Army Air Force in World War IIqv and attained the rank of warrant officer. He was awarded the Silver Star for bravery in action. He received his B.A. degree in political science from the New School for Social Research at Eugene Lang College in 1948 and his M.A. in political science from the same school in 1949. From 1947 to 1950 he was documents specialist in international law at Columbia University, where he received an additional M.A. degree in political history in 1950. He was head of the government department at Amarillo College from 1950 to 1952 and an instructor in government at Rice University from 1952 to 1956. He received his Ph.D. degree in political history from Rice University in 1956. He joined the government faculty at Lamar State College of Technology (now Lamar University) in Beaumont in 1957 as an assistant professor and advanced to the rank of full professor in 1962.

Professor Fornell wrote over twenty articles for professional journals and two major books, *The Galveston Era* (1961) and *The Unhappy Medium* (1964). He was a contributor to the *Encyclopaedia Britannica* and the *Handbook of Texas,* and shortly before his death he completed a manuscript on the Moodys of Galveston. In 1967 he was chosen a fellow of the Texas State Historical Association.qv He was also a member of the American Philosophical Society, the Galveston Historical Foundation,qv the Gulf Coast Historical Society, the American Association of University Professors, and the Foreign Policy Association.

Fornell was married to Martha Steinmetz on September 20, 1947. They resided in New York City before their move to Texas in 1950. Although he lived in Beaumont after 1957, he maintained a close interest in Galveston and Houston through research and writing. Fornell died on March 2, 1969, in Beaumont and was buried at Magnolia Cemetery in that city.

BIBLIOGRAPHY: Beaumont *Enterprise,* March 3, 1969. *Who's Who in the South and Southwest,* 11th ed.
Ralph A. Wooster

FORNEY, JOHN HORACE (1829–1902). John Horace Forney,

Confederate general, was born at Lincolnton, North Carolina, on August 12, 1829, and was appointed to the United States Military Academy at West Point from Alabama on July 1, 1848. He graduated twenty-second in his class on July 1, 1852, and was posted to the Seventh United States Infantry as a brevet second lieutenant. He was promoted to second lieutenant on October 24, 1853, and transferred to the Tenth Infantry on March 3, 1855. He was promoted to first lieutenant on August 25, 1855, but, with the secession^qv of the states of the lower South, he resigned his commission on January 23, 1861. He entered Confederate service as colonel of the Tenth Alabama Infantry and saw action at First Manassas. He was wounded at Dranesville, Virginia, in December 1861, and was promoted to brigadier general on March 10, 1862, and to major general on October 27—a rise in rank that probably outran his abilities. After brief service as commander of the departments of Alabama and Florida he was given a division of Lt. Gen. John C. Pemberton's army defending Vicksburg and was captured there when the city fell in July 1863. After being exchanged Forney was sent to the trans-Mississippi, where he superseded John George Walker^qv as commander of the Texas Division. At the end of the war he returned to Alabama, where he was a farmer and civil engineer until his death, at Jacksonville on September 13, 1902.

BIBLIOGRAPHY: Ezra J. Warner, *Generals in Gray* (Baton Rouge: Louisiana State University Press, 1959). Francis B. Heitman, *Historical Register and Dictionary of the United States Army* (2 vols., Washington: GPO, 1903; rpt., Urbana: University of Illinois Press, 1965).

Thomas W. Cutrer

FORNEY, TEXAS. Forney is on U.S. Highway 80, the Missouri Pacific Railroad, Buffalo Creek, and Mustang Creek, twenty-three miles east of Dallas in northwestern Kaufman County. When the earliest settlers arrived and established a community in this area they found a broad expanse of fertile blackland prairie covered with grass. By 1870 several of these settlers, including John C. McKellar, who established the first general store in the settlement, were calling their town Brooklyn, reportedly because several springs flowed together to form a brook nearby. Soon after McKellar's store was opened, a saloon and a blacksmith shop began operation in Brooklyn.

The citizens applied for a post office in 1873, but it was discovered that there was a Brooklyn in Shelby County. That same year the promoters of the Texas and Pacific Railway, having failed to interest the residents of either the county seat, Kaufman, or Cedar Grove in the rail line, chose to build between these communities and through the Brooklyn settlement. In honor of the railroad and in hopes of winning federal approval for the local post office, the residents of Brooklyn renamed their community Forney, on December 29, 1873, after the Pennsylvania journalist, politician, and member of the board of directors of the T&P line, John Wien Forney, then employed as a civil engineer to direct the Texas and Pacific in the area. Forney was officially incorporated in 1884, and soon afterward a mayor-alderman form of local government was established.

The railroad and fertile soil attracted settlers to Forney after 1873, and the town grew as a farm center and residential community. The population increased slowly for the next century, to more than 3,000 residents by 1960. The surrounding land is used as ranchland and for the production of cotton, corn, grain, and onions. Although situated in a predominantly agricultural area, Forney has been a small manufacturing community since 1936. Its factories have produced such goods as cottonseed oil, ice, athletic supplies, paper products, and plastics. In 1964 Forney Reservoir was constructed on the East Fork of the Trinity River four miles north of Forney. The reservoir, impounded to provide water for Dallas, was later renamed Lake Ray Hubbard.

The population of Forney in 1980 was 2,483. The increase was partly a result of the growth of Dallas. Three local manufacturers produced plastics, recycled-paper products, and insulation products. The Forney *Messenger*, first published in 1881, continued to serve as the community's weekly newspaper. Forney's first public school was built in 1874. A black school opened in 1890, and Forney Academy, a private coeducational school, was established by 1894. Just north of the town, along Highway 80, are located some fifteen warehouses that sell antiques and antique reproductions. In 1990 the population was 4,070.

BIBLIOGRAPHY: Robert Richard Butler, History of Kaufman County, Texas (M.A. thesis, University of Texas, 1940). *Farm and Ranch*, October 15, 1885, June 14, 1913. Kaufman County Historical Commission, *History of Kaufman County* (Dallas: Taylor, 1978).

Brian Hart

FORREST, S. LAMAR (1892–1948). S. Lamar Forrest, lumber merchant, was born on November 23, 1892, in Madison County, Texas, the son of Sidney Samuel and Ora Celia (Robinson) Forrest. He attended Clarendon College from 1908 to 1910 and graduated from Seth Ward College in Plainview in 1912. He married Myrtle Robertson on October 13, 1916, and they had three children. Lamar developed a prosperous network of building-supply stores in West Texas and gained national recognition for his merchandising skill. In 1934 he became a director of the Lumbermen's Association of Texas and during 1937–38 served as its president. The following year he was made a director in the National Retail Lumber Dealers' Association, of which he was president in 1944. During World War II^qv he was a member of the War Production Board and held the position of industrial advisor to the Office of Price Administration. He died of a heart attack on February 28, 1948.

BIBLIOGRAPHY: Seymour V. Connor, ed., *Builders of the Southwest* (Lubbock: Southwest Collection, Texas Technological College, 1959).

Roy Sylvan Dunn

FORRESTON, TEXAS. Forreston is on U.S. Highway 77 and the Missouri, Kansas and Texas tracks eight miles south of Waxahachie in south central Ellis County. At first the site was called Howe's Settlement, after William R. Howe, who arrived around 1843 and is credited as being the area's first settler. Thus Forreston can lay claim to being the oldest settlement in Ellis County. By the mid-1840s a community had been established under the name Chambers Creek, so named by Gen. Edward H. Tarrant^qv in honor of his friend Gen. Thomas J. Chambers.^qv Chambers had received a large land grant in the area as a gift from Mexico for his services as a judge. The community received a post office in 1846 and served as the original county seat of Navarro County until the organization of Ellis County in 1850 placed Forreston within the new county's boundaries. From its beginnings the community provided a school for area farmers. Over the next three decades a church, two cotton gins, and several stores were added. The arrival of the Katie Railroad by the early 1890s stimulated rapid population growth, and gradually businesses moved closer to the tracks. Capt. Carr Forrest, a prominent local businessman and Forreston's first postmaster, donated land for the railway depot. At that time the town, already frequently referred to as Forrest or as Forrest's Store, was renamed Forreston. By 1904 it had well over 200 residents. Throughout the twentieth century Forreston served farmers as a shipping point and as a school and church community. Its population peaked at a reported high of 350 by the mid-1940s. Later the population declined somewhat, diminishing to 300 by 1986, when Forreston supported eleven businesses. The population continued to be reported as 300 in 1990.

BIBLIOGRAPHY: Edna Davis Hawkins et al., *History of Ellis County, Texas* (Waco: Texian, 1972). *Memorial and Biographical History of Ellis County* (Chicago: Lewis, 1892; rpt., as *Ellis County History*, Fort Worth: Historical Publishers, 1972). Kathleen E. and Clifton R. St. Clair, eds., *Little Towns of Texas* (Jacksonville, Texas: Jayroe Graphic Arts, 1982).

David Minor

FORSAN, TEXAS. Forsan, on Farm Road 461 in southeastern Howard County, was established in 1929, after Clayton Stewart, the first settler in the area, gave land for the townsite in 1928. The community was named for the four oil sands believed to be located nearby. Drillers later discovered they had underestimated, and there were actually at least five sands. Forsan experienced boomtown growth and by 1931 reported a population of 350, a post office, and twenty-five commercially rated businesses. In 1936 it had 400 residents. This figure remained constant through 1956, but the number of businesses dropped from eighteen to twelve. Between 1960 and 1966 the town became incorporated. By 1980 its population had fallen to 239, but Forsan retained its post office, several businesses, and its incorporated status. In 1990 its population was reported as 256.

BIBLIOGRAPHY: John R. Hutto, *Howard County in the Making* (Big Spring, Texas: Jordan's, 1938).
Noel Wiggins

FORSHEY, CALEB GOLDSMITH (1812–1881). Caleb Goldsmith Forshey, engineer, scientist, and founder of the Texas Military Institute, was born on July 18, 1812, in Somerset County, Pennsylvania. He attended Kenyon College in Ohio (1831–33) and the United States Military Academy at West Point (1833–36) but apparently did not graduate. He was professor of mathematics and civil engineering from 1836 to 1838 at Jefferson College in Washington, Mississippi. Forshey was then employed in engineering projects along the Mississippi River. He lived in Vidalia, Louisiana, from about 1840 to 1848, while serving as the city engineer of Natchez, Mississippi, across the river from Vidalia. In 1848 he constructed at Carrollton, Louisiana, a hydrologic station that measured the flow of the river from 1848 to 1855 for the federal government's Mississippi Delta Survey.

In 1853 Forshey moved to Texas to become chief engineer of the newly chartered Galveston, Houston and Henderson Railroad. On November 16, 1853, he officiated at the railroad's ground-breaking ceremonies, at Virginia Point on Galveston Bay. He planned the construction of the line and has been credited with the design of the original West Bay Bridge, which was eventually constructed in 1859 and carried the first train from Virginia Point on the mainland across to Galveston on February 1, 1860.

Forshey published scientific articles in many of the leading journals of the 1840s and 1850s. He made astronomical observations in Texas and collected biological specimens, primarily in Fayette County in 1856–59, for the Smithsonian Institution and for academies and museums in Boston and Philadelphia. He contributed articles on the meteorology and climate of Texas to the Texas Almanac[qv] in 1860 and 1861.

Forshey founded the Texas Military Institute, Galveston,[qv] in 1854. In 1856 the school was moved to Rutersville, in Fayette County, where it was consolidated with Rutersville College and the Texas Monumental Committee of La Grange. Forshey served as superintendent at Rutersville until 1861, when the school closed at the onset of the Civil War.[qv]

In 1861–62 he worked in the Engineering Corps, C.S.A., on the defense of the Texas coast. As chief engineer on the staff of Gen. John B. Magruder,[qv] he played an important role in the fall of 1862 in planning the recapture of Galveston. On December 25, 1862, he issued the order for the outfitting of the Confederate "cotton-clad" gunboats that were used successfully at the battle of Galveston[qv] on January 1, 1863. Forshey supervised the building of Fort Esperanza, near Saluria on Matagorda Island, early in 1863. He then planned Confederate fortifications near Orange and at other points along the Sabine River. Three Civil War songs by Forshey were included in Francis D. Allan's collection of *Allan's Lone Star Ballads* (1874).

After the war Forshey was an engineering consultant to the city of Galveston. In 1866 he published a report proposing a system of railroads designed to lead from the port of Galveston into the interior of Texas. In 1870 he was chairman of a committee that suggested improvements to the channels and harbors of Galveston Bay. He worked along the Red River in 1874–75 and eventually returned to the Mississippi River delta, where he died, at Carrollton, Louisiana, on July 25, 1881.

BIBLIOGRAPHY: *Appleton's Cyclopaedia of American Biography* (7 vols., New York: Appleton, 1888–91). David S. Evans and Donald W. Olson, "Early Astronomy in Texas," *Southwestern Historical Quarterly* 93 (April 1990). S. W. Geiser, "Men of Science in Texas, 1820–1880," *Field and Laboratory* 26–27 (July–October 1958–October 1959).
Donald W. Olson

FORSYTH, CONSTANCE (1903–1987). Constance (Connie) Forsyth, printmaker, painter, and teacher, was born on August 18, 1903, in Indianapolis, Indiana, the second of three daughters of William and Alice (Atkinson) Forsyth. Her father was one of Indiana's leading artists during the early part of the twentieth century, and from a young age Forsyth and her sisters accompanied him when he taught outdoor painting classes during the summer. Both parents encouraged their children to observe nature, which subsequently became the enduring theme of Connie Forsyth's art.

After completing a B.A. degree in chemistry at Butler University in Indianapolis in 1925, Forsyth began formal art training at the John Herron Art Institute. There she studied with Clifton Wheeler, Myra Richards, and her father; she received a diploma in 1929. In 1927–28 and in the spring of 1930 she attended the Pennsylvania Academy of Fine Arts, where she studied with Henry McCarter, George Harding, and Albert Laessle. In the summers of 1932 and 1934 she studied at the Broadmoor Art Academy (later the Colorado Springs Fine Arts Center), where she studied under Boardman Robinson and John Ward Lockwood.[qv] She attended the first lithography class offered there in the summer of 1932 and developed an enthusiasm for printmaking, which became her primary medium. She also assisted Thomas Hart Benton on the Indiana murals for the Century of Progress International Exposition in Chicago in 1933.

Forsyth first gained experience in teaching by offering private art lessons in Indianapolis. From 1931 to 1935 she was an instructor at the John Herron Art Institute, and in 1937 she enrolled in education courses at Butler University. She taught art at Western College in Oxford, Ohio, in the spring of 1939. In 1940 her former teacher, Ward Lockwood, hired her to help develop a program in printmaking in the University of Texas art department. Forsyth's efforts to teach printmaking were hampered by what she referred to as the "World War II Battle for Supplies." Carborundum, essential for the preparation of lithographic stones, and proper paper were often unavailable, but she made do with available materials. In the summer of 1945 she spent a week in Burlington, Vermont, with the renowned printer George C. Miller, an invaluable opportunity to observe an expert at work and to develop a dependable printing method for classroom use.

During her thirty-three years of teaching at the University of Texas Forsyth supervised many graduate students and served on numerous committees. Her teaching activities extended beyond the university campus; she gave lectures and demonstrations on printmaking for the Texas Fine Arts Association[qv] and local and state museums and served on juries for major statewide competitive exhibitions. She was a member of the Indiana Art Association, the Indiana Society of Printmakers, and the Printmakers' Guild, a group of women printmakers in the Southwest. She was also a member of the Texas Fine Arts Association, the Texas Association of College Teachers,[qv] Texas Printmakers, and the National Association of Women Artists.

She most characteristically composed semiabstract studies of natural forms such as waves, mountains, and especially clouds. Her early work was primarily lithography, but during the 1940s and 1950s she frequently combined aquatint, drypoint, and lithographic processes to achieve a variation in textures and tones. Occasionally she added a single color as an accent. In *Sun Cloud* (1972), for example, drypoint lines swirl around a woodcut golden sun; aquatint was used to achieve fluid background swirls. Forsyth excelled in capturing subtleties found in nature; in *Sky and Goat Mountain* (n.d.), for example, the cluster of inky mountains at a low horizon are dominated by curving drypoint lines that suggest air currents. She also painted watercolors in bright, earthy colors in a style influenced by John Marin. In later years she became increasingly nonobjective and experimented with collages of torn, colored papers, often combined with overpainting. She used acrylics in patterns, texture, and calligraphy meant to suggest natural processes.

Forsyth exhibited her work widely, beginning in 1928, when she won a prize at the Hoosier Salon. She won awards at exhibitions sponsored by the John Herron Art Museum (1936, 1938, 1961), the Dallas Printmaker Society (1945), the Joslyn Memorial Museum in Omaha, Nebraska (1949), the Indiana State Fair (1941, 1946–47, 1950, 1956–57), the Indiana Society of Printmakers (1949, 1953), the Eighth Texas General Exhibition (1946), the Texas Fine Arts Association (1946–47, 1951, 1954, 1956, 1961, 1972), and the National Association of Women Artists (1955, 1961), among others. She exhibited her work at the Witte Museum[qv] in San Antonio; the Museum of Fine Arts, Houston;[qv] the Dallas Museum of Art;[qv] the Laguna Gloria Art Museum and Elisabet Ney Museum,[qqv] both in Austin; an invitational Printmaking Exhibition at Texas Tech University in Lubbock; and annual art-faculty exhibitions at the University of Texas. The Laguna Gloria Art Museum mounted a solo exhibition of her paintings and drawings in 1946; galleries in Austin, San Antonio, and Indianapolis also sponsored solo exhibitions of her work. Nationally her work was exhibited at the Philadelphia Academy of Fine Arts, the San Francisco Museum of Art, the Cincinnati Art Museum, the National Academy of Design and the 1939 World's Fair (both in New York), the Kansas City Art Institute, the Library of Congress, the Denver Art Museum, and the Seattle Art Museum. She also exhibited her work in Italy, France, Switzerland, Germany, Scotland, England, Japan, and India.

Forsyth retired with the rank of professor emeritus in 1973. Her contributions were honored a year later by a joint retrospective with William L. Lester[qv] organized by the Archer M. Huntington Art Gallery.[qv] She continued to contribute work to the annual faculty exhibition until 1985. On March 22, 1985, the Southern Graphics Council presented her with the Printmaker Emeritus Award in recognition for her outstanding achievement in that field. Constance Forsyth died on January 22, 1987. Her work is represented in the Archer M. Huntington Art Gallery, Austin; the Witte Museum, San Antonio; the Dallas Museum of Art; the Texas Fine Arts Association, Austin; Texas Wesleyan College, Fort Worth; the Indianapolis Museum of Art, Indiana; Ball State Teachers College, Muncie, Indiana; and Joslyn Memorial Museum in Omaha, Nebraska, among others. Forsyth also illustrated two books, Charles Garrett Vannest's *Lincoln the Hoosier: Abraham Lincoln's Life in Indiana* (1928), and *The Friends* (1951), a children's book by Esther Buffler.

BIBLIOGRAPHY: Clinton Adams, *American Lithographers, 1900–1960: The Artists and Their Printers* (Albuquerque: University of New Mexico Press, 1983). Jim L. Collins, *Women Artists in America, Eighteenth Century to the Present* (1973; rev. and enlarged ed., Poughkeepsie, New York: Apollo, 1980). Peter Haskins Falk, ed., *Who Was Who in American Art* (Madison, Connecticut: Sound View, 1985). David Farmer, "Constance Forsyth: Printmaker," in *The Tamarind Papers*, Vol. 12, ed. Clinton Adams (Albuquerque, New Mexico: Tamarind Institute, 1989). Retrospective Exhibition of Constance Forsyth and William Lester, Huntington Art Gallery Archives, University of Texas at Austin, 1974. Vertical Files, Barker Texas History Center, University of Texas at Austin.
Kendall Curlee

FORSYTH, JOHN HUBBARD (1797–1836). John Hubbard Forsyth, defender of the Alamo, son of Alexander and Mary (Treat) Forsyth, was born at Avon, New York, on August 10, 1797. He was raised on his father's farm in Livingston County, New York. He studied medicine but never practiced. On April 3, 1822, he married Deborah Smith. He left New York in late December 1828 after the death of his wife, leaving his son, Edmund Augustus, with his father's family. Forsyth traveled to Texas from Kentucky in 1835 as the captain of a volunteer company. In Texas he obtained a commission as a captain in the Regular Texan Cavalry and used all of his available cash to outfit and supply his company. Forsyth and his men traveled to the Alamo with Lt. Col. William B. Travis[qv] and arrived in San Antonio de Béxar in early February 1836. He died in the battle of the Alamo[qv] on March 6, 1836.

BIBLIOGRAPHY: Daughters of the American Revolution, *The Alamo Heroes and Their Revolutionary Ancestors* (San Antonio, 1976). Sylvia Van Voast Ferris and Eleanor Sellers Hoppe, *Scalpels and Sabers* (Austin: Eakin Press, 1985). Bill Groneman, *Alamo Defenders* (Austin: Eakin, 1990). John H. Jenkins, ed., *The Papers of the Texas Revolution, 1835–1836* (10 vols., Austin: Presidial Press, 1973). Pat Ireland Nixon, *The Medical Story of Early Texas, 1528–1853* (Lancaster, Pennsylvania: Lupe Memorial Fund, 1946).
Bill Groneman

FORT ANAHUAC. Fort Anahuac is located in a Chambers County park on State Highway 564 one mile south of Anahuac. It was the site of the first armed confrontation between Anglo-Texans and Mexican troops, on June 10–12, 1832. In November 1830 Col. Juan Davis Bradburn[qv] chose the site for the fort and its town on a bluff, called Perry's Point since 1816, overlooking the entrance to the Trinity River. The garrison was one of six new outposts located at strategic entrances to Texas and designed to enforce the Law of April 6, 1830.[qv] All the garrisons carried Mexican names. Anáhuac, the name of the ancient home of the Aztecs, was borrowed for the Chambers County fort. Bradburn brought plans and a cardboard fort with him.

The garrison lived temporarily in a fortified wooden barracks a half mile north of the bluff in the center of the site of modern Anahuac. The barracks was later used as the jail that held William B. Travis[qv] and others. Bricks for the walls and buildings of the permanent fort were made by convict soldiers on-site, beginning in March 1831. A Masonic and military ceremony marked completion of the foundation on May 14, 1831. The exterior walls were 100 by seventy feet and enclosed two redoubts diagonally opposite on the southwest and northeast corners. Inside the perimeter was a reinforced-brick building about fifty by thirty-five feet. The southwest redoubt, overlooking Trinity Bay, was named Fort Davis (for Bradburn); it was manned by a maximum of fifty men and defended by a six-pound cannon, while its twin on the northeast guarded the land approach. The cavalry tethered its horses between the two redoubts. An excavated passage connected the enclosure with the powder magazine on the east side, where two bulwarks named Hidalgo and Morelos (for martyrs of the Mexican independence movement) near the sites of the brick kilns, each with a sixteen-pound cannon, guarded the compound.

The garrison grew from forty men and four officers in November 1830 to a maximum of 285 men and ten officers in May 1832. After March 1832 about 100 of the men were stationed at Velasco, at the mouth of the Brazos, under Col. Domingo de Ugartechea.[qv] The troops were from the Eleventh and Twelfth battalions; the boatmen came from the battalion of Pueblo Viejo de Tampico; La Bahía supplied twenty-five cavalrymen and one officer.

Texan insurgents under Col. Francis White Johnson[qv] attacked the fort on June 10–12, 1832, to rescue Travis. The troops dismantled the fort when they left in July 1832, and a fire in November gutted the wooden parts. The wooden calaboose was burned in December 1832, and practical residents removed bricks for fireplaces and foundations.

In January 1835 Capt. Antonio Tenorio[qv] arrived with about forty troops to reopen the fort, but it was in such disrepair that he asked his superiors for wood to make repairs. The wood arrived in May but was burned by irate Texans. Tenorio had no artillery when Travis and his volunteers attacked on June 29, so his troops fled into the woods. He capitulated the next day, and the small garrison sailed to Harrisburg and retreated to Bexar.

The fort was never used again; the land became private property. In 1938 the county surveyor made field notes of the existing foundations. Erosion caused by rechanneling the Trinity River sometime after the 1930s caused the remains of the southwestern redoubt to fall into the water. Chambers County acquired the site for a park in 1946, and officials ordered it cleared and the rubble buried for safety reasons and to prevent vandalism. An amateur excavation was made in 1968 before preservation laws went into effect, but no in-depth archeological study has been made of the site.

See also ANAHUAC DISTURBANCES.

BIBLIOGRAPHY: Margaret S. Henson, *Anahuac in 1832: The Cradle of the Texas Revolution* (Anahuac, Texas: Fort Anahuac Committee of the Chambers County Historical Commission, 1982). Margaret S. Henson, *Juan Davis Bradburn: A Reappraisal of the Mexican Commander of Anahuac* (College Station: Texas A&M University Press, 1982). James Wright Steely, comp., *A Catalog of Texas Properties in the National Register of Historic Places* (Austin: Texas Historical Commission, 1984).
Margaret Swett Henson

FORT BELKNAP. Fort Belknap, a United States Army post three miles south of Newcastle in Young County, was founded on June 24, 1851, at the site of present Newcastle by Bvt. Brig. Gen. William G. Belknap.qv After the commanding officer, Capt. C. L. Stephenson, Fifth Infantry, found no water in shafts dug sixty-six feet deep at the location of the water tower now in Newcastle, he moved the fort two miles south, where adequate water was found in springs by the Brazos River. The present well was dug in 1857 under the direction of Capt. Gabriel R. Paul of the Seventh Infantry. The first buildings were jacals. Some were later replaced with stone.

Fort Belknap was a four-company post. Among the companies stationed there during its existence were some from the Fifth United States Infantry, the Second United States Dragoons, the Seventh United States Infantry, the Second United States Cavalry,qv and the Sixth United States Cavalry. Among the commanding officers were Col. Gustavus Loomis, Maj. Enoch Steen, Captain Paul, Maj. George H. Thomas,qv Maj. Samuel Henry Starr, Lt. Col. Samuel Davis Sturgis, and Capt. Richard W. Johnson.

Fort Belknap was the northern anchor of a chain of forts founded to protect the Texas frontier from the Red River to the Rio Grande. It was a post without defensive works. From it troops pursued raiding bands of Indians, and on occasion mounted expeditions from the fort carried the war to the enemy on the plains as far north as Kansas. The fort gave confidence to citizens, who came in such numbers that surrounding counties were organized. Fort Belknap became the hub of a network of roads stretching in every direction; the most notable of these was the Butterfield Overland Mailqv route from St. Louis to San Francisco.

In early 1861, believing that war was imminent, Gen. David E. Twiggsqv ordered Col. William H. Emoryqv to gather all federal troops and move them north to Fort Leavenworth. On February 9, 1861, General Twiggs, in San Antonio, surrendered all United States forts and military equipment in Texas. Although it was abandoned before the Civil War,qv the fort was occupied from time to time by state troops of the Frontier Regimentqv under Col. James M. Norris.qv Major Starr, with troops of the Sixth United States Cavalry, reoccupied Fort Belknap on April 28, 1867. When Fort Griffin was founded in Shackelford County, Fort Belknap was abandoned for the last time, in September of 1867.

During the Texas Centennial,qv Senator Benjamin G. Onealqv and local citizens restored and rebuilt some of the buildings. During the 1970s the Fort Belknap Archives, with some assistance from the Young County Commissioners Court, rebuilt Infantry Quarters Number Four to house the records of North Texas. Since its restoration Fort Belknap has become a cultural and recreational center. Senator Oneal and others organized the Fort Belknap Society to supervise the maintenance of the fort. The Young County Commissioners Court supports it financially. Professional and learned societies, as well as family groups, use the facilities, and around 30,000 visitors register their attendance annually.

BIBLIOGRAPHY: Roger N. Conger, et al., *Frontier Forts of Texas* (Waco: Texian Press, 1966). Carrie J. Crouch, *Fort Belknap* (Graham, Texas: Graham *Leader*, n.d.) Barbara Neal Ledbetter, *Fort Belknap Frontier Saga: Indians, Negroes and Anglo-Americans on the Texas Frontier* (Burnet, Texas: Eakin Press, 1982). Kenneth F. Neighbours, *Robert Simpson Neighbors and the Texas Frontier, 1836–1859* (Waco: Texian Press, 1975). Robert B. Roberts, *Encyclopedia of Historic Forts: The Military, Pioneer, and Trading Posts of the United States* (New York: Macmillan, 1988). Bill Winsor, *Texas in the Confederacy* (Hillsboro, Texas: Hill Junior College Press, 1978).
Kenneth F. Neighbours

FORT BEND. Fort Bend was a blockhouse built in a large bend of the Brazos River in what is now Fort Bend County to provide protection against Indian raids. It was erected in November 1822 by several members of Stephen F. Austin'sqv Old Three Hundred,qv including William W. Little and Joseph Polley,qqv and is described as a "little log shanty." The location was reportedly selected by Austin, and a settlement soon grew up around the post. As the site provided one of the more favorable fords of the Brazos River, it became important during the Texas Revolution.qv The Fort Bend crossing was briefly defended in April 1836 by a rear guard detachment led by Wiley Martin.qv After Martin was maneuvered out of the position Gen. Antonio López de Santa Annaqv transported a portion of his Mexican army across the Brazos at the crossing. After Santa Anna's defeat at the battle of San Jacintoqv the site was used briefly by the Texas army. Troops under Thomas Jefferson Green,qv who were in pursuit of retreating Mexican forces led by Gen. Vicente Filisola,qv halted for a short time in mid-May 1836 at Fort Bend. Because Fort Bend had been the center of activity in the area its name was given to the county when it was established in 1837. The next year nearby Richmond was selected as the county seat and soon absorbed the smaller Fort Bend settlement. In 1936 the Texas Centennialqv Commission erected a monument to commemorate Fort Bend's role in the Texas Revolution.

BIBLIOGRAPHY: Gerald S. Pierce, *Texas Under Arms: The Camps, Posts, Forts, and Military Towns of the Republic of Texas* (Austin: Encino, 1969). Harold Schoen, comp., *Monuments Erected by the State of Texas to Commemorate the Centenary of Texas Independence* (Austin: Commission of Control for Texas Centennial Celebrations, 1938). Frank X. Tolbert, *The Day of San Jacinto* (New York: McGraw-Hill, 1959; 2d ed., Austin: Pemberton Press, 1969). Clarence Wharton, *Wharton's History of Fort Bend County* (San Antonio: Naylor, 1939).
Stephen L. Hardin

FORT BEND COUNTY. Fort Bend County (K-21) is in the coastal plains of southeastern Texas. Richmond, the county seat, at 29°35′ north latitude and 95°45′ west longitude, is twenty-eight miles east-southeast of Houston and at the approximate center of the county. The county comprises 869 square miles of level to slightly rolling terrain with an elevation ranging from eighty to 250 feet above sea level. Temperatures range from an average high of 94° F in July to an average low of 44° in January; rainfall averages slightly more than forty-five inches a year, and the growing season lasts 296 days. The Brazos River flows diagonally northwest to southeast through the county and drains the broad central valley via numerous creeks and bayous. The San Bernard River, which forms the west boundary, drains the western quarter of the county. Major streams include Big Creek, which flows east into the Brazos River; Oyster Creek, which winds parallel to and east of the Brazos River; and Buffalo Bayou, which rises in the northern tip of the county and flows east into Harris County. Soils vary from rich alluvial in the Brazos valley to sandy loams and clay on the prairies. Native trees include pecan, oak, ash, and cottonwood; there are some timberlands in the north and along streams. Mineral resources include natural gas, oil, and sulfur; sand, clay, and gravel are also produced in commercial quantities.

The settlement of Fort Bend County began in the early 1820s as part of the Anglo-American colonization[qv] of Texas under the auspices of the Spanish government. Authorization to settle 300 families in the valleys of the Brazos and Colorado rivers was initially granted to Moses Austin,[qv] but plans were delayed by his death in June 1821 and Mexican independence from Spain. Stephen F. Austin[qv] assumed the responsibility of leadership from his father and gained confirmation of the original Spanish grants from the newly established Mexican government in 1823. Following arrangements with Austin, a group of colonists sailed from New Orleans in November 1821 on the schooner *Lively*[qv] and anchored near the mouth of the Brazos River on the Texas coast. In 1822 a small party of men from this group left the ship and traveled inland some ninety miles and, on a bluff near a deep bend in the river, built a two-room cabin. As the settlement grew, the cabin became known as both Fort Settlement and Fort Bend; the latter name, in time, prevailed. In 1824 the Mexican government issued documents officially granting to the colonists their leagues of land. Of the 297 grants, fifty-three were issued to Fort Bend settlers (*see* OLD THREE HUNDRED). The presence of the Karankawa Indians near the new colonial settlements proved to be a comparatively minor problem. The first settlers had a few skirmishes, but as the colonies increased, the Karankawas began moving out of the area and by the 1850s had migrated as far south as Mexico.

In May 1837 the Congress of the Republic of Texas[qv] passed an act incorporating nineteen towns, including Richmond. Robert Eden Handy[qv] of Pennsylvania and William Lusk of Richmond, Virginia, both of whom had arrived in Texas shortly before the war for independence from Mexico, founded and named the town with eight other proprietors, including Branch T. Archer, Thomas Freeman McKinney, and Samuel May Williams.[qqv] An act establishing Fort Bend County and fixing its boundaries was passed on December 29, 1837; Wyly Martin[qv] was appointed the first chief justice. On January 13, 1838, the citizens voted to make Richmond the county seat. The county was taken from portions of Austin, Brazoria, and Harris counties. Its irregular shape was, in part, the result of using waterways to form the west and segments of the south and east boundaries. Several efforts have been made to change the lines but with little success.

Some of the first settlers in Fort Bend County played prominent roles in early Texas history. Nathaniel F. Williams[qv] and Matthew R. Williams cultivated and milled sugar on their Oakland Plantation near Oyster Creek in the early 1840s, thus laying the groundwork for an industry that continued to develop and thrive in Sugar Land (*see* IMPERIAL SUGAR COMPANY); in 1837 Jane Long[qv] opened a boarding house in Richmond, where she lived until her death in 1880; and Mirabeau B. Lamar[qv] moved to Richmond in 1851 and built a plantation home on land purchased from Jane Long. Both Mrs. Long and Lamar are buried in Morton Cemetery, Richmond. During the Texas Revolution[qv] many of the people of Fort Bend fled in great haste as Antonio López de Santa Anna's[qv] army marched through the area. Part of this army camped at Thompson's Ferry on the Brazos River while part marched on to meet defeat at the battle of San Jacinto.[qv] Fort Bend settlers returned from the Runaway Scrape[qv] to find their homes plundered or burned and their livestock scattered or dead.

Soon after its founding, Richmond developed into a prosperous trade center for the surrounding agricultural region of the lower Brazos valley. Barges and steamboats plied the Brazos River, transporting cotton and other products to the port at Galveston, as merchants of Richmond and other river towns vied with Houston for the lucrative agricultural trade. Transportation facilities were greatly improved in 1853, when the Buffalo Bayou, Brazos and Colorado Railway was completed to Stafford's Point from Harrisburg, which was located on Buffalo Bayou's navigable channel to Galveston. The prosperity of the 1840s and 1850s, however, ended with the Civil War.[qv]

In antebellum Texas[qv] slaves were essential to the development of the valley plantations. As early as 1840 there were already 572 slaves in Fort Bend County, and by 1845 that number had risen to 1,172, placing Fort Bend near the top of counties with the largest slave populations. In 1850, Fort Bend was one of only six counties in the state with a black majority. The labor provided by the burgeoning slave population made possible the growth of the plantation economy. In 1860 there were 159 farms in Fort Bend County, with about 12,000 acres in cotton, 7,000 acres in corn, and 1,000 acres in sugarcane; the slave population totaled 4,127, more than twice that of the 2,016 whites. Fort Bend planters, believing that their economic and social successes, among other reasons, justified the institution of slavery,[qv] strongly supported the Confederacy, and, in 1861, voted 486 to 0 for secession[qv] from the United states. The majority of county men volunteered for Confederate service; many joined the Eighth Texas Cavalry[qv] (Terry's Texas Rangers),[qv] a regiment organized by Benjamin Franklin Terry,[qv] a wealthy sugar planter from Sugar Land.

Although battle never reached Fort Bend, the war's duration and ultimate loss imposed economic hardships and social and political stress on the community. During Reconstruction,[qv] efforts to live in peace with politics dominated by Radical Republicans and black officeholders brought no more than an uneasy compromise. White Democrats, outnumbered by blacks more than two to one, were unable to regain control of local government until the late 1880s, when their all-out campaign to attract black as well as white votes led to the Jaybird-Woodpecker War.[qv] This brief but violent conflict, which took place on August 16, 1889, abruptly ended the Republican, or "Woodpecker" rule, and the Democrats quickly formed the Jaybird Democratic Association. With a constitution that declared as its purpose the "protection of the white race" and "an honest and economical government," the association controlled local politics mainly through the white primary,[qv] which excluded blacks until the United States Supreme Court, in 1953, supported a lower court's ruling forbidding the practice. The Jaybird Association accepted the ruling, continued for a few years, then disbanded in 1959.

Fort Bend County remained a state Democratic party[qv] stronghold until the 1970s, when the combination of population growth and the growing association of conservative political ideas with the Republican party[qv] broke the trend. In a special election held in April 1976 the people of the county elected Ron Paul, a physician from Lake Jackson in Brazoria County, as congressman, the first Republican elected to office in Fort Bend County since Reconstruction. Paul focused his campaign on the evils of "big government" and the "ultraliberalism" of his Democratic opponent.

New towns and a new demography began to develop in the last quarter of the nineteenth century as railroads branched out across the county. In 1878 the Gulf, Colorado and Santa Fe line from Galveston crossed the Galveston, Harrisburg and San Antonio (the former Buffalo Bayou, Brazos and Colorado) one mile west of Richmond. This junction, called Rosenberg, became a community when the developers of the New York, Texas, and Mexican Railway made it their headquarters in 1882. With the addition of the San Antonio and Aransas pass and the Texas and New Orleans railroads, all parts of the county were served. The new lines, with routes passing through potentially productive farmlands, attracted new settlers, many of whom were immigrants from Central Europe. Germans,[qv] Austrians, and Bohemians (*see* CZECHS) comprised 400 of the 5,259 new residents entering the county from 1890 to 1900. They were primarily agrarian in orientation—small farmers or merchants serving farmers—and many were Catholic. Their distinctly different cultural and linguistic characteristics added a new dimension to the established Anglo-Protestant community, and their agricultural achievements contributed to the county's economic stability and development. Among the many towns founded in the 1890s by or for these immigrants were Beasley, Needville, and Orchard, which still exist as small rural communities serving farmers.

Missouri City, on the far eastern edge of the county near Houston, was founded in 1894; Katy, a tri-county town in Fort Bend, Waller, and Harris counties, developed after the Missouri, Kansas and Texas (Katy) Railroad was completed to that point. In the 1890s, a million-dollar refinery was built at Sugar Land and a new cane mill was constructed; in 1907, they were purchased by the Imperial Sugar Company (see IMPERIAL HOLLY SUGAR CORPORATION) a major industry in the county and the only cane-sugar refinery in Texas.

In 1920 Rosenberg's population edged past Richmond's by the thin margin of 1,273 to 1,279; by 1950 Rosenberg residents overshadowed those of Richmond 6,210 to 2,030. Two decades later, Rosenberg-Richmond, as the "twin cities" population center, had counts of 12,098 and 5,777, respectively, in a county of 52,134 residents. Fort Bend County population declined between 1940 and 1950; however, in the same period, Rosenberg grew by nearly a third and Richmond held steady, a fact that reflects the national rural-to-urban movement.

Fort Bend County produces substantial minerals. Throughout the county subterranean salt domes hold concentrated deposits of oil, gas, sulfur, and salt that made early development possible. Gulf Oil Company brought in the first commercially producing oil well in 1919 at Blue Ridge and, three years later, located another major field at Big Creek. Thompsons had a major oilfield in 1921. In 1926 Gulf discovered a major sulfur and gas deposit in Orchard; the Humble Oil Company (now Exxon Company, U.S.A.) opened a high-producing gas field near Katy in 1935 and later built a gas plant that produced 450 million cubic feet of gas daily in the mid-1980s. Between 1954 and 1957 oil production in the county averaged 30,000 barrels a day, as compared to the 21,600 barrels a day in 1963. As demand for petroleum increased in the mid-1970s, developers managed to bring in forty new wells in 1976 and 1977, providing the county with $121 million from the sale of crude oil. Since that time a recession in the petroleum industry has caused development in the county to drop sharply. In 1976 the top three taxpayers in the county were, in order, Exxon, Gulf, and Houston Lighting and Power Company; in 1983 the top three taxpayers were Houston Lighting and Power, Exxon, and Utility Fuels. Gulf dropped to fourth place.

Farming and ranching have been the central focus of Fort Bend County economic and social life since its inception. The influx of new settlers in the 1880s and 1890s helped county agriculture to change from antebellum plantations to productive small farms. The county had 2,365 farms with 183 acres each in 1900, in contrast to 995 farms with 154 acres each in 1890. The national recession of the 1890s, a major flood on the Brazos River in June 1899, and the great Galveston hurricane of 1900 qv forced many farmers into tenancy. By 1910, 61 percent of the county's farmers were working as cash or share tenants. By 1925, of the 3,659 farms in the county, approximately 72 percent were operated by tenants, a partial result of a statewide economic recession and adverse summer weather from 1919 to 1922. During the World War II qv years, with the rural to urban movement and military service, farm tenancy dropped, and full ownership of farms increased. Since the 1960s, home developments, industry, business, and commerce in the county have forced a trend toward fewer commercial farms. The 1974 Census of Agriculture reported 1,340 farms in the county, but only 758 of these reported cash sales in excess of $2,500. Among the four top agricultural commodities for cash income in the mid-1980s were cotton, sorghum, beef cattle, and rice. Cotton culture, qv a source of income for nearly 700 families in the county, varies greatly with seasonal weather, allocated acreage, and selling prices. Sorghum culture qv has increased in recent years due to favorable selling prices and more consistent profit. Total value of the crop in the county in 1976 was $11 million. Rice culture qv began as early as 1901 with plantings on acreage once considered worthy only of grazing; rice yielded eighteen to twenty bags an acre in 1903. The 1990 annual acreage was just above 25,000 acres, with a yield of 4,488 pounds per acre. In 1982 agriculture provided more than $90 million in average annual income for the county.

Ample grazing land and free-roaming herds of longhorn cattle qv encouraged the first settlers in Fort Bend County to combine cattle raising with farming. The Fort Bend County Book of Brands indicates that landowners with minimal acreage tried to turn a profit in the cattle business. As elsewhere in Texas, the boom years of the 1870s and early 1880s culminated in the bottom falling out of the market by 1886. Local cattlemen began fencing their pastures and upgrading their herds with shorthorns, Brahmans, and Herefords. Today, more farms in the county produce cattle than any other cash crop.

Transportation facilities for Fort Bend County include the Southern Pacific and the Santa Fe railroad systems, two commercial lines of motor-freight services, and two airports for private and commercial aircraft. Major highways are Interstate 59, which joins U.S. Highway 90 Alternate in the county and runs northeast to southwest; Interstate 10, an east-west route through Katy; State Highway 6, north-south through Sugar Land; and State Highway 36, north-south through Rosenberg. Numerous farm roads serve the rural areas.

Until the last decade commerce and industry have been associated with the development and transport of oil, gas, and sulfur in the county. Local businesses provided agricultural needs and products and services for the communities. As the population increased in east Fort Bend County, a result of Houston's westward expansion, industry and commerce became more diverse. Among the top ten commercial taxpayers in Fort Bend County in 1983 were three property-development corporations and two high-technology corporations.

In the last decades of the twentieth century Fort Bend was among the fastest-growing counties in the United States. Between 1980 and 1990 the population nearly doubled, from 130,960 to 225,421. In 1990, 62.6 percent of the population was white, 20.7 percent black, 19.5 percent Hispanic, 6.4 percent Asian, and 0.2 percent American Indian. The largest communities were Rosenberg (20,183), Houston (with 27,027 in Fort Bend County), Missouri City (32,219 in Fort Bend County), and Sugar Land (24,529). Two major social and cultural events characteristic of the county and its people are the Fort Bend County Fair, first held in 1933 and still held annually each October, and the Fort Bend County Czech Fest, first held in 1976 as a spring tourist attraction and continued annually each May.

BIBLIOGRAPHY: S. A. McMillan, comp., *The Book of Fort Bend County* (Richmond, Texas, 1926). Pamela A. Puryear and Nath Winfield, Jr., *Sandbars and Sternwheelers: Steam Navigation on the Brazos* (College Station: Texas A&M University Press, 1976). Clarence Wharton, *Wharton's History of Fort Bend County* (San Antonio: Naylor, 1939). Pauline Yelderman, *The Jay Bird Democratic Association of Fort Bend County* (Waco: Texian Press, 1979). *Virginia Laird Ott*

FORT BIRD. After the battle of Village Creek qv in May 1841, Gen. Edward H. Tarrant qv ordered the construction and garrisoning of a fort near the site to protect the extreme northwest corner of the Texas frontier. Fort Bird (or Bird's Fort), constructed by a hundred volunteers of the Fourth Brigade of Texas Militia under Maj. Jonathan Bird in September and October 1841, consisted of a blockhouse and several smaller buildings enclosed in a picket stockade. Bird's company and that of Capt. Alexander W. Webb occupied the fort until March 1842, when it was apparently abandoned. The Sniveley expedition qv was disbanded at Fort Bird in August 1843, and in September the fort housed a council between representatives of the Republic of Texas qv and nine Indian tribes. Fort Bird subsequently became the site of the Tarrant County community of Birdville, now part of northeast Fort

Worth. In Arlington a stone marker, seven miles to the south, commemorates the fort.

BIBLIOGRAPHY: Austin *Daily Bulletin*, December 15, 1841. Gerald S. Pierce, *Texas Under Arms: The Camps, Posts, Forts, and Military Towns of the Republic of Texas* (Austin: Encino, 1969).

Thomas W. Cutrer

FORT BLISS. After the end of the Mexican War[qv] the need to defend the new border, to maintain law and order, to protect settlers and California-bound migrants from Indian attacks, and to survey for a new transcontinental railroad compelled the United States government to establish a military post on the Rio Grande in the area of El Paso del Norte (now Ciudad Juárez, Chihuahua). On November 7, 1848, the War Department instructed the Third Infantry to take up quarters at the pass, and Bvt. Maj. Jefferson Van Horne[qv] led 257 soldiers, including the regimental staff, six infantry companies, and a howitzer battery, west from San Antonio. They arrived in the area on September 8; on September 14, four companies were quartered on Coons' Rancho,[qv] formerly Ponce's Ranch, in downtown El Paso. About one-third of the troops occupied the presidio at San Elizario, an old Spanish garrison twenty miles southeast of El Paso.

The War Department closed the post and presidio in September 1851 and withdrew the troops to Fort Fillmore, forty miles to the north. A military post was reestablished on the Rio Grande in January 1854 when Lt. Col. Edmund Brooke Alexander, with four companies of the Eighth United States Infantry,[qv] rented quarters at Magoffinsville, a hacienda three miles east of Coons' Rancho. On March 8, 1854, the official name of the post became Fort Bliss, in memory of Lt. Col. William Wallace Smith Bliss, Gen. Zachary Taylor's[qv] chief of staff during the Mexican War and later his son-in-law.

Lt. Col. Isaac V. D. Reeve was in command of Fort Bliss on March 31, 1861, when it was surrendered to the Confederate authorities of Texas. Confederate lieutenant colonel John Robert Baylor[qv] then occupied the post with elements of the Second Regiment of Texas Mounted Rifles. Brig. Gen. Henry Hopkins Sibley[qv] used Fort Bliss as a base from which to invade New Mexico but was repulsed in mid-1862 and driven from West Texas. Elements of the California Volunteers commanded by Col. James H. Carleton[qv] reoccupied Fort Bliss for the Union. Under Carleton's protection Mexican president Benito Juárez[qv] survived in El Paso del Norte in 1865–66 and received supplies from north of the border before driving the French from Mexico.

In 1867 the post at Magoffinsville was swept away by a Rio Grande flood. The troops moved three miles north and named their post Camp Concordia in March 1868. On March 23, 1869, the camp was renamed Fort Bliss. The War Department closed the post in January 1877, just before the Salt War of San Elizario[qv] flared. A military board, however, convened to investigate the reopening of the post as a result of the violence; the board recommended in 1878 that Fort Bliss be reestablished, and the post was moved to downtown El Paso, which soldiers called Garrison Town.

In late 1879 the government purchased land at Hart's Mill, three miles west of downtown El Paso, and Fort Bliss became a way station for troops pursuing renegade Indians. After Geronimo surrendered in 1886, the government began to abolish small, isolated posts and replaced them with new facilities near railroads. Fort Bliss was almost supplanted by Fort Selden, eighteen miles north of Las Cruces, New Mexico, but was kept in El Paso by community leaders, who contributed about $7,000 for the purchase of land on Lanoria Mesa, five miles east of town. Congress then committed $300,000 for new facilities. Fort Bliss moved to its sixth and final home in late 1893.

After the Mexican Revolution[qv] started in 1910, the army gradually increased its troop strength at Fort Bliss. Eventually 50,000 men, mostly national guardsmen, were based at the facility. Fort Bliss also changed from an infantry station to the largest cavalry post in the United States. Gen. Hugh Scott commanded briefly in 1914, and Gen. John J. Pershing[qv] took charge from 1914 through much of 1916. When Francisco (Pancho) Villa[qv] attacked Columbus, New Mexico, in March 1916, Pershing led a punitive expedition south, and Fort Bliss became Pershing's primary supply base.

The First Cavalry Division was activated in 1921. With the arrival of the Eighty-second Field Artillery Battalion in 1921, Fort Bliss hosted its first artillery unit. During the 1940s the fort grew from a few thousand acres to more than one million, becoming roughly seventy-five miles long and fifty-four miles wide. Most of its area lies in New Mexico. By June 1943 Fort Bliss had phased out horses, and the cavalry had become mechanized. With the First Cavalry Division's departure in 1943, the fort became primarily an artillery post.

William Beaumont General Hospital opened at Fort Bliss on July 1, 1921. On July 1, 1972, the hospital dedicated a twelve-story facility, and on April 1, 1973, the hospital became the center of a three-state government medical complex known as William Beaumont Army Medical Center.[qv] In 1919 the Fort Bliss Flying Field was established. In 1925 it was renamed Biggs Field, an army flying field used by the Border Air Patrol; in 1947 it became Biggs Air Force Base. During its service, the base handled blimps, DH4s, B-17s, B-29s, B-50s, B-36s, B-47s, and B-52s. In July 1966 the air force base reverted to Fort Bliss, becoming Biggs Army Air Field.[qv]

Fort Bliss became an antiaircraft training center in September 1940. German rocket experts, including Wernher von Braun, lived and worked there shortly after World War II.[qv] In 1946 Fort Bliss became the United States Army Anti-aircraft Artillery and Guided Missile Center and later the United States Army Air Defense Center. The base hosted in succession Nike-Ajax, Nike-Hercules, Hawk, Sprint, Chaparral, and Redeye missiles and other antiaircraft weapons.

Fort Bliss played a significant role in training international military students after World War II. Approximately 10 percent of Fort Bliss Air Defense School graduates were from foreign countries. The Third Armored Cavalry has been stationed at Fort Bliss since 1972. In the 1990s Fort Bliss personnel comprised about 20,000 military people and 8,000 civilians. The fort contributed more than $500 million annually to the El Paso economy. In addition, retired service people and their dependents in El Paso numbered in the thousands. From 1977 until his death in 1981 Omar N. Bradley, latest five-star general of the United States Army, lived and worked at Fort Bliss. A cluster of adobe[qv] buildings representing the original 1848 post was built and donated to the post by the city of El Paso during the Fort Bliss centennial in 1948. The replica serves as the post museum.

BIBLIOGRAPHY: Martin Hardwick Hall, *The Confederate Army of New Mexico* (Austin: Presidial Press, 1978). Richard Keith McMaster, comp., *Musket, Saber and Missile: A History of Fort Bliss* (El Paso, 1962). Leon C. Metz, *Fort Bliss* (El Paso: Mangan, 1981).

Leon C. Metz

FORT BOGGY. Fort Boggy was a two-story log blockhouse built by a company of Texas Rangers[qv] in 1839 to protect the settlers between the Navasota and Trinity rivers in what is now Leon County. It was on the north bank of Boggy Creek two miles north of the site of present Leona. The first settlements on the Leon Prairie grew up around Fort Boggy, and the first store in the area was opened there by Moses Campbell. A Thomas Garner built the first sawmill. The community had been dropped from maps by 1941. In 1936 the Texas Centennial[qv] Commission erected a marker at the site of the old fort.

BIBLIOGRAPHY: Thomas Clarence Richardson, *East Texas: Its History and Its Makers* (4 vols., New York: Lewis Historical Publishing, 1940). Harold Schoen, comp., *Monuments Erected by the State of Texas to Commemorate the Centenary of Texas Independence* (Austin: Commission of Control for Texas Centennial Celebrations, 1938).

Fort Brown, Brownsville. Carte de visite by R. H. Wallis. Courtesy Lawrence T. Jones III Collection, Austin. This building is probably one of those erected by the U.S. Army, after it reoccupied Fort Brown in 1867.

W. D. Wood, "History of Leon County," *Quarterly of the Texas State Historical Association* 4 (January 1901). Art Leatherwood

FORT BROWN (Cameron County). Fort Brown, originally called Fort Texas, was established when Zachary Taylor^{qv} and the United States forces of occupation arrived on the Rio Grande on March 26, 1846, to establish the river as the southern boundary of Texas. In April 1846 Taylor built an earthen fort of 800 yards perimeter, with six bastions, walls more than nine feet high, a parapet of fifteen feet, and the whole surrounded by a ditch fifteen feet deep and twenty feet wide. Armament was four eighteen-pound guns. The Seventh Infantry, with Company I of the Second Artillery and Company E, Third Artillery, commanded by Maj. Jacob Brown,^{qv} garrisoned the fort. Mexican troops led by Mariano Arista^{qv} intercepted United States troops as they brought supplies from Fort Polk at Point Isabel to Fort Brown, leading to the opening battles of the war, Palo Alto and Resaca de la Palma,^{qqv} fought on May 8 and 9, 1846. On May 9 Major Brown died from injuries received during the bombardment of the fort by Mexican forces in Matamoros. Shortly after his death he was buried within the fortifications, and the post was named in his honor. The fort was held by a strong force during the Mexican War.^{qv} In 1848 quarters for officers and enlisted men and a permanent post were built a quarter mile north of the first site. The land was purchased from heirs of José Salvador de la Garza, recipient of the Potrero del Espíritu Santo land grant and one of José de Escandón's^{qv} colonists.

A brick wall, called the Quarter Master's Fence, divided the fort and the community that became the city of Brownsville. Rumors that the fort was to be abandoned started circulating in 1848; however, Indian raids in 1852 made it a necessary fortification for the town, and from one to four companies of troops were stationed there for protection from Indians and as a show of force against potential incursions into Texas by Mexico. In 1859 Juan Nepomuceno Cortina^{qv} occupied the fort as a refuge. In 1860 Robert E. Lee^{qv} was stationed at Fort Brown on assignment to quell border disturbances. The post was abandoned by United States troops in March 1861 and occupied by troops of the state of Texas. Fort Brown was garrisoned by a small force of Confederates until November 1863. On the approach of Union forces, the Confederates retreated and burned all stored cotton and the fort buildings. Union forces occupied the fort until July 1864, when it was again taken by Confederates forces, who held it until November 1865. During Confederate occupation the fort was described as a field work of six bastion fronts with a defense line of 950 yards garrisoned by 2,000 men with an armament of guns of different calibers. The fort was reoccupied by federal forces after the Civil War,^{qv} again as a protection against Mexican invasion. Fort Brown was rebuilt with brick buildings starting in 1869. Among the buildings were the post hospital, an administration building, a large officers' quarters, and the chapel. In 1882 Dr. William Crawford Gorgas^{qv} was sent to the post in response to the last and worst yellow fever epidemic at Fort Brown.

The Brownsville raid of 1906^{qv} occurred on August 13, when a group of black soldiers from the fort allegedly attacked the city. The consequences included a federal investigation, the demand of the removal of black troops from the fort by Brownsville citizens, the court-martial of the black troops, and the transfer of the fort from the War Department to the Department of the Interior by President Theodore Roosevelt. This department converted the fort into an experimental garden for spineless cacti. In 1914, because of increased racial and economic tensions in the Lower Rio Grande valley, Fort Brown was reactivated and made headquarters for the Brownsville Military District under Gen. James Parker. Within a few months 50,000 state guards were mobilized in the district. The first wireless station was established about 1916. From World War I^{qv} to February

1941 Fort Brown was headquarters for the Twelfth Cavalry. That unit was replaced by the 124th Cavalry, which trained there until May 1944, when the fort was deactivated. Official deactivation was declared by the War Department in 1945, at which time the fort was turned over to the army engineers; it was certified to the War Assets Administration for disposal on May 15, 1946, and assigned to the Federal Works Agency on July 7. The agency then turned the land over to the Federal Land Bank for farming purposes. On July 22, 1948, the front 162 acres of Fort Brown was deeded to the city of Brownsville, and the old post hospital was granted to the Brownsville schools for the use of Texas Southmost College. The fort buildings were sold or donated to various organizations and schools in the Brownsville area. In the early 1990s much of what was left of Fort Brown buildings and land were used by the University of Texas–Pan American at Brownsville and Texas Southmost College.

BIBLIOGRAPHY: Helen Chapman, *The News From Brownsville: Helen Chapman's Letters from the Texas Military Frontier, 1848–1852*, ed. Caleb Coker (Austin: Texas State Historical Association, 1992). Garna L. Christian, "The Brownsville Raid's 168th Man: The Court-Martial of Corporal Knowles," *Southwestern Historical Quarterly* 93 (July 1989). Vertical Files, Barker Texas History Center, University of Texas at Austin.

Elizabeth Pettit Davenport

FORT BROWN (Houston County). Fort Brown was built around 1834 in northeastern Houston County by Reuben Brown for his wife Sarah (Parker) Brown and family and for others of the Daniel Parker qv family. Sarah was one of Daniel's daughters. Around 1833 the Parker family group had started from Illinois for Texas with the intention of organizing the Pilgrim Church there. The congregation settled for a time at the Reuben Brown Fort before moving on to the north and west, settling in what was still at that time Houston County (near what is now Elkhart in Anderson County). The Parkers were also associated with Fort Houston in Palestine and eventually settled at Fort Parker, Limestone County. Reuben and family remained in northeastern Houston County, establishing a community named Refuge. The Refuge cemetery remains and Reuben and wife and other settlers of Fort Brown are buried there.

BIBLIOGRAPHY: *Houston County Cemeteries* (Crockett, Texas: Houston County Historical Commission, 1977; 3d ed. 1987). Houston County Historical Commission, *History of Houston County, Texas, 1687–1979* (Tulsa, Oklahoma: Heritage, 1979).

Eliza H. Bishop

FORT BUFFALO SPRINGS. Fort Buffalo Springs was at Buffalo Springs, thirty miles north of Jacksboro, Texas, in Clay County. It was occupied by two companies of the Sixth Calvary deployed from Jacksboro in 1867, with orders to erect substantial buildings. Inadequate water and timber forced the troops to abandon the site, possibly in the same year, and return to Jacksboro, where they established a new post to be named Fort Richardson.

BIBLIOGRAPHY: William Curry Holden, Frontier Problems and Movements in West Texas, 1846–1900 (Ph.D. dissertation, University of Texas, 1928). H. H. McConnell, *Five Years a Cavalryman, or Sketches of Regular Army Life on the Texas Frontier* (Jacksboro, Texas: J. N. Rogers, 1889). Joseph Carroll McConnell, *West Texas Frontier* (Vol. 1, Jacksboro, Texas, 1933; Vol. 2, Palo Pinto, Texas, 1939). Theronne Thompson, "Fort Buffalo Springs, Texas Border Post," *West Texas Historical Association Year Book* 36 (1960). Vertical Files, Barker Texas History Center, University of Texas at Austin.

Art Leatherwood

FORT CHADBOURNE. Fort Chadbourne was on Oak Creek near what is now U.S. Highway 277 eleven miles northeast of Bronte in extreme northeast Coke County. The post was established on October 28, 1852, by companies A and K of the Eighth United States Infantry for frontier protection and named for 2d Lt. Theodore Lincoln Chadbourne, who was killed at the battle of Resaca de la Palma in the Mexican War.qv Much Indian activity occurred in the area during the 1850s, including a skirmish inside the fort in 1856. The fort was a defense for a station on the Butterfield Overland Mailqv route from 1858 to 1861. It was surrendered to Confederate Col. Henry E. McCullochqv on February 28, 1861. Chadbourne was occupied briefly by United States troops after the Civil War,qv but lack of water, wood, and adequate facilities forced its abandonment in 1868. The site, near the present town of Fort Chadbourne, is designated by a Texas historical marker near the old cemetery south of Highway 277.

BIBLIOGRAPHY: Arrie Barrett, "Western Frontier Forts of Texas, 1845–1861," *West Texas Historical Association Year Book* 7 (1931). M. L. Crimmins, "Experiences of an Army Surgeon at Fort Chadbourne," *West Texas Historical Association Yearbook* 15 (1939). John Leeds Kerr and Frank Donovan, *Destination Topolobampo: The Kansas City, Mexico & Orient Railway* (San Marino, California: Golden West, 1968). Jewell G. Pritchett, *From the Top of Old Hayrick: A Narrative History of Coke County* (Abilene, Texas: Pritchett, 1980).

Charles G. Davis

FORT CHADBOURNE, TEXAS. The Fort Chadbourne community is on a local road and the Atchison, Topeka and Santa Fe line, about eight miles north of Bronte and four miles southwest of old Fort Chadbourne in northeastern Coke County. A small settlement grew up in the area during the 1850s, and a post office operated there from January 1859 to November 1866. After the Civil War,qv settlers first gathered around the fort but soon established a new town some four miles to the southwest. The Fort Chadbourne post office was reinstated in October 1879. In 1892 the town reported the post office, a general store, and twenty-five citizens. The community was moved about one mile east to a new townsite donated by W. D. McDonald when the Kansas City, Mexico and Orient built through the county about 1910. Soon the settlement had a newspaper, a hotel, a store, a bank, a gin, a school, and two churches; by 1917 it reported a population of sixty-five. By the 1940s, however, only two businesses and a population of fifty were reported. Eventually the school was consolidated with that of Bronte, and the post office closed for good in 1942. Fort Chadbourne had a population of fifty during the 1950s and 1960s; by the 1980s county maps showed only a railroad station at the site, with a cemetery nearby.

BIBLIOGRAPHY: M. L. Crimmins, "Experiences of an Army Surgeon at Fort Chadbourne," *West Texas Historical Association Year Book* 15 (1939). John Leeds Kerr and Frank Donovan, *Destination Topolobampo: The Kansas City, Mexico & Orient Railway* (San Marino, California: Golden West, 1968). Jewell G. Pritchett, *From the Top of Old Hayrick: A Narrative History of Coke County* (Abilene, Texas: Pritchett, 1980).

Charles G. Davis

FORT CHAMBERS. Fort Chambers, built during the Civil War,qv was a small Confederate mud fortification located about halfway between the site of Fort Anahuacqv and the town of Anahuac in Chambers County. It was built in late 1862 under the direction of Heinrich Mueller of Galveston, who was in the Confederate military service. Its construction came after an inspection of coastal defenses by Commander William W. Hunter of the Confederate Navy in January 1862. The small fort, which was named for Thomas Jefferson Chambers,qv included two cannons, a twenty-four pounder and a thirty-two pounder. They were later mounted outside the doors of Galveston's Artillery Hall.

BIBLIOGRAPHY: Jewel Horace Harry, A History of Chambers County (M.A. thesis, University of Texas, 1940; rpt., Dallas: Taylor, 1981). Margaret S. Henson and Kevin Ladd, *Chambers County: A Pictorial*

History (Norfolk, Virginia: Donning, 1988). Adele B. Looscan, "The Old Fort at Anahuac," *Quarterly of the Texas State Historical Association* 2 (July 1898).
Kevin Ladd

FORT CIBOLO. Fort Cibolo is located on Cibolo Creek four miles northwest of Shafter at the southeast end of the Chinati Mountains in central Presidio County. The private fort was constructed in the late 1850s by Presidio County's first Anglo-American rancher, Milton Faver,qv on his headquarters ranch. Fort Cibolo offered protection from Indian raids, an outpost for army detachments from Fort Davis, and subsistence for its inhabitants. The one-story adobeqv structure had a flat roof of cottonwood poles and was surrounded by walls twenty feet high and three to four feet thick, set with broken bottles to prevent attackers from scaling them. Loopholes allowed defenders to shoot from behind the walls. Circular towers at the north and south corners aided defense. The building was fitted with heavy paneled doors and wood-grilled windows. During the 1860s, when Fort Davis was abandoned during the Civil War,qv Indians raided the Fort Cibolo area with little resistance other than that of Faver and his men. After the war Fort Davis lent a cannon and stationed troops at Fort Cibolo. Fort Davis patrols were resupplied from the quartermaster's stored goods at Fort Cibolo when they passed through the area.

Fort Cibolo, named for the Spanish word meaning "buffalo," was self-sufficient. Nearby, Big Springs Cibolo provided enough water for irrigation, and enough vegetables were produced to be sold. Cattle, horses, mules, goats, and sheep were raised on the rangeland near the fort. A peach orchard grew nearby, and Faver kept a still at the fort to make brandy from the fruit. He traded the brandy to the Indians for hides, leather goods, horses, and mules. When Faver died in December 1889, the fort became the property of his wife, who sold the livestock and gave the money to a faith healer. In the 1970s the Cibolo Ranch was part of the J. E. White and Sons Ranch.

BIBLIOGRAPHY: Leavitt Corning, Jr., *Baronial Forts of the Big Bend* (Austin: Trinity University Press, 1967). John Ernest Gregg, History of Presidio County (M.A. thesis, University of Texas, 1933). Cecilia Thompson, *History of Marfa and Presidio County, 1535–1946* (2 vols., Austin: Nortex, 1985).
Julia Cauble Smith

FORT CIENEGA. Fort Cienega, a private fort near the source of Cienega Creek six miles east of Shafter in central Presidio County, was built between 1855 and 1857 by Presidio County's first Anglo-American rancher, Milton Faver.qv It served as a stronghold during Indian attacks, an outpost for army patrols from Fort Davis, and a self-sufficient home to ranch workers. The adobeqv structure was built for protection. It had one story, a flat roof, and twenty-foot-high walls three to four feet thick. The living quarters were thirteen-foot rooms along the south and west sides. Animals were stockaded within the enclosure. Two square defensive towers stood at the northeast and southwest corners. The main gate was the only entrance.

As formidable as the fort must have appeared to Indians, it was not spared from attacks. During the Civil Warqv Fort Davis was abandoned, and Indian raids increased in the Fort Cienega area. In 1871 Fort Cienega was attacked by Indians who dug a trench under the wall. Faver and his men discovered the plan in progress and killed the first Indian when he appeared in the opening. Fort Cienega served as a quasimilitary post when troops from Fort Davis were garrisoned there in times of need. Army provisions were stored there to resupply patrols that came through the area.

Fort Cienega, named for the Spanish word *ciénaga* ("marshland") was self-sufficient. Its abundant water supply, derived from nearby Cienega Spring, allowed the cultivation of many vegetables. Cattle, horses, mules, goats, and sheep were raised on the open range near the fort. Peach trees growing near the spring provided the fruit for Faver's homemade brandy, which he bartered to Indians for hides, leather goods, horses, and mules. After Faver's death in December 1889, ownership of Cienega passed to his son, Juan. John A. Pool bought the ranch from the Faver descendants, and at the end of the 1980s it was home to the fourth generation of Pool's family.

BIBLIOGRAPHY: Leavitt Corning, Jr., *Baronial Forts of the Big Bend* (Austin: Trinity University Press, 1967). John Ernest Gregg, History of Presidio County (M.A. thesis, University of Texas, 1933). Historic American Buildings Survey, *Texas Catalog*, comp. Paul Goeldner (San Antonio: Trinity University Press, 1974?). Ray Miller, *Ray Miller's Texas Forts* (Houston: Cordovan, 1985). Carlysle Graham Raht, *The Romance of the Davis Mountains and Big Bend Country* (Odessa, Texas: Rahtbooks, 1963). Cecilia Thompson, *History of Marfa and Presidio County, 1535–1946* (2 vols., Austin: Nortex, 1985).
Julia Cauble Smith

FORT CLARK. Fort Clark was established on June 20, 1852, at Las Moras Springsqv in Kinney County by companies C and E of the First Infantry under the command of Maj. Joseph H. LaMotte. The name Las Moras ("the mulberries") was given by Spanish explorers to the springs and the creek they feed. The site was long favored by Coahuiltecan Indians and later by the Comanches, Apaches, and other tribes. During the late eighteenth and early nineteenth centuries the big spring was a stopping place on the eastern branch of the great Comanche Trailqv into Mexico. In 1849 Lt. W. H. C. Whiting,qv during his reconnaissance for a practicable wagon route between San Antonio and El Paso, recognized its military potential and recommended the location as a site for a fort. The post was originally named Fort Riley in honor of the commanding officer of the First Infantry, but on July 15, 1852, at Riley's request, it was renamed in honor of Maj. John B. Clark, a deceased officer who had served in the Mexican War.qv A formal military lease for Fort Clark was made on July 30, 1852, when Lt. Col. D. C. Tompkins signed an agreement with Samuel A. Maverick,qv who owned the land, for a period not to exceed twenty years. The fort was strategically located as anchor to the cordon of army posts that had been established along the southwest Texas border after the Mexican War. It was at Eagle Pass on the Rio Grande, forty-five miles north of Fort Duncan and 145 miles west of San Antonio. The fort's purpose was to guard the Mexican border, to protect the military road to El Paso, and to defend against Indian depredations arising from either side of the Rio Grande. By November 1852 Fort Clark had two companies of the First Infantry under the command of Capt. W. E. Prince, and for the next three years officers of the First Infantry and Mounted Rifles served as post commanders.

Bvt. Lt. Col. W. G. Freeman inspected Fort Clark on August 1, 1853, as a part of his tour of the Eighth Military Department, and reported it to be "a point of primary importance . . . from its salient position looking both to the Rio Grande and Indian frontiers." Freeman was the first to recommend the fort as being "well fitted for a Cavalry station." The quartermaster, according to Freeman, had only eight wagons available for hauling the materials needed to build the post. This was an inadequate number since the depot at Corpus Christi was 280 miles distant and wagons required thirty days, under favorable conditions, to make the round trip. Mail came to the post from San Antonio, "being brought weekly by special express." From their campsite near the spring and from tents pitched along the banks of Las Moras Creek, soldiers began construction of the fort on an adjacent high limestone ridge. The first barracks and houses were Mexican-type jacals and crude log huts of palisade construction. A few buildings of limestone, some of which are still standing, were begun in 1856–57. The ruins of the old post headquarters building has the date 1857 over the doorway. With the establishment of Fort Clark, a neighboring settlement of Las Moras came into existence when Oscar B. Brackettqv established a supply village for the fort. The town's name was changed to Brackett in 1856 and later to Brackettville. The stage from San Antonio to El Paso ran through the settlement, and for almost a century the town and the fort remained closely identified. In the summer of 1854 the Indian menace in Texas prompted Gen. Persifor F. Smith,qv the department commander, to make a requisition to Governor Elisha M. Peaseqv for six companies of Texas Rangersqv to conduct a campaign against the raiders. Two companies of these Texas military volunteers, under captains Charles E. Travisqv and William Henry, were sent to Fort Clark, where they assisted the regulars in patrolling the road. Col. J. K. F. Mansfield inspected the post in early June 1856 and reported the presence of one company of the First Artillery and two companies of Mounted Rifles under the command of Bvt. Lt. Col. J. B. ("Prince John") Magruder.qv Mansfield observed that although the adjutant's office, guardhouse, bakery, and magazine were built of stone, the other buildings were of log construction. He recommended that "stone quarters for the officers of these Companies be immediately commenced."

In February 1861 Texas voted to secede from the Union, and almost immediately state troops began demanding the surrender of United States posts in Texas. On March 19 Capt. W. H. T. Brooks, with three companies of United States Third Infantry, surrendered Fort Clark to a small company of the Provisional Army of Texas. In June 1861, after the outbreak of the Civil War,qv Fort Clark was garrisoned by companies C and H, Second Regiment of Texas Mounted Rifles, with Capt. H. A. Hamner as post commander. In August 1862 all Confederate troops were withdrawn from Fort Clark. After the war the fort was regarrisoned in December 1866 by Troop C, Fourth United States Cavalry,qv under the command of Capt. John A. Wilcox,qv with the task of protecting the road to El Paso. Although the post was dilapidated and required extensive repairs, a program for new construction was not begun, perhaps in part because the government was still leasing the land. In fact, a deed to the fort property was not secured until 1884, when Mary A. Maverickqv was paid $80,000 for the 3,965-acre tract. Despite efforts at patchwork repairs, more than five years went by before any significant progress was made. Between 1873 and 1875 most of the buildings, still in use in the historic district in 1990, were built of quarried limestone in an ambitious rebuilding project. A twenty-acre post was developed with the construction of barracks, officers' quarters, hospital, bakery, stables, and guardhouse. By 1875 the fort had quarters built of stone for more than 200 officers and men, including a commanding officer's house and eight officers' row duplexes accommodating sixteen families, as well as four previously built log quarters.

Especially significant during the Indian campaigns in the last half of the nineteenth century were the Black Seminole scouts,qv who served at Fort Clark from 1872 until 1914. The Black Seminoles had spent twenty years protecting the northern Mexican frontier state of Coahuila before being recruited by the United States Army to serve as scouts. Under Lt. John L. Bullis,qv who commanded them from 1873 to 1881, the scouts played a decisive role in the Indian campaigns. Among the roster of scouts are four who were awarded the Medal of Honor. During the Civil War the southwest Texas frontier was left relatively unprotected, and Indian depredations, particularly by Indians using Mexico as a sanctuary, were widespread and devastating. After the war attempts by federal troops to curtail Indian raiders coming from Mexico met with little success until early 1873, when Col. Ranald S. Mackenzieqv and the Fourth United States Cavalry were ordered to Fort Clark. On May 18 Mackenzie led six companies of the Fourth Cavalry, along with a contingent of Black Seminole scouts, across the border into Mexico on a punitive expedition against Kickapoo and Lipan Apache Indians at Remolino. It was a daring raid that resulted in the destruction of three villages, the killing of nineteen warriors, and the capture of forty prisoners, including the aged Lipan chief Costillitto. Despite Mexico's protests that the United States was violating its sovereignty, other sorties by Mackenzie soon followed. As a result, Indian forays from Mexico into Texas declined dramatically. Mackenzie was succeeded by Lt. Col. William Rufus Shafterqv in 1876. Shafter followed Mackenzie as one of the most successful of Fort Clark's Indian-fighting commanding officers. Under Shafter, Fort Clark became the garrison for the Tenth United States Cavalry and the Twenty-fourth and Twenty-fifth United States Infantryqqv regiments. These were mounted regiments of blacks, called "buffalo soldiers"qv by the Indians. The buffalo soldiers, for long mostly unacclaimed, left a distinguished record of service in ridding Southwest Texas of Indians.

Mackenzie's raid in 1873 had stopped Indian activity for almost three years, but, as the lesson of Remolino dimmed, violence once more came to the Rio Grande border area. In the fall of 1875 department commander Gen. Edward O. C. Ordqv established the District of the Nueces, with Fort Clark as headquarters and with Shafter in control. When, in April and May 1876, Lipan warriors killed twelve Texans in an unusually bloody raid, Ord authorized Shafter to go after the offenders in their Mexican villages. Shafter took five companies of cavalry, along with Bullis's scouts, and established a base camp near the mouth of the Pecos River. In the first of a long succession of border violations, Shafter's cavalrymen splashed across the Rio Grande and drove deep into the mountains of northern Coahuila. For two years Shafter's determined thrusts into Mexico in pursuit of the marauding Indians and their chief, Washa Lobo, aroused Mexican animosity and caused tensions between the United States and Mexican governments. Shafter's extensive campaign on the Texas borderlands frontier not only earned him the sobriquet "Pecos Bill" but boldly implemented the army's aggressive policy toward hostile Indians, which was one of removal or extermination. By the end of the decade the Indian problem along the border had finally been brought under control.

As the country became settled, the role of the fort was reduced to a routine of garrison duty and border patrol. In 1882 Gen. William T. Sherman,qv after making a tour of inspection, described Fort Clark as the "largest and most costly military post in Texas if not in the United States." Because of the new railroad being constructed nine miles south, he thought Fort Clark was obsolete and should be closed. The War Department decided otherwise, and, instead of closing the fort, launched a new program of construction and expansion. A large storehouse and granary, capable of holding 3,000 bushels of grain, was built. Three years later the eight officers' row duplexes were enlarged, and a new two-story bachelor officers' quarters was built on the site of the original post hospital. In 1888 a fine new duplex for staff officers was also added to the line of stone quarters on Officers' Row. During the late 1880s and early 1890s the fort was home for the Third Cavalry, the Eighteenth and Nineteenth Infantry, and occasional elements of the Seventh United States Cavalry. After the fort was again threatened with closure, it revived briefly during the Spanish-American War, when it was garrisoned by the Third Texas Infantry. With American entrance into World War Iqv in 1917, a period of reconstruction and enlargement was begun that continued after the war ended. Many infantry regiments and practically all of the cavalry regiments were stationed at Fort Clark at various times. For twenty-one years, from 1920 to November 1941, Fort Clark was home of the Fifth Cavalry. The regiment, first organized in 1855 as the Second United States Cavalry,qv had been associated with the fort as early as 1856. Col. George S. Patton, Jr., served at Fort Clark in 1938 as regimental commander of the Fifth Cavalry.

At the outbreak of World War IIqv the 112th Cavalry Division of the Texas National Guard,qv under command of Col. Julian Cunningham, was assigned to Fort Clark, where it trained until it was deployed for combat in the Pacific. Just before the 112th Cavalry left, the black Ninth United States Cavalryqv arrived at Fort Clark from Fort Riley. Elements of the regiment had first served at Fort Clark in 1875, when the fort was a frontier outpost. In 1942 Col. William C. Chase and the 113th Cavalry spent a short stay guarding the Southern Pacific Railroad. On February 25, 1943, the Second Cavalry Division, the army's last horse-mounted unit, was activated under command of Maj. Gen. Harry H. Johnson. More than 12,000 troops were stationed there until their deployment in February 1944 to the European Theater of Operations. The war added another feature to the history of Fort Clark, that of having a German prisoner of war subcamp on the 4,000-acre reservation (*see* PRISONERS OF WAR). Finally, in June 1944, nearly three years after the beginning of World War II, and after full mechanization of the cavalry, the government ordered the closure of Fort Clark, one of the last horse-cavalry posts in the country. The fort was officially inactivated in early 1946, and later that year it was sold to the Texas Railway Equipment Company of Houston, a subsidiary of Brown and Root Company, for salvage and later use as a "Guest Ranch" (*see* DUDE RANCHING).

In 1971 Fort Clark was purchased by North American Towns of Texas and developed into a private recreation and retirement community. Since many famous officers served at Fort Clark, a number of the streets and buildings at the fort honor their names, including those of Mackenzie, Shafter, Bullis, Bliss, Wainright, and Patton. The Seminole-Negro Indian Scout Cemetery, where four Medal of Honor recipients have specially marked graves, may be visited on Farm Road 3348 west of the fort and three miles south of U.S. Highway 90. In 1990 Fort Clark encompassed about 2,700 acres. The large spring still fed Las Moras Creek, as well as the adjacent large swimming pool, which has sixty-eight-degree year-round water temperature. The grove of ancient oak and pecan trees next to the spring, where emigrants bound for California camped on the overland trail, is now a beautiful picnic area. Below the spring are seven miles of wooded creekfront. The historic district of the fort remains much as it was planned and built in the 1870s, with the old parade ground now a well-groomed par-three golf course. Much of the fort's military history is on display in the Old Fort Clark Guardhouse Museum, which is maintained by the Fort Clark Historical Society. In September 1979 Fort Clark was entered on the National Register of Historic Places.

BIBLIOGRAPHY: Roger N. Conger, et al., *Frontier Forts of Texas* (Waco: Texian Press, 1966). M. L. Crimmins, "W. G. Freeman's Report on the Eighth Military Department," *Southwestern Historical Quarterly* 51–54 (July 1947–October 1950). Ben E. Pingenot, ed., *Paso del Águila . . . Memoirs of Jesse Sumpter* (Austin: Encino, 1969). Kenneth Wiggins Porter, "The Seminole Negro-Indian Scouts, 1870–1881," *Southwestern Historical Quarterly* 55 (January 1952). George F. Price, *Across the Continent with the Fifth Cavalry* (New York: Van Nostrand, 1883; rpt., New York: Antiquarian, 1959). Carl Coke Rister, *Comanche Bondage: Dr. John Charles Beales's Settlement of La Villa de Dolores on Las Moras Creek in Southern Texas of the 1830s* (Glendale, California: Clark, 1955).

Ben E. Pingenot

FORT COLORADO. Fort Colorado stood on high ground on the north bank of the Colorado River just west of Walnut Creek within the bounds of what later became Travis County. The fort was a key post in the chain of defensive positions established by the Republic of Texas[qv] from the San Antonio River to east of the Trinity. Other links in the barrier against raiding Plains Indians included Little River Fort, Fort Milam, and Fort Houston (Houston County). Fort Colorado and its ranger garrison contributed materially to the lull in border warfare between white settlers and Comanches and Kiowas during 1837 and early 1838.

Fort Colorado, popularly known as Coleman's Fort or Fort Coleman and also officially known as Fort Houston, consisted of two two-story blockhouses and a number of cabins enclosed within a high stockade wall. It was built during the fall of 1836 by Col. Robert M. Coleman[qv] and first garrisoned by two or three companies of his ranger battalion. Soon after the fort's completion, however, Coleman was relieved of command by Maj. William H. Smith, but he did not turn over command of the fort until Capt. Micah Andrews arrived there in January 1837. In the summer or fall of 1837 Andrews was in turn relieved by Capt. William M. Eastland,[qv] who retained command until March 2, 1838. Lt. William H. Moore was the fort's last commander before it was abandoned, in April 1838. Settlers in the area, pleased to have a source of dressed logs, lumber, and hardware, soon stripped the fort, and today the site, 2½ miles northeast of the Montopolis Bridge in Austin, is marked only by a state historical marker. Noah Smithwick[qv] served as a ranger at Fort Colorado and left a fine description of life in a frontier fort in his notable memoir, *Evolution of a State* (1900).

BIBLIOGRAPHY: George B. Erath, "The Memoirs of George B. Erath, 1813–1891," *Southwestern Historical Quarterly* 26–27 (January–October 1923; rpts., Austin: Texas State Historical Association, 1923; Waco: Heritage Society of Waco, 1956). "F. A. Sawyer to Colonel Robert M. Coleman, August 12, 1836," *Texana* 1 (Winter 1963). Gerald S. Pierce, *Texas Under Arms: The Camps, Posts, Forts, and Military Towns of the Republic of Texas* (Austin: Encino, 1969). Noah Smithwick, *The Evolution of a State, or Recollections of Old Texas Days* (Austin: Gammel, 1900; rpt., Austin: University of Texas Press, 1983).

Thomas W. Cutrer

FORT CONCHO. Fort Concho, in San Angelo, was one of a number of United States military posts built to establish law and order in West Texas as settlers began to move in after the Civil War.[qv] A site at the juncture of the Main and North Concho rivers was selected in November 1867 for a new post to replace Fort Chadbourne, which lacked an adequate water supply. Company H of the Fourth United States Cavalry[qv] arrived there in December. The post's first commanding officer, Capt. George Gibson Huntt, named the post Camp Hatch after the commander of his regiment, Maj. John Porter Hatch.[qv] Later it was called Camp Kelly for the recently deceased Maj. Michael J. Kelly,[qv] and in March 1868 the post became Fort Concho, named after the Middle and North Concho rivers, which converge in San Angelo to form the Concho.

Fort Concho's commissary storehouse (today the oldest building in San Angelo) and its twin, the quartermaster storehouse, were constructed in 1868. Subsequent construction progressed slowly because building materials not available locally had to be hauled from the Gulf Coast by oxcart. An official report in 1876 stated that "a flat, treeless, dreary prairie" surrounded the fort, but Capt. Robert G. Carter[qv] recalled Fort Concho in the 1870s as "one of the most beautiful and best ordered posts on the Texas border. Its arrangement was artistic and every feature bespoke comfort and convenience. On the south side of the ample parade grounds stood the officers' quarters, tasty, elegant, imposing; on the north, the commodious and handsome barracks; on the east side the commissary and quartermaster's buildings, while the west side of the grounds was closed with an ornamental fence with a large gateway in the center." Civilian stonemasons and carpenters from the Fredericksburg area were employed in the early years of construction, and soldiers built the later buildings. The government did not buy the land on which the fort was built but leased it from private owners.

By 1879 Fort Concho was an eight-company post with some forty permanent structures built of locally quarried limestone around a parade ground that measured about 500 by 1,000 feet. Besides the buildings mentioned by Carter, the fort's stone buildings included stables, blacksmith and carpenter shops, a forage house, an ordnance storehouse, a guardhouse, a powder magazine, a pump house, a bakery, a hospital, an administration building, and a schoolhouse that was used also as a chapel. A number of temporary frame buildings—married soldiers' quarters, telegraph office, and post trader's store—were built adjacent to the fort. The fort was not stockaded, but stone walls surrounded the hospital and the backyards of the officers' quarters. A belvedere on the post hospital afforded a distant view in every direction.

Food from the commissary was sometimes supplemented from the post garden at nearby Bismarck Farm or purchased from the sutler's store. Grain and meat were contracted from local suppliers. Hunting parties killed buffalo and turkeys when possible. Drinking water came from a clear-running spring three miles south of Fort

Concho, and water for cooking, washing, and animals was abundant in the nearby rivers.

Fort Concho was commanded by such famous officers as William R. Shafter, Ranald S. Mackenzie, Benjamin H. Grierson,[qqv] John P. Hatch, and Wesley Merritt. While in command of Fort Concho, Colonel Grierson also commanded the District of the Pecos throughout the existence of that military jurisdiction in far western Texas (1878–81). Fort Concho served as regimental headquarters for the Tenth United States Cavalry,[qv] known as the Buffalo Soldiers, from 1875 until 1882. The Fourth Cavalry headquarters was at Fort Concho for several brief periods between 1868 and 1873. The Eleventh Infantry was headquartered at Fort Concho in 1870 and the Sixteenth Infantry from 1882 until 1887. Units of the Third, Eighth, and Ninth United States Cavalry[qv] regiments and of the Tenth, Eleventh, Nineteenth, Twenty-fourth,[qv] and Twenty-fifth[qv] United States Infantry regiments also served the garrison, along with signal corps personnel, who managed telegraph and weather service.

Soldiers from Fort Concho scouted and mapped large portions of West Texas; built roads and telegraph lines; escorted stagecoaches, cattle drives, and railroad survey parties; and served generally as a police force. At times Fort Concho troops were stationed at semipermanent subposts at Grierson's Spring, Camp Charlotte,[qv] and the head of the North Concho. Among the numerous temporary field camps were several former Butterfield Overland Mail[qv] stops such as Johnson's Station, Grape Creek Station, and old Fort Chadbourne.

In the early years of the fort's existence, its soldiers skirmished with numerous small parties of Indians. Fort Concho also furnished personnel and supplies for three major Indian campaigns: Mackenzie's 1872 campaign, the 1874 Red River War,[qv] and the Victorio[qv] campaign of 1879–80. In 1872–73 more than 100 Indian women and children captured by Mackenzie were imprisoned in a stone corral at Fort Concho for six months. Other important Fort Concho events include the 1875 exploration of the Llano Estacado[qv] by Colonel Shafter and Capt. Nicholas Nolan's expedition of 1877 (see NOLAN EXPEDITION).

In 1870 a town, which later became San Angelo, began to form across the river from the fort. As civilian law enforcement improved, Fort Concho ceased to be of any value as a military post; from 1882 to 1889 the fort was mainly a holding point for soldiers awaiting reassignment. The army abandoned the fort on June 20, 1889. Most of its buildings escaped demolition by being converted into civilian housing and commercial storage space. In 1929 Ginevra Wood Carson headed a fund-raising campaign to buy the former Fort Concho administration building. She had established the West Texas Museum in 1928 in a room of the county courthouse. In 1930 she moved her museum into the newly acquired building and changed the name to Fort Concho Museum. The city of San Angelo took over the operation of the museum in 1935 and began a program of land acquisition and building restoration. By the mid-1950s the city had acquired several fort properties and had rebuilt two barracks and two mess halls from ruins. The fort was designated a National Historic Landmark in 1961, and its first master plan for reconstruction was prepared by the National Park Service in 1967. Besides museum exhibits and living history programs, Fort Concho hosts a variety of community activities. See also FORT CONCHO NATIONAL HISTORIC LANDMARK.

BIBLIOGRAPHY: Robert G. Carter, *On the Border with Mackenzie, or Winning West Texas from the Comanches* (Washington: Eynon Printing, 1935). *Fort Concho Report.* J. Evetts Haley, *Fort Concho and the Texas Frontier* (San Angelo *Standard-Times*, 1952). Frank M. Temple, "Colonel B. H. Grierson's Administration of the District of the Pecos," West Texas Historical Association *Year Book* 38 (1962).

Wayne Daniel and Carol Schmidt

FORT CONCHO NATIONAL HISTORIC LANDMARK. Fort Concho[qv] was abandoned as an active military post in 1889. In 1905 C. A. Broome formed the Fort Concho Realty Company and parceled off lots in his Fort Concho addition to San Angelo. At about the same time J. L. Millspaugh, another real-estate developer who had been a post trader during the fort's active years, attempted to persuade the newly incorporated city of San Angelo to purchase the old fort as a park site. Although Millspaugh's initial efforts were unsuccessful, the eastern third of the parade ground and other pieces of property were donated to the city in 1913. The Pocahontas Chapter of the Daughters of the American Revolution[qv] sought to have Fort Concho designated a state historic site, a goal accomplished in 1924, when a bronze plaque was placed on the parade ground.

By 1929 Ginevra Wood Carson had founded the organization that became the Fort Concho Museum. She launched her campaign to save the fort by purchasing, for $6,000, the original headquarters building, built in 1876 by request of Col. Benjamin H. Grierson,[qv] who was then the post commander. Over the next thirty years Mrs. Carson spearheaded efforts to develop and expand public ownership of the museum. During that time several projects were undertaken, including the purchase and renovation of the schoolhouse-chapel, the reconstruction of two enlisted-men's barracks in 1951, and the acquisition of the Ruffini office building. In 1961 Fort Concho was registered as a National Historical Landmark through the Historic Preservation Office of the National Park Service. At about the same time the fort was placed on the National Register of Historic Places and designated a Texas Historic Landmark. Then in 1967 Franklin G. Smith, an NPS staff member, submitted a three-phase master plan for long-range development, financing, and interpretation of the site. Under Smith's plan, a museum director was employed, additional staff positions and several new programs were established, and a consistent preservation and acquisition program was carried on. Although local businesses and clubs continued to occupy and use some of the old fort buildings, such as the barracks, the officers' quarters, and the old commissary, the grounds contained seventeen surviving period structures, and the two barracks reconstructions. Some of these were at least partially restored and used for museum exhibits by 1980.

In 1980 a new master plan was published by the Bell, Klein, and Hoffman architectural firm in Austin. The old post hospital, which had been damaged by fire in 1911 and subsequently demolished, was reconstructed. It is now part of the John and Sally Meadows Historical Complex. By 1989 the museum complex included sixteen original structures, six reconstructions, and a stabilized ruin, making it one of the best preserved frontier forts in the United States.

The Fort Concho Museum contains over 35,000 artifacts in its collections. Equipment and furnishings in one of the officers' quarters and a barracks replicate the interiors of such buildings during the post's active years. The restored post chapel is often utilized by area school children, who relive the days of the McGuffy readers and one-room schoolhouses. The museum maintains an education department and an archive and research library. Conventions are often held in the restored commissary building. The Fort Concho Museum Press produces a monthly periodical, the Fort Concho *Members' Dispatch*, and other publications. Living-history groups reenact the lives of white infantry and white and black cavalry units on the Texas frontier. These units can be seen at Fort Concho during Fiesta Frontier Day (third Saturday in June), Fiestas Patrias (second weekend in September), Christmas at Old Fort Concho (first weekend in December), and special events throughout the year.

BIBLIOGRAPHY: David Hoffman, comp., *Fort Concho National Historic Landmark: A Master Plan for Development* (Austin: Bell, Klein, and Hoffman, 1980). Jack Lowery, "Fort Concho: Outpost on the Texas Frontier," *Texas Highways*, March 1989.

H. Allen Anderson

FORT CROCKETT. Fort Crockett, named after David Crockett,[qv] was a United States military reservation on Galveston Island. It was built in 1897 for coast artillery training and harbor defense. Its batteries, which fronted the Gulf of Mexico, held ten-inch guns, mortars, and rapid-fire guns. It was first occupied by Battery G, First Artillery, and relieved by Battery C in 1900. A seawall constructed along the Gulf shore of the military reservation in 1904–05 tied into the gun emplacements. After the Galveston hurricane of 1900,qv Fort Crockett's batteries were transferred to the United States Army Corps of Engineers. The fort was not garrisoned again until 1911.

Between 1917 and 1926 Battery G, Thirteenth Coast Artillery, organized as the Third Company, manned the fort. The installation eventually became headquarters for the Sixty-ninth Coast Artillery, and Battery G was transferred to the Twentieth Coast Artillery. Both were harbor-defense units. When the Third Attack Group was stationed at Fort Crockett in the mid-1920s, an aerodrome was built nearby. Until 1940 the fixed batteries at Fort Crockett remained on caretaker status. The next year the Twentieth and 265th Coast Artillery units were activated to man the defenses. A number of German prisoners of warqv were interned at the post from 1941 to 1946. Adjunct operations during World War IIqv included a laundry, a bakery, and a hospital, as well as signal corps, engineer, and ordnance detachments.

From the late 1940s to the mid-1950s Fort Crockett served as a recreational facility for active and reserve military personnel and their families. In 1955 the General Services Administration declared the post surplus and began disposing of its property and buildings. Only one of the batteries, completed in 1942, remained in 1986.

BIBLIOGRAPHY: Galveston *Daily News*, April 11, 1942.

Maury Darst

FORT CROGHAN. Fort Croghan, a United States military post, was established at the site of a frontier post known as McCulloch's Station, on Hamilton Creek three miles south of the site of present Burnet in Burnet County. Henry E. McCullochqv and his rangers were stationed there when the place was chosen for the fort on March 13, 1849, by Lt. C. H. Tyler, commander of Company A of the Second Dragoons. McCulloch was not relieved of his duty until March 18, when the site became officially a federal post. On October 12 a new location was chosen, and the fort was built across Hamilton Creek three miles above the first site. The post was known as Camp Croghan, then Camp Hamilton, and finally as Fort Croghan, in honor of Col. George Croghan. The buildings were of oak covered with shingles; officers' quarters were four log houses, each with two rooms separated by a hall. The hospital was a large four-room log house. The fort became headquarters of the Second Dragoons in 1852, but the government started removing its troops in 1853, and only a small guard remained when orders were issued to abandon the fort in 1855. The buildings were used as residences; the old hospital, long the home of W. P. Fry, was torn down in 1922. In 1940 only the foundations remained as evidence of the military occupation.

During the late 1950s and early 1960s the Burnet County Historical Society began the reconstruction of Fort Croghan. Since all original buildings had been destroyed, old buildings in the area that had been built at the time of the fort were moved from their original locations to the site. They included typical frontier log houses and one stone building that had been one of the original homes of Hamilton valley. Descendants of the first settlers in the area contributed authentic nineteenth-century articles to furnish the relocated buildings. By 1967 three buildings had been completely restored and were open to the public from April to November. The society in that year was also in the process of restoring a store building.

BIBLIOGRAPHY: Arrie Barrett, Federal Military Outposts in Texas, 1845–1861 (M.A. thesis, University of Texas, 1927). Malvin George Bowden, History of Burnet County (M.A. thesis, University of Texas, 1940). Mike Cox, "Old Fort Croghan," *Texas Military History* 5 (Spring 1965). Joseph Carroll McConnell, *West Texas Frontier* (Vol. 1, Jacksboro, Texas, 1933; Vol. 2, Palo Pinto, Texas, 1939). Vertical Files, Barker Texas History Center, University of Texas at Austin.

FORT D. A. RUSSELL. In 1911 the Mexican Revolutionqv in progress alarmed the citizens of Presidio County, Texas, who feared that Mexican forces might raid across the border. To provide protection the United States government sent military forces to the Mexican border areas, including Marfa, Texas, where several cavalry troops were sent. The post at Marfa, first named Camp Albert and then renamed Camp Marfa, also was the base for Signal Corps biplanes that patrolled the Rio Grande during the crisis. From 1913 to 1916 cavalry units from Fort Bliss rotated to Marfa for garrison and field duties. During World War I,qv Camp Marfa was expanded to accommodate numerous units, including federal, state, and national guard troops. In 1920 the post was designated as headquarters for the Marfa Command, which replaced the Big Bend District. Between 1923 and 1936, the War Department took advantage of the remote location of Camp Marfa to conduct simulated combat maneuvers on a large tract of land made available by local ranchers.

On January 1, 1930, Secretary of War Patrick Hurley announced that Camp Marfa was to be renamed Fort D. A. Russell in honor of Gen. David Allen Russell, a native New Yorker who served in the Mexican War and Civil Warqqv and was killed fighting for the Union at Winchester, Virginia, in 1864. A Wyoming fort had previously borne the name, but it had been renamed Fort Warren. Hurley also announced that the post was to be a permanent installation instead of a temporary army post. When the government began to consider abandoning the fort in 1931, the Marfa Chamber of Commerce and civic and political leaders tried to retain the installation. The 650 officers and men, maintenance for 400 horses and mules, and payroll of $480,000 a year added greatly to the Marfa economy during the Great Depression.qv However, in 1932 Marfa lost its fight, and on January 2, 1933, Fort Russell was left in the hands of caretakers.

In 1935 the post was regarrisoned by 700 men of the Seventy-seventh Field Artillery. In 1938 the first group scheduled for officer training arrived. Training continued at the fort for several years. During the prewar and World War IIqv years, Fort Russell added 2,400 acres donated by the citizens of Marfa, planted 1,000 trees, improved existing buildings, and built new ones. By this time 1,000 men were stationed at the fort. In 1944 the first woman officer was assigned to the post, and civilian women replaced soldiers as drivers of cars and trucks. During the war a camp for prisoners of warqv also was established at Marfa. Fort D. A. Russell was deactivated in 1945, closed on October 23, 1946, and transferred from the army to the Corps of Engineers in preparation for transfer to the Texas National Guard.qv In 1949 most of the fort area and facilities were sold to private citizens.

BIBLIOGRAPHY: *Post History* (Fort D. A. Russell, 1944). *Voice of the Mexican Border*, Centennial ed., 1936.

Lee Bennett

FORT DAVIS (Jeff Davis County). Fort Davis, at the eastern base of the Davis Mountains, was founded in response to War Department interest in a route through the Southwest with available water. It was established by order of Secretary of War Jefferson Davisqv in 1854 on Limpia Creek, on land leased from John James,qv a San Antonio surveyor. The army post guarded the Trans-Pecos segment of the southern route to California as the key member of a line of forts reaching from San Antonio to El Paso, and played a significant role in the defense and development of West Texas. In its history thirteen regiments were headquartered at Fort Davis, including nine infantry and four cavalry.

Westward expansion to the Pacific was assured with the end of the Mexican Warqv in 1848, when a vast territory comprising the present states of New Mexico, Arizona, and California was added to the United States, and with the discovery of gold in California in 1849. Thousands of migrants and, later, mail and freight wagons avoiding the snows and mountainous terrain of northerly routes pushed their way west over southern trails. The San Antonio–El Paso road was an important part of the most southern of these routes. Indian trails leading southward to Mexico intersected the El Paso road, however, and Apache and Comanche raiders preyed on travelers until the Civil War.^{qv} By 1854 military authorities found it necessary to construct a fort in West Texas.

In October 1854 Bvt. Gen. Persifor F. Smith,^{qv} commanding the Department of Texas, personally selected the site of Fort Davis for its "pure water and salubrious climate." Smith named the post after Jefferson Davis. Six companies of the Eighth United States Infantry under Lt. Col. Washington Seawell, ordered to build and garrison the post, arrived at Painted Comanche Camp on Limpia Creek on October 7 of that year.

With the beginning of the Civil War, United States troops evacuated Fort Davis under orders from Brig. Gen. David E. Twiggs,^{qv} commander of the Eighth United States Military District, and were quickly replaced by Col. John R. Baylor's^{qv} Confederate cavalry forces in April 1861. Confederate troops occupied the post for almost a year, then retreated to San Antonio after failing to take New Mexico. For the next five years Fort Davis lay abandoned, and Indians used the wood from its buildings for fuel.

Federal troops, led by Lt. Col. Wesley Merritt, reoccupied Fort Davis in June 1867 and began construction of a new post. By the mid-1880s Fort Davis was a major installation with quarters for more than 600 men and more than sixty adobe^{qv} and stone structures. From 1867 to 1885 the post was garrisoned primarily by units composed of white officers and black enlisted men of the Ninth and Tenth United States Cavalry^{qqv} regiments and the Twenty-fourth and Twenty-fifth United States Infantry^{qqv} regiments, who compiled a notable record of military achievements against the Apaches and Comanches.

In September 1879 Apache chief Victorio^{qv} and Mescalero Apache warriors began a series of attacks in the area west of Fort Davis. Col. Benjamin H. Grierson^{qv} led troops from Fort Davis and other posts against the raiders. After several hard-fought engagements, Victorio retreated to Mexico, where he and many of his followers were killed in a battle with Mexican troops in October 1880. After the Victorio campaign, life at Fort Davis settled into a quiet routine, and large numbers of cattlemen moved into the area. The soldiers were kept busy drilling on the parade ground, patrolling the surrounding area, and repairing roads and telegraph lines. The military usefulness of Fort Davis had come to an end, however, and the post was ordered abandoned in 1891. *See also* FORT DAVIS NATIONAL HISTORIC SITE.

BIBLIOGRAPHY: Barry Scobee, *Fort Davis, Texas, 1583–1960* (Fort Davis, Texas, 1963). Barry Scobee, *Old Fort Davis* (San Antonio: Naylor, 1947). Vertical Files, Barker Texas History Center, University of Texas at Austin.
Douglas C. McChristian

FORT DAVIS (Stephens County). When Camp Cooper closed in February 1861 as Union troops were withdrawn from the frontier, several white families remained along the Clear Fork of the Brazos River in what is now northern Shackelford and southern Throckmorton counties. After the Elm Creek Raid^{qv} by Comanches in October of 1864, in which several people were killed and three were kidnapped, several families decided to gather in a common location for protection against the Indians. On October 20, 1864, a stronghold called Fort Davis was established just across the county line in Stephens County. It was only one of several such "forts" along the frontier.

The post was located on the east side of the Clear Fork about fifteen miles downriver from Camp Cooper. It measured about 300 by 325 feet, and a street ran through it from east to west. About twenty picket-style houses with dirt roofs were set so as to form a loose stockade. A picket stockade fence around the entire fort was begun but never completed. A large stone house built earlier at the location served to anchor one corner of the works and provided protection for women and children in case of attack. Although an attack never materialized, inhabitants did have several confrontations with the hostiles in the area around the outpost. In 1865 Sam Newcomb opened a school in a structure on the northeast corner. Supplies for the inhabitants had to be freighted in by wagon from Weatherford, to the east, a dangerous journey of some days over poor roads. Originally, the flag of the Confederacy flew over Fort Davis but was destroyed by lightning and not replaced.

Fort Davis was abandoned in 1867 when Union troops returned to the area to establish Fort Griffin on the Clear Fork about ten miles upriver, a site much preferred to the unsatisfactory one further upriver where Camp Cooper was earlier located. Today the site of Fort Davis is owned jointly by H. G. Law and the Jones Company of Albany. The stone structure has been restored by Joe Carlton as a hunting lodge. The tombstone of Sam Newcomb is still visible near the site.

BIBLIOGRAPHY: Mrs. L. E. Farmer, "Fort Davis on the Clear Fork of the Brazos," West Texas Historical Association *Year Book* 33 (1957). Marilynne Housely, "Forting Up on the Texas Frontier during the Civil War," West Texas Historical Association *Year Book* 17 (1941). John Chadbourne Irwin, Autobiography (MS, Richardson Library, Hardin-Simmons University). Sallie Reynolds Matthews, *Interwoven: A Pioneer Chronicle* (Houston: Anson Jones, 1936; 4th ed., College Station: Texas A&M University Press, 1982). Samuel Newcomb, Diary (MS, Southwest Collection, Texas Tech University). Susan Newcomb, Diary (MS, Southwest Collection, Texas Tech University).
Lawrence Clayton

FORT DAVIS, TEXAS. Fort Davis, the county seat of Jeff Davis County, is on Limpia Creek at the intersection of State highways 17 and 118, eighty miles northeast of Presidio and 175 miles southeast of El Paso in south central Jeff Davis County. The precursor of the town was a rough-and-tumble settlement known as Chihuahua, which formed just southwest of the military post of Fort Davis^{qv} after it was established in 1854. The fort was on the site of an earlier Indian village, which the earliest Anglo-American explorers of the area called Painted Comanche Camp. When Henry Skillman^{qv} contracted to carry the mail from San Antonio to El Paso in 1850, a stage stand was established near the site of the future town. E. P. Webster, a native of Illinois, and Diedrick Dutchover, a Belgian immigrant who had fought in the Mexican War,^{qv} rode with W. A. (Big Foot) Wallace^{qv} to escort the first mail coach to the site, by way of Fort Concho. Webster remained in Limpia Canyon as the first master of the stage station there and may have been the first white settler in the area. Dutchover rode as a guard for two more years before settling at Fort Davis. During the Civil War,^{qv} when Confederate troops withdrew from the fort, they left Dutchover, who had maintained strict neutrality while establishing a small sheep ranch near the post, in charge. Almost immediately the Apache chief Nicolás attacked the settlement. Dutchover, a Mexican woman with two children, and four Americans hid on the roof for three days while the Apaches looted the fort. On the third night Dutchover and all the others, except one of the Americans, who had fallen ill, slipped out and began the long trek to Presidio, eighty miles away. One day later the stage arrived to find a ravaged fort and the American dead on the roof, apparently of natural causes. Dutchover and the others staggered into Presidio four days later. The Belgian later returned to Fort Davis and was employed as a hauling contractor.

After 1867, when troops of the Ninth United States Cavalry^{qv} reoccupied the fort, the town of Fort Davis became "the most important town in the Trans-Pecos country," by virtue of its position at the crossroads of two important trails and its status as a base for travelers and hunters. A. J. Buckoz was given permission to serve as post trader in 1867, although he was unceremoniously replaced four years later. Other settlers who came with the return of the troops included storekeeper Dan Murphy, butcher Sam R. Miller, and baker Whitaker Keesey, who later became the most influential merchant in Fort Davis. Sgt. Charles Mulhern, a native of County Donegal, Ireland, arrived in the late 1870s and eventually acquired a substantial amount of land in the area; he and Gen. Benjamin Grierson,qv who retired to Fort Davis in 1890, were the only military men who became important local landowners. In the 1880s Fort Davis became a ranching center, as ambitious cattlemen poured into the Trans-Pecos, many of them seeking to escape the Texas feverqv epidemic raging in other parts of the state.

Although one local historian insisted that "Fort Davis never was a wild town," the place had its share of colorful legends. One involved Dolores Gavino Doporto, who as a young woman became engaged to a goatherd named José. While José was out tending his goats she would communicate with him by building a fire every Thursday night on the low mountain just south of town. Shortly before their wedding day José was killed and scalped by Mescaleros while tending his goats in or near Musquiz Canyon. Dolores, overcome with grief, continued to climb the mountain and build her fire every Thursday night for some thirty or forty years. When she died in 1893 she was buried near the path she had worn on her lonely trips up the mountain, which became known as Dolores Mountain.

When Presidio County was organized in April 1871 it included the areas of present Jeff Davis and Brewster counties. Fort Davis was selected as the county seat, but the courthouse later burned and all records of the election were destroyed. Twelve years later, when the Southern Pacific Railroad built through Marfa, twenty-three miles southwest, many felt that the latter town ought to replace Fort Davis as county seat. They disputed the results of the earlier election, for which no records remained. In July 1885 another election was held, and Marfa was proclaimed the victor. The losers immediately began a movement to organize a new county, with Fort Davis as the seat. By this time the town had an estimated 2,000 inhabitants, three lawyers, a milliner, two saloons, two churches, gristmills and cotton gins, and a weekly newspaper called the *Apache Rocket*. Jeff Davis County was established by an act of the legislature on March 15, 1887, and Fort Davis was once again a county seat.

By the early 1890s, after the army abandoned the fort, the town's population fell to an estimated 1,200, and by 1896 it was 500. It grew again in the early twentieth century to 1,061 in 1904 and 1,100 in 1914, by which time the Fort Davis Commercial Club had been established. Beginning in the late 1920s the population fluctuated between an estimated 700 in 1928, 1,200 in 1931, 668 in 1933, and 1,000 in 1936. It remained at the latter figure until the late 1940s, when it again rose to 1,200. In the early 1960s it was down to 850 but by the mid-1970s had grown to 900. In 1990 Fort Davis had a population of 1,212 and sixteen businesses.

Around 1900 the mild climate and location amid the Davis Mountains made Fort Davis a popular summer resort for wealthy Gulf Coast families. Around 1908 the Kansas City, Mexico and Orient Railway proposed building a line to Fort Davis, but the locals protested that it would attract low-class people, and the line was never built. In the late 1920s a group of Oklahoma oilmen decided to turn Fort Davis into a Western movie center, with Jack Hoxie as featured player, but the Great Depressionqv ended that plan. Later attempts to attract visitors met with more success. In May 1946 David A. Simmonsqv of Houston, former president of the American Bar Association, bought the property on which the old fort stood with the intention of restoring it and opening it to the public as a year-round resort. Simmons died in 1951, before his plan could be realized, but in September 1961 Fort Davis National Historic Siteqv came into being; the 460-acre site was formally dedicated in April 1966. A few years later the Chihuahuan Desert Research Institute,qv headquartered in Alpine, opened an arboretum on a 300-acre tract of land on State Highway 118 just southeast of Fort Davis. Both these attractions, as well as the nearby Davis Mountains State Park and the University of Texas McDonald Observatory,qqv have helped make tourism an important part of the Fort Davis economy.

BIBLIOGRAPHY: Barry Scobee, *Old Fort Davis* (San Antonio: Naylor, 1947). Barry Scobee, *The Story of Fort Davis: Jeff Davis County and the Davis Mountains* (Fort Davis, Texas: Marvin Hunter, 1936).

Martin Donell Kohout

FORT DAVIS NATIONAL HISTORIC SITE. Fort Davis National Historic Site, located on the northern edge of Fort Davis, Jeff Davis County, was authorized by Congress in 1961 and established as part of the national park system on July 4, 1963. The 460-acre site, near U.S. Highway 290 on the north and U.S. 90 on the south, includes more than twenty original stone and adobeqv structures of early Fort Davis,qv now restored to their 1880 appearance. A visitors' center and museum, lieutenant's quarters, and post hospital are open daily, and audio programs, a slide show, and self-guided tours of the grounds are among services provided year-round. Summer seasons are highlighted by costumed employees and volunteers who explain the refurnished quarters and present cavalry and infantry demonstrations. A picnic grove and extensive nature-trail system are located on the site. Camping, motel, restaurant, and shopping facilities are available within a short distance of the fort.

BIBLIOGRAPHY: Robert M. Utley, *Fort Davis National Historic Site* (Washington: National Park Service, 1965). Robert M. Utley, *Special Report on Fort Davis* (Santa Fe: National Park Service, Region 3, 1960). Vertical Files, Barker Texas History Center, University of Texas at Austin.

Douglas C. McChristian

FORT DEFIANCE. Fort Defiance was the name given by James W. Fannin, Jr.,qv to the La Bahíaqv presidio, Nuestra Señora de Loreto, at Goliad in February 1836, when the fort was repaired and strengthened, primarily under the direction of Joseph M. Chadwick,qv in preparation for the Mexican advance during the Texas Revolution.qv Fannin drew the name by lottery; the two losing choices were Milam and Independence. The presidio was called Fort Goliad during the earlier command of George M. Collinsworth,qv whose volunteers initially overpowered the Mexican garrison in October 1835, and also by his successors, Philip Dimmitt and Francis W. Thornton,qqv whose forces held the presidio until Fannin took charge in February 1836. Many continued to call the sanctuary Fort Goliad during Fannin's tenure (*see also* GOLIAD CAMPAIGN OF 1835, GOLIAD CAMPAIGN OF 1836).

BIBLIOGRAPHY: Kathryn Stoner O'Connor, *The Presidio La Bahía del Espíritu Santo de Zúñiga, 1721 to 1846* (Austin: Von Boeckmann–Jones, 1966). Ruby C. Smith, "James W. Fannin, Jr., in the Texas Revolution," *Southwestern Historical Quarterly* 23 (October 1919, January, April 1920). Dudley Goodall Wooten, ed., *A Comprehensive History of Texas* (2 vols., Dallas: Scarff, 1898; rpt., Austin: Texas State Historical Association, 1986).

Craig H. Roell

FORT DUNCAN. Fort Duncan, on the east side of the Rio Grande above Eagle Pass in Maverick County, was established by order of Maj. Gen. William J. Worthqv on March 27, 1849, when Capt. Sidney Burbank occupied the site with companies A, B, and F of the First United States Infantry. John Twohigqv owned the 5,000-acre site. At the start of the Mexican Warqv in 1846 a temporary post called Camp Eagle Pass had been established at the site. Roads ran from there to Fort Inge and Fort McIntosh, and mail was received from San Antonio. On November 14, 1889, the post was named Fort Duncan, after James Duncan, a hero of the Mexican War. The post consisted of a storehouse, two magazines, four officers' quarters, and a stone hospital, in addition to quarters for enlisted men. Construction was done half by the troops and half by hired workers. There was ample stone but no timber for building, and the men suffered from exposure. Company C, First Artillery, asked permission to construct quarters at its own expense. The fort was significant because of the trade crossing into Mexico at Eagle Pass, its location on the California Road, and its position for scouting against Indians in the 1850s.

Fort Duncan became involved in the Callahan expedition of 1855, when James H. Callahan^{qv} led an effort to repel attacks of Lipan Apaches and to capture runaway slaves. Callahan seized and burned the Mexican town of Piedras Negras, and the commanders at the fort ultimately refused to help him recross the Rio Grande into the United States. Secretary of War John B. Floyd ordered the post abandoned in May 1859, and troops were transferred to Camp Verde^{qv} on June 18. Because of Juan N. Cortina's^{qv} disturbances on the Rio Grande, Robert E. Lee^{qv} ordered the fort regarrisoned in March 1860, and in August 1860 Maj. D. H. Vinton leased the site from Twohig. With the outbreak of the Civil War^{qv} the post was again abandoned when the federal troops evacuated on March 20, 1861, and John C. Crawford received the property as agent for the state of Texas. During the war the post was known as Rio Grande Station^{qv} and served the Frontier Regiment.^{qv} It was also an important customs point for Confederate cotton and munitions trade with Mexico. On June 19, 1864, the fort was attacked by a force of about 100 Mexicans from the surrounding area and Piedras Negras, but they managed to capture only a few horses.

Federal troops reoccupied Fort Duncan on March 23, 1868. In 1870 Seminole Indians were attached to the command as guides. The post was abandoned in 1883, when the government could not secure its purchase. Fort Duncan was renamed the Camp at Eagle Pass that year and served as a subpost of Fort Clark, housing Company A of the Third Cavalry. In 1894, however, the government finally bought the site. From 1890 to 1916, when disturbances in Mexico took national guard units to the river, the fort had a skeleton caretaking detachment. However, in 1916 the number of troops at the fort was increased to 16,000. Troop activity continued throughout World War I,^{qv} when the fort served as a training facility, but by 1920 only a small detail remained. In 1933 the city of Eagle Pass began maintaining the old fort as a public park on the condition that the federal government could reclaim the post for military or other reasons. The city formally acquired the property in 1935 and converted it into Fort Duncan Park. In 1942 the mayor offered the fort to the military for use during World War II.^{qv} The government accepted and used the Fort Duncan Country Club as an officers' club and the swimming pool for commissioned personnel stationed at Eagle Pass Army Air Field.^{qv} The site was listed in the National Register of Historic Places in 1971. Seven of the original buildings were extant and had been restored. The old headquarters building became a museum.

BIBLIOGRAPHY: Arrie Barrett, Federal Military Outposts in Texas, 1846–1861 (M.A. thesis, University of Texas, 1927). M. L. Crimmins, "Old Fort Duncan: A Frontier Post," *Frontier Times*, June 1938. Fort Duncan Papers, Barker Texas History Center, University of Texas at Austin. Robert W. Frazer, *Forts of the West* (Norman: University of Oklahoma Press, 1965). S. Rolando Rodriguez, "Historic Fort Duncan," *Junior Historian*, September 1967. Rosella R. Sellers, The History of Fort Duncan, Eagle Pass, Texas (M.A. thesis, Sul Ross State College, 1960).

FORT ELLIOTT. Fort Elliott was the United States Army outpost in the eastern Texas Panhandle from 1875 to 1890. Though never involved in a major military engagement, it helped transform the Panhandle^{qv} from Indian hunting territory into a settlement area. Troops from Fort Elliott patrolled the borders of Indian Territory to the east, policed cattle drives headed north to Kansas railroad depots, and in other ways protected and encouraged settlement of the region.

In 1874 the army undertook a major offensive to clear the Panhandle of Indians after a Cheyenne attack on a camp of white buffalo hunters at Adobe Walls (see ADOBE WALLS, SECOND BATTLE OF). In December 1874 Col. Nelson A. Miles^{qv} decided to establish an advance supply post for his forces from Camp Supply on the North Fork of the Red River. It was to be near a point where troops led by Lt. Col. George P. Buell had found a good campsite in September. By late January 1875 the camp was provisioned and garrisoned by 422 officers and men of the Fifth Infantry and Sixth Cavalry under the command of Maj. James Biddle. Within a month the Panhandle campaign ended, but the army ordered Biddle to select a site for a permanent post from which surveillance of the western boundary of Indian Territory could be maintained. He chose a low plateau overlooking Sweetwater Creek, twenty-seven miles west of the 100th meridian. Maj. H. C. Bankhead confirmed the choice in May when he relieved Biddle with 263 men of the Fourth United States Cavalry^{qv} and Nineteenth Infantry. The new site was occupied in June. At first known simply as Cantonment on the Sweetwater, the post was renamed Fort Elliott the following February, in honor of Maj. Joel A. Elliott, who had died at the battle of the Washita.

Construction of permanent facilities began in July 1875. Stables, storehouses, and the guardhouse were built with cottonwood posts, adobe,^{qv} and thatch available locally, but for more substantial buildings lumber had to be brought by wagon from Dodge City, 196 miles to the north. The post commander's residence, six sets of officers' quarters, five company barracks, a twelve-bed hospital, the post headquarters, and a combined chapel and school, all one-story frame buildings on stone foundations, were erected by 1878. There was little additional construction, although the headquarters was replaced after it burned in 1879 in the post's only serious fire. Enclosing the post within a stockade was not considered necessary.

Except during its first months, when more than 400 troops were stationed there, Fort Elliott's strength was normally slightly fewer than 200 men. After 1883 a company of forty Indian scouts was also stationed at the post. In 1879 a company of the black Tenth United States Cavalry^{qv} was assigned to the garrison, and between 1880 and 1888 other black units, companies of the Twenty-fourth United States Infantry and Ninth United States Cavalry,^{qqv} served there. From November 1881 until February 1884 all of Fort Elliott's troops were black. The commissioned officers were all white, however, with the exception of Lt. Henry O. Flipper,^{qv} the first black graduate of West Point.

Troops from Fort Elliott patrolled both the Panhandle and western Indian Territory. Their main task was to stop small hunting parties of Indians from entering the Panhandle, but on several occasions during the late 1870s they pursued bands seeking to escape the reservation. By the mid-1880s the garrison's attention had shifted to policing the range cattle industry, keeping Panhandle stock off the reservation, and supervising southern Texas herds being driven north through Indian land.

The fort provided for the Panhandle not only security but also economic stimulation. Under its protection, numerous large ranches were quickly established, and by 1880 nearly 300,000 cattle grazed the Panhandle. Settlement was clustered near Fort Elliott. Civilians were employed in the fort's construction and thereafter as teamsters or skilled laborers. Post supplies were, whenever possible, purchased locally. Sweetwater City, a buffalo hide dealer's trading post one mile from the fort, grew into Mobeetie, with a population of 150 by 1880. Wheeler County, in which the post office stood, was the first among the twenty-five Panhandle counties to have a large enough population to organize its own government, and for several years it administered the other counties as well. The census of 1880 showed 512 of the Panhandle's 1,379 residents in Wheeler County.

In 1887, when the first railroad to enter the Panhandle bypassed Fort Elliott eighteen miles to the north and provided a new source of security and prosperity, the fort's central role in the region's growth ended. In 1890 the army decided to close the fort, and an outbreak of typhoid that summer speeded its abandonment. On October 2 most of the garrison departed, and on the twentieth the fort was formally closed. In the next sixteen years the Interior Department sold the buildings and land. Little remains today of the post that helped transform the Panhandle from a frontier into a settled region.

BIBLIOGRAPHY: John Q. Anderson, "Fort Elliott, Texas, Last Guard of the Plains Indians," *Texas Military History* 2 (November 1962).

David E. Kyvig, "Policing the Panhandle: Fort Elliott, Texas, 1875–1890," *Red River Valley Historical Review* 1 (1974). James M. Oswald, "History of Fort Elliot," *Panhandle-Plains Historical Review* 32 (1959).
David E. Kyvig

FORT ESPERANZA. Fort Esperanza, a Civil War qv earthwork fortification on the eastern shore of Matagorda Island, was constructed to guard Cavallo Pass,qv the entry to Matagorda Bay. The fort was also known as Fort DeBray, in honor of Col. Xavier Blanchard DeBray,qv commander of the Sub-Military District of Houston. Building of the fort began in late December 1861, when it was determined that the location of Fort Washington, a small fort put up near the lighthouse in 1842–43 on the extreme southeast corner of Matagorda Island, was too exposed. Confederate colonel R. R. Garland chose a new position farther up the pass, at about the halfway point of the island's frontage on the pass, and ordered Capt. Dan Shea to begin the construction. Additional fortifications were added by Maj. Caleb G. Forsheyqv in February 1862. The fort, itself armed with nine guns including eight twenty-four-pounders and one 128-pounder, was out of range of the guns of large federal vessels in the Gulf but had the same command of the channel as the older Fort Washington. The Confederate assessment was that the shallow water, only ten feet deep, on the bar would prevent vessels larger than gunboats from attempting to enter the bay. This proved correct, but the new fort still did not stop the Union navy from forcing the pass.

On October 25, 1862, less than a month after capturing Galveston, William B. Renshaw, captain of the USS Westfield,qv sailed past Fort Esperanza. Much impressed by the federals' gunnery, the defenders of the fort retreated to Indianola before they could be cut off. The Union forces seized Indianola after a brief battle. Port Lavaca was extensively bombarded, but a Confederate battery of two guns put up a determined resistance. In early November the Union fleet withdrew from Matagorda Bay, and since they had no ground forces to leave behind to secure their gains, the Confederates reoccupied Indianola and Fort Esperanza.

After the Union debacle in the battle of Sabine Passqv in September 1863, the federal invasion plans for Texas shifted south. The Rio Grande valley was invaded in early November. Corpus Christi and Aransas Pass fell in the middle of the month. Union troops advanced up St. Joseph's Island. Their crossing to Matagorda Island was unsuccessfully challenged, and a battle took place on November 23 at Cedar Bayou, which separates the two islands. After Union forces under Gen. T. E. G. Ransom reached Fort Esperanza on November 27 and dug in, a two-day battle followed. On the night of November 29 the Confederates, outnumbered and outflanked, evacuated the fort after spiking the guns, firing their stores, and blowing up their magazines. The fort was occupied and repaired by the Union forces, who used it as their base of operations for further campaigns in the area. In the spring of 1864 the Union troops were withdrawn from Matagorda Bay to participate in the proposed invasion of Texas from northeast Louisiana. After the last of the federals left Matagorda Island on June 15, Fort Esperanza was reoccupied by the Confederates and held until the end of the war.

The eastern walls of the fort were destroyed as the shoreline was eroded by a storm in 1868. By 1878 the rest of the nine-foot-high, twenty-foot-thick, turf-covered walls had eroded away, but the shore was accreting again. The outlying emplacements and rifle pits can still be traced in some areas.

BIBLIOGRAPHY: J. Barto Arnold III, *A Matagorda Bay Magnetometer Survey and Site Test Excavation Project* (Texas Antiquities Committee Publication 9, Austin, 1982). Brownson Malsch, *Indianola—The Mother of Western Texas* (Austin: Shoal Creek, 1977).
J. Barto Arnold III

FORT EWELL. Fort Ewell was on the south bank of the Nueces River at the Nueces River crossing of the road from San Antonio to Laredo in what is now La Salle County. It was established on May 18, 1852, and was garrisoned by Companies E, G, and I of the regiment of Mounted Riflemen. Capt. John Smith Simonson was the commanding officer of the fort, which was named for Capt. Richard S. Ewell, a veteran of the Mexican War.qv

According to Col. W. G. Freeman's inspection report in June 1853 the fort was in a poor location. The river was seventy-five feet wide and only four feet deep, and it frequently overflowed its banks, covering the nearby bottoms and salt marshes and making the fort inaccessible. There was no suitable timber for construction within ten to fifteen miles, nor was there good grazing for the animals. The buildings had been constructed by troop labor of soft adobe, which was not strong enough to support a roof without bracing. Most buildings were covered with canvas. Attempts to grow kitchen gardens for food were unsuccessful due to lack of rainfall. Food and clothing were sometimes at a premium, and troops were often sick. For two years after July 1852 every officer and man was sick on the average of once every three months. Scurvy was frequent. Many soldiers deserted the fort and went to Mexico. In December 1853 the base was ordered abandoned, and in October 1854 it was deserted.

The post office for Fort Ewell continued to serve the area from the settlement of Guajoco, a mile from the old fort. By 1886, when the Fort Ewell post office was decommissioned, the community too had faded away.

BIBLIOGRAPHY: Arrie Barrett, *Federal Military Outposts in Texas, 1846–1861* (M.A. thesis, University of Texas, 1927). M. L. Crimmins, "W. G. Freeman's Report on the Eighth Military Department," *Southwestern Historical Quarterly* 51-54 (July 1947–October 1950). Annette Martin Ludeman, *La Salle: La Salle County* (Quanah, Texas: Nortex, 1975). Ray Miller, *Ray Miller's Texas Forts* (Houston: Cordovan, 1985).
Art Leatherwood

FORT EWELL CREEK. Fort Ewell Creek rises at the junction of its east and west prongs, two miles east of Chacon Reservoirqv and 3½ miles north of Natalia in southeastern Medina County (at 29°14′ N, 98°51′ W), and runs south for 4½ miles to its mouth on Chacon Creek, a mile southeast of Natalia (at 29°12′ N, 98°52′ W). The stream traverses an area of rolling prairie surfaced by clay loams that support mesquite and grasses.

FORT FISHER. Fort Fisher, at a site on the west bank of the Brazos River now within the Waco city limits, was built in February 1837 by Capt. Thomas H. Barron'sqv company of Maj. William H. Smith's battalion of Texas Rangers.qv In 1837, wrote ranger George B. Erath,qv "Waco was in the possession of buffalo, and only a short time before had been vacated by the Waco Indians." According to Erath, the rangers "built some shanties for barracks near the big spring of the river" and named the post for Secretary of War William S. Fisher.qv The fort was garrisoned first by Barron's men and later by other rangers, including Capt. Daniel Monroe's company, and Smith for a time maintained his headquarters there. The men "were too far out to do good service," however, and so the fort was abandoned in June 1837 or soon thereafter. The post was reconstructed in 1968 as a home for the Colonel Homer Garrisonqv Museum and serves as headquarters for a company of Texas Rangers. The reconstructed fort displays works of contemporary Western artists and maintains an excellent collection of weapons connected with the history of the Texas Rangers. The Texas Ranger Hall of Fame and Museumqv is located nearby.

BIBLIOGRAPHY: Gerald S. Pierce, *Texas Under Arms: The Camps, Posts, Forts, and Military Towns of the Republic of Texas* (Austin: Encino, 1969). John Sleeper and J. C. Hutchins, comps., *Waco and McLennan County* (Waco: Golledge, 1876; rpt., Waco: Kelley, 1966).
Thomas W. Cutrer

FORT FITZHUGH. Fort Fitzhugh, three miles southeast of Gainesville, was one in a series of military outposts built from Preston to the Rio Grande for the protection of settlers from Indian raids. Around it was the first settlement in Cooke County. The fort was constructed in 1847 by volunteers of the Texas Rangers[qv] from nearby Collin County under the command of William F. Fitzhugh.[qv] The outpost was a small log stockade consisting of a single row of blockhouses with a nearby stable. Cooke County chose the fort as the site of the county seat and renamed it Liberty, but that name had already been taken. Meanwhile a new site for the county seat near the banks of nearby Elm Creek was completed and named Gainesville. The fort was abandoned by 1850. In 1948 a plaque donated by the local Boy Scout unit marked the spot where the fort once stood. Twenty years later the only remnant of Fort Fitzhugh was a well that had been about thirty feet northwest of the stockade and a caved-in ammunition dump that may have been part of the original military outpost.

BIBLIOGRAPHY: Gainesville *Daily Register*, August 30, 1948. A. Morton Smith, *The First 100 Years in Cooke County* (San Antonio: Naylor, 1955).

David Minor

FORT GATES. Fort Gates, originally Camp Gates, was established by Capt. William R. Montgomery[qv] on October 26, 1849, as a stockaded United States cantonment on the north bank of the Leon River above Coryell Creek, about five miles east of the site of present Gatesville. The installation was named for Bvt. Maj. Collinson Reed Gates of New York, who won distinction in the battles of Palo Alto and Resaca de la Palma.[qqv] As the last of a cordon of posts established in 1849 to protect settlers on the frontier from Indians, Fort Gates was authorized by Gen. George Mercer Brooke,[qv] commander of the Eighth Military Department. The establishment had eighteen buildings—four for officers' quarters, two for company quarters, three for laundresses, one for muleteers and employees, a hospital, a stable, a forage house, two storehouses, a guardhouse, a bakehouse, and a blacksmith shop. Quarters for a third company were half completed before orders for the building were revoked. Supplies were transported from Washington-on-the-Brazos, Houston, and Indianola. Commanding officers at Fort Gates were Montgomery (1849–50), James G. S. Snelling[qv] (1850–51), Carlos Adolphus Waite[qv] (1851–52), and Horace Haldeman (1852). The 1850 census enumerated six officers and ninety-four men at the garrison. The personnel included men of companies D, I, F, and H of the Eighth United States Infantry.[qv] In April 1851, 256 enlisted men and forty-five officers were stationed at Fort Gates, the most reported in a single month. Lt. George Pickett, later a Confederate general and leader of "Pickett's Charge" at Gettysburg, was stationed at Fort Gates in 1850–51.

Lt. W. H. C. Whiting of the Corps of Engineers, ordered by General Brooke to make a reconnaissance of the cordon of forts, reported early in 1850 that Fort Gates was good only for the protection of its immediate neighborhood, that it needed at least two companies to operate within a radius of sixty or seventy miles, and that the nature of the country was such that the Indians could move in all directions. The district lay in the northern part of Tonkawa country and was visited by the Waco, Comanche, and Lipan Apache Indians. But the Indian menace was soon removed, and the fort was abandoned in March 1852, the first of the line of posts to be evacuated. Though for a time after the removal of the garrison settlers continued to look upon the fort as a refuge from Indian raids, the buildings soon disintegrated until only the rock of the fireplaces remained. Lead Mountain, back of the ruins, was so named because of the number of lead bullets found there. The Cotton Belt railroad had a flag station named Fort Gates near the site of the old post, and a community called Fort Gates prospered there after the construction of Fort Hood in the 1940s.

BIBLIOGRAPHY: Thomas C. Lemmons, Fort Gates and the Central Texas Frontier, 1849–1852 (M.A. thesis, Abilene Christian College, 1967). Mildred Watkins Mears, *Coryell County Scrapbook* (Waco: Texian, 1963). Mildred Watkins Mears, "Three Forts of Coryell County," *Southwestern Historical Quarterly* 67 (July 1963). Zelma Scott, *History of Coryell County* (Austin: Texas State Historical Association, 1965).

Zelma Scott

FORT GATES, TEXAS. The Fort Gates community is on State Highway 36 a mile southeast of Gatesville in east central Coryell County. It grew up around Fort Gates,[qv] a frontier outpost established in 1849, and was the first settlement in Coryell County. Although the fort was officially abandoned in 1852, the community remained, serving as county seat from February 4 to May 27, 1854, when the county government was moved to Gatesville. Most residents moved their homes and businesses to Gatesville as well, and the Fort Gates community all but died. It was revived in the 1940s after the establishment of the Fort Hood[qv] military reservation in southern Coryell County. The town was incorporated in February 1966, when its population was 250. In the 1980s Fort Gates had several residential areas, a business district consisting primarily of service industries, and an estimated population of 755. In 1990 its population was 818.

BIBLIOGRAPHY: Coryell County Genealogical Society, *Coryell County, Texas, Families, 1854–1985* (Dallas: Taylor, 1986).

Vivian Elizabeth Smyrl

FORT GRAHAM. Fort Graham, a United States Army post, was established in March 1849 and was occupied on April 17 of that year by Maj. Ripley A. Arnold[qv] and companies F and I of the Second Dragoons under command of Bvt. Brig. Gen. William S. Harney,[qv] commander of the Frontier District of Texas. The site was near the eastern bank of the Brazos River at Little Bear Creek fourteen miles west of the site of present Hillsboro. According to material in the National Archives, the post was named for James D. Graham of the Corps of Topographical Engineers. Other sources, however, state that it was named for Lt. Col. William M. Graham of the Second Dragoons, who was killed in 1847 at the Mexican War[qv] battle of Molino del Rey.

The annexation[qv] of Texas and the other territorial gains made by the United States as a result of the Treaty of Guadalupe Hidalgo[qv] had given the United States Army the responsibility for frontier defense and communication in the Southwest. Fort Graham was intended to help anchor the northern frontier defense line between the Towash Indian village and Fort Washita. Arnold's orders directed him to provide escorts for supply trains and travelers, to patrol the countryside as far as the forks of the Trinity, to protect the citizens from hostile incursions by Indians, and to attempt to conciliate the local Indians. During the first months, the men began construction of a number of log and clapboard structures including a commissary, officers' quarters, and a stable. Meanwhile, civilian laborers built a hospital, a carpenter and wheelwright shop, a blacksmith shop, three corncribs, a wagon and mule yard, and a quartermaster's storehouse.

Building and patrol duties, however, were hindered by a lack of adequate manpower. Arnold was assigned a complement of eighty-nine officers and men, but according to post returns filed by Arnold in April, he had only fifty-five men, including five officers and seven noncommissioned officers. This number was further reduced in June, when Arnold turned the command at Fort Graham over to Lt. Fowler Hamilton and moved north with F Company to the West Fork of the Trinity River to establish Fort Worth. Soon after Arnold's departure, Graham's new commanding officer reported that he had only one officer and forty-six men available for duty. The situation did not improve until early fall, when Gen. George M. Brooke,[qv] the new commander of the Eighth Military Department, was able to send two companies of the Eighth United States Infantry[qv] under command of Bvt. Lt. Col. James V. Bomford to the northwestern posts. Bomford and Company H remained at Fort Graham, where the colonel assumed command, while the other company proceeded to the Trinity to reinforce Fort Worth.

In October 1849 Brooke ordered Lt. W. H. C. Whiting of the corps of engineers to make a general reconnaissance of the frontier posts. According to Whiting, Fort Graham was one of the most important posts on the upper frontier. The post was near a recognized council spot and close to the villages and camps of many Indian groups. Fort Graham was thus in an excellent position to serve as a frontier "listening post" in the Northwest. The fort also served as headquarters for Indian agents during their missions to the upper Brazos and provided escorts for the agents during councils and periodic visits to the Indian camps. Moreover, it was located near George Barnard's^{qv} trading post, a target for criticism from Indian agents and departmental commanders, who accused the traders of selling liquor and firearms to the Indians. Thus Fort Graham's position, both geographically and militarily, was so important that Whiting recommended, and Brooke concurred, that about 200 men should be stationed there.

Unfortunately, Brooke did not have such forces. Bomford's arrival did bring the strength of the post up to five officers and seventy-five men, however, and during 1850 and 1851 the garrison was able to carry out patrol and escort duties and complete the building of two sets of quarters, a log house for the commanding officer, a second stable, a guardhouse, a bakehouse, and a powder magazine. During June 1851 troops from Graham under command of Maj. Henry H. Sibley^{qv} provided escorts for acting adjutant general Samuel Cooper's inspection of the upper Brazos Indian villages. During the fall the post served as a base for Indian agent Jesse Stem's^{qv} meetings with various tribal delegations in the region.

During 1852 Fort Graham continued to serve as a listening post along the northern frontier, but by 1853 the line of settlement had advanced far to the west, and Graham's location ceased to be strategic. In August 1853 Bvt. Maj. Gen. Persifor F. Smith^{qv} ordered Fort Graham closed and the troops moved to other posts. Before the order could be carried out, the post surgeon, Josephus M. Steiner,^{qv} shot and killed Major Arnold, who had returned to Graham to help close it. Despite this disruption the troops began leaving Fort Graham in October, and the post was closed by November 9, 1853.

Fort Graham was fairly typical of Texas frontier posts of the 1845–60 period. No hostilities occurred between the army and the Indians in or near it, and the post was far more important as a scouting and reporting station than as a defensive outpost. Its strategic location near the upper Brazos villages, however, and its role in the affairs of the Indian agents indicate that Graham may well have been one of the most important pre–Civil War ports in Northwest Texas.

By offering protection against Indian raids, Fort Graham helped open the Hill County area to settlement. It also provided a market for local goods and labor, stimulated economic growth, and helped attract settlers to the region. The post was not in existence long enough, however, to build up a large community in the immediate vicinity. Although a hamlet called Fort Graham developed near the post, attempts to develop a major townsite there after 1853 were unsuccessful. By 1890 the population of the settlement had dropped to 250, and it soon disappeared. In 1936 the Texas Centennial^{qv} Commission arranged for the state to buy the site, erect a marker, and reconstruct the barracks, though it is doubtful that a reconstruction was ever built. With the development of Lake Whitney in the 1970s, the site was flooded, and the remains of the post disappeared beneath the waters of the lake.

BIBLIOGRAPHY: Sandra L. Myres, "Fort Graham, Listening Post on the Texas Frontier," West Texas Historical Association *Year Book* 59 (1983). *Sandra L. Myres*

FORT GRIFFIN (Jefferson County). The Jefferson County Fort Griffin was a Confederate fort located in the southeastern part of the county on what is now Farm Road 3322, fifteen miles south of Port Arthur. Hoping to block Union threats to the upper Texas Gulf Coast, Gen. John B. Magruder^{qv} dispatched Maj. Julius Kellersberg to build a fort at Sabine Pass^{qv} in March 1863. With thirty engineers and 500 slaves Kellersberg constructed a triangular fort on an eminence overlooking the Sabine River. The installation housed six gun emplacements and bombproofs built into a sawtooth front, and timber and railroad iron reinforced the earthwork position. The fort was named for the commander of the Twenty-first Texas Battalion, Col. William H. Griffin.

In September 1863 four Union gunboats, leading a strong amphibious invasion force, attacked Fort Griffin. At the battle of Sabine Pass^{qv} Lt. Richard Dowling^{qv} and a forty-six-man garrison, with two of their six guns put out of action, disabled two of the attacking vessels and scattered the remainder of the Union ships. In anticipation of another possible federal assault, Fort Griffin was strengthened with several captured Parrott rifles and temporarily reinforced. By January 1, 1864, however, the garrison, one of the last coastal positions remaining in Southern hands, had been reduced to 268 men. Confederate troops spiked the five remaining cannons and abandoned Fort Griffin by May 24, 1865.

Erosion and the channelization of Sabine Pass have removed evidence of Fort Griffin's exact location. However, a statue and a plaque at Sabine Pass Battleground State Historical Park^{qv} mark what is thought to have been the site of the fort.

BIBLIOGRAPHY: W. T. Block, A History of Jefferson County, Texas, from Wilderness to Reconstruction (M.A. thesis, Lamar University, 1974; Nederland, Texas: Nederland Publishing, 1976). *Sabine Pass Battleground State Historical Park* (brochure, Austin: Texas Parks and Wildlife Department, 1986). *Robert Wooster*

FORT GRIFFIN (Shackelford County). Fort Griffin, a strategic unit in the string of border and frontier outposts defending Texas settlers against hostile Indians and outlaws, was established in 1867. Its location is on the Clear Fork of the Brazos River in northeast Shackelford County. Lt. Col. Samuel D. Sturgis chose the site and led four companies of the Sixth United States Cavalry (F, I, K, and L) there on July 31. On June 3, 1868, companies of the Seventeenth Infantry under Lt. Col. S. B. Hayman joined the garrison. The new post was first called Camp Wilson but was soon renamed Fort Griffin after Gen. Charles Griffin,^{qv} commander of the Military District of Texas, 1866–67 (see FIFTH MILITARY DISTRICT). Stone buildings were planned to replace the original picket, log, and frame structures, but soldiers' quarters, stables, and even the hospital were always temporary, some mere canvas-covered shelters.

The older posts of Belknap, Phantom Hill, and Chadbourne became subposts of the new Fort Griffin, which supplied garrisons for the first two. These subposts furnished escorts for stagecoaches, wagon trains, and surveying parties. In time, Griffin was the nucleus of the border-defense line from Fort Richardson^{qv} at Jacksboro to the Big Bend country. Law enforcement at Fort Griffin was strengthened in 1877 by the arrival of over two dozen Texas Rangers^{qv} led by Capt. G. W. Campbell. In July 1878 Campbell was replaced by Lt. George W. Arrington,^{qv} whose Indian-fighting talents were preferred over those of the United States Army by the townspeople.

By 1879 the southern buffalo^{qv} herd was depleted, and the fort and its outposts were within a settled area. On May 31, 1881, Capt. J. B. Irvine closed Fort Griffin and marched the single remaining army unit, Company A, Twenty-Second Infantry, southward to Fort Clark.^{qv} Exodus from the town proper soon followed. Now only the ruins of Fort Griffin stand in Fort Griffin State Historical Park,^{qv} fifteen miles north of Albany on U.S. Highway 283.

BIBLIOGRAPHY: Vernon Lynch, "1879 in the *Echo*: A Year at Fort Griffin on the Texas Frontier," West Texas Historical Association *Year Book* 41 (1965). Rupert N. Richardson, *The Frontier of Northwest Texas, 1846 to 1876* (Glendale, California: Clark, 1963). Carl Coke Rister, *Fort Griffin on the Texas Frontier* (Norman: University of Oklahoma Press, 1956). University of Texas School of Architecture, *Texas*

Historic Forts: Architectural Research (5 vols., Austin: Texas Parks and Wildlife Department, 1968).   *Vernon Lynch*

FORT GRIFFIN, TEXAS. The town of Fort Griffin grew up on the level bottomland between the military fort bearing the same name and the Clear Fork of the Brazos River. The fort stood on a hill, and the townsite was frequently called the Bottom or the Flat. U.S. Highway 283 runs by the site about fifteen miles north of Albany in northern Shackelford County. The town, begun in the late 1860s, grew and quickly gained the reputation of a lawless frontier outpost that attracted such women as Lottie Deno[qv] and Mollie McCabe; lawmen Patrick F. Garrett,[qv] Doc Holiday, and Wyatt Earp; outlaws such as John Wesley Hardin;[qv] and men such as John Selman and John M. Larn,[qqv] who lived on both sides of the law. By 1874 the lawlessness of the community had become so extreme that the commander of the fort placed the town under government control and forced a number of undesirable residents to leave; this situation lasted until the organization of Shackelford County later in the year. The community served as a major supply source for buffalo[qv] hunters, especially during the busy seasons from 1874 to 1876–77. The sale of hides and salted meat was brisk during this period. The Butterfield Overland Mail[qv] route passed west and north of the townsite at Clear Fork Crossing, and herds on the Western Trail[qv] after 1875 passed it en route to Kansas railheads. A newspaper, the Fort Griffin *Echo,* was published from 1879 to 1882, and a local academy operated for several years. At its height, Fort Griffin had a permanent population of about 1,000 and an estimated transient population of nearly twice that. With the buffalo gone, the trail drivers' needs served by Albany to the south, and the contingent of soldiers greatly reduced, the town declined. When the fort closed in 1881 and the Texas Central Railroad laid tracks through Albany instead of Fort Griffin, the end came rapidly. Although it survived into the twentieth century as a rural community with a school and country store, virtually nothing remains of this once riotous, flourishing town. The site is preserved as Fort Griffin State Historical Park.[qv]

BIBLIOGRAPHY: T. Lindsay Baker, *Ghost Towns of Texas* (Norman: University of Oklahoma Press, 1986). Roscoe P. and Margaret B. Conkling, *The Butterfield Overland Mail, 1857–1869* (3 vols., Glendale, California: Clark, 1947). Frances Mayhugh Holden, *Lambshead Before Interwoven: A Texas Range Chronicle, 1848–1878* (College Station: Texas A&M University Press, 1982). Sallie Reynolds Matthews, *Interwoven: A Pioneer Chronicle* (Houston: Anson Jones, 1936; 4th ed., College Station: Texas A&M University Press, 1982). Carl Coke Rister, *Fort Griffin on the Texas Frontier* (Norman: University of Oklahoma Press, 1956). Edgar Rye, *The Quirt and the Spur: Vanishing Shadows of the Texas Frontier* (Chicago: Conkey, 1909; facsimile ed., Austin: Steck-Vaughn, 1967).   *Lawrence Clayton*

FORT GRIFFIN FANDANGLE. The Fort Griffin Fandangle is an annual outdoor musical drama produced in Albany, Texas, on Thursday, Friday, and Saturday evenings of the last two weeks in June. Its focus is the historical and cultural development of the area along the Clear Fork of the Brazos River in northern Shackelford County near Fort Griffin, the military outpost that from 1867 to 1881 provided protection for settlers in the region and gave rise to a community in the flat between the fort on the hill and the Clear Fork. The story is recalled through the memory of an old-timer of the region, a cattleman who sits on the porch of a ranchhouse to reveal the past as he remembers it. The production consists of a series of segments, each based on historical material introduced by the narrators and then interpreted by one or more songs and dancing.

The Fandangle had its inception in 1937 when C. B. Downing, superintendent of the Albany schools, asked Alice Reynolds, a local music teacher, if she would write an outdoor musical play for the senior class to present the next spring. She declined but asked another native of Albany, Robert Edward Nail, Jr.,[qv] who responded enthusiastically with *Dr. Shackelford's Paradise,* produced in 1938. The play was so well received that it was expanded to include adults in the cast and was produced that summer as the Fort Griffin Fandangle. A sponsoring organization, the Fandangle Association, was first incorporated in 1947. Nail established three rules: first, anybody with ties in Shackelford County could be in the show; second, the show would have to be publicized by word of mouth, not by paid publicity; and third, there would be no profanity in the show. Alice Reynolds was active from the beginning in writing songs, in designing sets and the numerous banners associated with the play, particularly the steerhead and fiddle emblem that represents the Fandangle, and in sketching some of the elaborate costumes. For many years she also played the organ for the performances. She died in May 1984.

The title was chosen for its alliteration and euphony. Fandangle is a provincial version of Spanish fandango, a fast dance. Originally only traditional or folk music and dances were used, but as the show was repeated in later years by popular demand, new material was written and included in the performances, a practice that is still followed. Although material is repeated from year to year, each season's version varies from any previous show in both content and focus.

In addition to Nail and Reynolds, numerous other citizens have contributed significantly. Songs written by James Ball, Elsa Turner, and later Luann George, who replaced Reynolds as organist in 1983, have increased the store available to the production. Marge Bray, long-time choreographer for the show, assumed the directorship after James Ball, who served for four years after Nail's death in 1968. Of particular significance to the development of the Fandangle over the years is the work of G. P. Crutchfield, local craftsman, who built the authentic replica of the Butterfield stagecoach, the machine representing the Texas Central Railroad train, a self-contained blacksmith shop on wheels, and the steam calliope, which is still played regularly before performances. All of these works and many other entries, bands, and horse units appear in the annual parade held on Thursday afternoon of the second week.

Although early performances were held at the local football stadium, the Prairie Theatre west of town was constructed in 1965, on land leased for a dollar a year from the John Alexander Matthews[qv] estate. Performances have been held there since that time. Full-scale productions are held only in Albany, but short versions have been given in many locations over the years. These are usually performed in the spring and serve as the core around which the major show is built during late May and early June. These "samplers" were performed in Europe in 1967 and 1976 and in Washington, D.C., in 1984.

BIBLIOGRAPHY: Albany *News,* 45th Annual Fandangle Souvenir Edition, June 1983. Fane Downs, "Fandangle: Myth as Reality," *West Texas Historical Association Yearbook* 54 (1978). *Fort Griffin Fandangle* (Program, June 1983). Vertical Files, Barker Texas History Center, University of Texas at Austin.   *Lawrence Clayton*

FORT GRIFFIN STATE HISTORICAL PARK. Fort Griffin State Historical Park, deeded to the state by Shackelford County in 1935, is located just off U.S. Highway 283 fifteen miles north of Albany. It offers picnicking, overnight camping facilities, and fishing from the banks of the Clear Fork of the Brazos River, as well as nature beauty and displayed artifacts. In the 506-acre park the ruins of several buildings of old Fort Griffin, plus the restored post bakery and replicas of enlisted men's huts, are located on a bluff overlooking the townsite of Fort Griffin. The townsite is not in the park boundaries. The park is the original home of the official state longhorn cattle[qv] herd.

BIBLIOGRAPHY: Ross A. Maxwell, *Geologic and Historic Guide to the State Parks of Texas* (Bureau of Economic Geology, University of Texas at Austin, 1970). George Oxford Miller, *Texas Parks and Campgrounds: Central, South, and West Texas* (Austin: Texas Monthly Press, 1984).   *H. Allen Anderson*

FORT GRIGSBY. Fort Grigsby was on the Neches River at the site of present Port Neches, eleven miles southeast of Beaumont in eastern Jefferson County. It was called Grigsby's Bluff, when Maj. Julius Kellersberg built a small defensive installation in October 1862 on the bluff of that name. Fort Grigsby was part of a series of river defenses designed to block a possible Union advance up the Neches after the fall of Fort Sabine. The fort's two twenty-four-pound guns overlooked a bend in the river. Kellersberg confidently predicted that the battery would "blow anything out of the water" that crossed the bar he had made by sinking shell-laden ships downstream in the Sabine River. The fort itself consisted of mud and clamshell embankments reinforced by upright, pointed logs. It was occupied by Capt. K. D. Keith's company from October to December 1862 and was no longer necessary after the construction of Fort Manhassett.qv Fort Grigsby seems to have been abandoned sometime after July 1863.

BIBLIOGRAPHY: W. T. Block, A History of Jefferson County, Texas, from Wilderness to Reconstruction (M.A. thesis, Lamar University, 1974; Nederland, Texas: Nederland Publishing, 1976). W. T. Block, "Where Was Fort Grigsby?" *East Texas Historical Journal* 9 (October 1971). "The Memoirs of Captain Kosciuszko D. Keith," *Texas Gulf Historical and Biographical Record* 10 (1974). *The War of the Rebellion: A Compilation of the Official Records of the Union and Confederate Armies.*
Robert Wooster

FORT HANCOCK. Fort Hancock, originally designated Camp Rice, was a military installation established on April 15, 1881, as a subpost of Fort Davis to defend against Indians and bandits from across the Rio Grande. On July 9, 1882, it was moved from its initial location six miles northwest of Fort Quitman to a site on the Southern Pacific Railroad. The next month it was moved again to higher ground nearby. Commanding general William T. Shermanqv believed the fort would be permanent because of its proximity to the railroad, and it was one of the few Texas forts to be purchased by the United States War Department (for $2,370 in 1883). On July 1, 1884, Camp Rice became an independent post in order to establish more efficient administration, and on July 17 Congress authorized major improvements that cost $47,000. On May 14, 1886, the fort's name was changed to Fort Hancock, in honor of Maj. Gen. Winfield Scott Hancock,qv who had died on February 9.

Capt. Theodore A. Baldwin and Company I, Tenth United States Cavalry,qv formed the first garrison of the independent post. Thereafter, it was generally garrisoned by mixed detachments of infantry and cavalry rarely numbering more than sixty men. These troops patrolled the Rio Grande to prevent illegal crossings by smugglers, Mexican bandits, or insurrectionists. Post commanders included ethnologist and author Capt. John G. Bourkeqv (June–August 1885) and Maj. S. B. M. Young (August 1885–November 1887).

Fort Hancock suffered at various times from the ravages of both water and fire. Under Bourke, soldiers of the Third Cavalry constructed dikes to protect the post from overflow from the Rio Grande. On the night of May 31, 1886, the western dike broke and the lower portion of the fort was flooded. The break was repaired and the dike strengthened, but four nights later a heavy gale pushed water over the retaining wall and flooded the entire post to a depth of eighteen inches to three feet. In the mid-afternoon of February 14, 1889, the carpenter and blacksmith shops were burned, and on the morning of March 30 the blacksmith and wheelwright's shop followed. Fires on May 4 and May 11 burned the post gymnasium, the quartermaster's stable, and the haystack. By this time Fort Hancock had virtually outlived its usefulness. It was turned over to the Department of the Interior on November 1, 1895, and abandoned by the army on December 6. A marker on U.S. Highway 80, fifty-two miles southeast of El Paso, marks the site.

BIBLIOGRAPHY: Herbert M. Hart, *Tour Guide to Old Western Forts* (Boulder, Colorado: Pruett, 1980). George Ruhlen, "Fort Hancock—Last of the Frontier Forts," *Password,* January 1959.
Bruce J. Dinges

FORT HANCOCK, TEXAS. The town of Fort Hancock is on State Highway 20 and the Southern Pacific Railroad thirty miles northwest of Sierra Blanca in southwestern Hudspeth County. It developed just east of the military installation of the same name, which was originally established as Camp Rice in 1881. Camp Rice was renamed Fort Hancock in May 1886, in honor of Maj. Gen. Winfield Scott Hancock,qv who had died earlier that year. Also in 1886 a post office was established with Albert Warren as postmaster. In 1887 a new railroad depot was built at Fort Hancock, and in 1890 the town had a population of 200, a general store, a hotel, and a meat market. The army abandoned the fort in 1895, and by 1914 the population of the town had dropped to fifty. In the late 1920s, however, its population was estimated at 400. By the mid-1930s the number of residents had declined to 136, but in the 1940s it rose to 500. By the early 1970s it was an estimated 400 and remained at that level through the early 1990s. During the late 1980s Fort Hancock had five churches and two schools.
Martin Donell Kohout

FORT HENDERSON. Fort Henderson was built by Maj. William H. Smith's Texas Ranger battalion early in 1837 and commanded by Capt. Lee C. Smith as part of the defensive line established by the Republic of Texasqv against marauding plains Indians. The fort was named for Gen. James Pinckney Henderson,qv secretary of state. It was on the upper Navasota River near the present boundaries of Robertson and Leon counties, deep in Indian territory and therefore difficult to supply and of questionable defensive utility. For those reasons the fort was abandoned soon after its construction, probably in the fall of 1837.

BIBLIOGRAPHY: Gerald S. Pierce, *Texas Under Arms: The Camps, Posts, Forts, and Military Towns of the Republic of Texas* (Austin: Encino, 1969).
Thomas W. Cutrer

FORT HOOD. Fort Hood is located in southwestern Bell and southeastern Coryell counties in Central Texas. Most of the 218,000 acres owned by the United States Army is located in Coryell County. On January 14, 1942, at the beginning of United States involvement in World War II,qv it was announced that a tank destroyer tactical and firing center would be established near Killeen, Texas. Gen. Andrew D. Bruceqv was selected as the first commander. The first major unit, the 893d Tank Destroyer Battalion, arrived from Fort Meade, Maryland, on April 2, 1942. As other troops began arriving, some 300 farming and ranching families were required, on very short notice, to give up their land. Camp Hood was officially opened on September 18, 1942, and has been continuously used for armored training ever since. The installation was named in honor of Gen. John Bell Hood.qv The mission at Camp Hood was almost immediately expanded to include a replacement and basic training center at North Fort Hood. At times as many as 100,000 soldiers were being trained for the war effort. During the later part of the war some 4,000 German prisoners of warqv were interned at Camp Hood.

The postwar years saw a significant reduction of activity, and the post's population dropped to about 1,700. By 1950 the temporary camp was designated the permanent status of Fort Hood. Basic facilities for a permanent army installation were constructed. The demands for training brought about by the Korean War accelerated military activities. The installation acquired an additional 49,578 acres in 1953 and former United States Air Force and Department of Defense landholdings in the 1950s and 1960s. Major army units stationed at one time or another at Fort Hood included the First, Second, and Fourth Armored divisions. In 1954 Fort Hood was the nation's only two-division installation, and the Third Corps was transferred from Camp

Roberts, California. In 1990 the installation was the headquarters of the Third Corps under United States Army Forces command. Fort Hood was located in the Fifth United States Army area. The two active army divisions, the Second Armored Division^qv ("Hell on Wheels") and the First Cavalry Division, were stationed there. Other commands at Fort Hood included the Sixth Cavalry Brigade (Air Combat), Corps Support Command, the Third Signal Brigade, and several tenant organizations including MEDDAC (Medical Department Activity), Test and Experimentation Command, and more than a dozen other smaller support or tenant commands including two major airfields. Reserve units such as the Forty-ninth and Fiftieth Armored divisions and the Thirty-sixth Airborne Brigade of the Texas National Guard^qv and other smaller regular and reserve units of the army, air force, and marine corps used the Fort Hood facility.

Fort Hood is one of the largest military installations in the world. The primary mission of Fort Hood is to maintain a state of readiness for combat missions, and the dominant activity is the training of the Third Armored Corps. A significant portion of the combat-ready air and ground forces of the United States Army is stationed at Fort Hood. The combat readiness of the Third Armored Corps distinguishes Fort Hood from many other installations, which do not have the same rapid and massive military response capability. With the end of the Cold War, military cutbacks became common throughout the United States. The Second Armored Division was deactivated for a short period, during which time the Fifth Infantry Division (Mechanized) was assigned to Fort Hood. However, operations Desert Shield and Desert Storm in 1990–91 halted this deactivation, and more than 25,000 troops were sent from Fort Hood to the Middle East. Of these, 17,000 were from the Second Armored Division and the First Cavalry Division. Three soldiers from Fort Hood were killed and nine wounded. On April 12, 1991, following the Gulf War, the Department of Defense labeled Fort Hood a top fighting installation and stationed 12,000 additional troops there. In December 1992 the Fifth Infantry Division was inactivated and redesignated the Second Armored Division; it was scheduled to be renamed the Fourth Infantry Division (Mechanized) in December 1995.

The installation has been a critical social and economic reality in the Central Texas region. Prior to the establishment of Fort Hood the region was cotton and cattle country. The shift from a low-population agrarian environment to a densely populated cosmopolitan environment has had both positive and negative features. On the one hand, Fort Hood has stimulated the growth of educational institutions, commercial conveniences, and professional services such as health care. Local communities have benefited from a military population with a pool of experienced teachers and professionals not found in most rural areas. On the other hand, the large number of transitory personnel has resulted in a community characterized by a sense of impermanence and highly focused economic interests not generally found in communities with more social and economic diversity. The installation offers excellent public recreational opportunities, including two museums and many ponds and lakes suitable for fishing. Hunting is also allowed in designated areas. Outdoor recreation in most areas is subject to certain constraints and requires permission from Fort Hood Area Access Control.

Fort Hood is the largest solely federally owned Texas landholding and has taken an initiative in the stewardship of cultural resources on public lands. More than 2,000 archeological sites dating from the Ice Age to historic times have been recorded. The archeological record at Fort Hood contains a diversity of resources including more than 1,000 sites of hunting and gathering people from all major time periods in Texas prehistory and the nineteenth and early twentieth centuries. More than fifty historic communities, most of them now extinct, are represented in the Fort Hood archeological inventory. In November 1973 the skeletal remains of forty-five Indians were reinterred at Fort Hood. Archeological sites are protected by federal law from unauthorized damage, destruction, collecting, or excavation, and records provide resources for anthropological research and public appreciation.

BIBLIOGRAPHY: Dan Cragg, *The Guide to Military Installations* (Harrisburg, Pennsylvania: Stackpole, 1983; 2d ed. 1988). Sylvia Ann Edwards, Land Acquisition in Coryell County, Texas, for the Formation of Camp Hood, 1942–1945: A Civilian Perspective (M.A. thesis, Baylor University, 1988). Duncan Gra'Delle, *Killeen: Tale of Two Cities, 1882–982* (Killeen, Texas, 1984). Oscar Lewis, *On the Edge of the Black Waxy: A Cultural Survey of Bell County* (Washington University Studies, St. Louis, 1948). Mildred Watkins Mears, *Coryell County Scrapbook* (Waco: Texian, 1963).

Frederick L. Briuer

FORT HOUSTON. Fort Houston was a stockade and blockhouse of the Republic of Texas^qv at a site that is now on Farm Road 1990 two miles west of Palestine. It was built on the public square of Houston, Anderson County, by Capt. Michael Costley's Company of Texas Rangers^qqv and completed before May 19, 1836. It covered an acre of the townsite. Tradition says the blockhouse was built by the rangers and the stockade by the settlers. Although it was an important point of frontier defense from 1836 to 1839, it was never attacked by an Indian force; there were Indian raids on the settlements nearby, however. After the fort was abandoned in 1841 or 1842, Houston became known as Fort Houston, but the settlement declined when Palestine became the county seat. In 1857 John H. Reagan^qv bought 600 acres, which included the old site of the fort and town, and his home became known as Fort Houston. The Texas Centennial^qv Commission erected a marker near the townsite in 1936. State historical markers were later placed near the site and at the nearby Fort Houston Cemetery.

BIBLIOGRAPHY: Gerald S. Pierce, *Texas Under Arms: The Camps, Posts, Forts, and Military Towns of the Republic of Texas* (Austin: Encino, 1969). Harold Schoen, comp., *Monuments Erected by the State of Texas to Commemorate the Centenary of Texas Independence* (Austin: Commission of Control for Texas Centennial Celebrations, 1938). Jimmy Valentine, "The Original Houston, Texas, and the First Fort Sam Houston," *Junior Historian*, September 1944.

Mrs. Harmon Watts

FORT INGE. Fort Inge (Camp Leona) is on the east bank of the Leona River a mile south of Uvalde in southern Uvalde County. The site is dominated by Mount Inge, a 140-foot volcanic plug of Uvalde phonolite basalt. Archeological evidence indicates the place has been intermittently occupied since the Pre-Archaic period, about 6,000 B.C. It is possible that ranching occurred there in the Spanish colonial and Mexican periods (*see* SPANISH TEXAS, MEXICAN TEXAS). On March 13, 1849, frontier artist Capt. Seth Eastman^qv and fifty-six soldiers of companies D and I, First United States Infantry, established camp on the Leona, four miles above Woll's Crossing. In December 1849 the post was renamed Fort Inge in honor of Lt. Zebulon M. P. Inge, United States Second Dragoons, a West Point officer killed at the Mexican War^qv battle of Resaca de la Palma.^qv

Fort Inge was established as a part of the first federal line of frontier forts in Texas. It was to serve as a base of operations for army troops and Texas militia. The missions of the soldiers included security patrols for the construction of the San Antonio–El Paso military road, escorts for supply trains and mail, protection for frontier settlements from bandits and Indian raiders, and guarding the international boundary with Mexico. The fort was a typical one-company, fifty-man post for most of its history. For a brief period in 1854 it was the regimental headquarters for the United States Mounted Rifle Regiment with a garrison of 200. One staff inspector reported that Fort Inge "is justly regarded as one of the most important and desirable positions in Texas. No station of the line possesses so many advantages as this . . . in point of wood, water, and soil . . . It is pre-eminent as a military site. [It is in] a state of constant warfare and constant service."

Army units and officers of the post include the First Infantry Regiment (1849); Capt. William J. Hardee and Company C, Second Dragoons (1849–52); William A. A. (Bigfoot) Wallace's^qv Texas Ranging Company (1850); the United States Mounted Rifle Regiment, under Col. William Wing Loring and captains Gordon Granger^qv and John G. Walker^qv (1852–55); and the Second United States Cavalry,^qv with Capt. Edmund Kirby Smith^qv and lieutenants Fitzhugh Lee, Zenas R. Bliss, and William B. (Wild Bill) Hazen^qqv (1856–61). During the Civil War^qv the post was occupied by Confederate and state units including Walter P. Lane's^qv rangers; Company A, C.S.A. Cavalry; and John J. Dix's^qv company, Norris Frontier Regiment. The fort was reoccupied by federal troops in 1866, and its final garrisons included Company K, Fourth United States Cavalry^qv (1866–68); Company L, Ninth United States Cavalry;^qv and Lt. John L. Bullis^qv and Company D, Forty-first Infantry (1868–69). The Ninth Cavalry and Forty-first Infantry were black units.

The dozen buildings of the post were arranged around the rectangular parade ground with an enclosed stable at the south end of the post. The most substantial building was constructed of cut limestone and was used as a hospital and later as a storehouse. Most structures were of jacal construction—upright log pickets plastered with mud and whitewashed. A low, dry-stacked stone wall was built around the fort during or after the Civil War.

The establishment of the post in 1849 immediately attracted a number of farmers to the area. In 1853 Reading Wood Black^qv bought land a mile upstream and began the settlement of Encina in 1855. The community was renamed Uvalde in 1856. Fort Inge was closed for federal service on March 19, 1869, and the garrison transferred to Fort McKavett. In 1871 United States troops returned to tear down some of the buildings and recover the timber and stone to be used in construction at Fort Clark. The site was used as a camp by the Texas Rangers^qv until 1884. It was farmland until 1961, when it became Fort Inge Historical Site County Park. From 1980 to 1982 the Uvalde County Historical Commission and local donors sponsored archival research and an archeological project to establish an accurate and detailed history of Fort Inge.

BIBLIOGRAPHY: Arrie Barrett, Federal Military Outposts in Texas, 1846–1861 (M.A. thesis, University of Texas, 1927). George Collins, "Fort Inge," *Junior Historian*, September 1950. George S. Nelson, *Preliminary Archaeological Survey and Testing of Fort Inge, Texas* (Uvalde, Texas: Uvalde County Historical Commission, 1981). Thomas Tyree Smith, *Fort Inge* (Austin: Eakin Press, 1993). *Thomas T. Smith*

FORT INGLISH. During the early years of the Republic of Texas^qv Fannin County residents lived in constant danger of Indian attack, and Fort Inglish was a frequent refuge for settlers on the western edge of the Red River frontier. It was built in the summer of 1837 by Bailey Inglish^qv in the form of a single blockhouse, sixteen feet square and topped by an overhanging story twenty-four feet square, probably surrounded by a log stockade. Fort Inglish was on grounds now occupied by a Veterans Administration center, north of East Ninth Street and east of Lynn street, in downtown Bonham. Although it was private, Fort Inglish played a role in several official campaigns against the Indians by the Army of the Republic of Texas.^qv In November 1838 it served as the rendezvous point for the militia brigade of Gen. John H. Dyer during the Rusk-Dyer Indian expedition, and in October 1840 Col. William G. Cooke's^qv troops straggled into Fort Inglish after the near-disaster of the Military Road^qv expedition. After the removal of the Indian threat to white settlement in Northeast Texas in the early 1840s, however, Fort Inglish fell into disrepair and was eventually dismantled.

BIBLIOGRAPHY: Gerald S. Pierce, *Texas Under Arms: The Camps, Posts, Forts, and Military Towns of the Republic of Texas* (Austin: Encino, 1969). Rex Wallace Strickland, "History of Fannin County, Texas, 1836–1843," *Southwestern Historical Quarterly* 33, 34 (April, July 1930). "William G. Cooke to B. T. Archer, November 14, 1840," *Journals of the House of Representatives of the Republic of Texas: Fifth Congress, First Session, 1840–1841* (Austin: Cruger and Wing, 1841).
Thomas W. Cutrer

FORT JOHNSTON. Fort Johnston (or Johnson), a small, transient fort of the Republic of Texas,^qv was between Coffee's Station^qv and Basin Springs at a site now in northern Grayson County. It was established in November 1840. The site was selected by William G. Cooke,^qv commander of the Military Road^qv expedition, immediately after his arrival on the Red River. The post was constructed by First Infantry companies D (commanded by John Holliday) and E (commanded by James P. Goodall) under the command of Holliday. It was to be the upper post in a line of frontier forts proposed by Albert Sidney Johnston.^qv In March 1841 the post was abandoned. After learning of the disbanding of the Army of the Republic of Texas,^qv Holliday left Coffee's Station on April 19. He joined Capt. William D. Houghton, from Camp Jordan, and arrived in Austin on May 3. About this time the post was used as a rendezvous for Gen. Edward H. Tarrant and James Bourland,^qqv in preparation for their Village Creek campaign (*see* VILLAGE CREEK, BATTLE OF).

In 1842 commissioners Esther Stroud and Leonard H. Williams^qv met at the fort during their preparation for a Texas Indian treaty. The community at the site became known as Georgetown, after George R. Reeves,^qv who lived in the area. The Snively expedition^qv mustered and departed from Fort Johnston in 1843. In the winter of 1845–46, Lyman Wight,^qv leading a congregation of defecting Mormons^qv into Texas, used the fort as his headquarters. The commissioners' journey to Comanche Peak in connection with the Comanche treaty of 1846 (*see* INDIAN RELATIONS) passed through Georgetown, as did that of Randolph B. Marcy^qv on his return from Dona Ana in 1849. The old road became the upper part of the military road from Preston to Fort Belknap. The community is mentioned in the log of the Leach wagon train. The site is now just west of Fink, a few miles from Lake Texoma. A Texas Centennial^qv historical marker located there says that the post was named for Francis W. Johnson.^qv It now seems more likely, however, that the fort was named Fort Johnston in honor of Albert Sidney Johnston. It is called by both names in historical sources.

BIBLIOGRAPHY: Gerald S. Pierce, "The Military Road Expedition of 1840–41," *Texas Military History* 6 (Summer 1967). Gerald S. Pierce, *Texas Under Arms: The Camps, Posts, Forts, and Military Towns of the Republic of Texas* (Austin: Encino, 1969). *Morris L. Britton*

FORT LANCASTER. Fort Lancaster was on the left bank of Live Oak Creek above its confluence with the Pecos River. It is now a state historic site off old U.S. Highway 290 ten miles east of Sheffield in Crockett County. The post was established as Camp Lancaster on August 20, 1855, by Capt. Stephen D. Carpenter and manned by companies H and K of the First United States Infantry. Camp Lancaster became Fort Lancaster on August 21, 1856. Carpenter was succeeded in command by Capt. R. S. Granger, who served from February 1856 to March 31, 1858. Carpenter resumed command after March 31 and was succeeded again by Granger in January 1859. Granger commanded until the removal of federal troops in March 1861 after the secession^qv of Texas from the Union. During the Civil War^qv the post was occupied from December 1861 to April 1862 by Walter P. Lane's^qv rangers, who became a part of Company F, Second Regiment, of the Texas Mounted Rifles. After the war the fort was reoccupied in 1871 as a subpost by a company of infantry and a detachment of calvary. Personnel changed monthly. The post was apparently abandoned in 1873 or 1874 and much of its masonry was used for buildings in Sheffield.

Fort Lancaster protected the lower road from San Antonio to El Paso in the years following the discovery of gold in California. The duties of the men stationed at Fort Lancaster were to escort mail and freight trains, pursue Mescalero Apaches and Comanches, and patrol their segment of road to keep track of Indian movements. The post was originally constructed of picket canvas and portable Turnley prefabricated buildings. By the time it was abandoned all its major structures were made of stone or adobe. The Butterfield Overland Mail[qv] changed its route west from the upper road between San Antonio and El Paso to the lower road in August 1859. Mail on the lower road had previously been contracted to George H. Giddings[qv] and John Birch. Three coaches per month passed over the road. In June of 1860 Lt. William E. Echols and his "camel corps" visited the fort (see CAMELS).

The site of Fort Lancaster was deeded to Crockett County in 1965 and donated to the Texas Parks and Wildlife Department[qv] in 1968. Archeological exploration had been begun two years earlier by T. R. Hays and Edward B. Jelks; their project involved excavating one barracks and three latrines and testing two other barracks and two commissary structures. Three structures—an officers' quarters, the commissary, and the hospital kitchen—and the flagpole location were entirely excavated in 1971 by John W. Clark. Dessamae Lorraine did additional mapping of the site and work on the flagpole site shortly after Clark's excavation. In 1974 Wayne Roberson excavated two enlisted men's barracks and two officers' quarters. The excavations produced large numbers of artifacts and a great deal of architectural information for interpreting the site. Much of this material is presented at the visitors' center at Fort Lancaster State Historic Site and in state archeological reports. Because of a budget shortfall the state yielded management of the site to Texas Rural Communities, Incorporated, in 1993.

BIBLIOGRAPHY: Art Black, *Fort Lancaster State Historic Site, Crockett County, Texas: Archeological Investigations* (Archeological Report 8 [Austin: Texas Parks and Wildlife Department, Parks Division, Historic Sites and Restoration Branch, 1975?]). John W. Clark, Jr., *Archeological Investigations at Fort Lancaster State Historic Site, Crockett County, Texas* (Texas Archeological Salvage Project Research Report 12 [Austin: University of Texas, 1972]). John W. Clark, Jr., "The 'Digs' at Fort Lancaster, Texas, 1966 and 1971," *Military History of Texas and the Southwest* 12 (1974). T. R. Hays and Edward B. Jelks, *Archeological Exploration at Fort Lancaster, 1966* (Austin: State Building Commission, 1966). University of Texas School of Architecture, *Texas Historic Forts: Architectural Research* (5 vols., Austin: Texas Parks and Wildlife Department, 1968).
John W. Clark, Jr.

FORT LE DOUT. Fort Le Dout, reportedly located in what is now Wood County, was probably established during the eighteenth century by the French as a post for trade with the Caddo and Wichita Indians. Le Dout, which means "redoubt," or "fortification," may have been located on the Sabine River or possibly on Lake Fork Creek, a fork of the Sabine. A 1989 archeological study suggested that the Woldert Site, located about five miles from the confluence of Lake Fork Creek and the Sabine River, might be the site of Fort Le Dout.

BIBLIOGRAPHY: Timothy K. Perttula and Bob D. Skiles, "Another Look at an Eighteenth-Century Archaelogical Site in Wood County, Texas," *Southwestern Historical Quarterly* 92 (January 1989).

FORT LEATON. Fort Leaton (Old Fortín, El Fortín, Fortin) is on Farm Road 170 five miles southeast of Presidio in southern Presidio County. The fort sits on a bluff overlooking the Rio Grande and what has been called the Chihuahua Trail. Fort Leaton was listed as the first seat of Presidio County in 1850. It was the private citadel of a Chihuahua Trail freighter and the first Anglo-American farmer in Presidio County, Ben Leaton. Leaton built on the ruins of a Spanish fort founded in 1773 and known as El Fortín de San José at La Junta. After El Fortín was abandoned in 1810, the structure stood unoccupied until Juan Bustillos took it as his home in 1830. By August 1848 Leaton had bought El Fortín from Bustillos and established Fort Leaton as his home, trading post, and private fort. During that month an expedition led by John C. (Jack) Hays[qv] to find a practicable road from San Antonio to Chihuahua via El Paso spent ten days at Fort Leaton.

The fort was built in an L-shape with the long side running east and west for 200 feet, parallel to the river. The measurement across the base of the structure was 140 feet. The walls were made of adobe bricks, eighteen inches long, five inches thick, and twelve inches wide. By laying the bricks crosswise, the builders made the walls eighteen inches thick. A stockade for animals was made at the base of the L. Large doors allowed teams and wagons to drive inside the structure. A crenellated parapet surrounded the rooms and fortified the structure.

Because of its desolate location and the constant threat of Indian attack, Fort Leaton offered much-needed frontier defense. The private bastion was the only fortification on the American side of the Rio Grande between Eagle Pass and El Paso before and during the building of Fort Davis (Jeff Davis County), and the United States Army made Fort Leaton its unofficial headquarters. Even after the completion of Fort Davis, eighty miles to the north, the army used the private fort as an outpost for military patrols. Military maps of the 1850s listed Fort Leaton along with official army posts.

There is no record of any Indian attack on Fort Leaton. The reason may be found in an accusation made by the Mexican inspector for the military colonies at El Paso del Norte,[qv] Emilio Langberg, who accused Leaton of trading guns to Indians for horses they had stolen in Mexico. Such illegal trading with the Indians might have gained him their favor and protected his fort from attack. Before any legal charges could be brought against him, Leaton died in 1851.

Leaton's farm, with eight to ten American workers and a gravity irrigation ditch, produced vegetables, wheat, and livestock to supply the fort's inhabitants and needy travelers. At his death his widow faced large debts. Eventually, the fort was acquired by John Burgess, who had held the mortgage. Burgess lived there until Leaton's son Bill killed him in 1875. The fort then fell into disuse. In 1934 and 1935 some restoration work was completed there under a government project. In 1967 the state acquired a five-acre tract around the old fort, and the partially restored structure became Fort Leaton State Historic Site.[qv]

BIBLIOGRAPHY: Leavitt Corning, Jr., *Baronial Forts of the Big Bend* (Austin: Trinity University Press, 1967). Virginia Madison and Hallie Stillwell, *How Come It's Called That? Place Names in the Big Bend Country* (Albuquerque: University of New Mexico Press, 1958). Elton Miles, *Tales of the Big Bend* (College Station: Texas A&M University Press, 1976). Cecilia Thompson, *History of Marfa and Presidio County, 1535–1946* (2 vols., Austin: Nortex, 1985).
Julia Cauble Smith

FORT LEATON STATE HISTORIC SITE. Fort Leaton State Historic Site is on Farm Road 170, the Rio Grande, and what has been called the Chihuahua Trail five miles southeast of Presidio in Presidio County. At various times Fort Leaton[qv] was called Old Fortin, El Fortin, and Fortin. Because the area around the fort has been continuously occupied since 1500 B.C., tradition has given it a romantic past. Fort Leaton has been named as the site of both El Apostol Santiago, a Spanish mission established in 1684 and rebuilt in 1773, and as Presidio del Norte de la Junta de los Rios, built in 1760. However, recent archeological investigations at Fort Leaton do not substantiate these claims and set the site's earliest possible human occupation as the 1820s. Indications suggest that the building was used from the 1840s to the 1920s.

The structure, called the largest adobe[qv] structure in Texas, was probably built by Juan Bustillos as his home in the 1830s. In August 1848 Ben Leaton,[qv] a Chihuahua Trail freighter and the first Anglo-American farmer in Presidio County, bought the property from Bustillos. Leaton established Fort Leaton as his home, trading post, and private fort. It was the first seat of the unorganized Presidio County. The L-shaped fort was built with the long side running east and west, parallel to the river, for 200 feet. The base of the building measured 140 feet. A crenellated parapet surrounded the rooms, allowing a stockade for animals and fortification for the site. Large doors gave access to teams and wagons.

Leaton died between January 1 and August 15, 1851, leaving his wife with large debts. The fort passed to John Burgess, who held the mortgage. Burgess's descendants lived at Fort Leaton into the 1920s. After the Burgesses left, the fort fell into disuse. In 1934 T. C. Mitchell and the Marfa State Bank acquired the old structure and donated it to the county as a historic site. Restoration work began under a county works project, but inadequate funding prevented its completion. A. C. Skidmore bought the property later and donated it to the state. In 1968 it became Fort Leaton State Historic Site. Archeological work done in 1969 revealed that the adobe walls were built in three phases. Excavations in 1971 uncovered nine new rooms, a ramada, a corral, various living floors, and the limits of the north wall. The site has been restored to conform with the archeological findings.

BIBLIOGRAPHY: Leavitt Corning, Jr., *Baronial Forts of the Big Bend* (Austin: Trinity University Press, 1967). Daniel E. Fox, *Traces of Texas History: Archeological Evidence of the Past 450 Years* (San Antonio: Corona Press, 1983). Elton Miles, *Tales of the Big Bend* (College Station: Texas A&M University Press, 1976). *Julia Cauble Smith*

FORT LINCOLN. Fort Lincoln, on the west bank of Seco Creek a mile north of D'Hanis in west central Medina County, was named for Capt. George Lincoln, an officer of Company E, Eighth Infantry, who lost his life in the Mexican War qv battle of Buena Vista. The fort was one of eight that formed the first line of permanent federal frontier defense in Texas from Eagle Pass on the Rio Grande to Coffee's Bend on the Red River. In 1848, at the conclusion of the Mexican War, a Texas Ranger company commanded by Charles S. DeMontel qv established a camp on Seco Creek a mile north of D'Hanis. On July 7, 1849, Fort Lincoln was established at the site used the year before by DeMontel. The 1,476-acre plot had been patented to the heirs of Milton Anderson on August 27, 1846.

The fort was built on the west bank of Seco Creek on high, open ground that provided a commanding view of the surroundings. Companies E and G of the Eighth United States Infantry, qv commanded by Maj. James Longstreet, were stationed at Fort Lincoln to repel and track down Indian raiders in protection of newly arrived European and American settlers and the commercial and military property transported on the Woll Road, an important trade route from San Antonio to Fort Duncan on the Rio Grande and points west. Longstreet's second in command, Lt. Richard Irving Dodge, was the man for whom Dodge City, Kansas, was named.

Water for the post was hauled from Seco Creek, at that time no more than a succession of standing pools. The builders of the fort made use of the locally abundant gray limestone in construction. In 1851 the installation had buildings for two companies, a commissary store, a storehouse for company property, a storehouse for the quartermaster's depot, and a hospital. The temporary buildings were of logs or poles, with roofs of shingles, thatch, or tarpaulins. Though the number of officers and men stationed at the fort was usually between 90 and 120, it reached 141 at one time. Longstreet was succeeded by Maj. Pitcairn Morrison, who was succeeded by Bvt. Capt. William Steel qv and Capt. Washington G. Newton.

Fort Lincoln was abandoned on July 20, 1852, after the frontier line had advanced westward. The buildings remained intact for some time, and the Texas Rangers qv made headquarters at the site. The barracks were torn down and transformed into residences east of Seco Creek at D'Hanis after being purchased by Irishman Richard Reily, who used the hospital building to raise his family. None of the buildings remains. On May 26, 1936, a dedication ceremony was held for the unveiling of a marker placed by the Texas Centennial qv Commission at the site.

BIBLIOGRAPHY: Castro Colonies Heritage Association, *The History of Medina County, Texas* (Dallas: National Share Graphics, 1983). Cornelia and Garland Crook, "Fort Lincoln, Texas," *Texas Military History* 4 (Fall 1964). La Coste *Leader*, May 22, 1936. *H. E. Haass*

FORT LIPANTITLÁN. Fort Lipantitlán (meaning "Lipan land") was conceived about 1825 by José M. J. Carbajal.qv The site, now in northwestern Nueces County, was that of camping grounds of the Lipan Apache Indians on the west bank of the Nueces River about three miles upstream from the old town of San Patricio, which is on the east side of the river. At the site a number of ancient trails beaten by game animals, Indians, and explorers crossed. An old presidio was also reportedly there as early as 1734 but had completely vanished. Mexican general Manuel de Mier y Terán,qv acting on the orders to restrict Anglo immigration into Texas, commissioned the fort and placed Capt. Enrique Villareal qv in command. He served until 1835, when he was relieved by Capt. Nicolás Rodríguez.

Author John Linn qv wrote, "The fort was a simple embankment of earth, lined within by fence-rails to hold the dirt in place, and would have answered tolerably well, perhaps, for a second-rate hog pen." After its construction it was garrisoned with from eighty to 120 men; however, many times the complement was much less. Each of the four parapets was designed for one cannon, but it is doubtful if the fort was ever fully armed. Evidently several buildings and at least one barracks were built surrounding the embankments. James McGloin,qv in his account of the battle of Lipantitlán qv (November 4, 1835), makes reference to burning several houses, including a barracks.

The Mexican armies, coming north by land out of Mexico, headed to Goliad, Refugio, and East Texas during the Texas Revolution qv and crossed the Nueces at either the De Leon Crossing at the fort or Paso de Santa Margarita near San Patricio. During this period Mexican troops were in almost constant occupancy of the fort. Captain Rodríguez was in command of the Mexican forces when Capt. Ira J. Westover qv and a force of about seventy Texans defeated the Mexicans on November 4, 1835. Since the Texans did not occupy the fort after their victory, Mexican forces continued to use the old fort on occasion.

Fort Lipantitlán played an important role in the years immediately after the war, when Federalist forces under Gen. Antonio Canales qv sought refuge on the Nueces River to regroup and to seek assistance from Americans. Gen. James Davis qv repulsed Mexican troops under Canales at Lipantitlán on July 7, 1842. After the Mexican War qv put an end to Mexican armies in Texas, Lipantitlán was abandoned and grew up in brush.

In the mid-1980s digs on private land uncovered a number of artifacts in a rather large camp adjacent to the old fort where families and army women lived. A population of 300 or more in the camp is considered likely. The site of the old fort is a state park, but no traces of the earthen embankments remain. The archeological digs confirmed Indian presence before the Spanish and Mexican eras, as well as occupancy by Texas forces in 1842. Aboriginal ceramics, Indian artifacts, personal items, all types of military buttons and ordnance (Spanish, Mexican, and Texan), money, and miscellaneous hardware were among the hundreds of artifacts recovered.

BIBLIOGRAPHY: Eugene C. Barker, ed., *The Austin Papers* (3 vols., Washington: GPO, 1924–28). William Campbell Binkley, ed., *Official Correspondence of the Texan Revolution, 1835–1836* (2 vols., New York: Appleton-Century, 1936). Bethel Coopwood, "The Route of Cabeza de Vaca," *Quarterly of the Texas State Historical Association* 3 (October 1899, January, April 1900). Charles Adams Gulick, Jr., Harriet Smither, et al., eds., *The Papers of Mirabeau Buonaparte Lamar* (6 vols., Austin: Texas State Library, 1920–27; rpt., Austin: Pemberton Press, 1968). Hobart Huson, *Refugio: A Comprehensive History of Refugio County from Aboriginal Times to 1953* (2 vols., Woodsboro, Texas: Rooke Foundation, 1953, 1955). Hobart Huson, *Captain Philip Dimmitt's Commandancy of Goliad, 1835–1836* (Austin: Von Boeckmann–Jones, 1974). Hobart Huson, *Souvenir Program, Refugio County Centennial Celebration* (Refugio: Refugio *Timely Remarks*,

1936?). John J. Linn, *Reminiscences of Fifty Years in Texas* (New York: Sadlier, 1883; 2d ed., Austin: Steck, 1935; rpt., Austin: State House, 1986). Joseph Milton Nance, *Attack and Counterattack: The Texas-Mexican Frontier, 1842* (Austin: University of Texas Press, 1964).

Keith Guthrie

FORT LYDAY. Fort Lyday, also known as Lyday's Fort and Fort DeKalb, was built by Isaac Lyday three-fourths of a mile east and a half mile north of Lyday's Crossing on the North Sulphur River in what is now extreme southwestern Lamar County. The site is near Dial in Fannin County. Typical of small private forts on the Texas frontier, Lyday's covered about a quarter acre, with several ten-by-twelve-foot storerooms against its north wall and similarly sized living quarters ranged against the other three. The fort was surrounded by a picket palisade and had a large well in the middle of the parade ground. A livestock corral was located outside the stockade. The fort was constructed in 1836 for the defense of settlers on the river and Cypress Creek and garrisoned late in 1838 by the Red River County Rangers under the command of Capt. William B. Stout. Under the orders of Gen. John H. Dyer, commander of the Fourth Militia Brigade, Stout's men repaired the dilapidated fort and brought in fourteen families for protection from marauding Indians. The fort saw sporadic activity until about 1843, when troubles with Indians in the area at last subsided. Thereafter Fort Lyday was allowed to fall into decay.

BIBLIOGRAPHY: Charles Adams Gulick, Jr., Harriet Smither, et al., eds., *The Papers of Mirabeau Buonaparte Lamar* (6 vols., Austin: Texas State Library, 1920–27; rpt., Austin: Pemberton Press, 1968). Gerald S. Pierce, *Texas Under Arms: The Camps, Posts, Forts, and Military Towns of the Republic of Texas* (Austin: Encino, 1969).

Thomas W. Cutrer

FORT MCINTOSH. Fort McIntosh, on the Rio Grande near Laredo, was established in the aftermath of the Mexican War[qv] and abandoned after World War II.[qv] American occupation of the former Spanish presidio dates from the arrival in November 1846 of Capt. Mirabeau B. Lamar,[qv] former president of the Republic of Texas,[qv] with the Laredo Guard of the Texas Volunteers. Pursuant to the ratification of the Treaty of Guadalupe Hidalgo,[qv] which terminated the war with Mexico and settled the boundary question in favor of the United States, the government dispatched Lt. Egbert Ludovicus Vielé, subsequent designer of Central Park in New York City, from Ringgold Barracks (*see* FORT RINGGOLD) with a company of the First United States Infantry. On March 3, 1849, the unit reached the banks of the Rio Grande in Webb County, where they set up a camp of tents on a bluff to the west of Laredo. They named the post Camp Crawford, in honor of Secretary of War George W. Crawford. In January 1850 the site became Fort McIntosh, in tribute to Lt. Col. James S. McIntosh, killed three years earlier in the battle of Molino Del Rey.

Fort McIntosh formed a key link in the dual chain of forts that lined the Rio Grande and the western frontier. Its geographical location, intense summer heat, and scarcity of rainfall and tillable soil made the location undesirable, but the post nevertheless provided the area a measure of military and economic security. Comanches and Lipan Apaches harassed the region; the adjacent river ford was popularly known as Indian Crossing. An inspection by Col. J. K. F. Mansfield in 1856 confirmed McIntosh's strategic value, and the temporary removal of the garrison three years later depressed the local economy.

The fort was initially a star-shaped earthwork built by army engineers and troop labor. The Indian problem expanded the normally small garrison at times to over 400 men, including prominent officers Philip H. Sheridan and Randolph B. Marcy and Texas Ranger John S. Ford.[qqv] The outbreak of the Civil War[qv] resulted in Union abandonment and Confederate occupation of the fort. During the war Fort McIntosh sustained several unsuccessful Northern assaults. In 1865 federal soldiers returned and inaugurated a period of stability. Permanent construction began three years later, and within the next decade the installation was greatly enhanced. In 1875, after a series of leases, Laredo ceded to the federal government 208 acres adjoining the considerably larger original site. Barracks and temporary structures were erected during World War II. Infantry, cavalry, field artillery, an engineer squadron, and national guard units operated in turns from the premises.

Black troops garrisoned McIntosh without notable incident in the 1870s, but their return after the Spanish-American War started a racial conflict that presaged later outbursts at Brownsville and Houston. Complaining of police brutality, an undetermined number of soldiers from Company D of the Twenty-fifth Infantry beat and clubbed a peace officer in October 1899. Governor Joseph Sayers[qv] responded to the public outcry by demanding the removal of all black troops from the state. The furor subsided with the arrest of several infantrymen and the growing alarm of the citizenry that Washington might close the post altogether.

The Mexican Revolution[qv] and two world wars prolonged the utility of Fort McIntosh long after transportation improvements rendered the old frontier posts obsolete. The war department discontinued the installation on May 31, 1946, when the Boundary Commission acquired the northern half of the property and the city of Laredo reclaimed the remainder. Laredo Junior College occupies a portion of the latter.

BIBLIOGRAPHY: Garna L. Christian, "The Twenty-fifth Regiment at Fort McIntosh: Precursor to Retaliatory Racial Violence," West Texas Historical Association *Yearbook* 55 (1979). Kathleen Da Camara, *Laredo on the Rio Grande* (San Antonio: Naylor, 1949). Robert W. Frazer, *Forts of the West* (Norman: University of Oklahoma Press, 1965). Jerry Don Thompson, *Sabers on the Rio Grande* (Austin: Presidial, 1974). J. B. Wilkinson, *Laredo and the Rio Grande Frontier* (Austin: Jenkins, 1975).

Garna L. Christian

FORT MANHASSETT. Fort Manhassett was located six miles west of Sabine Pass near State Highway 87 in southeastern Jefferson County. After the battle of Sabine Pass[qv] Confederate authorities feared that another Union invasion force might strike the upper Texas Gulf Coast near Sabine Pass. To block this threat, a series of five earthen redoubts was built on the ridges west of the city, thus preventing either a Union attack on the rear of Fort Griffin or a flanking movement aimed at Beaumont. The defenses were named Fort Manhassett after the Union coal schooner Manhassett, which was beached nearby during a storm on September 29, 1863. Seven companies, commanded by Maj. Felix McReynolds, held Fort Manhassett in October 1863; the force had been reduced to 266 men by January 1, 1864. As late as March 1865 the post still had six heavy guns and two field pieces. Forts Griffin and Manhassett were both abandoned shortly before May 24. Excavations at the latter reveal that the Confederates buried their shells and gunpowder before the evacuation. A plaque now marks the location of the abandoned fort.

BIBLIOGRAPHY: W. T. Block, *A History of Jefferson County, Texas, from Wilderness to Reconstruction* (M.A. thesis, Lamar University, 1974; Nederland, Texas: Nederland Publishing, 1976).

Robert Wooster

FORT MARCY. Fort Marcy, named for William L. Marcy,[qv] secretary of war under President James Buchanan, was probably established when Zachary Taylor[qv] moved United States troops, infantry, dragoons, and artillery to Corpus Christi from St. Joseph's Island on August 15, 1845. The engineers laid out Bay View Cemetery that month, and the first burials were probably those of eight soldiers killed en route from the island to the mainland. Taylor proposed abandoning the Corpus Christi area in February 1846 and began moving his troops to the Rio Grande on March 11. There may have been no other federal troops in the area until June 1849, when part of a company of dragoons was stationed there. A depot for military supplies was set up at Corpus Christi in August 1849; Gen. Persifor Smith^qv moved the army headquarters there in 1853 and may have used the name Fort Marcy. The supply depot was probably abandoned in 1857. Whether or not defense works were ever erected at Corpus Christi is not certain, but in 1863 Confederate troops were reported to be positioned behind Taylor's old earthworks.

BIBLIOGRAPHY: Vertical Files, Barker Texas History Center, University of Texas at Austin.

J. E. Conner

FORT MARTIN SCOTT. On December 5, 1848, Capt. Seth Eastman,^qv commander of Companies D and H, First United States Infantry, established Camp Houston as one of the first United States Army posts on the western frontier of Texas. The post was two miles southeast of Fredericksburg on Barons Creek, a tributary of the Pedernales River. This fort, part of the army's effort to protect Texan settlers and travelers from Indian depredations, served the Fredericksburg–San Antonio road and the local region. Eastman remained in Fredericksburg until February 1849, when he was ordered to move to establish a camp on the Leona River (Fort Inge). Camp Houston, or "the Camp near Fredericksburg," began with two companies, originally both infantry, then alternated between a company of infantry and one of dragoons. The German settlers in Fredericksburg had established a lasting treaty with the local Comanches in 1847; the influx of more settlers into the rich valleys of the Pedernales and its tributaries led to skirmishes but not open warfare.

The Eighth Military Department renamed the camp in December 1849 for Maj. Martin Scott (Fifth United States Infantry), who was killed at the battle of Molina del Rey in 1847. Fort Martin Scott served as a first line of defense, keeping the peace and minimizing possible friction caused by an active trade between the Comanches and German settlers. The soldiers also represented the one constant source of hard cash for businessmen in this rural community. The influx of new settlers, soldiers, and other whites traversing the range led to the brink of open warfare in 1850, when several tribes of Indians met near the San Saba River. Indian agent John Rollins, under escort by Capt. Hamilton W. Merrill^qv and troopers of the Second Dragoons from Fort Martin Scott, met with the Indians. This meeting culminated in the Fort Martin Scott Treaty, which improved the situation enough to prevent open hostilities.

As the settlers pushed farther west, Fort Martin Scott lost any strategic significance it might have had and became economically unjustified and militarily unnecessary because of its distance from the front line of forts. From late 1852 through 1853 the fort assumed the role of forage depot. In his report, filed in the fall of 1853, Col. W. G. Freeman recommended that the fort be closed. Consequently, the Eighth Military Department ordered that Fort Martin Scott close in December 1853.

During the Civil War^qv the fort had no strategic position. Except as a possible site of a Confederate mustering station to serve notice against the populace of Gillespie County who had voted against secession,^qv the Confederate Army did not occupy Fort Martin Scott. In September 1866 Gen. Philip H. Sheridan^qv ordered elements of the Fourth United States Cavalry^qv to Fort Martin Scott to secure the frontier once again from possible Indian depredations. By the end of 1866 the fort was finally abandoned by military units.

Though it held an important position as frontier guardian for only a short time, Fort Martin Scott served the country and state well. Many of its commanders fought in the Civil War, including William R. Montgomery, Eugene B. Beaumont,^qqv William Steele, Edward D. Blake, James Longstreet, and Theodore Fink. The Fredericksburg Heritage Association now leases the land on which Fort Martin Scott was located from the city of Fredericksburg. The association has developed the property as a park and historic site and continues with archeological projects and historic renovations.

BIBLIOGRAPHY: M. L. Crimmins, "The First Line of Army Posts Established in West Texas in 1849," *West Texas Historical Association Year Book* 19 (1943). M. L. Crimmins, "W. G. Freeman's Report on the Eighth Military Department," *Southwestern Historical Quarterly* 51–54 (July 1947–October 1950). Robert W. Frazer, *Forts of the West* (Norman: University of Oklahoma Press, 1965). Robert B. Roberts, *Encyclopedia of Historic Forts: The Military, Pioneer, and Trading Posts of the United States* (New York: Macmillan, 1988). *A Seth Eastman Sketchbook* (Austin: University of Texas Press, 1961). Robert Wooster, "Military Strategy in the Southwest, 1848–1860," *Military History of Texas and the Southwest* 15 (1979).

Paul R. M. Brooks, Jr.

FORT MASON. After the Mexican War^qv and the annexation^qv of Texas by the United States, the population of the state began to increase rapidly, but the increasing numbers were crowded into a limited area because Indians controlled the majority of the state. To open new areas and provide protection for settlers, in 1848 the United States War Department authorized a line of army forts from the Rio Grande to the Red River. Fort Mason's location on Post Oak Hill near Comanche and Centennial creeks in the northern part of what was then called Gillespie County was chosen by Lt. Col. William J. Hardee, assisted by Richard Austin Howard,^qv on July 6, 1851. Hardee left the actual establishment of the post to Bvt. Maj. Hamilton W. Merrill^qv and companies A and B of the Second Dragoons. The post was most likely named either for Lt. George T. Mason, who was killed at Brownsville during the Mexican War, or for Gen. Richard Barnes Mason, who died only a year before the fort was established.

During the next ten years, or until the beginning of the Civil War,^qv the fort played an important part in settlement of the area. Settlers at first stayed close to the fort, but as the aggressive attitude of the military became apparent, additional settlers located farther from the post. The Indians—Kiowas, Lipan Apaches, and Comanches—were driven farther away and began making fewer raids into the settlements. The fort was closed several times during that decade, first in January 1854. It was reoccupied by Company A, First Dragoons, from March to May and was occupied by various companies of the Second United States Cavalry^qv from January 14, 1856, to March 29, 1861, when it passed into the hands of the secessionists. The fort reached its maximum population in January 1856, when the headquarters and companies B, C, D, G, H, and I of the Second Cavalry were all stationed there, with Col. Albert Sidney Johnston^qv in command. Twenty officers stationed at Fort Mason before the Civil War became generals. Twelve fought for the Confederacy, eight for the Union. Among these generals were Earl Van Dorn, Fitzhugh Lee, E. Kirby Smith, George H. Thomas, Robert E. Lee, John Bell Hood,^qqv William J. Hardee, and Philip St. George Cooke. Fort Mason was designated regimental headquarters for the Second Cavalry several times.

For a short period during 1862 the Confederate Army held 215 men prisoner, mostly civilians accused of being Union sympathizers, in the fort. During August 1862 they were marched to Austin. Indian depredations during the Civil War and immediately afterward were worse than they had ever been. The area was terrorized by killings, thefts, and nuisance raids. Texas state troops and minutemen had been unable to cope with the problem. The United States Army, in the form of the Headquarters Company with field staff and officers and the regimental band and Company F of the Fourth United States Cavalry,^qv reoccupied the fort on December 24, 1866. Gen. John Porter Hatch^qv was the commanding officer.

The fort was repaired and improved through the use of civilian artisans and military labor. Reconstruction^qv lawlessness also affected military personnel; a large number of desertions and courts-martial were reported. Cavalry were replaced with soldiers from the Thirty-fifth Infantry over a period of time. The last inspection of the fort occurred on January 13, 1869. The report listed twenty-five buildings, mostly vacant and in need of repair; only sixty-nine men were present. The order to close the fort was carried out on March 23, 1869.

During 1870 the state of Texas organized several companies of frontier forces. Fort Mason was reopened in September of that year as headquarters for Companies A and B, Frontier Forces. Capt. James M. Hunter, later county judge of Mason County, was in command for most of that year. During the next year the forces were disbanded or moved, and for the last time the fort was closed.

Although the fort buildings and land became private property, the rock buildings were gradually dismantled by local citizens. Many early homes in the town of Mason contained material from the fort. In 1975 a local group of citizens began reconstructing one of the officers' quarters at the site. Many people contributed and assisted in the building. Today, this building belongs to the Mason County Historical Society.

BIBLIOGRAPHY: Margaret Bierschwale, *Fort Mason, Texas* (1968). Margaret Bierschwale, "Mason County, Texas, 1845–1870," *Southwestern Historical Quarterly* 52 (April 1949). Kathryn Burford Eilers, A History of Mason County, Texas (M.A. thesis, University of Texas, 1939). Harold B. Simpson, *Cry Comanche: The Second U.S. Cavalry in Texas* (Hillsboro, Texas: Hill Junior College Press, 1979).

Julius E. DeVos

FORT MCKAVETT. Fort McKavett, twenty-two miles southwest of Menard in southwestern Menard County, was established by the United States War Department as Camp San Saba (not to be confused with Camp San Saba in McCulloch County) in March 1852. The camp covered about 2,373 acres near the right bank of the San Saba River. Several infantry companies were stationed there in an effort to protect frontier settlers from Comanche Indians. The post was abandoned in March 1859 but reoccupied in April 1868 under the name Fort McKavett. The new name was probably chosen in honor of Capt. Henry McKavett, who was killed in the battle of Monterrey in 1846 (see MEXICAN WAR).

Much of the post was in ruins when Fort McKavett reopened, and the troops lived in tents for the next year or two while the facilities were rebuilt under the command of Gen. Ranald S. Mackenzie.[qv] The completed fort had four barracks, twelve officers' quarters, a magazine, a hospital, a guardhouse, a bakery, two storehouses, a post office, three stables, a headquarters building, a forage house, and a thirty-acre garden. Supplies for the fort were hauled by wagon from San Antonio. After the second battle of Adobe Walls[qv] in 1874, the Indians presented little threat to settlers, and the military presence at Fort McKavett was no longer essential. The fort was closed on June 30, 1883. Most of the buildings either were used by townspeople for other purposes or fell into ruin. Fort McKavett State Historical Park[qv] opened in 1968, and many of the buildings were acquired by the state and restored.

BIBLIOGRAPHY: M. L. Crimmins, "Fort McKavett, Texas," *Southwestern Historical Quarterly* 38 (July 1934). Menard County Historical Society, *Menard County History—An Anthology* (San Angelo: Anchor, 1982). Vertical Files, Barker Texas History Center, University of Texas at Austin.

Vivian Elizabeth Smyrl

FORT MCKAVETT, TEXAS. Fort McKavett, is at the intersection of Farm roads 864 and 1674, twenty miles southwest of Menard in southwestern Menard County. It began in the 1850s as a community of civilians associated with a military post then known as Camp San Saba (not to be confused with Camp San Saba in McCulloch County). The civilian community, at a site about a mile north of the post, was supposed to be named Lehnesburg, in honor of a German merchant, but it was called Scabtown instead. When Camp San Saba closed in 1859, some civilians chose to remain, but most withdrew to more protected areas. After the military reactivated the post as Fort McKavett in 1868, the civilian community began to grow again and adopted the less obnoxious name of the new post. By 1880 the town had a school, a church, and a variety of shops. In 1883 the closing of the fort hurt the Fort McKavett community economically, but because residents no longer had to fear for their safety in the absence of troops, they did not scatter as they had when Camp San Saba closed. By the mid-1890s the community had three churches, two hotels, a broom and mattress factory, a weekly newspaper, and eighty residents. The Fort McKavett school had twenty-eight students and two teachers in 1904; it was later consolidated with the Menard Independent School District. The population of Fort McKavett was estimated at 150 in the late 1920s; the number of residents fell to 136 in the early 1930s and remained at that level through the mid-1960s. The population was reported at 103 in the 1970s and at forty-five in 1990. Efforts to restore the old military post at Fort McKavett began in the late 1960s, and the site became Fort McKavett State Historical Park.[qv]

BIBLIOGRAPHY: Menard County Historical Society, *Menard County History—An Anthology* (San Angelo: Anchor, 1982). Vertical Files, Barker Texas History Center, University of Texas at Austin.

Vivian Elizabeth Smyrl

FORT MCKAVETT STATE HISTORICAL PARK. Fort McKavett State Historical Park is twenty-two miles southwest of Menard in southwestern Menard County. It is the site of Fort McKavett, a military post built in 1852 as Camp San Saba (not to be confused with Camp San Saba in McCulloch County). The post closed in 1859 but reopened in 1868 as Fort McKavett. It was named in honor of Capt. Henry McKavett, who was killed at the Mexican War[qv] battle of Monterrey. The fort was abandoned in 1883 after the threat of Indian attacks had diminished, and the buildings either fell into disrepair or were purchased by area residents. The state of Texas acquired the old school and one of the barracks in 1968 and placed them under the control of the Texas Parks and Wildlife Department.[qv] The restoration project continued as more former building sites came under state control; by 1990 seventeen buildings had been restored. Fort McKavett State Historical Park covers about eighty-two acres. It is a day-use park and has picnic facilities and a visitor center. In 1993, because of budget cuts, the park was taken over by a nonprofit firm, Texas Rural Communities, Incorporated.

BIBLIOGRAPHY: Vertical Files, Barker Texas History Center, University of Texas at Austin.

Vivian Elizabeth Smyrl

FORT MERRILL. Fort Merrill, located on the right bank of the Nueces River where the Corpus Christi to San Antonio road crossed the river, fifty miles above its mouth, was founded on March 1, 1850, by Capt. Samuel M. Plummer and companies H and K of the First United States Infantry. Lumber and logs used in the construction of the fort were shipped in from New Orleans, and the soldiers of the garrison erected the buildings. The fort probably was named in honor of Capt. Moses E. Merrill, who was killed in the Mexican War[qv] battle of Molino del Rey on September 8, 1847. Companies I and E of the Rifle Regiment were the regular garrison until April 26, 1853, when they were transferred to Fort Ewell,[qv] leaving only two noncommissioned officers and thirteen men at Fort Merrill. After 1853 the fort was garrisoned only intermittently. When W. G. Freeman inspected it on June 21, 1853, Lt. Alexander McRae was in command, but the garrison was so small that it could do no more than night sentinel duty. The fort was abandoned on December 1, 1855. Fort Merrill is off U.S. Highway 281, three miles northwest of Dinero in Live Oak County.

BIBLIOGRAPHY: M. L. Crimmins, "W. G. Freeman's Report on the Eighth Military Department," *Southwestern Historical Quarterly* 51–54 (July 1947– October 1950). Robert W. Frazer, *Forts of the West* (Norman: University of Oklahoma Press, 1965). Francis Paul Prucha, *A Guide to the Military Posts of the United States, 1789–1895* (Madison: State Historical Association of Wisconsin, 1964). Robert Wooster, *Soldiers, Sutlers and Settlers: Garrison Life of the Texas Frontier* (College Station: Texas A&M University Press, 1987).

Thomas W. Cutrer

FORT MILAM. The first Fort Milam, on the west bank of the Brazos River in central Falls County, was built in 1834 and called Fort Viesca. In December 1835 it was renamed in honor of Benjamin R. Milam,qv who had died at the siege of Bexarqv earlier that month. The fort was built for the protection of the settlers of the Robertson's colonyqv community of Sarahville de Viesca at the falls of the Brazos. It was abandoned during the Runaway Scrapeqv in March 1836. As settlers began to return to the area in the spring, however, Col. Edward Burlesonqv organized three ranger companies to garrison the fort and provide protection to that exposed region. Burleson's volunteers were replaced on the Brazos frontier in the fall by Col. Robert M. Coleman'sqv rangers, and Capt. Thomas H. Barron'sqv company of Coleman's battalion took up garrison duty at Fort Milam on October 1. Barron was relieved by Capt. Daniel Monroe in January 1837. From Fort Milam detachments were sent to construct Little River Fortqv in 1836 and forts Fisher and Hendersonqqv in 1837. Ranger enlistments began to expire during the late summer of 1837; the Fort Milam garrison, once again under Barron's command, began to evaporate, and the fort soon stood vacant. Its site is now marked only by a stone monument four miles southwest of Marlin.

BIBLIOGRAPHY: George B. Erath, "The Memoirs of George B. Erath, 1813–1891," *Southwestern Historical Quarterly* 26-27 (January–October 1923; rpts., Austin: Texas State Historical Association, 1923; Waco: Heritage Society of Waco, 1956). Charles Adams Gulick, Jr., Harriet Smither, et al., eds., *The Papers of Mirabeau Buonaparte Lamar*, Vols. 2 and 4. Adele B. Looscan, "Capt. Joseph Daniels," *Quarterly of the Texas State Historical Association* 5 (July 1901). Gerald S. Pierce, *Texas Under Arms: The Camps, Posts, Forts, and Military Towns of the Republic of Texas* (Austin: Encino, 1969). Lillian S. St. Romain, *Western Falls County, Texas* (Austin: Texas State Historical Association, 1951). George Tyler, *History of Bell County* (San Antonio: Naylor, 1936).
Thomas W. Cutrer

FORT MILAM. A second Fort Milam, later known as Fort Burleson, was constructed in January and February of 1839 on the east bank of the Brazos near the home of John Marlin, a few miles east of the old Fort Milam and two miles south of the site of present Marlin in Falls County. The new fort was a response to a devastating Indian attack that winter. It was built and temporarily garrisoned by Capt. Joseph Daniels'sqv Milam Guardsqv company from Houston, "150 feet square, built of Cedar pickets doubl[e] banked, eleven feet high with bastions at each angle." Daniels's men departed in mid-February, and Lt. William G. Evans marched thirty-four Houston volunteers—the Travis Spies—into the fort on April 3; in the Austin colony Capt. John Birdqv raised an additional company that arrived at Fort Milam on May 6. These two companies remained through the spring and summer. At their discharge the government planned to garrison the fort with regulars from the First Infantry. On August 26, 1839, Lt. Col. William S. Fisherqv ordered the name of the post changed to Fort Burleson, in honor of Edward Burleson,qv commander of the Army of the Republic of Texas,qv and from that time until late in the spring of 1840 the fort was manned by Company D of the regulars, commanded first by Capt. George T. Howardqv and later by Capt. John Holliday. The company was moved to Camp Chambers that spring, however. The fort passed into private hands and was maintained by local citizens until danger of Indian attack had passed.

BIBLIOGRAPHY: Charles Adams Gulick, Jr., Harriet Smither, et al., eds., *The Papers of Mirabeau Buonaparte Lamar*, Vols. 2 and 4. Adele B. Looscan, "Capt. Joseph Daniels," *Quarterly of the Texas State Historical Association* 5 (July 1901). Gerald S. Pierce, *Texas Under Arms: The Camps, Posts, Forts, and Military Towns of the Republic of Texas* (Austin: Encino, 1969). George Tyler, *History of Bell County* (San Antonio: Naylor, 1936).
Thomas W. Cutrer

FORT MOORE. Fort Moore, a Confederate installation at Eagle Grove on Galveston Island, Galveston County, was established soon after the battle of Galvestonqv on January 1, 1863. It was an earthen fortification defended by two thirty-two-pound smoothbores and two eighteen-pound howitzers. The fort was dismantled after the city surrendered to federal troops on June 19, 1865.

BIBLIOGRAPHY: Bill Winsor, *Texas in the Confederacy* (Hillsboro, Texas: Hill Junior College Press, 1978).
Maury Darst

FORT MORITAS. Fort Moritas or El Morita, near the site of Shafter in Presidio County, was a private fortress built by Milton Faverqv in the 1850s for protection of his ranch against depredations by Apache Indians. After 1865 the quadrangular adobeqv structure was captured by Apaches and its inhabitants killed or taken captive. In the late 1940s all that was left was a one-room adobe house and the walls of a small stone house.

BIBLIOGRAPHY: Leavitt Corning, Jr., *Baronial Forts of the Big Bend* (Austin: Trinity University Press, 1967). Evelyn Davis and Thomas Clement, *Spirit of the Big Bend* (San Antonio: Naylor, 1948). Harold Schoen, comp., *Monuments Erected by the State of Texas to Commemorate the Centenary of Texas Independence* (Austin: Commission of Control for Texas Centennial Celebrations, 1938).

FORT OLDHAM. Fort Oldham, a mile east of Farm Road 1362 in central Burleson County, was a private fort and stopping place on the Independence–Tenoxtitlán road during the Republic of Texas.qv It was located on land belonging to Maj. William Oldham,qv who purchased it from Hendrick Arnoldqv in September 1837. Fort Oldham was probably a fortified house built by Major Oldham on his property. Settlers in the area took refuge there during Indian alarms around 1837–38, but no record survives of the fort's actually having been attacked. By July 1838 a post office was operating at the site, and in 1841 Fort Oldham was a station on post office route 22 (the route connecting Independence and Franklin via Mound Prairie, Fort Oldham, Tenoxtitlán, and Nashville). The site is on land still owned by black descendants of Major Oldham.

BIBLIOGRAPHY: Malcolm H. Addison, *Reminiscences of Burleson County, Texas* (Caldwell, Texas, 1886; rpt., Caldwell: Caldwell Printing, 1971). Burleson County Historical Society, *Astride the Old San Antonio Road: A History of Burleson County, Texas* (Dallas: Taylor, 1980). Gerald S. Pierce, *Texas Under Arms: The Camps, Posts, Forts, and Military Towns of the Republic of Texas* (Austin: Encino, 1969).
Catherine G. Alford

FORT OLDHAM, TEXAS. Fort Oldham was a community in Washington County during the Republic of Texasqv era. Its post office was established on January 24, 1838, with Claiborne Fitch as postmaster. Fitch served until the post office was closed on January 11, 1842. The settlement disappeared soon afterwards and left no trace.

BIBLIOGRAPHY: Ed Ellsworth Bartholomew, *The Encyclopedia of Texas Ghost Towns* (Fort Davis, Texas, 1982). James M. Day, comp., *Post Office Papers of the Republic of Texas* (2 vols., Austin: Texas State Library, 1966–67).
Carole E. Christian

FORT PARKER. Fort Parker was a private fort built by Silas M. and James W. Parkerqqv near the headwaters of the Navasota River in Limestone County, between old Springfield and the present site of Groesbeck, in 1834 or 1835. It may have also been known as Fort Sterling. Cabins were built at the fort to be occupied by nearby families in case of Indian attack. The outer walls of the cabins were part of a surrounding stockade perforated with loopholes for defense. On May 19, 1836, the fort was attacked by 500 to 700 Caddo and Comanche Indians. Silas was killed, and his nine-year-old daughter, Cynthia Ann, and six-year-old son, John, Mrs. Rachel Plummerqv and her son James, and Mrs. Elizabeth Kellogg were captured by the Indians. A replica of the fort was erected at Fort Parker State Recreation Area,qv eight miles southwest of Mexia on State Highway 14 in Limestone County.

See also PARKER, CYNTHIA ANN, *and* PARKER, JOHN.

BIBLIOGRAPHY: James T. DeShields, *Border Wars of Texas*, ed. Matt Bradley (Tioga, Texas, 1912; rpt., Waco: Texian Press, 1976). Joseph Carroll McConnell, *West Texas Frontier* (Vol. 1, Jacksboro, Texas, 1933; Vol. 2, Palo Pinto, Texas, 1939). Ray Miller, *Ray Miller's Texas Forts* (Houston: Cordovan, 1985).

Art Leatherwood

FORT PARKER STATE RECREATION AREA. Fort Parker State Recreation Area is off State Highway 14 six miles south of Mexia in Limestone County. The 1,458.78-acre park, named for the nearby stockade of the Parker family built in 1834 (*see* FORT PARKER), features a 750-acre lake on the Navasota River. The land was donated to the state by the city of Mexia and three individual property owners in 1935 and 1936. The Civilian Conservation Corpsqv constructed the dam for the lake and the park's other structures during the mid-1930s. The heavily wooded area is home to a variety of wildlife, ranging from raccoons and opossums to great blue herons and great egrets. Facilities include a hiking trail, a dining hall, camping and picnicking areas, and playgrounds.

BIBLIOGRAPHY: Ray Miller, *Texas Parks* (Houston: Cordovan, 1984).

Christopher Long

FORT PHANTOM HILL. Fort Phantom Hill was one of the second line of forts laid out in the early 1850s to protect the westward-moving frontier of Texas settlement. In 1849 the federal government sent Capt. Randolph B. Marcyqv to explore and mark the best route through the Comanchería, the vast region to the north and west of Austin inhabited by the warlike Comanche Indians. This was meant to give safer passage to immigrants headed for the California gold fields. The advanced cordon of forts, including Fort Phantom Hill, was established as a result of Marcy's recommendations.

Acting on orders from Gen. Persifor F. Smith,qv Lt. Col. John J. Abercrombie arrived at the Clear Fork of the Brazos in the area of present Jones County with five companies of the Fifth Infantry on November 14, 1851. Smith had recently taken command of the newly organized Texas (Eighth Military) Department from the ailing Gen. William G. Belknap,qv who had been supervising construction of the fort on the upper Brazos that was named for him. Originally, Belknap's orders had been to build a second fort on Pecan Bayou, at a site now in Coleman County. Smith, who was unfamiliar with this area, changed the locale to the Clear Fork near its junction with Elm Creek.

This unreasoned alteration affected the post's future, for the lack of an adequate water supply and the scarcity of building timbers added greatly to the hardships of the garrison. Though Lt. Clinton W. Lear, writing to his wife at Fort Washita, deemed the Clear Fork valley beautiful and abundant with game, he felt that it was never intended "for white man to occupy such a barren waste." Nevertheless, the troops dutifully began work on the new fort. A suitable stone quarry was located on Elm Creek about two miles south. Blackjack oak logs for the officers' quarters and hospital had to be brought in by ox wagon from as far away as forty miles. The company quarters and other buildings were of jacal construction. All of the buildings had stone chimneys, but only the magazine, guardhouse, and commissary storehouse were built entirely of stone.

Oddly enough, Fort Phantom Hill was never officially named; military records usually refer to it as the "Post on the Clear Fork of the Brazos." Although there are several legends about the origin of the unofficial designation Phantom Hill, the name probably derives from the fact that from a distance the hill on which it was built rises sharply from the plains but seems to level out as it is approached, vanishing like a phantom.

Life at the fort was difficult. Elm Creek was often dry, and the waters of the Clear Fork were brackish. At one time an eighty-foot-deep, walk-in well was dug near the guardhouse, but even it was not always reliable. More often than not, it was necessary to haul barrels of water in wagons from a spring about four miles upriver from the post.

Although the isolated fort was vulnerable to attacks, its garrison had only peaceful encounters with the Indians. Certainly, it would have been a tactical blunder to match infantry against the Comanche horsemen of the plains. A band of Penateka Comanches led by Buffalo Humpqv occasionally came calling, as did groups of Lipans, Wichitas, Kiowas, and Kickapoos. Mrs. Emma Johnson Elkins, who as a child lived with her parents at the fort, recalled a ritual held by a group of friendly Delawares in preparation for a hunt. Jim Shawqv and Black Beaver were among the noted Delaware scouts employed by the garrison as interpreters and guides.

Colonel Abercrombie turned command of the post over to Lt. Col. Carlos A. Waiteqv on April 27, 1852. In turn, Waite was succeeded by Maj. Henry H. Sibleyqv on September 24, 1853. By this time four of the five companies had been withdrawn, and the remaining company was reinforced by Company I of the Second Dragoons. Lt. Newton C. Givensqv assumed command of the post on March 26, 1854, and was commander at the time it was first abandoned twelve days later, on April 6.

The decline in rank of its commanders shows the fort's decline in importance. Its initial occupation had been relatively uneventful. At the time of its evacuation, the purpose of curbing the Indian menace had momentarily been attained by the establishment of the reservations on the upper Brazos and the Clear Fork to the northeast near Fort Belknap. Shortly after the soldiers left Phantom Hill, the fort buildings mysteriously burned to the ground, an event variously attributed to everyone from an irate officer's wife to Indians and later to Union sympathizers. The scanty evidence points inconclusively to members of the departing garrison as the arsonists.

In 1858 the remaining structures of the fort were repaired and utilized as Way Station Number 54 by the Southern Overland (Butterfieldqv) Mail. The station was managed by a man named Burlington, whose wife prepared meals for the stage passengers. Most travelers agreed with New York Herald correspondent Waterman L. Ormsby that Phantom Hill was "the cheapest and best new station on the route." During the Civil War,qv when the frontier was patrolled by Ranger companies and subsequently by the Frontier Battalion,qv Col. James B. (Buck) Barryqv or some of the units under his command used Fort Phantom Hill as a base of field operations. Beginning in 1871, the post served as a subpost of Fort Griffin, near the site of present Albany. Gen. William T. Shermanqv made an overnight stop here during his inspection tour of the Department of Texas. Capt. Theodore Schwan led one column of Col. Ranald S. Mackenzie'sqv raiders from the post in the first series of Indian campaigns into West Texas between January and March 1872.

After the Indian wars subsided, a town grew up around the fort ruins. In 1876–77, it was a buying and shipping point for buffaloqv hides taken during the slaughter of the Southern Plains herds. By 1880 the community had a population of 546; it was made Jones county seat in May 1881 but lost that distinction to Anson on November 14, 1881, thirty years after the establishment of the post. The Texas and Pacific Railway routed its tracks through Abilene, fourteen miles to the south. A letter written to the San Antonio Express in 1892 commented that Fort Phantom contained nothing but "one hotel, one saloon, one general store, one blacksmith shop, and 10,000 prairie dogs."

Fort Phantom Hill is on private land. The owners have improved the fort and made it available to the public. At the site, three stone buildings and more than a dozen chimneys and foundations remain. Only two miles south of the fort is a manmade reservoir, Fort Phantom Hill Reservoir,qv which supplies the water for about 100,000 people in Taylor and Jones counties. The remains of Fort Phantom

Hill have been celebrated in verse by the cowboy poet William L. Chittenden^qv and in the prose of other western writers.

BIBLIOGRAPHY: H. Allen Anderson, "Fort Phantom Hill: Outpost on the Clear Fork of the Brazos," *Museum Journal* 16 (1976). Robert G. Carter, *On the Border with Mackenzie, or Winning West Texas from the Comanches* (Washington: Eynon Printing, 1935). William Lawrence Chittenden, *Ranch Verses* (New York: Putnam, 1893; 16th ed. 1925). A. C. Greene, *A Personal Country* (New York: Knopf, 1969). Waterman L. Ormsby, *The Butterfield Overland Mail* (San Marino, California: Huntington Library, 1942; rpt. 1955). Rupert N. Richardson, *The Frontier of Northwest Texas, 1846 to 1876* (Glendale, California: Clark, 1963). Ernest Wallace, ed., *Ranald S. Mackenzie's Official Correspondence Relating to Texas* (2 vols., Lubbock: West Texas Museum Association, 1967, 1968).
H. Allen Anderson

FORT PHANTOM HILL RESERVOIR. Fort Phantom Hill Reservoir (Lake Fort Phantom Hill) is between Farm roads 600 and 2833 five miles south of Nugent in the extreme southeast corner of Jones County (at 32°37′ N, 99°40′ W). The lake, impounded by a dam on Elm Creek, a tributary of the Clear Fork of the Brazos River, covers a surface area of 4,246 acres and provides a storage capacity of 74,310 acre-feet. The reservoir's drainage basin of about 470 square miles is bordered on the north by a rolled-earth dam 3,700 feet long and seventy feet high. The city of Abilene owns and operates the lake for municipal and recreational purposes. Construction began in June 1937 and was finished in October 1938. Since that time Abilene has developed parks on the lake and has diverted water from the Clear Fork and Deadman Creek to the lake in order to meet the needs of the area's growing population. In July 1974 West Texas Utility Company began operating a power plant on the reservoir.

BIBLIOGRAPHY: U.S. Geological Survey, *Water Resources Data: Texas, Water Year 1983* (3 vols., Washington: GPO, 1984).
Connie Ricci

FORT PICKETVILLE, TEXAS. Fort Picketville, also called Picketville, was founded about 1854 on Gunsolus (now Gonzales) Creek, about two miles north of the site of what is now Breckenridge in northeastern Stephens County. The settlement was used by area pioneers during the 1850s and 1860s for collective defense against Indian raids. Picketville was named either for area rancher Bill Picket or for the fact that houses in the community were built from picket posts. The town served as the first county seat, from 1858 to 1864. During its short existence and in spite of substantial Indian activity, the town maintained a school and was the community center for the surrounding region. After Breckenridge was established as county seat in the 1870s, Fort Picketville was abandoned.

BIBLIOGRAPHY: Betty E. Hanna, *Doodle Bugs and Cactus Berries: A Historical Sketch of Stephens County* (Quanah, Texas: Nortex, 1975). Loy W. Hartsfield, A History of Stephens County (M.A. thesis, University of Texas, 1929).
Charles G. Davis

FORT POLK. In 1840 the government of the Republic of Texas^qv debated the construction of a fort on the north end of Brazos Island in what is now Cameron County, six miles north of the Rio Grande at Brazos Santiago Pass. This installation would not only have controlled navigation through the vital pass between Padre and Brazos islands, but would also have established a Texas military presence in the disputed territory below the Nueces River. Since the site lay 120 miles to the south of the nearest white Texan settlement, however, only nominally in Texas territory and on the site of Brazos de Santiago, a customhouse and outpost of the Mexican army, the planned fort never materialized. But in 1846, with the heightening of international tension after the annexation^qv of Texas to the United States, Maj. Gen. Zachary Taylor's^qv army of observation marched to the Rio Grande and established itself opposite Matamoros, from where it drove the Mexican garrison at Brazos Santiago back across the Rio Grande while converting the Mexican installation to an arsenal. On March 6 Taylor's men established a military depot near the Brazos Santiago arsenal and named it Fort Polk, in honor of the president of the United States. The fort was also known as Fort Brazos Santiago. Fort Polk was garrisoned from 1848 until 1850 by Capt. F. C. Hunt's company of the Fourth United States Artillery regiment. By January 1849, however, the buildings were being moved to different locations on the Rio Grande, and on February 9, 1850, the post was abandoned. The location was used as a transit depot for materials for Fort Brown in 1852, and on February 21, 1861, at the outbreak of the Civil War,^qv it was seized by a Confederate artillery company from Galveston. Long afterward, the United States Army Corps of Engineers straightened the channel and installed jetties in the pass, obliterating the site of both the Mexican fort at Brazos Santiago and Fort Polk.

BIBLIOGRAPHY: K. Jack Bauer, *The Mexican War, 1846–1848* (New York: Macmillan, 1974). Gerald S. Pierce, *Texas Under Arms: The Camps, Posts, Forts, and Military Towns of the Republic of Texas* (Austin: Encino, 1969).
Thomas W. Cutrer

FORT PRAIRIE, TEXAS. Fort Prairie was five miles east of Austin near the Missouri, Kansas and Texas Railroad in Travis County. It formed in the 1880s. A post office called John, for John Grove, the first postmaster, was established at Fort Prairie in 1895; it was discontinued in 1901. The community reported a population of 102 in 1904 and ten in 1910. In the early 1930s Fort Prairie reported having two businesses.

BIBLIOGRAPHY: John J. Germann and Myron Janzen, *Texas Post Offices by County* (1986).
Vivian Elizabeth Smyrl

FORT QUITMAN. Fort Quitman was eighty miles below El Paso and twenty miles southeast of the site of present-day McNary in far southern Hudspeth County. On September 28, 1858, Capt. Arthur T. Lee^qv and companies C and H, Eighth Infantry, established the post on a barren and sandy plain 400 yards east of the Rio Grande to protect travelers and mail along the route from San Antonio to El Paso. It was named for Mexican War^qv general John A. Quitman,^qv who had died on July 17. Federal troops evacuated Fort Quitman on April 5, 1861. During the Civil War^qv the post was intermittently garrisoned by Confederate and Union detachments and quickly fell into disrepair. Capt. Henry Carroll and Company F, Ninth United States Cavalry,^qv reoccupied the crumbling adobe buildings on January 1, 1868, and on February 25 orders from headquarters of the District of Texas reestablished the fort. Over the next decade companies and detachments of black soldiers of the Ninth Cavalry and the Twenty-fifth United States Infantry^qv guarded the mails and scouted for hostile Indians.

Fort Quitman had a reputation as one of the most uncomfortable military installations in Texas. Lydia Spencer Lane described it in 1869 as "forlorn and tumble-down" and was surprised to observe a sergeant, in full-dress uniform, jumping rope outside the guardhouse. "If any one at Quitman could feel cheerful enough to enjoy so innocent a pastime," she concluded, "he was to be congratulated." Surgeon John J. Culver was more blunt in his assessment of conditions at Fort Quitman (1870), which he found "entirely unworthy of the name of fort, post, or station for United States troops." The adobe^qv buildings had been stripped of all wood, including roofs, doors, and window frames. "The dormitories of the barracks," he sarcastically commented, "having neither doors or windows, have abundant ventilation." The sandy soil and dry hot climate frustrated attempts to cultivate a post garden. Consequently, milk and fresh vegetables had to be hauled in at exorbitant prices from San Elizario, El Paso, or San Ignacio, Chihuahua. Soldiers at Fort Quitman spent considerable time repairing the buildings, which by 1876 consisted of barracks for two companies, five sets of double officers' quarters, an adjutant's office, a hospital, a guardhouse, two storehouses, a bakery, workshops, and wooden cavalry and quartermaster's stables.

Fort Quitman was vacated on January 5, 1877, but was regarrisoned in 1880–82, during the campaign against the Apache chief Victorio,^{qv} as a subpost of Fort Davis. Despite the efforts of Capt. Nicholas Nolan and troopers of the Tenth United States Cavalry,^{qv} during the summer of 1880 Victorio's warriors crossed and recrossed the Rio Grande in the vicinity of the post. Also, on August 9, Mescaleros attempting to return to their reservation in New Mexico attacked a stagecoach near the fort, mortally wounding Maj. Gen. James J. Byrne,^{qv} an employee of the Texas and Pacific Railway. Although Victorio was killed in Mexico in the fall of 1880, Fort Quitman continued to be garrisoned through April 1882. The post was abandoned later that year, partly because it was not on a railroad. Fort Hancock (originally Fort Rice) was established in 1882 at a better site nearby. Today only a cemetery remains near the site of Fort Quitman.

BIBLIOGRAPHY: James C. Cage and Tommy Powell, *Fort Quitman* (McNary, Texas, 1972). John J. Culver and D. Hershey, "Fort Quitman, Texas," in *A Report on the Hygiene of the United States Army, with Descriptions of Military Posts* (Washington: GPO, 1875). Robert W. Frazer, *Forts of the West* (Norman: University of Oklahoma Press, 1965). Herbert M. Hart, *Old Forts of the Southwest* (Seattle, Washington: Superior, 1964). George Ruhlen, "Quitman's Owners: A Sidelight on Frontier Reality," *Password*, April 1960. George Ruhlen, "Quitman: 'The Worst Post at Which I Ever Served'," *Password*, Fall 1966.
Bruce J. Dinges

FORT QUITMAN, TEXAS. The Fort Quitman community was on Farm Road 192 some sixteen miles southwest of Sierra Blanca in southwestern Hudspeth County. It grew up around the military installation of the same name, which was established in 1858 to protect travelers on the San Antonio–San Diego Mail Route^{qv} from the Mescalero Apaches. A local post office opened in 1868 with Veronica Stovall as postmistress and closed in 1876. The fort was permanently abandoned in the spring of 1881, after the death of the Mescalero chief Victorio.^{qv} A second post office operated four miles south of the ruins of the fort from 1926 until either 1937 or the late 1940s. In 1940 the residents of Fort Quitman numbered less than twenty-five, and by the mid-1950s the town was no longer shown on maps of the area.
Martin Donell Kohout

FORT RAMÍREZ. Fort Ramírez was a fortified ranchhouse built by the Ramírez family on the west bank of the Nueces River in southern Live Oak County. The building was never a fort, but it was the first permanent structure in Live Oak County. The Ramirez family left the area in 1813. Local legends of buried treasure nearby resulted in destruction of the house.

BIBLIOGRAPHY: J. Frank Dobie, *Coronado's Children: Tales of Lost Mines and Buried Treasures of the Southwest* (New York: Garden City, 1930). J. Frank Dobie, *Some Part of Myself* (Austin: University of Texas Press, 1967). Ray Miller, *Ray Miller's Texas Forts* (Houston: Cordovan, 1985).
Art Leatherwood

FORT RICHARDSON. Fort Richardson was officially established in February 1868 in order to provide protection against marauding bands of Comanche and Kiowa Indians on the North Texas frontier and named for Union general Israel Bush (Fighting Dick) Richardson. The unstockaded reservation occupied some 300 acres on Lost Creek, a tributary of the Trinity River, one-half mile south of Jacksboro, in Jack County. Eventually fifty-five stone, picket, and cottonwood-lumber buildings were constructed at an estimated cost to the government of $800,000. Located seventy miles from the Indian Territory and 120 miles from Fort Sill, Richardson was the northernmost army outpost in Texas and the anchor of a defensive line of fortifications that included forts Griffin and Concho. For a brief period from 1868 to 1873 Richardson was strategically the most important post in Texas, and in 1872 it had the largest garrison (666 officers and men) among military installations in the United States.

During its ten-year history the fort served as the regimental headquarters for the Sixth United States Cavalry (1868–71), the Fourth United States Cavalry^{qv} (1871–73), and the Eleventh Infantry (1873–76), as well as home for various elements of the Tenth United States Cavalry^{qv} and Twenty-fourth United States Infantry.^{qv} The soldiers of Richardson maintained the post, helped local law officers keep the peace, pursued criminals and deserters, escorted wagon trains, oversaw elections, protected cattle herds, and, most importantly, patrolled for Indians. During the prime raiding months of April through September, scouting parties were in the field constantly. Although most of these excursions were fruitless, occasionally the soldiers had bloody encounters with bands of hostile Indians; in July 1879, for instance, Capt. Curwin B. McClellan and fifty-six officers and men of the Sixth Cavalry were ambushed near the Little Wichita River by some 250 Kiowas and Comanches led by the Kiowa chief Kicking Bird.^{qv} After a desperate fight McClellan and his men were able to hold off the Indians and retreat to safety. Thirteen men of the Sixth won the Medal of Honor for gallantry in action in the battle of the Little Wichita.

In May of 1871 Gen. William T. Sherman^{qv} visited Fort Richardson as part of a fact-finding tour of the Texas frontier. While there, he received word that a freight-hauling wagon train had been attacked by a large party of Indians on the Salt Creek Prairie twenty miles from the fort (*see* WARREN WAGON TRAIN RAID). At Fort Sill, Sherman personally arrested the ringleaders of the raid and ordered them taken to Jacksboro to stand trial. The Kiowa chiefs Satanta and Big Tree^{qqv} were held in custody at Fort Richardson and in July 1871 had the dubious honor of becoming the first Indians to be tried in a Texas civil court. After sensational hearings that received nationwide publicity, the chiefs were found guilty of murder and sentenced to hang.

In response to these events, General Sherman authorized Fort Richardson's commanding officer, Col. Ranald S. Mackenzie,^{qv} Fourth Cavalry, to begin offensive operations against any Indians not on the reservation. Over a fifteen-month period Mackenzie led four major expeditions from Richardson into the Panhandle^{qv} of Texas. In late 1871 he fought a running battle with the Quahadi Comanches, led by their famous war chief, Quanah Parker.^{qv} In the summer of 1872 Mackenzie explored the unmapped Llano Estacado,^{qv} and late that year, on the North Fork of the Red River, he located and attacked the encampment of the Comanche chief Mow-way,^{qv} killing fifty warriors and capturing 130 women and children.

During the Red River War^{qv} (1874–75) Fort Richardson served as a major staging base for the columns of cavalry and infantry that swept the plains and inflicted final military defeat on the Comanche and Kiowa Indians. With the North Texas frontier secure, there was no longer any need for a military presence in Jack County, and in May 1878 the army abandoned the post. Most of the buildings quickly fell into ruins, but the city of Jacksboro maintained some of them, especially the hospital and one of the officers' quarters. In 1963 Fort Richardson was declared a national historic landmark, and in 1968 the Texas Parks and Wildlife Department^{qv} assumed control of the grounds and began extensive renovations. Fort Richardson State Historic Park^{qv} opened in 1973.

BIBLIOGRAPHY: William Weatherford Dennis, *Fort Richardson, Texas (1867–1878) and the Mackenzie Trail* (Jacksboro, Texas, 1964). Orion Knox, et al., *Preservation Plan and Program for Fort Richardson State Historical Park* (Austin: Texas Parks and Wildlife Department, 1975). Ernest Wallace, *Ranald S. Mackenzie on the Texas Frontier* (Lubbock: West Texas Museum Association, 1964).
Allen Lee Hamilton

FORT RICHARDSON SPRINGS. The Fort Richardson Springs are a group of strongly flowing freshwater springs on Lost Creek near Jacksboro in Jack County (at 33°12′ N, 98°10′ W). The springs flow from cavities in the Cisco limestone at an elevation of 1,082 feet above sea level. They provided water for the fort that was at a site nearby from 1866 to 1878. Individual springs in this group are called Murphy, Rumbling, McConnell, Stone, and Dennis. On May 11, 1979, the combined flow from the springs was more than eleven gallons per second. In recent years the water has occasionally become contaminated from human activities in the area.

BIBLIOGRAPHY: Gunnar Brune, *Springs of Texas*, Vol. 1 (Fort Worth: Branch–Smith, 1981). *Gunnar Brune*

FORT RICHARDSON STATE HISTORICAL PARK. Fort Richardson State Historical Park is off U.S. Highway 281 a half mile south of Jacksboro in Jack County. The 396.1-acre park was the site of Fort Richardson, a United States Army installation built in 1867 in an attempt to pacify the Indians on the Western frontier. After the army abandoned the facility in 1878 the buildings were left to the elements, and many of the structures collapsed. The city of Jacksboro acquired title to the fort and deeded it to the Texas Parks and Wildlife Department[qv] in 1968. The department purchased the adjoining 347 acres in 1970 and 1974. The fort hospital now serves as a museum; it and several other buildings have been restored. The ruins of many of other structures can also be seen. Facilities include a hiking trail, camping and picnicking areas, and restrooms.

BIBLIOGRAPHY: Ray Miller, *Texas Parks* (Houston: Cordovan, 1984). *Christopher Long*

FORT RINGGOLD. Fort Ringgold, the southernmost installation of the western tier of forts constructed at the end of the Mexican War,[qv] stood guard for nearly a century over the Rio Grande and Rio Grande City. On October 26, 1848, Bvt. Maj. Joseph H. LaMotte led two companies of the First United States Infantry to Davis Landing, near the newly established Rio Grande City in Starr County. The army leased thirty-three acres from Henry Clay Davis, the town founder, whose heirs sold 350 acres to the government for $20,000 in 1878. Known initially as the Post at Davis Landing, the fort bore the names Camp Ringgold and Ringgold Barracks before being named Fort Ringgold in the year of the purchase. The name was in honor of Bvt. Maj. Samuel Ringgold, the first United States Army officer to die from wounds received during the battle of Palo Alto[qv] on May 8, 1846. The military chose the site to protect the area from Indian and Mexican attacks.

The ninety-six-year occupancy of the post was marked by several interruptions, at times when the government considered it redundant, followed by regarrisoning when the region was threatened. Major periods of occupation were from 1848 until the Civil War[qv] intervened in 1861; from 1865 until military exigencies in the Philippines closed it in 1906; and from 1917 to 1944. The army declared the fort surplus and disposed of the property in 1944. The installation was of flimsy construction until after the Civil War. Construction began on a new post in 1869 at the same location, and by the mid-1870s it took on a permanent look with the erection of frame and brick structures along a palm-lined parade ground. Ringgold was one of the most attractive posts along the border. Congress appropriated additional funds for improvements in 1917. In the nineteenth century Ringgold hosted a number of prominent military figures, including Robert E. Lee, John J. Pershing, and possibly Jefferson Davis.[qq,qv] In 1875 Capt. Leander H. McNelly[qv] and a contingent of Texas Rangers[qv] garrisoned the post.

Fort Ringgold assured permanence for the isolated Rio Grande City and socially and economically affected the life of the community while it safeguarded the citizenry from border violence. The post housed the area's first telegraph office, fueled the local economy through federal appropriations, and waged protracted warfare on smugglers, rustlers, and insurrectionists who ravaged the region. The Cortina War and the unrest along the border during the Mexican Revolution[qv] particularly emphasized the importance of the garrison. Ringgold troops under the command of Maj. Samuel P. Heintzelman[qv] ended the threat of the former by joining forces with John Salmon Ford[qv] and the Texas Rangers to rid the area of Juan N. Cortina[qv] in 1860.

The most serious rift between Fort Ringgold and Rio Grande City occurred in 1899 when Troop D of the Ninth United States Cavalry[qv] briefly garrisoned the installation. The black troops, returning triumphantly from the Cuban campaign, quickly grew impatient at racial restrictions and harassment. Tensions heightened amid conflicting reports of impending attacks on the fort and town. On the night of November 20 post commander 2d Lt. E. H. Rubottom responded to a presumed assault on the garrison by ordering Gatling gunfire on the area between the post and town. Only one minor injury resulted, but Rubottom's action succeeded in quelling the disturbance. Ensuing federal, state, and grand jury investigations failed to specify culpability or motivation, although many townspeople and other Texans insisted that soldiers feigned an attack on the fort in order to wreak havoc on the community. Lt. Col. Cyrus S. Roberts of the United States Army and Thomas Scurry,[qv] adjutant general of Texas, concluded that Rubottom had acted unwisely but recommended no charges against him or others. Governor Joseph Sayers[qv] favored the locals' demand that the Ninth Cavalry be moved, and the residents requested that a white garrison be retained.

In 1947 remains from the abandoned Fort Ringgold post cemetery were reinterred at Fort Sam Houston National Cemetery in San Antonio. The Rio Grande Consolidated Independent School District purchased the fort property in 1949. In 1988 the district maintained the standing buildings, the most renowned of which is the Lee House, where Lee resided in 1860 while he was investigating Cortina's intrusions.

BIBLIOGRAPHY: Garna L. Christian, "Rio Grande City: Prelude to the Brownsville Raid," West Texas Historical Association *Year Book* 57 (1981). Robert W. Frazer, *Forts of the West* (Norman: University of Oklahoma Press, 1965). Herbert M. Hart, *Old Forts of the Southwest* (Seattle, Washington: Superior, 1964). Kathleen E. and Clifton R. St. Clair, eds., *Little Towns of Texas* (Jacksonville, Texas: Jayroe Graphic Arts, 1982). J. Lee and Lillian J. Stambaugh, *The Lower Rio Grande Valley of Texas* (San Antonio: Naylor, 1954). *Garna L. Christian*

FORT SABINE. Fort Sabine was off Farm Road 3322 and State Highway 87 one mile south of the Sabine Pass Battleground State Historical Park[qv] and fifteen miles south of Port Arthur in southeastern Jefferson County. Fearing a Union invasion during the Civil War,[qv] the citizens of Sabine Pass decided to build a fort to protect their town. Local residents, including many slaves, constructed a dirt and timber earthwork overlooking the Sabine River. The post was garrisoned by local militia, the Sabine Pass Guard, and later by the Sixth Texas Infantry Battalion. On September 24, 1862, the fort was shelled by Union gunboats and severely damaged. With the fort's ability to continue functioning already in doubt, yellow fever broke out among the remaining troops, and Maj. Josephus S. Irvine[qv] ordered the guns spiked and the position abandoned. The following March, Maj. Julius Kellersberg inspected the remains of Fort Sabine and determined that the site was no longer useful. Consequently, he ordered the construction of a new fort, several miles away, which became Fort Griffin. Fort Griffin was completed in August 1863, when the two thirty-two-pound guns from Fort Sabine were installed and reactivated.

BIBLIOGRAPHY: W. T. Block, *A History of Jefferson County, Texas, from Wilderness to Reconstruction* (M.A. thesis, Lamar University, 1974; Nederland, Texas: Nederland Publishing, 1976). *Robert Wooster*

FORT SAM HOUSTON. Fort Sam Houston is a major military installation in the northeast section of San Antonio. As early as 1846 the city was attempting to secure the establishment of a permanent United States military installation. During the Mexican War^qv the United States Army established a quartermaster depot at San Antonio and a training camp at San Pedro Springs.^qv In 1849 San Antonio was named headquarters of the United States Army Eighth Military District with forces at Nuestra Señora de la Purísima Concepción Mission and San Pedro Springs. The Alamo was taken on lease from the Catholic Church^qv and used for storage. The Vance house, a two-story stone house where the Gunter Hotel now stands, was leased for army headquarters. The city made several offers of free land, but all were refused except for a small parcel on Flores Street, which was used for an arsenal.

A formal proposal for a permanent army post was made in 1870, but it met with political opposition in Washington. Secretary of War W. W. Belknap illegally held up funding until 1875. He resigned in 1876 rather than face impeachment, partly over his refusal to fund congressional appropriations for the San Antonio base. On June 7, 1876, construction was finally begun on ninety-three acres of city-donated land known as Government Hill. The contract was with the Edward Braden Construction Company for $83,900 and $15,247 for extras. Construction of the quadrangle included a one-story north wall 624 feet long, east and west walls 499½ feet long, and a two-story south wall with the only entry gate. Work was completed in February 1873.

In 1870 the Texas Department of the United States Army had moved to San Antonio. In 1879 the depot that had been occupying space in the Alamo^qv moved to the new post. Almost immediately expansion began with the construction of officers' quarters, a 10,830-square-foot commander's home later named the Pershing House, and a tent hospital, which was replaced by a permanent post hospital in 1885. Between 1885 and 1891 forty-three acres and sixty buildings were added to what was to become the infantry post. In 1890 the military post at San Antonio was designated Fort Sam Houston, in honor of Gen. Sam Houston,^qv by President Benjamin Harrison. Prominent visitors to the post included Chief Geronimo, who was held there in 1886 before his exile to Florida, and Theodore Roosevelt, who stopped with his men at the base to receive provisions before leaving for Cuba in 1898 (*see* FIRST UNITED STATES VOLUNTEER CAVALRY).

In 1907 the first chapel was built, with donated funds; it was nicknamed "Gift Chapel." In 1908 a new hospital was built at the artillery post. It was enlarged in 1910 and again in 1915 to provide 1,000 beds. On February 15, 1910, Lt. Benjamin Foulois brought the army's first airplane to Fort Sam Houston. There he learned to fly with instruction through correspondence with the Wright brothers. He instigated the first experimental flights in United States military aviation and gave the first public demonstration flights on March 2. There were four flights that day, and the last one crashed during landing. After the crash, experimental flights and the aviation program were temporarily suspended at the post. Foulois's airplane, United States Army Aeroplane Number One, is in the National Air and Space Museum in Washington, D.C.

By 1912 the military units at Fort Sam Houston included an infantry regiment, a regiment of calvary, each with a headquarters and band, two batteries of field artillery, and signal and engineer troops. By 1917 the installation had been raised to general depot status and was supplying the Mexican frontier, including Gen. John J. Pershing's^qv pursuit of Francisco (Pancho) Villa.^qv The First Aero Squadron, consisting of nine airplanes and fifteen pilots, was ordered from Fort Sam to Columbus, New Mexico, to support Pershing.

During World War I^qv an addition of 1,280 acres northeast of the fort was called Camp Travis. More than 208,000 soldiers passed through this new addition, where the epidemic of 1918 claimed 11,372 cases of influenza, resulting in 201 deaths. By the early 1920s Camp Travis was deserted and dilapidated. Most of the buildings were torn down by 1928. That year $6 million was appropriated for some 500 permanent buildings at the fort. They were built in Spanish Colonial style and still provided a Moorish atmosphere in the 1990s. By 1933 Fort Sam Houston was supporting the Civilian Conservation Corps.^qv In 1937 the largest maneuvers since World War I were held, and many of the tactical principles used during World War II^qv were developed, including the "Triangular Division." The Eighth Corps and the Eighth Service Command were organized at Fort Sam Houston. It was headquarters for the Southern Defense Command. In 1940 the fort was the largest army post in the United States. The post served as a major internment center for prisoners of war^qv during World War II.^qv By 1949 Fort Sam Houston had 1,500 buildings on more than 3,300 acres of land and was headquarters for the Fourth United States Army.

Some of the great military strategists and commanders of World War II came from Fort Sam Houston. Among them were Lt. Gen. Walter Krueger,^qv United States Third Army; Lt. Gen. Courtney Hodges, who took the Third Army to England; Lt. Gen. William Simpson, United States Fourth Army; and Gen. Dwight Eisenhower,^qv who became the commander of Allied Forces in Europe and later president of the United States. After the war Gen. Jonathan Wainwright^qv commanded the Fourth Army at Fort Sam Houston.

In the mid-1930s $3 million was appropriated to build a new base hospital. It opened in 1938 and was named for Gen. Roger Brooke.^qv It had 425 beds, and an additional wing of 200 beds was added soon after. In 1946 the Institute of Surgical Research was moved to Fort Sam from Halloran General Hospital in New York. The institute specialized in trauma surgery. The Burn Center was established in 1949. During the Korean conflict Fort Sam Houston became a major training center with its Medical Field Service School. In 1973 the fort acquired a major military command devoted to medical service, known as the Health Services Command.

In 1991 Fort Sam Houston comprised the headquarters of the Fifth United States Army, the Health Services Command, the Academy of Health Services, Brooke Army Medical Center, the Institute of Surgical Research, the United States Army Dental Laboratory, the 902nd Military Intelligence Group, and the Joint Military Readiness Center, among other organizations. In addition the fort hosts the real estate projects office of the Fort Worth District, United States Army Corps of Engineers, the West Point Admissions Office, and the United States Army Medical Department Museum and Fort Sam Houston Museum. The fort is the site of Fort Sam Houston National Cemetery. It also supports all of the National Guard and Army Reserve units in Texas, as well as the Texas high school and college reserve officer training corps units.

BIBLIOGRAPHY: Eldon Cagle, Jr., *Quadrangle: The History of Fort Sam Houston* (Austin: Eakin Press, 1985). Paul Ebers, *San Antonio: The Metropolis and Garden Spot of Texas and Fort Sam Houston* (San Antonio, 1909). Robert W. Frazer, *Forts of the West* (Norman: University of Oklahoma Press, 1965). Mary Olivia Handy, *History of Sam Houston* (San Antonio: Naylor, 1951). San Antonio *Express*, November 26, 1940. Nevin Otto Winter, *Texas the Marvellous: The State of Six Flags* (Boston: Page, 1916; centennial ed., Garden City, New York: Garden City Publishing Company, 1936). Art Leatherwood

FORT SAN JACINTO. Fort San Jacinto, formerly a United States coastal-defense fortification on the eastern end of Galveston Island, was constructed by the United States government in 1898. The site was first reserved for public purposes by an act of the Republic of Texas^qv on December 9, 1836. After construction was completed in 1901, Fort San Jacinto, named in honor of the Texan victory over Mexican troops, became the first headquarters for Galveston's harbor defenses. It contained three gun batteries and a direction-finder control station. A seventeen-foot-high seawall fronting the Gulf of Mexico was constructed at the military reservation between 1918 and 1926. The guns of San Jacinto were manned by both the 265th Coast Artillery and the Twentieth Coast Artillery. After the end of World War II[qv] the reservation was maintained by the United States Coast Guard as an electronic repair shop. In 1986 it was used by the United States Army Corps of Engineers, who were dredging silt from the Galveston Ship Channel.

BIBLIOGRAPHY: Margaret Garcia, "The Three Forts in Galveston County," *Junior Historian*, January 1968. *Maury Darst*

FORT SHERMAN (Titus County). Fort Sherman, established by Capt. W. B. Stout in December 1838, was on the Cherokee Trail a mile north of the Cherokee Crossing of Cypress Creek and thirteen miles southwest of the site of Mount Pleasant in Titus County. After trouble between settlers and Indians, Stout established the fort to protect families living in that area. It was used until the Cherokee Indians were moved out of East Texas. In 1967 only a large abandoned cemetery remained at the site.

BIBLIOGRAPHY: Charles Adams Gulick, Jr., Harriet Smither, et al., eds., *The Papers of Mirabeau Buonaparte Lamar* (6 vols., Austin: Texas State Library, 1920–27; rpt., Austin: Pemberton Press, 1968). Traylor Russell, *History of Titus County* (2 vols., Waco: Morrison, 1965, 1966; rpt., Walsworth, Texas, 1975). *Traylor Russell*

FORT SMITH. Fort Smith was one of a series of forts established by the Republic of Texas[qv] to protect its citizens from Indian attacks. It was located at the headwaters of Richland Creek in what was then Navarro County but today is the northeastern corner of Hill County. Its garrison was under the command of Capt. Thomas I. Smith,[qv] for whom the fort was named and who oversaw its construction in 1847. Smith, however, died later that year. J. C. Connor replaced him and remained in command until 1848. That year the company of dragoons abandoned the stockade and moved farther west to a new garrison, Fort Graham. The site of Fort Smith later was the home of Iverson School. In 1936 the Texas Centennial[qv] Commission placed a marker at the site.

BIBLIOGRAPHY: Hill County Historical Commission, *A History of Hill County, Texas, 1853–1980* (Waco: Texian, 1980). Harold Schoen, comp., *Monuments Erected by the State of Texas to Commemorate the Centenary of Texas Independence* (Austin: Commission of Control for Texas Centennial Celebrations, 1938). *David Minor*

FORT SPUNKY, TEXAS. The remnants of the Fort Spunky community are on Farm roads 199 and 2174 and Lake Granbury in the southeastern corner of Hood County. The settlement was originally named Barnardville. In 1849 George Barnard[qv] built one of a chain of Torrey trading houses[qv] on the Brazos River at what is now the site of Fort Spunky. George and his brother Charles Barnard,[qv] the Torrey brothers, and Sam Houston,[qv] president of the former Republic of Texas,[qv] invested in this enterprise, thinking that it would improve Indian relations. The post itself, run by Charles Barnard, was built near a spring and beside a settlement of peaceable, agricultural Indians. The trading post lay near well-traveled Indian highways and the prominent landmark Comanche Peak, used by the Indians, especially the Comanches, as a lookout, rallying point, and campground. George and Charles Barnard procured thousands of acres near Comanche Peak and along the Brazos River. A tributary of the Brazos nearby was called George's Creek, and a community by the same name developed in the 1850s as a companion settlement near the trading post. In the mid-1850s the Indians were moved to Fort Belknap by the United States government, and the Barnards' trading post declined. The community acquired the colorful name Fort Spunky because sporadic fistfights broke out in town. The community's post office opened in 1886. The settlement was predominantly an agricultural trade center that took the place of the defunct trading post. About forty residents lived there in 1896. In the early 1900s John D. Armstrong, the postmaster, owned virtually all the businesses, namely the cotton gin, gristmill, general store, blacksmith shop, and feed store. The businesses and post office were gone in the 1980s. The population of Fort Spunky was sixty-five in 1964 and was reported as fifteen from 1966 to 1990.

BIBLIOGRAPHY: Viola Block, *History of Johnson County and Surrounding Areas* (Waco: Texian Press, 1970). Raymond Elliott and Mildred Padon, *Of a People and a Creek* (Cleburne, Texas: Bennett Printing, 1979). Thomas T. Ewell, *History of Hood County* (Granbury, Texas: Gaston, 1895; rpt., Granbury Junior Woman's Club, 1956). W. C. Nunn, *Somervell: Story of a Texas County* (Fort Worth: Texas Christian University Press, 1975). *Dorothy Leach*

FORT ST. LOUIS. René Robert Cavelier, Sieur de La Salle,[qv] established Fort St. Louis of Texas in the summer of 1685 on the Texas coast. The site has long been in controversy. Period maps and documents support Herbert E. Bolton's[qv] conclusion that it was on the right bank of Garcitas Creek "a league and a half" from its mouth in Lavaca Bay, in what is now Victoria County. Yet archeologists have been unable to substantiate that location, and evidence continues to be offered in favor of the Lavaca River in Jackson County, rather than Garcitas Creek.

The previous February La Salle, seeking the mouth of the Mississippi River, had landed his 280 colonists, including 100 soldiers, at the mouth of Matagorda Bay in Spanish-claimed territory. A temporary camp was made on Matagorda Island while he sought a more secure location farther up the bay. Staking the site on an eminence overlooking the "Rivière aux Boeufs"—so named for the numerous buffalo[qv] on the surrounding prairie—in April, he put men to felling timber.

Early in June La Salle sent word for the colonists to proceed overland to the new site. The bark *Belle* plied between the temporary camp and a supply dump at Indian Point (now in Calhoun County), bringing supplies and timbers from the storeship *Aimable*,[qv] which had been wrecked in Cavallo Pass, between Matagorda Bay and the Gulf of Mexico. The cargo was transshipped to canoes for the rest of the journey.

During the building of the fort disease and overwork took a heavy toll. By the end of July the colony had been reduced by more than half. La Salle saw the building well under way, then set out in autumn 1685 to explore the surrounding country. When he departed in January 1687 on his last journey, he left at the fort scarcely more than twenty men, women, and children in the charge of the Sieur de Barbier.[qv]

With La Salle himself dead from an assassin's bullet, the end came for Fort St. Louis in late 1688 or early 1689, when the Karankawa Indians gained entry under guise of friendship and murdered all the occupants but five children. These were kept by the tribe until rescued later by the Spanish expeditions of Alonso De León and Domingo Terán de los Ríos.[qqv] One of the children, Jean-Baptiste Talon, nine years old at the time, gave the only eyewitness account.

The best description of the fort comes from the De León expedition, which found the ruins on April 22, 1689. Of six buildings, the one nearest the creek served as the fort. Solidly built of ship timbers, it had a gabled roof covered with planking and stood four varas high, with an attic storeroom above the four rooms at ground level. The other houses, "not very large," were built of poles plastered with mud and roofed with buffalo hides. A picket fence enclosed a corn patch and an herb garden.

In 1721 the Marqués de Aguayo[qv] claimed to have built Nuestra Señora de Loreto de la Bahía Presidio on the same site, where he turned up various French artifacts while digging the foundation. The presidio was situated on the Garcitas Creek site favored by Bolton.

Ft. Stockton, Tex. Town from East. *Courtesy Lawrence T. Jones III Collection, Austin. This view shows the courthouse (with cupola), which was built in 1883.*

Yet archeologists have failed to find conclusive evidence that Fort St. Louis was at the same place. The question may never be settled to everyone's satisfaction.

BIBLIOGRAPHY: Herbert Eugene Bolton, ed., *Spanish Exploration in the Southwest, 1542–1706* (New York: Scribner, 1908; rpt., New York: Barnes and Noble, 1959). Pierre Margry, ed., *Découvertes et établissements des Français dans l'ouest et dans le sud de l'Amérique septentrionale, 1614–1754* (6 vols., Paris: Jouast, 1876–86). Walter J. O'Donnell, trans., *La Salle's Occupation of Texas* (Preliminary Studies of the Texas Catholic Historical Society 3.2 [April 1936]). Robert S. Weddle, *Wilderness Manhunt: The Spanish Search for La Salle* (Austin: University of Texas Press, 1973).
Robert S. Weddle

FORT STOCKTON. Fort Stockton, constructed of adobe^{qv} and named for Robert Field Stockton,^{qv} was established by the United States Army on March 23, 1859, at Comanche Springs, which was within the site of the present city of Fort Stockton, for the protection of the mail service, travelers, and freighters. Comanche Springs was on the Comanche war trail into Mexico, the upper and lower San Antonio–El Paso–San Diego roads, the Butterfield Overland Mail^{qv} route, and the San Antonio–Chihuahua Trail, and near the Pecos River–New Mexico road. Capt. Arthur T. Lee,^{qv} commanding Company C, Eighth Infantry, on order of Col. Carlos A. Waite,^{qv} who commanded all federal troops in Texas, abandoned the post in April 1861. On June 26 the post was reoccupied by Capt. Charles L. Pyron,^{qv} in command of Company B, Second Regiment, Texas Mounted Rifles. It was abandoned by the Confederates in August 1862, after Gen. Henry H. Sibley's^{qv} defeat in New Mexico.

On July 21, 1867, Fort Stockton, in ruins after the Civil War,^{qv} was reoccupied by Gen. Edward Hatch, who made it the headquarters for the Ninth United States Cavalry,^{qv} a regiment of black troops. Hatch built a new post nearby at a cost of $82,000 on land the federal government neither owned nor had leased. Except for the stone guardhouse, the buildings had stone foundations, adobe walls, and dirt roofs. The troops quartered at the post were used for patrols, escorts, and scouts, largely against the Apaches. In 1882, after the Apaches had been defeated, the army began withdrawing the troops. The last contingent, a company of the Third Cavalry and two companies of the Sixteenth Infantry, commanded by Maj. George A. Purington, left on June 26–27, 1886.

By providing protection to travelers and settlers, a market for stockmen, irrigation farmers, and merchants, and employment for freighters, mechanics, and laborers, Fort Stockton promoted the establishment and development of a thriving community. Since their abandonment by the military, some of the officers' quarters have been used continuously for residences. In 1936 the state erected a marker at the site of the fort on the grounds of the Pecos County Courthouse.

BIBLIOGRAPHY: Clayton W. Williams, *Texas' Last Frontier: Fort Stockton and the Trans-Pecos, 1861–1895* (College Station: Texas A&M University Press, 1982).
Ernest Wallace

FORT STOCKTON, TEXAS. Fort Stockton, the county seat of Pecos County, is on Interstate Highway 10, U.S. highways 67, 290, and 385, and the Santa Fe Railroad, 329 miles northwest of San Antonio and 245 miles east of El Paso. It grew up around Comanche Springs,^{qv} at one time the third largest source of spring water in Texas, and near the military fort founded in 1859 and named for Robert Field Stockton.^{qv} Comanche Springs was a favorite rest stop on the Comanche Trail^{qv} to Chihuahua, the Old San Antonio Road,^{qv} the Butterfield Overland Mail^{qv} route, and the San Antonio–Chihuahua freight-wagon road. The Confederates took possession of the fort at the outbreak of the Civil War^{qv} but abandoned it the next year. In 1867 the army rebuilt the fort on a larger and more permanent basis to protect travelers and settlers from Indians. Until abandoned in 1886, the fort provided employment for freighters and laborers and a market for farmers, stockmen, and merchants.

San Antonio entrepreneurs, convinced that the water from Comanche and nearby Leon springs could be used for irrigation, purchased large tracts of land for agricultural development. In 1868 Peter Gallagher^{qv} bought the land that included the military garrison and Comanche Springs, platted 160 acres for a townsite named Saint

Gall, and established two stores at Comanche Springs. Later, Gallagher and John James purchased 5,500 acres along Comanche Creek. By 1870 the Saint Gall region had a population of 420 civilians, predominantly Irish, German, and Mexican Catholics who had come by way of San Antonio. The first church in Saint Gall was Catholic. When Pecos County was organized in 1875, Saint Gall became the county seat. The name, however, was never popular with the citizens, and on August 13, 1881, it was changed officially to Fort Stockton.

By 1870 some settlers were using the water from the Pecos River for irrigation.qv Seven years later irrigated farmland comprised 7,000 acres, and by 1945 the total reached 12,900 acres. After the military post was abandoned on June 30, 1886, and both the Texas and Pacific and the Southern Pacific railroads had bypassed it, Fort Stockton experienced a decline. By then, however, it was rapidly becoming the center for an extensive sheep and cattle ranching industry, and in 1926 the opening of the nearby Yates oilfieldqv brought on an economic boom.

In 1980 Fort Stockton had a broad-based economy and a population of 8,868. In addition to its irrigated agriculture and extensive ranches, it had become a major center for the production, processing, and distribution of oil, gas, and sulfur. Its historic sites, including Comanche Springs, the remains of the old fort, and the Annie Riggs Memorial Museum, are tourist attractions. In 1990 the population was 8,524.

BIBLIOGRAPHY: Clayton W. Williams, *Texas' Last Frontier: Fort Stockton and the Trans-Pecos, 1861–1895* (College Station: Texas A&M University Press, 1982).

Ernest Wallace

FORT SULLIVAN. Fort Sullivan, near Port Sullivan in Milam County, was established by Augustus W. Sullivan in 1835 as a trading post at the intersection of the Houston–Waco and the Austin–East Texas roads. In 1936 the Texas Centennialqv Commission placed a marker at the site.

BIBLIOGRAPHY: Harold Schoen, comp., *Monuments Erected by the State of Texas to Commemorate the Centenary of Texas Independence* (Austin: Commission of Control for Texas Centennial Celebrations, 1938).

FORT TENOXTITLÁN. Fort Tenoxtitlán, constructed in 1830 in what is now northeastern Burleson County, was part of a chain of military garrisons designed to Mexicanize Texas and stanch immigration from the United States pursuant to the Law of April 6, 1830.qv On June 25, 1830, Lt. Col. José Francisco Ruizqv was dispatched from Bexar in command of 100 cavalrymen of the presidial company of Álamo de Parras (*see* SECOND FLYING COMPANY OF SAN CARLOS DE PARRAS), with orders from Gen. Manuel de Mier y Teránqv to establish a fort at the strategic point halfway down the Old San Antonio Road,qv where the thoroughfare crossed the Brazos River en route to Nacogdoches. Ruiz reached the Brazos on July 13 and established temporary headquarters on the east bank about a half mile below the Old San Antonio Road. On October 17, 1830, the garrison moved to a permanent site on a high bluff on the west bank of the Brazos twelve miles above the San Antonio crossing, opposite the spot where the present Brazos-Robertson county line strikes the river. The small spring-fed creek nearby was subsequently known as Dam Creek, probably because its water was diverted into the settlement. Although Mier y Terán, who envisioned Tenoxtitlán as a future capital of Texas, issued elaborate instructions from Matamoros for the design of the fort, most were eventually disregarded; the fortifications themselves were likely of conventional log construction.

One of the garrison's most important duties was to assist in the transportation of military funds from Bexar to Nacogdoches. Despite the ban on American settlement, the nearby farming community included an undetermined number of American immigrants; as early as July 1831, for example, Francis Smith operated a thriving general merchandise store at the fort, trading manufactured goods to the Indians for beaver pelts and buffalo robes. On December 31, 1830, the ayuntamientoqv of San Felipe de Austin, acknowledging the importance of the garrison, established a commission to construct a road from San Felipe to Tenoxtitlán.

In late October 1830 Maj. Sterling C. Robertsonqv of the Texas (or Nashville) Association, appeared at Tenoxtitlán requesting permission to select a settlement site for fifty American families accompanying him, provided by the colonization contract that his group had made with the province of Coahuila and Texas.qv Three months later official announcement of the provincial government's invalidation of this contract reached the fort. However, Colonel Ruiz, Texas-born himself and sympathetic to the American settlers, evaded orders to apprehend the colonists and turn them over to the authorities in Nacogdoches, thus permitting them to scatter into various parts of Texas.

On July 13, 1832, despondent over the failure of his grand scheme to settle Mexicans in the Texas wilderness, Mier y Terán committed suicide. Thereupon the demoralized Colonel Ruiz decided to abandon Tenoxtitlán. He began evacuation of the garrison and entire Mexican settlement to Bexar on August 22, 1832. By December only a handful of Americans remained in occupation of the site. A trading post and settlement continued in the vicinity for many years but disappeared after 1860.

In 1936 a granite commemorative marker was erected by the Texas Centennialqv Commission near the site of the fort, fourteen miles northeast of Caldwell off Farm Road 1362. Another was erected in 1970 five miles east of Caldwell on State Highway 21. Tenoxtitlán, or "Prickly Pear Place" was the Aztec name for what became known as Mexico City.

BIBLIOGRAPHY: Burleson County Historical Society, *Astride the Old San Antonio Road: A History of Burleson County, Texas* (Dallas: Taylor, 1980). Malcolm D. McLean, "Tenoxtitlán, Dream Capitol of Texas," *Southwestern Historical Quarterly* 70 (April 1967).

Charles Christopher Jackson

FORT TERAN. Fort Teran was a Mexican military encampment or station established in 1831 at a Neches River crossing that Spanish government representatives in Nacogdoches at the beginning of the nineteenth century had referred to as the "pass to the south." Three important trails crossed the Neches River at this point, underscoring the significance of this strategic site. The fort was named in honor of Gen. Manuel de Mier y Terán,qv commandant general of the eastern division of the Provincias Internasqv (which included Texas), and constructed at this location as part of a program to control the flow of smugglers and illegal immigrants into Texas.

The site was in what is now Tyler County about a half mile downstream from the mouth of Shawnee Creek and three miles west of Rockland. The crossing at this point provided access to a feasible route across the Kisatchie Wold,qv a ridge that extends from the Mississippi River to the lower Rio Grande valley of Texas and that was a formidable obstacle for north-south travel. In northern Tyler County this ridge reaches heights of 400 to 450 feet above sea level at several of its peaks and has forced the Neches River to run eastward along the northern boundary of Tyler County.

Construction of a fort on the Neches River was a result of General Terán's inspection tour of East Texas in 1829. He observed that immigrants and smugglers were coming into Texas from Louisiana by using unguarded trails such as the Coushatta Trace, the Alabama Trace,qqv and the Nacogdoches-Orcoquisac Road, all of which crossed the Neches River at the future site of Fort Teran. When Terán returned to Mexico, he helped to draft Anastasio Bustamante'sqv Law of April 6, 1830,qv forbidding American immigrants to settle in Mexican territory.

Responsibility for enforcing this law was assigned to a "director of colonization," and Terán was the first to hold this office. His program for closing Texas to immigrants from the United States included establishing garrisons on the Neches and several other rivers. He chose Peter Ellis Bean,qv a colonel in the Mexican army, to construct Fort Teran on the Neches. On September 25, 1831, Bean departed from Nacogdoches to establish the fort. Apparently construction proceeded very slowly, since the military commandant at Nacogdoches, José de las Piedras,qv on April 19, 1832, reported the need for additional carpenters and other craftsmen to assist in building the fort. When completed, this project consisted of approximately ten wooden cabins to provide housing for Colonel Bean and his small garrison. The Mexican government, however, found itself unable to support its Texas forts adequately, and later in 1832 transferred most of the troops.

After Fort Teran was abandoned by the remaining troops in 1834, the population in the immediate area was about a dozen persons. Samuel T. Belt opened a trading post at the fort site. A post office operated there in 1856–66, and this small community, sometimes called Fort Turan, continued as a trading and shipping point until the railroads came to Tyler and Angelina counties in the 1880s. Until 1878 steamboats continued to land near the fort, which was at the head of navigation on the Neches River. When Texas counties were organized after 1845, Fort Teran was used as a point of reference in describing the boundaries of Angelina and Jasper counties.

Another of Belt's enterprises was the operation of a ferry at the Fort Teran crossing. Stagecoaches used this crossing for many years. The ferry operated first as Belt's Ferry, then Boone's Ferry and Duncan Ferry, until the completion of a state highway through Rockland in 1917.

BIBLIOGRAPHY: Juan N. Almonte, "Statistical Report of Texas," *Southwestern Historical Quarterly* 28 (January 1925). Wallace W. Atwood, *The Physiographic Provinces of North America* (Boston: Ginn, 1940). Eugene C. Barker, *Readings in Texas History* (Dallas: Southwest Press, 1929). David J. Weber, *The Mexican Frontier, 1821–1846* (Albuquerque: University of New Mexico Press, 1982). James E. Wheat, "The Story of Fort Teran on the Neches," *It's Dogwood Time in Tyler County,* March 1951. James E. and Josiah Wheat, "Tyler County under Mexico," *It's Dogwood Time in Tyler County,* March 1966. Amelia W. Williams and Eugene C. Barker, eds., *The Writings of Sam Houston, 1813–1863* (8 vols., Austin: University of Texas Press, 1938–43; rpt., Austin and New York: Pemberton Press, 1970).

Howard N. Martin

FORT TRAVIS. The first Fort Travis, on the eastern end of Galveston Island, was the first fort established by the Republic of Texasqv in 1836 to protect the Galveston harbor entrance. It was an octagonal structure mounted with six and twelve pound guns from the *Cayuga*qv and was commanded by James Morgan.qv The fort, originally called Fort Point, was renamed for William Barrett Travis,qv commander at the Alamo. When building began in April 1836, the nearby construction camp was called Camp Travis. The garrison was withdrawn in 1844. Two other installations, the earthworks of James Longqv and later fortifications of the Civil Warqv and Reconstructionqv period, were west of the fort site. Neither is still standing today.

The later Fort Travis was across the harbor entrance at the southern end of Bolivar Peninsula. There the federal government purchased a ninety-seven-acre site in 1898 for $36,000; other parcels were added later. Federal construction began in 1898 and ended in 1943. The fort was turned over to the coast artillery on October 25, 1899. It was defended by four batteries: Ernst and Davis, completed in 1898; Kimball in 1925; and No. 236, finished in 1943. Its firepower ranged from two twelve-inch guns mounted on barbette carriages to three-inch rapid-fire guns. There were twenty-seven buildings, including barracks for enlisted men, officers, and noncommissioned officers; a mess hall; and ancillary frame buildings. All have been demolished. After the Galveston hurricane of 1900,qv a seventeen-foot seawall was constructed on the Gulf side of the fort. Fort Travis was occupied by troops in both world wars, and a number of German prisoners of warqv were interned there during World War II.qv In 1949 the reservation was declared war surplus and sold to the M and M Building Corporation, a private developer, with the stipulation that the former batteries would be made available to the public during hurricane emergencies. In 1960 the fort was designated an official civil-defense shelter and sold to C. Pat Lumpkin Associates of Houston. In 1973 the Galveston County Commissioners Court purchased the site for a public park.

BIBLIOGRAPHY: Lynn M. Alperin, *Custodians of the Coast: History of the United States Army Engineers at Galveston* (Galveston: U.S. Army Corps of Engineers, 1977). Galveston *Daily News,* February 11, 1962, October 25, 1965, May 20, 1975. Charles Waldo Hayes, *Galveston: History of the Island and the City* (2 vols., Austin: Jenkins Garrett, 1974). Ray Miller, *Ray Miller's Texas Forts* (Houston: Cordovan, 1985).

Maury Darst

FORT WAUL. Fort Waul, located on Waldrip Hill, a high, wide hill on the northern edge of Gonzales in Gonzales County, is one of the few remaining Confederate earthwork fortifications in Texas. The fort was intended to be a supply depot for the Confederate Army in the Western Subdistrict of Texas, as well as a defensive post on the Guadalupe River. This site was chosen because of its central location between Austin, San Antonio, Houston, and Victoria. In addition, it is at the confluence of the Guadalupe and San Marcos rivers, both of which could be used to transport goods and supplies. Col. Albert Miller Lea,qv chief engineer for the Confederate Army, and Capt. H. Wickeland, topographical engineer, were responsible for the construction of the fort, which was designed to have outside walls eight feet high, four to six feet thick at the top, and twelve feet thick at the bottom. The entire compound was to have a defensive entrenchment, eight feet wide by four feet deep, surrounding it. A large, square bastion for cannons was to be situated on each of the four corners, with a redan in the middle of the western wall. The blockhouse was designed to be underground in the center of the fort. In December of 1863 Colonel Lea was instructed to use slave labor from the surrounding counties to aid in the construction, which continued throughout 1864. But as the threat of a Union invasion of Texas declined, so did the defensive need of the Gonzales post and its importance as a central supply depot. Construction had ceased by November of 1864, and the fort was soon abandoned. It had never been completed or officially named.

The unfinished fort fell into decay, and the stones from the blockhouse were used to rebuild the Gonzales College dormitory. Not until the late 1870s was the site named Fort Waul, in honor of Confederate general Thomas N. Waul, who had lived in the area. The city of Gonzales currently owns the site but has made no use of it. Most of the land has been put under the protection of the Gonzales County Historical Committee. The outer walls of the original fort and a portion of the defensive ditch along the western wall are still plainly visible. In 1991 an unofficial attempt was made to rebuild the northern portion of the fort.

BIBLIOGRAPHY: Compiled Service Records of Confederate Soldiers Who Served in Organizations from the State of Texas, National Archives and Record Service, Washington. *The War of the Rebellion: A Compilation of the Official Records of the Union and Confederate Armies.*

James B. McCrain

FORT WOLTERS. Fort Wolters, established as Camp Wolters in 1925, is four miles east of Mineral Wells in Parker and Palo Pinto counties. It was named for Brig. Gen. Jacob F. Wolters,qv commander of the Fifty-sixth Brigade of the National Guard, and designated a summer training site for his units. Mineral Wells donated fifty acres, leased 2,300 acres, and in World War IIqv provided land to increase the camp's area to 7,500 acres. The camp became an important infantry-replacement training center with a troop capacity that reached a peak of 24,973. Six months after the end of the war the camp was deactivated.

Local businessmen purchased the land and facilities and converted them to private use. The tensions of the cold war, however, resulted in the reopening of the camp in early 1951, under the authority of the United States Air Force. At the installation, then named Wolters Air Force Base, was housed the newly formed Aviation Engineer Force. Special-category army and air force personnel were trained there.

In September 1956 the base became the Primary Helicopter Center directed by the United States Army. In June 1963 it was renamed Fort Wolters. At the time all army rotary-wing aviators received basic and primary flight training there. The Vietnam War increased the need for pilots, and the base became the home for training not just army personnel, but also helicopter pilots for the Marine Corps in 1968 and for the Air Force in 1970. By 1970 Fort Wolters covered 8,500 acres and leased an additional 1,700 to help handle the 1,200 helicopters used at the camp. By January 1, 1973, 40,000 students had completed the twenty-week training program. The base was also the home of the Beach Army Hospital, the Eighty-fourth Military Police Detachment, the 328th United States Army Band, and United States Army Reserve Detachment 20, Sixteenth Weather Squadron.

In 1975 orders deactivating the base were issued. Part of the land and facilities became the property of the city and private businessmen; ninety acres and thirteen buildings became the Education Center of Weatherford College. A portion of the land was also transferred by the United States government to the state of Texas for development as part of Lake Mineral Wells State Park.qv

BIBLIOGRAPHY: Parker County Historical Commission, *History of Parker County* (Dallas: Taylor, 1980). *Texas Almanac*, 1970–71, 1972–73, 1975–76.   David Minor

FORT WORTH. Fort Worth, originally Camp Worth, was established at the end of the Mexican War,qv when Gen. Winfield Scott sent forty-two men of Company F of the Second Dragoons under command of Maj. Ripley A. Arnoldqv to North Texas to establish a post to guard East Texas settlements from the Indians. Acting on the advice of scouts who had camped there during the winter of 1848, Arnold chose a position on the south side of the confluence of the Clear Fork and West Fork of the Trinity River. The camp was established on June 6, 1849, and named for Brig. Gen. William Jenkins Worth.qv Its designation was changed to Fort Worth on November 14, 1849. The project was successful, for there were no Indian raids east of Parker County after the establishment of the camp. The only threat to the post came from a band of Taovaya warriors who were dispersed by a shot from a howitzer, the camp's only artillery. On June 17, 1851, Capt. J. V. Bamford of companies F and H of the Eighth Infantry assumed command, relieving Arnold. The post was abandoned on September 17, 1853, and troops who had been stationed there were sent to Fort Belknap. No permanent fort had been erected, and the abandoned barracks were used as store buildings by the early merchants of the new city of Fort Worth.

BIBLIOGRAPHY: Buckley B. Paddock, *History of Texas: Fort Worth and the Texas Northwest Edition* (4 vols., Chicago: Lewis, 1922).

FORT WORTH, CATHOLIC DIOCESE OF. The Catholic diocese of Fort Worth comprises twenty-eight counties of north central Texas—Archer, Baylor, Bosque, Clay, Comanche, Cooke, Denton, Eastland, Erath, Foard, Hardeman, Hill, Hood, Jack, Johnson, Knox, Montague, Palo Pinto, Parker, Shackelford, Stephens, Somervell, Tarrant, Throckmorton, Wichita, Wilbarger, Wise, and Young—an episcopal region embracing 23,900 square miles. On August 22, 1969, Pope Paul VI separated this area from the Catholic Diocese of Dallasqv and established it as the Diocese of Fort Worth. Two months later, on October 21, Bishop John J. Cassata,qv a native of Galveston, was installed in St. Patrick Cathedralqv as Fort Worth's first ordinary.

In 1890 the Catholic population of the area of the Brazos and Trinity rivers had grown large enough that Pope Leo XIII established the Diocese of Dallas. As early as 1870 Claude Marie Dubuis,qv the second bishop of Galveston (which diocese encompassed all of Texas at that time), had begun sending Father Vincent Perrier twice a year to visit Fort Worth. At that time several Catholic families were meeting in the Carrico home. Fort Worth's first parish church was a frame structure built at 1212 Throckmorton Street and called St. Stanislaus Church. It stood until 1907. The cornerstone of St. Patrick's Church, which eventually became St. Patrick Cathedral, was laid in 1888; the church was built just north of St. Stanislaus Church and dedicated in 1892. When Dallas was made a diocese the region that eventually became the Diocese of Fort Worth had seven parishes—in Fort Worth, Cleburne, Gainesville, Henrietta, Hillsboro, Muenster, and Weatherford. The decade of the 1870s witnessed the earliest Catholic education in the area. In 1879 Father Thomas Loughrey, pastor of St. Stanislaus Church, opened a boys' school that operated in the church until 1907. In 1885 the Sisters of Saint Mary of Namurqv established Saint Ignatius Academy in Fort Worth and Xavier Academy in Denison. In 1910 the same order of nuns founded Fort Worth's first Catholic college, Our Lady of Victory College. Other Catholic schools opened in Denton (1874), Weatherford (1880), Muenster (1890 and 1895), Gainesville (1892), Pilot Point (1893), and Cleburne (1896). St. Joseph's Infirmary (now St. Joseph Hospitalqv) opened in 1885 in Fort Worth. In 1953 Pope Pius XII changed the name of the Diocese of Dallas to Diocese of Dallas–Fort Worth, and Saint Patrick's Church in Fort Worth was elevated to the status of a cocathedral. In 1985 St. Patrick Cathedral, St. Ignatius Church, and the St. Ignatius rectory were added to the National Register of Historic Places.

From 1969, when the Diocese of Fort Worth was established, to 1986 the Catholic population increased from 67,000 to 120,000. Meanwhile, in 1981 Bishop Cassata retired, and Pope John Paul II named as his successor a native of Massachusetts who had previously worked in Brownsville, Bishop Joseph P. Delaney. Under this well-liked prelate the diocese continued to mature. In 1986 it had fourteen primary schools, three secondary schools, the Cassata Learning Center (dedicated in 1975 as an institution offering nontraditional, personalized instruction to the underprivileged of Fort Worth), and a new Catholic Center. The center, a 20,000-square-foot edifice, brought together under one roof all of the pastoral and administrative offices of the diocese. Guided by Bishop Delaney, the diocese continued to underscore the principles of the Second Vatican Council, especially a commitment to the poor, to ecumenism, and to an increased role in the church for the laity.

BIBLIOGRAPHY: Sister Joseph A. Dederichs and Sister Rose Mary Cousins, *Catholic Schools: Dawn of Education in Texas* (Beaumont: Beaumont Printing and Lithographing, 1986). William R. Hoover, *St. Patrick's: The First 100 Years* (Fort Worth: St. Patrick Cathedral, 1988).   *Patrick Foley*

FORT WORTH, TEXAS. Fort Worth is on Interstate highways 35W, 20, and 30 and the Clear Fork of the Trinity River in central Tarrant County. In January 1849 United States Army General William Jenkins Worth,qv hero of the Mexican War,qv proposed a line of ten forts to mark the western Texas frontier from Eagle Pass to the confluence of the West Fork and Clear Fork of the Trinity River. Upon the death of Worth, Gen. William S. Harneyqv assumed the command and ordered Maj. Ripley S. Arnold[qv] to find a new fort site near the West Fork and Clear Fork. This site was suggested by Middleton Tate Johnson,[qv] who once commanded a detachment of Texas Rangers[qv] and founded Johnson Station, just southeast of what is now Fort Worth. On June 6, 1849, Arnold established a camp on the bank of the Trinity River and named the post Camp Worth in honor of General Worth. In August 1849 Arnold moved the camp to the north-facing bluff which overlooked the mouth of the Clear Fork. The United States War Department officially named the post Fort Worth on November 14, 1849. Although Indians were still a threat in the area, pioneers were already settling near the fort. When relocating the camp, Arnold found George "Press" Farmer living on the bluff and allowed him to open the first sutler's store. Other early settlers were Ephraim M. Daggett,[qv] George W. Terrell, Ed Terrell, and Howard W. Peak. But when a new line of forts was built further west, the army evacuated Fort Worth on September 17, 1853. Settlers then took uncontested possession of the site. John Peter Smith[qv] opened a school with twelve students in 1854; Henry Daggett and Archibald Leonard started department stores. Julian Feild[qv] ran a general store and flour mill in 1856, and the Butterfield Overland Mail[qv] and the Southern Pacific Stage Line used the town as a western terminus on the way to California. In 1855 the county seat war erupted. Since 1849 the county seat had been Birdville, but in 1855 Fort Worth citizens decided that this honor belonged to their town. After a long bitter fight Fort Worth became the county seat in April 1860, and construction began on a stone county courthouse. After a delay due to the Civil War[qv] the courthouse was finished in the 1870s, although it burned in 1876.

During the 1860s Fort Worth suffered from the effects of the Civil War and Reconstruction.[qv] The population dropped as low as 175, and money, food, and supply shortages burdened the residents. Gradually, however, the town began to revive. By 1872 Jacob Samuels, William Jesse Boaz, and William Henry Davis had opened general stores. The next year Khleber M. Van Zandt[qv] established Tidball, Van Zandt, and Company, which became Fort Worth National Bank in 1884. Barrooms such as Tom Prindle's Saloon and Steele's Tavern welcomed many travelers. Weekly newspapers were prominent, including the Fort Worth *Chief* and the *Democrat*. Schools gradually reopened, and in 1869 Addison and Randolph Clark,[qqv] along with Ida Clark, taught six pupils in a local church. It was the developing cattle industry, however, that really began the community's economic boom. Known as Cowtown, Fort Worth offered cowboys a respite from the cattle drives to Abilene, Kansas. Northern cattle buyers established their headquarters in the town, and new businesses included Pendery and Wilson's Liquor Wholesale, B. C. Evans dry goods, and Martin B. Loyd's Exchange Office. In 1873 the city was incorporated with a mayor-council[qv] government, and W. P. Burts became the first mayor. During this time the *Democrat*, owned by K. M. Van Zandt and under the editorial leadership of Buckley B. Paddock,[qv] successfully campaigned for a fire department and other civic improvements. Transportation and communication were an important part of Fort Worth and its growth. In 1874 the first westbound stage arrived, and in 1878 the Yuma Stage Line made Fort Worth the eastern terminus to Yuma, Arizona. The Texas and Pacific Railway designated Fort Worth as the eastern terminus for the route to San Diego, California. After a delay caused by the panic of 1873 the Texas and Pacific was finally completed to Fort Worth on July 19, 1876; by 1900 the Missouri, Kansas and Texas (the "Katy"), the Santa Fe, the Fort Worth and New Orleans, the Fort Worth and Brownwood, the Fort Worth and Rio Grande, the Fort Worth and Denver City, the Fort Worth, Corsicana and Beaumont, and the St. Louis Southwestern (the "Cotton Belt") served the town. The Fort Worth Street Railway Company ran a mile-long route down Main Street. Early newspapers were the Fort Worth *Standard* (1873–78), the *Greenback Tribune* (1878–89; later the Fort Worth *Tribune*), the *Democrat* (1876), the *Democrat-Advance* (1881), the *Gazette* (1882–98), and the Fort Worth *Star-Telegram*[qv] (1909–).

One of the most popular gathering places was the Texas Spring Palace,[qv] an agricultural exhibition hall built in 1889 and destroyed by fire in 1890. The palace was not only a form of entertainment but also an important part of the town's strategy for boosting commercial expansion. It was advertised throughout the nation, and special trains brought visitors from as far away as Boston and Chicago. Hell's Half Acre[qv] provided saloons and bawdy houses for cowboys and havens for desperadoes. By 1876 Fort Worth residents were demanding that the lawlessness be controlled, and they elected Timothy I. "Jim" Courtright[qv] as marshal. By the 1890s the Queen City of the Prairie, as Fort Worth liked to be known, was becoming a dressed-beef center. In North Fort Worth businessmen founded the Texas Dressed Beef and Packing Company, the Union Stockyards Company, and the Fort Worth Stockyards[qv] Company. When Swift and Company[qv] and Armour and Company began to look for Texas sites for branch plants, Fort Worth citizens pledged a bonus of $100,000 for the two companies if they would locate there. Because of this incentive, and because the town was served by railroads, Armour and Swift decided to locate a meat-packing plant in Fort Worth. The venture was successful and, combined with the stockyards, helped Fort Worth become a leading packing-house center. In 1903 the first livestock was slaughtered in the new plants. The rise of the stockyards and packing plants stimulated other livestock-related businesses. J. B. Buchanan and C. E. Lee issued the *Livestock Reporter* and the *North Fort Worth News*. In 1896 the first Fat Stock Show was held, and in 1908 the Northside Coliseum was built to house the Southwestern Exposition and Fat Stock Show (later the Southwestern Exposition and Livestock Show[qv]). The city decided to begin the construction of new county courthouse in 1893. The leaders of Fort Worth also caught the reform spirit of the Progressive era,[qv] and in 1907 the city government was restructured to the commission form.[qv] In 1909 a devastating fire motivated the construction of a dam on the West Fork; the resulting Lake Worth provided a reliable water supply. The city limits were expanded to 16.83 square miles in 1909.

During World War I[qv] the United States Army established Camp Bowie (in the Arlington Heights area), which trained 100,000 men, and the United States Army Air Force converted three airfields into centers of aviation training. With the discovery of oil in Texas, refinery and pipeline companies such as Sinclair Refining Company, Texaco,[qv] and Humble Oil and Refining Company (later Exxon Company, U.S.A.[qv]) converged on Fort Worth, which also developed into a center for oil stock exchanges. In 1927 Meacham Field[qv] opened, offering commercial and passenger service from locally operated Braniff Airways[qv] and American Airlines (*see* AMR CORPORATION). Medical care was provided by several hospitals—Fort Worth Children's, St. Joseph's, John Peter Smith, and Harris. In 1924 the city government was changed to the council-manager form,[qv] and the city limits were expanded to 61.57 square miles. The major additions were Arlington Heights, Riverside, Niles City, and Polytechnic. During the Great Depression[qv] of the 1930s Fort Worth was able to secure federal money for many construction projects, including the Will Rogers Memorial Coliseum and Auditorium, as well as the renovation and building of public schools. With the outbreak of World War II[qv] the aviation industry came to Fort Worth. Consolidated Vultee Aircraft Corporation,[qv] the largest manufacturer in Fort Worth, was later bought by General Dynamics Corporation. Next to the bomber factory the Army Air Force located the Tarrant Field Air Drome, which in 1948 became Carswell Air Force Base,[qv] a part of the Strategic Air Command and a station for the B–36. Because the Trinity River had flooded severely in 1922 and 1949, Fort Worth residents secured federal money to build the Trinity River Floodway. The project was completed in 1956. Texas Christian University, Texas Wesleyan College, and Southwestern Baptist Theological Seminary provided higher education.

By the 1950s the downtown area had deteriorated, and in 1956 the Gruen Plan was introduced. This plan called for a freeway loop around the central business district, the construction of underground tunnels, and the elimination of vehicular traffic inside the loop. Although the plan was never accepted, it emphasized the necessity of planning for the city's future needs. During the 1960s and 1970s Fort Worth was filled with economic activity. The Tarrant County Convention Center, the Dallas–Fort Worth International Airport,qv the Amon Carter Museum,qv and the Kimbell Art Museumqv were constructed. Amon Carter, Sr.,qv publisher of the Fort Worth *Star-Telegram*, worked diligently to promote the city's growth. He was also a successful oil operator and owned much real estate in the area. He worked hard to publicize the city and secured government installations and projects. During this time the city limits expanded to 272 square miles. Over the past century the city population has boomed—6,663 in 1880, 26,668 in 1900, 277,047 in 1950, 385,164 in 1980, and 447,619 in 1990, but in spite of increasing urbanization Fort Worth has retained its western flavor as the city "Where the West Begins."

BIBLIOGRAPHY: Verana E. Berrong, History of Tarrant County: From Its Beginnings until 1875 (M.A. thesis, Texas Christian University, 1938). David Ross Copeland, Emerging Young Giant: Fort Worth, 1877–1880 (M.A. thesis, Texas Christian University, 1972). Macel D. Ezell, Progressivism in Fort Worth Politics, 1935–38 (M.A. thesis, Texas Christian University, 1963). James Farber, *Fort Worth in the Civil War* (Belton, Texas: Peter Hansborough Bell Press, 1960). Fort Worth *Star-Telegram*, October 30, 1969. Julia Kathryn Garrett, *Fort Worth: A Frontier Triumph* (Austin: Encino, 1972). Thomas Albert Harkins, A History of the Municipal Government of Fort Worth, Texas (M.A. thesis, Texas Christian University, 1937). Donald Alvin Henderson, Fort Worth and the Depression, 1929–33 (M.A. thesis, Texas Christian University, 1937). Delia Ann Hendricks, The History of Cattle and Oil in Tarrant County (M.A. thesis, Texas Christian University, 1969). Oliver Knight, *Fort Worth, Outpost on the Trinity* (Norman: University of Oklahoma Press, 1953). Richard G. Miller, "Fort Worth and the Progressive Era: The Movement for Charter Revision, 1899–1907," in *Essays on Urban America*, ed. Margaret Francine Morris and Elliot West (Austin: University of Texas Press, 1975). Ruth Gregory Newman, The Industrialization of Fort Worth (M.A. thesis, North Texas State University, 1950). Buckley B. Paddock, *History of Texas: Fort Worth and the Texas Northwest Edition* (4 vols., Chicago: Lewis, 1922). J'Nell Pate, *Livestock Legacy: The Fort Worth Stockyards, 1887–1987* (College Station: Texas A&M University Press, 1988). Warren H. Plasters, A History of Amusements in Fort Worth from the Beginning to 1879 (M.A. thesis, Texas Christian University, 1947). Leonard Sanders, *How Fort Worth Became the Texasmost City* (Fort Worth: Amon Carter Museum, 1973). Robert H. Talbert, *Cowtown-Metropolis: Case Study of a City's Growth and Structure* (Fort Worth: Texas Christian University, 1956). Joseph C. Terrell, *Reminiscences of the Early Days of Fort Worth* (Fort Worth, 1906). Mack H. Williams, *In Old Fort Worth: The Story of a City and Its People as Published in the News-Tribune in 1976 and 1977* (1977). Mack H. Williams, comp., *The News-Tribune in Old Fort Worth* (Fort Worth: News-Tribune, 1975).
Janet Schmelzer

FORT WORTH BELT RAILWAY. The Fort Worth Belt Railway was a terminal line with 3.2 miles of mainline track and 15.27 miles of yard track and sidings. It was incorporated as the Fort Worth Stockyards and Belt Railway Company on November 26, 1895, and the name was changed to Fort Worth Belt on January 22, 1903. The business office was located at Fort Worth. Members of the first board of directors included George B. Robbins, J. B. Googins, O. W. Matthews, W. B. King, W. B. Robbins, W. O. Johnson, and H. C. Gardner.

The company laid thirteen miles of track in Fort Worth in 1904–05 and two miles in 1913. Although it was originally intended as a belt railway, the railroad operated as a switching line for the Fort Worth railroads and a plant facility for industries. It served several large meat, provision, grain, and produce companies in north Fort Worth, but its primary customers were the Fort Worth Stockyardsqv Company and the Armour and Swift packing companies. In 1931, in compliance with a United States Supreme Court ruling that required all packing concerns to dispose of their interest in terminal railroads and stockyards, the Fort Worth Stockyards Company made arrangements to sell the railway. On May 31, 1931, an agreement was signed, subject to the approval of the Interstate Commerce Commission, by which the road was acquired by the Republic National Company, which then contracted to sell 60 percent interest, valued at $900,000, to the Texas and Pacific Railway Company. Application for approval was filed on August 19, 1931, but the application was denied in March 1932, when the commission ruled that the price was too high. Sale was authorized, however, at $700,000. The Fort Worth Belt was merged into the Missouri Pacific Railroad Company on November 1, 1978.
Harold D. Conner

FORT WORTH CHRISTIAN COLLEGE. Fort Worth Christian College, Fort Worth, a private, coeducational junior college of the Church of Christ,qv offered standard liberal arts courses and a strong Bible program. In 1956 the college obtained a forty-eight-acre campus. On January 21, 1957, a board of trustees was established. A state charter was granted on May 13, and Roy Deaver, first president of the college, began a campaign that produced $254,000 for construction of administration and classroom buildings. The college began classes in the fall of 1959 and expanded annually. Thomas B. Warren was appointed president that year, and during his administration a cafeteria-auditorium and a library-classroom building were added. Claude A. Guild succeeded Warren in 1961. Between 1961 and 1964 two dormitories, a president's home, and a gymnasium-auditorium were completed. Enrollment for the 1962–63 year was 100.

By 1965 twelve departments offered work leading to the associate in arts or associate in science degree. All work offered conformed to standards of accreditation agencies. In 1969 the faculty numbered eighteen, and the library holdings reached 13,500 volumes. Enrollment during the 1968–69 regular term was 220. Curtis E. Ramey served as president in 1965.

Due to financial difficulties Fort Worth Christian College ceased to exist in 1971 and became a branch of Abilene Christian College (now Abilene Christian University). Thomas A. Shaver was executive dean. Enrollment was 104 during 1970–71, and the faculty numbered fourteen. In 1973 the branch merged with the former Christian College of the Southwest to form the ACC Metrocenter. By 1976 the Metrocenter had become Abilene Christian University in Dallas (now Amber University), and classes were discontinued at the Fort Worth campuses.

BIBLIOGRAPHY: Donald W. Whisenhunt, *The Encyclopedia of Texas Colleges and Universities* (Austin: Eakin, 1986).

FORT WORTH AND DENVER NORTHERN RAILWAY. The Fort Worth and Denver Northern Railway Company was chartered by the Burlington system on May 20, 1929. The road was to build from Childress north to Shamrock in Wheeler County and then northwest to Pampa in Gray County, a distance of 110 miles. The initial capital was $110,000, and the business office was in Childress. Members of the first board of directors included John A. Hulenqv of Houston; F. E. Williamson and C. E. Spens, both from Chicago, Illinois; and Khleber M. Van Zandt,qv F. E. Clarity, T. B. Yarbrough, J. H. Barwise, W. C. Logan, and W. O. Hamilton, all from Fort Worth. The 110 miles of track from Childress north to Shamrock in Wheeler County and then northwest to Pampa in Gray County was completed on July 15, 1932. The road was leased to the Fort Worth and Denver City for operation and merged into that company on June 13, 1952. The section between Wellington and Pampa was abandoned in 1970.
Chris Cravens

FORT WORTH AND DENVER RAILWAY. The Fort Worth and Denver Railway Company was chartered on May 26, 1873, as the Fort Worth and Denver City Railway Company; the name was changed on August 7, 1951. The line's promoters, particularly Warren H. H. Lawrence, had begun advocating a line from the Gulf of Mexico to Colorado by way of Fort Worth as early as 1869. The financial panic of 1873 delayed construction of the railroad until 1881, when Grenville M. Dodge became interested in the project. Dodge organized the Texas and Colorado Railway Improvement Company to build and equip the Fort Worth and Denver City in return for $20,000 in stock and $20,000 in bonds for each mile of track laid. In April 1881 the Fort Worth and Denver City and the Denver and New Orleans Railroad Company agreed to connect at the Texas–New Mexico border. Dodge began construction at Hodge Junction, just north of Fort Worth, on November 27, 1881, and by September 1882 had completed 110 miles of track to Wichita Falls. Construction resumed in 1885, when the line was extended from Wichita Falls to Harrold, a distance of thirty-four miles. In 1886 the line was extended thirty-one miles from Harrold to Chilicothe. The following year 194 miles of track were built from Chilicothe to the Canadian River, and in 1888 the line was extended to the Texas state line. The Denver, Texas and Fort Worth Railroad, organized to build the section south of Pueblo, Colorado, had not arrived at the state line, and the Fort Worth and Denver City construction forces continued to build into New Mexico Territory, where the railheads met at Union Park, 528 miles from Fort Worth, on March 14, 1888.

The Fort Worth and Denver City had been built with no state subsidy other than the right-of-way across state-owned lands totaling 2,162 acres. Service between Fort Worth and Denver began on April 1, 1888. During that year the Denver, Texas and Fort Worth acquired stock control of the Fort Worth and Denver City. In 1890 the Denver, Texas and Fort Worth became part of the Union Pacific, Denver and Gulf Railway Company, but both it and its Texas connection entered receivership during the panic of 1893. The Fort Worth and Denver City was reorganized in 1895 under the same name and charter, with Dodge as president. Since the charter of the Fort Worth and Denver City prohibited the construction of branch lines, new companies were formed to do any new work. The first of these companies was the Panhandle Railway Company, chartered on December 13, 1887, to build between Washburn and Panhandle City, where connection was made with the Southern Kansas Railway Company of Texas (Santa Fe). This fifteen-mile line was leased to the Santa Fe in 1898 and sold in 1900. The Fort Worth and Denver Terminal Railway Company was chartered on March 24, 1890, to give the Fort Worth and Denver City its own entrance into and terminal facilities in Fort Worth. Another company, the Acme Tap Railroad Company, was incorporated on January 7, 1889, when it became necessary to condemn a right-of-way from Acme to Agatite in order to construct an industrial spur to serve the Salina Cement Plaster Company. Other feeder lines were built at Wichita Falls, but these were not directly promoted by the Fort Worth and Denver City. Morgan Jones[qv] and Dodge were among the parties who incorporated the Wichita Valley Railway Company on February 8, 1890. This company constructed a line from Wichita Falls to Seymour. Jones was also active in the Wichita Falls and Oklahoma Railway Company, chartered on October 12, 1903, to build a line to Byers, as well as in the Wichita Valley Railway Company, which ran from Seymour to Stamford and was completed by January 1, 1907. Another company, the Abilene and Northern Railway Company, built between Stamford and Abilene. These feeders were all acquired by the Colorado and Southern Railway Company, successor to the Union Pacific, Denver and Gulf. The Colorado and Southern also constructed the Stamford and Northwestern Railway Company between Stamford and Spur in 1909. These feeders were all leased to the Wichita Valley Railway Company. In the 1920s the Colorado and Southern expanded its service area by building several new railroads. The Wichita Falls and Oklahoma Railway Company of Oklahoma was formed to extend the Wichita Falls and Oklahoma line to Waurika, Oklahoma. On March 6, 1925, the Fort Worth and Denver South Plains Railway Company was chartered to tap the growing agricultural market in the South Plains. This line began at Estelline and by mid-1928 had completed 206 miles to Lubbock and Plainview with branches to Silverton and Dimmit. The Fort Worth and Denver Northern Railway Company, chartered on May 29, 1929, completed its 110-mile line between Childress and Pampa in July 1932. Both the Fort Worth and Denver South Plains and the Fort Worth and Denver Northern were leased to the Fort Worth and Denver City for operation. Elsewhere during the 1920s the Fort Worth and Denver City extended service from Fort Worth to Dallas in 1925 by acquiring trackage rights over the Chicago, Rock Island and Gulf. In June of 1925 the Fort Worth and Denver City purchased the one-eighth interest in the Union Terminal Company at Dallas owned by the Trinity and Brazos Valley.

As the first rail line to penetrate Northwest Texas, the Fort Worth and Denver City influenced the area's growth. The construction of stockyards at Wichita Falls and later railheads ended the necessity for long cattle drives. The Fort Worth and Denver City actively promoted the growth of towns and farming to increase traffic for the line; "No settlers, no trains" was the company's rule. The line is given credit for promoting winter wheat as food for cattle. The railroad pioneered control of wind erosion by furnishing trees and tree seedlings to use as windbreaks. The road urged the introduction of cotton to the plains country, actively supporting the work of agriculturist Seamann A. Knapp.[qv] The Fort Worth and Denver City cooperated with ranchers and land developers in experimental farms to show potential settlers the value of West Texas as farm country and was instrumental in lobbying for the first federally funded experimental farm in the Panhandle.[qv] The line also furnished seed for experimental plots on private lands to encourage agricultural diversity. Some of the line's major stockholders were closely associated with land development firms that provided land at extremely liberal terms to attract settlers to the region. During the drought years of the 1890s the railroad provided free seed for farmers to keep them in business. In other years the line acted as a banker for the farmers and accepted crop liens as collateral for loans. During the Centennial Year of 1936 the Fort Worth and Denver City and the Burlington–Rock Island cooperated in operating the first streamlined train in Texas, the Sam Houston Zephyr, between Houston and Dallas–Fort Worth. In 1931 the Fort Worth and Denver City and the Rock Island jointly leased the Burlington–Rock Island between Waxahachie and Teague and expanded the lease to the entire property in 1950. On June 13, 1952, all of the other Colorado and Southern properties in Texas, with the exception of the Burlington–Rock Island, were merged into the Fort Worth and Denver. In 1965 the Colorado and Southern and Rock Island absorbed the Burlington–Rock Island, with each owner acquiring an undivided one-half interest in the property. The Colorado and Southern's interest was also merged into the Fort Worth and Denver. Other acquisitions included the purchase of Wichita Falls terminal properties from the abandoned Wichita Falls and Southern in 1954. In 1973 the Fort Worth and Denver acquired forty-two miles between Stamford and Rotan from the Texas Central. However, this line was abandoned in 1976. Other abandonments included the line between Stamford and Spur in 1967, the Wellington to Pampa line in 1970, the track from Teague to Mexia in 1976, and the Sterley to Silverton section in 1978. When the Colorado and Southern was merged into the Burlington Northern Railroad on December 31, 1981, the Fort Worth and Denver expanded to operate the track between Texline and Denver. The Fort Worth and Denver, in turn, was merged into the BN on December 31, 1982. In 1989 the BN abandoned the former Fort Worth and Denver South Plains between Estelline and Lubbock in favor of trackage rights over the Santa Fe. Sixty-four miles of the right-of-way between Estelline and South Plains were opened in 1993 as a hike-and-bike trail as part of the Caprock Canyons State Park[qv] Trailway System. *William C. Billingsley*

FORT WORTH AND DENVER SOUTH PLAINS RAILWAY. The Fort Worth and Denver South Plains Railway Company was chartered on March 6, 1925, to build from Estelline in Hall County to a point in Castro County, with a branch from Briscoe County to Lubbock County, about 200 miles. The line came out of an attempt by the Fort Worth and Denver City to build branches into the lower Panhandle[qv] to handle the shipping of cotton. The initial capital was $200,000, and the business office was in Fort Worth. Members of the first board of directors included Hale Holden and C. G. Burnham of Chicago, Illinois, and Khleber M. Van Zandt,[qv] F. E. Clarity, W. F. Sterley, T. B. Yarbrough, Joseph H. Barwise, Jr., W. C. Logan, and W. O. Hamilton, all from Fort Worth. In 1928 the road completed 206 miles of track from Estelline through Sterley and Plainview to Dimmit, and from Lubbock through Sterley to Silverton. The route required the construction of two tunnels near Quitaque. The line was leased to the Fort Worth and Denver City for operation and merged into that company on June 13, 1952. In 1989 the Burlington Northern, successor to the Fort Worth and Denver, abandoned much of the former Fort Worth and Denver South Plains. During the summer of 1993 64½ miles of right-of-way from Estelline to South Plains opened as a hike-and-bike trail as part of the Caprock Canyons State Park[qv] Trailway System.

BIBLIOGRAPHY: W. D. Jeter, The Fort Worth and Denver South Plains Railway (M.A. thesis, Texas Technical College, 1949).

Chris Cravens

FORT WORTH *GUIDE*. The Fort Worth *Guide*, a black daily newspaper, was published in 1888 by Moore and Smith, but most probably appeared for little more than a year.

Diana J. Kleiner

FORT WORTH *MIND*. The Fort Worth *Mind*, a weekly black newspaper, was published by Raymond L. Melton and C. R. Wise from 1944 until 1945.

Diana J. Kleiner

FORT WORTH MUSEUM OF SCIENCE AND HISTORY. The Fort Worth Museum of Science and History, formerly the Fort Worth Children's Museum, began with the ideas and work of the Council of Administrative Women in Education in 1939. The museum, chartered in 1941, was originally housed in a classroom of De Zavala Elementary School. In 1947 growth required a move to the old Harding home on Summit Avenue. In 1953 a new building was constructed through public funding, and the museum was moved to its present location in Amon Carter Square. The Amon G. Carter Foundation provided donations for two major wings added in 1961 and 1964. Changing programs and exhibits came to appeal to all ages, and it became apparent that the museum was no longer exclusively for children; in 1968 its name was changed. In 1983, 30,000 additional feet was added for the Omni Theater, bringing the size of the museum to 118,000 square feet. The museum was one of the first to achieve accreditation from the American Association of Museums.

A twenty-six-member board of trustees governs the museum, which has an executive director. William G. Hassler was director from 1953 to 1962, followed by Helmuth J. Naumer, who held the position until 1976, when Donald R. Otto took over. The Fort Worth Museum of Science and History is funded by income from the museum school, gift shop, Noble Planetarium, and Omni Theater, and by the city of Fort Worth and Tarrant County.

From its inception, the museum was devoted to implementing programs that would foster a better understanding and appreciation of history, science, and culture. There are five permanent exhibits in the museum. Medicine and Man is divided into two sections, the Hall of Medical Science and the Hall of Physiology. The Hall of Texas History includes dioramas and six period rooms: a general store, blacksmith shop, Victorian parlor, school room, log cabin, and barbershop. Man and His Possessions presents world cultures through such artifacts as clothing, tools, pottery, baskets, and masks. Rocks and Fossils includes the basics of geological formation and prehistoric life. Technological exhibits have included one on lasers and a semipermanent IBM exhibit named Antique Calculators and Computer Technology. Other exhibits represent a variety of subjects such as world dolls and live Texas animals. The museum also acquires temporary exhibits from around the world.

A collection of over 100,000 artifacts and specimens in both the science and history departments is used for research, exhibition, and teaching. The disciplines represented in the collections include archeology, ethnology, malacology, Texas and American history, entomology, mineralogy, herpetology, mammalogy, meteoritics, and paleontology.

The museum has a preschool for children three to five and general classes and workshops for all ages. The Noble Planetarium in the museum was named for Charlie Mary Noble,[qv] who taught the museum's astronomy classes for many years. The planetarium provides many different multimedia programs on history, geology, and meteorites, as well as on astronomy; it also presents laser-light shows. The museum houses its own curatorial library. In 1983 the museum opened the Omni Theater, which seats 356 people and features an eighty-foot tilted dome. The Omnimax film projector produces 180-degree images that surround the audience.

BIBLIOGRAPHY: Fort Worth *Press*, May 14, 1953. Fort Worth *Star-Telegram*, March 10, 1968. Paula and Ron Tyler, *Texas Museums: A Guidebook* (Austin: University of Texas Press, 1983).

Carol E. Williams

FORT WORTH AND NEW ORLEANS RAILWAY. The Fort Worth and New Orleans Railway Company was chartered on June 13, 1885, by J. J. Roche, Thomas Roche, M. C. Hurley, and other citizens of Fort Worth to build from Fort Worth to a point on the Sabine River in Newton County and thence to New Orleans by the most practical route. The capital was $300,000, and the business office was in Fort Worth. Members of the first board of directors included J. J. Roche, M. C. Hurley, Thomas Roche, Eugene Roche, John Hurley, W. S. Pendleton, and Charles C. Allen. Although New Orleans was the stated destination of the road, the first major objective was to connect with the Central Texas and Northwestern Railway, which had built to Waxahachie in 1879. Citizens of Fort Worth raised $75,000, and construction of forty-two miles of track to Waxahachie began in September 1885. The line was completed in 1886. In December 1886 the Fort Worth and New Orleans was acquired by the Houston and Texas Central Railway Company. On January 6, 1887, Charles Dillingham took formal possession of the road for the H&TC after his firm reportedly paid $500,000 for the FW&NO. In 1892 the company owned fifty-five freight cars and earned $34,911 in passenger revenue and $88,991 in freight revenue. Earnings for 1895 were $193,767. In 1899 the FW&NO built 1.92 additional miles of track, bringing the total length of mainline track to 41.97 miles. In 1901 the Texas legislature authorized the consolidation of the road with the Houston and Texas Central Railroad, which occurred on August 22, 1901. As the Fort Worth and New Orleans, the line hauled freight, including grain, lumber, livestock, and flour. In 1934 the Houston and Texas Central was merged into the Texas and New Orleans Railroad Company, which was subsequently merged into Southern Pacific Company in 1961. The Southern Pacific continued to operate the track in 1994.

W. Kellon Hightower

FORT WORTH QUARTERMASTER DEPOT. Fort Worth Quartermaster Depot served as a distribution point and supply center for the United States Army during World War II.[qv] Fort Worth was chosen as the site because of its proximity to area army camps, large packing plants, highways, and railroad lines. Construction of the $10 million depot began in the winter of 1941–42 and included extension of lines of the Missouri, Kansas and Texas and the Santa Fe railroads to the site. The army activated the supply point on May 4, 1942. Within two months the eighty-four-building depot also became a distribution center for the armed forces. In December of that year the army designated the site as an emergency supply point for troop trains. The Fort Worth Quartermaster Depot's supply area covered all or parts of Texas, Oklahoma, Arkansas, New Mexico, Louisiana (excluding New Orleans), and Arizona. By the end of 1943 it was the second or third largest military supply center (according to the number of troops supplied) in the nation. The depot continued to operate after the end of World War II, but at a greatly reduced level of activity. In the early 1960s the supply center ceased operations.

David Minor

FORT WORTH AND RIO GRANDE RAILWAY. The Fort Worth and Rio Grande Railway Company was chartered on June 1, 1885, to build from Fort Worth to Brownwood, a distance of 127 miles. A branch was also proposed from Logan's Gap in Comanche County to Coleman in Coleman County, a distance of forty miles. The capital was $200,000, and the business office was in Fort Worth. Members of the first board of directors included Edmund A. Morse of Rutland, Vermont; W. D. Nichols, Thomas G. Rigney, and S. B. Bostwick, all of New York; and W. W. H. Lawrence, Buckley B. Paddock,qv Thomas Roche, W. L. Lase, and Charles Swasey, all of Fort Worth. Work on the line began on November 23, 1886, after Paddock persuaded the Vanderbilt railroad syndicate to fund its construction. Both Fort Worth boosters and the Vanderbilts dreamed of building a transcontinental route linking New York City, Fort Worth, and Topolobampo Harbor on the Pacific coast in Mexico. Fort Worth businessmen also believed the Fort Worth and Rio Grande would strengthen the local economy by bringing foreign trade, the Southwest Texas livestock business, and additional service and distribution facilities to Fort Worth. In actual operation, the road fell far short of these goals. Construction was slow, and the route was changed many times before the tracks reached Granbury, forty miles away, in October 1887. The line was extended seventy-four more miles to Comanche by early 1890, and an additional thirty miles to Brownwood in 1891, bringing the total miles of track to 144. In 1892 the company owned ten locomotives, ninety-nine freight cars, and nine passenger cars and earned $64,990 in passenger revenue, $164,435 in freight revenue, and $11,364 in other revenue.

The road was acquired in 1901 by the St. Louis and San Francisco Railway Company (Frisco), which financed a fifty mile extension to Brady that opened in 1903 and an additional twenty-seven miles to Menard in 1911. Although other extensions were considered, Menard remained the end of the line. In order to increase its livestock traffic once it reached Brady, the Fort Worth and Rio Grande built a 100 mile long fenced and watered cattle trail between Sonora Brady. This trail was cut back to Menard once the railroad reached that point. The company also explored for coal in Coleman County.

The railway's immigration policy, which aided in the development of Southwest Texas through establishment of the Luverne Colony in Crockett County, cosponsorship of the Texas Spring Palace,qv and organization of the "Karporama Car" (the state's first traveling immigration exhibit), was the company's only success. (*Karporama* is a "Texas Greek" formation on the Greek word for "fruit," which is here generalized to mean "resources" or "products"; hence "resources exhibit car.") In 1931 the Fort Worth and Rio Grande was classified as a Class I railroad by the Railroad Commission.qv Earnings for that year were $670,502 but, as in most other years, the railroad operated at a deficit. Although the road was controlled by the Frisco, it was independently operated until March 1, 1937, when it was sold to the Atchison, Topeka and Santa Fe Railway Company for $1,519,325. The Fort Worth and Rio Grande was then leased to the Gulf, Colorado and Santa Fe Railway Company for operation, until it was merged into that company on December 31, 1948. The acquisition of the Fort Worth and Rio Grande shortened the Santa Fe route from West Texas to Fort Worth by 117 miles. Several sections of the former Fort Worth and Rio Grande were abandoned by the Santa Fe, including the forty-four miles between Brownwood and Brady in 1959 and the thirty-one miles between Brady and Menard in 1972. The remainder of the line was acquired by the Cen-Tex Rail Link on May 20, 1994.

BIBLIOGRAPHY: Patricia L. Duncan, Enterprise: B. B. Paddock and Fort Worth—A Case Study of Late Nineteenth Century American Boosterism (M.A. thesis, University of Texas at Arlington, 1982). William Curry Holden, *Alkali Trails, or Social and Economic Movements of the Texas Frontier, 1846–1900* (Dallas: Southwest, 1930). Buckley B. Paddock, *History of Texas: Fort Worth and the Texas Northwest Edition* (4 vols., Chicago: Lewis, 1922).

Patricia L. Duncan

FORT WORTH SCHOOL. The Fort Worth School of artists, most active as a group between 1945 and 1955, cannot be defined by a common aesthetic, as can the Dallas Nine,qv but by their support of one another and their development of an art community in Fort Worth. The group emerged in the aftermath of World War II,qv when the industrial, financial, and cultural sectors of Fort Worth grew rapidly. The Fort Worth Art Association had reorganized in 1939 and implemented a policy to exhibit the work of local artists. Under the leadership of Sam Cantey III and Sallie M. Gillespie, and later Dan Defenbacher, the association's annual solo exhibition and "Local Artists Show" became important stimuli to artists and patrons alike.

A varied group of men and women was part of the Fort Worth School; some of the best-known artists were Blanche McVeigh, E. Dickson Reeder, Veronica Helfensteller,qqv Evaline Sellors, Flora Blanc Reeder (who painted under the name Flora Blanc), Kelly Fearing, Cynthia Brants, Bill Bomar, McKie Trotter, and Bror Utter. Also prominent in the group were Emily Guthrie Smith, Charles T. Williams,qqv George Grammer, Lia Cuilty, David Brownlow, Marjorie Johnson Lee, Ann Williams Boynton, Jack Boynton, and John Erickson. Although the styles of these artists were quite distinct from one another, common influences shaped the work of many in the group. Cubism, with flattened, shifting planes, structural grid, and roots in primitive art, colored the works of Dickson Reeder, George Grammer, Bill Bomar, Cynthia Brants, Bror Utter, and David Brownlow, among others. Surrealist interest in fantastic and dreamlike imagery influenced the work of Veronica Helfensteller, Kelly Fearing, and Flora Blanc, as well as that of Reeder, Bomar, and Utter. Although some of the Fort Worth artists worked in a number of modes, including realism, the group as a whole moved beyond the painstaking representation and earthy subject matter of Regionalism, which had dominated Texas art since the early 1930s.

The Fort Worth artists' awareness of European trends was fostered in part by the Fort Worth School of Fine Arts, founded in 1931 by McVeigh, Sellors, and Wade Jolly, and attended by many of the artists in the group. Flora Reeder was born in New York and often summered in Paris, where she studied with Leon Kroll, George Gross, Yasuo Kuniyoshi, Fernand Leger, and S. W. Hayter. Dickson Reeder also studied in Paris, with Alexandra Exter and S. W. Hayter. The faculty of the Fort Worth School of Fine Arts organized an exhibition program and brought to Fort Worth the first show of such School of Paris artists as Pablo Picasso, Henri Matisse, Georges Braque, and André Derain. The Fort Worth Art Association also brought in many exhibitions from New York galleries that exposed local artists to the work of leading contemporaries. Perhaps most influential, however, were Dickson and Flora Reeder, whose home became a forum for the exchange of new ideas that they gathered on their travels. The Reeders were particularly generous in sharing printmaking techniques that they learned at Stanley William Hayter's Atelier 17, thus encouraging a number of other artists to experiment with the intaglio process.

Other activities that united the group included work on sets for the Reeder School,^qv established by the Reeders in 1945. This school's annual productions prompted interactions among artists, actors, musicians, and dancers until it closed in 1958. The local artists were also active in the Fort Worth Art Association. Many of them spoke or demonstrated painting techniques for local organizations, donated works for auction, and decorated debutante balls in order to raise money for the new museum, which opened in 1954. Several of the artists associated with the Fort Worth School displayed their work nationally and internationally. The Fort Worth Art Center (later the Modern Art Museum of Fort Worth^qv) subsequently shifted its emphasis to national and international art, and the "Local Show" was discontinued after 1965.

The Fort Worth School dispersed after the mid-1950s; many artists moved away, and those who chose to stay promoted their art elsewhere. However, the activities of the Fort Worth artists had effected a change in the national perception of Texan art, both through positively received group shows in New York galleries and enthusiastic reviews of Texas exhibitions in the New York *Times*. Closer to home, the Fort Worth artists were instrumental in raising funds for the city's first independent art museum and in cultivating art patrons. Such collectors as Kay and Velma F. Kimbell and Amon G. Carter, Jr.,^qqv subsequently established outstanding museums, the activities of which contributed to Fort Worth's importance as a national art center.

BIBLIOGRAPHY: *Beyond Regionalism: The Fort Worth School (1945–1955): A Texas Sesquicentennial Exhibition* (Albany, Texas: Old Jail Art Center, 1986). Jerry Bywaters, *Texas Painting and Sculpture: 20th Century* (Dallas: Broadax Printing, 1971). Floyd Durham, "An Exploration of Some of the Causes of a Developing Painter's Colony in Fort Worth, Texas," *Journal of Cultural Economics* 1 (December 1977). *New York Times*, November 15, 1953.
Kendall Curlee

FORT WORTH *STAR-TELEGRAM*. The Fort Worth *Star* was founded in 1906 by a group of newsmen including Col. Louis J. Wortham (as publisher), Amon G. Carter, Sr.^qqv (as advertising manager), and D. C. McCaleb and A. G. Dawson; they also had the help of wholesale grocer and major investor Col. Paul Waples. The *Star* was first published in sixteen pages for a 4,500-copy free delivery. By 1908 the *Star* was in financial difficulty, and Carter and Wortham decided to buy out their rival, the *Telegram*, an evening newspaper that dated back to the Fort Worth *Evening Mail* and the Fort Worth *Mail Telegram* and other papers beginning around 1879. The new paper, known as the *Star-Telegram*, began publication in 1909, and was later identified in the 1920s by a phrase on its masthead reading "Where the West Begins." Carter and the paper stressed local news and served eighty-four counties, with some papers delivered in the Panhandle^qv by stagecoach. The *Star-Telegram* had a preelectronic distribution area of 350,000 square miles, and daily home delivery as far as 700 miles west of Fort Worth. Carter and the paper successfully resisted takeover attempts by William Randolph Hearst, who sold the Fort Worth *Record* to the *Star-Telegram* in 1925. In 1922 the paper began the first Fort Worth radio station, WBAP, "We Bring A Program." The *Star-Telegram* established the first television station in the southern half of the United States in the early fall of 1948 and did a remote broadcast of President Harry Truman's whistle-stop campaign visit to Fort Worth. In 1954, WBAP–TV also did the first colorcast in Texas, at a time when there were no more than 100 color television sets in Fort Worth and Dallas. Carter was majority owner and publisher of the paper until his death in 1955, when he was succeeded by his son, Amon G. Carter, Jr.,^qv who died in 1982. The paper, an active participant in the Fort Worth community, supported numerous local causes as well as efforts to create Big Bend National Park^qv in far west Texas and to establish Texas Technological College, now Texas Tech University. The paper was sold in 1974 to Capital Cities Communications, Incorporated. The circulation at that time was 235,000 daily papers and 224,000 on Sundays.

Under Capital Cities, which later became Capital Cities/ABC, Incorporated, when it purchased the ABC television network in 1986, the *Star-Telegram* won two Pulitzer Prizes. The first was in 1981 for photographer Larry Price's photos of Liberian officials being slain by a firing squad. The second (1985) was the coveted gold-medal Pulitzer for meritorious public service; it was awarded for a news series that exposed a flaw in Bell helicopters that was a factor in numerous crashes over a seventeen-year period. In the 1980s the *Star-Telegram* pioneered the establishment of an electronic information service and built one of the most modern newspaper printing and distribution plants in the nation. StarText, an "electronic newspaper" begun in 1982, complemented the printed newspaper with updated news and information; it was available on computer via a local telephone call in the Fort Worth and Dallas area. In 1986 the newspaper opened a new state-of-the-art printing facility that enabled it to produce one of the most colorful and visually attractive newspapers anywhere. In the early 1990s, under publisher Richard L. Connor, circulation climbed above 290,000 daily and more than 350,000 on Sundays.

BIBLIOGRAPHY: Jimmy Donaldson, "The Voice of the West," *Texas Historian*, March 1981. Phillip J. Meek, *Fort Worth Star Telegram: "Where the West Begins"* (New York: Newcomen Society in North America, 1981). *Texas Newspaper Directory* (Austin: Texas Press Service, 1991).
Diana J. Kleiner

FORT WORTH STOCKYARDS. The Fort Worth Stock Yards were officially incorporated on March 23, 1893, and the corporation was dissolved on May 31, 1944, but those who purchased it at the later date continued operations under the same name until November 1, 1981, when they leased the facilities to a company that continued using the same name. The Fort Worth livestock market became the largest in Texas and the Southwest, the biggest market south of Kansas City, and ranked between third and fourth consistently among the nation's large terminal livestock markets for five decades, from about 1905 to the mid-1950s. Texans started calling Fort Worth "Cowtown" soon after the Civil War,^qv when drovers began herding cattle from South Texas northward to connect with the Chisholm Trail^qv in Indian Territory and stopping in Fort Worth for supplies. Not until the Texas and Pacific Railway arrived on July 19, 1896, did promoters build pens to hold cattle, but business leaders of Fort Worth already dreamed of packing plants and stockyards to make their community a permanent focus of the cattle industry. By 1886 four stockyards had been built near the railroads. Businessmen chartered the Union Stock Yards on July 26, 1887, and opened their 258-acre facility north of the Trinity River in midsummer 1889. They also chartered a packing company. Local interests invited Boston capitalist Greenleaf W. Simpson to visit, with the hope that he would invest. Simpson, with a half dozen Boston and Chicago associates, incorporated the Fort Worth Stock Yards Company in West Virginia because of more favorable tax laws there, and purchased the Union Stock Yards and the Fort Worth Packing Company in April 1893. A neighbor of Simpson in Boston, Louvulle V. Niles, bought half the shares. The investors struggled because of the financial panic of 1893 and other problems, but in 1896 the company began a fat-stock show that has survived to the present as one of the largest livestock shows in the nation, the Southwestern Exposition and Livestock Show.^qv In 1896 stockyard owners also began a market newspaper that still exists today under independent ownership as the *Weekly Livestock Reporter*, the largest livestock newspaper in the Southwest. In 1897–98 the company, in connection with the Bureau of Animal Industry, gained nationwide attention by experimenting with cattle dipping to kill ticks (*see* TEXAS FEVER).

An agreement Simpson and Niles made in 1902 with Armour and Swift brought in two of the nation's largest meatpackers, which constructed modern plants adjacent to the stockyards. In a stock reorganization, each packer received a third interest in the stockyards company, and Simpson, Niles, and smaller investors retained a third. In exchange for stock and land on which to build their plants, the packers agreed that each animal they slaughtered would pass through the stockyards at a standard fee. Boom years followed for the Fort Worth Stock Yards Company after the arrival of Armour and Swift. Immigrants came from Central Europe to work in the plants and settled in a community that stockyard officials incorporated in 1902 under the name North Fort Worth.

The first decade of the twentieth century saw great growth in livestock-related industries in Fort Worth—grain elevators, livestock-pharmaceutical companies, and other meatpackers. The Fort Worth Stock Yards Company constituted the hub around which everything else revolved. The reorganized company spent $125,000 for a two-story Spanish-style exchange building and constructed brick-floored pens with a capacity of 24,500 animals. By 1905 the Fort Worth market had grown to fifth in the nation. In 1906 the calf market at Fort Worth ranked second only to Chicago. Because of rapid growth, the yards kept expanding. In March 1908, when a new $175,000 coliseum for the fat-stock show opened, the company hosted the first cutting-horse contest ever held indoors under electric lights. Population in Fort Worth tripled during the first decade after Armour and Swift came. The larger city extended its city limits to include the smaller North Fort Worth in 1909 but left the actual stockyards and other factories outside as a tax-free industrial district. Two years later, when Fort Worth planned to annex the district, the stockyard interests incorporated another small community, Niles City, which lasted as a separate entity until 1922. During those years it called itself "the richest little city in the United States" because in its one-half square mile it comprised a $30 million stockyard and meatpacking industry.

To stimulate more hog receipts for its market the Fort Worth Stock Yards Company sent its public-relations agent, Charles C. French, to rural areas in Texas and the South from 1909 to 1914, to establish "pig clubs" among rural youth. His efforts preceded and assisted in the spread of Four-H clubs after the Smith-Lever Act established the United States Extension Service in 1914 (see TEXAS AGRICULTURAL EXTENSION SERVICE). New horse and mule barns, completed in March 1912 with a capacity of 5,000 animals, enabled Fort Worth to become the largest horse and mule market in the country during the early days of World War I,[qv] when agents of foreign governments purchased cavalry animals at the yards. The year 1917 set records that stood for nearly thirty years; more than a million cattle and a million hogs arrived, for a total of 3.5 million animals in all categories—cattle, calves, hogs, sheep, and horses and mules. In 1921 a Packers and Stockyards Act decreed that the nation's large meatpackers divest themselves of stockyards, so Armour and Swift had to begin the sale of Fort Worth Stock Yards Company stock. The Armour Company established General Stockyards to purchase the stock they owned in numerous stockyards, and Swift established United Stockyards. Eventually United Stockyards bought the Fort Worth Stock Yards Company stock belonging to General Stockyards and others. During the Great Depression,[qv] though receipts declined, the company paid consistent dividends. It provided round-the-clock service, retained nearly 200 employees, and had a capacity of 30,000 cattle, 18,000 sheep, 12,000 hogs, and 4,000 horses and mules on its 253-acre site. By 1936 Texas had become the largest-producing state for both cattle and sheep. In May 1937, for the first time in history, total receipts in Fort Worth topped the nation, exceeding even Chicago and Kansas City. The year 1937 proved to be the largest since 1917, with over three million animals received.

By 1944 United Stockyards had purchased all Fort Worth Stock Yards Company stock. United dissolved the corporation calling itself the Fort Worth Stock Yards, and the yards became a wholly owned subsidiary of United. Little changed, for as a division of United the company continued under the same leadership and name. Sometime in the 1940s the company began to write *Stockyards* as one word. The war decade shattered old records. Fort Worth had developed into the nation's largest sheep market, as two million sheep a year arrived. The total receipts in all categories in 1944 surpassed 5.25 million animals, and 1944 remained the largest year ever in the history of the market. Forty-eight commission companies operated on the yards during the peak years of the 1940s, along with numerous other speculators and traders. In that decade, however, aircraft manufacturing replaced livestock and meatpacking as the largest industry in Fort Worth (see AERONAUTICS AND AEROSPACE INDUSTRY).

During the 1950s receipts declined to two million animals a year because country auctions in small towns drew away trade. The shift from rail transportation to trucks, as well as the long distances from Texas ranches to Fort Worth, caused producers to sell closer to home. The Armour plant closed in 1962, and a more rapid decline in receipts came in the following years. A few small independent packers and Swift remained, but the latter closed in 1971. Commission companies dwindled to fewer than a dozen. Changes in ownership also took place. In 1959 Canal-Randolph, a large real estate–development corporation, gained control of United Stockyards. To make the yards more efficient, officials reduced pens from railroad size to truck size, laid off employees, and curtailed operations. Feedlots, particularly in the Panhandle,[qv] became the new phenomenon of the 1960s. Cattle feeding[qv] accelerated a decentralization process in livestock marketing that already had made great gains.

Receipts had dropped to a few more than 300,000 animals as the 1970s began. In 1972 the city of Fort Worth named a Stockyards Area Restoration Committee to supervise the private and public redevelopment of the area. By early 1978 some $4.4 million of public funds, mostly from the Economic Development Administration, had brought nearly $7 million in private investment. Canal-Randolph spent $500,000 to remodel pens, build new ones, and move the unloading dock. The company also spent $750,000 to renovate the Livestock Exchange Building to lease as office space. Stockyard personnel, members of the North Fort Worth Historical Society, and numerous other Fort Worth citizens celebrated at the yards on July 26, 1987, the centennial of the date that the Fort Worth Union Stock Yards was incorporated. The society, with offices and a museum in the Livestock Exchange Building, promotes the stockyards area and preserves its heritage. Several historical markers dot the area. The Chisholm Trail Days celebration in June and Pioneer Days in September testify to great interest in the area. Promoters of rodeos, restaurants, hotels, and nightclubs are capitalizing on the Western heritage that brings thousands of tourists to the Fort Worth Stockyards annually. Livestock receipts on the yards continued to dwindle. Consequently, the Fort Worth Stockyards held its last auction in December 1992, and the grand old market shut down. Tourists frequent the area for its restaurants, shops, and Western atmosphere. See also CATTLE TRAILING, HORSE AND MULE INDUSTRY, SHEEP RANCHING, SOUTHWESTERN EXPOSITION AND LIVESTOCK SHOW, SWIFT AND COMPANY, SWINE RAISING.

BIBLIOGRAPHY: E. C. Barksdale, *The Meat Packers Come to Texas* (Austin: Bureau of Business Research, University of Texas, 1959). Fort Worth Stockyards Company Collection, University of North Texas Archives. Delia Ann Hendricks, The History of Cattle and Oil in Tarrant County (M.A. thesis, Texas Christian University, 1969). J'Nell Pate, *Livestock Legacy: The Fort Worth Stockyards, 1887–1987* (College Station: Texas A&M University Press, 1988). Robert H. Talbert, *Cowtown-Metropolis: Case Study of a City's Growth and Structure* (Fort Worth: Texas Christian University, 1956). Clarence Arnold Thompson, Some Factors Contributing to the Growth of Fort Worth (M.A. thesis, University of Texas, 1933).

J'Nell L. Pate

FORT WORTH UNIVERSITY. Fort Worth University was chartered as Texas Wesleyan College by the Northern Methodist Church on June 6, 1881, and authorized to maintain the usual curricula and departments of a college and to confer the corresponding degrees. It opened in temporary quarters in Fort Worth on September 7, 1881, and was moved five years later to a site south of the city, where three stone buildings were erected on a ten-acre campus. The institution was affiliated with the Methodist Episcopal Church from 1881 to 1911. William Fielder was president. In June 1889 the trustees secured an amended charter under the name of Fort Worth University. The school of law was organized under the new charter in August 1893, and the school of medicine in July 1894. The institution belonged to the University Senate and offered courses in the arts and sciences that led to A.B., B.S., B.Litt., and Ph.D. degrees; in professional courses four years in medicine led to the M.D., and three years in law led to the LL.B. In 1910 an unsuccessful attempt was made to consolidate Fort Worth University with Polytechnic College. In 1911 the institution was joined with the Methodist Episcopal University at Oklahoma City.

BIBLIOGRAPHY: Walter N. Vernon et al., *The Methodist Excitement in Texas* (Dallas: Texas United Methodist Historical Society, 1984). Donald W. Whisenhunt, *The Encyclopedia of Texas Colleges and Universities* (Austin: Eakin Press, 1986).
Clay Sandidge

FORT WORTH AND WESTERN RAILROAD. The Fort Worth and Western Railroad Company was chartered on May 13, 1988, to acquire trackage in Fort Worth from the Burlington Northern Railroad Company. This track had been owned by the St. Louis–San Francisco Railway Company prior to its merger into the Burlington Northern. The new road was capitalized at $100,000, and the business office was in Fort Worth. Members of the first board of directors included Edward M. McLaughlin of Euless, Jerry Brannon of Granbury, and William S. Davis, Sr., Robert Robertson, and Bradford Farrar, all of Fort Worth. The company began operating in October 1988 over 6.5 miles of track. It is controlled by the Tarantula Corporation. The Tarantula Train, an excursion passenger train, operates over the Fort Worth and Western between Eighth Avenue and the Fort Worth Stockyards.qv The Tarantula Corporation also controls the Fort Worth and Dallas Railroad Company with 1.25 miles of track at Dallas. This line, acquired from the Union Pacific, began operating in November 1988.
Chris Cravens

FORTIER, HONORÉ (1764–1826). Francis Honoré (Honorato) Fortier, merchant, Spanish viceregal emissary, and soldier, was born in New Orleans in 1764, the son of Michel and Perrine (Langlois) Fortier. He was engaged in the mercantile business with his brother, Jacques, and made several voyages from Louisiana to Europe in ships carrying tobacco and other colonial products. In 1801 he went to Mexico and asked permission of the viceroy to carry a portion of Louisiana's subsidy overland through the Provincias Internasqv to New Orleans because of the insecurity of maritime travel. He was accompanied on the trip by Honorato Celestino de St. Maxent.qv The travelers journeyed from Veracruz to Mexico City by way of Puebla on April 15, 1801, and on June 10 they left Mexico City for the frontier. By June 19 they were in San Luis Potosí, where they rested until August 4. They reached Reynosa on September 8 and ascended the Rio Grande toward Camargo because of the swollen river. They swam their 700 mules and 215 horses over the river. A stampede on September 26 delayed the travelers until October 1. On October 7 they were forced to ford the Nueces River, and they continued toward the settlement at La Bahíaqv and then toward San Antonio and Natchitoches. They described crossing the Guadalupe, Colorado, Trinity, and Sabine rivers, and by November 28 they had reached the Red River in Louisiana. They descended that river through the Spanish posts of Avoyelles and Pointe Coupée and arrived at New Orleans on the evening of December 5, having traveled 922 leagues in seventy-seven days of actual travel. Fortier fought with the Fourth Regiment of the First Division of Louisiana militia as a corporal during the War of 1812. He was married to Marie Asunción Brulé, a native of New Orleans, and they had two children. Fortier died in 1826.

BIBLIOGRAPHY: Stanley Faye, "Privateersmen of the Gulf and Their Prizes," *Louisiana Historical Quarterly* 22 (October 1939). Jack D. L. Holmes, "De México a Nueva Orleans en 1801: el diario inédito de Fortier y St. Maxent," *Historia Mexicana* 16 (Julio–Septiembre 1966).
Jack D. L. Holmes

FORTO, EMILIO (1856–?). Emilio Forto, politician and businessman, was born in Gerona, Spain, in 1856. He moved with his family to New Orleans when he was twelve, then followed his older brother, Frederick, to Brownsville by the early 1870s. Like his older brother, who served as a county commissioner, Emilio Forto became involved in Cameron County politics. He was elected county judge in 1882 and served for ten years. In 1892 he was elected Cameron County sheriff for several terms. He also served as mayor of Brownsville and was on the City Board of Education for sixteen years. As a businessman Forto served as an agent for two British steamships that landed at Brazos Santiago, and he and his brother were responsible for a canal built in Brownsville. In 1900 Forto became the personal representative for banker James Stillman,qv who was chairman of the board for New York's National City Bank. Forto remained Stillman's representative for many years, overseeing the operations of the financier's numerous interests in Brownsville and throughout the lower Rio Grande Valley. Forto himself became very wealthy and owned many interests in the Brownsville area. One publication listed his home as "one of the most comfortable homes in Brownsville."

But Forto was not without his detractors. Like most politicians in South Texas during the early 1900s, Forto belonged to the Democratic political machine headed by James B. Wells, Jr.qv Many Hispanic ranchers in Cameron County opposed Forto's nomination for sheriff because of his apparent approval of the Texas Rangers'qv tactics, which often included harassing Mexican-American ranchers in the area. These ranchers also claimed that Forto had built a close alliance with smugglers in the Rio Grande Valley. A split within the Cameron County Democratic partyqv occurred before the election of 1900, and Forto left the party and joined the fledgling Republican ticket as candidate for sheriff. Forto's opponent was former county treasurer Celedonio Garza, who also was a part of the Wells machine. However, Jim Wells refused to throw his support behind either candidate. Although unsuccessful in his bid for sheriff, within a few years Forto had become a leader in the Cameron County Republican partyqv and even expressed outrage when a Mexican-American rancher was brutally murdered by a Texas Ranger. Unfortunately for Forto, Jim Wells resolidified his Democratic machine, and Forto's support dwindled. In 1908 Emilio Forto helped form the Independent Party of Cameron County, which accused Well's Democratic machine of graft, corruption, and patronage. This call for political reform was well received among the growing number of Anglo farmers who were moving to the Valley from the Midwest. These newcomers resented the hegemony ranchers held over South Texas politics, and sought to sever the patronage system to disable machine politics. Following the Independent Party's success during the election of 1910 and Rentfro B. Creager'sqv rise to power within the ranks of the party, Forto returned to the Democratic fold. He was vice president of the First National Bank of Brownsville in 1914. No information is available on his death.

BIBLIOGRAPHY: Evan Anders, *Boss Rule in South Texas: The Progressive Era* (Austin: University of Texas Press, 1982). W. H. Chatfield, *The Twin Cities of the Border and the Country of the Lower Rio Grande* (New Orleans: Brandao, 1893; rpt., Brownsville: Brownsville Historical Association, 1959). Frank W. Johnson, *A History of Texas and Texans* (5 vols., ed. E. C. Barker and E. W. Winkler [Chicago and New York: American Historical Society, 1914; rpt. 1916]).
Gene B. Preuss

FORTY. The Forty, or the Fortiers, a fraternity of German students with chapters at the universities of Giessen and Heidelberg and at the industrial academy of Darmstadt, was patterned in part on Étienne Cabet's qv Icarian dream of a communistic utopia and Charles Fourier's idea of social inventiveness. Most members were born to families in government, business, and the sciences in the Grand Duchy of Hesse-Darmstadt. Named *Die Vierziger,* either for the size of their membership or the 1840s, the group was recruited in early 1847 by Prince Carl of Solms-Braunfels,qv former commissioner-general of the Adelsverein qv in Texas, to encourage the young professionals (among others, two musicians, an engineer, a theologian, an agriculturalist, two architects, seven lawyers, four foresters, and a lieutenant of artillery) to find new markets for their talents and also to boost the emigration society's sagging reputation and to focus German emigration on Texas. Count Carl of Castell-Castell,qv another officer of the society, wrote that the Forty "have the trust of their German countrymen, and if their settlement succeeds, there can be no doubt that the stream of emigration will be directed toward Texas." After crossing the Atlantic and reaching Texas, the Forty succeeded in establishing a short-lived settlement, named Bettina, in the Fisher-Miller Land Grant qv in the summer of 1847. Although this utopian venture organized around the principles of "friendship, freedom, and equality" lasted less than a year and two later attempts to establish the communes of Darmstädter Farm and Tusculum near New Braunfels and Sisterdale, respectively, were equally short-lived, many individuals in the fraternity became highly successful, notably San Antonio physician Ferdinand Ludwig Herff;qv Gustav Schleicher,qv engineer and legislator; and Jacob Kuechler,qv a local Unionist who became commissioner of the General Land Office in Austin. Others, like Christoph Flach and Johannes Hoerner, founded large and prominent Hill Country families which for four or five generations maintained freethinking practices, like secular funerals. The writings of members Louis Reinhardt and Phillip Friedrich Schenck qv illustrate the everyday experiences of the group in Texas; Herff wrote a political treatise in which he touches on the colony and generalizes on the founding principles; journalist Emma Murck Altgelt, geologist Ferdinand von Roemer, editor Ferdinand J. Lindheimer qqv and others not directly associated with the fraternity also commented on the group as a whole and on individual members. Vera Flach wrote a moving twentieth-century account of the acculturation of one of the Forty families.

BIBLIOGRAPHY: Rudolph L. Biesele, *The History of the German Settlements in Texas, 1831–1861* (Austin: Von Boeckmann–Jones, 1930; rpt. 1964). Vera Flach, *A Yankee in German-America: Texas Hill Country* (San Antonio: Naylor, 1973). Ferdinand von Herff, *The Regulated Emigration of the German Proletariat with Special Reference to Texas,* trans. Arthur L. Finck (San Antonio: Trinity University Press, 1978). H. T. Edward Hertzberg, trans., "A Letter from Friedrich Schenck in Texas to His Mother in Germany, 1847," *Southwestern Historical Quarterly* 92 (July 1988). Glen E. Lich and Dona B. Reeves, eds., *German Culture in Texas* (Boston: Twayne, 1980). Glen E. Lich, *The German Texans* (San Antonio: University of Texas Institute of Texan Cultures, 1981). Louis Reinhardt, "The Communistic Colony of Bettina," *Quarterly of the Texas State Historical Association* 3 (July 1899).
Glen E. Lich

FORTY-EIGHTERS. Forty-Eighters is a collective term for supporters of the European revolutions of 1848–49, which in Germany culminated in the meeting of a constitutional parliament in March 1848 and the Frankfurt National Assembly from May 1848 through June 1849. A prominent Forty-Eighter in Germany and the first president of the National Assembly was Prince Carl of Leiningen,qv a half-brother of Queen Victoria and promoter of the Adelsverein,qv the society which directed the settlement of New Braunfels and Fredericksburg and five other colonies. In addition to thousands of Forty-Eighters like Leiningen who stayed in Europe, about 4,000 came to the United States. Of these, at least 100 moved to Texas, where many settled in Sisterdale in Kendall County (*see* LATIN SETTLEMENTS OF TEXAS) and others temporarily in larger German towns and in San Antonio, before they moved on to American cultural and political centers.

In Germany, the Forty-Eighters favored unification, constitutional government, and guarantees of human rights. In Texas and elsewhere in the United States, they provided the leadership to oppose nativism and to support a continental foreign policy. They almost universally opposed slavery, some arguing for immediate emancipation, even at the price of war, and other gradualists suggesting subsidies to slave holders over a longer transition to non-slavery. Several Forty-Eighters, including Friedrich Kapp, who lived briefly in Texas, supported the new Republican party.qv Many were subsequently prominent during the Civil War,qv most as Unionists and several as military leaders, and even larger numbers took active public roles during Reconstruction.qv Throughout the second half of the nineteenth century Forty-Eighters in the United States supported improved labor laws and working conditions. They also advanced the country's cultural and intellectual development in such fields as education, the arts, journalism, medicine, and business—notably insurance.

Forty-Eighters in Sisterdale, Texas, included Ottomar von Behr,qv the son of a German prime minister and a published agricultural theorist regarding Texas; Carl Daniel Adolph Douai,qv introducer of the kindergarten system to the United States; Julius Froebel, mineralogist and educator; Ernst Kapp,qv geographer and early philosopher of environment and technology); and August Siemering,qv writer, journalist, and editor. In addition to settling in Sisterdale, Comfort, New Braunfels, and San Antonio, Forty-Eighters dispersed as well to many other settlements in the two German population areas of Central Texas, where, after a period of activism during the 1850s, Civil War, and Reconstruction, they lived in relative obscurity as teachers, civil servants, merchants, farmers, and ranchers. A few of these wrote memoirs, most of which have apparently been identified, translated, and published. Some Texas Forty-Eighters and their sons died at the battle of the Nueces.qv The most vocal and prominent—and intolerant—Forty-Eighters who lived in or passed through Texas soon moved to more liberal parts of the country, where they had better prospects as educators, scientists, writers, and speakers.

BIBLIOGRAPHY: Rudolph L. Biesele, *The History of the German Settlements in Texas, 1831–1861* (Austin: Von Boeckmann–Jones, 1930; rpt. 1964). Glen E. Lich and Dona B. Reeves, eds., *German Culture in Texas* (Boston: Twayne, 1980). Carl Wittke, *Refugees of Revolution: The German Forty-Eighters in America* (Philadelphia: University of Pennsylvania Press, 1952). Adolph E. Zucker, ed., *The Forty-Eighters: Political Refugees of the German Revolution of 1848* (New York: Columbia University Press, 1950).
Glen E. Lich

FORTYONE CANYON CREEK. Fortyone Canyon Creek, also known as T Fortyone (or T41) Canyon Creek, rises four miles south of U.S. Highway 82 in east central Dickens County (at 33°33′ N, 100°35′ W) and runs southwest for four miles to its mouth on Little Croton Creek, fourteen miles northeast of Spur (at 33°32′ N, 100°38′ W). The stream rises at an elevation of about 2,200 feet above sea level and drops almost 300 feet as it runs through an area of dissected gullies, low hills, and steep slopes. In some areas there is no topsoil; in other places silt loams support grasses and mesquite. The canyon and creek were named for the T41 cattle brand.

BIBLIOGRAPHY: Dickens County Historical Commission, *Dickens County: Its Land and Its People* (Lubbock: Craftsman Printers, 1986).

FORWARD, TEXAS. Forward, a farming community in western Lamar County, was established by 1904, when a post office and a general store opened there. The store remained the community's only business, and the post office closed in 1909. Forward reported a population of forty in 1933, when some residents were leaving in search of jobs. By 1936, though the population had reportedly stabilized at twenty-five, Forward was no longer labeled on maps. The settlement reported twenty-five citizens and one business in 1948, the last year for which statistics were available. *Vista K. McCroskey*

FOSSIL KNOBS. The Fossil Knobs are two miles northwest of Terlingua in southwestern Brewster County (centered at 29°20′ N, 103°38′ W). They rise 3,234 feet above sea level and 430 feet above Farm Road 170, a mile south. The shallow, stony soils on the Fossil Knobs support oak, juniper, and some mesquite. The Fossil Knobs, like many other peaks in the area, are dotted with mines dating from the glory days of the Terlingua Mining District in the early 1900s.

FOSSIL RIM WILDLIFE CENTER. Fossil Rim Wildlife Center is on U.S. Highway 67 just southwest of Glen Rose in Somervell County. The 3,000-acre park, which opened in 1986, is operated by the nonprofit Fossil Rim Foundation to manage and breed endangered species, conduct research, and provide education. It is an accredited member of the American Association of Zoological Parks. Fossil Rim has thirty species of exotic animals from Africa, Asia, and South and North America, including giraffes, cheetahs, addaxes, and red wolves. In 1990 the preserve maintained more than 1,000 animals. Visitors can view the animals on a ten-mile internal roadway or spend "safari" weekends at the park. Facilities include a petting pasture, a nature trail, a picnic area, a gift shop and restaurant, and six tent-like bungalows. *Christopher Long*

FOSTER, ANDREW (1879–1930). Andrew (Rube) Foster, founder of the Negro baseball leagues and member of the Baseball Hall of Fame, was born in Calvert, Texas, on September 17, 1879, the son of Andrew and Sarah Foster. His father was the presiding elder of the African Methodist Episcopal Church in Calvert, and his half-brother, Willie, was also a prominent Negro League player.

Foster began a barnstorming career at age seventeen pitching with the traveling Waco Yellow Jackets. By 1902 his abilities enabled him to move north, where he pitched for some of the foremost black teams of his era, including the Chicago Union Giants and the Philadelphia Giants. In 1902 he won the nickname Rube for defeating white Hall of Fame pitcher Rube Wadell in an exhibition game. In 1903 he won four games of the first of what was called the Colored World Series.

After an illustrious playing career Foster became a baseball manager and businessman. He helped form the Chicago American Giants in 1911 and in February 1920 organized the Negro League. He was selected its first president. Foster's Chicago American Giants were the most prominent team in the early years of the league. They traveled in a private Pullman car and barnstormed the nation, playing both exhibition and regular league games. At a time when there were few opportunities for blacks, Foster and his team held celebrity status in black America and were followed avidly through nationally circulated black newspapers.

Foster married Sarah Watts. He left baseball due to mental illness in 1926 and died in an Illinois asylum on December 9, 1930. At his well-attended, highly emotional funeral, he was eulogized as the "father of Negro baseball." He was elected to the Baseball Hall of Fame in 1981, in acknowledgment of the role the Negro leagues played in American life before the integration of baseball and of his own role in baseball history.

BIBLIOGRAPHY: Rayford W. Logan and Michael R. Winston, eds., *Dictionary of American Negro Biography* (New York: Norton, 1982). Robert Peterson, *Only the Ball Was White* (Englewood Cliffs, New Jersey: Prentice-Hall, 1970; rpt., New York: McGraw-Hill, 1984). Donn Rogosin, *Invisible Men: Life in Baseball's Negro Leagues* (New York: Atheneum, 1983). *W. Donn Rogosin*

FOSTER, ISAAC (?–?). Isaac Foster, one of Stephen F. Austin's[qv] Old Three Hundred[qv] colonists, was probably the son of John Foster and the brother of Randolph Foster.[qqv] He came from Mississippi to Texas in 1822. As one of the Old Three Hundred he received title to one sitio[qv] of land in what is now Matagorda County on August 10, 1824. On February 1, 1830, he was ordered to appear before the ayuntamiento[qv] at San Felipe de Austin to testify concerning the improvements on his land. On March 1, 1830, the ayuntamiento reported that Foster had cultivated the land and lived in the country since the land was granted to him but had recently died in the colony, leaving many relatives. Though one Isaac Foster's will was probated in March 1839, in 1859 another Isaac Foster or his estate was given a bounty warrant for 320 acres of land for military service from March to June 1836.

BIBLIOGRAPHY: Eugene C. Barker, ed., *The Austin Papers* (3 vols., Washington: GPO, 1924–28). Eugene C. Barker, ed., "Minutes of the Ayuntamiento of San Felipe de Austin, 1828–1832," 12 parts, *Southwestern Historical Quarterly* 21–24 (January 1918–October 1920). Lester G. Bugbee, "The Old Three Hundred: A List of Settlers in Austin's First Colony," *Quarterly of the Texas State Historical Association* 1 (October 1897). Matagorda County Historical Commission, *Historic Matagorda County* (3 vols., 1986–88).

Andrew (Rube) Foster. Courtesy Negro Leagues Baseball Museum, Kansas City.

FOSTER, JAMES M. (1815?–?). James M. Foster, Calhoun County cattleman, had homes on Chocolate Bayou, at Old Town, and at other places in the county. By 1849 or earlier he shipped beef by steamship from Indianola to New Orleans, thus opening the first reliable market for Texas beef. Thomas O'Connor[qv] sold him one of his first shipments at ten dollars a head, a price that increased by 1857 to between sixteen and twenty dollars a head. The 1860 census lists Foster as a native of Kentucky, aged forty-five, with a wife, Mary. The beef trade ceased in 1861 but resumed after the Civil War.[qv] Foster conducted the business through purchasing agents who visited ranches across the county. He shipped his cattle by the Morgan Lines,[qv] on which he secured by charter the entire carrying capacity north to Texas ports. He later used the Vanderbilt line. In competition with Silvanus Hatch, Foster also provided animal pens and hotel service for drovers across Chocolate Creek from Hatch's property.

BIBLIOGRAPHY: Paul H. Freier, *A "Looking Back" Scrapbook for Calhoun County and Matagorda Bay, Texas* (Port Lavaca, Texas: Port Lavaca *Wave*, 1979).

Diana J. Kleiner

FOSTER, JOHN (?–1837). John Foster, one of Stephen F. Austin's[qv] Old Three Hundred[qv] colonists, moved to Texas from Mississippi in 1822. He was the father of two sons, John R. and Randolph Foster.[qv] On July 15, 1824, he received title to 2½ sitios and three labors in present Fort Bend County. In April 1826 John Foster or possibly John R. Foster, his son, carried a message from Stephen F. Austin to the Cherokee Indians. In November of that same year he was commissioned to buy a steel mill in New Orleans for William Cooper.[qv] William B. Travis[qv] had Foster's power of attorney in January 1834. Foster died in Woodville, Mississippi, in January 1837, and his property passed to his heirs. Randolph Foster was living on the original headright at the time of his father's death.

In February 1830 another John Foster moved to the Austin colony from Carolina.

John R. Foster, probably the son of the Old Three Hundred settler, fought with the Texas army during the siege of Bexar.[qv] He appears to have been part of Travis's cavalry detachment that captured a herd of Mexican horses outside of San Antonio. In mid-November 1835 Travis dispatched the captured herd to Gonzales under the charge of John R. Foster. In 1837 this Foster petitioned for the organization of Fort Bend County.

BIBLIOGRAPHY: Eugene C. Barker, ed., *The Austin Papers* (3 vols., Washington: GPO, 1924–28). Eugene C. Barker, "General Austin's Order Book for the Campaign of 1835," *Southwestern Historical Quarterly* 11 (July 1907). Lester G. Bugbee, "The Old Three Hundred: A List of Settlers in Austin's First Colony," *Quarterly of the Texas State Historical Association* 1 (October 1897). John H. Jenkins, ed., *The Papers of the Texas Revolution, 1835–1836* (10 vols., Austin: Presidial Press, 1973). William Barret Travis, *Diary*, ed. Robert E. Davis (Waco: Texian Press, 1966). Clarence Wharton, *Wharton's History of Fort Bend County* (San Antonio: Naylor, 1939).

FOSTER, JOSEPH BEVERLY (1895–1949). Joseph Beverly (Joe B.) Foster, orthopedic surgeon, was born at Ennis, Texas, on January 28, 1895, the son of James Everett and Ann (Treadway) Foster. He attended Sterling City public schools, Abilene Christian College (now Abilene Christian University), and Austin College in Sherman. He received an M.D. from the University of Texas Medical Branch in 1920 and served an internship at St. Joseph's Infirmary in Houston. He then became a partner in the Houston Clinic. From 1927 to 1930 he attended Harvard Medical School for training in orthopedic surgery.

In Boston, Foster had appointments at both Massachusetts General Hospital and Children's Hospital. Upon returning to Houston, he established a private practice in orthopedic surgery. He was chief surgeon at Arabia Temple Shrine Crippled Children's Clinic, orthopedic consultant at M. D. Anderson Hospital for Cancer Research (now the University of Texas M. D. Anderson Cancer Center[qv]) and the Veterans Administration Hospital in Houston (now the Veterans Affairs Medical Center[qv]), consultant in orthopedic surgery at Brooke General Hospital (now Brooke Army Medical Center[qv]) at Fort Sam Houston in San Antonio, and an active member of the staff at Methodist, Hermann,[qqv] and Memorial hospitals in Houston, as well as at St. Joseph's Infirmary. From 1943 until his death he was professor of orthopedic surgery and chairman of the Department of Orthopedics at Baylor University College of Medicine.

Foster was the chairman of the advisory committee for the Harris County Chapter of the National Foundation for Infantile Paralysis, the Texas Society for Crippled Children, and the Crippled Children's Division of the State Department of Health. He was a charter member of the Houston Surgical Society, as well as a charter member and president of the Texas Orthopedic Association. He belonged to the American Academy of Orthopedic Surgeons, the Harris County Medical Society, the Texas Medical Association,[qv] the American Medical Association, and the Texas Surgical Society.

Throughout his life he was active in the Church of Christ; he served many years as an elder at his church in Houston. He married Lucile Parrish of Sherman, whom he met at Abilene Christian College. They had no children. Foster died from a coronary thrombosis at his home in Houston on June 25, 1949.

BIBLIOGRAPHY: Houston *Post*, June 26, 1949. Reference Folder, Houston Academy of Medicine–Texas Medical Center Library, Harris County Medical Archive. *Texas State Journal of Medicine*, September 1949.

Patricia L. Jakobi

FOSTER, LAFAYETTE LUMPKIN (1851–1901). Lafayette Lumpkin Foster was born on November 27, 1851, in Cumming, Forsyth County, Georgia. He moved to Texas at the age of eighteen and lived successively in the Limestone County communities of Horn Hill and Springfield. He worked at cotton picking or bricklaying until he had saved enough money to attend Waco University. Foster moved to Groesbeck in 1873 and began the publication of a newspaper there, the *Limestone New Era*, in 1876. He left the *New Era* when his political activities became too time-consuming. In 1880 he was a representative in the Seventeenth Legislature; in the Nineteenth Legislature he was the speaker of the House, the youngest man to hold the position at that time. Governor Lawrence S. Ross[qv] appointed him commissioner of insurance, statistics, and history, and later of agriculture. As commissioner, he helped Attorney General James S. Hogg[qv] to harry illegally operated insurance companies out of Texas. On May 4, 1891, Hogg appointed Foster to the first Railroad Commission.[qv] However, Foster resigned to become vice president and general manager of the Velasco Terminal Railway. He became president of Texas Agricultural and Mechanical College (now Texas A&M University) in 1898 and held the position until his death. He helped plan Texas A&M. Foster married Laura Pender on January 2, 1875, and they had five sons and two daughters. The family belonged to the First Baptist Church in Groesbeck. Foster was a member of the Groesbeck Masonic Lodge, where he served for a time as worshipful master. He died of pneumonia on December 2, 1901, and was buried on the Texas A&M campus.

BIBLIOGRAPHY: Lewis E. Daniell, *Personnel of the Texas State Government, with Sketches of Representative Men of Texas* (Austin: City Printing, 1887; 3d ed., San Antonio: Maverick, 1892). *Presiding Officers of the Texas Legislature, 1846–1982* (Austin: Texas Legislative Council, 1982). Marker Files, Texas Historical Commission, Austin.

Stephanie Panus

FOSTER, MARCELLUS ELLIOT (1870–1942). Marcellus Elliot Foster [pseud. Mefo], newspaperman and businessman, was born at Pembroke, Christian County, Kentucky, on November 29, 1870, the son of Mariella (Fitzhugh) and Marcellus Aurelius Foster. The elder Foster had been a Confederate captain in Archer's Tennessee Brigade.

The family moved to Huntsville, Texas, in 1873. After attending the public schools of Huntsville, Foster graduated from Sam Houston Normal Institute (now Sam Houston State University) in 1890. He also studied at the University of Texas in 1891–92. At the age of fifteen he began his newspaper career as an apprentice printer on the staff of the Huntsville *Item*. He received his first payment for a story he wrote about Sam Houston's grave. Foster moved to Houston around 1895 and joined the Houston *Post*.qv William Sydney Porter qv was on the *Post* staff at the time, and Foster's salary of twenty-four dollars a week exceeded that of Porter's by four dollars. Foster became the youngest managing editor of a Texas newspaper in 1899, when he was twenty-eight years old. His paper covered the Galveston hurricane of 1900.qv He ingeniously published the names of some survivors, all registered at Galveston's Tremont Hotel, instead of listing the dead.

Foster left the *Post* and founded the Houston *Chronicle*qv in October 1901. He invested $25,000, part of which he had received from a venture at the Spindletop oilfield qv near Beaumont, and initially edited a six-page afternoon daily, which reached a circulation of 7,000. By 1926 the paper reached nearly 75,000 readers each weekday and 85,000 on Sundays. Foster's *Chronicle* reputedly was the first Texas paper to sell for two cents a copy and to reject front-page advertising. Foster achieved great acclaim for his fight against the Ku Klux Klan qv during the 1920s. The Klan burned a cross on his lawn and tapped his telephone line. "During that time," he recalled, "I went straight from home to the office and from the office home. My life wouldn't have been worth five cents any place else." Foster, who wrote under the pen name Mefo, entitled his daily column "Our City."

Foster sold 50 percent of his ownership in the *Chronicle* to Jesse Holman Jones qv in 1908 in order to finance the construction of a new building to house the publication. Jones purchased Foster's remaining interest in the paper on June 26, 1926, when Foster retired. By that time the publication's estimated value was $2.5 million. Foster became editor of the Houston *Press*,qv a Scripps Howard newspaper, in February 1927. He maintained his reputation as a combative journalist through his column "Why." He attacked the state prison system qv and blamed a prisoner overcrowding crisis in 1930 on Governor Daniel J. Moody,qv whom he had formerly supported. He argued that Moody's refusal to grant pardons to deserving inmates caused the prison to grow beyond its capacity. Unique among Texas newspapers of the period, the *Press* criticized the frequently praised management of the prison system by Marshall Lee Simmons qv in the 1930s. Foster contended that Simmons condoned atrocities and concealed the deaths of prisoners. Because of the *Press*'s derogatory stories, Simmons banned the publication from the prison.

Foster retired as editor of the Houston *Press* on January 13, 1937, but continued writing his "Why" column as editor emeritus. After a journalism career that spanned nearly fifty years, he definitively retired in March 1941. At a farewell dinner attended by former governors William Hobby and James Allred,qqv Foster voiced his conviction that "Texas could be no great success without the work of the little men. Those who go to the factories or to the great stores of the country earn their small wages and return to their families satisfied and contented." Noting that twelve Texas governors had held office during his career, Foster remarked in a final "Why" column on March 21, 1941: "Sometimes it has occurred to you and me that we didn't pick them very carefully."

Due to his support for former governor James E. Ferguson's qv fight against the Ku Klux Klan, Miriam Amanda Ferguson qv named Foster to the University of Texas Board of Regents when she became governor in 1925. Foster, who served as president of the Southern Newspaper Publishers Association and the Texas Editorial Association, also owned the Journal Publishing Company of Beaumont in 1909–10. In Houston, Foster served as president of the Texas Avenue Realty Company, the University Land Company, and the M. E. Foster Properties Company and was director of the City National and Seaport National banks and the Standard Fire Insurance Company. He was an Episcopalian and a Democrat and belonged to the Elks Club, Kappa Sigma fraternity, the Yacht Club, and the Houston Riding and Polo Club. Foster published four books. *The Town Tattler* (1920) contained his speeches, *South and Southeast Texas* (1928) was a biographical reference work, *Mefo Wanders and Wonders* (1929) recounted his travels in Europe, and *Words* (1920s) included a number of his poems.

Foster married Zaidee L. Lochhead of Houston on September 6, 1905, and the couple had three children. He married Claire Collier LaBarge of Meridian, Mississippi, on March 9, 1919. He died at his home in Houston after suffering a heart attack on April 1, 1942. He was buried in Houston.

BIBLIOGRAPHY: Houston *Post*, April 2, 1942. Huntsville *Item*, March 6, 1941. Vertical Files, Barker Texas History Center, University of Texas at Austin. Clarence R. Wharton, ed., *Texas Under Many Flags* (5 vols., Chicago: American Historical Society, 1930).

Paul M. Lucko

FOSTER, RANDOLPH (1790–1878). Randolph Foster, one of Stephen F. Austin's qv Old Three Hundred qv colonists, the son of John Foster,qv was born in Mississippi on March 12, 1790. During the War of 1812 he served with Randal Jones,qv later his Texas neighbor for fifty years. Foster married Lucy Hunter in Mississippi, and they became the parents of seven children. In 1822 the couple joined John Foster and Isaac Foster qv to move to Texas and establish a camp in what became Fort Bend County. On July 16, 1824, Foster received title to a league of land in an area that is now Waller and Fort Bend counties. On October 11, 1835, Richardson Royster Royall qv dispatched Foster to retrieve 800 pounds of lead reported to be at William Stafford's qv plantation. Foster later helped supply the army with meat and furnished food and escort for his family and neighbors during the Runaway Scrape.qv In 1836 he made a trip back to Mississippi, then returned to Texas to establish permanent residence in Fort Bend County. In December 1845 he signed a proclamation at Richmond commending Sam Houston qv for his work for the annexation qv of Texas and inviting him to dinner at Richmond. As a fellow Mississippian, Foster, in August 1865 wrote David G. Burnet qv requesting him to go to Washington, D.C., to ask President Andrew Johnson to release Jefferson Davis qv from prison. On August 18, 1878, Foster died in Fort Bend County at the home of his daughter, Mrs. Mary L. Blakely.

BIBLIOGRAPHY: Lester G. Bugbee, "The Old Three Hundred: A List of Settlers in Austin's First Colony," *Quarterly of the Texas State Historical Association* 1 (October 1897). Dallas *Herald*, September 9, 1865. Clarence Wharton, *Wharton's History of Fort Bend County* (San Antonio: Naylor, 1939).

FOSTER, TEXAS (Fort Bend County). Foster, on Farm Road 359 ten miles northwest of Richmond in northwestern Fort Bend County, sits on land that was part of the 1824 grant to John and Randolph Foster.qqv Before the Civil War qv the Foster plantation produced rice and sugarcane. The settlement was established by 1882, when the community of Foster acquired a post office. In 1884 Foster had semi-weekly mail delivery, a steam gristmill and cotton gin, a physician, and a population of sixty. In 1892 the town had daily mail delivery and three gristmills. By 1896 a general store and a flour mill had been added, and by 1897 the community had two schools, one for white students and one for black. In 1914 the town was noted for its pecan production. By 1925, however, the community's population had dwindled to forty; in 1931 only one business was reported, and no population figures were listed. Foster still had two community schools and was served by a blacktop road in 1936. The post office and schools were closed by the 1940s, but Foster still existed in 1990.

Stephen L. Hardin

FOSTER, TEXAS (Terry County). Foster is on Farm Road 403 eight miles south of Brownfield in south central Terry County. Early ranchers in the area, such as Monroe Brown Sawyer,qv lived in virtual isolation; the mail was delivered on horseback. Foster was founded in 1928. By 1930 there were thirty schools in Terry County, including the Foster school. It was consolidated with the Wellman Independent School District by 1943 and was located in the Union Independent School District by the mid-1960s. In 1936 Foster had a church, a school, and a number of scattered dwellings. In 1966 the community reported a population of four, a general store, and a gin. The 1982 county highway map showed one industry, an additional business, and a church at Foster.

BIBLIOGRAPHY: Terry County Historical Survey Committee, *Early Settlers of Terry* (Hereford, Texas: Pioneer, 1968).

Jeanne F. Lively

FOSTER ARMY AIR FIELD. Foster Army Air Field, an advanced single-engine flying school for fighter pilots six miles northeast of Victoria, was established in the summer of 1941. A local funding campaign led by E. J. Dysart the previous spring had raised some $17,000 to locate the base at Victoria as an economic asset. Subsequent government construction cost more than $4 million. The initial class of cadets arrived in September 1941 and served under Lt. Col. Warren R. Carter, the first commander. WACs began to arrive the following May. The base was known until January 15, 1942, as Victoria Field and then renamed in memory of Lt. Arthur L. Foster, a United States Army Air Corps instructor killed in a crash at Brooks Field in 1925. Foster's son received his training and commission at the base in the spring of 1942. Cadets used the North American AT-6 "Texas" and Curtis P-40 trainers to drill in aerial gunnery, though actual practice took place on ranges located on Matagorda Island and Matagorda Peninsula. The local influence of the base was social as well as economic. In 1941 the Victoria County Courthouse recorded a 25 percent increase in marriage licenses issued. After World War IIqv the Foster Field site returned to its owners, the Buhler and Braman estates.

In the fall of 1951 the government purchased 1,376 acres at the site, and Foster Field was reactivated for single-engine jet training during the Korean War. The first cadets graduated in March 1953 after three months of duty using T-28 propeller and T-33 jet trainers. Foster Air Force Base was designated a permanent military installation in 1954 and began housing F-86F Sabrejet fighter planes. Col. Frank L. Dunn became the new commander, replacing Col. C. C. Sonnkalb. The following year Foster AFB was designated headquarters for the Nineteenth Air Force, a new branch of the Tactical Air Command, under Gen. Henry Viccellio. Base personnel increased to about 6,000, with new F-100C Super-Sabre jets replacing the F-86s. Foster Field's Nineteenth Air Force carried out the first overseas deployment of a complete tactical force as a unit in a training flight to Europe in 1956. The next year three Foster-based F-100s flew the first TAC single-engine, nonstop, round-trip mission over a great distance when they "attacked" Panama in a training maneuver.

Washington surprised both Victorians and base commanders with the announcement in August 1957 that it was closing Foster AFB, especially since President Eisenhower had just appropriated finances for new construction. Despite a rigorous "Save Foster" campaign led in Washington by senators Lyndon B. Johnsonqv and Ralph Yarborough and Congressman Clark W. Thompson,qv the base was deactivated and closed in December 1958. The local economy suffered greatly. In the summer of 1960, however, the General Services Administration approved the exchange of Aloe Fieldqv for Foster Field, and Victoria County Airport was moved to the latter site. The growth of the county airport slowly replaced the loss of Foster AFB as numerous businesses located there. Two of the largest in 1968 were the Devereux Foundation, a therapeutic-education center, and Gary Aircraft, which repaired C-54 planes for the military. In 1976 Foster became the site of Victoria Regional Airport, which provides passenger service and connections with major carriers.

BIBLIOGRAPHY: Roy Grimes, ed., *300 Years in Victoria County* (Victoria, Texas: Victoria *Advocate*, 1968; rpt., Austin: Nortex, 1985). Robert W. Shook and Charles D. Spurlin, *Victoria: A Pictorial History* (Norfolk, Virginia: Donning, 1985). Victoria *Advocate*, Historical Edition, May 12, 1968. *Life*, June 19, 1942. *Craig H. Roell*

FOSTER BRANCH. Foster Branch rises three miles east of Moody in southern McLennan County (at 31°19′ N, 97°19′ W) and runs east for 4½ miles to its mouth on the South Fork of Cow Bayou, two miles north of Bruceville–Eddy (at 31°20′ N, 97°16′ W). The stream traverses flat to rolling prairie with locally steep slopes, surfaced by expansive clays and clay loams that support juniper, oak, mesquite, and grasses.

FOSTERS STORE, TEXAS. Fosters Store is a farming community on the west bank of the Brazos River two miles north of Snook in eastern Burleson County. Settlement in the area began during the mid-1820s. After the Civil Warqv the Foster family operated a plantation, one of the largest in the county, on the rich Brazos bottomlands. In the early 1890s a number of Italian immigrants took up farming on and around the Foster plantation. The community known as Fosters Store coalesced during the early 1900s on the banks of Middle Bayou near the plantation. Farm Road 166 was extended through the community in the mid-1900s. By the 1950s the community had a business and a church. The population of the Fosters Store community was estimated at ten in 1966, after which no further population statistics were available. In the early 1980s county highway maps showed one business at Fosters Store.

BIBLIOGRAPHY: Burleson County Historical Society, *Astride the Old San Antonio Road: A History of Burleson County, Texas* (Dallas: Taylor, 1980). *Charles Christopher Jackson*

FOSTERVILLE, TEXAS. Fosterville is near Indian Creek at the intersection of a country road and Farm Road 315, seventeen miles northeast of Palestine in northeastern Anderson County. The community was founded sometime before 1870 and had a post office from 1870 to 1905. In 1884 Fosterville had an estimated population of seventy. At that time it also had Baptist, Colored Baptist, and Christian churches, four blacksmith shops, two water-powered cotton gins and sawmills, two doctors, a district school, and a general store. The population of the community was estimated at forty in 1890 and at fifty in 1896. By the 1930s the Fosterville school was gone, but the townsite still had a sawmill and a number of dwellings. The 1985 county highway map did not name the community but showed one business at the site. *Mark Odintz*

FOSTORIA, TEXAS. Fostoria is at the intersection of the Atchison, Topeka and Santa Fe Railway and State Highway 105, seventeen miles east of Conroe in Montgomery County. In the early 1900s the town was called Clinesburg after the owner of a mill there. In 1901 the mill was sold to the Foster Lumber Company of Kansas City, Missouri, and the settlement was renamed Fostoria after the lumber firm in 1903. Between 1910 and 1920 the population was reportedly 1,000, most of whom were employed in the mill. The town reached its peak population of 1,500 between 1915 and 1925. In 1941 the mill produced 20 million board feet of lumber and was thus one of the largest providers of Southern pine in the United States.

Fostoria was a company town. The company store sold employees clothing, groceries, furniture, and saddles and owned a hotel and barber shop for which company scrip was accepted. The scrip was not redeemable anywhere else. Only the post office was not run by the company, but it was closed after 1930. The Foster Lumber Company closed in June 1957. After the mill closed, the company homes were sold, primarily to former employees, and the business district was shut down. From the 1940s to the 1960s the population was 500.

In the 1980s only a few scattered dwellings, a cemetery, a pumping station, and a radio tower south of the city remained.

BIBLIOGRAPHY: Montgomery County Genealogical Society, *Montgomery County History* (Winston-Salem, North Carolina: Hunter, 1981). Robin Navarro Montgomery, *The History of Montgomery County* (Austin: Jenkins, 1975).

Rebecca L. Borjas

FOUKE, TEXAS. Fouke is on Farm Road 2869 three miles northeast of Crow and less than a mile west of Lake Hawkins in southeast Wood County. A community called Center was said to exist in the southern part of the county as early as 1866, and sometime around 1873 the inhabitants built a log building, which was used for church, school, lodge, and community meetings. In 1879 a two-acre site for a Methodist Episcopal church was bought for six dollars, and a frame building was eventually constructed. At that time the pastor usually also taught the school, which was attended by black children only. The community's few white children went to subscription schools in Redland or Hawkins. A Center school district for blacks was established when Wood County was divided into public school districts in 1884, though by 1896 no records for that school exist. The predominantly black community never had a post office. The name was changed to Fouke sometime after 1885, when George W. Fouke's lumber company built a large sawmill in the area.

By the 1930s Fouke had a number of dwellings concentrated at the intersection of several bladed earth roads two miles north of U.S. Highway 80. The community also had a business, two churches, and a school, which in 1932 had an enrollment of seventeen white students and 111 black students. By 1960 the community had two churches and a few widely scattered dwellings. Sometime after 1960 Lake Hawkins was formed by a dam on the Little Sandy Creek, and by 1981 a number of new dwellings had appeared in the community, which supported two churches, two businesses, and a town hall or community center.

BIBLIOGRAPHY: *Wood County, 1850–1900* (Quitman, Texas: Wood County Historical Society, 1976).

Rachel Jenkins

FOUNDATION SCHOOL PROGRAM. The foundation school program was established by the Gilmer-Aikin Laws[qv] in 1949. The state distributes funds from the Available School Fund[qv] to local school districts through the two-tiered program. Tier One of the FSP provides funds to meet the costs of basic education programs that meet state accreditation standards. Tier Two provides schools with equal access to revenue for educational enrichment. Both tiers contain a state and local share, with the latter depending on the property wealth of each district. Under Tier One of FSP, additional funding is made available to school districts for special, vocational, compensatory, bilingual, and gifted and talented programs. In 1993 the state spent close to $7 billion on the public schools. This constituted roughly 48 percent of revenues generated for public schools. The remaining $7.1 billion came from local tax revenues.

BIBLIOGRAPHY: Legislative Budget Board, *Fiscal Size-up of Texas State Services, 1992–1993 Biennium* (Austin, 1993). Rae Files Still, *The Gilmer-Aikin Bills* (Austin: Steck, 1950).

Tracé Etienne-Gray

FOUNDATION FOR WOMEN'S RESOURCES. The Foundation for Women's Resources (formerly known as the Texas Foundation for Women's Resources), a private, nonprofit, educational organization with headquarters in Austin, develops programs and projects to advance and improve the personal, economic, and professional status of women. It was originally incorporated on December 28, 1973, in San Antonio under the name Texas Women's Caucus with Josephine Hall, Marilyn Cazort, and Janice McCoy as the founding board of directors. On June 25, 1974, the name of the corporation was changed to Womanpower, An Educational Fund. At a meeting of the board of directors chaired by Liz Parker on September 19, 1976, Sarah Weddington, Jane Hickie, Ann Richards, Cathy Bonner, Judith Guthrie, and Martha Smiley were elected as the board of the corporation. The board's first educational project was the publication, in 1977, of a book entitled *Texas Women in Politics*. On April 6, 1977, the name of the corporation was formally changed to the Foundation for Women's Resources, and in March 1978, under the leadership of Ann Richards, president, the board of directors launched its first major statewide project, "Texas Women: A Celebration of History," with Mary Beth Rogers as project director. The project was the first large-scale effort to document and publicize the contributions of women to the state's history. The project included an exhibition that toured museums in San Antonio, Dallas, Austin, Amarillo, El Paso, and Houston in 1981 and 1982. The exhibit was given to Texas Woman's University for permanent display in its library in 1983. TWU is also the repository of the 6,000-plus items collected during the development of the project. The project included an exhibit catalog (reprinted as a sesquicentennial project in 1986); a set of seven traveling exhibits circulated by the University of Texas Institute of Texan Cultures[qv] (two new sets were circulated in 1987); a bibliography of resources on Texas women's history; a book for young people, *We Can Fly: Stories of Katherine Stinson and Other Gutsy Texas Women* (1983), and the 1990 publication of a multicultural instructional guide to *Texas Women: A Celebration of History*, compiled by Candace O'Keefe. Mary Beth Rogers was named executive director of the foundation in 1981 and became a member of the board in 1983. Ellen C. Temple and Katherine B. (Chula) Reynolds were elected to the board of directors in 1981. In 1982 board president Cathy Bonner proposed the establishment of Leadership Texas,[qv] a program to identify and develop Texas's women leaders. The program combines education in leadership skills with information on state policy issues and an examination of the philosophies and programs of the state's business, cultural, educational, community, and political leaders. Martha P. Farmer was appointed director of Leadership Texas and executive director of the Texas foundation in 1982.

In 1986 the foundation became a national organization. Additional members elected to the board from 1986–88 include Rosie Zamora-Cope, Cassandra Carr, Pat Bailey, Shirley Hoskins, Judith Ford, and Patricia Diaz-Dennis. Also in 1986 the board approved a nationwide program called Leadership America, which expanded the original statewide program to the national level and was launched the following year. Farmer was named national director of both the foundation and Leadership America, headquartered in Alexandria, Virginia. Mary Love Henderson became director for Texas operations. In 1989 Mandy Dealey became executive director of Leadership Texas, followed in 1991 by Candace O'Keefe. Upon retiring from her staff role with the foundation, Martha Farmer was elected to the foundation board of directors in 1991. In 1994 the thousandth woman graduated from the Leadership Texas program at the conclusion of its twelfth year of programming. The foundation has also helped establish similar women's leadership programs in other states, including California, Kentucky, Missouri, and Tennessee. Other foundation projects have included Leadership Texas and America alumnae organizations; the Texas Capital Network entrepreneurial program; Friends of the Foundation; cosponsorship of numerous Texas women's history and women's issues conferences; a three-year Women's History Research Fellowship for the Texas State Historical Association's[qv] *Handbook of Texas* revision; a statewide conference on women and technology; and the 1992 publication of an anthology on science and math education entitled *Options for Girls—a Door to the Future*.

BIBLIOGRAPHY: Texas Foundation for Women's Resources, Minutes, Austin.

Ellen C. Temple and Candace O'Keefe

FOUNTAIN, ALBERT JENNINGS (1838–1896). Albert Jennings Fountain, lawyer, legislator, and Indian fighter, was born on Staten

Island, New York, on October 23, 1838, the son of Solomon Jennings, a sea captain. His mother was from a colonial Huguenot family. Fountain was reared in the Episcopal faith and educated in New York public schools and at Columbia College. He moved to California in the 1850s and worked as a reporter for the Sacramento Union. While he was with the newspaper, he went to Nicaragua to cover the filibuster expedition of William Walker. Fountain read law in the office of N. Greene Curtis and was admitted to the California bar in 1860.

In 1861 he enlisted in the First California Infantry Volunteers, commanded by Col. James H. Carleton. Fountain advanced from private to lieutenant in this Union force as it marched from the Pacific coast over mountains and deserts of the Southwest to the Rio Grande. After arriving too late to intercept Gen. Henry H. Sibley's qv retreating Confederate army, the California Column qv became an army of occupation for New Mexico and Arizona territories. Fountain was assigned to the garrison at Franklin (El Paso) and at nearby Mesilla in the New Mexico Territory. At Mesilla he met Marianna Pérez, whom he married on October 26, 1862. They had four sons and two daughters. Fountain participated in the Mescalero Indian roundup and the relocation of this group to Bosque Redondo under the guns of Fort Sumner and then commanded volunteer New Mexico cavalry against the Mimbreño and Chiricahua Apaches. Wounds received in the Western Apache campaigns led to Fountain's hospitalization at Fort Bliss, El Paso, where he recovered and was discharged from federal service.

After the Civil War qv he and his wife made their home in El Paso, where he established a law practice and became a civic leader, a founder of the local Episcopal church, and a leading organizer of the Republican party qv in western Texas. Articulate and forceful, Fountain advocated "militant Republicanism" during the Reconstruction qv of Texas. His early political appointments included county surveyor and collector of customs for El Paso.

Fountain's oratory at the Radical Republican convention at Corpus Christi in 1868 led to his election as vice chairman of the convention and a major role in drafting the Texas Radical Republican platform. When the military governor of Texas authorized elections in 1868, Fountain supported Radical Republican Edmund J. Davis qv for governor and was himself elected state senator from the El Paso district. When the Twelfth legislature convened in Austin, Fountain was elected majority leader of the Senate. He assisted in drafting Governor Davis's radical program for reconstructing Texas, and he worked for local needs, including the "frontier protection bill" to reactivate the Texas Rangers.qv As the acknowledged political kingpin of western Texas, Fountain regularly was challenged by adversaries at El Paso. He killed political enemy Frank Williams in a duel after Williams insulted him in a saloon.

At the second session of the Twelfth Legislature Fountain was elected president of the Senate; in the Thirteen Legislature he served as Senate minority leader. His legislative proposals included extension of suffrage to women, which was defeated, and incorporation for the town of El Paso, which was approved. As the force of Reconstruction in Texas diminished, Fountain's political base at El Paso evaporated. In 1873 he moved his family back to Mesilla.

He became a powerful Republican leader in New Mexico Territory, where he served as speaker of the New Mexico House of Representatives. In 1879 he became captain of the Mesilla Scouts, a militia unit raised to defend the town against Indian raids. Fountain published the Mesilla *Independent* and was one of New Mexico's most prominent attorneys for nearly twenty-five years. His success in obtaining indictments and convictions of rustlers in southern New Mexico—he had twenty convictions in 1894 alone—earned him a number of enemies. On February 1, 1896, Fountain and his eight-year-old son Henry disappeared between Tularosa and Las Cruces; their bodies were never found. Three men were tried for the murders but acquitted. The disappearance is still the most famous unsolved murder case in that region.

BIBLIOGRAPHY: Robert J. Casey, *The Texas Border and Some Borderliners* (Indianapolis: Bobbs-Merrill, 1950). Arrell Morgan Gibson, *The Life and Death of Colonel Albert Jennings Fountain* (Norman: University of Oklahoma Press, 1965).
Arrell Morgan Gibson

FOUNTAIN CREEK. Fountain Creek rises two miles southwest of Groveton in central Trinity County (at 31°03′ N, 95°10′ W) and runs southwest for nine miles to its mouth on the Lake Livingston reservoir, two miles west of Chita (at 30° 58′ N, 95° 13′ W). Before the construction of the reservoir in the 1960s, the stream entered the Trinity River just west of Sebastopol. Fountain Creek traverses flat to rolling terrain surfaced by clay and sandy loams that support conifers, water-tolerant hardwoods, and grasses.

FOUR CORNERS, TEXAS (Montgomery County). Four Corners is on Farm Road 3083 on the northern edge of the Conroe oilfield in southeastern Montgomery County. In the late 1940s the community had six businesses and fourteen dwellings. By 1965 the area was incorporated into the Conroe Independent School District. The townsite had only a few scattered dwellings and businesses by the late 1980s. The community still existed in 1990.

BIBLIOGRAPHY: Montgomery County Genealogical Society, *Montgomery County History* (Winston-Salem, North Carolina: Hunter, 1981).
Rebecca L. Borjas

FOUR CORNERS, TEXAS (Motley County). Four Corners, sometimes known as Frog Hollow, was on a branch of the Middle Pease River at the intersection of two local roads two miles east of what is now Whiteflat in central Motley County. During the 1920s and 1930s the settlement was on a through road running north from Matador and had a filling station, a mercantile store, a general store, a gin, and an icehouse. However, because a low area near the community tended to flood after heavy rains, construction for what is now State Highway 70 bypassed Four Corners in 1934. One store and the gin remained active at the townsite until about 1946. By the early 1980s no evidence of the community was shown on county highway maps.
Charles G. Davis

FOURMILE CREEK (Jasper County). Fourmile Creek rises 11½ miles west of Harrisburg in northern Jasper County (at 31°01′ N, 94°00′ W) and runs southeast for 4½ miles to its mouth on Sandy Creek, just over three miles north of Jasper (at 30°58′ N, 93°58′ W). The stream cuts through undulating to hilly terrain surfaced by deep sandy soil that supports heavy woodlands. Dominant trees in the area include loblolly, shortleaf, and longleaf pine.

_____ (Kent County). Fourmile Creek rises at an elevation of 2,200 feet above sea level, seven miles southwest of Clairemont in central Kent County (at 33°09′ N, 100°52′ W), and travels northeast for eight miles, dropping 300 feet before reaching its mouth on the Salt Fork of the Brazos River, four miles northwest of Clairemont (at 33°12′ N, 100°47′ W). The stream traverses isolated ranchland with moderately steep slopes and locally high relief, surfaced by shallow to moderately deep silt loams that support mesquite and grasses.

FOURMILE DRAW (Pecos County). Fourmile Draw rises at the intersection of Upper Fourmile Draw and Lower Fourmile Draw, near Interstate Highway 10 in eastern Pecos County (at 30°46 N, 102°20′ W), and runs southeast for eight miles to its mouth on the Pecos River (at 30°45′ N, 101°49′ W). The draw crosses Interstate 10 six miles northwest of Sheffield and State Highway 349 further east. The local terrain varies from flat, with local deep and dense dissection, to sloping and is surfaced by shallow stony soils that support oak, juniper, mesquite, and scrub brush.

_____ (Reeves County). Fourmile Draw, a valley with an intermittent stream, begins 1½ miles southeast of Cottonwood Tank in western

Reeves County (at 31°35′ N, 103°58′ W) and runs northeast for nineteen miles to its mouth on the Pecos River, 2½ miles south of Mason Station on the northeastern edge of the county (at 31°46′ N, 103°49′ W). Threemile Draw joins Fourmile Draw two miles northeast of TP Tank in northwestern Reeves County. Fourmile Draw crosses an area of steep to gentle slopes with alluvial fans and mountain wash materials of sand, gravel, and mud. Local vegetation includes scrub brush, sparse grasses, and cacti. Fourmile Draw may have been named for the width of its flow at flood stage.

FOUR MILE PRAIRIE, TEXAS. Four Mile Prairie, on Farm Road 90 twelve miles southwest of Canton in western Van Zandt County, was founded in 1847 when the Norwegian colony led by Johan R. Reiersen^{qv} moved there from Henderson County. The community, one of three Norwegian settlements in the area, takes its name from a sandy prairie ten miles long that begins on the north shore of Cedar Creek Reservoir^{qv} in southeastern Kaufman County and runs northeast into Van Zandt County; in width it is bounded by two streams four miles apart, Cedar Creek on the west and Lacy Fork on the east. The settlement was in both Van Zandt County and Kaufman County. Until it became the major Norwegian settlement in the area, the community used the post office at Prairieville, three miles west in Kaufman County; a Four Mile Prairie post office was established in 1849 and operated until 1866. Fourteen Norwegian families arrived in 1850 and brought the population of Four Mile Prairie and Prairieville to a total of 105. Many survivors of an epidemic in the 1850s moved for their health to Bosque County. Fourmile Lutheran Church was established in 1848; it built successive buildings in 1854, 1875, 1941, and 1955. The settlement's first Lutheran pastor, Rev. E. A. Fredrickson, came from Norway in 1855. Aanenson Cemetery was started 1853. In 1884 Four Mile Prairie had a population of 200 and was a rural market center, but the population declined to eighty by 1890, when a school operated there. The number of residents rose again to 300 in 1914, then dwindled. At one time four schools were in operation on Four Mile Prairie, two in each county. In 1936 state highway maps showed Fourmile Church and scattered dwellings at the site, and in 1981 a business, the church, a cemetery, and residences made up the small community.

BIBLIOGRAPHY: C. A. Clausen, ed., *The Lady with the Pen: Elise Wærenskjold in Texas* (Northfield, Minnesota: Norwegian-American Historical Association, 1961; rpt., New York: Arno Press, 1979). Margaret Elizabeth Hall, *A History of Van Zandt County* (Austin: Jenkins, 1976). Darwin Payne, "Early Norwegians in Northeast Texas," *Southwestern Historical Quarterly* 45 (October 1961). Terrell *Times-Star*, May 3, 1890. Terrell *Weekly Transcript*, January 5, 12, 19, 1899. Lyder L. Unstad, "Norwegian Migration to Texas," *Southwestern Historical Quarterly* 43 (October 1939). Van Zandt County History Book Committee, *History of Van Zandt County* (Dallas, 1984).   *Jack Stoltz*

FOUR POINTS, TEXAS. Four Points, also called Four Corners or Hickmuntown, was at the intersection of Farm roads 620 and 2222, twelve miles northeast of downtown Austin in northern Travis County. A school, a church, a few businesses, and several scattered houses marked the community on county highway maps in the 1940s. By the 1980s it was not labeled on county maps. The community still existed in 1990.   *Vivian Elizabeth Smyrl*

FOUR-SECTION ACT. The so-called Four-Section Act of April 4, 1895, allowed the sale and lease of a maximum of four sections of school, asylum, or public lands in all Texas counties except El Paso, Pecos, and Presidio. The act was an extension of laws made as early as 1887 allowing settlers to purchase four sections of pastureland from the public domain. A law passed in 1881, which allowed the purchase of as much as seven sections of grassland in certain localities, had been modified in 1883, after an orgy of land speculation, by an increase in the price of school lands from one dollar to two dollars an acre. According to the 1895 act the sales were directed by the commissioner of the General Land Office,^{qv} and three-year residence and improvements were required. Although the object of the law was to attract ranchers to unsettled regions, many farmers moved into the western plains and started wheat farms. The law was later modified and extended, particularly by the Eight-Section Act.^{qv}

BIBLIOGRAPHY: Hans Peter Nielsen Gammel, comp., *Laws of Texas, 1822–1897* (10 vols., Austin: Gammel, 1898). *General Laws of the State of Texas Passed by the Thirty-eighth Legislature at Its First, Second and Third Sessions, 1923* (Austin: Secretary of State, 1923). *Revised Civil Statutes of the State of Texas* (Austin: Baldwin, 1925).

Jeanne Dibrell

FOUR SIXES RANCH. The Four Sixes (6666) brand was established by Samuel Burk Burnett^{qv} in the early 1870s. Although legend persists that Burnett's brand was devised to honor a winning poker hand of four sixes that he once held, sources indicate that Burnett, after successfully completing his first drive to Kansas as trail boss for his father's herd in 1867, saved his earnings and in 1871 used them to buy 100 cattle bearing the Four Sixes brand from Frank Crowley in Denton County. Burnett's brother Bruce used the brand in reverse (9999) for his ranching operation, which he moved to Knox County in 1889. In 1874 Burnett moved his cattle to the region of the Wichita River, bought land, and established his ranch headquarters near the site of present Wichita Falls. Due to the drought of 1881 Burnett was forced to drive his cattle to the Red River to survive. He subsequently leased 300,000 acres of Comanche-Kiowa reservation land. In 1893 he began the process of purchasing the Old Eight Ranch, 140,000 acres and 1,500 head of stock, from the Louisville Land and Cattle Company of Kentucky. The purchase was finalized in 1900, and Burnett moved his 6666 Ranch headquarters to King County.

By 1900, when the government opened the Kiowa-Comanche reservation for settlement and ordered the cattlemen to vacate their leases, Burnett obtained from President Theodore Roosevelt a two-year extension to enable him and his fellow cattlemen to move out and dispose of their herds in an orderly fashion. In 1902 Burnett bought 107,520 acres in Carson and Hutchinson counties from the British-owned White Deer Lands (*see* FRANCKLYN LAND AND CATTLE COMPANY) for $2.65 per acre. This choice Panhandle^{qv} range, which had previously been leased to Al Popham and J. L. Harrison, was located along Dixon Creek and contained abundant water. It became known as the Burnett–Dixon Creek–6666 Ranch. Over the next few years Burnett acquired sufficient adjoining range land to constitute an operation totaling almost a third of a million acres.

On his Four Six ranges Burnett began improving his cattle by careful culling of cows and importation of purebred Hereford^{qv} and Durham bulls. The resultant offspring soon became consistent winners as feeder cattle in livestock shows nationwide. The Dixon Creek Division, sometimes known as the Stocker Ranch, was set up to receive calves produced on the other Burnett properties. Gradually, the Four Sixes became a strictly Hereford operation, and Burnett's cattle were among the first to be spayed to better fatten them prior to slaughter. The Four Sixes acquired its first cow horses from Burnett's father-in-law, Col. M. B. Lloyd of Fort Worth; since then all horses on the ranch have been branded with the letter L on the left shoulder. Burnett's purebred quarter horses^{qv} likewise became well known throughout the Southwest. Outstanding Four Six employees during its early years, some of whom had worked for the Eight Ranch before Burnett bought it, included John Humphreys, Jim Gibson, Sid Williams, Charlie Hart, Joe Crystal, and Oak (Coley) Owens. Bud Arnett was retained as the first foreman. The Four Sixes brand was used on the Burnett properties in Wichita County, headquartered at Iowa Park, until 1910, when Burnett leased them to his son Thomas L. Burnett,^qv who subsequently adopted Colonel Lloyd's Triangle brand as his own.

Although Burk Burnett at first utilized the Old Eight Camp as his headquarters in King County, he later moved it west to the county seat of Guthrie and in 1917 built his magnificent $100,000 stone ranch house on a hill overlooking the town. Barns, corrals, a bunkhouse, and other outbuildings were erected around it. In 1918 a severe Panhandle blizzard wiped out 2,000 cattle on the Dixon Creek Division, but the losses were practically forgotten in 1921, when the first seven of Carson County's oil and gas wells, including Eugene S. Blasdel's^qv Gulf No. 1 and No. 2, were drilled on the ranch.

After Burnett's death in 1922 the Four Sixes was inherited by his granddaughter, Anne Burnett Tandy.^qv Known affectionately among the ranch people as "Miss Anne," she became nationally famous as a judge and breeder of horses; among the well-known champion racers and show horses acquired by or bred on the Four Sixes were Grey Badger II and Hollywood Gold. The ranch and its overseers were prime movers in the organization of the American Quarter Horse Association. When Bud Arnett retired as foreman in 1930, his son-in-law filled the position for two years and then was succeeded by a second-generation Four Sixes cowhand, George P. Humphreys. By 1936 around 20,000 Hereford cattle stocked the Four Six ranges, ably run by the S. B. Burnett Estate in Fort Worth, of which John C. Burns served as trustee for many years. In 1961 John Boyce (Jay) Humphrey III was appointed as trustee and general manager; he held the position until 1980.

The Four Sixes Ranch, which occupies some 208,000 acres, continues to be the primary economic mainstay of King County. The imposing ranch house, occupied by the foreman and his family, stands at the end of a paved driveway just off U.S. Highway 82. A rock watertower stands behind it, and other ranch facilities, including barns and corrals, a dining room, and a bunkhouse for single employees, cover about eighteen acres. Four line camps, the South, North, Old Eight, and Taylor, are located on the ranch. Each camp is run by an overseer, who looks after an allotted number of acres and cattle. Living quarters are furnished for him and his family. The wagon boss and other married ranch employees reside with their families in Guthrie, in furnished, rent-free housing. The town's high school and nondenominational church are supported by tax money from the ranch, and the Four Sixes Supply Store is another well-known landmark. The ranch continues to use the old horse-drawn chuckwagon, where cowboys and visitors are welcome to a Western-style meal out on the range at roundup time. The Dixon Creek Division (108,000 acres) in Carson and Hutchinson counties contains several producing oil and gas wells and a spacious stone headquarters house, which is easily spotted from State Highway 207 north of Panhandle.

After Miss Anne's death in 1980, the Four Sixes was passed on to her daughter Anne V. (Little Anne) Windfohr Sowell and granddaughter Windi Phillips. George Humphreys, known in later years as the "Little Sheriff" of King County, remained as foreman until his retirement in 1970. His successor was another second-generation employee, James J. Gibson, Jr. In addition to conducting an extensive brush-control project, Gibson's main contribution in recent years has been the introduction and crossbreeding of Brangus cattle with ranch Herefords to produce the Black Baldie, a hardy breed more resilient to cedar flies, a common pest in the cedar brakes of West Texas. Champion quarter horses continue to reap profits for the Four Sixes. George (Coon) Jeffers became foreman of the Dixon Creek Division in 1949. In the 1980s Gibson became general manager of the ranch. Mike Gibson was the foreman in 1994.

In addition to its high-grade livestock, the Four Sixes has won fame as a setting for several Marlboro cigarette television ads during the 1960s, with certain ranch employees posing as the "Marlboro Man." Portions of the movie *Mackintosh and T. J.*, which starred Roy Rogers, were filmed at the Old Eight Camp in 1975. The ranch has likewise been a favorite subject for paintings by area artists such as Tom Ryan and Mondel Rogers. One of the original red Four Sixes barns, which was for years a prominent landmark in Guthrie, is now on the grounds of the Ranching Heritage Center^qv in Lubbock.

BIBLIOGRAPHY: James Cox, *Historical and Biographical Record of the Cattle Industry* (2 vols., St. Louis: Woodward and Tiernan Printing, 1894, 1895; rpt., with an introduction by J. Frank Dobie, New York: Antiquarian, 1959). Dallas *Morning News*, September 4, 1991. C. L. Douglas, *Cattle Kings of Texas* (Dallas: Baugh, 1939; rpt., Fort Worth: Branch-Smith, 1968). Gus L. Ford, ed., *Texas Cattle Brands* (Dallas: Cockrell, 1936). King County Historical Society, *King County: Windmills and Barbed Wire* (Quanah, Texas: Nortex, 1976). Dorothy Abbott McCoy, *Texas Ranchmen* (Austin: Eakin Press, 1987). Jo Stewart Randel, ed., *A Time to Purpose: A Chronicle of Carson County* (4 vols., Hereford, Texas: Pioneer, 1966–72). Mondel Rogers, *Old Ranches of the Texas Plains* (College Station: Texas A&M University Press, 1976). Jesse Wallace Williams, *The Big Ranch Country* (Wichita Falls: Terry, 1954; 2d ed., Wichita Falls: Nortex, 1971).   *H. Allen Anderson*

FOURTH CREEK. Fourth Creek rises sixteen miles southwest of Darrouzett in north central Lipscomb County (at 36°21′ N, 100°22′ W) and runs south for seven miles to its mouth on Wolf Creek, seven miles west of Lipscomb (at 36°14′ N, 100°21′ W). It traverses flat to rolling terrain with some local escarpments, surfaced by deep, fine sandy loams that support mesquite, brush, and grasses. The creek's lower portion was within the Seven K Ranch^qv range.

FOURTH TEXAS INFANTRY. The Fourth Texas Infantry was one of the three Texas Civil War^qv regiments in the Texas Brigade of Gen. Robert E. Lee's^qv Army of Northern Virginia. In 1861 Governor Edward Clark^qv established a camp of instruction on the San Marcos River in Hays County. The first units that later formed the Fourth Texas Infantry enlisted there in April 1861. Originally the Texans planned to enlist for a period of one year, but after the outbreak of war at Fort Sumter on April 12, 1861, the Confederate government announced that it would accept only regiments enlisted for the duration of the war. In July 1861 twenty companies of Texas infantry were transferred to a camp near Harrisburg and promptly shipped to Virginia. Soon after their arrival in Richmond the Texas units were officially organized into regiments, on September 30, 1861. The ten companies that made up the Fourth Texas were Company A, the Hardeman Rifles, recruited in Gonzales County; Company B, the Tom Green Rifles, Travis County; Company C, the Robertson Five Shooters, Robertson County; Company D, the Guadalupe Rangers, Guadalupe County; Company E, the Lone Star Guards, McLennan County; Company F, the Mustang Grays, Bexar County; Company G, the Grimes County Grays; Company H, the Porter Guards, Walker County; Company I, the Navarro Rifles, Navarro County; and Company K, the Sandy Point Mounted Rifles, Henderson County.

Contrary to the prevailing custom, the Texans were not allowed to elect their own field officers but had them appointed by the Confederate War Department. The first commander of the regiment was Robert T. P. Allen,^qv former superintendent of the Bastrop Military Academy (*see* TEXAS MILITARY INSTITUTE, AUSTIN), who because of his harsh discipline was extremely unpopular and was forced to resign his position in October. Allen was replaced by Texan John Bell Hood,^qv who was assigned to command the Fourth with the rank of colonel. John F. Marshall,^qv editor of the Austin based *Texas State Gazette* and one of the principle organizers of the regiment, was appointed to the post of lieutenant colonel, and Virginian Bradfute Warwick was given the rank of major.

The Fourth was formally assigned to Brig. Gen. Louis T. Wigfall's^qv Texas Brigade shortly after Hood assumed command and was subsequently stationed at Dumfries, Virginia, in November 1861. As the regiment drilled and prepared for active duty it was plagued with a great deal of sickness, a rather typical ordeal for Civil War units. In

October 1861 the chaplain of the Fourth, Nicholas A. Davis,^qv reported that more than 400 of the regiment's original 1,187 men were sick. This served to weed out many who were unfit for service and reduce the unit to a fighting trim. In March 1862 Hood was promoted to command of the Texas Brigade, Marshall became a colonel, and Capt. J. C. G. Key of Company A advanced to the post of major.

The regiment first saw combat on the Virginia peninsula on May 7, 1862, at Eltham's Landing, but its introduction to real battle came on June 27, 1862, at the battle of Gaines' Mill. Here both the Texas Brigade and the Fourth Texas established their reputation for hard fighting by successfully breaking the Union line on Turkey Hill, which had resisted all previous Confederate attempts to do so. Taking only 500 men into the battle, the Fourth lost eighty-five men: twenty-one killed, sixty-three wounded, and one captured. Marshal and Warwick were both killed, and Key was wounded.

The Fourth Texas was not engaged again until the battle of Second Manassas on August 30, 1862. Under the command of Lt. Col. B. F. Carter it participated in the Confederate attack on the second day of the fighting, taking a federal battery of artillery in the process. Losses in this engagement totaled thirty-one (eleven killed, twenty wounded). On September 14, 1862, the regiment was engaged in combat at the battle of South Mountain, where it had six men killed and two wounded in the delaying action before the battle of Sharpsburg (Antietam), fought on September 17, 1862. At Antietam the Fourth Texas was involved in some of the stiffest fighting on the Confederate left flank and suffered its greatest number of losses for any single battle of the war, losing 210 men (57 killed, 130 wounded, and 23 captured).

The regiment was only marginally engaged at the battle of Fredericksburg in December 1862 and was not present with Lee's army during the battle of Chancellorsville in May 1863. After that, however, it took part in every major action of the Army of Northern Virginia during the rest of the war as well as in the battle of Chickamauga, during the temporary transfer of Lt. Gen. James Longstreet's First Corps to the Confederate Army of Tennessee in September 1863. At Gettysburg on July 2, 1863, the Fourth Texas participated in the attack against the Union left flank and in the fighting for Little Round Top, losing 140 men (twenty-five killed, fifty-seven wounded, and fifty-eight captured), including Lieutenant Colonel Carter, who was mortally wounded.

At Chickamauga, Georgia, on September 19 and 20, 1863, the regiment, now under the command of Lt. Col. John P. Bane,^qv was part of the rebel force that broke the federal line on the second day of fighting and helped to rout the Union Army of the Cumberland. The Fourth's losses at Chickamauga totaled seventy-seven (thirty-four killed, forty wounded, and three captured). At the battle of Wauhatchie, during the siege of Chattanooga, Tennessee, on October 28, 1863, the Fourth was routed by the enemy for the only time during the war. Upon the unit's return to Virginia in April 1864 with the rest of Longstreet's corps, the Texans once again acquitted themselves admirably, by plugging a gap torn in the Confederate line at the battle of the Wilderness, May 7, 1864. Here the regiment took part in the famous "Lee to the rear" episode and suffered 124 casualties (twenty-six killed, ninety-five wounded, and three captured) out of only 207 men engaged. Subsequently, the Fourth was marginally involved in the fighting at Spotsylvania and helped to repel the Union attack at Cold Harbor on June 3, 1864. During the fall and winter of 1864–65 the regiment fought around Petersburg and Richmond before taking part in the Southern retreat that ended in the surrender of Lee's army at Appomattox Court House on April 9, 1865.

Throughout its existence 1,343 men were assigned to the Fourth Texas Infantry. Of that number 256 (19 percent) were killed or mortally wounded in battle. Another 486 men (35.9 percent) were wounded, many more than once, for the total number of wounds suffered by the regiment in four years of fighting amounted to 606. The total number of battle casualties suffered by the Fourth Texas Infantry was 909 (67.7 percent). The number of prisoners lost by the regiment was 162 (12 percent). Of the regiment, 161 died of diseases (11.9 percent), 251 (18 percent) were discharged due to sickness, wounds, etc., and 51 deserted (3 percent). At the time of its surrender the Fourth Texas mustered only fifteen officers and 143 men. Despite such heavy losses, or perhaps because of them, the Fourth Texas Infantry and its parent Texas Brigade won a reputation as one of the hardest fighting and most reliable units in the Confederate Army of Northern Virginia.

BIBLIOGRAPHY: Nicholas A. Davis, *Chaplain Davis and Hood's Texas Brigade*, ed. Donald E. Everett (San Antonio: Principia Press of Trinity University, 1962). Mary Lasswell, comp. and ed., *Rags and Hope: The Memoirs of Val C. Giles* (New York: Coward-McCann, 1961). Joseph Benjamin Polley, *Hood's Texas Brigade* (New York: Neale, 1910; rpt., Dayton, Ohio: Morningside Bookshop, 1976). Harold B. Simpson, *Hood's Texas Brigade* (Waco: Texian Press, 1970). Harold B. Simpson, *Hood's Texas Brigade: A Compendium* (Hillsboro, Texas: Hill Junior College Press, 1977).
Jeffrey William Hunt

FOURTH UNITED STATES CAVALRY. The Fourth United States Cavalry regiment, one of the most effective units of the United States Army against Indians on the Texas frontier, was organized on March 26, 1855, at Jefferson Barracks, Missouri, as the First Cavalry Regiment. It was redesignated on August 3, 1861, as the Fourth United States Cavalry. Its first commanders were Col. Edwin V. Sumner and Lt. Col. Joseph E. Johnston.^qv From 1855 to 1861 the First Cavalry served against hostile Plains Indians, sought to keep peace between the opposing factions in Kansas, and fought against Confederates in Missouri, Arkansas, and Indian Territory. In 1861–62 two companies served with distinction in Virginia before being reunited with the regiment in Tennessee. The regiment fought gallantly and continuously in the western theater from Shiloh to Macon.

In August 1865 the Fourth Cavalry was sent to Texas. At various times during the next thirteen years units of its twelve companies occupied the military posts between the Rio Grande and Jacksboro and between San Antonio and San Angelo. Before 1871 the operations of the regiment were limited to guarding the mail and settlements against Indians and to desultory attempts to overtake bands of Indian raiders. Col. Lawrence Pike Graham never led a major campaign, and none of the regiment's fourteen skirmishes with Indians was of major significance.

In December 1870 Col. Ranald S. Mackenzie^qv was given command of the Fourth Cavalry, with orders to put a stop to Comanche and Kiowa raids along the Texas frontier. On February 25, 1871, Mackenzie took command of the Fourth Cavalry at Fort Concho. A month later he moved the headquarters of the regiment to Fort Richardson, near Jacksboro; companies of the Fourth remained at Fort Griffin and Fort Concho. In May, while Gen. William T. Sherman,^qv commander in chief of the army, was at Fort Richardson, the Kiowas brutally mutilated some teamsters with a wagon train on nearby Salt Creek Prairie (*see* SALT CREEK MASSACRE). A few days later at Fort Sill, Sherman had three leaders of the raid, Satanta, Satank, and Big Tree,^qqv arrested and had Mackenzie return them to Jacksboro for trial for murder. On the way a trooper killed Satank when he tried to escape; Satanta and Big Tree were sentenced to life imprisonment.

In August Mackenzie led an expedition into Indian Territory against the Comanches and Kiowas who had left the agency, but he was later ordered to return to Texas. He then led eight companies of the Fourth Cavalry and two companies of the Eleventh Infantry, about 600 men, in search of Quahadi Comanches, who had refused to go onto the reservation and were plundering the Texas frontier. On October 10 he skirmished with a group in Blanco Canyon, near the site of present Crosbyton, but the entire band escaped across the plains. The following summer Mackenzie, with six companies of the Fourth Cavalry, renewed his search for the Quahadis. After establishing his supply camp on the Freshwater Fork of the Brazos (now the White River) southeast of present Crosbyton, Mackenzie with five companies of cavalry followed a cattle trail across the unexplored High Plains into New Mexico and returned by another well-watered Comanchero^{qv} road from Fort Bascom, near the site of present Tucumcari, New Mexico, to the site of present Canyon. At the head of 222 cavalrymen on September 29 he surprised and destroyed Chief Mow-way's^{qv} village of Quahadi and Kotsoteka Comanches on the North Fork of the Red River about six miles east of the site of present Lefors. An estimated fifty-two Indians were killed and 124 captured, with a loss of three cavalrymen killed and three wounded. For almost a year both the Kiowas and Comanches remained at peace.

In March 1873 Mackenzie and five companies (A, B, C, E, and K) of the Fourth Cavalry were transferred to Fort Clark with orders to put an end to the Mexican-based Kickapoo and Apache depredations in Texas, which had cost an alleged $48 million. On May 18, 1873, Mackenzie, with five companies of the Fourth Cavalry, surprised and burned three villages of the raiders near Remolino, Coahuila; the cavalrymen killed nineteen Indians and captured forty-one, with a loss of one trooper killed and two wounded. The soldiers recrossed the Rio Grande into Texas at daybreak the next morning, some of the men having ridden an estimated 160 miles in forty-nine hours. The raid and an effective system of border patrols brought temporary peace to the area.

When the Southern Plains Indians opened the Red River War^{qv} in June 1874, the Grant administration discarded its Quaker peace policy and authorized the military to take control of the reservations and subdue all hostile Indians. Gen. Philip H. Sheridan,^{qv} commander of the Division of the Missouri, ordered five military expeditions to converge on their hideouts along the upper Red River country. In the ensuing campaign the Fourth Cavalry was the most successful. On September 26–27 it staved off a Comanche attack at the head of Tule Canyon and on the morning of September 28 descended by a narrow trail to the bottom of Palo Duro Canyon. There it completely destroyed five Comanche, Kiowa, and Cheyenne villages, including large quantities of provisions, and captured 1,424 horses and mules, of which 1,048 were slaughtered at the head of Tule Canyon. Afterward, Mackenzie, with detachments of the regiment, made two other expeditions onto the High Plains. On November 3, near the site of Tahoka, in their last fight with the Comanches, the cavalrymen killed two and captured nineteen. In spring 1875 Mackenzie and the units of the Fourth Cavalry from various posts in Texas were sent to Fort Sill to take control of the Southern Plains Indians.

Meanwhile, the Indians in Mexico had renewed their marauding in Texas. In 1878 General Sherman, at the insistence of the Texans, transferred Mackenzie and six companies of the Fourth Cavalry to Fort Clark. This time Mackenzie led a larger and more extensive expedition into Mexico, restored a system of patrols, and reestablished peace in the devastated region of South Texas.

Outside Texas, Mackenzie and the Fourth Cavalry administered and controlled the Kiowa-Comanche and the Cheyenne-Arapaho reservations for several years, and after the annihilation of George A. Custer's^{qv} command on the Little Big Horn in June 1876 forced Red Cloud and his band of Sioux and the Northern Cheyennes to surrender. In the autumn of 1879 Mackenzie with six companies of the Fourth Cavalry subdued the hostile Utes in Southern Colorado without firing a shot and in August 1880 forced them to move to a reservation in Utah. Immediately thereafter, the Fourth Cavalry was transferred to Arizona, where Mackenzie was to assume full command of all military forces in the department and subdue the hostile Apaches. Within less than a month the Apaches had surrendered or fled to Mexico, and on October 30 Mackenzie and the Fourth Cavalry were transferred to the new District of New Mexico. By November 1, 1882, when W. B. Royall replaced Mackenzie as colonel, the Fourth Cavalry had forced the White Mountain Apaches, Jicarillas, Navajos, and Mescaleros to remain peacefully on their respective reservations.

From 1884 to 1886 the Fourth Cavalry operated against the Apaches in Arizona. In 1890 the regimental headquarters was moved to Walla Walla, Washington. During World War I^{qv} the Fourth Cavalry remained in the United States in case hostilities should erupt along the Mexican border. In 1942 the unit was reorganized and redesignated the Fourth Cavalry Mechanized and sent to Europe, where it participated throughout the remainder of World War II.^{qv} Afterward in Vietnam the unit served with undiminished valor.

BIBLIOGRAPHY: James M. Merrill, *Spurs to Glory: The Story of the U.S. Cavalry* (Chicago: Rand McNally 1966). Ernest Wallace, *Ranald S. Mackenzie on the Texas Frontier* (Lubbock: West Texas Museum Association, 1964).

Ernest Wallace

FOURTH WARD, HOUSTON. The Fourth Ward in Houston, also sometimes referred to as Freedmen's Town, is one of that city's most important African-American historic communities. During the late nineteenth and early twentieth centuries, it was the center of black cultural and professional life in the city. By the early twentieth century it housed prominent educational institutions and the majority of the black physicians and attorneys, while at night its bars and night spots attracted whites and blacks who came to hear great blues and jazz^{qv} musicians. Blues guitarist B. B. King later termed the Fourth Ward night life the "breeding ground" for musicians Arnett Cobb and Sam (Lightnin') Hopkins.^{qv} The Houston city charter of 1839 organized the city into four wards. The fourth is located just southwest of downtown Houston, along the south bank of Buffalo Bayou. It extended south of Congress Avenue and west of Main Street to the city limits. Although the Fourth Ward was established as a political subdivision, and although at least through the nineteenth century it housed more whites than blacks, the area is best known as one of Houston's oldest and most important black neighborhoods. Initially it encompassed most of what is now downtown Houston west of Main Street, as well as the residential areas along San Felipe Street (now West Dallas) and West Grey that still are referred to as the Fourth Ward and are today almost exclusively black in population.

The Fourth Ward emerged as Houston's most prominent African-American neighborhood when thousands of freed slaves flooded into the city after emancipation. These newcomers settled on the fringes of the third, fifth, and fourth wards. The Freedmentown area north of San Felipe and the streets west of downtown not only attracted the largest number of the new black residents but also housed the first black churches, schools, and political organizations. Several factors combined to facilitate the subsequent growth of the Fourth Ward's black community. First, its location—southwest of downtown and on the San Felipe road, which connected the city with the Brazos River plantations—meant that it was situated on the major route that brought freedmen into the city. In addition, in the aftermath of the war many whites who owned farmland on the outskirts of the city recognized the economic advantage of subdividing their land to provide housing lots or rental houses for the rapidly growing black population. One former slave recalled that his owner, Charles S. Longcope, had assembled all of his slaves in June 1865, and, standing in his door of his Second Ward mansion, read them the proclamation that gave them their freedom; he then offered each of his former slaves a building lot in the Fourth Ward. Finally, the Fourth Ward provided a home to early black religious and educational institutions. It had, in fact, achieved this distinction even before emancipation. In 1851 black Methodists began worshiping in their own church, adjacent to the white Methodist church on Milam Street in the Fourth Ward. This black church briefly housed a school for blacks in the late 1850s. After the Civil War the Fourth Ward attracted two of the city's most important African American churches, the Trinity Methodist Episcopal Church on Travis at Bell, and Antioch Baptist Church, located initially at Rusk and Bagby and later on Robin Street. The Fourth Ward's role as a center of education was strengthened in 1870, when the various Freedmen's Bureau^qv schools in the city were consolidated at Gregory School, the first public school for blacks in Houston.

As the black population of Houston grew in the late nineteenth and early twentieth century, the nature of black Houston and the Fourth Ward began to take shape. Lacking a single concentrated area of black population, Houston, like many other Southern cities, had several black enclaves. The Fourth Ward was one of these. In the late nineteenth century the community spread slowly out of the downtown area around the present site of the City Hall and Houston Public Library,^qv south and west down San Felipe Street and adjacent areas of the Old Freedmentown area. By 1907 the shotgun residences that are today characteristic of the Ward began to be commonplace (see FOLK BUILDING); they were joined by T-shaped houses, L-shaped houses, and several two-story tenements. Along the major streets commercial buildings, churches, and schools appeared while many of the residential blocks had a commercial building, usually a cafe, grocery, or bar, on the corner.

Throughout the late nineteenth and early twentieth century the Fourth Ward maintained its position as the economic, cultural, and intellectual center of black Houston. Although never more than 36 percent of the city's black population resided in the ward, it continued to house a disproportionate share of its professionals and was home to most of its significant institutions. For example, in 1869 black churches were instrumental in the organization of the Harris County Republican Club, an integrated political organization that held most of its meetings in Antioch Baptist Church. Rev. Jack Yates and other black ministers successfully campaigned for a permanent park site for Houston blacks. In 1872 they established Emancipation Park, in the Third Ward. Yates and Antioch also took the lead in promoting black education. After failing to attract Bishop College to the city, in 1885 they established Houston College (also known as Houston Baptist Academy) in the Third Ward. The college moved to a three-acre wooded tract on the western edge of the Fourth Ward in 1894. Until the mid-1920s the Fourth Ward was home to the only black high school in Houston (Colored High School, later renamed Booker T. Washington High School), and Ernest O. Smith^qv began the movement that resulted in the establishment of the black branch of the Carnegie Library, located in the Fourth Ward across the street from Colored High School. Finally, in 1915 all but one of the black doctors and dentists in Houston, as well as 75 percent of the black lawyers, had offices in the Fourth Ward; in 1910 a group of black physicians established Houston's first black hospital, Union Hospital, on Andrews Street near San Felipe. Development of the Fourth Ward was capped by the construction of the Pilgrim Life Insurance Building, an imposing structure that housed offices, clubrooms, ballrooms, and a rooftop roller rink; during his trip through Houston in 1930, Lorenze Greene described the building as "an imposing office building, The most beautiful, Owned by Negroes, I have yet seen." On the other hand, in 1917 the Fourth Ward was the scene of Houston's worst race riot (see HOUSTON RIOT OF 1917).

The Fourth Ward lost its preeminence in the 1920s as the Third Ward passed it in population and began to attract more black institutions, including Houston Negro Hospital (now Riverside General Hospital), Yates High School (the second black high school in Houston), and Houston Colored Junior College (the antecedent of Texas Southern University). The Fourth Ward also faced other difficulties. First, its ability to expand was severely limited. Unlike the other two early centers of black population, the Third Ward and the Fifth Ward, the Fourth Ward was hemmed in on the south and west by other developments. In the 1920s it failed to continue to attract as many new residents as did the other wards, and it began to lose its more affluent residents to new housing developments. Second, beginning in the 1930s, white institutions and downtown businesses encroached on the Fourth Ward. Black residents were displaced in that decade as land was cleared for the City Hall complex. More damaging still, in the early 1940s land north of San Felipe was cleared to build San Felipe Courts (now Allen Parkway Village), a housing development for white defense workers. (Housing projects for blacks were built in the Fifth Ward and the Third Ward.) The construction of Interstate 45 southwest of downtown Houston eliminated many of the ward's most important buildings and destroyed the geographical integrity of the community. Finally, in the 1960s a large area of the Fourth Ward in the vicinity of Antioch Baptist Church was cleared to make way for the construction of office buildings; today Antioch stands, cut off from its community and surrounded by office towers.

By 1980 the only residential area left in the old Fourth Ward, along West Dallas (formerly San Felipe) and West Grey just a few blocks west of downtown, had become the poorest black area in the city. Its population had declined to fewer than 4,400, down from almost 17,000 in 1910. Almost 50 percent of its residents lived below the poverty level, and only 5 percent owned their own homes. In the 1980s and 1990s the continued future of the Fourth Ward as a black community came under serious attack. Plans to tear down Allen Parkway Village and redevelop the area with office buildings and upper-income housing were presented, only to be delayed by citizen opposition—and, more importantly, by the economic downturn of the mid-1980s. The viability of the community has been undermined by the disappearance through neglect of much of its housing, the reluctance of investors to put capital in the ward, and doubts about the future of the neighborhood. Allen Parkway Village and the absentee landlords are still waiting for the bonanza that redevelopment would bring.

BIBLIOGRAPHY: Howard Beeth and Cary D. Wintz, eds., *Black Dixie: Afro-Texan History and Culture in Houston* (College Station: Texas A&M University Press, 1992). Houston Metropolitan Research Center Files, Houston Public Library. Howard Jones, *The Red Diary: A Chronological History of Black Americans in Houston and Some Neighboring Harris County Communities—122 Years Later* (Austin: Nortex Press, 1991). James Martin SoRelle, The Darker Side of 'Heaven': The Black Community in Houston, Texas, 1917–1945 (Ph.D. dissertation, Kent State University, 1980). Vertical Files, Barker Texas History Center, University of Texas at Austin (Houston—Neighborhoods). Cary D. Wintz, "The Emergence of a Black Neighborhood: Houston's Fourth Ward, 1865–1915," in *Urban Texas: Politics and Development*, ed. Char Miller and Heywood T. Sanders (College Station: Texas A&M University Press, 1990).
Cary D. Wintz

FOUR WAY, TEXAS. Four Way, four miles north of Masterson in southern Moore County, is named for its position on the spot where U.S. Highway 87 from Dumas to Masterson crosses the route from Channing to Lake Meredith and Stinnett. Four Way is a hamlet allied with Masterson and the Colorado International Gas Company plant. After natural gas was discovered in the vicinity in the late 1920s, a man named Anthony and his wife opened a grocery store, filling station, and dance hall. Music for this popular roadhouse was furnished during the 1930s by "Little Ham" Hamilton's band from Amarillo. Later, after the highway was paved, a family named Atchison opened a store and cafe on the east side of the road. The dance hall expanded into a cafe and tourist court. By the early 1970s only one store and service station remained. The community was still listed in 1990.

BIBLIOGRAPHY: Fred Tarpley, *1001 Texas Place Names* (Austin: University of Texas Press, 1980).
H. Allen Anderson

FOUTS, TEXAS. Fouts was on the Trinity Valley and Northern Railway ten miles north of Dayton in west central Liberty County. The railroad, completed from Dayton through Fullerton to Fouts in 1909, was extended another eight miles by 1911. Fouts was presumably named for L. Fouts, one of the railroad's incorporators. It was in a heavily forested area crossed by logging roads for the lumbering operations and at one time had a population of fifty. It had a post office from 1909 to 1917. The Dayton Lumber Company's logging facilities at Fouts were sold in 1917. Presumably because logging had become less profitable, the Trinity Valley and Northern abandoned its line north of Fullerton in 1929. Fouts is not shown on county highway maps in the mid-1980s.

BIBLIOGRAPHY: S. G. Reed, *A History of the Texas Railroads* (Houston: St. Clair, 1941; rpt., New York: Arno, 1981). Charles P. Zlatkovich, *Texas Railroads* (Austin: University of Texas Bureau of Business Research, 1981).

Robert Wooster

FOWLER, ANDREW JACKSON (1815–1885). Andrew Jackson (Jack) Fowler, jurist, teacher, legislator, and Confederate Army officer, was born near the Caldwell County, Kentucky, town of Princeton on November 11, 1815, the youngest son of Clara (Wright) and Godfrey Fowler, Jr. In 1836 he graduated from LaGrange College in Alabama, then regarded as the finest Methodist college in the south. He read law in the office of his brother Wyley Paul Fowler in Smithfield, Kentucky, before moving to Clarksville, Texas, late in 1837 to join two other brothers, John H. Fowler,qv who had settled Pecan Point in Red River County in 1817, and Bradford C. Fowler, who served as a sergeant in one of James W. Fannin, Jr.'s,qv companies during the Texas Revolution.qv Sam Houston Dixon and Louis W. Kempqqv credit Andrew Fowler with having served at the battle of San Jacinto,qv but their conclusion is almost certainly based upon a mistranscription of the name Andrew Fogle.

Fowler was living in Clarksville when he was appointed chief justice of Red River County on June 27, 1839, by Mirabeau B. Lamar.qv He was reappointed on January 30, 1840. At that time he owned no taxable property. On February 10, 1840, he married Martha Susan Glenn at old Fort Houston near Palestine; the couple had nine children. Fowler moved to Paris in 1840 and represented Lamar County in the House of Representatives of the Sixth Congress, 1841–42. He took part in a number of Indian campaigns between 1838 and 1841. In the fall of 1841 he commanded a company of volunteers in Col. Edward H. Tarrant'sqv regiment, through the Cross Timbersqv as far as the Clear Fork of the Brazos River. In 1845 he was appointed by his brother Littleton Fowlerqv to the post of professor of mathematics and ancient languages at Wesleyan Male and Female College in San Augustine, where he taught for a year. In 1848 he was appointed chief justice of Henderson County, and on December 25 of that year became the first district attorney of Van Zandt County, then the Ninth Judicial District. The 1850 census listed him as a farmer in Anderson County with real estate worth $1,000. He later founded Hill College near Athens and Rusk Creek Academy in Navarro County and taught courses in the sciences until the latter school was closed in 1861 by the coming of war.

Although a Whig, a Unionist, and supporter of Sam Houston,qv during the Civil Warqv Fowler served as lieutenant colonel of Col. Thomas Coke Bass'sqv Twentieth Texas Cavalry; he saw duty in Arkansas, Indian Territory, and Texas before being exempted due to his age. He subsequently returned to Lamar County and became tax assessor and collector. After the war, Governor Edmund J. Davisqv appointed him judge of the Tenth Judicial District, which encompassed Anderson, Kaufman, Henderson, and Van Zandt counties, a position he held until replaced under the Constitution of 1876.qv Fowler died at his home in Lindale, Smith County, on March 31, 1885. He was survived by two of his children.

BIBLIOGRAPHY: Mrs. James J. Arthur, ed., *Annals of the Fowler Family* (Austin, 1901). *Compiled Index to Elected and Appointed Officials of the Republic of Texas, 1835–1846* (Austin: State Archives, Texas State Library, 1981). Wentworth Manning, *Some History of Van Zandt County* (Des Moines, Iowa: Homestead, 1919; rpt., Winston-Salem, North Carolina: Hunter, 1977). Texas House of Representatives, *Biographical Directory of the Texan Conventions and Congresses, 1832–1845* (Austin: Book Exchange, 1941).

Thomas W. Cutrer

FOWLER, HOMER THOMAS WILSON (1909–1972). Homer T. (Wick) Fowler, reporter and producer of Wick Fowler's Two-Alarm Chili, was born in Big Sandy, Texas, in 1909, the son of Isaac Dudley and Lola Viola (Glass) Fowler. He was reared in Victoria, attended the University of Texas, and began his career in 1932 as a crime reporter for the Austin *Statesman* (see AUSTIN AMERICAN-STATESMAN). He worked as a Capitol correspondent for the International News Service and the Austin *American* before turning to employment as a city detective and highway patrolman. He also spent three years as an investigator for the Senate Committee on Un-American Activities.

In 1943 Fowler joined the Dallas *Morning News*qv and became the first Texas reporter to go overseas in World War II.qv His assignment was to cover Texans, but his role extended to that of goodwill ambassador, and he was occasionally called in to give the troops a laugh. He traveled to Italy and France and followed Gen. George S. Patton into Germany. In Italy, Fowler worked with Ernie Pyle at Anzio and received a Purple Heart when the press building was bombed. He also followed the Pacific island fighting to Japan and was one of the first journalists to enter Hiroshima after the United States bombed that city. After he returned to the Dallas *Morning News*, his editor asked him for an expense account. Fowler reluctantly obliged after several months. On the back of an envelope, he wrote, 'Covering war—$2,000.' The editor paid him.

When the war ended, Fowler was in great demand as a speaker, making an estimated 282 speeches in one year. He loved to be in the public eye, a characteristic that served him well when he was leader of the Chili Appreciation Society International. During the decade after the war he worked as a roving correspondent for the News, as executive assistant to Governor Allan Shivers,qv as administrative assistant to Senator William Blakley, and as managing editor of the Midland *Reporter Telegram*. In 1954 Fowler started his own newspaper, called the *State Journal*, which reported legislative news. That year the masthead included the modest subheading, "Published at the State Capitol by Wick Fowler." The next year, the subhead read, "Published in the interest of sound, conservative government."

The war in Vietnam brought Fowler back to wartime reporting. In 1965 he asked the editor of the Denton *Record-Chronicle*qv to send him to Vietnam, thus ending publication of his weekly *News Digest*, which had seen only forty-three issues. He came back from Vietnam feeling that too many Americans thought of the war as a false alarm. He dubbed himself the military-affairs editor of the Denton paper. On his next trip to Vietnam in 1969, he took with him several cases of chili mix, which put him in the position to start the Da Nang Branch of the Chili Appreciation Society International. During his second trip he syndicated his stories to fifteen newspapers to get greater circulation for his articles, but the motive was hardly financial. One daily offered him fifteen dollars per article, but Fowler said, "Based on your circulation, you have no business paying that much. Make it $10." In 1970 Fowler was back in Vietnam, this time with Texas businessman H. Ross Perot, to seek the release of American prisoners of war. In 1971 he ran for Place Five on the Austin City Council on a law-and-order platform and placed second in a run-off election.

In 1964 Fowler started his chili company, called Wick Fowler's Two-Alarm Chili. The renowned chili competition at Terlingua began in 1967 when a humorist from Mount Kisco, New York, named H. Allen Smith, challenged Francis Tolbertqv of the Dallas *Morning News* to a cook-off. Smith claimed that no one in Texas could make proper chili. A reader suggested that Fowler answer the challenge, which he did. Two-hundred fifty persons attended the first contest, which ended in a tie. Fowler was in his element at an event like this; he arrived wearing a huge sombrero and carrying his chili secrets in a crumpled paper bag.

In 1937 he married Margaret Elizabeth O'Farrell; the couple had two children. They were divorced in 1964, and in 1968 Fowler married Zelda Bess Blailock Reed. He received the Press Award from the Press Club of Dallas in 1966. Fowler was a member of Sigma Delta Chi, the professional journalism society. He died of amyotrophic lateral sclerosis (Lou Gehrig's disease) on September 22, 1972. Ernie Pyle had written about Fowler to George B. Dealey,qv "He fit in quicker than any other correspondent who has ever showed up in the war zone, and everybody likes him instantly."

BIBLIOGRAPHY: Austin *American-Statesman*, September 27, 1972. Ginger Banks, "Chili King 'Escapes'," *Texas Parade*, June 1969. Frank X. Tolbert, "Tolbert's Texas" Scrapbook, Barker Texas History Center, University of Texas at Austin. Vertical Files, Barker Texas History Center, University of Texas at Austin. *Alice M. Shukalo*

FOWLER, JOHN HOPKINS (1796–1873). John H. Fowler, early settler, soldier, and legislator, the son of Godfrey and Clara (Wright) Fowler, Jr., was born on December 23, 1796, in Tennessee. The name of his first wife is not known, but his second wife was Mrs. Elizabeth Alexander, whom he married in Hempstead County, Arkansas, on September 26, 1837. Fowler moved to the Red River area in 1817 and settled on the north side of the river. By 1819 he had moved into what is now Red River County near Pecan Point. During the Texas Revolutionqv he served with Col. Robert M. Coleman'sqv First Regiment, Texas Rangers.qv He represented Red River County in the House of the Third Congress (1838–39). As a wealthy landowner, he was one of a group of prominent men involved in founding the College of DeKalb. He was a frequent contributor to area newspapers. During the secessionqv crisis he was a staunch Unionist. He died in Paris, Texas, on October 12, 1873.

BIBLIOGRAPHY: Mrs. James J. Arthur, ed., *Annals of the Fowler Family* (Austin, 1901). Sam Houston Dixon and Louis Wiltz Kemp, *The Heroes of San Jacinto* (Houston: Anson Jones, 1932). Texas House of Representatives, *Biographical Directory of the Texan Conventions and Congresses, 1832–1845* (Austin: Book Exchange, 1941). *Cecil Harper, Jr.*

FOWLER, LITTLETON (1803–1846). Littleton Fowler, Methodist minister, fourth son of Godfrey and Clara (Wright) Fowler, was born in Smith County, Tennessee, on September 12, 1803. In 1806 the family moved to Caldwell County, Kentucky. Converted at age sixteen, Fowler joined the Methodist Episcopal Church and was licensed to preach in 1826. He was admitted to the Kentucky Conference in 1826 and ordained a deacon in 1828 and an elder in 1830. After transferring to the Tennessee Conference in 1832 he served a year at Tuscumbia, Alabama, and three years as agent of LaGrange College. In 1837 he volunteered to go to the Republic of Texasqv as a missionary, along with Robert Alexander and Martin Ruter.qqv

Although he was delayed by illness, Fowler set out for Texas on August 22. he recruited John B. Dentonqv in Arkansas, and they crossed the Red River into Texas in late September. Having preached in Clarksville and Nacogdoches, Fowler reached San Augustine on October 19 and held a week's meeting. He obtained a lot and raised a subscription of $3,500 for a church building. By mid-November he had obtained two more lots in Washington-on-the-Brazos. Continuing southwest, he joined Robert Alexander in a meeting at John Wesley Kenney'sqv home, a center of Methodist activities. Fowler arrived in Houston on November 19 and was soon elected chaplain of the Senate. In December Ruter visited Houston, and the two missionaries formed the first Sunday school society in Texas. Ruter assigned Fowler responsibility for Houston and East Texas. After obtaining a church lot near the Capitol in Houston, Fowler returned to San Augustine, where, on January 17, 1838, he and Gen. Thomas J. Ruskqv laid the cornerstone of the Methodist church, believed to be the first Protestant church in Texas. Fowler also organized congregations near Crockett and Nacogdoches and obtained a lot and raised a subscription for a church in Nacogdoches. At the first regular meeting of the Grand Lodge of Texas Masons in April 1838, Fowler served as grand chaplain. After Ruter's death in May 1838 Fowler was appointed superintendent of the Texas Mission. His recruitment of Jesse Hord,qv Samuel A. Williams, and Isaac L. G. Strickland from the Tennessee conference, as well as several local preachers, assured the future of Methodism in Texas.

When the Texas Annual Conference was organized in 1840 Fowler was appointed presiding elder of the San Augustine District. He served as agent of Rutersville College in 1841–42. From December 1842 to January 1845 he was presiding elder of the Lake Soda District. During that period, he assisted Francis A. Wilsonqv and Daniel Poe in the founding of Wesleyan College in San Augustine and served as a trustee. As a delegate to the General Conference in 1844, Fowler submitted the resolution that led to the establishment of two annual conferences in Texas and voted in favor of the Plan of Separation that divided American Methodism (*see* METHODIST CHURCH). When the newly formed Eastern Texas Conference met for its first session in January 1845, Fowler was appointed to the Sabine District and elected a delegate to the convention that formed the Methodist Episcopal Church, South, the following May.

On June 21, 1838, Fowler married Mrs. Missouri M. Lockwood Porter of Nacogdoches, a native of Kentucky. They had a daughter and a son, Littleton Morris Fowler, who became a prominent Methodist minister. Fowler died on January 29, 1846, at his farm home in Sabine County and was buried beneath the pulpit of McMahan's Chapel. The Fowler Institute, a Methodist school established at Henderson in 1847, was named in his honor.

BIBLIOGRAPHY: Dora Fowler Arthur, "Jottings from the Old Journal of Littleton Fowler," *Quarterly of the Texas State Historical Association* 2 (July 1898). Dora Fowler Arthur, "The Reverend Littleton Fowler: Missionary to the Republic of Texas," *Texas Methodist Historical Quarterly* 1 (October 1909). Littleton Fowler Papers, Bridwell Library, Perkins School of Theology, Southern Methodist University. Walter N. Vernon et al., *The Methodist Excitement in Texas* (Dallas: Texas United Methodist Historical Society, 1984). Laura Fowler Woolworth, comp., *Littleton Fowler* (Shreveport, Louisiana, 1936).
Norman W. Spellmann

FOWLER, THOMAS W. (1921–1944). Thomas W. Fowler, Medal of Honor recipient, was born at Wichita Falls, Texas, on October 31, 1921, the son of Mrs. A. H. Fowler. On May 23, 1944, he was a second lieutenant with the First Armored Division, United States Army, near Carano, Italy. During an armored-infantry attack he came upon two disorganized infantry platoons held back by a minefield. Although a tank officer, he reorganized the platoons, cleared a path through the mines with his bare hands, led his tanks into a position to cover the infantry, then led the two platoons to reach their objectives. The enemy began an armored counterattack on Fowler's position. One of his tanks was set afire. He ran through the enemy tank fire and for a half hour, still under intense fire, attempted to save the lives of the wounded tank crew. Finally forced to retreat, but still under incoming fire, he gave first aid to nine wounded infantrymen. Fowler was killed in combat ten days later. He is buried in Crestview Memorial Park, Wichita Falls.

BIBLIOGRAPHY: Dallas *Morning News*, August 26, 1944. Committee on Veterans' Affairs, United States Senate, *Medal of Honor Recipients, 1863–1973* (Washington: GPO, 1973). *Art Leatherwood*

FOWLER INSTITUTE. The Fowler Institute, planned by the Methodists of the Henderson area in 1849, was a school during the early 1850s in Rusk County. It was housed in a brick structure on a site in the northwest part of present Henderson. The Eastern Texas Conference of the Methodist Episcopal Church, South, chartered the school and named it for Littleton Fowlerqv on January 26, 1850. Presidents of the school included W. P. Bewley, J. M. Price, and Napoleon W. Burks. The school and the building were later used by Henderson Male and Female College. The building was torn down in 1900.

BIBLIOGRAPHY: Henderson *Times*, November 21, 1893, July 4, 1976. Benjamin Wiley Martin, Some Early Educational Institutions of East Texas (M.A. thesis, University of Texas, 1924). Dorman H. Winfrey, *A History of Rusk County* (Waco: Texian, 1961).

Megan Biesele

FOWLERTON, TEXAS. Fowlerton is on State Highway 97 twenty-five miles east of Cotulla in northeastern La Salle County. The Fowler Brothers Land Company (James and Charles) founded and developed the town in the early twentieth century in an ambitious attempt to develop a 100,000-acre tract that had once belonged to the Dull Ranch. They induced the San Antonio, Uvalde and Gulf Railway to extend its lines into the planned town, built two dams to provide water for irrigation and a new hotel, and laid 200 miles of public roads. They also built a cotton gin, installed an expensive water system, and conducted an aggressive advertising campaign to attract settlers and investors.

The land surrounding the townsite was divided into tracts of ten to 160 acres; for $25 dollars down and $10 a month an aspiring farmer could buy farmland and a receive a complimentary town lot. Land seekers (some called them "land suckers") responded by moving to Fowlerton by the hundreds. By October 1911, when the SAU&G made its first trip into Fowlerton, the town already had two hotels, three general stores, a bank, twenty-five miles of streets, a telephone system, and 1,200 residents. By 1914 Fowlerton's population was estimated at 2,000, and that year the town became the home of a summer normal school.

After 1917, however, the town rapidly declined; most of the farmers had suffered financial reverses due to a draught, low commodity prices, and marketing problems. Meanwhile, the Fowler brothers were targeted by a number of lawsuits accusing them of fraudulent marketing practices. The town thereafter "literally seemed to fall apart," according to a former resident. By 1925 Fowlerton's population had dropped to 600, and by 1931 only six businesses were reported there. By 1949 the community had 300 residents and four businesses and by 1964 200 people and two businesses. In 1972 the population was 100. In 1986 one newspaper called Fowlerton a "near-ghost town." In 1990 Fowlerton reported a population of 100 and had a post office.

BIBLIOGRAPHY: Annette Martin Ludeman, *La Salle: La Salle County* (Quanah, Texas: Nortex, 1975). San Antonio *Express*, June 6, 1986. Paul S. Taylor, "Historical Note on Dimmit County, Texas," *Southwestern Historical Quarterly* 34 (October 1930). Laura Knowlton Tidwell, *Dimmit County Mesquite Roots* (Austin: Wind River, 1984).

John Leffler

FOWLKES, TEXAS. Fowlkes is on State Highway 477 two miles southeast of Electra in western Wichita County. It was established in the early 1880s as a loading station on the Fort Worth and Denver City Railway and was originally called Day, or Day Station, after James Monroe Day,[qv] founder of the Day Land and Cattle Company.[qv] South of the railroad tracks, Day laid out a main street, along which were constructed several false-fronted buildings, some houses, and a school. While the community apparently remained little more than a loading station, a post office operated there under the name Day from 1890 to 1894, and in 1905 its one-teacher school registered eighteen students. During the early twentieth century Day sold his holdings in Wichita County, including the land for the settlement, to I. L. Fowlkes, an area landowner, cotton gin owner, and real estate investor, and the name of the community was changed. With the discovery of oil in and around nearby Electra in 1911, and more particularly following several small discoveries near Fowlkes, additional people began moving into the area. From 1911 to 1915 a post office operated there under the name Fowlkes. Despite the oil discoveries Fowlkes remained a small settlement. In 1940 it had a service station, a school, and scattered residences. In 1947 the Fowlkes school was consolidated with the Electra Independent School District. By the 1980s only the railroad siding marked the community on county highway maps.

BIBLIOGRAPHY: Louise Kelly, *Wichita County Beginnings* (Burnet, Texas: Eakin Press, 1982).

Brian Hart

FOX, JOSEPHINE MARSALIS CLARDY (1881–1970). Josephine Marsalis Clardy Fox, art collector and benefactor, was born in Liberty Township, Missouri, on August 13, 1881, the only child of Zeno Blanks and Allie (Davis) Clardy. In 1882 her family moved to El Paso, where her father established a legal business. His frequent acceptance of valuable property in lieu of money for legal services formed the foundation for a considerable fortune. Josephine Clardy attended public schools until 1895, when she enrolled in a private girls' school in St. Louis. Her enjoyment of drama and music classes there prompted a lifelong interest in the arts.

After her father's death in 1901, she studied music in El Paso, San Francisco, and New York City and traveled in the United States and in Europe. Although she had a fine voice, she gave up singing entirely in later years. As a young woman she suffered an eye injury that eventually led to a partial loss of sight. On January 20, 1916, Josephine Clardy married Eugene Emmett Fox, a railroad executive, in New York City; they had no children. They settled in El Paso, where Mrs. Fox began collecting fine furniture and art for their home at 1119 Montana Street.

The thirties were difficult years for her. She was in a serious car accident in the early thirties that left her back permanently damaged, and she suffered serious financial setbacks, frequently finding it difficult to pay the taxes on her family's land. Financial obligations kept her in El Paso while her husband worked in Washington, D.C. He died in 1934, and in 1940 her mother, to whom she was very close, also died. After the depression, however, her fortunes began to improve, and she participated in El Paso's social and cultural events until poor health intervened in the 1960s. She was a supporter of the El Paso Museum of Art,[qv] the El Paso Symphony Orchestra, the El Paso Community Concert Association, and the Dallas Civic Opera. She was a member of the El Paso County Historical Society,[qv] the National Society of Arts and Letters, and numerous other social and charitable clubs. She was named to the Advisory Committee of the National Arts Foundation in 1953.

In the mid-forties, with the help of William J. Elliott, Josephine Fox began developing large tracts of land formerly used to grow cotton. This development, together with two profitable land sales in the late 1950s, made her a wealthy woman. Her increased affluence enabled her to buy a number of paintings and other art objects from Count Ivan Podgoursky and Count Louis von Cseh in the late fifties and sixties. She paid high prices for works falsely attributed to Antoine Watteau, Peter Paul Rubens, Thomas Gainsborough, Diego Velázquez, and Bartolomé Esteban Murillo, but did acquire a valuable painting by Jean Baptiste Camille Corot and a portrait of George Washington by a follower of Gilbert Stuart. She was more successful in assembling an extensive collection of decorative art objects; her home was filled with fine antique furniture, a large collection of beautiful and historic fans, rare silver boxes and flatware, fine porcelain, a large collection of antique clocks, and Limoges enamels. She also gave land to the city of El Paso to establish a school in memory of her father and a branch library in her name. She made charitable gifts to the El Paso Symphony, the Hotel Dieu School of Nursing, the Salvation Army, the United Fund, and a number of other churches, schools, and charities.

In 1959 Fox fell and broke her hip, necessitating surgery and a long convalescence. She broke the same hip in 1964, and spent the rest of her life in the hospital. She was a Presbyterian for most of her life but was converted to Catholicism shortly before her death. She died on May 11, 1970, and left her entire estate, valued at more than $3 million, to the University of Texas at El Paso, the largest gift to the institution at that time. Her collection of 1,000 books, some very old and rare, went to the University of Texas at El Paso library. Hundreds of the picture hats that Fox loved to wear were given to the university's drama department for use in costumes. Some of the oil paintings, antique furniture, and fine art objects from her home are exhibited in various places on the University of Texas at El Paso campus, including Hoover House, the president's home, and the conference room and faculty dining room at the Centennial Museum. In addition, the Centennial Museum has lent many of her decorative art objects and furniture to the Quinta Gameras Museum at the University of Chihuahua.

BIBLIOGRAPHY: Ruby Burns, *Josephine Clardy Fox: Traveler, Opera-Goer, Collector of Art, Benefactor* (El Paso: Texas Western Press, 1973). Josephine Clardy Fox Collection, Special Collections Department, University of Texas at El Paso. "Texas Women: A Celebration of History" Archives, Texas Woman's University, Denton.

Kendall Curlee

FOX, OSCAR JULIUS (1879–1961). Oscar J. Fox, composer of Western songs, was born on a ranch in Burnet County, Texas, on October 11, 1879, son of Bennie and Emma (Kellersberger) Fuchs and grandson of Adolph Fuchs.qv His mother died five months after his birth, and he was reared in the home of an uncle, Hermann T. Fuchs. He attended school in Marble Falls until 1893, when he went to San Antonio and began to study music. In 1896 he was sent to Zürich, Switzerland, by his grandfather, Getuli Kellersberger, to study piano, violin, and choral direction for three years. He subsequently studied in New York City for two years before going to Galveston in 1902 as choirmaster of the First Presbyterian Church and later of St. Mary's Cathedral.qv He resigned in 1904 to accept a similar position at the First Presbyterian Church in San Antonio, where he served for ten years. He was conductor of the San Antonio Choir Club (1913–15) and director of the men's and girls' glee clubs and the University Choral Society at the University of Texas (1925–28). Fox was a member of the Texas Music Teachers Association, the Sinfonia Fraternity of America, the American Society of Composers, Authors, and Publishers, the Composers-Authors Guild, and the Sons of the Republic of Texas.qv

He published the first of his more than fifty songs in 1923. He first achieved fame through setting to music the cowboy songs collected by John A. Lomax.qv He never wrote lyrics but set existing poems to music. He drew strongly on his Texas background, and some of his best-known compositions were "The Hills of Home" (1925), "Old Paint" (1927), "The Old Chisholm Trail" (1924), "Whoopee Ti Yi Yo, Git Along, Little Dogies" (1927), "Will You Come to the Bower?" (1936), and "The Cowboy's Lament" (1923).

Fox married Nellie Tuttle in 1905; they had three daughters. The last fifteen years of his life he taught voice and was organist and choir director at Christ Episcopal Church, San Antonio. He died on July 29, 1961, while visiting in Charlottesville, Virginia, and was buried in Mission Burial Park in San Antonio. On May 27, 1962, the state honored him by placing a red granite marker a mile south of Marble Falls on Highway 181. Inscribed on the marker beneath his name is the first line of "The Hills of Home," his own favorite song and one that has continued to be popular around the world.

BIBLIOGRAPHY: *Daily Texan*, October 18, 1925. Dallas *Morning News*, July 30, 1961. San Antonio *Express*, December 8, 1931. Lota M. Spell, *Music in Texas* (Austin, 1936; rpt., New York: AMS, 1973). Vertical Files, Barker Texas History Center, University of Texas at Austin. Carl Weaver, "Oscar J. Fox and His Heritage," *Junior Historian*, December 1963.

S. W. Pease

FOX, RUTH (ca. 1902–1978). Ruth Fox, social worker, was born in Celeste, Hunt County, Texas, around 1902. Her father was a rural physician. She graduated from Baylor University and then studied two years at the New York School of Social Work, where she completed her work in criminology early in the 1920s. She then served as supervisor of classification and parole at the Federal Correctional Institution in Seagoville, Texas, where she was credited with obtaining probation and parole privileges for adult offenders. Later, through relief work she supervised in rural areas during the Great Depression,qv Fox became involved with the western part of Dallas. This work impressed upon her the indignities suffered by people who lacked proper food and other necessities.

In the early 1950s, after a bout with tuberculosis, she continued her service to West Dallas when she joined the staff of the Dallas Housing Authority. As a self-described "little ol' do-gooder," she used her position with DHA for twenty-two years to wage a war on poverty in West Dallas and to set an example for other endeavors of this nature across the state. Acknowledging that the authority was not strictly a welfare agency, she nonetheless made welfare her priority there, spending most of her time making referrals for needy people. Officially, she served as the authority's liaison to city, county, and state offices through her role as agency relations supervisor and management aide. Unofficially, she consistently fought to lower discrepancies in living standards between West Dallas and more affluent areas of the city and to encourage the rest of Dallas to recognize and assist West Dallas. She also engineered several beautification projects in West Dallas before retiring from the agency in 1974.

Fox's interest in social work was supplemented by a variety of efforts in civic affairs. She served as president of the Texas Federation of Business and Professional Women, as well as president of the Dallas chapter of this group. She supported the Equal Rights Amendment in the 1970s and was a close associate of the leader for that movement in Texas, attorney Hermine Tobolowsky. Fox also assisted Edna Gladneyqv in her efforts to have the word "illegitimate" kept off public birth records. As the first woman to serve on the Dallas County grand jury commission, Fox was instrumental in having the first two women in the county named to a grand jury. She also was a member of the county welfare board and the board of the Dallas Civic Opera and received numerous community service awards.

She was married to Phil E. Fox, an advertising and public relations executive, who preceded her in death. She died in Gilmer, Texas, on November 23, 1978, and was buried in Grovehill Cemetery in Dallas. She was survived by one son and one sister.

BIBLIOGRAPHY: Dallas *Morning News*, November 24, 1978. Dallas *Times Herald*, December 26, 1965, October 18, 1973.

Debbie Mauldin Cottrell

FOX, TEXAS (Gonzales County). Fox, nineteen miles southwest of Gonzales in Gonzales County, appears to have been established in the 1880s. The settlement had a post office from 1890 to 1892. In 1892 Fox had a population of twenty and served as a judicial seat as well as a banking and shipping point for the area. Fox was not shown on the 1936 county highway map.

Stephen L. Hardin

FOX, TEXAS (Henderson County). Fox was 11½ miles southwest of Athens in southern Henderson County. A post office operated there from 1900 to 1901. After 1900 a mill and a church were in the area, but by the mid-1930s the settlement was no longer shown on maps. In the early 1990s only a few scattered houses remained in the area.

Christopher Long

FOX MOUNTAIN. Fox Mountain stands five miles north of Llano in central Llano County (at 30°49′ N, 98°42′ W). Its summit, at an elevation of 1,354 feet above sea level, rises 150 feet above the surrounding terrain, which ranges from rolling to flat to steep and is surfaced variously with sandy and clay loams or shallow stony soil. Local vegetation includes open stands of live oak and mesquite.

FOY, FREDERICK (ca. 1778–1854). Frederick Foy, farmer and early settler, was born in South Carolina around 1778. He grew up and married there and subsequently moved to the area of Monroe, Louisiana. In 1828 he moved to Texas and probably settled originally in the Tenehaw District (now in Shelby County), which he represented in the Convention of 1832.qv By 1837 he was living in San Augustine, where he became senior warden in the local Masonic lodge in 1837. By 1845 he had moved to Sabine County, where he was a farmer. Foy and his family moved from Sabine County to the Prairie Lea area of Caldwell County in 1851 or 1852; there he continued farming until his death, in 1854.

BIBLIOGRAPHY: *Memorial and Genealogical Record of Southwest Texas* (Chicago: Goodspeed, 1894; rpt., Easley, South Carolina: Southern Historical Press, 1978). Texas House of Representatives, *Biographical Directory of the Texan Conventions and Congresses, 1832–1845* (Austin: Book Exchange, 1941). *Cecil Harper, Jr.*

FOYLE CREEK. Foyle Creek rises five miles north of Albany in northeastern Shackelford County (at 32°51′ N, 99°24′ W) and runs northeast for twenty-two miles to its mouth on the Clear Fork of the Brazos River, six miles southeast of Fort Griffin State Historical Parkqv (at 32°53′ N, 99°08′ W). The creek is dammed in its upper reaches. It initially traverses an area of steep slopes and benches surfaced by shallow clay loams that support juniper, live oak, mesquite, and grasses. In the creek's lower reaches the terrain becomes flat with local shallow depressions and is surfaced by clay and sandy loam soils that support water-tolerant hardwoods, conifers, and grasses.

FRAME SWITCH, TEXAS. Frame Switch, a small stock-raising community with a railroad flag stop, is on U.S. Highway 79 and the Missouri Pacific line, three miles west of Taylor in east central Williamson County. The site in 1882 had a sheep ranch run by Solomon George Yakey. In 1884 Yakey married an Ohio woman, Mattie Frame, and persuaded her parents to join him at the settlement; the community was named for David Frame, Mattie's father. A number of Danish immigrants settled in the area in the 1880s and 1890s. In 1890 Yakey built a school on land donated by the Frames, and in 1903 the school had fifty-eight pupils. Frame Switch remained a small community throughout the twentieth century, with a population of twenty reported from 1933 to 1990. Two businesses were reported there in 1943. In 1988 there remained one business, a locally popular bar called the Frame Switch Tavern. The tavern, for some time a community center of sorts, had in the 1980s one of the few jukeboxes anywhere with a recording of Moon Mullican's classic country song "Pipe Liner Blues."

BIBLIOGRAPHY: Clara Stearns Scarbrough, *Land of Good Water: A Williamson County History* (Georgetown, Texas: Williamson County Sun Publishers, 1973). *Mark Odintz*

FRANCIS, CHARLES INGE (1893–1969). Charles Inge Francis, attorney, was born in Denton, Texas, on September 1, 1893, the third son of Mr. and Mrs. William Byrne Francis. He attended the University of Texas, where he earned a B.A. in 1915 and bachelor's and master's degrees in law in 1917. He played shortstop and third baseman on the Longhorn baseball team that, coached by William J. (Billy) Disch,qv won both the Texas Intercollegiate and the Southwest Association championships. Francis then joined the army and served in France in World War I,qv after which he moved to Wichita Falls and became a partner in Weeks and Weeks, a law firm. He was also in on the discovery of a Permian Basinqv oil well, which he and his partner sold to Magnolia Petroleum Companyqv in 1924 for $2 million.

In 1933 Francis was appointed special assistant to the United States Attorney General in Washington and served as counselor to the Petroleum Administration Board. In 1934 he moved to Houston, where he spent sixteen years as a partner in Vinson, Elkins, Weems, and Francis. In 1940 he was appointed special assistant to the secretary of war. In 1946 he and E. Holley Poe, of Tulsa, Oklahoma, and New York, purchased the "Big Inch" and "Little Inch"qv pipelines from the government for $143,127,000. They called their new company Texas Eastern Transmission Corporation. Francis eventually became vice president, general counsel, and director of the company. In 1950 he opened his own Houston law office. He retired from the board of Texas Eastern in 1967, whereupon he was made director emeritus.

He served on the University of Texas Board of Regents from 1929 through 1935 and from 1931 through 1933 was president of the Texas Ex-Students' Association. In 1952 he helped form the UT Law School Foundation, of which he was president from 1952 until 1967. In 1958 he was named the most distinguished alumnus of the law school, the first person to receive that award. That same year the Law Day Program was dedicated in his name. In 1964 he was again honored as a distinguished alumnus. In 1968–69 he donated a professorship in law for a professor who had achieved excellence in lecture and other classroom skills. Francis was also a regent for North Texas State University (later the University of North Texas) and a member of the Centennial Board of the University of Michigan. He was director of the Reed Roller Bit Company and vice president of Southland Life Insurance Company.qv He served on the state Democratic executive committee and was a consultant to the United States Department of the Interior as an expert on oil and gas. He married Adelle Adickes of Wichita Falls in 1920, and they had two daughters. Francis died on November 11, 1969, after suffering a stroke, and was buried at Glenwood Cemetery in Houston.

BIBLIOGRAPHY: Vertical Files, Barker Texas History Center, University of Texas at Austin (Charles Inge Francis). *Sheana Dempsey*

FRANCIS, MARK (1863–1936). Mark Francis, first dean of the School of Veterinary Medicine at the Agricultural and Mechanical College of Texas (now Texas A&M University), the son of Abner and Martha Ann (Vaughan) Francis, was born on March 19, 1863, in Shandon, Ohio. He received a degree in veterinary medicine from Ohio State University in 1877. He later studied at the American Veterinary College in New York, at the University of Michigan, and in Germany. He was awarded an honorary doctorate by Miami University of Ohio in 1929. Francis became professor of veterinary science at Texas A&M in 1888. He became dean of the School of Veterinary Medicine in 1916 and was chief of the division of veterinary science in the Agricultural Experiment Station System.qv His fight against the fever tick and his work in developing the subcutaneous injection method of immunizing cattle against Texas feverqv gave him an international reputation and the cognomen "Father of the Texas Cattle Industry." In 1930 Francis was nominated to receive the Capper Award for Distinguished Service to American Agriculture. He also received the first honorary lifetime fellowship in the Texas Academy of Scienceqv and was honorary vice president of the 1935 Southwestern Exposition and Fat Stock Show in Fort Worth during the 1930s. He married Anna J. Scott on September 10, 1890; they had two children. He died at his home in College Station on June 23, 1936, and was buried in Shandon, Ohio.

BIBLIOGRAPHY: Patton W. Burns, *Veterinary Medicine at Texas A&M University, 1958–1975* (College Station: Texas A&M University College of Veterinary Medicine, 1975). Hubert Schmidt, *Eighty Years of Veterinary Medicine at the Agricultural and Mechanical College of Texas* (College Station: Texas A&M Archives, 1958). *Who Was Who in America*, Vol. 1. *James D. McCrady*

FRANCISCANS. Franciscans is the popular name of the priests and brothers of the Order of Friars Minor, founded by St. Francis of Assisi in 1209. In 1517 Pope Leo X divided the order into two autonomous branches, Observant Friars Minor and Conventual Friars Minor. A third branch, the Capuchin Friars Minor, begun in 1525, became autonomous in 1619. Within the ranks of the Observants, three stricter groups were formed in the sixteenth century: the Discalced or Alcantarine, the Reformati, and the Recollect Friars Minor. All the Franciscans in New Spain, except those who belonged to the Discalced Province of San Diego in Mexico beginning in 1599, were Observants. A Franciscan province comprises a number of conventos or friaries in a certain area, and these are under the jurisdiction of a minister provincial. No fewer than six provinces were established in Mexico between 1534 and 1606. The Franciscan missionary colleges, of which seven were founded in Mexico between 1683 and 1860, did not belong to a province but were the equivalent of a small province; each consisted of only one large convento or colegio, governed by a father guardian. The colleges ceased to exist in the latter part of the nineteenth century. The members of the colleges wore a grey Franciscan habit, while those of the Observant provinces had a habit of a bluish color; the Discalced Friars' habit was light brown. In 1897 Pope Leo XIII reunited the Discalced, Reformati, and Recollect Franciscans with the Observants in one Order of Friars Minor, simply so-called; and dark brown was made the common color of the habit of all its members.

The Franciscans who made journeys into what is now Texas or served as missionaries there during the Spanish period belonged to different units of the order, both provinces and colleges. If the Indian missions they maintained formed a group in a certain area, they were organized into a presidency with a father president as superior, or in the case of a province, if there were many missions, into a custody that remained dependent on the province until it could be made a new and separate province.

If the Quivira[qv] province of 1540 was not in Texas but in Kansas, on the north side of the Arkansas River near Great Bend, as is now considered quite certain, the first mission in Texas was founded in 1632 near the site of present San Angelo by Franciscan missionaries from the custody of San Pablo de Nuevo México, which was a part of the Province of Santo Evangelio or Mexico City. The same custody also founded the missions in the El Paso del Norte[qv] area in 1659 and 1680, the two near the site of Presidio, Texas, in 1683, and another short-lived Jumano mission, east or west of the San Angelo area, in 1684. Later missions founded in 1715 in the Presidio area were established by Franciscans of the Province of San Francisco de Zacatecas, which had charge of numerous missions in the area of the present Mexican state of Chihuahua.

Most of the Spanish missions in what is now Texas were established and staffed by Franciscans from two missionary colleges, the College of Santa Cruz de Querétaro (founded 1683) and the College of Guadalupe de Zacatecas (founded 1703–07).[qq,qv] Fr. Damián Massanet[qv] and his companions of the college of Querétaro founded the first two missions in East Texas in 1690—San Francisco de los Tejas, which was abandoned in 1693, and Santísimo Nombre de María, which was destroyed by a flood in 1692. The first permanent missions in East Texas, six in number, were a joint project of the two colleges of Querétaro and Zacatecas. In 1716 Father President Isidro Félix de Espinosa[qv] of Querétaro founded three missions, which were temporarily abandoned in 1719, restored in 1721, moved in 1730 to a site on the Colorado River now in Zilker Park in Austin, and reestablished on the San Antonio River in 1731. In the meantime, Queretaran Father Antonio de Olivares,[qv] called the founder of San Antonio, had established San Antonio de Valero Mission in 1718; it became the Alamo[qv] after its secularization in 1793. Nearby San Francisco Xavier de Nájera Mission was staffed from Valero from 1722 to 1726 and then merged with it.

"Unsuccessful" missions were also founded by missionaries of the college of Querétaro: the three missions on the San Xavier (now San Gabriel) River in 1746–49, two of them moved to the San Marcos River in 1755 and one to the Guadalupe in 1756 (*see* SAN XAVIER MISSIONS); the Apache mission of Santa Cruz on the San Saba River in 1757, destroyed the next year by hostile Indians; and San Lorenzo de Santa Cruz and Nuestra Señora de la Candelaria missions to the Apaches on the Nueces River in 1762. The three Apache missions belonged not to the presidency that had been moved from East Texas to San Antonio in 1731, but to that of the Rio Grande missions of San Juan Bautista,[qv] which was begun there in 1700. For the mission of Santa Cruz and others planned in the San Saba River area, besides the missionaries supplied by the college of Querétaro, three were sent by the College of San Fernando or Mexico City (founded 1730–34).

In 1772 the college of Querétaro surrendered its four remaining missions on the San Antonio River to the college of Zacatecas and left Texas so it could undertake the care and further development of the former Jesuit missions of Pimería Alta (northernmost Mexico and southern Arizona) into a chain of successful missions, resembling and contemporary with the "Old Missions of California" (that is, Alta California), which were begun in 1769 by Fr. Junípero Serra and his companions from the College of San Fernando.

Five of the Texas missions of the College of Guadalupe de Zacatecas were founded by Father President Antonio Margil de Jesús,[qv] either personally or through a companion friar who represented him. They were Guadalupe Mission at Nacogdoches, founded in 1716; Dolores Mission near San Augustine; Los Adaes Mission near Robeline, Louisiana, founded in 1717; San José y San Miguel de Aguayo Mission on the San Antonio River, founded in 1720; and Nuestra Señora del Espíritu Santo Mission, near Lavaca Bay, founded in 1721–22, moved to its second site on the Guadalupe River in 1726 and to its third site at La Bahía,[qv] the present Goliad, in 1749. A second mission founded near La Bahía in 1754 was that of Nuestra Señora del Rosario. Near the mouth of the Trinity River, Nuestra Señora de la Luz de Orcoquisac Mission was established in 1756; and the last of the Texas missions, Nuestra Señora del Refugio, was founded on the coast south of La Bahía in 1793. To these must be added a mission that was such in a somewhat wider sense, which had two sites. Missionaries of the College of Zacatecas ministered to the Spanish villa of Bucareli[qv] from 1774 to 1779 and its successor, the Villa de Nacogdoches, from 1779 to 1834, as well as to former mission Indians who lived in East Texas during those years. Father José Francisco Mariano de la Garza, who conducted refugees from Bucareli to Nacogdoches in 1775, shares with Antonio Gil Ibarvo[qv] the title of founder of the city of Nacogdoches. The last Spanish Franciscan in Texas was Fr. José Antonio Díaz de León,[qv] who had his headquarters at Nacogdoches and was murdered in 1834 while making one of his missionary trips in East Texas.

The College of Guadalupe de Zacatecas also supplied seventeen missionaries for the nineteen villas and fifteen missions established by José de Escandón[qv] in the new civil province of Nuevo Santander between 1749 and 1755. This province extended across the lower Rio Grande into what is now Texas. Two of its villas, Laredo and Dolores, were on the Texas side of the river, and four on the Mexican side—Revilla, Mier, Camargo, and Reynosa—extended across the river since their settlers had ranchos on the Texas side. From the settlements south of the Rio Grande, the Zacatecan missionaries occasionally also visited the four groups of ranchos and for a short time also the two villas in Texas. In 1766 the college of Zacatecas surrendered the care of the villas and missions in Nuevo Santander to fellow Franciscans from the provinces in Mexico.

Of the thirty-eight Spanish missions in Texas (including the one in Louisiana) and the six visitas on the lower Rio Grande, sixteen missions were staffed by the college of Querétaro, nine missions and six visitas by the college of Zacatecas, eight missions by the Nuevo México custody of the Holy Gospel Province, and four missions by the Franciscan province of Zacatecas. One, Santa María de las Caldas, below Socorro, had a diocesan priest as its missionary from 1730 to 1749. A biographical dictionary published in 1973 contains sketches of 121 Franciscans of the college of Zacatecas who served as missionaries in Texas between 1716 and 1834. Of this number thirty-two died in Texas. Seventy Texas missionaries are known to have come from the college of Querétaro, but the list is incomplete.

To the Spanish Franciscans who were Texas missionaries must be added the three Recollect Franciscans who were among the six priests with La Salle^{qv} in his expedition of 1684. All of them except the Recollect father Anastase Douay died when Fort St. Louis was destroyed by Karankawas in January 1689. Father Douay accompanied La Salle on his last trip, reached the Illinois country, returned to France, traveled back to Louisiana, and celebrated the first Mass at the site of New Orleans, where a monument has been erected in his honor.

From 1852 to 1859 a group of five German Conventual Franciscans worked among their countrymen at New Braunfels, Fredericksburg, and other towns in the vicinity of San Antonio. The Conventual Franciscan father Leopold Moczygemba,^{qv} who went to San Antonio in 1851, led 100 families of immigrants from Poland to the junction of the San Antonio River and Cibolo Creek on December 24, 1854, and founded the first Polish settlement in the United States at Panna Maria. He was succeeded at the Panna Maria parish by a confrere from London who remained till 1860.

Franciscan father Bartholomew (Augustine) D'Asti^{qv} and four other friars, who resided at St. Vincent's Friary in Houston during the years 1859–66, made such an impression on the people of that city that their memory is still kept alive more than a century later. Father D'Asti belonged to a group of Italian Franciscans who moved to Buffalo, New York, in 1855, and were organized into a custody in 1861 and into the Province of the Immaculate Conception (New York) in 1911.

Franciscans of the St. Louis–Chicago province came in 1931 to San José Mission in San Antonio, and in 1967 to the two missions of San Juan Capistrano and San Francisco de la Espada. They have also established new "missions," that is, parishes of Mexican Americans,^{qv} in the southern part of San Antonio: St. Joseph, Our Lady of Angels, St. Leonard, St. Bonaventure, and St. Clare. They have the care of the parishes in Von Ormy and Macdona south of the city, and attend the mission station of St. Ann in Southton from San Juan Capistrano and that of St. Frances Cabrini from Espada. In 1984 a total of twenty-eight friars of the St. Louis–Chicago Province were residing in six south San Antonio friaries.

The St. Louis–Chicago Province of Franciscans has also had the temporary care of several parishes in the Dallas–Fort Worth area. A friary opened at Paris, Texas, in the summer of 1949 was closed a year later. In 1955 Holy Family parish at Vernon, with missions at Quanah and Crowell, and two years later St. Peter's parish in Fort Worth were committed to the province; but they were relinquished on January 6, 1961.

On the shore of Lake Benbrook, near Fort Worth, St. Francis Village, a village with double cottages for retired persons, was established in 1936 under the sponsorship of the National Fraternity of the Secular Franciscan Order (formerly called the Third Order Secular of St. Francis, founded in 1209). At various times during the years from 1924 to 1969 Franciscans of the Province of St. John Baptist (Cincinnati) had the care of nineteen parishes and one chaplaincy in sixteen different cities or towns of Texas. After an interval of about a decade, Franciscans of the Cincinnati Province returned to Texas and began in 1980 to administer Our Lady of Guadalupe parish in Galveston.

BIBLIOGRAPHY: Carlos E. Castañeda, *Our Catholic Heritage in Texas* (7 vols., Austin: Von Boeckmann–Jones, 1936–1958; rpt., New York: Arno, 1976). Catholic Archives of Texas, Files, Austin. Marion A. Habig, *The Alamo Chain of Missions* (Chicago: Franciscan Herald Press, 1968; rev. ed. 1976). Marion A. Habig, "The Franciscan Provinces of Spanish North America," *The Americas* 1 (July, October 1944, January 1945). Marion A. Habig, *San Antonio's Mission San José* (San Antonio: Naylor, 1968). Benedict Leutenegger and Marion A. Habig, *The Zacatecan Missionaries in Texas, 1716–1834* (Austin: Texas Historical Survey Committee, 1973). Alexander C. Wangler, ed., *Archdiocese of San Antonio, 1874–1974* (San Antonio, 1974).

Marion A. Habig, O.F.M.

FRANCISCO PEREZ CREEK. Francisco Perez Creek, also known as San Francisco, San Francisco Perez, and Francisco Creek, rises two miles north of Highway 90 West and five miles northwest of Castroville in Medina County (at 29°23′ N, 98°58′ W) and runs south for twenty-five miles to its mouth on Chacon Creek, near the Frio county line (at 29°05′ N, 98°56′ W). Together Francisco Perez and Chacon creeks form San Miguel Creek. According to local tradition Francisco Perez Creek was named for Mexican trader Francisco Perez, who often camped on the creek before there was any settlement in the area. The creek rises in an area of flat to rolling prairie, surfaced by clays that support grasses, mesquite, and chaparral. Further along the stream's course the terrain changes to low-rolling hills and then to a flat area with local shallow depressions. Vegetation near the creek's mouth includes water-tolerant hardwoods, conifers, and grasses.

FRANCITAS, TEXAS. Francitas is on Farm Road 616 and the Missouri Pacific line in southeastern Jackson County. A small colony of French families settled in the area during the late 1890s, and soon thereafter railroad employees named the community Francitas. In 1909 representatives of the Valley Fruit Farm and Garden Company promoted the community by a public sale of town lots. In 1910 acreage purchased from Lafayette Ward, a local rancher, was surveyed into additional town lots and opened for settlement. The next year officials granted a post office to the community, and C. O. Hardy served as the first postmaster. By 1914 the community was a stop on the St. Louis, Brownsville and Mexico Railway. It had hardware and furniture stores, a bank, a weekly newspaper, and a telephone connection. The reported population of the community peaked at 300 in 1940, when the town also had three businesses. Its population fell to around 100 in the 1950s, grew to 200 by 1962, and then declined by 1988 to thirty, where it remained in 1990.

Stephen L. Hardin

FRANCKLYN LAND AND CATTLE COMPANY. The Francklyn Land and Cattle Company was an English syndicate chartered in 1881 to invest in the "Beef Bonanza." It was headed by and named for Charles G. Francklyn, a son-in-law of E. G. Cunard, owner of the Cunard Steamship Line, who helped finance the venture. The syndicate purchased a total of 631,000 acres of land in the Panhandle^{qv} counties of Carson, Gray, Roberts, and Hutchinson, and also in Greer County, Oklahoma, then considered a part of Texas. The purchase price was $880,000; Francklyn bought with a partial down payment. Later the company issued mortgage bonds for $1,450,000, the greatest part subscribed by Cunard and other British citizens. For a resident manager the syndicate acquired the services of B. B. Groom,^{qv} a relative of Francklyn, who for several years had bred cattle in Kentucky. Groom decided to make a stock ranch of the Greer County holdings and start a steer ranch in the Panhandle, where he would fatten cattle for market. Always an optimist, he took out a ten-year lease on 529,920 acres in the four Panhandle counties, to begin on February 10, 1882, and already paid up to August 9, 1883. Among the smaller outfits he bought out was D. C. Cantwell's Key-No Ranch^{qv} on White Deer Creek. With approval from the Francklyn Company, Groom designed the Diamond F brand for the Panhandle range and turned it over to his son Harrison T. Groom, while he took personal charge of the Bar X in Greer County, which he had bought from E. B. Harrold and William S. Ikard.^{qv} Harrison Groom and his wife made their home in Cantwell's cottonwood log cabin in northeastern Carson County. Because Mrs. Groom never liked living in such isolation, with the post office thirty miles away in Mobeetie, after three years B. B. Groom hired a Swiss immigrant, Henry Thut,^{qv} to assist in managing the Diamond F. The ranch grew as the Grooms added other herds to their ranges, and employment reached a peak of forty-five men on the Diamond F and ninety on the Bar X. Perry LeFors, Rip Arnold, and Billy Frazier served successively as foreman. Between the two ranges the Francklyn Company owned 700,000 acres and controlled 1,000 sections. The combined herds of cattle numbered between 70,000 and 100,000 at the highest count. Among these was a herd of polled Angus that B. B. Groom imported from Scotland. From Kentucky he brought in several shorthorns and thoroughbred horses. Although the cattle carried several brands, which the company registered, they were all eventually rebranded with the Diamond F in the Panhandle and the Bar X in Greer County. Since the Diamond F was a dry range, Groom was one of the first to hire well-drillers to fill his cattle tanks. The colonel's extravagance was further exemplified in the fine corrals, sheds, and living quarters he constructed, and also in the miles of barbed wire[qv] he had shipped in from Dodge City to enclose a pasture twenty-eight miles wide and forty-two miles long.

Such liberal spending, in addition to the terrible January blizzard, was partially responsible for the bankruptcy of the ranch in 1886. That year the Francklyn Company failed to pay bonds due ($2,182,330, including interest), and bondholders brought suit in the federal court at Dallas, asking that the land be sold and payments foreclosed. The syndicate was thus reorganized as the White Deer Lands Trust, which soon became known as White Deer Land Company or simply as White Deer Lands, although still branding the Diamond F. Two New York capitalists, Frederic de P. Foster and Cornelius C. Cuyler, came into possession of the lands. Other names associated with this new venture through the ensuing years included Russell Benedict, who was made trustee of the White Deer Lands, Sir Robert Williams, and Sir Gordon Cunard. George Tyng[qv] served as resident manager until his resignation in 1903, when he was succeeded by Timothy Dwight Hobart.[qv]

As manager of the White Deer Lands, Hobart was in charge of settling them with farmers. Henry Thut and Perry LeFors were among the first settlers to buy. Agricultural communities like LeFors and Groom were founded, and the company office was located in the new rail town of Pampa. Beginning in the 1890s the Diamond F Ranch, then consisting of 630,000 acres, sold its cattle and leased its land to various cattle outfits, including the Frying Pan, the Matador, and the N Bar N ranches.[qqv] By the turn of the century the White Deer Lands had succeeded in selling most of the remaining 400,000 acres of land. Among the buyers was Samuel Burk Burnett[qv] of the Four Sixes Ranch, who bought 107,520 acres of former Diamond F land and established his Dixon Creek division headquarters in Carson County south of present Borger. After the discovery of oil on Burnett's ranch in 1921, White Deer Lands adopted a policy of reserving one-half or all of the mineral rights on lands sold. During the Dust Bowl[qv] era the company remained stable and deposited $150,000 with the stipulation that it be lent to area farmers affected by the drought. With the prosperity brought on by World War II,[qv] increasing oil income, along with income tax problems involving foreign investments in the company, drove taxes sometimes as high as 90 percent. Finally in 1949 a change in the Texas corporation laws, plus the purchase of most of the remaining British interests by Cecil V. P. Buckler[qv] and other United States citizens, enabled the company to reduce taxes to about 50 percent. The White Deer Corporation was formed with Williston Benedict in New York City as president and Buckler as vice president and Texas agent. By 1957 the directors decided to liquidate the corporation by paying the stockholders and prorating the mineral rights among them. M. K. Brown[qv] bought the remainder of the property, including the red brick office building in Pampa, for $70,000. Since then this building, which dates from 1916, has been converted into the White Deer Land Museum. The company records are housed in the Panhandle-Plains Historical Museum[qv] in Canyon.

BIBLIOGRAPHY: Sylvia Grider, "'He's for Progress': C. P. Buckler and the White Deer Land Company," *West Texas Historical Association Year Book* 43 (1967). Laura V. Hamner, *Short Grass and Longhorns* (Norman: University of Oklahoma Press, 1943). Lester Fields Sheffy, *The Francklyn Land & Cattle Company* (Austin: University of Texas Press, 1963). Lester Fields Sheffy, *The Life and Times of Timothy Dwight Hobart* (Canyon, Texas: Panhandle-Plains Historical Society, 1950).

H. Allen Anderson

FRANCO, TEXAS. Franco was a railroad switch and loading station on the Weatherford, Mineral Wells and Northwestern Railway six miles northwest of Weatherford in central Parker County. The loading station was named for the Franco-Texan Land Company,[qv] which owned land in the area. In the early 1890s a small community developed there. It had a post office branch in 1892 and 1893. The community was apparently abandoned sometime in the early 1900s.

David Minor

FRANCO-TEXAN LAND COMPANY. The Franco-Texan Land Company, chartered under the laws of Texas on August 4, 1876, owned about 600,000 acres of land in Parker, Palo Pinto, Stephens, Callahan, Shackelford, Mitchell, Taylor, Nolan, Jones, and Fisher counties. The company had its origin in a land grant made by the Texas legislature to the Memphis, El Paso and Pacific Railroad. The charter, granted in 1856, authorized the building of a railroad from a point on the eastern boundary of the state between Sulphur Fork and the Red River to a point on the Rio Grande opposite or near the city of El Paso. The state donated sixteen sections of 640 acres each for every mile of road constructed and placed in running order, on the completion of a minimum of ten miles, and eight sections per mile for the grading of a minimum of twenty-five miles of roadbed. By 1861 the Memphis, El Paso and Pacific directors, originally a group of sincere and earnest Texans, had surveyed the center line of the road as far as the Brazos River and graded fifty-five miles on which they were ready to lay the track. The Civil War[qv] suddenly halted all operations, and the company could do no more than retain its corporate form for the duration of the war. In 1866 the legislature passed a relief act that extended the limitations on the company's contract for ten years. Interest revived, and the Texas directors, in search of capital, brought John Charles Frémont into the company. Frémont, envisioning a transcontinental road on the thirty-second parallel, beginning at San Diego and connecting with the East at Memphis, took control and promptly executed three mortgages secured by the road itself and the land grants yet to be received from the state of Texas. Frémont sold his securities in France and collected some $5 million after he had succeeded, by highly questionable methods, in getting his "puffed-up" bonds quoted on the Paris Bourse.

Because the "French Bond Scandal" was widely publicized at home and abroad, and because little of the money was spent on the railroad, Congress refused to grant Frémont a transcontinental charter. He therefore compromised with the rival Texas and Pacific Company, which, since it had to have the Memphis, El Paso and Pacific to get across Texas, agreed to buy the embryonic railroad and take over its liens. Ultimately Frémont was frozen out of the successor company, but the French bondholders did become the owners of the Texas land that secured their bonds, subject, however, to rules and regulations imposed by John A. C. Gray, the agent who put the Memphis, El Paso and Pacific into receivership and sold it to the Texas and Pacific.

The French bondholders received thirteen acres of land for each $100 bond, and this land constituted the capital stock of the Franco-Texan Land Company. The incorporators were H. E. Alexander and S. Pinkney Tuck of New York, and Claiborne S. West and Harry C. Withers[qv] of Austin, Texas. Tuck, the company's secretary, traveled to Weatherford, Texas, and began the sale of land in 1878. Henry P. du Bellet, vice secretary residing in Paris, staged a coup in which the New York officers were ousted and Sam H. Milliken of Weatherford was elected president. Du Bellet then came to Texas and had a hand in the company's affairs until he too was ousted. Successive presidents were V. G. Frost of Palo Pinto, A. Chaptive of Paris, France, R. W. Duke and A. J. Hood of Weatherford, Texas, and George P. Levy of Paris,

France. With the gradual increase in the value of Texas land, the Franco-Texan Land Company developed into something of a bonanza for the French and American directors, who bought stock certificates for a few cents on the dollar and conspired to riddle the company's coffers. The losers were the French peasants who had invested their life savings in the Memphis, El Paso and Pacific bonds. In 1896, after years of local rivalry and dissension, the charter of the Franco-Texan Land Company expired by limitation. On request, the legislature allowed the company three additional years to liquidate its assets and conclude its business.

BIBLIOGRAPHY: Virginia H. Taylor, *The Franco-Texan Land Company* (Austin: University of Texas Press, 1969).   *Virginia H. Taylor*

FRANCO-TEXIAN BILL. The Franco-Texian Bill, introduced into the Texas Congress on January 12, 1841, was proposed by two Frenchmen, Jean Pierre Hippolyte Basterrèche and Pierre François de Lassaulx. The bill, "An Act to Incorporate the Franco Texian Commercial and Colonization Company," called for the company to introduce 8,000 families and establish and maintain twenty forts for twenty years in return for a grant of three million acres from the Republic of Texas qv and exemption of the settlers from all taxes and tariffs for a period of twenty years. The land under consideration lay along Texas rivers and was not in one contiguous plot. The proposal specified that the company was to have exclusive trading privileges with the New Mexico settlements. The company was also to develop mines within the territory and pay the republic 15 percent of the gross returns. The bill, urged by both Dubois de Saligny,qv French chargé d'affaires to Texas, and Sam Houston,qv was approved by the House on January 23, 1841, but the measure was never presented in the Senate because its sponsors saw that a two-thirds majority could not be mustered to pass it over the threatened veto of acting president David G. Burnet.qv

BIBLIOGRAPHY: Nancy Nichols Barker, trans. and ed., *The French Legation in Texas*, Vol. 1: *Recognition, Rupture, and Reconciliation* (Austin: Texas State Historical Association, 1971); Vol. 2: *Mission Miscarried* (1973). Herbert Rook Edwards, "Diplomatic Relations between France and the Republic of Texas, 1836–1845," *Southwestern Historical Quarterly* 20 (January 1917).   *Curtis Bishop*

FRANK, TEXAS. Frank, on Farm Road 1553 eight miles southwest of Bonham in southwestern Fannin County, had a post office from 1895 to 1910. In the mid-1930s, when it reported its first population statistics, the community had one business and ten residents. By the mid-1940s its population had increased to twenty-five. No population was reported for the community from the 1950s through the 1970s. In the early 1990s Frank reported three residents.
    Brian Hart

FRANKEL CITY, TEXAS. Frankel City, at the junction of Farm roads 181 and 1967 in western Andrews County, began with the county's oil boom. It was established as Fullerton in 1941 with the drilling of a discovery well by the Fullerton Oil Company. During World War IIqv other wells were drilled, and by 1945 there were reportedly 100 rigs drilling in a five-by-eight-mile area. Several companies opened oilfield supply stores and built camps on the sand hills in the area for about 750 workers and their families. Students were bused to Andrews, which had the only school in the county. A post office opened in 1948 with G. W. Blanchard as postmaster, and the town was renamed Frankel City after the Frankel Brothers Oil Company. Skeet Morris was the community's first and only mayor. As drilling was completed in the area the town began to decline, and on March 12, 1976, its post office closed. At one time the town had several stores and filling stations, two cafés, two churches, and a telephone exchange. By the 1980s Frankel City comprised a café, a house, a mobile home, and an estimated population of eleven.

BIBLIOGRAPHY: *Andrews County History, 1876–1978* (Andrews, Texas: Andrews County Heritage Committee, 1978).
    Tracey L. Compton

FRANKELL, TEXAS. Frankell, on Farm Road 207 some twelve miles southeast of Breckenridge in southeastern Stephens County, originated with the Ranger oil boom of 1916 (*see* RANGER, DESDEMONA, AND BRECKENRIDGE OILFIELDS). It became a station on the Wichita Falls and Southern Railway in 1920, when it was named for Frank Kell,qv the president of that line. Between 1920 and 1935 it had a population of 250, chiefly oilfield workers. In 1936 the town had two schools and a church. By 1940 Frankell had a post office, a store, and a population of fifty. The 1984 county highway map identified Frankell but did not show any buildings at its site.
    Claudia Hazlewood

FRANKEN, ROSE DOROTHY LEWIN (1895–1988). Rose Lewin Franken, author and playwright, was born on December 28, 1895, in Gainesville, Texas, the youngest child of Michael and Hannah (Younker) Lewin. She was educated there until age twelve, when she moved with her mother and siblings to New York. She attended New York's Ethical Culture School, but did not graduate. In 1914 Lewin married Dr. Sigmund W. A. Franken, an oral surgeon. She began writing to amuse Franken, and he encouraged her efforts. At first she wrote short stories for newspapers and popular magazines. She had three sons, born in 1920, 1925, and 1928. She continued writing while raising the children (she was assisted by a housekeeper). The noted editor Maxwell Perkins of Charles Scribner's and Sons arranged the publication of her first novel, *Pattern*, in 1925. *Twice Born*, her second, followed in 1926. Franken's first play, *Another Language*, met with immediate success in 1932, running for more than 450 performances and setting a Broadway record for a first play. In December 1932, soon after the play opened in London, Sigmund Franken died of tuberculosis. Rose Franken moved her family to Hollywood, and between 1932 and 1941 she turned out stories, film scripts, and novels. The 1933 Metro-Goldwyn-Mayer film *Another Language,* based on her play, starred the young Helen Hayes. United Artists obtained a Franken script for the studio's 1936 movie *Beloved Enemy.* Her books included *Of Great Riches* (1937), *Strange Victory* (1939), *Claudia: The Story of A Marriage* (1939), and *When Doctors Disagree* (1940). In 1937 Franken married writer and attorney William Brown Meloney, Jr. They returned to New York and continued writing, both individually and collaboratively, for magazines, including *Harper's Bazaar* and *Collier's.* They sometimes wrote together under the pseudonym Franken Meloney. From her novel *Claudia* and a *Redbook Magazine* serial story, "Claudia and David," Franken developed a play, a radio series, and two films. In 1941 she directed the play *Claudia*, starring Dorothy McGuire, in its first Broadway run. The story of a naive young wife's maturing, *Claudia* had a total of 722 New York performances. Franken sold the screen adaptation to 20th Century Fox for $187,500, an enormous amount at the time, on the condition that the producer keep McGuire in the leading role. This 1943 film, also titled *Claudia,* led to Franken's screenplay for *Claudia and David*, a 1946 sequel from 20th Century Fox. She also wrote the script for Metro-Goldwyn-Mayer's *The Secret Heart* (1946).

While overseeing British, Australian, and American touring productions of the play *Claudia,* Franken wrote the novel *Another Claudia* (1943). *Young Claudia* was completed in 1946, *The Marriage of Claudia* in 1948, and *From Claudia to David* in 1949. Two more Claudia novels followed in 1952, and Doubleday and Company released an omnibus edition, *The Complete Book of Claudia,* in 1958. Like most of Franken's stories, the Claudia series explored the challenges and delights of family relationships that foster personal growth. Franken wrote and directed two additional commercially successful plays, both produced by Meloney. *Outrageous Fortune,* a psychological drama, opened on Broadway in 1943. It was soon followed by *Soldier's Wife,* which concerned a family's adjustments after wartime separation. Meloney and Franken encountered little enthusiasm for a 1944 stage adaptation of her 1940 novel, retitled *Doctors Disagree,* nor for *The Hallams,* a 1948 sequel to *Another Language.* In January 1953, NBC-TV premiered a series based on *Claudia: The Story of a Marriage,* but it was dropped three months later. Returning to the novel form, Franken wrote *Rendezvous,* published in 1954 and sold in the United Kingdom under the title *The Quiet Heart.* After another novel, *Intimate Story,* was published in 1955, her writing pace slowed. She and Meloney spent more time at their Connecticut mountain home and eventually retreated from New York entirely. In 1963 Doubleday published her autobiography, *When All Is Said and Done.* Three years later she completed a whimsical novelette, *You're Well Out of the Hospital.* William Meloney died in 1970. Franken returned to New York and wrote another play, but never saw it produced. Although she continued to write, the changing tastes of audiences caused editors and producers to reject most of her manuscripts after the 1960s. Discouraged, she spent her last years organizing her papers and tending to family affairs. In 1984 she moved to Tucson, Arizona, where her youngest son lived. Franken died in Tucson on June 22, 1988.

BIBLIOGRAPHY: *New York Times,* June 24, 1988. Alice M. Robinson et al., *Notable Women in the American Theatre: A Biographical Dictionary* (New York: Greenwood Press, 1989). *Who's Who 1986* (London: A&C Black).

Sherilyn Brandenstein

FRANKFORD, TEXAS. Frankford was nine miles northwest of Richardson in extreme southwestern Collin County. Settlement of the area began around a campsite on the Shawnee Trail qv near a small spring on Halls Branch, used in the 1850s and 1860s as a stopping point and watering hole for traildrivers and other travelers. A small town developed after the Civil War qv at the nearby crossing of the Addison and Weber roads (later known respectively as the Dallas North Tollroad and Hilton Head Road), and a post office opened on May 11, 1880, under the name Frankford. By 1890 the town had a population of eighty-three, a steam gristmill, a corn mill, a cotton gin, a blacksmith shop, two general stores, and three churches. The St. Louis Southwestern Railway bypassed the town in the late 1880s, however, and many Frankford residents moved to Addison, Plano, and other nearby communities. In 1904 the Frankford post office was closed, and in 1907 its lodge hall, which had served as a nondenominational church, was moved to Addison. A second church, built in the 1890s, continued to serve a predominantly Methodist congregation until 1924. By the mid-1930s the town was no longer shown on county highway maps. Its church building was restored in 1963 by the Frankford Cemetery Association, which arranged for the Episcopal Church of the Holy Communion to worship there. The city of Dallas annexed the area in 1975, and in 1990 local children attended the Plano schools. All that remained of the community in 1990 was the Frankford Church and Cemetery, adjoined by residences on three sides and by the Bent Tree Country Club to the south.

BIBLIOGRAPHY: J. Lee and Lillian J. Stambaugh, *A History of Collin County* (Austin: Texas State Historical Association, 1958).

Frances B. Wells

FRANKLIN, BENJAMIN CROMWELL (1805–1873). Benjamin Cromwell Franklin, judge and legislator, the eldest son of Abednego (?) and Mary Graves (Cleveland) Franklin, was born in Georgia on April 25, 1805. He was educated at Franklin College in Athens, Georgia, and admitted to the bar in 1827. In 1835 he traveled to Velasco, Texas, and shortly afterward joined an expedition against Indians. In December 1835 at a public meeting at Columbia he was among those who favored immediate declaration of war against Mexico. On April 7, 1836, he was commissioned a captain in the Texas army by President David G. Burnet,qv but since he was not assigned to the command of a company at San Jacinto, he fought there as a private in Capt. Robert J. Calder's qv company. On April 23, 1836, Secretary of War Thomas J. Ruskqv directed Franklin to proceed to Galveston Island and inform President Burnet and his cabinet of the victory at San Jacinto. Franklin later received a bounty warrant for 320 acres for his service and was among the first to purchase land at the future site of Houston.

He was the first man to hold a judicial position in the Republic of Texas.qv The *Pocket,*qv a brig owned by a citizen of the United States, was captured in March 1836 by the *Invincible,*qv a Texas armed schooner. Realizing that the affair might alienate the United States, the government of Texas took immediate steps to have the matter thoroughly investigated. The judiciary not having been organized, the government established the judicial district of Brazoria in which to try the case, and Burnet appointed Franklin district judge. The exact date of his appointment has not been ascertained, but it was before June 15, 1836. The position had been tendered to James Collinsworth qv on April 12, but he declined.

On December 20, 1836, Franklin was appointed judge of the Second or Brazoria Judicial District by President Sam Houston.qv The appointment automatically made Franklin a member of the Supreme Court of the republic, of which James Collinsworth was chief justice. Franklin held his first court at Brazoria on March 27, 1837. He resigned from his judgeship on November 29, 1839, and moved to Galveston to practice law. He was elected to represent Galveston County in the House of Representatives of the Third, Fifth, and Eighth state legislatures. At the outbreak of the Civil Warqv he was too old for military service and was suffering from rheumatism. He retired to a small farm near Livingston, Polk County, and remained until 1870, when he returned to Galveston. Governor E. J. Davis qv appointed him commissioner to revise the laws of Texas, but he declined the appointment.

Franklin's first wife was Eliza Carter Brantly, whom he married on October 31, 1837; they had two children. After her death on September 24, 1844, Judge Franklin married Estelle B. Maxwell of Illinois, on November 3, 1847. He died unexpectedly on December 25, 1873, after several weeks of illness and was buried in Galveston. The act establishing Franklin County does not state for whom the county was named, but it is generally accepted as having been named for Judge Benjamin C. Franklin.

BIBLIOGRAPHY: DeWitt Clinton Baker, comp, *A Texas Scrap-Book* (New York: Barnes, 1875; rpt. 1887; facsimile rpt., Austin: Steck, 1935). Henry Lewis Bentley, *Experiments in Range Improvement in Central Texas* (U.S. Department of Agriculture, Bureau of Plant Industry Bulletin No. 13 [Washington: GPO, 1902]). Daughters of the Republic of Texas, *Founders and Patriots of the Republic of Texas* (Austin, 1963–). William DeRyee and R. E. Moore, *The Texas Album of the Eighth Legislature, 1860* (Austin: Miner, Lambert, and Perry, 1860). Sam Houston Dixon and Louis Wiltz Kemp, *The Heroes of San Jacinto* (Houston: Anson Jones, 1932). Zachary T. Fulmore, *History and Geography of Texas As Told in County Names* (Austin: Steck, 1915; facsimile, 1935). James D. Lynch, *The Bench and Bar of Texas* (St. Louis, 1885).

L. W. Kemp

FRANKLIN, IONE RUTH (1893–1985). Ione Ruth Franklin, sculptor and teacher, was born in Poetry, Texas, on January 16, 1893, the eldest of three daughters of Nathaniel Timothy and Bertha Melora (Smith) Franklin. She exhibited artistic ability from an early age. After graduating from high school in San Angelo in 1912, she attended Texas State College for Women (later Texas Woman's University) in Denton, where she earned a bachelor of science degree with honors in household arts and sciences in 1923. She subsequently received a bachelor of science in fine and applied arts with honors from the same institution in 1926 and completed a master of arts degree at Columbia University in 1927. In the late 1930s she attended the Art Students' League in New York City, where she studied with Robert Laurent and William Zorach. Under the influence of the latter, Franklin adopted direct carving, a reaction against more complicated traditional techniques such as casting. She completed a year of private instruction with William Palmer before returning to Texas in 1939.

From 1928 to 1955 Ione Franklin taught art at East Texas State Teachers College (later East Texas State University) in Commerce, where she was chairman of the art department from 1936 until her retirement. She participated in a number of competitive exhibitions and won prizes in Texas General exhibitions (1941, 1945) and Southern States Art League exhibitions (1936, 1946). The marble Young Mother (1944), in which Franklin deftly evoked the tender relationship between a mother and the chunky infant cradled on her shoulder, typifies her sensitive approach to sculpture; the work is now in the collection of Marcelle and David Orman. Franklin exhibited her work at the Dallas Museum of Art, the Museum of Fine Arts in Houston, the Witte Museum qqv in San Antonio, the University of Texas at Austin, the Rockhill-Nelson Gallery in Kansas City, the University of Georgia in Athens, and the High Museum of Art in Atlanta, Georgia. She was a member of the Southern States Art League and the Texas Sculptors Group. Franklin has been associated with such artists as Dorothy Austin, Evaline Sellors, Mabel Fairfax Karl, and Bess Bigham Hubbard,qv a group of women who popularized modern sculpture styles and techniques in Texas in the 1930s and 1940s.

Franklin retired from teaching in 1955 and returned to San Antonio to care for an aged aunt. Although she joined the River Art Group and exhibited with them and the San Antonio Art League, her nursing duties left her little time for sculpting. She became an accomplished embroiderer in later years. She died in San Antonio on January 11, 1985, and was buried in Mission Park Cemetery. Her work was included in A Century of Sculpture in Texas, 1889–1989 (1989), an exhibition organized by the Archer M. Huntington Art Galleryqv in Austin that traveled to several museums throughout the state.

BIBLIOGRAPHY: Peter Haskins Falk, ed., *Who Was Who in American Art* (Madison, Connecticut: Sound View, 1985). Jerry Bywaters Collection on the Art of the Southwest, Southern Methodist University.

Kendall Curlee

FRANKLIN, TEXAS (Lamar County). Franklin was on the Red River 1½ miles west of Arthur City in northern Lamar County. The area was originally settled by Samuel Moore Fultonqv as a trading post—first called the U. S. Factory—and steamboat landing. In 1842 a post office called Franklin opened there, with Fulton as postmaster. The settlement declined when the importance of river transportation lessened and the area became more settled. In 1886 the St. Louis and San Francisco bypassed Franklin, and most business was transferred to the new railroad town, nearby Arthur City. Franklin was no longer shown on maps by 1936.

BIBLIOGRAPHY: A. W. Neville, *The History of Lamar County, Texas* (Paris, Texas: North Texas, 1937; rpt. 1986). *Vista K. McCroskey*

FRANKLIN, TEXAS (Liberty County). Franklin was on the east side of the Trinity River sixteen miles north of Liberty in northern Liberty County. In 1845 there was a steamboat landing at Franklin and the community had a population of fifty. It was subsequently abandoned.

BIBLIOGRAPHY: Miriam Partlow, *Liberty, Liberty County, and the Atascosito District* (Austin: Pemberton, 1974). *Robert Wooster*

FRANKLIN, TEXAS (Robertson County). Franklin, the county seat of Robertson County, is on U.S. Highway 79 and the Missouri Pacific line near the geographical center of the county. The community was originally established in 1872, and took its first name, Morgan, from that of an International Railway Company official; in its first year the community had a depot and three stores. By 1879 it had 200 residents, and voters transferred the county seat from Calvert to Morgan. When the community applied for its post office, another Texas post office was named Morgan, so residents changed the name to Franklin, after the name of the original county seat. The first county judge to preside in the new Franklin was T. J. Simmons. The post office of the new county seat opened in 1880 with J. C. Mitchell as postmaster. The next year the community's first school building, a frame structure, was built; it burned in 1894, and another was erected which served the district until 1924, when a brick building was constructed. A stone courthouse was completed on January 7, 1882. By then J. A. Keigewin was publishing the town's first newspaper, the Franklin *Weekly*. By 1885 Franklin had three hotels, three churches, two gristmills, a school, and a harness and saddle plant operated by Elias Reynolds. A fourth church opened in 1892, but all the church structures were destroyed by a 1913 windstorm that also damaged every public building in the county. In 1890 Isaac R. Overall advertised a mineral springs, attracting visitors to his hotel and spa for the next several years. Franklin reported a population of 250 in 1882, of about 1,000 in 1890, and of 1,087 in 1942. In 1905 the First National Bank of Franklin was chartered, and the First State Bank was established in 1913. By the 1970s Franklin, an incorporated community, had a mayor-council form of city government.qv In 1989 it had a population estimated at 1,462 and twenty businesses. In 1990 its population was reported as 1,336.

BIBLIOGRAPHY: J. W. Baker, *History of Robertson County, Texas* (Franklin, Texas: Robertson County Historical Survey Committee, 1970). Ivory Freeman Carson, Early Development of Robertson County (M.A. thesis, North Texas State College, 1954).

James L. Hailey

FRANKLIN COLLEGE. Franklin College was a private nondenominational school chartered on February 2, 1856, by the Sixth Legislature of the State of Texas to be located at Palestine in Anderson County as a school of learning consisting of male and female departments. Seventeen trustees were named, their duties and powers were stipulated, and the role of the college was stated as purely literary and scientific. The school succeeded the Palestine Masonic Institute. An issue of the Corsicana Prairie Blade of June 1855 states that two large houses, one for the men's school and one for the women's, had been built by the Masons in 1851. Together the schools constituted Franklin College. Reverend John Van Epps Coveyqv was named as the president of the college. The male school, located in the old section of Palestine, ended after one year of operation. By 1858 the female school had been moved to a 3.7-acre tract donated for its use, and that November a new frame building was completed. Elisha Pettit was appointed president, and the school was called the Palestine Female Academy. The female academy was called Palestine Female College by 1876. In 1881 the property was transferred to the trustees of the newly inaugurated public school system in Palestine.

BIBLIOGRAPHY: James David Carter, *Education and Masonry in Texas, 1846 to 1861* (Waco Grand Lodge of Texas, 1964). Hans Peter Nielsen Gammel, comp., *Laws of Texas, 1822–1897* (10 vols., Austin: Gammel, 1898).

Georgia Kemp Caraway

FRANKLIN COUNTY. Franklin County (C-21) is located in northeast Texas, one county removed from Oklahoma and three counties removed from Arkansas. Mount Vernon, the county seat, is on Interstate Highway 30 seventy-two miles southwest of Texarkana and ninety-six miles northeast of Dallas. With a 1990 population of 2,219, Mount Vernon is the largest town situated entirely within the boundaries of the county, but Winnsboro, in southwestern Franklin and northwestern Wood counties, had a 1990 population of 2,904. The county's center lies at 33°09′ north latitude and 95°14′ west longitude. The county comprises 294 square miles of the post oak belt and is heavily wooded; post oak, blackjack oak, and pine trees predominate. The terrain varies from nearly level to rolling, and the soils are predominantly loam with clay subsoils. The county is drained by the Sulphur River, which forms its northern boundary, and Big Cypress Creek, which runs through the southern portion. Mineral resources include oil, gas, limestone, and lignite coal. Pine and hardwood production in 1981 totaled 1,073,412 cubic feet. Wildlife native to the area once included buffalo, bear, deer, beaver, and turkey. Temperatures range from an average high of 94° F in July to an average low of 35° in January. Rainfall averages almost forty-five inches a year, and the growing season averages 234 days annually.

Archeological evidence to the north in Red River County indicates that the area was occupied by Indians as early as the Late Archaic Period, around 1500 B.C. At the time of first European contact, the area was occupied by the Caddo Indians, an agricultural people with a highly developed culture. During the last decade of the eighteenth century, due to epidemics that decimated the tribe and problems with the Osages, most of the Caddos abandoned the villages they had occupied for centuries. During the early 1820s bands of Shawnee, Delaware, and Kickapoo Indians immigrated to the area. These Indians stayed for only a brief period, then generally abandoned their settlements in the mid-1830s. The time of earliest European exploration of the area has not been conclusively determined. The Moscoso expedition[qv] of 1542 may have passed through or very near what is now Franklin County. It could be, however, that the first European contact with the area did not occur until after 1719, when the French founded Le Poste des Cadodaquious[qv] in what is now Bowie County. Although the French occupied the post for more than fifty years, little is known about their activities. It seems probable, however, that they did explore as far to the southwest as Franklin County. White settlement began in the late 1830s along the eastern edge of what became Franklin County; most of the early settlers came from the upper southern states, predominantly Tennessee. The Cherokee Trace passed through the area, and by the late 1840s the central part of the county was also settled. By 1870 Mount Vernon had a population of 223. The county was marked off by the legislature in March 1875 and named for Judge Benjamin C. Franklin,[qv] an early Red River County settler. An election was held on April 30, 1875, to select the county seat. Mount Vernon won by a large majority, and the matter was never again contested.

In 1880 the county had a population of 5,280. The most important factor inhibiting growth was the lack of adequate transportation. The county had no navigable waterways and before 1876 no railroad. This deficiency, coupled with the availability of equally suitable croplands nearer Jefferson, the major market for Northeast Texas, prevented the area from becoming dominated by plantation agriculture in antebellum Texas.[qv] As a consequence the county was predominantly white. The 614 blacks present in 1880 were less than 12 percent of the total population. The state's growing rail network finally reached the county in 1876, when the East Line and Red River Railroad was constructed across the southeastern corner of the county. This railroad, although still inconveniently located for those in the northern and western portions of the county, undoubtedly made it somewhat easier for farmers to transport their crops to market. Its effects on the population are impossible to measure because no census of the county was taken until 1880. In 1887 the St. Louis, Arkansas and Texas Railway was built across the center of the county and became the major access to market for most farmers. Between 1884 and 1890 Mount Vernon, the largest town and major shipping point, grew from an estimated 350 to an estimated 700 residents. The county as a whole was also growing, though at a much slower rate. Its population expanded from 5,280 in 1880 to 6,481 by 1890, at which time the 819 black residents constituted 13 percent of the population.

The county was overwhelmingly rural and agricultural and remained so for more than seventy subsequent years. Two crops dominated the agricultural economy—cotton, the principal cash crop, and corn, the principal food crop (see COTTON CULTURE, CORN CULTURE). Together these two crops accounted for three out of every four acres of cropland harvested in 1880. From 1880 through 1950 the acreage planted in these dominant crops varied from six out of ten acres to more than eight out of ten acres harvested. Although farmers seem to have devoted enough acreage to the corn crop to maintain self-sufficiency, cotton absorbed an increasing amount of their time and land during the years 1880 through 1929. In 1879 the county's 706 farms had 8,660 acres of cotton, an average of slightly over twelve acres per farm. In 1929 there were 1,678 farms with 37,969 acres of cotton, an average of more than twenty-two acres per farm. In fact, during the 1929 crop season, about one in five acres in the entire county was planted in cotton. During this same period the average acres per farm devoted to corn dropped from thirteen to nine. Truck farming provided some diversity to county agriculture, and farmers shipped cane syrup, peaches, and melons around the turn of the century. For most farmers the ever-larger cotton fields did not mean a rising standard of living. As they planted successive cotton crops on the same land and extended the fields into areas that were less fertile, the yield per acre dropped steadily. In 1879 the average yield was almost half a bale of cotton per acre planted; in 1929 the yield was one-fifth of a bale. Additionally, farm tenancy[qv] had risen through the years. In 1880, 34 percent of all farmers were tenants; by 1930 the figure was 62 percent.

The county was hit hard by the Great Depression[qv] in the 1930s, which had actually begun for farmers in the mid-1920s. The average farm in Franklin County in 1930 was worth $2,085, compared to the 1920 average of $4,172. But while the value had dropped drastically, the average farm size had increased from seventy to seventy-five acres. For most citizens the depression meant harder times, but it did not bring poverty, since most residents were already poor. The population had grown steadily between 1880 and 1910, from 5,280 to 9,331, but dropped to 9,304 by 1920 and to 8,494 by 1930. During the 1920s the number of farms also fell, declining from 1,844 in 1920 to 1,678 in 1930. Hard times in agriculture, in a county with an economy that was almost exclusively agricultural, were responsible for the decline. During the 1930s the programs of the New Deal helped to alleviate some of the worst effects of the depression. A local development also provided some economic opportunities; oil was discovered near Talco in northwestern Titus County in 1936, and it was soon ascertained that the oil deposit extended into the northeastern portion of Franklin County. Since that time, oil has been discovered in various portions of the county, but all of the fields are comparatively small. The discoveries, particularly those of the 1930s when conditions were so bad for farmers, directly benefited those who owned land in or around the fields, but the overall impact seems to have been minimal. As a 1939 issue of the local newspaper put it, the oil boom had helped the county, but it was "not large enough to disrupt the economic structure nor disturb the way of living."

By 1940 the number of farms had fallen to 1,310. The average farm size had increased to 105 acres, and the average value per farm had fallen to $1,870. While the drop in value was a sign of continuing problems in the agricultural sector of the economy, there were also signs of a more positive trend. For the first time since 1900, more than half of all farmers owned the land they worked. Although cotton was still the principal cash crop in 1940, the number of acres in cotton had fallen from 37,969 acres in 1930 to 16,582 acres in 1940. Although partly due to increasing diversity in crops, the most important cause of the decline in cotton was the beginning of a move away from staple-crop agriculture. The programs of the New Deal reimbursed farmers for letting land lie fallow, while the emphasis on livestock production increased. Although the number of farms had fallen, production of dairy and beef cattle and poultry had risen. The value of farms began to rise in the 1940s, but the other trends that were evident in 1940 continued through the 1970s. The number of farms steadily declined until 1982, when there were just 478 farms. Those farms had an average size of 245 acres and an average value of $204,630. By 1982 livestock production dominated the agricultural economy, accounting for 96 percent of total cash receipts in agriculture. Tenant farming had also virtually disappeared by 1982, when just 9 percent of farms were occupied by tenants. In the 1990s hay was the principal crop, and farmers also grew blueberries, blackberries, and peaches. Poultry production increased to meet the needs of the Pilgrim plants in nearby Pittsburg and Mount Vernon. Fewer people made their living in agriculture, and consequently the population fell, since the county had no cities and a very small industrial base. The decline that began in the 1920s continued until 1960, when the population was reported as 5,101, the lowest figure ever recorded. During the 1960s citizens, particularly in Mount Vernon, worked to bring industry and jobs into the county. They established the Franklin County Industrial Foundation and purchased an industrial-park site. In 1964 three plastics industries built plants in Mount Vernon. In 1958 only 57 laborers had been employed in manufacturing; that number had risen to 300 by 1972 and 400 by 1982. Increases in the industrial sector were probably responsible for the turnaround in the population trend. The population was reported as 5,291 in 1970 and 6,893 in 1980. The county remained predominantly white; the 409 blacks in the county in 1980 constituted less than 6 percent of the total population. The county continued its modest but steady growth in the 1980s, reaching a population of 7,802 in 1990.

Because Mount Vernon had a population of fewer than 2,500 in 1980, the county was still defined as almost exclusively rural by the Bureau of the Census. Only the 862 Franklin County residents who lived within the city limits of Winnsboro were considered urban residents. Still, the county had undergone drastic changes. In 1981 nonfarm income totaled more than $47 million, and total farm cash receipts were less than $29 million. The dirt roads that had crossed the county for generations had been paved beginning in 1916, when voters approved a $200,000 bond issue for road improvement. Improving transportation and the changing nature of employment opportunities made it easier and more advantageous for citizens to obtain more formal education. In 1896 the county had been divided into thirty-one school districts, twenty-eight of which were completely within the county. Most of these districts had only one teacher, a one-room school, and a session of fewer than 120 days. Most children dropped out of school before reaching high school. By 1980 the county had just one school district completely within its boundaries, but that district had almost twice as many teachers as the twenty-eight districts had in 1896. In 1980 more than 75 percent of students aged sixteen to nineteen graduated from high school; for the first time more than half the citizens the county over the age of twenty-five had received a high school diploma.

Franklin County voters have consistently supported Democratic presidential candidates since the county's inception in 1875. In 1896 the Populist party^{qv} candidates, William Jennings Bryan and Tom Watson, received 391 votes for president and vice president. The Democratic ticket, Bryan and Arthur Sewall, won 971 votes for each office, and the Republicans, William McKinley and Garret A. Hobart, came in third with 76 votes. In 1968 and 1992 third-party candidates George Wallace and Ross Perot made strong showings in the county, but Democratic candidates carried the county through 1992, with the exception of 1984, when Republican Ronald Reagan defeated Walter Mondale by a vote of 1,836 to 1,104.

Recreation facilities in Franklin County are primarily geared toward outdoor pursuits. Opportunities for boating and fishing abound. Cypress Springs Reservoir, the largest lake in the county, covers 3,400 acres. Several other lakes dot the landscape. In addition to the Sulphur River several streams run through the county. Various species of animals are available for hunting, including deer, squirrel, and quail. State Highway 37 and Farm Road 21 are scenic drives through the southern part of the county. The Rogers-Drummond House, near Mount Vernon, is listed on the National Register of Historic Places. Mount Vernon hosts a rodeo in June, a county fair in October, and a Christmas Parade in December. The Franklin County Museum Complex in Mount Vernon offers a variety of exhibits on local and natural history.

BIBLIOGRAPHY: *Comprehensive Overall Economic Development Study and Plan for Franklin County* (Mount Vernon, Texas: Franklin County Study and Planning Committee, 1962). Millard F. Fleming, Reorganization of the Public Schools of Franklin County, Texas (M.A. thesis, University of Texas, 1938). Billy Hicks and Doris Meek, comps., *Historical Records of Franklin County, Texas* (Mount Vernon, Texas: Franklin County Historical Survey Committee, 1972). Ina M. O. McAdams, A Study of the Mount Vernon *Optic-Herald*, 1906–1931, and Its Community (M.A. thesis, University of Texas, 1960). Rex W. Strickland, Anglo-American Activities in Northeastern Texas, 1803–1845 (Ph.D. dissertation, University of Texas, 1937).

Cecil Harper, Jr.

FRANKLIN MOUNTAIN. Franklin Mountain is fifteen miles northeast of Lampasas in eastern Lampasas County (at 31°15′ N, 98°03′ W). Its summit, at an elevation of 1,402 feet above sea level, rises 250 feet above nearby Bear Branch. The mountain stands in an area of the Grand Prairies region characterized by flat terrain with some local dissections, surfaced by stony shallow clays and loams. Local vegetation includes grasses and open stands of oak, mesquite, and juniper.

FRANKLIN MOUNTAINS. The Franklin Mountains extend from just north of downtown El Paso in El Paso County into southern Doña Ana County, New Mexico; their center is at 32°01′ north latitude, 106°32′ west longitude. They are roughly three miles wide by twenty-three miles long and rise to an elevation of 7,192 feet above sea level at North Franklin Mountain. The mountains divide the city of El Paso and have influenced its shape and growth. This range comprises the bulk of the second largest state park in Texas and what is said to be the largest urban park in the nation, Franklin Mountains State Park.^{qv}

The Franklin Mountains are composed primarily of sedimentary rock with some igneous intrusions. Geologists refer to them as tilted-block fault mountains, and in them can be found billion-year-old Precambrian rocks, the oldest in Texas. The Franklins were formed during the Laramide mountain-building period in late Cretaceous time, 60 million to 70 million years ago. Typical Chihuahuan Desert plants and animals are found in the Franklins and some, such as the large barrel cactus, are found nowhere else in Texas. El Pasoans are especially fond of the native Mexican poppies and introduced California poppies that tint the rocky slopes each spring. Animals range from many species of rodents to deer, mountain lions, and occasionally black bears. Though the mountains look arid, a number of springs can be found during periods of adequate moisture. These springs are particularly conducive to plant and animal life. Stands of cottonwood, hackberry, oak, and juniper grow in some of the more remote areas of the park.

The name Franklin may have been derived from that of Franklin, Texas, in El Paso County, which in turn was named for Benjamin Franklin Coons^{qv} (*see also* EL PASO, TEXAS). Other sources suggest that the profile of Benjamin Franklin can be seen in some of the rocky crests. Early Spanish maps referred to the range as Las Sierras de los Mansos (an Indian tribe the Spanish found along the river at El Paso) or Las Sierras de los Organos (for the organ-pipe shapes of some of the cliffs). Early Spanish and Mexican settlers usually avoided the mountains because Apache and Comanche raiders used them as bases for their raids upon the river settlements.

Outlaws also used the rugged isolation of the Franklins. At Fussell- man Canyon, in an encounter with rustlers in 1890, deputy United States marshall Charles H. Fussellman was killed in a shootout. The outlaw Gerónimo Parra was later hanged for the shooting.

The only tin mine in the United States was located in the Franklin Mountains, where its ruins are visible today. The mine, founded in

1909 and operated by the El Paso Tin Mining and Smelting Company, proved unsuccessful; work was stopped in 1915 after the project yielded only 160 100-pound pigs of tin (see TIN SMELTING). The legendary Lost Padre Mine is said to be hidden somewhere in the mountains. The tale says that some 300 burro loads of silver were left by Jesuits,qv who filled in the shaft before fleeing the area. Other versions state that 5,000 silver bars, 4,336 gold ingots, nine burro loads of jewels, and four priceless Aztec codices were hidden in the shaft by Juan de Oñate.qv Local newspapers periodically report someone's claiming to have found the fabled treasure, only to lose it again or run out of capital before it can be recovered.

BIBLIOGRAPHY: Charles H. Binion, *An Introduction to El Paso's Scenic and Historic Landmarks* (El Paso: Texas Western Press, 1970). J. Frank Dobie, *Coronado's Children: Tales of Lost Mines and Buried Treasures of the Southwest* (New York: Garden City, 1930). C. L. Sonnichsen, *Pass of the North: Four Centuries on the Rio Grande* (2 vols., El Paso: Texas Western Press, 1968, 1980).   *Robert W. Miles*

FRANKLIN MOUNTAINS STATE PARK. The Franklin Mountains,qv in El Paso County, were seen as worthy of preservation as far back as 1925, but attempts to establish a park there were unsuccessful until 1979. In that year, after a land developer cut a road to the top of North Franklin Mountain, a group of environmentalists formed the Wilderness Park Coalition and succeeded in getting the Texas legislature to direct the Texas Parks and Wildlife Departmentqv to acquire the Franklin Mountains for a state park. The original bill prohibited any funds being spent to operate or maintain the park, but that prohibition was removed in 1985, and the park master plan was begun soon after. In 1988 facilities were limited to picnic facilities in Tom Mays Park, formerly a county park, and McKelligon Canyon Park, operated by the city. The Woodrow Bean Transmountain Highway bisects the state park and offers limited access for hikers, although several sections of the land bordering this road are still a part of the United States Army Castner Range, and unexploded artillery rounds make the area hazardous. The Franklin Mountains State Park is ideal for nature studies, backpacking, hiking, and rock climbing (although much of the rock found in the Franklins is unstable). Studies have yet to be made concerning the archeological and historical aspects of the area. The park includes a number of prehistoric sites, including locations of rock paintings, as well as signs of early prospecting and mining.   *Robert W. Miles*

FRANK PHILLIPS COLLEGE. Frank Phillips College, in Borger, Texas, was established as Borger City Junior College in 1948. C. A. Cryer served as first president of the college and as superintendent of the Borger schools. The board requested and received permission from Frank Phillips, founder of Phillips Petroleum Company, which had extensive holdings in the Borger area, to rename the college in his honor. J. W. Dillard served as dean in the planning stage of the school and as president from 1955 to 1974. The college and Borger High School shared a physical plant that was completed in time for occupancy in the fall of 1948. During that year 250 students enrolled in the college, and its faculty numbered ten. In 1955 the college bought thirty acres in the southwestern part of the city for a new campus, and facilities were ready for classes by the fall semester of 1956. Enrollment that year was 450, and the faculty had grown to twenty-nine. In 1960 a fine-arts building was completed, with an auditorium, a cafeteria, a student lounge, and a bookstore, as well as classrooms and offices. A $450,000 library opened in 1966, and by 1970 it had more than 21,000 volumes. The college was accredited by the Southern Association of Colleges and Schools in 1969. With the addition of twenty acres to the campus, the college physical plant was valued at $3 million. In 1973 the Texas Education Agencyqv approved vocational training programs to begin at the college. Because of the growth of the vocational programs, and with the help of a grant from Phillips Petroleum, a new vocational campus began operation in 1976. This campus, three miles west on State Highway 136, housed the agriculture, drafting, and welding schools and an expanded adult continuing-education department until a new building for vocational education was completed on the main campus in 1983. In 1984 Andrew Hicks was president of the college, which that year had ten buildings on a sixty-acre campus valued at more than $12 million. That year the administration, faculty, and staff totaled eighty-one; academic and vocational student enrollment totaled more than 1,000; and continuing-education students totaled about 1,700. For the 1992–93 regular session there were fifty-two faculty members and 1,031 students with 898 continuing-education or extension students.
  Thomas T. Brooks, Kathleen Ann Cornelius, and Julia Ann Kasch

FRANKS, L. B. (?–?). L. B. Franks, commander of the Texan artillery during the siege of Bexar,qv was in Robertson's colonyqv as early as 1834. There he owned a league on the Brazos River on what became the Falls-McLennan county line and served as an assistant surveyor under John G. W. Pierson.qv On November 27, 1835, Gen. Edward Burleson,qv commander of the Texas forces, appointed Franks lieutenant colonel of the Texan artillery—comprising two cannons and fifteen gunners—and, due to the illness of James C. Neill,qv Franks served as artillery commander at the siege of Bexar, December 5–9, 1835. His one twelve-pounder, however, became unmounted, and the artillery did little effective service in the fight. Although fearful that the enemy had received a large-caliber mortar that would be damaging to the assaulting troops, Franks advised that the Texans not retreat but press home their attack on the Alamo. His irritation at Burleson's aide-de-camp, Peter W. Grayson,qv for failing to forward reinforcements to the troops assaulting the Mexican fortifications caused him, on the third day of the battle, to send an intemperate note to Grayson, who thereupon withdrew from the army. Later that month Grayson and Franks met at San Felipe, and as a result of the meeting Franks published an apology to Grayson acknowledging that his note "was an unjust and wanton attack upon his feelings and character," for which Franks asked Grayson's pardon. The note, however, also drew the wrath of General Burleson, who, when Grayson was running for the presidency in 1838, attacked Franks as having held "a temporary but undeserved standing in the army." Franks considered the attack mere "electioneering."

On March 8, 1836, Franks wrote from the Nashville (Robertson) colony informing the convention at Washington-on-the-Brazos that he had formed a volunteer company of thirty men to take the field against Indian raiders on the northern frontier. With this force, mounted at his own expense, Franks pursued the raiders to the headwaters of the Little River. There he hoped to induce them to attack his force, which he disguised to resemble an immigrant wagon train. His letter was referred to the Committee on Indian Affairs. On April 23 George P. Digges reported to Sam Houstonqv that he had organized two spy companies, one under Franks, which was to patrol between Robbins' Ferryqv and Gonzales.

About May 1, 1838, Franks left his Washington County home for a trip into West Texas. On May 26, 1838, he, R. R. Royal,qv and three other San Antonio men offered a reward of $1,000 for the arrest and conviction of the persons who broke into and robbed San Fernando de Béxar Cathedralqv of its plate, crucifix, and candlesticks, valued at $1,000. Most of the time that he was away from Washington County, however, was spent "in the woods." He returned to San Antonio on or about July 25 to learn of and respond to Burleson's "misrepresentation" of his actions at the storming of Bexar. Franks returned in the fall of 1838 to the west, where he remained for two or three months.

A Littleberry B. Franks was charged with the murder of a Henry Castledine but escaped custody of Milam county sheriff Ordera Watson "during the storms and darkness of the night" on July 10, 1842. A fifty-dollar reward was offered for his recapture. He was said to have been six feet tall, of a fair complexion, with red whiskers and sandy colored hair, and of "thin visage."

BIBLIOGRAPHY: Clarksville *Northern Standard*, July 27, 1843. John H. Jenkins, ed., *The Papers of the Texas Revolution, 1835–1836* (10 vols., Austin: Presidial Press, 1973). Malcolm D. McLean, comp. and ed., *Papers Concerning Robertson's Colony in Texas* (19 vols., Arlington: University of Texas at Arlington Press, 1974–93). *Telegraph and Texas Register*, December 16, 1836, June 9, 18, December 15, 1838.

Thomas W. Cutrer

FRANKS CREEK. Franks Creek rises just north of Ginger in east central Rains County (at 32°51′ N, 95°43′ W) and runs southeast for ten miles to its mouth on the Sabine River, two miles south of Farm Road 779 (at 32°44′ N, 95°41′ W). The creek traverses flat to rolling terrain surfaced by sandy and clayey loams that support water-tolerant hardwoods, conifers, and grasses.

FRANKSTON, TEXAS. Frankston is at the intersection of U.S. Highway 175 and State Highway 155, near Lake Palestine and within a twenty-five-mile radius of Tyler, Jacksonville, Palestine, and Athens in far northeastern Anderson County. The town was founded when the Texas and New Orleans Railroad was built through the area. Most of its first residents moved there from Kickapoo, two miles to the southeast on an old Indian battleground site. The community was founded in January 1902. The town and post office, originally called Ayers, were renamed after Miss Frankie Miller, who donated land for the downtown city park. Lumber was the first industry of Frankston, and some lumber businesses still operated in the 1980s. Cotton was the basis of the economy around 1925; other crops such as peaches and tomatoes were raised extensively well into the early 1950s. Most of the community's businesses were on the town square or a few blocks away. The railroad station, south of the square, was a center of town activity. At one time Frankston had three hotels, a variety of stores, several gas stations and cafes, a basket factory, a Masonic hall, a livery stable, and a movie house. After 1925 the town's population ranged from 818 to 1,500. It was reported as 1,459 in 1988, when the major local employer was the Class AA school system. By the 1980s the town was incorporated with the mayor-council form of city government.[qv] Businesses and resources in the 1980s included assorted stores and cafes, several gas stations, two automobile dealerships, the Fairway oilfield, the Frankston Box Factory, a bank, a savings and loan association, a rest home, a newspaper, and a funeral home. The town also had a doctor in a well-equipped medical clinic, a dentist, and several churches. Most of the economy centered around ranching and the fishing and other tourist attractions in the forested, rolling countryside. The old rail depot was converted into the Depot Library, which in the 1980s had more than 7,000 volumes, tape cassettes, and other materials. Ellis Mercantile, a tourist attraction, provided a "trip into the past." In the early 1990s the population of Frankston was reported as 1,149, with ninety-eight rated businesses.

BIBLIOGRAPHY: Frankston Bicentennial Committees, *The Story of Frankston, Texas, and Neighboring Communities, 1900–1976* (Frankston: Jayroe Graphic Arts, 1976). Kathleen E. and Clifton R. St. Clair, eds., *Little Towns of Texas* (Jacksonville, Texas: Jayroe Graphic Arts, 1982).

Jack Dempsey

FRANQUIS DE LUGO, CARLOS BENITES (1691–?). Carlos Benites Franquis de Lugo, Spanish governor of Texas, was born at Ortoba, Tenerife, in the Canary Islands in 1691. In early manhood he moved to Havana, Cuba, where he married Ángela de Alarcón y Ocaña. In 1736 the king of Spain appointed him governor of the province of Tlaxcala. But when Franquis arrived in Mexico, that office was still held by his predecessor, so the viceroy, Archbishop Vizarron, appointed him governor ad interim of Texas to succeed Manuel de Sandoval.[qv] He arrived in San Antonio on September 26, 1736. Having "a stormy, petulant, and precipitous temper," Franquis refused to show his credentials, insulted both civil and religious authorities, and lost the respect of the missionaries at San Antonio and Los Adaes.[qv] In little more than a year as governor, 1736–37, he came near to ruining the province of Texas. He placed Sandoval under arrest, seized his papers, and brought criminal charges against him. In the ensuing investigation, Franquis himself was arrested, on July 9, 1737, for his overbearing conduct. In September 1737 he was removed from the office of governor and was retired to San Juan Bautista,[qv] where he deserted and went to Mexico City. After his trial, which lasted for several years, he became an officer of the garrison of Veracruz. He eventually returned to service in the regiment of Savoya in Spain. The date of his death is unknown, and sources conflict as to his place of death as Mexico or Spain.

BIBLIOGRAPHY: Carlos E. Castañeda, *Our Catholic Heritage in Texas* (7 vols., Austin: Von Boeckmann–Jones, 1936–1958; rpt., New York: Arno, 1976). Margaret McGill, The Administration of Carlos Franquis de Lugo, Governor of Texas, 1736–1737 (M.A. thesis, University of Texas, 1928).

Robert Bruce Blake

FRANTZ, DALIES ERHARDT (1908–1965). Dalies Erhardt Frantz, pianist and teacher, was born on January 9, 1908, in Lafayette, Colorado, the son of William Henry and Amalia (Lueck) Frantz. He grew up in Denver, where he studied piano at an early age and became known as a child prodigy. Later he learned to play the organ and helped support himself by serving as organist and choirmaster in churches. He studied at Huntington Preparatory School in Boston and under Guy Maier at the University of Michigan from 1926 to 1930. He received the bachelor of music degree with highest honors from that university; subsequently, he studied in Europe with Artur Schnabel and Vladimir Horowitz.

Following his debut with the Philadelphia Orchestra under Leopold Stokowski in 1934, Frantz was signed by Columbia Concerts Corporation and began a long and brilliant career that took him from coast to coast in recitals and in appearances with most of the major orchestras in the United States. During this period he also taught two summer sessions at the University of Washington in Seattle and returned for further study at the University of Michigan. In 1934 he married Martha King of Detroit. They were separated five years later.

Frantz's eminence as a pianist attracted Hollywood's attention, and he appeared in several motion pictures. During World War II[qv] he served for a time as an intelligence officer in a West Coast fighter squadron but was given a medical discharge before the end of the war. In 1943 he joined the University of Texas music department. In spite of physical misfortunes that continued to plague him, he pursued his teaching until the time of his death and was recognized as one of the outstanding music teachers in the country. He inspired a large number of student pianists, some of whom won national and international acclaim, and well-known professional pianists came to Austin to work with him. Some of his experiences and convictions about piano teaching were passed on to music teachers all over the United States through a series of articles in a publication of the National Piano Guild. Frantz died in Austin on December 1, 1965, and was buried at Capital Memorial Gardens, Austin.

BIBLIOGRAPHY: Vertical Files, Barker Texas History Center, University of Texas at Austin.

Kent Kennan

FRANTZ, EZRA ALLEN (1875–1964). Ezra Allen Frantz, manufacturer, inventor, and businessman, was born in the Pleasant Hill community, Macoupin County, Illinois, on August 6, 1875, the son of Michael and Barbara (Brubaker) Frantz. In 1896 he married Mary Lavanna Buckley of Parker County, Texas; they became the parents of two sons and three daughters. Frantz and his brother Peter manufactured heavy machinery and chain stay fences in Sterling, Illinois. In 1900 they dissolved the partnership, and Ezra and his wife moved to Texas. Except for three years in the 1920s, when Frantz joined his brother in the real estate business in Miami, Florida, he remained in Texas until his death.

In 1902 Frantz perfected a wire buckle for tying compressed cotton bales; W. C. Ragsdale had patented the device but failed to fix protruding wire ends, which were dangerous for workers handling the bales. Frantz purchased the rights to the buckle and took over the Standard Bale Wire Buckle Company. The buckle made possible high-density compressing and dominated the cotton-buckle market until the close of World War II.qv Frantz also held about a dozen other patents, including one for an improved piston ring and another for the first successful scratcher for oil drilling rigs. At one time he was president of seven different companies. He spent most of his career in Weatherford, although he maintained his chief manufacturing plant in Memphis, Tennessee. He lived from 1923 to 1932 in Fort Worth, where he reorganized distressed business firms and designed oilfield machinery, particularly an improved pump jack. He served as general superintendent for the American Manufacturing Company during World War II, when it received huge contracts for manufacturing naval shells. Frantz was also active in various philanthropic religious organizations of several denominations. He died in San Angelo on August 31, 1964, and was buried in Weatherford.

BIBLIOGRAPHY: Ezra Allen Frantz Papers, Barker Texas History Center, University of Texas at Austin. Parker County Historical Commission, *History of Parker County* (Dallas: Taylor, 1980).

FRANTZ, JOE BERTRAM (1917–1993). Joe B. Frantz, historian, adopted son of Ezra A. and Mary (Buckley) Frantz, was born in Dallas, Texas, on January 16, 1917. He grew up in Weatherford, graduated from Weatherford High School in 1934, attended Weatherford College for two years, transferred to the University of Texas, and graduated in 1938 with a bachelor's degree in journalism. He completed a master's degree in history in 1940 at the University of Texas and worked as archivist and acting director of the San Jacinto Museum before joining the United States Navy in 1943. Lieutenant Frantz served in the South Pacific as a communications officer in eight major engagements during World War II qv and then returned to the University of Texas as a teaching fellow. In 1948 he finished Ph.D. work under the direction of Walter Prescott Webb.qv His dissertation, published as *Gail Borden, Dairyman to a Nation* by the University of Oklahoma Press in 1951, won the Texas Institute of Letters qv prize. Hired by the history department at the University of Texas as an assistant professor in 1949, Frantz became an associate professor in 1953 and full professor in 1959. With Julian E. Choate as a coauthor, his *The American Cowboy: The Myth and the Reality,* published by the University of Oklahoma Press in 1955, established his reputation as an historian of the American West. This was followed in 1961 with *6,000 Miles of Fence: Life on the XIT Ranch of Texas,* written with Cordelia Sloan Duke.qv Meanwhile, Frantz became noted as an outstanding teacher and speaker. He served as chair of the history department, 1959–65, became director of the Texas State Historical Association qv and editor of the Southwestern Historical Quarterly,qv 1966–77, and was honored as the first holder of the Walter Prescott Webb Chair of History and Ideas at the University of Texas, 1977–80. He retired as professor emeritus in 1986. During his tenure at the University of Texas he wrote thirteen books and supervised more than fifty graduate students. He also worked as the director of the Lyndon B. Johnson qv Oral History Project, 1967–74, which produced 1,000 oral history interviews to supplement the collection of materials at the Johnson presidential library. Frantz served, in addition, as president of various organizations—Phi Alpha Theta, the international honor society for history, 1962–64; Southwestern Social Science Association,qv 1963–64; Texas Institute of Letters, 1967–69; Southern Historical Association, 1977–78; and Western History Association, 1978–79. Following his retirement from the University of Texas Frantz taught at Corpus Christi State University as Turnbull Professor in History until 1993. There he continued oral history work, facilitated the quincentennial voyage of the Columbian replica ships, and finished in 1988 a final book, *Lure of the Land: Texas County Maps and the History of Settlement,* written with Mike Cox. The book won awards from the Texas Historical Commission qv and from the Sons of the Republic of Texas.qv Two daughters were born in his marriage to Helen Andrews Boswell of Weatherford, 1939–79. During the next decade he was married twice. In 1990 he married Betsy Chadderdon of Houston. Frantz was a strong Democrat with a preference for the Methodist Church. He died on November 13, 1993, in Houston.

BIBLIOGRAPHY: W. Eugene Hollon, "Remembering Joe Frantz," *Southwestern Historical Quarterly* 97 (January 1994). David G. McComb, "In Memory of Joe B. Frantz," *Southwestern Historical Quarterly* 97 (January 1994).
David G. McComb

FRANZHEIM, KENNETH (1890–1959). Kenneth Franzheim, architect, was born on October 28, 1890, in Wheeling, West Virginia, the son of Charles W. and Lida Riddle (Merts) Franzheim. He graduated from Lawrenceville School and Massachusetts Institute of Technology (B. A. 1913), then worked from 1913 until 1917 for the Boston architect Welles Bosworth. He subsequently served for two years at Ellington Field qv outside Houston, Texas, as a first flight lieutenant in the United States Army Air Corps. On May 12, 1919, he married Elizabeth Frances Simms; they had three children, one of whom, Kenneth Franzheim II, served as ambassador to New Zealand, Western Samoa, Fiji, and Tonga during President Richard M. Nixon's administration. Franzheim became a partner of the Detroit architect C. Howard Crane in 1920. He worked for Crane in Chicago, then in Boston. In 1925 he began independent practice in New York, where he specialized in the design of large commercial buildings and airports. He was retained in 1928 by Jesse H. Jones qv to collaborate with Alfred C. Finn on the design of the thirty-seven-story Gulf Building, Houston qv (1929), and to design a temporary coliseum for the Democratic national convention in Houston. Also for Jones, Franzheim designed a forty-two-story office building (1930) and a twenty-story apartment building (1931) in midtown Manhattan. A second round of major projects in Houston, undertaken with John F. Staub,qv led Franzheim to move his practice from New York to Houston in 1937, although he maintained a New York office until 1940. From 1941 until 1944 Franzheim worked in Washington, D.C. Upon returning to Houston he established himself as the foremost commercial architect in the city, a position he held until his death. Most of the buildings that he produced in Houston were examples of modernistic architecture. Ben A. Dore, another former partner of C. Howard Crane, was his chief designer.

Franzheim's major buildings in Houston were the seventeen-story Humble Tower (1936, with Staub); the second Hermann Hospital qv and the Hermann Professional Building (1949, with Hedrick and Lindsley); the eighteen-story Prudential Building (1952); the twenty-one-story Texas National Bank building (1955); and the twenty-four-story Bank of the Southwest building (1956). Franzheim was also responsible for the twenty-one-story National Bank of Commerce building in San Antonio (1957, with Atlee B. and Robert M. Ayres qqv). Franzheim's best known Houston building was Foley's Department Store (1947, 1957), for which he won an Award of Merit from the American Institute of Architects in 1950.

Franzheim was particularly interested in incorporating works of art in his architecture, and this led to collaboration with the artists Wheeler Williams, Peter Hurd,qv Leo Friedlander, and Rufino Tamayo. Franzheim was the first chairman of the board of the Allied Arts Association of Houston and was an honorary member of the National Sculpture Society. In 1949 he was elected to fellowship in the American Institute of Architects, the same year that he served as chairman of the institute's annual convention, which was held in Houston, and as president of the Houston Chapter of the AIA. Franzheim also was an honorary member of the Mexican Society of Architects; after 1945 he maintained a second home in Mexico City. He was a member and deacon of the First Presbyterian Church of Houston. He belonged to the Bayou Club, the Houston Country Club, the Coronado Club, and the Ramada Club. Franzheim died in Mexico on March 13, 1959, and is buried in Glenwood Cemetery, Houston.

BIBLIOGRAPHY: *American Architects Directory*, 1955. Joseph L. Clark, *Texas Gulf Coast: Its History and Development* (4 vols., New York: Lewis Historical Publishing, 1955). *Who Was Who in America*, Vol. 3.

Stephen Fox

FRAPS, GEORGE STRONACH (1876–1955). George Stronach Fraps, agricultural chemist, son of Anton Wenzel and Margaret Lumley (Stonebanks) Fraps, was born in Raleigh, North Carolina, on September 9, 1876. He attended North Carolina College of Agriculture and Mechanical Arts (now North Carolina State University) and graduated with a B.S. in 1896. After serving as an assistant chemist, Fraps attended Johns Hopkins University, where he received a Ph.D. in 1899. He returned to his alma mater that year and remained until 1903 as assistant professor of chemistry, conducting experiments on the improvement of fertilizers and soils and the adulteration of coffee, tea, and flour. He also served as assistant chemist at the North Carolina Experiment Station during this period and wrote *The Principles of Dyeing*, published in 1903.

Fraps married Ellen Hale Saunders on June 17, 1903; they had three children. The year of his marriage Fraps accepted the position of assistant chemist at the Texas Agricultural Experiment Station (*see* AGRICULTURAL EXPERIMENT STATION SYSTEM). In 1905 he was promoted to state chemist. He became chief of chemistry at the Texas Agricultural Experiment Station in 1914 and held this and his state post until his retirement in 1945. He also taught courses in basic and agricultural chemistry at the Texas Agricultural and Mechanical College (now Texas A&M University) from 1903 to 1913.

In 1913 Fraps wrote Principles of Agricultural Chemistry. His most important writings appeared as bulletins of the Texas Agricultural Experiment Station and articles in scientific journals. His principal interests were the composition of soils, especially Texas soils; feeds, irrigation waters, fertilizers, and seeds; cottonseed; forage grasses; digestibility and productive energy in chickens; vitamins; and insecticides and fungicides. In his time Fraps was the most prolific author in the history of the Texas Agricultural Experiment Station. During his career his major contributions laid the basic foundation for understanding Texas soils. By applying the principles of chemistry to agricultural problems, he began to develop the present vast and diversified area of agricultural chemistry in Texas. In the process he defined many terms in animal nutrition and contributed to a better understanding of human nutrition. He discovered that even a total chemical analysis of the soil provided insufficient information about the soil's productive capacity and, building on this base of knowledge, developed methods for estimating soil fertility. For these contributions Fraps has been called the "father of Texas soil chemistry."

He was honored with the presidencies of the Association of Official Agricultural Chemists and the Association of American Feed Control Officials. In 1927 he served as the United States delegate to the First International Congress of Soil Science. He was a member of Phi Beta Kappa and a fellow of the American Association for the Advancement of Science. He died on November 28, 1955, in Bryan and is buried in the Bryan City Cemetery.

BIBLIOGRAPHY: Frank Carter Adams, ed., *Texas Democracy: A Centennial History of Politics and Personalities of the Democratic Party, 1836–1936* (4 vols., Austin: Democratic Historical Association, 1937). Dallas *Morning News*, November 29, 1955. George S. Fraps, Scientific Articles, Texas A&M University Archives. A. D. Jackson, *Publications of G. S. Fraps* (Texas Agricultural Experiment Station Progress Report 958 [College Station, September 1945]). Irvin M. May, Jr., Science and Technology for Texas Farmers: A History of the Texas Agricultural Experiment Station (MS, Texas A&M University Library, 1981).

Irvin M. May, Jr.

FRATT, TEXAS. Fratt was a flag station on the Missouri, Kansas and Texas Railroad six miles north of downtown San Antonio in northern Bexar County. The community was first settled by German farmers before 1900. In the mid-1930s Fratt had a general store, a church, and a station house. Its population was reported as twenty-five in 1946. The settlement declined after World War II,[qv] and by the 1960s it was no longer shown on maps.

Christopher Long

FRAZER, HUGH MCDONALD (?–1836). Hugh McDonald Frazer, captain of the Refugio Militia and scout to James W. Fannin, Jr.,[qv] was a native of Nova Scotia. He immigrated to Texas as a member of the McMullen-McGloin colony,[qv] but like others at San Patricio he was unable to agree with the empresarios and in 1835 moved to the Refugio colony, where he went into the cattle-raising and trading business. He was elected a delegate from Refugio Municipality to the Consultation,[qv] but apparently he never took his seat, for he was with Capt. Ira J. Westover[qv] on October 9, 1835, in the capture of Goliad. As a member of the Lipantitlán expedition[qv] he incurred the ire of Capt. Philip Dimmitt[qv] over unauthorized sale of government tobacco and was kept under arrest. Dimmitt finally came to the conclusion that Frazer was "principally guilty of being in bad company" and released him.

On February 2, 1836, Frazer, elected captain of the Refugio Militia, recruited a company of some thirty or thirty-five men, which operated as an auxiliary of Fannin's regiment at Goliad, scouting and guarding supply trains. Although Fannin had been warned of José de Urrea's[qv] approach, he did not desire to abandon Goliad until he had some word regarding the fate of Amon King and William Ward[qqv] and their men, whom he had detached to Refugio. Frazer volunteered to ride to Refugio to secure information. He gave Fannin a true account of the defeat and annihilation of King's and Ward's forces and with the Refugio Militia accompanied Fannin on the retreat and took part in the battle of Coleto.[qv] Frazer distinguished himself for his bravery, and although he was painfully wounded, he remained on the battlefield to attend the needs of other Texans.

Most of the reliable accounts state that Frazer was massacred with Fannin's men at Goliad on March 27, 1836 (*see* GOLIAD MASSACRE). There was, however, a Hugh Frazier who served as a private at the battle of San Jacinto[qv] and who has been identified with Capt. Hugh M. Frazer. The Nova Scotia heirs of Frazer thought that Frazer was among the Goliad victims.

BIBLIOGRAPHY: William Campbell Binkley, ed., *Official Correspondence of the Texan Revolution, 1835–1836* (2 vols., New York: Appleton-Century, 1936). Harbert Davenport, Notes from an Unfinished Study of Fannin and His Men (MS, Harbert Davenport Collection, Texas State Library, Austin; Barker Texas History Center, University of Texas at Austin). Hobart Huson, *Refugio: A Comprehensive History of Refugio County from Aboriginal Times to 1953* (2 vols., Woodsboro, Texas: Rooke Foundation, 1953, 1955). John H. Jenkins, ed., *The Papers of the Texas Revolution, 1835–1836* (10 vols., Austin: Presidial Press, 1973). John J. Linn, *Reminiscences of Fifty Years in Texas* (New York: Sadlier, 1883; 2d ed., Austin: Steck, 1935; rpt., Austin: State House, 1986). Kathryn Stoner O'Connor, *The Presidio La Bahía del Espíritu Santo de Zúñiga, 1721 to 1846* (Austin: Von Boeckmann–Jones, 1966). Texas House of Representatives, *Biographical Directory of the Texan Conventions and Congresses, 1832–1845* (Austin: Book Exchange, 1941).

Hobart Huson

FRAZIER, JAMES (?–ca. 1832). James Frazier came to Texas probably with David Fitzgerald^{qv} as early as March 1822. In April 1824 Frazier voted for the Baron de Bastrop^{qv} as elector for the colony of Stephen F. Austin.^{qv} Frazier was a partner of David Shelby and John McCormick^{qqv} as one of Austin's Old Three Hundred^{qv} settlers. They received title to a league of land on the west bank of the Brazos River two miles below the site of San Felipe de Austin in what is now southeast Austin and northwest Fort Bend counties on July 24, 1824. The census of March 1826 listed Frazier as a farmer, a single man aged between twenty-five and forty. Evidently he married between 1826 and 1832 and died before February 1832. Thomas Barnett^{qv} offered land of the James Frazier estate for sale in February 1832, and a land title on Buckner's Creek in Fayette County was granted in 1832 to Peggy Browne, widow of James Frazier.

Another James Frazier, an early resident of Texas, claimed prize money from the capture of the brig *Pocket*^{qv} in 1836. A James Fraizer enlisted in Col. Robert M. Coleman's^{qv} rangers to serve from November 1, 1836, to December 31, 1836. A James Frazier was an agent in Monclova for the estate of Dr. James Grant^{qv} in 1838.

BIBLIOGRAPHY: Eugene C. Barker, ed., *The Austin Papers* (3 vols., Washington: GPO, 1924–28). Lester G. Bugbee, "The Old Three Hundred: A List of Settlers in Austin's First Colony," *Quarterly of the Texas State Historical Association* 1 (October 1897). QSMNH, *Telegraph and Texas Register*, November 2, 12, 1836. *Texas Gazette*, February 18, 1832. Clarence Wharton, *Wharton's History of Fort Bend County* (San Antonio: Naylor, 1939).

FRAZIER, TEXAS. Frazier was just north of State Highway 49 and fifteen miles northeast of Jefferson in eastern Marion County. The Frazier school had thirty nine black pupils and one teacher in 1899. In 1938 the community had a one-room schoolhouse that accommodated forty-five black elementary school students and one teacher. The Frazier school was consolidated with those of Jefferson by 1955, and in 1967 all that remained of Frazier was two cemeteries named for the Coore family, who owned the original land grants at the site.

BIBLIOGRAPHY: Jack Reed Harvey, Survey and Proposed Reorganization of the Marion County Schools (M.A. thesis, University of Texas, 1940).
Mark Odintz

FRAZIER CANYON. Frazier Canyon begins just east of Mount Locke and nine miles northwest of Fort Davis in central Jeff Davis County (at 30°40′ N, 103°59′ W) and extends east for thirteen miles to its mouth on Limpia Canyon, just east of State Highway 17 and ten miles northeast of Fort Davis (at 30°41′ N, 103°47′ W). Through Frazier Canyon flows an intermittent stream. The surrounding rugged canyon terrain is surfaced by shallow, stony soils that support Mexican buckeye, walnut, persimmon, desert willow, scrub brush, and sparse grasses. Both Frazier Canyon and Horse Thief Canyon were named for Walt Frazier, who reportedly stole horses from a ranch north of Fort Stockton in 1896 and fled south toward Mexico. His two young accomplices were killed in a shootout with Texas Rangers^{qv} in what came to be called Horse Thief Canyon, but Frazier eluded his pursuers in the canyon that now bears his name. Though he rode on to the Texas and Pacific Railway, where he abandoned his horse and hopped a westbound freight train, he was subsequently caught and imprisoned.

FRAZIER CREEK (Cass County). Frazier Creek rises five miles southwest of Douglassville in northern Cass County (at 33°09′ N, 94°26′ W) and runs southeast for thirty-one miles before joining Jims Bayou to form James Bayou fifteen miles northeast of Jefferson in northeastern Marion County (at 32°52′ N, 94°07′ W). The stream, which is intermittent in its upper reaches, runs through nearly level to gently rolling flood-prone terrain with loamy soils that support water-tolerant hardwoods, conifers, and grasses. The creek was probably named for James and Ebenezer Frazier, both of whom owned land near its upper reaches.

FRAZIERVILLE, TEXAS. Frazierville or Frazier was on Farm Road 3267 some three miles southeast of Hillsboro in Hill County. In 1852 Richard Cason Frazier and his wife Agnes Clark Frazier received a land grant in Hill County, including what came to be known as Frazier Springs, a popular campground for Indians. Eventually settlers in the area wanted a school, and in 1883 John Frazier, Richard's son, donated two acres of land for a school and nondenominational church. When it was built it was used as a church and school and also for Sunday school and the debating society. In the 1905–06 school year the Frazier school had nineteen students and one teacher, but eventually it closed. In the 1980s members of the Frazier family still resided on the original land grant.

BIBLIOGRAPHY: Claude W. Dooley, comp., *Why Stop?* (Odessa: Lone Star Legends, 1978; 2d ed., with Betty Dooley and the Texas Historical Commission, Houston: Lone Star, 1985). Hill County Historical Commission, *A History of Hill County, Texas, 1853–1980* (Waco: Texian, 1980).
Lisa C. Maxwell

FRED, TEXAS. Fred is seven miles south of Spurger in extreme southeastern Tyler County. The Fred post office was established in 1881 with Wiley Cunningham as the first postmaster. In 1883 the community had a population of thirty, along with two churches, a general store, and a school. The principal shipments from the town were cotton and hides. The community's population had risen to seventy-five by 1913. In 1917 the Shilo Independent School District operated near Fred. In the 1920s, with population growth and improved transportation routes in the county, the number of local school districts began to decline, but the Fred district existed until at least the mid-1950s. By the late 1960s Fred had 349 residents, and from the early 1970s through 1990 it reported a population of 239. The Fred post office was one of only three post offices extant in Tyler County in the 1960s, and it was still in operation in 1985. In the mid-1980s the Fred Elementary School was part of the Warren Independent School District.

BIBLIOGRAPHY: *It's Dogwood Time in Tyler County* (Woodville, Texas), 1955, 1962.
Megan Biesele

FREDERICKSBURG, TEXAS. Fredericksburg, the county seat of Gillespie County, is seventy miles west of Austin in the central part of the county. The town was one of a projected series of German settlements from the Texas coast to the land north of the Llano River, originally the ultimate destination of the German immigrants sent to Texas by the Adelsverein.^{qv} In August 1845 John O. Meusebach^{qv} left New Braunfels with a surveying party to select a site for a second settlement en route to the Fisher-Miller Land Grant.^{qv} He eventually chose a tract of land sixty miles northwest of New Braunfels, where two streams met four miles above the Pedernales River; the streams were later named Barons Creek, in Meusebach's honor, and Town Creek. Meusebach was impressed by the abundance of water, stone, and timber and upon his return to New Braunfels arranged to buy 10,000 acres on credit. The first wagontrain of 120 settlers arrived from New Braunfels on May 8, 1846, after a sixteen-day journey, accompanied by an eight-man military escort provided by the Adelsverein. Surveyor Hermann Wilke laid out the town, which Meusebach named Fredericksburg after Prince Frederick of Prussia, an influential member of the Adelsverein. Each settler received one town lot and ten acres of farmland nearby. The town was laid out like the German villages along the Rhine, from which many of the colonists had come, with one long, wide main street roughly paralleling Town Creek. The earliest houses in Fredericksburg were built simply, of post oak logs stuck upright in the ground. These were soon replaced by *Fachwerk* houses, built of upright timbers with the spaces between filled with rocks and then plastered or whitewashed over (*see* GERMAN VERNACULAR ARCHITECTURE).

The colonists planted corn, built storehouses to protect their provisions and trade goods, and prepared for the arrival of more immigrant trains, which came throughout the summer. Within two years Fredericksburg had grown into a thriving town of almost 1,000, despite an epidemic that spread from Indianola and New Braunfels and killed between 100 and 150 residents in the summer and fall of 1846. The first two years also saw the opening of a wagon road between Fredericksburg and Austin; the signing of the Meusebach-Comanche Treaty,^{qv} which effectively eliminated the threat of Indian attack; the opening of the first privately owned store, by J. L. Ransleben; the construction of the Vereins-Kirche,^{qv} which served for fifty years as a church, school, fortress, and meeting hall; the formal organization of Gillespie County by the Texas legislature, which made Fredericksburg the county seat; the founding of Zodiac, a nearby settlement, by a group of Mormons under Lyman Wight;^{qv} the construction of the Nimitz Hotel;^{qv} and the establishment by the United States Army of Fort Martin Scott, which became an important market for the merchants and laborers of Fredericksburg, two miles east of town. After the signing of the Treaty of Guadalupe Hidalgo^{qv} in 1849, Fredericksburg also benefited from its situation as the last town before El Paso on the Emigrant or Upper El Paso Road.

Religion played an important part in the lives of the German settlers of Gillespie County. Devout farmers drove as much as twenty miles into town for religious services and built Fredericksburg's characteristic Sunday houses^{qv} for use on weekends and religious holidays. Though most of the original colonists were members of the Evangelical Protestant Church, there were also Lutherans, Methodists, and Catholics. Initially, all communions held services in the Vereins-Kirche, but in 1848 the Catholics built their own church, which was supplanted in 1860 by the Marienkirche (old St. Mary's Church). Also in 1848 the German missionary Father Menzel erected a large wooden cross on Cross Mountain^{qv} just north of Fredericksburg. The Methodists withdrew from the Vereins-Kirche around the same time, and another group left the Evangelical Protestants in 1852 and formed Zion's Evangelical Lutheran Church under Rev. Philip F. Zizelman. Their church building, completed the following year, was the first Lutheran church in the Hill Country.^{qv}

The German settlers were also passionate believers in the importance of education. The first school in Fredericksburg was established under Johann Leyendecker, in whose home Catholic services were held immediately after the town's founding. Leyendecker was succeeded as teacher a year later by Jacob Brodbeck,^{qv} who was in turn succeeded by Rev. Gottlieb Burchard Dangers.^{qv} In 1852 Heinrich Ochs^{qv} replaced Dangers; Ochs remained an important figure in the community until his death in 1897. The first public school, with August Siemering as teacher, and the first official Catholic school in Fredericksburg were established in 1856.

Fredericksburg, like many of the German communities in south central Texas, generally supported the Union in the Civil War.^{qv} Still, despite widespread opposition to slavery and secession^{qqv} on philosophical grounds, a number of Fredericksburg residents supported the Confederacy. Charles H. Nimitz^{qv} organized the Gillespie Rifles for the Confederate Army and was later appointed enrolling officer for the frontier district. The Fredericksburg Southern Aid Society subscribed more than $5,000 in food and clothing for Confederate soldiers in 1861. In general, however, the people of Fredericksburg and Gillespie County suffered under Confederate martial law, imposed in 1862, and from the depredations of such outlaws as James P. Waldrip. Waldrip, the leader of a notorious gang, was shot by an unknown assassin beneath a live oak tree outside the Nimitz Hotel in 1867.

The bitter experience of the Civil War strengthened the traditional German determination not to get involved in state and national affairs. The Germans tried to maintain their independence by steadfastly refusing to learn or use English. The first newspaper in the county was the German-language Fredericksburg *Wochenblatt*, established in 1877, and a teamster who drove freight from Austin to Fredericksburg in the 1880s claimed that the local sheriff, who spoke German and broken English, was the only person in Fredericksburg who could act as an interpreter for him. The most authoritative history of early Fredericksburg was *Fest-Ausgabe zum fuenfzig-jaehrigen Jubilaeum der deutschen Kolonie Friedrichsburg*, written by Robert G. Penniger^{qv} for the town's fiftieth-anniversary celebration in 1896. Not until after 1900 were the first purely English-speaking teachers employed in Fredericksburg's public schools.

As the town grew in size and importance, however, its self-imposed isolation was beginning to break down. The first Gillespie County Fair was held in 1881 at Fort Martin Scott and moved to Fredericksburg in 1889. The fair, celebrated as the first in Texas, soon attracted relatively large numbers of visitors to Fredericksburg. The town got its first electric-light company in 1896 and its first ice factory in 1907; by 1904 the estimated population had risen to 1,632. Another factor in Fredericksburg's decreasing insularity was the construction of the San Antonio, Fredericksburg and Northern Railway, the first train of which rolled into Fredericksburg on November 17, 1913, and was greeted with a three-day celebration. The railroad was reorganized as the Fredericksburg and Northern in 1917 and remained in operation until July 25, 1942, when it died, a victim of improved roads and automobiles.

By World War I^{qv} a number of residents of Fredericksburg considered Penniger's editorial newspaper too pro-German. Another symbol of change was the spring 1928 vote to incorporate, a move the people of Fredericksburg had resisted for eighty-two years because they preferred to use the county as the unit of local government: why, they reasoned, pay two sets of public officials when one would suffice? At the time of the vote Fredericksburg was the largest unincorporated town in the United States, and the increasing size and complexity of both the town and the county made a change necessary. The 1930 United States census, the first in which Fredericksburg was included, gave the town's population as 2,416. Thereafter the population grew slowly but steadily, reaching 3,544 in 1940, 3,847 in 1950, 4,629 in 1960, 5,326 in 1970, and 6,412 in 1980. As Fredericksburg grew it became the principal manufacturing center of Gillespie County. At various times it has had a furniture factory, a cement plant, a poultry-dressing plant, granite and limestone quarries, a mattress factory, a peanut-oil plant, a sewing factory, a metal and iron works, and a tannery. As early as 1930, however, the town was also becoming known as a resort center, with a tourist camp and hunting and fishing opportunities; a significant part of the town's economy continues to depend upon its ability to attract the tourist trade. One of the organizations that has helped make Fredericksburg an important tourist center is the Gillespie County Historical Society, founded in 1934 to preserve local history and traditions. Its immediate goal was the completion, with the help of the Civil Works Administration, of a replica of the Vereins-Kirche, which had been torn down in 1897. When it was completed in 1936 for the Texas Centennial^{qv} celebration, the structure became the home of the Pioneer Museum. After the museum was moved in 1955 the new Vereins-Kirche became the home of the Gillespie County archives. Another local structure of some historical significance is the Admiral Nimitz Center in the old Nimitz Hotel, commemorating native son Adm. Chester W. Nimitz,^{qv} a hero of World War II^{qv} (*see* ADMIRAL NIMITZ STATE HISTORICAL PARK).

In the 1980s Fredericksburg had thirty-eight restaurants, thirteen motels, a resort farm, a campground, three art galleries, and twenty antique stores. In addition, the town was the site of a number of annual events, many of which recall Fredericksburg's German pioneer past, which attracted visitors from throughout the state. Among these events were the Wild Game Dinner (for men only) in March and the

Damenfest (for women only) in October, both of which benefit the Fredericksburg Heritage Foundation; the Easter Fires qv Pageant; the Founders Day celebration, on the Saturday nearest May 8, which benefits the Gillespie County Historical Society; A Night in Old Fredericksburg, in July; Oktoberfest; and the Kristkindl Market and Candlelight Homes Tour, both in December. The Gillespie County Fair is held in Fredericksburg on the third weekend in August; the fairgrounds are also the site of racing meets on Memorial Day and the Fourth of July and a hunter-jumper horse show in June. In 1990 the population was 6,934. *See also* GERMANS.

BIBLIOGRAPHY: Don Hampton Biggers, *German Pioneers in Texas* (Fredericksburg, Texas: Fredericksburg Publishing, 1925). Sara Kay Curtis, A History of Gillespie County, Texas, 1846–1900 (M.A. thesis, University of Texas, 1943). Gillespie County Historical Society, *Pioneers in God's Hills* (2 vols., Austin: Von Boeckmann–Jones, 1960, 1974). Ella Amanda Gold, The History of Education in Gillespie County (M.A. thesis, University of Texas, 1945). Sarah Sam Gray, The German-American Community of Fredericksburg, Texas and Its Assimilation (M.A. thesis, University of Texas, 1929). Richard Zelade, *Hill Country* (Austin: Texas Monthly Press, 1983).

Martin Donell Kohout

FREDERICKSBURG COLLEGE. Fredericksburg College was founded in 1876 by the German Methodist Church of Fredericksburg. Its original purpose was to teach adult students, but financial difficulties soon forced the college to admit students of all ages. Total enrollment at the college was about 150, including some boarding students from Houston, Galveston, Llano, and Mason. W. J. R. Thoenssen, the first principal, was succeeded by Charles F. Tansill. Courses were offered in the arts and sciences, with emphasis on foreign languages. When the college was discontinued in 1884, the building and property were sold to the Fredericksburg Independent School District.

BIBLIOGRAPHY: Ella Amanda Gold, The History of Education in Gillespie County (M.A. thesis, University of Texas, 1945).

Clinton P. Hartmann

FREDERICKSBURG AND NORTHERN RAILWAY. The Fredericksburg and Northern Railway Company was chartered on December 26, 1917. It connected Fredericksburg with Fredericksburg Junction, twenty-four miles to the south on the San Antonio and Aransas Pass Railway in Kendall County. The capital was $25,000, and the principal place of business was Fredericksburg. Members of the first board of directors were James M. Dobie qv of Cotulla; C. B. Lucas of Berclair; and Richard R. Russell, qv Thomas E. Mathis, W. W. Collier, J. H. Haile, and J. L. Browne, all of San Antonio. The Fredericksburg and Northern acquired the twenty-four miles of the San Antonio, Fredericksburg and Northern Railway Company, which was sold under foreclosure on December 31, 1917. Under the ownership of Mrs. R. F. Spenser the new railroad faired better than the old. In 1919 it grossed $15,353 and showed a profit of $3,003. In 1925 it showed a profit of $5,970. In 1926 it reported passenger earnings of $4,000 and freight earnings of $56,000 and owned two locomotives and one car; it was listed as a Class III railroad. Over the next several years revenue increased at a healthy rate, and operating expenses were kept at acceptable levels. But the railroad was still unable to service the debt incurred to purchase the railroad. The projected Gulf and West Texas Railway was to have included the Fredericksburg and Northern as part of its route, but the failure of this project left the company on its own. Train service ended July 27, 1942. *Victoria S. Murphy*

FREDONIA, TEXAS (Gregg County). Fredonia was on the south bank of the Sabine River in northern Rusk County. The site is now in central Gregg County on Farm Road 2087 and Interstate Highway 20, 4½ miles southwest of the county courthouse in Longview. The town was established by Haden Edwards, qv whose earlier colonization efforts had been beset by controversy (*see* FREDONIAN REBELLION) and whose colonization contract of 1825 had been canceled. Fredonia was located on land that Edwards acquired through a first-class headright. He filed the survey for the site on March 20, 1838. On November 14, 1839, he issued a broadside printed in Nacogdoches advertising the sale of lots in each of two new townsites on the Sabine. The planned towns were Fredonia, some sixty miles north of Nacogdoches, and Cotton-Plant, about forty miles from Fredonia. The territory, "lately occupied by the Northern Indians," was a tract that had been claimed by the Cherokees who first entered Texas in 1819–20 and who numbered about 800 in the early 1830s. The district was also inhabited by members of allied groups from the eastern United States and by two indigenous Caddo groups.

Borders of the district included the Old San Antonio Road qv to the south, the Sabine River to the north, and the Neches and Angelina rivers to the west and east. Despite repeated attempts, the Cherokees had never been able to establish a secure title to this land, and in the summer of 1839 the Indians living there had been driven out of Texas by President Mirabeau B. Lamar qv and others antagonistic to their presence (*see* CHEROKEE WAR). Fredonia was located very near the northeast corner of what had been the Cherokee claim.

Edwards received a patent for the league including the site of Fredonia on February 10, 1843. On July 7 he was issued a license to operate a ferry across the Sabine at Fredonia, at a spot then known as Cotton's Crossing. Travel to and from Fredonia was accomplished by roads north and south to Gilmer and Nacogdoches. The north road crossed the Shreveport-Tyler Road (Red Rock Road) near Pine Tree. It was a long time before a direct east-west route was established. One had to go either north or south before reaching a road going east and west. Later the Longview-Fredonia road, beginning in Longview as Fredonia Street, was cleared, as was the Wallings Ferry Road.

Very little documentary evidence of the town has been found. No plat of Fredonia can be found nor one showing the "2,000 lots" advertised in Edwards's 1839 broadside. Outlines of the town can be seen on early maps of the Edwards league. Deeds of record establish the existence of Fredonia, and at least fifty-five documents from 1851 to 1883 in the Rusk County Courthouse refer to the town of Fredonia. Deed Record Books B, C, D, and E of Rusk County were destroyed in a fire at Henderson in 1877.

River traffic to and from the Gulf of Mexico, especially from New Orleans, stopped at Fredonia. The first steamship to reach town was the *Buffalo* in 1848. At one time the Sabine was navigable for 300 miles, but travel was not regular or necessarily year-round; it was said to have been "informal." The steamboats had very shallow drafts, no more than eighteen inches; the boilers on the decks resulted in many fires and accidents. The boats often went aground in shallow water, and on these occasions they would either have to turn around and go back downstream or wait until upstream rains raised the river level. The captains always kept themselves informed as to the river conditions, though communications were poor. The boats were equipped with "snag-cutting" booms, winches, and other means with which to extricate themselves from riverbank and bottom troubles. An alternate route for river traffic was used when the Sabine was not navigable to Fredonia. Shipments could be sent up the Red River, through Caddo Lake to Port Caddo, the official port of entry to Texas in this area, then freighted by wagon to Fredonia. This, however, meant an overland trip of more than fifty miles.

By the 1850s Fredonia had developed into a thriving town. It had three warehouses, principally for cotton, forty to fifty buildings including houses, and a cemetery. A post office operated there from 1849 to 1855 and from 1856 to 1859. Waide and Wilson, an apparently successful general store, sold such commodities as combs of many types and fine champagne. Most of the inventory came up the Sabine from New Orleans. This firm, in all probability, was the first retail establishment in what is now Gregg County. Some financial difficulties must have developed; a New Orleans wholesale supplier complained about delays in Mr. Waide's remittances, which had not occurred in previous transactions.

Fredonia's advantage was that of having good transportation by means of a river. The location already had a well-known river crossing. This subsequently became known as Fredonia Crossing. In 1871 the Texas legislature granted the authority to operate the ferry to J. H. Jones and Henry Miller. In May 1884 the commissioners' court of Gregg County contracted for construction of the Fredonia Bridge, which was used for seventy-one years, until the completion of the present bridge in 1955 on the Old Longview–Kilgore Highway, Farm Road 2087. The Civil War and Reconstruction qqv hurt Fredonia as it did all of the South. In 1870 the town was not listed in the post office directory. After the Civil War, a new settlement named Fredonia, formed by freed blacks, grew up about two miles south of the original townsite. This community was still listed, without population statistics, in 1990.

BIBLIOGRAPHY: Mary Whatley Clarke, *Chief Bowles and the Texas Cherokees* (Norman: University of Oklahoma Press, 1971). Richard B. Levy, History of the Creation of Gregg County, Texas (MS, Genealogy Department, Longview Public Library, Longview, Texas). Eugene W. McWhorter, *Traditions of the Land: The History of Gregg County* (Longview, Texas: Gregg County Historical Foundation, 1989). Vertical Files, Barker Texas History Center, University of Texas at Austin (Haden Harrison Edwards). E. W. Winkler, "The Cherokee Indians in Texas," *Quarterly of the Texas State Historical Association* 7 (October 1903). Louis J. Wortham, *A History of Texas* (5 vols., Fort Worth: Wortham-Molyneaux, 1924).
Norman W. Black

FREDONIA, TEXAS (Mason County). Fredonia is just south of the junction of State Highway 71 and Farm Road 386, near the McCulloch–San Saba county line in northern Mason County. Nearby is the 200-foot-high granite formation known as Spy Rock. Early settlers began arriving in southwestern San Saba and northern Mason counties in the late 1850s. Among the earliest were Jack and Caroline Lathum and Chaney and Isabella Couch, who settled near Deer Creek with their families around 1858 or 1859. After the Civil War qv the population increased. An early school, called Hayes and Lathum School, was established, and in 1874 a church and school building were erected. That same year the community petitioned the county to rename the school Deer Creek School. To achieve this, it was necessary for the community to reorganize as a school community called Deer Creek and to provide a stone school building and other facilities. A school was erected and furnished in 1877 for approximately $800, and its name was legally changed in 1878.

The first post office in the area, named Deerton, was established in San Saba County in the home of William L. Hays on March 17, 1879, by his brother, Samuel Parker Hays, who was the first postmaster. William renamed the office Fredonia on June 8, 1880, as there was another Deerton in Texas. John C. Calhoun built one of the community's first stores, which later housed the post office, and became postmaster in 1882. He eventually moved the post office two miles across Lost Creek into Mason County, and the community thereafter became centered in that county.

This rural market community was a stage stop in the late 1880s. An early gristmill-gin was established by J. A. Williams and Sons, and the community once had a cooperative store run by the Grange.qv In addition, at one time the town had several churches, a general store, a drugstore, and a blacksmith shop. The community also had its own newspaper, the Fredonia *Kicker*, which was published by a man named Robertson in his home for a short time. The paper was absorbed by the *Mason County News* in 1910. Telephone service was established by 1914.

In the twentieth century Fredonia's economy gradually changed its emphasis from cotton farming to peanut farming, and numerous small landholdings were gradually consolidated into larger ones. The population peaked at an estimated 200 in the 1920s and dropped to 110 by the mid-1960s. It was 74 in 1968 and 50 in 1990. In the mid-1980s the town had a post office, a church, and a filling station.

BIBLIOGRAPHY: Kathryn Burford Eilers, A History of Mason County, Texas (M.A. thesis, University of Texas, 1939). Stella Gipson Polk, *Mason and Mason County: A History* (Austin: Pemberton Press, 1966; rev. ed., Burnet, Texas: Eakin Press, 1980).
Alice J. Rhoades

FREDONIAN REBELLION. The Fredonian Rebellion was a dispute between the Mexican government and the Edwards brothers, Haden and Benjamin.qqv Haden Edwards received his empresarial grant on April 14, 1825. It entitled him to settle as many as 800 families in a broad area around Nacogdoches in eastern Texas. Like all empresarios he was to uphold land grants certified by the Spanish and Mexican governments, provide an organization for the protection of all colonists in the area, and receive a land commissioner appointed by the Mexican government. He arrived in Nacogdoches on September 25, 1825, and posted notices on street corners to all previous landowners that they would have to present evidence of their claims or forfeit to new settlers. This naturally offended the older settlers.

Edwards's grant was located in a difficult part of the country. To the east was the Neutral Ground,qv inhabited mostly by fugitives; to the north and west were Indians; to the south was Austin's colony; and in Nacogdoches itself were the remnants of previous filibuster expeditions that had failed. The number of grants actually in question was probably very low. According to General Land Officeqv records, thirty-two had been made before 1825. Furthermore, in only one case was someone's land actually sold to someone else. But Edwards's behavior was threatening and served to polarize the old inhabitants against the new.

An election for alcaldeqv in December provided the occasion for the factions to express their opposition. Samuel Norrisqv was the candidate for the old settlers, and Chichester Chaplin,qv Edwards's son-in-law, was supported by the new. After the voting Edwards certified Chaplin's election to political chief José Antonio Saucedoqv in San Antonio. Norris's supporters challenged his claim and charged that the voters in Chaplin's support had come from unqualified voters. Saucedo reversed the election in March 1826 and ordered archives and duties to be surrendered to Norris. The controversy did not settle down, and by the time the news reached Saltillo and federal authorities in Mexico, Edwards appeared to be unwilling to abide by their terms, so in mid-year 1826 the grant was declared forfeit. Edwards was outraged, and he found support in the settlers he had brought.

On November 22, 1826, Martin Parmer, John S. Roberts,qqv and Burrell J. Thompson led a group of thirty-six men from the Ayish Bayou to Nacogdoches, where they seized Norris, Haden Edwards, José Antonio Sepulveda, and others and tried them for oppression and corruption in office. Haden was released, and in fact his inclusion in the group may have been to cover up his participation in the attack. The others were tried, convicted, and told they deserved to die but would be released if they relinquished their offices. Parmer turned the enforcement of the verdict over to Joseph Durstqv and proclaimed him alcalde.

As soon as Mexican authorities heard of the incident, Lt. Col. Mateo Ahumada, principal military commander in Texas, was ordered to the area. He left San Antonio on December 11 with twenty dragoons and 110 infantrymen. It was clear to Haden Edwards that his only chance to make good the time and estimated $50,000 he had already expended on his colony was to separate from Mexico. He and Parmer began preparations to meet the Mexican force in the name of an independent republic they called Fredonia. Since they planned to include the Cherokees in their move for independence, the flag they designed had two parallel bars, red and white, symbolizing Indian and white. In fact, although a treaty was signed with the Indian leaders, Richard Fields and John Dunn Hunter,[qqv] that support never materialized. The flag was inscribed "Independence, Liberty, Justice." The rebels signed it and flew it over the Old Stone Fort.[qv] Their Declaration of Independence was signed on December 21, 1826.

Haden Edwards designated his brother Benjamin commander in chief and appealed to the United States for help. Ahumada enlisted Stephen F. Austin,[qv] who sided with the government, and Peter Ellis Bean,[qv] the Mexican Indian agent, headed for Nacogdoches. When the Mexican officers and militia and members of Austin's colony reached Nacogdoches on January 31, 1827, the revolutionists fled and crossed the Sabine River. The Indians killed Hunter and Fields for involving them in the venture.

BIBLIOGRAPHY: Jordan Holt, The Edwards Empresarial Grant and the Fredonia Rebellion (M.A. thesis, Stephen F. Austin State University, 1977). Archie P. McDonald, comp., Nacogdoches: Wilderness Outpost to Modern City, 1779–1979 (photocopy, Barker Texas History Center, University of Texas at Austin). C. F. Sheley, "Whence Came the Name Fredonia?": The Bicentennial Commemorative History of Nacogdoches (Nacogdoches Jaycees, 1976).

Archie P. McDonald

FRED YARBROUGH SITE. The Fred Yarbrough Site, in east central Van Zandt County, is located four miles northeast of Grand Saline in an area of rolling plains spotted with growths of hardwood trees. The site consists of two unconnected parts. Area A is a low knoll some fifty yards south of the Sabine River with stone artifacts on and in it, and Area B is a circular place in a plowed field with many prehistoric earthenware shards, 300 yards to the south of the knoll. Both areas were completely excavated by the Work Projects Administration[qv] from April through September of 1940. In the middle 1940s Alex D. Krieger examined the collection of artifacts, and in 1962 LeRoy Johnson, Jr., analyzed the specimens and published a lengthy study. Because the site had several stratified prehistoric Indian occupations, it became the key prehistoric pottery site of East Texas.

The knoll, Area A, is a natural rise ten feet above the Sabine floodplain capped with a zone of sandy soil three feet deep containing chipped-stone debris. In Area A several periods of occupation were mixed together, although there was also some stratigraphic separation. The earliest period, Paleo-Indian, is represented by a few lance-shaped flint and quartzite spear points of the Clovis, San Patrice, Meserve, and other types. Occupation from around 7000 B.C. by early Archaic Age people is evidenced by quartzite gouges or adzes, rounded and grooved net weights, and slightly barbed spear points of the Yantis type or other types.

Later Archaic Age people were at the site from 6000 to 2500 B.C. and left spear points with long rectangular tangs, among which the Morrill and Wells points were common, as well as sandstone grinding slabs and hand-held milling stones. The Yarbrough Site is the key representative of the early La Harpe Culture, which existed from 3000 or 2000 B.C. to the time of Christ. The sandy pottery, Gary points, and spear points with pointed tangs characteristic of late La Harpe Culture are also found at Area A. Finally, a few potsherds of still later pottery makers, dating to A.D. 1300 or 1400, were found on the knoll.

In the knoll was fair separation by depth of the early La Harpe spear points, which were most common in lower levels; the late La Harpe points, which dominated higher levels; and the potsherds, which were higher yet. The pre–La Harpe periods were recognized by resemblance of specific artifacts to related, well-dated specimens from other archeological sites. At the end of Archaic times, Area A was also used as a small cemetery.

Area B may have been a house site. The spot producing potsherds was about twenty feet in diameter and represents a much later group of people, whose cultural remains are called the Sanders Focus. The inhabitants practiced corn agriculture and were potters who made beakers, cups, large flat bowls, and deep bowls with shoulders below the rim. Deer ulnas made into punches or awls were almost the only other artifacts found in Area B besides the pottery, which may date to A.D. 800–1000. By this time the Indian population of the region had probably reached its peak. A few potsherds of even later pottery makers, dating to A.D. 1300 or 1400, were found on the knoll, Area A. The potters of both areas A and B were ancestors of the Caddo Indians who lived in East Texas in historic times directly east of what is now Van Zandt County. The artifacts and records of the Yarbrough Site are now housed at the Texas Archeological Research Laboratory of the University of Texas at Austin.

BIBLIOGRAPHY: LeRoy Johnson, Jr., The Yarbrough and Miller Sites of Northeastern Texas, with a Preliminary Definition of the La Harpe Aspect," *Bulletin of the Texas Archeological Society* 32 (1962). Alex D. Krieger, *Culture Complexes and Chronology in Northern Texas, with Extension of Puebloan Datings to the Mississippi Valley* (University of Texas Publication 4640 [Austin, 1946]). Dee Ann Suhm et al., "An Introductory Handbook of Texas Archeology," *Bulletin of the Texas Archeological Society* 25 (1954).

LeRoy Johnson, Jr.

FREE, TEXAS. Free was on Independence Canyon in northwestern Terrell County. It began in 1900, before Terrell County was created from Pecos County, as a post office and trading point for local ranchers. The first post office was on the Mansfield ranch in the Tarver home; Paul Tarver drove the mail hack twice a week. The post office was later moved to the Wakefield home and eventually to the Edwards Ranch, where Frank Edwards was postmaster. Edwards also ran a small store for those who came for their mail. After automobiles came into use between 1910 and 1920, local ranchers drove into larger towns for supplies and mail, and the post office at Free was no longer needed. It closed in 1921, and the small community, which was named for the surrounding open landscape, was soon abandoned.

BIBLIOGRAPHY: Terrell County Heritage Commission, *Terrell County, Texas* (San Angelo: Anchor, 1978). *Julia Cauble Smith*

FREE BLACKS. Free blacks in Texas experienced freedom under four different governments—those of Spain, Mexico, the Republic of Texas,[qv] and Texas as the twenty-eighth state of the Union. Free blacks were never a large population in Texas; in the 1860 census they numbered less than 400, but may have been twice that many. Free blacks, nevertheless, made a significant contribution to the early history of Texas. Blacks often accompanied Spanish expeditions to the Texas area. It was not uncommon for succeeding expeditions to find people of African and mixed ancestry living within Indian communities. In permanent settlements established in Texas by the Spanish, blacks and persons of mixed ancestry constituted a large segment of the outposts. As of 1792 the black and mulatto population constituted 15 percent of the 2,992 people living in Spanish Texas.[qv] Within the Spanish empire, the legal status of free blacks resembled that of the Indian population. The law required free blacks to pay tribute, forbade them to carry firearms, and restricted their freedom of movement. In practice Spanish officials ignored such restrictions, often encouraging the manumission of slaves. The small number of Spanish subjects in Texas and the vast distances between settlements also brought about the intermarriage of whites, blacks, and Indians. While most free blacks in Texas before 1800 were born there, thereafter an increased emigration to Texas of free blacks and some escaped slaves from the southern United States began to take place. After the Mexican War of Independence[qv] (1821), the Mexican government offered free blacks full rights of citizenship, allowing land ownership and other privileges. Mexico accepted free blacks as equals to white colonists. Favorable conditions for free blacks in Texas in the 1830s led one noted abolitionist, Benjamin Lundy,^{qv} to seek authorization for the establishment of a black colony from the United States. While the Mexican government expressed interest in the idea, opposition from whites in Texas and the United States precluded its implementation. Free blacks, as did other frontiersmen, continued to emigrate to Texas seeking an opportunity for advancement and a better life. One such free black was William Goyens,^{qv} who migrated to Texas from North Carolina in the early 1820s and later became a prominent blacksmith near Nacogdoches. From 1835 to 1838 Goyens would act as an interpreter for Sam Houston^{qv} with the East Texas^{qv} Indians.

Numerous free blacks fought for Texas independence—some fearing Anglo retribution if they did not serve, and others sharing Anglo beliefs about the Mexican government. Free black Samuel McCulloch, Jr.,^{qv} appears to have been the first casualty of the Texas Revolution,^{qv} receiving a shoulder wound when the Texans captured the Mexican fort at Goliad in October 1835. Hendrick Arnold^{qv} served with Erastus (Deaf) Smith^{qv} at the capture of San Antonio and later in the battle of San Jacinto.^{qv} Wyly Martin's^{qv} slave Peter gained his freedom after he voluntarily carried military supplies with his own wagon. Several landed free black families contributed money and supplies to the cause. Even with these and many other sacrifices, free blacks in Texas saw many fundamental changes in their lives after the revolution. While the Mexican government treated free blacks as equal citizens and began to pursue the abolition^{qv} of slavery,^{qv} the Republic of Texas sought to restrict the freedoms they already enjoyed and strengthened the institution of slavery. The Constitution of the Republic of Texas^{qv} designated people of one-eighth African blood as a separate and distinct group, took away citizenship, sought to restrict property rights, and forbade the permanent residence of free blacks without the approval of the Congress of the Republic of Texas.^{qv} Interracial marriages were also legally prohibited. Ironically, local communities and legislators that favored the new provisions often did not want them enforced within their districts. Documents show that prominent whites were known to intercede on behalf of free blacks in danger of being prosecuted by the new regulations. A stricter law passed in 1840, which gave free blacks two years to leave Texas or risk being sold into slavery, was effectively postponed by President Sam Houston. Throughout the 1840s and 1850s manumitted slaves who remained in Texas without seeking legal sanction from the legislature formed a third category of blacks in Texas—those who were neither free nor enslaved. After annexation,^{qv} the legislature passed stricter laws governing the lives of free blacks. These new laws called for harsh punishments usually reserved only for slaves, including branding, whipping, and forced labor on public works. In 1858 the legislature even passed a law that encouraged free blacks to reenter slavery voluntarily by allowing them to choose their own masters. The increased restrictions and the rise in white hostility resulted in a virtual halt to additional free black immigration to Texas and may have caused a reduction in the Texas population of free blacks. The United States census reported 397 free blacks in Texas in 1850 and 355 in 1860, though there may have been an equal number of free blacks not counted.

BIBLIOGRAPHY: Alwyn Barr, *Black Texans: A History of Negroes in Texas, 1528–1971* (Austin: Jenkins, 1973). Randolph B. Campbell, *An Empire for Slavery: The Peculiar Institution in Texas, 1821–1865* (Baton Rouge: Louisiana State University Press, 1989). Lyle N. McAlister, *Spain and Portugal in the New World, 1492–1700* (Minneapolis: University of Minnesota, 1984). Harold Schoen, "The Free Negro in the Republic of Texas," *Southwestern Historical Quarterly* 39–41 (April 1936–July 1937).

Douglas Hales

FREED, FRANK (1906–1975). Frank Freed, painter, was born in San Antonio, Texas, on February 6, 1906, to Louis and Fannie (Goodman) Freed. In 1913 his family moved to Houston, where Freed drew cartoons for his high school yearbook and the Rice *Owl*, the campus humor magazine, during a year of study at Rice University. From 1924 to 1927 he attended Harvard University, where he received a B.S. in English literature. After graduation he published several articles and began a forty-two-year career as a life-insurance salesman. He enlisted in the United States Army in 1943 and from 1944 to 1946 served in Normandy with the United States Corps of Engineers. He visited museums and exhibitions in Brussels and Paris. At the Museum of Modern Art in New York City he was impressed by a retrospective of the social realist painter Ben Shahn. In 1948 Freed began to paint; his earliest paintings, such as the jubilant *Liberation of Paris* (1948), were based on the war.

Although he studied briefly with Robert Preusser, he quickly developed an idiosyncratic style that changed little over the years. Certain qualities in his art, such as his reliance on outlining, attention to detail, flat compositions, anatomical irregularities, and use of bright colors, have led critics to categorize him as a "naive" painter. He used cartoon-like, simplified forms and a dry humor to satirize the modern world in works such as *Urban Landscape* (1973), a canvas filled with labyrinthine highways choked with cars, and *Climate of Opinion* (1970), in which people peering around and above a maze of walls and partially opened doors depict paranoia. *Cocktail Party* (1970) is filled with gesturing, exclaiming people, none of whom seems to hear anyone else. In other works he focused on a single person, generally expressing a contemplative or melancholy mood; in the ink drawing *Bar Fly*, for example, the dejection of a woman seated at a bar is captured by the single line that traces the shape of her back. Freed also focused on some historic events. Between 1965 and 1969 he represented student protests against the Vietnam War in *Confrontation*, and in *Auschwitz*, a group of inmates walking towards a distant funnel of smoke is dwarfed by the ominous silhouettes of a helmeted soldier and spotlights in the foreground.

Freed's work elicited interest from critics soon after he began to paint. He was included in two group shows in Houston galleries in 1949 and participated in annual group shows of Houston artists sponsored by the Museum of Fine Arts^{qv} in 1950–52 and 1958–59. He also participated in group shows sponsored by the Contemporary Arts Museum^{qv} in Houston in 1953, 1956, and 1964. In 1956 the Alley Theatre^{qv} in Houston hosted his first solo exhibition; his work was featured in shows at the Carol Lane Gallery (1969), at the Meredith Long Galleries (1972), and at the Fiftieth Anniversary of the Alliance Française of Houston, in the Shamrock Hilton (1973). Freed participated in many of the Dimension/Houston group shows sponsored by the Art League of Houston. His work was exhibited throughout Texas: at the Dallas Museum of Art^{qv} (1966–67), the Junior Service League invitational show in Longview (1966–69), the El Paso Museum of Art^{qv} (1968–69), and the Laguna Gloria Art Museum^{qv} in Austin (1968–69). He received national attention in exhibitions at the National Academy of Design, New York (1951); the Fogg Museum, Cambridge, Massachusetts (1952); the New Orleans Museum of Art (1967); and the Butler Institute of American Art, Youngstown, Ohio (1968, 1973). Ten of his paintings were exhibited in the Kyoto Municipal Museum in Japan (1966). Among the more significant exhibitions of his work was a 1970 solo show in Mexico City, where Mexicans accustomed to an art of social protest responded to his vision of the "American Scene distorted by the . . . social and political chaos which prevails everywhere today."

In an article on his art Freed categorized a naive painter as "one who expects to make a living at it." He stressed that he was mainly interested in conveying ideas and noted a sense of kinship with Pieter Brueghel, William Hogarth, Honoré Daumier, Ben Shahn, and Edward Hopper, all of whom used art to comment upon or respond to their respective societies. He was aware of the abstract and minimalist styles practiced by his contemporaries, but preferred his own style of simplified realism to communicate ideas.

In 1950 Freed married Eleanor Kempner, who later became an art critic for the Houston Post.qv They had no children. Their travels in the United States, Europe, Mexico, and Israel provided additional material for Freed's art. He was a member of the Congregation Emanu Elqv and served as president of the Houston chapters of the American Jewish committee and the American Association of United Nations. He was diagnosed as having cancer in 1973, but he taped several interviews and continued to paint between cycles of treatment. He died on December 23, 1975. His work has been included in several exhibitions since his death, and in 1983 the Contemporary Arts Museum in Houston commemorated his work in the exhibition Frank Freed: People and Places. Freed's work is represented in the collections of the Museum of Fine Art, Houston; the Marion Koogler McNay Art Museumqv in San Antonio; the Harry Ransom Humanities Research Centerqv at the University of Texas, Austin; and the Israel Museum in Jerusalem.

BIBLIOGRAPHY: Eleanor Freed, "Frank Freed's Visual Reflections on the Human Comedy," *University of Houston Forum* 2 (Spring 1973). Frank Freed, "Artist on Art," *Southwest Art Gallery Magazine*, March 1972. Houston *Post*, December 24, 1975. Cecilia Steinfeldt, *Texas Folk Art: One Hundred Fifty Years of the Southwestern Tradition* (Austin: Texas Monthly Press, 1981).

Kendall Curlee

FREEDMEN'S BUREAU. The Bureau of Refugees, Freedmen, and Abandoned Lands, commonly known as the Freedmen's Bureau, was established by Congress in March 1865 as a branch of the United States Army. It was to be a temporary agency. Its functions were to provide relief to the thousands of refugees, black and white, who had been left homeless by the Civil War;qv to supervise affairs related to newly freed slaves in the southern states; and to administer all land abandoned by Confederates or confiscated from them during the war. Since the profits from administering the lands were to provide funds for the operation of the bureau, the bill establishing the agency did not appropriate money for it. President Andrew Johnson, however, returned most of the confiscated property to its owners, and Congress was forced to appropriate funds for the bureau's operations after the first year. Gen. Oliver Otis Howard was commissioner of the bureau throughout its existence. Under Howard was an extensive hierarchy of assistants and subassistants. Officers working with the bureau at the state level were headed by an assistant commissioner and included a superintendent of education, a traveling inspector, and, during the early months of the bureau's activities, a surgeon-in-chief.

The Freedmen's Bureau operated in Texas from late September 1865 until July 1870. During that time five men served as assistant commissioner: Edgar M. Gregory,qv from September 1865 until May 14, 1866; Joseph Kiddoo,qv until January 14, 1867; Charles Griffin,qv until his death on September 15, 1867; Joseph J. Reynolds,qv until January 1869; and Edward R. S. Canby,qv briefly, until he was replaced by Reynolds. In the beginning, at least, Howard regarded Texas as his most difficult sphere of operations. Much later in his Autobiography he recalled that the job of assistant commissioner for Texas, to which he was appointing Gregory, "seemed at the time . . . to be the post of greatest peril."

The men who served as assistant commissioners in Texas were convinced that the two keys to providing long-term protection for freedmen and promoting peace and goodwill were the establishment of a free agricultural labor system and the founding of good schools for the freedmen. They reasoned that once the planters realized that fair treatment and pay would motivate blacks to work, then planters would offer those incentives, and freedmen would willingly work hard in their own best interest. Education would provide blacks with the tools they needed to function effectively in a literate society. Although the five commissioners shared to some extent the racial views prevalent among most contemporary Americans, they insisted that the courts accord blacks the same legal rights that whites enjoyed. When, for example, a subassistant commissioner aided local authorities in disarming blacks who were in town, Kiddoo ordered the agent to return the weapons unless the law also disarmed whites.

For implementation of their objectives the assistant commissioners relied on the subassistant commissioners, who operated on the local level. The nature of their responsibilities made these local authorities powerful, at least theoretically. They were to monitor all legal cases involving blacks and take control of the legal process if necessary to ensure justice to them. They were to supervise all labor contracts and void those that were signed by freedmen under duress or were patently unfair to the black laborer. They were to do their utmost to protect black lives and property and to aid in the apprehension of those who committed crimes against freedmen. They were to aid blacks in organizing schools and ensure the safety of their teachers. They toured their respective districts urging freedmen to work hard and fulfill their contracts. Agents also tried to help blacks to find relatives from whom they had been separated while slaves. Although not always successful, the bureau provided a network through which information about missing relatives could be circulated throughout the South.

From the beginning, the effort to build a truly effective organization in Texas was defeated by the size of the state, its poor transportation and communication facilities, and the hostility of most white Texans to the bureau's efforts. The bureau had only limited resources at its disposal. Between September 1865 and May 1866, when he was relieved, Gregory placed subassistant commissioners in stations across East Texas. By May 1, 1866, he had established branches of the bureau in thirty counties, staffed by thirty-one subassistant commissioners. Kiddoo petitioned Howard for more military officers, but he was not successful in enlarging the bureau's operations. The number of subassistant commissioners varied from a high of thirty-four to a low of twenty-seven during his tenure. When Griffin took over in January 1867 the positions of assistant commissioner and commander of troops were combined, and thus he had greater control over the assignment of soldiers to bureau posts. By April 1867 Griffin had forty-nine agents in the field. At its largest, the bureau had fifty-nine subassistants and ten assistant subassistant commissioners. Each of the fifty-nine agents was responsible for a clearly defined district.

Though the increased number of agents did increase the amount of supervision bureau agents could provide on the local level, the number was still quite inadequate. In the first place, Griffin had ordered that every commander of troops in an area where no bureau existed act as an agent of the bureau. Therefore, some of the men officially designated as subassistant commissioners were stationed at places such as Fort Inge, Camp Verde, and Fort Belknap, where there were few or no freedmen. Second, the size and shape of the districts were determined by the ability of the bureau to provide protection to the agents rather than by the ability of the agents to fulfill their duties in their districts. Matthew Young, stationed at Belton in August 1867, for example, was responsible only for Bell County. Lt. Adam G. Malloy, on the other hand, stationed the same month at Marshall, was responsible for Harrison, Marion, Panola, Rusk, Davis, and Upshur counties.

The bureau could draw subassistant commissioners from three sources: the army, Northern citizens, and Texans. Of these three the assistant commissioners clearly preferred army officers. Army officers received army pay while serving with the bureau; they had training, experience, and credentials that the assistant commissioners, as army officers themselves, were familiar with; and, as Kiddoo put it, army officers were "amenable to the Articles of War and military discipline." The problem that the assistant commissioners faced was finding enough officers willing to serve as agents. Gregory lamented that "but few . . . manifest that interest in the advancement of the freedmen that they should." The use of civilians presented problems for the assistant commissioners, particularly before 1867, when the bureau had neither funds nor authority to pay them. Civilians who served before 1867 did so on a voluntary basis. Even afterward, assistant commissioners hesitated to use civilians because they had less control over them. Of the civilians willing to serve in the bureau, assistant commissioners were most suspicious of former Texans, who were assumed to have no sympathy for the freedmen. Nonetheless, there were always at least a few civilians employed, and at the height of the bureau's activities, from April 1867 through December 1868, about half the agents were civilians. A few Texans were generally serving at any given time in the bureau's history.

Because the Freedmen's Bureau was an agency of the United States Army white Texans generally viewed it as an extension of the army of occupation imposed on them by the victorious North, as further evidence of the Northern desire for revenge. Not only that, but the bureau's objectives envisioned a role for blacks in Texas society that whites had steadfastly maintained they were incapable of filling. Under such conditions, when a bureau officer made a mistake, it glared. Through a system of traveling inspectors, the assistant commissioners endeavored to prevent problems, but they were not totally successful. Although the vast majority of subassistant commissioners appear to have been competent and dedicated individuals, a few were clearly incompetent, and some were little more than criminals. There were enough of these latter types to prove to Texans what they already wanted to believe. To make the situation worse, the military generally would not allow bureau officers to be tried locally. Cases involving misdeeds by bureau agents were investigated and tried by the military.

The role of local agents in Texas was enlarged considerably after the passage of the Reconstruction qv acts in March 1867. As the military took charge of politically reconstructing the state, they often relied on local bureau agents for information and advice. This process began on March 30, 1867, when Griffin ordered bureau agents to supply him reports of the population of their counties, convenient polling places ("as few as possible"), and the names of "undoubted union men (white and black)" who could serve as voter registrars and election judges. Later that year, when the removal of county officials as "impediments to Reconstruction" began, local agents often supplied the proof of the officials' wrongdoing. Agents were also called on to recommend replacement officials and to investigate the suitability of candidates whose names had been suggested by others. Agents were now charged with the responsibility of seeing that blacks' right to register and vote was not impeded. In 1866 Texans had refused to ratify the thirteenth and fourteenth amendments to the United States Constitution, had passed a series of "black codes" qv restricting the freedom of former slaves, and had refused to allow blacks even limited political participation. It seemed obvious, therefore, that in a free election the majority of blacks would vote for the Republican, the Northern, party. For most white Texans then, the agents were not only guilty of trying to force black political equality on the south, but also of trying to turn the machinery of state government over to a despised political party.

After the expansion of the bureau staff, many agents were forced to operate with little or no military support. In some areas, the results were violent. Two agents were killed on duty and a third was killed en route to his post. At least three others were shot and wounded, two more escaped attempted assassinations without serious injury, and two others, finding themselves surrounded by a hostile populace and threatened with death, ran. These problems were compounded by the yellow fever epidemic in the late summer and early fall of 1867. The fever forced several local offices to close and caused the death of General Griffin and four of his subassistant commissioners. In December 1868 the bureau halted all but its educational efforts in Texas, and the local offices were closed.

Evaluations of the bureau are fraught with controversy. Earlier accounts, generally based on documents of contemporary white Texans, portray the bureau negatively. More recent accounts have revised the picture somewhat. But on any account the bureau failed to achieve its long-term objectives. Shortly after Reconstruction ended, black political participation was effectively limited, and segregation became entrenched by custom and law. Still, while it was operating the bureau probably provided positive benefits to blacks. At least many blacks clearly believed that it did, for hundreds monthly turned to the agency for protection, advice, or help in finding lost relatives.

The bureau was most successful in its educational effort. At the end of 1865, sixteen schools were serving just over 1,000 black pupils. By July of 1870, the last month of the bureau's activities, 150 schools enrolled 9,086 black students. As in other areas of their work, the bureau had faced fierce and determined opposition on the part of some white Texans, who burned school buildings, harassed teachers, and otherwise obstructed progress. Gradually, however, the opposition declined. In his last report, the superintendent of the Texas schools reported that "The burning of school houses and maltreatment of teachers so common at the commencement of the Bureau operations, have almost entirely ceased." Even historians generally critical of the Freedmen's Bureau have conceded that the education of blacks in Texas would not have been possible so soon without its efforts. *See also* AFRICAN AMERICANS *and* SLAVERY.

BIBLIOGRAPHY: Ira Christopher Colby, The Freedmen's Bureau in Texas and Its Impact on the Emerging Social Welfare System and Black-White Social Relations, 1865–1885 (D.S.W. dissertation, University of Pennsylvania, 1984). Barry A. Crouch, *The Freedmen's Bureau and Black Texans* (Austin: University of Texas Press, 1992). Barry A. Crouch, "The Freedmen's Bureau and the Thirtieth Sub-District in Texas: Smith County and Its Environs during Reconstruction," *Chronicles of Smith County,* Spring 1972. Barry A. Crouch and Larry Madaras, "Reconstructing Black Families: Perspectives from the Texas Freedmen's Bureau Records," *Prologue* 18 (Summer 1986). Barry A. Crouch, "View from Within: Letters of Gregory Barrett, Freedmen's Bureau Agent," *Chronicles of Smith County,* Winter 1973. Ross Nathaniel Dudney, Texas Reconstruction: The Role of the Bureau of Refugees, Freedmen and Abandoned Lands, 1865–1870, Smith County, (Tyler) Texas (M.S. thesis, Texas A&I University, 1986). Claude Elliott, "The Freedmen's Bureau in Texas," *Southwestern Historical Quarterly* 56 (July 1952). Alton Hornsby, Jr., "The Freedmen's Bureau Schools in Texas, 1865–1870," *Southwestern Historical Quarterly* 76 (April 1963). Nora Estelle Owens, Presidential Reconstruction in Texas: A Case Study (Ph.D. dissertation, Auburn University, 1983). Charles W. Ramsdell, *Reconstruction in Texas* (New York: Columbia University Press, 1910; rpt., Austin: Texas State Historical Association, 1970). William L. Richter, *The Army in Texas during Reconstruction, 1865–1870* (College Station: Texas A&M University Press, 1987). Robert W. Shook, Federal Occupation and Administration of Texas, 1865–1870 (Ph.D. dissertation, North Texas State University, 1970). James Smallwood, "Black Education in Reconstruction Texas: The Contributions of the Freedmen's Bureau and Benevolent Societies," *East Texas Historical Journal* 19 (Spring 1981). James Smallwood, "Charles E. Culver, a Reconstruction Agent in Texas," *Civil War History* 27 (December 1981). James Smallwood, "The Freedmen's Bureau Reconsidered," *Texana* 11 (Fall 1973). James Smallwood, *Time of Hope, Time of Despair: Black Texans during Reconstruction* (London: Kennikat, 1981). Esther Lane Thompson, The Influence of the Freedmen's Bureau on the Education of the Negro in Texas (M.A. thesis, Texas Southern University, 1956).
Cecil Harper, Jr.

FREELAND, TEXAS. Freeland was thirteen miles southwest of Cleburne in southwestern Johnson County. It was established by and named for George Freeland, a county pioneer. The settlement, which served as a school community for area ranch families, was founded around 1880. That year a local post office opened. By 1890 Freeland's population had risen to fifty, and community life centered around the local Baptist church. The railroads bypassed Freeland during the 1880s. In the 1904–05 school year Freeland's school had one teacher and fifty-six students. The community's post office closed in 1911, and by 1925 Freeland had ceased to exist.

BIBLIOGRAPHY: Viola Block, *History of Johnson County and Surrounding Areas* (Waco: Texian Press, 1970). Johnson County History Book Committee, *History of Johnson County, Texas* (Dallas: Curtis Media, 1985).

Brian Hart

FREEMAN, GEORGE R. (1830–1910). George R. Freeman, Confederate officer and lawyer, son of Dandridge Claiborne and Martha (Fox) Freeman, was born on June 25, 1830, near Frankfort, Kentucky. He may have attended Georgetown College in Kentucky before joining his grandfather in Texas in the 1840s. During the Civil War qv he served as captain of Company D, Twenty-third Texas Cavalry. On June 11, 1865, he was captain of the Treasury Guards, a group of about thirty former Confederate soldiers, who on the night of June 11, 1865, saved the state treasury some $30,000 when it was attacked by a band of robbers called "Missouri roughs." About 1875 Freeman moved to Hamilton, where he practiced law and became a landowner. With income from his Austin and Hamilton property he endowed a Bible chair at Baylor University. He died on December 14, 1910, and was buried at Hamilton. His body was reinterred at Oakwood Cemetery, Austin, about 1915. His correspondence and legal documents are collected in the Barker Texas History Center,qv University of Texas at Austin.

BIBLIOGRAPHY: George R. Freeman Papers, Barker Texas History Center, University of Texas at Austin. Adam R. Johnson, *The Partisan Rangers of the Confederate Army*, ed. William J. Davis (Louisville: George G. Fetter, 1904).

W. A. Flachmeier

FREEMAN, JACOB E. (ca.1841–?). Jacob E. Freeman, who represented Waller, Fort Bend, and Wharton counties in the Fourteenth and Sixteenth legislatures, was born a slave in Alabama around 1841. He arrived in Texas at the age of eleven and apparently assisted his master in the Confederate Army during the Civil War.qv Freeman was a mechanic in the Hempstead area by 1873, when he served on the Waller County grand jury. In July 1873 he participated in the Colored Men's Convention at Brenham, which sought to enhance the status of African Americansqv in Texas politics. He won election to the Texas House of Representatives for the Fourteenth Legislature, 1874, and served on the Penitentiary Committee. He was elected to the Sixteenth Legislature in 1879. He ran unsuccessfully for the legislature as a People's party candidate in 1886. Although he was a member of the Republican party,qv Freeman campaigned for a Greenback partyqv candidate for governor in 1878 and for a Democratic gubernatorial candidate in 1892. At the time of the Fourteenth Legislature Freeman was married.

BIBLIOGRAPHY: J. Mason Brewer, *Negro Legislators of Texas and Their Descendants* (Dallas: Mathis, 1935; 2d ed., Austin: Jenkins, 1970). Merline Pitre, *Through Many Dangers, Toils and Snares: The Black Leadership of Texas, 1868–1900* (Austin: Eakin, 1985). Lawrence D. Rice, *The Negro in Texas, 1874–1900* (Baton Rouge: Louisiana State University Press, 1971). Frank M. Spindler, "Concerning Hempstead and Waller County," *Southwestern Historical Quarterly* 59 (April 1956).

Paul M. Lucko

FREEMAN, JOHN HENRY (1886–1980). John Henry Freeman, attorney, the son of James D. and Rose (Phelps) Freeman, was born on October 23, 1886, in San Antonio, Texas, and grew up in Houston's Fifth Ward,qv where his father was shop foreman for the Southern Pacific. He went to public schools in Houston and worked five years for a title company before graduating from the University of Chicago Law School, which he attended from 1908 to 1910. He then returned to Houston, resumed title-office work, and secured a law license in 1913. Freeman practiced law from 1916 through 1923 with the firm of Campbell, Meyers, and Freeman before becoming a partner in Fulbright, Crooker, and Freeman on January 1, 1924. As Fulbright and Jaworski (*see* FULBRIGHT, RUFUS CLARENCE *and* JAWORSKI, LEON), the firm developed into one of the nation's largest law partnerships. Freeman's contribution to the firm was primarily in banking, real estate, and corporate practice. In addition he was Houston city attorney in 1928–29, president of the Houston Bar Association in 1933, a member of the board of directors of the First City National Bank of Houston, and general counsel for the cotton firm of Anderson, Clayton and Company, whose partners included Monroe D. Andersonqv and his brother, Frank.

In 1936 Freeman prepared the legal documents establishing the M. D. Anderson Foundation,qv and along with his law partner William B. Batesqv joined Monroe Anderson as an original trustee of the foundation. Anderson died in 1939, leaving the foundation, with assets worth over $19 million, the first of Houston's large general-purpose foundations. In 1942 Freeman, Bates, and new trustee Horace M. Wilkins contributed foundation funds to the University of Texas cancer hospital in Houston. This was the start of the Texas Medical Center,qv which the Anderson Foundation has continued to support ever since. Freeman remained one of the trustees of the foundation until his death. He also administered the $500,000 Max Krost Charitable Trust, established in 1946, which made contributions to the Shriners Hospital for Crippled Children and the University of Houston Law School before the school was terminated and its assets given to Texas Lutheran College in 1978. Freeman was a Democrat, a member of Holland Masonic Lodge, and an Episcopalian. He married Edna Stewart on December 5, 1912, and they had two children. Freeman died in Houston on July 13, 1980, and was buried in Glenwood Cemetery, Houston.

BIBLIOGRAPHY: N. Don Macon, *Mr. John H. Freeman and Friends: A Story of the Texas Medical Center and How It Began* (Houston: Texas Medical Center, 1973).

Newton Gresham and James A. Tinsley

FREEMAN, TEXAS. Freeman was a post office community sixteen miles southwest of Carthage in southwestern Panola County. In 1888 a post office opened there, with Joseph W. Freeman as postmaster. In the early 1890s the settlement had a general store and a number of scattered houses. Its post office closed in 1892, and mail for the community was sent to Caledonia. By the mid-1930s Freeman was no longer shown on county highway maps.

BIBLIOGRAPHY: John Barnette Sanders, *Postoffices and Post Masters of Panola County, Texas, 1845–1930* (Center, Texas, 1964).

Christopher Long

FREEMASONRY. The Masonic fraternity, brought to the American colonies in the mid-eighteenth century, was well established in all of the United States by 1820. Among the first Americans to migrate to Texas in the 1820s were a number of Masons, including Stephen F. Austin.qv Austin attempted to organize a Masonic lodge in 1828, when he and six other Masons met at San Felipe and petitioned the Grand York Lodge of Mexico for a charter dispensation. The petition evidently reached Mexico at the height of a quarrel between the "Yorkinos" and "Escoceses" (adherents of the Scottish Rite) and disappeared. A more successful effort occurred in the spring of 1835 when Dr. Anson Jonesqv and five others, fearing Mexican reprisals, met secretly under the Masonic Oak near Brazoria and petitioned the Grand Lodge of Louisiana for a charter. The grand master of that state, John Henry Holland,qv issued the dispensation, and Holland Lodge No. 36 met for the first time on December 27, 1835, with Jones presiding as worshipful master. The Holland Lodge struggled for several months until overwhelmed during the Texas Revolutionqv by the Mexican army of Gen. José de Urrea,qv which destroyed all the lodge's records and equipment. Because of a scattering of the membership the brethren decided not to reopen the lodge at Brazoria. Instead, they opened it at Houston in October 1837. The Grand Lodge of Louisiana issued two additional charters to Texas lodges during this period: Milam No. 40 at Nacogdoches and McFarland No. 41 at San Augustine. In December 1837 delegates from these three lodges convened at Houston to organize the Grand Lodge of the Republic of Texas.qv President Sam Houston qv presided over this meeting, which resulted in the election of Anson Jones as the first grand master. Between 1838 and 1845 the Texas Grand Lodge issued charters to twenty-one more lodges, and membership increased from seventy-three to 357. In addition, there were probably some 1,100 Masons from other jurisdictions living in Texas at this time. Although constituting only 1½ percent of the population, Masons filled some 80 percent of the republic's higher offices. All of the presidents, vice presidents, and secretaries of state were Masons. After annexation qv Masons continued to be equally prominent in the state government, and between 1846 and 1861 five of the six governors were members of the fraternity. Masonry continued to prosper; by 1860 Texas had 226 active lodges and 9,000 members. The Civil War qv saw between one-third and one-half of the membership in military service. During the war the Grand Lodge issued dispensations for thirty-two traveling military lodges established within army units. Meager records, however, make it impossible to determine exactly how many such lodges were actually formed. The Grand Lodge experienced severe financial difficulties during these years. Many lodges were unable to pay their annual assessments, and in 1861 the grand treasurer was directed to sell all United States government bonds and invest the money in Confederate bonds. The Grand Lodge was thus rendered penniless by the defeat of the Confederacy. Reconstruction qv brought continued financial problems as local lodges sought remission of their annual dues. Although the Grand Lodge frequently complied, it also canceled over fifty charters between 1865 and 1880 for financial reasons. Prosperity gradually returned, and by 1878 the Grand Lodge was solvent and membership had reached 17,000. This trend continued for many years except for brief downturns. As after most wars, Masonic membership showed a dramatic increase after World War I;qv in Texas it climbed from 94,000 in 1920 to more than 134,000 in 1929. The Great Depression qv brought an equally dramatic decline, to a low of 95,000 in 1937. A number of local lodges lost their temples, constructed during the prosperous 1920s, and their membership declined by as much as 60 percent. The waning of the depression and the onset of World War II qv produced the reinstatement of many former members, and after 1945 thousands of new members joined the lodge. Postwar membership reached 245,000 in 1961. A magnificent new Grand Lodge Temple was constructed at Waco in 1948–49. This building, supposedly patterned after King Solomon's biblical temple, contains 135,000 square feet and includes a library and museum of Texas memorabilia, open to the public.

The charitable and benevolent activities of Texas Masonry fall into two categories. Before 1900 most of the money and effort was directed to education, especially in those years before establishment of a viable public school system. The Grand Lodge established an education fund in 1847 and appointed a superintendent of education the following year. Between 1850 and 1873 the legislature chartered seventeen Masonic-sponsored schools. Texas Masons also helped establish more than 100 other unchartered schools. In addition, many of the early public schools initially met in lodge buildings. In the twentieth century Texas Masons have broadened the scope of their philanthropic efforts. Those limited to the Masonic family include the Masonic Home and School in Fort Worth, the Home for Aged Masons in Arlington, and the Scottish Rite Dormitory for Women at the University of Texas at Austin. Among the Masonic charities serving the public are the Texas Scottish Rite Hospital for Crippled Children in Dallas and the Shriners Burns Institute qv at Galveston. Since the early 1960s Texas Masonry, like other fraternal organizations, has faced a serious membership decline. From the 1961 high of 245,000, the number of Masons dropped to 201,000 by the end of 1985, when 960 working lodges were reported. Changes in modes of living and moral values are among the reasons given for the failure to attract more new members.

BIBLIOGRAPHY: James David Carter, *Masonry in Texas: Background, History and Influence to 1846* (Waco: Grand Lodge of Texas, 1955). Joseph W. Hale, "Masonry in the Early Days of Texas," *Southwestern Historical Quarterly* 49 (January 1946). *Proceedings of the Most Worshipful Grand Lodge of Texas* (1837–).

William Preston Vaughn

FREEMOUND, TEXAS. Freemound is just east of the Cooke-Montague county line and eighteen miles southwest of Gainesville in southwestern Cooke County. The community had a post office from 1894 through 1907. Ten people reportedly lived in Freemound during the 1940s, when highway maps showed a few scattered residences and one empty business building at the site. In the 1960s there were a number of scattered dwellings in the area, and in 1990 Freemound remained a small farming community.

Brian Hart

FREEPORT, TEXAS (Brazoria County). Freeport, on the Missouri Pacific tracks some sixteen miles south of Angleton in southern Brazoria County, is a deepwater port three miles from the mouth of the Brazos River on the Gulf of Mexico. The community's post office has been in continuous operation since 1898, but the town itself was officially founded by the Freeport Sulphur Company and formally dedicated in November 1912. Freeport was at the site of the world's largest sulfur mines and was the home of the Houston and Brazos Valley Railway. The community also provided storage tanks for the Freeport and Mexico Oil Company. A one-room school was in operation there by 1913, and by 1914 the community had a hotel, a bank, a fish and oyster plant, and a church. The weekly Freeport *Facts* was established in 1912, when the community's population numbered 300. Freeport incorporated with on February 10, 1917, and by 1929 the local population had reached 3,500. In 1937 the area was served by two schools for white students, one school for black students, and a high school; by 1939 the Freeport school district had twenty-seven teachers. Between 1931 and 1939 the town reached 4,100 residents and seventy-five businesses; from 1941 to 1950 it declined to about 2,579 residents but had 135 businesses. Growth was spurred by construction of the Dow Chemical Company facilities, beginning in 1939, and the town's participation in the Brazosport industrial area by 1944. By 1952 Freeport had a population of 6,008 and 195 businesses. On July 27, 1957, Velasco, one of the oldest towns in Texas, was incorporated into Freeport. In 1961 Freeport had 11,619 residents and 280 businesses, and in 1984 it had 13,444 residents and 513 businesses. It is home to one of the Gulf's largest commercial shrimp trawler fleets (more than 500 boats). In 1990 the population was 11,389.

BIBLIOGRAPHY: Brazoria County Federation of Women's Clubs, *History of Brazoria County* (1940). Brazosport *Facts*, March 26, 1991. James A. Creighton, *A Narrative History of Brazoria County* (Angleton, Texas: Brazoria County Historical Commission, 1975). Kathleen E. and Clifton R. St. Clair, eds., *Little Towns of Texas* (Jacksonville, Texas: Jayroe Graphic Arts, 1982). Vertical Files, Barker Texas History Center, University of Texas at Austin.

Diana J. Kleiner

FREEPORT, TEXAS (Hale County). Freeport, about two miles north of the site of what is now Plainview in northeastern Hale County, consisted mainly of a post office, established on July 10, 1909, with Clarence C. Smith as postmaster. The office, intended to serve the nearby Central Plains College and Conservatory of Music, was discontinued and moved to Plainview on May 14, 1910, around the time the school was renamed Seth Ward College. By the early 1980s Freeport was no longer shown on county highway maps, although there was a Seth Ward subdivision of Plainview, located northwest of Farm Road 400.

BIBLIOGRAPHY: Mary L. Cox, *History of Hale County, Texas* (Plainview, Texas, 1937).
Charles G. Davis

FREER, TEXAS. Freer is at the intersection of U.S. Highway 59 and State highways 16, 44, and 339, twenty-four miles northwest of San Diego and twenty-three miles northwest of Benavides in northwestern Duval County. It is the second largest town in the county. The area was originally called Las Hermanitas ("the Sisters"), for two hills south of the present townsite, and then became known as Government Wells, for a water well dug by United States Cavalry troops in 1876 on the property of A. J. Wiederkehr, north of the site of present Freer. When Norman G. Collins, who moved to Duval County in 1867 and later became the county's leading sheep rancher, bought 35,000 acres, the future townsite became part of his Rancho Americano. The German immigrant William Hubberd became one of the first settlers at Government Wells when he arrived to manage Collins's ranch; Hubberd bought his own land in 1876. Among the first settlers in the area may have been the brothers Paul and Joe White, who around 1900 settled in the valley of Rosita Creek, near the site of future Freer, to dig water wells for the local ranchers. Others followed them, including Harry and Arthur Lundell in 1905 and August H. Kramer in 1908. Jot Gunter[qv] also owned several thousand acres in the Government Wells area; in April 1904 the San Diego rancher Doss Seago had made a homestead application on the section of land that included the future townsite; in July 1905 he sold it to Encarnacion Rodriguez, who sold it in 1907 to Roxana Gunter. Five years later she sold twenty sections of land, including the site of future Freer, to a Houston real-estate promoter named C. W. Hahl.

Hahl advertised his land for sale in newspapers throughout the southwest and set up a sales office in San Diego with J. M. Momeny, who was later the superintendent of schools in Benavides, as manager. Hahl sold the land in eighty-acre sections for a dollar down per acre and fifteen dollars per acre with fourteen years to pay; to entice potential buyers, he reportedly hung apples on the mesquite trees. The first family on Hahl's Rosita Valley Rancho was the John W. Riley family, who arrived from Binger, Oklahoma, in April 1916. The Rileys pitched a tent three-fourths of a mile west of the current townsite. Several other settlers arrived the next year, including J. A. Powers, who built the first house on the site in 1917 but who left the Rosita valley three years later; William Patton Norton; and Daniel J. Freer. In 1917 Riley, Powers, and John Short built a one-room schoolhouse; nine pupils attended that first school in the Freer area. Virgil Guffey, another settler, was the teacher. The Daniel J. Freer family had been neighbors of the Rileys in Binger and came to visit them in Duval County. Daniel Freer liked the area so much that he took out an option on 160 acres adjoining the Riley property, but did not pay until his son Charles had looked the place over thoroughly. J. T. Johnson and his brother-in-law George Pricer arrived in 1919 and bought adjoining properties on which they built two-room houses, but they did not bring their families. In 1925 Johnson bought out Pricer and brought his family to the Rosita valley. That same year he and Charles Freer sent in an application for a post office. They submitted three names; Riley, Wendt, and Freer. Since the first two were already in use in Texas, Freer was selected. The first postmaster was Minnie Freer, wife of Charles Freer.

The single most important event in the history of Freer occurred three years later, in 1928. Three wildcatters drilling on the W. P. Norton property just southwest of what is now the Freer townsite struck one of the nation's largest oil reserves. The discovery of oil soon turned Freer into what *Life* magazine called "the last of the tough frontier oil towns." Shortly after the discovery of oil, Hahl sold the section of land on which the town would rise to D. L. Tipton, who laid out a townsite with lots fronting north and south. Tipton sold the property in January 1929 to A. H. (Big Boy) Compton, who had built a two-story hotel, a cafe, and a barbershop nearby in 1927. On December 20, 1930, Charles Freer bought the townsite from Compton and laid it out with lots fronting east and west. The town grew rapidly thereafter. The Great Depression[qv] and the discovery of oil in East Texas (*see* EAST TEXAS OILFIELD) in 1930 put an end to the first oil boom in Freer, but when the Heller-Suttle Number One well came in during the spring of 1932 it set off a second, even bigger, boom. By 1933 Freer was the second-largest oilfield in the United States and had attracted a flood of settlers from Oklahoma, Kansas, and other midwestern states.

The 1930s were a decade of phenomenal growth in Freer. The town had two businesses in 1931, but by the spring of 1933, when a fire that started in the Bluebonnet Cafe on Main Street came close to destroying the town, it had five cafes, four grocery stores, three drugstores, two each of meat markets, filling stations, pool halls, barbershops, and rooming houses, and one cleaner, one dance hall, one dry goods store, and some tourist cottages. The fire merely provided the citizens of Freer with an opportunity to display their resilience. In 1933 C. L. Day established the weekly Freer *Enterprise*, which ceased publication in 1972, and in 1934 the first chamber of commerce was founded. By 1936, when the community's population was estimated at 1,200, Freer had sixty businesses and was incorporated for a time. Two years later both the population and the number of businesses had doubled. The town quickly attracted a colorful cast of prostitutes, gamblers, drifters, and drunks, and a certain boomtown raffishness prevailed. At this time Freer had no jail, so the town constable used to chain drunks to the nearest telephone pole overnight. "Dr." B. F. Floyd, who had served as the first president of the chamber of commerce, later proved to be a pharmacist masquerading as a physician. He was arrested by federal agents but skipped his bail and disappeared.

Freer's main streets were not paved until 1938, which meant that when it rained, the trucks carrying bread and milk from Alice and San Diego could not reach the town. The town also had no potable water, no sewage system, and no bank, despite a monthly payroll estimated at $500,000. Not surprisingly, outsiders tended to sneer at Freer. In January 1938 *Life* headlined a two-page spread on the town with a reference to its "Squat[ting] in the Mud of Texas" and implied that vice ran rampant in Freer. The accompanying photographs emphasized the town's more squalid and ramshackle aspects. Yet such attacks only drew the residents of the town closer together. In 1975, when the town celebrated its fiftieth anniversary, a booklet put out to commemorate the occasion included several poems by Freer residents that acknowledged the town's lack of physical beauty but praised its warmth and unity. The town has continued to depend on the petroleum industry for much of its prosperity. Beginning in the mid-1950s a number of major petrochemical corporations, including at various times Coastal States, Exxon, Goliad Corporation, Mobil Oil, Phillips Petroleum, Texas Eastern, and Valero, have had plants in Freer. In 1990 Valero Hydrocarbons was still operating a small plant at Freer producing butane, propane, and natural gas. The estimated population of Freer had declined to 2,280 by the mid-1950s, but by the early 1960s it had begun a gradual increase that continued into the late 1980s, when the town had 3,735 residents and 103 businesses. In 1990 Freer reported 3,271 residents.

BIBLIOGRAPHY: Dorothy Abbott McCoy, *Oil, Mud, and Guts* (Brownsville, Texas, 1977).
Martin Donell Kohout

FREESE, SIMON WILKE (1900–1990). Simon W. Freese, civil engineer, was born at Blossom, Texas, on December 4, 1900, son of Wilke Harm and Leonora Novella (Hancock) Freese. His father was a building contractor. Freese finished high school at Paris, Texas, in 1917, attended Southern Methodist University two years, and earned a bachelor of science degree in civil engineering in 1921 from Massachusetts Institute of Technology. In 1923–24 he pursued postgraduate studies in bacteriology and chemistry at Cambridge University in England.

Freese joined the consulting engineering firm of John B. Hawley^qv at Fort Worth in 1922. Hawley made Freese a partner in 1927. In 1930 Marvin C. Nichols^qv joined the firm, which was called Hawley, Freese, and Nichols until Hawley retired in 1937. Under the name of the successor organization, Freese and Nichols, the firm incorporated in 1977 with senior partner Freese as chairman of the board.

Freese was a specialist in hydraulic and sanitary, or "environmental," engineering, as the speciality was dubbed during the 1960s. He conceived and designed approximately 100 municipal water and sewerage systems for Texas cities, including Fort Worth, Dallas, Houston, Beaumont, Austin, San Antonio, Corpus Christi, Lubbock, and Amarillo. He was responsible for his firm's involvement in more than 200 dam and reservoir projects, including lakes Fort Phantom Hill, Mackenzie, J. B. Thomas, E. V. Spence, Cedar Creek, Greenbelt, Hubbard Creek, White River, Conroe, and Richland Creek.

After floods killed thirty-seven people at Fort Worth in April 1922, Freese and Hawley recommended construction of lakes Eagle Mountain and Bridgeport. Freese designed both dams. When completed (Bridgeport in December 1931 and Eagle Mountain in October 1932), the two lakes were the first large dual-purpose reservoirs in the United States to provide separate reservoir capacities for flood control and water supply.

Freese helped pioneer the modern activated sludge process in American sewage-treatment plant design. At Cambridge in 1923–24 he studied the early English activated sludge plants, the most advanced in the world at that time. He incorporated the process into his design for San Antonio's first sewage-treatment plant, built in 1929–30. The San Antonio plant, which treated thirty million gallons a day, was one of the earliest activated sludge plants in the United States and was among the largest constructed before 1931.

The firm was active during World War II^qv as architect-engineers of twenty-one major installations for the army, air force, and navy, including camps Hulen, Barkeley, Swift, and Fannin. In 1943 Freese entered the United States Army and was on Gen. Dwight D. Eisenhower's^qv staff, Supreme Headquarters, Allied Expeditionary Force. He was economics officer for the military government and public works administrator in Germany and the occupied territories. He was the United States member of the Quadripartite Committee for Central German Administrative Agencies and aided in setting policy for a central German government under Allied control. He was discharged in March 1946 with the rank of lieutenant colonel.

Between 1946 and 1949 Freese helped establish the Colorado River Municipal Water District,^qv the state's first multi-city water district. The project introduced the concept of joint water-supply facilities to serve a group of cities. He chaired the Texas section of the American Society of Civil Engineers' 1951 Committee on State Water Policy, which wrote the state's first comprehensive water policy. Freese was principal author of *A Water Policy for Texans* (1952), precursor to the Texas Water Plan of 1968.

He was a member of the American Society of Civil Engineers, American Water Works Association, National Society of Professional Engineers, and Texas Water Conservation Association. He published professional papers on sewerage and water treatment. In 1975 the American Society of Civil Engineers established the national Simon W. Freese Environmental Engineering Award and Lecture. Texas Wesleyan University awarded Freese an honorary doctor of science degree in 1980. In 1981 he received the Texas Section, ASCE, Award of Honor. In 1984 the parent society made him an Honorary Member, ASCE's highest national honor. He was cited for "exceptional service as an engineer and a citizen of the state of Texas, and for his major role in enabling Texas to meet water resource needs." In May 1990 the Colorado River Municipal Water District dedicated the dam impounding the O. H. Ivie Reservoir near Ballinger as S. W. Freese Dam.

Freese was a Methodist and a Democrat. He married Eunice Elizabeth Brooks in Dallas on June 30, 1927. They had three children. Mrs. Freese died in Fort Worth on November 28, 1985. Freese died on July 27, 1990, in Fort Worth. He was active in engineering until a few months before his death and participated in writing a centennial history of Freese and Nichols, Incorporated.

BIBLIOGRAPHY: Fort Worth *Press*, November 6, 1933. Fort Worth *Star-Telegram*, January 23, 1989, July 28, 1990. Vertical Files, Barker Texas History Center, University of Texas at Austin.

Deborah Lightfoot Sizemore

FREE STATE OF VAN ZANDT. Several explanations have been proposed for the origin of the name Free State of Van Zandt for Van Zandt County. The first is that when Van Zandt and Kaufman counties were formed from Henderson County, all debts for the area were retained by Henderson County, and consequently Van Zandt County became known as a debt-free territory. Resentful politicians of Henderson County thereafter referred to Van Zandt County as a free state. Another explanation states that in 1861 some 350 residents attended a meeting to protest secession.^qv They reasoned that if Texas could leave the Union, then Van Zandt County could leave the state of Texas. These people tried to organize a government until they were threatened with military intervention. In another story, a slaveowner from out of the state came through Van Zandt County seeking a place to keep his slaves after Confederate setbacks. Asked if Van Zandt County would suffice, the man replied, "Hell no, I had as soon think of taking them to a free state. I came all the way from Quitman and never so much as saw a slave." In yet another tale, during Reconstruction^qv residents declared Van Zandt County independent of state and national authority. Gen. Philip H. Sheridan^qv sent troops, eventually captured the perpetrators, and imprisoned them near Canton. Although the rebels had temporarily routed the United States troops, in their eagerness to celebrate they drank too much and failed to post a guard. All eventually escaped.

BIBLIOGRAPHY: Margaret Elizabeth Hall, *A History of Van Zandt County* (Austin: Jenkins, 1976). William Samuel Mills, *History of Van Zandt County* (Canton, Texas, 1950).   *Gerald F. Kozlowski*

FREESTONE, TEXAS. Freestone is at the junction of Farm roads 489 and 80, six miles south of Teague in southwestern Freestone County. The area was known as Bond's Prairie in 1905, when the Trinity and Brazos Valley Railway was built through the area. That same year W. T. Hopson opened a general store there. Mrs. Allie Beene renamed the community Freestone in 1906, probably after the county. Also in 1906 a cotton gin was built, and a post office opened with Thomas T. Chester, a railway agent, as postmaster. The town also had a blacksmith shop. A school opened there in 1907. By 1914 Freestone had a population of 100, five businesses, and two churches. In 1918 an oil well was brought in near the town, and a townsite was laid out two years later. In 1936 Freestone comprised a school, two churches, and a population of 100. The Freestone school was consolidated with the Teague Independent School District in 1955, and by 1969 the community reported thirty residents and two businesses. Its post office was closed in 1976, and local mail was rerouted through Teague. Freestone's population was estimated at thirty-five from 1970 to 1990.

BIBLIOGRAPHY: Freestone County Historical Commission, *History of Freestone County, Texas* (Fairfield, Texas, 1978).   *Chris Cravens*

FREESTONE COUNTY. Freestone County (F-19) is located in east central Texas in the center of a group of counties once known as the Trinity Star. It is bounded on the east by Anderson County, on the south by Leon County, on the west by Limestone County, and on the north by Navarro and Henderson counties. The county's center lies at 31°43′ north latitude and 96°07′ west longitude; Fairfield, the county seat, is about eighty miles southeast of Dallas. Freestone County covers 888 square miles of coastal plain upland with an elevation ranging from 600 to 900 feet above sea level. The topography is generally a smooth, even plain with a gentle slope from northwest to southeast. The area is timbered with mesquite on the west, while the eastern half has almost every variety of oak, hickory, and walnut; there is a also scattering of pine groves on the western bank of the Trinity River, which provides drainage for the entire county, with the exception of a small area in the southwest, where runoff finds its way to the Navasota River. Most of the soil is fine sandy loam; springs are common in the deep sandy areas. Rainfall averages about thirty-eight inches per year, and temperatures range from an average high of 94° F in July to an average low of 36° in January. The growing season extends for 263 days. Interstate Highway 45 and State Highway 75 run north-south through the county, while U.S. Route 84 runs northwest to southeast.

Archeological evidence indicates that the area that is now Freestone County was inhabited from the late Holocene era to the arrival of the Spanish. In the historic period the area was inhabited by Caddoan Indians; in the 1830s these included the Kichais, who had a small settlement near what is now Butler, and the Tawakonis, who lived around Tehuacana Creek. Many other tribes also appear to have used the area for hunting and trading. While both the French and Spanish were familiar with the area, the French seem to have had more influence with these Indians, which limited the Spanish presence in the region. In the mid-1820s the Mexican government opened Texas to American colonization through the national colonization law of 1824 and through a law passed by the state of Coahuila and Texas,qv in 1825, which opened uninhabited tracts to contractors and empresarios (see MEXICAN COLONIZATION LAWS). One of the first to secure a grant was David G. Burnet,qv whose land lay in the area that later became Freestone County. Under the terms of his grant, Burnet was authorized to settle 300 families in the area within six years. Little progress was made in executing the provisions of the contract, however, until after 1830, when Burnet joined with other empresarios to form the Galveston Bay and Texas Land Company.qv In 1833 at least seven Mexican citizens received eleven-league grants, and another twenty-four titles to land were granted between 1834 and 1835. It is unclear how many of these landholders actually took up residence in the area; according to one account, in 1835 the only white inhabitant was James Hall, a fur trader. After the establishment of the Republic of Texas qv in 1836, the land company's rights to land in the area were terminated, and all lands not previously assigned became part of the public domain. During the early years of the republic period the area that is now Freestone County was considered Indian land and therefore dangerous; very few whites ventured into it until the Indian Treaty of 1843 (see INDIAN RELATIONS). So many settlers moved into the region in the years immediately following the treaty, however, that by 1846 every county now bordering Freestone County had been organized. One of these, Limestone County, included the land that would later comprise Freestone County. By the 1840s the white population of the northeastern half of Limestone County had grown significantly. By 1846 a fairly large settlement, later called Troy, had been established along the west side of the Trinity River near Pine Bluff, and in 1848 a few isolated settlers appeared in the southern and central sections of what is now Freestone County. Sometime around 1847 the steamboat *Roliance* made its way up the Trinity River. Others soon followed, bringing supplies for the many settlers moving into the area. Often the heads of families arrived on prospecting missions, then returned home to bring their families back with them. Since the population of Limestone County was rapidly expanding, in 1850 the Texas legislature divided it to form Freestone County. By 1851 the county had been organized; the town of Mound Prairie, in the center of the county, was chosen to be the county seat, and its name was changed to Fairfield. Some other early towns were Cotton Gin, Avant Prairie, Butler, and Bonner Community. By 1860 the agricultural economy was rapidly developing toward the model provided by slaveholding areas to the east; of the county's total population of 6,881, more than half (3,613) were slaves. The United States agricultural census found 417 farms, encompassing 282,803 acres, in Freestone County that year. More than half of these farms were smaller than 100 acres in size (and only two were larger than 1,000 acres), but already a few extensive plantations had been established. Two local landholders owned more than 100 slaves each, and four owned 70 to 100 slaves; all told, there were fifty-seven slaveholders in the county who owned twenty slaves or more. Though corn was the county's most important crop at this time, cotton production was also becoming well established. Over 6,900 bales of cotton were ginned in 1860, and local farmers also produced 5,200 pounds of tobacco, along with other crops such as wheat, oats, and sweet potatoes. Ranching was also an important part of the economy; the agricultural census listed almost 19,300 cattle and 7,700 sheep in 1860. By the early 1860s the residents had also begun to found cultural institutions. A combination school and Masonic lodge was built in Fairfield in 1853, and at least two colleges were established before or during the Civil War,qv including Fairfield Female Academy,qv (chartered in 1860) and Woodland College for Boys (established in 1863). Thirteen churches, mostly Methodist and Baptist, had also been established by 1860.

At the Secession Convention qv of 1861 Freestone County, represented by John Gregg and W. M. Peck,qqv voted to secede. After the convention county residents voted 585 to 3 in favor of secession.qv Preparations for military action were undertaken with 529 men available for duty. The Freestone contingent served well in the war, although there were many casualties. The loss of slave labor and the lack of a good transportation system slowed the economy in the years just after the Civil War,qv and in 1870 the area's production of corn (about 197,400 bushels) and cotton (6,465 bales) was lower than it had been in 1860. Nevertheless, the county experienced a good deal of growth during this period. By 1870 the agricultural census counted 1,029 farms in the area, more than double the number ten years earlier, and the population had increased to 8,139. The lack of good transportation persisted into the early twentieth century. In the early 1870s, for example, local farmers lost valuable opportunities to link directly to national markets when two railroads, the Houston and Texas Central and the International–Great Northern, skirted the county to the west and south. The local economy profited by the proximity of these railways, however, and the county grew significantly between 1870 and 1900. The number of farms nearly doubled (to 2,111) between 1870 and 1880, then increased to 2,728 by 1890 and to 3,518 by 1900; the number of "improved" acres of farmland more than tripled during this period, rising from 47,558 in 1870 to more than 159,000 by 1900. The population mirrored this growth, reaching 14,921 by 1880, 15,987 by 1890, and 18,910 by 1900.

Much of the county's growth during the late nineteenth century can be attributed to a significant rise in cotton production. About 31,300 acres were devoted to raising cotton in 1880 and about 49,300 acres in 1890; by 1900 that number had risen to almost 72,700 acres. Other aspects of the agricultural economy also developed during this time. By 1900 more than 48,000 acres were devoted to corn production. Sheep ranching declined significantly during this period (by 1900 there were only 346 sheep counted), but cattle ranching continued to flourish, and by 1900 almost 22,700 cattle were counted. Poultry had also become significant in the local economy; by the turn of the century farmers owned almost 112,000 chickens, which produced about 387,000 dozens of eggs that year. Agricultural activity was further encouraged in 1906, when the Trinity and Brazos Valley Railway was built across the county and partially solved the transportation problem, and the economy continued to grow during the first two decades of the twentieth century despite a boll weevilqv infestation that plagued farmers beginning in 1903. The number of farms increased to 3,518 by 1910 and to 3,587 by 1920. At the same time farm acreage rose from about 324,000 to almost 564,500 acres. By 1920 almost 100,000 acres were devoted to cotton, and more than 50,600 acres were planted in cereal crops, primarily corn. At that time the U.S. census found 23,264 people living in Freestone County.

Agriculture declined dramatically during the early 1920s, however. The county lost 777 farms between 1920 and 1925, when only 2,910 farms remained. One of the most lucrative enterprises during the 1920s, when prohibition^qv was in effect, was bootlegging, centered around the community of Young (or Young's Mill). Illegal whiskey known as Freestone County Bourbon Deluxe was transported out of the county by car, boat, truck, and plane and helped offset the downturn in the economy; according to one source, a number of local families "became wealthy, directly or indirectly," from the liquor trade. More farms were established in the late 1920s—by 1929 there were 3,559 farms in the area—but the rate of farm tenancy^qv among local farmers also rose significantly during this period, from 46 percent in 1920 to 65 percent in 1930. The economy never fully recovered. By 1929 the land devoted to cotton production had dropped to about 93,400 acres, and by 1930 the population had declined to 22,589.

The economic slump continued during the Great Depression^qv of the 1930s. Partly due to newly imposed federal crop restrictions, cropland harvested in the county dropped from 135,700 acres in 1929 to 112,700 in 1940; land in cotton declined by more than 50 percent during the depression years, with only about 44,000 acres left by 1940. Hundreds of farmers left, and by 1940 the county had only 2,761 farms and 21,138 residents. Due partly to farm consolidations, the population continued to decline, to 15,696 by 1950, to 12,525 by 1960, and to 11,116 by 1970. It rose significantly in the 1970s and 1980s, however, as new businesses moved in. While farming and the livestock business remained important, the biggest gains were in the mining industry, which by 1988 employed over 500 workers in the county, up from 20 in 1970. A new electric generating plant just outside of Fairfield caused the public utilities to more than double their work force from 1980 to 1986. Service and retail industries also grew significantly, and the population increased from 14,830 in 1980 to 20,946 by 1990. The majority of county voters supported Democratic candidates in every presidential election through 1992, except for 1972 and 1984, when the majorities went with Republicans Richard Nixon and Ronald Reagan. Communities in Freestone County include Teague (1992 estimated population, 3,816), Kirvin (117), Streetman (455, partly in Navarro County), and Wortham (1,317). Fairfield (4,068) is the largest town and county seat. Lake Fairfield, in the north central part of the county, provides recreation for residents and visitors, and many historic sites are preserved throughout the county. Blues artist Blind Lemon Jefferson^qv was born in Coutchman and buried in Wortham.

BIBLIOGRAPHY: Freestone County Historical Commission, *History of Freestone County, Texas* (Fairfield, Texas, 1978).

John Leffler

FREETHINKERS. Freethinkers (German *Freidenker*) is a term used to describe some nineteenth-century German intellectuals. The term had special currency in the Kendall County communities of Sisterdale and Comfort, where freethinkers formed the majority. Apart from its literal meaning, which suggests an attitude of liberalism unencumbered by dogma and the status quo, the term is also understood to connote agnosticism, if not atheism. However, many of the early freethinkers in Texas were neither true agnostics nor true atheists. Better stated, they considered the notion of Deity irrelevant and opposed clerics and churches; if they acknowledged the existence of a traditional Judeo-Christian God, they did not do so with friendliness or affection but as the impatient successors of such belief systems. A Freethinkers' Society held regular meetings in Sisterdale during the 1850s. Freethinking, which had various sources, among them early nineteenth-century Romanticism and science as well as the Turner movement and early communism, lasted in Comfort until the 1970s.

BIBLIOGRAPHY: Glen E. Lich and Dona B. Reeves, eds., *German Culture in Texas* (Boston: Twayne, 1980). Glen E. Lich, *The German Texans* (San Antonio: University of Texas Institute of Texan Cultures, 1981).

Glen E. Lich

FREIHEIT, TEXAS. Freiheit, northeast of New Braunfels in eastern Comal County, originated in 1891 as the San Geronimo School community. The school, named for a nearby creek, was on land donated by Henry A. Rose and served the blacklands farming area 3½ miles northeast of New Braunfels. In 1906 a store opened near the school at the intersection of Eberling Lane and Prairie Lea Road. In 1910 Alonzo Nolte, owner of the store, organized the Freiheit Bowling Club, which lent its name to the crossroads community. In the reorganization of Comal County schools after World War II,^qv the San Geronimo School was consolidated with the Goodwin Rural High School. The crossroads on Farm Road 1101 leading to New Braunfels Municipal Airport was still known as Freiheit (German for "freedom") in 1985.

BIBLIOGRAPHY: Oscar Haas, *History of New Braunfels and Comal County, Texas, 1844–1946* (Austin: Steck, 1968). New Braunfels *Herald*, July 6, 1954.

Daniel P. Greene

FRELS, WILLIAM (1810–1870). William Frels, founder of Frelsburg, was born in 1810 in the grand duchy of Oldenburg, Germany. In response to a letter from Friedrich Ernst,^qv one of the first German settlers in Texas, printed in the Oldenburg newspaper, Frels joined Robert Kleberg^qv and Louis von Roeder^qv and immigrated to Texas. Frels arrived in Galveston in December 1834 and first located near Ernst's settlement, Industry, but within a year moved westward to the fledgling community of Kraewinkel (Crows Nest) in what is now Colorado County. He participated in the siege of Bexar^qv and commanded a company of German volunteers in the revolutionary army.^qv He was a survivor of the battle of San Jacinto.^qv Afterward he and Peter Pieper^qv laid out a community that was opened to settlement in 1837. Frels donated land for a Lutheran church, school, parsonage, and cemetery, and under the name Frelsburg, the community flourished. On January 25, 1851, Frels married Louisa Frerichs. They had four children. Louisa Frels died in 1859. William Frels died on March 20, 1870, and is buried in the cemetery he donated to the community.

BIBLIOGRAPHY: Rudolph L. Biesele, *The History of the German Settlements in Texas, 1831–1861* (Austin: Von Boeckmann-Jones, 1930; rpt. 1964). Colorado County Historical Commission, *Colorado County Chronicles from the Beginning to 1923* (2 vols., Austin: Nortex, 1986). Frelsburg Historical Committee, *The History of Frelsburg* (New Ulm, Texas: Enterprise, 1986). Galveston *Daily News*, April 6, 1870.

Jeff Carroll

FRELSBURG, TEXAS. Frelsburg (Frelsburgh) is at the intersection of Farm roads 109 and 1291 in the northern corner of Colorado County. The community was founded around 1837 by Capt. William Frels^qv and his brother John, who immigrated to Texas from Germany in 1834 on the ship *Congress*. Captain Frels served in the revolutionary army^qv and, after independence, donated the land for the townsite, a school, a parsonage, and a Protestant church and cemetery. Original settlers were Germans from the area around Holstein and Oldenburg. By 1847 the population had increased enough to require a post office, and new immigrants from the Rhineland organized Sts. Peter and Paul Catholic Church. Community life, supported by an economy based on small farms similar to those in Germany, reflected both the German heritage and the influence of the Texas frontier. By 1852 the community had several stores, a cotton gin, and a number of service businessmen, such as blacksmiths and harnessmakers. After the Civil War qv Frelsburg continued to prosper, and much of the local land was devoted to the production of cotton. Area farmers credit Frank Walls, Sr., as the inventor of the first automatic cotton distributor and cleaner for use in gins. In 1870 Frelsburg was chosen by the state as the site of Hermann University, but after completion of the building there were not enough subscribers to keep the school in operation, and the building was subsequently sold to the local school district. During the 1870s the main line of the Galveston, Harrisburg and San Antonio Railway passed through Columbus twelve miles south of Frelsburg, and later the Missouri, Kansas and Texas passed several miles to the north. In 1884 Frelsburg had a population estimated at 300 and five cotton gins, four gristmills, three churches, and a sawmill. Even after it was bypassed by the railroads, Frelsburg remained prosperous through the first half of the 1900s. Its post office closed in 1908. After the 1950s most of the local small farms shifted to the production of beef cattle. Discovery of the nearby Frelsburg gas field removed more land from crop production and encouraged absentee ownership. The population of Frelsburg was reported as seventy-five from 1933 to 1990.

BIBLIOGRAPHY: *Colorado County Sesquicentennial Commemorative Book* (La Grange, Texas: Hengst Printing, 1986).   *Jeff Carroll*

FRENCH. France was given a claim to Texas by the explorations of René Robert Cavelier, Sieur de La Salle qv and his establishment, in 1685, of Fort St. Louis. In 1700 Louis Juchereau de St. Denis qv made an expedition up the Red River, and in 1714 he crossed Texas from Natchitoches, Louisiana, to San Juan Bautista qv on the Rio Grande in an attempt to open an overland trade route with the Spanish in Mexico. Later at Natchitoches he traded with Indians of the Red River and East Texas area. In August 1718 Jean Baptiste Bénard de La Harpe qv established a trading post among the Caddo Indians in the area of present Red River County. He and his party entered a bay on August 27, 1721, which they thought to be San Bernardo but was probably Galveston Bay. Hostile Indians forced La Harpe to withdraw. Another French trader at Natchitoches, Joseph Blancpain, qv also engaged in trade with the Indians of Texas until his capture in 1754. In April 1817 the French pirate Jean Laffite qv set up a "republic" on Galveston Island. His settlement grew to more than 1,000 persons, reached its peak of prosperity in 1818, and was abandoned early in May 1820. In 1818 a group of Napoleonic exiles under Gen. Charles Lallemand qv attempted to make a settlement at Champ d'Asile, qv on the Trinity River near the site of present Liberty, but the settlement had to be abandoned because of food shortages and threats from Spanish authorities.

On February 14, 1840, a commercial treaty was made between France and the Republic of Texas, qv and with the making of the treaty French interest in Texas increased. A French chargé or minister was sent to the republic, and plans were made for sending French colonists to Texas. One such plan, the Franco-Texian Bill, qv proposed sending 8,000 French soldiers to the Texas frontier. The bill was introduced in the Texas Congress in 1841 but failed because of popular opposition. Snider de Pellegrini, qv director of a French colonization company, arrived with fourteen immigrants at Matagorda in July 1842, but his efforts to found a colony failed. The most successful of French colonization projects was that of Henri Castro, qv who in September 1844 founded Castroville, west of the line of the frontier. From 1843 to 1846 Castro brought a few more than 2,000 immigrants to Texas and was instrumental in establishing Quihi, Vandenburg, and D'Hanis. Victor Prosper Considérant qv founded, near the site of present Dallas, a socialistic colony named La Réunion, qv which flourished briefly in the middle 1850s but ultimately failed because of poor soil, inexperienced farmers, poor financing, and too much unsocialistic individualism.

The French who came to Texas in search of better social, political, and economic conditions contributed to the state in extending the frontier and in encouraging cultural development. The census of 1850 showed 647 French-born men in Texas; that of 1860 listed 1,883. In 1930 the census showed 10,185 persons of French nationality in the state. In 1990 there were 571,175 people of French descent in Texas.

BIBLIOGRAPHY: Eugéne Maissin, *The French in Mexico and Texas, 1838–1839* (Salado, Texas: Anson Jones Press, 1961). Robert S. Weddle, *The French Thorn: Rival Explorers in the Spanish Sea, 1682–1762* (College Station: Texas A&M University Press, 1991). Vertical Files, Barker Texas History Center, University of Texas at Austin.

FRENCH, GEORGE H. (?–1843?). George H. French, newspaperman, came to Texas probably in 1838, when he joined his brother-in-law, Samuel Bangs, qv in the publication of the *Galvestonian*. qv In the early 1840s the two men were in Houston publishing the *Mosquito;* qv they apparently returned to Galveston and were association with the *Daily News*, for on April 19, 1842, the earliest extant copy of this predecessor of the Galveston *News* qv was printed in Bangs's shop and listed George H. French as publisher. In April 1840 French and Bangs founded the *Daily Courier* at Galveston, with Joel T. Case qv as editor. For publishing remarks offensive to Judge Anthony B. Shelby, who presided over the Galveston and Houston district court, French was arrested, sentenced to a year in jail, and fined $1,000. The incident aroused the citizenry, and French's sentence was remanded, but ultimately he left Houston. In March 1841 French and Bangs issued the *Daily Galvestonian*, with French as editor. In 1843 French and G. L. Hamlin, probably still in association with Bangs, took over another Galveston Island paper, the *San Luis Advocate*, qv which was renamed *Texas Times*. French died shortly thereafter in a yellow fever epidemic.

BIBLIOGRAPHY: Sam Hanna Acheson, *35,000 Days in Texas: A History of the Dallas "News" and Its Forbears* (New York: Macmillan, 1938). Joe B. Frantz, Newspapers of the Republic of Texas (M.A. thesis, University of Texas, 1940). Douglas C. McMurtrie, "Pioneer Printing in Texas," *Southwestern Historical Quarterly* 35 (January 1932). Marilyn M. Sibley, *Lone Stars and State Gazettes: Texas Newspapers before the Civil War* (College Station: Texas A&M University Press, 1983).

FRENCH, HENRY R. (?–?). Henry R. French, Galveston newspaperman, the brother of George H. French and brother-in-law of Samuel Bangs, qqv entered the newspaper business with his brother and worked as editor on the daily *Galvestonian* qv after the death of John Gladwin. qv When the paper ceased publication in early 1840, he moved the operation to the office of the *Civilian*, and in March founded another *Galvestonian*, which he left in 1842 to become the proprietor of a bakery shop.

BIBLIOGRAPHY: Joe B. Frantz, Newspapers of the Republic of Texas (M.A. thesis, University of Texas, 1940). Douglas C. McMurtrie, "Pioneer Printing in Texas," *Southwestern Historical Quarterly* 35 (January 1932). Marilyn M. Sibley, *Lone Stars and State Gazettes: Texas Newspapers before the Civil War* (College Station: Texas A&M University Press, 1983).   *Diana J. Kleiner*

FRENCH, JAMES HENRY (1835–1893). James Henry French, mayor of San Antonio, was born on March 26, 1835, in Warrenton, Virginia, to James and Sarah Butler (Henry) French. He attended Columbia College in Washington, D.C., before he moved to San Antonio, Texas, in October 1851. On October 15, 1856, he married Sarah L. Webb; they eventually had five children. French and his wife moved in 1856 to Atascosa County, where he served two terms as sheriff and managed a ranch. He returned to San Antonio in 1859 and in May 1861 enlisted in the Confederate Army. He served in the adjutant general's office until October 1861, then was appointed captain and assigned to the commissary department under Gen. Paul O. Hébert.qv He served this assignment on the Rio Grande under Gen. Hamilton P. Bee.qv In January 1863 French was transferred to the purchasing department at San Diego, Texas, and in March 1865 took charge of the reserve department of supplies for the forces operating under Col. John S. Port.

After the war he made his home in San Antonio, where he instituted many reforms in city government during his period as mayor (1875–1885) and alderman (1885–89). These reforms included a system of street names and house numbering, increased city control of public schools, and an increase in the school tax by 10 percent. In addition, during his tenure the International–Great Northern Railroad was built into San Antonio. French died on September 6, 1893, and was buried in the City Cemetery in San Antonio.

BIBLIOGRAPHY: *Biographical Encyclopedia of Texas* (New York: Southern, 1880). *Memorial and Genealogical Record of Southwest Texas* (Chicago: Goodspeed, 1894; rpt., Easley, South Carolina: Southern Historical Press, 1978). Vertical Files, Barker Texas History Center, University of Texas at Austin.

Carolyn Hyman

FRENCH, JOHN C. (ca. 1820s–1889). John C. French, businessman, was born in New Jersey or Pennsylvania in the 1820s. He and his brother Samuel moved to San Antonio in the 1840s. French entered the employ of Lewis and Groesbeck, dealers in groceries and banking. The firm became Groesbeck and French in 1854 and later was run by French alone. In 1858 the French Building was completed; in 1868 it became the Bexar County Courthouse and in 1879 housed the city government. San Antonio's first regular bank was organized by French and Erasmus André Florian; it operated until the Civil Warqv forced French to withdraw from active business, though he still retained large interests in San Antonio. He helped promote the Gulf, Western Texas and Pacific Railway Company (see SAN ANTONIO AND MEXICAN GULF RAILWAY). French married Sally Roberts. He died in Cuero on May 16, 1889, and was buried beside his daughter in Philadelphia, Pennsylvania.

BIBLIOGRAPHY: Frederick Charles Chabot, *With the Makers of San Antonio* (Yanaguana Society Publications 4, San Antonio, 1937).

S. W. Pease

FRENCH, TEXAS. French, on Farm Road 667 some sixteen miles west of Corsicana in western Navarro County, was probably established in the 1880s. A post office may have operated there from 1888 to 1889. In the mid-1930s the community had a church, a cemetery, and a number of houses. The church was later disbanded, and by the mid-1960s only a cemetery and a few widely scattered houses were left in the area.

Christopher Long

FRENCH CREEK (Bexar County). French Creek rises just east of Helotes in northwestern Bexar County (at 29°35' N, 98°41' W) and runs southeast for six miles to its mouth on Leon Creek, just west of State Highway 16 (at 29°29' N, 98°38' W). It traverses flat to rolling terrain surfaced by shallow, stony soils that support mesquite and grasses.

_____ (Uvalde County). French Creek rises a half mile east of the West Nueces River and seven miles north of Cline in west central Uvalde County (at 29°22' N, 100°04' W) and runs north, then east, then south, for a total of 7½ miles before reaching its mouth on the Nueces River, two miles south of Laguna (at 29°24' N, 100°01' W). The stream traverses flat terrain with local shallow depressions, surfaced by shallow and stony clays and loams that grow deeper toward the stream's mouth. Local vegetation includes water-tolerant hardwoods, conifers, and grasses.

FRENCH EXPEDITION. Parker H. French was born about 1826 in Kentucky and after the death of his parents was raised by a Judge Edwards. He ran away from home at the age of fifteen and worked five years as a cabin boy on an English man-of-war. He then returned to Kentucky and married Judge Edwards's daughter. After an unsuccessful attempt at shipbuilding in St. Louis, Missouri, French conceived of a scheme for raising money by organizing an express wagon train across Texas to California for gold seekers. He placed a large ad in the New York newspapers and set up an office in Tammany Hall. The ad promised fast and safe travel to the California gold fields, across the easy terrain and mild weather of Texas, under the protection of sixty Texas Rangers.qv French hinted of a stopover on the Gila River, where gold was to be found. All supplies, including food, wagons, mules, tents, cooks, and a physician, would be provided. The cost was $250 per passenger, with a promised rebate of five dollars for each day exceeding sixty days. Enlisted men who worked for their passage enrolled for $100 each. A total of 120 passengers and sixty enlisted men signed up. The group left New York on a crowded steamboat on May 13, 1850, and after a stopover in Cuba arrived in New Orleans, where members of the group were presented with the opportunity to join the López Revolution in Cuba as mercenaries. Offers of free land were made, but the group declined to go to Cuba. The passengers enjoyed a week of high living in New Orleans at the St. Charles Hotel, paid for by French, then sailed to the Texas coast and began a difficult overland trip from Port Lavaca to San Antonio, Uvalde, and finally to El Paso, where the bogus expedition disintegrated.

The overland trip across Texas was replete with disasters. Wild mules had to be broken to harness, the men fought swarms of mosquitos, and the group ran out of food, all within the first seven days. It took them that long to travel twenty-five miles to Victoria. French replenished supplies in San Antonio by using forged bank drafts and claiming that he was an agent of the United States government, and the military opened its stores to him. The expedition left San Antonio on July 15. Between San Antonio and El Paso the travelers crossed the Devil's River a number of times, watched a Texas Ranger named Black Warrior shoot and scalp a thieving Indian, crossed the muddy Pecos River, where they lost four horses to the swift water, and were frequently robbed by Indians. One of the men was accidently shot and killed. At one point French got into a serious confrontation with a wagon master, Durand, over moving the wagon train in the hot sun. The argument almost resulted in a duel. After 130 days of travel from New York, the expedition finally reached Franklin (El Paso) on September 18, 1850.

The weary men had already suspected that French was a fraud for passing forged bank drafts in New Orleans, San Antonio, and Franklin (James W. Magoffinqv had sold French fresh mules). They mutinied, secured a key to French's safe, and found it empty. Henry, French's body servant, told them that French had deposited the money in a New Orleans bank. French had avoided mutiny during the overland trip across Texas by claiming to be an agent of the government, by reminding the men of mysterious gold deposits on the Gila River, and by promising to refund some of their money since sixty days had long since passed. The men finally realized that they had been victimized. French avoided arrest in Franklin by crossing the Rio Grande into Mexico. The expedition was then divided into four groups, with two going to California and two into Mexico and to California by ship. French attempted a raid on one group near Corralitos, Chihuahua, Mexico, but he was shot and had to have his right arm amputated. After an adventurous sojourn in Mexico, he traveled to California, where he proclaimed himself a lawyer and replaced his law partner (who had suddenly died) in the 1854 California legislature. He later traveled to Nicaragua, sent by William Walker as

"Minister Plenipotentiary and Envoy Extraordinary," but United States authorities refused to recognize him. He was kicked out of the office of the United States secretary of state. During the Civil War[qv] French was arrested in Connecticut, probably for outfitting a privateer for the Confederacy, and was held in Boston from November 8, 1861, to February 21, 1862. He had used the aliases Carlisle Murray and Charles Maxey. He worked for the Knights of the Golden Circle[qv] (Confederacy) and the Knights of the Golden Square (Union). French was last seen in the winter of 1876–77 in Washington, D.C. He filed a claim with the Commission for the Adjustment of American and Mexican Claims on March 23, 1870. No record exists of his death. In an 1893 list of California legislators the one-word notation "dead" is entered after the name Parker H. French.

BIBLIOGRAPHY: Michael Baldridge, *A Reminiscence of the Parker H. French Expedition Through Texas and Mexico to California in the Spring of 1850* (Los Angeles, 1959; first pub. in the San Jose *Pioneer*, August–December 1895). Kenneth M. Johnson, "A Little Bit More on Parker H. French," *Southern California Quarterly* 49 (September 1967). Edward McGowan, *The Strange Eventful History of Parker H. French* (Los Angeles: Glen Dawson Book Shop, 1958). William Miles, *Journal of the Sufferings and Hardships of Capt. Parker H. French's Overland Expedition to California* (Chambersburg, Pennsylvania: Valley Spirit Office, 1851; rpt., New York: Cadmus Book Shop, 1916).

Albert Briggs Tucker

FRENCH JOHN CREEK. French John Creek rises near the intersection of State Highway 29 and Ranch Road 1431 in eastern Llano County (at 30°44′ N, 98°27′ W) and runs southwest for four miles to its mouth on Pennington Creek, 1½ miles west of the intersection of Ranch roads 1431 and 3404 (at 30°42′ N, 98°29′ W). The stream traverses an area of the Llano basin characterized by flat to rolling terrain with local dissections, surfaced by sandy to clay loam soils that support open stands of live oak and mesquite.

FRENCH LEGATION. The term *French Legation* refers both to the diplomatic mission of Alphonse Dubois de Saligny[qv] to the Republic of Texas[qv] from 1840 to 1846 and to the house in Austin built for him in late 1840 and early 1841. The legation has frequently been referred to as the "French Embassy," but Dubois de Saligny was merely a chargé d'affaires, considerably lower than an ambassador or minister in the diplomatic hierarchy. The French government first expressed interest in recognizing the Republic of Texas in 1839, when it sent Dubois de Saligny, then a secretary in the French legation in Washington, on a mission of exploration. He stayed in Texas only briefly but wrote a strongly favorable report encouraging his government to recognize the new republic. King Louis Philippe did so on September 25, 1839, when he signed a treaty of amity, navigation, and commerce. Dubois de Saligny was promoted to chargé d'affaires and sent to establish a legation in Texas.

One of the principal objectives of Dubois's mission was the passage of the Franco-Texian bill,[qv] under which substantial portions of West Texas would be settled by French colonists. Texans at first looked favorably upon the bill, but Dubois's relations with the administration of acting president David G. Burnet[qv] began to deteriorate rapidly in early 1841. Suspicions arose that Dubois and certain French entrepreneurs would profit handsomely by the Franco-Texian bill, and matters were made worse by the so-called Pig War.[qv] In April 1841 Secretary of State James S. Mayfield[qv] requested that the French government recall its agent, but before Mayfield's letter reached Paris, Dubois asked for his passport and left Austin for good. He continued to observe affairs in Texas from New Orleans, where he stayed until March 1842.

When Sam Houston[qv] won the Texas presidential election of 1841, Dubois de Saligny hoped for better relations with the Texas government; he spent part of 1842 in Galveston and Houston. The controversies of 1841, however, had severely damaged his credibility. He took a leave of absence in 1843 and returned to France, ostensibly for reasons of health. Jules Edouard de Cramayel[qv] served as chargé d'affaires ad interim. When Dubois resumed his position in 1844, he spent most of his time in New Orleans, making only occasional visits to Houston, Galveston, and Washington-on-the-Brazos. Thinking that French interests would be better served if Texas remained independent, he encouraged Texas to seek recognition from Mexico instead of annexation[qv] to the United States. The legation was recalled in May 1846, after annexation was accomplished.

The house called the French Legation was built in Austin by Dubois de Saligny on the crest of a hill in the middle of twenty-one acres purchased from Anson Jones[qv] in 1840. Illness, bad weather, shortages of workmen and materials, and the necessity of digging a cellar delayed completion of the house until the middle of 1841. By then Dubois had left for New Orleans, so it seems unlikely that he ever occupied the house in its finished state. The carpenters who built the house apparently had worked in East Texas and possibly Louisiana, for they blended the Greek Revival, by then an American vernacular style, and Mississippi Valley French architecture. The house, made of loblolly pine from Bastrop, was raised some two feet off the ground, as if it were on a Louisiana bayou rather than in the Hill Country[qv] of Texas.

Possibly Dubois ran out of money before the house was finished. On December 31, 1840, he sold it to Father Jean Marie Odin,[qv] later the first bishop of the Catholic Diocese of Galveston. Dubois agreed to complete the house, to build a separate kitchen and stable, and to fence the property. In return, he could occupy the house until April 1, 1842. When Odin took possession on that date, the city of Austin was rapidly losing population because of the government's move to Washington-on-the-Brazos. The house remained vacant for several years, and Odin finally sold it to Gen. Moseley Baker[qv] on October 30, 1847. Baker in turn sold it on May 16, 1848, to Dr. Joseph W. Robertson,[qv] whose family kept the house for a hundred years. Around 1880 a fire destroyed the original kitchen, and the Robertsons built a new attached kitchen, dining room, and bathroom. On August

The French Legation, by Julia Robertson, ca. 1858. Oil on canvas. 15¼″ × 19¼″. Courtesy French Legation Museum and the Daughters of the Republic of Texas. When Julia Robertson painted this view, her family had been living in the residence for about ten years. Here she shows a woman pushing a baby carriage past the house, which then stood on the outskirts of Austin.

11, 1948, the house was sold to the state of Texas and placed in the custody of the Daughters of the Republic of Texas.qv Between 1953 and 1956 the DRT built the present stone wall around the compound, extensively landscaped the grounds, and restored the house to its 1841 appearance. This entailed not only the removal of the Robertson wing, but also the reconstruction—on extremely limited evidence—of a freestanding kitchen and stable. Raiford Stripling of San Augustine was the architect of the kitchen (1966) and the carriage house (1974), both of which were larger and fancier than the original outbuildings would have been.

The French Legation Museum opened on April 5, 1956, under the auspices of the DRT. Its contents included an armchair and sofa thought to have belonged to Dubois de Saligny, a substantial collection of Robertson family furniture ranging in date from the 1820s to the 1880s, and various donated items. The kitchen was stocked with a large number of cooking antiques, mostly French and mostly made before 1840. In the 1980s the carriage house was converted into an office, gift shop, and meeting facility.

BIBLIOGRAPHY: Nancy Nichols Barker, trans. and ed., *The French Legation in Texas* (2 vols., Austin: Texas State Historical Association, 1971, 1973). *Diplomatic Correspondence of the Republic of Texas*, ed. George Pierce Garrison (3 parts, Washington: GPO, 1908-11). Kenneth Hafertepe, *A History of the French Legation* (Austin: Texas State Historical Association, 1989). *Kenneth Hafertepe*

FRENCHMAN HILLS. The Frenchman Hills are a mile west of Perdiz Creek in central Presidio County (at 30°01′ N, 104°07′ W). Their peaks, at elevations of 4,564 and 4,636 feet above sea level, rise 367 and 439 feet above the road running along their eastern edge. The Frenchman Hills are formed of conglomerates, sandstone, and tuff and stand in an area of desert mountain terrain with rugged canyons that dissect volcanic rock. Local vegetation includes sparse grasses, cacti, and desert shrubs of conifers and oaks.

FRENCHTOWN, TEXAS. Frenchtown was a neighborhood of four square blocks in Houston's Fifth Wardqv in Harris County. It comprised 500 blacks of French and Spanish descent from Louisiana, who came to northeastern Houston and organized a community in 1922. Many Frenchtown skilled or semiskilled workers, including mechanics, carpenters, sawmill workers, and bricklayers, were employed by the Southern Pacific Railroad. Their community of largely French-speaking Catholics was centered around Our Mother of Mercy Roman Catholic Church and had a rich Creole culture distinguished by its colorful patois, unique cuisine, and characteristic zydeco music. The women of the community refused to take employment as cooks, despite the appeal of their cooking. With no further influx of new residents, Frenchtown gradually merged into the larger community.

BIBLIOGRAPHY: Marie Phelps McAshan, *A Houston Legacy: On the Corner of Main and Texas* (Houston: Gulf, 1985). James Martin SoRelle, *The Darker Side of 'Heaven': The Black Community in Houston, Texas, 1917–1945* (Ph.D. dissertation, Kent State University, 1980). Cary Wintz, *Blacks in Houston* (Houston Center for the Humanities, 1982). WPA Writers Program, *Houston* (Houston: Anson Jones, 1942). *Diana J. Kleiner*

FRENSTAT, TEXAS. Frenstat, also known as Friendsted, is on Big Creek and Farm Road 2774 some seven miles northwest of Somerville in southern Burleson County. Settlement in the area began in the mid-1830s. The community was founded by Czech Catholic families, who first arrived in the area in 1884. Two years later about forty Czech families were established there, some from Caldwell, eleven miles to the north. The community was named Frenstat in the summer of 1886, after the town of Frenštát, Moravia, from which most of the original inhabitants had emigrated. A school was soon erected, and by 1889 the settlers had constructed Holy Rosary Catholic Church, the first Catholic church in Burleson County. Land for the school, church, and a cemetery was donated by Adolph Polansky. A local post office was established in 1891, and a cotton gin and a general store were located in the settlement during the late 1800s. A population estimate of twenty-five was reported in 1892 and again in the 1940s, the last time for which a population figure is available. In 1931 some eighty-five Czech families lived in the vicinity. The community's post office was discontinued in 1908, and in 1948 the local school was consolidated with the Somerville Independent School District. In the late 1900s the community comprised a handful of farm dwellings scattered around the church and recreation center.

BIBLIOGRAPHY: Burleson County Historical Society, *Astride the Old San Antonio Road: A History of Burleson County, Texas* (Dallas: Taylor, 1980). National Alliance of Bohemian Catholics of America, *History of the Czech-Moravian Catholic Communities of Texas* (Waco: Texian Press, 1974; trans. by V. A. Svrcek of *Naše Dejiny* [Granger, Texas: Našinec, 1939]). *Charles Christopher Jackson*

FRESH WATER SUPPLY DISTRICTS. Fresh water supply districts have been established in Texas since 1919, when the Texas legislature authorized them under the conservation amendment of 1917 for the exclusive purpose of providing and distributing water for domestic and commercial use. The districts are organized on much the same basis as the water improvement districtsqv and have no limitation on bonds or taxation. Through petitions, local commissioners' courts or individuals can request hearings and elections for new districts. A board of five elected supervisors directs the affairs of each district. The board fixes rates paid by water users, decides the terms on which water can be furnished, and makes rules regarding water use and distribution. The revenue earned is used for operation and maintenance expenses or to help pay debts or interest on bonds. The board also has the power to acquire rights-of-way for the construction of pipelines, levees, sewer systems, bridges, and other structures through private and public land, and it awards contracts to the lowest and best bidders for such construction. In 1992 Texas had a total of thirty-eight fresh water supply districts.

BIBLIOGRAPHY: Gwendolyn Lea Gilchrist, *Texas Water Resources Management by Water Districts and River Authorities* (M.A. thesis, University of Texas at Austin, 1992). *West's Texas Statutes and Codes*, Vol. 4 (St. Paul, Minnesota: West, 1984).

FRESNO, TEXAS (Collingsworth County). Fresno, southeast of Wellington in southeastern Collingsworth County, was the site of the first homesteads in the county. John Elliott and Philo W. Myers were the first to file claims on land there, in August 1888. Others soon followed, and by 1889 a small settlement had developed south of the Rocking Chair Ranchqv pasture. Initially the community was called both Elliott Flats and the South Side, but when a post office opened there at the home of P. W. Myers in July 1889, it was named Fresno. A school was built out of lumber hauled from Childress and opened in the summer of that year, with thirteen pupils taught by Mrs. W. O. Richards. In 1890 the Fresno settlers pushed for the county's organization, while the "Rockers" (Rocking Chair Ranch employees) initially sought to delay it. The settlers soon prevailed, and after the community of Wellington was elected to be the county seat, Fresno was rapidly eclipsed. Fresno's post office was discontinued in November 1893, with mail thereafter sent to Arlie in Childress County. During the mid-1980s a few scattered farms remained in the area.

BIBLIOGRAPHY: Clyde Chestnut Brown, *A Survey History of Collingsworth County, Texas* (M.A. thesis, University of Colorado,

1934). Estelle D. Tinkler, ed., *Archibald John Writes the Rocking Chair Ranche Letters* (Burnet, Texas: Eakin Press, 1979). Estelle D. Tinkler, "Nobility's Ranche: A History of the Rocking Chair Ranche," *Panhandle–Plains Historical Review* 15 (1942).
H. Allen Anderson

FRESNO, TEXAS (Fort Bend County). Fresno is on Farm Road 521 twenty miles northeast of Richmond in northeastern Fort Bend County. A settler from Fresno, California, reportedly chose the name. The town is on land patented in 1824, once surrounded by cotton plantations. Fresno acquired a post office in 1910. In 1914 it had a telephone connection, a general store, a hardware store, and a population of thirty-two. By 1933 the town had only ten inhabitants and one business. In 1936 it had three rows of dwellings on both sides of a paved highway and was served by the International–Great Northern Railroad. By 1946 the population had risen to 100, a level maintained throughout the 1960s. In 1970 the figure had increased to 120; two years later it had grown to 161. During the 1970s and 1980s the population of Fresno increased more rapidly as the area was affected by growth of Houston. In 1990 Fresno had a population of 3,182.
Stephen L. Hardin

FRESNO CREEK (Brewster County). Fresno Creek rises two miles southwest of Emory Peak in Big Bend National Park[qv] in south central Brewster County (at 29°13′ N, 103°19′ W) and runs southeast for twenty-one miles to its mouth on the Rio Grande, twelve miles southwest of Boquillas (at 29°04′ N, 103°06′ W). The stream is intermittent for its first eight and last eleven miles. It rises in an area of rugged terrain with numerous box canyons and shallow, stony soils that support Mexican buckeye, walnut, persimmon, desert willow, scrub brush, and sparse grasses. In the creek's lower reaches the terrain changes to steep to gentle slopes with variable soils that support scrub brush and sparse grasses. *Fresno* is Spanish for "ash tree."

_____ (Presidio County). Fresno Creek, a major intermittent stream, rises on the west flank of the Solitario[qv] dome near Post Mountain in southeastern Presidio County (at 29°30′ N, 103°49′ W) and runs south for sixteen miles to its mouth on the Rio Grande, six miles west of Lajitas (at 29°17′ N, 103°51′ W). It rises in an area of Cretaceous limestones, crosses Tertiary deposits of sandstone, tuff, and igneous rocks, and ends in a Quaternary alluvium on the Rio Grande. The local terrain is surfaced by generally light reddish-brown to brown sands, clay loams, and rough stony areas. Sparse desert shrubs are the main vegetation in the vicinity.

FRESNO PEAK. Fresno Peak is in southeastern Presidio County three miles west of the Brewster county line (at 29°26′ N, 103°50′ W). Its summit, with an elevation of 5,131 feet above sea level, rises 1,331 feet over Fresno Canyon, which runs along its eastern edge. Fresno Peak is a Tertiary intrusion that stands in the Solitario,[qv] a domal uplift with a nine-mile diameter and a prominent limestone rim. The area topography is desert mountain terrain of basalt deposits. Local vegetation includes sparse grasses, cacti, desert shrubs, and scrub brush.

BIBLIOGRAPHY: *Geology of the Big Bend Area and Solitario Dome, Texas* (Midland: West Texas Geological Society, 1986). *Geology of the Big Bend Area, Texas* (Midland: West Texas Geological Society, 1965). Ronnie C. Tyler, *The Big Bend* (Washington: National Park Service, 1975).

FREYBURG, TEXAS. Freyburg is at the intersection of Farm roads 956 and 2238, twelve miles southwest of La Grange in southwestern Fayette County. It was founded about 1868 by Germans[qv] and named for a town in Germany. By 1886 Freyburg had a blacksmith shop and C. F. Thulemeyer's general store. A post office was opened in 1889, and by 1896 the community had fifty inhabitants, a saloon, a grocery store, and a general store. In the early 1900s the Order of Sons of Hermann[qv] had a dance hall in the community. The post office closed in 1907, and in 1940 Freyburg had forty inhabitants, one business, and a number of scattered dwellings. In the 1970s it comprised an old store, an old gin, several cemeteries, scattered homes, several cemeteries, and Lutheran and Methodist churches. By the 1980s there were no longer any businesses in the community, and in 1990 Freyburg had a population of forty-five.

BIBLIOGRAPHY: La Grange High School, *Fayette County: Past and Present* (La Grange, Texas, 1976).
Mark Odintz